CASSELL'S
ENGLISH DICTIONARY

CASSELL'S
ENGLISH
DICTIONARY

CASSELL&CO

Cassell & Co
Wellington House
125 Strand
London
WC2R 0BB

First published as *The Cassell Compact Dictionary*, 1998

© Cassell 2000

British Library Cataloguing in Publication Data
A catalogue entry for this book is available from the British Library

ISBN 0–304–35732–4

Printed and bound in Great Britain by Mackays of Chatham PLC, Kent

Contents

Acknowledgements

Consultant Editor	Lesley Brown
Project editor	Alex Williams
Proof-reader	Alice Grandison
Database technology	Librios
Typesetting	Gem Graphics

How to use the Dictionary

The entry

Each entry in the dictionary begins with the headword in bold type. For most words this is immediately followed by the pronunciation, any variant spellings or forms, then the (first) relevant part of speech. Inflections (plurals of nouns, parts of verbs etc.) which are irregular or which may cause spelling difficulty follow the part-of-speech label.

Where the headword has more than one meaning, senses are numbered **1, 2** etc. and ordered on a basis of current frequency or importance. Closely related uses may share a number, subdivided as **a, b** etc. Sense numbering starts afresh for second or subsequent parts of speech.

Any usage note on the headword, or applying to one of its nested entries, follows the final definition or part-of-speech, marked off on a separate line. However, in very long entries, containing a number of nested headwords, usage notes are sometimes included immediately after the relevant headword and definition.

Other types of entry give expansions for abbreviations, or direct the user to words elsewhere in the dictionary.

Arrangement of entries

By no means all words included in the dictionary are headwords. Many words or expressions which are derived from the same root are grouped or 'nested' together, e.g. **applicable** is under **apply**. This not only demonstrates at a glance the relationship of words but also allows many more words to be included than would otherwise be the case. The majority of such words are easy to find since their positions in the dictionary are very close alphabetically to the points they would have been entered at as separate headwords. Where this is not the case cross-reference entries are generally included, e.g. **mangy** is cross-referred to **mange**.

Organization of entries

Many headwords have more than one meaning and more than one derived or related word. Nested words and expressions are arranged in two categories – idioms/phrases and compounds/derivatives.

The idioms group consists of phrases that include the headword, e.g. **to bring about**, **over and above**, and some cross-references to compound words not beginning with the headword. Idioms are placed immediately after the last meaning of the last part of speech of the headword, and are in strict alphabetical order.

The compound and derivative group comprises single units beginning with the headword or its root, either in combination with another word or words, e.g. **airport**, **brother-in-law**, **office hours**, or with a suffix, e.g. **happily**, **strangeness**. Compounds and derivatives are placed immediately after the last meaning of the last idiom (or of the headword if no idioms are included). Those with predictable meanings are generally not defined, in order to save space. Compounds and derivatives may have their own idioms and secondary compounds/derivatives, and these follow the appropriate nested word, organized as they would be for a headword. This means some deviation from strict alphabetical order to show relationships, e.g. **simplification** follows its root verb **simplify**.

Usage notes relevant to individual idioms or compounds/derivatives may either follow the whole entry or the nested entry itself, on a new line.

Spellings

The recommended modern British spellings are given first. North American alternatives are specified where applicable.

Where a variant spelling is provided, the alternative is generally given only once, but can be assumed to be possible for any nested words or phrases in the entry.

Compounds given in only one form (solid, e.g. **eyesight**, hyphenated, e.g. **basket-maker**, as two, e.g. **sleeping bag**) may often quite correctly be spelt in one of the other styles.

Some common misspellings are entered in alphabetical positions where users may try to look a particular word up.

Labels

Descriptive labels in brackets have been added where appropriate. They fall into three main categories – stylistic labels, e.g. (*coll.*), (*poet.*), (*offensive*), geographical labels, e.g. (*N Am.*), (*New Zeal.*), and field or subject labels, e.g. (*Law*), (*Comput.*). A list of abbreviations used appears on pp. ix–x.

Cross-references

The word cross-referred to appears with small capitals for usual lower case, e.g. **am** BE, **saintpaulia** *n.* AFRICAN VIOLET.

Symbols

Obsolete and archaic words, phrases and meanings are preceded by a dagger sign † Misspellings are preceded by a cross ☒

Pronunciation

See pp. xi–xiii.

Chief Abbreviations

All are given here in roman, though some of them may also appear in italics as labels.

Other standard abbreviations used, such as those for books of the Bible, points of the compass, units of measurement etc. will be found in their alphabetical places in the main text.

a.	adjective	conn.	connected
abbr.	abbreviation	constr.	construction, constructed;
abl.	ablative		construed
acc.	accusative; according	contr.	contraction
adapt.	adaptation	corr.	corruption; corresponding
adv.	adverb	cp.	compare
alln.	allusion		
alt.	altered, alteration; alternative	d.	died
anal.	analogous, analogy	dat.	dative
Ang.-Ind.	Anglo-Indian	def.	definition
Ang.-Ir	Anglo-Irish	deriv.	derivation, derivative
appar.	apparently	derog.	derogatory
Archit.	Architecture	dial.	dialect, dialectal
assim.	assimilated, assimilation	dim.	diminutive
Astrol.	Astrology		
Astron.	Astronomy	ellipt.	elliptical, elliptically
at. no.	atomic number	emphat.	emphatic, emphatically
attrib.	attributive, attribute	erron.	erroneous, erroneously
augm.	augmentative	esp.	especially
Austral.	Australia, Australian	etym.	etymology
aux.	auxiliary	euphem.	euphemistic, euphemistically
		exc.	except
b.	born		
Biol.	Biology	f.	feminine
Bot.	Botany	facet.	facetious, facetiously
		fam.	familiar
c.	circa, about	fem.	feminine
Can.	Canada, Canadian	fig.	figurative, figuratively
cent.	century	freq.	frequentative
cents.	centuries	fut.	future
Chem.	Chemistry	fut.p.	future participle
chem.	chemical		
cogn.	cognate	gen.	genitive
coll.	colloquial; collateral	Geol.	Geology
collect.	collective	Geom.	Geometry
comb.	combination	ger.	gerund, gerundive
comb. form	combining form	Gram.	Grammar
comp.	comparative		
Comput.	Computing	Her.	Heraldry
cond.	conditional	Hist.	History
conf.	confusion		
confs.	confusions	ident.	identical; identified
conj.	conjunction; conjugation	imit.	imitative, imitatively

imper.	imperative	poss.	possessive; possibly
impers.	impersonal	p.p.	past participle
incept.	inceptive	pred.	predicative
ind.	indicative	pref.	prefix
inf.	infinitive	prep.	preposition
influ.	influenced	pres.	present
instr.	instrumental	pres.p.	present participle
int.	interjection	pret.	preterite
intens.	intensive	Print.	Printing
interrog.	interrogative, interrogatively	priv.	privative
intr.	intransitive	prob.	probably
Ir.	Irish	pron.	pronoun; pronounced
iron.	ironical, ironically	pronun.	pronunciation
irreg.	irregular, irregularly	prop.	proper, properly
		prov.	provincial
L	Latin	Psych.	Psychology
lit.	literal, literally		
		redupl.	reduplication, reduplicative
m.	masculine	ref.	reference, referring
Math.	Mathematics	reflex.	reflexive
Med.	Medicine	rel.	related
med.	medieval	rel. pron.	relative pronoun
Mil.	Military		
Mineral.	Mineralogy	S Afr.	South Africa, South African
mod.	modern	Sc.	Scottish
Mus.	Music	Shak.	Shakespeare
		sing.	singular
n.	noun	sl.	slang
N Am.	North America, North American	subj.	subjunctive
		suf.	suffix
Naut.	Nautical	superl.	superlative
neg.	negative, negatively	syl.	syllable
neut.	neuter		
New Zeal.	New Zealand	Theol.	Theology
nom.	nominative	tr.	transitive
North.	Northern	trans.	translation
NT	New Testament		
		ult.	ultimately
obj.	objective	US	United States of America
obs.	obsolete	usu.	usually
onomat.	onomatopoeic		
opp.	opposed, opposition	v.	verb
orig.	originally, origin	var.	variant
OT	Old Testament	verb.a.	verbal adjective
		verb.n.	verbal noun
part.	participle, participial	v.i.	verb intransitive
pass.	passive	voc.	vocative
perf.	perfect	v.refl.	verb reflexive
perh.	perhaps	v.t.	verb transitive
pers.	person; personal		
Philos.	Philosophy	W	West
phr.	phrase	W Ind.	West Indian
pl.	plural		
poet.	poetical, poetry	Zool.	Zoology
pop.	popular, popularly		

Guide to Pronunciation

Introduction

The respelling scheme used for pronunciation is designed to provide a compromise between accuracy and understanding by the majority of users. As few specialized phonetic symbols and additional accents or marks on letters are used as will fulfil this aim. A full list of symbols/letters and their equivalents follows below, with transcriptions given alongside the words used as examples.

The particular variety of pronunciation aimed for is that of the 'ordinary educated English speaker', which some users will recognize under the label of 'Received Pronunciation'.

Where variant spellings or nested headwords differ in pronunciation (and this includes stress) from the main headword, partial or full pronunciations are also given for these. Where partial pronunciations appear, it should be assumed that the remaining (untranscribed) part of the word concerned is pronounced as before, or with only predictable (and often unconscious) slight vowel modifications associated with the new pronunciation pattern.

In longer entries, there may be more than one variety of difference in pronunciation from the headword. In such cases, any nested word *not* given a transcription should be assumed to revert to the pronunciation pattern of the headword. The exceptions to this are variants and secondary derivatives of a nested word which closely follow it and usually have minimal difference from it in form; for example, under **drama** (drah´mə), nested **dramatic** has the partial pronunciation (drəmat´-), and is followed immediately by **dramatical** and after its meanings by **dramatically**, in which case **dramatical** and **dramatically** follow **dramatic** in pattern and *not* **drama**.

It can also be seen from this illustration that derivatives formed by adding suffixes (e.g. **-ly**, **-ness**) or including other formative elements which are consistently pronounced, are assumed to be known by the user.

Stress

Stress (´) is shown in pronunciations immediately *after* the syllable which is stressed, e.g. (tī´gə) = **tiger**. Stress is *not* given on words of one syllable nor, usually, on compounds composed of two or more separate words.

Usage notes

A small number of usage notes comment on pronunciation: usually where an individual meaning has an idiosyncratic pronunciation or where North American practice seems particularly noteworthy.

Symbols

Vowel sounds

ah	far	(fah)		ī	bite	(bīt)
a	fat	(fat)		o	not	(not)
ā	fate	(fāt)		ō	note	(nōt)
aw	fall	(fawl)			sower	(sō´ə)
	north	(nawth)		oo	blue	(bloo)
	paw	(paw)		ŭ	sun	(sŭn)
	soar	(saw)		u	foot	(fut)
e	bell	(bel)			bull	(bul)
ē	beef	(bēf)		ū	muse	(mūz)
œ	her	(hœ)		ə	again	(əgen´)
	fur	(fœ)			silent	(sī´lənt)
i	bit	(bit)			sailor	(sā´lə)
	happy	(hap´i)			amaze	(əmāz´)

Note: the natural sound of many unstressed vowels is represented, as shown above, by the symbol ə; some unstressed vowels in this dictionary are (more accurately) transcribed as (-i-), as in (ilek´trik).

Diphthongs

(i) Vowel sounds incorporating the final unpronounced 'r' of standard British English:

(ii) Others:

eə	fair	(feə)		ow	bout	(bowt)
	mare	(meə)			cow	(kow)
	mayor	(meə)		oi	join	(join)
iə	fear	(fiə)				
	seer	(siə)				
īə	fire	(fīə)				
ūə	pure	(pūə)				
uə	poor	(puə)				

Foreign vowels not dealt with by the main system

(i) Nasalized

ã	(vēvã´)	(bon) viv*ant*
ĩ	(īzhānü´)	*ing*énue
õ	(bõ)	b*on* (vivant)

(ii) Rounded

ü	(vü´)	(déjà) *vu*
	(īzhānü´)	ingé*nue*

Consonants

b	bit	(bit)		ng	sing	(sing)
ch	church	(chœch)		p	pit	(pit)
d	dance	(dahns)		r	run	(rŭn)
dh	this	(dhis)		s	sit	(sit)
f	fit	(fit)		sh	ship	(ship)
g	get	(get)		t	tin	(tin)
h	hit	(hit)		th	thin	(thin)
j	just	(jŭst)		v	van	(van)
k	kit	(kit)		w	win	(win)
kh	loch	(lokh)		y	yet	(yet)
l	lid	(lid)		z	haze	(hāz)
m	man	(man)		zh	measure	(mezhʹə)
n	nut	(nŭt)				

Note: where a sound represented by two symbols, e.g. (-ng-), is followed by another syllable which begins with the second symbol, here (-g-), and where the stress mark falls elsewhere, a centred dot is used to show where the syllable break occurs, for example as in (ang·glōəmerʹikən).

Proprietary Terms

This book includes some words which are or are asserted to be proprietary names. The presence or absence of such assertions should not be regarded as affecting the legal status of any proprietary name or trade mark.

THE DICTIONARY

A¹ (ā), **a** (*pl.* **As, A's**) the first letter of the English and other versions of the Roman alphabet, corresponding to the Greek alpha (α, A), derived from the Phoenician. It has five principal sounds: (1) open as in *far, father, mikado*, marked in this dictionary ah; (2) short as in *fat, man, ample*, left unmarked, a; (3) long, as in *fate, fame*, marked ā; (4) broad as in *fall, appal*, marked aw; (5) the long sound historically modified by the letter *r*, as in *fair, bear*, marked eə. In unstressed syllables *a* is often obscured, as in *desperate, amidst*, marked ə. In conjunction with other vowels *a* also represents a variety of sounds, as in *death, hair, pea, boat* etc. ~**symbol 1** the first in a series, the highest in a range, e.g. of marks, etc. **2** (*Math.*) the first known quantity in an algebraic expression. **3** (*Mus.*) **a** the sixth note in the diatonic scale of C major. **b** the scale of a composition in which the keynote is A. **4** a blood type in the ABO system. **from A to B** from one point or position to another. **from A to Z** from beginning to end. **A1** *a.* **1** first-class. **2** (*coll.*) excellent, first-rate. **3** (*Naut.*) first-class in Lloyd's Register of ships. **A3** *n.* a standard paper size, 420 x 297 mm. **A4** *n.* a standard paper size, 297 x 210 mm. **A5** *n.* a standard paper size, 210 x 148 mm. **A-bomb** *n.* an atomic bomb, as distinct from a hydrogen bomb. **A-frame** *n.* **1** a frame shaped like a capital A. **2** (*esp. N Am.*) a house constructed on a framework of this shape. ~*a.* having an A-frame. **A level** *n.* (a pass in) an examination in a subject at the Advanced level of the General Certificate of Education. **A-line** *a.* (esp. of a dress or skirt) that is wide at the bottom and close-fitting at the top. **A-side** *n.* the side of a gramophone record or tape that is usu. played first or that has the more important material recorded on it. **A-team** *n.* **1** the first or best team in a sport. **2** a team of skilled capable people brought together for a specific task.

A² *abbr.* **1** ampere. **2** answer.

Å *abbr.* ångstrom(s).

a¹ (ə, ā), **an** (ən, an) *a.* a weakened form of *one*, sometimes called the indefinite article, used before singular nouns or noun phrases to denote an individual of a class. *A* is used before words beginning with a consonant, *h* aspirate, or *eu* or *u*, with the sound of *yu*, also before *one* (wŭn). *An* is used before vowels and sometimes before *h* in an unaccented syllable, e.g. *an historian*. In such phrases as *50 pence a pound, twice a week*, it has a distributive force. In such phrases as *all of a piece* it means 'the same'. Also used

before collective phrases like *a hundred men, a dozen eggs, a few, a good many*, i.e. a hundred of men etc.

a² *abbr.* **1** ante (before). **2** are (metric unit of area).

a-¹ (ə) *pref.* **1** on, in, engaged in, as in *afoot, aboard, adying.* **2** away, out, intensifying the action of verbs, as in *arise, awake.* **3** of, from, as in *akin, athirst.*

a-² (ə) *pref.* **1** from, as in *avert.* **2** at, to, as in *amass, ascent.* **3** out of, utterly, as in *amend, abash.*

a-³ (ā, a, ə) *pref.* not, without, as in *achromatic, amoral.*

-a¹ (ə) *suf.* forming nouns from Greek, Latin and Romance feminine singulars, esp. in ancient or Latinized names for plants and animals, as in *calendula, amoeba*; in geographical names, as in *Asia*; in names of oxides, as in *magnesia*; in ancient or Latinized feminine forenames, as in *Gloria, Claudia.*

-a² (ə) *suf.* forming plural nouns as in the Greek or Latin neuter plural for words ending in *-on*, as in *criteria*, or *-um*, as in *errata*, and for the names of zoological groups, as in *Carnivora, Lepidoptera.*

-a³ (ə) *suf.* (*coll.*) representing elided forms used in colloquial speech, esp. of *of*, as in *sorta, pinta*; of *to*, as in *gotta, gonna*; of *have*, as in *musta, shoulda.*

AA *abbr.* **1** Alcoholics Anonymous. **2** (*Mil.*) anti-aircraft. **3** Automobile Association.

AAA *abbr.* **1** Amateur Athletic Association. **2** American Automobile Association. **3** Australian Automobile Association.

A and M *abbr.* (Hymns) Ancient and Modern.

A and R *abbr.* **1** artists and recording. **2** artists and repertoire.

aardvark (ahd´vahk) *n.* the African anteater, *Orycteropus afer.*

aardwolf (ahd´wulf) *n.* (*pl.* **aardwolves** (-wulvz)) a hyena-like carnivorous mammal, *Proteles cristatus*, of southern Africa.

Aaronic (eəron´ik), **Aaronical** (-əl) *a.* of or relating to Aaron, his descendants, or the Jewish priesthood. **Aaron's beard** *n.* **1** rose of Sharon or large flowered St-John's wort, *Hypericum calycinum.* **2** a Chinese herb, *Saxifraga sarmentosa*, with hanging stems bearing clusters of hairy leaves. **Aaron's rod** *n.* any of certain plants that flower on long stems, e.g. great mullein, *Verbascum thapsus*, and golden rod.

A'asia *abbr.* Australasia.

aasvogel (ahs´fōgəl) *n.* (*S Afr.*) a vulture.

AAU *abbr.* (*US*) Amateur Athletic Union.

AB *abbr.* **1** able(-bodied) seaman; able rating. **2** (*US*) Bachelor of Arts.

Ab *abbr.* antibody.

ab-[1] (ab, əb) *pref.* off, from, away, apart, as in *abrogate, abuse* (cp. Gr. *apo*, Eng. *of, off*, G *ab*); in L and F derivatives often assimilated to a subsequent consonant or reduced to *a*, as in *assoil, avert, abstract*.

ab-[2] (əb) *pref.* to, as in *abbreviate*.

aback (əbak´) *adv.* **1** by surprise (*I was taken aback by the news*). **2** (*Naut.*) with the sails pressed against the mast. **3** †backwards. **4** †behind.

abacus (ab´əkəs) *n.* (*pl.* **abaci** (-sī)) **1** a counting-frame; an apparatus of beads sliding on wires for facilitating arithmetical calculations. **2** (*Archit.*) a flat stone crowning the capital of a column and supporting the architrave.

abaft (əbahft´) *adv., prep.* **1** (*Naut.*) in, on or towards the rear of a ship. **2** behind.

abalone (əbəlō´ni) *n.* an edible gastropod mollusc of the genus *Haliotis*, that has an ear-shaped shell, perforated with breathing holes.

abandon (əban´dən) *v.t.* **1** to give up completely (*abandon hope*). **2** to desert or forsake (a person); to leave or leave behind (a ship, possessions). **3** to surrender (oneself) unreservedly, e.g. to indolence or vice. **4** to give up (something) before it is completed or ended. **5** to yield to the control of another person. ~*n.* freedom from conventional restraint, careless freedom of manner. **abandoned** *a.* **1** (of a person) deserted or forsaken; left behind, left empty, left unused. **2** uninhibited, unrestrained. **3** wholly given up to wickedness, profligate. **abandonment** *n.*

abase (əbās´) *v.t.* to lower, humble or degrade. **abasement** *n.*

abash (əbash´) *v.t.* to embarrass or put to shame by exciting a sense of guilt, mistake or inferiority. **abashed** *a.*

abate (əbāt´) *v.t.* **1** to lessen, esp. to make less violent or intense. **2** to deduct or subtract (from a price or sum). **3** (*Law*) to annul (a writ); to terminate (a nuisance). ~*v.i.* to lessen or diminish, esp. to become less violent or intense. **abatable** *a.* **abatement** *n.*

abatis (ab´atis, -tē) *n.* (*pl.* **abatis, abatises, abattis, abattises**) a defence work made of felled trees with their boughs directed outwards.

abattoir (ab´ətwah) *n.* a public slaughterhouse.

abbacy (ab´əsi) *n.* (*pl.* **abbacies**) the office and jurisdiction of an abbot. **abbatial** (əbā´shəl) *a.* of or relating to an abbey or abbot.

abbé (ab´ā) *n.* **1** a French abbot. **2** in France, a title used in addressing any cleric; any man entitled to wear clerical dress.

abbess (ab´is, -es) *n.* the lady superior of an abbey.

abbey (ab´i) *n.* **1** a monastic community governed by an abbot or abbess. **2** a building either now or formerly inhabited by a body of monks or nuns. **3** a church attached to an abbey.

abbot (ab´ət) *n.* **1** the superior of an abbey. **2** the superior of a monastery. **abbotship** *n.*

abbreviate (əbrē´viāt) *v.t.* to shorten (esp. a word or phrase) by omitting certain parts of it. **abbreviation** (-ā´shən) *n.* **1** the act of abridging or contracting. **2** an abridged or shortened form, esp. of a word. **3** an abridgement.

ABC[1] *n.* (*pl.* **ABCs, ABC's**) **1** (*usu. pl. in US*) the alphabet. **2** (*pl. in US*) rudiments, first principles. **3** an alphabetical guide.

ABC[2] *abbr.* **1** American Broadcasting Company. **2** Australian Broadcasting Commission.

abdicate (ab´dikāt) *v.t.* to resign, to renounce formally, to give up. ~*v.i.* to abandon or relinquish a throne, or other dignity or privilege. **abdication** (-ā´shən) *n.* **abdicator** *n.*

abdomen (ab´dəmən) *n.* **1** the part of the body which lies between the thorax and the pelvis and contains the stomach, bowels etc. **2** the belly. **3** (*Zool.*) the posterior division of the body in the higher Arthropoda. **abdominal** (-dom´-) *a.*

abduct (əbdŭkt´) *v.t.* **1** to kidnap; to take away illegally (esp. a woman or child) by guile or force. **2** (of muscles) to draw (a limb) away from the central line of the body. **abduction** *n.* **abductor** *n.*

abeam (əbēm´) *adv.* on a line at right angles to the keel of a ship or the length of an aircraft; opposite the middle (of a ship etc.).

†abed (əbed´) *adv.* in bed, gone to bed.

abele (əbēl´, ā´bəl) *n.* the white poplar, *Populus alba.*

abelia (əbē´liə) *n.* a shrub of the genus *Abelia*, that is evergreen and has pink or white flowers.

abelian (əbē´liən) *a.* (*Math.*) (of a group) whose members are commutative in binary operations.

Aberdeen (əbədēn´) *n.* a breed of rough-haired Scotch terrier. **Aberdeen Angus** *n.* a breed of hornless, black Scottish beef cattle. **Aberdonian** (-dō´-) *n.* a native or inhabitant of Aberdeen. ~*a.* belonging to Aberdeen.

aberrant (əber´ənt) *a.* **1** (*Biol.*) deviating from the normal type. **2** inconsistent with the usual or accepted standard. **aberrance** *n.* **aberrancy** *n.*

aberration (əbərā´shən) *n.* **1** deviation from, or inconsistency with, the norm. **2** a departure from a person's normal behaviour or way of thinking, that often seems strange or inexplicable. **3** (*Biol.*) deviation from the normal type. **4** (*Astron.*) the difference between the true and observed position of a heavenly body, due to the observer's velocity caused by the earth's rotation. **5** the failure of focused rays to unite in a point due to a defect in a lens or mirror.

abet (əbet´) *v.t.* (*pres.p.* **abetting**, *past, p.p.* **abetted**) **1** to encourage or aid (a person) in crime or wrongdoing by word or deed. **2** to countenance, stimulate or instigate (chiefly in a bad sense). **abetment** *n.* **abetter, abettor** *n.* **1** an accessory to a crime. **2** a person who encourages or instigates another.

abeyance (əbā´əns) *n.* the state of being suspended or temporarily unused. **abeyant** *a.*

ABH *abbr.* actual bodily harm.

abhor (əbhaw´, əbaw´) *v.t.* (*pres.p.* **abhorring**, *past, p.p.* **abhorred**) to hate extremely, loathe, detest. **abhorrence** (-hor´-), **abhorrency** *n.* **1** extreme hatred, aversion, repugnance, loathing. **2** an abhorred thing. **abhorrent** *a.* **1** exciting repugnance, loathing or hatred. **2** opposed to, inconsistent with. **abhorrer** *n.*

abide (əbīd´) *v.t.* (*past, p.p.* **abided**, (*rare*) **abode** (əbōd´)) **1** to endure, bear, tolerate. **2** to submit to. **3** †to await, encounter, withstand. *~v.i.* **1** to dwell or live in a place. **2** to stay, wait. **3** to continue, remain firm. **to abide by 1** to comply with, act upon (terms, a decision). **2** to stay faithful to (a promise). **abidance** *n.* **abiding** *a.* continuing, permanent, durable. *~n.* continuance, residence. **abidingly** *adv.*

ability (əbil´iti) *n.* (*pl.* **abilities**) **1** the capacity or power (to do something). **2** physical or mental capacity or talent. **3** (*pl.*) special talents or competence.

-ability -ABLE.

ab initio (ab inish´iō) *adv.* from the beginning.

abiogenesis (ābīōjen´əsis) *n.* the theoretical process by which animate matter can be produced from something inanimate; the supposed spontaneous generation of animate matter. **abiogenic** *a.*

abiotic (ābīot´ik) *a.* not living, not produced by living organisms.

✗ abismal common misspelling of ABYSMAL (under ABYSM).

abject (ab´jekt) *a.* **1** miserable and wretched. **2** very humble and submissive (*an abject apology*). **3** servile, degraded, contemptible. **abjectly** *adv.* **abjectness, abjection** *n.*

abjure (əbjooə´) *v.t.* **1** (*formal*) to renounce, recant, retract or abrogate upon oath. **2** to vow to avoid or refrain from (*to abjure the company of women*).

Usage note The verbs *abjure* and *adjure* should not be confused: *abjure* means to renounce under oath, and *adjure* to urge or entreat solemnly.

ablation (əblā´shən) *n.* **1** the surgical removal of any body tissue or part. **2** (*Geol.*) the wearing away of rock, glaciers etc., esp. by the action of water. **3** (*Astron.*) the melting away of expendable parts of a spacecraft on re-entry into the earth's atmosphere. **ablate** *v.t.*

ablative (ab´lətiv) *a.* **1** taking away, separating, subtractive. **2** (*Gram.*) of or in the case called ablative. *~n.* (*Gram.*) the case in Latin and other languages expressing separation, instrumentality, and other relations expressed in English by the prepositions from, by, with etc. **ablatival** (ablətī´-) *a.*

ablaut (ab´lowt) *n.* a vowel change in the middle of a word indicating modification in meaning, as *sit, set, rise, raise, ring, rang, rung.*

ablaze (əblāz´) *a., adv.* **1** on fire, in a blaze. **2** brilliant. **3** excited.

able (ā´bəl) *a.* (*comp.* **abler**, *superl.* **ablest**) **1** having sufficient physical, mental, moral or spiritual power, or acquired skill, or sufficient financial and other resources to do something indicated. **2** gifted, vigorous, active. **able-bodied** *a.* **1** having a sound, strong body. **2** experienced, skilled. **able-bodied rating, able-bodied seaman** *n.* (*Naut.*) a rating able to perform the full range of duties. **abled** *a.* having all the usual abilities or abilities of a certain kind (*differently abled*). **ableism, ablism** *n.* discrimination in favour of able-bodied people. **ableist** *a.*, *n.* **able rating, able seaman** *n.* (*Naut.*) an able-bodied rating. **ably** (ā´bli) *adv.* **1** in an able manner. **2** with ability.

-able (əbəl) *suf.* **1** that may be, is fit or suitable for, as in *eatable, movable, saleable.* **2** causing or showing, as in *comfortable, reasonable.* **3** that is subject to, as in *taxable, indictable.* **4** †that may, as in *suitable.* **-ability** (əbil´iti) *suf.* forming nouns. **-ably** (əbli) *suf.* forming adverbs.

ablution (əbloo´shən) *n.* **1** (*often pl.*) the act of washing, cleansing or purifying by means of water or other liquids. **2** a ceremonial or symbolic washing or cleansing, esp. carried out by a priest. **3** a building containing washing facilities, as in a military camp. **ablutionary** *a.*

ABM *abbr.* antiballistic missile.

abnegate (ab´nigāt) *v.t.* to deny oneself, to refuse, to renounce, to abjure. **abnegation** (-ā´shən) *n.* **1** denial, renunciation. **2** self-sacrifice. **abnegative** (-gā´-) *a.* implying denial, negative. **abnegator** *n.*

abnormal (abnaw´məl) *a.* **1** not normal, usual or typical, anomalous, departing from the ordinary type. **2** relating to, or dealing with, abnormal phenomena. **abnormality** (-mal´-) *n.* (*pl.* **abnormalities**) **1** departure from the normal, usual or typical. **2** an abnormal thing or event. **3** irregularity, deformity. **abnormally** *adv.*

Abo (ab´ō) *n.* (*pl.* **Abos**) (*offensive*) an Australian Aborigine. *~a.* Aboriginal.

aboard (əbawd´) *adv., prep.* **1** on board, on or in (a boat, ship, train, aircraft etc.). **2** into or on to (a boat, ship, train, aircraft etc.). **3** (*Naut.*) (of a ship) alongside (another vessel).

abode[1] ABIDE.

abode[2] (əbōd´) *n.* (*formal or facet.*) home, place of residence; a habitation.

abolish (əbol´ish) *v.t.* **1** to do away with, put an end to, destroy. **2** to annul, cancel or revoke (used of laws, customs, institutions or offices). **abolishable** *a.* **abolisher** *n.* **abolishment** *n.* **abolition** (abəlish´-) *n.* **1** the act of abolishing or doing away with. **2** the state of being abolished. **abolitionism** *n.* **abolitionist** *n.* a person who entertains views in favour of the abolition of a law, institution etc., esp. one who favoured the abolition of slavery during the movement against it in the 18th and 19th cents.

abomasum (abəmā´səm) *n.* (*pl.* **abomasa** (-sə)) the fourth stomach in a ruminating animal.

abominate (əbom´ināt) *v.t.* to loathe, to detest, to hate exceedingly. **abominable** *a.* **1** very loathsome, physically or morally, hateful and repellent. **2** (*coll.*) very bad, awful (*abominable luck*). **abominableness** *n.* **abominable snowman** *n.* the yeti. **abominably** *adv.* **abomination** (-ā´shən) *n.* **1** extreme hatred or loathing. **2** something that is vile, hateful or repellent. **3** an object of extreme hatred, loathing or aversion.

aborigine (abərij´ini), **Aborigine** *n.* **1** an indigenous or original inhabitant of a continent, country or district. **2** an aboriginal inhabitant of Australia. **3** (*pl.*) the earliest fauna and flora of an area. **aboriginal, Aboriginal** *a.* **1** original, indigenous, inhabiting a place from the earliest times. **2** of or relating to the Aboriginal inhabitants of Australia. ~*n.* **1** an original inhabitant. **2** an aboriginal inhabitant of Australia. **3** a member of the original fauna or flora. **4** any one of the languages of the Australian Aboriginals. **aboriginally** *adv.* **1** from the beginning, from the first. **2** originally.

Usage note Both *Aborigine(s)* and *Aboriginal(s)* are acceptable as nouns for the indigenous people of Australia. Use of *Aborigine* as an adjective, however, is best avoided.

abort (əbawt´) *v.t.* **1** to cause (a foetus) to be expelled from the womb before it is able to survive independently; to cause (a mother) to undergo an abortion. **2** to give birth to before the proper time; to miscarry. **3** to terminate prematurely or in the early stages. **4** to abandon (a military or space mission) before it is completed, because of technical or other difficulties. **5** (*Biol.*) to cause to undergo partial or total arrest of development. ~*v.i.* **1** (of a foetus) to be expelled from the womb prematurely; (of a mother) to miscarry. **2** to end prematurely or unsuccessfully. **3** (*Biol.*) (of an organism) to undergo partial or entire arrest of development. ~*n.* **1** an undertaking, esp. a space flight, that is terminated prematurely. **2** the act of terminating an undertaking prematurely. **abortifacient** (-tifā´shənt) *n.* a device or drug to induce abortion. ~*a.* inducing abortion.

abortion (əbaw´shən) *n.* **1** a procedure to induce the premature expulsion of a foetus. **2** the expulsion of a foetus before the proper time. **3** the act of miscarrying. **4** an aborted foetus. **5** anything that fails or is terminated prematurely. **6** (*Biol.*) arrest in the development of an organism. **7** a monster, a misshapen creature. **abortionist** *n.* **1** a person who performs abortions. **2** a supporter of the right of women to have an abortion.

abortive (əbaw´tiv) *a.* **1** fruitless, ineffectual, failing in its effect. **2** resulting in or intended to result in abortion. **3** brought forth in an immature or rudimentary state. **4** (*Biol.*) arrested in development. **abortively** *adv.*

ABO system (ābēō´) *n.* a system for typing human blood according to the presence or absence of certain antigens.

aboulia (əboo´liə), **abulia** (-oo´-, -ū´-) *n.* loss of will-power, as a symptom of mental illness. **aboulic, abulic** *a.*

abound (əbownd´) *v.i.* **1** to be present in great quantities. **2** to be rich (in), to be copiously supplied (with).

about (əbowt´) *prep.* **1** concerning, in connection with; in the nature or content of; so as to affect or change. **2** near in time or space. **3** surrounding, so as to surround, around the outside of. **4** in various directions from, or at various points surrounding (a central point) (*The garden lay about us in ruins*). **5** here and there within (*wandering about the house*). **6** engaged in (*be about one's business*). ~*adv.* **1** (*coll.*) approximately; nearly, almost (*felt about done in*). **2** (*coll.*) here and there, in no particular direction; in different places and, usu., having various experiences (*been about a bit*). **3** nearby or present in a particular locality. **4** all around, in every direction. **5** to face in the opposite direction. **6** in succession or rotation. **7** (*Naut.*) to or on the opposite tack. **to be about to** to be on the point of (doing something). **to be (all) about to** to be essentially, to have as its main point. **about-face, about-turn** *v.i.* (*orig. Mil.*) to turn right round, face the opposite way. ~*n.* **1** a turn to face the opposite way. **2** a complete change in attitude etc.

above (əbŭv´) *prep.* **1** over, at or to a higher point than. **2** in excess of, more than. **3** superior to, more important than. **4** too virtuous or noble for; untouched by because of (one's) reputation, honesty, skill etc. (*above suspicion*). **5** beyond the understanding of. **6** despite the noise or loudness of (*heard above the noise of the crowd*). **7** (*formal*) more than and in preference to (*loved his country above everything*). **8** upstream of. **9** †to a period or time before. ~*adv.* **1** overhead, in a higher place or position; upstairs, on a higher floor (*the apartment above*). **2** at a previous point. **3** on the upper side. **4** in heaven. **5** upstream. ~*n.* **1** the aforesaid. **2** an upper part or side. ~*a.* above mentioned, given at a previous point in something written. **above all 1** principally. **2** before everything else. **above oneself** arrogant; conceited. **above board, above-board** *adv., a.* (done) openly; without dishonesty or trickery. **above ground, above-ground** *adv., a.* **1** (situated, working etc.) on the surface of the earth, not buried, not underground. **2** (*facet.*) alive.

ab ovo (ab ō´vō) *adv.* from the beginning.

abracadabra (abrəkədab´rə) *int.* a word used as a magic word by conjurors when performing tricks.

abrade (əbrād´) *v.t.* to rub or wear away by friction. **abrader** *n.*

abrasion (əbrā´zhən) *n.* **1** the act of rubbing away or wearing down. **2** the state of being rubbed away or worn down. **3** a superficial lesion of the skin; an area of damage caused by rubbing or wearing away. **abrasive** (-siv) *a*. **1** tending to rub or wear away; able to polish by abrading. **2** (of a person's manner) causing friction or irritation. ~*n*. a substance, such as emery, used for grinding or rubbing down.

abreaction (abriak´shən) *n*. (*Psych*.) the ridding oneself of a complex by reliving in feeling or action repressed fantasies or experiences. **abreact** *v.t.* to rid oneself of in this way.

abreast (əbrest´) *adv*. **1** side by side with the fronts in line. **2** up to the standard (of). **3** up to date, aware (of).

⊠ **abreviate** common misspelling of ABBREVIATE.

abridge (əbrij´) *v.t.* **1** to reduce the length of (a book) by excision or recasting. **2** to shorten, curtail. **abridgeable, abridgable** *a*. **abridgement, abridgment** *n*. **1** a condensed version; an abstract, a summary. **2** the act of abridging. **3** the state or process of being abridged. **abridger** *n*.

abroad (əbrawd´) *adv*. **1** in or to a foreign country. **2** widely, at large, far and wide. **3** (*formal*) (of news, rumour) circulating. **from abroad** from a foreign country.

abrogate (ab´rəgāt) *v.t.* to annul by an authoritative act; to repeal, to make void. **abrogation** (-ā´shən) *n*. **abrogator** *n*.

Usage note The verbs *abrogate* and *arrogate* should not be confused: *abrogate* means to annul or repeal, and *arrogate* to claim unjustifiably.

abrupt (əbrŭpt´) *a*. **1** sudden, unexpected. **2** brusque, curt. **3** very steep, precipitous. **4** (*Bot*.) truncated, shaped as if cut off below or above. **5** (*Geol*.) (of strata) suddenly emerging above ground. **abruptly** *adv*. **abruptness** *n*.

ABS *abbr*. anti-lock braking system.

abs- (abs) *pref*. away, off, from, as in *abstain*, *absterge*, *abstruse*.

abscess (ab´ses) *n*. a gathering of pus in any tissue or organ, accompanied by pain and inflammation. **abscessed** *a*.

abscise (absīz´) *v.t., v.i.* to separate from the stem of a plant by abscission. **abscisic acid** (-sī´zik) *n*. a plant hormone that inhibits germination and promotes the shedding of leaves, fruit etc. **abscission** (-sish´ən) *n*. **1** (*Bot*.) the natural process whereby leaves, fruit, branches etc. detach themselves from the stem of a plant. **2** the act of cutting off; the state of being cut off.

abscissa (əbsis´ə) *n*. (*pl*. **abscissas, abscissae** (-ē)) (*Math*.) the x co-ordinate that shows the distance of a point from a vertical axis along a horizontal line.

abscond (əbskond´) *v.i.* **1** to go away secretly or in a hurry. **2** to go out of the jurisdiction of a court, to hide oneself to avoid legal proceedings. **absconder** *n*.

abseil (ab´sāl) *v.i.* to descend a vertical or steeply sloping surface, such as a rock face, using a rope attached at the top and wound round the body. ~*n*. a descent involving abseiling.

absence (ab´səns) *n*. **1** the state of being absent from a place, event etc. **2** a period of being absent. **3** a lack (of); the non-existence (of). **absence of mind** *n*. inattention to what is happening.

absent[1] (ab´sənt) *a*. **1** away from or not present in a place; not in attendance. **2** lacking, missing, not present where it is expected to be found. **3** inattentive to what is happening around one. **absentee** (-tē´) *n*. **1** a person who is habitually absent from duty, work, school or home. **2** a landlord who lets an estate and lives away. ~*a*. habitually absent from duty etc. or from one's estate. **absenteeism** *n*. the fact or practice of being a habitual absentee, esp. from work. **absently** *adv*. in an absent-minded way. **absent-minded** *a*. inattentive, abstracted in mind from immediate objects or business. **absent-mindedly** *adv*. **absent-mindedness** *n*.

absent[2] (absent´) *v.t.* (*reflex*.) to keep oneself away.

absinthe (ab´sinth, absīt´), **absinth** *n*. **1** wormwood. **2** a liqueur flavoured with wormwood.

absolute (ab´səloot) *a*. **1** complete, utter (*an absolute scandal*; *absolute bliss*). **2** independent, unlimited, under no restraint (*absolute power*). **3** arbitrary, despotic. **4** universally valid, not relative or conditional (*an absolute standard*). **5** not subject to doubt or uncertainty (*the absolute truth*). **6** (*Gram*.) **a** (applied to a grammatical case) not determined by any other word in a sentence. **b** (of an adjective) used as a noun as in 'the poor'. **c** (of a transitive verb) used without a direct object, as in 'if looks could kill'. **7** (*Philos*.) existing independently of any other cause. **8** (*Chem*.) free from mixture. **9** (of a legal decree) final. ~*n*. something, such as a standard or value, that is universally valid and not relative or conditional. **absolute alcohol** *n*. (*Chem*.) ethanol that contains 1% or less of water or other impurities. **absolutely** *adv*. **1** totally, unconditionally. **2** used to express agreement or assent. **absolute magnitude** *n*. the magnitude of a star at a distance of 32.6 light years (10 parsecs) from the earth. **absolute majority** *n*. a number of votes polled which exceeds the combined total for all other candidates. **absoluteness** *n*. **absolute pitch** *n*. (*Mus*.) **1** the ability to recognize the pitch of any note, or to reproduce any note, without reference to any other note. **2** a fixed standard of pitch defined by vibrations per second. **absolute temperature** *n*. temperature measured from the absolute zero. **absolute zero** *n*. the zero of the absolute scale of temperature, equal to -273.15° C. **absolutism** *n*. **1** despotic government. **2** the theological doctrine of absolute predestination. **absolutist** *n*. a person who is in favour of arbitrary government. ~*a*. of or relating to absolutism or despotism.

absolution (absəloo´shən) *n*. **1** acquittal, remission, forgiveness. **2** the declaration of pardon of sins by a priest to a penitent or a congregation after private or general public confession.

absolve (əbzolv´) *v.t.* **1** to set free from obligation etc.; to release, pardon; acquit, pronounce not guilty. **2** to pronounce forgiveness of sins to (a penitent). **3** to pardon or pronounce forgiveness for.

absorb (absawb´, -zawb´) *v.t.* **1** to suck or soak up, drink in. **2** to imbibe by capillarity. **3** to incorporate. **4** to fully occupy the attention of, to engross. **5** to take in and transform (radiant energy, sound) without transmission or reflection. **6** to reduce or deaden the force of (impact, a blow). **7** to use up or consume (energy, income, resources). **absorbable** *a.* **absorbability** (-bil´-) *n.* **absorbance** *n.* (*Physics*) capacity to absorb light. **absorbed** *a.* fully engrossed. **absorbedly** *adv.* **absorbent** *a.* absorbing, capable of or tending to absorb, absorptive. ~*n.* **1** a vessel in an organism which takes nutritive matter into the system. **2** a substance which has the power of absorbing gases or liquids. **absorbency** *n.* **absorber** *n.* **1** something which absorbs. **2** the part of a caloric-engine that absorbs heat. **absorbing** *a.* occupying one's complete attention. **absorbingly** *adv.* **absorption** (-sawp´-, -z-) *n.* **1** the act of absorbing. **2** the process of being absorbed. **absorptive** (-sawp´-, -z-) *a.*

abstain (əbstān´) *v.i.* **1** to keep oneself away, refrain (from). **2** to refrain voluntarily from intoxicating liquors. **3** to refrain from voting. **abstainer** *n.*

abstemious (əbstē´miəs) *a.* sparing, not self-indulgent, esp. in the use of food and strong liquors. **abstemiously** *adv.* **abstemiousness** *n.*

abstention (əbsten´shən) *n.* **1** the act of abstaining or refraining, esp. from exercising one's right to vote. **2** a formally recorded instance of a person's not using their vote.

abstinence (ab´stinəns) *n.* **1** the act or practice of refraining from some indulgence. **2** continence, fasting. **abstinent** *a.* practising abstinence. ~*n.* an abstainer. **abstinently** *adv.*

abstract[1] (əbstrakt´) *v.t.* **1** to draw or take away, remove. **2** (*euphem.*) to steal. **3** to separate mentally, to consider apart from other things. **4** to epitomize, summarize. **5** to separate by chemical distillation. **6** to extract. **abstracted** (-strak´-) *a.* absent-minded, inattentive, withdrawn in thought. **abstractedly** *adv.* **1** absent-mindedly. **2** in the abstract, separately.

abstract[2] (ab´strakt) *a.* **1** not related to tangible, concrete or particular instances, theoretical, ideal. **2** (of a noun) denoting an intangible. **3** abstruse. **4** (of art) non-representational, achieving its effect by geometrical design or patterns of shape and colour. ~*n.* **1** an abstract term. **2** a summary, an epitome. **3** an abstract work of art. **abstractly** *adv.* **abstractness** *n.*

abstraction (əbstrak´shən) *n.* **1** the act of abstracting or separating. **2** taking away. **3** (*euphem.*) stealing. **4** the state of being engrossed

in thought; absent-mindedness. **5** the process of considering separately the quality of an object. **6** a mental conception so formed. **7** an abstract idea. **8** the faculty by which people form abstract ideas. **9** an abstract work of art. **abstractionism** *n.* **1** the theory and practice of abstract art. **2** the love of abstract ideas. **abstractionist** *n.*

abstruse (əbstroos´) *a.* **1** difficult to understand, recondite, profound. **2** wilfully difficult to understand. **abstrusely** *adv.* **abstruseness** *n.*

absurd (əbsœd´) *a.* **1** incongruous, ridiculous, ludicrous. **2** contrary to or inconsistent with reason; nonsensical, logically contradictory. **the absurd** existence as regarded in absurdism. **absurdism** *n.* artistic expression of the philosophical idea of absurdity. **absurdist** *n.*, *a.* **absurdity** *n.* (*pl.* **absurdities**) **1** the quality or state of being absurd. **2** folly, extremely inappropriate or ridiculous behaviour. **3** an absurd notion, statement or action. **absurdly** *adv.* **absurdness** *n.*

ABTA (ab´tə) *abbr.* Association of British Travel Agents.

abulia ABOULIA.

abundance (əbŭn´dəns) *n.* **1** a more than sufficient quantity or number (of). **2** wealth, affluence. **abundant** *a.* **1** plentiful, fully sufficient, more than sufficient, ample. **2** overflowing with, having a plentiful supply of (*abundant in mineral resources*). **abundantly** *adv.*

abuse[1] (əbūz´) *v.t.* **1** to put to an improper use, misuse. **2** to insult, to use coarse language to. **3** to use in an illegitimate sense, to pervert the meaning of. **4** to maltreat, act cruelly to. **5** to subject to physical, esp. sexual, assault or mistreatment. **abuser** *n.*

abuse[2] (əbūs´) *n.* **1** improper treatment or employment, misuse. **2** a corrupt practice or custom. **3** insulting or scurrilous language. **4** perversion from the proper meaning. **5** physical maltreatment; sexual assault or mistreatment. **abusive** *a.* **1** scurrilous or insulting (language); using such language. **2** subjecting others to physical or sexual abuse. **3** improper, incorrectly used, misapplied. **abusively** *adv.*

abut (əbŭt´) *v.i.* (*pres.p.* **abutting**, *past, p.p.* **abutted**) **1** to be contiguous. **2** to border (on or upon). **3** to form a point or line of contact. **4** (of a building) to lean (on or upon). ~*v.t.* to be contiguous with, to border on. **abutment** *n.* **1** the state of abutting. **2** something which abuts or borders. **3** a pier or wall, or the part of a pier or wall, against which an arch rests. **4** the junction between a supporting structure and the thing supported. **abutter** *n.* **1** a person who or something which abuts. **2** (*Law*) the owner of property that abuts. **abutting** *a.*

abuzz (əbŭz´) *a.*, *adv.* buzzing with activity, conversation etc.

abysm (əbiz´m) *n.* (*poet.*) an abyss. **abysmal** *a.* **1** extremely bad. **2** profound, immeasurable. **3** of or relating to an abyss. **abysmally** *adv.*

abyss (əbis´) *n.* **1** a vast physical depth, chasm or cavity. **2** anything conceived of as immensely deep and unfathomable or difficult to get out of (*an abyss of despair*). **3** catastrophe, a catastrophic situation (*drew back from the abyss*). **4** primeval chaos; hell. **abyssal** *a.* **1** of or relating to the lowest depths of the sea beyond 300 fathoms (about 550 m). **2** (*Geol.*) of or relating to the depths below the surface of the earth; plutonic.

AC *abbr.* **1** aircraftman. **2** alternating current. **3** ante Christum (before Christ). **4** appellation contrôlée. **5** athletic club. **6** Companion of the Order of Australia.

Ac *chem. symbol* actinium.

a/c *abbr.* account.

ac- (ək) *pref.* AD-, assim. to *c*, *k*, *qu*, as in *accommodate*, *accord*, *acquire*.

-ac (ak) *suf.* of or relating to, as in *cardiac*, *demoniac* (adjectives so formed are often used as nouns).

acacia (əkā´shə) *n.* **1** a tree of the extensive genus *Acacia*, with pinnated leaves or else phyllodes, and small flowers in balls or spikes: some species yield catechu and others gum arabic. **2** the N American locust tree or false acacia, *Robinia pseudoacacia*. **acacia tree** *n.*

academe (ak´ədēm, -dēm´) *n.* **1** academia. **2** (*poet.*) an academy. **academia** (akədē´miə) *n.* **1** the world of academics; the life of scholarship. **2** universities etc. collectively.

academic (akədem´ik) *a.* **1** of or relating to an academy, college or university. **2** scholarly, relating to the more advanced levels of esp. theoretical subjects. **3** impractical, unrelated to practical concerns. **4** (of art and artists) conforming to conventionally taught rules and techniques. **5** (**Academic**) of or relating to the Platonic school of philosophy. ~*n.* **1** a member of the staff of an academy, college or university etc. **2** a person belonging to the academy of Plato, or adhering to the Academic philosophy. **academical** *a.* **1** academic. **2** unpractical. ~*n.* (*pl.*) academical dress, cap and gown. **academically** *adv.* **academician** (əkadəmish´ən) *n.* **1** a person belonging to an academy or association for the promotion of science, literature or art. **2** (**Academician**) a Royal Academician. **academicism** (akadem´-) *n.* **1** conformity with rules and tradition in art. **2** neglect of the easily accessible in favour of the more academic or abstruse. **academic year** *n.* a period of a year or less, measured from the time of the arrival or return of students to an institution to the end of the final term or semester.

academy (əkad´əmi) *n.* (*pl.* **academies**) **1** a society or institution for promoting literature, science or art. **2** a place of higher education or training in a specialized subject (*academy of music*). **3** any school or place of study, now used mainly in the names of particular schools. **academism** *n.* **1** academicism. **2** Platonism.

-acal (əkəl) *suf.* **1** adjectives ending in *-ac* being often used as nouns, *-al* was added to distinguish the adjective, e.g. *demoniacal*, *maniacal*. **2** *-al* is also added to adjectives to show a less intimate connection with the original noun, e.g. *cardiacal*.

acanthus (əkan´thəs) *n.* **1** any plant or shrub of the genus *Acanthus*, which is native to the Mediterranean but widely grown for its large spiny leaves and white or purple flowers. **2** (*Archit.*) a conventional ornament resembling the foliage of the acanthus, used to decorate the capitals of the Corinthian and Composite orders.

a cappella (a kəpel´ə, ah kəpel´ə), **alla cappella** (ala) *a.*, *adv.* (*Mus.*) (of choral music) without instrumental accompaniment.

acarus (ak´ərəs) *n.* a mite of the genus *Acarus*. **acariasis** (akərī´əsis) *n.* disease caused by mites. **acaricide** (əkar´isīd) *n.* a substance that kills mites, a remedy for itching. **acarid** (ak´ərid), **acaridan** (-kar´-), **acaridean** (-rid´i-) *a.* belonging to the order Acarina, which includes mites and ticks. ~*n.* any small arachnid of the order Acarina. **acarology** (-ol´-) *n.*

ACAS (ā´kas) *abbr.* Advisory, Conciliation and Arbitration Service.

acausal (ākaw´zəl) *a.* not causal.

accede (əksēd´) *v.i.* **1** to agree (to), assent (to). **2** to become a party to (a treaty, agreement). **3** to come to or attain (an office or dignity).

accelerando (əcheləran´dō) *a.*, *adv.* (*Mus.*) with increasing speed. ~*n.* (*pl.* **accelerandos**, **accelerandi** (-dē)) a passage to be performed in this way.

accelerate (əksel´ərāt) *v.t.* **1** to increase the speed or rate of progress. **2** to hasten, to bring nearer in point of time. ~*v.i.* to increase in velocity or rate of progress, to move faster. **acceleratedly** *adv.* **acceleration** (-ā´shən) *n.* **1** the act of accelerating, or the state of being accelerated. **2** progressive increase of speed or rate of progress. **3** the ability to gain speed rapidly. **4** (*Physics*) rate of increase of velocity, measured by time-units. **accelerative** *a.* **accelerator** *n.* **1** (in vehicles) a device for increasing the supply of fuel into the carburettor, thus causing the engine to run at an accelerated speed. **2** (*Chem. etc.*) any chemical or apparatus for speeding up a process or reaction, such as the development of photographic film or the setting of concrete. **3** (*Physics*) an electrical appliance for accelerating charged particles such as electrons or protons to high velocities or energies. **accelerator board**, **accelerator card** *n.* (*Comput.*) a circuit board which can increase the speed of a small computer. **accelerometer** (-om´itə) *n.* an instrument for measuring acceleration.

accent[1] (ak´sənt) *n.* **1** a manner of speaking or pronunciation peculiar to an individual, a locality or a nation. **2** a particular prominence given to a syllable by means of stress or higher musical pitch. **3** a mark used in writing or printing to direct the stress of the voice. **4** a mark used in writing or printing certain languages, usu. placed over particular letters, to show how those letters are to be pronounced or to distinguish a word from a homograph. **5** particular prominence, emphasis or attention given to something (*with the accent on quality*). **6** (*esp. Mus.*) musical stress; metrical or rhythmical stress. **7** (*pl.*) words, language.

accent² (əksent´) *v.t.* **1** to lay stress upon (a syllable or word, or a note or passage of music). **2** to mark with emphasis, make conspicuous. **3** to mark with a written or printed accent. **accentual** *a.* **accentuate** *v.t.* **1** to pronounce or mark with an accent. **2** to lay stress on, to emphasize. **accentuation** (-ā´shən) *n.*

accept (əksept´) *v.t.* **1** to consent to take (something offered). **2** to give a positive response to (an invitation, recommendation). **3** to behave in a friendly or approving way towards (*accepted her as a member of the family*). **4** to admit the truth of, to receive as valid or adequate. **5** to admit, to be willing to acknowledge. **6** to be willing to submit to (a referee's decision). **7** to undertake the responsibilities or duties of. **8** to regard as suitable or valid as a means of payment (*don't accept credit cards*). **acceptable** *a.* **1** adequate, satisfactory. **2** welcome, pleasing. **acceptability** (-bil´-), **acceptableness** *n.* **acceptably** *adv.* **acceptance** *n.* **1** the act of receiving a thing offered or due. **2** a positive response. **3** agreement to terms or proposals; an act of accepting an invitation etc. **4** friendly or approving behaviour towards. **5** general approval or belief. **6** admission, acknowledgement. **7** an accepted bill of exchange. **8** the act of subscribing, or the subscription to, a bill of exchange. **acceptant** *a.* willingly receiving. **acceptation** (-tā´shən) *n.* the recognized sense or meaning of an expression. **accepted** *a.* generally recognized or approved. **acceptor** *n.* **1** a person who accepts a bill of exchange. **2** (*Physics*) an impurity added to a semiconductor to increase the number of positively charged current carriers and hence the conductivity. **3** (*Chem.*) a molecule etc. which receives electrons when a bond is formed. **4** an electric circuit which resonates at a particular frequency.

access (ak´ses) *n.* **1** admission to a place or person. **2** freedom to obtain or use something. **3** approach. **4** a means of approach or entry, a passage, channel. **5** a sudden, usu. violent, attack of a disease or emotion. ~*v.t.* (*Comput.*) **1** to gain access to, esp. to retrieve (data) from computer storage. **2** to place data in (computer storage). ~*a.* designating, of or relating to radio and television programmes made by the general public. **accessible** (-ses´-) *a.* **1** capable of being approached or reached; easy to approach, reach or obtain. **2** (of a person) readily available (esp. to subordinates); approachable. **3** not difficult to

understand. **accessibility** (-bil´-) *n.* **accessibly** *adv.* **access road** *n.* a road that gives access to a particular place.

accession (aksesh´ən) *n.* **1** coming to the throne; becoming the holder of an office, rank or dignity; entering upon a particular condition or status. **2** the act of acceding to a treaty, agreement etc. **3** an increase, addition, esp. a book added to the stock of a library. **4** (*Law*) an improvement or addition to property by growth or labour expended; the owner's right to the increased value of property so improved. ~*v.t.* to enter in an accession book; to record the acquisition of (for a library, museum etc.). **accession book** *n.* a register of additions to the stock of books in a library.

accessory (akses´əri), **accessary** *n.* (*pl.* **accessories, accessaries**) **1** a supplementary thing, esp. an additional part designed to improve the appearance, performance, comfort etc. of a vehicle, appliance etc. **2** an item, e.g. a scarf, gloves, that accompanies and usu. matches a woman's dress. **3** a person who is involved in, and shares the guilt of, a crime without actually being present when it is committed. ~*a.* **1** supplementary, additional; accompanying. **2** contributive to some effect; acting in subordination to a principal. **3** assisting in the commission of a crime. **accessorial** (-aw´-) *a.* **accessorize, accessorise** *v.t.* to add accessories to (a dress).

acciaccatura (əchakətoo´rə) *n.* (*pl.* **acciaccaturas, acciaccature** (-rä)) (*Mus.*) a short grace note played rapidly.

accidence (ak´sidəns) *n.* that part of grammar which deals with the inflection of words.

accident (ak´sidənt) *n.* **1** an event proceeding from an unknown cause; the unforeseen effect of a known cause. **2** something that happens unexpectedly or by chance. **3** a mishap, esp. one that results in danger or injury. **4** chance. **5** (*coll.*) an instance of involuntary urination or defecation. **6** (*Geol.*) a surface irregularity in a formation. **7** (*Philos.*) a property or quality of a thing not essential to our conception of it. **by accident 1** unintentionally. **2** by chance, fortuitously. **accidental** (-den´-) *a.* **1** occurring by chance or unexpectedly. **2** not according to the usual order of things. **3** adventitious, non-essential. ~*n.* **1** a non-essential property. **2** (*Mus.*) a sharp, flat or natural sign occurring in music before a particular note, and that is not in the key-signature. **accidentally** *adv.* **accident-prone** *a.* apparently more liable than other people or things to suffer mishaps.

accidie (ak´sidi), **acedia** (əsē´diə) *n.* an abnormal mental condition characterized by extreme apathy and listlessness.

acclaim (əklām´) *v.t.* **1** to applaud loudly; to greet or receive with great enthusiasm. **2** to announce publicly and with great enthusiasm (that someone has obtained a particular office or honour) (*acclaimed him as emperor*). ~*v.i.* to applaud or shout loudly. ~*n.* **1** enthusiastic applause, praise or approval. **2** a shout of joy. **acclaimer** *n.* **acclamation** (akləmā´shən) *n.* **1** the act of acclaiming; enthusiastic applause or approval. **2** the expression of approval (of a proposal) by shouts and applause. **3** (*usu. pl.*) a shout of approval or enthusiasm. **by acclamation** by a large majority or unanimously, without a ballot.

acclimatize (əklī´mətīz), **acclimatise** *v.t.* **1** to habituate to a new climate or environment. **2** to adapt for existence and propagation in a new climate. **acclimation** (aklīma´shən), **acclimatation** (-mətā´-) *n.* (*Biol.*) acclimatization by nature, spontaneous accommodation to new conditions as distinguished from acclimatization by humans. **acclimatization** (-zā´shən) *n.*

acclivity (əkliv´iti) *n.* (*pl.* **acclivities**) **1** an upward slope, as distinct from *declivity*. **2** the talus of a rampart. **acclivitous** *a.* characterized by an acclivity or acclivities.

accolade (ak´əlād) *n.* **1** an award or honour, (an expression of) praise and approval. **2** the ceremony of conferring knighthood by an embrace, putting hand on neck, or a gentle stroke with the flat of a sword.

accommodate (əkom´ədāt) *v.t.* **1** to provide lodging for. **2** to have or provide space for. **3** to fit, adapt or adjust. **4** to bring into harmony or concord, reconcile. **5** to do a favour for, oblige. **6** to supply or furnish (with). **accommodating** *a.* obliging, complying, yielding to others' desires. **accommodatingly** *adv.* **accommodation** (-ā´shən) *n.* **1** (*usu. pl.*, *N Am.*) a place to live or stay, lodgings. **2** space, or a place, to keep or store something. **3** adjustment, adaptation; the state of being fitted or adapted. **4** a reconciliation or compromise, a mutually convenient or agreeable arrangement. **5** the act of doing someone a favour or of supplying or furnishing something. **accommodation address** *n.* an address to which mail may be sent, used by a person or business unable or unwilling to give a permanent address. **accommodation ladder** *n.* a light ladder fixed outside a vessel for access to a small boat, jetty etc. **accommodation road** *n.* a road giving access to a place that is not a public road.

✗ **accomodate** common misspelling of ACCOMMODATE.

accompany (əkŭm´pəni) *v.t.* (*3rd pers. sing. pres.* **accompanies**, *pres.p.* **accompanying**, *past, p.p.* **accompanied**) **1** to go with, escort, attend as a companion. **2** to exist along with; to be a characteristic or result of. **3** to supplement (*accompanied by a bottle of decent claret*). **4** (*Mus.*) to play the instrumental accompaniment for. **accompanier** *n.* **accompaniment** *n.* **1** something superadded to or attendant upon another thing. **2** something which gives greater completeness to. **3** (*Mus.*) the part or parts performed by instruments accompanying the soloist. **accompanist** *n.* the performer who plays the instrumental accompaniment. **accompanying** *a.*

accomplice (əkŭm´plis) *n.* a partner, esp. in crime.

accomplish (əkŭm´plish) *v.t.* **1** to complete, to finish. **2** to carry out, fulfil, achieve. **accomplished** *a.* **1** complete, finished. **2** highly skilled, consummate. **3** having the graces and social skills perfecting one for society. **accomplisher** *n.* **accomplishment** *n.* **1** the act of accomplishing or fulfilling. **2** the state of being accomplished. **3** something achieved. **4** an acquirement, attainment, esp. a social skill.

accord (əkawd´) *v.t.* **1** to grant, to bestow. **2** to adapt, to make consistent, to adjust. ~*v.i.* to agree, to correspond or be in harmony (with). ~*n.* **1** agreement, assent. **2** harmony or harmonious correspondence; mutual adjustment or conformity. **3** a treaty. **according as** in proportion to. **according to 1** in proportion or relation to (*according to age and experience*). **2** as stated or reported by. **3** depending on. **4** in conformity with (*went according to plan*). **of one's own accord** voluntarily. **with one accord** with the assent of all. **accordance, accordancy** *n.* agreement, harmony. **in accordance with** in conformity with, in such a way as to correspond to (*carried out in accordance with your instructions*). **accordant** *a.* agreeing, consonant, harmonious, in tune. **accordingly** *adv.* **1** suitably, in accordance. **2** therefore, consequently.

accordion (əkaw´diən) *n.* a small portable keyed instrument in which the notes are produced by bellows acting on metallic reeds. **accordionist** *n.* **accordion-pleating** *n.* pleats with very narrow folds resembling the bellows of an accordion.

accost (əkost´) *v.t.* **1** (*formal*) to approach, to speak to, to address. **2** (*formal*) (of a prostitute) to solicit.

account (əkownt´) *v.t.* **1** to regard as, to deem, consider. **2** †to reckon, compute, count. ~*n.* **1** a recital, description or narrative. **2** an explanation or justification of one's own conduct given usu. to someone in authority. **3** a facility at a bank etc. that enables a customer to deposit, hold and withdraw money; the amount of money in such an account. **4** a business arrangement whereby a supplier, shop etc. allows a customer to buy goods on credit (*have an account at the chemist's*). **5** (*often pl.*) a statement of monetary transactions or receipts and expenditure showing a balance. **6** a statement of goods or services supplied with a calculation of money due, a bill, an invoice. **7** on the Stock Exchange, the fortnightly period from one settlement to another. **8** a regular client or customer, or the work or business associated with that client; an area of business assigned to some other person or company. **9** (*pl.*) the practice of counting or reckoning. **10** profit, advantage (*turn to account*). **11** importance, consequence (*of little account*). **12** behalf, sake. **by all accounts** according to what most people say, in most people's opinion.

of no account valueless, negligible. **on account 1** on credit. **2** as an interim payment. **on account of** for the sake of, because of. **on no account** by no means. **on one's own account 1** for one's own purpose or benefit. **2** at one's own risk; on one's own responsibility. **to account for 1** to give, or to serve as, an explanation of. **2** to render an account for (expenditure, payments made etc.). **3** to give a formal explanation or justification of. **4** to kill or destroy or defeat (an enemy, opponent). **to bring to account** to call to account. **to call to account 1** to require an explanation from. **2** to reprimand. **to give a good account of** to be successful, do (oneself) credit. **to hold to account** to hold responsible. **to keep account of** to keep a record of. **to leave out of account** to disregard. **to make account of 1** to set a value upon. **2** to consider. **to settle accounts with** to have one's revenge on. **to square accounts with** to settle accounts with. **to take account of 1** to pay attention to, to consider. **2** to make allowance for. **to take into account** to take account of. **to turn to (good) account** to derive advantage from. **accountable** *a.* **1** liable to be called on to give an account of something. **2** responsible. **accountability** (-bil´-) *n.* **accountableness** *n.* **account day** *n.* a day of reckoning. **account executive** *n.* a person in a business, esp. in advertising, who manages a client's account. **accounting** *n.* the practice or skill of keeping and checking accounts. **account rendered** *n.* a bill that has been sent to a client but for which payment has not been received. **accounts payable** *n.pl.* money that a company owes. **accounts receivable** *n.pl.* money that is owing to a company.

Usage note It is best not to use *as* after the verb and its object. *She accounted it to be wrong* and *She accounted it wrong* are generally acceptable, but *She accounted it as wrong* is not.

accountant (əkown´tənt) *n.* **1** a person whose occupation is the keeping or preparation of business accounts. **2** a public officer charged with the duty of keeping and inspecting accounts. **accountancy** *n.* the profession or business of an accountant. **accountantship** *n.*

accoutre (əkoo´tə), (*N Am.*) **accouter** *v.t.* **1** to dress, to equip. **2** to array in military dress. **3** to equip for military service. **accoutrement** (-trəmənt), (*N Am.*) **accouterment** (-təmənt) *n.* **1** (*Mil.*) a soldier's equipment, excepting arms and dress. **2** (*usu. pl.*) dress, outfit, equipment.

accredit (əkred´it) *v.t.* **1** to attribute (a saying, discovery etc.) (to a person). **2** to credit (a person) (with a saying, discovery etc.). **3** to give official recognition to, sanction. **4** to send with credentials (as an ambassador). **accreditation** (-ā´shən) *n.* **accredited** *a.* **1** recognized officially, generally accepted. **2** conforming to an official standard of quality.

accrete (əkrēt´) *v.i.* **1** to grow together. **2** to combine round a nucleus. ~*a.* (*Bot.*) grown together

by adhesion (of parts normally separate). **accretion** *n.* **1** increase by organic growth. **2** increase in growth by external additions. **3** the growing together of parts naturally separate, as the fingers. **4** the result of such growth. **5** a part added by one of these processes. **6** (*Law*) the accession or adhesion of foreign matter to something (chiefly used of land deposited from a river or the sea). **7** (*Law*) an increase in a beneficiary's share of an estate due to another beneficiary's failing to claim a share.

accrue (əkroo´) *v.i.* **1** to grow, to increase. **2** to arise, to fall, come (to) as a natural growth. ~*v.t.* to amass. **accrual** *n.*

acculturate (əkŭl´chərət) *v.i.* to adopt the values and traits of another culture. ~*v.t.* to cause to do this. **acculturation** (-ā´shən) *n.*

accumulate (əkū´mūlāt) *v.t.* **1** to heap up, pile one thing above another. **2** to bring together by degrees, to amass. ~*v.i.* to grow in size, number or quantity, by repeated additions. **accumulation** (-lā´shən) *n.* **1** the act of accumulating or amassing; the state of being accumulated. **2** something that has been accumulated. **3** a mass. **4** the increase of capital by the retention of earned interest. **accumulative** *a.* **1** cumulative, arising by accumulation. **2** organized in such a way as to accumulate. **3** acquisitive; tending to amass or to hoard. **accumulatively** *adv.* **accumulator** *n.* **1** a person who or something that accumulates. **2** an apparatus for storing hydraulic or electric energy, esp. a rechargeable electric cell or battery. **3** a bet, usu. on four or more races, in which the winnings from one race are staked on the next. **4** a location in a computer where numbers are stored or arithmetic operations are performed.

accurate (ak´ūrət) *a.* **1** in precise accordance with a rule or standard or with the truth. **2** without error or defect. **3** careful, precise, exact. **accuracy** (-rəsi) *n.* (*pl.* **accuracies**) **1** exactness; correctness resulting from care; precision. **2** conformity to a standard. **3** precision of fit. **accurately** *adv.* **accurateness** *n.*

accursed (əkœ´sid, əkœst´), **accurst** (əkœst´) *a.* **1** lying under a curse. **2** execrable, detestable.

accusative (əkū´zətiv) *a.* (*Gram.*) **1** of or belonging to the formal case of direct objects in inflected languages. **2** denoting a word representing a direct object in uninflected languages. ~*n.* **1** the accusative case. **2** a word or form in this case.

accuse (əkūz´) *v.t.* **1** to charge with a crime, offence or fault, to indict. **2** to lay the blame formally on (a person or thing). **accusal** *n.* **accusation** (akūzā´shən) *n.* **1** the act of accusing. **2** the state of being accused. **3** a charge brought against someone. **accusatorial** (-taw´-) *a.* (*Law*) involving accusation or indictment in a case in which judge and prosecutor are distinct (contrasted with *inquisitorial*). **accusatory** *a.*

containing or involving an accusation. **accused** *a.* **the accused** the defendant or defendants in a criminal case. **accuser** *n.* **accusingly** *adv.*

accustom (əkŭs´təm) *v.t.* to habituate (oneself, someone) (to), to make familiar by use. **accustomed** *a.* **1** used (to), inured (to) (*become accustomed to army life*). **2** in the habit of (*I'm accustomed to take wine with my dinner*). **3** often practised, usual, familiar, ordinary, habitual. **accustomedness** *n.*

AC/DC (āsēdē´sē) *a.* (*sl.*) bisexual.

ace (ās) *n.* **1** the single point on cards or dice. **2** a card or domino with only one mark upon it. **3** a person who is particularly skilful or successful in any activity, esp. sport. **4** a fighter-pilot who has brought down many hostile aircraft. **5** in tennis, a service or stroke which one's opponent cannot return. **6** (*N. Am*) in golf, a hole in one. *~a.* (*sl.*) excellent, brilliant, first-rate. **within an ace of** very close to, within a hair's breadth of (*came within an ace of colliding with a truck*). **ace in the hole** *n.* (*N Am.*) an ace up one's sleeve. **ace up one's sleeve** *n.* an unsuspected advantage, something effective kept in reserve.

-acean (ā´shən) *suf.* used to form singular nouns or adjectives corresponding to collective nouns in *-acea*, e.g. *crustacean, cetacean.*

acedia ACCIDIE.

acellular (āsel´ūlə) *a.* (*Biol.*) **1** not having or consisting of cells. **2** (esp. of protozoa) consisting of a single cell.

-aceous (ā´shəs, ā´siəs) *suf.* of the nature of, belonging to, like: forming adjectives from nouns in natural science, e.g. *crustaceous, cretaceous, farinaceous, filaceous.*

acephalous (əsef´ələs, əkef´-) *a.* **1** without a head. **2** having no superior or ruler. **3** short of the beginning (as in a verse or manuscript). **4** (*Zool.*) with no distinct head, as in one division of the Mollusca.

acerbic (əsœb´ik) *a.* **1** sour, astringent. **2** bitter or harsh in speech or manner. **acerbically** *adv.*

acerbity (əsœ´biti) *n.* (*pl.* **acerbities**) **1** sourness, with roughness or astringency, as of unripe fruit. **2** harshness of speech, action or temper. **3** bitterness of suffering.

⊠ acessory common misspelling of ACCESSORY.

acet- (əset´, əset´), **aceto-** (-tō) *comb. form* **1** of the nature of vinegar. **2** (*Chem.*) **a** acetic. **b** acetic acid.

acetabulum (əsətab´ūləm) *n.* (*pl.* **acetabula** (-lə)) **1** (*Anat.*) a cavity in any bone designed to receive the protuberant head of another bone, e.g. the socket of the hip-joint in man. **2** any one of the suckers on the arms of a cuttlefish.

acetal (as´ital) *n.* (*Chem.*) any of a class of compounds formed by the reaction of an alcohol with an aldehyde.

acetaldehyde (əsətal´dəhīd) *n.* (*Chem.*) a volatile liquid aldehyde used in the manufacture of organic compounds.

acetate (as´ətāt) *n.* **1** a salt of acetic acid. **2** cellulose acetate. **3** a photographic film or a textile made from cellulose acetate.

acetic (əsē´tik, əset´-) *a.* **1** of or relating to vinegar, akin to vinegar. **2** sour. **acetic acid** *n.* (*Chem.*) the acid which imparts sourness to vinegar.

acetone (as´itōn) *n.* (*Chem.*) an inflammable liquid obtained by distilling acetated or organic substances and used in the manufacture of chloroform and as a solvent.

acetous (as´itəs), **acetose** (-ōs) *a.* **1** having the character of vinegar, sour. **2** causing the process of making into vinegar, or of rendering sour.

acetyl (as´itil, asē´-) *n.* (*Chem.*) the radical of acetic acid. **acetylcholine** (-kō´lēn, -līn) *n.* (*Chem.*) a chemical released at nerve endings that transmits nerve impulses. **acetylsalicylic acid** (asitilsalisil´ik) *n.* (*Chem.*) the chemical name for aspirin.

acetylene (əset´əlēn) *n.* (*Chem.*) a gas composed of carbon and hydrogen, which burns with an intensely brilliant flame; ethyne.

ache (āk) *v.i.* **1** to suffer continuous dull pain; to be the source of an ache. **2** to long (for or to do). *~n.* **1** continuous dull pain (in contradistinction to a twinge). **2** mental distress or longing. **aching** *a.* **achingly** *adv.* with great desire or longing. **achy** *a.* suffering from or subject to an ache or aches.

⊠ acheive common misspelling of ACHIEVE.

achene (əkēn´), **achaene** *n.* (*Bot.*) a small dry carpel, with a single seed, which does not open when ripe.

achieve (əchēv´) *v.t.* **1** to perform, accomplish, finish. **2** to attain, acquire, or bring about by an effort. **achievable** *a.* **achievement** *n.* **1** the act of accomplishing. **2** the thing achieved. **3** a heroic deed, an exploit. **4** (*Psych.*) performance in a standardized test. **5** (*Her.*) a complete heraldic composition. **6** a funeral escutcheon. **achiever** *n.*

achillea (akil´iə, akilē´ə) *n.* any plant of the genus *Achillea*, such as the milfoil or yarrow, which are aromatic and have white, yellow or purple flowers.

Achillean (akilē´ən) *a.* **1** like Achilles. **2** heroic, invincible. **3** invulnerable. **Achilles heel** (əkil´iz) *n.* a person's vulnerable point or fatal weakness (Achilles' mother Thetis having held him by the heel when she dipped him in the river Styx to make him invulnerable). **Achilles' tendon** *n.* the tendon or ligature connecting the muscles of the calf to the heel-bone.

achondroplasia (əkondrəplā´ziə, ā-) *n.* (*Med.*) a hereditary bone disorder in which cartilage fails to ossify into long bones, resulting in very short limbs.

achromatic (akrəmat´ik) *a.* **1** colourless. **2** transmitting light without decomposing it into its primary colours. **achromatically** *adv.* **achromatism** (əkrō´-), **achromaticity** (əkrōmətis´-) *n.*

achy ACHE.

acid (as´id) *a*. **1** sour, tart, sharp to the taste. **2** sharp or sour in manner or speech. **3** (*Chem*.) having the properties of an acid, reacting as an acid. **4** (*Geol*.) (of rocks) having a large proportion of silica. **5** (of colours) intensely bright. ~*n*. **1** (*Chem*.) a compound of hydrogen in which the hydrogen can be replaced by a metal, or with a basic metallic oxide, to form a salt of that metal and water. **2** a sour substance. **3** (*sl*.) LSD. **to put on the acid** (*Austral*.) to scrounge, to cadge. **acid drop** *n*. a boiled sweet with a sour taste. **acid head** *n*. (*sl*.) a person who uses LSD. **acid house** *n*. **1** a youth cult concerned with highly electronically synthesized disco or pop music (and the taking of psychedelic drugs). **2** disco or pop music of this kind. **acidic** (-sid´-) *a*. acid. **acidify** (əsid´ifī) *v.t*. (*3rd pers. sing. pres*. **acidifies**, *pres.p*. **acidifying**, *past, p.p*. **acidified**) **1** to render acid or sour. **2** to convert into an acid. ~*v.i*. to become acid. **acidification** (-fikā´shən) *n*. **acidimeter** (asidim´itə) *n*. an instrument for measuring the strength of acids. **acidimetry** (-dim´itri) *n*. **acidity** (-sid´-) *n*. (*pl*. **acidities**) **1** the quality of being acid. **2** sourness, tartness, sharpness. **3** hyperacidity. **acid rain** *n*. precipitation made acidic and thus harmful to crops etc. by the release of (industrial) pollutants, esp. sulphur and nitrogen compounds, into the atmosphere. **acid rock** *n*. rock music featuring unusual amplified instrumental effects. **acid test** *n*. **1** an absolute and definite test. **2** a critical ordeal.

acidosis (asidō´sis) *n*. (*Med*.) a condition characterized by the appearance of excess acid in the urine and bloodstream. **acidotic** (-dot´-) *a*.

acidulous (əsid´ūləs) *a*. **1** a little sour or acid, moderately sharp to the taste, subacid. **2** sharp or sour in manner or speech. **acidulate** *v.t*. **1** to render slightly acid. **2** to flavour with an acid.

-acious (ā´shəs) *suf*. **1** abounding in, characterized by, inclined to. **2** added to verbal stems to form adjectives, e.g. *loquacious, tenacious*.

-acity (as´iti) *suf*. the quality of: forming nouns of quality from adjectives in -ACIOUS.

ack-ack (ak´ak) *a*. (*coll*.) anti-aircraft. ~*n*. (*coll*.) anti-aircraft guns or fire.

ackee (ak´ē), **akee** *n*. **1** a tropical African tree, *Blighia sapida*, also cultivated in the West Indies. **2** the red, pear-shaped fruit of this tree, which is edible when cooked.

†ack-emma (akem´ə) *n*. (*coll*.) morning, a.m.

acknowledge (əknol´ij) *v.t*. **1** to admit the truth of, to recognize, accept. **2** to confess, to admit. **3** to recognize the authority of. **4** to give a receipt for, confirm receipt (of something). **5** to express appreciation or gratitude for. **6** to show awareness or recognition of, e.g. by a gesture. **acknowledgeable** *a*. **acknowledged** *a*. **acknowledgement, acknowledgment** *n*. **1** the act of acknowledging. **2** recognition, acceptance; confession, admission. **3** a receipt for money or goods; a letter confirming receipt of a letter, invoice etc. **4** an expression of gratitude, esp.

(*usu. in pl*.) an author's expression of gratitude to other people. **5** something given or done in return for a service or message.

aclinic (əklin´ik) *a*. not dipping, situated where the magnetic needle does not dip. **aclinic line** *n*. the magnetic equator.

acme (ak´mi) *n*. **1** the top or highest point, the culmination, peak or perfection (of achievement, excellence etc.). **2** the maturity of life. **3** the crisis or turning-point of a disease.

acne (ak´ni) *n*. **1** a skin condition characterized by pimples. **2** a pimple on the skin. **acned** *a*.

🔀 **acolade** common misspelling of ACCOLADE.

acolyte (ak´əlīt) *n*. **1** a person assisting a priest in a service or procession. **2** an attendant, ministrant. **3** a faithful follower.

aconite (ak´ənīt) *n*. **1** a plant of the genus *Aconitum*, esp. *A. napellus*, the common monk's-hood or wolf's-bane. **2** a poison drug used medicinally, obtained from the root of this plant. **aconitine** (əkon´itīn) *n*. (*Chem*.) a poisonous alkaloid substance derived from the genus *Aconitum*.

acorn (ā´kawn) *n*. the fruit of the oak. **acorn barnacle, acorn shell** *n*. **1** a barnacle of the family Balanidae. **2** a multivalve cirriped, *Balanus balanoides*, allied to the barnacles.

acotyledon (əkotilē´dən) *n*. **1** any plant of the class *Acotyledones*. **2** a plant without distinct seed-lobes.

acoustic (əkoos´tik), **acoustical** (-əl) *a*. **1** of or relating to hearing, sound or acoustics. **2** of or relating to the ear, constituting part of the physical apparatus for hearing (*acoustic nerve*). **3** of or relating to musical instruments whose sound is not electronically amplified. **4** (of building materials) designed to absorb or control sound. **5** (*Mil*.) (of a mine) that can be detonated by sound waves. ~*n*. the acoustics of a room or building. **acoustically** *adv*. **acoustic coupler** *n*. (*Comput*.) a modem that enables computer data to be transmitted along a telephone line by converting it into acoustic form. **acoustician** (-tish´ən) *n*. **1** an expert in acoustics. **2** a person who investigates the phenomena of sound. **acoustics** *n*. **1** the science of sound and its phenomena. **2** the phenomena of hearing. **2** (*as pl*.) the properties of a room or building that determine sound quality.

acquaint (əkwānt´) *v.t*. to make (someone, oneself) aware of or familiar with (usu. followed by *with*). **acquaintance** *n*. **1** knowledge of any person or thing. **2** the state of knowing, or becoming known to, a person. **3** a person, or the persons collectively, whom one knows, but with whom one is not intimate. **to make the acquaintance of** to get to know. **acquaintanceship** *n*.

acquiesce (akwies´) *v.i*. **1** to submit or remain passive. **2** to assent, to accept tacitly, to concur (in). **acquiescence** *n*. **acquiescent** *a*.

acquire (əkwīə´) *v.t*. **1** to gain, or obtain possession of, by one's own exertions or abilities. **2** to come into possession of. **acquirable** *a*.

acquired *a.* **acquired characteristic** *n.* (*Biol.*) a characteristic of an organism that is attained through environmental influences rather than genetically. **acquired immune deficiency syndrome** *n.* Aids. **acquired taste** *n.* something which one learns to like. **acquirement** *n.* **1** the act of acquiring. **2** the object gained. **3** a personal attainment, esp. a mental one.

acquisition (akwizish´ən) *n.* **1** the act of acquiring. **2** the object acquired. **3** a gain, an acquirement. **acquisitive** (əkwiz´-) *a.* eager to acquire possessions; materialistic. **acquisitively** *adv.* **acquisitiveness** *n.*

acquit (əkwit´) *v.t.* (*pres.p.* **acquitting**, *past, p.p.* **acquitted**) **1** to declare not guilty. **2** to release from an obligation, suspicion or charge. ~*v.refl.* **1** to conduct (oneself) in a particular way. **2** to discharge (oneself) of (the duties of one's position). **acquittal** *n.* **1** a deliverance from a charge by legal process; being declared not guilty. **2** discharge or release from a promise, debt or other obligation. **3** performance. **4** discharge of duty. **acquittance** *n.* **1** the act of releasing from a charge or debt. **2** a receipt in full. **3** discharge of duty. **acquitter** *n.*

acre (ā´kə) *n.* **1** a measure of land containing 4840 sq. yd. (0.4 ha). **2** (*pl.*) large areas or amounts (of). **acreage** *n.* **1** the area of any piece of land in acres. **2** acres taken collectively or in the abstract. **acred** *a.*

acrid (ak´rid) *a.* **1** sharp, pungent, biting to the taste. **2** irritating, corrosive. **3** bitterly irritating to the feelings. **4** of irritating temper and manners. **acridly** *adv.* **acridness, acridity** (əkrid´-) *n.*

acriflavine (akriflā´vin, -vēn) *n.* an aniline dye, solutions of which form a strong antiseptic.

acrimony (ak´riməni) *n.* (*pl.* **acrimonies**) **1** bitter, bad-tempered and accusatory feeling or speech. **2** sharpness, bitterness of feeling, manner or speech. **acrimonious** (-mō´-) *a.* bitter, bad-tempered and recriminating and reproachful. **acrimoniously** *adv.*

acro- (ak´rō) *comb. form* situated on the outside, beginning, termination, extremity, point or top, e.g. *acrobat, acrogenous.*

acrobat (ak´rəbat) *n.* **1** a performer of daring gymnastic feats, such as a tumbler or a tightrope walker. **2** a person who rapidly changes their opinions or loyalties. **acrobatic** (-bat´-) *a.* **acrobatically** *adv.* **acrobatics** *n.pl.* **1** the feats performed by an acrobat. **2** the skill required to perform these. **3** any agile performance.

acromegaly (akrōmeg´əli) *n.* (*Med.*) a disease the chief feature of which is the enlargement of the face and of the extremities of the limbs. **acromegalic** (-gal´-) *a.*

acronym (ak´rənim) *n.* a word formed from initials, e.g. *NATO, laser.*

acrophobia (akrəfō´biə) *n.* (*Psych.*) an abnormal dread of high places. **acrophobic** *a.*

acropolis (əkrop´əlis) *n.* the citadel or elevated part of a Greek town, esp. that of Athens.

across (əkros´) *prep.* **1** from one side to the other of (*go across the road*). **2** on the other side of (*lives across the street*). **3** spanning, covering, extending etc. from one side of to the other (*a bridge across the river*). **4** transversely in relation to, forming a cross with. **5** so as to cross (boundaries, divisions etc.) (*across the political and religious divide*). ~*adv.* **1** to the other side. **2** on the other side. **3** from one side to the other. **4** (in a crossword puzzle) relating to the horizontal series of squares. **across the board** affecting or applying in all cases.

acrostic (əkros´tik) *n.* a composition in which the lines are so disposed that their initial letters taken in order constitute a word or short sentence.

acrylic (əkril´ik) *a.* (*Chem.*) denoting or made from polymers of acrylic acid or its derivatives. ~*n.* **1** an acrylic textile fibre. **2** paint containing an acrylic resin. **3** a painting executed in acrylic paint. **acrylic acid** *n.* (*Chem.*) an acid used in the manufacture of acrylic resins. **acrylic resin** *n.* a resin consisting of a polymer of acrylic acid or one of its derivatives, used in making paints, adhesives, and for cast and moulded goods.

ACT *abbr.* Australian Capital Territory.

act (akt) *n.* **1** something that is done or being done, a deed. **2** the process of doing (*in the act of*). **3** a statute, law or edict of a legislative or judicial body. **4** any one of the principal divisions of a play, usu. subdivided into smaller portions called scenes. **5** a short entertainment, such as in a variety show, given by a particular performer or group of performers, esp. one that is particularly associated with and repeatedly given by the performer. **6** a group who give such a performance. **7** a document proving the truth of some transaction. **8** (*usu. pl.*) a record of the proceedings, decisions etc. of a committee, society etc. **9** (*pl.* **Acts**) the Acts of the Apostles, the book of the New Testament which follows the four Gospels and relates the history of the early Church. ~*v.t.* **1** to perform (a play). **2** to play the part of. **3** to impersonate or pretend. **4** to demonstrate or pretend using gestures. ~*v.i.* **1** to take action, to do something. **2** to be in action or operation. **3** to produce an effect, to exert power. **4** to behave, to conduct oneself. **5** to perform as an actor. **6** to pretend to be (*act stupid*). **to act for** to be the (esp. legal) representative of. **to act on/ upon 1** to follow, to carry out (advice, recommendation). **2** to have an effect on, to influence. **to act out** (*esp. Psych.*) to represent (a scene, one's desires) in physical action or by performance. **to act up 1** (*coll.*) to behave badly. **2** (*coll.*) to function badly, to give trouble. **to get in on the act** (*coll.*) to become involved in an undertaking, esp. so as to benefit. **to get one's act together 1** (*coll.*) to organize or prepare oneself properly. **2** (*coll.*) to start to behave in a more responsible or more appropriate way. **to put on an act** (*coll.*) to pretend. **actable** *a.* **acting** *a.*

1 performing dramatically. **2** operating. **3** doing temporary duty. *~n.* **1** performance, execution, action. **2** dramatic performance. **acting pilot officer** *n.* an RAF rank immediately below pilot officer. **act of God** *n.* the operation of uncontrollable natural forces in causing an event. **actor** *n.* **1** a performer. **2** a person who represents a character on the stage. **3** a doer. **actress** (-tris) *n.* a female actor.

ACTH *abbr.* adrenocorticotrophic hormone.

actinia (aktin´iə) *n.* (*pl.* **actiniae** (-ē), **actinias**) a sea anemone of the genus *Actinia*.

actinic (aktin´ik) *a.* **1** of or relating to rays, esp. the radiation from the sun. **2** (of rays) that can produce a photochemical effect. **actinism** (ak´-) *n.* **1** the property in rays of light by which chemical changes are produced. **2** the radiation of light or heat.

actinide (ak´tinīd), **actinoid** (-oid) *n.* (*Chem.*) any of a series of radioactive elements beginning with actinium and ending with lawrencium.

actinium (aktin´iəm) *n.* (*Chem.*) a radioactive metallic element, at. no. 89, chem. symbol Ac, found in pitchblende.

actino- (ak´tinō), **actin-** *comb. form* **1** indicating a radial shape or structure. **2** of or relating to radiation, esp. solar radiation, and radioactivity.

actinozoan ANTHOZOAN.

action (ak´shən) *n.* **1** the state, condition or fact of acting or doing. **2** anything done or performed; a deed, an exploit. **3** energetic activity or forcefulness, esp. as a characteristic of a person (*a man of action*). **4** the exertion of a force, effect or influence (*the action of sunlight on the surface of the leaf*). **5** (*coll.*) exciting activity. **6** (*Mil.*) **a** combat, fighting. **b** a small-scale military engagement. **7** the way in which something operates or works; the mechanism of a machine or of a musical instrument, esp. a piano or an organ; the sensitivity to the player's touch of a keyboard instrument. **8** the events constituting the main storyline, or the main source of interest and suspense, in a play, novel etc. **9** a legal process, a lawsuit. **10** the particular style of movement of an animal, esp. a horse, or of an athlete. **11** industrial action. *~int.* a command, given by the director of a film, to begin the shooting of a scene. *~v.t.* **1** to implement, to put into effect. **2** to take action concerning. **3** to take legal action against. **out of action** not working, unable to operate. **the action** (*coll.*) the principal or most lively activity. **to go into action 1** to begin to take action, esp. energetically. **2** to go into battle. **to take action** to do something, esp. something energetic or decisive or something intended as a protest. **actionable** *a.* furnishing ground for an action at law. **action committee, action group** *n.* a body formed to take positive action to achieve an end. **action-packed** *a.* full of exciting events. **action painting** *n.* abstract expression using spontaneous actions of smearing, throwing etc.

to apply paint. **action replay** *n.* the repetition, often in slow motion, of a small piece of film showing an important or decisive (sporting) incident. **action stations** *n.pl.* the positions taken by military personnel in readiness for or during battle. *~int.* a command to take up these positions.

activate (ak´tivāt) *v.t.* **1** to make active, to induce activity in. **2** (*Physics*) to make radioactive. **3** (*Chem.*) to make (more) reactive. **activated** *a.* **activated carbon** *n.* carbon in the form of an absorbent powder used for purifying liquids and gases. **activated sludge** *n.* aerated sewage that contains anaerobic bacteria and is used to promote decomposition and purification in untreated sewage. **activation** (-ā´shən) *n.* **activator** *n.*

Usage note The meanings of the verbs *activate* and *actuate* overlap, but *activate* is more common of physical effects, and *actuate* of feelings or abstract qualities.

active (ak´tiv) *a.* **1** characterized by action, work or the performance of business; continually employed, busy (*an active life*; *like to keep active*). **2** that involves the performance of actual work or the making of an actual contribution; involved or participating in something in this way (*active assistance*; *active support*; *active member*). **3** able to move about and perform tasks (*less active since her illness*). **4** physically energetic (*very active children*). **5** communicating action or motion, initiating or furthering a process (*active ingredient*). **6** in actual operation or capable of actual operation. **7** (of a volcano) still liable to erupt. **8** radioactive. **9** (*Gram.*) (of a form of a verb) attributing the action expressed by the verb to the person or thing that performs it (as opposed to *passive*). **active birth** *n.* an approach to childbirth that encourages the mother to remain active, to move around and to adopt whatever position feels comfortable. **active carbon** *n.* ACTIVATED CARBON (under ACTIVATE). **active duty** *n.* (*N Am.*) ACTIVE SERVICE (under ACTIVE). **actively** *adv.* **active matrix** *n.* an electronic display system with individually controlled pixels. **active service** *n.* military duty in an operational area. **activism** *n.* the policy of taking decisive or militant action. **activist** *n.* a person who takes decisive, sometimes militant, action in support of a (political or social) cause. **activity** (-tiv´-) *n.* (*pl.* **activities**) **1** the quality or state of being active. **2** exertion of energy; liveliness, vigorous action. **3** a pursuit, occupation, recreation. **4** radioactivity.

actor, actress ACT.

actual (ak´chuəl) *a.* **1** existing in act or reality, real, genuine. **2** present, current. **actual bodily harm** *n.* physical injury intentionally caused and giving grounds for criminal prosecution, but less serious than grievous bodily harm. **actuality** (-al´-) *n.* (*pl.* **actualities**) **1** the state of being actual. **2** reality. **3** (*usu. pl.*) an existing condition. **actualize, actualise** *v.t.* **1** to make actual. **2** to describe realistically. **actualization** (-zā´shən) *n.* **actually** *adv.* **1** in fact, in reality. **2** as a matter of fact. **3** at present.

actuary (ak´chuəri) *n.* (*pl.* **actuaries**) an officer of a mercantile or insurance company, skilled in statistics, esp. on the expectancy of life and the average proportion of losses by fire and other accidents. **actuarial** (-ea´ri-) *a.*

actuate (ak´chuāt) *v.t.* **1** to put in action, to cause to operate. **2** to impart motion to. **3** to motivate, to induce. **actuation** (-ā´shən) *n.* **actuator** *n.*

Usage note See note under ACTIVATE.

acuity (əkū´iti) *n.* sharpness, acuteness (of a point, an acid, disease or wit).

acumen (ak´ūmən) *n.* acuteness of mind, shrewdness, keen penetration.

acupressure (ak´ūpreshə) *n.* massage using the fingertips applied to the points of the body used in acupuncture.

acupuncture (ak´ūpŭngkchə) *n.* a system of medical treatment in which the body surface is punctured by needles at specific points to relieve pain, cure disease or produce anaesthesia.

⊠ **acurate** common misspelling of ACCURATE.

acute (əkūt´) *a.* **1** sharp, keen, penetrating. **2** quick to perceive minute distinctions, sensitive to detail. **3** (of pain) sharp, piercing. **4** (of an illness) attended with violent symptoms, and coming speedily to a crisis. **5** (of an angle) less than a right angle. **6** (of a problem, shortage) critical, very serious, requiring urgent attention. **7** shrill, high in pitch. *~n.* an acute accent. **acute accent** *n.* a mark (´) placed over some vowels in certain languages to indicate the quality of the vowel or the degree of stress to be given to it. **acutely** *adv.* **acuteness** *n.*

ACW *abbr.* Aircraftwoman.

-acy (əsi) *suf.* forming nouns of quality, state, condition etc., e.g. *fallacy, infancy, magistracy, piracy.*

acyclovir (āsī´kləvēə) *n.* an antiviral drug used in the treatment of Aids and herpes.

acyl (ā´sīl) *n.* (*Chem.*) the monovalent radical of a carboxylic acid.

AD *abbr.* in the year of our Lord.

Usage note AD comes before dates which are cardinal numerals (AD 91), but may follow ordinals (*the third century* AD).

ad (ad) *n.* (*coll.*) short for ADVERTISEMENT (under ADVERTISE).

ad- (əd) *pref.* signifying motion towards, direction to, adherence etc., e.g. *adduce, adhere, adjacent, admire* (this prefix undergoes many alterations to assimilate it with the initial consonant of the root, examples of which will be found in their respective places).

-ad[1] (ad) *suf.* **1** forming nouns denoting a group or unit of a specific number, as in *monad, triad.*

2 forming female patronymics, as in *naiad.* **3** (in the titles of epic or mock-epic poems) of or relating to, as in *Iliad.*

-ad[2] (əd) *suf.* forming nouns, as in *salad, ballad.*

-ad[3] (ad) *suf.* forming adverbs, esp. in anatomical descriptions, indicating direction towards a specified part, as in *caudad.*

adage (ad´ij) *n.* a proverb; a pithy maxim handed down from old time.

adagio (ədah´jiō, -zhiō) *adv.* (*Mus.*) slowly, gracefully. *~a.* slow, graceful. *~n.* (*pl.* **adagios**) a slow movement or passage of a soft, tender, elegiac character.

Adam (ad´əm) *n.* **1** the first man, in the Bible and in the Koran. **2** the unregenerate state of man. **Adam's ale** *n.* water. **Adam's apple** *n.* a protuberance on the forepart of the throat formed by the thyroid cartilage.

adamant (ad´əmənt) *a.* immovably resolved, stubbornly determined. *~n.* a legendary stone of impenetrable hardness, often taken to be the lodestone or the diamond. **adamancy** *n.* **adamantine** (-man´tin), †**adamantean** (-man´tiən) *a.* (*poet.*) **1** made of adamant. **2** incapable of being broken. **adamantly** *adv.*

adapt (ədapt´) *v.t.* to fit, to adjust, to make suitable for a new purpose or conditions. *~v.i.* to change so as to become fit or suitable for new conditions. **adaptable** *a.* **1** capable of being adapted. **2** able to adapt easily. **adaptability** (-bil´-) *n.* **adaptation** (adəptā´shən) *n.* **1** the act of adapting; the state of being adapted. **2** anything which has been adapted. **3** (*Biol.*) the process of modification that enables an organism to survive better in its environment. **adaptedness** *n.* **adaptive** *a.* **1** tending to adapt. **2** suitable. **adaptively** *adv.* **adaptor, adapter** *n.* **1** a person or thing that adapts. **2** an accessory for connecting a plug etc. fitted with terminals of one type to a supply point fitted with terminals of another type, or for connecting several appliances to a single supply point. **3** any device for connecting differing parts or making pieces of equipment compatible with one another.

ADC *abbr.* **1** aide-de-camp. **2** analog-digital converter.

add (ad) *v.t.* **1** to put together with, join with or put into (*add a spoonful of milk*). **2** to combine (numbers) in order to make a total. **3** to say or write in addition. *~v.i.* to perform the operation of addition. **to add in** to include. **to add on** to attach as a supplement or extension. **to add to to** increase (*You're simply adding to my difficulties*). **to add up 1** to perform the operation of addition. **2** to produce a correct total when added. **3** to make sense, to show a consistent pattern. **to add up to** to amount to. **added** *a.* **adder**[1] *n.* **addition** *n.* **1** the process of combining two or more numbers or quantities into one sum. **2** a person or thing that is added. **in addition** as well, also. **additional** *a.* added; supplementary. **additionally** *adv.* **additive** *a.* **1** that may be or is to be added. **2** characterized by addition. *~n.* something added, esp. a substance added to food to preserve or enhance it. **add-on** *n.* **1** something supplementary. **2** a computer peripheral.

addax (ad´aks) *n.* (*pl. in general* **addax,** *in particular* **addaxes**) a species of antelope, *Oryx nasomaculata.*

addendum (əden´dəm) *n.* (*pl.* **addenda** (-də)) **1** a thing to be added, an addition. **2** an appendix.

Usage note *Addenda* is sometimes used as a singular noun (*an addenda*), but it should always be a plural.

adder[1] ADD.

adder[2] (ad´ə) *n.* **1** the common viper, *Vipera berus.* **2** (with epithet) any of various other venomous snakes of the family Viperidae, as puffadder, death-adder. **adder's tongue** *n.* a fern of the genus *Ophioglossum.*

addict[1] (ədikt´) *v.t.* to cause (someone, oneself) to become dependent on something, esp. a narcotic drug. **addicted** *a.* **1** dependent, esp. on a narcotic drug. **2** enthusiastically devoted to something. **addictedness** *n.* **addiction** *n.* **1** a condition of physical dependence on something, esp. a narcotic drug. **2** the act of addicting. **3** (*coll.*) an extreme devotion to something. **addictive** *a.* **1** that causes addiction. **2** (*coll.*) compulsively pleasurable, attractive, watchable etc.

addict[2] (ad´ikt) *n.* **1** a person who has become addicted to some habit, esp. the taking of drugs. **2** (*coll.*) a person who is extremely devoted to something, esp. a pastime or sport (*a football addict*).

addition, additive ADD.

addle (ad´əl) *a.* **1** (of an egg) putrid, bad. **2** (*in comb.*) muddled, confused (*addle-headed*). **3** empty, vain. *~v.t.* **1** to make addle or addled. **2** to cause to become confused or deranged. *~v.i.* (of an egg) to become putrid. **addled** *a.* **1** (of an egg) rotten. **2** mentally confused or deranged.

address (ədres´) *n.* **1** the place where a person lives or a business, an organization etc. has its premises. **2** the written form of this used on letters etc. **3** a speech or discourse delivered to an audience. **4** tact, skill, adroitness. **5** a number that identifies a location in a computer memory where a particular piece of data is stored. **6** (*pl.*) a man's attentions to a woman whom he wishes to woo, courtship. **7** bearing in conversation. *~v.t.* **1** to write the address on (a letter, envelope). **2** to speak to. **3** to deliver a speech or discourse to. **4** to direct (a message, protest etc.) to. **5** to direct one's attention to; to deal with. **6** to adopt a position facing (the ball, target), when preparing to hit, shoot etc. *~v.i.* to present a formal address. **to address oneself to 1** to speak to. **2** to apply oneself to; to deal with. **addressable** *a.* (*Comput.*) able to be accessed by means of an address. **addressee** (-ē´) *n.* a person to whom a letter, parcel or communication is addressed. **addresser** *n.* **1** ADDRESSOR (under ADDRESS). **2** a

machine for addressing envelopes, wrappers etc. **addressor** *n.* **1** the person who addresses (a letter, envelope etc.). **2** a person who speaks to someone else.

adduce (ədūs´) *v.t.* to bring forward as a proof or illustration, to cite, to quote. **adducer** *n.* **adducible** *a.* **adduct** (ədŭkt´) *v.t.* to draw (a body part) inwards or towards another part. **adduction** *n.* **1** the act of leading or drawing to or together. **2** the act of citing. **adductive** *a.* **adductor** *n.*

-ade (ād) *suf.* forming nouns denoting action, e.g. *cannonade, ambuscade*; a person or body involved in action, e.g. *brigade, cavalcade*; product of action, e.g. *masquerade*; sweet drink, e.g. *lemonade.*

adenine (ad´ənēn, -nin) *n.* one of the four purine bases in DNA and RNA.

adeno- (ad´ənō), **adeni-** (-i), **aden-** *comb. form* connected with a gland or glands, glandular; used in medical terms, e.g. *adenitis, adenopathy.*

adenoid (ad´ənoid) *a.* having the form of a gland, glandular. *~n.pl.* (*Med.*) **1** adenoid tissue. **2** a spongy growth at the back of the nose and throat, impeding respiration and speech. **adenoidal** (-oi´dəl) *a.*

adenoma (adənō´mə) *n.* (*pl.* **adenomas, adenomata** (-ətə)) a benign tumour formed of glandular tissue.

adenosine (aden´əsēn, -sin) *n.* a compound of adenine and the sugar ribose, that forms part of RNA and various compounds that provide energy in cells.

adept[1] (adept´, ad´ept) *a.* thoroughly versed, highly skilled. **adeptly** *adv.* **adeptness** *n.*

adept[2] (ad´ept) *n.* a person who is completely versed in any science or art.

adequate (ad´ikwət) *a.* **1** equal to a requirement, sufficient; competent. **2** barely sufficient, just good enough. **3** proportionate, commensurate. **adequacy** *n.* **adequately** *adv.*

adhere (əd·hiə´, ədiə´) *v.i.* **1** to stick (to). **2** to remain firmly attached (to). **3** to continue to give support to. **4** not to deviate (followed by *to*).

adherence (əd·hiə´rəns, ədiə´-) *n.* **1** the state or quality of adhering. **2** firm attachment. **3** continuing support or loyalty. **4** continuing and precise observance. **adherent** *a.* **1** sticking. **2** tenaciously attached. *~n.* **1** a supporter, a partisan, a follower. **2** a devotee.

Usage note The meanings of *adherence* and *adhesion* overlap, but *adherence* particularly corresponds to figurative or abstract senses of *adhere*, and *adhesion* to the more literal or physical.

adhesion (əd·hē´zhən, ədē´-) *n.* **1** the act or state of sticking, attaching oneself to, or joining. **2** the union of structures or tissues that are normally separate. **3** (*Med.*) the fusion of two surfaces, as the two opposing surfaces of a wound in healing. **adhesive** (-siv, -ziv) *a.* **1** having the power of adhering. **2** sticky, clinging. *~n.* a substance

used for sticking things together. **adhesively** *adv.*
adhesiveness *n.*

Usage note See note under ADHERENCE.

adhibit (əd·hib´it) *v.t.* (*pres.p.* **adhibiting**, *past*,
p.p. **adhibited**) **1** to apply, to administer (a
remedy). **2** to append, to affix. **adhibition**
(ad·hibish´ən, -adi-) *n.*

ad hoc (ad hok´) *a.*, *adv.* for a particular
purpose only, specially.

ad hominem (ad hom´inem) *a.*, *adv.* **1** directed
to or against the person, not disinterested. **2** (of
an argument) based on or appealing to emotion
rather than reason.

adiabatic (adiəbat´ik) *a.* (*Physics*) **1** impervious,
esp. to heat. **2** without loss or gain of heat. **adia-
batically** *adv.*

☒ **adict** common misspelling of ADDICT.

adieu (ədū´, ədyœ´) *int.*, *n.* (*pl.* **adieux** (-z)) God
be with you, good-bye, farewell.

ad infinitum (ad infinī´təm) *adv.* to infinity,
without end.

adipocere (ad´ipəsiə, -ōs-) *n.* a greyish-white
fatty or soapy substance, into which the flesh of
dead bodies buried in moist places is converted.

adipose (ad´ipōs) *a.* of or relating to animal fat,
fatty. ~*n.* animal fat, esp. the fat on the kidneys.
adiposity (-pos´-) *n.*

adit (ad´it) *n.* **1** an approach, entrance, passage.
2 a more or less horizontal entrance to a mine.

Adj., **Adjt** *abbr.* adjutant.

adjacent (əjā´sənt) *a.* lying near (to); contiguous;
neighbouring, bordering. **adjacency** *n.* **ad-
jacently** *adv.*

adjective (aj´iktiv) *a.* **1** added to. **2** dependent.
3 forming an adjunct to a noun substantive. ~*n.*
a word or phrase joined to, or grammatically
linked to, a substantive to define and limit its
signification. **adjectival** (-tī´-) *a.* **adjectivally** *adv.*

adjoin (ajoin´) *v.t.* **1** to be next to and contiguous
with. **2** †to join or add, to unite. ~*v.i.* to be
contiguous.

adjourn (əjœn´) *v.t.* **1** to put off or defer till a
later period. **2** to suspend (a meeting) in order to
meet at a later period or elsewhere. **3** to postpone
till a future meeting. ~*v.i.* **1** to cease proceedings
till a later period. **2** to move elsewhere. **adjournment** *n.* **1** the act of adjourning. **2** the time during
which or to which business or a meeting (esp. of
a public body) is postponed.

adjudge (əjŭj´) *v.t.* **1** to pronounce officially or
formally (*adjudged to be at fault*). **2** to award by a
judicial decision. **3** to adjudicate. **adjudgement**,
adjudgment *n.*

adjudicate (əjoo´dikāt) *v.t.* **1** to give a decision
regarding, to judge, to determine. **2** to pronounce. ~*v.i.* **1** to sit as a judge. **2** to act as a judge
in a competition. **adjudication** (-ā´shən) *n.* **1** the
act of adjudicating. **2** the decision or judgement
of a judge or court. **adjudicator** *n.*

adjunct (aj´ŭngkt) *n.* **1** any thing joined to another without being an essential part of it. **2** an

associate, assistant or subordinate. **3** (*Gram.*) an
extension of the subject or predicate. **4** (*Logic*) a
non-essential attribute. ~*a.* **1** added to, or con-
joined with, any person or thing. **2** auxiliary;
subordinate. **adjunctive** (əjŭngk´-) *a.*, *n.*

adjure (əjooə´) *v.t.* **1** to charge upon oath, or on
pain of divine displeasure. **2** to entreat with great
earnestness.

Usage note See note under ABJURE.

adjust (əjŭst´) *v.t.* **1** to regulate; to make slight
alteration to, esp. to achieve greater accuracy.
2 to arrange; to put in the correct order or position. **3** to make suitable or correspondent (to).
4 to accommodate, settle or harmonize (differences). **5** to assess (insurance claims). ~*v.i.*
to adapt or conform (to a new situation, environment etc.). **adjustable** *a.* **adjuster** *n.* **adjustment** *n.*

adjutant (aj´ətənt) *n.* **1** (*Mil.*) an officer in each
regiment who assists the commanding officer in
matters of business, duty and discipline. **2** an
assistant. **3** an adjutant bird. **adjutancy** *n.* the
office of adjutant. **adjutant bird** *n.* either of
two large wading birds of the stork family,
Leptoptilos dubius or *L. jauanicus*, natives of
SE Asia. **adjutant general** *n.* (*pl.* **adjutants general**, **adjutant generals**) (*Mil.*) **1** a senior officer
of the general staff with administrative functions. **2** the executive officer to a general.

adjuvant (aj´əvənt) *a.* **1** helping. **2** (*Med.*) (of
cancer therapy) applied after the initial treatment, esp. to prevent the development of secondaries. ~*n.* **1** an assistant, helper, auxiliary.
2 (*Med.*) **a** an auxiliary, enhancing ingredient in
a prescription. **b** a substance, injected with an
antigen, to enhance the body's immune response
to it.

ad lib (ad lib´), **ad libitum** (lib´itum, lībē´təm)
adv. **1** at pleasure, to any extent. **2** (*Mus.*) at the
performer's discretion to change time or omit
passages. **ad-lib** *v.t.* (*pres.p.* **ad-libbing**, *past*, *p.p.*
ad-libbed) to say, perform, interject etc. without
notes or preparation. ~*v.i.* to extemporize. ~*a.* improvised, extempore. ~*n.* an improvised speech,
line etc. **ad-libber** *n.*

Adm. *abbr.* admiral.

adman (ad´man) *n.* (*pl.* **admen** (-men)) (*coll.*) a
person who works in advertising.

admeasure (admezh´ə) *v.t.* to measure out, to
apportion. **admeasurement** *n.*

admin (ad´min) *n.* (*coll.*) administration, administrative work.

adminicle (ədmin´ikəl) *n.* **1** an aid, support.
2 (*Sc. Law*) corroborative evidence, esp. of the
contents of a missing document. **adminicular**
(adminik´ūlə) *a.*

administer (ədmin´istə) *v.t.* **1** to manage or conduct as chief agent. **2** to superintend the execution of (e.g. laws). **3** to direct the taking of (an
oath). **4** to dispense, supply or perform the rites
of (a sacrament). **5** to give (medicine, remedy).

6 to deliver (a rebuke). **7** to manage and dispose of (the estate of a deceased person). *~v.i.* **1** to act as administrator. **2** to minister (to). **administrable** *a.* **administrate** *v.t., v.i.* **administration** (-trā´shən) *n.* **1** the act of administering. **2** the management of the affairs of a business, organization etc. **3** the people entrusted with this. **4** the management of public affairs, the conduct of government. **5** a government. **6** the period in office of a government, president etc. **7** (**Administration**) (in the US) a government board or agency. **8** (*Law*) the management and distribution of the estate of a deceased person, esp. an intestate. **administrative** (-trə-) *a.* **administratively** *adv.* **administrator** (-trā-) *n.* **1** a person who administers, manages, dispenses or furnishes. **2** (*Law*) a person who administers the estate of an intestate. **administratorship** *n.* **administratrix** (-triks) *n.* (*pl.* **administratrices** (-sēz)) a female administrator.

admirable (ad´mirəbəl) *a.* **1** worthy of admiration. **2** excellent, highly satisfactory. **admirably** *adv.*

admiral (ad´mirəl) *n.* **1** the commander of a fleet or a division of a fleet (a rank having four grades in the Royal Navy: Admiral of the Fleet, Admiral, Vice-Admiral and Rear-Admiral). **2** either of two butterflies, *Vanessa atalanta*, the red, and *Limenitis sibylla*, the white admiral butterfly.

admiralty (ad´mirəlti) *n.* (*pl.* **admiralties**) **1** the office of admiral. **2** (*Law*) the maritime branch of the administration of justice. **the Admiralty** the Government department that formerly dealt with the British navy.

admire (ədmīə´) *v.t.* **1** to have a high opinion of, to respect. **2** to regard with pleasure and approval. **3** to express admiration of. *~v.i.* to feel admiration, to wonder, to be astonished. **admiration** (-mirā´shən) *n.* **1** pleasure or respect excited by anything pleasing or excellent. **2** pleased contemplation. **3** a person or thing that is admired. **admirer** *n.* **1** a person who feels admiration. **2** a suitor, lover. **admiring** *a.* **admiringly** *adv.*

admissible (ədmis´ibəl) *a.* **1** fit to be considered as an opinion or as evidence. **2** (*Law*) allowable as evidence. **3** capable of being admitted. **admissibility** (-bil´-) *n.* **admissibly** *adv.* **admission** (-shən) *n.* **1** permission or the right to enter. **2** a charge made or paid for entry. **3** an acknowledgement, a confession. **4** a concession made in an argument. **5** a person admitted to a hospital.

admit (ədmit´) *v.t.* (*pres.p.* **admitting**, *past, p.p.* **admitted**) **1** to concede, to acknowledge. **2** to accept as valid or true. **3** to allow to enter. **4** to allow to become a member or to participate or share. **5** (of a hospital) to accept (a patient) for residential treatment. **6** (of a space) to have room for, to accommodate. *~v.i.* to give access (*admits into the dining room*). **to admit of** to allow of, to be capable of. **to admit to** to acknowledge one's

guilt or responsibility in respect of. **admittable** *a.* **admittance** *n.* **1** the act of admitting. **2** entrance given or permitted. **3** a measure of the ease of flow of an alternating current, the reciprocal of impedance. **admittedly** *adv.* I admit, it is true.

admix (admiks´) *v.t.* **1** to mix, to mingle. **2** to add as a further ingredient. **admixture** (admiks´chə, ad´-) *n.* **1** the act of mixing. **2** something added to something else; an alloy; a foreign element.

admonish (ədmon´ish) *v.t.* **1** to reprove gently. **2** to urge, exhort. **3** to warn, caution. **admonishment** *n.* **admonition** (admənish´ən) *n.* **1** (a) gentle reproof. **2** a friendly caution or warning. **admonitory** *a.*

ad nauseam (ad naw´ziam, -si-) *adv.* to the point of producing disgust or nausea.

adnominal (adnom´inəl) *a.* (*Gram.*) attached to a noun.

ado (ədoo´) *n.* **1** activity. **2** trouble, difficulty, fuss. **without further/more ado** straight away, without delay.

-ado (ah´dō, ā´dō) *suf.* forming nouns, e.g. *desperado, renegado, tornado* (*bravado, gambado, strappado,* and some other terms, are alterations of words in *-ade*).

adobe (ədō´bi) *n.* **1** a sun-dried brick. **2** a clay used in making such bricks. **3** a building made of adobe bricks.

adolescent (adəles´ənt) *a.* **1** growing up; between puberty and maturity. **2** typical of people of this age. **3** immature; silly. *~n.* a person in the age of adolescence. **adolescence** *n.*

Adonis (ədō´nis) *n.* (*pl.* **Adonises**) **1** a handsome young man; a beau, a dandy. **2** a butterfly, *Polyommatus adonis.*

adopt (ədopt´) *v.t.* **1** to take into any relationship, as child, heir, citizen, candidate etc. **2** to take (a child) as one's own. **3** to embrace, to espouse (a principle, cause etc.). **4** to take over (an idea, argument etc.) as if it were one's own. **5** to accept (a report, accounts) officially. **6** (of a local authority) to accept responsibility for the maintenance of (a road etc.). **adopter** *n.* **adoption** *n.* **adoptional** *a.* **adoptive** *a.* due to or by reason of adoption. **adoptively** *adv.*

adore (ədaw´) *v.t.* **1** to regard with the utmost respect and affection. **2** to worship as a god. **3** (*coll.*) to like very much. **4** (in the Roman Catholic Church) to offer reverence to. *~v.i.* to offer worship. **adorable** *a.* **1** charming, delightful, fascinating. **2** worthy of the utmost love and respect. **adorableness** *n.* **adorably** *adv.* **adoration** (adərā´shən) *n.* **1** ardent love or esteem. **2** worship, veneration. **adoring** *a.* **adoringly** *adv.*

adorn (ədawn´) *v.t.* **1** to decorate, ornament, embellish. **2** to add attractiveness to. **adorner** *n.* **adornment** *n.* **1** a decoration, ornament or embellishment. **2** the act of adorning.

ADP *abbr.* **1** adenosine diphosphate. **2** automated data processing.

adrenal (ədrē´nəl) *a.* near the kidneys. **adrenal gland** *n.* (*Anat.*) a small gland adjacent to each kidney that secretes adrenalin and steroid hormones.

adrenalin (ədren´əlin), **adrenaline** *n.* **1** a hormone secreted by the adrenal glands that stimulates the heart muscle and increases blood pressure. **2** a crystalline substance derived from the adrenal glands of cattle and sheep, used as a stimulant.

✗ **adress** common misspelling of ADDRESS.

adrift (ədrift´) *a.*, *adv.* **1** drifting; unable to steer. **2** detached from its moorings; unfastened. **3** wandering, at a loss, at the mercy of circumstances. **4** inaccurate; not keeping to a course, guideline, schedule etc. **5** (*coll.*) out of touch; not well informed. **6** (*coll.*) absent without leave.

adroit (ədroit´) *a.* dexterous, active, clever, mentally or physically resourceful. **adroitly** *adv.* **adroitness** *n.*

adsorb (ədsawb´, -z-) *v.t.* to take up and cause to adhere in a thin film on the surface. ~*v.i.* to concentrate and adhere to the surface of a solid. **adsorbable** *a.* **adsorbent** *n.* a solid substance that adsorbs gases, vapours or liquids that contact it. ~*a.* capable of adsorbing. **adsorption** (-sawp´-, -z-) *n.* concentration of a substance on a surface. **adsorptive** *a.*

adsuki ADZUKI.

ADT *abbr.* Atlantic Daylight Time.

aduki ADZUKI.

adulate (ad´ūlāt) *v.t.* to fawn upon, to flatter servilely. **adulation** (-lā´shən) *n.* **adulator** *n.* **adulatory** *a.*

adult (ad´ult, ədult´) *a.* **1** grown to maturity. **2** grown up, full-grown. **3** of or for adults. **4** (*euphem.*) containing sexually explicit material, pornographic. ~*n.* **1** a person, animal or plant that has grown to maturity. **2** (*Law*) a person who has reached the age of majority. **adulthood, adultness** *n.*

adulterate (ədul´tərāt) *v.t.* to corrupt or debase (anything) by mixing it with an inferior substance. ~*a.* **1** adulterated. **2** spurious, debased by admixture. **adulterant** *n.* anything which adulterates or is used to adulterate. ~*a.* adulterating. **adulteration** (-ā´shən) *n.* **adulterator** *n.* **adulterine**[1] (-īn) *a.* **1** spurious, counterfeit. **2** illegal, unlicensed.

adulterine[1] ADULTERATE.

adulterine[2] ADULTERY.

adultery (ədul´təri) *n.* (*pl.* **adulteries**) **1** voluntary sexual intercourse on the part of a married person with someone other than their spouse. **2** an instance of this. **adulterer** *n.* a person who has committed adultery. **adulteress** *n.* a woman who has committed adultery. **adulterine**[2] (-rīn) *a.* conceived in adultery. **adulterous** *a.* of or relating to adultery, having committed adultery. **adulterously** *adv.*

adumbrate (ad´əmbrāt) *v.t.* **1** to outline, to sketch out. **2** to indicate faintly as if by a shadow.

3 to foreshadow. **4** to overshadow. **adumbration** (-brā´shən) *n.* **adumbrative** (ədŭm´brətiv) *a.*

advance (ədvahns´) *v.t.* **1** to bring or move forward or upwards. **2** to supply before or on credit. **3** to promote, to further. **4** to put forward for attention. **5** to set to an earlier time; to bring forward to an earlier date or time. **6** to raise. ~*v.i.* **1** to move forward. **2** to progress. **3** (of prices) to rise. ~*n.* **1** the act or process of moving forward. **2** progress; an example of progress, development or increased sophistication. **3** a payment made beforehand; a loan. **4** a rise (in price). **5** (*pl.*) amorous overtures. **6** promotion. ~*a.* **1** done, supplied etc. beforehand. **2** (of position) forward. **in advance 1** beforehand. **2** in front. **to advance on** to move towards menacingly. **advanced** *a.* **Advanced level** *n.* A LEVEL (under A¹). **Advanced Supplementary level** *n.* AS LEVEL. **advance guard** *n.* a detachment which precedes the advance of the main body of an army. **advance man** *n.* (*pl.* **advance men**) (*NAm.*) a person who visits a place before a visit by a political or public figure in order to make suitable arrangements. **advancement** *n.* **1** the act of advancing; the state of being advanced. **2** preferment. **3** furtherance, improvement. **4** the application beforehand of property to which children are prospectively entitled; the property so applied. **advancer** *n.*

advantage (ədvahn´tij) *n.* **1** a favourable condition or circumstance. **2** superiority of any kind; superior or better position. **3** profit, benefit. **4** in tennis, the next point scored after deuce. ~*v.t.* **1** to benefit. **2** to further, to promote the interests of. **to advantage** so as to display the best points. **to take advantage of 1** to make good use of; to profit by. **2** to exploit or abuse unscrupulously or unfairly. **3** (*euphem.*) to seduce. **advantageous** (advəntā´jəs) *a.* **1** conferring advantage. **2** profitable, beneficial. **advantageously** *adv.* **advantageousness** *n.*

advection (advek´shən) *n.* the transfer of heat by the horizontal movement of air.

advent (ad´vent) *n.* **1** (**Advent**) the season of the Christian year including the four Sundays before Christmas. **2** the Incarnation of Christ; the Second Coming. **3** any arrival, a coming. **Advent Calendar** *n.* a calendar for Advent, usu. with numbered doors or windows to be opened one a day. **Adventism** (-vən-) *n.* **Adventist** (-vən-) *n.* a person who believes that the Second Coming of Christ is imminent.

adventitious (advəntish´əs) *a.* **1** accidental, casual. **2** extraneous, foreign. **3** (*Biol.*) developing in an unusual position. **4** (*Law*) coming otherwise than by direct succession. **adventitiously** *adv.* **adventitiousness** *n.*

adventure (ədven´chə) *n.* **1** an enterprise in which hazard or risk is incurred and for which enterprise and daring are required. **2** any novel or unexpected event. **3** enterprise and daring. **4** a speculation. ~*v.t.* to risk, to hazard, to put in danger. *~v.i.* **1** to venture. **2** to dare. **adventure playground** *n.* a children's playground containing objects that can be built with, climbed on and used in creative play. **adventurer** *n.* **1** a person who seeks adventures. **2** a person who seeks to gain social position by false pretences. **adventuresome** (-səm) *a.* adventurous. **adventuresomeness** *n.* **adventuress** *n.* a female adventurer, a woman who seeks to gain social position by false pretences. **adventurism** *n.* hasty, ill-considered, opportunistic action, esp. in politics. **adventurous** *a.* **1** fond of adventure. **2** venturesome, daring, rash. **3** involving risk; perilous, hazardous. **adventurously** *adv.* **adventurousness** *n.*

adverb (ad´vœb) *n.* a word or phrase qualifying a verb, an adjective or another adverb. **adverbial** (-vœ´-) *a.* **adverbially** *adv.*

adversary (ad´vəsəri) *n.* (*pl.* **adversaries**) **1** an opponent. **2** an enemy, a foe. **adversarial** *a.* **1** involving conflict or opposition. **2** antagonistic, hostile. **3** (of a legal process) involving parties or interests that are in opposition to one another.

Usage note Pronunciation as (advœ´səri), with stress on the second syllable, is best avoided.

---

adverse (ad´vœs) *a.* **1** unpropitious, unfavourable. **2** hostile, inimical. **3** acting in a contrary direction; opposite in position. **adversely** *adv.* **adverseness** *n.* **adversity** (-vœ´-) *n.* (*pl.* **adversities**) **1** adverse circumstances, misfortune, calamity, trouble. **2** an instance of this.

Usage note The adjectives *adverse* and *averse* should not be confused: *adverse* means inimical or unfavourable, and *averse* unwilling or disinclined.

---

advert[1] (ədvœt´) *v.i.* **1** to refer (to). **2** to direct attention to.

advert[2] (ad´vœt) *n.* (*coll.*) short for ADVERTISEMENT (under ADVERTISE).

advertise (ad´vətīz) *v.t.* **1** to publicly describe (a product, service, vacancy etc.) in order to promote awareness, increase sales, invite applications etc. **2** to give public notice of; to make publicly known. **3** to inform. *~v.i.* **1** to issue advertisements. **2** to give public notice of a wish or need (for). **advertisement** (-vœ´tiz-) *n.* **1** a paid announcement in a newspaper or on radio, television etc. **2** the act of advertising. **3** a public notice. **advertiser** *n.*

advice (ədvīs´) *n.* **1** counsel, opinion as to a course of action. **2** a formal or official notice. **3** (*usu. pl.*) information or notice. **4** news.

advise (ədvīz´) *v.t.* **1** to counsel (a person). **2** to recommend (a course of action). **3** to inform, to notify. *~v.i.* **1** to give advice. **2** (*esp. N Am.*) to consult. **advisable** *a.* **1** right, proper, to be recommended, expedient. **2** capable of being advised. **advisability** (-bil´-) *n.* **advisably** *adv.* **advised** *a.* **1** acting with deliberation. **2** well

considered, deliberate. **advisedly** (-zid-) *adv.* with mature deliberation. **advisement** *n.* (*N Am.*) consideration, deliberation. **adviser, advisor** *n.* a person who advises, esp. in a professional capacity. **advisory** *a.* **1** having the function or power to advise. **2** containing advice.

advocaat (ad´vəkah) *n.* a sweet thick liqueur containing raw egg and brandy.

advocate[1] (ad´vəkət) *n.* **1** a person who defends or promotes a cause. **2** a person who pleads a cause in a civil or criminal court. **3** (*Sc.*) a barrister. **4** an intercessor. **advocacy** *n.* (*pl.* **advocacies**) **1** verbal support or argument in favour (of). **2** judicial pleading. **3** the office of advocate. **advocateship** *n.*

advocate[2] (ad´vəkāt) *v.t.* to plead in favour of, recommend.

adze (adz), (*also N Am.*) **adz** *n.* a cutting tool with an arched blade at right angles to the handle. *~v.t.* to shape by means of an adze.

adzuki (ədzoo´ki), **adsuki** (-soo´-), **aduki** (ədoo´-) *n.* **1** a plant, *Phaseolus angularis*, grown esp. in China and Japan. **2** the small round reddish-brown edible seed of this plant. **adzuki bean** *n.* the adzuki plant or its seed.

-ae (ē) *suf.* forming the plural of non-naturalized Latin words, e.g. *laminae, Rosaceae, Homeridae*.

aegis (ē´jis) *n.* protection, a protective influence. **under the aegis of** under the auspices of.

aegrotat (ī´grətat) *n.* **1** a note certifying that a student is sick. **2** a degree awarded to a student unable to sit the relevant examinations because of illness.

-aemia (ē´miə), (*esp. N Am.*) **-emia**, **-haemia** (hē´-), (*esp. N Am.*) **-hemia** *comb. form* of, relating to or denoting blood, esp. a specified condition of the blood.

Aeolian (ēō´liən), (*esp. N Am.*) **Eolian** *a.* **1** of or relating to Aeolus (god of the winds in Greek myth). **2** (**aeolian, eolian**) wind-borne. **Aeolian harp, aeolian harp** *n.* a stringed instrument played by a current of air.

aeon (ē´ən, -on), (*esp. N Am.*) **eon** *n.* **1** a period of immense duration. **2** an age of the universe. **3** (*Astron.*) a period of a thousand million years.

aerate (eə´rāt) *v.t.* **1** to subject to the action of atmospheric air. **2** to charge with carbon dioxide. **3** to oxygenate (the blood) by respiration. **aeration** (-rā´shən) *n.* the act of aerating. **aerator** *n.*

aerial (eə´riəl) *a.* **1** of or relating to the air. **2** occurring, moving, growing, operating in or inhabiting the air. **3** of, for or using aircraft, effected by or operating from or against aircraft. **4** airy, thin, gaseous. **5** atmospheric. **6** high, elevated. **7** imaginary, immaterial, refined. *~n.* a collector or radiator of electromagnetic waves for radio, television etc. **aerialist** *n.* a trapeze artist or tightrope walker. **aeriality** (-al´-) *n.* **aerially** *adv.* **aerial torpedo** *n.* a torpedo launched from an aircraft.

aerie EYRIE.

aero- (eə´rō), **aer-** comb. form **1** of or relating to the air or atmosphere, e.g. aerodynamics. **2** of or relating to aircraft, aeronautics, e.g. aerodrome.

aerobatics (eərəbat´iks) n.pl. spectacular flying or stunts by an aircraft.

aerobe (eə´rōb) n. an organism that requires oxygen for life. **aerobic** (-rō´-) a. **1** (Biol.) using or requiring oxygen, occurring in the presence of oxygen. **2** of or involving aerobes. **3** of or relating to aerobics. **aerobically** adv. **aerobics** n.pl. physical exercises designed to improve heart and lung function, esp. (often sing. in constr.) a system of exercises consisting of routines of rhythmic dancelike movements and stretches, usu. performed to music.

aerobiology (eərōbīol´əji) n. the study of airborne microorganisms.

aerodrome (eə´rədrōm), (N Am.) **airdrome** (eə´drōm) n. an area, with any buildings attached, for the operation of esp. light aircraft.

aerodynamics (eərōdīnam´iks) n. the science which deals with the forces exerted by gases in motion. **aerodynamic** a. **1** of or involving aerodynamics. **2** designed so as to minimize wind resistance. **aerodynamically** adv.

aero-engine (eə´rōenjin) n. an engine used to power an aircraft.

aerofoil (eə´rəfoil), (N Am.) **airfoil** (eə´foil) n. a winglike structure constructed to obtain reaction on its surfaces from the air; one of the flying surfaces of an aeroplane.

aerogram (eə´rəgram) n. **1** a radiogram, a wireless message. **2** (also **aerogramme**) a single sheet of lightweight paper with a printed postage stamp that folds up for sending by airmail; a letter written on this.

aerolite (eə´rəlīt), **aerolith** (-lith) n. **1** a stone which falls through the air to the earth. **2** a meteoric stone.

aerology (eərol´əji) n. the department of science that deals with the atmosphere. **aerological** (-loj´-) a.

aeronaut (eə´rənawt) n. a person who pilots, navigates or flies in a balloon or airship. **aeronautic** (-naw´-), **aeronautical** a. of or relating to aeronautics. **aeronautics** n. the science or art of travel through the air.

aeronomy (eəron´əmi) n. the science of the upper atmosphere of the earth and other planets. **aeronomist** n.

aeroplane (eə´rəplān) n. a mechanically-driven heavier-than-air flying-machine with fixed wings as lifting surfaces.

aerosol (eə´rəsol) n. **1** a suspension of fine particles in air or gas, as in smoke or mist. **2** a substance dispersed as an aerosol from a pressurized metal container. **3** such a container.

aerospace (eə´rəspās) n. **1** the earth's atmosphere and the space beyond. **2** the science or industry concerned with aerospace. ~a. of or relating to aerospace, to travel or operation in aerospace, or to vehicles used in aerospace.

aerostat (eə´rəstat) n. an aircraft that is supported in the air statically, i.e. lighter-than-air.

aerotowing (eə´rōtōing) n. the towing of gliders by powered aircraft.

aerotrain (eə´rōtrān) n. a train that glides above its track supported on a cushion of air.

aery EYRIE.

Aesculapian (ēskūlā´piən), **Esculapian** a. **1** of or belonging to Aesculapius, the Greek god of medicine. **2** medical; medicinal.

aesthete (ēs´thēt, es´-), (esp. N Am.) **esthete** (es´-) n. a person who professes a special appreciation of the beautiful, esp. in the arts. **aesthetic** (əsthet´-), **aesthetical** a. **1** of or relating to aesthetics. **2** appreciating the beautiful in nature and art. **3** in accord with the laws of the beautiful, or with principles of taste. ~n. a set of principles defining beauty or good taste in art. **aesthetically** adv. **aesthetician** (-tish´-) n. **1** a person who studies aesthetics. **2** (N Am.) a beautician. **aestheticism** n. **1** the quality of being aesthetic. **2** devotion to the study of the beautiful. **aestheticize, aestheticise** v.t. **aesthetics** n. the theory or philosophy of the perception of the beautiful.

aestival (ēs´tivəl, es´-), (esp. N Am.) **estival** (es´-) a. (formal) **1** of or belonging to the summer. **2** produced in the summer. **aestivate** v.i. **1** (formal) to remain in a place during the summer. **2** (Zool.) (of an animal) to fall into a summer sleep or torpor. **aestivation** (-ā´shən) n. **1** (Bot.) the internal arrangement of a flower bud, prefloration. **2** (Zool.) the act of remaining torpid in the summer.

aether, aethereal ETHER.

aetiology (ētiol´əji), (esp. N Am.) **etiology** n. (pl. **aetiologies, etiologies**) **1** the study of causation. **2** an investigation into the cause of anything. **3** (Med.) the study of the cause of disease; the cause of a specific disease. **aetiologic** a. **aetiologically** adv.

AF abbr. audio frequency.

af- (əf) pref. AD-, assim. to f, e.g. afford.

afar (əfah´) adv. at or to a (great) distance. **from afar** from a great distance away.

AFC abbr. **1** Air Force Cross. **2** Association Football Club.

AFDCS abbr. Association of First Division Civil Servants.

affable (af´əbəl) a. good-natured, friendly, approachable. **affability** (-bil´-) n. **affably** adv.

affair (əfeə´) n. **1** a matter, a concern, something that is to be done. **2** a sexual or romantic relationship, esp. an extramarital one. **3** an event or sequence of events, esp. one that attains public fame or notoriety. **4** (coll.) a thing. **5** (pl.) public or private business. **6** (pl.) finances. **7** (pl.) circumstances.

affect[1] (əfekt´) v.t. **1** to act upon, have an effect upon, exert an influence upon. **2** (of a disease) to attack. **3** to touch or stir emotionally. **affecting** *a.* touching, moving. **affectingly** *adv.*

Usage note The verbs *affect* and *effect* should not be confused: *affect* means to have an effect on, and *effect* to bring about.

affect² (əfekt´) *v.t.* **1** to make a pretence of, to feign; to pretend (*affect unconcern*). **2** to imitate or assume (*affect an air of indifference*). **3** to pose as. **4** to make a show of liking. **affectation** (afektā´shən) *n.* **1** pretentiousness. **2** a mannerism, form of behaviour etc. adopted or contrived in order to impress. **3** assumption, adoption. **4** pretence. **affected** *a.* **1** pretentious, given to affectation. **2** artificially adopted, contrived. **affectedly** *adv.* **affectedness** *n.*

affection (əfek´shən) *n.* **1** fondness, love. **2** a state of the body due to any cause, malady, disease. **3** (*usu. pl.*) an emotion. **4** a psychological disposition. **5** the act of affecting; the state of being affected. **affectional** *a.* **affectionate** (-nət) *a.* **1** of a loving disposition. **2** tenderly disposed. **3** indicating or expressing love. **affectionately** *adv.* **affectionateness** *n.*

affective (əfek´tiv) *a.* of or relating to the affections, emotional. **affectivity** (-tiv´-), **affectiveness** *n.*

affenpinscher (af´ənpinshə) *n.* **1** a European breed of dog, resembling the griffon, that has tufts of hair on the face. **2** a dog of this breed.

afferent (af´ərənt) *a.* bringing or conducting inwards or towards, esp. conducting nerve impulses towards the brain or spinal cord.

affiance (əfī´əns) *v.t.* (*formal*) to promise solemnly in marriage, to betroth.

affiant (əfī´ənt) *n.* (*N Am.*) a person who makes an affidavit.

affidavit (afidā´vit) *n.* a voluntary affirmation sworn before a person qualified to administer an oath.

affiliate¹ (əfil´iāt) *v.t.* **1** (*usu. pass.*) to connect with a larger organization. **2** to receive as a member or branch. *~v.i.* to become connected or associated, combine (with). **affiliable** *a.* **affiliation** (-ā´shən) *n.* **affiliation order** *n.* a legal order requiring the father of an illegitimate child to make maintenance payments.

affiliate² (əfil´iət) *n.* a person, company, branch etc. that is affiliated to an organization. *~a.* that is an affiliate.

affinity (əfin´iti) *n.* (*pl.* **affinities**) **1** a natural attraction or inclination to, or liking for, something. **2** relationship, esp. relationship by marriage as opposed to consanguinity or relationship by blood. **3** a close connection or structural resemblance. **4** a resemblance due to, or suggesting, common origin. **5** (*Chem.*) chemical attraction, the property by which elements unite to form new compounds. **affinity card** *n.* a bank card linked with a particular charity to which the issuing bank pays

a proportion of the money spent using the card.

Usage note After *affinity* the prepositions *with* and *between* are preferred to *to* and *for*, which do not imply the necessary mutual relationship.

affirm (əfœm´) *v.t.* **1** to assert positively or solemnly; to allege confidently. **2** (*esp. Law*) to confirm, to ratify. **3** to declare the existence or worth of something, or one's commitment to it. **4** (*Logic*) to state affirmatively. *~v.i.* (*Law*) to make a solemn affirmation in lieu of oath. **affirmant**, **affirmer** *n.* **affirmation** (afəmā´shən) *n.* **1** the act of affirming anything; something which is affirmed. **2** (*Law*) a solemn declaration made under penalties, in lieu of oath. **3** a statement or declaration of the existence, truth, worth etc. of something. **affirmative** *a.* **1** (*Gram.*) containing an assertion that something is true or valid. **2** expressing agreement, approval, consent. *~n.* **1** an affirmative statement or reply. **2** (*Gram.*) a word or phrase that indicates agreement, approval or consent. *~int.* (*esp. N Am.*) yes. **in the affirmative** so as to indicate agreement, approval, consent; yes. **affirmative action** *n.* (*N Am.*) a policy designed to favour and assist persons or groups who are often discriminated against, positive discrimination. **affirmatively** *adv.*

affix¹ (əfiks´) *v.t.* **1** to fix, fasten, attach. **2** to annex, to subjoin. **3** to impress (a stamp). **affixation** (-ā´shən) *n.*

affix² (af´iks) *n.* **1** an addition. **2** (*Gram.*) a word or syllable added to the beginning or the end of, or inserted in a word or root to produce a derived word or inflection, a prefix, suffix or infix.

afflatus (əflā´təs) *n.* **1** inspiration. **2** poetic impulse.

afflict (əflikt´) *v.t.* to inflict bodily or mental pain on; to cast down; to trouble. **afflicted to be afflicted with** to suffer from. **affliction** *n.* **1** the state of being afflicted. **2** calamity, trouble, misery, distress. **3** a mental or bodily ailment. **afflictive** *a.*

Usage note The verbs *afflict* and *inflict* should not be confused: *afflict* refers to the immediate source of pain and trouble, and *inflict* to a secondary cause of the source of pain: a torturer inflicts pain *on* or *upon* their victim, who is afflicted *by* or *with* pain.

affluent (af´luənt) *a.* **1** wealthy, prosperous. **2** abundant, copious. **3** flowing freely. *~n.* a tributary. **affluence** *n.* wealth, prosperity. **affluently** *adv.*

afford (əfawd´) *v.t.* **1** to be able to bear the expense of, to have the money, the means etc. to. **2** to be able to ignore the disadvantages of (*We can't afford to offend them*). **3** to provide, furnish, supply. **affordable** *a.* **affordability** (-bil´-) *n.*

afforest (əfor´ist) *v.t.* to plant trees on; to convert into forest. **afforestation** (-ā´shən) *n.* the act of converting waste or other land into forest.

affranchise (əfran´chīz) *v.t.* to make free; to set at liberty physically or morally. **affranchisement** (-chiz-) *n.*

affray (əfrā´) *n.* a breach of the peace, a fight or disturbance involving two or more persons in a public place.

affricate (af´rikət) *n.* a speech sound, such as *ch* in *church*, combining an initial plosive with a following fricative or spirant.

affront (əfrŭnt´) *v.t.* 1 to insult openly. 2 to offend the dignity or modesty of. 3 to confront, esp. in a hostile way, to accost. ~*n.* 1 an open insult. 2 contemptuous, rude treatment.

Afghan (af´gan) *a.* of or belonging to Afghanistan. ~*n.* 1 a native or inhabitant of Afghanistan. 2 the language of Afghanistan, Pashto. 3 an Afghan hound. 4 (**afghan**) a knitted or crocheted thick woollen blanket or shawl. 5 an Afghan coat. **Afghan coat** *n.* a type of sheepskin coat with the skin outside, often embroidered and with a shaggy border. **Afghan hound** *n.* a tall slim hunting dog with long silky hair.

aficionado (əfishənah´dō) *n.* (*pl.* **aficionados**) a keen follower or fan.

afield (əfēld´) *adv.* 1 away, at a distance, abroad. 2 to or in the field.

afire (əfīə´) *adv., pred.a.* 1 on fire. 2 intensely or passionately aroused.

aflame (əflām´) *adv., pred.a.* 1 flaming. 2 feeling passionate emotion or intense excitement.

aflatoxin (af´lətoksin) *n.* (*Chem.*) a carcinogenic toxin produced in badly stored peanuts, maize etc. by the mould *Aspergillus flavus.*

afloat (əflōt´) *a., adv.* 1 floating. 2 at sea, aboard ship. 3 out of debt, solvent. 4 in circulation, current. 5 covered with liquid. 6 in full swing. 7 moving about, adrift.

▣ **affluent** common misspelling of AFFLUENT.

afoot (əfut´) *adv.* 1 on foot. 2 in progress, in action.

afore (əfaw´) *adv., prep.* †1 (*also dial.*) a before. **b** in front (of). 2 (*Naut.*) †in or towards the front part of a ship. **aforementioned** *a.* mentioned earlier. **aforesaid** *a.* said or mentioned before. **aforethought** *a.* premeditated, prepense.

a fortiori (ā fawtiaw´ri, ah) *adv.* with still more reason, much more, still more conclusively.

afoul (əfowl´) *a., adv.* fouled, entangled, in collision. **to fall/ run afoul of** (*NAm.*) to fall foul of.

afraid (əfrād´) *a.* 1 filled with fear, terrified. 2 apprehensive. 3 regretfully admitting or of the opinion.

afresh (əfresh´) *adv.* again, anew, freshly.

African (af´rikən) *a.* of or relating to Africa. ~*n.* 1 a native or inhabitant of Africa. 2 a person, wherever born, who belongs ethnologically to one of the African peoples. **African-American** *n.* a black American. ~*a.* of or relating to black Americans. **African elephant** *n.* the species of elephant, *Loxodonta africana,* found in Africa,

which is larger than the Indian elephant and never domesticated. **Africanist** *n.* a person who specializes in the study of African culture, affairs etc. **Africanize, Africanise** *v.t.* 1 to make African. 2 to bring under black African influence or control. **Africanization** (-zā´shən) *n.* **African violet** *n.* a tropical African plant, *Saintpaulia ionantha,* with velvety leaves and pink, white or violet flowers.

Africander AFRIKANDER.

Afrikaans (afrikahns´) *n.* the language, descended from and similar to Dutch, spoken by Afrikaners and some people of mixed descent in South Africa (one of the official languages of the Republic of South Africa).

Afrikander (afrikan´də), **Africander** *n.* 1 a breed of longhorn, humpbacked cattle originating from southern Africa; an animal of this breed. 2 a breed of southern African fat-tailed sheep; an animal of this breed.

Afrikaner (afrikah´nə) *n.* 1 a person born in South Africa of white parents whose mother tongue is Afrikaans. 2 a S African gladiolus.

Afro (af´rō) *a.* (of a hairstyle) characterized by thick, bushy hair. ~*n.* (*pl.* **Afros**) an Afro hairstyle.

Afro- (af´rō) *comb. form* of or relating to Africa or Africans.

Afro-American (afrōəmer´ikən) *n., a.* AFRICAN-AMERICAN (under AFRICAN).

Afro-Caribbean (afrōkaribē´ən, -kərib´iən) *n.* a person of African descent from the Caribbean. ~*a.* of or relating to Afro-Caribbeans.

Afrocentric (afrōsen´trik) *a.* 1 centred on African or Afro-American history and culture, esp. in order to promote a sense of cultural pride and identity in black Americans. 2 regarding African affairs, culture etc. as pre-eminent.

afrormosia (afrəmō´ziə) *n.* 1 any tree of the African genus *Afrormosia,* with dark hard wood used for furniture. 2 this wood.

aft (ahft) *a., adv.* 1 (*Naut.*) towards or at the stern of a vessel. 2 abaft.

after (ahf´tə) *prep.* 1 at a later time than. 2 behind. 3 in pursuit or search of. 4 in view of, considering. 5 in spite of. 6 concerning. 7 (of a name) with reference to. 8 next in rank or importance to. 9 in imitation of; from an original by. 10 according to. ~*a.* 1 later, subsequent. 2 (*Naut.*) located (further) towards the rear or stern. ~*adv.* 1 later, subsequently. 2 behind. ~*conj.* at a later time than that when. **after you** a polite formula inviting someone to go ahead. **afterbirth** *n.* the placenta, the secundine. **afterburner** *n.* a device that initiates afterburning in a jet engine. **aftercare** *n.* 1 care or supervision following a person's discharge from hospital, prison etc. 2 after-sales service to a customer. 3 subsequent care or maintenance. **afterdamp** *n.* choke damp; carbon dioxide gas resulting from the combustion of firedamp in coal mines. **after-effect** *n.* an effect that follows some time after the cause. **afterglow**

n. **1** a glow in the western sky after sunset. **2** (*coll.*) a feeling of pleasure after an enjoyable experience. **after-hours** *a.* occurring after normal working, business etc. hours. **after-image** *n.* the image that remains for a moment after looking away from an object at which one has been gazing steadily. **afterlife** *n.* **1** life after death. **2** a person's life subsequent to the time in question. **aftermarket** *n.* **1** the market in components and spares. **2** (on the Stock Exchange) the market in shares subsequent to their original issue. **afters** *n.pl.* (*coll.*) what follows the main course at a meal. **after-school** *a.* occurring after normal school hours. **aftershave** *n.* a cosmetic, usu. astringent, lotion applied to the face after shaving. **aftershock** *n.* a tremor occurring after the main shock of an earthquake. **aftertaste** *n.* **1** a taste that persists after eating or drinking. **2** an impression or feeling that remains. **afterthought** *n.* **1** something that one thinks of or does after the original or proper occasion for it is past. **2** a belated addition. **afterward, afterwards** *adv.* **1** subsequently. **2** at a later period.

aftermath (ahf'təmahth) *n.* **1** consequences or after-effects. **2** (*dial.*) a second crop of grass springing up after the first has been mowed.

aftermost (ahf'təməst) *a.* nearest the stern.

afternoon (ahftənoon') *n.* **1** the latter part of the day between noon or lunchtime and evening. **2** the later part of something. *~a.* occurring during the afternoon. *~int.* (*coll.*) good afternoon.

Ag *chem. symbol* silver.

ag- (ag, əg) *pref.* AD-, assim. to *g*, e.g. *aggravate, aggrieve.*

Aga® (ah'gə) *n.* a type of stove with several ovens which is permanently lit. **Aga saga** *n.* (*facet.*) a novel featuring middle-class country life.

aga (ah'gə), **agha** *n.* a Turkish civil or military officer of high rank. **Aga Khan** *n.* the nominated hereditary spiritual head of the Ismaili sect of Muslims.

again (əgen', əgān') *adv.* **1** a second time, once more; afresh, anew. **2** in addition. **3** moreover, besides. **4** on the other hand.

against (əgenst', əgānst') *prep.* **1** in opposition to, opposite to, in contrast to. **2** in contact with, in preparation or provision for.

agama (ag'əmə, əgah'mə) *n.* any land lizard of the Old World genus *Agama.*

agamic (əgam'ik), **agamous** (ag'əməs) *a.* characterized by absence of sexual action, asexual, parthenogenetic.

agamospermy (agəməspœ'mi) *n.* (*Bot.*) the formation of seeds without fertilization by division of the ovule.

agapanthus (agəpan'thəs) *n.* an ornamental plant with bright blue flowers, of the African genus *Agapanthus* and of the order Liliaceae.

agape[1] (əgāp') *a., adv.* in an attitude or condition of wondering expectation.

agape[2] (ag'əpē) *n.* (*pl.* **agapes, agapae** (-pē)) **1** a 'love-feast', a kind of feast of fellowship held by the early Christians in connection with the Lord's Supper. **2** (*Theol.*) Christian love.

agar-agar (āgah-ā'gah), **agar** *n.* a gelatinous substance obtained from seaweeds and used for the artificial cultivation of bacteria.

agaric (əgar'ik) *n.* any fungus of the family *Agaricaceae,* which have a cap and a stalk and include the edible mushroom.

agate (ag'ət, -āt) *n.* any semi-pellucid variety of chalcedony, marked with bands or clouds, or infiltrated by other minerals, and used for seals, brooches etc.

agave (əgā'vi) *n.* any of a genus of spiny-leaved plants, *Agave,* that includes the century plant.

age (āj) *n.* **1** the length of time that a person or thing has existed. **2** a period or stage of life. **3** (*Geol. etc.*) a distinct period of the past, an epoch; a period of geological time; a generation. **4** (*usu. pl., coll.*) a long time. **5** the latter portion of life. **6** (*Law*) (legal) maturity, majority. *~v.i.* (*pres.p.* **ageing, aging,** *past, p.p.* **aged**) **1** to show the signs of becoming older. **2** to grow old. **3** to mature. *~v.t.* to cause to grow old or to show signs of age. **of age** (*Law*) having reached the full legal age (18). **aged** (ājd, ā'jid) *a.* **1** (*pred.*) of a certain age. **2** old. **3** that has been subject to ageing. **4** (of a horse) over six years old. *~n.pl.* (**the aged**) old people. **age group** *n.* a group of people or things classed together by virtue of their age. **ageing, aging** *a.* **1** becoming or appearing older. **2** (esp. of an item of dress) making the wearer appear older. *~n.* **1** growing older. **2** maturing; the process of developing or being allowed to develop its full strength, taste etc. **3** giving the appearance of greater age. **4** a change in the properties of certain metals that occurs after heat treatment or cold working. **ageism** *n.* discrimination on grounds of age. **ageist** *a.* supporting or practising ageism. *~n.* an ageist person. **ageless** *a.* never growing aged, never coming to an end. **age-long** *a.* lasting a very long time. **age of consent** *n.* (*Law*) the age at which a person's consent is legally valid, esp. a person's consent to sexual intercourse. **age-old** *a.* that has been in existence for a very long time. **age-range** *n.* the span of ages between two particular points.

-age (ij) *suf.* forming nouns, denoting actions, as in *breakage, passage;* a collection, group or set, as in *acreage, peerage;* a state or condition, as in *dotage, bondage;* a charge or fee payable, as in *postage;* the result of an action, as in *damage, wreckage;* a place or house, as in *anchorage, orphanage.*

agenda (əjen'də) *n.* **1** (*pl.* **agendas**) a list of the business to be transacted. **2** (*pl.*) things to be done, engagements to be kept. **agendum** *n.*

agent (ā'jənt) *n.* **1** a person who acts or transacts business on behalf of another. **2** a person or company that offers a specific service or acts as a broker. **3** a person who or something which exerts power; something that produces an effect;

the material cause or instrument. **4** a travelling salesperson. **5** a spy. **agency** *n.* (*pl.* **agencies**) **1** a commercial organization offering a specific service. **2** a place where an agent conducts business. **3** the business, functions etc. of an agent. **4** causative action, instrumentality. **5** active working, operation. **6** immediate or intervening action. **7** (*esp. N Am.*) an administrative department of a government. **8** a place of business, office, commercial organization. **agent noun** *n.* a noun that denotes the person or thing that performs a particular action e.g. *speaker, accelerator.*

agent provocateur (azhā provokatœ') *n.* (*pl.* **agents provocateurs** (azhā provokatœ')) a person employed to detect suspected political offenders by leading them on to some overt action.

agglomerate¹ (əglom'ərāt) *v.t.* to heap up or collect into a ball or mass. *~v.i.* to gather in a mass. **agglomeration** (-ā'shən) *n.* **agglomerative** *a.*

agglomerate² (əglom'ərət) *a.* collected into a mass; heaped up. *~n.* **1** a mass. **2** (*Geol.*) a mass of volcanic fragments united by heat.

agglutinate (əgloo'tināt) *v.t.* **1** to cause to adhere; to glue together. **2** (*Biol.*) to cause (bacteria, blood cells etc.) to collect into clumps. **3** to compound (simple words or roots) with little change into more complex terms. *~v.i.* **1** to unite, cohere. **2** to form compound words. **agglutination** (-ā'shən) *n.* **agglutinative** (-nə-) *a.*

aggrandize (əgran'dīz), **aggrandise** *v.t.* **1** to make great in power, wealth, rank or reputation. **2** to cause to appear greater than in reality; to exaggerate. **3** to exalt. **aggrandizement** (-diz-), **aggrandization** (-zā'shən) *n.*

aggravate (ag'rəvāt) *v.t.* **1** to make worse or more severe. **2** (*coll.*) to exasperate, to provoke, to irritate. **aggravating** *a.* **aggravatingly** *adv.* **aggravation** (-ā'shən) *n.* **1** the act of aggravating; the state of being aggravated. **2** something which aggravates. **3** an addition to a burden, wrong, crime, abuse or charge.

aggregate¹ (ag'rigāt) *v.t.* **1** to collect together. **2** to bring together into a mass or whole. *~v.i.* **1** to form an aggregate. **2** to unite. **aggregation** (-ā'shən) *n.* **1** the act of collecting together; the state of being aggregated. **2** an aggregate. **aggregative** *a.*

aggregate² (ag'rigət) *a.* **1** collected together; collected into a mass. **2** formed of separate parts combined into a mass or whole. **3** consisting of florets united together. **4** (*Bot.*) consisting of individuals united in a compound organism. **5** (*Mineral.*) composed of distinct minerals. *~n.* **1** a mass formed by the union of individual units or particles; the total, the whole. **2** material, esp. crushed particles, to be bonded together with cement to form concrete. **3** (*Geol.*) a rock that consists of a number of different minerals. **in the aggregate** collectively.

aggress (əgres') *v.i.* to begin an attack or quarrel. *~v.t.* to attack, to assault. **aggression** (-shən) *n.*

1 (an) unprovoked attack or injury. **2** vigour, forcefulness or self-assertiveness. **3** violation of a country's territorial integrity or sovereignty by another country. **4** (*Psych.*) a hostile attitude or outlook. **aggressive** *a.* **1** involving an act of aggression. **2** offensive, pugnacious. **3** vigorous, forceful or self-assertive. **4** making the first attack. **aggressively** *adv.* **aggressiveness** *n.* **aggressor** *n.* the person, country etc. that begins hostilities, a quarrel etc.

aggrieve (əgrēv') *v.t.* **1** to cause grief, annoyance or pain to. **2** to perpetrate injustice against. **aggrieved** *a.* having a grievance. **aggrievedly** *adv.*

aggro (ag'rō) *n.* (*coll.*) **1** aggressive, annoying behaviour; troublemaking. **2** trouble, problems.

aghast (əgahst') *a.* **1** dismayed; appalled, horrified. **2** struck with terror.

agile (aj'īl) *a.* **1** having the ability to move quickly and gracefully. **2** mentally quick, nimble, active. **agilely** *adv.* **agility** (əjil'-) *n.*

aging AGEING (under AGE).

agio (aj'iō) *n.* (*pl.* **agios**) **1** the difference in value between one kind of currency and another. **2** money-changing. **3** the charge for changing notes for cash, or one kind of money for another.

agist (əjist') *v.t.* to provide pasture for (the cattle of others) at a certain rate.

agitate (aj'itāt) *v.t.* **1** to shake or move briskly. **2** to excite, to disturb, to perturb. *~v.i.* to arouse public feeling or opinion for or against something. **agitation** (-ā'shən) *n.* **1** the act of agitating; the state of being agitated. **2** commotion, perturbation. **agitator** *n.* **1** a person who or something which agitates. **2** a mechanical contrivance for shaking and mixing.

agitato (ajitah'tō) *adv., a.* (*Mus.*) in an agitated manner.

aglet (ag'lit), **aiglet** (ā'-), **aiguillette** (āgwilet') *n.* **1** the metal tag of a lace. **2** a taglike ornament on a uniform.

aglow (əglō') *a., adv.* in a glow.

AGM *abbr.* annual general meeting.

agnail (ag'nāl) *n.* a piece of torn skin or a sore at the root of a toe- or fingernail.

agnate (ag'nāt) *n.* **1** a descendant through the male line from the same male ancestor. **2** a relative on the father's side. *~a.* **1** related by descent from a common male ancestor. **2** related on the father's side. **3** allied, akin. **agnatic** (-nat'-) *a.* **agnation** (-nā'shən) *n.*

agnolotti (agnəlot'i) *n.* small pieces of pasta stuffed with meat etc.

agnosia (agnō'siə) *n.* (*Med.*) loss of the ability to recognize familiar things or people, esp. after brain damage.

agnostic (əgnos'tik) *n.* **1** a person who believes that knowledge of the existence of God is impossible. **2** a person who denies that humans have any knowledge except of material phenomena. **3** a person who professes uncertainty about any subject; a sceptic. *~a.* of or relating to agnostics or their teachings. **agnostically** *adv.* **agnosticism** (-sizm) *n.*

Agnus Dei (agnŭs dā´ē) *n.* **1** a figure of a lamb bearing a flag or cross. **2** a part of the Mass beginning with the words *Agnus Dei.* **3** a musical setting of this part of the Mass.

ago (əgō´) *adv.* before this time.

Usage note It is best to avoid the use of *since* rather than *that* or *when* after *ago*, as both *since* and *ago* imply an earlier period (so *It is 3 days since it happened, but 2 days ago that I was told*).

agog (əgog´) *a., adv.* in a state of eager expectation.

agogic (əgoj´ik) *a.* (*Mus. etc.*) of or characterized by variations of stress in speech or musical rhythm produced by the lengthening of a syllable or note. **agogics** *n.* variation of stress by lengthening of duration.

à gogo (ə gō´gō) *adv.* in abundance, galore.

agonic (əgon´ik) *a.* having no dip, denoting an imaginary line on the earth's surface, drawn through the two magnetic poles.

agonist (ag´ənist) *n.* **1** any muscle whose action is opposed by another muscle. **2** a substance which, when combined with a receptor, triggers a physiological response. **3** a competitor in an agon; a person engaged in a struggle. **agonistic** (-nis´-), **agonistical** *a.* **1** of or relating to a chemical agonist. **2** combative, argumentative, very competitive. **3** (*Zool.*) (of animal behaviour) relating to conflict. **agonistically** *adv.*

agonize (ag´ənīz), **agonise** *v.t.* to subject to extreme pain; to torture. *~v.i.* **1** to suffer agony. **2** to make desperate or convulsive efforts. **3** (*coll.*) to struggle desperately to come to a decision or conclusion (over). **agonized** *a.* expressing agony. **agonizing** *a.* causing agony. **agonizingly** *adv.*

agony (ag´əni) *n.* (*pl.* **agonies**) **1** anguish of mind. **2** extreme physical pain. **3** the death struggle. **agony aunt** *n.* **1** the person who writes the replies for an agony column. **2** a woman who gives sympathetic advice. **agony column** *n.* **1** the part of a newspaper or magazine dealing with readers' problems. **2** the column in a newspaper devoted to advertisements for missing friends and other matters of a personal kind. **agony uncle** *n.* a man who writes the replies for an agony column.

agora (agərah´) *n.* (*pl.* **agorot** (-rot´)) a monetary unit of Israel equal to one hundredth of a shekel.

agoraphobia (agərəfō´biə) *n.* (*Psych.*) abnormal dread of open spaces. **agoraphobe** (ag´-) *n.* a person who suffers from agoraphobia. **agoraphobic** *a., n.*

AGR *abbr.* advanced gas-cooled reactor.

agrarian (əgreə´riən) *a.* **1** of or relating to the land and cultivation. **2** of or relating to landed property or cultivated land. *~n.* a person in favour of the redistribution of landed property. **agrarianism** *n.*

☒ **agravate** common misspelling of AGGRAVATE.

agree (əgrē´) *v.i.* **1** to be of one mind, to hold the same opinion. **2** to consent, to accede (to). **3** to live in concord. **4** to reach an agreement or settlement. **5** to harmonize, to coincide (with). **6** to suit; to have a beneficial effect, be good for. **7** (*Gram.*) to be in grammatical concord (with). *~v.t.* **1** to admit, to concede. **2** to reach agreement about. **3** to give consent or approval to. **4** to concert, to reconcile, to render consistent with one another. **to be agreed** to have reached agreement.

agreeable (əgrē´əbəl) *a.* **1** affording pleasure, pleasing, pleasant. **2** favourable, disposed to. **3** corresponding, conformable, suitable to. **agreeability** (-bil´-), **agreeableness** *n.* **agreeably** *adv.*

agreement (əgrē´mənt) *n.* **1** the fact of being of one mind; concurrence in the same opinion. **2** an arrangement mutually acceptable; a contract duly executed and legally binding. **3** conformity, correspondence. **4** (*Gram.*) grammatical concord.

☒ **agression** common misspelling of AGGRESSION (under AGGRESS).

agribusiness (ag´ribiznis) *n.* **1** agriculture conducted as a strictly commercial enterprise, esp. using advanced technology. **2** an organization engaged in this. **3** the businesses involved in producing and marketing farm produce taken as a whole.

agriculture (ag´rikŭlchə) *n.* the science and practice of cultivating the soil, growing crops and rearing livestock. **agricultural** (-kŭl´-) *a.* **agriculturalist** (-kŭl´-), **agriculturist** *n.* **agriculturally** *adv.*

agrimony (ag´riməni) *n.* (*pl.* **agrimonies**) **1** any plant of the genus *Agrimonia*, one species of which (*A. eupatoria*) was formerly valued as a tonic. **2** any of various other similar plants, e.g. hemp agrimony.

agro- (ag´rō) *comb. form* of or relating to fields, soil or agriculture.

agrochemical (agrōkem´ikəl) *n.* a chemical for use on the land or in farming. *~a.* of or producing agrochemicals.

agroforestry (agrōfor´istri) *n.* farming that incorporates the cultivation of trees.

agronomy (əgron´əmi) *n.* the science of land management, cultivation and crop production. **agronomic** (-nom´-), **agronomical** *a.* **agronomist** *n.*

aground (əgrownd´) *a., adv.* on the shallow bottom of any water.

ague (ā´gū) *n.* **1** a malarial fever, marked by successive hot and cold paroxysms, the latter attended with shivering. **2** any fit of shivering or shaking. **agued** *a.* affected with ague. **aguish** *a.*

AH *abbr.* in the year of the Hegira (AD 622), from which is dated the Muslim era.

ah (ah) *int.* used to express various emotions, according to the manner in which it is uttered, e.g. sorrow, regret, fatigue, relief, surprise, admiration, appeal, remonstrance, aversion, contempt, mockery.

aha (əhah´) *int.* an exclamation of surprise, triumph or mockery.

ahead (əhed´) *adv.* 1 in front, further on. 2 forward, esp. in a straight line. 3 in the future. **ahead of 1** in front of, in the line of progress of. 2 further on than, making better progress than. 3 in advance of (*ahead of his time*). 4 awaiting (someone) in the future.

ahem (əhem´) *int.* an exclamation used to attract attention or merely to gain time.

-aholic (əhol´ik), **-oholic** *comb. form* (a person) having an addiction.

ahoy (əhoi´) *int.* (*Naut.*) used in hailing another ship or to attract attention.

AI *abbr.* 1 artificial insemination. 2 (*Comput.*) artificial intelligence.

AID *abbr.* artificial insemination by donor.

aid (ād) *v.t.* to assist, to help; to give financial assistance to. ~*n.* 1 help, assistance. 2 anything, e.g. an implement, machine, book, that assists in the performance of a task. 3 financial or material assistance given by one country to another. **in aid of 1** in support of, so as to help. 2 (*coll.*) intended for.

aide (ād) *n.* an assistant, a help. **aide-de-camp** (ād-dəkamp´, -kā´, ed-) *n.* (*pl.* **aides-de-camp** (-kamp´, -kā´)) an officer who receives and transmits the orders of a general or other senior officer. **aide-mémoire** (ādmemwah´) *n.* (*pl.* **aides-mémoire, aides-mémoires** (ādmemwah´)) an aid to memory, a memorandum, a memorandum-book.

Aids (ādz), **AIDS** *n.* a condition in which the body's immune system is attacked by a virus, leaving the body defenceless against disease.

aiglet AGLET.

aigrette (ā´grit, āgret´) *n.* 1 an ornamental feather or plume, esp. from the egret. 2 a spray of gems worn on the head.

aiguille (āgwēl´, ā´-) *n.* a slender, needle-shaped peak of rock.

aiguillette AGLET.

AIH *abbr.* artificial insemination by husband.

aikido (īkē´dō) *n.* a Japanese martial art using throws, locks and twisting techniques to turn an opponent's own momentum against them.

ail (āl) *v.i.* to be in pain, trouble or ill health. ~*tv.t.* to trouble, to cause pain or uneasiness of body or mind to. **ailing** *a.* affected with illness, sick, suffering. **ailment** *n.* a (slight) disorder or illness, sickness, indisposition.

aileron (ā´leron) *n.* the hinged portion on the rear edge of the wing-tip of an aeroplane that controls lateral balance.

aim (ām) *v.t.* 1 to point at a target with (a missile or weapon), to level (a gun) at a target. 2 to direct (a blow, remark, criticism) at. ~*v.i.* 1 to point a weapon, direct a blow etc. (at). 2 to intend, to endeavour (to do). 3 to try to achieve or

attain. 4 to take aim. ~*n.* 1 an intention, a purpose. 2 the fact of aiming a weapon, missile etc. 3 the point or object aimed at. 4 the direction in which a missile travels. **to take aim** to direct a gun, missile etc. (at). **aimer** *n.* **aimless** *a.* purposeless, objectless. **aimlessly** *adv.* **aimlessness** *n.*

ain't (ānt) *contr.* (*coll.*) 1 are not. 2 is not, am not. 3 have not, has not.

aioli (īō´li), **aïoli** *n.* mayonnaise flavoured with garlic.

air (eə) *n.* 1 the mixture of gases which envelops the earth, chiefly consisting of oxygen and nitrogen; the atmosphere. 2 open space. 3 the medium of broadcasting, airwaves. 4 (the operation of, or transportation by) aircraft. 5 a distinctive quality, an aura, atmosphere. 6 manner, appearance, mien, gesture. 7 (*usu. pl.*) affectation, haughtiness. 8 a light wind, a breeze. 9 (*Mus.*) a tune, melody, either solo or in harmony. ~*v.t.* 1 to expose to open or fresh air, to ventilate. 2 to dry or warm (as clothes) by exposing to heat. 3 to express publicly (a grievance, an opinion). 4 to show off, to parade. ~*v.i.* to become aired. **in the air 1** (of an opinion, feeling) perceptible; current or becoming current. 2 (of a project, plan) as yet unsettled, in the process of being decided. **to tread/ walk on air** to feel elated. **up in the air** as yet unsettled, in the process of being decided. **air bag** *n.* a safety device in a car consisting of a bag that inflates automatically in a collision, cushioning the passengers against the impact. **air base** *n.* a place used as a base for operations by, or for the housing of, military aircraft. **air-bed**, (*N Am.*) **air mattress** *n.* a bed or mattress inflated with air. **air bladder** *n.* a vesicle containing air, esp. the swimming-bladder of fishes. **airborne** *a.* 1 (of troops etc.) carried by air. 2 (of an aircraft) in the air, in flight. **air brake** *n.* 1 a brake worked by compressed air. 2 a device, esp. a movable flap, to reduce the speed of an aircraft. **airbrick** *n.* a perforated brick or iron grating for admitting air through a wall. **air bridge** *n.* a service by air transport between two places. **airbrush** *n.* a device for spraying paint by compressed air. ~*v.t.* to paint with an airbrush. **Air Chief Marshal** *n.* an officer in the RAF corresponding in rank to a general in the Army. **Air Commodore** *n.* an officer in the RAF corresponding in rank to a brigadier in the Army. **air-condition** *v.t.* to equip (e.g. a building) with an air-conditioning system. **air-conditioned** *a.* **air-conditioner** *n.* **air-conditioning** *n.* an apparatus for, or the process of, purifying the air circulating in a room or building and controlling its temperature and humidity. **air corridor** *n.* a path for air traffic in an area where flying is restricted. **aircraft** *n.* (*pl.* **aircraft**) a flying-machine of any type, whether heavier or lighter than air. **aircraft carrier** *n.* a ship designed for the housing and servicing of aircraft, with a deck where they can take off and land. **aircraftman, aircraftwoman** *n.* (*pl.* **aircraftmen, aircraftwomen**) (a person of) the lowest rank in the RAF. **aircrew** *n.* **1** (*pl.* **aircrews**) the crew of an aircraft. **2** (*usu. as pl.* **aircrew**) a member of such a crew. **air cushion** *n.* **1** a cushion or pillow inflated to make it resilient. **2** the body of air supporting a hovercraft. **airdrome** AERODROME. **airdrop** *n.* a delivery of supplies or troops by parachute from an aircraft. ~*v.t.* (*pres.p.* **airdropping**, *past, p.p.* **airdropped**) to drop (supplies etc.) by parachute. **airer** *n.* a clothes-horse. **airfield** *n.* a field specially prepared for the landing and taking-off of aircraft. **airflow** *n.* the flow of air past a moving surface or vehicle, or as created in a wind tunnel. **airfoil** AEROFOIL. **air force** *n.* the branch of a country's armed forces organized for warfare in the air. **airframe** *n.* the structure and external surfaces of an aircraft or rocket, excluding the engines. **airgun** *n.* a gun from which missiles are projected by compressed air. **airhead** *n.* **1** (*Mil.*) a base inside enemy territory for aircraft operations. **2** (*sl.*) a stupid person. **airhole** *n.* **1** an opening to admit air. **2** a flaw in a casting. **3** an air pocket. **air hostess** *n.* (*dated*) an air stewardess. **airing** *n.* **1** exposure to the free action of the air, or to a fire or heat. **2** a walk or ride in the open air. **air lane** *n.* a path regularly used by aircraft. **airless** *a.* **1** not open to the air. **2** close, musty. **3** calm, still. **airlessness** *n.* **air letter** *n.* AEROGRAM. **airlift** *n.* the transport of supplies, goods etc. by air, esp. in an emergency. **airline** *n.* **1** a commercial organization operating regular transport by air. **2** a pipe through which air is supplied to a diver. **airliner** *n.* a passenger-carrying aeroplane flying along a regular air route. **airlock** *n.* **1** a chamber that has airtight doors and allows entrance to or exit from an area where the air is under pressure. **2** an obstruction in a pipe caused by a bubble of air. **airmail** *n.* **1** mail conveyed by aircraft. **2** the postal system of conveying mail by air. **airman** *n.* (*pl.* **airmen**) **1** a pilot or a member of the crew of an aircraft. **2** a non-commissioned member of the RAF. **Air Marshal** *n.* an officer in the RAF corresponding in rank to a lieutenant-general in the Army. **air mile** *n.* **1** a nautical mile used for measuring distances flown by aircraft. **2** (*usu. pl.*) a point entitling the buyer of an airline ticket or other product to free air travel for a certain distance. **airmiss** *n.* a near-collision of aircraft. **airplane** *n.* (*N Am.*) an aeroplane. **air plant** *n.* an epiphyte. **air pocket** *n.* **1** an area of rarefied atmosphere where an aircraft is apt to drop unexpectedly. **2** an air-filled space, e.g. in a pipe. **airport** *n.* a place where civil aircraft take off and land, often with extensive passenger facilities, customs, freight terminals etc. **air raid** *n.* an attack on a town, troops etc. by hostile aircraft. **air rifle** *n.* a rifle which operates by compressed air. **air sac** *n.* **1** a tiny air cell in the lungs, an alveolus. **2** an air-filled space connecting with the lungs in

birds. **airs and graces** *n.pl.* would-be elegant or genteel mannerisms intended to impress. **airship** *n.* a lighter-than-air flying-machine driven by an engine. **airsick** *a.* affected by airsickness. **airsickness** *n.* nausea caused by the motion of aircraft. **airside** *n.* the part of an airport complex beyond the passport control, customs etc., where the aircraft are boarded or loaded (cp. LANDSIDE (under LAND)). **airspace** *n.* the atmosphere above (a certain part of) the earth, esp. above a particular country. **air speed** *n.* the speed of an aeroplane or airship relative to the air, as distinct from its speed relative to the ground. **airstream** *n.* a current of air. **airstrip** *n.* a strip of even ground where aircraft can take off or land. **air terminal** *n.* a building where passengers assemble to be taken to an airport. **airtight** *a.* **1** not allowing air to pass in or out. **2** unassailable. **airtime** *n.* broadcasting time, esp. on radio, allotted to a particular topic, record etc. **air-to-air** *a.* between aircraft in flight. **air-traffic control** *n.* the ground-based organization which determines the altitudes, routes etc. to be used by aircraft in a particular area. **air-traffic controller** *n.* **Air Vice-Marshal** *n.* an officer in the RAF corresponding in rank to a major-general in the Army. **airwaves** *n.pl.* (radio) broadcasting channels. **airway** *n.* **1** a passage for air into the lungs; a tubelike device inserted into the throat to enable air to reach the lungs. **2** a fully organized air route. **3** a tunnel in a mine, fitted with valve-like doors, for the passage of air in one direction. **airwoman** *n.* (*pl.* **airwomen**) **1** a female pilot or member of an aircraft crew. **2** a female non-commissioned member of the RAF. **airworthy** *a.* (of an aeroplane) examined and passed as fit for flying. **airworthiness** *n.*

Airedale (eə′dāl) *n.* a large breed of terrier with a rough-haired, tan-coloured coat; a dog of this breed.

⊠ **aeroplane** common misspelling of AEROPLANE.

airy (eə′ri) *a.* (*comp.* **airier**, *superl.* **airiest**) **1** well-ventilated. **2** spacious; uncluttered or unconstricted. **3** nonchalant; flippant; offhand. **4** light as air. **5** light and graceful in movement. **6** visionary; unreal. **7** situated high up in the air, lofty. **airily** *adv.* **airiness** *n.* **airy-fairy** *a.* (*coll.*) fanciful, unrealistic.

aisle (īl) *n.* **1** a division of a church, esp. one parallel to, and separated by pillars from, the nave. **2** a passage between the seats in a church, theatre, cinema etc. **3** a passage between rows of shelving in a supermarket.

ait (āt), **eyot** (āt, ā′ət) *n.* a small island, esp. one in a river or lake.

aitch (āch) *n.* the letter *h*.

aitchbone (āch′bōn) *n.* **1** the rump bone. **2** the cut of beef over this bone.

ajar¹ (əjah′) *a., adv.* (of a door) partly open.

ajar² (əjah′) *adv.* in a jarring state, at discord.

aka, AKA *abbr.* also known as.

akee ACKEE.

Akela (ahkā´lə) *n.* the adult leader of a group of Cub Scouts.

akimbo (əkim´bō) *adv.* with the hands resting on the hips and the elbows turned outwards.

akin (əkin´) *a.* **1** allied by blood relationship. **2** allied in properties or character.

☒ **acknowledge** common misspelling of ACKNOWLEDGE.

akvavit AQUAVIT.

Al *chem. symbol* aluminium.

al- (əl) *pref.* AD-, assim. to *l*, e.g. *alliteration*.

-al¹ (əl) *suf.* forming adjectives: *annual, equal, mortal*.

-al² (əl) *suf.* forming nouns, esp. denoting the enactment of the action of a verb: *arrival, acquittal*.

ala (ā´lə) *n.* (*pl.* **alae** (-ē)) a wing or winglike anatomical or plant part. **alar** (ā´lə), **alary** (-əri) *a.* **1** of or relating to a wing. **2** winglike, wing-shaped. **alate** (-āt), **alated** *a.* having wings or winglike processes.

à la (a´ la) *prep.* **1** in the fashion of, after the manner of, after. **2** (*of food*) prepared with or in the style of.

alabaster (al´əbastə) *n.* a fine, soft, usu. white or semi-transparent form of gypsum, widely used for making ornaments. ~*a.* **1** made of alabaster. **2** white and translucent like alabaster. **alabastrine** (-bas´trin, -trīn) *a.*

à la carte (a la kaht´) *a., adv.* **1** (of a menu) having each dish priced separately. **2** (of a dish) priced separately, not part of a set menu.

†**alack** (əlak´) *int.* used to express sorrow. †**alackaday** *int.*

alacrity (əlak´riti) *n.* **1** briskness, eagerness. **2** vivacity, sprightliness.

à la mode (a la mōd´) *adv., a.* **1** fashionable. **2** (of meat) braised in wine. **3** (*N Am.*) served with ice cream.

alar ALA.

alarm (əlahm´) *n.* **1** warning of approaching danger. **2** a device for waking people from sleep or arousing attention. **3** terror mingled with surprise. ~*v.t.* **1** to frighten; to startle or agitate. **2** to rouse to a sense of danger. **alarm clock** *n.* a clock that can be set to make a loud noise at a particular hour. **alarmed** *a.* **alarming** *a.* frightening, disturbing. **alarmingly** *adv.* **alarmist** *n.* **1** a person who needlessly spreads alarm, a scaremonger. **2** a person who is easily alarmed. ~*a.* that needlessly spreads alarm. **alarmism** *n.*

alas (əlas´) *int.* used to express sorrow, grief, pity or concern.

alate, alated ALA.

alb (alb) *n.* a long white surplice with close sleeves worn by priests and servers at some church services.

albacore (al´bəkaw) *n.* **1** a large long-finned species of tuna, *Thunnus alalunga*. **2** any of various allied species.

Albanian (albā´niən) *a.* of or relating to Albania or its inhabitants. ~*n.* **1** a native or inhabitant of Albania. **2** the language of Albania.

albatross (al´bətros) *n.* **1** any long-winged large-bodied bird of the family *Diomedeidae*, esp. *Diomedea exulans*, the largest known seabird, the great albatross. **2** a burden or handicap from which a person cannot escape. **3** in golf, a score of three under par for a hole.

albedo (albē´dō) *n.* (*pl.* **albedos**) the fraction of incident light reflected by a planet or other body or surface.

albeit (awlbē´it) *conj.* although, even though, notwithstanding.

albert (al´bət) *n.* a short kind of watch-chain, fastened to a waistcoat buttonhole.

albescent (albes´ənt) *a.* becoming or passing into white; whitish. **albescence** *n.*

albino (albē´nō) *n.* (*pl.* **albinos**) **1** a human being, or animal, having the colour pigment absent from the skin, the hair and the eyes, so as to be abnormally light in colour. **2** a plant in which little or no chlorophyll is developed. **albinism** (al´bi-) *n.* **albinotic** (-binot´-) *a.*

albite (al´bīt) *n.* white feldspar, soda feldspar.

album (al´bəm) *n.* **1** a blank book for the insertion of photographs, poetry, drawings or the like. **2** (*N Am.*) a visitors' book. **3** a collection of pieces of recorded music issued on one or more long-playing records, cassettes, CDs etc.

albumen (al´būmin) *n.* **1** the white of an egg. **2** (*Bot.*) the substance interposed between the skin and embryo of many seeds; the endosperm or perisperm.

albumin (al´būmin) *n.* any of several water-soluble proteins existing in animals, in the white of egg, in blood serum and in plants. **albuminoid** (-bū´minoid), **albuminoidal** (-oi´-) *a.* resembling or of the nature of albumin. ~*n.* a scleroprotein. **albuminous** (-bū´-), **albuminose** (-nōs) *a.* consisting of, resembling or containing albumin. **albuminuria** (-nū´riə) *n.* **1** the presence of albumin in the urine. **2** the diseased condition causing this.

alburnum (albœ´nəm), **alburn** (al´bœn) *n.* the sapwood in exogenous stems, between the inner bark and heartwood.

alchemy (al´kəmi) *n.* (*pl.* **alchemies**) **1** the chemistry of the Middle Ages, the search for an alkahest, the philosophers' stone, and the panacea. **2** a magic power of transmutation. **alchemic** (-kem´-), **alchemical** *a.* **alchemically** *adv.* **alchemist** *n.* **alchemize, alchemise** *v.t.* to transmute.

alcohol (al´kəhol) *n.* **1** (*Chem.*) **a** a colourless liquid produced by fermenting sugars and constituting the intoxicating agent in various drinks. **b** any of a class of compounds analogous to common alcohol that contain one or more hydroxyl groups. **2** any intoxicating drink containing alcohol. **alcohol-free** *a.* **1** (of a drink) containing no alcohol. **2** (of a bar etc.) serving no alcoholic drinks. **alcoholic** (-hol´-) *n.* a person who is addicted to alcohol. ~*a.* of, relating to or containing alcohol. **alcoholism** *n.* **1** addiction to or excessive use of alcohol. **2** the action of (excessive) alcohol on the human system. **alcoholometer** (-om´itə) *n.* an instrument for measuring the proportion of pure alcohol in a liquor. **alcoholometrical** (-met´-) *a.* **alcoholometry** (-om´itri) *n.*

alcopop (al´kōpop) *n.* an alcoholic drink tasting and packaged like a soft drink.

alcove (al´kōv) *n.* **1** a recess in a wall. **2** a vaulted recessed area, as in a garden wall.

aldehyde (al´dihīd) *n.* (*Chem.*) **1** a volatile liquid that can be obtained from alcohol by oxidation; acetaldehyde, ethanal. **2** any of an extensive class of organic compounds of the same type. **aldehydic** (-hī´-) *a.*

al dente (al den´ti, -tā) *a.* (esp. of cooked pasta) firm when bitten.

alder (awl´də) *n.* **1** a tree, *Alnus glutinosa*, growing in moist places. **2** any of various other plants whose leaves more or less resemble those of the alder. **alder buckthorn** *n.* a shrub, *Frangula alnus*, with small black berry-like fruits. **alder fly** *n.* any neuropterous insect of the genus *Sialis*, that are found near streams.

alderman (awl´dəmən) *n.* (*pl.* **aldermen**) **1** (*Hist.*) (in England and Wales) a civic dignitary, elected from among members of a council, ranking next below the mayor. **2** (in the US, Canada, Australia etc.) a male elected member of the city council. **aldermanic** (-man´-) *a.* **aldermanship** *n.* **alderperson** *n.* (*N Am.*) an alderman or alderwoman (non-sexist use). **alderwoman** *n.* (*pl.* **alderwomen**) (in the US, Canada, Australia etc.) a female elected member of a city council.

aldosterone (aldos´tərōn) *n.* a steroid hormone produced by the adrenal glands that regulates salt levels.

aldrin (awl´drin, al´-) *n.* an extremely poisonous chlorine containing insecticide.

ale (āl) *n.* **1** an intoxicating drink made from malt by fermentation, orig. distinguished from beer in not being flavoured with hops. **2** beer. **3** (*N Am.*) a type of beer fermented rapidly at high temperature. **alehouse** *n.* a tavern licensed to sell ale.

aleatory (ā´liətəri), **aleatoric** (-tor´ik) *a.* **1** depending upon an uncertain event or chance. **2** (*Mus.*) (of music) allowing the performer a random choice of certain elements.

alec (al´ik), **aleck** *n.* (*Austral., sl.*) a stupid person.

☒ **aledge** common misspelling of ALLEGE.

alee (əlē´) *a., adv.* **1** on the lee side. **2** to leeward.

alembic (əlem´bik) *n.* a vessel made of glass or copper formerly used for distilling.

alert (əlœt´) *a.* **1** watchful, vigilant. **2** brisk, lively. ~*n.* **1** warning of danger. **2** a period during which a state of enhanced preparedness to defend against or respond to an attack is in force. **3** a warning by siren or otherwise of a threatened air raid. ~*v.t.* **1** to warn. **2** to put on guard. **3** to arouse. **on the alert 1** on the watch. **2** on one's guard. **3** ready, prepared. **alertly** *adv.* **alertness** *n.*

aleuron (əlū´ron), **aleurone** (-rōn) *n.* a protein found in the form of grains in ripening seeds.

alewife (āl´wīf) *n.* (*pl.* **alewives** (-wīvz)) a N American fish, *Clupea serrata*, resembling the shad but smaller.

alexanders (aligzahn´dəz) *n.* (*pl.* **alexanders**) a European plant, *Smyrnium olusatrum*, formerly used as a vegetable.

alexandrine (aligzahn´drīn) *n.* a verse line containing twenty syllables in French, or six iambic feet in English prosody, usu. divided by a caesura.

alexandrite (aligzahn´drīt) *n.* a dark green chrysoberyl.

alexia (əlek´siə) *n.* (a brain defect resulting in) the inability to understand written or printed words, word-blindness.

alfalfa (alfal´fə) *n.* a plant, *Medicago sativa*, with flowers and leaves similar to those of clover, that is widely cultivated as forage, a salad vegetable and a commercial source of chlorophyll.

alfresco (alfres´kō) *a., adv.* in the open air, open-air.

alga (al´gə) *n.* (*pl.* **algae** (-gē)) a seaweed or other plant belonging to the Algae, a major group of simple aquatic or subaquatic plants, including the seaweeds, that lack differentiation into stems, roots and leaves. **algal** *a.* **algicide** (-jisīd) *n.* a substance that destroys algae. **alginate** (-jināt) *n.* (*Chem.*) a salt of alginic acid used as a stabilizing and thickening agent in pharmaceuticals, food and plastics. **alginic** (-jin´-) *a.* of, relating to or obtained from seaweed. **alginic acid** *n.* (*Chem.*) an insoluble acid found in some algae, such as kelp. **algology** (-gol´-) *n.* the branch of botany dealing with algae. **algological** (-gəloj´-) *a.* **algologist** (-gol´-) *n.*

algebra (al´jibrə) *n.* **1** the branch of mathematics in which letters are used as symbols for quantities, and signs represent arithmetical processes. **2** any of a number of systems which use symbols to denote basic operations and relationships. **algebraic** (-brā´-), **algebraical** *a.* **algebraically** *adv.* **algebraist** (-brā´ist), **algebrist** *n.*

-algia (al´jiə) *comb. form* (*Med.*) denoting pain (in a particular place), e.g. *neuralgia*.

algolagnia (algəlag´niə) *n.* sexual gratification derived from inflicting or suffering pain. **algolagnic** *n., a.*

Algonquian (algong´kwiən), **Algonkian** (-kiən) *n.* **1** a family of N American Indian languages. **2** a member of a people speaking an Algonquian language. ~*a.* of these languages or people.

Algonquin (algong´kwin), **Algonkin** (-kin) *n.* (*pl.* **Algonquin, Algonquins, Algonkin, Algonkins**) **1** a member of a N American Indian people formerly living in the valley of the Ottawa and around the northern tributaries of the St Lawrence. **2** their language, a dialect of Ojibwa. **3** Algonquian. ~*a.* **1** of or relating to the Algonquins or their language. **2** Algonquian.

algorithm 31 **all**

algorithm (al´gəridhm) *n.* (*Math.*) a rule or set procedure for solving a mathematical problem, esp. using a computer. **algorithmic** (-ridh´mik) *a.* **algorithmically** *adv.*

alias (ā´liəs) *adv.* otherwise (named or called). ~*n.* (*pl.* **aliases**) an assumed name.

alibi (al´ibī) *n.* (*pl.* **alibis**) **1** the plea (of a person accused) of having been elsewhere when the offence was committed; the evidence to support such a plea. **2** (*coll.*) an excuse for failing to do something). ~*v.t.* (*3rd pers. sing. pres.* **alibis**, *pres.p.* **alibiing**, *past*, *p.p.* **alibied**) to provide with an alibi. ~*v.i.* to provide an alibi.

alicyclic (alisī´klik) *a.* (*Chem.*) (of an organic compound) having aliphatic properties but containing a ring of carbon atoms.

alidad (al´idad), **alidade** (-dād) *n.* an arm or index showing degrees on a circle in an astrolabe, quadrant, theodolite etc.

alien (ā´liən) *a.* **1** unfamiliar; strange, incongruous. **2** foreign, of foreign extraction; belonging to a foreign country. **3** unacceptable, repugnant to; not compatible or consistent. **4** extraterrestrial, coming from another world. **5** (*Bot.*) (of a species) naturalized after introduction from elsewhere. ~*n.* **1** a foreigner; a foreign-born non-naturalized resident. **2** a being from another world. **3** an alien species.

alienate (ā´liənāt) *v.t.* **1** to cause to become unfriendly or hostile, to estrange. **2** to cause to feel isolated or estranged. **3** (*formal*) to take away, divert (someone's affections). **4** (*Law*) to transfer to the ownership of another. **alienation** (-nā´shən) *n.* **1** the act of alienating; state of being alienated. **2** the feeling of being estranged from one's social environment. **alienator** *n.*

aliform (ā´lifawm) *a.* shaped like a wing.

alight¹ (əlīt´) *v.i.* (*past*, *p.p.* **alighted**) **1** to get down, descend, dismount. **2** to reach the ground, to settle. **3** to come by chance, to happen (on).

alight² (əlīt´) *a.*, *adv.* **1** on fire. **2** illuminated.

align (əlīn´), **aline** *v.t.* **1** to range or place in a line. **2** to place in a position of agreement with others. ~*v.i.* to fall into line. **alignment** *n.*

alike (əlīk´) *a.* similar. ~*adv.* equally, in the same manner, similarly.

aliment (al´imənt) *n.* (*formal*) **1** nutriment, food. **2** support, sustenance. **3** mental nutriment. **alimental** (-men´-) *a.* **alimentary** *a.* **1** of or relating to aliment or nutrition; nutritious, nourishing. **2** sustaining, supporting. **alimentary canal** *n.* (*Anat.*) the great tube or duct from mouth to anus conveying food to the stomach and carrying off solid excreta from the system. **alimentation** (-tā´shən) *n.* **1** the act or quality of affording nourishment. **2** sustenance, support.

alimony (al´iməni) *n.* (*esp. N Am.*) payment of means of support, esp. the proportional part of a person's income allowed for the support of a spouse after legal separation or divorce, or for other causes.

aliphatic (alifat´ik) *a.* (*Chem.*) belonging or relating to a class of organic compounds containing open chains of carbon atoms in the molecular structure, not aromatic.

aliquot (al´ikwot) *a.* (*Math.*) of or relating to a number that is contained an integral number of times by a given number. ~*n.* an integral factor, an aliquot part. **aliquot part** *n.* a part that is a division of the whole without remainder, as 50p of £1, 10 g of 1 kg.

alive (əlīv´) *adv.* **1** living, existent. **2** in force or operation; of current interest, topical. **3** lively, active, full of life. **4** sensitive, responsive (to). **5** swarming or teeming (with); full of. **6** (of an electric circuit) live. **alive and kicking** (*coll.*) in a very lively state. **alive and well** still alive (esp. despite contrary assumptions).

alizarin (əliz´ərin) *n.* the red colouring matter of madder. ~*a.* (of a dye) derived from this.

alkali (al´kəli) *n.* (*pl.* **alkalis**, **alkalies**) **1** (*Chem.*) **a** a compound of hydrogen and oxygen with sodium, potassium or other substances, which is soluble in water, and produces caustic and corrosive solutions capable of neutralizing acids and changing the colour of litmus to blue. **b** any water-soluble chemical base. **2** alkaline products, such as caustic potash and caustic soda. **3** any soluble salt present to excess in soil. **alkali metal** *n.* each of the metals, the hydroxides of which are alkalis (potassium, sodium, caesium, lithium, rubidium, francium). **alkalimetry** (-lim´ətri) *n.* the measurement of the strength of alkalis. **alkalimetrical** (-met´-) *a.* **alkaline** (-līn) *a.* **1** having the properties of an alkali. **2** containing an alkali. **alkaline earth** *n.* (an oxide of) any of the alkaline earth metals. **alkaline earth metal** *n.* each of the metals calcium, strontium, magnesium, radium and beryllium. **alkalinity** (-lin´iti) *n.* **alkaloid** (-oid) *a.* resembling an alkali in properties. ~*n.* any of a large group of natural organic nitrogenous bases derived from plants, some of which are used as medicinal drugs. **alkalosis** (-ō´sis) *n.* (*Med.*) an abnormal increase in the alkalinity of body fluids or tissue.

alkane (al´kān) *n.* (*Chem.*) any of a series of aliphatic hydrocarbons including methane, ethane, butane and octane.

alkanet (al´kənet) *n.* **1** a red dye material obtained from *Alkanna tinctoria.* **2** the plant itself.

alky (al´ki), **alkie** *n.* (*pl.* **alkies**) (*sl.*) an alcoholic.

alkyd (al´kid) *n.* (*Chem.*) any of a group of synthetic resins derived from alkyls and acids, used in paints, protective coatings and adhesives.

alkyl (al´kil) *n.* (*Chem.*) any monovalent hydrocarbon radical of the alkane series, e.g. methyl, ethyl, butyl. **alkylation** (-ā´shən) *n.* the introduction of an alkyl into a compound.

all (awl) *a.* **1** the whole (quantity, duration, extent, amount, quality or degree) of. **2** every one of. **3** any whatever. **4** the greatest possible. ~*pron.* **1** all the persons or things concerned; everyone, everything. **2** the whole. ~*n.* **1** one's entire strength or resources. **2** the whole, the totality. ~*adv.* **1** wholly, entirely, completely. **2** (in scoring for games) each, apiece. **3** (*coll.*) very. **after all 1** when everything has been taken into account. **2** in spite of everything that was done, said etc. **3** against expectation or probability. **all about it** the whole of the matter. **all along** throughout, all the time. **all and sundry** everyone, anyone who cares to do something. **all around** (*N Am.*) all round. **all but** almost. **all for** (*coll.*) very much in favour of. **all hands** (*Naut.*) the entire crew. **all in 1** including everything. **2** (*coll.*) exhausted. **all in all** all things considered. **all of** as much, far etc. as, no less than (*all of thirty miles to Bath*). **all one** of no importance (to). **all out** with maximum effort. **2** at full speed. **all over 1** completely; everywhere. **2** finished (*all over with*; *it's all over*). **3** (*coll.*) typical of (*that's him all over*). **4** (*coll.*) excessively attentive to (*was all over her*). **all round 1** all things considered; in most respects. **2** for everyone (present) (*drinks all round*). **all set** (*coll.*) ready to start. **all the better/ more/ worse** so much the better/ more/ worse. **all the same 1** nevertheless; in spite of what has been said; in spite of this. **2** a matter of indifference. **all together** in a body, altogether. **all very well** used to express rejection of or scepticism about a positive or consolatory statement. **and all** (*coll.*) too, as well. **and all that** with all the rest of it. **at all 1** in any respect, to any extent, in any degree. **2** of any kind, whatever. **in all** in total, altogether. **to be all up with** to be hopeless for. **all-American** *a.* **1** representing the whole of America or of the US. **2** typifying US ideals (*all-American boy*). **3** selected (by a panel of journalists) as one of the top amateur sportsmen in the US. ~*n.* an all-American sportsman. **all clear** *n.* a signal indicating that danger has passed or that one can proceed safely. **all comers** *n.pl.* anyone who accepts a challenge. **All Hallows** *n.* All Saints' Day. **All Hallows' Eve** *n.* Hallowe'en. **all-important** *a.* of utmost importance. **all-in** *a.* in which everything is included. **all-in wrestling** *n.* a form of wrestling with almost no restrictions. **all-inclusive** *a.* in which everything is included. **all-in-one** *a.* combining two or more functions, items etc. in a single thing. **all-out** *a.* **1** with maximum effort. **2** at full speed. **all-over** *a.* covering the whole surface of something. **all-party** *a.* involving all the political parties concerned. **all-powerful** *a.* supremely or overwhelmingly powerful. **all right, alright** *a.*, *adv.* (*coll.*) **1** correct, satisfactory, in good condition, safe etc. **2** satisfactorily. **3** yes.

Usage note The spelling *alright* for *all right* is best avoided.

all-round *a.* good in all respects. **all-rounder** *n.* **1** a person who is generally competent or versatile. **2** a person who is good at several sports or several aspects of one sport, esp. cricket. **All**

Saints' Day *n.* a church festival (1 Nov.) in honour of the saints collectively. **all-seater** *a.* (of a stadium, football ground) having no standing accommodation for spectators. **all-singing-all-dancing** *a.* (*facet.*) lavishly or comprehensively equipped, accessorized etc. **All Souls' Day** *n.* the day (2 Nov.) on which the Roman Catholic Church commemorates all the faithful departed. **all-star** *a.* composed of star performers. **all-ticket** *a.* (of an event) for which admission is exclusively by ticket bought in advance. **all-time** *a.* exceeding all others, as yet unsurpassed. ~*n.* a record high or low level. **all-up weight** *n.* the total weight of an aircraft with its load when in the air.

alla breve (alə brā′vi) *n.* (*Mus.*) a time signature including two or four minims to the bar.

alla cappella A CAPPELLA.

allay (əlā′) *v.t.* **1** to quiet, to still, to calm (fear); to diminish (suspicion). **2** to abate, to alleviate, to relieve (pain).

allegation (aligā′shən) *n.* **1** the act of alleging. **2** an assertion without proof, a statement of what one undertakes to prove.

allege (əlej′) *v.t.* **1** to affirm positively but without or before proof. **2** to adduce as an authority, to plead as an excuse. **alleged** *a.* **allegedly** (-jid-) *adv.* as has been alleged or stated.

allegiance (əlē′jəns) *n.* **1** the obligation of subjects to their sovereign or citizens to their country or government. **2** loyalty, devotion.

allegory (al′igəri) *n.* (*pl.* **allegories**) **1** a story, play, picture etc. in which the characters and events depicted are meant to be understood as representing other, usu. abstract spiritual or psychological, entities. **2** the genre which comprises such works. **3** the technique of symbolic representation. **4** a person or thing invested with symbolic meaning. **allegoric** (-gor′-), **allegorical** *a.* **1** of, relating to or consisting of allegory. **2** resembling an allegory. **allegorically** *adv.* **allegorist** *n.* **allegorize, allegorise** *v.t.* to convert into an allegory, to interpret allegorically.

allegro (əleg′rō) *a.* (*Mus.*) brisk, lively. ~*adv.* briskly, quickly. ~*n.* (*pl.* **allegros**) a movement or passage in allegro time or manner. **allegretto** (aləgret′ō) *adv.* (*Mus.*) a little slower than allegro. ~*n.* (*pl.* **allegrettos**) a movement or passage to be performed allegretto.

allele (əlēl′, al′-) *n.* an allelomorph. **allelic** *a.*

allelomorph (əlē′ləmawf, əlel′-) *n.* **1** any of two or more contrasted characteristics, inherited as alternatives, and assumed to depend on genes in homologous chromosomes. **2** any of two or more genes determining such alternative characteristics. **allelomorphic** (-maw′-) *a.*

alleluia (aliloo′ya), **alleluya, hallelujah** (hal-) *int.* praise be to God. ~*n.* **1** an utterance of 'alleluia', an offering of praise to God. **2** a song of praise to God. **3** the part of a Mass containing this.

Allen screw (al´ən) *n.* a screw with a hexagonal socket in the head. **Allen key** *n.* an L-shaped tool designed to fit and unscrew an Allen screw.

allergy (al´əji) *n.* (*pl.* **allergies**) **1** (*Med.*) **a** an abnormal response or reaction to some food or substance innocuous to most people. **b** hypersensitiveness to certain substances inhaled or touched. **2** (*coll.*) an aversion, antipathy. **allergen** (-jən) *n.* a substance that induces allergy. **allergenic** (-jen´-) *a.* **allergic** (-lœ´-) *a.* **1** caused by allergy. **2** having an allergic response (to). **3** (*coll.*) averse (to). **allergist** *n.*

alleviate (əlē´viāt) *v.t.* to lighten, lessen, mitigate. **alleviation** (-ā´shən) *n.* **alleviative** *n.* **alleviator** *n.* **alleviatory** *a.*

alley[1] (al´i) *n.* (*pl.* **alleys**) **1** a passage, esp. between or behind buildings. **2** a narrow street or lane. **3** a bordered walk in a garden or park. **4** a narrow enclosure for playing at skittles etc.

alley[2] ALLY[3].

alliaceous (aliā´shəs) *a.* **1** of or relating to the plant genus *Allium*, which contains the onion and garlic. **2** having the taste or smell of onion or garlic.

alliance (əli´əns) *n.* **1** the act of allying; the state of being allied. **2** agreement committing two or more states, individuals etc. to act together. **3** union by such a treaty or agreement. **4** the parties allied. **5** union or connection of interests. **6** union by marriage, affinity. **7** (*Bot.*) a group of related families.

alligator (al´igātə) *n.* **1** a large reptile, native to America and China, that resembles a crocodile but differs from it esp. by having a broader snout. **2** the skin of this animal used as leather, or a material resembling it. **3** (*pl.*) shoes made from this. **alligator clip** *n.* a clip with serrated edges for gripping. **alligator pear** *n.* an avocado.

alliterate (əlit´ərāt) *v.i.* **1** to commence with the same letter or sound. **2** to practise alliteration. **alliteration** (-ā´shən) *n.* commencement of two or more words or accented syllables, in close connection, with the same letter or sound. **alliterative** *a.* **alliteratively** *adv.*

allium (al´iəm) *n.* a plant of the genus *Allium*, containing garlic, leeks, onions etc.

allo- (al´ō) *comb. form* different, other, as in *allomorph*, *allopathy*.

allocate (al´əkāt) *v.t.* **1** to assign, allot, apportion. **2** to localize. **allocable** (-əkəbəl) *a.* **allocation** (-ā´shən) *n.* **allocator** *n.*

allogamy (əlog´əmi) *n.* (*Bot.*) cross-fertilization. **allogamous** *a.* reproducing by cross-fertilization.

allograft (al´əgrahft) *n.* a tissue graft from a genetically unrelated donor.

allograph (al´əgrahf) *n.* a signature written by one person on behalf of another.

allomorph (al´əmawf) *n.* any of the two or more forms of a morpheme. **allomorphic** (-maw´-) *a.*

allopathy (əlop´əthi) *n.* the treatment of disease by including effects of a different kind from those produced by the disease; ordinary medical practice, as opposed to homoeopathy. **allopathic** (aləpath´-) *a.* **allopathist** *n.*

allopatric (aləpat´rik) *a.* (*Biol.*) occurring in geographically separated areas.

allophone (al´əfōn) *n.* any of the two or more forms of a phoneme. **allophonic** (-fon´-) *a.*

allot (əlot´) *v.t.* (*pres.p.* **allotting**, *past, p.p.* **allotted**) to distribute, to grant, to bestow, to assign as one's share. **allotment** *n.* **1** the act of allotting. **2** the share assigned. **3** a small plot of land let, usu. by a local authority, for cultivation.

allotropy (əlot´rəpi) *n.* variation of physical properties without change of substance (e.g. diamond, graphite and charcoal are allotropic forms of carbon). **allotrope** (al´ətrōp) *n.* any one of the forms in which a substance exhibiting allotropy exists. **allotropic** (alətrop´ik) *a.*

allow (əlow´) *v.t.* **1** to permit. **2** to assign, set aside for a purpose. **3** to give, grant or provide (a limited quantity or sum). **4** to acknowledge, concede. **5** to take into account, give credit for. **to allow for** to make allowance or deduction for. **to allow of** to accept, to admit. **allowable** *a.* **allowably** *adv.* **allowance** *n.* **1** a fixed quantity or sum allowed to a particular person or for a specific purpose. **2** a deduction or discount, made in consideration of something. **3** an amount of income not subject to income tax. **4** the act of allowing; tolerance. **5** (*N Am.*) pocket money. ~*v.t.* to put upon allowance. **to make allowance/ allowances for** to take (mitigating circumstances) into account.

alloy[1] (al´oi) *n.* **1** an inferior metal mixed with one of greater value. **2** a mixture of metals. **3** an amalgam. **4** any base admixture.

alloy[2] (əloi´) *v.t.* **1** to mix with a baser metal. **2** to mix (metals). **3** to mix with anything base or inferior. **4** to diminish, to impair.

☒ **allready** common misspelling of ALREADY.

allseed (awl´sēd) *n.* any of various many-seeded plants, esp. *Radiola linoides* of the flax family.

allspice (awl´spīs) *n.* **1** (a spice prepared from) the berry of the pimento, said to combine the flavour of cinnamon, cloves and nutmeg. **2** any of various other aromatic shrubs.

allude (əlood´, əlūd´) *v.i.* **1** to make indirect reference (to), to hint at. **2** (*loosely*) to mention, to refer (to). **allusion** (-zhən) *n.* **1** a reference to anything not directly mentioned. **2** a hint. **allusive** *a.* **1** containing an allusion. **2** hinting at an implied meaning, characterized by allusion. **allusively** *adv.* **allusiveness** *n.*

Usage note (1) *Allude* and *allusion* imply indirectness, and should not be used simply for refer, a reference. (2) *Allusion* and *illusion* should not be confused: an illusion is a deception.

allure (əlūə´) *v.t.* **1** to attract or tempt by the offer of some real or apparent good. **2** to entice.

3 to fascinate, to charm. ~n. charm, sex appeal. **allurement** n.

alluvion (əloo´viən) n. (Law) the formation of new land by the action of flowing water.

alluvium (əloo´viəm) n. (pl. **alluvia**) (a fine-grained fertile soil derived from) transported matter which has been washed away and later deposited by rivers, floods or similar causes. **alluvial** a.

ally¹ (əlī´) v.t. (3rd pers. sing. pres. **allies**, pres.p. **allying**, past, p.p. **allied**) **1** to unite by treaty, confederation, marriage or friendship. **2** to connect; to combine.

ally² (al´ī) n. (pl. **allies**) **1** a state, person, group etc. that has an alliance with another. **2** something akin to another in structure or properties.

ally³ (al´i), **alley** n. (pl. **allies**, **alleys**) a superior kind of playing-marble or taw.

almacantar (alməkan´tə), **almucantar** n. (Astron.) a smaller circle of the celestial sphere parallel to the horizon, a parallel of altitude.

alma mater (almə mā´tə, mah´-), **Alma Mater** n. the university, college or school that a person attended.

almanac (awl´mənak), †**almanack** n. **1** a register of the days of the year, with astronomical data and calculations, civil and ecclesiastical festivals etc. **2** an annual directory or compendium of information.

almandine (al´məndīn) n. a precious deep red garnet.

almighty (awlmī´ti) a. **1** omnipotent. **2** possessed of unlimited ability, strength or power. **3** (coll.) very great, very loud. ~adv. (coll.) exceedingly. **the Almighty** God. **almightiness** n.

almond (ah´mənd) n. **1** a small widely cultivated tree of the rose family, Prunus dulcis. **2** the edible kernel of the fruit of this tree. **almond-eyed** a. having narrow, almond-shaped eyes. **almond paste** n. marzipan.

almoner (al´mənə, ah´-) n. **1** (Hist.) an official distributor of alms or bounty. **2** (Hist.) a medico-social worker attached to a hospital.

almost (awl´mōst) adv. nearly, very nearly, well-nigh.

alms (ahmz) n.pl. **1** anything given out of charity to the poor. **2** charity. **almshouse** n. a house where poor people are lodged and provided for by charitable endowment.

almucantar ALMACANTAR.

aloe (al´ō) n. **1** a succulent plant of the genus Aloe, having fleshy, toothed leaves and bitter juice. **2** any of various other plants, e.g. the American aloe. **3** (pl.) the inspissated juice of plants of the genus Aloe, a purgative drug. **aloe vera** (veə´rə) n. a Caribbean aloe whose juice is used in various medical and cosmetic preparations.

aloft (əloft´) adv. **1** high up, on high. **2** upwards.

alogical (əloj´ikəl) a. **1** not logical, not rational. **2** opposed to logic.

alone (əlōn´) a., adv. **1** with no other present.

2 without help from others. **3** lonely. **4** only, solely (He alone knew the truth). **5** without others of the same opinion (was alone in believing). **6** without equal, unique.

along (əlong´) prep. **1** from one end to the other of. **2** over or through the length, or part of the length of. **3** beside and extending over the length of. ~adv. **1** forward, onward. **2** into a more advanced state. **3** in company with someone or oneself (bring him along). **4** to or at a particular place. **5** over the length of something; lengthwise. **along with** in company or together with. **alongshore** adv. **1** in a line with, and nearly parallel to, the shore. **2** along and on the shore. **alongside** adv. **1** by the side of something. **2** to the side of something. ~prep. **1** by the side of. **2** to the side of. **alongside of** side by side with.

aloof (əloof´) adv. away, at a distance, apart. ~a. distant or unsympathetic in manner. **aloofness** n.

alopecia (aləpē´shə) n. (Med.) baldness.

aloud (əlowd´) adv. audibly.

alp (alp) n. **1** a high mountain. **2** pasture ground on the side of a mountain. **alpenstock** (al´pənstok) n. a long stick shod with iron, used in mountaineering. **Alpine** (al´pīn) a. of, relating to or growing on the Alps. **alpine** a. **1** of, relating to or growing on any high mountain. **2** growing above the tree line. **3** of or relating to ski events such as slalom and downhill racing. ~n. **1** a plant native or suited to high mountains. **2** a plant suitable for rockeries. **alpinism** (-pin-) n. mountain-climbing. **alpinist** (-pin-) n. a mountaineer, esp. one who climbs in the Alps.

alpaca (alpak´ə) n. **1** the domesticated llama of Peru. **2** the wool of the domesticated llama. **3** cloth made from this wool.

alpargata (alpahgah´tə) n. a light, rope-soled canvas shoe, an espadrille.

alpenstock ALP.

alpha (al´fə) n. **1** the first letter of the Greek alphabet (α, A). **2** a first-class mark for a piece of work, in an examination etc. **alpha and omega** n. the beginning and the end; the essential or most important part, point etc. **alpha decay** n. the process of radioactive decay that results in the emission of alpha particles. **alpha particle** n. a positively-charged particle emitted by certain radioactive substances, e.g. radium. It has been identified as a doubly-ionized helium atom. **alpha rays** n.pl. rays consisting of streams of alpha particles. **alpha test** n. a test of a new product, esp. in computer software, carried out by the developer before release for beta testing. ~v.t. to put (a product) through such a test.

alphabet (al´fəbet) n. **1** the letters or characters used in writing a language, arranged in order. **2** a set of signs or symbols representing letters. **alphabetic** (-bet´-), **alphabetical** a. **1** of or relating to the alphabet. **2** arranged in the order of the letters of the alphabet. **alphabetically** adv.

alphabetize, alphabetise *v.t.* to arrange in alphabetical order. **alphabetization** (-zā´shən) *n.*

alphabet soup *n.* a confusing mass or string of initials, acronyms, abbreviations etc., as found in some official or technical documents.

alphanumeric (alfənūmer´ik), **alphameric** (-mer´ik), **alphamerical** *a.* consisting of or using both letters and numbers.

already (awlred´i) *adv.* **1** beforehand, before some specified time. **2** in anticipation.

alright ALL RIGHT (under ALL).

Alsatian (alsā´shən) *a.* belonging to Alsace, a region of E France. ~*n.* **1** a native or inhabitant of Alsace. **2** a breed of large, German wolflike dog, the German shepherd dog; a dog of this breed.

alsike (al´sīk, -sik) *n.* a species of clover, *Trifolium hybridum.*

also (awl´sō) *adv., conj.* **1** in addition, as well. **2** likewise, in like manner, besides. **also-ran** *n.* **1** an unplaced horse in a race. **2** (*coll.*) an unimportant person, a failure.

alstroemeria (alstrəmē´riə) *n.* a plant of the originally S American genus *Alstroemeria*, of the amaryllis family, cultivated for their brightly coloured orchid-like flowers.

altar (awl´tə) *n.* **1** a sacrificial block or table; a place of sacrifice, commemoration or devotion. **2** the communion table. **to lead to the altar** to marry (a woman). **altar boy** *n.* a boy who assists the priest during a service. **altarpiece** *n.* a picture or ornamental sculpture over the altar (or communion table) in a church.

altazimuth (altaz´iməth) *n.* an instrument for measuring altitude and azimuth.

alter (awl´tə) *v.t.* **1** to cause to vary or change in some degree. **2** to modify. **3** (*N Am., Austral., euphem.*) to castrate or spay. ~*v.i.* to undergo some change. **alterable** *a.* **alterability** (-bil´-) *n.* **alteration** (-ā´shən) *n.* **alterative** *a., n.*

altercate (awl´təkāt) *v.i.* **1** to dispute hotly. **2** to wrangle. **altercation** (-ā´shən) *n.*

alter ego (awltər ē´gō, al-, eg´-) *n.* (*pl.* **alter egos**) **1** a second self. **2** a trusted friend. **3** a plenipotentiary.

alternate[1] (awl´tənāt) *v.t.* **1** to arrange or perform by turns. **2** to cause to succeed by turns or reciprocally. **3** to interchange. ~*v.i.* **1** to happen or succeed one another by turns. **2** to change repeatedly from one condition or state to another. **3** (of an electric current, voltage etc.) to change from positive to negative and back again by turns. **alternating** *a.* that alternate(s) or interchange(s); changing from positive to negative and back. **alternating current** *n.* an electric current that changes from positive to negative regularly and frequently. **alternation** (-ā´shən) *n.* the act of alternating; the state of being alternate. **alternation of generations** *n.* (*Biol.*) the alternation of different forms of reproduction (sexual and parthenogenetic, haploid and diploid, etc.) in a life cycle.

alternate[2] (awltœ´nət) *a.* **1** done or happening by turns, first one and then the other. **2** every other, every second. **3** (of a sequence) consisting of alternate things. **4** (*Bot.*) (of plant parts) placed on opposite sides of an axis at successive levels. **5** (of angles) formed at opposite ends and on opposite sides of a straight line that cuts two other lines. **alternately** *adv.*

Usage note The adjectives *alternate* and *alternative* should not be confused: *alternate* means ovory other, and *alternative* offering a choice of two.

alternative (awltœ´nətiv) *a.* **1** offering a choice of two things. **2** being the other of two things open to choice. **3** denoting or relating to a lifestyle, practice, art form etc. which functions outside, and constitutes an alternative to, conventional or institutionalized methods or systems. ~*n.* **1** the permission or opportunity to choose between two things. **2** either of two courses which may be chosen. **alternative comedy** *n.* comedy that rejects conventional (racial and sexual) stereotypes as a source of humour. **alternative energy** *n.* energy fuelled from renewable or environment-friendly sources. **alternatively** *adv.* **alternative medicine** *n.* any system of medicine or medical treatment, such as homoeopathy or osteopathy, that does not use orthodox practices or substances. **alternative society** *n.* a group that rejects the values and forms of conventional society.

Usage note See note under ALTERNATE[2].

alternator (awl´tənātə) *n.* a dynamo for generating an alternating electric current.

althorn (alt´hawn) *n.* an instrument of the saxhorn family, esp. the E flat alto or tenor saxhorn.

although (awldhō´) *conj.* though, notwithstanding, however.

altimeter (al´timētə, altim´itə) *n.* an instrument that indicates height above a given datum, usu. sea level.

altitude (al´titūd) *n.* **1** vertical height. **2** height above sea level. **3** (*Geom.*) elevation of an object above its base. **4** (*Astron.*) the elevation of a heavenly body above the horizon.

alto (al´tō) *n.* (*pl.* **altos**) **1** the lowest female voice, contralto. **2** the highest adult male voice, countertenor. **3** a singer possessing such a voice. **4** the part of the music sung by persons possessing the alto voice. **5** an alto instrument, esp. an alto saxophone. ~*a.* **1** to be sung by altos. **2** being the second- or third-highest in pitch of a family of instruments (*alto clarinet*). **alto clef** *n.* the clef which establishes middle C on the third line of the stave.

altocumulus (altōkū´mūləs) *n.* in meteorology, intermediate-altitude cloud in rounded masses with a level base.

altogether (awltəgedh´ə) *adv.* **1** wholly, completely, entirely. **2** inclusive of everything. **3** on the whole, in view of all things. **the altogether** (*coll.*) the nude.

Usage note In writing, it is conventional to distinguish between *altogether* and *all together*, which means 'all at one place' or 'all at one time'.

alto-relievo (altōrəlyä´vō) *n.* (*pl.* **alto-relievos**) **1** high relief, standing out from the background by more than half the true proportions of the figures carved. **2** a sculpture of this type.

altostratus (altōstrah´təs) *n.* in meteorology, intermediate-altitude cloud forming a continuous level layer.

altrices (al´trisēz) *n.pl.* birds whose young are very immature after hatching and depend entirely on the parents for food. **altricial** (altrish´əl) *a.* hatching immature young. ~*n.* an altricial bird.

altruism (al´trooizm) *n.* devotion to the good of others (as opposed to *egoism*). **altruist** *n.* **altruistic** (-is´-) *a.* **altruistically** *adv.*

alum (al´əm) *n.* **1** (*Chem.*) **a** a double sulphate of aluminium and potassium. **b** any of a series of double sulphates of a monovalent metal or group. **c** a family of analogous compounds. **2** (*Mineral.*) any of various minerals, alums or pseudo-alums.

alumina (əloo´minə) *n.* (*Chem.*) the oxide of aluminium occurring as corundum and a constituent of all clays.

aluminium (alūmin´iəm), (*N Am.*) **aluminum** (əloo´minəm) *n.* (*Chem.*) a white, ductile metallic element, at. no. 13, chem. symbol Al, with good resistance to corrosion, used as a basis for many light alloys. **aluminium bronze** *n.* a compound of aluminium and copper. **aluminize** (-loo´-), **aluminise** *v.t.* to coat with aluminium.

aluminosilicate (əlūminōsil´ikāt) *n.* a silicate containing a proportion of aluminium, esp. a rock-forming silicate such as feldspar.

aluminum ALUMINIUM.

alumnus (əlŭm´nəs) *n.* (*pl.* **alumni** (-nī)) **1** a former pupil or student (of a particular place of education). **2** (*N Am.*) a graduate. **alumna** (-nə) *n.* (*pl.* **alumnae** (-nē)) a female alumnus.

alveolus (alvē´ələs, -viō´ləs) *n.* (*pl.* **alveoli** (-lī)) **1** a little cavity. **2** an air sac in the lungs. **3** a tooth socket. **alveolar** *a.* **1** of, relating to or having alveoli or an alveolus. **2** (of a consonant) produced with the tip of the tongue touching the roof of the mouth behind the front teeth. **alveolate** (-lət) *a.*

always (awl´wāz), †**alway** *adv.* **1** on all occasions, in all cases. **2** repeatedly, regularly. **3** in any event, whatever the circumstances. **4** forever; till the end of one's life.

alyssum (əlis´əm) *n.* **1** a plant of the cruciferous genus *Alyssum*, that includes *A. saxatile*. **2** a related plant, *Lobularia maritima*, sweet alyssum.

AM *abbr.* **1** amplitude modulation. **2** anno mundi (in the year of the world). **3** associate member. **4** (*esp. N Am.*) Master of Arts (L *Artium Magister*).

Am *chem. symbol* americium.

am BE.

a.m. *abbr.* ante meridiem (before noon).

amadavat AVADAVAT.

amadou (am´ədoo) *n.* a tinder prepared from a dried fungus steeped in saltpetre, used as a match and a styptic.

amah (ah´mə) *n.* (in the Far East and India) a maidservant or nanny.

amalgam (əmal´gəm) *n.* **1** a compound of different things. **2** a mixture of any other metal with mercury. **amalgamate** *v.t.* **1** to mix, unite, combine, to compound into one mixture. **2** to combine (another metal) with mercury. ~*v.i.* to combine, to blend, to merge into one. **amalgamation** (-ā´shən) *n.*

amanuensis (əmanūen´sis) *n.* (*pl.* **amanuenses** (-sēz)) a person employed to write what another dictates or to copy manuscripts.

amaranth (am´əranth), †**amarant** (-ant) *n.* **1** an imaginary flower supposed never to fade. **2** a purple colour. **3** any of a genus of plants, *Amaranthus*, that includes love-lies-bleeding and prince's feather. **amaranthine** (-an´thīn) *a.*

amaryllis (aməril´is) *n.* an autumn-flowering bulbous plant.

amass (əmas´) *v.t.* **1** to make or gather into a heap. **2** to collect together, to accumulate. **amasser** *n.*

amateur (am´ətə, -chə) *n.* **1** a person who practises anything as a pastime, as distinguished from one who does so professionally. **2** a person who competes in a sport for enjoyment rather than payment. **3** a person who is fond of an art, pastime etc., a devotee. **4** (*derog.*) a person who dabbles or is unskilled in a subject. ~*a.* **1** engaging in something for enjoyment; not professional, not receiving payment. **2** involving or for amateurs. **3** amateurish. **amateurish** *a.* not up to the professional standard. **amateurishly** *adv.* **amateurishness** *n.* **amateurism** *n.*

amatory (am´ətəri) *a.* of or relating to love or sexual desire.

amaurosis (amawrō´sis) *n.* (*Med.*) partial or total blindness from disease of the optic nerve, usu. without visible defect.

amaze (əmāz´) *v.t.* to astound, to overwhelm with wonder, to bewilder. **amazement** *n.* **1** overwhelming surprise. **2** the state of being amazed. **amazing** *a.* **amazingly** *adv.*

Amazon (am´əzən) *n.* **1** any of a fabled race of Scythian female warriors. **2** (**amazon**) a tall, strong woman; a virago. **amazon ant** *n.* an ant of the genus *Polyergus*, the neuters of which enslave the young of other species. **Amazonian** (-zō´-), **amazonian** *a.* **1** of or relating to the fabled Amazons; warlike, strong. **2** of or relating to the river Amazon (named from the female warriors recorded there by the early Spaniards).

ambassador (ambas´ədə) *n.* **1** a high-ranking diplomat sent by a state as its permanent representative in another country or on a particular mission abroad. **2** a representative, messenger; a promoter (e.g. of peace). **ambassador-at-large** *n.*

(*pl.* **ambassadors-at-large**) a US ambassador not accredited to a particular foreign government. **ambassadorial** (-daw´-) *a.* **ambassadorship** *n.* **ambassadress** (-dris) *n.* **1** a female ambassador. **2** the wife of an ambassador.

amber (am´bə) *n.* **1** a yellowish translucent fossil resin, found chiefly on the southern shores of the Baltic, used for ornaments, mouthpieces of pipes, and in the manufacture of some varnishes. **2** the colour of amber, an orange yellow or brownish yellow. **3** a warning light of this colour, esp. a traffic light. ~*a.* made of or coloured like amber.

ambergris (am´bəgrēs) *n.* a light, fatty, inflammable substance, ashy in colour, found floating in tropical seas (a secretion from the intestines of the cachalot or sperm whale, it is used in perfumery, and was formerly used in cookery and medicine).

ambiance AMBIENCE (under AMBIENT).

ambidextrous (ambidek´strəs), **ambidexterous** *a.* using both hands with equal facility. **ambidexterity** (-ster´-) *n.* **ambidextrously** *adv.* **ambidextrousness** *n.*

ambient (am´biənt) *a.* surrounding, encompassing on all sides; of or relating to the immediate surroundings. **ambience** (am´biəns, ābiās´), **ambiance** *n.* a surrounding atmosphere or influence, an environment.

ambiguous (ambig´ūəs) *a.* **1** susceptible to two or more meanings. **2** of doubtful meaning, equivocal, obscure. **3** of uncertain position or classification. **ambiguity** (-bigū´-) *n.* (*pl.* **ambiguities**) **1** the state or an instance of being ambiguous; an ambiguous expression. **2** uncertainty of meaning. **ambiguously** *adv.* **ambiguousness** *n.*

Usage note See note under AMBIVALENT (under AMBIVALENCE).

ambisonics (ambison´iks) *n.* a system of multichannel high-fidelity sound reproduction which surrounds the listener with sound.

ambit (am´bit) *n.* **1** scope, extent. **2** boundary, limit.

ambition (ambish´ən) *n.* **1** a desire for power, success, superiority or excellence. **2** a strong desire to achieve anything, usu. something advantageous or creditable. **3** the object of such desire. **ambitious** *a.* **1** actuated by or indicating ambition. **2** highly desirous (of); eager and determined (to do). **3** necessitating great effort, resources, skill etc. **ambitiously** *adv.* **ambitiousness** *n.*

ambivalence (ambiv´ələns), **ambivalency** (-si) *n.* the simultaneous existence in the mind of two incompatible feelings or wishes. **ambivalent** *a.* **ambivalently** *adv.*

Usage note The adjectives *ambivalent* and *ambiguous* should not be confused: *ambivalent* refers to uncertainty of attitude, and *ambiguous* to different possible meanings or interpretations.

amble (am´bəl) *v.i.* **1** to walk at a leisurely relaxed pace. **2** (of a horse, mule) to move by lifting the two feet on one side alternately with the two feet on the other. **3** to ride an ambling horse. ~*n.* **1** an easy relaxed pace. **2** a leisurely walk, a stroll. **3** a pace like that of an ambling horse. **ambling** *a.*

amblyopia (ambliō´piə) *n.* dimness of vision without any obvious defect in the eye. **amblyopic** (-op´-) *a.* affected with or relating to amblyopia.

ambrosia (ambrō´ziə) *n.* **1** the fabled food of the gods. **2** anything very pleasant to the taste or the smell. **3** bee-bread. **4** a composite plant of the genus *Ambrosia*, allied to wormwood. **ambrosial** *a.* **ambrosially** *adv.*

ambulance (am´būləns) *n.* **1** a vehicle for the transport of wounded, injured or sick people. **2** a moving hospital which follows an army in the field. **ambulance-chaser** *n.* (*coll.*, *derog.*) a person who tries to profit from another's tragedy, grief etc., esp. a lawyer who offers to pursue a claim for damages on behalf of accident victims. **ambulance man** *n.* a male member of an ambulance crew. **ambulance woman** *n.* a female member of an ambulance crew.

ambulate (am´būlāt) *v.i.* (*formal*) to walk about. **ambulant** *a.* **1** walking or moving about. **2** (*Med.*) (of a patient) able to walk. **3** (*Med.*) (of a treatment) not confining the patient to bed.

ambulatory (am´būlətəri) *a.* **1** of or relating to walking. **2** fitted for walking. **3** not confined or confining to bed. **4** movable, temporary. ~*n.* (*pl.* **ambulatories**) a place to walk in, esp. an aisle or a cloister in a church or a monastery.

ambush (am´bush) *n.* **1** a surprise attack by forces. **2** the concealment of forces for such an attack; the locality chosen; or force employed. **3** any lying in wait. ~*v.t.* **1** to lie in wait for. **2** to attack from ambush. ~*v.i.* to lie in wait. **ambush television** *n.* (*esp. N Am.*) television in which members of the public participating in a show are confronted with unexpected personal information.

ameba AMOEBA.

ameer AMIR.

ameliorate (əmē´liərāt) *v.t.* (*formal*) to make better, to improve. ~*v.i.* to grow better. **amelioration** (-ā´shən) *n.* **ameliorative** *a.* **ameliorator** *n.*

amen (ahmen´, ā´men) *int.* so be it, may it be as it has been asked, said or promised (said esp. at the end of a prayer or hymn). ~*n.* an utterance of the word 'Amen', an expression of assent.

amenable (əmēn´əbəl) *a.* **1** willing to cooperate, readily persuaded, tractable, responsive. **2** (*Law*) (of a person) answerable, liable. **3** (*Law*) (of a thing) subject, liable. **amenability** (-bil´-) *n.* **amenableness** *n.* **amenably** *adv.*

amend (əmend´) *v.t.* **1** to alter (a person or thing) for the better, to improve. **2** to remove errors from, to correct. **3** to formally alter (a bill or resolution). ~*v.i.* to abandon evil courses, grow better. **amendable** *a.* **amendment** *n.* **1** a change for the better. **2** something added to a bill or motion; an addition to the US constitution. **3** improvement in health. **4** reformation. **5** a correction of error in a writ or process. **amends** *n.* reparation, satisfaction, compensation. **to make amends** to compensate or make up (for).

Usage note See note under EMEND.

amenity (əmē´niti, -men´-) *n.* (*pl.* **amenities**) **1** the quality of being pleasant or agreeable; attractions, charms. **2** a feature or facility conducive to the usefulness or attractiveness of something. **amenity bed** *n.* a bed in a hospital for which the patient pays a charge in order to enjoy certain amenities, e.g. privacy.

ament (əment´), **amentum** (-təm) *n.* (*pl.* **aments**, **amenta** (-tə)) (*Bot.*) a catkin.

amentia (əmen´shiə) *n.* (*Med.*) severe congenital mental deficiency.

Amerasian (amərā´shən, -zhən) *a.* of mixed American and Asian parentage. ~*n.* an Amerasian person, esp. someone fathered by an American serviceman in Korea or Vietnam.

amerce (əmœs´) *v.t.* **1** (*Law*) to punish by fine. **2** to punish. **amercement** *n.* **amerciable** *a.*

American (əmer´ikən) *a.* of or relating to the continent of America, esp. to the US. ~*n.* **1** a native or inhabitant of N, S or Central America. **2** a native or inhabitant of the US. **3** the English language as spoken in the United States. **Americana** (-rikah´nə) *n.pl.* objects typical of or relating to America, esp. in the form of a collection. **American aloe** *n.* the century plant. **American dream** *n.* the notion that America offers the possibility of success to any individual. **American football** *n.* a football game somewhat resembling rugby, played with an oval ball and teams of 11 players. **American Indian** *n.* a member of any of the indigenous peoples of N, S or Central America, usu. with the exception of the Inuit people. **Americanism** *n.* **1** anything characteristic of the US, esp. a word or phrase peculiar to or borrowed from the US. **2** attachment to or political sympathy with the US. **Americanize, Americanise** *v.t.* **1** to naturalize as an American. **2** to assimilate political customs or institutions to those of the US. ~*v.i.* to become American in character, manners or speech. **Americanization** (-zā´shən) *n.* **American plaice** *n.* a N Atlantic fish, *Hippoglossoides platessoides.*

Usage note The term *Native American* is now sometimes preferred to *American Indian*, though not by all the peoples to whom the names are applicable.

americium (aməris´iəm) *n.* (*Chem.*) an artificially-created, metallic radioactive element, at. no. 95, chem. symbol Am.

Amerind (am´ərind), **Amerindian** (-rin´diən) *n.* an American Indian. ~*a.* of or relating to American Indians.

amethyst (am´əthist) *n.* a violet-blue variety of crystalline quartz, supposed by the ancients to prevent intoxication. **amethystine** (-tīn) *a.*

Amharic (amhar´ik) *n.* the official language of Ethiopia. ~*a.* of or relating to this language.

amiable (ā´miəbəl) *a.* **1** friendly, kindly-disposed, likeable. **2** possessed of qualities fitted to evoke friendly feeling. **amiability** (-bil´-) *n.* **amiably** *adv.*

amicable (am´ikəbəl) *a.* **1** friendly. **2** resulting from friendliness. **amicability** (-bil´-) *n.* **amicableness** *n.* **amicably** *adv.*

amice¹ (am´is) *n.* a piece of white linen worn on the neck and shoulders at Mass by Roman Catholic and some Anglican priests.

amice² (am´is) *n.* a hood, cap or cape worn by members of certain religious orders.

amid (əmid´), **amidst** (əmidst´) *prep.* in the midst or middle, among. **amidships**, (*N Am. also*) **amidship** *adv.* in the middle part of a ship.

amide (am´īd) *n.* (*Chem.*) any of various compounds formed by substitution of another element or radical for an atom of hydrogen in ammonia.

amine (am´īn, -ēn, ā´-) *n.* (*Chem.*) any of various organic compounds derived from ammonia by the substitution of one or more univalent hydrocarbon radicals for one or more atoms of hydrogen. **amino** (əmē´nō) *a.* (*Chem.*) containing the characteristic amine group of ammonia with one hydrogen atom replaced by a hydrocarbon radical. **amino acid** *n.* an organic acid containing one or more amino groups, esp. any of those that occur as the constituents of proteins.

amir (əmiə´), **ameer** *n.* the title of several Muslim rulers, esp. formerly in India and Afghanistan.

Amish (ā´mish, ah´-, am´-) *a.* of or belonging to a strict US Mennonite sect. ~*n.pl.* the members of this sect.

amiss (əmis´) *a.* faulty, unsatisfactory, wrong. ~*adv.* wrongly, astray, in a faulty manner, unsatisfactorily. **to take amiss** to be offended by.

amitosis (amitō´sis, āmī-) *n.* (*Biol.*) cell division without mitosis.

amity (am´iti) *n.* friendship, concord, mutual good feeling, friendly relations.

ammeter (am´ətə) *n.* an instrument for measuring the strength of the electric current in a circuit.

ammo (am´ō) *n.* (*coll.*) short for AMMUNITION.

ammonia (əmō´niə) *n.* (*Chem.*) **1** a pungent volatile gas, powerfully alkaline, a compound of nitrogen and hydrogen first obtained from sal ammoniac. **2** a solution of ammonia in water, containing ammonium hydroxide. **ammoniac** (əmən´ak), **ammoniacal** *a.* of, relating to or possessing the properties of ammonia. **ammoniated** (-ātid) *a.* combined with ammonia. **ammonium** (-əm) *n.* the ion or radical derived from ammonia by addition of a hydrogen ion or atom.

ammonite (am´ənīt) *n.* the shell of a genus of

fossil cephalopods, curved like the ram's horn on the statue of Jupiter Ammon.

ammunition (amŭnish´ən) n. **1** any projectiles, e.g. bullets, shells, rockets, that can be discharged from a weapon. **2** offensive missiles generally. **3** anything that can be used to advantage in a dispute or argument.

amnesia (amnē´ziə, -zhə) n. loss of memory. **amnesiac** (-ziak), **amnesic** (-zik) n. a person suffering from amnesia. ~a. of or relating to amnesia.

amnesty (am´nəsti) n. (pl. **amnesties**) **1** a general pardon. **2** a period during which offences may be admitted without incurring punishment. ~v.t. (3rd pers. sing. pres. **amnesties**, pres.p. **amnestying**, past, p.p. **amnestied**) to grant amnesty to.

amniocentesis (amniōsentē´sis) n. (Med.) the removal of a sample of amniotic fluid from the womb, by insertion of a hollow needle, in order to test for chromosomal abnormalities in the foetus.

amnion (am´niən) n. (pl. **amnions, amnia** (-niə)) (Zool., Anat.) the innermost membrane with which the foetus in the womb is surrounded. **amniote** (-ōt) n. (Zool.) any of the group of vertebrates (reptiles, birds and mammals) which possess an amnion in the foetal state. ~a. of or relating to these animals. **amniotic** (-ot´-) a. **amniotic fluid** n. the fluid contained by the amnion in which the foetus is suspended.

amoeba (əmē´bə), (N Am.) **ameba** n. (pl. **amoebas, amoebae** (-bē), (N Am.) **amebas, amebae**) a microscopic organism of the simplest structure, consisting of a single protoplasmic cell, which is extensile and contractile so that its shape is continually changing. **amoebiasis** (-bī´ə-) n. (pl. **amoebiases**) (Med.) infection with amoebas, esp. so as to cause dysentery. **amoebic** a. **amoebic dysentery** n. (Med.) dysentery caused by intestinal infection with certain types of amoebae. **amoeboid** a.

amok (əmok´), **amuck** (əmŭk´) adv. in a frenzy, esp. as below. **to run amok** to rush about in a wild, uncontrollable rage, attacking people indiscriminately.

among (əmŭng´), **amongst** (əmŭngst´) prep. **1** in the midst of; surrounded by. **2** in the number of. **3** in the category or class of. **4** by sharing or dividing between a group of. **5** involving a group of.

amontillado (əmontilah´dō) n. (pl. **amontillados**) a kind of medium dry sherry.

amoral (āmor´əl, ə-) a. not concerned with morals; having no moral principles. **amoralism** n. **amoralist** n.

Usage note The adjectives amoral and immoral should not be confused: amoral means having no reference to morality, and immoral contrary to morality.

amorist (am´ərist) n. a person who makes a study of or writes about love.

amorous (am´ərəs) a. **1** naturally inclined to love. **2** in love. **3** lecherous. **4** relating to, or belonging to, love. **amorously** adv. **amorousness** n.

amorphous (āmaw´fəs, ə-) a. **1** shapeless. **2** irregularly shaped. **3** (Biol.) not conforming to a normal standard. **4** (Chem., Mineral.) not crystalline, uncrystallized. **5** ill-arranged, unsystematic, unorganized. **amorphousness** n.

amortize (əmaw´tīz), **amortise** v.t. **1** to liquidate (a debt) by instalments or by regular transfers to a sinking fund. **2** to write off (an asset) by gradual transfers to a sinking fund. **amortization** (-zā´shən) n.

amount (əmownt´) v.i. **1** to run into an aggregate by the accumulation of particulars; to mount up (to), to add up (to). **2** to be equivalent (to). ~n. **1** a (numerical) quantity. **2** the sum total.

amour (əmuə´) n. a love affair, esp. a secret one; an amorous intrigue.

amour propre (amuə prop´rə) n. self-esteem.

amp (amp) n. **1** short for AMPERE. **2** short for AMPLIFIER (under AMPLIFY).

ampere (am´peə) n. a unit by which an electric current is measured, the current sent by 1 volt through a resistance of 1 ohm. **amperage** n. the strength of an electric current measured in amperes.

ampersand (am´pəsand) n. the sign '&'.

amphetamine (amfet´əmēn, -min) n. (a derivative of) a synthetic drug which has a stimulant action on the brain.

amphi- (am´fi) comb. form **1** both. **2** of both kinds. **3** on both sides. **4** around.

amphibian (amfib´iən) n. **1** (Zool.) any vertebrate animal of the class Amphibia, that have an aquatic gill-breathing larval stage followed by a terrestrial lung-breathing adult stage. **2** any animal that can live either on land or in water. **3** an aircraft, tank or other vehicle adapted for both land and water. ~a. **1** (Zool.) of or relating to the Amphibia. **2** amphibious. **amphibious** a. **1** capable of living both on land and in water. **2** designed for operation on land and in water. **3** (Mil.) of, relating to or trained for the invasion of foreign shores via the sea. **4** of mixed nature. **amphibiousness** n.

amphibole (am´fibōl) n. (Geol.) any of a group of silicate and aluminosilicate minerals including hornblende and tremolite that usu. occur in the form of long slender dark-coloured crystals. **amphibolite** (-līt) n. a rock consisting essentially of amphibole. **amphibolitic** (-lit´-) a.

amphibology (amfibol´əji), **amphiboly** (-fib´əli) n. (pl. **amphibologies, amphibolies**) **1** an ambiguous expression, esp. a sentence composed of unambiguous words that is susceptible to a double meaning because of its construction. **2** the use of such expressions; ambiguity; equivocation.

amphimixis (amfimik´sis) n. (Biol.) **1** sexual reproduction. **2** the fusion of gametes.

amphipod (am´fipod) n. any small sessile-eyed crustacean of the order Amphipoda, having two kinds of feet, one for walking and one for swimming.

amphisbaena (amfisbē´nə) *n.* (*pl.* **amphisbaenas, amphisbaenae** (-nē)) **1** (*esp. poet.*) a fabled snake said by the ancients to have a head at each end, and to be able to move in either direction. **2** (*Zool.*) a serpentiform lizard of the genus *Amphisbaena*, having the tail short and blunt so that it resembles a second head.

amphitheatre (am´fithiətə), (*N Am.*) **amphitheater** *n.* **1** an oval or circular building with rows of seats rising one above another round an open space. **2** a place of public contest. **3** a semi-circular gallery in a theatre. **4** a valley surrounded by hills.

amphora (am´fərə) *n.* (*pl.* **amphoras, amphorae** (-ē)) an ancient two-handled vessel for holding wine, oil etc.

amphoteric (amfəter´ik) *a.* (*Chem.*) able to react as both an acid and a base.

ampicillin (ampisil´in) *n.* a semisynthetic penicillin used to treat infections esp. of the urinary and respiratory tract.

ample (am´pəl) *a.* (*comp.* **ampler**, *superl.* **amplest**) **1** of large dimensions, wide, great. **2** more than enough, fully sufficient, liberal. **3** (*euphem.*) (of a person) large; fat. **ampleness** *n.* **amply** *adv.*

amplify (am´plifī) *v.t.* (*3rd pers. sing. pres.* **amplifies**, *pres.p.* **amplifying**, *past, p.p.* **amplified**) **1** to increase, make greater, esp. to increase the strength of (a signal) or the loudness of (sound). **2** to enlarge or dilate upon. ~*v.i.* to speak or write at greater length or in greater detail. **amplification** (-fikā´shən) *n.* **amplifier** *n.* **1** an electrical or electronic circuit or system to amplify signals, esp. in sound reproduction. **2** a complete unit which performs this function.

amplitude (am´plitūd) *n.* **1** extent, size, bulk, greatness. **2** abundance. **3** breadth or scope. **4** (*Physics*) the magnitude of the variation from a main position or value of a vibration or oscillation, or of an alternating current or wave. **amplitude modulation** *n.* (transmission of a signal by) modulation of the amplitude of a radio carrier wave in accordance with the characteristics of the signal carried.

ampoule (am´pool), (*N Am.*) **ampule** (-pūl) *n.* a sealed phial containing one dose of a drug.

ampulla (ampul´ə) *n.* (*pl.* **ampullae** (-ē)) **1** a nearly globular flask with two handles, used by the ancient Romans. **2** a vessel for holding consecrated oil, wine etc. **3** (*Biol.*) the dilated end of any vessel.

amputate (am´pūtāt) *v.t.* to cut off (a limb or part of a limb) from an animal body by surgical operation. **amputation** (-tā´shən) *n.* **amputator** *n.* **amputee** (-tē´) *n.* a person who has had a limb surgically removed.

amtrac (am´trak), **amtrak** *n.* (*N Am.*) an amphibious tracked vehicle for landing assault troops.

amu *abbr.* atomic mass unit.

amuck AMOK.

amulet (am´ūlət) *n.* anything worn about the person as an imagined preservative against sickness, witchcraft etc.

amuse (əmūz´) *v.t.* **1** to cause to laugh, smile or feel cheerful. **2** to keep pleasantly occupied, to entertain. **amusement** *n.* **1** anything which amuses; play, diversion. **2** the act of amusing, the excitement of laughter. **3** the state of being amused. **4** a mechanical device, sideshow etc. providing entertainment at a fairground, amusement arcade etc. **amusement arcade** *n.* a covered space containing coin-operated game and gambling machines. **amusement park** *n.* an outdoor area with permanent fairground rides and other amusements. **amusing** *a.* **amusingly** *adv.*

amygdala (əmig´dələ) *n.* (*pl.* **amygdalae** (-lē)) an almond-shaped body part, such as a tonsil or a lobe of the cerebellum. **amygdaloid** (əmig´dəloid) *a.* almond-shaped. **amygdaloid nucleus** *n.* a mass of grey matter, shaped roughly like an almond, found inside each cerebral hemisphere and associated with the sense of smell.

amyl (am´il) *n.* (*used attrib., Chem.*) a monovalent group, C_5H_{11}, derived from pentane. **amylase** (-ās) *n.* any of various enzymes that break down starch and glycogen. **amyloid** (-oid) *a.* (*Med.*) resembling or containing starch; starchy. ~*n.* a non-nitrogenous starchy substance deposited in tissues in certain degenerative diseases. **amylopsin** (-op´sin) *n.* an enzyme in pancreatic juice that converts starch into sugar.

an A[1].

an- (an, ən) *pref.* **1** AD- assim. to *n*, as in *annex, announce*. **2** ANA-. **3** A-[3] before a vowel, as in *anaesthetic, anarchy*; not, without.

-an (ən) *suf.* of, belonging or relating to, e.g. *human, pagan, publican, Christian, Unitarian, European* etc.

ana (ah´nə) *n.* (*pl.* **ana**) **1** (*as pl.*) literary gossip or anecdotes, usu. of a personal or local kind. **2** (*as pl.*) a collection of reminiscences, gossip or memorable sayings.

ana- (an´ə), **an-** (an) *pref.* **1** up, as in *anadromous*. **2** back, backwards, as in *anachronism, anatropous*. **3** again, as in *Anabaptism*.

-ana (ah´nə), **-iana** (iah´nə) *suf.* **1** objects relating to, as in *Africana, Americana, Victoriana*. **2** sayings of, anecdotes concerning, as in *Johnsoniana, Virgiliana*.

Anabaptism (anəbap´tizm) *n.* the doctrine that baptism should only be given to adults. **Anabaptist** *n., a.*

anabatic (anəbat´ik) *a.* (of wind or air currents) moving upwards.

anabiosis (anəbiō´sis) *n.* (*Biol.*) **1** a state of suspended animation or greatly reduced metabolism. **2** the ability to return to life from this state or from apparent death. **anabiotic** (-biot´ik) *a.*

anabolism (ənab´əlizm) *n.* the building up of complex substances by assimilation of nutriment, with storage of energy. **anabolic** (anəbol´-)

a. **anabolic steroid** *n.* any of a group of synthetic steroid hormones that cause rapid growth in body tissues, esp. skeletal muscle, and are sometimes (illegally) taken by athletes.

anabranch (an´əbrahnch) *n.* (*Austral.*) a tributary rejoining the main stream of a river and thus forming an island.

anachronism (anak´rənizm) *n.* **1** the assigning of an event, custom or circumstance to a wrong period or date. **2** anything out of date or incongruous with the present. **anachronistic** (-nis´-) *a.* **anachronistically** *adv.*

anacoluthon (anəkəloo´thon) *n.*(*pl.* **anacolutha** (-thə)) **1** lack of grammatical sequence in a sentence. **2** a change of structure in a sentence that renders it ungrammatical.

anaconda (anəkon´də) *n. Eunectes murinus*, a very large semiaquatic S American boa.

anadromous (ənad´rəməs) *a.*(of fish) ascending rivers to deposit spawn.

anaemia (ənē´miə), (*esp. N Am.*) **anemia** *n.* lack of haemoglobin or red corpuscles in the blood, leading to pallor and lack of energy. **anaemic**, (*N Am.*) **anemic** *a.* **1** of, relating to or suffering from anaemia. **2** lacking vitality. **3** pale.

anaerobe (əneə´rōb, an´ə-) *n.* an organism that thrives best, or only, in the absence of oxygen. **anaerobic** (anərō´bik) *a.*

anaesthesia (anəsthē´ziə), (*NAm.*) **anesthesia** *n.* **1** loss of bodily sensation due to nerve damage or other abnormality. **2** general or local loss of sensation, artificially induced for surgical purposes. **anaesthetic** (-thet´-) *a.* producing anaesthesia. ~*n.* a substance which produces anaesthesia (during surgical operations). **anaesthetist** (-nēs´thə-), (*N Am.*) **anesthesiologist** (-thēziol´əjist) *n.* a person who administers an anaesthetic, a person skilled in producing anaesthesia. **anaesthetize** (-nēs´thətīz), **anaesthetise** *v.t.* to administer an anaesthetic to. **anaesthetization** (-zā´shən) *n.*

anaglyph (an´əglif) *n.* **1** a composite photograph in superimposed complementary colours which gives a stereoscopic image when viewed through special glasses. **2** a figure cut or embossed in low relief. **anaglyphic** (-glif´-), **anaglyptic** (-glip´-) *a.*

anagram (an´əgram) *n.* a word or sentence formed by transposing the letters of another word or sentence. **anagrammatic** (-mat´-), **anagrammatical** *a.* **anagrammatically** *adv.* **anagrammatize** (-gram´-), **anagrammatise** *v.t.* to transpose so as to form into an anagram.

anal (ā´nəl) *a.* of, relating to or situated near the anus. **anally** *adv.* **anal-retentive** *a.*(of a person or personality type) excessively fussy and concerned about tidiness (supposedly on account of conflicts over toilet training in infancy). ~*n.* an anal-retentive person.

analeptic (anəlep´tik) *a.* restorative, increasing the strength. ~*n.* a restorative medicine.

analgesia (anəljē´ziə) *n.* loss of sensibility to pain. **analgesic** *n.* a drug that relieves pain. ~*a.* insensible to pain.

analogous (ənal´əgəs) *a.* presenting some analogy or resemblance. **analogously** *adv.*

Usage note Pronunciation with (-j-) (after *analogy*) is best avoided.

analogue (an´əlog), (*Comput., N Am.*) **analog** *n.* **1** an analogous word or thing, a parallel. **2** a physical object or quantity, such as a hand on a watch or a voltage, used to measure or represent another quantity. **3** something that has a similar function to, but a different origin from, something else. **4** (*Chem.*) a chemical compound related to another one by the replacement of hydrogen atoms by alkyl groups. ~*a.* **1** (*Comput., usu.* analog) **a** of or relating to information having a continuous range of values. **b** measuring or displaying information on a continuous scale. **2** (of a watch) having a dial and hands.

analogy (ənal´əji) *n.* (*pl.* **analogies**) **1** similitude of relations, conformity, similarity; a comparison used to demonstrate this. **2** reasoning from a parallel case. **3** (*Biol.*) the relation between anatomical parts agreeing in function but not in origin. **4** imitation of existing words or linguistic patterns in forming new words, inflectional forms etc. **analogic** (-loj´-), **analogical** *a.* **analogically** *adv.* **analogize**, **analogise** *v.t.* to represent or explain by analogy. ~*v.i.* to reason from analogy.

analyse (an´əlīz), (*NAm.*) **analyze** *v.t.* **1** to take to pieces, resolve into its constituent elements. **2** to examine minutely. **3** (*Chem.*) to determine the elements of (a chemical compound). **4** to examine critically. **5** (*Gram.*) to resolve (a sentence) into its grammatical elements. **6** to psychoanalyse. **analysable** *a.* **analysand** (-and´) *n.* a person undergoing psychoanalysis. **analyser** *n.*

analysis (ənal´isis) *n.* (*pl.* **analyses** (-sēz)) **1** the process of analysing; a report or statement of the results of this process. **2** (*Chem.*) **a** separation into constituent elements. **b** resolution of a chemical compound into its elements to ascertain composition, purity etc. **3** (*Math.*) resolution of mathematical problems by reducing them to equations. **4** psychoanalysis. **in the final/ last/ ultimate analysis** in the end, when everything has been taken into consideration.

analyst (an´əlist) *n.* **1** a person who analyses. **2** a psychoanalyst.

analytic (anəlit´ik) *a.* **1** of or relating to analysis. **2** capable of, given to or skilled in analysing. **3** resolving anything into its constituent parts. **4** (of languages) using separate words instead of inflections. **5** (*Logic*) (of a statement) true or false by definition. **analytical** *a.* **analytical geometry** *n.* geometry that uses coordinates to determine the position of a point. **analytically** *adv.*

analyze ANALYSE.

anamnesis (anəmnē´sis) *n.* (*pl.* **anamneses** (-sēz)) **1** recollection. **2** the doctrine of recollection of a previous existence. **3** (*formal*) a patient's medical history. **4** the part of the Eucharist that recalls the Passion, Resurrection and Ascension of Christ. **anamnestic** (-nes´-) *a.*

anamorphosis (anəmaw´fəsis) *n.* (*pl.* **anamorphoses** (-sēz)) a distorted projection of any object so contrived that if looked at from one point of view, or reflected from a suitable mirror, it will appear properly proportioned. **anamorphic** *a.*

anandrous (ənan´drəs) *a.* (*Bot.*) lacking stamens.

anapaest (an´əpest, -pēst), (*esp. N Am.*) **anapest** *n.* a metrical foot consisting of three syllables, the first two short and the third long, a reversed dactyl. **anapaestic** (-pes´-) *a.*, *n.*

anaphora (ənaf´ərə) *n.* **1** (*Gram.*) **a** the commencement of successive sentences or clauses with the same word or words. **b** the use of a word, such as a pronoun, to refer to a preceding word or phrase without repetition. **2** the consecration and offering of the elements at the Eucharist. **anaphoric** (ənəfor´-) *a.* **anaphorically** *adv.*

anaphrodisiac (ənafrədiz´iak) *a.* that suppresses or decreases sexual desire. ~*n.* an anaphrodisiac drug or thing.

anaphylaxis (ənəfilak´sis) *n.* (*Med.*) a condition of increased or extreme sensitivity to a foreign substance introduced into the body following previous contact. **anaphylactic** *a.*

anarchy (an´əki) *n.* **1** disorder, lawlessness. **2** absence of government; lack of settled government. **3** political anarchism or the utopian society resulting from this. **anarchic** (-ah´-), **anarchical** *a.* **anarchically** *adv.* **anarchism** *n.* the doctrine that government should be abolished; a theory of government based on the free agreement of individuals rather than on submission to law and authority. **anarchist** *n.* **1** a person who aims at producing anarchy. **2** a person opposed to all forms of government, a supporter of anarchism.

anastigmat (anəstig´mat), **anastigmat lens** *n.* a lens free from astigmatism, which refers every point on the scene accurately to a corresponding point image. **anastigmatic** (-mat´-) *a.* free from astigmatism.

anastomose (ənas´təmōz) *v.i.* **1** to communicate by anastomosis. **2** to interosculate, to intercommunicate. **anastomosis** (-mō´-) *n.* (*pl.* **anastomoses** (-sēz)) the uniting of vessels, such as veins, arteries, sap-vessels etc., by connecting branches.

anathema (ənath´əmə) *n.* (*pl.* **anathemas**, **anathemata** (-them´ətə)) **1** an object of loathing. **2** the formal act by which a person or thing is cursed, excommunication. **3** the person or thing cursed. **4** a curse, denunciation. **anathematize**, **anathematise** *v.t.* to excommunicate, to curse, to put under a ban. ~*v.i.* to curse.

anatomy (ənat´əmi) *n.* (*pl.* **anatomies**) **1** the science of the structure of organized bodies. **2** the physical structure of an animal or plant or of one of its parts. **3** the art of dissecting an

organized body so as to discover its structure and the make-up, arrangement and interrelation of its parts. **4** the act of dissecting. **5** (*coll.*) the human body. **6** a minute examination, reduction to parts or elements, analysis. **anatomic** (anətom´-), **anatomical** *a.* **1** of or relating to anatomy. **2** of or relating to a bodily structure. **anatomically** *adv.* **anatomist** *n.* a person who practises or is skilled in anatomy. **anatomize**, **anatomise** *v.t.* **1** to examine minutely, analyse. **2** to dissect, to make a dissection of.

anatta, anatto ANNATTO.

ANC *abbr.* African National Congress.

-ance (əns) *suf.* forming nouns denoting a state or action, as in *distance*, *fragrance*, *parlance*, *riddance*.

ancestor (an´sestə) *n.* **1** any person from whom another person is descended; a progenitor. **2** an organism of low type from which others of higher type have been developed. **3** any thing or person regarded as the forerunner of a later thing or person. **ancestral** (-ses´-) *a.* **1** of or relating to ancestors. **2** derived from or possessed by ancestors. **ancestress** *n.* a female ancestor. **ancestry** (-tri) *n.* (*pl.* **ancestries**) **1** a line of ancestors. **2** high birth, honourable lineage. **3** ancient descent.

anchor (ang´kə) *n.* **1** a heavy hooked iron instrument dropped from a ship to grapple the bottom and prevent drifting. **2** anything shaped like an anchor. **3** something that holds an object in place. **4** a source of security or confidence. **5** an anchorperson. ~*v.t.* **1** to secure by means of an anchor. **2** to fix firmly. ~*v.i.* **1** to come to anchor. **2** to take up a position. **3** to settle, rest, to sit down. **at anchor 1** held by an anchor. **2** at rest. **to cast anchor 1** to drop the anchor into the sea. **2** (of a person) to settle down. **to weigh anchor** to raise the anchor preparatory to sailing. **anchorage** (ang´kərij) *n.* **1** a place suitable for anchoring in; any place where a vessel is anchored. **2** the act of anchoring. **3** a source of security. **4** something that offers a secure hold to something else. **anchorman, anchorwoman** *n.* (*pl.* **anchormen, anchorwomen**) **1** a television or radio broadcaster who introduces and links the various reports etc. making up a (news) programme. **2** in sport, the last team member to compete, esp. in a relay race. **3** in sport, the person at the back of a tug-of-war team. **anchorperson** *n.* (*pl.* **anchorpersons, anchorpeople**) an anchorman or anchorwoman. **anchor plate** *n.*

anchorite (ang´kərīt) *n.* **1** a religious recluse, a hermit; an early Christian recluse. **2** a person of solitary habits. **anchoress, ancress** (-kris) *n.* a female anchorite. **anchoret** (-ret) *n.* an anchorite. **anchoretic** (-ret´-), **anchoretical** *a.* **anchoritic** (-rit´-), **anchoritical** *a.*

anchovy (an´chəvi, anchō´vi) *n.* (*pl.* **anchovies**) any of various small fish of the herring family, esp. *Engraulis encrasicolus*, caught in the Mediterranean, pickled for exportation, and used in sauces etc. **anchoveta** (-chəvet´ə) *n.* a small Pacific anchovy, *Cetengraulis mysticetus*, used as bait.

anchusa (ankū´zə, anchū´zə) *n.* any Eurasian plant of the genus *Anchusa*, similar to borage.

anchylose, anchylosis ANKYLOSE.

ancien régime (āsyā rāzhēm´) *n.* (*pl.* anciens régimes) **1** the political and social system of France before the French Revolution. **2** any superseded order.

ancient[1] (ān´shənt) *a.* **1** of or belonging to time long past. **2** very old. **the ancients** those who lived in former (esp. classical) times. **ancient Greek** *n.* the Greek language as recorded until about 300 BC. **ancient history** *n.* **1** history of ancient times, esp. to the end of the Western Empire, AD 476. **2** (*coll.*) information, gossip etc. that is widely known. **ancient lights** *n.pl.* windows that have acquired by long usage (not less than 20 years) the right to light from adjoining property. **anciently** *adv.* in ancient times; long ago. **ancient monument** *n.* a historic building or ruin dating from the Middle Ages or earlier, preserved by government order. **ancientness** *n.* **ancient world** *n.* the history of the civilizations of the Mediterranean and the Near East, up to the time of the fall of the Western Roman Empire in AD 476.

ancient[2] (ān´shənt) *n.* (*Hist.*) **1** a flag, a standard. **2** a standard-bearer, an ensign.

ancillary (ansil´əri) *a.* **1** auxiliary, supplementary, esp. providing support to a central service or industry. **2** subservient, subordinate. ~*n.* (*pl.* ancillaries) **1** a person who assists or supplements. **2** an ancillary device or thing.

ancon (ang´kon) *n.* (*pl.* ancones (-kō´nēz)) (*Archit.*) **1** a bracket or console supporting a cornice. **2** either of a pair of projections on a block of stone by which it can be lifted or moved.

ancress ANCHORITE.

-ancy (ənsi) *suf.* forming nouns expressing quality or state, e.g. *constancy, elegancy, infancy, vacancy*.

and (and, ənd) *conj.* **1** the copulative which joins words and sentences: connecting words that are to be considered together or in relation to each other; implying consequence; implying a sequence in time; used to join identical words with an intensifying force; used to join identical words but implying a contrast (*fish and chips*; *Antony and Cleopatra*; *One move and I'll shoot*; *She married and started a family*; *It gets worse and worse*; *for days and days*; *There are helpers and there are helpers*). **2** plus. **3** (*coll.*) to, after *try, go* etc. **and/ or** indicating that either or both of two possibilities may occur, be chosen etc.

-and (and) *suf.* forming nouns meaning a person or thing that is about to undergo a specified process (*analysand, graduand, multiplicand*).

Andalusian (andəloo´ziən) *a.* of or relating to Andalusia, a region of S Spain. ~*n.* **1** a native

or inhabitant of Andalusia. **2** the language or dialect of Andalusia.

andante (andan´ti) *a., adv.* (*Mus.*) moderately slow. ~*n.* a moderately slow movement, piece or passage. **andantino** (-tē´nō) *a., adv.* (*Mus.*) rather quicker than andante. ~*n.* (*pl.* andantinos) a movement or piece of this character.

Andean (andē´ən) *a.* of or relating to the Andes mountains. **Andean condor** *n.* a large S American vulture, *Vultur gryphus.*

andesite (an´dəsīt) *n.* a fine-grained volcanic rock.

andiron (an´dīən) *n.* a horizontal bar raised on short legs with an ornamental upright in front, placed on each side of the hearth to support logs in a wood fire; a firedog.

androecium (andrē´siəm, -shi-) *n.* (*pl.* androecia (-ə)) (*Bot.*) the stamens of a flower collectively.

androgen (an´drəjən) *n.* **1** a male sex hormone. **2** any substance with male sex hormone activity. **androgenic** (-jen´-) *a.*

androgyne (an´drəjīn) *n.* **1** a hermaphrodite. **2** an androgynous plant. **androgynous** (-droj´i-) *a.* **1** presenting the characteristics of both sexes in the same individual. **2** bearing both stamens and pistils in the same flower or on the same plant. **androgyny** (-droj´ini) *n.* (*Biol.*) hermaphroditism, the presence of male and female organs in one individual.

android (an´droid) *n.* a robot having human form.

-androus (an´drəs) *suf.* (*Bot.*) having male organs or stamens, e.g. *diandrous, monandrous.* **-andry** (an´dri) *suf.* forming nouns.

-ane (ān) *suf.* **1** forming adjectives, e.g. *humane, mundane, urbane.* **2** (*Chem.*) forming names of hydrocarbons, e.g. *methane, pentane, hexane.*

anecdote (an´ikdōt) *n.* a brief account of an interesting or amusing fact or incident, esp. a biographical one. **anecdotage** (-dō´tij) *n.* **1** (*facet.*) garrulous old age (as if from DOTAGE). **2** anecdotes collectively. **anecdotal** (-dō´-) *a.* **anecdotic** (-dot´-), **anecdotical** *a.* **anecdotist** *n.*

anechoic (anikō´ik) *a.* free from echoes.

anemia ANAEMIA.

anemograph (ənem´əgrahf) *n.* an instrument which automatically records the velocity and direction of the wind. **anemographic** (-graf´-) *a.* of or relating to an anemograph.

anemometer (anəmom´itə) *n.* an instrument for measuring the velocity of wind, a wind gauge. **anemometric** (-met´-) *a.* **anemometry** (-tri) *n.*

anemone (ənem´əni) *n.* any of a genus of plants, *Anemone*, with brilliantly-coloured flowers, esp. *Anemone nemorosa*, sometimes called the windflower, common in Britain.

Usage note Pronunciation as (ənen´əmi), with transposition of the *m* and second *n*, is best avoided.

anemophilous (anəmof´iləs) *a*. wind-fertilized; having the pollen carried away by the wind.

-aneous (ā´niəs) *suf*. forming adjectives, e.g. *extraneous, instantaneous.*

aneroid (an´əroid) *a*. operating without liquid. *~n*. an aneroid barometer. **aneroid barometer** *n*. a barometer which measures the pressure of air by its action on a springy metallic box from which the air has been partially exhausted.

anesthesia, anesthetic etc. ANAESTHESIA.

aneurin (ənūə´rin, an´ūrin), **aneurine** *n*. thiamine.

aneurysm (an´ūrizm), **aneurism** *n*. an abnormal dilatation in an artery, particularly of the aorta. **aneurysmal** (-riz´-) *a*.

anew (ənū´) *adv*. **1** again; once again. **2** afresh; in a different way.

anfractuose (anfrak´tūōs), **anfractuous** (-əs) *a*. winding, sinuous, tortuous. **anfractuosity** (-os´-) *n*. **1** circuitousness, tortuousness. **2** intricacy.

angel (ān´jəl) *n*. **1** a messenger from God. **2** a ministering spirit. **3** a guardian or attendant spirit. **4** a member of the lowest order of the celestial hierarchy. **5** a benign, innocent or adorable creature. **6** a conventional representation of the heavenly messenger. **7** (*coll*.) a financial backer, esp. of a theatrical production. **8** (*coll*.) an unexplained radar echo. **angel cake**, (*esp. N Am*.) **angel food cake** *n*. a light sponge cake made with egg whites. **angel dust** *n*. the hallucinogenic drug phencyclidine. **angelfish** *n*. (*pl. in general* **angelfish**, *in particular* **angelfishes**) **1** any of several brightly-coloured tropical fishes with laterally compressed bodies. **2** a small tropical American fish with black and silver stripes, often kept in aquariums. **angelic** (anjel´ik), **angelical** *a*. **1** resembling or of the nature of an angel. **2** supremely good, beautiful, innocent etc. **angelically** *adv*. **angel shark** *n*. a fish of the family *Squatinidae*, allied to the rays and sharks and named from the winglike expansion of the pectoral fins (also called *monkfish*). **angels-on-horseback** *n*. oysters rolled in bacon.

Angeleno (anjəle´nō) *n*. (*pl.* **Angelenos**) a native or inhabitant of Los Angeles, California.

angelica (anjel´ikə) *n*. **1** an umbelliferous plant, *Angelica archangelica*, used in medicine, and as a preserve or sweet. **2** candied angelica root.

angelus (an´jələs) *n*. (*pl.* **angeluses**) **1** a short devotional exercise in the Roman Catholic Church in honour of the Incarnation. **2** the angelus bell. **angelus bell** *n*. a bell rung early in the morning, at noon and in the evening, as a signal to say the angelus.

anger (ang´gə) *n*. rage, fierce displeasure, passion excited by a sense of wrong. *~v.t*. to make angry, to enrage. *~v.i*. to become angry. **angry** (ang´gri) *a*. (*comp*. **angrier**, *superl*. **angriest**) **1** wrathful, expressing anger. **2** inflamed, painful. **3** suggesting anger, threatening. **angrily** *adv*.

angina (anjī´nə) *n*. **1** any disease causing inflammation or constriction of the throat, esp. quinsy. **2** angina pectoris. **anginal** *a*.

angina pectoris (anjīnə pek´təris) *n*. a heart condition marked by paroxysms of intense pain due to over-exertion when the heart is weak or diseased.

angio- (an´jiō), **angi-** *comb. form* vascular; of or relating to the vessels of organisms.

angiography (anjiog´rəfi) *n*. X-ray photography of the blood vessels. **angiograph** (an´-), **angiogram** *n*. a photograph made by angiography.

angioma (anjiō´mə) *n*. (*pl.* **angiomas, angiomata** (-tə)) a tumour composed of blood or lymph vessels.

angioplasty (an´jiōplasti) *n*. (*pl.* **angioplasties**) an operation undertaken to repair or unblock a blood vessel, e.g. by laser or by the insertion and inflation of a balloon.

angiosperm (an´jiəspœm) *n*. a plant of the class Angiospermae, that has its seed enclosed in a vessel or ovary. **angiospermous** (-spœ´-) *a*. having the seeds enclosed in an ovary.

Angle (ang´gəl) *n*. a member of one of the Low German tribes that settled in Northumbria, Mercia and East Anglia. **Anglian** (-gli-) *a*., *n*.

angle[1] (ang´gəl) *n*. **1** the inclination of two lines towards each other. **2** the space between the lines or planes inclined to each other. **3** a corner. **4** an angular projection. **5** a point of view from which something is considered, an approach. **6** the direction from which something is looked at or photographed. *~v.t*. **1** to move, place, turn, direct at an angle. **2** to present (a report, news story etc.) in a particular way or from a particular point of view. *~v.i*. to proceed or turn at an angle. **angle brackets** *n.pl*. printed or written brackets in the form < >. **angle-iron** *n*. an angular piece of iron used to strengthen a framework of any kind. **angle of attack** *n*. the angle between the chord line of an aerofoil and the relative airflow, or of a hydrofoil and the relative flow of water surrounding it. **angle of reflection** *n*. (*Physics*) the angle made by a ray of light reflecting from a surface and a line perpendicular to that surface. **angle of refraction** *n*. (*Physics*) the angle at which a ray of light is turned from its direct course in passing through a given medium. **angle of repose** *n*. the slope at which a mass of loose material comes to rest if left to itself. **Anglepoise**® *n*. a desk lamp with an adjustable, jointed arm that holds its position by means of a spring.

angle[2] (ang´gəl) *v.i*. **1** to fish with rod and line. **2** (*fig*.) to fish (for), to try to elicit, as a compliment. **3** to get something by craft. *~v.t*. to fish (a stream) with rod and line. **angler** *n*. **angler fish** *n*. *Lophius piscatorius*, a small British fish which attracts its prey by filaments attached to its head.

Anglican (ang´glikən) *a*. of or belonging to the Church of England or any Church in communion with it. ~*n.* a member of the Anglican Church. **Anglicanism** *n.*

Anglicism (ang´glisizm) *n.* **1** an English idiom. **2** an English custom or characteristic. **3** English political principles. **4** attachment to what is English. **Anglicist, Anglist** *n.* a student or specialist in English language, literature or culture. **Anglicize, Anglicise** *v.t.* **1** to make English. **2** to give an English form to.

Anglo (ang´glō) *n.* (*pl.* **Anglos**) **1** an Anglo-American. **2** any white North American who is not of Latin extraction. **3** a Scots, Irish or Welsh player who plays for an English club in any sport. ~*a.* of or relating to Anglos.

Anglo- (ang´glō) *comb. form* **1** English; of or belonging to England or the English. **2** partially English (the meaning completed by another word).

Anglo-American (ang-glōəmer´ikən) *n.* an American of English parentage or descent. ~*a.* **1** of or belonging to Anglo-American people. **2** of, relating to or between England or Britain and the US.

Anglo-Catholic (ang-glōkath´lik) *a.* Anglican, but of Catholic not Protestant tendencies. ~*n.* a High Church member of the Church of England. **Anglo-Catholicism** (-thol´-) *n.*

Anglocentric (ang-glōsen´trik) *a.* considering England as the centre or English customs, practices etc. as the norm.

Anglo-French (ang-glōfrensh´) *a.* **1** of, relating to or between England or Britain and France. **2** of or relating to Anglo-French. ~*n.* the French language of medieval England.

Anglo-Indian (ang-glōin´diən) *n.* **1** an English person born, or long resident, in the Indian subcontinent. **2** a person of mixed British and Indian descent. ~*a.* **1** of or belonging to Anglo-Indians. **2** of, relating to or between England or Britain and India. **3** (of a word) adopted into English from an Indian language.

Anglo-Irish (ang-glōī´rish) *a.* **1** of or between Britain and Ireland, esp. the Republic of Ireland. **2** of the Anglo-Irish people. ~*n.* **1** the English language as used in Ireland. **2** (*collect.*) the section of Irish people of English Protestant descent. **3** (*collect.*) the people of mixed English and Irish parentage.

Anglomania (ang-glōmā´niə) *n.* excessive fondness for English manners and customs.

Anglo-Norman (ang-glōnaw´mən) *a.* **1** of or relating to the Normans in England after the Norman Conquest. **2** of, relating to or between England and Normandy. **3** of or relating to the Anglo-French language. ~*n.* the Anglo-French language.

Anglophile (ang´glōfīl), **Anglophil** (-fil) *n.* an admirer of England or of the English. ~*a.* showing admiration of England or the English.

Anglophobe (ang´glōfōb) *n.* a hater of England or of the English. **Anglophobia** (-fō´-) *n.* fear or distrust of England.

anglophone (ang´glōfōn) *n.* a person who speaks English. ~*a.* of or belonging to an English-speaking nation.

Anglo-Saxon (ang-glōsak´sən) *a.* **1** of or relating to the English people before the Norman Conquest. **2** of or relating to English people of European descent. **3** of or relating to Old English. **4** of or belonging to the English Saxons as distinct from the Continental Saxons. ~*n.* **1** a member of the Anglo-Saxon peoples. **2** Old English.

angora (ang-gaw´rə) *n.* **1** a goat with long silky hair. **2** the hair itself, or a fabric made of it. **3** a long-haired variety of the domestic cat. **4** a breed of rabbit with long, fine fur. **5** a yarn or fabric made from angora rabbit hair.

angostura (ang-gəstū´rə) *n.* a febrifugal bark, used also in the preparation of bitters. **Angostura Bitters®** *n.pl.* a brand of aromatic bitters used in flavouring alcoholic drinks.

angry, angrily ANGER.

angst (angst) *n.* a nonspecific feeling of anxiety and guilt produced esp. by considering the imperfect human condition.

ångström unit (ang´strəm) *n.* a unit of length used to express the wavelengths of different kinds of radiations, equivalent to 1/254,000,000 in. (10^{-10}m).

anguish (ang´gwish) *n.* excessive pain or distress of body or mind. ~*v.t.* to afflict with extreme pain or grief. **anguished** *a.*

angular (ang´gūlə) *a.* **1** having angles or sharp corners. **2** forming an angle. **3** in an angle. **4** measured by an angle. **5** bony, lacking in plumpness or smoothness. **6** stiff, formal, unaccommodating, crotchety. **angularity** (-lar´-) *n.* **angularly** *adv.*

anhedral (anhē´drəl) *n.* the downward angle between the wing of an aircraft and the horizontal. ~*a.* having an anhedral.

anhinga (anhing´gə) *n.* a darter, esp. the American *Anhinga anhinga.*

anhydride (anhī´drīd) *n.* (*Chem.*) a chemical substance formed from another, esp. an acid, by removing the elements of water.

anhydrite (anhī´drīt) *n.* (*Chem.*) a colourless, orthorhombic mineral, calcium sulphate or anhydrous gypsum.

anhydrous (anhī´drəs) *a.* (*Chem.*) **1** having no water in the composition. **2** esp. destitute of water of crystallization.

ani (ah´ni) *n.* (*pl.* **anis**) any of various S and Central American birds of the genus *Crotophaga* of the cuckoo family, that have black plumage, a curved bill and a long tail.

❌ **anihilate** common misspelling of ANNIHILATE.

aniline (an´ilin) *n.* (*Chem.*) a chemical base used in the production of many beautiful dyes, and orig. obtained from indigo, now chiefly from nitrobenzene. **aniline dye** *n.* any synthetic dye, esp. one made from aniline.

anima (an´imə) *n.* **1** (*Psych.*) a person's true inner self, as opposed to the *persona.* **2** the feminine aspect of the male personality.

animadvert (animədvœt´) v.i. **1** to criticize or censure (with on or upon). **2** to direct attention to. **animadversion** (-shən) n.

animal (an´iməl) n. **1** an organized being possessing life, sensation and the power of voluntary motion. **2** any one of the lower animals as distinct from humans, esp. a mammal or quadruped. **3** a human being whose animal nature is abnormally strong, a brute. **4** (coll.) a person, thing or organization. ~a. **1** of, belonging to or derived from animals, their nature or functions. **2** carnal. **3** of or relating to animals as distinguished from vegetables or minerals. **animal husbandry** n. the breeding and care of domestic animals. **animalism** n. **1** behaviour or a characteristic typical of animals. **2** the theory which views mankind as merely animal. **3** sensuality. **animalist** n. **1** a believer in animalism. **2** a supporter of animal rights. **animality** (-mal´-) n. **1** animal nature. **2** the phenomena of animal life, animal life as distinct from vegetable life. **animalize, animalise** v.t. **1** to make into an animal. **2** to make into animal substance. **3** to brutalize. **animalization** (-zā´shən) n. **animal liberation** n. a movement aimed at securing animal rights. **animal magnetism** n. **1** the quality of being attractive esp. to members of the opposite sex. **2** MESMERISM. **animal rights** n.pl. the rights of animals to live without being exploited by humans (often used attrib., as in animal rights protest). **animal spirits** n.pl. liveliness, cheerfulness or exuberance.

animalcule (animal´kūl), **animalculum** (-ləm) n. (pl. **animalcules, animalcula** (-lə)) an animal so small as to be invisible to the naked eye. **animalcular** a.

animate[1] (an´imāt) v.t. **1** to give life or spirit to; to enliven, to vivify. **2** to actuate, to inspire. **3** to stir up. **4** to give the appearance of movement to. **5** to produce as an animated cartoon. **animated** a. **1** possessing life. **2** full of life or spirits; vivacious, lively. **3** moving as if alive. **animated film** n. a film produced by photographing a series of drawings or objects, each varying slightly in position from the preceding one, to give the illusion of movement. **animatedly** adv. **animation** (-ā´shən) n. **1** the act of animating. **2** the state of being animated, vitality. **3** life, vivacity. **4** (the techniques used in the production of) an animated cartoon. **animator** n. an artist who prepares material for animated cartoons.

animate[2] (an´imət) a. **1** living, endowed with life. **2** lively.

animateur (animətœr´) n. a person who is the animating force behind something; a promoter, a sponsor.

animatronics (animətron´iks) n. **1** the technique of making and using lifelike, esp. animal, robots. **2** the technique of editing and processing filmed images of real animals to produce particular effects, e.g. the simulation of spontaneous speech.

animism (an´imizm) n. **1** the attribution of a living soul to inanimate objects and to natural phenomena. **2** a spiritual (not a materialist) theory of the universe. **animist** n. **animistic** (-mis´-) a.

animosity (animos´əti) n. (pl. **animosities**) hostility, enmity; extreme dislike.

animus (an´iməs) n. **1** animosity. **2** a motive, intention or spirit actuating feeling, usu. of a hostile character. **3** (Psych.) the masculine part of the female personality.

anion (an´īən) n. (Chem.) an ion that moves towards the anode, a negatively charged ion; cp. cation. **anionic** (anīon´ik) a. **1** of or relating to anions. **2** having an active anion.

anise (an´is) n. an umbelliferous plant, Pimpinella anisum, cultivated for its aromatic seeds, which are carminative, anciently confused with the dill. **aniseed** (-sēd) n. the seed of the anise, used as a flavouring. **anisette** (-zet´) n. a liqueur made from aniseed.

anisotropy (anīsot´rəpi) n. the fact of possessing different physical properties in different directions, as with wood along and across the grain. **anisotropic** (-trop´-) a.

ankh (angk) n. a cross with a loop above the crosspiece, that was in ancient Egypt the emblem of life, or male symbol of generation.

ankle (ang´kəl) n. **1** the joint by which the foot is united to the leg. **2** the part of the leg between foot and calf. ~v.i. **1** to use the ankles to increase the force exerted on the pedals when cycling. **2** (sl.) to walk. **ankle-bone** n. the talus, the bone that forms the ankle joint. **ankle sock** n. a short sock that just covers the ankle. **anklet** n. **1** an ornamental chain or band worn round the ankle. **2** a fetter, strap or band for the ankle. **3** (N Am.) an ankle sock.

ankylosaur (angkī´ləsaw) n. a member of a suborder of dinosaurs, Ankylosauria, which were heavily armoured, short-legged, herbivorous quadrupeds.

ankylose (ang´kilōz), **anchylose** v.t. **1** to stiffen (a joint) by ankylosis. **2** to consolidate (two separate bones). ~v.i. **1** to become stiff. **2** to grow together. **ankylosis** (-lō´-) n. **1** the formation of a stiff joint by the fusion of bones or fibrous tissue. **2** the fusion of two bones. **ankylotic** (-lot´-) a.

annals (an´əlz) n.pl. **1** a narrative of events arranged in years. **2** historical records. **annal** n. **1** the record of one year's events. **2** in a chronicle, a record of a single item. **annalist** n. a person who writes annals. **annalistic** (-lis´-) a.

annatto (ənat´ō), **anatta** (ənat´ə), **anatto** (-ō) n. **1** an orange-red dye used to colour food, fabric etc. **2** the tropical American tree, Bixa orellana, from whose pulpy seeds this dye is obtained.

anneal (ənēl´) v.t. **1** to temper (glass or metals) by subjecting them to intense heat, and then allowing them to cool slowly. **2** (fig.) to temper or toughen. **3** to recombine a nucleic acid in its duplex form. ~*v.i.* (of a nucleic acid) to undergo annealing. ~*n.* the process of annealing.

annelid (an´elid) *n.* any of the Annelida, a class of invertebrate animals with elongated bodies composed of annular segments that includes the earthworm. **annelidan** *a.* of or relating to the Annelida. ~*n.* an annelid.

annex (eneks´) *v.t.* **1** to unite to, add on to, esp. to something larger; to append to a book or document. **2** to take possession of (territory). **3** to append as a condition, qualification or consequence. **4** (*coll.*) to steal. **annexable** *a.* **annexation** (aneksā´shen) *n.* **annexe** (an´eks), (*esp. N Am.*) **annex** *n.* **1** an appendix. **2** a supplementary or subsidiary building; an extension to a main building.

annihilate (eni´elāt) *v.t.* **1** to reduce to nothing, to blot out of existence, to destroy completely. **2** (*coll.*) to defeat comprehensively, to trounce, to thrash. **annihilation** (-ā´shen) *n.* **1** the act of annihilating; the state of being annihilated. **2** (*Physics*) the combining of an elementary particle and its antiparticle with spontaneous transformation into energy. **annihilator** *n.*

anniversary (anive´seri) *n.* (*pl.* **anniversaries**) **1** the annual return of any remarkable date. **2** the celebration of such an annually recurring date.

Anno Domini (anō dom´inī) *adv.* in the year of Our Lord (indicating a date reckoned from the beginning of the Christian era). ~*n.* (*coll.*) old age.

annotate (an´etāt) *v.t.* to make notes or comments upon. ~*v.i.* to write notes or comments. **annotatable** *a.* **annotation** (-ā´shen) *n.* **1** the act of annotating. **2** an explanatory note. **annotative** *a.* **annotator** *n.*

announce (enowns´) *v.t.* **1** to make known, to proclaim. **2** to declare officially, or with authority. **3** to make known the approach or arrival of. **announcement** *n.* **announcer** *n.* a person who announces the items of a broadcasting programme, reads news summaries etc.

annoy (enoi´) *v.t.* **1** to cause to feel irritated, displeased or angry. **2** to tease, to molest, to trouble, to put to inconvenience by repeated or continued acts. **annoyance** *n.* **1** the act of annoying. **2** the state of being annoyed. **3** something which annoys. **annoyer** *n.* **annoying** *a.* **annoyingly** *adv.*

annual (an´ūel) *a.* **1** returning or happening every year. **2** reckoned by or done or performed in a year. **3** (*Bot.*) lasting only a single year or season. ~*n.* **1** a book published every year, a year-book. **2** a plant which lives for a year only. **annual general meeting** *n.* a yearly, statutory meeting of the shareholders of a company, members of a society etc., at which reports are presented and officers elected. **annualize, annualise** *v.t.* to adjust or calculate according to a yearly rate. **annually** *adv.* **annual ring** *n.* a ring of wood seen in the cross-section of a plant stem or root, indicating one year's growth.

annuity (enū´iti) *n.* (*pl.* **annuities**) **1** a sum of money payable annually. **2** an investment insuring fixed annual payments for a specified period. **annuitant** *n.* a person who receives an annuity.

annul (enŭl´) *v.t.* (*pres.p.* **annulling**, *past, p.p.* **annulled**) **1** to render void, cancel, abolish. **2** to declare the invalidity of (a marriage). **annulment** *n.*

annular (an´ūle) *a.* ring-shaped.

annunciate (enŭn´siāt) *v.t.* **1** to announce, to proclaim the approach or arrival of. **2** to bring tidings of. **annunciation** (-ā´shen) *n.* the act of announcing. **the Annunciation 1** the announcement of the Incarnation made by the angel Gabriel to the Virgin Mary. **2** the church festival (Lady Day, 25 March) in honour of that event. **annunciator** *n.* **1** a person who or something that announces. **2** a visual indicator, e.g. for electric bells or telephones, to show which of several electrical circuits has been activated. **3** a visual or audible device indicating the position of a train.

annus mirabilis (anes, anus mirah´bilis) *n.* (*pl.* **anni mirabiles** (anē mirah´bilēz)) a remarkable year (usu. applied in English history to 1666, year of the Great Fire of London etc.). **annus horribilis** (horib´ilis) *n.* a year of personal or general misfortune and calamity.

anode (an´ōd) *n.* **1** the positive electrode or pole in an electrolytic cell. **2** the negative electrode of a primary cell delivering current. **3** the positive electrode which collects electrons in an electronic valve. **anodal, anodic** (-nod´-) *a.* **anodize, anodise** *v.t.* to give a protective surface coating of an oxide to (a metal) by making it the anode of an electrolytic cell. **anodizer** *n.*

anodyne (an´edīn) *a.* **1** assuaging pain. **2** alleviating distress of mind, soothing to the feelings. **3** bland, undemanding; uncontroversial. ~*n.* **1** a medicine which assuages pain. **2** anything which alleviates distress of mind or soothes the feelings.

anoint (enoint´) *v.t.* **1** to smear with oil or an ointment, esp. to pour oil on as a religious ceremony. **2** to consecrate with oil. **anointer** *n.*

anomaly (anom´eli) *n.* (*pl.* **anomalies**) **1** (an) irregularity. **2** (a) deviation from the common or established order, abnormality. **3** (*Astron.*) the angular distance of a planet or satellite from its last perihelion or perigee. **anomalistic** (-lis´-) *a.* irregular, abnormal. **anomalous** *a.* **1** deviating from rule. **2** irregular, abnormal. **anomalously** *adv.* **anomalousness** *n.*

anomie (an´omi), **anomy** *n.* the breakdown or absence of moral and social standards in an individual or society. **anomic** (enom´ik) *a.*

anon (enon´) *adv.* (*dated, poet. or facet.*) **1** immediately, thereupon. **2** soon after, in a little while.

anon. (ənon´) *abbr.* **1** anonymous. **2** an anonymous author.

anonymous (ənon´iməs) *a.* **1** nameless. **2** having no name attached. **3** of unknown or unavowed authorship or origin. **4** lacking distinctive characteristics, nondescript. **anonym** (an´ənim) *n.* **1** a person whose name is not made known. **2** a pseudonym. **anonymity** (anənim´iti) *n.* **anonymously** *adv.* **anonymousness** *n.*

anopheles (ənof´əlēz) *n.* any of a genus of mosquitoes, *Anopheles*, that includes the malarial mosquito *A. maculipennis.*

anorak (an´ərak) *n.* **1** a warm waterproof jacket, usu. with a hood. **2** (*coll., derog.*) a person who is considered boring and socially inept, usu. for devotion to some unfashionable, solitary or very studious pursuit.

anorexia (anərek´siə) *n.* **1** loss of appetite. **2** anorexia nervosa. **anorexia nervosa** (nœvō´sə) *n.* a psychological disorder characterized by an aversion to eating and fear of gaining weight. **anorexic, anorectic** (-rek´-) *a.* **1** suffering from anorexia (nervosa). **2** causing loss of appetite. **3** (*coll.*) extremely thin. ~*n.* **1** a person suffering from anorexia (nervosa). **2** a substance that causes loss of appetite.

anorthosite (ənaw´thəsīt) *n.* (*Geol.*) a coarse-grained rock that consists almost entirely of plagioclase feldspar.

anosmia (ənoz´miə) *n.* absence or loss of the sense of smell.

another (ənŭdh´ə) *a.* **1** an additional, one more. **2** one of the same kind as (*She's another Navratilova*). **3** a different (*try another brand*). **4** any other. ~*pron.* **1** an additional one. **2** a different one. **3** some other unnamed person, esp. an additional party to a legal action. **A. N. Other** (ā en ŭdh´ə) *n.* in a team list etc., a player or person who has yet to be selected or named. **another place** *n.* the other House (of Parliament).

ANOVA (an´əvə) *n.* a statistical procedure to divide the variations in a set of observations into particular components.

anovulant (anov´ūlənt) *n., a.* (a drug) that inhibits ovulation.

anoxia (ənok´siə) *n.* (*Med.*) deficiency of oxygen to the tissues. **anoxic** *a.*

ansate (an´sāt) *a.* having a handle.

anserine (an´sərīn) *a.* **1** of or belonging to the goose. **2** gooselike, stupid, silly.

ANSI *abbr.* American National Standards Institution.

answer (ahn´sə) *n.* **1** a reply to a question, appeal, objection or charge. **2** the solution to a problem. **3** something done in return. **4** a practical reply. **5** (*Law*) a written reply to a bill of charges. ~*v.t.* **1** to reply or respond to. **2** to act on a signal or summons from (*answer the door*). **3** to solve; to reply correctly to. **4** to be sufficient for or suitable to. ~*v.i.* **1** to reply, to respond. **2** to be suitable or satisfactory. **to answer back** to reply rudely or cheekily. **to answer for**

to be responsible or answerable for. **to answer to 1** to correspond, to suit. **2** to be responsible or answerable to. **answerable** *a.* **1** liable to be called to account, responsible (for, to). **2** capable of being answered. **answerability** (-bil´-) *n.* **answerer** *n.* **answering** *n.* **answering machine** *n.* a recording device that answers telephone calls and allows the caller to leave a message. **answering service** *n.* a business that receives and answers telephone calls on its clients' behalf. **answerphone** *n.* a telephone answering machine.

ant (ant) *n.* a small, social, hymenopterous insect of the family Formicidae. **to have ants in one's pants** (*coll.*) to be extremely fidgety and restless. **ant-bear** *n.* an aardvark. **anteater** *n.* **1** an edentate mammal, with a long extensile tongue, which it thrusts into anthills and withdraws covered with ants. **2** an echidna. **3** an aardvark. **antheap, anthill** *n.* **1** the mound or hillock raised by a community of ants. **2** a very crowded or busy place. **anting** *n.* the placing by birds of live ants in their plumage. **ant-lion** *n.* a neuropterous insect, the larvae of which construct a kind of pitfall for ants and other insects. **ant's eggs, ant-eggs** *n.pl.* (*coll.*) the pupae of ants. **antsy** (ant´si) *a.* (*N Am., coll.*) excited, agitated, fidgety.

ant- ANTI-.

-ant (ənt) *suf.* **1** forming adjectives, as *distant, elegant, trenchant.* **2** denoting an agent, a person who or thing that produces an effect, as in *accountant, merchant.*

antacid (antas´id) *a.* counteracting acidity. ~*n.* a medicine that counteracts acidity of the stomach.

antagonist (antag´ənist) *n.* **1** an opponent; a person who contends or strives with another. **2** a muscle which counteracts another, and is in turn counteracted by it. **3** (*Biol.*) a drug that counteracts the action of another or of a substance occurring naturally in the body. **antagonism** *n.* **1** opposition. **2** conflict, active disagreement. **3** (an) opposing force, action or principle. **antagonistic** (-nis´-) *a.* **antagonistically** *adv.* **antagonize, antagonise** *v.t.* **1** to arouse hostility or opposition in. **2** to counteract, to make antagonistic, put in active opposition.

Antarctic (antahk´tik) *a.* **1** of or belonging to the S Pole or the region within the Antarctic Circle. **2** opposite to the Arctic. ~*n.* the Antarctic regions. **Antarctic Circle** *n.* a parallel of the globe, 23° 28´ distant from the S Pole, which is its centre.

Usage note Pronunciation as (antah´tik), without the (k) before the (t), is best avoided.

---

ante (an´ti) *n.* **1** the stake which a poker player puts down after being dealt a hand, but before drawing. **2** (*coll.*) amount paid, price. ~*v.t.* (*3rd pers. sing. pres. antes, pres.p. anteing, past, p.p. anted*) **1** to stake. **2** to pay.

ante- (an´ti) *pref.* before in time or position.

Usage note The spellings of words beginning with *ante-* (before) and *anti-* (against, pronounced the same in British English) should not be confused.

ante-bellum (antibel´əm) *a.* existing before the war, esp. the American Civil War.

antecede (antisēd´) *v.t.* **1** to precede. **2** to go before or in front of. **antecedence** *n.* **1** a going before in point of time. **2** precedence, anteriority. **antecedent** *a.* **1** going before in time, prior, anterior. **2** presumptive, a priori. ~*n.* **1** something which goes before. **2** (*Gram.*) the word phrase, clause etc. to which another word, esp. a relative pronoun, refers. **3** (*pl.*) past circumstances, background. **4** (*Logic*) the conditional clause of a hypothetical proposition. **antecedently** *adv.*

antechamber (an´tichāmbə) *n.* an anteroom.

antechapel (an´tichapəl) *n.* the part of a chapel between the western wall and the choir screen.

antedate (an´tidāt) *n.* a date preceding the actual date. ~*v.t.* **1** to happen earlier than, precede. **2** to date before the true date. **3** to assign to an earlier date. **4** to cause to happen prematurely.

antediluvian (antidiloo´viən) *a.* **1** of or relating to the period before the biblical Flood. **2** old-fashioned, antiquated.

antelope (an´tilōp) *n.* (*pl. in general* **antelope**, *in particular* **antelopes**) **1** an animal of the genus *Antilope*, of the family Bovidae, containing ruminants akin to the deer and the goat. **2** leather made from the skin of such an animal.

ante meridiem (anti mərid´iem) *adv.* before noon.

antenatal (antinā´təl) *a.* **1** happening or existing before birth. **2** dealing with pregnancy or pregnant women.

antenna (anten´ə) *n.* (*pl.* **antennae** (-nē), **antennas**) **1** (*Zool.*) (*pl.* **antennae**) a sensory organ occurring in pairs on the heads of insects and crustaceans; a palp, a feeler. **2** (*pl.* **antennas**) an aerial.

antenuptial (antinŭp´shəl, ŭchəl) *a.* happening before marriage.

antepenult (antipənŭlt´) *n.* the last syllable but two. **antepenultimate** (-imət) *a.* last but two. ~*n.* the last but two.

ante-post (antipōst´) *a.* (of betting) done in advance of the event concerned, esp. before the runners' numbers are posted.

anterior (antiə´riə) *a.* **1** at the front, more to the front. **2** preceding, prior. **anteriority** (-or´-) *n.* **anteriorly** *adv.*

anteroom (an´tirum) *n.* a room leading into or forming an entrance to another.

anthelion (anthē´liən) *n.* (*pl.* **anthelia** (-ə)) a mock sun, a luminous ring projected on a cloud or fog bank opposite the sun.

anthelmintic (anthəlmin´tik), **anthelminthic** (-thik) *a.* destroying or remedial against parasitic,

esp. intestinal, worms. ~*n.* a remedy for intestinal worms.

anthem (an´thəm) *n.* **1** a portion of Scripture or of the Liturgy set to music, often in an elaborate choral setting. **2** a national anthem. **3** a song that is particularly associated with a group, institution etc. **4** a song of gladness or triumph. **5** a hymn in alternate parts.

anthemion (anthē´miən) *n.* (*pl.* **anthemia** (-ə)) a palmette, honeysuckle or conventional leaf or floral design.

anther (an´thə) *n.* (*Bot.*) the pollen-bearing organ of flowering plants. **antheral** *a.*

antheridium (anthərid´iəm) *n.* (*pl.* **antheridia** (-diə)) (*Bot.*) the male spore-bearing organ, analogous to an anther, of cryptogams.

anthology (anthol´əji) *n.* (*pl.* **anthologies**) **1** any collection of selected poems or other literary pieces. **2** a collection of songs, paintings etc. **anthological** (-loj´-) *a.* **anthologist** *n.* **anthologize**, **anthologise** *v.t.* to put into an anthology. ~*v.i.* to compile an anthology.

anthozoan (anthəzō´ən), **actinozoan** (aktinō-) *n.* any of a class, Anthozoa or Actinozoa, of radiated animals containing the sea anemones and coral polyps.

anthracene (an´thrəsēn) *n.* a crystalline substance with blue fluorescence obtained from tar, used in the manufacture of chemicals.

anthracite (an´thrəsīt) *n.* a non-bituminous coal, burning with intense heat, without smoke, and with little flame. **anthracitic** (-sit´-) *a.*

anthracnose (anthrak´nōs) *n.* a fungal disease of plants that causes dark, sunken spots to appear.

anthrax (an´thraks) *n.* an infectious, often fatal bacterial disease of sheep and cattle transmissible to humans.

anthropic (anthrop´ik) *a.* of or relating to human beings. **anthropic principle** *n.* a principle of cosmology which maintains that theories of the origin of the universe must necessarily take into account the development of individual human existence.

anthropo- (an´thrəpō), **anthrop-** *comb. form* **1** human. **2** of or relating to mankind.

anthropocentric (anthrəpōsen´trik) *a.* **1** centring on human beings. **2** regarding mankind as the measure and aim of the universe.

anthropogeny (anthrəpoj´əni), **anthropogenesis** (-jen´əsis) *n.* the science or study of the origin of human beings. **anthropogenic**, **anthropogenetic** (-net´-) *a.*

anthropoid (an´thrəpoid) *a.* **1** resembling human beings, of human form. **2** belonging to the suborder Anthropoidea which includes the higher apes and man. **3** (of a person) apelike. ~*n.* a creature, esp. one of the higher apes, resembling a human being in form.

anthropology (anthrəpol´əji) *n.* **1** the study of human beings, esp. in regard to the customs, societies, rituals etc. they have evolved. **2** the study of the physical and mental evolution of human beings in the widest sense. **anthropological** (-loj´-) *a.* **anthropologist** *n.*

anthropometry (anthrəpom´ətri) *n.* the scientific measurement of the human body. **anthropometric** (-met´-), **anthropometrical** *a.*

anthropomorphic (anthrəpəmaw´fik), **anthropomorphous** (-fəs) *a.* **1** possessed of a form resembling that of a human being. **2** of or relating to anthropomorphism. **anthropomorphism** *n.* the attribution of a human form or character to the Deity, or of human characteristics to the lower animals. **anthropomorphize, anthropomorphise** *v.t.* to give a human shape or attribute human characteristics to.

anthropophagous (anthrəpof´əgəs) *a.* feeding on human flesh, cannibal. **anthropophagy** *n.*

anti (an´ti) *prep.* opposed to. *~n.* (*pl.* **antis**) an opponent of a policy, political party etc.

anti- (an´ti), **ant-** *pref.* forming nouns and adjectives indicating opposition to something, as in *anti-apartheid*; the prevention of something, as in *anticoagulant*; the opposite of something, as in *anticlockwise*; a rival, as in *antipope*; something that is unlike the conventional form, as in *anti-hero*.

Usage note See note under ANTE-.

anti- (+ a– words) **anti-abortion** *a.* opposed to the practice or legalization of abortion. **anti-abortionist** *n.* **anti-aircraft** *a.* employed against hostile aircraft.

anti- (+ b–c words) **antibacterial** *a.* that combats the action of or destroys bacteria. **antibiosis** (antibīō´sis) *n.* antagonistic association between two organisms or between one organism and a substance produced by the other. **antibiotic** (-ot´-) *a.* inimical to life, esp. bacteria. *~n.* a substance produced synthetically or by a microorganism which inhibits the growth of or kills another microorganism. **antibody** (an´ti-) *n.* (*pl.* **antibodies**) a substance produced in the blood in response to the presence of an antigen and capable of counteracting toxins. **anticathode** (antikath´ōd) *n.* the target electrode for a stream of electrons in an X-ray tube, from which the X-rays are emitted. **anticlerical** *a.* opposed to (the political influence of) the clergy. **anticlericalism** *n.* **anticlimax** *n.* **1** the opposite of climax. **2** a descent or decrease in impressiveness; bathos. **anticlimactic** *a.* **anticlinal** (antiklī´nəl) *a.* (*Geol.*) forming a ridge so that the strata lean against each other in opposite directions. **anticline** (an´-) *n.* (*Geol.*) an anticlinal fold. **anticlockwise** *a., adv.* in the reverse direction from that taken by the hands of a clock. **anticoagulant** *a., n.* (a drug) that hinders blood clotting. **anticodon** *n.* a unit of genetic code in a transfer RNA molecule, that corresponds to a particular codon in messenger RNA and consists of a sequence of three nucleotides. **anticonvulsant** *a., n.* (a drug) used in treating or controlling

(epileptic) convulsions. **anticyclone** *n.* the rotary outward flow of air from an atmospheric region of high pressure. **anticyclonic** (-klon´-) *a.*

antic (an´tik) *n.* **1** (*pl.*) grotesque, ridiculous or troublesome behaviour. **2** a ludicrous action.

Antichrist (an´tikrīst) *n.* **1** a personal antagonist of Christ spoken of in the New Testament. **2** an opponent of Christ. **antichristian** (-kris´-) *a.* **1** opposed to Christ or to Christianity. **2** of or relating to Antichrist. *~n.* **1** a person opposed to Christ or to Christianity. **2** an adherent of Antichrist.

anticipate (antis´ipāt) *v.t.* **1** to foresee and act in advance of (*anticipates my every move*). **2** to expect (*I don't anticipate any problems*). **3** to forestall, to thwart by acting first. **4** to cause to happen earlier, to hasten. **5** to look forward to. **anticipation** (-ā´shən) *n.* **1** the act of anticipating. **2** expectation, presentiment, foresight. **3** (*Mus.*) the introduction of a note before the chord about to be played. **anticipative** *a.* **anticipator** *n.* **anticipatory** *a.*

Usage note The use of *anticipate* to mean expect is best avoided.

anti- (+ d– words) **antidepressant** *a., n.* (a drug) used in treating or preventing mental depression. **antidiuretic** *a., n.* (a substance) that decreases the flow of urine. **antidiuretic hormone** *n.* vasopressin.

antidote (an´tidōt) *n.* **1** a medicine designed to counteract poison or disease. **2** anything intended to counteract something harmful or unpleasant. **antidotal** (-dō´-) *a.*

anti- (+ e–g words) **anti-establishment, anti-Establishment** *a.* opposed to the Establishment in a particular society and its practices, values etc. **antifreeze** (an´ti-) *n.* a substance added to the water in car radiators to lower the freezing point. **anti-g** (antijē´) *a.* (*Physics*) designed to counteract the gravitational forces experienced during high acceleration.

antigen (an´tijən) *n.* a substance introduced into the body which stimulates the production of antibodies.

anti- (+ h–l words) (an´ti-) **anti-hero** *n.* (*pl.* **anti-heroes**) a principal character in a play, novel etc. who lacks noble or traditional heroic qualities. **antihistamine** *n.* a drug that counteracts the effects of histamine in allergic reactions. **antiknock** *n.* a compound which is added to petrol to prevent knocking. **anti-lock** *a.* (of a braking system) designed to prevent locking and skidding when the brakes are suddenly applied. **antilogarithm, antilog** (an´-) *n.* the number represented by a logarithm. **antilogarithmic** (-ridh´-) *a.*

antilogy (antil´əji) *n.* (*pl.* **antilogies**) contradiction in terms or in ideas.

anti- (+ m– words) **antimacassar** *n.* a covering for chairs, sofas etc. to prevent their being soiled by (macassar) oil on the hair, or as an ornament. **antimatter** (an´ti-) *n.* (*Physics*) hypothetical matter composed of antiparticles. **antimetabolite** (anti mitab´əlīt) *n.* any drug that disrupts the normal metabolic processes within cells, esp. one used against cancer.

antimony (an´timəni) *n.* (*Chem.*) a bright bluish-white brittle metallic element, at. no. 51, chem. symbol Sb, occurring naturally and used esp. in the manufacture of alloys and semiconductors. **antimonial** (-mō´-) *a., n.* **antimonic** (-mon´-) *a.* **antimonious** (-mō´-) *a.*

anti- (+ n–o words) antinode (an´ti-) *n.* (*Physics*) a region of maximum vibration between two nodes. **anti-nuclear** *a.* opposed to the use of nuclear power or weapons. **antioxidant** *n.* **1** (*Chem.*) any substance that prevents deterioration due to oxidization, esp. in stored foodstuffs. **2** (*Biol.*) any substance that removes oxidizing agents from a living organism, e.g. vitamin C or E.

antinomian (antinō´miən) *a.* **1** opposed to the moral law. **2** of or relating to the Antinomians. ~*n.* **1** a person who holds that the moral law is not binding on Christians. **2** (**Antinomian**) a member of a German sect of the 16th cent. said to hold this opinion. **antinomianism** *n.*

antinomy (antin´əmi) *n.* (*pl.* **antinomies**) **1** a contradiction between two laws. **2** a conflict of authority. **3** intellectual contradiction, opposition between laws or principles that appear to be equally founded in reason; paradox.

anti- (+ p– words) antiparticle (an´tipahtikəl) *n.* (*Physics*) an elementary particle with the same mass as but opposite charge to another particle. **anti-personnel** *a.* (of a weapon etc.) designed to kill or injure people. **antiperspirant** *n., a.* (a substance) used to reduce perspiration. **antipole** *n.* **1** the opposite pole. **2** the direct opposite. **antipope** *n.* a pope elected in opposition to the one canonically chosen. **antiproton** *n.* (*Physics*) a particle having the same mass as a proton and an equal but negative charge. **antipruritic** *a., n.* (a drug or agent) that relieves itching. **antipyretic** *a., n.* (a medicine) that prevents or allays fever.

antipasto (antipas´tō) *n.* (*pl.* **antipastos**, **antipasti** (-tē)) an hors d'oeuvre.

antipathic (antipath´ik) *a.* of contrary character or disposition.

antipathy (antip´əthi) *n.* (*pl.* **antipathies**) **1** hostile feeling towards; aversion, dislike. **2** a person or thing that is the object of such feeling. **antipathetic** (-thet´-), **antipathetical** *a.* **antipathetically** *adv.*

antiphon (an´tifon) *n.* **1** a sentence sung by one choir in response to another. **2** a series of such responsive sentences or versicles. **3** a short sentence said or sung before the psalms, canticles etc., in the Roman Catholic Church, an anthem. **4** an answer. **antiphonal** (-tif´-) *a.* **1** sung or recited alternately. **2** consisting of antiphons. ~*n.* an antiphonary. **antiphonally** *adv.* **antiphonary** (-tif´-) *n.* (*pl.* **antiphonaries**) a book containing a collection of antiphons. **antiphony** (-tif´-) *n.* (*pl.*

antiphonies) **1** alternate chanting or singing by a choir divided into two parts. **2** any musical or sound effect that echoes or answers another. **3** an antiphon.

antipodes (antip´ədēz) *n.pl.* **1** a place on the surface of the globe diametrically opposite to another. **2** a pair of places diametrically opposite. **3** the direct opposite of some other person or thing. **the Antipodes** Australia and New Zealand. **antipodal** *a.* **1** of or relating to the antipodes. **2** situated on the opposite side of the globe. **antipode** (an´tipōd) *n.* an exact opposite. **antipodean** (-dē´-) *a.* of, relating to or from the antipodes. ~*n.* (**Antipodean**) a person from the Antipodes.

antiquary (an´tikwəri) *n.* (*pl.* **antiquaries**) **1** a student, investigator, collector or seller of antiquities or antiques. **2** a student of ancient times. **antiquarian** (-kweə´riən) *a.* **1** of, relating to or dealing in antiques or rare and ancient books. **2** of or relating to the study of antiquities. ~*n.* an antiquary. **antiquarianism** *n.*

antiquated (an´tikwātid) *a.* old-fashioned, out of date, obsolete.

antique (antēk´) *a.* **1** ancient, old, that has been in existence for a long time. **2** old-fashioned, antiquated. ~*n.* **1** a piece of furniture, ornament etc., made in an earlier period and valued by collectors. **2** a relic of antiquity. **3** any very old thing or person. ~*v.t.* (*3rd pers. sing. pres.* **antiques**, *pres.p.* **antiquing**, *past, p.p.* **antiqued**) to give an antique appearance to.

antiquity (antik´witi) *n.* (*pl.* **antiquities**) **1** the state of being ancient, great age. **2** ancient times, esp. the period of European history before the Middle Ages. **3** (*usu. pl.*) a relic of ancient times. **4** (*usu. pl.*) manners, customs, events etc. of ancient times. **5** the ancients.

anti- (+ r– words) anti-racism *n.* opposition to all forms of prejudice or persecution on grounds of race. **anti-racist** *a., n.* **antirust** *a.* intended to prevent or treat rust.

antirrhinum (antirī´nəm) *n.* any plant of a genus, *Antirrhinum*, that includes the snapdragon.

anti- (+ s– words) antiscorbutic *n., a.* (a medicine or remedy) used in treating or preventing scurvy. **anti-Semite** *n.* a person who is hostile towards or prejudiced against Jews. **anti-Semitic** *a.* **anti-Semitism** *n.* **antiseptic** *a.* **1** counteracting sepsis, or putrefaction, by inhibiting the growth of micro-organisms. **2** free from contamination. **3** lacking interest, warmth or excitement, sterile. ~*n.* an antiseptic substance. **antisepsis** *n.* the principle of antiseptic treatment. **antiserum** *n.* (*pl.* **antiserums**, **antisera**) a serum containing antibodies. **antishock** *a.* designed or intended to resist shocks. **antiskid** *a.* intended to prevent skidding. **antisocial** *a.* **1** opposed to the interest of society, or to the principles on which society is constituted. **2** unsociable. **antistatic** (antistat´ik) *a., n.* (an agent) that counteracts the effects of static electricity. **anti-submarine** *a.* designed to destroy submarines or to defend against submarine attack.

antistrophe (antis´trəfi) *n.* **1** the return movement from left to right of a Greek chorus, answering the movement of a strophe. **2** the poem or choral song recited during this movement.

anti- (+ t– words) anti-tank *a.* designed to destroy tanks or defend against tank attacks. **antiterrorism** *n.* opposition to terrorism; procedures to combat terrorism. **antiterrorist** *a.* **antitetanus** *a.* preventing tetanus. **antitheft** *a.* intended to prevent something from being stolen. **antitoxin** *n.* an antibody or antiserum formed in the body which neutralizes the action of toxins. **antitoxic** *a.* **antitrade** *a.*, *n.* (a wind) blowing in an opposite direction to that of the trade winds. **antitrust** *a.* (*N Am.*) opposing trusts or monopolies which adversely affect competition.

antithesis (antith´əsis) *n.* (*pl.* **antitheses** (-sēz)) **1** the direct opposite. **2** opposition, contrast. **3** sharp opposition or contrast between words, clauses, sentences or ideas. **antithetic** (-thet´-), **antithetical** *a.* **1** of, relating to or marked by antithesis. **2** contrasted. **3** sharply opposed. **antithetically** *adv.*

antitype (an´titīp) *n.* **1** the thing or person that is represented by a type or symbol. **2** an opposite type. **antitypical** (-tip´-) *a.*

anti- (+ v– words) antiviral *a.* effective against viruses. **antivivisection** *a.* opposed to vivisection. **antivivisectionism** *n.* **antivivisectionist** *n.*, *a.*

antivenin (antiven´in) *n.* serum obtained from animals immunized against snake venom, used as an antidote against snake-bite.

antler (ant´lə) *n.* **1** a branch of the horns of a stag or other deer. **2** either of the branched horns of a deer. **antlered** *a.*

antonomasia (antənəmā´ziə) *n.* **1** the substitution of an epithet for a proper name, e.g. *the Corsican* for Napoleon. **2** the use of a proper name to describe one of a class, e.g. a *Cicero* for an orator.

antonym (an´tənim) *n.* a term expressing the reverse of some other term, as 'good' to 'bad'.

antrum (an´trəm) *n.* (*pl.* **antra** (-trə)) (*Anat.*) a natural anatomical cavity, particularly one in bone.

anuran (ənū´rən) *n.* any tailless amphibian vertebrate of the order Anura which includes the frogs and toads. ~*a.* of or relating to this order.

anus (ā´nəs) *n.* (*Anat.*) the lower, excretory opening of the intestinal tube.

anvil (an´vil) *n.* **1** the iron block, usu. with a flat top, concave sides and a point at one end, on which smiths hammer and shape their work. **2** anything resembling a smith's anvil in shape or use, esp. a bone in the ear, the incus.

anxious (angk´shəs) *a.* **1** troubled or fearful about some uncertain or future event. **2** inspiring

anxiety, distressing, worrying. **3** eagerly desirous (to do something). **anxiety** (angzī´əti) *n.* (*pl.* **anxieties**) **1** the state of being anxious. **2** trouble, solicitude or mental distress. **3** eager desire. **4** a cause of anxiety. **5** (*Psych.*) a mental disorder symptomized by chronic uneasiness. **anxiolytic** (angziōlit´ik) *n.*, *a.* (a drug) that alleviates anxiety. **anxiously** *adv.*

any (en´i) *a.*, *pron.* **1** one, unspecified, among several (*pick any card*). **2** some or an unspecified number (*Read any good books lately?*). **3** a minimal amount (*makes hardly any difference*). **4** whichever, whatever (*any day will suit me*). ~*adv.* (*usu. with a negative*) at all, to an appreciative degree (*hasn't made it any better*). **any day now** very soon, very shortly. **any longer** for any further length of time; now, from this point on. **any minute now** very soon, very shortly. **anymore** (*N Am.*) any more. **any more** for any further length of time; now, from this point on. **any old** (*coll.*) any, no matter which or what. **anytime** (*N Am.*) any time. **any time** (*coll.*) whenever, at any time. **any time now** very soon, very shortly. **not having any** (*coll.*) unwilling to tolerate or put up with something; unwilling to participate in something. **anybody** *n.*, *pron.* **1** any person; any one. **2** a person of little importance (*I'm not just anybody!*). **3** a person of some importance (*is she anybody?*). **anybody's 1** (of a game, contest) evenly balanced. **2** (*coll.*) (of a person) able to be seduced, bribed etc. by anybody. **anyhow** *adv.* **1** anyway. **2** in a disorderly fashion, imperfectly, haphazardly. **anyone** *n.*, *pron.* any person, anybody. **anyplace** *adv.* (*N Am.*) anywhere. **any road** *adv.* (*dial.*) anyway, in any case. **anything** *pron.*, *n.* any object, thing, event, action of any kind . (*be prepared for anything*). ~*adv.* in any way (*if you're anything like me*). **anything but** not at all (*it's anything but easy*). **like anything** (*coll.*) very fast, vigorously, intensely etc. **anyway** *adv.* **1** nevertheless, in any case, in any event. **2** in any manner or fashion. **3** to resume. **anyways** *adv.* (*N Am.*, *coll.* or *dial.*) anyway. **anywhere** *adv.* in or to any place.

Usage note In writing, it is conventional to distinguish between *anyone* and *any one*: *any one* means any individual one (as in *I could kill any one of you*), while *anyone* means anybody at all (*I couldn't kill anyone*).

Anzac (an´zak) *n.* **1** a soldier in the Australian or New Zealand forces, in the war of 1914–18. **2** any Australian or New Zealander, esp. a soldier. **Anzac Day** *n.* 25 April, a public holiday in Australia and New Zealand to commemorate the Anzac landing at Gallipoli in 1915.

AO *abbr.* Officer of the Order of Australia.

AOB *abbr.* any other business.

AOC *abbr.* appellation d'origine contrôlée.

A-OK (āōkā´) *a.* in good or perfect working order.

aorist (ā´ərist) n. (Gram.) a Greek tense expressing indefinite past time. ~a. aoristic. **aoristic** (-ris´-) a.

aorta (āaw´tə) n. (pl. **aortas**) **1** the largest artery in the body. **2** the main trunk of the arterial system proceeding from the left ventricle of the heart. **aortic** a.

AP abbr. Associated Press.

ap-¹ (ap) pref. AD-, assim. to p, e.g. appear, approve.

ap-² APO-.

apace (əpās´) adv. at a quick pace, speedily, fast.

Apache (əpach´i) n. (pl. **Apache, Apaches**) **1** a member of a N American Indian people of the SW US and N Mexico. **2** the language of this people. ~a. of or relating to this people or their language. **apache** (əpash´) n. (pl. **apaches** (əpash´)) a hooligan or street ruffian or robber, originally from Paris.

❌ **apall** common misspelling of APPAL.

❌ **aparent** common misspelling of APPARENT.

apart (əpaht´) adv. **1** parted, at a distance from one another. **2** into two or more pieces or parts. **3** to or on one side. **4** not being taken into account. **5** independently. **6** distinct from others. **apart from 1** with the exception of, leaving out. **2** in addition to. **apartness** n.

apartheid (əpah´tāt, -tīt) n. (a policy of) racial segregation.

apartment (əpaht´mənt) n. **1** (pl.) a suite of rooms, lodgings. **2** (esp. N Am.) a flat. **3** a single room in a house. **apartment building, apartment house** n. (N Am.) a block of flats. **apartment hotel** n. (N Am.) a hotel that lets furnished suites of rooms on a short- or long-term basis.

apathy (ap´əthi) n. **1** absence of feeling or passion. **2** lack of interest, indifference. **apathetic** (-thet´-) a. characterized by apathy; listless, emotionless, indifferent. **apathetically** adv.

apatosaurus (əpatəsaw´rəs) n. (pl. **apatosauruses**) a very large herbivorous dinosaur of the genus Apatosaurus, formerly Brontosaurus, having a long neck and tail, a small head and trunklike legs.

APB abbr. (N Am.) all-points bulletin.

ape (āp) n. **1** a tailless primate, esp. one of the Pongidae (a gorilla, chimpanzee, orang-outan or gibbon). **2** (loosely) any monkey. **3** a mimic, an imitator. **4** a clumsy, coarse or brutish person. ~v.t. to imitate or mimic. **to go ape** (N Am.) to go berserk; to go crazy. **apeman** n. (pl. **apemen**) any of various extinct primate species thought to have been intermediate between the higher apes and humans. **apery** (ā´pəri) n. (pl. **aperies**) mimicry, esp. if silly or pretentious. **apish** a. **1** silly, foolish. **2** of the nature of or like an ape. **apishly** adv. **apishness** n.

❌ **apear** common misspelling of APPEAR.

aperçu (apœsoo´) n. **1** a concise exposition, an outline, a brief summary. **2** an insight.

aperient (əpiə´riənt) a. laxative, purgative, deobstruent. ~n. a laxative medicine.

aperiodic (āpiəriod´ik) a. **1** not occurring regularly. **2** (Physics) **a** not having a periodic motion. **b** (of an instrument) sufficiently damped to reach equilibrium without oscillation. **aperiodicity** (-dis´-) n.

aperitif (əperitēf´) n. a short drink, usu. alcoholic, taken as an appetizer.

aperture (ap´əchə) n. **1** an opening, a hole, a gap, a passage. **2** (the diameter of) the space through which light passes in an optical instrument. **3** the diameter of a lens.

apetalous (əpet´ələs) a. (Bot.) without petals

APEX¹ abbr. Association of Professional, Executive, Clerical and Computer Staff.

APEX², Apex n. a discounted fare on some air, sea and rail journeys paid for no later than a specified number of days before departure.

apex (ā´peks) n. (pl. **apexes, apices** (ā´pisēz)) **1** the tip, top, vertex or summit of anything. **2** the culmination, climax. **apical** (-pikəl) a. **1** of or relating to an apex. **2** placed at the summit. **apically** adv. **1** at the apex. **2** towards the apex.

aphasia (əfā´ziə) n. (Med.) (partial) loss of the power to express or understand anything in words. **aphasic** a.

aphelion (əfē´liən) n. (pl. **aphelia** (-ə)) the point most distant from the sun in the orbit of a planet or a comet.

aphid (ā´fid) n. **1** any of a family of minute insects, Aphididae, which are very destructive to vegetation, comprising among others the greenfly, black fly, American blight etc. **2** a plantlouse.

aphis (ā´fis, af´-) n. (pl. **aphides** (-dēz)) an aphid, esp. of the genus Aphis.

aphonia (əfō´niə), **aphony** (af´əni) n. (Med.) inability to speak or loss of voice caused by disease of the vocal tract. **aphonic** (əfon´-) a.

aphorism (af´ərizm) n. a detached, pithy sentence, containing a maxim or wise precept. **aphorist** n. a person who writes or utters aphorisms. **aphoristic** (-ris´-) a. **aphoristically** adv. **aphorize, aphorise** v.i. to utter or write aphorisms.

aphrodisiac (afrədiz´iak) a. exciting sexual desire. ~n. a drug that arouses or increases sexual desire.

aphyllous (əfil´əs) a. (Bot.) without leaves.

apian (ā´piən) a. of or relating to bees.

apiarian (āpieə´riən) a. relating to bees or beekeeping. ~n. an apiarist. **apiarist** (ā´-) n. a person who rears bees, a bee-keeper. **apiary** (ā´-) n. (pl. **apiaries**) a place where bees are kept.

apical, apices see APEX.

apiculture (ā´pikŭlchə) n. bee-keeping; bee-rearing.

apiece (əpēs´) adv. for or to each, severally.

apish see APE.

aplanatic (aplənat´ik) a. (of a lens etc.) free from spherical aberration. **aplanat** (ap´lənat) n. an aplanatic surface or instrument.

aplasia (əplā´ziə) n. (Med.) defective or arrested development in a body tissue or organ. **aplastic** (-plas´-) a.

aplenty (əplen´ti) adv. in plenty, in abundance.

aplomb (əplom´) n. self-possession, coolness.

apnoea (apnē´ə), (N Am.) **apnea** n. (Med.) a breakdown or cessation of breathing.

apo- (ap´ō), **ap-** pref. away, detached, separate, as in apology, apostrophe.

Apoc. abbr. **1** Apocalypse. **2** Apocrypha, apocryphal.

apocalypse (əpok´əlips) n. **1** any revelation or prophetic disclosure, esp. relating to the end of the world. **2** a vast decisive or cataclysmic event or confrontation. **the Apocalypse 1** the revelation granted to St John the Divine. **2** the book of the New Testament in which this is recorded. **apocalyptic** (-lip´-), **apocalyptical** a. **1** of or relating to the revelation of St John. **2** of the nature of a revelation or apocalypse. **3** prophesying disaster or doom. **apocalyptically** adv.

apocarpous (apəkah´pəs) a. (Bot.) having the carpels wholly or partly distinct.

apochromat (apəkrō´mat) n. a lens that reduces chromatic aberrations. **apochromatic** (-krəmat´ik) a.

apocrine (ap´əkrīn, -in) a. (Biol.) (of a gland) whose secretions include parts of the cells of the gland.

apocrypha (əpok´rifə) n.pl. writings or statements of doubtful authority. **the Apocrypha** a collection of 14 books in the Old Testament, included in the Septuagint and the Vulgate (not written in Hebrew originally and not recognized by the Jews or inserted in the Authorized Version of the Bible). **apocryphal** a. **1** of or relating to the Apocrypha. **2** spurious, fabulous. **apocryphally** adv.

apod (ap´əd), **apode** (ap´ōd) n. a footless creature, a bird, fish or reptile in which the feet or corresponding members are absent or undeveloped. **apodal** a. (Zool.) **1** footless. **2** having no ventral fin.

apodictic (apədik´tik), **apodeictic** (-dīk´-) a. **1** clearly demonstrative. **2** established on uncontrovertible evidence.

apogee (ap´əjē) n. **1** the point in the orbit of the moon or any planet or satellite which is at the greatest distance from the earth. **2** the furthest point, the highest point, the culmination. **apogean** (-je´-) a.

apolitical (āpəlit´ikəl) a. **1** uninterested in political affairs, politically neutral. **2** without political significance.

apologetic (əpoləjet´ik), **apologetical** a. **1** regretfully acknowledging or excusing an offence. **2** of or relating to a reasoned defence or vindication. **3** hesitant, diffident. **apologetically** adv. **apologetics** n. defensive argument, esp. the argumentative defence of Christianity.

apologia (apəlō´jiə) n. a vindication or formal defence of one's conduct, views etc.

apologue (ap´əlog) n. a fable designed to impress some moral truth upon the mind, esp. a beast-fable or a fable of inanimate things.

apology (əpol´əji) n. (pl. **apologies**) **1** a regretful acknowledgement of offence. **2** an explanation, excuse. **3** a defence, vindication. **4** a wretched substitute for the real thing. **apologist** n. a person who defends or vindicates by reasoned argument. **apologize**, **apologise** v.i. to make an apology or excuses, to express regret.

apolune (ap´əloon, ap´ō-) n. the point in a body's lunar orbit where it is furthest from the moon.

apomixis (apəmik´sis) n. (pl. **apomixes** (-sēz)) (Biol.) reproduction without fertilization. **apomictic** a.

apophthegm (ap´əthem), (NAm.) **apothegm** n. a terse pointed saying, a maxim expressed in few but weighty words. **apophthegmatic** (-thegmat´-) a.

apoplexy (ap´əpleksi) n. **1** (Med.) a sudden loss of sensation and of power of motion, generally caused by rupture or obstruction of a blood vessel in the brain, a stroke. **2** (coll.) a violent fit of anger. **apoplectic** (-plek´-) a. **1** of, relating to or tending to cause apoplexy. **2** predisposed to apoplexy. **3** violently angry.

apoptosis (apəptō´sis) n. (Biol.) the death of cells as part of the normal growth and development of an organism. **apoptotic** (-tot´ik) a.

aporia (əpaw´riə, əpor´iə) n. **1** in rhetoric, a real or affected doubt about what to do. **2** a difficulty, a puzzling thing.

aposematic (apəsimat´ik) a. (Zool.) (of the colouring of some animals) providing protection against predators.

apostasy (əpos´təsi) n. (pl. **apostasies**) **1** (a) renunciation of religious faith, moral allegiance or political principles. **2** in the Roman Catholic Church, renunciation of religious vows.

apostate (əpos´tāt) n. a person who apostatizes. ~a. **1** unfaithful to creed or principles. **2** rebel, rebellious. **apostatic** (əpəstat´-), **apostatical** a. **apostatize** (-tə-), **apostatise** v.i. to abandon one's creed, principles or party, to commit apostasy.

a posteriori (a postiəriaw´ri, ah) a., adv. reasoning from consequences, effects, things observed to causes; inductive, as opposed to a priori or deductive.

apostle (əpos´əl) n. **1** (**Apostle**) any one of the twelve men appointed by Christ to preach the gospel. **2** a first Christian missionary to any region, or a missionary who has pre-eminent success. **3** the leader of, or an outstanding figure in, a movement, esp. of reform. **4** a member of a council of twelve appointed to preside over the Mormon Church. **apostle-bird** n. an Australian babbler which forms flocks of about twelve. **Apostles' Creed** n. a Christian creed, each clause of which is said to have been contributed by one of the Apostles. **apostleship** n. **apostolate** (-tələt) n. **1** the office of apostle. **2** leadership, esp. in the propagation of a doctrine. **apostolic** (apəstol´-), **apostolical** a. **1** of or relating to the Apostles. **2** derived directly from or agreeable to the doctrine or practice of the Apostles. **3** of the character or nature of an apostle. **4** of or relating to the Pope as St Peter's successor, papal. **apostolically** adv. **apostolic succession** n. uninterrupted transmission of spiritual authority through bishops, from the Apostles.

apostrophe[1] (əpos´trəfi) n. the sign (') used to denote the omission of a letter or letters, and as the sign of the English possessive case.

apostrophe[2] (əpos´trəfi) n. a rhetorical figure in which the speaker addresses one person in particular, or turns away from those present to address the absent or dead. **apostrophic** (apəstrof´ik) a. **apostrophize, apostrophise** v.t. to address in or with apostrophe.

apothecary (əpoth´ikəri) n. (pl. **apothecaries**) **1** †a person who prepares and sells medicines, a druggist or pharmaceutical chemist. **2** a licentiate of the Apothecaries' Society. **apothecaries' measure** n. a system of liquid capacity measure formerly used in pharmacy, based on the minim, fluid drachm and fluid ounce. **apothecaries' weight** n. a system of weights formerly used in pharmacy, based on the grain, scruple, drachm and troy ounce.

apothegm APOPHTHEGM.

apotheosis (əpothiō´sis) n. (pl. **apotheoses** (-sēz)) **1** deification, transformation into a god. **2** a sublime example of something. **3** a deified ideal. **4** enrolment among the saints. **apotheosize** (-poth´-), **apotheosise** v.t. to deify, to exalt, to glorify.

apotropaic (apətrəpā´ik) a. intended or supposed to avert evil influences.

app. abbr. (Comput.) application.

appal (əpawl´), (esp. N Am.) **appall** v.t. (pres.p. **appalling**, past, p.p. **appalled**) to horrify, to shock, to dismay. **appalling** a. **1** horrifying, shocking. **2** unsatisfactory. **3** unpleasant. **appallingly** adv.

apparat (apərat´, ap´-) n. (Hist.) the party organization of the Communist party in the Soviet Union and similar states. **apparatchik** (-chik) n. **1** a member of an apparat. **2** a bureaucrat or official in any political party or other organization, esp. a zealous one. **3** a Communist agent.

apparatus (apərā´təs, -rah´-) n. (pl. **apparatuses**, **apparatus**) **1** equipment generally. **2** the instruments employed in scientific or other research. **3** equipment or a machine used for a specific function. **4** the administrative workings of a (political) system or organization. **5** materials for critical study. **6** (Anat.) the organs by which any natural process is carried on.

apparel (əpar´əl) n. **1** (N Am. or formal) dress, attire, clothes. **2** ornamental embroidery on ecclesiastical vestments. ~†v.t. (pres.p. **apparelling**, (N Am.) **appareling**, past, p.p. **apparelled**, (N Am.) **appareled**) to dress, to clothe.

apparent (apar´ənt, -peə´-) a. **1** to be seen, visible, in sight. **2** plain, obvious, indubitable. **3** appearing (in a certain way), seeming. **apparent horizon** n. SENSIBLE HORIZON (under SENSIBLE). **apparently** adv. **apparent magnitude** n. the brightness of a star etc. as observed. **apparent time** n. SOLAR TIME (under SOLAR).

apparition (apərish´ən) n. **1** the fact of appearing or becoming visible, esp. suddenly or strangely. **2** a strange appearance. **3** a spectre, phantom, ghost. **apparitional** a.

appeal (əpēl´) v.i. **1** to make an earnest request (for) or a formal or earnest request (to). **2** to attract or be of interest (to). **3** to refer to some person or thing for corroboration or support. **4** (Law) to refer one's case to a superior court for reconsideration. **5** in cricket, to ask the umpire for a decision on whether a batsman is out; to shout out something for this purpose. **6** to challenge a decision given by an umpire, referee etc. ~v.t. (Law) to refer (a case, conviction) for review to a superior court. ~n. **1** the act of appealing. **2** a request for aid, esp. for money for charitable purposes. **3** reference or recourse to another person or authority, esp. a higher court. **4** power of attracting or interesting. **5** entreaty. **appealable** a. that may be appealed against. **appealing** a. attractive, arousing interest. **appealingly** adv.

appear (əpiə´) v.i. **1** to become or be visible. **2** to be manifest. **3** to seem. **4** to present oneself. **5** to be published; to come before the public. **appearance** n. **1** the act of appearing. **2** the act of appearing formally or publicly. **3** the outward or visible form of a person or thing. **4** external show, pretence. **to all appearances** so far as could be ascertained, apparently. **to keep up appearances 1** to keep up an outward show of affluence, respectability etc. **2** to conceal the absence of something desirable. **to make an appearance** to put in an appearance. **to put in an appearance** to attend a function or to visit a person, usu. briefly and often.

appease (əpēz´) v.t. **1** to quiet, to pacify, to calm, to assuage, to allay. **2** to conciliate by acceding to demands. **3** to satisfy (an appetite, thirst etc.). **appeasable** a. **appeasement** n. **appeaser** n.

appellant (əpel´ənt) n. (Law) a person who appeals to a higher tribunal or authority. **appellate** (-ət) a. (Law) of, relating to or dealing with appeals. **appellation** (apəlā´shən) n. (formal) **1** a name, designation. **2** naming, nomenclature. **appellative** a. **1** (Gram.) (of a noun) common as opposed to proper; designating a class. **2** of or relating to the giving of names.

appellation contrôlée (apəlasyō kōtrō´lā), **appellation d'origine contrôlée** (dorēzhēn) n. a guarantee, in the labelling of some French wines and foodstuffs, that the product conforms to statutory regulations in respect of its origin, quality, strength etc.

append (əpend´) v.t. **1** to add or subjoin. **2** to hang on to or upon. **appendage** (-dij) n. **1** something added or appended. **2** (*Zool.*, *Bot.*) a subordinate or subsidiary organ or process, such as a limb or branch. **appendant** *a.* attached, annexed, joined on. ~*n.* **1** that which is attached or annexed. **2** an appendix, a corollary.

appendectomy (apəndek´təmi), **appendicectomy** (əpendisek´təmi) *n.* (*pl.* **appendectomies, appendicectomies**) the excision of the vermiform appendix.

appendicitis (əpendisī´tis) *n.* inflammation of the vermiform appendix.

appendix (əpen´diks) *n.* (*pl.* **appendixes, appendices** (-disēz) **1** a supplement to a book or document containing useful material. **2** (*Anat.*) a small process arising from or prolonging any organ, esp. the vermiform appendix of the intestine.

apperceive (apəsēv´) *v.t.* **1** to be conscious of perceiving. **2** (*Psych.*) to assimilate by reference to previous experience. **apperception** (-sep´shən) *n.* **apperceptive** *a.*

appertain (apətān´) *v.i.* **1** to relate (to). **2** to belong (as a part to a whole, as a possession, or as a right or privilege). **3** to be suitable or appropriate (to).

appetence (ap´itəns), **appetency** *n.* (*pl.* **appetences, appetencies**) instinctive desire, craving, appetite.

appetite (ap´ətīt) *n.* **1** desire for food. **2** the desire to satisfy a natural function. **3** inclination, disposition or desire for something. **appetitive** (əpet´i-) *a.* **appetize, appetise** *v.t.* **1** to give an appetite to. **2** to make (one) feel hungry or relish one's food. **appetizer, appetiser** *n.* a stimulant to appetite, esp. food (or drink) served before or at the beginning of a meal. **appetizing, appetising** *a.* stimulating appetite or hunger; tasty, delicious. **appetizingly** *adv.*

applaud (əplawd´) *v.i.* to express approbation, esp. by clapping the hands. ~*v.t.* to approve, commend or praise in an audible and significant manner. **applause** (əplawz´) *n.* **1** the act of applauding. **2** praise or approval emphatically expressed.

apple (ap´əl) *n.* **1** the round, firm, fleshy fruit of the apple tree. **2** any similar fruit. **3** a tree, genus *Malus*, that bears apples. **apple brandy** *n.* a spirit made from apples. **apple-cart** *n.* a cart of or for apples. **to upset the apple-cart** to disrupt plans or arrangements. **apple-cheeked** *a.* having chubby rosy cheeks. **applejack** *n.* (*N Am.*) apple brandy. **apple of one's eye** *n.* anything very dear or precious. **apple-pie bed** *n.* a bed prepared as a practical joke, with sheets folded short or tucked in hard so as to prevent one stretching one's full length. **apple-pie order** *n.* perfect order. **apples and pears** *n.pl.* (*sl.*) stairs.

appliqué (ap´likā) *n.* ornamental work laid on some other material. **appliquéd** *a.* treated with work of this kind.

apply (əplī´) *v.t.* (*3rd pers. sing. pres.* **applies**, *pres.p.* **applying**, *past*, *p.p.* **applied**) **1** to put to

(practical) use, to employ. **2** to bring to bear, to bring into operation (a rule, law). **3** to operate (a brake). **4** to put or rub on. ~*v.i.* **1** to offer oneself for a job, position etc. **2** to make a formal request (for). **3** to be relevant (to). **4** to have recourse (to). **to apply oneself** to work, study etc. in a concentrated and diligent fashion. **appliance** (-plī´-) *n.* an apparatus, device or contrivance. **applicable** (ap´li-, əplik´-) *a.* **1** capable of being applied. **2** fit, suitable, appropriate; relevant. **applicability** (-bil´-) *n.* **applicant** (ap´li-) *n.* a person who applies, esp. for a job. **application** (aplikā´shən) *n.* **1** the act of applying, esp. an ointment; the thing applied. **2** (a) petition, request. **3** the use to which something is put. **4** relevance. **5** disciplined and sustained work or study. **6** close attention. **application program** *n.* a computer program that performs a specific task for a user. **applied** *a.* **1** practical. **2** put to practical use. **applied mathematics** *n.* the application of mathematics to branches of physical research, as mechanics, astronomy etc.

appoggiatura (əpojətoo´rə) *n.* (*Mus.*) a grace note before a significant note.

appoint (əpoint´) *v.t.* **1** to nominate, designate (to a position, office). **2** to decide on, to fix (a time, place). **3** to decree, ordain. **4** (*Law*) **a** to assign, to grant (a thing to a person). **b** to declare (a person) to have an interest in a property. **appointed** *a.* furnished, equipped. **appointee** (-tē´) *n.* **1** a person who receives an appointment. **2** (*Law*) a person in whose favour an appointment is executed. **appointment** *n.* **1** an arrangement to meet at a specific time. **2** the act of appointing, esp. to a position or office. **3** the job or position to which someone is appointed. **4** a person who is appointed to something. **5** (*pl.*) equipment, fixtures and fittings. **6** (*Law*) the official declaration of the destination of any specific property. **7** decree, ordinance.

☒ **appology** common misspelling of APOLOGY.

apport (apawt´) *n.* **1** in spiritualistic terminology, a material object made to appear without material agency. **2** the production of such an object.

apportion (əpaw´shən) *v.t.* to share out in just or suitable proportions. **apportionment** *n.* the act of apportioning; the state of being apportioned.

apposite (ap´əzit) *a.* fit, apt, appropriate. **appositely** *adv.* **appositeness** *n.* **apposition** (-zish´-) *n.* **1** the act of putting together or side by side; juxtaposition, addition. **2** (*Gram.*) the placing together of two words, esp. of two nouns, one being a complement to the other. **appositional** *a.*

appraise (əprāz´) *v.t.* **1** to estimate the worth, value or quality of. **2** to set a price on, to value. **3** to make an official assessment of the performance of (an employee). **appraisable** *a.* **appraisal** *n.* **1** an authoritative valuation. **2** an estimate of worth. **3** a formal assessment of an employee's performance. **appraisee** (-zē´) *n.* a person whose performance is appraised. **appraiser** *n*. **1** a person who appraises. **2** a person authorized to fix the value of property. **appraisive** *a*.

Usage note The verbs *appraise* and *apprise* should not be confused: *appraise* means to estimate or assess, and *apprise* to inform.

appreciate (əprē´shiāt, -si-) *v.t.* **1** to esteem highly. **2** to feel gratitude for. **3** to understand. **4** to be sensitive to (delicate impressions). **5** to form an estimate of the value, merit, quality or quantity of. **6** to raise in value. ~*v.i.* to rise in value. **appreciable** (-shə-) *a*. capable of being appreciated; significant, considerable. **appreciation** (-ā´shən) *n*. **1** gratitude or grateful recognition. **2** an estimate or assessment of the worth or value of something. **3** understanding of or sensitivity to something. **4** a rise in value. **5** a critical study or review, esp. a favourable one. **appreciative** (-shə-) *a*. **appreciatively** *adv*. **appreciativeness** *n*. **appreciator** *n*. **appreciatory** (-shə-) *a*.

apprehend (aprihend´) *v.t.* **1** to seize, grasp or lay hold of mentally. **2** to seize, to arrest. **3** to fear, to dread, to anticipate with anxiety. ~*v.i.* to understand. **apprehensible** *a*. capable of being perceived. **apprehensibility** (-bil´-) *n*. **apprehension** (-shən) *n*. **1** fear, dread of what may happen. **2** power to perceive or grasp mentally. **3** the act of laying hold of, seizing or arresting. **4** conception, idea. **apprehensive** *a*. **1** anticipative of something unpleasant or harmful, fearful, anxious. **2** characterized by or fitted for (mental) apprehension. **apprehensively** *adv*. **apprehensiveness** *n*.

apprentice (əpren´tis) *n*. **1** a person who is bound by a formal agreement or indentures to work for an employer in order to learn some trade or craft which the employer agrees to teach. **2** a learner, a tyro, a novice. ~*v.t.* to bind as an apprentice. ~*v.i.* (*N Am*.) to work as an apprentice. **apprenticeship** *n*.

apprise (əprīz´) *v.t.* to inform, to make aware, to bring to the knowledge or notice of.

Usage note See note under APPRAISE.

appro (ap´rō) *n*. (*coll*.) short for APPROVAL (under APPROVE). **on appro** on approval.

approach (əprōch´) *v.i.* **1** to come, go or draw near or nearer. **2** (of an aircraft) to prepare to land. ~*v.t.* **1** to come near to. **2** to accost or communicate with (a person) with a view to making a proposal, securing something etc. **3** to begin to deal with (a task, problem). **4** to resemble; to be equal to. **5** to approximate to, to be close to. ~*n*. **1** the act of drawing near. **2** avenue, entrance, access. **3** a way of dealing with a person or thing. **4** (*often pl*.) communication with a person for a particular purpose; sexual advances. **5** an approximation. **6** the course taken by an aircraft in preparation for landing. **approachable** *a*.

1 capable of being approached. **2** easy to deal with. **3** friendly. **approachability** (-bil´-) *n*. **approach road** *n*. a road that gives access to a motorway.

approbate (ap´rəbāt) *v.t.* (*esp. N Am*.) to express approval of.

approbation (aprəbā´shən) *n*. **1** the act of approving. **2** approval, commendation, praise. **approbatory** (aprəbā´təri, ap´-) *a*.

appropriate¹ (əprō´priāt) *v.t.* **1** to take as one's own, esp. unlawfully or without permission. **2** to take possession of. **3** to devote to or set apart for a special purpose or use. **appropriation** (-ā´shən) *n*. **appropriator** *n*.

appropriate² (əprō´priət) *a*. **1** suitable, fit, becoming. **2** (*formal*) set apart for a particular person or use; particular, peculiar. **3** annexed or attached to. **appropriately** *adv*. **appropriateness** *n*.

approve (əproov´) *v.t.* **1** to commend, sanction, confirm. **2** to esteem, accept or pronounce as good. ~*v.i.* to express a favourable opinion or to feel approbation (of). **approval** *n*. **1** favourable opinion. **2** an act or the act of sanctioning. **on approval** (of goods) to be returned if not suitable. **approved** *a*. **1** officially sanctioned. **2** regarded with approval. **3** tried, proved, tested. **approved school** *n*. formerly in Britain, a state boarding school for juvenile offenders (boys under 15, girls under 17). **approving** *a*. **approvingly** *adv*.

Usage note When *approve* refers to feeling or expressing approval, *approve of* is preferred to the use with a direct object (so *They approved the decision* should mean that they confirmed or sanctioned it, rather than that they thought it good).

approx. (əproks´) *abbr*. approximate, approximately.

approximate¹ (əproks´simāt) *v.t.* **1** to cause to approach (esp. in number or quantity), to make almost the same as. **2** to draw or bring near. ~*v.i.* **1** to be more or less identical or equal (to). **2** to draw near, to approach. **approximation** (-ā´shən) *n*.

approximate² (əproks´simət) *a*. **1** nearly approaching accuracy. **2** rough, inexact. **3** very close to. **approximately** *adv*.

appurtenance (əpœ´tinəns) *n*. (*formal*) a thing which belongs to something else; an adjunct, an accessory, an appendage. **appurtenant** *a*. of or relating to, belonging to, pertinent.

APR *abbr*. annual percentage rate (of credit etc.).

Apr. *abbr*. April.

☒ appreciate common misspelling of APPRECIATE.

après-ski (apreskē´) *n., a.* (of or intended for) the social time following a day's skiing.

apricot (ā´prikot, ap´-) *n*. **1** a soft-fleshed, yellow to orange stone-fruit allied to the plum. **2** the tree, *Prunus armeniaca*, on which it grows. **3** the colour of the ripe fruit.

April (ā´prəl) *n.* the fourth month of the year. **April Fool** *n.* a victim of a practical joke on 1 April.

a priori (ā priaw´ri, -rī, ah) *adv.* from the cause to the effect; from abstract ideas to consequences; deductively. ~*a.* **1** deductive; derived by reasoning from cause to effect. **2** prior to experience. **3** abstract and unsupported by actual evidence. **apriorism** (āprī´ərizm), **apriority** (āprīor´əti) *n.*

apron (ā´prən) *n.* **1** a garment worn in front of the body to protect the clothes, or as part of a distinctive dress, e.g. of bishops, Freemasons. **2** anything resembling an apron in shape or function, such as a leather covering for the legs in an open carriage. **3** the extension of the stage in some theatres beyond the proscenium. **4** the surfaced area on an airfield. **5** an endless conveyor belt formed of metal slats. **aproned** *a.* **apronful** *n.* (*pl.* **apronfuls**) **apron string** *n.* the string of an apron. **tied to the apron strings** unduly controlled by a wife, mother etc.

apropos (aprəpō´) *adv.* **1** opportunely, seasonably. **2** by the way. ~*a.* **1** bearing on the matter in hand; to the point. **2** appropriate. **3** opportune, seasonable. **apropos of** with regard to, concerning.

apse (aps) *n.* **1** a semicircular, or polygonal, and generally dome-roofed, recess in a building, esp. at the east end of a church. **2** an apsis. **apsidal**[1] (apsī´dəl, ap´sidəl), **absidal** (ab-) *a.*

apsidal[2] APSE.

apsidal[2] APSIS.

apsis (ap´sis) *n.* (*pl.* **apsides** (-sidēz)) either one of two points at which a planet or satellite is at its greatest or least distance from the body around which it revolves. **apsidal**[2] (apsī´dəl, ap´sidəl) *a.*

apt (apt) *a.* **1** fit, suitable, proper, relevant. **2** having a tendency (to), likely. **3** quick, ready. **aptly** *adv.* **aptness** *n.*

apterous (ap´tərəs) *a.* **1** (*Zool.*) (of insects) wingless, or having only rudimentary wings. **2** (*Bot.*) without membranous winglike expansions.

apteryx (ap´təriks) *n.* the kiwi, a bird from New Zealand, about the size of a goose, with rudimentary wings.

aptitude (ap´titūd) *n.* **1** a natural talent or ability. **2** fitness, suitability, adaptation.

aqua (ak´wə) *n.* water, liquid, solution. **2** the colour aquamarine. ~*a.* aquamarine.

aquaculture (ak´wəkŭlchə), **aquiculture** (ak-´wi-) *n.* the cultivation of aquatic organisms for human use.

aqua fortis (akwəfaw´tis), **aquafortis** *n.* (*Chem.*) nitric acid.

❌ **aquaint** common misspelling of ACQUAINT.

aqualeather (akwəledh´ə) *n.* tanned fishskin.

aqualung (ak´wəlŭng) *n.* a portable diving apparatus, strapped on the back and feeding air to the diver as required. ~*v.i.* to dive with an aqualung.

aquamarine (akwəmərēn´) *n.* **1** a bluish-green variety of beryl, named from its colour. **2** this colour. ~*a.* bluish-green.

aquanaut (ak´wənawt) *n.* **1** a skin-diver. **2** a person who lives or explores under water.

aquaplane (ak´wəplān) *n.* a board on which one is towed, standing, behind a motorboat. ~*v.i.* **1** to ride on an aquaplane. **2** (of a car etc.) to slide on a film of water on a road surface.

aqua regia (akwə rē´jə) *n.* (*Chem.*) a mixture of nitric and hydrochloric acids, capable of dissolving gold and platinum.

aquarelle (akwərel´) *n.* a kind of painting in Chinese ink and very thin transparent watercolours.

aquarium (əkweə´riəm) *n.* (*pl.* **aquariums**, **aquaria** (-riə)) **1** an artificial tank, pond or vessel in which aquatic animals and plants are kept alive. **2** a place in which such tanks are exhibited.

Aquarius (əkweə´riəs) *n.* (*Astron.*, *Astrol.*) a zodiacal constellation giving its name to the 11th sign, which the sun enters on 21 Jan. **Aquarian** *a.* of or relating to Aquarius. ~*n.* a person born under Aquarius.

aquarobics (akwərō´biks) *n.* (*sing. or pl. in constr.*) exercises performed in water to music.

aquatic (əkwat´ik) *a.* **1** living or growing in or near water. **2** played or performed on or in water. **3** of or relating to water. ~*n.* an aquatic animal or plant. **aquatics** *n.pl.* sports or athletic exercises on or in the water.

aquatint (ak´wətint) *n.* **1** a method of etching on copper to produce tones similar to those of watercolour. **2** a design so produced.

aquavit (ak´wəvēt, -vit), **akvavit** (ak´və-) *n.* alcoholic spirit flavoured with caraway seeds.

aqua vitae (akwə vē´tī) *n.* strong spirits, brandy etc.

aqueduct (ak´widŭkt) *n.* **1** an artificial channel, esp. an artificial channel raised on pillars or arches for the conveyance of (drinking) water from place to place. **2** a bridge carrying a canal. **3** a small canal, chiefly in the heads of mammals.

aqueous (ak´wiəs, ā´-) *a.* **1** consisting of, containing, formed in or deposited from water. **2** watery. **aqueous humour** *n.* (*Anat.*) the watery fluid in the eye between the cornea and the lens.

❌ **aquiesce** common misspelling of ACQUIESCE.

aquifer (ak´wifə) *n.* (*Geol.*) a water-bearing layer of rock, gravel etc.

aquilegia (akwilē´jə) *n.* a plant of the genus Aquilegia, having backward-pointing spurs, commonly known as COLUMBINE.

aquiline (ak´wilīn) *a.* **1** of or relating to an eagle; eagle-like. **2** (esp. of noses) hooked, curved, like an eagle's bill.

❌ **aquire** common misspelling of ACQUIRE.

❌ **aquit** common misspelling of ACQUIT.

Ar *chem. symbol* argon.

ar- (ə) *pref.* AD-, assim. to *r*, e.g. *arrest*, *arrogate*.

-ar[1] (ə) *suf.* **1** forming adjectives, as in *angular*, *linear*, *lunar*. **2** forming nouns, as in *scholar*, *exemplar*.

-ar[2] (ə) *suf.* forming nouns, as in *pillar*.

-ar[3] (ə) *suf.* forming nouns, meaning the agent, e.g. *bursar*, *mortar*, *vicar*.

-ar[4] (ə) *suf.* forming nouns, var. of -ER[1], -OR, assim. to -AR[3], e.g. *beggar*, *liar*.

ARA *abbr.* Associate of the Royal Academy.

Arab (ar´əb) *n.* **1** a member of a Semitic people orig. inhabiting Arabia and now much of the Middle East. **2** a horse of a breed originating from Arabia. ~*a.* of or relating to the Arabs, or to Arabia. **Arabian** (ərā´biən) *a.* of or relating to Arabia or to Arabs. ~*n.* **1** a native or inhabitant of Arabia. **2** (*esp. N Am.*) an Arab. **Arabian camel** *n.* a camel with one hump, *Camelus dromedarius*, of the N African and Near Eastern deserts; also called *dromedary*. **Arabic** *a.* of or relating to Arabia, the Arabs, or to Arabic. ~*n.* the language of the Arabs. **Arabic numeral** *n.* any of the figures, 1, 2, 3 etc., as opposed to a Roman numeral.

arabesque (arəbesk´) *n.* **1** surface decoration composed of flowing lines fancifully intermingled, usu. representing foliage in a conventional manner, without animal forms. **2** a posture in ballet dancing with one leg raised behind and the arms extended.

arabica (ərab´ikə) *n.* **1** coffee or coffee beans from the tree *Coffea arabica*, widely grown in South America. **2** this tree.

arabis (ar´əbis) *n.* a plant of the genus *Arabis* of cruciferous plants largely grown on rockwork, also called *rock cress*.

arable (ar´əbəl) *a.* **1** (of land) ploughed or capable of being ploughed, fit for tillage. **2** of or relating to tillage.

arachnid (ərak´nid) *n.* any individual of the class Arachnida, which contains the spiders, scorpions, ticks and mites. **arachnidan** *n., a.* **arachnoid** (-noid) *a.* **1** (*Bot.*) cobweb-like, covered with long filamentous hairs. **2** of, belonging to or resembling the Arachnida. **3** of or relating to the arachnoid membrane. ~*n.* (*Anat.*) the arachnoid membrane. **arachnoid membrane** *n.* (*Anat.*) the transparent membrane lying between the pia mater and the dura mater, that is the middle of the three membranes enveloping the brain and spinal cord. **arachnophobia** (əraknəfō´biə) *n.* abnormal fear of spiders. **arachnophobe** (-nəfōb) *n.* **arachnophobic** (-nəfō´bik) *a.*

arak ARRACK.

Aramaean (ərəmē´ən) *a.* of or relating to ancient Aram, or Syria, or its language. ~*n.* **1** a Syrian. **2** the Syrian language. **Aramaic** (-mā´ik) *a.* applied to the ancient northern branch of the Semitic family of languages, including Syriac and Chaldean. ~*n.* the Aramaic language, still spoken in parts of Syria and Lebanon, the lingua franca of the Near East from the 6th cent. BC.

Aran (ar´ən) *a.* knitted in a style that originated in the Aran Islands off the W coast of Ireland, typically with a thick cream-coloured wool.

arapaima (ərapī´mə) *n.* a very large primitive freshwater fish of S America.

arational (ārash´ənəl) *a.* not concerned with reason, non-rational.

araucaria (arawkeə´riə) *n.* a tree of the coniferous genus *Araucaria*, one species of which (*A. imbricata*), the monkey-puzzle, is common in Britain as an ornamental tree. **araucarian** *a.*

arb (ahb) *n.* (*sl.*) ARBITRAGEUR (under ARBITRAGE).

arbalest (ah´bəlest), **arbalist** (-list), **arblast** (-blahst) *n.* a large, medieval crossbow for firing arrows and other missiles.

arbiter (ah´bitə) *n.* **1** a judge. **2** a person appointed to arbitrate between contending parties. **3** an umpire. **4** a person who has power to decide according to their absolute pleasure.

arbitrage (ah´bitrij) *n.* traffic in bills of exchange or stocks so as to take advantage of rates of exchange in different markets. **arbitrageur** (-trahzhœ´) *n.*

arbitral ARBITRATE.

arbitrament (ahbit´rəmənt) *n.* **1** decision by arbitrators. **2** power or liberty of deciding. **3** the award or decision given by arbitrators.

arbitrary (ah´bitrəri) *a.* **1** (apparently) random, irrational. **2** determined by one's own will or caprice, capricious. **3** subject to the will or control of no other, despotic. **arbitrarily** (ah´-, -treə´rə-) *adv.* **arbitrariness** *n.*

arbitrate (ah´bitrāt) *v.t.* **1** to hear and judge as an arbitrator. **2** to decide, to settle. ~*v.i.* to act as arbitrator or umpire. **arbitral** *a.* of or relating to arbitration. **arbitration** (-rā´shən) *n.* the hearing or determining of a dispute by means of an arbitrator. **arbitrator** *n.* **1** a person chosen or appointed to hear and settle impartially a dispute between two or more parties, esp. an industrial dispute. **2** an umpire, an arbiter. **arbitratorship** *n.*

arbitress (ah´bitris) *n.* **1** a female arbiter in a dispute etc. **2** a woman who has absolute power.

arblast ARBALEST.

arbor[1] (ah´bə) *n.* **1** a main shaft or axle on which something, e.g. a cutting or milling tool, rotates in a machine. **2** a rotating mandrel in a lathe on which the piece to be worked on is fitted.

arbor[2] ARBOUR.

arboraceous (ahbərā´shəs) *a.* **1** resembling a tree. **2** woody, wooded.

arboreal (ahbaw´riəl) *a.* **1** of or relating to trees. **2** connected with or living in trees. **arboreous** (-riəs) *a.* **1** thickly wooded. **2** arborescent.

arborescent (ahbəres´ənt) *a.* **1** having treelike characteristics. **2** branching like a tree, dendritic. **arborescence** *n.*

arboretum (ahbərē´təm) *n.* (*pl.* **arboretums**, **arboreta** (-tə)) a botanical garden for the rearing and exhibition of rare trees.

arboriculture (ah´bərikŭlchə, ahbaw´-) *n.* the systematic culture of trees and shrubs. **arboricultural** (-kŭl´-) *a.* **arboriculturist** (-kŭl´-) *n.*

arborization (ahbərīzā´shən), **arborisation** *n.* treelike appearance.

arbor vitae (ahbaw vē´tī) *n.* any of several Asian and N American evergreens of the genus *Thuja.*

arbour (ah´bə), (*N Am.*) **arbor** *n.* a bower formed by trees or shrubs planted close together or trained on lattice-work; a shady retreat. **arboured** *a.*

arbovirus (ah´bəvīrəs) *n.* (*pl.* **arboviruses**) (*Med.*) any of a group of viruses transported by mosquitoes, ticks etc. that cause diseases such as yellow fever.

arbutus (ah´būtəs) *n.* (*pl.* **arbutuses**) an evergreen shrub or tree of the genus *Arbutus,* of which *A. unedo,* the strawberry tree, is cultivated as an ornamental tree in Britain.

ARC (ahk) *n.* Aids-related complex.

arc (ahk) *n.* **1** a portion of the circumference of a circle or other curve. **2** something curved in shape. **3** the luminous arc or bridge across a gap between two electrodes when an electric current is sent through them. ~*v.i.* (*3rd pers. sing. pres.* **arcs,** *pres.p.* **arcing, arcking,** *past, p.p.* **arced, arcked**) to form an (electric) arc. **arc lamp, arc light** *n.* an electric lamp in which such an arc or bridge is the source of illumination. **arc weld** *v.t.* to weld (metal) by means of an electric arc. **arc welding** *n.*

arcade (ahkād´) *n.* **1** a walk or passage with an arched roof. **2** a covered passage with shops on each side. **3** (*Archit.*) a series of arches and their columns or piers. **4** an amusement arcade. **arcaded** *a.*

Arcadian (ahkā´diən) *a.* **1** of or relating to Arcadia, a district of the Peloponnesus, the ideal region of rural happiness. **2** (*poet.*) ideally rustic or pastoral. ~*n.* **1** an inhabitant of Arcadia. **2** (*poet.*) an idealized peasant or country-dweller. **Arcadianism** *n.* an ideal rustic condition, pastoral simplicity.

arcane (ahkān´) *a.* secret, esoteric.

arcanum (ahkā´nəm) *n.* (*pl.* **arcana** (-nə)) a mystery, a secret, esp. one of the supposed secrets of the alchemists.

arch[1] (ahch) *n.* **1** a curved structure arranged so that the parts support each other by mutual pressure, used as an opening or a support, e.g. for a bridge. **2** anything resembling this, a vault, a curve. **3** a curved anatomical structure, as of the bony part of the foot. **4** an archway. ~*v.t.* **1** to cover with or form into an arch or arches. **2** to overarch, to span. ~*v.i.* to assume an arched form. **archway** *n.* an arched entrance or vaulted passage.

arch[2] (ahch) *a.* **1** self-consciously teasing, roguish or mischievous. **2** knowing. **archly** *adv.* **archness** *n.*

arch- (ahch), **archi-** (-i) *pref.* **1** chief, principal, as in *archbishop, archdeacon, archdiocese.* **2** leading, pre-eminent, esp. in a bad sense, as in *arch-enemy; arch-hypocrite.*

Archaean (ahkē´ən), (*N Am.*) **Archean** *a.* of, relating to or belonging to the earliest geological period or the rocks formed in this time.

archaeology (ahkiol´əji), (*N Am. also*) **archeology** *n.* the science or special study of antiquities, esp. of prehistoric remains. **archaeologic** (-loj´-), **archaeological** *a.* **archaeologically** *adv.* **archaeologist** *n.* **archaeologize, archaeologise,** (*N Am.*) **archeologize** *v.i.*

archaeopteryx (ahkiop´təriks) *n.* a bird of the fossil genus *Archaeopteryx,* containing the oldest known bird.

archaic (ahkā´ik) *a.* **1** old-fashioned, antiquated. **2** (of a word) belonging to an earlier period, no longer in general use. **3** of or belonging to a much earlier period, ancient. **4** primitive. **archaism** (ah´-) *n.* **1** an old-fashioned habit or custom. **2** an archaic word or expression. **3** affectation or imitation of ancient style or idioms. **archaistic** (-is´-) *a.*

archaize (ah´kāiz), **archaise** *v.i.* to imitate or affect ancient manners, language or style. ~*v.t.* to make archaic.

archangel (ahk´ānjəl) *n.* **1** an angel of the highest rank. **2** an angel of the eighth order in the celestial hierarchy. **archangelic** (-anjel´-) *a.*

archbishop (ahchbish´əp) *n.* a chief bishop; a metropolitan; the spiritual head of an archiepiscopal province. **archbishopric** *n.* **1** the office of archbishop. **2** the district under the jurisdiction of an archbishop.

archdeacon (ahchdē´kən) *n.* **1** a church dignitary next below a bishop in the care of the diocese. **2** a chief deacon. **archdeaconry** *n.* (*pl.* **archdeaconries**) **archdeaconship** *n.*

archdiocese (ahchdī´əsis, -sēs) *n.* the see of an archbishop.

archduke (ahchdūk´) *n.* a chief duke, esp. a son of an Emperor of Austria. **archducal** *a.* **archduchess** (-dŭch´-) *n.* **1** the wife of an archduke. **2** a daughter of an Emperor of Austria. **archduchy** *n.* (*pl.* **archduchies**).

Archean ARCHAEAN.

archegonium (ahkigō´niəm) *n.* (*pl.* **archegonia** (-iə)) (*Bot.*) the female sex organ in mosses, ferns and some conifers.

arch-enemy (ahchen´əmi) *n.* (*pl.* **arch-enemies**) **1** a principal enemy. **2** Satan, the Devil.

archeology, archeological etc. ARCHAEOLOGY.

archer (ah´chə) *n.* a person who uses the bow and arrow, a bowman. **the Archer** the constellation of Sagittarius. **archeress** (-ris) *n.* a female archer. **archer fish** *n.* a fish, *Toxotes jaculator,* from SE Asia, that has the power of projecting water from its mouth to a considerable distance. **archery** *n.* the act or art of shooting with bow and arrow.

archetype (ah´kitīp) *n.* **1** the primitive or original type, model or pattern on which anything is formed, or assumed to be formed. **2** a typical or perfect example of something. **3** (*Psych.*) an inherited mental image, supposed by Jung to constitute part of the collective unconscious. **4** a recurrent symbol or motif in art or literature. **archetypal** (ah´-, -tī´-), **archetypical** (-tip´-) *a.*

archi- ARCH-.

archidiaconal (ahkidīak´ənəl) *a.* of, relating to or holding the office of an archdeacon. **archidiaconate** (-nət) *n.*

archiepiscopal (ahkiəpis´kəpəl) *a.* of or relating to an archbishop or an archbishopric. **archiepiscopate** (-pət) *n.*

archil ORCHIL.

archimandrite (ahkiman´drīt) *n.* the superior of a monastery or convent in the Greek Church, corresponding to an abbot in the Roman Catholic Church.

Archimedean (ahkimē´diən) *a.* of, relating to or invented by Archimedes, a Greek mathematician (*c.*287–212 BC). **Archimedean screw**, **Archimedes' screw** *n.* an instrument for raising water, formed by a tube wound into the form of a screw inside or around a long cylinder.

archipelago (ahkipel´əgō) *n.* (*pl.* **archipelagoes**, **archipelagos**) **1** any area of sea or water studded with islands. **2** these islands collectively.

architect (ah´kitekt) *n.* **1** a person who plans and draws the designs of buildings, and superintends their erection. **2** a naval architect. **3** a contriver or a designer of something. **architecture** *n.* **1** the art or profession of designing buildings. **2** a style of building. **3** architectural work, buildings and structures collectively. **4** the design and structural arrangement of the hardware components of a computer or computer system. **architectural** (-tek´-) *a.* **architecturally** *adv.*

architectonic (ahkitekton´ik), **architectonical** *a.* **1** of or relating to architecture or architects. **2** of or relating to the organization of knowledge. **architectonics** *n.* **1** the science of architecture. **2** the systematization of knowledge. **3** construction or systematic design in a literary or other artistic work.

architrave (ah´kitrāv) *n.* **1** the lowest portion of the entablature of a column, immediately resting on the column itself. **2** the ornamental moulding round a door or window.

archive (ah´kīv) *n.* **1** (*usu. pl.*) a place in which (historical) records are kept. **2** (historical) records officially preserved. ~*v.t.* **1** to store (records) in an archive. **2** (*Comput.*) to transfer (data) to a less-used file. **archival** (-kī´-) *a.* **archivist** (-ki-) *n.* **1** a person who has charge of archives. **2** a keeper of records.

archivolt (ah´kivōlt) *n.* **1** the inner contour of an arch. **2** the mouldings and ornaments on this inner contour.

archlute (ahch´loot) *n.* a large bass lute with a double neck.

-archy (ah´ki) *comb. form* denoting government

or rule of a particular type or by a particular group, as in *oligarchy, monarchy.*

arcology (ahkol´əji) *n.* (*pl.* **arcologies**) an ideal city where architecture and ecology are harmoniously combined.

Arctic (ahk´tik) *a.* of or relating to the north, the North Pole, or the region within the Arctic Circle. ~*n.* **1** the North Pole. **2** Arctic regions. **arctic** *a.* **1** designed for use in very cold conditions. **2** (*coll.*) extremely cold. ~*n.* (*N Am.*) a waterproof overshoe with buckles. **Arctic Circle** *n.* a parallel of the globe, 23° 28´ distant from the North Pole, which is its centre.

Usage note Pronunciation as (ah´tik), without the (k) before the (t), is best avoided.

---

arcuate (ah´kūat), **arcuated** (-tid) *a.* **1** curved like a bow. **2** arched.

arcus senilis (ahkəs senē´lis) *n.* a bow- or ring-shaped opaque area around the cornea of the eye, often seen in elderly people.

-ard (əd, ahd) *suf.* **1** denoting disposition to do something to excess, e.g. *drunkard, sluggard.* **2** forming other nouns, e.g. *poniard, Spaniard.*

ardent (ah´dənt) *a.* **1** glowing, fierce, intense, eager, zealous, fervid. **2** burning, on fire. **ardency** *n.* **ardently** *adv.*

ardour (ah´də), (*N Am.*) **ardor** *n.* **1** intensity of emotion, fervour, passion. **2** zeal, enthusiasm, eagerness.

arduous (ah´dūəs) *a.* **1** laborious, difficult. **2** involving much labour, strenuous, energetic. **3** steep and lofty, hard to climb. **arduously** *adv.* **arduousness** *n.*

are¹ (ah) *n.* a metric unit of area equal to 100 square metres (1076.44 sq. ft.).

are² BE.

area (eə´riə) *n.* **1** a particular extent of surface, a region, a tract of country. **2** a section of a larger space or surface or of a building etc., esp. one designated for a particular purpose. **3** the measurable extent of a surface. **4** a geographical or administrative division. **5** a sphere of interest or study. **6** the sunken court, partly enclosed by railings, giving access to the basement of some dwelling-houses; a space left open round a basement to obviate damp. **the area** in football, the penalty area. **areaway** *n.* (*N Am.*) an area giving access to a basement.

areca (ar´ikə, ərē´-) *n.* a tree of a genus of palms, *Areca*, esp. *A. catechu*, which yields the betelnut. **areca nut** *n.* the betel-nut.

areg ERG².

arena (ərē´nə) *n.* **1** an area enclosed by seating in which sports events or entertainments take place, an amphitheatre. **2** a field of conflict. **3** a sphere of action. **arenaceous** (arənā´shəs) *a.* **1** sandy. **2** in the form of sand. **3** composed partly or entirely of sand. **arena stage** *n.* a stage completely surrounded by seats.

aren't (ahnt) *contr.* **1** (*coll.*) are not. **2** (in questions) am not.

areola (ərē´ələ) *n.* (*pl.* **areolae** (-lē)) **1** (*Anat.*) **a** a dark circle round the human nipple. **b** a similar circle round a pustule. **2** any minute space enclosed by lines or markings. **3** any one of the interstices in organized tissue. **areolar** *a.*

arête (əret´) *n.* a sharp ascending ridge of a mountain.

argali (ah´gəli) *n.* (*pl.* **argalis, argali**) the wild sheep of Asia, *Ovis ammon.*

argent (ah´jənt) *n.* (*Her.*) the white colour representing silver. ~*a.* **1** (*poet.*) silver. **2** silvery-white. **argentiferous** (-tif´-) *a.* producing silver.

Argentine (ah´jəntīn), **Argentinian** (-tin´iən) *a.* of or relating to Argentina. ~*n.* a native or inhabitant of Argentina.

argentine (ah´jəntīn) *a.* **1** of or containing silver. **2** silvery.

argil (ah´jil) *n.* white clay, potter's earth. **argillaceous** (-ā´shəs) *a.*

arginine (ah´jinīn) *n.* one of the essential amino acids found in plant and animal proteins.

argol (ah´gol) *n.* **1** an impure acid potassium tartrate deposited from wines. **2** crude cream of tartar.

argon (ah´gon) *n.* (*Chem.*) an inert gas, at. no. 18, chem. symbol Ar, one of the gaseous constituents of the atmosphere, discovered in 1894.

argosy (ah´gəsi) *n.* (*pl.* **argosies**) (*poet.*) a large vessel for carrying merchandise.

argot (ah´gō) *n.* **1** the phraseology or jargon of a class or group. **2** thieves' slang.

argue (ah´gū) *v.t.* (*3rd pers. sing. pres.* **argues**, *pres.p.* **arguing**, *past, p.p.* **argued**) **1** to (try to) exhibit or prove by reasoning. **2** to discuss, debate. **3** to convince by logical methods. ~*v.i.* **1** to quarrel, to exchange views heatedly. **2** to bring forward reasons (for or against). **to argue the toss** (*coll.*) to continue to dispute about a matter that has already been decided. **arguable** *a.* **argufy** *v.i.* (*3rd pers. sing. pres.* **argufies**, *pres.p.* **argufying**, *past, p.p.* **argufied**) (*coll.*) to argue.

argument (ah´gūmənt) *n.* **1** an exchange of views, esp. an angry or passionate one. **2** (a) debate, discussion. **3** a reason, series of reasons or demonstration put forward. **4** the process of reasoning. **5** an abstract or summary of a book. **6** the subject of a discourse. **7** (*Math.*) a mathematical variable whose value determines that of a dependent function. **argumentation** (-tā´shən) *n.* **1** the act or process of methodical reasoning. **2** a systematic argument. **argumentative** (-men´-) *a.* **1** having a natural tendency to argue, disputatious. **2** controversial. **3** consisting of or relating to argument or reasoning. **argumentatively** *adv.* **argumentativeness** *n.*

Argus (ah´gəs) *n.* **1** a vigilant watcher or guardian. **2** an Asian pheasant, having the plumage marked with eyelike spots. **3** a butterfly of the genus *Polyommatus*, which has eyelike spots on the wings. **Argus-eyed** *a.* very observant, sharp-sighted.

argute (ahgūt´) *a.* **1** shrill, sharp. **2** quick, keen, shrewd.

argy-bargy (ahjibah´ji), **argie-bargie** *n.* (*pl.* **argy-bargies, argie-bargies**) (*coll., esp. facet.*) (a) dispute, argument. ~*v.i.* (*3rd pers. sing. pres.* **argy-bargies, argie-bargies**, *pres.p.* **argy-bargying, argie-bargying**, *past, p.p.* **argy-bargied, argie-bargied**) (*coll.*) to have a noisy quarrel or fight.

aria (ah´riə) *n.* (*Mus.*) a song, esp. in an opera or oratorio, for one voice supported by instruments.

Arian ARYAN.

-arian (eə´riən) *suf.* forming adjectives meaning belonging to, believing in, or nouns meaning a person who belongs to, believes in, or is associated with: e.g. *humanitarian, sabbatarian, sexagenarian, trinitarian.*

arid (ar´id) *a.* **1** dry, parched, without moisture. **2** barren, bare. **3** dry, uninteresting. **aridity** (ərid´-), **aridness** *n.* **aridly** *adv.*

ariel (eə´riəl) *n.* a Middle Eastern and African gazelle.

Aries (eə´rēz) *n.* (*Astrol.*) **1** (*Astron.*) the Ram, the first of the zodiacal constellations, which the sun enters in the month of March. **2** a person born under this sign. **Arian** *a.* of or relating to Aries. ~*n.* a person born under Aries.

aright (ərīt´) *adv.* **1** right, rightly, properly, becomingly. **2** correctly, without failure or mistake.

aril (ar´il) *n.* (*Bot.*) an accessory seed-covering, more or less incomplete but often brightly coloured and fleshy, formed by a growth near the hilum. **arillate** (əril´āt), **arilled** *a.*

arioso (ahriō´zō) *a., adv.* (*Mus.*) in a songlike style, melodious(ly). ~*n.* (*pl.* **ariosos**) a piece or passage played arioso.

-arious (eə´riəs) *suf.* forming adjectives meaning connected with, belonging to, e.g. *gregarious, vicarious.*

arise (ərīz´) *v.i.* (*past* **arose** (ərōz´), *p.p.* **arisen** (əriz´ən)) **1** to appear, to come into being, notoriety etc. **2** to originate (from), to occur as a result. **3** to come to notice. **4** (*poet.*) to assume an upright position after lying or sitting, to get up. **5** to rise up, to ascend. **arisings** *n.pl.* materials which constitute the secondary or waste products of industrial processes.

aristocracy (aristok´rəsi) *n.* (*pl.* **aristocracies**) **1** the nobility. **2** a ruling body of nobles. **3** government by the highest class of citizens or by the nobles. **4** a state so governed. **5** the highest or best of any class or group. **aristocrat** (ar´istəkrat) *n.* **1** a noble. **2** a member of an aristocracy. **3** a person who has aristocratic tastes or style. **aristocratic** (-krat´-), **aristocratical** *a.* **aristocratically** *adv.*

Aristotelian (aristətē´liən), **Aristotelean** *a.* of or relating to Aristotle (384–322 BC), the famous Greek philosopher, or his philosophy. ~*n.* a follower or student of the philosophy of Aristotle. **Aristotelianism** *n.* **Aristotle's lantern**

(ar´istotəlz) *n.* (*Zool.*) a cone-shaped framework of muscles and calcareous plates that supports the teeth of sea urchins.

arithmetic[1] (ərith´mətik) *n.* **1** the science of numbers. **2** computation by figures. **3** arithmetical knowledge or skill. **arithmetician** (ərithmətish´ən) *n.*

arithmetic[2] (arithmet´ik), **arithmetical** (-əl) *a.* of or relating to arithmetic. **arithmetic mean** *n.* the average value of a set of numbers or terms, found by dividing the sum of the terms by the number. **arithmetic progression** *n.* **1** a series of numbers that increase or decrease consecutively by a constant quantity. **2** increase or decrease by a constant quantity. **arithmetic series** *n.* a series showing arithmetic progression.

-arium (eə´riəm) *suf.* forming nouns meaning place for or connected with, as in *aquarium*, *herbarium*, *sacrarium*.

ark (ahk) *n.* **1** a ship, a boat, esp. Noah's ark. **2** †a chest, a box. **out of the ark** (*coll.*) extremely old or old-fashioned. **Ark of the Covenant, Ark of the Testimony** *n.* the cupboard containing the scrolls or tables of the Law in a synagogue.

arm[1] (ahm) *n.* **1** the upper limb of the human body on either side, from the shoulder to the hand. **2** anything resembling the human arm. **3** a sleeve. **4** the forelimb of any of the lower mammals. **5** a flexible limb or appendage, with armlike functions, in invertebrates. **6** the part of a chair etc. on which a person's arm rests. **7** a branch of a tree; a projecting branch of the sea, a mountain, river etc.; a projecting or armlike part of a machine, instrument etc. **8** a division of a service or organization. **9** power, authority. **10** in sport, the ability to throw or pitch effectively. **11** either of the parts of a yard on each side of the mast. **an arm and a leg** (*coll.*) a great amount of money. **arm in arm** with the arms interlinked. **at arm's length 1** at a distance. **2** at a sufficient distance to avoid undue familiarity. **3** (of negotiations) such that each party preserves its freedom of action. **in arms** (of a baby) needing to be carried, too young to walk. **in someone's arms** being embraced by someone. **on someone's arm** (of a person) walking arm in arm with someone or supported by someone's arm. **under one's arm** held between the arm and the body. **armband** *n.* a band of material encircling the coat-sleeve, usu. black to indicate mourning. **armchair** *n.* a chair, usu. a comfortably upholstered one, with arms to support the elbows. ~*a.* **1** (of a critic, strategist etc.) having no practical involvement with or knowledge of something. **2** participated in from the comfort of one's own home. **armful** *n.* (*pl.* **armfuls**) **armhole** *n.* the hole in a garment to admit the arm. **armless**[1] *a.* **armlock** *n.* a wrestling hold in which part of the opponent's body is gripped tight by the arm or arms. **armpit** *n.* the hollow under the arm at the shoulder. **armrest** *n.* a support for the arm. **arm-twisting** *n.* the use of force or psychological pressure to persuade

someone to do something. **arm-wrestling** *n.* a contest in which two people sitting opposite each other with their elbows on a table and their arms vertical, clasp hands and attempt to force their opponent's arm down flat on to the table.

arm[2] (ahm) *n.* **1** (*usu. in pl.*) a weapon. **2** any branch of the military service. **3** (*pl.*) the military profession. **4** (*pl.*) heraldic bearings. **5** (*pl.*) armour. **6** (*pl.*) war. ~*v.t.* **1** (*also reflex.*) to furnish or equip with offensive or defensive weapons. **2** to furnish with a protective covering. **3** to equip with tools or other appliances. **4** to make ready (a bomb etc.) for explosion. ~*v.i.* **1** to take up weapons, put on armour etc. **2** to prepare for war. **to lay down one's arms 1** to cease fighting. **2** to surrender. **to take (up) arms 1** to prepare to fight. **2** to begin to fight. **under arms 1** bearing arms. **2** ready for service. **3** in battle array. **up in arms 1** (*coll.*) angry, indignant, protesting. **2** in revolt. **armed** *a.* **armed forces** *n.pl.* the military personnel of a country; its army, navy, air force etc. **armless**[2] *a.* **arms race** *n.* rivalry between nations, esp. (formerly) between the US and USSR, in building up stocks of (nuclear) weapons.

armada (ahmah´də) *n.* **1** an armed fleet, esp. the fleet sent by Philip II of Spain against England in 1588. **2** any large (armed) force.

armadillo (ahmədil´ō) *n.* (*pl.* **armadillos**) any of several small burrowing edentate animals of the family Dasypodidae, native to S America, encased in bony armour, and capable of rolling themselves into a ball.

armament (ah´məmənt) *n.* **1** the arms and munitions of war, esp. the weapons with which a warship, aircraft etc. is equipped. **2** the act of arming a fleet or army for war.

armamentarium (ahməmenteə´riəm) *n.* (*pl.* **armamentariums, armamentaria** (-iə)) the equipment, medicines etc. collectively, that are available to a doctor or other medical practitioner.

armature (ah´məchə) *n.* **1** the revolving part, wound with coils, of an electric motor or dynamo. **2** the moving part of an electromagnetic device. **3** a piece of soft iron placed in contact with the poles of a magnet to preserve and increase its power. **4** (*Biol.*) the protective outer covering of an animal or plant. **5** the supportive framework for a model in clay etc.

Armenian (ahmē´niən) *a.* of or relating to Armenia. ~*n.* **1** a native or inhabitant of Armenia. **2** the language spoken by the Armenians.

armiger (ah´mijə) *n.* **1** an esquire. **2** a person entitled to heraldic bearings.

armistice (ah´mistis) *n.* a cessation of fighting for a stipulated time during war; a truce.

armless[1] ARM[1].

armless[2] ARM[2].

armlet (ahm´lit) *n.* **1** a small ornamental band worn on the arm. **2** a badge on a band around the arm. **3** a small arm of the sea, a lake etc.

armoire (ahmwah´) *n.* a chest, a cupboard.

armor ARMOUR.

armory[1] (ah´məri) *n.* (*pl.* **armories**) the science of heraldry. **armorial** (-maw´-) *a., n.*

armory[2] ARMOURY (under ARMOUR).

armour (ah´mə), (*N Am.*) **armor** *n.* **1** a defensive covering worn by a person in combat, esp. by a medieval warrior. **2** a defensive covering, usu. of metal plates, protecting a vehicle, warship etc. **3** tanks and other armoured vehicles collectively. **4** a protective covering enclosing an animal or plant. **5** heraldic bearings. ~*v.t.* to equip, cover or protect with armour. **armoured** *a.* **1** (*Mil.*) protected by armour. **2** (*Mil.*) consisting of units using armour or armoured vehicles. **3** (of glass) strengthened. **armourer** *n.* **1** a person who makes or repairs arms or armour. **2** an officer in charge of the arms of a regiment, ship etc. **armour plate** *n.* tough, heavy steel, often surface-hardened, used as a defensive covering for tanks, warships etc. **armour-plated** *a.* **armoury**, (*N Am.*) **armory** *n.* (*pl.* **armouries**, (*N Am.*) **armories**) **1** a place for keeping arms, an arsenal. **2** a large stock or an array of weapons, defensive materials etc. **3** a stock of resources such as arguments, objections etc. on which one can draw. **4** (*N Am.*) a place where arms are manufactured. **5** (*N Am.*) a place where people are trained in the use of arms and military drill, a drill hall. **6** (*pl., Can.*) a drill hall used as a headquarters by a reserve unit of the armed forces.

army (ah´mi) *n.* (*pl.* **armies**) **1** a body of people organized for land warfare. **2** a large subdivision of the land forces of a nation. **3** a multitude, a very large number. **4** any large organized body, esp. one with a military structure (e.g. the *Salvation Army*). **the army** the military profession. **army ant** *n.* any of various ants which travel in vast numbers destroying animals and plants. **Army List** *n.* an official list of the serving and reserve officers of the British army. **army worm** *n.* any of the larvae of various flies and moths, esp. in America and Africa, that move about in swarms destroying crops.

arnica (ah´nikə) *n.* **1** a tincture prepared from *Arnica montana*, mountain tobacco, and used as an application for bruises, sprains etc. **2** any composite plant of the genus *Arnica*.

aroid (eə´roid), **araceous** (ərā´shəs) *a.* belonging to the family Araceae, which includes the *Arum* genus of plants.

aroma (ərō´mə) *n.* **1** the fragrance in a plant, spice, fruit, wine etc. **2** an agreeable odour or smell. **3** a subtle pervasive quality. **aromatherapy** *n.* the use of (massage with) essential plant oils to promote physical and mental wellbeing and in healing. **aromatherapeutic** *a.* **aromatherapist** *n.*

aromatic (ərəmat´ik) *a.* **1** of or relating to an aroma. **2** fragrant, spicy. **3** (*Chem.*) belonging to or of or relating to a class of organic compounds containing a benzene ring in the molecular structure. ~*n.* **1** a fragrant drug, a spice. **2** (*Chem.*) a benzene-type additive to motor fuel. **aromatically** *adv.* **aromaticity** (ərōmətis´-) *n.* **aromatize** (ərō´-), **aromatise** *v.t.* (*Chem.*) to convert (a compound) to an aromatic structure. **aromatization** (-zā´shən) *n.*

arose ARISE.

around (ərownd´) *prep.* **1** surrounding, round about. **2** on all sides of; enveloping. **3** along the circuit of. **4** at various points within or surrounding (*dotted around the arena*). **5** from place to place in. **6** passing or having passed on a curved course (*around the corner*). **7** (*esp. N Am.*) approximately at or in. ~*adv.* **1** on all sides, all round; in a circle. **2** here and there, at various points; at random. **3** (*coll.*) in existence; in circulation; available (*been around for years*). **4** (*coll.*) in the vicinity, at hand (*It's lucky you were around*). **5** approximately. **6** (*coll.*) in many different places or situations acquiring experience. **to have been around 1** (*coll.*) to have acquired a wide experience. **2** (*coll.*) to be worldly-wise and shrewd.

arouse (ərowz´) *v.t.* **1** to raise, stir up, awaken. **2** to excite, stimulate. **3** to stimulate sexually. **arousable** *a.* **arousal** *n.* **arouser** *n.*

arpeggio (ahpej´iō) *n.* (*pl.* **arpeggios**) (*Mus.*) **1** a chord played on a keyed instrument by striking the notes in rapid succession instead of simultaneously. **2** the notes of a chord played or sung in ascending or descending progression, esp. as an exercise.

arquebus HARQUEBUS.

arr. *abbr.* **1** (*Mus.*) arranged. **2** arrives.

arrack (ar´ək), **arak** *n.* a distilled spirit from the East, esp. one distilled from coconut or rice.

arraign (ərān´) *v.t.* **1** to cite before a tribunal to answer a criminal charge. **2** to accuse, to charge with wrongdoing. **3** to find fault with. **arraigner** *n.* **arraignment** *n.*

arrange (ərānj´) *v.t.* **1** to adjust, to put in proper order. **2** to plan or settle circumstances in readiness for. **3** to work out or agree the order or circumstances of. **4** (*Mus.*) to adapt (a musical composition) for other voices or instruments. **5** to adapt (a play etc.) for broadcasting. ~*v.i.* **1** to make plans or preparations (for, to). **2** to come to an agreement (with). **arrangeable** *a.* **arrangement** *n.* **1** the act of arranging, the state of being arranged. **2** the manner in which things are arranged. **3** settlement, disposition, preparation. **4** a grouping or combination of things in a particular way. **5** (*pl.*) dispositions in advance, preparations. **6** (*Mus.*) the adaptation of a musical composition for instruments or voices for which it was not written; a piece of music so adapted. **arranger** *n.*

arrant (ar´ənt) *a.* **1** notorious, downright, unmitigated. **2** complete, thorough. **arrantly** *adv.*

arras (ar´əs) *n.* **1** a rich tapestry. **2** a wall-hanging made of this, esp. one concealing an alcove.

array (ərā´) n. **1** an impressive display or collection. **2** an orderly arrangement or disposition, esp. of troops for battle. **3** (poet.) dress, attire. **4** (Math.) an arrangement of numbers or mathematical symbols in rows and columns. **5** (Comput.) a set of storage locations etc., referenced by a single identifier. **6** (Law) a panel of jurors. ~v.t. **1** to deck, to adorn, to dress up. **2** to set in order; to marshal (troops) for battle. **3** (Law) to draw up (a panel of jurors).

arrears (əriəz´) n.pl. that which remains unpaid or undone. **in arrear/ arrears 1** behindhand, esp. in payment. **2** unpaid; undone, uncompleted. **arrearage** (-rij) n.

arrest (ərest´) v.t. **1** to apprehend, esp. to apprehend and take into legal custody. **2** to stop, check. **3** to seize and fix (the sight, mind etc.). **4** to seize (a ship) by legal authority. **5** to stay (legal proceedings etc.). ~n. **1** seizure, detention, esp. by legal authority. **2** a stoppage, stay, check. **under arrest** in legal custody. **arrestable** a. **1** (of an offence) making the offender liable to be arrested without a warrant. **2** liable to arrest. **arrester** n. **1** a person who or something which arrests. **2** a contrivance for slowing or stopping something, esp. a wire or arrangement of wires on the deck of an aircraft carrier. **arresting** a. striking, catching the attention. **arrestingly** adv. **arrestment** n. **1** (Law) seizure of property by legal authority. **2** (Sc. Law) the process by which a creditor detains the effects of a debtor, which are in the hands of third parties, till the money owing is paid. **arrest of judgement** n. staying of proceedings after a verdict on the grounds of possible error.

arrhythmia (əridh´miə, ā-) n. (Med.) an irregularity or alteration in the rhythm of the heartbeat.

arris (ar´is) n. (pl. **arris, arrises**) (Archit.) the line in which two straight or curved surfaces forming an exterior angle meet each other.

arrive (əriv´) v.i. **1** to come to a place, position, during a journey or movement; to reach a destination. **2** (of an object) to be brought. **3** (coll.) (of a baby) to be born. **4** (of an event, time) to occur. **5** (coll.) to attain fame, success or recognition. **to arrive at 1** to reach, to get to. **2** to agree upon (a decision); to attain to (a conclusion). **arrival** n. **1** the act of coming to a place, a journey's end or destination. **2** the coming to a position, state of mind etc. **3** a person who or thing which has arrived. **4** (coll.) a newborn child.

arriviste (arēvēst´) n. **1** a social climber, a parvenu. **2** a self-seeker, esp. in politics.

arrogance (ar´əgəns), **arrogancy** (-si) n. **1** the act or quality of being arrogant. **2** undue assumption.

arrogant (ar´əgənt) a. **1** insolent, assuming, overbearing, haughty. **2** claiming or assuming too much. **arrogantly** adv.

arrogate (ar´əgāt) v.t. to make unduly exalted claims or baseless pretensions to (a thing) for oneself or someone else. **arrogation** (-ā´shən) n.

Usage note See note under ABROGATE.

arrow (ar´ō) n. **1** a slender, straight, sharp-pointed missile shot from a bow. **2** anything resembling an arrow in shape or function, esp. a sign indicating direction. **3** (pl., coll.) darts. ~v.t. to indicate or mark with an arrow or arrows. ~v.i. to move swiftly like an arrow. **arrow-grass** n. any plant of the genus Triglochin. **arrowhead** n. **1** the pointed head of an arrow. **2** anything shaped like an arrowhead, esp. a decorative mark. **3** a water plant of the genus Sagittaria, the leaves of which resemble arrowheads. **arrowroot** n. **1** a nutritious starch extracted from the tubers of several species of Maranta. **2** a plant of the genus Maranta, which includes M. arundinacea, the tubers of which were used to absorb poison from wounds, esp. those made by poisoned arrows. **arrow worm** n. a marine worm with a ring of bristles around the mouth, a chaetognath.

arroyo (ərō´yō) n. (pl. **arroyos**) (N Am.) a dried-up watercourse, a rocky ravine.

arse (ahs), (esp. N Am.) **ass** (as) n. (taboo sl.) **1** the buttocks, the rump, the hind parts. **2** the anus. **to arse about/ around** (taboo sl.) to act in a stupid or irritating manner. **arsehole**, (esp. N Am.) **asshole** n. **1** (taboo) the anus. **2** (sl., offensive) a stupid or worthless person. **arselicker** n. (taboo sl.) a sycophant, toady. **arselicking** n., a.

arsenal (ah´sənəl) n. **1** a place for the storage, or manufacture and storage, of naval and military weapons and ammunition. **2** (fig.) a stock or supply of things, e.g. arguments, that can be compared with weapons.

arsenic[1] (ahs´nik) n. (Chem.) **1** a brittle, semi-metallic steel-grey element, at. no. 33, chem. symbol As. **2** white arsenic.

arsenic[2] (ahsen´ik) a. (Chem.) of or containing arsenic, esp. applied to compounds in which arsenic combines as a pentavalent element.

arson (ah´sən) n. the wilful setting on fire of another's house or other property, or of one's own with intent to defraud the insurers. **arsonist** n.

art (aht) n. **1** creative activity concerned with the production of aesthetic objects or of beauty in general. **2** any of the branches of this activity, e.g. music, painting, writing. **3** the products of this collectively. **4** creative activity specifically of a visual or representational kind; visual works of art. **5** human skill or workmanship as opposed to nature. **6** skill in the production of aesthetic objects; excellent workmanship. **7** a method, technique. **8** a facility, knack. **9** (pl.) the academic subjects concerned with creative or critical skills rather than scientific or technical ones. **Art Deco** (dek´ō) n. a style of decorative art of the 1920s and 1930s characterized by bold geometrical forms. **art form** n. **1** a medium of artistic expression. **2** an established form in music or literature.

artful *a.* **1** crafty, cunning. **2** characterized by art or skill. **artfully** *adv.* **artfulness** *n.* **artless** *a.* **1** guileless, simple, unaffected. **2** without art. **3** unskilful, clumsy. **4** uncultured, natural. **artlessly** *adv.* **artlessness** *n.* **Art Nouveau** (noovō´) *n.* a style of decorative art of the late 19th and early 20th cents. characterized by sinuous curving forms. **art paper** *n.* paper coated with a composition of china clay, making it suitable for fine printing. **arts and crafts** *n.pl.* decorative design and handicraft. **artwork** *n.* the illustrative material in a magazine, book etc. **arty,** (*esp. N Am.*) **artsy** *a.* (*comp.* **artier, artsier,** *superl.* **artiest, artsiest**) (*coll.*) self-consciously or pretentiously affecting the artistic. **arty-crafty** *a.* more showily artistic than functional. **arty-farty, artsy-fartsy** *a.* (*coll.*) pretentiously artistic.

artefact (ah´tifakt), **artifact** *n.* **1** a product of human skill or workmanship. **2** a simple object of archaeological importance or interest. **3** (*Biol.*) a feature not naturally present introduced during the preparation or examination of something. **artefactual** *a.*

artemisia (artimiz´iə) *n.* any herbaceous, perennial plant of the genus *Artemisia*, that includes wormwood, mugwort and sagebrush.

artery (ah´təri) *n.* (*pl.* **arteries**) **1** any of the membranous pulsating vessels conveying blood from the heart to all parts of the body. **2** a main channel of communication or transport. **arterial** (-tiə´-) *a.* **1** of, relating to or contained in an artery or arteries. **2** constituting an important channel for communications or transport. **arterialize** *v.t.* **arterialise** *v.t.* **1** to convert (venous blood) into arterial blood by exposing to the action of oxygen in the lungs. **2** to provide with arteries. **arterialization** (-zā´shən) *n.* **arteriole** (ahtiə´riōl) *n.* a small branch of an artery. **arteriosclerosis** (ahtiəriōsklərō´sis) *n.* thickening and loss of elasticity in the walls of the arteries. **arteriosclerotic** (-rot´-) *a.*

artesian well (ahtē´ziən, -zhən) *n.* a well in which water is obtained by boring through an upper retentive stratum to a subjacent water-bearing stratum, the water being forced to the surface by natural pressure.

arthritic (ahthrit´ik) *a.* of or suffering from arthritis. ~*n.* a person with arthritis. **arthritis** (-thrī´-) *n.* (painful) inflammation of one or more joints causing stiffness.

arthropod (ah´thrəpod) *n.* (*Zool.*) a member of the Arthropoda, a phylum of invertebrate animals with segmented bodies and jointed limbs, including the insects, arachnids and crustaceans.

Arthurian (ahthuə´riən) *a.* of or relating to King Arthur, the legendary early medieval king of Britain, or his knights.

☒ **Artic** common misspelling of ARCTIC.

artic (ah´tik) *n.* short for ARTICULATED LORRY (under ARTICULATE[1]).

☒ **artical** common misspelling of ARTICLE.

artichoke (ah´tichōk) *n.* **1** a composite plant, *Cynara scolymus*, somewhat like a large thistle: the receptacle and fleshy bases of the scales are eaten as a vegetable. **2** JERUSALEM ARTICHOKE.

article (ah´tikəl) *n.* **1** an item, a piece, a distinct element. **2** a commodity, a thing, an object. **3** a prose composition, complete in itself, in a newspaper, magazine, encyclopedia etc. **4** a point of faith or duty. **5** a distinct statement, clause or provision in an agreement, statute, indictment, code or other document. **6** (*Gram.*) each of the adjectives, *a*, *an*, *the*, or their equivalents in other languages, when these are considered to form a separate part of speech. ~*v.t.* to bind (an apprentice), indenture. **articled** *a.* (esp. of a lawyer's clerk) bound under article of apprenticeship.

articular (ahtik´ūlə) *a.* of or relating to the joints.

articulate[1] (ahtik´ūlāt) *v.t.* **1** to utter (words) distinctly. **2** to express (an idea, thought) clearly and coherently. **3** to connect by means of a joint. **4** to join together in proper order. **5** to joint. ~*v.i.* **1** to speak distinctly, to utter intelligible sounds. **2** to form a joint (with). **articulated** *a.* **articulated lorry** *n.* a long lorry with separate tractor and trailer sections connected so as to allow the tractor to turn at an angle to the remainder. **articulation** (-lā´shən) *n.* **1** the act or process of speaking. **2** articulate sound, utterance, speech. **3** the process or method of jointing. **4** the state of being jointed; a jointed structure. **5** a joint. **articulator** *n.*

articulate[2] (ahtik´ūlət) *a.* **1** able to express oneself clearly and coherently; clearly and coherently expressed. **2** formed by the distinct and intelligent movements of the organs of speech. **3** (*Biol.*) jointed; composed of segments. **articulately** *adv.* **articulateness** *n.*

artifact ARTEFACT.

artifice (ah´tifis) *n.* **1** a clever expedient, a contrivance. **2** cunning, trickery. **3** a cunning trick. **4** skill, dexterity. **artificer** (-tif´-) *n.* **1** a maker, a contriver. **2** a craftsman. **3** a mechanic employed to make and repair military stores.

artificial (ahtifish´əl) *a.* **1** made or produced by human agency, not natural. **2** not real, factitious, fake. **3** affected in manner, insincere. **artificial insemination** *n.* artificial injection of semen into a female. **artificial intelligence** *n.* **1** the ability of a computer, robot etc. to perform as an intelligent being. **2** the area of study dealing with the development of machines capable of imitating intelligent human-like mental processes. **artificiality** (-al´-) *n.* **artificial kidney** *n.* a machine that performs the functions of a human kidney outside the body. **artificially** *adv.* **artificialness** *n.* **artificial respiration** *n.* **1** any of various methods of manually or mechanically resuscitating a person who has stopped breathing. **2** any method of maintaining breathing by means of a machine. **artificial silk** *n.* synthetically produced filaments that resemble natural silk in appearance.

artillery (ahtil´əri) *n.* (*pl.* **artilleries**) **1** large-calibre guns, cannons, mortars etc., with their equipment for use in land warfare. **2** the branch of the military service in charge of those weapons. **artillerist** *n.* an artilleryman. **artilleryman** *n.* (*pl.* **artillerymen**) **1** an artillery soldier. **2** a person practically acquainted with the principles of gunnery.

artisan (ah´tizan, -zan´) *n.* a skilled manual worker; a handicraftsman, a mechanic.

artist (ah´tist) *n.* **1** a person who practises any of the fine arts, esp. that of painting. **2** any artistic performer, an artiste. **3** a person who works at anything with the devotion and skill associated with an artist. **4** (*sl.*) a person who frequently practises, or is proficient in, a particular, esp. dubious, activity (*piss artist*). **artistic** (-tis´-) *a.* **1** of or relating to art or artists. **2** made or done with particular skill or taste; aesthetically pleasing. **3** having a natural talent for one or other of the arts, esp. painting. **artistically** *adv.*

artiste (ahtēst´) *n.* **1** a public performer, an actor, dancer, musician, acrobat etc. **2** a highly proficient cook, hairdresser etc.

artsy ARTY (under ART).

arugula (əroo´gülə) *n.* (*N Am.*) rocket, a Mediterranean plant used in salads.

arum (eə´rəm) *n.* **1** a plant of the European genus *Arum*, usu. with a white spathe and arrow-shaped leaves, e.g. the cuckoo pint. **2** any of several other plants of the family Araceae. **arum lily** *n.* an African plant of the genus *Zantedeschia*, with a large ornamental white spathe and yellow spadix (also called *calla lily*).

arvo (ah´vo) *n.* (*pl.* **arvos**) (*Austral., coll.*) afternoon.

-ary¹ (əri) *suf.* **1** forming adjectives meaning of or relating to, connected with, belonging to, engaged in, as in *elementary, necessary, voluntary.* **2** forming nouns meaning a thing connected with or used in or a place for, as in *antiquary, statuary, aviary, granary.*

-ary² (əri) *suf.* equivalent to -AR¹ and sometimes to -ARY¹ e.g. *exemplary, military, contrary.*

Aryan (eə´riən), **Arian** *n.* **1** a member of any of the peoples speaking a language of the Indo-European family, esp. the Indo-Iranian branch. **2** the parent language of the family, Indo-European. **3** in Nazi terminology, a Caucasian, non-Jewish person, esp. of the Nordic type. ~*a.* **1** of or belonging to any of the Aryan peoples. **2** of or relating to the Aryan language. **3** in Nazi terminology, Caucasian, non-Jewish.

aryl (ar´il) *n.* (*Chem.*) any monovalent aromatic hydrocarbon radical, e.g. phenyl.

AS *abbr.* Anglo-Saxon.

As *chem. symbol* arsenic.

as (az) *adv.* in or to the same degree (followed by *conj.* governing pronoun, n. phr. or relative clause) (*as happy as we/us, as pretty as a picture, not as clever as she is*). ~*conj.* **1** while; at the time that. **2** since, because. **3** expressing manner (*viewed as a mistake*). **4** (preceded by *so*) expressing result (*so small as to be invisible*). **5** expressing concession (*good as it is*). **6** in the role, position or state of (*speaking as one who knows the situation*). **7** for instance (*herbs, as thyme, parsley etc.*). ~*pron.* **1** that, who, which (*I go to the same doctor as he does*). **2** a fact that (*it's not easy, as you know*). **as and when** to the degree and at the time that. **as for/ regards/ to** regarding, concerning. **as from/ of** from (the specified time or date). **as if/ though** as it would be if. **as it is** in the present state, actually. **as it were** in a certain way, to some extent, so to speak. **as was** (*coll.*) in a previous state.

Usage note After the second *as* in the comparisons *as...as, so...as, the same...as*, the objective pronoun (*him, us* etc.) is the everyday choice. The subjective (*he, we* etc.), though required by strict grammatical rule, is now considered rather pedantic.

as- (əs) *pref.* AD-, assim. to *s*, as *assimilate, assume.*

ASA *abbr.* **1** Advertising Standards Authority. **2** Amateur Swimming Association. **3** American Standards Association.

a.s.a.p. *abbr.* as soon as possible.

❌ **asassin** common misspelling of ASSASSIN.

asbestos (asbes´təs, az-) *n.* a fibrous form of certain minerals that is practically incombustible and resistant to chemicals, formerly widely used as a heat-resistant or insulating material. **asbestine** (-tīn) *a.* **asbestosis** (-tō´sis) *n.* a lung disease caused by breathing in asbestos particles.

ascarid (as´kərid), **ascaris** (-ris) *n.* (*pl.* **ascarids, ascarides** (-dēz)) any of the genus *Ascaris* of intestinal nematode worms.

ascend (əsend´) *v.i.* **1** to go or come from a lower to a higher place, position or degree, to rise, to be raised. **2** to slope upwards. **3** to proceed from a lower to a higher plane of thought, quality, degree, rank. **4** to go back in order of time. **5** (*Mus.*) to rise in pitch. **6** (of a letter) to have a part projecting upward. ~*v.t.* **1** to climb or go up, to go to a higher position upon; to go to the top or summit of. **2** to follow (a river) upstream or towards its source. **3** to mount. **to ascend the throne** to become king or queen. **ascendant, ascendent** *a.* **1** moving upwards, rising. **2** predominating, ruling. **3** (*Astrol.*) just above the eastern horizon. **4** (*Astron.*) moving towards the zenith. ~*n.* **1** (*Astrol.*) the point of the ecliptic which is rising in the eastern horizon at a particular moment. **2** the sign of the zodiac that contains this point. **3** superiority, supremacy. **in the ascendant 1** dominant, predominant, supreme. **2** rising. **ascendancy** *n.* **1** controlling influence. **2** governing power. **ascender** *n.* **1 a** part of a lower-case letter, e.g. *b* or *d*, that rises above the body of the letter. **b** a letter having this. **2** a person or thing that ascends.

ascension (əsen´shən) *n.* **1** the act of ascending. **2** (**Ascension**) the ascent of Christ to heaven. **3** (**Ascension**) Ascension Day; Ascensiontide. **4** the rising of a celestial body above the horizon. **ascensional** *a.*

ascent (əsent´) *n.* **1** the act or process of ascending, upward motion. **2** a slope. **3** a way by which one may ascend. **4** advancement, rise. **5** a movement back in time or ancestry.

ascertain (asətān´) *v.t.* **1** to discover, learn or verify by investigation, examination or experiment. **2** to find out. **3†** to make sure of. **ascertainable** *a.* **ascertainment** *n.*

ascesis (əsē´sis) *n.* (*pl.* **asceses** (-sēz)) the practice of self-discipline.

ascetic (əset´ik) *a.* **1** severely abstinent, austere, practising rigorous self-discipline, esp. for spiritual or religious ends. **2** of or relating to the ascetics or their mode of life. **~***n.* any person given to rigorous self-denial and mortification. **ascetically** *adv.* **asceticism** *n.* the mode of life of an ascetic.

ascidian (əsid´iən) *n.* (*Zool.*) a tunicate of the order Ascidiacea, the adults of which are sedentary, e.g. the sea squirt.

ASCII (as´ki) *n.* (*Comput.*) a standard system for representing alphanumeric symbols as binary numbers, used in data processing.

ascites (əsī´tēz) *n.* (*Med.*) dropsy causing swelling of the abdomen.

ascorbic acid (əskaw´bik) *n.* vitamin C, occurring in vegetables, fruits etc.

ascribe (əskrīb´) *v.t.* **1** to attribute, to impute, to assign (to). **2** to consider as belonging (to). **ascribable** *a.*

ascription (əskrip´shən) *n.* **1** the act of ascribing; a thing which is ascribed. **2** a statement ascribing glory or praise to God at the end of a sermon.

-ase (āz) *suf.* forming nouns denoting enzymes, such as *amylase.*

ASEAN (ā´siən) *abbr.* Association of South East Asian Nations.

aseismic (āsīz´mik) *a.* **1** free of, or virtually free of, earthquakes. **2** (of buildings) proof or protected against earthquake shocks.

ⓧ asend common misspelling of ASCEND.

asepsis (āsep´sis) *n.* **1** the condition of being aseptic. **2** the process of making aseptic. **aseptic** *a.* **1** not liable to or free from contamination by harmful micro-organisms. **2** preventing such contamination. **~***n.* an aseptic substance.

asexual (asek´sūəl, -shəl) *a.* **1** without sex, sexual organs or sexual functions. **2** (*Biol.*) (of reproduction) without union of gametes. **3** without sexual content or interest. **asexuality** (-sūal´-, -shūal´-) *n.* **asexually** *adv.*

ASH (ash) *abbr.* Action on Smoking and Health.

ash[1] (ash) *n.* **1** the residuum left after the burning of anything combustible. **2** powdery mineral matter ejected from volcanoes. **3** (*pl.*) the remains of anything burnt, esp. the remains of a cremated dead body preserved in an urn or coffin. **ash bin** *n.* a receptacle for ashes and other household refuse. **ash blond** *n.* **1** a very pale blond colour. **2** a person with hair of this colour. **~***a.* of or having hair of this colour. **ash blonde** *n.,* *a.* (a woman) having ash blond hair. **ashcan** *n.* (*N Am.*) a dustbin. **ash heap** *n.* a collection of ashes and other refuse. **ashpan** *n.* a pan beneath a furnace or grate for the reception of ashes. **ashtray** *n.* a small container for tobacco ash, cigarette butts etc. **ashy** *a.* **1** of or composed of ashes. **2** covered with ashes. **3** whitish-grey. **4** pale.

ash[2] (ash) *n.* **1** (*also* **ash-tree**) a forest tree, *Fraxinus excelsior,* with grey bark, pinnate leaves and tough, close-grained wood. **2** the wood of the ash-tree. **~***a.* made from ash. **ash-key** *n.* the winged seed-vessel of the ash. **ashplant** *n.* an ash-tree sapling used as a walking stick.

ashamed (əshāmd´) *a.* **1** feeling shame, either abashed by consciousness of one's own error or guilt or on account of some other person or thing. **2** unwilling or hesitant. **ashamedly** (-mid-) *adv.*

ashen[1] (ash´ən) *a.* **1** ash-coloured, between brown and grey. **2** pale. **3** of or relating to ashes.

ashen[2] (ash´ən) *a.* of or relating to the ash-tree.

ashet (ash´it) *n.* (*Sc., North., New Zeal.*) a large flat plate or dish.

Ashkenazi (ashkənah´zi) *n.* (*pl.* **Ashkenazim** (-zim)) **1** an E European or German Jew. **2** a Jew of E European or German descent (cp. SEPHARDI).

ashlar (ash´lə), **ashler** *n.* **1** a square-hewn stone used in a building. **2** masonry built of these. **3** thin masonry built as a facing to rubble or brick work. **ashlaring** *n.* **1** upright boards that form a wall in garrets, by cutting off the angle between roof and floor. **2** ashlar masonry.

ashore (əshaw´) *adv.* **1** to the shore. **2** on the shore. **3** on land.

ashram (ash´rəm) *n.* **1** (in India) a hermitage for a holy man or place of retreat for a religious community. **2** any place of religious or communal life modelled on an Indian ashram.

Asian (ā´shən, -zhən) *a.* of, relating to or belonging to Asia or its people. **~***n.* **1** a native or inhabitant of Asia. **2** a person of Asian descent, esp. (in Britain) from the Indian subcontinent.

Asiatic (āshiat´ik, -zhi-) *a.* Asian. **~***n.* (*offensive*) an Asian.

Usage note Because of a supposed association with racist ideology, the use of *Asiatic* to refer to people has come to be considered highly offensive, and is best avoided.

aside (əsīd´) *adv.* **1** at, to or towards one side. **2** away. **3** to a place that is out of hearing or more private. **4** apart, not entering into consideration. **5** as an aside. **~***n.* **1** something spoken so as to be audible only to the person addressed, esp. a speech by an actor, which others on stage are not supposed to hear. **2** a digression. **aside from** apart from.

asinine (as´inīn) *a.* **1** stupid, ridiculous. **2** of, relating to or resembling asses. **asininity** (-nin´-) *n.*

ask (ahsk) *v.t.* **1** to put a question to, to enquire of; to put (a question). **2** to seek to obtain by words, to request. **3** to enquire concerning, to request to be informed about. **4** to invite. **5** to solicit or state (a price required). **6** to demand, to require. ~*v.i.* **1** to make a request, petition or demand. **2** to enquire, to request to be informed (about). **if you ask me** in my opinion. **to ask after** to request information about, esp. about (the health of) another person. **to ask for** to behave in such a way as to invite (trouble etc.). **to ask for it** (*coll.*) to act in such a way as to make trouble, unpleasant consequences etc. inevitable. **asker** *n.* **1** a person who asks or enquires. **2** a petitioner, a suppliant, a beggar. **asking for the asking** (obtainable) for nothing or for very little effort. **asking price** *n.* the price set by a seller.

askance (əskans´), **askant** (əskant´) *adv.* **1** obliquely, sideways, askew, squintingly. **2** with mistrust, suspicion or disapproval.

askew (əskū´) *adv.* **1** in an oblique direction. **2** out of true, awry. ~*a.* oblique, awry, skew.

aslant (əslahnt´) *adv.*, *a.* in a slanting or oblique direction. ~*prep.* across in a slanting direction.

asleep (əslēp´) *adv.*, *pred.a.* **1** in or into a state of sleep. **2** inactive, inattentive, unresponsive. **3** numb. **4** (*euphem.*) dead.

AS level (āes´) *n.* (a pass in) an examination in a subject at the Advanced Supplementary level of the General Certificate of Education, equivalent to half an A level.

aslope (əslōp´) *a.* sloping, oblique. ~*adv.* **1** with a slope. **2** aslant, obliquely, crosswise.

☒ **asma** common misspelling of ASTHMA.

asocial (āsō´shəl) *a.* **1** not social. **2** antisocial; inconsiderate or hostile towards others. **3** hostile to society as such or life in society.

asp (asp), †**aspic** (as´pik) *n.* **1** a small venomous hooded serpent, *Naja haje*, the Egyptian cobra. **2** a European viper, *Vipera aspis*.

asparagine (əspar´əjīn) *n.* an amino acid occurring in proteins, found in asparagus and other vegetables.

asparagus (əspar´əgəs) *n.* **1** any plant of the genus *Asparagus*, esp. *A. officinalis*, a culinary plant, the tender shoots of which are eaten. **2** the edible shoots of this plant. **asparagus fern** *n.* a decorative fernlike plant, *Asparagus setaceus*.

aspartame (əspah´tām) *n.* an artificial sweetener derived from aspartic acid.

aspartic acid (əspah´tik) *n.* a nonessential amino acid present in many proteins, that acts as a neurotransmitter.

aspect (as´pekt) *n.* **1** a particular element or feature of something. **2** a way of regarding or viewing something. **3** (of a building) a position facing in a particular direction; outlook. **4** the appearance or visual effect. **5** (*formal*) a facial expression. **6** (*Gram.*) a verbal form that expresses such features as continuity, repetition etc. **7** (*Astrol.*) the situation of one planet with respect to another. **aspect ratio** *n.* **1** the ratio of the width to the height of the picture on a television or cinema screen. **2** the ratio of the span of an aerofoil to its mean chord. **aspectual** (aspek´chuəl) *a.*

aspen (as´pən), †**asp** *n.* a poplar, *Populus tremula*, remarkable for its quivering leaves; also called *trembling poplar*. ~*a.* **1** of or relating to the aspen. **2** made of the wood of the aspen.

asperity (əspor´iti) *n.* **1** harshness of manner, acrimony. **2** roughness of surface. **3** (*pl.* **asperities**) a rugged excrescence.

asperse (əspœs´) *v.t.* **1** (*formal*) to spread disparaging reports about, to defame. **2** to scatter or strew upon, to besprinkle. **aspersion** (-shən) *n.* **1** calumny, slander, a false report or insinuation. **2** the act of sprinkling. **3** something which is sprinkled. **to cast aspersions on** to make disparaging or slanderous remarks about.

asphalt (as´falt) *n.* **1** a bituminous pitch that occurs naturally or as a residue from petroleum distillation. **2** a mixture of this with gravel or other material, used for roofing, road surfacing etc. ~*v.t.* to cover, surface or line with asphalt. **asphaltic** (-fal´-) *a.*

asphodel (as´fədel) *n.* **1** (*esp. poet.*) a mythical undying flower, said to bloom in the Elysian fields. **2** a plant of the S European liliaceous genus *Asphodelus*, or related genera.

asphyxia (əsfik´siə, ā-) *n.* **1** a lack of oxygen in the blood, leading to unconsciousness or death. **2** suffocation. **asphyxial** *a.* **asphyxiant** *a.*, *n.* (something) that causes asphyxia. **asphyxiate** *v.t.* **1** to affect with asphyxia. **2** to suffocate. ~*v.i.* **1** to undergo asphyxia. **2** to suffocate. **asphyxiation** (-ā´shən) *n.*

aspic (as´pik) *n.* a savoury jelly used as a garnish or in which game, hard-boiled eggs, fish etc., may be embedded.

aspidistra (aspidis´trə) *n.* a plant of the liliaceous genus *Aspidistra*, formerly often grown as a house plant.

aspirant ASPIRE.

aspirate[1] (as´pirāt) *v.t.* **1** to pronounce with an exhalation of breath. **2** to prefix the letter *h* or its equivalent to. **aspiration**[1] (-ā´shən) *n.* **1** the act of breathing. **2** the act of aspirating. **3** an aspirated sound. **aspirator** *n.* **1** (*Med.*) an instrument for evacuating a cavity by means of an exhausted receiver. **2** an instrument for drawing air or gas through a tube.

aspirate[2] (as´pirət) *a.* **1** pronounced with an exhalation of breath. **2** prefixed by or blended with the sound of *h*. ~*n.* a consonant pronounced with an exhalation or the sound of *h*.

aspiration[1] ASPIRATE[1].

aspiration[2] ASPIRE.

aspire (əspiə´) *v.i.* **1** to long, desire eagerly. **2** to seek to attain (to). **aspirant** (as´pir-) *a.* aspiring, aiming at a higher position. ~*n.* **1** a person who aspires. **2** a candidate. **aspiration**[2] (aspirā´shən) *n.* **1** the act of aspiring. **2** steadfast desire or ambition. **3** a seeking for better things.

aspirin (as´prin) *n.* (*pl.* **aspirin, aspirins**) (*Med.*) (a tablet containing) acetylsalicylic acid, used as a painkiller.

asquint (əskwint´) *adv.* **1** out of the corner of the eye, obliquely. **2** with a squint. **3** with distrust, suspicion. **4** with crafty designs, furtively.

ass[1] (as) *n.* (*pl.* **asses**) **1** either of two wild quadrupeds, *Equus africanus* (of Africa) and *E. hemionos* (of Asia), allied to the horse, but of smaller size, with long ears and a tufted tail. **2** a donkey. **3** a stupid person. **to make an ass of** to treat as an ass, to render ridiculous. **to make an ass of oneself** to make oneself appear foolish, play the fool.

ass[2] ARSE.

assagai ASSEGAI.

assai (əsī´) *adv.* (*Mus.*) very, as *largo assai*, very slow.

assail (əsāl´) *v.t.* **1** to attack violently by physical means. **2** to attack with argument, abuse, censure, questioning etc. **3** to approach with intent to overcome. **4** to beset, disturb. **assailable** *a.* **assailant** *a.* assailing, attacking. ~*n.* a person who attacks another physically.

Assamese (asəmēz´) *a.* of or relating to Assam, its people or its language. ~*n.* (*pl.* **Assamese**) **1** a native or inhabitant of Assam. **2** (*as pl.*) the people of Assam. **3** the official Indic language of Assam.

assassin (əsas´in) *n.* a person who kills by surprise or secret assault (generally for money or for fanatical, political etc. motives). **assassinate** *v.t.* **1** to kill by surprise or secret assault. **2** to murder (esp. a political or religious leader) by sudden violence. **3** to injure or destroy (a person's character or reputation). **assassination** (-ā´shən) *n.* **assassinator** *n.* **assassin bug** *n.* a predatory or bloodsucking insect of the family Reduviidae.

assault (əsawlt´) *n.* **1** a violent physical or verbal attack. **2** (*Law*) a threatening word or act. **3** (*euphem.*) an act of or attempt at rape. **4** the charge of an attacking body on a fortified place. **5** a determined attempt. ~*v.t.* **1** to make a violent physical or verbal attack on. **2** to attack (a fortified place) by sudden rush; to storm. **3** (*Law*) to attack with threatening words or with blows. **4** (*euphem.*) to rape or attempt to rape. **assaultable** *a.* **assault and battery** *n.* (*Law*) an assault followed by a physical attack. **assault course** *n.* an obstacle course used for training soldiers.

assay (əsā´, as´ā) *n.* **1** the scientific determination of the quantity of metal in an ore, alloy, bullion or coin. **2** (*Chem.*) the chemical analysis of a substance to determine its content. **3** a metal or other substance analysed. **4** a trial, examination. ~*v.t.* **1** to determine the amount of metal in (an ore, alloy, bullion or coin). **2** to subject to chemical analysis. **3** to show (content) as a result of assaying. **4** to try, to test. ~*v.i.* to attempt, to

endeavour. **assayer** *n.* **assay office** *n.* an office which assays precious metals and awards hallmarks.

assegai (as´əgī), **assagai** *n.* (*pl.* **assegais, assagais**) a slender lance of hard wood, esp. that of the southern African tribes.

assemble (əsem´bəl) *v.t.* **1** to call or bring together. **2** to arrange in order. **3** to fit together the component parts of. **4** (*Comput.*) to convert (a program) from assembly language to machine code. ~*v.i.* to meet or come together; to gather, to congregate. **assemblage** (-blij) *n.* **1** a gathering, assembling; a concourse. **2** a collection. **3** the act or process of putting together; something made from assembled pieces. **assembler** *n.* **1** a person who or thing which assembles. **2** (*Comput.*) **a** a computer program that automatically translates assembly language into machine code. **b** an assembly language. **assembly** *n.* (*pl.* **assemblies**) **1** the act of assembling; the state of being assembled. **2** a body of people met together for some common purpose. **3** a meeting of all or some of the members of a school. **4** a deliberative, legislative or religious body. **5** a lower house in some legislatures. **6** the conversion of assembly language into machine code. **7** (*Mil.*) a signal, esp. a drumbeat, summoning soldiers to prepare to march. **assembly language** *n.* a low-level computer language in which instructions written in mnemonics correspond directly to instructions in machine code. **assembly line** *n.* a sequential arrangement of workers and machines operating from stage to stage in assembling some product. **assembly room** *n.* a room in which public assemblies, balls, concerts etc. are held.

assent (əsent´) *v.i.* **1** to express agreement. **2** to agree to or sanction something proposed. ~*n.* **1** the act of admitting, agreeing to or concurring in; agreement, acquiescence. **2** sanction. **assentient** (-shənt) *a.* assenting to. ~*n.* a person who assents or agrees. **assentor** *n.*

assert (əsœt´) *v.t.* **1** to affirm, to declare positively, to maintain. **2** to insist on (a claim etc.). **3** (*refl.*) to put (oneself) forward, insist on one's rights etc. **assertable** *a.* **assertion** *n.* **1** the act of asserting. **2** a positive statement, an affirmation. **assertive** *a.* **1** characterized by assertion, forthright. **2** self-assertive. **3** dogmatic. **assertively** *adv.* **assertiveness** *n.* **assertor, asserter** *n.*

assess (əses´) *v.t.* **1** to estimate, to judge the quality or worth of; to value. **2** to value (property, income etc.) for the purpose of taxation. **3** to fix by authority the amount of (a tax, fine etc. for a person or community). **4** to tax, fine etc. (in or at a specified sum). **assessable** *a.* **assessment** *n.* **assessor** *n.* **1** a person who makes an assessment, esp. of the value of property for taxation or of the performance of students. **2** a person who evaluates insurance claims. **3** a person who sits near and advises a judge or magistrate on technical points, commercial usage, navigation etc.

assets (as´ets) *n.pl.* **1** all the property of a person or company which may be liable for outstanding debts. **2** property in general. **3** (*Law*) **a** goods sufficient to satisfy a testator's debts and legacies. **b** property or effects that may be applied for this purpose. **asset** *n.* a useful or valuable resource. **asset-stripping** *n.* the practice of buying a company and selling off its assets to make a profit. **asset-stripper** *n.*

asseverate (əsev´ərāt) *v.t.* **1** to affirm with solemnity. **2** to assert positively. **asseveration** (-ā´shən) *n.*

assibilate (əsib´ilāt) *v.t.* to pronounce (a sound) with or as a sibilant. **assibilation** (-ā´shən) *n.*

assiduous (əsid´ūəs) *a.* hard-working, persevering; conscientious. **assiduity** (asidū´-) *n.* **1** constant or close application to the matter in hand, perseverance, diligence. **2** (*pl.*) persistent endeavours to please, constant attentions. **assiduously** *adv.* **assiduousness** *n.*

assign (əsīn´) *v.t.* **1** to allot, to apportion. **2** to designate for a specific purpose. **3** to name, to fix. **4** to ascribe, to attribute. **5** (*Law*) to transfer, to surrender. ~*n.* a person to whom a property or right is transferred. **assignable** *a.* **assignation** (asignā´shən) *n.* **1** a meeting, esp. an illicit one between lovers. **2** an appointment to meet, esp. illicitly. **3** the act of assigning. **4** attribution of origin. **5** (*Sc. Law*) a transference of property or right. **assignee** (-nē´) *n.* **1** an agent, a representative. **2** (*Law*) a person to whom a right or property is transferred. **assignment** *n.* **1** the act of assigning; allotment, allocation. **2** a specific task or mission. **3** a position or job to which one is assigned. **4** a legal transference of right or property. **5** the instrument by which such transference is effected. **6** the right or property transferred. **7** attribution. **assignor** (-naw´) *n.* a person who transfers a right or property.

assimilate (əsim´ilāt) *v.t.* **1** to take as nutriment and convert into living tissue, to incorporate in the substance of an organism. **2** to take in (information) and comprehend. **3** to absorb into a population or group. **4** to incorporate. **5** to make similar or alike. **6** to adapt (a speech sound) so as to resemble an adjacent sound. ~*v.i.* **1** to become absorbed or incorporated. **2** to be incorporated in the substance of a living organism. **3** to become similar. **assimilable** *a.* **assimilation** (-ā´shən) *n.* **assimilationist** *n.* a person who advocates or promotes racial or cultural integration. ~*a.* of, relating to or promoting the views of assimilationists. **assimilative** *a.* **assimilator** *n.* **assimilatory** (-lə-) *a.*

assist (əsist´) *v.t.* **1** to help, to aid, to give support or succour to. **2** to act as a subordinate to. ~*v.i.* **1** to give help or aid. **2** to be present (at). ~*n.* (*NAm.*) **1** an act of assisting. **2** in sport, an action that helps a team to score, put out an opponent etc. **3** a credit awarded for this. **assistance** *n.* **assistant** *n.* **1** a person who assists another. **2** an auxiliary. **3** SHOP ASSISTANT (under SHOP). ~*a.*

aiding, helping, auxiliary. **assisted place** *n.* (in the UK) a place as a student at a fee-paying school, the cost of which is partly or wholly paid by the state.

assize (əsīz´) *n.* (*pl.*) from 1815 to 1971, the sessions held periodically by the judges of the Supreme Court in each county in England and Wales for the administration of civil and criminal justice.

associate[1] (əsō´shiāt, -sō´si-) *v.t.* **1** to connect in the mind or imagination. **2** to join, to unite, to combine, to connect. **3** to connect (oneself) with a partner, supporter, friend, companion etc. (with). ~*v.i.* **1** to unite or combine for a common purpose. **2** to keep company or mix (with). **associable** *a.* capable of being (mentally) associated. **associability** (-bil´-) *n.* **association** (-ā´shən) *n.* **1** the act of combining for a common purpose. **2** a society formed for the promotion of some common object. **3** fellowship, intimacy, cooperation, connection. **4** mental connection of ideas, memories, sensations etc. **5** a memory, thought or feeling connected with some object, place etc. and recalled to the mind in connection with it. **6** (*Bot*) a plant community growing in a uniform habitat and forming part of a larger ecological unit. **7** (*Chem.*) the formation of loosely held aggregates of molecules, ions etc. **associational** *a.* **Association Football** *n.* football played between two teams of eleven players, with a round ball which may not be touched with the hands except by the goalkeepers. **associative** (-ətiv) *a.*

associate[2] (əsō´shiət, -sō´si-) *a.* **1** connected or joined in a common enterprise. **2** having equal rank or status. **3** in the same group or category. **4** having less than full status. ~*n.* **1** a partner, colleague, esp. in business. **2** a friend, ally or companion. **3** a person who has partial membership or subordinate status in an association or institution. **4** something generally found with something else. **associateship** *n.*

assonant (as´ənənt) *a.* **1** corresponding in sound. **2** rhyming in the accented vowels, but not in the consonants, as *keep* and *seen*. **3** corresponding in consonant sounds, but with different vowels, as *lick* and *lack*. **assonance** *n.* **1** the quality of being assonant. **2** a word or syllable that is assonant with another. **3** correspondence or resemblance in other respects. **assonate** (-āt) *v.i.*

assort (əsawt´) *v.t.* to arrange or dispose in groups of the same type, to classify. ~*v.i.* to suit, to agree, to match, to be in congruity or harmony (with). **assortative** *a.* **assorted** *a.* **1** of various sorts, miscellaneous. **2** arranged in groups, sorts. **3** (*usu. preceded by adv.*) matched. **assortment** *n.* **1** a collection of things of various kinds. **2** a collection of things assorted.

assuage (əswāj´) *v.t.* **1** to soothe, to lessen the violence or pain of, to allay, to mitigate. **2** to appease, satisfy. **3** to calm, to pacify.

assume (əsūm´) v.t. **1** to take for granted, to accept without proof or as a hypothesis. **2** to pretend, feign. **3** to take upon oneself, to undertake (a task, office). **4** to take on, adopt (a quality, characteristic). **5** to arrogate, appropriate, pretend to, to claim. **assumable** a. **assumed** a. **1** fictitious; feigned, false. **2** taken for granted. **3** usurped, pretended. **assumedly** (-mid-) adv. **assuming** a. arrogant, haughty.

Usage note Assume usually implies greater tentativeness (and less arrogance) than presume.

assumption (əsŭmp´shən) n. **1** the act of assuming. **2** the thing assumed; a supposition, a postulate. **3** arrogance. **4** (**Assumption**) the bodily reception of the Virgin Mary into heaven; the feast (15 Aug.) in honour of this event. **assumptive** a. **1** taken for granted. **2** arrogant.

assure (əshuə´) v.t. **1** to give confidence to, to convince. **2** to tell positively. **3** to ensure, guarantee. **4** to make safe or secure. **5** to ensure the payment of compensation in case of loss of (esp. life), to insure. **assurance** n. **1** the act of assuring. **2** a positive declaration. **3** certainty, security. **4** self-confidence, self-reliance, intrepidity. **5** audacity, impudence. **6** insurance, esp. a contract to pay a given sum on a person's death in return for an annual premium. **assured** a. **1** certain, guaranteed. **2** confident, convinced. **3** self-confident, full of assurance. **4** insured. **assuredly** (-rid-) adv. **assurer** n.

Assyrian (əsir´iən) a. of or relating to the ancient kingdom of Assyria. ~n. **1** a native or inhabitant of Assyria. **2** the language of Assyria. **Assyriology** (-ol´-) n. the study of the history, language and antiquities of Assyria. **Assyriologist** n.

AST abbr. Atlantic Standard Time.

astable (āstā´bəl) a. **1** not stable. **2** (of an electrical circuit) switching spontaneously between two states.

astatic (əstat´ik, ā-) a. **1** not remaining fixed; unstable, unsteady. **2** (Physics) not having the tendency to assume a particular direction or orientation.

astatine (as´tətēn) n. (Chem.) a radioactive element, at. no. 85, chem. symbol At, formed in minute amounts by radioactive decay or made artificially.

aster (as´tə) n. any of a genus, Aster, of composite plants with showy, daisy-like heads.

-aster (as´tə) suf. forming nouns meaning an inferior practitioner of an art, as in criticaster, poetaster.

asterisk (as´tərisk) n. a mark (*) used in printing to call attention to a note, to mark omission etc. ~v.t. to mark with an asterisk.

asterism (as´tərizm) n. **1** a small cluster of stars. **2** three asterisks (⁂) to draw attention to something important.

astern (əstœn´) adv., a. (Naut.) **1** in, at or towards the stern of a ship. **2** behind a ship. **3** backwards.

asteroid (as´təroid) n. **1** (Astron.) any of the small celestial bodies that orbit the sun, esp. between the orbits of Mars and Jupiter, a planetoid, a minor planet. **2** (Zool.) a member of the class Asteroidea, a starfish. **asteroidal** (-roi´-) a.

asthenia (əsthē´niə) n. (Med.) absence of strength; debility, diminution or loss of vital power. **asthenic** (-then´-) a. **1** of, relating to or affected with asthenia. **2** (of a person's physique) characterized by a small trunk and long limbs. ~n. an asthenic person. **asthenosphere** (-then-´əsfiə) n. (Geol.) the semifluid upper layer of the earth's mantle that is thought to be capable of movement and to account for such phenomena of the lithosphere as continental drift.

asthma (as´mə) n. a respiratory disorder, usu. allergic in origin, characterized by wheezing, constriction of the chest, and usu. coughing. **asthmatic** (-mat´-) a. **1** of, relating to or affected with asthma. **2** wheezy, puffing. ~n. a person affected with asthma. **asthmatical** a. **asthmatically** adv.

astigmatism (əstig´mətizm) n. a defect of the eye or of a lens as a result of which a point source of light tends to be focused as a line. **astigmatic** (astigmat´ik) a.

astilbe (əstil´bi) n. any plant of the perennial saxifragaceous genus Astilbe, having spikes or plumes of tiny red or white flowers.

astir (əstœ´) a., adv. **1** in motion. **2** in commotion, in excitement. **3** out of bed.

astonish (əston´ish) v.t. to strike with sudden surprise or wonder, to amaze, to surprise. **astonishing** a. **astonishingly** adv. **astonishment** n.

astound (əstownd´) v.t. to strike with amazement, to shock with alarm, wonder, or surprise. **astounding** a. **astoundingly** adv.

astraddle (əstrad´əl) adv. **1** in a straddling position. **2** astride.

astragal (as´trəgəl) n. (Archit.) a small semicircular moulding or bead, round the top or the bottom of a column. **astragalus** (əstrag´-) n. **1** (Anat.) the talus, the bone with which the tibia articulates below. **2** any of a large genus of leguminous plants, Astragalus, containing the milk-vetch.

astrakhan (astrəkan´, -kahn´) n. **1** the tightly curled, usu. black or grey fleece obtained from lambs orig. from Astrakhan. **2** a fabric with a pile in imitation of this.

astral (as´trəl) a. **1** of or relating to the stars. **2** starry. **3** of or relating to the supposed astral body or material composing it. **astral body** n. (pl. **astral bodies**) a supposed kind of spiritual body coexisting with the physical body and surrounding it like an aura, which some occultists claim to be able to perceive, to project to a distance etc.

astray (əstrā´) a., adv. **1** in or into sin, crime or error. **2** out of or away from the right way.

astride (əstrīd´) a., adv. **1** with a leg on either side. **2** with legs apart. ~prep. **1** with a leg on either side of. **2** extending across.

astringent (əstrin´jənt) *a.* **1** causing contraction of body tissues. **2** styptic. **3** stern, severe, harsh. ~*n.* an astringent substance. **astringency** *n.* **astringently** *adv.*

astro- (as´trō) *comb. form* **1** of or relating to the heavenly bodies, planets or stars, as in *astrology, astronomy.* **2** of or relating to outer space, as in *astronaut.*

astrochemistry (astrōkem´istri) *n.* the study of the chemistry of celestial bodies and particles in interstellar space.

astrodome (as´trədom) *n.* **1** (*Astron.*) a dome window in an aircraft to enable astronomical observations to be made. **2** a large sports stadium covered by a translucent domed roof.

astrohatch (as´trəhach) *n.* (*Astron.*) an astrodome in an aircraft.

astroid (as´troid) *n.* (*Math.*) a hypocycloid with four cusps (resembling a square with concave sides).

astrolabe (as´trəlāb) *n.* an instrument, usu. consisting of a graduated disc with a sighting device, formerly used to measure the altitude of celestial bodies and as an aid to navigation.

astrology (əstrol´əji) *n.* the study of a supposed connection between the changing aspects of the heavenly bodies and the changing course of human life, with predictions of events and advice on conduct. **astrologer** *n.* **astrological** (astrəloj´-), **astrologic** *a.* **astrologically** *adv.*

astronautics (astrənaw´tiks) *n.* the science of travel through space. **astronaut** (as´-) *n.* a person who travels or is trained to travel into space beyond the earth's atmosphere in a spacecraft. **astronautical** *a.*

astronomy (əstron´əmi) *n.* the science which studies all phenomena of the heavenly bodies, space and the physical universe. **astronomer** *n.* **astronomic** (astrənom´-) *a.* **1** of or relating to astronomy. **2** enormously large or great. **astronomical** *a.* astronomic. **astronomically** *adv.* **astronomical unit** *n.* a unit of length equal to the mean distance of the earth from the sun, about 93 million miles (150 million km), used for measuring distances in the solar system. **astronomical year** *n.* a year determined by astronomical observations, as opposed to a civil year.

astrophysics (astrōfiz´iks) *n.* the branch of astronomy concerned with the physics and chemistry of celestial objects and their origin and evolution. **astrophysical** *a.* **astrophysicist** *n.*

Astroturf® (as´trōtœf) *n.* an artificial grass surface, esp. for sports fields.

astute (əstūt´) *a.* **1** acute, discerning, shrewd. **2** clever, wily, cunning. **astutely** *adv.* **astuteness** *n.*

asunder (əsŭn´də) *adv.* (*formal*) apart, separately, in different pieces or places.

asylum (əsī´ləm) *n.* **1** protection from extradition given by one country to a person, esp. a political refugee, from another. **2** (a) shelter, (a) refuge.

3 an institution formerly affording relief and shelter to the afflicted, unfortunate or destitute, esp. an institution for the treatment of the mentally ill.

asymmetry (əsim´ətri) *n.* (*pl.* **asymmetries**) lack of symmetry, or of proportion; an instance of this. **asymmetric** (asimet´-, ā-), **asymmetrical** *a.* **asymmetrically** *adv.*

asymptomatic (āsimptəmat´ik, ā-) *a.* (of a disease) not exhibiting symptoms.

asymptote (as´imtōt) *n.* a straight mathematical line continually approaching some curve but never meeting it within a finite distance. **asymptotic** (-tot´-), **asymptotical** *a.* **asymptotically** *adv.*

asynchronous (əsing´krənəs, ā-) *a.* not coincident in point of time. **asynchronously** *adv.*

At *chem. symbol* astatine.

at (at) *prep.* **1** denoting nearness or precise position in time or space or on a scale. **2** denoting direction to or towards. **3** denoting engagement in (an occupation, activity) or a state of being in (a condition, relation). **4** denoting a value or rate. **5** denoting the object of an emotion. **at it 1** at work, engaged, busy. **2** (*coll.*) engaged in a habitual (usu. disapproved of) activity. **3** (*coll.*) having sexual intercourse. **at one** in harmony. **at that** moreover. **where it's at 1** where the really important or fashionable activity is taking place. **2** where the real significance lies. **at-home** *n.* a gathering or party held in one's own home.

at- (ət) *pref.* AD-, assim. to *t*, e.g. *attain, attend.*

ataraxia (atərak´siə), **ataraxy** (at´-) *n.* impassiveness, calmness, indifference, stoicism. **ataractic, ataraxic** *a.* calming, tranquillizing. ~*n.* an ataractic substance or drug.

atavism (at´əvizm) *n.* **1** recurrence of some characteristic of a more or less remote ancestor. **2** reversion to a primitive or ancestral form. **atavistic** (-vis´-) *a.* **atavistically** (-vis´-) *adv.*

ataxia (ətak´siə), **ataxy** (ətak´si, at´-) *n.* (*Med.*) loss of the power of coordination of the muscles, resulting in irregular, jerky movements. **ataxic, atactic** *a.*

ATC *abbr.* **1** air-traffic control. **2** Air Training Corps.

ate EAT.

-ate[1] (āt, ət) *suf.* **1** forming nouns of office or function, e.g. *curate, episcopate.* **2** forming nouns denoting a group, e.g. *electorate.* **3** (*Chem.*) **a** forming nouns denoting the salts of acids, e.g. *acetate, carbonate.* **b** forming nouns denoting the product of a process, e.g. *condensate, filtrate.*

-ate[2] (āt, ət) *suf.* **1** forming participial adjectives, e.g. *desolate, separate, situate.* **2** forming other adjectives by analogy, e.g. *roseate, ovate.*

-ate[3] (āt) *suf.* forming verbs, e.g. *desolate, separate,* corresponding to adjectives in the same form, or others produced on the same model, e.g. *fascinate, isolate.*

atelier (ətel´yā, at´-) *n.* a workshop, an artist's studio.

a tempo (a tem´pō) *adv., a.* (*Mus.*) in the original tempo or time.

atheism (ā´thiizm) *n.* disbelief in the existence of a God or gods. **atheist** *n., a.* **atheistic** (-is´-), **atheistical** *a.*

athematic (athimat´ik) *a.* 1 (*Mus.*) not based on themes. 2 (*Gram.*) having a suffix attached to the stem without an intervening vowel.

athenaeum (athənē´əm), (*N Am.*) **atheneum** *n.* 1 a literary or scientific club or institution. 2 a literary club-room, a public reading-room or library.

Athenian (əthē´niən) *n., a.* (a native or inhabitant) of Athens.

atherosclerosis (athərōsklərō´sis) *n.* arteriosclerosis characterized by deposits of fatty material in the arteries. **atherosclerotic** (-rot´-) *a.*

athirst (əthœst´) *a.* (*poet.*) 1 thirsty, oppressed with thirst. 2 eager, eagerly desirous.

athlete (ath´lēt) *n.* 1 a person trained to compete in events, such as running, weight-throwing and jumping, requiring strength, agility, speed or stamina. 2 a healthy, vigorous person, esp. one with a natural aptitude for sports and physical activities. **athlete's foot** *n.* a fungal infection of the foot affecting the skin between the toes. **athletic** (-let´-) *a.* 1 of or for athletes or athletics. 2 physically strong, fit and active. 3 muscular, robust and well-proportioned. **athletically** *adv.* **athleticism** (-sizm) *n.* **athletics** *n.* 1 the type of competitive sporting events engaged in by athletes, esp. track and field events. 2 (*NAm.*) sports and games of any kind. 3 the practice of physical exercises by which muscular strength is developed.

-athon (əthon) *suf.* denoting an event or contest that continues for a long time, e.g. *talkathon*, *danceathon*.

athwart (əthwawt´) *prep.* 1 from side to side of, across. 2 against, opposing. ~*adv.* 1 transversely, from side to side, crosswise. 2 so as to thwart.

-atic (at´ik, ətik) *suf.* forming adjectives, e.g. *aquatic, fanatic, lunatic.*

-atile (ətīl) *suf.* forming adjectives chiefly denoting possibility or quality, e.g. *fluviatile, volatile.*

atilt (ətilt´) *a., adv.* tilted up.

-ation (ā´shən) *suf.* forming abstract nouns from verbs, e.g. *agitation, appreciation, ovation.*

-ative (ətiv, ā-) *suf.* forming adjectives, e.g. *demonstrative, representative, talkative.*

Atlantic (ətlan´tik) *a.* 1 of or occurring in or near the Atlantic Ocean. 2 of or relating to the Atlas mountains in N Africa. **the Atlantic** the Atlantic Ocean. **Atlanticism** (-sizm) *n.* belief in close co-operation and mutual support between the countries of W Europe and N America. **Atlanticist** *a., n.* **Atlantic Ocean** *n.* the ocean between Europe and Africa in the east and America in the west. **Atlantic Standard Time, Atlantic Time** *n.* the standard time, four hours behind GMT, in a time zone that includes the eastern parts of Canada.

atlas (at´ləs) *n.* (*pl.* **atlases**) 1 a book containing a collection of maps. 2 a book containing a collection of charts or plates. 3 (*Anat.*) the first cervical vertebra, in humans, that supports the skull.

ATM *abbr.* automated teller machine.

atm. *abbr.* 1 (*Physics*) atmosphere. 2 atmospheric.

atman (aht´mən) *n.* in Hinduism, the innermost self, the soul or the Universal Soul, the supreme spiritual principle.

atmo- (at´mō) *comb. form* of or relating to vapour or to the atmosphere.

atmosphere (at´məsfiə) *n.* 1 the gaseous envelope surrounding any of the celestial bodies, esp. that surrounding the earth. 2 the air in any given place. 3 mental or moral environment. 4 a prevailing mood or tone felt to be present in a place, work of art etc. 5 (*coll.*) a feeling of tension between people. 6 (*Physics*) a unit of pressure corresponding to the average pressure of the earth's atmosphere at sea level and equal to a pressure of about 15 lb. per square inch (101,325 N/m²). 7 a gaseous envelope surrounding any substance. **atmospheric** (-fer´-), **atmospherical** *a.* **atmospherically** *adv.* **atmospherics** *n.pl.* 1 (audible interference in communications produced by) electromagnetic waves generated by an electric discharge between two clouds or from a cloud to earth. 2 effects deliberately intended to create a particular mood. 3 such a deliberately created atmosphere.

at. no. *abbr.* atomic number.

atoll (at´ol) *n.* a coral island, consisting of an annular reef surrounding a lagoon.

atom (at´əm) *n.* 1 the smallest particle taking part in chemical action, the smallest particle of matter possessing the properties of an element. 2 such a particle as a source of nuclear energy. 3 the smallest conceivable portion of anything. 4 a body or particle of matter originally thought to be incapable of further division. **atom bomb** *n.* a bomb in which the explosion is due to atomic energy released when atoms of uranium, plutonium etc. undergo nuclear fission. **atomic** (ətom´-) *a.* 1 of or relating to an atom or atoms. 2 of, relating to or using atomic energy or atom bombs. 3 extremely small. **atomically** *adv.* **atomic bomb** *n.* ATOM BOMB (under ATOM). **atomic clock** *n.* an electronic apparatus which makes use of molecular or atomic resonances to generate precise intervals of time. **atomic energy** *n.* the energy liberated when the nucleus of an atom undergoes change, e.g. by fission of uranium or by fusion of hydrogen, nuclear energy. **atomicity** (-is´-) *n.* 1 the number of atoms in a molecule of an element or of a compound. 2 the fact of being made up of atoms. 3 valency. **atomic mass** *n.* the mass of an atom measured in atomic mass units. **atomic mass unit** *n.* a unit of mass used to express atomic and molecular weight that is equal to one twelfth of the mass of an atom of carbon-12. **atomic number** *n.* the number of protons in the nucleus of an atom (the atomic number determines the chemical properties of an atom). **atomic physics** *n.* the branch of physics that is concerned with atomic structure and the nature and properties of subatomic particles. **atomic pile** *n.* a nuclear reactor. **atomic power** *n.* nuclear power. **atomic spectrum** *n.* the emission or absorption spectrum characteristic of an element that arises from electron transitions within the atom. **atomic structure** *n.* the structure of the atom conceived as a central positively charged nucleus, made up of protons and neutrons, surrounded by negatively charged orbiting electrons. **atomic theory** *n.* 1 (*Physics*) the theory that atoms are composed of subatomic particles. 2 the theory that all matter is made up of atoms, that all atoms of the same element are alike and that they combine with atoms of other elements to form compounds in a definite proportion. **atomic warfare** *n.* warfare with nuclear weapons. **atomic weight** *n.* RELATIVE ATOMIC MASS (under RELATIVE). **atomism** *n.* 1 (*Philos.*) the doctrine that the ultimate constituents of the universe are tiny, individual particles. 2 (*Psych.*) the theory that experiences and mental states are composed of elementary units. **atomist** *n.* **atomistic** (-mis´tik) *a.* **atomize, atomise** *v.t.* 1 to reduce to atoms. 2 to reduce to fine particles or to a spray. **atomization** (-zā´shən) *n.* **atomizer** *n.* an instrument for reducing a liquid, such as a disinfectant or perfume, into spray. **atom smasher** *n.* (*coll.*) an accelerator for increasing the energy of charged particles.

atonal (ātō´nəl) *a.* (*Mus.*) without a fixed key. **atonality** (-nal´-) *n.*

atone (ətōn´) *v.i.* to make expiation or satisfaction for some crime, sin or fault. **atonement** *n.* 1 the act of atoning. 2 reparation, expiation, amends. 3 the propitiation of God by the expiation of sin. **the Atonement** (*Theol.*) the expiation of the sin of humankind by the suffering and death of Christ. **atoningly** *adv.*

atonic (əton´ik) *a.* 1 without an accent, unaccented. 2 (*Med.*) lacking physiological or muscular tone. ~*n.* an unaccented word or syllable. **atony** (at´-) *n.*

atop (ətop´) *adv.* on or at the top. ~*prep.* (*also* **atop of**) on or at the top of.

-ator (ā´tə) *suf.* forming nouns denoting a person or thing performing an action e.g. *equator, agitator, commentator.*

-atory (ətəri, ā´təri) *suf.* forming adjectives meaning related to or involving a verbal action, e.g. *commendatory.*

ATP *abbr.* adenosine triphosphate.

atrabilious (atrəbil´iəs), **atrabiliar** (-bil´iə) *a.* 1 melancholic, hypochondriacal. 2 splenetic, bitter-tempered.

atrium (at´riəm, ā´-) *n.* (*pl.* **atria, atriums**) 1 the central court in an ancient Roman house. 2 a central hall rising the whole height of a large building and usu. with a glass roof and galleries on the upper floors. 3 a central hall or glazed court with rooms opening off it. 4 a forecourt or vestibule in front of a church. 5 (*Anat.*) a body cavity esp. either of the two upper chambers of the heart into which the veins pour the blood. **atrial** *a.*

atrocious (ətrō´shəs) *a.* 1 very bad, execrable. 2 savagely and wantonly cruel, characterized by heinous wickedness. 3 fierce, violent. **atrociously** *adv.* **atrociousness** *n.* **atrocity** (ətros´-) *n.* (*pl.* **atrocities**) 1 an act of extreme cruelty or ruthlessness, esp. against defenceless victims. 2 excessive cruelty or other flagrant wickedness. 3 something that shows execrable taste, workmanship etc.

atrophy (at´rəfi) *n.* (*pl.* **atrophies**) 1 a wasting of the body, or (one of) its organs, through lack of nourishment or disease. 2 mental or spiritual starvation. ~*v.t.* (*3rd pers. sing. pres.* **atrophies**, *pres.p.* **atrophying**, *past, p.p.* **atrophied**) to affect with atrophy, to cause to waste away. ~*v.i.* to waste away. **atrophied** *a.*

atropine (at´rəpēn, -pin), **atropin** *n.* a poisonous alkaloid obtained from deadly nightshade, *Atropa belladonna*, used in the treatment of intestinal spasm and to counteract the slowing of the heart.

attach (ətach´) *v.t.* 1 to fasten on, connect. 2 to affix. 3 to attribute (importance, significance etc.). 4 to include or append (a condition). 5 (*reflex.*) to join, to become a member of, to take part in. 6 to appoint to an organization, military, police etc. unit, temporarily. 7 (*Law*) to lay hold on, arrest, indict, esp. to seize (a person or goods) by a writ of attachment. ~*v.i.* 1 to adhere; to be connected. 2 to be inherent in or attributable (to). **attachable** *a.* **attached** *a.* 1 joined, fastened. 2 fond of; joined by bonds of love, friendship or sympathy. 3 incident, connected. 4 (*coll.*) married, engaged or in a long-term relationship. **attachment** *n.* 1 the act of attaching. 2 the means by which anything is attached. 3 a thing that is or can be attached, esp. a device that can be fitted to a machine to perform a special function. 4 fidelity, affection, devotion. 5 a temporary posting or secondment. 6 (*Law*) **a** apprehension, esp. for contempt of court. **b** the seizure of goods or estate to secure a debt or demand.

attaché (ətash´ā) *n.* 1 a junior member of an ambassador's staff. 2 a specialist attached to an ambassador's staff. 3 (*N Am.*) an attaché case. **attaché case** *n.* a flat rectangular case for carrying papers etc.

attack (ətak´) *v.t.* 1 to launch a physical or armed assault on. 2 to subject to hostile words or writings; to criticize or abuse strongly. 3 to begin (a piece of work) with determination. 4 (of a physical agent, disease etc.) to exert a destructive or harmful influence on. 5 to take the initiative in trying to score points, goals etc. against. ~*v.i.* 1 to make an attack. 2 to take offensive action in a game or sport. ~*n.* 1 the act of attacking; an onset, an assault. **2** violent abuse or injury. **3** a sudden fit of illness, panic etc. **4** the beginning of active work on something. **5** vigour and decisiveness in undertaking something. **6** (*Mus.*) a (crisp and decisive) manner of beginning a musical piece or passage. **7** an offensive or scoring move in a game or sport. **8** the players in a team who attack. **attackable** *a.* **attacker** *n.*

attain (ətān′) *v.i.* to arrive at some object. ~*v.t.* **1** to reach, gain; to arrive at. **2** to accomplish. **attainable** *a.* **attainability** (-bil′-) *n.* **attainableness** *n.* **attainment** *n.* **1** the act of attaining. **2** something which is attained. **3** a personal achievement or accomplishment.

attar (at′ə), **otto** (ot′ō) *n.* a fragrant essence, or essential oil, esp. of roses.

attempt (ətempt′, ətemt′) *v.t.* **1** to try, endeavour (to do, achieve, effect etc.). **2** to make an effort to achieve. **3** to set out to climb (a mountain). ~*n.* **1** an endeavour, effort, undertaking. **2** something produced or achieved as a result of trying; something imperfect as contrasted with something perfect. **3** an assault (on life, honour etc.). **attemptable** *a.*

attend (ətend′) *v.t.* **1** to be present at. **2** to go regularly to (church, a school etc.). **3** to accompany, escort. **4** to look after, wait upon. **5** (*chiefly pass.*) to result from. ~*v.i.* **1** to pay attention, apply the mind (to). **2** to apply one's efforts or energies (to). **3** to be present. **4** to be in attendance. **5** to wait upon or for a person. **attendance** *n.* **1** the act of attending. **2** presence. **3** the (number of) persons attending. **attendance allowance** *n.* a state benefit in the UK paid to people, esp. the disabled, who need frequent or continual care and supervision. **attendance centre** *n.* (in the UK) a place which young offenders must attend regularly as a minor penalty. **attendant** *a.* **1** following as a consequence. **2** accompanying, waiting (on), ministering. ~*n.* **1** a person who attends or accompanies another; a servant. **2** a person employed to assist, guide etc. the general public. **attendee** (ətendē′) *n.* an attender at an event. **attender** *n.*

attention (ətenʹshən) *n.* **1** the act or state of directing the mind to, or concentrating the mind on, some object. **2** the mental faculty of attending. **3** consideration, notice (*brought to my attention*). **4** watchful care. **5** (*usu. pl.*) an act of courtesy or kindness; an act indicating love or the desire to woo. **6** (*Mil.*) a position in which the body is held rigidly erect with the feet together and hands by the sides. ~*int.* **1** (*Mil.*) a command to stand at attention. **2** used as a means of attracting or commanding attention, usu. so that an announcement can be made. **attentional** *a.*

attentive (ətenʹtiv) *a.* **1** paying attention; listening carefully. **2** polite, courteous. **3** heedful, regardful. **attentively** *adv.* **attentiveness** *n.*

attenuate[1] (ətenʹūāt) *v.t.* **1** to make thin or slender. **2** to reduce the strength, intensity or force of, to weaken. **3** to dilute, diminish the density of.

4 to reduce the amplitude of (an electric current). ~*v.i.* to become thin or weak. **attenuated** *a.* **attenuation** (-ā′shən) *n.* **attenuator** *n.*

attenuate[2] (ətenʹūət) *a.* **1** slender. **2** tapering. **3** thin in consistency.

attest (ətest′) *v.t.* **1** to vouch for, to certify. **2** to give evidence or proof of. **3** to testify, bear witness that. ~*v.i.* to bear witness. **attestation** (atestā′shən) *n.* **attestor** *n.*

Attic (at′ik) *a.* of or belonging to Attica, its capital, Athens, or the Greek dialect spoken there.

attic (at′ik) *n.* **1** the top storey of a house. **2** a room in this storey. **3** a low storey placed above an entablature or cornice.

attire (ətīə′) *v.t.* (*formal*) **1** to dress, esp. in fine or formal clothing. **2** to array, adorn. ~*n.* dress, clothes.

attitude (at′itūd) *n.* **1** a mental position or way of thinking with respect to someone or something. **2** behaviour indicating opinion and sentiment. **3** bearing or gesture, expressing action or emotion. **4** a posture or position taken by a person, animal or object. **5** the posture in which a figure is represented in painting or sculpture. **6** the position of an aircraft or spacecraft in relation to a plane of reference. **7** (*sl.*) a provocatively insolent, truculent or non-cooperative manner or mode of behaviour. **8** (*sl.*) very self-confident style, swagger. **9** a position in ballet in which the body is held upright with one leg raised and bent behind. **attitude of mind** *n.* habitual mode of thinking and feeling. **attitudinize** (-tū′din-), **attitudinise** *v.i.* **1** to practise or assume attitudes; to pose. **2** to behave or act affectedly.

attn. *abbr.* attention, for the attention of.

atto- (at′ō) *comb. form* (*Math.*) denoting a factor of 10^{-18}.

attorney (ətœ′ni) *n.* (*pl.* **attorneys**) (*Law*) **1** a legally authorized agent or deputy. **2** (*N Am.*) a lawyer, a barrister, a solicitor, esp. one qualified to act for another in legal proceedings. **Attorney-General** *n.* (*pl.* **Attorneys-General, Attorney-Generals**) the chief law officer in England, the US and other countries, and legal adviser to the government. **attorneyship** *n.*

attract (ətrakt′) *v.t.* **1** to draw to oneself or itself or cause to approach (physically or in an immaterial sense). **2** to cause to desire; to arouse interest or fascination in. **3** (of a magnet, gravity) to exert an influence on that causes a thing to approach. ~*v.i.* to exert the power of attraction, to be attractive. **attractable** *a.* **attractant** *a.* that attracts. ~*n.* a substance that attracts (esp. insects). **attraction** *n.* **1** the action or power of attracting. **2** a person, thing, quality or characteristic that attracts. **3** (*Physics*) a force causing two objects, molecules etc. to be drawn together or to resist separation. **attractive** *a.* **1** pleasing to the senses, appealing, alluring. **2** that appears advantageous, profitable etc. **3** that has the ability to pull something towards itself. **attractively** *adv.* **attractiveness** *n.* **attractor** *n.*

attribute¹ (at´ribūt) *n.* **1** a quality ascribed or imputed to any person or thing, as an essential characteristic. **2** a characteristic, a feature. **3** a symbolic or other object recognized as appropriate to a person, office, rank etc. **4** an attributive word.

attribute² (ətrib´ūt) *v.t.* **1** (*with to*) to regard as caused by. **2** to regard as having been produced or created by. **3** to regard as possessing. **4** to regard as characteristic of. **attributable** *a.* **attribution** (atribū´shən) *n.* **1** the act of attributing. **2** something which is ascribed. **attributive** (ətrib´-) *a.* (*Gram.*) (of an adjective) expressing an attribute of a noun and usu. immediately preceding it. **attributively** *adv.*

attrit (ətrit´) *v.t.* (*pres.p.* **attritting**, *past*, *p.p.* **attritted**) (*N Am.*, *coll.*) **1** to wear down (an enemy, opponent) by constant (small-scale) action. **2** to kill.

attrition (ətrish´ən) *n.* **1** the act or process of wearing away, esp. by friction. **2** abrasion. **3** a constant wearing down or weakening, as of an adversary. **4** (*esp. N Am.*, *Austral.*) reduction in the size of the workforce by natural wastage. **5** (*Theol.*) sorrow for sin on account of the punishment due to it.

attune (ətūn´) *v.t.* **1** to accustom, acclimatize. **2** to bring (an instrument) to the right pitch; to put (instruments) in tune with one another. **3** (*poet.*) to make tuneful.

Atty. *abbr.* attorney.

ATV *abbr.* all-terrain vehicle.

atypical (ātip´ikəl) *a.* not typical, not conforming to type. **atypically** *adv.*

AU *abbr.* **1** ångström unit. **2** astronomical unit.

Au *chem. symbol* gold.

aubergine (ō´bəzhēn) *n.* **1** the eggplant, *Solanum melongena*. **2** its ovoid, characteristically dark purple fruit used as a vegetable and in stews. **3** a dark purple colour.

aubrietia (awbrē´shə) *n.* a plant of a genus, *Aubretia*, of dwarf, perennial, spring-flowering rock plants of the family Cruciferae.

auburn (aw´bən) *a.* **1** reddish-brown. **2** †yellowish. **~n.** a reddish-brown colour.

AUC *abbr.* (in Roman dates) from the foundation of the city.

auction (awk´shən) *n.* **1** a public sale of goods, usu. one in which each bidder offers a higher price than the preceding. **2** auction bridge; the sequence of bids made in a game of auction bridge. **~v.t.** to sell by auction. **auction bridge** *n.* a version of bridge in which the players bid for the advantage of choosing trump suit. **auctioneer** (-niə´) *n.* a person who sells goods by auction, or conducts auctions. **~v.t.**, *v.i.* to sell by auction.

audacious (awdā´shəs) *a.* **1** bold, daring, spirited. **2** impudent, shameless. **audaciously** *adv.* **audaciousness** *n.* **audacity** (-das´-) *n.*

✗ **audiance** common misspelling of AUDIENCE.

audible (aw´dibəl) *a.* **1** capable of being heard.

clear or loud enough to be heard. **audibility** (-bil´-) *n.* **audibleness** *n.* **audibly** *adv.*

audience (aw´diəns) *n.* **1** an assembly of hearers or spectators at a meeting, play, concert etc. **2** the people who read a book. **3** the people who regularly watch or listen to a particular television or radio programme, performer etc. **4** a formal interview granted by a superior to an inferior.

audile (aw´dīl) *a.* **1** of or relating to sound or hearing. **2** characterized by awareness and retention of sounds.

audio (aw´diō) *a.* **1** of or relating to sound or its reproduction, transmission or broadcasting. **2** of, relating to or using audio frequencies. **~n.** the (electronic) reproduction and transmission of sound. **Audio-Animatronics®** *n.* ANIMATRONICS. **audio cassette** *n.* a cassette of audiotape. **audio conference** *n.* a conference conducted using audio telecommunications. **audio frequency** *n.* a frequency in the range corresponding to that of audible sound waves. **audiotape** *n.* **1** magnetic tape for recording and reproducing sound. **2** a length or cassette of this tape. **3** a recording made on this tape. **~v.t.** to make a recording on audiotape of. **audiotypist** *n.* a typist trained to type directly from material on a dictating machine. **audiotyping** *n.*

audio- (aw´diō) *comb. form* **1** of or relating to hearing. **2** of or relating to sound or sound reproduction.

audiology (awdiol´əji) *n.* the science of hearing. **audiological** (-loj´-) *a.* **audiologist** *n.*

audiometer (awdiom´itə) *n.* an application of the telephone for testing the sense of hearing. **audiometric** (-met´-) *a.* **audiometry** (-tri) *n.*

audiophile (aw´diōfīl) *n.* a person with an enthusiastic interest in high-fidelity sound reproduction.

audiovisual (awdiōvizh´uəl) *a.* (esp. of teaching methods or aids) directed at or involving hearing and sight.

audit (aw´dit) *n.* **1** an official examination of accounts. **2** any formal review or examination. **3** (*N Am.*) an audited account. **~v.t.** **1** to examine officially and pronounce as to the accuracy of (accounts). **2** (*N Am.*) to attend (a class) without working for credits or intending to sit an examination.

audition (awdish´ən) *n.* **1** a trial performance by a singer, musician, actor etc. applying for a position or role. **2** (*formal*) the act or faculty of hearing. **~v.t.** to test by an audition. **~v.i.** to give a trial performance. **auditive** (aw´-) *a.* of or relating to hearing.

auditor (aw´ditə) *n.* **1** a person appointed to audit accounts. **2** a hearer, a member of an audience. **3** (*N Am.*) a person who audits a class. **auditorial** (-taw´-) *a.*

auditorium (awditaw´riəm) *n.* (*pl.* **auditoriums**, **auditoria** (-riə)) **1** the part of a building occupied by the audience. **2** (*N Am.*) a building with a large hall for public meetings, sports events etc. **3** (*N Am.*) a large room or hall, e.g. in a school.

auditory (aw´ditəri) *a.* of or relating to the organs or sense of hearing, perceived by the ear.

AUEW *abbr.* Amalgamated Union of Engineering Workers.

au fait (ō fā´) *a.* **1** having up-to-date knowledge, fully informed. **2** familiar, well acquainted (with).

Aug. *abbr.* August.

auger (aw´gə) *n.* **1** a carpenter's tool, somewhat resembling a very large gimlet, worked with both hands, for boring holes in wood. **2** a similar instrument of larger size, for boring into soil or rock.

†**taught**[1] (awt), **ought** *n.* **1** anything whatever. **2** a whit, a jot or tittle. ~*adv.* in any respect.

aught[2] OUGHT[2].

augite (aw´gīt) *n.* a greenish, brownish-black or black variety of aluminous pyroxene found in igneous rocks.

augment (awgment´) *v.t.* **1** to increase, to make larger or greater in number, degree, intensity etc.; to extend, to enlarge. **2** (*Mus.*) to increase (an interval) by a semitone. ~*v.i.* to increase, to become greater in size, number, degree etc. **augmentation** (-tā´shən) *n.* **1** the act of augmenting. **2** the state of being augmented. **3** the thing added. **4** increase, addition. **5** the reproduction of a melody or passage in notes of greater length than those in which it was first treated. **augmentative** (-men´-) *a.* **1** having the power or quality of augmenting. **2** (*Gram.*) **a** (of an affix) increasing the force of the original word. **b** (of a word) formed by an augmentative affix. ~*n.* an augmentative element or word.

au gratin (ō grat´ī) *a.* (of a dish) with a light crust, usu. made by browning breadcrumbs and cheese.

augur (aw´gə) *v.t.* **1** to foretell from signs or omens. **2** to betoken, portend. ~*v.i.* **1** to make predictions of future events from signs or omens. **2** to be a sign or foreboding. ~*n.* **1** a religious official among the Romans who professed to foretell future events from omens derived chiefly from the actions of birds, inspection of the entrails of slaughtered victims etc. **2** a soothsayer, a diviner. **augural** (-gū-) *a.* of or relating to an augur or to augury. **augury** (-gū-) *n.* (*pl.* **auguries**) **1** the art or practice of the augur; divination. **2** an omen, prognostication, foreboding.

August (aw´gəst) *n.* the eighth month of the year, named in honour of Augustus Caesar.

august (awgŭst´) *a.* **1** majestic, stately, inspiring reverence and admiration. **2** dignified, worshipful. **augustly** *adv.* **augustness** *n.*

Augustan (awgŭs´tən) *a.* **1** of or belonging to Augustus Caesar or his age, (63 BC–AD 14), in which Latin literature reached its highest development. **2** classical, refined, distinguished by correct literary taste. **3** of or relating to a period

in the literature of any language, e.g. the eighteenth century in English literature, marked by a striving for classical refinement. ~*n.* a writer of the Augustan period of any literature.

Augustine (awgŭs´tin, aw´gəstin) *n.* an Augustinian friar. **Augustinian** (-tin´-) *a.* **1** of or relating to St Augustine (354–430), Bishop of Hippo (396–430), or to his doctrine of grace and predestination. **2** belonging or relating to a religious order whose rule derives from the writings of St Augustine. ~*n.* **1** an adherent of the doctrines of St Augustine. **2** a member of an Augustinian order.

auk (awk) *n.* a northern seabird of the family Alcidae, with black and white plumage, heavy body and short wings, esp. the great auk (now extinct), the little auk and the razorbill. **auklet** *n.* any of various small auks, esp. as found in N Pacific.

auld (awld) *a.* (*Sc.*, *North.*) old. **auld lang syne** *n.* long ago, the (good) times long gone by.

aumbry (awm´bri), **ambry** (am´-) *n.* (*pl.* **aumbries**, **ambries**) a niche or cupboard in a church for books and sacred vessels.

au naturel (ō natürel´) *a.*, *adv.* **1** in the natural state. **2** uncooked or plainly cooked. **3** (*coll.*, *euphem.*) naked.

aunt (ahnt) *n.* **1** the sister of one's father or mother. **2** one's uncle's wife. **3** (*coll.*) a woman friend of a child. **my sainted aunt** (*coll.*) used to express surprise, disbelief etc. **aunthood** *n.* **auntie**, **aunty** *n.* (*pl.* **aunties**) a familiar form of AUNT. **Aunt Sally** *n.* **1** a game in which a figure, often with a pipe in its mouth, is set up, and the players endeavour to knock the figure down or break the pipe by throwing sticks or balls at it. **2** an object of ridicule. **auntship** *n.*

au pair (ō peə´) *n.* a person, esp. a girl, from a foreign country who performs domestic tasks in exchange for board and lodging. ~*v.i.* to work as an au pair.

aura (aw´rə) *n.* (*pl.* **auras**, **aurae** (-rē)) **1** a distinctive atmosphere or quality. **2** a subtle emanation from any body, esp. a mystic light produced by and surrounding the body of a living creature which is said to be visible to people of supernormal sensitivity. **3** (*Med.*) a sensation (as of a current of cold air rising to the head) that precedes an attack in epilepsy, hysteria etc. **aural**[1] *a.* of or relating to an aura.

aural[1] AURA.

aural[2] (aw´rəl) *a.* **1** of or relating to the ear. **2** received by the ear. **aurally** *adv.*

Usage note See note under ORAL.

aureate (aw´riət) *a.* **1** golden, gold-coloured. **2** brilliant, splendid. **3** (of language or literary style) over-elaborate and embellished.

aureole (aw´riōl), **aureola** (-rē´ələ) *n.* **1** the gold disc surrounding the head in early pictures of religious figures, and denoting glory, a nimbus. **2** the halo round the moon in total eclipses of the sun, a corona. **3** a halo of radiating light round the sun or moon.

au revoir (ō rəvwah´) *int.* farewell, goodbye.

auric (aw´rik) *a.* of or relating to gold, applied to compounds in which gold is trivalent. **aurous** *a.* of or relating to gold, applied to compounds in which gold is univalent.

auricle (aw´rikəl) *n.* (*Anat.*) **1** an atrium of the heart. **2** an earlike sac on the surface of each atrium of the heart. **3** the external ear, that part which projects from the head.

auricula (awrik´ūlə) *n.* a garden flower, *Primula auricula*, sometimes called bear's ear, from the shape of its leaves.

auricular (awrik´ūlə) *a.* **1** of, relating to, using or known by the sense of hearing. **2** shaped like an auricle. **3** of or relating to an auricle of the heart. **auriculate** (-lət) *a.* having ears, or appendages resembling ears.

auriferous (awrif´ərəs) *a.* yielding or producing gold.

aurochs (aw´roks) *n.* (*pl.* **aurochs**) the extinct wild ox, *Bos primigenius*.

aurora (awraw´rə) *n.* (*pl.* **auroras, aurorae** (-rē)) **1** a peculiar illumination of the night sky common within the polar circles, consisting of streams of light ascending towards the zenith. **2** (*poet.*) morning twilight, dawn. **aurora australis** (ostrah´lis) *n.* the aurora seen in the southern hemisphere. **aurora borealis** (bawriah´lis) *n.* the aurora seen in the northern hemisphere. **auroral** *a.*

aurous AURIC.

AUS *abbr.* Australia (IVR).

auscultation (awskəltā´shən) *n.* **1** listening with the ear or stethoscope to the sounds made by the internal organs, to judge their condition. **2** the act of listening. **auscultate** (aws´-) *v.t.* to examine by auscultation. **auscultatory** (-kŭl´-) *a.*

auspice (aw´spis) *n.* **1** (*usu. pl.*) patronage, protection. **2** (*often pl.*) a (favourable) portent, sign or omen. **3** an omen drawn from the actions of birds. **under the auspices of** under the leadership, encouragement or patronage of. **auspicious** (-spish´-) *a.* **1** having favourable omens, auguring good fortune. **2** conducive to prosperity or success. **auspiciously** *adv.* **auspiciousness** *n.*

Aussie (oz´i), **Ozzie** *n.* (*coll.*) **1** an Australian. **2** Australia. ~*a.* Australian.

austere (ostiə´) *a.* **1** severely simple, unadorned. **2** ascetic, abstemious. **3** severe, stern, rigorous. **austerely** *adv.* **austereness** *n.* **austerity** (-ter´-) *n.* (*pl.* **austerities**) **1** severe simplicity and lack of adornment. **2** self-denial, asceticism. **3** (*pl.*) ascetic or penitential practices. **4** sternness, severity. **5** a policy of reducing the availability of luxury goods and maintaining strict financial controls.

Austin (os´tin) *a., n.* (an) Augustinian.

austral (os´trəl) *a.* **1** southern. **2** (**Austral**) of or relating to Australia or Australasia.

Australasian (ostrələā´zhən) *a.* of or relating to Australasia, a general name for Australia, New Zealand, Tasmania and the surrounding islands. ~*n.* a native or inhabitant of Australasia.

Australian (ostrāl´yən) *a.* of or belonging to Australia. ~*n.* **1** a native or inhabitant of Australia. **2** a person of Australian descent. **Australian bear** *n.* the koala. **Australianism** *n.* **1** an Australian idiom or characteristic. **2** devotion to Australia, its culture, political independence etc. **Australian Rules (football)** *n.* a game similar to rugby football played in Australia on an oval pitch with an oval ball between teams of 18 players. **Australian salmon** *n.* a large green and silver marine fish, *Arripis trutta*. **Australian terrier** *n.* a short-legged breed of terrier, small and wire-haired. **Australoid** (os´trəl-) *a.* of, relating to or denoting a racial group including and typified by the Aborigines of Australia. ~*n.* a member of this group.

Austrian (os´triən) *n.* **1** a native or inhabitant of Austria. **2** a person of Austrian descent. ~*a.* of or relating to Austria. **Austrian blind** *n.* a window blind with several vertical lines of shirring in the fabric, that forms a series of ruches when raised.

Austro-[1] (os´trō) *comb. form* **1** southern. **2** Australian.

Austro-[2] (os´trō) *comb. form* Austrian (*Austro-Hungarian*).

AUT *abbr.* Association of University Teachers.

aut- AUTO-.

autarch (aw´tahk) *n.* an absolute sovereign, an autocrat. **autarchic** (-tah´-), **autarchical** *a.* **autarchy** *n.* (*pl.* **autarchies**) **1** absolute sovereignty, autocracy. **2** despotism. **3** a country under autarchic rule.

autarky (aw´tahki) *n.* (*pl.* **autarkies**) **1** self-sufficiency, esp. national economic self-sufficiency. **2** a state that is economically self-sufficient. **autarkic** (-tah´-), **autarkical** *a.* **autarkist** *n.*

auteur (ōtœ´, aw-) *n.* a film director who is thought of as having a more than usually dominant role in the creation of their films and a unique personal style.

authentic (awthen´tik) *a.* **1** of undisputed origin, genuine, really proceeding from the professed source. **2** entitled to acceptance or belief, trustworthy, credible. **3** vested with all legal formalities and legally attested. **4** (*Mus.*) (of performances, recordings) played on instruments of the composer's time and in a manner appropriate to that time and to the composer's expectations. **5** (*Mus.*) (of a mode) having the notes between the final and the octave above. **authentically** *adv.* **authenticate** *v.t.* **1** to establish the genuineness, truth or credibility of. **2** to verify the authorship of. **3** to render authentic or valid. **authentication** (-ā´shən) *n.* **authenticator** *n.* **authenticity** (-tis´-) *n.*

author (aw´thə) *n.* **1** the composer of a literary work. **2** a person whose profession is writing, esp. books. **3** the works of an author. **4** the originator, producer or efficient cause of anything. ~v.t. **1** to be the author of (something written). **2** to be the originator or cause of. **authoress** (-ris) n. (often felt to be derog.) a female author. **authorial** (-thaw´-) a. **authoring** n. (Comput.) the writing of programs, creation of databases etc. for computer applications, esp. educational ones, and multimedia products. **authorship** n. **1** the profession of a writer of books. **2** the origin of a literary work.

authority (awthor´əti) n. (pl. **authorities**) **1** legitimate power to command or act. **2** (often pl.) a person or body exercising this power. **3** delegated power or right to act. **4** power, weight or influence, derived from character, station, mental superiority and the like. **5** weight of testimony, credibility. **6** the standard book or work of reference on any subject. **7** an expert, one entitled to speak with authority on any subject. **8** the author or the source of a statement. **9** confidence resulting from the possession of skill. **authoritarian** (-teə´-) n. **1** a person who places obedience to authority above personal liberty. **2** a domineering or dictatorial person. ~a. **1** believing in, favouring or enforcing strict obedience to authority. **2** of, relating to or favouring government by a small group with wide powers. **3** domineering, dictatorial. **authoritative** a. **1** accepted as possessing authority, as being true, valid, reliable etc. **2** (of a person, manner) commanding, assertive, self-confident. **3** supported by authority, official. **authoritatively** adv. **authoritativeness** n.

Usage note The adjectives authoritarian and authoritative should not be confused: authoritarian means favouring or enforcing obedience to authority, and authoritative deserving respect or obedience as an authority.

authorize (aw´thərīz), **authorise** v.t. **1** to give authority to, to empower. **2** to sanction. **3** to warrant legally. **4** to justify, afford just ground for. **authorizable** a. **authorization** (-zā´shən) n. **1** the act of authorizing. **2** a document etc. that authorizes something. **authorized** a.

autism (aw´tizm) n. a disorder of mental development, usu. evident from childhood, marked by complete self-absorption, lack of social communication and inability to form relationships. **autistic** (-tis´-) a.

auto (aw´tō) n. (pl. **autos**) (esp. N Am.) short for AUTOMOBILE.

auto- (aw´tō), **aut-** comb. form **1** self. **2** one's own. **3** from within or by oneself. **4** operating independently; self-propelling, self-regulating.

autobahn (aw´təbahn) n. a motorway in Germany, Austria or Switzerland.

autobiography (awtəbīog´rəfi) n. (pl. **autobiographies**) **1** a memoir of one's life, written by oneself. **2** the writing of one's own memoirs. **autobiographer** n. **autobiographic** (-graf´-), **autobiographical** a. **autobiographically** adv.

autocar (aw´təkah) n. a vehicle driven by its own mechanical power, a motor vehicle.

autocephalous (awtōsef´ələs, -kef´-) a. **1** (of an eastern Church) having the power to appoint its own synod, bishop etc. **2** (of a bishop, Church) independent. **autocephaly** n.

autochthon (awtok´thən, -thōn) n. (pl. **autochthons**, **autochthones** (-thənēz)) **1** any one of the original or earliest known inhabitants. **2** an aboriginal animal or plant. **autochthonous** a. **1** native, indigenous. **2** (esp. Geol.) occurring, formed or originating in the place where found.

autoclave (aw´təklāv) n. **1** a sealed vessel used for chemical reactions at high temperature and pressure. **2** an apparatus using superheated steam for sterilizing, cooking etc.

autocracy (awtok´rəsi) n. (pl. **autocracies**) **1** absolute government by a single person. **2** the power wielded by an autocrat. **3** a country under autocratic rule.

autocrat (aw´təkrat) n. **1** a sovereign with uncontrolled authority. **2** a dictatorial person. **autocratic** (-krat´-) a. **autocratically** adv.

autocross (aw´tōkros) n. the sport of motor racing across country or on unmade roads.

Autocue® (aw´təkū) n. a device that displays the text to be spoken by a person on television.

auto-da-fé (awtōdafā´) n. (pl. **autos-da-fé** (awtō-)) **1** a sentence pronounced by the Inquisition. **2** the execution of this judgement. **3** the burning of a heretic.

autodidact (awtōdī´dakt) n. a self-taught person. **autodidactic** (-didak´-) a.

auto-erotism (awtōer´ətizm), **auto-eroticism** (-irot´-) n. (Psych.) self-produced sexual pleasure or emotion, e.g. masturbation. **auto-erotic** (-irot´-) a.

autofocus (aw´tōfōkəs) n. a facility in some cameras for automatically focusing the lens.

autogamy (awtog´əmi) n. (Bot.) self-fertilization. **autogamous** a.

autogenous (awtoj´ənəs) a. **1** self-engendered, self-produced, independent. **2** (of a graft, vaccine) originating from sources within the patient's own body.

autogiro (aw´tōjīrō), **autogyro** n. (pl. **autogiros**, **autogyros**) an aircraft in which the lifting surfaces are the freely-rotating blades of a large horizontal airscrew.

autograft (aw´təgrahft) n. a surgical graft that moves tissue from one point to another in the same individual's body.

autograph (aw´təgrahf) n. **1** a signature written esp. by a celebrity for an admirer. **2** a person's own handwriting. **3** a manuscript in an author's own handwriting. ~a. written by the author. ~v.t. **1** to write one's signature on or in, esp. at the request of an admirer. **2** to write with one's own hand. **autographic** (-graf´-), **autographical** a. **1** written by one's own hand. **2** of or relating to autographs or autography. **autography** (-tog´-) n. **1** writing with one's own hand. **2** one's own handwriting. **3** a process of reproducing handwriting or drawing in facsimile.

Autoharp® (aw'tōhahp) *n.* a zither-like instrument having dampers which stop selected strings from sounding and allow chords to be played.

autoimmune (awtōimūn´) *a.* (*Med.*) of or caused by antibodies that attack the molecules, cells etc. normally present in the organism producing them. **autoimmunity** *n.*

autointoxication (awtōintoksikā´shən) *n.* (*Med.*) reabsorption of toxic matter produced by the body.

autolysis (awtol´isis) *n.* the breakdown of cells by the action of enzymes produced in the cells themselves. **autolytic** (-lit´-) *a.*

automat (aw´təmat) *n.* **1** a vending machine. **2** (*N Am.*) a restaurant or room equipped with automatic machines for supplying food etc.

automatic (awtəmat´ik) *a.* **1** self-acting, self-regulating; operating without direct or continuous human intervention. **2** (of actions, behaviour) spontaneous, involuntary, reflex. **3** (*derog.*) (of actions, behaviour) habitual, merely mechanical. **4** (*Psych.*) carried on unconsciously. **5** (of a firearm) repeatedly ejecting the empty shell, introducing a new one and firing, until the trigger is released. **6** (of a vehicle) having automatic transmission. ~*n.* **1** an automatic firearm. **2** a motor vehicle with automatic transmission. **automatically** *adv.* **automaticity** (-tis´-) *n.* **automatic pilot** *n.* a device which automatically maintains an aircraft or spacecraft on a predetermined course. **automatic transmission** *n.* power transmission in a motor vehicle in which the gears change automatically.

automation (awtəmā´shən) *n.* **1** the use of self-regulating or automatically programmed machines in the manufacture of goods. **2** the introduction of such machinery to save labour. **automate** (aw´-) *v.t.* to make automatic; to bring automation to. ~*v.i.* to apply automation.

automatism (awtom´ətizm) *n.* **1** the quality of being automatic. **2** involuntary action. **3** (*Psych.*) the performance of actions without conscious control. **4** automatic routine. **automatize, automatise** *v.t.* **1** to make automatic. **2** to automate. **automatization** (-zā´shən) *n.*

automaton (awtom´ətən) *n.* (*pl.* **automatons, automata** (-tə)) **1** a machine that is activated by a concealed mechanism and power source within itself, a robot. **2** a machine of this kind that simulates human or animal actions. **3** a person who acts mechanically or leads a life of monotonous routine.

automobile (awtəməbēl´, aw´-) *n.* (*esp. N Am.*) a motor car.

automotive (awtəmō´tiv) *a.* **1** self-propelling. **2** of or relating to motor vehicles.

autonomy (awton´əmi) *n.* (*pl.* **autonomies**) **1** the right of self-government. **2** an independent state or community. **3** freedom to act as one pleases. **4** in Kantian philosophy, freedom of the will. **5** organic independence. **autonomic** (-nom´-) *a.* **1** (*Biol.*) occurring involuntarily, spontaneous. **2** of, relating to or mediated by the autonomic nervous system. **autonomic nervous system** *n.* the part of the vertebrate nervous system that regulates the involuntary actions of the heart, glands and some muscles. **autonomist** *n.* an advocate of autonomy. **autonomous** *a.* **1** of or possessing autonomy. **2** self-governing or partially self-governing. **3** able to act or acting independently. **autonomously** *adv.*

autopilot (aw´tōpīlət) *n.* AUTOMATIC PILOT (under AUTOMATIC).

autopista (awtōpēs´tə) *n.* a motorway in Spain.

autopsy (aw´topsi, -top´-) *n.* (*pl.* **autopsies**) **1** a post-mortem examination. **2** a critical examination. **3** a personal observation. ~*v.t.* (*3rd pers. sing. pres.* **autopsies,** *pres.p.* **autopsying,** *past, p.p.* **autopsied**) to perform a post-mortem examination on.

autoradiograph (awtōrā´diəgrahf) *n.* a photograph produced by radiation from, and showing the distribution of, radioactive particles in a body. **autoradiographic** (-graf´ik) *a.* **autoradiography** (-og´rəfi) *n.*

autorotation (awtōrōtā´shən) *n.* rotation resulting from the shape or structure of an object in an airflow, not from a power source. **autorotate** *v.i.*

autoroute (aw´tōroot) *n.* a motorway in France.

autostrada (aw´tōstrahdə) *n.* a motorway in Italy.

autosuggestion (awtōsəjes´chən) *n.* suggestion arising from oneself, esp. the unconscious influencing of one's own beliefs, physical condition etc.

autotelic (awtōtel´ik, awtə-) *a.* that is an end in itself.

autotimer (aw´tōtīmə) *n.* a device that can be set to turn an appliance, e.g. a cooker, on or off at a predetermined time.

autotomy (awtot´əmi) *n.* (*Zool.*) voluntary separation of a part of the body, e.g. the tail, as in certain lizards.

autotoxic (awtətok´sik) *a.* self-poisoning. **autotoxin** *n.* a poisonous substance produced within the organism it attacks.

autotrophic (awtətrof´ik) *a.* (*Biol.*) (of or relating to organisms) capable of manufacturing organic foods from inorganic sources, as by photosynthesis.

autotype (aw´tōtīp) *n.* **1** a facsimile. **2** a photographic printing process for reproducing photographs in monochrome; a print made by this process. **3** a true impress.

autowinder (aw´tōwīndə) *n.* an electrically powered device that automatically winds on the film in a camera after a photograph has been taken.

autoxidation (awtoksidā´shən) *n.* (*Chem.*) oxidation that occurs spontaneously on exposure to atmospheric oxygen.

autumn (aw´təm) *n*. **1** (*Astron*.) the season of the year between summer and winter – astronomically, it extends from the autumnal equinox to the winter solstice; popularly, it comprises the months from September to November in the northern hemisphere and from March to May in the southern. **2** the stage of late maturity or incipient decline, e.g. in human life. **autumnal** (-tŭm´nəl) *a*. **1** relating to, characteristic of or produced in autumn. **2** of or relating to the declining period of life. **autumnal equinox, autumn equinox** *n*. (*Astron*.) the time when the sun crosses the equator in autumn (this happens about 22 Sept. in the northern hemisphere and about 21 March in the southern). **autumn crocus** *n*. a plant of the genus *Colchicum*, meadow saffron.

auxiliary (awgzil´yəri) *a*. **1** helping, aiding. **2** subsidiary (to). **3** applied to verbs used in the conjugation of other verbs. ~*n*. (*pl*. **auxiliaries**) **1** a person who or something which helps or assists. **2** (*Gram*.) an auxiliary verb. **3** (*pl., Mil*.) foreign or allied troops in the service of a nation at war. **4** (*N Am*.) a group that helps or assists, esp. with charitable activities. **auxiliary verb** *n*. (*Gram*.) a verb used in the conjugation of other verbs.

auxin (awk´sin) *n*. any of a group of growth-promoting plant hormones. **auxology** (-sol´-) *n*. the study of growth, esp. in humans. **auxologist** *n*.

AV *abbr*. **1** audiovisual. **2** Authorized Version (of the Bible).

Av. *abbr*. avenue.

avadavat (av´ədəvat, avədəvat´), **amadavat** (am-) *n*. an Indian and SE Asian waxbill of the genus *Amandava*.

avail (əvāl´) *v.i*. **1** to be of value, use, profit or advantage. **2** to be helpful. **3** to be effectual or sufficient. ~*v.t*. to be of use or advantage to. ~*n*. worth, value, profit, advantage, use. **of no avail** ineffectual, in vain. **to avail oneself of** to take advantage of, make use of.

available (əvā´ləbəl) *a*. **1** capable of being employed; at one's disposal. **2** at hand, accessible. **3** (of a person) unoccupied, contactable. **4** (*coll*.) free for a sexual relationship. **availability** (-bil´-) *n*. **availableness** *n*. **availably** *adv*.

avalanche (av´əlahnsh) *n*. **1** a mass of snow, ice and debris falling or sliding from the upper parts of a mountain. **2** a sudden overwhelming arrival or build-up. ~*v.i*. to descend or arrive like an avalanche. ~*v.t*. to overwhelm as or like an avalanche.

avant-garde (avägahd´) *a*. **1** in advance of contemporary artistic tastes or trends; experimental, progressive. **2** radical, daring. ~*n*. the people who create or take up avant-garde or experimental ideas, esp. in the arts. **avant-gardism** *n*. **avant-gardist** *n*.

avarice (av´əris) *n*. excessive desire for wealth; greed, covetousness. **avaricious** (-rish´əs) *a*. **avariciously** *adv*.

avast (əvahst´) *int*. (*Naut*.) stay! stop! desist!

avatar (av´ətah) *n*. **1** in Hinduism, the descent of a god or released soul to earth. **2** the incarnation of a Hindu god; incarnation. **3** a manifestation, a phase. **4** an archetypal example of a concept or principle.

Ave., ave. *abbr*. avenue.

ave (ah´vā) *int*. hail! welcome! farewell! (in allusion to the classical custom of greeting the dead). ~*n*. **1** an Ave Maria. **2** any one of the small beads on a rosary on which prayers are counted. **3** a shout of welcome or adieu. **Ave Maria, Ave Mary** *n*. the Hail Mary; the angelical salutation (Luke i.28) with that of St Elisabeth (i.42), to which a prayer is added, the whole being used as a form of devotion.

avenge (əvenj´) *v.t*. **1** to execute vengeance on account of or on behalf of. **2** to take vengeance for. ~*v.i*. to execute vengeance. **to be avenged** to execute vengeance on one's own behalf. **avenger** *n*.

Usage note *Avenge* implies greater justification and less purely personal motivation than *revenge*.

avens (av´əns) *n*. (*pl*. **avens**) **1** a rosaceous plant of the genus *Geum*, esp. the wood avens or herb bennet, *G. urbanum*, and the water avens, *G. rivale*. **2** a related alpine plant, the mountain avens, *Dryas octopetala*.

aventurine (əven´churin), **aventurin** *n*. **1** a gold-spangled Venetian glass (made by a process which was discovered accidentally, hence the name). **2** a quartz of similar appearance spangled with scales of mica or some other mineral.

avenue (av´inū) *n*. **1** a way or means of approaching an objective or gaining an end. **2** a broad street or road, typically lined with trees. **3** an approach to a country house or similar building, lined with trees; a way or path lined with trees. **4** (*N Am*.) a road in a grid system running perpendicular to another.

aver (əvœ´) *v.t*. (*pres.p*. **averring**, *past, p.p*. **averred**) (*formal*) to assert or declare positively. **averment** *n*. **1** the act of averring; affirmation, positive assertion. **2** (*Law*) an affirmation alleged to be true, and followed by an offer to verify.

average (av´ərij) *n*. **1** the typical or prevailing number, quantity, proportion, level or degree; the general standard. **2** the value obtained by adding together a set of numbers and dividing the result by the number of members of the set. **3** (*Law*) **a** loss arising from damage to a ship or cargo at sea. **b** appointment of such loss among the parties interested. ~*v.t*. **1** to calculate the average of. **2** to assess the ordinary standard of. **3** to divide proportionately to the number involved. **4** to be or consist of on average. **5** to do, have or take as a mean rate or value. ~*v.i*. to be or amount to as an average. ~*a*. **1** ascertained by taking a mean proportion between given quantities. **2** medium, ordinary, usual. **3** mediocre. **on**

(an) average 1 usually, typically. **2** taking the mean calculated from a number of examples. **to average out** to attain an acceptable level in the long run. **to average out at** to come to (a certain figure) when the average is calculated. **average adjuster** *n.* (*Law*) an assessor who deals with claims for losses at sea. **averagely** *adv.*

averse (əvœs´) *a.* **1** unwilling, disinclined, reluctant (to). **2** feeling repugnance or dislike. **aversely** *adv.* **averseness** *n.* **aversion** (-shən) *n.* **1** disinclination, dislike, repugnance. **2** an object of dislike. **aversion therapy** *n.* therapy designed to stop undesirable behaviour by associating it with an unpleasant sensation (e.g. an electric shock). **aversive** *a.*

Usage note See note under ADVERSE.

avert (əvœt´) *v.t.* **1** to turn away. **2** to ward off, to prevent. **avertible** *a.*

Usage note The verbs *avert* and *avoid* should not be confused: *avert* implies some definite action taken in advance, while *avoid* means simply to escape or evade.

avian (ā´viən) *a.* of or relating to birds. **aviarist** *n.*

aviary *n.* (*pl.* **aviaries**) a large cage or building in which birds are kept.

aviation (āviā´shən) *n.* **1** the subject of aircraft; the practice of operating aircraft. **2** the design and manufacture of aircraft. **3** the art or skill of flying or travelling in the air. **aviate** (ā´-) *v.i.* to fly in or pilot an aircraft. ~*v.t.* to pilot (an aircraft). **aviator** *n.* a person who flies, or is a member of the crew of, an aircraft. **aviatrix** (āviā´triks) *n.* a female aviator.

aviculture (ā´vikŭlchə) *n.* the breeding and rearing of birds. **aviculturist** (-kŭl´-) *n.*

avid (av´id) *a.* **1** very keen, enthusiastic. **2** ardently desirous (of); extremely eager (for). **avidity** (-vid´-) *n.* **1** great keenness, enthusiasm; eagerness. **2** the strength of the interaction between an antibody and antigen. **avidly** *adv.*

avifauna (ā´vifawnə) *n.* the birds in any district taken collectively. **avifaunal** *a.*

avionics (āvion´iks) *n.* (the science concerned with) the development and use of electronic and electric equipment in aircraft and spacecraft.

avitaminosis (āvitəminō´sis) *n.* (*pl.* **avitaminoses** (-sēz)) (*Med.*) (a) disease resulting from vitamin deficiency.

avocado (avəkah´dō) *n.* (*pl.* **avocados**) **1** (*also* **avocado pear**) the pear-shaped fruit of a Central American tree, *Persea americana*. **2** this tree. **3** a green colour, either a dull green resembling the skin or a light green resembling the flesh of the fruit. ~*a.* of the colour avocado.

avocation (avəkā´shən) *n.* **1** a minor employment or occupation. **2** a person's ordinary employment, a calling, a vocation.

avocet (av´əset), **avoset** *n.* a wading bird of the genus *Recurvirostra*, having a long slender bill curved upwards.

avoid (əvoid´) *v.t.* **1** to keep at a distance from, to shun. **2** to refrain from. **3** to escape, evade. **4** (*Law*) to nullify, to invalidate, to quash. **avoidable** *a.* **avoidably** *adv.* **avoidance** *n.* **avoider** *n.*

Usage note See note under AVERT.

avoirdupois (avwahdoopwah´, avədəpoiz´) *n.* **1** a system of weights based on the unit of a pound of 16 ounces, equal to 7000 grains (0.4536 kg). **2** (*esp. N Am.*) weight, heaviness. **avoirdupois weight** *n.* weight reckoned by this system.

avow (əvow´) *v.t.* **1** to own, to acknowledge, to admit (of one's free will). **2** to state, allege, declare. **avowable** *a.* **avowal** *n.* **avowed** *a.* **1** acknowledged. **2** self-acknowledged. **avowedly** (-id-) *adv.*

avulsion (əvŭl´shən) *n.* **1** the act of tearing away or violently separating. **2** (*Law*) sudden removal of land (without change of ownership) by flood, alteration in the course of a river etc. **avulse** *v.t.* to remove by avulsion.

avuncular (əvŭng´kūlə) *a.* **1** of or relating to an uncle. **2** benevolent or friendly like an uncle.

aw (aw) *int.* (*esp. N Am. or Sc.*) used to express sympathy, disapproval, appeal etc. **aw-shucks** *a.* (*N Am.*, *coll.*) self-deprecating, self-conscious, apologetic.

await (əwāt´) *v.t.* **1** to wait for, look out for, expect. **2** to be in store for.

awake (əwāk´) *v.i.* (*past* **awoke** (əwōk´), **awaked**, *p.p.* **awoken** (əwō´kən), *past*, *p.p.* **awaked**) **1** to wake from sleep, cease sleeping. **2** to become active or alert. **3** to become conscious of or alive to something. ~*v.t.* **1** to arouse from sleep, or from lethargy or inaction. **2** to excite to action or new life; to stir up, revive (*awoke feelings of compassion*). ~*a.* **1** not asleep; roused from sleep. **2** vigilant, aware, alive (to). **to be awake up** (*Austral.*, *coll.*) to be aware, to be alert. **awaken** *v.t.* **1** to arouse from sleep, awake. **2** to make aware or conscious. ~*v.i.* to awake. **awakenment** *n.* an awakening.

award (əwawd´) *v.t.* **1** to grant or confer, esp. as a prize for merit or as something needed. **2** to adjudge, to assign by judicial sentence. ~*n.* **1** a prize, sum of damages, or other thing awarded. **2** the decision of a judge, arbitrator or umpire. **awarder** *n.*

aware (əweə´) *a.* **1** apprised, cognizant, conscious. **2** well informed in a specified field (*environmentally aware*). **3** (*coll.*) sensitive and perceptive. **awareness** *n.*

awash (əwosh´) *adv.* **1** on a level with the water. **2** afloat and at the mercy of the waves. ~*a.* covered with water; flooded. **awash with** full of, having an abundance of; having too much or too many of.

away (əwā´) *adv.* **1** from a place, person, cause or condition. **2** absent, at another place. **3** apart, at a distance. **4** in the other direction. **5** into another place; until gone or removed. **6** continuously, constantly. **7** directly, without hesitation, freely. **8** at a sporting opponent's ground. ~*a.* **1** absent. **2** distant. **3** played at a sporting opponent's ground. ~*n.* a (football) match played or won at an opponent's ground. **away from it all** in or to a place without the stresses of everyday life. **far and away** beyond comparison, by a large margin.

awe (aw) *n.* **1** dread mingled with veneration. **2** solemn, reverential wonder. ~*v.t.* **1** to inspire with solemn fear or reverence. **2** to restrain or profound respect or reverential fear. **awe-inspiring** *a.* **1** exciting awe or wonder. **2** (*sl.*) marvellous, impressive. **awesome** (-səm) *a.* **1** inspiring awe. **2** full of or displaying awe. **3** (*sl.*) marvellous, impressive. **awesomely** *adv.* **awesomeness** *n.* **awe-stricken**, **awe-struck** *a.* overwhelmed with awe.

aweary (əwiə´ri) *a.* (*poet.*) tired, weary.

☒ **aweful** common misspelling of AWFUL.

aweigh (əwā´) *adv.* (*Naut.*) (of an anchor) raised vertically just off the bottom.

awful (aw´fəl) *a.* **1** extremely disagreeable, frightful, terrible, monstrous; very bad of its kind. **2** (*coll.*) very great, excessive. **3** (*poet.*) inspiring awe; worthy of profound reverence. **4** †filled with awe. **awfully** *adv.* **1** in an awful manner. **2** (*coll.*) exceedingly, very. **awfulness** *n.*

awhile (əwīl´) *adv.* for some time; for a little.

awkward (awk´wəd) *a.* **1** lacking dexterity, bungling, clumsy. **2** ungraceful, ungainly. **3** unhandy, ill-adapted for use. **4** embarrassed, ill at ease. **5** embarrassing. **6** not easy to manage or deal with; requiring care and tact. **7** deliberately uncooperative or unhelpful. **awkwardly** *adv.* **awkwardness** *n.*

awl (awl) *n.* a hand tool with a cylindrical tapering blade, sharpened at the end, for making holes for stitches in leather.

awn (awn) *n.* any one of the bristles springing from a bract in the inflorescence of some cereals and grasses. **awned** *a.* having awns. **awnless** *a.*

awning (aw´ning) *n.* **1** a covering of tarpaulin, canvas or other material used as a protection from sun or rain, as above the deck of a ship. **2** a shelter resembling an awning.

awoke, awoken AWAKE.

AWOL (ā´wol) *a.*, *adv.* absent without authorization from one's post or position of duty. ~*n.* a member of the armed forces who is absent without authorization.

awry (əri´) *adv.* **1** obliquely, crookedly. **2** erroneously, amiss. ~*a.* **1** crooked, distorted, oblique. **2** wrong.

axe (aks), (*esp. N Am.*) **ax** *n.* (*pl.* **axes**) **1** a hand tool for cutting or chopping, consisting of an iron or steel blade with a sharp edge fitted to a handle or helve. **2** any similar tool or weapon, such as a battleaxe. **3** a stone-dressing hammer. **4** (*sl.*) a guitar. ~*v.t.* **1** to chop or cut with an axe. **2** to dismiss (staff) for reasons of economy. **3** to make

drastic reductions in (expenditure, services etc.); to abandon (an enterprise). **the axe 1** (*sl.*) dismissal from employment. **2** drastic reduction in expenditure, staff etc.; abandonment of an enterprise. **axe-breaker** *n.* an Australian tree, *Notelaea longifolia*, whose timber is very hard. **axeman** *n.* (*pl.* **axemen**) **1** a woodman. **2** a warrior armed with a battleaxe. **3** a psychopath who kills with an axe. **4** (*sl.*) a guitarist. **axe to grind** *n.* **1** an ulterior motive. **2** a grievance to air.

axel (ak´səl) *n.* a jump in ice-skating incorporating one and a half turns.

axenic (āzē´nik) *a.* uncontaminated by undesirable microorganisms.

axes[1] AXE.

axes[2] AXIS[1].

axil (ak´sil) *n.* (*Bot.*) the hollow where the base of a leaf joins the stem or where a branch leaves the trunk. **axilla** (-sil´ə) *n.* (*pl.* **axillae** (-lē), **axillas**) **1** (*Anat.*) the armpit. **2** (*Bot.*) an axil. **axillar**, **axillary** *a.* **1** (*Anat.*) of or relating to the armpit. **2** (*Bot.*) of, relating to or arising from the axil.

axiom (ak´siəm) *n.* **1** a self-evident or generally accepted truth. **2** (*Math.*, *esp. Geom.*) a self-evident proposition, assented to as soon as enunciated. **axiomatic** (-mat´-), **axiomatical** *a.* **1** self-evident, containing an axiom or axioms. **2** full of maxims. **axiomatically** *adv.*

axis[1] (ak´sis) *n.* (*pl.* **axes** (-sēz)) **1** a real or imaginary straight line round which a body revolves, or round which its parts are arranged, or to which they have a symmetrical relation. **2** a fixed reference line used, as on a graph, in locating a point. **3** (*Anat.*) the second cervical vertebra. **4** the central stem, core or main skeletal support of (a part of) an organism. **5** (*Bot.*) the central shaft of growth of a plant. **6** a core alliance between countries etc. to which others may become allied. **axial** *a.* **1** of or relating to an axis. **2** forming an axis. **3** round an axis. **axially** *adv.* in the direction of the axis.

axis[2] (ak´sis), **axis deer** *n.* (*pl.* **axis**, **axises**, **axis deer**) a S Asian deer with a white-spotted coat, *Cervus axis*.

axle (ak´səl) *n.* **1** the pin or bar on which a wheel revolves or wheels revolve, or which revolves with a wheel. **2** a pivot or support. **3** an axle tree. **axled** *a.* provided with an axle. **axle tree** *n.* a beam or bar connecting the wheels of a vehicle, on the ends of which the wheels revolve.

axolotl (aksəlot´əl) *n.* a salamander of the genus *Ambystoma* that retains the larval form when fully grown, esp. a small Mexican salamander, *A. mexicanum*.

axon (ak´son) *n.* (*Anat.*, *Zool.*) the projection from a nerve cell that typically conducts impulses away from the cell.

axonometric (aksənōmet´rik) *a.* (of a drawing etc.) showing vertical and horizontal lines projected to scale but inclined to the principal axes of the object represented.

ay AYE[1].

ayah (ī´ə) *n.* a nurse for European children or a maidservant in a European household in the Indian subcontinent or in other former British territories.

ayatollah (īətol´ə) *n.* a leader of the Shiite Muslims in Iran.

aye[1] (ī), **ay** *adv., int.* (*also dial.*) †yes. ~*n.* **1** an affirmative vote in the House of Commons. **2** (*pl.*) those who vote in the affirmative.

†**aye**[2] (ā) *adv.* **1** always, ever. **2** in all cases, on all occasions. **for (ever and) aye** for ever, to all eternity.

aye-aye (ī´ī) *n.* a small lemur found in Madagascar, *Daubentonia madagascariensis*.

Ayrshire (eə´shə) *n.* a breed of cattle highly prized for dairy purposes.

ayurveda (ahyəvā´də, -vē´də) *n.* an ancient Hindu system of medicine, health and healing. **ayurvedic** *a.*

az. *abbr.* azimuth.

azalea (əzāl´yə) *n.* any of various shrubby plants of the genus *Rhododendron*, with showy and occasionally fragrant flowers.

azeotrope (ā´ziətrōp, əzē´ə-) *n.* (*Chem.*) a mixture of liquids in which the boiling point remains constant during distillation at a given pressure. **azeotropic** (-trō´pik, -trop´ik) *a.*

Azerbaijani (azəbījah´ni) *n.* (*pl.* **Azerbaijanis**) **1** a native or inhabitant of Azerbaijan in the Caucasus. **2** the Turkic language of Azerbaijanis. ~*a.* of or relating to the Azerbaijanis or their language.

azide (ā´zīd) *n.* (*Chem.*) a salt or ester of hydrazoic acid, containing the monovalent group or ion N_3. **azidothymidine** (āzīdōthī´midēn) *n.* AZT.

azimuth (az´iməth) *n.* **1** an angular distance from a point of the horizon to the intersection with the horizon of a vertical circle passing through a celestial body. **2** the horizontal angle or direction of a compass bearing. **azimuthal** (-imū´-) *a.* **azimuthally** *adv.* **azimuthal projection** *n.* a type of map projection in which a region of the earth is projected on to a plane tangential to it.

azine (ā´zēn) *n.* (*Chem.*) an organic compound with more than one nitrogen atom in a six-atom ring.

azo- (ā´zō) *comb. form* (*Chem.*) having two adjacent nitrogen atoms. **azo dye** *n.* a dye whose molecules have two adjacent nitrogen atoms between carbon atoms.

azoic (əzō´ik) *a.* **1** having no trace of life. **2** (*Geol.*) destitute of organic remains, in the time that antedates life.

AZT (āzedtē´) *n.* an antiviral drug derived from thymine, used in the treatment of HIV.

Aztec (az´tek) *a.* **1** denoting, of or relating to the leading Mexican Indian people at the time of the Spanish invasion (1519). **2** (*loosely*) of or relating to Mexico before the Spanish invasion. ~*n.* **1** a member of the Aztec people. **2** their language.

azure (azh´ə, ā´-) *n.* **1** the deep blue of the sky. **2** (*poet.*) the vault of heaven. ~*a.* **1** resembling the deep blue of the sky. **2** (*poet.*) clear, unclouded.

azygous (az´igəs) *a.* (*Biol.*) unpaired, occurring singly, not as one of a pair. ~*n.* a structure occurring singly.

B

B¹ (bē), **b** (*pl.* **Bs, B's, Bees**) the second letter of the English and other versions of the Roman alphabet, corresponding to the Greek beta (β, B) and the Phoenician and Hebrew beth. It is pronounced as a voiced bilabial plosive. ~*symbol* **1** the second of a series, the second highest in a range, e.g. of marks, etc. **2** (*Math.*) the second known quantity in an algebraic expression. **3** (*Mus.*) **a** the seventh note of the diatonic scale of C major. **b** the scale of composition in which the keynote is B. **4** (*Med.*) a blood type in the ABO system. **5** (*Physics*) magnetic flux density. **B film** *n.* **1** a supporting film. **2** a low-budget film. **B-lymphocyte, B-cell** *n.* a lymphocyte originating in bone marrow that produces antibodies. **B movie, B picture** *n.* B FILM (under B¹). **B road** *n.* a road of secondary importance. **B-side** *n.* the side of a gramophone record or tape cassette that is usually played second or that has the least important material recorded on it.

B² *abbr.* **1** (*Physics*) bel. **2** bishop (in chess). **3** (of pencil lead) black. **4** Blessed.

B³ *chem. symbol* boron.

b *abbr.* **1** billion. **2** born. **3** bowled. **4** bye.

BA *abbr.* **1** Bachelor of Arts. **2** British Academy. **3** British Airways. **4** British America. **5** British Association (for the Advancement of Science).

Ba *chem. symbol* barium.

BAA *abbr.* British Airports Authority.

baa (bah) *n.* (*pl.* **baas**) the cry or bleat of a sheep. ~*v.i.* (*past* **baaed, baa'd**) to cry or bleat as a sheep. **baa-lamb** *n.* a lamb (used to or by children).

baas (bahs) *n.* (*S Afr.*) boss, overseer. **baasskap** (bah´skap) *n.* domination, esp. by whites.

baba (bah´bah) *n.* (**rum baba**) a small cake soaked in rum.

babacoote (bab´əkoot) *n.* the indri, a short-tailed woolly lemur, *Indri indri*, from Madagascar.

Babbitt (bab´it) *n.* a dull, complacent businessman (or other person) with orthodox views and little interest in cultural values. **Babbittry** *n.*

babbitt (bab´it) *n.* **1** babbitt metal. **2** a bearing-lining made of this. **babbitt metal, babbitt's metal** *n.* an alloy of tin, antimony and copper, used in bearings to diminish friction.

babble (bab´əl) *v.i.* **1** to talk incoherently; to make inarticulate sounds. **2** to talk childishly or in-opportunely; to prattle. **3** (of streams, birds etc.) to murmur. **4** (of hounds) to give tongue without reason. ~*v.t.* to prate; to utter; to blab. ~*n.* **1** incoherent talk. **2** shallow, foolish talk; prattle. **3** confused murmur, as of a running brook.

4 background noise on a telephone line caused by conversations on other lines. **babblement** *n.* **babbler** *n.* **1** an unintermitting and shallow talker. **2** a gossip. **3** a person who tells secrets. **4** a long-legged thrush, of the family Timaliidae.

babe (bāb) *n.* **1** a young child, a baby. **2** a foolish or childish person. **3** (*sl., sometimes derog.*) a girl, a woman.

babel (bā´bəl) *n.* **1** noisy confusion, tumult, disorder. **2** a noisy gathering.

Babi (bah´bē), **Babee** *n.* a follower of the Bab (1819–50), who forbade polygamy, begging and alcohol (and was executed for heresy). **Babism** (bah´bizm) *n.* a Persian religious movement founded by Mirza Ali Mohammed (the Bab) in 1844.

babirusa (babiroo´sə), **babiroussa** *n.* the wild hog of eastern Asia, *Babyrousa babyrussa*, in the male of which the upper canines grow through the lip and turn backwards like horns.

baboon (bəboon´) *n.* **1** a monkey of the genera *Papio* and *Mandrillus*, with long doglike snout, great canine teeth, callosities on the buttocks, and capacious cheek-pouches. **2** an ungainly or ugly person; an unintelligent person.

babu (bah´boo), **baboo** *n.* (*pl.* **babus, baboos**) **1** in the Indian subcontinent, Hindu gentleman, a respectful title corresponding to English Mr. **2** (*Ang.-Ind., offensive*) an Indian clerk who writes English; a Bengali with a superficial English education.

babushka (bəboosh´kə) *n.* **1** a grandmother, an old woman. **2** a Russian triangular headscarf.

baby (bā´bi) *n.* (*pl.* **babies**) **1** an infant; a child in arms. **2** the youngest person in a family, group etc. **3** a foolish, childish person. **4** (*coll.*) a girl, a girlfriend. **5** (*sl.*) a pet project; a person or thing in which one has a special personal interest. ~*a.* **1** small or smaller than usual. **2** newly born, young. ~*v.t.* (*3rd pers. sing. pres.* **babies**, *pres.p.* **babying**, *past, p.p.* **babied**) to make a baby of, to treat like a baby. **baby boom** *n.* (*coll.*) a sharp increase in the birthrate of a population. **baby boomer** *n.* (*coll.*) a person born during a baby boom, esp. in the years following World War II. **baby-bouncer** *n.* a seat or harness on springs, in which a baby can bounce. **baby buggy** *n.* (*pl.* **baby buggies**) **1** a light pushchair. **2** (*N Am.*) a pram. **baby carriage** *n.* (*N Am.*) a pram. **baby-face** *n.* **1** a face like a baby's. **2** a person with a face like this. **baby-faced** *a.* **baby-farmer** *n.* a person who takes in infants to nurse for payment. **baby grand** *n.* a small grand piano. **Babygro®**

(-grō) *n.* (*pl.* **Babygros**) an all-in-one baby garment made of a stretch fabric. **babyhood** *n.* **babyish** *a.* **babyishly** *adv.* **babyishness** *n.* **baby's breath, babies' breath** *n.* **1** a tall plant, *Gypsophila paniculata*, which bears very small white or pink flowers. **2** any of several other plants bearing small fragrant flowers. **babysitter** *n.* a person who looks after a child while the parents are out. **babysit** *v.i.* (*pres.p.* **babysitting**, *past, p.p.* **babysat**). **baby-snatcher** *n.* **1** a person who abducts an infant. **2** a person who marries or goes out with someone much younger. **baby talk** *n.* **1** the speech of young children. **2** an adult's attempt to speak like this. **baby tooth** *n.* (*pl.* **baby teeth**) MILK TOOTH (under MILK). **baby walker** *n.* a frame on wheels for supporting a baby learning to walk. **baby wipe** *n.* a wet tissue or cloth used for cleaning a baby's bottom or the face, hands etc.

Babylon (bab´ilon) *n.* **1** Rome, the papacy (regarded as corrupt by some Protestants). **2** a great and dissolute city. **3** white society (regarded as corrupt by some blacks). **Babylonian** (-lō´-) *a.* of or relating to Babylon.

Bacardi® (bəkah´di) *n.* (*pl.* **Bacardis**) a Caribbean rum.

bacca (bak´ə), **baccy** (-i) *n.* short for TOBACCO.

baccalaureate (bakəlaw´riət) *n.* **1** an examination qualifying successful candidates for higher education in more than one country. **2** the university degree of bachelor.

baccarat (bak´ərah), **baccara** *n.* a gambling card game between banker and punters.

bacchanal (bak´ənəl) *a.* **1** of or relating to Bacchus, the god of wine, or his festivities. **2** characterized by drunken revelry. ~*n.* **1** a votary of Bacchus. **2** a drunken reveller. **3** (*pl.*) a festival in honour of Bacchus. **4** an orgy. **bacchanalia** (-nā´liə) *n.pl.* **1** the festival of Bacchus. **2** bacchanals. **3** drunken revelry. **bacchanalian** *a.* **1** of or relating to bacchanals. **2** bacchanal. ~*n.* **1** a bacchanal. **2** a drunken reveller. **bacchant** *n.* (*pl.* **bacchants, bacchantes** (bəkan´tēz)) **1** a votary of Bacchus. **2** a drunken reveller. ~*a.* **1** worshipping Bacchus. **2** fond of drinking. **bacchante** (-kan´ti) *n.* a priestess of Bacchus. **bacchantic** (-kan´-) *a.* **bacchic** *a.* **1** of or relating to Bacchus or his worship. **2** frenzied; riotously festive.

baccy *n.* BACCA.

bachelor (bach´ələ) *n.* **1** an unmarried man. **2** (*also* **bachelor girl**) an unmarried woman. **3** a holder of the first degree of a university etc., ranking below master or doctor. **4** †a young knight who followed the banner of another. **bachelorhood** *n.* **bachelor's buttons** *n.pl.* **1** the double buttercup *Ranunculus acris*. **2** any of several other plants with button-like flowers. **bachelorship** *n.*

bacillus (bəsil´əs) *n.* (*pl.* **bacilli** (-ī)) a microscopic, rodlike (disease-causing) bacterium. **bacillary** *a.* **1** of, relating to or consisting of little rods. **2** of, relating to or caused by bacilli. **bacilliform** (-ifawm) *a.* rod-shaped.

back (bak) *n.* **1** the hinder part of the human body, from the neck to the lower extremity of the spine. **2** the corresponding portion in the lower vertebrates, and the analogous part in the invertebrates. **3** the spine (*broke her back*). **4** the surface of any object opposite to the face or front; the side or part normally facing away. **5** the outer surface of the hand, the convex part of a book, the thick edge of a knife etc. **6** the hinder part, the rear, the part away from the actor or speaker. **7** the ridge or upper surface of a hill. **8** the keel of a ship. **9** a diagonal parting in a seam of coal. **10** that side of an inclined mineral ore nearest the surface. **11** any one of the players whose duty it is to defend the goal in football and other field games; the position of such a player. ~*a.* **1** situated behind or in the rear. **2** coming back, turned back, reversed. **3** behind in time. **4** remote, distant, inferior. ~*adv.* **1** in a direction to the rear. **2** to the place from which one came. **3** to a former state, position or condition. **4** behind, not advancing, behindhand. **5** in return, in retaliation. **6** in a position behind, away from the front. **7** in a state of check. **8** in time past. **9** again. **10** in returning. ~*v.t.* **1** to furnish with a back or backing. **2** to be at the back of. **3** to support materially or morally, to second, to uphold. **4** to bet in favour of. **5** to mount or get on the back of. **6** to write on the back of, to countersign, to endorse. **7** to cause to move back. **8** to push back. **9** to reverse the action of. ~*v.i.* **1** to retreat, to recede. **2** to move in a reversed direction. **at the back of one's mind** not consciously thought of. **back of** (*N Am.*) behind. **back of beyond** an extremely remote place. **behind someone's back** secretly, surreptitiously. **on one's back 1** floored. **2** at the end of one's tether. **3** laid up. **on the back of 1** weighing as a heavy burden on. **2** in addition to. **to back down/ out 1** to move backwards. **2** to retreat from a difficult situation. **to back into 1** to knock into (someone or something) with a backward motion. **2** (of a train) to run backwards into a station or siding. **to back off 1** to withdraw, to retreat. **2** to stop pursuing a course. **to back on to** to have its back next to. **to back up 1** to support. **2** to render support to (a team-mate) in cricket and other games. **3** (*Comput.*) to duplicate (a computer data file) as security against damage to the original. **4** (of water) to build up behind something. **5** to reverse (a vehicle) to an intended position. **6** to build up into a queue on account of traffic etc.). **to back water** to reverse the motion of the oars when rowing. **to get off someone's back** to stop harassing someone. **to go back on** to fail to abide by or honour. **to put/ get someone's back up 1** to offer resistance. **2** to cause resentment. **3** to feel resentment and show it. **to put one's back into** to make a strenuous effort to perform (a task). **to see the back of** to get rid of. **to turn one's back** to turn away, to flee. **to turn one's back on/ upon 1** to abandon, to forsake. **2** to ignore. **with one's back to the wall** in a critical position. **backache** n. a pain in one's back. **back-band** n. a strap or chain put across the cart saddle of a horse to support the shafts. **backbar** n. a shelving unit for bottles etc. behind a bar. **backbeat** n. (*Mus.*) an accent on a normally un-accented beat. **backbench** n. the seat of a back-bencher. **backbencher** n. a member of Parliament without portfolio. **backbite** v.t., v.i. to slander, censure or speak ill (of). **backbiter** n. **backbiting** n., a. making malicious comments. **backblocks** n.pl. (*Austral.*, *New Zeal.*) the interior parts of the continent or a station, esp. those far from a river. **backblocker** n. a person who lives there. **backboard** n. 1 a board strapped across the back to prevent stooping. 2 a board forming the back of anything. 3 a board behind the basket used in basketball, off which the ball can rebound. 4 a board attached to the rim of a waterwheel to pre-vent the water running off the floats. **back boiler** n. a boiler built into the back of a domestic fireplace. **backbone** n. 1 the bony framework of the back, the spine, the spinal column. 2 a main support or axis. 3 strength of character, firmness, decision. 4 (*N Am.*) the spine of a book. **back-breaker** n. (*coll.*) an arduous task. **back-breaking** a. physically exhausting. **backchat** n. (*coll.*) flip-pant retort, answering back. **backcloth** n. 1 the curtain at the back of a stage. 2 the background. **backcomb** v.t. to comb backwards with short, sharp strokes, making (the hair) fuzzy. **back-country** n. thinly populated districts. **back-crawl** n. the backstroke in swimming. **backcross** v.t. (*Biol.*) to mate (a hybrid) with one of its parents. ~n. 1 the product of this. 2 an instance of this. **backdate** v.t. 1 to apply retrospectively from a particular date (e.g. a pay rise). 2 to put an earlier date on than the real one. **back door** n. 1 a back or private entrance. 2 an indirect or circuitous way or means. **back-door** a. clandestine. **back-down** n. an act of backing down. **back-draught** n. a backward draught of air. **backdrop** n. a back-cloth. **backer** n. **backfield** n. 1 the area of play behind the scrimmage line in American football. 2 (the positions of) the players in this area. **back-fill** v.t. to refill (a hole or excavation) with earth. **backfire** n. 1 premature combustion in the cylinder. 2 a controlled fire set to make a barrier of scorched earth against the advance of a forest fire. ~v.i. 1 to emit a loud noise as a result of premature combustion in the cylinder. 2 (*coll.*) to fail and have the opposite effect. **backflip** n. a backward somersault with straight arms and legs. **back-formation** n. 1 the formation of a new word as if it were formed, e.g. by con-traction, from an existing one (as *burgle* from *burglar*). 2 a new word so formed. **background** n. 1 the ground or surface behind the chief objects of contemplation. 2 that part of a picture, stage-scene or description which represents this. 3 the setting; relevant information about preceding events etc. 4 (*fig.*) an inferior or obscure position. 5 a person's upbringing, education and history.

6 unwanted electrical noise. **background music** n. music intended to be played while something more important is happening or being done. **background radiation** n. low-level radiation present in the soil and atmosphere. **backhand** n. 1 a stroke in tennis etc. played with the hand turned backwards towards the opponent. 2 handwriting sloped backwards. ~a. executed with a backhand. **backhanded** a. 1 with the back of the hand. 2 directed backwards. 3 indirect (*a backhanded compliment*). 4 executed with a backhand. **backhander** n. 1 a blow with the back of the hand. 2 a backhand stroke. 3 (*coll.*) an in-direct attack. 4 (*coll.*) a bribe. **backhoe** n. (*N Am.*) a type of mechanical excavator. **backing** n. 1 sup-porting, seconding. 2 the thing or the body of persons which forms a back or support. 3 money supplied for a project by an investor. 4 musical accompaniment, esp. for a popular song. 5 a piece forming the back or lining the back. **back-ing group** n. a group that provides a musical backing. **backing store** n. a computer storage de-vice that supplements the main memory. **back-ing track** n. a track of recorded musical backing. **backlash** n. 1 a strong adverse reaction. 2 a jar-ring reaction in a piece of mechanism. 3 excess-ive play between parts of a mechanism. **backless** a. **backlight** n. a light projected on a subject from a source behind the camera. **backlist** n. a list of a publisher's books that are still in print. **backlit** a. illuminated from behind. **backlog** n. 1 reserves or arrears of unfulfilled orders, unfinished work etc. 2 an accumulation of business. **backmarker** n. the competitor at the back or with the least chance in a race. **backmost** a. furthest back. **back number** n. 1 a past issue of a newspaper or magazine. 2 (*sl.*) an out-of-date person or thing. **backpack** n. 1 a rucksack. 2 the oxygen supply etc. carried by an astronaut. ~v.i. to hike with a rucksack. **backpacker** n. **backpacking** n. **back passage** n. (*coll.*) the rectum. **backpay** n. arrears of pay. **back-pedal** v.i. (*pres.p.* **back-pedalling**, (*N Am.*) **back-pedaling**, *past, p.p.* **back-pedalled**, (*N Am.*) **back-pedaled**) 1 to press back the pedals of a cycle. 2 to reverse a course of action. 3 to restrain one's enthusiasm. **back-projection** n. the projection of a picture from behind a screen. **backrest** n. a support or rest for the back. **back-room boys** n.pl. (*coll.*) scientists and others who work in the background unrecognized. **back-scatter** n. (*Physics*) the scattering of radiation by deflection. ~v.t. to scatter (radiation) by deflec-tion. **backscattering** n. the reverse scattering of radiation. **back-scratcher** n. 1 a hand-shaped ap-pliance with out-stretched fingers for scratching the back. 2 a flatterer; a person who does favours for another in the expectation of gain. **back-scratching** n. 1 flattery. 2 toadyism; the doing of mutual favours. ~a. that toadies or does favours in the expectation of gain. **back seat** n. 1 the seat at the back of anything, such as a car or theatre. 2 a position of less importance. **back-seat driver**

n. **1** a passenger in a car who offers unwanted advice. **2** a person who offers advice on matters which do not concern them. **backside** *n.* **1** (*coll.*) the buttocks. **2** the back or hinder portion of anything. **backsight** *n.* **1** a sight taken backwards in land surveying. **2** the sight of a rifle near the stock. **back slang** *n.* a peculiar kind of slang in which ordinary words are pronounced backwards (such as, *Cool the eslop* (or *slop*), Look, the police). **backslapping** *a.* hearty in a demonstrative or vigorous way. **backslash** *n.* a reverse solidus. **backslide** *v.i.* (*past, p.p.* **backslid**, *p.p.* **backslidden**) **1** to fall into wrongdoing or false opinions. **2** to relapse. **backslider** *n.* **backspace** *v.i.* to move a typewriter carriage or a cursor back one space using a key. ~*n.* a typewriter or computer key that does this. **backspin** *n.* in tennis, golf etc., the spin of a ball against the direction it is moving in, imparted to dull the bounce. **backstage** *a., adv.* **1** behind the scenes. **2** out of public view. **backstairs** *n.pl.* **1** stairs at the back of a house. **2** the private stairs in a large house or palace for the use of servants etc. ~*a.* clandestine, underhand, scandalous. **backstair** *a.* clandestine, backstairs. **backstitch** *n.* a method of sewing with stitches that are made to overlap. ~*v.t., v.i.* to sew in this manner. **backstop** *n.* **1** a fielder in cricket or baseball who stands behind the person batting. **2** this fielding position. **3** a screen or barrier used to stop the ball in some sports. **backstreet** *n.* **1** a street away from the centre of the town. **2** (*pl.*) the poorer streets of a town. **back-street abortion** *n.* an abortion performed by an unqualified person. **backstroke** *n.* a swimming stroke performed on the back. **back talk** *n.* (*N Am., coll.*) backchat. **back to back** *adv.* **1** with backs facing each other. **2** (*N Am.*) consecutively. **back-to-back** *a.* **1** (of a house) with its back adjoining another so that they face in opposite directions. **2** (*N Am.*) consecutive. ~*n.* a back-to-back house. **back to front** *a., adv.* **1** in reverse, the wrong way round. **2** in disorder. **backtrack** *v.i.* **1** to retrace one's steps. **2** to reverse an opinion, attitude etc. **backup** *n.* **1** support. **2** reinforcement, reserve. **3** (*Comput.*) **a** the act or process of duplicating a computer data file for security. **b** a duplicate copy of a computer data file. **4** a queue of traffic etc. built up. **backup light** *n.* (*N Am.*) a reversing light. **backveld** *n.* (*S Afr.*) country far removed from towns. **backwash** *n.* **1** the wash from the oars of a boat in front. **2** the dragging motion of a receding wave. **3** a backward current. **4** eddy or swirl caused by a ship's propeller. **5** the rush of air from an aircraft engine. **6** reaction; aftermath. **backwater** *n.* **1** a remote place out of touch with mainstream or advanced thought or behaviour. **2** water dammed back or that has overflowed. **3** a piece of water without current fed by the back flow of a river. **backwoods** *n.pl.* **1** remote, uncleared forest land. **2** (*derog.*) a remote, uncultured area. **backwoodsman** *n.* (*pl.* **backwoodsmen**) **1** a settler in the backwoods.

2 an uncultivated person. **3** (*coll.*) a peer who rarely attends the House of Lords. **backyard** *n.* **1** a yard behind a house etc. **2** (*N Am.*) a back garden. **in one's own backyard** near one's own home, close by, locally.

backgammon (bak´gamən) *n.* **1** a game played by two persons on a table with pieces moved according to the throw of dice. **2** the highest win in backgammon. ~*v.t.* to defeat at backgammon.

backsheesh BAKSHEESH.

backwards (bak´wodz), **backward** *adv.* **1** with the back foremost. **2** towards the back or rear. **3** behind, towards the starting-point. **4** towards past time. **5** towards a worse state or condition. **6** in reverse order. **backward** *a.* **1** directed to the back or rear. **2** directed the way from which one has come, reversed. **3** reluctant, unwilling. **4** behind in progress; mentally handicapped. **5** towards or into past time. **6** in cricket, denoting the position of a fielder behind a line through the stumps at right angles to the wicket. **backward and forward 1** to and fro. **2** in an uncertain or vacillating manner. **backwards and forwards** backward and forward. **to bend/ fall/ lean over backwards** to go to great pains, esp. to help. **backwardation** (-ā´shən) *n.* a consideration paid by a seller of stock for the privilege of delaying its delivery. **backwardness** *n.*

baclava BAKLAVA.

bacon (bā´kən) *n.* the cured back and sides of a pig. **to bring home the bacon 1** (*coll.*) to succeed. **2** (*coll.*) to provide a living.

Baconian (bəkō´niən) *a.* of or relating to Bacon or his inductive philosophy. ~*n.* **1** a follower of the inductive system of natural philosophy. **2** a believer in the conceit that Bacon was really the author of Shakespeare's works.

bacteria BACTERIUM.

bactericide (baktiəri´sīd) *n.* an agent that destroys bacteria. **bactericidal** *a.*

bacteriology (baktiəriol´əji) *n.* the scientific study of bacteria. **bacteriological** (-loj´-) *a.* **bacteriologically** *adv.* **bacteriologist** *n.*

bacteriolysis (baktiəriol´isis) *n.* the destruction of bacteria. **bacteriolytic** (-lit´-) *a.*

bacteriophage (baktiə´riəfāj) *n.* a virus which destroys bacteria.

bacteriostasis (baktiəriəstā´sis) *n.* inhibition of the growth of bacterial cells. **bacteriostat** (-tiə´riəstat) *n.* any substance which stops the growth of bacteria without killing them. **bacteriostatic** (-stat´-) *a.*

bacterium (baktiə´riəm) *n.* (*pl.* **bacteria**) a member of a large group of microscopic unicellular organisms found in soil, water and as saprophytes or parasites in organic bodies. **bacterial** *a.*

Usage note *Bacteria* is commonly used as a singular noun (*a bacteria*), but it should always be a plural, with *bacterium* as the singular.

Bactrian (bak´triən) *a.* of or relating to Bactria in central Asia. **Bactrian camel** *n.* a camel with two humps, *Camelus ferus.*

bad (bad) *a.* (*comp.* **worse,** *superl.* **worst**) **1** not good, worthless; unsatisfactory; unpleasant. **2** defective, faulty, incorrect. **3** evil, hurtful, harmful; wicked, morally depraved, offensive. **4** noxious, painful, dangerous, pernicious. **5** in ill-health, sick. **6** injured, diseased. **7** sorry for what one has done, guiltily responsible. **8** (*Law*) invalid. **9** (*NAm., sl.*) very good. ~*n.* **1** that which is bad. **2** a bad state or condition. **from bad to worse** to a worse state from an already bad one. **in a bad way** ill, seriously out of sorts. **not (so) bad** quite good. **to go bad** to decay. **to go to the bad** to go to ruin, to go to the dogs. **to the bad 1** to ruin. **2** to the wrong side of an account. **badass** (bad´as) *n.* (*esp. NAm., sl.*) **1** an aggressive person. **2** a troublemaker. ~*a.* **1** aggressive. **2** bad or worthless. **3** excellent. **bad blood** *n.* mutual hostility or ill feeling. **bad break** *n.* (*coll.*) **1** bad luck. **2** a mistake. **bad breath** *n.* breath that smells. **bad company** *n.* **1** a person who is boring or not fun to be with. **2** a person who is not suitable as a friend, or a group of such people. **bad debt** *n.* a debt that cannot be recovered. **baddish** *a.* **baddy, baddie** *n.* (*pl.* **baddies**) (*coll.*) a criminal or wrong-doer, esp. an evil character in fiction, cinema, television or radio. **bad egg, bad penny** *n.* **1** a bad speculation. **2** a ne'er-do-well. **bad faith** *n.* intent to deceive. **bad form** *n.* **1** bad manners. **2** lack of breeding. **bad hair day** *n.* (*sl.*) a day on which one would rather not face the world, a day on which everything seems to go wrong for one. **bad job** *n.* (*coll.*) a sad or unfortunate turn of affairs. **badlands** *n.pl.* **1** tracts of arid country in the western states of America. **2** unsafe parts of a country. **bad lot** *n.* a disreputable person, a person of bad character. **badly** *adv.* (*comp.* **worse,** *superl.* **worst**) **1** in a bad manner. **2** improperly, wickedly, evilly. **3** unskilfully, imperfectly. **4** defectively. **5** faultily. **6** dangerously, disastrously. **7** (*coll.*) very much, by much. **bad mouth** *n.* (*coll.*) malicious gossip, abuse. **bad-mouth** *v.t.* (*coll.*) to abuse, to criticize. **badness** *n.* **bad news** *n.* (*coll.*) a person who or thing that is undesirable. **bad temper** *n.* an angry mood, a tendency to anger. **bad-tempered** *a.* irritable or ungracious. **bad-temperedly** *adv.*

bade BID.

badge (baj) *n.* **1** a distinctive mark, sign or token. **2** an emblem sewn on clothing. **3** (*Her.*) a cognizance. **4** a feature or quality that characterizes. ~*v.t.* to mark with or as with a badge.

badger (baj´ə) *n.* **1** a nocturnal plantigrade mammal of the weasel family, with thick body and short legs and a head with two stripes, *Meles meles,* found in Britain, Europe and Asia. **2** a related mammal, *Taxidea taxus,* found in N America. **3** a painter's brush, or angler's fly, made of badgers' hair. ~*v.t.* to worry, to tease, to annoy like dogs baiting a badger.

badinage (bad´inahzh, -nij) *n.* light good-humoured, playful talk, banter.

badminton (bad´mintən) *n.* **1** a game resembling tennis, but played, usu. indoors, with shuttlecocks instead of balls. **2** a kind of claret-cup.

baffle (baf´əl) *v.t.* **1** to bewilder, perplex, confound. **2** to thwart, defeat. **3** to frustrate, elude, escape, circumvent. **4** to regulate the volume or flow of. ~*n.* **1** a defeat. **2** a rigid appliance that regulates the distribution of sound-waves from a producer. **baffle board** *n.* a device to prevent the carrying of noise, esp. to prevent sound from spreading in different directions. **bafflement** *n.* **baffler** *n.* **baffling** *a.* **bafflingly** *adv.*

BAFTA (baf´tə) *abbr.* British Academy of Film and Television Arts.

bag (bag) *n.* **1** a pouch, small sack or other flexible receptacle. **2** a measure of quantity, varying with different commodities. **3** the contents of such a measure. **4** a game-bag, the result of a day's sport or of a hunting expedition. **5** a purse, a money-bag. **6** an item of luggage; a handbag. **7** a sac or baglike receptacle in animal bodies containing some secretion; an udder. **8** (*pl.*) folds of skin under the eyes. **9** (*pl.*) loose clothes, esp. trousers. **10** (*pl., coll.*) quantities. **11** (*sl., derog.*) a slovenly, bad-tempered or ugly woman, often in *old bag.* ~*v.t.* **1** to put into a bag. **2** to take, seize, appropriate. **3** (*coll.*) to steal. **4** (*coll.*) to claim by speaking first (*Bags I get breakfast first tomorrow*). **5** to shoot or catch for a game-bag. ~*v.i.* (*pres.p.* **bagging,** *past, p.p.* **bagged**) **1** to swell as a bag. **2** to hang loosely. **3** (*Naut.*) to drop away from the direct course. **in the bag** (*coll.*) secured or as good as secured. **bag and baggage** *n.* **1** with all belongings. **2** entirely, completely. **bagful** *n.* (*pl.* **bagfuls**) **baggy** *a.* (*comp.* **baggier,** *superl.* **baggiest**) **1** loose. **2** bulging out like a bag. **3** (of trousers etc.) stretched by wear. **baggily** *adv.* **bagginess** *n.* **bag lady** *n.* (*pl.* **bag ladies**) (*coll.*) a female vagrant. **bagman** *n.* (*pl.* **bagmen**) **1** (*coll.*) a travelling salesman. **2** a vagrant. **3** (*NAm., sl.*) a person who collects and transports money for gangsters. **4** (*Can.*) a fund-raiser for a political party. **bag of bones** *n.* a living skeleton, someone very thin. **bag of nerves** *n.* (*coll.*) BUNDLE OF NERVES (under BUNDLE). **bagworm** *n.* a caterpillar or larva of the family Psychidae, which forms a protective covering from silk, leaves etc. **bagworm moth** *n.* a moth of the bagworm family.

❌ **bagage** common misspelling of BAGGAGE.

bagasse (bəgas´) *n.* the refuse products in sugar-making.

bagatelle (bagətel´) *n.* **1** a game played on a nine-holed board with pins obstructing the holes, with nine balls to be struck into them. **2** a trifle, a negligible amount. **3** (*Mus.*) a light piece of music.

bagel (bā´gəl) *n.* a ring-shaped bread roll.

baggage (bag´ij) *n.* **1** luggage; belongings packed for travelling. **2** portable belongings, esp. the tents, furniture, utensils and other necessaries of an army. **3** knowledge and experience as encumbrances. **4** a woman of loose character. **5** (*facet. or derog.*) a playful arch young woman.

bagnio (han´yō) *n.* (*pl.* **bagnios**) **1** a brothel. **2** an oriental prison for slaves.

bagpipe (bag´pīp) *n.* a musical instrument of great antiquity, now chiefly used in the Scottish Highlands, consisting of a windbag and several reed-pipes into which the air is pressed by the player. **bagpiper** *n.*

baguette (baget´), **baguet** *n.* **1** a narrow stick of French bread. **2** a precious stone cut into a rectangular shape. **3** (*Archit.*) a small semicircular moulding.

bah (bah) *int.* expressing contempt.

bahadur (bəhah´duə) *n.* a ceremonious title formerly given in India to officers and distinguished officials.

Baha'i (bəhah´ī) *n.* (*pl.* **Baha'is**) a follower of a religious movement originating in Iran in the 19th cent., which stresses the validity of all world religions and the spiritual unity of all humanity. **Baha'ism** *n.* **Baha'ist** *n.*

Bahamian (bəhā´miən) *n.* **1** a native or inhabitant of the Bahamas. **2** a person descended from Bahamians. ~*a.* of or relating to the Bahamas.

baht (baht) *n.* (*pl.* **baht**) the standard unit of currency in Thailand.

Bahutu HUTU.

bail¹ (bāl) *n.* **1** (*Law*) **a** the temporary release of a prisoner from custody on security given for their due surrender when required. **b** the money security, or the person or persons giving security, for the due surrender of a prisoner temporarily released. **2** security, guarantee. ~*v.t.* **1** to procure the liberation of (a prisoner) by giving sureties. **2** to admit to or release on bail. **3** to deliver (goods) in trust on an expressed or implied contract. **to bail out 1** (*Law*) to procure release on bail from prison. **2** to rescue from difficulty. **bailable** *a.* **bail bandit** *n.* an offender who breaks the law while on bail. **bailment** *n.* **1** delivery of goods. **2** delivery in trust. **3** the bailing of a prisoner. **bailout** *n.* financial help given to a person or company to prevent collapse. **bailsman** *n.* (*pl.* **bailsmen**) a person who gives bail.

bail² (bāl) *n.* **1** in cricket, either of the crosspieces laid on top of the wicket. **2** a division between the stalls of a stable. **3** (*Austral., New Zeal.*) a framework for securing the head of a cow while she is being milked. **4** a bar on a typewriter that holds the paper in position. ~*v.i.* to surrender by throwing up the arms. ~*v.t.* **1** to make (a person) surrender by throwing up their arms. **2** (*Austral., New Zeal.*) to fasten (up) the head of (a cow) for milking. **3** to buttonhole.

bail³ (bāl), **bale** *v.t.* **1** to throw (water) out of a boat with a shallow vessel. **2** to empty (a boat) of water. **to bail out** BALE³. **bailer** *n.* a person or thing that bails water out of a boat etc.

bailee (bālē´) *n.* (*Law*) a person to whom goods are entrusted for a specific purpose.

bailey (bā´li) *n.* (*pl.* **baileys**) **1** the wall enclosing the outer court of a feudal castle. **2** the outer court itself. **3** any other courts or enclosures of courts (*the outer bailey; the inner bailey*).

Bailey bridge (bā´li) *n.* (*Mil.*) a bridge of lattice steel construction made of standard parts for rapid erection and transport.

bailie (bā´li) *n.* **1** a Scottish municipal magistrate corresponding to an English alderman. **2** †a Scottish magistrate with duties corresponding to those of an English sheriff.

bailiff (bā´lif) *n.* **1** a sheriff's officer who executes writs and distrains. **2** an agent or steward to a landowner. **3** (*Law*) **a** (*N Am.*) a courtroom official who keeps order etc. **b** an officer appointed for the administration of justice in a certain bailiwick or district.

bailiwick (bā´liwik) *n.* **1** (*Law*) the district within which a bailie or bailiff possesses jurisdiction. **2** (*coll., esp. facet.*) the range of a person's interest or authority.

bailor (bā´lə) *n.* (*Law*) a person who entrusts another person with goods for a specific purpose.

bain-marie (bāmərē´) *n.* (*pl.* **bains-marie** (bāmərē´)) a vessel of boiling water into which saucepans are put for slow heating; a double saucepan.

Bairam (bīram´) *n.* either of two Muslim festivals following the Ramadan, the *Lesser* lasting three days, the *Greater*, which lasts seventy days later, lasting four days.

bairn (beən) *n.* (*Sc. or North.*) a child.

bait (bāt) *v.t.* **1** to furnish (a hook, gin, snare etc.) with real or sham food to entice prey. **2** to tempt, entice, allure. **3** to set dogs to worry (an animal). **4** to worry, harass, torment. **5** to give food to (a horse) on a journey, to feed. ~*v.i.* to stop on a journey for rest or refreshment. ~*n.* **1** an attractive morsel put on a hook, gin, snare etc., to attract fish or animals. **2** worms, insects, grubs, small fish etc., so used. **3** food, refreshment on a journey. **4** a halt for refreshment. **5** a temptation, allurement. **6** BATE¹.

baize (bāz) *n.* a coarse woollen material something like felt.

bajra (bahj´rə) *n.* a type of Indian millet.

bake (bāk) *v.t.* **1** to cook by dry conducted (as opposed to radiated) heat, to cook in an oven or on a heated surface. **2** to dry and harden by means of fire or by the sun's rays. ~*v.i.* **1** to cook food by baking. **2** to undergo the process of baking. **3** to become dry and hard by heat. **4** (of a person, weather etc.) to be very hot, be affected by the heat of the sun. **baked** *a.* that has been baked. **baked Alaska** *n.* a dessert of ice-cream covered with meringue baked in an oven. **baked beans** *n.pl.* haricot beans baked and usu. tinned in tomato sauce. **bakehouse** *n.* a house or building in which baking is carried on. **baker** *n.* a person whose occupation is to bake bread, biscuits etc. **baker's dozen** *n.* thirteen. **bakery** *n.* (*pl.* **bakeries**) **1** the trade or calling of a baker. **2** a bakehouse. **3** a baker's establishment. **baking** n. **1** the action of cooking by dry heat. **2** the quantity baked at one operation. **baking powder** n. a powder of bicarbonate of soda and tartaric acid used as a raising agent. **baking soda** n. sodium bicarbonate.

Bakelite® (bā´kəlīt) n. a synthetic resin made from formaldehyde and phenol, used for insulating purposes and in the manufacture of plastics, paints and varnishes.

Bakewell tart (bāk´wel) n. an open tart with a pastry base, containing jam and almond paste.

baklava (bəklah´və), **baclava** n. a cake made from layered pastry strips with nuts and honey.

baksheesh (bak´shēsh), **bakhshish, backsheesh** n. a gratuity, a tip (used without the article).

balaclava (baləklah´və), **balaclava helmet** n. a tight woollen covering for the head, ears, chin and neck.

balalaika (baləlī´kə) n. a three-stringed triangular-shaped musical instrument resembling a guitar.

balance (bal´əns) n. **1** (often pl.) a pair of scales. **2** any other instrument used for weighing. **3** equipoise, an equality of weight or power; stability. **4** the amount necessary to make two unequal amounts equal. **5** the difference between the debtor and creditor side of the account. **6** (esp. Mus.) harmony of design, perfect proportion; desirable relative volume. **7** (coll.) the remainder, the residue. **8** a contrivance for regulating the speed of a clock or watch. **9** an impartial state of mind. **10** that which renders weight or authority equal. **11** a zodiacal constellation, Libra. **12** the seventh sign of the zodiac, which the sun enters at the autumnal equinox. ~v.t. **1** to weigh. **2** to compare by weighing. **3** to compare. **4** to bring to an equipoise, to equalize, to steady. **5** to adjust an account, to make two amounts equal. **6** to sway backwards and forwards. ~v.i. **1** to be in equipoise, to have equal weight or force. **2** to have the debtor and creditor side equal. **3** to oscillate. **in the balance** in an uncertain or undecided state. **on balance** taking all factors into consideration. **to strike a balance** to reckon up the balance on a statement of credit and indebtedness. **balanced** a. **1** having good balance. **2** sane, sensible (often in comb., such as well-balanced). **balance of payments** n. the difference over a period of time between the total payments (for goods and services) to, and total receipts from, abroad. **balance of power** n. **1** a condition of equilibrium among sovereign states, supposed to be a guarantee of peace. **2** a condition of having power because other greater powers are equal. **balance of trade** n. the difference between the imports and exports of a country. **balancer** n. **balance sheet** n. a tabular statement of accounts, showing receipts and expenditure. **balance wheel** n. the wheel regulating the beat in clocks, watches etc. **balancing act** n. the act of achieving a balance between different needs or situations

(*Trying to keep all the children happy required quite a balancing act*).

balata (bal´ətə) n. **1** any of various Central American trees which yield latex, esp. *Mankara bidentata*. **2** the dried latex of this.

balboa (balbō´ə) n. the unit of currency in Panama.

balcony (bal´kəni) n. (pl. **balconies**) **1** a gallery or platform projecting from a house or other building. **2** in theatres, a tier of seats between the dress circle and the gallery. **3** (*NAm.*) the dress circle. **balconied** a.

bald (bawld) a. **1** without hair upon the crown of the head. **2** (of species of birds, animals etc.) having no feathers or hair on the head. **3** bare, treeless, leafless. **4** (coll.) (of a tyre etc.) having a worn-away surface. **5** (of horses) streaked or marked with white. **6** trivial, meagre. **7** destitute of ornament or grace. **8** undisguised, shameless. **bald eagle** n. the American white-headed eagle, *Haliaeetus leucocephalus*, the emblem of the US. **baldhead** n. a person who is bald. **bald-headed** a. with a bald head. **balding** a. going bald. **baldish** a. **baldly** adv. **1** in a bald manner. **2** nakedly, shamelessly, inelegantly. **3** plainly. **baldmoney** n. (pl. **baldmoneys**) SPIGNEL. **baldness** n. **baldy, baldie** n. (pl. **baldies**) (coll.) a person who is bald. ~a. bald.

balderdash (bawl´dədash) n. **1** rubbish, nonsense. **2** confused speech or writing.

baldric (bawl´drik), **baudric** (bawd´-) n. a richly ornamented girdle or belt, passing over one shoulder and under the opposite, to support dagger, sword, bugle etc.

bale¹ (bāl) n. **1** a package. **2** a certain quantity of goods or merchandise, wrapped in cloth or baling-paper and corded for transportation. ~v.t. to pack in a bale or bales. **baler** n. a machine that makes bales of hay, straw etc.

†bale² (bāl) n. (also poet.) **1** evil, mischief, calamity. **2** pain, sorrow, misery. **baleful** a. **1** full of evil. **2** pernicious, harmful, deadly. **balefully** adv. **balefulness** n.

bale³ (bāl), **bail** v.i. (followed by out) to abandon an aeroplane in the air and descend by parachute. ~v.t. (followed by out) to help out of a difficulty.

baleen (bəlēn´) n. whalebone. ~a. of whalebone. **baleen whale** n. a whale of the suborder Mysticeti having plates of whalebone in its mouth, with which it filters plankton.

☒ **balence** common misspelling of BALANCE.

Balinese (bahlinēz´) n. (pl. **Balinese**) **1** a native or inhabitant of Bali. **2** (as pl.) the people of Bali. **3** the language spoken by the people of Bali. ~a. of or relating to Bali.

balk BAULK.

Balkan (bawl´kən) a. of or relating to the region of SE Europe which includes the Balkan Peninsula. **the Balkans** the Balkan countries. **Balkanize** (bawl´kənīz), **Balkanise** v.t. to split (a region) into a number of smaller and often mutually hostile states, as occurred in the Balkan Peninsula during the 19th and early 20th cents. **Balkanization** (-zā´shən) n.

ball[1] (bawl) n. **1** a spherical body of any dimensions, a globe. **2** such a body, differing in size, make and hardness, used in games. **3** anything made, rolled or packed into a spherical shape. **4** a rounded natural object or part of the body; a planetary or celestial body (usu. with qualifying adjective). **5** (pl., taboo sl.) testicles. **6** (pl., sl.) courage, nerve. **7** (pl., sl.) a mess, a bungle. **8** a globular body of wood, ivory or other substance used for voting by ballot. **9** a throw, delivery, pass or cast of the ball in games. ~v.t. **1** to make, roll or pack into a ball. **2** to clog (as a horse's foot with a collection of snow). ~v.i. **1** to gather into a ball. **2** to become clogged. **3** (of bees) to cluster round the queen when they swarm. **on the ball 1** alert. **2** in control. **to balls up** to mess up or botch (a situation). **to keep/ start the ball rolling** to keep the conversation, debate, work or game from flagging. **to make a balls of** (sl.) to make a mess of; to botch, to do badly. **to play ball** (coll.) to cooperate (I've asked him, but he just won't play ball). **ball-and-socket joint** n. **1** a joint formed by a ball playing in a socket, and admitting of motion in any direction. **2** joints like those of the human hip and shoulder. **ball-bearing** n. **1** (usu. pl.) a bearing containing loose metallic balls for lessening friction. **2** a metal ball used in such a bearing. **ballboy** n. a boy who retrieves the balls that go out of play in a game of tennis. **ballcock, balltap** n. a self-acting tap which is turned off or on by the rising or falling of a hollow ball on the surface of the water in a cistern, boiler etc. **ballgame** n. **1** a game played with a ball. **2** (N Am.) baseball. **a different ballgame** (coll.) something quite different. **ballgirl** n. a girl who retrieves the balls that go out of play in a game of tennis. **ball lightning** n. floating luminous balls sometimes seen during thunderstorms. **ballpark** n. **1** a park or field where ballgames are played. **2** (N Am.) a baseball field. **3** (coll.) a sphere of activity. **in the right ballpark** (coll.) approximately right, on the right lines. **ballpark figure** n. (coll.) an approximate amount. **ballpoint (pen)** n. a pen with a tiny ball in place of a nib as its writing point. **balls!** int. (sl.) nonsense. **balls-up** n. (taboo sl.) **1** a mess. **2** a botched situation. **ballsed-up** a. **ballsy** (bawl´zi) a. (comp. **ballsier**, superl. **ballsiest**) (sl.) manly or brave, gutsy. **ball valve** n. a valve opened or closed by the rising of a ball.

ball[2] (bawl) n. a social assembly for dancing. **to have a ball** (coll.) to have a good time. **ballroom** n. a room used for balls. **ballroom dancing** n. formal social dancing to dances such as the foxtrot, tango and two-step.

ballad (bal´əd) n. **1** a light simple song, esp. a slow sentimental one. **2** a popular song, generally of a personal or political character, formerly printed as a broadside. **3** a simple spirited poem usu. narrating some popular or patriotic story.

balladeer (-diə´) n. a ballad-singer, a composer of ballads. **ballad metre** n. common metre. **balladry** n. **1** the ballad style of composition. **2** ballads collectively.

ballade (bəlahd´) n. **1** a poem consisting of three eight-lined stanzas rhyming a b a b b c b c, each having the same line as a refrain, and with an envoy of four lines, an old form revived in the 19th cent. **2** (Mus.) a short lyrical piano piece or similar composition.

ballast (bal´əst) n. **1** stones, iron or other heavy substances placed in the bottom of a ship or boat to lower the centre of gravity and make her steady. **2** gravel or other material laid as foundation for a railway, or for making roads. **3** a mixture containing coarse gravel for making concrete. **4** a device for stabilizing an electric current. **5** something which tends to give intellectual or moral stability. **6** (coll.) solid foods, food containing carbohydrate. ~v.t. **1** to furnish with ballast; to lay or pack with ballast. **2** to steady, to give stability to.

ballerina (balərē´nə) n. (pl. **ballerinas**, **ballerine** (-nā)) a female ballet dancer; a female dancer taking a leading part in a ballet.

ballet (bal´ā, -li) n. **1** a form of dramatic representation consisting of dancing and mime to set steps. **2** an example of this. **3** a piece or suite of music for this. **4** a company performing this. **ballet dancer** n. a dancer esp. in ballet. **ballet dancing** n. **balletic** (-et´-) a. **balletomane** (bəlet´əmān) n. an enthusiast for the ballet. **balletomania** (-mā´niə) n.

ballista (bəlis´tə) n. (pl. **ballistae** (-ē), **ballistas**) a military engine used in ancient times for hurling stones, darts and other missiles.

ballistic (bəlis´tik) a. **1** of or relating to the hurling and flight of projectiles. **2** moving by gravity alone. **to go ballistic** (sl.) to become explosively angry, lose one's temper. **ballistically** adv. **ballistic missile** n. (Mil.) a missile guided over the first part of its course but then descending according to the laws of ballistics. **ballistics** n. the science of the flight of projectiles.

ballocks BOLLOCKS.

ballon d'essai (balõ desā´) n. (pl. **ballons d'essai** (balõ)) a trial balloon.

balloon (bəloon´) n. **1** a spherical or pear-shaped bag of light material, which when filled with heated air or gas rises and floats in the air (to the larger kinds a car is attached, capable of containing several persons, and these balloons are used for scientific observations, reconnoitring etc.). **2** an inflatable rubber bag used as a child's toy or for decoration. **3** a spherical glass receiver, used in distilling; a large spherical drinking glass. **4** a frame or trellis on which trees or plants are trained. **5** the shape into which fruit trees are trained. **6** a line enclosing the words or thoughts of a cartoon character. ~v.i. **1** to go up in a balloon. **2** to swell out. ~v.t. to kick high in the air in a wide arc. **when the balloon goes up** when

the action begins, when the troubles start.
balloon-fish *n.* (*pl. in general* **balloon-fish,** *in particular* **balloon-fishes**) a fish belonging to the genus *Diodon*, members of which are able to distend their bodies with air. **balloonist** *n.*

ballot (bal'ət) *n.* **1** the method or system of secret voting. **2** the total votes recorded. **3** a ticket, paper or other instrument (*orig.* a ball) used to give a secret vote. **4** drawing of lots by means of balls or otherwise. ~*v.t.* (*pres.p.* **balloting,** *past, p.p.* **balloted**) **1** to select by drawing lots. **2** to ask to vote secretly, to take a ballot of. ~*v.i.* **1** to vote secretly, to hold a ballot. **2** to draw lots. **ballot box** *n.* a box into which ballots are put in voting, or from which balls are taken in drawing lots. **ballot paper** *n.* a voting-paper used in voting by ballot.

bally (bal'i) *a.* (*sl., euphem.*) bloody.

ballyhoo (balihoo') *n.* **1** noisy and unprincipled propaganda. **2** a great fuss about nothing.

ballyrag (bal'irag), **bullyrag** (bul'irag) *v.t.* (*pres.p.* **ballyragging, bullyragging,** *past, p.p.* **ballyragged, bullyragged**) (*sl.*) **1** to revile, abuse, assail with violent language. **2** to victimize with practical jokes.

balm (bahm) *n.* **1** the fragrant juice, sap or gum of certain trees or plants. **2** fragrant ointment or oil. **3** anything which soothes pain, irritation or distress. **4** perfume, fragrance. **5** a plant of the genus *Balsamodendron*, which yields balm. **6** any of several fragrant garden herbs. ~*v.t.* **1** to anoint or impregnate with balm. **2** to soothe, to assuage. **Balm of Gilead** (gil'iad) *n.* **1** a resin formerly in use as an antiseptic and soothing ointment. **2** any tree of the genus *Commiphora*, from which such resin may be obtained. **3** the balsam fir or balsam poplar. **balmy** *a.* (*comp.* **balmier,** *superl.* **balmiest**) **1** producing balm. **2** impregnated with or having the qualities of balm. **3** soft, soothing, healing. **4** fragrant, mild. **5** (*sl.*) rather idiotic, daft, silly. **balmily** *adv.* **balminess** *n.*

Balmoral (balmor'əl) *n.* **1** (*also* **Balmoral bonnet**) a kind of Scottish cap. **2** (*pl.*) heavy walking boots, laced in front.

balneology (balniol'əji) *n.* the science of treating diseases by bathing and medicinal springs. **balneological** (-loj'-) *a.* **balneologist** *n.*

baloney (bəlō'ni), **boloney** *n.* (*pl.* **baloneys, boloneys**) **1** (*sl.*) idiotic talk, nonsense. **2** (*NAm.*) BOLOGNA.

balsa (bawl'sə) *n.* **1** an American tropical tree, *Ochroma lagopus*. **2** balsa wood. **balsa wood** *n.* light, strong wood from this tree used for rafts, model aircraft etc.

balsam (bawl'səm) *n.* **1** a vegetable resin with a strong fragrant odour, balm. **2** a tree or shrub yielding a resin of this kind. **3** any plant of the genus *Impatiens*, as garden balsam, *I. balsamina*. **4** a medicinal preparation made with oil or resin for applying to wounds or soothing pain. **5** any of other various preparations of resins mixed with volatile oils. **6** anything that possesses

healing or soothing qualities. **balsam fir** *n.* a N American fir, *Abies balsamea*, which yields Canada balsam. **balsamic** (-sam'-) *a.* having the qualities of balsam. **balsamic vinegar** *n.* a dark, sweet, Italian vinegar used esp. in salad dressings. **balsam poplar** *n.* a N American poplar, *Populus balsamifera*, that yields balsam.

Balti (bal'ti) *n.* a type of curry composed of meat and vegetables cooked in an iron pot.

Baltic (bawl'tik) *a.* **1** denoting, of or relating to a sea in N Europe or its bordering countries. **2** of or denoting Baltic as a group of languages. ~*n.* **1** the area around the Baltic sea. **2** a branch of the Indo-European languages comprising Latvian, Lithuanian, Lettish and Old Prussian.

baluster (bal'əstə) *n.* **1** a small column, usu. circular, swelling towards the bottom, and forming part of a series called a balustrade. **2** a post supporting a handrail, a banister. **balustrade** (-strād) *n.* a range of balusters, resting on a plinth, supporting a coping or rail, and serving as a protection, barrier, ornament etc. **balustraded** *a.*

bambino (bambē'nō) *n.* (*pl.* **bambinos, bambini** (-ni)) **1** a child, a baby. **2** an image of the infant Jesus in the crib, exhibited at Christmas in Roman Catholic churches.

bamboo (bamboo') *n.* (*pl.* **bamboos**) **1** any giant tropical grass of the subfamily Bambusidae. **2** the stem of such grass used as a stick, thatch, building material etc. **bamboo shoot** *n.* an edible shoot of young bamboo.

bamboozle (bamboo'zəl) *v.t.* **1** to mystify for purposes of fraud; to cheat, to swindle. **2** to bewilder, confuse. **bamboozler** *n.*

ban (ban) *v.t.* (*pres.p.* **banning,** *past, p.p.* **banned**) **1** to interdict, to proscribe. **2** †to curse, anathematize. ~*v.i.* to utter curses. ~*n.* **1** a formal prohibition. **2** a public proclamation. **3** an edict of excommunication, an interdict. **4** a curse, a formal anathematization.

banal (bənahl') *a.* commonplace, trite, petty. **banality** (-nal'-) *n.* (*pl.* **banalities**) **1** a commonplace, trite remark. **2** commonplaceness, triviality.

banana[1] (bənah'nə) *n.* **1** a tropical and subtropical treelike plant, *Musa sapientum*, closely allied to the plantain. **2** the fruit of this, a large, elongated berry, growing in clusters. **to be/ go bananas** (*sl.*) to be or go insane. **banana republic** *n.* (*derog.*) a small tropical country, politically unstable, economically dependent on the export of fruit, and dominated by foreign capital. **banana skin** *n.* **1** the skin of a banana. **2** any episode or occurrence which leads to humiliation or embarrassment, esp. in a political context. **banana split** *n.* a dessert consisting of a banana sliced length-wise and filled with ice-cream, cream etc. **banana tree** *n.*

banana[2] (bənah'nə) *n.* (*coll.*) an opponent of all further construction on and development of land.

banausic (bɘnaw´sik) *a.* (*derog.*) **1** mechanical, considered merely fit for a mechanic; uncultured. **2** materialistic.

Banbury cake (ban´bɘri) *n.* a kind of pastry cake filled with mincemeat, supposed to be made at Banbury in Oxfordshire.

banc (bangk), **banco** (-ō) *n.* (*Law*) the judicial bench. **in banc** sitting (as a Superior Court of Common Law) as a full court.

band[1] (band) *n.* **1** a flat slip or band (BAND[2]), used to bind together, encircle or confine, or as part of an article of apparel. **2** a transverse stripe. **3** a specific range of frequencies or wavelengths. **4** a classificatory range or division. **5** a simple gold ring. **6** a broad, endless strap for communicating motion. **7** a track of a record or magnetic tape. **8** a division of pupils according to ability. **9** (*pl.*) a pair of linen strips hanging down in front of the collar and forming part of clerical, legal or academical dress. **10** the collar of a shirt, a collar or ruff. **11** a bandage. **12** (*Geol.*) a bandlike stratum. **13** (*Bot.*) a space between any two ribs on the fruit of umbellifers. **14** a slip of canvas used to strengthen the parts of a sail most liable to pressure. **Band-Aid**® *n.* a small adhesive plaster with a medicated gauze pad. **band-aid** *n.* a stopgap, a thing used as a temporary solution. ~*a.* (of measures etc.) temporary. **bandbox** *n.* a box of cardboard or other thin material for holding collars, hats, millinery etc., originally used for bands or ruffs. **bandpass** *n.* the range of frequencies transmitted through a filter. **bandsaw** *n.* an endless steel saw, running rapidly over wheels. **bandwidth** *n.* **1** the range of frequencies used for a particular radio transmission. **2** the range of frequencies within which an amplifier (or other electronic device) operates most efficiently.

†**band**[2] (band) *n.* that which binds, confines or restrains.

band[3] (band) *n.* **1** a company of musicians playing together. **2** an organized company; a confederation. **3** an assemblage of people. **4** (*N Am.*) a herd, a flock. **bandleader** *n.* the leader of a band of musicians. **bandmaster** *n.* the leader or conductor of a band of musicians. **bandsman** *n.* (*pl.* **bandsmen**) a member of a band of musicians. **bandstand** *n.* an elevated platform for the use of a band of musicians. **bandwagon** *n.* the musicians' wagon in a circus parade. **to climb/ jump on the bandwagon** to try to be on the winning side.

band[4] (band) *v.t.* **1** to bind or fasten with a band. **2** to mark with a band. **3** to form into a band, troop or society. ~*v.i.* to unite, to assemble.

bandage (ban´dij) *n.* **1** a strip of flexible material used to bind up wounds, fractures etc. **2** the operation of bandaging. **3** a strip of flexible material used to cover up something. ~*v.t.* to bind up with a bandage.

bandanna (bandan´ɘ), **bandana** *n.* **1** a silk handkerchief of a type orig. of Indian manufacture, having white or yellow spots on a coloured ground. **2** a cotton handkerchief or neckerchief similarly printed.

B. & B., **b. and b.** *abbr.* bed and breakfast.

bandeau (ban´dō) *n.* (*pl.* **bandeaux** (-dōz)) a narrow band or fillet for the head.

banderilla (bandɘrē´yɘ, -rēl´-) *n.* a little dart ornamented with ribbons, which bullfighters stick in the neck of the bull. **banderillero** *n.* (*pl.* **banderilleros**) a bullfighter who sticks banderillas into the bull.

banderole (ban´dɘrōl), **banderol** *n.* **1** a long narrow flag with a cleft end flying at a masthead. **2** any small ornamental streamer. **3** a flat band with an inscription, used in the decoration of buildings of the Renaissance period.

bandicoot (ban´dikoot) *n.* **1** (*also* **bandicoot rat**) a large Asian rat of the genus *Bandicota*. **2** a marsupial of the family Peramelidae, which has some resemblance to this.

banding (ban´ding) *n.* **1** the action of binding or marking with a band. **2** the formation of bands; the state of being banded. **3** a banded pattern or structure.

bandit (ban´dit) *n.* (*pl.* **bandits, banditti** (-dit´ē)) **1** a person who is proscribed, an outlaw. **2** a brigand. **banditry** *n.*

bandog (ban´dog) *n.* an aggressive cross-breed fighting dog.

bandolier (bandɘliɘ´), **bandoleer** *n.* a belt worn over the right shoulder and across the breast, with little leather loops to receive cartridges.

bandy[1] (ban´di) *v.t.* (*pres.p.* **bandying**, *past, p.p.* **bandied**) **1** to beat or throw to and fro as at the game of tennis or bandy. **2** to toss to and fro or toss about like a ball. **3** to give and take, to exchange (esp. blows, arguments etc.). ~*n.* **1** the game of hockey. **2** a club, bent and rounded at the lower end, used in this game for striking the ball.

bandy[2] (ban´di) *a.* (*comp.* **bandier**, *superl.* **bandiest**) **1** crooked, bent outwards. **2** bandy-legged. **bandy-legged** *a.* having legs that bend outwards.

bane (bān) *n.* **1** a cause of ruin or mischief. **2** (*poet.*) ruin, destruction, mischief, woe. **3** poison (*chiefly in comb.*, such as *henbane*, *rat's bane* etc.). **baneberry** *n.* (*pl.* **baneberries**) **1** herb Christopher, *Actaea spicata*. **2** the black berries of this, which are very poisonous. **baneful** *a.* **banefully** *adv.*

bang[1] (bang) *v.t.* **1** to slam (a door), fire (a gun), beat (a musical instrument) with a loud noise. **2** to beat with loud blows. **3** to thrash, to thump; to handle roughly, to drub. **4** to cut (the front hair) square across. **5** to beat, to surpass. **6** (*taboo sl.*) to have sexual intercourse with. **7** (*sl.*) to inject (heroin). ~*v.i.* **1** to resound with a loud noise. **2** to jump or bounce up noisily. ~*n.* **1** a sudden explosive noise. **2** a resounding blow, a thump. **3** impulsive motion, a dash. **4** (*taboo sl.*) an act of sexual intercourse. **5** (*sl.*) an injection of heroin. **6** the front hair cut straight across. ~*adv.* **1** with a violent blow or noise. **2** suddenly, abruptly, all at once. **3** (*coll.*) exactly. **bang off** (*sl.*) immediately. **bang on** (*coll.*) exactly right. **to bang away at** to do something violently or noisily. **to bang on** (*coll.*) to talk loudly or at great length. **to bang up** (*sl.*) to imprison or lock up. **to go (off) with a bang** to go very well, to succeed. **banger** *n.* **1** a sausage. **2** (*coll.*) a decrepit old car. **3** a small explosive firework. **4** (*sl.*) a very fine and exceptional specimen. **5** a cudgel. **bangtail** *n.* a horse with tail cut off square. **bangtail muster** *n.* (*Austral.*) the counting of cattle in which each one has its tail docked as it is counted. **bang-up** *a.* (*sl.*) fine, first-rate.

Bangladeshi (bang-glədesh´i) *n.* (*pl.* **Bangladeshi, Bangladeshis**) **1** a native or inhabitant of Bangladesh. **2** (*as pl.*) the people of Bangladesh. ~*a.* of or relating to Bangladesh.

bangle (bang´gəl) *n.* a ring-bracelet or anklet.

banian BANYAN.

banish (ban´ish) *v.t.* **1** to condemn to exile. **2** to drive out or away, to expel. **banishment** *n.*

banister (ban´istə) *n.* **1** a shaft or upright supporting a handrail at the side of a staircase. **2** (*pl.*) the whole railing protecting the outer side of a staircase.

banjo (ban´jō) *n.* (*pl.* **banjos, banjoes**) a stringed musical instrument, having a head and neck like a guitar and a body like a tambourine, and played with the fingers. **banjoist** *n.*

bank¹ (bangk) *n.* **1** a raised shelf or ridge of ground. **2** a mound with steeply sloping sides. **3** a shelving elevation of sand, gravel etc., in the sea or in a river. **4** the margin or shore of a river. **5** the ground near a river. **6** an embankment. **7** the sides of a road, cutting or any hollow. **8** an incline on a railway. **9** a bed of shellfish. **10** a long flat-topped mass, as of ice, snow, cloud or the like. ~*v.t.* **1** to form a bank to. **2** to confine within a bank or banks; to embank. **3** to form into a bank. **4** to cause (an aircraft) to incline inwards at a high angle in turning. **5** to bring to land. ~*v.i.* **1** to rise into banks. **2** (of an aircraft etc.) to incline inwards at a high angle in turning. **to bank up** to make up (a fire) by putting on and pressing down fuel.

bank² (bangk) *n.* **1** an establishment which deals in money, receiving it on deposit from customers and investing it. **2** a building operated by such an establishment. **3** in gaming, the money which the proprietor of the table, or player who plays against the rest, has before them. **4** any store or reserve of material or information (*blood bank*). **5** a child's box for saving money in, a piggy bank. ~*v.i.* **1** to keep a bank. **2** to act as a banker. **3** to be a depositor in a bank. **4** in gaming, to form a bank, to challenge all comers. **5** (*coll.*) to count or depend (on). ~*v.t.* **1** to deposit in a bank. **2** to realize, convert into money. **to break the bank** to win the limit set by the management of a gambling house for a particular period. **bankable** *a.* **1** capable of being banked. **2** guaranteed to

produce a profit. **3** guaranteed to be trustworthy. **bank account** *n.* a facility at a bank etc. that enables a customer to deposit, hold and withdraw money. **bank balance** *n.* the amount of money in a bank account. **bank bill** *n.* **1** (*Hist.*) a bill drawn by one bank on another, payable on demand or at some specified time. **2** (*N Am.*) a bank note. **bankbook** *n.* a passbook in which the cashier enters the debits and credits of a customer. **bank card** *n.* CHEQUE CARD (under CHEQUE). **banker** *n.* **1** a proprietor of a bank. **2** a person involved in banking. **3** a person who keeps the bank at a gaming-table. **4** the dealer in certain card games. **5** a gambling card game. **6** an identical result forecast in several entries on a football-pool coupon. **banker's card** *n.* a card issued by a bank guaranteeing payment of cheques up to a certain limit. **banker's order** *n.* an instruction to a bank to pay money etc., signed by a representative of the bank. **bank holiday** *n.* a day on which all banks are legally closed, usu. observed as a national holiday. **banking** *n.* the business engaged in by a bank. **bank machine** *n.* a cash dispenser. **bank manager** *n.* a person who is in charge of a branch of a bank. **bank note** *n.* a note issued by a bank and payable on demand. **bankroll** *n.* (*orig. N Am.*) **1** a supply of money. **2** a sum of money used to buy or invest in something. ~*v.t.* to supply the funding for (a purchase or investment). **bank statement** *n.* a list showing the transactions carried out by the holder of a bank account. **bank stock** *n.* the capital stock of a bank.

bank³ (bangk) *n.* **1** the bench for rowers, or a tier of oars, in a galley. **2** a bench or table used in various trades. **3** a row of keys on an organ.

bankrupt (bangk´rŭpt) *n.* **1** (*Law*) **a** a person who, becoming insolvent, is judicially required to surrender their estates to be administered for the benefit of their creditors. **b** an insolvent debtor. **2** a person lacking in some necessary or desirable quality or at the end of their resources. ~*a.* **1** (*Law*) **a** judicially declared a bankrupt. **b** insolvent. **2** without credit, lacking some necessary or desirable quality; at the end of one's resources. ~*v.t.* **1** to render (a person) bankrupt. **2** to render insolvent. **3** to reduce to beggary; to discredit. **bankruptcy** (-si) *n.* (*pl.* **bankruptcies**) **1** the state of being bankrupt. **2** the act of declaring oneself bankrupt.

banksia (bangk´siə) *n.* an Australian flowering shrub or tree of the genus *Banksia* of the family Proteaceae. **banksia rose** *n.* a Chinese climbing rose, *Rosa banksiae*.

banner (ban´ə) *n.* **1** an ensign or flag painted with some device or emblem. **2** a flag, generally square, painted or embroidered with the arms of the person in whose honour it is borne. **3** the standard of a feudal lord, used as a rallying-point in battle. **4** an ensign or symbol of principles or fellowship. ~*a.* (*attrib., N Am.*) notable, excellent. **bannered** *a.* **1** furnished with banners.

2 borne on a banner. **banner headline** *n*. a head-line in heavy type running across the entire page of a newspaper.

banneret (ban´ərit) *n*. (*Hist*.) **1** a knight entitled to lead a company of vassals under his banner, ranking above other knights and next below a baron. **2** a title conferred for deeds done in the king's presence on a field of battle.

bannister BANISTER.

bannock (ban´ək) *n*. a flat round cake made of pease- or barley-meal or flour, usu. unleavened.

banns (banz) *n.pl.* proclamation in church of an intended marriage, so that any impediment may be made known and inquired into. **to forbid the banns** to allege an impediment to an intended marriage.

banquet (bang´kwit) *n*. a sumptuous feast, usu. of a ceremonial character and followed by speeches. ~*v.t.* (*pres.p.* **banqueting**, *past, p.p.* **banqueted**) to entertain at a sumptuous feast. ~*v.i.* to take part in a banquet, to feast luxuriously. **banqueter** *n*.

banquette (bāket´) *n*. **1** a built-in cushioned seat along a wall. **2** a bank behind a parapet on which soldiers mount to fire.

banshee (ban´shē) *n*. a supernatural being, supposed in Ireland and the Scottish Highlands to wail round a house when one of the inmates is about to die.

bantam (ban´təm) *n*. **1** a small domestic fowl, of which the cocks are very aggressive. **2** a small and conceited or very pugnacious person. **bantamweight** *n*. **1** a boxer, wrestler, weightlifter etc. in the weight category intermediate between flyweight and featherweight. **2** this weight category.

banter (ban´tə) *v.t.* to ridicule good-humouredly; to rally, to chaff. ~*v.i.* to indulge in good-natured raillery. ~*n.* good-natured raillery, chaff. **banterer** *n*.

Bantu (ban´too) *n*. (*pl.* **Bantu, Bantus**) **1** a group of languages of S and Central Africa. **2** (*Hist., or offensive*) a black S African. **3** (*offensive*) a Bantu speaker. ~*a.* **1** of or relating to these languages. **2** (*offensive*) of or relating to these peoples. **Bantustan** *n*. (*S Afr., coll., derog.*) a S African homeland.

Usage note Because of its association with apartheid, the use of *Bantu* to refer to people has come to be considered highly offensive in South Africa, and is best avoided.

banyan (ban´yan), **banian** (-yən) *n*. **1** a Hindu merchant or shop-keeper, a Bengali broker or hawker. **2** a loose morning-gown or jacket. **3** the banyan tree. **banyan tree** *n*. the Indian fig tree, *Ficus indica*, the branches of which drop shoots to the ground, which taking root support the parent branches and in turn become trunks, so that one tree covers a very large extent of ground.

banzai (ban´zī, -zī´) *int.* a Japanese battle-cry, patriotic salute or cheer. ~*a.* reckless.

baobab (bā´əbab) *n*. **1** an African tree, *Adansonia digitata*, bearing large pulpy fruit. **2** an Australian tree, *Adansonia gregorii*.

bap (bap) *n*. a large soft bread roll.

baptize (baptīz´), **baptise** *v.t.* **1** to sprinkle with or immerse in water as a sign of purification and consecration, esp. into the Christian Church. **2** to christen, to give a name or nickname to. ~*v.i.* to administer baptism. **baptism** (bap´tizm) *n*. **1** the act of baptizing. **2** the ceremony of sprinkling with or immersion in water, by which a person is admitted into the Christian Church. **3** a ceremonial naming of ships, church bells etc. **4** an initiation (ceremony). **baptismal** (-tiz´-) *a.* **baptism of fire** *n*. **1** a soldier's first experience of actual war. **2** a difficult or frightening introduction to something. **baptist** (bap´tist) *n*. **1** a person who baptizes. **2** (**Baptist**) a member of a Christian body who hold that baptism should be administered only to adult believers, and by immersion. **baptistery** (-təri), **baptistry** (-tri) *n*. (*pl.* **baptisteries, baptistries**) **1** the place where baptism is administered, originally a building adjoining the church. **2** the tank used for baptism in Baptist churches.

bar[1] (bah) *n*. **1** a piece of wood, iron or other solid material, long in proportion to breadth; a pole. **2** a transverse piece in a gate, window, door, fire-grate etc. **3** a connecting piece in various structures. **4** a straight stripe, a broad band. **5** an ingot of gold or silver cast in a mould. **6** a similar block of chocolate, soap etc. **7** any thing that constitutes a hindrance or obstruction. **8** a bank of silt, sand or gravel deposited at the mouth of a river or harbour. **9** any immaterial or moral barrier or obstacle. **10** (*Law*) a plea or objection of sufficient force to stop an action. **11** the counter in a public house, hotel or other house or place of refreshment, across which liquors etc. are sold. **12** the room containing this. **13** a rail or barrier, a space marked off by a rail or barrier. **14** a counter or place where foods, goods or services are sold or provided. **15** in a law court, the barrier at which prisoners stand during trial. **16** the railing separating ordinary barristers from Queen's (or King's) Counsel, hence the profession of a barrister. **17** barristers collectively. **18** any tribunal. **19** the barrier cutting off a space near the door in both Houses of Parliament, to which non-members are admitted. **20** (*Mus.*) **a** a vertical line drawn across the stave to divide a composition into parts of equal duration, and to indicate periodical recurrence. **b** the portion contained between two such lines. **21** (*Her.*) two horizontal lines across a shield. **22** a metal strip attached to a medal, indicative of an additional award. ~*v.t.* (*pres.p.* **barring**, *past, p.p.* **barred**) **1** to fasten with a bar or bars. **2** to obstruct, to exclude. **3** to take exception to. **4** to hinder, to prevent. **5** to mark with or form into bars. **6** (*Law*) to stay by objection. **7** to cancel (a claim or right). **8** in betting, to exclude. **9** (*sl.*) to object to, dislike.

behind bars in jail. **to be called within the bar** to be made a Queen's (or King's) Counsel. **to call to the bar** to admit as a barrister. **barbell** *n.* a metal bar with heavy discs at each end used for weight-lifting and exercising. **bar billiards** *n.* a game played esp. in pubs, in which balls are pushed into holes in a special table using a short cue. **bar chart, bar graph** *n.* a graph containing vertical or horizontal bars representing comparative quantities. **bar code** *n.* a compact arrangement of lines of varied lengths and thicknesses which is machine-readable, e.g. printed on supermarket goods or books, giving coded details of price, quantity etc. **barfly** *n.* (*pl.* **barflies**) (*coll.*) a person who spends time in bars. **barfly jumping** *n.* the sport of jumping up and sticking on to a special wall covered in Velcro. **barkeep** *n.* (*N Am.*) **1** a bartender. **2** the owner of a bar. **barkeeper** *n.* (*N Am.*) **1** a bartender. **2** the owner of a bar. **bar line** *n.* (*Mus.*) a vertical line that divides bars. **barmaid** *n.* **1** a female bartender. **2** (*N Am.*) a drinks waitress. **barman** *n.* (*pl.* **barmen**) a male bartender. **bar person** *n.* (*pl.* **bar persons**) a person who works in a pub or bar. **bar room** *n.* the room in a public house in which the bar is situated. **bar stool** *n.* a tall stool at a bar. **bartender** *n.* a person who serves at the bar of a public house, hotel etc. **bartracery** *n.* window tracery characteristic of later Gothic in which the stonework resembles a twisted bar.

bar[2] (bah) *n.* a unit of atmospheric pressure which is equivalent to 10^6 dynes per square centimetre (10^5 newton per square metre).

bar[3] (bah) *prep.* except, apart from. **bar none** without exception.

barathea (barəthē′ə) *n.* a fabric made from wool mixed with silk or cotton, used esp. for coats and suits.

barb (bahb) *n.* **1** the appendages on the mouth of the barbel and other fishes. **2** part of a woman's head-dress, still worn by some nuns. **3** a recurved point, as in a fish-hook or arrow. **4** a point, a sting. **5** a biting or pointed remark or comment. **6** any of the lateral filaments from the shaft of a feather. ~*v.t.* to furnish (fish-hooks, arrows etc.) with barbs. **barbed** *a.* having a barb or barbs; pointed, biting, hurtful. **barbed wire**, (*N Am.*) **barb wire** *n.* wire armed with sharp points, used for fences, to protect front-line trenches or to enclose prison camps. **barbless** *a.*

Barbadian (bahbā′diən) *n.* a native or inhabitant of Barbados. ~*a.* of or relating to Barbados.

barbarian (bahbeə′riən) *n.* **1** a savage, a person belonging to some uncivilized people. **2** a person destitute of pity or humanity. ~*a.* **1** rude, uncivilized, savage. **2** cruel, inhuman. **barbaric** (-bar′-) *a.* **1** of or relating to barbarians. **2** rude, uncouth, uncivilized. **3** cruel, inhuman. **barbarism** (bah′bə-) *n.* **1** absence of civilization. **2** lack of culture or refinement, brutality, cruelty. **3** an impropriety of speech, a solecism, a foreign idiom. **4** an act of barbarism. **barbarity** (-bar′-) *n.*

(*pl.* **barbarities**) **1** brutality, inhumanity, cruelty. **2** an act of brutality or cruelty. **3** the state or quality of being barbaric. **barbarize** (bah′bə-), **barbarise** *v.t.* to render barbarous. ~*v.i.* to grow barbarous. **barbarization** (-zā′shən) *n.* **barbarous** (bah′bə-) *a.* **1** uncivilized. **2** uncultured, unpolished; uncouth. **3** cruel. **barbarously** *adv.* **barbarousness** *n.*

Barbary (bah′bəri) *a.* of or relating to Barbary, an extensive region in the north of Africa. **Barbary ape** *n.* a tailless ape, *Macaca sylvana*, found in the north of Africa, with a colony on the rock of Gibraltar.

barbastelle (bahbəstel′) *n.* a bat of the genus *Barbastella* which roosts in trees or caves.

barbecue (bah′bikū) *n.* **1** an outdoor meal at which food is prepared over a charcoal fire. **2** food, esp. meat, so cooked. **3** a framework on which food is cooked for a barbecue or meat is smoked; a very large grill or gridiron. ~*v.t.* (*pres.p.* **barbecuing**, *past, p.p.* **barbecued**) to cook on a barbecue; to smoke or dry (meat etc.) on a framework over a fire. **barbecue sauce** *n.* a spicy or strong sauce added to barbecued food.

barbel (bah′bəl) *n.* **1** a European freshwater fish, *Barbus vulgaris*, allied to the carp, named from the fleshy filaments which hang below the mouth. **2** the small fleshy filament hanging from the mouth of some fishes, probably organs of touch.

barber (bah′bə) *n.* a person who shaves and cuts beards and hair; a men's hairdresser. ~*v.t.* to shave or dress the hair of. **barber-shop** *n., a.* (denoting) a type of close harmony singing orig. for male voices, usu. quartets. **barber's pole** *n.* a pole, usu. striped spirally, exhibited as a sign in front of a barber's shop.

barberry (bah′bəri), **berberry** (bœ′-) *n.* (*pl.* **barberries**, **berberries**) **1** a shrub of the genus *Berberis*, esp. *B. vulgaris*. **2** the red acid berry of this tree.

barbican (bah′bikən) *n.* an outer fortification to a city or castle, designed as a cover to the inner works, esp. over a gate or bridge and serving as a watchtower.

barbie (bah′bi) *n.* (*esp. Austral., sl.*) a barbecue.

barbituric (bahbitū′rik) *a.* (*Chem.*) denoting an acid obtained from malonic and uric acids. **barbital, barbitone** (bah′bitōn) *n.* (*N Am.*) a derivative of barbituric acid used as a sedative, veronal. **barbiturate** (-bit′ūrət) *n.* any compound with hypnotic and sedative properties derived from barbituric acid.

barbola (bahbō′lə), **barbola work** *n.* **1** the attachment of small flowers etc. in paste to embellish vases etc. **2** articles decorated by this means.

barbule (bah′būl) *n.* a hooked or serrated filament given off from the barb of a feather.

barcarole (bahkərōl′), **barcarolle** *n.* **1** a song sung by Venetian gondoliers. **2** a composition of a similar kind.

barchan (bah´kən) *n.* a shifting sand dune in the shape of a crescent.

bard[1] (bahd) *n.* **1** a Celtic minstrel. **2** a member of an order whose function it was to celebrate heroic achievements, and to perpetuate historical facts and traditions in verse. **3** a poet generally. **4** a poet honoured at a Welsh eisteddfod. **bardic** *a.* **bardolatry** (-dol´ətri) *n.* the worship of Shakespeare.

bard[2] (bahd) *n.* a slice of bacon put on meat or game before roasting. ~*v.t.* to cover with slices of bacon before roasting.

bardy (bah´di) *n.* (*pl.* **bardies**) (*Austral.*) an edible wood-boring grub.

bare (beə) *a.* **1** unclothed, naked, nude. **2** with the head uncovered as a mark of respect. **3** destitute of natural covering, such as hair, fur, flesh, leaves, soil etc. **4** napless. **5** unsheathed. **6** poor, indigent, ill-furnished, empty. **7** simple, mere, unsupported, undisguised, open. **8** bald, meagre. **9** unadorned. ~*v.t.* **1** to strip, to make bare. **2** to uncover, unsheathe. **3** to make manifest. **bare of** without. **with one's bare hands** without using tools or weapons. **bareback** *a., adv.* without a saddle on the horse etc. being ridden. **barefaced** *a.* unconcealed, impudent, shameless. **barefacedly** (-sid-) *adv.* **barefacedness** *n.* **barefoot** *a., adv.* with the feet naked. **barefoot doctor** *n.* a villager, esp. in Asia, who has been trained in basic health care to meet the simple medical needs of the community. **barefooted** *a.* **bareheaded** *a.* **bare-knuckle, bare-knuckled** *a.* **1** (of boxing) without gloves. **2** making no concessions. **barely** *adv.* **1** nakedly, poorly. **2** hardly, scarcely. **bareness** *n.*

Usage note When *barely* refers to time ('only just'), a following *when* is preferable to *than* (so *She had barely got in when the phone rang*).

---

barège (barezh´) *n.* a light gauzy dress fabric originally made at Barèges, Hautes-Pyrénées, France.

barf (bahf) *v.i.* (*sl.*) to vomit, to retch. ~*n.* an act of vomiting or retching.

bargain (bah´gin) *n.* **1** an agreement between parties, generally concerning a sale. **2** an advantageous purchase. ~*v.i.* to haggle over terms. **into/ in the bargain** over and above what is stipulated. **to bargain away** to exchange for something of less value. **to bargain on/ for** to count on, to expect. **bargain basement, bargain counter** *n.* a basement or counter in a store where goods are sold which have been marked down in price. **bargainer** *n.*

barge (bahj) *n.* **1** a flat-bottomed freight-boat, with or without sails, used principally on canals or rivers. **2** the second boat of a man-of-war. **3** a large ornamental state or pleasure boat, an ornamental houseboat. ~*v.i.* to lurch (into), rush (against). ~*v.t.* to transport by barge. **bargee** (-jē´) *n.* a bargeman, a person in charge of a barge. **bargeman** *n.* (*pl.* **bargemen**) a person working on

a barge. **bargepole** *n.* the pole with which a barge is propelled or kept clear of banks etc. **would not touch with a bargepole** would not come near or associate with on account of dirt, disease or ill temper etc.

barge- (bahj) *comb. form* used as below. **bargeboard** *n.* a projecting horizontal board at the gable-end of a building, concealing the barge-couples and warding off the rain. **barge-couples** *n.pl.* two beams mortised and tenoned together to increase the strength of a building.

barilla (boril´ə) *n.* **1** an impure alkali obtained from the ash of *Salsola soda* and allied species. **2** an impure alkali obtained from kelp. **3** a plant, *Salsola soda*, common on the seashore in Spain, Sicily and the Canaries.

barite BARYTES (under BARYTA).

baritone (bar´itōn), **barytone** *n.* **1** a male voice intermediate between a bass and a tenor. **2** a singer having such a voice. **3** a part for such a voice. **4** the smaller bass saxhorn in B flat or C. ~*a.* **1** having a compass between tenor and bass. **2** of or relating to such a compass.

barium (beə´riəm) *n.* **1** (*Chem.*) a metallic divalent element, at. no. 56, chem. symbol Ba, the metallic base of baryta. **2** (*Med.*) barium sulphate as administered in a barium meal. **barium meal** *n.* a mixture of barium sulphate, administered to allow X-ray examination of a patient's stomach or intestines.

bark[1] (bahk) *v.i.* **1** to utter a sharp, explosive cry, like that of a dog. **2** to speak in a peevish, explosive manner. **3** to cough. **4** (*N Am.*) to tout or advertise as a barker. ~*n.* **1** a sharp, explosive cry, orig. of dogs, hence of other animals. **2** the report of a firearm. **3** a cough. **to bark up the wrong tree 1** to be on a false scent. **2** to accuse the wrong person. **barker** *n.* **1** an auction tout; a vocal advertiser for a circus, fun-fair etc. **2** a person who or animal which barks. **barking** *a.* **1** that barks. **2** (*sl.*) mad, crazy. **barking mad** *a.* (*coll.*) completely mad, crazy.

bark[2] (bahk) *n.* **1** the rind or exterior covering of a tree, formed of tissues parallel to the wood. **2** spent bark, tan. **3** an outer covering. ~*v.t.* **1** to strip the bark from (a tree). **2** to cut a ring in the bark so as to kill (the tree). **3** to steep in a solution of bark, to tan. **4** to graze, to abrade (the shins, elbows etc.). **5** to cover with or as with bark, to encrust. **6** to strip or scrape off. **bark beetle** *n.* a small wood-boring beetle of the family Scolytidae, which cause great damage to trees.

bark[3] (bahk), **barque** *n.* **1** (*poet.*) a ship or boat, esp. a small sailing vessel. **2** (*usu.* **barque**) a sailing vessel with three or more masts, square-rigged on the fore and main masts, schooner rigged on the mizzen or other masts. **barkentine** *n.* BARQUENTINE.

barley (bah´li) *n.* **1** a plant of the genus *Hordeum*, a hardy, awned cereal. **2** the grain of this used for soups, malt liquors and spirits, animal feeds etc. **barleycorn** *n.* **1** a grain of barley. **2** a former measure, the third part of an inch (about 0.8 cm).

barleymow n. a stack of barley. **barley sugar** n. a hard confection, prepared by boiling down sugar, formerly with a decoction of barley. **barley water** n. a soothing drink made from pearl barley. **barley wine** n. a strong kind of ale.

barm (bahm) n. 1 the frothy scum which rises to the surface of malt liquor in fermentation, used as a leaven. 2 (also dial.) †yeast. **barmy** a. (comp. **barmier,** superl. **barmiest**) (sl.) crazy, cracked, silly (cp. BALMY (under BALM)). **barmily** adv. **barminess** n.

barmbrack (bahm´brak), **barnbrack** (bahn´-) n. sweet, spicy bread containing currants, dried peel etc.

Barmecide (bah´misīd) n. a person who gives illusory benefits. ~a. barmecidal.

bar mitzvah (bah mits´və) n. 1 a Jewish boy who has reached the age of religious responsibility, usu. on his 13th birthday. 2 the ceremony and celebration marking this event.

barn (bahn) n. 1 a covered building for the storage of grain and other agricultural produce. 2 (derog.) a barnlike building. 3 (N Am.) a stable, a cowshed. 4 (N Am.) a covered building for the storage of large vehicles. 5 (Physics) a unit of area, 10^{-28} square metres. **barn dance** n. 1 a dance, orig. US, somewhat like a schottische. 2 a country dance held in a barn or similar building. **barn owl** n. an owl which frequents barns, Tyto alba. **barnstorm** v.i. 1 to tour the country giving theatrical performances. 2 (N Am.) to tour rural areas giving political speeches at election time. 3 (N Am.) to perform aerobatic tricks, give flying displays. **barnstormer** n. **barnstorming** a. characteristic of a barnstormer, showy. **barnyard** n. 1 the yard adjoining a barn. 2 a farmyard, a barton.

barnacle (bah´nəkəl) n. 1 the barnacle goose. 2 any of various cirriped crustaceans that live attached to rocks, ship bottoms etc. 3 a constant attendant. **barnacled** a. **barnacle goose** n. (pl. **barnacle geese**) a species of wild goose, Branca leucopsis, formerly supposed to be developed from the common barnacle.

barnbrack BARMBRACK.

barney (bah´ni) n. (pl. **barneys**) (coll.) a noisy argument or fight.

barograph (bar´əgrahf) n. an aneroid barometer recording the variations of atmospheric pressure.

barometer (bərom´itə) n. 1 an instrument used for measuring the atmospheric pressure, thus indicating probable weather change, and also for measuring altitudes reached. 2 any indicator of change (e.g. in public opinion). **barometric** (barəmet´-), **barometrical** a. 1 of or relating to the barometer. 2 measured or indicated by a barometer. **barometrically** adv. **barometry** (-om´-) n. the art or practice of taking barometrical observations.

baron (bar´ən) n. 1 a member of the lowest rank of nobility. 2 a noble, a peer. 3 a powerful head

of a business or financial organization. 4 (Hist.) a person who held land by military service from the king. **baronage** (-nij) n. 1 the whole body of barons, the peerage. 2 a published list of barons. **baroness** n. 1 the wife or widow of a baron. 2 a lady who holds the baronial dignity in her own right. **baronial** (-rō´-) a. **baron of beef** n. a joint consisting of the two sirloins. **barony** n. (pl. **baronies**) 1 the lordship, or fee, of a baron. 2 the rank or dignity of a baron. 3 a subdivision of a county of Ireland. 4 a large manor in Scotland.

baronet (bar´ənit) n. a hereditary titled order of commoners ranking next below barons, instituted by James I in 1611. **baronetage** (-nij) n. 1 baronets collectively. 2 a list of the baronets. **baronetcy** n. (pl. **baronetcies**) the title or rank of a baronet.

baroque (bərōk´, -rok´) n. 1 a style of artistic or architectural expression prevalent esp. in 17th-cent. Europe, characterized by extravagant ornamentation. 2 a similar style in music or literature. ~a. 1 baroque in style. 2 grotesque. 3 gaudy. 4 flamboyant.

baroreceptor (bar´ōriseptə) n. (Biol.) a collection of nerve endings in the body that are sensitive to changes in pressure.

barouche (bəroosh´) n. a double-seated four-wheeled horse-drawn carriage, with a movable top, and a seat outside for the driver.

barque BARK³.

barquentine (bah´kəntēn), **barkentine** n. a three-masted vessel, with the foremast square-rigged, and the main and mizen fore-and-aft rigged. -

barrack¹ (bar´ək) n. 1 a temporary hut. 2 (pl., pl. or sing. in constr.) buildings used to house troops. 3 any large building resembling or used like barracks. ~v.t. 1 to provide with barracks. 2 to put in barracks. **barrack-room lawyer** n. 1 a soldier who argues with those in authority. 2 a person who gives advice in a pompous or insistent way, esp. when not qualified to do so. **barrack square** n. a drill ground near a barracks.

barrack² (bar´ək) v.i. 1 to jeer. 2 (orig. Austral.) to cheer (for). ~v.t. 1 to shout or cheer derisively at (e.g. a sports side). 2 (orig. Austral.) to shout support or encouragement for (a team).

barracouta (barəkoo´tə) n. (pl. in general **barracouta**, in particular **barracoutas**) 1 a large edible fish of the Pacific, Thyrsites atun. 2 (New Zeal.) a thin loaf of bread.

barracuda (barəkū´də) n. (pl. in general **barracuda**, in particular **barracudas**) a predatory tropical fish of the family Sphyraenidae.

barrage (bar´ahzh) n. 1 an artificial bar or dam formed to raise the water in a river. 2 (Mil.) a screen of artillery fire behind which troops can advance, or which can be laid down to hinder an enemy advance. 3 heavy or continuous questioning or criticism. 4 a deciding heat. **barrage balloon** n. (Hist.) an anchored balloon intended to prevent hostile aircraft making machine-gun attacks.

barramundi (barəmŭn´di), **burramundi** *n.* (*pl. in general* **barramundi**, *in particular* **barramundis**) any of various percoid fishes found in Australian rivers, esp. *Lates calcarifer.*

barrator (bar´ətə), **barrater** *n.* a person who out of malice or for their own purposes stirs up litigation or discord. **barratrous** *a.* **barratry** (-tri) *n.* **1** (*Law*) fraud or criminal negligence on the part of a master of a ship to the owners' detriment. **2** (*Hist.*) the offence of vexatiously exciting or maintaining lawsuits.

barre (bah) *n.* a wall-mounted horizontal rail used for ballet exercises.

barré (bar´ā) *n.* (*Mus.*) the laying of a finger across a particular fret of a guitar etc., to raise the pitch for the chord being played.

barrel (bar´əl) *n.* **1** a cask; a cylindrical wooden vessel bulging in the middle, formed of staves held together by hoops, and with flat ends. **2** the capacity or contents of such a vessel. **3** anything resembling such a vessel, as the tube of a firearm, through which the bullet or shot is discharged. **4** the belly and loins of a horse, ox etc. **5** a measure of capacity for liquid and dry goods, varying with the commodity. **6** a revolving cylinder or drum round which a chain or rope is wound. **7** the revolving cylinder studded with pins in a musical box or barrel organ. **8** the cavity behind the drum of the ear. ~*v.t.* (*pres.p.* **barrelling**, (*N Am.*) **barreling**, *past, p.p.* **barrelled**, (*N Am.*) **barreled**) to draw off into, or put or stow in barrels. ~*v.i.* (*N Am.*) to drive fast. **to have someone over a barrel 1** to have power over someone. **2** to have someone at a disadvantage. **to scrape the barrel 1** to get the last remaining bit. **2** to obtain the last scrap. **barrel-chested** *a.* having a rounded chest. **barrel drain** *n.* a cylindrical drain. **barrel of fun, barrel of laughs** *n.* a source of entertainment or amusement; a person who is a great deal of fun to be with. **barrel organ** *n.* a musical instrument in which the keys are mechanically acted on by a revolving cylinder (barrel) studded with pins. **barrel roll** *n.* a manoeuvre in aerobatics in which an aircraft rolls about its longitudinal axis. **barrel vault** *n.* (*Archit.*) a semi-cylindrical vault. **barrel-vaulted** *a.*

barren (bar´ən) *a.* **1** incapable of producing offspring. **2** not producing, unfertile; bearing no fruit or vegetation. **3** fruitless, unprofitable. **4** not productive intellectually, uninventive, dull. ~*n.* **1** a tract of barren land. **2** (*pl., esp. US*) elevated land on which small trees grow but not timber. **barrenly** *adv.* **barrenness** *n.*

barrette (bəret´) *n.* (*N Am.*) a hair-clasp.

barricade (barikād´, bar´-), †**barricado** (-kā´dō) *n.* (*pl.* **barricades**, †**barricados**, †**barricadoes**) **1** a hastily-formed rampart erected across a street or passage to obstruct an enemy or an attacking party. **2** any bar or obstruction. ~*v.t.* **1** to block or

defend with a barricade. **2** to obstruct in any way by physical obstacles.

barrier (bar´iə) *n.* **1** an obstacle which hinders approach or attack. **2** any material or immaterial obstruction. **3** a gate at a border where customs are collected or papers examined. **4** a bar that is raised to give access. **5** an enclosing fence. **6** a limit, a boundary. **7** the sound barrier. **barrier cream** *n.* a cream used to protect the hands from dirt, oils and solvents. **barrier reef** *n.* a coral reef running nearly parallel to the land, with a lagoon between.

barring (bah´ring) *prep.* (*coll.*) except, omitting.

barrio (bar´iō) *n.* (*pl.* **barrios**) a Spanish speaking community or district, usu. sited in the poorer areas of cities in the Southwestern US.

barrister (bar´istə), **barrister-at-law** *n.* (*pl.* **barristers(-at-law)**) a member of the legal profession who has been admitted to practise as an advocate at the bar; a counsellor-at-law.

barrow[1] (bar´ō) *n.* a prehistoric grave mound, a tumulus.

barrow[2] (bar´ō) *n.* **1** a shallow cart with two wheels pushed by hand. **2** a wheelbarrow. **barrow boy** *n.* a street trader in fruit, vegetables or other goods with a barrow. **barrowful** *n.* **barrowload** *n.*

Bart. *abbr.* Baronet.

barter (bah´tə) *v.t.* **1** to give (anything except money) in exchange for some other commodity. **2** to exchange. ~*v.i.* to traffic by exchanging one thing for another. ~*n.* traffic by exchanging one commodity for another. **barterer** *n.*

bartizan (bah´tizan, -zan´) *n.* (*Archit.*) **1** a battlement on top of a house or castle. **2** a small overhanging turret projecting from the angle on the top of a tower.

barton (bah´tən) *n.* **1** the part of an estate which the lord of the manor kept in his own hand. **2** a farmyard.

baryon (bar´ion) *n.* (*Physics*) any member of the heavier class of subatomic particles that have a mass equal to or greater than that of the proton.

barysphere (bar´isfiə) *n.* the solid, heavy core of the earth, probably consisting of iron and other metals.

baryta (bərī´tə) *n.* barium oxide or barium hydroxide. **barytes** (-tēz), **barite** (bā´rīt), **baryte** *n.* native sulphate of barium, heavy spar (used as white paint). **barytic** (-rit´-) *a.*

barytone BARITONE.

basal BASE[1].

basalt (bas´awlt) *n.* **1** a dark igneous rock of a black, bluish or leaden grey colour, of a uniform and compact texture, consisting of augite, feldspar and iron intimately blended, olivine also being often present. **2** a black stoneware first used by Wedgwood. **basaltic** (-sawl´-) *a.* **basaltiform** (-sawl´tifawm) *a.*

bascule (bas´kūl) *n.* an apparatus on the principle of the lever, in which the depression of one end raises the other. **bascule bridge** *n.* a kind of drawbridge balanced by a counterpoise which falls or rises as the bridge is raised or lowered.

base¹ (bās) *n.* **1** the lowest part on which anything rests. **2** (*Archit.*) **a** the part of a column between the bottom of the shaft and the top of the pedestal. **b** a plinth with its mouldings constituting the lower part of the wall of a room. **3** a pedestal. **4** the bottom of anything. **5** (*Bot.*) the extremity of a part by which it is attached to the trunk. **6** (*Geom.*) the side on which a plane figure stands or is supposed to stand. **7** (*Mil.*) the imaginary line connecting the two salient angles of adjacent bastions. **8** the middle part of a transistor. **9** (*Her.*) the width of a bar parted off from the lower part of a shield by a horizontal line. **10** a starting point of an expedition etc.; a place to which a person or group returns. **11** (*Mil.*) that line or place from which a combatant draws reinforcements of men, ammunition etc. **12** the place from which a commencement is made in some ball-games. **13** the starting-post. **14** any one of the points that must be reached in scoring a run in baseball, rounders etc. **15** (*Chem.*) **a** a substance with which an acid can combine to form a salt. **b** a substance which can accept or neutralize hydrogen ions. **c** a purine or pyrimidine group. **16** the fundamental principle, groundwork; that on which something essentially depends, a basis. **17** any substance used in dyeing as a mordant. **18** a substance used as a foundation for another substance or process. **19** (*Gram.*) the original stem of a word; the word from which another is formed. **20** (*Math.*) **a** the line from which trigonometrical measurements are calculated. **b** the number on which a system of calculations depends. **21** the datum or basis for any process of reckoning, measurement or argument. *~v.t.* **1** to found, to secure. **2** to station as a base for operations etc. **to make/ get to first base 1** (*N Am., coll.*) to complete the initial stage in a process. **2** (*N Am., coll., Geom.*) to seduce. **to touch base** to make esp. prearranged contact (with) again. **basal** *a.* **1** of or relating to, situated at or constituting the base of anything. **2** fundamental. **basal ganglia** *n.pl.* (*Anat.*) a group of ganglia at the base of the brain, linked to the thalamus. **basal metabolism** *n.* the amount of energy consumed by an individual in a resting state for functions such as respiration and blood circulation. **baseball** *n.* **1** the national ballgame of America, akin to English rounders. **2** the ball used in this. **baseboard** *n.* **1** (*N Am.*) a skirting board. **2** a board that functions as the base of anything. **basecamp** *n.* a camp used as the base for an expedition, military operation etc. **basehead** *n.* (*N Am., sl.*) a person who takes the drugs freebase or crack. **base hospital** *n.* (*Austral.*) a hospital that serves a rural area. **baseless** *a.* **baselessly** *adv.* **baselessness** *n.* **baseline** *n.* **1** a line used as a base. **2** the common section of a picture and the geometrical plane. **3** the back line at each end of a tennis or volleyball court etc. **baseload**

n. the load on an electrical power supply that is more or less constant. **baseman** *n.* (*pl.* **basemen**) in baseball, a fielder who is positioned next to a base. **basement** *n.* **1** the lowest or fundamental portion of a structure. **2** the lowest inhabited storey of a building, esp. when below the ground level. **basement membrane** *n.* (*Anat.*) a thin membrane that separates the epithelium from the tissue beneath it. **base pairing** *n.* the hydrogen bonding that occurs in a DNA molecule between complementary nitrogenous bases. **base rate** *n.* the rate of interest on which a bank bases its lending rates. **base unit** *n.* a basic unit in a system of measurement, such as a second, metre or kilogram. **basic** *a.* **1** of, relating to or constituting a base, fundamental. **2** without luxury, extras etc. **3** unrefined, vulgar. **4** (*Chem.*) being a base, having the base in excess. **5** (*Geol.*) (of igneous rock) with little silica present in its composition. **6** in metallurgy, prepared by the basic process. **basically** *adv.* **1** fundamentally. **2** in fact. **basic dye** *n.* a dye consisting of salts of organic bases. **Basic English** *n.* a fundamental selection of 850 English words, designed by C. K. Ogden as a common first step in English teaching and as an auxiliary language. **basic industry** *n.* an industry on which the economy depends. **basicity** (-sis´-) *n.* the combining power of an acid. **basic process** *n.* a method of making steel or homogeneous iron by means of a Bessemer converter lined with non-siliceous materials. **basics** *n.pl.* fundamental principles. **basic slag** *n.* a by-product of the manufacture of steel, used as manure. **basic wage** *n.* **1** a wage earned before overtime or other extra payments are added. **2** (*Austral., New Zeal.*) the minimum living wage. **basilar** *a.* (*Zool., Bot.*) growing from, or situated near, the base.

base² (bās) *a.* **1** low in the moral scale; unworthy, despicable. **2** menial, inferior in quality. **3** alloyed, debased, counterfeit. **basely** *adv.* **base metals** *n.pl.* those which are not noble or precious metals. **baseness** *n.*

base jump (bās), **BASE jump** *n.* a parachute jump from a fixed point such as a high building. **base jumper** *n.*

basenji (bəsen´ji) *n.* (*pl.* **basenjis**) a small central African hunting dog which cannot bark.

bases BASIS.

bash (bash) *v.t.* **1** to strike, so as to smash or hurt. **2** (*N Am.*) to criticize heavily. *~v.i.* to strike violently; to collide. *~adv.* **1** with force. **2** with a smash or bang. *~n.* **1** a heavy blow, a bang. **2** (*sl.*) a social entertainment.

bashful (bash´fəl) *a.* **1** shamefaced, shy. **2** characterized by excessive modesty. **bashfully** *adv.* **bashfulness** *n.*

basho (bash´ō) *n.* (*pl.* **basho, bashos**) a tournament in sumo wrestling.

basic BASE¹.

basidium (bəsid´iəm) *n.* (*pl.* **basidia**) (*Bot.*) a mother cell carried on a stalk and bearing spores characteristic of various fungi.

basil (baz´əl) *n.* any herb of the genus *Ocimum*, species of which are used as culinary herbs, e.g. the sweet basil, *O. basilicum*.

basilar BASE[1].

basilica (bəsil´ikə) *n.* (*pl.* **basilicas**) **1** a large oblong building with double colonnades and an apse, used as a court of justice and an exchange. **2** such a building used as a Christian church. **3** a church having special privileges granted by the Pope. **basilican** *a.*

basilisk (baz´ilisk, bas´-) *n.* **1** a fabulous reptile, said to be hatched by a serpent from a cock's egg – its look and breath were reputedly fatal. **2** (*Her.*) a cockatrice. **3** a tropical American lizard of the genus *Basiliscus* (named from its inflatable crest).

basin (bā´sən) *n.* **1** a hollow (usu. circular) vessel for holding food being prepared or water, esp. for washing; a bowl. **2** the quantity contained by such a vessel, a basinful. **3** a washbasin. **4** a hollow. **5** a pond, a dock, a reservoir; a land-locked harbour. **6** the tract of country drained by a river and its tributaries. **7** (*Geol.*) **a** a depression in strata in which beds of later age have been deposited. **b** a circumscribed formation in which the strata dip on all sides inward. **basinful** *n.* (*pl.* **basinfuls**)

basipetal (bāsip´itəl) *a.* (*Bot.*) proceeding in the direction of the base. **basipetally** *adv.*

basis (bā´sis) *n.* (*pl.* **bases** (-sēz)) **1** the base or foundation. **2** the fundamental principle, groundwork, ingredient or support. **3** the starting point.

bask (bahsk) *v.i.* **1** to expose oneself to the influence of genial warmth; to sun oneself. **2** (*fig.*) to luxuriate (in love, good fortune etc.). **basking shark** *n.* a large shark, *Cetorhinus maximus* (from its often lying near the surface of the sea).

basket (bahs´kit) *n.* **1** a wickerwork vessel of plaited osiers, twigs or similar flexible material. **2** as much as will fill a basket; a basketful. **3** the net or hoop used as a goal in basketball. **4** a goal scored in basketball. **5** a group or range (of currencies etc.) considered together. **6** (*euphem.*, *coll.*, *derog.*) a bastard. **~v.t.** to put in a basket. **basketball** *n.* **1** a game consisting in dropping a large ball into suspended nets or hoops. **2** the ball used in the game. **basket case** *n.* (*coll.*, *offensive*) **1** a person who has had their arms and legs amputated. **2** a person who is incapacitated or useless. **basketful** *n.* (*pl.* **basketfuls**) **basket-maker** *n.* a person who makes baskets. **basket-making** *n.* **basketry** *n.* **1** the making of baskets; basketwork. **2** baskets collectively. **basketwork** *n.* **1** wickerwork. **2** the making of baskets or wickerwork.

basmati rice (basmah´ti) *n.* a type of rice with a slender grain, delicate fragrance and nutty flavour.

Basque (bahsk) *n.* **1** a member of a people occupying both slopes of the western Pyrenees. **2** the language spoken by this people. **~a.** of or relating to this people or their language. **basque** *n.* a woman's jacket, often extended below the waist to form a kind of skirt.

bas-relief (bahrəlēf´, bas-) *n.* **1** low relief, a kind of sculpture in which the figures project less than one-half of their true proportions above the plane forming the background. **2** a carving in low relief.

bass[1] (bās) *n.* **1** the lowest part in harmonized musical compositions; the deepest male voice. **2** a part for such a voice. **3** the lowest tones of an instrument. **4** a person who sings the bass part, a singer with such a voice. **5** a bass string. **6** a bass instrument, esp. the bass guitar or double bass. **7** the player of a bass instrument. **8** the frequency output of audio equipment corresponding to the musical bass. **~a.** **1** of or relating to the lowest part in harmonized musical composition or the lowest pitch of voice; deep. **2** (of an instrument) being the lowest in pitch in its family. **bass clef** *n.* (*Mus.*) the F clef on the fourth line. **bassist** *n.* **1** a double-bass player. **2** a bass-guitar player. **bass viol** *n.* **1** a viola da gamba. **2** (*N Am.*) double bass. **3** a player of either of these instruments in a mixed group of musicians.

bass[2] (bas), **basse** *n.* (*pl. in general* **bass**, *in particular* **basses**) **1** the common European perch, *Perca fluviatilis*. **2** a sea fish resembling this, *Disentrarchus labrax*, of European waters. **3** a N American fish of the genus *Morone*. **4** SEA BASS (under SEA). **5** BLACK BASS (under BLACK).

bass[3] (bas) *n.* **1** the inner bark of the lime tree or any similar vegetable fibre. **2** an article made from this fibre. **basswood** *n.* **1** an American linden tree, *Tilia americana*. **2** the wood of this tree.

basset (bas´it), **basset hound** *n.* a short-legged breed of dog, orig. used to drive foxes and badgers from their earths.

basset-horn (bas´it) *n.* a tenor clarinet with a recurved mouth.

bassinet (basinet´) *n.* an oblong wicker basket with a hood at the end, used as a cradle.

basso (bas´ō) *n.* (*pl.* **bassos**, **bassi** (-si)) a bass singer. **basso profundo** (profun´dō) *n.* (*pl.* **basso profundos**, **bassi profundi** (-di)) **1** the lowest bass voice. **2** a singer with such a voice.

bassoon (bəsoon´) *n.* **1** a wooden double-reed instrument, the bass to the clarinet and oboe. **2** a bassoonist in an orchestra etc. **3** an organ stop of similar tone, a similar series of reeds on a harmonium etc. **bassoonist** *n.*

basso-rilievo (basōrilyā´vō) *n.* (*pl.* **basso-rilievos**) **1** low relief, bas-relief. **2** a sculpture in low relief.

bast (bast) *n.* **1** the inner bark of the lime or linden tree. **2** any similar fibrous bark.

bastard (bahs´təd) *n.* **1** (*now often offensive*) an illegitimate child or person. **2** (*sl.*, *often considered taboo*) an obnoxious or disagreeable person. **3** (*sl.*, *often considered taboo*) any person in general. **4** (*sl., often considered taboo*) something annoying or unpleasant. **5** anything spurious, counterfeit or false. ~*a.* **1** (*now often offensive*) born out of wedlock, illegitimate. **2** spurious, not genuine. **3** having the resemblance of something of a higher quality or kind, inferior. **bastardize, bastardise** *v.t.* **1** to declare (a person) to be illegitimate. **2** to debase. **bastardization** (-zā´shən) *n.* **bastardy** *n.* illegitimacy.

baste¹ (bāst) *v.t.* to moisten (a roasting joint etc.) with liquid fat, gravy etc.

baste² (bāst) *v.t.* to beat with a stick, to thrash, cudgel.

baste³ (bāst) *v.t.* to sew slightly, to tack, to fasten together with long stitches.

bastille (bastēl´) *n.* (*Hist.*) **1** a fortified tower. **2** a prison, a workhouse.

bastinado (bastinā´dō) *n.* (*pl.* **bastinadoes**) a method of corporal punishment or torture inflicted with a stick on the soles of the feet. ~*v.t.* (*3rd pers. sing. pres.* **bastinadoes,** *pres.p.* **bastinadoing,** *past, p.p.* **bastinadoed**) to beat with a stick, esp. on the soles of the feet.

bastion (bas´tyən) *n.* **1** a projecting work at the angle or in the line of a fortification, having two faces and two flanks. **2** (*fig.*) a defence. **3** a rock formation resembling the fortifying work.

bat¹ (bat) *n.* **1** a wooden instrument with a cylindrical handle and broad blade used to strike the ball at cricket or similar games. **2** a blow with a bat or club. **3** a batsman. **4** a spell of batting at cricket. **5** an object with a round flat face and a handle, used to guide taxiing or landing aircraft. ~*v.t.* (*pres.p.* **batting,** *past, p.p.* **batted**) to strike with a bat. ~*v.i.* to take an innings as batsman. **off one's own bat** on one's own initiative, by one's own exertions. **right off the bat** (*N Am., coll.*) straightaway. **to bat around 1** (*sl.*) to potter. **2** to discuss (an idea). **batsman** *n.* (*pl.* **batsmen**) **1** a person who uses the bat at cricket and other ball games. **2** the person on an airfield or aircraft carrier who guides taxiing or landing aircraft by waving a round, plainly visible bat in each hand.

bat² (bat) *n.* **1** a small nocturnal mouselike mammal of the order Chiroptera, having the digits extended to support a wing-membrane stretching from the neck to the tail, by means of which it flies. **2** (*derog.*) a woman (*the silly old bat!*). **like a bat out of hell** (*coll.*) extremely quickly. **to have bats in the belfry** (*coll.*) to be crazy; to suffer from delusions. **bats** *a.* (*coll.*) crazy, batty. **batty** *a.* (*comp.* **battier,** *superl.* **battiest**) **1** (*coll.*) mentally unstable; crazy. **2** batlike. **batwing sleeve** *n.* a sleeve shaped like a bat's wing.

bat³ (bat) *n.* (*only in combs.*) a packsaddle. **batman** *n.* (*pl.* **batmen**) (*Mil.*) the military servant of an officer. **batwoman** *n.* (*pl.* **batwomen**) the female military servant of a female military officer.

bat⁴ (bat) *v.t.* (*pres.p.* **batting,** *past, p.p.* **batted**) to blink. **not to bat an eyelid/ eyelash/ eye 1** not to blink. **2** to show no surprise or emotion.

☒ **batallion** common misspelling of BATTALION.

batch (bach) *n.* **1** any quantity produced at one operation or treated together. **2** as much bread as is produced at one baking. **3** a sort, lot, set, crew. ~*v.t.* **1** to collect into batches. **2** to treat as a batch or in batches. **batch processing** *n.* **1** an industrial process that performs on batches. **2** (*Comput.*) a system by which a number of jobs submitted by users are run through a computer as a single batch.

☒ **batchelor** common misspelling of BACHELOR.

bate¹ (bāt), **bait** *n.* (*sl.*) a rage.

bate² (bāt) †*v.t., v.i.* ABATE. **with bated breath 1** with breath held in check. **2** in suspense, anxiously.

bateau (bat´ō) *n.* (*pl.* **bateaux** (-z)) a long, light, flat-bottomed river-boat, tapering at both ends, used in Canada.

bateleur (batəlœ´), **bateleur eagle** *n.* an African eagle, *Terathopius ecaudatus,* having a short tail and a crest.

Batesian mimicry (bāt´siən) *n.* (*Zool.*) mimicry in which a species is protected by its resemblance to one that is harmful or inedible.

Bath (bahth) *n.* used as below. **Bath bun** *n.* a rich bun, generally with currants. **bath chair** *n.* an old kind of wheel chair.

bath (bahth) *n.* (*pl.* **baths** (bahdhz)) **1** the act of washing or immersing the body in water or other fluid. **2** a (usu. large) container for water for immersing the body for washing. **3** the water or other fluid used for bathing. **4** (*usu. pl.*) a building with baths or a swimming pool. **5** (*N Am.*) a bathroom. **6** a wash, a lotion. **7** the action of immersing any substance in a solution for scientific, art or trade purposes. **8** a vessel containing such a solution. **9** a solution used in such a process. ~*v.t.* to wash or put (usu. a child) in a bath. **bath cube** *n.* a cube of bath salts. **bathhouse** *n.* a building which has baths for the public to use. **bath mat** *n.* **1** a mat put next to a bath. **2** a rubber mat put in a bath to make it less slippery. **bath-oil** *n.* (perfumed) oil for use in bathwater. **bathrobe** *n.* (*esp. N Am.*) a dressing gown. **bathroom** *n.* **1** a room containing a bath or shower. **2** (*esp. N Am.*) a lavatory. **3** a set of fitments for a bathroom. **bath salts** *n.pl.* perfumed crystals used for softening bathwater. **bathtub** *n.* (*esp. N Am.*) a vessel containing water for bathing, a movable bath. **bathwater** *n.* the water in a bath.

bathe (bādh) *v.i.* **1** to swim in a body of water for pleasure. **2** (*esp. N Am.*) to take a bath. ~*v.t.* **1** to cleanse or soothe (a wound etc.) by applying liquid. **2** to suffuse, to moisten, to wet copiously. **3** to immerse in or as in a bath; to plunge or dip. ~*n.* the act of immersing the body to take a swim (esp. in the sea, a river etc.) or a bath. **bather** *n.* a person who bathes, esp. in the sea, a river or a swimming bath. **bathers** *n.pl.* (*Austral.*) a swimming costume or swimming trunks. **bathing** *n.* **bathing costume, bathing dress, bathing**

suit *n.* a garment for swimming or sunbathing in. **bathing hut** *n.* a hut for bathers to undress and dress in.

batholith (bath'əlith), **batholite** (-līt) *n.* a great mass of intrusive igneous rock, esp. granite. **batholithic** (-lith'-), **batholitic** (-lit'-) *a.*

bathometer (bəthom'itə) *n.* an instrument used to ascertain the depths reached in soundings.

bathos (bā'thos) *n.* **1** ridiculous descent from the sublime to the commonplace in writing or speech. **2** anticlimax. **bathetic** (bəthet'-) *a.*

bathymetry (bəthim'itri) *n.* the art or method of taking deep soundings. **bathymeter** *n.* **bathymetric** (bathimet'-), **bathymetrical** *a.*

bathyscaphe (bath'iskāf), **bathyscape** (-skāp), **bathyscaph** (-skaf) *n.* a submersible vessel for deep-sea observation and exploration.

bathysphere (bath'isfiə) *n.* a strong steel deep-sea observation chamber.

batik (bat'ik, bətēk') *n.* **1** a method of printing designs on fabric by masking areas to be left undyed with wax. **2** fabric or a piece of cloth produced by this method.

batiste (bətēst') *n.* a fine cotton or linen fabric. ~*a.* made of batiste.

baton (bat'on, bat'ən) *n.* **1** the wand used by a conductor of an orchestra etc. in beating time. **2** a short stick transferred between successive team-mates in a relay-race. **3** a knobbed staff carried and swung into the air at the head of a parade or twirled by majorettes etc. **4** a truncheon used as a badge or symbol of authority or as an offensive weapon. **5** a bar marking divisions on the face of a clock etc. **6** (*Her.*) a diminutive of the bend sinister, used in English coats of arms as a badge of bastardy. **baton charge** *n.* a charge by police or troops with batons. **baton round** *n.* a rubber or plastic bullet used esp. to control rioters.

batrachian (bətrā'kiən) *a.* of or relating to the order Anura (formerly Batrachia), which includes frogs and toads. ~*n.* any individual of this order, a frog or toad.

bats BAT².

battalion (bətal'yən) *n.* **1** a main division of an army. **2** an assemblage of companies of infantry. **3** the tactical and administrative unit of infantry, consisting of from four to eight companies, and generally about 1000 strong on a war footing. **4** a large group of people acting together.

batten¹ (bat'ən) *n.* **1** a strip of sawn wood used for flooring. **2** a piece of wood for clamping together the boards of a door. **3** (*Naut.*) a thin piece of wood nailed on masts etc. to prevent chafing, or to fasten down the edges of tarpaulins over the hatches. ~*v.t.* to fasten or strengthen with battens. **to batten down the hatches 1** to secure the hatches of a ship. **2** to prepare for action, trouble, danger etc.

batten² (bat'ən) *v.i.* to thrive, to prosper (on).

Battenberg (bat'ənbœg) *n.* a kind of oblong cake made with sponge of two colours.

batter¹ (bat'ə) *v.t.* **1** to strike with successive blows so as to bruise, shake or demolish. **2** to wear or impair by beating or rough usage. **3** to subject to hard, crushing attack. ~*v.i.* to hammer (at) a door. ~*n.* **1** in cooking, a mixture of several ingredients, esp. eggs, flour and milk, well beaten together. **2** (*Print.*) a damaged area of type. **battered** *a.* **1** (of a person) subjected to violent attack, esp. regularly. **2** (of food) covered in batter and fried. **batterer** *n.* **battering ram** *n.* **1** an ancient military engine used for battering down walls, and consisting of a heavy beam shod with iron, which was originally in the form of a ram's head. **2** a similar beam used to break down doors. **3** a forcible means of getting something done.

batter² (bat'ə) *v.i.* to incline (as walls, parapets, embankments etc.) from the perpendicular with a receding slope. ~*n.* a receding slope (of a wall etc.); a talus.

batter³ (bat'ə) *n.* a batsman; a player who is batting.

battery (bat'əri) *n.* (*pl.* **batteries**) **1** a connected series of electric cells, dynamos or Leyden jars, forming a source of electrical energy. **2** any apparatus for providing voltaic electricity. **3** a series of nesting-boxes in which hens are confined to increase laying. **4** (*Mil.*) a number of pieces of artillery for combined action, with men, transport and equipment. **5** the tactical unit of artillery. **6** a ship's armament. **7** (*Law*) an unlawful attack by beating, or even touching in a hostile manner. **8** a combination of instruments and general apparatus for use in various arts or sciences. **9** an embankment. **10** a connected series of tests. **11** the pitcher and catcher in baseball.

batting (bat'ing) *n.* **1** using a bat, hitting with a bat. **2** cotton fibre prepared for quilting. **batting average** *n.* a batter's or batsman's average score of runs or hits. **batting order** *n.* the order in which batters or batsmen bat.

battle (bat'əl) *n.* **1** a fight or hostile engagement between opposing armies etc. **2** fighting, hostilities, war. **3** a persistent struggle. ~*v.i.* **1** to fight, to contend (with or against). **2** (*esp. Austral.*) to struggle for a living. ~*v.t.* (*esp. N Am.*) to assail in battle, to fight against. **battleaxe**, (*N Am.*) **battle-ax** *n.* **1** a weapon like an axe, formerly used in battle. **2** a halberd. **3** (*coll.*) a formidable woman. **battlebus** *n.* a bus used as a mobile headquarters during an election campaign. **battlecruiser** *n.* a large, heavily-armed cruiser. **battle-cry** *n.* (*pl.* **battle-cries**) a war cry, a slogan. **battledress** *n.* comfortable, loose-fitting uniform worn by soldiers in battle. **battle fatigue** *n.* combat fatigue. **battlefield**, **battleground** *n.* the scene of a battle. **battler** *n.* **battle royal** *n.* (*pl.* **battles royal**) **1** a general engagement. **2** a free fight, a general row. **battleship** *n.* **1** a warship. **2** a ship adapted by armament for line of battle, as opposed to a cruiser.

battledore (bat´əldaw) *n.* **1** the light racket used to strike a shuttlecock in an old racket game. **2** the game in which this is used. **3** (*Hist.*) a wooden bat used for washing. **battledore and shuttlecock** *n.* the game of battledore.

battlement (bat´əlmənt) *n.* **1** a parapet with openings or embrasures, on the top of a building, orig. for defensive purposes, afterwards used as an ornament. **2** a roof having a battlement. **battlemented** *a.*

battue (batoo´) *n.* **1** driving game from cover by beating the bushes. **2** a shoot on this plan. **3** a wholesale slaughter.

batty BAT².

bauble (baw´bəl) *n.* **1** a gew-gaw, a showy trinket. **2** a piece of childish folly. **3** a mere toy. **4** a thing of no value. **5** a short stick or wand having a head with asses' ears carved at the end of it, carried by the fools or jesters of former times. **6** a foolish, childish person.

baud (bawd) *n.* (*pl.* **baud, bauds**) (*Comput. etc.*) a unit which measures the rate of telegraphic or electronic transmission, equal to one information unit or (loosely) one bit of data per second.

baudric BALDRIC.

baulk (bawlk, bawk), **balk** *n.* **1** an obstacle, a hindrance, a check; a disappointment. **2** the part of a billiard or snooker table behind a transverse line behind which the cue ball is placed at the beginning of the game. **3** a beam of timber. **4** a tie-beam of a house. **5** an illegal action of a pitcher in baseball. **6** a ridge of land left (deliberately or accidentally) unploughed. ~*v.i.* to turn aside, to swerve, to refuse to leap or to proceed; to hesitate (at). ~*v.t.* **1** to check, hinder; to disappoint. **2** to avoid, let slip. **3** to pass over intentionally; to refuse. **4** to evade, frustrate. **baulky** *a.* (*comp.* **baulkier,** *superl.* **baulkiest**) **1** (of a horse) prone to baulk or swerve. **2** perverse, unwilling.

bauxite (bawk´sīt), **beauxite** (bō´zīt) *n.* a clay which is the principal source of aluminium. **bauxitic** (-sit´ik) *a.*

Bavarian (bəveə´riən) *n.* **1** a native or inhabitant of Bavaria. **2** the German dialect spoken in Bavaria. ~*a.* of or relating to Bavaria or its inhabitants.

bawd (bawd) *n.* **1** a procuress, a brothel-keeper. **2** a prostitute. **3** a go-between, a pander. **bawdy** *a.* (*comp.* **bawdier,** *superl.* **bawdiest**) **1** obscene, lewd. **2** of or befitting a bawd. **3** dirty. ~*n.* bawdiness. **bawdily** *adv.* **bawdiness** *n.* **bawdy house** *n.* a brothel.

bawl (bawl) *v.i.* **1** to cry loudly, howl, bellow. **2** to shout at the top of one's voice. ~*v.t.* **1** to shout aloud. **2** to utter with bawling. ~*n.* a loud, prolonged shout or cry. **to bawl out** (*coll.*) to reprove fiercely.

bay¹ (bā) *n.* **1** an arm or inlet of the sea extending into the land, with a wide mouth. **2** a recess or cirque in a range of hills.

bay² (bā) *n.* **1** an opening or recess in a wall. **2** a main compartment or division, like the interval between two pillars. **3** a division of a barn or other building. **4** an internal recess in a room formed by the outward projection of the walls. **5** a platform on a railway station with a cul-de-sac, forming the terminus of a sideline. **6** a compartment or division in a ship or in the fuselage of an aircraft. **bay window** *n.* an angular window structure forming a recess in a room.

bay³ (bā) *n.* **1** barking. **2** the prolonged hoarse bark of a dog. **3** the barking of a pack that has tracked down its prey. **4** the final encounter between hounds and their prey. **5** the position of a hunted animal defending itself at close quarters. ~*v.i.* to bark hoarsely, as a hound at its prey. ~*v.t.* **1** to bark at. **2** to bring to bay. **at bay** in a position of defence, in great straits, in the last extremity. **to bring/ drive to bay 1** to come to close quarters with (the animal hunted). **2** to reduce to extremities. **to hold/ keep at bay** to keep back (assailing hounds or other pursuers) from attacking. **to stand at bay** to turn to face assailing hounds or one's pursuers.

bay⁴ (bā) *n.* **1** the bay tree or bay laurel, *Laurus nobilis*. **2** (*pl.*) leaves or twigs of this tree, woven into a garland as a reward for a conqueror or poet. **bayberry** *n.* (*pl.* **bayberries**) the candleberry or its fruit. **bay laurel** *n.* the tree *Laurus nobilis*. **bay leaf** *n.* a leaf from the bay tree, dried and used in cooking to flavour sauces, stews etc. **bay rum** *n.* an aromatic, spiritous liquid, used in medicines and cosmetics, and prepared by distilling rum in which bay leaves have been steeped. **bay tree** *n.* the tree *Laurus nobilis*.

bay⁵ (bā) *a.* reddish-brown in colour, approaching chestnut. ~*n.* a horse of that colour.

bayonet (bā´ənit) *n.* **1** a weapon for stabbing or thrusting, attached by a band to the muzzle of a rifle, so as to convert that into a kind of pike. **2** a type of connection used to secure light-bulbs, camera lenses etc. in which pins are engaged in slots in a cylindrical fitting. ~*v.t.* (*pres.p.* **bayoneting,** (*N Am.*) **bayonetting,** *past, p.p.* **bayoneted,** (*N Am.*) **bayonetted**) to stab with a bayonet.

bayou (bī´yoo) *n.* (*N Am.*) **1** the outlet of a lake or river. **2** a sluggish watercourse.

bazaar (bəzah´) *n.* **1** an Eastern market-place, where goods of all descriptions are offered for sale. **2** a sale of useful or ornamental articles, often handmade or second-hand, in aid of charity. **3** a shop where a variety of (ornamental) goods are sold.

bazooka (bəzoo´kə) *n.* an anti-tank or rocket-firing gun.

BB *abbr.* (on lead pencils) double black.

BBC *abbr.* British Broadcasting Corporation. **BBC English** *n.* the English language supposedly spoken by BBC announcers and newsreaders.

bbl. *abbr.* barrels.

BBQ *abbr.* barbecue.
BC *abbr.* before Christ.

BCD *abbr.* (*Comput.*) binary-coded decimal.
BCE *abbr.* before the Common Era.
BCG *abbr.* Bacillus Calmette-Guérin, used in anti-tuberculosis vaccine.
BD *abbr.* Bachelor of Divinity.
Bde. *abbr.* Brigade.
bdellium (del´iəm) *n.* **1** a tree of any of several species of *Balsamodendron*, which produces gum resin. **2** the gum resin of these trees.
Bdr. *abbr.* Bombardier.
BDS *abbr.* Bachelor of Dental Surgery.
BE *abbr.* **1** Bachelor of Engineering. **2** Bachelor of Education. **3** bill of exchange.
be (bē) *v.*, *often aux.* (*pres. ind. 1st pers. sing.* **am** (am), *2nd pers. sing.* **are** (ah), †**art** (aht), *3rd pers. sing.* **is** (iz), *pl.* **are** (ah), *pres. subj.* **be**, *pres.p.* **being**, *past ind.*, *1st*, *3rd pers.* **was** (woz), *2nd pers. sing.* **were** (wœ), †**wast** (wost), †**wert** (wœt), *pl.* **were**, *past subj.* **were**, *p.p.* **been** (bēn)) **1** to exist, to live, to have a real state of existence, physical or mental. **2** to become, remain, continue. **3** to happen, occur, come to pass. **4** to have come or gone to or to occupy a certain place. **5** to have a certain state or quality. **6** used as a copula, asserting the connection between the subject and the predicate (*They are old*; *It was a fox*; *Yesterday was my birthday*; *The tickets were £6 each*; *You are everything to your parents*). **7** (*aux. v.*) used in complex verb phrases expressing mood, aspect, or tense, such as passive, continuous, future or (*literary or dial.*) perfect (*He was killed*; *They were singing*; *You are to sit here*; *She is gone*). **been (and gone) and** (*sl.*) used to express surprise or annoyance at what someone has done. **to be at** to occupy oneself with. **be-all** *n.* **1** all that is to be. **2** the consummation, the finality. **be-all and end-all** *n.* the sole object or idea in view.

be- (bi) *pref.* **1** about, by, e.g. *besmear*, to smear all over, *bedaub*, to daub about, *before*, about the front of, *below*, on the low side of, *besiege*, to sit around. **2** making intransitive verbs transitive or reflexive, e.g. *bemoan*, *bespeak*, *bethink*. **3** forming verbs from nouns or adjectives, e.g. *befool*, *befriend*, *benumb*. **4** having a privative force, as in *behead*, *bereave*. **5** compounded with nouns, signifying to call this or that, as in *bedevil*, *belady*, *bemadam*. **6** intensive, e.g. *becrowd*, *bedrug*, *bescorch*. **7** making adjectives, e.g. *bejewelled*, *bewigged*.

beach (bēch) *n.* **1** a sandy or pebbly seashore. **2** the strand on which the waves break. *~v.t.* to haul or run (a ship or boat) on a beach. **beach ball** *n.* an inflatable ball that is used on the beach. **beach buggy** *n.* a low motor vehicle that can be driven on sand. **beachcomber** *n.* **1** a long wave rolling in from the ocean. **2** a settler in the Pacific Islands, living by pearl-fishing and other means. **3** a loafer in these conditions. **beachfront** *n.* (*esp. N Am.*) SEAFRONT (under SEA). **beachhead** *n.* (*Mil.*) a fortification established on a beach by landing forces. **beach plum** *n.* **1** a N American shrub, *Prunus maritima*, which grows in coastal regions. **2** the fruit of this. **beachside** *attrib. a.* next to the beach (*a beachside café*). **beachwear** *n.* clothes that are designed for wearing on the beach.

beacon (bē´kən) *n.* **1** a burning cresset fixed on a pole or on a building. **2** a signal-fire on an eminence. **3** a conspicuous hill. **4** a watchtower. **5** a lighthouse. **6** a fixed signal to give warning of a shoal or rock, or to indicate the fairway. **7** a transmitter concentrating its radiation in a narrow beam, to act as a guide to aircraft. **8** a Belisha beacon.

bead (bēd) *n.* **1** a small globular perforated body of glass, coral, metal or other material. **2** a bead-like drop threaded on a string to form a rosary. **3** the same used as an ornament. **4** a beadlike drop of a liquid, a bubble. **5** the front sight of a gun. **6** the inner edge of a tyre. **7** (*Archit.*) a narrow semicircular moulding. **8** an ornament resembling a string of beads. **9** (*pl.*) a necklace. **10** (*pl.*) a rosary. *~v.t.* **1** to ornament with beads or beading. **2** to thread beads. *~v.i.* to form beads. **to draw a bead on** to aim at. **to tell/ say one's beads** to count the rosary, to say one's prayers. **beaded** *a.* **beading** *n.* **1** the formation of beads. **2** beadwork. **3** (*Archit.*) a bead (moulding). **4** a bead of a tyre. **beadsman, beadswoman, bedesman, bedeswoman** *n.* (*pl.* **beadsmen, beadswomen, bedesmen, bedeswomen**) (*Hist.*) **1** a person appointed to pray for another. **2** an almsman or almswoman. **beadwork** *n.* ornamental work in beads. **beady** *a.* (*comp.* **beadier**, *superl.* **beadiest**) **1** (of eyes) small and bright like beads. **2** covered with beads or bubbles, foaming. **beadily** *adv.* **beadiness** *n.* **beady-eyed** *a.* **1** having eyes like beads. **2** watchful, observant.

beadle (bē´dəl) *n.* **1** a messenger, crier or usher of a court. **2** a petty officer of a church, parish, college, city company etc. **beadledom** *n.* **beadleship** *n.*

beagle (bē´gəl) *n.* **1** a small dog orig. bred for hunting hares by members of the hunt on foot. **2** a person who scents out or hunts down. **3** (*Hist.*) an officer of the law. **beagler** *n.* **beagling** *n.*

beak (bēk) *n.* **1** the pointed bill of a bird. **2** any beaklike process, such as the mandibles of a turtle or an octopus. **3** (*coll.*) a hooked or prominent nose. **4** (*Naut.*) the prow of an ancient war-galley, often sheathed with brass, and used as a ram. **5** a promontory of land etc. **6** a spout. **7** (*sl.*) a magistrate. **8** (*sl.*) a headmaster or headmistress. **beaked** *a.* **beaky** *a.* (*comp.* **beakier,** *superl.* **beakiest**).

beaker (bē´kə) *n.* **1** a large wide-mouthed drinking vessel. **2** the contents of a beaker. **3** an open-mouthed glass vessel with a lip, used in scientific experiments.

beam (bēm) *n.* **1** a large, long piece of timber squared on its sides, esp. one supporting rafters in a building. **2** a ray or collection of rays of light or radiation. **3** a series of radio or radar signals. **4** the direction indicated by such signals. **5** a broad smile. **6** the part of a balance from which the scales are suspended. **7** the pole of a carriage. **8** the part of a loom on which the warp is wound. **9** a cylinder on which cloth is wound as it is woven. **10** the main piece of a plough to which the handles are fixed. **11** the main trunk of a stag's horn. **12** a transverse piece of timber, supporting the deck and staying the sides of a ship. **13** the width of a ship or boat. **14** the shank of an anchor. ~*v.t.* **1** to emit or direct in rays, to radiate. **2** to transport in a beam of energy. ~*v.i.* **1** to send out rays of light. **2** to shine radiantly. **3** to smile brightly. **4** to be transported in a beam of energy. **broad across/ in the beam 1** (of a ship) wide. **2** (of a person) having wide hips, having large buttocks. **beam-compass, beam-compasses** *n.* an instrument for describing large circles, consisting of a beam of wood or brass, with sliding sockets bearing steel or pencil points. **beamer** *n.* (*coll.*) in cricket, a fast ball bowled at the batsman's head. **beamy** *a.* (*comp.* **beamier,** *superl.* **beamiest**) **1** (of ships) massive, broad in the beam. **2** shining, radiant, brilliant.

bean (bēn) *n.* **1** the kidney-shaped seed in long pods of *Faba vulgaris* and allied plants. **2** the seeds of other plants in some way resembling those of the common bean. **3** (*sl.*) the head. **4** (*pl.*, *N Am.*, *sl.*) anything at all (*You don't know beans*). ~*v.t.* (*esp. N Am.*, *sl.*) to hit on the head. **full of beans** energetic and vigorous. **not a bean** (*sl.*) no money. **beanbag** *n.* **1** a small cloth bag filled with dried beans used in games. **2** a large cushion filled with foam or polystyrene beads, used as a seat. **bean-counter** *n.* (*orig. N Am.,coll.*, *derog.*) **1** an accountant. **2** a miser, a pennypincher. **bean curd** *n.* an extract of soya bean in the form of jelly, custard or cake, which is used in Chinese and other Asian cooking. **beanery** *n.* (*pl.* **beaneries**) (*N Am.*, *sl.*) a cheap restaurant. **beanfeast** *n.* (*coll.*) **1** an annual dinner given by an employer to employees. **2** a celebration. **bean goose** *n.* a migratory goose, *Anser fabalis.* **beanie, beany** *n.* (*pl.* **beanies**) a small close-fitting cap like a skullcap. **beano** (-ō) *n.* (*pl.* **beanos**) (*coll.*) a treat, a spree, a beanfeast. **bean paste** *n.* a fermented paste made from soybeans and various other ingredients, used in Chinese and other Asian cooking. **beanpole** *n.* **1** a tall, thin pole

used to support bean plants. **2** (*coll.*) a tall thin person. **bean sprout** *n.* a young shoot of the mung bean used as a vegetable in Chinese cooking, and in salads. **beanstalk** *n.* the stem of the bean.

bear[1] (beə) *n.* (*pl. in general* **bear,** *in particular* **bears**) **1** a plantigrade mammal of the family Ursidae, with a large head, long shaggy hair, hooked claws and a stumpy tail. **2** a rough unmannerly man. **3** either of the northern constellations, the Great or the Little Bear. **4** a person who sells stock for future delivery in the expectation that prices will fall, a speculator for the fall. **5** a teddy bear. **6** (*esp. N Am.*, *sl.*) a police officer, the police. ~*v.i.* to speculate for a fall in stocks. ~*v.t.* to produce a fall in the price of (stock etc.). **like a bear with a sore head** in a very bad mood, irritable. **bear-baiting** *n.* (*Hist.*) the sport of baiting a chained bear with dogs. **bearberry** *n.* (*pl.* **bearberries**) an evergreen trailing shrub of the genus *Arctostaphylos.* **beargarden** *n.* a rude, turbulent assembly. **bear-hug** *n.* a tight hug. **bearish** *a.* **1** bearlike. **2** rough, rude, uncouth. **3** in the stock market, characterized by a fall in prices. **bear market** *n.* on the Stock Exchange, a market with falling prices, as distinct from *bull market.* **bearpit** *n.* **1** a sunken area in a zoo for bears to live in. **2** a rowdy scene or place. **bear's breech** *n.* a plant of the genus *Acanthus,* esp. *A. mollis.* **bear's ear** *n.* the common auricula, *Primula auricula.* **bear's foot** *n.* stinking hellebore, *Helleborus fetidus.* **bearskin** *n.* **1** the skin of a bear. **2** a shaggy woollen cloth, used for overcoats. **3** the tall fur cap worn by some regiments in the British Army.

bear[2] (beə) *v.t.* (*past* **bore** (baw), *p.p.* **borne** (bawn)) **1** to carry, to wear, to show or display (e.g. armorial bearings). **2** to bring. **3** to sustain, to support the weight of (material or immaterial things). **4** to be responsible for, to wield. **5** to suffer, to endure, to tolerate. **6** to admit of. **7** to thrust, to press. **8** to give birth to. **9** to produce, to yield. **10** (*reflex.*) to behave. ~*v.i.* **1** to incline, take a certain direction (as to the point of the compass) with respect to something else. **2** to suffer, to be patient. **to bear arms 1** to be a soldier. **2** (*Her.*) to be entitled to a coat of arms. **to bear away 1** to carry off. **2** to win. **to bear down 1** to overwhelm, to crush, to subdue. **2** to use the abdominal muscles to assist in giving birth. **to bear down on 1** to sail in the direction of. **2** to approach purposefully. **to bear fruit** (*fig.*) to have a successful outcome. **to bear hard/ heavily on** to oppress. **to bear in mind** to remember, to take into account. **to bear off 1** to carry off. **2** to win. **to bear on 1** to press against. **2** to be relevant to. **to bear out** to confirm, to justify. **to bear up** to endure cheerfully. **to bear upon** to be relevant to. **to bear with** to put up with, to endure. **to bring to bear** to apply, bring into operation. **bearable** *a.* **bearability** (-bil´-) *n.* **bearableness** *n.* **bearably** *adv.* **bearer** *n.* **1** a person who or thing which bears, carries or supports. **2** a person who helps to carry a corpse to the grave or to hold the pall. **3** a porter. **4** a person who holds or presents a cheque. **5** a bringer of anything. **6** the holder of any rank or office. **7** (*Hist.*) in India, Africa etc., a personal or domestic servant. **bearing** *n.* **1** endurance, toleration. **2** mien, deportment, carriage, manner, behaviour. **3** relation, connection. **4** the space between the two fixed extremities of a piece of timber, or between one of the extremities and a post or wall. **5** a carrier or support for moving parts of any machine. **6** any part of a machine that bears the friction. **7** (*Her.*) a charge, a device. **8** relation, relevance, aspect. **9** the direction in which an object lies from a ship. **10** (*pl.*) relative position; one's sense of this. **bearing-rein** *n.* a fixed rein for holding a horse's head up.

beard (biəd) *n.* **1** the hair on the lower part of a man's face, esp. on the chin. **2** the analogous hairy appendage in animals. **3** the hairy appendages in the mouth of some fishes, gills of some bivalves etc.; a byssus. **4** the awn of grasses. ~*v.t.* **1** to oppose with resolute effrontery; to defy. **2** to take hold of by the beard. **bearded** *a.* **bearded tit** *n.* a small Eurasian songbird, *Panurus biarmicus*, which is common in reed-beds (also called the *reedling*). **beardie** *n.* (*coll.*) a man with a beard. **beardless** *a.*

Béarnaise sauce (bāənāz´) *n.* a rich sauce made with egg yolks, lemon juice or wine vinegar, herbs and shallots.

beast (bēst) *n.* **1** any of the animals other than man. **2** a quadruped esp. a large wild one. **3** an animal to ride or drive. **4** a domestic animal, esp. ox or cattle. **5** a brutal person. **6** an objectionable person. **7** an objectionable thing. **the beast** man's carnal or brutal instincts. **beast fable** *n.* **beastie** *n.* **1** (*Sc. or facet.*) a small animal. **2** (*coll.*) an insect. **beastlike** *a.* **beastly** *a.* (*comp.* **beastlier,** *superl.* **beastliest**) **1** like a beast in form or nature. **2** brutal, filthy, coarse. **3** disgusting, offensive. **4** disagreeable. ~*adv.* **1** in a beastly manner. **2** (*coll.*) exceedingly, very. **beastliness** *n.* **beast of burden** *n.* an animal used for carrying loads, esp. a mule. **beast of prey** *n.* a carnivorous animal.

beat (bēt) *v.t.* (*past* **beat,** *p.p.* **beaten**) **1** to strike with repeated blows; to thrash. **2** to bruise or break by striking or pounding. **3** to work (metal etc.) by striking. **4** to strike (bushes etc.) in order to rouse game. **5** to mix or agitate by beating. **6** (of water, wind etc.) to strike or impinge on, to dash against. **7** to conquer, overcome, master. **8** to perplex. **9** to tread, as a path. **10** to play (an instrument or tune) by striking. **11** to indicate (time) with a baton or by gestures etc. **12** to cause to move rhythmically. ~*v.i.* **1** to strike against some obstacle. **2** to pulsate, throb. **3** to knock. **4** to move rhythmically. **5** to mark time in music. **6** (*Naut.*) to make way against the wind. ~*n.* **1** a strong musical accent or rhythm. **2** the rise or fall of the hand or foot in regulating time. **3** a stroke

or blow. **4** a stroke upon the drum, the signal given by such a blow. **5** a pulsation, a throb. **6** (*Physics*) a periodic variation in amplitude caused by the combination of oscillations of different frequencies. **7** a certain assigned space regularly traversed at intervals by patrols, police etc. **8** sphere, department, range. **9** a beatnik. ~*a.* BEATEN (under BEAT). **to beat about the bush 1** to approach a matter in a roundabout way. **2** to shilly-shally. **to beat a retreat** to retire to avoid confrontation. **to beat around the bush** (*N Am.*) to beat about the bush. **to beat back** to compel to retire in a confrontation. **to beat down 1** to throw or cast down. **2** to force down (a price) by haggling. **3** to force (a seller) to lower a price by haggling. **4** to come down from the sky strongly. **to beat it** (*sl.*) to go away. **to beat off** to drive away by blows. **to beat one's brains** to puzzle, to ponder laboriously. **to beat one's breast** to show grief or sorrow. **to beat out 1** to extend by beating, to hammer out. **2** to extinguish by beating. **to beat the bounds** to mark the boundary of a parish by striking it with light rods. **to beat the clock** to complete a task within the allotted time. **to beat the tattoo** (*Mil.*) to beat to quarters. **to beat up 1** to injure seriously by beating. **2** to bring to a fluid or semi-fluid mass by beating. **3** to make way against wind or tide. **beatable** *a.* **beaten** *a.* **1** subjected to repeated blows. **2** defeated, vanquished, weary, exhausted. **3** trodden smooth, plain or bare. **4** prostrated by the wind. **beaten track** *n.* **1** the usual method. **2** the ordinary way. **beater** *n.* **1** a person who beats. **2** a person employed to rouse game, esp. grouse or pheasant. **3** an instrument for beating, pounding or mixing. **4** (*N Am., coll.*) an old vehicle. **beat generation** *n.* young people of the 1950s and early 1960s characterized by unconventional attitudes and self-conscious bohemianism in behaviour and dress. **beating** *n.* **1** the action of striking repeated blows. **2** a punishment or chastisement by blows. **3** pulsation, throbbing. **4** an overthrow, defeat. **5** sailing against the wind. **to take some/a lot of beating** to be difficult to improve upon. **beatnik** (-nik) *n.* (*often derog.*) a member of the beat generation. **beat-up** *a.* (*coll.*) damaged with long or rough use.

beatify (biat´ifi) *v.t.* (*3rd pers. sing. pres.* **beatifies,** *pres. p.* **beatifying,** *past, p.p.* **beatified**) **1** in the Roman Catholic Church, to declare (a deceased person) blessed in heaven. **2** to render supremely blessed or happy. **beatific** (bēətif´-) *a.* **1** making one supremely blessed or happy. **2** suggesting blessedness. **beatifically** *adv.* **beatification** (-fikā´shən) *n.* **1** the Pope's declaration that a deceased person is blessed in heaven and that definite forms of public reverence should be paid to them, the first step towards canonization. **2** the act of making blessed; the state of being blessed. **beatitude** (-tūd) *n.* **1** supreme felicity. **2** heavenly bliss. **3** any of the states of special blessedness announced in the Sermon on the

Mount. **4** a title of the patriarchs in the Orthodox Church.

beau (bō) *n.* (*pl.* **beaus** (bōz), **beaux** (bō, bōz)) **1** a suitor, lover, sweetheart. **2** a man unduly attentive to dress and social fashions and etiquette; a fop, a dandy. ~*v.t.* **1** to act as beau to. **2** to escort. **beau geste** (zhest´) *n.* (*pl.* **beaux gestes** (bō zhest´)) a gracious gesture. **beau idéal** (ēdāal´) *n.* (*pl.* **beaux idéals** (bōz ēdāal´)) the highest conceivable type of excellence. **beau monde** (mōd´) *n.* the fashionable world.

Beaujolais (bō´zhəlā) *n.* a usu. red, light Burgundy wine from the Beaujolais district. **Beaujolais Nouveau** (noovō´) *n.* Beaujolais wine in the first year of its vintage.

beauty (bū´ti) *n.* (*pl.* **beauties**) **1** that quality or assemblage of qualities which gives the eye or the other senses intense pleasure. **2** that characteristic in a material object or an abstraction which gratifies the intellect or the moral feeling. **3** a beautiful person, esp. a woman. **4** a beautiful feature or characteristic. **5** embellishment, grace, charm. **6** a particular aspect that gives satisfaction or (*iron.*) the reverse. **7** a very fine example of its kind. ~*v.t.* **1** to adorn. **2** to beautify. **beaut** *n.* (*esp. Austral., sl.*) something or someone outstanding. ~*int., a.* great, excellent. **beauteous** *a.* (*poet.*) endowed with beauty; beautiful. **beauteously** *adv.* **beauteousness** *n.* **beautician** (-tish´-) *n.* a person who administers or who operates an establishment administering beauty treatment. **beautiful** *a.* **1** full of beauty; possessing the attributes that constitute beauty. **2** satisfactory, palatable, delicious. **3** (*iron.*) egregious. **beautifully** *adv.* **beautifulness** *n.* **beautify** (-fī) *v.t.* (*3rd pers. sing. pres.* **beautifies**, *pres.p.* **beautifying**, *past, p.p.* **beautified**) to make beautiful. ~*v.i.* to grow beautiful. **beautification** (-fikā´shən) *n.* **beautifier** *n.* **beauty parlour**, (*N Am.*) **beauty parlor** *n.* a shop specializing in beauty treatments. **beauty queen** *n.* a woman picked as the most attractive in a contest. **beauty salon** *n.* a beauty parlour. **beauty sleep** *n.* sleep before midnight. **beauty spot** *n.* **1** a beautiful place or landscape. **2** a small mark such as a mole on the face, considered to be attractive. **3** a patch or spot placed upon the face to heighten some beauty. **4** a foil. **beauty treatment** *n.* improvement of a person's appearance by artificial means.

beaux arts (bōz ah´) *n.pl.* fine arts.

beaver[1] (bē´və) *n.* (*pl. in general* **beaver**, *in particular* **beavers**) **1** an amphibious rodent mammal, of the genus *Castor*, with broad tail, soft fur and habits of building huts and dams. **2** the fur of this animal. **3** a hat made of such fur. **4** beaver cloth. **5** (*sl.*) a man with a beard. **6** (**Beaver**) a six- or seven-year-old child who is a member of a group affiliated to the Scout Association. **to beaver away at** to work hard at. **beaverboard** *n.* a building board of wood-fibre material. **beaver cloth** *n.* a felted cloth for overcoats. **beaver lamb** *n.* lambskin made to resemble beaver fur.

beaver[2] (bē´və) *n.* the lower part of a visor.

bebop (bē´bop) *n.* a variety of jazz music which developed in the 1940s, distinguished from the earlier jazz tradition by its more complex melodies and harmonies and faster tempos (see BOP[1]). **bebopper** *n.*

becalm (bikahm´) *v.t.* **1** to deprive (a ship) of wind. **2** to render calm or still. **3** to quiet, to tranquillize, to soothe.

became BECOME.

because (bikoz´) *conj.* **1** by cause of, by reason of, on account of, for. **2** for this reason, inasmuch as.

Usage note See note under REASON.

béchamel (bā´shəmel) *n.* a white sauce made with cream or milk and flavoured with onions and herbs.

bêche-de-mer (beshdəmeə´) *n.* (*pl.* **bêche-de-mer, bêches-de-mer** (besh-)) the sea-slug or trepang, *Holothuria edulis*, an echinoderm eaten by the Chinese.

beck[1] (bek) *n.* **1** a nod, a gesture of the finger or hand. **2** (*poet.*) a mute signal of assent or command. **at someone's beck and call 1** ready to obey someone's orders instantly. **2** subject to someone's every whim.

beck[2] (bek) *n.* **1** a brook, a rivulet. **2** a mountain or moorland stream.

becket (bek´it) *n.* (*Naut.*) anything used to confine loose ropes, tackle or spars, such as a large hook, a rope with an eye at one end; a bracket, pocket, loop etc.

beckon (bek´ən) *v.i.* to make a signal by a gesture of the hand or a finger or by a nod. ~*v.t.* to summon or signal to by a motion of the hand, a nod etc.

becloud (biklowd´) *v.t.* **1** to cover with or as with a cloud. **2** to obscure.

become (bikŭm´) *v.i.* (*pres.p.* **becoming**, *past* **became** (-kām´), *p.p.* **become**) **1** to pass from one state or condition into another. **2** to come into existence. **3** to come to be. ~*v.t.* **1** to be suitable to, befit, be proper to or for. **2** to be in harmony with. **3** to look well upon. **to become of** to happen to, befall. **becoming** *a.* **becomingly** *adv.* **becomingness** *n.*

becquerel (bek´ərel) *n.* (*Physics*) a unit which measures the activity of a radioactive source.

B.Ed. *abbr.* Bachelor of Education.

bed (bed) *n.* **1** an article of domestic furniture to sleep on. **2** the resting-place of an animal; any impromptu resting-place. **3** the use of a bed in marriage, conjugal rights, childbirth. **4** a plot of ground in a garden. **5** the flat surface on which anything rests. **6** the channel of a river. **7** the bottom of the sea. **8** a horizontal course in a wall. **9** a stratum, a layer of rock. **10** an aggregation of small animals disposed in a bedlike mass. **11** a layer of oysters. **12** the foundation of a road, street or railway. **13** the bottom layer or support on which a mechanical structure or machine is laid. ~*v.t.* (*pres.p.* **bedding**, *past*, *p.p.* **bedded**) **1** to put in bed. **2** to plant in a bed or beds. **3** to have sexual intercourse with. **4** to fix in a stratum or course. **5** to place in a matrix of any kind, to embed. ~*v.i.* **1** to form a stratum or course. **2** to go to bed. **to bed out** to plant out in beds. **to get out of bed on the wrong side** to begin the day in a foul mood. **to go to bed 1** to retire at the end of the day. **2** to have sexual intercourse (with). **to lie in the bed one has made** to suffer for one's own misdeeds or mistakes. **to make a bed** to put a bed in order after it has been used. **to make up a bed** to prepare sleeping accommodation at short notice. **to put to bed 1** to settle (a child etc.) in bed for the night. **2** to complete work on (a newspaper) so that it can go to press. **bed and board** *n.* **1** lodgings and food. **2** connubial relations. **bed and breakfast** *n.* **1** in a hotel etc., overnight accommodation with breakfast. **2** a hotel etc. providing this. **bed-and-breakfast** *v.t.* to sell (shares) and buy them back the next morning. **bedbug** *n.* a bloodsucking insect of the genus *Cimex*, which infests filthy bedding. **bedchamber** *n.* **1** a sleeping apartment. **2** a bedroom. **bedclothes** *n.pl.* sheets, blankets and coverlets for a bed. **bedcover** *n.* a bedspread. **beddable** *a.* (*coll.*) sexually attractive. **bedder** *n.* a plant for bedding-out. **bedding** *n.* **1** a bed with the clothes upon it. **2** bedclothes. **3** litter for domestic animals. **4** a bottom layer or foundation. **5** (*Geol.*) the stratification of rocks. **bedding plant, bedding-out plant** *n.* a plant intended to be set in a bed. **beddy-byes** *n.* bed, sleep (used by or to children). **bedfellow** *n.* **1** a person who sleeps in the same bed with another. **2** an associate. **bedhead** *n.* the head end of a bed. **bed-hop** *v.i.* (*pres.p.* **bed-hopping**, *past*, *p.p.* **bed-hopped**) (*coll.*) to have casual sexual affairs. **bedjacket** *n.* a jacket to be worn in bed, e.g. in hospital. **bedlinen** *n.* sheets and pillow cases etc. for a bed. **bedmaker** *n.* **1** a person who makes beds. **2** a person who makes students' beds and cleans the rooms in a college. **bed of roses** *n.* a comfortable place. **bedpan** *n.* a chamber utensil for urination and defecation when confined to bed. **bedpost** *n.* any one of the upright supports of a bedstead. **bedrest** *n.* (of an invalid) confinement to bed. **bedrid, bedridden** *a.* confined to bed through age or sickness. **bedrock** *n.* **1** the rock underlying superficial formations. **2** the bottom, foundation, fundamental principles. **bedroll** *n.* bedding rolled up so as to be carried by a camper etc. **bedroom** *n.* a sleeping apartment. **bedside** *n.* the space beside a bed, esp. a sickbed. **bedside manner** *n.* a doctor's manner in attending a patient. **bed-sitting room, bedsit, bedsitter** *n.* a bedroom and sitting room combined, usu. with cooking facilities. **bedsock** *n.* a thick sock to be worn in bed. **bedsore** *n.* a sore produced by long confinement to bed. **bedspread** *n.* a counterpane, a coverlet. **bedstead** (-sted) *n.* a framework on which a mattress is placed. **bedstraw** *n.* **1** straw covered with a sheet

and used as a bed or palliasse. **2** any herbaceous plant of the genus *Galium*, esp. lady's bedstraw *G. verum*. **bedtable** *n.* a table or tray designed to be used in bed. **bedtime** *n.* the usual hour for going to bed. **bed-wetting** *n.* the act of involuntarily urinating in bed. **bed-wetter** *n.*

bedabble (bidab´əl) *v.t.* to sprinkle, to wet; to splash, to stain.

bedaub (bidawb´) *v.t.* to daub over, to besmear, to bedizen.

bedazzle (bidaz´əl) *v.t.* to confuse by dazzling. **bedazzlement** *n.*

bedeck (bidek´) *v.t.* to deck out, to adorn.

bedeguar (bed´igah) *n.* a mossy growth on rose briers.

bedevil (bidev´əl) *v.t.* (*pres.p.* **bedevilling**, (*esp. N Am.*) **bedeviling**, *past*, *p.p.* **bedevilled**, (*esp. N Am.*) **bedeviled**) **1** to torment. **2** to confound, confuse; to obstruct. **3** to treat with diabolical violence or ribaldry. **4** to bewitch. **bedevilment** *n.*

bedew (bidū´) *v.t.* to moisten or sprinkle with dewlike drops.

bedim (bidim´) *v.t.* (*pres.p.* **bedimming**, *past*, *p.p.* **bedimmed**) (*poet.*) **1** to render dim. **2** to obscure.

bedizen (bidī´zən, -diz´ən) *v.t.* (*poet.*) to deck out in gaudy vestments or with tinsel finery.

bedlam (bed´ləm) *n.* **1** a scene of wild uproar. **2** madness, lunacy. **3** †an asylum.

Bedlington terrier (bed´lingtən) *n.* a breed of grey, crisp-haired terrier.

Bedouin (bed´uin), **Beduin** *n.* (*pl.* **Bedouin, Beduin**) **1** a nomadic Arab, as distinguished from one living in a town. **2** a gypsy, a wanderer. ~*a.* **1** of or relating to the nomadic Arabs. **2** nomad.

bedraggle (bidrag´əl) *v.t.* to soil by trailing in the wet or mire. **bedraggled** *a.*

Beds. (bedz) *abbr.* Bedfordshire.

bee (bē) *n.* **1** a four-winged insect of the genus *Apis*, which collects nectar and pollen and is often kept in hives for the honey and wax it produces. **2** any closely allied insect of the superfamily Apoidea, e.g. *carpenter bee*, *bumble-bee*. **3** a busy worker. **4** (*N Am.*) a social meeting for work usu. on behalf of a neighbour. **the bee's knees** (*coll.*) (someone or something) wonderful, admirable. **to have a bee in one's bonnet** to have a crazy fancy or be cranky on some point. **beebread** *n.* a mixture of honey and pollen, on which bees feed their larvae. **bee-eater** *n.* a tropical Old World bird of the genus *Merops*, esp. *M. apiaster*. **beehive** *n.* **1** a receptacle (usu. of wood or straw and dome-shaped) for bees. **2** a hive of activity. **3** a hairstyle in which the hair is piled up. **bee-keeping** *n.* the occupation of keeping bees. **bee-keeper** *n.* **beeline** *n.* the shortest route between two places, that which a bee is assumed to take. **to make a beeline for** to make straight for. **bee-master, bee-mistress** *n.* a person who keeps bees. **bee orchid, bee orchis** *n.* a British orchid, *Ophrys apifera*, the flower of which resembles a bee. **beeswax** *n.* the wax secreted by bees for their cells, used to make polishes. ~*v.t.* to rub or polish with beeswax. **beeswing** *n.* the second crust, a fine filmy deposit in an old port wine.

beech (bēch) *n.* **1** a forest tree of the genus *Fagus*, esp. *F. sylvatica*, the common beech, with smooth bark and yielding nuts or mast. **2** the wood of this tree. **3** (*Austral.*) any of various Australian trees resembling this. **beech-fern** *n.* any of several ferns, esp. *Phegopteris connectilis*. **beech marten** *n.* a stone marten. **beechmast** *n.* (*pl.* **beechmast**) the fruit of the beech tree. **beechnut** *n.* the nut of the beech, two of which lie in the prickly capsule. **beech tree** *n.* **beechwood** *n.* the wood of the beech tree.

beef (bēf) *n.* (*pl.* **beeves** (bēvz), **beefs**) **1** the flesh of the ox, cow or bull, used as food. **2** (*pl.* **beeves**) an ox, esp. one fatted for the market (*usu. in pl.*). **3** flesh, muscle. **4** (*sl.*) (*pl.* **beefs**) a complaint. ~*v.i.* to grumble, to grouse. **to beef up** (*coll.*) to strengthen, reinforce. **beefburger** *n.* a hamburger. **beefcake** *n.* (*sl.*) men with muscular physiques, esp. as displayed in photographs. **beefeater** *n.* a warder of the Tower of London, a Yeoman of the Guard. **beefsteak** *n.* a thick slice of beef from the hindquarters. **beefsteak fungus** *n.* an edible reddish bracket fungus, *Fistulina hepatica*, that grows on oak trees. **beefsteak tomato** *n.* (*esp. N Am.*) a beef tomato. **beef tea** *n.* the nutritive juice extracted from beef by simmering. **beef tomato** *n.* a large variety of tomato. **beefwood** *n.* **1** any of various trees that produce very hard wood, esp. *Casuarina equisetifolia*. **2** the wood of these trees. **beefy** *a.* (*comp.* **beefier**, *superl.* **beefiest**) **1** like beef. **2** fleshy. **3** stolid. **4** muscular. **beefily** *adv.* **beefiness** *n.*

been BE.

beep (bēp) *n.* a short sound as made by a car horn or an electronic device, usu. as a warning. ~*v.i.* to make such a sound. ~*v.t.* **1** to cause (e.g. a car horn) to sound. **2** (*esp. N Am.*) to summon with a beeper. **beeper** *n.* a device that emits a beeping sound. **2** (*N Am.*) a bleeper.

beer (biə) *n.* **1** an alcoholic drink brewed from fermented malt, hops, water and sugar. **2** any malt liquor prepared by brewing, including ale and porter. **3** any of various other fermented liquors, such as *ginger-beer*, *spruce-beer* etc. **4** a drink of any of these. **beer and skittles** *n.* enjoyment or pleasure; all one could wish. **beer belly** *n.* a protruding stomach, caused by much beer-drinking. **beer cellar** *n.* **1** an underground room where beer is stored. **2** a basement where beer is sold or drunk. **beer garden** *n.* a garden or outdoor area with tables where beer and other refreshments may be consumed. **beer gut** *n.* (*sl.*) BEER BELLY (under BEER). **beer hall** *n.* a large room where beer is sold and drunk. **beer mat** *n.* a small mat made of card, to be put under a glass. **beery** *a.* (*comp.* **beerier**, *superl.* **beeriest**) **1** abounding in beer. **2** like beer. **3** under the influence of beer. **4** fuddled. **beerily** *adv.* **beeriness** *n.*

beest (bēst) *n.* the first milk drawn from a cow after calving. **beestings, beastings** *n.pl.* (*also constr. as sing.*) beest.

beet (bēt) *n.* any plant of the genus *Beta*, whose root is used as a salad and in sugar-making. **beetroot** *n.* the root of the beet used as a salad. **beet sugar** *n.* sugar from sugar beet.

beetle[1] (bē´təl) *n.* **1** an insect of the order Coleoptera, the upper wings of which have been converted into hard wing-cases, the under ones being used for flight, if it is able to fly, the name being popularly confined to those of black colour and large size. **2** any insect resembling these, such as the cockroach. **3** a game in which the players attempt to complete a beetle-shaped drawing according to the throw of a dice. **to beetle along/ off** to hurry, scuttle along. **beetle-crusher** *n.* (*sl.*) **1** a large foot. **2** a heavy boot.

beetle[2] (bē´təl) *n.* **1** a maul; a heavy wooden mallet for driving stones, stakes or tent-pegs into the ground, hammering down paving-stones and other ramming and crushing operations. **2** a machine with rollers, used to give lustre to cloth. ~*v.t.* **1** to beat with a beetle. **2** to give lustre to (cloth) with a beetle.

beetle[3] (bē´təl) *v.i.* to jut out, hang over. ~*a.* projecting, overhanging, scowling. **beetle-browed** *a.* having projecting or overhanging brows.

beeves BEEF.

befall (bifawl´) *v.t.* (*past* **befell** (-fel´), *p.p.* **befallen**) (*poet.*) to happen to. ~*v.i.* to happen.

befit (bifit´) *v.t.* (*pres.p.* **befitting**, *past*, *p.p.* **befitted**) **1** to be suitable to or for. **2** to become, suit. **3** to be incumbent upon. **befitting** *a.* **befittingly** *adv.*

befog (bifog´) *v.t.* (*pres.p.* **befogging**, *past*, *p.p.* **befogged**) **1** to obscure, to confuse. **2** to involve in a fog.

befool (bifool´) *v.t.* **1** to make a fool of. **2** to dupe, delude.

before (bifaw´) *prep.* **1** in front of, in time, space, rank or degree. **2** in the presence or sight of. **3** under the cognizance of. **4** under the influence or impulsion of. **5** in preference to. ~*adv.* **1** ahead, in front. **2** beforehand, already, in the past. **3** on the front. ~*conj.* **1** earlier than. **2** sooner than, rather than. **before Christ** (of a date) before the birth of Christ (e.g. 1000 BC). **before God** with the knowledge or in the sight of God. **beforehand** *adv.* in anticipation, in advance, before the time. **to be beforehand 1** to forestall. **2** to be earlier than expected.

befoul (bifowl´) *v.t.* (*poet.*) **1** to make dirty, to soil. **2** to defile, to degrade.

befriend (bifrend´) *v.t.* to become a friend of, to favour, help.

befuddle (bifŭd´əl) *v.t.* **1** to confuse, baffle. **2** to stupefy with drink. **befuddlement** *n.*

beg (beg) *v.i.* (*pres.p.* **begging**, *past*, *p.p.* **begged**) **1** to ask for alms, to live by asking alms. **2** to make an earnest request or entreaty. **3** (of a dog)

to sit up on the hind quarters expectantly. ~v.t.
1 to ask or supplicate in charity. **2** to ask earnestly, to crave, entreat. **3** to ask politely or formally for. **to beg off** to seek to be released from
some obligation. **to beg pardon** to apologize. **to
beg the question 1** to assume the thing to be
proved. **2** to raise the question. **3** (coll.) to avoid
facing the difficulty. **to go begging 1** to be acceptable to nobody. **2** to be left after everyone has
eaten etc. **beggar** n. **1** a person who begs. **2** a
person who lives by asking alms. **3** a person in
indigent circumstances. **4** (coll.) a fellow; a
youngster. ~v.t. **1** to reduce to want. **2** to impoverish. **3** to exhaust, to outdo. **beggarly** a. **1** like a
beggar. **2** poverty-stricken. **3** mean, contemptible. **beggarliness** n. **beggar-my-neighbour** n. **1** a
game of cards in which players try to deprive
other players of cards. **2** the making of profits at
the expense of others. **beggary** n. **1** the state or
condition of a habitual beggar. **2** extreme indigence. **begging** n. **begging bowl** n. **1** a bowl held
out by a beggar for money or food. **2** an appeal
for help. **begging letter** n. a letter asking for
money.

Usage note The use of beg the question to mean
raise the question is commonly seen as a misunderstanding, and is best avoided.

began BEGIN.
beget (biget´) v.t. (pres.p. **begetting**, past **begot**
(-got´), †**begat** (-gat´), p.p. **begotten**) **1** to engender, to generate, to procreate. **2** to cause to
come into existence.
begin (bigin´) v.i. (pres.p. **beginning**, past **began**
(-gan´), p.p. **begun** (-gŭn´)) to come into existence, to arise, to start; to commence. ~v.t. to
be the first to do, to do the first act of, to enter
on, to commence. **to begin with 1** to take first.
2 firstly. **beginner** n. **1** a person who originates
anything. **2** a person who is the first to do anything. **3** a young learner or practitioner. **beginner's luck** n. good luck shown by someone new
to a game etc. **beginning** n. **1** the first cause, the
origin. **2** the first state or commencement. **3** first
principles, rudiments. **the beginning of the
end** the point at which the outcome becomes
clear.

Usage note In standard English, the past tense
of begin is began, not begun.

begone (bigon´) int. (poet.) get you gone, go
away, depart.
begonia (bigō´niə) n. a plant of the genus
Begonia, cultivated chiefly for their ornamental
foliage.
begorra (bigor´ə) int. (Ir.) by God!
begrime (bigrīm´) v.t. to blacken or soil with
grime.
begrudge (bigrŭj´) v.t. **1** to grudge. **2** to envy (a
person) the possession of. **begrudgingly** adv.
beguile (bigīl´) v.t. **1** to deceive, cheat, deprive of
or lead into by fraud. **2** to charm away the

tedium or weariness of, to amuse. **3** to bewitch.
beguilement n. **beguiler** n. **beguiling** a. **beguil-
ingly** adv.
beguine (bigēn´) n. music or dance in bolero
rhythm, of S American or W Indian origin.
begum (bā´gəm) n. **1** a queen, princess or lady of
high rank in the Indian subcontinent. **2** (**Begum**)
the title of a married Muslim woman.
begun BEGIN.
behalf (bihahf´) n. interest, lieu, stead. **in behalf
of** (N Am.) on someone's behalf, on behalf of.
on behalf of 1 on account of, for the sake of,
2 representing. **3** (coll.) on the part of.

Usage note The use of on behalf of to mean
on the part of (done by, proceeding from) is best
avoided. There are two participants or sets of
participants when something is done or felt on
behalf of another. The distinction can be seen in
a terrific effort on the part of the team on behalf of
their fans.

behave (bihāv´) v.refl. to conduct, to demean.
~v.i. **1** to conduct oneself or itself. **2** to conduct oneself well, to display good manners. **3** to
function properly. **behaviour** (-yə), (esp. N Am.)
behavior n. **1** outward deportment, carriage.
2 manners, conduct, demeanour. **3** the manner
in which a thing acts. **4** (Psych.) response to a
stimulus. **behavioural** a. **behaviouralist** n. a be-
haviourist. **behavioural science** n. the scientific
study of the behaviour of human beings and
other organisms. **behaviourism** n. (Psych.) **1** the
guiding principle of certain psychologists who
hold that the proper basis of psychological science is the objective study of behaviour under
stimuli. **2** the practice of this principle. **behavi-
ourist** n. **behaviouristic** (-ris´-) a. **behaviour
therapy** n. a method of treating neurotic disorders (e.g. a phobia) by gradually conditioning
the patient to react normally.
behead (bihed´) v.t. to cut the head off, to kill by
decapitation.
beheld BEHOLD.
behemoth (bē´əmoth, bihē´-) n. a huge person or
thing.
behest (bihest´) n. (formal) **1** a command. **2** an
injunction.
behind (bihīnd´) prep. **1** at the back of. **2** inferior
to. **3** after, later than. **4** in support of. **5** responsible for the existence or doing of. **6** in the rear of.
7 past in relation to. ~adv. **1** at the back, in the
rear. **2** towards the rear. **3** in the past. **4** backwards, out of sight, on the further side. **5** in reserve. **6** in arrears. ~n. **1** the back part of a person
or garment. **2** the posterior. **3** in Australian Rules
football, a kick etc. from which the ball crosses
the behind line; a score from this. **behind someone's back** without someone's knowledge. **behind the times** old-fashioned, out of date. **to put
behind one 1** to get on with one's life after. **2** to
refuse to think about. **behindhand** a., adv. **1** dilatory, tardy. **2** backward, unfinished. **3** in arrears.

behind line *n.* in Australian Rules football, the line between an inner and outer goalpost.

behold (bihōld´) *v.t.* (*past, p.p.* **beheld** (-held´)) **1** to see. **2** to look attentively at, observe with care. **beholden** *a.* obliged, indebted, under obligation of gratitude (with *to*). **beholder** *n.*

behoof (bihoof´) *n.* advantage, use, profit, benefit.

behove (bihōv´), (*N Am.*) **behoove** (-hoov´) *v.t.* (*formal*) **1** to befit, to be due to, to suit. **2** to be needful to. **3** to be incumbent on.

beige (bāzh) *n.* a light brownish yellow colour. ~*a.* of a light brownish yellow.

being (bē´ing) *n.* **1** the state of existing; existence. **2** lifetime. **3** nature, essence. **4** a thing or person existing. **5** a thing or person imagined as existing. **in being** existing.

bejabers (bijā´bəz), **bejabbers** (bijab´əz) *int.* (*Ir.*) used to express surprise.

bejewelled (bijoo´əld), (*N Am.*) **bejeweled** *a.* decorated with jewels.

bel (bel) *n.* (*Physics*) a measure for comparing the intensity of noises, currents etc., the logarithm to the base 10 of the ratio of one to the other being the number of bels.

belabour (bilā´bə), (*NAm.*) **belabor** *v.t.* **1** to beat, to thrash. **2** to assault verbally. **3** to dwell unduly on.

belated (bilā´tid) *a.* **1** very late; behind time. **2** too late. **3** overtaken by night, benighted. **belatedly** *adv.* **belatedness** *n.*

belay (bilā´) *v.t.* **1** to fasten (a running rope) by winding it round a cleat or belaying-pin. **2** to turn a rope round (an object). **3** to secure (a climber) to a rope. ~*n.* **1** a turn of a rope round an object. **2** that around which a climber's rope is belayed. ~*int.* (*Naut.*) stop; enough. **belaying-pin** *n.* **1** a stout pin to which running ropes may be belayed. **2** a projection round which a rope can be tied or hitched.

bel canto (bel kan´tō) *n.* a style of operatic singing characterized by purity of tone and exact phrasing.

belch (belch) *v.i.* **1** to eject wind noisily by the mouth from the stomach. **2** to issue out, as by eructation. ~*v.t.* **1** to expel from the mouth noisily or with violence. **2** to eject (smoke etc.), to throw out. **3** to utter in a noisy or drunken manner. ~*n.* **1** the act of belching, an eructation. **2** an eruption, a burst (of smoke or fire).

†**beldam** (bel´dəm), **beldame** *n.* **1** an old woman. **2** a hag, a witch.

beleaguer (bilē´gə) *v.t.* **1** to besiege. **2** to harass.

☒ **beleive** common misspelling of BELIEVE.

belemnite (bel´əmnīt) *n.* **1** a conical, sharply pointed fossil shell of a cephalopod of the order Belemnoidea, allied to the cuttlefish. **2** any such cephalopod.

belfry (bel´fri) *n.* (*pl.* **belfries**) **1** a bell tower attached to or separate from a church or other building. **2** the chamber for the bells in a church tower.

Belgian (bel´jən) *a.* of or relating to Belgium or to the Belgians. ~*n.* **1** a native or inhabitant of Belgium. **2** a kind of canary. **Belgian hare** *n.* a large breed of domestic rabbit, dark red in colouring. **Belgic** *a.* of the ancient Belgae or of Belgium.

belie (bilī´) *v.t.* (*pres.p.* **belying**, *past, p.p.* **belied**) **1** to tell lies about, to slander. **2** to misrepresent. **3** to be faithless to. **4** to fail to perform or justify.

belief (bilēf´) *n.* **1** religion, religious faith. **2** reliance, confidence. **3** the mental act or operation of accepting a fact or proposition as true. **4** a thing believed to be true. **5** an opinion firmly held, a persuasion. **beyond belief** incredible.

believe (bilēv´) *v.t.* **1** to accept as true. **2** to be of the opinion that. **3** to have confidence in or reliance on. **4** to give credence to. ~*v.i.* **1** to have faith. **2** to have religious faith. **to believe in 1** to trust in, to rely on. **2** to believe in the existence of. **to make believe** to pretend. **believable** *a.* **believability** (-bil´-) *n.* **believableness** *n.* **believably** *adv.* **believer** *n.*

☒ **beligerent** common misspelling of BELLIGERENT.

Belisha beacon (bilē´shə) *n.* a flashing orange globe on a post to indicate a street crossing for pedestrians.

belittle (bilit´əl) *v.t.* **1** to depreciate or undermine verbally. **2** to make little. **3** to dwarf. **belittlement** *n.* **belittler** *n.* **belittlingly** *adv.*

bell[1] (bel) *n.* **1** a hollow body of cast metal, usu. in the shape of an inverted cup with recurved edge, so formed as to emit a clear musical sound when struck by a hammer. **2** a buzzer or ringing device that functions as a signal like a bell. **3** the sound of a bell, esp. as a signal. **4** (*Naut.*) **a** the bell struck on board ship every half-hour to indicate time. **b** a space of half an hour. **5** any object in nature and art of a form similar to that of a bell. ~*v.i.* **1** to have the shape of a bell. **2** (of hops) to be in flower. ~*v.t.* **1** to provide with a bell. **2** to give the shape of a bell to. **3** to utter loudly. **to give someone a bell** to telephone someone. **to ring a bell 1** to revive a memory. **2** to sound familiar. **bellbird** *n.* a bird with a bell-like song, as any Central or S American bird of the genus *Procnias*, an Australian flycatcher, *Oreoica gutturalis*, or a New Zealand honeyeater, *Anthornis melanura*. **bell-bottom** *n.* **1** a flare below the knee of a trouser leg. **2** (*pl.*) trousers with this type of flare. **bell-bottomed** *a.* **bellboy**, **bellhop** *n.* (*NAm.*) a hotel page-boy. **bell-buoy** *n.* a buoy to which a bell is attached, rung by the motion of the waves. **bellflower** *n.* a bell-shaped flower or plant with such flowers, of the genus *Campanula*. **bell-founder** *n.* a caster of bells. **bell-founding** *n.* **bell-glass** *n.* a bell-shaped glass for protecting plants. **bell jar** *n.* a bell-shaped glass cover used in laboratories to protect apparatus or contain gases in experiments etc. **bellman** *n.* (*pl.* **bellmen**) a public crier who attracts attention by ringing a bell. **bell metal** *n.* an alloy of copper and tin, usu.

with a little zinc, used for bells. **bell pull** n. a cord or handle by which a bell is rung. **bell punch** n. a ticket punch in which a bell is rung each time it is used. **bell push** n. a button which operates an electric bell. **bell-ringer** n. a person whose business it is to ring a church or public bell at stated times. **bell-ringing** n. **bells and whistles** n.pl. (esp. Comput., coll.) showy but inessential accessories or additional features. **bell tent** n. a conical tent. **bell-wether** n. **1** the sheep that wears a bell and leads a flock. **2** (fig.) a leader.

bell² (bel) n. the cry of a stag at rutting time. ~v.i. (of a stag) to bellow.

belladonna (belədon´ə) n. **1** deadly nightshade or dwale, Atropa belladonna. **2** (Med.) a drug prepared from the leaves and root of this plant. **belladonna lily** n. a bulbous plant, Amaryllis belladonna, which grows in S Africa, and has white or pink flowers.

belle (bel) n. **1** a beautiful woman. **2** a reigning beauty. **belle laide** (lād´) n. (pl. **belles laides** (bel lād´)) a woman who is attractive in spite of being ugly.

belles-lettres (bellet´rə) n.pl. (also constr. as sing.) polite literature, the humanities, pure literature. **belletrism** n. devotion to belles-lettres. **belletrist** n. **belletristic** (-letris´tik) a.

bellicose (bel´ikōs) a. warlike; inclined to war or fighting. **bellicosity** (-kos´-) n. inclination to war.

belligerent (bilij´ərənt) a. **1** carrying on war. **2** of or relating to persons or nations carrying on war. **3** aggressive. ~n. a nation, party or individual engaged in war. **belligerence, belligerency** n. **1** the state of being at war. **2** aggressive or warlike behaviour. **belligerently** adv.

bellow (bel´ō) v.i. **1** to emit a loud hollow sound (as a bull). **2** to raise an outcry or clamour, to bawl, to vociferate. **3** to emit a loud hollow sound (as the sea, the wind, artillery etc.). ~v.t. to utter with a loud hollow voice. ~n. the roar of a bull, or any similar sound.

bellows (bel´ōz) n.pl. (also constr. as sing.) **1** an instrument or machine for supplying a strong blast of air to a fire or a wind instrument. **2** the expansible portion of a photographic camera. **3** (fig.) the lungs.

belly (bel´i) n. (pl. **bellies**) **1** that part of the human body in front which extends from the breast to the insertion of the lower limbs. **2** the corresponding part of a four-legged animal. **3** the part containing the stomach and bowels. **4** the stomach, the womb. **5** appetite, gluttony. **6** the front or lower surface of an object. **7** anything swelling out or protuberant. **8** the bulging part of a violin or a similar instrument. ~v.t. (3rd pers. sing. pres. **bellies**, pres.p. **bellying**, past, p.p. **bellied**) to cause to swell out, to render protuberant. ~v.i. to swell or bulge out, to become protuberant. **bellyache** n. a pain in the stomach. ~v.i. (coll.) to express discontent, to whine.

bellyacher n. **bellyband** n. a band passing under the belly of a horse, ass or other beast of burden to keep the saddle in place. **belly button** n. (coll.) the navel. **belly dance** n. an erotic solo dance involving undulating movements of the abdomen. **belly dancer** n. **belly dancing** n. **bellyflop** n. an awkward dive into the water on to the front of the body and flat against the surface. ~v.i. (pres.p. **bellyflopping**, past, p.p. **bellyflopped**) to perform a bellyflop. **bellyful** n. (pl. **bellyfuls**) **1** as much as fills the belly, as much food as satisfies the appetite. **2** (coll.) a sufficiency, more than enough. **belly landing** n. a landing of an aircraft without using the landing wheels. **belly laugh** n. a deep, hearty laugh.

belong (bilong´) v.i. **1** to be the property, attribute, appendage, member, right, duty, concern or business (of) (The book belongs to me; He belongs to several clubs). **2** to be a native or resident of (I belong to Glasgow). **3** to be rightly placed in (It belongs in the cupboard; You belong in jail). **belonging** n. **1** anything belonging to one (usu. in pl.). **2** a quality or endowment. **3** (pl., coll.) one's possessions. **belongingness** n.

Belorussian (belōrŭsh´ən), **Byelorussian** (byelō-) a. **1** of Belarus in eastern Europe. **2** of its language or people. ~n. **1** the Slavonic language of Belarus. **2** a native or citizen of Belarus, also called White Russian.

beloved (bilŭvd´, -lŭv´id) a. loved greatly. ~n. a person who is greatly loved.

below (bilō´) prep. **1** under in place. **2** under the surface of. **3** downstream from. **4** lower on a scale than. **5** inferior to in rank, degree or excellence. **6** unworthy of, unsuitable to. ~adv. **1** in or to a lower place, rank or station. **2** downstairs. **3** downstream. **4** lower on the same page, or on a following page. **5** on the lower side or surface. **6** on earth (as opposed to heaven). **7** in hell (as opposed to earth).

belt (belt) n. **1** a broad, flat strip of leather or other material worn around the waist or over the shoulder, esp. to hold clothes in place, to hold a weapon, as a safety restraint, or as a badge of rank or distinction. **2** anything resembling a belt in shape. **3** a broad strip or stripe. **4** a strait. **5** a zone or region. **6** a flat endless strap passing round two wheels and communicating motion from one to the other. **7** a strap carrying cartridges for a machine gun. **8** (coll.) a blow. ~v.t. **1** to encircle with or as with a belt. **2** to fasten on with a belt. **3** to invest with a belt. **4** to deck with a zone of colour. **5** to thrash with a belt. ~v.i. (sl.) to move at speed, to rush. **belt and braces** offering double security. **to belt out** to sing or emit (a sound) vigorously or with enthusiasm. **to belt up 1** (sl.) to stop talking (often imper.). **2** to fasten with a belt. **3** to put a seat belt on. **to hit below the belt** to act unfairly in a contest (from boxing). **to tighten one's belt** to make economies, to reduce expenditure. **under one's belt** secured in one's possession. **belt drive** n. a transmission system using a flexible belt. **belted** a. belted **galloway** n. a variety of a breed of usu. black beef cattle, having a broad white band. **belter** n. **beltman** n. (pl. **beltmen**) (Austral.) the member of a beach life-saving team who swims out with a line attached to their belt. **beltway** n. (N Am.) a ring road.

beluga (biloo'gə) n. **1** a large sturgeon, Huso huso, from the Black and Caspian Seas. **2** caviar obtained from this sturgeon. **3** the white whale, Delphinapterus leucas.

belvedere (bel'vidiə) n. **1** a turret, lantern or cupola, raised above the roof of a building to command a view. **2** a summer house built on an eminence for the same purpose.

belying BELIE.

BEM abbr. British Empire Medal.

bemire (bimīə') v.t. to cover or soil with mire. **bemired** a. stuck or sunk in mire.

bemoan (bimōn') v.t. to moan over, to deplore.

bemuse (bimūz') v.t. to make utterly confused or dazed. **bemusedly** (-zidli) adv. **bemusement** n.

ben (ben) n. a mountain peak in Scotland etc.

bench (bench) n. **1** a long seat or form. **2** a carpenter's or other mechanic's work table. **3** (Law) **a** the office of judge. **b** a seat where judges and magistrates sit in court. **c** judges or magistrates collectively, or sitting as a court. **4** other official seats and those who have a right to occupy them. **5** (pl.) groups of seats in the Houses of Parliament. **6** a terrace or ledge in masonry, quarrying, mining, earthwork etc. **7** a platform for exhibiting dogs. ~v.t. **1** to exhibit (dogs) at a show. **2** (N Am.) to remove (a player) from a game. **3** to furnish with benches. **bencher** n. **1** (Law) any one of the senior members of an Inn of Court who collectively govern the Inn, and have power of 'calling to the bar'. **2** (in comb.) a person who sits on a particular bench in Parliament. **benchmark** n. **1** a mark cut in some durable material in a line of survey for reference at a future time. **2** anything that serves as a standard of comparison or point of reference. ~v.t. to test or assess using a benchmark. **benchmark test** n. a test using a benchmark. **bench test** n. (esp. Comput.) a test of a new component, device etc. before it is installed, to check its condition. ~v.t. to run a bench test on.

bend (bend) v.t. (past, p.p. **bent** (bent), **bended**) **1** to bring into a curved shape (as a bow) by pulling the string. **2** to render curved or angular. **3** to deflect. **4** to direct to a certain point. **5** to apply closely. **6** to bring into operation. **7** to incline from the vertical. **8** to subdue. **9** to fasten, to make fast. **10** to tie into a knot. ~v.i. **1** to assume the form of a curve or angle. **2** to incline from an erect position, to bow, stoop. **3** to surrender, submit. **4** to turn in a new direction. ~n. **1** a bending curve or flexure. **2** a sudden turn in a road or river. **3** (Her.) an ordinary formed by two parallel lines drawn across from the dexter chief to the sinister base point of an escutcheon.

4 a knot. **on bended knees 1** with the knees bent. **2** as a suppliant. **round the bend** (coll.) crazy, insane. **the bends** (coll.) caisson disease, decompression sickness. **bendable** a. **bender** n. (sl.) **1** a bout of heavy drinking. **2** (offensive) a homosexual. **bendy** a. (comp. **bendier**, superl. **bendiest**). **bendiness** n.

beneath (binēth') prep. **1** below, under in place or position. **2** unworthy of. ~adv. in a lower place, below.

benedicite (benidī'siti) int. bless you, good gracious. ~n. **1** the invocation of a blessing. **2** grace before meat.

Benedictine (benidik'tēn, -tin) a. of or relating to St Benedict, 480–543, or to the order of monks founded by him. ~n. **1** a monk or nun of the order founded (529) by St Benedict. **2** a liqueur first made by Benedictine monks (a registered name).

benediction (benidik'shən) n. **1** a blessing pronounced officially. **2** the act of blessing or invoking a blessing. **3** grace before or after meals. **4** blessedness, grace, blessing. **benedictory** a. of or relating to or expressing benediction.

benefaction (benifak'shən) n. **1** a gift or endowment for charitable purposes. **2** the conferring of a benefit. **3** a benefit conferred. **benefactor** (ben'ifaktə) n. **1** a person who gives another help or friendly service. **2** a person who gives to a religious or charitable institution. **benefactress** (-tris) n. a female benefactor.

benefice (ben'ifis) n. **1** an ecclesiastical living. **2** the property attached to such a living. **beneficed** a. possessed of a benefice.

beneficent (binef'isənt) a. **1** kind, generous, doing good. **2** characterized by benevolence. **beneficence** n. **beneficently** adv.

beneficial (benifish'əl) a. **1** advantageous, helpful. **2** remedial. **3** (Law) **a** of or belonging to usufruct. **b** enjoying the usufruct of property. **beneficially** adv.

beneficiary (benifish'əri) n. (pl. **beneficiaries**) **1** a person who receives a favour. **2** the holder of a benefice, a person who benefits under a trust.

benefit (ben'ifit) n. **1** profit, advantage, gain. **2** advantage, something favourable. **3** (usu. pl.) money or services provided under government social security or private pension schemes etc. **4** a theatrical, music-hall or other performance, the receipts from which, with certain deductions, are given to some person or charity. **5** (Law) the advantage of belonging to some privileged order. ~v.t. (pres.p. **benefiting**, (N Am.) **benefitting**, past, p.p. **benefited**, (N Am.) **benefitted**) **1** to do good to. **2** to be of advantage or profit to. ~v.i. to derive advantage. **benefit club, benefit society** n. a society whose members, in return for a certain periodical payment, receive certain benefits in sickness or old age. **benefit of clergy** n. **1** sanction by the Church. **2** (Hist.) a privilege that put the clergy outside secular jurisdiction. **benefit of the doubt** n. the assumption of innocence in the absence of clear evidence of guilt.

benevolent (binev´ələnt) *a.* **1** disposed to do good, kind, generous. **2** charitable. **benevolence** *n.* **benevolently** *adv.*

B.Eng. *abbr.* Bachelor of Engineering.

Bengali (bengaw´li, beng·gaw´li) *a.* of or relating to Bengal, a region coinciding with Bangladesh and the Indian state of W Bengal, formerly an Indian province, its people or language. ~*n.* (*pl.* **Bengalis**) **1** a native or inhabitant of Bengal; a person whose family came from Bengal. **2** the language of Bengalis.

benighted (binī´tid) *a.* **1** involved in moral or intellectual darkness; ignorant; uncivilized. **2** overtaken by night. **benightedness** *n.*

benign (binīn´) *a.* **1** kind-hearted, gracious, mild. **2** favourable, propitious. **3** agreeable, salubrious. **4** (*Med.*) (of a tumour etc.) not malignant. **benignant** (-nig´nənt) *a.* **1** gracious, kind, benevolent. **2** favourable, propitious. **3** (*Med.*) (of a tumour etc.) not malignant. **benignancy** *n.* **benignantly** *adv.* **benignity** (-nig´ni-) *n.* (*pl.* **benignities**) **1** kindly feeling. **2** kindness, a favour bestowed. **benignly** *adv.* **benign neglect** *n.* neglect that is intended to benefit the subject.

benjamin (ben´jəmin) *n.* benzoin.

bent[1] (bent) *n.* **1** an inclination, a bias. **2** a disposition, a propensity. **3** tension, extent, capacity. ~*a.* **1** curved. **2** intent (on), resolved (to). **3** (*sl.*) dishonest. **4** crooked. **5** (*sl.*) stolen. **6** (*sl., offensive*) homosexual. **bentwood** *n.* wood steamed and curved in moulds for making furniture.

bent[2] (bent) *n.* **1** stiff, rushlike grass, esp. of the genus *Agrostis*. **2** old grass stalks.

bent[3] BEND.

benthos (ben´thos), **benthon** (-thon) *n.* the sedentary animal and plant life on the ocean bed or at the bottom of a lake. **benthal, benthic** *a.*

bentonite (ben´tənīt) *n.* an absorbent clay used in various industries as a filler, bonding agent etc.

benumb (binŭm´) *v.t.* **1** to render torpid or numb. **2** to deaden, to paralyse.

Benzedrine® (ben´zidrēn) *n.* amphetamine.

benzene (ben´zēn) *n.* (*Chem.*) an aromatic hydrocarbon obtained from coal tar and some petroleum fractions, used in industry in the synthesis of organic chemical compounds, as a solvent and insecticide. **benzene ring** *n.* a closed chain of six carbon atoms each bound to a hydrogen atom in the benzene molecule. **benzenoid** *a.* **benzine** (-zēn), **benzin** (-zin) *n.* a mixture of liquid hydrocarbons, distilled from petroleum, used esp. as a solvent and motor fuel. **benzodiazepine** (-zōdīā-´zəpīn, -az´-) *n.* any of a group of synthetic drugs used as sedatives and tranquillizers. **benzol** (-zol), **benzole** (-zōl) *n.* unrefined benzene used as a fuel.

benzoin (ben´zoin, -zōin) *n.* **1** a resin obtained from trees of the genus *Styrax*, used in medicine and in perfumery, also called (*gum*) *benjamin*. **2** a ketone present in the resin benzoin. **benzoic** (-zō´-) *a.* **benzoic acid** *n.* an acid present in

benzoin and other natural resins, used in medicines, dyes, as a food preservative and in organic synthesis.

bequeath (bikwēdh´) *v.t.* **1** to leave by will or testament. **2** to transmit to future generations. **bequeathable** *a.* **bequeathal, bequeathment** *n.* **bequeather** *n.* **bequest** (-kwest´) *n.* **1** the act of bequeathing. **2** that which is bequeathed; a legacy.

berate (birāt´) *v.t.* to rebuke or scold vehemently.

Berber (bœ´bə) *n.* **1** a member of the Hamitic peoples of N Africa. **2** their language. ~*a.* of or relating to this people or their language.

berberis (bœ´bəris) *n.* (*pl.* **berberises**) **1** any shrub of the genus *Berberis*. **2** the berry of this shrub.

berceuse (beəscez´) *n.* (*pl.* **berceuses** (beəscez´)) **1** a lullaby, a cradle song. **2** a piece of lulling instrumental music.

bereave (birēv´) *v.t.* (*past, p.p.* **bereaved, bereft** (-reft´)) **1** to deprive, rob or spoil of anything. **2** to render desolate (*usu. in p.p.*). **bereaved** *a.* deprived of a near relative or friend by death. **bereavement** *n.* **bereft** *a.* deprived (esp. of something abstract, as hope, dignity etc.).

beret (ber´ā) *n.* a round, brimless flat cap fitting the head fairly closely.

berg[1] (bœg) *n.* an iceberg.

berg[2] (bœg) *n.* (*S Afr.*) a mountain or hill (often used in place names). **berg wind** *n.* a hot dry wind in South Africa blowing from the north to the coast.

bergamot[1] (bœ´gəmot) *n.* **1** a citrus tree, *Citrus bergamia*, which yields a fragrant essential oil used in perfumery. **2** the oil itself. **3** a kind of mint, *Mentha citrata*, which yields an oil somewhat similar.

bergamot[2] (bœ´gəmot) *n.* a juicy kind of pear.

bergschrund (beəg´shrŭnd) *n.* a crevasse or fissure between the base of a steep slope and a glacier or névé.

beribboned (birib´ənd) *a.* decorated with ribbons.

beriberi (beribˈer´i, ber´-) *n.* a degenerative disease due to a deficiency of vitamin B_1.

berk (bœk), **burk** *n.* (*sl.*) an idiot.

berkelium (bœkē´liəm) *n.* (*Chem.*) an artificially produced radioactive element, at. no. 97, chem. symbol Bk.

Berks. (bahks) *abbr.* Berkshire.

Berliner (bœlin´ə) *n.* **1** a native or inhabitant of Berlin in Germany. **2** a lightly-fried iced bun with jam inside.

berm (bœm) *n.* **1** a narrow ledge at the foot of the exterior slope of a parapet. **2** the bank of a canal opposite the towing-path.

Bermuda shorts (bəmū´də), **Bermudas** *n.pl.* tight-fitting knee-length shorts.

berry (ber´i) *n.* (*pl.* **berries**) **1** any smallish, round, fleshy fruit. **2** any one of the eggs of a fish or lobster. **3** (*Bot.*) a many-seeded, indehiscent, pulpy fruit, the seeds of which are loosely scattered through the pulp. **4** a coffee bean. ~*v.i.* (3rd *pers. sing. pres.* **berries,** *pres.p.* **berrying,** *past,* *p.p.* **berried) 1** to go berry-gathering. **2** to bear or produce berries. **berried** *a.*

berserk (bəsœk´), **baresark** (beə´sahk´) *n.* (*also* **berserker**) a Norse warrior possessed of preternatural strength and fighting with desperate fury and courage. ~*a.,* *adv.* frenzied; filled with furious rage. **to go berserk** to lose control of one's actions in violent rage.

berth (bœth) *n.* **1** a sleeping place on board ship. **2** a sleeping place in a railway carriage. **3** a place for a ship at a wharf. **4** sea room. **5** a convenient place for mooring. **6** a situation on board ship. **7** a room in a ship where any number of officers mess and reside. **8** a permanent job or situation of any kind. **9** a suitable place for keeping anything. ~*v.t.* **1** to moor in a berth. **2** to furnish with a berth. **to give a wide berth to 1** to keep away from. **2** to steer clear of.

bertha (bœ´thə) *n.* **1** a wide, deep collar, often of lace. **2** a small cape on a dress.

beryl (ber´il) *n.* **1** a gem nearly identical with the emerald, but varying in colour from pale green to yellow or white. **2** a silicate of aluminium and beryllicum, occurring usu. in hexagonal prisms.

beryllium (biril´iəm) *n.* (*Chem.*) a light metallic element, at. no. 4, chem. symbol Be, used as a component in nuclear reactors and to harden alloys etc.

beseech (bisēch´) *v.t.* (*past, p.p.* **besought** (-sawt´), **beseeched) 1** to ask earnestly, implore, supplicate. **2** to ask earnestly for. **beseeching** *a.* **beseechingly** *adv.*

beset (biset´) *v.t.* (*pres.p.* **besetting,** *past, p.p.* **beset) 1** to set upon, to fall upon, to assail. **2** to set or surround (with). **besetting sin** *n.* the sin that particularly tempts a person.

beside (bisīd´) *prep.* **1** by the side of, side by side with. **2** in comparison with. **3** near, hard by, close to. **4** away from, wide of. ~*adv.* besides. **beside oneself** out of one's wits with worry etc. **besides** *prep.* **1** in addition to, over and above. **2** other than, except. ~*adv.* **1** moreover, further, over and above, in addition. **2** otherwise.

besiege (bisēj´) *v.t.* **1** to surround (a place) with intent to capture it by military force. **2** to crowd round. **3** to assail importunately. **besieger** *n.*

besmear (bismiə´) *v.t.* **1** to cover or daub with something unctuous or viscous. **2** to soil, to defile, to sully the reputation of.

besmirch (bismœch´) *v.t.* **1** to soil, discolour. **2** to sully the reputation of, to dishonour.

besom (bē´zəm) *n.* **1** a broom made of twigs or heath bound round a handle. **2** anything that sweeps away impurity. **3** (*North., Sc., derog. or facet.*) a term of reproach for a woman.

besot (bisot´) *v.t.* (*pres.p.* **besotting,** *past, p.p.* **besotted) 1** to make sottish. **2** to stupefy, to muddle. **3** to cause to dote on. **besotted** *a.*

besought BESEECH.

bespangle (bispang´gəl) *v.t.* to cover over with or as with spangles.

bespatter (bispat´ə) *v.t.* **1** to spatter over or about. **2** to load with abuse.

bespeak (bispēk´) *v.t.* (*past* **bespoke** (-spōk´), *p.p.* **bespoken** (-ən)) **1** to speak for, to arrange for, to order beforehand. **2** to ask. **3** to request. **4** to give evidence of. **5** to betoken, to foreshow. **bespoke** *a.* **1** made-to-measure. **2** (of a suit etc.) made to a customer's specific requirements. **3** making or selling such articles.

bespectacled (bispek´təkəld) *a.* wearing spectacles.

besprinkle (bispring´kəl) *v.t.* **1** to sprinkle or scatter over. **2** to bedew.

best (best) *a.* **1** of the highest excellence. **2** surpassing all others. **3** most desirable. ~*adv.* **1** in the highest degree. **2** to the most advantage. **3** with most ease. **4** most intimately. ~*n.* **1** the best thing. **2** the utmost. **3** (*collect.*) the best people. **4** the deciding majority (*play the best of seven games*). ~*v.t.* **1** to get the better of. **2** to cheat, outwit. **at best** as far as can be expected. **at one's best** in prime condition, in one's prime. **to be (all) for the best** to have a happy or successful outcome, though immediately unpleasant. **to get the best of** to get the advantage or victory over. **to give best to** to concede defeat to, to give way to. **to have the best of** to have the advantage or victory over. **to make the best of 1** to make the most of. **2** to be content with. **to the best of** to the utmost extent of. **with the best of them** without having to be ashamed of one's ability etc. **best-before date** *n.* **1** the date marked on the packaging of a perishable product indicating the date before which it should be used. **2** (*coll.*) the optimum age of a person, machine etc., before decline sets in. **best bib and tucker** *n.* (*coll.*) one's best clothing, one's best outfit. **best bower** *n.* the starboard bower. **best boy** *n.* the assistant to the chief electrician of a film crew. **best buy** *n.* a recommended item, a bargain. **best end** *n.* the rib end (of a neck of lamb etc.). **best man** *n.* a groomsman. **best part** *n.* the largest part (of), the most. **best-seller** *n.* **1** a popular book which has sold in large numbers. **2** a writer of such a book. **best-sell** *v.i.* to be or become a best-seller.

bestial (bes´tiəl) *a.* **1** brutish, sensual, obscene, sexually depraved. **2** resembling a beast. **3** of or relating to the lower animals, esp. the quadrupeds. **bestiality** (-tial´-) *n.* (*pl.* **bestialities) 1** bestial behaviour. **2** sexual relations between a person and an animal. **3** a bestial act. **bestialize,** **bestialise** *v.t.* **bestially** *adv.*

bestiary (bes´tiəri) *n.* (*pl.* **bestiaries)** a moralized natural history of animals.

bestir (bistœ´) *v.t.* (*pres.p.* **bestirring,** *past, p.p.* **bestirred)** to rouse into activity.

bestow (bistō´) *v.t.* **1** to give as a present. **2** to stow, to lay up. **3** to stow away, to lodge, provide with quarters. **4** to expend, to lay out. **bestowal** *n.* **bestower** *n.*

bestrew (bistroo´) *v.t.* (*p.p.* **bestrewed, bestrewn) 1** to strew over. **2** to lie scattered over.

bestride (bistrīd´) *v.t.* (*past* **bestrode** (-strōd´), *p.p.* **bestridden** (-strid´ən)) **1** to sit upon with the legs astride. **2** to span, overarch.

bet (bet) *n.* **1** an act of betting, a wager. **2** a sum staked on a contingent event. ~*v.t.* (*pres.p.* **betting**, *past, p.p.* **bet, betted**) **1** to lay a wager against. **2** to stake on a contingency. ~*v.i.* to risk a sum of money or belonging against another's on a contingent event, to lay a wager. **better**[1], **bettor** *n.* a person who makes bets. **betting** *n.* **1** gambling by risking money on contingent events. **2** the odds on an event. **what's the betting?** I think it very likely (that). **betting shop** *n.* a bookmaker's.

beta (bē´tə) *n.* **1** the second letter of the Greek alphabet (β, B). **2** a second-class mark given to a student's work. **3** the second of a series of numerous compounds and other enumerations. **beta blocker** *n.* a drug that reduces the heart rate, esp. used to treat high blood pressure, but also used illegally by some sports competitors to improve their concentration and performance. **beta decay** *n.* (*Physics*) radioactive decay accompanying the emission of an electron. **beta particle** *n.* (*Physics*) a negatively-charged particle emitted by certain radioactive substances, identified as an electron. **beta rhythm, beta waves** *n.* the normal electrical activity of the brain. **beta test** *n.* a test of a new product, esp. in computer software, carried out by an external tester (typically a customer or potential customer) before final release (cp. ALPHA TEST (under ALPHA)). ~*v.t.* to put (a product) through such a test. **betatron** (-tron) *n.* (*Physics*) an electrical apparatus for accelerating electrons to high energies.

betake (bitāk´) *v.refl.* (*past* **betook** (-tuk´), *p.p.* **betaken**) **1** to take oneself (to). **2** to have recourse (to).

betel (bē´təl) *n.* **1** a shrubby Asian plant with evergreen leaves, *Piper betle*. **2** its leaf, used as a wrapper to enclose a few slices of the areca nut with a little shell lime, which are chewed by people in the East. **betel-nut** *n.* the nut of the betel-tree. **betel-tree** *n.* an Asian palm, *Areca catechu* (so called because its nut is chewed with betel leaves).

bête noire (bet nwah´) *n.* (*pl.* **bêtes noires** (bet nwah´)) a bugbear, pet aversion.

betide (bitīd´) *v.t.* (*past* **betided, betid** (-tid´), *p.p.* **betid**) (*esp. poet.*) to happen to. ~*v.i.* to happen, to come to pass.

betoken (bitō´kən) *v.t.* **1** to foreshow, to be an omen of, to indicate. **2** to be a type of.

betony (bet´əni) *n.* (*pl.* **betonies**) **1** a labiate plant, *Stachys officinalis*, with purple flowers. **2** any of various similar plants.

betook BETAKE.

betray (bitrā´) *v.t.* **1** to deliver up a person or thing treacherously. **2** to be false to. **3** to disclose treacherously. **4** to disclose against one's will or intention; to reveal incidentally. **5** to lead astray. **betrayal** *n.* **betrayer** *n.*

betroth (bitrōdh´) *v.t.* to contract (two persons) in an engagement to marry, to engage, to affiance. **betrothal, betrothment** *n.* **betrothed** *a.* engaged to be married, affianced. ~*n.* a person engaged to be married.

better[1] BET.

better[2] (bet´ə) *a.* **1** superior, more excellent. **2** more desirable. **3** greater in degree. **4** improved in health. ~*adv.* **1** in a superior, more excellent or more desirable manner. **2** more correctly or fully. **3** with greater profit. **4** in a greater or higher degree. **5** more. ~*n.pl.* social superiors. ~*v.t.* **1** to make better. **2** to excel, to surpass, to improve on. ~*v.i.* to become better, to improve. **better off** in better circumstances. **for better (or) for worse** whatever the circumstances. **for the better** in the way of improvement. **had better** would be wiser to (do), would be advised to (do). **to get the better of** to defeat, to outwit. **to think better of** to reconsider. **better feelings** *n.pl.* one's moral sense; the kindlier side of one's nature. **better half** *n.* one's wife. **betterment** *n.* **1** amelioration. **2** an improvement of property. **3** improvements made on new lands.

betting, bettor BET.

between (bitwēn´) *prep.* **1** in, on, into, along or across the place, space or interval of any kind separating (two points, lines, places or objects). **2** intermediate in relation to. **3** related to both of. **4** related so as to separate. **5** related so as to connect, from one to another of. **6** among. **7** in shares among, so as to affect all. ~*adv.* **1** intermediately. **2** in an intervening space or time. **3** in relation to both. **4** to and fro. **5** during or in an interval. **between ourselves** in confidence. **betwixt and between 1** (*coll.*) neither one thing nor the other. **2** (*coll.*) half and half. **3** (*coll.*) middling. **in between** intermediate(ly). **betweenwhiles, betweentimes** *adv.* **1** now and then. **2** at intervals.

†**betwixt** (bitwikst´) *prep., adv.* between.

BeV *abbr.* billion electronvolt(s) in the US: equivalent to gigaelectronvolt(s), GeV.

bevatron (bev´ətron) *n.* an electrical apparatus for accelerating protons to high energies.

bevel (bev´əl) *n.* **1** a tool consisting of a flat rule with a movable tongue or arm for setting off angles. **2** a slope from the right angle, an inclination of two planes, except one of 90°. ~*v.t.* (*pres.p.* **bevelling**, (*N Am.*) **beveling**, *past, p.p.* **bevelled**, (*N Am.*) **beveled**) to cut away to a slope, to give a bevel angle to. ~*v.i.* to recede from the perpendicular, to slant. ~*a.* **1** oblique, sloping, slanting. **2** at more than a right angle. **bevel gear, bevel gearing** *n.* a gear or gearing for transmitting motion from one shaft to another by means of bevel wheels. **bevel square** *n.* a bevel (the tool). **bevel wheel** *n.* a cogged wheel, the axis of which forms an angle (usu. 90°) with the shaft.

beverage (bev´ərij) *n.* (*esp. formal*) any drink other than water. **bevvy** *n.* (*pl.* **bevvies**) (*sl.*) an alcoholic drink.

bevy (bev´i) *n.* (*pl.* **bevies**) **1** a flock of larks or quails. **2** a company of women.

bewail (biwāl´) *v.t.* to wail over, to lament for. ~*v.i.* to express grief. **bewailer** *n.*

beware (biwee´) *v.i.* **1** to be wary, to be on one's guard. **2** to take care. ~*v.t.* **1** to be wary of, on guard against. **2** to look out for.

bewhiskered (biwis´kəd) *a.* **1** having whiskers. **2** very old.

Bewick's swan (bū´iks) *n.* a small white swan, native to E Asia and NE Europe, a race of *Cygnus columbianus.*

bewig (biwig´) *v.t.* (*pres.p.* **bewigging**, *past*, *p.p.* **bewigged**) to adorn with a wig. **bewigged** *a.*

bewilder (biwil´də) *v.t.* to perplex, confuse, lead astray. **bewilderedly** *adv.* **bewildering** *a.* **bewilderingly** *adv.* **bewilderment** *n.*

bewitch (biwich´) *v.t.* **1** to charm, to fascinate, to allure. **2** to practise witchcraft against. **bewitching** *a.* **bewitchingly** *adv.*

beyond (biyond´) *prep.* **1** on, to or towards the farther side of. **2** past, later than. **3** exceeding in quantity or amount, more than. **4** surpassing in quality or degree, outside the limit of. **5** in addition to, over and above. ~*adv.* **1** at a greater distance. **2** farther away. ~*n.* that which lies beyond human experience or after death.

bezant (bizant´, bez´-), **byzant** *n.* **1** a gold coin struck at Constantinople by the Byzantine emperors, varying greatly in value. **2** (*Her.*) a gold roundel borne as a charge.

bezel (bez´əl) *n.* **1** a sloping edge like that of a cutting tool. **2** any one of the oblique sides of a cut gem. **3** the groove by which a watch-glass or a jewel is held.

bezique (bizēk´) *n.* **1** a game of cards for two players, using a double pack. **2** the combination of the jack of diamonds and queen of spades in this game.

bezoar (bē´zaw, bez´ōə) *n.* a calculous concretion found in the stomach of certain animals and supposed to be an antidote to poisons.

bf *abbr.* **1** bloody fool. **2** (*Print.*) bold face. **3** brought forward.

BG *abbr.* Brigadier General.

bhaji (bah´ji) *n.* (*pl.* **bhajis**) **1** an Indian vegetable dish (*mushroom bhaji*). **2** a small cake or ball of vegetables mixed with gram flour and deep-fried (*onion bhaji*).

bhang (bang), **bang** *n.* the dried leaves of hemp, *Cannabis sativa.*

bhangra (bang´grə) *n.* music based on a fusion of Asian and contemporary pop music.

b.h.p. *abbr.* brake horsepower.

Bi *chem. symbol* bismuth.

bi (bī) *a.* (*sl.*) bisexual. ~*n.* (*pl.* **bis** (bīz)) a bisexual.

bi- (bī), (*also before a vowel*) **bin-** (bin) *pref.* **1** double, twice. **2** doubly. **3** with two. **4** in two. **5** every two, once in every two, lasting for two.

biannual (bīan´ūəl) *a.* half-yearly, twice a year. **biannually** *adv.*

bias (bī´əs) *n.* **1** a leaning of the mind, inclination, prejudice, prepossession. **2** a distortion of a statistical result due to a factor not allowed for. **3 a** in the game of bowls, the irregular shape of a bowl, imparting oblique motion. **b** the oblique motion of a bowl. **4** a voltage applied to an electrode of a transistor or valve. **5** an edge cut slantwise across a strip of material. ~*v.t.* (*pres.p.* **biasing, biassing**, *past*, *p.p.* **biased, biassed**) **1** to cause to incline to one side. **2** to prejudice, to prepossess. **on the bias** (of material) cut diagonally, slanting obliquely. **bias binding** *n.* a strip of material cut slantwise, used for binding hems in sewing. **bias-ply** *a.* (*N Am.*) CROSS-PLY (under CROSS).

biathlon (bīath´lon) *n.* an athletic event combining either cross-country skiing and rifle shooting or cycling and running. **biathlete** *n.*

biaxial (bīak´siəl), **biaxal** (-səl) *a.* having two (optical) axes.

bib (bib) *n.* **1** a cloth or piece of shaped plastic put under a child's chin to keep the front of the clothes clean. **2** the front section of a garment (e.g. an apron, dungarees) above the waist. **3** the whiting pout, *Trisopterus luscus*, a food fish with a chin barbel. ~†*v.i.* (*pres.p.* **bibbing**, *past*, *p.p.* **bibbed**) **1** to drink. **2** to drink frequently; to tipple. †**bibber** *n.* **bibcock** *n.* a tap with the nozzle bent downwards.

bibelot (bib´əlō) *n.* a small article of virtu, a knick-knack.

Bible (bī´bəl), **bible** *n.* **1** the sacred writings of the Christian religion, comprising the Old and New Testaments. **2** the Hebrew Scriptures. **3** a copy of these, a particular edition of these. **4** a textbook, an authority. **5** a sacred book. **Bible-basher, Bible-puncher, Bible-thumper** *n.* **1** an aggressive preacher. **2** an ardent exponent of the Bible. **Bible-bashing, Bible-punching, Bible-thumping** *n.* **Bible belt** *n.* those regions of southern and central US characterized by fervent religious fundamentalism. **Bible oath** *n.* an oath administered on the Bible. **Bible paper** *n.* **1** a thin opaque paper used for Bibles, reference books etc. **2** INDIA PAPER (under INDIAN). **biblical** (bib´li) *a.* **1** of or relating to the Bible. **2** characteristic of the Bible. **biblically** *adv.*

biblio- (bib´liō) *comb. form* of or relating to books.

bibliography (bibliog´rəfi) *n.* (*pl.* **bibliographies**) **1** the methodical study of books, authorship, printing, editions, forms etc. **2** a book dealing with this. **3** a systematic list of books of any author, printer or country, or on any subject. **4** a systematic list of works quoted or referred to in a scholarly publication. **bibliographer** *n.* **bibliographical** (-graf´-), **bibliographic** *a.* **bibliographically** *adv.* **bibliographize** (-og´rəfiz), **bibliographise** *v.t.*

bibliomancy (bib´liōmansi) *n.* divination by books or verses of the Bible.

bibliomania (bibliōmā´niə) *n.* a mania for collecting and possessing books. **bibliomaniac** (-ak) *n.* a person who has such a mania. ~*a.* having or exhibiting such a mania.

bibliophile (bib´liōfīl) *n.* a lover or collector of books. **bibliophilic** (-fil´ik) *a.* **bibliophilist** (-of´-) *n.* **bibliophily** (-of´ili) *n.*

bibliopole (bib´liōpōl) *n.* a bookseller, esp. one dealing in rare books.

bibulous (bib´ūləs) *a.* **1** addicted to alcohol. **2** readily absorbing moisture. **bibulously** *adv.* **bibulousness** *n.*

bicameral (bīkam´ərəl) *a.* having two legislative chambers or assemblies. **bicameralism** *n.*

bicarbonate (bīkah´bənət) *n.* (*Chem.*) a salt of carbonic acid. **bicarbonate of soda,** (*coll.*) **bicarb** (bī´-) *n.* sodium bicarbonate used as a raising agent in baking or as an antacid.

bice (bīs) *n.* **1** any of various pigments made from blue or green basic copper carbonate. **2** a pale blue or green pigment made from smalt. **3** a pale blue or green colour.

bicentenary (bīsəntē´nəri) *n.* (*pl.* **bicentenaries**) a 200th anniversary. ~*a.* **1** of or relating to a bicentenary. **2** consisting of or relating to 200 years. **bicentennial** (-ten´-) *a.* **1** occurring every 200 years. **2** lasting 200 years. **3** of or relating to a bicentenary. ~*n.* a bicentenary.

bicephalous (bīsef´ələs, -kef´-) *a.* having two heads.

biceps (bī´seps) *n.* (*pl.* **biceps**) **1** the large muscle in front of the upper arm. **2** the corresponding muscle of the thigh. ~*a.* having two heads, points or summits, esp. of muscles having two attachments.

bicker (bik´ə) *v.i.* **1** to dispute, quarrel, wrangle or squabble over petty issues. **2** to quiver, glisten, flicker. **3** (*poet.*) to patter. **bickerer** *n.*

bicky (bik´i), **bikky** *n.* (*pl.* **bickies, bikkies**) (*childish and coll.*) a biscuit.

bicolour (bī´kŭlə), (*N Am.*) **bicolor** *a.* having two colours. ~*n.* a bicolour blossom or animal.

biconcave (bīkon´kāv) *a.* concave on both sides.

biconvex (bīkon´veks) *a.* convex on both sides.

bicultural (bīkŭl´chərəl) *a.* having or consisting of two cultures. **biculturalism** *n.*

bicuspid (bīkŭs´pid) *a.* having two points or cusps. ~*n.* a bicuspid tooth, one of the premolars in humans. **bicuspidate** (-dāt) *a.*

bicycle (bī´sikəl) *n.* a two-wheeled pedal-driven vehicle, with the wheels one behind the other and usu. with a saddle for the rider mounted on a metal frame. ~*v.i.* to ride on a bicycle. **bicycle clip** *n.* a thin metal clip worn around the ankles by cyclists to prevent their trousers from catching on the chain. **bicycle pump** *n.* a hand pump for filling bicycle tyres with air. **bicycler, bicyclist** *n.*

bicyclic (bīsī´klik, -sik´-) *a.* (*Chem.*) having two rings of atoms in the molecular structure.

bid (bid) *v.t.* (*pres.p.* **bidding,** *past* **bid,** †**bade** (bād), *p.p.* **bid,** †**bidden** (bid´ən)) **1** to offer, to make a tender of (a price), esp. at an auction or for work to be undertaken. **2** to call (a certain number of tricks) at bridge. **3** †to command. **4** †to invite, to ask. ~*v.i.* **1** to make an offer at an auction. **2** to tender. **3** to state before a game of bridge the number of tricks one intends to make. ~*n.* **1** an offer of a price, esp. at an auction or for work to be undertaken. **2** the call at bridge whereby a player contracts to make a certain number of tricks. **3** (*coll.*) an attempt to achieve or acquire something. **to bid fair** to seem likely, to promise well. **to make a bid for** to make an attempt to gain. **biddable** *a.* obedient, willing. **biddability** (-hil´-) *n.* **bidder** *n.* **bidding** *n.* **1** a bid at an auction. **2** in cards, the act of making a bid or bids. **3** invitation, command. **bidding prayer** *n.* a prayer in which the congregation is exhorted to pray for certain objects.

biddy (bid´i) *n.* (*pl.* **biddies**) (*derog.*) an old woman.

bide (bīd) *v.t.* (*past* **bided,** †**bode** (bōd), *p.p.* **bided**) †(*also dial.*) to abide, await. **to bide one's time** to await an opportunity patiently.

bidet (bē´dā) *n.* a low basin for bathing the genital and anal area.

bidirectional (bīdirek´shənəl) *a.* functioning in two directions.

biennial (bīen´iəl) *a.* **1** happening every two years. **2** lasting two years. **3** (*Bot.*) (of a plant) taking two years to reach maturity, ripen its seeds and die. ~*n.* (*Bot.*) a biennial plant. **2** a two-yearly event. **biennially** *adv.* **biennium** (-əm) *n.* (*pl.* **bienniums, biennia**) a period of two years.

bier (biə) *n.* a stand or litter on which a corpse is placed, or on which the coffin is borne to the grave.

biff (bif) *v.t.* (*coll.*) to strike, to cuff. ~*n.* a blow.

bifid (bī´fid) *a.* split into two lobes by a central cleft.

bifocal (bīfō´kəl) *a.* **1** with two foci. **2** having bifocal lenses. ~*n.pl.* bifocal spectacles. **bifocal lenses** *n.pl.* spectacle lenses divided for near and distant vision.

bifold (bī´fōld) *a.* twofold, double.

bifurcate[1] (bī´fəkāt) *v.i.* to divide into two branches, forks or peaks. **bifurcation** (-kā´shən) *n.* **1** division into two parts or branches. **2** the point of such division. **3** either of two forks or branches.

bifurcate[2] (bī´fəkāt, -fœ´kət) *a.* divided into two forks or branches.

big (big) *a.* (*comp.* **bigger,** *superl.* **biggest**) **1** large or great in bulk, quantity or intensity. **2** grown up. **3** pregnant, advanced in pregnancy. **4** important. **5** (*coll., often iron.*) magnanimous. **6** (*coll.*) boastful, pompous, pretentious. **7** most important, dominant. ~*adv.* **1** in a big way. **2** (*coll.*) boastfully. **3** pretentiously. **in a big way 1** (*coll.*) to a considerable degree. **2** (*coll.*) very enthusiastically. **to come/ go over big** to impress. **to talk big** to boast. **to think big** to have high ambitions. **big band** *n.* a large jazz or dance band. **big bang** *n.* **1** in cosmology, the cataclysmic explosion of superdense matter from which one theory maintains the universe evolved. **2** (*fig.*) any fundamental change in organization. **Big Brother** *n.* a sinister and ruthless person or organization that exercises totalitarian control (from George Orwell's novel *1984* (1949)). **big bud** *n.* a disease of plants, esp. of blackcurrants, caused by a mite. **big bug** *n.* (*sl.*) BIGWIG (under BIG). **big business** *n.* large commercial organizations, esp. when exploitative, sinister or socially harmful. **Big Chief, Big Daddy** *n.* (*sl.*) BIGWIG (under BIG). **big deal** *int.* (*sl., iron.*) a derisory exclamation or response. **big dipper** *n.* **1** (*orig. N Am.*) ROLLER COASTER (under ROLL). **2** (*N Am.* **Big Dipper**) the constellation Great Bear. **big end** *n.* the crankpin end of the connecting rod in an internal-combustion engine. **Bigfoot** *n.* (*pl.* **Bigfeet**) an animal like a yeti, supposed to live in NW America (from its big footprints). **big game** *n.* large animals hunted or fished for sport. **biggie** *n.* (*coll.*) something or someone important or large. **big gun** *n.* (*sl.*) an important person. **big-head** *n.* (*coll.*) a conceited individual. **big-headed** *a.* **big-headedness** *n.* **big-hearted** *a.* generous. **bighorn** *n.* the Rocky Mountain sheep, *Ovis montana.* **big house** *n.* **1** the largest or most important house in a village or town. **2** (*sl.*) a prison. **big idea** *n.* (*often iron.*) a grand plan or scheme. **big league** *n.* (*N Am.*) a top league in a sport, esp. baseball. **big-league** *a.* (*coll.*) major, top. **big lie** *n.* (*esp. N Am.*) an intentional distortion of facts, esp. by a politician. **big money** *n.* large amounts of money, profit or pay. **bigmouth** *n.* (*sl.*) a loud, indiscreet, boastful person. **big name** *n.* a famous person, celebrity. **bigness** *n.* **big noise, big pot, big shot** *n.* (*coll.*) a person of importance. **big stick** *n.* (*coll.*) brutal force. **big talk** *n.* boasting, bragging. **big time** *n.* (*coll.*) the highest rank in a profession, esp. in entertainment. **big-timer** *n.* **big top** *n.* a large circus tent. **big tree** *n.* (*N Am.*) the giant sequoia, *Sequoiadendron giganteum.* **big wheel** *n.* **1** a Ferris wheel. **2** (*N Am., sl.*) BIGWIG (under BIG). **bigwig** *n.* (*coll.*) a person of importance (from the large wigs formerly worn).

bigamy (big´ami) *n.* (*pl.* **bigamies**) marriage with another person while a legal spouse is living. **bigamist** *n.* **bigamous** *a.* **bigamously** *adv.*

bight (bīt) *n.* **1** a bending, a bend. **2** a small bay, the space between two headlands. **3** the loop of a rope.

bigot (big´ət) *n.* a person unreasonably and intolerantly devoted to a particular creed, system or party. **bigoted** *a.* affected with bigotry. **bigotry** (-ri) *n.* (*pl.* **bigotries**)

bijou (bē´zhoo) *n.* (*pl.* **bijoux** (bē´zhoo)) **1** a jewel, a trinket. **2** anything that is small, pretty or valuable. ~*a.* small, pretty or valuable. **bijouterie** (-zhoo´təri) *n.* jewellery, trinkets.

bike (bīk) *n.* **1** (*coll.*) a bicycle. **2** (*coll.*) a motorcycle. **3** (*Austral., sl.*) a prostitute. ~*v.i.* to ride a bicycle. **biker** *n.* (*coll.*) **1** a motorbike enthusiast. **2** a cyclist.

bikini (bikē´ni) *n.* (*pl.* **bikinis**) a brief, two-piece swimming costume. **bikini briefs** *n.pl.* brief underpants for women. **bikini line** *n.* the area of skin at the top of the legs, as revealed by someone wearing a bikini.

bikky BICKY.

bilabial (bīlā´biəl) *a.* of or denoting a consonant produced with both lips, e.g. b, p, w.

bilateral (bīlat´ərəl) *a.* **1** having, arranged on, of or relating to two sides. **2** affecting two parties. **bilaterally** *adv.* **bilateral symmetry** *n.* symmetry if cut in only one plane.

bilberry (bil´bəri) *n.* (*pl.* **bilberries**) **1** the fruit of a dwarf moorland shrub, *Vaccinium myrtillus,* also called *whortleberry* and *blaeberry.* **2** the shrub itself. **3** any of various other shrubs of the genus *Vaccinium.*

bile (bīl) *n.* **1** a bitter yellowish fluid which is secreted by the liver and aids digestion. **2** a medical disorder caused by faulty secretion of bile. **3** anger, choler. **bile duct** *n.* the duct which conveys bile to the duodenum. **biliary** (bil´i-) *a.* of or relating to the bile, the ducts which convey the bile, the small intestine, or the gall bladder. **bilious** (bil´yəs) *a.* **1** biliary. **2** produced or affected by bile. **3** peevish, ill-tempered. **biliously** *adv.* **biliousness** *n.*

bi-level (bī´levəl) *a.* **1** having or operating on two levels. **2** arranged on two planes. **3** (*N Am.*) (of a house) having the lower storey partially below ground level. ~*n.* (*N Am.*) a bi-level house.

bilge (bilj) *n.* **1** that part on which a ship rests when aground, where the vertical sides curve in. **2** (*pl.*) the bottom of a ship's floor. **3** the dirt which collects in the bottom of the hold of a ship; bilge water. **4** (*sl.*) worthless nonsense. ~*v.i.* to spring a leak in the bilge. ~*v.t.* to stave in, to cause to spring a leak in the bilge. **bilge keel** *n.* a timber fixed under the bilge to hold a vessel up when ashore and to prevent rolling. **bilge water** *n.* the foul water that collects in the bilge of a ship.

bilharzia (bilhah´ziə), **bilharziasis** (-ī´əsis), **bilharziosis** (-iō´sis) *n.* **1** a disease caused by blood flukes, characterized by blood loss and tissue damage, which is endemic to Asia, Africa and S America (also known as *schistosomiasis*). **2** a blood fluke.

biliary BILE.

bilingual (bīling´gwəl) *a.* **1** knowing or speaking two languages. **2** written or composed in two languages. ~*n.* a person who knows or speaks two languages. **bilingualism** *n.*

bilious BILE.

bilirubin (biliroo´bin) *n.* the chief pigment of bile, a derivative of haemoglobin.

bilk (bilk) *v.t.* **1** to cheat, to defraud. **2** to escape from, to elude. **3** to evade payment of. **4** to spoil (an opponent's score) in cribbage. **bilker** *n.*

bill[1] (bil) *n.* **1** a statement of particulars of goods delivered or services rendered. **2** a draft of a proposed law. **3** an advertisement or public announcement printed and distributed or posted up. **4** a theatre programme. **5** (*N Am.*) a banknote. **6** (*Law*) a written statement of a case. ~*v.t.* **1** to announce by bills or placards, to cover with bills or placards. **2** to put into a programme. **3** to present an account for payment to. **to fill/ fit the bill** to prove satisfactory, to be what is required. **billable** *a.* **billboard** *n.* (*N Am.*) a street hoarding. **billfold** *n.* (*N Am.*) a wallet for notes. **billhead** *n.* a business form with the name and address of the firm etc. at the top. **bill of exchange** *n.* a written order from one person to another to pay a sum on a given date to a designated person. **bill of fare** *n.* **1** a list of dishes, a menu. **2** a programme. **bill of goods** *n.* (*N Am.*) a batch of goods. **to sell someone a bill of goods** to deceive someone. **bill of health** *n.* (*Naut.*) a document testifying to the state of health of a ship's company. **bill of indictment** *n.* an accusation in writing, submitted to a grand jury. **bill of lading** *n.* (*Naut.*) **1** a master of a ship's acknowledgment of goods received. **2** a list of goods to be shipped. **Bill of Rights** *n.* (*Law*) a summary of rights and liberties claimed by a people and guaranteed by the state, esp. the English statute of 1689 and the first ten amendments to the US Constitution protecting the freedom of the individual. **bill of sale** *n.* a legal document for the transfer of personal property. **billposter** *n.* a person who sticks bills on walls etc. **billposting** *n.* **billsticker** *n.* **billsticking** *n.*

bill² (bil) *n.* **1** the horny beak of birds or of the platypus. **2** a beaklike projection or promontory. **3** (*Naut.*) the point of the fluke of an anchor. ~*v.i.* **1** (of doves) to lay the bills together. **2** to exhibit affection. **to bill and coo 1** to kiss and fondle. **2** to make love. **billed** *a.*

bill³ (bil) *n.* **1** an obsolete weapon resembling a halberd. **2** a billhook. **billhook** *n.* a thick, heavy knife with a hooked end, used for chopping brushwood etc.

billabong (bil´əbong) *n.* **1** a stream flowing from a river to a dead end. **2** a creek that fills seasonally.

billet¹ (bil´it) *n.* **1** quarters assigned to a soldier or others, esp. in a civilian household. **2** a ticket requiring a householder to furnish food and lodgings for a soldier or others. **3** (*coll.*) a situation, an appointment. ~*v.t.* (*pres.p.* **billeting**, *past, p.p.* **billeted**) **1** to quarter (soldiers or others), esp. on a civilian household. **2** to provide quarters for (soldiers or others) in one's household. **billetee** (-tē´) *n.* **billeter** *n.*

billet² (bil´it) *n.* **1** a small log or faggot for firing. **2** a bar, wedge or ingot of gold or silver. **3** (*Archit.*) a short cylindrical piece placed lengthwise at regular intervals in a hollow moulding in Norman work.

billet-doux (bilādoo´) *n.* (*pl.* **billets-doux** (bilā dooz´)) (*often facet.*) a love letter.

billiards (bil´yədz) *n.* a game with three balls, which are driven about on a cloth-lined table

with a cue. **billiard ball** *n.* **billiard cue** *n.* **billiard table** *n.*

billion (bil´yən) *n.* (*pl.* **billions**, **billion**) **1** one thousand million, i.e. 1,000,000,000 or 10⁹. **2** †in Britain, one million million, i.e. 1,000,000,000,000 or 10¹². **3** (*pl.*) any very large number. ~*a.* amounting to a billion. **billionaire** (-neə´) *n.* a person having a billion pounds, dollars etc. or more. **billionth** *a.*, *n.*

billon (bil´ən) *n.* base metal, esp. silver alloyed with copper.

billow (bil´ō) *n.* **1** a great swelling wave of the sea. **2** anything sweeping onward like a mighty wave. **3** anything curved or swelling like a wave. ~*v.i.* **1** to surge. **2** to rise in billows. **billowy** *a.*

billy (bil´i), **billie** *n.* (*pl.* **billies**) (*esp. Austral.*) a metal can or pot for boiling water etc. over a campfire. **billycan** *n.* (*esp. Austral.*) a billy. **billy goat** *n.* a male goat.

billy-o (bil´iō) *n.* used only as below. **like billy-o** (*sl.*) vigorously, strongly.

biltong (bil´tong) *n.* (*S Afr.*) strips of lean meat dried in the sun.

bimbo (bim´bō) *n.* (*pl.* **bimbos**) (*sl., usu. derog.*) **1** an attractive person, esp. a woman, who is naive or of limited intelligence. **2** a foolish or stupid person.

bi-media (bīmē´diə) *a.* using or relating to two media, such as radio and television.

bimetallism (bīmet´əlizm) *n.* the employment of two metals (gold and silver) in the currency of a country, at a fixed ratio to each other, as standard coin and legal tender. **bimetallic** (-mital´-) *a.* **1** composed of two metals. **2** of or relating to bimetallism. **bimetallic strip** *n.* a strip of two metals bonded together which expand by different amounts when heated. **bimetallist** *n.* a supporter or advocate of bimetallism.

bimillenary (bīmilen´əri) *n.* (*pl.* **bimillenaries**) **1** a period of 2000 years. **2** a 2000th anniversary. ~*a.* **1** consisting of or relating to 2000 years. **2** of or relating to a bimillenary.

bimodal (bīmō´dəl) *a.* having two modes (*bimodal distribution*).

bimonthly (bīmŭnth´li) *a.* **1** occurring once in two months. **2** occurring twice a month. **3** lasting two months. ~*adv.* **1** once every two months. **2** twice a month. ~*n.* (*pl.* **bimonthlies**) a bimonthly publication.

Usage note It is often impossible to tell in a particular context whether *bimonthly*, *biweekly* and *biyearly* mean every two months, weeks etc. or twice a month etc. It is safer to use *two-monthly* and *twice-monthly* or their equivalents, or to paraphrase in some other way.

bin (bin) *n.* **1** a box or other receptacle for bread, corn, wine etc. **2** a container for rubbish. **3** wine from a particular bin. ~*v.t.* (*pres.p.* **binning**, *past, p.p.* **binned**) **1** to stow in a bin. **2** to throw away as rubbish. **bin-end** *n.* a bottle of wine sold off cheaply because there are so few left of the bin.

bin liner n. a plastic bag used to line a rubbish bin. **binman** n. (pl. **binmen**) a refuse collector.

bin- BI-.

binary (bī´nəri) a. 1 consisting of a pair or pairs. 2 double, dual. ~n. (pl. **binaries**) 1 something having two parts. 2 a binary number. 3 a binary star. **binary code** n. (Comput.) a system that uses the binary digits 0 and 1 to represent characters. **binary compound** n. (Chem.) a chemical compound of two elements. **binary digit** n. either of two digits, 0 or 1, used in a binary system of notation. **binary fission** n. the division of a cell into two parts. **binary notation** n. a number system using the base two (instead of base ten), numbers being represented as combinations of one and zero: because the two digits can be represented electronically as on and off, the system is used in computers. **binary number** n. a number expressed in binary notation. **binary star**, **binary system** n. a system of two stars revolving around a common centre of gravity. **binary tree** n. a diagram used for classification or decision-making, which represents choices by right- or left-branching paths.

binaural (bīnaw´rəl) a. 1 relating to, having or using two ears. 2 employing two channels in recording or transmitting sound.

bind (bīnd) v.t. (past, p.p. **bound** (bownd)) 1 to tie, or fasten together, to or on something. 2 to put in bonds, confine. 3 to wrap or confine with a cover or bandage. 4 to form a border to. 5 to cover, secure or strengthen, by means of a band. 6 to sew (a book) and put into a cover. 7 to tie up. 8 to cause to cohere. 9 to make constipated. 10 to oblige to do something by contract. 11 to oblige, to engage, to compel. ~v.i. 1 to cohere. 2 to grow stiff and hard. 3 to tie up. 4 to be obligatory. 5 (sl.) to complain. ~n. 1 a band or tie. 2 a bine. 3 (coll.) an annoying or frustrating predicament, a bore. **to bind over** (Law) to place under legal obligation. **to bind up** to bandage. **binder** n. 1 a cover or folder for loose papers, correspondence etc. 2 something which binds or fastens. 3 a person who binds. 4 a reaping machine that binds grain into sheaves. 5 a bookbinder. 6 a cementing agent. **bindery** n. (pl. **binderies**) a bookbinder's workshop. **binding** a. obligatory. ~n. 1 the act of binding. 2 something which binds. 3 the state of being bound. 4 the act, art or particular style of bookbinding. 5 a book cover, braid or other edging. **bindweed** n. 1 a plant of the genus Convolvulus. 2 any of several other climbing plants, such as honeysuckle.

bindi-eye (bin´dīī) n. a small Australian herbaceous plant, Calotis cuneifolia, with burlike fruits.

bine (bīn) n. a flexible shoot or stem, esp. of the hop (cp. WOODBINE (under WOOD)).

binge (binj) n. (coll.) 1 a drinking spree. 2 overindulgence in anything. ~v.i. (pres.p. **bingeing**, **binging**, past, p.p. **binged**) 1 to indulge in a drinking spree. 2 to overindulge in anything.

bingo (bing´gō) n. 1 a game in which random numbers are called out and then marked off by players on a card with numbered squares, the winner being the first to mark off all or a predetermined sequence of numbers. 2 an exclamation made by the winner of a bingo game. 3 an exclamation expressing the suddenness of an event.

binnacle (bin´əkəl) n. the case in which the ship's compass is kept.

binocular (binok´ūlə) a. 1 having two eyes. 2 suited for use by both eyes. **binoculars** n.pl. a field or opera glass with tubes for both eyes. **binocular vision** n. vision using both eyes, which gives good depth perception.

binomial (bīnō´miəl) a. 1 binominal. 2 of or relating to binomials. ~n. a mathematical expression consisting of two terms united by the signs + or -. **binomial distribution** n. a statistical distribution of the possible number of successful outcomes in a specified number of trials in an experiment with a constant probability of success in each. **binomially** adv. **binomial nomenclature** n. a system of classifying plants and animals using two names, the first one indicating the genus and the second the species. **binominal** (-nom´inəl) a. having two names, the first denoting the genus, the second the species.

bint (bint) n. (sl., offensive) a girl or woman.

bio- (bī´ō) comb. form of or relating to life or living things.

bioassay (bīōəsā´, bīōas´ā) n. the measuring of the strength and effect of a substance such as a drug by testing it on living cells or tissues.

biochemistry (bīōkem´istri) n. the chemistry of physiological processes occurring in living organisms. **biochemical** a. **biochemist** n.

biocide (bī´ōsīd) n. 1 a chemical which kills living organisms. 2 the destruction of life. **biocidal** (-sī´-) a.

biocoenosis (bīōsēnō´sis), (N Am.) **biocenosis** n. (pl. **biocoenoses, biocenoses**) 1 the relationship between plants and animals that are ecologically interdependent. 2 an association of ecologically interdependent organisms. **biocoenology** (-nol´əji) n. **biocoenotic** (-not´ik) a.

biodegradable (bīōdigrā´dəbəl) a. capable of being broken down by bacteria. **biodegradability** (-bil´-) n. **biodegradation** (-degrədā´shən) n.

biodiversity (bīōdīvœ´sitī) n. the existence of a wide variety of plant and animal species.

bioengineering (bīōenjinē´ring) n. 1 the provision of aids such as artificial limbs, hearts etc. to restore body functions. 2 the design, construction and maintenance of equipment used in biosynthesis. **bioengineer** n., v.t.

bioethics (bīōeth´iks) n. the study of ethical issues arising from advances in medicine and science. **bioethical** a. **bioethicist** (-sist) n.

biofeedback (bīōfēd´bak) n. a method of regulating involuntary body functions, e.g. heartbeat, by conscious mental control.

bioflavonoid (bīōflā´vənoid) *n.* a group of substances found in citrus fruits and blackcurrants, also called *citrin* and *vitamin P*.

biogas (bī´ōgas) *n.* gas, such as methane, that is produced by the action of bacteria on organic waste matter.

biogenesis (bīōjen´isis), **biogeny** (-oj´əni) *n.* the doctrine that living matter originates only from living matter. **biogenetic** (-jinet´-), **biogenic** (-jen´-) *a.*

biogeography (bīōjiog´rəfi) *n.* the study of the distribution of plant and animal life over the globe. **biogeographer** *n.* **biogeographical** (-jēəgraf´-) *a.*

biography (bīog´rəfi) *n.* (*pl.* **biographies**) **1** the history of the life of a person. **2** literature dealing with personal history. **biographer** *n.* **biographic** (bīəgraf´-), **biographical** *a.* **biographically** *adv.*

biohazard (bīōhaz´əd) *n.* a risk to human health or the environment from biological research.

biology (bīol´əji) *n.* the science of physical life or living matter in all its phases. **biological** *a.* of or relating to biology. **biological clock** *n.* the inherent mechanism that regulates cyclic physiological processes in living organisms. **biological control** *n.* the control of pests etc. by using other organisms that destroy them. **biological warfare** *n.* warfare involving the use of disease germs. **biologist** *n.*

bioluminescence (bīōloomines´əns) *n.* the production of light by living organisms such as insects, marine animals and fungi. **bioluminescent** *a.*

biomass (bī´ōmas) *n.* the total weight of living organisms in a unit of area.

biomathematics (bīōmathəmat´iks) *n.* the study of the application of mathematics to biology.

biome (bī´ōm) *n.* **1** a large ecological community, having flora and fauna which have adapted to the particular conditions in which they live. **2** the geographical region containing an ecological community.

biomechanics (bīōmikan´iks) *n.* the study of the mechanics of movement in living creatures.

biomedicine (bīōmed´sin, -isin) *n.* the study of the medical and biological effects of stressful environments, esp. space travel. **biomedical** (-ikəl) *a.*

biometry (biom´itri) *n.* the statistical measurement of biological data. **biometric** (-met´-) *a.* **biometrical** *a.* **biometrician** (-trish´ən) *n.* **biometrics** *n.*

biomorph (bī´ōmawf) *n.* a decoration representing a living thing. **biomorphic** (-maw´fik) *a.*

bionics (bīon´iks) *n.* **1** the science of applying knowledge of biological systems to the development of electronic equipment. **2** the replacement of parts of the body or enhancement of physiological functions by electrical or mechanical equipment. **bionic** *a.* **1** of or relating to bionics. **2** in science fiction, having exceptional powers

through the electronic augmentation of physical processes. **bionically** *adv.*

bionomics (bīonom´iks) *n.* ecology. **bionomic** *a.*

biophysics (bīōfiz´iks) *n.* the application of physics to living things. **biophysical** *a.* **biophysicist** (-sist) *n.*

biopic (bī´ōpik) *n.* a film, often giving a glamorized and uncritical account of the life of a celebrity.

biopsy (bī´opsi) *n.* (*pl.* **biopsies**) the removal and diagnostic examination of tissue or fluids from a living body.

biorhythm (bī´ōridhm) *n.* **1** a supposed biological cycle governing physical, emotional and intellectual moods and performance. **2** any periodic change in an organism's behaviour or physiology. **biorhythmic** (-ridh´mik) *a.* **biorhythmically** *adv.*

bioscope (bī´ōskōp) *n.* **1** a cinematograph. **2** (*S Afr.*) a cinema.

biosphere (bī´ōsfiə) *n.* the portion of the earth's surface and atmosphere which is inhabited by living things.

biosynthesis (bīōsin´thəsis) *n.* the production of chemical compounds by living organisms. **biosynthetic** (-thet´-) *a.*

biota (bī´ō´tə) *n.* the flora and fauna of a region.

biotechnology (bīōteknol´əji) *n.* the use of microorganisms and biological processes in industry.

biotic (bīot´ik) *a.* **1** relating to life or living things. **2** (of a factor in an ecosystem) of biological origin.

biotin (bī´ōtin) *n.* a vitamin of the B complex (also known as vitamin H) found esp. in liver and egg yolk.

biotite (bī´ətīt) *n.* a black or dark-coloured micaceous mineral.

bipartisan (bīpahtizan´, -pah´-) *a.* involving or supported by two or more (political) parties. **bipartisanship** (-zan´-) *n.*

bipartite (bīpah´tīt) *a.* **1** comprising or having two parts. **2** (*Law*) (of an agreement) affecting or corresponding to two parties. **3** (of leaves) divided into two corresponding parts from the apex almost to the base.

biped (bī´ped) *a.* having two feet. ~*n.* an animal having only two feet, such as man and birds. **bipedal** (-pē´-) *a.* **bipedalism** *n.* **bipedality** (-pidal´iti) *n.*

biphenyl (bīfē´nil) *n.* (*Chem.*) an organic compound which contains two phenyl groups.

bipinnate (bīpin´ət), **bipinnated** (-ātid) *a.* (of a pinnate leaf) having pinnated leaflets.

biplane (bī´plān) *n.* an aircraft with two sets of wings, one above the other.

bipolar (bīpō´lə) *a.* having two poles or opposite extremities. **bipolarity** (-lar´iti) *n.*

birch (bœch) *n.* **1** any tree of the genus *Betula*, with slender limbs and thin, tough bark. **2** the wood of any of these trees, also called birchwood. **3** a birch-rod. **4** (*New Zeal.*) any of various similar trees. ~v.t. to chastise with a birch-rod, to flog. **birch-bark** n. **1** the bark of *Betula papyracea.* **2** (*N Am.*) a canoe made from this. **birchen** a. composed of birch. **birch-rod** n. a rod made from birch twigs for flogging.

bird (bœd) n. **1** any feathered vertebrate animal of the class Aves. **2** a game bird. **3** (*sl.*) a girl, young woman. **4** (*coll.*) a person. **5** (*sl.*) a prison. **6** (*sl.*) a prison term. (**strictly**) **for the birds** worthless, not serious. **the birds and the bees** (*euphem.*) reproduction; the facts of life. **to get the bird 1** to be hissed. **2** to be fired or dismissed. **bird bath** n. a small usu. ornamental basin for birds to bathe in. **birdbrained** a. (*coll.*) stupid, silly. **birdbrain** n. **birdcage** n. a wire or wicker cage for holding birds. **bird call** n. **1** the cry of a bird. **2** an instrument for imitating the cry of birds. **bird cherry** n. a wild cherry, *Prunus padus*, which has clusters of white flowers. **birder** n. (*esp. N Am.*) a birdwatcher. **bird-fancier** n. a person who collects, breeds or rears birds. **birdie** n. **1** a little bird (used as a term of endearment). **2** a hole in golf made in one under par. ~v.t. (*3rd pers. sing. pres.* **birdies**, *pres.p.* **birdying**, *past, p.p.* **birdied**) to play (a hole) in a birdie. **birding** n. **1** bird-catching. **2** fowling. **3** birdwatching. **bird in the hand** n. something in one's possession (alluding to the proverb a bird in the hand is worth two in the bush). **birdlime** n. a sticky substance used to snare birds. **bird-nesting**, **bird's nesting** n. seeking birds' nests to steal the eggs. **bird of paradise** n. any of the New Guinea Paradiseidae which have brilliantly coloured plumage. **bird of passage** n. **1** a migratory bird. **2** a person who travels frequently and rarely stays long in one place. **bird of prey** n. a bird such as the hawk or vulture which feeds on carrion or hunts other animals for food. **bird sanctuary** n. an area where birds are protected. **birdseed** n. special seed (hemp, canary seed etc.) given to cagebirds. **bird's-eye** a. **1** of, belonging to or resembling a bird's eye. **2** having eye-like markings. **3** seen from above, as by the eye of a bird, esp. in *bird's-eye view.* ~n. **1** any of several plants with small, round, bright flowers. **2** the germander speedwell. **3** a pattern used for fabric, made up of small diamond shapes with a spot in the centre of each. **bird's-foot, bird-foot** n. (*pl.* **bird's-foots, bird-foots**) any plant which has a part like the foot of a bird, esp. *Ornithopus perpusillus.* **bird's-foot trefoil** n. a British wild flower, *Lotus corniculatus*, which has yellow flowers streaked with red. **bird's nest** n. **1** the nest of a bird. **2** an edible bird's nest. ~v.i. to search for birds' nests. **bird's nest soup** n. a rich Chinese soup made from the dried coating of the nests of swifts and other birds. **birds of a feather** n.pl. people of similar character or interests. **bird song** n. the musical call of a bird or birds. **bird-strike** n. a collision of a bird with an aircraft. **bird table** n. a small elevated platform for wild birds to feed from. **birdwatcher** n. a person who observes wild birds in their natural habitat. **bird-watching** n.

birefringence (bīrifrin´jəns) n. (*Physics*) the formation of two unequally refracted rays of light from a single unpolarized ray. **birefringent** a.

bireme (bī´rēm) n. (*Hist.*) a Roman galley with two banks of oars. ~a. having two banks of oars.

biretta (biret´ə), **berretta** n. a square cap worn by clerics of the Roman Catholic and Anglican Churches.

biriani (biriah´ni), **biryani** n. an Indian dish of spiced rice mixed with meat or fish.

Biro® (bī´rō), **biro** n. (*pl.* **Biros, biros**) a type of ballpoint pen.

birth (bœth) n. **1** the act of bringing forth. **2** the bearing of offspring. **3** the act of coming into life or being born. **4** that which is brought forth. **5** parentage, extraction, lineage, esp. high extraction, high lineage. **6** condition resulting from birth. **7** origin, beginning, product, creation. ~v.t. (*N Am., coll.*) **1** to give birth to. **2** to help (a woman) give birth. **birth certificate** n. an official document giving particulars of a person's birth. **birth control** n. the artificial control of reproduction, esp. by means of contraceptives. **birth control pill** n. a contraceptive pill. **birthday** n. the day on which a person was born, or its anniversary. **birthday suit** n. (*coll., facet.*) one's bare skin, nudity. **birthing** n. the act or process of giving birth. **birthing pool** n. a pool in a hospital or in a woman's home in which she can give birth or experience labour. **birthmark** n. a mark or blemish formed on the body of a child at or before birth. **birth mother** n. the woman who has given birth to a child, not the adoptive mother. **birth pill** n. a contraceptive pill. **birthplace** n. the place at which someone or something was born. **birth rate** n. the percentage of live births to the population. **birthright** n. rights belonging to an eldest son, to a member of a family, order or people, or to a person as a human being. **birthstone** n. a gemstone associated with the month of someone's birth. **birthweight** n. a baby's weight at birth.

biryani BIRIANI.

biscuit (bis´kit) n. **1** a thin flour-cake baked until it is highly dried. **2** pottery moulded and baked in an oven, but not glazed. **3** a light brown colour. ~a. light brown in colour. **biscuity** a.

bisect (bīsekt´) v.t. to divide into two (equal) parts. ~v.i. to fork. **bisection** n. **bisector** n.

bisexual (bīsek´sūəl, -shəl) a. **1** (*Biol.*) having both sexes combined in one individual. **2** attracted sexually to both sexes. **3** of or relating to both sexes. ~n. a bisexual individual. **bisexuality** (-sūal´-, -sh-) n.

bish (bish) n. (*sl.*) a mistake.

bishop (bish´əp) n. **1** a dignitary presiding over a diocese, ranking beneath an archbishop, and above the priests and deacons. **2** a spiritual superintendent in the early Christian Church.

3 a piece in chess, having the upper part shaped like a mitre. **4** a beverage composed of wine, oranges and sugar. **bishopric** (-rik) *n.* the diocese, jurisdiction or office of a bishop.

bismuth (biz´məth) *n.* **1** (*Chem.*) a reddish white crystalline metallic element, at. no. 83, chem. symbol Bi, used in alloys and in medicine. **2** (*Med.*) any compound of this element used medicinally.

bison (bī´sən) *n.* (*pl.* **bison**) either of two large bovine mammals of the genus *Bison*, with a shaggy coat and a large hump, the European bison, *B. bonasus*, now very rare, and the American bison, *B. bison*, commonly called buffalo, once found in great numbers in the mid-Western prairies.

bisque¹ (bisk), **bisk** *n.* a rich soup made by boiling down fish, birds or the like.

bisque² (bisk) *n.* in tennis, golf etc., a stroke allowed at any time to the weaker party to equalize the players.

bisque³ (bisk) *n.* a kind of unglazed white porcelain used for statuettes.

bistable (bīstā´bəl) *a.* (of a valve or electrical circuit) having two stable states.

bistort (bis´tawt) *n.* a plant with a twisted root and spike of flesh-coloured flowers, *Polygonum bistorta*.

bistre (bis´tə), (*esp. N Am.*) **bister** *n.* a transparent brownish yellow pigment prepared from soot. ~*a.* coloured like this pigment. **bistred** *a.* coloured with or as with bistre.

bistro (bēs´trō) *n.* (*pl.* **bistros**) a small bar or restaurant.

bisulphate (bīsŭl´fāt), (*esp. N Am.*) **bisulfate** *n.* (*Chem.*) a salt or ester of sulphuric acid.

bit¹ (bit) *n.* **1** a small portion. **2** a morsel, a fragment. **3** the smallest quantity, a whit, a jot. **4** a brief period of time. **5** a small coin (usu. with the value expressed, as a threepenny bit). **6** (*N Am., coll.*) an eighth of a dollar. **7** (*coll.*) a poor little thing. **8** somewhat or something (of). **9** BIT PART (under BIT¹). **a bit 1** a little. **2** rather, somewhat. **bit by bit** gradually, piecemeal. **not a bit** not at all. **to bits 1** into pieces, completely apart. **2** (*coll.*) very much. **to do one's bit** to do one's share. **bit of all right** *n.* (*sl.*) a sexually attractive woman. **bit of crackling, bit of crumpet, bit of fluff, bit of skirt, bit of stuff, bit of tail** *n.* (*sl., offensive*) an attractive woman regarded as a sexual object. **bit of rough** *n.* (*sl.*) a man who is sexually attractive because of his lack of sophistication. **bit on the side** *n.* (*sl.*) **1** a sexual relationship outside one's marriage. **2** the person with whom one is having an affair. **bit part** *n.* a small role in a play. **bit player** *n.* an actor who plays small parts. **bits and pieces, bits and bobs** *n.pl.* odds and ends, incidental tasks. **bitty** *a.* (*comp.* **bittier**, *superl.* **bittiest**) **1** scrappy, disjointed, piecemeal. **2** lacking unity. **3** (*N Am., coll.*) tiny. **bittily** *adv.* **bittiness** *n.*

bit² (bit) *n.* **1** the iron part of the bridle inserted in the mouth of a horse. **2** the cutting part of a tool.

3 the movable boring-piece in a drill. **4** the part of the key at right angles to the shank. **5** the copper head of a soldering iron. ~*v.t.* to furnish with, or accustom (a horse) to, a bit. **to champ at the bit** to be impatient. **to take the bit between one's teeth 1** to become unmanageable. **2** to act decisively.

bit³ (bit) *n.* (*Comput.*) in binary notation, either of the two digits, 0 or 1, a unit of information in computers and information theory representing either of two states, such as *on* and *off*. **bitmap** *n.* (*Comput.*) a method of creating a graphic image in which a bit is assigned to each dot that forms the image. ~*v.t.* (*pres.p.* **bitmapping**, *past, p.p.* **bitmapped**) to represent or manipulate (data) using a bitmap.

bit⁴ BITE.

bitch (bich) *n.* **1** the female of the dog. **2** a female of allied species. **3** (*sl., offensive*) an offensive, malicious or spiteful woman. **4** (*sl.*) a complaint. **5** (*sl.*) an awkward problem or situation. ~*v.i.* (*sl.*) to moan, complain. ~*v.t.* (*sl.*) **1** to mess up, botch. **2** to be spiteful or unfair to. **bitchy** *a.* (*comp.* **bitchier**, *superl.* **bitchiest**) **1** of or like a bitch, spiteful. **2** ill-tempered. **bitchily** *adv.* **bitchiness** *n.*

bite (bīt) *v.t.* (*past* **bit** (bit), *p.p.* **bitten** (bit´ən)) **1** to seize, nip, rend, cut, pierce or crush with the teeth. **2** to cut, to wound. **3** to affect with severe cold. **4** to cause to smart. **5** to inflict sharp physical or mental pain on. **6** to wound with reproach or sarcasm. **7** to hold fast, as an anchor or screw. **8** to corrode. ~*v.i.* **1** to have a habit, or exercise the power, of biting. **2** to sting, to be pungent. **3** to take a bait. **4** to act upon something (of weapons, tools etc.). ~*n.* **1** the act of biting. **2** a wound made by the teeth. **3** a mouthful, a small quantity. **4** a piece seized or detached by biting. **5** pungency. **6** sharpness. **7** a hold, a grip. **8** the angle of contact between the top and bottom teeth when the mouth is closed. **to bite back** to avoid saying (e.g. something hurtful). **to bite off more than one can chew** to undertake more than one can manage. **biter** *n.* **bite-size, bite-sized** *a.* **1** small enough to be eaten in one mouthful. **2** very small. **biting** *a.* **1** sharp, keen. **2** acrid, pungent. **3** stinging, caustic, sarcastic. **bitingly** *adv.*

bitten BITE.

bitter (bit´ə) *a.* **1** sharp or biting to the taste. **2** acrid, harsh, virulent, piercingly cold. **3** painful, distressing, mournful. ~*n.* **1** anything bitter. **2** bitterness. **3** (*coll.*) bitter beer. **4** (*pl.*) liquors flavoured with bitter herbs etc., used as appetizers or in cocktails. ~*v.t.* to make bitter. **bitter aloes** *n.pl.* the purgative drug aloes. **bitter end** *n.* **1** the last extremity. **2** the loose end of a belayed rope. **bitterly** *adv.* **bitterness** *n.* **bitter orange** *n.* a Seville orange. **bitter pill** *n.* something which is unwelcome or difficult to accept. **bitter-sweet** *a.* **1** sweet with a bitter aftertaste. **2** pleasant with admixture of pain or sadness. ~*n.* **1** a mixture of sweet and bitter. **2** woody nightshade.

bitterling (bit´əling) *n.* a small brightly coloured freshwater fish, *Rhodeus amarus.*

bittern[1] (bit´ən) *n.* any of the wading birds of the heron family, esp. of the genus *Botaurus.*

bittern[2] (bit´ən) *n.* (*Chem.*) the liquid obtained when sea water is evaporated to extract the salt.

bitumen (bit´ūmin) *n.* **1** any of various solid or sticky mixtures of hydrocarbons that occur naturally or as a residue from petroleum distillation, e.g. tar, asphalt. **2** (*Austral., coll.*) a tarred road. **bituminize** (-tū´-), **bituminise** *v.t.* to impregnate with or convert into bitumen. **bituminization** (-zā´shən) *n.* **bituminous** (-tū´-) *a.* of the nature of, resembling, or impregnated with bitumen. **bituminous coal** *n.* coal that flames when it burns.

bivalent (bīvā´lənt, biv´ə-) *a.* **1** (*Chem.*) having a valency of two. **2** (*Biol.*) (of homologous chromosomes) associated in pairs. ~*n.* (*Biol.*) any pair of homologous chromosomes. **bivalency** *n.*

bivalve (bī´valv) *a.* (*Biol.*) having two shells or valves which open and shut. ~*n.* a mollusc which has its shell in two opposite directions connected by a ligament and hinge, such as the oyster.

bivouac (biv´uak, biv´wak) *n.* **1** a temporary encampment in the field without tents etc. **2** the scene of such an encampment. ~*v.i.* (*pres.p.* **bivouacking**, *past, p.p.* **bivouacked**) to remain in the open air without tents or other covering.

biweekly (bīwēk´li) *a., adv.* **1** occurring once a fortnight. **2** occurring twice a week. ~*n.* (*pl.* **biweeklies**) a periodical appearing every two weeks.

Usage note See note under BIMONTHLY.

biyearly (bīyiə´li) *a., adv.* **1** occurring every two years. **2** occurring twice a year.

Usage note See note under BIMONTHLY.

biz (biz) *n.* (*coll.*) business, work, employment.

bizarre (bizah´) *a.* **1** odd, whimsical, fantastic, eccentric. **2** of mixed or discordant style. **bizarrely** *adv.* **bizarreness** *n.* **bizarrerie** (-zah´rəri) *n.* bizarreness.

Bk *chem. symbol* berkelium.

bk *abbr.* book.

BL *abbr.* **1** Bachelor of Law. **2** bill of lading. **3** British Library.

bl *abbr.* **1** barrel. **2** black.

blab (blab) *v.t.* (*pres.p.* **blabbing**, *past, p.p.* **blabbed**) **1** to tell or reveal indiscreetly. **2** to betray. ~*v.i.* **1** to talk indiscreetly, to tell tales or secrets. **2** to prattle. ~*n.* **1** a chatterer, babbler. **2** a tell-tale. **blabber** *n.* **1** a person who blabs. **2** a telltale, a tattler. ~*v.i.* to talk at length, often aimlessly. **blabbermouth** *n.* a blab.

black (blak) *a.* **1** intensely dark in colour (the opposite of white). **2** denoting total absence of colour due to absence or entire absorption of light. **3** (*also* **Black**) dark-skinned, esp. of African or Australian Aboriginal descent. **4** of or

relating to black people. **5** (of the sky) heavily overcast. **6** angry. **7** implying disgrace or dishonour. **8** atrociously wicked. **9** sombre, gloomy, dirty. **10** disastrous, dismal, mournful. **11** dirty. **12** (of humour) macabre. **13** subject to a trade union ban. **14** wearing black clothes, uniform or armour. **15** destitute of light. **16** obscure. **17** dark in colour as distinguished from a lighter variety (*black bread*). ~*n.* **1** the darkest of all colours (the opposite of white). **2** a black pigment or dye. **3** (*also* **Black**) a member of a dark-skinned people, esp. of African or Australian Aboriginal descent. **4** mourning garments. **5** a minute particle of soot or dirt. **6** in a game, a black piece, ball etc. **7** the player using the black pieces. **8** the credit side of an account. ~*v.t.* **1** to blacken. **2** to soil. **3** to place under a trade union ban. **4** to polish with blacking. **black and blue** *a.* **1** discoloured by beating. **2** livid. **black and white** *n.* **1** printed or written matter. **2** a photograph, drawing etc., in black and white or shades of grey. **3** visual images reproduced in black and white, esp. by photography or television. ~*a.* **1** monochrome as opposed to colour (of film or television). **2** recorded in writing or print. **3** divided into two extremes, not admitting of compromise. **black art** *n.* magic, necromancy. **blackball** *n.* a vote of rejection in a ballot (from the black ball sometimes used to indicate a vote against in a ballot). ~*v.t.* **1** to vote against. **2** to exclude. **3** to dislike, bar. **black bass** *n.* a N American freshwater fish of the genus *Micropterus.* **black beetle** *n.* a cockroach, *Blatta orientalis.* **black belt** *n.* **1** a belt awarded for highest proficiency in judo, karate etc. **2** a person entitled to wear this. **blackberry** *n.* (*pl.* **blackberries**) **1** the common bramble, *Rubus fruticosus* or *discolor.* **2** its fruit. ~*v.i.* (*3rd pers. sing. pres.* **blackberries**, *pres.p.* **blackberrying**, *past, p.p.* **blackberried**) to gather blackberries. **blackberrying** *n.* gathering blackberries. **blackbird** *n.* **1** a species of European thrush, *Turdus merula*, the male of which has black plumage and an orange beak. **2** any of several dark plumaged American birds. **blackboard** *n.* a board painted black, used by teachers and lecturers to write and draw on. **black book** *n.* a book recording the names of persons liable to censure or punishment. **black box** *n.* **1** a closed unit in an electronic system whose circuitry remains hidden from the user and is irrelevant to understanding its function. **2** a flight recorder in an aircraft. **black bread** *n.* coarse, dark rye bread. **black bryony** *n.* a climbing plant, *Tamus communis*, which has poisonous red berries and small green flowers. **blackbuck** *n.* a common Indian gazelle, *Antilope cervicapra*, also called sasin. **black cap** *n.* any English bird having the top of the head black. **blackcap warbler** *n.* a small warbler, *Sylvia atricapilla.* **blackcock** *n.* the male of the black grouse. **black coffee** *n.* coffee without milk or cream. **blackcurrant** *n.* a garden bush, *Ribes nigrum*, or its fruit. **black**

disc *n.* a long-playing gramophone record, as opposed to a compact disc. **black earth** *n.* a fertile soil covering regions in S Russia north of the Black Sea. **black economy** *n.* illegal and undeclared economic activity. **blacken** *v.t.* **1** to make black, to darken. **2** to sully, to defame. *~v.i.* to become black. **black English** *n.* the form of English spoken by some black people, esp. in the US. **black eye** *n.* **1** discoloration produced by a blow upon the parts round the eye. **2** an eye of which the iris is very dark. **black-eyed bean, black-eye bean,** (*N Am.*) **black-eyed pea** *n.* a variety of bean, *Vigna sinensis*. **black-eyed Susan** *n.* any of several flowers, esp. of the genus *Rudbeckia*, which have a dark centre and yellow petals. **blackface** *n.* **1** a black-faced sheep or other animal. **2** the make-up used by a white performer playing a black role. **blackfellow** *n.* (*derog., offensive*) an Aboriginal of Australia. **blackfish** *n.* (*pl. in general* **blackfish,** *in particular* **blackfishes**) **1** a salmon just after spawning. **2** any of several species of dark-coloured fish. **black flag** *n.* a flag of black cloth used as a sign that no quarter will be given or taken, as an ensign by pirates, and as the signal for an execution. **blackfly** *n.* (*pl.* **blackflies**) **1** any black aphid, esp. *Aphis fabae*, that infests beans and other plants. **2** a biting fly of the genus *Simulium* or the family Simuliidae. **Black Forest gateau,** (*N Am.*) **Black Forest cake** *n.* a thick chocolate cake containing whipped cream and morello cherries in layers. **Black Friar** *n.* a Dominican friar. **black frost** *n.* frost without snow or white dew. **black ginger** *n.* unscraped ginger. **black grouse** *n.* a European grouse, *Tetrao tetrix*. **blackguard** (blag'ahd, blag'əd) *n.* **1** a scoundrel. **2** a low, worthless fellow. *~v.t.* to revile in scurrilous language. **blackguardly** (-gəd-) *a., adv.* **blackhead** *n.* a pimple with a black head. **black hole** *n.* **1** a hypothetical celestial region formed from a collapsed star, surrounded by a strong gravitational field from which no matter or energy can escape. **2** a punishment cell. **3** the guardroom. **black horehound, black hoarhound** *n.* the labiate herb, *Ballota nigra*. **black ice** *n.* a thin layer of transparent ice on roads. **blacking** *n.* **1** the action of making black. **2** a composition for giving a shining black polish to boots and shoes, harness etc. **blackish** *a.* **blackjack** *n.* **1** (*N Am.*) a loaded stick, a bludgeon. **2** pontoon or a similar card game. **blacklead** (-led) *n.* plumbago or graphite, made into pencils, also used to polish ironwork. *~v.t.* to colour or rub with blacklead. **blackleg** *n.* (*derog.*) a worker who works for an employer when other employees are on strike, a scab. *~v.i.* (*pres.p.* **blacklegging,** *past, p.p.* **blacklegged**) to act as a blackleg. **black leopard** *n.* a leopard with black fur. **black letter** *n.* the Old English or Gothic as distinguished from the Roman character. **black light** *n.* invisible infra-red or ultraviolet light. **blacklist** *n.* a list of persons in disgrace, or who have incurred censure or punishment. *~v.t.* to ban or prohibit (books etc.). **blackly** *adv.* **black magic** *n.* BLACK ART (under BLACK). **blackmail** *n.* **1** any payment extorted by intimidation or pressure. **2** the use of threats or pressure to influence someone's actions. *~v.t.* **1** to levy blackmail on. **2** to threaten. **blackmailer** *n.* **Black Maria** (mərī'ə) *n.* (*coll.*) a prison van. **black mark** *n.* a note of disgrace put against a person's name. **black market** *n.* illegal buying and selling of rationed goods. **black marketeer** *n.* **black mass** *n.* a travesty of the Mass performed by diabolists. **Black Monk** *n.* a Benedictine monk (from the colour of the habit). **black Muslim** *n.* a member of a black Islamic sect in the US who want to establish a new black nation. **black nationalism** *n.* the advocacy of black self-determination and civil rights. **blackness** *n.* **black nightshade** *n. Solanum nigrum*, with white flowers and poisonous black berries. **blackout** *n.* **1** a temporary loss of consciousness, sight or memory. **2** an electrical power failure or cut. **3** the extinguishing or concealment of lights against air attack. **4** an interruption or suppression of broadcasting, communications etc. **5** the sudden darkening of the stage in a theatre. *~v.t.* **1** to cause to blackout. **2** to obscure (windows), extinguish (lights etc.) to protect against air attack. *~v.i.* to suffer a temporary loss of consciousness, sight or memory. **Black Panther** *n.* a member of the militant black political party in the US. **black pepper** *n.* the whole or ground berries of *Piper nigrum*, the common pepper, used as a condiment. **black power** *n.* a black civil rights movement, esp. in the US and Australia. **black pudding** *n.* a kind of sausage made with blood, rice and chopped fat. **black salsify** *n.* scorzonera. **black sheep** *n.* a bad member of a group or family. **blackshirt** *n.* a member of a Fascist organization in Europe before and during World War II, esp. in Italy. **blacksmith** *n.* **1** a smith who works in iron. **2** (*N Am.*) a person who treats horses. **black spot** *n.* **1** an area of a road where accidents are common. **2** any dangerous area. **3** any of various plant diseases that cause black blotches on the leaves, esp. of roses. **black swan** *n.* **1** an Australian swan, *Cygnus atratus*, that has black plumage and a red bill. **2** something that is very rare. **black tea** *n.* **1** tea that is fully fermented before it is dried. **2** tea without milk. **blackthorn** *n.* **1** the sloe, *Prunus spinosa* (so called from the dark colour of the bark). **2** a walking stick or cudgel of its wood. **blackthorn winter** *n.* a spell of cold weather in the spring, at the time when the blackthorn is flowering. **black tie** *n.* **1** a black bow tie worn with a dinner jacket for a formal occasion. **2** (*coll.*) formal evening dress. **blacktop** *n.* (*esp. N Am.*) **1** a type of bituminous material for surfacing roads. **2** a road surfaced with this. *~v.t.* to surface (a road) with blacktop. **black tracker** *n.* (*Austral.*) an Aboriginal used in tracking escaped criminals or lost travellers. **black velvet** *n.*

a mixture of stout and champagne or cider.
blackwater fever *n*. a form of malaria in which
the urine is very dark in colour. **black widow** *n*.
a venomous American and Far Eastern spider,
Latrodectus mactans, of which the female has a
black body.

Usage note *Black* is now the term least likely to
give offence in referring to members of a dark-
skinned people.

bladder (blad´ə) *n*. **1** a membranous bag in the
animal body which receives the urine. **2** any
similar membranous bag (usu. with distinctive
epithet, as *gall-bladder*, *swim-bladder* etc.). **3** the
prepared (urinary) bladder of an animal. **4** an
inflated pericarp. **5** a vesicle. **6** anything inflated
and hollow. **bladderwort** *n*. an aquatic plant of
the genus *Utricularia*. **bladderwrack** *n*. a seaweed, *Fucus vesiculosus*, which has air bladders
in its fronds.

blade (blād) *n*. **1** the thin cutting part of a knife,
sword etc. **2** any broad, flattened part, as of a
paddle, bat, oar etc. **3** (*Bot.*) **a** a leaf of a plant.
b the culm and leaves of a grass or cereal. **c** the
expanded part of the leaf as distinguished from
the petiole. **d** the corresponding part of a petal.
4 the front part of the tongue. **5** (*poet.*) a sword.
6 (*dated coll.*) a dashing, reckless fellow. **7** in
archaeology, a piece of hard stone used as a tool.
8 BLADE-BONE (under BLADE). **blade-bone** *n*. the
shoulder blade in man and the lower mammals.
bladed *a*.

blaeberry (blā´bəri), **bleaberry** *n*. (*pl.* **blae-
berries, bleaberries**) (*Sc., North.*) **1** the bilberry
or whortleberry. **2** any of various similar fruits or
plants.

blag (blag) *n*. (*sl.*) robbery, esp. violent robbery.
~*v.t., v.i.* (*pres.p.* **blagging**, *past*, *p.p.* **blagged**) to
rob. **blagger** *n*.

blague (blahg) *n*. pretentiousness, humbug.
blagueur (blahgœ´) *n*. a person given to blague.

blah (blah), **blah-blah** *n*. foolish talk, chatter,
exaggeration.

blain (blān) *n*. a pustule, a blister or sore.

blame (blām) *v.t.* **1** to censure, to find fault with,
to reproach. **2** to hold responsible. ~*n*. **1** the
act of censuring. **2** the expression of censure.
3 responsibility, accountability. **to be to blame** to
be culpable. **blamable, blameable** *a*. deserving
blame, culpable. **blamableness** *n*. **blamably** *adv*.
blameful *a*. deserving blame. **blamefully** *adv*.
blameless *a*. free from blame. **blamelessly** *adv*.
blamelessness *n*. **blameworthy** *a*. deserving
blame. **blameworthiness** *n*.

blanch (blahnch) *v.t.* **1** to whiten by taking out
the colour. **2** to bleach, to make pale. **3** to take off
the outward covering of (almonds, walnuts etc.).
4 to whiten (a plant) by the deprivation of light.
5 to plunge (vegetables, fruit, meat etc.) briefly
into boiling water. ~*v.i.* **1** to lose colour. **2** to
become white. **to blanch over** to try to conceal or
misrepresent (e.g. a fault).

blancmange (bləmonzh´) *n*. milk (usu. sweetened) thickened with cornflour or gelatine to
form a jelly-like dessert.

bland (bland) *a*. **1** mild, soft, gentle. **2** genial,
balmy. **3** dull, insipid. **blandly** *adv*. **blandness** *n*.

blandish (blan´dish) *v.t.* **1** to flatter gently. **2** to
coax, to cajole. **blandishment** *n*. **1** flattering
speech or action. **2** cajolery, charm, allurement.

blank (blangk) *a*. **1** empty, void, vacant. **2** not
written or printed on. **3** not filled up. **4** confused,
dispirited, nonplussed. **5** pure, unmixed, downright, sheer. **6** (*euphem.*) (*also* **blankety, blanky**)
used instead of an offensive adjective. ~*n*. **1** a
blank space in a written or printed document.
2 a blank form. **3** a blank cartridge. **4** a vacant
space, a void. **5** an uneventful space of time. **6** a
piece of metal before stamping. **7** a dash written
to replace an obscenity. **8** (*euphem.*) (*also* **blankety, blanky**) used instead of an offensive noun.
9 a domino with one or both halves blank. **10** a
lottery ticket that draws no prize. **11** the white
point in the centre of a target. ~*v.t.* **1** to render
blank. **2** to block out. **3** (*N Am.*) to defeat without allowing (one's opponent) to score. ~*int*.
a mild execration. **blank cartridge** *n*. a cartridge containing no bullet. **blank cheque** *n*. **1** a
cheque with the amount left for the payee to
insert. **2** complete freedom of action. **blankly**
adv. **blankness** *n*. **blank verse** *n*. unrhymed verse,
esp. the iambic pentameter or unrhymed heroic.

blanket (blang´kət) *n*. a piece of woollen or
other warm material, used as bed-covering or
for covering an animal etc. ~*a*. covering all conditions or cases (*blanket medical screening*).
~*v.t.* (*pres.p.* **blanketing**, *past*, *p.p.* **blanketed**) **1** to
cover with or as with a blanket. **2** to stifle.
3 (*Naut.*) to obstruct (a ship) by preventing wind
reaching it. **blanket bath** *n*. a wash given to a
bedridden person. **blanket bog** *n*. an extensive
flat peat bog found in cold wet climates. **blanket
stitch** *n*. a reinforcing stitch for the edge of
blankets and other thick material.

blare (bleə) *v.i.* **1** to roar, bellow. **2** to sound as a
trumpet. ~*v.t.* to utter with a trumpet-like sound.
~*n*. **1** sound as of a trumpet. **2** roar, noise,
bellowing.

blarney (blah´ni) *n*. **1** smooth, flattering speech.
2 cajolery. **3** nonsense. ~*v.t.* (*3rd pers. sing. pres.*
blarneys, *pres.p.* **blarneying**, *past*, *p.p.* **blar-
neyed**) to wheedle, to cajole. ~*v.i.* to talk in a
wheedling way.

blasé (blah´zā) *a*. **1** dulled in sense or emotion.
2 worn out through over-indulgence, used up.

blaspheme (blasfēm´) *v.t.* to utter profane language against (God or anything sacred). ~*v.i.* to
utter blasphemy, to rail. **blasphemer** *n*. **blasphemous** (blas´fə-) *a*. uttering or containing
blasphemy. **blasphemously** *adv*. **blasphemy**
(blas´fəmi) *n*. (*pl.* **blasphemies**) **1** profane language towards God or about sacred things. **2** irreverent or abusive speaking about any person or
thing held in high esteem.

blast (blahst) *n*. **1** a violent gust of wind. **2** the sound of a trumpet or the like. **3** the strong current of air used in iron-smelting. **4** a blowing by gunpowder or other explosive. **5** a violent gust of air caused by the explosion of a bomb. **6** (*coll.*) a severe reprimand. *~v.t.* **1** to blow or breathe on so as to wither. **2** to injure by some pernicious influence. **3** to blight, to ruin. **4** to blow up with gunpowder or other explosive. **5** to curse (often used as an imprecation). **6** to reprimand. **7** to shoot or shoot at. *~v.i.* **1** to blow. **2** to use explosives. **3** to curse. **4** to emit a blast. *~int.* used to express annoyance. **at full blast** hard at work. **to blast off** (of a missile or space vehicle) to be launched. **blasted** *a*. blighted, confounded, cursed. **blaster** *n*. **blast freezing** *n*. the use of a rapid current of chilled air to freeze foods. **blast freeze** *v.t.* **blast from the past** *n*. a nostalgic song, event etc. **blast furnace** *n*. a furnace into which a current of air is introduced to assist combustion. **blast-off** *n*.

-blast (blast) *comb. form* (*Biol.*) used in biological terms to indicate an embryonic cell or cell layer, as *mesoblast, statoblast*.

blastula (blas´tūlə) *n*. (*pl.* **blastulas, blastulae** (-lē)) (*Biol.*) a hollow sphere composed of a single layer of cells, produced by the cleavage of an ovum.

blatant (blā´tənt) *a*. **1** very obvious, palpable. **2** loud, clamorous. **blatancy** *n*. the quality of being blatant. **blatantly** *adv*.

blather, blatherskite BLETHER.

blaze[1] (blāz) *n*. **1** a bright glowing flame. **2** a glow of bright light or colour. **3** an outburst of display, glory, splendour. **4** an outburst of passion. *~v.i.* **1** to burn with a bright flame. **2** to shine, to glitter. **3** to be bright with colour. **4** to be eminent or conspicuous from character, talents etc. **5** to be consumed with anger. **like blazes** (*sl.*) furiously. **to blaze away 1** to fire continuously (with guns). **2** to work continuously and enthusiastically. **to blaze up 1** (of a fire) suddenly to burst into flames. **2** to burst into anger. **what the blazes!** (*sl.*) what the hell! **blazer** *n*. **1** a flannel jacket of bright colour worn at cricket, tennis etc. **2** a jacket used in school uniform. **3** a man's plain jacket worn with non-matching trousers. **blazing** *a*. **1** emitting flame or light. **2** radiant, lustrous. **3** very angry. **blazingly** *adv*.

blaze[2] (blāz) *n*. **1** a white mark on the face of a horse or other animal. **2** a white mark made on a tree by chipping off bark. *~v.t.* **1** to mark (a tree). **2** to indicate (a path or boundary) by such marks. **to blaze a trail 1** to mark out a route. **2** to pioneer something.

blaze[3] (blāz) *v.t.* to proclaim. **to blaze abroad** to spread (news).

blazon (blā´zən) *n*. **1** the art of describing and explaining coats of arms. **2** renown, reputation (of virtues or good qualities). *~v.t.* **1** to proclaim, to trumpet. **2** (*Her.*) **a** to describe or depict according to the rules of heraldry. **b** to decorate with heraldic devices. **blazonment** *n*. **blazonry** *n*. (*pl.* **blazonries**) **1** (*Her.*) **a** the art of depicting or describing a coat of arms. **b** armorial bearings. **2** brilliant display.

bleach (blēch) *v.t.* to make white by exposure to the sun or by chemical agents. *~v.i.* to grow white. *~n.* **1** a bleaching agent. **2** the process or act of bleaching. **bleacher** *n*. **1** a person who or something which bleaches. **2** a vessel used in bleaching. **3** (*usu. pl., esp. NAm.*) a cheap bench seat at a sports ground.

bleak[1] (blēk) *a*. **1** bare of vegetation. **2** cold, chilly, desolate, cheerless. **bleakly** *adv*. **bleakness** *n*.

bleak[2] (blēk) *n*. any of various small river fishes, esp. *Alburnus alburnus*.

†blear (bliə) *a*. dim, indistinct, misty. *~v.t.* **1** to make (the eyes) dim. **2** to blur with or as with tears. **bleary** *a*. (*comp.* **blearier,** *superl.* **bleariest**). **blearily** *adv*. **bleariness** *n*. **bleary-eyed** *a*.

bleat (blēt) *v.i.* to cry like a sheep, goat or calf. *~v.t.* **1** to utter in a bleating tone. **2** to say feebly and foolishly. *~n.* **1** the cry of a sheep, goat or calf. **2** a complaint, whine. **bleater** *n*. **bleatingly** *adv*.

bleb (bleb) *n*. **1** (*Med.*) a small blister or bladder. **2** a bubble in glass or anything similar.

bleed (blēd) *v.i.* (*past, p.p.* **bled** (bled)) **1** to emit, discharge or run with blood. **2** to emit sap, resin or juice from a cut or wound. **3** to be wounded. **4** to die from a wound. **5** to lose money. **6** to have money extorted. **7** (*coll.*) to feel acute mental pain. *~v.t.* **1** to draw blood from. **2** (*coll.*) to extort money from. **3** in bookbinding, to cut margins too much and trench on the print. **4** to extract liquid, air or gas from (a container or closed system such as hydraulic brakes). *~n.* an act of bleeding. **bleeder** *n*. **1** a person who bleeds. **2** (*coll.*) a person with haemophilia. **3** (*sl.*) a contemptible person. **bleeding** *a*. **1** running with blood. **2** (*sl.*) bloody. **3** accursed. **bleeding heart** *n*. **1** any of various plants, esp. *Dicentra spectabilis*, characterized by heart-shaped flowers. **2** (*coll.*) someone who is a do-gooder or too softhearted.

bleep (blēp) *n*. an intermittent, high-pitched sound from an electronic device. *~v.i.* to emit this sound. *~v.t.* **1** to cause to make this sound. **2** to summon with a bleeper. **bleeper** *n*. a small radio receiver emitting a bleeping sound, often carried by doctors, police officers, business people, allowing them to be contacted.

blemish (blem´ish) *v.t.* to impair, tarnish, sully. *~n.* a physical or moral defect or stain, an imperfection, a flaw, a fault.

blench (blench) *v.i.* **1** to shrink back, to draw back. **2** to turn aside, to flinch.

blend (blend) *v.t.* to mix, to mingle (esp. teas, wines, spirits, tobacco etc. so as to produce a certain quality). *~v.i.* **1** to become mingled or indistinguishably mixed. **2** to form a harmonious union or compound. **3** to pass imperceptibly into each other. *~n.* **1** a mixture of various qualities (of teas, wines, spirits, tobacco etc.). **2** a port-manteau word. **blender** *n.* **1** a type of electric liquidizer used in the preparation of food esp. for mixing and puréeing. **2** a person or thing which blends.

blende (blend) *n.* a native sulphide of zinc.

blenny (blen´i) *n.* (*pl. in general* **blenny**, *in particular* **blennies**) any of a family of small, spiny-finned sea fishes, esp. of the genus *Blennius*.

blepharitis (blefərī´tis) *n.* inflammation of the eyelids.

blesbok (bles´bok), **blesbuck** (-bŭk) *n.* (*pl. in general* **blesbok**, **blesbuck**, *in particular* **blesboks**, **blesbucks**) (*S Afr.*) a subspecies of bontebok, a S African antelope, having a white blaze on its forehead.

bless (bles) *v.t.* **1** to consecrate, to hallow. **2** to invoke God's favour on, to render happy or prosperous, as by supernatural means. **3** to wish happiness to. **4** to extol, magnify, worship. **5** (*euphem.*) to curse. **to bless one's stars** to be very thankful. **without a penny to bless oneself with** penniless (with allusion to the cross on a silver penny). **blessed** (bles´id, blest), (*poet.*) **blest** (blest) *a.* **1** consecrated by religious rites. **2** worthy of veneration. **3** (*often iron.*) happy, fortunate, beatified, enjoying the bliss of heaven. **4** joyful, blissful. **5** (*euphem.*) cursed. ~*n.* (*collect.*) the saints in heaven. **blessedly** (-id-) *adv.* **blessedness** (-id-) *n.* **blessing** *n.* **1** consecration. **2** divine favour. **3** an invocation of divine favour or happiness. **4** a cause of happiness. **5** a gift. **6** grace before or after meat. **blessing in disguise** *n.* something that turns out to be unexpectedly advantageous.

blether (bledh´ə), **blather** (bladh´ə) *v.i.* (*coll.*) to talk nonsense volubly. ~*n.* **1** voluble nonsense. **2** a person who blethers, a prattler. **bletherskate** (-skāt), **blatherskite** (-skīt) *n.* a person who talks blatant nonsense.

blew[1] BLOW[1].

blew[2] BLOW[2].

blewits (bloo´its) *n.* any fungus of the genus *Tricholoma*, with edible purplish tops.

blight (blīt) *n.* **1** a disease caused in plants by fungoid parasites and various insects, mildew, smut, rust, aphids etc. **2** any baleful atmospheric influence affecting the growth of plants. **3** any obscure malignant influence. **4** an area of urban decay. ~*v.t.* **1** to affect with blight. **2** to exert a baleful influence on. **3** to mar, frustrate. **blighter** *n.* (*sl.*) a nasty fellow, a blackguard.

Blighty (blī´ti) *n.* **1** (*sl.*) (used by soldiers) Britain, home. **2** (*Mil.*) a wound that invalids one home.

blimey (blī´mi) *int.* (*sl.*) an exclamation of astonishment.

blimp (blimp) *n.* **1** a small airship used for observation. **2** (*coll.*) someone who is narrow-minded and conservative. **3** a diehard army officer. **blimpish** *a.*

blind (blīnd) *a.* **1** unseeing. **2** destitute of sight either naturally or by deprivation. **3** unseen,

dark, admitting no light, having no outlet. **4** of, relating to or for the use or benefit of the sight-less. **5** destitute of understanding, judgement or foresight. **6** undiscerning, obtuse. **7** reckless, heedless. **8** drunk. **9** purposeless, random. **10** (of letters) imperfectly addressed. **11** (*Bot.*) having no buds, eyes or terminal flower. **12** (of a bud) abortive. ~*n.* **1** a blind person. **2** (*pl.*) blind persons collectively. **3** anything which obstructs the light or sight. **4** a blinker for a horse. **5** (*coll.*) a pretence, a pretext. **6** a window-screen or shade, esp. one on rollers for coiling up, or of slats on strips of webbing. **7** (*sl.*) a drunken fit. ~*v.t.* **1** to make blind, to deprive of sight (permanently or temporarily). **2** to darken, make dim. **3** (*coll.*) to deceive. **4** to darken the understanding of. ~*v.i.* **1** to drive blindly and recklessly. **2** (*sl.*) to swear. **blind to** incapable of appreciating. **not a blind bit of** (*sl.*) not any; not the slightest. **to bake blind** to bake (pastry intended for a pie or flan) before adding the filling. **to fly blind** to fly by the use of instruments only. **to go it blind** to act recklessly. **blind alley** *n.* **1** a street, road or alley walled-up at the end. **2** a situation leading nowhere. **blind coal** *n.* a flameless anthracite. **blind corner** *n.* a corner around which one cannot see. **blind date** *n.* **1** a social engagement arranged between two people previously unknown to one another. **2** a person on a blind date. **blind drunk** *a.* too drunk to be able to see straight. **blinder** *n.* **1** a person who or thing which blinds. **2** (*N Am.*) a horse's blinker. **3** (*coll.*) an excellent performance, esp. in cricket, football etc. **blindfold** *v.t.* **1** to cover the eyes of, esp. with a bandage. **2** to dull or obstruct the understanding of. ~*a.* **1** having the eyes bandaged. **2** devoid of foresight. **blind gut** *n.* the caecum. **blinding** *n.* **1** the process of laying sand or grit on a road to cover cracks. **2** sand or grit used in this way. ~*a.* **1** causing blindness; very bright (*blinding snow*). **2** noticeable; brilliant (*a blinding show of skill*). **blindingly** *adv.* **blindly** *adv.* **blind man's buff** *n.* a game in which a player has their eyes bandaged, and has to catch and identify one of the others. **blindness** *n.* **blind screening** *n.* the testing of unidentified samples (of blood) without the patient's knowledge. **blind side** *n.* the direction in which one is most easily assailed. **blind spot** *n.* **1** (*Anat.*) a part of the retina insensitive to light, owing to the passage through it of the optic nerve. **2** a point within the service area of a radio station where signals are received very faintly. **3** a tendency to overlook faults etc. **4** a failure of understanding or judgement. **blind stitch** *n.* sewing that does not show, or that shows at the back only. **blind-stitch** *v.t.*, *v.i.* to sew in blind stitch. **blindworm** *n.* an aberrant British lizard, *Anguis fragilis*, also called the slow-worm (erroneously supposed to be blind, from the small size of its eyes).

blink (blingk) *v.i.* **1** to move the eyelids. **2** to open and shut the eyes. **3** to look with winking eye-lids, to look unsteadily. **4** to shine fitfully. **5** to peep, to wink, to twinkle. ~*v.t.* **1** to shut the eyes to. **2** to evade, to shirk. ~*n.* **1** an act of blinking. **2** a gleam, a glimmer, a twinkle (cp. ICEBLINK (under ICE)). **3** a glance, a twinkling. **on the blink** (*coll.*) (of a machine) not functioning properly. **blinker** *n.* **1** a person who blinks. **2** (*pl.*) screens on a bridle to prevent a horse from seeing sideways. **3** a device that blinks, esp. an indicator on a vehicle. **to wear blinkers** (*coll.*) not to see or understand what is going on around one. **blinkered** *a.* **1** wearing blinkers. **2** not understanding what is going on around one. **3** having a distorted or biased view or opinion. **blinking** *a.* (*coll.*) a euphemism for BLOODY (under BLOOD) used for emphasis.

blip (blip) *n.* (*coll.*) **1** an irregularity in the linear trace on a radar screen indicating the presence of an aircraft, vessel etc. **2** an intermittent, high-pitched sound from an electronic device, a bleep. **3** a temporary movement in the performance of something, esp. in an unexpected and unwelcome direction. ~*v.i.* (*pres.p.* **blipping**, *past, p.p.* **blipped**) to make a blip. ~*v.t.* to strike or tap sharply.

bliss (blis) *n.* **1** happiness of the highest kind. **2** the perfect joy of heaven. **blissful** *a.* **1** full of bliss. **2** causing bliss. **blissfully** *adv.* **blissfully ignorant of** quite unaware of. **blissfulness** *n.*

blister (blis'tə) *n.* **1** a pustule or thin vesicle raised on the skin by some injury, burn etc. and containing a watery fluid or serum. **2** any similar swelling on a plant, metal, a painted surface etc. **3** a blistering agent. **4** (*Med.*) anything applied to raise a blister. **5** (*sl.*) an irritating person. ~*v.i.* **1** to rise in blisters. **2** to be covered with blisters. ~*v.t.* **1** (*Med.*) to raise blisters on. **2** to criticize spitefully. **blister gas** *n.* a poison gas which causes the skin to blister. **blister pack** *n.* a type of clear plastic and cardboard packaging for small products.

blithe (blīdh) *a.* (*poet.*) **1** gay, cheerful, joyous. **2** merry, sprightly. **3** casual, indifferent. **blithely** *adv.* **blitheness** *n.* **blithesome** (-səm) *a.*

blithering (blidh'əring) *a.* **1** (*sl.*) nonsensical, contemptible. **2** jabbering, talking senselessly.

B. Litt. *abbr.* Bachelor of Letters.

blitz (blits) *n.* (*coll.*) **1** intense enemy onslaught, esp. an air raid. **2** an intensive campaign against. **3** intensive activity or action. ~*v.t.* **1** to make an enemy onslaught on. **2** to mount an intensive campaign against. **3** to subject to intensive activity. **blitzkrieg** (-krēg) *n.* an intense military attack intended to defeat the opposition quickly.

blizzard (bliz'əd) *n.* a furious storm of snow and wind.

bloat (blōt) *v.t.* **1** to cause to swell. **2** to puff up. **3** to make vain or conceited. ~*v.i.* **1** to swell. **2** to grow turgid. **bloated** *a.*

bloater (blō'tə) *n.* a herring partially cured by steeping in dry salt and smoking.

blob (blob) *n.* **1** a globular drop of liquid. **2** a spot of colour. **3** any vague, soft form. **4** (*sl.*) in cricket,

a score of nought. **blobby** *a.* (*comp.* **blobbier**, *superl.* **blobbiest**).

bloc (blok) *n.* a combination of parties, or of nations.

block (blok) *n.* **1** a solid mass of wood or stone; a log, a tree stump. **2** a solid unshaped mass of any material. **3** a large building, esp. one that is divided. **4** a compact or connected group of buildings, esp. when bounded by intersecting streets, regarded in the US as a method of measuring distances. **5** an obstruction, a hindrance, an impediment or its effects. **6** a pulley, or system of pulleys, mounted in a frame or shell. **7** a solid cube, used as a child's toy. **8** a piece of wood or metal on which figures are engraved for printing from. **9** a mould on which a thing is shaped. **10** (*sl.*) the head. **11** a dull, unemotional or hard-hearted person. **12** a quantity of things treated as a unit. **13** a pad of writing or drawing paper. **14** in cricket, the position in which a batsman blocks balls. **15** a starting block. **16** in American football, a blocking action. **17** (*Austral.*) a tract of land used for farming or settlement. **18** (*Austral.*) a building plot. ~*v.t.* **1** to stop up, to obstruct. **2** to impede (progress or advance). **3** to shape (a hat) on the block. **4** in bookbinding, to emboss (a cover) by impressing a device. **5** in cricket, to stop (a ball) dead without attempting to hit it. **6** in American football, to obstruct (another player) with one's body. **on the block** (*N Am.*) being auctioned. **to block in** to sketch roughly the broad masses of (a picture or drawing). **to block out 1** to mark out (work) roughly. **2** to exclude (something painful) from memory. **to block up 1** to confine. **2** to infill (a window or doorway) with bricks. **to put the blocks on** to prevent from going ahead. **blockage** *n.* an obstruction. **block and tackle** *n.* a system of pulleys and ropes used for lifting. **blockboard** *n.* board made from thin strips of wood with plywood veneer. **block-booking** *n.* the reserving of a number of seats or places at a single booking. **blockbuster** *n.* (*coll.*) **1** a particularly effective or successful thing or person. **2** a very heavy and effective aerial bomb. **3** a very successful and profitable film or book. **blockbusting** *a.* **block capital** *n.* BLOCK LETTER (under BLOCK). **block diagram** *n.* a diagram showing interconnected parts of a process, structure etc. **blocker** *n.* **blockhead** *n.* a stupid, dull person. **blockheaded** *a.* **blockhouse** *n.* **1** a detached fort covering some strategical point. **2** (*Hist.*) a one-storeyed timber building, with loopholes for musketry. **3** a house of squared timber. **blockish** *a.* **1** stupid. **2** dull. **3** rough, clumsy. **4** like a block. **blockishly** *adv.* **blockishness** *n.* **block letter** *n.* **1** a wood type of large size used in printing. **2** (*pl.*) the imitation in handwriting of printed capital letters. **block mountain** *n.* (*Geol.*) a mountain formed by natural faults. **blockship** *n.* (*Naut.*) a warship used defensively, e.g. to block a channel. **block system** *n.* a system by which a railway line is divided into sections, and no train is allowed to pass into any section till it is signalled clear. **block tin** *n.* tin cast into ingots. **block vote** *n.* a system used esp. at a trade union conference, whereby the value of a delegate's vote is based on the number of people represented.

blockade (blokād´) *n.* **1** the investment of a place by sea or land, so as to compel surrender by starvation or prevent communication with the outside. **2** anything that prevents access or progress. **3** imprisonment by weather or other causes. ~*v.t.* to block up, esp. by troops or ships. **to run a blockade** to pass through a blockading force.

bloke (blōk) *n.* (*coll.*) a man, a fellow.

blond (blond) *a.* **1** fair or light in colour. **2** having light hair and a fair complexion. ~*n.* a person who has light hair and a fair complexion. **blonde** *a.* (of a woman or girl) blond. ~*n.* a blond woman or girl. **blondish** *a.* **blondness** *n.*

blood (blŭd) *n.* **1** the red fluid circulating by means of veins and arteries, through the bodies of man and other vertebrates. **2** any analogous fluid in the invertebrates. **3** lineage, descent. **4** honourable or high birth, family relationship, kinship. **5** slaughter, murder, bloodshed. **6** temperament, passion. **7** a man of a fiery spirit, a rake, a dandy, a dissipated character. **8** (*sl.*) a leader of fashion. ~*v.t.* **1** to cause blood to flow from, to bleed. **2** to inure to blood (as a hound). **3** to initiate (a person) to war or experience. **in one's blood** inborn; in one's character. **out for someone's blood 1** wanting revenge on someone. **2** wanting to kill someone. **to make one's blood boil** to make one furious. **to make one's blood run cold** to horrify one. **to taste blood** to want to repeat something enjoyable or successful. **blood-and-thunder** *a.* sensational, melodramatic. **blood bank** *n.* the place where blood for transfusion is stored. **bloodbath** *n.* a massacre. **blood blister** *n.* a blister containing blood, caused e.g. by a bruise. **blood brother** *n.* **1** a brother by both parents. **2** a man linked to another in a ceremony by the mixing of blood. **blood cell** *n.* any of the cells that circulate in the blood. **blood count** *n.* **1** a calculation of the number of red and white corpuscles in a sample of blood. **2** the number of these. **blood-curdling** *a.* horrifying. **blood donor** *n.* a person from whom blood is taken for transfusion. **blood feud** *n.* a feud arising out of murder or homicide; a vendetta. **blood fluke** *n.* any parasitic flatworm, such as a schistosome, that lives in the blood of man and other vertebrates. **blood group** *n.* any one of four types into which human blood has been classified for purposes of blood transfusion. **blood-heat** *n.* the ordinary heat of blood in a healthy human body (about 98°F or 37°C). **bloodhound** *n.* a variety of hound remarkable for keenness of scent, used for tracking fugitives. **bloodless** *a.* **1** without blood. **2** spiritless. **3** unfeeling. **bloodlessly** *adv.* **bloodlessness** *n.* **bloodletting** *n.* **1** the act, process or art

of taking blood from the body, phlebotomy. **2** bloodshed. **3** excessive financial demands. **bloodline** *n.* (of animals) all the individuals in a family line regarded over generations, esp. regarding characteristics; pedigree. **blood money** *n.* **1** money paid for evidence or information leading to a conviction on a murder charge. **2** money paid to the next of kin as compensation for the murder of a relative. **3** money paid to a hired murderer. **blood orange** *n.* an orange having pulp and juice of a reddish hue. **blood plasma** *n.* blood from which all red corpuscles have been removed. **blood poisoning** *n.* a diseased condition set up by the entrance of septic matter into the blood. **blood pressure** *n.* pressure of the blood on the walls of the containing arteries. **blood relation, blood relative** *n.* a relation by descent, not merely by marriage. **blood serum** *n.* blood plasma from which the clotting factors have been removed. **bloodshed** *n.* **1** the act of shedding blood. **2** murder. **3** slaughter in war. **bloodshot** *a.* **1** red and inflamed. **2** (of the eye) suffused with blood. **blood sport** *n.* a sport entailing the killing of animals, such as fox-hunting. **bloodstain** *n.* a stain produced by blood. **bloodstained** *a.* **1** stained by blood. **2** guilty of bloodshed. **bloodstock** *n.* (*collect.*) thoroughbred horses. **bloodstone** *n.* heliotrope, a variety of quartz with bloodlike spots of jasper. **bloodstream** *n.* **1** the blood circulating in the body. **2** the circulatory movement of the blood in the body. **bloodsucker** *n.* **1** any animal which sucks blood, esp. the leech. **2** an extortioner. **bloodsucking** *a.* **blood sugar** *n.* the amount of glucose circulating in the blood. **blood test** *n.* the examination of a sample of blood for medical disorders. **bloodthirsty** *a.* (*comp.* **bloodthirstier**, *superl.* **bloodthirstiest**) **1** eager to shed blood. **2** delighting in sanguinary deeds. **bloodthirstily** *adv.* **bloodthirstiness** *n.* **blood-transfusion** *n.* transference of blood from the vein of a healthy person to the vein of a person whose blood is deficient in quantity or quality. **blood vessel** *n.* a vessel in which blood circulates in the animal body; an artery or a vein. **bloodworm** *n.* **1** the red wormlike larva of several midges, such as *Chironomus plumosus*, which live in stagnant pools and ditches. **2** a freshwater worm of the genus *Tubifex*. **blood-wort** *n.* any of various plants, either from their red leaves or roots, or from the notion that they were efficacious in staunching blood. **bloody** *a.* (*comp.* **bloodier**, *superl.* **bloodiest**) **1** of or relating to blood. **2** stained or running with blood. **3** attended with bloodshed. **4** cruel, murderous. **5** (*sl.*) damned, devilish. **6** very, exceedingly (prob. from the bloods or hooligans of rank in the 17th or 18th cent.). **7** (*sl.*) annoying, wretched etc. ~*v.t.* (*3rd pers. sing. pres.* **bloodies**, *pres.p.* **bloodying**, *past, p.p.* **bloodied**) to make bloody; to stain with blood. **bloodily** *adv.* **bloodiness** *n.* **Bloody Mary** *n.* a drink consisting of tomato juice and vodka. **bloody-minded** *a.* of an obstinate or unhelpful disposition. **bloody-mindedly** adv. **bloody-mindedness** n. **bloody murder** n. (NAm.) BLUE MURDER (under BLUE).

bloom[1] (bloom) n. **1** a blossom, a flower. **2** the delicate dust on newly gathered plums, grapes etc. **3** the yellow sheen on well-tanned leather. **4** lustre, efflorescence. **5** flush, glow. **6** prime, perfection. **7** WATER-BLOOM (under WATER). **8** the coloured scum formed by this. ~v.i. **1** to blossom, to come into flower. **2** to be at the highest point of perfection or beauty. **to take the bloom off** to make stale. **blooming** a. **1** in a state of bloom, flourishing. **2** bright, lustrous. **3** (sl.) euphemistic for bloody. ~adv. (sl.) used as an intensifier.

bloom[2] (bloom) n. a mass of iron that has undergone the first hammering. ~v.t. to hammer or squeeze (the ball, or lump of iron, from the puddling furnace into a bloom). **bloomery** n. (pl. **bloomeries**) **1** the apparatus for making blooms out of puddled iron. **2** a furnace for making malleable iron by a direct process.

bloomer[1] (bloo´mə) n. **1** (Hist.) a style of dress for ladies, consisting of a shorter skirt, and loose trousers gathered round the ankles. **2** (pl.) bloomer trousers. **3** (pl.) baggy knickers.

bloomer[2] (bloo´mə) n. **1** a plant that blooms (esp. in comb., as early-bloomer). **2** (NAm.) a person who develops in a specified way (late bloomer). **3** (sl.) a mistake, a foolish blunder.

bloomer[3] (bloo´mə) n. an oblong crusty loaf with rounded ends and notches on the top.

blooper (bloo´pə) n. (esp. NAm., coll.) a blunder; a silly mistake.

blossom (blos´əm) n. **1** the flower of a plant, esp. considered as giving promise of fruit. **2** a flower. **3** the mass of flowers on a fruit tree. **4** promise of future excellence or development. ~v.i. **1** to put forth flowers. **2** to bloom. **3** to flourish. **blossomy** a.

blot (blot) n. **1** a spot or stain of ink or other discolouring matter. **2** a blotting out by way of correction. **3** a dark patch. **4** a blemish, disgrace, disfigurement, defect. **5** in biochemistry, a procedure for analysing molecules, esp. proteins, in which they are separated by gel electrophoresis. ~v.t. (pres.p. **blotting**, past, p.p. **blotted**) **1** to spot or stain with ink or other discolouring matter. **2** to obliterate. **3** to dry with blotting paper, to apply blotting paper to. **4** to darken, to disfigure, to sully. **5** in biochemistry, to transfer by means of a blot. ~v.i. to make blots, to become blotted. **to blot one's copybook 1** (coll.) to commit an indiscretion. **2** (coll.) to spoil one's good record. **to blot out** to obliterate, to efface. **blot on the escutcheon** n. a stain on the reputation of a person, family etc. **blotter** n. **1** a person or thing which blots. **2** a paper pad or book for absorbing superfluous ink from paper after writing. **3** (NAm.) a record sheet in e.g. a police station.

blotch (bloch) n. **1** a pustule, boil, botch. **2** a blot. **3** a patch. **4** a clumsy daub. ~v.t. to blot. **blotched** a. marked with blotches. **blotchy** a. (comp. **blotchier**, superl. **blotchiest**)

blotto (blot´ō) a. (sl.) unconscious with drink.

blouse (blowz) n. a light, loose, upper garment. ~v.t. to make (a garment) hang in loose folds. ~v.i. to hang in loose folds.

blouson (bloo´zon) n. a short, loose jacket fitted or belted in at the waist.

blow[1] (blō) v.i. (past **blew** (bloo), p.p. **blown** (blōn)) **1** to move as a current of air. **2** to send a current of air from the mouth. **3** to pant, to puff. **4** to sound, to give forth musical notes (as a horn). **5** to eject water and air from the spiracles (as cetaceans). **6** to boast, to talk big. **7** (of a fuse) to melt from overloading. ~v.t. **1** to drive a current of air upon. **2** to inflate with air. **3** to drive by a current of air. **4** to put out of breath. **5** to sound (a wind instrument or a note on it). **6** to taint by depositing eggs upon (as flies). **7** to shatter by explosives. **8** to spread (a report etc.). **9** to inflate, to puff up, to enlarge. **10** (sl.) (past, p.p. **blowed**) to curse, confound. **11** to cause (a fuse) to melt by overloading. **12** (sl.) to spoil (an opportunity). **13** (sl.) to squander. ~n. **1** a blowing, a blast of air. **2** a breath of fresh air. **3** (coll.) a spell of playing jazz. **to blow a kiss** to kiss one's hand and blow the air towards someone. **to blow away 1** (sl.) to kill or destroy. **2** (sl.) to defeat. **3** (sl.) to amaze. **to blow hot and cold 1** to vacillate. **2** to do one thing at one time, and its opposite at another. **to blow in 1** to break inwards. **2** to make an unexpected visit. **to blow off 1** to escape with a blowing noise, as steam. **2** to discharge (steam, energy, anger etc.). **3** to break wind. **to blow one's lid** (coll.) to lose one's temper. **to blow one's mind** (sl.) to give one drug-induced hallucinations or a similar experience. **to blow one's own trumpet** to boast, to sing one's own praises. **to blow one's stack** (NAm., coll.) to lose one's temper. **to blow one's top** (coll.) to lose one's temper. **to blow out 1** to extinguish by blowing. **2** to clear by means of blowing. **3** (of a tyre) to burst. **4** (of a fuse) to melt. **5** (NAm., sl.) to defeat soundly. **6** (NAm., sl.) to break. **blow over** to pass away, to subside. **to blow the whistle on** (coll.) to inform on (someone) or bring (something) to an end. **to blow up 1** to inflate. **2** to scold, to censure severely. **3** to ruin. **4** to explode, to fly in fragments. **5** (coll.) to enlarge (a photograph). **6** (coll.) to exaggerate. **7** (coll.) to arise. **8** (coll.) to lose one's temper. **blow-by-blow** a. (of a storyline or description) very detailed. **blow-dry** n. a method of styling hair while drying it with a small hairdryer. ~v.t. (3rd pers. sing. pres. **blow-dries**, pres.p. **blow-drying**, past, p.p. **blow-dried**) to arrange (hair) while drying it in this way. **blow-dryer, blow-drier** n. **blower** n. **1** a person who or thing which blows. **2** a cetacean, a whale. **3** a contrivance for creating an artificial current of air. **4** (coll.) a telephone, speaking-tube etc. **blowfish** n. (pl. in general **blowfish**, in particular **blowfishes**) any of several kinds of fish which inflate their bodies when they are frightened. **blowfly** n. (pl. **blowflies**) a fly of the family Calliphoridae, such as the bluebottle, which lays its eggs on meat. **blowgun** n. (N Am.) a tube used by American Indians for shooting darts; a blowpipe. **blowhard** n. a boastful person. ~a. boastful. **blowhole** n. 1 an airhole. 2 a hole in the ice to which seals and whales come to breathe. 3 (pl.) the spiracles of a cetacean. **blow job** n. (taboo sl.) an act of fellatio. **blowlamp, blowtorch** n. 1 a lamp used in soldering, brazing etc. 2 a burner used to remove paint. **blow-out** n. (sl.) 1 a hearty meal. 2 a celebration. 3 an explosion of oil and gas from an oil well. 4 the puncturing of a tyre. 5 the burning out of an electrical fuse or a valve. 6 (N Am.) a defeat or failure. **blowpipe** n. 1 a tube used for increasing combustion by directing a current of air into a flame. 2 a pipe used in glass-blowing. 3 a tube used by American Indians for shooting darts by means of the breath. **blow-up** n. 1 the enlargement of part or whole of a photograph. 2 (coll.) an explosion. 3 (coll.) a burst of anger, a heated argument. **blowy** a. (comp. **blowier**, superl. **blowiest**) 1 windy. 2 exposed to the wind.

blow[2] (blō) n. 1 a stroke with the fist or any weapon or instrument. 2 an act of hostility. 3 a severe shock. 4 a sudden and painful calamity. **at one blow** in one action.

†**blow**[3] (blō) v.i. (past **blew** (bloo), p.p. **blown** (blōn)) 1 to blossom. 2 to bloom, to flourish. ~n. the state of blossoming.

blowze (blowz) **blowse** n. 1 a red-faced, bloated woman. 2 a woman with disordered hair. **blowzy** a. (comp. **blowzier**, superl. **blowziest**) 1 having a red, bloated face. 2 untidy, sluttish. **blowzily** adv. **blowziness** n.

BLT abbr. bacon, lettuce and tomato.

blub (blŭb) v.i. (pres.p. **blubbing**, past, p.p. **blubbed**) (sl.) to weep noisily, shed tears.

blubber (blŭb´ə) n. 1 the fat underlying the skin in whales and other cetaceans, from which trainoil is prepared. 2 (coll.) excess body fat. 3 noisy weeping. ~a. (of the lips etc.) swollen, pouting. ~v.i. to weep noisily. ~v.t. 1 to wet and disfigure with weeping. 2 to utter with sobs and tears. **blubberer** n. **blubbery** a.

bludge (blŭj) v.i. (Austral., New Zeal., sl.) 1 to evade work. 2 to scrounge from someone. ~v.t. to cadge, scrounge. ~n. an easy task. **to bludge on** to impose on (someone). **bludger** n.

bludgeon (blŭj´ən) n. a short, thick stick, sometimes loaded; a blackjack. ~v.t. 1 to strike with this. 2 to coerce verbally, or by physical force.

blue (bloo) a. (comp. **bluer**, superl. **bluest**) 1 of the colour of the cloudless sky or deep sea. 2 of the similar colour of smoke, vapour, distant landscape, steel etc. 3 (coll.) miserable, low-spirited. 4 (sl.) obscene, smutty. 5 with bluish skin because of cold etc. 6 belonging to the political party which adopts blue for its colour (in Britain, usu. the Conservatives). 7 having blue as a

distinguishing colour. 8 dressed in blue. 9 (of women) learned, pedantic. ~n. 1 a blue colour. 2 a blue pigment. 3 a blue substance, object or animal (as explained by context). 4 blue clothes. 5 a person who plays for their university in sport or athletics. 6 a supporter of a political party which has blue for its colour, such as the Conservative Party. 7 any of various small blue butterflies of the family Lycaenidae. 8 a blue powder used in laundries. 9 (Austral., sl.) an argument. 10 (Austral., sl.) (as a nickname) someone with red hair. 11 a blue ball, piece etc. in a game. 12 the sky. 13 the sea. ~v.t. (pres.p. **blueing, bluing**, past, p.p. **blued**) 1 to make blue. 2 to treat with (laundry) blue. 3 (sl.) to squander (money). **out of the blue** unexpectedly. **blue baby** n. a baby with a bluish discoloration of the skin due to a shortage of oxygen in the blood. **Bluebeard** n. 1 a man who murders his wives. 2 a person with a horrible secret. **bluebell** n. 1 a woodland plant, Hyacinthoides nonscripta, which has blue bell-shaped flowers, also called wild hyacinth or wood hyacinth. 2 (Sc.) the harebell, Campanula rotundifolia. 3 any of several other plants which have blue bell-shaped flowers. **blueberry** n. (pl. **blueberries**) 1 any of several plants of the genus Vaccinium, which have blue-black edible berries, also called huckleberry. 2 the fruit of these plants. **blue bice** n. a shade of blue between ultramarine and azure. **bluebird** n. 1 any N American songbird of the genus Sialia, which have blue plumage on the back or head. 2 (fig.) a symbol of happiness. **blue-black** a. of a blue colour that is almost black. ~n. black with a tinge of blue. **blue blood** n. 1 aristocratic descent. 2 a person of aristocratic descent. **blue-blooded** a. **blue book** n. 1 an official report of Parliament (bound in volumes which have blue covers). 2 (N Am.) a list of Government officials with their salaries etc. **bluebottle** n. 1 the blue cornflower, Centaurea cyanus. 2 any of several other blue flowers. 3 the meat-fly or blowfly, Calliphora vomitoria. 4 †a beadle. 5 (coll.) a police officer. 6 (Austral.) a Portuguese man-of-war. **blue box** n. 1 (esp. N Am.) an electronic device used to gain illegal access to long-distance telephone lines. 2 (esp. Can.) a blue plastic box for storing materials to be recycled. **blue cheese** n. a cheese threaded by blue veins of mould induced by the insertion of copper wires during its making. **blue chip** n. an issue of stocks or shares believed to be dependable in maintaining or increasing its value. **blue-chip** a. **blue-collar** a. of or relating to manual work and manual workers in contrast to desk work and office employees (see WHITE-COLLAR (under WHITE)). **blue ensign** n. a blue flag flown by the naval reserve and by some yachts and merchant vessels. **blue eye** n. an eye with a blue iris. **blue-eyed** a. **blue-eyed boy, blue-eyed girl** n. (coll., usu. derog.) someone especially favoured by a person or group. **blue film, blue movie** n. a sexually explicit or pornographic film. **bluefish** *n.* (*pl. in general* **bluefish,** *in particular* **bluefishes**) a large voracious fish, *Pomatomus saltatrix*, which inhabits tropical and temperate waters. **blue funk** *n.* **1** abject terror. **2** (*N Am.*) a state of despondency or depression. **bluegrass** *n.* (*N Am.*) **1** the rich grass of the limestone lands of Kentucky and Tennessee (bluegrass country). **2** a kind of folk music originating from these regions. **blue-green alga** *n.* a cyanobacterium. **blue ground** *n.* KIMBERLITE. **bluegum, bluegum tree** *n.* any tree of the genus *Eucalyptus*, esp. *E. regnans*. **blueish** BLUISH (under BLUE). **bluejacket** *n.* (*sl.*) a sailor in the British Navy. **blue line** *n.* in ice hockey, either of the two lines midway between the centre of the rink and each goal. **bluely** *adv.* **blue metal** *n.* broken blue stone used to make roads. **blue moon** *n.* **1** a very rare or unknown occurrence. **2** never. **once in a blue moon** very rarely, seldom; never. **blue mould** *n.* a blue-coloured fungus which grows on rotting food and other vegetable matter, and is induced in blue cheese. **blue movie** BLUE FILM (under BLUE). **blue murder** *n.* a loud noise; a great commotion. **blueness** *n.* **blue-pencil** *v.t.* (*pres.p.* **bluepencilling,** (*N Am.*) **blue-penciling,** *past, p.p.* **blue-pencilled,** (*N Am.*) **blue-penciled**) (*coll.*) to censor, edit or mark with corrections (traditionally using a blue pencil). **Blue Peter** *n.* a small blue flag with a white square in the centre, used as a signal for sailing. **blueprint** *n.* **1** a plan or drawing printed on specially sensitized paper: the print is composed of white lines on a blue background, and is much used for scale and working drawings of engineering designs, electrical circuits etc. **2** any original plan or guideline for future work. *~v.t.* (*N Am.*) to work out (a plan, programme etc.). **blue ribbon** *n.* **1** the ribbon of the Garter. **2** the greatest distinction, the first prize. **blue rinse** *n.* a rinse for tinting grey hair. **blue roan** *a.* black mixed with white. *~n.* an animal of this colour. **blue rock** *n.* ROCK DOVE (under ROCK[1]). **blues** *n.pl.* **1** (**the blues**) low spirits, depression. **2** (**the blues**) a form of melancholy, black American folk song originating in the deep south, usu. consisting of three, four-bar phrases in 4/4 time. **3** (*sing.*) a blues song. **bluesy** *a.* **bluestocking** *n.* a woman affecting learning or literary tastes. **bluestone** *n.* **1** any of various bluegrey building stones. **2** any of the smaller stones used at Stonehenge, made of dolerite. **bluet** *n.* a N American blue-flowered plant of the genus *Hedyotis*. **blue tit** *n.* a common tit, *Parus caeruleus*, which has a blue crown, wings and tail and yellow underparts. **blue vitriol** *n.* hydrous sulphate of copper. **blue water** *n.* the open sea. **blue whale** *n.* the largest known living mammal, *Balaenoptera musculus*, a bluish-grey rorqual. **bluey**[1] *n.* (*pl.* **blueys**) (*Austral., coll.*) **1** a bundle carried by a bushman. **2** a blanket. **bluey**[2] *a.* having a tinge of blue. **bluish, blueish** *a.* having a tinge of blue. **bluishly** *adv.* **bluishness** *n.*

bluff[1] (blŭf) *a.* **1** (of a cliff, or a ship's bows) having a broad, flattened face or front. **2** abrupt, blunt, frank, outspoken. *~n.* a cliff or headland with a broad, precipitous front. **bluffly** *adv.* **bluffness** *n.*

bluff[2] (blŭf) *n.* **1** (*sl.*) an excuse, a blind. **2** the action of bluffing at cards. **3** boastful language. **4** empty threats or promises. *~v.t.* **1** to impose upon (one's adversary at cards) by making them believe one's hand is stronger than it is, and inducing them to throw up the game. **2** (*fig.*) to treat rivals (political opponents, or foreign powers) in this way. *~v.i.* to make one's adversary believe that one is strong or confident. **to call someone's bluff** to challenge someone who is bluffing; to expose someone. **bluffer** *n.*

bluish BLUE.

blunder (blŭn'də) *v.i.* **1** to err grossly. **2** to act blindly or stupidly. **3** to flounder, to stumble. *~v.t.* to mismanage. *~n.* a gross mistake, a stupid error. **blunderer** *n.* **blundering** *a.* **blunderingly** *adv.*

blunderbuss (blŭn'dəbŭs) *n.* (*Hist.*) a short gun, of large bore, widening at the muzzle.

blunt (blŭnt) *a.* **1** dull, stupid, obtuse. **2** without edge or point. **3** abrupt, unceremonious. **4** rough, unpolished. *~v.t.* **1** to make less sharp, keen, or acute. **2** to deaden, to dull. *~v.i.* to become blunt. **bluntish** *a.* **bluntly** *adv.* **bluntness** *n.*

blur (blœ) *n.* **1** a smear, a blot, a stain. **2** a dim, misty effect. *~v.t.* (*pres.p.* **blurring,** *past, p.p.* **blurred**) **1** to smear, to blot. **2** to stain, to sully. **3** to render misty and indistinct. **4** to dim. *~v.i.* to become indistinct. **blurry** *a.* (*comp.* **blurrier,** *superl.* **blurriest**).

blurb (blœb) *n.* a description of a book, usu. printed on the dust jacket, intended to advertise and promote it.

blurt (blœt) *v.t.* to utter abruptly (*usu. with out*).

blush (blŭsh) *v.i.* **1** to become red in the face from shame or other emotion, to assume a bright red colour. **2** to be ashamed. **3** to bloom. *~n.* **1** the reddening of the face produced by shame, modesty or any similar cause. **2** a crimson or roseate hue. **3** a flush of light. **at (the) first blush** at the first glance; at first sight. **to spare someone's blushes** to avoid embarrassing someone by praising them too much. **blusher** *n.* **1** a person who blushes. **2** a cosmetic for reddening the cheeks.

bluster (blŭs'tə) *v.i.* **1** to blow boisterously. **2** to play the bully, to swagger, to boast. *~n.* **1** boisterous, blowing, inflated talk, swaggering. **2** empty vaunts and threats. **blusterer** *n.* **blustery** *a.*

BM *abbr.* **1** Bachelor of Medicine. **2** British Museum.

B. Mus. *abbr.* Bachelor of Music.

BMX *abbr.* **1** bicycle motocross, bicycle stunt riding over an obstacle course. **2** (BMX®) a bicycle designed for this.

Bn. *abbr.* **1** battalion. **2** billion.

BO *abbr.* **1** body odour. **2** box office.

bo (bō), **boh** *int.* an exclamation intended to surprise or frighten.

boa (bō´ə) *n.* **1** a genus of large S American snakes of the family Boidae, which kill their prey by crushing. **2** any such snake, e.g. a python. **3** a long fur or feather stole worn round the neck. **boa constrictor** *n.* **1** a Brazilian serpent, *Boa constrictor*, which kills its prey by crushing it. **2** any very large snake which kills its prey by constriction.

boar (baw) *n.* **1** the uncastrated male of the domesticated swine. **2** (**wild boar**) the male of the wild swine, *Sus scrofa*. **3** a male guinea pig.

board (bawd) *n.* **1** a piece of timber of considerable length, and of moderate breadth and thickness. **2** a flat slab of wood, used as a table, for exhibiting notices, and other purposes. **3** a table or frame on which games (such as chess, draughts etc.) are played. **4** a thick substance formed of layers of paper etc., pasted or squeezed together. **5** a piece of stout pasteboard or millboard used as one of the sides of a bound book. **6** a table, esp. for meals. **7** †a table spread for a meal. **8** daily provisions. **9** one's keep, or money in lieu of keep. **10** a council table. **11** the members of a council. **12** the persons who have the management of some public trust or business concern. **13** (*pl.*) the stage. ~*v.t.* **1** to furnish or cover with boards. **2** to provide with daily meals (and now usu. with lodging). **3** to attack and enter (a ship) by force. **4** to go on a ship, to embark. ~*v.i.* to have one's meals (and usu. lodging) at another person's house. **by the board 1** overboard, by the ship's side. **2** ignored, rejected or disused. **on board** in or into a ship, train, bus or aeroplane. **boarder** *n.* **1** a person who has their food at the house of another. **2** a scholar who is boarded and lodged at a school. **3** a person who boards an enemy's ship. **board game** *n.* a game, such as chess, which is played with pieces or counters on a special board. **boarding** *n.* **1** the action of the verb to BOARD. **2** a structure of boards. **boarding house** *n.* a house in which board may be had. **boarding kennel** *n.* a place where dogs are boarded. **boarding pass** *n.* a ticket authorizing one to board an aeroplane, ship etc. **boarding school** *n.* a school in which pupils are boarded as well as taught. **boardroom** *n.* the meeting place of a company's board of directors. **boardsailing** *n.* **1** sailing on a surf board propelled by a sail mounted with a steering bar. **2** windsurfing. **boardsailor, boardsailer** *n.* **boardwalk** *n.* **1** a seaside promenade made of planks. **2** (*N Am.*) a wooden walkway over sand, marsh etc.

boast (bōst) *n.* **1** proud, vainglorious assertion, a vaunt, a brag. **2** an occasion of pride. **3** laudable exultation. ~*v.i.* to brag, to praise oneself, to speak ostentatiously or vaingloriously. ~*v.t.* **1** to extol, to speak of with pride. **2** to have as worthy of pride. **boaster** *n.* **boastful** *a.* **1** full of boasting. **2** vainglorious. **boastfully** *adv.* **boastfulness** *n.* **boastingly** *adv.*

boat (bōt) *n.* **1** a small vessel, generally undecked and propelled by oars or sails. **2** a fishing vessel, mailboat or passenger ship. **3** a vessel or utensil resembling a boat, such as a sauce-boat. ~*v.i.* to sail in a boat, to row in a boat. **in the same boat** in the same circumstances or position. **to push the boat out** (*coll.*) to celebrate expensively. **to rock the boat** to disrupt existing conditions, to cause trouble. **boat-building** *n.* the occupation of building boats. **boat-builder** *n.* **boater** *n.* **1** a person who boats. **2** a man's stiff straw hat. **boatful** *n.* (*pl.* **boatfuls**) **boat-hook** *n.* a pole with an iron point and hook, used to push or pull a boat. **boathouse** *n.* a house by the water in which boats are kept. **boatie** *n.* (*esp. Austral., New Zeal.*) a boating enthusiast. **boating** *n.* the art, sport or practice of sailing or rowing. **boatload** *n.* **1** enough to fill a boat. **2** (*coll.*) a large number of people. **boatman** *n.* (*pl.* **boatmen**) **1** a person who lets out boats on hire. **2** a person who rows or sails a boat for hire. **boat people** *n.pl.* refugees (usu. Vietnamese) who have fled from their country in small boats. **boat race** *n.* a race between rowing boats. **boat-train** *n.* a train conveying passengers to or from a ship.

boatel (bōtel´), **botel** *n.* **1** a floating hotel, a moored ship functioning as a hotel. **2** a waterfront hotel accommodating boaters.

boatswain (bō´sən), **bo's'n, bosun, bo'sun** *n.* the foreman of the crew (in the RN a warrant officer) who looks after the ship's boats, rigging, flags, cables etc. **boatswain's chair** *n.* a wooden seat suspended from ropes, used by someone working on a ship's side.

bob (bob) *n.* **1** a short jerking action, a curtsy. **2** a peal of courses or set of changes in bell-ringing. **3** a short hairstyle. **4** a weight or pendant at the end of a cord, chain, plumb line, pendulum etc. **5** a bobsleigh. **6** the docked tail of a horse. **7** a short line at the end of a stanza. **8** a knot or bunch of hair, a short curl, a bobwig. **9** (*Hist., sl.*) a shilling or 5 pence. ~*v.t.* (*pres.p.* **bobbing**, *past, p.p.* **bobbed**) **1** to move with a short jerking motion. **2** to cut short (as a horse's tail). **3** to cut (hair) in a bob. **4** to rap, to strike lightly. ~*v.i.* **1** to have a short jerking motion. **2** to move to and fro or up and down. **3** to dance, to curtsy. **4** to catch with the mouth. **5** to ride on a bobsleigh. **to bob up** to emerge suddenly. **bobber** *n.* a person who rides on a bobsleigh. **bobble** (bob´əl) *n.* **1** a fabric or wool ball used as decorative trimming, a pompon. **2** (*N Am.*) a mistake; a fumble. ~*v.t., v.i.* (*N Am.*) to fumble, handle ineptly or bungle. **bobbly** *a.* **bobcat** *n.* a N American lynx, *Felix rufus*, which has reddish-brown fur with dark spots or stripes, and a short tail. **bobsled** *n.* **1** a conveyance formed of two sleds or sleighs coupled together, used to transport large timber. **2** (*N Am.*) a bobsleigh. **bobsledding** *n.* **bobsleigh** *n.* a sleigh with two pairs of runners, one behind the other, often used for racing. **bobsleighing** *n.* **bobtail** *n.* **1** a tail (of a horse) cut short. **2** a horse or dog with its tail cut short. **bobwig** *n.* a wig having the bottom turned up in bobs or curls, in contradistinction to a full-bottomed wig.

bobbie pin (bob´i), **bobby pin** *n.* (*esp. N Am.*) a hairgrip.

bobbin (bob´in) *n.* **1** a spool or pin with a head on which thread for making lace, cotton, yarn, wire etc., is wound and drawn off as required. **2** a piece of wood with a string for actuating a door latch. **bobbinet** (-net´) *n.* machine-made cotton net, orig. imitated from bobbin lace. **bobbin lace, bobbinwork** *n.* work woven with bobbins.

bobbitt (bob´it) *v.t.* to sever the penis of (one's husband or lover).

bobble BOB.

bobby[1] (bob´i) *n.* (*pl.* **bobbies**) (*coll.*) a policeman, a police officer.

bobby[2] (bob´i), **bobby calf** *n.* (*pl.* **bobbies, bobby calves**) a calf slaughtered for veal because it has been weaned.

bobby-dazzler (bobidaz´lə) *n.* (*coll.*) an excellent striking person or thing, esp. an attractive girl.

bobby sox (bob´i), **bobby socks** *n.* (*esp. N Am.*) ankle socks usu. worn by young girls. **bobby-soxer** *n.* an adolescent girl.

bobolink (bob´əlingk) *n.* a N American songbird, *Dolichonyx oryzivorus.*

Boche (bosh) *n.* (*derog.*) a German, esp. a soldier. ~*a.* German. **the Boche** Germans, esp. German soldiers, collectively.

bock (bok) *n.* a strong German beer.

BOD *abbr.* biochemical oxygen demand.

bod (bod) *n.* (*coll.*) **1** a person. **2** (*N Am.*) a body.

bodacious (bədā´shəs) *a.* (*sl., esp. N Am.*) excellent, wonderful.

bode (bōd) *v.t.* **1** to foretell. **2** to presage. **3** to give promise of. **4** to forebode. ~*v.i.* to portend (well or ill).

bodega (bədē´gə) *n.* a shop selling wine, esp. in a Spanish-speaking country.

bodice (bod´is) *n.* **1** a tight-fitting outer vest for women. **2** the upper part of a woman's dress, for the body above the waist. **3** (*Hist.*) an inner vest worn by women over the corset. **bodice-ripper** *n.* (*coll.*) a romantic historical novel involving sex and violence. **bodice-ripping** *a.*

bodiless, bodily BODY.

bodkin (bod´kin) *n.* **1** a large-eyed and blunt-pointed needle for leading a tape or cord through a hem, loop etc. **2** a pin for fastening up women's hair. **3** an instrument for piercing holes.

body (bod´i) *n.* (*pl.* **bodies**) **1** the material frame of man or the lower animals. **2** the main trunk, excluding the head and limbs. **3** the upper part of a dress, a bodice. **4** a corpse, a dead body. **5** the main or central part of a building, ship, document, book etc. **6** the part of a car in which the driver and passengers sit. **7** a collective mass of persons, things or doctrine, precepts etc. **8** matter, substance, as opposed to spirit. **9** a human being, a person, an individual. **10** a society,

a corporate body, a corporation. **11** a military force. **12** (*Philos.*) matter, substance, that which has sensible properties. **13** any substance, simple or compound. **14** (*Geom.*) a figure of three dimensions. **15** strength, substantial quality. **16** a figure-hugging woman's garment resembling a swimsuit or leotard fastened beneath the crotch (and worn under a skirt or trousers). ~*v.t.* (*3rd pers. sing. pres.* **bodies,** *pres.p.* **bodying,** *past, p.p.* **bodied**) **1** to clothe with a body. **2** to embody. **in a body** all together. **over my dead body** (*coll.*) without my agreement, against my opposition. **to keep body and soul together** to survive, to maintain life. **bodiless** *a.* **bodily** *a.* **1** of, relating to or affecting the body or the physical nature. **2** corporeal. ~*adv.* **1** corporeally, united with matter. **2** wholly, completely, entirely. **body bag** *n.* a strong plastic bag in which a dead body (esp. of a soldier killed in battle) is transported home. **body blow** *n.* **1** in boxing, a punch landing between the breast bone and navel. **2** a harsh disappointment or setback, a severe shock. **bodybuilder** *n.* **1** a person who develops their muscles through exercise and/or eating high protein food. **2** an exercising machine. **bodybuilding** *n., a.* **body-check** *n.* in sports such as lacrosse or hockey, a deliberate obstruction of one player by another. ~*v.t.* to obstruct in this way. **body colour** *n.* **1** a pigment having a certain degree of consistency and tingeing power as distinct from a wash. **2** a colour rendered opaque by the addition of white. **body double** *n.* in films, a person who stands in for an actor during a nude scene or a stunt, where the face is not seen. **bodyguard** *n.* **1** a guard for the person of a sovereign or dignitary. **2** a retinue, following. **body language** *n.* a form of non-verbal communication by means of conscious or unconscious gestures, postures and facial expressions. **body odour** *n.* the smell of the human body, esp. the smell of sweat. **body piercing** *n.* the piercing of holes in a person's body, so that jewellery can be worn. **body politic** *n.* **1** organized society. **2** the state. **body-popping** *n.* (*orig. N Am.*) dancing with jerky, robotic movements. **body scanner** *n.* (*Med.*) an X-ray or ultrasound machine that uses a computer to produce cross-sectional pictures of the body. **body search** *n.* a search of a person's body in order to find drugs, weapons etc. **body shop** *n.* a vehicle-body repair shop. **body stocking** *n.* a clinging all-in-one undergarment for women, often of a sheer material. **bodysuit** *n.* **1** a top worn by girls or women which fastens beneath the crotch. **2** an undergarment worn by babies. **body warmer** *n.* a padded or quilted jacket without sleeves. **body wave** *n.* a soft light permanent wave for the hair. **body weight** *n.* the weight of a person's or animal's body. **bodywork** *n.* the metal shell of a motor vehicle. **body wrap** *n.* a beauty treatment in which the body is wrapped in hot bandages in order to cleanse the skin or improve the figure.

Boer (buə, bō´ə, baw) *n.* a S African of Dutch birth or extraction. ~*a.* of or relating to the Boers.

boffin (bof´in) *n.* (*coll.*) a scientist, esp. one employed by the armed services or the government.

bog (bog) *n.* **1** a marsh, a morass. **2** wet, spongy soil, a quagmire. **3** (*sl.*) a lavatory. ~*v.t.* (*pres.p.* **bogging**, *past, p.p.* **bogged**) to sink or submerge in a bog. **to bog down 1** to overwhelm, as with work. **2** to hinder. **to bog off** (*sl.*) to go away. **bog asphodel** *n.* a yellow-flowered marsh plant, *Narthecium ossifragum*, which has grasslike leaves. **bogbean** *n.* BUCKBEAN. **bog cotton** *n.* COTTON GRASS (under COTTON). **boggy** *a.* (*comp.* **boggier**, *superl.* **boggiest**) **1** of or characterized by bogs. **2** swampy. **bogginess** *n.* **bog moss** *n.* the genus *Sphagnum*. **bog myrtle** *n.* a deciduous shrub, *Myrica gale*, with catkins and grey-green leaves, also called *sweet gale*. **bog oak** *n.* oak found preserved in bogs, black from impregnation with iron. **bog standard** *a.* (*sl.*) basic. **bogtrotter** *n.* **1** a person used to traversing boggy country. **2** (*offensive*) an Irish person.

bogey[1] (bō´gi) *n.* (*pl.* **bogeys**) in golf, one stroke over par on a hole. ~*v.t.* (*3rd. pers. sing. pres.* **bogeys**, *pres.p.* **bogeying**, *past, p.p.* **bogeyed**) to complete (a hole) in one stroke over par.

bogey[2] (bō´gi), **bogy** *n.* (*pl.* **bogeys, bogies**) **1** a spectre, a bugbear. **2** an awkward thing or circumstance. **3** (*sl.*) a piece of nasal mucus. **bogeyman** *n.* (*pl.* **bogeymen**) an evil person or spirit, used to menace children.

boggle (bog´əl) *v.i.* **1** (*coll.*) to be astounded. **2** (*coll.*) to be unable to imagine or understand. ~*v.t.* to overwhelm (mentally).

bogie (bō´gi), **bogy** *n.* (*pl.* **bogies**) a revolving undercarriage.

bogle (bō´gəl) *n.* **1** a hobgoblin, a spectre, a bugbear. **2** a scarecrow.

bogus (bō´gəs) *a.* sham, counterfeit, spurious, fictitious.

bogy BOGEY[2].

Bohemian (bəhē´miən) *a.* of or relating to Bohemia, its people or their language. ~*n.* a native or inhabitant of Bohemia.

bohemian (bəhē´miən) *n.* **1** a gypsy. **2** a person who leads a free, irregular life, despising social conventionalities. ~*a.* of or characteristic of the gypsies or of social bohemians. **bohemianism** *n.*

boho (bō´hō) *n.* (*pl.* **bohos**) (*coll.*) a bohemian. ~*a.* bohemian.

boil[1] (boil) *v.i.* **1** to be agitated by the action of heat, as water or other fluids. **2** to reach the temperature at which these are converted into gas. **3** to be subjected to the action of boiling, as meat etc., in cooking. **4** to bubble or seethe like boiling water (also of the containing vessel). **5** to be agitated with passion. ~*v.t.* **1** to cause (a liquid) to bubble with heat. **2** to bring to the boiling point. **3** to cook by heat in boiling water. **4** to prepare in a boiling liquid. ~*n.* **1** an act of boiling. **2** the state of boiling. **3** boiling point. **to boil down 1** to

lessen the bulk of by boiling. **2** to condense. **to boil down to** to amount to; to mean. **to boil over 1** to bubble up, so as to run over the sides of the vessel. **2** to be effusive. **3** to lose one's temper. **boiled** *a.* **boiled shirt** *n.* (*coll.*) a dress shirt. **boiled sweet** *n.* a hard sweet made from boiled sugar. **boiler** *n.* **1** a person who boils. **2** a vessel in which anything is boiled. **3** the large vessel in which anything is boiled. **3** the large vessel in a steam engine in which water is converted into steam. **4** a tank in which water is heated for domestic use. **5** (*Hist.*) a vessel for boiling clothes in a laundry, a copper. **6** a tough chicken etc. that needs to be cooked by boiling. **boilermaker** *n.* **1** a person who makes boilers. **2** a welder or plater, working in heavy industry. **boiler room** *n.* the room in a building that contains the boiler and other heating equipment. **boiler suit** *n.* a combined overall garment, esp. for dirty work. **boiling** *a.* **1** in a state of ebullition by heat. **2** inflamed, greatly agitated. **3** (*coll.*) (*also* **boiling hot**) very hot. ~*n.* the action of boiling. **boiling point** *n.* **1** the temperature at which a fluid is converted into the gaseous state, esp. the boiling point of water at sea level (100°C). **2** a peak of excitement.

boil[2] (boil) *n.* a hard, inflamed, suppurating tumour.

boisterous (boi´stərəs) *a.* **1** wild, unruly, intractable. **2** stormy, roaring, noisy. **boisterously** *adv.* **boisterousness** *n.*

bold (bōld) *a.* **1** courageous, daring, confident, fearless. **2** planned or executed with courage. **3** vigorous, striking. **4** audacious, forward, presumptuous. **5** steep, prominent, projecting (of a cliff or headland). **6** BOLDFACE (under BOLD). **to make/be so bold** to venture, to presume. **boldface** *a.* (of type) heavy, conspicuous. **boldfaced** *a.* **1** impudent, shameless. **2** boldface. **boldly** *adv.* **boldness** *n.*

bole[1] (bōl) *n.* the stem or trunk of a tree.

bole[2] (bōl) *n.* a brownish, yellowish or reddish, soft unctuous clay, containing more or less iron oxide.

bolero (bəleə´rō, bol´ərō) *n.* (*pl.* **boleros**) **1** a lively Spanish dance. **2** (*Mus.*) music for or in the time of this dance. **3** a short jacket worn over a bodice.

Usage note The pronunciation (bol´ərō) is used only of the jacket.

boletus (bəlē´təs) *n.* a mushroom or toadstool of the genus *Boletus*, having the undersurface of the pileus full of pores instead of gills.

bolivar (bol´ivah) *n.* (*pl.* **bolivars, bolivares** (-ah´res)) the standard unit of currency in Venezuela.

boliviano (bəliviah´nō) *n.* (*pl.* **bolivianos**) the standard unit of currency in Bolivia, equal to 100 centavos.

boll (bōl) *n.* a rounded seed vessel or pod. **bollweevil** *n.* a weevil, *Anthonomus grandis*, that infests the flowers and bolls of the cotton plant.

bollard (bol´əd, -ahd) *n.* **1** (*Naut.*) a large post or bitt on a wharf, dock or on shipboard for securing ropes or cables. **2** a short post preventing motor vehicle access.

bollocks (bol´əks), **ballocks** *n.pl.* **1** (*taboo sl.*) testicles. **2** rubbish, nonsense, a mess. **bollocking** *n.* (*sl.*) a strong rebuke.

bologna (bəlō´nyə, bəlon´yə), **Bologna sausage** *n.* a large smoked sausage of mixed meats, also called a *polony*.

Bolognese (bolənyāz´, -nāz´) *a.* of or relating to Bologna. ~*n.* a native or inhabitant of Bologna.

boloney BALONEY.

Bolshevik (bol´shəvik), **Bolshevist** (bol´shəvist) *n.* **1** (*Hist.*) a member of the Russian majority Socialist party which came to power under Lenin in 1917. **2** a political revolutionary. **3** (*often derog.*) a political agitator. ~*a.* that is a Bolshevik; of or relating to Bolsheviks. **Bolshevism** *n.* **bolshie** (-shi), **bolshy** *n.* (*pl.* **bolshies**) **1** (*coll.*) (*also* **Bolshie, Bolshy**) a Russian Bolshevik. **2** (*often derog.*) a political agitator. ~*a.* (*sl.*) stubborn and argumentative. **bolshiness** *n.*

bolster (bōl´stə) *n.* **1** a long underpillow, used to support the pillows in a bed. **2** a pad, cushion or anything resembling a pad or cushion, in an instrument, machine, ship, architecture or engineering. **3** a short timber cap on a post to increase the bearing area. ~*v.t.* **1** to support with or as with a bolster. **2** to pad, stuff. **to bolster up 1** to support, to prevent from falling. **2** to aid, abet, countenance. **bolsterer** *n.*

bolt¹ (bōlt) *n.* **1** a short thick arrow with a blunt or thick head. **2** a discharge of lightning. **3** a measured roll of woven fabric, esp. canvas. **4** a sliding piece of iron for fastening a door, window etc. **5** a metal pin for holding objects together, frequently screw-headed at one end to receive a nut. **6** that portion of a lock which engages with the keeper to form a fastening. **7** a sudden start, a sudden flight. **8** the act of suddenly breaking away. ~*v.t.* **1** to shut or fasten by means of a bolt or iron. **2** to fasten together with a bolt or bolts. **3** to gulp, to swallow hastily and without chewing. ~*v.i.* **1** to start suddenly forward or aside. **2** to run away (as a horse). **3** (of a plant) to run to seed. **bolt from the blue 1** lightning from a cloudless sky. **2** an unexpected sudden event. **to bolt on 1** to fasten by bolts. **2** to add on. **bolter**¹ *n.* **bolt-hole** *n.* **1** a hole by which or into which one escapes. **2** an escape. **3** a means of escape. **bolt-on** *a.* **1** able to be attached with bolts. **2** able to be added. ~*n.* a thing that can be added or bolted on. **bolt upright** *a., adv.* straight upright.

bolt² (bōlt), **boult** *n.* a sieve for separating bran from flour. ~*v.t.* to pass through a bolt or bolting cloth. **bolter**² *n.* **1** a sieve. **2** a bolting cloth. **3** a sifting machine. **bolting cloth** *n.* a fine cloth used in sifting meal.

bolter¹ BOLT¹.

bolter² BOLT².

bolus (bō´ləs) *n.* (*pl.* **boluses**) **1** medicine in a round mass larger than a pill. **2** a round lump of anything.

bomb (bom) *n.* **1** an explosive device triggered by impact or a timer usu. dropped from the air, thrown or placed by hand. **2** (*coll., often iron.*) a great success. **3** (*coll.*) a large amount of money. **4** (*coll.*) (of a play etc.) an utter failure, a flop. **5** (*sl.*) a drugged cigarette. ~*v.t.* to attack, destroy or harm with bombs. ~*v.i.* **1** to throw, drop or detonate bombs. **2** (*coll.*) to fail utterly, to flop. **the bomb 1** the atom or hydrogen bomb. **2** nuclear arms. **bomb bay** *n.* a compartment in an aircraft for bombs. **bomb disposal** *n.* the detonation or diffusing of an unexploded bomb rendering it harmless. **bombed** *a.* **1** subject to bombing. **2** (*sl.*) drunk, or under the influence of drugs. **bombed-out** *a.* **1** (of a person) made homeless by bombing. **2** (of a building etc.) destroyed by bombing. **3** (*sl.*) drunk, or under the influence of drugs. **bomber** *n.* **1** a person who throws, drops, places or triggers bombs. **2** an aircraft used for bombing. **bomber jacket** *n.* a waist-length jacket elasticated at the wrists and waist. **bombproof** *a.* (of a shelter etc.) affording safety from the explosion of a bomb. **bombshell** *n.* **1** a bomb thrown by artillery. **2** a total (often unpleasant) surprise. **3** (*sl.*) a very attractive woman. **bombsight** *n.* a device for aiming a bomb from an aircraft. **bomb-site** *n.* an area where buildings have been destroyed by bombing. **bomb squad** *n.* a division of a police force dealing with crimes involving bombs.

bombard (bəmbahd´, bom-) *v.t.* **1** to attack with shot and shell. **2** to assail with arguments or invective. **3** (*Physics*) to subject (atoms) to a stream of high-speed particles. **bombardier** (bombədiə´) *n.* **1** a non-commissioned artillery officer ranking as corporal. **2** (*N Am.*) a member of a bomber crew responsible for releasing bombs. **bombardment** *n.*

bombasine (bom´bəzēn, -zēn´), **bombazine** *n.* a twilled dress fabric of silk and worsted, cotton and worsted, or of worsted alone.

bombast (bom´bast) *n.* **1** high-sounding words. **2** inflated speech, fustian. **bombastic** (-bas´-) *a.* **bombastically** *adv.*

Bombay duck (bom´bā) *n.* a small S Asian fish, *Harpodon nehereus*, when salted and dried eaten as a relish; also called *bummalo*.

bombazine BOMBASINE.

bombe (bomb, bōb) *n.* an ice-cream dessert moulded into a rounded, bomb shape.

bombora (bombaw´rə) *n.* (*Austral.*) dangerous broken water, usu. at the base of a cliff.

bona fide (bōnə fī´di) *adv.* in good faith. ~*a.* genuine. **bona fides** (-dēz) *n.* **1** (*Law*) good faith, sincerity. **2** (*treated as pl., coll.*) documentary evidence of acceptability.

bonanza (bənan´zə) *n.* **1** a rich mine. **2** a successful enterprise. **3** a run of luck. ~*a.* **1** very successful. **2** highly profitable.

bon-bon (bon´bon, bŏ´bŏ) *n.* a sweet, esp. of fondant.

bonce (bons) *n.* **1** (*sl.*) the head. **2** a large marble.

bond[1] (bond) *n.* **1** a thing which binds or confines, as a cord or band. **2** (*pl.*) chains, imprisonment, captivity. **3** that which restrains or cements. **4** a binding agreement or engagement. **5** that which impedes or enslaves. **6** a document by which a government or a public company undertakes to repay borrowed money, a debenture. **7** adhesiveness. **8** (*Law*) a deed by which one person (the obligor) binds themselves, their heirs, executors and assigns, to pay a certain sum to another person (the obligee), their heirs etc. **9** (*Chem.*) a linkage between atoms in a chemical compound. **10** a mode of overlapping bricks in a wall so as to tie the courses together (as with English bond and Flemish bond). ~*v.t.* **1** to put into a bonded warehouse. **2** to mortgage. **3** to bind or connect (as bricks or stones) by overlapping or by clamps. ~*v.i.* to become emotionally attached. **in bond** in a bonded warehouse and liable to customs duty. **bonded** *a.* **1** bound by a bond. **2** put in bond. **bonded warehouse** *n.* a warehouse in which imported goods are stored until the duty is paid. **bonder** *n.* **bondholder** *n.* a person holding a bond or bonds granted by a private person or by a government. **bond paper** *n.* a good-quality paper. **bond-washing** *n.* dividend stripping.

bond[2] (bond) *a.* in serfdom or slavery. **bondsman, bondman** *n.* (*pl.* **bondsmen**) **1** a slave. **2** a surety. **bondswoman, bondwoman** *n.* (*pl.* **bondswomen, bondwomen**) a female slave.

bondage (bon´dij) *n.* **1** slavery, captivity, imprisonment. **2** subjection, restraint, obligation. **3** sadomasochistic practices involving restraints.

bone (bōn) *n.* **1** the hard material of the skeleton of mammals, birds, reptiles and some fishes. **2** any separate and distinct part of such a skeleton. **3** the substance of which the skeleton consists. **4** an article made (or formerly made) of bone or ivory, whalebone etc. **5** a stiffening material for garments. **6** a small joint of meat. **7** (*pl.*) dice. **8** a domino. **9** (*pl.*) castanets made of bone. **10** (*pl.*) the body. **11** (*pl.*) mortal remains. **12** (*pl.*) the essential part of a thing. ~*a.* **1** of or relating to bone. **2** made of bone. ~*v.t.* **1** to take out the bones of (for cooking). **2** (*sl.*) to steal. **3** to stiffen (a garment). **a bone to pick with someone** a cause of quarrel with or complaint against someone. **close to/ near the bone 1** tactless. **2** indecent. **3** destitute; hard up. **to bone up (on)** (*sl.*) to study hard, to swot. **to make no bones about 1** to do or speak about without hesitation or scruple. **2** to present no difficulty or opposition to. **to point a/ the bone 1** (*Austral.*) in Aboriginal magic, to will the death of an enemy. **2** (*Austral.*) to put a jinx on someone. **to the bone 1** to the inmost part. **2** to the minimum. **bone china** *n.* porcelain made with china clay (kaolin) and bone ash (calcium phosphate). **bone**

dry *a.* quite dry. **bonefish** *n.* (*pl. in general* **bonefish**, *in particular* **bonefishes**) any of several species of large game fish, esp. *Albula vulpes.* **bonehead** *n.* (*sl.*) a dolt. **boneheaded** *a.* **bone idle, bone lazy** *a.* utterly idle; idle to the bone. **boneless** *a.* **bone marrow** *n.* a fatty substance contained in the cavities of bones. **bonemeal** *n.* bone dust used as animal feed or fertilizer. **bone of contention** *n.* a subject of dispute. **boner** *n.* (*N Am.*) a gross mistake, a howler. **bone-setter** *n.* a non-qualified practitioner who sets fractured and dislocated bones. **boneshaker** *n.* **1** an old-fashioned bicycle without india-rubber tyres. **2** any dilapidated or old-fashioned vehicle. **bony** *a.* (*comp.* **bonier**, *superl.* **boniest**) **1** of, relating to or of the nature of bone or bones. **2** big-boned. **boniness** *n.*

bonfire (bon´fīə) *n.* **1** a large fire lit in the open air on an occasion of public rejoicing. **2** a fire for burning up garden rubbish.

bong (bong) *n.* a low-pitched reverberating sound. ~*v.i.* to make such a sound.

bongo[1] (bong´gō) *n.* (*pl.* **bongos, bongoes**) a small hand drum of a type often played in pairs. **bongo drum** *n.*

bongo[2] (bong´gō) *n.* (*pl. in general* **bongo**, *in particular* **bongos**) a rare antelope, *Tragelaphus euryceros*, which has spiralled horns and a red-brown coat with narrow cream stripes.

bonhomie (bonəmē´) *n.* good nature, geniality. **bonhomous** *a.*

bonito (bonē´tō) *n.* (*pl. in general* **bonito**, *in particular* **bonitos**) **1** any of various striped tuna. **2** any of various other fish of the mackerel family.

bonk (bongk) *v.t.* **1** (*coll.*) to hit. **2** (*taboo sl.*) to have sexual intercourse with. ~*v.i.* **1** to bang or bump. **2** (*taboo sl.*) to have sexual intercourse. ~*n.* an act of bonking.

bonkers (bong´kəz) *a.* (*sl.*) crazy, mad.

bon mot (bŏ mō´) *n.* (*pl.* **bons mots** (bŏ mō´, bŏ mōz´)) a witticism.

bonne bouche (bon boosh´) *n.* (*pl.* **bonne bouches** (bon boosh´), **bonnes bouches**) a tasty titbit.

bonnet (bon´it) *n.* **1** a hat tied beneath the chin, of various shapes and materials, formerly worn by women out of doors and now usu. by babies. **2** (*esp. Sc.*) a flat cap. **3** a hat without a brim for men and boys. **4** the front part of a motor vehicle covering the engine. **5** a feathered headdress worn by American Indians. **6** a chimney cowl. **7** a protective covering to a machine etc. **8** (*Naut.*) an additional piece of canvas laced to the bottom of a sail to enlarge it. **bonnethead** *n.* a hammerhead shark, *Sphyrna tiburo*, with a narrow head, also called **shovelhead**. **bonnet monkey** *n.* an Indian macaque, *Macaca radiata*, with a tuft of hair like a bonnet.

bonny (bon´i) *a.* (*comp.* **bonnier**, *superl.* **bonniest**) **1** beautiful, handsome, pretty. **2** healthy-looking. **3** good, pleasant. **bonnily** *adv.* **bonniness** *n.*

bonsai (bon´sī) n. (pl. **bonsai**) **1** (also **bonsai tree**) a potted tree or shrub cultivated into a dwarf variety by skilful pruning of its roots. **2** the art or practice of cultivating trees or shrubs in this manner.

bontebok (bon´təbok), **bontbok** n. (pl. in general **bontebok, bontbok,** in particular **bonteboks, bontboks**) a large antelope, Damaliscus dorcas, which has a deep reddish-brown coat, a white tail and white patches on its head and rump.

bonus (bō´nəs) n. (pl. **bonuses**) **1** something over and above what is due. **2** a premium given for a privilege or in addition to interest for a loan. **3** an extra dividend. **4** a distribution of profits to policyholders in an insurance company. **5** a gratuity over and above a fixed salary or wages.

Usage note The phrase added bonus is best avoided: bonus already implies addition.

bon vivant (bō vēvã´) n. (pl. **bon vivants** (bō vēvã´), **bons vivants**) a person fond of good living, a gourmand.

bon viveur (bō vēvœ´) n. (pl. **bon viveurs** (bō vēvœ´), **bons viveurs**) BON VIVANT.

bon voyage (bon voiahzh´, bō vwayahzh´) n., int. a pleasant journey, farewell.

bony BONE.

bonza (bon´zə), **bonzer** a. (Austral., sl.) excellent.

bonze (bonz) n. a Buddhist religious teacher in Japan, China and adjacent regions.

boo (boo) int., n. (pl. **boos**) **1** a sound used to express contempt, displeasure, aversion etc. (imitating the lowing of oxen). **2** a sound intended to surprise, esp. a child. ~v.i. (3rd pers. sing. pres. **boos,** pres.p. **booing,** past, p.p. **booed**) **1** to say or call 'boo', to jeer. **2** (of an ox) to low. ~v.t. to say or call 'boo' to, to jeer at. **would not say boo to a goose** would never venture to say anything, is very timid. **boohoo** (-hoo´) int., n. **1** the sound of noisy weeping. **2** a sound used to express contempt. ~v.i. (3rd pers. sing. pres. **boohoos,** pres.p. **boohooing,** past, p.p. **boohooed**) **1** to weep noisily. **2** to bellow, to roar.

boob[1] (boob) n. (coll.) **1** an error, a blunder. **2** a simpleton. ~v.i. to err, commit a blunder.

boob[2] (boob) n. (usu. in pl., sl.) a woman's breast. **boob tube** n. **1** (sl.) a woman's elasticated, strapless top. **2** (N Am.) television.

booboo (boo´boo) n. (pl. **booboos**) (sl.) a mistake.

booby (boo´bi) n. (pl. **boobies**) **1** a dull, stupid person; a dunce. **2** a gannet, esp. Sula fusca. **booby-hatch** n. (N Am., sl., offensive) a psychiatric hospital. **booby prize** n. the prize, usu. a worthless one, given in ridicule to the player who makes the lowest score, esp. in whist drives, or the competitor who comes last. **booby trap** n. **1** a trap placed as a practical joke, consisting of e.g. books etc. placed on the top of a door left ajar, so that the whole tumbles on the head of the first person entering. **2** (Mil.) a bomb so disposed that it will explode when some object is touched. ~v.t. (pres.p. **booby-trapping,**

past, p.p. **booby-trapped**) to set a booby trap in or on.

boodle (boo´dəl) n. (sl.) money, capital, stock in trade.

boogie (boo´gi) v.i. (pres.p. **boogieing,** past, p.p. **boogied**) (sl.) to dance to pop music. ~n. **1** BOOGIE-WOOGIE (under BOOGIE). **2** a dance to pop music. **boogie-woogie** (boogiwoo´gi) n. a jazz piano style of a rhythmic and percussive nature based on 12-bar blues.

boohoo BOO.

book (buk) n. **1** a collection of sheets printed, written on or blank, bound in a volume. **2** a literary composition of considerable extent. **3** a set of tickets, cheques, forms of receipt, stamps or the like, fastened together. **4** (pl.) a set of accounts. **5** a main division of a literary work. **6** a libretto, a script. **7** (fig.) anything that can be read or that conveys instruction. **8** a telephone directory. **9** bets on a race or at a meeting taken collectively. **10** an imaginary record or list. ~v.t. **1** to enter or register in a book. **2** to reserve by payment in advance (as a seat in a conveyance, theatre or the like). **3** to hand in or to receive for transmission (as a parcel, goods etc.). **4** to take the name and details of (an offender or rule-breaker), prior to making a charge. **5** to engage the services of (a performer etc.) in advance. ~v.i. to make a reservation. **in my book** according to my view of things. **in someone's bad/ black books** regarded with disfavour by someone. **in someone's good books** regarded with favour by someone. **like a book** formally, pedantically, as if one were reciting from a book. **not in the book** not allowed. **on the books** on the official list of names. **to book in** to register one's arrival. **to book up** to buy tickets in advance. **to bring to book** to convict, call to account. **to go by the book** to proceed according to the rules. **to make a book** in racing, to pay out and take winnings. **to make book** (N Am.) in racing, to take bets and pay out winnings. **to suit one's book** to be agreeable or favourable to one. **to throw the book at** **1** (coll.) to charge with every offence possible. **2** (coll.) to punish severely. **without book** **1** from memory. **2** without authority. **bookable** a. **1** that may be reserved in advance. **2** in football, (of an offence) serious enough to be entered in the referee's notebook. **bookbinder** n. a person who binds books. **bookbinding** n. **bookcase** n. **1** a case with shelves for books. **2** a bookcover. **book club** n. **1** an association of persons who buy and lend each other books. **2** a business which sells to its members a choice of books at below publishers' prices. **booked up** a. with all the places reserved; full up. **bookend** n. a prop placed at the end of a row of books to keep them upright. **booker** n. **bookie** n. (coll.) a bookmaker who takes bets. **booking** n. a reservation. **booking clerk** n. a person who issues tickets or takes bookings. **booking hall** n. a room at a station where tickets are issued. **booking office** n. an office where tickets are issued or bookings are made. **bookish** *a.* **1** learned, studious. **2** acquainted with books only. **3** (of a word, language etc.) literary. **bookishly** *adv.* **bookishness** *n.* **bookkeeper** *n.* a person who keeps the accounts in an office etc. **bookkeeping** *n.* **book learning** *n.* **1** learning derived from books. **2** theory, not practical knowledge or experience. **booklet** *n.* a little book, a pamphlet. **booklouse** *n.* (*pl.* **book-lice**) an insect, belonging to the Psocoptera, found amongst books, papers etc. **bookmaker** *n.* **1** a person who takes bets, principally in relation to horse races, and pays out to winners as a profession. **2** a person who makes or compiles books. **bookmaking** *n.* **bookman** *n.* (*pl.* **bookmen**) **1** a literary man. **2** a bookseller. **bookmark, bookmarker** *n.* a piece of ribbon, paper, leather etc. put in a book to mark a place. **bookmobile** *n.* (*N Am.*) a mobile library. **book of words** *n.* a libretto, script etc. **bookplate** *n.* a label with a name or device, pasted in a book to show the ownership. **bookrest, bookstand** *n.* a support for a book. **bookseller** *n.* a person whose trade it is to sell books. **bookshelf** *n.* (*pl.* **bookshelves**) a shelf for books. **bookshop** *n.* a shop where books are sold. **booksie** (-si), **booksy** *a.* (*coll.*) would-be literary. **bookstall, bookstand** *n.* a stall or stand at which books and periodicals are sold. **bookstore** *n.* (*N Am.*) a bookshop. **book token** *n.* a gift token exchangeable for books. **book value** *n.* the value of an asset, commodity or enterprise as it is recorded on paper (not always the same as its market value). **bookwork** *n.* study of textbooks, as opposed to practice and experiment. **bookworm** *n.* **1** any worm or insect which eats holes in books. **2** (*coll.*) an avid reader.

Boolean (boo'liən) *a.* being or relating to a logical system using symbols to represent relationships between entities. **Boolean logic** *n.* (*Comput.*) the use of the logical operators 'and', 'or' and 'not' in retrieving information.

boom[1] (boom) *n.* **1** a loud, deep, resonant sound. **2** a sudden demand for a thing. **3** a burst of commercial activity and prosperity. ~*v.i.* **1** to make a loud, deep, resonant sound. **2** to go off with a boom. **3** to become very important, prosperous or active. ~*v.t.* to utter with a booming sound. **boom box** *n.* (*sl.*) a ghetto blaster. **boom town** *n.* a town undergoing rapid expansion or enjoying sudden commercial prosperity.

boom[2] (boom) *n.* **1** (*Naut.*) a long spar to extend the foot of a particular sail. **2** a bar, chain or line of connected spars forming an obstruction to the mouth of a harbour. **3** a movable overhead pole carrying a microphone used in television, film and videotape recordings.

boomer (boo'mə) *n.* **1** (*Austral.*) a large kangaroo. **2** a large wave.

boomerang (boo'mərang) *n.* **1** an Aboriginal Australian missile weapon, consisting of a curved flat stick so constructed that it returns to the thrower. **2** an action, speech or argument that recoils on the person who makes it. ~*v.i.* **1** to

return to the thrower. **2** (of a plan etc.) to rebound on the originator, to have the opposite of the desired effect.

boon[1] (boon) *n.* **1** a benefit, a blessing. **2** †a prayer, a petition, an entreaty. **3** †a favour, a gift.

boon[2] (boon) *a.* close, intimate. **boon companion** *n.* **1** a person who is convivial or congenial. **2** a close or special friend.

boondock (boon'dok) *n.* **1** (*usu. in pl., N Am., sl.*) remote or uncultivated country. **2** (*sl.*) a provincial area.

boondoggle (boon'dogəl) *n.* **1** work of little practical value. **2** a dishonest undertaking; a fraud. ~*v.i.* to do work of little practical value.

boonies (boo'niz) *n.pl.* (*N Am., sl.*) the boondocks.

boor (booə) *n.* a rude, awkward or insensitive person. **boorish** *a.* **boorishly** *adv.* **boorishness** *n.*

boost (boost) *v.t.* **1** to push or shove upwards. **2** to advertise on a big scale. **3** to promote or encourage. **4** to enlarge or increase (e.g. the voltage in an electric circuit). **5** to elevate or raise (e.g. the pressure of an internal-combustion engine). **booster** *n.* **1** a contrivance for intensifying the strength of an alternating current. **2** an auxiliary motor in a rocket that usu. breaks away when exhausted. **3** any thing or person that boosts. **4** (*Med.*) a supplementary vaccination.

boot[1] (boot) *n.* **1** a covering (usu. of leather) for the foot and part of the leg. **2** a luggage compartment in a car. **3** (*sl.*) a kick. **4** (*preceded by the, sl.*) summary dismissal, e.g. from employment. **5** a covering to protect the lower part of a horse's leg. **6** (*derog.*) a person. **7** a heavy sports shoe, e.g. football boot. **8** (*pl.*) a hotel servant who cleans boots, runs errands etc. ~*v.t.* **1** to kick. **2** to start (a computer program) running. **3** to equip with boots. **to bet one's boots** to be absolutely certain. **to boot out** (*sl.*) to eject, dismiss, sack. **to put/ stick the boot in 1** to kick brutally. **2** (*sl.*) to cause further upset or harm to one already in distress. **bootblack** *n.* a person who cleans and polishes shoes. **bootboy** *n.* **1** a hooligan, a bovver boy. **2** a boy employed to clean shoes. **bootee** (-tē') *n.* **1** a knitted boot for infants. **2** a short boot. **bootjack** *n.* a device for removing boots. **bootlace** *n.* a string for fastening boots. **bootleg** *a.* **1** illicit, smuggled (e.g. of alcohol). **2** (of a recording) pirated. ~*n.* **1** an illicit or smuggled commodity. **2** a pirated musical recording. ~*v.i.* (*pres.p.* **bootlegging**, *past, p.p.* **bootlegged**) to act as a bootlegger. **bootlegger** *n.* a person who makes, deals in or transports an illicit commodity esp. liquor. **bootlegging** *n.* **bootlicker** *n.* a sycophant. **bootmaker** *n.* a person who makes boots. **bootstrap** *n.* **1** a looped strap on a boot-top enabling it to be pulled up. **2** (*Comput.*) a technique for loading the first few program instructions so that the rest of the program can be introduced from an input device. **to pull oneself up by the bootstraps** to achieve or improve one's situation by one's own efforts.

boot² (boot) *n.* advantage, profit (used only as below). **to boot** into the bargain, besides, in addition. **bootless** *a.* profitless, unavailing. **bootlessly** *adv.* **bootlessness** *n.*

booth (boodh, booth) *n.* **1** a stall, tent or other temporary erection at a fair, in a market, polling station etc. **2** a compartment or structure containing a telephone, a table in a restaurant etc.

booty (boo´ti) *n.* **1** spoil taken in war. **2** property carried off by thieves. **3** (*coll.*) a gain, a prize.

booze (booz), **boose, bouse** *n.* (*coll.*) **1** an alcoholic drink. **2** a drinking bout. ~*v.i.* to drink to excess, to tipple. **boozer** *n.* (*coll.*) **1** a heavy drinker. **2** a public house. **booze-up** *n.* (*sl.*) a drinking session. **boozy** *a.* (*comp.* **boozier**, *superl.* **booziest**) drunk, tipsy. **boozily** *adv.* **booziness** *n.*

bop¹ (bop) *n.* **1** an innovative style of jazz music dating from the 1940s. **2** a spell of dancing, esp. to pop music. **3** a dance. ~*v.i.* (*pres.p.* **bopping**, *past, p.p.* **bopped**) to dance to bop or pop music. **bopper** *n.*

bop² (bop) *v.t.* (*pres.p.* **bopping**, *past, p.p.* **bopped**) to hit, to strike. ~*n.* a hit, a blow.

☒ **boquet** common misspelling of BOUQUET.

boracic BORAX.

borage (bŭr´ij, bor´-) *n.* a hairy, blue-flowered plant of the genus *Borago*, esp. *B. officinalis*, formerly esteemed as a cordial, and used to flavour claret cup etc.

borak (baw´rak) *n.* (*Austral., New Zeal., sl.*) chaff, banter.

borax (baw´raks) *n.* **1** the mineral salt sodium borate. **2** the purified form of this, used as an antiseptic, and in the manufacture of glass and china. **boracic** (-ras´ik), **boric** *a.* of, relating to or derived from borax or boron. **boracic acid, boric acid** *n.* an acid obtained from borax. **borate** (-rāt) *n.* a salt of boracic acid.

borborygmus (bawbərig´məs) *n.* (*pl.* **borborygmi** (-mī)) rumbling of the stomach. **borborygmic** *a.*

Bordeaux (bawdō´) *n.* (*pl.* **Bordeaux** (-dōz)) a red, white or rosé wine from Bordeaux. **Bordeaux mixture** *n.* a preparation of sulphate of copper and lime for destroying fungi and other garden pests.

bordello (bawdel´ō) *n.* (*pl.* **bordellos**) a brothel.

border (baw´də) *n.* **1** a brim, edge, margin. **2** a boundary line or region. **3** a frontier or frontier region. **4** an edging designed as an ornament. **5** an edging to a plot or flower bed. ~*v.t.* **1** to put a border or edging to. **2** to form a boundary to. ~*v.i.* **1** to lie on the border. **2** to be contiguous. **3** to approximate, resemble. **Border collie** *n.* a breed of collie commonly used as a sheepdog. **bordered** *a.* **borderer** *n.* a person who dwells on a border or frontier, esp. on that between England and Scotland. **borderland** *n.* **1** land near the border between two countries or districts. **2** an indeterminate region. **3** an area for debate. **borderless** *a.* **borderline** *n.* a line of demarcation.

~*a.* on the borderline (*a borderline case*). **Border terrier** *n.* a type of small rough-haired terrier.

bore¹ (baw) *v.t.* **1** to perforate or make a hole through. **2** to hollow out. ~*v.i.* **1** to make a hole. **2** to drill a well. **3** to push forward persistently. **4** (of a horse) to thrust the head straight forward. **5** to push a horse, boat or other competitor out of the course. **6** to drive a boxing adversary on to the ropes by sheer weight. ~*n.* **1** a hole made by boring. **2** the diameter of a tube. **3** the cavity of a gun barrel. **bore hole** *n.* a shaft or pit cut by means of a special tool, esp. one made to find water, oil etc. **borer** *n.* **1** a person, tool or machine that bores or pierces. **2** a horse that bores. **3** any of various insects, insect larvae, molluscs or crustaceans that bore into rock, wood etc.

bore² (baw) *n.* a tidal wave of great height and velocity, caused by the meeting of two tides or the rush of the tide up a narrowing estuary.

bore³ (baw) *n.* a tiresome person, a wearisome twaddler. ~*v.t.* to weary with twaddle or dullness. **to bore to tears** to weary greatly. **boredom** *n.* the condition of being bored. **boring** *a.* **boringly** *adv.* **boringness** *n.*

bore⁴ BEAR².

boreal (baw´riəl) *a.* **1** of or relating to the north or the north wind. **2** northern.

boric BORAX.

born (bawn) *a.* **1** brought into the world. **2** brought forth, produced. **3** having certain characteristics from birth. **born again** regenerate. **born and bred** by birth and upbringing. **born to** destined to. **born with a silver spoon in one's mouth** born in luxury. **in all one's born days** (*coll.*) in all one's life so far. **not born yesterday** (*coll.*) not inexperienced, not gullible. **born-again** *a.*

borne (bawn) *a.* carried by (*waterborne*). **borne in upon one 1** having become one's firm conviction. **2** realized by one.

borné (baw´nā) *a.* narrow-minded, limited.

boron (baw´ron) *n.* (*Chem.*) the element, at. no. 5, chem. symbol B, present in borax and boracic acid. **borosilicate** *n.* any of several substances containing boron, silicon and oxygen.

boronia (bərō´niə) *n.* (*Austral.*) any shrub of the genus *Boronia*.

borough (bŭr´ə) *n.* **1** a town possessing a municipal corporation. **2** (*Hist.*) a town which sends a representative to Parliament. **3** an administrative division of London or New York. **4** a municipal corporation of a US state. **5** a county in Alaska.

borrow (bor´ō) *v.t.* **1** to obtain and make temporary use of. **2** to obtain under a promise or understanding to return. **3** to adopt, to assume, to derive from other people. **4** to copy, imitate, feign. ~*v.i.* **1** to obtain money temporarily. **2** in golf, to play a ball uphill in order that it may roll back. **borrowed time** *n.* time that one did not expect to have, esp. additional days to live.

borrower *n.* **borrow-pit** *n.* an excavation dug to provide material elsewhere.

borsch (bawsh), **borscht, bortsch** (bawch) *n.* Russian beetroot soup.

Borstal (baw´stəl) *n.* (*Hist.*) a place of detention and corrective training for juvenile offenders, now called *youth custody centre.*

bortsch BORSCH.

borzoi (baw´zoi) *n.* (*pl.* **borzois**) **1** a Russian wolfhound of a breed with a long silky coat. **2** this breed.

boscage (bos´kij), **boskage** *n.* **1** wood, woodland. **2** underwood or ground covered with it. **3** thick foliage. **4** wooded landscape.

bosh (bosh) *n.* (*sl.*) empty talk, nonsense, folly. ~*int.* stuff! rubbish! humbug!

bosk (bosk) *n.* a bush, a thicket, a small forest. **bosky** *a.* (*comp.* **boskier**, *superl.* **boskiest**) **1** bushy, woody. **2** covered with boscage.

bo's'n BOATSWAIN.

Bosnian (boz´niən) *a.* of or relating to Bosnia in SE Europe. ~*n.* **1** a native or inhabitant of Bosnia. **2** a person of Bosnian descent.

bosom (buz´m) *n.* **1** the breast of a human being, esp. of a woman. **2** that part of the dress which covers this. **3** the breast as the seat of emotions or the repository of secrets. **4** embrace. **the bosom of one's family** the midst of one's family. **bosom friend** *n.* a dearest and most intimate friend. **bosomy** *a.* (of a woman) having large breasts.

boson (bō´son, -zon) *n.* (*Physics*) a particle, or ·member of a class of particles, with an integral or zero spin, which behaves in accordance with the statistical relations laid down by Bose and Einstein.

boss[1] (bos) *n.* **1** a protuberant part. **2** an ornamental stud. **3** the knob in the centre of a shield. **4** (*Archit.*) an ornamental projection at the intersection of the ribs in vaulting. **5** (*Geol.*) a large mass of igneous rock.

boss[2] (bos) *n.* **1** a foreman, manager. **2** a chief, leader or master. **3** the manager or dictator of a party machine. ~*a.* **1** chief, best, most highly esteemed. **2** first-rate, excellent. ~*v.t.* to manage, to direct, to control. **bossy** *a.* (*comp.* **bossier**, *superl.* **bossiest**) **1** managing. **2** domineering. **bossily** *adv.* **bossiness** *n.* **bossy-boots** *n.* (*coll.*) a domineering person.

boss[3] (bos) *n.* **1** a miss, a bad shot, a bungle. **2** a short-sighted person. **3** a person who squints. **boss-eyed** *a.* (*coll.*) **1** having only one eye. **2** having one eye injured. **3** squinting. **boss-shot** *n.* (*sl., dial.*) **1** a miss. **2** an unsuccessful attempt.

bossa nova (bosə nō´və) *n.* **1** a Brazilian dance resembling the samba. **2** the music for such a dance.

bossy BOSS[2].

bosun, bo'sun BOATSWAIN.

bot (bot), **bott** *n.* a parasitic worm, the larva of the genus *Oestrus.* **botfly** *n.* (*pl.* **botflies**) **1** a fly of the genus *Oestrus.* **2** a gadfly.

botany (bot´əni) *n.* the science which treats of plants and plant life. **botanic** (bətan´-), **botanical** *a.* **botanically** *adv.* **botanic garden** *n.* (*often in pl.*) a garden laid out for the scientific culture and study of plants. **botanist** *n.* **botanize, botanise** *v.i.* **1** to collect plants for scientific study. **2** to study plants. ~*v.t.* to explore botanically. **Botany wool** *n.* merino wool from Botany Bay.

botch (boch) *n.* **1** a clumsy patch. **2** a bungled piece of work. ~*v.t.* **1** to mend or patch clumsily. **2** to put together in an unsuitable or unskilful manner. **3** to ruin. **botcher** *n.*

botel BOATEL.

both (bōth) *a., pron.* the one and also the other, the two. ~*adv.* **1** as well the one thing as the other. **2** equally in the two cases.

bother (bodh´ə) *v.t.* **1** to tease, to vex. **2** to annoy, to pester. ~*v.i.* **1** to make a fuss, to be troublesome. **2** to worry oneself. **3** to take trouble. ~*int.* used to express annoyance, fuss. **cannot be bothered** will not make an effort. **botheration** (-ā´shən) *n.* **1** the act of bothering. **2** bother. ~*int.* bother. **bothersome** (-səm) *a.* troublesome, annoying.

bothy (both´i), **bothie** *n.* (*pl.* **bothies**) (*esp. Sc.*) **1** a rough kind of cottage. **2** a hut, a hovel, esp. a lodging place for unmarried labourers on a Scottish farm.

bo tree (bō), **bodhi tree** (bō´di) *n.* the peepul or pipla tree, a fig tree, *Ficus religiosa*, held sacred by the Buddhists and planted beside their temples.

botryoid (bot´rioid), **botryoidal** (-oi´-) *a.* resembling a bunch of grapes in form.

bott BOT.

bottle (bot´əl) *n.* **1** a vessel with a narrow neck for holding liquids (usu. of glass). **2** the quantity in a bottle. **3** a baby's feeding bottle. **4** a hot-water bottle. **5** a metal cylinder for liquefied gas. **6** (*sl.*) temerity, courage, strength of will. ~*v.t.* **1** to put into bottles. **2** to preserve (fruit etc.) in jars or bottles. **on the bottle** drinking (alcohol) heavily. **to bottle out** (*sl.*) to fail to do something because of fear. **to bottle up 1** to conceal. **2** to restrain, repress (one's emotions). **to hit the bottle** (*sl.*) to drink a great deal of alcoholic drink. **bottle bank** *n.* a public repository for empty glass jars and bottles which are to be recycled. **bottle-brush** *n.* **1** a brush for cleaning bottles. **2** any of various plants with a flower shaped like this, such as the genus *Equisetum* or *Hipparis vulgaris.* **3** (*Austral.*) a genus of trees bearing brushlike flowers. **bottled** *a.* **1** stored in jars or bottles. **2** bottle-shaped. **3** (*sl.*) drunk. **bottle-feed** *v.t., v.i.* to feed (a baby) from a bottle instead of the breast. **bottle-glass** *n.* coarse green glass for making bottles. **bottle green** *n.* dark green, like bottle-glass. **bottle-green** *a.* of this colour. **bottleneck** *n.* **1** a constricted outlet. **2** an obstruction; something that holds up progress. **3** in guitar playing, a device that produces sliding effects on the strings. **4** the style of playing that uses this. **5** (*in* *full* **bottleneck guitar**) a guitar played like this. **bottlenose** *n.* **1** a large thick or swollen nose. **2** a whale of the genus *Hyperodon.* **bottlenose dolphin, bottlenosed dolphin** *n.* a dolphin, *Tursiops truncatus*, which has a bottle-shaped snout. **bottle party** *n.* a drinking party to which each person brings their own alcoholic drink. **bottler** *n.* **1** a person who or machine which bottles. **2** (*Austral., New Zeal., sl.*) an excellent person or thing. **bottle tree** *n.* any of various Australian trees of the genus *Brachychiton* with a bulbous trunk resembling the shape of a bottle. **bottle-washer** *n.* **1** a person or machine that washes bottles. **2** a general factotum, an understrapper.

bottom (bot´əm) *n.* **1** the lowest part of anything, the part on which anything rests. **2** the buttocks, the posterior. **3** the seat of a chair. **4** the bed or channel of any body of water. **5** an alluvial hollow. **6** low-lying land. **7** the lowest point. **8** the inmost part, the furthest point of a recess, gulf or inland sea. **9** the end of a table remote from a host, chairperson etc. **10** the lowest rank. **11** (*Naut.*) **a** the keel of a ship, the part near and including the keel, the hull. **b** a ship as receptacle for cargo. **12** (*pl.*) dregs of liquor, sediment. **13** foundation, base. **14** source, basis. ~*v.t.* **1** to put a bottom to. **2** to examine exhaustively, to sound, to fathom. **3** to base or ground. **4** to touch the bottom or the lowest point of. ~*v.i.* **1** (of a ship) to touch the bottom. **2** to be based or founded (on). ~*a.* **1** of or relating to the bottom. **2** lowest. **3** fundamental. **at bottom 1** in reality. **2** at heart. **to be at the bottom of** to be the cause of. **to bottom out** to drop to, and level out at, the lowest point (as of prices). **to get to the bottom of** to investigate and discover the real truth about. **to knock the bottom out of 1** to refute (an argument). **2** to destroy the usefulness of. **bottom dog** *n.* UNDERDOG (under UNDER- (+ A–S WORDS)). **bottom dollar** *n.* one's last coin. **to bet one's bottom dollar** to predict with the utmost confidence. **bottom drawer** *n.* a drawer in which a woman keeps her new clothes etc. before marriage. **bottom gear** *n.* FIRST GEAR (under FIRST). **bottomless** *a.* **1** without a bottom. **2** fathomless, unfathomable. **bottomless pit** *n.* **1** hell. **2** (*coll.*) a very hungry or greedy person. **bottom line** *n.* **1** the concluding line in a statement of accounts, giving net profit or loss figures. **2** the final word (on). **3** the crux of a matter. **bottommost** *a.* lowest of all. **bottomry** (-ri) *n.* (*Naut.*) borrowing money on the security of a ship. ~*v.t.* (*3rd pers. sing. pres.* **bottomries,** *pres.p.* **bottomrying,** *past, p.p.* **bottomried**) to pledge (a ship) in this manner. **bottoms up!** *int.* (*coll.*) a drinking toast. **bottom-up** *a., adv.* upside-down.

botulism (bot´ūlizm) *n.* a form of food poisoning caused by eating preserved food infected by *Clostridium botulinum.*

bouclé (boo´klā) *n.* **1** a looped yarn. **2** the thick, curly material woven from such yarn. ~*a.* woven from looped yarn.

boudoir (boo´dwah) *n.* a small, elegantly furnished room, used as a lady's private apartment.

bouffant (boo´fā) *a.* full, puffed out, as a hairstyle.

bougainvillaea (boogənvil´iə), **bougainvillea,** **bougainvillia** *n.* any tropical plant of the genus *Bougainvillaea*, the red or purple bracts of which almost conceal the flowers.

bough (bow) *n.* a large arm or branch of a tree.

bought BUY.

bougie (boo´zhi) *n.* **1** a wax candle. **2** (*Med.*) smooth, flexible, slender cylinder used for exploring or dilating passages in the human body.

bouillabaisse (booyəbes´) *n.* a rich fish stew or chowder, popular in the south of France.

bouilli (booyē´) *n.* meat gently simmered.

bouillon (booyō´) *n.* broth, soup.

boulder (bōl´də) *n.* **1** a water-worn, rounded stone, a cobble. **2** a large rounded block of stone transported to a lesser or greater distance from its parent rock. **3** a large detached piece of ore. **boulder clay, boulder drift** *n.* a clayey deposit of the glacial period. **bouldery** *a.*

boule[1] (bool), **boules** *n.pl.* a French game resembling bowls, played with metal balls.

boule[2] BUHL.

boulevard (boo´ləvahd) *n.* **1** a broad street planted with trees. **2** (*esp. N Am.*) an arterial road, trunk road.

boulle BUHL.

boult BOLT[2].

bounce (bowns) *v.i.* **1** to rebound. **2** to bound like a ball. **3** to come or go unceremoniously. **4** to exaggerate, to brag. **5** (of a cheque) to be returned to the drawer. ~*v.t.* **1** to slam, to bang. **2** to bully. **3** (*sl.*) to throw or turn out. ~*n.* **1** rebound. **2** a leap, a spring. **3** swagger, self-assertion. **4** impudence. **to bounce back** to recover quickly or easily. **bouncer** *n.* **1** anything large and bouncing. **2** a boaster, a swaggerer. **3** a big lie. **4** someone employed to eject (undesirable) people from a public place. **5** in cricket, a short, fast ball that rises sharply off the ground. **bouncing** *a.* **1** big, heavy. **2** stout, strong. **bouncy** *a.* (*comp.* **bouncier,** *superl.* **bounciest**) **1** (of a ball) that bounces well. **2** vivacious. **3** resilient, springy. **bouncily** *adv.* **bounciness** *n.* **bouncy castle** *n.* a children's play area consisting of an inflatable base (for bouncing on) and high inflatable sides decorated to look like (usu.) a castle.

bound[1] (bownd) *n.* a leap, a spring, a rebound. ~*v.i.* **1** to leap, to spring. **2** to rebound, to bounce. **by leaps and bounds** with astonishing speed. **bounder** *n.* **1** a person or something which leaps. **2** (*sl.*) an ill-bred person. **3** (*dated or facet.*) a scoundrel.

bound[2] (bownd) *n.* **1** a limit, a boundary. **2** limitation, restriction. **3** territory. ~*v.t.* **1** to set bounds to. **2** to confine. **3** to form the boundary of. **out of bounds** (of an area, topic or person) forbidden, prohibited. **boundary** *n.* (*pl.* **boundaries**) **1** a mark indicating limit. **2** the limit thus marked.

3 in cricket, a hit that crosses the limits of the field. **boundary layer** n. the layer of fluid that immediately surrounds a solid object immersed in fluid. **boundary umpire** n. in Australian Rules, an umpire who signals when the ball is out. **boundless** a. **1** without bounds. **2** limitless. **boundlessly** adv. **boundlessness** n.

bound³ (bownd) a. **1** under obligation, compelled, obliged, certain (to). **2** in a cover, esp. in a cover of leather or other permanent material as distinguished from paper covers. †**bounden** a. obliged, under obligation. **bounden duty** n. obligatory duty.

bound⁴ (bownd) a. **1** prepared, ready. **2** starting, destined. **3** directing one's course.

bounty (bown'ti) n. (pl. **bounties**) **1** goodness, gracious liberality. **2** an act of generosity, a gift. **3** a premium for joining the army or navy, or to encourage commerce or industry. **bounteous** (-tiəs) a. (poet.) **1** full of bounty. **2** liberal, beneficent. **3** generously given. **bounteously** adv. **bounteousness** n. **bountiful** a. **1** full of bounty. **2** liberal, munificent. **3** plenteous, abundant. **bountifully** adv. **bounty hunter** n. a person who does something, esp. catches a criminal, for the reward.

bouquet (bukā´, buk´ā, bō-) n. **1** a nosegay, a bunch of flowers. **2** the perfume exhaled by wine. **3** a compliment. **bouquet garni** (bukā gah´nē) n. (pl. **bouquets garnis** (bukāz gah´nē)) a bunch (traditionally five sprigs) of herbs for flavouring meat dishes and soups.

bourbon (bœ´bən, buə´bən) n. an American whisky made of wheat or Indian corn.

bourdon (buə´dən) n. (Mus.) **1** a bass stop on an organ. **2** a bass reed in a harmonium. **3** the lowest bell in a peal of bells. **4** the drone of a bagpipe.

bourgeois (buə´zhwah) n. (pl. **bourgeois**) (sometimes derog.) a person of the mercantile, shopkeeping or middle class. ~a. of or relating to the bourgeoisie, middle-class or capitalist as distinguished from working-class. **bourgeoisie** (-zē´) n. **1** (sometimes derog.) the mercantile or shopkeeping class. **2** the middle class as opposed to the proletariat.

bourn¹ (bawn) n. a small stream, esp. a stream that runs periodically from springs in chalk.

bourn² BOURNE.

†**bourne** (bawn), **bourn** n. a bound, a limit, a goal.

bourree (boo´rā), **bourrée** n. **1** a folk dance from the Auvergne and Basque provinces. **2** a musical composition in this rhythm.

bourse (buəs) n. a (French) foreign exchange for the transaction of commercial business.

boustrophedon (boostrəfē´dən, bow-) a., adv. written alternately from left to right and from right to left.

bout (bowt) n. **1** a turn, a round, a set-to. **2** trial, essay, attempt. **3** a spell of work. **4** a fit of drunkenness or of illness.

boutique (bootēk´) n. **1** a fashionable clothes shop. **2** any small specialist shop. **3** a shop within in a department store, hotel, airport lounge etc.

boutonnière (bootonyeə´) n. a flower or flowers worn in the buttonhole.

❌ **bouyant** common misspelling of BUOYANT (under BUOY).

bouzouki (buzoo´ki) n. a Greek stringed instrument similar to the mandolin.

bovine (bō´vīn) a. **1** of or resembling oxen. **2** sluggish. **3** dull, stupid. **bovinely** adv. **bovine spongiform encephalopathy** n. a disease of the central nervous system in cattle, usu. fatal, also called mad cow disease.

bovver (bov´ə) n. (sl.) a boisterous or violent commotion, a street fight. **bovver boot** n. (sl.) a heavy workboot worn esp. by teenage thugs. **bovver boy** n. (sl.) a member of a violent teenage gang, a hooligan.

bow¹ (bō) n. **1** the doubling of a string in a slipknot. **2** a single-looped knot. **3** an ornamental knot in which neckties, ribbons etc. are tied. **4** a necktie, ribbon or the like, tied in such a knot. **5** a stringed weapon for discharging arrows. **6** a curve, a rainbow. **7** the appliance with which instruments of the violin family are played. **8** a single stroke of such an appliance. **9** any of various simple contrivances in shape like a bow. **10** a saddle bow, an oxbow. **11** (N Am.) the side piece of a pair of spectacles. **12** in archery, a bowman. ~v.t. to play with or use the bow on (a violin etc.). **two strings to one's bow** more resources, plans or opportunities than one. **bow-compasses, bow-compass** n. compasses with the legs jointed, so that the points can be turned inwards. **bowfin** n. an American freshwater bony fish, Amia calva. **bowhead** n. an Arctic whale, Balaena mysticetus. **bow-legged** a. having the legs bowed or bent. **bow-legs** n.pl. **bowman**¹ n. (pl. **bowmen**) a person who shoots with the bow, an archer. **bowsaw** n. a saw fitted in a frame like a bowstring in a bow. **bowshot** n. the distance to which an arrow can be shot. **bowstring** n. the string by which a bow is stretched. **bow tie** n. a necktie in the form of a bow. **bow window** n. a bay window segmentally curved. **bowyer** (bō´yə) n. **1** a bowmaker. **2** a seller of bows.

bow² (bow) v.i. **1** to bend forward as a sign of assent, submission or salutation. **2** to incline the head. **3** to bend under a yoke. **4** to submit, to yield. ~v.t. **1** to cause to bend. **2** to incline, to influence. **3** to crush. **4** to express by bowing. **5** to usher (in or out). ~n. an inclination of the body or head, as a salute or token of respect. **to bow and scrape** to be obsequious. **to bow down 1** to bend or kneel in submission or reverence. **2** to crush, to make stoop. **to bow out 1** to make one's exit. **2** to retire, to retreat. **to make one's bow** to exit or enter formally. **to take a bow** to acknowledge applause.

bow³ (bow) n. **1** (often in pl.) the rounded fore-end of a ship or boat. **2** the rower nearest this. **on the**

bow (*Naut.*) within 45° of the point right ahead. **bowline** (bō´lin, -līn), **bolin** *n*. (*Naut.*) a rope fastened to the middle part of the weather side of a sail to make it stand close to the wind. **on a bowline** close-hauled, sailing close to the wind. **bowline knot** *n*. a kind of non-slipping knot. **bowman**² *n*. (*pl*. **bowmen**) the rower nearest the bow. **bowsprit** (bō´sprit) *n*. (*Naut*.) a spar running out from the bows of a vessel to support sails and stays. **bow wave** *n*. a wave set up at the bows of a ship, or in front of a body moving through a fluid.

bowdlerize (bowd´lərīz), **bowdlerise** *v.t.* to expurgate (a book). **bowdlerism, bowdlerization** (-zā´shən) *n.*

bowel (bow´əl) *n*. **1** each of the intestines, a gut. **2** (*pl*.) the entrails, the intestines. **3** (*fig*.) the seat of tender emotions. **4** the interior, the centre. ~*v.t.* (*pres.p.* **bowelling**, (*NAm*.) **boweling**, *past, p.p.* **bowelled**, (*NAm*.) **boweled**) to disembowel. **bowel movement** *n*. **1** defecation. **2** the faeces discharged.

bower¹ (bow´ə) *n*. **1** an arbour, a shady retreat, a summer house. **2** (*poet*.) a dwelling. **3** (*poet*.) an inner room, a boudoir. **4** the run of a bowerbird. **bowerbird** *n*. **1** any of various Australian birds of the family Ptilonorhynchidae, which build bowers or runs, adorning them with feathers, shells etc. **2** (*Austral., sl*.) a person who collects odds and ends.

bower² (bow´ə) *n*. either of the two knaves in euchre.

bower³ (bow´ə) *n*. (*Naut*.) **1** either of the two anchors carried in the bows. **2** the cable attached to either.

bowie knife (bō´i, boo´i) *n*. a long knife with the blade double-edged towards the point, used as a weapon in the south and south-west of US.

Usage note The pronunciation (boo´i) is used in the US.

bowl¹ (bōl) *n*. **1** a hollow (usu. hemispherical) vessel for holding liquids, a basin. **2** the contents of such a vessel. **3** a drinking-vessel. **4** a basin-shaped part or concavity. **5** in geography, a natural basin. **6** (*esp. NAm*.) a stadium. **7** (*NAm*.) (*in full* **bowl game**) an American football game played after the main season. **bowlful** *n*. (*pl*. **bowlfuls**).

bowl² (bōl) *n*. **1** a solid ball, generally made of wood, slightly biased or one-sided, used to play various games with. **2** (*pl*.) a game with bowls. ~*v.i.* **1** to play at bowls. **2** to roll a bowl along the ground. **3** to deliver the ball at cricket. **4** to move rapidly and smoothly (usu. with *along*). ~*v.t.* **1** to cause to roll or run along the ground. **2** to deliver (as a ball at cricket). **3** to strike the wicket and put (a player) out. **to bowl out** to put (a player) out at cricket by bowling the bails off. **to bowl over 1** to knock over. **2** (*coll*.) to impress. **bowler**¹ *n*. **1** a person who plays at bowls. **2** the player

who delivers the ball at cricket. **bowling** *n*. **1** playing at bowls. **2** the act of delivering a ball at cricket. **bowling alley** *n*. a covered space for playing skittles or tenpin bowls. **bowling green** *n*. a level green on which bowls are played.

bowler¹ BOWL².

bowler² (bō´lə), **bowler hat** *n*. an almost-hemispherical stiff felt hat. **bowler-hat** *v.t.* (*pres.p.* **bowler-hatting**, *past, p.p.* **bowler-hatted**) (*sl*.) to retire, discharge, dismiss.

bowman¹ BOW¹.

bowman¹ BOW¹.

bowser (bow´zə) *n*. **1** a tanker used for refuelling aircraft on an airfield, or for supplying water. **2** (*Austral., New Zeal*.) a petrol pump.

bow-wow (bowwow´, bow´wow) *int*. used to represent the bark of a dog. ~*n*. **1** the bark of a dog. **2** a dog (used by or to children).

Usage note The pronunciation with stress on the first syllable applies to the sense a 'dog'.

bowyer BOW¹.

box¹ (boks) *n*. **1** a case or receptacle usu. with a lid and rectangular or cylindrical, adapted for holding solids, not liquids. **2** the contents of such a case. **3** a Christmas box. **4** a compartment partitioned off in a theatre, tavern, coffee house, or for animals in a stable, railway truck etc. **5** an enclosure, e.g. *telephone box, sentry box*. **6** a facility at a newspaper office where replies to advertisements may be sent. **7** a hut, a small house. **8** a rectangle enclosing print on a page. **9** a case for the protection of some piece of mechanism from injury. **10** a protective pad for the genitals worn by cricketers. **11** the penalty area in football. **12** the place where the batter or pitcher stands in baseball. **13** the driver's seat on a coach. ~*v.t.* **1** to enclose in or furnish with a box. **2** to deposit (a document) in court. **3** (*Austral., New Zeal*.) to allow (sheep that should be kept separate) to run together. **the box 1** television. **2** a television set. **to box the compass** to name the points of the compass in proper order. **to box up 1** to shut in. **2** to squeeze together. **box camera** *n*. a simple box-shaped camera with an elementary lens, shutter and viewfinder. **boxcar** *n*. (*NAm*.) a goods van. **boxful** *n*. (*pl*. **boxfuls**) **box girder** *n*. a rectangular or square hollow girder. **box junction** *n*. a road junction with a box-shaped area painted with criss-crossed yellow lines into which traffic is prohibited from entering until there is a clear exit. **box kite** *n*. a box-shaped kite composed of open-ended connected cubes. **boxlike** *a*. **box mattress, box spring mattress** *n*. a mattress consisting of spiral springs contained in a wooden frame and covered with ticking. **box number** *n*. a number in a newspaper office to which replies to advertisements may be sent. **box office** *n*. **1** an office in a theatre or concert hall for booking seats. **2** the commercial appeal of an actor, production etc. **box pleat** *n*. a double fold or pleat. **boxroom** *n*. a room for

box 150 **bracket**

storing boxes etc. **box spanner** *n.* a tubular spanner with the ends shaped to fit the nuts and turned by a tommy bar inserted into a transverse hole. **boxy** *a.* (*comp.* **boxier,** *superl.* **boxiest**) 1 shaped like a box. 2 (of clothes) having a square cut. 3 (of reproduced music) lacking the high and low tones. **boxiness** *n.*

box[2] (boks) *n.* 1 a genus of small evergreen shrubs, *Buxus,* esp. the common box tree, *Buxus semper-virens.* 2 boxwood. **box elder** *n.* an American ash-leaved maple, *Acer negundo.* **box tree** *n.* the common box, *Buxus sempervirens.* **boxwood** *n.* the wood of the box tree.

box[3] (boks) *n.* a blow with the open hand on the ear or side of the head. *~v.t.* to strike (on the ear etc.) with the open hand. *~v.i.* to fight or spar with fists or with gloves. **to box clever** (*coll.*) to act in a clever or cunning way. **boxer** *n.* 1 a person who boxes, a pugilist. 2 (*Hist.*) (**Boxer**) a member of a secret society in China, ostensibly devoted to athletics, which took the leading part in the movement for the expulsion of foreigners, which came to a head in the rising of 1900. 3 a large, smooth-haired mastiff of a breed derived from the German bulldog. 4 this breed. **boxer shorts** *n.pl.* men's baggy underpants resembling the shorts worn by boxers. **boxing** *n.* the sport of fist fighting with gloves. **boxing glove** *n.* either of a pair of protective leather mittens worn by boxers. **boxing weight** *n.* each of a series of weight ranges at which boxers fight.

Box and Cox (boks ənd koks´) *n.* two people who share a job or a room but never meet. *~a., adv.* alternating. *~v.i.* to share accommodation or work in this manner.

boxer BOX[3].

boy (boi) *n.* 1 a male child. 2 a lad, a son. 3 a slave. 4 (*offensive*) a black man in a country colonized by Europeans, a black male servant or labourer. 5 (*offensive*) any male servant. 6 (*pl.*) grown-up sons. 7 (*pl., coll.*) a group of male friends. *~int.* used to express surprise, appreciation etc. **oh boy!** used to express surprise, appreciation, delight or derision. **boyfriend** *n.* (*coll.*) a male friend, esp. a regular partner or lover. **boyhood** *n.* **boyish** *a.* **boyishly** *adv.* **boyishness** *n.* **boyo** (boi´ō) *n.* (*pl.* **boyos**) (*Welsh, Ir., coll.*) boy, fellow. **Boy Scout** *n.* a member of the Scout Association. **boys in blue** *n.pl.* policemen; the police.

boycott (boi´kot) *v.t.* 1 to combine to ostracize (a person) on account of their political opinions. 2 to refuse to have dealings with. *~n.* the action of boycotting. **boycotter** *n.*

boyla (boi´lə) *n.* a sorcerer.

boysenberry (boi´zənberi) *n.* (*pl.* **boysenberries**) an edible hybrid fruit related to the loganberry and the raspberry.

BP *abbr.* 1 before the present (era). 2 British Pharmacopoeia.

bp *abbr.* 1 boiling point. 2 blood pressure.

BPC *abbr.* British Pharmaceutical Codex.

B.Phil. *abbr.* Bachelor of Philosophy.

bpi *abbr.* (*Comput.*) bits per inch (of computer tape).

bps *abbr.* (*Comput.*) bits per second.

Bq *abbr.* becquerel.

BR *abbr.* British Rail.

Br *chem. symbol* bromine.

Br. *abbr.* 1 British. 2 Brother.

bra (brah) *n.* (*pl.* **bras**) a women's undergarment that supports the breasts. **braless** *a.*

brace (brās) *n.* 1 that which clasps, tightens, connects or supports. 2 a timber or scantling to strengthen the framework of a building. 3 (*pl.*) straps to support the trousers. 4 a wire dental appliance for straightening crooked teeth. 5 two taken together, a couple, a pair. 6 a rope attached to a yard for trimming the sail. 7 (*esp. Printing, Mus.*) a sign in writing, printing or music uniting two or more words, lines, staves etc. *~v.t.* 1 to encompass. 2 to gird. 3 to bind or tie close. 4 to tighten or make tense. 5 to strengthen, to fill with energy or firmness. 6 to trim (sails) by means of braces. **brace and bit** *n.* a tool used by carpenters for boring, consisting of a kind of crank in which a bit or drill is fixed. **bracer** *n.* 1 something which braces. 2 (*coll.*) a stiff drink or tonic. **bracing** *a.* imparting tone or strength. **bracingly** *adv.* **bracingness** *n.*

bracelet (brās´lit) *n.* 1 an ornamental ring or band for the wrist or arm. 2 (*pl., sl.*) handcuffs.

brachial (brā´kiəl, brak´-) *a.* 1 of or belonging to the arm. 2 resembling an arm. **brachiate**[1] (-ət) *a.* (*Biol.*) 1 having branches in pairs, nearly at right angles to a stem and crossing each other alternately. 2 having arms. **brachiate**[2] (-āt) *v.i.* (of various arboreal mammals) to move along by swinging from each arm alternately. **brachiation** (-ā´shən) *n.* **brachiator** *n.*

brachiopod (brak´iəpod) *n.* (*pl.* **brachiopods, brachiopoda** (-op´ədə)) a bivalve mollusc of the phylum Brachiopoda, with tentacles on each side of the mouth.

brachiosaurus (brakiəsaw´rəs) *n.* (*pl.* **brachiosauruses**) a herbivorous dinosaur of the genus *Brachiosaurus,* characterized by the length of its front legs and its huge size.

brachistochrone (brəkis´təkrōn) *n.* the curve between two points through which a body moves in a shorter time than any other curve.

brachycephalic (brakisifal´ik, -kefal´ik) *a.* having a skull in which the breadth is at least four-fifths of the length. **brachycephalous** (-sef´ələs, -kef´-) *a.*

brachylogy (brəkil´əji) *n.* (*pl.* **brachylogies**) 1 concision of speech. 2 abridged or condensed expression. 3 inaccuracy caused by excess of brevity.

bracken (brak´ən) *n.* 1 a fern, esp. *Pteridium aquilinum.* 2 a mass of such ferns.

bracket (brak´it) *n.* 1 a projection with a horizontal top fixed to a wall. 2 a shelf with a wall underneath for hanging against a wall. 3 an angular support. 4 (*Mil.*) the cheek of a gun carriage, holding the trunnion. **5** a gas pipe projecting from a wall. **6** a mark used in printing to enclose words or mathematical symbols. **7** (*Mil.*) the distance between two artillery shots fired either side of the target. ~*v.t.* (*pres.p.* **bracketing,** *past, p.p.* **bracketed**) **1** to furnish with a bracket or brackets. **2** to place within brackets. **3** to connect (names of equal merit) in an honours list. **4** to associate, categorize or group (like things) together. **5** (*Mil.*) to find the range of (a target) by dropping shots alternately short of and over it. **bracket fungus** *n.* a fungus of the family Polyporaceae, which grow as shelflike projections on tree trunks.

brackish (brak´ish) *a.* **1** partly fresh, partly salt. **2** of a saline taste. **brackishness** *n.*

bract (brakt) *n.* (*Bot.*) a small modified leaf or scale on the flower stalk. **bracteal** (-tiəl) *a.* **bracteate** (-tiət) *a.*

brad (brad) *n.* a thin, flattish nail, with a small lip or projection on one side instead of a head.

bradawl (brad´awl) *n.* a small boring-tool.

bradycardia (bradikah´diə) *n.* (*Med.*) a slow heartbeat.

brae (brā) *n.* (*Sc.*) **1** a slope bounding a river valley. **2** a hill.

brag (brag) *v.i.* (*pres.p.* **bragging,** *past, p.p.* **bragged**) to boast. ~*v.t.* **1** to boast about. **2** to challenge. ~*n.* **1** a boast. **2** boasting. **3** a game of cards. **bragger** *n.* **braggingly** *adv.*

braggadocio (bragədō´chiō) *n.* **1** an empty boaster. **2** empty boasting.

braggart (brag´ət) *n.* a boastful person. ~*a.* given to bragging; boastful.

brahma (brah´mə), **brahmaputra** (-poo´trə) *n.* **1** any bird of an Asian breed of domestic fowl. **2** this breed.

Brahmin (brah´min), **Brahman** (-mən) *n.* **1** a member of the highest Hindu caste, the priestly order. **2** (*N Am.*) a person of superior intellectual or social status, a highbrow. **3** a breed of Indian cattle. **Brahminic** (-min´-), **Brahminical** *a.* **Brahminism** *n.*

braid (brād) *n.* **1** anything plaited or interwoven. **2** a narrow band. **3** a woven fabric for trimming or binding. ~*v.t.* **1** to intertwine, to plait. **2** to dress (the hair) in plaits or bands. **3** to tie (ribbon or bands) into the hair. **4** to trim or bind with braid. **braiding** *n.* **1** the action of plaiting or interweaving. **2** embroidery.

brail (brāl) *n.* (*pl.*) ropes used to gather up the foot and leeches of a sail before furling. ~*v.t.* to haul up by means of the brails.

Braille (brāl) *n.* a system of writing or printing for the blind, by means of combinations of points stamped in relief. ~*v.t.* to print or transcribe in Braille.

brain (brān) *n.* **1** the soft, whitish, convoluted mass of nervous substance contained in the skull of vertebrates. **2** any analogous organ in the invertebrates (*sing.* the organ, *pl.* the substance). **3** the seat of intellect, thought etc. **4** the centre of

sensation. **5** intellectual power. **6** (*coll.*) an intelligent person. **7** (*usu. in pl., coll.*) the cleverest person in a group. **8** (*usu. in pl.*) the person who thinks up a plan. ~*v.t.* to dash out the brains of, to kill in this way. **brainbox** *n.* (*coll.*) a clever person. **brainchild** *n.* (*pl.* **brainchildren**) a plan or project which is the product of creative thought. **brain coral** *n.* coral resembling the convolutions of the brain. **brain death** *n.* the cessation of brain function, taken as an indication of death. **braindead** *a.* **1** having suffered brain death. **2** (*coll., derog.*) lacking intelligence. **brain drain** *n.* (*coll.*) the emigration of academics or scientists looking for better pay or conditions. **brain fever** *n.* inflammation of the brain. **brainless** *a.* **1** destitute of brain. **2** silly, witless. **brainstem** *n.* the stalk-shaped part of the brain which connects it to the spinal cord. **brainstorm** *n.* a sudden, violent mental disturbance. **brainstorming** *n.* intensive discussion, e.g. to generate ideas. **brains trust** *n.* a bench of persons before the microphone answering impromptu selected questions from an audience. **brain-teaser, brain-twister** *n.* (*coll.*) a perplexing problem or puzzle. **brainwashing** *n.* the subjection of a victim to sustained mental pressure, or to indoctrination, in order to extort a confession or to induce them to change their views. **brainwash** *v.t.* **brainwave** *n.* (*coll.*) a (sudden) brilliant idea. **brainy** *a.* (*comp.* **brainier,** *superl.* **brainiest**) **1** having brains. **2** acute, clever. **brainily** *adv.* **braininess** *n.*

braise (brāz) *v.t.* to cook slowly in little liquid in a tightly closed pan.

brake[1] (brāk) *n.* **1** an appliance to a wheel to check or stop motion. **2** anything that stops or hinders something. ~*v.t.* to retard by means of a brake. ~*v.i.* to apply a brake. **brake block** *n.* **1** a block applied to a wheel as a brake. **2** a block used to hold a brake shoe. **brake disc** *n.* a disc attached to a wheel, on which the brake pad presses. **brake drum** *n.* a drum attached to the hub of a wheel of a motor vehicle which has drum brakes. **brake fluid** *n.* an oily liquid used in a hydraulic brake or clutch system. **brake horsepower** *n.* the measurement of an engine's power calculated from its resistance to a brake. **brakeless** *a.* **brake light** *n.* the red light on the rear of a vehicle which indicates braking. **brake lining** *n.* a thin strip of fabric attached to a brake shoe to increase its friction. **brakeman,** (*N Am.*) **brakesman** *n.* (*pl.* **brakemen, brakesmen**) a person in charge of a brake, a railway guard. **brake pad** *n.* a flat metal block which presses on the brake disc. **brake shoe** *n.* the curved metal block which presses on the brake drum. **brakevan** *n.* a railway carriage containing a brake.

brake[2] (brāk) *n.* **1** an instrument for breaking flax or hemp. **2** (*in full* **brake harrow**) a heavy harrow for breaking up clods. **3** (*also* **break**) a large estate car. ~*v.t.* to crush (flax or hemp).

brake[3] (brāk) *n.* a mass of brushwood, a thicket.

brake[4] (brāk) *n.* bracken.

bramble (bram´bəl) *n.* **1** the blackberry bush, *Rubus fructicosus*, or any allied thorny shrub. **2** the edible berry of these. **3** any of various other shrubs of the rose family, esp. the dog rose, *Rosa canina*. **bramble finch, brambling** (-bling) *n.* the mountain finch, *Fringilla montifringilla*. **brambly** *a.* (*comp.* **bramblier,** *superl.* **brambliest**)

Bramley (bram´li) *n.* (*pl.* **Bramleys**) (*in full* **Bramley's seedling**) a large green variety of cooking apple which has firm flesh.

bran (bran) *n.* the husks of ground corn separated from the flour by bolting. **bran tub** *n.* a lucky dip with presents hidden in a container full of bran.

branch (brahnch) *n.* **1** a shoot or limb of a tree or shrub, esp. one from a bough. **2** anything considered as a subdivision or extension of a main trunk, as of a mountain range, river, road, railway, family, genus, system of knowledge, legislature, commercial organization etc. **3** any offshoot, member, part or subdivision of an analogous kind. ~*v.i.* **1** to shoot out into branches or subdivisions. **2** to diverge from a main direction. **3** to divide, to ramify. **to branch out** to broaden one's interests or activities. **branched** *a.* **branchlet** *n.* a small branch, a twig. **branchlike** *a.* **branchy** *a.* (*comp.* **branchier,** *superl.* **branchiest**)

branchia (brang´kiə), **branchiae** (-ē) *n.pl.* the gills of fishes and some amphibians. **branchial** *a.* **branchiate** (-ət) *a.*

brand (brand) *n.* **1** a trade mark, a particular kind of manufactured article. **2** class, quality. **3** a mark made by or with a hot iron; an instrument for stamping a mark. **4** a piece of burning wood. **5** a piece of wood partially burnt. **6** (*poet.*) a torch. **7** a stigma. **8** (*poet.*) a sword. **9** a kind of blight. ~*v.t.* **1** to mark with a brand. **2** to imprint on the memory. **3** to stigmatize. **brander** *n.* **brand leader** *n.* the best-selling product within its category. **brand name** *n.* a trade name for the commodities of a particular manufacturer. **brand new, bran new** *a.* as if just from the furnace, totally new.

brandish (bran´dish) *v.t.* to wave or flourish about (a weapon etc.). **brandisher** *n.*

brandling (brand´ling) *n.* a small red worm with vivid rings, used as bait in angling.

brandy (bran´di) *n.* (*pl.* **brandies**) a spirit distilled from wine. **brandy ball** *n.* a kind of sweet. **brandy butter** *n.* a sweet sauce made with brandy, butter and sugar. **brandy snap** *n.* a thin, crisp, waferlike gingerbread, usu. scroll-shaped.

brank-ursine (brangkœ´sin) *n.* the acanthus or bear's-breech.

bran new BRAND NEW (under BRAND).

brant BRENT.

brash¹ (brash) *a.* **1** impertinent, cheeky. **2** vulgarly assertive or pushy. **3** rash. **brashly** *adv.* **brashness** *n.*

brash² (brash) *n.* loose, disintegrated rock or rubble.

brass (brahs) *n.* **1** a yellow alloy of copper and zinc. **2** anything made of this alloy. **3** an en-graved sepulchral tablet of this metal. **4** musical wind instruments of brass. **5** (*also pl., Mus.*) the section in an orchestra composed of brass instruments. **6** (*sl.*) money. **7** effrontery, impudence. **8** HORSE BRASS (under HORSE). **9** (*coll.*) those in authority or of high military rank, TOP BRASS (under TOP¹). **10** a brass block or die used in bookbinding. ~*a.* made of brass. **brassed off** (*sl.*) fed up. **brass band** *n.* a band performing chiefly on brass instruments. **brass hat** *n.* (*coll.*) a staff officer. **brass neck** *n.* (*coll.*) impudence, audacity. **brass rubbing** *n.* **1** the transfer of an image from a brass tablet to paper by placing the paper over the original and rubbing it with crayon or chalk. **2** the image copied by this method. **brass tacks** *n.pl.* (*coll.*) **1** details. **2** the essential facts of the matter. **brassy** *a.* (*comp.* **brassier,** *superl.* **brassiest**) **1** resembling brass. **2** unfeeling, impudent, shameless. **3** debased, cheap, pretentious. **brassily** *adv.* **brassiness** *n.*

brassard (bras´ahd) *n.* **1** a badge worn on the arm. **2** an armband, armlet.

brasserie (bras´əri) *n.* a (usu. small) restaurant, orig. one serving beer as well as wine etc. with the food.

brassica (bras´ikə) *n.* any plant belonging to the genus *Brassica* of the Cruciferae family (turnip, cabbage etc.).

brassière (braz´iə, bras´-) *n.* a women's undergarment for supporting the breasts.

brat (brat) *n.* (*usu. derog.*) a child, an infant, usu. one who is badly behaved or ragged and dirty. **brat pack** *n.* (*sl.*) a group of young celebrities, such as film stars or writers. **brat packer** *n.* **bratty** *a.*

brattice (brat´is) *n.* **1** a partition for ventilation in a mine. **2** a partition. **3** a lining of timber. **bratticing** *n.* **bratticing** *n.* **1** bratticework. **2** (*Archit.*) open carved work.

bratwurst (brat´vœst) *n.* a kind of German sausage.

bravado (brəvah´dō) *n.* (*pl.* **bravadoes**) **1** ostentatious defiance. **2** swaggering behaviour.

brave (brāv) *a.* **1** daring, courageous. **2** gallant, noble. **3** (*formal*) **a** showy, merry. **b** excellent, fine. ~*n.* a N American Indian warrior. ~*v.t.* **1** to defy, to challenge. **2** to meet with courage. **to brave it out** to bear oneself defiantly in the face of blame or suspicion. **bravely** *adv.* **braveness** *n.* **bravery** (-vəri) *n.* **1** courage. **2** display, splendour. **3** finery.

bravo¹ (brahvō´, brah´vō) *int.* (*fem.* **brava,** *superl.* **bravissimo** (-vis´imō), **bravissima** (-mə)) capital! well done! ~*n.* (*pl.* **bravoes, bravos**) **1** a cry of approval. **2** a cheer.

bravo² (brah´vō) *n.* (*pl.* **bravoes, bravos**) **1** a hired assassin. **2** a bandit, a desperado.

bravura (brəvūə´rə) *n.* **1** (*Mus.*) brilliance of execution. **2** a display of daring and skill in artistic execution. **3** a piece of music that calls out all the powers of an executant. ~*a.* requiring or showing bravura.

brawl (brawl) *v.i.* **1** to quarrel noisily. **2** to babble (as running water). *~n.* a noisy quarrel, disturbance, a tumult. **brawler** *n.*

brawn (brawn) *n.* **1** muscle, flesh. **2** a potted meat dish usu. made from pig's head. **3** strength, muscularity. **brawny** *a.* (*comp.* **brawnier**, *superl.* **brawniest**) muscular, strong, hardy. **brawnily** *adv.* **brawniness** *n.*

bray (brā) *v.i.* to make a harsh, discordant noise, like an ass. *~v.t.* to utter harshly or loudly (often with *out*). *~n.* **1** a loud cry. **2** the cry of the ass. **3** a harsh, grating sound.

braze[1] (brāz) *v.t.* to solder with an alloy of brass and zinc. *~n.* **1** a brazed joint. **2** the alloy used for brazing.

braze[2] BRAZEN.

brazen (brā′zən) *a.* **1** made of brass. **2** resembling brass. **3** shameless, impudent. *~v.t.* **1** to face impudently (often with *out*). **2** to harden, make shameless. **braze**[2] (brāz) *v.t.* **1** to make, cover or ornament with brass. **2** to colour like brass. **3** to make hard like brass. **brazenly** *adv.* **brazenness**, **brazenry** *n.* **brazier**[1] (-ziə) *n.* a worker in brass. **braziery** *n.* brasswork.

brazier[1] BRAZEN.

brazier[2] (brā′ziə), **brasier** (brā′zhə) *n.* **1** a large pan to hold lighted charcoal. **2** (*N Am.*) a charcoal grill.

brazil (brəzil′), **brazil wood** *n.* a red dyewood produced by the genus *Caesalpinia*, which gave its name to the country in S America. **brazil nut** *n.* the triangular, edible seed of the S American tree *Bertholletia excelsa*.

breach (brēch) *n.* **1** the act of breaking. **2** a break, a gap. **3** (*Law etc.*) violation, whether by a definite act or by omission, of a law, duty, right, contract or engagement. **4** a rupture of friendship or alliance. **5** alienation, a quarrel. **6** a gap, esp. one made by guns in a fortification. *~v.t.* **1** to make a breach or gap in. **2** (*Law etc.*) to break (a law, contract etc.). **to step into the breach** to help out, esp. by replacing someone. **breach of promise** *n.* failure to keep a promise, esp. a promise to marry. **breach of the peace** *n.* **1** violation of the public peace. **2** a riot, an affray.

bread (bred) *n.* **1** a food, made of flour or other meal kneaded into dough, generally with yeast, made into loaves and baked. **2** food. **3** livelihood. **4** (*sl.*) money. *~v.t.* to dress with breadcrumbs before cooking. **to take the bread out of someone's mouth** to take away someone's means of living. **bread and butter** *n.* **1** a slice of buttered bread. **2** livelihood. *~a.* **1** plain, practical. **2** routine, basic. **3** giving thanks for hospitality (of a letter). **breadbasket** *n.* **1** a basket for holding bread. **2** (*sl.*) the stomach. **3** rich grain lands. **bread bin** *n.* a container for storing bread in. **breadboard** *n.* **1** a board on which bread is sliced. **2** an experimental arrangement of electronic circuits. **bread buttered on both sides** *n.* **1** fortunate circumstances. **2** ease and prosperity. **breadcrumb** *n.* **1** a fragment of the soft part of

bread. **2** (*pl.*) bread crumbled for culinary purposes. **breadfruit** *n.* **1** (*also* **breadfruit tree**) a S Sea tree, *Artocarpus altilis*. **2** the farinaceous fruit of this tree. **breadline** *n.* **1** subsistence level. **2** (*N Am.*) a queue of people waiting to be given free food. **bread sauce** *n.* a sauce made with breadcrumbs, milk and onions. **breadstick** *n.* a long thin stick of bread dough which has been baked until crisp, sometimes with flavouring such as sesame seeds or garlic added. **breadwinner** *n.* the member of a family who supports it with their earnings.

breadth (bredth) *n.* **1** measure from side to side. **2** a piece of material of full breadth. **3** width, extent, largeness. **4** broad effect. **5** liberality, catholicity, tolerance. **6** in art, harmony of the whole. **breadthways**, **breadthwise** *adv.* by way of the breadth, across.

break (brāk) *v.t.* (*past* **broke** (brōk), †**brake** (brāk), *p.p.* **broken** (brō′kən), **broke**) **1** to part by violence. **2** to rend apart, to shatter, to rupture, to disperse, to impair. **3** to destroy the completeness or continuity of. **4** to subdue, to tame, to train. **5** to ruin financially. **6** (*Mil.*) to cashier, to reduce to the ranks. **7** to disable, to wear out, to exhaust the strength or resources of. **8** to disconnect, to interrupt. **9** to intercept, to lessen the force of. **10** to infringe, to transgress, to violate. **11** to fail to rejoin (one's ship) after an absence on leave. **12** to disprove (an alibi). *~v.i.* **1** to separate into two or more portions. **2** to burst, to burst forth. **3** to appear with suddenness. **4** to become bankrupt. **5** to decline in health. **6** to change direction. **7** to twist, as a ball at cricket. **8** to make the first stroke at billiards or snooker. **9** to alter the pace (as a horse). **10** to alter (as a boy's voice at the age of puberty). **11** in boxing, (of two fighters) to come out of a clinch. **12** (of prices) to fall sharply. *~n.* **1** the act of breaking. **2** an opening, gap, breach. **3** interruption of continuity in time or space. **4** the twist of a ball at cricket. **5** a number of points scored continuously in billiards etc. **6** (*coll.*) a lucky opportunity. **7** (*Mus.*) a short unaccompanied passage played by a soloist, often improvised. **8** a discontinuity in an electric circuit. **to break away 1** to remove by breaking. **2** to start away. **3** to revolt. **to break camp** to take down one's tent in preparation for leaving. **to break cover** to dart out from a hiding place. **to break down 1** to destroy, to overcome. **2** to collapse, to fail. **3** to analyse costs etc. into component parts. **to break even** to emerge without gaining or losing. **to break fresh/ new ground 1** to do something not previously done. **2** to make a start. **3** to cut the first sod. **to break in 1** to tame, to train to something. **2** to wear in (e.g. shoes). **3** (*Austral., New Zeal.*) to bring (land) into cultivation. **to break in on** to disturb or interrupt. **to break into 1** to enter by force. **2** to interrupt. **3** to suddenly burst out with. **4** to suddenly change to (a faster pace). **to break news** to tell something that has just happened. **to break off 1** to detach from. **2** to cease, to desist. **to break open 1** to force a door or cover. **2** to penetrate by violence. **to break out 1** to burst loose, to escape. **2** to burst forth (as a war). **3** to appear (as an eruption on the skin). **4** to exclaim. **5** to release (a flag). **6** to open (a container) and remove the contents. **to break someone's serve** to win a game of tennis in which the opposing player served. **to break the back 1** to break the keel of a ship. **2** to get through the greater part of. **to break the ice 1** to prepare the way. **2** to take the first steps, esp. towards overcoming formality or shyness at a gathering. **to break the mould 1** to make unique. **2** to effect a fundamental change. **to break up 1** to disintegrate. **2** to lay open (as ground). **3** to dissolve into laughter. **4** to disband, to separate. **5** to start school holidays. **6** (esp. N Am.) to be upset or excited. **to break with 1** to cease to be friends with. **2** to quarrel with. **breakable** a. **breakage** (-ij) n. **1** the act of breaking. **2** the state of being broken. **3** loss or damage from breaking. **4** an interruption. **breakaway** n. **1** (Austral.) a stampede of cattle or sheep. **2** any person, thing or group which breaks away from a main body. **3** a false start in a race. **4** in rugby, each of the two flank forwards on the outsides of the second row of a scrum. ~a. that is or involves a breakaway. **break crop** n. a crop grown as a change from cereal crops. **break-dancing** n. an energetic type of modern dancing characterized by spinning on various parts of the body (the hands, back etc.). **breakdown** n. **1** downfall, collapse. **2** total failure resulting in stoppage. **3** an analysis. **breaker** n. **1** a person who or something which breaks. **2** a person who breaks in a horse. **3** a heavy wave breaking against the rocks or shore. **break-in** n. an illegal forced entry into premises, esp. for criminal purposes. **breaking** n., a. **breaking and entering** n. (Law) illegal forced entry into premises for criminal purposes. **breaking point** n. the limit of endurance. **breakline** n. (Print.) the last line of a paragraph, usu. one of less than full length. **breakneck** a. **1** endangering the neck, hazardous. **2** (of speed) very fast. **break of day** n. dawn. **breakout** n. an escape, esp. from prison. **break point** n. **1** a place or time of a break. **2** (Comput.) **a** an instruction to interrupt a sequence of instructions. **b** the point in a program at which this happens. **3** in tennis, a point which would allow the player receiving service to win the game. **4** the situation when this happens. **5** breaking point. **breakthrough** n. **1** penetration of enemy lines. **2** an advance, a discovery. **break-up** n. **1** disruption, dispersal into parts or elements. **2** disintegration, decay, dissolution. **3** dispersal. **breakwater** n. a pier, mole or anything similar, to break the force of the waves and protect shipping.

breakfast (brek'fəst) n. the first meal of the day. ~v.i. to have breakfast. ~v.t. to provide with or entertain at breakfast. **to have someone for breakfast** to crush or destroy someone. **breakfaster** n. **breakfast television** n. early-morning television.

bream (brēm) n. **1** a freshwater fish of the genus Abramis, esp. A. brama. **2** a marine fish of the family Sparidae, a sea bream.

breast (brest) n. **1** either of the organs for the secretion of milk in women. **2** the rudimentary part corresponding to this in men. **3** the forepart of the human body between the neck and the abdomen. **4** the analogous part in the lower animals. **5** the upper forepart of a coat or other article of dress. **6** (fig.) a source of nourishment. **7** the seat of the affections. **8** the affections. **9** the front, the forepart. ~v.t. **1** to apply or oppose the breast to. **2** to stem, to oppose, to face. **3** to reach the top of (a hill). **to make a clean breast** to confess all that one knows. **breastbone** n. the flat bone in front of the chest to which certain ribs are attached; the sternum. **breasted** a. **breastfeed** v.t., v.i. to feed (a baby) from the breast instead of the bottle. **breast-pin** n. **1** a pin worn on the breast or in a scarf. **2** a brooch. **breastplate** n. armour worn upon the breast. **breast pocket** n. the inside pocket of a jacket. **breast-rail** n. the upper rail on a balcony. **breaststroke** n. a swimming stroke involving wide circling motions of the arms and legs while facing forward on one's breast. **breastsummer** (bres'əmə), **bressummer** n. (Archit.) a beam supporting the front of a building after the manner of a lintel. **breastwork** n. **1** a hastily constructed parapet thrown up breast-high for defence. **2** the parapet of a building.

breath (breth) n. **1** the air drawn in and expelled by the lungs in respiration. **2** the act or power of breathing. **3** a single respiration. **4** in phonetics, the expulsion of air without vibrating the vocal cords. **5** a very slight breeze. **6** (fig.) the time of a single respiration. **7** respite. **8** an instant. **9** a whiff, an exhalation. **10** a rumour, a whisper, a murmur. **in the same breath** done or said at the same time. **out of breath** gasping for air after exercise. **to catch one's breath 1** to cease breathing momentarily. **2** to regain even breathing after exertion or a shock. **to hold one's breath** to stop breathing for a short time. **to save one's breath** (coll.) to avoid talking to someone on purpose. **to take breath** to pause. **to take one's breath away** to astonish, delight. **to waste one's breath** to talk to no avail. **breathalyse** (-əlīz), (N Am.) **breathalyze** v.t. to test for the level of alcohol in the breath of (a driver) with a breathalyser. **breathalyser, Breathalyzer®** n. an instrument containing crystals for measuring the level of alcohol in the breath. **breathless** a. **1** out of breath. **2** dead, lifeless. **3** panting. **4** without a movement of the air. **5** excited, eager. **breathlessly** adv. **breathlessness** n. **breath of fresh air** n. **1** a small amount of fresh air. **2** a refreshing change. **breathtaking** a. astonishing, marvellous. **breathtakingly** adv. **breath test** n. a test to determine the amount of alcohol in the breath. **breathy** a. (comp. **breath-**

ier, *superl.* **breathiest**) **1** aspirated. **2** giving the sound of breathing. **breathily** *adv.* **breathiness** *n.*

breathe (brēdh) *v.i.* **1** to inhale or exhale air, to respire. **2** to live. **3** to take breath. **4** to move or sound like breath. **5** to be exposed to air. **6** (of fabric) to let air or moisture through. ~*v.t.* **1** to inhale or exhale (as air). **2** to emit, to send out, by means of the lungs. **3** to utter. **4** to utter softly. **5** to express, to manifest. **6** to allow breathing space to. **not to breathe a word** to keep silent, keep a secret. **to breathe down someone's neck** to cause someone discomfort with one's close supervision or constant attention. **breather** *n.* **1** a person who or thing which breathes. **2** (*coll.*) a rest in order to gain breath. **3** a vent in an air-tight container. **breathing** *a.* **1** living. **2** lifelike. ~*n.* **1** the action of breathing. **2** either of the two signs in Greek grammar, (') or (') placed over the first vowel of a word to mark the presence or absence of the aspirate. **breathing-place, breathing-space** *n.* a pause, place or opening for breathing.

breccia (brech'iə) *n.* a rock composed of angular, as distinguished from rounded, fragments cemented together in a matrix. **brecciated** (-ātid) *a.* **brecciation** (-ā'shən) *n.*

bred *a.* BREED.

☒ **bredth** common misspelling of BREADTH.

breech (brēch) *n.* (*pl.* **breeches** (brē'chiz, brich'iz)) **1** the portion of a gun behind the bore. **2** the hinder part of anything. **3** †the buttocks, the posterior. **4** (*pl.*) a garment worn by men, covering the loins and thighs, and reaching just below the knees. **5** (*pl., coll.*) any trousers. **breech birth, breech delivery** *n.* a birth in which the baby's buttocks or feet emerge first. **breech-block** *n.* a movable piece to close the breech of a gun. **breeches-buoy** (brē-) *n.* a life-saving device run on a rope stretched from a wrecked vessel to a place of safety. **breech-loader** *n.* a firearm loaded at the breech. **breech-loading** *a.* loaded at the breech.

Usage note The plural pronunciation (brē'chiz) is used where there is a corresponding singular, (brich'iz) where the plural is the fixed form.

breed (brēd) *v.t.* (*past, p.p.* **bred** (bred)) **1** to bring forth. **2** to give birth to. **3** to raise (cattle etc.), to rear. **4** to give rise to, to yield, to produce. **5** to engender, to cause to develop. **6** to train up, to educate, to bring up. **7** (*Physics*) to create (fissile material) by nuclear reaction. ~*v.i.* **1** to produce offspring. **2** to come into being, to arise, to spread. **3** to be produced or engendered. ~*n.* **1** a line of descendants from the same parents or stock. **2** family, race, offspring. **3** a sort, kind. **bred in the bone** hereditary. **breeder** *n.* a person who breeds, esp. one who breeds cattle and other animals. **breeder reactor** *n.* a nuclear reactor which produces more plutonium than it consumes. **breeding** *n.* **1** the act of giving birth to. **2** the raising of a breed. **3** bringing-up, nurture, rearing. **4** education, deportment, good manners.

breeze[1] (brēz) *n.* **1** a gentle gale, a light wind. **2** a wind of force 2 to 6 on the Beaufort scale (4–31 m.p.h) (7–50 k.p.h). **3** a wind blowing from land at night or sea during the day. **4** a disturbance, a row. **5** (*coll.*) something which can be done or got with ease. ~*v.i.* **1** to move in a lively way. **2** (*coll.*) to do or achieve something easily. **breezy** *a.* (*comp.* **breezier**, *superl.* **breeziest**) **1** open, exposed to breezes, windy. **2** lively, brisk, jovial. **breezily** *adv.* **breeziness** *n.*

breeze[2] (brēz), **brize** *n.* a gadfly.

breeze[3] (brēz) *n.* **1** small cinders and cinder dust. **2** small coke, siftings of coke. **breeze-block, breeze-brick** *n.* a brick or block made of breeze and cement.

brent (brent), (*N Am.*) **brant** (brant) *n.* the smallest of the wild geese, *Branta bernicla*, which visits Britain in the winter. **brent-goose** *n.* (*pl.* **brent-geese**).

brethren BROTHER.

Breton (bret'ən) *n.* **1** a native of Brittany. **2** the Celtic language of Brittany. ~*a.* of or relating to Brittany or its language.

breve (brēv) *n.* **1** a sign (˘) used in printing to mark a short vowel. **2** (*Mus.*) a note of time equal to two semibreves. **3** (*Hist.*) a papal letter.

brevet (brev'it) *n.* **1** an official document conferring certain privileges. **2** a warrant conferring nominal rank of an officer without the pay. **3** the wing-badge a flying member of the RAF may put on his uniform. ~*v.t.* (*pres.p.* **breveting**, **brevetting**, *past, p.p.* **breveted**, **brevetted**) to confer (a certain rank) by brevet.

breviary (brē'viəri) *n.* (*pl.* **breviaries**) in the Roman Catholic Church, a book containing the divine office.

brevity (brev'iti) *n.* **1** briefness, shortness. **2** conciseness.

brew (broo) *v.t.* **1** to make (beer, ale etc.) by boiling, steeping and fermenting. **2** to convert into (beer, ale etc.) by such processes. **3** to prepare (other beverages) by mixing or infusion. **4** to prepare. **5** to concoct. **6** to contrive, to plot. **7** to bring about. ~*v.i.* **1** to make beer etc. by boiling, fermenting etc. **2** to undergo these or similar processes. **3** to be in preparation. ~*n.* **1** the action, process or product of brewing. **2** the quantity brewed at one process. **3** the quality of the thing brewed. **to brew up** (*coll.*) to make tea. **brewer** *n.* a person whose trade is to brew malt liquors. **brewer's yeast** *n.* a yeast, *Saccharomyces cerevisiae*, used in brewing and as a source of vitamin B. **brewery** (-əri) *n.* (*pl.* **breweries**) a place where beer is brewed. **brewhouse** *n.* a brewery. **brew-up** *n.* (*coll.*) an instance of making tea.

briar[1] BRIER[1].

briar[2] BRIER[2].

bribe (brīb) *n.* a gift or consideration of any kind offered to anyone to influence their judgement or conduct. ~*v.t.* to influence in action or opinion of by means of a gift or other inducement. ~*v.i.* to practise bribery. **bribable** *a.* **briber** *n.* **bribery**

(-əri) *n.* (*pl.* **briberies**) the act of giving or receiving bribes.

bric-a-brac (brik´əbrak), **bric-à-brac, bricabrac** *n.* fancy ware, curiosities, knick-knacks.

brick (brik) *n.* **1** a block of clay and sand, usu. oblong, moulded and baked, used in building. **2** a brick-shaped block of any material. **3** a child's block for toy building. **4** a brick-shaped loaf. **5** (*sl.*) a good person. ~*a.* **1** made of brick. **2** of a dull red colour. ~*v.t.* to lay or construct with bricks. **like a ton of bricks** (*coll.*) with great force. **to brick up** to block up with brickwork. **to drop a brick** to say the wrong thing, to commit a blunder. **to see through a brick wall** to be unusually discerning; to have extraordinary insight. **brickbat** *n.* **1** a broken piece of brick, esp. for use as a missile. **2** (*coll.*) a critical remark. **brick-built** *a.* built of bricks. **brick-field** *n.* a field in which brickmaking is carried on. **brickie** *n.* (*coll.*) a bricklayer. **bricklayer** *n.* a person who lays or sets bricks. **bricklaying** *n.* **brick red** *n.* the colour of a red brick. **brick-red** *a.* **brickwork** *n.* **1** builder's work in brick. **2** bricklaying. **bricky** *a.* **brickyard** *n.* a place where bricks are made, stored or sold.

bride (brīd) *n.* a woman newly married or on the point of being married. **bridal** *a.* of or relating to a bride or a wedding. **bridally** *adv.* **bridegroom** *n.* a man about to be married or recently married. **bride price** *n.* (in some societies) money or goods given to a bride's family by the bridegroom's family. **bridesmaid, bridemaid** *n.* an unmarried girl or woman who attends the bride at her wedding.

bridge[1] (brij) *n.* **1** a structure thrown over a body of water, a ravine, another road etc. to carry a road or path across. **2** anything more or less resembling a bridge in form or function. **3** the upper bony part of the nose. **4** (*Mus.*) the thin wooden bar over which the strings are stretched in a violin or similar instrument. **5** a support for a billiard cue in an awkward stroke. **6** a partial deck extending from side to side of a steam vessel amidships. **7** an electrical circuit used for the accurate measurement of electrical quantities, e.g. resistance. **8** a partial denture. ~*v.t.* to span or cross with or as with a bridge. **to cross a bridge when one comes to it** to cope with a difficulty only when it occurs, not to anticipate difficulties unnecessarily. **bridgeable** *a.* **bridge-building** *n.* **1** the activity of building bridges. **2** the use of diplomacy to restore friendly relations. **bridge-builder** *n.* **bridgehead** *n.* (*Mil.*) a fortification protecting the end of a bridge nearest the enemy. **bridge of boats** *n.* a bridge supported on a number of boats moored abreast. **bridge passage** *n.* (*Mus. etc.*) a linking passage in a piece of music or literary or dramatic work. **bridgework** *n.* **1** a partial denture. **2** the technique of making such dentures.

bridge[2] (brij) *n.* a card game descended from whist, played by partners one of whose hand is

exposed at a particular point in the game. **bridge roll** *n.* a long thin soft bread roll.

bridle (brī´dəl) *n.* **1** a headstall, bit and bearing or riding rein, forming the headgear of a horse or other beast of burden. **2** a curb, a check, a restraint. **3** (*Naut.*) a mooring cable. ~*v.t.* **1** to put a bridle on. **2** to control with a bridle. **3** to hold in, to check, to control. ~*v.i.* to hold up the head and draw in the chest in pride, scorn or resentment (with *up*). **bridle path, bridle road, bridleway** *n.* a horse track, a path for horseriders.

Brie (brē) *n.* a soft white cheese orig. produced in France.

brief (brēf) *a.* **1** short in duration. **2** expeditious. **3** short, concise. **4** curt. ~*n.* **1** a papal letter of a less solemn character than a bull. **2** instructions. **3** a short statement. **4** (*Law*) **a** a writ, a summons. **b** a summary of facts and points of law given to counsel in charge of a case. **c** (*N Am.*) pleadings. **5** (*pl.*) close-fitting pants, underpants or knickers without legs. ~*v.t.* **1** (*Law*) **a** to reduce to the form of a counsel's brief. **b** to instruct or retain (a barrister) by brief. **2** to give detailed instructions to. **in brief** briefly. **to hold a brief for 1** to argue in support of. **2** to be retained as counsel for. **briefcase** *n.* a flat hand-held bag for carrying papers. **briefing** *n.* the imparting of instructions or information. **briefless** *a.* **briefly** *adv.* **briefness** *n.*

brier[1] (brī´ə), **briar** *n.* **1** a thorny or prickly shrub, esp. a wild rose. **2** the stem of a wild rose on which a garden rose is grafted. **brier rose** *n.* the dog rose or other wild roses. **briery** *a.* **1** full of briers. **2** thorny.

brier[2] (brī´ə), **briar** *n.* **1** the white or tree heath, *Erica arborea.* **2** a tobacco pipe made from the root of this.

Brig. *abbr.* Brigadier.

brig (brig) *n.* **1** a square-rigged vessel with two masts. **2** a US Navy prison. **3** (*sl.*) any prison.

brigade (brigād´) *n.* **1** (*Mil.*) a subdivision of an army, varying in composition in different countries and at different dates. **2** an organized body of workers, often wearing a uniform. **3** (*coll.*) a group of people who share some characteristic, belief etc. ~*v.t.* to form into one or more brigades. **brigadier** (-ədiə´) *n.* (*Mil.*) **1** the officer in command of a brigade. **2** the rank below that of major general. **brigadier general** *n.* (*pl.* **brigadier generals**) (*Mil.*) an officer ranking above colonel in the US army, air force and marine corps.

brigalow (brig´əlō) *n.* any acacia tree, esp. *Acacia harpophylla.*

brigand (brig´ənd) *n.* a robber, a bandit, an outlaw. **brigandage, brigandry** *n.*

brigantine (brig´əntēn) *n.* a two-masted vessel square-rigged on both masts but with a fore-and-aft mainsail, and mainmast much longer than the foremast.

bright (brīt) *a.* **1** lighted up, full of light. **2** emitting or reflecting abundance of light. **3** shining. **4** unclouded. **5** cheerful, happy, sanguine. **6** witty, clever. ~*adv.* (*esp. poet.*) brightly. ~*n.* **1** (*pl.*) bright colours. **2** (*pl.*, *N Am.*) headlights on full beam. **bright and early** very early in the morning. **to look on the bright side** to be optimistic. **brighten** *v.t.* **1** to make bright. **2** to make happy, hopeful etc. ~*v.i.* **1** to become bright. **2** (of the weather) to clear up. **brightish** *a.* **bright lights** *n.pl.* **1** the area of a city where places of entertainment are concentrated. **2** the city. **brightly** *adv.* **brightness** *n.* **bright spark** *n.* (*coll.*) a witty or lively person.

brill[1] (bril) *n.* a flat sea fish, *Scophthalmus rhombus*, allied to the turbot.

brill[2] (bril) *a.* (*coll.*) excellent, very pleasing.

brilliant (bril´yənt) *a.* **1** shining, sparkling. **2** lustrous. **3** illustrious, distinguished. **4** extremely clever and successful. **5** (*coll.*) excellent. ~*n.* a diamond or other gem of the finest cut, consisting of lozenge-shaped facets alternating with triangles. **brilliance**, **brilliancy** *n.* **brilliantine** *n.* **1** a cosmetic for making the hair glossy. **2** (*NAm.*) a glossy fabric. **brilliantly** *adv.*

brim (brim) *n.* **1** the upper edge, margin or brink of a vessel, hollow or body of water. **2** the rim of a hat. ~*v.t.* (*pres.p.* **brimming**, *past, p.p.* **brimmed**) to fill to the brim. ~*v.i.* to be full to the brim. **to brim over** to overflow. **brim-full, brimful** *a.* full to the brim. **brimless** *a.* **brimmed** *a.*

brimstone (brim´stōn) *n.* **1** †sulphur, esp. in the biblical context of the lake of brimstone. **2** the butterfly *Goneptery rhamni*, or moth *Opisthographtis luteolata*, which have yellow wings. **3** a spitfire, a termagant.

brindle (brin´dəl), **brindled** *a.* **1** tawny, with bars of darker hue. **2** streaked, spotted.

brine (brīn) *n.* **1** water strongly impregnated with salt. **2** the sea. ~*v.t.* to treat with brine, to pickle. **brine shrimp** *n.* a small crustacean of the genus *Artemia.* **briny** *a.* (*comp.* **brinier**, *superl.* **briniest**) **1** full of brine. **2** very salty. ~*n.* (*coll.*) the sea. **brininess** *n.*

bring (bring) *v.t.* (*past, p.p.* **brought** (brawt)) **1** to cause to come along with oneself. **2** to bear, to carry, to conduct, to lead. **3** to induce, to prevail upon, to influence, to persuade. **4** to produce, yield, result in. **to bring about 1** to cause, to bring to pass. **2** to reverse (the ship). **to bring around** (*N Am.*) to bring round. **to bring back** to recall to memory. **to bring down 1** to humble, to abase. **2** to shoot, to kill. **3** to lower (a price). **4** to carry on (a history) to a certain date. **5** to depose, to overthrow. **6** (*sl.*) to make unhappy. **7** (*coll.*) to demean. **to bring forth 1** to bear, to produce, to give birth to. **2** to cause. **to bring forward 1** to produce, to adduce. **2** to carry on (a sum) from the bottom of one page to the top of the next (in bookkeeping). **3** to move to an earlier date or time. **to bring home to** to cause to realize. **to bring in 1** to produce, to yield. **2** to introduce (as an action or bill). **3** to return (as a verdict). **to bring into play** to cause to operate. **to bring low 1** to overcome. **2** to humiliate. **3** to depress. **to**

bring off to accomplish. **to bring on** to cause to develop (more quickly). **to bring out 1** to express, to exhibit, to illustrate. **2** to publish. **3** to expose. **to bring over 1** to convert. **2** to cause to change sides. **to bring round 1** to revive. **2** to convert. **to bring the house down** to create tumultuous applause. **to bring through** to help (someone) through a crisis, illness etc. **to bring to 1** to restore to health or consciousness. **2** to check the course of (a ship). **to bring to pass** to cause to happen. **to bring under** to subdue. **to bring up 1** to educate, to rear. **2** to lay before a meeting. **3** to vomit. **4** to come to a stop. **to bring upon oneself** to be responsible for (one's own problems). **bring-and-buy sale** *n.* a sale, usu. for charity, at which people bring items to sell and buy those that other people have brought. **bringer** *n.*

brinjal (brin´jəl), **brinjall** *n.* esp. in the Indian subcontinent, an aubergine.

brink (bringk) *n.* **1** the edge or border of a precipice, pit, chasm or the like. **2** the margin of water. **3** the verge. **on the brink of** on the point of; in danger of. **brinkmanship** *n.* the art of maintaining one's position on the brink of a decision or crisis.

briny BRINE.

brio (brē´ō) *n.* spirit, liveliness.

brioche (briosh´, brē´-) *n.* a kind of light sweet bread.

briquette (briket´), **briquet** *n.* a block of compressed coal dust.

brisk (brisk) *a.* **1** lively, animated, active. **2** keen, stimulating, bracing. ~*v.t.* to make brisk. ~*v.i.* to move briskly. **brisken** *v.t., v.i.* **briskly** *adv.* **briskness** *n.*

brisket (bris´kit) *n.* **1** that part of the breast of an animal which lies next to the ribs. **2** this joint of meat.

brisling (briz´ling, bris´-), **bristling** (bris´-) *n.* (*pl. in general* **brisling, bristling**, *in particular* **brislings, bristlings**) a small herring, a sprat.

bristle (bris´əl) *n.* **1** a short, stiff, coarse hair, esp. on the back and sides of swine, in a beard or on a plant. **2** a similar hair in a brush etc. ~*v.t.* **1** to cause to stand up (as hair). **2** to cover with bristles. ~*v.i.* **1** to stand erect (as hair). **2** to show indignation or defiance (with *up*). **3** to be thickly beset (with difficulties, dangers etc.). **bristlecone pine** *n.* a shrubby pine, *Pinus aristata*, which is the longest-lived known tree. **bristletail** *n.* any small primitive wingless insect of the order Thysanura or Diplura, such as a silverfish. **bristling** *a.* **bristling with** full of, with many of. **bristly** *a.* **1** thickly covered with or as with bristles. **2** (*coll.*) quick to anger, touchy. **bristliness** *n.*

bristols (bris´təlz) *n.pl.* (*sl.*) a woman's breasts.

Brit (brit) *n.* (*coll., sometimes derog.*) a Briton, a British subject.

Britannia (britan´yə) *n.* Britain personified, esp. as a female figure in a helmet with a shield and trident. **Britannia metal** *n.* a white alloy of tin, copper and antimony. **Britannia silver** n. silver that is at least 95.8 per cent pure. **Britannic** a. British (*Her Britannic Majesty*).

British (brit′ish) a. **1** of or relating to Great Britain or the United Kingdom or its inhabitants. **2** of or relating to the British Commonwealth or (earlier) the British Empire. **3** of or relating to ancient Britain. ~n. (*as pl.*) the people of Britain. **British English** n. English employed in Britain and not in the US or elsewhere. **Britisher** n. a Briton, a British subject. **Britishism, Briticism** (-sizm) n. an idiom employed in Britain and not in the US or elsewhere. **Britishness** n. **British Summer Time** n. the official time of one hour in advance of Greenwich Mean Time that comes into force between March and October. **British thermal unit** n. the quantity of heat required to raise the temperature of 1 lb (0.45 kg) of water by 1°F, equivalent to 1055.06 joules.

Briton (brit′ən) n. **1** a member of the people inhabiting S Britain at the Roman invasion. **2** a native or inhabitant of Britain or (formerly) of the British Empire; a British subject.

Britpop (brit′pop) n. a type of pop music giving prominence to melody and often imitating 1960s British songs.

brittle (brit′əl) a. **1** liable to break or be broken, fragile. **2** not malleable. ~n. a brittle sweet (e.g. *peanut brittle*). **brittle-bone disease** n. **1** a disease which causes the bones to break easily. **2** OSTEOPOROSIS. **brittlely** adv. **brittleness** n. **brittle-star** n. a type of starfish of the class Ophiuroidea, with long flexible arms.

bro. abbr. brother.

broach (brōch) v.t. **1** to open, to moot, to make public. **2** to pierce (as a cask), so as to allow liquor to flow. **3** to tap. **4** (to cause a ship) to turn suddenly to windward. ~v.i. (of a ship) to veer suddenly windward. ~n. **1** a mason's chisel, a boring-bit. **2** a roasting-spit. **3** (*also* **broach spire**) a spire rising from a tower without a parapet.

broad (brawd) a. **1** wide, large, extended across. **2** extensive, expansive. **3** of wide range, general. **4** expanded, open, clear. **5** tolerant, liberal. **6** rough, strong, rustic. **7** coarse, obscene. **8** bold, vigorous, free in style or effect. **9** (of speech) markedly regional. ~n. **1** the broad portion of a thing. **2** (*N Am., sl., offensive*) a woman. **3** (*sl.*) a prostitute. ~adv. **1** in breadth. **2** broadly, widely. **broad arrow** n. a mark resembling an arrowhead cut or stamped on British Government property. **broadband** a. receiving, transmitting or involving a wide range of frequencies. **broad bean** n. **1** a leguminous plant, *Vicia faba*, with edible seeds in a pod. **2** one of these seeds. **broad-brush** a. (*attrib.*) general; not worked out in detail. **broadcast** a. **1** transmitted by radio or television. **2** widely disseminated. **3** scattered by the hand (as seed). ~n. **1** anything transmitted to the public by radio or television. **2** broadcast sowing. ~adv. by scattering widely. ~v.t. (*past* **broadcast**,

p.p. **broadcast, broadcasted**) **1** to sow by scattering with the hand. **2** to transmit by radio or television. **3** to disseminate widely. **broadcaster** n. **broadcasting** n. **Broad Church** n. **1** a party in the Church of England interpreting formularies and dogmas in a liberal sense. **2** any group that is similarly broad-minded or liberal. ~a. of or relating to the Broad Church. **broadcloth** n. **1** a fine, wide, dressed black cloth, used for men's coats etc. **2** poplin. **broaden** v.i. to become broader, to spread. ~v.t. to make broader. **broad gauge** n. a railway track that has a greater distance between the lines than the standard gauge. **broadleaf** n. a non-coniferous tree. ~a. having a (relatively) broad leaf, non-coniferous. **broadleafed** a. **broadleaved** a. **broadloom** n. carpet woven on a wide loom. ~a. woven on a wide loom. **broadly speaking** speaking in a general way. **broad-minded** a. tolerant, having an open mind. **broad-mindedly** adv. **broadmindedness** n. **broadness** n. **broadsheet** n. **1** a large sheet printed on one side only. **2** a large format newspaper. **broadside** n. **1** the side of a ship above the water. **2** a volley from all the guns on one side of a ship of war. **3** a broadsheet. **4** a political attack on a person or policy. ~v.t. (*N Am.*) to collide with the side of (a vehicle etc.). **broadside on** sideways on. **broad spectrum** a. (of antibiotics etc.) wide-ranging. **broadsword** n. a sword with a broad blade. **broadtail** n. **1** the karakul sheep. **2** the black wavy fur from karakul lambs. **broadway** n. a wide road, a main thoroughfare. **broadways, broadwise** adv. in the direction of the breadth.

brocade (brəkād′) n. silken material with raised figures. ~v.t. to weave or work with raised patterns.

broccoli (brok′əli) n. **1** a variety of cabbage which has greenish flower heads. **2** the stalk and head of this eaten as a vegetable.

broch (brokh, brok) n. a prehistoric circular tower, common in Scotland.

brochette (broshet′) n. **1** a skewer. **2** small pieces of food grilled together on a skewer (like a kebab).

brochure (brō′shə) n. a small pamphlet.

brock (brok) n. a badger.

✗ brocoli common misspelling of BROCCOLI.

broderie anglaise (brōdəri äglez′) n. open embroidery on cambric or linen.

brogue (brōg) n. **1** a sturdy shoe. **2** (*Hist.*) a coarse, rough shoe, usu. of untanned leather. **3** a dialectal pronunciation, esp. Irish.

broil[1] (broil) n. a tumult, disturbance, contention.

broil[2] (broil) v.t. **1** to cook on a gridiron; to grill. **2** to scorch. ~v.i. **1** to be very hot. **2** to grow hot. **broiler** n. **1** a person who or thing which broils. **2** a gridiron. **3** a chicken 8–10 weeks old for broiling or roasting. **4** (*coll.*) a very hot day.

broke[1] (brōk) a. (*coll.*) ruined, penniless. **to go for broke** (*sl.*) to risk everything in a venture.

broke[2] BREAK.

broken[1] (brō´kən) a. **1** in pieces. **2** not whole or continuous. **3** weakened, infirm. **4** crushed, humbled. **5** transgressed, violated. **6** interrupted, incoherent, ejaculatory. **7** shattered, bankrupt, ruined. **broken chord** n. (Mus.) a chord in which the notes are played successively. **broken-down** a. **1** decayed. **2** worn-out. **3** ruined in health, in character or financially. **broken English** n. halting or defective English as spoken by a foreigner. **broken-hearted** a. crushed in spirit by grief or anxiety. **broken-heartedness** n. **broken home** n. the home of children with separated or divorced parents. **brokenly** adv. **brokenness** n. **broken reed** n. an unreliable or weak person. **broken wind** n. a chronic respiratory disease of horses. **broken-winded** a.

broken[2] BREAK.

broker (brō´kə) n. **1** an agent, a factor, a middleman. **2** a person who buys and sells for others. **brokerage** (-rij) n. **1** the business of a broker. **2** a broker's commission on sales etc. **broker-dealer** n. a person who works as a broker and jobber on the Stock Exchange. **broking** n. the trade of broker.

brolga (brol´gə) n. a large Australian crane, *Grus rubicunda*, which has a red-and-green head and a trumpeting call.

brolly (brol´i) n. (pl. **brollies**) **1** (coll.) an umbrella. **2** (sl.) a parachute.

brome grass (brōm) n. any grass of the genus *Bromus*, esp. *B. inermis*, a cultivated fodder-grass.

bromelia (brəmēl´yə), **bromeliad** (-liad) n. any plant of the family Bromeliaceae, esp. of the genus *Bromelia*, which have short stems and stiff spiny leaves, such as the pineapple.

bromine (brō´mēn, -min) n. (Chem.) a non-metallic, dark red, liquid element, at. no. 35, chem. symbol Br, with a strong, irritating odour. **bromate** (-māt) n. a salt or ester of bromic acid. **bromic** a. **1** of or relating to bromine. **2** having bromine in its composition. **bromic acid** n. a strong acid used as an oxidizing agent. **bromide** (-mīd) n. **1** a combination of bromine with a metal or a radical, esp. bromide of potassium, which is used as a sedative. **2** (coll.) a commonplace remark, a platitude. **3** a reproduction or proof on bromide paper. **bromide paper** n. a sensitized paper used in printing a photograph from a negative.

bronc (brongk) n. (N Am., coll.) a bronco.

bronchi, bronchial BRONCHUS.

bronchiole (brong´kiōl) n. any of the tiny branches of the bronchi. **bronchiolar** (-ō´lə) a.

bronchitis (brongkī´tis) n. inflammation of the bronchial tubes. **bronchitic** (-kit´-) a.

bronchodilator (brongkōdīlā´tə) n. a substance which causes widening of the bronchi, used by people with asthma.

bronchopneumonia (brongkōnūmō´niə) n. pneumonia originating in the bronchial tubes.

bronchoscope (brong´kəskōp) n. an instrument which is inserted in the bronchial tubes for the purpose of examination or extraction. **bronchoscopy** (-kos´kəpi) n.

bronchus (brong´kəs) n. (pl. **bronchi** (-kī)) **1** any of the main divisions of the windpipe. **2** any of the ramifications into which these divide within the lungs. **bronchia** (-kiə) n.pl. the bronchial tubes. **bronchial** a. of or relating to the bronchi. **bronchial tree** n. the branching system of the bronchial tubes. **bronchial tubes** n.pl. the bronchi and bronchioles.

bronco (brong´kō) n. (pl. **broncos**) a wild or half-tamed horse of California or New Mexico. **broncobuster** n. (N Am., sl.) a breaker-in of broncos.

brontosaurus (brontəsaw´rəs), **brontosaur** (bron´-) n. (pl. **brontosauruses, brontosaurs**) APATOSAURUS.

bronze (bronz) n. **1** a brown alloy of copper and tin, sometimes with a little zinc or lead. **2** a brown colour, like that of bronze. **3** a work of art in bronze. **4** a bronze medal. ~a. made or of the colour of bronze. ~v.t. **1** to give a bronzelike appearance to (wood, metal, plaster etc.). **2** to brown, to tan. ~v.i. to become brown or tanned. **Bronze Age, Bronze Period** n. a period after the Stone and before the Iron Age when weapons and implements were made of bronze. **bronzelike** a. **bronze medal** n. a medal made of bronze, or bronze-coloured, awarded for third place in a contest. **bronzy** a. (comp. **bronzier**, superl. **bronziest**)

brooch (brōch) n. an ornamental clasp with a pin, worn on or to fasten clothing.

brood (brood) n. **1** a family of birds hatched at once. **2** offspring, progeny. **3** (coll.) the children in a family. **4** bee or wasp larvae. **5** a race, a species. **6** a swarm, a crowd. ~v.i. **1** to sit on eggs. **2** to hang close overhead (as clouds). **3** to meditate moodily. ~v.t. to sit upon (eggs) to hatch them. **brooder** n. **1** a cover for sheltering young chickens. **2** a person who broods. **brood hen, brood mare** n. a hen or a mare kept for breeding. **broodingly** adv. **broody** a. (comp. **broodier**, superl. **broodiest**) **1** inclined to sit on eggs. **2** sullen, morose. **3** inclined to brood over matters. **4** (coll.) wanting to have a baby. **broodily** adv. **broodiness** n.

brook[1] (bruk) n. a small stream, a rivulet. **brooklet** n. **brooklime** n. a kind of speedwell, *Veronica beccabunga*, growing in watery places. **brookweed** n. a small white-flowered plant, *Samolus valerandi*, growing in wet ground. **brooky** a. abounding in brooks.

brook[2] (bruk) v.t. (formal) to endure, to support, to put up with.

broom (broom) n. **1** a shrub with yellow flowers belonging to the genus *Sarothamnus* or *Cytisus*, esp. *Cytisus scoparius*. **2** a besom for sweeping, orig. made of broom. **3** a long-handled brush. **broomrape** n. a plant of the parasitic genus *Orobanche*. **broomstick, broomstaff** n. the handle of a broom.

Bros. (bros) *abbr.* Brothers.

broth (broth) *n.* **1** the liquor in which anything, esp. meat, has been boiled. **2** thin soup. **3** (*Biol.*) a medium for growing cultures (e.g. of bacteria).

brothel (broth´əl) *n.* premises where prostitutes sell their services.

brother (brŭdh´ə) *n.* (*pl.* **brothers, brethren** (bredh´rən)) **1** a son of the same parents or parent. **2** a person closely connected with another. **3** a person of the same community, country, city, church, order, profession or society. **4** a fellow man, a fellow creature. **brother german** *n.* a brother on both sides. **brotherhood** *n.* **1** the relationship of a brother. **2** a fraternity, an association for mutual service. **3** (*N Am.*) a trade union. **4** brotherly affection or feeling. **brother-in-law** *n.* (*pl.* **brothers-in-law**) **1** the brother of one's husband or wife. **2** one's sister's husband. **3** one's sister-in-law's husband. **brotherless** *a.* **brotherlike** *a.* **brotherly** *a.* **1** becoming to a brother. **2** fraternal. ~*adv.* fraternally. **brotherliness** *n.* **brother uterine** *n.* a brother born of the same mother but not the same father.

Usage note *Brethren* is used in more solemn senses.

brougham (broom, broo´əm, brō´əm) *n.* (*Hist.*) **1** a close, four-wheeled carriage drawn by one horse. **2** an early motor vehicle with an open driver's seat.

brought BRING.

brouhaha (broo´hah·hah) *n.* a tumult, a row.

brow (brow) *n.* **1** the ridge over the eye. **2** the forehead. **3** the countenance generally. **4** (*fig.*) aspect, appearance. **5** the projecting edge of a cliff or hill. **6** the top of a hill. ~*v.t.* **1** to be at the edge of. **2** to form a brow to. **to knit one's brows** to frown. **browbeat** *v.t.* (*past* **browbeat,** *p.p.* **browbeaten**) to intimidate arrogantly, to bully. **browbeater** *n.* **browed** *a.* (*in comb.*, as *beetle-browed*).

brown (brown) *a.* **1** of the colour of dark wood, scorched paper or dark soil; of the compound colour produced by a mixture of red, black and yellow. **2** dusky, dark, suntanned. **3** (of bread) made from wholemeal or wheatmeal flour. **4** (of species) having brown coloration. ~*n.* **1** a brown colour; a compound colour produced by a mixture of red, black and yellow. **2** a pigment of this colour. **3** a brown butterfly. **4** brown clothes. **5** (in a game) a brown piece etc. ~*v.i.* to make brown. ~*v.i.* to become brown. **brown ale** *n.* a dark, mild bottled beer. **brown bag** *n.* (*N Am.*) a brown paper bag. **brown-bagger** *n.* a person who carries their lunch in this. **brown bear** *n.* a brown bear, *Ursus arctos*, common to Europe, Asia and N America. **brown coal** *n.* lignite. **brown fat** *n.* a dark fatty tissue which generates body heat. **brown goods** *n.pl.* household appliances, usu. brownish in colour, such as TV sets, record players etc., as opposed to *white goods*. **brown holland** *n.* unbleached holland linen. **Brownie, Brownie Guide** *n.* a junior Guide from 8 to 11 years of age. **Brownie Guider** *n.* the adult leader of a Brownie pack. **Brownie point** *n.* (*sometimes derog.*) a supposed mark to one's credit for some achievement. **brownie** (-ni) *n.* **1** (*orig. N Am.*) a kind of nutty, dark chocolate cake cut into flat squares. **2** (*Austral.*) a kind of currant loaf. **3** a kindly domestic elf. **browning** *n.* colouring material for gravy. **brownish** *a.* **brownness** *n.* **brown-nose** *n.* (*N Am., sl.*) (*also* **brown-noser**) a sycophant. ~*v.i.* to curry favour. ~*v.t.* to curry favour with. **brown owl** *n.* **1** any of various owls, esp. the tawny owl *Strix aluco.* **2** (*coll.*) (**Brown Owl**) a Brownie Guider. **brown rice** *n.* husked rice left unpolished. **Brownshirt** *n.* (*Hist.*) a uniformed member of the Nazi party in Germany. **brownstone** *n.* (*N Am.*) **1** a dark-brown sandstone. **2** a building of this material. **brown study** *n.* a reverie, daydream. **brown sugar** *n.* coarse, half-refined sugar. **brown trout** *n.* a common European trout, *Salmo trutta*, with a dark spotted back. **browny** *a.*

browse (browz) *v.t.* **1** to nibble and eat off (twigs, young shoots etc.). **2** (*Comput.*) to read or survey (data files etc.). **3** to read in a desultory way, to leaf through. ~*v.i.* **1** to feed on twigs, young shoots etc. **2** to graze. **3** to look or read among articles in an idle manner. **4** (*Comput.*) to read through data files etc. ~*n.* **1** the tender shoots of trees and shrubs fit for cattle to feed on. **2** an act of browsing. **browser** *n.*

brucellosis (broosəlō´sis) *n.* an infectious bacterial disease in animals, caused by bacteria of the genus *Brucella*, which is also contagious to humans (also called *contagious abortion, Malta* or *undulant fever*).

brucite (broo´sīt) *n.* a mineral form of magnesium hydroxide.

Bruin (broo´in) *n.* (a personal name for) the brown bear.

bruise (brooz) *v.t.* **1** to crush, indent or discolour, by a blow from something blunt and heavy. **2** to injure without breaking skin or bone, usu. with discoloration. **3** to batter, pound, grind up. **4** to hurt, disable. ~*v.i.* **1** to be susceptible to bruising. **2** to display the effects of a blow. ~*n.* **1** an injury caused by something blunt and heavy. **2** a discoloured area of the skin caused by rupture of underlying blood vessels. **3** a damaged area on a fruit. **bruiser** *n.* **1** a person who or thing which bruises. **2** (*coll.*) a large strong man, a prizefighter or boxer.

bruit (broot) *v.t.* to rumour, to noise abroad. ~*n.* **1** an abnormal sound heard in auscultation. **2** †noise, tumult, rumour, report.

Brum (brŭm) *n.* (*coll.*) Birmingham, England. **Brummie** (-i), **Brummy** *n.* (*pl.* **Brummies**) a person from Birmingham. ~*a.* of or relating to Birmingham.

brumby (brŭm´bi) *n.* (*pl.* **brumbies**) (*Austral.*) a wild horse.

brume (broom) *n.* mist, fog, vapour. **brumal** *a.*
1 of or relating to winter. 2 wintry. **brumous** *a.*
wintry, foggy.

Brummagem (brŭm´əjəm), **brummagem** *a.*
1 cheap and ostentatious. 2 sham, spurious.

brunch (brŭnch) *n.* (*coll.*) a meal which combines a late breakfast with an early lunch. ~*v.i.* to
eat brunch.

brunette (brunet´), (*N Am.*) **brunet** *n.* a girl or
woman with dark hair and a dark complexion.
~*a.* 1 brown-haired. 2 of dark complexion.

brunt (brŭnt) *n.* the shock, impetus or stress of an
attack, danger or crisis.

brush[1] (brŭsh) *n.* 1 an instrument for sweeping
or scrubbing, generally made of bristles, twigs or
feathers. 2 an instrument consisting of hair or
bristle attached to a handle, for colouring, whitewashing, painting etc. 3 a brushing. 4 an attack,
a skirmish. 5 a bushy tail, as of a fox. 6 a piece
of metal or carbon or bundle of wires or plates,
forming a good electrical conductor. 7 a brushlike appearance produced by polarized light.
8 brushwood, underwood, a thicket of small
trees. 9 loppings, faggots of brushwood. 10 (*Austral.*) dense forest. ~*v.t.* 1 to sweep or scrub with
a brush. 2 to remove by brushing. 3 to touch
lightly, as in passing. ~*v.i.* 1 to move with a
sweeping motion. 2 to pass lightly. **to brush
aside** to dismiss curtly. **to brush off** to dismiss
curtly. **to brush over** to paint lightly. **to brush up**
1 to clean by brushing. 2 to revive, to tidy one's
appearance. 3 to refresh one's memory. **brushed**
a. **brushed aluminium** *n.* aluminium that has
been treated so that the surface is matt. **brusher**
n. **brushless** *a.* not needing a brush. **brushlike** *a.*
brush-off *n.* (*coll.*) a brusque rebuff. **brush turkey**
n. (*Austral.*) any of several birds of New Guinea
and Australia, esp. *Alectura lathami*. **brush-up**
n. an act of brushing up; a tidying of one's
appearance. **brushwood** *n.* 1 a thicket, underwood. 2 low scrubby thicket. 3 loppings. **brush-
work** *n.* 1 a painter's manipulation of the brush.
2 style of manipulation of the brush. **brushy** *a.*
(*comp.* **brushier,** *superl.* **brushiest**)

brush[2] (brŭsh) *n.* (*Austral., New Zeal., sl.*) a young
woman, a girl.

brusque (brŭsk, broosk) *a.* rough or blunt in
manner, unceremonious. **brusquely** *adv.* **brusque-
ness** *n.* **brusquerie** (-kəri) *n.*

Brussels (brŭs´əlz) *a.* made at or derived from
Brussels. **Brussels sprout** *n.* a small sprout
springing from the stalk of a variety of cabbage,
and used as a vegetable.

brut (broot) *a.* (of wine) dry, unsweetened.

brute (broot) *n.* 1 an animal as opposed to a
human being; a beast. 2 a person resembling a
brute in lack of intelligence etc.; a violent person
or animal. 3 the animal nature in humans. ~*a.*
1 stupid, irrational. 2 beastlike, sensual. 3 unconscious, material. **brutal** *a.* 1 resembling a
brute. 2 savage, cruel. 3 coarse, unrefined, sen-
sual. **brutalism** *n.* brutality. **brutalist** *n.* **brutality**

(-tal´-) *n.* (*pl.* **brutalities**) 1 the quality of being
brutal. 2 a brutal action. **brutalize, brutalise** *v.t.*
1 to make brutal. 2 to treat brutally. **brutalization**
(-zā´shən) *n.* **brutally** *adv.* **brutehood** *n.* **brutish** *a.*
brutishly *adv.* **brutishness** *n.*

bruxism (brŭk´sizm) *n.* the unconscious habit of
grinding the teeth.

bryology (brīol´əji) *n.* the science of mosses.
bryological (-əloj´-) *a.* **bryologist** *n.*

bryony (brī´əni), **briony** *n.* 1 a climbing plant of
the genus *Bryonia*, esp. *B. dioica*, with whitish
flowers. 2 BLACK BRYONY (under BLACK).

bryophyte (brī´ōfīt) *n.* a cryptogamous plant of
the division Bryophyta, consisting of the liver-
worts and mosses. **bryophitic** (-fit´ik) *a.* of the
phylum Bryozoa.

bryozoan (brīəzō´ən) *n.* any one of the lowest
class of the mollusca, of the phylum Bryozoa,
also called *polyzoan*. **bryozoology** (-zōol´əji,
-zoo-ol´-) *n.*

BS *abbr.* 1 (*N Am.*) Bachelor of Science. 2 Bachelor
of Surgery. 3 Blessed Sacrament. 4 British
Standard(s).

B.Sc. *abbr.* Bachelor of Science.

BSE *abbr.* bovine spongiform encephalopathy.

BSI *abbr.* British Standards Institution.

BST *abbr.* 1 bovine somatotrophin. 2 British
Summer Time.

Bt. *abbr.* Baronet.

btu, BTU, B.th.U *abbr.* British thermal unit.

bu. *abbr.* bushel.

bub (bŭb) *n.* (*N Am., coll.*) (as a form of address)
boy.

bubal (bū´bəl) *n.* the hartebeest.

bubble (bŭb´əl) *n.* 1 a vesicle of water or other
liquid filled with air or other gas. 2 a cavity in
a solidified material, such as ice, amber, glass
etc. 3 anything unsubstantial or unreal. 4 a fraud,
a swindling project. ~*a.* 1 visionary, unreal.
2 fraudulent, fictitious. ~*v.i.* 1 to rise up in or as
in bubbles. 2 to make a noise like bubbling water.
to bubble over to boil over with laughter, anger,
etc. **bubble and squeak** *n.* meat and vegetables
fried together. **bubble bath** *n.* 1 a foaming bath
preparation. 2 a bath containing this. **bubble car**
n. a midget motor car with rounded line and
transparent top. **bubble chamber** *n.* (*Physics*) an
apparatus for tracking the path of a charged
particle by the stream of bubbles left in its wake.
bubblegum *n.* a kind of chewing gum that can
be blown up into a bubble. **bubble memory** *n.*
(*Comput.*) a data storage system in computers
composed of tiny areas of bubbles of magnetism.
bubble pack *n.* BLISTER PACK (under BLISTER).
bubble wrap *n.* plastic packaging material made
up of air-filled pockets. **bubbly** *a.* (*comp.* **bub-
blier,** *superl.* **bubbliest**) 1 full of bubbles. 2 excited, vivacious. ~*n.* (*coll.*) champagne.

bubo (bū´bō) *n.* (*pl.* **buboes**) an inflamed swelling
of the lymphatic glands, esp. in the groin or armpit. **bubonic** (-bon´-) *a.* **bubonic plague** *n.* a type
of plague characterized by buboes.

buccal (bŭk´əl) *a.* of or relating to the cheek or the mouth.

buccaneer (bŭkəniə´) *n.* 1 a piratical rover, orig. on the Spanish Main. 2 a brazen adventurer. ~*v.i.* to act the part of a buccaneer. **buccaneering** *a.* **buccaneerish** *a.*

buccinator (bŭk´sinātə) *n.* the flat, thin muscle forming the wall of the cheek, used in blowing.

buck[1] (bŭk) *n.* 1 the male of the fallow deer, reindeer, goat, hare and rabbit. 2 †a dashing young fellow. 3 (*offensive*) a male N American Indian or black. 4 (*N Am., Austral., sl.*) a dollar. 5 (*sl.*) cheek. 6 (*sl.*) a marker in poker which indicates the next dealer. 7 an object used as a reminder. ~*a.* (*attrib., sl.*) 1 male (*a buck antelope*). 2 (*Mil., N Am.*) of the lowest rank (*a buck private*). ~*v.i.* to buckjump. ~*v.t.* 1 to throw (a rider) by buckjumping. 2 (*esp. N Am.*) to oppose, resist. **to buck up** 1 to hurry. 2 to improve. 3 to become cheerful or lively. **to pass the buck** (*sl.*) to shift responsibility to someone else. **bucked** *a.* (*coll.*) 1 invigorated. 2 pleased. **buckeye** *n.* 1 the horse chestnut of the US, of the genus *Aesculus*. 2 the shiny brown fruit of this. **buck fever** *n.* (*N Am.*) nervousness, such as that felt by inexperienced hunters. **buck-horn** *n.* 1 the horn of a buck. 2 the material of a buck's horn used for knife handles etc. **buck-hound** *n.* a small variety of the staghound. **buck-passing** *n.* shifting of responsibility to someone else. **buck rarebit** *n.* Welsh rarebit with a poached egg on top. **buckshot** *n.* a kind of coarse lead shot. **buckskin** *n.* 1 the skin of a buck. 2 a soft yellowish deerskin or sheepskin. 3 (*pl.*) buckskin breeches. **buckthorn** *n.* any thorny shrub of the genus *Rhamnus*, esp. *R. cathartica*, berries of which yield sap green. **buck-tooth** *n.* a large, protruding tooth. **bucktoothed** *a.*

buck[2] (bŭk) *n.* the body of a wagon or cart. **buckboard** *n.* 1 a projecting board or ledge over the wheels of a cart. 2 (*N Am.*) a light four-wheeled vehicle.

buck[3] (bŭk) *n.* 1 (*N Am.*) a sawhorse. 2 a vaulting horse.

buckbean (bŭk´bēn) *n.* a water plant having pinkish-white flowers, of the genus *Menyanthes*, esp. *M. trifoliata*, also called the *bogbean*.

bucket (bŭk´it) *n.* 1 a vessel with a handle, for drawing or carrying water. 2 a scoop or receptacle for lifting mud, gravel, coal, grain etc. in a dredger or elevator. 3 as much as a bucket will hold. 4 the piston of a pump. 5 (*in pl.*) large quantities of liquid (*raining buckets*). ~*v.t.* (*pres.p.* **bucketing**, *past, p.p.* **bucketed**) 1 to lift or draw in buckets. 2 to hurry or jerk while rowing. ~*v.i.* 1 to hurry the forward swing of an oar. 2 (*coll.*) to rain heavily. **to kick the bucket** (*sl.*) to die. **bucketful** *n.* (*pl.* **bucketfuls**) **bucket seat** *n.* a round-backed seat for one person in a vehicle or aeroplane. **bucket shop** *n.* 1 the office of unofficial brokers who deal in trashy stock. 2 (*coll.*) a place where cheap airline tickets are sold.

buckle (bŭk´əl) *n.* 1 a link of metal etc., with a tongue or catch, for fastening straps etc. 2 a bow, a curl, a twist. 3 the state of being crisped, curled or twisted. ~*v.t.* 1 to fasten with or as with a buckle. 2 to bend, to twist. 3 to equip with a buckle. ~*v.i.* to bend, to be put out of shape. **to buckle down** to make a determined effort. **to buckle to** to set to work, to set about energetically. **to buckle under** to give way under stress. **buckler** *n.* (*Hist.*) a small round shield. **buckler fern** *n.* (*Bot.*) any of the shield ferns of the genus *Dryopteris*.

Buckley's (bŭk´liz), **Buckley's chance** *n.* (*Austral., New Zeal., coll.*) no chance at all.

buckling (bŭk´ling) *n.* a smoked herring.

bucko (bŭk´ō) *n.* (*pl.* **buckoes**) (*Naut., sl.*) a swaggering or bullying person. ~*a.* swaggering, bullying.

buckram (bŭk´rəm) *n.* a strong coarse kind of linen cloth, stiffened with gum.

Bucks. (bŭks) *abbr.* Buckinghamshire.

Buck's Fizz (bŭks) *n.* a cocktail of champagne or sparkling wine mixed with orange juice.

buckshee (bŭkshē´) *n.* (*sl.*) 1 something for nothing, a windfall. 2 something in addition to the agreed allowance. ~*a.* free, gratuitous.

buckwheat (bŭk´wēt) *n.* a cereal plant of the genus *Fagopyrum*, esp. *F. esculentum*, the three-cornered seeds of which are given to horses and poultry, and in the US are used for cakes.

bucolic (būkol´ik) *a.* (*often derog.*) pastoral, rustic. ~*n.* 1 a pastoral poem. 2 a pastoral poet. 3 a peasant. **bucolically** *adv.*

bud[1] (bŭd) *n.* 1 the germ of a branch, cluster of leaves or flower, usu. arising from the axil of a leaf. 2 an unexpanded leaf or flower. 3 (*Biol.*) a gemmule which develops into a complete animal. 4 something undeveloped. ~*v.i.* (*pres.p.* **budding**, *past, p.p.* **budded**) 1 (*Bot., Zool.*) to put out buds. 2 to begin to grow. 3 to develop. ~*v.t.* 1 to graft (on) by inserting a bud under the bark. 2 to produce by germination. **in bud** about to flower or grow leaves. **to nip in the bud** to put a stop to at the outset.

bud[2] (bŭd) *n.* (*N Am., coll.*) buddy; pal.

Buddha (bud´ə) *n.* 1 the title given to Gautama, the founder of Buddhism, by his disciples. 2 a statue or picture of the Buddha. **Buddhism** *n.* the religious system founded in India in the 5th cent. BC by Sakyamuni, Gautama or Siddartha, teaching the existence of suffering and the way to release from suffering. **Buddhist** *n.* a follower of Buddha. ~*a.* of or connected with Buddhism. **Buddhistic** (-is´-), **Buddhistical** *a.*

buddleia (bŭd´liə) *n.* any shrub of the genus *Buddleia*, which have fragrant lilac, orange or white flowers.

buddy (bŭd´i) *n.* (*pl.* **buddies**) 1 (*coll.*) a close friend, pal. 2 a person who visits and counsels (in a voluntary capacity) someone suffering from Aids. ~*a.* (of a film or story) dealing with the adventures of and relationship between usu. two male partners. ~*v.i.* (*3rd pers. sing. pres.* **buddies,** *pres.p.* **buddying,** *past, p.p.* **buddied**) to act as a buddy to a someone suffering from Aids. **to buddy up** to become friendly.

budge (bŭj) *v.i.* **1** to move from one's place. **2** to change one's opinion. ~*v.t.* to cause one's opinion to budge. **to budge over/up** to move along to make room for someone.

budgerigar (bŭj´ərigah) *n.* **1** an Australian green parakeet, *Melopsittacus undulatus.* **2** a coloured variety of this, bred as a cage bird.

budget (bŭj´it) *n.* **1** an estimate of receipts and expenditure, esp. the annual financial statement of the Chancellor of the Exchequer in the House of Commons. **2** the amount of money allowed (for a specific item etc.). ~*v.i.* (*pres.p.* **budgeting,** *past, p.p.* **budgeted**) to prepare a budget or estimate (for). ~*v.t.* to make provision for in a budget. ~*a.* (*attrib.*) inexpensive. **on a budget** with a restricted amount of money to spend. **budgetary** *a.*

budgie (bŭj´i) *n.* (*coll.*) a budgerigar.

buff (bŭf) *n.* **1** the colour of buff leather, light yellow. **2** (*coll.*) an expert on or devotee of a subject. **3** soft, stout leather prepared from the skin of the buffalo. **4** the skins of other animals similarly prepared. **5** (*coll.*) the bare skin. **6** an instrument for polishing with. ~*v.t.* **1** to polish with a buff. **2** to give a velvety surface to (leather). **in the buff** (*coll.*) naked.

buffalo (bŭf´əlō) *n.* (*pl. in general* **buffalo,** *in particular* **buffaloes**) **1** an Asiatic ox of the genus *Babulus,* esp. *B. arnee,* the water buffalo. **2** a wild ox, *Syncerus caffer,* the Cape buffalo. **3** a N American bison, *Bison bison.* ~*v.t.* (*3rd pers. sing. pres.* **buffaloes,** *pres.p.* **buffaloing,** *past, p.p.* **buffaloed**) (*N Am., sl.*) to overcome or outwit. **buffalo grass** *n.* prairie grass such as *Buchloe dactyloides* of N America, or *Stenotaphrum secundatum* of Australia and New Zealand.

buffer (bŭf´ə) *n.* **1** a mechanical apparatus for deadening or sustaining the force of a concussion. **2** an apparatus fixed to railway carriages for this purpose. **3** a fellow. **4** (*Chem.*) a chemical compound which maintains the balance of acidity/alkalinity in a solution. **5** (*Comput.*) a short-term storage unit in a computer. ~*v.t.* **1** to add or treat with a buffer. **2** to protect with a buffer. **buffer state** *n.* a small neutral state separating two larger rival states and tending to prevent hostilities. **buffer stock** *n.* a reserve of a commodity held to minimize the effect of fluctuations in price. **buffer zone** *n.* a neutral zone separating two others.

buffet[1] (bŭf´it) *n.* **1** a blow with the hand or fist, a cuff. **2** a blow of fate, a disaster, a misfortune. ~*v.t.* (*pres.p.* **buffeting,** *past, p.p.* **buffeted**) **1** to strike with the hand. **2** to thump, to cuff. **3** to beat back, to contend with. ~*v.i.* to struggle, to contend. **buffeting** *n.* **1** repeated blows; a beating. **2** air turbulence affecting an aircraft.

buffet[2] (buf´ā) *n.* **1** a cupboard or sideboard for the display of plate, china etc. **2** a refreshment

bar. **3** dishes of food set out on a table from which diners help themselves. **buffet car** *n.* a coach in a train where refreshments are served.

buffoon (bəfoon´) *n.* **1** a person who indulges in jests and antics. **2** a vulgar, clowning fool. **buffoonery** *n.* **buffoonish** *a.*

bug[1] (bŭg) *n.* **1** any insect of the order Hemiptera, esp. the blood-sucking, evil-smelling insect, *Cimex lectularius,* found in bedsteads etc. **2** any small insect. **3** (*sl.*) a virus. **4** (*sl.*) a viral infection. **5** a secreted radio receiver. **6** a technical hitch, a flaw, esp. in a computer program. **7** (*coll.*) an obsession, a temporary craze or fashion. ~*v.t.* (*pres.p.* **bugging,** *past, p.p.* **bugged**) **1** to plant a hidden microphone in or on. **2** (*sl.*) to pester or irritate. **to bug off** (*esp. N Am., sl.*) to go away. **to bug out 1** (*esp. N Am., sl.*) (of eyes) to protrude. **2** (*esp. N Am., sl.*) to depart hurriedly. **bug-eyed** *a.* with bulging eyes. **buggy**[1] *a.* (*comp.* **buggier,** *superl.* **buggiest**) infested with bugs.

bug[2] (bŭg) *n.* †a hobgoblin, a bugbear. **bugaboo** (-əboo) *n.* a bugbear, a bogey. **bugbear** (bŭg´beə) *n.* **1** an imaginary object of terror. **2** a nuisance.

bugger (bŭg´ə) *n.* **1** a sodomite. **2** (*sl.*) an unpleasant, difficult or brutish person. **3** (*sl.*) something difficult, disliked, unwanted etc., a nuisance. ~*int.* (*often considered taboo*) used to express annoyance, frustration etc. ~*v.t.* **1** to have anal intercourse with. **2** (*sl.*) to exhaust. **3** (*sl.*) to destroy or spoil. **bugger all** (*sl.*) nothing. **to bugger about** (*sl.*) to muddle about, to interfere with a thing. **to bugger around** (*sl.*) to muddle about, to interfere with a thing. **to bugger off** (*sl.*) to leave. **buggery** *n.* sodomy, anal intercourse.

buggy[1] BUG[1].

buggy[2] (bŭg´i) *n.* (*pl.* **buggies**) **1** a light, four-wheeled or two-wheeled vehicle, having a single seat. **2** a pushchair, a baby buggy. **3** any such light vehicle or carriage (e.g. *beach buggy*).

bugle[1] (bū´gəl) *n.* **1** (*also* **bugle-horn**) a hunting-horn, orig. made from the horn of a wild ox. **2** a small military trumpet used to sound signals for the infantry. ~*v.t.* **1** to sound by bugle. **2** to call by bugle. ~*v.i.* to sound a bugle. **bugler** *n.*

bugle[2] (bū´gəl) *n.* a long, slender glass bead, usu. black, for trimming dresses.

bugle[3] (bū´gəl) *n.* a creeping plant of the genus *Ajuga,* esp. *A. reptans.*

bugloss (bū´glos) *n.* **1** any of various plants of the borage family, esp. of the genus *Anchusa,* with rough, hairy leaves. **2** viper's bugloss, *Echium vulgare.*

buhl (bool), **boule, boulle** *n.* **1** brass, tortoiseshell etc. cut into ornamental patterns for inlaying. **2** work so inlaid. ~*a.* (*attrib.*) inlaid with buhl.

build (bild) *v.t.* (*past, p.p.* **built** (bilt)) **1** to construct, to erect, to make by putting together parts and materials. **2** to have constructed or erected. **3** to establish, to develop. ~*v.i.* **1** to erect a building or buildings. **2** to make a nest. ~*n.* **1** form, style or mode of construction. **2** shape, proportions, figure. **to build in** to incorporate (into a structure etc.). **to build on 1** to found or rely on (as a basis). **2** to add (to a building). **to build up 1** to establish or strengthen by degrees. **2** to block up. **3** to erect many buildings in an area. **4** to praise. **builder** *n*. **1** a person who builds. **2** a master builder or contractor who erects buildings under the direction of the architect. **builder's merchant** *n*. a tradesperson who supplies building materials to builders. **building** *n*. **1** the act of constructing or erecting. **2** a structure erected to form an enclosure, an edifice. **building site** *n*. an area where building is taking place. **building society** *n*. an organization lending money to contributors enabling them to purchase residences. **build-up** *n*. **1** a creation of favourable publicity. **2** the leading to the climax in a speech etc. **3** an increase. **built** *a*. constructed, erected, fashioned, formed (*in comb.*, as *well-built*). **built-in** *a*. **1** part of the main structure, e.g. cupboards, wardrobe. **2** fixed, included. **built-up** *a*. **1** having many buildings (of an urban area). **2** increased in height etc. (*built-up heels*). **3** composed of separately prepared parts.

bulb (bŭlb) *n*. **1** a subterranean stem or bud sending off roots below and leaves above, as in the onion or lily. **2** a bulbil. **3** a spherical dilatation of a glass tube, as in the thermometer. **4** a light bulb. **5** a spherical swelling of any cylindrical organ or structure. ~*v.i.* to take or grow into the form of a bulb. **bulbil** (-bil) *n*. (*Bot*.) a small bulb developed at the side of a larger one, or in an axil. **bulbous** *a*. **1** of or relating to a bulb. **2** having a bulb or bulbs. **3** bulb-shaped.

☒ **bulettin** common misspelling of BULLETIN.

bulgar (bŭl′gə), **bulgur** *n*. wheat that has been boiled and then dried.

Bulgarian (bŭlgeə′riən) *n*. **1** a native or inhabitant of Bulgaria. **2** the language of Bulgaria. ~*a*. of or relating to Bulgaria, its people or language.

bulge (bŭlj) *n*. **1** a swelling on a flat or flattish surface. **2** (*coll.*) a temporary increase in volume or numbers. **3** (*Naut.*) the bilge of a ship. **4** (*Mil.*) a projection in a line of military attack or defence. **5** the protuberant part of a cask. ~*v.i.* **1** to swell irregularly. **2** to be protuberant. **3** to be full. ~*v.t.* **1** to swell out (a bag). **2** to push out of shape. **bulging** *a*. protuberant. **bulgingly** *adv*. **bulgy** *a*.

bulgur BULGAR.

bulimia (būlim′iə, bul′-), **bulimy** (bū′limi) *n*. (*Med.*) **1** a medical condition characterized by overeating. **2** bulimia nervosa. **bulimarexia** (-ərek′siə) *n*. (*esp. N Am.*) bulimia nervosa. **bulimarexic** *a.*, *n*. **bulimia nervosa** (nœvō′sə) *n*. an emotional disorder in which the sufferer alternately overeats and induces vomiting or purging. **bulimic** *a.*, *n*.

bulk (bŭlk) *n*. **1** magnitude of three dimensions. **2** size, great size, mass. **3** the greater portion, the main mass. **4** (*Naut.*) **a** cargo. **b** a ship's hold or hull. **5** anything of great size. **6** the trunk of the body, esp. if large. ~*v.i.* **1** to appear relatively big

or important. **2** to amount. ~*v.t.* **1** to pile in heaps. **2** to pack in bulk. **3** to make thicker or larger. **in bulk 1** (of cargo) loose in the hold. **2** in large quantities. **bulk buying** *n*. **1** the purchase of goods in large quantities in order to obtain cheaper prices. **2** the purchase by one customer of the whole of a producer's output. **bulk-buy** *v.t.* **bulky** *a*. (*comp.* **bulkier**, *superl.* **bulkiest**) **1** of great bulk or dimensions. **2** large. **bulkily** *adv*. **bulkiness** *n*.

bulkhead (bŭlk′hed) *n*. an upright partition dividing a ship, aircraft etc. into compartments.

bull[1] (bul) *n*. **1** the uncastrated male of any bovine mammal, esp. of the domestic species, *Bos taurus*. **2** the male of some other large animals, such as the elk, the elephant, the whale. **3** a person who speculates for a rise in stocks (see also BEAR[1]). **4** (**the Bull**) the constellation and sign Taurus. **5** a bull's-eye, a hit in the bull's-eye. **6** (*sl.*) rubbish, nonsense. ~*a*. **1** of large size. **2** thickset. **3** coarse. **4** male. ~*v.i.* to speculate for a rise (in stocks). ~*v.t.* to produce a rise in (stocks etc.). **to take the bull by the horns** to grapple with a difficulty boldly. **bull ant** *n*. BULLDOG ANT (under BULL[1]). **bull at a gate** *n*. a person who does something in a clumsy way. **bulldog** *n*. **1** a powerful breed of dogs formerly used to bait bulls. **2** a person who possesses obstinate courage. **bulldog ant** *n*. (*Austral.*) a large red or black Australian ant with a poisonous bite. **Bulldog clip** *n*. a metal spring clip for fastening papers together or on to a board. **bull-fiddle** *n*. (*N Am.*, *coll.*) a double bass. **bullfight** *n*. a Spanish sport in which a bull is baited and then killed. **bullfighter** *n*. **bullfighting** *n*. **bullfinch** *n*. a European songbird of the genus *Pyrrhula*, with handsome plumage. **bullfrog** *n*. a large American frog, *Rana catesbiana*, with a deep voice. **bullhead** *n*. the miller's thumb, a small river fish *Cottus gobio*, with a big head. **bull-headed** *a*. **1** with a massive head. **2** stupid. **3** obstinate, impetuous. **bull-headedly** *adv*. **bull-headedness** *n*. **bullhorn** *n*. a loudspeaker. **bull in a china shop** *n*. an indelicate or tactless person, a blunderer. **bullish** *a*. **1** resembling a bull. **2** obstinate. **3** on the Stock Exchange, optimistic. **bullishly** *adv*. **bullishness** *n*. **bull market** *n*. on the Stock Exchange, a market with rising prices, as distinct from *bear market*. **bull-nose, bull-nosed** *a*. (*attrib.*) having a rounded end. **bullock** (-ək) *n*. a castrated bull. **bullring** *n*. an arena for a bullfight. **bull session** *n*. (*N Am.*) an informal discussion, esp. between men. **bull's-eye** *n*. **1** the centre of a target. **2** something that achieves its aim. **3** a hard, peppermint-flavoured sweet. **4** a hemispherical disc of glass in the side or deck of a ship to give light below. **5** a small round window. **6** a hemispherical lens in a lantern. **7** a lantern with such a lens. **8** a boss of glass in the middle of a blown sheet. **bullshit** *n*. (*taboo sl.*) rubbish, deceptive nonsense. ~*v.i.* (*pres.p.* **bullshitting**, *past*, *p.p.* **bullshitted**) to talk rubbish, to attempt to deceive with nonsense.

~*v.t.* to talk nonsense to. **bullshitter** *n.* **bull terrier** *n.* a breed of dog that is a cross between a bulldog and a terrier. **bulltrout** *n.* a variety of sea trout, *Salmo trutta.*

bull² (bul) *n.* a papal edict.

bull³ (bul) *n.* **1** a ludicrous contradiction in terms, supposed to be characteristic of the Irish, an Irish bull. **2** (*sl.*) rubbish, deceptive nonsense. **3** (*N Am., sl.*) a bad blunder.

bullace (bul´əs) *n.* a wild plum, *Prunus insititia,* having two varieties, one with white, the other with dark fruit.

bulldoze (bul´dōz) *v.t.* **1** to level or clear (ground) using a bulldozer. **2** (*coll.*) to force or bully. **to bulldoze one's way** (*coll.*) to make one's way by force. **bulldozer** *n.* **1** a power-operated machine with a large blade, employed for removing obstacles, levelling ground and spreading material. **2** a person who bulldozes, a bully.

bullet (bul´it) *n.* **1** a metal ball or cone used in firearms of small calibre. **2** a small circle used at the start of a printed line, for emphasis. **to bite (on) the bullet 1** to submit to an unpleasant situation. **2** to face up to something. **bullet-head** *n.* **1** a round-shaped head. **2** (*esp. N Am.*) an obstinate person. **bullet-headed** *a.* **bullet-proof** *a.* impenetrable to bullets. **bullet train** *n.* a high-speed passenger train.

bulletin (bul´ətin) *n.* **1** an official report of some matter of public interest, e.g. of the condition of an invalid. **2** a brief news item on radio or television, a news bulletin. **3** a periodical publication of an organization, society etc. **bulletin board** *n.* **1** a noticeboard. **2** a system which allows computer users to leave messages and access information.

bullion (bul´yən) *n.* **1** uncoined gold and silver in the mass. **2** solid gold or silver.

bully¹ (bul´i) *n.* (*pl.* **bullies**) **1** a blustering, overbearing person. **2** a cowardly tyrant; a person who intimidates or hurts those who don't stand up for themselves. ~*a.* jolly, first-rate, capital. ~*v.t.* (*3rd pers. sing. pres.* **bullies,** *pres.p.* **bullying,** *past, p.p.* **bullied**) **1** to treat in a tyrannical manner. **2** to tease, oppress, terrorize. ~*v.i.* to act as a bully. **bully for you!** (*sometimes iron.*) well done! bravo! **bully boy** *n.* a thug, a hired ruffian.

bully² (bul´i), **bully beef** *n.* tinned beef.

bully³ (bul´i) *n.* (*pl.* **bullies**) (*also* **bully off**) in hockey, the starting of a game by striking sticks on the ground and then above the ball three times and then attempting to hit the ball. ~*v.i.* (*3rd pers. sing. pres.* **bullies,** *pres.p.* **bullying,** *past, p.p.* **bullied**) to start a game of hockey.

bullyrag BALLYRAG.

bully tree (bul´i) *n.* BALATA.

bulrush (bul´rush) *n.* **1** either of two tall rushes growing in water, *Scirpus lacustris* and *Typha latifolia,* the reed mace or cat's-tail. **2** (*Bible*) the papyrus.

bulwark (bul´wək) *n.* **1** a rampart or fortification. **2** a mole, a breakwater. **3** any shelter, protection,

screen. **4** that part of the sides of a ship which rises above the upper deck.

bum¹ (bŭm) *n.* (*sl.*) the buttocks. **bumbag** *n.* (*coll.*) a pouch, usu. fastened with a zip, for holding money and other small personal belongings, worn on a belt round the waist or hips. **bumboy** *n.* (*sl.*) a young male homosexual, esp. a prostitute. **bum fluff** *n.* (*sl.*) a young man's first beard growth. **bum-sucker** *n.* (*taboo sl.*) a toady. **bum-sucking** *n.*

bum² (bŭm) *n.* (*esp. N Am., coll.*) **1** a tramp. **2** an idler, a loafer. **3** a scrounger. ~*a.* **1** useless, broken. **2** worthless. ~*v.i.* (*pres.p.* **bumming,** *past, p.p.* **bummed**) **1** to live like a tramp. **2** to idle. **3** to scrounge. ~*v.t.* to acquire by scrounging. **on the bum** scrounging, begging. **bummer** *n.* (*esp. N Am., sl.*) **1** a person who or thing which bums. **2** an unpleasant experience. **bum rap** *n.* (*N Am., sl.*) a false charge. **bum's rush** *n.* (*N Am., sl.*) **1** (*preceded by the*) forcible ejection, as from a gathering. **2** (*preceded by the*) dismissal (of an idea or person). **bum steer** *n.* misleading information.

bumble (bŭm´bəl) *v.i.* **1** to buzz, to boom. **2** to bustle and blunder. **3** to grumble (at). ~*n.* **1** a jumble, a confused heap. **2** a blunderer, an idler. **bumble-bee** *n.* a large bee of the genus *Bombus.* **bumbler** *n.*

bumboat (bŭm´bōt) *n.* a boat used to carry provisions to vessels.

bumf (bŭmf), **bumph** *n.* (*sl.*) **1** toilet paper. **2** (*derog.*) official documents. **3** any unwanted paperwork.

bump (bŭmp) *n.* **1** a thump, a dull, heavy blow, an impact or collision. **2** a swelling. **3** (*Hist.*) a protuberance on the skull, said by phrenologists to indicate distinct faculties or affections. **4** a touch in a bumping race. **5** a sudden movement of an aircraft caused by currents. ~*v.t.* **1** to cause to strike forcibly against anything hard or solid. **2** to hurt by striking against something. **3** to hit (against). **4** in boat racing, to strike the boat in front with the prow of one's own boat. **5** (*N Am.*) to displace (esp. a passenger on a flight). ~*v.i.* **1** to strike heavily. **2** to collide. **3** to move along with a bump or succession of bumps. ~*adv.* **1** with a bump. **2** with a sudden shock. **the bumps** the act of lifting someone up by the arms and legs and dropping them down to the ground. **to bump into** to meet unexpectedly, to encounter accidentally. **to bump off** (*coll.*) to murder. **to bump up 1** to increase (prices). **2** to raise. **bumper** *n.* **1** a person or thing which bumps. **2** a glass filled to the brim, esp. for drinking a toast. **3** the fender of a motor vehicle. **4** a buffer. **5** (*coll.*) anything very large or wonderful or full. **6** in cricket, a bouncer. ~*a.* (*coll.*) **1** extraordinary, startling, fine. **2** full to the brim. **bumper car** *n.* a dodgem. **bump-start** *v.t.* **1** to start (a motor vehicle) by pushing it while engaging the gears. **2** to jump-start. ~*n.* **1** a push-start. **2** a jump-start. **bumpy** *a.* (*comp.* **bumpier,** *superl.* **bumpiest**) full of bumps, uneven, jolty. **bumpily** adv. **bumpiness** n.

bumph BUMF.

bumpkin (bŭmp´kin) n. **1** a country lout. **2** a clumsy, thickheaded person.

bumptious (bŭmp´shəs) a. disagreeably self-assertive or self-opinionated. **bumptiously** adv. **bumptiousness** n.

bun (bŭn) n. **1** a small sweet roll or cake. **2** a compact ball of hair worn at the back of the head. **3** (pl., N Am., sl.) the buttocks. **to have a bun in the oven** (sl.) to be pregnant. **bun fight** n. a crowded tea-party.

bunch (bŭnch) n. **1** a cluster of several things of the same kind growing or tied together. **2** a tuft, a knot, a bow. **3** a lot, a collection, a pack, a herd. ~v.t. **1** to tie up or form into a bunch. **2** to gather into folds. ~v.i. to come or grow into a cluster or bunch. **bunch grass** n. (N Am.) a clumped grass, esp. of the genus Poa or Festuca. **bunch of fives** n. a fist. **bunchy** a. (comp. **bunchier**, superl. **bunchiest**)

buncombe BUNKUM.

bundle (bŭn´dəl) n. **1** a number of things or a quantity of anything bound together loosely. **2** a package, a parcel. **3** a set of rods, wires, fibres, nerves etc., bound together. **4** a group of characteristics. **5** (sl.) a large amount of money, a bundle of bank notes. ~v.t. **1** to tie up in a bundle. **2** to throw hurriedly together. **3** to hustle. **4** (Comput.) to sell as a package. ~v.i. to prepare for departure, to pack up, to start hurriedly (in, off, away or out). **to bundle off 1** to send away hurriedly or unceremoniously. **2** to dismiss. **to bundle up 1** to gather into a bundle. **2** to clothe warmly. **to go a bundle on** (sl.) to like enormously. **bundle of nerves** n. (coll.) a very timid, anxious person. **bundler** n.

bung (bŭng) n. a large cork stopper for a bunghole. ~v.t. **1** to stop with a bung. **2** to close, to shut up. **3** (sl.) to throw, to sling. **bunged up** a. closed, blocked. **bung-hole** n. the hole in the bulge of a cask through which it is filled.

bungalow (bŭng´gəlō) n. a one-storeyed house.

bungee (bŭn´ji), **bungee cord, bungee rope** n. an elasticated cord. **bungee jumping** n. the sport of jumping off high places with a rubber rope tied round one's ankles or attached to a body harness, the rope stretching to break one's fall only a few feet above the ground. **bungee jump** n. **bungee jumper** n.

bungle (bŭng´gəl) v.t. **1** to botch. **2** to manage clumsily or awkwardly. ~v.i. **1** to act clumsily or awkwardly. **2** to fail in a task. ~n. **1** botching. **2** mismanagement. **bungler** n.

bunion (bŭn´yən) n. a swelling on the foot, esp. of the joint of the big toe.

bunk[1] (bŭngk) n. **1** a box or recess serving for a bed. **2** a sleeping berth. ~v.i. to sleep in a bunk. **bunk bed** n. either of a pair of narrow beds built one above the other. **bunker** n. **1** a container or bin usu. for coal or fuel, e.g. on a ship.

2 an underground bombproof shelter. **3** a sandy hollow or other obstruction on a golf course. ~v.t. **1** to fill with fuel. **2** to play into a bunker.

bunkhouse n. a building for labourers to sleep in.

bunk[2] (bŭngk) v.i. (sl.) to make off, to bolt. ~n. a bolt, a making off, an escape. **to bunk off** to play truant. **to do a bunk** to run away.

bunk[3] (bŭngk) n. BUNKUM.

bunkum (bŭng´kəm), **buncombe** n. **1** political claptrap. **2** tall talk, humbug.

bunny (bŭn´i) n. (pl. **bunnies**) **1** a rabbit (used by or to children). **2** (Austral., sl.) a dupe. **bunny girl** n. a waitress in a nightclub who wears a sexually provocative costume including rabbit ears and tail.

Bunsen burner (bŭn´sən), **Bunsen lamp** n. a burner or lamp in which air is mingled with gas to produce an intense flame.

bunt[1] (bŭnt) n. **1** the middle part of a sail, formed into a cavity to hold the wind. **2** the baggy part of a fishing net. **buntline** n. a rope passing from the foot-rope of a square sail in front of the canvas to prevent bellying.

bunt[2] (bŭnt) n. a fungus, Tilletia caries, which attacks wheat.

bunt[3] (bŭnt) v.t. (N Am.) in baseball, to hit (a ball) very gently. ~n. an instance of bunting.

buntal (bŭn´təl) n. straw obtained from the leaves of the talipot palm.

bunting[1] (bŭn´ting) n. a bird of the family Emberizidae, related to the finches.

bunting[2] (bŭn´ting) n. **1** a thin woollen material of which flags are made. **2** flags collectively (e.g. strung up as decoration).

bunya bunya (bŭnyə bŭn´yə), **bunya** n. (Austral.) a large conifer, Araucaria bidwilli, with edible seeds.

bunyip (bŭn´yip) n. (Austral.) **1** the fabulous rainbow serpent that lives in pools. **2** an impostor.

buoy (boi) n. **1** an anchored float indicating a fairway, reef, shoal etc. **2** a lifebuoy. ~v.t. to place a buoy upon, to mark with a buoy. **to buoy up 1** to keep afloat. **2** to bear up. **3** to bring to the surface. **buoyancy** (-ənsi) n. **1** the ability to float. **2** power of resisting or recovering from depression, elasticity. **3** lightheartedness. **4** tendency to rise (of stocks, prices etc.). **buoyancy aid** n. a sleeveless jacket lined with buoyant material. **buoyant** a. **1** tending to float. **2** tending to keep up. **3** elastic, light. **4** easily recovering from depression. **5** light-hearted. **buoyantly** adv.

bur (bœ), **burr** n. **1** any prickly or spinous fruit, calyx or involucre. **2** a person or thing hard to get rid of. **3** a small drill used by dentists and surgeons. **burdock** (-dŏk) n. a coarse plant with prickly flower heads, of the genus Arctium, esp. A. lappa. **bur oak** n. a N American oak, Quercus macrocarpa. **bur walnut** n. walnut wood containing knots, used as veneer.

burb (bœb) n. (usu. in pl., N Am., coll.) a suburb.

burble (bœ´bəl) v.i. **1** to talk inconsequentially or excitedly. **2** (of the airflow around a body) to become turbulent. ~n. **1** a murmuring noise. **2** excited speech. **burbler** n.

burbot (bœ´bət) n. an eel-like flat-headed freshwater fish, *Lota lota*.

burden (bœ´dən), †**burthen** (-dhən) n. **1** something borne or carried; a load. **2** a load of labour, sin, sorrow, care, obligation, duty, taxation, expense, fate etc. **3** the principal theme, the gist of a composition of any kind. **4** the carrying capacity of a vessel, tonnage. **5** a refrain, a chorus. ~v.t. **1** to load. **2** to lay a burden on. **3** to oppress, to encumber. **burden of proof** n. the obligation of proving a contention or assertion. **burdensome** a.

burdock BUR.

bureau (bū´rō) n. (pl. **bureaux** (-rōz), **bureaus**) **1** a writing table with drawers for papers. **2** (NAm.) a chest of drawers. **3** an office. **4** a public office. **5** a government department.

bureaucracy (būrok´rəsi) n. (pl. **bureaucracies**) **1** government by departments of state. **2** centralization of government. **3** officials as a body. **4** rigid adherence to procedure, inflexible government. **bureaucrat** (bū´rəkrat) n. **1** a government official. **2** a bureaucratic person. **bureaucratic** (-krat´-) a. **1** of, relating to or constituting a bureaucracy. **2** tending towards bureaucracy. **bureaucratically** adv. **bureaucratize** (-rok´rə-), **bureaucratise** v.t. to make into a bureaucracy. **bureaucratization** (-zā´shən) n.

burette (būret´), (NAm.) **buret** n. a graduated glass tube for measuring small quantities of liquid.

burg (bœg) n. (NAm., coll.) a town.

burgee (bœ´jē) n. a triangular or swallow-tailed flag.

burgeon (bœ´jən), **bourgeon** v.t. **1** to sprout, to bud. **2** to begin to grow or develop. ~n. (poet.) a bud, a shoot.

burger (bœ´gə) n. **1** a flat round cake of minced meat or vegetables which is grilled or fried, e.g. *hamburger*, *beefburger*. **2** a burger served in a bread roll or bun often with a topping, e.g. *cheeseburger*, *chilliburger*.

burgess (bœ´jis) n. **1** an inhabitant of a borough possessing full municipal rights, a citizen. **2** a freeman of a borough. **3** (Hist.) a Member of Parliament for a borough or a university. **4** (NAm.) a borough magistrate or governor.

burgh (bŭr´ə) n. **1** a Scottish town holding a charter. **2** (Hist.) a borough. **burghal** (bœ´gəl) a. **burgher** (bœ´gə) n. a citizen or inhabitant of a burgh, borough or corporate town, esp. of a Continental town.

burglar (bœ´glə) n. (Law) a person who breaks into premises with intent to commit a felony, esp. theft. **burglarious** (-gleə´ri-) a. **burglariously** adv. **burglarize, burglarise** v.t. (NAm.) to enter or rob burglariously. **burglary** n. (pl. **burglaries**). **burgle** (-gəl) v.i. to commit burglary. ~v.t. to commit burglary on.

burgomaster (bœ´gəmahstə) n. the chief magistrate of a municipal town in Austria, Germany, the Netherlands or Belgium.

burgrave (bœ´grāv) n. (Hist.) **1** the commandant of a castle or fortified town. **2** a hereditary noble ruling such a town and the adjacent domain.

burgundy (bœ´gəndi) n. (pl. **burgundies**) **1** red or white wine made in Burgundy, France. **2** a similar wine from another place. **3** the red colour of burgundy wine. ~a. of this colour.

burial (ber´iəl) n. **1** the act of burying, esp. of a dead body in the earth; interment. **2** a funeral with burying of the body. **burial ground, burial place** n. a place for burying the dead.

burin (bū´rin, byaw´-) n. **1** the cutting tool of an engraver on copper. **2** an early Stone Age flint tool.

burk BERK.

burka (bœ´kə) n. the long veil or veiled, loose overgarment worn by Muslim women.

burl (bœl) n. **1** a knot or lump in wool or cloth. **2** a knot in wood.

burlap (bœ´lap) n. **1** a coarse kind of canvas used for sacking, upholstering etc. **2** a similar, lighter material used for dressmaking and wallcoverings.

burlesque (bœlesk´) a. **1** drolly or absurdly imitative. **2** mock-serious or mock-heroic. ~n. **1** mockery, grotesque imitation. **2** literary or dramatic representation caricaturing other work. **3** (NAm.) a form of theatrical variety show characterized by lewd humour, singing and dancing and striptease. ~v.t. (pres.p. **burlesquing**, past, p.p. **burlesqued**) **1** to produce a grotesque imitation of. **2** to travesty. **burlesquely** adv. **burlesquer** n.

burly (bœ´li) a. (comp. **burlier**, superl. **burliest**) stout, lusty, corpulent. **burliness** n.

Burmese (bœmēz´) n. (pl. **Burmese**) **1** a native or inhabitant of Burma (Myanmar). **2** (as pl.) the people of Burma (Myanmar). **3** the language spoken by the people of Burma (Myanmar). ~a. of or relating to Burma (Myanmar). **Burman** (bœ´mən) n., a. **Burmese cat** n. a breed of shortcoated domestic cat, often dark-brown or blue-grey in colour.

burn¹ (bœn) v.t. (past, p.p. **burnt** (-t), **burned** (-d)) **1** to consume, destroy, scorch or injure by fire. **2** to subject to the action of fire. **3** to produce an effect on (anything) similar to the action of fire. **4** to treat with heat for some purpose of manufacture etc. **5** to corrode, eat into. **6** to combine with oxygen. **7** to make use of the nuclear energy of (uranium etc.). **8** to cauterize. **9** (NAm., sl.) to anger. ~v.i. **1** to be on fire. **2** to be or become intensely hot. **3** to emit light, to shine. **4** to act with destructive effect. **5** to be bright, to glow with light or colour. **6** to rage, to be inflamed. ~n. **1** the effect of burning. **2** a burnt place. **3** a firing of a space rocket engine to obtain thrust. **4** (N Am., Austral., New Zeal.) the clearing of vegetation by burning; an area cleared in this way. **5** (*sl.*) a cigarette. **6** (*sl.*) a car race. **to burn a hole in one's pocket** (of money) to cause one to want to spend it immediately. **to burn down** to reduce to ashes. **to burn in** to render indelible by or as by burning. **to burn one's boats/ bridges** to commit oneself to something without possibility of retreat. **to burn out 1** to consume the inside or contents of. **2** (*coll.*) to exhaust or render inoperative through overwork or overheating. **3** to eradicate or expel by burning. **to burn up 1** to destroy, to get rid of, by fire. **2** to blaze, to flash into a blaze. **3** (*coll.*) to drive fast. **4** (*N Am.,sl.*) to be furious or make furious. **burnable** *a.* **burned up** *a.* (*N Am., sl.*) angry. **burner** *n.* that part of a lamp or gas-jet from which the flame issues. **on the back burner** having low priority. **on the front burner** having high priority. **burning** *a.* **1** in a state of heat. **2** ardent, glowing. **3** vehement, exciting. **burning bush** *n. Dictamnus albus*, various species of *Euonymus*, and other shrubs with vivid foliage, fruit etc. (from the bush that burned and was not consumed in Exod. iii.2). **burning-glass** *n.* a convex lens used for causing intense heat by concentrating the sun's rays. **burningly** *adv.* **burn-out** *n.* **1** exhaustion. **2** depression or disillusionment. **burnt-out** *a.* physically or emotionally exhausted. **burnt ochre** *n.* the deep yellow or reddish-brown colour of roasted ochre. **burnt offering, burnt sacrifice** *n.* an offering or sacrifice to a deity by fire, esp. one offered to God by the Jews. **burnt sienna** *n.* the reddish-brown colour of roasted sienna. **burnt umber** *n.* **1** umber heated so as to produce a much redder brown. **2** the colour of this. **burn up** *n.* **1** (*coll.*) a fast drive in a motor vehicle. **2** the consumption of nuclear fuel in a reactor.

burn[2] (bœn) *n.* (*chiefly Sc.*) a small stream, a brook.

burnet (bœ´nit) *n.* a plant of the genus *Sanguisorba*, with pinkish flower heads. **burnet fly, burnet moth** *n.* a crimson-spotted, greenish-black moth of the family Zygaenidae. **burnet saxifrage** *n.* a plant, *Pimpinella saxifraga*, with leaves like burnet.

burnish (bœ´nish) *v.t.* to polish, esp. by rubbing. ~*v.i.* to become bright or glossy. **burnisher** *n.*

burnous (bənoos´), **burnouse** (-ooz´) *n.* a mantle or cloak with a hood, worn by Arabs.

burnt BURN[1].

burp (bœp) *n.* a belch. ~*v.i.* to belch. ~*v.t.* to make (a baby) burp by massaging or patting on the back. **burp gun** *n.* (*N Am.,sl.*) an automatic pistol or sub-machine gun.

burpee (bœ´pē) *n.* an exercise that consists of a squat thrust from standing position, and back to this position.

burr[1] (bœ), **bur** *n.* **1** a whirring noise. **2** a rough sounding of the letter *r*. **3** a rough ridge or edge left on metal or other substances after cutting, punching etc. **4** an electric rotary filing tool. **5** siliceous rock occurring in bands or masses among softer formations. **6** the round, knobby

base of a deer's horn. **7** the roughness made by the graver on a copper plate. **8** a triangular hollow chisel. **9** a clinker, a mass of semi-vitrified brick. ~*v.t.* to pronounce with a rough sounding of the *r*. ~*v.i.* **1** to speak with a burr. **2** to speak indistinctly. **3** to make a whirring noise.

burr[2] BUR.

burrawang (bŭr´əwang) *n.* (*Austral.*) **1** any of several palmlike trees of the genus *Macrozamia*. **2** a nut from these trees.

burrito (bərē´tō) *n.* (*pl.* **burritos**) a tortilla with a filling of beef, cheese, chicken or beans.

burro (bŭr´ō) *n.* (*pl.* **burros**) (*esp. N Am.*) a donkey.

burrow (bŭr´ō) *n.* a hole in the ground made by rabbits, foxes etc., for a dwelling-place. ~*v.i.* **1** to excavate a burrow for shelter or concealment. **2** to live in a burrow. **3** to hide oneself. **4** to bore or excavate. **5** to investigate (into). **6** to nestle (into). **7** to dig deep while searching (e.g. in a pocket). ~*v.t.* to make by means of excavation. **burrower** *n.*

bursa (bœ´sə) *n.* (*pl.* **bursas, bursae** (-sē)) (*Anat.*) a synovial sac found among tendons in the body and serving to reduce friction. **bursal** *a.* **bursitis** (-sī´tis) *n.* (*Med.*) inflammation of a bursa.

bursar (bœ´sə) *n.* **1** a treasurer, esp. of a college. **2** a person who holds a bursary. **bursarial** (-seə´riəl) *a.* **bursarship** *n.* **bursary** *n.* (*pl.* **bursaries**) **1** the treasury of a college or a monastery. **2** a scholarship.

burst (bœst) *v.t.* (*past, p.p.* **burst**) to break, split or rend asunder with suddenness and violence. ~*v.i.* **1** to be broken suddenly from within. **2** to fly open. **3** to issue or rush forth with suddenness and energy or force. ~*n.* **1** a sudden and violent breaking forth. **2** a sudden explosion. **3** an outbreak. **4** a spurt, a vigorous fit of activity. **5** a drinking-bout, a spree. **6** a volley of bullets. **to burst in 1** to enter suddenly. **2** to interrupt. **to burst out 1** to break out. **2** to exclaim. **burster** *n.* **burstproof** *a.* (of a door lock) able to withstand an impact.

Burton (bœ´tən) *n.* a beer from a brewery in Burton-on-Trent. **gone for a burton 1** (*sl.*) dead. **2** (*sl.*) absent, missing.

burton (bœ´tən), **barton** (bah´-), **burton-tackle** *n.* a small tackle consisting of two or three pulleys.

bury (ber´i) *v.t.* (*3rd. pers. sing. pres.* **buries**, *pres.p.* **burying**, *past, p.p.* **buried**) **1** to place (a corpse) under ground, to inter, to consign to the grave (whether earth or sea). **2** to perform funeral rites for. **3** to put under ground. **4** to consign to obscurity, oblivion etc. **5** to hide, to cover up, to embed. **to bury one's head in the sand** to ignore the facts. **buried** *a.* **1** that has been buried. **2** occupied deeply, engrossed, absorbed. **burying** *n.* burial. **burying beetle** *n.* a sexton beetle. **burying ground, burying place** *n.* BURIAL GROUND (under BURIAL).

bus (bŭs), **'bus** *n.* (*pl.* **buses**, (*N Am.*) **busses**) **1** a large passenger vehicle for transporting members of the public, hotel guests, employees etc., usu. on a set route. **2** (*coll.*) an aeroplane, car etc. **3** (*Comput.*) a series of conductors in a computer which carry information or power. ~*v.i.* (*3rd pers. sing. pres.* **buses**, (*N Am.*) **busses**, *pres.p.* **bussing**, *past, p.p.* **bussed**) to go by bus. ~*v.t.* **1** to transport by bus. **2** (*N Am.*) to carry or clear away (dishes) in a café or restaurant. **busbar** *n.* **1** in an electric system, a conductor or series of conductors connecting several circuits. **2** (*Comput.*) a bus. **busboy, busgirl** *n.* (*N Am.*) a restaurant employee who clears tables etc. **bus lane** *n.* a traffic lane restricted to the use of buses (i.e. the lane closest to the verge or pavement). **busman** (-mən) *n.* (*pl.* **busmen**) the conductor or driver of a bus. **busman's holiday** *n.* (*coll.*) a holiday spent doing one's everyday work. **bus shelter** *n.* a shelter erected at a bus stop to protect waiting passengers against the weather. **bus station** *n.* the place in a town where buses or coaches arrive and leave from. **bus stop** *n.* a place marked by a sign at which buses stop to pick up or let off passengers.

busby (bŭz′bi) *n.* (*pl.* **busbies**) **1** the tall fur cap worn by hussars. **2** a bearskin hat worn by the Guards.

bush[1] (bush) *n.* **1** a thick shrub. **2** a clump of shrubs. **3** a thicket. **4** (*Hist.*) a bunch of ivy used as a tavern sign. **5** uncleared land, more or less covered with wood, esp. in Australasia. **6** anything resembling a bush. **7** the hinterland, the interior, the wild. **8** a thick growth of hair. ~*v.t.* **1** to set with bushes in order to prevent poaching. **2** to cover or decorate with bushes. ~*v.i.* to grow bushy. **to go bush** (*Austral.*) to go into the bush; to leave civilization. **bushbaby** *n.* (*pl.* **bushbabies**) a small nocturnal African primate of the family Lorisidae; a galago. **bush basil** *n.* a herb, *Ocimum minimum*, used in cooking. **bushbuck** *n.* a small bush-dwelling African antelope, *Tragelaphus scriptus*. **bushcat** *n.* the serval. **bushed** *a.* **1** (*Austral., New Zeal.*) lost in the bush. **2** (*sl.*) confused. **3** (*sl.*) exhausted. **bushfire** *n.* a usu. fast-spreading fire in the bush. **bush jacket, bush shirt** *n.* a belted upper garment of a lightweight material equipped with large pockets. **bush lawyer** *n.* **1** (*Austral., New Zeal.*) an irregular legal practitioner. **2** (*New Zeal.*) a bramble. **bush league** *n.* (*N Am.*) a minor league. ~*a.* (*attrib., coll.*) inferior, unsophisticated. **bushleaguer** *n.* **bushman** *n.* (*pl.* **bushmen**) **1** a person who lives in the Australian bush. **2** (**Bushman**) a member of a disappearing nomadic people in S Africa. **3** the language of the Bushmen. **bushmaster** *n.* a large venomous snake of tropical America, *Lachesis muta*. **bushranger** *n.* (*Hist.*) a person who has taken to the Australian bush and lives by robbing travellers etc. **bush sickness** *n.* a disease of animals caused by a mineral deficiency in old bush country. **bush telegraph** *n.* the rapid dissemination of rumours, information etc. **bushveld, bosveld, boschveld** *n.* wooded

S African grasslands. **bushwhack** *v.i.* **1** (*N Am., Austral., New Zeal.*) to clear bush. **2** to live or travel in the bush. ~*v.t.* (*N Am.*) to ambush. **bushwhacker** *n.* **1** (*N Am.*) a backwoodsman. **2** a person who clears woods and bush country. **3** (*Austral.*) an inhabitant of the outback, a country bumpkin. **4** (*N Am.*) a guerrilla fighter. **bushy** *a.* (*comp.* **bushier**, *superl.* **bushiest**) **1** abounding with bushes. **2** shrubby, thick. **3** growing like a bush. ~*n.* (*pl.* **bushies**) (*Austral., New Zeal., coll.*) a person who lives in the bush. **bushily** *adv.* **bushiness** *n.*

bush[2] (bush) *n.* (*also* **bushing**) the metal lining of an axle-hole or similar orifice. ~*v.t.* to furnish with a bush.

bushel (bush′əl) *n.* **1** a dry measure of 8 gal. (36.37 litres). **2** (*N Am.*) a measure of 64 US pints (35.24 litres) used for dry goods. **to hide one's light under a bushel** to conceal one's skills or talents. **bushelful** *n.* (*pl.* **bushelfuls**).

bushido (bushē′dō) *n.* the code of honour of the Japanese samurai.

busily BUSY.

business (biz′nis) *n.* **1** employment, occupation, trade, profession. **2** serious occupation, work. **3** duty, concern, province. **4** a particular matter demanding attention. **5** (*coll., often derog.*) an affair, a matter, a concern, a contrivance. **6** commercial, industrial or professional affairs. **7** commercial activity. **8** buying and selling, bargaining. **9** a commercial establishment. **10** a shop, with stock, fixtures etc. **11** in the theatre, action, as distinct from speech. **on business** with a particular (esp. work-related) purpose. **the business** (*coll.*) exactly what is needed. **to have no business** to have no right to. **to make it one's business** to undertake to do something. **to mean business** to be in earnest. **to mind one's own business 1** to attend to one's own affairs. **2** to refrain from meddling. **to send someone about their business** to send someone off brusquely or summarily. **business card** *n.* a card printed with a company's name, address and phone number, and the identity of the employee or executive who carries it. **business end** *n.* (*coll.*) the point (of a tool or weapon). **businesslike** *a.* **1** suitable for or befitting business. **2** methodical, practical. **3** prompt, punctual. **4** energetic. **businessman** (-mən), **businesswoman** *n.* (*pl.* **businessmen**, **businesswomen**) a person who deals with matters of commerce etc., a person who runs a business. **business park** *n.* an area where businesses and light industry are accommodated. **business person** *n.* a businessman or businesswoman. **business studies** *n.pl.* a college or university course comprising courses relating to business. **business suit** *n.* a lounge suit.

busk (bŭsk) *v.i.* to perform in the street or in a public place, esp. beside a queue in order to collect money. **busker** *n.* **busking** *n.*

buskin (bŭs′kin) *n.* **1** (*Hist.*) a kind of high boot reaching to the calf or knee. **2** the thick-soled boot worn by actors in Athenian tragedy. **3** the tragic vein. **4** tragedy. **buskined** *a*.

buss (bŭs) *n.* (*esp. N Am., coll.*) a loud kiss. ~*v.t.* to kiss.

bust[1] (bŭst) *n.* **1** a sculptured representation of the head, shoulders and breast of a person. **2** the upper front part of the body, the breast, the bosom, esp. of a woman. **busty** *a.* (*comp.* **bustier**, *superl.* **bustiest**) (*coll.*) having large breasts. **bustiness** *n*.

bust[2] (bŭst) *v.i.* (*past, p.p.* **busted, bust**) (*coll.*) to break or burst. ~*v.t.* **1** (*sl.*) to raid or arrest, esp. for a drug offence. **2** (*esp. N Am.*) to reduce to a lower rank; to dismiss. ~*n.* **1** (*sl.*) a drinking spree. **2** a police raid. **3** a bankruptcy. **4** (*esp. N Am.*) a punch or hit. **5** a worthless thing. **6** a bad hand in a card game. ~*a.* **1** broken, burst. **2** (*also* **busted**) bankrupt. **to bust up 1** to quarrel and separate. **2** to bring or come to collapse. **buster** *n.* **1** something big, something astonishing. **2** (*Austral.*) a gale. **3** (*coll., sometimes derog.*) a form of address to a boy or man. **bust-up** *n.* **1** a quarrel. **2** a collapse.

bustard (bŭs´təd) *n.* any large bird of the family Otididae, allied to the plovers and the cranes.

bustier (bŭs´tiā, bus´-) *n.* a strapless bodice.

bustle[1] (bŭs´əl) *n.* **1** activity with noise and excitement. **2** stir, agitation, fuss. ~*v.i.* **1** to be active, esp. with excessive fuss and noise. **2** to make a show of activity. ~*v.t.* to make hurry; to hustle, to cause to move quickly or work hard. **bustler** *n*.

bustle[2] (bŭs´əl) *n.* (*Hist.*) a pad, cushion or framework, worn under a woman's dress to expand the skirts behind.

busy (biz´i) *a.* (*comp.* **busier**, *superl.* **busiest**) **1** fully occupied. **2** actively employed. **3** characterized by activity, unresting, always at work. **4** fussy, officious, meddlesome. **5** (of a phone line) engaged. ~*v.i.* (*3rd pers. sing. pres.* **busies**, *pres.p.* **busying**, *past, p.p.* **busied**) to occupy oneself (about, in etc.). ~*v.t.* to make or keep busy. ~*n.* (*pl.* **busies**) (*sl.*) a detective; a police officer. **busily** *adv.* **busy bee** *n.* a busy worker. **busybody** *n.* (*pl.* **busybodies**) **1** an officious person. **2** a meddler. **3** a mischief-maker. **busy Lizzie** (liz´i) *n.* a popular flowering house plant, *Impatiens walleriana*, with red, pink or white flowers. **busyness** *n*.

but (bŭt) *prep.* except, barring. ~*conj.* **1** yet still. **2** notwithstanding which. **3** except that. **4** otherwise than, not that. **5** on the contrary, nevertheless, however. ~*n.* a verbal objection. ~*adv.* **1** only. **2** (*Austral., New Zeal., Sc.*) though, however. ~*v.t.* to raise as an objection. **but for** were it not for. **but that** were it not that. **but yet** however, on the other hand.

butane (bū´tān) *n.* (*Chem.*) an inflammable gaseous compound; a hydrocarbon of the paraffin series found in petroleum.

butch (buch) *a.* (*sl.*) masculine in manner or appearance. ~*n.* (*derog.*) **1** a lesbian with masculine

manners or appearance. **2** a tough, aggressive man.

butcher (buch´ə) *n.* **1** a person whose trade it is to slaughter domestic animals for food. **2** a person who sells the flesh of such animals. **3** a person who delights in killing. **4** (*used possessively, sl.*) a look (rhyming slang, *butcher's hook*). ~*v.t.* **1** to slaughter (animals) for food. **2** to put to death in a wanton or sanguinary fashion. **3** to spoil by bad playing, acting, reading, editing etc. **4** to criticize savagely. **butcher-bird** *n.* **1** a shrike (family Laniidae). **2** a similar bird of the Australasian family Cracticidae. **butcher meat, butcher's meat** *n.* the flesh of animals killed for food, sold fresh by butchers. **butcher's broom** *n.* a prickly, evergreen British shrub, *Ruscus aculeatus*. **butchery** *n.* (*pl.* **butcheries**) **1** the business of a butcher. **2** a slaughterhouse. **3** cruel and remorseless slaughter, carnage.

butler (bŭt´lə) *n.* **1** a servant in charge of the wine, plate etc. **2** a head servant. **butlership** *n*. **buttle** (bŭt´əl), **butle** *v.i.* (*facet.*) to work as a butler.

butt[1] (bŭt) *n.* **1** the hinder, larger or blunter end of anything, esp. of a tool, weapon and the like. **2** the square end of a piece of timber coming against another piece. **3** the bole of a tree. **4** (*N Am., sl.*) the buttocks. ~*v.i.* **1** (of timber, planks etc.) to abut, to meet with the end (against). **2** to meet end to end. **butt-end** *n.* **1** the thick and heavy end. **2** the remnant. **butt weld** *n.* a weld formed by forcing together flat iron or steel bars.

butt[2] (bŭt) *n.* **1** a large cask. **2** a measure of 126 gall. (572.8 litres) of wine, or 108 gall. (490.98 litres) of beer.

butt[3] (bŭt) *n.* **1** a goal. **2** a target, a mark for shooting. **3** the mound behind targets, the shelter for the marker. **4** (*pl.*) the distance between the targets, the shooting-range. **5** aim, object. **6** a target for ridicule, criticism or abuse.

butt[4] (bŭt) *v.i.* to strike, thrust or push with the head or as with the head. ~*v.t.* to strike or drive away with or as with the head or horns. ~*n.* a push with the head. **to butt in** to interfere, interrupt. **to butt out 1** (*esp. N Am., sl.*) to stop interfering. **2** (*N Am., sl.*) to stop doing something.

butte (būt) *n.* (*N Am.*) an abrupt, isolated hill or peak.

butter (bŭt´ə) *n.* **1** the fatty portion of milk or cream solidified by churning. **2** a substance of the consistency or appearance of butter. **3** gross flattery. ~*v.t.* **1** to spread or cook with butter. **2** to flatter grossly. **to butter up** (*coll.*) to flatter. **to look as if butter wouldn't melt in one's mouth** to look innocent. **butter-and-eggs** *n.* any of several plants with two shades of yellow in the flower, esp. yellow toadflax. **butterball** *n.* **1** a piece of butter shaped into a ball. **2** (*N Am., sl.*) a chubby or fat person. **butter-bean** *n.* **1** a variety of lima bean. **2** a yellow-podded bean. **butter bur, butter burdock** *n.* a plant of the genus *Petasites*, which has large soft leaves. **butter-cream** *n.* a mixture of butter and sugar used as icing or cake-filling. **buttercup** *n.* a plant of the genus *Ranunculus*, esp. those species with yellow cup-shaped flowers. **butterfat** *n.* the fat in milk from which butter is made. **butter-fingered** *a.* apt to let things fall, as if the hands were greasy. **butter-fingers** *n.* (*coll.*) a person who is butter-fingered. **butter-icing** *n.* butter-cream. **butter knife** *n.* a small knife with a rounded blade for cutting butter. **buttermilk** *n.* that part of the milk which remains when the butter is extracted. **butter muslin** *n.* a fine loosely woven, cotton material used for protecting food from insects. **butternut** *n.* 1 the N American white walnut tree, *Juglans cinerea*, and its fruit. 2 the S American genus *Caryocar*. **butterscotch** *n.* a kind of toffee made with butter. **butterwort** *n.* a British bog plant belonging to the genus *Pinguicula*, esp. *P. vulgaris*. **buttery**[1] *a.* having the qualities or appearance of butter. **butteriness** *n.*

butterfly (bŭt´əflī) *n.* (*pl.* **butterflies**) 1 an insect with erect wings and knobbed antennae belonging to the diurnal Lepidoptera. 2 a showily dressed, vain, giddy or fickle person. 3 (*in full* **butterfly stroke**) a swimming stroke performed on the front and characterized by simultaneous wide, upward strokes of the arms. 4 (*pl.*, *coll.*) nervous tremors. **butterfly bush** *n.* a buddleia, esp. *Buddleia davidii*. **butterfly fish** *n.* a fish resembling a butterfly, esp. *Blennius ocellatus*, or any brightly coloured fish of the family Chaetodontidae. **butterfly net** *n.* a fine net attached to a pole, used for catching butterflies. **butterfly nut, butterfly screw** *n.* a screw with a thumb-piece, a wing nut. **butterfly valve** *n.* a valve with two hinged pieces.

buttery[1] BUTTER.

buttery[2] (bŭt´əri) *n.* (*pl.* **butteries**) a room in which liquor and provisions are kept.

buttie BUTTY.

buttle BUTLER.

buttock (bŭt´ək) *n.* (*usu. in pl.*) either of the protuberant parts of the rump, the posterior.

button (bŭt´ən) *n.* 1 a knob or disc used for fastening or ornamenting garments. 2 a small bud. 3 a small handle, knob, fastener, catch etc. for securing doors, actuating electrical apparatus etc. 4 the knob on a foil. 5 a small disc-shaped object. ~*a.* (of mushrooms, blooms etc.) having a small round shape. ~*v.t.* 1 to fasten or furnish with buttons. 2 to secure by means of buttons or a buttoned garment. ~*v.i.* to fasten up the clothes with buttons. **not to care a button** to be quite indifferent about something. **not worth a button** of no value. **on the button** (*esp. N Am.*, *sl.*) precisely. **to button one's lip** (*sl.*) to stay silent. **button-back** *n.* a chair or sofa with a quilted back set with buttons. **buttonball tree** *n.* the N American plane tree, *Platanus occidentalis*. **button-down** *a.* (of a collar) with points buttoned to the shirt. **buttoned** *a.* **buttoned up 1** (*coll.*) formal

and inhibited. 2 (*coll.*) silent. **buttonhole** *n.* 1 a hole, slit or loop to admit a button. 2 a small bouquet for the buttonhole of a coat. ~*v.t.* 1 to hold by the buttonhole. 2 to detain in conversation. 3 to make buttonholes in. **buttonholer** *n.* **buttonhole stitch** *n.* a looped stitch used on buttonholes. **buttonhook** *n.* a hook for drawing buttons through buttonholes. **buttons** *n.* (*coll.*) a page in buttoned livery. **button-through** *a.* (of a garment) having button fastenings from top to bottom. **buttonwood tree** *n.* BUTTONBALL TREE (under BUTTON). **buttony** *a.*

buttress (bŭt´ris) *n.* 1 a structure built against a wall to strengthen it. 2 a prop, support. 3 a spur or supporting ridge of a hill. ~*v.t.* to support by or as by a buttress.

butty (bŭt´i), **buttie** *n.* (*pl.* **butties**) (*dial.*) a sandwich, a snack.

butyl (bū´tĭl, -til) *n.* (*Chem.*) any of four isomeric forms of the chemical group C_4H_9. **butyl rubber** *n.* a synthetic rubber used in tyres and as a waterproofing material.

butyraceous (būtirā´shəs) *a.* of the nature or consistency of butter. **butyrate** (bū´tirət) *n.* a salt of butyric acid. **butyric** (-tir´-) *a.* of or relating to butter. **butyric acid** *n.* (*Chem.*) a colourless acid occurring in butter and other fats.

buxom (bŭk´səm) *a.* 1 (of women) plump and comely. 2 (of women) full-bosomed. **buxomness** *n.*

buy (bī) *v.t.* (*past, p.p.* **bought** (bawt)) 1 to purchase, to procure by means of money or something paid as a price. 2 to gain by bribery. 3 to redeem. 4 (*sl.*) to believe. ~*n.* (*coll.*) a purchase. **to buy in 1** to buy back for the owner (at an auction). 2 to obtain a stock of (anything) by purchase. 3 to purchase (stock) and charge the extra cost to the person who had undertaken to deliver it. **to buy into** to purchase a share of or interest in (e.g. a company). **to buy it** (*sl.*) to be killed. **to buy off 1** to pay a price to, for release or non-opposition. 2 to get rid of by a payment. **to buy out 1** to purchase the release of (a member of the forces) from service. 2 to buy a majority share in or complete control over (e.g. a property, a company), thereby dispossessing the original owner(s). 3 to buy off. **to buy over** to bribe. **to buy time** to delay something. **to buy up** to purchase all the available stock of (e.g. a company). **buyable** *a.* **buy-back** *n.* the buying back of something by agreement. **buyer** *n.* a person who buys, esp. one who buys stock for a mercantile house. **buyer's market, buyers' market** *n.* a market favourable to buyers, i.e. when supply exceeds demand. **buy-in** *n.* an act of buying something in. **buyout** *n.* an act of buying somebody or something out.

buzz (bŭz) *n.* 1 a sibilant hum, like that of a bee. 2 a confused, mingled noise. 3 stir, bustle, movement. 4 (*coll.*) report, rumour. 5 (*sl.*) a telephone call. 6 (*sl.*) a euphoric feeling, a boost. ~*v.i.* 1 to make a noise like humming or whirring. 2 to whisper, to circulate a rumour. 3 to signal by electric buzzer. ~*v.t.* **1** to tell in a low whisper. **2** to spread abroad secretly. **3** (*coll.*) in aviation, to interfere with by flying very near to. **4** to make a telephone call to. **5** to signal with a buzzer. **6** (*coll.*) to throw with some violence. **to buzz about** to hover or bustle about in an annoying manner. **buzzer** *n.* **1** an apparatus for making a loud humming noise. **2** an electric warning apparatus that makes a buzzing sound. **buzz off** *int.* (*sl.*) go away! **buzz-saw** *n.* (*NAm.*) a circular saw. **buzzword** *n.* (*sl.*) a vogue word adopted from the jargon of a particular subject or discipline.

buzzard (bŭz´əd) *n.* **1** a bird of prey, esp. of the genus *Buteo*. **2** (*NAm.*) a vulture, esp. the turkey buzzard *Cathartes aura.*

BVM *abbr. Beata Virgo Maria*, Blessed Virgin Mary.

b/w *abbr.* black and white.

bwana (bwah´nə) *n.* (in Africa) sir, master.

BWR *abbr.* boiling water reactor.

by (bī) *prep.* **1** near, at, in the neighbourhood of, beside, along, through, via. **2** with, through (as author, maker, means, cause). **3** according to, by direction, authority or example of. **4** in the ratio of. **5** to the amount of. **6** during, not later than, as soon as. **7** concerning, with regard to. **8** sired by. ~*adv.* **1** near at hand. **2** in the same place. **3** aside, in reserve. **4** past. ~*a.* **1** side, subordinate, secondary, of minor importance. **2** private, secret, clandestine, sly. ~*n.* (*pl.* **byes**) BYE¹. **by and by 1** soon, presently. **2** later on. **3** (*NAm.*) the future, time to come. **by and large** on the whole. **by oneself 1** alone, without help. **2** of one's own initiative. **by the by/bye** by the way. **by the way** casually, apart from the main subject. **by-** *pref.* **1** (*also* **bye-**) subordinate, secondary. **2** near. **by-blow** *n.* **1** a side blow. **2** the illegitimate child of a man. **by-election** *n.* an election caused by the death or resignation of a member. **bygone** *a.* past. ~*n.* **1** a past event. **2** (*pl.*) the past. **3** (*pl.*) past injuries. **byline** *n.* **1** a sideline. **2** the name of the author of a newspaper or magazine article printed beside it. **3** in football, a touchline. **byname** *n.* a nickname. **bypass** *n.* **1** a road for the purpose of diverting traffic from crowded areas. **2** a pipe passing round a tap or valve, so as to leave a gas burner etc. alight. **3** a passage that allows blood to avoid blocked or damaged arteries. ~*v.t.* **1** to avoid, evade. **2** to go around. **3** to supply with a bypass. **bypath** *n.* **1** a private or unfrequented path. **2** an obscure branch of a subject. **byplay** *n.* action carried on aside while the main action is proceeding. **by-product** *n.* **1** a secondary product. **2** a secondary result. **byroad** *n.* a road little frequented. **bystander** *n.* **1** a person standing near. **2** an onlooker, an eyewitness. **byway** *n.* a bypath. **byword** *n.* **1** a person or thing noted for a particular characteristic. **2** a common saying. **3** a proverb.

bye¹ (bī) *n.* **1** in cricket, a run scored when the ball passes the batsman and wicket-keeper. **2** in golf, holes left over after the end of contest and played as a new game. **3** an individual left without a competitor when the rest have been drawn in pairs, an odd man. **4** the case of being odd man.

bye² (bī), **bye-bye** (-bī´) *int.* (*coll.*) goodbye.

bye-byes (bī´bīz) *n.* sleep, bedtime, bed (used by or to children).

Byelorussian BELORUSSIAN.

by-law (bī´law), **bye-law** *n.* **1** a private statute made by the members of a corporation or local authority. **2** a rule adopted by an incorporated or other society.

BYOB *abbr.* bring your own bottle.

byre (bīə) *n.* a cowshed.

byssus (bis´əs) *n.* (*pl.* **byssuses, byssi** (-ī)) **1** a textile fabric of various substances. **2** the tuft of fibres by which molluscs of the genus *Pinna* attach themselves to other bodies. **byssinosis** (-inō´sis) *n.* (*Med.*) a lung disease contracted by cotton workers.

byte (bīt) *n.* (*Comput.*) a series of usu. eight binary digits treated as a unit.

Byzantine (bīzan´tīn, biz´əntīn, -tēn) *a.* **1** of or relating to Byzantium or Istanbul (formerly Constantinople). **2** hierarchical, inflexible. **3** convoluted, complex. **4** (*Archit.*) belonging to the style of architecture developed in the Eastern Empire, characterized by the round arch, the circle, the dome and ornamentation in mosaic. ~*n.* an inhabitant of Byzantium. **Byzantinism** *n.* **Byzantinist** *n.* a specialist in Byzantine history, arts etc.

C

C¹ (sē), **c** (*pl.* **Cs, C's**) the third letter of the English and other versions of the Roman alphabet. Before *a, o, u, l* and *r* it is pronounced as a voiceless velar plosive like *k*, and before *e, i* and *y* like the voiceless dental fricative or soft sibilant *s* (when it has this sound before other letters it is marked *ç* in some other European alphabets). ~*symbol* **1** the third in a range of series, the third highest in the range, e.g. of marks, etc. **2** (*Math.*) the third known quantity in an algebraic expression. **3** (*Mus.*) the first note of a diatonic scale in a composition where the keynote is C; the natural major mode. **4** 100 in Roman numerals.

C² *abbr.* **1** capacitance. **2** Cape. **3** Celsius, Centigrade. **4** century. **5** Conservative. **6** (*also* ©) copyright. **7** coulomb.

C³ *chem. symbol* carbon.

c *abbr.* **1** caught. **2** cent. **3** centi-. **4** century. **5** chapter. **6** cold. **7** colt. **8** cubic.

c., ca. *abbr.* about.

c/- *abbr.* (*Austral., New Zeal.*) care of.

Ca *chem. symbol* calcium.

cab (kab) *n.* **1** a taxi. **2** the driver's compartment in a lorry, crane or locomotive. **3** a public, covered, horse-drawn carriage with two or four wheels. **cabbie, cabby** *n.* (*pl.* **cabbies**) (*coll.*) a cab-driver. **cabman** *n.* (*pl.* **cabmen**) the driver of a horse-drawn cab.

cabal (kəbal´) *n.* **1** a small body of persons closely united for some secret purpose; a junta, a clique. **2** a plot, a conspiracy. **3** the five ministers of Charles II who signed the Treaty of Alliance in 1672, the initials of whose names (Clifford, Ashley, Buckingham, Arlington and Lauderdale) happened to form the word *cabal*.

cabala CABBALA.

cabana (kəbah´nə) *n.* (*esp. N Am.*) a small hut, cabin or tent on the beach or at a swimming-pool, used for changing by bathers.

cabaret (kab´ərā) *n.* **1** an entertainment or floor show consisting of singing, dancing etc. **2** a restaurant or nightclub where such entertainment is provided.

cabbage (kab´ij) *n.* **1** any of the plain-leaved, hearted varieties of *Brassica oleracea.* **2** the terminal bud of some palm trees. **3** (*coll., derog.*) an inert or apathetic person. **cabbage butterfly** *n.* either of two species of butterfly, *Pieris brassicae* or *P. rapae*, the larvae of which cause injury to cabbages. **cabbage rose** *n.* a double red rose, *Rosa centifolia*, with large, compact flowers. **cabbage tree** *n.* a palm tree with an edible terminal bud. **cabbage white** *n.* the cabbage butterfly. **cabbagy** *a.*

cabbala (kəbah´lə), **cabala, kabala, kabbala** *n.* **1** a traditional exposition of the Pentateuch attributed to Moses. **2** mystic or esoteric doctrine. **cabbalism** (kab´ə-) *n.* **cabbalist** (kab´ə-) *n.* **cabbalistic** (kabəlist´-), **cabbalistical** *a.*

caber (kā´bə) *n.* a pole, the roughly-trimmed stem of a young tree, used in the Highland sport of tossing the caber.

cabin (kab´in) *n.* **1** a small hut or house. **2** a temporary shelter. **3** a room or compartment in a ship or aircraft for officers or passengers. **4** a driver's cab. ~*v.i.* (*pres. p.* **cabining**, *past, p.p.* **cabined**) to live in a cabin. ~*v.t.* to shelter or confine in or as in a cabin. **cabin boy** *n.* a boy who waits on the officers or passengers of a ship. **cabin crew** *n.* the crew in an aircraft responsible for looking after passengers. **cabin cruiser** *n.* a motor-boat with living accommodation.

cabinet (kab´init) *n.* **1** a piece of furniture with drawers, shelves etc., in which to keep or display curiosities or articles of value. **2** an outer case for a television set etc. **3** (*also* **Cabinet**) a deliberative committee of the principal members of government. **4** the advisory council of a sovereign, president etc. **cabinetmaker** *n.* a person who makes household furniture of fine quality. **cabinetmaking** *n.* **cabinet minister, Cabinet minister** *n.* a member of a cabinet. **cabinetry** *n.*

cable (kā´bəl) *n.* **1** a strong, thick rope of hemp or wire. **2** (*Naut.*) **a** the rope or chain to which an anchor is fastened. **b** a nautical unit of length, about 202 yds. (185 m) or one-tenth of a nautical mile. **3** a wire or bundle of wires insulated and in a sheath, used to conduct electricity. **4** (*Archit.*) a cable-like moulding. **5** a cablegram. **6** cable television. **7** cable stitch. ~*v.t.* **1** to send (a message) by cable. **2** to inform by cablegram. **3** to fasten with a cable. **4** to fill (the lower part of the flutings in a column) with convex mouldings. **cable car** *n.* **1** a passenger cabin suspended from an overhead cable and moved by it, esp. up and down a mountain. **2** a carriage on a funicular railway. **cablegram** *n.* a telegraphic message by submarine cable, communications satellite etc. **cable-laid** *a.* (of a rope) having three strands twisted like a cable. **cable railway** *n.* a funicular railway. **cable release** *n.* in photography, a cable that can be used to operate the shutter of a camera, to avoid the risk of camera movement while the shutter is open.

cable stitch *n.* a series of stitches in knitting that produces a pattern resembling twisted rope.

cable television *n.* a television service transmitted by an underground cable connected to subscribers' television sets. **cableway** *n.* a transport system for freight or passengers using containers or cable cars suspended from overhead cables.

cabochon (kab´əshon) *n.* a precious stone polished, and having the rough parts removed, but without facets.

caboodle (kəboo´dəl) *n.* (*coll.*) crowd, lot. **the whole caboodle** the whole lot.

caboose (kəboos´) *n.* **1** the cook's house or galley on a ship. **2** (*N Am.*) the guard's van in a goods train. **3** (*N Am.*) a car on a train for the use of workmen or crew.

cabriole (kab´riōl) *a.* (of table and chair legs) shaped in a reflex curve. ~*n.* in ballet, a leap in which one leg is stretched out and the other is struck against it.

cabriolet (kabriōlā´, kab´-) *n.* **1** a covered, horse-drawn carriage with two wheels. **2** a type of motor-car with a folding top.

cacao (kəkah´ō, -kā´ō) *n.* a tropical American tree, *Theobroma cacao*, from the seeds of which chocolate and cocoa are prepared.

cachalot (kaṣh´əlot, -lō) *n.* a member of a genus of whales having teeth in the lower jaw, esp. the sperm whale.

cache (kash) *n.* **1** a place in which provisions, arms, treasure etc. are hidden. **2** the hidden provisions, arms, treasure etc. ~*v.t.* to hide or conceal in a cache. **cache memory** *n.* (*Comput.*) a memory store from which data can be retrieved at very high speed. **cachepot** (kash´pō) *n.* an ornamental holder for a plant-pot.

cachet (kash´ā) *n.* **1** a stamp, a characteristic mark. **2** prestige. **3** (*Med.*) a flat capsule in which unpleasant-tasting drugs can be administered.

cachexia (kəkek´siə), **cachexy** (-si) *n.* (*Med.*) a loss of weight from and weakness of the body resulting from chronic disease. **cachectic** (-kek´-tik) *a.*

cachinnate (kak´ināt) *v.i.* (*formal*) to laugh immoderately. **cachinnation** (-ā´shən) *n.* **cachinnatory** (-ā´təri) *a.*

cacholong (kach´əlong) *n.* a white or opaque variety of opal or quartz.

cachou (kash´oo, -shoo´) *n.* **1** a small pill-like sweet for perfuming the breath. **2** catechu.

Usage note The spellings of the sweet *cachou* and the nut *cashew* (pronounced the same) should not be confused.

cachucha (kəchoo´chə) *n.* a lively Spanish dance in triple time.

cacique (kəsēk´), **cazique** *n.* **1** a chief of the indigenous inhabitants of the W Indies or the neighbouring parts of America. **2** a local political leader in this area.

cack (kak) *n.* (*dial.*) excrement. **cack-handed** *a.*

(*sl.*) **1** left-handed. **2** clumsy. **cack-handedly** *adv.* **cack-handedness** *n.*

cackle (kak´əl) *n.* **1** the cackling of a hen. **2** silly chatter. ~*v.i.* **1** (of a hen) to make a squawking or clucking noise. **2** to make a similar noise. **3** to chatter in a silly manner. **4** to giggle. **to cut the cackle** to get down to business. **cackler** *n.*

cacoethes (kakōē´thēz) *n.* **1** a bad habit. **2** an irresistible urge.

cacography (kəkog´rəfi) *n.* **1** bad spelling. **2** bad handwriting. **cacographer** *n.* **cacographic** (kakō-graf´-), **cacographical** *a.*

cacology (kəkol´əji) *n.* **1** bad choice of words. **2** incorrect pronunciation.

cacomistle (kak´əmisəl), **cacomixle** (-miksəl) *n.* a ring-tailed American mammal, *Bassariscus astutus*, related to the raccoon.

cacophony (kəkof´əni) *n.* (*pl.* **cacophonies**) **1** a rough, discordant sound or mixture of sounds. **2** (*Mus.*) a discord. **cacophonous** *a.*

cactus (kak´təs) *n.* (*pl.* **cacti** (kak´tī), **cactuses**) any succulent spiny plant of the family *Cactaceae*. **cactaceous** (-tā´shəs) *a.* **cactus dahlia** *n.* a variety of dahlia with double flowers resembling those of a cactus.

CAD *abbr.* **1** computer-aided design. **2** compact audio disc.

cad (kad) *n.* (*dated*) an ill-mannered person, a person guilty of ungentlemanly conduct. **caddish** *a.* **caddishly** *adv.*

cadaver (kədav´ə, -dahv´ə, -dā´və) *n.* (*Med.*) a corpse, a dead body. **cadaveric** *a.* **cadaverous** *a.* **1** corpselike. **2** deathly pale. **cadaverously** *adv.* **cadaverousness** *n.*

caddie (kad´i), **caddy** *n.* (*pl.* **caddies**) a person who assists a golfer, esp. by carrying clubs. ~*v.i.* (*3rd pers. sing. pres.* **caddies**, *pres.p.* **caddying**, *past, p.p.* **caddied**) to act as a caddie. **caddie car, caddie cart** *n.* a two-wheeled cart for carrying golf clubs.

caddis (kad´is) *n.* the larva of the caddis fly, which lives in water in a protective case of sand, stones, sticks, leaves etc. **caddis fly** *n.* (*pl.* **caddis flies**) any insect of the order *Trichoptera*, resembling a small moth. **caddis worm** *n.* a caddis larva.

caddy[1] (kad´i) *n.* (*pl.* **caddies**) a small box in which tea is kept.

caddy[2] CADDIE.

cadence (kā´dəns) *n.* **1** the sinking of the voice, esp. at the end of a sentence. **2** modulation of the voice, intonation. **3** rhythmical beat or movement. **4** poetical rhythm or measure. **5** (*Mus.*) the close of a movement or phrase. ~*v.t.* to put into rhythmical measure. **cadenced** *a.* **cadential** (kədən´shəl) *a.* of or relating to a cadence or a cadenza.

cadenza (kədən´zə) *n.* (*pl.* **cadenzas**) (*Mus.*) a vocal or instrumental flourish of indefinite form at the close of a movement.

cadet (kədet´) *n.* **1** a young trainee in the army, navy, air force or police. **2** a young volunteer who receives military training while at school. **3** (*New Zeal.*) a sheep-farming apprentice or trainee. **cadetship** *n.*

cadge (kaj) *v.t.* to get by begging. ~*v.i.* to beg. **cadger** *n.* a person who cadges.

cadi (kah´di, kā´-), **kadi, qadi** *n.* (*pl.* **cadis, kadis, qadis**) the judge of a Muslim town or village.

cadmium (kad´miəm) *n.* (*Chem.*) a bluish-white metallic element, at. no. 51, chem. symbol Cd. **cadmium cell** *n.* **1** a type of photocell with a cadmium electrode. **2** a primary electrical cell used as a standard. **cadmium yellow** *n.* a yellow or orange pigment prepared from cadmium sulphide.

cadre (kah´də, kah´dri) *n.* **1** the permanent establishment or nucleus of a regiment; the skeleton of a regiment. **2** any similar nucleus or basic structure, esp. of key personnel. **3** a group of revolutionary activists. **4** a member of such a group.

CAE *abbr.* computer-aided engineering.

caecilian (sēsil´iən), **coecilian** *n.* any wormlike legless amphibian of the order Apoda (or Gymnophiona) which burrows in moist soil.

caecum (sē´kəm), (*N Am.*) **cecum** *n.* (*pl.* **caeca** (-kə), (*N Am.*) **ceca**) **1** (*Anat.*) the first part of the large intestine, which is prolonged into a blind pouch. **2** any similar structure in animals or plants that ends in a blind pouch. **caecal** *a.* **caecitis** (-sī´-) *n.* (*Med.*) inflammation of the caecum.

Caerphilly (keəfil´i) *n.* a mild-flavoured white cheese.

Caesar (sē´zə) *n.* **1** (*Hist.*) the title of the Roman emperors down to Hadrian, and of the heirs presumptive of later emperors. **2** (*Med., coll.*) a Caesarean section. **Caesarean** (sizeə´-), **Caesarian** *a.* of or belonging to Caesar. ~*n.* (*N Am.* **Cesarian, Cesarean**) a Caesarean section. **Caesarean section** *n.* the delivery of a child through the walls of the abdomen (as Julius Caesar is said to have been brought into the world). **Caesar salad** *n.* a salad of cos lettuce and croutons with a dressing made from olive oil, raw egg, lemon juice and Worcester sauce (from Caesar Cardini, Mexican restaurateur). **Caesar's wife** *n.* a woman of spotless reputation.

caesium (sē´ziəm), (*N Am.*) **cesium** *n.* (*Chem.*) a highly-reactive, silvery-white metallic element, at. no. 55, chem. symbol Cs, similar to sodium in many properties.

caesura (sizūə´rə), (*N Am.*) **cesura** *n.* (*pl.* **caesuras, caesurae** (-rē), (*N Am.*) **cesuras, cesurae**) **1** in classical prosody, the division of a metrical foot between two words, esp. in the middle of a line. **2** in modern prosody, a pause about the middle of a line. **caesural** *a.*

CAF *abbr.* (*esp. N Am.*) cost and freight.

cafard (kafah´, kaf´ah) *n.* depression, low spirits.

café (kaf´ā), **cafe** (kāf, kaf) *n.* **1** a small restaurant serving coffee, tea etc. and light inexpensive meals or snacks. **2** a coffee house or coffee bar. **3** coffee. **café au lait** (ō lā´) *n.* coffee with milk.

café bar *n.* a café which also sells alcoholic drinks. **café noir** (nwah´) *n.* black coffee. **café society** *n.* fashionable society; people who frequent fashionable restaurants, nightclubs, etc.

cafeteria (kafitiə´riə) *n.* (*pl.* **cafeterias**) a restaurant in which customers fetch their own food and drinks from the counter.

cafetière (kafətyeə´, -tiə´), **cafetiere** *n.* a type of coffee-pot fitted with a plunger that forces the grounds to the bottom and holds them there while the coffee is poured.

caff (kaf) *n.* (*sl.*) a café or cafoteria.

caffeine (kaf´ēn), **caffein** *n.* a vegetable alkaloid derived from the coffee and tea plants.

caftan KAFTAN.

cage (kāj) *n.* **1** a box or enclosure wholly or partly of wire or iron bars, in which animals or birds are kept. **2** any framework or structure resembling this. **3** the cabin of a lift. **4** (*Mining*) an iron structure used as a lift in a shaft. **5** a prison, prison cell or prison camp. ~*v.t.* **1** to shut up in a cage. **2** to confine. **cagebird** *n.* **1** a bird kept in a cage. **2** a type of bird normally kept in a cage.

cagey (kā´ji), **cagy** *a.* (*comp.* **cagier**, *superl.* **cagiest**) (*coll.*) **1** uncommunicative, secretive. **2** wary, cautious. **3** sly. **cagily** *adv.* **caginess, cageyness** *n.*

cagoule (kəgool´), **kagoule** *n.* a lightweight weatherproof jacket, usu. hooded.

cahoots (kəhoots´) *n.pl.* (*sl.*) partnership, collusion (*in cahoots*).

CAI *abbr.* computer-aided instruction, computer-assisted instruction.

caiman CAYMAN.

Cain (kān) *n.* a murderer, a fratricide. **to raise Cain** (*sl.*) to make a disturbance, to make trouble.

Cainozoic CENOZOIC.

caïque (kah´ik, kī´-), **caique** *n.* **1** a light rowing boat used on the Bosporus. **2** a small sailing vessel of the eastern Mediterranean.

cairn (keən) *n.* **1** a pyramidal heap of stones, esp. one raised over a grave or to mark a summit, track or boundary. **2** a cairn terrier. **cairn terrier** *n.* a small rough-haired terrier orig. from Scotland.

cairngorm (keəngawm´, keən´-) *n.* a yellow or brown variety of rock crystal (found in the Cairngorm mountains in NE Scotland).

caisson (kā´sən, kəsoon´) *n.* **1** a large, watertight case or chamber used in laying foundations under water. **2** a similar apparatus used for raising sunken vessels. **3** a floating vessel used as a dock gate. **4** an ammunition chest or wagon. **caisson disease** *n.* symptoms resulting from a sudden return from high air pressure to normal pressure conditions; decompression sickness.

cajole (kəjōl´) *v.t.* to persuade by flattery or fair speech (*He cajoled me into staying*). ~*v.i.* to use artful flattery. **cajolement** *n.* **cajoler** *n.* **cajolery** *n.* **cajolingly** *adv.*

Cajun (kā´jən) *n.* a descendant of the French-speaking Acadians deported to Louisiana in the

18th cent. ~*a.* of or relating to the Cajuns or their music, cookery etc.

cake (kāk) *n.* **1** a mixture of flour, butter, eggs, sugar and other ingredients, baked usu. in a tin. **2** a small mass of baked dough. **3** a flat mass of food or any solidified or compressed substance. ~*v.t.* (*usu. pass.*) to make into a solidified or compressed mass. ~*v.i.* to assume a solidified or compressed form. **to go/ sell like hot cakes** to be sold very quickly. **to have one's cake and eat it** to take advantage of two alternatives, one of which excludes the other (*You can't have your cake and eat it*). **cake-hole** *n.* (*sl.*) the mouth. **cakes and ale** *n.pl.* a good time. **cakewalk** *n.* **1** a dance with high marching steps, which originated among American blacks (formerly performed for the prize of a cake). **2** (*sl.*) something easily accomplished. **3** a moving promenade at a fairground.

CAL *abbr.* computer-aided learning, computer-assisted learning.

Cal. *abbr.* Calorie (kilocalorie).

cal. *abbr.* (small) calorie.

Calabar bean (kal'əbah) *n.* the highly poisonous seed of the climbing plant *Physostigma venenosum* of W Africa, a source of physostigmine.

calabash (kal'əbash) *n.* **1** a kind of gourd, esp. the fruit of the calabash tree. **2** the calabash tree. **3** the shell enclosing the fruit of this tree, used for drinking vessels and other domestic utensils, and tobacco pipes. **calabash tree** *n.* a tropical American tree, *Crescentia cujete.*

calaboose (kaləboos', kal'-) *n.* (*N Am. dial.*) a prison.

calabrese (kaləbrā'zi) *n.* a type of green broccoli.

calamander (kaləman'də) *n.* a hard wood, marked with black and brown stripes, from India and Sri Lanka.

calamari (kaləmah'ri) *n.pl.* squid, esp. in Mediterranean cookery.

calamine (kal'əmīn) *n.* **1** a pinkish powder of zinc carbonate and ferric oxide used in a lotion to soothe the skin. **2** (*Hist.*) zinc carbonate.

calamint (kal'əmint) *n.* an aromatic herb of the genus *Clinopodium* (formerly *Calamintha*) of the mint family.

calamity (kələm'iti) *n.* (*pl.* **calamities**) **1** extreme misfortune or adversity; disaster. **2** great distress or misery. **calamitous** *a.* **calamitously** *adv.* **calamitousness** *n.* **calamity Jane** *n.* (*coll.*) a person who heralds or brings disaster.

calando (kəlan'dō) *a., adv.* (*Mus.*) gradually becoming softer and slower.

calash (kəlash') *n.* **1** a light horse-drawn carriage, with low wheels and removable top. **2** (*Can.*) a two-wheeled horse-drawn vehicle for two, with seat for the driver on the splashboard. **3** a woman's silk hood supported by a framework of whalebone.

calc- (kalk) *comb. form* lime, calcium. **calc-spar** *n.* calcite.

calcaneum (kalkā'niəm), **calcaneus** (-niəs) *n.*

(*pl.* **calcanea** (-niə), **calcanei** (-niī)) the bone of the heel. **calcaneal** *a.*

calcareous (kalkeə'riəs), **calcarious** *a.* of or containing calcium carbonate; chalky or limy.

calceolaria (kalsiəleə'riə) *n.* (*pl.* **calceolarias**) any plant of the genus *Calceolaria*, with slipper-like flowers; slipperwort.

calceolate (kal'siəlāt) *a.* (*Bot.*) shaped like a slipper.

calces CALX.

calciferol (kalsif'ərol) *n.* a compound found in dairy products, vitamin D$_2$.

calciferous (kalsif'ərəs) *a.* (*Chem.*) yielding or containing calcium salts.

calcify (kal'sifī) *v.t.* (*3rd pers. sing. pres.* **calcifies,** *pres.p.* **calcifying,** *past, p.p.* **calcified**) **1** to convert into lime. **2** to harden by the deposition of calcium salts. ~*v.i.* to become calcified. **calcific** (-sif'ik) *a.* **calcification** (-ikā'shən) *n.*

calcine (kal'sin, -sīn) *v.t.* **1** to reduce to calcium oxide by heat. **2** to expel water and other volatile matter from, to desiccate by heat. **3** to purify or refine. **4** to burn to ashes. ~*v.i.* to undergo calcination. **calcination** (-sinā'shən) *n.*

calcite (kal'sīt) *n.* natural crystallized calcium carbonate.

calcium (kal'siəm) *n.* (*Chem.*) a silver-white metallic element, at. no. 20, chem. symbol Ca. **calcium carbonate** *n.* a white crystalline compound occurring in limestone, chalk, marble etc. **calcium hydroxide** *n.* a white powder used in the production of cement, plaster etc.; slaked lime. **calcium oxide** *n.* lime, quicklime. **calcium phosphate** *n.* a compound that occurs in bones and is used in fertilizers.

calcrete (kal'krēt) *n.* (*Geol.*) a rock made up of particles of sand and gravel held together with calcium carbonate.

calculate (kal'kūlāt) *v.t.* **1** to compute, to determine by mathematical process, to estimate. **2** to ascertain beforehand. **3** to plan beforehand. ~*v.i.* **1** to reckon, to form an estimate. **2** to rely (on). **3** (*N Am.*) to think, to suppose. **calculable** *a.* **calculability** (-bil'-) *n.* **calculably** *adv.* **calculated** *a.* **1** prearranged, intended. **2** premeditated, cold-blooded. **3** suitable, designed (to). **calculatedly** *adv.* **calculating** *a.* **1** that calculates. **2** shrewd, acting with forethought. **3** scheming. **calculatingly** *adv.* **calculation** (-lā'shən) *n.* **1** the act of computing or calculating. **2** the result of this. **3** reckoning, a forecast or projection, an estimation. **4** careful planning, esp. selfish. **calculative** *a.* **calculator** *n.* **1** an electronic device, usu. small and portable, which can carry out mathematical calculations. **2** a person who calculates. **3** a series of tables for use in calculating.

calculus (kal'kūləs) *n.* (*pl.* **calculuses, calculi** (-lī)) **1** (*Med.*) a stony concretion formed in various organs of the body, such as the kidney. **2** (*Math.*) a method of calculation. **calculous** *a.* (*Med.*) affected with or of the nature of a calculus.

caldera (kaldeə´rə) *n*. (*pl*. **calderas**) a large, deep volcanic crater.

caldron CAULDRON.

Caledonian (kalidō´niən) *a*. **1** of or relating to Scotland; Scottish. **2** (*Geol*.) denoting a mountain building period in the Palaeozoic era. ~*n*. (*poet*.) a Scotsman or Scotswoman.

calefacient (kalifā´shənt) *a*. (*Med*.) causing heat or warmth. ~*n*. a medicine or other substance for increasing the heat of the body.

calendar (kal´ində) *n*. **1** a list of the months, weeks and days of the year, with the civil and ecclesiastical holidays, festivals and other dates. **2** the system by which the beginning, length and subdivisions of the year are defined, esp. the Gregorian calendar adopted in England in 1752. **3** a table giving the times of sunrise and sunset, with other astronomical phenomena; an almanac. **4** a list or schedule of forthcoming events, appointments etc. **5** any list or register, e.g. of saints, cases awaiting trial etc. ~*v.t*. to register or enter in a list or calendar. **calendar month** *n*. a month according to the calendar, as distinct from *lunar month* etc. **calendar year** *n*. the period of 365 days, from 1 Jan. to 31 Dec., divided into 12 months and adopted as the legal year, with one day being added every fourth year to form a bissextile or leap year. **calendric** (-len´-), **calendrical** *a*.

calender (kal´ində) *n*. a press or machine in which cloth or paper is passed between rollers to make it glossy. ~*v.t*. to glaze by passing between rollers.

calends (kal´əndz), **kalends** *n.pl*. the first day of any month in the ancient Roman calendar.

calendula (kəlen´dülə) *n*. a marigold, or any other plant of the genus *Calendula*.

calf¹ (kahf) *n*. (*pl*. **calves** (kahvz)) **1** the young of any bovine animal, esp. of the domestic cow. **2** leather made from the skin of a calf; calfskin. **3** the young of some large animals, as of the elephant, rhinoceros, whale etc. **4** (*Naut*.) a small iceberg detached from a larger one. **in calf** (of cow, elephant, rhinoceros etc.) pregnant. **with calf** in calf. **calf love** *n*. romantic attachment between a boy and a girl. **calfskin** *n*. leather made from the skin of a calf, used in bookbinding and for boots and shoes.

calf² (kahf) *n*. (*pl*. **calves** (kahvz)) the thick fleshy part of the back of the leg below the knee. **calf-length** *a*. (of a skirt, coat etc.) reaching down to the middle of the calves.

calibre (kal´ibə), (*N Am*.) **caliber** *n*. **1** the internal diameter of the bore of a gun or any tube. **2** the diameter of a bullet, shell etc. **3** quality, ability, character, standing. **calibrate** *v.t*. **1** to ascertain the calibre of. **2** to test the accuracy of (an instrument) against a standard. **3** to graduate (a gauge etc.). **calibration** (-rā´shən) *n*. **1** the act of calibrating. **2** any of the marks on a graduated scale. **calibrator** *n*. **calibred** *a*. (*also in comb*.)

caliche (kalē´chi) *n*. **1** a deposit of sand, gravel or clay containing minerals (esp. Chile saltpetre), found in very dry regions. **2** a crust of sand cemented with calcium carbonate on the surface of soil in very dry regions.

calico (kal´ikō) *n*. (*pl*. **calicoes, calicos**) **1** cotton cloth formerly imported from the East. **2** white or unbleached cotton cloth. **3** (*esp. N Am*.) printed cotton cloth. ~*a*. **1** made of calico. **2** (*N Am*.) brightly coloured, multicoloured.

Californian (kalifaw´niən) *a*. of or relating to the N American state of California. ~*n*. a native or inhabitant of California. **California condor** (kalifaw´niə) *n*. a rare vulture of California, *Cymnogyos californianus*. **California poppy** *n*. a plant of the genus *Eschscholtzia*, with bright yellow or orange flowers.

californium (kalifaw´niəm) *n*. (*Chem*.) an artificially-produced radioactive element, at. no. 98, chem. symbol Cf.

caliper CALLIPER.

caliph (kā´lif, kal´-), **calif, kalif, khalif** *n*. the chief ruler in certain Muslim countries, who is regarded as the successor of Muhammad. **caliphate** (-fāt) *n*.

calisthenics, calisthenic CALLISTHENICS.

calk CAULK.

call (kawl) *v.t*. **1** to name, to designate. **2** to describe as. **3** to regard or consider as. **4** to summon, esp. in a loud voice. **5** to communicate with or summon by telephone or radio. **6** to invite. **7** to command. **8** to announce or cause to happen (*to call a strike*). **9** to appeal to. **10** to rouse from sleep. **11** to nominate, invite or summon (to a profession etc.). **12** to lure (birds etc.) by imitating their cry. **13** (*Comput*.) to transfer control to (a subroutine) by means of a calling sequence. **14** to call over (a list of names) to ascertain that all are present (*to call the roll*). ~*v.i*. **1** to speak in a loud voice; to cry aloud, to shout. **2** (of a bird etc.) to make a characteristic sound or cry. **3** to pay a short visit. **4** to make a telephone call. **5** in bridge, to make a bid. **6** in poker, to ask an opponent to show their cards. **7** in whist, to show by special play that trumps are wanted. ~*n*. **1** a loud cry. **2** a vocal address or supplication. **3** a communication by telephone or radio. **4** the cry of a bird or animal. **5** a whistle to imitate the cry of a bird or animal. **6** a short visit. **7** a summons, an invitation. **8** an invitation to become minister to a congregation. **9** a summons or signal on a bugle, whistle etc. **10** a requirement or demand. **11** duty, necessity, justification, occasion. **12** demand for payment of instalments due (of shares etc.). **at call** on call. **on call 1** (of a doctor etc.) available to be summoned if required. **2** (of a loan etc.) to be repaid on demand. **to call away** to summon away, to divert. **to call back 1** to revoke, to withdraw. **2** to visit again. **3** to call later by telephone. **to call down** to invoke. **to call for 1** to desire the attendance of. **2** to appeal for, to demand. **3** to require, necessitate. **4** to visit a place to bring (a person or thing) away. **5** to signal for (trumps). **to call forth 1** to elicit. **2** to summon to action. **to call in 1** to summon to one's aid. **2** to withdraw (money) from circulation. **3** to order the return of. **4** to pay a short visit (on, at etc.). **to call into being** to give existence to, to create. **to call off 1** to summon away, to order (an animal or person) to stop attacking etc. **2** to cancel. **to call on 1** to invoke, to appeal to. **2** to pay a short visit to. **to call one's own** to regard as one's possession, to own. **to call out 1** to say loudly, to shout. **2** to summon (troops etc.) to service. **3** to order (workers) to strike. **4** to elicit. **5** to challenge to a duel or fight. **to call over** to read aloud. **to call up 1** (*Mil.*) to mobilize. **2** to make a telephone call to. **3** to rouse from sleep. **4** to cause to remember or imagine. **5** to summon to appear. **6** to require payment of. **to pay a call** (*coll.*) to urinate or defecate. **within call** within hearing. **call-box** *n.* a public telephone box. **call-boy** *n.* **1** a person who calls actors when they are wanted on the stage. **2** a male prostitute who makes appointments by telephone. **caller** *n.* a person who calls, esp. one who telephones or visits. **call-girl** *n.* a female prostitute who makes appointments by telephone. **calling** *n.* **1** an occupation, trade or profession. **2** a vocation. **3** a solemn summons to duty, faith etc. **calling card** *n.* (*N Am.*) a visiting card. **call of nature** *n.* a need to urinate or defecate. **call-out** *n.* an instance of summoning someone to do repairs, provide emergency services, etc. **call-over** *n.* **1** a roll-call. **2** a recital of betting prices. **call sign, call signal** *n.* a set of numbers and/or letters identifying a radio transmitter or station. **call-up** *n.* (*Mil.*) mobilization.

calla (kal´ə), **calla lily** *n.* **1** the arum lily, *Zantedeschia aethiopica.* **2** a marsh plant, *Calla palustris.*

calligraphy (kəlig´rəfi) *n.* **1** the art of beautiful handwriting. **2** handwriting. **calligrapher, calligraphist** *n.* **calligraphic** (-graf´-) *a.*

calliope (kəli´əpi) *n.* (*N Am.*) a series of steam-whistles that produce musical notes when played by a keyboard.

calliper (kal´ipə), **caliper** *n.* **1** (*pl.*) compasses with bow legs for measuring convex bodies, or with points turned out for measuring calibres. **2** a calliper splint. ~*v.t.* to measure by means of callipers. **calliper splint** *n.* a form of splint for the leg which takes pressure off the foot when walking.

callisthenics (kalisthen´iks), (*esp. N Am.*) **calisthenics** *n.pl.* gymnastics promoting fitness and grace. **callisthenic** *a.*

callop (kal´əp) *n.* an Australian freshwater fish, *Plectroplites ambiguus*, used as food.

callous (kal´əs) *a.* **1** unfeeling, insensitive, unsympathetic. **2** (of skin) hardened. **callosity** (-los´-) *n.* (*pl.* **callosities**) hardened or thickened skin, caused by friction, pressure, disease, injury etc. **callously** *adv.* **callousness** *n.*

callow (kal´ō) *a.* youthful, immature, inexperienced. **callowly** *adv.* **callowness** *n.*

calluna (kəloo´nə) *n.* the heather, *Calluna vulgaris.*

callus (kal´əs) *n.* (*pl.* **calluses**) **1** an area of hard or thick skin caused by friction, pressure etc. **2** (*Bot.*) a hard formation.

calm (kahm) *a.* **1** still, quiet. **2** tranquil, undisturbed. ~*n.* **1** the state of being calm. **2** (*Naut.*) complete absence of wind. ~*v.t.* to make calm. ~*v.i.* to become calm. **to calm down** to make or become calm. **calmative** *a.* tending to calm. ~*n.* (*Med.*) a sedative medicine. **calmly** *adv.* **calmness** *n.*

calomel (kal´əmel) *n.* mercurous chloride, an active purgative.

Calor gas® (kal´ə) *n.* a type of bottled gas used for cooking etc.

caloric (kəlor´ik) *a.* of or relating to heat or calories.

calorie (kal´əri) **calory** *n.* **1** a unit of heat, equalling 4.1868 joules; the quantity of heat required to raise the temperature of 1 gram of water by 1°C, a small calorie. **2** (Calorie) a unit of heat equalling 1000 (small) calories, used in measuring the energy content of food. **calorific** (-rif´-) *a.* of, relating to or producing heat. **calorifically** *adv.* **calorific value** *n.* the amount of heat produced by the complete combustion of a given amount (usu. 1 kg) of fuel. **calorimeter** (-rim´itə) *n.* an instrument for measuring actual quantities of heat, or the specific heat of a body. **calorimetric** (-met´-) *a.* **calorimetry** (-rim´-) *n.*

calque (kalk) *n.* a loan translation, a literal translation of a foreign expression.

caltrop (kal´trəp), **calthrop** (-thrəp), **caltrap** (-trap) *n.* **1** an instrument formed of four iron spikes joined at the bases, thrown on the ground to impede the advance of cavalry. **2** any of several trailing plants of the genus *Tribulus* etc., with spiny fruit, that entangle the feet. **3** the star thistle, *Centaurea calcitrapa.* **4** a water weed, such as *Potamogeton densus*, *P. crispus* or *Trapa natans*; water caltrop.

calumet (kal´ūmet) *n.* the tobacco-pipe of the N American Indians, used as a symbol of peace and friendship; the peace pipe.

calumny (kal´əmni) *n.* (*pl.* **calumnies**) **1** a malicious misrepresentation of the words or actions of another. **2** slander. **3** a false charge. ~*v.t.* (*3rd pers. sing. pres.* **calumnies**, *pres.p.* **calumnying**, *past,p.p.* **calumnied**) to utter calumnies about, to slander. **calumniate** (kəlŭm´niāt) *v.t.* (*formal*) to slander. **calumniation** (-ā´shən) *n.* **calumniator** *n.* **calumniatory** *a.* **calumnious** *a.*

calvados (kal´vədos) *n.* apple brandy made in Normandy.

calve (kahv) *v.i.* **1** to give birth to a calf. **2** to bring forth young. **3** (of icebergs) to detach and cast off a mass of ice. ~*v.t.* to bear, bring forth.

calves[1] CALF[1].

calves[2] CALF[2].

Calvinism (kal´vinizm) *n.* the tenets of John Calvin, esp. his doctrine of predestination and election. **Calvinist** *n.* **Calvinistic, Calvinistical** (-nist´-) *a.*

calx (kalks) *n.* (*pl.* **calxes, calces** (kal´sēz)) **1** ashes or fine powder remaining from metals, minerals etc. after they have undergone calcination. **2** calcium oxide.

calycine (kal´isīn), **calycinal** (kəlis´inəl) *a.* of, belonging to, or in the form of a calyx.

calypso (kəlip´sō) *n.* (*pl.* **calypsos**) a W Indian narrative song, usu. performed to a syncopated accompaniment and made up as the singer goes along.

calyx (kā´liks, kal´-) *n.* (*pl.* **calyces** (-sēz), **calyxes**) **1** (*Bot.*) the whorl of leaves or sepals (usu. green) forming the outer integument of a flower. **2** (*Biol.*) a cuplike body cavity or organ.

calzone (kaltsō´nā) *n.* (*pl.* **calzones, calzoni** (-ni)) a folded pizza containing a filling.

CAM *abbr.* computer-aided manufacture, computer-assisted manufacturing.

cam (kam) *n.* an eccentric projection attached to a revolving shaft for the purpose of giving linear motion to another part. **camshaft** *n.* a shaft bearing cams which operate the valves of internal-combustion engines.

camaraderie (kamərah´dəri) *n.* **1** comradeship. **2** good fellowship and loyalty among intimate friends.

Camb. *abbr.* Cambridge.

camber (kam´bə) *n.* **1** the curvature given to a road surface to make water run off it. **2** any similar slight convexity, as on a ship's deck, the wing of an aircraft, etc. **3** a slight upward slope towards the outside of a bend in a road, racetrack, etc. ~*v.t., v.i.* to bend, to arch.

Camberwell beauty (kam´bəwel) *n.* a butterfly, *Nymphalis antiopa*, having deep purple wings with yellow or cream borders.

cambium (kam´biəm) *n.* (*pl.* **cambiums, cambia** (-biə)) (*Bot.*) the cellular tissue which annually increases the girth of exogenous trees and other plants. **cambial** *a.*

Cambodian (kambō´diən) *a.* of or relating to Cambodia (Kampuchea) in SE Asia. ~*n.* a native or inhabitant of Cambodia.

Cambrian (kam´briən) *a.* **1** of or belonging to Wales. **2** (*Geol.*) of or relating to the first period of the Palaeozoic era, or the geological system formed in this period. ~*n.* **1** a Welshman or Welshwoman. **2** (*Geol.*) the Cambrian period or system.

cambric (kam´brik) *n.* a type of very fine white linen or cotton.

Cambridge blue (kām´brij) *n., a.* pale blue.

Cambs. *abbr.* Cambridgeshire.

camcorder (kam´kawdə) *n.* a video camera and recorder combined in one unit.

came COME.

camel (kam´əl) *n.* **1** a large, hornless, humpbacked ruminant with long neck and padded feet, used in Africa and the East as a beast of burden. There are two species, the Arabian camel, *Camelus dromedarius*, with one hump, and the Bactrian camel, *C. bactrianus*, with two humps. **2** a watertight float attached to a boat to raise it in the water. **3** a pale brownish-yellow colour. ~*a.* **1** of this colour. **2** made of camel-hair fabric. **cameleer** (-liə´) *n.* a camel-driver. **camel-hair, camel's hair** *n.* **1** the hair of a camel used to make various fabrics. **2** an artist's paintbrush made of hairs from squirrels' tails.

camellia (kəmē´liə) *n.* an evergreen shrub, of the genus *Camellia*, with beautiful flowers.

Camembert (kam´əmbeə) *n.* a soft rich cheese from Normandy.

cameo (kam´iō) *n.* (*pl.* **cameos**) **1** a precious stone with two layers of colours, the upper being carved in relief, the lower serving as background. **2** a similar carving using other materials. **3** a piece of jewellery using such carving. **4** a short literary piece. **5** a small part in a play or film, esp. one played by a famous actor. ~*a.* **1** of a cameo or cameos. **2** small and perfect.

camera (kam´ərə) *n.* (*pl.* **cameras**) **1** an apparatus for taking photographs, which records an image (or a series of images in a cinecamera) on a light-sensitive surface. **2** an apparatus which records (moving) images and converts them to electrical signals for TV transmission. **in camera 1** in private. **2** (*Law*) in a judge's chamber, or with the public excluded from the court. **off camera** not being filmed. **on camera** being recorded on film. **camera lucida** (loo´sidə) *n.* (*pl.* **camera lucidas**) an instrument (often attached to a microscope) by which the rays of light from an object are reflected to produce an image of the object on a piece of paper or other drawing surface. **cameraman** *n.* (*pl.* **cameramen**) a person who operates a film or television camera. **camera obscura** (əbskū´rə) *n.* (*pl.* **camera obscuras**) a dark box, or small room, admitting light through a pinhole or a double-convex lens which projects an image of external objects on an internal screen. **camera-ready copy** *n.* (*Print.*) textual and/ or illustrative material that is ready to be photographed for the production of printing plates. **camerawork** *n.* the technique or process of using a camera, esp. a film or television camera.

camisole (kam´isōl) *n.* an underbodice. **camiknickers** *n.pl.* an undergarment comprising a camisole and knickers in one piece.

camomile (kam´əmīl), **chamomile** *n.* an aromatic creeping plant belonging to the genera *Anthemis* or *Matricaria*, esp. *A. nobilis* or *M. chamomilla*. **camomile tea** *n.* a medicinal drink made from dried flowers of these plants.

camouflage (kam´əflahzh) *n.* **1** disguise, esp. the concealment of guns, camps, buildings, vehicles etc., from the enemy by means of deceptive painting, a covering of boughs etc. **2** the natural colouring or markings of some animals, which resemble their surroundings and thus conceal them from predators. **3** concealment of one's actions. ~*v.t.* to disguise.

camp[1] (kamp) *n.* **1** the place where an army is lodged in tents or other temporary structures. **2** a station for training troops. **3** a body of troops in tents; an army on campaign. **4** military life. **5** the temporary quarters of gypsies, holidaymakers, Scouts or Guides, explorers, refugees etc., usu. in tents, caravans or similar structures. **6** the occupants of such quarters. **7** a body of adherents; a side. **8** a ruined prehistoric fort. **9** (*Austral.*) a halting-place for cattle. ~*v.i.* to encamp; to lodge temporarily in a tent etc., to camp out. **to camp out 1** to lodge in a tent etc. in the open. **2** to sleep outdoors. **camp-bed** *n.* a light folding bed. **camper** *n.* **1** a person who camps, esp. a holidaymaker. **2** a vehicle having living accommodation in the back. **campfire** *n.* an open fire at the centre of a camp. **camp follower** *n.* **1** a civilian who follows an army in the field. **2** a hanger-on. **campsite, campground** *n.* a place set aside, or suitable, for camping.

camp[2] (kamp) *a.* **1** affectedly homosexual. **2** effeminate. **3** exaggerated, theatrical, artificial. ~*v.i.* to behave in a camp manner. ~*n.* camp behaviour. **to camp it up** to act in an exaggeratedly camp manner; to overact. **campy** *a.* **campily** *adv.*

campaign (kampān´) *n.* **1** a series of military operations aimed at a single objective. **2** military service in the field. **3** a series of operations aimed at raising public awareness, achieving reform etc., as in politics or advertising. ~*v.i.* to organize or take part in a campaign. **campaigner** *n.*

campanile (kampənē´li) *n.* (*pl.* **campaniles, campanili** (-li)) a bell-tower, esp. a detached one.

campanology (kampənol´əji) *n.* **1** the art of bell-ringing. **2** the study of bells. **campanologer, campanologist** *n.* **campanological** (-loj´-) *a.*

campanula (kampan´ūlə) *n.* any plant of the genus *Campanula* with bell-shaped flowers, such as the bluebell of Scotland, the Canterbury bell etc. **campanular, campanulate** (-lət) *a.* (*Bot., Zool.*) bell-shaped.

camphor (kam´fə) *n.* a whitish, translucent, volatile, crystalline substance with a pungent odour, obtained from *Camphora officinarum, Dryobalanops aromatica* and other trees, used as an insect repellent, in liniment and in the manufacture of celluloid. **camphoric** (kamfo´rik) *a.* of, relating to or containing camphor.

camphorate (kam´fərāt) *v.t.* to wash or impregnate with camphor.

campion (kam´piən) *n.* any flowering plant of the genera *Lychnis* or *Silene*.

campus (kam´pəs) *n.* (*pl.* **campuses**) **1** the buildings and grounds of a university or college. **2** a geographically separate part of a university or college. **3** the academic world in general.

campylobacter (kampilōbak´tə, kam´-) *n.* a bacterium that can cause gastroenteritis and other disorders.

camshaft CAM.

camwood (kam´wud) *n.* barwood; a hard red wood from a W African tree, *Baphia nitida.*

Can. *abbr.* **1** Canada. **2** Canadian.

can[1] (kan) *v.aux.* (*pres.* **can,** †**canst** (kanst), *neg.* **cannot** (kan´ət, -not´), **can't** (kahnt), *past* **could** (kud)) **1** to be able to (*I can't swim*). **2** to be allowed to (*Can I go now?*). **3** to be possible to (*It can't be done*). **4** (*in past, coll.*) to want to (*I could murder a drink*). **can-do** *a.* (of an attitude, approach etc.) positive and determined.

Usage note See note under MAY[1].

can[2] (kan) *n.* **1** a metal vessel for holding liquid. **2** a metal vessel in which meat, fruit, vegetables, fish etc. are hermetically sealed up for preservation; a tin. **3** a canful. **4** a shallow metal container for film. **5** (*sl.*) prison. **6** (*sl.*) a lavatory. **7** (*pl., sl.*) headphones. ~*v.t.* (*pres.p.* **canning,** *past, p.p.* **canned**) to put in cans for preservation. **in the can 1** filmed or recorded, processed and ready for release. **2** (*fig.*) arranged. **to carry the can** (*coll.*) to take responsibility, to accept blame. **canful** *n.* **canned** *a.* **1** preserved in a can. **2** (*sl.*) drunk. **3** (of music or laughter) recorded in advance. **canner** *n.* **cannery** *n.* (*pl.* **canneries**) a place where food is canned. **can of worms** *n.* (*coll.*) a complicated and potentially problematic issue or situation. **can-opener** *n.* a tin-opener.

Canaan (kā´nən) *n.* **1** (*fig.*) a land of promise. **2** heaven. **Canaanite** *n.* **1** an inhabitant of the land of Canaan. **2** a descendant of Canaan, the son of Ham.

Canadian (kənā´diən) *a.* of or relating to Canada. ~*n.* a native or inhabitant of Canada. **Canada goose** *n.* a large N American wild goose, *Branta canadensis*, grey and brown in colour. **Canadian French** *n.* the form of the French language used in French-speaking parts of Canada. ~*a.* of or relating to this language. **Canadian pondweed** *n.* a N American aquatic plant, *Elodea canadensis* or *Anacharis canadensis*, used in ponds and aquariums.

canaille (kanī´) *n.* the rabble, the mob.

canal (kənal´) *n.* **1** an artificial watercourse, esp. one used for navigation. **2** (*Anat., Bot.*) a duct or tubular passage. **3** (*Zool.*) a siphonal groove. **canal boat** *n.* a long narrow boat used on canals. **canalize** (kan´-), **canalise** *v.t.* **1** to make a canal across or through. **2** to convert (a river) into a navigable waterway. **3** to provide with canals. **4** to give a desired direction to; to channel. **canalization** (-zā´shən) *n.* **canals of Mars** *n.pl.* (*Astron.*) apparent linear markings on the surface of the planet Mars, formerly supposed by some astronomers to be waterways or zones of vegetation.

canapé (kan´əpā), **canape** *n.* **1** a small thin piece of bread or toast topped with cheese, fish etc. **2** a sofa.

canard (kanahd´) *n.* **1** an absurd story, a hoax, a false report. **2** an aircraft having a tailplane mounted in front of the wings.

Canarese KANARESE.

canary (kənee´ri) n. (pl. **canaries**) a small yellow cagebird, *Serinus canaria*, from the Canary Islands. **canary-coloured, canary yellow** a. bright yellow. **canary creeper** n. a climbing plant, *Tropaeolium peregrinum*, with bright yellow flowers. **canary grass** n. a grass of the genus *Phalaris*, esp. *Phalaris canariensis*, the source of canary seed. **canary seed** n. the seed of the canary grass, used as food for canaries and other cagebirds.

canasta (kənas´tə) n. a card game similar to rummy, played by two to six players, using two packs of playing cards.

canaster (kənas´tə) n. a coarse kind of tobacco (so named from the rush baskets in which it was orig. brought from America).

cancan (kan´kan) n. a stage dance of French origin performed by female dancers, involving high kicking of the legs.

cancel (kan´səl) v.t. (pres.p. **cancelling**, (N Am.) **canceling**, past, p.p. **cancelled**, (N Am.) **canceled**) **1** to annul, countermand, revoke. **2** to withdraw or discontinue. **3** to obliterate by drawing lines across. **4** (*Math.*) to strike out common factors. **5** to mark (a stamp, ticket) to prevent reuse. ~n. **1** a cancellation or countermand. **2** the deletion and reprinting of a part of a book. **3** a page or sheet substituted for a cancelled one. **to cancel out** to neutralize, counterbalance or compensate for (one another). **cancellate** (-lət), **cancellated** (-lātid), **cancellous** a. **1** (*Zool., Bot.*) cross-barred; reticulated. **2** (*Anat.*) (of bones) spongy, formed of cancelli. **cancellation** (-ā´shən) n. **1** the act of cancelling. **2** something cancelled, such as a reservation. **canceller**, (N Am.) **canceler** n.

Cancer (kan´sə) n. (*Astrol.*) **1** the fourth of the 12 signs of the zodiac, the Crab. **2** a person born under this sign. **Cancerian** (-siə´riən, -seə´-) n., a.

cancer (kan´sə) n. **1** a malignant spreading growth affecting parts of the body. **2** the disease that results from this. **3** any evil that spreads uncontrollably. **cancered, cancerous** a. **cancer stick** n. (*sl.*) a cigarette. **cancroid** a. **1** crablike. **2** resembling cancer. ~n. **1** a crustacean belonging to the crab family. **2** a type of skin cancer.

candela (kandel´ə, -dē´-) n. a unit of luminous intensity.

candelabrum (kandəlah´brəm), **candelabra** (-brə) n. (pl. **candelabrums, candelabra, candelabras**) a high, ornamental candlestick or lampstand, usually branched. **candelabrum tree** n. an African tree, *Euphorbia candelabrum*, with branches arranged in the form of a candelabrum.

Usage note *Candelabra* is quite commonly used as a singular noun (*a candelabra*), but it should always be a plural, with *candelabrum* as the singular.

candid (kan´did) a. **1** frank, sincere, open. **2** outspoken, freely critical. **candid camera** n. a small camera used to take photographs of people unposed or without their knowledge. **candidly** adv. **candidness** n.

candida (kan´didə) n. a yeastlike fungus of the genus *Candida*, esp. *C. albicans*, which causes thrush. **candidiasis** (kandidī´əsis) n. thrush.

candidate (kan´didət, -dāt) n. **1** a person who seeks or is proposed for some office or appointment (so named because such persons in ancient Rome wore white togas). **2** a person or thing considered likely for a particular end (*a candidate for redundancy*). **3** a person taking an examination. **candidacy** n. **candidature** (-chə), **candidateship** n.

candle (kan´dəl) n. **1** a cylindrical body of tallow, wax etc. with a wick in the middle, used for lighting or ornament. **2** a candela. ~v.t. to test (eggs) by holding before a candle. **not fit to hold a candle to** not to be comparable with; to be greatly inferior to. **not worth the candle** not worth the trouble, expense etc. **to burn the candle at both ends** to expend one's energies or exhaust oneself, esp. by staying up late and getting up early. **candleberry** n. (pl. **candleberries**) **1** a N American shrub, *Myrica cerifera*, yielding wax used for candle-making; the wax myrtle or bayberry. **2** its fruit; a bayberry or waxberry. **candleholder** n. a candlestick. **candlelight** n. **1** the light of a candle. **2** dusk; evening. **candlepower** n. the intensity of light emitted, expressed in candelas. **candler** n. **candlestick** n. a utensil for holding a candle. **candlewick** n. a cotton fabric with a pattern of raised tufts, used to make bedspreads, dressing gowns etc.

candour (kan´də), (N Am.) **candor** n. candidness, frankness, sincerity, openness.

C. and W. abbr. Country and Western.

candy (kan´di) n. (pl. **candies**) **1** sugar crystallized by boiling and evaporation. **2** (N Am.) a sweet or sweets; confectionery. ~v.t. (3rd pers. sing. pres. **candies**, pres.p. **candying**, past, p.p. **candied**) **1** to preserve with sugar, to coat with crystallized sugar. **2** to crystallize. **candy apple** n. (N Am.) a toffee apple. **candyfloss** n. coloured spun sugar on a stick. **candy-stripe** n. a pattern of alternate narrow stripes of white and a colour. **candy-striped** a.

candytuft (kan´dituft) n. **1** a herbaceous plant, *Iberis umbellata*. **2** any other plant of the genus *Iberis*, esp. *I. sempervivum*, the perennial candytuft.

cane (kān) n. **1** a slender, hollow, jointed stem of the bamboo, sugar cane or other reeds or grasses. **2** the thin stem of the rattan or other palms. **3** such a stem used as a walking stick or an instrument of punishment. **4** any (slender) walking stick. **5** the stem of a raspberry and other plants. ~v.t. **1** to beat with a cane. **2** to fit or repair (a chair etc.) with interwoven strips of cane. **cane-brake** n. (N Am.) a thicket of canes. **cane chair** n. a chair with a seat of interwoven strips of cane. **caner** n. **cane sugar** n. sugar made from

sugar cane, as distinguished from beet sugar.
cane toad *n.* a large toad, *Bufo marinus*, found in
America and Australia. **cane-trash** *n.* the refuse
of sugar cane. **caning** *n.* **1** a beating with a cane.
2 a thorough defeat.
canine (kā´nīn) *a.* **1** of or relating to dogs or the
family Canidae. **2** doglike. ~*n.* **1** a canine tooth.
2 a dog or other mammal of the family Canidae.
canine tooth *n.* (*pl.* **canine teeth**) either of two
pointed teeth in each jaw, one on each side,
between the incisors and the premolars.
canister (kan´istə) *n.* **1** a metal case or box for
holding tea, coffee etc. **2** canister shot, or the
metal case in which it is packed. **canister shot** *n.*
bullets packed in metal cases which burst when
fired; case-shot.
canker (kang´kə) *n.* **1** (*Med.*) an ulceration in the
human mouth. **2** (*Zool.*) **a** an ulcerative ear disease of animals, esp. the dog or cat. **b** a fungous
excrescence in a horse's foot. **3** (*Bot.*) a fungus
growing on and injuring fruit trees and other
plants. ~*v.t.* **1** to infect or rot with canker, to eat
into like a canker. **2** to corrupt. **cankered** *a.* **1** infected by canker. **2** crabbed, peevish. **cankerous**
a. **canker-worm** *n.* a caterpillar that feeds on
buds and leaves.
canna (kan´ə) *n.* any of a genus of ornamental
plants with brightly coloured flowers.
cannabis (kan´əbis) *n.* **1** any plant of the genus
Cannabis, esp. the Indian hemp. **2** a narcotic
drug obtained from the leaves and flowers of
plants of this genus, esp. *C. sativa* and *C. indica*.
cannabinol *n.* (*Chem.*) a phenol, a crystalline
constituent of the drug cannabis. **cannabis resin**
n. a sticky resin, the active principle of the drug
cannabis.
canned CAN².
cannel (kan´əl), **cannel-coal** *n.* a hard, bituminous coal, burning with a bright flame.
cannelloni (kanəlō´ni) *n.pl.* rolls of sheet pasta
filled with meat etc. and baked.
cannelure (kan´əlüə) *n.* a groove round a
projectile.
canner, cannery CAN².
cannibal (kan´ibəl) *n.* **1** a human being who
feeds on human flesh. **2** any animal that feeds on
its own kind. ~*a.* **1** of or relating to cannibalism.
2 like a cannibal; ravenous, bloodthirsty. **cannibalism** *n.* **cannibalistic** (-lis´-) *a.* **cannibalist-
ically** *adv.* **cannibalize, cannibalise** *v.t.* to
dismantle (a machine etc.) for its spare parts,
usu. to repair a similar machine.
cannikin (kan´ikin), **canikin, canakin** (-əkin) *n.*
a small can or cup.
cannily, canniness CANNY.
cannon¹ (kan´ən) *n.* **1** a heavy mounted gun.
2 an automatic aircraft gun. **3** artillery, ordnance. **4** a hollow sleeve or cylinder revolving
independently on a shaft. **cannonade** (-nād´)
n. a continued attack with artillery against a
town, fortress etc. ~*v.t.* to attack or bombard
with cannon. ~*v.i.* to discharge heavy artillery.

cannonball *n.* a solid shot fired from a cannon.
cannon bit *n.* a smooth round bit for a horse.
cannon-bone *n.* the metacarpal or metatarsal
bone of a horse, ox etc. **cannon fodder** *n.* (*facet.*)
soldiers, esp. infantrymen, regarded as expendable. **cannon-proof** *a.*
cannon² (kan´ən) *n.* a billiards stroke by which
two balls are hit successively. ~*v.i.* **1** to make a
cannon. **2** to come into violent contact; to collide
(*He cannoned into a tree*).
cannot CAN¹.
cannula (kan´ūlə), **canula** *n.* (*pl.* **cannulas, can-
nulae** (-lē), **canulas, canulae**) a small tube introduced into a body cavity to withdraw a fluid.
cannulate (-lāt) *v.t.* to insert a cannula into.
canny (kan´i) *a.* (*comp.* **cannier**, *superl.* **canniest**)
1 knowing, shrewd, wise. **2** artful, crafty. **3** prudent, cautious. **4** frugal, thrifty. **5** (*Sc., North.*)
nice, good. **cannily** *adv.* **canniness** *n.*
canoe (kənoo´) *n.* a light narrow boat (orig. made
from a hollowed-out tree trunk) propelled by
paddles. ~*v.i.* (*pres.p.* **canoeing**, *past, p.p.* **canoed**)
to go in a canoe. **to paddle one's own canoe** to be
independent. **canoeist** *n.*
canon (kan´ən) *n.* **1** a rule, a regulation, a general
law or principle. **2** a standard, test or criterion.
3 a decree of the Church. **4** the catalogue of
canonized saints. **5** the portion of the Roman
Catholic Mass in which the words of consecration are spoken. **6** a list of the books of sacred
writings officially accepted as genuine; the
books themselves. **7** a list of literary works, esp.
an author's recognized works; the works themselves. **8** a resident member of a cathedral chapter. **9** a member of a religious body (from the fact
that some cathedral canons lived in community).
10 (*Mus.*) a musical composition in which the
several parts take up the same theme in succession. **canoness** *n.* a member of a female religious
community living by rule but not bound by
vows. **canonical** (-non´-), **canonic** *a.* **1** of, relating to or according to canon law. **2** included in
the canon of sacred writings. **3** authoritative,
accepted, approved. **4** of, relating to or belonging
to a cathedral chapter. **5** (*Mus.*) in canon form.
canonical hours *n.pl.* **1** the time from 8 a.m. to
6 p.m. during which marriages may legally be
celebrated. **2 a** the times of the day set for prayer,
according to canon law. **b** the services set for
these times. **canonically** *adv.* **canonicals** *n.pl.* the
full robes of an officiating clergyman as appointed by the canons. **canonicate** (-non´ikət)
n. the dignity or office of a canon. **canonicity**
(-nis´-) *n.* the quality of being canonical, esp. the
authority of a canonical book. **canonist** *n.* a
person versed in canon law. **canonize, canonise**
v.t. **1** to enrol in the canon or list of saints. **2** to
recognize officially as a saint. **3** to recognize
as canonical. **4** to sanction as conforming to the
canons of the Church. **canonization** (-zā´shən) *n.*
canon law *n.* ecclesiastical law as laid down by
popes and councils. **canon regular** *n.* a member

of the Augustinian or Premonstratensian orders, who live as monks but also perform the duties of the clergy. **canonry** n. (pl. **canonries**) **1** the dignity or office of a canon. **2** a canon's benefice.

cañon CANYON.

canoodle (kənoo´dəl) v.i. (coll.) to kiss and cuddle amorously.

canopy (kan´əpi) n. (pl. **canopies**) **1** a rich covering suspended over an altar, throne, bed, person etc. **2** any similar covering, esp. providing shelter. **3** the sky. **4** (Archit.) an ornamental projection over a niche or doorway. **5** the transparent roof of an aircraft cockpit. **6** the fabric portion of a parachute. **7** the topmost layer of branches and leaves in a forest. ~v.t. (3rd pers. sing. pres. **canopies**, pres.p. **canopying**, past, p.p. **canopied**) to cover with or as with a canopy.

canorous (kənaw´rəs) a. (formal) tuneful, melodious, resonant.

cant[1] (kant) n. **1** hypocritical talk; hypocritical sanctimoniousness. **2** slang or jargon. **3** (often derog.) a method of speech or phraseology peculiar to any sect or group. ~a. of, relating to or of the nature of cant. ~v.i. to use cant. **canting arms** n. (Her.) armorial bearings containing a punning device or other allusion to the name of the family.

cant[2] (kant) n. **1** a slope, a slant, an inclination. **2** a jerk producing a slant or inclination. **3** an external angle. **4** a bevel. **5** a sloping or slanting position. ~v.t. **1** to tip, tilt or throw, esp. with a jerk. **2** to bevel, to give a bevel to. ~v.i. (Naut.) to swing round. **cant-dog, cant-hook** n. a metal hook on a pole, used esp. for handling logs. **cant-rail** n. a bevelled plank placed along the top of the uprights in a railway carriage to support the roof.

can't CAN[1].

Cantab. (kan´tab) a. of Cambridge (University).

cantabile (kantah´bilā) a., adv. (Mus.) in an easy, flowing style. ~n. a piece or passage in cantabile style.

Cantabrigian (kantəbrij´iən) a. of or relating to the town or University of Cambridge, England or of Massachusetts. ~n. **1** a member of Cambridge or Harvard Universities. **2** a native of inhabitant of Cambridge.

Cantal (kan´tal), **cantal** n. a hard strong-flavoured French cheese.

cantaloupe (kan´təloop), **cantaloup** n. a small, round, ribbed musk-melon.

cantankerous (kantang´kərəs) a. disagreeable, bad-tempered; quarrelsome, crotchety. **cantankerously** adv. **cantankerousness** n.

cantata (kantah´tə) n. (pl. **cantatas**) (Mus.) a poem, a short lyrical drama or (usu.) a biblical text, set to music, with solos and choruses.

canteen (kantēn´) n. **1** a restaurant or cafeteria in a factory or office where meals and light refreshments are sold at low prices to the employees. **2** a place where school meals are served. **3** a small shop or cafeteria for soldiers at a military

camp or barracks. **4** a bottle or flask for carrying liquid refreshments. **5** a chest for cutlery. **6** a chest or box in which a soldier's mess utensils, cutlery etc., are carried.

canter (kan´tə) n. an easy gallop. ~v.t. to cause (a horse) to go at this pace. ~v.i. to ride or move at this pace. **in/ at a canter** easily.

canterbury (kan´təbəri) n. (pl. **canterburies**) a light stand with divisions for music portfolios etc. **Canterbury bell** n. a plant of the genus Campanula, esp. C. medium, with bell-shaped flowers.

cantharis (kan´tharis) n. (pl. **cantharides** (-thar´idēz)) Spanish fly, a coleopterous insect having vesicatory properties. **cantharides** n.pl. Spanish flies dried and used to raise blisters or internally, also used as an aphrodisiac.

canthus (kan´thəs) n. (pl. **canthi** (-thī)) the angle made at the corner of the eye where the eyelids meet.

canticle (kan´tikəl) n. a brief song, a chant, esp. one of certain portions of Scripture said or sung in churches. **Canticles, Canticle of Canticles** n. (Bible) the Song of Solomon.

cantilena (kantilā´nə) n. (pl. **cantilenas**) (Mus.) a simple flowing melody or style.

cantilever (kan´tilēvə) n. **1** a projecting beam, girder or bracket for supporting a balcony or other structure. **2** a beam, girder etc. that is fixed at one end only. ~v.i. to project as or like a cantilever. ~v.t. **1** to support by a cantilever. **2** to fix as a cantilever. **cantilever bridge** n. a bridge formed with cantilevers, resting in pairs on piers of masonry or ironwork, the ends meeting or connected by girders.

cantillate (kan´tilāt) v.t. to chant or intone as in synagogues. **cantillation** (-ā´shən) n.

cantina (kantē´nə) n. (pl. **cantinas**) a bar or wine shop, esp. in Spanish-speaking countries.

canto (kan´tō) n. (pl. **cantos**) any one of the principal divisions of a poem.

canton[1] (kan´ton, -ton´, kan´tən) n. **1** a division of a country, a small district. **2** a political division of Switzerland. **3** (Her.) a small division in the corner of a shield. **cantonal** (kan´-) a.

Usage note (kan´tən) is the usual pronunciation in heraldry.

canton[2] (kanton´, -toon´) v.t. **1** to divide into troops or cantons. **2** to billet (troops); to provide with quarters. **cantonment** n. **1** temporary or winter quarters for troops. **2** (Hist.) a permanent military station in British India.

Usage note (kanton´) is the usual pronunciation for dividing into cantons, (kantoon´) for providing with quarters.

Cantonese (kantənēz´) a. **1** of the city of Canton in S china, or its inhabitants. **2** of the dialect of Chinese spoken there. ~n. (pl. **Cantonese**) **1** a native or inhabitant of Canton. **2** the Cantonese dialect.

cantor (kan´taw) n. **1** a precentor; a person who leads the singing in church. **2** the Jewish religious official who sings the liturgy. **cantorial** (-taw´-) a. **1** of or relating to a precentor. **2** of or relating to the north side of the choir, where the precentor has his seat, as distinct from *decanal*. **cantoris** (-taw´ris) a. (*Mus.*) sung by the cantorial side of the choir, as distinct from *decani*.

Canuck (kənŭk´) n. **1** (*N Am.*, *coll.*) a Canadian. **2** (*Can. coll.*) a French Canadian. ~a. Canadian.

canvas (kan´vəs) n. **1** a coarse unbleached cloth, made of hemp or flax, used for sails, tents, paintings, embroidery etc. **2** the sails of a ship or boat. **3** a sheet of canvas for oil-painting etc. **4** a painting. **5** a covered part at the ends of a racing-boat. **6** the floor of a boxing or wrestling ring. ~a. made of canvas. ~v.t. (*pres.p.* **canvassing**, (*N Am.*) **canvasing**, *past*, *p.p.* **canvassed**, (*N Am.*) **canvased**) to cover with canvas. **to win by a canvas** in boat-racing, to win by a small margin. **under canvas 1** in a tent or tents. **2** with sails set. **canvas-back** n. a N American duck, *Aythya valisineria*.

canvass (kan´vəs) v.t. **1** to solicit votes, interest, support, orders etc. from. **2** to ascertain the opinions and feelings of. **3** to examine thoroughly, to discuss. ~v.i. to solicit votes etc. ~n. **1** the act of soliciting votes. **2** close examination, discussion. **canvasser** n.

canyon (kan´yən), **cañon** n. a deep gorge or ravine with precipitous sides, esp. of the type formed by erosion in the western plateaus of the US.

caoutchouc (kow´chook) n. raw rubber, the coagulated juice of certain tropical trees, which is elastic and waterproof.

CAP abbr. Common Agricultural Policy (of the EU).

cap (kap) n. **1** a covering for the head, usu. soft and close-fitting, with or without a peak at the front. **2** a natural or artificial covering resembling this in form or function. **3** a special form of head-covering distinguishing the holder of an office, a member of a sports team etc. **4** the lid of a bottle, covering for the point of a pen etc. **5** the top part of anything. **6** a porcelain crown set on the stump of a tooth. **7** a Dutch cap, a form of contraceptive device. **8** a block pierced to hold a mast or spar above another. ~v.t. (*pres.p.* **capping**, *past. p.p.* **capped**) **1** to cover the top of with a cap. **2** to put a cap on. **3** to protect or cover with or as with a cap. **4** (*Sc.*, *New Zeal.*) to confer a university degree upon. **5** to select (a player) for a sports team, esp. a national team. **6** to put a limit on (spending, charges etc.). **7** to be on the top of. **8** to complete, to surpass or outdo (*to cap a story*). **9** to put a percussion cap on (a gun). **cap in hand** in a humble or servile manner. **to set one's cap at** to try to attract or win (a particular person, esp. a man) for love or marriage. **cap of liberty** n. a soft conical cap, usu. red, given to freed Roman slaves and subsequently adopted as a symbol of freedom or republicanism, esp.

during the French Revolution; a Phrygian cap. **cap of maintenance** n. a cap or other head-covering worn as a symbol of office or carried before the sovereign at the coronation. **capper** n. **cap rock** n. a hard impervious layer of rock which overlies a gas or oil deposit. **cap sleeve** n. a short sleeve just covering the shoulder. **capstone** n. **1** the top stone. **2** a coping-stone. **3** a coping.

cap. (kap) abbr. **1** capacity. **2** capital (letter). **3** chapter.

capable (kā´pəbəl) a. **1** competent, able, skilful, qualified, fitted. **2** susceptible (of). **capability** (-bil´-) n. (*pl.* **capabilities**) **1** the quality of being capable. **2** capacity. **3** (*pl.*) resources, abilities, intellectual attainments. **capableness** n. **capably** adv.

capacious (kəpā´shəs) a. able to hold or contain much. **capaciously** adv. **capaciousness** n.

capacitate (kəpas´itāt) v.t. **1** to make capable. **2** to qualify. **3** to render competent.

capacity (kəpas´iti) n. (*pl.* **capacities**) **1** the power of containing, receiving, absorbing, producing etc. **2** room, cubic extent, volume. **3** the amount that can be contained etc. **4** capability, ability. **5** opportunity, scope. **6** relative position, character or office. **7** legal qualification or competence. **8** a measure of the output of a piece of electrical apparatus. **to capacity** fully; to the limit. **capacitance** n. **1** the ability of a conductor, system etc. to store electric charge. **2** the amount stored, measured in farads. **capacitative** a. **capacitive** a. **capacitor** n. a device for storing electric charge in a circuit.

caparison (kəpar´isən) n. **1** (*often pl.*) ornamental coverings or trappings for a horse or other beast of burden. **2** outfit, equipment. **3** rich clothing, finery. ~v.t. (*pres.p.* **caparisoning**, *past*, *p.p.* **caparisoned**) **1** to furnish with caparisons. **2** to deck out; to adorn.

cape[1] (kāp) n. **1** a sleeveless cloak. **2** a covering for the shoulders, sometimes attached to another garment. **caped** a.

cape[2] (kāp) n. a headland projecting into the sea. **Cape buffalo** n. a type of ox, *Syncercus caffer*, of southern and eastern Africa. **Cape Coloured** n. in the Cape Province of S Africa, a person of mixed white and non-white descent. ~a. of or relating to such a person. **Cape gooseberry** n. **1** a tropical plant, *Physalis peruviana*, with a small yellow edible fruit. **2** this fruit. **capeskin** n. a soft leather made from the skins of S African sheep or lambs.

capelin (kap´əlin), **caplin** (kap´lin) n. a small Newfoundland fish, *Mallotus villosus*, of the smelt family, used as food or as bait for cod.

caper[1] (kā´pə) n. **1** a frolicsome leap, a playful or frisky movement. **2** a prank; a light-hearted or high-spirited escapade. **3** (*sl.*) any activity, esp. of questionable legality. ~v.i. **1** to leap. **2** to skip about, to frolic. **caperer** n.

caper[2] (kā´pə) n. **1** a prickly shrub, *Capparis*

spinosa, of S Europe. **2** (*pl.*) the flower-buds of this, usu. pickled and used for flavouring.

capercaillie (kapəkā´li), **capercailzie** (-kāl´zi, -kā´li) *n.* the woodgrouse, *Tetrao urogallus*, also called the *cock of the wood.*

capillary (kəpil´əri) *a.* **1** resembling a hair, esp. in fineness. **2** (of a tube etc.) having a minute bore. **3** of or relating to the hair. **4** of or relating to the capillaries, capillary action etc. ~*n.* (*pl.* **capillaries**) **1** any of the minute blood vessels in which the arterial circulation ends and the venous circulation begins. **2** a capillary tube. **capillary action** *n.* the tendency of a fluid to ascend or descend in a capillary tube, absorbent material etc., caused by surface tension.

capital[1] (kap´itəl) *a.* **1** principal, chief, most important. **2** (*coll.*) excellent, first-rate. **3** involving or affecting the head. **4** punishable by death. **5** very serious or fatal. **6** (of letters) of the large size and shape used for initials, the first letter of a proper name etc. **7** relating to the main fund or stock of a corporation or business firm. ~*n.* **1** the most important city or town of a country, state etc. **2** a capital letter. **3** money used to start a business or industry. **4** money employed in earning interest or profits. **5** the main fund or stock of a corporation or business firm. ~*int.* (*coll.*) used to express great satisfaction or approval. **to make capital out of** to make profit from, to turn to one's advantage. **capital assets** *n.pl.* buildings, machinery, tools etc. used in business or industry; fixed assets. **capital gain** *n.* profit made from the sale of shares or other property. **capital gains tax** *n.* a tax levied on capital gain. **capital goods** *n.pl.* raw materials and tools used in the production of consumer goods. **capitalism** *n.* the economic system under which individuals use capital and employees to produce wealth. **capitalist** *n.* **1** a person who possesses capital. **2** a person who uses capital and employees to produce wealth. **3** a person who advocates capitalism. **capitalistic** (-lis´tik) *a.* **capitalistically** (-lis´-) *adv.* **capitalize, capitalise** *v.t.* **1** to convert into capital. **2** to use as capital. **3** to calculate or realize the present value of (periodical payments). **4** to write or print with a capital letter. **to capitalize on** to use to one's advantage. **capitalization** (-zā´shən) *n.* **capital levy** *n.* a levy on capital. **capital punishment** *n.* the death penalty. **capital sum** *n.* a lump sum of money, esp. payable on an insurance policy. **capital territory** *n.* the area of a country, state etc. where the capital is situated.

capital[2] (kap´itəl) *n.* (*Archit.*) the head of a pillar.

capitation (kapitā´shən) *n.* a tax, fee or grant per person. **capitation grant, capitation allowance** *n.* a subsidy or allowance calculated on the number of persons fulfilling specified conditions.

capitula CAPITULUM.

capitular (kəpit´ūlə) *a.* **1** of or relating to a cathedral chapter. **2** of or relating to a capitulum.

3 (*Anat.*) of or relating to the protuberant head of a bone.

capitulary (kəpit´ūləri) *n.* (*pl.* **capitularies**) a collection of ordinances, esp. those of the Frankish kings.

capitulate (kəpit´ūlāt) *v.i.* to surrender, esp. on stipulated terms. **capitulation** (-lā´shən) *n.* **1** the act of capitulating. **2** the document containing the terms of surrender. **3** a summary of the main divisions of a subject. **capitulator** *n.* **capitulatory** *a.*

capitulum (kəpit´ūləm) *n.* (*pl.* **capitula** (-lə)) (*Bot.*) a close cluster or head of sessile flowers.

caplin CAPELIN.

cap'n (kap´ən) *n.* (*coll.*) captain.

capo (kap´ō) *n.* (*pl.* **capos**) **1** the head of a branch of the Mafia. **2** (*Mus.*) a capo tasto.

capon (kā´pən) *n.* a castrated cock, esp. fattened for cooking. ~*v.t.* to caponize. **caponize, caponise** *v.t.* to castrate.

caponier (kapəniə´), **caponiere** *n.* a covered passage across the ditch of a fortified place.

capot (kəpot´) *n.* the winning of all the tricks at piquet by one player. ~*v.t.* (*pres. p.* **capotting**, *past, p.p.* **capotted**) to win all the tricks from.

capo tasto (kapō tas´tō) *n.* (*pl.* **capo tastos**) (*Mus.*) a bar fitted across the fingerboard of a guitar or similar instrument, to alter the pitch of all the strings simultaneously.

capote (kəpōt´) *n.* a long cloak or overcoat, usu. with a hood.

capper, capping CAP.

cappuccino (kapuchē´nō) *n.* (*pl.* **cappuccinos**) **1** white coffee, esp. from an espresso machine, often topped with whipped cream or powdered chocolate. **2** a drink of this.

capriccio (kəprē´chō, -chiō) *n.* (*pl.* **capriccios**, **capricci** (-chē)) **1** (*Mus.*) a lively composition, more or less free in form. **2** a fanciful work of art. **capriccioso** (-chō´sō, -chiō´sō) *adv.* (*Mus.*) in a free, fanciful style.

caprice (kəprēs´) *n.* **1** a sudden impulsive change of opinion, mood or behaviour. **2** a whim, a fancy. **3** a disposition to this kind of behaviour. **4** a capriccio. **capricious** (-rish´əs) *a.* **1** influenced by caprice. **2** whimsical, uncertain, fickle, given to unexpected and unpredictable changes. **capriciously** *adv.* **capriciousness** *n.*

Capricorn (kap´rikawn) *n.* **1** (*Astron.*) the zodiacal constellation of the Goat. **2** (*Astrol.*) **a** the tenth sign of the zodiac. **b** a person born under this sign. **Capricornian** (-kaw´-) *n.*, *a.*

caprine (kap´rīn) *a.* like a goat.

capriole (kap´riōl) *n.* **1** a leap made by a horse without advancing. **2** in ballet, a leap made from bent knees. ~*v.i.* to perform a capriole.

Capri pants (kaprē´), **Capris** *n.pl.* women's tight-fitting trousers, tapering towards and ending above the ankle.

caps. *abbr.* capital letters.

capsicum (kap´sikəm) *n.* (*pl.* **capsicums**) **1** a plant of the genus *Capsicum*, with mild or pungent fruit and seeds. **2** the fruit of a capsicum used as a vegetable or ground to produce the condiments chilli, cayenne etc.

capsid[1] (kap´sid) *n.* any bug of the family Miridae, feeding on plants.

capsid[2] (kap´sid) *n.* the outer casing of some viruses, made of protein.

capsize (kapsīz´) *v.t.* to upset, to overturn. ~*v.i.* to be upset, to overturn. ~*n.* an instance of capsizing. **capsizal** *n.*

capstan (kap´stən, -stan) *n.* **1** a revolving pulley or drum, either power- or lever-driven, used to wind in a rope or cable. **2** a revolving shaft in a tape recorder, which draws the tape past the head. **capstan lathe** *n.* a lathe with a revolving turret, so that several different tools can be used in rotation.

capsule (kap´sūl) *n.* **1** a small envelope of gelatin containing medicine. **2** (*Anat.*) a sac or enveloping membrane. **3** (*Bot.*) a dry dehiscent seed-vessel. **4** a metallic cover for a bottle. **5** a part of a spacecraft, aircraft etc., usu. housing the instruments and crew, that can be detached or ejected. **capsular** *a.* **capsulate** (-lət), **capsulated** (-lātid) *a.* **capsulize, capsulise** *v.t.* to put (information) into a very condensed form.

Capt. *abbr.* Captain.

captain (kap´tin) *n.* **1** a leader, a commander. **2** in the army, a rank between major and lieutenant; a similar rank in the air force in N America. **3** in the navy, a rank between commodore or rear admiral and commander. **4** the master of a merchant ship. **5** the pilot of a civil aircraft. **6** (*N Am.*) a police officer in charge of a precinct. **7** the leader of a side or team. **8** (*N Am.*) a head waiter or the supervisor of bell boys in a hotel. **9** the chief boy or girl in a school. **10** a general, a strategist, a great soldier, a veteran commander. **11** (*coll.*) a Guide Guider. ~*v.t.* **1** to act as captain of. **2** to lead, to head. **Captain Cooker** *n.* (*New Zeal., coll.*) a wild boar (descended from swine landed there by Capt. Cook). **captaincy** *n.* (*pl.* **captaincies**). **captain-general** *n.* an honorary officer. **captainship** *n.*

caption (kap´shən) *n.* **1** the wording under an illustration, cartoon etc. **2** a subtitle or other printed or graphic material in a television broadcast or cinematograph film. **3** the heading of a chapter, section or newspaper article. **4** (*Law*) **a** the heading or descriptive preamble of a legal document. **b** apprehension by judicial process. ~*v.t.* to provide with a caption.

captious (kap´shəs) *a.* **1** fault-finding, carping, cavilling. **2** sophistical, quibbling. **captiously** *adv.* **captiousness** *n.*

captivate (kap´tivāt) *v.t.* to fascinate, to charm. **captivating** *a.* **captivatingly** *adv.* **captivation** (-ā´shən) *n.*

captive (kap´tiv) *n.* a person or animal taken prisoner or held in confinement. ~*a.* **1** taken prisoner. **2** held in confinement, restraint or control. **3** unable to move away, refuse, exercise choice etc. (*a captive audience, a captive market*). **4** of or relating to captivity. **5** captivated, fascinated. **captive balloon** *n.* a balloon held by a rope from the ground. **captivity** (-tiv´-) *n.* (*pl.* **captivities**) **1** the state of being captive. **2** a period of being captive. **captor** *n.*

capture (kap´chə) *v.t.* **1** to take as a captive. **2** to take control of; to seize as a prize. **3** to succeed in describing in words or by drawing (a likeness etc.). **4** (*Physics*) (of an atom, molecule etc.) to acquire or absorb (an additional particle). **5** (*Comput.*) to cause (data) to be stored. ~*n.* **1** the act of capturing. **2** the person or thing captured. **capturer** *n.*

capuchin (kap´əchin, -ū-) *n.* **1** (**Capuchin**) a Franciscan friar of the reform of the 1520s. **2** a hooded cloak, like the habit of the Capuchins, worn by women. **3** a capuchin monkey or pigeon. **capuchin monkey** *n.* an American monkey, *Cebus capucinus*, with thick hair like a cowl on the head. **capuchin pigeon** *n.* a variety of pigeon with cowl-like feathers in the head and neck.

capybara (kapibah´rə), **capibara** *n.* (*pl.* **capybaras, capibaras**) a S American mammal, *Hydrochoerus hydrochaeris*, the largest living rodent, allied to the guinea pig.

car (kah) *n.* **1** a small road vehicle propelled by an internal-combustion engine, usu. having four wheels and seats for two to five passengers; a motor-car. **2** a wheeled vehicle (*esp. in comb.*, as *tramcar*). **3** (*Ir.*) a jaunting-car. **4** a railway carriage (*esp. in comb.* as *dining car*). **5** (*N Am.*) any railway coach or wagon. **6** the passenger carriage below an airship, balloon, cable railway etc. **7** (*esp. N Am.*) a lift cage. **8** (*poet.*) a chariot. **car bomb** *n.* an explosive device hidden in or below a parked car, which destroys the car and usu. kills any occupants. **car boot sale** *n.* a sale of second-hand goods, from the boots of cars or from tables. **car-coat** *n.* a short coat which can be worn comfortably in a car. **car ferry** *n.* (*pl.* **car ferries**) a ferry that transports motor vehicles. **carful** *n.* (*pl.* **carfuls**) **carhop** *n.* (*coll., N Am.*) a waiter or waitress at a drive-in restaurant. **carjack** *v.t.* to hijack (a car). **carjacker** *n.* **carjacking** *n.* **carload** *n.* as much as a car will hold. **car park** *n.* a place where cars may be left for a limited period. **carphone** *n.* a cellular telephone suitable for operating in a car. **carport** *n.* an open-sided shelter for a car beside a house. **carsick** *a.* suffering from nausea or vomiting brought on by the motion of a car. **carsickness** *n.* **car-wash** *n.* an establishment with equipment for the automatic washing of cars.

carabine, carabineer CARBINE.

carabiniere (karəbinyeə´rā) *n.* (*pl.* **carabinieri** (-ri)) a member of the national police force in Italy.

caracal (kar´əkal) *n.* a lynx, *Felis caracal*, of N Africa and S Asia, having black-tufted ears.

caracara (karəkah´rə) *n.* (*pl.* **caracaras**) any of

various American birds of prey that feed on carrion.

caracol (kar´əkol), **caracole** (-kōl) *n.* a half turn or wheel made by a horse or its rider. ~*v.i.* (*pres.p.* **caracoling**, *past, p.p.* **caracoled**) to perform a caracol. ~*v.t.* to make (a horse) caracol.

caracul KARAKUL.

carafe (kəraf´, -rahf´, kar´əf) *n.* **1** a wide-mouthed glass container for wine or water at table. **2** as much wine or water as a carafe will hold.

carambola (karəmbō´lə) *n.* (*pl.* **carambolas**) **1** the star fruit. **2** the SE Asian tree, *Averrhoa carambola*, that bears this fruit.

caramel (kar´əmel, -məl) *n.* **1** burnt sugar used for flavouring and colouring food and drink. **2** a kind of toffee. **3** the colour of caramel, a pale brown. **caramelize, caramelise** *v.t., v.i.* to turn into caramel. **caramelization** (-zā´shən) *n.*

carangid (kəran´jid, -rang´gid), **carangoid** (-rang´goid) *n.* any fish of the family Carangidae, including the scads, pilot fishes etc. ~*a.* of or relating to this family.

carapace (kar´əpās) *n.* **1** the upper shell of an animal of the tortoise family. **2** any analogous covering in other animals, such as the crab.

carat (kar´ət) *n.* **1** a weight (standardized as the International Carat of 0.200 g) used for precious stones, esp. diamonds. **2** (*N Am.* **karat**) a proportional measure of gold content, 24-carat gold being pure gold.

caravan (kar´əvan) *n.* **1** a mobile home, a vehicle for living in that can be towed by a car or (esp. formerly) by a horse. **2** a covered wagon used by gypsies, showmen etc. **3** a company of merchants or pilgrims, travelling together (esp. in desert regions) for mutual security. ~*v.i.* (*pres.p.* **caravanning**, *past, p.p.* **caravanned**) to travel or live in a caravan, esp. while on holiday. **caravanette** (-et´) *n.* a large motor vehicle having living accommodation at the back. **caravanner** *n.* **caravan site, caravan park** *n.* a place where holidaymakers etc. can live temporarily in caravans.

caravanserai (karəvan´sərī), **caravansary** (-ri), **caravansera** (-rə) *n.* (*pl.* **caravanserais, caravansaries, caravanseras**) an Oriental inn with a large courtyard for the accommodation of caravans of merchants or pilgrims.

caravel (kar´əvel) *n.* any of various small light ships, such as a swift Spanish or Portuguese merchant vessel of the 15th–17th cents.

caraway (kar´əwā), **carraway** *n.* a European umbelliferous plant, *Carum carvi.* **caraway seed** *n.* the small dried fruit of this plant used as a flavouring.

carb (kahb) *n.* (*coll.*) a carburettor.

carbamate (kah´bəmāt) *n.* (*Chem.*) a salt or ester of carbamic acid, esp. carbaryl. **carbamic acid** (-bam´ik) *n.* an amide of carbonic acid.

carbide (kah´bīd) *n.* (*Chem.*) a compound of carbon with a metal, esp. calcium carbide.

carbine (kah´bīn), **carabine** (kar´əbīn) *n.* a short rifle used by cavalry. **carbineer** (-biniə´), **carabineer, carabinier** *n.* a soldier armed with a carbine.

carbo- (kah´bō), **carb-** *comb. form* of, with, containing, or relating to carbon.

carbohydrate (kahbəhī´drāt) *n.* an organic compound of carbon, hydrogen and oxygen, usu. having two atoms of hydrogen to every one of oxygen, as in starch, glucose etc.

carbolic (kahbol´ik) *a.* derived from coal or coal tar. ~*n.* carbolic acid. **carbolic acid** *n.* an antiseptic and disinfectant acid; phenol. **carbolic soap** *n.* soap containing carbolic acid.

carbon (kah´bən) *n.* **1** (*Chem.*) a non-metallic element, at. no. 6, chem. symbol C, found in nearly all organic substances, in carbon dioxide and the carbonates, and occurring naturally as diamond, graphite and charcoal. **2** carbon paper. **3** a carbon copy. **4** a rod of fine charcoal used in arc-lamps. **carbonaceous** (-nā´-) *a.* **1** like coal or charcoal. **2** containing carbon. **carbonate**[1] (-nət) *n.* a salt of carbonic acid. **carbonate**[2] (-āt) *v.t.* **1** to impregnate with carbonic acid. **2** to aerate (water etc.). **3** to form into a carbonate. **carbonation** (-nā´shən) *n.* **carbon black** *n.* a fine black carbon powder, used in the production of rubber, ink etc. **carbon copy** *n.* **1** a duplicate of something typed, written or drawn, made by placing carbon paper between two or more sheets of paper before typing etc. **2** a person, thing or event etc. that is identical or very similar to something else. **carbon cycle** *n.* (*Biol.*) the biological cycle in which carbon compounds are circulated between living organisms and their environment. **carbon dating** *n.* a method of calculating the age of organic material (wood, bones etc.) by measuring the decay of the isotope carbon-14. **carbon dioxide** *n.* a gaseous combination of one atom of carbon with two of oxygen, a normal constituent of the atmosphere and a product of respiration. **carbon disulphide** *n.* a colourless liquid with an unpleasant smell, used as a solvent and in the production of artificial fibres. **carbon fibre**, (*N Am.*) **carbon fiber** *n.* a very strong thread of pure carbon, used for reinforcing plastics, metals etc. **carbonic** (-bon´-) *a.* of, relating to or containing carbon. **carbonic acid** *n.* a weak acid; the compound formed by carbon dioxide and water. **carboniferous** (-nif´-) *a.* producing coal or carbon. **Carboniferous period** *n.* (*Geol.*) the fifth period of the Palaeozoic era, between the Devonian and the Permian. **carbonize, carbonise** *v.t.* **1** to convert into carbon by the action of heat or acid. **2** to cover with carbon, charcoal, lamp-black, or the like. **carbonization** (-zā´shən) *n.* **carbon monoxide** *n.* a poisonous gas containing one atom of oxygen for each atom of carbon; a constituent of motor vehicle exhaust gases. **carbon paper** *n.* a dark-coated paper used for making carbon copies by transferring an impression of what is typed, written or drawn on the top sheet to a lower sheet. **carbon steel** *n.* any of several types of steel containing carbon in varying amounts. **carbon tax** *n.* a suggested tax on fossil fuels, esp. petrol, aimed at reducing their use and so protecting the environment. **carbon tetrachloride** *n.* a colourless toxic liquid, used as a dry-cleaning solvent. **carbonyl** (-īl, -il) *a.* (*attrib.*) of or containing the divalent radical: C=O.

carbonado (kahbənä´dō, -nah´-) *n.* (*pl.* **carbonados, carbonadoes**) a black, opaque diamond of poor quality, used industrially in drills etc.

Carborundum® (kahbərŭn´dəm) *n.* an abrasive material, esp. a silicon carbide used for grinding-wheels etc.

carboxyl (kahbok´sīl, -sil) *a.* (*attrib.*, *Chem.*) of or containing the monovalent radical -COOH. **carboxylic acid** (-sil´ik) *n.* an organic acid containing the carboxyl group.

carboy (kah´boi) *n.* a large globular bottle of green or blue glass, protected with wickerwork, used for holding corrosive liquids.

carbuncle (kah´bŭngkəl) *n.* **1** a hard, painful boil without a core, caused by bacterial infection. **2** a precious stone of a bright red colour. **3** (*coll.*) an ugly building etc. which defaces its surroundings. **carbuncular** (-bŭng´kū-) *a.*

carburation (kahbūrā´shən), **carburetion** (-resh´ən) *n.* the process of mixing the correct proportions of hydrocarbon fuel and air in an internal-combustion engine etc.

carburet (kah´būret, -ret´) *v.t.* (*pres.p.* **carburetting**, (*N Am.*) **carbureting**, *past, p.p.* **carburetted**, (*N Am.*) **carbureted**) to combine (another element) with carbon. **carburettor, carburetter**, (*N Am.*) **carburetor** *n.* an apparatus designed to atomize a liquid, esp. petrol in an internal-combustion engine, and to mix it with air in the correct proportions to ensure ready ignition and complete combustion. **carburize, carburise** *v.t.* **1** to carburet. **2** to add carbon to (wrought iron). **carburization** (-zā´shən) *n.*

carcajou (kah´kəzhoo) *n.* the glutton or wolverine.

carcass (kah´kəs), **carcase** *n.* **1** the dead body of an animal. **2** the trunk of a slaughtered animal without the head and offal. **3** (*derog. or facet.*) the human body, dead or alive. **4** the framework or skeleton of a building, ship etc. **5** a mere shell or husk. **carcass meat** *n.* raw meat as sold in a butcher's shop.

carcinogen (kahsin´əjən) *n.* a substance that can give rise to cancer. **carcinogenic** (-jen´-) *a.* **carcinogenicity** (-is´iti) *n.*

carcinoma (kahsinō´mə) *n.* (*pl.* **carcinomas, carcinomata** (-tə)) **1** a malignant tumour. **2** the disease cancer. **carcinomatous** *a.*

Card. *abbr.* Cardinal.

card[1] (kahd) *n.* **1** stiff paper or thin cardboard. **2** a flat, rectangular piece of this for writing or drawing on etc. **3** a small piece of card, usu. printed, such as a visiting card, a business card, a membership card, an identity card etc. **4** a folded piece of card with a picture on the front, used to send greetings (*a birthday card*; *a Christmas card*). **5** a postcard. **6** any one of a pack of oblong pieces of card, marked with symbols and pictures, used in playing games of chance or skill; a playing-card. **7** (*pl.*) a game or games played with cards; card-playing. **8** a programme, a menu, a list of events at races, regattas etc. **9** (*pl., coll.*) a worker's employment documents. **10** (*Comput.*) a punchcard. **11** a small oblong piece of plastic used for financial transactions etc., often bearing personal details that can be read electronically (*a cheque card*; *a credit card*). **12** a similar piece of plastic used for other purposes, such as a phonecard. **13** the piece of card on which the points are marked in the mariner's compass; a compass card. **14** (*sl.*) a character, an eccentric. **a card up one's sleeve** a plan or resource held secretly in reserve or in readiness; an undisclosed advantage. **on the cards** possible; not improbable. **to play one's cards close to one's chest** to be secretive about one's intentions, resources etc. **to play one's cards well/ right** etc. to be a good strategist; to take the appropriate action to gain an advantage. **to put one's cards on the table** to disclose one's situation, plans etc. **to stack the cards 1** to interfere with a deck of playing-cards secretly for the purpose of cheating. **2** to arrange matters to the disadvantage or advantage of someone (*The cards are stacked against us*). **cardboard** *n.* fine pasteboard used for making light boxes and other articles. ~*a.* **1** made of cardboard. **2** without substance or reality. **cardboard city** *n.* an area of a city where homeless people set up makeshift shelters constructed from cardboard boxes etc. **card-carrying** *a.* (*attrib.*) being a full member of (a political party etc.). **card game** *n.* a game played with cards. **cardholder** *n.* a person who has a credit card, membership card etc. **card index** *n.* an index in which each item is entered on a separate card. **card-index** *v.t.* to make a card index of. **cardphone** *n.* a public telephone where a phonecard is inserted rather than coins. **card-playing** *n.* the playing of card games. **card-sharp, card-sharper** *n.* a person who swindles by means of card games or tricks with cards. **card table** *n.* a table to play cards on. **card vote** *n.* a ballot where the vote of each delegate counts for the number of their constituents.

card[2] (kahd) *n.* a toothed instrument for combing wool, flax etc. or raising a nap. ~*v.t.* **1** to comb (wool, flax or hemp) with a card. **2** to raise a nap on. **carder** *n.* **carding-wool** *n.* short-stapled wool.

cardamom (kah´dəməm), **cardamum, cardamon** (-ən) *n.* **1** an aromatic plant of SE Asia, *Elettaria cardamomum*. **2** a spice obtained from the seed capsules of this plant or of various species of *Amomum* and other genera.

cardan joint (kah´dən) *n.* in engineering, a type of universal joint which can rotate when out of alignment. **cardan shaft** *n.* a shaft with a universal joint at either end.

cardiac (kah´diak) *a.* **1** of or relating to the heart. **2** of or relating to the upper part of the stomach. ~*n.* **1** a stimulant for the heart. **2** a person suffering from heart disease. **cardiac tamponade** *n.* abnormal pressure on the heart caused by excessive fluid in the pericardial sac.

cardie (kah´di), **cardy, cardi** *n.* (*pl.* **cardies**) (*coll.*) a cardigan.

cardigan (kah´digən) *n.* a knitted jacket buttoned up the front.

cardinal (kah´dinəl) *a.* **1** fundamental, chief, principal. **2** of the colour of a cardinal's cassock, deep scarlet. **3** of or relating to a hinge. ~*n.* **1** any of the ecclesiastical dignitaries of the Roman Catholic Church who elect a new pope, usu. from among their own number. **2** a cardinal number. **3** a cardinal-bird. **4** (*Hist.*) a short cloak (orig. of scarlet) for women. **cardinalate** (-āt), **cardinalship** *n.* **cardinal-bird** *n.* a N American songbird, *Cardinalis cardinalis*, with scarlet plumage in the male. **cardinal flower** *n.* the scarlet lobelia, *Lobelia cardinalis*. **cardinally** *adv.* **cardinal number** *n.* any of the numbers 1, 2, 3, etc., as distinguished from the *ordinal numbers* 1st, 2nd, 3rd etc. **cardinal point** *n.* any of the four points of the compass: north, south, east and west. **cardinal virtues** *n.pl.* **1** (*Philos.*) prudence, temperance, justice and fortitude. **2** (*Theol.*) faith, hope and charity.

cardio- (kah´diō), **cardi-** *comb. form* (*Anat.*) of or relating to the heart.

cardiogram (kah´diəgram) *n.* a reading from a cardiograph.

cardiograph (kah´diəgrahf) *n.* an instrument for registering the activity of the heart. **cardiographer** (-og´-) *n.* **cardiography** (-og´-) *n.*

cardioid (kah´dioid) *n.* (*Math.*) a heart-shaped curve. ~*a.* heart-shaped.

cardiology (kahdiol´əji) *n.* the branch of medicine concerned with the heart. **cardiological** (-əloj´-) *a.* **cardiologist** *n.*

cardiomyopathy (kahdiōmīop´əthi) *n.* (*Med.*) a disease of the heart muscle.

cardiopulmonary (kahdiōpŭl´mənəri) *a.* (*Med.*) of or relating to the heart and lungs.

cardiovascular (kahdiōvas´kūlə) *a.* of or relating to the heart and blood-vessels.

cardoon (kahdoon´) *n.* a thistle-like plant, *Cynara cardunculus*, allied to the artichoke, the leaf stalks of which are eaten as a vegetable.

cardy CARDIE.

care (keə) *n.* **1** anxiety, concern. **2** a cause of these. **3** caution, serious attention, heed. **4** supervision, protection. **5** attention or services provided for the sick etc. ~*v.i.* **1** to be concerned, interested, emotionally affected etc. **2** to have affection, respect or liking (for). **3** to be desirous, willing or inclined (to). **care of** at or to the address of. **in care** (of a child) in the guardianship of the local authority. **to care for** to provide for; to look after. **to have a care** to take care. **to take care 1** to be careful, cautious or vigilant.

2 (*coll.*) to look after oneself. **to take care of 1** to look after (*takes care of his elderly mother*). **2** to provide or pay for (*put money aside in order to take care of the bills*). **3** to deal with. **carefree** *a.* free from responsibility, light-hearted. **careful** *a.* **1** cautious, watchful, circumspect. **2** painstaking, attentive, exact. **3** done with care. **4** solicitous, concerned. **5** not neglecting, omitting, failing etc. (*He was careful to spell her name right*). **carefully** *adv.* **carefulness** *n.* **caregiver** *n.* a carer. **care label** *n.* a label bearing washing or cleaning instructions, attached to a garment etc. **careless** *a.* **1** not taking care. **2** heedless, thoughtless, unconcerned. **3** inattentive, negligent (of). **4** done without care; inaccurate. **5** casual. **carelessly** *adv.* **carelessness** *n.* **carer** *n.* a person who looks after someone, e.g. an invalid, dependent relative etc. **caretaker** *n.* a person in charge of an unoccupied house, a public building etc. ~*a.* (*attrib.*) interim. **care-worn** *a.* **caring** *a.* **1** showing care or concern. **2** providing medical care or social services (*the caring professions*).

✕ **carecter** common misspelling of CHARACTER.

careen (kərēn´) *v.t.* to turn (a ship) on one side in order to clean, caulk or repair it. ~*v.i.* (of a ship) to heel over. **careenage** *n.*

career (kəriə´) *n.* **1** a course or progress through life, esp. a person's working life. **2** a person's chosen profession, business or other occupation. **3** the progress and development of a nation, party etc. **4** a running, a swift course. ~*a.* (*attrib.*) having a specified career; professional (*a career diplomat*). ~*v.i.* **1** to move in a swift, headlong course. **2** to gallop at full speed. **careerism** *n.* making personal advancement one's main objective. **careerist** *n.*, *a.* **career structure** *n.* a pattern or system of advancement within a profession or organization.

caress (kəres´) *n.* **1** a gentle touch, an embrace, a kiss. **2** an act of endearment. ~*v.t.* **1** to fondle, to pet, to stroke affectionately. **2** to touch gently. **caressing** *a.* **caressingly** *adv.*

caret (kar´ət) *n.* in writing or printing, a mark (∧) used to show that something, which may be read above or in the margin, is to be inserted.

cargo (kah´gō) *n.* (*pl.* **cargoes, cargos**) **1** freight carried by ship or aircraft. **2** a load of such freight.

Carib (kar´ib) *n.* **1** a member of the aboriginal people of the southern islands of the W Indies. **2** the language spoken by these people. ~*a.* of or relating to these people or their language. **Caribbean** (-bē´ən) *a.* denoting, of or relating to the Caribbean Sea, its islands or their inhabitants. ~*n.* a West Indian or Carib.

caribou (kar´iboo) *n.* (*pl.* **caribou**) the N American reindeer.

caricature (kar´ikəchə, -tūə) *n.* **1** a representation of a person or thing exaggerating characteristic traits in a ludicrous way. **2** a burlesque, a parody. **3** a laughably inadequate person or thing. ~*v.t.* **1** to represent in this way. **2** to burlesque, to parody. **caricatural** *a.* **caricaturist** (-tūə'rist) *n.*

caries (keə'riēz) *n.* (*pl.* **caries**) decay of the bones or teeth. **cariogenic** (-ōjen'-) *a.* producing caries. **carious** *a.*

carillon (kəril'yən, kar'ilən) *n.* **1** a set of bells played by the hand or by machinery. **2** a tune played on such bells. **3** a musical instrument (or part of one) imitating such bells.

carina (kərē'nə, -rī'-) *n.* (*pl.* **carinas, carinae** (-nē)) (*Bot., Zool.*) a ridgelike or keel-shaped structure. **carinate** (kar'ənāt), **carinated** *a.*

caring CARE.

carioca (kariō'kə) *n.* **1** a S American dance like the samba. **2** music for this dance. **3** (*coll.* **Carioca**) a native or inhabitant of Rio de Janeiro.

cariogenic CARIES.

cariole CARRIOLE.

carious CARIES.

❌ **carisma** common misspelling of CHARISMA.

carline (kah'lin) *n.* any plant of the genus *Carlina*, allied to the thistle, esp. *C. vulgaris.*

Carlovingian CAROLINGIAN.

Carmelite (kah'məlīt) *n.* **1** a member of an order of mendicant friars, founded in the 12th cent. on Mount Carmel; a White Friar. **2** a nun of a corresponding order. ~*a.* of or relating to the Carmelites.

carminative (kah'minətiv, -min'-) *a.* relieving flatulence. ~*n.* a carminative drug or medicine.

carmine (kah'mīn, -min) *n.* **1** a vivid red or crimson pigment obtained from cochineal. **2** this colour. ~*a.* of this colour.

carnage (kah'nij) *n.* butchery, slaughter, esp. of human beings.

carnal (kah'nəl) *a.* **1** fleshly, bodily, sensual, sexual. **2** temporal, secular. **3** worldly, unspiritual. **carnalism** *n.* **carnality** (-nal'-) *n.* **carnal knowledge** *n.* (*esp. Law*) sexual intercourse. **carnally** *adv.*

carnassial (kahnas'iəl) *n.* in carnivores, a large tooth adapted for tearing flesh, the first lower molar or the last upper premolar. ~*a.* relating to such a tooth.

carnation[1] (kahnā'shən) *n.* the cultivated clove pink, *Dianthus caryophyllus*, with sweet-scented double flowers of various colours.

carnation[2] (kahnā'shən) *n.* **1** a light rose-pink colour. **2** a flesh tint. **3** a part of a painting representing human flesh. ~*a.* of this colour.

carnauba (kahnow'bə) *n.* **1** a Brazilian palm, *Copernicia cerifera.* **2** (*also* **carnauba wax**) a yellow wax obtained from its leaves, used in polishes.

carnelian CORNELIAN.

carnet (kah'nā) *n.* **1** a document allowing the transport of vehicles or goods across a frontier. **2** a book of vouchers, tickets etc.

carnival (kah'nivəl) *n.* **1** a festival, esp. annual, usu. marked by processions and revelry. **2** the season immediately before Lent, in many Roman Catholic countries devoted to pageantry

and riotous amusement. **3** riotous amusement, revelry. **4** a travelling funfair.

carnivore (kah'nivaw) *n.* **1** any animal of the order Carnivora, a large order of mammals subsisting on flesh. **2** a carnivorous animal or plant. **carnivorous** (-niv'ərəs) *a.* **1** feeding on flesh. **2** (of plants) feeding on insects. **carnivorously** *adv.* **carnivorousness** *n.*

carob (kar'əb) *n.* **1** the Mediterranean locust tree, *Ceratonia siliqua.* **2** its fruit, with an edible pulp, used as a substitute for chocolate.

carol (kar'əl) *n.* **1** a joyous song or hymn, esp. sung at Christmas. **2** joyous warbling of birds. ~*v.i.* (*pres.p.* **carolling**, (*N Am.*) **caroling**, *past, p.p.* **carolled**, (*N Am.*) **caroled**) **1** to sing carols. **2** to warble. ~*v.t.* to celebrate with songs. **caroller**, (*N Am.*) **caroler** *n.* **carol-singer** *n.* a person who sings carols at Christmas, esp. for money outside private houses or in public places. **carol-singing** *n.*

Caroline (kar'əlīn), **Carolean** (-lē'ən), **Carolinian** (-lin'iən) *a.* **1** of or relating to the reigns of Charles I and II of Britain. **2** of or relating to any king called Charles. **3** Carolingian.

Carolingian (karəlin'jiən), **Carlovingian** (kah-ləvin'iən) *a.* of or belonging to the dynasty of French kings founded by Charlemagne. ~*n.* a member of this dynasty.

Carolinian (karəlin'iən) *a.* of or relating to either of the US states of North Carolina and South Carolina. ~*n.* a native or inhabitant of either of these states.

carom (kar'əm) *n.* (*N Am.*) in billiards, a cannon. ~*v.i.* **1** to make a cannon. **2** to rebound after striking.

carotene (kar'ətēn), **carotin** (-tin) *n.* an orangered pigment found in plants, e.g. carrots, a source of vitamin A. **carotenoid** (kərot'inoid), **carotinoid** *n.* any of a group of pigments, including carotene, found in plants and some animals.

carotid (kərot'id) *a.* of or related to either of the arteries (one on each side of the neck) supplying blood to the head. ~*n.* a carotid artery.

carouse (kərowz') *n.* a carousal. ~*v.i.* **1** to have a carousal. **2** to drink freely. **carousal** *n.* **carouser** *n.*

carousel (karəsel'), (*esp. N Am.*) **carrousel** *n.* **1** (*N Am.*) a merry-go-round. **2** a rotating conveyor belt for luggage at an airport. **3** a rotating container which delivers slides to a projector.

carp[1] (kahp) *n.* any freshwater fish of the genus *Cyprinus*, esp. *C. cyprio*, the common carp.

carp[2] (kahp) *v.i.* **1** to talk querulously, to complain. **2** to find fault, to cavil. **carper** *n.*

carpaccio (kahpach'iō) *n.* an Italian hors d'oeuvre comprising thin slices of raw meat or fish, sometimes served with a dressing.

carpal CARPUS.

carpel (kah'pəl) *n.* (*Bot.*) the female reproductive organ of a flower, comprising ovary, style and stigma. **carpellary** *a.*

carpenter (kah´pintə) n. **1** a person who prepares and fixes the woodwork of houses, ships etc.; a skilled woodworker. **2** (esp. N Am.) a joiner. ~v.i. to do carpentry. ~v.t. to make by carpentry. **carpenter ant** n. any ant of the genus Campanotus, which bores into wood to make its nest. **carpenter bee** n. any bee that bores into wood or plant stems, e.g. the genus Xylocopa. **carpentry** n. **1** the trade of a carpenter. **2** carpenter's work, esp. the kind of woodwork prepared at the carpenter's bench.

carpet (kah´pit) n. **1** a woollen or other thick fabric, usu. with a pile, for covering floors and stairs (fitted carpet). **2** a large piece of this, used to cover all or part of the floor of a room. **3** any similar covering, e.g. of snow, leaves etc. ~v.t. (pres.p. **carpeting**, past, p.p. **carpeted**) **1** to cover with or as with a carpet. **2** (coll.) to reprimand. **on the carpet** under consideration. **2** (coll.) being reprimanded. **to sweep under the carpet** to conceal or ignore deliberately (a problem etc.). **carpet-bag** n. a travelling-bag orig. made with sides of carpet. **carpet-bagger** n. **1** (esp. N Am.) a person who seeks political office in a place where the person has no local connections. **2** an unscrupulous opportunist or profiteer. **carpet beetle**, (N Am.) **carpet bug** n. any of several beetles of the genus Anthrenus, whose larvae feed on carpets and other fabrics. **carpet bombing** n. bombing of a whole area, rather than of selected targets. **carpeting** n. **1** the material of which carpets are made. **2** carpets in general. **3** the action of covering with or as with carpet. **4** (coll.) a severe reprimand. **carpet slippers** n.pl. comfortable slippers orig. made of carpet-like fabric. **carpet tile** n. a small square of carpeting which can be laid with others to cover a floor.

carpology (kahpol´əji) n. the branch of botany which deals with fruits and seeds.

carpus (kah´pəs) n. (pl. **carpi** (-pī)) **1** the wrist, the part of the human skeleton joining the hand to the forearm, comprising eight small bones. **2** the corresponding part in other animals. **carpal** a. of the wrist. ~n. a wrist bone.

carr (kah) n. **1** an area of marshy ground or fen where willow, alder or similar trees or shrubs are found. **2** a copse of such trees or shrubs in marshy ground.

carrageen (kar´əgēn), **carragheen** n. an edible seaweed, Chondrus crispus, found on N Atlantic shores; Irish moss. **carrageenan, carrageenin, carragheenin** n. an extract of carrageen used in food processing.

carrel (kar´əl), **carrell** n. a cubicle for private study in a library.

☒ **carress** common misspelling of CARESS.

carriage (kar´ij) n. **1** a passenger vehicle in a train. **2** a wheeled vehicle, esp. a horse-drawn vehicle for carrying passengers. **3** carrying, transporting, conveyance, esp. of merchandise. **4** the cost of conveying. **5** the manner or means of carrying. **6** mien, bearing, deportment. **7** the moving part of a machine which carries another part (a typewriter carriage). **8** the wheeled support of a cannon. **9** the wheeled framework of a vehicle as distinguished from the body. **carriage and pair** n. a four-wheeled private vehicle drawn by two horses. **carriage clock** n. a portable clock in an oblong metal case with a handle on top. **carriage dog** n. (dated) a Dalmatian (from its former use as a guard dog running behind a carriage). **carriage return key** n. a key that returns the carriage of a typewriter to its original position. **carriageway** n. the part of a road used for vehicular traffic.

☒ **Carribean** common misspelling of CARIBBEAN (under CARIB).

carrier (kar´iə) n. **1** a person, thing or organization conveying goods or passengers for payment. **2** any person or thing that carries. **3** a person or animal that transmits a disease, esp. without suffering from it. **4** a carrier bag. **5** a framework on a bicycle for holding luggage. **6** an aircraft carrier. **7** (Physics) an electron or hole that carries charge in a semiconductor. **8** a substance that supports a catalyst, conveys radioactive material etc. **9** any of various parts of machines or instruments which act as transmitters or bearers. **carrier bag** n. a strong plastic or paper bag with handles. **carrier pigeon** n. a pigeon of a breed trained to carry communications. **carrier wave** n. an electromagnetic wave which is modulated for the radio transmission etc. of a signal.

carriole (kar´iōl), **cariole** n. **1** a small open carriage. **2** a light covered cart. **3** (Can.) an ornamental sledge.

carrion (kar´iən) n. **1** dead, putrefying flesh. **2** garbage, filth. ~a. **1** feeding on carrion. **2** putrid. **3** loathsome. **carrion crow** n. a species of crow, Corvus corone, that feeds on small animals and carrion. **carrion flower** n. the stapelia.

carrot (kar´ət) n. **1** a plant, Daucus carota, with an orange-coloured tapering root, used as a vegetable. **2** this vegetable. **3** an incentive. **4** (pl., coll.) a person with red hair. **carroty** a.

carry (kar´i) v.t. (3rd pers. sing. pres. **carries**, pres.p. **carrying**, past, p.p. **carried**) **1** to bear, transport or convey from one place to another by supporting and moving with the thing conveyed. **2** to convey or take with one. **3** to conduct or transmit. **4** to bring, to enable to go or come. **5** to transfer, as from one book, page or column to another. **6** to bear or support. **7** to have in or on. **8** to imply or involve. **9** to bear or hold (oneself) in a particular way. **10** to extend or cause to move in any direction in time or space. **11** to effect, to accomplish. **12** to win, to capture. **13** to wear (clothes). ~v.i. **1** to act as bearer. **2** to extend or travel a distance. **3** to bear the head in a particular manner, as a horse. ~n. (pl. **carries**) **1** the act of carrying. **2** the distance travelled by a golf ball between being struck and touching the ground. **3** the range of a firearm. **4** (N Am.) a portage. **to carry all before one 1** to bear off all the honours. **2** to win or gain complete success, unanimous support etc. **to carry away 1** to remove. **2** (*usu. pass.*) to excite, to inspire, to deprive of self-control. **3** (*Naut.*) to break or lose (a rope, mast etc.). **to carry forward** to transfer to another page or column. **to carry it off** to succeed, esp. under difficult circumstances. **to carry off 1** to remove. **2** to win. **3** to do or handle successfully. **4** to cause to die. **to carry on 1** to conduct or engage in (a business, a conversation etc.). **2** to continue. **3** to behave in a particular way, esp. to flirt outrageously. **4** to make a fuss. **to carry oneself** to behave (in a particular way). **to carry out 1** to perform. **2** to accomplish. **to carry over 1** to carry forward. **2** to postpone to a future occasion. **to carry through 1** to accomplish. **2** to bring to a conclusion in spite of obstacles. **to carry with one 1** to bear in mind. **2** to convince. **carry-all** *n.* **1** (*N Am.*) a holdall. **2** (*N Am.*) a type of car with seats facing sideways. **3** a four-wheeled carriage for several persons. **carrycot** *n.* a light portable cot for a baby. **carrying trade** *n.* the transport of goods, esp. by water or air. **carry-on** *n.* **1** a fuss. **2** an instance of questionable behaviour or flirtation. **carry-out** *n.*, *a.* (*Sc.*, *N Am.*) (a) takeaway. **carry-over** *n.* **1** the act of carrying over. **2** something carried over.

cart (kaht) *n.* **1** a strong two-wheeled vehicle for heavy goods etc., usu. drawn by a horse. **2** a light two-wheeled vehicle (*usu. with attrib.*, as *dog cart*). **3** a light vehicle pulled or pushed by hand. **4** (*N Am.*) a supermarket trolley. ~*v.t.* **1** to carry or convey in a cart. **2** (*coll.*) to carry or pull with difficulty. ~*v.i.* to carry or convey goods in a cart. **to cart off** (*coll.*) to remove by force. **to put the cart before the horse** to reverse the natural or proper order. **cartage** *n.* **1** the act of carting. **2** the price paid for this. **carter** *n.* **cartful** *n.* (*pl.* **cartfuls**) **carthorse** *n.* any of a breed of horses used for drawing carts and other heavy work. **cartload** *n.* **1** a cartful. **2** a large number or amount. **cart road**, **cart track** *n.* a rough road on a farm etc. **cartwheel** *n.* **1** the wheel of a cart. **2** a sideways somersault made with the arms and legs outstretched. **cartwright** *n.* a person whose trade is to make carts.

carte¹ (kaht) *n.* **1** a card. **2** a menu. **carte blanche** (blãsh´) *n.* (*pl.* **cartes blanches** (kaht blãsh´)) unlimited power to act (*The new manager was given carte blanche*).

carte² QUARTE.

cartel (kahtel´) *n.* **1** an agreement (often international) among manufacturers to keep prices high, to control production etc. **2** in politics, an alliance between two parties to further common policies. **cartelize** (kah´təlīz), **cartelise** *v.t.*, *v.i.* to form into a cartel. **cartelization** (-zā´shən) *n.*

Cartesian (kahtē´ziən, -zhən) *a.* of or relating to the French philosopher and mathematician René Descartes (1596–1650), or his philosophy or mathematical methods. **Cartesian coordinates**

n.pl. a system for locating a point in space by specifying its distance from two lines or three planes intersecting at right angles. **Cartesianism** *n.*

Carthusian (kahthū´ziən) *a.* of or belonging to an order of monks founded by St Bruno in 1084. ~*n.* a Carthusian monk.

cartilage (kah´tilij) *n.* **1** an elastic, pearly-white animal tissue; gristle. **2** a cartilaginous structure. **cartilaginoid** (-laj´in-) *a.* **cartilaginous** (-laj´in-) *a.* **cartilaginous fish** *n.* any fish with a cartilaginous skeleton, such as the shark or ray.

cartogram (kah´təgram) *n.* a map showing statistical information in diagrammatic form.

cartography (kahtog´rəfi), **chartography** (chah-) *n.* the art or practice of making maps and charts. **cartographer** *n.* **cartographic** (-graf´-), **cartographical** *a.*

cartomancy (kah´təmansi) *n.* fortune-telling from a selection of playing cards.

carton (kah´tən) *n.* **1** a cardboard box. **2** a box made of waxed paper for holding liquids.

cartoon (kahtoon´) *n.* **1** an illustration, esp. comic, usu. dealing with a topical or political subject. **2** a comic strip. **3** an animated film, esp. one produced from a series of drawings. **4** a preliminary design on strong paper for a painting, tapestry, mosaic etc. **cartoonish** *a.* **cartoonist** *n.* **cartoon strip** *n.* a comic strip. **cartoony** *a.*

cartouche (kahtoosh´), **cartouch** *n.* **1** (*Archit.*) a scroll on the cornice of a column. **2** an ornamental tablet in the form of a scroll, for inscriptions etc. **3** an elliptical figure containing the hieroglyphics of Egyptian royal or divine names or titles.

cartridge (kah´trij) *n.* **1** a case, esp. of metal, holding the explosive charge of a gun etc., with or without a bullet (*a blank cartridge*; *a ball cartridge*). **2** a removable, sealed container holding film for a camera, magnetic tape for a tape recorder, ribbon for a typewriter or printer etc. **3** a removable part of the pick-up arm of a record player, containing the stylus etc. **4** a replaceable container holding ink for a pen etc. **cartridge belt** *n.* a belt with pockets for cartridges. **cartridge paper** *n.* a type of stout, rough-surfaced paper, orig. used for cartridge-making, now used for drawing, making strong envelopes etc.

caruncle (kar´ŭngkəl, kərŭng´-) *n.* **1** a small, fleshy excrescence. **2** (*Zool.*) a wattle, comb or similar outgrowth. **3** (*Bot.*) a protuberance round or near the hilum. **caruncular** (-rŭng´-) *a.*

carve (kahv) *v.t.* **1** to cut (solid material) into the shape of a person, thing etc. **2** to make or shape by cutting. **3** to decorate or inscribe by cutting. **4** to cut (letters, patterns etc.) into the surface of hard material. **5** to cut (esp. meat) into slices. ~*v.i.* **1** to carve wood, stone etc. as an art or profession. **2** to carve meat. **to carve out 1** to take (a piece) from something larger. **2** to create or establish by one's own effort (*to carve out a career*). **to carve up 1** to divide into pieces or portions, to subdivide (esp. land). **2** to drive into the path of (another vehicle), esp. in an aggressive or dangerous manner after overtaking. **carver** *n.* **1** a person who carves. **2** a carving knife. **3** (*pl.*) a carving knife and fork. **4** a dining chair with arms. **carvery** *n.* (*pl.* **carveries**) a restaurant providing a type of buffet service, where roast meat is carved to the customers' requirements. **carve-up** *n.* (*sl.*) the act of sharing out or distributing booty etc. **carving** *n.* **1** the act of carving. **2** a carved object or ornament. **carving knife** *n.* a large knife for carving meat.

carvel (kah´vəl) *n.* CARAVEL. **carvel-built** *a.* (*Naut.*) having the planks flush at the edges, as distinct from *clinker-built.*

caryatid (kariat´id) *n.* (*pl.* **caryatids, caryatides** (-dēz)) (*Archit.*) a figure of a woman in long robes, serving to support an entablature.

caryo- KARYO-.

caryopsis (kariop´sis) *n.* (*pl.* **caryopses** (-sēz), **caryopsides** (-sidēz)) (*Bot.*) a fruit with a single seed, to which the pericarp adheres throughout, as in grasses.

carzey (kah´zi), **carsey, karsey, karzy, kazi** *n.* (*sl.*) a lavatory.

Casanova (kasənō´və) *n.* a man notorious for his amorous or sexual adventures.

casbah KASBAH.

cascade (kaskād´) *n.* **1** a small waterfall, esp. one of a series of waterfalls. **2** anything resembling this, such as a loose, wavy fall of lace or hair. **3** a series of actions or processes, each triggered or fuelled by the previous one. ~*v.i.* to fall in or like a cascade.

cascara (kaskah´rə) *n.* (*also* **cascara sagrada** (səgrah´də)) the bark of a N American buckthorn, *Rhamnus purshiana,* used as a laxative.

case[1] (kās) *n.* **1** an instance, an occurrence. **2** a state of affairs, situation, position, circumstances. **3** a set of arguments for or against a particular action or cause. **4** a question at issue. **5** a particular instance of any disease etc. **6** the patient suffering from the disease etc. **7** a solicitor's or social worker's client. **8** a matter for police investigation. **9** (*Law*) **a** a cause or suit in a court of law. **b** a statement of facts or evidence for submission to a court. **c** the evidence and arguments considered collectively. **d** a cause that has been decided and may be quoted as a precedent. **10** (*Gram.*) **a** the form of a declinable word used to express relation to some other word in the sentence. **b** the system of changes in termination involved. **11** (*sl.*) an eccentric or difficult character. **in any case** in any event, whatever may happen. **in case 1** if, supposing that. **2** (*Take a map in case you get lost*). **in case of** in the event of. **in no case** under no circumstances. **in that case** if that should happen, if that is true. **in the case of** regarding. **casebook** *n.* a book describing (medical or legal) cases for record or for instruction. **case history** *n.* a record of a person's background, history etc., esp. used

for clinical purposes. **case law** *n.* (*Law*) law as settled by precedent. **caseload** *n.* the number of cases assigned to a doctor or social worker. **case of conscience** *n.* a matter in which conscience must make the decision between two principles. **case study** *n.* **1** a study or analysis of the background, history etc. of a particular person or institution. **2** the written record of such a study. **casework** *n.* medical or social work concentrating on individual cases. **caseworker** *n.*

case[2] (kās) *n.* **1** a box, chest or other container. **2** a covering or sheath; that which contains or encloses something else. **3** a protective outer shell or cover. **4** a suitcase. **5** a glass box for exhibits. **6** a container and its contents (*a case of wine*). **7** (*Print.*) an oblong frame, with divisions, for type (*lower case; upper case*). ~*v.t.* **1** to cover with or put into a case. **2** (*sl.*) to reconnoitre (a building etc.) with a view to burglary (*to case the joint*). **case-bound** *a.* (of a book) hardbacked. **case-harden** *v.t.* **1** to harden the outside surface of (esp. iron, by converting into steel). **2** to make callous. **case-shot** *n.* CANISTER SHOT (under CANISTER). **casing** *n.* **1** an outer shell or skin; a protective case or covering. **2** material used to make this.

casein (kā´siin, -sēn) *n.* the protein in milk, forming the basis of cheese.

casemate (kās´māt) *n.* an armoured vault or chamber in a fortress or ship, containing an embrasure.

casement (kās´mənt) *n.* **1** a window or part of a window opening on hinges. **2** (*poet.*) a window.

cash (kash) *n.* **1** coins and banknotes, as opposed to cheques etc. **2** immediate payment, as opposed to credit. **3** (*coll.*) money, wealth. ~*a.* involving cash, paid for or paying in cash (*a cash deposit*). ~*v.t.* to turn into or exchange for cash. **cash down** with money paid on the spot. **to cash in** to exchange for money. **to cash in on** (*coll.*) to profit from. **to cash in one's checks** (*sl.*) to die. **to cash up** to add up the money taken (in a shop etc.) at the end of the day. **cashable** *a.* **cash-and-carry** *a., adv.* sold for cash, without a delivery service. ~*n.* (*also* **cash and carry**) a shop which trades in this way, usu. selling goods in large quantities at wholesale prices. **cash book** *n.* a book in which money transactions are entered. **cash box** *n.* a box in which money is kept. **cash card** *n.* a plastic card used to obtain money from a cash dispenser. **cash crop** *n.* a crop grown for sale, not for consumption. **cash desk** *n.* the desk in a shop where payments are made by customers. **cash dispenser** *n.* an electronic machine operated by a bank, which dispenses cash on insertion of a special card. **cash flow** *n.* the flow of money into and out of a business in the course of trading. **cashless** *a.* **cash on delivery** *n.* a system by which goods are paid for on delivery. **cashpoint** *n.* a cash dispenser. **cash price** *n.* the price for payment in cash. **cash register** *n.* a calculating machine used in a shop etc., which has a drawer for money and displays or records the amount received.

cashew (kash´oo, -shoo´) *n.* **1** (*also* **cashew nut**) the kidney-shaped nut of a tropical tree, *Anacardium occidentale.* **2** (*also* **cashew tree**) this tree. **cashew apple** *n.* the fleshy fruit of the cashew tree, to which the cashew nut is attached.

Usage note See note under CACHOU.

---

cashier[1] (kashiə´) *n.* a person who has charge of the cash or of financial transactions in a bank, shop etc.

cashier[2] (kashiə´) *v.t.* to dismiss from service, esp. from the armed forces, in disgrace.

cashmere (kash´miə), **kashmir** *n.* **1** a fine soft wool from the hair of the Himalayan goat. **2** a soft material made from this or similar fine wool.

casing CASE[2].

casino (kəsē´nō) *n.* (*pl.* **casinos**) a public establishment, or part of one, used for gambling.

cask (kahsk) *n.* **1** a barrel. **2** the quantity contained in a cask.

casket (kahs´kit) *n.* **1** a small case for jewels etc. **2** (*esp. N Am.*) a coffin.

casque (kask) *n.* **1** (*poet.*) a helmet. **2** (*Zool.*) a horny cap or protuberance on the head or beak of some birds.

Cassandra (kəsan´drə) *n.* a person who prophesies evil or takes a gloomy view of the future, esp. one who is not listened to.

cassata (kəsah´tə) *n.* a type of ice cream containing nuts and candied fruit.

cassation (kəsā´shən) *n.* (*Mus.*) an 18th-cent. instrumental composition similar to a divertimento.

cassava (kəsah´və) *n.* **1** a W Indian plant, the manioc, of the genus *Manihot,* esp. *M. esculenta,* the bitter cassava, or *M. dulcis,* the sweet cassava. **2** a nutritious flour obtained from its roots.

casserole (kas´ərōl) *n.* **1** an earthenware, glass etc. cooking pot with a lid. **2** the food cooked in such a pot, esp. a meat dish cooked slowly in the oven. *~v.t.* to cook in such a pot.

cassette (kəset´) *n.* **1** a small plastic case containing a length of audiotape, to be inserted into a cassette deck or cassette recorder; an audio cassette. **2** a similar container of videotape; a video cassette. **3** a similar container of photographic film, to be inserted into a camera. **cassette deck** *n.* a tape deck on which audio cassettes can be played or recorded. **cassette player** *n.* a machine used to play back a recorded audio cassette. **cassette recorder** *n.* a tape recorder on which audio cassettes can be played or recorded. **cassette tape** *n.* a cassette, esp. a prerecorded audio cassette.

cassia (kas´iə, kash´ə) *n.* **1** any plant of the genus *Cassia,* including the senna. **2** (*also* **cassia bark**) the cinnamon-like bark of *Cinnamomum cassia.*

cassingle (kasing´gəl) *n.* (*coll.*) a prerecorded audio cassette containing a single item of music, esp. pop or rock music, on each side.

cassis (kas´ēs) *n.* a usu. alcoholic cordial made from blackcurrants.

cassiterite (kəsit´ərīt) *n.* a black or brown mineral, stannic dioxide, a source of tin.

cassock (kas´ək) *n.* a long, close-fitting garment worn by clerics, choristers, vergers etc. **cassocked** *a.*

cassoulet (kas´əlā) *n.* a dish consisting of haricot beans stewed with bacon, pork etc.

cassowary (kas´əweri) *n.* (*pl.* **cassowaries**) a large flightless bird of the Australasian genus *Casuarius.*

cast (kahst) *v.t.* (*past, p.p.* **cast**) **1** to throw, to fling, to hurl. **2** to emit or throw by reflection. **3** to cause to fall, to direct (*to cast a glance*). **4** to throw off, to shed. **5** to dismiss, to reject. **6** to throw (a fishing line). **7** to assign the parts in (a play, film etc.). **8** to assign a particular role to (an actor) (*She was cast as Ophelia*). **9** to found, to mould. **10** to add up, compute, calculate. **11** to record or register (a vote etc.). *~v.i.* **1** to throw a fishing line. **2** to reckon accounts, to add up figures. **3** to warp. *~a.* **1** thrown. **2** made by founding or casting. *~n.* **1** the act of casting or throwing. **2** a throw. **3** the thing thrown. **4** the distance thrown. **5** the set of actors allocated roles in a play, film etc. **6** a mould. **7** the thing or shape moulded. **8** a plaster cast. **9** a throw of dice, or the number thrown. **10** chance, fortune. **11** a motion or turn of the eye. **12** a squint. **13** a twist. **14** feathers, fur etc. ejected from the stomach by a bird of prey. **15** the end portion of a fishing line, carrying hooks etc. **16** a tinge, a characteristic quality or form. **17** an adding up, a calculation. **to cast about** to make an extensive mental, visual or physical search (*to cast about for inspiration*). **to cast adrift** to cause or leave to drift. **to cast around** to cast about. **to cast aside 1** to reject. **2** to give up. **to cast away 1** to reject. **2** to shipwreck. **to cast down 1** to throw down. **2** to deject. **to cast off 1** to discard. **2** to untie (a rope), to unmoor (a boat). **3** in knitting, to finish by looping together the last row of stitches. **4** (*Print.*) to estimate the amount of space a piece of copy will occupy. **to cast on** in knitting, to make the first row of loops or stitches. **to cast out** to expel. **castaway** *a.* shipwrecked. *~n.* a shipwrecked person. **caster**[1] *n.* a person or thing that casts. **caster sugar** *n.* finely ground white sugar. **casting** *n.* **1** the act of allotting parts in a play, film etc. **2** anything formed by casting or founding, esp. a metal object as distinguished from a plaster cast. **casting couch** *n.* (*sl.*) a couch on which actresses are allegedly seduced by their casting director, in return for a role in his film, play etc. **casting vote** *n.* the deciding vote of a chairperson etc. when the votes are equal. **cast iron** *n.* an alloy of iron, cast in a mould. **cast-iron** *a.* **1** made of cast iron. **2** hard, rigid, unyielding, unchangeable. **3** incontestable, unchallengeable (*a cast-iron alibi*). **cast-off** *a.* discarded, rejected. ~*n.* a person or thing cast off, esp. a discarded garment.

castanet (kastənet´) *n.* (*usu. pl.*) a small spoon-shaped concave instrument of ivory or hard wood, a pair of which is fastened to each thumb and rattled or clicked as an accompaniment to music.

caste (kahst) *n.* **1** any one of the hereditary classes of society in India. **2** any hereditary, exclusive class. **3** the caste or class system. **4** dignity or social influence due to position. **5** (*Zool.*) a type of specialized individual among social insects, such as the worker bee. **to lose caste 1** to descend in the social scale. **2** to lose favour or consideration. **casteism** *n.* **casteless** *a.* **caste mark** *n.* a red mark on the forehead showing one's caste.

castellan (kas´tələn) *n.* (*Hist.*) the governor of a castle.

castellated (kas´təlātid) *a.* **1** having turrets and battlements. **2** resembling a castle. **castellation** (-lā´shən) *n.*

caster[1] CAST.

caster[2] CASTOR[1].

castigate (kas´tigāt) *v.t.* (*formal*) **1** to chastise, to punish. **2** to rebuke or criticize severely. **castigation** (-ā´shən) *n.* **castigator** *n.* **castigatory** (-ā´təri) *a.*

Castilian (kastil´iən) *n.* **1** a native or inhabitant of Castile in Spain. **2** the language of Castile, standard European Spanish. ~*a.* **1** of or relating to Castile or its inhabitants. **2** of or relating to Castilian or standard European Spanish.

castle (kah´səl) *n.* **1** a fortified building, a fortress. **2** a mansion that was formerly a fortress. **3** a chess piece in the shape of a tower, a rook. ~*v.i.* in chess, to move the king two squares to the right or left and bring up the castle to the square the king has passed over. ~*v.t.* to move (the king) thus. **castled** *a.* **castles in Spain** *n.pl.* castles in the air. **castles in the air** *n.pl.* visionary or unrealizable projects, daydreams.

castor[1], **caster** (kahs´tə) *n.* **1** a small swivelled wheel attached to the leg of a table, sofa, chair etc. **2** a small container with a perforated top for sprinkling the contents, esp. at table. **castor sugar** *n.* CASTER SUGAR (under CAST).

castor[2] (kahs´tə) *n.* an oily compound secreted by the beaver, used in medicine and perfumery.

castor oil (kahstəroil´) *n.* **1** an oil, used as a cathartic and lubricant, obtained from the seeds of the plant *Ricinus communis*. **2** (*also* **castor oil plant**) this plant, also grown as a house plant. **castor bean** *n.* **1** the seed of the castor oil plant. **2** (*N Am.*) the castor oil plant. **castor oil bean** *n.* the seed of the castor oil plant.

castrate (kastrāt´) *v.t.* **1** to remove the testicles of, to geld. **2** to deprive of reproductive power. **3** to deprive of force or vigour. **castration** *n.* **castrator** *n.*

castrato (kastrah´tō) *n.* (*pl.* **castrati** (-tē)) (*Hist.*) a male soprano castrated before puberty to retain the pitch of his voice.

casual (kazh´ūəl, kaz´ūəl) *a.* **1** happening by chance; accidental. **2** offhand (*a casual remark*). **3** occasional, temporary. **4** careless, unmethodical. **5** unconcerned, apathetic. **6** informal (*casual clothes*). ~*n.* **1** an occasional or temporary worker. **2** (*pl.*) flat-heeled shoes that slip on without lacing. **3** (*pl.*) informal clothes. **casualization** (-zā´shən), **casualisation** *n.* the re-employment of regular workers on a casual basis. **casual labour** *n.* workers employed irregularly. **casually** *adv.* **casualness** *n.*

casualty (kazh´ūəlti, kaz´ūəlti) *n.* (*pl.* **casualties**) **1** a person who is killed or injured in a war or in an accident. **2** anything lost or destroyed in a similar situation. **3** a casualty department (*She was taken to casualty*). **4** an accident, esp. one involving personal injury or loss of life. **casualty department, casualty ward** *n.* the department in a hospital for receiving the victims of accidents.

casuarina (kasūərī´nə) *n.* (*pl.* **casuarinas**) any tree of the genus *Casuarina*, of Australia and SE Asia, with jointed leafless branches.

casuist (kaz´ūist, kazh´-) *n.* **1** a person who studies or resolves moral problems, esp. one who uses plausible but false reasoning. **2** a sophist, a hair-splitter. **casuistic** (-is´-), **casuistical** *a.* **casuistically** *adv.* **casuistry** *n.*

CAT *abbr.* **1** computer-assisted testing, computer-aided testing. **2** (*Med.*) computerized axial tomography.

cat[1] (kat) *n.* **1** any mammal of the genus *Felis*, comprising the lion, tiger, leopard etc., esp. *F. catus*, the domestic cat. **2** any catlike animal. **3** (*coll.*) a spiteful woman. **4** (*sl.*) a man. **5** (*sl.*) a jazz enthusiast. **6** a cat-o'-nine-tails. **7** (*Naut.*) **a** the cathead. **b** a strong tackle used to hoist the anchor to the cathead. **8** the game of tipcat. **9** the tapered stick used in this game. ~*v.t.* (*pres.p.* **catting**, *past, p.p.* **catted**) **1** (*Naut.*) to hoist to the cathead. **2** (*coll.*) to vomit. **the cat's whiskers/ pyjamas** (*sl.*) the best or greatest person or thing (*He thinks he's the cat's whiskers*). **to let the cat out of the bag** to give away a secret, esp. unintentionally. **to play cat and mouse with** to tease or toy with an opponent or victim, esp. before defeating or destroying them. **to put/ set the cat among the pigeons** to stir up trouble. **to rain cats and dogs** (*coll.*) to rain very heavily. **cat-and-dog** *a.* quarrelsome. **catbird** *n.* **1** a N American bird, *Dumetalla carolinensis*, with a call like the mewing of a cat. **2** any other bird with a catlike call. **cat burglar** *n.* a thief who enters a house by climbing up the outside. **catcall** *n.* a whistle or cry of disapproval at a public meeting, show etc. ~*v.i.* to make a catcall. ~*v.t.* to deride with a catcall. **catfish** *n.* (*pl. in general* **catfish**, *in particular* **catfishes**) any of various esp. freshwater fish with barbels resembling a cat's whiskers around the mouth. **cat flap, cat door** *n.* a small flap set into a door to allow a cat to pass through. **catgut** *n.* a cord made from the intestines of animals, used for the strings of musical instruments and for surgical sutures. **cathead** *n.* (*Naut.*) a beam projecting from a ship's bows to which the anchor is secured. **cat-ice** *n.* thin white ice over shallow places where the water has receded. **cat-lick** *n.* (*coll.*) a perfunctory wash. **catlike** *a.* **cat-mint** *n.* a European labiate plant, *Nepeta cataria*, with scented leaves attractive to cats. **catnap** *n.* a short sleep. ~*v.i.* (*pres.p.* **catnapping**, *past, p.p.* **catnapped**) to have a catnap. **catnip** *n.* catmint. **cat-o'-nine-tails** *n.* a whip or scourge with nine lashes, formerly used as an instrument of punishment. **cat's cradle** *n.* a children's game played with a loop of string held between the fingers. **Catseye®** *n.* a reflector stud on a road. **cat's-eye** *n.* a precious stone from Sri Lanka, Malabar etc., a vitreous variety of quartz. **cat's-foot** *n.* (*pl.* **cat's-feet**) **1** a European plant, *Antennaria dioica*, with woolly leaves. **2** the ground ivy. **cat's paw** *n.* **1** a dupe used as a tool (from the fable of the monkey who used the cat's paw to pick chestnuts out of the fire). **2** a light wind which just ripples the surface of the water. **cat's-tail** *n.* **1** the reed mace. **2** a catkin. **catsuit** *n.* a one-piece trouser suit. **cat's whisker** *n.* a very fine wire in contact with a crystal receiver to rectify current and cause audibility. **cattery** *n.* (*pl.* **catteries**) a place where cats are bred or boarded. **cattish** *a.* catty. **cattishly** *adv.* **cattishness** *n.* **catty** (kat´i) *a.* (*comp.* **cattier**, *superl.* **cattiest**) **1** spiteful, malicious. **2** catlike. **cattily** *adv.* **cattiness** *n.* **catwalk** *n.* **1** a narrow walkway high above the ground, as above the stage in a theatre. **2** a narrow walkway used by the models in a fashion show.

cat² (kat) *n.* **1** a catalytic converter. **2** a catamaran.

catabolism (kətab´əlizm), **katabolism** *n.* the process of change by which complex organic compounds break down into simpler compounds, destructive metabolism. **catabolic** (katəbol´ik) *a.*

catachresis (katəkrē´sis) *n.* (*pl.* **catachreses** (-sēz)) **1** the wrong use of one word for another. **2** the misuse of a trope or metaphor. **catachrestic** (-kres´-, -krē´-), **catachrestical** *a.*

cataclasis (katəklā´sis) *n.* (*pl.* **cataclases** (-sēz)) (*Geol.*) the crushing of rocks by pressure. **cataclastic** (-klas´-) *a.*

cataclasm (kat´əklazm) *n.* a violent break or disruption.

cataclysm (kat´əklizm) *n.* **1** a violent upheaval or disaster. **2** a vast and sudden social or political change. **3** a deluge, esp. the Flood. **4** a geological catastrophe. **cataclysmal** (-kliz´-), **cataclysmic** *a.* **cataclysmically** *adv.*

catacomb (kat´əkoom) *n.* **1** (*often pl.*) a subterranean burial place, with niches for the dead, esp. the subterranean galleries at Rome. **2** any similar excavation or subterranean construction. **3** a cellar, esp. a wine-cellar.

catadromous (kətad´rəməs) *a.* (of fish) descending periodically to spawn (in the sea or the lower waters of a river).

catafalque (kat´əfalk) *n.* a temporary stage or tomblike structure for the coffin during a state funeral service.

Catalan (kat´ələn) *a.* of or relating to Catalonia, its people or their language. ~*n.* **1** a native or inhabitant of Catalonia. **2** the language of Catalonia.

catalase (kat´əlāz) *n.* an enzyme involved in the decomposition of hydrogen peroxide.

catalectic (katəlek´tik) *a.* having an incomplete metrical foot at the end of a line. ~*n.* a catalectic line.

catalepsy (kat´əlepsi) *n.* a state of trance or suspension of voluntary sensation. **cataleptic** (-lep´tik) *a.* affected by or subject to catalepsy. ~*n.* a person subject to attacks of catalepsy.

catalogue (kat´əlog), (*N Am.*) **catalog** *n.* **1** a methodical list, arranged alphabetically or under class headings, e.g. of items for sale, books in a library etc. **2** (*N Am.*) a university calendar or list of courses. ~*v.t.* (*pres.p.* **cataloguing**, (*N Am.*) **cataloging**, *past, p.p.* **catalogued**, (*N Am.*) **cataloged**) **1** to enter in a catalogue. **2** to make a catalogue of. **cataloguer**, (*N Am.*) **cataloger** *n.*

catalpa (kətal´pə) *n.* (*pl.* **catalpas**) any tree of the chiefly N American genus *Catalpa*, with long, thin pods.

catalysis (kətal´isis) *n.* (*pl.* **catalyses** (-sēz)) (*Chem.*) the acceleration of a chemical reaction by a catalyst. **catalyse** (kat´əlīz), (*N Am.*) **catalyze** *v.t.* to subject to catalysis. **catalyser** *n.* a catalytic converter. **catalyst** (kat´əlist) *n.* **1** any substance that changes the speed of a chemical reaction without itself being permanently changed. **2** any person or thing that causes change. **catalytic** (katəlit´-) *a.* relating to or involving catalysis. **catalytic converter** *n.* a device fitted to the exhaust pipe of a motor vehicle to remove toxic impurities from the exhaust gases. **catalytic cracker** *n.* an industrial apparatus used to break down the heavy hydrocarbons of crude oil and yield petrol, paraffins etc.

catamaran (kat´əmaran) *n.* **1** a double-hulled boat. **2** a raft made by lashing two boats together. **3** a raft made by lashing logs together. **4** (*coll.*) a vixenish woman.

catamite (kat´əmīt) *n.* a boy kept for homosexual purposes.

cataplexy (kat´əpleksi) *n.* temporary paralysis brought on suddenly by shock. **cataplectic** (-plek´-) *a.*

catapult (kat´əpŭlt) *n.* **1** a device for propelling small stones, made from a forked stick with elastic between the prongs. **2** (*Hist.*) a military machine for hurling darts or stones. **3** a device or machine used to launch aircraft from a ship. ~*v.t.* to throw or launch with or as with a catapult. ~*v.i.* to shoot from or as from a catapult.

cataract (kat'ərakt) *n.* **1** a large, rushing waterfall. **2** a deluge of rain. **3** any violent rush of water. **4** (*Med.*) a disease of the eye in which the crystalline lens or its envelope becomes opaque and vision is impaired or destroyed.

catarrh (kətah') *n.* **1** inflammation of a mucous membrane, esp. of the nose, causing a watery discharge. **2** this discharge. **catarrhal, catarrhous** *a.*

catarrhine (kat'ərīn) *a.* (*Zool.*) (of Old World monkeys) having the nostrils in a close, oblique position. ~*n.* such a monkey.

catastrophe (kətas'trəfi) *n.* **1** a great misfortune or disaster. **2** a change that brings about the conclusion of a drama; the denouement. **3** a final event, esp. one that brings disaster or ruin. **4** (*Geol.*) a violent convulsion of the earth's surface, producing changes in the relative extent of land or water. **catastrophic** (katəstrof'-) *a.* **catastrophically** *adv.* **catastrophism** *n.* (*Geol.*) the theory that geological changes have been produced by the action of catastrophes. **catastrophist** *n.*

catatonia (katətō'niə) *n.* **1** a syndrome often associated with schizophrenia, marked by periods of catalepsy. **2** (*loosely*) catalepsy, or a state of apathy or stupor. **catatonic** (-ton'-) *a.*

catawba (kətaw'bə) *n.* **1** a N American variety of grape, *Vitis abrusca*. **2** wine made from this grape.

catch (kach) *v.t.* (*past, p.p.* **caught** (kawt)) **1** to grasp, to take hold of. **2** to seize, esp. in pursuit. **3** to take in a snare, to entrap. **4** to take by angling or in a net. **5** to intercept and hold (a ball or other moving object). **6** in cricket, to dismiss (a batsman) by catching the ball. **7** to come upon suddenly, to surprise, to detect. **8** to receive by infection or contagion. **9** to be in time for (*to catch a train*). **10** to check, to interrupt. **11** to cause to become fastened or entangled. **12** to grasp, to perceive, to apprehend (*I didn't catch your name*). **13** to attract, to gain, to win. ~*v.i.* **1** to become fastened or entangled. **2** to ignite. **3** to take hold. **4** to spread epidemically. **5** to communicate. ~*n.* **1** the act of catching. **2** a thing or amount caught. **3** the act of catching the ball at cricket. **4** a fastening device. **5** a contrivance for checking motion. **6** an acquisition. **7** an opportunity. **8** (*coll.*) a person worth catching, esp. in marriage. **9** a trap, a snare. **10** an unexpected or concealed difficulty or drawback. **11** a game in which a ball is thrown and caught. **12** (*Mus.*) a type of round, esp. humorous. **to catch at** to attempt to seize. **to catch it** (*sl.*) to get a scolding. **to catch on 1** (*coll.*) to become popular. **2** to understand. **to catch out 1** to discover (someone) in error or wrongdoing. **2** in cricket, to dismiss (a batsman) by catching the ball. **to catch up 1** to reach (a person, vehicle etc. that is ahead). **2** to make up arrears. **3** (*often pass.*) to involve (*He was caught up in a plot to assassinate the president*). **4** to raise and hold. **catch-22** *n.* a situation

from which escape is impossible because rules or circumstances frustrate effort in any direction (from such a situation in a novel of this title by J. Heller). **catchable** *a.* **catch-all** *a.* (of a rule etc.) which covers all situations, or any not previously covered. **catch-as-catch-can** *n.* a style of wrestling in which most holds are allowed. ~*a.* (*esp. N Am.*) using whatever comes to hand. **catch crop** *n.* a quick-growing green crop sown between main crops. **catcher** *n.* **catchfly** *n.* (*pl.* **catchflies**) any plant of the genera *Lychnis* or *Silene*, from their glutinous stems which often retain small insects. **catching** *a.* **1** infectious. **2** attractive. **catchline** *n.* (*Print.*) a short line of type, esp. as a headline. **catchment** *n.* **1** the act of collecting water. **2** a surface on which water may be caught and collected. **catchment area** *n.* **1** (*also* **catchment basin**) an area from which water, esp. rainfall, drains into a river system. **2** the area from which a particular school, hospital etc. officially takes its pupils, patients etc. **catchpenny** *a.* worthless, but superficially attractive, in order to be quickly sold. **catchphrase** *n.* a phrase which comes into fashion and is much used, esp. one associated with a particular person or group. **catchweight** *a.* in wrestling etc., unrestricted with regard to weight. ~*n.* unrestricted weight. **catchword** *n.* **1** a word or phrase in frequent or popular use, esp. temporarily; a slogan. **2** an actor's cue. **3** a word printed under the last line of a page, being the first word of the next page. **4** the first word in a dictionary entry. **catchy** *a.* (*comp.* **catchier**, *superl.* **catchiest**) **1** (of a tune etc.) easy to pick up or remember; pleasant or attractive. **2** tricky, deceptive. **3** irregular, fitful. **4** catching. **catchily** *adv.* **catchiness** *n.*

catechetic (katəket'ik), **catechetical** (-əl) *a.* consisting of questions and answers; of or relating to catechism. **catechetically** *adv.*

catechism (kat'əkizm) *n.* **1** a form of instruction by means of question and answer, esp. the authorized manuals of doctrine of a Christian Church. **2** any series of interrogations. **catechismal** (-kiz'-) *a.* **catechist** *n.* a person who teaches by catechizing.

catechize (kat'əkīz), **catechise** *v.t.* **1** to instruct by means of questions and answers. **2** to instruct in the Church catechism. **catechizer** *n.*

catechu (kat'əchoo) *n.* a brown astringent gum, obtained chiefly from the Asian tree *Acacia catechu*, used in tanning.

catechumen (katikū'mən) *n.* a person who is under Christian instruction preparatory to receiving baptism.

category (kat'igəri) *n.* (*pl.* **categories**) an order, a class, a division. **categorial** (-gaw'riəl) *a.* **categorical** (-gor'ikəl), **categoric** *a.* **1** of or relating to a category or categories. **2** absolute, unconditional. **3** explicit, direct. **categorically** *adv.* **categorize, categorise** *v.t.* to place in a category or categories. **categorization** (-zā'shən) *n.*

catena (kətē´nə) n. (pl. **catenas, catenae** (-nē)) **1** a chain. **2** a connected series. **catenate** (kat´ənāt) v.t. to link together. **catenation** (-ā´shən) n.

catenary (kətē´nəri, kat´ə-) n. (pl. **catenaries**) a curve formed by a chain or rope of uniform density hanging from two points of suspension not in the same vertical line. ~a. of, resembling or relating to a chain, a catena or a catenary. **catenary bridge** n. a suspension bridge hung from catenary chains.

cater[1] (kā´tə) v.i. **1** to supply food, entertainment etc. (for). **2** to provide´ what is needed (for). **3** to pander (to). ~v.t. (N Am.) to provide food etc. for (a party etc.). **caterer** n. a person who provides food etc. for social functions, esp. as a trade. **catering** n. **1** the trade of a caterer. **2** the food etc. for a social function.

cater[2] (kā´tə) adv. (dial.) diagonally. **cater-cornered, catty-cornered** (kat´i-), **kitty-cornered** (kit´i-) a. (N Am.) placed diagonally; diagonal; not square. ~adv. diagonally.

caterpillar (kat´əpilə) n. the larva of a butterfly or other lepidopterous insect. **Caterpillar track**® n. an articulated belt revolving round two or more wheels, used to propel a motor vehicle over soft or rough ground. **Caterpillar tractor**®, **Caterpillar tank**® n. a tractor or tank fitted with a Caterpillar track.

caterwaul (kat´əwawl) v.i. to make the loud howling noise of a cat on heat. ~n. such a noise.

catharsis (kəthah´sis) n. (pl. **catharses** (-sez)) **1** the purging of the emotions by tragedy; emotional release achieved through dramatic art. **2** (Psych.) the bringing out of repressed ideas and emotions. **3** (Med.) purgation of the body. **cathartic** a. **1** purgative. **2** causing or resulting in catharsis. ~n. a purgative medicine. **cathartical** a. **cathartically** adv.

cathectic CATHEXIS.

cathedral (kəthē´drəl) n. the principal church in a diocese, containing the bishop's throne. **cathedral city** n. a city where there is a cathedral.

Catherine wheel (kath´ərin) n. **1** a firework that rotates like a wheel. **2** an ornamental circular window with spokelike mullions or shafts.

catheter (kath´itə) n. (Med.) a tube used to introduce fluids to, or withdraw them from, the body, esp. to withdraw urine from the bladder. **catheterize, catheterise** v.t. to insert a catheter into.

cathetometer (kathitom´itə) n. an instrument consisting of a telescope mounted on a vertical graduated support, used for measuring small vertical distances.

cathexis (kəthek´sis) n. (pl. **cathexes** (-sēz)) (Psych.) concentration of mental or emotional energy on a single object. **cathectic** a.

cathode (kath´ōd), **kathode** n. **1** the negative electrode in an electrolytic cell. **2** the source of electrons in an electronic valve. **3** the positive terminal of a primary cell. **cathode ray** n. a stream of electrons emitted from the surface of a cathode during an electrical discharge. **cathode**

ray tube n. a vacuum tube in which a beam of electrons, which can be controlled in direction and intensity, is projected on to a fluorescent screen thus producing a point of light. **cathodic** (-thod´-), **cathodal** a. **cathodic protection** n. the protection from corrosion of a metal structure, esp. underwater, by making the structure act as the cathode in an electrolytic cell.

catholic (kath´əlik) a. **1** universal, general, comprehensive. **2** liberal, large-hearted, tolerant. **3** (Catholic) of or relating to the Church of Rome; Roman Catholic. **4** (Catholic) of or relating to the whole Christian Church. **5** (Catholic) not heretical. ~n. (Catholic) a Roman Catholic. **catholically** (-thol´-), **catholicly** adv. **Catholicism** (-thol´-) n. Roman Catholic Christianity. **catholicity** (-lis´-) n. the quality of being catholic (in all senses). **catholicize** (-thol´-), **catholicise** v.t. to make catholic or Catholic. ~v.i. to become catholic or Catholic.

cation (kat´īən), **kation** n. the positive ion which in electrolysis is attracted towards the cathode. **cationic** (-on´-) a.

catkin (kat´kin) n. the pendulous inflorescence of the willow, birch, poplar etc.

catsup KETCHUP.

cattalo (kat´əlō), **catalo** n. (pl. **cattaloes, cattalos, cataloes, catalos**) a hardy cross between domestic cattle and American bison.

cattery, cattish CAT[1].

cattle (kat´əl) n.pl. **1** domesticated animals, esp. bovine mammals such as cows, bulls, oxen and bison. **2** †livestock, including horses, sheep, pigs etc. **cattle cake** n. a concentrated processed food for cattle. **cattle grid** n. a grid covering a trench in a road which prevents cattle etc. from crossing but allows vehicles to pass over. **cattle guard** n. (N Am.) a cattle grid. **cattleman** n. (pl. **cattlemen**) **1** a person who looks after cattle. **2** (N Am.) a person who breeds and rears cattle, a ranch owner. **cattle-plague** n. any of several diseases to which cattle are subject, esp. rinderpest. **cattle stop** n. (New Zeal.) a cattle grid.

cattleya (kat´liə) n. any epiphytic orchid of the genus Cattleya, with brightly coloured flowers.

catty CAT[1].

catty-cornered CATER-CORNERED (under CATER[2]).

Caucasian (kawkā´zhən) a. **1** (also **Caucasoid**) of or belonging to one of the main ethnological divisions of humankind, native to Europe, W Asia, and N Africa, with pale skin. **2** of or relating to the Caucasus Mountains or the district adjoining. ~n. a Caucasian person.

caucus (kaw´kəs) n. (pl. **caucuses**) **1** (N Am.) a preparatory meeting of representatives of a political party to decide upon a course of action, party policy etc. **2** (N Am.) a party committee controlling electoral organization. **3** (N Am.) the system of organizing a political party as a machine. **4** (often derog.) **a** a small group within a larger organization, esp. a political party. **b** a meeting of such a group, esp. in secret. ~v.i.

(*pres.p.* **caucusing**, *past*, *p.p.* **caucused**) to hold a caucus.

caudal (kaw´dəl) *a.* of or relating to the tail or the posterior part of the body. **caudally** *adv.* **caudate** (-dāt), **caudated** *a.* having a tail or tail-like process.

caudillo (kowdē´lyō, kaw-) *n.* (*pl.* **caudillos**) in Spanish-speaking countries, a military leader or head of state.

caught CATCH.

caul (kawl) *n.* **1** a part of the amnion, sometimes enclosing the head of a child when born. **2** a membrane enveloping the intestines, the omentum. **3** (*Hist.*) a net or other covering for the hair. **4** (*Hist.*) the rear part of a woman's cap.

cauldron (kawl´drən), **caldron** *n.* a large, deep, bowl-shaped vessel with handles, for boiling.

cauliflower (kol´iflowə) *n.* **1** a variety of cabbage with an edible white flowering head. **2** this head eaten as a vegetable. **cauliflower cheese** *n.* a dish of cauliflower with cheese sauce. **cauliflower ear** *n.* a permanently swollen or misshapen ear, usu. caused by boxing injuries.

caulk (kawk), **calk** *v.t.* **1** to fill or seal with waterproof material. **2** (*Naut.*) **a** to stuff (the seams of a ship) with oakum. **b** to make (a ship) watertight by caulking the seams. ~*n.* waterproof material used to fill or seal. **caulker** *n.*

cause (kawz) *n.* **1** that which produces or contributes to an effect. **2** (*Philos.*) the condition or aggregate of circumstances and conditions that is invariably accompanied or immediately followed by a certain effect. **3** the person or other agent bringing about something. **4** the reason, motive or ground that justifies some act or state. **5** a side or party. **6** a movement, set of principles or ideals etc. (*the feminist cause*). **7** a matter in dispute. **8** (*Law*) **a** the grounds for an action. **b** a suit, an action. ~*v.t.* **1** to produce; to be the cause of. **2** to act as an agent in producing. **3** to effect. **4** to make or induce to (*What caused you to change your mind?*). **in the cause of** in order to defend or support. **to make common cause** to unite for a specific purpose. **causable** *a.* **causal** *a.* **1** of, being or expressing a cause. **2** of or relating to cause and effect. **causality** (-zal´-) *n.* **1** the operation of a cause. **2** the relation of cause and effect. **3** (*Philos.*) the theory of causation. **causally** *adv.* **causation** (-zā´shən) *n.* **1** the act of causing. **2** the connection between cause and effect. **3** (*Philos.*) the theory that there is a cause for everything. **causative** (kaw´zə-) *a.* **1** that causes. **2** effective as a cause. **3** (*Gram.*) expressing cause. **causatively** *adv.* **cause célèbre** (kōz sāleb´rə) *n.* (*pl.* **causes célèbres** (kōz sāleb´rə)) a famous or notorious lawsuit or controversy. **causeless** *a.* **causelessly** *adv.* **causer** *n.*

'cause (koz, kəz) *conj.* (*coll.*) because.

causeway (kawz´wā), (*also dial.*) †**causey** (kaw´zi) *n.* **1** a raised road across marshy ground or shallow water. **2** a raised footway beside a road. **3** a paved road or path.

caustic (kaws´tik, kos´-) *a.* **1** burning, hot, corrosive. **2** bitter, sarcastic. **3** (*Physics*) of or relating to rays of light reflected or refracted by a curved surface. ~*n.* **1** a substance that burns or corrodes organic matter. **2** (*Physics*) a caustic surface. **caustically** *adv.* **causticity** (-tis´-) *n.* **caustic potash** *n.* (*Chem.*) potassium hydroxide, an alkaline solid used in the manufacture of soap, detergents etc. **caustic soda** *n.* (*Chem.*) sodium hydroxide, an alkaline solid used in the manufacture of rayon, paper, soap etc.

cauterize (kaw´tərīz), **cauterise** *v.t.* **1** (*Med.*) to burn or sear (a wound etc.) with a hot iron or a caustic substance. **2** (*fig.*) to sear. **cauterization** (-zā´shən) *n.* **cautery**, **cauter** *n.* (*pl.* **cauteries**, **cauters**) (*Med.*) **1** the act or operation of cauterizing. **2** an instrument for cauterizing.

caution (kaw´shən) *n.* **1** wariness, prudence; care to avoid injury or misfortune. **2** a warning. **3** a reprimand and injunction. **4** a formal warning to a person under arrest that what is said may be taken down and used in evidence. **5** (*coll.*) something extraordinary, a strange or amusing person. ~*v.t.* **1** to warn. **2** to administer a caution to. **cautionary** *a.* **1** containing, or serving as, a warning. **2** given as security. **caution money** *n.* money lodged by way of security or guarantee. **cautious** *a.* heedful, careful, wary. **cautiously** *adv.* **cautiousness** *n.*

cavalcade (kavəlkād´) *n.* **1** a company or procession of riders on horseback. **2** a procession of motor vehicles.

cavalier (kavəliə´) *n.* **1** (**Cavalier**) a supporter of Charles I during the Civil War; a Royalist. **2** a lady's escort; a gallant or lover. **3** †a horseman, a knight. ~*a.* offhand, haughty, supercilious. **cavalierly** *adv.*

cavalry (kav´əlri) *n.* (*pl.* **cavalries**) **1** (*esp. Hist.*) a body of soldiers on horseback, part of an army. **2** a body of soldiers in armoured vehicles, part of the armed forces. **cavalryman** *n.* (*pl.* **cavalrymen**) a member of the cavalry. **cavalry twill** *n.* a strong woollen twill fabric, used esp. for trousers.

cavatina (kavətē´nə) *n.* (*pl.* **cavatinas**) **1** a short, simple song. **2** a similar instrumental composition.

cave¹ (kāv) *n.* **1** a hollow place in a rock or underground. **2** a den. ~*v.t.* **1** to hollow out. **2** to cause to cave in. ~*v.i.* **1** to give way, to cave in. **2** to explore caves as a sport or pastime. **to cave in 1** to fall in; to collapse. **2** to give in, to yield. **cave bear** *n.* an extinct species of bear, *Ursus spelaeus.* **cave dweller** *n.* a prehistoric caveman or cavewoman. **cave-in** *n.* the act or instance of caving in. **cavelike** *a.* **caveman** *n.* (*pl.* **cavemen**) **1** a prehistoric man who dwelt in caves. **2** (*facet.*) a man of primitive instincts. **cave painting** *n.* a prehistoric picture on the wall of a cave. **caver** *n.* **cavewoman** *n.* (*pl.* **cavewomen**) a prehistoric woman who dwelt in caves. **caving** *n.* the sport or pastime of exploring caves.

cave[2] (kā´vi) *int.* look out! **to keep cave** to keep watch, to act as lookout.

caveat (kav´iat) *n.* 1 a warning, a caution. 2 (*Law*) a process to stop or suspend proceedings. **caveat emptor** (emp´taw) let the buyer beware; the purchaser is responsible for the quality of the purchase.

cavern (kav´ən) *n.* 1 a large cave or underground chamber. 2 a place resembling this, such as a large dark room. **cavernous** *a.* **cavernously** *adv.*

caviar (kav´iah, -ah´), **caviare** *n.* the salted roes of various fish, esp. the sturgeon, eaten as a delicacy.

cavil (kav´il) *n.* (*formal*) a petty or frivolous objection. ~*v.i.* (*pres.p.* **cavilling**, (*N Am.*) **caviling**, *past, p.p.* **cavilled**, (*N Am.*) **caviled**) to argue captiously; to make trivial objections (*to cavil at the price*). **caviller** *n.*

caving CAVE[1].

cavitation (kavitā´shən) *n.* 1 the formation of a cavity or cavities. 2 the formation of a cavity or partial vacuum between a solid and a liquid in rapid relative motion, e.g. on a propeller.

cavity (kav´iti) *n.* (*pl.* **cavities**) 1 a hollow space or part. 2 a decayed hole in a tooth. **cavity wall** *n.* a wall consisting of two layers of bricks with a space between.

cavort (kəvawt´) *v.i.* to prance about; to caper or frolic.

cavy (kā´vi) *n.* (*pl.* **cavies**) a S American rodent of the family Cavidae, esp. any of the genus *Cavia*, including *C. cobaya*, the guinea pig.

caw (kaw) *v.i.* to cry like a rook, crow or raven. ~*n.* this cry.

cay (kā, kē) *n.* a reef or bank of sand, coral etc.

cayenne (kāen´), **cayenne pepper** *n.* the powdered fruit of various species of capsicum, a very hot, red condiment.

cayman (kā´mən), **caiman** *n.* (*pl.* **caymans, caimans**) a tropical American reptile similar to an alligator, esp. any of the genus *Caiman*.

CB *abbr.* 1 citizen's band. 2 Companion of the Order of the Bath.

Cb *chem. symbol* columbium.

CBD *abbr.* cash before delivery.

CBE *abbr.* Commander of the Order of the British Empire.

CC *abbr.* 1 City Council. 2 Companion of the Order of Canada. 3 County Council. 4 County Councillor. 5 Cricket Club.

cc, c.c. *abbr.* 1 carbon copy. 2 cubic centimetre.

CCD *abbr.* charge-coupled device.

CCTV *abbr.* closed-circuit television.

CD *abbr.* 1 Civil Defence. 2 compact disc. 3 Corps Diplomatique.

Cd *chem. symbol* cadmium.

Cd. *abbr.* Command Paper.

cd *abbr.* candela.

CD-I *abbr.* compact disc interactive (a compact disc that allows the user to interact with the images on the screen).

Cdr *abbr.* (*Mil.*) Commander.

Cdre *abbr.* Commodore.

CD-ROM (sēdērom´) *n.* a compact disc used with a computer system.

CDT *abbr.* 1 (*N Am.*) Central Daylight Time. 2 craft, design and technology.

CE *abbr.* 1 Church of England. 2 civil engineer. 3 Common (or Christian) Era.

Ce *chem. symbol* cerium.

ceanothus (seənō´thəs) *n.* (*pl.* **ceanothuses**) any N American shrub of the genus *Ceanothus*, with small ornamental flowers.

cease (sēs) *v.i.* 1 to come to an end, to stop. 2 to desist (from). ~*v.t.* 1 to put a stop to. 2 to discontinue. ~*n.* 1 a stopping, an end. 2 cessation. **without cease** without pausing or stopping. **ceasefire** *n.* (*Mil.*) 1 a command to stop firing. 2 an agreement to stop fighting, a period of truce. **ceaseless** *a.* incessant, unceasing. **ceaselessly** *adv.* **ceaselessness** *n.*

cecum CAECUM.

cedar (sē´də) *n.* 1 any evergreen coniferous tree of the genus *Cedrus*, with durable and fragrant wood, including the cedar of Lebanon. 2 (*also* **cedarwood**) the wood of any of these trees. **cedared** *a.* covered with cedars. **cedarn** (-dən) *a.* (*poet.*) **cedar of Lebanon** *n.* the tree *Cedrus libani*, of SW Asia.

cede (sēd) *v.t.* 1 to give up, to surrender. 2 to yield, to grant.

cedi (sē´di, sā´-) *n.* (*pl.* **cedi, cedis**) the standard unit of currency in Ghana.

cedilla (sədil´ə) *n.* 1 a mark (,) placed under a *c* in French, Portuguese etc., to show that it has the sound of *s*. 2 a similar mark used in other languages, such as Turkish, to denote other sounds.

ceilidh (kā´li) *n.* an informal gathering, esp. in Scotland or Ireland, for music, dancing etc.

ceiling (sē´ling) *n.* 1 the inner, upper surface of a room. 2 the plaster or other lining of this. 3 the upper limit of prices, wages etc. 4 the maximum height to which an aircraft can climb. 5 the base of the cloud layer or its height above the ground.

celadon (sel´ədon) *n.* 1 a pale grey-green colour. 2 a glaze of this colour on pottery. 3 pottery with such a glaze. ~*a.* of this colour.

celandine (sel´əndīn) *n.* 1 a yellow-flowered plant related to the poppy, *Chelidonium majus*, the greater celandine. 2 a yellow-flowered plant related to the buttercup, *Ranunculus ficaria*, the lesser celandine also called *pilewort*.

-cele (sēl), **-coele** *comb. form* (*Med.*) a tumour or hernia.

celeb (sileb´) *n.* (*coll.*) a celebrity.

celebrate (sel´ibrāt) *v.t.* 1 to observe, to mark (a festival, special occasion etc.) with festivities or ceremonies. 2 to perform (a religious service or ceremony), to say or sing (Mass), to administer (Communion). 3 to praise, to extol. 4 to make famous. 5 to commemorate. ~*v.i.* 1 to mark an occasion with festivities. 2 to officiate at the Eucharist. **celebrant** *n.* a priest who officiates, esp. at the Eucharist. **celebrated** *a.* famous, renowned. **celebration** (-rā´shən) n. **celebrator** n. **celebratory** a. **celebrity** (-leb´-) n. (pl. **celebrities**) 1 a famous person. 2 fame, renown.

celeriac (səler´iak) n. a variety of celery with a turnip-like root eaten as a vegetable.

celerity (səler´iti) n. (formal or poet.) speed, swiftness, promptness.

celery (sel´əri) n. a plant, Apium graveolens, the blanched leaf-stalks of which are eaten cooked or raw. **celery pine** n. a tree of Australia and New Zealand, Phyllocladus trichomanoides, with shoots resembling celery.

celesta (səles´tə) n. (pl. **celestas**) a keyboard instrument in which steel plates are struck by hammers. **celeste** (-est´) n. 1 a celesta. 2 a voix céleste.

celestial (səles´tiəl) a. 1 of or relating to heaven; spiritual, angelic, divine. 2 of or relating to the sky or outer space (a celestial body). **celestial equator** n. the great circle on the celestial sphere, the plane of which is perpendicular to the earth's axis. **celestial horizon** n. the great circle parallel to the sensible horizon, the centre of which is the centre of the earth. **celestially** adv. **celestial navigation** n. navigation by the stars etc. **celestial sphere** n. an imaginary sphere with the observer at its centre and all celestial objects on its surface.

celiac COELIAC.

celibate (sel´ibət) a. 1 unmarried. 2 devoted or committed to a single life, esp. by religious vows. 3 abstaining from sexual activity. ~n. a celibate person. **celibacy** n.

cell (sel) n. 1 a small room, esp. one in a prison or monastery. 2 (Hist.) a small religious house dependent on a larger one. 3 a subsidiary unit of a political organization, esp. a proscribed or revolutionary one. 4 (Biol.) the smallest unit of living matter in animals or plants. 5 a small cavity or compartment. 6 a cavity in the brain, formerly supposed to be the seat of a particular faculty. 7 a compartment in a honeycomb. 8 the cuplike cavity containing an individual zoophyte in a compound organism. 9 a device for producing electrical energy, usually containing two electrodes in an electrolyte. 10 a small area covered by a cellular radio transmitting station. **cell block** n. a block of cells in a prison. **celled** a. **cell-like** a. **cellphone** n. a portable telephone suitable for use with the cellular radio system. **cell wall** n. (Biol.) the surface layer of a cell.

cellar (sel´ə) n. 1 an underground room or vault beneath a house used for storage (a coal cellar). 2 a place for storing wine. 3 a stock of wine. ~v.t. 1 to put in a cellar. 2 to store in a cellar. **cellarage** n. 1 cellars collectively. 2 space for storage in a cellar. 3 a charge for cellar storage. **cellarer** n. 1 a monk in charge of the stores. 2 an officer of a chapter in charge of the provisions. **cellaret** (-ret´), (N Am.) **cellarette** n. 1 a small case with compartments for holding bottles. 2 a sideboard

for storing wine. **cellarman** n. (pl. **cellarmen**) a person employed in a wine or beer cellar.

cello (chel´ō) n. (pl. **cellos**) a four-stringed bass instrument of the violin family rested on the ground between the legs. **cellist** n.

Cellophane® (sel´əfān) n. a transparent paper-like material made of viscose, chiefly used for wrapping.

cellular (sel´ūlə) a. 1 of, relating to or resembling a cell or cells. 2 (Biol.) composed of cells. 3 (of textiles) woven with a very open texture. **cellular blanket** n. a blanket with a very open texture. **cellularity** (-lar´iti) n. **cellular plant** n. a plant having no distinct stem or leaves. **cellular radio** n. a type of radio communication, used esp. for mobile telephones, which connects directly to the public telephone network and uses a series of transmitting stations, each covering a small area or cell. **cellular telephone** n. a cellphone. **cellule** n. (Biol.) a little cell or cavity. **cellulite** (-līt) n. subcutaneous fat which gives the skin a dimpled appearance. **cellulitis** (-lī´tis) n. inflammation of subcutaneous tissue, caused by bacterial infection. **cellulous** a.

celluloid (sel´ūloid) n. 1 a transparent flammable thermoplastic made from cellulose nitrate, camphor and alcohol, used e.g. in cinema film. 2 cinema film.

cellulose (sel´ūlōs) n. 1 a carbohydrate of a starchy nature that forms the cell walls of all plants. 2 (Chem.) a solution of cellulose acetate or cellulose nitrate. **cellulose acetate** n. (Chem.) a chemical compound formed by the action of acetic acid on cellulose, used in the manufacture of photographic film, varnish, some textile fibres etc. **cellulosic** (-lō´-) a.

celom COELOM.

Celsius (sel´siəs) a. of or denoting a temperature scale in which the freezing point of water is designated 0° and the boiling point 100°.

Celt (kelt, selt), **Kelt** (k-) n. a member or descendant of an ancient people comprising the Welsh, Cornish, Manx, Irish, Gaels and Bretons, inhabiting parts of England, Scotland, Ireland, Wales and northern France. **Celtic** a. of or relating to the Celts or their language. ~n. the language of the Celts; a group of languages including Gaelic, Welsh, Cornish and Breton. **Celtic cross** n. a Latin cross with a circle round the intersection of the arms. **Celtic fringe** n. 1 the inhabitants of the Scottish Highlands, Ireland, Wales and Cornwall, as opposed to the rest of the British people. 2 the Scottish Highlands, Ireland, Wales and Cornwall. **Celticism** (-sizm) n.

celt (selt) n. a prehistoric cutting or cleaving implement of stone or bronze.

cement (siment´) n. 1 a powdery substance, esp. used in building to make mortar or concrete and hardening like stone. 2 any analogous material, paste, gum etc. for sticking things together. 3 a substance for filling teeth. 4 cementum. 5 anything that unites, binds or joins. ~v.t. 1 to unite with or as with cement. **2** to line or coat with cement. **3** to unite firmly or closely (*to cement a relationship*). **cementation** (sēmentā´shən) *n.* **1** the act of cementing. **2** the conversion of iron into steel by heating the former in a mass of charcoal. **cementer** *n.* **cement mixer** *n.* a machine in which cement is mixed with water. **cementum** (-təm) *n.* the bony substance forming the outer layer of the root of a tooth.

cemetery (sem´ətri) *n.* (*pl.* **cemeteries**) a public burial ground, esp. one that is not a churchyard.

C. Eng. *abbr.* chartered engineer.

cenobite COENOBITE.

cenotaph (sen´ətahf) *n.* a sepulchral monument raised to a person buried elsewhere.

Cenozoic (sēnəzō´ik), **Caenozoic, Cainozoic** (kī-) *a.* (*Geol.*) of or relating to the third and most recent geological era. ~*n.* the Cenozoic era.

cense (sens) *v.t.* to burn incense near or in front of. **censer** *n.* a vessel for burning incense, esp. at religious ceremonies; a thurible.

censor (sen´sə) *n.* **1** a public officer appointed to examine books, films etc., before they are published or released, to see that they contain nothing obscene, seditious etc. **2** a person whose duty it is in wartime to see that nothing is published, or passes through the post, that might give information to the enemy. **3** (*Hist.*) a Roman officer who registered the property of the citizens, imposed the taxes, and watched over manners and morals. **4** any person given to reproof or censure of other people. **5** (*Psych.*) the superego, an unconscious mechanism in the mind that excludes disturbing factors from the conscious. ~*v.t.* **1** to act as a censor of. **2** to expurgate or delete objectionable matter from. **censorial** (-saw´-), †**censorian** (-saw´-) *a.* **censorious** (-saw´-) *a.* expressing or given to criticism or censure. **censoriously** *adv.* **censoriousness** *n.* **censorship** *n.*

Usage note The verbs *censor* and *censure* should not be confused: *censoring* involves suppression or removal, and *censuring* simply criticizing a work or rebuking an author severely.

censure (sen´shə) *n.* **1** blame, reproach. **2** disapproval, condemnation. **3** an expression of this. ~*v.t.* to blame; to criticize harshly; to find fault with. **censurable** *a.*

census (sen´səs) *n.* (*pl.* **censuses**) **1** an official enumeration of the inhabitants of a country. **2** the statistical result of such enumeration. **3** any similar official enumeration (*a traffic census*).

cent (sent) *n.* **1** a hundredth part of the basic unit of many currencies, e.g. of the US dollar. **2** a coin of this value. **3** an insignificant coin. **4** (*coll.*) a very small sum of money (*I haven't got a cent*).

cent. *abbr.* century.

centaur (sen´taw) *n.* a Greek mythological figure, half man, half horse.

centaury (sen´tawri) *n.* (*pl.* **centauries**) any of various plants once used medicinally, esp. those of the genus *Centaurium*, such as *C. erythraea*.

centavo (sentah´vō) *n.* (*pl.* **centavos**) **1** a hundredth part of the basic unit of currency of Portugal and some Latin American countries. **2** a coin of this value.

centenarian (sentənee´riən) *n.* a person who has reached the age of 100 years. ~*a.* being at least 100 years old. **centenary** (səntē´nəri, -ten´əri) *n.* (*pl.* **centenaries**) the hundredth anniversary of any event, or the celebration of this. ~*a.* **1** of or relating to a centenary. **2** recurring once in 100 years. **centennial** (-ten´-) *a.* **1** lasting for or completing 100 years. **2** centenary. ~*n.* a centenary.

center CENTRE.

centesimal (sentes´iməl) *a.* **1** hundredth. **2** by hundredth parts. ~*n.* **1** a hundredth part. **2** (*coll.*) a tiny part. **centesimally** *adv.*

centi- (sen´ti-), **cent-** *comb. form* **1** a hundred. **2** a hundredth part, esp. of a metric unit, as *centigram, centilitre, centimetre*.

centigrade (sen´tigrād) *a.* **1** Celsius. **2** divided into 100 degrees.

centigram (sen´tigram), **centigramme** *n.* a metric unit of weight, a hundredth part of a gram.

centilitre (sen´tilētə), (*N Am.*) **centiliter** *n.* a metric unit of capacity, a hundredth part of a litre.

centime (sä´tēm) *n.* **1** a hundredth part of the basic unit of many currencies, e.g. the French franc. **2** a coin of this value.

centimetre (sen´timētə), (*N Am.*) **centimeter** *n.* a metric unit of length, a hundredth part of a metre. **centimetre-gram-second** *a.* of or denoting a metric system of measurement based on the centimetre, gram and second, now superseded by the SI system in science and technology.

centipede (sen´tipēd) *n.* an arthropod of the class Chilopoda with many segments, each bearing a pair of legs.

cento (sen´tō) *n.* (*pl.* **centos**) **1** a composition of verses from different authors. **2** a string of quotations etc.

central (sen´trəl) *a.* **1** relating to, containing, proceeding from, or situated in the centre. **2** principal, of chief importance. **Central American** *a.* of or relating to Central America, the isthmus that joins N America and S America. **central bank** *n.* a national bank that regulates the money supply, carries out government policy etc. **central heating** *n.* a system of warming a whole building from a single source of heat by means of pipes, ducts etc. **centralism** *n.* a system or policy of centralization. **centralist** *n.* **centrality** (-tral´-) *n.* **centralize, centralise** *v.t.* **1** to bring to a centre; to concentrate. **2** to bring under central control. ~*v.i.* to come to a centre. **centralization** (-zā´shən) *n.* **central locking** *n.* a system whereby all the doors of a motor vehicle can be locked simultaneously. **centrally** *adv.* **central nervous system** *n.* (*Anat.*) the nerve tissue that controls the activities of the body, esp. that part of the nervous system of vertebrates consisting of the brain and spinal cord. **centralness** *n.* **central processing unit, central processor** *n.* the part of a computer which performs arithmetical and logical operations on data. **central reservation** *n.* the strip of ground that separates the carriageways of a motorway or other major road.

centre (sen´tə), (*N Am.*) **center** *n.* **1** the middle point or part. **2** the middle or central object. **3** the point round which something revolves, the pivot or axis. **4** the principal point; the most important point. **5** the nucleus, the source from which anything radiates or emanates. **6** the main area for a specified activity (*the shopping centre*). **7** a political party or group occupying a place between two extremes. **8** a player in the middle position in some sports. ~*v.t.* **1** to place in the centre. **2** to collect to a point. **3** to find the centre of. ~*v.i.* **1** to be fixed on a centre. **2** to be collected at one point. **3** to have as a centre, central theme etc. (*The report centred on the incompetence of the management*). ~*a.* at or of the centre. **centre back** *n.* in sport, a player or position in the middle of the back line. **centre bit** *n.* a carpenter's tool consisting of a bit fixed in a brace, for boring large round holes. **centreboard** *n.* a sliding keel which can be raised or lowered. **centred** *a.* **centrefold** *n.* **1** the two facing pages at the centre of a newspaper or magazine. **2** an illustration or article occupying these pages, esp. a photograph of a nude or scantily clad person. **centre forward** *n.* in sport, a player or position in the middle of the front line. **centre half** *n.* in sport, a player or position in the middle of the defence. **centre line** *n.* a real or imaginary line that divides something into two equal halves. **centremost** *a.* **centre of attention, centre of attraction** *n.* **1** a person who draws general attention. **2** (*Physics*) the point towards which bodies gravitate. **centre of gravity** *n.* the point about which all the parts of a body exactly balance each other. **centre of inertia, centre of mass** *n.* a point through which a body's inertial force acts coincident with the centre of gravity. **centrepiece** *n.* an ornament for the middle of a table, ceiling etc. **centre spread** *n.* a centrefold. **centre stage** *n.* **1** the centre of the stage in a theatre, show etc. **2** the centre of attention. ~*adv.* in or to this position. **centric, centrical** *a.* central. **centrically** *adv.* **centricity** (-tris´-) *n.* **centring, centreing** *n.* the woodwork or framing that supports an arch or vault during construction. **centrism** *n.* the holding of moderate political opinions. **centrist** *n.*

Usage note The use of *centre about*, *centre around* (rather than *centre in*, *centre on*) is sometimes disapproved of, on the grounds that a centre is a definite point but 'about' and 'around' are vague and indefinite.

-centric (sen´trik) *comb. form* having a specified centre, as *heliocentric*.

centrifugal (sentrif´ugəl, sen´-, -fū´-) *a.* tending to move away from the centre. **centrifugal force**

n. an apparent force that acts outwards on a revolving body. **centrifugally** *adv.* **centrifuge** (sen´trifūj) *n.* a centrifugal machine for separating liquids of different density, such as cream and milk. ~*v.t.* to subject to centrifugal force or the action of a centrifuge. **centrifugation** (-fūgā´shən) *n.*

centriole (sen´triōl) *n.* (*Biol.*) a small rodlike part of an animal cell, which forms one of the poles of the spindle during cell division.

centripetal (sentrip´ətəl, sen´tripētəl, -pē´-) *a.* tending to move towards the centre. **centripetal force** *n.* the force that draws a revolving body towards the centre. **centripetally** *adv.*

centrism, centrist CENTRE.

centromere (sen´trəmiə) *n.* (*Biol.*) the part of a chromosome by which it is attached to the spindle during cell division.

centrosome (sen´trəsōm) *n.* (*Biol.*) a small body of protoplasm near a cell nucleus, containing a centriole.

centuple (sen´tūpəl) *n.* a hundredfold. ~*a.* multiplied a hundredfold. ~*v.t.* to multiply a hundredfold.

centurion (sentū´riən, sen´-) *n.* a Roman military officer commanding a company of a hundred men.

century (sen´chəri) *n.* (*pl.* **centuries**) **1** a period of a hundred years. **2** a score of a hundred, esp. a hundred runs in cricket. **3** a group of a hundred things. **4** a division of the Roman people for the election of magistrates etc. **5** a division of a Roman legion, consisting originally of a hundred men. **century plant** *n.* the American aloe, *Agave americanus*, formerly thought to flower only once in 100 years.

Usage note The first century AD was 1–100, so centuries in the traditionally Christian world properly start in a year 01. Popularly, however, a century has come to be identified with all the years beginning with the same number, so that the 19th century is 1800–99 and not 1801–1900.

cep (sep) *n.* a type of edible mushroom, *Boletus edulis*, with a brown shiny cap.

cephalic (sifal´ik, kef-), **kephalic** (kef-) *a.* of or relating to the head. **cephalic index** *n.* the ratio of the greatest transverse to the greatest longitudinal diameter of the skull.

-cephalic (sifal´ik, kef-), **-cephalous** (sef´ələs, kef´-) *comb. form* -headed, as *brachycephalic, microcephalous*.

cephalo- (sef´əlō, kef´-), **cephal-** *comb. form* of or relating to the head.

cephalopod (sef´ələpod, kef´-) *n.* a mollusc of the class Cephalopoda, having a distinct head with prehensile and locomotive organs attached.

cephalothorax (sefəlōthaw´raks, kef-) *n.* (*pl.* **cephalothoraxes, cephalothoraces** (-rəsēz)) (*Anat.*) the anterior division of the body, consisting of the coalescence of head and thorax in spiders, crabs and other arthropods.

-cephalous -CEPHALIC.

cepheid (sē´fiid, sef´-), **cepheid variable** n. (*Astron.*) a variable star with a regular cycle of variations in brightness, which allows its distance to be estimated.

ceramic (səram´ik), **keramic** (kər-) a. **1** of or relating to pottery. **2** of or relating to any substance made by applying great heat to clay or another non-metallic mineral. ~n. **1** such a substance. **2** an article made from this. **ceramics** n.pl. **1** (*usu. sing. in constr.*) the art of pottery. **2** ceramic articles. **ceramist** (ser´-), **ceramicist** (-sist) n.

cerastes (siras´tēz) n. (*pl.* **cerastes**) any snake of the genus *Cerastes*, esp. the horned viper.

cerastium (siras´tiəm) n. any plant of the genus *Cerastium*, with horn-shaped capsules.

cercaria (sœkeə´riə) n. (*pl.* **cercariae** (-riē)) (*Zool., Med.*) a trematode worm or fluke in its second larval stage.

cercus (sœ´kəs) n. (*pl.* **cerci** (-kī)) (*Zool.*) either of a pair of tail-like sensory appendages at the tip of the abdomen in some arthropods.

cere (siə) n. the patch of waxlike skin at the base of the upper beak in many birds. **cerecloth** n. a cloth dipped in melted wax, used to wrap dead bodies in. **cerement** n. **1** a cerecloth. **2** (*usu. pl.*) any burial clothes. **ceresin** (ser´isin) n. a type of hard, whitish wax.

cereal (siə´riəl) a. of or relating to wheat or other grain. ~n. **1** any edible grain. **2** a breakfast food made from a cereal.

cerebellum (serəbel´əm) n. (*pl.* **cerebellums**, **cerebella** (-lə)) a portion of the brain situated beneath the posterior lobes of the cerebrum, responsible for balance and muscular coordination. **cerebellar**, **cerebellous** a.

cerebral CEREBRUM.

cerebrospinal (serəbrōspī´nəl) a. (*Anat.*) of or relating to the brain and to the spinal cord. **cerebrospinal fluid** n. the clear fluid that fills the spaces around the brain and spinal cord.

cerebrovascular (serəbrōvas´kūlə) a. of or relating to the brain and its blood vessels.

cerebrum (ser´əbrəm) n. (*pl.* **cerebrums**, **cerebra** (-rə)) the main part of the brain, filling the upper cavity of the skull. **cerebral** a. **1** of or relating to the brain or the intellect. **2** intellectual rather than emotional. **3** (of sounds) made by touching the roof of the mouth with the tip of the tongue. **cerebral hemisphere** n. either of the two halves of the cerebrum. **cerebrally** adv. **cerebral palsy** n. a disability caused by brain damage before or during birth, characterized by lack of balance and muscular coordination, often with speech impairment. **cerebrate** v.i. to think. **cerebration** (-rā´shən) n. the action of the brain, whether conscious or unconscious.

cerement CERE.

ceremonial (serəmō´niəl) a. of, relating to or performed with ceremonies or rites. ~n. **1** the prescribed order for a ceremony or function.

2 observance of etiquette. **3** in the Roman Catholic Church, the rules for rites and ceremonies. **4** the book containing these. **ceremonialism** n. **ceremonialist** n. **ceremonially** adv.

ceremony (ser´əməni) n. (*pl.* **ceremonies**) **1** a prescribed rite or formality, esp. in accordance with religion or tradition. **2** an occasion when such rites or formalities are performed. **3** formality (*with ceremony*). **to stand on ceremony** to be rigidly punctilious, to insist on observing formalities. **without ceremony** informally. **ceremonious** (-mō´-) a. **1** punctiliously observant of ceremony according to prescribed form. **2** of or involving ceremony; ceremonial. **ceremoniously** adv. **ceremoniousness** n.

cereus (siə´riəs) n. (*pl.* **cereuses**) any cactus of the genus *Cereus*, esp. *C. jamacaru* of Brazil, which can grow to a height of 40 ft. (13 m).

cerise (sərēs´, -rēz´) n. a red colour, cherry red. ~a. of this colour.

cerium (siə´riəm) n. (*Chem.*) a malleable grey metallic element of the rare earth group, at. no. 58, chem. symbol Ce.

cermet (sœ´mit) n. an alloy of a heat-resistant ceramic and a metal.

cero- (siə´rō) comb. form of, relating to or composed of wax.

ceroc (serok´) n. a jive dance for two people, originating in France.

cerography (siərog´rəfi) n. **1** the art or technique of writing, engraving etc. on or with wax. **2** printing from an engraved wax plate.

ceroplastic (siərəplas´tik) a. **1** modelled in wax. **2** of or relating to modelling in wax.

cert (sœt) n. (*sl.*) a certainty (*a dead cert*).

cert. abbr. **1** certificate. **2** certification. **3** certified.

certain (sœ´tən) a. **1** sure, convinced, assured, confident. **2** established beyond a doubt, undoubtedly true. **3** absolutely determined or fixed. **4** bound, destined, inevitable (*It is certain to go wrong*). **5** unfailing, reliable, unerring. **6** not particularized (*on a certain day*). **7** some (*a certain amount*). ~pron. (*as pl.*) an indefinite number or quantity (*Certain of the books were missing*). **for certain** definitely. **to make certain** to ensure, to secure. **certainly** adv. **1** assuredly. **2** without doubt. **3** without fail. **4** yes. **certainty** n. (*pl.* **certainties**) **1** that which is certain. **2** absolute assurance. **for a certainty** without doubt.

Usage note See note on *certainty* under CERTITUDE.

Cert. Ed. abbr. Certificate in Education.

certificate[1] (sətif´ikət) n. a written testimony or document, esp. of status or ability (*a birth certificate*; *an examination certificate*).

certificate[2] (sətif´ikāt) v.t. **1** to give a certificate to. **2** to license by certificate. **certificated** a. possessing a certificate from some examining body. **certification** (-kā´shən) n.

certify (sœ´tifī) v.t. (*3rd pers. sing. pres.* **certifies**, *pres.p.* **certifying**, *past, p.p.* **certified**) **1** to attest or testify to, esp. in writing. **2** to give a certificate to (*She is certified as a first aider*). **3** to declare legally or officially insane. **certifiable** *a.* **1** able to be certified. **2** (*coll.*) insane. **certifiably** *adv.* **certified** *a.* **certified cheque** *n.* a cheque guaranteed valid by a bank. **certified mail** *n.* (*N Am.*) recorded delivery. **certified milk** *n.* milk guaranteed free from the tuberculosis bacillus. **certifier** *n.*

certiorari (sœtiərea˘rī, -rah˘rē) *n.* (*Law*) a writ issuing from a superior court calling for the records of or removing a case from a court below.

certitude (sœ˘titūd) *n.* the state of being certain; certainty, conviction.

Usage note The meanings of the nouns *certitude* and *certainty* overlap, but in general *certitude* refers to subjective feeling or conviction, and *certainty* to objective fact.

---

cerulean (sərooˊliən), **caerulean** *n.* **1** a deep blue colour. **2** sky blue. ~*a.* of this colour.

cerumen (sərooˊmen) *n.* the waxlike secretion of the ear. **ceruminous** *a.*

ceruse (siəˊroos, sirooosˊ) *n.* **1** white lead. **2** an ointment or cosmetic made from this.

cervelat (sœˊvəlat, -lah) *n.* a kind of smoked sausage made from pork or beef.

cervical (sœˊvikəl, -vīˊ-) *a.* (*Anat.*) **1** of or relating to the neck (*the cervical vertebrae*). **2** of or relating to the cervix of the uterus (*cervical cancer*). **cervical screening** *n.* the routine examination of women for the early signs of cervical cancer. **cervical smear** *n.* a specimen of cells taken from the cervix of the uterus to test for the presence of cancer.

cervine (sœˊvīn) *a.* **1** of or relating to the deer family. **2** of or like a deer.

cervix (sœˊviks) *n.* (*pl.* **cervixes, cervices** (-sēz)) (*Anat.*) a necklike part of the body, esp. the passage between the uterus and the vagina.

Cesarean, Cesarian CAESAREAN (under CAESAR).

cesium CAESIUM.

cess[1] (ses) *n.* (*Sc., Ir.*) a tax.

cess[2] (ses), **sess** *n.* (*Ir., sl.*) luck. **bad cess to you** may ill luck befall you.

cessation (səsaˊshən) *n.* **1** the act of ceasing. **2** a pause.

cession (seshˊən) *n.* **1** a yielding, a surrender; a ceding of territory, rights or property. **2** something that is ceded. **cessionary** *n.* (*pl.* **cessionaries**) (*Law*) a person who is the recipient of an assignment; an assign or assignee.

cesspit (sesˊpit) *n.* **1** a cesspool. **2** a pit for refuse.

cesspool (sesˊpool) *n.* **1** an underground container or a hole in the ground for sewage to drain into. **2** any corrupt or filthy place.

cestode (sesˊtōd) *a.* ribbon-like. ~*n.* any intestinal worm of the class Cestoda, including the tapeworms. **cestoid** (-toid) *n.* a cestode.

cesura CAESURA.

cetacean (sitaˊshən) *a.* of, relating to or belonging to the Cetacea, an order of marine mammals including whales, dolphins etc. ~*n.* any mammal of this order.

cetane (sēˊtān) *n.* (*Chem.*) an oily, colourless hydrocarbon found in petroleum. **cetane number** *n.* a measure of the ignition quality of diesel fuel.

cetology (sitolˊəji) *n.* the study of whales.

Ceylon moss (silonˊ) *n.* a red seaweed, *Gracilaria lichenoides*, of the E Indian Ocean, from which agar is obtained. **Ceylon satinwood** *n.* **1** a tree, *Chloroxylon swietenia*, of India and Sri Lanka. **2** the wood of this tree.

CF *abbr.* Chaplain to the Forces.

Cf *chem. symbol* californium.

c.f. *abbr.* carried forward.

cf. *abbr.* compare.

CFC *abbr.* chlorofluorocarbon.

CFE *abbr.* College of Further Education.

cg *abbr.* centigram.

CGS *abbr.* Chief of General Staff.

cgs *abbr.* centimetre-gram-second.

CH *abbr.* Companion of Honour.

ch. *abbr.* **1** champion (of dogs). **2** chapter. **3** chestnut (of horses). **4** church.

cha (chah), **char** *n.* (*coll.*) tea.

cha-cha (chahˊchah), **cha-cha-cha** (chahchahchahˊ) *n.* (*pl.* **cha-chas, cha-cha-chas**) **1** a ballroom dance of Latin American origin. **2** music for this dance. ~*v.i.* (*pres.p.* **cha-chaing**, *past, p.p.* **cha-chaed, cha-cha'd**) to dance the cha-cha.

chaconne (shəkonˊ) *n.* **1** (*Mus.*) a set of variations over a continuously repeated ground bass. **2** (*Hist.*) a Spanish dance in triple time; music for this dance.

chador (chŭdˊə), **chadar, chuddar** *n.* a large veil, worn over the head and body by Muslim women.

chaeto- (kēˊtō), **chaet-** *comb. form* characterized by bristles or a mane.

chaetognath (kēˊtənath, -təgnath) *n.* any marine worm of the phylum Chaetognatha, such as the arrow worm, with a ring of bristles around the mouth.

chafe (chāf) *v.t.* **1** to rub so as to make sore or worn. **2** to make warm by rubbing. **3** to irritate. ~*v.i.* **1** to be made sore or worn by rubbing. **2** to fret. ~*n.* **1** a sore caused by rubbing. **2** irritation, a fit of rage. **chafing dish** *n.* **1** a vessel for keeping food warm or cooking at the table. **2** any vessel for heating.

chafer (chāfˊə) *n.* a beetle of the family Scarabaeidae, such as the cockchafer.

chaff[1] (chaf, chahf) *n.* **1** the husks of grain. **2** hay or straw cut fine for fodder. **3** the scales and bracts of grass and other flowers. **4** anything worthless. **5** thin strips of metal foil thrown from an aeroplane to confuse enemy radar. **chaff-cutter** *n.* a machine for cutting straw and hay for fodder. **chaffy** *a.*

chaff[2] (chaf) *n.* **1** banter. **2** teasing. ~*v.t.* **1** to banter. **2** to tease. ~*v.i.* to indulge in banter or teasing.

chaffer (chafˊə) *v.i.* to dispute about price; to haggle; to bargain. ~*n.* the act of haggling or bargaining. **chafferer** *n.*

chaffinch

chalk

chaffinch (chaf'inch) *n.* a common European bird, *Fringilla coelebs*.

chagrin (shəgrin´) *n.* vexation, disappointment, mortification. ~*v.t.* (*pres.p.* **chagrining**, *past, p.p.* **chagrined**) to vex, to disappoint, to mortify.

chain (chān) *n.* **1** a series of links or rings fitted into or connected with each other, for binding, joining, holding, hauling etc. or for decoration, esp. as jewellery. **2** anything resembling this in form or function. **3** (*pl.*) bonds, fetters; bondage, restraint. **4** a connected series, a sequence, a range. **5** a group of shops, hotels etc. under the same ownership and run in a similar style. **6** (*Chem.*) a series of atoms linked together in a molecule. **7** a measure of 100 links, or 66 ft. (20.12 m), used in land surveying. **8** (*pl., Naut.*) strong plates of iron bolted to a ship's sides and used to secure the shrouds. ~*v.t.* **1** to fasten or bind with a chain or chains (*The dogs were chained up*). **2** to fasten or restrict as if with a chain or chains (*She was chained to her desk*). **chain armour** *n.* chain mail. **chain bridge** *n.* a suspension bridge. **chain drive** *n.* an endless chain used as a system of transmission. **chain gang** *n.* a gang of convicts working in chains, esp. chained together. **chain gear** *n.* a gear that transmits motion by means of an endless chain, usu. passing over sprocket-wheels. **chainless** *a.* **chainlet** *n.* a small chain. **chain letter** *n.* a circular letter each recipient of which forwards a copy to a number of other people. **chain link** *a.* (of fencing etc.) made of wire twisted into a diamond-shaped mesh. **chain mail** *n.* armour of interwoven links. **chain reaction** *n.* **1** (*Chem., Physics*) a self-perpetuating chemical or nuclear reaction, producing energy etc., which initiates another, identical reaction. **2** any analogous series of events. **chainsaw** *n.* a power saw whose teeth are in a continuous revolving chain. **chain-smoke** *v.i., v.t.* (*coll.*) to smoke continuously, lighting one cigarette from another. **chain-smoker** *n.* **chain stitch** *n.* **1** an ornamental stitch resembling a chain. **2** a looped stitch made by a sewing machine. **chain store** *n.* one of a series of retail stores under the same ownership and selling the same kind of goods. **chain-wale** *n.* CHANNEL[2]. **chain wheel** *n.* a toothed wheel which receives or transmits power by means of an endless chain.

chair (cheə) *n.* **1** a movable seat with a back and usu. four legs for one person. **2** a seat of authority or office. **3** a professorship. **4** a chairmanship or mayoralty. **5** the person presiding at a meeting; a chairperson. **6** this person's seat. **7** a sedan chair, a wheelchair, the electric chair etc. **8** an iron socket to support and secure the rails in a railway. ~*v.t.* **1** to act as chairperson of. **2** to carry publicly in a chair in triumph. **3** to install in a seat of authority or office. **to take a chair** to sit down. **to take the chair** to preside at a meeting. **chair-bed** *n.* a bed that folds up and becomes a chair. **chair-borne** *a.* (*coll.*) working at a desk,

rather than having a more active job. **chair-car** *n.* a railway carriage with individual chairs rather than long seats. **chairlift** *n.* a series of seats suspended from an endless cable, used to carry people up and down a mountain etc. **chairman** *n.* (*pl.* **chairmen**) **1** a chairperson. **2** (*Hist.*) a person who carried a sedan chair, wheeled a bath chair etc. **chairmanship** *n.* **chairperson** *n.* the president of a meeting or the permanent president of a society, committee, board of directors etc. **chairwoman, chairlady** *n.* (*pl.* **chairwomen, chairladies**) a female chairperson.

chaise (shāz) *n.* **1** a light horse-drawn carriage for travelling or pleasure. **2** a post-chaise. **3** a chaise longue. **chaise longue** (lõg) *n.* (*pl.* **chaise longues, chaises longues** (shāz lõg)) **1** a type of sofa for reclining on, with a back and armrest at one end only. **2** a chair with support for the legs. **chaise lounge** *n.* (*N Am.*) a chaise longue.

chalaza (kəlā´zə) *n.* (*pl.* **chalazas, chalazae** (-zē)) **1** either of the two twisted albuminous threads holding the yolk in position in an egg. **2** an analogous part of a plant ovule.

chalcedony (kalsed´əni), **calcedony** *n.* (*pl.* **chalcedonies, calcedonies**) a cryptocrystalline variety of quartz. **chalcedonic** (-don´-) *a.*

chalcolithic (kalkəlith´ik) *a.* of or relating to a prehistoric period when both stone and copper or bronze implements were in use.

chalcopyrite (kalkōpī´rīt) *n.* a yellow mineral, a sulphide of copper and iron; copper pyrites, a copper ore.

chalet (shal´ā) *n.* **1** a small house or hut on a mountainside, esp. in Switzerland. **2** a small low house with projecting eaves. **3** a small dwelling, usu. of wood, used esp. for holiday accommodation.

chalice (chal´is) *n.* **1** (*poet.*) a cup, goblet or other drinking vessel. **2** the cup used in the Eucharist.

chalk (chawk) *n.* **1** soft white limestone or calcium carbonate, chiefly composed of the remains of marine organisms. **2** a piece of this or a coloured substance prepared from it, used for writing and drawing. **3** any similar substance, such as French chalk. ~*v.t.* to rub, mark or write with chalk. **as different/ alike/ like as chalk and cheese** completely or fundamentally different. **by a long chalk** by a great deal, by far. **to chalk out** to sketch out, to plan. **to chalk up 1** to record or register (*to chalk up a high score*). **2** to charge to an account, to give or take credit for (*Chalk it up!*). **chalk and talk** *n.* formal or traditional teaching methods, using a blackboard and oral instruction from the front of the class. **chalkboard** *n.* (*N Am.*) a blackboard. **chalk pit** *n.* a chalk quarry. **chalk-stone** *n.* a chalky concretion in the joints, occurring in chronic gout. **chalkstripe** *n.* a pattern of narrow white stripes on a dark-coloured background. **chalk-striped** *a.* **chalk talk** *n.* (*N Am.*) an informal lecture using notes, diagrams etc. chalked on a blackboard. **chalky** *a.* (*comp.* **chalkier**, *superl.* **chalkiest**)

1 containing chalk (*chalky soil*). **2** as white as chalk. **3** containing or resembling chalk-stones.

challah (khahlah´, hah´lə), **hallah** *n.* (*pl.* **challah, challoth** (-lot´), **hallahs, halloth**) a loaf of white bread, usu. plaited, eaten by Jews on the Sabbath.

challenge (chal´inj) *n.* **1** a summons or invitation to fight a duel. **2** an invitation to take part in a contest of any kind. **3** a difficult task which stretches one's abilities. **4** a calling in question, a demand for proof or justification. **5** (*Law*) exception taken to a juror or voter. **6** the call of a sentry in demanding a password etc. **7** (*Med.*) a test of immunity after immunization. ~*v.t.* **1** to summon or invite to a duel. **2** to invite to take part in a contest of any kind. **3** to call on to answer or to prove or justify something. **4** to call into question. **5** to object to, to dispute, to contest. **6** to stimulate, to stretch. **challengeable** *a.* **challenged** *a.* (*euphem. or facet.*) handicapped (*usu. in comb.*, as *visually challenged*). **challenger** *n.* **challenging** *a.* demanding, stimulating. **challengingly** *adv.*

challis (shal´is, shal´i, chal´is), **challie** (shal´i) *n.* a light fabric of wool or cotton, used for clothing.

chalybeate (kəlib´iət) *a.* impregnated with iron. ~*n.* a mineral water or spring so impregnated.

chamber (chām´bə) *n.* **1** the place where a legislative assembly meets. **2** the assembly itself. **3** any similar meeting place, such as a hall of justice. **4** an association of persons for the promotion of some common object (*the Chamber of Agriculture*). **5** (*Law*) **a** (*pl.*) the office or rooms of a barrister in an Inn of Court. **b** (*pl.*) a judge's private room in court. **6** (*poet.*) a room, esp. a bedroom. **7** a cave or underground cavity. **8** a hollow cavity or enclosed space. **9** that part of the bore of a gun or other firearm where the charge lies. **10** a chamber pot. **chambered** *a.* **1** enclosed. **2** divided into compartments or sections. **chambermaid** *n.* **1** a woman who cleans the bedrooms at a hotel. **2** (*N Am.*) a housemaid. **chamber music** *n.* (*Mus.*) music adapted for performance by a small group of instruments (orig. for performance in a room, as distinguished from that intended for theatres, churches etc.). **Chamber of Commerce** *n.* a board or committee appointed to promote the interests of business in a district. **Chamber of Horrors** *n.* a place full of horrifying objects (from a room in Madame Tussaud's waxwork exhibition devoted to famous criminals). **chamber orchestra** *n.* (*Mus.*) a small orchestra suitable for playing chamber music. **chamber pot** *n.* a bedroom receptacle for urine etc.

chamberlain (chām´bəlin) *n.* **1** an officer in charge of the household of a sovereign or nobleman. **2** the treasurer of a city or corporation. **chamberlainship** *n.*

chambray (sham´brā) *n.* a light cotton or linen fabric with a white weft and coloured warp.

chambré (shom´brā) *a.* (of wine) warmed to room temperature.

chameleon (kəmēl´yən), **cameleon** *n.* **1** a small African lizard having the power of changing colour. **2** a changeable person. **chameleonic** (-lion´-) *a.*

chamfer (cham´fə) *n.* **1** in carpentry, an angle slightly pared off. **2** a bevel, a groove, a fluting. ~*v.t.* **1** to groove. **2** to bevel off.

chamois (sham´wah) *n.* (*pl.* **chamois** (-wah, -wahz)) **1** a goatlike European antelope, *Rupicapra rupicapra.* **2** CHAMOIS LEATHER (under CHAMOIS). **chamois leather** (sham´i, sham´wah) *n.* **1** soft, pliable leather, orig. prepared from the skin of the chamois. **2** a piece of this, used for polishing etc.

chamomile CAMOMILE.

champ[1] (champ), **chomp** (chomp) *v.t., v.i.* to bite with a crunching or grinding noise; to chew or munch noisily. ~*n.* **1** champing. **2** the noise of champing.

champ[2] (champ) *n.* (*coll.*) a champion.

champagne (shampān´) *n.* **1** a white sparkling wine made in the province of Champagne, France. **2** a pale yellow colour.

champaign (shampān´, sham´-) *n.* (*esp. poet.*) **1** flat, open country. **2** an expanse of this.

champers (sham´pəz) *n.* (*coll.*) champagne.

champerty (cham´pəti) *n.* (*pl.* **champerties**) (*Law*) an illegal agreement to finance a party in a suit on condition of sharing the property at issue if recovered. **champertous** *a.*

champion (cham´piən) *n.* **1** a person, animal or exhibit that defeats all competitors. **2** a person who argues on behalf of or defends a person or a cause. **3** (*Hist.*) a person who engaged in single combat on behalf of another. ~*v.t.* **1** to defend as a champion. **2** to support (a cause). ~*a.* **1** superior to all rivals. **2** (*dial.*) first class, splendid, excellent. ~*adv.* (*dial.*) very well, splendidly, excellently. **championless** *a.* **championship** *n.* **1** a contest to find a champion. **2** the fact or status of being a champion. **3** the act of championing or defending.

champlevé (shā´ləvā) *n.* enamelling by the process of inlaying vitreous powders into channels cut in the metal base. ~*a.* of or relating to this process.

chance (chahns) *n.* **1** a risk, a possibility, an opportunity. **2** (*usu. pl.*) likelihood, probability (*What are the chances?*). **3** an accident, an unplanned result or occurrence. **4** fortune, luck. **5** fate, the indeterminable course of events, fortuity. ~*v.t.* (*coll.*) to risk. ~*v.i.* to happen, to come to pass (*He chanced to notice it*). ~*a.* fortuitous, accidental, unforeseen. **by any chance 1** as it happens. **2** perhaps. **by chance** accidentally; undesignedly. **on the chance 1** on the possibility. **2** in case. **to chance it** to take the risk. **to chance one's arm** to make a speculative attempt, to try something not very likely to succeed. **to chance on/ upon** to come upon accidentally. **to stand**

a **chance** to have a prospect of success (*She doesn't stand a chance!*). **to take a chance** to take a risk, to risk failure. **to take chances** to behave in a risky manner. **to take one's chances** to trust to luck. **chancer** *n.* (*sl.*) a person who takes risks in order to make a profit. **chancy, chancey** *a.* (*comp.* **chancier,** *superl.* **chanciest**) risky, doubtful. **chancily** *adv.* **chanciness** *n.*

chancel (chahn´səl) *n.* the eastern part of a church, usu. separated from the nave by a screen or by steps.

chancellery (chahn´sələri), **chancellory** *n.* (*pl.* **chancelleries, chancellories**) **1** a chancellor's court or council and official establishment. **2** the building or room occupied by a chancellor's office. **3** the position or rank of chancellor.

chancellor (chahn´sələ) *n.* **1** the president of a court, public department, or university. **2** an officer who seals the commissions etc. of an order of knighthood. **3** a bishop's law officer or a vicar-general. **Chancellor of the Exchequer** *n.* the principal finance minister of the British Government. **chancellorship** *n.*

chancery (chahn´səri) *n.* (*pl.* **chanceries**) **1** the court of the Lord Chancellor, the highest English court of justice next to the House of Lords, comprising a court of common law and a court of equity, now a division of the High Court of Justice. **2** (*N Am.*) a court of equity. **3** a court or office for the deposit of records. **4** an office or department attached to an embassy or consulate. **5** a chancellery. **in chancery** in boxing, having one's head under an opponent's arm.

chancre (shang´kə) *n.* (*Med.*) a hard syphilitic lesion. **chancroid** *n.* a soft ulcer caused by venereal infection.

chancy CHANCE.

chandelier (shandəliə´) *n.* a hanging branched frame for a number of lights.

chandler (chahnd´lə) *n.* **1** a retail dealer in oil, soap, groceries etc. **2** a dealer in a specified commodity (*a ship's chandler*). **chandlery** *n.* (*pl.* **chandleries**) the establishment or the merchandise of a chandler.

change (chānj) *v.t.* **1** to make different, to alter. **2** to give up or substitute for something else (*to change one's clothes*). **3** to give or take an equivalent for in other coins or currency. **4** to exchange (*to change places*). ~*v.i.* **1** to become different. **2** to be altered in appearance. **3** to put on different clothes (*to change for dinner; to change into a dress*). **4** to pass from one state or phase to another. **5** to get off one train etc. and board another (*change at Manchester for Bolton*). **6** to become tainted, to deteriorate. ~*n.* **1** alteration, variation. **2** an instance of this. **3** shifting, transition. **4** the substitution of one thing for another; exchange. **5** an exchange; something substituted for another. **6** small coins or foreign currency given in return for other money. **7** the balance of money paid beyond the value of

goods purchased. **8** novelty, variety (*for a change*). **9** (*coll.*) the change of life. **10** alteration in order, esp. of a peal of bells in bell-ringing. **11** the passing of the moon from one phase to another. **12** (*Hist.*) (also **'change**) a place where merchants met or transacted business. **to change down** in driving etc., to engage a lower gear. **to change over** to change from one state, position, situation, system etc. to another. **to change up** in driving etc., to engage a higher gear. **to get no change out of 1** (*coll.*) to fail to gain information from. **2** (*coll.*) not to be able to take any advantage of. **to ring the changes** to vary the ways of doing something. **changeable** *a.* **1** liable to change, variable. **2** inconstant, fickle. **changeability** (-bil´-) *n.* **changeableness** *n.* **changeably** *adv.* **changeless** *a.* **1** free from change. **2** unchanging. **changelessly** *adv.* **changelessness** *n.* **changeling** *n.* **1** a child substituted for another, esp. by fairies. **2** anything substituted for another. **change of heart** *n.* a change of attitude, opinion etc., which often results in the reversal of a decision. **change of life** *n.* (*coll.*) the menopause. **changeover** *n.* **1** an alteration or reversal from one state to another. **2** in a relay race, the passing of the baton from one runner to the next. **changer** *n.* **1** a person who changes anything. **2** a money changer. **change-ringing** *n.* a form of bell-ringing in which a set of bells is rung repeatedly but in slightly varying order. **change-ringer** *n.* **changing** *a.*

channel[1] (chan´əl) *n.* **1** the bed of a stream or an artificial watercourse. **2** the deep or navigable part of an estuary, river etc.; a fairway. **3** a narrow piece of water joining two seas. **4** a tube or duct, natural or artificial, for the passage of liquids or gases. **5** any means of passing, conveying or transmitting. **6** a course, line or direction. **7** a band of frequencies on which radio and television signals can be transmitted without interference from other such bands. **8** a path for an electrical signal. **9** a furrow, a groove, a fluting. **10** a gutter. ~*v.t.* (*pres.p.* **channelling,** (*N Am.*) **channeling,** *past, p.p.* **channelled,** (*N Am.*) **channeled**) **1** to guide or direct (*to channel information*). **2** to cut a channel or channels in. **3** to groove. **channelize, channelise** *v.t.* to channel. **channelization** (-zā´shən) *n.* **channel surfing** *n.* (*coll.*) moving swiftly from one television channel to another, using a remote control device.

channel[2] (chan´əl) *n.* (*Naut.*) a plank fastened horizontally to the side of a ship to spread the lower rigging.

chant (chahnt) *v.t.* **1** to speak or sing rhythmically or repetitively (*to chant a slogan*). **2** to recite to music or musically, to intone. ~*v.i.* **1** to sing in an intoning fashion. **2** to perform a chant. ~*n.* **1** a song, a melody. **2** (*Mus.*) **a** a composition consisting of a long reciting note and a melodic phrase. **b** a psalm, canticle or other piece sung in this manner. **3** a monotonous song. **4** a rhythmic or repetitive phrase, usu. spoken or sung in

unison by a crowd (*a football chant*). **chanter** *n.*
1 a person who chants. **2** (*Mus.*) the pipe on a
bagpipe that plays the tune.

chanterelle (shahntərel´) *n.* an edible fungus,
Cantharellus cibarius.

chanteuse (shãtœz´) *n.* a female nightclub
singer.

Chantilly (shantil´i) *n.* **1** (*also* **Chantilly lace**) a
delicate type of lace. **2** (*also* **Chantilly cream**)
whipped cream, usu. sweetened or flavoured.

chantry (chahn´tri) *n.* (*pl.* **chantries**) **1** an
endowment for a priest or priests to say mass
daily for some person or persons deceased. **2** the
chapel or the part of a church used for this purpose. **3** the body of priests who perform this
duty.

chanty SHANTY².

chaos (kā´os) *n.* **1** confusion, disorder. **2** the void,
the confusion of matter said to have existed
before the creation of the universe. **chaos theory**
n. the theory that apparently random or unpredictable phenomena observed in the universe
or in various branches of science are based on
complex underlying principles. **chaotic** (-ot´-) *a.*
chaotically *adv.*

chap¹ (chap) *v.t.* (*pres.p.* **chapping**, *past, p.p.*
chapped) to cause to crack or open in long slits.
~*v.i.* to crack or open in long slits. ~*n.* (*usu. pl.*) a
longitudinal crack, cleft or seam on the surface
of the skin, the ground etc. **chapped** *a.*

chap² (chap), **chappie** (chap´i) *n.* (*coll.*) a man, a
fellow.

chap³ (chap) *n.* **1** (*pl.*) the jaws (usu. of animals),
the mouth and cheeks; the chops. **2** the lower
part of the cheek. **chap-fallen** *a.* **1** having the
lower jaw depressed. **2** downcast, dejected,
dispirited.

chap. *abbr.* chapter.

chaparajos (chaparā´khõs, sha-), **chaparejos**,
chaps (chaps) *n.pl.* leather leggings worn by
cowboys.

chaparral (shap´əral) *n.* (*N Am.*) a thicket of
low evergreen oaks, or of thick undergrowth and
thorny shrubs. **chaparral cock** *n.* the roadrunner.

chapati (chəpat´i), **chapatti**, **chupatty** *n.* (*pl.*
chapatis, chapattis, chupatties) in Indian cookery, a round, thin loaf of unleavened bread.

chape (chāp) *n.* **1** the catch or piece by which an
object is attached, such as the tongue of a buckle.
2 the transverse guard of a sword. **3** the hook or
tip of a scabbard.

chapel (chap´əl) *n.* **1** a place of worship connected with and subsidiary to a church. **2** a part
containing an altar in a church. **3** a place of worship other than a church or cathedral, esp. one in
a palace, mansion or public institution. **4** a Nonconformist place of worship. **5** a service, or the
sort of service, at a chapel. **6** a printing office
(from the legend that Caxton set up his printing
press in Westminster Abbey). **7** a printers' or
journalists' trade union, or a branch of it. **8** a
meeting of such a trade union or branch. ~*a.*

belonging to a Nonconformist church. **chapel of
ease** *n.* a subordinate church in a parish. **chapel
of rest** *n.* an undertaker's mortuary. **chapel royal**
n. the chapel of a royal palace. **chapelry** *n.* (*pl.*
chapelries) the district or jurisdiction of a
chapel.

chaperone (shap´ərōn), **chaperon** *n.* **1** a married
or elderly woman who accompanies a young unmarried woman on social occasions or in public
places. **2** any person who accompanies or
supervises young people in public places. ~*v.t.* to
act as chaperone to. **chaperonage** *n.*

chaplain (chap´lin) *n.* a clergyman who officiates in a private chapel, in the armed forces, or
in some other establishment or institution (*a
prison chaplain*). **chaplaincy** *n.* (*pl.* **chap-
laincies**). **chaplainship** *n.*

chaplet (chap´lit) *n.* **1** a wreath or garland for the
head. **2** a string of beads, esp. one-third of a
rosary. **3** a necklace. **4** a round moulding carved
into beads, olives etc.

†chapman (chap´mən) *n.* (*pl.* **chapmen**) an
itinerant merchant, a pedlar, a hawker.

chapped CHAP¹.

chappie CHAP².

chaps CHAPARAJOS.

chapter (chap´tə) *n.* **1** a division of a book. **2** a
part of a subject. **3** a piece of narrative, an episode. **4** a period of time (*another chapter in the
nation's history*). **5** a series or sequence of events.
6 a numbered division of the Acts of Parliament
arranged in chronological order for reference.
7 the council of a bishop, consisting of the clergy
attached to a cathedral or collegiate church. **8** a
meeting of the members of a religious order. **9** a
branch or meeting of certain other orders and
societies. **10** a chapter house. ~*v.t.* to divide into
chapters. **chapter and verse** a full and precise
reference in order to verify a fact or quotation.
chapter house *n.* **1** the place in which a chapter
is held, esp. part of a cathedral or collegiate
church. **2** (*N Am.*) the meeting place of a college
fraternity or sorority.

char¹ (chah) *v.t.* (*pres.p.* **charring**, *past., p.p.*
charred) **1** to burn slightly, to blacken with fire.
2 to reduce to charcoal. ~*v.i.* to become blackened with fire.

char² (chah), **charr** *n.* (*pl. in general* **char, charr**,
in particular **chars, charrs**) any small fish of the
genus *Salvelinus*, of the salmon family, esp. *S.
alpinus*.

char³ (chah) *n.* a charwoman. ~*v.i.* (*pres.p.*
charring, *past, p.p.* **charred**) **1** to work as a charwoman. **2** to do small jobs. **charwoman, char-
lady** *n.* (*pl.* **charwomen, charladies**) a woman
employed to do cleaning in houses, offices etc.

char⁴ CHA.

charabanc (shar´əbang) *n.* (*dated*) a coach for
day trippers.

characin (kar´əsin), **characid** (-sid) *n.* any freshwater fish of the family Characidae, including
the piranha.

character (kar´iktə) *n.* 1 the distinctive qualities or traits peculiar to a person or thing. 2 the sum of a person's mental and moral qualities. 3 moral excellence, moral strength. 4 reputation or standing, esp. good reputation. 5 a certificate of a person's capacity, moral qualities and conduct; a testimonial. 6 position, rank, capacity. 7 a person, a personage. 8 (*coll.*) an eccentric person (*She's quite a character*). 9 a personality created by a novelist, poet or dramatist. 10 a part in a play, an actor's role. 11 a letter, symbol or other mark made by writing, printing, engraving etc. 12 (*Comput.*) a symbol, e.g. a letter, punctuation mark etc., that can be used in representing data. 13 style of handwriting. 14 a characteristic (of a species etc.) (*generic characters*). 15 an inherited characteristic. **in character** typical of a person, consistent with a person's character. **out of character** not in character. **character actor** *n.* an actor who specializes in portraying eccentric or unusual characters. **character assassination** *n.* the destruction of a person's good reputation, e.g. by spreading malicious rumours. **characterful** *a.* **characterfully** *adv.* **characteristic** (-ris´-) *n.* 1 a typical or distinctive quality or feature. 2 (*Math.*) the whole number or integral part of a logarithm. ~*a.* constituting or exhibiting a characteristic. **characteristically** *adv.* **characterize, characterise** *v.t.* 1 to give character to, to stamp, to distinguish. 2 to describe as. 3 to be characteristic of. **characterization** (-zā´shən) *n.* **characterless** *a.*

charade (shərahd´) *n.* 1 (*pl., usu. sing. in constr.*) a game in which a word is guessed from actions or utterances representing each syllable and the whole word. 2 any of the clues in this game. 3 a ridiculous pretence.

charbroil (chah´broil) *v.t.* to grill (meat etc.) over charcoal.

charcoal (chah´kōl) *n.* 1 an impure form of carbon prepared from vegetable or animal substances, esp. wood partially burnt under turf. 2 a stick of this used for drawing. 3 a drawing made with such a stick. 4 charcoal grey. ~*a.* charcoal grey. **charcoal biscuit** *n.* a biscuit containing wood charcoal. **charcoal grey** *n.* a dark grey colour. ~*a.* of this colour.

charcuterie (shahkoo´təri) *n.* 1 a shop selling cold cooked meats and similar products. 2 these products.

chard (chahd) *n.* a variety of beet, *Beta vulgaris*, with stalks and leaves eaten as a vegetable, also called *Swiss chard*.

charge (chahj) *v.t.* 1 to ask as a price. 2 to debit (to). 3 to accuse. 4 to enjoin, to command, to exhort. 5 to give directions to, as a judge to a jury or a bishop to his clergy. 6 to entrust. 7 to rush on and attack. 8 to put the proper load or quantity of material into; to load (a gun), to accumulate electricity in (a battery) etc. 9 to give an electric charge to. 10 to load, to fill. 11 to saturate, to pervade. ~*v.i.* 1 to make an attack or onrush. 2 (*coll.*) to demand high prices or

payments. ~*n.* 1 a price demanded, a cost. 2 a financial liability, a tax. 3 an entry on the debit side of an account. 4 (*Law*) an accusation, esp. a formal accusation of crime. 5 an office, duty or obligation. 6 a command, a commission. 7 care, custody (*in your charge*). 8 a thing or person under one's care; a minister's congregation. 9 attack, onrush. 10 the quantity with which any apparatus, esp. a firearm, is loaded. 11 the electrical property of matter, negative or positive. 12 the amount or accumulation of electricity, e.g. in a battery. 13 instructions, directions, esp. those of a judge to a jury or of a bishop to clergy. 14 (*Her.*) anything borne on an escutcheon. 15 a load, a burden. **in charge** 1 on duty. 2 in command. **in charge of** responsible for. **on a charge** having been charged with a crime. **to give in charge** 1 to commit to the care of another. 2 to hand over to the custody of a police officer. **to lay to the charge of** to accuse of. **to take charge** to assume control, command, responsibility etc. **to take in charge** to arrest, to take into custody. **chargeable** *a.* **charge account** *n.* a credit account at a shop. **charge card** *n.* a credit card issued by a shop or retail chain for use in its own outlets. **charge-coupled device** *n.* (*Comput.*) a storage device built into a chip which can be used only so long as it has an electric charge. **chargehand** *n.* a worker in charge of several others. **charge nurse** *n.* a nurse in charge of a ward. **charger** *n.* 1 a person who charges. 2 a horse, esp. a cavalry horse. 3 a device for charging a battery. **charge sheet** *n.* a list of offenders taken into custody, with their offences, for the use of a magistrate.

chargé d'affaires (shahzhā dafeə´), **chargé** (shah´zhā) *n.* (*pl.* **chargés d'affaires** (shah´zhā), **chargés**) 1 a diplomatic agent acting as deputy to an ambassador. 2 an ambassador to a country of minor importance.

charily, chariness CHARY.

chariot (char´iət) *n.* 1 (*Hist.*) a carriage used in war, public triumphs and racing. 2 (*Hist.*) a light, four-wheeled carriage used for pleasure and on ceremonial. 3 (*esp. poet.*) any vehicle, esp. a stately kind of vehicle. ~*v.t.* (*pres.p.* **charioting**, *past, p.p.* **charioted**) (*poet.*) to convey in a chariot. **charioteer** (-tiə´) *n.* a chariot driver.

charisma (kəriz´mə), **charism** (kar´izm) *n.* (*pl.* **charismata** (-mətə), **charisms**) 1 personal magnetism or charm enabling one to inspire or influence other people. 2 a quality which inspires admiration or devotion. 3 a divinely given power or talent. **charismatic** (karizmat´-) *a.* 1 having charisma. 2 of or relating to the charismatic movement. **charismatically** *adv.* **charismatic movement** *n.* a Christian movement characterized by speaking in tongues, spontaneity, communal prayer, healing etc.

charity (char´iti) *n.* (*pl.* **charities**) 1 generosity to those in need, alms-giving. 2 the money etc. so given. 3 a foundation or institution for assisting those in need. 4 kindness, goodwill. 5 an act of kindness. **6** leniency, tolerance of faults and offences, liberality of judgement. **7** love of one's fellow human beings, one of the theological virtues. **charitable** *a.* **1** of, relating to or supported by charity (*a charitable organization*). **2** generous to those in need. **3** benevolent, kindly, lenient, large-hearted. **4** dictated by kindness. **charitableness** *n.* **charitably** *adv.*

charivari (shahrivah´ri), (*esp. N Am.*) **shivaree** *n.* (*pl.* **charivaris, shivarees**) **1** a mock serenade of discordant music. **2** a confusion of sounds, a hubbub.

charlatan (shah´lətən) *n.* a person who pretends to have skill or knowledge; a quack; an impostor. **charlatanism, charlatanry** *n.*

Usage note Pronunciation with (ch-) rather than (sh-) is best avoided.

Charles's wain (chahl´ziz) *n.* seven stars in the constellation the Great Bear; the Plough.

charleston (chahl´stən), **Charleston** *n.* a strenuous dance in 4/4 time with characteristic kicking outwards of the lower part of the legs.

charley horse (chah´li) *n.* (*N Am., sl.*) muscle stiffness or cramp, esp. in the arm or leg after exercise.

charlie (chah´li) *n.* (*sl.*) **1** an utterly foolish person (*a proper charlie*). **2** (*pl.*) a woman's breasts.

charlock (chah´lok) *n.* a type of wild mustard, *Sinapis arvensis*; the field mustard.

charlotte (shah´lət) *n.* a kind of pudding made with fruit and thin slices of bread or layers of breadcrumbs etc. **charlotte russe** (roos) *n.* custard or whipped cream enclosed in sponge cake or sponge fingers.

charm (chahm) *n.* **1** a power or gift of alluring, pleasing, fascinating etc. **2** a pleasing or attractive feature. **3** a spell, an enchantment. **4** a thing, act or formula having magical power. **5** an article worn to avert evil or ensure good luck, an amulet. **6** a small trinket worn on a bracelet. **7** (*Physics*) a property of some elementary particles. ~*v.t.* **1** to attract, to delight, to please. **2** to enchant, to fascinate, to bewitch. **3** (*usu. pass.*) to protect with occult power (*a charmed life*). **4** to gain or influence by charm. **like a charm** perfectly. **charm bracelet** *n.* a bracelet hung with charms. **charmer** *n.* **charming** *a.* highly pleasing; delightful. ~*int.* (*iron.*) used to express disapproval. **charmingly** *adv.* **charmingness** *n.* **charmless** *a.* **charmlessly** *adv.* **charmlessness** *n.* **charm offensive** *n.* the excessive use of charm to get what one wants, achieve a goal etc.

charnel (chah´nəl) *a.* deathlike; sepulchral. **charnel house** *n.* a place where dead bodies or the bones of the dead are deposited.

charpoy (chah´poi) *n.* (*Ang.-Ind.*) a light Indian bedstead.

charr CHAR².

chart (chaht) *n.* **1** a map of some part of the sea, with coasts, islands, rocks, shoals etc., for the use of sailors. **2** a statement of facts in tabular form. **3** a projection of relative facts, statistics or observations in the form of a graph. **4** a skeleton map for special purposes (*a heliographic chart*). **5** (*often pl.*) a weekly list of best-selling records. ~*v.t.* **1** to make a chart of. **2** to map. **chartbuster** *n.* (*coll.*) a best-selling record.

charter (chah´tə) *n.* **1** an instrument in writing granted by the sovereign or parliament, incorporating a borough, company or institution, or conferring certain rights and privileges. **2** a deed, an instrument. **3** a special privilege or exemption. **4** a contract for the hire of a ship, aircraft or other means of transportation. ~*a.* **1** (of an aircraft) hired by charter. **2** (of a flight) made in a charter aircraft. ~*v.t.* **1** to establish by charter. **2** to license by charter. **3** to hire (a ship, aircraft etc.) esp. by charter. **chartered** *a.* (of an accountant, engineer etc.) qualified to the standards set by a professional body that has a royal charter. **charterer** *n.* **Charter Mark** *n.* an award granted to an organization or institution providing a high standard of public service under the Citizen's Charter. **charter member** *n.* an original member of a society or organization.

Chartism (chah´tizm) *n.* the principles of an English reform movement of 1838–48, including universal suffrage, vote by ballot, annual parliaments, payment of members, equal electoral districts and the abolition of property qualifications for members. **Chartist** *n.*

chartography CARTOGRAPHY.

chartreuse (shahtrœz´) *n.* **1** a pale green or yellow liqueur made with aromatic herbs. **2** the colour of this. **3** a dish of fruit in jelly. ~*a.* of the colour of chartreuse.

chary (cheə´ri) *a.* (*comp.* **charier,** *superl.* **chariest**) **1** wary, prudent, cautious. **2** frugal, sparing. **charily** *adv.*

chase¹ (chās) *v.t.* **1** to pursue, esp. at speed. **2** to hunt. **3** to drive away. **4** to put to flight. **5** (*coll.*) to try to achieve or obtain. ~*v.i.* to move rapidly, esp. in pursuit. ~*n.* **1** the act of chasing (*a car chase*). **2** the hunting of wild animals (*the thrill of the chase*). **3** an animal etc. that is chased. **4** an open hunting ground or preserve for game. **5** a steeplechase. **to chase up** (*coll.*) to pursue or investigate in order to obtain information etc. **chaser** *n.* **1** a person or thing that chases. **2** a horse used for steeplechasing. **3** (*coll.*) a drink taken after one of another kind, esp. spirits after beer.

chase² (chās) *v.t.* to engrave, to emboss.

chase³ (chās) *n.* a rectangular iron frame in which type is locked for printing.

chase⁴ (chās) *n.* **1** a wide groove. **2** the part of a gun in front of the trunnions.

chasm (kaz´m) *n.* **1** a deep cleft or fissure in the ground; a yawning gulf. **2** a breach or division between persons or parties. **3** a gap or void. **chasmic** *a.*

chassé (shas´ā) *n.* a gliding step in dancing. ~*v.i.*

(*pres.p.* **chasséing**, *past, p.p.* **chasséd**) to perform this step.

chasseur (shasœ´) *n.* a huntsman. ~*a.* cooked in a sauce of white wine and mushrooms (*chicken chasseur*).

chassis (shas´i) *n.* (*pl.* **chassis** (-iz)) **1** the framework of a motor vehicle, aeroplane etc. **2** a framework supporting a piece of electronic equipment. **3** the base-frame of a cannon or gun carriage.

chaste (chāst) *a.* **1** abstaining from all sexual intercourse, or from sex outside marriage. **2** modest, innocent, virginal. **3** free from obscenity. **4** pure in style. **5** simple, unadorned, unaffected. **chastely** *adv.* **chasteness** *n.* **chaste tree** *n.* an ornamental flowering shrub, *Vitex agnus-castus*. **chastity** (chas´-) *n.* **1** the state of being chaste. **2** virginity. **3** celibacy. **4** purity of taste and style. **chastity belt** *n.* a beltlike garment designed to prevent a woman from having sexual intercourse.

chasten (chā´sən) *v.t.* **1** to punish with a view to reformation; to correct; to discipline. **2** to subdue; to moderate; to restrain. **chastener** *n.*

chastise (chastīz´) *v.t.* **1** to punish, esp. physically. **2** to reprimand severely. **chastisement** (chas´tiz-, -tīz´-) *n.* **chastiser** *n.*

chasuble (chaz´ūbəl) *n.* a sleeveless vestment worn by a priest over the alb while celebrating Mass.

chat[1] (chat) *v.i.* (*pres.p.* **chatting**, *past, p.p.* **chatted**) **1** to talk easily and familiarly. **2** to gossip. ~*n.* **1** easy, familiar talk. **2** an informal conversation. **3** gossip. **to chat up** (*sl.*) to chat to in order to establish a (sexual) relationship. **chatline** *n.* a telephone service that enables a number of callers to engage in conversation together. **chat show** *n.* a television show or radio programme in which invited celebrities are interviewed informally. **chatty** *a.* (*comp.* **chattier**, *superl.* **chattiest**) **1** talkative. **2** informal (*a chatty letter*). **chattily** *adv.* **chattiness** *n.* **chat-up** *n.* (*coll.*) an instance of chatting someone up. ~*a.* used in chatting someone up (*a chat-up line*).

chat[2] (chat) *n.* any of various birds, mostly songbirds or warblers, such as the stonechat or the whinchat.

chateau (shat´ō), **château** *n.* (*pl.* **chateaux** (-tōz), **châteaux**) a castle or country house in French-speaking countries.

chateaubriand (shatōbrē´ā) *n.* a thick steak of beef cut from the fillet.

chatelain (shat´əlān) *n.* the lord of a castle. **chatelaine** *n.* **1** a female chatelain. **2** a chain worn on a woman's belt, to which may be attached a watch, keys, trinkets, etc.

chattel (chat´əl) *n.* (*usu. pl.*) **1** (*Law*) moveable property. **2** (*Law*) any property except freehold land. **3** any personal possession (*goods and chattels*).

chatter (chat´ə) *v.i.* **1** to talk idly and thoughtlessly. **2** to jabber, to prattle. **3** (of a bird etc.) to utter rapid, inharmonious sounds. **4** (of the teeth) to make a noise by rattling together. **5** to make a noise resembling this. ~*n.* **1** the sound of chattering. **2** idle talk. **3** the vibration of a tool. **the chattering classes** (*derog. or facet.*) intellectuals etc. considered as a social group enjoying political, social or cultural discussion. **chatterbox** *n.* an incessant talker. **chatterer** *n.* **chattery** *a.*

chatty CHAT[1].

chauffeur (shō´fə, -fœ´) *n.* a person employed to drive a motor car. ~*v.t.* to drive (a car or a person) as a chauffeur. **chauffeuse** (shōfœz´) *n.* a female chauffeur.

chaulmoogra (chawlmoo´grə) *n.* **1** any of various trees of the family Flacourtiaceae, of tropical Asia, esp. *Hydnocarpus kurzii*. **2** oil from the seeds of this tree, used in the treatment of leprosy and other skin diseases.

chauvinism (shō´vinizm) *n.* **1** exaggerated patriotism of an aggressive kind; jingoism. **2** an exaggerated and excessive attachment to any cause, such as sexism (*male chauvinism*). **chauvinist** *n.* **1** a person who believes their own ethnic group, sex etc. to be superior and despises all others. **2** a male chauvinist. **chauvinistic** (-nis´-) *a.* **chauvinistically** *adv.*

ChB *abbr.* Bachelor of Surgery.

cheap (chēp) *a.* **1** low in price. **2** worth more than its price or cost. **3** charging low prices. **4** of poor quality. **5** easy to get; requiring little effort. **6** despicable (*a cheap trick*). ~*adv.* at a low price or cost. **on the cheap 1** cheaply. **2** in a miserly way. **cheap and cheerful** *a.* low in price but not unattractive. **cheap and nasty** *a.* low in price and quality. **cheapen** *v.t.* **1** to reduce the price or value of. **2** to depreciate. ~*v.i.* **1** to become cheap. **2** to depreciate. **cheapie** *n.* (*N Am., sl.*) a cheap product. ~*a.* cheap. **cheapish** *a.* **cheapjack** *n.* a person who sells cheap goods of inferior quality. ~*a.* **1** cheap. **2** inferior. **cheaply** *adv.* **cheapness** *n.* **cheapo** *a.* (*sl.*) low in price and usu. of poor quality (*cheapo trainers*). **cheapskate** *n.* (*coll.*) a miserly person.

cheat (chēt) *v.t.* **1** to defraud, to deprive. **2** to deceive, to trick. **3** to avoid or escape, esp. by luck or skill (*to cheat death*). ~*v.i.* to gain unfair advantage in a game, examination etc. by using trickery or deception or by breaking rules. ~*n.* **1** a person who cheats. **2** a trick or deception. **3** a fraud, a swindle. **cheater** *n.* **1** a person who cheats or defrauds. **2** (*pl., N Am., sl.*) spectacles. **to cheat on** (*coll.*) to be unfaithful to (one's wife, husband, lover etc.).

check[1] (chek) *n.* **1** a test for accuracy, quality etc. **2** a sudden stoppage or restraint of motion. **3** a person or thing that stops or restrains motion. **4** a reverse, a repulse, a rebuff. **5** a pause, a halt. **6** restraint, repression. **7** in chess, the situation of a king exposed to direct attack, from which it must be moved or protected. **8** a mark put against names or items in going over a list. **9** a token by which the correctness or authenticity of a document etc. may be ascertained. **10** a token serving for identification. **11** a pass entitling to readmission to a theatre. **12** (*NAm.*) a bill at a restaurant etc. **13** (*NAm.*) a token at cards. **14** (*NAm.*) a left-luggage ticket. ~*v.t.* **1** to test the accuracy, quality etc. of. **2** to confirm, to verify (*Check that the lid is shut*). **3** to cause to stop or slow down. **4** to restrain, to curb. **5** to rebuke. **6** in chess, to put an opponent's king in check. **7** to ease off (a rope etc.). **8** (*NAm.*) to mark with a tick etc. **9** (*NAm.*) to deposit (left-luggage etc.). ~*v.i.* **1** to pause, to halt. **2** to agree, to correspond (with). **3** to make sure. ~*int.* **1** used in chess when an opponent's king is in check. **2** used to express agreement or correspondence. **in check 1** under control or restraint. **2** (of a king in chess) exposed to direct attack. **to check in** to register on arrival at a hotel, at work etc. **to check off** to mark or tick (an item on a list etc.). **to check on 1** to keep watch on. **2** to check up on. **to check out 1** to leave a hotel, place of work etc. **2** to test for accuracy, quality etc. **3** to investigate. **4** (*NAm., sl.*) to die. **to check over** to examine for faults, errors etc. **to check through** to examine carefully (a series of items) (*to check through the records*). **to check up 1** to investigate. **2** to make sure. **to check up on** to investigate. **checkable** *a.* **checker**[1] *n.* **check-in** *n.* **1** the act of checking in. **2** a place where one's arrival is registered. **checklist** *n.* **1** a list used in checking for accuracy, completeness etc. **2** an inventory. **checkout** *n.* **1** the act of checking out. **2** a cash desk at a supermarket. **checkpoint** *n.* a place (as at a frontier) where documents etc. are checked. **checkroom** *n.* (*NAm.*) **1** a cloakroom. **2** a left-luggage office. **check-up** *n.* a general examination (esp. medical).

check[2] (chek) *n.* **1** a chequered pattern, a cross-lined pattern. **2** a fabric having such a pattern. ~*a.* having such a pattern (*a check shirt*). **checked** *a.* **checky** *a.*

check[3] CHEQUE. **checking account** (chek´ing) *n.* (*NAm.*) a current account.

checker[1] CHECK[1].

checker[2] CHEQUER.

checkerberry (chek´əberi) *n.* (*pl.* **checkerberries**) **1** a N American shrub, *Gaultheria procumbens*, with white flowers and edible red fruit. **2** the fruit of this plant.

checkerman, checkers CHEQUER.

checkmate (chek´māt) *n.* **1** in chess, the winning move or situation when one king is in check and cannot escape from that position. **2** a complete defeat. **3** a position from which there is no escape. ~*int.* used in chess when an opponent's king is put into this position. ~*v.t.* **1** to give checkmate to. **2** to defeat utterly, to frustrate.

Cheddar (ched´ə) *n.* a hard, strong-flavoured yellow cheese.

cheek (chēk) *n.* **1** the side of the face below the eye. **2** impudent speech. **3** (*coll.*) impudence,

sauciness. **4** effrontery, assurance (*He had the cheek to excuse me of lying*). **5** a side-post of a door, the side of a pulley. **6** either of two corresponding sides of a frame, machine, or implement. **7** (*sl.*) a buttock. ~*v.t.* to be impudent to. **cheek by jowl 1** side by side. **2** in the closest proximity. **to turn the other cheek** to accept a physical or verbal attack without retaliation. **cheekbone** *n.* the prominence of the malar bone. **cheeky** *a.* (*comp.* **cheekier,** *superl.* **cheekiest**) impudent, saucy. **cheekily** *adv.* **cheekiness** *n.*

cheep (chēp) *v.i.* to chirp feebly. ~*n.* the feeble cry of a young bird. **cheeper** *n.* a young bird.

cheer (chiə) *n.* **1** a shout of joy, encouragement or applause. **2** disposition, frame of mind, mood (*of good cheer*). **3** a state of gladness or joy. ~*v.t.* **1** to make glad or cheerful. **2** to applaud or encourage with cheers. ~*v.i.* **1** to grow cheerful. **2** to utter a cheer or cheers. **to cheer up 1** to make more cheerful. **2** to become more cheerful. **cheerful** *a.* **1** contented. **2** full of good spirits. **3** lively, animated. **4** willing. **5** hopeful. **cheerfully** *adv.* **cheerfulness** *n.* **cheerio** (-riō´), **cheer-ho** (-hō´) *int.* goodbye. **cheerleader** *n.* (*N Am.*) a person who leads organized cheering at a rally, football game etc. **cheerless** *a.* dull, gloomy, dispiriting. **cheerlessly** *adv.* **cheerlessness** *n.* **cheers** *int.* (*coll.*) **1** a drinking toast. **2** thank you. **3** goodbye. **cheery** *a.* (*comp.* **cheerier,** *superl.* **cheeriest**) lively, sprightly, full of good spirits, genial. **cheerily** *adv.* **cheeriness** *n.*

cheese[1] (chēz) *n.* **1** the curd of milk pressed into a solid mass and ripened by keeping. **2** a cylindrical or spherical block of this. **3** anything of cheeselike form or consistency. **cheeseboard** *n.* **1** a board on which cheese is served at table. **2** the variety of cheeses on such a board. **cheeseburger** *n.* a hamburger with a slice of cheese on top. **cheesecake** *n.* **1** a kind of tart made of pastry or biscuit crumbs with a filling of cream cheese, sugar etc. **2** (*sl.*) young and attractive women, esp. scantily clad or nude. **3** pictures of such women. **cheesecloth** *n.* thin cotton cloth loosely woven. **cheese-fly** *n.* (*pl.* **cheese-flies**) a fly, *Piophila casei*, bred in cheese. **cheese-head** *a.* (of a screw or bolt) having a slotted head shaped like a short thick cylinder. **cheesemaker** *n.* **cheesemaking** *n.* **cheese-mite** *n.* any mite of the genus *Tyroglyphus*, infesting old cheese and other foodstuffs. **cheesemonger** *n.* a person who deals in cheese, butter etc. **cheese-paring** *a.* niggardly, mean, miserly. ~*n.* **1** meanness, stinginess. **2** (*pl.*) scraps of cheese. **3** (*pl.*) odds and ends. **cheese plant** *n.* SWISS CHEESE PLANT (under SWISS). **cheese-skipper** *n.* the cheese-fly. **cheese straw** *n.* a long thin strip of cheese-flavoured pastry. **cheesewood** *n.* **1** an Australian tree of the genus *Pittosporum* with a hard wood of a yellowish colour. **2** the wood of this tree. **cheesy** *a.* (*comp.* **cheesier,** *superl.* **cheesiest**) **1** resembling or tasting like cheese. **2** (*sl.*) corny. **cheesiness** *n.*

cheese[2] (chēz) *n.* (*sl.*) an important person.

cheese³ (chēz) *v.t.* (*sl.*) to annoy or exasperate. **cheesed off** (*coll.*) bored, annoyed.

cheetah (chē´tə), **chetah** *n.* a leopard-like mammal, *Acinonyx jubatus*, the swiftest land animal.

chef (shef) *n.* a professional cook, esp. the head cook of a restaurant etc.

chef-d'oeuvre (shādœv´rə) *n.* (*pl.* **chefsd'oeuvre** (shādœv´rə)) a masterpiece.

☒ cheif common misspelling of CHIEF.

chela (kē´lə) *n.* (*pl.* **chelae** (-lē)) a claw (as of a lobster or crab), a modified thoracic limb. **chelate** (-lāt) *n.* (*Chem.*) a compound with molecules that contain a closed ring of atoms, including one metal atom. ~*a.* **1** (*Zool.*) of, relating to or having chelae. **2** (*Chem.*) of, relating to or forming a chelate. ~*v.i.* (*Chem.*) to form a chelate. **chelation** (-lā´-) *n.*

chelonian (kilō´niən) *n.* any reptile of the order Chelonia, containing the turtles and tortoises. ~*a.* of or relating to this order.

Chelsea bun (chel´si) *n.* a bun made of a roll of sweet dough with raisins. **Chelsea pensioner** *n.* an old or disabled ex-soldier, an inmate of the Chelsea Royal Hospital. **Chelsea ware** *n.* a type of 18th-cent. china.

chem-, chemi- CHEMO-.

chemical (kem´ikəl) *a.* **1** of or relating to chemistry, its laws or phenomena. **2** of or produced by chemical process. ~*n.* a substance or agent produced by or used in chemistry or chemical processes. **chemical bond** *n.* a mutual attraction that holds atoms together in a molecule etc. **chemical engineer** *n.* a specialist in chemical engineering. **chemical engineering** *n.* the branch of engineering concerned with the design and building of industrial chemical plants. **chemically** *adv.* **chemical reaction** *n.* the process of changing one substance into another. **chemical symbol** *n.* a letter or letters used to represent an atom of a chemical element. **chemical warfare** *n.* war waged using poisonous chemicals (gases, sprays, etc.). **chemical weapon** *n.* a weapon used in chemical warfare.

chemiluminescence (kemiloomines´əns) *n.* luminescence occurring as a result of a chemical reaction, without production of heat. **chemiluminescent** *a.*

chemin de fer (shəmī də feə´) *n.* a variety of baccarat.

chemise (shəmēz´) *n.* **1** an undergarment of linen or cotton worn by women. **2** a straight, loose-fitting dress.

chemisorption (kemisawp´shən) *n.* a process of adsorption involving chemical bonds.

chemist (kem´ist) *n.* **1** a scientist specializing in chemistry. **2** a person qualified to dispense drugs, a pharmacist. **3** a shop where drugs, toiletries etc. are sold.

chemistry (kem´istri) *n.* (*pl.* **chemistries**) **1** the science which investigates the elements of which bodies are composed, the combination of these elements, and the reaction of these chemical compounds on each other (*organic chemistry*; *inorganic chemistry*). **2** the practical application of this science. **3** the chemical composition, properties etc. of a substance. **4** any process or change conceived as analogous to chemical action, esp. emotional attraction.

chemo- (kē´mō), **chemi-** (kem´i), **chem-** *comb. form* chemical.

chemoreceptor (kēmōrisep´tə, kem-) *n.* (*Biol.*) a sensory nerve ending which responds to a chemical stimulus.

chemosynthesis (kēmōsin´thəsis, kem-) *n.* the production of organic material by some bacteria, using chemical reactions.

chemotherapy (kēmōthe´rəpi, kem-) *n.* the treatment of disease, esp. cancer, by drugs. **chemotherapist** *n.*

chenille (shənēl´) *n.* **1** a round tufted or fluffy cord of silk or worsted. **2** a pile fabric made with similar yarn.

cheongsam (chongsam´, chiong-) *n.* a Chinese woman's long, tight-fitting dress with slit sides.

cheque (chek), (*N Am.*) **check** *n.* **1** a draft on a bank for money payable to the bearer. **2** the printed form bearing such an order. **chequebook** *n.* a book containing cheques. **chequebook journalism** *n.* sensational journalism using stories bought at high prices. **cheque card** *n.* a card issued by a bank, guaranteeing payment of cheques up to a specified limit.

chequer (chek´ə), (*N Am.*) **checker** *n.* **1** (*usu. pl.*) a pattern made of squares in alternating colours, like a chessboard. **2** (*pl., usu. sing. in constr.*) the game of draughts. **3** any of the pieces used in the game of Chinese chequers. ~*v.t.* **1** to form into a pattern of small squares. **2** to variegate. **3** to diversify, to fill with vicissitudes (*a chequered career*). **checkerman** *n.* (*pl.* **checkermen** (*N Am.*)) any of the pieces used in the game of draughts. **checkers** *n.pl.* (*usu. sing. in. constr.*, *N Am.*) the game of draughts. **chequer-board** *n.* **1** a chessboard. **2** a pattern resembling this. **chequered flag** *n.* a flag with black and white squares used to signal the finish in a motor race.

cherish (cher´ish) *v.t.* **1** to hold dear, to treat with affection, to protect lovingly. **2** to hold closely to, to cling to (*to cherish hopes of success*).

chernozem (chœ´nəzem), **tschernosem** *n.* a dark-coloured, very fertile soil found in temperate climates.

cheroot (shəroot´) *n.* a cigar with both ends cut square off.

cherry (cher´i) *n.* (*pl.* **cherries**) **1** a small stone-fruit of the plum family. **2** any tree of the genus *Prunus* on which this fruit grows. **3** the wood of this tree. **4** the colour of a red cherry. **5** (*taboo sl.*) virginity. ~*a.* of the colour of a red cherry. **cherry brandy** *n.* a red liqueur made from brandy in which cherries have been steeped. **cherry laurel** *n.* an evergreen shrub, *Prunus laurocerasus*, with white flowers and small fruits resembling cherries. **cherry-pick** *v.i.* to select or take the best people, items etc. from a group. **cherry red** *n.* the colour of a red cherry. ~*a.* of this colour. **cherry tomato** *n.* (*pl.* **cherry tomatoes**) a strong-flavoured miniature tomato. **cherry tree** *n.* the tree on which the cherry grows. **cherrywood** *n.* the wood of the cherry tree.

chert (chœt) *n.* a flinty type of quartz; hornstone. **cherty** *a.* resembling or containing chert.

cherub (cher´əb) *n.* (*pl.* **cherubs**, **cherubim** (-im)) **1** a celestial spirit next in order to the seraphim. **2** a beautiful child. **3** in art, the winged head of a child. **cherubic** (-roo´-) *a.* **1** of or relating to cherubs. **2** angelic. **3** full-cheeked and ruddy. **cherubically** *adv.*

chervil (chœ´vil) *n.* a garden herb, *Anthriscus cerefolium*, used in soups, salads etc.

Cheshire (chesh´ə), **Cheshire cheese** *n.* a mild-flavoured white or red cheese with a firm but crumbly texture, originally made in Cheshire. **to grin like a Cheshire cat** to grin broadly.

chess (ches) *n.* a game played by two persons with 16 pieces each on a board divided into 64 squares. **chessboard** *n.* the board on which chess is played. **chessman** *n.* (*pl.* **chessmen**) any of the pieces used in chess. **chess set** *n.* a set comprising 32 chessmen and a chessboard.

chest (chest) *n.* **1** a large strong box. **2** a case for holding particular commodities (*a tea chest*). **3** the quantity such a case holds. **4** a small cabinet (*a medicine chest*). **5** the fore part of the human body from the neck to the waist. **6** the treasury or funds of an institution. **to get off one's chest 1** (*coll.*) to unburden oneself of (a secret etc.). **2** (*coll.*) to admit, to declare. **-chested** *comb. form* having a chest of a specified kind. **chest freezer** *n.* a large freezer, opening at the top. **chest of drawers** *n.* a movable wooden frame containing drawers. **chest voice** *n.* the lowest singing or speaking register of the voice. **chesty** *a.* (*comp.* **chestier**, *superl.* **chestiest**) (*coll.*) **1** suffering from, or subject to, bronchitis etc. **2** having a large chest or large breasts. **3** (*N Am.*) arrogant, self-important. **chestily** *adv.* **chestiness** *n.*

chesterfield (ches´təfēld) *n.* **1** a deeply upholstered sofa with curved arms and back of the same height. **2** a loose kind of overcoat.

chestnut (ches´nŭt) *n.* **1** any tree of the genus *Castanea*, esp. the Spanish or sweet chestnut, *C. sativa*. **2** the edible fruit of this tree. **3** the reddish-brown colour of this fruit. **4** a horse of this colour. **5** the horse chestnut tree or its fruit. **6** (*coll.*) a stale joke or anecdote. **7** in horses, a knob on the inside of the forelegs. ~*a.* reddish-brown.

cheval glass (shəval´) *n.* a large swinging mirror mounted on a frame.

chevalier (shevəliə´) *n.* **1** a member of some foreign orders of knighthood or of the French Legion of Honour. **2** †a knight. **3** a chivalrous man.

chevet (shəvā´) *n.* an apse.

chèvre (shev´rə) *n.* a type of cheese made from goats' milk.

chevron (shev´rən) *n.* **1** a V-shaped badge on the sleeve of a uniform, esp. of a non-commissioned officer in the armed forces. **2** (*Her.*) an inverted V shape, an honourable ordinary representing two rafters meeting at the top. **3** (*Archit.*) a zigzag moulding. **4** any V-shaped stripe or pattern.

chevrotain (shev´rətān), **chevrotin** (-tin) *n.* a small animal of the family Tragulidae, resembling a deer.

chevy CHIVVY.

chew (choo) *v.t.* **1** to masticate, to grind with the teeth. **2** to ruminate on, to digest mentally. ~*v.i.* **1** to masticate food. **2** to chew tobacco or gum. **3** to meditate. ~*n.* **1** the act of chewing. **2** something to be chewed, esp. a sweet. **to chew on 1** to grind continuously with the teeth. **2** to ruminate on. **to chew out** (*N Am.*, *coll.*) to reprimand. **to chew over 1** to discuss. **2** to think about. **to chew the fat 1** (*sl.*) to chat. **2** (*sl.*) to grumble, to complain. **to chew the rag** (*sl.*) to chew the fat. **chewable** *a.* **chewing gum** *n.* a preparation of flavoured insoluble gum for chewing. **chewy** *a.* (*comp.* **chewier**, *superl.* **chewiest**) firm-textured, suitable for or requiring much chewing. **chewiness** *n.*

chez (shā) *prep.* at the house of.

chi (kī) *n.* the 22nd letter of the Greek alphabet (χ, Χ).

Chianti (kian´ti) *n.* (*pl.* **Chiantis**) a dry red wine from Tuscany.

chiaroscuro (kiahrəskoo´rō, -skuə´-) *n.* (*pl.* **chiaroscuros**) **1** the treatment or effects of light and shade in drawing, painting etc. **2** variety or contrast in a literary work etc. ~*a.* half-revealed.

chic (shēk) *n.* **1** smartness, style. **2** the best fashion or taste. ~*a.* (*comp.* **chic-er**, *superl.* **chic-est**) stylish, elegant, fashionable. **chicly** *adv.*

Chicana CHICANO.

chicane (shikān´) *n.* **1** an artificial obstacle on a motor-racing circuit. **2** in bridge or whist, a hand of cards containing no trumps. **3** chicanery. **chicanery** (-nəri) *n.* (*pl.* **chicaneries**) **1** artifice, deception or subterfuge, esp. legal trickery. **2** quibbling, pettifogging.

Chicano (chikah´nō, -kā´nō) *n.* (*pl.* **Chicanos**) a person of Mexican origin living in the US. **Chicana** *n.* (*pl.* **Chicanas**) a female Chicano.

chichi (shē´shē) *a.* **1** showy, affectedly pretty or fashionable. **2** (of a person) fussy; pretentious; affected. ~*n.* **1** the quality of being chichi. **2** something that is chichi.

chick (chik) *n.* **1** a young bird about to be hatched or newly hatched. **2** (*coll.*) a young child. **3** (*sl.*) a young woman. **chickweed** *n.* **1** a garden weed, *Stellaria media*, with small white flowers. **2** any of various similar plants.

chickadee (chik´ədē) *n.* any of various N American songbirds of the tit family, such as *Parus atricapillus*.

chicken (chik´ən) *n.* **1** the young of the domestic fowl. **2** a domestic fowl prepared for the table. **3** the flesh of this. **4** a young or inexperienced person. **5** (*coll.*) a coward. **6** (*coll.*) a game involving a test of courage or recklessness. ~*a.* (*coll.*) cowardly. **to chicken out** (*coll.*) to lose one's nerve. **chicken-and-egg** *a.* of or denoting a situation in which it is impossible to distinguish between cause and effect. **chicken brick** *n.* an earthenware cooking vessel in two halves, in which a chicken can be roasted in its own fat. **chicken feed** *n.* **1** food for poultry. **2** (*coll.*) an insignificant sum of money. **3** (*coll.*) a trifling amount or matter. **chicken-hearted, chicken-livered** *a.* timid, cowardly. **chickenpox** *n.* an infectious disease, usually occurring in childhood, characterized by fever and a rash of small blisters. **chicken wire** *n.* wire netting with a small hexagonal mesh.

chickpea (chik´pē) *n.* **1** a dwarf species of pea, *Cicer arietinum*. **2** the edible seed of this plant.

chicle (chik´əl) *n.* the juice of the sapodilla, used in the making of chewing gum.

chicory (chik´əri), **chiccory** *n.* (*pl.* **chicories, chiccories**) **1** a blue-flowered plant, *Cichorium intybus*, the succory. **2** the root of this plant, roasted and ground for use as a coffee additive. **3** the endive.

chide (chīd) *v.t.* (*past* **chided, chid** (chid), *p.p.* **chided, chid, chidden**) to find fault with, to reprove. ~*v.i.* to scold. **chider** *n.* **chidingly** *adv.*

chief (chēf) *a.* **1** principal, first. **2** highest in authority. **3** most important, leading, main. ~*n.* **1** a leader or commander, esp. the leader of a tribe or clan. **2** the head of a department. **3** the principal thing. **4** the largest part. **5** (*Her.*) the upper third of a shield. **Chief Constable** *n.* the officer in charge of the police force of a county or other area. **chiefdom** *n.* **chiefly** *adv.* **1** principally, especially. **2** for the most part. **Chief of Staff** *n.* the senior officer of a division of the armed forces. **chiefship** *n.* **chief technician** *n.* a noncommissioned officer in the Royal Air Force ranking between sergeant and flight sergeant.

chieftain (chēf´tən) *n.* **1** a general, a leader. **2** the head of a tribe or a Highland clan. **chieftaincy** *n.* (*pl.* **chieftaincies**). **chieftainry, chieftainship** *n.*

chiffchaff (chif´chaf) *n.* a European warbler, *Phylloscopus collybita*.

chiffon (shif´on) *n.* a gauzy semi-transparent fabric. ~*a.* **1** made of chiffon. **2** (of puddings) having a fine, light consistency. **chiffonier** (-niə´), **chiffonnier** *n.* **1** a movable piece of furniture serving as a cupboard and sideboard. **2** (*esp. NAm.*) a tall chest of drawers.

chigger (chig´ə) *n.* **1** a small W Indian and S American flea, *Tunga penetrans*. **2** (*NAm.*) a harvest mite or its larva.

chignon (shēn´yō) *n.* a coil or knot of long hair at the back of the head.

chigoe (chig´ō) *n.* the flea *Tunga penetrans*, a chigger.

chihuahua (chiwah´wah) *n.* (*pl.* **chihuahuas**) **1** a very small dog with big eyes and pointed ears. **2** this breed of dog.

chilblain (chil´blān) *n.* an inflamed swelling of the hands or feet caused by bad circulation and cold. **chilblained** *a.* **chilblainy** *a.*

child (chīld) *n.* (*pl.* **children** (chil´drən)) **1** a boy or girl. **2** a son or daughter. **3** an infant, a baby. **4** an unborn baby. **5** a young person. **6** an inexperienced or childish person. **7** (*pl.*) descendants. **8** a person whose character is the result (of a specified environment etc.) (*a child of nature*). **child abuse** *n.* ill-treatment or neglect of a child, esp. physical or sexual abuse. **child allowance** *n.* **child benefit. childbearing** *n.* the act of carrying and giving birth to children. ~*a.* of or relating to this (*of childbearing age*). **child benefit** *n.* a sum of money paid regularly by the state to the parent of a child. **childbirth** *n.* the time or act of giving birth to a child. **childcare** *n.* **1** daytime care and supervision provided for children while their parents are working. **2** residential care provided for children whose parents are unable to look after them. **child-centred** *a.* centred on the needs, interests etc. of the child (*child-centred education*). **childhood** *n.* **1** the state of being a child. **2** the period from birth to puberty. **childish** *a.* **1** of or befitting a child. **2** silly, puerile. **childishly** *adv.* **childishness** *n.* **childless** *a.* **childlessness** *n.* **childlike** *a.* **1** resembling or befitting a child. **2** docile, simple, innocent, frank. **childminder** *n.* a person who looks after other people's children for payment. **child molester** *n.* a person who sexually abuses a child. **childproof** *a.* designed to be impossible for a child to operate or damage (*a childproof lock*). **child's play** *n.* easy work.

chile CHILLI.

Chilean (chil´iən) *n.* a native or inhabitant of Chile in S America. ~*a.* of or relating to Chile.

chili CHILLI.

chill (chil) *n.* **1** coldness, a fall in bodily temperature. **2** a cold (*to catch a chill*). **3** a cold, shivering sensation preceding fever. **4** coldness of the air etc. **5** coldness of manner etc. **6** a check, a discouragement. **7** disappointment, depression. ~*v.t.* **1** to make cold. **2** to preserve (meat etc.) by cold. **3** to cool (wine etc.). **4** to cool (metal) suddenly so as to harden. **5** to depress, to dispirit, to discourage. **6** to frighten. ~*v.i.* **1** to become cold. **2** (*esp. NAm., coll.*) to hang around. ~*a.* chilly. **to chill out** (*esp. NAm., coll.*) to relax. **chiller** *n.* **1** a chilled container for food or drink. **2** (*coll.*) a frightening novel, film etc., a spine-chiller. **chill factor** *n.* the lowering of the perceived air temperature, esp. by the wind. **chilling** *a.* **chillingly** *adv.* **chillness** *n.* **chilly** *a.* (*comp.* **chillier,** *superl.* **chilliest**) **1** rather cold. **2** sensitive to the cold. **3** cold or distant in manner; unfriendly; unemotional. **chilliness** *n.*

chilli (chil´i), **chili, chile** *n.* (*pl.* **chillies, chilies, chiles**) the hot-tasting ripe pod of a species of capsicum, esp. *Capsicum anuum*, used to flavour, sauces, pickles etc. **chilli con carne** (kon kah´ni) *n.* a Mexican dish of minced meat with beans in a chilli sauce. **chilli powder** *n.* ground dried chillies, sometimes mixed with other spices. **chilli sauce** *n.* a hot-tasting sauce made from tomatoes, chillies etc.

chimaera CHIMERA.

chime (chīm) *n.* **1** the harmonic or consonant sounds of musical instruments or bells. **2** a number of bells tuned in diatonic succession. **3** the sounds so produced. **4** tune, rhythm. **5** harmony, accord. **6** agreement, correspondence. *~v.i.* **1** to sound in harmony or accord. **2** (of bells) to ring, to strike the hour etc. **3** to accord, to agree. **4** to be in rhyme. *~v.t.* **1** to ring (a series of bells). **2** to ring (a chime) on bells. **3** to sound (the hour etc.) by chiming. **to chime in 1** to join in. **2** to express agreement. **chimer** *n.*

chimera (kimiə´rə, kī-), **chimaera** *n.* **1** a fabulous fire-eating monster, with a lion's head, a serpent's tail, and the body of a goat. **2** any incongruous conception of the imagination. **3** an imaginary terror. **4** any cartilaginous fish of the family Chimaeridae. **5** (*Biol.*) a hybrid of genetically dissimilar tissues. **chimeric** (-mer´-), **chimerical** *a.* purely imaginary. **chimerically** *adv.*

chimichanga (chimichang´gə) *n.* a deep-fried rolled tortilla with a savoury filling.

chimney (chim´ni) *n.* (*pl.* **chimneys**) **1** the flue, vent or passage through which smoke etc. escapes from a fire into the open air. **2** the top part of this, projecting above a roof. **3** a glass tube placed over the flame of a lamp to intensify combustion. **4** a vent from a volcano. **5** a vertical or nearly vertical fissure in rock. **chimney breast** *n.* the projecting part of the wall of a room containing the fireplace. **chimney piece** *n.* a mantelpiece. **chimney pot** *n.* a tube of pottery or sheet metal above the shaft of a chimney to increase the updraught. **chimney stack** *n.* **1** a series of chimneys united in a block of masonry or brickwork. **2** a chimney top. **chimney sweep** *n.* a person whose business is to sweep chimneys. **chimney top** *n.* the part of a chimney projecting above a roof.

chimp (chimp) *n.* (*coll.*) a chimpanzee.

chimpanzee (chimpanzē´) *n.* **1** a large intelligent African anthropoid ape, *Pan troglodytes*. **2** the pygmy chimpanzee.

chin (chin) *n.* the front part of the lower jaw. **to keep one's chin up** (*coll.*) to remain cheerful in adversity. **to take it on the chin** to face up to (misfortune, defeat etc.) courageously. **chinless** *a.* (*coll.*) **1** having a receding chin. **2** weakspirited, ineffectual. **chinless wonder** *n.* (*coll.*) an ineffectual person, esp. of the upper class. **chinstrap** *n.* a strap passing under the chin. **chin-up** *n.* (*esp. N Am.*) an exercise in which the body is raised by the arms, a pull-up. **chinwag** *n.* (*coll.*) a chat, a talk. *~v.i.* (*pres.p.* **chinwagging**, *past, p.p.* **chinwagged**) to chat, to gossip.

china (chī´nə) *n.* **1** fine porcelain, first brought from China. **2** porcelain or ceramic ware. **3** household tableware, esp. made of china. **4** (*sl.*) one's husband or wife, a friend (from *china plate*, mate). *~a.* made of china. **china clay** *n.* kaolin. **Chinagraph®** *n.* a coloured pencil used to write on china, glass etc. **china stone** *n.* a type of granite rock. **chinaware** *n.* articles made of china.

China aster (chī´nə) *n.* a Chinese garden plant, *Callistephus chinensis*, with showy aster-like flowers. **Chinaman** *n.* (*pl.* **Chinamen**) **1** (*derog.*, *usu. offensive*) a native of China, or a person of Chinese descent. **2** in cricket, a ball bowled by a left-handed bowler, spinning from off to leg. **china-root** *n.* the root of a Chinese plant, *Smilax china*, used medicinally. **China tea** *n.* a smoky-flavoured tea from China. **Chinatown** *n.* the Chinese quarter of a town.

chinch (chinch), **chinch bug** *n.* **1** a N American insect, *Blissus leucopterus*, destructive to cereal crops. **2** (*N Am.*) the bedbug.

chincherinchee (chinchərinchē´) *n.* a S African plant of the lily family, *Ornithogalum thyrsoides*, with white flowers.

chinchilla (chinchil´ə) *n.* (*pl.* **chinchillas**) **1** any S American rodent of the genus *Chinchilla*. **2** its soft silver-grey fur. **3** a breed of rabbit or cat.

chin-chin (chinchin´) *int.* (*coll.*) a familiar form of salutation or drinking toast.

chine¹ (chīn) *n.* **1** the backbone or spine of any animal. **2** part of the back of an animal cut for cooking. **3** a ridge. *~v.t.* to cut (meat) along or across the backbone. **chined** *a.* (*usu. in comb.*) having a backbone; backboned.

chine² (chīn) *n.* (*dial.*) a deep and narrow ravine.

chine³ (chīn) *n.* the join between the side and bottom of a ship or boat.

chiné (shēnā´, shē´-) *a.* (of fabric) having a mottled pattern.

Chinese (chīnēz´) *n.* (*pl.* **Chinese**) **1** a native or inhabitant of China, or a person of Chinese descent. **2** (*as pl.*) the people of China. **3** the language of the Chinese. *~a.* of or relating to China. **Chinese burn** *n.* (*coll.*) a burning sensation, produced by placing both hands on a person's arm and twisting the skin in the opposite direction. **Chinese cabbage** *n.* a cabbage-like vegetable, *Brassica chinensis*, with crisp leaves. **Chinese chequers**, (*N Am.*) **Chinese checkers** *n.pl.* (*usu. sing. in constr.*) a board game played with marbles on a star-shaped board. **Chinese gooseberry** *n.* (*pl.* **Chinese gooseberries**) the kiwi, or the plant on which it grows. **Chinese lantern** *n.* **1** a collapsible lantern made of thin paper. **2** a plant, *Physalis alkekengi*, with round orange fruits in a papery calyx. **Chinese leaf, Chinese leaves** *n.* Chinese cabbage. **Chinese puzzle** *n.* a complicated or intricate puzzle or problem. **Chinese water chestnut** *n.* a variety of sedge, *Eleocharis tuberosa*, or its edible corm. **Chinese white** *n.* an opaque white paint.

Chink (chingk) *a., n.* (*offensive*) (a) Chinese.
chink[1] (chingk) *n.* **1** a narrow cleft or crevice. **2** a small longitudinal opening.
chink[2] (chingk) *n.* a jingling sound as of coins or glasses. ~*v.t.* to cause to make this sound. ~*v.i.* to make this sound.
Chinky (ching'ki) *n.* (*pl.* **Chinkies**) **1** (*offensive*) a Chinese person. **2** (*sl.*) a Chinese restaurant. ~*a.* (*offensive*) Chinese.
Chino- (chī'nō) *comb. form* Chinese; of or relating to China.
chino (chē'nō) *n.* (*pl.* **chinos**) **1** a tough, twilled cotton fabric. **2** (*pl.*) trousers, often off-white, made of this fabric.
chinoiserie (shinwah'zəri, shē-, -rē') *n.* **1** a style of Western art and architecture using Chinese motifs. **2** an object or objects in this style.
chinook (chinook') *n.* **1** a warm dry wind blowing east of the Rocky Mountains. **2** a warm wet wind blowing west of the Rocky Mountains. **chinook salmon** *n.* a large Pacific salmon, *Oncorhynchus tshawytscha*.
chintz (chints) *n.* a printed cotton cloth with floral devices etc., usu. glazed. **chintzy** *a.* (*comp.* **chintzier**, *superl.* **chintziest**) **1** of or resembling chintz. **2** cheap, tawdry, gaudy. **3** typical of the decor associated with chintz soft furnishings. **chintzily** *adv.* **chintziness** *n.*
chip (chip) *n.* **1** a small piece of wood, stone etc. detached or chopped off. **2** the place from which such a piece has been removed. **3** (*usu. pl.*) a deep-fried strip of potato. **4** (*pl.*, *N Am.*) thin slices of potato, potato crisps. **5** a counter used in gambling games. **6** a very small piece of semiconducting material, esp. silicon, with an integrated circuit printed on it; a microchip. **7** a thin strip of wood for making such hats or baskets. **8** a basket made from such strips. **9** any thin fragment. **10** a chip shot. ~*v.t.* (*pres.p.* **chipping**, *past*, *p.p.* **chipped**) **1** to cut into chips. **2** to cut or break a chip or chips off. **3** to hit or kick (the ball) with a chip shot. ~*v.i.* **1** to break or fly off in chips. **2** to play a chip shot. **to chip in 1** (*coll.*) to cut into a conversation. **2** (*coll.*) to contribute (money). **to have had one's chips 1** (*coll.*) to be defeated. **2** (*coll.*) to be unable to avoid death. **when the chips are down** (*coll.*) at a moment of crisis; when it comes to the point. **chipboard** *n.* a thin board of compressed wood fragments. **chip off the old block** *n.* a person resembling one of their parents, esp. in character or in behaviour. **chip on one's shoulder** *n.* a grievance, a disposition to feel badly treated. **chipping** *n.* **1** a chip of wood, stone etc. **2** (*pl.*) such chips used to surface roads, roofs etc. **chippy** *a.* (*comp.* **chippier**, *superl.* **chippiest**) **1** (*sl.* or *dial.*) irritable. **2** (*N Am.*) belligerent. ~*n.* (*pl.* **chippies**) (*coll.*) **1** a chip shop. **2** a carpenter. **chippiness** *n.* **chip shop** *n.* a shop selling fish and chips and similar prepared meals to take away. **chip shot** *n.* in football or golf, a short high shot.

chipmunk (chip'mŭngk) *n.* a N American rodent of the genus *Tamias lysteri*, resembling a squirrel.
chipolata (chipəlah'tə) *n.* (*pl.* **chipolatas**) a small sausage.
chipper (chip'ə) *a.* (*esp. N Am.*, *coll.*) **1** energetic and cheerful. **2** smart.
chiral (kīə'rəl) *a.* (*Chem.*) (of an optically active chemical compound) asymmetric, having a left-handed or right-handed structure. **chirality** (-ral'-) *n.*
chiro- (kī'rō), **cheiro-**, **chir-**, **cheir-** *comb. form* **1** manual. **2** having hands and handlike organs.
chirograph (kī'rəgrahf) *n.* a written or signed document. **chirographer** (-rog'-) *n.* a person skilled in handwriting. **chirographic** (-graf'-), **chirographical** *a.* of, relating to or in handwriting. **chirography** (-rog'-) *n.* **1** the art of writing; calligraphy. **2** character and style in handwriting.
chiromancy (kī'rəmansi) *n.* divination by means of the hand; palmistry.
chiropodist (kirop'ədist, shi-) *n.* a person skilled in the care of the feet, esp. in the removal of corns etc. **chiropody** *n.*

Usage note The pronunciation (sh-) is sometimes disapproved of, though it is quite common. Historically *ch* here represents the Greek letter chi, which was pronounced hard, as (k).

chiropractic (kīrəprak'tik) *n.* spinal manipulation as a method of curing disease, disorders of the joints etc. **chiropractor** (kī'-) *n.*
chiropteran (kīrop'tərən) *n.* any mammal of the order Chiroptera, with membranes connecting their fingers and used as wings, consisting of the bats. **chiropterous** *a.*
chirp (chœp) *v.i.* **1** (of a bird, insect etc.) to make a quick, sharp sound. **2** to talk cheerfully. ~*v.t.* to utter or sing with a sharp, quick sound. ~*n.* **1** a sharp, quick sound of a bird. **2** a sound resembling this. **chirper** *n.* **chirpy** *a.* (*comp.* **chirpily**, *superl.* **chirpiest**) **1** cheerful. **2** vivacious. **chirpily** *adv.* **chirpiness** *n.*
chirr (chœ), **churr** *v.i.* to make a trilling monotonous sound like that of the grasshopper. ~*n.* this sound.
chirrup (chir'əp) *v.i.* (*pres.p.* **chirruping**, *past*, *p.p.* **chirruped**) to chirp, to make a twittering sound. **chirruper** *n.* **chirrupy** *a.*
chisel (chiz'əl) *n.* an edged tool for cutting wood, iron or stone, operated by pressure or striking. ~*v.t.* (*pres.p.* **chiselling**, (*N Am.*) **chiseling**, *past*, *p.p.* **chiselled**, (*N Am.*) **chiseled**) **1** to cut, shape or engrave with a chisel. **2** (*sl.*) to take advantage of, to cheat. ~*v.i.* to cheat. **chiselled** *a.* **1** cut with or as with a chisel. **2** clear-cut (*finely chiselled features*). **chiseller** *n.*
chit[1] (chit) *n.* **1** a child. **2** (*derog. or facet.*) a young girl.
chit[2] (chit), **chitty** (chit'i) *n.* (*pl.* **chits, chitties**) **1** a voucher for money owed. **2** a requisition. **3** a receipt. **4** a memorandum.

chit-chat (chit´chat) *n*. chat, gossip, trifling talk. ~*v.i.* (*pres.p.* **chit-chatting**, *past, p.p.* **chit-chatted**) to chat, to gossip.

chitin (kī´tin) *n*. (*Biol*.) the horny substance that gives firmness to the exoskeleton of arthropods and to the cell wall of fungi. **chitinous** *a*.

chitterlings (chit´əlingz), **chitlings** (chit´lingz) *n.pl*. the smaller intestines of animals, esp. as prepared for food.

chitty CHIT².

chivalry (shiv´əlri) *n*. **1** the knightly system of the Middle Ages. **2** the ideal qualities which inspired it, nobleness and gallantry of spirit, courtesy, respect for and defence of the weak. **3** gallantry, devotion to the service of women. **4** †knights collectively. **chivalric** *a*. **chivalrous** *a*. **1** gallant, noble. **2** courteous. **chivalrously** *adv*.

chive (chīv), **cive** (sīv) *n*. a small onion-like herb, *Allium schoenoprasum*.

chivvy (chiv´i), **chivy, chevy** (chev´i) *v.t.* (*3rd pers. sing. pres.* **chivvies, chivies, chevies,** *pres.p.* **chivvying, chivying, chevying,** *past, p.p.* **chivvied, chivied, chevied**) to hurry; to pester or nag.

chlamydia (kləmid´iə) *n*. (*pl.* **chlamydiae** (-mid´iē)) **1** any disease-causing microorganism of the genus *Chlamydia*, resembling both bacteria and viruses. **2** a sexually transmitted disease caused by such a microorganism.

chloracne (klawrak´ni) *n*. (*Med*.) a skin disease that results from exposure to chlorinated chemicals.

chloral (klaw´rəl) *n*. **1** a liquid made from chlorine and alcohol. **2** chloral hydrate. **chloral hydrate** *n*. a white crystalline substance obtained from chloral, used as a hypnotic and anaesthetic.

chlorate (klaw´rāt) *n*. (*Chem*.) a salt of chloric acid.

chlorella (klərel´ə) *n*. any green freshwater alga of the genus *Chlorella*.

chloric (klaw´rik) *a*. (*Chem*.) of, relating to or containing pentavalent chlorine. **chloric acid** *n*. an acid containing hydrogen, chlorine and oxygen.

chloride (klaw´rīd) *n*. (*Chem*.) **1** a compound of chlorine with another element. **2** chloride of lime, or a similar substance. **chloride of lime** *n*. a compound of chlorine with lime, used as a disinfectant and for bleaching.

chlorine (klaw´rēn) *n*. (*Chem*.) a yellow-green, poisonous, gaseous element, at. no. 17, chem. symbol Cl, obtained from common salt, used as a disinfectant and for bleaching. **chlorinate** (-rin-) *v.t.* to combine or treat with chlorine. **chlorination** (-rinā´shən) *n*. **1** the sterilization of water with chlorine. **2** the extraction of gold by exposure of ore to chlorine gas.

chlorite (klaw´rīt) *n*. a green silicate mineral.

chlorofluorocarbon (klawrōfluərōkah´bən) *n*. any of various compounds of carbon, hydrogen, chlorine and fluorine, used in refrigerators, aerosols etc., some of which are harmful to the ozone layer; a CFC.

chloroform (klor´əfawm) *n*. (*Chem*.) a volatile fluid formerly used as an anaesthetic. ~*v.t.* **1** to administer chloroform to. **2** to render unconscious with chloroform.

chlorophyll (klor´əfil, klaw´-), (*esp. N Am*.) **chlorophyl** *n*. (*Biol*.) the green colouring matter of plants which absorbs the energy from sunlight, used in producing carbohydrates from water and carbon dioxide. **chlorophyllous** (klawrəfil´əs) *a*.

chlorosis (klawrō´sis) *n*. **1** (*Med*.) a disease affecting young people due to deficiency of iron in the blood. **2** (*Bot*.) etiolation, a blanching of plants through the non-development of chlorophyll. **chlorotic** (-rot´-) *a*.

chlorous (klaw´rəs) *a*. (*Chem*.) of, relating to or containing trivalent chlorine. **chlorous acid** *n*. an acid containing hydrogen, chlorine and oxygen.

ChM *abbr*. Master of Surgery.

choc (chok) *n*. (*coll*.) a chocolate (*a box of chocs*). **choc ice** *n*. a bar of (vanilla) ice cream coated with chocolate.

chock (chok) *n*. a wood block, esp. a wedge-shaped block used to prevent a cask, wheel, boat etc. from shifting. ~*v.t.* **1** to wedge, support or make fast, with a chock or chocks. **2** to cram full. ~*adv*. **1** as close as possible. **2** tightly, fully. **chock-a-block**, (*coll*.) **chocka** *a., adv*. chock-full. **chocker** *a*. **1** (*coll*.) full up, crammed. **2** (*sl*.) annoyed, fed up. **chock-full** *a., adv*. **1** crammed full. **2** full to overflowing. **chockstone** *n*. in mountaineering, a stone wedged in a chimney or crack.

chocoholic (chokəhol´ik), **chocaholic** *n*. a person who is very fond of or addicted to chocolate. ~*a*. of or relating to such people.

chocolate (chok´lit) *n*. **1** a usu. sweet food made from the roasted and ground seeds of the cacao tree (*milk chocolate; plain chocolate*). **2** a sweetmeat made of or coated with this. **3** a drink made with chocolate, usu. dissolved in hot water or milk. **4** chocolate brown. ~*a*. **1** made of or flavoured with chocolate. **2** chocolate brown. **chocolate-box** *a*. sentimentally pretty. **chocolate brown** *n*. a dark brown colour. ~*a*. dark brown. **chocolate vermicelli** *n*. small thin pieces of chocolate used for cake decoration. **chocolatey, chocolaty** *a*.

choice (chois) *n*. **1** the power or act of choosing. **2** the person or thing chosen. **3** the range to choose from. **4** selection, preference. **5** an alternative; the opportunity to choose (*I had no choice but to go*). **6** the best part. ~*a*. **1** selected, picked, chosen with care. **2** of great value or superior quality. **choicely** *adv*. **choiceness** *n*.

choir (kwīə) *n*. **1** an organized body of singers. **2** a band of singers, in a church or chapel. **3** the part of the church or chapel allotted to the singers. **4** the chancel of a cathedral or large church. **5** (*Mus*.) a group of musical instruments of the same family playing together. **6** a group of birds, angels etc. singing together. **choirboy** *n*. a boy singer in a church choir. **choirgirl** *n*.

a girl singer in a church choir. **choirman** *n.* (*pl.* **choirmen**) a male singer in a choir. **choirmaster** *n.* a person who trains or conducts a choir. **choir organ** *n.* the least powerful section of a compound organ, used chiefly for accompaniments. **choir stall** *n.* a seat in the choir of a large church.

choke (chōk) *v.t.* **1** to block or compress the windpipe (of), so as to prevent breathing. **2** to suffocate (as by gas, water etc.). **3** to smother, to stifle. **4** to repress, to silence. **5** to stop up, to block, to obstruct, to clog. **6** to reduce the intake of air to (a carburettor, engine etc.) and thereby enrich the fuel mixture. ~*v.i.* **1** to have the windpipe blocked or compressed. **2** to be wholly or partially suffocated; to be unable to breathe. **3** to be blocked up. **4** (*sl.*) to die. ~*n.* **1** the act of choking. **2** a sound of choking. **3** a device to reduce the air supply to a carburettor and thereby enrich the fuel mixture. **4** an inductance coil constructed to prevent high-frequency currents from passing. **5** the centre of an artichoke. **to choke back** to suppress (*He choked back his anger*). **to choke down 1** to swallow with difficulty. **2** to choke back. **to choke up** to fill up until blocked. **chokeberry** *n.* (*pl.* **chokeberries**) **1** any of various shrubs of the genus *Aronia*, of the rose family. **2** its red or purple berry-like fruit. **choke chain** *n.* a collar-like chain attached to a dog's lead, designed to tighten around the dog's neck if it pulls on the lead. **choke cherry** *n.* (*pl.* **choke cherries**) **1** any of various N American cherry trees, esp. *Prunus virginiana*. **2** its astringent dark-coloured fruit. **choked** *a.* (*coll.*) **1** disappointed. **2** angry. **choke-damp** *n.* carbon dioxide generated in mines, wells etc. **choker** *n.* **1** a necklace that fits closely round the neck. **2** a clerical collar. **choky**[1] *a.* (*comp.* **chokier**, *superl.* **chokiest**) **1** that causes choking. **2** having a sensation of choking.

choky[1] CHOKE.

choky[2] (chō'ki), **chokey** *n.* (*pl.* **chokies, chokeys**) (*sl.*) a prison.

cholecalciferol (kolikalsif'ərol) *n.* a compound that occurs in fish-liver oils; vitamin D_3.

choler (kol'ə) *n.* (*also poet.*) †anger; tendency to anger. **choleric** *a.* irascible, angry. **cholerically** *adv.*

cholera (kol'ərə) *n.* (*Med.*) an acute, often fatal, bacterial infection, spread by contaminated water supplies, in which severe vomiting and diarrhoea cause dehydration. **choleraic** (-rā'-) *a.*

cholesterol (kəles'tərol), †**cholesterin** (-in) *n.* a steroid alcohol occurring in body tissues, including blood and bile (high levels of cholestrol in the blood are thought to be a cause of arteriosclerosis and heart disease).

chomp CHAMP[1].

choo-choo (choo'choo), **choo-choo train** *n.* (*coll.*) a railway train or steam engine (used by or to children).

chook (chuk), **chookie** (chuk'i) *n.* (*Austral., New Zeal.*) (*coll.*) a chicken or other domestic fowl.

choose (chooz) *v.t.* (*past* **chose** (chōz), *p.p.* **chosen** (chō'zən)) **1** to take by preference, to select from a number. **2** to feel inclined, to prefer (to do something rather than something else). **3** to decide willingly (to do). ~*v.i.* **1** to make one's choice. **2** to have the power of choice. **chooser** *n.* **choosy** *a.* (*comp.* **choosier**, *superl.* **choosiest**) (*coll.*) hard to please, particular. **choosily** *adv.* **choosiness** *n.* **chosen** *a.* **1** selected, esp. for some special quality (*the chosen few*). **2** (*Theol.*) destined to be saved (*the chosen people*).

chop[1] (chop) *v.t.* (*pres.p.* **chopping**, *past, p.p.* **chopped**) **1** to cut with a sharp blow. **2** to cut or strike off. **3** to cut (meat, vegetables etc.) into parts or small pieces. **4** to strike (a ball) with backspin. **5** (*coll.*) to reduce or abolish. ~*v.i.* to do anything with a quick motion like that of a sharp blow. ~*n.* **1** the act of chopping. **2** a cutting stroke or blow. **3** a piece chopped off. **4** a thick slice of meat, esp. pork or lamb, usu. including a rib or other bone. **5** (*pl.*) broken waves of the sea. **the chop 1** (*sl.*) dismissal (from a job etc.). **2** (*sl.*) killing or being killed. **3** (*sl.*) (of a project etc.) cancellation. **chopper** *n.* **1** a person or thing that chops. **2** a butcher's cleaver. **3** an axe. **4** (*coll.*) a helicopter. **5** (*coll.*) a motorcycle or bicycle with very high handlebars. **6** a device that periodically interrupts an electric current, light beam etc. **7** (*pl., sl.*) teeth. **choppy** *a.* (*comp.* **choppier**, *superl.* **choppiest**) (of the sea) rough, with short quick waves. **choppily** *adv.* **choppiness** *n.*

chop[2] (chop) *v.i.* (*pres.p.* **chopping**, *past, p.p.* **chopped**) (of the wind etc.) to change direction suddenly. **to chop and change 1** to vary continuously; to fluctuate. **2** to vacillate. **to chop logic** to wrangle pedantically.

chop[3] (chop) *n.* (*usu. pl.*) the jaw of an animal.

chop-chop (chopchop') *adv., int.* at once, quickly.

chopstick (chop'stik) *n.* either of two small sticks of wood or ivory used by the Chinese to eat with.

chop suey (chop soo'i) *n.* (*pl.* **chop sueys**) a Chinese dish of shredded meat and vegetables served with rice.

choral[1] (kaw'rəl) *a.* of, for or sung by a choir or chorus. **chorally** *adv.* **choral society** *n.* a group of people who meet to sing choral music together.

choral[2] CHORALE.

chorale (kərahl') **choral** *n.* **1** a simple choral hymn or song, usually of slow rhythm. **2** (*esp. N Am.*) a choir.

chord[1] (kawd) *n.* (*Mus.*) the simultaneous and harmonious sounding of notes of different pitch. **chordal**[1] *a.*

chord[2] (kawd) *n.* **1** (*Math. etc.*) a straight line joining the extremities of an arc or two points in a curve. **2** (*Anat.*) a cord. **3** in engineering, one of the principal members of a truss. **4** (*poet.*) †the string of a musical instrument. **to strike a chord**

1 to cause someone to recall something. **2** to elicit an emotional response, esp. sympathy. **to touch the right chord** to elicit an appropriate emotional response. **chordal**² a. **chordate** (-dāt) n. any member of the Chordata, a phylum of animals with a backbone or notochord. ~a. of or relating to this phylum.

chordal¹ CHORD¹.

chordal² CHORD².

chore (chaw) n. **1** a small regular task, esp. a household job. **2** a boring task.

chorea (kərē´ə) n. (Med.) a nervous disorder characterized by irregular convulsive movements of an involuntary kind.

choreography (koriog´rəfi) n. the arrangement of steps (of a stage dance or ballet). **choreograph** (kor´iəgrahf) v.t. to compose or arrange the steps of (a stage dance or ballet). **choreographer** (-og´-) n. **choreographic** (-graf´-) a. **choreographically** adv.

choreology (koriol´əji) n. the study of the movements of dancing. **choreologist** n.

choric CHORUS.

chorine (kaw´rēn) n. a chorus girl.

chorion (kaw´riən) n. the outer membrane which envelops the embryo of a reptile, bird or mammal. **chorionic** (-on´-) a. **choroid** a. resembling the chorion. ~n. the vascular portion of the retina. **choroid coat, choroid membrane** n. the choroid.

chorister (kor´istə), †**chorist** (kaw´rist) n. **1** a person who sings in a choir, esp. a choirboy or choirgirl. **2** (N Am.) the leader of a choir or congregation, a precentor.

chorizo (chawrē´zō) n. (pl. **chorizos**) a highly seasoned pork sausage made in Spain or Mexico.

chortle (chaw´təl) v.i. to make a loud chuckle. ~v.t. to utter with a loud chuckle. ~n. a loud chuckle.

chorus (kaw´rəs) n. (pl. **choruses**) **1** a large choir. **2** a piece of music for a large choir. **3** a group of people singing or dancing in concert in a musical comedy, opera etc. **4** the refrain of a song in which the company joins the singer. **5** a group of people or animals producing a simultaneous utterance. **6** this utterance. **7** a band of dancers and singers in ancient Greek drama. **8** the song or recitative between the acts of a Greek tragedy. **9** (the speaker of) the prologue and epilogue in an Elizabethan play. ~v.t. (pres.p. **chorusing**, past, p.p. **chorused**) to utter simultaneously. ~v.i. to speak simultaneously. **in chorus** in unison; together. **choric** (kor´-) a. **chorus girl** n. a young woman who sings or dances in the chorus in a musical comedy etc.

chose, chosen CHOOSE.

chough (chŭf) n. a large black bird of the crow family, Pyrrhocorax pyrrhocorax, with red legs and bill.

choux pastry (shoo pā´stri) n. a rich light pastry made with eggs.

chow (chow) n. **1** (coll.) food. **2** a chow-chow.

chow-chow (chow´chow) n. a dog of an orig. Chinese breed with thick coat and curled tail.

chowder (chow´də) n. (esp. N Am.) a thick soup or stew made of fish, bacon etc.

chow mein (chow mān´) n. a Chinese dish of meat and vegetables served with fried noodles.

chrism (kriz´m) n. consecrated oil, used in the Roman Catholic and Greek Orthodox Churches in administering baptism, confirmation, ordination and extreme unction. **chrisom** (-zəm) n. **1** chrism. **2** a chrisom-cloth. **chrisom-cloth** n. a white cloth, anointed with chrism, formerly placed over the face of a child after baptism.

Christadelphian (kristədel´fiən) n. a member of a millenarian Christian sect claiming apostolic origin. ~a. of, relating to or belonging to this sect.

christen (kris´ən) v.t. **1** to receive into the Christian Church by baptism; to baptize. **2** to give a Christian name to at baptism. **3** to name. **4** to nickname. **5** (coll.) to use for the first time. ~v.i. to administer baptism. **christener** n. **christening** n.

Christendom (kris´əndəm) n. **1** Christians collectively. **2** that portion of the world in which Christianity is the prevailing religion.

Christian (kris´chən) n. **1** a person who believes in or professes the religion of Christ. **2** a person whose character is consistent with the teaching of Christ. ~a. **1** of or relating to Christ or Christianity. **2** professing the religion of Christ. **3** (coll.) kind, charitable. **Christianity** (-tian´-) n. **1** the doctrines and precepts taught by Christ. **2** the religion based on these. **3** faith in Christ and his teaching. **4** Christian character and conduct. **5** the state of being a Christian. **6** Christians collectively. **Christianize, Christianise** v.t. to convert to Christianity. ~v.i. to be converted to Christianity. **Christianization** (-zā´shən) n. **Christianly** a., adv. **Christian name** n. a forename, esp. one given in baptism. **Christian Science** n. the religious system of the Church of Christ Scientist, including the belief that diseases can be healed without medical treatment. **Christian Scientist** n.

Christie (kris´ti), **Christy** n. (pl. **Christies**) in skiing, a turn in which the skis are kept parallel, used esp. for stopping or turning sharply.

Christingle (kris´ting-gəl) n. a lighted candle held by children at Advent services etc., representing Christ as the light of the world.

Christmas (kris´məs) n. **1** the festival of the nativity of Jesus Christ celebrated on 25 Dec. **2** Christmastide. ~a. of, relating to or appropriate to Christmas or its festivities. ~int. (sl.) used to express surprise, dismay etc. **Christmas box** n. a present or tip given at Christmas, esp. to tradesmen. **Christmas cake** n. a rich fruit cake, usu. iced, eaten at Christmas. **Christmas card** n. an ornamental card sent as a Christmas greeting. **Christmas carol** n. a song of praise sung at Christmas. **Christmas pudding** n. a rich pudding eaten at Christmas. **Christmas rose** n. a white-flowered plant, *Helleborus niger*, flowering in winter. **Christmas stocking** *n.* a stocking that children hang up on Christmas Eve for Father Christmas to fill with presents. **Christmassy, Christmasy** *a.* **Christmastide, Christmastime** *n.* the season of Christmas. **Christmas tree** *n.* an evergreen or artificial tree kept indoors and decorated at Christmas.

Christo- (kris′tō) *comb. form* of or relating to Christ.

Christology (kristol′əji) *n.* the branch of theology concerned with Christ. **Christological** (-loj′-) *a.*

chroma (krō′mə) *n.* purity or intensity of colour.

chromate (krō′māt) *n.* (*Chem.*) a salt of chromic acid.

chromatic (krəmat′ik) *a.* **1** of or relating to colour. **2** coloured. **3** (*Mus.*) including notes not belonging to the diatonic scale. **chromatic aberration** *n.* the failure of different wavelengths of refracted light to focus at the same distance, causing a blurred image. **chromatically** *adv.* **chromaticism** *n.* **chromaticity** (-tis′-) *n.* the purity and dominant wavelength of colour or light. **chromatic scale** *n.* (*Mus.*) a succession of notes a semitone apart.

chromatid (krō′mətid) *n.* (*Biol.*) either of the two strands into which a chromosome divides during cell division.

chromatin (krō′mətin) *n.* the portion of the nucleus of a cell, consisting of nucleic acids and protein, which readily takes up a basic stain.

chromato- (krō′mətō), **chromat-** *comb. form* of or relating to colour.

chromatography (krōmətog′rəfi) *n.* (*Chem.*) a technique for separating or analysing the components of a mixture which relies on the differing capacity for adsorption of the components in a column of powder, strip of paper etc. **chromatograph** (-mat′əgrahf) *n.* **chromatographic** (-grăf′ik) *a.*

chromatopsia (krōmətop′siə) *n.* (*Med.*) abnormal coloured vision.

chrome (krōm) *n.* **1** (*Chem.*) chromium, esp. chromium-plating. **2** anything plated with chromium. **3** a pigment containing chromium. ~*v.t.* **1** to plate with chromium. **2** to treat with a chromium compound. **chrome leather** *n.* leather prepared by tanning with chromium salts. **chrome steel** *n.* a hard steel containing chromium. **chrome yellow** *n.* a brilliant yellow pigment containing lead chromate.

chromic (krō′mik) *a.* (*Chem.*) of, relating to or containing trivalent chromium. **chromic acid** *n.* an acid containing hydrogen, chromium and oxygen.

chrominance (krō′minəns) *n.* in television, the difference between a given colour and a reference colour of equal luminance.

chromite (krō′mīt) *n.* **1** (*Mineral.*) a mineral consisting of chromium and iron oxide. **2** (*Chem.*) a salt of divalent chromium.

chromium (krō′miəm) *n.* (*Chem.*) a bright grey metallic element, at. no. 24, chem. symbol Cr, remarkable for the brilliance of colour of its compounds, used as a protective or decorative plating. **chromium-plate** *v.t.* to electroplate with chromium to give a shiny decorative or protective coating. ~*n.* such a coating. **chromium-plated** *a.* **1** electroplated with chromium. **2** showy. **chromium steel** *n.* chrome steel.

chromo- (krō′mō), **chrom-** *comb. form* **1** of or relating to colour. **2** (*Chem.*) of or relating to chromium.

chromolithograph (krōmōlith′əgrahf) *n.* a picture printed in colours by lithography. ~*v.t.* to print in this way. **chromolithographer** (-og′-) *n.* **chromolithographic** (-graf′-) *a.* **chromolithography** (-og′-) *n.*

chromosome (krō′məsōm) *n.* (*Biol.*) any of the rod-shaped structures in a cell nucleus that carry the genes which transmit hereditary characteristics. **chromosomal** (-sō′-) *a.* **chromosome map** *n.* a plan of the relative positions of genes on a chromosome.

chronic (kron′ik) *a.* **1** (of a disease, social problem etc.) of long duration, or apt to recur. **2** (*coll.*) habitual (*a chronic smoker*). **3** (*coll.*) very bad, severe. **chronically** *adv.* **chronic fatigue syndrome** *n.* myalgic encephalomyelitis, ME. **chronicity** (-nis′-) *n.*

chronicle (kron′ikəl) *n.* **1** a register or history of events in order of time. **2** a narrative account. ~*v.t.* to record in or as if in a chronicle. **chronicler** *n.*

chrono- (kron′ō), **chron-** *comb. form* of or relating to time or dates.

chronograph (kron′əgrahf) *n.* **1** an instrument for measuring and registering very small intervals of time with great precision. **2** a stopwatch. **chronographic** (-graf′-) *a.*

chronology (krənol′əji) *n.* (*pl.* **chronologies**) **1** the study of historical records etc. in order to determine the sequence of past events. **2** an arrangement of dates of historical events. **chronological** (kronəloj′-) *a.* **1** in order of occurrence in time (*in chronological order*). **2** of or relating to chronology. **chronologically** *adv.* **chronologist, chronologer** *n.* **chronologize, chronologise** *v.t.*

chronometer (krənom′itə) *n.* an instrument that measures time with great precision, esp. one used in navigation at sea. **chronometric** (kronōmet′-), **chronometrical** *a.* **chronometrically** *adv.* **chronometry** *n.*

chrysalis (kris′əlis), **chrysalid** (-əlid) *n.* (*pl.* **chrysalises, chrysalides** (-dēz), **chrysalids**) **1** the last stage through which a lepidopterous insect passes before becoming a perfect insect. **2** the pupa, the shell or case containing the imago. **3** an undeveloped or transitional state.

chrysanth (krisanth′, -zanth′) *n.* (*coll.*) a cultivated chrysanthemum.

chrysanthemum (krisan′thəməm, -zan′-) *n.*

any cultivated plant of the genera *Chrysanth-emum* or *Dendranthema*, with brightly coloured flowers.

chrysoberyl (kris´əberəl, -ber´-) *n.* a gem of a yellowish-green colour, composed of beryllium aluminate.

chrysolite (kris´əlīt) *n.* a yellowish-green or brown translucent orthorhombic mineral, a variety of olivine.

chrysoprase (kris´əprāz) *n.* **1** an apple-green variety of chalcedony. **2** in the New Testament, a variety of beryl.

chrysotile (kris´ətīl) *n.* a fibrous mineral, a source of asbestos.

chthonian (thō´niən), **chthonic** (thon´-) *a.* of or relating to the underworld.

chub (chŭb) *n.* (*pl. in general* **chub**, *in particular* **chubs**) **1** a coarse river fish, *Leuciscus cephalus*. **2** any of various N American fishes.

chubby (chŭb´i) *a.* (*comp.* **chubbier,** *superl.* **chubbiest**) fat, plump, rounded (*a chubby child*; *chubby cheeks*). **chubbily** *adv.* **chubbiness** *n.*

chuck[1] (chŭk) *v.t.* **1** (*coll.*) to fling, to throw. **2** (*coll.*) to reject, to give up (*He chucked his girl-friend*). **3** to strike gently under the chin. ~*n.* **1** a slight tap or blow under the chin. **2** a toss or throw. **the chuck** (*sl.*) dismissal (from a job etc.). **to chuck out 1** (*coll.*) to eject forcibly from a meeting, building etc. **2** (*coll.*) to throw away. **chucker-out** *n.* (*coll.*) a bouncer, a person employed to eject undesirable people.

chuck[2] (chŭk) *n.* **1** a device for holding the work to be turned on a lathe, or for holding the bit in a drill. **2** a cut of beef from the neck and shoulder. **3** (*esp. N Am., dial.*) food. ~*v.t.* to fix on a lathe or drill by means of a chuck. **chuck steak** *n.* beef steak from the neck and shoulder. **chuckwagon** *n.* (*N Am.*) **1** a wagon carrying food, cooking utensils etc. **2** a roadside eating place.

chuck[3] (chŭk) *n.* (*dial.*) darling, dear.

chuckle (chŭk´əl) *v.i.* **1** to laugh to oneself. **2** to make a half-suppressed sound of laughter. ~*n.* such a laugh or noise.

chuff (chŭf) *v.i.* **1** (of a steam locomotive etc.) to make a short puffing sound. **2** to move while making such sounds. ~*n.* such a sound. **chuff-chuff** *n.* a steam engine or train (used by or to children).

chuffed (chŭft) *a.* (*sl.*) pleased, happy.

chug (chŭg) *n.* a short dull explosive sound, as of an engine. ~*v.i.* (*pres.p.* **chugging,** *past, p.p.* **chugged**) **1** to make such a noise. **2** to move while making such a noise.

chukka (chŭk´ə), **chukker** *n.* any of the periods into which a polo game is divided.

chum[1] (chŭm) *n.* (*coll.*) a close friend. ~*v.i.* (*pres.p.* **chumming,** *past, p.p.* **chummed**) to share rooms with another. **to chum up** to become friendly (with). **chummy** *a.* (*comp.* **chummier,** *superl.* **chummiest**). **chummily** *adv.* **chummi-ness** *n.*

chum[2] (chŭm) *n.* (*N Am.*) **1** chopped fish used by anglers as bait. **2** refuse from fish.

chump (chŭmp) *n.* **1** (*sl.*) a silly person. **2** a cut of meat from the loin and hind leg. **3** a short, thick piece of wood. **4** (*sl.*) the head. **off one's chump** (*sl.*) crazy. **chump chop** *n.* a thick meat chop from the chump.

chunder (chŭn´də) *v.i.* (*Austral., sl.*) to vomit. ~*n.* vomit. **chunderous** *a.* nauseating.

chunk (chŭngk) *n.* **1** a short, thick lump of anything. **2** a large portion. **chunky** *a.* (*comp.* **chunkier,** *superl.* **chunkiest**) **1** containing or consisting of chunks. **2** short and thick. **3** small and sturdy. **4** (of clothes etc.) made of thick material (*a chunky sweater*). **chunkiness** *n.*

chunter (chŭn´tə) *v.i.* (*coll.*) **1** to talk at length and meaninglessly. **2** to mutter or grumble.

chupatty CHAPATI.

church (chœch) *n.* **1** a building set apart and consecrated for public worship, esp. Christian worship. **2** a body of Christian believers worshipping in one place, with the same ritual and doctrines. **3** (*usu.* **Church**) Christians collectively. **4** (*usu.* **Church**) a section of Christians organized for worship under a certain form (*the Roman Catholic Church*). **5** (*usu.* **Church**) the whole organization of a religious body or association. **6** (*usu.* **Church**) the clergy as distinct from the laity. **7** (*usu.* **Church**) ecclesiastical authority or influence (*the conflict between Church and State*). **8** (*N Am.*) the communicants of a congregation. **9** a meeting for Christian worship in a church (*to go to church*; *after church on Sunday*). **churchgoer** *n.* a person who goes regularly to church. **churchgoing** *n.* the practice of regularly going to church. ~*a.* habitually going to church. **churchman** *n.* (*pl.* **churchmen**) **1** a cleric, an ecclesiastic. **2** a member of the Church of England. **3** a member of any Church. **4** a supporter of the Church. **Church Militant** *n.* Christians on earth, regarded as warring against evil, as distinct from the *Church Triumphant*. **church parade** *n.* a parade by Scouts, Guides etc. or by members of the armed forces in conjunction with attendance at a church service. **church school** *n.* a school controlled or supported by a particular Church, esp. the Church of England. **Church Triumphant** *n.* Christians in heaven, as distinct from the *Church Militant*. **churchwarden** *n.* **1** in an Anglican parish either of two officers who protect church property, superintend the performance of divine worship etc. and act as the legal representatives of the parish generally. **2** a long clay pipe with a large bowl. **churchwoman** *n.* (*pl.* **churchwomen**) **1** a female member of the clergy. **2** a female member of Church, esp. the Church of England. **3** a female supporter of the Church. **churchy** *a.* (*comp.* **churchier,** *superl.* **churchiest**) **1** making a hobby of church work and church matters. **2** aggressively devoted to the Church and intolerant of dissenters. **3** like a church. **churchiness** *n.* **churchyard** *n.* the ground adjoining a church consecrated for the burial of the dead.

churinga (chəring′gə) n. (pl. **churinga, churingas**) (Austral.) a sacred amulet.

churl (chœl) n. a surly, rude or ill-bred person. **churlish** a. **1** surly, rude, ill-bred. **2** mean, miserly. **churlishly** adv. **churlishness** n.

churn (chœn) n. **1** a large can for carrying milk long distances. **2** a vessel in which milk or cream is agitated or beaten in order to produce butter. ~v.t. **1** to agitate (milk or cream) in a churn for the purpose of making butter. **2** to make (butter) in this way. **3** to agitate with violence or continued motion (often with up). **4** to upset (often with up). ~v.i. **1** to perform the operation of churning butter. **2** (of waves etc.) to foam, to swirl about. **3** to move or turn out in an agitated way. **to churn out** to produce rapidly and prolifically, usu. without concern for quality.

churr CHIRR.

chute[1] (shoot) n. **1** an inclined trough for conveying water, timber, grain etc. to a lower level. **2** an inclined watercourse. **3** a slide into a swimming pool.

chute[2] (shoot) n. (coll.) a parachute. **chutist** n.

chutney (chŭt′ni) n. (pl. **chutneys**) a hot seasoned condiment or pickle.

chutzpah (khuts′pə, huts′-) n. (sl.) barefaced audacity.

chyle (kīl) n. the milky fluid separated from the chyme by the action of the pancreatic juice and the bile, absorbed by the lacteal vessels, and assimilated with the blood. **chylous** a.

chyme (kīm) n. the pulpy mass of digested food before the chyle is separated from it. **chymous** a.

Ci abbr. curie.

ciabatta (chəbat′ə) n. (pl. **ciabattas**) **1** a moist type of Italian bread made with olive oil. **2** a loaf of this bread.

ciao (chow) int. (coll.) used to express greeting or leave-taking.

ciborium (sibaw′riəm) n. (pl. **ciboria** (-riə)) **1** a vessel with an arched cover for the Eucharist. **2** a shrine or tabernacle to receive this. **3** (Archit.) a baldachin canopy or shrine.

cicada (sikah′də), **cicala** (-lə), **cigala** (-gah′lə) n. (pl. **cicadas, cicadae** (-dē), **cicalas, cicale** (-lā), **cigalas**) any homopterous insect of the family Cicadidae, with stridulating organs.

cicatrice (sik′ətris), **cicatrix** (-triks) n. (pl. **cicatrices** (-trī′sēz)) **1** the mark or scar left after a wound or ulcer has healed. **2** (Bot.) a mark on a stem or branch of a plant where a leaf was attached. **cicatricial** (-trish′-) a. **cicatrize, cicatrise** v.t. to heal a wound or ulcer by scar formation. ~v.i. (of a wound or ulcer) to heal in this way. **cicatrization** (-zā′shən) n.

cicely (sis′əli) n. (pl. **cicelies**) any of several umbelliferous plants, esp. sweet cicely.

cichlid (sik′lid) n. any tropical freshwater fish of the family Cichlidae, often kept in aquaria.

CID abbr. Criminal Investigation Department.

-cide (sīd) comb. form **1** a person or substance that kills, as fratricide, insecticide. **2** a killing, as homicide.

cider (sī′də), **cyder** n. **1** an alcoholic drink made from the fermented juice of apples. **2** (NAm.) an unfermented apple-juice drink. **cider press** n. a press for squeezing the juice from crushed apples.

❌ **cieling** common misspelling of CEILING.

c.i.f. abbr. cost, insurance, freight.

cig (sig), **ciggy** (sig′i) n. (pl. **cigs, ciggies**) (coll.) a cigarette.

cigala CICADA.

cigar (sigah′) n. a roll of tobacco leaves for smoking. **cigarillo** (sigəril′ō) n. (pl. **cigarillos**) a very small cigar. **cigar-shaped** a. cylindrical, with tapering ends.

cigarette (sigəret′), (NAm.) **cigaret** n. a cylinder of cut tobacco or aromatic herbs rolled in paper for smoking. **cigarette card** n. a picture card enclosed in cigarette packets. **cigarette end** n. the unsmoked part of a cigarette. **cigarette holder** n. a mouthpiece for holding a cigarette. **cigarette paper** n. a piece of thin paper for wrapping the tobacco in a cigarette.

cilium (sil′iəm) n. (pl. **cilia** (-iə)) **1** (Anat.) an eyelash. **2** (Biol.) a flagellum in a unicellular organism. **ciliary** a. **ciliary body** n. (Anat.) the part of the eye that connects the iris to the choroid, containing the muscle that controls the shape of the lens. **ciliate** (-ət) a. having cilia. ~n. a ciliate protozoan of the phylum Ciliophora. **ciliated** (-ātid) a. **ciliation** (-ā′shən) n.

cill SILL.

cimbalom (sim′bələm) n. a Hungarian type of dulcimer.

C.-in-C. abbr. Commander-in-Chief.

cinch (sinch) n. **1** (coll.) a certainty. **2** (coll.) an easy task. **3** a firm grip or hold. **4** (NAm.) a broad kind of saddle girth. ~v.t. **1** to furnish, fasten or tighten with or as if with a cinch. **2** to hold firmly. **3** (sl.) to make certain of.

cinchona (singkō′nə) n. (pl. **cinchonas**) **1** any S American tree of the genus Cinchona, whose bark yields quinine. **2** the bark of such a tree. **3** a medicinal substance derived from this bark. **cinchonic** (-kon-′) a. **cinchonine** (sing′kōnēn) n. an organic alkaloid contained in cinchona bark.

cincture (singk′chə) n. **1** (poet.) a belt, a girdle. **2** (Archit.) the fillet at the top and bottom of a column.

cinder (sin′də) n. **1** a piece of coal that has ceased to burn but retains heat. **2** a piece of partly burnt coal or other combustible. **3** light slag. **4** (pl.) the refuse of burnt coal or wood; the remains of anything that has been subject to combustion. **5** (pl.) scoriae ejected from a volcano. **to burn to a cinder** to burn thoroughly; to render useless, inedible etc. by burning. **cindery** a.

Cinderella (sindərel′ə) n. **1** a person whose merits are unrecognized. **2** a despised or neglected person or thing.

cine- (sin´i), **ciné-** (sin´ā) *comb. form* **1** cinema. **2** cinematographic, as *cine-projector.* **cine-camera** *n.* a camera for taking motion pictures. **cine-film** *n.* film suitable for use in a cine-camera.

cineaste (sin´iast), **cineast** *n.* **1** a cinema enthusiast. **2** a person who makes films.

cinema (sin´əmə) *n.* (*pl.* **cinemas**) **1** a theatre where cinematographic films are shown. **2** films collectively. **3** the making of films as an art form or industry. **cinema organ** *n.* an organ with special effects etc. **cinematheque** (-tek) *n.* **1** a film archive or library. **2** a small, intimate cinema. **cinematic** (-mat´-) *a.* **cinematically** *adv.*

cinematograph (sinəmat´əgrahf), **kinematograph** (kin-) *n.* an apparatus for projecting very rapidly onto a screen a series of photographs, so as to create the illusion of continuous motion. **cinematographer** (-tog´rəfə) *n.* **cinematographic** (-graf´-) *a.* **cinematographically** *adv.* **cinematography** (-tog´-) *n.*

cinéma-vérité (sēnāmə vā´rētā), **ciné-vérité** (sēnā-) *n.* cinema which approaches a documentary style by using realistic settings, characters etc.

cinephile (sin´ifil) *n.* a person who likes the cinema.

cineraria (sinəreə´riə) *n.* (*pl.* **cinerarias**) a garden or hothouse plant, *Pericallis cruenta*, cultivated for its brightly coloured daisy-like flowers.

cinerary (sin´ərəri) *a.* of or relating to ashes. **cinerary urn** *n.* an urn used to hold the ashes of the dead. **cinereous** (-niə´-) *a.* ash-coloured, ash-grey.

cingulum (sing´gūləm) *n.* (*pl.* **cingula** (-lə)) (*Anat., Zool.*) a girdle-like part or structure, such as the ridge that surrounds the base of a tooth.

cinnabar (sin´əbah) *n.* **1** a bright red form of mercuric sulphide. **2** vermilion. **3** a large moth, *Tyria jacobaeae*, with red and black markings. ~*a.* bright red in colour.

cinnamon (sin´əmən) *n.* **1** a spice obtained from the aromatic inner bark of a SE Asian tree, *Cinnamomum zeylanicum*. **2** this or any other tree of the genus *Cinnamomum*. **3** the bark of any of these trees. **4** a light brownish-yellow colour. ~*a.* of this colour.

cinquefoil (singk´foil) *n.* **1** a plant of the genus *Potentilla*, with five-lobed leaves. **2** (*Archit.*) an ornamental foliation in five compartments, used in tracery etc.

cion SCION.

cipher (sī´fə), **cypher** *n.* **1** a code or alphabet used to carry on secret correspondence, designed to be intelligible only to the persons concerned. **2** anything written in this. **3** a key to it. **4** the arithmetical symbol 0. **5** a person or thing of no importance. **6** a monogram, a device. **7** a character of any kind used in writing or printing. **8** an Arabic numeral.

circa (soe´kə) *prep.* about, around (often used with dates) (*circa 1830*). ~*adv.* about, nearly.

circadian (soekā´diən) *a.* (of biological cycles etc.) recurring or repeated (approximately) every 24 hours.

circle (soe´kəl) *n.* **1** a plane figure bounded by a curved line, called the circumference, every point in which is equidistant from the centre. **2** a ring, a round figure or object. **3** a round enclosure. **4** a tier of seats at a theatre (*the dress circle*). **5** a number of people or things gathered or arranged in a ring (*standing in a circle; a circle of stones*). **6** a number of people with a common interest or bond (*the family circle*). **7** a class, a set, a coterie. **8** a sphere of action or influence. **9** a circular route. **10** any series ending as it begins and perpetually repeated (*a vicious circle*). **11** a period, a cycle. **12** an inconclusive argument in which two or more statements are brought forward to prove each other. **13** in hockey, a striking-circle. **14** (*N Am.*) a circle of buildings or circular open space at the intersection of streets; a circus. **15** (*loosely*) a round body, a sphere. ~*v.t.* **1** to move round. **2** to surround. ~*v.i.* **1** to revolve; to move in a circle. **2** to form a circle. **3** to be passed round. **to circle back** to go back to the starting point following a circular or indirect route. **to come full circle** to come round to where one started. **to go round in circles** to make no progress in spite of one's efforts. **to run round in circles** (*coll.*) to be very active without achieving much. **circler** *n.* **circlet** (-lit) *n.* **1** a small circle. **2** a ring or circular band worn on the finger, head etc.

circlip (soe´klip) *n.* a split metal ring fitted into a slot or groove on a bar, shaft etc. to hold something in place.

circs (soeks) *n.pl.* (*coll.*) circumstances.

circuit (soe´kit) *n.* **1** the line enclosing a space, the distance round about. **2** the space enclosed in a circle or within certain limits. **3** the act of revolving or moving round, a revolution. **4** the periodical visitation of judges for holding assizes. **5** the district thus visited. **6** the barristers making the circuit. **7** a continuous electrical communication between the poles of a battery. **8** a series of conductors, including the lamps, motors etc., through which a current passes. **9** a motor-racing track. **10** a series of sporting tournaments visited regularly by competitors. **11** a group of theatres or cinemas under the same ownership, putting on the same entertainment in turn. **12** a circular route or itinerary followed by a salesman, politician etc. (*the election circuit*). **13** a series of athletic exercises. **14** a group of Methodist churches associated together for purposes of government and organization of the ministry. **circuit board** *n.* a board on which an electronic circuit is built, with a connector to plug into a piece of equipment. **circuit-breaker** *n.* a device which stops the electric current in the event of a short circuit etc. **circuitous** (-kū´i-) *a.*

indirect, roundabout. **circuitously** *adv.* **circuitousness** *n.* **circuitry** *n.* (*pl.* **circuitries**) **1** electric or electronic circuits collectively. **2** the design of an electric or electronic circuit. **circuit training** *n.* a form of athletic training consisting of repeated cycles of exercises.

circular (sœ´kūlə) *a.* **1** in the shape of a circle, round. **2** of or relating to a circle. **3** moving in a circle. **4** cyclic. **5** (of a letter etc.) addressed in identical terms to a number of people. **6** (*Logic*) (of an argument) inconclusive, consisting of two or more statements brought forward to prove each other. ~*n.* a letter or printed notice of which a copy is sent to many people. **circularity** (-lar´-) *n.* **circularize, circularise** *v.t.* **1** to send circulars to. **2** (*N Am.*) to canvass by means of questionnaires. **circularization** (-zā´shən) *n.* **circularly** *adv.* **circular saw** *n.* a power tool with a rotating disc notched with teeth for cutting timber etc.

circulate (sœ´kūlāt) *v.i.* **1** to pass from place to place or person to person. **2** (of blood in the body etc.) to pass through certain channels and return to the starting point. **3** to move round. **4** to move from person to person at a social gathering; to be sociable. ~*v.t.* **1** to cause to pass from place to place or person to person. **2** to spread, to diffuse. **circulating** *a.* **1** that circulates. **2** current. **3** (*Math.*) recurring. **circulating capital** *n.* raw materials, money, goods etc. which are constantly changing hands in business or industry. **circulating library** *n.* (*Hist.*) a small lending library, esp. one for which subscribers paid a small fee. **circulating medium** *n.* the currency of a country. **circulation** (-lā´shən) *n.* **1** the act of circulating. **2** the state of being circulated. **3** the motion of the blood in a living animal, by which it is propelled by the heart through the arteries to all parts of the body, and returned to the heart through the veins. **4** the analogous motion of sap in plants. **5** the free movement of water, air etc. **6** distribution of books, newspapers, news etc. **7** the amount of distribution, the number of copies sold. **8** a medium of exchange, currency. **9** the movement of this. **in circulation 1** (of money) serving as currency. **2** in general use. **3** participating in social or business activities. **out of circulation** not in circulation. **circulatory** (sœ´kūlətəri, -lā´-) *a.* of or relating to circulation, esp. of blood or sap (*the circulatory system*).

circum- (sœ´kəm) *pref.* **1** round, about. **2** surrounding. **3** indirectly. **4** of or relating to the circumference.

circumambulate (sœkəmam´būlāt) *v.t.* (*formal*) to walk or go round. ~*v.i.* to walk about. **circumambulation** (-lā´shən) *n.* **circumambulatory** *a.*

circumcircle (sœ´kəmsœkəl) *n.* (*Geom.*) a circle that surrounds a triangle or other polygon, touching all the vertices.

circumcise (sœ´kəmsīz) *v.t.* to remove surgically or by ritual the prepuce or foreskin of (a male), or the clitoris of (a female). **circumcision** (-sizh´ən) *n.*

circumference (səkŭm´fərəns) *n.* **1** the line that bounds a circle. **2** a periphery. **3** the distance round a space or a body. **4** a circuit. **circumferential** (-ren´-) *a.* **circumferentially** *adv.*

circumflex (sœ´kəmfleks) *n.* (*also* **circumflex accent**) a mark (ˆ, or ˆ in Greek) placed above a vowel to indicate accent, quality, length or contraction. ~*a.* **1** marked with such accent. **2** (*Anat.*) bent, turning, or curving round something.

circumlocution (sœkəmləkū´shən) *n.* **1** a roundabout phrase or expression. **2** the use of roundabout, indirect or evasive language. **3** the use of many words where few would suffice. **circumlocutional, circumlocutionary** *a.* **circumlocutionist** *n.* **circumlocutory** (-lok´ū-) *a.*

circumnavigate (sœkəmnav´igāt) *v.t.* to sail or fly completely round. **circumnavigation** (-ā´shən) *n.* **circumnavigator** *n.*

circumpolar (sœkəmpō´lə) *a.* **1** situated round or near one of the earth's poles. **2** (*Astron.*) revolving about the pole, not setting.

circumscribe (sœ´kəmskrīb) *v.t.* **1** to draw a line around. **2** to limit, to define by bounds, to restrict. **3** (*Geom.*) to surround with a figure that touches at every possible point. **circumscribable** (-skrī´bəbəl) *a.* **circumscriber** *n.* **circumscription** (-skrip´-) *n.*

circumspect (sœ´kəmspekt) *a.* **1** cautious, wary. **2** taking everything into account. **circumspection** (-spek´-), **circumspectness** *n.* **circumspectly** *adv.*

circumstance (sœ´kəmstəns) *n.* **1** an incident, an occurrence. **2** something relative to a fact or case. **3** a concomitant. **4** (*pl.*) the facts, relations, influences and other conditions that affect an act or an event. **5** (*pl.*) the facts, conditions etc. that affect one's way of life. **6** ceremony, pomp, fuss. ~*v.t.* to place in a particular situation. **in/ under no circumstances** not at all, never, in no case. **in/ under the circumstances** in the particular situation for which allowance should be made (*He did very well under the circumstances*). **circumstanced** *a.*

circumstantial (sœkəmstan´shəl) *a.* **1** depending on circumstances. **2** incidental, not essential. **3** detailed, minute. **circumstantiality** (-shial´-) *n.* **circumstantially** *adv.*

circumvent (sœkəmvent´, sœ´-) *v.t.* **1** to go round, to avoid or evade. **2** to deceive, to outwit, to cheat. **circumvention** (-ven´-) *n.*

circumvolution (sœkəmvəloo´shən) *n.* **1** the act of rolling round. **2** a coil, a convolution. **3** a revolution. **4** a winding or tortuous movement.

circus (sœ´kəs) *n.* (*pl.* **circuses**) **1** a travelling company of clowns, acrobats, trained animals etc. **2** the place, usu. a circular tent, where they perform. **3** such a performance. **4** a set of people who travel together and put on displays, engage in sporting activities etc. **5** a circle of buildings or circular open space at the intersection of streets. **6** an amphitheatre in ancient Rome, such as the Circus Maximus, for sports and games. **7** a performance given there. **8** (*coll.*) a scene of noisy, disorganized activity. **9** a circular hollow with hills on all sides.

cire perdue (siə pœdū´) *n.* a method of casting bronze, using wax which is subsequently melted and replaced by the metal.

cirque (sœk) *n.* (*Geol.*) a semicircular basin in a hillside or valley, caused by erosion.

cirrhosis (sirō´sis) *n.* (*Med.*) a disease of the liver in which it becomes yellowish and nodular because of the death of liver cells and the growth of fibrous tissue. **cirrhotic** (-rot´-) *a.*

cirri CIRRUS.

cirro- (sir´ō) *comb. form* denoting cloud formed at high altitudes.

cirrocumulus (sirōkū´mūləs) *n.* a cloud at high altitude broken up into small fleecy masses.

cirrostratus (sirōstrah´təs) *n.* a horizontal or slightly inclined sheet of cloud more or less broken into fleecy masses.

cirrus (sir´əs) *n.* (*pl.* **cirri** (-rī)) **1** a lofty feathery cloud. **2** (*Bot.*) a tendril. **3** (*Zool.*) a slender locomotive filament. **4** a barbule. **cirrose** (-rōs), **cirrous** *a.*

cis- (sis) *pref.* **1** on this side of. **2** closer to the present time than. **3** (*Chem.*) having two groups of atoms on the same side of a given plane or double bond.

cisalpine (sisal´pīn) *a.* south of the Alps.

cisatlantic (sisətlan´tik) *a.* on the speaker's side of the Atlantic, as distinct from *transatlantic*.

cisco (sis´kō) *n.* (*pl.* **ciscoes, ciscos**) any of several freshwater whitefish of the genus *Coregonus* of N America.

cislunar (sisloo´nə) *a.* between the moon and the earth.

cissy SISSY (under SIS).

Cistercian (sistœ´shən) *n.* a member of a monastic order founded in 1098. ~*a.* of or relating to the Cistercians.

cistern (sis´tən) *n.* **1** a tank for storing water, esp. a water tank for a lavatory. **2** an underground reservoir.

cistus (sis´təs) *n.* (*pl.* **cistuses**) any plant of the genus *Cistus*, a rock rose.

citadel (sit´ədəl) *n.* **1** a castle or fortified place in a city. **2** a Salvation Army hall.

cite (sīt) *v.t.* **1** to quote, to allege as an authority. **2** to quote as an instance. **3** to refer to. **4** to mention in dispatches etc. **5** (*Law*) to summon to appear in court. **citable** *a.* **citation** (-tā´shən) *n.* **1** a quotation. **2** a mention in dispatches etc. **3** an official commendation, for bravery etc. **4** a summons. **citatory** *a.*

citified CITY.

citizen (sit´izən) *n.* **1** a member of a state having political rights (*a French citizen*). **2** a dweller in a town or city. **3** a freeman of a city or town. **4** (*esp. N Am.*) a civilian. **citizenhood** *n.* citizen of the world *n.* a cosmopolitan. **citizenry** *n.* citizens collectively. **Citizens' Advice Bureau** *n.* an office providing free advice and information to

members of the public. **citizen's arrest** *n.* an arrest made by a member of the public. **citizens' band** *n.* a band of radio frequencies designated for use by private citizens for communication between individuals. **citizenship** *n.*

citrate (sit´rāt, sī´-) *n.* (*Chem.*) a salt of citric acid. **citric** (sit´-) *a.* derived from citrus fruits.

citric acid (sitric as´id) *n.* the acid found in lemons, citrons, limes, oranges etc.

citrine (sit´rin) *a.* **1** like a citron. **2** greenish-yellow. ~*n.* (*Mineral.*) a yellow, pellucid variety of quartz, false topaz. **citrinous** *a.* lemon-coloured.

citron (sit´rən) *n.* **1** a tree, *Citrus medica*, bearing large lemon-like fruit. **2** this fruit.

citronella (sitrənel´ə) *n.* **1** any S Asian grass of the genus *Cymbopogon*. **2** a fragrant oil derived from this, used to drive away insects and in perfumery.

citrus (sit´rəs) *n.* (*pl.* **citruses**) **1** any tree of the genus *Citrus*, including the orange, lemon, citron etc. **2** (*also* **citrus fruit**) the fruit of any of these trees; an orange, lemon, lime, citron, grapefruit etc. **citrous** *a.*

cittern (sit´ən), **cither** (sith´ə), **cithern** (sith´ən) *n.* a medieval instrument resembling a lute, with wire strings.

city (sit´i) *n.* (*pl.* **cities**) **1** a town incorporated by a charter. **2** a large and important town. **3** a cathedral town. **4** the inhabitants of a city. ~*a.* **1** of or relating to a city. **2** characteristic of a city. **citified, cityfied** *a.* (*usu. derog.*) **1** townish. **2** having the characteristics of city-dwellers. **City Company** *n.* a London livery company representing one of the medieval guilds. **city desk** *n.* **1** the editorial department of a newspaper dealing with financial news. **2** (*N Am.*) the department of a newspaper dealing with local news. **city editor** *n.* an editor in charge of a city desk. **city fathers** *n.pl.* people in charge of the administration of a city. **city hall** *n.* **1** a town hall. **2** (*N Am.*) **a** municipal offices. **b** municipal officers. **city manager** *n.* (*N Am.*) an official in charge of the administration of a city. **city page** *n.* the part of a newspaper containing financial news. **cityscape** *n.* an urban landscape. **city slicker** *n.* (*usu. derog.*) **1** a sophisticated city dweller. **2** a smooth, plausible rogue. **city-state** *n.* (*esp. Hist.*) an independent state comprising a city and its surrounding territory. **City Technology College** *n.* a type of senior secondary school, partly funded by industry, specializing in science and technology. **cityward, citywards** *adv.*

civet (siv´it) *n.* **1** a civet cat. **2** a resinous musky substance obtained from the anal pouch of this animal, used as a perfume. **civet cat** *n.* a carnivorous quadruped of the family Viverridae from Asia and Africa, esp. *Viverra civetta*.

civic (siv´ik) *a.* **1** of or relating to a city or citizens. **2** urban. **3** municipal. **4** civil. **civically** *adv.* **civic centre** *n.* a group of buildings including the town hall and local administrative offices.

civics *n.* the study of citizenship and municipal government.
civil (siv´əl) *a.* **1** of or relating to citizens. **2** domestic, not foreign. **3** municipal, commercial, legislative. **4** of or relating to social, commercial and administrative affairs, not military or naval. **5** (*Law*) of or relating to private matters, not criminal (*a civil action; a civil process*). **6** civilized, polite, courteous. **civil aviation** *n.* civilian, non-military airlines and their operations, esp. commercial aviation. **civil commotion** *n.* (*Law*) a riot or similar disturbance. **civil defence** *n.* a civilian service for the protection of lives and property in the event of enemy attack. **civil disobedience** *n.* a political campaign taking the form of refusal to pay taxes or perform civil duties. **civil engineer** *n.* an engineer dealing with the design, construction and maintenance of roads, railways, bridges, harbours etc. **civil engineering** *n.* **civilian** (-vil´yən) *n.* a person engaged in civil life, not belonging to the armed forces. ~*a.* of or relating to civilians. **civilianize, civilianise** *v.t.* to make civilian. **civilianization** (-zā´shən) *n.* **civility** (-vil´-) *n.* (*pl.* **civilities**) **1** the quality of being civil. **2** politeness, courtesy. **3** an act of politeness or courtesy. **civil law** *n.* **1** the law dealing with private rights, as distinct from *criminal law*. **2** Roman law, non-ecclesiastical law. **civil liberty** *n.* (*pl.* **civil liberties**) (a) personal freedom, e.g. freedom of speech, within the framework of the state. **civil libertarian** *n.* **civil list** *n.* the yearly sum granted for the support of a sovereign or ruler. **civilly** *adv.* **civil marriage** *n.* a marriage performed by a civil official, not by a member of the clergy. **civil parish** *n.* a civil district for the purposes of local government etc. **civil rights** *n.pl.* the rights of an individual or group within a state to certain freedoms, e.g. from discrimination. **civil servant** *n.* a member of the civil service. **civil service** *n.* the non-military branch of the public service, dealing with public administration. **civil state** *n.* marital status. **civil war** *n.* a war between citizens of the same country. **civil year** *n.* the calendar or legal year, as distinct from an *astronomical year*.
civilize (siv´əlīz), **civilise** *v.t.* **1** to bring out of barbarism, to bring to a state of civilization. **2** to instruct in the arts and refinements of civilized society. **civilizable** *a.* **civilization** (-zā´shən) *n.* **1** an advanced stage of social and cultural development. **2** societies or peoples at such a stage of development. **3** a civilized society or people of the past (*the Inca civilization*). **4** the act or process of civilizing. **5** the state of being civilized. **civilizer** *n.*
civvy (siv´i) *n.* (*pl.* **civvies** (-iz)) **1** (*pl.*) civilian clothes, as opposed to uniform (*in civvies*). **2** a civilian. ~*a.* civilian. **Civvy Street** *n.* (*sl.*) civilian life.
CJ *abbr.* Chief Justice.
CJD *abbr.* Creutzfeldt–Jakob disease.

Cl *chem. symbol* chlorine.
cl. *abbr.* **1** centilitre. **2** class.
clack (klak) *v.i.* **1** to make a sharp, sudden noise like a clap or crack. **2** to chatter rapidly and noisily. ~*n.* **1** a sudden, sharp sound. **2** a device making such a sound. **3** rapid and noisy chattering. **4** a chatterbox. **clacker** *n.* **clackety** (-əti) *a.*
clad[1] (klad) *v.t.* (*pres.p.* **cladding**, *past, p.p.* **cladded, clad**) to provide with cladding. **cladding** *n.* a protective coating, e.g. of stone on a building or insulating material on a hot-water pipe.
clad[2] CLOTHE.
clade (klād) *n.* (*Biol.*) a group of organisms sharing a unique characteristic because of evolution from a common ancestor. **cladism** (klad´-) *n.* **cladistic** *a.* **cladistics** (klədis´tiks) *n.* (*Biol.*) a method of classifying organisms based on clades.
claim (klām) *v.t.* **1** to demand, or challenge, as a right. **2** to assert that one has or is (something) or has done (something). **3** to affirm, to maintain. **4** to be deserving of. **5** to take or have as a consequence (*The floods claimed many lives*). ~*v.i.* to make a claim on an insurance policy (*to claim for a broken windscreen*). ~*n.* **1** a demand for something due. **2** a request for payment under the terms of an insurance policy. **3** an assertion. **4** a real or supposed right. **5** a title. **6** something claimed. **7** a piece of land allotted to one. **8** (*esp. Mining*) a piece of land marked out by a settler or miner with the intention of buying it when it is offered for sale. **to lay claim to** to assert that one owns or has a right to. **claimable** *a.* **claimant** *n.* a person who makes a claim. **claimer** *n.*
clairaudience (kleəraw´diəns) *n.* the (supposed) faculty of hearing voices and other sounds not perceptible to the senses. **clairaudient** *n., a.*
clairvoyance (kleəvoi´əns) *n.* **1** the (supposed) power of perceiving future events or objects not present to the senses. **2** unusual sensitivity or insight. **clairvoyant** *n.* a person having the power of clairvoyance. ~*a.* of, relating to or having the power of clairvoyance. **clairvoyante** *n.* a female clairvoyant. **clairvoyantly** *adv.*
clam (klam) *n.* **1** any of several edible bivalve molluscs, esp. *Venus mercenaria*, the hard clam, and *Mya arenaria*, the soft clam. **2** (*coll.*) a taciturn person. ~*v.i.* (*pres.p.* **clamming**, *past, p.p.* **clammed**) to gather clams. **to clam up** to become silent. **clamshell** *n.* **1** the shell of a clam. **2** something resembling this, such as a hinged dredging bucket, aircraft cockpit canopy, takeaway food container etc.
clamber (klam´bə) *v.i.* to climb with hands and feet, to climb with difficulty. ~*n.* a climb of this nature.
clammy (klam´i) *a.* (*comp.* **clammier**, *superl.* **clammiest**) **1** moist, damp. **2** sticky. **3** (of weather) humid. **clammily** *adv.* **clamminess** *n.*

clamour (klam´ə), (*N Am.*) **clamor** *n.* **1** a loud and continuous shouting or calling out. **2** a continued and loud expression of complaint, demand or appeal. ~*v.t.* **1** to shout. **2** to utter or express with loud noise. ~*v.i.* **1** to cry out loudly and earnestly. **2** to demand or complain noisily (*The crowd clamoured for his release*). **clamorous** *a.* **clamorously** *adv.* **clamorousness** *n.*

clamp[1] (klamp) *n.* **1** a frame with two tightening screws to hold pieces of wood etc. together. **2** a piece of timber or iron used to fasten things together. **3** a wheel clamp. ~*v.t.* **1** to unite, fasten or strengthen with a clamp or clamps. **2** to put or hold firmly. **3** to immobilize with a wheel clamp. **to clamp down (on)** to impose (heavier) restrictions (on); to attempt to suppress. **clampdown** *n.* an act of clamping down (on something). **clamper** *n.*

clamp[2] (klamp) *n.* **1** a heap, mound or stack of turf, rubbish, potatoes etc. **2** a pile of bricks for firing.

clan (klan) *n.* **1** a tribe or number of families bearing the same name, descended from a common ancestor, and united under a chieftain representing that ancestor (*the Highland clans*). **2** a large extended family. **3** a clique, a set. **4** a genus or species. **5** a group of animals. **clannish** *a.* (*usu. derog.*) **1** (of a family etc.) united closely together. **2** cliquish. **3** of or relating to a clan. **clannishly** *adv.* **clannishness** *n.* **clanship** *n.* **1** the system of clans. **2** loyalty to a clan. **clansman, clanswoman** *n.* (*pl.* **clansmen, clanswomen**) a member of a clan.

clandestine (klandes´tin, klan´-) *a.* secret, surreptitious, underhand. **clandestinely** *adv.* **clandestineness** *n.*

clang (klang) *v.t.* to strike together, so as to cause a sharp, ringing sound. ~*v.i.* **1** to emit a sharp, ringing sound. **2** to resound. ~*n.* a sharp, ringing sound, as of two pieces of metal struck together. **clanger** *n.* (*sl.*) **1** a foolish mistake. **2** a social blunder. **to drop a clanger** to make a conspicuous mistake or blunder. **clangour** (-gə), (*N Am.*) **clangor** *n.* **1** a sharp, ringing sound or series of sounds. **2** an uproar. **clangorous** *a.* **clangorously** *adv.*

clank (klangk) *n.* a sound as of solid metallic bodies struck together (usu. a deeper sound than *clink*, and a less resounding one than *clang*). ~*v.t.* to strike together so as to make such a sound. ~*v.i.* to make such a sound. **clankingly** *adv.*

clannish CLAN.

clap[1] (klap) *v.t.* (*pres.p.* **clapping**, *past, p.p.* **clapped**) **1** to strike together noisily (*to clap one's hands*). **2** to applaud, by striking the hands together. **3** to strike quickly or slap with something flat. **4** to put or place suddenly, hastily or firmly. **5** (of a bird) to flap (the wings) noisily. ~*v.i.* to strike the hands together, esp. in applause. ~*n.* **1** the noise made by the collision of flat surfaces. **2** a sudden loud noise. **3** a peal of thunder. **4** applause shown by clapping. **5** a heavy slap. **a clap**

on the back congratulations. **to clap up** to make hastily. **clapped out,** (*attrib.*) **clapped-out** *a.* (*sl.*) **1** worn out; of no more use. **2** finished, exhausted. **clapper** *n.* **1** a person or thing that claps. **2** the tongue of a bell. **like the clappers** (*sl.*) extremely fast. **clapperboard** *n.* a pair of hinged boards clapped together at the start of a take during film shooting to help synchronize sound and vision. **claptrap** *n.* **1** pretentious or insincere talk. **2** showy words or deeds designed to win applause or public favour.

clap[2] (klap) *n.* (*taboo sl.*) gonorrhoea.

clapboard (klap´bawd) *n.* (*N Am.*) a feather-edged board used to cover the roofs and sides of houses.

claque (klak) *n.* a body of hired applauders.

claret (klar´it) *n.* **1** a light red Bordeaux wine. **2** any light red wine resembling Bordeaux. **3** a reddishviolet colour. ~*a.* claret-coloured. **claret-coloured** *a.* reddish-violet.

clarify (klar´ifī) *v.t.* (*3rd pers. sing. pres.* **clarifies**, *pres.p.* **clarifying**, *past, p.p.* **clarified**) **1** to make clearer or easier to understand. **2** to clear from visible impurities (*to clarify butter*). **3** to make transparent. ~*v.i.* to become transparent. **clarification** (-fikā´shən) *n.* **clarificatory** (-fikā´-) *a.* **clarifier** *n.*

clarinet (klarinet´) *n.* **1** a keyed woodwind instrument with a single reed. **2** a clarinet player, esp. in an orchestra. **3** an organ stop giving a clarinet-like sound. **clarinettist,** (*esp. N Am.*) **clarinetist** *n.*

clarion (klar´iən) *n.* **1** (*Hist.*) a kind of trumpet, with a narrow tube, producing a loud and clear note. **2** a sound of or resembling that of a clarion. **3** an organ stop giving a similar tone. ~*a.* loud and clear.

clarity (klar´əti) *n.* clearness.

clash (klash) *v.i.* **1** to make a loud noise by striking together. **2** to come into collision. **3** to disagree; to conflict. **4** (of colours) to be in disharmony. **5** (of dates etc.) to coincide, esp. inconveniently. ~*v.t.* to cause one thing to strike against another so as to produce a loud noise. ~*n.* **1** the noise produced by the violent collision of two bodies. **2** opposition, disagreement, conflict. **3** a collision. **4** disharmony of colours. **clasher** *n.*

clasp (klahsp) *n.* **1** a catch, hook or interlocking device for fastening. **2** a buckle or brooch. **3** any fastening. **4** a close embrace. **5** a grasp. **6** a metal bar attached to a ribbon carrying a medal commemorating a battle or other exploit. ~*v.t.* **1** to fasten or shut with or as if with a clasp or buckle. **2** to embrace. **3** to grasp. **4** to cling to by twining or encircling. **to clasp one's hands** to put one's hands together with the fingers interlaced. **clasper** *n.* **1** a person or thing that clasps. **2** (*pl.*) a pair of organs in some insects and fishes by which the male holds the female. **clasp-knife** *n.* (*pl.* **clasp-knives**) a pocket knife in which the blade shuts into the hollow part of the handle.

class (klahs) *n.* **1** a number of persons or things

ranked together. **2** a social rank (*the middle classes*). **3** the system of social caste or social ranking. **4** a number of pupils or students taught together. **5** an occasion when they are taught (*an evening class; a tap-dancing class*). **6** (*N Am.*) the students taken collectively who expect to graduate at the same time (*the class of 1988*). **7** a division according to quality. **8** (*sl.*) high quality or merit. **9** a number of individuals having the same essential qualities. **10** (*Biol.*) a division of animals or plants next above an order. *~v.t.* to assign to a class or classes. *~a.* (*sl.*) of good quality. **in a class of one's/ its own** of matchless excellence. **class-conscious** *a.* oversensitive to social differences. **class-consciousness** *n.* **classism** *n.* discrimination on the ground of social class. **classist** *a., n.* **classless** *a.* **1** not divided into classes. **2** not belonging to any class. **classlessness** *n.* **class-list** *n.* a classified list of candidates issued by examiners. **classmate** *n.* a person who is or has been in the same class, esp. at school. **classroom** *n.* a room in a school etc. in which classes are taught. **class war, class warfare** *n.* conflict between the social classes in a community. **classy** *a.* (*comp.* **classier**, *superl.* **classiest**) (*coll.*) **1** genteel. **2** of superior quality. **3** stylish, elegant. **classily** *adv.* **classiness** *n.*

classic (klas´ik) *n.* **1** an author, artist etc. of the first rank. **2** a Greek or Latin writer of the first rank. **3** a literary or artistic work by any of these. **4** any recognized masterpiece. **5** (*pl.*) ancient Greek and Latin literature. **6** (*pl., sing. in constr.*) the study of these. **7** anything in classic style. *~a.* **1** of the first rank, esp. in literature or art. **2** outstandingly typical (*a classic example*). **3** of or relating to the art or literature of the ancient Greeks and Romans. **4** in the style of these. **5** of standard authority. **classicism** (-sizm) *n.* **1** a classic style or idiom. **2** devotion to or imitation of the classics. **3** classical scholarship. **4** advocacy of classical education. **classicist** *n.* **classicize, classicise** *v.t.* to make classic. *~v.i.* to affect or imitate a classic or classical style. **classic races** *n.pl.* the five principal horse races of the British season, being the 2000 Guineas, 1000 Guineas, Derby, Oaks and St Leger.

classical (klas´ikəl) *a.* **1** belonging to or characteristic of the ancient Greeks and Romans or their civilization or literature. **2** (of education) based on a study of Latin and Greek. **3** (of any of the arts) influenced by Roman or Greek models, restrained, simple and pure in form. **4** (of music) serious or traditional in style or composition, esp. of orchestral music, opera etc. rather than pop, jazz etc. **5** of or relating to music composed esp. in the 18th and 19th cents., simple and restrained in style. **6** outstanding; exemplary; of lasting merit. **7** (of physics) not involving relativity or quantum mechanics. **classicalism** *n.* **classicalist** *n.* **classicality** (-kal´-) *n.* **classical Latin** *n.* Latin of the golden age of Latin literature (*c.*75 BC to AD 175). **classically** *adv.*

classify (klas´ifī) *v.t.* (*3rd pers. sing. pres.* **classifies**, *pres.p.* **classifying**, *past, p.p.* **classified**) **1** to distribute into classes or divisions. **2** to assign to a class. **3** to restrict the availability of (information), esp. for security reasons. **classifiable** *a.* **classification** (-fikā´shən) *n.* **classificatory** (-kā´-) *a.* **classified** *a.* **1** arranged in classes. **2** (of information) of restricted availability, esp. for security reasons. **3** (of printed advertisements) arranged according to the type of goods or services offered or required. **4** (of a road) belonging to one of the categories of the national road system. *~n.* (*pl.*) classified advertisements. **classifier** *n.*

clatter (klat´ə) *v.i.* **1** to make a sharp rattling noise. **2** to fall or move with such a noise. **3** to talk idly and noisily. *~v.t.* to cause to make a rattling sound. *~n.* **1** a sharp rattling noise. **2** loud, tumultuous noise. **3** noisy, empty talk. **clatterer** *n.* **clatteringly** *adv.* **clattery** *a.*

clause (klawz) *n.* **1** (*Gram.*) **a** a complete grammatical unit, usu. including a subject and predicate. **b** a subdivision of a compound or complex sentence (*a subordinate clause; a main clause*). **2** a separate and distinct portion of a document. **3** a particular stipulation. **clausal** *a.*

claustral (klaws´trəl) *a.* **1** of or relating to a cloister or monastic foundation. **2** narrowminded.

claustrophobia (klawstrəfō´biə) *n.* an abnormal fear of being in a confined space. **claustrophobe** (klaws´-) *n.* a person who suffers from claustrophobia. **claustrophobic** *a.* **1** suffering from claustrophobia. **2** causing claustrophobia. *~n.* a claustrophobe. **claustrophobically** *adv.*

clave (klāv, klahv) *n.* (*Mus.*) either of a pair of hardwood sticks that make a hollow sound when struck together.

clavicembalo (klavichem´bəlō) *n.* (*pl.* **clavicembalos**) a harpsichord.

clavichord (klav´ikawd) *n.* a soft-toned musical instrument, one of the first stringed instruments with a keyboard, a predecessor of the pianoforte.

clavicle (klav´ikəl) *n.* the collarbone. **clavicular** (-vik´ū-) *a.*

clavier (klav´iə, kləviə´) *n.* **1** the keyboard of an organ, pianoforte etc. **2** a keyboard instrument.

claw (klaw) *n.* **1** the sharp hooked nail of a bird or animal. **2** the foot of any bird or animal armed with such nails. **3** the pincer of a crab, lobster or crayfish. **4** an implement for grappling or holding. *~v.t.* **1** to tear or scratch with the claws. **2** to clutch or drag with or as with claws. *~v.i.* to scratch with the claws. **to claw back 1** to get back by clawing or with difficulty. **2** to take back (part of a benefit or allowance etc.) by extra taxation etc. **clawback** *n.* **1** the act of clawing back. **2** money etc. clawed back. **clawed** *a.* **claw hammer** *n.* **1** a hammer with claws at the back of the head to extract nails. **2** (*sl.*) a dress coat (from its shape). **clawless** *a.*

clay (klā) *n.* **1** heavy, sticky earth. **2** a hydrated silicate of aluminium, with a mixture of other substances, used to make bricks, pottery etc. **3** (*poet.*) the human body. **4** (*coll.*) a clay pipe. **clayey** *a.* **clayish** *a.* **claylike** *a.* **clay-pan** *n.* (*Austral.*) a hollow (often dry in summer) where water collects after rain. **clay pigeon** *n.* a clay disc thrown into the air as a target for shooting. **clay pipe** *n.* a tobacco pipe made of baked clay, usu. long. **claystone** *n.* a compact fine-grained rock.

claymore (klā′maw) *n.* **1** a two-edged sword used by the Scottish Highlanders. **2** a basket-hilted broadsword. **3** a type of explosive mine.

clean (klēn) *a.* **1** free from dirt, stain, contamination, disease etc. **2** clear, unobstructed, unused (*a clean page*). **3** free from errors, defects etc. **4** pure, holy, free from ceremonial defilement. **5** attentive to personal cleanliness. **6** free from evidence of criminal activity. **7** (of a driving licence) free from endorsements or penalty points. **8** (*sl.*) not carrying or containing a gun, drugs, illegal or incriminating articles etc. **9** free from sexual references, innuendo etc. **10** producing relatively little radioactive fallout. **11** smooth, streamlined, shapely (*clean lines*). **12** adroit, dexterous, unerring. *~v.t.* **1** to make clean. **2** to cleanse, to purify. **3** to gut (fish, poultry etc.). **4** to remove (marks etc.). *~v.i.* **1** to become clean. **2** to make oneself clean. *~adv.* **1** quite, completely. **2** without qualification, absolutely. **3** in a clean manner, cleanly. **4** dexterously, cleverly. *~n.* **1** an act of cleaning (*This carpet needs a clean*). **2** in weightlifting, the raising of a weight from the floor to shoulder level in a single movement (*clean and jerk*). **to clean one's plate** to eat all the food on one's plate. **to clean out 1** to clean thoroughly. **2** to strip. **3** (*sl.*) to deprive of all money. **to clean up 1** to clear away a mess. **2** to put tidy. **3** to make oneself clean. **4** to collect all the money, profits etc. **to come clean** (*coll.*) to confess. **cleanable** *a.* **clean bill of health** *n.* **1** a document certifying the health of a ship's company. **2** a statement that a person is in good health or a thing in good condition. **clean break** *n.* a quick and complete separation. **clean-cut** *a.* **1** sharply defined; clear-cut. **2** clean, neat. **cleaner** *n.* **1** a person who cleans, esp. one paid to clean the interior of a house, office, factory etc. **2** a device or substance that cleans. **3** (*pl.*) a dry-cleaners' shop. **to take to the cleaners 1** (*sl.*) to deprive of all one's money, goods etc. **2** (*sl.*) to criticize severely. **cleanish** *a.* **clean-living** *a.* upright, decent, respectable. **cleanly**[1] *adv.* **cleanness** *n.* **clean-shaven** *a.* without beard or moustache. **clean sheet, clean slate** *n.* a new start, all debts etc. written off. **clean-up** *n.* an act of cleaning up.

cleanly[1] CLEAN.

cleanly[2] (klen′li) *a.* (*comp.* **cleanlier**, *superl.* **cleanliest**) clean in person and habits. **cleanlily** *adv.* **cleanliness** *n.*

cleanse (klenz) *v.t.* **1** (*usu. formal*) to make clean. **2** to purge, to purify. **cleanser** *n.* **cleansing** *n.* **cleansing cream** *n.* a cream used to remove dirt, make-up etc. from the face or hands. **cleansing department** *n.* the department of a local authority that deals with refuse collection, street cleaning etc.

clear (kliə) *a.* **1** free from darkness, dullness or opacity. **2** luminous, bright. **3** transparent, translucent. **4** (of the sky etc.) free from clouds or mist (*on a clear day*). **5** distinctly audible. **6** evident, easy to see. **7** lucid, easy to understand. **8** indisputable, unambiguous. **9** brightly intelligent. **10** certain, unmistaken (*I'm not clear about this*). **11** irreproachable, guiltless. **12** unobstructed (*a clear road*). **13** free, unshackled, unentangled. **14** free from commitments etc. **15** free from deduction; net, not curtailed. **16** complete (*two clear days*). *~adv.* **1** clearly. **2** completely, quite, entirely. **3** apart, free from risk of contact (*to stand clear*). *~v.t.* **1** to make clear; to free from darkness, opacity, obstruction etc. **2** to empty. **3** to remove trees, buildings etc. from (land), esp. in order to cultivate it. **4** to liberate, to disengage. **5** to acquit, to exonerate. **6** to obtain authorization for. **7** to pass through (customs etc.). **8** to pass or leap over without touching. **9** to gain, to realize as profit. **10** to pass (a cheque etc.) through a clearing house. **11** in football, to send (the ball) out of the defence area. *~v.i.* **1** to become clear, bright or unclouded. **2** to become free from obstruction. **3** to dissipate, disappear etc. (*The fog gradually cleared*). **in clear** not in code. **in the clear** free from suspicion. **out of a clear sky** as a complete surprise. **to clear away 1** to remove. **2** to clear plates etc. after a meal. **3** to disappear. **4** to melt away. **to clear off 1** to remove. **2** (*coll.*) to depart. **to clear one's throat** to make one's voice clear with a slight cough. **to clear out 1** to empty. **2** to eject. **3** (*coll.*) to depart. **to clear the air 1** to make the air cooler, fresher etc. **2** to remove misunderstandings or suspicion. **to clear the way 1** to remove obstacles (*to clear the way for negotiations*). **2** to stand aside, to get out of the way. **to clear up 1** to become bright and clear. **2** to elucidate. **3** to tidy up. **4** to disappear. **clearable** *a.* **clear-cut** *a.* **1** regular, finely outlined, sharply defined. **2** obvious, evident. *~v.t.* (*pres.p.* **clear-cutting**, *past, p.p.* **clear-cut**) to clear-fell (an area). **clearer** *n.* **1** a person or thing that clears. **2** a clearing bank. **clear-fell** *v.t.* to remove all trees from (an area). **clear-headed** *a.* **1** acute, sharp, intelligent. **2** sensible (*a clear-headed decision*). **clear-headedness** *n.* **clearly** *adv.* **1** in a clear manner. **2** distinctly, audibly. **3** plainly, evidently. **4** certainly, undoubtedly. **clearness** *n.* **clear-out** *n.* an act of clearing out. **clear-sighted** *a.* **1** acute, discerning, far-seeing. **2** seeing clearly. **clear-sightedness** *n.* **clearstory** CLERESTORY. **clear-up** *n.* an act of clearing up, tidying or solving. **clearway** *n.* a road on which stopping or parking is forbidden.

clearance (kliə´rəns) n. **1** the act of clearing. **2** the state of being cleared. **3** the removal of people, buildings etc. from an area. **4** authorization. **5** the clearing of cheques etc. **6** clear profit. **7** a certificate that a ship etc. has been cleared at the custom house. **8** the distance between the moving and the stationary part of a machine. **9** any similar clear space allowed between parts. **clearance sale** n. a sale of stock at reduced prices to make room for new stock.

clearing (kliə´ring) n. **1** the act of making clear, free from obstruction etc. **2** a tract of land cleared for cultivation. **3** the passing of cheques etc. through a clearing house. **clearing bank** n. a bank which is a member of a clearing house. **clearing house** n. **1** a financial establishment where cheques, transfers, bills etc. are exchanged between member banks, so that only outstanding balances have to be paid. **2** a person or agency acting as a centre for the exchange of information etc.

cleat (klēt) n. **1** a strip of wood secured to another one to strengthen it. **2** a strip fastened on steps etc. to prevent slipping. **3** a wedge.

cleave[1] (klēv) v.t. (past **clove** (klōv), **cleft** (kleft), **cleaved**, p.p. **cloven** (klō´vən), **cleft**, **cleaved**) (poet.) **1** to split apart, esp. with violence, to cut through, to divide forcibly. **2** to make one's way through. ~v.i. **1** to come apart. **2** to split, to crack. **cleavable** a. **cleavage** n. **1** the hollow between a woman's breasts, esp. as revealed by a low-cut dress or top. **2** an act of cleaving. **3** the particular manner in which a mineral with a regular structure may be cleft or split. **cleaver** n. **1** a person or thing that cleaves. **2** a butcher's instrument for cutting meat into joints.

cleave[2] (klēv) v.i. (past **cleaved**, †**clave** (klāv)) (poet.) to stick, to adhere.

clef (klef) n. (Mus.) a symbol at the beginning of a stave denoting the pitch and determining the names of the notes according to their position on the stave.

cleft[1] (kleft) a. divided, split. **cleft lip** n. a congenital fissure of the upper lip. **cleft palate** n. a congenital fissure of the hard palate. **cleft stick** n. a stick split at the end. **in a cleft stick** in a difficult situation, esp. one where going forward or back is impossible.

cleft[2] (kleft) n. a split, a crack, a fissure.

cleg (kleg) n. a gadfly, a horsefly.

clematis (klem´ətis, kləmā´-) n. any ranunculaceous plant of the genus Clematis, including the traveller's joy, C. vitalba.

clement (klem´ənt) a. **1** (of weather) mild. **2** merciful. **3** gentle. **clemency** n. **clemently** adv.

clementine (klem´əntīn, -tēn) n. a small, bright orange citrus fruit with a sweet flavour.

clench (klench) v.t. **1** to close (the hands, teeth etc.) firmly. **2** to grasp firmly. **3** to fasten (a nail etc.) firmly by bending the point; to clinch. **4** to rivet. ~n. **1** the act or action of clenching. **2** the state of being clenched.

clerestory (kliə´stawri), (esp. N Am.) **clearstory** n. (pl. **clerestories, clearstories**) the upper part of the nave, choir or transept of a large church containing windows above the roofs of the aisles.

clergy (klœ´ji) n. (pl. **clergies**) **1** the body of people set apart by ordination for the service of the Christian Church. **2** ecclesiastics collectively. **3** the clergy of a church, district or country. **clergyman** n. (pl. **clergymen**) a member of the clergy, esp. of the Church of England. **clergywoman** n. (pl. **clergywomen**) a female member of the clergy.

cleric (kler´ik) a. clerical. ~n. a member of the clergy.

clerical (kle´rikəl) a. **1** of or relating to the clergy. **2** of or relating to a clerk or office worker. **clerical collar** n. a stiff, white collar fastening at the back, as worn by clergymen. **clerical error** n. an error in copying. **clericalism** n. **clericalist** n. **clerically** adv.

clerihew (kler´ihū) n. a satirical or humorous poem, usu. biographical, consisting of four rhymed lines of uneven length.

clerk (klahk) n. **1** a person employed in an office, bank, shop etc. to assist in correspondence, bookkeeping etc. **2** a person who keeps the records, accounts etc. of a court, council etc. **3** a person who has charge of an office or department, subject to a higher authority, such as a board. **4** the lay officer of a parish church. **5** (N Am.) a shop assistant. **6** (N Am.) a hotel receptionist. ~v.i. to be a clerk. **clerkdom** n. **clerkish** a. **clerkly** a. **clerk of the course** n. an official in charge of administration of a motor- or horse-racing course. **clerk of (the) works** n. a surveyor appointed to supervise building work and test the quality of materials etc. **clerkship** n.

clever (klev´ə) a. **1** intelligent. **2** dexterous, skilful. **3** talented. **4** ingenious. **clever-clever** a. clever in a superficial or showy way. **clever clogs, clever Dick** n. (coll.) a person who shows off their own cleverness. **cleverish** a. **cleverly** adv. **cleverness** n.

clew (kloo) n. (Naut.) **1** the lower corner of a square sail. **2** the aftermost corner of a triangular sail. **3** the cords by which a hammock is suspended. ~v.t. to clew up or down. **to clew down** to unfurl (a sail) by letting down the clews. **to clew up** to truss (a sail) by drawing the clews up to the yard or mast.

clianthus (klian´thəs) n. (pl. **clianthuses**) any plant of the Australian genus Clianthus, with clusters of red flowers.

cliché (klē´shā), **cliche** n. **1** a hackneyed phrase. **2** anything hackneyed or overused. **3** (Print.) a stereotype, esp. a stereotype or electrotype from a block. **clichéd, cliché'd, cliched** a.

click (klik) v.i. **1** to make a slight, sharp noise, as of small hard objects knocking together. **2** (coll.) to fall into place, to make sense (It didn't click until I read her note). **3** (coll.) to be successful.

4 (*coll.*) to become friendly with someone, esp. of the opposite sex (*We clicked the first time we met*). **5** (of horses) to strike shoes together. ~*v.t.* **1** to cause to click (*to click one's fingers*). **2** (*Comput.*) **a** to press (one of the buttons of a computer mouse). **b** to click on. ~*n.* **1** a slight, sharp sound. **2** a sharp clicking sound used in some languages, esp. of southern Africa. **3** the act or action of clicking. **4** a catch for a lock or bolt. **5** a latch. **to click on** to select (an item on a computer screen) by pressing one of the buttons of a computer mouse. **click beetle** *n.* any beetle of the family Elateridae, which can right itself with a click when turned on its back. **clicker** *n.*

client (klī´ənt) *n.* **1** a person who entrusts any business to a lawyer, accountant, architect etc. **2** a customer. **3** a person who is receiving help from a social worker or charitable agency. **clientless** *a.* **client-server** *a.* denoting a computer system in which networked workstations receive data from a central server. **clientship** *n.*

clientele (klēontel´) *n.* **1** clients collectively. **2** customers, patients, the patrons of a theatre or restaurant.

cliff (klif) *n.* a high, steep rock face, esp. on the coast. **cliffhanger** *n.* **1** a story, film etc. that has one in suspense till the end. **2** a highly dramatic, unresolved ending to an instalment of a serial. **3** any similarly suspenseful or exciting situation, such as a sporting contest. **cliffhanging** *a.* **cliff-like** *a.* **cliffy** *a.*

climacteric (klīmak´tərik, -ter´-) *n.* **1** a critical period in human life. **2** the menopause in women, or a corresponding period in men. ~*a.* **1** of or relating to a climacteric. **2** critical. **3** (*Med.*) occurring late in life. **climacterical** (-ter´-) *a.*

climactic CLIMAX.

climate (klī´mət) *n.* **1** the temperature of a place, and its meteorological conditions generally, with regard to their influence on animal and plant life. **2** a region considered with reference to its weather. **3** a prevailing character (*the current economic climate*). **climatic** (-mat´-) *a.* **climatical** (-mat´-) *a.* **climatically** *adv.* **climatology** (-tol´-) *n.* the science of climate. **climatological** (-loj´-) *a.* **climatologist** (-tol´-) *n.*

Usage note See note on *climatic* under CLIMAX.

climax (klī´maks) *n.* **1** the highest point, culmination. **2** an orgasm. **3** a rhetorical figure in which the sense rises gradually in a series of images, each exceeding its predecessor in force or dignity. **4** a stable final stage in the development of a plant or animal community. ~*v.i.* to reach a climax. ~*v.t.* to bring to a climax. **climactic** (-mak´-) *a.* **climactically** *adv.*

Usage note The adjectives *climactic* and *climatic* should not be confused: the first is related to *climax*, and the second to *climate*.

climb (klīm) *v.t.* (*past, p.p.* **climbed,** †**clomb** (klōm)) **1** to ascend, esp. by means of the hands

and feet. **2** (of a plant) to ascend, esp. by means of tendrils. ~*v.i.* **1** to ascend. **2** to move in any direction by grasping or with effort (*He climbed along the ledge*). **3** (of a plant) to grow up a wall, trellis etc., esp. by means of tendrils. **4** to slope upwards. **5** to rise (*The temperature continued to climb*). **6** to rise in rank or prosperity. ~*n.* **1** an ascent. **2** the act of climbing or ascending. **3** a place climbed. **to climb down 1** to descend, esp. using hands and feet. **2** to abandon one's claims, to withdraw from a position, opinion etc. **to climb into 1** to enter, esp. with effort or by climbing (*They climbed into the truck*). **2** to put on (clothes). **climbable** *a.* **climbdown** *n.* a withdrawal from a position, opinion etc. **climber** *n.* **1** a person or thing that climbs, esp. a mountaineer. **2** a creeper or climbing plant. **3** a social climber. **climbing** *n.* mountaineering. ~*a.* that climbs (*a climbing plant*). **climbing frame** *n.* a framework of bars for children to climb on.

clime (klīm) *n.* (*poet.*) **1** a region, a country. **2** a climate.

clinch (klinch) *v.t.* **1** to drive home or settle (an argument, deal etc.). **2** to secure (a nail etc.) by hammering down the point. **3** (*Naut.*) to make (a rope) fast with a clinch. ~*v.i.* **1** to hold an opponent by the arms in boxing etc. **2** (*coll.*) to embrace. ~*n.* **1** the act of clinching. **2** (*Naut.*) a method of fastening large ropes by a half-hitch. **3** a grip or hold, esp. in boxing etc. **4** (*coll.*) an embrace. **clincher** *n.* **1** a person or thing that clinches. **2** (*coll.*) a conclusive argument or statement. **clincher-built** *a.* CLINKER-BUILT (under CLINKER²). **clinch nail** *n.* a nail with a malleable end adapted for clinching.

cline (klīn) *n.* **1** (*Biol.*) a gradation of forms seen in a single species over a given area. **2** a series of gradations forming a continuum. **clinal** (klī´nəl) *a.*

cling (kling) *v.i.* (*past, p.p.* **clung** (klŭng)) **1** to adhere closely and tenaciously, esp. by twining, grasping or embracing. **2** to be stubbornly or tenaciously faithful (to). ~*n.* a clingstone. **clinger** *n.* **cling film** *n.* a kind of thin polythene film which clings to itself or anything else, used for airtight wrapping. **clingingly** *adv.* **clingstone** *n.* a kind of peach in which the pulp adheres closely to the stone. **clingy** *a.* (*comp.* **clingier,** *superl.* **clingiest**) **1** clinging. **2** showing great emotional dependence. **clinginess** *n.*

clinic (klin´ik) *n.* **1** a private hospital, or one specializing in one type of ailment or treatment. **2** a specialist department in a general hospital, esp. for outpatients. **3** medical and surgical instruction, esp. in hospitals. **4** a session in which advice and instruction are given on any topic. **clinical** *a.* **1** (*Med.*) of or relating to a patient in bed, or to instruction given to students in a hospital ward. **2** detached, unemotional. **3** (of a room etc.) bare or plainly furnished; simple and functional. **clinical death** *n.* death judged by observing the condition of the patient. **clinically**

adv. **clinical medicine** *n.* the branch of medicine which deals with the treatment of patients. **clinical thermometer** *n.* a thermometer for taking the temperature of a patient. **clinician** (-nish´ən) *n.*

clink[1] (klingk) *n.* a sharp, ringing sound, as when glasses or metallic bodies are struck lightly together. ~*v.i.* to make this sound. ~*v.t.* to cause to clink. **clinkstone** *n.* a feldspathic rock that clinks when struck.

clink[2] (klingk) *n.* (*sl.*) a prison (*in clink*).

clinker[1] (kling´kə) *n.* **1** vitrified slag. **2** fused cinders. **3** (*sl.*) anything outstanding or remarkable. **4** (*N Am., coll.*) a mistake.

clinker[2] (kling´kə) *n.* (*North.*) a clinch nail. **clinker-built** *a.* (*Naut.*) built with overlapping planks fastened with clinched nails, as distinct from *carvel-built.*

clip[1] (klip) *v.t.* (*pres.p.* **clipping**, *past, p.p.* **clipped**) **1** to cut with shears or scissors. **2** to trim. **3** to cut away, to cut out (*to clip a coupon from a magazine*). **4** to pare the edges of (a coin etc.). **5** to cut (a word) short by omitting letters, syllables etc. **6** to cancel (a ticket) by snipping a piece out. **7** (*coll.*) to hit sharply. **8** (*sl.*) to swindle. ~*v.i.* to run or go swiftly. ~*n.* **1** an act of clipping, a shearing or trimming. **2** an extract from a film. **3** (*coll.*) a sharp blow. **4** all the wool clipped from a sheep or flock in a season. **5** (*sl.*) a fast rate. **clip joint** *n.* (*sl.*) a nightclub etc. which overcharges. **clippable** *a.* **clipper** *n.* **1** a person or thing that clips. **2** (*pl.*) a tool for clipping hair, nails etc. **3** a fast sailing vessel with a long sharp bow and raking masts. **clipping** *n.* **1** a piece clipped off. **2** (*esp. N Am.*) a press cutting.

clip[2] (klip) *n.* an appliance for gripping, holding or attaching (*a paper clip*). ~*v.t.* (*pres.p.* **clipping**, *past, p.p.* **clipped**) **1** to fasten with a clip. **2** to clasp, to embrace. **3** to encircle, to surround closely. **clipboard** *n.* a flat board with a spring clip at one end, to hold paper for writing. **clip-on** *a.* that can be attached by a clip (*clip-on sunglasses*).

clip-clop CLOP.

clique (klēk) *n.* an exclusive set. **cliquey, cliquy** *a.* (*comp.* **cliquier**, *superl.* **cliquiest**). **cliquish** *a.* **cliquishness** *n.* **cliquism** *n.*

C.Lit. *abbr.* Companion of Literature.

clitoris (klit´əris) *n.* (*pl.* **clitorises, clitorides** (-dēz)) a small erectile body situated at the apex of the vulva and corresponding to the penis in the male. **clitoral** *a.* **clitoridectomy** (-dek´təmi) *n.* (*pl.* **clitoridectomies**) surgical removal of the clitoris.

Cllr *abbr.* Councillor.

cloaca (klōā´kə) *n.* (*pl.* **cloacae** (-sē, -kē)) **1** the excretory cavity in certain animals, birds, insects etc. **2** a sewer. **cloacal** *a.*

cloak (klōk), †**cloke** *n.* **1** a loose, wide, outer garment, usu. sleeveless. **2** a covering. **3** a disguise, a blind, a pretext. **4** (*pl.*) a cloakroom. ~*v.t.* **1** to cover with or as with a cloak. **2** to disguise. **3** to hide. **under the cloak of** hidden by; using as a

disguise or pretext. **cloak-and-dagger** *a.* involving mystery and intrigue. **cloakroom** *n.* **1** a room where coats, small parcels etc. can be deposited. **2** (*euphem.*) a lavatory.

clobber (klob´ə) *n.* (*sl.*) clothes. ~*v.t.* **1** to beat, to batter. **2** to defeat overwhelmingly. **3** to criticize harshly. **clobberer** *n.*

cloche (klosh) *n.* **1** a glass cover, orig. bell-shaped, put over young or tender plants to preserve them from frost. **2** a close-fitting bell-shaped hat.

clock[1] (klok) *n.* **1** an instrument for measuring and indicating time (*an alarm clock; a digital clock*). **2** (*coll.*) a taximeter or speedometer. **3** the seed-head of a dandelion or similar flower. **4** (*sl.*) a person's face. ~*v.t.* **1** to time using a clock or stopwatch. **2** (*sl.*) to hit. **3** (*sl.*) to see, notice. **against the clock 1** (of a task etc.) to be finished by a certain time. **2** (of a race etc.) timed by a stopwatch or similar device. **to clock in/ on** to register on a specially constructed clock the time of arrival at work. **to clock out/ off** to register on a specially constructed clock the time of departure from work. **to clock up** to register (a specified time, speed etc.). **clock golf** *n.* a putting game played on a lawn marked out like the dial of a clock. **clockmaker** *n.* a person who makes or repairs clocks. **clockmaking** *n.* **clock radio** *n.* an alarm clock combined with a radio, which uses the radio instead of a bell. **clock tower** *n.* a tower with a large clock at the top, esp. as part of a church or a public building. **clockwise** *adv.* in the direction of the hands of a clock. **clockwork** *n.* **1** the mechanism of a clock. **2** a train of wheels producing motion in a similar fashion. **like clockwork** with unfailing regularity; mechanically, automatically; very smoothly (*to go like clockwork*).

clock[2] (klok) *n.* an ornamental pattern on the side of the leg of a stocking. **clocked** *a.*

clod (klod) *n.* **1** a lump of earth or clay. **2** a mass of earth and turf. **3** the shoulder part of the neck of beef. **4** (*coll.*) a foolish person. **cloddish** *a.* loutish, coarse, clumsy, foolish. **cloddishly** *adv.* **cloddishness** *n.* **clodhopper** *n.* (*coll.*) **1** an awkward rustic, a bumpkin. **2** a foolish or clumsy person. **3** (*usu. pl.*) a large, heavy shoe. **clodhopping** *a.*

clog (klog) *n.* **1** a kind of shoe with a wooden sole. **2** a boot with a metal rim. **3** a block of wood attached to a person or animal to hinder free movement. ~*v.t.* (*pres.p.* **clogging**, *past, p.p.* **clogged**) **1** to obstruct. **2** to choke up. **3** to hinder. **4** to encumber or hamper with a weight. ~*v.i.* to be obstructed or encumbered with anything heavy or adhesive. **cloggy** *a.* (*comp.* **cloggier**, *superl.* **cloggiest**) **1** clogging. **2** adhesive, sticky.

cloisonné (klwazonã´, klwah´-, klwahzon´-) *a.* partitioned, divided into compartments. ~*n.* cloisonné enamel. **cloisonné enamel** *n.* enamel-work in which the coloured parts are separated by metallic partitions.

cloister (klois´tə) n. **1** a series of covered passages usu. arranged along the sides of a quadrangle in monastic, cathedral or collegiate buildings. **2** a place of religious seclusion. **3** a religious house or convent. ~v.t. to shut up in or as in a cloister or convent. **cloistered** a. **1** secluded. **2** sheltered from the world, reality etc. **3** monastic. **cloistral** a.

clomp (klomp) v.i. to walk or tread in a heavy and clumsy fashion.

clone (klōn) n. **1** a number of organisms produced asexually from a single progenitor. **2** any such organism. **3** (coll.) an exact copy. ~v.t. to produce a clone of. **clonal** a. **clonally** adv.

clonk (klongk) v.i. to make a short dull sound, as of two solid objects striking each other. ~v.t. (coll.) to hit. ~n. a short dull sound.

clonus (klō´nəs) n. a muscular spasm with alternate contraction and relaxation, as opposed to tonic spasm. **clonic** (klon´-) a.

clop (klop), **clip-clop** (klip-) n. the sound of a horse's hoof striking the ground. ~v.i. (pres.p. **clopping**, **clip-clopping**, past, p.p. **clopped**, **clip-clopped**) to make such a sound.

close[1] (klōs) a. **1** near in time or space. **2** intimate, familiar (a close friend). **3** nearly alike. **4** almost equal (a close contest). **5** solid, dense, compact. **6** concise, compressed. **7** attentive, concentrated (a close examination). **8** following the original closely. **9** accurate, precise, minute. **10** without ventilation, oppressive, stifling. **11** (of the weather) warm and damp. **12** closed, shut fast. **13** pronounced with the lips or mouth partly shut (a close vowel). **14** confined, shut in. **15** restricted, limited, reserved. **16** retired, secret, reticent. **17** difficult to obtain, scarce. **18** parsimonious, miserly. ~adv. **1** near. **2** closely, tightly, thickly or compactly. ~n. **1** an enclosure or enclosed place. **2** a road that is closed at one end. **3** a narrow passage or street. **4** the precincts of a cathedral or abbey. **5** a small enclosed field or yard. **6** (Sc.) an entry from the street to building or courtyard. **close on/ upon** nearly (We lived there close on twenty years). **close-cropped** a. cut very short (close-cropped hair). **close-fisted**, †**close-handed** a. niggardly, miserly. **close-fistedness** n. **close-fitting** a. (of clothes) fitting tightly to the outline of the body. **close-grained** a. (of wood etc.) with fibres or particles densely packed. **close harmony** n. a kind of singing in which all the parts lie close together. **close-hauled** a. (Naut.) kept as near as possible to the point from which the wind blows. **close-in** a. **1** at short range. **2** close to the centre. **close-knit** a. closely united (a close-knit family). **closely** adv. **closeness** n. **close quarters** n.pl. **1** direct contact. **2** proximity. **at close quarters 1** in direct contact, esp. with an enemy. **2** very near. **close-range** a. **1** at a short distance. **2** from a short distance. **close-run** a. won by a narrow margin (a close-run election). **close season** n. the breeding season, during which it is illegal to kill

certain fish or game. **close-set** a. close together. **close shave** n. a narrow escape. **close-up** n. **1** a view taken with the camera at very close range. **2** any intimate view or examination. **closish** a.

close[2] (klōz) v.t. **1** to shut. **2** to fill (up) an opening. **3** to enclose, to shut in. **4** to bring or unite together. **5** to be the end of, to conclude. **6** to complete, to settle (to close a deal). ~v.i. **1** to shut. **2** to come to an end, to cease. **3** to stop doing business, esp. at the end of the working day (The bank closes at five). **4** to agree, to come to terms. **5** to grapple, to come to hand-to-hand fighting. **6** to coalesce. ~n. **1** the act of closing. **2** an end, a conclusion. **3** (Mus.) a cadence. **to close down 1** (of a factory, shop etc.) to cease work or business, esp. permanently. **2** (of a radio or television station) to go off the air. **to close in 1** to shut in, to enclose. **2** to come nearer. **3** to get shorter (The days are closing in). **to close on 1** to shut over. **2** to grasp. **3** to catch up with. **to close out** to terminate (a business, an account etc.). **to close up 1** to block up, to fill in. **2** to come together. **to close with 1** to agree or consent to. **2** to unite with. **3** to grapple with (to close with the enemy). **closable** a. **closed** a. **1** shut. **2** not doing business, esp. temporarily (Most of the shops were closed). **3** restricted, exclusive (a closed society). **4** self-contained. **closed book** n. **1** a subject one knows nothing about. **2** a matter that has been concluded. **closed circuit** n. an electrical circuit with a complete, unbroken path for the current to flow through. **closed-circuit television** n. a television system for a restricted number of viewers in which the signal is transmitted to the receiver by cable. **closed-end** a. limited, finite; not open-ended. **closed-in** a. **1** enclosed. **2** restricted. **closed season** n. CLOSE SEASON (under CLOSE[1]). **closed shop** n. a workplace where all employees must be union members. **closed syllable** n. a syllable that ends in a consonant. **close-down** n. the act of closing down.

closet (kloz´it) n. **1** a small room for privacy and retirement. **2** a water closet. **3** (esp. N Am.) a cupboard. ~a. **1** secret. **2** private. ~v.t. (pres.p. **closeting**, past, p.p. **closeted**) to shut away in a private room for consultation etc.

closure (klō´zhə) n. **1** the act of closing. **2** the state of being closed. **3** something that closes or seals a container etc. **4** the power of terminating debate in a legislative or deliberative assembly. ~v.t. to apply this power to (a debate, speaker or motion).

clot (klot) n. **1** a small coagulated mass of soft or fluid matter, esp. of blood. **2** a clod, a lump, a ball. **3** (sl.) a silly person. ~v.t. (pres.p. **clotting**, past, p.p. **clotted**) to cause to form clots. ~v.i. to form into clots. **clotted cream** n. cream produced in clots on new milk when it is simmered, orig. made in Devon. **clotty** a.

cloth (kloth) n. (pl. **cloths** (kloths, klodhz)) **1** a woven fabric of wool, cotton, silk etc. used for garments or other coverings. **2** any textile fabric, material. **3** a piece of this. **4** a tablecloth. **5** woven woollen fabric. **6** the dress of a profession, esp. the clergy (from their usu. wearing black cloth). **7** this profession, the clergy. **cloth cap** *n.* a flat cap with a peak. **cloth-cap** *a.* (*sometimes derog.*) belonging to or characteristic of the working class. **cloth-eared** *a.* (*coll.*) **1** deaf. **2** inattentive.

clothe (klōdh) *v.t.* (*past, p.p.* **clothed,** (*poet.*) **clad** (klad)) **1** to provide or cover with or as with clothes. **2** to invest (with a quality). **clothes** (klōdhz, klōz) *n.pl.* **1** garments, dress. **2** bedclothes. **clothes horse** *n.* **1** a frame for drying clothes on. **2** (*coll.*) a fashionably dressed person. **clothes line** *n.* a line for drying clothes on. **clothes-peg,** (*N Am.*) **clothes-pin** *n.* a wooden or plastic clip used to fasten clothes on a line. **clothes prop** *n.* a pole for supporting a clothes line. **clothing** *n.* clothes, dress.

clothier (klō´dhiə) *n.* **1** a manufacturer of cloth. **2** a person who deals in cloth or clothing.

cloud (klowd) *n.* **1** a mass of visible vapour condensed into minute drops and floating in the upper regions of the atmosphere. **2** a volume of smoke or dust resembling a cloud. **3** a great number of birds, insects, snowflakes, arrows etc., moving in a body. **4** a dimness or patchiness in liquid. **5** the dusky veins or markings in marble, precious stones etc. **6** a veil which obscures or darkens. **7** obscurity, bewilderment, confusion of ideas. **8** suspicion, trouble. **9** any temporary depression. ~*v.t.* **1** to cover with clouds, to darken. **2** to mark with cloudlike spots or patches. **3** to make gloomy or sullen. **4** to sully, to stain. **5** to impair. ~*v.i.* to grow cloudy (*The sky clouded over*). **in the clouds 1** mystical, unreal. **2** absent-minded. **on cloud nine** (*coll.*) very happy, elated. **under a cloud** in temporary disgrace or misfortune; under suspicion. **cloud base** *n.* the lowest layer of cloud or clouds. **cloudburst** *n.* a sudden and heavy fall of rain. **cloud chamber** *n.* an apparatus in which high-energy particles are tracked as they pass through a vapour. **cloud cover** *n.* **1** a mass of unbroken cloud or clouds. **2** the extent of this. **cloud-cuckoo-land, cloud-land** *n.* **1** a utopia. **2** a fantastic scheme for social, political or economic reform. **clouded leopard** *n.* a leopard-like arboreal mammal, *Neofelis nebulosa*. **cloudless** *a.* **cloudlessly** *adv.* **cloudlessness** *n.* **cloudlike** *a.* **cloudscape** *n.* a view or picture of clouds. **cloudy** *a.* (*comp.* **cloudier,** *superl.* **cloudiest**) **1** consisting of or covered with clouds. **2** not transparent (*a cloudy liquid*). **3** marked with veins or spots. **4** obscure, confused. **cloudiness** *n.*

clout (klowt) *n.* **1** a blow, esp. on the head. **2** (*coll.*) power, influence. **3** (*dial.*) a piece of cloth, rag etc. **4** (*dial.*) a piece of clothing. **5** a clout-nail. ~*v.t.* **1** to strike, esp. heavily. **2** to patch, to mend roughly. **clout-nail** *n.* a short nail with a large flat head for fastening metal to wood, or to stud the soles of heavy boots and shoes.

clove[1] (klōv) *n.* **1** a dried, unexpanded flower bud of the tree *Eugenia aromatica*, used as a spice. **2** this tree. **clove gillyflower, clove pink** *n.* any sweet-scented double variety of *Dianthus caryophyllus*.

clove[2] (klōv) *n.* a small bulb forming one part of a compound bulb, as in garlic, the shallot etc.

clove[3] CLEAVE[1].

clove hitch (klōv hich´) *n.* a knot used to fasten a rope round a spar or another rope.

cloven[1] (klō´vən) *a.* **1** divided into two parts. **2** cleft, split. **cloven hoof, cloven foot** *n.* **1** a hoof divided in the centre, as those of the ruminants. **2** an emblem of the god Pan or the Devil. **3** an indication of guile or evil (*to show the cloven hoof*). **cloven-hoofed, cloven-footed** *a.*

cloven[2] CLEAVE[1].

clover (klō´və) *n.* any plant of the genus *Trifolium*, with dense flower heads and usu. trifoliate leaves, used for fodder. **in clover 1** in enjoyable circumstances. **2** in luxury.

clown (klown) *n.* **1** a comic entertainer, usu. with traditional make-up and costume, in a circus or pantomime. **2** a buffoon. **3** a clumsy or foolish person. **4** a rough, ill-bred person. ~*v.i.* to play silly jokes, to act the buffoon. ~*v.t.* to perform in the manner of a clown. **clownery** *n.* **clownish** *a.* **clownishly** *adv.* **clownishness** *n.*

cloy (kloi) *v.t.* **1** to satiate, to glut. **2** to tire with sweetness, richness or excess. **cloyingly** *adv.*

cloze test (klōz) *n.* a test of readability or comprehension in which words omitted from the text must be supplied by the reader.

club[1] (klŭb) *n.* **1** a piece of wood with one end thicker and heavier than the other, used as a weapon. **2** a stick bent and usu. weighted at the end for driving a ball, esp. in golf. **3** (*pl.*) one of the four suits at cards denoted by a black trefoil. **4** a card of this suit. **5** a club-shaped structure or organ. ~*v.t.* (*pres.p.* **clubbing,** *past, p.p.* **clubbed**) to beat with a club. **club foot** *n.* a short deformed foot. **club-footed** *a.* **clubmoss** *n.* a species of moss of the family Lycopodiaceae, with seed vessels pointing straight upwards. **clubroot** *n.* a disease of plants of the *Brassica* (cabbage) genus in which the lower part of the stem becomes swollen and misshapen owing to the attacks of larvae. **club sandwich** *n.* a sandwich made with three slices of bread and two different fillings.

club[2] (klŭb) *n.* **1** an association of persons combined for some common object, such as social intercourse, politics, sport etc., governed by self-imposed regulations. **2** the building in which such an association meets; a clubhouse. **3** the body of members collectively. **4** a commercial organization that offers discounts etc. to subscribers (*a book club*). **5** a nightclub. ~*v.t.* (*pres.p.* **clubbing,** *past, p.p.* **clubbed**) to contribute for a common object or to a common stock. ~*v.i.* **1** to join (together) for a common object (*We clubbed together to buy him a present*). **2** (*coll.*) to go to nightclubs. **in the club** (*sl.*) pregnant. **clubbable**

a. sociable. **clubbability** (-bil´-), **clubbableness** *n.* **clubber** *n.* **clubby** *a.* (*comp.* **clubbier,** *superl.* **clubbiest**) (*esp. N Am.*) sociable. **club car** *n.* (*N Am.*) a railway coach designed like a lounge, usu. with a bar. **club class** *n.* a class of air travel designed for business people. **clubhouse** *n.* the building occupied by a club, or in which it holds its meetings. **clubmate** *n.* a fellow member of a club, esp. a sports club. **club soda** *n.* (*N Am.*) soda water.

cluck (klŭk) *n.* **1** the guttural call of a hen. **2** any similar sound. **3** (*sl.*) a foolish person. *~v.i.* to utter a cluck. *~v.t.* to call or express with a cluck. **clucky** *a.* broody.

clue (kloo) *n.* **1** anything that serves as a guide, direction or hint for the solution of a problem or mystery, or as evidence in the detection of crime. **2** the thread of a story. *~v.t.* (*pres.p.* **cluing, clue-ing,** *past, p.p.* **clued**) to provide with a clue. **not to have a clue 1** (*coll.*) to have no idea whatever. **2** (*coll.*) to be utterly incompetent. **to clue in/ up** (*sl.*) to inform. **clued-up** *a.* (*coll.*) well informed. **clueless** *a.* (*coll.*) **1** ignorant. **2** stupid. **cluelessly** *adv.* **cluelessness** *n.*

clump (klŭmp) *n.* **1** a thick cluster of trees, shrubs or flowers. **2** a thick mass of small objects, organisms, cells etc. **3** a thick piece of leather fastened onto the sole of a boot. **4** a heavy blow. *~v.i.* **1** to walk or tread in a heavy and clumsy fashion. **2** to form or gather into a clump or clumps. *~v.t.* **1** to make a clump of. **2** (*sl.*) to beat. **clumpy** *a.* (*comp.* **clumpier,** *superl.* **clumpiest**).

clumsy (klŭm´zi) *a.* (*comp.* **clumsier,** *superl.* **clumsiest**) **1** awkward, ungainly. **2** ill-constructed, difficult to use. **3** rough, rude, tactless. **clumsily** *adv.* **clumsiness** *n.*

clung CLING.

clunk (klŭngk) *v.i.* to make a short, dull sound, as of metal striking a hard surface. *~n.* such a sound. **clunker** *n.* (*N Am., coll.*) **1** a useless or dilapidated machine. **2** a failure. **clunky** *a.* (*comp.* **clunkier,** *superl.* **clunkiest**) **1** clunking. **2** (*N Am.*) heavy, unwieldy.

cluster (klŭs´tə) *n.* **1** a number of things of the same kind growing or joined together. **2** a bunch. **3** a number of persons or things gathered or situated close together. **4** a group, a crowd. *~v.i.* to come or to grow into a cluster or clusters. *~v.t.* to bring or cause to come into a cluster or clusters. **cluster bomb** *n.* a bomb which explodes to scatter a number of smaller bombs. **cluster fly** *n.* a dipterous fly, *Pollenia rudis,* that gathers in large numbers in the autumn. **cluster pine** *n.* the pinaster.

clutch[1] (klŭch) *n.* **1** a snatch, a grip, a grasp. **2** (*pl.*) claws, grasping hands, tyrannical power. **3** a device for connecting and disconnecting two revolving shafts in an engine. **4** the pedal that operates this device in a motor vehicle. **5** a gripping device. *~v.t.* **1** to seize, clasp or grip with the hand. **2** to snatch. **clutch bag** *n.* a woman's handbag, without a handle, carried in the hand.

clutch[2] (klŭch) *n.* **1** a set of eggs to be hatched. **2** a brood of chickens.

clutter (klŭt´ə) *v.t.* to fill or strew with clutter. *~n.* a mess, a disorderly collection of things. **to clutter up** to fill untidily.

clypeus (klip´iəs) *n.* (*pl.* **clypei** (-iī)) the shield-like part of an insect's head, which joins the labrum. **clypeal, clypeate** (-ət), **clypeiform** (klip´-ifawm) *a.*

Cm *chem. symbol* curium.

cm *abbr.* centimetre(s).

Cmdr. *abbr.* Commander.

Cmdre. *abbr.* Commodore.

CMG *abbr.* Companion of (the Order of) St Michael and St George.

CNS *abbr.* central nervous system.

CO *abbr.* **1** Commanding Officer. **2** conscientious objector.

Co *chem. symbol* cobalt.

Co. *abbr.* **1** company. **2** county.

co. (kō) *n.* (*coll.*) the others, similar or related people or things; only in *and co.* (*I've invited Rachel and co.*).

c/o *abbr.* care of.

co- (kō) *pref.* **1** with, together, jointly, mutually, as in *coalesce, cooperate.* **2** joint, mutual, as in *co-author, co-heir.* **3** (*Math.*) of the complement of an angle, as in *cosecant, cosine.*

coach (kōch) *n.* **1** a long-distance bus. **2** a railway carriage. **3** a large, closed, four-wheeled, horse-drawn vehicle, used for purposes of state, or formerly for travelling. **4** a person who trains sports players. **5** a tutor who prepares students for examinations. **6** any specialized instructor (*a drama coach*). **7** (*N Am.*) the economy class area of an aircraft. *~v.t.* **1** to train. **2** to prepare for an examination. **3** to instruct or advise in preparation for any event. *~v.i.* **1** to travel in a coach. **2** to work as a coach. **coachbuilder** *n.* a person who builds or repairs the bodywork of road or rail vehicles. **coach-built** *a.* (of vehicles) built individually by craftsmen. **coachful** *n.* as many as a coach will hold. **coach house** *n.* an outhouse to keep a horse-drawn coach or carriage in. **coachload** *n.* a coachful (*a coachload of tourists*). **coachman** *n.* (*pl.* **coachmen**) the driver of a horse-drawn coach. **coach station** *n.* a terminus or stopping place for long-distance buses. **coachwork** *n.* the bodywork of a road or rail vehicle.

coadjutor (kōaj´ətə) *n.* an assistant, a helper, esp. to a bishop.

coagulate (kōag´ūlāt) *v.t., v.i.* **1** to curdle, to clot. **2** to change from a fluid into a semi-solid mass. **3** to solidify. **coagulable** *a.* **coagulant** *n.* a substance which causes coagulation. **coagulation** (-lā´shən) *n.* **coagulative** *a.* **coagulator** *n.* **coagulum** (-ləm) *n.* (*pl.* **coagula** (-lə)) a coagulated mass.

coal (kōl) *n.* **1** a black, solid, opaque carbonaceous substance of vegetable origin, obtained from the strata usu. underground, and used for fuel. **2** a piece of this. **3** a piece of wood or other combustible substance, ignited, burning or charred. **4** a cinder. ~*v.t.* to supply with coal. ~*v.i.* to take in a supply of coal. **to carry coals to Newcastle** to bring things to a place where they abound; to do anything superfluous or unnecessary. **to haul over the coals 1** to call to account. **2** to reprimand. **coal-black** *a.* as black as coal. **coal dust** *n.* powdered coal. **coaler** *n.* a ship that transports coal. **coalface** *n.* the exposed surface of a coal-seam. **coalfield** *n.* an area where coal abounds. **coal-fired** *a.* (of a furnace, heating system etc.) fuelled by coal. **coalfish** *n.* (*pl. in general* **coalfish,** *in particular* **coalfishes**) the saithe or coley, *Pollachius virens,* an edible fish resembling the cod. **coal gas** *n.* a mixture of gases obtained from coal and used for lighting and heating. **coal-hole** *n.* a small cellar for storing coal. **coalhouse** *n.* a building where coal is stored. **coalless** *a.* **coalman** *n.* (*pl.* **coalmen**) a person who sells, carries or delivers coal. **coal mine** *n.* a mine from which coal is obtained. **coal miner** *n.* **coal mining** *n.* **coal scuttle** *n.* a fireside utensil for holding coal. **coal-seam** *n.* a stratum of or containing coal. **coal tar** *n.* tar produced in the destructive distillation of bituminous coal. **coal tit** *n.* COALMOUSE. **coaly** *a.*

coalesce (kōəles´) *v.i.* **1** to fuse into one. **2** to combine, to grow together. **3** to form a coalition. **coalescence** *n.* **coalescent** *a.*

coalition (kōəlish´ən) *n.* **1** a combination of persons, parties or states, having different interests. **2** a union of separate bodies into one body or mass. **coalitionist** *n.*

coalmouse (kōl´mows), **colemouse** *n.* (*pl.* **coalmice** (-mīs), **colemice**) a small dark bird, *Parus ater,* also called *coal tit* or *cole tit.*

coaming (kō´ming) *n.* (*Naut.*) a raised border round a hatch etc. for keeping water out of the hold.

coarse (kaws) *a.* **1** large in size or rough in texture. **2** rude, rough, vulgar. **3** unpolished, unrefined. **4** indecent, obscene. **5** common, of average or inferior quality. **coarse fish** *n.* any freshwater fish not of the salmon family. **coarse fishing** *n.* **coarse-grained** *a.* **1** having a coarse grain. **2** unrefined, vulgar. **coarsely** *adv.* **coarsen** *v.t.* to make coarse. ~*v.i.* to become coarse. **coarseness** *n.* **coarsish** *a.*

coast (kōst) *n.* **1** that part of the border of a country where the land meets the sea. **2** the seashore. **3** the seaside. **4** a swift rush downhill on a bicycle or in a car, without using motive power or applying brakes. **5** (*NAm.*) a toboggan slide. ~*v.t.* **1** to sail by or near to. **2** to keep close to. ~*v.i.* **1** to descend an incline on a bicycle or in a motor vehicle without applying motive power or brakes. **2** to proceed without any positive effort. **3** (*NAm.*) to slide down snow or ice on a toboggan. **4** to sail near or in sight of the shore. **5** to sail from port to port in the same country. **coastal** *a.* **coaster** *n.* **1** a ship that sails from port to port in the same country. **2** a small tray for a bottle or

decanter on a table. **3** a small mat under a glass. **4** (*NAm.*) a toboggan. **5** (*NAm.*) a roller coaster. **coastguard** *n.* **1** a member of a body of people who watch the coast to save those in danger, give warning of wrecks, and prevent the illegal landing of persons and goods. **2** this body of people. **coastline** *n.* the line or outline of a coast. **coast to coast** *a., adv.* from coast to coast, across a whole continent. **coastwise** *a., adv.* along the coast.

coat (kōt) *n.* **1** an outer garment with sleeves; an overcoat or jacket. **2** the hair, fur or natural external covering of an animal. **3** any integument, tunic or covering. **4** a layer of any substance covering and protecting another (*a coat of paint*). ~*v.t.* **1** to cover. **2** to spread with a layer of anything. **coat check** *n.* (*NAm.*) a cloakroom with an attendant. **coat checker** *n.* (*NAm.*) a cloakroom attendant. **coat dress** *n.* a woman's dress styled like a coat. **coat-hanger** *n.* a piece of shaped wood, wire, plastic etc. for hanging up clothes. **coating** *n.* **1** a covering, layer or integument. **2** the act of covering. **3** a substance spread over as a cover or for protection. **4** cloth for coats. **coatless** *a.* **coat of arms** *n.* the armorial bearings of a family, corporation etc. **coat of mail** *n.* armour worn on the upper part of the body, consisting of iron rings or scales fastened on a stout linen or leather jacket. **coat-stand** *n.* a stand with hooks or pegs for hanging coats etc. on. **coat-tail** *n.* either of the long, tapering flaps at the back of a tailcoat.

coati (kōah´ti), **coatimundi** (-mŭn´di) *n.* (*pl.* **coatis, coatimundis**) a racoon-like carnivorous mammal of the genera *Nasua* or *Nasuella,* with a long flexible snout, from Central or S America.

co-author (kōaw´thə) *n.* a person who writes a book together with someone else. ~*v.t.* to be a co-author of.

coax[1] (kōks) *v.t.* **1** to persuade by tenderness or flattery. **2** to wheedle, to cajole. **3** to obtain by coaxing (*They coaxed the truth out of her*). **4** to handle or manipulate with care and patience (*to coax a machine to work*). **coaxer** *n.* **coaxingly** *adv.*

coax[2] (kō´aks) *n.* (*coll.*) coaxial cable.

coaxial (kōak´siəl), **coaxal** (-səl) *a.* having a common axis. **coaxial cable** *n.* a cable having a central conductor within an outer tubular conductor. **coaxially** *adv.*

cob (kob) *n.* **1** a lump or ball of anything, esp. coal. **2** a small round loaf. **3** a spike of maize; a corn cob. **4** a cobnut. **5** a short stout horse for riding. **6** a male swan. **cob loaf** *n.* a small round loaf. **cobnut** *n.* a variety of the cultivated hazel.

cobalt (kō´bawlt) *n.* **1** (*Chem.*) a greyish-white, brittle, hard metallic element, at. no. 27, chem. symbol Co. **2** cobalt blue. ~*a.* deep blue. **cobalt blue** *n.* **1** a deep blue pigment containing cobalt aluminate. **2** the colour of this pigment. **cobaltic** (-bawl´-) *a.* **cobaltous** (-bawl´-) *a.*

cobber (kob´ə) *n.* (*Austral., New Zeal., coll.*) a friend, a mate.

cobble (kob´əl) n. 1 (also **cobblestone**) a rounded stone or pebble used for paving. 2 (usu. pl.) a roundish lump of coal. ~v.t. to pave with cobbles.

cobbler (kob´lə) n. 1 a person who mends shoes. 2 a mender or patcher. 3 a clumsy worker. 4 a type of pie with a topping of scones or a thick, crunchy crust. 5 a cooling drink of wine, sugar, lemon and ice. 6 (pl., sl.) nonsense. **cobble** (kob´əl) v.t. 1 to mend or patch (esp. shoes). 2 to make or do clumsily (to cobble together a meal).

co-belligerent (kōbəlij´ərənt) a. waging war jointly with another. ~n. a nation that joins another in waging war. **co-belligerence, co-belligerency** n.

cobra (kō´brə, kob´-) n. (pl. **cobras**) any venomous snake of the genus Naja, from tropical Africa and Asia, which distends the skin of the neck into a kind of hood when excited.

cobweb (kob´web) n. 1 the web or net spun by a spider for its prey. 2 the material or a thread of this. 3 anything flimsy and worthless. 4 (pl.) old musty rubbish. **to blow away the cobwebs** to refresh oneself in the open air. **cobwebbed** a. **cobwebby** a.

coca (kō´kə) n. 1 the dried leaves of a S American plant, Erythroxylum coca chewed as a narcotic stimulant. 2 the plant itself.

cocaine (kōkān´) n. a drug prepared from coca leaves or synthetically, used as a narcotic stimulant and medicinally as a local anaesthetic.

coccus (kok´əs) n. (pl. **cocci** (kok´sī)) a spherical bacterium. **coccal** a. **coccoid** a.

coccyx (kok´siks) n. (pl. **coccyxes, coccyges** (-sijēz)) the lower solid portion of the vertebral column, the homologue in human of the tail of the lower vertebrates. **coccygeal** (koksij´iəl) a.

cochineal (kochinēl´) n. a red substance obtained from the dried bodies of the female cochineal insect, used in dyeing, as a food colouring and in the manufacture of scarlet and carmine pigments. **cochineal insect** n. the insect, Dactylopius coccus, from which cochineal is obtained.

cochlea (kok´liə) n. (pl. **cochleae** (-liē)) the anterior spiral division of the internal ear. **cochlear** a.

cock[1] (kok) n. 1 the male of birds, particularly of the domestic fowl. 2 a male salmon, lobster or crab. 3 a vane in the form of a cock, a weathercock. 4 (sl.) a friend, a good fellow. 5 (taboo sl.) the penis. 6 (taboo sl.) nonsense. 7 the hammer of a gun or pistol, which strikes against a piece of flint or a percussion cap to produce a spark and explode the charge. 8 the position of this when ready to fire. 9 a tap or valve for regulating the flow through a spout or pipe. ~v.t. to raise the cock of (a firearm). **cock-a-doodle-doo** (-ədoodəldoo´) n., int. the crow of the domestic cock. **cock-a-hoop** a. triumphant, exultant; strutting or crowing. ~adv. exultantly, with crowing and boastfulness. **cock and bull story** n. a silly, exaggerated story. **cockcrow, cockcrowing** n. early

dawn. **cock-eye** n. (coll.) an eye that squints. **cock-eyed** a. (coll.) 1 having squinting eyes. 2 irregular, ill-arranged. 3 askew. 4 eccentric, absurd (a cock-eyed scheme). **cockfight** n. a battle or match of gamecocks as a sport. **cockfighting** n. **cock-of-the-walk** n. 1 a masterful person. 2 a leader, a chief. **cockpit** n. 1 the part of the fuselage of an aircraft where the pilot and crew are accommodated. 2 the driver's compartment of a racing car. 3 a sheltered space in a sailing yacht or other small boat, where the helm is situated. 4 a part of the lower deck of a man-of-war, used as a hospital in action. 5 an area where many battles take place (Belgium, the cockpit of Europe). 6 a pit or area where gamecocks fight. **cockscomb** n. 1 the comb or crest of a cock. 2 a garden plant, Celosia cristata, with a plume of tiny flowers. **cocksfoot** n. any pasture grass of the genus Dactylis, esp D. glomerata. **cockshy, cockshot** n. (pl. **cockshies, cockshots**) 1 a rough-and-ready target for sticks or stones. 2 a throw at this. 3 a butt of ridicule, criticism etc. **cock sparrow** n. 1 a male sparrow. 2 a pert or quarrelsome person. **cocksure** a. 1 self-confident, arrogantly certain. 2 perfectly sure, absolutely certain. **cocksurely** adv. **cocksureness** n.

cock[2] (kok) n. 1 the act of turning or sticking anything upward, such as a hat, the ears etc. 2 the turn so given. ~v.t. 1 to set erect. 2 to cause to stick up. 3 to set (the hat) jauntily on one side. 4 to turn up (the nose). 5 to turn (the eye) in an impudent or knowing fashion. 6 to raise (the ears) or tilt (the head) in an attentive manner. **to cock up** (sl.) to ruin by incompetence; to bungle. **cocked hat** n. 1 a pointed triangular hat. 2 (Hist.) a hat with the brim turned up. **cock-up** n. (sl.) a bungled failure.

cock[3] (kok) n. a small conical pile of hay. ~v.t. to put into cocks.

cockade (kəkād´) n. 1 a knot of ribbons worn in the hat as a badge. 2 a rosette worn in the hat by the male servants of naval and military officers etc. **cockaded** a.

cock-a-leekie (kokəlē´ki), **cocky-leeky** (koki-), **cockie-leckie** (-lek´i) n. soup made from a fowl boiled with leeks.

cockatiel (kokətēl´), **cockateel** n. a small crested parrot, Nymphicus hollandicus, of Australia.

cockatoo (kokətoo´) n. 1 a large crested parrot of the Cacatuidae, usu. white, from Australasia. 2 (Austral., New Zeal., coll.) a small farmer.

cockatrice (kok´ətris, -trīs) n. 1 the basilisk, a deadly mythical reptile. 2 (Her.) a cock with a serpent's tail.

cockboat (kok´bōt) n. a small ship's boat.

cockchafer (kok´chāfə) n. a large brown beetle, Melolontha melolontha, whose larvae feed on the roots of crops.

cockerel (kok´ərəl) n. a young cock.

cocker spaniel (kok´ə), **cocker** n. 1 a small spaniel of a breed used in shooting snipe etc. 2 this breed.

cockle[1] (kok´əl) *n.* **1** a bivalve mollusc of the genus *Cardium*, esp. *C. edule*. **2** its ribbed shell. **3** a cockleboat. **cockleboat** *n.* a small shallow boat. **cockleshell** *n.* **1** a cockleboat. **2** the shell of a cockle or scallop worn as the badge of a pilgrim. **cockles of the heart** *n.pl.* the inmost feelings (*to warm the cockles of one's heart*).

cockle[2] (kok´əl) *n.* **1** the corncockle. **2** any of various other weeds. **3** a disease of wheat. **cocklebur** *n.* a weed of the genus *Xanthium*, having bristly burs.

cockle[3] (kok´əl) *v.i.* to pucker up. ~*v.t.* to curl, pucker up, crease or cause to bulge. ~*n.* a pucker, crease or wrinkle in paper, cloth, glass etc.

cockney (kok´ni) *n.* (*pl.* **cockneys**) **1** a native of London (traditionally, a person born within sound of the bells of St-Mary-le-Bow, Cheapside). **2** the London accent or dialect. **3** a person who speaks with it. **4** (*Austral.*) a young snapper fish, *Chrysophrys auratus*. ~*a.* of or relating to cockneys, their accents or their dialect. **cockneyism** *n.*

cockroach (kok´rōch) *n.* an orthopterous insect, *Blatta orientalis* or *Periplaneta americana*, resembling a beetle, and a pest in kitchens.

cocktail (kok´tāl) *n.* **1** a drink taken esp. before a meal, usu. spirit mixed with fruit juice, bitters, other alcoholic liquor etc. **2** a dish consisting of a mixture of cold foods (*a prawn cocktail*). **3** any mixture of assorted ingredients, e.g. drinks, drugs. **cocktail dress** *n.* a short dress suitable for wearing at cocktail parties and other semi-formal occasions. **cocktail stick** *n.* a thin pointed stick for serving snack foods.

cocky[1] (kok´i) *a.* (*comp.* **cockier,** *superl.* **cockiest**) **1** arrogant, self-important, conceited. **2** †impudent, pert, saucy. **cockily** *adv.* **cockiness** *n.*

cocky[2] (kok´i) *n.* (*pl.* **cockies**) (*Austral., New Zeal., coll.*) a small farmer.

cocky-leeky COCK-A-LEEKIE.

coco (kō´kō), **cocoa, coker** (kō´kə) *n.* (*pl.* **cocos, cocoas, cokers**) a tropical palm tree, *Cocos nucifera*, the coconut palm. **coconut** *n.* **1** the fruit of this tree, a large, rough, hard-shelled nut with a white edible lining and containing a sweet white liquid. **2** the tree itself. **3** the lining of the coconut, used in cakes, sweets etc. (*desiccated coconut*). **4** (*sl.*) the human head. **coconut butter** *n.* the solid oil obtained from the lining of the coconut. **coconut ice** *n.* a sweet made from desiccated coconut and sugar. **coconut matting** *n.* coarse matting made from the fibrous husk of the coconut. **coconut milk** *n.* the sweet white liquid found inside the coconut. **coconut palm, coconut tree** *n.* the coco. **coconut shy** *n.* a fairground game in which the aim is to knock coconuts off sticks.

cocoa[1] (kō´kō) *n.* **1** a preparation from the seeds of the cacao tree, *Theobroma cacao*. **2** a drink made from this. **cocoa bean** *n.* the seed of the cacao. **cocoa butter** *n.* a buttery substance extracted from the cocoa nut in the manufacture of cocoa.

cocoa[2] COCO.

cocoon (kəkoon´) *n.* **1** a silky covering spun by the larvae of certain insects in the chrysalis state. **2** any analogous case made by other animals. **3** any protective covering. **4** a preservative coating sprayed onto machinery etc. ~*v.t.* **1** to wrap in, or as if in, a cocoon. **2** to spray with a preservative coating. ~*v.i.* to make a cocoon. **cocooned** *a.*

cocotte (kəkot´) *n.* a small dish in which food is cooked and served.

COD *abbr.* **1** cash on delivery. **2** (*N Am.*) collect on delivery.

cod[1] (kod) *n.* (*pl. in general* **cod,** *in particular* **cods**) any large deep-sea food fish, of the family Gadidae, esp. *Gadus morrhua*. **codfish** *n.* (*pl. in general* **codfish,** *in particular* **codfishes**) the cod. **codling**[1] (-ling) *n.* a young cod. **cod liver oil** *n.* oil from the liver of the cod, rich in vitamins A and D.

cod[2] (kod) *n.* (*taboo*) †the scrotum. **codpiece** *n.* (*Hist.*) a baggy appendage in the front of breeches or the tight hose worn in the 15th and 16th cents. to cover male genitals.

cod[3] (kod) *n.* **1** (*sl.*) a parody. **2** (*sl.*) a hoax. ~*a.* (*sl.*) intended to deceive or burlesque; mock (*cod Latin*). ~*v.t.* (*pres.p.* **codding,** *past, p.p.* **codded**) (*sl. or dial.*) **1** to hoax. **2** to parody. ~*v.i.* to perform a hoax.

cod[4] (kod) *n.* (*sl.*) nonsense.

coda (kō´də) *n.* (*pl.* **codas**) **1** (*Mus.*) an adjunct to the close of a composition to enforce the final character of the movement. **2** in ballet, the concluding part of a dance. **3** any concluding part, event etc.

coddle (kod´əl) *v.t.* **1** to treat as an invalid or baby, to pamper. **2** to cook (esp. eggs) gently in water. **coddler** *n.*

code (kōd) *n.* **1** a series of symbols, characters, letters or words used for the sake of brevity or secrecy. **2** a system of signals used for similar reasons. **3** (*Comput.*) a piece of program text. **4** a collection of statutes, a body of laws or regulations systematically arranged. **5** a collection of rules or canons. **6** the principles accepted in any sphere of art, taste, conduct etc. (*a code of practice; a code of conduct*). ~*v.t.* to put into a code. ~*v.i.* to be the genetic code (for). **code-breaker** *n.* a person who solves or interprets a code. **code-breaking** *n.* **code name, code number** *n.* a short name or number used for convenience or secrecy. **code-named** *a.* **coder** *n.* **codify** *v.t.* (*3rd pers. sing. pres.* **codifies,** *pres.p.* **codifying,** *past, p.p.* **codified**) **1** to collect or arrange (laws etc.) as a systematic body. **2** to put into a code. **codification** (-fikā´shən) *n.* **codifier** *n.*

codeine (kō´dēn) *n.* an alkaloid obtained from morphine and used as a narcotic and analgesic.

codependency (kōdipen´dənsi) *n.* mutual dependency for the fulfilment of emotional needs within a relationship. **codependent** *a., n.*

co-determination (kōditœminā´shən) n. co-operation between management and employees, or their trade union representatives, in decision-making.

codex (kō´deks) n. (pl. **codexes**, **codices** (kō´disēz, kod´-)) 1 a manuscript volume, esp. of the Bible or of texts of classics. 2 (Med.) a list of prescriptions.

codger (koj´ə) n. (coll.) an odd old person.

codicil (kod´isil, kō´-) n. an appendix to a will, treaty etc. **codicillary** (-sil´-) a.

codify CODE.

codling[1] COD[1].

codling[2] (kod´ling), **codlin** n. 1 a long, tapering kind of apple, used for cooking. 2 a codling moth. **codling moth** n. the moth Carpocapsa pomonella, whose larvae feed on apples and cause them to fall prematurely. **codlings-and-cream** n. the hairy willowherb, Epilobium hirsutum.

codomain (kō´dəmān) n. (Math.) the set of values that a function can take in all possible expressions.

codon (kō´don) n. a set of three nucleotides in DNA or RNA that specifies a particular amino acid.

co-driver (kō´drīvə) n. a person who shares the driving of a motor vehicle, esp. a rally car, with another.

codswallop (kodz´woləp) n. (sl.) nonsense.

coed (kō´ed, -ed´), **co-ed** n. (coll.) 1 a co-educational school. 2 (N Am.) a girl being educated in a co-educational establishment. ~a. co-educational.

co-education (kōedūkā´shən) n. education of the two sexes together. **co-educational** a.

coefficient (kōifish´ənt) n. 1 (Math.) the numerical or constant factor of an algebraical number, as 4 in 4ab. 2 (Physics) a number denoting the degree of a quality (the coefficient of expansion).

coelacanth (sē´ləkanth) n. a large bony sea fish, Latimeria chalumnae, the only known living representative of the primitive subclass Crossopterygii thought to be extinct until 1938.

-coele -CELE.

coelenterate (sēlen´tərāt, -rət) n. any invertebrate of the phylum Coelenterata, containing the jellyfish, corals, sea anemones etc. ~a. of or belonging to the Coelenterata.

coeliac, (N Am.) **celiac** a. 1 of or relating to the abdomen. 2 (Med.) of, relating to or suffering from coeliac disease. **coeliac disease** n. (Med.) a condition involving defective digestion caused by sensitivity to gluten.

coelom (sē´ləm), (N Am.) **celom** n. (pl. **coeloms**, **coelomata** (-lō´mətə), (N Am.) **celoms**, **celomata**) (Zool.) a body cavity, esp. the space between the body wall and the intestines. **coelomate** a., n.

coeno- (sē´nō), **ceno-**, **coen-**, **cen-** comb. form common.

coenobite (sē´nəbīt), **cenobite** n. a monk living in a monastic community. **coenobitic** (-bit´-), **coenobitical** a.

coenzyme (kōen´zīm, kō´-) n. in biochemistry, a non-protein organic molecule that is necessary for the activity of certain enzymes.

co-equal (kōē´kwəl) a. (poet. or formal) 1 equal with another. 2 of the same rank, dignity etc. ~n. a person of the same rank, as an equal. **co-equality** (-ikwol´-) n. **co-equally** adv.

coerce (kōœs´) v.t. 1 to restrain by force. 2 to compel to obey. 3 to enforce by compulsion. **coercible** a. **coercion** (-œ´shən) n. 1 the act of coercing. 2 government by force. **coercive** a. 1 having power or authority to coerce. 2 compulsory. **coercively** adv. **coerciveness** n.

coeval (kōē´vəl) a. 1 of the same age. 2 having the same date of birth or origin. 3 existing at or for the same period. ~n. a contemporary. **coevality** (-val´-) n. **coevally** adv.

coexist (kōigzist´) v.i. 1 to exist together at the same time or in the same place. 2 (of nations, regimes etc.) to be in a state of peaceful coexistence. **coexistence** n. **coexistent** a.

coextend (kōikstend´) v.i. to extend equally in time or space. **coextensive** a.

C of E abbr. Church of England.

coffee (kof´i) n. 1 a beverage made from the ground roasted seeds of a tropical Asiatic and African shrub, of the genus Coffea, esp. C. arabica. 2 a cup of this beverage. 3 the seeds of the shrub. 4 the shrub itself. 5 a pale brown colour, like milky coffee. ~a. pale brown. **coffee bag** n. a small perforated bag containing ground coffee. **coffee bar** n. a café where coffee, snacks etc. are served. **coffee bean** n. a coffee seed. **coffee cup** n. a small cup from which coffee is drunk. **coffee essence** n. a concentrated coffee extract, often containing chicory. **coffee grinder** n. a coffee mill. **coffee grounds** n.pl. the sediment or lees of coffee after infusion. **coffee house** n. a house where coffee and other refreshments are sold, esp. one that was popular in 18th-cent. London. **coffee-maker** n. a machine for making coffee from ground coffee beans, esp. a percolator. **coffee mill** n. a machine for grinding roasted coffee beans. **coffee morning** n. a social gatherings held at mid-morning, where coffee is served. **coffeepot** n. a vessel in which coffee is made. **coffee shop** n. a coffee bar, esp. in a department store. **coffee table** n. a low table in a sitting room. **coffee-table book** n. a large and expensively produced illustrated book.

coffer (kof´ə) n. 1 a chest or box for holding valuables. 2 (pl.) a treasury, funds, financial resources. 3 a sunken panel in a ceiling etc. ~v.t. to enclose or store in a coffer. **coffer-dam** n. a watertight enclosure pumped dry to expose a river bed etc., used in laying foundations of piers, bridges etc. **coffered** a.

coffin (kof´in) n. 1 the box in which a corpse is enclosed for burial or cremation. 2 the hoof of a horse below the coronet. ~v.t. (pres.p. **coffining**, past, p.p. **coffined**) **1** to put into a coffin. **2** to put out of sight. **coffin-bone** n. the spongy bone in a horse's hoof around which the horn grows. **coffin corner** n. in American football, the corner between the goal line and the sideline. **coffin-joint** n. the joint above the coffin-bone. **coffin-nail** n. (sl.) a cigarette.

cog (kog) n. **1** a tooth or projection in the rim of a wheel or other gear for transmitting motion to another part. **2** a person playing a small and unimportant part in any enterprise. **cogged** a. **cogwheel** n. a wheel furnished with cogs.

cogent (kō´jənt) a. powerful, constraining, convincing (a cogent argument). **cogency** n. **cogently** adv.

cogitate (koj´itāt) v.i. to think, to reflect, to meditate. ~v.t. to meditate, to devise. **cogitable** a. **1** capable of being thought. **2** conceivable by the reason. **cogitation** (-tā´shən) n. **cogitative** (-tətiv) a. **cogitator** n.

cognac (kon´yak) n. French brandy of fine quality, esp. that distilled in the neighbourhood of Cognac, in SW France.

cognate (kog´nāt) a. **1** akin, related. **2** of common origin. **3** of the same kind or nature. **4** derived from the same linguistic family or from the same word or root. ~n. **1** a blood relation. **2** a cognate word. **cognately** adv. **cognateness** n. **cognate object** n. (Gram.) an object governed by an etymologically related verb, as song as in to sing a song.

cognition (kognish´ən) n. **1** the act of apprehending. **2** the faculty of perceiving, conceiving, and knowing, as distinguished from the feelings and the will. **3** a sensation, perception, intuition, or conception. **cognitional** a. **cognitive** (kog´-) a. **cognitively** adv. **cognitivism** n. a tendency to emphasize the similarities between linguistic knowledge and non-linguistic knowledge. **cognitivist** a.

cognizance (kog´nizəns), **cognisance** n. **1** knowledge, notice, recognition. **2** the range of one's perception or concern. **3** (Law) the right of a court to deal with a cause. **4** (Her.) a badge, a coat, a crest. **to have cognizance of** to know. **to take cognizance of** to take into consideration. **cognizant** a. having cognizance or knowledge (of).

cognize (kogniz´), **cognise** v.t. (Philos.) to have knowledge or perception of. **cognizable** (kog´-niz-) a. **1** knowable, perceptible. **2** (Law) liable to be tried and determined. **cognizably** adv.

cognomen (kognō´mən) n. (pl. **cognomens**, **cognomina** (-nom´inə)) **1** the last of the three names of an ancient Roman citizen. **2** a nickname.

cognoscente (konyəshen´ti) n. (pl. **cognoscenti** (-ti)) a connoisseur.

cohabit (kōhab´it) v.i. (pres.p. **cohabiting**, past, p.p. **cohabited**) to live together, esp. as husband and wife without being legally married. **cohabitant** n. **cohabitation** (-ā´shən) n. **cohabitee** (-tē´-) n. **cohabiter** n.

cohere (kəhiə´) v.i. **1** to stick together. **2** to hold together, remain united. **3** to be logically consistent. **coherence, coherency** n. **coherent** a. **1** that coheres. **2** articulate, intelligible. **3** logically connected, consistent. **4** (of electromagnetic waves) having the same frequency or phase. **coherently** adv.

cohesion (kəhē´zhən) n. **1** coherence. **2** the act or state of sticking or holding together. **3** a tendency to stick or hold together. **4** (Physics) the force uniting molecules of the same nature. **cohesive** (-siv) a. **cohesively** adv. **cohesiveness** n.

coho (kō´hō), **cohoe** n. (pl. **cohos, cohoes**) a Pacific salmon, Oncorhynchus kisutch.

cohort (kō´hawt) n. **1** a tenth part of a Roman legion, containing three maniples or six centuries. **2** a body of soldiers. **3** any band of associates. **4** a set of people in a population sharing a common attribute, e.g. age or class. **5** (coll.) a colleague or accomplice.

Usage note The use of cohort of an individual, in the sense 'colleague, accomplice', is sometimes disapproved of, though it is quite common, especially in North America.

---

coif (koif) n. **1** a close-fitting cap, esp. worn by nuns under a veil. **2** (Hist.) a protective cap worn under chain mail. **3** (N Am.) coiffure. ~v.t. (pres.p. **coiffing**, (N Am.) **coifing**, past, p.p. **coiffed**, (N Am.) **coifed**) **1** to cover with a coif. **2** to arrange (the hair). **3** to arrange the hair of. **coiffed** a.

coiffeur (kwafœ´) n. a hairdresser. **coiffeuse** (-fœz´) n. a female hairdresser. **coiffure** (-füə´) n. a method of dressing the hair, a hairstyle. **coiffured** a.

coign (koin) n. **1** a quoin. **2** †a corner. **coign of vantage** n. a projecting corner affording a good view; an advantageous position.

coil (koil) v.t. **1** to wind (a rope etc.) into rings. **2** to twist into a spiral shape. ~v.i. (of a snake, a climbing plant etc.) to wind itself. ~n. **1** a series of concentric rings into which anything is coiled up. **2** a length of anything coiled up. **3** a single turn of anything coiled up. **4** a coiled lock of hair. **5** a wire wound round a bobbin to form a resistance or an inductance. **6** a transformer in an internal-combustion engine. **7** a metal or plastic coil inserted in the uterus as a contraceptive device. **8** a roll of postage stamps.

coin (koin) n. **1** a piece of metal stamped and current as money. **2** money, esp. coins. ~v.t. **1** to mint or stamp (money). **2** to invent, to fabricate (to coin a new word). **to coin a phrase** (iron.) said before or after using a cliché. **to coin it in** (sl.) to make money rapidly. **to coin money** (sl.) to make money rapidly. **coin box** n. **1** a coin-operated telephone or other machine. **2** the receptacle for coins in such a machine. **coiner** n. **1** a person who coins money, esp. one who makes counterfeit coin. **2** a person who coins a word, phrase etc. **coin-op** n. a launderette etc. with coin-operated machines. **coin-operated** a. (of a machine) operated by inserting a coin.

coinage (koi´nij) n. **1** the act of coining. **2** the pieces coined, coins collectively. **3** the monetary system in use (*decimal coinage*). **4** invention, fabrication. **5** something invented, esp. a new word or expression.

coincide (kōinsīd´) v.i. **1** to correspond in time, place, nature etc. **2** to happen at the same time. **3** to occupy the same position in space. **4** to agree, to concur. **coincidence** (-in´sidəns) n. **1** the act, fact, or condition of coinciding. **2** an instance of this. **3** a remarkable instance of apparently fortuitous concurrence. **4** (*Physics*) the simultaneous presence of two or more signals in a circuit etc. **coincident** (-in´sidənt) a. that coincides. **coincidental** (-siden´təl) a. **1** coincident. **2** characterized by, of the nature of or resulting from coincidence. **coincidentally** adv. **coincidently** adv.

coir (koiə) n. **1** coconut fibre. **2** ropes or matting manufactured from this.

coition (kōish´ən) n. (*Med.*) copulation. **coital** a. **coitus** (kō´itəs) n. (*Med.*) the act of copulation. **coitus interruptus** (intərŭp´təs) n. coitus deliberately interrupted before ejaculation into the vagina.

coke[1] (kōk) n. **1** coal from which gas has been extracted. **2** a residue in a car engine etc. formed by the incomplete combustion of petrol or other fuel. ~v.t. to convert into coke.

coke[2] (kōk) n. (*sl.*) cocaine.

Col. abbr. Colonel.

col (kol) n. **1** a depression in a mountain ridge; a saddle or elevated pass. **2** an area of low pressure between two anticyclones.

col. abbr. column.

cola (kō´lə), **kola** n. **1** a tropical African tree of the genus *Cola*, bearing a nut which contains caffeine. **2** a soft drink flavoured with cola-nuts. **cola nut** n. the fruit of the cola tree.

✗ colaborate common misspelling of COLLABORATE.

colander (kol´əndə, kŭl´-), **cullender** (kŭl´-) n. a culinary strainer having the bottom perforated with small holes.

colchicum (kol´chikəm, -ki-) n. **1** any plant of the genus *Colchicum*, esp. the meadow saffron, the corm and seeds of which are used in medicine. **2** the corm or seeds of the meadow saffron. **colchicine** (-sēn) n. an alkaloid obtained from meadow saffron, used to treat gout.

cold (kōld) a. **1** low in temperature, esp. in relation to normal or bodily temperature. **2** lacking heat or warmth. **3** causing a sensation of loss of heat. **4** suffering from a sensation of lack of heat. **5** without ardour or intensity, indifferent, unconcerned. **6** lacking friendliness, unwelcoming. **7** sad, dispiriting, depressing. **8** not hasty or violent, spiritless. **9** (of a scent in hunting) weak. **10** in children's games etc., far from guessing or finding something. **11** frigid, sexually

unresponsive. **12** dead. **13** (*coll.*) unconscious. **14** (*coll.*) at one's mercy. **15** unrehearsed. ~adv. **1** without rehearsal or preparation. **2** (*esp. N Am.*) absolutely. ~n. **1** absence of warmth. **2** the sensation produced by absence of warmth. **3** a viral infection of the mucous membranes of the respiratory tract, accompanied by sneezing and coughing. **4** cold weather. **in cold blood 1** without feeling, callously or ruthlessly. **2** without passion or excitement, deliberately. **out in the cold** ignored or neglected (*I was left out in the cold*). **to catch a cold 1** to contract a cold. **2** (*coll.*) to run into difficulties. **to throw/ pour cold water on** to discourage. **cold-blooded** a. **1** having a body temperature which varies with that of the environment. **2** unfeeling, callous. **cold-bloodedly** adv. **cold-bloodedness** n. **cold calling** n. the practice of making unsolicited telephone calls or visits to potential customers in order to sell products or services. **cold cathode** n. a cathode which emits electrons at normal temperatures. **cold chisel** n. a chisel for cutting cold metals. **cold comfort** n. poor consolation, depressing reassurance. **cold cream** n. a creamy ointment for cooling, cleansing or softening the skin. **cold cuts** n.pl. cold sliced meat. **cold feet** n.pl. (*coll.*) loss of courage or confidence (*to get cold feet*). **cold frame** n. an unheated glass frame to protect seedlings etc. **cold front** n. in meteorology, the front edge of an advancing mass of cold air. **cold-hearted** a. unfeeling, indifferent. **cold-heartedly** adv. **cold-heartedness** n. **coldish** a. **coldly** adv. **coldness** n. **cold shoulder** n. **1** a rebuff (*to give someone the cold shoulder*). **2** studied indifference. **cold-shoulder** v.t. to treat with studied coolness or neglect, to rebuff. **cold snap** n. a sudden short spell of cold weather. **cold sore** n. a blister or cluster of blisters around the lips, caused by herpes simplex. **cold start** n. **1** the starting of an engine etc. at the ambient temperature. **2** the starting of any process without preparation. **cold-start** v.t. to start (an engine, process etc.) in this way. **cold steel** n. cutting weapons, such as sword and bayonet, as opposed to firearms. **cold storage** n. **1** the preservation of perishable foodstuffs by refrigeration. **2** abeyance (*to put a project into cold storage*). **cold sweat** n. sweating accompanied by chill, caused esp. by fear. **cold table** n. a selection of cold dishes. **cold turkey** n. (*sl.*) the physical and psychological symptoms caused by sudden and complete withdrawal of drugs from an addict. **cold war** n. a state of psychological tension between two countries without actual fighting.

cold-short (kōld´shawt) a. (of a metal) brittle when cold.

cole (kōl) n. **1** the cabbage. **2** any of various other edible plants of the genus *Brassica*, esp. the rape. **coleseed** n. rapeseed. **coleslaw** n. a salad made of shredded raw cabbage, carrot, etc.

colemouse COALMOUSE.

coleopteran (koliop´tərən) n. any insect of the order Coleoptera, including the beetles and weevils, having the forewings converted into sheaths for the hind wings. **coleopterist** n. **coleopterous** a.

coleoptile (koliop´tīl) n. (Bot.) a protective sheath around the shoot tip in grasses.

cole tit (kōl´ tit) n. COALMOUSE.

coleus (kō´liəs) n. (pl. **coleuses**) any plant of the genus Solenostemon, cultivated for their variegated coloured leaves.

coley (kō´li) n. (pl. **coleys**) the coalfish.

colic (kol´ik) n. acute spasmodic pain in the intestines. **colicky** a.

coliseum COLOSSEUM.

colitis (kəli´tis) n. (Med.) inflammation of the colon.

Coll. abbr. College.

collaborate (kəlab´ərāt) v.i. 1 to work jointly with another, esp. in literary, artistic or scientific work. 2 to cooperate with an enemy in occupation of one's own country. **collaboration** (-ā´shən) n. **collaborationist** n., a. **collaborative** a. **collaboratively** adv. **collaborator** n.

collage (kolahzh´) n. 1 a picture made of pieces of paper, fabric etc., glued on to a surface. 2 the art form in which such pictures are made. 3 any collection of diverse things or ideas. **collagist** n.

collagen (kol´əjen) n. a fibrous protein that yields gelatin when boiled.

collapsar (kəlap´sah) n. (Astron.) 1 a black hole. 2 a star that has collapsed to form a white dwarf or black hole.

collapse (kəlaps´) v.i. 1 to fall in, to give way, to fall down. 2 to fold together, to be collapsible. 3 to break down, to suffer from physical or nervous prostration. 4 to come to nothing. ~v.t. to cause to collapse. ~n. 1 the act or an instance of collapsing. 2 complete failure. 3 general prostration. **collapsible** a. **collapsibility** (-bil´-) n.

collar (kol´ə) n. 1 something worn round the neck, esp. the part of a garment that goes round the neck. 2 a band of leather etc. for a dog's neck. 3 a leather loop round a horse's neck to which the traces are attached. 4 a ring or round flange. 5 anything shaped like a collar or ring. 6 a marking resembling a collar round the neck of a bird etc. 7 a cut of meat, esp. bacon, from the neck. 8 a piece of meat rolled and tied. ~v.t. 1 to seize by the collar. 2 to put a collar on. 3 to capture. 4 (coll.) to seize. 5 (coll.) to accost. 6 (sl.) to steal. **collar-beam** n. a tie-beam. **collarbone** n. either of the bones that join the shoulder blades to the breastbone; the clavicle. **collared** a. **collared dove** n. a dove, Streptopelia decaocto, with a collar-like marking at the back of the neck. **collarless** a.

collate (kəlāt´) v.t. 1 to bring together in order to compare. 2 to examine critically in order to ascertain by comparison points of agreement and difference. 3 to place in order (printed sheets for binding etc.). 4 to assemble or merge (information etc. from different sources). 5 to appoint (a clergyman) to a benefice. **collation** n. 1 the act of collating. 2 a light meal (from treatises being read in monasteries at meal-times). 3 a light meal permitted on fast days in the Roman Catholic Church. **collator** n.

collateral (kəlat´ərəl) a. 1 having the same common ancestor but not lineally related. 2 side by side, parallel. 3 being by the side. 4 subsidiary, subordinate. ~n. 1 collateral security. 2 a collateral relation. **collateral damage** n. damage over and above that intended, esp. in military operations. **collaterality** (-ral´iti) n. **collateralize, collateralise** v.t. to secure (a loan etc.) with collateral security. **collaterally** adv.

colleague (kol´ēg) n. a person associated with another in any office or employment; a fellow worker.

collect[1] (kəlekt´) v.t. 1 to gather together into one body, mass or place. 2 to gather (money, taxes, subscriptions, books, works of art, curiosities etc.) from a number of sources. 3 to call for, to fetch. 4 to concentrate, to bring under control. 5 to gather from observation, to infer. ~v.i. 1 to come together. 2 to meet together. 3 (coll.) to receive money, esp. a large amount of money. ~a., adv. (N Am.) (of a telephone call etc.) paid for by the recipient. **to collect oneself** to recover one's self-possession. **collectable, collectible** a. 1 worth collecting (collectable works of art). 2 that can be collected. ~n. a collectable item. **collectability** (-bil´-) n. **collected** a. 1 gathered, brought together. 2 cool, self-possessed, composed. **collectedly** adv. **collectedness** n. **collector** n. 1 a person who collects money etc. (a tax collector). 2 a person who collects works of art, curiosities etc. (a stamp collector). 3 any person or thing that collects. 4 the terminal of a transistor. **collector's item, collector's piece** n. an item of interest to a collector, esp. because of its value or rarity.

collect[2] (kol´ekt) n. a brief comprehensive form of prayer, adapted for a particular day or occasion.

collection (kəlek´shən) n. 1 the act of collecting. 2 that which is collected. 3 an assemblage of books, works of art etc. 4 money contributed for religious, charitable or other purposes. 5 an accumulation. 6 the act of removing mail from a postbox, refuse for disposal etc.

collective (kəlek´tiv) a. 1 tending to collect, forming a collection. 2 collected, aggregated, formed by gathering a number of things or persons together. 3 joint or common; cooperative (collective action). ~n. 1 a cooperative or collectivized organization or enterprise. 2 a collective noun. **collective bargaining** n. a method whereby employer and employees (or their representatives) determine the conditions of employment. **collective farm** n. a group of smallholdings, usu. state-owned or state-controlled, operated on a cooperative basis. **collectively** adv. **collectiveness**

n. **collective noun** *n.* (*Gram.*) a noun in the singular that denotes a group of individuals, such as *family, herd.* **collective ownership** *n.* ownership of land, capital, and other means of production by those engaged in the production. **collectivism** *n.* an economic theory based on collective ownership. **collectivist** *n.* **collectivistic** (-is´tik) *a.* **collectivity** (kolektiv´-) *n.* **collectivize, collectivise** *v.t.* to organize on the lines of collectivism. **collectivization** (-zā´shən) *n.*

colleen (kolēn´) *n.* (*Ir.*) a girl, a lass.

college (kol´ij) *n.* **1** an institution for further or higher education. **2** an institution providing specialized education, professional training etc. **3** an independent corporation of scholars, teachers, and fellows forming one of the constituent bodies of a university. **4** a similar foundation independent of a university. **5** a large and important secondary school, esp. a private school. **6** a body or community of persons, having certain rights and privileges, and devoted to common pursuits. **college of education** *n.* a training college for teachers. **collegial** (-lē´jiəl) *a.* **1** of or relating to a college. **2** constituted as a college. **3** of or involving shared responsibility, as among colleagues. **collegiality** (-al´-) *n.* **collegian** (-lē´jən) *n.* **1** a member of a college. **2** a student at a university.

collegiate (kəlē´jət) *a.* **1** of or relating to a college. **2** instituted or regulated as a college. **3** (of a university) made up of various colleges. **4** of or for college students. **collegiate church** *n.* a church which, though not a cathedral, has an endowed chapter of canons. **collegiately** *adv.*

collenchyma (kəleng´kimə) *n.* (*Bot.*) plant tissue composed of elongated cells with thickened walls, occurring immediately under the epidermis in leaf-stalks, stems etc.

collet (kol´ət) *n.* **1** a band or ring. **2** a flange or socket. **3** the part of a ring in which a stone is set. **4** in engineering, a sleeve that can be tightened round a shaft to grip it. **5** a small collar in a clock that supports the lower end of a balance spring.

collide (kəlīd´) *v.i.* to come into collision or conflict. **collider** *n.* (*Physics*) a particle accelerator in which two beams of particles are caused to collide.

collie (kol´i) *n.* **1** a sheepdog with long silky hair and a pointed nose. **2** this breed of sheepdog, originating in Scotland.

collier (kol´yə) *n.* **1** a person who works in a coal mine. **2** a ship employed in the coal trade. **3** a member of its crew. **colliery** *n.* (*pl.* **collieries**) a coal mine.

colligate (kol´igāt) *v.t.* **1** to bind together. **2** to bring into connection. **colligation** (-ā´shən) *n.*

collimate (kol´imāt) *v.t.* **1** to adjust the line of sight of (a telescope). **2** to make the axes of (lenses or telescopes) collinear. **3** to make parallel. **collimation** (-ā´shən) *n.* **collimator** *n.* **1** a small telescope used to adjust the line of sight of a larger optical instrument. **2** a tube attached to a

spectroscope for making parallel the rays falling on the prism.

collinear (kəlin´iə) *a.* (*Geom.*) in the same straight line. **collinearity** (-ar´-) *n.*

Collins (kol´inz), **collins** *n.* a drink made of spirits mixed with soda water, fruit juice, ice etc.

collision (kəlizh´ən) *n.* **1** the act of striking violently together. **2** the state of being struck violently together. **3** opposition, antagonism, conflict. **4** the clashing of interests. **5** a harsh combination of sounds etc. **6** (*Physics*) the striking or coming together of particles. **collision course** *n.* a course which will result inevitably in a collision.

collocate (kol´əkāt) *v.t.* **1** to place together. **2** to arrange. **3** to set in a particular place. **4** to juxtapose or associate (a particular word) with another, esp. habitually. **collocation** (-ā´shən) *n.*

collocutor (kəlok´ūtə, kol´ə-) *n.* a person who takes part in a conversation or conference.

collodion (kəlō´diən) *n.* a syrupy solution of pyroxylin in ether and spirit, used in photography and medicine.

collogue (kəlōg´) *v.i.* (*pres.p.* **colloguing**, *past*, *p.p.* **collogued**) to talk confidentially or plot together.

colloid (kol´oid) *n.* **1** (*Chem.*) an uncrystallizable, semi-solid substance, capable of only very slow diffusion or penetration. **2** (*Med.*) a gelatinous substance of homogeneous consistency. **colloidal** (kəloi´dəl) *a.*

collop (kol´əp) *n.* **1** a slice of meat. **2** a small piece or slice of anything.

colloquial (kəlō´kwiəl) *a.* of, relating to or used in common or familiar conversation, not used in formal writing or in literature. **colloquialism** *n.* **1** a colloquial word or expression. **2** the use of such words or expressions. **colloquially** *adv.*

colloquium (kəlō´kwiəm) *n.* (*pl.* **colloquiums**, **colloquia** (-kwiə)) **1** an academic conference. **2** a seminar.

colloquy (kol´əkwi) *n.* (*pl.* **colloquies**) (*formal*) **1** a conference, conversation or dialogue between two or more persons. **2** a gathering to discuss religious or theological matters.

collotype (kol´ətīp) *n.* **1** a method of lithographic printing in which the film of gelatin that constitutes the negative is used to produce prints. **2** a print obtained in this way.

collude (kəlood´) *v.i.* to act in concert, to conspire. **colluder** *n.*

collusion (kəloo´zhən) *n.* **1** secret agreement for a fraudulent or deceitful purpose. **2** (*Law*) such agreement between opponents in a lawsuit. **collusive** *a.* **collusively** *adv.*

collywobbles (kol´iwobəlz) *n.pl.* (*coll.*) **1** a stomach-ache, an upset stomach. **2** extreme nervousness (*to have the collywobbles*).

colobus (kol´əbəs) *n.* (*pl.* **colobuses**) a leaf-eating African monkey of the genus *Colobus*, with short or absent thumbs.

cologne (kəlōn´) *n.* eau-de-Cologne. **Cologne water** *n.* eau-de-Cologne.

colon[1] (kō´lon) *n.* a punctuation mark (:) used to mark the start of a list, a long quotation etc.; also used in expressing an arithmetical ratio.

colon[2] (kō´lon) *n.* (*Anat.*) the largest division of the intestinal canal, extending from the caecum to the rectum. **colonic** (kəlon´ik) *a., n.* **colonoscope** (kəlon´əskōp) *n.* a flexible lighted tube used to examine the colon. **colonoscopy** (kolən-os´kəpi) *n.* (*pl.* **colonoscopies**)

colonel (kœ´nəl) *n.* **1** the commander of a regiment; an army officer ranking below a brigadier and above a lieutenant colonel. **2** an officer of similar rank in other armed forces, such as the US Air Force. **Colonel Blimp** *n.* a blimp. **colonelcy** *n.* (*pl.* **colonelcies**). **colonelship** *n.*

colonial (kəlō´niəl) *a.* **1** of or relating to a colony, esp. to those of the British Empire or to those in America that became the United States in 1776. **2** of or relating to colonialism. **3** (of architecture etc.) in a style characteristic of the British colonies in America before 1776. ~*n.* **1** a native or inhabitant of a colony. **2** a house in colonial style. **colonialism** *n.* a policy of tight control over, or exploitation of, colonies. **colonialist** *n.* **colonially** *adv.*

colonist (kol´ənist) *n.* a settler in or inhabitant of a colony.

colonize (kol´ənīz), **colonise** *v.t.* **1** to found a colony in. **2** to settle in. **3** to people with colonists. **4** (*Biol.*) (of animals and plants) to become established in (a new environment). ~*v.i.* to found a colony or colonies. **colonization** (-zā´shən) *n.* **colonizer** *n.*

colonnade (kolənād´) *n.* a series or range of columns at regular intervals. **colonnaded** *a.*

colony (kol´əni) *n.* (*pl.* **colonies**) **1** a settlement founded by emigrants in a foreign country, and remaining subject to the jurisdiction of the parent state. **2** a group of people of the same nationality in a foreign town. **3** a group of people following the same occupation in a town, esp. when they live in the same quarter. **4** (*Biol.*) a body of organisms living or growing together.

colophon (kol´əfon) *n.* **1** a publisher's identifying symbol. **2** a device or inscription formerly at the end of a book, giving the printer's name, place, date of publication etc.

colophony (kəlof´əni) *n.* a dark-coloured resin obtained from turpentine, rosin.

color COLOUR.

Colorado beetle (kolərah´dō) *n.* a small yellow and black striped beetle, *Leptinotarsa decemlineata*, very destructive to the potato plant.

colorant (kŭl´ərənt), **colourant** *n.* a substance used to impart colour, a pigment etc.

coloration (kŭlərā´shən), **colouration** *n.* **1** colouring, marking, arrangement of colours. **2** a method of putting on or arranging colours.

coloratura (koləratoo´rə) *n.* (*Mus.*) **1** the ornamental use of variation, trills etc. in vocal music. **2** a singer, esp. a soprano, capable of singing such ornamented music.

colorific (kŭlərif´ik) *a.* **1** producing colour, having the power of imparting colour to other bodies. **2** highly coloured.

colorimeter (kŭlərim´itə) *n.* an instrument for measuring the hue, brightness, and purity of colours. **colorimetric** (-met´rik) *a.* **colorimetry** *n.*

colosseum (koləsē´əm), **coliseum** (koli-) *n.* a large amphitheatre, stadium or other place of entertainment.

colossus (kəlos´əs) *n.* (*pl.* **colossuses, colossi** (-sī)) **1** a statue of gigantic size. **2** any gigantic person, animal or thing. **3** a person of great power or genius. **colossal** *a.* **1** of, relating to or resembling a colossus. **2** huge. **3** (*coll.*) remarkable. **colossally** *adv.*

colostomy (kəlos´təmi) *n.* (*pl.* **colostomies**) the surgical formation of an artificial anus by an incision made into the colon.

colostrum (kəlos´trəm) *n.* **1** the first secretion from the mammary glands after parturition. **2** beestings.

colour (kŭl´ə), (*N Am.*) **color** *n.* **1** the sensation produced by waves of resolved light upon the optic nerve. **2** that property of bodies by which rays of light are resolved so as to produce certain effects upon the eye. **3** any one of the hues into which light can be resolved, or a mixture of these. **4** any of these as distinguished from black or white. **5** that which is used for colouring, a pigment, a paint. **6** colouring; the use or effect of colour, and of light and shade in drawings, photography etc. **7** the complexion or hue of the face, esp. a healthy hue, ruddiness. **8** pigmentation of the skin, esp. dark pigmentation. **9** (*often pl.*) semblance, appearance, esp. false appearance. **10** (*pl.*) coloured ribbons etc. worn as a badge of membership of a team, party, society, club etc. **11** (*pl.*) a flag, standard, or ensign borne in an army or fleet. **12** pretence, excuse, pretext. **13** timbre, quality of tone. **14** general character, quality. **15** mood, temper, emotional quality. **16** vividness, animation. ~*v.t.* **1** to give or apply colour to. **2** to paint, to dye. **3** to give a new colour to. **4** to put in a false light, to misrepresent. **5** to exaggerate. **6** to influence. ~*v.i.* **1** to become coloured. **2** to turn red, to blush. **to show one's true colours** **1** to reveal one's opinions, feelings or designs. **2** to throw off disguise. **with flying colours** brilliantly, successfully, with credit or distinction. **colourable** *a.* **1** specious, plausible. **2** apparent, not real. **3** feigned, counterfeit. **colourably** *adv.* **colourant** COLORANT. **colouration** COLORATION. **colour bar** *n.* a social, political, or other discrimination against non-white people. **colour-blind** *a.* totally or partially unable to distinguish different colours, esp. the primary colours. **colour-blindness** *n.* **colour code** *n.* a system of marking different things, e.g. electric wires, in different colours for ease of identification. **colour-code** v.t. **Coloured** a. (*sometimes derog. or offensive*) **1** of other than Caucasian descent. **2** in S Africa, of mixed blood. ~n. a Coloured person. **coloured** a. **1** having a colour or colours, esp. marked by any colour except black or white. **2** having a specious appearance. **3** (*Bot.*) of any colour except green. ~n. (*pl.*) coloured items of laundry. **colour fast** a. dyed with colours that will not run, fade etc. **colour fastness** n. **colourful** a. **1** having bright colour or colours. **2** interesting. **3** exotic. **colourfully** adv. **colourfulness** n. **colouring** n. **1** the act of giving a colour to. **2** the colour applied. **3** the art or style of using colour. **4** a false appearance. **5** the colour of a person's skin, hair etc. **colourist** n. a person who colours, esp. a painter. **colouristic** (-ris´-) a. **colourless** a. **1** without colour. **2** pale, neutral-tinted, subdued in tone. **3** dull, lacking in life and vigour. **4** neutral, impartial. **colourlessly** adv. **colourlessness** n. **colour scheme** n. a set of colours used together in decorating. **colour-sergeant** n. a non-commissioned officer in the infantry ranking above an ordinary sergeant. **colour supplement** n. a (usu. weekly) supplement to a newspaper printed in colour and containing articles on lifestyle, entertainment etc. **colourway** n. a particular colour scheme in a fabric etc., esp. one of a number of different combinations of colours. **coloury** a. having a good colour.

Usage note The term *Coloured* is often associated with discrimination, segregation or apartheid, and can give offence. It is better to use black, Aboriginal, Asian or some other suitable alternative when referring to non-white people.

colposcope (kol´pəskōp) n. an instrument for examining the cervix and upper vagina. **colposcopy** (-pos´kəpi) n. (*pl.* **colposcopies**).

colt (kōlt) n. **1** a young horse, esp. a young male from its weaning until the age of four. **2** a young, inexperienced person. **3** in sport, a member of a junior team. **colthood** n. **coltish** a. **coltishly** adv. **coltishness** n. **coltsfoot** n. (*pl.* **coltsfoots**) a coarse-leaved, yellow-flowered plant, *Tussilago farfara*, formerly much used in medicine.

colter COULTER.

colubrid (kol´ūbrid) n. (*Zool.*) any snake of the family Colubridae, most of which are harmless. ~a. of or relating to this family. **colubrine** (-brīn) a. **1** of, relating to, or resembling a snake. **2** of or relating to the Colubrinae, a subfamily of colubrid snakes.

colugo (kəloo´gō) n. (*pl.* **colugos**) a flying lemur.

columbine (kol´əmbīn) n. any plant of the genus *Aquilegia*, with five-spurred flowers, supposed to resemble five doves clustered together, esp. *A. vulgaris*.

columbite (kəlŭm´bīt) n. (*Chem.*) an ore of niobium and tantalum, containing manganese and iron.

columbium (kəlŭm´biəm) n. (*esp. N Am.*) niobium.

column (kol´əm) n. **1** (*Archit.*) a pillar or solid body of wood or stone, of considerably greater length than thickness, usu. consisting of a base, a shaft and a capital, used to support or adorn a building, or as a solitary monument. **2** anything resembling this, such as the mercury in a thermometer, a cylindrical mass of water or other liquid, a vertical mass of smoke etc. **3** a perpendicular line of figures. **4** a perpendicular section of a page. **5** a regular article in a newspaper or magazine. **6** (*pl.*) the contents of a newspaper. **7** a support. **8** a solid body into which the filaments in some plants are combined. **9** (*Mil.*) a body of troops in deep files. **10** (*Naut.*) a line of ships behind each other. **to dodge the column** (*coll.*) to avoid work, duty, responsibility etc. **columnar** (kəlŭm´nə) a. **columned** a. **column-inch** n. a print measure, 1 in. (2.54 cm) deep and one column wide. **columnist** (-nist) n. a regular writer esp. on general subjects in a newspaper.

colure (kəlūə´, kol´-) n. (*Astron.*) either of two great circles passing through the equinoctial points, and cutting each other at right angles at the poles.

colza (kol´zə) n. **1** the rape plant. **2** rapeseed.

COM (kom) abbr. computer output on microfilm.

coma¹ (kō´mə) n. (*pl.* **comas**) a state of absolute unconsciousness, characterized by the absence of any response to external stimuli or inner need. **comatose** (-tōs, -tōz) a. **1** in a coma. **2** sleepy, sluggish.

coma² (kō´mə) n. (*pl.* **comae** (-mē)) **1** (*Astron.*) the nebulous covering of the nucleus of a comet. **2** (*Bot.*) the tuft of hairs terminating certain seeds.

comb (kōm) n. **1** a toothed instrument for separating, tidying and arranging the hair. **2** an ornamental toothed device for fastening the hair when arranged. **3** a rake-shaped instrument with a short handle for cleaning wool or flax. **4** anything resembling a comb. **5** the red, fleshy tuft on the head of a fowl, esp. the cock. **6** the crest of a bird. **7** the cellular substance in which bees deposit their honey, a honeycomb. ~v.t. **1** to separate, tidy or arrange with a comb. **2** to curry (a horse). **3** to dress (flax, hemp, wool etc.). **4** to make a thorough search of. **to comb out 1** to tidy or arrange with a comb. **2** to remove with a comb. **3** to find and remove. **4** to search thoroughly. **combed** a. **comber** n. **1** a person or thing that combs. **2** a machine for combing cotton or wool. **3** a wave that forms a long crest and rolls over. **combing** n. **1** a tidying or dressing with a comb. **2** (*pl.*) hair removed by a comb. **combing wool** n. wool suitable for combing, used to make worsted. **comb-jelly** n. a ctenophore.

combat (kom´bat) v.i. (*pres.p.* **combating**, *past, p.p.* **combated**) to contend, to fight, to struggle.

~*v.t.* to oppose, to strive against, to fight. ~*n.* a fight, a battle. **combatant** (-bə-) *a.* **1** engaged in combat. **2** bearing arms. **3** antagonistic. ~*n.* a person who engages in combat. **combat dress** *n.* the uniform worn by soldiers in combat and field training. **combat fatigue** *n.* **1** nervous disturbance occurring in a very stressful situation, such as on the battlefield. **2** (*pl.*, *N Am.*) clothing worn in battle. **combative** (-bə-) *a.* **1** inclined to combat. **2** pugnacious. **combatively** *adv.* **combativeness** *n.*

combe (koom), **coomb** *n.* **1** a valley on the side of a hill or mountain. **2** a valley running up from the sea (often used in place names, as *Ilfracombe*).

combi (kom´bi) *n.* a machine or device that has a combined function. ~*a.* having a combined function (*a combi oven*).

combination (kombinā´shən) *n.* **1** the act or process of combining. **2** the state of being combined. **3** a combined body or mass. **4** a group of things. **5** a union, an association. **6** the sequence of numbers that will open a combination lock. **7** combined action. **8** (*Chem.*) chemical union. **9** a motorcycle and sidecar. **10** (*pl.*) a long-sleeved undergarment covering the body and legs. **11** a sequence of chess moves. **12** (*pl.*, *Math.*) the different collections which may be made of certain given quantities in groups of a given number. **combinational** *a.* **combination lock** *n.* a lock which opens only when a set of dials is turned to show a particular combination of numbers. **combination oven** *n.* an oven with the combined function of a microwave and conventional oven. **combinative** (kom´binətiv) *a.* **combinatorial** (kombinətaw´riəl) *a.* (*Math.*) of or relating to combinations of quantities. **combinatory** (kom´binətəri) *a.*

combine[1] (kəmbīn´) *v.t.* **1** to cause to unite or coalesce. **2** to bring together. **3** to have at the same time (properties or attributes usu. separate). ~*v.i.* **1** to unite, to coalesce. **2** to be joined or united in friendship or plans. **3** (*Chem.*) to unite by chemical affinity. **combinable** *a.* **combining form** *n.* (*Gram.*) an element that occurs only in combination with another, as *micro-* in *microscope*.

combine[2] (kom´bīn) *n.* **1** a combination, esp. of persons or companies to further their own commercial interests. **2** a combine harvester. **combine harvester** *n.* a combined reaping and threshing machine.

combo (kom´bō) *n.* (*pl.* **combos**) (*coll.*) **1** a small band in jazz and popular music. **2** any combination.

combs (komz) *n.pl.* (*coll.*) combinations (the undergarment).

combust (kəmbŭst´) *v.t.* to burn, to consume with fire. **combustible** *a.* **1** capable of being set on fire, flammable. **2** irascible, hot-tempered. ~*n.* a combustible material or thing. **combustibility** (-bil´-) *n.* **combustibleness** *n.* **combustion**

(-bŭs´chən) *n.* **1** the act of burning, the state of being on fire or destroyed by fire. **2** (*Chem.*) the combination of a substance with oxygen or another element, accompanied by light and heat. **combustion chamber** *n.* a space in which combustion takes place, as in an internal-combustion engine. **combustive** *a.*

come (kŭm) *v.i.* (*past* **came** (kām), *p.p.* **come**) **1** to move from a distance to a place nearer to the speaker or hearer. **2** to approach. **3** to be brought to or towards. **4** to move towards. **5** to travel (a certain distance) towards (*Have you come far?*). **6** to reach, to extend. **7** to arrive. **8** to arrive at some state or condition. **9** to appear. **10** to happen, to befall. **11** to be in a specified position (*B comes before C*). **12** to be available (*The skirt comes in four colours*). **13** to become, to get to be. **14** to be (*It doesn't come easy*). **15** (*in subj.*) when (a specified time or event) arrives (*come February*; *come the revolution*). **16** to result, to arise, to originate (from). **17** to be descended (from). **18** to bud, to shoot. **19** (*taboo sl.*) to experience orgasm. ~*v.t.* (*sl.*) to act the part of, to produce. ~*n.* (*taboo sl.*) semen ejaculated at orgasm. ~*int.* used to excite attention or rouse to action (when repeated it expresses remonstrance or reserve). **as ... as they come** being the most typical or supreme example (*She's as lazy as they come*). **as it comes** without additions or alterations. **come again** say that again. **come along** make haste. **come off it** (*coll.*) stop behaving or talking so stupidly or pretentiously. **come on** **1** hurry up. **2** proceed. **3** used to express encouragement. **come to that** (*coll.*) in fact. **come what may** whatever happens. **if it comes to that** in that case. **to come** in the future (*in days to come*). **to come about** **1** to result, to come to pass. **2** (*Naut.*) to change direction, esp. by tacking. **3** to recover. **4** to be perceived (as). **to come across** **1** to meet with accidentally. **2** (*coll.*) to be perceived (as). **to come across with** (*sl.*) to provide or hand over. **to come along** to make progress. **to come apart** to separate or break into parts or pieces. **to come around** (*N Am.*) to come round. **to come at** **1** to reach, to attain, to gain access to. **2** to attack. **come away** **1** to move away, to leave. **2** to become parted or separated. **to come back** **1** to return. **2** to recur to memory. **3** to retort. **4** to become popular or fashionable again. **to come between** **1** to damage a relationship between (two people). **2** to separate. **to come by** **1** to pass near. **2** to call, to visit. **3** to obtain, to gain. **to come down** **1** to descend, to fall. **2** to be humbled. **3** to decide. **4** to be handed down. **to come down on** **1** to reprimand. **2** to chastise. **to come down to** **1** to amount to. **2** to have as result. **to come down with** to contract (an ailment). **to come for** **1** to come to fetch or receive. **2** to attack. **to come forward** **1** to make oneself known, to identify oneself. **2** to offer oneself. **3** to move forwards. **to come home to roost** to have undesirable consequences for the doer or initiator. **to come in**

1 to enter. **2** to advance or approach, to arrive at a destination. **3** to become fashionable. **4** to be received. **5** to prove to be (*to come in useful*). **6** to play a role, to have a function (*This is where the torch comes in*). **7** to accrue. **8** to assume power. **9** (*coll.*) to secure an advantage or chance of benefit. **to come in for 1** to arrive in time for. **2** to obtain, to receive. **to come into 1** to join with. **2** to comply with. **3** to acquire, to inherit. **to come of 1** to be descended from. **2** to proceed or result from. **to come of age** to reach the age of 18, to become an adult. **to come off 1** to part from. **2** to be detachable. **3** to fall off. **4** to take place. **5** (*coll.*) to be accomplished. **6** to fare (*to come off best*). **7** (*sl.*) to experience orgasm. **to come on 1** to advance. **2** to prosper. **3** to appear. **4** to begin to perform, speak, play, be broadcast etc. **5** to happen, to arise. **6** to come upon. **to come out 1** to emerge. **2** to be revealed, to become public. **3** to be introduced into society. **4** to be published. **5** to declare something openly, esp. one's homosexuality. **6** to go on strike. **7** to turn out. **8** to be covered (in) (*She came out in a rash*). **9** (*N Am.*) to make profession of religion. **10** to be removed or solved. **to come out with** to utter, to disclose. **to come over 1** to cross over. **2** to change sides. **3** to affect. **4** (*coll.*) to become (*I came over dizzy*). **5** to make a casual visit. **6** to be perceived (as). **to come round 1** to change one's opinion. **2** to recover consciousness. **3** to make a casual visit. **4** to recur. **to come through 1** to survive. **2** to be successful. **3** to be received. **to come to 1** to amount to. **2** to recover consciousness. **3** (*Naut.*) to cease moving. **4** to reach. **5** to consent. **to come to oneself** to recover one's senses. **to come to one's senses 1** to recover consciousness. **2** to become sensible. **to come to pass** to happen. **to come to rest** to stop, to cease moving. **to come under 1** to be classed as. **2** to be subject to (authority, influence etc.). **to come up 1** to ascend. **2** to arise. **3** to be introduced as a topic. **4** to happen. **to come up against** to encounter or confront (a difficulty etc.). **to come upon 1** to attack. **2** to befall. **3** to find, to discover. **4** to meet with unexpectedly. **to come up to 1** to approach. **2** to be equal to. **3** to amount to. **to come up with 1** to produce. **2** to overtake. **comeback** *n.* **1** a return to popular favour. **2** (*sl.*) a retort. **3** (*Austral.*) a sheep bred from purebred and cross-bred parents. **comedown** *n.* **1** a fall or decline. **2** a disappointment. **come-hither** *a.* (*coll.*) sexually alluring (*a come-hither look*). **come-on** *n.* (*sl.*) an invitation, encouragement, esp. sexual. **come-at-able** (kŭmat´əbəl) *a.* easy to reach, accessible. **comedian** (kəmē´diən) *n.* **1** an entertainer who tells jokes, humorous anecdotes etc. **2** an actor or writer of comedy. **comedienne** (kəmēdien´) *n.* a female comedian. **comedy** (kom´ədi) *n.* (*pl.* **comedies**) **1** a dramatic composition of a light and entertaining character

depicting and often satirizing the incidents of ordinary life, and having a happy ending. **2** an entertaining drama of ordinary life more serious and more realistic than farce. **3** such compositions as a dramatic genre. **4** life or any incident or situation regarded as an amusing spectacle. **5** humour. **comedic** (-mē´-) *a.* **comedist** *n.* a writer of comedies. **comedy of manners** *n.* a dramatic composition satirizing social behaviour.

comely (kŭm´li) *a.* (*comp.* **comelier**, *superl.* **comeliest**) pleasing in appearance or behaviour. **comeliness** *n.*

✗ **comemorate** common misspelling of COM-MEMORATE.

comer (kŭm´ə) *n.* **1** a person who comes or arrives. **2** (*coll.*) a potential success.

comestible (kəmes´tibəl) *n.* (*usu. pl., formal or facet.*) food.

comet (kom´it) *n.* a luminous heavenly body, consisting of a nucleus or head, a coma, and a train or tail, revolving round the sun in a very eccentric orbit. **cometary** *a.* **cometic** (-met´-) *a.*

come-uppance (kŭmŭp´əns) *n.* (*coll.*) retribution for past misdeeds (*to get one's come-uppance*).

comfort (kŭm´fət) *v.t.* **1** to console. **2** to cheer, to encourage. **3** to make comfortable. ~*n.* **1** consolation. **2** support or assistance in time of weakness. **3** encouragement. **4** a person or thing that provides consolation or encouragement. **5** ease, general well-being, absence of trouble or anxiety. **6** (*pl.*) the material things that contribute to this. **comfortable** *a.* **1** providing comfort or security. **2** at ease, in good circumstances, free from want, hardship, trouble or pain. **3** happy, contented. **4** with a wide margin (*a comfortable lead*). **comfortableness** *n.* **comfortably** *adv.* **comforter** *n.* **1** a person or thing that comforts. **2** †a long, narrow, woollen scarf. **3** (*N Am.*) a quilted coverlet. **4** a baby's dummy. **comforting** *a.* **comfortingly** *adv.* **comfortless** *a.* **1** without comfort. **2** cheerless. **comfortlessly** *adv.* **comfortlessness** *n.* **comfort station** *n.* (*N Am., euphem.*) a public convenience.

comfrey (kŭm´fri) *n.* (*pl.* **comfreys**) a tall wild plant of the genus *Symphytum*, esp. *S. officinale*, with rough leaves and white or purplish flowers, formerly used for healing wounds.

comfy (kŭm´fi) *a.* (*comp.* **comfier**, *superl.* **comfiest**) (*coll.*) comfortable (*a comfy chair*). **comfily** *adv.* **comfiness** *n.*

comic (kom´ik) *a.* **1** of or relating to comedy; laughable, absurd. **2** facetious, burlesque, intended to provoke laughter. ~*n.* **1** a comedian. **2** a droll or amusing person, a buffoon. **3** a magazine containing comic strips, esp. for children. **4** (*N Am.*) comic strips. **5** the comic aspect of things. **comical** *a.* **1** ludicrous, laughable. **2** funny, provoking mirth. **comicality** (-kal´-) *n.* **comically** *adv.* **comic opera** *n.* a type of opera with humorous episodes, a light, sentimental plot and usu. some spoken dialogue. **comic strip**

n. a usu. comic narrative told in a series of pictures.

Usage note The meanings of the adjectives *comic* and *comical* overlap, but in general *comic* is more usual where the humour is deliberate or where comedy is the main purpose, and *comical* where the humour is unintentional or unexpected.

coming (kŭm'ing) *a.* **1** approaching. **2** future, to come. **3** of potential or future importance. ~*n.* the act of approaching or arriving. **not to know whether one is coming or going** to be totally confused, esp. because very busy. **coming and going, comings and goings** *n.* activity, movement.

☒ **comitee** common misspelling of COMMITTEE[1].

comity (kom'iti) *n.* (*pl.* **comities**) **1** affability, friendliness, courtesy, civility. **2** an association of nations. **3** comity of nations. **comity of nations** *n.* the courtesy by which a nation allows another's laws to be recognized within its territory, so far as is practicable.

comma (kom'ə) *n.* **1** a punctuation mark (,), denoting the shortest pause in reading. **2** (*Mus.*) a minute difference of tone. **3** (*also* **comma butterfly**) a butterfly, *Polygonia c-album*, with a white comma-shaped mark beneath the hindwing. **comma bacillus** *n.* a comma-shaped bacterium, *Vibrio comma*, which causes cholera.

command (kəmahnd') *v.t.* **1** to order, to call for, to enforce. **2** to govern, to hold in subjection, to exercise authority over. **3** to control, to have at one's disposal. **4** to master, to subjugate. **5** (*esp. Mil.*) to dominate, to overlook. ~*v.i.* **1** to give orders. **2** to exercise supreme authority. ~*n.* **1** an order, a bidding, a mandate. **2** power, authority (*to be in command*). **3** control, mastery. **4** (*Mil.*) a naval or military force under the command of a particular officer. **5** (*Comput.*) an instruction. **6** a working knowledge (of). **at command 1** ready for orders. **2** at one's disposal. **under command of** commanded by. **commandant** (kom'əndant) *n.* the governor or commanding officer of a place, force etc. **commandantship** *n.* **command economy** *n.* an economy in which prices, incomes and industrial activity are determined by central government rather than by market forces. **commanding** *a.* **1** giving or entitled to give commands (*a commanding officer*). **2** dignified. **3** impressive. **4** dominating, overlooking. **commandingly** *adv.* **command module** *n.* the compartment of a spacecraft from which operations are controlled. **Command Paper** *n.* a government report presented to Parliament. **command performance** *n.* a theatrical or film performance given by royal command. **command post** *n.* a place used as temporary headquarters by a military commander.

commandeer (koməndiə') *v.t.* **1** (*Mil.*) to seize or make use of for military purposes. **2** to seize or make use of without permission or authority.

commander (kəmahn'də) *n.* **1** a person who commands or is in authority. **2** (*Mil.*) a general or leader of a body of troops etc. **3** a naval officer between a lieutenant and a captain. **4** a police officer in London in charge of a district. **5** a knight commander. **6** a large wooden mallet. **commander-in-chief** *n.* (*pl.* **commanders-in-chief**) (*Mil.*) the officer in supreme command of military forces, of a foreign expedition etc. **commandership** *n.*

commandment (kəmahnd'mənt) *n.* an order, a command, esp. a divine command.

commando (kəmahn'dō) *n.* (*pl.* **commandos**) (*Mil.*) **1** a body of men called out for military service; a body of troops. **2** a body of troops selected and trained to undertake a specially hazardous raid on or behind the enemy lines. **3** a member of such a body. **4** a mobile amphibious force.

commemorate (kəmem'ərāt) *v.t.* **1** to keep in remembrance by some solemn act. **2** to celebrate the memory of. **3** to be a memorial of. **commemorable** *a.* **commemoration** (-ā'shən) *n.* **1** the act of commemorating. **2** a service, ceremony or festival in memory of some person, deed or event. **commemorative** *a.* **commemoratively** *adv.* **commemorator** *n.*

commence (kəmens') *v.i.* (*formal*) **1** to start, to begin. **2** to originate. ~*v.t.* to start, to begin. **commencement** *n.* (*formal*) **1** a beginning, an origin. **2** the first instance or first existence. **3** the day when the degrees of Master and Doctor are conferred, at Cambridge, Dublin and N American universities.

commend (kəmend') *v.t.* **1** to commit to the charge of, to entrust. **2** to recommend as worthy of notice, regard or favour. **3** to praise, to approve. **commendable** *a.* worthy of commendation. **commendableness** *n.* **commendably** *adv.* **commendation** (komendā'shən) *n.* **1** the act of commending. **2** recommendation of a person to the consideration or favour of another. **3** praise. **commendatory** *a.*, *n.* (*pl.* **commendatories**)

commensal (kəmen'səl) *a.* **1** (*Biol.*) (of an organism) living in intimate association with, on the surface of or in the substance of another, without being parasitic. **2** eating at the same table, sharing the same food. ~*n.* **1** (*Biol.*) a commensal organism. **2** a person who eats at the same table or shares the same food as another. **commensalism** *n.* **commensality** (komənsal'-) *n.*

commensurable (kəmen'shərəbəl) *a.* **1** measurable by a common unit. **2** proportionate (to). **3** (*Math.*) having a common factor. **commensurability** (-bil'-), **commensurableness** *n.* **commensurably** *adv.*

commensurate (kəmen'shərət) *a.* **1** having the same measure or extent. **2** proportionate. **commensurately** *adv.* **commensurateness** *n.*

comment (kom'ent) *n.* **1** a remark, an opinion. **2** criticism. **3** commenting (*I let it pass without* *comment).* **4** a note interpreting or illustrating a work or portion of a work. *~v.i.* **1** to make a comment or comments. **2** to make explanatory or critical remarks or notes (on a book or writing). **3** to criticize or make remarks (on) unfavourably. **commentary** *n. (pl.* **commentaries) 1** a series of explanatory notes on a whole work. **2** a broadcast description of an event as it takes place. **commentate** *v.i.* to act as commentator (on). **commentator** *n.* **1** the broadcaster of a commentary. **2** the author of a commentary. **3** an annotator, an expositor. **4** a person who comments on current affairs *(a political commentator).* **commenter** *n.*

commerce (kom´œs) *n.* **1** trade, financial transactions. **2** the interchange of commodities between nations or individuals, buying and selling. **3** social intercourse.

commercial (kəmœ´shəl) *a.* **1** of or relating to commerce. **2** done for profit. **3** (of chemicals) of poor quality and produced in bulk for industry. *~n.* an advertisement broadcast on radio or television. **commercial art** *n.* graphic art used in advertising etc. **commercialism** *n.* **1** commercial practices. **2** excessive emphasis on profit. **commercialist** *n.* **commerciality** (-shiăl´-) *n.* **commercialize, commercialise** *v.t.* **1** to make commercial. **2** to exploit or spoil for the sake of profit. **commercialization** (-zā´shən) *n.* **commercially** *adv.* **commercial traveller** *n.* an agent sent out by a company to solicit orders from retailers, a travelling sales representative. **commercial vehicle** *n.* a vehicle used for the transport of goods or passengers.

commère (kom´eə), **commere** *n.* a female compère.

commie (kom´i) *n., a.* (*coll., often derog.*) (a) communist.

comminate (kom´ināt) *v.t.* to threaten, to denounce. **commination** (-ā´shən) *n.* **comminatory** (-ət-) *a.*

commingle (kəming´gəl) *v.t., v.i.* (*poet.*) to mingle or mix together, to blend.

comminute (kom´inūt) *v.t.* **1** to make smaller. **2** to reduce to minute particles or to powder. **3** to divide into small portions. **comminution** (-nū´-) *n.*

commis (kom´i) *n. (pl.* **commis** (kom´i, kom´iz)) an apprentice or assistant waiter or chef.

commiserate (kəmiz´ərāt) *v.i.* to feel or express sympathy (with). **commiseration** (-ā´shən) *n.* **commiserative** (-ətiv) *a.* **commiseratively** *adv.*

commissar (kom´isah) *n.* (*Hist.*) **1** the head of a department of government in the USSR. **2** a party official responsible for political education in the USSR.

commissariat (komiseə´riət) *n.* **1** (*Mil.*) the department of the army charged with supplying provisions and stores. **2** (*Hist.*) a government department in the USSR.

commissary (kom´isəri) *n. (pl.* **commissaries) 1** a commissioner. **2** a deputy. **3** (*Mil.*) an officer in charge of the commissariat. **4** (*N Am.*) a shop

for the supply of food, equipment etc. in a military camp. **commissarial** (-seə´-) *a.* **commissary-ship** *n.*

commission (kəmish´ən) *n.* **1** the entrusting of a task or duty to another. **2** the task or duty entrusted. **3** an order, command or instruction to do or produce something. **4** the delegation of authority. **5** a number of persons entrusted with authority. **6** (*Mil., Naut.*) a document conferring rank or authority, esp. that of military and naval officers. **7** the authority to act as a factor or agent. **8** a percentage paid to a factor or agent. **9** the act of committing. **10** a body of commissioners. **11** the office of a commissioner. *~v.t.* **1** to authorize, to empower, to appoint to an office. **2** (*Naut. etc.*) to put (a ship, a machine etc.) into service or operation. **3** to order (the painting of a picture, writing of a book etc.). **4** to give (an artist, a writer etc.) a commission. **in commission** (of a naval ship) prepared for active service. **out of commission** (of a ship, machine etc.) not in service or operation, not in working order. **commission agent** *n.* a bookmaker. **commissionaire** (-neə´) *n.* a uniformed doorman at a hotel, theatre etc. **commissioned** *a.* holding a commission, esp. in the armed forces. **commissioner** *n.* **1** a person empowered to act by a commission or warrant. **2** a member of a commission or government board. **3** the head of some department of the public service. **Commissioner for Oaths** *n.* (*Law*) a person authorized to receive affidavits and other sworn declarations. **commissionership** *n.*

commissure (kom´isūə) *n.* **1** a joint, a seam. **2** the point of junction of two sides of anything separated, or of two similar organs, such as the hemispheres of the brain. **3** a suture. **4** (*Anat.*) a line of closure, as of the eyelids, lips, mandibles etc. **5** (*Bot.*) the line of junction of two parts of a plant. **commissural** (-sūə´-) *a.*

commit (kəmit´) *v.t.* (*pres.p.* **committing**, *past, p.p.* **committed**) **1** to entrust, to deposit, to consign. **2** to perpetrate (*to commit a crime*). **3** to refer (a bill etc.) to a committee. **4** (*Law*) to send for trial or to prison. **5** to assign, to pledge. **to commit to memory** to learn by heart. **commitment** *n.* **1** the act of committing. **2** the state of being committed. **3** an engagement to carry out certain duties or meet certain expenses. **committable** *a.* **committal** *n.* **1** a sending for trial, to prison, to a mental hospital etc. **2** the burial or cremation of a corpse. **committed** *a.* **1** morally or politically dedicated. **2** obliged. **committer** *n.*

committee[1] (kəmit´i) *n.* a board elected or deputed to examine, consider, and report on any business referred to them. **committee man, committee woman** *n. (pl.* **committee men, committee women**) a member of a committee. **committee stage** *n.* in Parliament, the stage at which a bill is examined in detail and may be amended.

committee[2] (komitē´) *n.* (*Law*) a person to whom the care of another person or their property is committed.

commode (kəmōd´) *n.* **1** a night commode. **2** a chest of drawers. **3** a chiffonier. **4** (*N Am.*) a lavatory.

commodify (kəmod´ifī) *v.t.* (*3rd pers. sing. pres.* **commodifies**, *pres.p.* **commodifying**, *past, p.p.* **commodified**) to turn into or treat as a commodity. **commodification** (-fikā´shən) *n.*

commodious (kəmō´diəs) *a.* roomy. **commodiously** *adv.* **commodiousness** *n.*

commodity (kəmod´iti) *n.* (*pl.* **commodities**) **1** an article of commerce, a product or raw material that can be bought and sold. **2** something that is useful or convenient. **3** advantage, profit.

commodore (kom´ədaw) *n.* **1** an officer ranking above captain and below rear-admiral. **2** by courtesy, the senior captain when two or more warships are in company. **3** the president of a yacht club. **4** the leading ship or the senior captain of a fleet of merchantmen. **Commodore-in-Chief** *n.* the supreme officer of the Royal Air Force.

common (kom´ən) *a.* (*comp.* **commoner**, *superl.* **commonest**) **1** belonging equally to more than one. **2** open or free to all. **3** of, relating to or affecting the public. **4** often met with, ordinary, usual, familiar. **5** (*derog.*) **a** of low rank, position or birth. **b** vulgar. **c** inferior, mean. **6** (*Math.*) belonging to several quantities. **7** (*Gram.*) applicable to a whole class. **8** (of a syllable) variable in quantity. **9** (*Law*) of lesser importance. ~*n.* **1** a tract of open ground, the common property of all members of a community. **2** (*Law*) **a** conjoint possession. **b** right of common. **3** (*sl.*) common sense. **4** a religious service used on various occasions. **in common** shared with another or others (*They have nothing in common*). **in common with** the same way as, like. **out of the common** extraordinary, unusual. **common chord** *n.* (*Mus.*) a note accompanied by its third and fifth. **common cold** *n.* a viral infection of the mucous membranes of the respiratory tract, accompanied by sneezing and coughing. **common crier** *n.* the public or town crier. **common denominator** *n.* **1** (*Math.*) a number that can be divided by the denominators of each of a group of fractions without remainder. **2** a feature shared by all members of a group. **commoner** *n.* **1** any one of the common people. **2** a person having a joint right in common ground. **3** a student at certain universities or schools who does not have a scholarship. **Common Era** *n.* the Christian era. **common factor** *n.* (*Math.*) a number that is a factor of two or more given quantities. **commonish** *a.* **common jury** *n.* (*pl.* **common juries**) (*Law*) a petty jury to try all cases. **common law** *n.* law based on usage or precedent rather than statutes. **common-law husband**, **common-law wife** *n.* a person recognized as a husband or wife after long cohabitation. **common logarithm** *n.* a logarithm to the base ten. **commonly** *adv.* **1** usually, frequently. **2** in an ordinary manner. **3** in a vulgar manner. **common metre** *n.* a metre for hymns,

four lines of 8, 6, 8, 6 syllables. **common multiple** *n.* any number containing two or more numbers an exact number of times without a remainder. **commonness** *n.* common noun, **common name** *n.* (*Gram.*) the name of any one of a class of objects or concepts, as distinct from a *proper noun* or *proper name*. **common or garden** *a.* (*coll.*) ordinary. **common property** *n.* something generally known. **common room** *n.* **1** a room in a college or school used by teachers or students for social purposes. **2** the people who use such a room. **common salt** *n.* sodium chloride, used for seasoning and preserving food. **common seal**[1] *n.* a seal of northern oceans, *Phoca vitulina*. **common seal**[2] *n.* the official seal of a corporate body. **common sense** *n.* sound practical judgement. **common-sense**, **commonsensical** *a.* marked by common sense. **common soldier** *n.* a private or non-commissioned officer. **common stock** *n.* (*N Am.*) ordinary shares. **common time** *n.* (*Mus.*) time with two or four beats, esp. four crotchets. **common valerian** *n.* the plant *Valeriana officianalis*. **common weal** *n.* the welfare or prosperity of the community. **common year** *n.* a period of 365 days.

commonality (komənal´iti) *n.* (*pl.* **commonalities**) **1** commonness; being shared by a number of individuals. **2** a common occurrence. **3** commonalty.

commonalty (kom´ənəlti) *n.* (*pl.* **commonalties**) **1** the common people. **2** mankind in general. **3** a commonwealth. **4** a corporation.

commonplace (kom´ənplās) *a.* common, trivial, trite, unoriginal. ~*n.* **1** a trite remark, a platitude. **2** a general idea or topic. **3** anything occurring frequently or habitually. **4** a passage entered in a commonplace book. **commonplace book** *n.* a book in which thoughts, extracts from books etc. are entered for future use. **commonplaceness** *n.*

commons (kom´ənz) *n.pl.* **1** the common people, esp. as part of a political system. **2** (**Commons**) the House of Commons. **3** food, esp. shared in common. **4** a ration or allowance of food.

commonwealth (kom´ənwelth) *n.* **1** the whole body of citizens, the body politic. **2** a free or independent state. **3** a republic. **4** (*fig.*) a body of persons having common interests.

commotion (kəmō´shən) *n.* **1** violent motion. **2** agitation, excitement. **3** a noisy disturbance. **4** a popular tumult or insurrection.

commune[1] (kom´ūn) *n.* **1** a group of people, not related, living together and sharing property and responsibilities. **2** the house used by such a group. **3** a small territorial district, esp. in France or Belgium, governed by a mayor and council. **4** the inhabitants or members of the council of such a district. **communal** (kom´ūnəl, kəmū´nəl) *a.* **1** for common use or benefit; shared. **2** of or relating to a commune. **3** of or relating to the community. **4** between different communities. **communalism** *n.* **1** the theory of government by communes of towns and districts. **2** the theory or

practice of living in communes. **communalist** *n.*
communalistic (-lis´-) *a.* **communality** (-nal´-) *n.*
communalize, communalise *v.t.* **communaliza-**
tion (-zā´shən) *n.* **communally** *adv.* **communard**
(-nahd) *n.* **1** a person who lives in a commune.
2 (*Hist.*) an adherent of the Paris Commune.

commune[2] (kəmūn´) *v.i.* **1** to converse together
familiarly or intimately. **2** to be or feel spiritually
close to (*to commune with nature*). **3** (*N Am.*) to
receive Holy Communion. **communer** *n.*

communicate (kəmū´nikāt) *v.t.* **1** to pass on,
to transmit. **2** to convey (information etc.) by
speech, writing, signals etc. **3** to impart, to reveal. **4** to give Holy Communion to. ~*v.i.* **1** to convey information, esp. by speech or writing. **2** to
share feelings etc. **3** to establish mutual understanding (with someone). **4** to be connected
(with), esp. by a common door. **5** to receive Holy
Communion. **communicable** *a.* **communicability**
(-bil´-), **communicableness** *n.* **communicably**
adv. **communicant** *n.* **1** a person who receives
Holy Communion. **2** a person who communicates information etc. **communication** (-ā´shən) *n.*
1 the act of communicating. **2** that which is communicated. **3** news, information. **4** conversation
or correspondence. **5** a means of passing from
one place to another. **6** a connecting link. **7** (*pl.*)
the means of communicating considered
collectively (e.g. telecommunications, the press
etc.). **8** the science of this. **9** (*pl., Mil.*) a system of
routes and vehicles for transport. **communica-**
tion cord *n.* a device whereby a passenger can
stop a train in an emergency. **communications**
satellite, communication satellite *n.* an artificial
satellite orbiting the earth and relaying television, telephone etc. signals. **communicative** *a.*
1 inclined or ready to communicate. **2** talkative,
not reserved. **communicatively** *adv.* **communic-**
ativeness *n.* **communicator** *n.* **communicatory** *a.*

communion (kəmūn´yən) *n.* **1** the act of communicating or communing. **2** participation,
sharing. **3** fellowship, social intercourse. **4** (**Com-**
munion) **a** Holy Communion. **b** the act of participating in the Eucharist. **5** union in religious
faith. **6** a religious body.

communiqué (komū´nikā) *n.* an official announcement.

communism (kom´ūnizm) *n.* **1** a theory of
government based on common ownership of all
property and means of production. **2** (*usu.* **Com-**
munism) the system of government, based on
Marxist socialism, practised in the former
USSR etc. **3** communalism. **communist** *n.* **1** an
adherent or advocate of communism. **2** (*usu.*
Communist) a member of a Communist Party. ~*a.*
(*also* **Communist**) of or relating to communism.
communistic (-nis´-) *a.* **communize, communise**
v.t. to make communal or communistic. **com-**
munization (-zā´shən) *n.*

communitarian (kəmūnitəə´riən) *n.* a member
of a community, esp. a communist community.
~*a.* of or relating to such a community.

community (kəmū´niti) *n.* (*pl.* **communities**) **1** a
body of people living in a particular place. **2** a
body of individuals having common interests,
occupation, religion, nationality etc. **3** society at
large, the public. **4** an organized body, municipal, national, social or political. **5** a body of
individuals living in a common home. **6** (*also*
Community) a body of nations (*the European
Community*). **7** common possession or liability.
8 fellowship. **9** similarity of nature or character.
10 a set of interdependent plants and animals
inhabiting an area. **community centre** *n.* a building open to all residents in the locality for social,
recreational and educational activities. **com-**
munity charge *n.* (*Hist.*) a flat-rate tax levied on
all adults to raise money for local government, a
type of poll tax. **community chest** *n.* (*esp. N Am.*)
a fund for welfare work in a community raised
by voluntary contributions. **community college**
n. a centre providing educational facilities for all
members of the community. **community policing**
n. the policy of assigning police officers to an
area where they are known or with which they
are familiar. **community policeman, community**
policewoman *n.* **community service** *n.* work for
the benefit of the community, esp. as stipulated
under a community service order. **community**
service order *n.* a form of sentence ordering a
convicted person to work for a specified time for
the benefit of the community. **community sing-**
ing *n.* organized singing by the audience at a
social gathering etc. **community worker** *n.* a person who works for the welfare of a community.

commute (kəmūt´) *v.t.* **1** to exchange or interchange. **2** to substitute (one payment, punishment etc.) for another. **3** (*Law*) to reduce the
severity of (a punishment). **4** to commutate. ~*v.i.*
1 to travel some distance daily to and from one's
place of work. **2** (*Math.*) to have a commutative
relationship. **commutable** *a.* **1** that can be com-
muted. **2** within commuting distance. **com-**
mutability (-bil´-) *n.* **commutate** (kom´ūtāt) *v.t.*
1 to reverse the direction of (an electric current).
2 to convert (an alternating current) to a direct
current. **commutation** (-tā´shən) *n.* **1** the act of
commuting or commutating. **2** change, exchange.
3 a payment made in commuting. **4** (*Law*) the
substitution of a lesser penalty for a greater.
5 (*Math.*) the act of reversing the order of two
quantities. **commutative** (kəmū´-, kom´ū-) *a.* **1** of
or relating to commutation. **2** (*Math.*) giving the
same result when the order of quantities is reversed. **commutatively** *adv.* **commutator** (kom´-)
n. **commutator transformer** *n.* a device for converting direct current from low to high voltage
and vice versa. **commuter** *n.* a person who com-
mutes to and from work.

comp (komp) *n.* (*coll.*) **1** a competition. **2** (*Print.*)
a compositor. **3** (*Mus.*) an accompaniment. ~*v.i.*
1 (*Print.*) to work as a compositor. **2** (*Mus.*) to
play an accompaniment. ~*v.t.* **1** (*Print.*) to work
as a compositor on. **2** (*Mus.*) to accompany.

compact[1] (kəmpakt´) a. **1** closely packed or fitted together. **2** small and practical (a compact camera). **3** (of a person) small and well-proportioned. **4** solid. **5** succinct. ~v.t. **1** to consolidate. **2** to join or pack closely and firmly together. **3** to condense. **4** to compose. **compact disc** (kom´pakt) n. a small disc, read by laser beam, on which sound or information is stored digitally. **compacted** a. **compaction** n. **compactly** adv. **compactness** n.

compact[2] (kom´pakt) n. **1** a small flat case containing face powder, puff and mirror. **2** (N Am.) a middle-sized motor car. **3** a compact mass of powder.

compact[3] (kom´pakt) n. an agreement, a bargain, a covenant.

compadre (kompah´dri) n. (N Am., coll.) a friend.

✕ compair common misspelling of COMPARE.

companion[1] (kəmpan´yən) n. **1** a person who associates with or accompanies another (a travelling companion). **2** a person employed to live with another. **3** (**Companion**) a member of the lowest grade in some orders of knighthood. **4** a handbook. **5** a thing that matches or goes with another; one of a pair. **6** a piece of equipment with several uses. **7** (Astron.) a star that accompanies another; the fainter component of a double star. ~v.t. to accompany. ~v.i. to associate or keep company (with). **companionable** a. **1** fit to be a companion. **2** sociable. **companionableness** n. **companionably** adv. **companionate** a. **1** of, like or acting as a companion. **2** wellsuited; well-matched. **companion-in-arms** n. a fellow soldier. **companionless** a. **companionship** n. fellowship, association, company.

companion[2] (kəmpan´yən) n. (Naut.) **1** the raised window frame on the quarterdeck through which light passes to the cabins and decks below. **2** a companionway. **companion hatch** n. a covering over the entrance to a cabin. **companion hatchway** n. an opening leading to a cabin. **companion ladder** n. a ladder leading from a cabin to the quarterdeck. **companionway** n. a staircase between a cabin and the quarterdeck.

company (kŭm´pəni) n. (pl. **companies**) **1** society, companionship, fellowship. **2** a number of people associated together for carrying on a business. **3** a corporation. **4** a number of people assembled; an audience. **5** guests, visitors. **6** a body of actors etc. **7** (Mil.) a subdivision of an infantry regiment under the command of a captain. **in company** with others, not alone. **in company with** together with. **to keep company (with) 1** to associate (with). **2** to court. **to keep someone company** to go or be with someone. **company car** n. a car provided for the use of an employee on company business (and often also for private use). **company officer** n. a captain or a commissioned officer of lower rank. **company sergeant major** n. (Mil.) the highest-ranking non-commissioned officer of a company.

comparative (kəmpar´ətiv) a. **1** of or involving comparison. **2** estimated by comparison. **3** (Gram.) expressing comparison, expressing a higher or lower degree of a quality (a comparative adjective). ~n. (Gram.) the comparative degree or the word or inflection expressing it. **comparatively** adv.

compare (kəmpeə´) v.t. **1** to liken (one thing to another) (He has been compared to Nureyev). **2** to see how (one thing) agrees with or resembles another (Compare her essay with mine). **3** to see how (two things) resemble each other or are related. **4** (Gram.) to inflect according to degrees of comparison. ~v.i. to bear comparison (with). ~n. (poet.) **1** comparison. **2** an equal. **comparable** (kom´pə-) a. **1** capable of being compared (with). **2** worthy of being compared (to). **comparability** (kompərəbil´-, kəmpərəbil´-), **comparableness** n. **comparably** adv.

Usage note The pronunciation of comparable as (-par´-), with stress on the second syllable, is best avoided.

comparison (kəmpar´isən) n. **1** the act of comparing. **2** a comparative estimate. **3** a simile, contrast or illustration. **4** similarity. **5** (Gram.) the degrees of comparison. **in/ by comparison with** compared with. **to bear/ stand comparison (with)** to be as good (as) or better (than).

compartment (kəmpaht´mənt) n. **1** a division. **2** a portion of a railway carriage, room etc., separated from the other parts. **3** (Naut.) a portion of the hold of a ship shut off by a bulkhead and capable of being made watertight. **4** any part separated or kept separate from other parts, as in a desk, the mind etc. **compartmental** (kompahtmen´-) a. **compartmentalize, compartmentalise** v.t. to divide into separate units or categories. **compartmentalization** (-zā´shən) n. **compartmentally** adv.

compass (kŭm´pəs) n. **1** an instrument indicating magnetic north, used to ascertain direction, to determine the course of a ship or aeroplane etc. **2** (usu. pl.) a pair of compasses. **3** a circle, a circumference. **4** area, extent. **5** reach, capacity. **6** the range or power of the voice or a musical instrument. **7** a circuit, a roundabout course. ~v.t. **1** to go round. **2** to besiege, to surround, to hem in. **3** to comprehend. **4** to accomplish, to contrive. **compassable** a.

compassion (kəmpash´ən) n. pity, sympathy for the sufferings and sorrows of others. **compassionate** (-ət) a. merciful, inclined to pity, sympathetic. **compassionate leave** n. leave granted on account of bereavement, domestic difficulties etc. **compassionately** adv. **compassionateness** n.

compatible (kəmpat´ibəl) a. **1** able to co-exist, well-matched or well-suited. **2** congruous, consistent, harmonious. **3** (Comput.) (of electronic machinery of different types or by different manufacturers) able to work together without modification. ~n. a compatible piece of electronic machinery. **compatibility** (-bil´-) *n.* **compatibly** *adv.*

compatriot (kəmpat´riət) *n.* a fellow countryman. **compatriotic** (-ot´-) *a.*

compeer (kom´piə, kəmpiə´) *n.* **1** an equal, a peer. **2** a comrade, a companion.

compel (kəmpel´) *v.t.* (*pres.p.* **compelling**, *past,* *p.p.* **compelled**) **1** to force, to oblige (*We were compelled to agree*). **2** to cause or exact by force (*to compel obedience*). **compellable** *a.* (*Law*) (of a witness) who may be forced to give evidence. **compelling** *a.* arousing strong interest or admiration. **compellingly** *adv.*

compendium (kəmpen´diəm) *n.* (*pl.* **compendiums, compendia** (-diə)) **1** a handbook or reference book. **2** an abridgement. **3** an epitome, a summary. **4** a brief compilation. **5** a collection of board or card games in one box. **6** any similar collection or package. **compendious** *a.* comprehensive but brief. **compendiously** *adv.* **compendiousness** *n.*

compensate (kom´pənsāt) *v.t.* **1** to recompense. **2** to make amends for. **3** to counterbalance. **4** in mechanics, to provide with an equivalent weight or other device forming a compensation. *~v.i.* **1** to make amends (for). **2** (*Psych.*) to make up for a perceived or imagined deficiency by developing another aspect of the personality. **compensation** (-sā´shən) *n.* **1** the act of compensating. **2** payment, recompense, amends. **3** that which balances or is an equivalent for something else. **4** (*Psych.*) the act or result of compensating. **5** (*N Am.*) salary, wages. **compensational** *a.* **compensation balance, compensation pendulum** *n.* (*Physics*) a balance wheel or pendulum constructed so as to make equal time beats despite changes of temperature. **compensative** (kom´pənsətiv, kəmpen´-) *a.* compensating. *~n.* an equivalent. **compensator** *n.* **compensatory** (kəmpen´sətəri, kompənsā´-) *a.*

compère (kom´peə), **compere** *n.* a person who introduces the items in a stage or broadcast entertainment. *~v.t.* to act as compère of. *~v.i.* to act as compère.

compete (kəmpēt´) *v.i.* **1** to contend as a rival (with). **2** to strive in emulation. **3** to take part (in a race, contest etc.) (*to compete in marathon*).

competent (kom´pitənt) *a.* **1** qualified, capable, suitable. **2** sufficient, adequate. **3** (*Law*) legally qualified (*a competent witness*). **competence, competency** *n.* **1** the state of being competent. **2** ability, skill. **3** adequate income or financial support. **4** (*Law*) legal capacity or qualification. **5** (*Law*) admissibility (of evidence). **competently** *adv.*

competition (kompətish´ən) *n.* **1** the act of competing. **2** a competitive game, contest etc. **3** rivalry. **4** the struggle for existence or superiority in industry or commerce. **5** the people or organizations competing against one. **competitive** (-pet´-) *a.* **1** of, relating to or involving competition. **2** liking competition, keen to compete. **3** (of

prices etc.) giving one an advantage over rivals. **competitively** *adv.* **competitiveness** *n.* **competitor** (-pet´-) *n.*

compile (kəmpīl´) *v.t.* **1** to compose using material from various authors or sources (*to compile an anthology*). **2** to assemble (various items) as in a list or dictionary. **3** to accumulate. **4** (*Comput.*) to put (a program or instruction written in a high-level language) into machine code. **compilation** (kompilā´shən) *n.* **1** the act of compiling. **2** that which is compiled. **compiler** *n.* **1** a person who compiles. **2** (*Comput.*) a program that compiles.

complacent (kəmplā´sənt) *a.* **1** smug, self-satisfied. **2** satisfied, gratified. **complacency, complacence** *n.* **complacently** *adv.*

Usage note See note under COMPLAISANT.

complain (kəmplān´) *v.i.* **1** to express dissatisfaction or objection. **2** to state a grievance. **3** to make a charge. **4** to murmur, to find fault. **5** to express pain or suffering (*He complained of backache*). **6** to express grief, to moan or wail. *~v.t.* to state as a complaint. **complainant** *n.* **1** a person who complains or makes a complaint. **2** (*Law*) a plaintiff. **complainer** *n.* **complaining** *a., n.* **complainingly** *adv.* **complaint** *n.* **1** an expression of grievance or dissatisfaction (*to make a complaint*). **2** the subject or ground of such expression. **3** an ailment. **4** an accusation. **5** (*Law*) a formal allegation or charge.

complaisant (kəmplā´zənt) *a.* **1** courteous, deferential. **2** acquiescent, obliging. **complaisance** *n.* **complaisantly** *adv.*

Usage note The adjectives *complaisant* and *complacent* should not be confused: a complacent person is pleased with themselves, but a complaisant person is agreeable to others.

complement[1] (kom´plimənt) *n.* **1** that which is necessary to make something complete. **2** either of a pair of things that go together. **3** the full number required to man a vessel. **4** full quantity. **5** (*Gram.*) a word or phrase required to complete the predicate. **6** the class of things that do not belong to a given set. **complemental** (-men´-) *a.* **complementally** *adv.* **complementary** (-men´-) *a.* that forms a complement. **complementarity** (-tar´iti) *n.* (**complementarities**) a state or relationship involving complementary elements. **complementary angle** *n.* either of two angles that together make 90°. **complementary colour** *n.* either of two colours that produce white when mixed together. **complementary medicine** *n.* alternative medicine.

Usage note The spellings of *complement* and *compliment* (and their derivatives) should not be confused. The meanings related to *complete* are spelt *complEment* with an *e* like *complete*; the expression of praise or approval is a *complIment*.

complement[2] (kom´pliment) *v.t.* **1** to be a complement to. **2** to complete. **complementation** (-tā´shən) *n.*

complete (kəmplēt´) *a.* **1** finished (*The work is complete*). **2** entire, free from deficiency (*a complete set*). **3** absolute (*complete confidence*). **4** (*usu. facet.*) skilled, highly accomplished. ~*v.t.* **1** to finish. **2** to bring to a state of perfection. **3** to make whole, to make up the deficiencies of. **4** to fill in the required information on (a questionnaire, a form etc.). **5** (*Law*) to conclude (a sale of land, property etc.). **complete with** having (an important or desirable accessory). **completely** *adv.* **completeness** *n.* **completion** *n.* **completist** *n.* a person who collects things obsessively or without discrimination. ~*a.* of or relating to such a person. **completive** *a.*

complex (kom´pleks) *a.* **1** composed of several parts, composite. **2** complicated. ~*n.* **1** a set of interconnected buildings for related purposes, forming a whole. **2** any complicated whole. **3** a complicated system or network of parts. **4** a collection. **5** (*Psych.*) a group of emotions, ideas etc., partly or wholly repressed, which can influence personality or behaviour (*an inferiority complex*). **6** an obsession. **complexity** (-plek´siti) *n.* (*pl.* **complexities**). **complexly** *adv.* **complexness** *n.*

complexion (kəmplek´shən) *n.* **1** the colour and appearance of the skin, esp. of the face. **2** nature, character, aspect. **complexioned** *a.* (*usu. in comb.*). **complexionless** *a.*

compliance (kəmplī´əns) *n.* **1** the act of complying. **2** the capacity of a mechanical system to yield to an applied force. **in compliance with** in accordance with. **compliant** *a.* **compliantly** *adv.*

complicate (kom´plikāt) *v.t.* **1** to make complex or intricate. **2** to involve. **complicated** *a.* **complicatedly** *adv.* **complicatedness** *n.* **complication** (-ā´shən) *n.* **1** the act of complicating. **2** the state of being complicated. **3** a complicated or complicating matter or circumstance. **4** (*Med.*) a disease or condition arising in the course of another.

complicity (kəmplis´əti) *n.* participation, partnership, esp. in wrongdoing. **complicit** *a.*

compliment[1] (kom´plimənt) *n.* **1** an expression or act of praise, courtesy, respect or regard. **2** (*pl.*) ceremonious greetings, courtesies, respects. **3** (*pl.*) praise. **to pay a compliment** to utter or perform a compliment. **to return the compliment 1** to pay a compliment in return for one received. **2** to retaliate in kind. **complimental** (-men´-) *a.* **complimentary** (-men´-) *a.* **1** expressing praise. **2** given free of charge. **complimentarily** *adv.*

Usage note See note under COMPLEMENT[1].

compliment[2] (kom´pliment) *v.t.* **1** to pay compliments to. **2** to congratulate, to praise, to flatter courteously.

compline (kom´plin, -plīn) *n.* in the Roman Catholic Church, the last part of the divine office of the breviary, sung after vespers.

comply (kəmplī´) *v.i.* (*3rd pers. sing. pres.* **complies**, *pres.p.* **complying**, *past,p.p.* **complied**) **1** to act or be in accordance (with rules, wishes etc.) (*The design does not comply with our specifications*). **2** to assent, to agree.

component (kəmpō´nənt) *a.* serving to make up a compound or a larger whole, constituent. ~*n.* **1** a constituent part. **2** (*Math.*) any of a set of vectors equivalent to a given vector. **componential** *a.*

comport (kəmpawt´) *v.t.* (*usu. reflex.*) to conduct (oneself), to behave. **to comport with** to suit, to agree with. **comportment** *n.*

compos COMPOS MENTIS.

compose (kəmpōz´) *v.t.* **1** to make, arrange or construct, esp. by putting together several parts to form one whole. **2** to constitute, to make up by combination. **3** to write, construct or produce (a literary or musical work etc.). **4** to arrange or design artistically (*to compose a picture*). **5** to calm, to soothe (*to compose oneself*). **6** to settle, to adjust. **7** to arrange (type for printing) in proper order. ~*v.i.* to compose music. **composed** *a.* calm, tranquil, settled. **composed of** made up of, comprising. **composedly** (-zid-) *adv.* **composer** *n.* a person who composes, esp. the author of a musical work.

Usage note See note under COMPRISE.

composite[1] (kom´pəzit) *a.* **1** made up of distinct parts or elements. **2** compound. **3** (*Bot.*) of or relating to the Compositae, a large family of plants, so called because the heads are made up of many small flowers. ~*n.* **1** a composite substance or thing. **2** (*Bot.*) a composite plant. **compositely** *adv.* **compositeness** *n.* **Composite order** *n.* (*Archit.*) the last of the five orders, which combines elements of the Corinthian and Ionic. **composite resolution** (kom´pəzīt) *n.* a resolution made up from related resolutions from local branches (of a trade union etc.) and containing the main points of each of them.

composite[2] (kom´pəzīt) *v.t.* to merge (related motions from different branches of a trade union, political party etc.) for presentation to a national conference. ~*n.* a composited motion.

composition (kompəzish´ən) *n.* **1** the act of composing or putting together to form a whole. **2** the thing composed, esp. a literary or musical work. **3** an essay, a piece written for the sake of practice in literary expression. **4** orderly disposition of parts, structural arrangement, style. **5** a combination of several parts or ingredients, a compound. **6** constitution. **7** character, nature. **8** (*Print.*) the process of setting type. **9** settlement by compromise. **10** (*Math.*) the combination of functions in a series. **compositional** *a.* **compositionally** *adv.*

compositor (kəmpoz´itə) *n.* (*Print.*) a person who sets type.

compos mentis (kompos men´tis), (*coll.*) **compos** (kom´pos) *a.* in one's right mind.

compost (kom'post) n. **1** a fertilizing mixture of vegetable matter etc. **2** a mixture containing this, in which plants are grown (*potting compost*). **3** any mixture. ~*v.t.* **1** to make into compost. **2** to manure with compost. **compost heap, compost pile** n. a heap of waste plant material decomposing into compost.

composure (kəmpō'zhə) n. calmness, tranquillity, esp. of the mind.

compote (kom'pōt) n. fruit stewed or preserved in syrup.

compound[1] (kom'pownd) a. **1** composed of two or more ingredients or elements. **2** composed of two or more parts. **3** collective, combined, composite. **4** (*Biol., Zool.*) formed by a combination of parts or of several individual organisms. ~n. **1** a combination, a mixture. **2** a compound word. **3** (*Chem.*) a combination of two or more elements by chemical action. **compound eye** n. an eye made up of many separate light sensitive units, as in insects. **compound fracture** n. a fracture in which the surrounding skin is injured, usually by the protrusion of the bone. **compound fruit** n. a fruit formed from several carpels of the same flower, or the carpels of several flowers. **compound interest** n. **1** interest payable on both the principal and its accumulated interest. **2** the method of calculating such interest. **compound interval** n. (*Mus.*) an interval greater than one octave. **compound leaf** n. a leaf composed of leaflets on a branched leaf-stalk. **compound sentence** n. a sentence consisting of two or more clauses. **compound word** n. a word formed from two or more existing words, as *toothbrush*.

compound[2] (kəmpownd') *v.t.* **1** to make into one mass or whole by the combination of several constituent parts. **2** to make up or form (a composite). **3** to intensify or complicate (*The drought compounded the shortage of food*). **4** to settle amicably. **5** to adjust by agreement. **6** to compromise. **7** (*Law*) to forbear to prosecute (a crime etc.) for some valuable consideration (*to compound a felony*). ~*v.i.* to settle with creditors by agreement. **compoundable** a. **compounder** n.

compound[3] (kom'pownd) n. **1** an open enclosure where workers are housed, esp. in S African mines. **2** the yard or space surrounding a house or factory in India, China etc. **3** any similar walled or fenced space, as in a prison. **4** an enclosure for animals, a pound.

comprehend (komprihend') *v.t.* **1** to grasp mentally, to understand. **2** to comprise, to include. **comprehensible** a. **1** that may be comprehended. **2** clear, intelligible. **comprehensibility** (-bil'-) n. **comprehensibly** adv.

comprehension (komprihen'shən) n. **1** the act or power of comprehending or understanding. **2** (*also* **comprehension test**) an exercise to test a student's understanding of a given passage. **3** the act of comprising or including. **comprehensive** a. **1** including all or most things; thorough. **2** of or relating to understanding. **3** of or relating to a

comprehensive school (*comprehensive education*). **4** (of motor vehicle insurance) providing protection against all or most risks. ~n. a comprehensive school. **comprehensively** adv. **comprehensiveness** n. **comprehensive school** n. a secondary school serving all children of all abilities in an area.

compress[1] (kəmpres') *v.t.* **1** to squeeze or press together. **2** to bring into narrower limits. **compressed air** n. air at a higher pressure than atmospheric pressure. **compressible** a. **compressibility** (-bil'-) n. **compression** n. **1** the act of compressing. **2** the state of being compressed. **3** a reduction in volume of fuel, air etc. causing an increase in pressure, as in an engine. **compressive** a. **compressor** n. a device for compressing esp. air or other gases.

compress[2] (kom'pres) n. (*Med.*) **1** a soft pad used to maintain pressure on an artery to stop bleeding. **2** a wet cloth for reducing inflammation.

comprise (kəmprīz') *v.t.* **1** to contain, to include, to consist of. **2** to make up, to constitute. **3** to bring (within certain limits). **comprisable** a.

Usage note The meanings of *compose, comprise, consist* and *constitute* overlap, but the generally accepted uses are as follows: a whole comprises or consists of parts or material (so *The whole army comprised only two divisions*, *The whole army consisted of only two divisions*); parts compose or constitute a whole (so *Only two divisions composed/ constituted the whole army*); a whole is composed of or constituted of parts or material (so *The whole army was composed of/ constituted of only two divisions*). It is best to avoid the use of *comprise* instead of *compose* in expressions such as *Only two divisions comprised the whole army* and *The whole army was comprised of only two divisions*, and the use of *comprise* instead of *include* where not all the parts are specified, as in *The army comprised a Scottish division*.

compromise (kom'prəmīz) n. **1** a settlement by mutual concession. **2** adjustment of opposing opinions, principles or purposes by a partial surrender. **3** a medium between conflicting purposes or courses of action. ~*v.t.* **1** to place in a position of difficulty or danger. **2** to expose to risk of disgrace. ~*v.i.* to make a compromise. **compromiser** n. **compromisingly** adv.

comptroller (kəntrō'lə, komp-) n. a controller, a financial officer or executive.

compulsion (kəmpŭl'shən) n. **1** the act of compelling by moral or physical force. **2** constraint of the will. **3** (*Psych.*) an irresistible impulse to perform actions against one's will. **compulsive** (-siv) a. **1** involving or resulting from compulsion. **2** tending to compel. **3** irresistible. **compulsively** adv. **compulsiveness** n. **compulsory** (-səri) a. **1** obligatory, required by law, rules, regulations etc. **2** necessary, essential. **compulsorily** adv. **compulsoriness** n. **compulsory purchase** n. the purchase of land or property against the owner's wishes, for a public development.

compunction (kəmpŭngk´shən) n. 1 pricking or reproach of conscience. 2 remorse, contrition. 3 regret.

compute (kəmpūt´) v.t. 1 to determine by calculation. 2 to estimate. ~v.i. 1 to calculate. 2 to use a computer. **computable** a. **computability** (-bil´-) n. **computation** (kəmpūtā´shən) n. **computational** a. **computationally** adv.

computer (kəmpū´tə) n. 1 an electronic device which does complex calculations or processes data according to the instructions contained in a program. 2 a person who computes. **computerate** a. computer-literate. **computerize, computerise** v.t. 1 to perform or control by means of computer. 2 to install computers in (a business, etc.). 3 to store in a computer. **computerization** (-zā´shən) n. **computer literacy** n. the ability to understand and operate computers. **computer-literate** a. **computer programmer** n. a person who writes programs for computers. **computer science** n. the sciences connected with the construction and operation of computers. **computer virus** n. a self-replicating computer program which damages or destroys the memory or other programs of the host computer.

comrade (kom´rād) n. 1 a friend, a companion. 2 a fellow soldier. 3 a fellow socialist or communist. **comrade-in-arms** n. (pl. **comrades-in-arms**) a companion or workmate. **comradely** a. **comradeship** n.

❌ **comunicate** common misspelling of COMMUNICATE.

❌ **comunity** common misspelling of COMMUNITY.

con[1] (kon) n. (sl.) a fraud, a swindle. ~v.t. (pres.p. **conning**, past, p.p. **conned**) 1 to deceive. 2 to swindle. **conman** n. (pl. **conmen**) a confidence man, a swindler. **con-trick** n. a confidence trick.

con[2] (kon) n. (usu. pl.) a reason against (the pros and cons).

con[3] (kon) n. (sl.) a convict.

con[4] (kon), (N Am.) **conn** v.t. (pres.p. **conning**, past, p.p. **conned**) (Naut.) to direct the steering of (a ship). **conner** n. **conning tower** n. the armoured shelter in a warship or submarine from which the vessel is steered.

conation (kənā´shən) n. (Philos., Psych.) the faculty of desiring or willing. **conational** a. **conative** (kon´-) a.

con brio (kon brē´ō) adv. (Mus.) with vigour or spirit.

concatenate (kənkat´ənāt) v.t. to join or link together in a successive series. ~a. joined, linked. **concatenation** (-ā´shən) n.

concave (kon´kāv) a. having a curve or surface hollow like the inner side of a circle or sphere, as distinct from convex. **concavely** adv. **concavity** (-kav´-) n. (pl. **concavities**)

conceal (kənsēl´) v.t. 1 to hide or cover from sight or observation. 2 to keep secret. **concealable** a. **concealer** n. **concealment** n.

concede (kənsēd´) v.t. 1 to yield, to give up, to surrender. 2 to admit, to grant. 3 to allow to pass unchallenged. 4 to allow an opponent to win (to concede a goal). ~v.i. 1 to yield. 2 to make concessions. 3 to admit defeat. **conceder** n.

conceit (kənsēt´) n. 1 a vain opinion of oneself, overweening self-esteem. 2 a whim, a fanciful idea. 3 in literature, an elaborate or far-fetched image. **conceited** a. full of conceit, inordinately vain. **conceitedly** adv. **conceitedness** n.

conceive (kənsēv´) v.t. 1 to become pregnant with. 2 to form, as an idea or concept, in the mind. 3 to imagine or suppose as possible. 4 to think. 5 to formulate. ~v.i. 1 to become pregnant. 2 to form an idea or concept (of). **conceivable** a. capable of being conceived in the mind, imaginable, possible. **conceivability** (-bil´-) n. **conceivably** adv.

❌ **concensus** common misspelling of CONSENSUS.

concentrate (kon´səntrāt) v.t. 1 to bring to a common focus, centre or point. 2 to reduce to a greater density or strength by removing water etc. ~v.i. 1 to come to a common focus or centre. 2 to direct all one's thoughts or efforts to one end (to concentrate on one's work; I can't concentrate). ~n. 1 a product of concentration. 2 any concentrated substance, esp. a concentrated solution of a foodstuff. **concentrated** a. 1 intense. 2 having had water etc. removed (concentrated acid). **concentratedly** adv. **concentration** (-trā´-shən) n. 1 the act or process of concentrating. 2 mental application. 3 (Chem.) the degree of concentration, esp. of a solution. **concentration camp** n. a camp for housing political prisoners and interned persons. **concentrative** a.

concentric (kənsen´trik) a. having a common centre (concentric circles). **concentrically** adv. **concentricity** (konsəntris´-) n.

concept (kon´sept) n. 1 a general notion, an abstract idea. 2 (Philos.) a general notion or idea comprising all the attributes common to a class of things. 3 (coll.) an idea, invention or innovation. **conception** (-sep´shən) n. 1 the act of conceiving. 2 the impregnation of the ovum followed by implantation in the womb. 3 origin, beginning. 4 a concept. **to have no conception of** to be unable to imagine. **conceptional** a. **conceptive** (-sep´-) a.

conceptual (kənsep´tūəl) a. of or relating to mental concepts or conception. **conceptualism** n. (Philos.) the doctrine that universals exist only in the mind of the thinking subject (a doctrine intermediate between nominalism and realism). **conceptualize, conceptualise** v.t. to form a concept of. ~v.i. to form a concept. **conceptualization** (-zā´shən) n. **conceptually** adv.

concern (kənsœn´) v.t. 1 to relate or belong to. 2 to affect. 3 to be of importance to. 4 to interest. 5 to disturb, to worry. 6 (usu. reflex.) to involve (oneself) (She doesn't concern herself with the financial side of the business). ~n. 1 that which affects or is of interest or importance to a person.

2 interest, regard. **3** anxiety, solicitude. **4** a business, a firm, an establishment. **5** a matter of personal importance. **6** (*pl.*) affairs. **7** (*coll.*) an affair, a thing. **concerned** *a.* **1** interested, involved, engaged (with) (*the people concerned*; *I was concerned with finding out what had happened*). **2** anxious, solicitous (about). **as far as I am concerned** in my opinion, as regards my interests. **concernedly** (-nid-) *adv.* **concernedness** *n.* **concerning** *prep.* with respect to. **concernment** *n.* (*formal*) **1** that which interests or concerns. **2** an affair, a matter, business. **3** importance. **4** anxiety.

concert[1] (kon´sət) *n.* **1** a public musical entertainment. **2** harmony, accordance of plans or ideas. **3** concord, harmonious union of sounds. **in concert 1** acting together. **2** (of musicians) performing live on stage. **concert grand** *n.* a powerful grand piano for use at concerts. **concert master** *n.* (*esp. N Am.*) the leader of an orchestra. **concert pitch** *n.* (*Mus.*) the standard pitch, in which the A above middle C has a frequency of 440 hertz.

concert[2] (kənsœt´) *v.t.* **1** to plan, to arrange mutually. **2** to contrive, to adjust. **concerted** *a.* **1** mutually planned or devised; combined (*a concerted effort*). **2** (*Mus.*) arranged in parts.

concertante (konchətan´ti) *n.* (*pl.* **concertanti** (konchətan´ti)) (*Mus.*) a piece of music containing a number of solo passages.

concertina (konsətē´nə) *n.* (*pl.* **concertinas**) a portable instrument having a keyboard at each end with bellows between. *~v.i.* (*3rd pers. sing. pres.* **concertinas**, *pres.p.* **concertinaing**, *past*, *p.p.* **concertinaed**) to collapse or fold up like a concertina.

concerto (kənshœ´tō) *n.* (*pl.* **concertos, concerti** (-ti)) a composition for a solo instrument or solo instruments with orchestral accompaniment.

concession (kənsesh´ən) *n.* **1** the act of conceding. **2** the thing conceded. **3** a reduction in price granted to a particular group of people (*no concessions for senior citizens*). **4** a privilege or right granted by a government, esp. for the use of land or property. **5** the (exclusive) right to market a particular product or service in a particular area. **concessionaire** (-neə´), **concessionnaire** *n.* a person who holds a concession, esp. from the government. **concessional** *a.* **concessionary** *a.* **concessive** (-siv) *a.* **1** conceding. **2** implying concession. **3** (*Gram.*) **a** (of a phrase or clause) giving a reason why something might not have been so (in English introduced by a preposition or conjunction such as *although* or *in spite of*). **b** (of a preposition or conjunction) introducing such a phrase or clause.

conch (kongk, konch) *n.* (*pl.* **conchs, conches**) **1** a shellfish of the family Strombidae. **2** its large spiral shell. **3** a shell of this kind used as a trumpet. **4** (*Archit.*) the domed roof of an apse, or the apse itself. **concha** (kong´kə) *n.* (*pl.* **conchae**

(-kē)) (*Anat.*) the largest and deepest concavity in the external ear.

conchie (kon´shi), **conchy** *n.* (*pl.* **conchies**) (*coll.*, *derog.*) a conscientious objector.

conchology (kongkol´əji) *n.* (*Zool.*) the branch of zoology that deals with shells and the animals inhabiting them. **conchological** (-loj´-) *a.* **conchologist** *n.*

concierge (konsiœzh´) *n.* **1** a doorkeeper, a porter, a janitor. **2** a hotel employee who assists guests by booking tours etc.

❌ **concieve** common misspelling of CONCEIVE.

conciliar (kənsil´iə) *a.* of or relating to a council, esp. an ecclesiastical council.

conciliate (kənsil´iāt) *v.t.* **1** to win the regard or goodwill of, to win over. **2** to gain or win (regard, goodwill, favour etc.). **3** to pacify. **conciliation** (-ā´shən) *n.* **conciliative** *a.* **conciliator** *n.* **conciliatory** *a.* **conciliatoriness** *n.*

concise (kənsīs´) *a.* condensed, brief, terse. **concisely** *adv.* **conciseness** *n.* **concision** (-sizh´ən) *n.*

conclave (kon´klāv) *n.* **1** a secret assembly or private meeting. **2** the assembly of cardinals for the election of a pope. **3** the apartment where they meet.

conclude (kənklood´) *v.t.* **1** to bring to an end, to finish. **2** to determine, to settle. **3** to gather as a consequence from reasoning, to infer. *~v.i.* **1** to come to an end. **2** to come to a decision. **3** to draw an inference. **conclusion** (-zhən) *n.* **1** an end, a finish, a termination. **2** a result. **3** an inference. **4** a final decision or judgement. **5** the final part, a summing-up. **6** settlement (of terms etc.). **7** (*Logic*) the inferential proposition of a syllogism. **in conclusion** to conclude. **conclusive** (-siv) *a.* that puts an end to argument, decisive, final. **conclusively** *adv.* **conclusiveness** *n.* **conclusory** (-səri) *a.*

concoct (kənkokt´) *v.t.* **1** to prepare by mixing together. **2** to invent, to devise (*to concoct a lie*). **concocter** *n.* **concoction** *n.* **1** the act of concocting. **2** the thing concocted. **concoctive** *a.* **concoctor** *n.*

concomitant (kənkom´itənt) *a.* **1** accompanying. **2** existing in conjunction with. *~n.* a concomitant person or thing. **concomitance**, **concomitancy** *n.* **concomitantly** *adv.*

concord (kong´kawd, kon´-) *n.* **1** agreement. **2** union in opinions, feelings, or interests. **3** (*Gram.*) the agreement of one word with another in number, gender etc. **4** (*Mus.*) a combination of notes satisfactory to the ear. **5** a treaty. **concordance** (kənkaw´-) *n.* **1** the state of being concordant. **2** agreement. **3** a list of the words in a book (esp. in the Bible), with exact references to the places where they occur. **concordant** (kənkaw´-) *a.* **1** (*Mus.*) in concord or harmony. **2** agreeing, correspondent. **concordantly** *adv.*

concordat (kənkaw´dat) *n.* a convention or treaty, esp. between a pope and a secular government.

concourse (kong´kaws, kon´-) *n.* **1** a confluence, a gathering together. **2** an assembly. **3** a main hall or open space at an airport, railway station etc.

concrete[1] (kong´krēt, kon´-) *a.* **1** existing, real, not abstract. **2** (*Gram.*) denoting a thing as distinct from a quality, a state, or an action. **3** specific, definite. **4** individual, not general. **5** formed by the union of many particles in one mass. **6** made of concrete. ~*n.* cement, coarse gravel and sand mixed with water. ~*v.t.* **1** to treat or cover with concrete. **2** to construct or embed in concrete. **concretely** *adv.* **concrete music** *n.* music consisting of pieces of pre-recorded music or other sound put together and electronically modified. **concreteness** *n.* **concrete poetry** *n.* poetry which uses the visual shape of the poem to help convey meaning. **concretize** (-krə-), **concretise** *v.t.* to render concrete, solid, or specific. **concretization** (-zā´shən) *n.*

concrete[2] (kəngkrēt´, kən-) *v.i.* **1** to coalesce. **2** to grow together. ~*v.t.* **1** to form into a solid mass. **2** to make concrete rather than abstract.

concretion (kəngkrē´shən, kən-) *n.* **1** the act of coalescing into a solid mass. **2** the mass thus formed. **3** (*Geol.*) an aggregation of particles into a ball. **4** (*Med.*) a growth of solid matter in the body, a stone. **concretionary** *a.*

concubine (kong´kūbīn) *n.* **1** a woman who cohabits with a man without being married to him. **2** (in polygamous societies) a lawful wife of inferior rank. **concubinage** (konkū´bi-) *n.*

concupiscence (kənkū´pisəns) *n.* (*formal*) unlawful or excessive sexual desire. **concupiscent** *a.*

concur (kənkœ´) *v.i.* (*pres.p.* **concurring**, *past, p.p.* **concurred**) **1** to coincide. **2** to agree. **3** to act in conjunction (with). **concurrent** (-kŭr´-) *a.* **1** happening or existing at the same time. **2** acting in union or conjunction. **3** consistent, harmonious. **4** contributing to the same effect or result. **5** (*Geom.*) meeting at one point, converging. **concurrence** (-kŭr´-) *n.* **concurrently** *adv.*

concuss (kənkŭs´) *v.t.* **1** to cause concussion in. **2** to shake or agitate violently. **concussion** (-kŭsh´ən) *n.* **1** (*Med.*) a state of unconsciousness produced by a blow to the skull, usu. followed by amnesia. **2** shaking by sudden impact. **3** a shock. **concussive** *a.*

condemn (kəndem´) *v.t.* **1** to censure, to blame. **2** to pronounce guilty, to give judgement against. **3** to pass sentence on (*He was condemned to death*). **4** to pronounce incurable or unfit for use. **5** to doom (to), to force into a particular state. **condemnable** (-dem´ə-, -dem´nə-) *a.* **condemnation** (kondemnā´shən) *n.* **condemnatory** (-dem´nə-) *a.*

condense (kəndens´) *v.t.* **1** to make more dense or compact. **2** to compress. **3** to concentrate. **4** to reduce into a denser form, esp. from a gas into a liquid. ~*v.i.* **1** to become dense or compact. **2** to be reduced into a denser form. **condensable** *a.*

condensability (-bil´-) *n.* **condensate** (-den´sāt) *n.* something made by condensation. **condensation** (-sā´shən) *n.* **1** the act of condensing. **2** the state of being condensed. **3** a condensed mass or substance, esp. water on glass etc. **4** conciseness, brevity. **5** an abridgement. **6** (*Chem.*) a reaction in which molecules combine and eliminate water. **condensed milk** *n.* a thickened and usu. sweetened form of preserved milk. **condenser** *n.* **1** an apparatus for reducing steam to a liquid form. **2** a lens for concentrating light on an object. **3** a contrivance for accumulating or concentrating electricity, a capacitor. **4** a person or thing that condenses.

condescend (kondisend´) *v.i.* **1** to stoop or lower oneself voluntarily to an inferior position. **2** (*often iron.*) to deign (to) (*She condescended to join us for a drink*). **3** (*derog.*) to behave patronizingly. **condescending** *a.* marked by condescension. **condescendingly** *adv.* **condescension** *n.* **1** the act of condescending. **2** gracious behaviour to imagined inferiors. **3** patronizing behaviour.

condign (kəndīn´) *a.* (of a punishment) well-deserved. **condignly** *adv.*

condiment (kon´dimənt) *n.* **1** a seasoning or sauce. **2** anything used to give a relish to food. **condimental** (-men´-) *a.*

condition (kəndish´ən) *n.* **1** a stipulation, an agreement, a requirement. **2** that on which anything depends. **3** (*Gram.*) a clause expressing this. **4** (*pl.*) circumstances or external characteristics. **5** a state or mode of existence. **6** a (good) state of health or fitness. **7** a (long-standing) ailment (*a heart condition*). **8** high social position. ~*v.t.* **1** to put in a good or healthy condition. **2** to make fit. **3** to accustom. **4** to establish a conditioned reflex in (a person or animal). **5** to put in a certain condition. **6** to test, to examine. **7** to impose conditions on. **8** to stipulate, to agree on. **on condition that** provided that, with the stipulation that. **conditional** *a.* **1** containing, implying, or depending on certain conditions. **2** made with limitations or reservations. **3** not absolute. **4** (*Gram.*) expressing a condition. ~*n.* (*Gram.*) **1** a conditional word, phrase or clause. **2** the conditional mood. **conditional discharge** *n.* the discharge of an offender without sentence on condition that no further offence is committed within a specified period. **conditionality** (-nal´-) *n.* **conditionally** *adv.* **conditioned reflex, conditioned response** *n.* (*Psych.*) a natural response to a stimulus which, by much repetition, becomes attached to a different stimulus. **conditioner** *n.* a substance used to improve the condition of something (*a hair conditioner; fabric conditioner*).

condo (kon´dō) *n.* (*pl.* **condos**) (*N Am., coll.*) a condominium.

condole (kəndōl´) *v.i.* **1** to sorrow, to mourn, to lament. **2** to sympathize (with). **condolatory** *a.* **condolence** *n.* **1** (*often pl.*) an expression of sympathy (*to offer one's condolences*). **2** sympathy.

Usage note *Condoling with* a person and *consoling* them should not be confused: *condole* refers only to the expression of sympathy and not its result, whereas *console* refers to the beneficial and cheering effect of the sympathy offered.

---

condom (kon´dom) *n.* a contraceptive device, a rubber sheath worn over the penis during sexual intercourse.

condominium (kondəmin´iəm) *n.* **1** joint sovereignty over a state. **2** (*N Am.*) a group of dwellings (e.g. a block of flats) of which each unit is separately owned. **3** any such dwelling.

condone (kəndōn´) *v.t.* **1** to forgive, excuse or overlook (an offence etc.). **2** to approve, esp. with reluctance. **condonable** *a.* **condonation** (kondənā´shən) *n.* **condoner** *n.*

condor (kon´daw) *n.* either of two vultures, *Vultur gryphus*, the Andean condor, and *Cymnagyos californianus*, the California condor.

conduce (kəndūs´) *v.i.* **1** to contribute (to a result). **2** to tend (to). **conducive** *a.* contributing, leading, favourable (*The atmosphere was not conducive to study*). **conduciveness** *n.*

conduct[1] (kon´dŭkt) *n.* **1** the way in which anyone acts or lives, behaviour. **2** management, direction, control. **3** the act of leading or guiding.

conduct[2] (kəndŭkt´) *v.t.* **1** to lead, to guide. **2** to manage, to direct (*to conduct a business*). **3** (*Physics*) to transmit (heat, electricity etc.). **4** to direct the performance of an orchestra, choir etc. **5** (*reflex.*) to behave (*to conduct oneself badly*). ~*v.i.* to act as a conductor. **conductance** *n.* (*Physics*) the ability of a substance or system to conduct electricity, the reciprocal of electrical resistance. **conducted tour** *n.* a tour lead by a guide. **conductible** *a.* **conductibility** (-bil´-) *n.* **conduction** *n.* **1** the transmission of heat, electricity etc. by a conductor. **2** the conveyance of liquids, etc., as through a pipe or duct. **conductive** *a.* **1** able to conduct heat, electricity etc. **2** of or relating to conduction. **conductively** *adv.* **conductivity** (kondŭktiv´-) *n.* **1** the state of being conductive. **2** the ease with which a substance transmits electricity, the reciprocal of resistivity. **conductor** *n.* **1** the director of an orchestra or choir. **2** the person in charge of collecting fares on a bus. **3** (*N Am.*) the guard of a train. **4** (*Physics*) a body capable of transmitting heat, electricity, etc. **5** a leader, a guide. **6** a director, a manager. **conductorship** *n.* **conductress** *n.* a female conductor on a bus or train.

conduit (kon´dit, -dūit) *n.* **1** a channel, canal, or pipe, usu. underground, to convey water. **2** a tube or duct for protecting electric wires or cables. **3** a channel, a passage.

cone (kōn) *n.* **1** a solid figure described by the revolution of a right-angled triangle about the side containing the right angle. **2** anything

cone-shaped, such as a wafer holder for ice cream, a temporary marker for traffic on roads etc. **3** a strobilus or dry multiple fruit, such as that of the pine tree. **4** (*also* **cone-shell**) a marine mollusc of the family Conidae. **5** a cone-shaped cell in the retina of the eye. ~*v.t.* **1** to shape like a cone. **2** to mark (off) with traffic cones. **conoid** *n.* a cone-shaped object. ~*a.* cone-shaped. **conoidal** (-noi´-) *a.* conoid.

✖ conect common misspelling of CONNECT.

coney CONY.

confab (kon´fab) *n.* (*coll.*) a chat, a conversation, a confabulation. ~*v.i.* (*pres.p.* **confabbing**, *past*, *p.p.* **confabbed**) to confabulate.

confabulate (kənfab´ūlāt) *v.i.* **1** to talk familiarly, to chat, to gossip. **2** (*Psych.*) to compensate for loss of memory by inventing imaginary experiences. **confabulation** (-lā´shən) *n.* **confabulatory** *a.*

confect (kənfekt´) *v.t.* (*formal*) **1** to make by combining ingredients. **2** to construct, esp. in the imagination. **confection** *n.* **1** the act or result of mixing or compounding. **2** a sweet dish or delicacy, a sweet, a preserve. **3** a ready-made dress or article of dress. **confectioner** *n.* a person whose trade it is to prepare or sell confections, sweets etc. **confectioner's sugar** *n.* (*N Am.*) icing sugar. **confectionery** *n.* (*pl.* **confectioneries**) **1** sweets and other confections generally. **2** the art or work of making these.

confederate[1] (kənfed´ərət) *a.* **1** united in a league. **2** allied by treaty. **3** (**Confederate**) of, relating to or supporting the Confederate States. ~*n.* **1** a member of a confederation or confederacy. **2** an ally, esp. an accomplice. **3** (**Confederate**) a supporter of the Confederate States in the American Civil War (1861–65). **confederacy** *n.* (*pl.* **confederacies**) **1** a number of persons, parties, or states united for mutual aid and support; a confederation. **2** a league or compact by which several persons engage to support each other. **3** conspiracy, unlawful cooperation, collusion. **confederation** (-ā´shən) *n.* **1** the act of confederating. **2** the state of being confederated. **3** a league or alliance of states, parties etc. **confederative** *a.*

confederate[2] (kənfed´ərāt) *v.t.*, *v.i.* to unite in a league or alliance.

confer (kənfœ´) *v.t.* (*pres.p.* **conferring**, *past*, *p.p.* **conferred**) to bestow, to grant. ~*v.i.* **1** to consult together. **2** to compare views. **conferee** (-rē´) *n.* **1** a person who takes part in a conference. **2** a person on whom something is conferred. **conference** (kon´fə-) *n.* **1** the act of conferring; consultation, discussion. **2** a meeting for consultation or discussion. **3** (*esp. N Am.*) a league or association in sport, commerce etc. **4** the linking of a number of computers, telephones etc. for simultaneous communication. **conferencing** *n.* participation in a conference. **conferment**, (*esp. N Am.*) **conferral** *n.* the act or an instance of conferring a degree, honour etc. **conferrable** *a.* **conferrer** *n.*

confess (kənfes´) v.t. **1** to own, to acknowledge, to admit (to confess a crime). **2** to admit reluctantly, to grant, to concede (He confessed that he hadn't read the book). **3** to hear the confession of. **4** (poet.) to reveal, to make manifest. ~v.i. **1** to make confession, esp. to a priest. **2** to admit (to) (She confessed to having forgotten). **confessant** n. a person who confesses to a priest. **confessedly** (-sid-) adv. admittedly, avowedly. **confession** (-shən) n. **1** the act or an instance of confessing. **2** something confessed. **3** formal acknowledgement of sins to a priest in order to receive absolution. **confessional** n. **1** the place where a priest sits to hear confessions. **2** the practice of confession. ~a. of or relating to confession. **confession-ary** a. **confession of faith** n. a declaration of one's religious beliefs. **confessor** n. **1** a person who confesses. **2** a priest who hears confessions. **3** a person who suffers religious persecution but not martyrdom.

confetti (kənfet´i) n. bits of coloured paper thrown at weddings etc.

confidant (konfidant´, kon´-) n. a person entrusted with secrets, esp. with love affairs. **confidante** n. a female confidant.

confide (kənfīd´) v.i. **1** to have trust or confidence (in). **2** to talk confidentially to (He confided in his friend). ~v.t. **1** to entrust (to). **2** to reveal in confidence (to). **confidence** (kon´fi-) n. **1** trust, faith. **2** self-reliance, boldness, assurance. **3** the revelation of a private matter to a friend etc. **4** the matter revealed. **5** assuredness, certainty. **in confidence** as a secret. **in someone's confidence** entrusted with someone's secrets. **confidence game** n. (N Am.) a confidence trick. **confidence man** n. a person who practises confidence tricks. **confidence trick** n. a swindle in which someone is induced to trust the swindler and usu. part with valuable property for something worthless. **confidence trickster** n. **confident** (kon´fi-) a. **1** full of confidence. **2** assured, certain. **confidential** (konfiden´-) a. **1** told or given in confidence. **2** entrusted with the private concerns of another. **3** private, intimate. **confidentiality** (-shial´-) n. **confidentially** adv. **confider** n. **confiding** a. trusting. **confidingly** adv.

configure (kənfig´yə, -fig´ə) v.t. **1** to give shape or form to. **2** to arrange. **3** (Comput.) to lay out or interconnect the elements of a computer system. **configuration** (-ā´shən) n. **1** shape, form. **2** structural arrangement. **3** (Astron., Astrol.) the relative position of the planets at any given time. **4** (Comput.) **a** the layout or interconnection of the several items of hardware making up a computer system. **b** these items of hardware.

confine¹ (kənfīn´) v.t. **1** to shut up, to imprison. **2** to keep within bounds. **3** to limit in application. **to be confined** to be in labour or childbirth. **confinement** n. **1** the act of confining. **2** the state of being confined. **3** labour, childbirth.

confine² (kon´fīn) n. (usu. pl.) a boundary, a limit.

confirm (kənfœm´) v.t. **1** to establish or support the truth or correctness of. **2** to ratify, to make valid. **3** to strengthen. **4** to administer confirmation to. **confirmand** (kon´fœmand) n. a person being prepared for the rite of confirmation. **confirmation** (konfəmā´shən) n. **1** the act of confirming. **2** corroborative testimony. **3** the rite of admitting a baptized person into full membership of a Christian Church. **confirmative** a. **confirmatory** a. **confirmed** a. **1** established, settled. **2** beyond hope of recovery or help. **3** having received confirmation. **confirmedly** (-mid-) adv. **confirmedness** (-mid-, -fœmd´-) n.

confiscate (kon´fiskāt) v.t. **1** to take or seize, esp. as a penalty. **2** to adjudge to be forfeited, or to seize as forfeited, to the public treasury. **confiscable** (kənfis´kə-), **confiscatable** (-kā´-) a. **confiscation** (-kā´shən) n. **confiscator** n. **confiscatory** (kənfis´kə-) a.

conflagration (konfləgrā´shən) n. a large and destructive fire.

conflate (kənflāt´) v.t. **1** to fuse together. **2** to blend (two variant readings) into one. **conflation** n.

conflict¹ (kon´flikt) n. **1** a fight, a struggle, a contest. **2** a clash or the opposition of interests, opinions, or purposes. **3** (Psych.) the opposition of incompatible needs, desires etc. **4** mental strife. **in conflict** in opposition.

conflict² (kənflikt´) v.i. **1** to strive or struggle. **2** to differ, to disagree. **3** to be incompatible. **conflicting** a. contradictory, irreconcilable. **confliction** n. **conflictive** a. **conflictual** a.

confluent (kon´fluənt) a. **1** flowing or running together. **2** uniting in a single stream. ~n. a stream which unites with another. **confluence** n. **1** the point of junction of two or more streams or rivers. **2** a flowing together. **3** a multitude, an assembly.

conflux (kon´flŭks) n. confluence.

conform (kənfawm´) v.t. **1** to make like in form, to make similar (to). **2** to accommodate, to adapt. ~v.i. **1** to comply with rules, accepted standards etc. **2** to be in harmony, agreement or accordance (with). **conformable** a. **1** having the same shape or form. **2** corresponding, similar. **3** compliant, conforming. **4** consistent. **conformability** (-bil´-) n. **conformably** adv. **conformation** (-mā´shən) n. the manner in which a thing is formed; form, shape, structure. **conformer** n. **conformist** n. **1** a person who accepts the prevailing orthodoxy in matters of dress, opinion etc. **2** a person who conforms to the practices of the Church of England. ~a. orthodox, conventional. **conformism** n. **conformity** n. **1** resemblance, likeness. **2** agreement, congruity. **3** compliance with orthodoxy or convention.

confound (kənfownd´) v.t. **1** to throw into confusion. **2** to perplex, to bewilder. **3** to mix up, to confuse. ~int. used as a mild curse (Confound it!). **confounded** á. **1** confused. **2** (coll.) damned (this confounded weather). **confoundedly** adv.

confrère (kŏ´freə) n. a fellow-member of a profession, religion, association etc.

confront (kənfrŭnt´) v.t. 1 to face. 2 to face defiantly. 3 to oppose, to meet in hostility. 4 to face up to. 5 to bring face to face (with). 6 to stand facing. 7 to be opposite to. 8 to compare (with). **confrontation** (konfrŭntā´shən) n. **confrontational** a.

Confucian (kənfū´shən) a. of or relating to Confucius or his philosophical system. ~n. a follower of Confucius. **Confucianism** n. **Confucianist** n , a

confuse (kənfūz´) v.t. 1 to confound, to perplex. 2 to jumble up. 3 to mix or mingle so as to render indistinguishable. 4 to disconcert. 5 to mistake, to fail to distinguish between (She confused me with my brother). **confusable** a. **confusability** (-bil´-) n. **confused** a. 1 muddled, disordered. 2 perplexed, bewildered. 3 senile, suffering from confusion. **confusedly** (-zid-, -zd-) adv. **confusedness** (-zid-, -zd-) n. **confusion** n. 1 the act of confusing. 2 the state of being confused. 3 disorder. 4 perplexity. 5 embarrassment. 6 disturbance of consciousness characterized by impaired capacity to think or to respond in any way to current stimuli. 7 commotion.

confute (kənfūt´) v.t. 1 to overcome in argument. 2 to prove to be false. **confutable** a. **confutation** (konfūtā´shən) n. **confuter** n.

conga (kong´gə) n. 1 a Latin American dance performed by several people in single file. 2 the music for this dance. 3 a conga drum. ~v.i. (3rd. pers. sing. pres. **congas**, pres.p. **congaing**, past, p.p. **congaed** (-gəd)) to perform this dance. **conga drum** n. a narrow bass drum beaten by the hand.

congeal (kənjēl´) v.t. 1 to convert from the liquid to the solid state by cold; to freeze. 2 to coagulate. ~v.i. 1 to become hard with cold. 2 to coagulate. **congealable** a. **congealment** n.

congelation (konjəlā´shən) n. 1 the act or process of congealing. 2 the state of being congealed. 3 a congealed mass or substance.

congener (kon´jənə, -jē´-) n. 1 a person or thing of the same kind or class. 2 an organism of the same stock or family. 3 a by-product that gives a distinctive flavour, colour etc. to an alcoholic drink. **congenerous** (-jen´-) a.

congenial (kənjē´nyəl, -niəl) a. 1 pleasant, agreeable. 2 sympathetic, having similar tastes, character etc. 3 suitable. **congeniality** (-al´-) n. **congenially** adv.

congenital (kənjen´itəl) a. 1 existing from birth (congenital disease). 2 as if from birth (a congenital liar). **congenitally** adv.

Usage note The adjectives congenital and genetic should not be confused: congenital has no reference to genes and heredity, and means simply existing since birth.

conger (kong´gə), **conger eel** n. any marine eel of the family Congridae, esp. Conger conger.

congeries (kənjiə´rēz, -jer´iēz) n. (pl. **congeries**) a collection or heap of particles, things, ideas etc.

congest (kənjest´) v.t. 1 to crowd, to obstruct, to block. 2 to overcharge (with blood). ~v.i. to become congested. **congested** a. affected with congestion. **congestion** (-chən) n. 1 an abnormal accumulation of blood in the capillaries, mucus in the respiratory system etc. 2 any abnormal accumulation (of people, traffic etc.). **congestive** a.

conglomerate[1] (kənglom´ərət) a. 1 gathered into a round body. 2 (Geol.) (of rock) composed of small pieces of rock cemented together. ~n. 1 a mass or thing formed from heterogeneous elements. 2 (Geol.) a conglomerate rock. 3 a large firm formed by the merger of several smaller firms with diverse interests.

conglomerate[2] (kənglom´ərāt) v.t., v.i. 1 to gather into a ball. 2 to collect into a mass. **conglomeration** (-ā´shən) n.

Congolese (kong-gəlēz´) a. of or relating to the Congo or Zaire. ~n. (pl. **Congolese**) 1 a native or inhabitant of the Congo or Zaire. 2 any of the languages of the Congolese.

congrats (kəngrats´) n.pl., int. (coll.) congratulations.

congratulate (kəngrach´əlāt) v.t. 1 to express pleasure or praise to, on account of some event or achievement. 2 to compliment, to felicitate. 3 (reflex.) to consider (oneself) clever, fortunate etc. **congratulant** a., n. **congratulation** (-lā´shən) n. **congratulations** n.pl. an expression of pleasure or praise (We offered them our congratulations). ~int. used to express pleasure or praise. **congratulative** a. **congratulator** n. **congratulatory** a. expressing congratulations.

congregate (kong´grigāt) v.t. to gather or collect together into a crowd. ~v.i. to come together, to assemble. **congregant** n. a member of a congregation, esp. of a particular place of worship. **congregation** (-gā´shən) n. 1 the act of gathering together. 2 the body gathered together. 3 an assembly of persons for religious worship. 4 such an assembly habitually meeting in the same place. **congregational** a. 1 of or relating to a congregation. 2 (Congregational) of or relating to Congregationalism. **Congregationalize**, **Congregationalise** v.t. **Congregationalism** n. a system of church government in which each church is self-governed, and independent of any other authority. **Congregationalist** n., a.

congress (kong´gres) n. 1 a discussion, a conference. 2 a formal meeting of delegates or of envoys for the settlement of international affairs. 3 (Congress) a the legislature of the US, consisting of a Senate and a House of Representatives. b any similar legislative body or assembly. 4 a society, association or organization. **congressional** (-gresh´-) a. **Congressman**, **Congresswoman** n. (pl. **Congressmen**, **Congresswoman**) a member of the US Congress.

congruent (kon´gruənt) *a.* **1** agreeing, suitable, correspondent. **2** (*Geom.*) (of geometrical figures) having the same shape. **congruence, congruency** *n.* **congruently** *adv.* **congruity** (-groo´-) *n.* **congruous** *a.* suitable, conformable, appropriate, fitting. **congruously** *adv.*

conic (kon´ik) *a.* of, relating to or having the form of a cone. **~n.** a conic section. **conical** *a.* **conically** *adv.* **conicalness** *n.* **conic section** *n.* any of the curves formed by the intersection of a cone and a plane; a parabola, a hyperbola, an ellipse or a circle.

conidium (kənid´iəm) *n.* (*pl.* **conidia** (-nid´iə)) an asexual reproductive cell or spore in certain fungi.

conifer (kon´ifə, kō´nifə) *n.* **1** any tree or shrub of the Coniferae, an order of resinous trees, such as the fir, pine and cedar, bearing a cone-shaped fruit. **2** any cone-bearing plant or tree. **coniferous** (-nif´-) *a.* **coniform** (kō´nifawm) *a.* cone-shaped.

conjecture (kənjek´chə) *n.* **1** guessing, surmise. **2** an opinion based on inadequate evidence. **3** in textual criticism, a proposed reading involving conjecture. **~v.t., v.i.** to guess, to surmise. **conjecturable** *a.* **conjecturally** *adv.*

conjoin (kənjoin´) *v.t.* to cause to unite, to join. **~v.i.** to unite, to come together. **conjoint** *a.* united, associated, cooperating. **conjointly** *adv.*

conjugal (kon´jəgəl) *a.* of or relating to matrimony or to married life. **conjugality** (-gal´-) *n.* **conjugally** *adv.* **conjugal rights** *n.pl.* the rights of a husband or wife, esp. to sexual relations.

conjugate[1] (kon´jəgāt) *v.t.* (*Gram.*) to inflect (a verb) by going through the voices, moods, tenses etc. **~v.i.** **1** (*Gram.*) (of a verb) to be inflected. **2** (*Biol.*) to unite sexually. **3** (*Biol.*) to become fused. **4** (*Chem.*) to combine. **conjugation** (-ā´shən) *n.* **1** (*Gram.*) **a** the act or process of conjugating. **b** the inflection of a verb. **c** a class of verbs conjugated alike. **2** (*Biol.*) the fusion of two or more cells or distinct organisms into a single mass. **conjugational** *a.*

conjugate[2] (kon´jəgət) *a.* **1** joined in pairs, coupled. **2** agreeing in grammatical derivation. **3** (*Math.*) reciprocally related so as to be interchangeable. **4** (*Biol.*) united, fused. **5** (*Chem.*) (of an acid or base) related by the loss or gain of a proton. **~n.** a conjugate thing, substance, quantity etc.

conjunct (kənjŭngkt´) *a.* **1** joined. **2** closely connected. **3** in union. **4** conjoint. **conjunction** *n.* **1** union, association, connection. **2** combination. **3** (*Gram.*) a word connecting sentences or clauses or coordinating words in the same clause. **4** (*Astron., Astrol.*) (of two heavenly bodies) the state of being in apparent proximity or alignment. **in conjunction with** together with. **conjunctional** *a.* **conjunctive** *a.* **1** serving to unite or join. **2** (*Gram.*) connective, conjunctional, copulative. **~n.** a conjunctive word. **conjunctively** *adv.* **conjunctly** *adv.* **conjuncture** (-chə) *n.* **1** a combination of circumstances or events. **2** a crisis.

conjunctiva (konjŭngktī´və, kənjŭngk´tivə) *n.* (*pl.* **conjunctivas, conjunctivae** (-vē)) (*Anat.*) the mucous membrane lining the inner surface of the eyelids and the front of the eyeball. **conjunctival** *a.* **conjunctivitis** (kənjŭngktivī´tis) *n.* inflammation of the conjunctiva.

conjure[1] (kŭn´jə) *v.t.* **1** to effect by or as if by magical influence. **2** to cause to appear, disappear etc. by or as if by magic. **3** to effect by jugglery or sleight of hand. **~v.i.** to perform tricks by sleight of hand. **to conjure up 1** to cause to appear by or as if by magic. **2** to bring to the mind, to evoke (*to conjure up an image*). **conjuration** (-ā´shən) *n.* **1** the act of conjuring. **2** a magic spell, a charm. **conjuror, conjurer** *n.* **1** a person who performs tricks by sleight of hand. **2** a juggler.

conjure[2] (kənjuə´) *v.t.* to appeal to by a sacred name, or in a solemn manner.

conk (kongk) *n.* (*coll.*) **1** the head. **2** the nose. **3** a punch on the head or nose. **~v.t.** **1** (*sl.*) to hit (someone) on the head or nose. **2** (*coll.*) to conk out. **to conk out 1** (*coll.*) to break down, to fail. **2** (*coll.*) to die. **3** (*coll.*) to collapse from exhaustion.

conker (kong´kə) *n.* **1** the fruit of a horse chestnut. **2** (*pl.*) a game played with conkers threaded on strings.

conn CON[4].

connatural (kənach´ərəl) *a.* **1** inborn. **2** naturally belonging (to). **3** of the same nature. **connaturally** *adv.*

connect (kənekt´) *v.t.* **1** to join, link, or fasten together. **2** to conjoin, to unite, to correlate. **3** to associate in one's mind. **4** to establish telephone communication between. **~v.i.** **1** to be or become connected. **2** (*coll.*) to manage to hit something (with a punch, kick etc.). **3** (of a train etc.) to have its arrival and departure times synchronized with those of other trains etc. **connectable** *a.* **connected** *a.* **1** united, esp. by marriage. **2** closely related. **3** coherent. **4** associated (with). **5** joined or linked together. **connectedly** *adv.* **connectedness** *n.* **connecting rod** *n.* a rod that transmits power from one part of a machine to another, esp. from the piston to the crankshaft in an internal-combustion engine. **connective** *a.* connecting or able to connect. **~n.** **1** a connecting word. **2** anything that connects. **connective tissue** *n.* (*Anat.*) the fibrous tissue supporting and connecting the various parts throughout the body. **connectivity** (konektiv´-) *n.* **1** the state of being connected or interconnected. **2** (*Comput.*) the capacity for connection or interconnection. **connector** *n.*

connection (kənek´shən), **connexion** *n.* **1** the act of connecting. **2** the state of being connected. **3** the place where two parts or things are connected. **4** a person or thing that connects, a link. **5** a telephone link. **6** the apparatus used in linking up electric current by contact. **7** the synchronization of the departure and arrival of trains, aeroplanes etc. **8** a train, aeroplane etc., whose timetable is so synchronized (*I missed my connection*). **9** relationship (esp. by marriage). **10** a person so connected. **11** acquaintanceship. **12** a party, a religious body. **13** a business associate or contact, esp. one with influence. **in connection with** connected with. **in this connection** in relation to this matter. **connectional** *a*.

conner CON⁴.

conning tower CON⁴.

connive (kənīv´) *v.i.* to conspire (with). **to connive at** to disregard or tacitly encourage (a wrong or fault). **connivance** *n*. **1** passive cooperation in a fault or crime. **2** tacit consent. **conniver** *n*.

connoisseur (konəsœ´) *n*. a person skilled in judging, esp. in the fine arts. **connoisseurship** *n*.

connote (kənōt´) *v.t.* **1** to imply, to betoken indirectly. **2** to signify, to mean. **connotation** (konətā´-) *n*. **1** the act of connoting. **2** something implied in addition to the primary meaning. **connotative** (kon´-, -nō´-) *a*. **connotatively** *adv*.

connubial (kənū´biəl) *a*. of or relating to marriage. **connubiality** (-al´-) *n*. (*pl*. **connubialities**) **connubially** *adv*.

conoid, conoidal CONE.

conquer (kong´kə) *v.t.* **1** to win or gain, esp. by military force. **2** to vanquish, to overcome. **3** to gain dominion, sovereignty, or mastery over. **4** to subdue, to surmount (*to conquer a fear*). **5** to climb (a mountain), esp. for the first time. **conquerable** *a*. **conqueror** *n*. **1** a person who conquers. **2** a conker.

conquest (kong´kwest) *n*. **1** the act of conquering. **2** a thing, person etc. that is conquered. **3** a person whose affection or compliance has been gained.

conquistador (konkwis´tədaw, -kēstədaw´) *n*. (*pl*. **conquistadors, conquistadores** (-daw´rāz)) any of the Spanish conquerors of America in the 16th cent.

con-rod (kon´rod) *n*. (*coll*.) a connecting rod.

consanguine (kənsang´gwin), **consanguineous** (-gwin´iəs) *a*. **1** of the same blood. **2** related by birth. **consanguinity** (-gwin´-) *n*.

conscience (kon´shəns) *n*. **1** moral sense. **2** the sense of right and wrong. **3** an inner feeling of guilt or otherwise (*a guilty conscience*; *to have a clear conscience*). **4** conscientiousness. **on one's conscience** causing one to feel guilt or remorse. **conscience clause** *n*. (*Law etc*.) a clause in a law etc. to relieve persons with conscientious scruples from certain requirements. **conscienceless** *a*. **conscience money** *n*. money paid voluntarily (and often anonymously), as compensation for evasion of commitments, esp. evaded tax. **conscience-stricken, conscience-struck, conscience-smitten** *a*. stung by conscience on account of some misdeed.

conscientious (konshien´shəs) *a*. **1** scrupulous, diligent. **2** actuated by strict regard to the dictates of conscience. **conscientiously** *adv*. **conscientiousness** *n*. **conscientious objector** *n*. **1** a

person who refuses on principle to take part in war or in activities connected with it. **2** a person who takes advantage of the conscience clause.

conscious (kon´shəs) *a*. **1** aware of one's own existence. **2** fully aware of one's surroundings etc.; not asleep or comatose. **3** having knowledge, cognizant, aware (*conscious of her failings*). **4** intentional (*a conscious effort*). **5** present to consciousness, felt. *~n*. the conscious mind. **-conscious** *comb. form* very aware of, attaching importance to (*fashion-conscious*). **consciously** *adv*. **consciousness** *n*. **1** the state of being conscious. **2** knowledge, awareness, sense, perception. **3** (*Psych*.) the faculty by which one knows one's own existence, acts, feelings etc. **4** the intellectual faculties collectively or any class of them.

conscript¹ (kon´skript) *a*. enrolled, registered, enlisted compulsorily in the armed forces. *~n*. a person compelled to serve in the armed forces.

conscript² (kənskript´) *v.t.* to enlist compulsorily. **conscription** *n*. compulsory enrolment for military, naval or air service.

consecrate (kon´sikrāt) *v.t.* **1** to make sacred, to hallow. **2** to dedicate to a religious purpose. **3** to devote to a particular purpose. **4** to sanctify (the bread and wine of the Eucharist). **5** to ordain (a bishop etc.). **consecration** (-rā´shən) *n*. **consecrator** *n*. **consecratory** (-rā´-) *a*.

consecutive (konsek´ūtiv) *a*. **1** following without interval or break. **2** (*Gram*.) expressing logical or grammatical consequence. **consecutive intervals** *n.pl.* (*Mus*.) a succession of similar intervals in harmony, esp. consecutive fifths and octaves. **consecutively** *adv*. **consecutiveness** *n*.

consensus (kənsen´səs) *n*. **1** general agreement, unanimity. **2** an instance of this. **consensual** *a*. existing or happening by consent.

consent (kənsent´) *v.i.* to assent, to agree, to give permission. *~n*. **1** agreement. **2** permission. **3** compliance. **consenter** *n*. **consenting** *a*. **consenting adult** *n*. a person over the age of consent, esp. legally able to enter into a homosexual relationship. **consentingly** *adv*.

consentient (kənsen´shənt) *a*. **1** of one mind, unanimous. **2** consenting.

consequent (kon´sikwənt) *a*. **1** following as a natural or logical result. **2** consistent. *~n*. **1** that which follows as a natural and logical result. **2** (*Logic*) the correlative to an antecedent. **consequence** *n*. **1** a result or effect. **2** importance (*of no consequence*). **3** a conclusion or inference. **4** (*pl*., *usu. sing. in constr*.) a game in which stories are made up from lines contributed by individual players unaware of what has gone before. **in consequence** as a result. **consequential** (-kwen´shəl) *a*. **1** following as a result or a necessary deduction. **2** resulting indirectly (*consequential loss*). **3** important. **consequentiality** (-shial´-) *n*. **consequentially** *adv*. **consequently** *adv*. **1** as a consequence. **2** accordingly, therefore.

❌ **consern** common misspelling of CONCERN.

conservancy (kənsœ´vənsi) *n*. (*pl*. **conservancies**) **1** the official preservation of forests and other natural resources. **2** a body concerned with this. **3** a commission or court with jurisdiction over a particular river, port etc.

conservation (konsəvā´shən) *n*. **1** the act of conserving. **2** preservation from waste or decay. **3** protection of natural resources and the environment, esp. from destruction by human activity. **conservational** *a*. **conservation area** *n*. an area of architectural or historical interest protected by law against undesirable environmental changes. **conservationist** *n*. a person who supports or promotes environmental conservation.

conservative (kənsœ´vətiv) *a*. **1** tending or inclined to conserve what is established. **2** disposed to maintain existing institutions. **3** (**Conservative**) of or relating to the Conservative Party. **4** moderate, not extreme (*a conservative estimate*). **5** of or relating to conservatism. **6** conventional. ~*n*. **1** a person inclined to preserve established things. **2** a conventional person. **3** (**Conservative**) a member or supporter of the Conservative Party. **conservatism** *n*. **1** conservative character. **2** dislike of change. **3** (**Conservatism**) the political principles of the Conservative Party. **conservatively** *adv*. **conservativeness** *n*.

conservatoire (kənsœ´vətwah) *n*. a public school of music or other fine art.

conservator (kon´səvātə, kənsœ´və-) *n*. **1** a person who preserves something from damage or injury. **2** a custodian, a keeper, a curator.

conservatory (kənsœ´vətri) *n*. (*pl*. **conservatories**) **1** a greenhouse for exotic plants. **2** a glasshouse attached to a house, used for growing plants or as a sun lounge. **3** a conservatoire.

conserve (kənsœv´) *v.t*. **1** to preserve from injury, decay, or loss. **2** to preserve (fruit etc.), esp. with sugar. ~*n*. **1** a preserve. **2** a confection. **conserver** *n*.

❌ **consession** common misspelling of CONCESSION.

consider (kənsid´ə) *v.t*. **1** to think about, to contemplate, to ponder. **2** to observe and examine. **3** to bear in mind. **4** to estimate, to regard. **5** to have or show regard for. **6** to discuss. ~*v.i*. to reflect, to deliberate. **considerable** *a*. **1** large or great (*considerable difficulty*). **2** important, notable, worth consideration or regard. **considerably** *adv*. **considerate** (-rət) *a*. characterized by regard for others. **considerately** *adv*. **considerateness** *n*. **consideration** (-ā´shən) *n*. **1** the act of considering. **2** reflection, thought. **3** regard for others, thoughtfulness. **4** a motive or ground for action. **5** something to be taken into account. **6** a recompense, a reward. **7** (*Law*) the material equivalent given in exchange for something and forming the basis of a contract. **in consideration of 1** as a payment for, in return for. **2** because of. **to take into consideration** to bear in mind, to take into account. **under consideration 1** being

considered. **2** under discussion. **considering** *prep*., *conj*. taking into consideration, in view of. ~*adv*. (*coll*.) all in all (*She did quite well, considering*).

Usage note It is best to avoid the use of *consider as* (as in *His parents consider her as unsuitable*). The preferred constructions are with *to be* or a simple adjective (as in *His parents consider her to be unsuitable*, or *His parents consider her unsuitable*).

consign (kənsīn´) *v.t*. **1** to commit to the care, keeping or trust of another. **2** to send (goods etc.). **3** to relegate, to commit permanently. **consignable** *a*. **consignee** (-nē´) *n*. a person to whom goods are consigned. **consignment** *n*. **1** the act of consigning. **2** a batch of goods consigned. **consignor** *n*. a person who consigns goods to another.

consist (kənsist´) *v.i*. **1** to be composed (of). **2** to be founded or lie (in). **3** to be compatible or consistent (with). **consistency, consistence** *n*. (*pl*. **consistencies, consistences**) **1** degree of density, firmness or solidity. **2** the state of being consistent. **consistent** *a*. **1** congruous, harmonious. **2** uniform in opinion or conduct, not self-contradictory. **3** compatible. **consistently** *adv*.

Usage note See note under COMPRISE.

consistory (kənsis´təri, kon´-) *n*. (*pl*. **consistories**) **1** the court of a bishop for dealing with ecclesiastical causes arising in his diocese. **2** the college of cardinals at Rome. **3** an assembly of ministers and elders in certain Reformed Churches. **consistorial** (-taw´-) *a*.

console[1] (kənsōl´) *v.t*. to comfort or cheer in trouble or distress. **consolable** *a*. **consolation** (konsəlā´shən) *n*. **1** the act of consoling. **2** the state of being consoled. **3** a fact, thing or person that consoles. **consolation prize** *n*. a prize awarded to a runner-up. **consolatory** (-sol´-, -sō´-) *a*. **consoler** *n*. **consolingly** *adv*.

Usage note See note under CONDOLE.

console[2] (kon´sōl) *n*. **1** the control panel of an electric or electronic system. **2** the desk or cabinet holding this. **3** a free-standing cabinet for a television set etc. **4** (*Mus*.) the frame enclosing the keyboards, stops etc. of an organ when separate from the instrument. **5** an ornamental bracket to support a shelf, cornice etc. **console table** *n*. a table supported by a console or consoles.

consolidate (kənsol´idāt) *v.t*. **1** to form into a solid and compact mass. **2** to strengthen, to reinforce. **3** to combine, to unite in one whole. ~*v.i*. to become solid. **consolidated annuities** *n.pl*. British Government securities, consolidated into a single stock in 1751, with fixed annual interest and without a redemption date. **consolidation** (-ā´shən) *n*. **consolidator** *n*. **consolidatory** *a*.

consols (kon´səlz) *n.pl.* consolidated annuities.

consommé (kənsom´ā) *n.* a clear soup made by boiling meat and vegetables to form a concentrated stock.

consonant (kon´sənənt) *a.* **1** agreeing or according, esp. in sound. **2** congruous, in harmony. **3** (*Mus.*) producing harmony. ~*n.* **1** a letter of the alphabet which cannot be sounded by itself, as *b* or *p.* **2** a sound that is combined with a vowel sound in order to make a syllable. **consonance, consonancy** *n.* (*pl.* **consonances, consonancies**) **1** accord or agreement of sound. **2** agreement, harmony. **3** recurrence of sounds. **4** assonance. **5** pleasing agreement of sounds, concord. **consonantal** (-nan´-) *a.* **consonantly** *adv.*

consort[1] (kon´sawt) *n.* **1** a companion, an associate. **2** a husband or wife, esp. of royalty. **3** a vessel accompanying another.

consort[2] (kənsawt´) *v.i.* **1** to associate, to keep company (with). **2** to agree, to be in harmony (with). ~*v.t.* **1** to associate. **2** to unite in harmony. **3** to attend, to escort.

consort[3] (kon´sawt) *n.* (*Mus.*) a group of musical instruments of the same type playing together.

consortium (kənsaw´tiəm) *n.* (*pl.* **consortia** (-tiə), **consortiums**) an association of companies, financial interests etc.

conspecific (konspisif´ik) *a.* (*Biol.*) of or relating to the same species.

conspectus (kənspek´təs) *n.* (*pl.* **conspectuses**) **1** a general sketch or survey. **2** a synopsis.

conspicuous (kənspik´ūəs) *a.* **1** obvious, clearly visible. **2** remarkable, extraordinary. **conspicuous consumption** *n.* lavish spending as a display of wealth. **conspicuously** *adv.* **conspicuousness** *n.*

conspire (kənspīə´) *v.i.* **1** to combine secretly to do any unlawful act, esp. to commit treason, sedition, murder, or fraud. **2** to concur, to unite, to act together (*Circumstances conspired against us*). **conspiracy** (-spir´-) *n.* (*pl.* **conspiracies**) **1** the act of conspiring. **2** a secret agreement or plan between two or more persons to commit an unlawful act that may prejudice any third person; a plot. **conspirator** (-spir´-) *n.* **conspiratorial** (-spirətaw´-) *a.* **conspiringly** *adv.*

constable (kon´stəbəl, kŭn´-) *n.* **1** a police constable. **2** an officer charged with the preservation of the peace. **3** a warden, a governor. **4** (*Hist.*) the chief officer of a royal household. **constableship** *n.* **constabulary** (-stab´ū-) *n.* (*pl.* **constabularies**) a body of police under one authority. ~*a.* of or relating to the police.

constant (kon´stənt) *a.* **1** continuous, unceasing. **2** continual, occurring frequently. **3** unchanging, steadfast. ~*n.* **1** anything unchanging or unvarying. **2** (*Physics*) any property or relation, expressed by a number, that remains unchanged under the same conditions. **3** (*Math.*) a quantity not varying or assumed not to vary in value throughout a series of calculations. **constancy** *n.* **constantly** *adv.*

constellation (konstələ´shən) *n.* **1** a number of fixed stars grouped within the outlines of an imaginary figure in the sky. **2** an assemblage of brilliant people or things. **3** a grouping of related ideas etc. **constellate** (kon´-) *v.t.* **1** to set or adorn with or as with stars. **2** to combine into a constellation.

consternate (kon´stənāt) *v.t.* (*usu. pass.*) to frighten, to dismay. **consternation** (-ā´shən) *n.* anxiety, dismay.

constipate (kon´stipāt) *v.t.* **1** to affect with constipation. **2** to confine, to restrict. **constipated** *a.* suffering from constipation. **constipation** (-ā´shən) *n.* **1** an undue retention or difficult evacuation of the faeces. **2** a restricted state.

constituent (kənstit´ūənt) *a.* **1** forming part of a whole. **2** having power to elect or appoint, or to construct or modify a political constitution. ~*n.* **1** a person or thing that constitutes. **2** a component part. **3** a member of a body which elects a representative. **constituency** *n.* (*pl.* **constituencies**) **1** the whole body of constituents. **2** a body of electors. **3** the place or body of persons represented by a Member of Parliament. **4** a body of clients, customers, supporters etc.

constitute (kon´stitūt) *v.t.* **1** to make up or compose. **2** to form, to be (*This constitutes a major setback*). **3** to establish. **4** to give legal form to. **5** to give a definite nature or character to.

Usage note See note under COMPRISE.

constitution (konstitū´shən) *n.* **1** the act of constituting. **2** the nature, form, composition or structure of a system or body. **3** the physical health or strength of the body. **4** a person's mental qualities. **5** the established form of government in a state or other organization. **6** a system of fundamental rules or principles for the government of a state or other organization. **constitutional** *a.* **1** inherent in the physical or mental constitution. **2** of, relating to or in accordance with a political constitution. **3** legal. ~*n.* a walk or other exercise for the benefit of one's health. **constitutionalism** *n.* **1** government based on a constitution. **2** adherence to constitutional government. **constitutionalist** *n.* **constitutionality** (-nal´-) *n.* **constitutionalize, constitutionalise** *v.t., v.i.* **constitutionally** *adv.*

constitutive (kon´stitūtiv) *a.* **1** that constitutes or composes; component, essential. **2** that can constitute, establish or appoint. **constitutively** *adv.*

constrain (kənstrān´) *v.t.* **1** to compel, to oblige (to do or not to do). **2** to restrain, to keep down by force. **3** to confine, to repress. **constrained** *a.* **1** acting under compulsion. **2** forced. **3** embarrassed. **constrainedly** (-nid-) *adv.* **constraint** *n.* **1** the act of constraining. **2** restraint, restriction. **3** compulsion, necessity. **4** something that constrains. **5** a constrained manner. **6** reserve, self-control.

constrict (kənstrikt´) v.t. **1** to make smaller, narrower or tighter. **2** (esp. Biol.) to cause to contract. **3** to keep within limits, to restrain. **constriction** n. **constrictive** a. **constrictor** n. **1** anything that constricts. **2** (Anat.) a muscle which serves to contract or draw together. **3** a snake that kills its prey by coiling round it and squeezing it, esp. a boa constrictor.

construct[1] (kənstrŭkt´) v.t. **1** to build, to make by putting parts together. **2** to combine words to form (a clause or sentence). **3** (Geom.) to form by drawing (to construct a triangle). **4** to form mentally. **constructor** n. **constructorship** n.

construct[2] (kon´strŭkt) n. **1** something constructed. **2** (Psych.) a concept or idea built up from sense impressions etc.

construction (kənstrŭk´shən) n. **1** the act or process of constructing. **2** the thing constructed. **3** a style, mode, or form of structure. **4** (Gram.) the syntactical arrangement and connection of words in a clause or sentence. **5** explanation, interpretation (of words, conduct etc.) (to put a different construction on it). **constructional** a. **constructionally** adv. **construction site** n. a building site. **constructive** a. **1** having the ability or power to construct, tending to construct. **2** positive, tending to improve or be helpful, as opposed to destructive (constructive criticism). **3** structural, of or relating to construction. **4** inferential, virtual, implied by construction or interpretation. **constructive dismissal** n. action taken by an employer, such as the changing of duties, conditions etc., that forces an employee to resign. **constructively** adv. **constructiveness** n. **constructivism** n. an abstract style of art using geometric shapes, man-made materials, mechanical objects etc. **constructivist** n.

construe (kənstroo´) v.t. **1** to explain, to interpret. **2** to combine syntactically. **3** to analyse the syntactical structure of. **4** to translate. **construable** a. **construal** n.

consubstantial (konsəbstan´shəl) a. (Theol.) (esp. of the three persons of the Trinity) having the same substance or essence. **consubstantiality** (-shial´-) n.

consubstantiate (konsəbstan´shiāt) v.t., v.i. to unite in one substance. **consubstantiation** (-shiā´shən) n. (Theol.) the doctrine that the body and blood of Christ are present along with the elements of the Eucharist after consecration, as distinct from transubstantiation.

consul (kon´səl) n. **1** an official appointed by a state to reside in a foreign country to protect its mercantile interests and citizens there. **2** (Hist.) either of the two supreme magistrates of ancient Rome, invested with regal authority for one year. **3** (Hist.) each of the three supreme magistrates of the French Republic, 1799–1804. **consular** (-sū-) a. **consulate** (-sūlət) n. the official residence, jurisdiction, office, or term of office, of a consul. **consulship** n.

consult (kənsŭlt´) v.i. to take counsel together, to

confer (with). ~v.t. **1** to ask for advice, approval, an opinion etc. (to consult a doctor). **2** to refer to for information (to consult a dictionary). **3** to have regard for, to take into account. **consultable** a. **consultancy** n. (pl. **consultancies**) **1** an agency providing professional advice. **2** the position of a consultant. **consultant** n. **1** a person who is consulted, esp. an expert who is called on for advice and information. **2** a specialist holding the most senior appointment in a branch of medicine in a hospital. **consultation** (konsəltā´shən) n. **1** the act or an instance of consulting. **2** a meeting of or with experts to consider a point or case. **consultative, consultatory, consultive** a. **consultee** (konsəltē´) n. a person consulted. **consulter** n. **consulting** a. **1** giving advice, esp. professional advice. **2** used for consultation (a consulting room).

consume (kənsūm´) v.t. **1** to eat or drink. **2** to use up. **3** to destroy by fire, decomposition etc. **4** to dissipate, to waste, to squander. **5** (often pass.) to engross, to dominate, to obsess. **consumable** a. that may be consumed. ~n. (usu. pl.) a commodity that may be consumed, used up or worn out. **consumer** n. **1** a person who purchases goods and services for their own use. **2** a person or thing that consumes. **consumer durable** n. a manufactured product that lasts for a relatively long time, such as a domestic appliance. **consumer goods** n.pl. manufactured goods destined for purchase by consumers, as opposed to those used to produce other goods. **consumerism** n. **1** protection of the interests of consumers. **2** the economic theory that increased consumption of goods and services is desirable. **consumerist** n., a. **consumingly** adv.

consummate[1] (kon´səmət, kənsŭm´ət) a. **1** complete, perfect. **2** of the highest quality or degree. **consummately** adv.

consummate[2] (kon´səmāt) v.t. **1** to bring to completion, to perfect, to finish. **2** to complete (a marriage) by sexual intercourse. **consummation** (-ā´shən) n. **1** the act of consummating. **2** the end or completion of something already begun. **3** perfection, perfect development. **consummative** a. **consummator** n.

consumption (kənsŭmp´shən) n. **1** the act of consuming. **2** the state or process of being consumed. **3** the purchase and use by individuals of goods and services. **4** a wasting disease, esp. pulmonary tuberculosis. **5** an amount consumed. **consumptive** (-tiv) a. **1** consuming, destructive. **2** disposed to or affected with tuberculosis. ~n. a person suffering from tuberculosis. **consumptively** adv. **consumptiveness** n.

cont. abbr. **1** contents. **2** continued.

contact (kon´takt) n. **1** touch, the state of touching. **2** the act or state of meeting or communicating. **3** a business or other acquaintance who can provide one with introductions etc. **4** a person who has been exposed to an illness and is likely to carry contagion. **5** the touching of two lines or surfaces. **6** the touching of conductors, allowing electric current to flow. **7** the part of the conductor that touches the other. **8** (*usu. pl.*, *coll.*) a contact lens. *~v.t.* to establish contact or communication with. **contactable** (-tak´-) *a.* **contact lens** *n.* a lens worn in contact with the eyeball in place of spectacles. **contact print** *n.* a photographic print made by placing a negative directly on to photographic paper. **contact sheet** *n.* a sheet of contact prints. **contact sport** *n.* a sport in which players come into physical contact. **contactual** (-tak´-) *a.*

Usage note The verb is also pronounced (kəntakt´).

contagion (kəntā´jən) *n.* **1** communication of disease by contact with a person suffering from it. **2** contagious disease. **3** the transmission of social or moral qualities, emotions etc. **4** deleterious influence. **contagious** *a.* **1** communicable by contact, communicating disease by contact. **2** (*loosely*) infectious. **3** (of an emotion etc.) likely or tending to spread to others (*contagious laughter*). **contagious abortion** *n.* a contagious or infectious disease, esp. brucellosis, which causes abortion in some farm animals. **contagiously** *adv.* **contagiousness** *n.*

contain (kəntān´) *v.t.* **1** to hold within fixed limits. **2** to be capable of holding. **3** to comprise, to include. **4** (*Math.*) to be exactly divisible by. **5** (*Mil.*) to hem in. **6** to prevent (a problem etc.) from extending. **7** (*also reflex.*) to restrain. **containable** *a.* **container** *n.* **1** something designed or used to contain or hold, a vessel or receptacle. **2** a large rigid box of standard size and shape used for bulk transport and storage of goods. **containerize, containerise** *v.t.* **1** to put into or transport in containers. **2** to convert (a transportation system etc.) to the use of containers. **containerization** (-zā´shən) *n.* **container port** *n.* a port that specializes in handling containers. **container ship** *n.* a ship designed for the transport of containers. **containment** *n.* the act of containing or restraining, esp. hostilities to a small area, or radioactive emission to a permitted zone in a nuclear reactor.

contaminate (kəntam´ināt) *v.t.* **1** to pollute, esp. with radioactivity. **2** to corrupt, to infect. **contaminable** *a.* **contaminant** *n.* **contamination** (-ā´shən) *n.* **contaminator** *n.*

contemn (kəntem´) *v.t.* (*formal or poet.*) **1** to despise, to scorn. **2** to slight, to neglect. **contemner** (-tem´ə, -tem´nə) *n.*

contemplate (kon´templāt) *v.t.* **1** to look at, to study. **2** to meditate and reflect on. **3** to purpose, to intend. **4** to regard as possible or likely. *~v.i.* to meditate. **contemplation** (-plā´shən) *n.* **contemplative** (-tem´plətiv) *a.* **1** given to contemplation. **2** thoughtful, studious. *~n.* a member of a contemplative order. **contemplatively** *adv.* **contemplativeness** *n.* **contemplative order** *n.* a religious order whose members are engaged

wholly in worship and meditation. **contemplator** *n.*

contemporaneous (kəntempərā´niəs) *a.* **1** existing, living or happening at the same time. **2** lasting, or of, the same period. **contemporaneity** (-nē´iti) *n.* **contemporaneously** *adv.* **contemporaneousness** *n.*

contemporary (kəntem´pərəri) *a.* **1** living at the same time. **2** of the same age. **3** belonging to the same period. **4** up-to-date, modern. *~n.* (*pl.* **contemporaries**) **1** a person living at the same time as another (*Shakespeare and his contemporaries*). **2** any contemporary person or thing. **contemporarily** *adv.* **contemporariness** *n.*

contempt (kəntempt´) *n.* **1** scorn, disdain. **2** the state of being scorned. **3** shame, disgrace. **4** disregard of or disobedience to the rules, orders or regulations of a court, legislative body etc. **contemptible** *a.* worthy of contempt, despicable, mean. **contemptibility** (-bil´-) *n.* **contemptibly** *adv.* **contempt of court** *n.* (*Law*) disobedience or resistance to the orders or proceedings of a court of justice. **contemptuous** (-tū-) *a.* **1** expressive of contempt. **2** disdainful, scornful. **contemptuously** *adv.* **contemptuousness** *n.*

contend (kəntend´) *v.i.* **1** to strive in opposition. **2** to compete. *~v.t.* to maintain by argument (that). **contender** *n.*

content[1] (kəntent´) *a.* **1** satisfied, pleased. **2** willing. *~v.t.* to satisfy, to make content. *~n.* satisfaction, ease of mind, contentment, contentedness. **contented** *a.* satisfied with what one has. **contentedly** *adv.* **contentedness** *n.* **contentment** *n.* **1** the state of being contented or satisfied. **2** gratification, satisfaction.

content[2] (kon´tent) *n.* **1** capacity or power of containing; volume. **2** (*usu. pl.*) that which is contained in a vessel, bag, book, house etc. **3** the amount (of one substance) contained in a mixture, alloy etc. (*the fat content*). **4** (*pl.*) TABLE OF CONTENTS[1]. **5** the meaning (of an utterance etc.) as opposed to the form.

contention (kənten´shən) *n.* **1** the act of contending. **2** quarrel, strife, controversy. **3** emulation, rivalry. **4** a point contended for. **in contention** competing. **contentious** *a.* **1** disposed to or characterized by contention. **2** controversial, disputed. **contentiously** *adv.* **contentiousness** *n.*

conterminous (kontœ´minəs), **coterminous** *a.* **1** having a common boundary (with). **2** having the same limits, coextensive (in range, time or meaning). **conterminously** *adv.*

contest[1] (kəntest´) *v.t.* **1** to contend or compete for, to strive earnestly for. **2** to dispute, to call in question, to oppose. **3** to debate. **contestable** *a.* **contestant** *n.* a person who contests, a competitor. **contestation** (kontestā´shən) *n.* **1** disputation, controversy. **2** something contended for, a contention. **contester** *n.*

contest[2] (kon´test) *n.* **1** a struggle for victory or superiority, a competition. **2** a dispute, a controversy.

context (kon´tekst) *n.* **1** the parts of a piece of speech or writing immediately connected with a sentence or passage quoted. **2** setting, surroundings. **3** the relevant circumstances. **in context** with the connected words, circumstances etc. **out of context** without the connected words, circumstances etc. (*Her remarks were quoted out of context*). **contextual** (-teks´tū-) *a.* **contextualize, contextualise** *v.t.* to put into context. **contextualization** (-zā´shən) *n.* **contextually** *adv.*

contiguous (kəntig´ūəs) *a.* **1** touching, in contact. **2** adjoining, neighbouring. **contiguity** (kontigū´-) *n.* **contiguously** *adv.*

continent[1] (kon´tinənt) *n.* **1** a large continuous tract of land. **2** any of the main geographical divisions of land (Europe, Asia, Africa, Australia, the Americas and Antarctica). **3** a mainland. **continental** (-nen´-) *a.* **1** of or relating to a continent. **2** (*also* **Continental**) of or relating to the Continent. ~*n.* (*also* **Continental**) a native or inhabitant of the Continent. **continental breakfast** *n.* a light breakfast of rolls and coffee. **continental climate** *n.* a climate characteristic of the interior of a continent, with hot summers, cold winters and low rainfall. **continental day** *n.* a school day beginning early in the morning and ending early in the afternoon. **continental drift** *n.* the theory that the continents were orig. one landmass and have drifted apart slowly to their present positions. **continentally** *adv.* **continental quilt** *n.* a duvet. **continental shelf** *n.* an area of shallow water round a landmass before the water begins to slope sharply down to the ocean depths.

continent[2] (kon´tinənt) *a.* **1** able to control one's bladder and bowel movements. **2** abstaining from indulgence or overindulgence in sexual and other pleasures; self-restrained. **continence, continency** *n.* **continently** *adv.*

contingent (kəntin´jənt) *a.* **1** dependent on an uncertain issue, conditional. **2** of doubtful occurrence. **3** accidental. **4** that may or may not be true. **5** associated. ~*n.* a group of people representing or forming part of a larger body. **contingency** *n.* (*pl.* **contingencies**) **1** the state of being contingent. **2** a chance or possible occurrence. **3** something dependent on an uncertain issue. **4** (*pl.*) **a** incidental expenses. **b** money provided for these in an estimate. **contingency fund** *n.* a sum of money kept in reserve for incidental or unforeseen expenses. **contingency plan** *n.* a plan of action kept in reserve in case some situation should arise. **contingently** *adv.*

continual (kəntin´ūəl) *a.* **1** frequently recurring (*continual complaints*). **2** unbroken, incessant. **continually** *adv.*

Usage note The adjectives *continual* and *continuous* should not be confused: *continual* implies a series of frequent repetitions, and *continuous* absence of interruption.

continuance (kəntin´ūəns) *n.* **1** the act or state of continuing. **2** duration. **3** stay (*his continuance in office*). **continuant** *a.* **1** continuing. **2** prolonged. **3** of or relating to a continuant. ~*n.* a consonant whose sound can be prolonged, such as *f, v, s, r.*

continuation (kəntinūā´shən) *n.* **1** the act or an instance of continuing. **2** that by which anything is continued or carried on. **3** extension or prolongation. **continuative** (-tin´ūətiv) *a.* **1** causing continuation, tending to continue. **2** (*Gram.*) expressing continuation.

continue (kəntin´ū) *v.t.* **1** to carry on without interruption. **2** to keep up. **3** to take up again, to resume. **4** to extend, to complete. ~*v.i.* **1** to remain, to stay. **2** to last, to remain in existence. **3** to resume, to recommence. **4** to persevere. **continuable** *a.* **continuer** *n.* **continuing education** *n.* adult education, esp. part-time courses.

continuity (kontinū´iti) *n.* (*pl.* **continuities**) **1** the state of being continuous. **2** an uninterrupted succession. **3** a logical sequence. **4** the detailed description of a film in accordance with which the production is carried out. **5** the linking of television or radio programmes with broadcast announcements etc.

continuo (kəntin´ūō) *n.* (*pl.* **continuos**) (*Mus.*) bass part with harmony indicated by shorthand marks; thorough bass.

continuous (kəntin´ūəs) *a.* **1** connected without a break in space or time. **2** uninterrupted, unceasing. **3** (*Gram.*) (of a verb form) progressive. **continuous assessment** *n.* assessment of the progress of a pupil by means of checks carried out at intervals throughout the course of study. **continuously** *adv.* **continuousness** *n.* **continuous stationery** *n.* paper in a long strip with regular perforations, which can be fed through a printer.

Usage note See note under CONTINUAL.

continuum (kəntin´ūəm) *n.* (*pl.* **continua** (-ūə), **continuums**) **1** an unbroken mass, series or course of events. **2** a continuous series of component parts that pass into each other.

contort (kəntawt´) *v.t.* **1** to twist with violence, to wrench. **2** to distort, to twist out of shape. **contortion** *n.* **1** the act of twisting. **2** a writhing movement. **3** a twisted shape. **contortionist** *n.* an acrobat who bends their body into various shapes.

contour (kon´tuə) *n.* **1** the defining line of any figure or body, an outline. **2** the outline of a coast or other geographical feature. **3** a contour line. **4** a line that separates parts of different colour in a design etc. ~*v.t.* **1** to make an outline of. **2** to mark with contour lines. **3** to carry (a road or railway) round a valley or hill. **contour line** *n.* a line on a map joining points at the same height or depth. **contour map** *n.* a map showing the elevations and depressions of the earth's surface by means of contour lines.

contra (kon´trə) *n.* (*pl.* **contras**) a counter-revolutionary guerrilla fighter in Nicaragua.

contra- (kon'trə) *pref.* **1** against, opposite, contrary. **2** denoting resistance or opposition. **3** (*Mus.*) pitched below, as *contrabassoon*.

contraband (kon'trəband) *a.* **1** prohibited, unlawful. **2** forbidden to be exported or imported. **3** of or relating to contraband. **4** smuggled. ~*n.* **1** articles forbidden to be exported or imported. **2** smuggled articles. **3** prohibited trade. **contrabandist** *n.*

contrabass (kon'trəbās) *n.* (*Mus.*) a double bass.

contrabassoon (kon'trəbəsoon) *n.* a double-reeded woodwind instrument with a range an octave lower than a bassoon.

contraception (kontrəsep'shən) *n.* birth control, the taking of measures to prevent conception. **contraceptive** *n.* a device or drug for preventing conception. ~*a.* preventing conception.

contract[1] (kəntrakt') *v.t.* **1** to draw together. **2** to make smaller. **3** (*Gram.*) to abbreviate, to shorten. **4** to acquire, to develop. **5** to incur, to become liable for. **6** to catch (a disease) (*He contracted pneumonia*). **7** to agree to or settle by covenant. **8** to settle, to establish by contract. **9** to arrange or enter into (a marriage). ~*v.i.* **1** to become smaller or narrower. **2** to agree (to do or supply something). **3** to make or undertake a contract. **contractable** *a.* (of a disease) capable of being contracted. **contractible** *a.* capable of being drawn together. **contractile** (-tīl) *a.* **1** causing contraction. **2** having the power to shorten itself. **contractility** (-til'-) *n.* **contraction** *n.* **1** the act of contracting. **2** the state of being drawn together or shortened. **3** (*Gram.*) **a** the shortening of a word by the omission of a letter or syllable. **b** a word so shortened. **4** (*Med.*) the shortening of a muscle, esp. during childbirth. **contractive** *a.*

Usage note In *to contract in* and *to contract out* the verb is pronounced (kon'trakt).

contract[2] (kon'trakt) *n.* **1** a formal agreement, esp. one recognized as a legal obligation. **2** the writing by which such an agreement is entered into. **3** an undertaking to do certain work or supply certain articles for a specified sum. **4** an offer or promise which has been formally accepted. **5** in bridge etc., an undertaking to win a certain number of tricks. **contract bridge** *n.* a form of bridge in which points are gained only for tricks made as well as bid. **contractual** (-trak'chuəl) *a.* of or relating to a contract. **contractually** *adv.*

Usage note The form *contractural* for *contractual* is best avoided.

contractor (kəntrak'tə) *n.* **1** a person who undertakes a contract, esp. to do or supply something for a specified sum. **2** an employer of labour who contracts to do building work, usu. on a large scale.

contradict (kontrədikt') *v.t.* **1** to deny the truth of (a statement etc.). **2** to assert the opposite of (a statement etc.). **3** to contradict a statement made by (a person). **4** to oppose, to be inconsistent with. ~*v.i.* to deny the truth of a statement. **contradictable** *a.* **contradiction** *n.* **1** the act or an instance of contradicting. **2** denial. **3** a contrary statement. **4** inconsistency. **5** that which is inconsistent with itself. **contradictor** *n.*

contradictory *a.* **1** affirming the contrary. **2** inconsistent. **3** (*Logic*) mutually opposed, logically incompatible. **4** disputatious. **contradictorily** *adv.* **contradictoriness** *n.*

contradistinguish (kontrədisting'gwish) *v.t.* to distinguish by contrasting opposite qualities. **contradistinction** (-tingk'-) *n.*

contraflow (kon'trəflō) *n.* a form of motorway traffic regulation, two-way traffic being instituted on one carriageway so that the other may be closed.

contraindicate (kontrəin'dikāt) *v.t.* (*Med.*) to indicate the unsuitability of (a particular treatment or drug). **contraindicant** *n.* **contraindication** (-ā'shən) *n.*

contralto (kəntral'tō) *n.* (*pl.* **contraltos, contralti** (-tē)) **1** the lowest of the three principal varieties of the female voice, the part next above the alto in choral music. **2** a person who sings this part. **3** music written for this part.

contraption (kəntrap'shən) *n.* (*often derog.* or *facet.*) a contrivance, a strange or improvised device.

contrapuntal (kontrəpŭn'təl) *a.* (*Mus.*) of, relating to or in counterpoint. **contrapuntally** *adv.* **contrapuntist** *n.*

contrarily[1] CONTRARY[1].
contrarily[2] CONTRARY[2].
contrariness[1] CONTRARY[1].
contrariness[2] CONTRARY[2].
contrariwise[1] CONTRARY[1].
contrariwise[2] CONTRARY[2].

contrary[1] (kon'trəri) *a.* **1** opposite. **2** opposed, diametrically different. **3** contradictory. **4** (*Logic*) opposed as regards affirmation and negation. **5** (of wind etc.) unfavourable, adverse. ~*n.* (*pl.* **contraries**) **1** the opposite. **2** a thing that contradicts. **3** a thing of opposite qualities. ~*adv.* in an opposite manner or direction (*contrary to popular opinion*). **on the contrary 1** on the other hand. **2** quite the reverse. **to the contrary** to the opposite effect. **contrariety** (-ī'ə-) *n.* **1** the state of being contrary. **2** opposition. **3** disagreement. **4** inconsistency. **contrarily**[1] *adv.* **contrariness**[1] *n.* **contrariwise**[1] *adv.* on the other hand, conversely.

contrary[2] (kəntreə'ri) *a.* (*coll.*) wayward, perverse. **contrarily**[2] *adv.* **contrariness**[2] *n.* **contrariwise**[2] *adv.* perversely.

contrast[1] (kəntrahst') *v.t.* to set in opposition, so as to show the difference between, or the superiority or inferiority of (*Contrast the copy with the original*). ~*v.i.* to stand in contrast or opposition. **contrastingly** *adv.* **contrastive** *a.*

contrast[2] (kon'trahst) *n.* **1** opposition or unlikeness of things or qualities. **2** the presentation of opposite or unlike things with a view to comparison. **3** the degree of difference in tone between the light and dark parts of a photograph or television picture. **4** a person or thing that is notably unlike another. **contrasty** *a.* showing great contrast between light and dark tones.

contravene (kontrəvēn´) *v.t.* **1** to violate, to infringe (*to contravene the rules*). **2** to be in conflict with, to obstruct. **3** to oppose, to be inconsistent with. **contravention** (-ven´shən) *n.* **1** violation, infringement. **2** an instance of this. **in contravention of** violating, infringing.

☒ **contraversy** common misspelling of CONTRO-VERSY.

contretemps (kõ´trətä) *n.* (*pl.* **contretemps** (-täz)) **1** an unexpected event which throws everything into confusion. **2** a disagreement, a confrontation.

contribute (kəntrib´ūt, kon´-) *v.t.* **1** to give for a common purpose. **2** to pay as one's share. **3** to write (an article or chapter) for a publication. ~*v.i.* **1** to give a part. **2** to have a share in any act or effect (*These remarks contributed to her downfall*). **3** to write for a newspaper etc. **contribution** (kontribū´shən) *n.* **1** the act of contributing. **2** that which is contributed. **contributive** *a.* **contributor** *n.* a person who contributes, esp. to a publication. **contributory** *a.* **1** contributing to the same fund, stock or result. **2** promoting the same end. **3** of or involving a contribution or contributions (*a contributory pension scheme*). ~*n.* (*pl.* **contributories**) (*Law*) a person liable to contribute to the assets of a company if it is wound up.

Usage note The pronunciation (kon´-), with the stress on the first syllable, is sometimes disapproved of.

contrite (kəntrīt´, kon´-) *a.* **1** deeply sorry for wrongdoing, full of remorse. **2** showing or characterized by penitence. **contritely** *adv.* **contriteness** *n.* **contrition** (-trish´-) *n.*

contrive (kəntrīv´) *v.t.* **1** to devise, to invent. **2** to bring about, to effect, to manage. ~*v.i.* to plot or scheme (against). **contrivable** *a.* **contrivance** *n.* **1** the act of contriving. **2** the thing contrived. **3** a mechanical device or apparatus. **4** a plan; a plot. **5** a trick, an artifice. **6** inventiveness. **contrived** *a.* forced, artificial. **contriver** *n.*

control (kəntrōl´) *n.* **1** check, restraint. **2** restraining, directing and regulating power. **3** authority, command. **4** a person who controls. **5** a means of controlling. **6** a standard of comparison for checking the results of an experiment. **7** (*pl.*) the mechanisms which govern the operation of a vehicle or machine. **8** a place where something is controlled or checked. ~*v.t.* (*pres.p.* **controlling**, *past, p.p.* **controlled**) **1** to exercise power over, to govern, to command. **2** to restrain, to regulate, to hold in check. **3** to verify or check. **4** to operate or direct (a vehicle, machine etc.). **in control**

controlling. **out of control** not or no longer controlled. **under control** being controlled. **control group** *n.* a group used as a standard of comparison in an experiment. **controllable** *a.* **controllability** (-bil´-) *n.* **controllably** *adv.* **controller** *n.* **1** a person or thing that controls. **2** a person in charge of financial planning, expenditure etc. **controllership** *n.* **controlling interest** *n.* a shareholding sufficiently large to ensure some control over the running of a company. **control tower** *n.* a tower at an airport from which air traffic in and out is controlled.

controversy (kon´trəvœsi, kəntrov´əsi) *n.* (*pl.* **controversies**) **1** a dispute or debate, esp. one carried on in public over a long period of time. **2** disputation, disagreement. **controversial** (kontrəvœ´shəl) *a.* **1** of, relating to or arousing controversy (*a controversial decision*). **2** inclined to argue or dispute. **controversialism** *n.* **controversialist** *n.* **controversially** *adv.*

Usage note The pronunciation (-trov´-), with stress on the second syllable, is sometimes disapproved of.

controvert (kon´trəvœt, -vœt´) *v.t.* **1** to dispute. **2** to call in question. **3** to oppose or refute by argument. **controvertible** (-vœ´-) *a.*

contumacious (kontūmā´shəs) *a.* **1** perverse, obstinate, stubborn. **2** stubbornly opposing lawful authority. **contumaciously** *adv.* **contumaciousness** *n.* **contumacy** (kon´tūməsi) *n.*

contumely (kon´tūmli) *n.* **1** rude, scornful abuse or reproach. **2** insolence, contempt. **3** disgrace, ignominy. **contumelious** (-mē´liəs) *a.* contemptuous, insolent, abusive. **contumeliously** *adv.* **contumeliousness** *n.*

contuse (kəntūz´) *v.t.* to bruise without breaking the skin. **contusion** (-tū´zhən) *n.* **1** the act of contusing. **2** the state of being contused. **3** a bruise.

conundrum (kənŭn´drəm) *n.* (*pl.* **conundrums**) **1** a riddle. **2** a puzzling question.

conurbation (konəbā´shən) *n.* a cluster of towns and urban districts that merge to form a densely populated area.

conure (kon´ūə) *n.* any parrot of the genus *Pyrrhura*, with a long tail.

convalesce (konvəles´) *v.i.* to recover health after illness, surgery etc. **convalescence** *n.* **convalescent** *a.* recovering health. ~*n.* a person who is recovering health.

convection (kənvek´shən) *n.* **1** the propagation of heat or electricity through liquids and gases by the movement of the heated particles. **2** in meteorology, the upward movement of warm air and downward movement of cool air. **convectional** *a.* **convection current** *n.* circulation resulting from convection. **convective** *a.* **convector** *n.* a heater which works by the circulation of currents of heated air.

convene (kənvēn´) *v.t.* **1** to call together. **2** to convoke. **3** to summon to appear. **4** to arrange (a meeting). ~*v.i.* to meet together, to assemble. **convenable** *a.* **convener, convenor** *n.* **1** a person who calls a committee etc. together. **2** a senior trade union official.

convenient (kənvēn´yənt) *a.* **1** suitable, opportune (*a convenient moment*). **2** useful, handy. **3** at hand, close by. **convenience** *n.* **1** the quality or state of being convenient. **2** comfort, ease. **3** a cause or source of comfort or ease. **4** advantage. **5** a thing that is useful. **6** (*pl.*) things or arrangements that promote ease and comfort or save trouble. **7** a lavatory, esp. a public lavatory. **at one's convenience** at a time that is suitable to one. **convenience food** *n.* food bought already prepared so as to need very little further work before cooking or eating. **convenience store** *n.* a shop which sells a wide range of useful articles as well as food, and is open at times convenient to the public. **conveniently** *adv.*

convent (kon´vənt) *n.* **1** a community of religious persons, now usu. nuns. **2** the building occupied by such a community. **3** (*also* **convent school**) a school run by the members of a convent. **conventual** (-ven´tū-) *a.* belonging to a convent. ~*n.* a member of a convent.

conventicle (kənven´tikəl) *n.* **1** a clandestine gathering, esp. for worship. **2** a meeting or place of worship of dissenters in the 16th and 17th cents.

convention (kənven´shən) *n.* **1** an agreement, a treaty. **2** an accepted usage, code of conduct etc. **3** the act of convening. **4** a meeting, a conference. **5** the persons assembled. **6** (*esp. N Am.*) an assembly of representatives. **conventional** *a.* **1** of, relating to or in accordance with convention. **2** observing the customs of society. **3** (of painting) following traditional and accepted models. **4** (of energy sources, warfare etc.) not nuclear. **5** agreed on by convention. **conventionalism** *n.* **conventionalist** *n.* **conventionality** (-al´-) *n.* (*pl.* **conventionalities**) **1** the state of being conventional. **2** (*often pl.*) a convention or propriety. **conventionalize, conventionalise** *v.t.* **conventionally** *adv.* **conventioneer** *n.* (*N Am.*) a person who attends a convention.

converge (kənvœj´) *v.i.* **1** to tend towards one point. **2** to meet at one point. **3** (of opinions, ideas etc.) to tend towards the same conclusion. **to converge on** to approach and meet at (a place) from different directions (*The police and emergency services converged on the scene*). **convergent** *a.* **1** tending to converge. **2** (*Biol.*) developing similar characteristics in a similar environment. **3** (*Psych.*) (of thought) producing a logical or conventional result. **convergence, convergency** *n.*

conversant (kənvœ´sənt) *a.* **1** having knowledge acquired by study, use or familiarity. **2** well acquainted, familiar (with). **conversance, conversancy** *n.*

conversation (konvəsā´shən) *n.* **1** the act of conversing, informal talk. **2** an instance of this (*to have a conversation*). **conversational** *a.* **conversationalist** *n.* a person inclined to or skilled in conversation. **conversationally** *adv.*

converse[1] (kənvœs´) *v.i.* to talk easily and informally (with) etc. **converser** *n.*

converse[2] (kon´vœs) *n.* **1** something opposite or contrary. **2** a counterpart or complement. **3** (*Math.*) an inverted proposition. **4** (*Logic*) a converted proposition. ~*a.* **1** opposite, reversed, contrary. **2** reciprocal, complemental. **conversely** (kon´-, -vœs´-) *adv.*

conversion (kənvœ´shən) *n.* **1** the act or an instance of converting. **2** change from one state to another. **3** change to a new mode of life, religion, morals or politics. **4** the changing of one kind of unit, security etc. into another kind. **5** a change in the structure or use of a building. **6** a building so changed. **7** (*Theol.*) the act of turning from sin to godliness. **8** the transformation of fertile to fissile material in a nuclear reactor. **9** in rugby or American football, the scoring of a goal from the kick taken after a try etc. has been scored.

convert[1] (kənvœt´) *v.t.* **1** to change from one physical state to another, to transmute. **2** to cause to turn from one religion or party to another. **3** to change (one kind of securities) into another kind. **4** to convert the structure or use of (a building or part of a building) (*We converted the garage into a bedroom; They live in a converted oast house*). **5** in rugby, to complete (a try) by kicking a goal. **6** (*Logic*) to transpose the terms of (a proposition). ~*v.i.* **1** to be converted or convertible. **2** in American football, to make a conversion. **converter, convertor** *n.* **1** a person or thing that converts. **2** a device for changing alternating current to direct current or vice versa. **3** a device for changing a signal from one frequency to another. **4** (*also* **converter reactor**) a reactor that converts fertile to fissile nuclear material. **5** a vessel used in refining molten metal, esp. in making steel. **convertible** *a.* **1** that may be converted or changed. **2** (of currency etc.) exchangeable for another kind. **3** (of a car) having a roof that can be folded back or removed. ~*n.* a convertible car. **convertibility** (-bil´-) *n.* **convertibly** *adv.*

convert[2] (kon´vœt) *n.* a person who is converted from one religion, party, belief or opinion to another, esp. one who is converted to Christianity.

convex (kon´veks) *a.* having a curve or surface rounded like the outer side of a circle or sphere, as distinct from *concave*. **convexity** (-veks´-) *n.* **convexly** *adv.*

convey (kənvā´) *v.t.* **1** to carry, to transport, to transmit. **2** to impart, to communicate. **3** (*Law*) to transfer (property). **conveyable** *a.* **conveyance** *n.* **1** the act or process of conveying. **2** a means of conveying, a vehicle. **3** (*Law*) **a** the act of transferring real property from one person to another. **b** the document by which it is transferred. **conveyancer** *n.* (*Law*) a person who draws up conveyances. **conveyancing** *n.* (*Law*) the drawing up of conveyances. **conveyor, conveyer** *n.* **1** a person or thing that conveys. **2** (*also* **conveyor belt**) an endless mechanical belt or moving platform which carries goods, materials etc., esp. along a production line in a factory.

convict[1] (kənvikt´) *v.t.* **1** to prove guilty. **2** to return a verdict of guilty against. **conviction** *n.* **1** the act of convicting. **2** the state of being convicted. **3** an instance of being convicted. **4** the state of being convinced. **5** strong belief, persuasion. **6** the act of convincing.

convict[2] (kon´vikt) *n.* a criminal sentenced to a term in prison.

convince (kənvins´) *v.t.* **1** to satisfy the mind of. **2** to persuade, to cause to believe or realize. **convinced** *a.* persuaded, certain (*I'm convinced he was lying*). **convincer** *n.* **convincible** *a.* **convincing** *a.* **1** persuasive, dispelling doubt (*a convincing explanation*). **2** positive, decisive (*a convincing victory*). **convincingly** *adv.* **convincingness** *n.*

convivial (kənviv´iəl) *a.* festive, social, jovial. **conviviality** (-al´-) *n.* **convivially** *adv.*

convocation (konvəkā´shən) *n.* **1** the act of calling together. **2** an assembly, a meeting, a gathering. **convocational** *a.*

convoke (kənvōk´) *v.t.* (*formal*) to call or summon together.

convolute (kon´vəloot) *a.* rolled or coiled together. **convoluted** (-loo´tid) *a.* **1** intricate, complex. **2** convolute. **convolutedly** *adv.* **convolution** (-loo´shən) *n.* **1** the act of convolving. **2** the state of being convolved. **3** a fold, esp. in the surface of the brain. **4** a coil. **5** a winding motion. **6** intricacy, complexity. **convolutional** *a.* **convolve** (kənvolv´) *v.t.* **1** to roll or wind together. **2** to wind (one part) over another. **convolved** *a.* **convolvulus** (-vol´vūləs) *n.* (*pl.* **convolvuluses, convolvuli** (-lī)) any climbing plant of the genus *Convolvulus*, containing the bindweed.

convoy (kon´voi) *v.t.* to accompany in transit by land or sea, for the sake of protection, esp. with a warship. ~*n.* **1** the act of convoying or escorting. **2** a protecting force accompanying persons, goods, ships etc. **3** a company of merchant ships, goods vehicles etc. being convoyed or travelling together. **4** goods etc. being convoyed. **in convoy** travelling together, with or without an escort.

convulse (kənvŭls´) *v.t.* **1** to agitate violently. **2** to affect with convulsions. **3** (*coll.*) to excite uncontrollable laughter in. **convulsant** *a.* inducing convulsions. ~*n.* a drug that induces convulsions. **convulsion** (-vŭl´shən) *n.* **1** (*usu. pl.*) an involuntary action of the muscular tissues of the body characterized by violent contractions and alternate relaxations. **2** a violent agitation, disturbance or commotion. **3** (*pl., coll.*) uncontrollable laughter. **convulsionary** *a.* **convulsive** *a.* **1** characterized by convulsions. **2** producing convulsions. **3** affected with convulsions. **convulsively** *adv.*

cony (kō´ni), **coney** *n.* (*pl.* **conies, coneys**) (*Her.* or *dial.*) **1** a rabbit. **2** rabbit fur.

coo (koo) *v.i.* (*3rd pers. sing. pres.* **coos,** *pres.p.* **cooing,** *past, p.p.* **cooed**) **1** to make a soft low sound, like a dove or pigeon. **2** to speak lovingly. ~*v.t.* to say in cooing fashion. ~*n.* the characteristic sound of a dove or pigeon. ~*int.* used to express astonishment.

co-occur (kōəkœ´) *v.i.* (*pres.p.* **co-occurring,** *past, p.p.* **co-occurred**) to occur at the same time or in the same place. **co-occurrence** (-kŭr´əns) *n.*

cooee (koo´ē) *n.* a call used to attract attention. ~*int.* used to attract attention. ~*v.i.* (*3rd pers. sing. pres.* **cooees,** *pres.p.* **cooeeing,** *past, p.p.* **cooeed**) to make this call.

cook (kuk) *n.* a person who prepares food for the table with the use of heat. ~*v.t.* **1** to prepare (food) for the table by boiling, roasting etc. **2** (*coll.*) to garble, to falsify. **3** (*sl.*) to ruin. ~*v.i.* **1** to act as a cook. **2** to undergo the process of cooking. **to be cooking** (*coll.*) to be happening (*What's cooking?*). **to cook someone's goose** **1** (*coll.*) to ruin someone's chances. **2** (*coll.*) to spoil someone's plans. **to cook the books** (*coll.*) to falsify the accounts. **to cook up** (*coll.*) to concoct (an excuse, a story etc.). **cookable** *a.* **cookbook** *n.* a book containing recipes and advice on preparing food. **cook-chill** *a.* denoting convenience food that has been cooked and chilled by the manufacturer for subsequent reheating and serving (*a cook-chill meal*). **cooker** *n.* **1** a stove or other apparatus for cooking. **2** (*coll.*) a cooking apple or similar item. **cookery** *n.* (*pl.* **cookeries**) **1** the act or art of cooking. **2** (*N Am.*) a place for cooking. **cookery book** *n.* a cookbook. **cookhouse** *n.* **1** (*Naut.*) a galley. **2** a detached kitchen in warm countries. **3** a camp kitchen. **cooking** *a.* **1** used in cooking. **2** suitable for cooking rather than eating raw (*a cooking apple; cooking chocolate*). ~*n.* cookery. **cookout** *n.* (*N Am.*) a party at which food is cooked out of doors. **cookware** *n.* utensils used for cooking.

cookie (kuk´i) *n.* **1** (*N Am.*) (*also* **cooky,** *pl.* **cookies**) a sweet biscuit. **2** (*coll.*) a person (of a particular character) (*a smart cookie*). **the way the cookie crumbles** the way things are or happen, an unalterable state of affairs.

cool (kool) *a.* **1** slightly or moderately cold. **2** not retaining or causing heat. **3** (of colours) greenish or bluish, creating a feeling of coolness. **4** aloof, unfriendly. **5** apathetic, unenthusiastic, indifferent. **6** calm, dispassionate, not showing emotion. **7** calmly impudent or audacious. **8** (*coll.*) amounting to without exaggeration, as much as. **9** (*coll.*) very good, excellent. **10** (*coll.*) sophisticated, fashionable, smart, trendy. **11** (*coll.*) acceptable. **12** (*coll.*) relaxed. **13** (of jazz) controlled and restrained. ~*n.* **1** coolness, moderate temperature. **2** a cool place. ~*v.t.* **1** to cause to lose heat, to make cool or cooler. **2** to quiet, to calm, to allay. ~*v.i.* **1** to lose heat, to become cool or cooler. **2** (of excitement, enthusiasm etc.) to become less. **3** to become less angry. **to cool it** (*sl.*) to calm down. **to cool one's heels** (*coll.*) to be kept waiting. **to keep one's cool** (*coll.*) to remain calm. **to lose one's cool** (*coll.*) to become upset, flustered or angry. **coolant** *n.* a fluid used for cooling or lubricating. **cool bag, cool box** *n.* an insulated bag or box in which food is kept cold. **cooler** *n.* **1** that which cools. **2** an apparatus or container for cooling things. **3** (*N Am.*) something for keeping things cool, such as a refrigerator or cool bag. **4** a drink consisting of wine, soda water and fruit juice. **5** (*sl.*) prison. **cool-headed** *a.* remaining, or able to remain, calm in tense, dangerous etc. situations. **cooling-off period** *n.* a period of time during which one may reconsider a decision, arrangement etc. **cooling tower** *n.* a tower in which water is cooled by trickling over wooden slats, for industrial reuse. **coolish** *a.* **coolly** *adv.* **coolness** *n.* **coolth** *n.* (*dial. or facet.*) coolness.

coolabah (kooˈləbah), **coolibah** (-libah) *n.* (*Austral.*) any of several species of eucalyptus trees, esp. *Eucalyptus microtheca*.

coolie (kooˈli), **cooly** *n.* (*pl.* **coolies**) **1** an unskilled hired labourer in or from the East, esp. India and China. **2** (*offensive*) a person of Indian extraction living in South Africa. **coolie hat** *n.* a type of broad, round, conical straw hat, as formerly worn by Chinese coolies.

coomb, coombe COMBE.

coon (koon) *n.* **1** (*coll.*) a raccoon. **2** (*offensive*) a black.

coop (koop) *n.* **1** a cage or small enclosure for poultry or small animals. **2** a confined space, esp. a prison or prison cell. **3** a wickerwork trap for catching eels etc. ~*v.t.* to confine in or as if in a coop (often with *up, in*).

co-op (kōˈop), **coop** *n.* a cooperative society, business venture, or shop. ~*a.* (of a business venture etc.) cooperative.

cooper (kooˈpə) *n.* **1** a person whose trade is to make barrels, tubs etc. **2** a person who mends casks etc. on a ship. ~*v.t.* to make or repair (casks etc.). **cooperage** *n.* **1** the trade or workshop of a cooper. **2** the price paid for a cooper's work.

cooperate (kōopˈərāt), **co-operate** *v.i.* **1** to work or act with another or others for a common end. **2** to be helpful, obliging or accommodating. **3** to form a cooperative business association. **4** to contribute to an effect. **cooperant** *a.* **cooperation** (-āˈshən) *n.* **1** the act of cooperating. **2** helpfulness, willingness to oblige another. **3** a form of partnership or association for the production or distribution of goods, or the formation of such partnerships or associations. **cooperative** *a.* **1** working, or willing to work, with others for a common end or the common good. **2** helpful, obliging, accommodating. **3** (of a business venture etc.) owned jointly by the workers etc., for the economic benefit of them all. ~*n.* a cooperative business, shop etc. **cooperatively** *adv.* **cooperativeness** *n.* **cooperator** *n.*

co-opt (kōopt´) *v.t.* **1** to elect onto a committee etc. by the votes of the members of that committee etc., as opposed to by the votes of a larger body of voters. **2** to adopt or use for one's own ends. **3** to take into or cause to join another, esp. larger, group, such as a political party. **co-optation, co-option** *n.*

coordinate¹ (kōawˈdinət) *a.* **1** of the same order, rank, importance, power etc. **2** coordinated, involving coordination. **3** (*Chem.*) denoting a covalent bond in which the two shared electrons are provided by one of the atoms involved. ~*n.* **1** (*Math.*) any of two or more numbers used as elements of reference to determine the position of any point, line or plane. **2** (*pl.*) clothes in harmonizing colours and patterns, designed to be worn together. **3** any of two or more people or things of equal rank or status. **coordinately** *adv.*

coordinate² (kōawˈdināt) *v.t.* **1** to make coordinate. **2** to correlate, to bring into orderly relation of parts and whole. ~*v.i.* to work well together, to produce a good effect. **coordination** (-āˈshən) *n.* **1** the act of coordinating or state of being coordinated. **2** effectively coordinated activity. **3** well-balanced, dexterous, skilful etc. actions, or the ability to perform such. **coordinative** *a.* **coordinator** *n.*

coot (koot) *n.* **1** a small black British aquatic bird, *Fulica atra*, or any other bird of the same genus. **2** a stupid person.

co-own (kō-ōn´) *v.t.* to own jointly. **co-owner** *n.* **co-ownership** *n.*

cop (kop) *v.t.* (*pres.p.* **copping**, *past, p.p.* **copped**) **1** (*sl.*) to seize. **2** to arrest. **3** to catch or get (something unpleasant). **4** to obtain (drugs). ~*n.* **1** (*coll.*) a policeman. **2** (*sl.*) an arrest. **no cop** (*sl.*) worthless. **not much cop** (*sl.*) worthless. **to cop a plea** (*N Am., sl.*) to plea-bargain. **to cop it** (*sl.*) to be caught or punished. **2** (*sl.*) to be killed. **to cop out** **1** (*sl.*) to refuse or avoid responsibility or a task. **2** (*sl.*) to give up, stop. **3** (*sl.*) to break a promise. **cop-out** *n.* **copper**¹ (kopˈə) *n.* (*coll.*) **1** a policeman. **2** a person who cops or seizes. **cop-shop** *n.* (*sl.*) a police station.

copal (kōˈpəl) *n.* **1** a resin obtained from any of a number of tropical trees. **2** a varnish made from this.

copartner (kōpahtˈnə) *n.* **1** a partner, an associate. **2** a partaker. **copartnership, copartnery** *n.*

cope¹ (kōp) *v.i.* **1** to encounter, to contend successfully (with). **2** to deal (with), manage successfully.

cope² (kōp) *n.* **1** an ecclesiastical sleeveless vestment worn in processions and at solemn ceremonies. **2** (*poet.*) anything spread overhead, such as a cloud or the sky. ~*v.t.* to cover with or as if with a cope or coping. **copestone** *n.* **1** a coping-stone. **2** a finishing touch. **coping** *n.* the course projecting horizontally on the top of a wall. **coping-stone** *n.* **1** the topmost stone of a building. **2** a stone forming part of the coping.

copeck (kō´pek, kop´-), **kopeck, kopek** n. a Russian monetary unit and coin, the hundredth part of a rouble.

Copernican (kəpœ´nikən) a. (Astron.) of or relating to the astronomical system of the Polish astronomer Copernicus, 1473–1543, which has the sun as its centre.

copier COPY.

co-pilot (kō´pīlət) n. a second or assistant pilot of an aircraft.

coping COPE².

copious (kō´piəs) a. **1** plentiful, abundant, ample. **2** producing a plentiful supply. **3** profuse, prolific, rich in vocabulary. **4** providing a lot of information. **copiously** adv. **copiousness** n.

copita (kəpē´tə) n. (pl. **copitas**) a tulip-shaped sherry glass.

copolymer (kōpol´imə) n. (Chem.) a polymer consisting of random or repeated sequences of more than one type of molecule. **copolymerize, copolymerise** v.t., v.i. **copolymerization** (-zā´shən) n.

copper¹ COP.

copper² (kop´ə) n. **1** (Chem.) a reddish-brown malleable, ductile metallic element, at. no. 29, chem. symbol Cu. **2** (usu. pl.) a copper or bronze coin. **3** the colour of copper. **4** a large cooking pot, laundry boiler etc. (formerly made of copper). **5** any of various species of butterfly of the genus Lycaena or related genera, with copper-coloured wings. ~a. made of or like copper. ~v.t. to cover, coat etc. with copper. **copper beech** n. a variety of beech with copper-coloured leaves. **copper bit** n. a soldering iron with a copper point. **copper-bottomed** a. **1** (Naut.) sheathed with copper. **2** (financially) reliable. **copperhead** n. **1** a highly venomous N American snake, Agkistrodon contortrix, allied to the rattlesnake. **2** a reddish-brown venomous snake, Denisonia superba, found in southern Australia and Tasmania. **copperplate** n. **1** neat and elegant handwriting. **2** a polished plate of copper on which something is engraved for printing. **3** an impression from such a plate. ~a. **1** (of handwriting) neat and elegant. **2** of or relating to the art of engraving on copper. **copper pyrites** n. (Mineral.) CHALCOPYRITE. **coppersmith** n. a worker in copper. **copper sulphate** n. a copper salt, $CuSO_4$, usu. found as blue crystals, used as a fungicide, in dyeing etc. **copper vitriol** n. blue vitriol, hydrous copper sulphate. **coppery** a. made of, containing or resembling copper.

coppice (kop´is) n. a small wood of small trees and undergrowth, cut periodically for firewood. ~v.t. to cut (trees and bushes) to make a coppice. ~v.i. to grow new shoots from a cut stump. **coppiced** a. **coppicewood** n. COPSEWOOD (under COPSE).

copra (kop´rə) n. the dried kernel of the coconut, yielding coconut oil.

copro- (kop´rō) comb. form of or relating to or living on or among dung.

co-produce (kōprədūs´) v.t. to produce (a film, play etc.) jointly with one or more other people. **co-producer** n. **co-production** n.

coprolite (kop´rəlīt) n. the fossil dung of various extinct animals, chiefly saurians, largely used as fertilizer. **coprolitic** (-lit´-) a.

coprophilia (koprəfil´iə) n. morbid, esp. sexual, interest in excrement.

copse (kops) n. a coppice. ~v.t. **1** to plant or preserve for copsewood. **2** to cover with copses. **copsewood** n. undergrowth, brushwood.

Copt (kopt) n. **1** an Egyptian at the time of the ancient Greek and Roman empires. **2** a Coptic Christian. **Coptic** a. of or relating to the Copts, or to the monophysite Egyptian Church established in the 5th cent. ~n. the language of the Copts, now extinct except in Coptic Church liturgy.

copula (kop´ūlə) n. (pl. **copulas**) (Logic, Gram.) the word in a sentence or proposition which links the subject and predicate together. **copular** a.

copulate (kop´ūlāt) v.i. to have sexual intercourse. **copulation** (-lā´shən) n. **1** sexual intercourse. **2** (Logic, Gram.) connection. **copulative** a. **1** serving to unite. **2** (Gram.) acting as a copula. **3** (Gram.) having two or more words, phrases or predicates connected by a copulative conjunction. **4** of or relating to sexual union. **copulatively** adv. **copulatory** a.

copy (kop´i) n. (pl. **copies**) **1** a transcript or imitation of an original. **2** a thing made in imitation of or exactly like another. **3** an example of a particular work or book. **4** in journalism, material for reporting, writing articles etc. **5** the words, as opposed to the pictures or graphic material, in an advertisement etc. **6** an original, a model, a pattern. **7** a writing exercise. ~v.t. (3rd pers. sing. pres. **copies**, pres.p. **copying**, past, p.p. **copied**) **1** to make a copy of. **2** (often with out) to make a written copy of, to transcribe. **3** to follow as pattern or model. **4** (with to) to send or give a copy of (a letter etc.) to someone. ~v.i. to make a copy, esp. illicitly. **copiable** a. **copier** n. **1** a person who copies. **2** a photocopier. **3** an imitator, a plagiarist. **copybook** n. a book in which specimens of good handwriting, formerly usu. proverbs, maxims etc., are written clearly to be copied esp. by children learning to write. ~a. **1** conventional. **2** perfect. **copycat** n. (coll.) a person who imitates someone else. ~a. done in imitation. **copydesk** n. a desk in a newspaper office where copy is edited before being passed for printing. **copy editor** n. a person who prepares written material for printing by correcting its style, punctuation etc. **copy-edit** v.t., v.i. **copy-editing** n. **copyhold** n. (Law, Hist.) **1** a tenure for which the tenant has nothing to show but the copy of the rolls made by the steward of the lord's court. **2** property held by such tenure. ~a. held by such tenure. **copyholder** n. **copyist** n. **copyreader** n. (N Am.) a copy editor or newspaper subeditor. **copyread** v.t. (past, p.p.

copyread (-red)). **copyright** *n.* the exclusive right for the author of a literary or artistic production, or the author's heirs, to publish or sell copies of their work. ~*a.* protected by copyright. ~*v.t.* to secure copyright for (a book, music, picture etc.). **copy-typist** *n.* a person who types from written copy, rather than from shorthand or tape. **copywriter** *n.* a person who writes advertisements. **copywriting** *n.*

coquet (kəket') *v.i.* (*pres.p.* **coquetting,** *past, p.p.* **coquetted**) **1** to flirt (with). **2** to trifle. **coquetry** (kō´-, kok´-) *n.* (*pl.* **coquetries**) **1** the practices of a coquette; affectation of encouragement to an admirer; flirtation. **2** treating serious matters lightly or frivolously. **coquette** *n.* **1** a female flirt; a jilt. **2** a hummingbird of the genus *Lophornis.* **coquettish** *a.* **coquettishly** *adv.* **coquettishness** *n.*

coquina (kōkē´nə) *n.* a type of soft, whitish limestone formed from broken shells and coral.

coquito (kəkē´tō) *n.* (*pl.* **coquitos**) a Chilean nutbearing palm tree, *Jubaea chilensis.*

cor[1] (kaw) *int.* (*sl.*) expressing surprise, amazement etc. **cor blimey** (blī´mi) *int.* used to express surprise, irritation etc.

cor[2] (kaw) *n.* (*Mus.*) a horn. **cor anglais** (kawr ong´glā) *n.* (*pl.* **cors anglais** (kawz ong´glā, kawr)) **1** the English horn, a woodwind instrument of the oboe family, slightly lower in pitch than the oboe. **2** a person who plays the cor anglais in an orchestra. **3** an organ stop producing the sound of a cor anglais.

coracle (kor´əkəl) *n.* a light boat used in Wales and Ireland, made of wickerwork covered with leather or oiled cloth.

coral (kor´əl) *n.* **1** the calcareous skeletal structure secreted by certain marine polyps or zoophytes of the class Anthozoa, deposited in masses on the bottom of the sea. **2** the animal or colony of animals forming these structures. **3** a deep orange-pink colour. **4** the unfertilized eggs of a lobster or scallop (from their colour). ~*a.* made of or resembling coral. **coral island** *n.* an island formed by the growth and accumulation of coral. **coralline** (-līn) *a.* **1** of the nature of coral. **2** containing or resembling coral. ~*n.* **1** a seaweed of the genus *Corallina* with calcareous fronds. **2** any of various coral-like aquatic animals. **corallite** (-līt) *n.* **1** a coral-shaped petrifaction. **2** the skeleton or case of a polyp. **coralloid** *a.* resembling coral. ~*n.* an organism akin to or resembling coral. **coral reef** *n.* a ridge or series of ridges of coral, tending to form a coral island. **coralroot** *n.* **1** a purple-flowered cruciferous woodland plant, *Cardamine bulbifera.* **2** (*also* **coralroot orchid**) any of a number of almost leafless orchids of the genus *Corallorhiza,* living mostly on dead organic matter. **coral snake** *n.* any of a large number of snakes belonging to the cobra family Elapidae, most patterned with bright bands of red, yellow, black or white.

cor anglais COR[2].

corbel (kaw´bəl) *n.* (*Archit.*) **1** a bracket or projection of stone, wood or iron projecting from a wall to support some superincumbent weight. **2** a corbel block. ~*v.t.* (*pres.p.* **corbelling,** (*NAm.*) **corbeling,** *past, p.p.* **corbelled,** (*NAm.*) **corbeled**) **1** (*with off, out*) to support by means of corbels. **2** to lay (a stone etc.) to form a corbel. **3** (*with off, out*) to (cause to) project by constructing on corbels. **corbel block** *n.* a short timber helping to support a beam at either end. **corbel table** *n.* a projecting course, parapet etc. supported by corbels.

cord (kawd) *n.* **1** thick string or thin rope composed of several strands, or a piece of this. **2** an electric flex. **3** (*Anat.*) a cordlike structure. **4** (*pl.*) corduroy trousers. **5** ribbed cloth, esp. corduroy. **6** a raised rib in woven cloth. **7** anything which binds or draws together emotionally etc. ~*v.t.* **1** to bind with a cord. **2** to fit a cord to. **cordage** *n.* **1** a quantity or store of ropes. **2** the ropes or rigging of a ship collectively. **corded** *a.* **1** bound or fastened with cords. **2** made with cords. **3** ribbed or twilled (like corduroy). **4** (of muscles) standing out like cords. **cordless** *a.* (of an electrical appliance) operated by stored electricity, e.g. batteries, as in *cordless telephone.*

cordate (kaw´dāt) *a.* heart-shaped.

cordial (kaw´diəl) *a.* **1** sincere, hearty, warmhearted. **2** cheering or comforting the heart. ~*n.* **1** a sweetened drink made with fruit juice, usu. diluted before drinking. **2** a medicine used to increase the circulation or to raise the spirits. **3** anything which cheers or comforts. **4** a liqueur. **cordiality** (-al´-) *n.* (*pl.* **cordialities**). **cordially** *adv.*

cordite (kaw´dīt) *n.* a smokeless explosive, prepared in stringlike grains.

cordon (kaw´dən) *n.* **1** a line or series of persons, posts or ships placed so as to guard or blockade a place. **2** a ribbon or cord worn as an ornament, a mark of rank or the badge of an order. **3** a fruit-tree trained and closely pruned to grow as a single stem. **4** (*Archit.*) a projecting band of stones in a wall, a string-course. ~*v.t.* to separate (off) or surround with a cordon.

cordon bleu (kawdō blœ´) *a.* (of food or cookery) of the highest standard. ~*n.* (*pl.* **cordons bleus** (kawdō blœz´)) a cook or chef of the highest calibre.

cordon sanitaire (kawdō sanitea´) *n.* (*pl.* **cordons sanitaires** (kawdō sanitea´)) **1** a line of guards surrounding a disease-infected area, to cut off communication and so prevent the spread of the disease. **2** any similar preventative measure or set-up designed to isolate or protect.

corduroy (kaw´dəroi, -roi´) *n.* **1** a stout-ribbed cotton cloth made with a pile. **2** (*pl.*) corduroy trousers. ~*a.* made of this material. **corduroy road** *n.* a causeway of logs laid over a swamp.

core (kaw) *n.* **1** the heart or inner part of anything. **2** the hard middle of an apple, pear or similar fruit, containing the seeds. **3** the pith, the gist, the essence. **4** the insulated conducting wires of a cable. **5** the central strand of a rope. **6** (*also* **core curriculum**) the essential part of a school curriculum, studied by all pupils. **7** the central part of the earth. **8** the round mass of rock brought up by an annular drill. **9** a piece of magnetic material, such as soft iron, inside an induction coil. **10** the part of a nuclear reactor containing the fissile material. **11** a mass of sand or something similar put into a mould in order to create a space or hollow in a casting. **12** the central portion of a flint left after flakes have been struck off. ~*v.t.* to remove the core from. **coreless** *a*. **corer** *n*. **core subjects** *n.pl.* the subjects, such as maths or science, studied as part of a core curriculum. **core time** *n*. in a flexitime system, the central part of the day when everyone is at work.

corelation CORRELATION (under CORRELATE).

coreligionist (kŏrilij´ənist) *n*. a person of the same religion.

coreopsis (koriop´sis) *n*. (*pl*. **coreopsises**) any of the many annual or perennial garden plants of the genus *Coreopsis*, with bright, mostly yellow flowers.

✗ **corespond** common misspelling of CORRESPOND.

co-respondent (kŏrispon´dənt) *n*. a joint respondent in a lawsuit, esp. a divorce suit.

corgi (kaw´gi) *n*. (*pl*. **corgis**) a small, smooth-haired, short-legged dog, orig. from Wales.

coriander (korian´də) *n*. **1** an umbellifer, *Coriandrum sativum*, with aromatic and carminative seeds used as a spice in cooking. **2** the seeds of this plant.

Corinthian (kərin´thiən) *a*. **1** of or relating to Corinth, a city of Greece. **2** (of sport, players etc.) amateur. ~*n*. **1** a native or inhabitant of Corinth. **2** an amateur in sport, esp. if wealthy. **Corinthian order** *n*. (*Archit*.) the most elaborate and ornate of the three Grecian orders, the capital being enriched with graceful foliated forms added to the volutes of the Ionic capital.

corium (kaw´riəm) *n*. (*pl*. **coria** (-riə)) (*Anat*.) the innermost layer of the skin in mammals.

cork (kawk) *n*. **1** a stopper for a bottle or cask. **2** the very light outer layer of bark of the cork oak, from which stoppers for bottles, floats for fishing etc. are made. **3** a float for fishing. **4** (*Bot*.) a layer of close-fitting, dead, impermeable cells protecting the living internal tissues of plants against injury and loss of water. ~*a*. made of cork. ~*v.t.* **1** to close with a cork. **2** (*often with up*) to stifle or restrain (feelings etc.). **3** to blacken with burnt cork. **corkage** *n*. a charge levied at hotels and restaurants on wines consumed by guests but not supplied by the hotel. **corked** *a*. **1** stopped with a cork. **2** (of wine) supposedly tasting of the cork (but in fact tainted by a fungus growing on the cork). **3** blackened with burnt cork. **corker** *n*. (*coll*.) something or somebody astounding. **corking** *a*. (*coll*.) excellent, superb, magnificent. **corklike** *a*. **cork oak** *n*. an oak,

Quercus suber, much cultivated in Spain, Portugal and France for the sake of its bark. **corkscrew** *n*. a spirally twisted, screwlike device for drawing corks. ~*v.i.* to move in a spiral or zigzag fashion. ~*v.t.* to cause to move in a spiral or zigzag fashion. ~*a*. twisted to resemble a corkscrew, spiral. **corkwood** *n*. **1** light, porous wood. **2** a name given to various trees with light, porous wood. **corky** *a*. (*comp*. **corkier**, *superl*. **corkiest**) **1** resembling cork in nature or appearance. **2** (of wine) corked.

corm (kawm) *n*. (*Bot*.) a bulblike, fleshy underground stem, sometimes called a solid bulb.

cormorant (kaw´mərənt) *n*. any of the somewhat ducklike waterbirds of the genus *Phalacrocorax*, in Britain esp. *P. carbo*, a voracious seabird.

corn[1] (kawn) *n*. **1** grain. **2** the seed of cereals. **3** wheat. **4** (*Sc., Ir.*) oats. **5** (*N Am., Austral., New Zeal.*) maize, sweetcorn. **6** something corny, such as a song, joke etc. **7** a single seed or grain of certain plants. ~*v.t.* to preserve and season with salt. **cornbrash** *n*. (*Geol*.) a calcareous sandstone belonging to the Inferior Oolite. **cornbread** *n*. (*N Am.*) bread made from maize meal. **corn circle** *n*. CROP CIRCLE (under CROP). **corn cob** *n*. a spike of maize. **corncockle** *n*. a plant, *Agrostemma githago*, with reddish-purple flowers, related to the campions and once common in cornfields. **corncrake** *n*. a bird, *Crex crex*, of the rail family, with brown barred plumage and a harsh grating call, inhabiting hayfields, grassland etc. **corn dolly** *n*. a decorative figure made of plaited straw. **corned beef** *n*. tinned seasoned and cooked beef. **corn exchange** *n*. a market where corn is sold from samples. **cornfield** *n*. a field in which corn is growing. **cornflakes** *n.pl.* a breakfast cereal made from toasted flakes of maize. **cornflour** *n*. finely ground meal of maize or rice, used in cooking to sweeten sauces etc. **cornflower** *n*. any of several plants that grow amongst corn, esp. the blue-flowered, *Centaurea cyanus*. **corn marigold** *n*. a yellow-flowered composite plant, *Chrysanthemum segetum*. **corn on the cob** *n*. maize boiled or grilled and eaten direct from the cob. **cornrows** *n.pl.* a style of braiding the hair into tight plaits, adopted by some blacks. **corn spurrey** *n*. a white-flowered plant, *Spergula arvensis*, of the pink family, found in cornfields. **cornstarch** *n*. (*N Am.*) cornflour. **corny** *a*. (*comp*. **cornier**, *superl*. **corniest**) **1** trite. **2** old-fashioned and sentimental. **3** unsophisticated. **cornily** *adv*.

corn[2] (kawn) *n*. a horny excrescence on the foot or hand, produced by pressure over a bone.

cornea (kaw´niə) *n*. (*pl*. **corneas**, **corneae** (-niē)) the transparent forepart of the external coat of the eye, through which the rays of light pass. **corneal** *a*.

cornelian (kawnēl´yən), **carnelian** (kah´-) *n*. **1** a variety of semi-transparent chalcedony. **2** the reddish colour of this stone.

corner (kaw´nə) *n.* 1 the place where two converging lines or surfaces meet. 2 the space included between such lines or surfaces. 3 an angle. 4 a place enclosed by converging walls or other boundaries. 5 a place where two streets meet. 6 **a** either of two opposite angles of a boxing or wrestling ring where contestants go between rounds. **b** the contestant's coach etc. who give support between rounds at the contestant's corner. 7 a region, a quarter, esp. a remote place. 8 a nook. 9 a position of difficulty or embarrassment. 10 in football and hockey, a free kick or hit from a corner. 11 a combination to buy up the available supply of any commodity, in order to raise the price, a ring. 12 a triangular cut of ham etc. ~*v.t.* 1 to drive into a corner, or into a position of difficulty. 2 to buy up (a commodity) in order to control (the market). 3 to furnish with corners. ~*v.i.* 1 (esp. of vehicles) to turn a corner. 2 to form a corner (in a commodity). **just around/ round the corner** 1 (*coll.*) very close. 2 (*coll.*) imminent. **cornerback** *n.* 1 in American football, a defensive back. 2 the role or position of such a player. **corner shop** *n.* a small neighbourhood shop, often on a street corner, selling a variety of goods. **cornerstone** *n.* 1 the stone which unites two walls of a building. 2 the principal stone. 3 the foundation. 4 something of the first importance. **cornerwise** *adv.* diagonally, with the corner in front.

cornet (kaw´nit) *n.* 1 a three-valved brass musical instrument shaped like a small trumpet. 2 a cornetist. 3 an ice-cream cone. 4 an organ stop producing a cornet-like sound. **cornetist** (-net´-), **cornettist** *n.* a cornet-player.

cornice (kaw´nis) *n.* 1 (*Archit.*) **a** a moulded horizontal projection crowning a wall, entablature, pillar or other part of a building. **b** an ornamental band of plaster between a wall and ceiling. 2 a projecting mass of snow along the top of a precipice. **corniced** *a.* **cornicing** *n.*

corniche (kawnēsh´), **corniche road** *n.* a coast road, esp. one along the face of a cliff.

Cornish (kaw´nish) *a.* of or relating to Cornwall. ~*n.* the ancient Celtic language of Cornwall. **Cornish cream** *n.* CLOTTED CREAM (under CLOT). **Cornishman** *n.* (*pl.* **Cornishmen**). **Cornish pasty** *n.* a half-moon-shaped pasty filled with seasoned meat and vegetables.

cornucopia (kawnūkō´piə) *n.* (*pl.* **cornucopias**) 1 an abundant stock. 2 the horn of plenty, a goat's horn wreathed and filled to overflowing with flowers, fruit, corn etc., the symbol of plenty and peace. 3 a representation of a cornucopia. **cornucopian** *a.*

corolla (kərol´ə) *n.* (*pl.* **corollas**) (*Bot.*) the inner whorl of two series of floral envelopes occurring in the more highly developed plants, the petals.

corollary (kərol´əri) *n.* (*pl.* **corollaries**) 1 (*Logic*) an additional inference from a proposition. 2 something that follows as a deduction from

something else, a natural consequence. ~*a.* additional, supplementary, being or following as a corollary.

corona[1] (kərō´nə) *n.* (*pl.* **coronas, coronae** (-nē)) 1 (*Astron.*) **a** a disc or halo round the sun or the moon. **b** an anthelion or disc of light opposite the sun. **c** the zone of radiance round the moon in a total eclipse of the sun. 2 (*Archit.*) a broad projecting face forming the principal member of a cornice. 3 a circular chandelier hanging from the roof, esp. in churches. 4 the circumference or margin of a compound radiated flower. 5 (*Anat.*) any structure like a crown in shape. 6 a glowing electrical discharge round a charged conductor. **coronal**[1] *a.*

corona[2] (kərō´nə) *n.* (*pl.* **coronas**) a kind of long cigar with straight sides.

coronal[1] CORONA[1].

coronal[2] (kərō´nəl) *a.* 1 of or relating to a crown or the crown of the head. 2 (*Bot.*) of or relating to a corona. **coronal bone** *n.* the bone forming the forehead and front part of the skull. **coronally** *adv.* **coronal plane** *n.* an imaginary plane dividing the body vertically into front (ventral) and rear (dorsal) sections. **coronal suture** *n.* the suture extending over the crown of the skull and separating the frontal and parietal bones.

coronal[3] (kor´ənəl) *n.* 1 a circlet or coronet. 2 a wreath or garland.

coronary (kor´ənəri) *n.* (*pl.* **coronaries**) a coronary thrombosis. ~*a.* (*Anat.*) denoting or involving blood vessels, nerves etc. which lie round a part of the body. **coronary artery** *n.* either of two arteries springing from the aorta before it leaves the pericardium. **coronary bypass** *n.* the bypassing of a blocked or narrowed part of a coronary artery by means of a piece of healthy blood vessel taken from elsewhere in the body and grafted round the malfunctioning section. **coronary thrombosis** *n.* (*pl.* **coronary thromboses**) the formation of a clot in one of the arteries of the heart.

coronation (korənā´shən) *n.* the act or ceremony of solemnly crowning a sovereign.

coroner (kor´ənə) *n.* 1 an officer of the Crown whose duty it is to inquire into cases of sudden or suspicious death, and to determine the ownership of treasure-trove. 2 (*Hist.*) an officer in charge of the private property of the Crown. **coronership** *n.*

coronet (kor´ənit) *n.* 1 a little crown. 2 any of various types of small crown worn by princes, princesses and the nobility, varying in style according to the rank of the wearer. 3 an ornamental fillet worn as part of a woman's headdress. 4 the part of a horse's pastern where the skin turns to horn. 5 a bony ring round the base of the antler of a deer. **coroneted** *a.*

corp., Corp. *abbr.* 1 corporal. 2 corporation.

corpora CORPUS.

corporal[1] (kaw´pərəl, -prəl) *n.* 1 an army noncommissioned officer of the lowest grade. 2 a sailor who attends to police matters under the master-at-arms. **3** (*N Am.*) FALLFISH (under FALL).

corporal² (kaw´pərəl) *a.* **1** relating to the body. **2** material, corporeal. ~*n.* the fine linen cloth on which the elements are consecrated in the Eucharist. **corporality** (-ral´-) *n.* (*pl.* **corporalities**) **1** materiality. **2** (*pl.*) material things. **3** a body. **corporally** *adv.* **corporal punishment** *n.* punishment inflicted on the body.

corporate (kaw´pərət) *a.* **1** united in a body and acting as an individual. **2** collectively one. **3** of or relating to a corporation or group. **4** corporative. ~*n.* a big industrial corporation. **corporate body** *n.* a group of people legally empowered to act as an individual. **corporately** *adv.* **corporate raider** *n.* a person who clandestinely builds up a shareholding in a company in order to gain some control over it. **corporatism** (kaw´pərə-) *n.* **corporatist** *a.*, *n.* **corporative** (kaw´pərə-) *a.* **1** of or relating to a corporation. **2** involving, run by etc. trade and professional corporations. **corporativism** *n.*

corporation (kawpərā´shən) *n.* **1** a united body. **2** (*Law*) CORPORATE BODY (under CORPORATE). **3** (*loosely*) a company or association for commercial or other purposes. **4** an elected body charged with the conduct of civic business. **5** (*coll., facet.*) a prominent abdomen.

corporeal (kawpaw´riəl) *a.* **1** having a body. **2** of or relating to the body. **3** material, physical, as opposed to *mental.* **4** (*Law*) tangible, visible. **corporeality** (-al´-) *n.* **corporeally** *adv.*

corporeity (kawpərē´əti) *n.* **1** material existence. **2** corporeality.

corps (kaw) *n.* (*pl.* **corps** (kawz)) **1** (*Mil.*) **a** a body of troops having a specific function. **b** a grouping of two or more divisions of an army, forming a tactical unit in the field. **2** a group of people employed in the same job, working together or in the same place. **corps de ballet** (də bal´ā) *n.* a body of dancers in a ballet. **corps diplomatique** (diplōmatēk´) *n.* DIPLOMATIC CORPS (under DIPLOMACY).

corpse (kawps) *n.* **1** a dead body, esp. of a human being. **2** the body.

corpulent (kaw´pūlənt) *a.* excessively fat or fleshy. **corpulence, corpulency** *n.* **corpulently** *adv.*

corpus (kaw´pəs) *n.* (*pl.* **corpora** (-pərə), **corpuses**) **1** a body. **2** the mass of anything. **3** a collection of writings or of literature. **4** (*Anat.*) the main part of an organ or any part of an organism. **corpus delicti** (dilik´tī) *n.* (*Law*) the aggregation of facts which constitute a breach of the law. **corpus luteum** (loo´tiəm) *n.* (*pl.* **corpora lutea** (-iə)) (*Anat.*) a mass of tissue which develops in the ovary after the discharge of an ovum.

corpuscle (kaw´pəsəl), **corpuscule** (-pŭs´kūl) *n.* **1** a cell, esp. a *white* or *red corpuscle*, suspended in the blood. **2** a minute body or cell forming part of an organism. **3** a minute particle of matter. **corpuscular** (-pŭs´-) *a.*

corral (kərahl´) *n.* **1** an enclosure (orig. of emigrants' wagons in American Indian territory) for cattle, horses etc. or for defence. **2** an enclosure for capturing elephants and other animals. ~*v.t.* (*pres.p.* **corralling**, *past, p.p.* **corralled**) **1** to pen up. **2** to form into a corral. **3** (*N Am., sl.*) to get, to acquire, to lay hold of.

correct (kərekt´) *v.t.* **1** to set right. **2** to remove faults or errors from. **3** to mark errors in for rectification. **4** to admonish, to punish, to chastise. **5** to obviate, to counteract. **6** to eliminate an aberration. **7** to replace (something wrong) with the right thing. **8** to adjust or reset (a measuring instrument etc.) to register accurately. ~*a.* **1** true, exact, accurate. **2** right, proper, decorous. **3** conforming to a fixed standard or rule. **4** free from fault or imperfection. **correctable, correctible** *a.* **correction** *n.* **1** the act of correcting. **2** that which is substituted for what is wrong. **3** amendment, improvement. **4** a quantity added or taken away to make a reading, calculation etc. more accurate. **5** punishment, chastisement. **6** criticism. **correctional** *a.* **correction fluid** *n.* a liquid, usu. white, which can be painted over errors in writing etc., drying to form a hard surface which can be written etc. on again. **correctitude** *n.* correctness of behaviour. **corrective** *a.* **1** having power to correct. **2** tending to correct. ~*n.* **1** that which tends to correct or counteract. **2** an antidote. **correctively** *adv.* **correctly** *adv.* **correctness** *n.* **corrector** *n.* **1** a person who or something which corrects. **2** a censor. **3** a critic.

correlate (kor´əlāt) *v.i.* (*usu. with* with, to) to be reciprocally related. ~*v.t.* (*usu. with* with) to bring into mutual relation. ~*a.* mutually related. ~*n.* a correlative. **correlation** (-ā´shən), **corelation** *n.* **1** reciprocal relation. **2** the act of bringing into correspondence or interaction. **3** the state or degree of reciprocal dependence of usu. two variables, or a quantity indicating this. **correlational** *a.* **correlative** (-rel´ə-) *a.* **1** reciprocally connected or related to, or reciprocally implied. **2** (*Gram.*) corresponding to each other, as *either* and *or*, *neither* and *nor*. ~*n.* a person who or something which is correlated with another. **correlatively** *adv.* **correlativity** (-rolativ´-) *n.*

correspond (korəspond´) *v.i.* **1** to be similar, comparable or equivalent (to). **2** to be congruous. **3** to fit (with), to suit, to agree (with) etc. **4** to communicate by letters sent and received. **correspondence** *n.* **1** mutual adaptation. **2** congruity. **3** communication by means of letters. **4** the letters which pass between correspondents. **correspondence college, correspondence school** *n.* a college or school whose students do not attend directly, but whose courses are conducted by post. **correspondence course** *n.* any of the courses of study conducted by post by a correspondence college. **correspondent** *a.* **1** agreeing or congruous with. **2** answering. ~*n.* **1** a person with whom communication is kept up by letters. **2** a person who sends news from a particular place or on a particular subject, to a newspaper, radio or TV station etc. **3** a person or firm having business relations with another. **correspondently** *adv.* **corresponding** *a.* **1** suiting. **2** communicating by correspondence. **correspondingly** *adv.*

corrida (kərē′də) *n.* **1** a bullfight. **2** bullfighting.

corridor (kor′idaw) *n.* **1** a gallery or passage communicating with the apartments of a building. **2** a passageway along the side of a railway carriage with openings into the different compartments. **3** a narrow strip of territory belonging to one state, which passes through the territory of another state (e.g. to reach the sea). **4** a narrow strip of airspace within which aircraft must fly, e.g. over a foreign country. **5** a main traffic route. **6** a particular flight path along which a spacecraft can safely re-enter the earth's atmosphere. **corridors of power** *n.pl.* the higher ranks in any organization, seen as the seat of power and influence.

corrie (kor′i) *n.* a semicircular hollow or cirque in a mountainside, usu. surrounded in part by crags.

corrigendum (korijen′dəm) *n.* (*pl.* **corrigenda** (-ə)) an error needing correction, esp. in a book.

corrigible (kor′ijibəl) *a.* **1** capable of being corrected. **2** punishable. **3** submissive, docile. **corrigibly** *adv.*

corroborate (kərob′ərāt) *v.t.* **1** to strengthen, to confirm, to establish. **2** to bear additional witness to. **corroboration** (-ā′shən) *n.* **corroborative** *a.*, *n.* **corroborator** *n.* **corroboratory** (-ətəri) *a.*

corrode (kərōd′) *v.t.* **1** to consume gradually, esp. chemically. **2** to wear away by degrees. ~*v.i.* to be eaten away gradually. **corrodible** *a.* **corrosion** (-zhən) *n.* **1** the act or process of corroding. **2** a corroded state or area. **corrosive** (-siv) *a.* **1** tending to corrode. **2** fretting, biting, vexing, virulent. ~*n.* anything which corrodes. **corrosively** *adv.* **corrosiveness** *n.*

corrugate (kor′əgāt) *v.t.* to contract or bend into wrinkles or folds. ~*v.i.* to become wrinkled. **corrugated** *a.* **corrugated iron** *n.* sheet iron pressed into folds and galvanized. **corrugation** (-ā′shən) *n.* **1** the act of corrugating. **2** a wrinkle, a fold. **corrugator** *n.* (*Anat.*) a muscle which contracts the brow.

corrupt (kərŭpt′) *a.* **1** perverted by bribery or willing to be. **2** involving bribery or unethical practices. **3** depraved. **4** (of a computer program, or data held in a computer) containing errors caused by the hardware or software. **5** (of a text etc.) vitiated by additions or alterations. **6** putrid, decomposed. ~*v.t.* **1** to change from a sound to an unsound state. **2** to infect, to make impure or unwholesome. **3** (*Comput.*) to introduce errors into (data, a program etc.). **4** to bribe. **5** to falsify. **6** to vitiate or defile. **7** to debauch, to seduce. ~*v.i.* to become corrupt. **corrupter** *n.* **corruptible** *a.* **corruptibility** (-bil′-) *n.* **corruptibly**

adv. **corruption** *n.* **1** the act of corrupting. **2** the state of being corrupt. **3** bribery or fraud. **4** moral deterioration. **5** a corrupt reading or version. **6** decomposition, putrefaction. **7** putrid matter. **8** misrepresentation. **corruptive** *a.* **corruptly** *adv.* **corruptness** *n.* **corrupt practices** *n.pl.* (*Law*) direct or indirect bribery in connection with an election.

corsage (kawsahzh′) *n.* **1** a flower or small bouquet or spray of flowers, usu. worn by a woman on the bodice or lapel of her dress. **2** the bodice of a woman's dress.

corsair (kaw′seə) *n.* **1** a pirate or a privateer, esp. formerly on the Barbary coast. **2** a pirate authorized by the government of his country. **3** a pirate ship.

corselet[1] CORSLET.

corselet[2] CORSELETTE.

corselette (kawsəlet′), **corselet** (kaws′lit) *n.* a woman's one-piece supporting undergarment.

corset (kaw′sit) *n.* **1** a close-fitting stiffened or elasticated undergarment worn by women to give a desired shape to the body. **2** a similar undergarment worn by either sex to support a weakened or injured part of the body. ~*v.t.* (*pres.p.* **corseting**, *past*, *p.p.* **corseted**) to restrain or support with a corset. **corseted** *a.* **corsetière** (kawsityeə′) *n.* a woman who makes or sells corsets. **corsetry** *n.*

Corsican (kaw′sikən) *a.* of or relating to the Mediterranean island of Corsica. ~*n.* **1** a native or inhabitant of Corsica. **2** the Italian dialect spoken in Corsica.

corslet (kaws′lit), **corselet** *n.* **1** body armour. **2** a light cuirass.

cortege (kawtezh′), **cortège** *n.* **1** a procession, esp. at a funeral. **2** a train of attendants.

cortex (kaw′teks) *n.* (*pl.* **cortices** (-tisēz)) **1** (*Bot.*) **a** the layer of plant tissue between the vascular bundles and the epidermis. **b** bark. **2** (*Anat.*) the outer layer of an organ, such as the kidney or brain. **cortical** (-tik-) *a.* **corticate** (-kət), **corticated** (-kātid) *a.* **1** coated with bark. **2** resembling bark.

corticosteroid (kawtikōstiə′roid), **corticoid** (kaw′tikoid) *n.* a steroid (e.g. cortisone) produced by the adrenal cortex, or a synthetic drug with the same actions.

cortisol (kaw′tisol) *n.* HYDROCORTISONE.

cortisone (kaw′tizōn, -sōn) *n.* a corticosteroid, natural or synthetic, used to treat rheumatoid arthritis, allergies and skin diseases.

corundum (kərŭn′dəm) *n.* **1** a rhombohedral mineral of great hardness, allied to the ruby and sapphire. **2** a class of minerals including these, consisting of crystallized alumina.

coruscate (kor′əskāt) *v.i.* **1** to sparkle, to glitter in flashes. **2** to be bright, flashy or brilliant. **coruscation** (-kā′shən) *n.*

corvette (kawvet′) *n.* (*Naut.*) **1** a small, fast escort vessel armed with anti-submarine devices. **2** (*Hist.*) a flush-decked, full-rigged ship of war, with one tier of guns.

corvine (kaw´vīn) *a.* (*Zool.*) of or relating to the crows.

corymb (kor´imb) *n.* (*Bot.*) a raceme or panicle in which the stalks of the lower flowers are longer than those of the upper, so creating a flat-topped cluster. **corymbose** (-rim´bōs) *a.*

cos[1] (kos), **cos lettuce** *n.* a curly variety of lettuce introduced from the island of Cos in the Aegean.

cos[2] (koz) *abbr.* cosine.

cos[3] 'COS.

'cos (koz), **cos** *conj.* (*coll.*) short for BECAUSE.

cosec (kō´sek) *abbr.* cosecant.

cosecant (kōsē´kənt) *n.* (*Math.*) the secant of the complement of an arc or angle.

coset (kō´set) *n.* (*Math.*) a set which forms a given larger set when added to another one.

cosh[1] (kosh) *n.* a heavy blunt weapon for hitting people with, e.g. a length of metal or hard rubber. ~*v.t.* to hit with a cosh.

cosh[2] (kosh, kozäch´) *abbr.* (*Math.*) hyperbolic cosine.

co-signatory (kōsig´nətəri) *n.* (*pl.* **co-signatories**) a person who signs jointly with others.

cosine (kō´sīn) *n.* (*Math.*) the sine of the complement of an arc or angle.

cosmetic (kəzmet´ik) *a.* **1** beautifying. **2** used for dressing the hair or skin. **3** intended or used to make only superficial improvements. ~*n.* an external application for improving the complexion, beautifying esp. the face, etc. **cosmetical** *a.* **cosmetically** *adv.* **cosmetician** (kozmetish´ən) *n.* a person who makes, sells or is professionally skilled in the use of cosmetics. **cosmetic surgery** *n.* surgery to improve the appearance rather than to treat illness or injury.

cosmic (koz´mik) *a.* **1** of or relating to the universe, esp. as distinguished from the earth. **2** derived from some part of the solar system other than the earth. **3** of or used in space travel. **cosmical** *a.* **cosmically** *adv.* **cosmic dust** *n.* minute particles of matter distributed throughout space. **cosmic radiation** *n.* very energetic radiation falling on the earth from outer space, consisting chiefly of charged particles. **cosmic rays** *n.pl.* cosmic radiation.

cosmogony (kozmog´əni) *n.* (*pl.* **cosmogonies**) a theory, investigation or dissertation respecting the origin of the world. **cosmogonic** (-gon´-), **cosmogonical** *a.* **cosmogonist** *n.*

cosmography (kozmog´rəfi) *n.* (*pl.* **cosmographies**) a description or delineation of the features of the universe, or of the earth as part of the universe. **cosmographer** *n.* **cosmographic** (-graf´-), **cosmographical** *a.*

cosmology (kozmol´əji) *n.* (*pl.* **cosmologies**) **1** the science which investigates the evolution and structure of the universe as an ordered whole. **2** an account of the origin, evolution and structure of the universe. **cosmological** (-loj´-) *a.* **cosmologist** *n.*

cosmonaut (koz´mənawt) *n.* an astronaut, esp. in the former Soviet Union.

cosmopolitan (kozməpol´itən) *a.* **1** at home in any part of the world. **2** free from national prejudices and limitations. **3** sophisticated. **4** (of plants and animals) widely distributed throughout the world. ~*n.* a cosmopolitan person. **cosmopolitanism** *n.* **cosmopolitanize, cosmopolitanise** *v.t., v.i.* **cosmopolite** (-mop´əlīt) *n.* a cosmopolitan person. ~*a.* **1** worldwide in sympathy or experience. **2** devoid of national prejudice.

cosmos (koz´mos), **kosmos** *n.* **1** the universe regarded as an ordered system. **2** an ordered system of knowledge. **3** totality of experience.

co-sponsor (kōspon´sə) *n.* a joint sponsor. ~*v.t.* to sponsor jointly.

Cossack (kos´ak) *n.* a member of a people, probably of mixed Turkish origin, living on the southern steppes of Russia, and formerly furnishing light cavalry to the Russian army.

cosset (kos´ət) *v.t.* to pet, to pamper.

cossie (koz´i) *n.* (*esp. Austral., coll.*) SWIMMING COSTUME (under SWIM).

cost (kost) *v.t.* (*past, p.p.* **cost**) **1** to require as the price of possession or enjoyment. **2** to cause the expenditure of. **3** to result in the loss of or the infliction of. **4** to be costly to. **5** (*past, p.p.* **costed**) to calculate or set the price of (a job etc.). ~*v.i.* to be costly. ~*n.* **1** the price charged or paid for a thing. **2** expense, charge. **3** (*pl.*) expenses of a lawsuit, esp. those awarded to the successful against the losing party. **4** expenditure of any kind. **5** penalty, loss, detriment. **6** pain, trouble. **at all costs** regardless of the cost. **at any cost** regardless of the cost. **at cost** at cost price. **at the cost of** involving or resulting in the loss or sacrifice of. **to one's cost** with consequent loss, expense, disadvantage etc. **cost-conscious** *a.* very aware of costs and expenditure, and generally trying to minimize them. **cost-cutting** *n.* the cutting of costs. ~*a.* cutting costs, or intended to do so. **cost-effective** *a.* giving a satisfactory return on the initial outlay. **cost-effectively** *adv.* **cost-effectiveness** *n.* **cost-efficient** *a.* cost-effective. **cost-efficiency** *n.* **cost-efficiently** *adv.* **costing** *n.* **1** the system of calculating the exact cost of production, so as to ascertain the profit or loss entailed. **2** (*usu.pl.*) the results of such calculations. **costly** *a.* (*comp.* **costlier**, *superl.* **costliest**) **1** of high price. **2** valuable. **3** involving great loss or sacrifice. **costliness** *n.* **cost of living** *n.* the cost of those goods and services considered necessary to a reasonable standard of living. **cost-plus** *a.* used of a contract where work is paid for at actual cost, with an agreed percentage addition as profit. **cost price** *n.* the price paid by the dealer. **cost-push inflation** *n.* inflation caused by rising costs.

costa (kos´tə) *n.* (*pl.* **costae** (-tē)) **1** a rib. **2** any process resembling a rib in appearance or function. **costal** *a.* **costate** (-tāt) *a.*

co-star (kō´stah) *n.* a star appearing (in a film) with another star. ~*v.i.* (*pres.p.* **co-starring**, *past*, *p.p.* **co-starred**) to be a co-star. ~*v.t.* (of a film etc.) to have as co-star(s).

Costa Rican (kostə rē´kən) *n.* a native or inhabitant of Costa Rica in Central America. ~*a.* of or relating to Costa Rica.

coster (kos´tə), **costermonger** (kos´təmŭng-gə) *n.* a seller of fruit, vegetables etc., esp. from a street barrow.

costive (kos´tiv) *a.* **1** having the motion of the bowels too slow, constipated. **2** niggardly. **costively** *adv.* **costiveness** *n.*

costmary (kost´meəri) *n.* (*pl.* **costmaries**) an aromatic plant of the aster family, *Chrysanthemum balsamita*, cultivated for use in flavouring.

costume (kos´tūm, -chəm) *n.* **1** dress. **2** the customary mode of dressing. **3** the dress of a particular time or country. **4** fancy dress. **5** the attire of an actor or actress. **6** SWIMMING COSTUME (under SWIM). **7** clothing for some purpose or activity. **8** (*dated*) a woman's, usu. tailor-made, suit consisting of jacket and skirt. **9** a set of outer garments. ~*v.t.* to provide or dress with costume. **costume drama** *n.* **1** a drama in which the actors wear historical or foreign costume. **2** such dramas as a genre. **costume jewellery** *n.* cheap and showy jewellery worn to set off one's clothes. **costumer** (-tū´mə), **costumier** (-tu´miə) *n.* a maker of or dealer in costumes.

cosy (kō´zi), (*N Am.*) **cozy** *a.* (*comp.* **cosier**, (*N Am.*) **cozier**, *superl.* **cosiest**, (*N Am.*) **coziest**) **1** comfortable, snug. **2** complacent. **3** warm and friendly. **4** (*derog.*) having, showing or resulting from friendship or collaboration, usu. to the detriment of others. ~*n.* (*pl.* **cosies**) **1** a fabric covering for keeping something warm, esp. a tea cosy or egg cosy. **2** a canopied seat or corner for two people. ~*v.t.* (*3rd pers. sing. pres.* **cosies**, *pres.p.* **cosying**, *past, p.p.* **cosied**) (*usu. with along, coll.*) to reassure, often with lies and deception. **to cosy up 1** (*coll., esp. N Am.*) to try to ingratiate oneself (with). **2** (*coll., esp. N Am.*) to snuggle up (to). **cosily** *adv.* **cosiness** *n.*

cot[1] (kot) *n.* **1** a small bed with high barred sides for a young child. **2** a hospital bed. **3** (*N Am.*) a small folding bed, a camp bed. **4** a light or portable bedstead. **5** (*Naut.*) a swinging bed like a hammock. **cot death** *n.* the sudden and inexplicable death of a baby while sleeping.

cot[2] (kot) *n.* **1** (*poet.*) a cottage or hut. **2** a shelter for birds or animals. ~*v.t.* (*pres.p.* **cotting**, *past, p.p.* **cotted**) to put (sheep) in a cot or fold.

cot[3] (kot) *abbr.* (*Math.*) cotangent.

cotangent (kōtan´jənt, kō´-) *n.* (*Math.*) the tangent of the complement of an arc or angle.

cote (kōt) *n.* a sheepfold, or any small house or shelter for birds or animals.

coterie (kō´təri) *n.* **1** a set of people associated together for friendly conversation. **2** an exclusive circle of people in society; a clique.

coterminous CONTERMINOUS.

coth (koth, kotāch´) *abbr.* (*Math.*) hyperbolic cotangent.

cotoneaster (kətōnias´tə) *n.* an ornamental shrub of the genus *Cotoneaster*, belonging to the order Rosaceae.

cottage (kot´ij) *n.* **1** a small country or suburban residence. **2** a small house, esp. for labourers on a farm. **3** (*sl.*) a public toilet. ~*v.i.* (*sl.*) to engage in homosexual acts with a partner anonymously in a public toilet. **cottage cheese** *n.* a soft white cheese made from skimmed milk curds. **cottage garden** *n.* a garden informally laid out and planted with traditional British flowers and plants rather than modern or imported varieties. **cottage hospital** *n.* a small hospital without a resident medical staff. **cottage industry** *n.* a small-scale industry in which the workers, usu. self-employed, work at home. **cottage loaf** *n.* a loaf of bread made with two rounded masses of dough stuck one above the other. **cottage pie** *n.* shepherd's pie made with beef. **cottager** *n.* a person who lives in a cottage. **cottagey**, **cottagy** *a.*

☒ **cotten** common misspelling of COTTON.

cotter (kot´ə) *n.* **1** a key, wedge or bolt for holding part of a machine in place. **2** a cotter pin. **cotter pin** *n.* **1** a split pin that opens after being passed through a hole. **2** a tapered pin with a thread at the narrower end which allows it to be fastened in place with a nut.

cotton (kot´ən) *n.* **1** a downy substance resembling wool, growing in the fruit of the cotton plant, used for making thread, cloth etc. **2** thread made from this. **3** cloth made of cotton. **4** cotton plants collectively, as a crop. ~*a.* made of cotton. ~*v.i.* to get on, to agree well (with). **to cotton on** to begin to understand. **to cotton to** (*N Am., coll.*) to take a liking to. **cotton cake** *n.* cottonseed pressed into cakes as food for cattle. **cotton candy** *n.* (*N Am.*) candyfloss. **cotton gin** *n.* a device for separating the seeds from cotton. **cotton grass** *n.* any plant of the genus *Eriophorum*, growing in marshy ground and having a white downy head. **cotton-picking** *a.* (*esp. N Am., sl.*) despicable. **cotton plant** *n.* any of various species of plant of the genus *Gossypium*, whose seed pods yield cotton. **cottonseed** *n.* the seed of the cotton plant, yielding oil, and when crushed made into cotton cake. **cottontail** *n.* any of several common American rabbits of the genus *Sylvilagus*. **cotton waste** *n.* refuse cotton used for cleaning machinery. **cottonwood** *n.* **1** any of several kinds of N American poplar, esp. *Populus deltoides* and *P. angulata* (from the white cottony hairs on the seeds). **2** any of a number of Australian trees, esp. *Bedfordia salicina*, which has leaves covered with down. **cotton wool** *n.* **1** bleached and sterilized cotton formed into pads, balls etc. and used as dressings, for cleansing etc. **2** (*N Am.*) raw cotton. **cottony** *a.*

cotyledon (kotilē´dən) *n.* **1** (*Bot.*) the rudimentary leaf of an embryo in the higher plants, the seed-leaf. **2** (*Bot.*) any succulent plant of the southern African genus *Cotyledon*, or of the related European genus *Umbilicus*. **cotyledonary** *a*. **cotyledonous** *a*.

couch[1] (kowch) *n*. **1** a long upholstered seat with a back, for more than one person. **2** a similar piece of furniture with a headrest but no back for a doctor's or psychiatrist's patient to lie on. **3** a bed, or any place of rest. *~v.t.* **1** to express in words. **2** (*in p.p.*) to cause to lie. **3** to lay (oneself) down. **4** to deposit in a layer or bed. **5** (*Med.*) to treat (a cataract) by displacement of the lens of the eye. **6** to lower (a spear) to a horizontal position for attack. *~v.i.* **1** to lie down, to rest. **2** to lie in concealment. **couch potato** *n*. (*pl.* **couch potatoes**) (*sl.*) an inactive person who watches an excessive amount of television instead of taking part in other forms of entertainment or exercise.

couch[2] (kowch, kooch) *n*. couch grass. **couch grass** *n*. any of various grasses of the genus *Agropyron*, esp. *A. repens*, whose long, creeping roots make them difficult to get rid of.

couchette (kooshet´) *n*. **1** a seat in a continental train which converts into a sleeping berth. **2** a carriage with such seats. **3** a similar seat on a cross-channel ferry.

cougar (koo´gə) *n*. the puma.

cough (kof) *n*. **1** a convulsive effort, accompanied by noise, to expel foreign or irritating matter from the lungs. **2** an irritated condition of the organs of breathing that causes coughing. **3** a tendency to cough or habit of coughing. *~v.t.* to drive from the lungs by a cough. *~v.i.* **1** to expel air from the lungs in a convulsive and noisy manner, with a cough. **2** (of an engine) to make a similar noise when malfunctioning. **3** (of a gun etc.) to make a similar noise. **to cough up 1** to eject by coughing. **2** (*sl.*) to produce (money or information), esp. under duress. **cough drop** *n*. (*also* **cough lozenge, cough sweet**) a medicinal lozenge taken to cure or relieve a cough. **cough mixture** *n*. a liquid medicine taken to cure or relieve a cough.

could CAN[1].

couldn't (kud´ənt) *contr.* could not.

coulis (koo´lē) *n*. (*pl.* **coulis** (koo´lēz)) a thin purée.

coulomb (koo´lom) *n*. a unit of electrical charge, equal to the quantity of electricity transferred by one ampere in one second.

coulter (kōl´tə), (*N Am.*) **colter** *n*. the iron blade fixed in front of the share in a plough.

coumarin (koo´mərin) *n*. (*Chem.*) an aromatic crystalline substance extracted from the tonka bean and other plants, used in flavourings and as an anticoagulant.

coumarone (koo´mərōn) *n*. (*Chem.*) a colourless aromatic liquid obtained from coal tar, used in the production of synthetic resins for use in paints and varnishes, adhesives etc.

council (kown´səl) *n*. **1** a number of people met together for deliberation, advice or some administrative purpose. **2** people acting as advisers to a

sovereign, governor or chief magistrate. **3** an elected body in charge of local government in a county, parish, borough etc. **4** an ecclesiastical assembly attended by the representatives of various churches. **5** the governing body of a university. *~a.* **1** used by a council. **2** provided or maintained by a council. **council-chamber** *n*. the room where a council meets. **council house** *n*. **1** a house owned by a local council and rented out to tenants. **2** a building in which a council meets. **councillor**, (*N Am.*) **councilor** *n*. a member of a council. **councillorship** *n*. **councilman, councilwoman** *n*. (*pl.* **councilmen, councilwomen**) (*N Am.*) a councillor. **council of war** *n*. **1** a council of officers called together in time of difficulty or danger. **2** a meeting to decide on future action. **council tax** *n*. a tax for the financing of local government, introduced in 1993 as a replacement for the community charge, calculated on the capital value of the property.

Usage note The spellings of the nouns *council*, *councillor* and *counsel*, *counsellor* should not be confused: the first refer to an elected body or assembly, and the second to a barrister or other legal representative or professional adviser.

counsel (kown´səl) *n*. **1** advice. **2** opinion given after deliberation. **3** a consultation. **4** (*Law*) a barrister. **5** (*as pl.*) the advocates engaged on either side in a law-suit. **6** a plan of action. *~v.t.* (*pres.p.* **counselling**, (*N Am.*) **counseling**, *past, p.p.* **counselled**, (*N Am.*) **counseled**) **1** to give advice or counsel to. **2** to advise. **to keep one's own counsel** to keep a matter secret. **to take counsel (with)** to seek advice (from). **counselling**, (*N Am.*) **counseling** *n*. the giving of advice, esp. the giving of advice and information, in (difficult) personal situations by a qualified adviser; the advice and information given. **counsellor**, (*N Am.*) **counselor** *n*. **1** a person who gives counsel or advice. **2** (*N Am.*) (*also* **counselor-at-law**) a lawyer, esp. one who conducts a case in court. **3** a senior member of the diplomatic service. **counsellorship** *n*.

Usage note See note under COUNCIL.

count[1] (kownt) *v.t.* **1** to reckon up in numbers, to calculate or total. **2** to include. **3** to consider. **4** to esteem. *~v.i.* **1** to possess a certain value. **2** to say the numerals in order. **3** in music and dancing, to keep to the correct rhythm by counting the beats. *~n.* **1** a reckoning or numbering. **2** the sum (of). **3** (*Law*) a statement of the plaintiff's case. **4** one of several charges in an indictment. **5** any of the points in an argument or discussion. **6** in boxing and wrestling, a count of up to ten seconds by the referee, during which a boxer who has been knocked down must get up or a wrestler who has been pinned down raise part of their body or else lose the match. **not counting** excluding. **out for the count 1** unconscious. **2** fast asleep. **3** thoroughly dispirited or dejected. **4** in boxing, having been counted out. **to count against** to be a factor against. **to count down** to count in reverse order, towards zero, in preparing for a particular event. **to count for** to be a factor in favour of. **to count in** to include. **to count one's blessings** to be thankful for the good things one has. **to count on/ upon 1** to rely on. **2** to consider as certain. **to count out 1** to reckon one by one from a number of units by counting aloud. **2** to count aloud (the number one is taking from a larger amount). **3** (*coll.*) to exclude, to not count in. **4** to declare (a boxer) defeated upon their failure to stand up within 10 seconds of the referee beginning to count. **to count the cost 1** to calculate the damage or loss that has resulted or would result from some action. **2** to consider the risks entailed in some action. **to count up** to calculate the sum of. **to keep count** to keep an accurate record of a numerical series. **to lose count** to be unable to keep count. **countable** *a.* **countable noun, count noun** *n.* (*Gram.*) a noun which can be used in both the singular and the plural. **countback** *n.* a way of scoring in sporting competitions by which, in the event of a tie, a winner is declared on the basis of previous scores. **countdown** *n.* **1** the counting backwards of the time left before some event, esp. the launching of a spacecraft. **2** the period of such counting. **3** the checks and other procedures carried out during this period. **4** the period of time preceding any significant event. **counting house** *n.* the house, room or office appropriated to the business of keeping accounts etc. **countless** *a.* **1** innumerable. **2** beyond calculation. **count noun** COUNTABLE NOUN (under COUNT¹).

count² (kownt) *n.* a foreign title of rank corresponding to a British earl. **countess** *n.* **1** the wife of an earl or count. **2** a woman holding this rank in her own right. **Count Palatine** *n.* (*pl.* **Counts Palatine**) (*Hist.*) **1** a high judicial officer under the Merovingian kings. **2** the ruler of either of the Rhenish Palatinates. **countship** *n.*

countenance (kown'tənəns) *n.* **1** the face. **2** the features. **3** air, look or expression. **4** composure of look. **5** favour, support, corroboration. ~*v.t.* **1** to sanction, to approve, to permit. **2** to abet, to encourage. **in countenance 1** in favour. **2** confident, assured. **out of countenance 1** out of favour. **2** abashed, dismayed. **countenancer** *n.*

counter¹ (kown'tə) *n.* **1** a table or desk over which business is conducted (in a shop, bank, library, cafe etc.). **2** a piece of metal, plastic etc., used for reckoning, e.g. in games. **3** an imitation coin or token. **4** a person who or something which counts. **5** (*NAm.*) a kitchen worktop. **over the counter 1** (of medicines) sold without prescription. **2** (of the buying and selling of shares) through a broker, because the shares are not on the official list of a stock exchange. **under the counter 1** referring to trade in black market goods. **2** secret(ly). **3** surreptitious(ly). **countertop** *n.* (*NAm.*) a worktop.

counter² (kown'tə) *n.* **1** the opposite, the contrary. **2** a countermove. **3** in fencing, a circular parry. **4** in boxing, a blow dealt just as the opponent is striking. ~*a.* **1** contrary, adverse, opposed. **2** opposing. **3** duplicate. ~*adv.* **1** in the opposite direction. **2** wrongly. **3** contrarily. ~*v.t.* **1** to oppose, to contradict. **2** to make a countermove against. **3** to return (a blow) by dealing another one. ~*v.i.* **1** to make a countermove. **2** to say something in opposition or retaliation. **3** in boxing, to give a return blow.

counter- (kowntə) *comb. form* **1** in return, duplicating. **2** in answer, corresponding. **3** in opposition. **4** in an opposite direction.

counteract (kowntərakt') *v.t.* **1** to act in opposition to, so as to hinder or defeat. **2** to neutralize. **counteraction** *n.* **counteractive** *a.*

counter-attack (kown'tərətak) *v.t.*, *v.i.* to make an attack after an attack by an enemy or opponent. ~*n.* such an attack.

counter-attraction (kowntərətrak'shən) *n.* **1** attraction in an opposite direction. **2** a rival attraction. **counter-attractive** *a.*

counterbalance¹ (kowntəbal'əns) *v.t.* **1** to weigh against or oppose with an equal weight or effect. **2** to countervail.

counterbalance² (kown'təbaləns) *n.* an equal weight or force acting in opposition.

counterblast (kown'təblahst) *n.* an argument or statement in opposition.

counterchange (kown'təchanj) *n.* exchange, reciprocation. ~*v.t.* **1** to exchange, to alternate. **2** to interchange, to chequer. ~*v.i.* to change places or parts.

countercharge (kown'təchahj) *n.* **1** a charge in opposition to another. **2** a counter-claim. ~*v.t.* **1** to make a charge against in return. **2** to charge in opposition to (a charge of troops).

counter-claim (kown'təklām) *n.* (*Law*) a claim made against another claim, esp. a claim brought forward by a defendant against a plaintiff. ~*v.t.*, *v.i.* to make a counter-claim (for).

counter-clockwise (kowntəklok'wīz) *adv.* (*NAm.*) anticlockwise.

counter-culture (kown'təkŭlchə) *n.* a way of life deliberately contrary to accepted social usages.

counter-espionage (kowntəres'piənahzh) *n.* work of an intelligence service directed against the agents of another country.

counterexample (kown'tərigzahmpəl) *n.* an example or fact that does not fit a proposed theory, and which is used as an argument against it.

counterfeit (kown'təfit, -fēt) *a.* **1** made in imitation with intent to be passed off as genuine. **2** pretend; false. ~*n.* **1** a counterfeit thing. **2** a person who pretends to be what they are not, an impostor. ~*v.t.* **1** (*Law*) to make a counterfeit copy of, to forge. **2** to imitate, to mimic. **3** to pretend, to simulate. **4** to resemble. ~*v.i.* to make counterfeits. **counterfeiter** *n.*

counterfoil (kown´təfoil) *n.* the counterpart of a cheque, receipt or other document, retained by the giver.

counter-insurgency (kowntərinsœ´jənsi) *n.* actions taken by a government, police force, army etc. to counter rebellion etc.

counterintelligence (kowntərintel´ijəns) *n.* work of an intelligence service designed to prevent or damage intelligence gathering by an enemy intelligence service.

counter-intuitive (kowntərintū´itiv) *a.* going against what one intuitively feels to be right.

counterirritant (kowntərir´itənt) *n.* **1** (*Med.*) an irritant applied to the body to remove or lessen some other irritation. **2** anything with a similar purpose or effect. ~*a.* acting as a counterirritant.

countermand (kowntəmahnd´) *v.t.* **1** (*esp. Mil.*) **a** to revoke, to annul. **b** to recall. **2** to cancel. ~*n.* (*Mil.*) an order contrary to or revoking a previous order.

countermarch (kown´təmahch) *v.i.* to march in an opposite direction. ~*v.t.* to cause to countermarch. ~*n.* (*Mil.*) the action of countermarching.

countermeasure (kown´təmezhə) *n.* an action taken to counter a danger, thwart an enemy etc.

countermove (kown´təmoov) *n.* a movement in an opposite or contrary direction, or in opposition or retaliation. ~*v.i.* to make a countermove. **countermovement** *n.*

counter-offensive (kowntərəfen´siv) *n.* **1** (*Mil.*) a counter-attack. **2** any attack made by defenders.

counterpane (kown´təpān) *n.* **1** a bedcover. **2** a quilt.

counterpart (kown´təpaht) *n.* **1** a person who is exactly like another in character, role etc. **2** a corresponding part. **3** (*Law*) one of two corresponding copies of an instrument.

counterplot (kown´təplot) *n.* a plot to defeat another plot. ~*v.t.* (*pres.p.* **counterplotting**, *past*, *p.p.* **counterplotted**) to oppose or frustrate by another plot. ~*v.i.* to make a counterplot.

counterpoint (kown´təpoint) *n.* **1** a melodious part or combination of parts written to accompany a melody. **2** the art of constructing harmonious parts. **3** the art of harmonious composition. **4** a contrasting idea, theme, argument etc. ~*v.t.* **1** (*Mus.*) to add counterpoint to (a melody etc.). **2** to set (an idea, theme etc.) in contrast to another for effect.

counterpoise (kown´təpoiz) *n.* **1** a weight in opposition and equal to another. **2** a counterbalancing force, power or influence. **3** equilibrium. ~*v.t.* **1** to oppose with an equal weight so as to balance. **2** to oppose, check or correct with an equal force, power or influence. **3** to bring into or maintain in equilibrium.

counter-productive (kowntərprədŭk´tiv) *a.* producing an opposite, or undesired, result.

counterpunch (kown´təpŭnch) *n.* a punch given in return. ~*v.i.* to make a counterpunch or counterpunches.

counter-reformation (kowntərefəmā´shən) *n.* **1** a reformation of an opposite nature to or as a reaction to another. **2** (*Hist.*) (**Counter-Reformation**) the attempt of the Roman Church to counteract the results of the Protestant Reformation.

counter-revolution (kowntərevəloo´shən) *n.* a revolution opposed to a former one, and designed to restore a former state of things. **counter-revolutionary** *n.* (*pl.* **counter-revolutionaries**) an instigator or supporter of such a revolution. ~*a.* of or relating to such a revolution.

countersign (kown´təsīn) *v.t.* **1** to attest the correctness of by an additional signature. **2** to ratify. ~*n.* **1** a password, a secret word or sign by which one may pass a sentry, or by which the members of a secret association may recognize each other. **2** any identifying mark. **countersignature** (-sig´nəchə) *n.*

countersink (kown´təsingk) *v.t.* (*past, p.p.* **countersunk** (-sŭngk)) **1** to chamfer (a hole) for a screw or bolt head. **2** to sink (the head of a screw etc.) into such a hole. ~*n.* **1** a chamfered hole. **2** a tool for making such a hole.

counterstroke (kown´təstrōk) *n.* a stroke made in return.

countertenor (kown´tətenə) *n.* (*Mus.*) **1** (a singer with) a voice higher than tenor, a male alto voice. **2** a part written for such a voice.

countervail (kowntəvāl´) *v.t.* **1** to act against with equal effect or power. **2** to counterbalance. ~*v.i.* to be of equal weight, power or influence on the opposite side.

countervalue (kown´təvalū) *n.* an equivalent value.

counterweigh (kowntəwā´) *v.t.* to counterbalance. **counterweight** *n.*

countess COUNT².

country (kŭn´tri) *n.* (*pl.* **countries**) **1** a territory or state. **2** the inhabitants of any territory or state. **3** one's native land. **4** the rural part as distinct from cities and towns. **5** the rest of a land as distinguished from the capital. **6** a region or area. **7** country music. **across country** not using roads etc. **in the country** in cricket, far from the wickets, in the outfield. **to appeal to the country** to go to the country. **to go to the country** to hold a general election, to appeal to the electors. **up country** away from the coast or from the capital city. **countrified, countryfied** *a.* (*often derog.*) rustic in manners or appearance. **country and western** *n.* country music. **country club** *n.* a sporting or social club in country surroundings. **country cousin** *n.* (*often derog.*) a relation of countrified ways or appearance. **country dance** *n.* **1** a dance in which the partners are ranged in lines opposite to each other. **2** any rural English dance. **country dancing** *n.* **country gentleman** *n.* (*pl.* **country gentlemen**) a man who owns and lives on an estate in the country. **country house** *n.* a mansion in the country, esp. one belonging or having belonged for generations to a landowning family. **countryman, country-woman** n. (pl. **countrymen, countrywomen**) **1** a person who lives in a rural district. **2** an inhabitant of any particular region. **3** a fellow countryman or countrywoman. **country music** n. a style of popular music based on the folk music of rural areas of the US. **country rock** n. **1** (Geol.) the rock surrounding a mineral deposit or an igneous intrusion. **2** a blend of country music and rock music. **country seat** n. a country house, or the house plus the estate surrounding it. **countryside** n. **1** a rural district, or rural districts in general. **2** the inhabitants of this. **countrywide** a. extending right across a country.

county (kown´ti) n. (pl. **counties**) **1** a division of land for administrative, judicial and political purposes. **2** in England, Wales and Ireland, and formerly in Scotland, the chief civil unit and chief administrative division outside the seven largest conurbations. **3** in the US, the civil division next below a state. **4** county families collectively. ~a. **1** of or relating to a county. **2** characteristic of county families. **county council** n. the elected council administering the civil affairs of a county. **county councillor** n. **county court** n. a local court dealing with civil cases. **county cricket** n. cricket played between sides representing counties. **county family** n. a family belonging to the nobility or gentry with an ancestral seat in the county. **county town,** (N Am.) **county seat** n. the chief town of any county.

coup (koo) n. **1** a stroke, a telling or decisive blow. **2** a successful move, piece of strategy or revolution. **3** a coup d'état. **4** in billiards, a stroke putting a ball into a pocket without its touching another.

coup de grâce (koo də grahs´) n. (pl. **coups de grâce** (koo də grahs´)) **1** a finishing stroke; an action that puts an end to something. **2** a death blow administered to put an end to suffering.

coup d'état (koo dātah´) n. (pl. **coups d'état** (koo dātah´)) a sudden and violent change of government, esp. of an illegal and revolutionary nature.

coupé (koo´pā), (N Am.) **coupe** (koop) n. **1** (usu., N Am. **coupe**) a two-doored car with an enclosed body. **2** (Hist.) (**coupé**) a four-wheeled closed carriage.

couple (kŭp´əl) n. **1** two. **2** more or less two, a few. **3** two people who are engaged, married or in a steady relationship. **4** two people who are partners in a dance, sports match etc. **5** two of anything of the same kind considered together. **6** (pl. **couple**) a pair or brace, esp. in hunting or coursing, a pair of dogs. **7** (pl.) two dog collars joined by a leash. **8** in carpentry, a pair of rafters connected by a tie. **9** a pair of equal forces acting in parallel and opposite directions so as to impart a circular movement. ~v.t. **1** to connect or fasten together. **2** to unite persons together, esp. in marriage. **3** to associate. ~v.i. to copulate. **coupler** n. **1** a person who or something which

couples. **2** (Mus.) a connection between two or more organ manuals or keys, or manuals and pedals. **3** (Mus.) OCTAVE COUPLER (under OCTAVE). **4** (Physics) a transformer that connects electrical circuits. **couplet** n. two, usu. rhyming, lines of running verse. **coupling** n. **1** a device for connecting railway carriages etc. together. **2** a device for connecting parts of machinery and transmitting motion. **3** (Mus.) the arrangement of songs, pieces of music etc. on a gramophone record, or any one of these songs etc.

coupon (koo´pon) n. **1** a form that may be detached or cut out e.g. from an advertisement, and used as an order form, entry form for a competition etc. **2** a football pools entry form. **3** a piece of paper which can be exchanged for goods in a shop. **4** a detachable ticket or certificate entitling to food ration etc. **5** a detachable certificate for the payment of interest on bonds.

courage (kŭr´ij) n. bravery, boldness, intrepidity. **courage of one's convictions** the courage to act in accordance with one's beliefs. **to pluck up courage** to summon up boldness or bravery. **to take courage 1** to pluck up courage. **2** to derive courage (from a thought, piece of news etc.). **to take one's courage in both hands** to summon up the courage necessary to do something. **courageous** (-rā´-) a. **courageously** adv. **courageousness** n.

courgette (kuəzhet´) n. a small kind of vegetable marrow.

courier (kur´iə) n. **1** an employee of a private postal company offering a fast collection and delivery service usu. within a city or internationally. **2** a person employed by a travel agency to accompany a party of tourists or to assist them at a resort. **3** a person who conveys secret information for purposes of espionage, or contraband for e.g. a drug-smuggling ring. **4** a messenger sent in great haste, an express.

course (kaws) n. **1** continued progress, continued movement along a path. **2** the act of passing from one place to another. **3** the direction in which something moves. **4** the path passed along, the route. **5** the correct or intended route. **6** a period of time passed. **7** the ground on which a race is run or on which a game (such as golf) is played. **8** the act of running, a race. **9** a series (of lectures, lessons, medical treatments etc.). **10** a planned programme of study. **11** any one of a series of dishes served at one meal. **12** mode of procedure. **13** method of life or conduct. **14** a career. **15** (Archit.) a row or tier of bricks or stones in a building. **16** the bed, or the direction of flow, of a stream. **17** in coursing, a chase after a hare by one or more dogs. **18** (Naut.) any of the sails set on a ship's lower yards. ~v.t. **1** to run after, to pursue. **2** to use in coursing. **3** to traverse. ~v.i. **1** to chase hares with greyhounds. **2** to run or move quickly. **3** (of blood etc.) to flow or circulate. **in (the) course of 1** in the process of. **2** during. **in the course of time 1** as time passes. **2** eventually.

of course 1 naturally. **2** admittedly. **off course** not on course. **on course** following the correct course, on target, on schedule. **coursebook** *n.* a book for use by a student on a particular course of academic study. **courser** *n.* **1** (*poet.*) a swift horse, a warhorse. **2** a person who practises coursing. **3** a dog used in coursing. **4** a desert bird of the genus *Cursorius*, related to the pratincole, noted for swiftness in running. **coursework** *n.* work done, or to be done, by a student as part of an academic course, often used in assessment or grading. **coursing** *a.* that courses. ~*n.* the sport of hunting hares with greyhounds or lurchers.

court (kawt) *n.* **1** an enclosed piece of ground used for games. **2** a subdivision of a piece so enclosed or merely marked out. **3** (*Law*) **a** the chamber in which justice is administered. **b** the judges or persons assembled to hear any cause. **4** any meeting or body having jurisdiction. **5** a place enclosed by buildings, or enclosing a house. **6** a narrow street. **7** a quadrangle or courtyard. **8** a word used in the names of large houses, blocks of flats etc. **9** the sovereign and advisers regarded as the ruling power. **10** the residence of a sovereign. **11** the body of courtiers. **12** a State reception by a sovereign. **13** deferential attention paid in order to secure favour or regard. **14** the council of certain organizations. **15** a meeting of a court. ~*v.t.* **1** to seek the affections of, to woo. **2** to seek the favour of, to pay court to. **3** to look for, to try to gain. **4** to act in such a way as to bring (disaster etc.). ~*v.i.* to try to gain the affections of a woman. **in court** attending legal proceedings as one of the parties to a case or as counsel. **out of court 1** without the case being heard in a civil court. **2** not entitled to be heard in court. **3** not worth considering. **to go to court** to begin legal proceedings. **to pay court to** to behave flatteringly or amorously (towards someone). **court card** *n.* any king, queen or knave in a pack of cards. **court circular** *n.* an official daily report in a newspaper, of the activities and engagements of the royal family. **courthouse** *n.* **1** a house or building containing rooms used by any court. **2** (*N Am.*) the building in which the offices of a county government are found. **court martial** *n.* (*pl.* **courts martial**, (*coll.*) **court martials**) a court for the trial of members of the armed forces, composed of officers, none of whom must be of inferior rank to the prisoner. **court-martial** *v.t.* (*pres.p.* **court-martialling**, (*N Am.*) **court-martialing**, *past, p.p.* **court-martialled**, (*N Am.*) **court-martialed**) to try by court martial. **Court of Appeal**, (*N Am.*) **Court of Appeals** *n.* (*Law*) a law court in which appeals against the judgements of other courts are heard. **court of first instance** *n.* (*Law*) the law court in which legal proceedings are first heard. **court of law** *n.* (*Law*) **1** the judges and persons assembled to hear any cause. **2** a courthouse, a courtroom. **court of record** *n.* (*Law*) a court whose proceedings are officially recorded and preserved as

evidence. **court of review** *n.* (*Law*) a court to which sentences and decisions are submitted for judicial revision. **Court of Session** *n.* (*Sc. Law*) the supreme civil court of justice in Scotland. **court of summary jurisdiction** *n.* (*Law*) a court which has the authority to try cases, reach judgements and make convictions in summary proceedings. **court order** *n.* (*Law*) a directive or order given by a judge to do or refrain from doing something. **court roll** *n.* (*Hist.*) the record of a manorial court. **courtroom** *n.* the chamber in which justice is administered. **courtship** *n.* **1** the act or process of wooing. **2** the behaviour of male birds and animals by which they try to attract a mate. **3** a period of courting. **4** the act of seeking after anything, esp. by flattery. **court shoe** *n.* a woman's low-cut shoe without straps etc. **court tennis** *n.* real tennis. **courtyard** *n.* an open area round or within a large building.

courteous (kœ′tiəs) *a.* polite, affable, considerate. **courteously** *adv.* **courteousness** *n.*

courtesan (kaw′tizan), **courtezan** *n.* **1** a prostitute or mistress. **2** a promiscuous woman.

courtesy (kœ′təsi) *n.* (*pl.* **courtesies**) **1** courteousness, politeness, graciousness. **2** an act of civility. **3** gracious disposition. **4** favour, as opposed to right. **by courtesy of** with the permission or agreement of. **courtesy light** *n.* a small light in a motor vehicle which is switched on when a door is opened. **courtesy title** *n.* a title to which a person has no legal right (used esp. of the hereditary titles assumed by the children of peers).

courtier (kaw′tiə) *n.* a person who is in attendance or a frequenter at a royal etc. court.

courtly (kawt′li) *a.* (*comp.* **courtlier**, *superl.* **courtliest**) **1** polished, elegant, polite. **2** flattering, obsequious. **3** of or relating to a court. **courtliness** *n.*

couscous (koos′koos) *n.* **1** a N African dish of pounded wheat steamed over meat or broth. **2** the wheat used in this dish.

cousin (kŭz′ən) *n.* **1** the son or daughter of an uncle or aunt. **2** (*usu. pl.*) a person of a related people, nation or group. **3** (*Hist.*) a title used by a sovereign in addressing another sovereign or a noble. **cousin german** *n.* (*pl.* **cousins german**) a first cousin. **cousinhood** *n.* **cousinly** *a.* **cousinship** *n.*

couture (kətūə′, -tuə′) *n.* **1** dressmaking. **2** dress-designing. **couturier** (-riā) *n.* a dress-designer or dressmaker. **couturière** (-riēə) *n.* a female couturier.

covalent (kōvā′lənt) *a.* (*Chem.*) having atoms linked by a shared pair of electrons. **covalence**, **covalency** *n.* **covalently** *adv.*

cove[1] (kōv) *n.* **1** a small creek, inlet or bay. **2** a nook or sheltered recess. **3** (*Archit.*) **a** (*also* **coving**) a hollow in a cornice moulding. **b** the cavity of an arch or ceiling. ~*v.t.* (*Archit.*) **1** to arch over. **2** to cause to slope inwards. **3** to make a cove in.

cove² (kōv) *n.* (*esp. Austral., coll.*) a man, a fellow, a chap.

coven (kŭv´ən) *n.* an assembly of witches.

covenant (kŭv´ənənt) *n.* **1** an agreement on certain terms, a compact. **2** a document containing the terms of agreement. **3** (*Law*) a formal agreement to pay a stated sum of money to a charity for a certain period of time. **4** (*Law*) any formal agreement under seal. **5** a clause in an agreement. **6** (*Bible*) an agreement between God and a people or group. ~*v.t.* to grant or promise by covenant. ~*v.i.* to enter into a covenant. **covenantal** (-nan´-), **covenanted** *a.* **1** secured by or held under a covenant. **2** bound by a covenant. **covenanter, covenantor** *n.*

Coventry (kŭv´əntri, kov´-) *n.* used only as below. **to send to Coventry** to refuse to have communication or dealings with.

cover (kŭv´ə) *v.t.* **1** to overlay. **2** to overspread with something. **3** to clothe. **4** to hide, cloak or screen. **5** to lie over so as to shelter or conceal. **6** to include or deal with. **7** to be enough to defray. **8** to travel across. **9** to protect by insurance. **10** to take precautions to protect (oneself) from a possible future problem etc. **11** to report on for a newspaper, broadcasting station etc. **12** (of a sales representative) to have as a sales territory. **13** to extend over. **14** to have range or command over. **15** to hold under aim with a firearm. **16** (*Mil.*) to protect with troops. **17** to be able to reach or protect with gunfire. **18** to protect with gunfire. **19** (of a soldier) to stand behind (someone in the front rank). **20** in cricket, to stand behind so as to stop ·balls that are missed. **21** in football etc., to mark (an opponent). **22** to make a cover version of. **23** to play a higher card than (one already played). **24** (of an animal such as a stallion or bull) to copulate with (a female). **25** to incubate. ~*n.* **1** anything which covers or hides. **2** a lid. **3** (*often pl.*) the outside covering of a book. **4** one side or board of this. **5** anything which serves to conceal, screen or disguise. **6** pretence, pretext. **7** shelter, protection. **8** a shelter. **9** a thicket, woods which conceal game. **10** in commerce, sufficient funds to meet a liability or ensure against loss. **11** the coverage of an insurance policy. **12** (*usu. pl.*) a bed-covering, blanket. **13** an envelope or other wrapping for a packet in the post. **14** a place setting in a restaurant. **15** protective gunfire. **16** a supporting military force. **17** COVER VERSION (under COVER). **18 a** (*often pl.*) in cricket, the position of cover point. **b** a fielder in this position. **19** the outer casing of a tyre. **from cover to cover** from beginning to end (of a book). **to cover for** to substitute for or replace (an absent fellow worker). **to cover in 1** to fill in. **2** to finish covering, e.g. with a roof. **to cover one's tracks 1** to remove all signs of one's passing. **2** to remove all evidence of what one has done. **to cover up 1** to cover completely. **2** to conceal (esp. something illegal). **to take cover** to go into shelter in a place

of protection. **under cover 1** concealed; acting under an assumed identity. **2** protected; sheltered by a roof etc. **coverable** *a.* **coverage** *n.* **1** the act of covering. **2** the extent to which anything is covered. **3** the area or the people reached by a broadcasting or advertising medium. **4** the amount of protection provided by an insurance policy. **5** the amount of publicity received by a story etc. **coverall** *a.* covering everything. ~*n.* **1** (*usu. pl.*) a one-piece garment covering limbs and body, e.g. a boiler-suit. **2** anything that covers completely. **cover charge** *n.* the amount added to a restaurant bill to cover service. **cover crop** *n.* a crop grown between main crops to provide protective cover for the soil. **cover drive** *n.* in cricket, a drive past cover point. **covered** *a.* **1** sheltered, protected. **2** concealed. **3** roofed. **4** wearing a hat. **cover girl** *n.* a female model whose photograph is used to illustrate a magazine cover. **covering** *n.* **1** that which covers. **2** a cover. **covering letter, covering note,** (*N Am.*) **cover letter** *n.* a letter explaining an enclosure. **cover note** *n.* a note given to an insured person to certify that they have cover. **cover point** *n.* **1** in cricket, a fielder or the position behind point. **2** in lacrosse, a defending player, or the position occupied by such a player. **cover story** *n.* the main news item or story in a magazine, which has a picture or photograph relating to it on the front cover. **cover-up** *n.* **cover version** *n.* a version of a song etc., similar to the original, recorded by a different artist.

coverlet (kŭv´əlit), **coverlid** (-lid) *n.* an outer covering for a bed, a counterpane or bedspread.

covert¹ (kŭv´ət, kō´vœt) *a.* disguised, secret, private. **covertly** *adv.* **covertness** *n.*

covert² (kŭv´ət, kŭv´ə) *n.* **1** a place which covers and shelters. **2** a cover for game. **3** WING COVERT (under WING).

covet (kŭv´it) *v.t.* **1** to desire (something unlawful) inordinately. **2** to long for. **covetable** *a.* **covetous** *a.* **1** eagerly desirous (of). **2** eager to obtain and possess. **3** avaricious. **covetously** *adv.* **covetousness** *n.*

covey (kŭv´i) *n.* (*pl.* **coveys**) **1** a brood or small flock of birds (prop. of partridges). **2** a small company, a party.

coving COVE¹.

cow¹ (kow) *n.* (*pl.* **cows**, †**kine** (kīn)) **1** the female of any bovine species, esp. of the domesticated species *Bos taurus.* **2** a female domesticated cow that has calved, as opposed to *heifer.* **3** any member of any variety of domesticated cattle. **4** a female elephant, whale or seal. **5** (*sl., derog.*) a woman. **6** (*Austral., New Zeal., sl.*) a difficult or unpleasant situation, thing etc. **till the cows come home** (*coll.*) forever. **cowbane** *n.* water hemlock. **cowbell** *n.* **1** a bell hung round a cow's neck, which rings as the cow moves and so indicates its whereabouts. **2** a similar but clapperless bell used as a percussion instrument. **cowberry** *n.* (*pl.* **cowberries**) **1** the red whortleberry, *Vaccinium vitis-idaea*. **2** the bilberry or whortleberry, *V. myrtillus*. **3** the berry of either of these. **cowbird** *n.* (*N Am.*) a bird belonging to any of several species of the genus *Molothrus* (from their accompanying cattle). **cowboy** *n.* **1** a man in charge of cattle on a ranch. **2** a conventional character in stories of the Wild West, often fighting Indians and not necessarily looking after cattle. **3** (*sl.*) an unqualified or unscrupulous businessman or workman. **4** a boy who tends cattle. **cowcatcher** *n.* (*N Am.*) an inclined frame attached to the front of a locomotive etc., to throw obstructions from the track. **cowfish** *n.* **1** a sea cow or small cetacean. **2** a fish, *Lactophrys quadricornis*, with hornlike protuberances over the eyes. **cowgirl** *n.* a female equivalent of a cowboy, either as one who looks after cattle or as a conventionalized character. **cowhand** *n.* (*N Am.*) a cowboy on a ranch. **cowheel** *n.* the foot of a cow or ox used to make jelly. **cowherd** *n.* a person who tends cattle. **cowhide** *n.* **1** the hide of a cow. **2** leather made from this. **3** a whip made of cowhide. **cow-house** *n.* a house or shed in which cows are kept. **cow-lick** *n.* a tuft of hair that grows up over the forehead. **cowman** *n.* (*pl.* **cowmen**) **1** a man who looks after cows on a farm. **2** (*N Am.*) the owner of a cattle ranch. **cow-parsley** *n.* a hedgerow umbelliferous plant, *Anthriscus sylvestris*. **cow-pat** *n.* a small pile of cow dung. **cow-pock** *n.* a pustule or pock of cowpox. **cowpoke** *n.* (*N Am., sl.*) a cowboy. **cowpox** *n.* a disease affecting the udders of cows, capable of being transferred to human beings, and conferring immunity from smallpox. **cowpuncher** *n.* (*N Am.*) a cowboy. **cowshed** *n.* **1** a shed providing shelter for cattle. **2** a shed where cows are milked. **cow-tree** *n.* any of various trees with milky sap, esp. the S American *Brosimum utile*. **cow-wheat** *n.* melampyre, *Melampyrum pratense*, or any other plant of the genus.

cow² (kow) *v.t.* to intimidate, to deprive of spirit or courage, to terrify, to daunt. **cowed** *a.*

coward (kow´əd) *n.* **1** a person without courage. **2** a contemptible bully. **cowardice** (-dis) *n.* extreme timidity, lack of courage. **cowardly** *a.* craven, faint-hearted, spiritless. ~*adv.* in the manner of a coward. **cowardliness** *n.* **cowardy** *a.* (*coll.*) cowardly. ~*n.* (*pl.* **cowardies**) (*also* **cowardy custard**) a coward.

cower (kow´ə) *v.i.* **1** to stoop, to bend, to crouch. **2** to shrink or quail through fear.

cowl (kowl) *n.* **1** a hooded garment, esp. one worn by a monk. **2** a loose hood, esp. on such a garment. **3** a large pleated robe worn by English Benedictines. **4** a hoodlike chimney-top, usu. movable by the wind, to facilitate the exit of smoke. **5** COWLING (under COWL). **cowled** *a.* **cowling** *n.* a removable metal casing for an aircraft engine. **cowl neck** *n.* a style of neck on a woman's dress, sweater etc. consisting of a collar that hangs in folds like a monk's cowl.

co-worker (kōwœ´kə) *n.* a fellow worker.

cowrie (kow´ri), **cowry** *n.* (*pl.* **cowries**) a gastropod of the family Cypraeidae, esp. *Cypraea moneta*, with a small shell formerly used as money in many parts of southern Asia and Africa.

co-write (kōrīt´) *v.t.* (*past* **co-wrote** (-rōt´), *p.p.* **co-written** (-rit´ən)) to write something together with one or more other people. **co-writer** *n.*

cowslip (kow´slip) *n.* **1** a wild plant with fragrant flowers, *Primula veris*, growing in pastures. **2** (*N Am.*) a marsh marigold.

Cox (koks) *n.* COX'S ORANGE PIPPIN.

cox (koks) *n.* in rowing, the person who steers for a crew in a race. ~*v.t.* to be the cox of. ~*v.i.* to act as cox. **coxless** *a.*

coxcomb (koks´kōm) *n.* a conceited person, a fop, a dandy. **coxcombry** *n.* (*pl.* **coxcombries**).

Cox's orange pippin (koksiz orənj pip´in) *n.* a sweet-tasting variety of eating apple with a green skin tinged with reddish orange.

coxswain (kok´sən, kok´swān), **cockswain** *n.* **1** a person who steers a boat, esp. in a race, a cox. **2** the petty officer on board ship in charge of a boat and its crew. ~*v.t.* to be the coxswain of. ~*v.i.* to act as coxswain. **coxswainship** *n.*

coy (koi) *a.* **1** coquettish. **2** modest, shy, reserved, shrinking from familiarity. **3** annoyingly unforthcoming. **coyly** *adv.* **coyness** *n.*

coyote (koiō´ti, kīō´-) *n.* (*pl.* **coyotes, coyote**) the N American prairie wolf.

coypu (koi´poo) *n.* (*pl.* **coypus, coypu**) **1** a S American aquatic rodent, *Myocastor coypus*, naturalized in Europe. **2** its fur.

cozen (kŭz´ən) *v.t.* **1** to deceive, to cheat. **2** to persuade by deception or charm. ~*v.i.* to be deceitful. **cozenage** *n.* **cozener** *n.*

cozy COSY.

cp *abbr.* candlepower.

cp. *abbr.* compare.

cpl, Cpl *abbr.* corporal.

CPO *abbr.* chief petty officer.

cps *abbr.* **1** (*Comput.*) characters per second. **2** cycles per second.

CPU *abbr.* (*Comput.*) central processing unit.

Cr *chem. symbol* chromium.

crab¹ (krab) *n.* **1** a decapod crustacean of the group Brachyura, esp. the common crab, *Cancer pagurus*, and other edible species. **2** crabmeat. **3** (**Crab**) the zodiacal sign or the constellation Cancer. **4** a kind of crane. **5** (*often pl.*) a crab louse. **to catch a crab** in rowing, to sink an oar too deep and be pushed backwards by the resistance of the water, or to miss a stroke and fall backwards. **crabgrass** *n.* any of various species of creeping grasses of the genus *Digitaria*. **crablike** *a.* **crab louse** *n.* an insect, *Phthirus pubis*, found on the human body. **crabmeat** *n.* the flesh of crabs as meat. **crabwise** *adv.* sideways.

crab² (krab) *v.t.* (*pres.p.* **crabbing**, *past, p.p.* **crabbed**) **1** (*coll.*) to criticize savagely, to pull to pieces. **2** to hinder.

crab³ (krab) *n.* **1** a crab apple. **2** a crab tree. **3** a peevish, morose person. ~*a.* sour, rough, austere. ~*v.i.* (*pres.p.* **crabbing,** *past, p.p.* **crabbed**) (*coll.*) to complain, grumble. **crab apple** *n.* a wild apple, the sour-tasting fruit of any of various trees of the genus *Malus,* esp. *M. silvestris.* **crab tree, crab-apple tree** *n.*

crabbed (krab´id, krabd) *a.* **1** peevish, morose, sour-tempered. **2** perverse. **3** (of handwriting) cramped, indecipherable. **4** intricate, perplexing, abstruse. **crabbedly** (-id-) *adv.* **crabbedness** (-id-) *n.* **crabby** *a.* (*comp.* **crabbier,** *superl.* **crabbiest**) **1** (*coll.*) bad-tempered. **2** perverse. **crabbily** *adv.* **crabbiness** *n.*

crack (krak) *v.t.* **1** to break without entire separation of the parts. **2** to cause to give a sharp, sudden noise. **3** to cause to break with a sharp noise. **4** to cause to break down by stress, torture etc. **5** to solve (a problem, code etc.). **6** to say (a joke etc.). **7** to hit sharply and with force. **8** (*Chem.*) to break (molecules of a compound) down into simpler molecules by the application of heat, pressure or a catalyst. ~*v.i.* **1** to partly break apart. **2** to make a loud, sharp sound. **3** to break with a sharp noise. **4** to break down under pressure, e.g. of stress or torture; to fail. **5** (of the voice) to change in tone because of emotion. **6** (of the voice) to change at puberty. ~*n.* **1** a partial separation of parts. **2** the chink, fissure or opening so made. **3** any chink or fissure. **4** a sharp sudden sound or report. **5** a sharp blow. **6** a change in the tone of voice, e.g. because of emotion. **7** the change of voice at puberty. **8** (*coll.*) a sarcastic joke. **9** (*sl.*) a highly addictive form of cocaine. **10** something or someone first-rate. **11** (*dial.*) chat. **12** (*dial.*) gossip, news. **13** (*dial.*) fun, amusement. ~*a.* **1** having qualities to be boasted of. **2** excellent, superior, brilliant. **to crack down (on)** (*coll.*) to take very strict measures (against). **to crack up 1** to extol highly, to puff. **2** to suffer a mental or physical breakdown. **3** (*coll.*) to begin laughing uncontrollably. **to get cracking** to make a prompt and active start to something. **to have a crack at** (*coll.*) to have a try, to attempt. **crack-brained** *a.* (*coll.*) crazy, cracked. **crackdown** *n.* **cracked** *a.* **1** having a crack or cracks. **2** (*coll.*) insane, crazy. **cracked wheat** *n.* wheat that has been coarsely ground into small grains. **cracker** *n.* **1** a paper tube containing a toy etc., that gives a sharp report in being torn open. **2** a form of explosive firework. **3** a thin, brittle, hard-baked (savoury) biscuit. **4** (*sl.*) a person who or thing which is exceptional or excellent. **5** (*often pl.*) an implement for cracking. **6** a crisp biscuit made with rice flour or tapioca. **7** a person who or thing which cracks. **8** (*N Am., offensive*) a poor white. **cracker-barrel** *a.* (*N Am.*) (of a person, opinions, philosophy etc.) expressing or exemplifying a simple, unsophisticated view of life (supposedly typical of opinions expressed in discussions carried on beside the barrels of crackers in N American

small-town stores). **crackerjack** *n.* (*sl.*) an excellent person or thing. **crackers** *a.* (*sl.*) crazy. **crackhead** *n.* (*sl.*) a person addicted to crack (the drug). **cracking** *a.* (*coll.*) **1** vigorous. **2** very good. ~*adv.* exceptionally. **crack-jaw** *a.* applied to long or unpronounceable words. ~*n.* any such word. **crack of dawn** *n.* the first light of dawn. **crack of doom** *n.* the end of the world at Judgement Day, or the noise of thunder supposed to accompany this. **crack of the whip** *n.* an opportunity or chance. **crackpot** *n.* (*coll.*) a crazy person. ~*a.* (of persons ideas etc.) crazy, eccentric. **crack-up** *n.* **crack willow** *n.* a species of willow, *Salix fragilis,* which has branches that break easily, or any of a number of similar species of *Salix.* **cracky** *a.* (*comp.* **crackier,** *superl.* **crackiest**) having many cracks.

crackle (krak´əl) *v.i.* **1** to make short, sharp crackling noises. **2** to be energetic. ~*v.t.* **1** to cause to make a cracking noise. **2** to produce decorative cracks in (porcelain etc.). ~*n.* **1** a rapid succession of slight, sharp noises like cracks. **2** a small crack. **3** a series of such cracks. **4** porcelain, glass or paintwork with a decoration of tiny cracks. **5** the decorative cracked surface of such porcelain, glass or paintwork. **crackling** *n.* **1** the browned scored skin of roast pork. **2** (*sl., offensive*) women regarded as sexual objects. **crackly** *a.* (*comp.* **cracklier,** *superl.* **crackliest**)

cracknel (krak´nəl) *n.* a hard, brittle biscuit.

-cracy (krəsi) *comb. form* government or rule of, or influence of or dominance by, as in *aristocracy, democracy, plutocracy, theocracy.*

cradle (krā´dəl) *n.* **1** a baby's bed or cot, usu. rocking or swinging. **2** place of birth or early nurture. **3** infancy. **4** a frame to protect a broken or wounded limb in bed. **5** a bed or framework of timbers to support a vessel out of water. **6** a platform or trolley in which workers are suspended to work on a ceiling, the side of a building or boat, etc. **7** the part of a telephone on which the receiver rests when not in use. ~*v.t.* **1** to lay or place in a cradle. **2** to rock to sleep. **3** to nurture or rear from infancy. **4** to receive or hold in or as if in a cradle. **from the cradle** from infancy. **from the cradle to the grave** throughout one's life. **cradle-snatcher** *n.* BABY-SNATCHER (under BABY). **cradle song** *n.* a lullaby. **cradling** *n.* **1** the act of laying or rocking in a cradle. **2** (*Archit.*) in building, a framework of wood or iron.

craft (krahft) *n.* **1** dexterity, skill. **2** cunning, deceit. **3** an art, esp. one applied to useful purposes, a handicraft, occupation or trade. **4** the members of a particular trade. **5** (*pl.* **craft**) a boat. **6** (*pl.* **craft**) an aircraft or space vehicle. **7** (**Craft**) Freemasonry, or the brotherhood of Freemasons. ~*v.t.* to make with skill or by hand. **-craft** *comb. form* a profession, skill or art, as in *woodcraft, handicraft, priestcraft.* **craft-brother** *n.* a person in the same craft or guild. **craft guild** *n.* an association of workers in the same occupation or trade. **craftsman, craftswoman** *n.* (*pl.* **craftsmen,**

craftswomen) **1** (*also* **craftsperson**, *pl.* **crafts-people**) a person skilled in some art or handi-craft. **2** a time-served experienced worker in a skilled trade. **3** a qualified private in the REME. **craftsmanship** *n.* **craftwork** *n.* the work of or pro-duced by a craftsperson. **craftworker** *n.*

crafty (krahf′ti) *a.* (*comp.* **craftier**, *superl.* **crafti-est**) artful, sly, cunning, wily. **craftily** *adv.* **crafti-ness** *n.*

crag (krag) *n.* a rugged or precipitous rock. **craggy** *a.* (*comp.* **craggier**, *superl.* **craggiest**) **1** full of crags, rough. **2** (of a face) attractively rugged. **craggily** *adv.* **cragginess** *n.* **cragsman** *n.* (*pl.* **cragsmen**) a skilful rock-climber.

crake (krāk) *n.* **1** the corncrake. **2** any of various other birds of the same family, belonging to the genus *Porzana.* **3** the cry of any of these birds. ~*v.i.* to cry like a crake.

cram (kram) *v.t.* (*pres.p.* **cramming**, *past, p.p.* **crammed**) **1** to stuff, push or press in so as to fill to overflowing. **2** to thrust in or into by force. **3** to eat greedily. **4** to overfeed (with). **5** to coach for examination by storing the pupil's mind with formulas and answers to probable questions. ~*v.i.* **1** to eat greedily. **2** to stuff oneself. **3** to learn a subject hastily and superficially, esp. to under-go cramming for examination. **cram-full** *a.* abso-lutely full. **crammer** *n.* **1** a person who crams. **2** a coach who crams. **3** a school which special-izes in cramming.

cramp[1] (kramp) *n.* **1** a spasmodic contraction of some limb or muscle, accompanied by pain and numbness. **2** (*often pl.*) acute pain in the ab-domen. ~*v.t.* to affect with cramp. **cramped** *a.* **1** uncomfortably or inconveniently small. **2** (of handwriting) difficult to read. **3** contracted.

cramp[2] (kramp) *n.* **1** a cramp-iron. **2** a clamp. **3** a restraint, a hindrance. ~*v.t.* **1** (*often with up*) to confine closely. **2** to hinder, to restrain. **3** to fasten with a cramp-iron. **to cramp someone's style** to impede a person's actions or self-expression. **cramp-iron** *n.* an iron with bent ends binding two stones together in a masonry course.

crampon (kram′pon) *n.* **1** (*usu. pl.*) a plate with iron spikes worn on climbing boots to assist in climbing ice-slopes etc. **2** (*usu. pl.*) a grappling iron. **3** a hooked bar of iron.

cranberry (kran′bəri) *n.* (*pl.* **cranberries**) **1** any shrub of the genus *Vaccinium*, esp. the American *V. macrocarpon* and the British *V. oxycoccos*, both with a small, red, acid fruit used in sauces etc. **2** the fruit of these shrubs.

crane[1] (krān) *n.* a long-necked bird of the family Gruidae, esp. the common crane of Europe, *Grus grus*, a migratory wading bird. ~*v.t.* to stretch out (the neck) like a crane, esp. to see over or round an object. ~*v.i.* to stretch out the neck in this way. **crane-fly** *n.* (*pl.* **crane-flies**) any fly of the family Tipulidae, with long legs, a long body and long wings, a daddy-long-legs. **craner** *n.* a person who cranes. **cranesbill** *n.* any of various species of wild geranium.

crane[2] (krān) *n.* **1** a machine for hoisting and lowering heavy weights. **2** a moving platform for a film camera. ~*v.t.* to raise or move by means of a crane.

cranio- (krā′niō) *comb. form* of or relating to the skull. **craniology** (-ol′-) *n.* the scientific study of crania. **craniological** (-loj′-) *a.* **craniologist** (-ol′-) *n.* **craniometer** (-om′itə) *n.* an instrument for measuring the cubic capacity of skulls. **crani-ometric** (-met′-), **craniometrical** *a.* **craniometry** (-om′-) *n.* **craniotomy** (-ot′əmi) *n.* (*pl.* **crani-otomies**) **1** surgical incision into the skull or removal of a part of the skull. **2** crushing of the skull of a dead foetus to make delivery easier.

cranium (krā′niəm) *n.* (*pl.* **craniums**, **crania** (-niə)) the skull, esp. the part enclosing the brain. **cranial** *a.* **cranial nerve** *n.* (*Anat.*) any of the twelve (in mammals, birds and reptiles) or ten (in fish and amphibians) paired nerves that con-nect directly to the brain rather than the spinal cord. **craniate** *a.* (*Zool.*) having a cranium.

crank[1] (krangk) *n.* **1** an arm at right angles to an axis for converting rotary into reciprocating motion, or the converse. **2** an iron elbow-shaped brace for various purposes. **3** a handle which turns the shaft of a motor until the pistons reach the maximum of compression. ~*v.t.* **1** to move or start by means of a crank. **2** to fit or provide with a crank. **3** to fasten with a crank. **4** to shape like a crank. **to crank up 1** to start an engine with a crank handle. **2** (*coll.*) to increase (speed, power etc.). **crankcase** *n.* a metal casing for the crank-shaft, connecting-rods etc. in an engine. **crank-pin** *n.* a cylindrical pin parallel to a shaft and fixed at the outer end of a crank. **crankshaft** *n.* a shaft that bears one or more cranks.

crank[2] (krangk) *n.* **1** an eccentric, esp. someone who is obsessed with a theory or fad. **2** (*N Am.*) a crotchety person. **3** a whimsical turn of speech.

crank[3] (krangk) *a.* (*Naut.*) liable to capsize.

cranky (krang′ki) *a.* (*comp.* **crankier**, *superl.* **crankiest**) **1** eccentric, esp. obsessed with a theory or fad. **2** whimsical. **3** (*esp. N Am.*) irrit-able, fidgety. **4** (of a machine) liable to break down. **crankily** *adv.* **crankiness** *n.*

cranny (kran′i) *n.* (*pl.* **crannies**) **1** a crevice, a chink. **2** a corner, a hole. **crannied** *a.*

crap[1] (krap) *n.* **1** (*sl.*) rubbish. **2** (*sl.*) nonsense. **3** (*taboo*) excrement. **4** (*taboo*) an act of defecat-ing. ~*v.i.* (*pres.p.* **crapping**, *past, p.p.* **crapped**) (*taboo*) to defecate. ~*a.* (*sl.*) worthless, of poor quality. **to crap out** (*sl.*) to opt out through fear, exhaustion etc. **crappy** *a.* (*comp.* **crappier**, *superl.* **crappiest**) (*sl.*) **1** rubbishy, worthless. **2** disgusting.

crap[2] (krap) *n.* a losing throw in the game of craps.

crape (krāp) *n.* **1** a gauzy fabric of silk or other material, with a crisped, frizzly surface, formerly usu. dyed black, used for mourning. **2** a band of this material worn round the hat as mourning. ~*v.t.* to cover, dress or drape with crape. ~*a.* made of crape. **crape hair** *n.* artificial hair for use in theatrical costume. **crapy** *a.* (*comp.* **crapier,** *superl.* **crapiest**).

craps (kraps) *n.* a gambling game played with two dice, with fixed winning and losing numbers. **to shoot craps** to play craps.

crapulent (krap´ūlənt) *a.* (*formal*) **1** given to intemperance. **2** resulting from intemperance. **3** surfeited, drunken. **crapulence** *n.* **crapulous** *a.*

crash[1] (krash) *v.t.* **1** to cause (a vehicle etc.) to hit something with great force and loud noise. **2** to cause (an aircraft) to fall with great force to the ground or into the sea. **3** to hit, throw, drop etc. (something) so that it makes a loud smashing noise, and often so that it breaks. **4** (*Comput.*) to cause (a computer or computer program) to cease operating suddenly. **5** (*coll.*) to go to (a party etc.) uninvited. **6** (*coll.*) to go through (a red traffic light). ~*v.i.* **1** (of a vehicle etc.) to hit something with great force and loud noise. **2** (of an aircraft) to fall with great force to the ground or into the sea. **3** (of a person) to be in a vehicle, aircraft etc. which crashes. **4** to hit (into) or collide with great force. **5** to move (through etc.) with great force and violence. **6** to move, fall, come together etc. with a loud noise, and often also breaking. **7** (*Comput.*) (of a computer or computer program) to cease operating suddenly. **8** to fail, be ruined financially. **9** to be defeated. **10** (*sl.*) to sleep, esp. in an improvised bed in someone's house. ~*n.* **1** an act or instance of crashing. **2** a loud sudden noise, as of many things broken at once. **3** a violent smash. **4** a sudden failure, collapse, bankruptcy. ~*a.* done rapidly, with urgency, or with great intensity over a short time. ~*adv.* with a crash. **crash barrier** *n.* a metal barrier along the edge or centre of a motorway etc. to prevent crashes. **crash-dive** *n.* **1** (*Naut.*) a submarine's sudden and rapid dive, usu. to avoid an enemy. **2** (of an aircraft) a rapid, steep descent, ending in a crash. ~*v.i.* to perform such a dive. ~*v.t.* to cause (a submarine or an aircraft) to make such a dive. **crash helmet** *n.* a padded helmet to protect the head in the event of an accident. **crashing** *a.* (*coll.*) extreme. **crash landing** *n.* an emergency landing of an aircraft, resulting in damage. **crash-land** *v.i.* to make a crash landing. ~*v.t.* to cause (an aircraft) to make a crash landing. **crash pad** *n.* (*sl.*) a place to sleep in an emergency.

crash[2] (krash) *n.* a coarse linen cloth, sometimes with cotton or jute in it, used for towelling.

crass (kras) *a.* **1** loutish, boorish, vulgar. **2** very great, disgraceful. **3** extremely stupid, obtuse. **4** extremely tactless or insensitive. **5** (*poet.*) thick, coarse. **crassitude** (-itūd) *n.* **crassly** *adv.* **crassness** *n.*

-crat (krat) *comb. form* **1** a partisan or supporter of something denoted by a word ending in −*cracy*, as in *democrat*. **2** a member of or participant in something denoted by a word ending in -*cracy*, as in *aristocrat, autocrat.*

crate (krāt) *n.* **1** a large wicker case for packing crockery. **2** an open framework of wood for packing. **3** (*dated, sl.*) an old and unreliable car, aircraft etc. ~*v.t.* to pack in a crate. **crateful** *n.* (*pl.* **cratefuls**).

crater (krā´tə) *n.* **1** the mouth of a volcano. **2** a bowl-shaped cavity. **3** a large cavity formed in the ground by the explosion of a shell or bomb or the impact of a meteorite. ~*v.t.* to make a crater or craters in. **craterous** *a.*

cravat (krəvat´) *n.* a tie-like scarf worn in an open-necked shirt, esp. by men. **cravatted** *a.*

crave (krāv) *v.t.* **1** to long for. **2** to ask for earnestly and submissively; to beg, to beseech, to entreat. ~*v.i.* **1** to long (for). **2** to beg (for). **craver** *n.* **craving** *n.* an intense desire or longing.

craven (krā´vən) *a.* cowardly, faint-hearted. ~*n.* a coward, a recreant, a dastard. **cravenly** *adv.* **cravenness** *n.*

craw (kraw) *n.* (*Zool.*) the crop or first stomach of birds or insects. **to stick in one's craw** to be hard to accept.

crawfish CRAYFISH.

crawl (krawl) *v.i.* **1** to move slowly on one's hands and knees or with one's body close to the ground. **2** (of an insect, snake etc.) to move slowly with the body on or close to the ground. **3** to move slowly. **4** to assume an abject posture or manner. **5** to get on, e.g. in a career, by obsequious servility. **6** to have a sensation as though insects were creeping over one's skin. **7** to be covered with crawling things. **8** to do the crawl in swimming. ~*n.* **1** the act of crawling. **2** a slow rate of movement. **3** a swimming stroke consisting of alternate overarm movements of the arms and kicking movements of the legs. **4** (*coll.*) a trip round a number of places of the same type, esp. one to a series of pubs. **crawler** *n.* **1** (*coll.*) an obsequious person. **2** a creeping or crawling insect or animal. **3** a slow-moving vehicle, esp. one that moves on caterpillar tracks. **4** (*pl., esp. N Am.*) a romper suit. **crawlingly** *adv.* **crawl space** *n.* space under a floor or roof that is large enough to crawl through, e.g. for maintenance purposes. **crawly** *a.* (*comp.* **crawlier,** *superl.* **crawliest**).

cray (krā) *n.* (*Austral., New Zeal.*) CRAYFISH.

crayfish (krā´fish), **crawfish** (kraw´-) *n.* (*pl. in general* **crayfish, crawfish,** *in particular* **crayfishes, crawfishes**) **1** any of the many, mostly freshwater, species of lobster-like crustaceans of the families Astacidae and Parastacidae. **2** the spiny lobster. **3** any kind of crab.

crayon (krā´ən, -on) *n.* **1** a stick or pencil of coloured chalk or similar material. **2** a drawing made with crayons. ~*v.t.* to draw with crayons.

craze (krāz) *v.t.* **1** to make insane. **2** to make cracks or flaws in (china etc.). ~*v.i.* (of the glaze on pottery etc.) to become cracked. ~*n.* **1** a mania, an extravagant idea or enthusiasm, a rage. **2** madness. **3** a flaw, impaired condition. **crazy** *a.* (*comp.* **crazier,** *superl.* **craziest**) **1** mad, deranged. **2** ridiculous. **3** (*coll.*) very enthusiastic (about). **4** (*sl.*) wild, exciting. ~*n.* (*pl.* **crazies**) (*coll.*) a crazy person or thing. **like crazy** (*sl.*) extremely. **crazily** *adv.* **craziness** *n.* **crazy paving** *n.* paving of irregularly-shaped flat stones, e.g. on a path.

CRC *abbr.* camera-ready copy.

creak (krēk) *v.t.* **1** to make a continued sharp grating or squeaking noise. **2** to move with a creaking sound. **3** to move slowly and stiffly. **4** to show signs of weakness, inadequacy or wear and tear. ~*v.i.* to cause to make a creaking noise. ~*n.* a creaking sound. **creakingly** *adv.* **creaky** *a.* (*comp.* **creakier,** *superl.* **creakiest**) **1** which creaks or is liable to creak. **2** stiff, arthritic. **3** showing signs of weakness, inadequacy or wear and tear. **creakily** *adv.* **creakiness** *n.*

cream (krēm) *n.* **1 a** the fatty part of milk which rises and collects on the surface, often separated off and used in cakes, desserts etc. **b** an artificial substitute for this. **2** a dish prepared with or having the texture of cream. **3** a cosmetic, antiseptic etc. preparation with a thick consistency like cream. **4** any part of a liquid that rises to the top like the cream of milk. **5** a pale yellowish-white colour. **6** a group of the best things or people. **7** the best part of anything. **8** essence or quintessence. **9** the main point of a story. **10** a soup or sauce made with cream or milk. **11** a usu. chocolate-covered sweet with a creamy peppermint- or fruit-flavoured centre. **12** a biscuit with a creamy filling. **13** a rich, sweet sherry. ~*v.t.* **1** to skim cream from. **2** to add cream to. **3** (*often with off*) to remove (the best part) from something. **4** to make creamy, e.g. by beating. **5** to treat with a cream, put cream on. **6** (*N Am., coll.*) to beat. ~*v.i.* **1** to gather cream. **2** to form a scum or froth. ~*a.* **1** cream-coloured. **2** of sherry, rich and sweet. **cream bun, cream-cake** *n.* a bun or cake with a filling of real or artificial cream. **cream cheese** *n.* a soft cheese made from unskimmed milk and cream. **cream-coloured** *a.* **cream cracker** *n.* an unsweetened crisp biscuit. **creamer** *n.* **1** a flat dish used for skimming the cream off milk. **2** a cream separator. **3** (*N Am.*) a small jug for cream. **4** a substitute for milk or cream for adding to coffee or tea. **creamery** *n.* (*pl.* **creameries**) **1** a shop for the sale of dairy produce. **2** an establishment where milk and cream are made into butter and cheese. **cream of tartar** *n.* purified potassium hydrogen tartrate, used in baking etc. **cream puff** *n.* **1** a cake of puff pastry filled with cream. **2** (*coll.*) an ineffectual person. **3** (*coll.*) an effeminate man. **cream separator** *n.* a machine for separating cream from milk. **cream soda** *n.* a soft drink flavoured with vanilla. **cream tea** *n.* an afternoon meal at which scones with cream and jam are eaten. **creamware** *n.* earthenware with a cream-coloured glaze. **creamy** *a.* (*comp.* **creamier,** *superl.* **creamiest**). **creamily** *adv.* **creaminess** *n.*

crease (krēs) *n.* **1** a line or mark made by folding or doubling. **2** a wrinkle. **3** in cricket, a line on the ground marking the position of bowler and batsman at each wicket. **4** in ice hockey and lacrosse, an area marked out around the goal. ~*v.t.* **1** to make a crease or creases in. **2** to graze the skin of with a bullet. **3** (*sl.*) to exhaust. **4** (*coll.*) to crease up. ~*v.i.* **1** to become creased or wrinkled. **2** (*coll.*) to crease up. **to crease up** (*coll.*) to double up with laughter. **creaser** *n.* **creasy** *a.* (*comp.* **creasier,** *superl.* **creasiest**).

create (kriāt´) *v.t.* **1** to cause to exist. **2** to produce, to bring into existence. **3** to be the occasion of. **4** to be the first person to act (a character in a play etc.). **5** to invest with a new character, office or dignity. **6** to cause (a disturbance). ~*v.i.* (*coll.*) to make a fuss. **creatable** *a.* **creative** *a.* **1** having the ability to create. **2** imaginative. **3** original. **creatively** *adv.* **creativeness** *n.* **creativity** (krēətiv´-) *n.*

creatine (krē´ətin, -tēn) *n.* an organic compound found in muscular fibre.

creation (kriā´shən) *n.* **1** the act of creating. **2** that which is created or produced. **3** (**Creation**) God's act of creating the world or the universe. **4** (**Creation**) the universe, the world, all created things. **5** the act of appointing, constituting or investing with a new character or position. **6** a production of art, craft, or intellect. **creational** *a.* **creationism** *n.* the theory that the universe was brought into existence out of nothing by God, and that new forms and species are the results of special creations. **creationist** *n.* **creator** *n.* **1** a person who or something which creates. **2** (**Creator**) God, as the maker of the universe.

creature (krē´chə) *n.* **1** a living being. **2** an animal, esp. as distinct from a human being. **3** a person (as an epithet of pity or endearment). **4** a person who owes their rise or fortune to another. **5** that which is created. **6** an instrument. **creature comforts** *n.pl.* those of or relating to the body, esp. food and drink. **creaturely** *a.* **creature of habit** *n.* a person etc. who follows the same routine every day.

crèche (kresh) *n.* **1** a day nursery in which young children are taken care of. **2** a model of the scene of the birth of Jesus.

cred (kred) *n.* (*coll.*) credibility, as in *street cred.*

credence (krē´dəns) *n.* **1** belief, credit. **2** reliance, confidence. **3** that which gives a claim to credit or confidence. **4** a credence table. **to give credence to** to believe, accept. **credence table** *n.* a small table, shelf or niche near the (south) side of the altar (or communion table) to receive the eucharistic elements before consecration. **credential** (kriden´-) *n.* **1** anything which gives an entitlement to confidence, trust etc. **2** (*pl.*) certificates or letters introducing or accrediting any person or persons.

credible (kred´ibəl) *a*. **1** deserving of or entitled to belief. **2** convincing; seemingly effective. **credibility** (-bil´-) *n*. **credibly** *adv*.

Usage note The adjectives *credible* and *credulous* should not be confused: *credible* means believable, and *credulous* too ready to believe.

credit (kred´it) *n*. **1** belief, trust, faith. **2** credibility, trustworthiness. **3** a reputation inspiring trust or confidence, esp. a reputation for solvency or honesty. **4** an acknowledgement of merit or value, or something awarded for this. **5** the time given for payment of goods sold on trust. **6** a person's financial position, esp. with regard to money in a bank etc. account. **7** a source or cause of honour, esteem or reputation. **8** the side of an account in which payment is entered, opposed to debit. **9** an entry on this side of a payment received. **10** the sum or total entered on this side. **11** an acknowledgement that a student has completed a course of study. **12** a unit of study in a degree etc. course, or a point awarded for completing the unit. **13** the passing of an examination at a mark well above the minimum required. ~*v.t.* (*pres.p.* **crediting**, *past, p.p.* **credited**) **1** to believe. **2** to set to the credit of (*to* the person). **3** to give credit for (*with* the amount). **4** to believe (a person) to possess, be etc. something. **5** to ascribe to. **on credit** with an agreement to pay at some later time. **to do someone credit** to be a source or cause of honour, esteem or heightened reputation for. **to give someone credit for 1** to ascribe (a good quality or ability) to someone. **2** to enter (an amount) in a person's account. **to one's credit** as something which can be considered praiseworthy, honourable etc. **creditable** *a*. bringing credit or honour. **creditability** (-bil´-) *n*. **creditableness** *n*. **creditably** *adv*. **credit card** *n*. a card issued by a bank or credit company which allows the holder to buy goods and services on credit. **credit note** *n*. a note of an amount owed to a customer for goods returned, which can be exchanged for other goods. **creditor** *n*. a person to whom a debt is due, as distinct from *debtor*. **credit titles** *n.pl.* a list of acknowledgements of actors, participants, contributors etc. at the beginning or end of a film etc. **creditworthy** *a*. deserving credit because of income level, past record of debt repayment etc. **creditworthiness** *n*.

credo (krā´dō, krē´-) *n*. (*pl.* **credos**) **1** (**Credo**) the Apostles' Creed or the Nicene Creed. **2** (**Credo**) a musical setting of either of the creeds, esp. of the Nicene Creed. **3** the statement of a belief.

credulous (kred´ūləs) *a*. **1** disposed to believe, esp. without sufficient evidence. **2** characterized by or due to such disposition. **credulity** (-dū´-) *n*. **credulously** *adv*. **credulousness** *n*.

Usage note See note under CREDIBLE.

creed (krēd) *n*. **1** a brief summary of the articles of religious belief. **2** (**Creed**) the Apostles' Creed or the Nicene Creed. **3** any system or solemn profession of religious or other belief or opinions. **credal, creedal** *a*.

creek (krēk) *n*. **1** a small inlet, bay or harbour, on the coast. **2** a backwater or arm of a river or an inlet on a river bank. **3** (*N Am., Austral., New Zeal.*) a small river, esp. a tributary. **up the creek 1** (*sl.*) in trouble or difficulty. **2** (*sl.*) mad.

creel (krēl) *n*. **1** an osier basket. **2** a fisherman's basket.

creep (krēp) *v.i.* (*past, p.p.* **crept** (krept)) **1** to crawl along the ground. **2** (of a plant) to grow along the ground or up a wall. **3** to move slowly and imperceptibly, stealthily, or with timidity. **4** to behave with servility; to fawn. **5** (of a feeling etc.) to begin or develop slowly. **6** to have a sensation of shivering or shrinking, e.g. from fear or repugnance. **7** (of a metal) to become gradually deformed under stress. ~*n*. **1** creeping. **2** a slow, almost imperceptible movement. **3** (*pl.*) a feeling of shrinking horror or disgust. **4** (*sl.*) an unpleasant or servile person. **5** a low arch or passage for animals. **6** gradual deforming of a metal due to stress. **to creep up on 1** to approach slowly, stealthily and without being noticed. **2** to develop slowly and imperceptibly. **creeper** *n*. **1** a person who or something which creeps or crawls. **2** (*Bot.*) a plant with a creeping stem. **3** the name, or an element of the name, of various birds that run up trees etc., esp., in N America, the treecreeper. **4** (*sl.*) a soft-soled shoe. **creeping** *a., n*. **creeping barrage** *n*. (*Mil.*) a barrage that moves forward or backward at prearranged intervals. **creeping Jenny** *n*. any of various creeping plants, esp. the moneywort. **creeping Jesus** *n*. (*sl.*) a sly or sanctimonious person. **creepy** *a*. (*comp.* **creepier**, *superl.* **creepiest**) **1** having the sensation of creeping of the flesh. **2** causing this sensation. **3** characterized by or prone to creeping. **creepily** *adv*. **creepiness** *n*. **creepy-crawly** *a*. creepy. ~*n*. (*pl.* **creepy-crawlies**) a creeping insect or small animal.

cremate (krimāt´) *v.t.* **1** to dispose of a corpse by burning. **2** to burn. **cremation** *n*. **cremator** *n*. **crematorium** (kremətaw´riəm) *n*. (*pl.* **crematoriums, crematoria** (-iə)) a place where bodies are cremated. **crematory** (krem´-) *a*. employed in or connected with cremation. ~*n*. (*pl.* **crematories**) (*esp. N Am.*) a crematorium.

crème de la crème (krem də la krem´) *n*. the pick, best, most select, elite.

crème fraîche (krem fresh´) *n*. a type of thick, slightly soured cream.

crenate (krē´nāt), **crenated** (krinā´tid) *a*. **1** (*esp. Zool.*) notched. **2** (*Bot.*) (of a leaf) having the edge notched. **crenation** (krinā´shən) *n*. **crenature** (krē´nəchə, kren´-) *n*.

crenel (kren´əl), **crenelle** (-nel´) *n*. **1** a loophole through which to discharge musketry. **2** a battlement. **crenellate** (kren´-), **crenelate** *v.t.* to furnish with battlements or loopholes. **crenellation** (-ā´shən) *n*.

Creole (krē´ōl) *n.* **1** a person of European parentage in the W Indies or Spanish America. **2** in Louisiana, a person descended from French or Spanish ancestors. **3** a person of mixed European and black parentage. **4** (**creole**) the native language of a region, formed from prolonged contact between the original native language(s) and that of European settlers. ~*a.* relating to the Creoles or a creole language. **creolize, creolise** *v.t.* **creolization** (-zā´shən) *n.*

creosote (krē´əsōt) *n.* **1** (*also* **creosote oil**) a liquid distilled from coal tar, used for preserving wood etc. **2** an antiseptic liquid distilled from wood. ~*v.t.* to treat (woodwork, etc.) with creosote. **creosote bush, creosote plant** *n.* a Mexican shrub, *Larrea tridentata*, smelling of creosote.

crêpe (krāp, krep) *n.* **1** crape. **2** a crapy fabric other than mourning crape. **3** a thin pancake. **4** crêpe paper. **5** crêpe rubber. **crêpe de Chine** (də shēn´) *n.* crape manufactured from raw silk. **crêpe paper** *n.* thin crinkly paper, used in making decorations. **crêperie** (-əri) *n.* a restaurant or café specializing in crêpes. **crêpe rubber** *n.* rubber with a rough surface used for shoe soles etc. **crêpey, crêpy** *a.*

crepitate (krep´itāt) *v.i.* **1** to crackle. **2** to burst with a series of short, sharp reports, as salt does in fire. **3** to rattle. **4** (*Zool.*) (of a beetle) to eject an acrid fluid as a form of self-defence. **crepitant** *a.* **crepitation** (-ā´shən) *n.* **crepitus** (krep´itəs) *n.* **1** (*Med.*) a rattling sound heard in the lungs during pneumonia etc. **2** (*Med.*) the sound of the ends of a broken bone scraping against each other.

crept CREEP.

crepuscle (krep´əsəl), **crepuscule** (-əskūl) *n.* morning or evening twilight. **crepuscular** (-pŭs´kū-) *a.* **1** of or relating to or connected with twilight. **2** glimmering, indistinct, obscure. **3** (*Zool.*) appearing or flying about at twilight.

Cres. *abbr.* (in street names) Crescent.

cres., cresc. *abbr.* (*Mus.*) crescendo.

crescendo (krishen´dō) *n.* (*pl.* **crescendos, crescendi** (-di)) **1** (*Mus.*) (a musical passage performed with) a gradual increase in the force of sound. **2** a gradual increase in force or effect. **3** a climax, high point. ~*adv., a.* with an increasing volume of sound. ~*v.i.* (*3rd pers. sing. pres.* **crescendoes**, *pres.p.* **crescendoing**, *past, p.p.* **crescendoed**) to increase in loudness or intensity.

Usage note The use of *crescendo* to mean climax is best avoided: a crescendo is a gradual increase towards a climax, not the climax itself.

crescent (kres´ənt) *a.* **1** shaped like a new moon. **2** (*poet.*) increasing, growing. ~*n.* **1** a shape like the new moon. **2** a street or row of buildings in crescent form. **3** the increasing moon in its first quarter. **crescentic** (-sen´tik) *a.*

cress (kres) *n.* any of various cruciferous plants with a pungent taste, e.g. watercress, garden cress.

cresset (kres´it) *n.* (*Hist.*) a metal cup or vessel, usu. on a pole, for holding oil for a light.

crest (krest) *n.* **1** a plume or comb on the head of a bird. **2** any tuft on the head of an animal. **3** a plume or tuft of feathers, esp. affixed to the top of a helmet. **4** the apex of a helmet. **5** (*Her.*) any figure placed above the shield in a coat-of-arms. **6** the same printed on paper or painted on a building etc. **7** the summit of a mountain or hill. **8** the top of a ridge. **9** the line of the top of the neck in animals. **10** an animal's mane. **11** the ridge of a wave. **12** (*Anat.*) a ridge on a bone. ~*v.t.* **1** to ornament or furnish with a crest. **2** to serve as a crest to. **3** to attain the crest of (a hill). ~*v.i.* to rise into a crest or ridge. **on the crest of a wave** at the peak of one's success; enjoying prolonged success. **crested** *a.* **crestfallen** *a.* **1** dispirited, abashed. **2** with a drooping crest. **crestless** *a.*

cretaceous (kritā´shəs) *a.* of the nature of or abounding in chalk. **Cretaceous** *a., n.* (of or formed in) the last period of the Mesozoic era.

Cretan (krē´tən) *n.* a native or inhabitant of the Greek island of Crete. ~*a.* of or relating to Crete or the Cretans.

cretin (kret´in) *n.* **1** a person mentally and physically disabled because of a (congenital) thyroid malfunction. **2** (*coll.*) a very stupid person. **cretinism** *n.* **cretinize, cretinise** *v.t.* **cretinous** *a.*

cretonne (kreton´, kret´on) *n.* a cotton fabric with pictorial patterns, used for upholstering, frocks etc.

Creutzfeldt–Jakob disease (kroitsfeltyak´ob) *n.* (*Med.*) a disease of human beings, related to BSE and scrapie, which causes brain degeneration, leading to death.

crevasse (krəvas´) *n.* **1** a deep fissure in a glacier. **2** (*N Am.*) a break in an embankment or levee of a river.

Usage note The meanings of *crevasse* and *crevice* overlap, but in general a *crevasse* is a large crack, and a *crevice* a narrow one.

crevice (krev´is) *n.* a crack, a cleft, a fissure. **creviced** *a.*

Usage note See note under CREVASSE.

crew[1] (kroo) *n.* **1** the sailors on a ship or boat, esp. as distinct from the officers or the captain. **2** the personnel on board an aircraft, train or bus. **3** a number of persons associated for any purpose. **4** a gang, a mob. ~*v.t., v.i.* to act as, or serve in, a crew (of). **crew-cut** *n.* a very short style of haircut. **crewman** *n.* (*pl.* **crewmen**). **crew neck** *n.* a close-fitting round neckline on a jersey.

crew[2] CROW[2].

crewel (kroo´əl) *n.* **1** fine two-threaded worsted. **2** embroidery or tapestry worked with such thread. **crewel work** *n.*

crib (krib) *n.* **1** a child's cot. **2** a model of the Nativity scene (placed in churches at Christmas). **3** a plagiarism. **4** a translation of or key to an author, used by students. **5** something (such as a hidden list of dates, formulae etc.) used to cheat in an examination. **6** (*coll.*) anything stolen. **7** a rack or manger. **8** a timber etc. framework lining a mine shaft, forming foundations etc. **9** a small cottage, a hut, a hovel. **10** cribbage. **11** a hand at cribbage made up of two cards thrown out by each player and given to the dealer. **12** (*Austral.*, *New Zeal.*) food, esp. a light meal. ~*v.t.* (*pres.p.* **cribbing**, *past*, *p.p.* **cribbed**) **1** to plagiarize. **2** to copy from a translation. **3** (*coll.*) to steal, to appropriate. **4** to shut up in a crib. **5** to confine. ~*v.i.* **1** to cheat using a crib. **2** (*coll.*) to grumble. **cribber** *n*. **crib-biting** *n*. a bad habit in some horses of biting the crib.

cribbage (krib´ij) *n*. a card game for two, three or four players. **cribbage board** *n*. a board with holes and pegs on which the progress of the game is marked.

crick (krik) *n*. a spasmodic painful stiffness, esp. of the neck or back. ~*v.t.* to cause a crick in.

cricket[1] (krik´it) *n*. an open-air game played by two sides of 11 players, consisting of an attempt to strike, with a ball, wickets defended by the opponents with bats. ~*v.i.* (*pres.p.* **cricketing**, *past*, *p.p.* **cricketed**) to play cricket. **not cricket** unfair, not honest. **cricketer** *n*.

cricket[2] (krik´it) *n*. **1** any grasshopper-like insect of the family Gryllidae, the males being noted for their chirping. **2** any of various similar insects not belonging to the Gryllidae, such as the mole cricket.

cricoid (krī´koid) *a*. (*Anat.*) ringlike. **cricoid cartilage** *n*. the cartilage at the top of the trachea.

crier (krī´ə), **cryer** *n*. a person who cries or proclaims.

crikey (krī´ki) *int*. (*coll.*) used to express astonishment.

crim (krim) *n.*, *a*. (*esp. Austral.*, *New Zeal.*) (a) criminal.

crime (krīm) *n*. **1** an act contrary to human or divine law. **2** a charge, the grounds for accusation. **3** (*Mil.*) any offence or breach of regulations. **4** any act of wickedness or sin. **5** wrong-doing, sin. **6** (*coll.*) something to be deplored, deprecated, regretted or ashamed of. ~*v.t.* (*Mil.*) to charge with or convict of a crime. **crime fighter** *n*. a person who fights crime. **crime-fighting** *n*. **crime sheet** *n*. (*Mil.*) a record of offences. **crime wave** *n*. a sudden sharp increase in crimes committed. **crime writer** *n*. a person who writes fiction about crime and detection.

criminal (krim´inəl) *a*. **1** of the nature of a crime, relating to (a) crime. **2** contrary to duty, law or right. **3** guilty of a crime. **4** tainted with crime. **5** (*Law*) involved with or relating to criminal law as distinct from civil law etc. **6** (*coll.*) regrettable, deplorable, shameful. ~*n*. a person guilty of a crime. **criminalistic** (-lis´-) *a*. relating to criminals. **criminalistics** *n*. (*esp. N Am.*) forensic science. **criminality** (-nal´-) *n*. **criminalize**, **criminalise** *v.t.* **1** to make (an activity etc.) illegal. **2** to make (a person) a criminal, e.g. by criminalizing

their activities. **criminalization** (-zā´shən) *n*. **criminal law** *n*. the body of laws or practice of law dealing with criminal offences and punishment of offenders, as distinct from *civil law*. **criminal libel** *n*. (*Law*) (a) libel likely to provoke a breach of the peace. **criminally** *adv*. **criminal record** *n*. a record of crimes a person has committed.

criminology (kriminol´əji) *n*. the scientific study of crime and criminals. **criminological** (-loj´ikəl) *a*. **criminologically** *adv*. **criminologist** (-ol´-) *n*

crimp (krimp) *v.t.* **1** to curl or put waves into (hair). **2** to compress into ridges or folds, to frill. **3** to corrugate, to flute, to crease. ~*n*. something crimped or crimpy. **to put a crimp in** (*N Am.*, *coll.*) to obstruct, hinder or thwart. **crimper** *n*. **crimpy** *a*. (*comp.* **crimpier**, *superl.* **crimpiest**). **crimpily** *adv*. **crimpiness** *n*.

crimson (krim´zən) *n*. a deep red colour. ~*a*. of this colour. ~*v.t.* to dye with this colour. ~*v.i.* **1** to turn crimson. **2** to blush.

cringe (krinj) *v.i.* (*pres.p.* **cringing**) **1** to shrink back in fear. **2** to crouch, to bend humbly. **3** to fawn, behave obsequiously to. **4** (*coll.*) to wince in embarrassment. ~*n*. an act of cringing. **cringe-making** *a*. (*coll.*) acutely embarrassing or distasteful. **cringing** *a.*, *n*. **cringingly** *adv*.

cringle (kring´gəl) *n*. (*Naut.*) an iron ring on the bolt-rope of a sail for a rope to pass through.

crinkle (kring´kəl) *n*. a wrinkle, a crease. ~*v.i.* to form wrinkles or creases. ~*v.t.* to wrinkle or crease. **crinkle-cut** *a*. (of vegetables) cut with wavy or scalloped edges or sides. **crinkly** *a*. (*comp.* **crinklier**, *superl.* **crinkliest**).

crinoid (krin´oid, krī´-) *a*. (*Zool.*) lily-shaped. ~*n*. any animal belonging to the class Crinoidea of echinoderms. **crinoidal** (-noi´-) *a*.

crinoline (krin´əlin, -lēn) *n*. **1** a stiff fabric of horsehair formerly used for petticoats, etc. **2** a petticoat of this material. **3** any stiff petticoat used to expand the skirts of a dress.

cripple (krip´əl) *n*. **1** (*also offensive*) †a lame or disabled person. **2** (*coll.*) a person who is disabled or defective in some respect (*emotional cripple*). ~*v.t.* **1** to make lame. **2** to deprive of the use of the limbs. **3** to deprive of or lessen the power of action. **crippled** *a*. **crippledom** *n*. **crippler** *n*. **crippling** *a*. **cripplingly** *adv*.

Usage note Using *cripple* to refer to a permanently lame or disabled person can give offence, and is best avoided.

crisis (krī´sis) *n*. (*pl.* **crises** (-sēz)) **1** a momentous juncture in war, politics, commerce, domestic affairs etc. **2** a time of great danger or difficulty. **3** a turning point, esp. that of a disease indicating recovery or death. **crisis management** *n*. the policy or style of management which involves taking action only when a crisis develops.

crisp (krisp) *a*. **1** hard, dry and brittle. **2** (of vegetables etc.) firm, crunchy. **3** (of weather etc.) cold and invigorating. **4** (of a person's manner) brisk and decisive. **5** (of wording) concise and to the point. **6** (of a person's features) neat, clean-cut. **7** (of hair) closely curled. **8** (of paper) stiff and crackly. ~*v.t.* **1** to make something crisp. **2** to curl, to wrinkle, to ripple. ~*v.i.* **1** to become crisp. **2** to become curly. ~*n.* POTATO CRISP (under POTATO). **to burn to a crisp** to overcook something to the point where it is burnt and uneatable. **crispbread** *n.* thin, dry, unsweetened biscuits of rye or wheat flour, or one of such biscuits. **crisper** *n.* **1** a person who or something which curls or crisps. **2** a compartment in a refrigerator for vegetables to keep them crisp. **crisply** *adv.* **crispness** *n.* **crispy** *a.* (*comp.* **crispier**, *superl.* **crispiest**) **1** crisp. **2** wavy. **3** curled, curling. **4** brisk. **crispily** *adv.* **crispiness** *n.*

criss-cross (kris´kros) *a.*, *n.* **1** (a network of lines) crossing one another. **2** repeated(ly) crossing to and fro. ~*v.t.*, *v.i.* to move in, lie in, or mark with, a criss-cross pattern. ~*adv.* **1** in a criss-cross pattern. **2** at cross purposes.

☒ cristal common misspelling of CRYSTAL.

cristobalite (kristō´bəlīt) *n.* one of the main forms of silica, occurring e.g. as opal.

crit (krit) *n.* (*coll.*) **1** a critical study or examination. **2** a formal criticism. **3** (*Physics*) critical mass.

criterion (krītiə´riən) *n.* (*pl.* **criteria** (-ə)) a principle or standard by which anything is or can be judged.

Usage note *Criteria* is commonly used as a singular noun (a *criteria*) but it should always be a plural, with *criterion* as the singular.

critic (krit´ik) *n.* **1** a judge, an examiner. **2** a censurer, a caviller. **3** a person skilled in judging of literary or artistic merit. **4** a reviewer. **5** an expert in textual criticism. **critical** *a.* **1** of or relating to criticism. **2** expressing criticism; frequently making criticisms. **3** fastidious, exacting, captious. **4** indicating or involving a crisis. **5** decisive, vital. **6** attended with danger or risk. **7** in literature, involving textual criticism of a text. **8** (*Physics*) of or designating a point at which a chain reaction becomes self-sustaining. **9** (*Physics*) (of a nuclear reactor) able to sustain such a chain reaction. **10** (*Math.*) relating to points of coincidence or transition. **criticality** (-kal´-) *n.* (*esp. Math., Physics*) **critically** *adv.* **critical mass** *n.* the smallest amount of fissile material that can sustain a chain reaction. **criticalness** *n.* **critical path** *n.* the series of steps and procedures by which a complex operation can be carried out in the shortest time. **critical temperature** *n.* the temperature below which a gas cannot be liquefied. **criticism** (-sizm) *n.* **1** the act of judging, esp. literary or artistic works. **2** a critical essay or opinion. **3** the work of criticizing. **4** an unfavourable judgement. **criticize, criticise** *v.t.* **1** to examine critically and deliver an opinion on. **2** to censure. ~*v.i.* to make criticisms. **criticizable** *a.* **criticizer** *n.*

critique (kritēk´) *n.* a critical essay or judgement. ~*v.t.* to make a critique of.

critter (krit´ə) *n.* (*esp. N Am., coll.*) a creature (an animal or, as a term of pity, a person).

croak (krōk) *v.i.* **1** (of e.g. a frog or a raven) to make a hoarse low sound in the throat. **2** (*sl.*) to die. **3** to grumble. **4** to prophesy evil. ~*v.t.* **1** to utter in a low hoarse voice. **2** (*sl.*) to kill. **3** to utter dismally. ~*n.* **1** the low harsh sound made by a frog or a raven. **2** any hoarse sound similar to this. **croaker** *n.* **1** a person, animal or bird that croaks. **2** a querulous person. **3** (*sl.*) a dying person. **4** a person who prophesies evil. **croaky** *a.* (*comp.* **croakier**, *superl.* **croakiest**) croaking, hoarse. **croakily** *adv.* **croakiness** *n.*

Croat (krō´at) *n.* **1** a native or inhabitant of Croatia in SE Europe. **2** a person of Croatian descent; a person belonging to a Slav ethnic group of Croatia. **3** the language of Croatia, one of the two main dialects of Serbo-Croat. ~*a.* of or relating to the Croats or their language, Croatian. **Croatian** (krōā´shən) *a.* of or relating to Croatia, its people or their language. ~*n.* **1** a native or inhabitant of Croatia. **2** a Croat.

croc (krok) *n.* (*coll.*) short for CROCODILE.

crochet (krō´shā, -shi) *n.* a kind of knitting done with a hooked needle. ~*v.t.* to knit or make in crochet. ~*v.i.* to knit in this manner.

croci CROCUS.

crocidolite (krəsid´əlīt) *n.* **1** a silky fibrous silicate of iron and sodium, also called blue asbestos. **2** a yellow form of this used as a gem or ornament.

crock[1] (krok) *n.* **1** an earthenware vessel; a pot, a pitcher, a jar. **2** a potsherd. **crockery** *n.* **1** earthenware. **2** earthenware or china dishes, cups, plates etc.

crock[2] (krok) *n.* **1** (*coll.*) a sick, decrepit or old person. **2** (*coll.*) a broken-down machine or implement. ~*v.i.* to break down, collapse, become disabled etc. ~*v.t.* (*often with up*) to cause to break down, become disabled etc.

crocket (krok´it) *n.* (*Archit.*) a carved foliated ornament on a pinnacle, the side of a canopy etc.

crocodile (krok´ədīl) *n.* **1** a large amphibian reptile of the family Crocodylidae, with the back and tail covered with large, square scales. **2** (leather made from) the skin of the crocodile. **3** a string of schoolchildren walking two by two. **crocodile clip** *n.* a clip with interlocking serrated edges, used for making connections in electrical apparatus. **crocodile tears** *n.pl.* hypocritical tears like those with which the crocodile, according to fable, attracts its victims. **crocodilian** (-dil´-) *n.* any of the large amphibian reptiles of the order Crocodilia, including crocodiles, alligators, caymans and gharials. ~*a.* of or relating to the crocodilians.

crocus (krō´kəs) *n.* (*pl.* **crocuses, croci** (-kī, -kē)) a small bulbous plant of the genus *Crocus*, belonging to the Iridaceae, with yellow, white or purple flowers, extensively cultivated in gardens.

Croesus (krē´səs) *n.* a very wealthy man.

croft (kroft) *n.* **1** a piece of enclosed ground, esp. adjoining a house. **2** a small farm in the Highlands and islands of Scotland or northern England. *~v.i.* to live and work on a croft. **crofter** *n.* a person who farms a croft, esp. one of the joint tenants of a farm in Scotland. **crofting** *n.*

croissant (krwas´ã) *n.* a crescent-shaped roll of rich flaky pastry.

cromlech (krom´lekh) *n.* **1** a circle of standing stones. **2** a prehistoric structure in which a large flat stone rests horizontally on upright ones, a dolmen.

crone (krōn) *n.* (*derog.*) an old woman.

cronk (krongk) *a.* (*Austral., coll.*) **1** unwell. **2** unsound. **3** fraudulent.

crony (krō´ni) *n.* (*pl.* **cronies**) (*sometimes derog.*) an intimate friend.

crook (kruk) *n.* **1** a shepherd's or bishop's hooked staff. **2** a bent or curved instrument. **3** a curve, a bend, a meander. **4** (*coll.*) a thief, a swindler. **5** a short tube for altering the key on a brass wind instrument. *~a.* **1** crooked. **2** (*Austral., New Zeal., coll.*) **a** sick, unwell, injured. **b** unpleasant. **c** dishonest. **d** irritable, angry. *~v.t.* to make crooked or curved. *~v.i.* to be bent or crooked. **to go crook (at/ on)** (*Austral., New Zeal., coll.*) to become angry (with), to reprimand. **crooked** (-kid) *a.* (*comp.* **crookeder**, *superl.* **crookedest**) **1** bent, curved. **2** turning, twisting, winding. **3** deformed. **4** not straightforward. **5** perverse. **6** (*Austral., New Zeal., coll.*) crook. **7** (*with on, Austral., coll.*) hostile (to). **crookedly** *adv.* **crookedness** *n.* **crookery** *n.*

Usage note In Austral. coll. senses, *crooked* is usually pronounced (krukt).

---

croon (kroon) *v.i.* to sing in a low voice. *~v.t.* **1** to sing in a low voice. **2** to mutter. *~n.* singing in a low voice. **crooner** *n.*

crop (krop) *n.* **1** (*pl.*) plants grown for food. **2** the produce of such plants. **3** the amount cut or gathered from such plants, harvest. **4** a group of anything produced, appearing etc. at one time. **5** (*Zool.*) **a** the craw of a fowl, constituting a kind of first stomach. **b** an analogous receptacle in masticating insects. **6** the upper part of a whip, a fishing rod etc. **7** a short whipstock with a loop instead of a lash. **8** an entire tanned hide. **9** a short haircut. **10** a piece chopped off. *~v.t.* (*pres.p.* **cropping**, *past, p.p.* **cropped**) **1** to cut off the ends of. **2** to mow, to reap, to pluck, to gather. **3** (of an animal) to bite off and eat. **4** to cut off, to cut short. **5** to sow. **6** to plant and raise crops on. **7** to reduce the margin of (a book) unduly, in binding. *~v.i.* to yield a harvest, to bear fruit. **to crop out** (*Geol.*) (of an underlying stratum) to come out at the surface by the edges. **to crop up 1** to come up unexpectedly. **2** (*Geol.*) to crop out. **crop circle** *n.* a circle, or a pattern based on circles, appearing as flattened stalks in the middle of a field of standing corn. **crop-full** *a.*

1 having a full crop. **2** satiated. **cropper** *n.* **1** a grain or plant which yields a good crop. **2** (*coll.*) a heavy fall. **3** (*coll.*) a collapse or failure. **to come a cropper 1** (*coll.*) to fall. **2** (*coll.*) to fail.

croquet (krō´kā) *n.* **1** an open-air game played on a lawn with balls and mallets. **2** the act of croqueting an opponent's ball. *~v.t.* to drive (an opponent's ball) away in this game by placing one's own ball against it and striking. *~v.i.* to play croquet.

croquette (krəket´) *n.* a savoury ball made with meat, potato etc. fried in breadcrumbs.

crore (kraw) *n.* in the Indian subcontinent, ten millions, a hundred lakhs (of rupees, people etc.).

crosier (krō´zhə, -ziə), **crozier** *n.* **1** the hooked pastoral staff of a bishop or abbot. **2** a shepherd's crook.

cross (kros) *n.* **1** an ancient instrument of execution made of two pieces of timber set transversely at various angles. **2** (**Cross**) the cross on which Jesus Christ was executed. **3** a representation of this, generally in the shape of a Latin cross, as an emblem of Christianity. **4** a staff with a cross at the top. **5** the sign of the cross. **6** a monument usu. but not always in the shape of a Latin cross, set up in the centre of a town etc. **7** the place in a town or village where such a monument stands or has once stood, often a market place. **8** a sign or mark formed by two short lines crossing, a + or ×. **9** an emblem, ornament etc. in the shape of a Latin cross, Greek cross or any other cross. **10** the mixture of two distinct stocks in breeding animals or plants. **11** the animal or plant resulting from such a mixture. **12** a mixture. **13** a compromise. **14** anything that thwarts or obstructs. **15** trouble, affliction. **16** in football, a pass across the field, esp. towards the opposing goal. **17** in boxing, a punch made with the fist coming from the side. **18** a movement across a stage. *~a.* **1** peevish, angry. **2** transverse, oblique, lateral. **3** intersecting. **3** adverse, contrary, perverse. *~v.t.* **1** to draw a line or lines across. **2** to erase by cross lines, to cancel. **3** to mark parallel lines on the face of (a cheque) in order to make it payable only through a bank. **4** to pass across, to traverse. **5** to place one across another. **6** to cause to intersect. **7** to pass over or in front of. **8** to meet and pass. **9** to cause to interbreed. **10** to cross-fertilize. **11** in football etc., to pass (the ball etc.) across the pitch. **12** to thwart, to counteract. **13** (*sl.*) to cheat. **14** to make the sign of the cross on or over. *~v.i.* **1** to lie or be across or over something. **2** to pass across something, to intersect. **3** (of letters between two correspondents) to be in the process of being delivered at the same time. **4** (of a telephone line) to be connected in error to more than one telephone. **5** to move in a zigzag. **6** to interbreed. **7** in football etc., to pass the ball etc. across the pitch. **to cross one's fingers 1** to put one finger across an adjacent one as a sign of wishing for good luck. **2** to wish for or hope for good luck. **to cross one's mind** to occur to one's memory or attention. **to cross someone's palm (with silver)** to give money to (e.g. a fortune-teller) as payment. **to cross swords** to have a fight or argument (with). **to get one's wires crossed** to have a misunderstanding, to be at cross purposes. **cross-comb. form 1** across. **2** having a part that lies across or transverse to another. **3** cross-shaped. **4** denoting two-way action or influence. **crossbar** *n.* **1** the horizontal bar of a football etc. goal. **2** the bar between the handlebar support and saddle support on a bicycle. **3** any transverse bar. **crossbeam** *n.* a large beam running from wall to wall. **cross-bedding** *n.* (*Geol.*) false bedding. **crossbench** *n.* in parliament, one of the benches for those independent of the recognized parties. **cross-bencher** *n.* **crossbill** *n.* a bird of the genus *Loxia*, the mandibles of the bill of which cross each other when closed, esp. *L. curvirostra*, an irregular British visitor. **crossbones** *n.pl.* the representation of two thigh bones crossed as an emblem of mortality. **cross-border** *a.* occurring etc. across the border between two states. **crossbow** *n.* a weapon for shooting, formed by placing a bow across a stock. **crossbowman** *n.* (*pl.* **crossbowmen**). **cross-bred** *a.* of a cross-breed, hybrid. **cross-breed** *n.* **1** a breed produced from a male and female of different strains or varieties. **2** a hybrid. ~*v.t.* (*past, p.p.* **cross-bred**) **1** to produce a cross-breed. **2** to cross-fertilize. **cross-check** *v.t.* to check (a fact etc.) by referring to other sources of information. ~*n.* such a check. **cross-country** *a., adv.* **1** across fields etc. instead of along the roads. **2** on minor rather than direct main roads. ~*n.* (*pl.* **cross-countries**) a cross-country race. **cross-cultural** *a.* concerning two or more different cultures, or the differences between them. **cross-current** *n.* **1** a sea etc. current flowing across another current. **2** a trend or tendency running counter to another. **cross-cut** *n.* **1** a shortcut, a path diagonally across something. **2** a cut across. ~*a.* cut across the grain or main axis. **cross-cut saw** *n.* a large saw for cutting timber across the grain. **cross-dating** *n.* in archaeology, a method of dating one site, level etc., or objects found there, by comparison with other sites, levels etc. **cross-dresser** *n.* a transvestite. **cross-dress** *v.i.* **cross-dressing** *n.* **cross-examine** *v.t.* (*Law*) to examine systematically for the purpose of eliciting facts not brought out in direct examination, or for confirming or contradicting the direct evidence. **cross-examination** *n.* **cross-examiner** *n.* **cross-eye** *n.* a squinting eye. **cross-eyed** *a.* with both eyes squinting inwards. **cross-fade** *v.t.* in TV or radio, to fade out (one signal) while introducing another. ~*n.* the act of doing this. **cross-fertilize, cross-fertilise** *v.t.* **1** (*Bot.*) to apply the pollen of one flower to the pistil of (a flower of the same species). **2** to fertilize (an animal) with genes usu. from an individual of another species. **3** to cause an interchange of

ideas from different sources in. ~*v.i.* to undergo cross-fertilization. **cross-fertilization** *n.* **crossfire** *n.* **1** firing in directions which cross each other. **2** a rapid or lively argument. **3** criticism coming from several sources at one time. **cross-grain** *n.* the grain or fibres of wood running across the regular grain. **cross-grained** *a.* **1** having the grain or fibres running across or irregularly. **2** perverse, peevish. **3** intractable. **cross-hairs** *n.pl.* two fine wires or lines that cross each other at right angles in an optical instrument, used for focusing etc. **cross-hatch** *v.t.* to shade with parallel lines crossing regularly in drawing or engraving. **cross-head** *n.* **1** the block at the head of a piston rod communicating motion to the connecting rod. **2** (*also* **cross-heading**) a heading printed across the page or a column. **cross-legged** (-legd, -leg′id) *a.* having one leg over the other. **cross-link, cross-linkage** *n.* (*Chem.*) a bond between adjacent chains of atoms in a large molecule (such as a polymer), or the atom or atoms forming the bond. **crossmatch** *v.t.* (*Med.*) to test (e.g. blood samples from two people) for compatibility. **crossmatching** *n.* **crossness** *n.* **crossover** *n.* **1** the act of crossing over. **2** a place of crossing over. **3** a road which crosses over another. **4** a changing over from one style of music, genre of literature etc. to another. ~*a.* **1** combining two distinct styles of music, genres of literature etc. **2** involving or allowing a crossing over. **3** having parts that cross over each other. **crosspatch** *n.* (*coll.*) a cross, ill-tempered person. **crosspiece** *n.* **1** a transverse piece. **2** in shipbuilding, the flooring-piece resting on the keel. **cross-ply** *a.* (of motor-vehicle tyres) having the cords crossing each other diagonally to strengthen the tread. **cross-pollination** *n.* the transfer of pollen from one flower to the stigma of another. **cross-pollinate** *v.t.* **cross purpose** *n.* **1** a contrary purpose. **2** contradiction, inconsistency, misunderstanding. **to be at cross purposes** to misunderstand or unintentionally act counter to each other. **cross-question** *v.t.* to cross-examine. **cross-refer** *v.t., v.i.* (*pres.p.* **cross-referring**, *past, p.p.* **cross-referred**) to refer from one place in a book etc. to another. **cross-reference** *n.* a reference from one place in a book etc. to another. ~*v.t.* to provide cross-references for. **cross-rhythm** *n.* (*Mus.*) **1** the use of two or more rhythms together. **2** a rhythm used along with another. **crossroad** *n.* a road that crosses another or connects two others. **crossroads** *n.* a place where two roads cross. **at a/ the crossroads** at a point at which an important decision must be made or a new direction taken. **cross-ruff** *n.* in card-playing, the play in which partners trump different suits and lead accordingly. ~*v.i.* to play in this way. **cross-section** *n.* **1** a cutting across the grain or at right angles to the length. **2** the surface produced in this way, or a representation of it. **3** a representative sample. **4** (*Geol.*) a cutting which shows all the strata. **cross-sectional** *a.* **cross stitch** *n.* **1** a kind of stitch crossing others in series. **2** needlework done in this way. **crossstitch** *v.t.* to sew or embroider with cross stitches. **cross-subsidize, cross-subsidise** *v.t.* to subsidize out of profits made elsewhere. **cross-subsidy** *n.* (*pl.* **cross-subsidies**). **crosstalk** *n.* **1** unwanted signals in a telephone, radio etc. channel, coming in from another channel. **2** repartee. **crosstrees** *n.pl.* (*Naut.*) timbers on the tops of masts to support the rigging of the mast above. **crossvoting** *n.* (*N Am.*) voting for a party other than the one usually supported, or voting for more than one party. **crosswalk** *n.* (*N Am., Austral.*) a pedestrian crossing. **crossway** *n.* a road that crosses another or connects two others. **crossways, crosswise** *adv.* **1** across. **2** in the form of a cross. **crosswind** *n.* **1** an unfavourable wind. **2** a sidewind. **crossword, crossword puzzle** *n.* a puzzle in which blank squares are filled with the letters of intersecting words corresponding to clues provided. **crossing** *n.* **1** a place of crossing. **2** the intersection of two roads, railways etc. **3** a place where a road etc. may be crossed. **4** the place where the nave and transepts of a church intersect. **crossing over** *n.* (*Biol.*) the interchange of segments of homologous chromosomes during meiotic cell division. **crossly** *adv.* in an illhumoured manner.

crosse (kros) *n.* the long, hooked, racket-like stick used in the game of lacrosse.

crotch (kroch) *n.* **1** a forking. **2** the angle between the thighs where the legs meet the body, or the corresponding part of e.g. a pair of trousers.

crotchet (kroch´it) *n.* **1** (*Mus.*) a note, equal in length to one beat of a bar of 4/4 time. **2** a whimsical fancy, a conceit. **3** a hook. **crotchety** *a.* irritable. **crotchetiness** *n.*

croton (krō´tǝn) *n.* **1** a plant of the genus *Croton*, euphorbiaceous medicinal trees and shrubs from the warmer parts of both hemispheres. **2** any tree or shrub of the genus *Codiaeum*, of the same family as the genus *Croton*, esp. *C. variegatum*, a plant with brightly coloured leaves. **croton oil** *n.* a strong purgative oil expressed from *Croton tiglium*.

crouch (krowch) *v.i.* **1** to stoop, to bend low. **2** to lie close to the ground. **3** to cringe, to fawn. ~*n.* the action of crouching.

croup[1] (kroop) *n.* **1** the rump, the buttocks (esp. of a horse). **2** the part behind the saddle.

croup[2] (kroop) *n.* inflammation of the larynx and trachea, characterized by hoarse coughing and difficulty in breathing. **croupy** *a.* (*comp.* **croupier,** *superl.* **croupiest**).

croupier (kroo´piǝ) *n.* **1** a person who superintends a gaming table and collects the money won by the bank. **2** a vice-chairman or -chairwoman at a public dinner.

crouton (kroo´ton) *n.* a small cube of fried or toasted bread, served with soup or salads.

crow[1] (krō) *n.* **1** a large black bird of the genus *Corvus*, esp. the hooded crow, and the carrion crow *C. corione*. **2** any bird of the family Corvidae, including jays, magpies, jackdaws etc. **3** (*sl., derog.*) an objectionable, old or ugly woman. **as the crow flies** in a direct line. **to eat crow** (*coll.*) to (be made to) humiliate or abase oneself. **crowbar** *n.* a bar of iron bent at one end (like a crow's beak) and used as a lever. **crowberry** *n.* (*pl.* **crowberries**) **1** a heathlike plant, *Empetrum nigrum*, with black berries. **2** (*N Am.*) the cranberry. **3** the berry of either of these plants. **crowfoot** *n.* (*pl.* **crowfoots**) each of several species of buttercup, *Ranunculus bulbosus, R. acris* and *R. repens*. **crow's-foot** *n.* (*pl.* **crow's feet**) **1** a wrinkle at the corner of the eye. **2** (*Mil.*) a caltrop. **crow's-nest** *n.* a tub or box for the lookout on a ship's mast.

crow[2] (krō) *v.i.* (*past* **crew** (kroo), **crowed**) **1** to make a loud cry like a cock. **2** to make a cry of delight like an infant. **3** to exult. **4** to brag, to boast. ~*v.t.* to proclaim by crowing. ~*n.* **1** the cry of a cock. **2** the cry of delight of an infant.

crowd (krowd) *n.* **1** a number of persons or things collected closely and confusedly together. **2** the mass, the mob, the populace. **3** (*coll.*) a set, a party, a lot. **4** an audience. **5** a large number (of things). **6** any group of persons photographed in a film but not playing definite parts. ~*v.t.* **1** to cause to collect in crowds. **2** to press or squeeze closely together. **3** to fill by pressing. **4** to throng or press upon. **5** to press (into or through). **6** to come close to in an aggressive or threatening way. **7** (*coll.*) to pressurize (someone). ~*v.i.* **1** to press, to throng, to swarm. **2** to collect in crowds. **to crowd out 1** to force (a person or thing) out by leaving no room. **2** to fill to absolute capacity. **crowded** *a.* **crowdedness** *n.* **crowd-puller** *n.* an event that attracts a large audience.

crown (krown) *n.* **1** the ornamental headdress or hat worn on the head by emperors, kings or princes as a badge of sovereignty. **2** an ornament of this shape. **3** (**Crown**) royal power. **4** (**Crown**) the sovereign. **5** a garland of honour worn on the head. **6** the culmination, glory. **7** a reward, distinction. **8** the top of anything, such as a hat, a mountain or a tree. **9** the head. **10** the top of the head. **11** the vertex of an arch. **12** the upper member of a cornice. **13** the highest part of a road, bridge or causeway. **14** the portion of a tooth above the gum. **15** an artificial crown for a broken or discoloured tooth. **16** the part of a plant just above and below the ground, where root and stem meet. **17** the upper part of a cut gemstone. **18** (*Naut.*) the part of an anchor where the arms join the shank. **19** (*Hist.*) a five-shilling piece. **20** a foreign coin of certain values. **21** a size of paper, 15 in. × 20 in. (381 × 508 mm) (formerly with a crown for a watermark). ~*v.t.* **1** to invest with a crown, or regal or imperial dignity. **2** (*fig.*) to surround, or top, as if with a crown. **3** to form a crown, ornament or top to. **4** to dignify, to adorn. **5** to consummate. **6** to put a crown or cap on (a tooth). **7** (*coll.*) to hit on the head. **8** in draughts, to make (a piece) into a king. **crown cap, crown cork** *n.* an airtight lined metal cap used to seal beer bottles etc. **Crown Colony** *n.* a colony administered by the British Government. **Crown Court** *n.* in England and Wales, a local criminal court. **crown glass** *n.* **1** the finest kind of window glass, made in circular sheets without lead or iron. **2** glass used in optical instruments, containing potassium and barium in place of sodium. **crown green** *n.* a type of bowling green which slopes slightly from the sides up to the centre. **crown imperial** *n.* a tall garden flower, *Fritillaria imperialis*, with a whorl of florets round the head. **crown jewels** *n.pl.* the regalia and other jewels belonging to the sovereign. **crownless** *a.* destitute or deprived of a crown. **Crown Office** *n.* **1** a section of the Court of King's (or Queen's) Bench which takes cognizance of criminal cases. **2** the office which now transacts the common law business of the Chancery. **crown of thorns** *n.* a starfish of the genus *Acanthaster*, which feeds on coral. **Crown prince** *n.* in some countries, the heir apparent to the Crown. **Crown princess** *n.* **1** the wife of a Crown prince. **2** in some countries, the female heir apparent to the Crown. **crown roast** *n.* roast ribs of lamb or pork formed into a circular crownlike arrangement. **crown saw** *n.* a type of cylindrical saw for cutting a circular hole.

crozier CROSIER.

CRT *abbr.* cathode ray tube.

cruces CRUX.

crucial (kroo´shəl) *a.* **1** decisive. **2** searching. **3** (*Anat.*) in the form of a cross. **4** intersecting. **5** (*loosely*) very important. **6** (*sl.*) excellent. **cruciality** (-al´iti) *n.* (*pl.* **crucialities**). **crucially** *adv.*

crucian (kroo´shən), **crucian carp** *n.* a small colourful fish, *Carassius carassius*, without barbels.

cruciate (kroo´shiāt) *a.* (*Biol.*) cruciform. **cruciate ligament** *n.* either of a pair of ligaments in the knee which connect the femur and the tibia, and which cross each other.

crucible (kroo´sibəl) *n.* **1** a melting pot of earthenware, porcelain or refractory metal, adapted to withstand high temperatures without softening, and sudden and great alterations of temperature without cracking. **2** a searching test or trial.

crucifer (kroo´sifə) *n.* a plant belonging to the Cruciferae, a natural order of plants, the flowers of which have four petals disposed crosswise. **cruciferous** (-sif´-) *a.* (*Bot.*) belonging to the Cruciferae.

crucifix (kroo´sifiks) *n.* (*pl.* **crucifixes**) a cross bearing a figure of Christ. **crucifixion** (-fik´shən) *n.* **1** the act of crucifying. **2** punishment by crucifying. **3** (**Crucifixion**) the death of Christ on the cross. **4** (**Crucifixion**) a picture of this.

cruciform (kroo´sifawm) *a.* **1** cross-shaped. **2** arranged in the form of a cross.

crucify (kroo´sifī) *v.t.* (*3rd pers. sing. pres.* **crucifies**, *pres.p.* **crucifying**, *past, p.p.* **crucified**) **1** to inflict capital punishment on by affixing to a cross. **2** to torture. **3** to mortify, to destroy the influence of. **4** to subject to scathing criticism, obloquy or ridicule. **5** to defeat utterly. **crucifier** *n.*

crud (krŭd) *n.* (*sl.*) **1** any dirty, sticky or slimy substance. **2** a contemptible person. **3** rubbish, nonsense. **cruddy** *a.* (*comp.* **cruddier**, *superl.* **cruddiest**).

crude (krood) *a.* **1** raw, in a natural state, not cooked, not refined, not polished etc. **2** rude, vulgar. **3** offensively blunt. **4** coarse, rough, unfinished, hasty, approximate. **5** imperfectly developed, immature, inexperienced. **6** (of statistics) not classified or analysed. **7** not digested. ~*n.* crude oil. **crudely** *adv.* **crudeness** *n.* **crude oil** *n.* unrefined petroleum. **crudity** *n.* (*pl.* **crudities**).

cruel (kroo´əl) *a.* (*comp.* **crueller**, (*N Am.*) **crueler**, *superl.* **cruellest**, (*NAm.*) **cruelest**) **1** disposed to give pain to others. **2** inhuman, unfeeling, hard-hearted. **3** causing pain, painful. ~*v.t.* (*Austral., sl.*) to thwart, spoil, frustrate. **cruelly** *adv.* **cruelness** *n.* **cruelty** *n.* (*pl.* **cruelties**) **1** cruel disposition or temper. **2** a barbarous or inhuman act. **3** repeated cruel acts or behaviour. **4** (*Law*) mental or physical hurt, whether caused intentionally or unintentionally, esp. as grounds for divorce. **cruelty-free** *a.* (of household, pharmaceutical, cosmetic etc. products) produced without cruelty to animals; not tested on animals.

cruet (kroo´it) *n.* **1** a small container for pepper, salt etc. at table. **2** a cruet-stand. **3** a small bottle for holding the wine or water in the Eucharist. **cruet-stand** *n.* a frame or stand for holding cruets.

cruise (krooz) *v.i.* **1** to sail to and fro, for pleasure or in search of plunder or an enemy. **2** (of a motor vehicle or aircraft) to travel at a moderate but sustained speed. **3** to travel (about) at a moderate speed with no fixed purpose. **4** (*sl.*) to search the streets or other public places for a sexual partner. **5** to win or succeed without difficulty. ~*v.t.* **1** to sail about or over, visiting various places. **2** (*sl.*) to search (the streets etc.) for a sexual partner. ~*n.* the act or an instance of cruising, esp. a pleasure trip on a boat. **cruise control** *n.* an electronic device which keeps a motor vehicle travelling at a predetermined speed without the use of the accelerator. **cruise missile** *n.* a low-flying subsonic guided missile. **cruiser** *n.* **1** a person or ship that cruises. **2** a warship designed primarily for speed, faster and lighter than a battleship. **3** (*NAm.*) a police patrol car. **cruiserweight** *n.* in boxing, (a) light heavyweight. **cruising speed** *n.* a comfortable and economical speed for a motor vehicle to travel at.

crumb (krŭm) *n.* **1** a small piece, esp. of bread. **2** the soft inner part of bread. **3** a tiny portion, a particle. **4** (*sl.*) an unpleasant or contemptible person. *~v.t.* **1** to break into crumbs. **2** to cover with crumbs (for cooking). *~v.i.* to crumble. **crumby** *a.* (*comp.* **crumbier,** *superl.* **crumbiest**) **1** covered with crumbs. **2** (*sl.*) crummy.

crumble (krŭm'bəl) *v.t.* to break into small particles. *~v.i.* **1** to fall into small pieces. **2** to fall into ruin. *~n.* **1** a pudding or other dish topped with a crumbly mixture of flour, sugar and butter, e.g. *apple crumble.* **2** the crumbly topping itself. **3** anything crumbly or crumbled. **crumbly** *a.* (*comp.* **crumblier,** *superl.* **crumbliest**) apt to crumble. *~n.* (*pl.* **crumblies**) (*sl., offensive*) a very old person. **crumbliness** *n.*

crumbs (krŭmz) *int.* (*coll.*) used to express surprise or dismay.

crumhorn KRUMMHORN.

crummy (krŭm'i) *a.* (*comp.* **crummier,** *superl.* **crummiest**) (*sl.*) **1** unpleasant, worthless. **2** unwell. **crummily** *adv.* **crumminess** *n.*

crumpet (krŭm'pit) *n.* **1** a thin, light, spongy teacake, often eaten toasted. **2** (*sl., offensive*) women as objects of sexual desire. **3** (*sl., offensive*) an attractive woman, as an object of sexual desire.

crumple (krŭm'pəl) *v.t.* **1** to crush. **2** to draw or press into wrinkles. *~v.i.* **1** (of cloth, paper etc.) to become wrinkled, to shrink. **2** to collapse, give way. *~n.* a wrinkle or crease. **crumple zone** *n.* a part of a motor vehicle, generally at the front or back, that is designed to crumple easily and thereby absorb the shock of impact in the event of a crash. **crumpling** *n.* **crumply** *a.* (*comp.* **crumplier,** *superl.* **crumpliest**).

crunch (krŭnch) *v.t.* **1** to crush noisily with the teeth. **2** to grind with the foot. *~v.i.* **1** to make a noise like crunching. **2** to advance with crunching. *~n.* **1** a noise of or like crunching. **2** (*coll.*) the decisive or testing moment, crisis, difficulty etc. **crunchy** *a.* (*comp.* **crunchier,** *superl.* **crunchiest**). **crunchiness** *n.*

crupper (krŭp'ə) *n.* **1** a strap with a loop which passes under a horse's tail to keep the saddle from slipping forward. **2** the croup or hindquarters of a horse.

crusade (kroosād') *n.* **1** any of several expeditions undertaken by Christians in the Middle Ages to recover possession of the Holy Land, then in Muslim hands, or any similar expedition or war undertaken at the instigation of the Church, e.g. against heretics. **2** any campaign conducted in an enthusiastic or fanatical spirit. *~v.i.* to engage in a crusade. **crusader** *n.*

crush (krŭsh) *v.t.* **1** to press or squeeze together between two harder bodies so as to break, bruise or reduce to powder. **2** to crumple. **3** to overwhelm by superior power. **4** to oppress, to ruin. **5** to dismay or subdue. *~n.* **1** the act of crushing. **2** a crowd. **3** (*coll.*) an infatuation or the object of this. **4** a drink made by or as if by crushing fruit. **crushable** *a.* **crush bar** *n.* a bar in a theatre which patrons may use in the intervals of a play. **crush barrier** *n.* a temporary barrier to keep back, or to

separate, a crowd. **crusher** *n.* **crushing** *a., n.* **crushingly** *adv.*

crust (krŭst) *n.* **1** the hard outer part of bread. **2** a piece of crust with some bread attached. **3** the crusty end of a loaf. **4** a hard piece of bread. **5** any hard rind, coating, layer, deposit or surface covering. **6** the pastry covering a pie. **7** a scab or hard patch on the skin. **8** (*Geol.*) the solid outer portion of the earth. **9** a film deposited on the inside of a bottle of wine. **10** a (meagre) living. **11** (*sl.*) impertinence. **12** hardness of manner. *~v.t.* **1** to cover with a crust. **2** to make into crust. *~v.i.* to become encrusted. **crustal** *a.* of or relating to the earth's crust. **crusted** *a.* **1** having a crust. **2** antiquated, hoary, venerable. **3** denoting port or other wine that has deposited a crust in the bottle. **crustose** *a.* (*Bot.*) forming or like a crust. **crusty** *a.* (*comp.* **crustier,** *superl.* **crustiest**) **1** resembling or of the nature of crust. **2** having a crust. **3** harsh, peevish, morose. **crustily** *adv.* **crustiness** *n.*

crustacean (krŭstā'shən) *n.* any animal of the class or subphylum Crustacea, including lobsters, crabs, shrimps, woodlice etc., named from their hard shells. *~a.* of or relating to crustaceans. **crustaceology** (-shiol'-) *n.* **crustaceologist** *n.* **crustaceous** *a.*

crutch (krŭch) *n.* **1** a staff, with a crosspiece to fit under the armpit, to support a lame or injured person. **2** a support. **3** the crotch of a person. **4** the corresponding part of a garment. *~v.t.* to support on or as if on crutches. *~v.i.* to go on crutches.

crux (krŭks) *n.* (*pl.* **cruxes, cruces** (kroo'sēz)) **1** the real essential. **2** anything exceedingly puzzling.

cruzeiro (kroozeə'rō) *n.* (*pl.* **cruzeiros**) a coin and monetary unit of Brazil, equal to 100 centavos.

cry (krī) *v.i.* (*3rd pers. sing. pres.* **cries,** *pres.p.* **crying,** *past, p.p.* **cried**) **1** to weep. **2** to lament loudly. **3** to make a loud exclamation, esp. because of pain or grief. **4** to call loudly, vehemently or importunately, e.g. for help. **5** to exclaim. **6** (of animals and birds) to call, to make their natural sound. **7** to make a proclamation. *~v.t.* **1** to utter loudly. **2** to proclaim, to declare publicly. **3** to announce for sale. **4** to shed (tears). *~n.* (*pl.* **cries**) **1** a loud utterance, usu. inarticulate, expressive of intense joy, pain, suffering, astonishment or other emotion. **2** an importunate call or prayer. **3** proclamation, public notification. **4** weeping. **5** lamentation. **6** inarticulate noise. **7** (of hounds) yelping. **a far cry 1** a long way off (from). **2** something very different (from). **for crying out loud** (*coll.*) used to express impatience or annoyance. **in full cry** in hot pursuit. **to cry down 1** to decry, to depreciate. **2** to shout down. **to cry for the moon** to ask for something one cannot have. **to cry halves** to demand a share of something. **to cry off** to withdraw from something promised or agreed on. **to cry one's eyes out** to weep abundantly and bitterly. **to cry one's heart out** to cry one's eyes out. **to cry out** to shout, to clamour. **to cry out for** to require or demand. **to cry over spilt milk** to waste time regretting something that cannot be undone. **to cry stinking fish** to decry or condemn, esp. one's own wares. **to cry up** to extol, to praise highly. **cry-baby** n. (pl. **cry-babies**) (coll.) a child or person easily provoked to tears. **cryer** CRIER. **cry from the heart** n. an ardent and impassioned appeal. **crying** a. **1** that cries. **2** calling for notice or vengeance, flagrant.

cryo- (krī´ō) comb. form very cold.

cryobiology (krīobīol´əji) n. the study of the effects of cold on organisms. **cryobiological** (-loj´-) a. **cryobiologist** n.

cryogen (krī´əjen) n. (Physics) a freezing-mixture, a mixture of substances used to freeze liquids. **cryogenics** (-jen´-) n. the branch of physics which studies very low temperatures and the phenomena associated with them. **cryogenic** a.

cryolite (krī´əlīt) n. a brittle fluoride of sodium and aluminium from Greenland.

cryonics (krīon´iks) n. the practice of preserving a dead body by deep-freezing it, in order to keep it until the discovery of a cure for the condition which caused the death. **cryonic** a.

cryoprotectant (krīōprətek´tənt) n. (Biol.) a substance that stops tissues freezing or prevents damage by freezing.

cryopump (krī´əpŭmp) n. a vacuum pump which uses liquefied gases.

cryostat (krī´əstat) n. an apparatus for maintaining, or for keeping something at, a low temperature.

cryosurgery (krīōsœ´jəri) n. surgery involving the application of very low temperatures to specific tissues in order to cut or remove them.

crypt (kript) n. **1** a vault, esp. one beneath a church, used for religious services or for burial. **2** (Anat.) a small pit, cavity or depression, or a pitlike gland.

cryptanalysis (kriptənal´əsis) n. the art of deciphering codes and coded texts. **cryptanalyst** (-an´-) n. **cryptanalytic** (-lit´-), **cryptanalytical** a.

cryptic (krip´tik) a. **1** hidden, secret, occult. **2** hard to understand. **3 a** (of a crossword clue) so written that the solution is far from obvious. **b** (of a crossword) having cryptic clues. **4** (Zool.) (of animal coloration) serving as camouflage. **cryptically** adv.

crypto (krip´tō) n. (pl. **cryptos**) a secret member or supporter of some organization etc.

crypto- (krip´tō), **crypt-** comb. form **1** secret. **2** inconspicuous. **3** not apparent or prominent.

cryptocrystalline (kriptōkris´təlīn) a. (Mineral.) having a crystalline structure which is visible only under the microscope.

cryptogam (krip´tōgam) n. (Bot.) a plant without

pistils and stamens; any seedless plant such as a fern, lichen, moss, seaweed or fungus. **cryptogamic** (-gam´-), **cryptogamous** (-tog´ə-) a.

cryptogram (krip´təgram) n. a text in code. **cryptograph** (-grahf) n. a system of writing in cipher. **cryptographer** (-tog´-), **cryptographist** n. **cryptographic** (-graf´-) a. **cryptographically** adv. **cryptography** (-tog´-) n.

cryptology (kriptol´əji) n. **1** the study of codes. **2** the making and breaking of codes, cryptography and cryptanalysis together. **cryptological** (-loj´-) a. **cryptologically** adv. **cryptologist** (-tol´-) n.

cryptomeria (kriptəmiə´riə) n. a coniferous evergreen tree, Cryptomeria japonica, from the Far East, with many cultivated varieties.

crystal (kris´təl) n. **1** (Mineral.) **a** a clear transparent mineral, transparent quartz, also called rock crystal. **b** a piece of this. **2** (Chem.) an aggregation of atoms or molecules arranged in a definite pattern which often assumes the form of a regular solid terminated by a certain number of smooth plane surfaces. **3** a very clear kind of glass. **4** articles made of crystal. **5** a crystalline component in various electronic devices, used as an oscillator etc. ~a. **1** clear, transparent, as bright as crystal. **2** made of crystal. **crystal ball** n. a ball made of glass, used in crystal-gazing. **crystal class** n. in crystallography, any of the 32 different forms of crystal, classified according to their rotational symmetry about axes passing through a point. **crystal clear** a. absolutely clear. **crystal-gazing** n. looking into a crystal ball in order to foresee the future. **crystal lattice** n. in crystallography, the network of points, forming a regular repeating pattern, on which the atoms, ions or molecules of a crystal are centred. **crystalline** (-līn) a. **1** consisting of crystal. **2** resembling crystal. **3** clear, pellucid. **4** (Chem., Mineral.) having the form and structure of a crystal. **crystalline lens** n. a lenticular, white, transparent solid body enclosed in a capsule behind the iris of the eye, the lens of the eye. **crystallinity** (-lin´-) n. **crystallite** (-līt) n. **1** any small developing crystal. **2** a small crystal or particle in a metal etc. **3** (Bot.) a crystal-like section of cellulose etc. **crystallize, crystallise** v.t. **1** to cause to form crystals. **2** to coat (fruit) with sugar crystals. **3** to cause (thoughts, plans etc.) to assume a definite form. ~v.i. **1** to assume a crystalline form. **2** to form crystals. **3** to become coated with sugar. **4** (of thoughts, plans etc.) to assume a definite form. **crystallizable** a. **crystallization** (-zā´shən) n. **crystal system** n. in crystallography, any of the seven different categories crystals can be grouped into on the basis of how they rotate on axes.

crystallographer (kristəlog´rəfə) n. a person who describes or investigates crystals and their formation. **crystallographic** (-graf´-) a. **crystallographically** adv. **crystallography** n. the science which deals with the forms of crystals.

crystalloid (kris'təloid) *a.* like a crystal in appearance or structure. ~*n.* a substance that in solution can pass through a semi-permeable membrane.

CS *abbr.* **1** chartered surveyor. **2** civil service. **3** Court of Session.

Cs *chem. symbol* caesium.

c/s *abbr.* cycles per second.

CS gas (sēes') *n.* an irritant gas, causing tears, painful breathing etc., used in riot control.

CSI *abbr.* Companion of (the Order of) the Star of India.

CSM *abbr.* Company Sergeant-Major.

CST *abbr.* Central Standard Time.

CT *abbr.* Central Time.

ct *abbr.* **1** carat. **2** cent.

CTC *abbr.* city technology college.

ctenoid (tē'noid, ten'-) *a.* **1** having projections like the teeth of a comb. **2** having ctenoid scales. ~*n.* a ctenoid fish. **ctenoid scales** *n.pl.* (*Zool.*) scales with projections like the teeth of a comb on the lower edge.

ctenophore (ten'əfaw, tē-) *n.* (*Zool.*) a member of the Ctenophora, coelenterates with fringed or comblike locomotive organs.

CT scanner (sētē') *n.* a machine which produces X-ray photographs of sections of the body with the assistance of a computer. **CT scan** *n.*

Cu *chem. symbol* copper.

cu. *abbr.* cubic.

cub (kŭb) *n.* **1** the young of certain animals, e.g. the lion, bear or fox. **2** an uncouth, mannerless youth. **3** (*also* **Cub Scout**) a member of the junior section of the Scout Association. **4** a cub reporter. **5** (*N Am.*) an apprentice. **6** a novice. ~*v.i.* (*pres.p.* **cubbing**, *past, p.p.* **cubbed**) **1** to give birth to cubs. **2** to hunt young foxes. ~*v.t.* to give birth to (cubs). **cubhood** *n.* **cub reporter** *n.* an inexperienced newspaper reporter.

cub. *abbr.* cubic.

Cuban (kū'bən) *a.* of or relating to Cuba, an island and republic in the Caribbean Sea, or its people. ~*n.* a native or inhabitant of Cuba. **Cuban heel** *n.* a straight-fronted moderately high heel on a boot or shoe.

cubby (kŭb'i) *n.* (*pl.* **cubbies**) a cubby hole. **cubby hole** *n.* **1** a narrow or confined space. **2** a cosy place.

cube (kūb) *n.* **1** a solid figure contained by six equal squares, a regular hexahedron. **2** a cube-shaped block or piece. **3** (*Math.*) the third power of a number (as 8 is the cube of 2). ~*v.t.* **1** to raise to the third power, to find the cube of (a number). **2** to find the cubic content of (a solid figure). **3** to cut into cubes. **cube root** *n.* the number which, multiplied by itself, and then by the product, produces the cube; thus 3 is the cube root of 27, which is the cube of 3 ($3 \times 3 \times 3 = 27$). **2** the rule for the extraction of the cube root. **cubic** *a.* **1** (*also* **cubical**) having the properties or form of a cube. **2** being or equalling a cube, the edge of which is a given unit. **3** (*Math.*) involving the cube of one or more numbers, but no higher power. **4** (*also* **cubical**) in crystallography, having three equal axes at right angles to each other. **cubical** *a.* **cubically** *adv.* **cubic content** *n.* volume in cubic metres. **cubiform** (-ifawm) *a.* cube-shaped. **cubism** *n.* an early 20th-cent. school of painting which depicted surfaces, figures, tints, light and shade etc. by a multiplicity of representations of cubes. **cubist** *n.*, *a.* **cuboid** *a.* resembling a cube. ~*n.* **1** (*Geom.*) a solid like a cube but with the sides not all equal, a rectangular parallelepiped. **2** (*Anat.*) the cuboid bone. **cuboidal** *a.* **cuboid bone** *n.* a bone on the outer side of the foot.

cubicle (kū'bikəl) *n.* **1** a portion of a bedroom partitioned off as a separate sleeping apartment. **2** a compartment.

cubit (kū'bit) *n.* an old measure of length, from the elbow to the tip of the middle finger, but varying in practice at different times from 18 to 22 in. (0.46 to 0.5 m). **cubital** *a.* (*Anat., Zool.*) of or relating to the forearm or corresponding part of the leg in animals.

cuckold (kŭk'əld) *n.* a man whose wife is sexually unfaithful. ~*v.t.* to make (a man) a cuckold by having a sexual relationship with his wife. **cuckoldry** *n.*

cuckoo (kuk'oo) *n.* (*pl.* **cuckoos**) **1** a migratory bird of the family Cuculidae, esp. *Cuculus canorus*, which visits Britain in the spring and summer and lays its eggs in the nests of other birds. **2** (*coll.*) a foolish person. ~*a.* (*sl.*) crazy. **cuckoo bee, cuckoo wasp** *n.* a bee or wasp, the queen of which lays its eggs in the nests of other species. **cuckoo clock** *n.* a clock which announces the hours by emitting a sound like the note of the cuckoo. **cuckoo flower** *n.* any of various plants, esp. lady's smock, *Cardamine pratensis*, or ragged robin, *Lychnis floscuculi*. **cuckoo in the nest** *n.* an unwanted and alien person, an intruder. **cuckoo pint** *n.* the wild arum, *Arum maculatum*, lords and ladies. **cuckoo spit** *n.* an exudation on plants from the larvae of the froghopper.

cucumber (kū'kŭmbə) *n.* **1** the elongated fruit *Cucumis sativus*, extensively used as a salad and pickle. **2** the plant itself.

cucurbit (kūkœ'bit) *n.* **1** a gourd. **2** a gourd-shaped vessel used in distillation. **cucurbitaceous** (-ā'shəs) *a.*

cud (kŭd) *n.* food deposited by ruminating animals in the first stomach, from which it is drawn and chewed over again. **to chew the cud 1** to ruminate. **2** to reflect.

cuddle (kŭd'əl) *v.i.* **1** to lie close or snug together. **2** to join in an embrace. ~*v.t.* to embrace, to hug, to fondle. ~*n.* a hug, an embrace. **cuddlesome** *a.* **cuddly** *a.* (*comp.* **cuddlier**, *superl.* **cuddliest**) **1** attractive to cuddle. **2** given to cuddling.

cudgel (kŭj'əl) *n.* a short club or thick stick, a bludgeon. ~*v.t.* (*pres.p.* **cudgelling**, (*N Am.*) **cudgeling**, *past, p.p.* **cudgelled**, (*N Am.*) **cudgeled**) to beat with a cudgel. **to cudgel one's brains** to try hard to recollect or find out something. **to take up (the) cudgels (for) 1** to fight (for). **2** to defend vigorously.

cudweed (kŭd′wēd) *n.* **1** any plant of the genus *Gnaphalium*, esp. *G. sylvaticum*, a plant formerly administered to cattle that had lost their cud. **2** any plant of the genus *Filago*, esp. *F. germanica*.

cue[1] (kū) *n.* **1** the last words of a speech, a signal to another actor that they should begin. **2** any similar signal, e.g. in a piece of music. **3** a hint, reminder. **4** a facility for cueing audio equipment. *~v.t.* (*3rd pers. sing. pres.* **cues**, *pres.p.* **cueing, cuing,** *past, p.p.* **cued**) **1** to give a cue to. **2** to make (audio equipment) precisely ready to play something. **on cue** at the right time. **to cue in 1** to give a cue to. **2** to inform. **to take one's cue from** to follow the example of or take advice from. **cue-bid** *n.* in bridge, a bid designed to reveal the presence of a particular card in the bidder's hand.

cue[2] (kū) *n.* a long straight rod used by players of snooker, pool etc. *~v.t., v.i.* (*3rd pers. sing. pres.* **cues**, *pres.p.* **cuing, cueing,** *past, p.p.* **cued**) to strike (a ball) with a cue. **cue ball** *n.* the ball which is struck with a cue. **cueist** *n.*

cuff[1] (kŭf) *n.* **1** the fold or band at the end of a sleeve. **2** a linen band worn round the wrist. **3** (*pl., coll.*) handcuffs. **4** (*N Am.*) a trouser turn-up. **off the cuff** extempore, without preparation. **cuffed** *a.* **cuff link** *n.* a usu. ornamental device consisting of a button-like disc attached to a short bar with a pivoting endpiece or a pair of buttons linked by a short chain, used to fasten a shirt cuff.

cuff[2] (kŭf) *v.t.* to strike with the open hand. *~n.* a blow of this kind.

Cufic KUFIC.

cuirass (kwiras′, kū-) *n.* **1** (*Hist.*) armour for the body, consisting of a breastplate and a backplate strapped or buckled together. **2** an apparatus for artificial respiration. **cuirassier** (-siə′) *n.* a soldier wearing a cuirass.

cuisine (kwizēn′) *n.* **1** a style of cooking. **2** cookery.

cul-de-sac (kŭl′disak) *n.* (*pl.* **culs-de-sac** (kŭl-), **cul-de-sacs**) **1** a street or lane open only at one end. **2** a route or course of activity that leads nowhere. **3** (*Anat.*) a vessel, tube or gut open only at one end.

-cule (kūl) *comb. form* used to form nouns, esp. indicating smallness, as in *molecule*.

culinary (kŭl′inəri) *a.* relating to the kitchen or cooking. **culinarily** *adv.*

cull (kŭl) *v.t.* **1** to select, to choose as the best. **2** to pick, gather (flowers, fruit etc.). **3** to select (an animal) from a group, esp. as weak or superfluous, for killing. **4** to reduce the size of (a group) in this way. *~n.* an act of culling. **culler** *n.* **culling** *n.*

cullet (kŭl′it) *n.* broken glass for recycling.

culm[1] (kŭlm) *n.* (*Bot.*) a stem, esp. of grass or sedge.

culm[2] (kŭlm) *n.* **1** anthracite coal, esp. if in small pieces. **2** coaldust. **3** (*Geol.*) shales, sandstones, grit etc. of the Carboniferous period.

culminate (kŭl′mināt) *v.i.* **1** to reach the highest point. **2** (*Astron.*) to come to the meridian. **culminant** *a.* **1** at the highest point. **2** (*Astron.*) on the meridian. **culmination** (-ā′shən) *n.*

culottes (kūlots′) *n.pl.* women's flared trousers cut to resemble a skirt.

culpable (kŭl′pəbəl) *a.* **1** blamable, blameworthy. **2** guilty. **culpability** (-bil′-) *n.* **culpableness** *n.* **culpably** *adv.*

culprit (kŭl′prit) *n.* **1** a person who is at fault. **2** a person who is arraigned before a judge on a charge.

cult (kŭlt) *n.* **1** a system of religious belief. **2** the rites and ceremonies of any system of belief. **3** an intense devotion to a person, idea etc., usu. by a specific section of society. **4** the object of such devotion. **5** an intense fad or fashion. *~a.* **1** very fashionable (*a cult film*). **2** of or relating to a pagan cult. **cultic, cultish** *a.* **cultism** *n.* **cultist** *n.*

cultivar (kŭl′tivah) *n.* (*Bot.*) a variety of a naturally-occurring species, produced and maintained by cultivation.

cultivate (kŭl′tivāt) *v.t.* **1** to till, to prepare for crops. **2** to raise or develop by tilling. **3** to cherish, to foster, to seek the friendship of. **4** to improve by labour or study, to civilize. **cultivable** *a.* **cultivatable** *a.* **cultivated** *a.* cultured, educated. **cultivation** (-ā′shən) *n.* **cultivator** *n.* **1** an implement to break up the soil and remove weeds. **2** a person who cultivates.

culture (kŭl′chə) *n.* **1** a state of intellectual and artistic development. **2** an ethos reflecting this (*enterprise culture*). **3** the experimental growing of bacteria or other micro-organisms in a laboratory. **4** the group of micro-organisms so grown. **5** intellectual or moral discipline and training. **6** the act of tilling. **7** husbandry, farming. **8** breeding and rearing. *~v.t.* **1** to grow (micro-organisms) in a laboratory. **2** to cultivate. **cultural** *a.* **culture-bound** *a.* limited in outlook by virtue of belonging to a particular culture. **cultured** *a.* **1** having good education, style, manners, refinement etc. **2** grown artificially, as pearls or micro-organisms. **cultured pearl** *n.* a pearl formed by an oyster after it has been artificially stimulated. **culture shock** *n.* feelings of disorientation caused by the transition from one culture or environment to another. **culture vulture** *n.* (*often derog.*) a person eager to acquire culture and be involved with cultural activities. **culturist** *n.*

culvert (kŭl′vət) *n.* **1** a drain or covered channel for water beneath a road, railway etc. **2** an underground channel for electric wires or cables.

cum (kŭm) *prep.* combined with, together with (*bathroom cum cloakroom*).

cumber (kŭm´bə) *v.t.* (*poet.*) to hamper, to clog, to hinder, to impede. ~*n.* a hindrance, an impediment. **cumbersome** *a.* **1** unwieldy, unmanageable. **2** burdensome, troublesome. **cumbersomely** *adv.* **cumbersomeness** *n.* **cumbrous** *a.* **cumbrously** *adv.* **cumbrousness** *n.*

cumbia (kŭm´biə) *n.* **1** a type of dance music similar to salsa, orig. from Colombia. **2** a dance using this music.

Cumbrian (kŭm´briən) *a.* belonging to the county of Cumbria in NW England, to the former county Cumberland, or the ancient British kingdom of Cumbria. ~*n.* a native or inhabitant of (either) Cumbria or Cumberland.

cumin (kŭm´in), **cummin** *n.* **1** an umbelliferous plant of the parsley family, *Cuminum cyminum*, with aromatic and carminative seeds. **2** these seeds used as flavouring for curries etc.

cummerbund (kŭm´əbŭnd), **kummerbund** *n.* a waistband or sash, worn esp. by men with evening dress.

cumquat KUMQUAT.

cumulate[1] (kū´mūlāt) *v.t.*, *v.i.* to accumulate. **cumulation** (-lā´shən) *n.*

cumulate[2] (kū´mūlət) *a.* heaped up, accumulated. **cumulative** *a.* **1** increasing by additions. **2** tending to accumulate. **cumulative error** *n.* in statistics, an error which increases in magnitude with the size of the sample in which it is revealed. **cumulatively** *adv.* **cumulativeness** *n.* **cumulative preference shares** *n.pl.* shares on which arrears of interest are paid before ordinary shareholders are paid any on the current year. **cumulative voting** *n.* a method of voting by which the votes of the elector can be all given to a single candidate instead of being given singly to several candidates.

cumulo- (kū´mūlō) *comb. form* (of cloud) cumulus.

cumulonimbus (kūmūlōnim´bəs) *n.* (*pl.* **cumulonimbuses, cumulonimbi** (-bī)) a very thick, dark cumulus cloud, usu. a sign of thunder or hail.

cumulus (kū´mūləs) *n.* (*pl.* **cumuli** (-lī)) a round billowing mass of cloud, with a flattish base. **cumulous** *a.*

cuneate (kū´niət) *a.* wedge-shaped. **cuneiform** (-nifawm) *a.* **1** wedge-shaped. **2** of or relating to cuneiform writing. ~*n.* cuneiform writing. **cuneiform writing** *n.* writing in characters resembling wedges or arrowheads, used in Babylonian, Hittite, Ninevite and Persian inscriptions.

cunnilingus (kŭniling´gəs), **cunnilinctus** (-lingk´təs) *n.* stimulation of the female genitals by the lips and tongue.

cunning (kŭn´ing) *a.* (*comp.* **cunninger**, *superl.* **cunningest**) **1** knowing, skilful, ingenious, artful, crafty. **2** (*N Am.*) amusingly interesting, quaint. ~*n.* **1** skill, knowledge acquired by experience. **2** artfulness, subtlety. **cunningly** *adv.* **cunningness** *n.*

cunt (kŭnt) *n.* (*taboo sl.*) **1** the female genitalia.

2 (*offensive*) an unpleasant or disliked person. **3** a woman regarded as a sexual object.

cup (kŭp) *n.* **1** a vessel to drink from, usu. small and with one handle. **2** the liquor contained in it. **3** an ornamental drinking vessel, usu. of gold or silver, awarded as a prize or trophy. **4** anything shaped like a cup, such as an acorn, the socket for a bone. **5** either one of two cup-shaped supports for the breasts in a brassière. **6** in golf, the hole or its metal lining. **7** one's lot in life (*my cup overflows*). **8** the chalice used in the Holy Communion. **9** an alcoholic mixed drink, usu. with wine or cider as a basc. **10** in cooking, a measure of capacity equal to 8 fl. oz. (0.23 l). ~*v.t.* (*pres.p.* **cupping**, *past*, *p.p.* **cupped**) **1** (of hands) to make into a cup shape. **2** to hold as if in a cup. ~*v.i.* (*Bot.*) to form a cup or cups. **in one's cups** intoxicated. **one's cup of tea** one's preferred occupation, company etc. **cupbearer** *n.* a person who serves wine, esp. in royal or noble households. **cupcake** *n.* a small sponge cake baked in a paper or foil case. **cup final**, **Cup Final** *n.* the final match of a competition to decide who wins a cup. **cupful** *n.* (*pl.* **cupfuls**). **cup lichen, cup moss** *n.* a lichen, *Cladonia pyxidata*, with cup-shaped processes rising from the thallus. **cup-tie** *n.* a match in a knockout competition for a cup.

cupboard (kŭb´əd) *n.* **1** an enclosed case or recess with shelves to receive plates, dishes, food etc. **2** a wardrobe. **cupboard love** *n.* greedy or self-interested love.

Cupid (kū´pid) *n.* **1** the Roman god of love. **2** a picture or statue of Cupid, usu. as a naked boy with wings, carrying a bow and arrows. **Cupid's bow** *n.* a shape of the upper lip thought to resemble the bow carried by Cupid.

cupidity (kūpid´iti) *n.* an inordinate desire to possess, covetousness, avarice.

cupola (kū´pələ) *n.* **1** a little dome. **2** a lantern etc. on the summit of a dome. **3** a spherical covering to a building, or any part of it. **4** a cupola furnace. **5** a revolving dome or turret on a warship. **cupolaed** (-ləd) *a.* **cupola furnace** *n.* a furnace for melting metals.

cuppa (kŭp´ə), **cupper** *n.* (*coll.*) a cup of tea.

cupreous (kū´priəs) *a.* of, like or composed of copper. **cuprammonium** (kūprəmō´niəm) *n.* (*Chem.*) a solution of copper oxide and ammonia, able to dissolve cellulose. **cupric** *a.* (*Chem.*) having divalent copper in its composition. **cupriferous** (-prif´-) *a.* copper-bearing. **cuprite** (-prīt) *n.* red copper oxide, a mineral with cubic crystal structure. **cupro-nickel** (-prō-) *n.* an alloy of copper and nickel. **cuprous** *a.* (*Chem.*) having monovalent copper in its composition.

cupule (kū´pūl) *n.* **1** (*Bot.*) an inflorescence consisting of a cup, as in the oak or hazel. **2** (*Zool.*) a cuplike organ.

cur (kœ) *n.* **1** a mongrel, an aggressive dog. **2** (*coll.*) a surly or despicable man. **currish** *a.* **currishly** *adv.* **currishness** *n.*

curable CURE.

curaçao (kūrəsah´ō, koo-), **curaçoa** (-sō´ə) n. (pl. **curaçaos, curaçoas**) a liqueur flavoured with bitter orange peel, sugar and cinnamon, orig. from Curaçao.

curacy CURATE[1].

curare (kūrah´ri) n. the dried extract of plants from the genera *Strychnos* and *Chondodendron*, used by the Indians of S America for poisoning arrows, and formerly employed in physiological investigations as a muscle relaxant.

curassow (kū´rəsō) n. any turkey-like game bird of the family Cracidae, found in S and Central America.

curate[1] (kū´rət) n. a member of the Church of England clergy who assists the incumbent of a parish. **curacy** n. (pl. **curacies**) the office of curate. **curate-in-charge** n. a priest-in-charge. **curate's egg** n. something of which some parts are good and some parts bad.

curate[2] CURATOR.

curative (kū´rətiv) a. tending to cure. ~n. any medicine etc. that tends to cure.

curator (kūrā´tə) n. a person who has charge of a library, museum or similar establishment. **curate**[2] (kūrāt´) v.t. to act as a curator of (a museum exhibit etc.). ~v.i. to hold the office of curator. **curation** n. **curatorial** (-taw´ri-) a. **curatorship** n.

curb (kœb) n. 1 a check, a restraint. 2 a chain or strap passing behind the jaw of a horse in a curb bit. 3 (*N Am.*) a kerb. 4 a kerbstone. ~v.t. 1 to put a curb on. 2 to restrain, to keep in check. **curb roof** n. a mansard roof.

curcuma (kœ´kūmə) n. 1 any plant of the genus *Curcuma*, tuberous plants of the ginger family. 2 turmeric, obtained from its root.

curd (kœd) n. 1 the coagulated part of milk, used to make cheese. 2 the fatty matter found in the flesh of boiled salmon. 3 a cauliflower head. **curd cheese** n. a soft mild white cheese made from skimmed milk curds, smoother in consistency than cottage cheese. **curd soap** n. a white soap made from tallow and soda. **curdy** a.

curdle (kœ´dəl) v.t. 1 to break into curds. 2 to coagulate, to congeal. ~v.i. to become curdled. **to make someone's blood curdle** to terrify, as with a ghost story or the like. **curdler** n.

cure (kūə) n. 1 the act of healing or curing disease. 2 a remedy, a restorative. 3 a course of remedial treatment. 4 the state of being cured or healed. 5 the care or spiritual charge of souls. 6 a parish or other sphere in which to pursue this. 7 the process of vulcanizing rubber or hardening plastic etc. ~v.t. 1 to heal, to restore to health, to make sound or whole. 2 to preserve or pickle. 3 to eliminate or correct (a habit or practice). 4 to vulcanize (rubber), to harden (plastic etc.). ~v.i. 1 to effect a cure. 2 to be cured or healed. **curable** a. **curability** (-bil´-) n. **cure-all** n. a panacea, a universal remedy. **curer** n.

curé (kū´rā) n. a parish priest in France etc., a French rector or vicar.

curette (kūret´) n. (*Med.*) a surgeon's instrument used for scraping a body cavity. ~v.t., v.i. to scrape or clean with a curette. **curettage** (-ret´ij, -ritahzh´) n.

curfew (kœ´fū) n. 1 a military or civil regulation to be off the streets or indoors between stated hours. 2 the time at which this comes into force. 3 a signal announcing this.

Curia (kū´riə), **curia** n. (pl. **Curiae** (-ē), **curiae**) 1 the papal court. 2 the temporal administration of the Vatican. **Curial** a.

curie (kū´ri) n. 1 the standard unit of radioactivity, 3.7×10^{10} disintegrations per second. 2 a quantity of radioactive material representing this.

curio (kū´riō) n. (pl. **curios**) a curiosity, esp. a curious piece of art; a bit of bric-a-brac.

curious (kū´riəs) a. 1 inquisitive, desirous to know. 2 extraordinary, surprising, odd. **curiosity** (-os´-) n. (pl. **curiosities**) 1 a desire to know, inquisitiveness. 2 a rarity, an object of curiosity. 3 strangeness, the quality of being curious. **curiously** adv. **curiousness** n.

curium (kū´riəm) n. (*Chem.*) an artificially-produced transuranic metallic element, at. no. 96, chem. symbol Cm.

curl (kœl) n. 1 a ringlet or twisted lock of hair. 2 anything coiled, twisted or spiral. 3 the state of being curled. 4 a contemptuous curving of the lip. 5 a disease in potatoes and other plants, of which curled shoots and leaves are a symptom. ~v.t. 1 to twine. 2 to twist into curls. 3 to curve up (the lip) in contempt. ~v.i. 1 to twist, to curve up. 2 to play at the game of curling. **to curl up** 1 to go into a curled position. 2 (*coll.*) to be embarrassed or disgusted. **curler** n. 1 a person who or thing which curls. 2 a device for curling the hair. 3 a person who plays at curling. **curling** (kœ´ling) n. 1 the act of twining, twisting etc. 2 a game played on ice in which participants slide smooth stones towards a mark. **curling stone** n. the stone used in the game of curling. **curling tongs, curling irons, curling pins** n.pl. a heated device for curling the hair. **curly** a. (*comp.* **curlier,** *superl.* **curliest**) 1 having curls. 2 wavy, undulated. 3 (*Bot.*) having curled or wavy margins. **curliness** n. **curly kale** n. a variety of kale with curly leaves.

curlew (kœ´lū) n. (pl. in general **curlew,** in particular **curlews**) a migratory wading bird of the genus *Numenius*, esp. the European *N. arquatus*.

curlicue (kœ´likū) n. a decorative curl or twist, esp. in handwriting.

curmudgeon (kəmŭj´ən) n. a miserly or churlish person. **curmudgeonly** a.

currant (kŭr´ənt) n. 1 the dried fruit of a dwarf seedless grape orig. from the E Mediterranean. 2 the fruit of shrubs of the genus *Ribes*, bearing black, red or white berries. 3 such a shrub.

currency (kŭr´ənsi) *n.* (*pl.* **currencies**) **1** the circulating monetary medium of a country, whether in coin or paper. **2** the state of being current. **3** the period during which anything is current. **4** prevalence, general acceptance, e.g. of an idea or theory.

current (kŭr´ənt) *a.* **1** belonging to the present week, month, year. **2** passing at the present time. **3** in general circulation among the public, generally received or acknowledged. ~*n.* **1** a flowing stream, a body of water, air etc., moving in a certain direction. **2** a general drift or tendency. **3** electrical activity regarded as the rate of flow of electrical charge along a conductor. **to pass current** to be generally accepted as true, genuine etc. **current account** *n.* a bank account which usu. does not pay interest and on which one may draw cheques. **currently** *adv.* **1** at present. **2** generally.

curriculum (kərik´ūləm) *n.* (*pl.* **curricula** (-lə)) **1** a fixed course of study at a school etc. **2** a programme of activities. **curricular** *a.* **curriculum vitae** (vē´tī) *n.* (*pl.* **curricula vitae, curricula vitarum** (-tah´rəm)) a brief outline of one's education, previous employment, and other achievements.

currier (kŭr´iə) *n.* a person who curries, dresses and colours leather after it has been tanned.

currish CUR.

curry[1] (kŭr´i) *n.* (*pl.* **curries**) a highly-spiced orig. Indian dish of stewed meat, fish etc. in a sauce, usu. served with rice. ~*v.t.* (*3rd pers. sing. pres.* **curries**, *pres.p.* **currying**, *past, p.p.* **curried**) to flavour with curry. **curry paste, curry powder** *n.* a mixture of ginger, turmeric and other strong spices used in curries etc.

curry[2] (kŭr´i) *v.t.* (*3rd pers. sing. pres.* **curries**, *pres.p.* **currying**, *past, p.p.* **curried**) **1** to groom (a horse) with a curry-comb. **2** to dress (leather). **3** to thrash. **to curry favour** to ingratiate oneself with superiors by officiousness or flattery. **currycomb** *n.* a comb used for grooming horses.

curse (kœs) *v.t.* **1** to invoke harm or evil upon. **2** to blast, to injure, vex or torment (with). **3** to excommunicate. ~*v.i.* to swear, to utter imprecations. ~*n.* **1** a solemn invocation of divine vengeance (upon). **2** a profane oath. **3** an invocation of evil (upon). **4** the evil imprecated. **5** anything which causes evil, trouble or great vexation. **6** a sentence of excommunication. **the curse** (*coll.*) menstruation. **cursed** (-sid) *†***curst** *a.* **1** troubled, burdened (with or by). **2** execrable, accursed, deserving of a curse. **3** blasted by a curse, execrated. **4** vexatious, troublesome. **cursedly** *adv.* **cursedness** *n.* **curser** *n.*

cursive (kœ´siv) *a.* handwritten with joined characters, esp. with looped characters. ~*n.* cursive writing. **cursively** *adv.*

cursor (kœ´sə) *n.* **1** (*Comput.*) on a VDU screen, a movable point of light or other indicator showing the position of the next action, e.g. the beginning of an addition or correction. **2** (*Math.*

etc.) the moving part of a measuring instrument, e.g. the slide with the reference line in a slide rule.

cursory (kœ´səri) *a.* hasty, superficial, careless. **cursorily** *adv.* **cursoriness** *n.*

curt (kœt) *a.* short, concise, abrupt, esp. rudely terse. **curtly** *adv.* **curtness** *n.*

curtail (kœtāl´) *v.t.* to shorten, lessen or reduce. **curtailer** *n.* **curtailment** *n.*

curtain (kœ´tən) *n.* **1** a length of material hanging beside a window or door, or round a bed, which can be drawn across. **2** a partition, screen, cover or protection. **3** the cloth partition in a theatre, cinema etc. separating the stage or screen from the audience. **4** the end of a scene or play, marked by the closing of the curtains. **5** (*pl., sl.*) death, the end. ~*v.t.* **1** to enclose with or as with curtains. **2** to furnish or decorate with curtains. **curtain call** *n.* a round of applause for an actor which calls for a reappearance before the curtain falls. **curtain-raiser** *n.* **1** in a theatre, a short piece given before the main play. **2** any short preliminary event. **curtain wall** *n.* (*Archit.*) **1** a wall that is not load-bearing. **2** in a castle, a wall between two bastions.

☒ **curtesy** common misspelling of COURTESY.

curtsy (kœt´si), **curtsey** *n.* (*pl.* **curtsies, curtseys**) an act of respect or salutation, performed by women by slightly bending the body and knees at the same time. ~*v.i.* (*3rd pers. sing. pres.* **curtsies, curtseys**, *pres.p.* **curtsying, curtseying**, *past, p.p.* **curtsied, curtseyed**) to make a curtsy.

curvaceous (kœvā´shəs) *a.* (*coll.*) (of a woman's body) generously curved.

curvature (kœ´vəchə) *n.* **1** deflection from a straight line. **2** a curved form. **3** (*Geom.*) the continual bending of a line from a rectilinear direction.

curve (kœv) *n.* **1** a line of which no three consecutive points are in a straight line. **2** a continuously bending course. **3** something bent, a curved form. **4** in baseball, a ball pitched so as to deviate from a straight course. ~*v.t.* to cause to bend without angles. ~*v.i.* to form or be formed into a curve. **curved** *a.* **curvy** *a.* (*comp.* **curvier**, *superl.* **curviest**) (of a woman) having a shapely figure. **curviness** *n.*

curvet (kœvet´) *n.* a particular leap of a horse raising the forelegs at once, and, as the forelegs are falling, raising the hindlegs, so that all four are off the ground at once. ~*v.i.* (*pres.p.* **curvetting, curveting**, *past, p.p.* **curvetted, curveted**) **1** to make a curvet. **2** to frolic, to frisk.

curvi- (kœ´vi) *comb. form* curved.

curvilinear (kœvilin´iə) *a.* **1** bounded by curved lines. **2** consisting of curved lines. **curvilinearly** *adv.*

cuscus KHUS KHUS.

cusec (kū´sek) *n.* a unit of rate of flow of water, 1 cu. ft. (0.0283 m³) per second.

cush (kush) *n.* (*coll.*) in snooker, pool etc., the cushion.

cushion (kush´ən) *n.* **1** a kind of pillow or pad for sitting, kneeling or leaning on, stuffed with feathers, wool, hair or other soft material. **2** anything padded to protect against shock etc. **3** the lining at the side of a snooker or pool table which causes the balls to rebound. **4** (*Zool.*) a cushion-like organ, part or growth. **5** the body of air which supports a hovercraft etc. in motion. ~*v.t.* **1** to seat, support or protect with cushions. **2** to protect against shock. **3** to furnish with cushions. **4** to place or leave (a snooker ball) close up to the cushion. **5** to suppress or quietly ignore. **cushiony** *a.*

Cushitic (kushit´ik) *n.* a group of Hamitic languages of E Africa. ~*a.* belonging to this group.

cushy (kush´i) *a.* (*comp.* **cushier,** *superl.* **cushiest**) (*coll.*) **1** (of a job etc.) well paid and with little to do. **2** soft, easy, comfortable. **cushily** *adv.* **cushiness** *n.*

cusp (kŭsp) *n.* **1** a point, an apex, a summit. **2** (*Astrol.*) a division between signs of the zodiac. **3** (*Archit.*) a Gothic ornament consisting of a projecting point formed by the meeting of curves. **4** (*Geom.*) the point in a curve at which its two branches have a common tangent. **5** (*Bot.*) the pointed end of a leaf or other part. **6** (*Med.*) a projection on a molar tooth. **7** (*Astron.*) either of the two points of a crescent moon. **8** (*Anat.*) a flap or fold in a heart valve. **cuspate** *a.* **cusped** *a.* **cuspidal** *a.*

cuspidor (kŭs´pidaw) *n.* a spittoon.

cuss (kŭs) *n.* (*coll.*) **1** a curse. **2** (*derog.*) a person, a creature (*an awkward cuss*). ~*v.t.* to curse. **cussed** (-sid) *a.* stubborn, obstinate, perverse, resolute. **cussedly** *adv.* **cussedness** *n.* **cuss word** *n.* a swear word.

custard (kŭs´təd) *n.* **1** a composition of milk and eggs, sweetened and flavoured. **2** a sweet sauce made of milk, sugar and custard powder. **custard apple** *n.* a W Indian fruit, *Annona reticulata,* with a soft pulp. **custard pie** *n.* **1** an open pie filled with egg custard. **2** an open pie filled with foam etc., thrown in slapstick comedy. **custard powder** *n.* a composition of cornflour, colouring and flavouring, used in the making of custard.

custody (kŭs´tədi) *n.* (*pl.* **custodies**) **1** guardianship, security. **2** imprisonment, confinement. **custodial** (-ō´-) *a., n.* **custodian** (-ō´-) *n.* a person who has the custody or guardianship of anything. **custodianship** *n.*

custom (kŭs´təm) *n.* **1** a habitual use or practice, established usage, familiarity. **2** buying of goods, business, frequenting a shop to purchase. **3** (*Law*) long established practice constituting common law. ~*a.* (*esp. N Am.*) made to a customer's specifications. **custom duties, customs duties** *n.pl.* duties imposed on certain goods imported or exported. **customed** *a.* usual, accustomed. **custom house, customs house** *n.* the office where vessels enter and clear, and where custom duties are paid. **customize, customise** *v.t.*

to make to a customer's specifications. **custom-made, custom-built** *a.* made to measure, custom. **customs** *n.* **1** (*as pl.*) custom duties. **2** (*as sing.* or *pl.*) the department of government administering these. **3** (*as sing.* or *pl.*) the place at a border, port, airport etc. dealing with dutiable or illegal imports or exports.

customary (kŭs´təməri) *a.* **1** habitual, usual. **2** (*Law*) holding or held by custom, liable under custom. ~*n.* (*pl.* **customaries**) a written or printed record of customs. **customarily** *adv.* **customariness** *n.*

customer (kŭs´təmə) *n.* **1** a purchaser. **2** a person who purchases regularly from a particular shop or business. **3** (*coll.*) a person one has to do with, a fellow (*He's a strange customer*).

cut¹ (kŭt) *v.t.* (*pres.p.* **cutting,** *past, p.p.* **cut**) **1** to penetrate or wound with a sharp instrument. **2** to divide or separate with a sharp-edged instrument. **3** to sever, to detach, to hew, to fell, to mow or reap. **4** to carve, to trim or clip. **5** to form by cutting. **6** to reduce by cutting. **7** to mutilate or shorten (a play, article or book). **8** to edit (a film). **9** to intersect, to cross. **10** to divide into two (as a pack of cards). **11** to hit (a cricket ball) with a downward stroke and make it glance to one side. **12** to wound deeply. **13 a** to leave, to give up. **b** (*esp. N Am.*) not to attend, to play truant from. **14 a** to ignore deliberately a person that one might be expected to greet. **b** to renounce the acquaintance of. **15** to reduce as low as possible. **16** (*sl.*) to dilute (a drink or drug). **17** to record a song etc. on (a master tape, disc etc.). ~*v.i.* **1** to make a wound or incision with or as with a sharp-edged instrument. **2** to have a good edge. **3** (of teeth) to come through the gums. **4** to divide a pack of cards into two, esp. to establish the dealer. **5** to intersect. **6** to be able to be cut or divided (*It will cut into three*). **7** to change abruptly from one scene to another in a film. **8** (*sl.*) to move away quickly, to run (*Cut away, Flashman!*). **9** (*Med.*) to perform an operation by cutting, esp. in lithotomy. ~*int.* ordering film or television cameras to stop. **to be (not) cut out** to be (not) naturally fitted (for). **to cut across 1** to pass by a shorter course so as to cut off an angle. **2** to go contrary to (usual procedure etc.). **to cut a figure** (usu. qualified by an adjective) to look, appear or perform in a certain style (*He cuts a bold figure*). **to cut and run** to depart rapidly. **to cut back 1** to prune. **2** to reduce. **to cut both ways** to have both good and bad consequences. **to cut corners 1** to take short cuts. **2** to sacrifice quality in favour of speed. **to cut dead** to refuse to acknowledge the presence of. **to cut down 1** to fell. **2** to compress, to reduce. **to cut in 1** to interrupt, to intrude. **2** (*coll.*) to allow to have a share in. **3** to drive in front of another person's car so as to affect their driving. **4** (of an electrical device) to start working. **to cut into 1** to make a cut in (something). **2** to reduce or interfere with (*It cuts into her schedule*). **to cut it out**

to desist from doing something annoying. **to cut off 1** to remove by cutting, to eradicate. **2** to intercept. **3** to prevent from access. **4** to sever. **5** to discontinue. **6** to bring to an untimely end, to kill. **7** to disinherit. **to cut one's coat according to one's cloth** to adapt to one's personal (esp. financial) circumstances. **to cut one's eye-teeth** to become worldly-wise. **to cut one's teeth** to have the teeth come through the gums. **to cut one's teeth on** to gain experience through, to learn one's trade or profession through. **to cut out 1** to shape by cutting. **2** to remove or separate by cutting. **3** to excel, to outdo. **4** to supplant. **5** to cease doing, taking or indulging in something unpleasant or harmful. **6** to cease operating suddenly and unexpectedly or by the automatic intervention of a cut-out device. **to cut short 1** to hinder by interruption. **2** to abridge. **to cut someone down to size** to cause someone to feel less important or be less conceited by exposing their limitations. **to cut up 1** to cut in pieces. **2** to distress deeply. **3** in a vehicle, to drive across the line of travel of (another driver) unexpectedly and dangerously. **to cut up rough** (*sl.*) to become quarrelsome or savage. **cut-and-come-again** *n.* **1** an abundant supply. **2** an opportunity to help oneself (to food etc.) and return again at will. **cut and dried** *a.* **1** pre-arranged, already decided, inflexible. **2** (of opinions) unoriginal, trite. **cut-and-paste** *n.* **1** a technique of assembling a page layout, montage etc. by cutting material out and pasting it in place. **2** in word processing or desktop publishing, a technique that mimics this by which text and graphics can be moved around in a document or between windows. **cutaway** *a.* **1** denoting a drawing of an engine etc. in which part of the casing is omitted to show the workings. **2** (of a coat) having the front cut away in a diagonal direction from waist to knee. **cutback** *n.* **1** a reduction esp. in expenditure. **2** an instance of cutting back. **cut-down** *a.* reduced, shortened. **cut glass** *n.* glass in which a pattern is formed by cutting or grinding. **cut-in** *n.* something that is inserted within another thing, esp. a film or video sequence. **cut-line** *n.* **1** a caption. **2** the line on the wall of a squash court above which a serve must strike. **cut-off** *n.* **1** the point at which something ceases to apply, operate etc. **2** a device for cutting off a supply of electricity, water, steam etc. **3** (*N Am.*) a short cut. **4** (*pl.*) shorts with unsewn or unbound leg bottoms. **cut-out** *n.* **1** a shape etc. cut from cardboard, fabric, paper etc. **2** a device for automatic disconnection of power, release of exhaust gases etc. **3** a switch for shutting off a light or a group of lights from an electric circuit. **4** a device in a vehicle which automatically disconnects the battery from the dynamo. **cut-out box** *n.* (*N Am.*) a fuse box. **cut-price** *a.* at a reduced price. **cut-rate** *a.* CUT-PRICE (under CUT¹). **cutter** *n.* **1** a person who or something that cuts. **2** a person who cuts out men's clothes to measure. **3** (*N Am.*) a light

sledge. **4** (*Naut.*) **a** a small boat for official duties. **b** a one-masted vessel with fore-and-aft sails. **5** in cricket, a ball delivered with a sharp turn. **cut-throat** *n.* **1** a murderer, an assassin. **2** a cut-throat razor. ~*a.* **1** (of competition etc.) fierce, merciless. **2** murderous, barbarous. **cut-throat razor** *n.* a folding razor with a long single-edged blade. **cutting** *a.* **1** dividing by a sharp-edged instrument. **2** sharp-edged. **3** wounding the feelings deeply. **4** sarcastic, biting. ~*n.* **1** a piece cut off or out (of a newspaper etc.). **2** an excavation for a road, railway or canal. **3** in horticulture, a piece cut from a plant for propagation, a slip. **cutting edge** *n.* **1** the edge of a blade etc. **2** the forefront of a movement, technological development etc. **cutting-edge** *a.* leading, pioneering, innovative. **cuttingly** *adv.* **cutwater** *n.* (*Naut.*) the fore part of a ship's prow which cuts the water. **cutworm** *n.* a caterpillar which cuts off plants near the roots, esp. (*N Am.*) the larva of the genus of moths *Agrotis*.

cut² (kŭ) *n.* **1** the action of cutting. **2** a stroke or blow with a sharp-edged instrument. **3** an opening, gash or wound made by cutting. **4** anything done or said that hurts the feelings. **5** the omission of a part of a play. **6** a slit, a channel, a groove, a trench. **7** a part cut off. **8** the finished version of a film, edited in a particular way. **9** a stroke with a whip. **10** a particular stroke in various ball games. **11** the act of dividing a pack of cards. **12** the shape in which a thing is cut, style. **13** the act of ignoring a former acquaintance. **14 a** an engraved wood block. **b** an impression from such a block. ~*a.* **1** subjected to the act or process of cutting. **2** severed. **3** shaped by cutting. **4** castrated. **a cut above** (*fig.*) superior to. **cut and thrust** *n.* **1** in a debate etc., a lively exchange of opinions. **2** in a sword fight, cutting and thrusting. **3** hand-to-hand struggle.

cutaneous (kūtā´niəs) *a.* belonging to or affecting the skin.

cute (kūt) *a.* **1** delightful, attractive, amusing, pretty. **2** cunning, sharp, clever. **cutely** *adv.* **cuteness** *n.* **cutesy** *a.* (*comp.* **cutesier**, *superl.* **cutesiest**) (*coll.*) affectedly or excessively dainty, quaint etc. **cutie** (-ti) *n.* (*sl.*) a bright, attractive person, esp. a girl or woman.

cuticle (kū´tikəl) *n.* **1** the dead skin at the edge of fingernails and toenails. **2** the epidermis. **3** (*Zool.*) the outer layer of the protective covering of many invertebrates. **4** (*Bot.*) the thin external covering of the bark of a plant. **cuticular** (-tik´ū-) *a.*

cutis (kū´tis) *n.* (*Anat.*, *Zool.*) the true skin beneath the epidermis.

cutlass (kŭt´ləs) *n.* (*Hist.*) a broad curved sword, esp. that formerly used by sailors.

cutler (kŭt´lə) *n.* a person who makes or deals in cutting instruments. **cutlery** *n.* knives, spoons and forks used for eating.

cutlet (kŭt´lit) *n.* **1** a small slice of meat, usu. from the loin or neck, for cooking. **2** minced meat or meat-substitute shaped to look like a cutlet.

cutter, cutting CUT[1].

cuttle (kŭt'əl) *n.* a cuttlefish. **cuttle-bone** *n.* the internal skeleton of the cuttlefish, used as a polishing agent and as a dietary supplement for cage birds. **cuttlefish** *n.* **1** a 10-armed cephalopod, *Sepia officinalis*. **2** any of various other members of the genera *Sepia* and *Sepiola*.

CV *abbr.* curriculum vitae.

CVO *abbr.* Commander of the Royal Victorian Order.

CVS *abbr.* (*Med.*) chorionic villus sampling, a test to detect chromosome abnormalities in unborn babies.

cwm (kum) *n.* **1** a valley in Wales. **2** (*Geol.*) a cirque, a corrie.

c.w.o. *abbr.* cash with order.

cwt. *abbr.* hundredweight.

-cy (si) *suf.* forming nouns of quality from adjectives, and nouns of office (cp. -SHIP) from nouns, as in *idiocy, lunacy, tenancy, residency*.

cyan (sī'an) *n.* a bluish-green colour. ~*a.* of this colour.

cyanamide (sīan´əmīd) *n.* **1** (*Chem.*) a colourless crystalline weak acid, an amide of cyanogen. **2** any salt of this.

cyanic (sīan´ik) *a.* **1** derived from cyanogen. **2** blue. **cyanic acid** *n.* (*Chem.*) an unstable acidic compound of cyanogen and hydrogen.

cyanide (sī´ənīd) *n.* (*Chem.*) any (very poisonous) compound of cyanogen with a metallic element.

cyanobacterium (sīənōbaktiə´riəm) *n.* (*pl.* **cyanobacteria** (-riə)) (*Biol.*) any prokaryotic organism of the division *Cyanobacteria*, containing a blue photosynthetic pigment, blue-green alga.

cyanocobalamin (sīənōkəbal´əmin) *n.* a vitamin of the B complex occurring in the liver, the lack of which can lead to pernicious anaemia, Vitamin B_{12}.

cyanogen (sīan´əjən) *n.* (*Chem.*) a colourless, poisonous gas composed of carbon and nitrogen, burning with a peach-blossom flame, and smelling like almond. **cyanogenic** (-jen´-) *a.* capable of producing cyanide.

cyanosis (sīənō´sis) *n.* (*pl.* **cyanoses** (-sēz)) (*Med.*) a condition in which the skin becomes blue or leaden-coloured owing to the circulation of oxygen-deficient blood. **cyanotic** (-not´-) *a.*

cyber- (sī´bə) *comb. form* denoting computer control systems, electronic communication networks and virtual reality.

cybernetics (sībənet´iks) *n.* the comparative study of control and communication mechanisms in machines and living creatures. **cybernate** (sī´-) *v.t.* to control automatically, e.g. by means of a computer. **cybernation** (-ā´shən) *n.* **cybernetic** *a.* **cybernetician** (-tish´-) *n.* **cyberneticist** *n.*

cyberpunk (sī´bəpŭngk) *n.* **1** a style of science fiction writing that features rebellious computer hackers in a bleak future world controlled by computer networks. **2** a writer or devotee of this.

cyberspace (sī´bəspās) *n.* virtual reality, the notional environment created by computer in which people can physically interact.

cycad (sī´kad) *n.* a tropical or subtropical palm-like plant of the order Cycadeles, an order of gymnosperms, allied to the conifers.

cyclamate (sik´ləmāt, sī´-) *n.* any of several compounds derived from petrochemicals, formerly used as sweetening agents.

cyclamen (sik´ləmən) *n.* (*pl.* **cyclamen, cyclamens**) **1** any S European tuberous plant of the genus *Cyclamen*, having red, pink or white flowers. **2** the strong pink colour associated with these.

cycle (sī´kəl) *n.* **1** a series of years, events or phenomena recurring in the same order. **2** a series that repeats itself. **3** a complete series or succession. **4** the period in which a series of events is completed. **5** a bicycle. **6** a long period, an age. **7** a body of legend connected with some myth. **8** (*Physics*) each complete series of changes in a periodically varying quantity, e.g. an electric current. ~*v.i.* **1** to ride a bicycle. **2** to revolve in a circle. **cycle track, cycleway** *n.* a path, often beside a road, reserved for cyclists. **cyclic, cyclical** *a.* **1** moving or recurring in a cycle. **2** (*Bot.*) arranged in whorls. **3** (*Chem.*) (of an organic chemical compound) containing a ring of atoms. **4** (*Math.*) of a circle or cycle. **cyclically** *adv.* **cyclist** *n.* a person who rides a bicycle.

cyclo- (sī´klō) *comb. form* **1** circular. **2** of or relating to a circle, circles or cycles.

cyclo-cross (sī´klōkros) *n.* the sport of cross-country racing on a bicycle.

cyclograph (sī´klōgrahf) *n.* an instrument for describing the arcs of large circles.

cycloid (sī´kloid) *n.* (*Math.*) the figure described by a point in the plane of a circle as it rolls along a straight line till it has completed a revolution. **cycloidal** (-kloi´-) *a.*

cyclometer (sīklom´itə) *n.* an instrument for recording the revolutions of a wheel, esp. that of a bicycle, and hence the distance travelled.

cyclone (sī´klōn) *n.* **1** a tropical cyclone. **2** a disturbance in the atmosphere caused by a system of winds blowing spirally towards a central region of low barometric pressure. **cyclonic** (-klon´-) *a.* **cyclonically** *adv.*

cyclopedia (sīkləpē´diə), **cyclopaedia** *n.* an encyclopedia. **cyclopedic** *a.*

cyclopropane (sīklōprō´pān) *n.* (*Chem.*) a colourless hydrocarbon gas used as an anaesthetic.

cyclorama (sīklərah´mə) *n.* **1** a curved wall or cloth at the rear of a stage, film set etc. **2** (*Hist.*) a panorama painted on the inside of a large cylinder and viewed by the spectator from the middle.

cyclosporin (sīklōspaw´rin) *n.* (*Med.*) an immunosuppressant drug used after transplant surgery to prevent rejection of grafts and transplants.

cyclostome (sī´kləstōm) *n.* any fish of the subclass Cyclostomata, with a circular sucking mouth, e.g. the lamprey and hag. **cyclostomate** (-stom´-), **cyclostomous** (-klos´-) *a.*

cyclostyle (sī´kləstīl) *n.* (*Hist.*) a machine for printing copies of handwriting or typewriting by means of a sheet perforated like a stencil. ~*v.t.* to print using this machine.

cyclothymia (sīklōthī´miə) *n.* (*Psych.*) a psychological condition characterized by swings between elation and depression. **cyclothymic** *a.*

cyclotron (sī´klətron) *n.* (*Physics*) a particle accelerator designed to accelerate protons to high energies.

cyder CIDER.

cygnet (sig´nət) *n.* a young swan.

cylinder (sil´ində) *n.* **1** a straight roller-shaped body, solid or hollow, and of uniform circumference. **2** (*Geom.*) a solid figure described by the revolution of a right-angled parallelogram about one of its sides which remains fixed. **3** a cylindrical member of various machines, esp. the chamber in an engine in which the piston is acted upon by internal combustion, steam etc. **4** the roller used in machine-printing. **cylinder saw** *n.* a crown saw. **cylindrical** (-lin´dri-) *a.* having the form of a cylinder. **cylindrically** *adv.* **cylindriform** (-lin´drifawm) *a.* **cylindroid** (-droid) *n.* (*Geom.*) a solid body differing from a cylinder in having the bases elliptical instead of circular.

cyma (sī´mə) *n.* (*pl.* **cymas**, **cymae** (-mē)) **1** (*Archit.*) a convex and a concave curve forming the topmost member of a cornice. **2** (*Bot.*) a cyme.

cymbal (sim´bəl) *n.* (*Mus.*) a disc of brass or bronze more or less basin-shaped, clashed together in pairs or hit with a stick etc. to produce a sharp, clashing sound. **cymbalist** *n.*

cymbidium (simbid´iəm) *n.* (*pl.* **cymbidiums**, **cymbidia** (-iə)) any orchid of the genus *Cymbidium* having colourful, long-lasting flowers and a recess in the flower-lip.

cyme (sīm) *n.* (*Bot.*) an inflorescence in which the central terminal flower comes to perfection first, as in the guelder rose. **cymose** (-mōs) *a.*

Cymric (kim´rik) *a.* of or relating to the Welsh.

cynic (sin´ik) *n.* **1** a person who is pessimistic about human nature. **2** a person who is habitually morose and sarcastic. **3** (*Hist.*) (**Cynic**) a member of a rigid sect of Greek philosophers (of which Diogenes was the most distinguished member) founded at Athens by Antisthenes, a pupil of Socrates, who insisted on the complete renunciation of all luxury and the subjugation of sensual desires. ~*a.* (**Cynic**) of or belonging to the Cynics. **cynical** *a.* **1** bitter, sarcastic, misanthropic. **2** acting in disregard of accepted standards of conduct. **cynically** *adv.* **cynicism** (-sizm) *n.*

cynosure (sin´əzūə, -shuə) *n.* a centre of interest or attraction.

cypher CIPHER.

cypress (sī´prəs) *n.* **1** (*also* **cypress tree**) a tree of the coniferous genera *Cupressus* or *Chamaecyparis*, esp. *Cupressus sempervirens*, valued for the durability of its wood. **2** a branch of this as emblem of mourning.

cyprine (sip´rīn) *n.* of or belonging to the fish suborder Cyprinoidea, containing the carp. **cyprinoid** *a.* of or like a carp. ~*n.* a carp or related fish.

Cypriot (sip´riət), **Cypriote** (-ōt) *n.* a native or inhabitant of Cyprus. ~*a.* of, relating or belonging to Cyprus. **Cyprian** (sip´riən) *a.* of or belonging to Cyprus, esp. as a place where the worship of Venus especially flourished. ~*n.* a Cypriot.

cypripedium (sipripē´diəm) *n.* any orchid of the genus *Cypripedium*, esp. the lady's slipper, possessing two fertile stamens, the central stamen (fertile in other orchids) being represented by a shieldlike plate.

cypsela (sip´silə) *n.* (*pl.* **cypselae** (-lē)) (*Bot.*) the dry single-seeded fruit of the daisy and related plants.

Cyrillic (siril´ik) *a.* denoting the alphabet of the Slavonic nations who belong to the Orthodox Church, now esp. Russia and Bulgaria (from the fact that it was introduced by Clement, a disciple of St Cyril). ~*n.* the Cyrillic alphabet.

cyst (sist) *n.* **1** (*Biol.*) a bladder, vesicle or hollow organ. **2** (*Med.*) a sac or cavity of abnormal character containing fluid or semi-solid matter. **3** (*Biol.*) a thick protective membrane enclosing an organism. **cystic** *a.* **1** of, relating to or enclosed in a cyst, esp. the gall or urinary bladder. **2** having cysts, or of the nature of a cyst. **cystic fibrosis** *n.* a hereditary disease appearing in early childhood, marked by overproduction of mucus and fibrous tissue, with consequent breathing and digestive difficulties. **cystiform** (sis´tifawm) *a.*

cysteine (sis´tēn, -tiēn, -tān, -tiin) *n.* a sulphur-containing amino acid, present in proteins and essential in the human diet. **cystine** (sis´tīn) *n.* a sulphur-containing amino acid discovered in a rare kind of urinary calculus, formed by the oxidization of cysteine.

cystitis (sistī´tis) *n.* (*Med.*) inflammation of the urinary bladder.

cystoscope (sis´təskōp) *n.* an instrument or apparatus for the exploration of the bladder. **cystoscopic** (-skop´-) *a.* **cystoscopy** (-tos´-) *n.*

cystotomy (sistot´əmi) *n.* (*pl.* **cystotomies**) the surgical operation of cutting into the urinary bladder.

-cyte (sīt) *comb. form* (*Biol.*) a mature cell, as in *leucocyte.*

cytidine (sī´tidēn) *n.* a nucleoside obtained from RNA by the condensation of ribose and cytosine.

cyto- (sī´tō) *comb. form* (*Biol.*) **1** cellular. **2** of or relating to or composed of cells.

cytogenetics (sītōjənet´iks) *n.* the branch of

genetics concerned with inheritance where related to the structure and function of cells. **cytogenetic, cytogenetical** *a.* **cytogenetically** *adv.* **cytogeneticist** *n.*

cytology (sītol´əji) *n.* the study of cells. **cytological** (-loj´-) *a.* **cytologically** *adv.* **cytologist** *n.*

cytoplasm (sī´tōplazm) *n.* the protoplasm of a cell apart from the nucleus. **cytoplasmic** (-plaz´-) *a.*

cytosine (sī´təsēn) *n.* a pyrimidine occurring in all living tissues, being a component base of RNA and DNA.

cytotoxin (sītōtok´sin) *n.* a substance which is poisonous to cells. **cytotoxic** *a.*

czar, czaritza TSAR.

Czech (chek) *n.* **1** a native or inhabitant of the Czech Republic. **2** the Slavonic language of the Czechs. **3** (*Hist.*) a native or inhabitant of Czechoslovakia. ~*a.* of or relating to the Czechs, their language or the Czech Republic. **Czechoslovak** (chekōslō´vak), **Czechoslovakian** (-vak´iən) *n.* (*Hist.*) a native or inhabitant of Czechoslovakia (a former state in Central Europe). ~*a.* of or relating to Czechoslovakia.

D

D¹ (dē), **d** (*pl.* **Ds, D's**) the fourth letter of the English and other versions of the Roman alphabet, corresponding to the Greek delta (δ, Δ). It is pronounced as a voiced dental plosive, though after a voiceless consonant its reflex approaches or becomes the sound of *t*, especially in the past tenses and past participles of verbs in *-ed*. ~*symbol* **1** the fourth of a series, the fourth highest in a range, e.g. of marks, etc. **2** the fourth known quantity in an algebraic expression. **3** (*Mus.*) **a** the second note of the diatonic scale of C major. **b** the scale of a composition in which the keynote is D. **4** 500 in Roman numerals. **D-day** *n.* **1** the code name for the date of the invasion of France, 6 June 1944. **2** the date planned for the beginning of an important venture. **D region, D layer** *n.* the lowest part of the ionosphere, between 25 and 40 miles (40 and 65 km) above the earth's surface.

D² *abbr.* **1** defence (in *D-notice*). **2** Democrat. **3** density (of electric flux density). **4** deuterium. **5** dextrorotatory. **6** dimension. **D-notice** *n.* an official notice prohibiting publication of sensitive information.

d. *abbr.* **1** daughter. **2** deci-. **3** depart(s). **4** depth. **5** died. **6** diameter. **7** penny (before decimalization, L *denarius*).

'd (d) *contr.* (*coll.*) **1** had. **2** would.

-d (d) *suf.* forming the past tense and p.p. of some regular verbs, as in *died, heard, loved, proved*.

DA *abbr.* (*N Am.*) District Attorney.

D/A *abbr.* (*Comput.*) digital to analogue.

da *abbr.* deca-.

dab¹ (dab) *v.t.* (*pres.p.* **dabbing**, *past, p.p.* **dabbed**) **1** to strike gently with some moist or soft substance. **2** to pat. **3** to press with a soft substance. ~*n.* **1** a gentle blow. **2** a light stroke or wipe with a soft substance. **3** a small amount of a soft substance dabbed. **4** (*often pl., sl.*) fingerprints. **dabber** *n.* **dab hand** *n.* (*coll.*) an expert (at).

dab² (dab) *n.* a small flatfish, *Limanda limanda*.

dabble (dab´əl) *v.t.* **1** to wet by little dips. **2** to besprinkle, to moisten, to splash. ~*v.i.* **1** to play or splash about in water. **2** to do or practise anything in a superficial manner. **3** to dip into a subject. **dabbler** *n.* **dabblingly** *adv.* superficially, shallowly.

dabchick (dab´chik), **dobchick** (dob´-) *n.* the little grebe, *Tachybaptus ruficollis*.

dace (dās) *n.* a small river fish, *Leuciscus leuciscus*.

dacha (dach´ə), **datcha** *n.* (*pl.* **dachas, datchas**) a country house or cottage in Russia.

dachshund (daks´hund, dak´sənd) *n.* a short-legged long-bodied breed of dog.

dactyl (dak´til) *n.* a metrical foot consisting of one long followed by two short syllables, or of one stressed followed by two unstressed syllables. **dactylic** (-til´-) *a.* of or relating to dactyls. ~*n.* (*usu. pl.*) verse in dactyls.

dad (dad) *n.* (*coll.*) father. **dada** (dad´ə, -ah) *n.* (used by or to children). **daddy** *n.* (*pl.* **daddies**). **the daddy of them all** (*coll.*) the supreme example of something. **daddy-long-legs** *n.* (*pl.* **daddy-long-legs**) **1** any of various species of crane-fly. **2** (*US*) a harvestman.

Dada (dah´dah), **Dadaism** (-izm) *n.* an early 20th-cent. school of art and literature that aimed at suppressing any correlation between thought and expression. **Dadaist** *n., a.* **Dadaistic** (-is´tik) *a.*

dado (dā´dō) *n.* (*pl.* **dados, dadoes**) **1** an arrangement of wainscoting or decoration round the lower part of the walls of a room. **2** the cube of a pedestal between the base and the cornice.

daemon DEMON.

daff (daf) *n.* (*coll.*) short for DAFFODIL.

daffodil (daf´ədil) *n.* **1** the yellow narcissus, *Narcissus pseudonarcissus*. **2** any of various other species and garden varieties of the genus *Narcissus*. **daffodil yellow** *n., a.* (of) a pale yellow colour.

daffy (daf´i) *a.* (*comp.* **daffier**, *superl.* **daffiest**) (*coll.*) crazy, daft. **daffily** *adv.* **daffiness** *n.*

daft (dahft) *a.* **1** weak-minded, imbecile. **2** foolish, silly, thoughtless. **3** frolicsome. **daft about** (*coll.*) very fond of. **daftly** *adv.* **daftness** *n.*

dag (dag) *n.* (*Austral., New Zeal.*) **1** a daglock. **2** (*coll.*) an old-fashioned, unattractive person; a character. ~*v.t.* (*pres.p.* **dagging**, *past, p.p.* **dagged**) to remove daglock from (a sheep). **to rattle one's dags** (*coll.*) to hurry up. **dagger¹** *n.* **daggy** *a.* (*comp.* **daggier**, *superl.* **daggiest**) (*coll.*) old-fashioned and unattractive.

dagger¹ DAG.

dagger² (dag´ə) *n.* **1** a short two-edged weapon adapted for stabbing. **2** (*Print.*) a reference mark (†). **at daggers drawn 1** on hostile terms. **2** ready to fight. **to look daggers** to look with fierceness or animosity. **daggerboard** *n.* (*Naut.*) a sliding centreboard on a boat.

daglock (dag´lok) *n.* the dirt-covered clumps of wool around the hindquarters of a sheep.

dago (dā´gō) *n.* (*pl.* **dagos, dagoes**) (*offensive*) a Spaniard, Italian or Portuguese.

daguerreotype (dəger´ətīp) *n.* **1** the process of

photographing on copper plates coated with silver iodide, developed by exposure to mercury vapour. **2** a photograph by this process.

dahlia (dā′lyə) n. (pl. **dahlias**) a composite plant of the genus *Dahlia* from Mexico, cultivated for their flowers.

daily (dā′li) a. **1** happening, done or recurring every day. **2** published every weekday. **3** necessary for every day. **4** ordinary, usual. ~*adv.* **1** day by day. **2** often. **3** continually, always. ~*n.* (pl. **dailies**) **1** a newspaper published every weekday. **2** a woman employed daily for housework. **daily bread** n. necessary food and sustenance, means of living. **daily dozen** n. (coll.) daily physical exercises.

daimon (dī′mōn) n. a genius or attendant spirit. **daimonic** (-mon′-) a.

dainty (dān′ti) a. (comp. **daintier**, superl. **daintiest**) **1** pretty, delicate, elegant. **2** pleasing to the taste, choice. **3** fastidious, delicate. ~*n.* (pl. **dainties**) a delicacy; a choice morsel. **daintily** adv. **daintiness** n.

daiquiri (dak′əri, dī′-) n. (pl. **daiquiris**) a cocktail made of rum and lime-juice.

dairy (deə′ri) n. (pl. **dairies**) **1** the place or building or department of a farm where milk is kept and converted into butter or cheese. **2** a place where milk, cream and butter are sold. ~*a.* of or relating to the production of milk and its products. **dairy-farm** n. **dairy-farming** n. **dairying** n. dairy-farming. †**dairymaid** n. a woman employed in a dairy. **dairyman** n. (pl. **dairymen**) a man employed in a dairy or dealing with dairy products.

dais (dā′is) n. (pl. **daises**) **1** a platform. **2** the raised floor at the upper end of a medieval dining-hall.

daisy (dā′zi) n. (pl. **daisies**) **1** a small composite flower, *Bellis perennis*, with white petals and a yellow centre. **2** any of various other flowers resembling this. **3** (sl.) a first-rate person or thing. **pushing up (the) daisies** dead (and buried). **daisy-chain** n. a string of daisies joined together. **daisy-cutter** n. in cricket, a ball bowled so low that it rolls along the ground. **daisy-wheel** n. (Comput.) a wheel-shaped printer with characters on spikes round the circumference.

dal DHAL.

Dalai Lama (dalī lah′mə) n. the spiritual leader of Tibetan Buddhism, previously also the temporal ruler of Tibet.

dalasi (dəlah′si) n. (pl. **dalasi**, **dalasis**) the standard monetary unit of the Gambia.

dale (dāl) n. a valley, esp. from the English midlands to the Scottish lowlands. **dalesman** n. (pl. **dalesmen**) a (male) native or inhabitant of a dale, esp. in the northern counties of England. **daleswoman** n. (pl. **daleswomen**) a female native or inhabitant of a dale.

dally (dal′i) v.i. (3rd pers. sing. pres. **dallies**, pres.p. **dallying**, past, p.p. **dallied**) **1** to trifle (with), to flirt (with), to treat frivolously. **2** to

idle, to delay, to waste time. ~*v.t.* to fritter or waste (away). **dalliance** n.

Dalmatian (dalmā′shən) n. a variety of hound, white with numerous black or brown spots, formerly kept chiefly as a carriage dog.

dalton (dawl′tən) n. (Chem.) an atomic mass unit.

daltonism (dawl′tənizm) n. colour-blindness, esp. inability to distinguish between red and green.

dam[1] (dam) n. **1** a bank or mound raised to keep back water (by humans to form a reservoir etc. or by a beaver). **2** any barrier acting like a dam. **3** the water kept back by a dam. **4** a causeway. ~*v.t.* (pres.p. **damming**, past, p.p. **dammed**) **1** to keep back or confine by a dam. **2** to obstruct, to hinder.

dam[2] (dam) n. a female parent (chiefly of quadrupeds); used of a human mother in contempt.

damage (dam′ij) n. **1** hurt, injury, mischief or detriment to any person or thing. **2** loss or harm incurred. **3** (pl.) value of injury done. **4** (pl., Law) reparation in money for injury sustained. **5** (sl.) cost. ~*v.t.* **1** to cause damage to. **2** to injure the reputation of. ~*v.i.* to receive damage. **damaging** a. **damagingly** adv.

damascene (dam′əsēn, -sēn′) v.t. to ornament by inlaying or incrustation, or (as a steel blade) with a wavy pattern in welding. ~*a.* of or relating to this form of ornamentation. ~*n.* a damascened article or design.

damask (dam′əsk) n. **1** a rich silk stuff with raised figures woven in the pattern, orig. made at Damascus. **2** a linen fabric, with similar figures in the pattern, used for tablecloths, dinnernapkins etc. **3** a tablecloth made of this. **4** steel made with a wavy pattern by forging iron and steel together. ~*a.* **1** made of damask. **2** pink or red, like the damask rose. ~*v.t.* **1** to work with figured designs, to work flowers on. **2** to damascene, to give a wavy appearance to (steel work etc.). **damask rose** n. an old-fashioned rose, *Rosa gallica*, var. *damascena*, used to make attar of roses.

dame (dām) n. **1** a lady; a title of honour (now applied to the wives of knights and baronets). **2** (a title of honour given to) a female equivalent of the Knight Commander or holder of the Grand Cross. **3** a comic old woman in pantomime, usu. played by a man. **4** (sl., esp. N Am.) a woman.

damn (dam) int. (sl.) used to express annoyance. ~*v.t.* **1** to condemn, to criticize harshly. **2** to call down curses on. **3** to condemn to eternal punishment. **4** to reveal the guilt of; to cause the ruin of. ~*v.i.* to swear profanely. ~*n.* **1** a profane oath. **2** a negligible amount. ~*a.*, adv. damned. **not to give a damn** to be totally unconcerned. **to damn with faint praise** to praise with so little enthusiasm that it suggests dislike or disapproval. **damfool** a. (coll.) extremely foolish. **dammit** int. damn it! **damnable** (dam′nəbəl) a. **1** deserving damnation or condemnation. **2** atrocious, despicable.

damnably (-nə-) *adv.* **damn all** *n.* absolutely nothing. **damnation** (-nāʹshən) *n.* **1** condemnation to eternal punishment. **2** eternal punishment. **3** condemnation. *~int.* used to express anger. **damnatory** (-nə-) *a.* causing or implying condemnation. **damned** (damd) *a.* **1** condemned. **2** condemned to everlasting punishment. **3** hateful, execrable. *~adv.* (*coll.*) very. **to be damned if** certainly will not. **damnedest** (damʹdist), **damndest** *n.* (*coll.*) the best. **to do one's damnedest** to do one's very best. **damning** (damʹing) *a.* suggesting guilt. **damningly** *adv.* **damn well** *adv.* definitely; whether you like it or not.

damp (damp) *a.* slightly wet; clammy. *~n.* **1** humidity, moisture in a building or article of use or in the air. **2** dejection, depression. **3** subterranean gases met with in mines, firedamp. *~v.t.* **1** to stifle, to restrain. **2** to moisten. **3** to check, to depress. **4** to discourage, to deaden. **5** to make burn less strongly. **6** to make vibrate less. **to damp off** (of the stems of plants) to rot off from damp. **damp course** *n.* a layer of impervious material put between the courses of a wall to keep moisture from rising. **dampen** *v.t.* **1** to make damp. **2** to dull, to deaden. *~v.i.* to become damp. **dampener** *n.* **damper** *n.* **1** a person or something which damps. **2** a valve or sliding plate in a flue for regulating a fire. **3** (*Austral., New Zeal.*) bread or cake baked in hot ashes. **4** (*Mus.*) a pad in a piano for deadening the sound. **5** (*Mus.*) a mute in brass wind instruments. **to put a damper on 1** to discourage, to stifle. **2** to reduce the chances of success of. **dampish** *a.* **damply** *adv.* **dampness** *n.* **damp-proof** *a.* impenetrable to moisture. *~v.t.* to render impervious to moisture. **damp-proof course** *n.* a damp course. **damp squib** *n.* a failed attempt, a disappointing event.

damsel (damʹzəl), **†damosel** (damʹəzel) *n.* (*poet.*) a young unmarried woman. **damselfish** *n.* a small fish of the family Pomacentidrae, found around coral reefs. **damselfly** *n.* (*pl.* **damselflies**) an insect somewhat resembling a dragonfly, of the order Odonata.

damson (damʹzən) *n.* **1** a small dark purple plum. **2** the tree, *Prunus institia*, that bears this. **3** a dark purple colour. *~a.* damson-coloured.

dan¹ (dan) *n.* **1** in martial arts, any of the black-belt grades of proficiency. **2** a person who has reached such a level.

dan² (dan), **dan buoy** *n.* a type of small deep-sea buoy.

dance (dahns) *v.i.* **1** to move, usu. to music, with rhythmical steps, figures and gestures. **2** to skip, to frolic, to move in a lively or excited way. **3** to bob up and down. *~v.t.* **1** to express or accomplish by dancing. **2** to perform (a particular kind of dance). **3** to toss up and down, to dandle. **4** to cause to dance. *~n.* **1** a rhythmical stepping with motions of the body, usu. adjusted to the measure of a tune. **2** a figure or set of figures in dancing. **3** a dancing-party, a ball. **4** the tune by which dance movements are regulated. **5** a

dancing motion. **to dance attendance on** to pay assiduous court to; to be kept waiting by. **to lead someone a (merry) dance** to cause someone trouble or delay. **danceable** *a.* **dance band** *n.* a band that plays dance music. **dance floor** *n.* a floor or area of floor for dancing, usu. with a polished surface. **dance hall** *n.* a public hall for dancing. **dance music** *n.* music intended for dancing to. **dancer** *n.* a person who dances, esp. one who earns money by dancing in public. **dancesport** *n.* ballroom dancing as a competitive sport. **dancing** *n.*, *a.* **dancing dervish** *n.* a whirling dervish. **dancing girl** *n.* a professional female dancer.

D and C (dē ənd sēʹ) *n.* (*Med.*) dilatation of the cervix and curettage of the womb, performed for diagnostic or therapeutic purposes.

dandelion (danʹdiliən) *n.* a well-known composite plant, *Taraxacum officinale*, with a yellow rayed flower and toothed leaves. **dandelion clock** *n.* the globular seed-head of a dandelion, with downy tufts. **dandelion coffee** *n.* (a drink made from) dandelion roots, powdered.

dander (danʹdə) *n.* (*coll.*) temper, anger. **to get one's dander up** to become angry.

dandify (danʹdifi) *v.t.* (*3rd pers. sing. pres.* **dandifies**, *pres.p.* **dandifying**, *past, p.p.* **dandified**) to make smart, or like a dandy. **dandification** (-fikāʹshən) *n.*

dandle (danʹdəl) *v.t.* **1** to bounce (a child) up and down on one's knees or toss (it) in one's arms. **2** to pet. **dandler** *n.*

dandruff (danʹdrŭf) *n.* scaly scurf on the head.

dandy (danʹdi) *n.* (*pl.* **dandies**) a man extravagantly concerned with his appearance; a fop, a coxcomb. *~a.* (*comp.* **dandier**, *superl.* **dandiest**) (*esp. N Am.*) very good, superior. **dandy brush** *n.* a hard whalebone brush for cleaning horses. **dandyish** *a.* **dandyism** *n.* **dandy roll**, **dandy roller** *n.* a roller used to produce water marks on paper.

Dane (dān) *n.* **1** a native or inhabitant of Denmark. **2** (*Hist.*) any of the Northmen who invaded Britain in the Middle Ages.

danger (dānʹjə) *n.* **1** risk, peril, hazard; exposure to injury or loss. **2** anything that causes peril. **3** on a railway, risk in going on owing to obstruction; the signal indicating this. **in danger of** liable to. **danger list** *n.* a list of those dangerously ill (in hospital). **danger man** *n.* a man to beware of, esp. as a rival in a sporting event. **danger money** *n.* money paid in compensation for the risks involved in any unusually dangerous job. **dangerous** *a.* **dangerously** *adv.*

dangle (dangʹgəl) *v.i.* **1** to hang loosely. **2** to swing or wave about. *~v.t.* **1** to cause to dangle. **2** to hold out (a temptation, bait etc.). **dangler** *n.* **dangling** *a.* that dangles. **dangling participle** *n.* (*Gram.*) a participle without a subject or antecedent. **dangly** *a.* (*comp.* **danglier**, *superl.* **dangliest**).

Danish (dāʹnish) *a.* of or relating to Denmark. *~n.* **1** the language of Denmark. **2** (*as pl.*) the Danes. **3** (*coll.*) a Danish pastry (*coffee and a Danish*).

Danish blue *n.* a strong-tasting, blue-veined cheese. **Danish pastry** *n.* a flaky pastry, usu. filled with jam, almonds or apples, and often iced.

dank (dangk) *a.* **1** damp, moist. **2** chilly with moisture. **dankly** *adv.* **dankness** *n.*

danthonia (danthō'niə) *n.* (*Austral., New Zeal.*) a pasture grass of the genus *Danthonia.*

dap (dap) *v.i.* (*pres.p.* **dapping,** *past, p.p.* **dapped**) to fish by letting the bait fall gently into the water. ~*v.t.* **1** to let fall lightly. **2** to cause to bounce on the ground. ~*n.* a bounce (of a ball etc.).

daphne (daf'ni) *n.* any shrub of the genus *Daphne.*

dapper (dap'ə) *a.* **1** spruce, smart. **2** brisk, active. **dapperly** *adv.* **dapperness** *n.*

dapple (dap'əl) *n.* **1** a spot on an animal's coat. **2** a mottled marking. **3** a horse or other animal with a mottled coat. ~*a.* spotted; variegated with streaks or spots. ~*v.t.* to spot, to streak, to variegate. ~*v.i.* to become dappled. **dappled** *a.* **dapple-grey** *a., n.* (a horse etc.) with a mottled grey coat.

darbies (dah'biz) *n.pl.* (*sl.*) handcuffs.

Darby and Joan (dahbi ənd jōn') *n.* an elderly married couple living in domestic bliss. **Darby and Joan club** *n.* a club for elderly people.

dare (deə), (*Sc.*) **daur** (daw) *v.i.* (*past* **dared,** †**durst** (dœst)) to venture (to); to have the courage or impudence (to) (*I wouldn't dare contradict her*). ~*v.t.* **1** to attempt, to venture on. **2** to challenge, to defy. ~*n.* **1** a challenge to do something dangerous. **2** an act of boldness. **I dare say** I suppose. **daredevil** *n.* a fearless, reckless person. ~*a.* fearless, reckless. **daredevilry** *n.* **darer** *n.* **daring** *a.* courageous, bold; fearless, reckless. ~*n.* boldness, bravery. **daringly** *adv.*

Usage note It is still conventional to write *dare say* (as in *I dare say*) as two separate words, not one (*daresay*).

---

daren't (deənt) *contr.* dare not.

darg (dahg) *n.* (*Sc., North. or Austral.*) **1** the quantity of work done in a day. **2** a task.

dariole (dar'iōl) *n.* a dish cooked in a usu. flowerpot-shaped mould. **dariole mould** *n.* a usu. flowerpot-shaped mould used in cookery.

dark (dahk) *a.* **1** without light. **2** almost black. **3** shaded. **4** dark-haired or dark-skinned. **5** opaque. **6** gloomy, sombre. **7** blind, ignorant. **8** obscure, ambiguous. **9** hidden, concealed. **10** without spiritual or intellectual enlightenment. **11** wicked, evil. **12** cheerless. **13** sad, sullen, frowning. **14** unknown, untried (esp. used of a horse that has never run in public). ~*n.* **1** darkness. **2** absence of light. **3** night, nightfall. **4** shadow, shade. **5** dark tint, the dark part of a picture. **6** lack of knowledge. **7** doubt, uncertainty. **in the dark 1** without light. **2** in ignorance (about). **to keep something dark** to keep silent about something. **Dark Ages, Dark Age** *n.* **1** the Middle Ages, esp. the period from the 5th to the 10th

cent. (from an incorrect view of the ignorance then prevailing). **2** any period of supposed ignorance. **darken** *v.i.* **1** to become dark or darker. **2** to become obscure. ~*v.t.* **1** to make dark or darker. **2** to render gloomy, ignorant or stupid. **not to darken someone's door** not to appear as a visitor. **dark glasses** *n.pl.* sunglasses. **dark horse** *n.* (*fig.*) **1** a person who keeps their opinions and thoughts secret. **2** a person of unknown capabilities. **darkish** *a.* **darkly** *adv.* **dark matter** *n.* (*Astron.*) hypothetical non-luminous matter constituting a large part of the universe's mass but unable to be detected. **darkness** *n.* **darkroom** *n.* a room from which actinic light is shut out for developing photographs. **dark star** *n.* a star emitting no light, whose existence is known only from its radio waves, infrared spectrum or gravitational effect.

darkie (dah'ki), **darky** *n.* (*pl.* **darkies**) (*offensive*) a dark-skinned person, esp. of African origin.

darling (dah'ling) *n.* **1** a person who is dearly loved. **2** a favourite. **3** (*coll.*) a lovable, charming or pretty person or thing. ~*a.* **1** dearly loved. **2** (*coll.*) charming, delightful.

darn[1] (dahn) *v.t.* **1** to mend with stitches that cross or interweave. **2** to embroider with a type of running stitch. ~*n.* a place mended by darning. **darner** *n.* **1** a person who darns. **2** a needle used in darning. **darning** *n.* **1** the action of a darner. **2** garments etc. to be darned. **darning needle** *n.* a needle used in darning.

darn[2] (dahn), (*N Am.*) **durn** (dœn) *int., v.t.* (*coll., euphem.*) damn. **darned** *a.* damned.

darnel (dah'nəl) *n.* **1** a kind of grass, *Lolium temulentum,* formerly believed to be poisonous, which grows among corn. **2** any plant of the genus *Lolium.*

dart (daht) *n.* **1** a small pointed missile used in the game of darts. **2** a short-pointed missile weapon thrown by the hand. **3** (*pl.*) an indoor game of throwing darts at a dartboard. **4** a sudden leap or rapid movement. **5** (*Zool.*) an insect's sting. **6** in dressmaking, a V-shaped tuck. ~*v.t.* **1** to throw. **2** to shoot or send forth suddenly. ~*v.i.* to run or move swiftly. **dartboard** *n.* a circular marked target used in the game of darts. **darter** *n.* **1** a person who throws or hurls. **2** a person who moves with great rapidity. **3** any long-necked swimming bird of the genus *Anhinga.* **4** any bird of the order Jaculatores, comprising the kingfishers and bee-eaters. **5** any small N American freshwater fish of the family Percidae.

Darwinian (dahwin'iən) *a.* of or relating to Charles Darwin, 1809–82, English naturalist, or Darwinism. ~*n.* a believer in Darwinism. **Darwinianism** *n.* the teaching of Charles Darwin, esp. the doctrine of the origin of species by natural selection. **Darwinism** *n.* Darwinianism. **Darwinist** *n., a.*

dash (dash) *v.i.* **1** to rush, fall or throw oneself violently. **2** to strike against something and break. **3** (usu. with *up, off* or *away*) to run, ride or drive quickly. ~*v.t.* **1** (usu. with *to pieces*) to break by collision. **2** (usu. with *out*, *down*, *away* etc.) to smite, to strike, to knock. **3** to throw violently or suddenly. **4** to destroy; to frustrate; to confound, to abash, to discourage, to daunt. ~*int.* (*dated, coll., euphem.*) damn. ~*n.* **1** a sharp collision of two bodies. **2** the sound of this, the sound of water in commotion. **3** a rapid movement. **4** a rush, a hurry. **5** a small amount. **6** activity, daring; brilliancy, display, ostentation (*He performed with great dash*). **7** a mark (–) denoting a break in a sentence, a parenthesis or omission. **8** the long element in Morse code. **9** (*N Am.*) in athletics, a sprint. **10** (*coll.*) the dashboard of a car. **dash it (all)!** (*coll.*) used to express annoyance. **to cut a dash** to make a bold impression. **to dash down** to dash off. **to dash off** to write down or complete in a hurry. **dashboard** *n.* a fascia with instruments in front of the driver of a car or the pilot of an aircraft. **dashing** *a.* **1** daring, spirited. **2** showy, smart. **dashingly** *adv.* **dashingness** *n.*

dashiki (dah´shiki) *n.* (*pl.* **dashikis**) a type of loose shirt worn esp. by blacks in America.

dastardly (das´tədli) *a.* cowardly and nasty. **dastardliness** *n.*

DAT *abbr.* digital audio tape.

data (dā´tə) *n.pl.* (*often sing. in constr., pl. of* **datum**) **1** facts or information from which other things may be deduced. **2** the information operated on by a computer program. **data-bank, database** *n.* a large amount of information, usu. stored in a computer for easy access. **data capture** *n.* the conversion of information into a form which can be processed by a computer. **data processing** *n.* the handling and processing of data in computer files. **data processor** *n.* **data protection** *n.* the protection of the privacy of personal data stored in computer files.

Usage note (1) The use of *data* as a singular noun is sometimes disapproved of, though in computing etc. it is standard. (2) Pronunciation as (dah´tə) is best avoided.

date[1] (dāt) *n.* **1** a fixed point of time. **2** the time at which anything happened or is appointed to take place. **3** the specification of time in a book, inscription, document or letter. **4** (*coll.*) a social or other engagement (usu. with a romantic partner). **5** (*esp. N Am.*) a person with whom one has a date. ~*v.t.* **1** to affix the date to. **2** to note or fix the date of. **3** to reveal the age of. **4** (*esp. N Am.*) to have a romantic relationship with. ~*v.i.* **1** to begin (from). **2** to become dated. **to date** up till now. **to make/ have a date** (*coll.*) to make or have an appointment. **dated** *a.* old-fashioned. **dateless** *a.* **1** without a date. **2** very old. **3** timeless, unlikely to grow out of date. **date-line** *n.* **1** the line on either side of which the date differs, running meridionally across the western hemisphere from the poles and theoretically 180° from Greenwich. **2** the line with date and place

of sending printed above a newspaper dispatch. **date rape** *n.* the rape of a woman by a man during or after a date. **date-stamp** *n.* **1** an adjustable rubber stamp for imprinting a date. **2** a stamp on perishable goods showing the date before which they are best used or consumed. ~*v.t.* to mark (goods) with a date-stamp.

date[2] (dāt) *n.* **1** the fruit of the date palm, an oblong fruit with a hard seed or stone. **2** the date palm. **date palm, date tree** *n.* a tall tree, *Phoenix dactylifera*, common in N Africa and Asia Minor.

dative (dā´tiv) *a.* (*Gram.*) denoting the grammatical case used to represent the indirect object, or the person or thing interested in the action of the verb. ~*n.* (*Gram.*) the dative case. **datival** (-tī´-) *a.*

datum (dā´təm) *n.* (*pl.* **data**) a quantity, condition, fact or other premise, given or admitted, from which other things or results may be found.

datura (dətūə´rə) *n.* any solanaceous plant of the genus *Datura*, as the thorn apple, *D. stramonium*, which yields a powerful narcotic.

daub (dawb) *v.t.* **1** to smear or coat with a soft adhesive substance. **2** to paint coarsely. **3** to apply (colour) in a crude or inartistic style. **4** to stain, to soil. ~*v.i.* to paint in a crude or inartistic style. ~*n.* **1** a smear. **2** a crude or inartistic painting. **3** a plaster or mud wall-covering. **dauber** *n.*

daube (dawb) *n.* a stew of meat braised with wine etc.

daughter (daw´tə) *n.* **1** a female child in relation to a parent or parents. **2** a female descendant. **3** a form of address used by a confessor to a female penitent etc. **4** a female member of a family, people, city etc. **5** (*Biol.*) a cell derived from another of the same type. **6** (*Physics*) a nuclide formed from another by radioactive decay. **daughterhood** *n.* **daughter-in-law** *n.* (*pl.* **daughters-in-law**) a son's wife. **daughterly** *a.* **daughterliness** *n.*

daunt (dawnt) *v.t.* to intimidate, to dishearten (*Nothing daunted, she continued on her journey*). **daunting** *a.* **dauntingly** *adv.* **dauntless** *a.* fearless, intrepid. **dauntlessly** *adv.* **dauntlessness** *n.*

dauphin (dō´fā, daw´fin) *n.* (*Hist.*) the heir apparent to the French throne (from the fact that the principality of Dauphiné was an apanage of his).

davenport (dav´ənpawt), **devonport** (dev´ənpawt) *n.* **1** a small writing desk with drawers on both sides. **2** (*esp. N Am.*) a large sofa, a couch.

davit (dav´it) *n.* **1** a spar used as a crane for hoisting an anchor. **2** either of a pair of beams projecting over a ship's side, with tackles to hoist or lower a boat.

Davy (dā´vi), **Davy lamp** *n.* (*pl.* **Davies, Davy lamps**) a miner's wire-gauze safety lamp.

Davy Jones (dāvi jōnz´) *n.* (*sl.*) **1** an imaginary malign spirit with power over the sea. **2** (*also* **Davy Jones's locker**) the sea as the tomb of the drowned.

daw (daw) *n.* a jackdaw.

dawdle (daw′dəl) *v.i.* **1** to be slow, to linger. **2** to trifle; to idle about; to waste time. *~n.* the act of dawdling. **dawdler** *n.*

dawn (dawn) *n.* **1** the break of day. **2** the first rise or appearance. *~v.i.* **1** to grow light, to break (as day). **2** to begin to open, expand or appear. **to dawn upon** to be realized gradually by. **dawn chorus** *n.* the singing of birds at dawn. **dawning** *n.* **1** dawn. **2** the first beginning or unfolding.

day (dā) *n.* **1** the time the sun is above the horizon. **2** a space of twenty-four hours, esp. that commencing at midnight, a practice borrowed from the ancient Romans. **3** the average time interval between two successive returns of the sun to the meridian. **4** daylight; daytime. **5** the part of a day during which work is usually done. **6** any specified point in time; a date agreed on. **7** an age. **8** (*often pl.*) life, lifetime, period of vigour, activity or prosperity. **9** a day appointed to commemorate any event. **10** a contest, a battle; a victory. **11** today. **12** a period on another planet corresponding to a day on earth. **day by day** gradually, every day. **day in, day out** every day, constantly. **from day one** from the very start. **not one's day** a day on which things go wrong for one. **one day 1** shortly; in the near future. **2** at some unspecified time in the future. **one of these days 1** shortly; in the near future. **2** at some unspecified time in the future. **one of those days** a day on which things go wrong for one. **some day** one day. **to call it a day** to stop what one is doing, esp. work. **to name the day** to fix the date for one's wedding. **daybed** *n.* a couch or sofa for lying on during the day. **day-boarder** *n.* a pupil who has meals, but does not sleep, at a school. **daybook** *n.* a book in which the business transactions of the day are recorded. **day-boy** *n.* a boy attending a day-school, but differing from a day-boarder in not taking dinner there. **daybreak** *n.* the first appearance of daylight. **day-care** *n.* the daytime supervision by trained staff of pre-school children or elderly or handicapped people. **day-care centre,** (*NAm.*) **day-care center** *n.* a day centre. **day centre,** (*NAm.*) **day center** *n.* a place providing social amenities for the elderly, handicapped etc. **daydream** *n.* a romantic scheme or vain fancy voluntarily indulged in. *~v.i.* to have daydreams. **daydreamer** *n.* **dayfly** *n.* (*pl.* **dayflies**) an insect of the genus *Ephemera*. **day-girl** *n.* a girl attending a day-school, but differing from a day-boarder in not taking dinner there. **day labour,** (*N Am.*) **day labor** *n.* work paid for by the day. **day labourer,** (*NAm.*) **day laborer** *n.* **day lily** *n.* (*pl.* **day lilies**) a liliaceous plant of the genus *Hemerocallis*, the flowers of which last one day. **day-long** *a.* lasting all day. **day nursery** *n.* a children's playroom in the daytime; a crèche. **Day of Atonement** *n.* a Jewish day of fasting, ten days after the Jewish New Year; Yom Kippur. **day off** *n.* a day's holiday from work, school etc. **Day of Judgement** *n.* JUDGEMENT DAY (under JUDGE). **day of reckoning** *n.* **1** the day of settling accounts. **2** (*fig.*) the Day of Judgement. **day out** *n.* a day-trip, a day away from home. **day release** *n.* a system which frees people from work for some hours each week to follow part-time education relevant to their employment. **day return** *n.* a special cheap ticket for travel to a place, returning the same day. **day room** *n.* a communal living-room in a school, hospital etc. **day-school** *n.* **1** a school for pupils living at home, as distinct from *boarding school*. **2** a school held in the daytime on a weekday, as distinct from *night-school, Sunday school* etc. **dayside** *n.* **1** (*Astron.*) the side of a planet facing the sun. **2** (*NAm.*) those in an organization who work during the day, esp. on a newspaper. **daytime** *n.* day, as opposed to night. **day trip** *n.* an excursion made to and from a place in a single day. **day tripper** *n.*

daylight (dā′līt) *n.* **1** the light of day, as opposed to that of the moon or artificial light. **2** dawn. **3** light visible through an opening; an interval, a gap, a visible space. **4** openness, publicity. **to beat/ knock the living daylights out of** to beat severely. **to scare the living daylights out of** to frighten greatly. **to see daylight 1** to begin to understand. **2** to draw near to the end of a task. **daylight robbery** *n.* flagrant extortion or overpricing. **daylight saving** *n.* a system of advancing the clock by one hour in spring and setting back the time by one hour in autumn (introduced into Great Britain in 1919). **daylight time** *n.* (*esp. NAm.*) time adjusted for daylight saving.

daze (dāz) *v.t.* **1** to stupefy, to confuse. **2** to dazzle, to overpower with light. *~n.* the state of being dazed. **dazed** *a.* **dazedly** (dā′zidli) *adv.*

dazzle (daz′əl) *v.t.* **1** to overpower with a glare of light. **2** to daze or bewilder with rapidity of motion, brilliant display, stupendous number etc. *~n.* something which dazzles. **dazzlement** *n.* **dazzler** *n.* **dazzling** *a.* **dazzlingly** *adv.*

dB *abbr.* decibel(s).

DBE *abbr.* Dame Commander of the (Order of the) British Empire.

DBS *abbr.* direct broadcasting by satellite.

DC *abbr.* **1** direct current. **2** District of Columbia. **3** District Commissioner.

DCB *abbr.* Dame Commander of the Order of the Bath.

DCL *abbr.* Doctor of Civil Law.

DCM *abbr.* Distinguished Conduct Medal.

DCMG *abbr.* Dame Commander of the Order of St Michael and St George.

DCVO *abbr.* Dame Commander of the Royal Victorian Order.

DD *abbr.* Doctor of Divinity.

DDS *abbr.* Doctor of Dental Surgery.

DDT *abbr.* dichlorodiphenyltrichloroethane, an insecticide.

de- (dē) *pref.* **1** from. **2** down. **3** away. **4** out. **5** completely, thoroughly. **6** expressing undoing, deprivation, reversal or separation.

deaccession (dēaksesh´ən) v.t. (of a library, museum etc.) to dispose of and remove from the catalogue of holdings.

deacon (dē´kən) n. **1** a cleric in orders next below a priest. **2** a lay officer who superintends the secular affairs of a Presbyterian church. **3** a lay officer who admits persons to membership, and assists at communion in the Congregational Church. ~v.t. to appoint as a deacon. **deaconess** n. a female deacon. **deaconship, deaconry** n.

deactivate (dēak´tivāt) v.t. to render harmless or less radioactive. **deactivation** (ā´shən) n. **deactivator** n.

dead (ded) a. **1** having ceased to live. **2** having no life, lifeless. **3** benumbed, insensible, temporarily deprived of the power of action. **4** resembling death. **5** unconscious or unappreciative. **6** without spiritual feeling. **7** obsolete, effete, useless. **8** inanimate or inorganic, as distinct from organic. **9** extinct. **10** lustreless, motionless, soundless; not resonant. **11** flat, vapid, dull, opaque. **12** certain, unerring. **13** complete. **14** sudden. **15** faulty or used up and no longer transmitting sound, electric current etc. **16** no longer burning. **17** no longer effervescent. **18** (of a ball) out of play in a game. ~adv. **1** absolutely, quite, completely. **2** (coll.) very. ~n. **1** (as pl.) dead people. **2** the time when things are still, stillness. **dead-ball line** n. in rugby, a line behind the goal line beyond which the ball is out of play. **dead beat** a. **1** quite exhausted. **2** without recoil. **deadbeat** n. (coll.) a worthless lazy person; a person who is always in debt. **deadbolt** n. a bolt turned by a knob or key. **dead centre,** (N Am.) **dead center** n. **1** the exact centre. **2** either of the two points at which a crank assumes a position in line with the rod which impels it. **dead certainty,** (coll.) **dead cert** n. something sure to occur. **dead duck** n. (coll.) a person or idea doomed to failure. **dead-end** n. **1** a cul-de-sac. **2** a position from which no progress can be made. ~a. (of a job etc.) having no prospects. **dead hand** n. a stifling or restricting influence. **deadhead** n. **1** a withered bloom on a plant. **2** (coll.) a person who has a free pass. **3** a stupid, unimaginative person. ~v.t. to remove withered blooms from (flowers) to encourage future growth. ~v.i. (N Am., coll.) to finish a journey without any passengers. **dead heat** n. **1** a race resulting in a draw. **2** such a result. **dead-heat** v.i. to draw in a race. **dead language** n. a language no longer spoken, such as classical Latin. **dead letter** n. **1** a letter which cannot be delivered by the post office, and is opened and returned to the sender. **2** a law or anything that has become inoperative. **deadline** n. **1** the time of newspapers, books etc. going to press. **2** a fixed time or date terminating something. **deadlock** n. **1** a complete standstill, a position in which no progress can be made. **2** a lock worked on one side by a handle, and on the other by a key. ~v.t., v.i. to bring or come into a deadlock. **dead loss** n. **1** (coll.) a useless person,

thing or situation. **2** a loss with no compensation whatever. **dead man's fingers, dead men's fingers** n. a variety of orchis, *Orchis mascula*. **dead man's handle** n. a device for automatically cutting off the current of an electrically-driven vehicle if the driver releases his pressure on the handle. **dead march** n. a piece of solemn music played at funerals, esp. of soldiers. **deadness** n. **dead nettle** n. a non-stinging labiate plant, like a nettle, of several species belonging to the genus *Lamium*. **dead of night** n. the middle of the night. **dead on** a., adv. completely accurate. **deadpan** a., adv. with an expressionless face or manner. ~v.i. (pres.p **deadpanning,** past, p.p. **deadpanned**) to look or speak deadpan. ~v.t. to address in a deadpan manner. **dead reckoning** n. the calculation of a ship's position from the log and compass, when observations cannot be taken. **dead ringer** n. (coll.) a person or thing exactly resembling someone or something else. **dead set** n. a determined attack or try. **dead shot** n. a marksman who never misses. **dead stock** n. farm equipment. **dead weight** n. **1** a mass of inert matter, a burden that exerts no relieving force. **2** any very heavy weight or load. **3** the total weight carried on a ship. **dead wood** n. useless people or things.

deaden (ded´ən) v.t. **1** to diminish the vitality, brightness, force or power of. **2** to make insensible, to dull; to blunt. ~v.i. to lose vitality, strength, feeling, spirit etc. **deadener** n.

deadly (ded´li) a. (comp. **deadlier,** superl. **deadliest**) **1** causing or procuring death; fatal. **2** like death. **3** very boring. **4** implacable, irreconcilable. **5** intense. ~adv. **1** as if dead. **2** extremely, excessively, intensively. **deadliness** n. **deadly nightshade** n. a poisonous shrub with dark purple berries, *Atropa belladonna*. **deadly sin** n. (Theol.) any one of the seven mortal sins, leading to damnation.

deaf (def) a. **1** incapable or dull of hearing. **2** unwilling to hear, disregarding, refusing to listen, refusing to comply (They were deaf to my requests). **3** insensible (to) (tone-deaf). ~n. (as pl.) deaf people. **deaf-aid** n. a hearing-aid. **deaf-blind** a. both deaf and blind. **deafen** v.t. **1** to make wholly or partially deaf. **2** to stun with noise. **3** to render impervious to sound by pugging (as a floor, partition etc.). **deafening** a. **deafly** adv. **deaf mute** n. a person who is deaf and also unable to speak. **deaf-mutism** n. **deafness** n.

Usage note Organizations connected with the deaf prefer *sign language* to *deaf-and-dumb alphabet* or *language*.

deal[1] (dēl) n. **1** a bargain, a piece of business; a business transaction. **2** an indefinite quantity. **3** the distribution of cards to the players. **4** a player's turn to distribute the cards. **5** a round of play at cards. **6** the hands dealt to a card-player. **7** a share, a part, a portion. **8** a particular form of treatment at a person's hands. ~v.t. (past, p.p.

dealt (delt)) **1** to distribute; to award to someone as their proper share. **2** to distribute or give in succession (as cards). *~v.i.* to distribute cards to the players. **a good deal 1** a large quantity. **2** to a large extent; by much, considerably. **a great deal 1** a large quantity. **2** to a large extent; by much, considerably. **to deal by** to act towards. **to deal in** to be engaged in; to trade in. **to deal with 1** to take action in respect of, to handle. **2** to have to do with. **3** to behave towards. **4** to consider judicially. **dealer** *n.* **1** a trader, a merchant. **2** (*sl.*) a drug-pusher. **3** in a card game, the person who deals. **dealership** *n.* **1** a right or agreement to deal in something. **2** a dealer's premises. **dealings** *n.pl.* **1** conduct towards others. **2** intercourse in matters of business, trade. **to have dealings with** to deal or associate with.

deal² (dēl) *n.* **1** a plank of fir or pine of a standard size, not more than 3 in. (7.6 cm) thick, 7 in. (17.8 cm) wide, and 6 ft. (1.8 m) long. **2** fir or pine wood, esp. when sawn into such planks.

dean¹ (dēn) *n.* **1** an ecclesiastical dignitary presiding over the chapter of a cathedral or collegiate church. **2** a rural dean, a member of the clergy charged with jurisdiction over a part of an archdeaconry. **3** a resident fellow in a college with disciplinary and other functions; a university official with such functions. **4** the head of a university faculty or department; the head of a medical school. **5** a doyen. **deanery** *n.* (*pl.* **deaneries**) the office, district or official residence of a dean. **deanship** *n.*

dean² DENE¹.

dear (diə) *a.* **1** beloved, cherished; greatly esteemed; (a conventional form of address used in letter-writing). **2** precious, valuable. **3** costly, of a high price; available only at a high rate of interest. **4** characterized by high prices. **5** strongly felt (*dashed my dearest hopes*). *~n.* **1** a darling, a loved one. **2** a cherished person, a favourite. *~adv.* dearly, at a high price (*This will cost you dear*). *~int.* expressing distress, sympathy or mild astonishment and protest. **dearie me** *int.* used to express sympathy, surprise etc. **Dear John (letter)** *n.* (*esp. N Am., coll.*) a letter, esp. from a woman to a man, ending a relationship. **dearly** *adv.* **1** very much (*I would dearly love to have a holiday*). **2** with affection, sincerely. **3** at a high price. **dearness** *n.* **deary, dearie** *n.* (*dial., coll.*) dear one (a term of endearment).

dearth (dœth) *n.* a scarcity; lack; want, privation.

death (deth) *n.* **1** extinction of life; the act of dying. **2** the state of being dead. **3** decay, destruction. **4** a cause or instrument of death. **5** spiritual destruction, annihilation. **at death's door** close to death. **in at the death** present at the finish. **like death warmed up/ over** (*coll.*) very ill or tired. **to be the death of 1** to cause the death of. **2** (*coll.*) to make (someone) 'die of laughing'. **3** to be a source of great worry to. **to catch one's death of cold** to catch a very bad cold. **to death** to the greatest degree, as much as possible. **to dice with death** to take great risks. **to do to death 1** to overuse. **2** to kill. **to put to death** to execute. **death adder** *n.* any venomous snake of the genus *Acanthophis.* **deathbed** *n.* the bed on which a person dies. **death blow** *n.* **1** a mortal blow. **2** an event that brings utter ruin or destruction. **death camp** *n.* a prison or detention centre where many people die or are killed. **death-cap** *n.* a poisonous fungus, *Amanita phalloides.* **death certificate** *n.* a document issued by a doctor certifying death and giving the cause, if known. **death duties** *n.pl.* (*Hist.*) a tax levied on property when it passed to the next heir. **death-knell** *n.* **1** a passing-bell. **2** a ringing in the ears supposed to forebode death. **deathless** *a.* **deathlessness** *n.* **deathlike** *a.* **deathly** *a.* (*comp.* **deathlier,** *superl.* **deathliest**) **1** like death. **2** deadly. *~adv.* so as to resemble death. **death mask** *n.* a plaster cast of the face after death. **death penalty** *n.* the punishment of being executed for committing a very serious crime. **death rate** *n.* the proportion of deaths in a given period in a given district. **death-rattle** *n.* a gurgling sound in the throat of a person just before death. **death row** *n.* a section of condemned cells, esp. in a US prison. **death's head** *n.* a human skull, or a representation of one, as an emblem of mortality. **death's-head moth** *n.* a large European moth, *Acherontia atropos,* with markings on the back of the thorax faintly resembling a human skull. **death squad** *n.* an organized armed group engaged in systematic killings. **death toll** *n.* the number of people killed in battle, a natural disaster etc. **death-trap** *n.* **1** a place unsuspectedly dangerous to life through insanitary or other conditions. **2** a vehicle etc. in dangerous condition. **death warrant** *n.* **1** an order for the execution of a criminal. **2** an act or measure putting an end to something. **death-watch (beetle)** *n.* a wood-boring beetle, *Xestobium rufovillosum,* which makes a clicking sound formerly thought to presage death. **death wish** *n.* a desire for one's own death.

deb (deb) *n.* a debutante.

debacle (dābah'kəl, di-), **débâcle** (dā-) *n.* **1** a complete failure; a rout. **2** a stampede.

debag (dēbag') *v.t.* (*pres.p.* **debagging,** *past, p.p.* **debagged**) (*coll.*) to remove the trousers of (someone) by force.

debar (dibah') *v.i.* (*pres.p.* **debarring,** *past, p.p.* **debarred**) **1** to hinder or exclude from approach, enjoyment or action. **2** to prohibit, to forbid.

debark¹ (dibahk') *v.t., v.i.* to disembark. **debarkation** (dēbahkā'shən) *n.*

debark² (dēbahk') *v.t.* to remove the bark from.

debase (dibās') *v.t.* **1** to lower in condition, quality or value. **2** to adulterate. **3** to degrade. **debasement** *n.* **debaser** *n.*

debate (dibāt') *v.t.* to contend by words or arguments, esp. formally or publicly; to discuss. *~v.i.* to discuss or argue a point, esp. formally or publicly; to engage in argument. *~n.* a (formal or public) discussion of a question; an argumentative contest. **debatable** *a.* **1** open to discussion or argument. **2** contentious. **debatably** *adv.* **debater** *n.* **debating** *n.*, *a.* **debating point** *n.* a point made to score a point in a debate rather than further the argument.

debauch (dibawch´) *v.t.* **1** to corrupt in morals, to pervert. **2** to lead into sensuality or intemperance. **3** to debase. *~n.* an act or bout of debauchery; a carouse. **debauched** *a.* having loose morals. **debauchee** (-chē´) *n.* a person who indulges their sensual appetites. **debaucher** *n.* **debauchery** *n.* indulgence of the sensual appetites.

debenture (diben´chə) *n.* **1** a written acknowledgement of a debt. **2** a deed or instrument issued by a company or a public body as a security for a loan of money on which interest is payable till it is redeemed. **3** (*US*) a debenture bond. **debenture bond** *n.* (*US*) a fixed-interest bond issued by a company or corporation and backed by general credit. **debenture stock** *n.* debentures consolidated or created in the form of stock, the interest on which constitutes the first charge on the dividend.

debilitate (dibil´itāt) *v.t.* to weaken, to enfeeble; to enervate, to impair. **debilitation** (-ā´shən) *n.* **debility** *n.* (*pl.* **debilities**) (a) weakness, feebleness.

debit (deb´it) *n.* **1** an amount set down as a debt. **2** in book-keeping, the left-hand side of an account, in which debits are entered. *~v.t.* (*pres.p.* **debiting**, *past*, *p.p.* **debited**) **1** to charge to as a debt. **2** in book-keeping, to enter (an amount, a person owing) on the debit side. **debit card** *n.* a card issued by a bank which enables the holder to debit a purchase to their account at the point of purchase.

debonair (debəneə´), **debonnaire** *a.* **1** having self-assurance, carefree. **2** courteous, genial, pleasing in manner and bearing. **debonairly** *adv.* **debonairness** *n.*

debouch (dibowch´, -boosh´) *v.i.* **1** to march out from a confined place into open ground. **2** to flow out from a narrow ravine. **debouchment** *n.*

debrief (dēbrēf´) *v.t.* to gather information from (someone, such as a soldier, diplomat or spy) after a mission.

debris (deb´rē, dā´brē) *n.* **1** broken rubbish, fragments. **2** (*Geol.*) fragmentary matter detached by a rush of water.

debt (det) *n.* **1** something which is owing from one person to another, esp. a sum of money. **2** obligation, liability. **in a person's debt** under an obligation to a person. **debt of honour** *n.* a debt which is morally but not legally binding, such as a gambling debt. **debtor** *n.* a person who is indebted to another, as distinct from *creditor*.

debug (dēbŭg´) *v.t.* (*pres.p.* **debugging**, *past*, *p.p.* **debugged**) **1** to find and remove hidden microphones from. **2** (*Comput.*) to find and remove the faults in (a computer program, a system etc.).

3 to remove insects from. **debugger** *n.* (*Comput.*) a computer program which debugs other programs.

debunk (dēbŭngk´) *v.t.* to dispel false sentiment about, to destroy pleasing legends or illusions about. **debunker** *n.*

debut (dā´bū, deb´ū) *n.* **1** a first appearance before the public, esp. of a performer. **2** the presentation of a debutante at court. **debutant** (deb´ūtant), **débutant** *n.* a male performer making his debut. **debutante** (deb´ūtahnt), **débutante** *n.* **1** a young woman who makes a debut at court. **2** a female performer making her debut.

Dec. *abbr.* December.

deca- (dek´ə), **dec-** *comb. form* ten.

decade (dek´ād) *n.* **1** a period of ten years. **2** a group of ten.

decadence (dek´ədəns) *n.* moral or cultural decay, deterioration; a falling-off from a high standard of excellence. **decadent** *a.* **1** having low moral or cultural standards. **2** self-indulgent, affected. *~n.* a decadent writer or artist, esp. one having weaknesses and affectations indicating lack of strength and originality.

decaf (dē´kaf), **decaff** *n.* decaffeinated coffee. *~a.* decaffeinated.

decaffeinate (dikaf´ināt) *v.t.* **1** to remove the caffeine from (coffee, tea etc.). **2** to reduce the caffeine in.

decagon (dek´əgən) *n.* a plane figure with ten sides and ten angles. **decagonal** (dikag´-) *a.*

decahedron (dekəhē´drən) *n.* (*pl.* **decahedra** (-drə), **decahedrons**) a solid figure with ten sides. **decahedral** *a.*

decal (dē´kəl) *n.* a transfer, a decalcomania.

decalcify (dēkal´sifī) *v.t.* (*3rd pers. sing. pres.* **decalcifies**, *pres.p.* **decalcifying**, *past*, *p.p.* **decalcified**) to clear (bone etc.) of calcareous matter. **decalcification** (-fikā´shən) *n.*

decalcomania (dikalkəmā´niə) *n.* (*pl.* **decalcomanias**) **1** the process of transferring a design. **2** a design so transferred.

decalitre (dek´əlētə), (*N Am.*) **decaliter** *n.* a liquid measure of capacity containing 10 litres (nearly 2½ gallons).

decametre (dek´əmētə), (*N Am.*) **decameter** *n.* a measure of length, containing 10 metres (393.7 in).

decamp (dikamp´) *v.i.* **1** to break camp. **2** to depart quickly; to take oneself off. **decampment** *n.*

decanal (dikā´nəl, dek´ənəl) *a.* **1** of or relating to a dean or a deanery. **2** of or relating to the south side of the choir, where the dean has his seat, as distinct from *cantorial*.

decant (dikant´) *v.t.* **1** to pour off by gently inclining, so as not to disturb the sediment. **2** to pour (wine etc.) from one container into another. **3** to move (people) from one area to another to provide better housing etc. **decanter** *n.* a glass container with a stopper, for holding wine or spirits.

decapitate (dikap'itāt) *v.t.* **1** to behead. **2** to cut the top or end from. **decapitation** (-tā'shən) *n.* **decapitator** *n.*

decapod (dek'əpod) *n.* **1** any cephalopod of the order Decapoda, having two tentacles and four pairs of arms. **2** any crustacean of the order Decapoda, having five pairs of ambulatory limbs, the first pair chelate.

decarbonate (dēkah'bənāt), **decarbonize** (-īz), **decarbonise** *v.t.* to remove carbon from. **decarbonization** (-zā'shən) *n.*

decasyllable (dek'əsiləbəl) *n.* a word or line of ten syllables. **decasyllabic** (-lab'ik) *a.*

decathlon (dikath'lon) *n.* (*pl.* **decathlons**) an athletic contest consisting of ten events. **decathlete** *n.*

decay (dikā') *v.i.* **1** to rot. **2** to decline in excellence. **3** to fall away, to deteriorate. **4** (*Physics*) (of radioactive matter) to disintegrate. ~*v.t.* **1** to cause to rot. **2** to impair, to cause to fall away. ~*n.* **1** gradual failure or decline; deterioration. **2** a state of ruin. **3** wasting away, consumption, gradual dissolution. **4** decomposition of dead tissue, rot. **5** decayed matter. **6** (*Physics*) disintegration of radioactive matter.

decease (disēs') *n.* (*formal*) death, departure from this life. ~*v.i.* to die. **deceased** *a.* dead. ~*n.* a person who has recently died.

deceit (disēt') *n.* **1** the act of deceiving. **2** a tendency to deceive. **3** trickery, deception, duplicity. **4** a stratagem, a dishonest act. **deceitful** *a.* **1** given to deceit. **2** intended to deceive. **deceitfully** *adv.* **deceitfulness** *n.*

deceive (disēv') *v.t.* **1** to mislead deliberately or knowingly. **2** to cheat, to delude. **3** to be unfaithful to. ~*v.i.* to act deceitfully. **to be deceived** to be mistaken. **to deceive oneself** to ignore the truth. **deceivable** *a.* **deceiver** *n.*

decelerate (dēsel'ərāt) *v.i.* to reduce speed, to slow down. ~*v.t.* to cause to decelerate. **deceleration** (-rā'shən) *n.*

December (disem'bə) *n.* the twelfth and last month of the year (orig. the tenth and afterwards the twelfth month of the Roman year).

decennary (disen'əri) *n.* (*pl.* **decennaries**) a period of ten years. **decennial** *a.* **1** lasting ten years. **2** occurring every ten years. **decennially** *adv.*

decent (dē'sənt) *a.* **1** becoming, seemly. **2** modest; decorous. **3** respectable. **4** passable, tolerable. **5** (*coll.*) kind and honest. **decency** (dē'sənsi) *n.* (*pl.* **decencies**) **1** propriety. **2** respectable speech or behaviour. **3** freedom from immodesty or obscenity; decorum. **4** (*pl.*) accepted standards of good behaviour. **decently** *adv.*

decentralize (dēsen'trəlīz), **decentralise** *v.t.* **1** to break up (a centralized administration etc.), transfer from central control. **2** to organize on the principle of local management rather than central government. **decentralist** *n., a.* **decentralization** (-zā'shən) *n.* **decentre**, (*N Am.*) **decenter** *v.t.* to remove the centre of.

deception (disep'shən) *n.* **1** the act of deceiving. **2** the state of being deceived. **3** something which deceives; a deceit, a fraud. **deceptive** *a.* tending or apt to deceive, easy to mistake. **deceptively** *adv.* **deceptiveness** *n.*

deci- (des'i) *pref.* a tenth part of.

decibel (des'ibel) *n.* a unit to compare levels of intensity, esp. of sound, one-tenth of a bel.

decide (disīd') *v.t.* **1** to come to a decision about, to determine; to adjudge. **2** to settle by adjudging (victory or superiority). **3** to bring to a decision. ~*v.i.* **1** to come to a decision. **2** to give a judgement. **decidable** *a.* **decided** *a.* **1** settled; clear, evident, unmistakable. **2** determined, resolute, unwavering, firm. **decidedly** *adv.* distinctly, downright. **decidedness** *n.* **decider** *n.* **1** a deciding heat or game. **2** a person or something which decides.

deciduous (disid'ūəs) *a.* **1** (of leaves etc. which fall in autumn and trees which lose their leaves annually) falling, not perennial. **2** (of wings etc.) shed during the lifetime of an animal. **3** falling off, not permanent; having only a temporary existence. **deciduousness** *n.*

⊠ **decieve** common misspelling of DECEIVE.

decigram (des'igram), **decigramme** *n.* a weight equal to one-tenth of a gram (1.54 grain).

decilitre (des'ilētə), (*N Am.*) **deciliter** *n.* a fluid measure of capacity of one-tenth of a litre (0.176 pint).

decimal (des'iməl) *a.* **1** of or relating to ten or tenths. **2** counting by tens. ~*n.* a decimal fraction. **decimal fraction** *n.* a fraction having some power of ten for its denominator, esp. when it is expressed by figures representing the numerator of tenths, hundredths etc. following a point. **decimalize, decimalise** *v.t.* to reduce or adapt to the decimal system. **decimalization** (-zā'shən) *n.* **decimally** *adv.* **decimal place** *n.* a position of a figure in a decimal fraction to the right of the decimal point. **decimal point** *n.* the dot to the right of the unit figure in a decimal fraction.

decimate (des'imāt) *v.t.* **1** to destroy a tenth or a large proportion of. **2** (*Mil.*) to punish every tenth man with death. **decimation** (-ā'shən) *n.* **decimator** *n.*

decimetre (des'imētə), (*N Am.*) **decimeter** *n.* the tenth part of a metre (3.937 in).

decipher (disī'fə) *v.t.* **1** to turn from cipher into ordinary language. **2** to discover the meaning of (something written in cipher). **3** to read or explain (bad or indistinct writing). **decipherable** *a.* **decipherment** *n.*

decision (disizh'ən) *n.* **1** the act or result of deciding. **2** the determination of a trial, contest or question. **3** resolution, firmness of character. **decisive** (-sī'-) *a.* **1** determining the outcome of something. **2** able to make decisions quickly. **decisively** *adv.* **decisiveness** *n.*

deck (dek) *n.* **1** the plank or iron flooring of a ship, a platform forming a floor in a ship.

2 accommodation on a deck at a particular level. **3** the floor of a bus or tramcar. **4** (*sl.*) the ground. **5** a floor or platform for sunbathing etc. **6** the floor of a pier. **7** a piece of sound-recording equipment in or on which the disc, tape etc. to be played is placed. **8** (*esp. N Am.*) a pack (of cards). **9** (*US, sl.*) a packet of narcotic drugs. ~*v.t.* **1** to adorn, to beautify. **2** to cover, to put a deck to. **3** (*sl.*) to knock to the ground. **below deck** in or to the area below the main deck of a ship. **below decks** below deck. **on deck 1** on an uncovered deck on a ship. **2** (*esp. US*) ready for action etc. **to deck out** to adorn, to beautify. **deckchair** *n.* a collapsible chair, camp-stool or long chair for reclining in. **decked** *a.* **-decker** (dek´ə) *comb. form* having a specified number of decks, as *double-decker*. **deckhand** *n.* a sailor who works primarily on deck.

deckle (dek´əl) *n.* a frame used in paper-making to keep the pulp within the desired limits. **deckle edge** *n.* the rough, untrimmed edge of paper. **deckle-edged** *a.*

declaim (diklām´) *v.t.* to utter rhetorically or passionately. ~*v.i.* **1** to speak a set oration in public. **2** to protest forcefully (against). **3** to speak rhetorically or passionately. **declaimer** *n.* **declamation** (dekləmā´shən) *n.* **1** the act or art of declaiming according to rhetorical rules. **2** a formal oration. **3** impassioned oratory. **4** an impassioned speech. **declamatory** (-klam´-) *a.*

declaration (deklərā´shən) *n.* **1** the act of declaring or proclaiming. **2** something which is declared or proclaimed. **3** the document in which anything is declared or proclaimed. **4** a manifesto, an official announcement, esp. of constitutional or diplomatic principles, laws or intentions. **5** (*Law*) an affirmation in lieu of oath. **6** in card games, the act of naming the trump suit; an announcement of a combination in one's hand. **7** in cricket, a voluntary close of innings before all the wickets have fallen.

declare (diklea´) *v.t.* **1** to pronounce, to assert or affirm positively. **2** to announce publicly, to proclaim formally. **3** to state the possession of (dutiable articles). **4** in card games, to name the (trump suit). **5** in cricket, to close (an innings) voluntarily. ~*v.i.* **1** to make a declaration, to avow. **2** in card games, to name the trump suit. **3** in cricket, to announce an innings as closed before all the wickets have fallen. **I (do) declare!** used to express surprise, disbelief etc. **to declare oneself 1** to avow one's intentions. **2** to disclose one's character or attitude. **declarable** *a.* **declarant** *n.* (*Law*) a person who makes a declaration. **declarative** (-klar´-) *a.* **1** explanatory, declaratory. **2** (*Comput.*) (of a programming language) for use in problem-solving without specification of exact procedures. ~*n.* **1** a declaratory statement. **2** a declarative sentence. **declaratively** *adv.* **declarative sentence** *n.* (*Gram.*) a sentence taking the form of a simple statement. **declaratory** (-klar´-) *a.* **declared** *a.* self-confessed. **declaredly**

(-klee´rid-) *adv.* by one's own admission. **declarer** *n.*

declassify (dēklas´ifī) *v.t.* (*3rd pers. sing. pres.* **declassifies**, *pres.p.* **declassifying**, *past, p.p.* **declassified**) to remove (information) from the security list. **declassification** (-fikā´shən) *n.*

declension (diklen´shən) *n.* **1** (*Gram.*) **a** the variation of inflection of nouns, adjectives and pronouns. **b** a number of nouns declined in the same way. **c** the act of declining a noun etc. **2** declining, descent, deterioration, falling off. **declensional** *a.*

declination (deklinā´shən) *n.* **1** the act of bending or moving downwards. **2** (*Astron.*) the angular distance of a heavenly body north or south of the celestial equator. **declinational** *a.* **declination of the compass** *n.* the angle between the geographic and the magnetic meridians.

decline (diklīn´) *v.i.* **1** to sink, to fall off, to deteriorate, to decay. **2** to refuse something politely. **3** to slope downwards. **4** to droop, to stoop. **5** (*Gram.*) (of a noun) to inflect. **6** to approach the end. ~*v.t.* **1** to refuse politely, to turn away from; to reject. **2** (*Gram.*) to recite the inflections of (a noun etc.) in order. **3** to depress, to lower. ~*n.* **1** a falling-off. **2** deterioration, decay, diminution. **3** gradual failure of strength or health, formerly esp. due to tuberculosis. **4** a fall in prices. **5** setting of the sun. **6** gradual approach to extinction or death. **declinable** *a.* **declining years** *n.pl.* old age.

declivity (dikliv´iti) *n.* (*pl.* **declivities**) an inclination, a slope or gradual descent of the surface of the ground, as distinct from *acclivity*. **declivitous** *a.*

declutch (dēkluch´) *v.i.* to release the clutch of a vehicle.

decoct (dikokt´) *v.t.* to extract the essence of by boiling. **decoction** *n.* **1** the act of boiling a substance to extract its essence. **2** the liquor or substance obtained by boiling.

decode (dēkōd´) *v.t.* to translate from code symbols into ordinary language. **decodable** *a.* **decoder** *n.* a person or thing that decodes symbols.

decoke (dēkōk´) *v.t.* to remove carbon from, to decarbonize. ~*n.* an act of decoking an engine.

décolleté (dākol´tā) *a.* (*fem.* **décolletée**) **1** (of a dress) low-necked. **2** wearing a low-necked dress. ~*n.* a low-cut neckline. **décolletage** (-tahzh´) *n.* the low-cut neckline of a dress.

decolonize (dēkol´ənīz), **decolonise** *v.t.* to grant independence to (a colonial state). **decolonization** (-zā´shən) *n.*

decommission (dēkəmish´ən) *v.t.* **1** to close or dismantle (a nuclear reactor etc.) which is no longer to be used. **2** to take (a ship) out of service.

decompose (dēkəmpōz´) *v.t.* **1** to resolve into constituent elements. **2** to cause to rot. ~*v.i.* to become decomposed; to putrefy. **decomposition** (-kompəzish´ən) *n.*

decompress (dēkəmpres´) v.t. **1** gradually to relieve pressure on. **2** to return to normal atmospheric pressure conditions. **decompression** (-presh´ən) n. **decompression chamber** n. a chamber in which a person (e.g. a diver) is gradually returned to normal pressure conditions. **decompression sickness** n. severe pain and breathing problems caused by sudden change in atmospheric pressure. **decompressor** n. a device for relieving pressure on an engine.

decongestant (dēkənjes´tənt) a. relieving congestion. ~n. a drug or medicine relieving nasal or chest congestion.

deconsecrate (dēkon´sikrāt) v.t. to withdraw consecrated status from; to secularize. **deconsecration** (-rā´shən) n.

deconstruction (dēkənstrŭk´shən) n. a method of literary and philosophical analysis by breaking down the structure of the language on the assumption that words have no fixed meaning outside of their relation to other words. **deconstruct** (-strŭkt´) v.t. **deconstructionism** n. **deconstructionist** n., a.

decontaminate (dēkəntam´ināt) v.t. to clear of a poisonous substance or radioactivity. **decontamination** (-ā´shən) n.

decontrol (dēkəntrōl´) v.t. (pres.p. **decontrolling**, past, p.p. **decontrolled**) to terminate government control of (a trade etc.). ~n. the act of decontrolling something.

decor (dā´kaw), **décor** n. the setting, arrangement and decoration of a room or of a scene on the stage.

decorate (dek´ərāt) v.t. **1** to make more attractive by ornamentation. **2** to be an embellishment to. **3** to confer a medal or other badge of honour on. **4** to paint, paper etc. (a room or house). **decorated** a. **1** adorned, ornamented, embellished. **2** possessing a medal or other badge of honour. **3** denoting the middle pointed architecture in England (c.1300–1400). **decoration** (-ā´shən) n. **1** the act of decorating. **2** ornamentation, ornament. **3** a medal or other badge of honour. **4** (pl.) flags, flowers and other adornments put up on an occasion of public rejoicing etc. **decorative** (dek´ərətiv) a. **decoratively** adv. **decorativeness** n. **decorator** n. **1** a person who adorns or embellishes. **2** a person whose business it is to paint and paper rooms or houses.

decorous (dek´ərəs) a. **1** behaving in a polite and decent manner. **2** in good taste. **decorously** adv. **decorousness** n. **decorum** (dikaw´rəm) n. (pl. **decorums**) **1** decency and propriety of words and conduct. **2** etiquette, polite usage. **3** a requirement of decency or etiquette.

découpage (dākoopahzh´) n. the art of decorating furniture etc. with cut-out patterns.

decouple (dēkŭp´əl) v.t. **1** to separate, to end the connection between. **2** in electronics, to reduce unwanted distortion on (a circuit).

decoy (dē´koi, dikoi´) n. **1** a bait, an attraction. **2** a person employed to lure or entrap; a tempter. **3** a decoy-duck. **4** a pond or enclosed water into which wildfowl are lured by means of a decoy. ~v.t. **1** to lure into a trap or snare. **2** to allure, to entice. **decoy-duck** n. a tame or imitation duck, used to lure wildfowl into a trap.

decrease¹ (dikrēs´) v.i. to become less, to wane, to fail. ~v.t. to make less, to reduce in size gradually. **decreasingly** adv.

decrease² (dē´krēs) n. **1** lessening, a diminution. **2** the amount of diminution.

decree (dikrē´) n. **1** an edict, law or ordinance made by superior authority. **2** (Law) the decision in some courts, esp. in matrimonial and Admiralty cases. ~v.t. (3rd pers. sing. pres. **decrees**, pres.p. **decreeing**, past, p.p. **decreed**) **1** to command by a decree. **2** to ordain or determine. ~v.i. to make an edict. **decree absolute** n. (pl. **decrees absolute**) the final decree in divorce proceedings. **decree nisi** n. (pl. **decrees nisi**) a provisional decree in divorce proceedings.

decrement (dek´rimənt) n. **1** decrease, diminution. **2** the quantity lost by diminution. **3** (Physics) a measure of the speed of damping-out of damped waves.

decrepit (dikrep´it) a. **1** broken down by age and infirmities; feeble. **2** dilapidated, decayed. **decrepitude** (-tūd) n.

decrescendo (dēkrishen´dō) adv., a. (Mus.) diminuendo. ~n. (pl. **decrescendos**) a diminuendo.

decretal (dikrē´təl) n. **1** a decree, esp. of the Pope. **2** (pl.) a collection or body of papal decrees on points of ecclesiastical law or discipline.

decriminalize (dēkrim´inəlīz), **decriminalise** v.t. to make (an action) no longer illegal. **decriminalization** (-zā´shən) n.

decry (dikrī´) v.t. (3rd pers. sing. pres. **decries**, pres.p. **decrying**, past, p.p. **decried**) **1** to cry down; to clamour against. **2** to depreciate. **decrier** n.

decrypt (dēkript´) v.t. to decipher. **decryption** n.

dedicate (ded´ikāt) v.t. **1** to apply or give up wholly to some purpose, person or thing. **2** to inscribe or address (a work of art) to a friend or patron. **3** to set apart and consecrate solemnly to God or to some sacred purpose. **dedicated** a. **1** devoting one's time to one pursuit or cause. **2** (of computers etc.) designed to perform a specific function. **dedicatedly** adv. **dedicatee** (-kətē´) n. the person to whom something is dedicated. **dedication** (-ā´shən) n. **1** the act of dedicating. **2** devotion to a pursuit or cause. **3** the words in which a book, building etc. is dedicated. **4** a dedicatory inscription. **dedicative** a. **dedicator** n. **dedicatory** a.

deduce (didūs´) v.t. to draw as a conclusion by reasoning, to infer. **deducible** a. **deductive** (-dŭk´tiv) a. deduced, or capable of being deduced, from premises. **deductively** adv.

deduct (didŭkt´) v.t. to take away, to subtract. **deductible** a. that may be deducted. ~n. (US) the excess payment in an insurance claim. **deductibility** (-bil´-) n.

deduction (didŭk´shən) *n.* **1** the act of deducting. **2** that which is deducted. **3** the act of deducing. **4** an inference, a consequence.

dee (dē) *n.* (*pl.* **dees**) **1** the fourth letter of the alphabet, D, d. **2** anything shaped like the capital form of this letter, as a D-shaped loop or link in harness.

deed (dēd) *n.* **1** an action, a thing done with intention. **2** an illustrious exploit, an achievement. **3** fact, reality (*in deed*). **4** (*Law*) a document containing the terms of a contract and the evidence of its due execution. *~v.t.* (*NAm.*) to transfer or convey by deed. **deed of covenant** *n.* an undertaking to pay a regular specified sum to a charity etc. which can then also recover the tax paid on income which would provide that sum. **deed poll** *n.* (*Law*) a deed made by one person only, esp. to change their name (so called because the paper is cut or polled evenly, and not indented).

deejay (dē´jā) *n.* (*coll.*) a disc jockey.

deem (dēm) *v.t.* (*formal*) **1** to judge, to consider. **2** to suppose, to think. **deemster** (dem´stə), **dempster** (demp´stə) *n.* either of two officers who officiate as judges, one in the north and the other in the south part of the Isle of Man.

de-emphasize (dēem´fəsīz), **de-emphasise** *v.t.* **1** to remove the emphasis from. **2** to reduce the emphasis on.

deep (dēp) *a.* **1** extending far down. **2** extending far in from the surface or away from the outside. **3** having a thickness or measurement back or down (*two feet deep*). **4** dark-coloured, intensely dark. **5** profound, penetrating, abstruse. **6** heartfelt, grave, earnest. **7** intense, extreme, heinous. **8** from far down, sonorous, low in pitch, full in tone. **9** well-versed, sagacious. **10** (*coll.*) artful, scheming, secretive. **11** distant from the batsman on a cricket pitch. **12** distant from the attacking line of a football team. *~adv.* **1** deeply, far down. **2** far on. **3** profoundly, intensely. **4** distant from the batsman or the attacking line etc. in a game. *~n.* **1** anything deep. **2** (*poet.*) the sea (*the deep*). **3** the deep parts of the sea. **4** a deep place, an abyss, a gulf, a cavity. **5** (*poet.*) the bottom of the heart, the mysterious region of personality. **in deep water** in trouble. **deep breathing** *n.* taking long breaths, esp. for relaxation. **deep-drawn** *a.* (of metal) drawn through a die when cold. **deepen** *v.t.* to make deeper. *~v.i.* to become deeper. **deep end** *n.* the end of a swimming pool where the water is deepest. **to be thrown in at the deep end** to be given the most difficult part to do first, to be required to start without much experience. **to go (in) off the deep end** to give way to one's anger. **to jump in at the deep end** to start with the most difficult part, to start without much experience. **deep-freeze** *n.* **1** a type of refrigerator for the storage of foods and perishable goods at a very low temperature. **2** a temporary cessation. *~v.t.* (*pres.p.* **deep-freezing**, *past* **deep-froze**, *p.p.* **deep-frozen**) to freeze in a deep-freeze. **deep-fry** *v.t.* (*3rd pers. sing. pres.* **deep-fries,**

pres.p. **deep-frying**, *past, p.p.* **deep-fried**) to fry (food) submerged in fat or oil. **deep-laid** *a.* (of a plan) profoundly, secretly or elaborately schemed. **deeply** *adv.* **deepness** *n.* **deep-rooted** *a.* firmly established. **deep sea** *n.* the deeper parts of the sea. **deep-seated** *a.* profound; firmly seated. **deep space** *n.* that area of space beyond the earth and the moon or the solar system.

deer (diə) *n.* (*pl.* **deer**) any ruminant quadruped of the family Cervidae, the males having antlers, except in the one domesticated species, the reindeer. **deer fly** *n.* any bloodsucking fly of the genus *Chrysops*. **deerhound** *n.* a large greyhound with a rough coat, formerly used for hunting deer. **deerskin** *n.* **1** the skin of a deer. **2** leather made from the skin of a deer. *~a.* of this material. **deerstalker** *n.* **1** a person who hunts deer by stalking. **2** a cap with peaks in front and behind and earflaps.

de-escalate (dēes´kəlāt) *v.t.* to reduce the intensity of. **de-escalation** (-ā´shən) *n.*

deface (difās´) *v.t.* **1** to disfigure; to spoil the appearance or beauty of. **2** to erase, to obliterate. **defaceable** *a.* **defacement** *n.* **defacer** *n.*

de facto (dā fak´tō) *adv.* (*formal*) in fact. *~a.* existing in fact.

defalcate (dē´falkāt) *v.i.* to commit embezzlement. **defalcation** (-kā´shən) *n.* **1** (*Law*) **a** misappropriation of money, embezzlement. **b** a sum misappropriated. **2** a defect. **3** defection. **defalcator** *n.*

defame (difām´) *v.t.* to speak maliciously about; to slander, to libel. **defamation** (defəmā´shən) *n.* **defamatory** (-fam´-) *a.*

defat (dēfat´) *v.t.* (*pres.p.* **defatting**, *past, p.p.* **defatted**) to remove fat(s) from.

default (difawlt´) *n.* **1** (*esp. Law*) failure to do something, esp. to appear in court on the day assigned or to meet financial liabilities. **2** want, lack, absence. **3** an option adopted by a computer if no alternative instructions are given. *~v.i.* (*esp. Law*) to fail to do something, esp. to appear in court or to meet financial liabilities. *~v.t.* (*Law*) to enter as a defaulter and give judgement against, in case of non-appearance. **by default** (happening) only because something else has not happened (*Since no one else applied, he got the job by default*). **in default of** instead of (something wanting). **defaulter** *n.* **1** a person who defaults. **2** (*Mil.*) a soldier guilty of a military offence.

defeat (difēt´) *v.t.* **1** to overthrow, to discomfit. **2** to resist successfully, to frustrate. **3** to baffle. **4** to reject in a ballot. **5** (*Law*) to render null. *~n.* **1** overthrow, discomfiture, esp. of an army. **2** (*Law*) annulment. **defeatism** *n.* **1** persistent expectation of defeat. **2** behaviour reflecting this. **defeatist** *n.*, *a.*

defecate (def´əkāt), **defaecate** *v.i.* to eject faeces from the body. **defecation** (-ā´shən) *n.*

defect[1] (dē´fekt) *n.* **1** absence of something essential to perfection or completeness. **2** moral imperfection, failing. **3** blemish. **4** the degree to which something falls short. **defective** (difek´-) *a.* **1** imperfect, incomplete, faulty. **2** intellectually, physically or morally lacking. ~*n.* (*offensive*) a person with a mental handicap. **defectively** *adv.* **defectiveness** *n.*

Usage note The meanings of the adjectives *defective* and *deficient* overlap, but in general *defective* implies some specific fault or damage, and *deficient* a shortage of something possessed.

defect² (difekt´) *v.i.* to desert one's country or cause for the other side. **defection** *n.* **defector** *n.*

defence (difens´), (*esp. N Am.*) **defense** *n.* **1** the state or act of defending. **2** something which defends. **3** the military resources of a country. **4** (*pl.*) fortifications, fortified posts. **5** justification, vindication. **6** excuse, apology. **7** (*Law*) **a** the defendant's reply to the plaintiff's declaration, demands or charges. **b** the defendant's lawyers. **8** in team sports, the players who defend their team's goal. **defenceless** *a.* **defencelessly** *adv.* **defencelessness** *n.* **defenceman** *n.* (*pl.* **defencemen**) a defender in ice hockey or lacrosse. **defence mechanism** *n.* (*Psych.*) a usually unconscious mental adjustment for excluding from the consciousness matters the subject does not wish to receive.

defend (difend´) *v.t.* **1** to protect, to guard; to shield from harm. **2** to keep safe against attack. **3** to support, to maintain by argument, to vindicate. **4** (*Law*) to plead in justification of. **5** in team sports, to try to stop the opposing team scoring in (a goal etc.). **6** (of the current holder) to defend (a sports title or championship) against a challenge. ~*v.i.* **1** (*Law*) **a** to plead on behalf of the defendant. **b** to contest a suit. **2** in team sports, to play in defence. **defendable** *a.* **defendant** *n.* (*Law*) **1** a person summoned into court to answer some charge. **2** a person sued in a lawsuit. **defender** *n.* **defensible** *a.* **defensibility** (-bil´-) *n.* **defensibly** *adv.* **defensive** *a.* **1** serving to defend. **2** overanxious to defend oneself against (expected) criticism. **3** protective, not aggressive. **on the defensive 1** ready to defend oneself. **2** overanxious to defend oneself against (expected) criticism. **defensive end** *n.* either of two particular defensive players in American football. **defensively** *adv.* **defensiveness** *n.*

defenestration (dēfenistrā´shən) *n.* (*formal or facet.*) the action of throwing someone (or occasionally something) out of a window. **defenestrate** (-fen´-) *v.t.*

defer¹ (difœ´) *v.t.* (*pres.p.* **deferring**, *past, p.p.* **deferred**) **1** to put off; to postpone. **2** (*US*) to postpone the conscription of. ~*v.i.* to delay; to procrastinate. **deferment** *n.* **deferrable** *a.* **deferral** *n.* **deferred** *a.* **deferred payment** *n.* payment by instalments.

defer² (difœ´) *v.i.* (*pres.p.* **deferring**, *past, p.p.* **deferred**) to yield to the opinion of another. **deference** (def´ər-) *n.* **1** submission to the views or opinions of another; compliance. **2** respect,

regard. **deferential** (deferen´-) *a.* **deferentially** *adv.* **deferrer** *n.*

defiance, defiant DEFY.

defibrillator (dēfib´rilātə) *n.* (*Med.*) a machine used to apply an electric current to the chest and heart area to stop fibrillation of the heart. **defibrillation** (-ā´shən) *n.*

deficient (difish´ənt) *a.* **1** wanting, defective; falling short. **2** not fully supplied. **deficiency** (difish´ənsi) *n.* (*pl.* **deficiencies**) **1** a falling short; deficit, lack, want, insufficiency. **2** a thing lacking. **3** the amount lacking to make complete or sufficient. **deficiency disease** *n.* a disease caused by lack or insufficiency of one or more of the essential food constituents. **deficiently** *adv.*

Usage note See note under DEFECT¹.

deficit (def´isit) *n.* **1** a falling short of revenue as compared with expenditure. **2** the amount of this deficiency. **3** the amount required to make assets balance liabilities.

defier DEFY.

defile¹ (difīl´) *v.t.* **1** to make foul or dirty; to soil, to stain. **2** (*euphem.*) to deprive of virginity, to violate. **3** to pollute, to desecrate, to make ceremonially unclean. **defilement** *n.* **defiler** *n.*

defile² (dē´fīl, difīl´) *n.* **1** a long, narrow pass or passage, as between hills, along which people can march only in file. **2** a gorge. ~*v.i.* to march in a file or by files.

☒ **definately** common misspelling of DEFINITELY (under DEFINITE).

define (difīn´) *v.t.* **1** to give a definition of, to state the meaning of (a word etc.), to describe (a thing) by its qualities and circumstances. **2** to mark out, to fix with precision (as duties etc.). **3** to determine the limits of. **definable** *a.* **definably** *adv.*

Usage note The meanings of the adjectives *definite* and *definitive* overlap, but in general something *definitive* is regarded as final and authoritative, and something *definite* is exact but may be changed, and may even be misleading or untrue.

definite (def´init) *a.* **1** limited, determinate, fixed precisely. **2** exact, distinct, clear. **3** positive, sure. ~*n.* a definite thing; a noun with a definite referent. **definite article** *n.* (*Gram.*) the word *the* or its equivalent in other languages. **definitely** *adv.* **1** in a definite manner. **2** certainly. **definiteness** *n.* **definition** (-nish´ən) *n.* **1** the act of defining. **2** a statement of the meaning of a word etc.; an exact description of a thing by its qualities and circumstances. **3** distinctness, clearness of form, esp. of an image transmitted by a lens or a television image. **definitive** (-fin´-) *a.* **1** decisive; conclusive; positive. **2** being the best or most authoritative of its kind. **3** (of a postage stamp) of a design etc. always in use, standard. ~*n.* **1** a definitive postage stamp. **2** a word used to limit the application of a common noun, such as an adjective or pronoun. **definitively** *adv.*

deflate (diflāt´) v.t. **1** to let down (a pneumatic tyre, balloon etc.) by allowing the air or gas to escape. **2** to reduce the inflation of (currency). **3** to humiliate, to take away the confidence of. **4** to reduce the importance of. ~v.i. **1** to be emptied of air or gas. **2** to bring about economic deflation. **3** to lose confidence. **deflation** n. **1** reduction of size by allowing air or gas to escape. **2** the reduction and control of the issue of paper money to increase its value. **3** (Geol.) erosion of rock by the wind. **deflationary** a. **deflationist** n., a. **deflator, deflater** n.

deflect (diflekt´) v.i. **1** to turn or move to one side. **2** to deviate. ~v.t. **1** to cause to turn, bend, or deviate. **2** to ward off, to avoid (criticism etc.). **deflection** (diflek´shən), **deflexion** n. **1** the act of deflecting. **2** the fact of being deflected. **3** a turn or move to one side, a deviation. **deflector** n.

deflower (diflow´ə) v.t. **1** to deprive of virginity, to ravish. **2** to ravage, to despoil. **3** to strip of flowers. **deflowerer** n.

defoliate (dēfō´liāt) v.t. to deprive of leaves, esp. in warfare. **defoliant** n. a chemical used to remove leaves. **defoliation** (-ā´shən) n.

deforest (defor´ist) v.t. to clear of trees. **deforestation** (-tā´shən) n.

deform (difawm´) v.t. **1** to render ugly or unshapely. **2** to disfigure, to distort. ~v.i. to experience deformation. **deformable** a. **deformation** (dēfawmā´shən) n. **1** the act or process of deforming. **2** a disfigurement, perversion or distortion. **3** a change in shape; a quantification of this. **4** an altered form of a word. **deformational** a. **deformed** a. misshapen. **deformity** n. (pl. **deformities**) **1** the state of being deformed. **2** a disfigurement, a malformation.

defraud (difrawd´) v.t. to deprive of what is right by deception; to cheat. **defrauder** n.

defray (difrā´) v.t. to pay; to bear the charge of; to settle. **defrayable** a. **defrayal** n. **defrayment** n.

defrock (dēfrok´) v.t. to deprive (a priest etc.) of ecclesiastical status.

defrost (dēfrost´) v.t. **1** to remove frost or ice from. **2** to thaw. ~v.i. to become defrosted. **defroster** n.

deft (deft) a. neat in handling; dextrous, clever. **deftly** adv. **deftness** n.

defunct (difŭngkt´) a. **1** dead, deceased, extinct. **2** no longer in operation or use.

defuse (dēfūz´), (N Am.) **defuze** v.t. **1** to render (a bomb) harmless by removing the fuse. **2** to dispel the tension of (a situation).

Usage note The verbs *defuse* and *diffuse* should not be confused: *defuse* means to remove a fuse from, and *diffuse* to disperse.

defy (difī´) v.t. (3rd pers. sing. pres. **defies**, pres.p. **defying**, past, p.p. **defied**) **1** to disregard openly. **2** to baffle (*that defies description*). **3** to challenge to do or substantiate. **defiance** n. **1** open disobedience; opposition; contemptuous disregard. **2** challenge to battle, single combat or any contest. **in defiance of** in disobedience or disregard of, in opposition to. **defiant** a. **1** openly disobedient. **2** challenging; hostile in attitude. **defiantly** adv. **defier** n.

deg. abbr. degree(s) (of temperature).

degenerate[1] (dijen´ərət) a. **1** having fallen from a better to worse state. **2** having low moral standards. **3** (Biol.) having reverted to a lower type. ~n. a degenerate person or animal. **degeneracy** n. **degenerately** adv.

degenerate[2] (dijen´ərāt) v.i. **1** to fall off in quality from a better to a worse physical or moral state; to deteriorate. **2** (Biol.) to revert to a lower type. **degeneration** (-ā´shən) n. **1** the act or process of degenerating. **2** the state of being degenerated. **3** (Biol.) gradual deterioration of any organ or class of organisms.

degradation (degrədā´shən) n. **1** the act of degrading. **2** the state of being degraded; debasement, degeneracy. **3** the wearing away of higher lands, rocks etc.

degrade (digrād´) v.t. **1** to reduce in rank. **2** to remove from any rank, office or dignity. **3** to debase, to lower. **4** to bring into contempt. **5** (Geol.) to wear away; to disintegrate. **6** (Biol.) to reduce from a higher to a lower type. **7** (Chem.) to reduce to a simpler structure. **8** (Physics) to reduce to a less convertible form. ~v.i. **1** to degenerate. **2** (Chem.) to disintegrate. **degradable** a. **degradability** (-bil´-) n. **degradative** a. **degrader** n. **degrading** a. humiliating, debasing. **degradingly** adv.

degrease (dēgrēs´) v.t. to remove grease from. **degreaser** n.

degree (digrē´) n. **1** a step or stage in progression, elevation, quality, dignity or rank. **2** relative position or rank. **3** relative condition, relative quantity, quality or intensity. **4** the 90th part of a right angle; the 360th part of the circumference of the earth or of a circle. **5** the unit of measurement of temperature or hardness. **6** a rank or grade of academic proficiency conferred by universities after examination, or as a compliment to distinguished persons. **7** a certain distance or remove in the line of descent determining proximity of blood. **8** social, official or Masonic rank. **9** (Med.) any one of the (usu. three) grades of severity of burns. **10** a grade of severity of a crime. **11** (Mus.) a note's position in a scale. **12** (Math.) the highest power of unknowns or variables in an equation. **by degrees** gradually, step by step. **to a degree** (coll.) to a certain extent, somewhat. **degreeless** a. **degree of comparison** n. (Gram.) the positive, comparative or superlative form of an adjective or adverb. **degrees of frost** n.pl. (with number) degrees below freezing-point.

dehisce (dihis´) v.i. (of the capsules or anthers of plants) to gape, to burst open. **dehiscence** n. **dehiscent** a.

dehorn (dēhawn´) v.t. to remove the horns from.

dehumanize (dēhū´mənīz), **dehumanise** v.t. **1** to divest of human character, esp. of feeling or tenderness; to brutalize. **2** to make like an automaton. **dehumanization** (-īzā´shən) *n*.

dehumidify (dēhūmid´ifī) *v.t.* (*3rd pers. sing. pres.* **dehumidifies**, *pres.p.* **dehumdifying**, *past, p.p.* **dehumidified**) to remove humidity from. **dehumidification** (-fikā´shən) *n*. **dehumidifier** *n*.

dehydrate (dēhīdrāt´) *v.t.* to release or remove water or its elements from (the body, tissues etc.). **dehydration** *n*. **dehydrator** *n*.

dehydrogenate (dēhīdroj´ənāt) *v.t.* (*Chem.*) to remove hydrogen from. **dehydrogenation** (-ā´shən) *n*.

de-ice (dēīs´) *v.t.* **1** to disperse or remove ice (from the wings and control surfaces of an aircraft, the windows of a car). **2** to prevent the formation of ice on. **de-icer** *n*. an apparatus or substance used for this purpose.

deictic (dīk´tik) *a*. (*Gram., Logic*) proving or pointing directly; demonstrative as distinct from *indirect* or *refutative*. ~*n*. a deictic word. **deictically** *adv*.

deify (dē´ifī, dā´-) *v.t.* (*3rd pers. sing. pres.* **deifies**, *pres.p.* **deifying**, *past, p.p.* **deified**) **1** to make a god of. **2** to adore as a god; to idolize. **deification** (-fikā´shən) *n*.

deign (dān) *v.i.* to condescend (*He wouldn't deign to join us*).

deindustrialize (dēindŭs´trielīz), **deindustrialise** *v.t.* to make (a country etc.) less industrial. **deindustrialization** (-zā´shən) *n*.

deinstitutionalize (dēinstitū´shənəlīz), **deinstitutionalise** *v.t.* **1** to remove from an institution, esp. from a mental hospital. **2** to make less institutional in organization etc. **deinstitutionalization** (-zā´shən) *n*.

deionize (dēī´ənīz), **deionise** *v.t.* to remove ions from (water or air). **deionization** (-zā´shən) *n*. **deionizer** *n*.

deism (dē´izm, dā´-) *n*. the belief in the being of a god as the governor of the universe, on purely rational grounds, without accepting divine revelation. **deist** *n*. **deistic** (-is´-), **deistical** *a*.

deity (dē´əti, dā´-) *n*. (*pl.* **deities**) **1** divine nature, character or attributes. **2** the Supreme Being. **3** a god or goddess.

déjà vu (dāzhah vü´), **deja vu** *n*. **1** (*Psych.*) an illusion of already having experienced something one is experiencing for the first time. **2** lack of originality, familiarity through repetition.

deject (dijekt´) *v.t.* to depress in spirit; to dishearten. **dejected** *a*. **dejectedly** *adv*. **dejection** *n*. the state of being dejected; lowness of spirits.

de jure (dē joo´ri, dā joo´ri) *adv.* (*formal*) by right, legally. ~*a*. rightful.

dekko (dek´ō) *n*. (*pl.* **dekkos**) (*coll.*) a quick look (*Have a dekko at this*).

delay (dilā´) *v.t.* **1** to postpone, to put off. **2** to hinder, to make (someone) late. ~*v.i.* **1** to put off action. **2** to linger. ~*n*. **1** the act of delaying. **2** postponement, retardation. **3** time lost before action; hindrance. **delayed-action** *a*. timed to activate or operate some time after initiation (a

delayed-action bomb). **delayer** *n*. **delay line** *n*. a device for delaying the transmission of a signal.

delectable (dilek´təbəl) *a*. **1** (*often facet.*) delightful, highly pleasing. **2** delicious to the taste. **delectability** (-bil´-), **delectableness** *n*. **delectably** *adv*. **delectation** (dēlektā´shən) *n*. delight, pleasure, enjoyment.

delegate[1] (del´igət) *n*. **1** a person authorized to transact business as a representative. **2** a deputy, an agent. **3** a member of a deputation or committee. **delegacy** *n*. (*pl.* **delegacies**) **1** a delegation. **2** an appointment as a delegate. **3** the process of delegating.

delegate[2] (del´igāt) *v.t.* **1** to depute as a delegate, agent or representative, with authority to transact business. **2** to commit (authority to transact business) to a delegate. **3** to entrust the performance of or responsibility for (a task etc.) to another. **delegable** *a*. **delegation** (-ā´shən) *n*. **1** a body of delegates. **2** the act of delegating, a deputation. **delegator** *n*.

delete (dilēt´) *v.t.* to score out, to erase. **deletion** *n*.

deleterious (delitiə´riəs) *a*. harmful; injurious to health or mind. **deleteriously** *adv*.

delft (delft), **delf** (delf), **delph** *n*. glazed earthenware of a type orig. made at Delft, the Netherlands. **delftware** *n*.

deli (del´i) *n*. (*pl.* **delis**) short for DELICATESSEN.

deliberate[1] (dilib´ərət) *a*. **1** done or carried out intentionally. **2** weighing matters or reasons carefully. **3** circumspect, cool, cautious. **4** leisurely, not hasty. **deliberately** *adv*. **deliberateness** *n*.

deliberate[2] (dilib´ərāt) *v.i.* **1** to weigh matters in the mind, to ponder. **2** to consider, to discuss, to take counsel. ~*v.t.* to weigh in the mind. **deliberation** (-ā´shən) *n*. **1** calm and careful consideration. **2** discussion of reasons for and against; a debate. **3** freedom from haste or rashness. **4** leisurely, not hasty, movement. **deliberative** (-lib´ərətiv) *a*. of, relating to, proceeding from, or acting with, deliberation. **deliberatively** *adv*. **deliberativeness** *n*. **deliberator** *n*.

delicacy (del´ikəsi) *n*. (*pl.* **delicacies**) **1** the quality of being delicate. **2** anything that is subtly pleasing to the senses, the taste or the feelings. **3** a luxury, a choice morsel. **4** accuracy of perception. **5** fineness, sensitiveness, shrinking from coarseness and immodesty.

delicate (del´ikət) *a*. **1** exquisite in form or texture. **2** fine, smooth, not coarse. **3** subtle in colour, form or style. **4** easily injured, fragile, constitutionally weak or feeble. **5** requiring careful treatment; critical, ticklish. **6** sensitive, subtly perceptive or appreciative. **7** fastidious, tender, soft, effeminate. **8** refined, chaste, pure. **9** gentle, considerate. **10** skilful, ingenious, dexterous. **11** highly pleasing to the taste. **12** dainty, palatable. **delicately** *adv*. **delicateness** *n*.

delicatessen (delikətes´ən) *n*. **1** a shop or part of a shop selling cold meats and cheeses and specialist prepared foods. **2** (*pl.*) such products.

delicious (dilish´əs) *a.* giving great pleasure to the senses, to taste or to the sense of humour. **deliciously** *adv.* **deliciousness** *n.*

delight (dilīt´) *v.t.* to please greatly, to charm. ~*v.i.* to be highly pleased; to take great pleasure (in). ~*n.* **1** a state of great pleasure and satisfaction. **2** a source of great pleasure or satisfaction (*Your daughter is a delight to look after*). **delighted** *a.* **delightedly** *adv.* **delightful** *a.* **delightfully** *adv.* **delightfulness** *n.*

delimit (dilim´it) *v.t.* (*pres.p.* **delimiting**, *past*, *p.p.* **delimited**) to fix the boundaries or limits of. **delimitate** *v.t.* to delimit. **delimitation** (-ā´shən) *n.*

delineate (dilin´iāt) *v.t.* **1** to draw in outline; to sketch out. **2** to describe, to depict, to portray. **delineation** (-ā´shən) *n.* **delineator** *n.*

delinquent (diling´kwənt) *n.* an offender, a culprit. ~*a.* offending, failing, neglecting. **delinquency** *n.* (*pl.* **delinquencies**) **1** a fault, an offence. **2** guilt. **3** a failure or omission of duty. **delinquently** *adv.*

deliquesce (delikwes´) *v.i.* (*Chem.*) to liquefy, to melt away gradually by absorbing moisture from the atmosphere. **deliquescence** *n.* **deliquescent** *a.*

delirious (dilir´iəs) *a.* **1** suffering from delirium, wandering in the mind, as a result of fever etc. **2** raving, madly excited. **3** frantic with delight or other excitement. **deliriously** *adv.*

delirium (dilir´iəm) *n.* **1** a wandering of the mind, perversion of the mental processes, the results of cerebral activity bearing no true relation to reality, characterized by delusions, illusions or hallucinations, caused by fever etc. **2** frantic excitement or enthusiasm, rapture, ecstasy. **delirium tremens** (trem´enz) *n.* an acute phase in chronic alcoholism, in which hallucinations and trembling are experienced.

deliver (diliv´ə) *v.t.* **1** to distribute, to present. **2** to give over, to hand over or on. **3** to free from danger or restraint; to save, to rescue. **4** to assist at the birth of (a child); to give birth to; to assist in giving birth. **5** to discharge, to send out. **6** to utter, or pronounce formally or officially. **7** to surrender, to give up. **8** (*Law*) to hand over to the grantee. **9** to aim successfully (a blow to an opponent, a ball to a team-mate etc.). ~*v.i.* (*coll.*) to fulfil a promise, to carry out an undertaking, to live up to expectations. **to deliver the goods** (*coll.*) to fulfil a promise, to carry out an undertaking, to live up to expectations. **to deliver up** to surrender possession of. **deliverable** *a.* **deliverance** *n.* **1** the state of being saved or rescued; a rescue. **2** the act of delivering an opinion. **deliverer** *n.* **delivery** (-əri) *n.* (*pl.* **deliveries**) **1** the act of delivering. **2** setting free, rescue. **3** transfer, surrender etc. **4** a distribution of letters from the Post Office. **5** a batch of letters etc. delivered. **6** the utterance of a speech. **7** style or manner of speaking. **8** childbirth. **9** discharge of a blow or missile. **10** in cricket, the act or style of delivering a ball, style of bowling. **11** (*Law*) **a** the act

of putting someone in formal possession of property. **b** the handing over of a deed to the grantee.

dell (del) *n.* a hollow or small valley, usually wooded.

delocalize (dēlō´kəlīz), **delocalise** *v.t.* **1** to remove from its proper or usual place. **2** to remove a limitation on location from. **delocalization** (-zā´shən) *n.* **delocalized** *a.* (*Chem.*) (of an electron) shared among three or more atoms.

delouse (dēlows´) *v.t.* to rid (a person or place) of vermin, esp. lice.

Delphic (del´fik), **Delphian** (-fiən) *a,* **1** of or belonging to Delphi, a town of Greece, where there was a celebrated oracle of Apollo. **2** susceptible of two interpretations, ambiguous.

delphinium (delfin´iəm) *n.* (*pl.* **delphiniums**) any plant of the genus *Delphinium*, having tall blue flowers.

delphinoid (del´finoid) *a.* **1** (*Zool.*) of or relating to the division Delphinoidea, including dolphins, porpoises etc. **2** resembling a dolphin. ~*n.* **1** (*Zool.*) a member of the division Delphinoidea. **2** an animal resembling a dolphin.

delta (del´tə) *n.* (*pl.* **deltas**) **1** the fourth letter of the Greek alphabet (δ, Δ). **2** a delta-shaped alluvial deposit at the mouth of a river. **3** a fourth-class mark given to a student's work. **4** (*Math.*) an increment in a variable. **deltaic** (-tā´-) *a.* **delta rays** *n.pl.* electrons moving at relatively low speeds. **delta rhythm, delta wave** *n.* the normal activity of the brain during deep sleep. **delta wing** *n.* a triangular-shaped wing on an aeroplane. **deltoid** *a.* shaped like a delta; triangular. ~*n.* a triangular muscle of the shoulder, which moves the arm.

deltiology (deltiol´əji) *n.* the study and collecting of postcards. **deltiologist** *n.*

delude (dilood´) *v.t.* to deceive, to convince (someone) that something untrue is true. **deluder** *n.*

deluge (del´ūj) *n.* **1** a general flood or inundation, esp. the biblical flood in the days of Noah. **2** a heavy downpour of rain. **3** a torrent of words etc. ~*v.t.* **1** to flood, to inundate with a large number of things (*deluged with phone calls*). **2** to overflow with water.

delusion (diloo´zhən) *n.* **1** the act of deluding. **2** the state of being deluded. **3** an error, a fallacy. **4** (*Psych.*) an erroneous idea in which the subject's belief is unshaken by facts. **delusional** *a.* **delusions of grandeur** *n.pl.* a false belief that one is very grand or important. **delusive** (-siv) *a.* deceptive, misleading, unreal. **delusively** *adv.* **delusiveness** *n.* **delusory** *a.*

Usage note The meanings of the nouns *delusion* and *illusion* overlap, but in general a *delusion* is generated within the mind, and an *illusion* comes through the senses.

de luxe (di lŭks´) *a.* luxurious, of superior quality.

delve (delv) *v.i.* **1** to dip, to descend suddenly (into). **2** to carry on laborious research (into). ~*v.t.* (*poet.*) to dig, to open up with a spade. **delver** *n.*

Dem. *abbr.* Democrat.

demagnetize (dēmag´nitīz), **demagnetise** *v.t.* to remove magnetism from. **demagnetization** (-zā´shən) *n.* **demagnetizer** *n.*

demagogue (dem´əgog), (*N Am.*) **demagog** *n.* **1** an agitator who appeals to the passions and prejudices of the people. **2** a leader of the people. **demagogic** (-gog´-) *a.* **demagoguery** (-gog´-) *n.* **demagogy** *n.*

demand (dimahnd´) *n.* **1** an authoritative claim or request. **2** the thing demanded, esp. price. **3** a claim. **4** a peremptory question. **5** desire to purchase or possess. ~*v.t.* **1** to ask for or claim with authority or as a right. **2** to ask for in a peremptory or insistent manner. **3** to seek to ascertain by questioning. **4** to need, to require. **in demand** much sought after. **on demand** whenever requested. **demandable** *a.* **demander** *n.* **demand feeding** *n.* the feeding of a baby whenever it wants to be fed, not at fixed times. **demanding** *a.* **demand-led** *a.* brought about by consumer demand.

demarcation (dēmahkā´shən) *n.* **1** the fixing of a boundary or dividing line. **2** the division between different types of work done by members of trade unions on a single job. **demarcate** (dē´-) *v.t.* to fix the limits of. **demarcator** *n.*

dematerialize (dēmətiə´riəlīz), **dematerialise** *v.t.* to deprive of material qualities or characteristics; to spiritualize. ~*v.i.* **1** to lose material form. **2** to vanish. **dematerialization** (-zā´shən) *n.*

demean[1] (dimēn´) *v.t.* to debase (oneself), to lower (oneself).

demean[2] (dimēn´) *v.t.* to conduct (oneself), to behave. **demeanour** (-nə), (*N Am.*) **demeanor** *n.* conduct, carriage, behaviour, deportment.

dement (diment´) *v.t.* to madden; to deprive of reason. **demented** *a.* insane, mad. **dementedly** *adv.* **dementedness** *n.*

dementia (dimen´shə) *n.* (*Med.*) serious deterioration of the mental faculties, with memory loss, mood swings etc. **dementia praecox** (prē´koks) *n.* a mental disorder resulting from a turning inwards into oneself away from reality, schizophrenia.

demerara (demərah´rə, -eə´-), **demarara sugar** *n.* a type of brown sugar.

demerge (dēmœj´) *v.t.*, *v.i.* to split into separate companies again. **demerger** *n.* the separation of companies formerly acting as one.

demerit (dēmer´it) *n.* (*formal*) something which merits punishment. **demeritorious** (-taw´riəs) *a.*

demesne (dimēn´, -mān´), †**demain** (-mān´) *n.* **1** an estate in land. **2** a manor-house and the lands near it, which the owner keeps in his own hands. **3** the territory of the Crown or state. **4** a region, a territory, a sphere.

demi- (dem´i) *pref.* half, semi-, partial, partially.

demigod (dem´igod) *n.* **1** a being who is half a god. **2** the offspring of a god and a human being. **demi-goddess** *n.*

demijohn (dem´ijon) *n.* a glass bottle with a large body and small neck, enclosed in wickerwork.

demilitarize (dēmil´itərīz), **demilitarise** *v.t.* to end military involvement in and control of. **demilitarization** (-zā´shən) *n.*

demi-mondaine (dem´imondān) *n.* a prostitute. **demi-monde** (-mond´) *n.* **1** persons not recognized in society, women of dubious character. **2** the section of a profession etc. which is not wholly legal or above board.

demineralize (dēmin´ərəlīz), **demineralise** *v.t.* to remove salts or other minerals from. **demineralization** (-zā´shən) *n.*

demise (dimīz´) *n.* **1** (*formal*) death. **2** the end of something. **3** (*Law*) a transfer or conveyance by lease or will for a term of years or in fee simple. ~*v.t.* (*Law*) **1** to bequeath. **2** to transfer or convey by lease or will.

demisemiquaver (dem´isemikwāvə) *n.* (*Mus.*) a note with the value of half a semiquaver or one-fourth of a quaver.

demist (dēmist´) *v.t.* to make clear of condensation. **demister** *n.*

demo (dem´ō) *n.* (*pl.* **demos**) (*coll.*) a demonstration. ~*a.* (*attrib.*) serving to demonstrate something.

demob (dēmob´) *v.t.* (*pres.p.* **demobbing**, *past*, *p.p.* **demobbed**) (*coll.*) to demobilize. ~*n.* demobilization.

demobilize (dēmō´bilīz), **demobilise** *v.t.* to disband, to dismiss (troops) from a war footing. **demobilization** (-zā´shən) *n.*

democracy (dimok´rəsi) *n.* (*pl.* **democracies**) **1** the form of government in which the sovereign power is in the hands of the people, and exercised by them directly or indirectly. **2** a democratic state. **3** any more or less democratic organization or society. **democrat** (dem´əkrat) *n.* a person who is in favour of democracy. **Democrat** *n.* (*US*) a member of the Democratic Party. **democratic** (deməkrat´-) *a.* **1** of or relating to a democracy. **2** governed by or maintaining the principles of democracy; favouring equality. **democratically** *adv.* **democratization** (-zā´shən), **democratisation** *n.* the inculcation of democratic views and principles. **democratize** *v.t.*, *v.i.*

demodulate (dēmod´ūlāt) *v.t.* (*Physics*) **1** to extract the original audio signal from (the modulated carrier wave by which it is transmitted). **2** to separate a modulating signal from. **demodulation** (-lā´shən) *n.* **demodulator** *n.*

demography (dimog´rəfi) *n.* the study of population statistics dealing with size, density and distribution. **demographer** *n.* **demographic** (deməgraf´-) *a.* **demographical** *a.* **demographically** *adv.* **demographics** *n.pl.* demographical data.

demoiselle (demwahzel´) *n.* **1** a demoiselle crane. **2** a damselfly. **3** a damselfish. **demoiselle crane** *n.* a small N African and Asian crane, *Anthropoides virgo*, having a graceful form and bearing.

demolish (dimol´ish) *v.t.* **1** to pull down; to raze. **2** to ruin, to destroy. **3** to refute. **4** (*coll., facet.*) to eat up. **demolisher** *n.* **demolition** (deməlish´ən) *n.* **demolitionist** *n.*

demon (dē´mən), **daemon** *n.* **1** an evil spirit supposed to have the power of taking possession of human beings. **2** a malignant supernatural being, a fallen angel, a devil. **3** a very cruel or evil person. **4** (*usu. in comb., sl.*) an extremely clever or skilful person (*a demon bowler*). **5** in Greek mythology, a supernatural being, lesser divinity, genius or attendant spirit supposed to exercise guardianship over a particular individual, in many respects corresponding to the later idea of a guardian angel. **demoniac** (dimō´niak) *a.* **1** of, relating to or produced by demons. **2** possessed by a demon. **3** frantic, frenzied. ~*n.* a person possessed by a demon. **demoniacal** (dēmənī´əkəl) *a.* **demoniacally** *adv.* **demonic** (dimon´-) *a.* **1** like that of a person possessed by a demon, frenzied. **2** of or relating to a demon. **3** possessed by a demon. **4** devilish. **demonism** *n.* belief in demons. **demonist** *n.* **demonize, demonise** *v.t.* **1** to make into a demon. **2** to regard as evil. **demonization** (-zā´shən) *n.*

demonolatry (dēmonol´ətri) *n.* the worship of demons or evil spirits.

demonology (dēmənol´əji) *n.* the study of demons or of evil spirits. **demonologist** *n.*

demonstrate (dem´ənstrāt) *v.t.* **1** to show by logical reasoning. **2** to prove beyond the possibility of doubt. **3** to exhibit, describe and prove by means of specimens and experiments. **4** to display, to indicate. ~*v.i.* **1** to organize or take part in a public or military demonstration. **2** to act as a demonstrator. **demonstrable** (dimon´strəbəl, dem´ən-) *a.* that may be shown or proved beyond doubt. **demonstrability** (-bil´-) *n.* **demonstrably** *adv.* **demonstration** (-strā´shən) *n.* **1** the act of demonstrating. **2** clear, indubitable proof. **3** an outward manifestation of feeling etc. **4** a public exhibition or declaration of principles, feelings etc. by any party. **5** an exhibition and description of objects for the purpose of teaching or showing how something works. **6** (*Mil.*) a movement of troops as if to attack. **demonstrative** (-mon´-) *a.* **1** manifesting one's feelings strongly and openly. **2** having the power of exhibiting and proving. **3** being proof (of). **4** (*Gram.*) (of an adjective or pronoun) used to highlight the referent(s), e.g. *this* or *that*. ~*n.* (*Gram.*) a demonstrative adjective or pronoun. **demonstratively** *adv.* **demonstrativeness** *n.* **demonstrator** *n.* **1** a person who takes part in a public demonstration of political, religious or other opinions. **2** a person who demonstrates how a piece of equipment works. **3** a person who

teaches by means of exhibition and experiment. **4** a car used for test drives; a piece of equipment used in demonstrations. **demonstratorship** *n.*

demoralize (dimor´əlīz), **demoralise** *v.t.* to lower the morale of, to discourage. **demoralization** (-zā´shən) *n.* **demoralizing** *a.* **demoralizingly** *adv.*

demote (dimōt´) *v.t.* to reduce in status or rank. **demotion** *n.*

demotic (dimot´ik) *a.* **1** of or relating to the people. **2** popular, common, vulgar. **3** of or relating to demotic. ~*n.* **1** the spoken form of modern Greek. **2** a simplified form of ancient Egyptian writing.

demotivate (dēmō´tivāt) *v.t.* to cause to feel lack of motivation, to discourage. **demotivation** (-ā´shən) *n.*

demount (dēmownt´) *v.t.* **1** to remove from a mounting. **2** to disassemble. **demountable** *a.*

demur (dimœ´) *v.i.* (*pres.p.* **demurring**, *past, p.p.* **demurred**) **1** to have or express scruples, objections or reluctance. **2** (*Law*) to take exception to any point in the pleading as insufficient. ~*n.* **1** scruple, objection (*without demur*). **2** the act of demurring. **demurrable** *a.* liable to exception, esp. legal objection. **demurral** *n.* (a) demur. **demurrer** *n.* **1** (*Law*) an objection made to a point submitted by the opposing party on the grounds of irrelevance or legal insufficiency. **2** an objection.

demure (dimūə´) *a.* (*comp.* **demurer**, *superl.* **demurest**) **1** reserved and modest. **2** affectedly modest, coy. **demurely** *adv.* **demureness** *n.*

demystify (dēmis´tifī) *v.t.* (*3rd pers. sing. pres.* **demystifies**, *pres.p.* **demystifying**, *past, p.p.* **demystified**) **1** to remove the mystery from, to clarify. **2** to make less irrational. **demystification** (-fikā´shən) *n.*

demythologize (dēmithol´əjīz), **demythologise** *v.t.* to remove the mythological elements from (something, e.g. the Bible) to highlight the basic meaning. **demythologization** (-zā´shən) *n.*

den (den) *n.* **1** the lair of a wild beast. **2** a retreat, a lurking-place; a hideout created by children. **3** a place where vice or crime is indulged in (*a den of iniquity*). **4** a hovel; a miserable room. **5** (*coll.*) a study, a sanctum, a snuggery. ~*v.i.* (*pres.p.* **denning**, *past, p.p.* **denned**) **1** to live in a den. **2** to retreat to a den.

denarius (dinah´riəs) *n.* (*pl.* **denarii** (-riī)) a Roman silver coin, worth ten asses; a penny.

denary (dē´nəri) *a.* **1** containing ten. **2** based on the number ten, decimal.

denationalize (dēnash´ənəlīz), **denationalise** *v.t.* **1** to transfer from public to private ownership. **2** to deprive of the rights, rank or characteristics of a nation. **3** to deprive of nationality. **denationalization** (-zā´shən) *n.*

denaturalize (dēnach´ərəlīz), **denaturalise** *v.t.* **1** to render unnatural; to alter the nature of. **2** to deprive of naturalization or citizenship. **denaturalization** (-zā´shən) *n.*

denature

334

dentil

denature (dēnā´chə), **denaturize** (-rīz-), **denaturise** v.t. **1** to change the essential nature or character of (something) by adulteration etc. **2** to modify (a protein) by heat or acid. **3** to render (alcohol) unfit for human consumption. **denaturant** n. **denaturation** (dēnachərā´shən) n.

dendrite (den´drīt) n. **1** (Mineral.) **a** a stone or mineral with treelike markings. **b** branching or treelike markings (on a stone or mineral). **2** (Anat., Zool.) any one of the branched extensions of a nerve cell which conduct impulses to the body of the cell. **3** (Chem.) a crystal with branched treelike growth. **dendritic** (-drit´-), **dendritical** a. **1** like a tree; arborescent. **2** with treelike markings. **dendritically** adv.

dendrochronology (dendrōkrənol´əji) n. **1** the study of the annual growth rings in trees. **2** a system of dating timber and historical events for which timber is evidence, based on such rings. **dendrochronological** (-loj´-) a. **dendrochronologist** n.

dendrogram (den´drəgram) n. (Biol.) a type of tree diagram showing relationships between kinds of organism.

dendroid (den´droid) a. treelike, branching, tree-shaped.

dendrology (dendrol´əji) n. the natural history of trees. **dendrological** (-loj´-) a. **dendrologist** n.

dene¹ (dēn), **dean** n. **1** a valley. **2** a deep and narrow valley (chiefly in place names).

dene² (dēn) n. a sandy down or low hill, a tract of sand by the sea.

denegation (dēnigā´shən) n. contradiction, denial.

dengue (deng´gi) n. an acute fever common in the tropics, characterized by severe pains, a rash and swellings.

deniable, denial DENY.

denier¹ (den´iə) n. a unit for weighing and grading silk, nylon and rayon yarn, used for women's tights and stockings.

denier² DENY.

denigrate (den´igrāt) v.t. to defame. **denigration** (-rā´shən) n. **denigrator** n. **denigratory** a.

denim (den´im) n. **1** a coarse, twilled cotton fabric used for jeans, overalls etc. **2** (pl.) jeans made of denim.

denitrate (dēnī´trāt) v.t. to remove nitric or nitrous acid or nitrate from. **denitrification** (-fikā´shən) n. the removal of nitrogen from the soil by the agency of bacteria. **denitrify** v.t. (3rd. pers. sing. pres. **denitrifies**, pres.p. **denitrifying**, past, p.p. **denitrified**).

denizen (den´izən) n. **1** a citizen, an inhabitant, a dweller, a resident. **2** (Law) a foreigner who has obtained letters patent to give them some of the rights of a British subject. **3** a foreign word, plant or animal, that has become naturalized. **denizenship** n.

denominate (dinom´ināt) v.t. **1** to call, to designate. **2** to give a name, epithet or title to. **denominated in** expressed as a value in (a particular

monetary unit). **denomination** (-ā´shən) n. **1** a religious group or sect. **2** a class, a kind, esp. of particular units (such as coins or weights). **3** a designation, title or appellation. **4** the act of naming. **5** a playing card's rank in a suit, or a suit's in a pack. **denominational** a. of or relating to a particular religious denomination, sectarian. **denominationalism** n. **denominative** (-nətiv) a. giving or constituting a distinctive name. **denominator** n. (Math.) the number below the line in a fraction, which shows into how many parts the integer is divided, while the numerator, above the line, shows how many of these parts are taken.

denote (dinōt´) v.t. **1** to mark, to indicate, to signify. **2** (Logic) to be a name of, to be predicable of, as distinct from connote. **denotation** (dēnōtā´shən) n. **denotative** a.

denouement (dānoo´mä), **dénouement** n. **1** the unravelling of a plot or story. **2** the catastrophe or final solution of a plot. **3** an outcome.

denounce (dinowns´) v.t. **1** to accuse or condemn publicly. **2** to inform against. **3** to give formal notice of the termination of (a treaty or convention). **denouncement** n. **denouncer** n.

dense (dens) a. **1** thick, compact; having its particles closely united. **2** crowded close together. **3** (coll.) stupid, obtuse. **4** in photography, opaque, strong in contrast. **densely** adv. **denseness** n. **densitometer** (-om´itə) n. an instrument for measuring density in photography. **density** n. (pl. **densities**) **1** denseness. **2** (Physics) the mass per unit volume of a substance measured, for example, in grams per cubic centimetre. **3** a crowded condition. **4** a measure of the reflection or absorption of light by a surface. **5** (coll.) stupidity.

dent (dent) n. **1** a depression such as is caused by a blow with a blunt instrument; an indentation. **2** a lessening or diminution (The holiday made a dent in my savings). ~v.t. **1** to make a dent in; to indent. **2** to have a diminishing or harmful effect on (The rejection dented her self-confidence).

dental (den´təl) a. **1** of or relating to or formed by the teeth. **2** of or relating to dentistry. **3** (of a consonant) formed by placing the end of the tongue against the upper teeth or the ridge of the upper teeth. ~n. a dental consonant. **dental floss** n. thread used to clean between the teeth. **dental mechanic** n. a maker and repairer of false teeth. **dental surgeon** n. DENTIST.

dentate (den´tāt), **dentated** (-tātid) a. (Zool., Bot.) **1** toothed. **2** indented.

denticle (den´tikəl) n. **1** a small tooth. **2** a projecting point, a dentil. **denticulate** (-tik´ūlət), **denticulated** (-lātid) a.

dentifrice (den´tifris) n. powder, paste or other material for cleansing the teeth.

dentil (den´til) n. (Archit.) any one of the small square blocks or projections under the moulding of a cornice.

dentilingual (dentiling´gwəl) a. formed by the teeth and the tongue.

dentine (den´tēn), **dentin** (den´tin) n. the ivory tissue forming the body of a tooth. **dentinal** (den´tinəl) a.

dentist (den´tist) n. a person skilled in and qualified in treating and preventing disorders of the teeth and jaws. **dentistry** n. **dentition** (-tish´-) n. **1** teething. **2** the time of teething. **3** the arrangement of the teeth in any species of animal. **denture** (-chə) n. (often pl.) a plate or frame with an artificial tooth or teeth, a set of false teeth. **denturist** n. a maker of dentures.

denuclearize (dēnū´kliərīz), **denuclearise** v.t. to deprive of nuclear arms. **denuclearization** (-zā´shən) n.

denude (dinūd´) v.t. **1** to make bare or naked. **2** to strip of clothing, attributes, possessions, rank or any covering. **3** (Geol.) to lay bare by removing whatever lies above. **denudation** (-nūdā´shən) n. **denudative** a.

denumerable (dēnū´mərəbəl) a. (Math.) able to be put into a one-to-one correspondence with the positive integers; countable. **denumerability** (-bil´-) n. **denumerably** adv.

denunciate (dinūn´siāt) v.t. to denounce. **denunciation** (-ā´shən) n. **denunciative** (-siətiv) a. **denunciator** n. **denunciatory** a.

deny (dinī´) v.t. (3rd pers. sing. pres. **denies**, pres.p. **denying**, past, p.p. **denied**) **1** to assert to be untrue or non-existent. **2** to disown, to reject, to repudiate. **3** to refuse to grant, to withhold from. **4** to refuse access to. **to deny oneself** to refrain or abstain from pleasures, to practise self-denial. **deniable** a. **deniability** (-bil´-) n. **denial** n. **1** the act of denying, contradicting or refusing. **2** a refusal, a negative reply. **3** abjuration, disavowal. **4** self-denial. **5** (Psych.) (subconscious) suppression of unacceptable knowledge or feelings. **denier²** n.

deodar (dē´ōdah) n. a large Himalayan cedar, Cedrus deodara.

deodorize (diō´dərīz), **deodorise** v.t. to deprive of odour. **deodorant** n. **1** a substance used to mask the odour of perspiration. **2** a substance which counteracts any unpleasant smells. **deodorization** (-zā´shən) n. **deodorizer** n.

deoxygenate (dēok´sijənāt) v.t. to deoxidize. **deoxygenation** (-ā´shən) n. **deoxygenize** v.t. to deoxidize.

deoxyribonucleic acid (dēoksirībōnūklē´ik), **desoxyribonucleic acid** (des-) n. the full name for DNA. **deoxyribose** (-rī´bōz) n. a sugar found in DNA nucleosides.

dep. abbr. **1** depart(s). **2** deputy.

depart (dipaht´) v.i. **1** to go away, to leave. **2** to diverge, to deviate (from). **3** (formal) to pass away, to die. ~v.t. to go away from, to quit (to depart this life). **departed** a. **1** past, bygone. **2** (formal) dead. **the departed** (euphem.) a dead person or dead people.

department (dipaht´mənt) n. **1** a separate part or branch of business, administration or duty. **2** a branch of study or science. **3** (coll.) a matter one takes an interest in, an area of knowledge. **4** any one of the administrative divisions of a country, such as France. **departmental** (dēpahtmen´-) a. **departmentalism** n. **departmentalize, departmentalise** v.t. **departmentalization** (-zā´shən) n. **departmentally** adv. **departmental store** n. a department store. **department store** n. a large shop selling a great variety of goods.

departure (dipah´chə) n. **1** the act of departing; leaving. **2** the starting of a journey. **3** death. **4** divergence, deviation. **5** (Naut.) the distance of a ship east or west of the meridian she sailed from.

depend (dipend´) v.i. **1** to be contingent, as to the issue or result, on something else. **2** to rely for support or maintenance. **3** to rely, to trust, to reckon (on). **4** to be grammatically dependent on. **depending on** according to. **dependable** a. able to be depended upon. **dependableness** n. **dependably** adv. **dependant**, (N Am.) **dependent** n. **1** a person depending upon another for support or favour. **2** a retainer, a servant. **dependence** n. **1** the state of being dependent. **2** something on which one depends. **3** reliance, trust, confidence. **dependency** n. (pl. **dependencies**) **1** something dependent, esp. a country or state subject to another. **2** addiction to alcohol or drugs. **dependent** a. **1** depending on another. **2** subject to, contingent (on), relying (on) for support, benefit or favour. **3** addicted. **4** (Gram.) connected in a subordinate relationship. **dependently** adv.

depersonalize (dēpœ´sənəlīz), **depersonalise** v.t. **1** to divest of personality. **2** to regard as without individuality. **depersonalization** (-zā´shən) n. **1** the divesting of personality. **2** (Psych.) the experience of unreality feelings in relation to oneself.

depict (dipikt´) v.t. **1** to paint, to portray. **2** to describe or represent in words. **depicter** n. **depiction** n. **depictive** a. **depictor** n.

depilate (dep´ilāt) v.t. to remove hair from. **depilation** (-ā´shən) n. **depilator** n. **depilatory** (dipil´-) a. having the power to remove hair. ~n. (pl. **depilatories**) an application for removing superfluous hair.

deplane (dēplān´) v.i. (N Am.) to disembark from an aeroplane. ~v.t. to remove from an aeroplane.

deplete (diplēt´) v.t. **1** to reduce. **2** to empty, to exhaust. **depletion** n.

deplore (diplaw´) v.t. to express disapproval of, to censure. **deplorable** a. **deplorably** adv. **deploration** (dēplawrā´shən) n.

deploy (diploi´) v.t. **1** (Mil.) **a** to open out. **b** to extend from column into line. **2** to bring into action. ~v.i. to form a more extended front. **deployment** n.

depoliticize (dēpəlit´isīz), **depoliticise** v.t. to make non-political. **depoliticization** (-zā´shən) n.

depolymerize (dēpol´imərīz), **depolymerise** v.t.

(*Chem.*) to break a polymer down into monomers. ~*v.i.* (of a polymer) to break down into monomers. **depolymerization** (-zā´shən) *n.*
depone (dipōn´) *v.t.* to declare under oath; to testify. **deponent** *a.* (*Gram.*) (of a Latin or Greek verb) passive or middle in form but active in meaning. ~*n.* **1** (*Gram.*) a deponent verb. **2** (*Law*) **a** a witness. **b** a person who makes an affidavit to any statement of fact.
depopulate (dēpop´ūlāt) *v.t.* **1** to clear of inhabitants. **2** to reduce the population of. ~*v.i.* to become less populous. **depopulation** (-lā´shən) *n.*
deport (dipawt´) *v.t.* **1** to expel from one country to another. **2** to carry away, esp. to a foreign country. **3** to conduct or to behave (oneself etc.). **deportable** *a.* **deportation** (dēpawtā´shən) *n.* **deportee** *n.* a person who is deported. **deportment** *n.* conduct, demeanour, manners.
depose (dipōz´) *v.t.* **1** to remove from a throne or other high office. **2** (*Law*) to bear witness (that), to testify on oath to. ~*v.i.* (*Law*) to bear witness.
deposit (dipoz´it) *v.t.* (*pres.p.* **depositing**, *past*, *p.p.* **deposited**) **1** to lay down, to place. **2** to lodge for safety or as a pledge. **3** to lodge in a bank account. **4** to leave behind as precipitation or accumulation. **5** to lay (eggs etc.). ~*n.* **1** anything deposited or laid down. **2** a pledge, an earnest or first instalment, a trust, a security. **3** a sum of money lodged in a bank. **4** matter accumulated or precipitated and left behind. **on deposit 1** when buying on hire purchase, payable as a first instalment. **2** in a deposit account. **deposit account** *n.* a bank account earning interest, usu. requiring notice for withdrawals. **depositary** *n.* (*pl.* **depositaries**) a person with whom anything is deposited for safety; a trustee. **deposition** (depəzi´shən, dē-) *n.* **1** the act of depositing. **2** the act of deposing, esp. from a throne. **3** (*Law*) **a** a voluntary affirmation sworn before a person qualified to administer an oath. **b** the act of bearing witness on oath. **c** the evidence of a witness reduced to writing. **depositor** *n.* a person who makes a deposit, esp. of money. **depository** *n.* (*pl.* **depositories**) **1** a place where anything, esp. furniture, is placed for safety. **2** a place where some quality is to be found. **3** a depositary.

Usage note The spellings of the nouns *depositary* and *depository* should not be confused: a *depositAry* is a person and a *depositOry* a place.

depot (dep´ō) *n.* **1** a place of deposit, a storehouse. **2** a building for the storage and servicing of buses, trains or goods vehicles. **3** (*N Am.*) a railway or bus station. **4** (*Mil.*) the headquarters of a regiment.
deprave (diprāv´) *v.t.* to make bad or corrupt. **depravation** (deprəvā´shən) *n.* **depravity** (-prav´-) *n.* (*pl.* **depravities**) **1** viciousness, profligacy; perversion, degeneracy. **2** a vicious or degenerate act. **3** a state of corruption.

deprecate (dep´rikāt) *v.t.* **1** to express disapproval of or regret for. **2** to express regret or reluctance about. **3** to argue or plead earnestly against. **4** to depreciate. **deprecating** *a.* **deprecatingly** *adv.* **deprecation** (-ā´shən) *n.* **deprecative** (-prikətiv) *a.* **deprecator** *n.* **deprecatory** *a.*

Usage note The meanings of *deprecate*, *deprecation* and *deprecatory* and *depreciate*, *depreciation* and *depreciatory* overlap (especially in compounds with *self*-). The basic sense of *deprecate*, however, is to express reluctance about or disapproval of, and that of *depreciate* to lower in value.

depreciate (diprē´shiāt) *v.t.* **1** to lower the value of. **2** to disparage, to undervalue, to decry. **3** to reduce the price of. **4** to lower the exchange value of (money etc.). ~*v.i.* to fall in value. **depreciatingly** *adv.* **depreciation** (-ā´shən) *n.* **1** the act of depreciating. **2** the state of becoming depreciated. **3** a fall in value. **4** allowance for wear and tear. **depreciatory** (-shiətəri) *a.*

Usage note See note under DEPRECATE.

depredation (deprədā´shən) *n.* **1** plundering, spoliation. **2** an act of plundering. **depredator** (dep´-) *n.* a pillager, a plunderer. **depredatory** (dep´-, -pred´-) *a.*
depress (dipres´) *v.t.* **1** to press down. **2** to lower. **3** to dispirit, to make dejected. **4** to reduce or keep down the energy or activity of. **depressant** *a.* **1** lowering the spirits. **2** (*Med.*) sedative. ~*n.* **1** (*Med.*) a sedative. **2** a depressing event or influence. **depressed** *a.* (*esp. Psych.*) suffering from depression, low in spirits. **depressing** *a.* **depressingly** *adv.* **depression** (-shən) *n.* **1** the act of depressing; the state of being depressed. **2** (*Med.*) a mental disorder characterized by low spirits, reduction of self-esteem and lowering of energy. **3** slackness of business; a long economic crisis. **4** a hollow place on a surface. **5** (*Astron.*) the angular distance of a heavenly body below the horizon. **6 a** a low state of the barometer indicative of bad weather. **b** the centre of low pressure in a cyclone. **depressive** *a.* **1** causing depression. **2** (*Psych.*) characterized by depression. ~*n.* (*Psych.*) a person who is subject to periods of depression. **depressor** *n.* **1** (*Anat.*) a muscle which depresses the part to which it is attached. **2** a surgical instrument for reducing or pushing back an obtruding part. **3** (*Anat.*) a nerve that lowers blood pressure. **depressor muscle** *n.*
depressurize (dēpresh´ərīz), **depressurise** *v.t.* to reduce the atmospheric pressure in (a pressure-controlled area, such as an aircraft cabin). **depressurization** (-zā´shən) *n.*
deprive (diprīv´) *v.t.* **1** to take from, to dispossess (of). **2** to debar. **deprivable** *a.* **deprival** *n.* **deprivation** (deprivā´shən) *n.* **1** the act of depriving. **2** the state of being deprived. **3** loss, dispossession, bereavement. **deprived** *a.* lacking adequate social, educational and medical facilities.

Dept. *abbr.* Department.

depth (depth) *n.* 1 deepness. 2 measurement from the top or surface downwards or from the front backwards. 3 a deep place, an abyss. 4 (*pl.*) the deepest, innermost part. 5 the middle or height of a season. 6 (*pl.*) the sea, the deep part of the ocean, deep water. 7 abstruseness, profundity, mental penetration. 8 intensity of colour, shade, darkness or obscurity. 9 profundity of thought or feeling. 10 (*pl.*) the extremity, the extreme or innermost part of a region. 11 (*pl.*) a state of depression. **in depth** thoroughly, in detail. **out of one's depth** 1 in water deeper than one's height. 2 puzzled beyond one's knowledge or ability. **depth-charge, depth-bomb** *n.* a mine or bomb exploded under water, used for attacking submarines. **depthless** *a.* 1 without depth. 2 unfathomable.

depute[1] (diput´) *v.t.* 1 to appoint or send as a substitute or agent. 2 to give as a task. **deputation** (depūtā´shən) *n.* a person or persons deputed to act as representatives for others, a delegation. **deputize** (dep´-), **deputise** *v.t.* to appoint or send as a deputy. ~*v.i.* to act as a deputy.

depute[2] (dep´ūt) *n.* (*Sc.*) a deputy.

deputy (dep´ūti) *n.* (*pl.* **deputies**) 1 a person who is appointed or sent to act for another or others. 2 a member of the French and other legislative chambers. 3 a safety officer in a coalmine. **by deputy** by proxy. **deputy lieutenant** *n.* the deputy of a Lord Lieutenant. **deputyship** *n.*

deracinate (diras´ināt) *v.t.* 1 to tear up by the roots. 2 to destroy. **deracination** (-ā´shən) *n.*

derail (dirāl´) *v.t.* to cause to leave the rails. ~*v.i.* to run off the rails. **derailer** *n.* **derailment** *n.*

derailleur (dirā´lə) *n.* a bicycle gear in which the chain is moved between different sprockets.

derange (dirānj´) *v.t.* 1 to put out of line or order. 2 to disorganize. 3 to disturb, to unsettle, to disorder (esp. the intellect). **deranged** *a.* 1 insane. 2 mentally disturbed. **derangement** *n.*

derby (dah´bi) *n.* (*pl.* **derbies**) 1 any important sporting event. 2 a match between two teams from the same area. 3 (*N Am.*) a bowler hat.

derecognize (dērek´əgnīz), **derecognise** *v.t.* to cease to recognize the rights of (a trade union). **derecognition** (-nish´-) *n.*

deregulate (dēreg´ūlāt) *v.t.* to remove legal or other regulations from (transport services etc.), often so as to open up to general competition. **deregulation** (-lā´shən) *n.*

derelict (der´əlikt) *a.* 1 left, forsaken, abandoned. 2 dilapidated, showing neglect. 3 (*N Am.*) negligent. ~*n.* 1 a down-and-out. 2 anything abandoned (esp. a ship at sea), relinquished or thrown away. **dereliction** (dərəlik´-) *n.* 1 the act of abandoning. 2 the state of being abandoned. 3 omission or neglect (as of a duty). 4 the exposure of land by the retreat of sea. 5 land left dry by the sea.

derequisition (dērekwizish´ən) *v.t.* to free (requisitioned property).

derestrict (dēristrikt´) *v.t.* to free from restriction, e.g. to free a road from speed limits. **derestriction** *n.*

deride (dirīd´) *v.t.* to laugh at, to mock. **derider** *n.* **deridingly** *adv.* **derisible** (diriz´əbəl) *a.* **derision** (-rizh´ən) *n.* 1 the act of deriding. 2 ridicule, mockery, contempt. **to hold in derision** to hold in contempt, to make a laughing-stock. **derisive** (-siv), **derisory** *a.* 1 scoffing, deriding, ridiculing. 2 ridiculous. **derisively** *adv.* **derisiveness** *n.*

Usage note The uses of the adjectives *derisive* and *derisory* overlap, but in general *derisive* means scoffing, and *derisory* ridiculous.

---

de rigueur (də rigœ´) *a.* required by fashion.

derive (dirīv´) *v.t.* 1 to obtain, to get. 2 to deduce. 3 to draw, as from a source, root or principle. 4 to trace the origin of. 5 to deduce or determine from data. ~*v.i.* 1 to come, to proceed, to be descended. 2 to originate. **derivable** *a.* **derivation** (derivā´shən) *n.* 1 the act of deriving. 2 origin, extraction. 3 the etymology of a word, the process of tracing a word to its root. 4 (*Math.*) the process of deducing a function from another. **derivational** *a.* **derivative** (diriv´-) *a.* 1 derived. 2 copied from something else, unoriginal. 3 secondary, not original. ~*n.* 1 anything derived from a source. 2 a word derived from or taking its origin in another. 3 (*Math.*) a differential coefficient. **derivatively** *adv.*

derm (dœm), **derma** (dœ´mə), **dermis** (-mis) *n.* 1 skin. 2 (*Anat.*) true skin or corium lying beneath the epidermis. **dermal** *a.* **dermic** *a.*

dermatitis (dœmətī´tis) *n.* inflammation of the skin.

dermatology (dœmətol´əji) *n.* the science of the skin and its diseases. **dermatological** (-loj´-) *a.* **dermatologist** *n.*

derogate (der´əgāt) *v.i.* (*formal*) 1 to detract, to withdraw a part (from). 2 to become inferior, to lower oneself, to degenerate. **derogation** (-ā´shən) *n.* **derogative** (dirog´-) *a.* **derogatively** *adv.* **derogatory** *a.* tending to detract from honour, worth or character; disparaging, depreciatory. **derogatorily** *adv.*

derrick (der´ik) *n.* 1 a hoisting machine with a boom stayed from a central post, wall etc., for raising heavy weights. 2 the framework over an oil-well.

derrière (deriœ´) *n.* (*coll.*, *euphem.*) the buttocks, the behind.

derring-do (deringdoo´) *n.* (*poet.* or *facet.*) 1 courageous deeds. 2 bravery.

derringer (der´injə) *n.* a short-barrelled large-bore pistol.

derris (der´is) *n.* an extract of the root of tropical trees of the genus *Derris*, which forms an effective insecticide.

derv (dœv) *n.* diesel engine fuel oil.

dervish (dœ´vish) *n.* a member of one of the various Muslim ascetic orders, whose devotional exercises include meditation and often frenzied physical exercises.

desalinate (dēsal'ināt) *v.t.* to remove salt from (sea water). **desalination** (-ā'shən) *n.* **desalinize** (dēsal'inīz), **desalinise** *v.t.* (*N Am.*) to desalinate. **desalinization** (-zā'shən) *n.*

desalt (desawlt') *v.t.* DESALINATE.

descale (dēskāl') *v.t.* to remove scale or scales from.

descant[1] (des'kant), **discant** (dis'-) *n.* **1** (*poet.*) a song, a melody. **2** (*Mus.*) the upper part, esp. the soprano, in part music. **descant recorder** *n.* (*Mus.*) a recorder with a high pitch.

descant[2] (deskant'), **discant** (dis-) *v.i.* **1** to comment or discourse at length (on). **2** to sing in parts.

descend (disend') *v.i.* **1** to come or go down. **2** to sink, to fall. **3** to slope downwards. **4** to make an attack. **5** to originate, to descend (from); to be derived. **6** to be transmitted from one generation to the next. **7** to pass on, as from more to less important matters, from general to particular, or from more remote to nearer times. **8** to stoop; to condescend; to lower or abase. **9** (*Mus.*) to become lower. **10** (of a letter such as j, p or y) to have a part below the level of the line of type. ~*v.t.* to walk, move or pass along downwards. **descendant** *n.* a person who descends from an ancestor; offspring; issue. **descendent** *a.* **descender** *n.* the part of a letter (such as j, p or y) which is below the level of the line of type.

descent (disent') *n.* **1** the act of descending. **2** a slope downwards. **3** a way of descending, a path leading down. **4** downward motion. **5** decline in rank or prosperity. **6** a sudden attack, esp. from the sea. **7** a fall. **8** pedigree, lineage, origin. **9** (*Mus.*) a passing to a lower pitch.

descramble (dēskram'bəl) *v.t.* to convert (a scrambled signal) to intelligible form. **descrambler** *n.*

describe (diskrīb') *v.t.* **1** to set forth the qualities, features or properties of in words. **2** to call (*He was described as a family friend*). **3** to draw, to trace out. **4** to form or trace out by motion. **describable** *a.* **describer** *n.* **description** (-skrip'shən) *n.* **1** the act of describing. **2** an account of anything in words. **3** a kind, a sort, a species (*There was no food of any description*). **descriptive** (-skrip'-) *a.* **1** containing description. **2** capable of describing. **3** given to description. **descriptively** *adv.* **descriptiveness** *n.*

descry (diskrī') *v.t.* (*3rd pers. sing. pres.* **descries**, *pres.p.* **descrying**, *past, p.p.* **descried**) to make out, to espy.

desecrate (des'ikrāt) *v.t.* to divert from any sacred purpose; to profane. **desecration** (-rā'shən) *n.* **desecrator** *n.*

deseed (dēsēd') *v.t.* to remove the seeds from. **deseeder** *n.* a machine used for deseeding.

desegregate (dēseg'rigāt) *v.t.* to end racial segregation in (an institution, e.g. a school). **desegregation** (-ā'shən) *n.*

deselect (dēsilekt') *v.t.* **1** to refuse to readopt as a candidate, esp. as a prospective parliamentary candidate. **2** to drop from a group or team. **deselection** *n.*

desensitize (dēsen'sitīz), **desensitise** *v.t.* to make insensitive to (a chemical agent etc.). **desensitization** (-zā'shən) *n.* **desensitizer** *n.*

desert[1] (dez'ət) *n.* **1** a waste, uninhabited, uncultivated place, esp. a waterless and treeless region. **2** an uninteresting or dreary place. ~*a.* **1** uninhabited, waste. **2** untilled, barren. **desert boots** *n.pl.* suede ankle-boots with laces. **desertification** (dizœtifikā'shən) *n.* the process of turning from fertile land into desert. **desert island** *n.* a small, uninhabited, tropical island.

desert[2] (dizœt') *v.t.* **1** to forsake, to abandon. **2** to quit, to leave. **3** to fail (*His sense of humour deserted him*). ~*v.i.* (*Mil.*) to abandon the service without permission. **deserter** *n.* **desertion** *n.*

desert[3] (dizœt') *n.* **1** what one deserves, either as reward or punishment. **2** state of deserving, meritoriousness. **3** (*pl.*) deserved reward or punishment. **to get one's just deserts** to receive what one's behaviour merits.

deserve (dizœv') *v.t.* to be worthy of, to merit by conduct or qualities, good or bad, esp. to merit by excellence, good conduct or useful deeds. **deservedly** (-vid-) *adv.* **deservedness** *n.* **deserving** *a.* merited, worthy. **deserving of** having deserved (*deserving of praise*). **deservingly** *adv.* **deservingness** *n.*

desexualize (dēseks'ūəlīz), **desexualise**, **desex** *v.t.* **1** to castrate or spay. **2** to deprive of sexuality.

deshabille (dāzabē'), **déshabillé** (dezab'ēā), **dishabille** (disabē') *n.* state of undress, state of being partly or carelessly attired.

desiccate (des'ikāt) *v.t.* to dry, to remove moisture from. **desiccant** *n.* (*Chem.*) a drying agent. **desiccation** (-ā'shən) *n.* **desiccative** (-kətiv) *a.*

desideratum (dizidərah'təm) *n.* (*pl.* **desiderata** (-tə)) anything desired, esp. anything to fill a gap.

design (dizīn') *v.t.* **1** to contrive, to formulate, to project. **2** to draw, to plan, to sketch out. **3** to purpose, to intend. ~*v.i.* to work as a designer. ~*n.* **1** a plan, a scheme. **2** a purpose, an intention. **3** thought and intention as revealed in the correlation of parts or adaptation of means to an end. **4** an arrangement of forms and colours forming a pattern. **5** a preliminary sketch, a study. **6** the art of designing. **7** plot, construction, general idea. **8** an artistic creation. **by design** intentionally, deliberately. **to have designs on** to scheme to take possession of. **designer** *n.* **1** a person who designs. **2** a person who makes designs for clothing, stage or film sets etc. ~*a.* **1** (of clothes) produced by a famous designer. **2** of or relating to anything considered extremely fashionable, unusual or expensive (*designer chairs*). **designer drug** *n.* an illegal drug made up from a mixture of legal narcotics. **designing** *a.* crafty, scheming. **designingly** *adv.*

designate[1] (dez'ignāt) *v.t.* **1** to indicate, to mark.

2 to describe (as). **3** to select, to nominate, to appoint. **designation** (-nā´shən) *n.* **1** the act of designating. **2** appointment, nomination. **3** name, title, description. **designator** *n.*

designate² (dez´ignət) *a.* (*often placed after the noun*) nominated to but not yet holding an office (*president designate*).

desire (dizīə´) *v.t.* **1** to wish (to do). **2** to wish for the attainment or possession of. **3** to express a wish to have, to request, to beseech, to command. ~*v.i.* to have desire. ~*n.* **1** an eagerness of the mind to obtain or enjoy some object. **2** a request, an entreaty. **3** the object of desire. **4** sensual appetite, lust. **desirable** *a.* **1** worthy of being desired. **2** attractive. **3** agreeable. **desirability** (-bil´-) *n.* **desirableness** *n.* **desirably** *adv.* **desirous** *a.* desiring, wishful (*She is desirous of meeting with you*). **desirously** *adv.*

desist (dizist´) *v.i.* to cease, to forbear; to leave off.

desk (desk) *n.* **1** a table for a writer or reader, often with a sloping top. **2** the place from which prayers are read; a pulpit. **3** a counter for information or registration in a public place, such as a hotel. **4** a newspaper or broadcasting department (*the news desk*). **5** (*Mus.*) a stand for two players in an orchestra. **desk-bound** *a.* engaged in deskwork. **desktop computer** *n.* a computer small enough to use on a desk. **desktop publishing** *n.* the production of text at a desk equipped with a computer and printer capable of producing high-quality printed copy.

deskill (dēskil´) *v.t.* **1** to reduce the level of skill required for (a job), esp. by automation. **2** to cause (workers) to do work which does not use their skills.

desolate¹ (des´ələt) *a.* **1** forsaken, solitary, lonely. **2** uninhabited, deserted, barren, neglected, ruined. **3** forlorn, comfortless; upset. **desolately** *adv.* **desolateness** *n.*

desolate² (des´əlāt) *v.t.* **1** to deprive of inhabitants. **2** to lay waste. **3** to make very unhappy. **desolated** *a.* **desolation** (-ā´shən) *n.* **desolator** *n.*

despair (dispeə´) *v.i.* to be without hope. **2** to give up all hope. ~*n.* **1** hopelessness. **2** a person who or something which causes hopelessness. **despairingly** *adv.*

despatch DISPATCH.

desperado (despərah´dō) *n.* (*pl.* **desperadoes, desperados**) a desperate or reckless ruffian.

desperate (des´pərət) *a.* **1** hopeless, reckless, lawless, regardless of danger or consequences, fearless. **2** affording little hope of success, recovery or escape; tried as a last resource. **3** extremely dangerous. **4** very bad, awful. **5** wanting very badly to do or have to do something (*desperate for a drink*). **desperately** *adv.* **1** in a desperate manner. **2** very, extremely. **desperateness** *n.* **desperation** (-ā´shən) *n.*

despicable (dispik´əbəl, des´-) *a.* meriting contempt; vile, nasty. **despicably** *adv.*

despise (dispīz´) *v.t.* to look down on; to regard with contempt; to scorn. **despiser** *n.*

despite (dispīt´) *prep.* notwithstanding; in spite of.

despoil (dispoil´) *v.t.* **1** to strip or take away from by force; to plunder. **2** to spoil or destroy (a place). **despoiler** *n.* **despoilment, despoliation** (-spoliā´shən) *n.*

despond (dispond´) *v.i.* to be low in spirits, to lose hope. **despondent** *a.* very unhappy, disheartened. **despondency, despondence** *n.* **despondently** *adv.*

despot (des´pot) *n.* **1** an absolute ruler or sovereign. **2** a tyrant, an oppressor. **despotic** (dispot´-) *a.* tyrannical, unfair, cruel. **despotically** *adv.* **despotism** *n.* **1** absolute authority, tyranny. **2** arbitrary government, autocracy. **3** a country ruled by a despot.

des res (dez rez´) *n.* (*coll.*) a desirable residence (used by estate agents).

dessert (dizœt´) *n.* the last course of a meal, consisting of fruit or sweetmeats; the sweet course. **dessertspoon** *n.* **1** a medium-sized spoon holding half as much as a tablespoon and twice as much as a teaspoon. **2** the amount that a dessertspoon will hold. **dessertspoonful** *n.* (*pl.* **dessertspoonfuls**). **dessert wine** *n.* a sweet wine served with dessert.

❌ **dessicate** common misspelling of DESICCATE.

destabilize (dēstā´bilīz), **destabilise** *v.t.* **1** to make unstable. **2** to undermine the power of (a government). **destabilization** (-zā´shən) *n.*

destination (destinā´shən) *n.* the place to which a person is going or to which a thing is sent.

destine (des´tin) *v.t.* to appoint, fix or determine to a use, purpose, duty or position. **destined** *a.* foreordained.

destiny (des´tini) *n.* (*pl.* **destinies**) **1** the purpose or end to which any person or thing is appointed. **2** fate, fortune, lot, events as the fulfilment of fate.

destitute (des´titūt) *a.* **1** in want, deprived of the necessities of life. **2** lacking, bereft (of). **destitution** (-titū´-) *n.*

destock (dēstok´) *v.i.* to reduce one's stock.

destroy (distroi´) *v.t.* **1** to pull down or demolish; to pull to pieces. **2** to undo, to nullify. **3** to annihilate; to lay waste. **4** to ruin the life or situation of. **5** to kill (a sick animal) humanely. **6** to overthrow. **7** to put an end to. **destroyable** *a.* **destroyer** *n.* **1** a person who destroys. **2** (*Naut.*) a fast warship armed with torpedoes.

destruction (distrŭk´shən) *n.* **1** the act of destroying. **2** the state of being destroyed. **3** demolition, ruin. **4** something which destroys. **destruct** *v.t.* to destroy (a rocket or missile in flight) deliberately. ~*v.i.* to be destructed. ~*n.* the act of destructing. **destructible** *a.* **destructibility** (-bil´-) *n.* **destructive** *a.* **1** causing or tending to destruction; ruinous, mischievous, wasteful. **2** serving or tending to subvert or confute (arguments or opinions); negative, as distinct from *constructive*. **destructively** *adv.* **destructiveness** *n.* **destructor** *n.* a furnace for burning up refuse.

desuetude (disū´itūd, des´wi-) *n.* disuse; cessation of practice or habit (*to fall into desuetude*).

desulphurize (dēsŭl´fəriz), **desulphurise**, (*esp. NAm.*) **desulfurize** *v.t.* to free (an ore) from sulphur. **desulphurization** (-zā´shən) *n.*

desultory (des´əltəri) *a.* **1** passing quickly from one subject to another. **2** loose, disjointed, discursive. **desultorily** *adv.* **desultoriness** *n.*

detach (ditach´) *v.t.* **1** to disconnect, to separate; to disengage. **2** (*Mil.*) to separate from the main body for a special service. **detachable** *a.* **detached** *a.* **1** not personally involved, impartial. **2** (of a house) not joined to the house next door. **detachedly** (-tach´id-) *adv.* **detachedness** *n.* **detachment** *n.* **1** freedom from prejudice, self-interest or worldly influence; independence, isolation. **2** the act of detaching. **3** the state of being detached. **4** (*Mil.*) a body of troops or a number of ships detached from the main body and sent on a special service or expedition.

detail (dē´tāl) *n.* **1** an item. **2** a minute and particular account. **3** (*pl.*) a number of particulars. **4** small features of a work of art etc., or the treatment of these (*attention to detail*). **5** (*pl.*) minute parts of a picture, statue etc., as distinct from the work as a whole. **6** a minor matter. **7** (*Mil.*) **a** a list of names detailed for particular duties. **b** a body of men selected for a special duty. ~*v.t.* **1** to list the particular items of. **2** to relate minutely. **3** (*Mil.*) to appoint for a particular service. **in detail** minutely; item by item. **to go into detail** to mention all the particulars about something. **detailed** *a.* **1** related in detail. **2** minute, complete.

detain (ditān´) *v.t.* **1** to restrain; to keep in custody. **2** to delay, to hinder. **detainee** (-ē´) *n.* a person held in custody. **detainer** *n.* **detainment** *n.*

detect (ditekt´) *v.t.* **1** to discover or find out. **2** to bring to light. **3** (*Physics*) to observe (radiation or a signal) with a detector. **detectable** *a.* **detectably** *adv.* **detection** *n.* **detective** *n.* a police officer employed to investigate special cases of crime. ~*a.* employed in or suitable for detecting. **detector** *n.* **1** a person who detects. **2** the part of a radio receiver which demodulates the radio waves.

detent (ditent´) *n.* a pin, catch or lever forming a check to the mechanism in a watch, clock, lock etc.

détente (dātāt´) *n.* relaxation of tension between nations or other warring forces.

detention (diten´shən) *n.* **1** the act of detaining. **2** the state of being detained. **3** keeping in school after hours as a punishment. **detention centre** *n.* a place where young offenders are detained.

deter (ditœ´) *v.t.* (*pres.p.* **deterring**, *past, p.p.* **deterred**) **1** to discourage or frighten (from). **2** to hinder or prevent. **deterrence** (-ter´-), **determent** *n.* the act of deterring. **deterrent** (-ter´-) *a.* tending to deter. ~*n.* **1** something which deters. **2** (*coll.*) a nuclear weapon the possession of which is supposed to deter the use of a similar weapon by another power.

detergent (ditœ´jənt) *n.* **1** a chemical cleansing agent for washing clothes etc. **2** a medicine or application which has the property of cleansing. ~*a.* cleansing, purging.

deteriorate (ditiə´riərāt) *v.t.* **1** to make inferior. **2** to reduce in value. ~*v.i.* **1** to become worse. **2** to degenerate. **deterioration** (-rā´shən) *n.* **deteriorative** (-rət-) *a.*

Usage note Pronunciation as (ditiə´riāt), as though the word were *deteriate*, is best avoided.

determinant (ditœ´minənt) *a.* determinative, decisive. ~*n.* **1** a person who or something which determines or causes to fix or decide. **2** (*Math.*) the sum of a series of products of several numbers, the products being formed according to certain laws, used in the solution of equations and other processes.

determinate (ditœ´minət) *a.* **1** limited, definite. **2** positive, determined, resolute. **determinately** *adv.* **determinateness** *n.* **determinative** *a.* **1** that limits or defines. **2** directive, decisive. ~*n.* that which decides, defines or specifies. **determinatively** *adv.*

determination (ditœminā´shən) *n.* **1** fixed intention, resolution, strength of mind. **2** the act of determining or settling. **3** something which is determined on. **4** (*Law*) **a** settlement by a judicial decision. **b** final conclusion. **5** (*Law*) the termination of an estate or interest.

determine (ditœ´min) *v.t.* **1** to ascertain exactly. **2** to fix, to settle finally, to decide. **3** to fix the limits of, to define. **4** to cause to decide. **5** to direct, to condition, to shape. **6** (*Law*) to bring to an end. **7** to terminate, to conclude. **8** (*Geom.*) to specify the position of. ~*v.i.* **1** to decide, to resolve. **2** to end, to reach a termination. **determinable** *a.* **determined** *a.* **1** resolute. **2** having a fixed purpose. **determinedly** *adv.* **determiner** *n.* **1** a person who or thing which determines. **2** (*Gram.*) a word that limits or modifies a noun, such as *that, my, every.* **determinism** (-minizm) *n.* the doctrine that the will is not free, but is determined by antecedent causes, whether in the form of internal motives or external necessity, the latter being the postulate of fatalism. **determinist** *a., n.* **deterministic** (-nis´tik) *a.* **deterministically** *adv.*

detest (ditest´) *v.t.* to hate exceedingly, to abhor. **detestable** *a.* **detestably** *adv.* **detestation** (dētestā´shən) *n.* **1** extreme hatred; abhorrence, loathing. **2** a person or thing detested. **detester** *n.*

dethrone (dithrōn´) *v.t.* **1** to remove or depose from a throne. **2** to drive from power or pre-eminence. **dethronement** *n.*

detonate (det´ənāt) *v.t.* to cause to explode with a loud bang. ~*v.i.* to explode with a loud bang. **detonation** (-ā´shən) *n.* **1** the act or process of detonating. **2** an explosion with a loud bang. **3** the spontaneous combustion in a petrol engine of part of the compressed charge after sparking. **detonative** *a.* **detonator** *n.* **1** a person who or something which detonates. **2** a fog signal on a railway line. **3** a device for causing detonation.

detour (dē´tuə) *n.* **1** a roundabout way. **2** a deviation, a digression. **3** (*N Am.*) a road diversion. ~*v.t.* to send by an indirect route. ~*v.i.* to make a deviation from a direct route.

detox[1] (dē´toks) *n.* (*coll., esp. N Am.*) detoxification.

detox[2] (dētoks´) *v.t.* (*coll., esp. N Am.*) to detoxify. ~*v.i.* to undergo detoxification.

detoxify (dētok´sifī) *v.t.* (*3rd pers. sing. pres.* **detoxifies**, *pres.p.* **detoxifying**, *past, p.p.* **detoxified**) to remove poison or toxin from, esp. as a treatment for drug or alcohol addiction. **detoxification** (-fikā´shən) *n.*

detract (ditrakt´) *v.i.* **1** to diminish, to reduce (*The bad publicity will detract from his wholesome image*). **2** to speak disparagingly. ~*v.t.* to take (a part) away from something. **detraction** *n.* **detractive** *a.* **detractor** *n.*

detrain (dētrān´) *v.t.* to cause to alight from a train. ~*v.i.* to alight from a train. **detrainment** *n.*

detriment (det´rimənt) *n.* **1** harm, injury, damage; loss. **2** a cause of detriment. **detrimental** (-men´-) *a.* causing detriment. **detrimentally** *adv.*

detritus (ditrī´təs) *n.* **1** (*Geol.*) accumulated matter produced by the disintegration of rock. **2** debris, rubbish. **detrital** *a.* **detrition** (-trish´-) *n.* a wearing down or away by rubbing.

de trop (də trō´) *a.* superfluous, in the way.

detumescence (dētūmes´əns) *n.* the diminution of swelling.

detune (dētūn´) *v.t.* to adjust (a musical instrument, car engine etc.) so that it is not tuned.

deuce[1] (dūs) *n.* **1** a card or die with two spots. **2** in tennis, a score of 40 all, requiring two successive points to be scored by either party to win.

deuce[2] (dūs) *n.* **1** (*coll.*) the Devil, invoked as a mild oath. **2** an extreme instance of (*a/ the deuce of an argument*). **†deuced** (dū´sid) *a.* (*coll., euphem.*) damned. **deucedly** *adv.*

deus (dā´us) *n.* god. **deus ex machina** (eks mak´inə) *n.* a contrived denouement.

deuterium (dūtiə´riəm) *n.* (*Chem.*) heavy hydrogen, an isotope of hydrogen with double mass.

deuteron (dū´təron) *n.* (*Physics*) a heavy hydrogen nucleus.

Deutschmark (doich´mahk), **Deutsche Mark** (doich´ə) *n.* the standard unit of currency of Germany.

deutzia (dū´tsiə, doi´tsiə) *n.* a Chinese or Japanese shrub of the genus *Deutzia*, with clusters of pink or white flowers.

devalue (dēval´ū), **devaluate** (-āt) *v.t.* **1** to reduce the value of. **2** to stabilize (currency) at a lower level. **devaluation** (-ā´shən) *n.*

devastate (dev´əstāt) *v.t.* **1** to lay waste, to ravage. **2** to overwhelm, to upset greatly. **devastating** *a.* (*coll.*) overwhelming, very upsetting. **devastatingly** *adv.* **devastation** (-vəstā´shən) *n.* **devastator** *n.*

devein (dēvān´) *v.t.* to remove the main vein from.

develop (divel´əp) *v.t.* (*pres.p.* **developing**, *past, p.p.* **developed**) **1** to unfold or uncover, to bring to light gradually. **2** to work out. **3** to bring from a simple to a complex state. **4** to evolve. **5** to bring to completion or maturity by natural growth. **6** to begin to have (*He developed a bad cough*). **7** to render visible (as the picture latent in sensitized film). **8** to build on or change the use of (land). **9** in chess, to bring (a piece) into play. **10** (*Mus.*) to elaborate on (a musical theme). ~*v.i.* **1** to expand. **2** to progress. **3** to be evolved. **4** to come to light gradually. **5** to come to maturity. **developable** *a.* **developer** *n.* **1** a person who or something which develops, esp. a person who develops land. **2** a chemical agent used to expose the latent image on film or light-sensitive paper. **developing country** *n.* a poor country which is just beginning to become industrialized. **development** *n.* **1** the act of developing. **2** the state of being developed. **3** gradual growth and advancement. **4** an event which is likely to affect a situation. **5** evolution. **6** maturity, completion. **7** the process of bringing into distinctness the picture latent in sensitized film. **8** an area of land which has been developed. **9** (*Mus.*) the section of a sonata in which the themes are developed. **10** in chess, the act of bringing a piece into play. **developmental** (-men´-) *a.* **1** of or relating to development or growth. **2** evolutionary. **developmentally** *adv.*

deviate[1] (dē´viāt) *v.i.* **1** to turn aside. **2** to stray or swerve from the path of duty. **3** to err. ~*v.t.* to cause to stray or err. **deviance, deviancy** *n.* **deviant** *a.* deviating from what is socially acceptable. ~*n.* a person whose behaviour deviates from what is socially acceptable. **deviation** (-ā´shən) *n.* **1** the act of deviating. **2** in statistics, the difference between one number in a series and the mean of that series. **3** (*esp. Naut.*) the deflection of a compass from the true magnetic meridian. **deviator** *n.* **deviatory** (-viətəri) *a.*

deviate[2] (dē´viət) *n.* (*Psych.*) a person who deviates from the norm. ~*a.* deviant.

device (divīs´) *n.* **1** a contrivance, an invention. **2** an explosive, a bomb. **3** a plan, a scheme; a stratagem, a trick. **4** a design, a figure, a pattern. **5** (*Her.*) an emblem or fanciful design, a motto. **to leave someone to their own devices** to leave someone to do as they please.

devil (dev´əl) *n.* **1** (*usu.* **Devil**) Satan, the chief spirit of evil. **2** any evil spirit. **3** a wicked, malignant or cruel person. **4** a person (*You lucky devil!*). **5** something troublesome. **6** a person of extraordinary energy, ingenuity and self-will devoted to selfish or mischievous ends. **7** an unfortunate person, a wretch. **8** energy, dash, unconquerable spirit (*It's the devil in him that makes him irresistible*). **9** a person who does literary work for which someone else takes the credit. **10** a barrister who prepares a case for another, or who takes the case of another without fee in order to gain reputation. **11** the Tasmanian devil. **12** (*S Afr.*) a dust devil. *~v.t.* (*pres.p.* **devilling,** (*esp. N Am.*) **deviling,** *past, p.p.* **devilled,** (*esp. N Am.*) **deviled**) **1** to prepare (food) with highly-spiced condiments. **2** (*N Am.*) to harass, to torment. *~v.i.* to act as a literary or legal devil. **a devil of a** (*coll.*) difficult or trying (*a devil of a problem*). **like the devil** energetically or fast. **speak/ talk of the devil** said when the person who is the subject of conversation arrives. **the devil 1** a nuisance. **2** a dilemma, an awkward fix. **3** (*as an interjection*) an expression of surprise or annoyance (*What the devil was that?*). **the devil to pay** serious consequences. **to give the devil his due** to give a person one dislikes credit for their good qualities. **to go to the devil 1** to be damned. **2** (*imper.*) go away! **devilfish** *n.* (*pl.* **devilfish**) **1** a devil ray. **2** any of various other fish, such as the stonefish. **devilish** *a.* **1** befitting a devil; diabolical; damnable. **2** mischievous. *~adv.* (*coll.*) extraordinarily, very. **devilishly** *adv.* **devilishness** *n.* **devil-may-care** *a.* carefree and reckless. **devilment** *n.* mischief, roguery. **devil ray** *n.* any fish of the family Mobulidae. **devilry** *n.* (*pl.* **devilries**) **1** diabolical wickedness, esp. cruelty. **2** wild and reckless mischief, revelry or high spirits. **3** an act of devilry. **4** diabolism, black magic. **devil's advocate** *n.* **1** a person who puts the opposing view in a discussion without necessarily holding that view. **2** (*Hist.*) an official of the Roman Catholic Church appointed to oppose a proposed canonization or beatification. **devil's bit** *n.* a small dark blue scabious, *Succisa pratensis*. **devil's coachhorse** *n.* a large beetle, *Staphylinus olens*. **devil's darning-needle** *n.* a dragonfly. **devil's dozen** *n.* thirteen. **devils-on-horseback** *n.pl.* prunes wrapped in bacon.

devious (dē´viəs) *a.* **1** insincere and deceitful. **2** circuitous, rambling. **deviously** *adv.* **deviousness** *n.*

devise (diviz´) *v.t.* **1** to invent, to contrive; to form in the mind, to scheme, to plot. **2** (*Law*) to give or assign (property) by will. *~n.* **1** the act of devising. **2** a will or clause of a will bequeathing real estate. **devisable** *a.* **devisee** (-zē´) *n.* (*Law*) a person to whom anything is devised by will. **deviser** *n.* a person who devises. **devisor** *n.* (*Law*) a person who bequeaths by will.

devitalize (dēvī´təlīz), **devitalise** *v.t.* to deprive of vitality or of vital power. **devitalization** (-zā´shən) *n.*

devitrify (dēvit´rifī) *v.t.* (*3rd pers. sing. pres.* **devitrifies,** *pres.p.* **devitrifying,** *past, p.p.* **devitrified**) to deprive of vitreous qualities. **devitrification** (-fikā´shən) *n.*

devoid (divoid´) *a.* empty (of), lacking.

devolution (dēvəloo´shən) *n.* **1** transference or delegation of authority, esp. from central to regional government. **2** passage from one person to another. **3** descent by inheritance. **4** descent in natural succession. **5** (*Biol.*) degeneration of species. **6** lapse of a right, privilege, or authority through desuetude. **devolute** (dē´-) *v.t.* to transfer (power or authority). **devolutionary** *a.* **devolutionist** *n.*

devolve (divolv´) *v.t.* to pass, transfer (duties or power) to another. *~v.i.* **1** to be transferred, delegated or deputed. **2** (*Law*) to fall by succession, to descend. **devolvement** *n.*

Devonian (divō´niən) *a.* **1** of or relating to Devon. **2** of or relating to the fourth period of the Palaeozoic era, between the Silurian and Carboniferous periods. *~n.* a native or inhabitant of Devon.

devote (divōt´) *v.t.* to consecrate, to dedicate; to apply; to give wholly up (to). **devoted** *a.* **1** dedicated, ardently attached. **2** dedicated, consecrated (to). **devotedly** *adv.* **devotedness** *n.* **devotee** (devətē´) *n.* **1** an enthusiast of. **2** a religious zealot. **devotion** *n.* **1** deep, self-sacrificing attachment, intense loyalty. **2** (*pl.*) prayers, religious worship. **3** religious zeal. **devotional** *a.*

devour (divow´ə) *v.t.* **1** to eat up quickly and greedily. **2** (of fire) to destroy wantonly, to waste; to swallow up, to engulf. **3** to read eagerly. **4** to absorb, to overwhelm (*devoured by jealousy*). **devourer** *n.* **devouringly** *adv.*

devout (divowt´) *a.* **1** deeply religious. **2** pious, filled with devotion. **3** sincere, genuine. **devoutly** *adv.* **devoutness** *n.*

dew (dū) *n.* **1** moisture condensed from the atmosphere upon surface at evening and during the night. **2** freshness (*the dew of youth*). **3** dewy moisture, such as tears. *~v.t.* to wet with dew. **dewberry** *n.* (*pl.* **dewberries**) **1** a shrub, *Rubus caesius*, which yields berries resembling blackberries. **2** its fruit. **dewclaw** *n.* **1** one of the bones behind a deer's foot. **2** the rudimentary upper toe often found in a dog's foot. **dewdrop** *n.* **1** a drop of dew. **2** a drop of mucus at the end of one's nose. **dewfall** *n.* **1** the falling of dew. **2** the time when dew falls. **dew point** *n.* the temperature at which dew begins to form. **dew-pond** *n.* a shallow, artificial pond formed on high land where water collects at night through condensation. **dewy** *a.* (*comp.* **dewier,** *superl.* **dewiest**) **1** wet with or as if with dew. **2** like dew. **dewily** *adv.* **dewiness** *n.* **dewy-eyed** *a.* naive, innocent.

dewlap (dū´lap) *n.* **1** the flesh that hangs loosely from the throat of cattle and some dogs. **2** the flesh of a person's throat become flaccid through age. **dewlapped** *a.*

deworm (dēwœm´) *v.t.* to rid (an animal) of worms.

Dexedrine® (dek´sədrēn) *n.* a dextrorotatary isomer of amphetamine.

dexter (deks´tə) *a.* (*Her.*) situated on the right of a shield (to the spectator's left) etc.

dexterity (dekster´iti) *n.* **1** manual skill. **2** mental skill, cleverness. **3** right-handedness. **dexterous** (deks´-), **dextrous** *a.* having dexterity. **dexterously** *adv.* **dexterousness** *n.*

dextral (deks'trəl) a. 1 right-handed. 2 of or relating to the right. 3 (of a spiral shell) having the whorls turning towards the right. 4 (of a flatfish) having the right side uppermost. ~n. a right-handed person. **dextrality** (-tral'-) n. **dextrally** adv.

dextrin (deks'trin) n. (Chem.) a gummy substance obtained from starch, so called from its dextrorotatory action on polarized light.

dextro- (deks'trō) comb. form (Chem.) turning the plane of a ray of polarized light to the right, or in a clockwise direction (as seen looking against the oncoming light).

dextrorotatary (dekstrōrōtā'təri), **dextrorotary** (dekstrōrō'təri) a. (Chem.) turning the plane of polarization to the right. **dextrorotation** (-tā'-shən) n.

dextrorse (deks'traws) a. rising from left to right in a spiral line.

dextrose (deks'trōs) n. (Chem.) a form of glucose which rotates polarized light clockwise; grape sugar.

dextrous DEXTEROUS (under DEXTERITY).

DFC abbr. Distinguished Flying Cross.

DFM abbr. Distinguished Flying Medal.

dhal (dahl), **dal, dahl** n. 1 a split grain, pulse. 2 an Asian soup of or purée made from this.

dharma (dah'mə) n. in Hinduism and Buddhism, the fundamental concept of both natural and moral law, by which everything in the universe acts according to its essential nature or proper station.

dhoti (dō'ti) n. (pl. **dhotis**) a loincloth worn by male Hindus.

dhow (dow) n. a ship with one mast, a very long yard, and a lateen sail, used on the Arabian Sea.

dhurra DURRA.

DI abbr. 1 Defence Intelligence. 2 Detective Inspector.

di- (dī) pref. 1 twice, two, dis-, double. 2 (Chem.) containing two atoms or groups of atoms of a specified kind.

dia. abbr. diameter.

dia- (dī'ə) pref. 1 through. 2 apart, across.

diabase (dī'əbās) n. (Geol.) an igneous rock which is an altered form of basalt; it includes most greenstone and trap. **diabasic** (-bā'sik) a.

diabetes (dīəbē'tēz) n. a disease characterized by excessive discharge of urine containing glucose, insatiable thirst and emaciation. **diabetes mellitus** (mili'təs) n. diabetes characterized by a disorder of carbohydrate metabolism, caused by insulin deficiency. **diabetic** (-bet'-) a. 1 of or relating to diabetes. 2 (of food) suitable for diabetics. ~n. a person suffering from diabetes.

diabolic (dīəbol'ik) a. 1 of, relating to, proceeding from or like the devil. 2 outrageously wicked or cruel; fiendish, devilish, satanic, infernal. **diabolical** a. 1 diabolic. 2 (coll.) very bad, unpleasant. **diabolically** adv. **diabolism** (-ab'əl-) n. 1 devil-worship. 2 belief in the devil or in devils. 3 devilish conduct or character, devilry.

diabolist n. **diabolize, diabolise** v.t. 1 to make diabolical. 2 to represent as a devil.

diachronic (dīəkron'ik) a. of or relating to the study of the historical development of a subject, e.g. a language. **diachronically** adv. **diachronism** (-ak'-) n. **diachronistic** (-akrənis'-) a. **diachronous** a. **diachrony** (-ak'-) n.

diaconal (dīak'ənəl) a. of or relating to a deacon. **diaconate** (-nāt) n. 1 the office, dignity or tenure of the office of a deacon. 2 deacons collectively.

diacritic (dīəkrit'ik), **diacritical** (-əl) a. distinguishing, distinctive. ~n. a diacritical mark. **diacritical mark** n. a mark (e.g. accent, cedilla, umlaut) attached to letters to show modified phonetic value or stress.

diadem (dī'ə'dem) n. 1 a fillet or band for the head, worn as an emblem of sovereignty. 2 a crown, a wreath, a reward. 3 a crown of glory or victory. 4 supreme power, sovereignty. ~v.t. to adorn with a diadem.

diaeresis (dīer'əsis), (N Am.) **dieresis** n. (pl. **diaereses** (-sēz), (N Am.) **diereses**) 1 a mark placed over the second of two vowels to show that it must be pronounced separately, as naïve. 2 in prosody, a pause where the end of a foot coincides with the end of the word.

diagnosis (dīəgnō'sis) n. (pl. **diagnoses** (-nō'sēz)) 1 determination of diseases by their symptoms. 2 a summary of these. 3 a summary of the characteristics by which one species is distinguished from another. 4 differentiation of character, style etc. by means of distinctive marks. 5 an analysis of phenomena or problems in order to gain an understanding. **diagnose** (-nōz) v.t. 1 to distinguish, to determine. 2 to ascertain the nature and cause of (a disease) from symptoms. ~v.i. to make a diagnosis of a disease. **diagnosable** a. **diagnostic** (-nos'-) a. of or relating to diagnosis. ~n. a sign or symptom by which anything is distinguished from anything else. **diagnostically** adv. **diagnostician** (-tish'ən) n. **diagnostics** n. 1 (as pl., Comput.) computer programs used to identify faults in a system. 2 the science of diagnosing a disease.

diagonal (dīag'ənəl) a. 1 extending from one angle of a quadrilateral or multilateral figure to a nonadjacent angle, or from one edge of a solid to a nonadjacent edge. 2 oblique, crossing obliquely. 3 marked by oblique lines, ridges etc. ~n. 1 a straight line or plane extending from one angle or edge to a nonadjacent one. 2 a diagonal row, line, beam, tie etc. **diagonally** adv.

diagram (dī'əgram) n. 1 (Geom.) a drawing made to demonstrate or illustrate some proposition, statement or definition. 2 an illustrative figure drawn roughly or in outline. 3 a series of marks or lines representing graphically the results of meteorological, statistical or other observations, or symbolizing abstract statements. ~v.t. (pres.p. **diagramming**, (N Am.) **diagraming**, past, p.p. **diagrammed**, (N Am.) **diagramed**) to represent in a diagram. **diagrammatic** (-grəmat´-) a. **diagrammatically** adv.

dial (dī´əl) n. **1** the graduated and numbered face of a timepiece. **2** a similar plate on which an index finger marks revolutions, indicates steam-pressure etc. **3** an instrument for showing the time of day by the sun's shadow. **4** the control on a radio or television set for selecting wavelength or channel. **5** a control on a washing machine, cooker etc. **6** the rotating, numbered disc on a telephone. **7** (sl.) the human face. ~v.t. (pres.p. **dialling**, (N Am.) **dialing**, past, p.p. **dialled**, (N Am.) **dialed**) **1** to indicate (the telephone number) one wishes to call. **2** to measure or indicate with or as with a dial. ~v.i. to dial a telephone number. **dialler,** (N Am.) **dialer** n. **dialling** n. **dialling code** n. a group of numbers dialled to obtain an exchange in an automatic telephone dialling system. **dialling tone,** (N Am.) **dial tone** n. the sound given by a telephone to show that the line is clear.

dialect (dī´əlekt) n. a form of speech or language peculiar to a particular district or people. **dialectal** (-lek´-) a. **dialectally** adv. **dialectology** (-tol´-) n. the study of dialects. **dialectologist** n.

Usage note The adjectives *dialectal* and *dialectical* or *dialectic* should not be confused: *dialectal* refers to speech, and *dialectic(al)* to reasoning.

dialectic (dīəlek´tik) n. dialectics. ~a. **1** of or relating to logic. **2** logical, argumentative. **dialectical** a. dialectic. **dialectically** adv. **dialectical materialism** n. the economic, political and philosophical system developed by Marx and Engels, based on the idea of constant change through a dialectical process of thesis, antithesis and synthesis. **dialectician** (-tish´ən) n. **1** a person skilled in dialectics. **2** a logician; a reasoner. **dialectics** n.pl. **1** the rules and methods of reasoning. **2** discussion by dialogue. **3** the investigation of truth by analysis.

Usage note See note under DIALECT.

dialogue (dī´əlog), (N Am.) **dialog** n. **1** a conversation or discourse between two or more persons. **2** a literary composition in conversational form. **3** the conversational part of a novel etc. **4** a political discussion between two groups or nations. **dialogic** (-loj´-) a. of the nature of a dialogue. **dialogically** adv. **dialogist** (-al´əjist) n. **1** a person who takes part in a dialogue. **2** a writer of dialogues. **dialogue box** n. (Comput.) a small area on a computer screen prompting the user to enter data or make selections.

dialysis (dīal´isis) n. (pl. **dialyses** (-sēz)) **1** (Chem.) the process of separating crystalloid from colloid ingredients in soluble substances by passing through moist membranes. **2** (Med.) the filtering of blood to remove waste products, either by semi-permeable membranes in the body, or by a kidney machine in the case of kidney failure.

dialyse (dī´əlīz), (esp. N Am.) **dialyze** v.t. **dialyser** n. the apparatus in which the process of dialysis is performed. **dialytic** (-lit´-) a.

diamagnetic (dīəmagnet´ik) a. of, relating to or exhibiting diamagnetism. ~n. a diamagnetic body or substance. **diamagnetically** adv. **diamagnetism** (-mag´nit-) n. the force which causes certain bodies, when suspended freely and magnetized, to assume a position at right angles to the magnetic meridian, and point due east and west.

diamanté (dēəmon´tā) n. material covered with glittering particles, such as sequins. ~a. decorated with glittering particles.

diameter (dīam´itə) n. **1** a straight line passing through the centre of any object from one side to the other. **2** a straight line passing through the centre of a circle or other curvilinear figure, and terminating each way in the circumference. **3** the length of such a line. **4** transverse measurement, width, thickness. **5** in optics, the unit of measurement of magnifying power. **diametral** a. **diametrical** (dīəmet´-), **diametric** a. **1** of or relating to a diameter, diametral. **2** along a diameter, direct. **3** directly opposed. **4** as far removed as possible. **diametrically** adv.

diamond (dī´əmənd) n. **1** the hardest, most brilliant and most valuable of the precious stones, a transparent crystal of pure carbon, colourless or tinted. **2** a facet of this when cut. **3** a figure resembling this, a rhomb. **4 a** a playing card with red figures of this shape. **b** (pl.) a suit of such cards. **5** a baseball field or the square formed by the four bases. **6** a glazier's cutting tool with a diamond at the point. **7** a glittering point or particle. ~a. **1** made of or set with diamonds. **2** resembling a diamond or lozenge. ~v.t. to adorn with or as if with diamonds. **diamondback** n. **1** a N American terrapin, *Malaclemys terrapin*, with a diamond-patterned shell. **2** a deadly N American rattlesnake of the genus *Crotalus*, with diamond-shaped markings. **diamond-bird** n. PARDALOTE¹. **diamond jubilee** n. the 60th anniversary of a sovereign's accession. **diamond wedding** n. the 60th anniversary of a marriage.

diandrous (dīan´drəs) a. (Bot.) having only two stamens.

dianthus (dīan´thəs) n. (pl. **dianthuses**) any plant of the genus *Dianthus* including the pinks and carnations.

diapason (dīəpā´zən) n. **1** a harmonious combination of notes. **2** a melodious succession of notes. **3** either of the two foundation stops of an organ. **4** a harmonious burst of music. **5** a recognized standard of pitch among musicians. **6** range, pitch.

diaper (dī´əpə) n. **1** (N Am.) a baby's nappy. **2** a silk or linen cloth woven with geometric patterns. **3** a towel or napkin made of this. **4** a surface decoration consisting of square or diamond reticulations. ~v.t. **1** to decorate or embroider with this. **2** (N Am.) to change the nappy of.

diaphanous (dīaf´ənəs) *a.* (of a fabric) fine and almost transparent. **diaphanously** *adv.*

diaphragm (dī´əfram) *n.* 1 the large muscular partition separating the thorax from the abdomen. 2 the vibrating disc in the mouthpiece or earpiece of a telephone, or in the loudspeaker of a radio receiver. 3 a dividing membrane or partition. 4 an annular disc excluding marginal rays of light. 5 a thin rubber or plastic cap placed over the mouth of the cervix as a contraceptive. **diaphragmatic** (-fragmat´-) *a.* **diaphragm pump** *n.* a pump with a flexible diaphragm instead of a piston.

diapositive (dīəpoz´itiv) *n.* a positive photographic transparency; a slide.

diarchy (dī´ahki), **dyarchy, dinarchy** (-nah´-) *n.* (*pl.* **diarchies, dyarchies, dinarchies**) 1 government by two rulers. 2 an instance of diarchy. **diarchal** (-ah´kəl), **diarchic** *a.*

diarrhoea (dīərē´ə), (*N Am.*) **diarrhea** *n.* the excessive discharge of faecal matter from the intestines. **diarrhoeal, diarrhoeic** *a.*

diary (dī´əri) *n.* (*pl.* **diaries**) 1 an account of the occurrences of each day. 2 the book in which these are registered. 3 a daily calendar with blank spaces for notes. **diarist** *n.* a person who keeps a diary. **diaristic** (-ris´-) *a.*

diascope (dī´əskōp) *n.* an optical projector for showing transparencies.

Diaspora (dīas´porə) *n.* 1 (*Hist.*) the dispersion of the Jews after the Babylonian captivity. 2 Jews living outside Palestine, or now, outside Israel. 3 a dispersion or migration of any people.

diastase (dī´əstāz) *n.* a nitrogenous substance produced during the germination of all seeds, and having the power of converting starch into dextrine, and then into sugar. **diastasic** (-stā´-), **diastatic** (-stat´ik) *a.*

diastole (dīas´təli) *n.* dilatation of the heart and arteries alternating with systole. **diastolic** (dīə-stol´-) *a.*

diathermancy (dīəthœ´mənsi) *n.* (*pl.* **diathermancies**) the property of being freely pervious to heat. **diathermal** *a.* **diathermic** *a.* **diathermous** *a.*

diathermy (dī´əthœmi) *n.* (*Med.*) the employment of high-frequency currents for the production of localized heat in the tissues.

diathesis (dīath´əsis) *n.* (*pl.* **diatheses** (-sēz)) (*Med.*) a constitution of body predisposing to certain diseases.

diatom (dī´ətəm) *n.* a member of the class of algae *Bacillariophyceae*, which have siliceous coverings and which exist in immense numbers at the bottom of the sea, multiplying by division or conjugation, and occurring as fossils in such abundance as to form strata of vast area and considerable thickness. **diatomaceous** (-mā´shəs) *a.* **diatomic** (-tom´-) *a.* 1 (*Chem.*) containing only two atoms. 2 containing two replaceable univalent atoms.

diatonic (dīəton´ik) *a.* (*Mus.*) 1 of the regular scale without chromatic alteration. 2 applied to the major and minor scales, or to chords, intervals and melodic progressions. **diatonically** *adv.*

diatribe (dī´ətrīb) *n.* an angry speech; a piece of harsh criticism or denunciation.

diazepam (dīaz´ipam) *n.* a type of tranquillizer and muscle relaxant.

diazo (dīaz´ō) *a.* 1 (of a compound) having two nitrogen atoms and a hydrocarbon radical. 2 of a photocopying technique using a diazo compound exposed to light. ~*n.* (*pl.* **diazos, diazoes**) a copy made in this way. **diazotype** *n.* a diazo.

dib (dib) *v.i.* (*pres.p.* **dibbing**, *past, p.p.* **dibbed**) to dap. **dibber** *n.* a dibble.

dibasic (dībā´sik) *a.* (*Chem.*) containing two bases or two replaceable atoms.

dibble (dib´əl) *n.* a pointed instrument used to make a hole in the ground for seed. ~*v.t.* 1 to make holes in (soil) with a dibble. 2 to plant with a dibble. ~*v.i.* to use a dibble. **dibbler** *n.*

dice (dīs) *n.* (*pl.* **dice**) 1 a small cube marked with figures on the sides, used in gambling, being thrown from a box or cup. 2 (*as pl.*) more than one such cube. 3 a game played with these. 4 small cubes of food. ~*v.i.* to play at dice. ~*v.t.* 1 to chop (food) into small cubes. 2 to gamble (away) at dice. 3 to weave into a pattern with squares. 4 to trim or ornament with such a pattern. 5 (*Austral., sl.*) to leave, to reject. **no dice** an expression of refusal or lack of success. **dicer** *n.*

dicey (dī´si) *a.* (*comp.* **dicier**, *superl.* **diciest**) (*coll.*) risky, difficult.

dichloride (dīklaw´rīd) *n.* a compound having two atoms of chlorine with another atom.

dichotomy (dīkot´əmi) *n.* (*pl.* **dichotomies**) 1 a separation into two. 2 a marked contrast. 3 (*Logic*) distribution of ideas into two mutually exclusive classes. 4 (*Zool., Bot.*) a continued bifurcation or division into two parts. **dichotomic** (-kətom´-) *a.* **dichotomize, dichotomise** *v.t., v.i.* **dichotomous** *a.*

Usage note *Dichotomy* is sometimes used as though it meant dilemma or ambivalence, but both are best avoided.

dichroic (dīkrō´ik) *a.* assuming two or more colours, according to the direction in which light is transmitted. **dichroism** (dī´-) *n.*

dichromatic (dīkrəmat´ik) *a.* 1 characterized by or producing two colours, esp. of animals. 2 able to distinguish only two of the three primary colours. **dichromatism** (-krō´-) *n.*

dick (dik) *n.* 1 a fellow or person. 2 (*sl.*) a detective. 3 (*taboo sl.*) the penis. **dickhead** *n.* (*taboo sl.*) a stupid or contemptible person.

dicken (dik´ən) *int.* (*Austral., sl.*) used to express disbelief or disgust.

dickens (dik´ənz) *n.* (*coll.*) the devil, the deuce (*How the dickens did she do that?*).

Dickensian (diken´ziən) *a.* 1 of, relating to or in the style of Charles Dickens, 1812–70, British novelist. 2 applied to squalid conditions as described in Dickens's novels.

dicker (dik´ə) v.i. **1** to barter, to haggle; to carry on a petty trade. **2** to hesitate. ~v.t. to barter, to exchange. ~n. a deal or bargain. **dickerer** n.

dicky[1] (dik´i), **dickey** n. (pl. **dickies, dickeys**) (coll.) **1** a false shirt front. **2** a driver's seat. **3** a seat behind the body of a carriage or a motor-car. **dicky bird** n. (coll.) a little bird (used by or to children). **dicky bow** n. a bow tie.

dicky[2] (dik´i) a. (comp. **dickier**, superl. **dickiest**) (sl.) unsound, weak (a dicky heart).

dicotyledon (dīkotilē´dən) n. (pl. **dicotyledons**) any plant of the class Dicotyledones of flowering plants including all of those with two cotyledons. **dicotyledonous** a.

dicrotic (dīkrot´ik) a. (of a pulse in an abnormal state) double-beating.

dicta DICTUM.

Dictaphone® (dik´təfōn) n. an apparatus for recording sounds, used for taking down correspondence etc., to be transcribed afterwards.

dictate[1] (diktāt´) v.t. **1** to read or recite to another (words to be written or repeated). **2** to prescribe, to lay down with authority, to impose (terms etc.). ~v.i. **1** to give orders. **2** to utter words to be written or repeated by another. **dictation** n. **1** the dictating of material to be written down or recorded. **2** an instance of this, as a school exercise. **3** the material dictated. **4** the act or an instance of giving orders. **5** a command. **dictation speed** n. a rate of speaking which is slow enough for dictation. **dictator** n. **1** a person who dictates. **2** a person invested with supreme and often tyrannical authority. **dictatorial** (-tətaw´ri-) a. **1** of or relating to a dictator. **2** imperious, overbearing. **dictatorially** adv. **dictatorship** n.

dictate[2] (dik´tāt) n. an order, an injunction; a direction; a precept.

diction (dik´shən) n. **1** the use of words. **2** manner of expression; style.

dictionary (dik´shənəri) n. (pl. **dictionaries**) **1** a book containing the words of any language in alphabetical order, with their definitions, pronunciations, parts of speech, etymologies and uses, or with their equivalents in another language. **2** a book containing information on any subject under words arranged alphabetically.

dictum (dik´təm) n. (pl. **dicta** (-tə), **dictums**) **1** a positive or dogmatic assertion. **2** a maxim, a saying.

did DO[1].

didactic (didak´tik, dī-) a. **1** adapted or tending to teach, esp. morally. **2** containing rules or precepts intended to instruct. **3** in the manner of a teacher. **didactically** adv. **didacticism** (-sizm) n.

diddle (did´əl) v.t. to cheat; to swindle. ~v.i. (N Am.) to fritter away or waste time. **diddler** n.

diddly-squat (did´liskwot), **doodly-squat** (doo´dli-) n. (N Am., sl.) **1** anything at all (He doesn't know diddly-squat). **2** nothing.

diddums (did´əmz) int. used to express commiseration to a baby.

didgeridoo (dijəridoo´), **didjeridoo** n. (pl. **didgeridoos, didjeridoos**) an Australian musical instrument, a long, hollow wooden tube that gives a deep booming sound when blown.

didn't (did´ənt) contr. did not.

die[1] (dī) v.i. (3rd pers. sing. pres. **dies**, pres.p. **dying**, past, p.p. **died**) **1** to lose life, to expire; to depart this life. **2** to come to an end; to cease to exist. **3** to wither, to lose vitality, to decay. **4** to fail, to become useless, to cease to function. **5** to go out. **6** to cease or pass away gradually. **7** to faint, to fade away, to languish with affection. ~v.t. to undergo (a specified kind of death). **never say die** never give up. **to be dying** (fig.) to be eager (I'm dying for a drink). **to die away** to become gradually less distinct. **to die back** (of a plant) to die from the tip to the root. **to die down 1** (of plants) to die off above ground, with only the roots staying alive in winter. **2** to become less loud, intense etc., to subside. **to die for** extremely attractive (a figure to die for). **to die hard** to be difficult to eradicate or suppress (old habits die hard). **to die off** to die in large numbers. **to die out** to become extinct. **die-away** a. fainting or languishing. **die-back** n. a disease which causes trees or shrubs to die back. **diehard** n. a person who is resistant to change, or who holds an untenable position, esp. in politics.

die[2] (dī) n. (pl. **dice, dies**) **1** (pl. **dice**) a dice. **2** hazard, chance, lot. **3** (Archit.) (pl. **dies**) the cube or plinth of a pedestal. **4** (pl. **dies**) a machine for cutting out, shaping or stamping. **5** (pl. **dies**) a stamp for coining money, or for impressing a device upon metal, paper etc. **straight as a die 1** very straight. **2** completely honest. **die-cast** v.t. to shape (an object) by forcing molten lead or plastic into a reusable mould. **die-casting** n. **die-sinker** n. a person who cuts or engraves dies for coins, medals etc. **die-stamping** n. the act of embossing with a die.

dieffenbachia (dēfənbak´iə) n. any plant of the tropical American evergreen genus Dieffenbachia.

dieldrin (dēl´drin) n. an insecticide containing chlorine.

dielectric (dīilek´trik) a. nonconductive, insulating. ~n. any medium, such as glass, through or across which electric force is transmitted by induction; a nonconductor; an insulator. **dielectrically** adv. **dielectric constant** n. permittivity.

diene (dī´ēn) n. (Chem.) an organic compound which has two double bonds between carbon atoms.

dieresis DIAERESIS.

diesel (dē´zəl) n. **1** any vehicle driven by a diesel engine. **2** diesel oil. **diesel-electric** a. using power from a diesel-operated electric generator. ~n. a locomotive so powered. **diesel engine** n. a type of reciprocating internal-combustion engine which burns heavy oil. **dieselize, dieselise** v.t., v.i. **dieselization** (-zā´shən) n. **diesel oil, diesel fuel** n. a heavy fuel oil used in diesel engines.

diet[1] (dī´ət) *n.* **1** a prescribed course of food followed for health reasons, or to reduce or control weight. **2** the food and drink a person usually takes. **3** regular activities (*a diet of soaps and videos*). *~a.* with a low fat or sugar content (*diet cola*). *~v.i.* (*pres.p.* **dieting**, *past*, *p.p.* **dieted**) to take food, esp. according to a prescribed regimen or to reduce or control weight. *~v.t.* **1** to feed according to the rules of medicine. **2** to feed in a restricted way as a punishment. **dietary** *a.* of or relating to a rule of diet. *~n.* (*pl.* **dietaries**) a regimen; a prescribed course of diet. **dietary fibre** *n.* foodstuffs with a high fibre content; roughage. **dieter** *n.* **dietetic** (-tet´-), **dietetical** *a.* **1** of or relating to diet. **2** prepared according to special dietary needs. **dietetically** *adv.* **dietetics** *n.* **1** the science of diet. **2** rules of diet. **dietitian** (-tish´ən), **dietician** *n.* a professional adviser on dietetics.

diet[2] (dī´ət) *n.* **1** a legislative assembly or federal parliament holding its meetings from day to day (esp. as an English name for Continental parliaments). **2** (*Hist.*) a conference or congress, esp. on international affairs. **3** (*Sc.*) a session of a court or any assembly.

diethyl ether (dīē´thīl) *n.* (*Chem.*) ether.

differ (dif´ə) *v.i.* **1** to be dissimilar. **2** to disagree in opinion; to dissent; to be at variance; to quarrel.

difference (dif´rəns) *n.* **1** the state of being unlike or distinct. **2** the quality by which one thing differs from another. **3** disproportion between two things. **4** the remainder of a quantity after another quantity has been subtracted from it. **5** a distinction, a differential mark, the specific characteristic or differentia. **6** a point or question in dispute, a disagreement in opinion, a quarrel, a controversy. **to make a difference** to have an effect. **to make no difference** to have no effect. **with a difference** with something distinctive added.

different (dif´rənt) *a.* **1** unlike, dissimilar. **2** distinct, not the same (*coll.*) unusual. **differently** *adv.* **differently abled** *a.* (*euphem.*) disabled. **differentness** *n.*

Usage note *From* is the safest preposition to use after *different*: though well established, *different to* is still sometimes disapproved of, and *different than* is more usual in American than British English.

differentia (difərən´shiə) *n.* (*pl.* **differentiae** (-shiē)) something which distinguishes one species from another of the same genus.

differential (difərən´shəl) *a.* **1** differing; consisting of a difference. **2** making or depending on a difference or distinction. **3** (*Math.*) of or relating to infinitesimal difference. **4** of or relating to differentials. **5** (*Physics*) relating to the difference between sets of motions acting in the same direction, or between pressures etc. *~n.* **1** something distinguishing between two examples of the same kind. **2** (*Math.*) an infinitesimal difference between two consecutive states of a variable quantity. **3** a differential gear. **4** the amount of difference within a wages structure between rates of pay for different classes of work. **differential equation** *n.* an equation containing differentials. **differential gear** *n.* a device of bevelled planetary and other wheels which permits of the relative rotation of two shafts driven by a third; applied to a car, it enables the rear (driving) wheels to rotate at different speeds when rounding a corner. **differentially** *adv.*

Usage note The noun *differential* should not be used as though it simply meant difference (without comparison of levels of the same thing).

differentiate (difərən´shiāt) *v.t.* **1** to make different. **2** to constitute a difference between, of or in. **3** to discriminate by the differentia, to mark off as different. **4** (*Math.*) to obtain the differential coefficient of. *~v.i.* to develop so as to become different, to acquire a distinct character. **differentiation** (-ā´shən) *n.* **differentiator** *n.*

difficult (dif´ikəlt) *a.* **1** hard to do or carry out. **2** troublesome. **3** hard to please. **4** not easily managed. **5** hard to understand. **6** bad-tempered. **7** full of difficulties or problems (*a difficult time*). **difficultly** *adv.* **difficultness** *n.* **difficulty** *n.* (*pl.* **difficulties**) **1** the quality of being difficult. **2** anything difficult. **3** an obstacle; objection. **4** reluctance, scruple. **5** (*pl.*) financial problems. **with difficulty** awkwardly, not easily.

diffident (dif´idənt) *a.* **1** lacking confidence in oneself or one's powers. **2** bashful, modest, shy. **diffidence** *n.* **diffidently** *adv.*

diffract (difrakt´) *v.t.* **1** to break into parts. **2** (*Physics*) to bend or deflect (a ray of light) by passing it close to an opaque object. **diffraction** *n.* **diffractive** *a.* **diffractively** *adv.*

☒ **diffrent** common misspelling of DIFFERENT.

diffuse[1] (difūz´) *v.t.* **1** to pour forth. **2** to spread abroad by pouring out. **3** to circulate. **4** (*Physics*) to cause to intermingle by diffusion. *~v.i.* **1** to be diffused. **2** (*Physics*) to intermingle by diffusion. **diffuser** *n.* **diffusible** *a.* **diffusibility** (-bil´-) *n.* **diffusion** (-zhən) *n.* **1** the act of diffusing a liquid, fluid etc. **2** the spreading abroad of news etc. **3** the state of being widely dispersed. **4** (*Chem.*, *Physics*) the mingling of liquids, gases or solids through contact. **5** spread of cultural elements from one community to another. **diffusionist** *n.*

Usage note See note under DEFUSE.

diffuse[2] (difūs´) *a.* **1** diffused, scattered, spread out. **2** copious, verbose, not concise. **diffusely** *adv.* **diffuseness** *n.* **diffusive** *a.* spreading, circulating, widely distributed. **diffusively** *adv.* **diffusiveness** *n.*

dig (dig) *v.t.* (*pres.p.* **digging**, *past*, *p.p.* **dug** (dŭg)) **1** to excavate or turn up with a spade or similar instrument, or with hands, claws etc. **2** to thrust or push into something. **3** to obtain by digging. **4** to make by digging. **5** to poke. **6** (*dated sl.*) to approve of or like. ~*v.i.* **1** to work with a spade. **2** to excavate or turn up ground with a spade or other implement. **3** to search, make one's way, thrust, pierce or make a hole by digging. ~*n.* **1** a piece of digging (esp. archaeological). **2** a thrust, a poke. **3** a cutting remark. **to dig in** (*coll.*) to begin eating. **to dig out 1** to obtain by digging. **2** to obtain by research. **to dig up 1** to excavate. **2** to extract or raise by digging. **3** to break up (ground) by digging. **4** to obtain by research. **digger** *n.* **1** a person who digs, esp. a gold-miner. **2** an implement, machine or part of a machine that digs. **3** (*coll.*) an Australian or New Zealander, esp. a soldier. **4** (*Austral., coll.*) a fellow, a mate. **digger wasp** *n.* any of several wasps that dig a hole in the ground for a nest. **digging** *n.* **1** the act of excavating with a spade, etc. **2** (*pl.*) a goldmine or goldfield. **3** (*pl., coll.*) lodgings. **digs** *n.pl.* (*coll.*) lodgings.

digastric (dīgas´trik) *a.* having a double belly or protuberance. ~*n.* (*Anat.*) the digastric muscle. **digastric muscle** *n.* (*Anat.*) a double muscle which depresses the lower jaw.

digest[1] (dījest´, dij-) *v.t.* **1** to break (food) down in the stomach into forms which can be easily assimilated by the body; to promote the digestion of. **2** to assimilate, to understand. **3** to arrange under proper heads or titles, to classify; to reduce to system or order. **4** to arrange methodically in the mind; to think over. **5** (*Chem.*) to soften and prepare by heat etc. ~*v.i.* **1** to be digested. **2** to be prepared by heat. **digester** *n.* **digestible** *a.* **digestibility** (-bil´-) *n.* **digestibly** *adv.* **digestion** (-jes´chən) *n.* **1** the act or process of assimilating food in the stomach; the conversion of food into chyme. **2** the power of digesting. **3** the act of extracting the essence from a substance, stewing. **4** mental reduction to order and method. **digestive** *a.* of, relating to or promoting digestion. ~*n.* **1** any substance which aids or promotes digestion. **2** a digestive biscuit. **digestive biscuit** *n.* a semi-sweet biscuit made of wholemeal flour. **digestively** *adv.*

digest[2] (dī´jest) *n.* **1** a compendium or summary arranged under proper heads or titles. **2** a magazine containing summaries of articles etc. in current literature.

digit (dij´it) *n.* **1** (*Anat., Zool.*) a finger or toe. **2** any numeral under ten (so called from the primitive habit of counting on the fingers). **digital** *a.* **1** representing data in the form of a series of tiny signals. **2** showing information by displaying digits, rather than by pointers and a dial. **digitalize, digitalise** *v.t.* to digitize. **digitally** *adv.* **digitize, digitise** *v.t.* to put into digital form for use in a computer. **digitization** (-zā´shən) *n.*

digitalin (dijitā´lin), **digitalia** (-liə) *n.* an alkaloid obtained from the foxglove.

digitalis (dijitā´lis) *n.* the dried leaves of the foxglove, which act as a cardiac sedative.

digitate (dij´itāt), **digitated** (-ātid) *a.* **1** (*Zool.*) having finger-like processes. **2** (*Bot.*) branching into distinct leaves or lobes like fingers. **digitately** *adv.* **digitation** (-ā´shən) *n.*

dignify (dig´nifī) *v.t.* (*3rd pers. sing. pres.* **dignifies**, *pres.p.* **dignifying**, *past, p.p.* **dignified**) **1** to invest with dignity. **2** to make worthy or illustrious. **3** to give the appearance of dignity to. **dignified** *a.* invested with dignity; stately; gravely courteous. **dignifiedly** *adv.*

dignity (dig´niti) *n.* (*pl.* **dignities**) **1** a calm, serious and respectable manner, stateliness. **2** worth, nobility. **3** estimation, rank. **4** the importance due to rank or position. **5** a high office, a position of importance or honour. **beneath someone's dignity** degrading, in someone's own opinion. **to stand on one's dignity** to assume a manner showing one's sense of self-importance. **dignitary** *n.* (*pl.* **dignitaries**) a person who holds a position of dignity, esp. in the Church.

digraph (dī´grahf) *n.* a combination of two letters to represent one simple sound, such as *ea* in *mead* or *th* in *thin*. **digraphic** (-graf´-) *a.*

digress (dīgres´) *v.i.* to deviate, to wander from the main topic. **digresser** *n.* **digression** (-gresh´ən) *n.* **digressive** *a.* **digressively** *adv.* **digressiveness** *n.*

digs DIG.

dihedral (dīhē´drəl) *a.* (*Math.*) of the nature of a dihedron. ~*n.* a dihedral angle. **dihedral angle** *n.* an angle made by the wing of an aeroplane in relation to the horizontal axis. **dihedron** (-drən) *n.* (*pl.* **dihedra, dihedrons**) (*Geom.*) a figure with two sides or surfaces.

dihybrid (dīhī´brid) *n.* the offspring of parents that differ in two pairs of genes.

dihydric (dīhī´drik) *a.* (*Chem.*) containing two hydroxyl groups.

dik-dik (dik´dik) *n.* any of several small E African antelopes of the genus *Madoqua*.

dike DYKE.

diktat (dik´tat) *n.* an order or statement allowing no opposition.

dilapidate (dilap´idāt) *v.t.* to damage, to bring into decay or ruin. ~*v.i.* to fall into decay or ruin. **dilapidated** *a.* ruined; shabby. **dilapidation** (-ā´shən) *n.* **1** the process of decaying owing to lack of repair. **2** a state of partial ruin, decay. **3** the action of an incumbent in suffering ecclesiastical buildings etc. to fall into disrepair. **4** charge for making this good. **dilapidator** *n.*

dilate (dīlāt´) *v.t.* to expand, to widen, to enlarge in all directions. ~*v.i.* **1** to be extended or enlarged; to expand, to swell. **2** to speak at length on a subject. **dilatable** *a.* **dilatation** (-lətā´shən) *n.* **1** expansion. **2** the act of dilating. **dilatation and currettage** *n.* D AND C. **dilation** *n.* dilatation. **dilator** *n.* **1** (*Anat.*) a muscle that dilates the parts on which it acts. **2** a surgical instrument for dilating the walls of a cavity.

dilatory (dil´ətəri) *a.* **1** causing or tending to cause delay. **2** addicted to or marked by procrastination. **dilatorily** *adv.* **dilatoriness** *n.*

dildo (dil'dō) *n.* (*pl.* **dildos, dildoes**) an object serving as an erect penis, used as a sex aid.

dilemma (dilem'ə, dī-) *n.* **1** an argument in which a choice of alternatives is presented, each of which is unfavourable; a position in which a person is forced to choose between equally unfavourable alternatives. **2** inability to decide between two alternatives. **3** a difficult situation.

Usage note *Dilemma* should not simply be used to mean a problem.

dilettante (dilətan'ti) *n.* (*pl.* **dilettanti** (-ti), **dilettantes**) **1** a lover or admirer of the fine arts. **2** a superficial amateur, a would-be connoisseur, a dabbler. ~*a.* amateurish, superficial. **dilettantish** *a.* **dilettantism** *n.*

diligence (dil'ijəns) *n.* **1** steady application or assiduity in business of any kind. **2** care, heedfulness.

diligent (dil'ijənt) *a.* **1** assiduous in any business or task. **2** persevering, industrious, painstaking. **diligently** *adv.*

dill (dil) *n.* **1** an annual umbellifer, *Anethum graveolens*, cultivated for its aromatic seeds, and for its flavour. **2** the leaves or seeds, used as a herb in cooking. **3** (*Austral., New Zeal., sl.*) **a** a fool. **b** a dupe. **dill pickle** *n.* a pickled cucumber flavoured with dill.

dilly (dil'i) *n.* (*pl.* **dillies**) (*N Am., coll.*) a remarkable person or thing. ~*a.* (*comp.* **dillier,** *superl.* **dilliest**) (*Austral., coll.*) silly.

dilly-dally (dilidal'i) *v.i.* (*3rd pers. sing. pres.* **dilly-dallies,** *pres.p.* **dilly-dallying,** *past, p.p.* **dilly-dallied**) (*coll.*) **1** to loiter about; to waste time. **2** to hesitate.

dilute (dīloot', dil-) *v.t.* **1** to make (a liquid) thin or weaken by adding water. **2** to reduce the strength or power of; to water down. ~*a.* **1** diluted, weakened. **2** washed out, faded, colourless. **diluent** (dil'ūənt) *a.* making thin or liquid; diluting. ~*n.* something which dilutes. **dilution** *n.*

dim (dim) *a.* (*comp.* **dimmer,** *superl.* **dimmest**) **1** lacking in light or brightness; somewhat dark. **2** obscure; not clear, not bright. **3** faint, indistinct, misty. **4** not clearly seen. **5** (of eyes) unable to see clearly. **6** (*coll.*) stupid, unintelligent. ~*v.t.* (*pres.p.* **dimming,** *past, p.p.* **dimmed**) **1** to make dim. **2** (*N Am.*) to dip (headlights). ~*v.i.* to become dim. **to take a dim view of** (*coll.*) to regard pessimistically, to view with suspicion or disfavour. **dimly** *adv.* **dimmer** *n.* **1** a device whereby an electric lamp can be switched on and off gradually. **2** (*N Am.*) **a** a small parking light on a vehicle. **b** a dipped headlight. **dimmish** *a.* **dimness** *n.*

dim. *abbr.* diminuendo.

dime (dīm) *n.* a silver coin of the US, worth 10 cents, or one-tenth of a dollar. **dime novel** *n.* (*N Am.*) a sensational story.

dimension (dimen'shən, dī-) *n.* **1** measurable extent or magnitude, length, breadth, height, thickness, depth, area, volume etc. **2** (*pl.*) size. **3** (*Physics*) one of a number of unknown or variable quantities contained as factors in a given product (thus ab^2c^3 is a term of six dimensions). **4** an aspect. **dimensional** *a.* **dimensioned** *a.* **1** having dimensions. **2** (*usu. in comb.*) proportional. **dimensionless** *a.*

dimer (dī'mə) *n.* (*Chem.*) a chemical composed of two identical molecules. **dimeric** (-mer'ik) *a.* **dimerize, dimerise** *v.t.* to cause to form a dimer. ~*v.i.* to form a dimer. **dimerization** (-ā'shən) *n.*

dimerous (dim'ərəs) *a.* having two parts, joints, divisions etc., arranged in pairs.

dimeter (dim'ətə) *n.* a verse of two metrical feet.

diminish (dimin'ish) *v.t.* **1** to make smaller or less. **2** to reduce in quantity, power, rank etc. **3** to disparage, to degrade. ~*v.i.* to become less, to decrease. **diminishable** *a.* **diminished** *a.* **1** made less or smaller, reduced in size or quality. **2** (*Mus.*) lessened by a semitone. **diminished responsibility** *n.* a plea in law in which criminal responsibility is denied on the grounds of mental derangement. **diminution** (-nū'-) *n.* **1** the act of diminishing. **2** the amount subtracted. **3** the state of becoming less or smaller. **4** (*Mus.*) lessening by a semitone.

diminuendo (diminūen'dō) *a., adv.* (*Mus.*) gradually decreasing in loudness. ~*n.* (*pl.* **diminuendos, diminuendi** (-di)) **1** a gradual decrease in loudness. **2** a passage characterized by this.

diminutive (dimin'ūtiv) *a.* **1** small, tiny. **2** (*Gram.*) (of a word or suffix) expressing diminution. ~*n.* (*Gram.*) a word formed from another to express diminution in size or importance, or affection. **diminutival** (-tī'-) *a.* **diminutively** *adv.* **diminutiveness** *n.*

dimorphic (dīmaw'fik) *a.* (*Biol., Chem., Mineral.*) having or occurring in two distinct forms. **dimorphism** *n.* **dimorphous** *a.*

dimple (dim'pəl) *n.* a small natural depression on the cheek or chin. ~*v.t.* to mark with dimples. ~*v.i.* to form dimples. **dimply** *a.* (*comp.* **dimplier,** *superl.* **dimpliest**)

dim sum (dim sŭm'), **dim sim** (sim') *n.* a Chinese dish of small steamed dumplings with various fillings.

dimwit (dim'wit) *n.* (*coll.*) a stupid person. **dimwitted** (-wit'-) *a.*

DIN (din) *n.* a method of classifying the speed of photographic film by sensitivity to light (the greater the light sensitivity the higher the speed).

din (din) *n.* a loud and continued noise. ~*v.t.* (*pres.p.* **dinning,** *past, p.p.* **dinned**) to stun with a loud continued noise. ~*v.i.* to make a din. **to din into** to teach by constant repetition.

dinar (dē'nah) *n.* **1** the standard unit of currency in the countries which formerly made up Yugoslavia. **2** the standard unit of currency of various N African and Middle Eastern countries.

din-din (din'din), **din-dins** *n.* (*coll.*) dinner (used by or to children).

dine (dīn) *v.i.* to take dinner. *~v.t.* to give or provide a dinner for. **to dine on** to eat (something) for dinner. **to dine out on** to be popular socially because of (something interesting to recount). **diner** *n.* 1 a person who dines. 2 a railway dining car. 3 (*N Am.*) a small, inexpensive restaurant. 4 a small dining room. **dinette** (-net′) *n.* 1 an alcove or a small part of a room set aside for eating. 2 (*N Am.*) a dining table and chairs for a dinette. **dining** *n.* **dining car** *n.* a railway coach in which meals are cooked and served. **dining hall, dining room** *n.* a room for eating dinner in. **dining table** *n.* a table for eating dinner at.

dinero (dineə′rō) *n.* (*N Am., sl.*) money.

ding¹ (ding) *v.i.* to ring, keep sounding. *~n.* a ringing sound. **ding-a-ling** (ding′əling) *n.* 1 the sound made by a bell. 2 (*N Am.*) a mad or silly person.

ding² (ding) *n.* (*Austral., sl.*) a lively party.

dingbat (ding′bat) *n.* (*sl.*) 1 (*N Am., Austral.*) a stupid person. 2 (*pl., Austral., New Zeal.*) **a** madness. **b** an attack of nerves.

ding-dong (ding′dong) *n.* 1 the sound of a bell. 2 (*coll.*) a violent argument. 3 a wild party. *~a.* 1 (of a fight or contest) intense. 2 sounding like a bell; jingling. *~adv.* vigorously, intensely.

dinge (dinj) *n.* a dent. *~v.t.* to make a dent in.

dinghy (ding′gi) *n.* (*pl.* **dinghies**) 1 a small ship's boat. 2 any small boat. 3 a small inflatable rubber boat.

dingle (ding′gəl) *n.* a dell, a wooded valley between hills.

dingo (ding′go) *n.* (*pl.* **dingoes, dingos**) 1 the Australian wild dog, *Canis dingo*. 2 (*Austral., sl.*) a cowardly or despicable person.

dingy (din′ji) *a.* (*comp.* **dingier,** *superl.* **dingiest**) 1 soiled, grimy. 2 of a dusky, soiled or dun colour. **dingily** *adv.* **dinginess** *n.*

dinkum (ding′kəm) *a.* (*Austral., New Zeal., coll.*) good, genuine, satisfactory. **dinkum oil** *n.* the truth.

dinky (ding′ki) *a.* (*comp.* **dinkier,** *superl.* **dinkiest**) (*coll.*) 1 charming, dainty, pleasing. 2 (*N Am.*) insignificant.

dinner (din′ə) *n.* 1 the main meal of the day. 2 a feast, a banquet. **dinner dance** *n.* a dinner followed by dancing. **dinner jacket** *n.* a man's formal jacket, usu. black, less formal than a dress coat, without tails and worn with black tie. **dinner lady** *n.* a woman who cooks or serves school lunches. **dinnerless** *a.* **dinner party** *n.* a social gathering where guests are invited to someone's house for dinner. **dinner service, dinner set** *n.* the set of dishes, used for serving dinner.

dinoflagellate (dīnōflaj′əlāt) *n.* any of a group of unicellular aquatic organisms with two flagella.

dinosaur (dī′nəsaw) *n.* 1 a gigantic Mesozoic reptile. 2 an outdated person, thing or organization. **dinosaurian** (-saw′riən) *a., n.*

dint (dint) *n.* the mark or dent caused by a blow. *~v.t.* to mark with a dint. **by dint of** by force of; by means of.

diocese (dī′əsis) *n.* the district under the jurisdiction of a bishop. **diocesan** (-os′-) *a.* of or relating to a diocese. *~n.* a person who has ecclesiastical jurisdiction over a diocese; a bishop or archbishop.

diode (dī′ōd) *n.* 1 a simple electron tube in which the current flows in one direction only between two electrodes. 2 a semiconductor with two terminals.

dioecious (dīē′shəs) *a.* 1 (*Bot.*) having the stamens on one individual and the pistils on another. 2 (*Zool.*) having the sexes in separate individuals, as distinct from *monoecious*.

Dionysiac (dīəniz′iak), **Dionysian** (-iən) *a.* 1 of or relating to Dionysus (the Greek god of wine). 2 wild, unrestrained.

dioptre (dīop′tə), (*N Am.*) **diopter** *n.* a unit of refractive power, being the power of a lens with a focal distance of one metre. **dioptric** *a.* 1 affording a medium for assisting the sight in the view of distant objects. 2 refractive. 3 of or relating to dioptrics. **dioptrically** *adv.* **dioptrics** *n.* the part of optics which treats of the refraction of light in passing through different mediums, esp. through lenses.

diorama (dīərah′mə) *n.* 1 a painting in which natural phenomena are depicted by means of change of colour and light. 2 a scenic representation viewed through an aperture by means of reflected and transmitted light, various alterations of colour and lighting imitating natural effects. 3 a miniature set for a film or television programme. **dioramic** (-ram′-) *a.*

diorite (dī′ərīt) *n.* (*Geol.*) a granite-like rock, consisting principally of hornblende and feldspar. **dioritic** (-rit′-) *a.*

dioxan (dīok′san), **dioxane** (-ān) *n.* (*Chem.*) a colourless, insoluble, toxic liquid.

dioxide (dīok′sīd) *n.* (*Chem.*) one atom of a metal combined with two of oxygen.

dioxin (dīok′sin) *n.* (*Chem.*) a highly toxic substance found in some weedkillers which causes birth defects, cancers and various other diseases.

DIP (dip) *n.* (*Comput.*) a kind of integrated circuit consisting of two rows of pins in a small piece of plastic or ceramic. **DIP switch** *n.* an electronic device with switches used to select an operating mode.

Dip. *abbr.* Diploma.

dip (dip) *v.t.* (*pres.p.* **dipping,** *past p.p.* **dipped**) 1 to plunge into a liquid for a short time, to immerse. 2 to wash, to dye, to coat by plunging into a liquid. 3 to lower for an instant. 4 to put (the hand or a ladle) into liquid and scoop out. 5 to lower (the headlights). 6 (*Naut.*) to salute by lowering (the flag) and hoisting it again. 7 to make (a candle) by dipping the wick in tallow. 8 to scoop up. *~v.i.* 1 to plunge into liquid for a short time. 2 to sink, e.g. below the horizon. 3 to become lower or smaller, esp. briefly. 4 to bend downwards, to bow. 5 to slope or extend downwards. 6 to dip a hand or a ladle into a liquid and

scoop something out. ~n. **1** the act of dipping in a liquid. **2** a short swim. **3** a candle made by dipping a wick in melted tallow. **4** the quantity taken up at one dip or scoop. **5** a preparation for washing sheep. **6** sauce, gravy etc. into which something is to be dipped. **7** a savoury mixture into which biscuits or raw vegetables are dipped before being eaten. **8** depth or degree of submergence. **9** (*Geol.*) the angle at which strata slope downwards into the earth. **10** (*N Am., sl.*) a foolish person. **to dip into 1** to draw upon (e.g. resources). **2** to read from cursorily. **3** to take a brief interest in. **to dip out** (*Austral., sl.*) to miss out (on). **dip-net** *n.* a small fishing net with a long handle. **dip of the horizon** *n.* the apparent angular depression of the visible horizon below the horizontal plane through the observer's eye, due to his elevation. **dip of the needle** *n.* the angle which a magnetic needle makes with the horizontal. **dipper** *n.* **1** a person who dips. **2** popular name for several birds, esp. the water ouzel. **dipshit** *n.* (*N Am., sl.*) a despicable person. **dipstick** *n.* **1** a rod for measuring the level of liquid in a container, esp. oil in a vehicle's engine. **2** (*sl.*) a foolish or despicable person. **dip switch** *n.* a device in a car for dipping headlights.
Dip. A.D. *abbr.* Diploma in Art and Design.
Dip. Ed. *abbr.* Diploma in Education.
dipeptide (dīpep'tīd) *n.* a peptide with two amino acid molecules in its structure.
Dip. H.E. *abbr.* Diploma of Higher Education.
diphosphate (dīfos'fāt) *n.* (*Chem.*) a compound containing two phosphate groups in the molecule.
diphtheria (difthiə'riə) *n.* an infectious disease characterized by acute inflammation and the formation of a false membrane, chiefly on the pharynx, nostrils, tonsils and palate, causing breathing difficulties. **diphtherial, diphtheric** *a.* **diphtheritic** (-thərit'-) *a.* **diphtheroid** (dif'thər-) *a.*

Usage note Pronunciation as (dip-) is best avoided.

diphthong (dif'thong) *n.* **1** the union of two vowels in one syllable. **2** a digraph or combination of two vowel characters to represent a vowel sound. **3** either of the vowel ligatures æ or œ. **diphthongal** (-thong'gəl), **dipthongic** (-gik) *a.* **diphthongize, dipthongise** *v.t.* **diphthongization** (-zā'shən) *n.*
diplo- (dip'lō) *comb. form* double.
diplodocus (diplod'əkəs) *n.* a very large dinosaur of the genus *Diplodocus*, characterized by a large tail and a small head.
diploid (dip'loid) *a.* (*Biol.*) having the full number of paired homologous chromosomes. ~*n.* (*Biol.*) a diploid cell or organism. **diploidic** *a.* **diploidy** *n.* the state of being diploid.
diploma (diplō'mə) *n.* (*pl.* **diplomas**) **1** a certificate of a degree, licence etc. **2** a document conveying some authority, privilege or honour. **3** a

charter, a state paper. **diplomaed** (-məd), **diploma'd** *a.* **diplomate** (dip'ləmāt) *n.* a person who has a diploma.
diplomacy (diplō'məsi) *n.* **1** the art of conducting negotiations between nations. **2** the act of negotiating with foreign nations. **3** skill in conducting negotiations of any kind. **4** adroitness, tact. **diplomat** (dip'ləmat) *n.* **1** a professional diplomatist. **2** a person who is skilled or trained in diplomacy. **diplomatic** (-mat'-) *a.* **1** of or relating to diplomacy or ambassadors. **2** adroit, tactful. **3** (of an edition) being a faithful reproduction of the original. **diplomatically** *adv.* **diplomatic bag** *n.* a bag used for sending official mail, free of customs control, to and from embassies and consulates. **diplomatic corps** *n.* the body of diplomatic representatives accredited to any government. **diplomatic immunity** *n.* the immunity from taxation and local laws given to diplomats resident in a foreign country. **diplomatic pouch** *n.* (*N Am.*) a diplomatic bag. **diplomatic service** *n.* that part of the Civil Service which provides diplomats to represent Britain abroad. **diplomatist** *n.* a person skilled or engaged in diplomacy.
dipole (dī'pōl) *n.* **1** (*Physics*) two equal and opposite electric charges or magnetic poles a small distance apart. **2** (*Chem.*) a molecule in which the centres of positive and negative charge do not coincide. **3** an aerial made of a single metal rod with the connecting wire attached half-way down. **dipolar** (-pō'-) *a.* having two poles.
dipper DIP.
dippy (dip'i) *a.* (*comp.* **dippier,** *superl.* **dippiest**) (*sl.*) slightly mad.
dipso (dip'sō) *n.* (*pl.* **dipsos**) (*coll.*) a dipsomaniac, an alcoholic.
dipsomania (dipsəmā'niə) *n.* alcoholism; an irresistible craving for stimulants. **dipsomaniac** (-ak) *n.*
dipterous (dip'tərəs) *a.* **1** of or relating to the Diptera, an order of insects which have two wings and two small knobbed organs called poisers. **2** (*Bot.*) having two winglike appendages. **dipteran** *a.* of or related to the Diptera. ~*n.* a dipterous insect.
diptych (dip'tik) *n.* an altarpiece or other painting with hinged sides closing like a book.
dire (dīə) *a.* (*comp.* **direr,** *superl.* **direst**) **1** dreadful, fearful. **2** dismal, lamentable, sad. **3** (*coll.*) of poor quality; terrible. **direful** *a.* **direfully** *adv.* **direfulness** *n.* **direly** *adv.* **direness** *n.*
direct (direkt', dī-) *a.* **1** in a straight line from one body or place to another; not curved or crooked. **2** nearest, shortest. **3** tending immediately to an end or result. **4** not circuitous. **5** not collateral in the line of descent. **6** exact, diametrical. **7** (*Astron.*) not contrary or retrograde. **8** immediate; personal, not by proxy. **9** honest, to the point. **10** plain, to the point, straightforward, upright. **11** from east to west (applied to the motion of a planet when in the same direction as the movement of the sun amidst the fixed stars). ~*adv.*

1 (*coll.*) directly. **2** immediately. ~*v.t.* **1** to point or turn in a direct line towards any place or object. **2** to show the right road to. **3** to inscribe with an address or direction. **4** to address, to speak or write to. **5** to aim, to point. **6** to guide, to prescribe a course to, to advise. **7** to order, to command. **8** to manage, to control, to act as leader or head of (a group of musicians, a play, film etc.). ~*v.i.* to give orders or instructions. **direct action** *n.* the use of the strike as a weapon to force political or social measures on a government. **direct current** *n.* an electric current which flows in one direction only. **direct debit** *n.* a method by which a creditor is paid directly from the payer's bank account. **direct dialling**, (*N Am.*) **direct dialing** *n.* dialling a telephone number without going through the operator. **direct dial** *a.* **directive** *n.* an authoritative instruction or direction. ~*a.* having the power of directing. **directly** *adv.* **1** exactly. **2** immediately. **3** at once. **4** in a direct manner. ~*conj.* (*coll.*) as soon as. **direct mail** *n.* advertising leaflets and promotional material sent, unsolicited, by a company to potential customers. **direct mailing** *n.* **directness** *n.* **direct object** *n.* (*Gram.*) the word or group of words which is acted upon by a transitive verb. **direct proportion** *n.* a relation between quantities with a constant ratio. **direct question** *n.* **1** an unambiguous question going straight to the point. **2** (*Gram.*) a question that is reported in the exact words, as in *She asked me, 'Where do you live?'* **direct speech** *n.* (*Gram.*) the reporting of spoken or written discourse by repeating the exact words, as in *He said, 'I will be late.'* **direct tax** *n.* a tax levied on the person who ultimately bears the burden of it.

direction (direk'shən, dī-) *n.* **1** the act of directing. **2** the end or object aimed at. **3** the course taken. **4** the point towards which one looks. **5** (*often pl.*) **a** the name or address on a letter or parcel. **b** an order or instruction. **c** an instruction how to find a destination. **6** sphere, subject. **directional** *a.* **directional aerial** *n.* an aerial that transmits or receives radio waves from one direction. **directionality** (-nal´-) *n.* **directionally** *adv.* **direction-finder** *n.* an apparatus for finding the bearings of a transmitting station. **directionless** *a.*

director (direk'tə, dī-) *n.* **1** a person who directs or manages. **2** an instructor, a counsellor. **3** anything which controls or regulates. **4** a person appointed to direct the affairs of a company. **5** a spiritual adviser, a confessor. **6** a device for controlling the application of a knife, an electric current etc. **7** the person responsible for directing the actors etc. in a film or play. **directorate** (-rət) *n.* **1** the position of a director. **2** a body or board of directors. **director-general** *n.* (*pl.* **director-generals**) the head of a large, often noncommercial organization, such as the BBC. **directorial** (-taw´ri-) *a.* **director of public prosecutions** *n.* PUBLIC PROSECUTOR (under PUBLIC). **directorship** *n.*

directory (direk'təri, dī-) *n.* (*pl.* **directories**) **1** a book containing the names, addresses and telephone numbers of the inhabitants etc. of a district. **2** a list of all the files on a computer disc. **3** a book of direction for public worship. **4** a board of directors. ~*a.* directing, commanding, advising.

dirge (dœj) *n.* **1** a funeral song or hymn. **2** a mournful tune or song; a lament. **dirgeful** *a.*

dirham (diə'həm), **dirhem** *n.* the standard unit of currency of several N African and Middle Eastern countries.

dirigible (dir'ijibəl) *a.* able to be directed or steered. ~*n.* a balloon or airship which can be steered. **dirigibility** (-bil´-) *n.*

dirk (dœk) *n.* a dagger, esp. one worn by a Highlander. ~*v.t.* to stab with a dirk.

dirndl (dœn´dəl) *n.* **1** an Alpine peasant woman's dress with tight-fitting bodice and full gathered skirt. **2** any full skirt like this.

dirt (dœt) *n.* **1** foul or unclean matter, matter that soils. **2** mud, mire, dust. **3** faeces. **4** a worthless thing, trash, refuse. **5** dirtiness. **6** earth, soil. **7** obscene or malicious talk. **to do someone dirt** (*sl.*) to behave maliciously towards someone. **to eat dirt** **1** to put up with insult and abuse without retaliation. **2** (*N Am.*) to make an embarrassing confession. **to treat like dirt** to behave disrespectfully towards. **dirt bike** *n.* a motorcycle for use on unsurfaced roads or dirt tracks. **dirt cheap** *a.* (*coll.*) very cheap. **dirt track** *n.* a racing-track with a soft, loose surface, for motorcycle racing. **dirty** *a.* (*comp.* **dirtier**, *superl.* **dirtiest**) **1** full of, mixed, or soiled with dirt. **2** foul, nasty, unclean. **3** offensive, obscene, sordid. **4** mean; contemptible, unfair. **5** (of weather) rough, wet and gusty. **6** (of a colour) dull, not bright or clear. **7** (of nuclear weapons) producing much radioactive fallout. ~*adv.* (*sl.*) **1** extremely (*a dirty great bill*). **2** dishonestly, unfairly. ~*v.t.* (*3rd pers. sing. pres.* **dirties**, *pres.p.* **dirtying**, *past, p.p.* **dirtied**) to make dirty, to soil. ~*v.i.* to become dirty. **to do the dirty on** (*coll.*) to play an underhand trick on. **dirtily** *adv.* **dirtiness** *n.* **dirty look** *n.* (*coll.*) a glance of disapproval or dislike. **dirty old man** *n.* a lewd old man. **dirty trick** *n.* **1** a contemptible or unfair act. **2** (*pl.*) underhand politics or business methods, used to discredit rivals. **dirty weekend** *n.* a weekend holiday with a sexual partner. **dirty word** *n.* **1** (*coll.*) a swear word or taboo word. **2** something currently out of favour or very much disliked (*'Smoking' is a dirty word these days*). **dirty work** *n.* (*coll.*) dishonesty, trickery, foul play (*I won't do your dirty work for you*).

dis (dis), **diss** *v.t.* (*pres.p.* **dissing**, *past, p.p.* **dissed**) (*N Am.*, *sl.*) to treat disrespectfully, to put down.

dis- (dis), **dif-** (dif) *pref.* **1** asunder, apart, away. **2** between, separating, distinguishing. **3** separately. **4** utterly, exceedingly. **5** (forming negative compounds) not, the reverse of. **6** undoing, depriving or expelling from.

disability (disəbil´iti) n. (pl. **disabilities**) **1** weakness, incapacity, inability; handicap. **2** lack of physical or intellectual power, or pecuniary means. **3** legal disqualification.

disable (disā´bəl) v.t. **1** to render unable. **2** to deprive of adequate physical or intellectual power, to incapacitate. **3** to injure so as to incapacitate, to cripple. **disabled** a. **disablement** n. **disablist** a. discriminating against disabled people.

disabuse (disəbūz´) v.t. to free from error or misapprehension, to undeceive.

disaccharide (dīsak´ərīd) n. (Chem.) a sugar with two linked monosaccharides per molecule.

disadvantage (disədvahn´tij) n. **1** an unfavourable position or condition. **2** injury, detriment, hurt. ~v.t. to cause disadvantage to. **at a disadvantage** in an unfavourable situation or position. **disadvantaged** a. **1** deprived of social or economic resources. **2** discriminated against. **disadvantageous** (-advəntā´jəs) a. **1** prejudicial, detrimental; unfavourable to one's interest. **2** disparaging, depreciative. **disadvantageously** adv. **disadvantageousness** n.

disaffect (disəfekt´) v.t. (chiefly pass.) to estrange, alienate the affection or loyalty of. **disaffected** a. **disaffectedly** adv. **disaffection** n.

disaffiliate (disəfil´iāt) v.t. **1** to end an affiliation to. **2** to detach. ~v.i. to separate oneself (from). **disaffiliation** (-ā´shən) n.

disafforest (disəfor´ist) v.t. **1** to strip of forest. **2** to reduce from the legal status of forest to that of ordinary land. **disafforestation** (-tā´shən) n.

disagree (disəgrē´) v.i. **1** to differ in opinion. **2** to quarrel, to fall out. **3** to differ; to be different or unlike. **4** to be unsuitable or injurious to the health or digestion of (Pickled onions disagree with me). **disagreeable** a. **1** offensive, unpleasant, repugnant. **2** ill-tempered. **disagreeableness** n. **disagreeably** adv. **disagreement** n.

disallow (disəlow´) v.t. to refuse to sanction or permit; to refuse assent to; to disavow, to reject; to prohibit. **disallowance** n.

disambiguate (disambig´ūāt) v.t. to make unambiguous. **disambiguation** (-ā´shən) n.

disappear (disəpiə´) v.i. **1** to go out of sight; to become invisible. **2** to be lost. **3** to cease to exist. **to do a disappearing act** to leave suddenly, esp. in order to avoid something unpleasant. **disappearance** n.

disappoint (disəpoint´) v.t. **1** to defeat the expectations, wishes, hopes or desires of. **2** to frustrate, hinder (a plan). **disappointed** a. frustrated, thwarted, deceived or defeated in one's desires or expectations. **disappointedly** adv. **disappointing** a. **disappointingly** adv. **disappointment** n. **1** the failure of one's hopes. **2** something which or a person who disappoints.

disapprobation (disəprəbā´shən) n. disapproval, condemnation. **disapprobative** (-ap´-) a. **disapprobatory** (-ap´-) a.

disapprove (disəproov´) v.t. to condemn or to reject, as not approved of. ~v.i. to feel or express

disapproval (Her father disapproved of her boyfriend). **disapproval** n. **disapprover** n. **disapproving** a. **disapprovingly** adv.

disarm (disahm´) v.t. **1** to take the weapons away from. **2** to remove the means of defence from (a ship). **3** to defuse (a bomb). **4** to reduce to a peace footing. **5** to render harmless. **6** to subdue, to tame. ~v.i. **1** to reduce or abandon military and naval establishments. **2** to lay aside arms. **disarmament** n. reduction of armaments by mutual agreement between nations. **disarmer** n. **disarming** a. tending to allay hostility or criticism; charming. **disarmingly** adv.

disarrange (disərānj´) v.t. to put out of order. **disarrangement** n.

disarray (disərā´) n. **1** disorder, confusion. **2** disorderliness of dress. ~v.t. to throw into confusion, to rout.

disarticulate (disahtik´ūlāt) v.t. to separate the joints of, to disjoint. ~v.i. to become disjointed or separated at the joints. **disarticulation** (-lā´shən) n.

disassemble (disəsem´bəl) v.t. to take apart. **disassembler** n. (Comput.) a program which translates machine code into assembly language. **disassembly** n.

disassociate (disəsō´shiāt, -si-) v.t., v.i. DISSOCIATE. **disassociation** (-ā´shən) n.

disaster (dizah´stə) n. **1** a sudden misfortune, a calamity. **2** misfortune, ill luck. **3** (coll.) fiasco, flop. **disaster area** n. **1** an area which has suffered a disaster and needs emergency aid. **2** (coll.) a person who or a place or thing which is in disarray or is a failure. **disastrous** (-trəs) a. **1** causing or threatening disaster. **2** very unsuccessful. **disastrously** adv.

Usage note Pronunciation of disastrous as (dizahs´tərəs), with an extra syllable, is best avoided.

❌ **disatisfy** common misspelling of DISSATISFY.

disavow (disəvow´) v.t. to deny the truth of, to disown; to disapprove; to disclaim. **disavowal** n.

disband (disband´) v.i. to be disbanded; to separate, to disperse. ~v.t. to break up the association of a group of people who have worked together. **disbandment** n.

disbar (disbah´) v.t. (pres.p. **disbarring**, past, p.p. **disbarred**) to deprive of status as a barrister; to expel from membership of the bar. **disbarment** n.

disbelieve (disbilēv´) v.t. to refuse credit to, to refuse to believe in. ~v.i. to be a sceptic. **disbelief** n. **disbeliever** n. **disbelievingly** adv.

disbenefit (disben´ifit) n. a disadvantage, a drawback.

disbud (disbŭd´) v.t. (pres.p. **disbudding**, past, p.p. **disbudded**) to cut away (esp. superfluous) buds from.

disburden (disbœ´dən) v.t. **1** to remove a burden or encumbrance from. **2** to relieve, to get rid of.

disburse (disbœs´) *v.t.* **1** to pay out, to expend. **2** to defray. ~*v.i.* to pay money. **disbursal** *n.* **disbursement** *n.* **disburser** *n.*

disc (disk), (*Comput.*, *also N Am.*) **disk** *n.* **1** a flat circular plate or surface. **2** a gramophone record. **3** a compact disc. **4** any round, luminous and apparently flat object. **5** (*Astron.*) the face of a celestial body. **6** the central part of a radiate compound flower. **7** a layer of fibrocartilage between vertebrae. **8** (*Comput.* disk) **a** MAGNETIC DISK (under MAGNET). **b** OPTICAL DISK (under OPTIC). **disc brake** *n.* a brake consisting of a metal disc attached to the axle, on the opposite surfaces of which the pads press. **disc harrow** *n.* a harrow consisting of sharpened saucer-shaped discs for cutting clods of soil. **disc jockey** *n.* the presenter of a programme of popular recorded music. **disk drive** *n.* (*Comput.*) the electromechanical device in a computer which reads information from, and writes it on to, the disk. **diskette** *n.* (*Comput.*) a floppy disk. **diskless** *a.*

Usage note In general the spelling *disc* is preferred in Britain and *disk* in the United States, but in computing *disk* is standard everywhere, complicating the British spelling of cases such as *compact disc.*

discard[1] (diskahd´) *v.t.* **1** to throw aside or away as useless. **2** to get rid of, to reject; to cast aside; to dismiss. **3** in cards, to play (a particular card) that does not follow suit. ~*v.i.* to play a nontrump card that does not follow suit. **discardable** *a.*

discard[2] (dis´kahd) *n.* **1** the playing of useless cards. **2** a card so played. **3** rejection as useless. **4** anything so rejected.

discern (disœn´) *v.t.* **1** to perceive distinctly with the senses, to make out. **2** to recognize clearly or perceive mentally. ~*v.i.* to discriminate. **discerner** *n.* **discernible** *a.* **discernibly** *adv.* **discerning** *a.* having the power to discern; discriminating, acute, penetrating. **discerningly** *adv.* **discernment** *n.* **1** the act, power or faculty of discerning. **2** clear discrimination, accurate judgement.

discharge[1] (dischahj´) *v.t.* **1** to unload from a ship, vehicle etc.; to take (a load etc.) out or away. **2** to emit, to let fly. **3** to dismiss. **4** to release from confinement. **5** to relieve of a load. **6** to set free from something binding. **7** to fire (a gun). **8** to empty, to pour out. **9** to pay off; to settle. **10** to perform (a duty). **11** (*Physics*) to remove an electrical charge from. ~*v.i.* **1** (of a river) to unload or empty itself. **2** (of a gun) to be discharged. **3** to pour out. **dischargeable** *a.* **discharger** *n.*

discharge[2] (dis´chahj) *n.* **1** the act of discharging. **2** unloading. **3** firing (of a gun). **4** payment. **5** dismissal. **6** release, acquittal, liberation. **7** (of a duty) performance. **8** a paper certifying discharge. **9** emission (of a fluid). **10** a fluid discharged. **11** (*Physics*) neutralization or loss of electric charge.

disciple (disī´pəl) *n.* **1** a pupil or adherent of a philosopher, leader etc. **2** a follower or a particular cult, area of interest etc. **3** one of the early followers, esp. one of the twelve personal followers of Christ. **discipleship** *n.* **discipular** (-sip´ū-) *a.*

discipline (dis´iplin) *n.* **1** instruction, training, exercise, or practice of the mental, moral and physical powers to promote order, regularity and efficient obedience. **2** punishment, chastisement. **3** training supplied by adversity. **4** military training. **5** order, systematic obedience, methodical action, the state of being under control. **6** a branch of instruction. **7** in the Roman Catholic Church, penitential chastisement or the instrument by which this is applied physically. **8** control over the members of a church, the rules binding on the members of a church. ~*v.t.* **1** to bring into a state of discipline. **2** to teach, to train, to drill, esp. in obedience, orderly habits and methodical action. **3** to punish, to chastise, to bring into a state of order and obedience. **disciplinable** *a.* **disciplinal** (dis´-, -plī´nəl) *a.* **disciplinarian** (-neə´ri-) *n.* a person who rigidly enforces discipline. **disciplinary** (dis´iplinəri) *a.* of or relating to or promoting discipline. **discipliner** *n.*

disclaim (disklām´) *v.t.* **1** to deny, to repudiate. **2** to refuse to acknowledge, to disown, to disavow. **3** (*Law*) to renounce, to relinquish or to disavow. **disclaimer** *n.* **1** the act of disclaiming. **2** (*esp. Law*) renunciation, disavowal, repudiation.

disclose (disklōz´) *v.t.* **1** to make known, to reveal, to divulge. **2** to uncover; to lay bare or open. **discloser** *n.* **disclosure** (-zhə) *n.* **1** the act of disclosing. **2** something which is disclosed, a revelation.

disco (dis´kō) *n.* (*pl.* discos) (*coll.*) **1** a discotheque. **2** disco music. ~*a.* of or relating to discotheques, as *disco dancing.* **disco music** *n.* a type of dance music with a strong bass rhythm, suitable for disco dancing.

discography (diskog´rəfi) *n.* (*pl.* discographies) **1** a catalogue or list of gramophone records or compact discs, esp. by a particular artist or band. **2** the literature and study of gramophone records or compact discs. **discographer** *n.*

discoid (dis´koid), **discoidal** (-koi´-) *a.* having the shape of a disc.

discolour (diskŭl´ə), (*N Am.*) **discolor** *v.t.* **1** to alter the colour of. **2** to give an unnatural colour to. **3** to stain; to tarnish. ~*v.i.* **1** to become stained or tarnished in colour. **2** to fade. **discoloration, discolouration** *n.*

discombobulate (diskəmbob´ūlāt) *v.t.* (*N Am.*, *coll.*) to confuse, to disconcert.

discomfit (diskŭm´fit) *v.t.* (*pres.p.* **discomfiting**, *past*, *p.p.* **discomfited**) **1** to embarrass and confuse. **2** to thwart, to frustrate. **discomfiture** (-fichə) *n.*

discomfort (diskŭm´fət) *n.* **1** lack of ease or comfort. **2** uneasiness, disquietude, distress. ~*v.t.* **1** to cause pain or uneasiness to. **2** to deprive of comfort.

discommode (diskəmōd´) *v.t.* to cause inconvenience to. **discommodious** *a.*

discompose (diskəmpōz´) *v.t.* **1** to disturb, to destroy the composure of. **2** to agitate, to vex, to disquiet. **discomposure** (-zhə) *n.*

disconcert (diskənsœt´) *v.t.* **1** to discompose, to disquiet. **2** to throw (plans) into confusion. **disconcertedly** *adv.* **disconcerting** *a.* **disconcertingly** *adv.*

disconnect (diskənekt´) *v.t.* **1** to remove (an electrical device) from its source of power, esp. by unplugging it. **2** to separate; to disunite, to sever. **disconnected** *a.* **1** incoherent, ill-connected. **2** separated. **disconnectedly** *adv.* **disconnectedness** *n.* **disconnection, disconnexion** *n.* **1** the act of disconnecting. **2** the state of being separated, ill-connected or incoherent.

disconsolate (diskon´sələt) *a.* inconsolable, dejected, forlorn; unable to be consoled or comforted. **disconsolately** *adv.* **disconsolateness** *n.* **disconsolation** (-lā´shən) *n.*

discontent (diskəntent´) *n.* **1** lack of content; dissatisfaction. **2** cause of dissatisfaction, a grievance. ~*a.* not content, dissatisfied. ~*v.t.* to make discontented, dissatisfied or uneasy. **discontented** *a.* **discontentedly** *adv.* **discontentedness** *n.* **discontentment** *n.*

discontinue (diskəntin´ū) *v.t.* **1** to stop producing (*a discontinued line*). **2** to break off, to interrupt. **3** to leave off, to cease to use. **4** to give up. ~*v.i.* to cease. **discontinuance** *n.* **discontinuation** (-ā´shən) *n.* **discontinuity** (-kontinū´-) *n.* **discontinuous** *a.* **1** not continuous, disconnected. **2** intermittent, gaping. **discontinuously** *adv.*

discord[1] (dis´kawd) *n.* **1** lack of concord or agreement; disagreement, contention, strife. **2** disagreement or opposition in quality, esp. in sounds. **3** (*Mus.*) **a** a lack of harmony in a combination of notes sounded together. **b** the sounding together of two or more inharmonious or inconclusive notes. **c** the interval or the chord so sounded. **d** a note that is out of harmony with another.

discord[2] (diskawd´) *v.i.* **1** to be out of harmony (with). **2** to disagree (with). **3** to be inconsistent, to clash (with). **discordant** *a.* **1** disagreeing, not in accord, unpleasing, esp. to the ear. **2** opposite, contradictory. **3** inconsistent. **discordance, discordancy** *n.* **discordantly** *adv.*

discotheque (dis´kətek) *n.* **1** a club or public place where people dance to recorded pop music. **2** mobile apparatus for playing records at a discotheque. **3** a party.

discount[1] (dis´kownt) *n.* **1** a deduction from the amount of a price or an account for early or immediate payment. **2** a deduction at a certain rate from money advanced on a bill of exchange which is not yet due. **3** the act of discounting. **4** the rate of discount. **at a discount 1** depreciated. **2** below par. **3** not held in much esteem.

discount[2] (diskownt´) *v.t.* **1** to deduct a certain sum or rate per cent from (an account or price). **2** to lend or advance (an amount), deducting interest at a certain rate per cent from the principle. **3** to leave out of account. **discountable** *a.* **discounter** *n.*

discountenance (diskown´tənəns) *v.t.* **1** to disconcert, to abash. **2** to discourage; to express disapprobation of.

discourage (diskŭr´ij) *v.t.* **1** to deprive of courage; to dishearten, to dispirit. **2** to dissuade; to deter. **discouragement** *n.* **discourager** *n.* **discouraging** *a.* **discouragingly** *adv.*

discourse[1] (dis´kaws) *n.* **1** talk, conversation, exchange of ideas. **2** a dissertation, a formal treatise. **3** a lecture or sermon. **4** a text consisting of more than one sentence, used for linguistic analysis.

discourse[2] (diskaws´) *v.i.* **1** to talk, to speak, to converse. **2** to talk formally, to hold forth (on).

discourteous (diskœ´tiəs) *a.* impolite, uncivil, rude. **discourteously** *adv.* **discourteousness** *n.* **discourtesy** *n.* (*pl.* **discourtesies**) **1** discourteous behaviour. **2** a discourteous act.

discover (diskŭv´ə) *v.t.* **1** to gain the first sight of. **2** to find out by exploration. **3** to ascertain, to realize suddenly. **4** to detect. **5** to discover (an unknown entertainer) and help them to become successful. **discoverable** *a.* **discoverer** *n.*

discovery (diskŭv´əri) *n.* (*pl.* **discoveries**) **1** the act of discovering. **2** something which is made known for the first time. **3** something which is found out. **4** revelation; disclosure; manifestation. **5** (*Law*) compulsory disclosure of facts and documents essential to the proper consideration of a case.

discredit (diskred´it) *n.* **1** lack or loss of credit. **2** disrepute, disgrace. **3** the cause of disrepute or disgrace. **4** disbelief; lack of credibility. ~*v.t.* (*pres.p.* **discrediting**, *past, p.p.* **discredited**) **1** to disbelieve. **2** to bring into disrepute. **3** to deprive of credibility. **discreditable** *a.* tending to discredit; disreputable, disgraceful. **discreditably** *adv.*

discreet (diskrēt´) *a.* **1** prudent, wary, circumspect. **2** judicious, careful in choosing the best means of action. **3** subtle, unobtrusive (*discreet aftershave*). **discreetly** *adv.* **discreetness** *n.*

Usage note The spellings of the adjectives *discreet* (circumspect) and *discrete* (distinct) should not be confused.

discrepancy (diskrep´ənsi) *n.* (*pl.* **discrepancies**) a difference; an inconsistency, esp. between two figures or claims. **discrepant** *a.*

discrete (diskrēt´) *a.* distinct, discontinuous, detached, separate. **discretely** *adv.* **discreteness** *n.*

Usage note See note under DISCREET.

discretion (diskresh´ən) *n.* **1** the power or faculty of distinguishing things that differ, or discriminating correctly between what is right and wrong, useful and injurious. **2** discernment, judgement, circumspection. **3** freedom of judgement and action. **4** (*Law*) the authority of a court to decide sentences etc. **at the discretion of** according to the judgement of. **to use one's discretion** to make decisions based on one's own judgement. **discretional** *a.* **discretionally** *adv.* **discretionary** *a.*

X discribe common misspelling of DESCRIBE.

discriminate (diskrim´ināt) *v.i.* **1** to make a distinction or difference. **2** to treat (unfairly) a group of people either worse or better than other groups. **3** to mark the difference between things. ~*v.t.* **1** to distinguish. **2** to mark or observe the difference or distinction between. **3** to distinguish by marks of difference, to differentiate. **to discriminate against** to distinguish or deal with unfairly or unfavourably. **discriminating** *a.* **1** exercising discrimination, discerning. **2** distinguishing clearly, distinctive. **3** distinguishing unfairly or unfavourably. **discriminatingly** *adv.* **discrimination** (-ā´shən) *n.* **1** power or faculty of discriminating. **2** discernment, penetration, judgement. **3** the act of discriminating. **4** unfair treatment of an individual or group of people on the grounds of race, religion, sex, age etc. **discriminative** (-nət-) *a.* **discriminatively** *adv.* **discriminator** *n.* **discriminatory** (-nət-) *a.*

discursive (diskœ´siv) *a.* **1** passing from one subject to another; rambling, desultory. **2** (*Philos.*) rational, argumentative, as distinct from *intuitive*. **discursively** *adv.* **discursiveness** *n.* **discursory** *a.*

discus (dis´kəs) *n.* (*pl.* **discuses**) **1** in ancient Greece, a metal disc thrown in athletic sports, a quoit. **2** a similar disc, with a thick, heavy middle, thrown in modern field events.

discuss (diskŭs´) *v.t.* **1** to debate. **2** to consider or examine by argument. **discussant** *n.* **discusser** *n.* **discussible, discussable** *a.* **discussion** (-shən) *n.* consideration or investigation by argument for and against.

disdain (disdān´) *n.* scorn, a feeling of contempt combined with haughtiness and indignation. ~*v.t.* **1** to regard as unworthy of notice. **2** to despise or repulse as unworthy of oneself. **disdainful** *a.* **disdainfully** *adv.* **disdainfulness** *n.*

disease (dizēz´) *n.* **1** any alteration of the normal vital processes of humans, the lower animals or plants, under the influence of some unnatural or hurtful condition. **2** any disorder or morbid condition, habit or function, mental, moral, social etc. **diseased** *a.* **1** affected with disease. **2** morbid, unhealthy, deranged.

disembark (disimbahk´) *v.i.* to leave a ship, aircraft, train etc. at the end of a journey. ~*v.t.* to remove from a ship, aircraft, train etc. at the end of a journey. **disembarkation** (-embahkā´shən) *n.*

disembarrass (disimbar´əs) *v.t.* **1** to free from embarrassment or perplexity. **2** to disencumber (of); to liberate (from). **disembarrassment** *n.*

disembody (disimbod´i) *v.t.* (*3rd pers. sing. pres.*

disembodies, *pres.p.* **disembodying,** *past, p.p.* **disembodied**) to divest of body or the flesh; to free from a concrete form. **disembodiment** *n.*

disembogue (disimbōg´) *v.t.* (of a stream) to pour out or discharge (water) at the mouth; to pour forth or empty itself. ~*v.i.* to flow out.

disembowel (disimbow´əl) *v.t.* (*pres.p.* **disembowelling,** (*N Am.*) **disemboweling,** *past, p.p.* **disembowelled,** (*N Am.*) **disemboweled**) **1** to lacerate so as to let the bowels protrude. **2** to take out the bowels of, to eviscerate. **disembowelment** *n.*

disembroil (disimbroil´) *v.t.* to free from confusion or perplexity.

X disemminate common misspelling of DISSEMINATE.

disempower (disimpow´ə) *v.t.* to deprive of the power to act. **disempowerment** *n.*

disenchant (disinchahnt´) *v.t.* **1** to free from enchantment or glamour, to free from a spell. **2** to disillusion. **disenchantment** *n.*

disencumber (disinkŭm´bə) *v.t.* to free from encumbrance.

disendow (disindow´) *v.t.* to strip of endowments. **disendowment** *n.*

disenfranchise (disinfran´chīz) *v.t.* **1** to deprive of electoral privilege. **2** to withdraw the rights of citizenship from. **disenfranchisement** (-chiz-) *n.*

disengage (disingāj´) *v.t.* **1** to separate; to loosen, to detach. **2** (*Mil.*) to withdraw from a battle. **3** in fencing, to pass the point of one's foil to the other side of one's adversary's. **4** to release. **5** to set free from any engagement. ~*n.* in fencing, the act of disengaging. **disengaged** *a.* **1** at leisure, having the attention unoccupied. **2** free from any engagement. **3** detached, uncommitted. **disengagement** *n.* **1** the act of disengaging. **2** the state of being disengaged. **3** ease, freedom of manner. **4** dissolution of an engagement to be married. **5** in fencing, a disengage.

disentail (disintāl´) *v.t.* (*Law*) to free from or break the entail of.

disentangle (disintang´gəl) *v.t.* **1** to unravel, to free from entanglement. **2** to disengage, to disembarrass. ~*v.i.* to be disentangled. **disentanglement** *n.*

disentitle (disintī´təl) *v.t.* to deprive of a right. **disentitlement** *n.*

disequilibrium (disēkwilib´riəm, -ek-) *n.* a lack of balance or equilibrium, esp. in economic affairs.

disestablish (disistab´lish) *v.t.* **1** to annul the establishment of, esp. to deprive (a Church) of its connection with the state. **2** to depose from established use or position. **disestablishment** *n.*

disesteem (disistēm´) *n.* a lack of esteem or regard. ~*v.t.* to look upon without esteem; to despise.

disfavour (disfā´və), (*NAm.*) **disfavor** *n.* **1** a feeling of dislike or disapprobation. **2** disesteem; displeasure. ~*v.t.* to treat or regard with disfavour, to discountenance.

disfigure (disfig′ə) *v.t.* to spoil the beauty or appearance of; to deform, to mar. **disfigurement** *n.* **disfigurer** *n.*

disforest (disfor′ist) *v.t.* to disafforest, to clear of forest. **disforestation** (-ristā′shən) *n.*

disfranchise (disfran′chīz) *v.t.* to disenfranchise. **disfranchisement** (-chiz-) *n.*

disfrock (disfrok′) *v.t.* **1** to strip of clerical attire. **2** to depose from the clerical office.

disgorge (disgawj′) *v.t.* **1** to eject from the mouth or stomach; to vomit. **2** to pour forth, empty out. **disgorgement** *n.*

disgrace (disgrās′) *n.* **1** the state of being out of favour; disesteem, discredit, ignominy, shame; infamy. **2** the cause or occasion of discredit or shame. ~*v.t.* **1** to dishonour; to bring disgrace on. **2** to dismiss from favour; to degrade. **in disgrace** having lost respect, out of favour. **disgraceful** *a.* shameful, dishonourable. **disgracefully** *adv.* **disgracefulness** *n.*

disgruntle (disgrŭn′təl) *v.t.* to annoy, to disappoint. **disgruntled** *a.* (*coll.*) annoyed, disappointed, discontented. **disgruntlement** *n.*

disguise (disgīz′) *v.t.* **1** to conceal or alter the appearance of, with a mask or unusual dress. **2** (*fig.*) to hide by a counterfeit appearance; to alter, to misrepresent. ~*n.* **1** a dress, mask or manner put on to disguise or conceal. **2** a pretence or show. **in disguise** wearing a disguise. **disguisement** *n.*

disgust (disgŭst′) *v.t.* **1** to cause loathing or aversion in. **2** to offend the taste of. ~*n.* **1** aversion, loathing, repulsion. **2** a strong feeling of distaste or nausea. **in disgust** with a feeling of disgust. **disgustedly** *adv.* **disgustful** *a.* **1** causing disgust, disgusting. **2** full of or inspired by disgust. **disgusting** *a.* **disgustingly** *adv.* **disgustingness** *n.*

dish (dish) *n.* **1** a broad, shallow, open vessel for serving up food at table. **2** the food so served. **3** any particular kind of food. **4** (*pl.*) the dirty dishes, cutlery and pots and pans which have been used for a meal. **5** any dishlike utensil, receptacle or concavity. **6** a dish-shaped concave reflector used as a directional aerial for radio or TV transmissions. **7** (*sl.*) an attractive person. ~*v.t.* **1** to put into or serve in a dish. **2** to make concave. **3** (*coll.*) to foil, to disappoint, to frustrate. **to dish up 1** to serve up. **2** (*coll.*) to present in an attractive or new way. **dishcloth,** (*dial.*) **dishclout** *n.* a cloth used for washing up dishes etc. **dishcloth gourd** *n.* a loofah. **dishful** *n.* (*pl.* **dishfuls**) **dishwasher** *n.* **1** a machine for washing dishes and cutlery. **2** a person employed to wash dishes etc. **dishwater** *n.* water in which dishes, cutlery etc. have been washed. **dishy** *a.* (*comp.* **dishier,** *superl.* **dishiest**) (*sl.*) good-looking.

dishabille DESHABILLE.

disharmony (dis·hah′məni) *n.* lack of harmony; discord, incongruity. **disharmonious** (-mō′niəs) *a.* **disharmoniously** *adv.* **disharmonize, disharmonise** *v.t., v.i.*

dishearten (dis·hah′tən) *v.t.* to discourage, to

disappoint. **disheartening** *a.* **dishearteningly** *adv.* **disheartenment** *n.*

dishevel (dishev′əl) *v.t.* (*pres.p.* **dishevelling,** (*N Am.*) **disheveling,** *past, p.p.* **dishevelled,** (*NAm.*) **disheveled**) to disorder (the hair). ~*v.i.* to be spread in disorder. **dishevelled** *a.* **1** (of hair) flowing in disorder; hanging loosely and negligently. **2** (of a person) untidy, unkempt. **dishevelment** *n.*

dishonest (dison′ist) *a.* **1** destitute of honesty, probity or good faith. **2** fraudulent, deceitful, insincere, untrustworthy. **dishonestly** *adv.* **dishonesty** *n.* (*pl.* **dishonesties**) **1** lack of honesty or uprightness. **2** fraud, cheating, violation of duty or trust. **3** a dishonest act.

dishonour (dison′ə), (*NAm.*) **dishonor** *n.* **1** lack of honour. **2** disgrace, discredit, ignominy. **3** the cause of this. ~*v.t.* **1** to bring disgrace or shame on; to damage the reputation of. **2** to treat with indignity. **3** to refuse to accept or pay (a cheque or bill). **dishonourable** *a.* **1** causing dishonour; disgraceful, ignominious. **2** unprincipled, mean, base; without honour. **dishonourableness** *n.* **dishonourably** *adv.* **dishonourer** *n.*

disillusion (disiloo′zhən) *v.t.* to free or deliver from an illusion; to undeceive. ~*n.* disenchantment; release from illusion. **disillusionize, disillusionise** *v.t.* **disillusionment** *n.*

✗ disimilar common misspelling of DISSIMILAR.

disincentive (disinsen′tiv) *n.* **1** something which discourages. **2** in economics, something which discourages productivity. ~*a.* discouraging.

disincline (disinklīn′) *v.t.* to make averse or indisposed (to). **disinclination** (-klinā′shən) *n.* a lack of inclination, desire or propensity; unwillingness.

disinfect (disinfekt′) *v.t.* to free or cleanse from infection, often by chemical means. **disinfectant** *n.* a substance which removes infection by destroying its causes. **disinfection** *n.* **disinfector** *n.*

disinfest (disinfest′) *v.t.* to rid of vermin, e.g. rats or lice. **disinfestation** (-festā′shən) *n.*

disinflation (disinflā′shən) *n.* a return to normal economic conditions after inflation, without a reduction in production. **disinflationary** *a.*

disinformation (disinfəmā′shən) *n.* the deliberate propagation or leaking of misleading information.

disingenuous (disinjen′ūəs) *a.* **1** not ingenuous. **2** lacking in frankness, openness or candour. **disingenuously** *adv.* **disingenuousness** *n.*

disinherit (disinher′it) *v.i.* (*pres.p.* **disinheriting,** *past, p.p.* **disinherited**) to cut off from a hereditary right. **disinheritance** *n.*

disintegrate (disin′tigrāt) *v.t.* **1** to separate into component parts; to reduce to fragments or powder. **2** to cause to lose cohesion. ~*v.i.* **1** to fall to pieces, to crumble. **2** to lose cohesion. **3** to deteriorate mentally or emotionally. **disintegration**

(-rā´shən) *n.* **disintegrative** (-rətiv) *a.* **disintegrator** *n.*

disinter (disintœ´) *v.t.* (*pres.p.* **disinterring**, *past, p.p.* **disinterred**) **1** to dig up, esp. from a grave. **2** to discover, bring to light. **disinterment** *n.*

disinterest (disin´trist) *n.* **1** impartiality, disinterestedness. **2** (*loosely*) lack of interest. **disinterested** *a.* **1** without personal interest or prejudice; unbiased, impartial, unselfish. **2** (*loosely*) uninterested. **disinterestedly** *adv.* **disinterestedness** *n.*

Usage note *Disinterested* is often thought to mean the same as *uninterested*, but the commonly accepted distinction is that *disinterested* means impartial, while *uninterested* means not interested.

disinvest (disinvest´) *v.i.* to reduce or withdraw one's investment (in). **disinvestment** *n.*

disjoin (disjoin´) *v.t., v.i.* to separate, to part. **disjoinable** *a.*

disjoint (disjoint´) *v.t.* **1** to put out of joint, to dislocate. **2** to separate at the joints. **3** to put out of working order. **disjointed** *a.* **1** broken up, incoherent. **2** out of joint. **disjointedly** *adv.* **disjointedness** *n.*

disjunction (disjŭngk´shən) *n.* the act of disjoining; separation. **disjunctive** *a.* **1** separating, disjoining. **2** marking separation. **disjunctively** *adv.* **disjuncture** *n.* the state of being disjointed; a separation.

disk DISC.

dislike (dislīk´) *v.t.* to regard with repugnance or aversion. ~*n.* **1** a feeling of repugnance; aversion. **2** a person or thing disliked. **dislikable, dislikeable** *a.* **dislikeful** *a.* disagreeable, unpleasant.

dislocate (dis´ləkāt) *v.t.* **1** to put out of joint. **2** to disturb, derange. **3** to break the continuity of (strata), to displace. **dislocation** (-ā´shən) *n.*

dislodge (disloj´) *v.t.* to eject from a place of rest, retirement or defence. **dislodgement, dislodgment** *n.*

disloyal (disloi´əl) *a.* **1** not true to allegiance. **2** unfaithful to the sovereign, disaffected towards the government. **disloyalist** *n.* **disloyally** *adv.* **disloyalty** *n.*

dismal (diz´məl) *a.* **1** dark, cheerless, depressing, doleful, dreary. **2** depressingly poor (*a dismal record*). ~*n.pl.* low spirits, the blues. **dismally** *adv.* **dismalness** *n.*

dismantle (disman´təl) *v.t.* **1** to strip of covering, equipment or means of defence. **2** to take to pieces. **3** to remove the defences (of a fortress). **dismantlement** *n.* **dismantler** *n.*

dismast (dismahst´) *v.t.* to deprive (a ship) of a mast or masts.

dismay (dismā´) *v.t.* to deprive of courage; to dispirit. ~*n.* utter loss of courage or resolution.

dismember (dismem´bə) *v.t.* **1** to separate limb from limb. **2** to divide, to distribute, to partition. **dismemberment** *n.*

dismiss (dismis´) *v.t.* **1** to send away; to dissolve;

to disband; to allow to depart. **2** to discharge from office or employment. **3** to put aside, reject. **4** to cast off, discard. **5** (*Law*) to discharge from further consideration. **6** in cricket, to bowl out. ~*v.i.* (*imper., Mil.*) break ranks! disperse! **dismissal** *n.* **dismissible** *a.* **dismissive** *a.* **dismissively** *adv.* **dismissiveness** *n.*

dismount (dismownt´) *v.i.* to alight from a horse or bicycle. ~*v.t.* to throw down or remove (a cannon etc.) from a carriage or support.

disobedient (disəbē´diənt) *a.* refusing or neglecting to obey; refractory. **disobedience** *n.* **disobediently** *adv.*

disobey (disəbā´) *v.t.* **1** to neglect or refuse to obey. **2** to violate, to transgress. ~*v.i.* to be disobedient. **disobeyer** *n.*

disoblige (disəblīj´) *v.t.* **1** to act in a way contrary to the wishes or convenience of. **2** to inconvenience. **disobligement** *n.* **disobliging** *a.* **1** not obliging, not disposed to gratify the wishes of another. **2** churlish, ungracious.

❌ **disolve** common misspelling of DISSOLVE.

disorder (disaw´də) *n.* **1** lack of order; confusion, irregularity. **2** tumult, commotion. **3** (*Med.*) disease, illness. **4** neglect or infraction of laws or discipline. ~*v.t.* **1** to throw into confusion. **2** (*esp. Med.*) to derange the natural functions of. **disordered** *a.* **disorderly** *a.* **1** confused, disarranged. **2** unlawful, irregular. **3** turbulent, causing disturbance, unruly. **disorderliness** *n.* **disorderly house** *n.* (*Law*) a term including brothels, gaming-houses, betting-houses and certain unlicensed places of entertainment.

disorganize (disaw´gənīz), **disorganise** *v.t.* to throw into confusion; to destroy the systematic arrangement of. **disorganization** (-zā´shən) *n.* **disorganized** *a.* lacking order, confused.

disorientate (disaw´riəntāt), **disorient** (disaw´riənt) *v.t.* **1** to cause to lose one's sense of direction. **2** to confuse. **disorientation** (-tā´shən) *n.*

disown (disōn´) *v.t.* **1** to disclaim, to renounce, to repudiate. **2** to refuse to own. **disowner** *n.* **disownment** *n.*

❌ **dispair** common misspelling of DESPAIR.

disparage (dispar´ij) *v.t.* **1** to treat or speak of slightingly; to depreciate. **2** to discredit, to disgrace. **disparagement** *n.* **disparagingly** *adv.*

disparate (dis´pərət) *a.* **1** dissimilar, discordant. **2** having nothing in common, not coordinate. ~*n.* (*usu. pl.*) things so unlike that they admit of no comparison with each other. **disparately** *adv.* **disparateness** *n.*

disparity (dispar´iti) *n.* (*pl.* **disparities**) **1** (an) inequality. **2** (a) difference in degree. **3** unlikeness.

dispassionate (dispash´ənət) *a.* free from passion; calm, temperate; impartial. **dispassionately** *adv.* **dispassionateness** *n.*

dispatch (dispach´), **despatch** *v.t.* **1** to send off to some destination, esp. to send with celerity and haste. **2** to transact quickly; to settle, to finish. **3** to put to death. **4** to eat quickly. ~*n.* **1** the act of dispatching or being dispatched. **2** prompt action. **3** promptitude, quickness, speed. **4** a message or letter dispatched, esp. an official communication on state affairs. **5** the act or an instance of killing someone. **dispatch case** *n.* (*Mil.*) a leather case for carrying papers. **dispatcher** *n.* **dispatch rider** *n.* a motorcyclist who carries dispatches.

dispel (dispel´) *v.t.* (*pres.p.* **dispelling,** *past, p.p.* **dispelled**) to dissipate, to disperse; to drive away, to banish. **dispeller** *n.*

dispensable (dispen´səbəl) *a.* **1** able to be dispensed with, inessential. **2** (of a law etc,) able to be relaxed. **dispensability** (-bil´-) *n.*

dispensary (dispen´səri) *n.* (*pl.* **dispensaries**) **1** a place where medicines are dispensed. **2** an establishment where medicines and medical advice are given free to the poor.

dispensation (dispensā´shən) *n.* **1** the act of dispensing; distribution. **2** something distributed. **3** scheme, plan, economy. **4** (*Theol.*) God's dealings with humans, esp. the divine relation at a particular period (as the Mosaic dispensation). **5** a system of principles, rights and privileges enjoined. **6** in the Roman Catholic Church, a licence to omit or commit something enjoined or forbidden by canon law. **7** the act of dispensing with or doing without something. **dispensational** *a.*

dispense (dispens´) *v.t.* **1** to deal out, to distribute. **2** to administer. **3** to prepare and give out (medicine). **4** to grant a dispensation to. **to dispense with 1** to do without. **2** to grant exemption from. **dispenser** *n.* **1** a person who or something which dispenses. **2** a machine which dispenses money, soap etc. **3** (*Med.*) a person who dispenses medicines. **dispensing** *n., a.*

disperse (dispœs´) *v.t.* **1** to scatter; to send, drive or throw in different directions. **2** to dissipate, to cause to vanish. **3** to distribute, to diffuse. **4** to disseminate. **5** (*Physics*) to divide (white light) into its component colours. **6** (*Chem.*) to put (particles) into a colloidal state, to distribute evenly in a fluid. *~v.i.* **1** to be scattered in different directions. **2** to break up, to vanish. **3** to become spread over a wide area. **dispersable** *a.* **dispersal** *n.* **dispersant** *n.* (*Chem.*) a liquid or gas used to disperse particles in a medium. **disperser** *n.* **dispersible** *a.* **dispersive** *a.*

dispersion (dispœ´shən) *n.* **1** the act of dispersing. **2** the state of being dispersed. **3** (*Chem.*) a mixture containing one substance dispersed in another. **4** (*Med.*) the removal of inflammation. **5** (*Math.*) in statistics, the scattering of variables around the arithmetic mean or median. **6** in ecology, the pattern of distribution of an animal or plant population.

dispirit (dispir´it) *v.t.* to discourage, to dishearten, to deject. **dispirited** *a.* **dispiritedly** *adv.* **dispiritedness** *n.* **dispiriting** *a.* **dispiritingly** *adv.*

displace (displās´) *v.t.* **1** to remove from the usual

or proper place. **2** to remove from a position of dignity; to dismiss. **3** to take the place of, to put something in the place of, to supersede. **displaced persons** *n.pl.* refugees who for any reason cannot be repatriated. **displacement** *n.* **1** the act of displacing. **2** the state of being displaced. **3** the water displaced by a floating body, such as a ship, the weight of which equals that of the floating body at rest. **4** (*Physics*) the amount by which anything is displaced. **5** (*Psych.*) the unconscious transferring of strong emotions from the original object to another. **6** the state of being superseded by something else. **displacement ton** *n.* a unit used to measure the amount of water displaced by a vessel, equivalent to 2240 lbs or 35 cu. ft. (0.99 m³) of sea water.

display (displā´) *v.t.* **1** to exhibit, to expose, to show. **2** to exhibit ostentatiously, to parade. **3** to make known, to unfold, to reveal. **4** to make prominent. *~n.* **1** displaying. **2** show, exhibition. **3** the kind of behaviour displayed by some birds and fish, esp. to attract a mate. **4** (*Comput.*) **a** the information displayed on a screen. **b** the screen itself. **5** ostentatious behaviour. **6** setting in prominent type. **displayer** *n.*

displease (displēz´) *v.t.* to dissatisfy, to offend; to vex, to annoy; to be disagreeable to. **to be displeased at/ with** to be annoyed or vexed at or with; to disapprove. **displeasing** *a.* **displeasingly** *adv.*

displeasure (displezh´ə) *n.* **1** a feeling of annoyance, vexation, irritation or anger. **2** †injury, offence.

disport (dispawt´) *v.t.* to amuse (oneself), to divert (oneself); to enjoy (oneself). *~v.i.* to play, to amuse or divert oneself; to gambol.

disposal (dispō´zəl) *n.* **1** the act of disposing. **2** distributing, bestowing, giving away or dealing with things in some particular way. **3** control, management, command. **4** the order or arrangement in which things are disposed. **5** the act of getting rid of rubbish. **6** (*N Am.*) a waste disposal unit. **at the disposal of 1** available for the use of. **2** in the power of, at the command of.

dispose (dispōz´) *v.t.* **1** to arrange, to set in order; to place. **2** to settle. **3** to adjust, to direct, to incline. *~v.i.* to determine or arrange affairs. **to dispose of 1** to get rid of. **2** to sell. **3** to finish; to settle. **4** to kill. **5** to prove wrong. **6** to use up. **disposable** *a.* **1** capable of being disposed of. **2** designed for disposal after use, as *disposable razors.* *~n.* any item intended for disposal after use. **disposability** (-bil´-) *n.* **disposable income** *n.* net income after payment of tax, available for use. **disposed** *a.* inclined (*I didn't feel disposed to help her*). **disposer** *n.*

disposition (dispəzish´ən) *n.* **1** the act of disposing, ordering, arranging or bestowing. **2** disposal. **3** arrangement in general. **4** aptitude; inclination, temperament, natural tendency. **5** a humour, caprice, fancy. **6** (*Law*) any unilateral writing by which a person makes over to another a piece of heritable or movable property. **7** (*usu. pl.*) arrangement, plan, preparation. **8** (*usu. pl., Mil.*) the posting of troops in the most advantageous position.

dispossess (dispəzes´) *v.t.* **1** to oust from possession, esp. of real estate. **2** to eject, to dislodge. **3** to deprive (of). **dispossession** (-zesh´ən) *n.*

dispraise (disprāz´) *v.t.* to censure, to express disapprobation of. ~*n.* blame, disapprobation, disparagement.

disproof (disproof´) *n.* **1** refutation. **2** something which proves error or falsehood.

disproportion (disprəpaw´shən) *n.* **1** lack of proportion between things or parts. **2** an inadequacy, a disparity. **disproportional** *a.* **disproportionally** *adv.* **disproportionate** *a.* **1** not duly proportioned. **2** too large or too small in relation to something. **disproportionately** *adv.* **disproportionateness** *n.*

disprove (disproov´) *v.t.* to prove to be erroneous or unfounded; to refute. **disprovable** *a.*

dispute (disput´) *v.i.* **1** to contend in argument; to quarrel in opposition to another. **2** to debate, to discuss. ~*v.t.* **1** to contend about in argument; to oppose, to question, to challenge or deny the truth of. **2** to reason upon, to discuss, to argue. **3** to contend or strive for, to contest. **4** to strive against, to resist. ~*n.* **1** contention or strife in argument; debate, controversy. **2** a difference of opinion; a falling out, a quarrel. **3** a dispute between management and trade union. **disputable** *a.* open to dispute; questionable, uncertain. **disputably** *adv.* **disputant** *n.*, *a.* **disputation** (-tā´shən) *n.* **1** the act of disputing. **2** controversy, discussion. **3** an exercise in arguing both sides of a question for the sake of practice. **disputatious** *a.* given to dispute or controversy; cavilling, contentious. **disputatiously** *adv.* **disputatiousness** *n.* **disputer** *n.*

disqualify (diskwol´ifī) *v.t.* (*3rd pers. sing. pres.* **disqualifies**, *pres.p.* **disqualifying**, *past, p.p.* **disqualified**) **1** to render unfit, to disable, to debar. **2** to render or declare legally incompetent for any act or post. **3** to disbar from a competition on account of an irregularity. **disqualification** (-fikā´shən) *n.*

disquiet (diskwī´ət) *v.t.* to disturb, to make uneasy, to harass, to vex. ~*n.* lack of quiet or peace; uneasiness, restlessness, anxiety. **disquieting** *a.* **disquietingly** *adv.* **disquietude** (-tūd) *n.*

disquisition (diskwizish´ən) *n.* **1** a formal discourse or treatise. **2** a formal and systematic inquiry, an investigation. **disquisitional** *a.*

disregard (disrigahd´) *v.t.* **1** to take no notice of; to neglect. **2** to ignore as unworthy of regard. ~*n.* lack or omission of attention or regard; slight, neglect. **disregarder** *n.* **disregardful** *a.* **disregardfully** *adv.*

disrepair (disripeə´) *n.* a state of being out of repair; dilapidation.

disreputable (disrep´ūtəbəl) *a.* **1** not reputable; of bad repute, not respectable; discreditable,

mean. **2** dirty or shabby in appearance. **disreputableness** *n.* **disreputably** *adv.* **disrepute** (-riput´) *n.* a loss or lack of reputation; discredit.

disrespect (disrispekt´) *n.* lack of respect or reverence; rudeness, incivility. **disrespectful** *a.* lacking in respect; uncivil, rude. **disrespectfully** *adv.* **disrespectfulness** *n.*

disrobe (disrōb´) *v.t.* **1** to strip of a robe or dress; to undress (oneself). **2** to divest of authority. ~*v.i.* to undress.

disrupt (disrupt´) *v.t.* **1** to interrupt, to prevent from continuing. **2** to tear apart, to break in pieces. **disrupter** *n.* **disruption** (-shən) *n.* **disruptive** *a.* **disruptively** *adv.* **disruptiveness** *n.* **disruptor** *n.*

diss DIS.

❌ **dissapear** common misspelling of DISAPPEAR.

❌ **dissappoint** common misspelling of DISAPPOINT.

dissatisfy (disat´isfī) *v.t.* (*3rd pers. sing. pres.* **dissatisfies**, *pres.p.* **dissatisfying**, *past, p.p.* **dissatisfied**) **1** to make discontented, to displease. **2** to fall short of the expectations of. **dissatisfaction** (-fak´shən) *n.* **dissatisfactory** (-fak´-) *a.* **dissatisfiedly** *adv.*

dissect (disekt´, dī-) *v.t.* **1** to cut in pieces. **2** to anatomize; to cut up (an organism) so as to examine the parts and structure. **3** to analyse, to criticize in detail. **dissection** (-sek´shən) *n.* **dissector** *n.*

Usage note The pronunciation (dī-) is sometimes disapproved of.

dissemble (disem´bəl) *v.i.* to hide one's feelings, opinions or intentions; to play the hypocrite. ~*v.t.* to pretend, to feign, to simulate. **dissemblance** *n.* **dissembler** *n.* **dissemblingly** *adv.*

disseminate (disem´ināt) *v.t.* **1** to spread (information) about. **2** to scatter (seed) about with a view to growth or propagation. **disseminated** *a.* **disseminated sclerosis** *n.* multiple sclerosis. **dissemination** (-ā´shən) *n.* **disseminator** *n.*

dissension (disen´shən) *n.* disagreement of opinion; discord, contention, strife.

dissent (disent´) *v.i.* **1** to differ or disagree in opinion; to hold opposite views. **2** to withhold assent or approval. **3** to differ from an established Church, esp. from the Church of England. ~*n.* **1** difference or disagreement of opinion. **2** a declaration of disagreement or nonconformity. **dissenter** *n.* **1** a person who dissents or disagrees, esp. one who dissents from an established Church. **2** (**Dissenter**) a member of a sect that has separated from the Church of England.

dissentient (disen´shənt) *a.* disagreeing or differing in opinion; holding or expressing contrary views. ~*n.* a person who holds or expresses contrary views.

dissertation (disətā´shən) *n.* a formal discourse on any subject; a disquisition, treaty or exile.

disservice (disœ´vis) *n.* a harmful act, a bad turn.

dissever (disev´ə) *v.t.* to sever, to separate. **disseverance, disseveration** (-vərā´shən) *n.* **disseverment** *n.*

dissident (dis´idənt) *a.* not in agreement; disagreeing, dissenting. ~*n.* **1** a person who dissents from or votes against any motion. **2** a person who disagrees with the government; a dissenter. **dissidence** *n.*

dissimilar (disim´ilə) *a.* not similar; unlike in nature, properties or appearances; discordant. **dissimilarity** (-lar´-) *n.* (*pl.* **dissimilarities**). **dissimilarly** *adv.*

dissimulate (disim´ūlāt) *v.t., v.i.* to dissemble, to conceal, to disguise. **dissimulation** (-lā´shən) *n.* **dissimulator** *n.*

dissipate (dis´ipāt) *v.t.* **1** to scatter; to drive in different directions. **2** to disperse, to dispel. **3** to squander, to waste, to fritter away. ~*v.i.* **1** to be dispersed, to vanish. **2** to indulge in dissolute or frivolous enjoyment. **dissipated** *a.* **1** given to dissipation, dissolute. **2** wasted in dissipation. **3** scattered, dispersed. **dissipater** *n.* **dissipation** (-pā´shən) *n.* **1** the act of dissipating or scattering. **2** the state of being dispersed or scattered. **3** excessive indulgence in luxury, frivolity or vice; dissoluteness. **4** wasteful expenditure, extravagance. **5** disintegration, dispersion, diffusion. **dissipative** *a.* **dissipator** *n.*

dissociate (disō´shiāt, -si-) *v.t.* **1** to separate, to disconnect. **2** (*Chem.*) to decompose, esp. by the action of heat. ~*v.i.* to become separated or disconnected. **to dissociate oneself from** to deny any connection or association with. **dissociation** (-shiā´shən, -siā´-) *n.* **dissociative** (-shiətiv, -siətiv) *a.*

dissoluble (disol´ūbəl) *a.* able to be dissolved, decomposed or disconnected. **dissolubility** (-bil´-) *n.* **dissolubly** *adv.*

dissolute (dis´əloot) *a.* given to dissipation, loose in morals; licentious, debauched. **dissolutely** *adv.* **dissoluteness** *n.*

dissolution (disəloo´shən) *n.* **1** the act or process of dissolving, separating, disintegrating, decomposing; liquefaction. **2** death, the separation of soul and body. **3** separation of a meeting, assembly or body. **4** the official ending of a marriage, partnership or other relationship. **5** gradual disappearance. **6** dissoluteness, corruption, depravity.

dissolve (dizolv´) *v.t.* **1** to diffuse the particles of (a substance) in a liquid. **2** to convert from a solid to a liquid state by heat or moisture. **3** to cause to disappear gradually. **4** to put an end to (as a meeting etc.); to dismiss, to disperse. ~*v.i.* **1** to become liquefied. **2** to decompose, to disintegrate. **3** to fade away, to melt away. **4** to melt by the action of heat. **5** to vanish. **6** (*coll.*) to be emotionally overcome (*She dissolved into tears*). **dissolvable** *a.* **dissolvent** *a.* having the power to melt or dissolve. ~*n.* anything which has the power of dissolving or melting, a solvent. **dissolver** *n.*

dissonant (dis´ənənt) *a.* **1** (*Mus.*) discordant, inharmonious. **2** harsh, incongruous. **dissonance, dissonancy** *n.* **dissonantly** *adv.*

dissuade (diswād´) *v.t.* **1** to try to persuade not to do some act. **2** to divert from a purpose by argument. **dissuasion** (-zhən) *n.* **dissuasive** (-siv) *a., n.*

dissyllable DISYLLABLE.

dissymmetry (disim´itri) *n.* (*pl.* **dissymmetries**) **1** lack of symmetry between objects or parts. **2** an instance of dissymmetry. **3** the fact of two objects or parts of being mirror images of each other. **dissymmetrical** (-met´-) *a.*

distaff (dis´tahf) *n.* **1** a cleft stick about 3 ft. (0.91 m) long, on which wool or carded cotton is wound for spinning. **2** women's work. **distaff side** *n.* the female side of a family or descent.

distal (dis´təl) *a.* (*Anat.*) applied to the extremity of a bone or organ furthest from the point of attachment or insertion.

distance (dis´təns) *n.* **1** the space between two objects measured along the shortest line. **2** extent of separation however measured. **3** the quality of being distant, remoteness. **4** a distance point (*from a distance*). **5** a set interval. **6** the length of a course run in a competition. **7** reserve, coolness; avoidance of familiarity; unfriendliness. **8** remoteness in time (past or future). **9** the remoter parts of a view or the background of a picture. ~*v.t.* **1** to place far off. **2** to leave behind in a race; to outstrip, to outdo. **3** to cause to seem remote. **to go the distance 1** to complete something one has started. **2** to endure to the end of a game or bout in sport. **to keep one's distance 1** to behave respectfully. **2** to behave with reserve or coldness. **distance learning** *n.* an educational system by which students study at home, by means of a correspondence course, videos, etc. **distance runner** *n.* in athletics, a runner who competes in long-distance or middle-distance races.

distant (dis´tənt) *a.* **1** separated by intervening space. **2** remote in space, time (past or future), succession, relationship, resemblance, kind or nature. **3** at a certain distance (*four miles distant*). **4** not plain or obvious; faint, slight. **5** reserved, cool. **6** distracted, absent (*a distant look*). **distantly** *adv.* **distantness** *n.*

distaste (distāst´) *n.* **1** disrelish, aversion of the taste. **2** dislike, disinclination. **distasteful** *a.* **distastefully** *adv.* **distastefulness** *n.*

distemper[1] (distem´pə) *n.*, **destemper** *n.* **1** a method of painting with colours soluble in water, mixed with chalk or clay, and diluted with size instead of oil. **2** the coloured preparation used in this style of painting. ~*v.t.* to paint or colour with distemper.

distemper[2] (distem´pə) *n.* a catarrhal disorder affecting dogs, foxes etc.

distend (distend´) *v.t.* to spread or swell out; to inflate. ~*v.i.* to swell out. **distensible** *a.* **distensibility** *n.* **distension** (-shən) *n.*

distil (distil'), (*N Am.*) **distill** *v.t.* (*pres.p.* **distilling**, *past*, *p.p.* **distilled**) **1** (*Chem.*) **a** to extract by means of vaporization and condensation. **b** to make or obtain by this process. **c** to purify by this process. **2** to extract the essence of. **3** to let fall in drops, to shed. ~*v.i.* **1** to fall in drops; to trickle. **2** to flow forth gently, to exude. **3** to undergo the process of distillation. **distillable** *a.* **distillate** (dis'tilāt) *n.* the product of distillation. **distillation** (-ā'shən) *n.* **1** the act of distilling. **2** the product of this process, a distillate. **distillatory** *a.* **distiller** *n.* a person who distils, esp. a manufacturer of whisky or another spirit by distillation. **distillery** *n.* (*pl.* **distilleries**) a building where whisky or another spirit is produced by distillation.

distinct (distingkt') *a.* **1** clearly distinguished or distinguishable, different, separate. **2** standing clearly apart, not identical. **3** unmistakable, clear, plain, evident, definite. **4** (*coll.*) decided, positive. **distinction** (-tingk'shən) *n.* **1** a mark or note of difference. **2** a distinguishing quality, a characteristic difference. **3** the act of distinguishing, discrimination. **4** something which differentiates. **5** honour, title, rank. **6** eminence, superiority. **7** an examination grade signifying excellence (*a pass with distinction*). **distinctive** *a.* **1** serving to mark distinction or difference, characteristic. **2** separate, distinct. **distinctively** *adv.* **distinctiveness** *n.* **distinctly** *adv.* **distinctness** *n.*

Usage note The meanings of the adjectives *distinct* and *distinctive* overlap, but in general *distinct* means clearly distinguished or separate, and *distinctive* serving to distinguish or characteristic.

distingué (dēstāgā'), (*fem.*) **distinguée** *a.* having an air of nobility or dignity.

distinguish (disting'gwish) *v.t.* **1** to discriminate, to differentiate. **2** to indicate the difference of from others by some external mark. **3** to classify. **4** to tell apart, to discriminate between. **5** to perceive the existence of by means of the senses; to recognize. **6** to be a mark of distinction or characteristic property of. **7** to separate from others by some token of honour or preference. **8** to make eminent, prominent, or well known. ~*v.i.* to differentiate; to draw distinctions. **distinguishable** *a.* **distinguishably** *adv.* **distinguished** *a.* **1** having an air of nobility or dignity. **2** eminent, celebrated, remarkable.

distort (distawt') *v.t.* **1** to twist or alter the natural shape or direction of. **2** to pervert from the true meaning. **3** to distort (an electrical sign) during transmission or application. **distortedly** *adv.* **distortedness** *n.* **distortion** (-taw'shən) *n.* **1** the act of distorting. **2** the state of being distorted. **3** a perversion of meaning, a misrepresentation. **4** deviation from strict reproduction in a radio receiver or loudspeaker. **distortional** *a.* **distortionless** *a.*

distract (distrakt') *v.t.* **1** to draw or turn aside, to divert the mind or attention of. **2** to draw in different directions, to confuse, to bewilder, to perplex. **distracted** *a.* **1** disturbed mentally, crazed, maddened. **2** worried, harassed, perplexed. **distractedly** *adv.* **distraction** (-trak'shən) *n.* **1** diversion of the mind or attention. **2** the thing that diverts; an interruption, a diversion. **3** relaxation, relief, amusement. **4** a lack of concentration. **5** confusion, perplexity, agitation, violent mental excitement arising from pain, worry etc. **6** mental aberration, madness, frenzy. **distractor** *n.*

distrain (distrān') *v.t.* (*Law*) to seize for debt; to take the personal property of, in order to satisfy a demand or enforce the performance of an act. ~*v.i.* to levy a distress. **distrainable** *a.* **distrainer** *n.* **distrainment** *n.* **distrainor** *n.* **distraint** *n.* (*Law*) the act of seizing goods for debt.

distrait (distrā'), (*fem.*) **distraite** (-trāt') *a.* absentminded, abstracted, inattentive.

distraught (distrawt') *a.* bewildered, agitated, distracted.

distress (distres') *n.* **1** extreme anguish or pain of mind or body. **2** misery, poverty, destitution. **3** exhaustion, fatigue. **4** calamity, misfortune. **5** a state of danger. **6** (*Law*) **a** the act of distraining. **b** goods taken in distraint. ~*v.t.* **1** to afflict with anxiety, unhappiness or anguish, to vex. **2** to exhaust, to tire out. **in distress 1** in a state of anguish or danger. **2** (of a ship) in a disabled or perilous condition. **distressed** *a.* **1** afflicted with pain or anxiety. **2** destitute, poor. **3** (of furniture, fabric etc.) having been artificially made to look old or worn. **distressful** *a.* **distressing** *a.* **distressingly** *adv.*

distribute (distrib'ūt) *v.t.* **1** to divide or deal out amongst a number. **2** to spread about, to disperse. **3** in hot-metal printing, to separate and return (type) to the cases. **4** to arrange, to allocate, to classify. **5** (*Logic*) to use (a term) in its fullest extent, so as to include every individual of the class. **distributable** *a.* **distribution** (-bū'shən) *n.* **1** the act of distributing. **2** the dispersal of commodities among the consumers. **3** dispersal, arrangement of a number of scattered units. **4** an assigning to different positions, the act of dividing or arranging into classes etc. **distributional** *a.* **distributive** (-trib'ūtiv) *a.* **1** distributing or allotting the proper share to each. **2** of or relating to distribution. **3** (*Gram.*) expressing distribution, separation or division. **4** (*Logic*) indicating distribution, as distinguished from collective terms. ~*n.* a distributive word such as *each*, *every*, *either* or *neither*. **distributively** *adv.* **distributiveness** *n.* **distributor** *n.* **1** a person who or something which distributes. **2** a wholesaler or agent who distributes goods to retailers. **3** the device in a petrol engine which distributes current to the sparking plugs.

Usage note Pronunciation as (dis'-), with stress on the first syllable, is best avoided.

district (dis'trikt) *n.* **1** a portion of territory

specially defined for judicial, administrative, fiscal or other purposes. **2** a division having its own representative in a legislature, its own district council, a church or chapel of its own or a separate magistrate. **3** a region, tract of country. ~*v.t.* (*N Am.*) to divide into districts. **District Attorney** *n.* (*N Am.*) the prosecuting officer of a district. **district nurse** *n.* a nurse employed by a local authority to visit and look after patients in their own homes.

distrust (distrŭst´) *v.t.* **1** to have no confidence in. **2** to doubt, to suspect. ~*n.* **1** lack of confidence, reliance or faith (in). **2** suspicion, discredit. **distruster** *n.* **distrustful** *a.* **distrustfully** *adv.* **distrustfulness** *n.*

disturb (distœb´) *v.t.* **1** to agitate, to disquiet. **2** to change the position of. **3** to worry, unsettle, to make uneasy. **4** to hinder, to interrupt, to inconvenience. **disturbance** *n.* **1** interruption of a settled state of things. **2** agitation, public agitation or excitement, tumult, disorder, uproar, an outbreak. **3** (*Law*) the interruption of a right; the hindering and disquieting of a person in the lawful and peaceable enjoyment of their right. **disturbed** *a.* (*Psych.*) emotionally or mentally unstable. **disturber** *n.* **disturbing** *a.* **disturbingly** *adv.*

disulphide (dīsŭl´fīd), (*esp. N Am.*) **disulfide** *n.* (*Chem.*) a compound in which two atoms of sulphur are united to another element or radical.

disunion (disūn´yən) *n.* the state of being disunited; disagreement, discord.

disunite (disūnīt´) *v.t.* **1** to disjoin, to divide. **2** to put at variance. ~*v.i.* to become divided. **disunity** (-ū´ni-) *n.*

disuse[1] (disūs´) *n.* a cessation of use, practice or exercise; the state of being disused; desuetude. **to fall into disuse** to stop being used.

disuse[2] (disūz´) *v.t.* to cease to use.

disyllable (dīsil´əbəl), **dissyllable** (dis-) *n.* a word or metrical foot of two syllables. **disyllabic** (-lab´-) *a.*

dit (dit) *n.* a word representing the dot in Morse code when this is spoken.

ditch (dich) *n.* **1** a trench made by digging to form a boundary or for drainage. **2** a stream. **3** a trench or fosse on the outside of a fortress, serving as an obstacle to assailants. ~*v.t.* **1** to make a ditch, trench or drain in. **2** to surround with a ditch. **3** (*coll.*) to abandon, to get rid of. **4** (*coll.*) to make an emergency landing in (an aircraft). ~*v.i.* **1** to dig or repair ditches. **2** (of an aircraft) to be brought down by an emergency landing. **ditcher** *n.* **ditchwater** *n.* stagnant water in a ditch. **dull as ditchwater** very uninteresting or unentertaining.

dither (didh´ə) *v.i.* to be distracted or uncertain; to hesitate, to be indecisive. ~*n.* (*coll.*) **1** agitation. **2** indecisiveness. **all of a dither** (*coll.*) very agitated or indecisive. **ditherer** *n.* **dithery** *a.*

dithyramb (dith´iram, -ramb) *n.* any wild, impetuous poem or song. **dithyrambic** (-ram´bik) *a.*

ditsy DITZY.

dittany (dit´əni) *n.* (*pl.* **dittanies**) **1** a herb, *Origanum dictamnus*, which was prized by the ancients for its medicinal properties. **2** (*N Am.*) a small herb, *Cunila origanoides*, growing in the Eastern US. **3** the bastard dittany, *Dictamnus fraxinella*.

ditto (dit´ō) *n.* (*pl.* **dittos**) **1** what has been said before. **2** the same thing. **3** a similar thing. ~*a.* similar. ~*v.t.* (*3rd pers. sing. pres.* **dittoes**, *pres.p.* **dittoing**, *past, p.p.* **dittoed**) to repeat (what someone else has said or done). **to say ditto** to repeat, endorse. **ditto marks** *n.pl.* a mark consisting of two dots, placed under a word to show that it is to be repeated on the next line.

ditty (dit´i) *n.* (*pl.* **ditties**) a little poem, a song.

ditty bag (dit´i) *n.* (*Naut.*) a sailor's bag for needles, thread and odds and ends. **ditty box** *n.* a box similarly used by fishermen.

ditzy (dit´si), **ditsy** *a.* (*comp.* **ditzier, ditsier,** *superl.* **ditziest, ditsiest**) (*N Am., sl.*) **1** scatterbrained. **2** overelaborate.

diuresis (dīūrē´sis) *n.* (*Med.*) an excess of urine secretion. **diuretic** (-ret´ik) *a.* (*Med.*) causing the secretion of urine. ~*n.* a diuretic medicine.

diurnal (dīœ´nəl) *a.* **1** of or relating to a day or the day-time. **2** performed in a day. **3** daily, of each day. **4** of common occurrence. **5** (*Zool.*) of the day, as distinct from *nocturnal*. **diurnally** *adv.*

diva (dē´və) *n.* (*pl.* **divas**) a famous female singer, a prima donna.

divalent (dīvā´lənt) *a.* (*Chem.*) with a valency of two.

divan (divan´) *n.* a thickly-cushioned backless seat or sofa against the wall of a room. **divan-bed** *n.* a mattress bed that can be converted into a sofa by day.

dive (dīv) *v.i.* (*pres.p.* **diving**, *past, p.p.* **dived**, (*N Am.*) **dove** (dōv)) **1** to plunge, esp. head first, under water. **2** to descend quickly. **3** to descend quickly and disappear. **4** to thrust one's hand rapidly (into something). **5** (*fig.*) to enter deeply (into any question, science or pursuit). ~*v.t.* to thrust (one's hand) rapidly into something. ~*n.* **1** a sudden plunge head first into water. **2** a sudden plunge or dart. **3** (*coll.*) a disreputable bar or pub. **4** (*Naut.*) the submerging of a submarine. **5** (of an aircraft) a steep descent with the nose down. **6** (*sl.*) in boxing, a faked knockout. **divebomber** *n.* a military aeroplane which releases its bombs while in a steep dive. **dive-bombing** *n.* **diver** *n.* **1** a person who dives, esp. someone who dives for pearls, or to work on sunken vessels etc. **2** any waterbird of the family Gaviidae, remarkable for their habit of diving. **diving** *n., a.* **diving beetle** *n.* a water beetle of the family Dytiscidae, which has flattened hind legs, used for diving and swimming. **diving bell** *n.* a hollow vessel, orig. bell-shaped, in which one may remain for a time under water, air being supplied through a flexible tube. **diving board** *n.* a platform from which one may dive into a swimming pool. **diving duck** *n.* a duck which can dive and swim under water, esp. a member of the tribe Aythini. **diving suit** *n.* waterproof clothing and breathing-helmet for divers working at the bottom of the sea.

diverge (dīvœj´, div-) *v.i.* **1** to go in different directions from a common point or from each other; to branch off. **2** to vary from a normal form. **3** to deviate, to differ. ~*v.t.* to cause to diverge. **divergence, divergency** *n.* **divergent** *a.* **divergently** *adv.* **divergent series** *n.* an infinite series the sum of which becomes indefinitely greater as more terms are added.

diverse (dīvœs´) *a.* **1** different, unlike, distinct. **2** varying, made up of a variety of things. **diversely** *adv.* **diverseness** *n.* **diversify** *v.t.* (*3rd pers. sing. pres.* **diversifies**, *pres.p.* **diversifying**, *past, p.p.* **diversified**) **1** to make different from others; to give variety to; to variegate. **2** to invest in securities of different types of (enterprise). ~*v.i.* to be engaged in the manufacture of several types of manufactured goods etc. **diversification** (-fikā´shən) *n.* **diversity** *n.* (*pl.* **diversities**) **1** difference, unlikeness; variance. **2** variety, distinctness.

diversion (dīvœ´shən, div-) *n.* **1** the act of diverting or turning aside. **2** something which tends or serves to divert the mind or attention from care, business or study. **3** a relaxation, distraction, amusement. **4** a redirection of traffic owing to the temporary closing of a road. **5** (*Mil.*) the act of diverting the attention of the enemy from any design by demonstration or feigned attack. **diversional** *a.* **diversionary** *a.* **diversionist** *n.* a subversive person, a dissident.

divert (dīvœt´, div-) *v.t.* **1** to turn from any course or direction, to turn aside, to deflect. **2** to draw off, to distract. **3** to entertain, to amuse. **divertimento** (dīvœtimen´tō) *n.* (*pl.* **divertimenti** (-tē), **divertimentos**) (*Mus.*) a piece of entertaining music. **diverting** *a.* entertaining, amusing. **divertingly** *adv.*

diverticulum (dīvətik´ūləm) *n.* (*pl.* **diverticula** (-lə)) (*Anat.*) an abnormal sac or pouch on the wall of a tubular organ, esp. the intestine. **diverticular** *a.* **diverticular disease** *n.* (*Med.*) a condition characterized by abdominal pain caused by muscular spasms in diverticula.

divest (dīvest´, div-) *v.t.* **1** to strip of clothing. **2** to deprive, rid (of). **divestiture** (-chə) *n.* **divestment** *n.*

divi DIVVY.

divide (divīd´) *v.t.* **1** to cut or part in two; to sever, to partition. **2** to cause to separate, to break into parts. **3** to distribute, to deal out. **4** to form the boundary between. **5** to part or mark divisions on (mathematical instruments etc.). **6** to distinguish the different kinds of, to classify. **7** to share, to take a portion of with others. **8** to separate (Parliament or a meeting) by taking opinions on, for and against. **9** to destroy unity amongst, to disunite feelings. **10** (*Math*) **a** to separate into

factors. **b** to perform the operation of division. ~*v.i.* **1** to be parted or separated. **2** to share. **3** to diverge. **4** (of a legislative house) to express decision by separating into two parts. **5** (*Math.*) to be an exact division of a number. ~*n.* **1** a marked distinction between two groups of people (*the North South divide*). **2** (*Geol.*) a watershed.

divider *n.* **1** a person who or something which divides. **2** a screen, a partition. **3** (*pl.*) compasses used to divide lines into a given number of equal parts.

dividend (div´idend) *n.* **1** the share of the interest or profit which belongs to each shareholder in a company, bearing the same proportion to the whole profit that the shareholder's capital bears to the whole capital. **2** a sum of money paid to football-pools winners. **3** (*Law*) the fractional part of the assets of a bankrupt paid to a creditor, in proportion to the amount of the debt. **4** (*Math.*) a number to be divided by a divisor. **5** an advantage, a bonus.

divine[1] (divīn´) *a.* **1** of, relating to, proceeding from or of the nature of God, a god, or gods. **2** appropriated to the service of the Deity, religious, sacred. **3** above the nature of man, superhuman, godlike, celestial. **4** (*coll.*) wonderful. ~*n.* **1** a clergyman, an ecclesiastic. **2** a theologian. **the Divine** God. **divinely** *adv.* **divineness** *n.* **divine office** *n.* the office of the Roman breviary, consisting of matins with lauds, prime, tierce, sext, none, vespers and compline, the recitation of which is obligatory on all clerics holding a benefice, on all persons in Holy Orders and on all monastics of both sexes professed for the service of the choir. **divinize** (div´in-), **divinise** *v.t.* to treat as divine; to deify.

divine[2] (divīn´) *v.t.* **1** to find out by inspiration, intuition or magic. **2** to foresee, to presage. **3** to conjecture, to guess. ~*v.i.* to practise divination. **divination** (-vinā´shən) *n.* **1** the art of predicting or foretelling events, or of discovering hidden or secret things by real or by alleged supernatural means. **2** an omen, an augury. **3** a prediction or conjecture as to the future. **divinatory** (-vin´-) *a.* **diviner** *n.* **divining rod** *n.* a dowsing rod.

diving DIVING.

divinity (divin´iti) *n.* (*pl.* **divinities**) **1** the quality of being divine. **2** the Divine Being; God. **3** a deity, a god. **4** theology.

❌ **divise** common misspelling of DEVISE.

divisible (diviz´ibəl) *a.* **1** capable of division. **2** (*Math.*) able to be divided into equal parts by a divisor without a remainder. **divisibility** (-bil´-) *n.*

division (divizh´ən) *n.* **1** the act of dividing. **2** the state of being divided; separation. **3** distribution. **4** something which divides or separates. **5** a boundary, a partition. **6** a separate or distinct part. **7** a district, an administrative unit. **8** a separate group of people. **9** a distinct sect or body. **10** disunion, disagreement, variance. **11** each of the groups of teams of a similar standard which make up a football league. **12** (*Biol.*) a separate class, kind, species or variety; a distinction. **13** the part of a county or borough returning a Member of Parliament. **14** the separation of Members of Parliament for the purpose of voting. **15** a formal vote in Parliament. **16** (*Math.*) the process of dividing one number by another. **17** (*Logic*) the separation of a genus into its constituent species; classification; analysis of meaning. **18** (*Mil.*) a body of soldiers, usu. three brigades, under the command of a general officer, applied loosely to smaller bodies. **19** in the navy, a number of ships under one command. **divisional, divisionary** *a.* **divisionally** *adv.* **division sign** *n.* (*Math.*) the sign ÷, indicating division. **divisor** (-vī′zə) *n.* **1** (*Math.*) a number by which a dividend is divided. **2** a number that divides another without a remainder.

divisive (divī′siv) *a.* **1** forming or noting separation or division, analytical. **2** tending to division or dissension. **divisively** *adv.* **divisiveness** *n.*

divorce (divaws′) *n.* **1** the dissolution of the marriage tie by competent authority. **2** a separation of things closely connected. ~*v.t.* **1** to dissolve by legal process the bonds of marriage between. **2** to obtain a divorce from. **3** to remove, to separate. ~*v.i.* to become divorced. **divorcé** (-sā′) *n.* a man who has been divorced. **divorcée** (-sā′) *n.* a woman who has been divorced. **divorceable** *a.* **divorcee** (-sē′) *n.* a person who has been divorced. **divorcement** *n.* **divorcer** *n.*

divot (div′ət) *n.* a piece of turf torn up by the head of a golf club when driving.

divulge (dīvŭlj′, div-) *v.t.* to make known; to reveal, disclose. **divulgement** *n.* **divulgence** *n.* **divulger** *n.*

divvy (div′i), **divi** *n.* (*pl.* **divvies, divis**) (*coll.*) **1** a dividend; a share. **2** a distribution. ~*v.t.* (*3rd pers. sing. pres.* **divvies**, *pres.p.* **divvying**, *past, p.p.* **divvied**) to divide (up).

Diwali (diwah′li) *n.* a Hindu festival honouring Lakshmi, the goddess of wealth, celebrated from October to November and marked by the lighting of lamps.

Dixie (dik′si) *n.* the US southern states. **Dixieland** (dik′siland) *n.* **1** Dixie. **2** an early type of jazz music played by small combinations of instruments.

dixie (dik′si) *n.* a pot for cooking over an outdoor fire.

DIY *abbr.* do-it-yourself.

dizzy (diz′i) *a.* (*comp.* **dizzier**, *superl.* **dizziest**) **1** giddy, dazed, vertiginous. **2** causing dizziness, confusing. **3** whirling; reeling. **4** (*coll.*) foolish, scatterbrained. ~*v.t.* (*3rd pers. sing. pres.* **dizzies**, *pres.p.* **dizzying**, *past, p.p.* **dizzied**) **1** to make dizzy. **2** to confuse, to confound. **dizzily** *adv.* **dizziness** *n.*

DJ *abbr.* **1** dinner jacket. **2** disc jockey.

djellaba (jel′əbə), **djellabah, jellaba** *n.* a cloak with wide sleeves and a hood, worn by men in N Africa and the Middle East.

djibba, djibbah JIBBA.

dl *abbr.* decilitre(s).

D.Litt. *abbr.* Doctor of Literature, Doctor of Letters.

DM *abbr.* Deutschmark.

dm *abbr.* decimetre(s).

D-mark (dē′mahk) *n.* short for DEUTSCHMARK.

D. Mus. *abbr.* Doctor of Music.

DNA *abbr.* deoxyribonucleic acid, the main constituent of chromosomes, in the form of a double helix, which is self-replicating and transmits hereditary characteristics. **DNA fingerprinting** *n.* GENETIC FINGERPRINTING (under GENETIC).

DNase (dēenāz′) *n.* an enzyme which hydrolyses DNA.

do[1] (doo) *v.t.* (*2nd pers. sing. pres.* †**doest** (doo′ist), *aux.* †**dost** (dŭst), *3rd pers. sing. pres.* **does** (dŭz), †**doeth** (doo′ith), †**doth** (dŭth), *pres.p.* **doing**, *past* **did** (did), *2nd pers. sing. past* †**didst** (didst), *p.p.* **done** (dŭn)) **1** to execute, perform, effect, transact, carry out (a work, thing, service, benefit, injury etc., or the action of any verb understood). **2** to produce, to make. **3** to bring to an end, to complete, to finish, to accomplish. **4** to produce, to cause, to render (good, evil, honour, justice, injury etc.). **5** to work. **6** to deal with. **7** to translate. **8** to prepare, to cook. **9** to play the part of. **10** to satisfy, to be adequate for. **11** to travel at a speed of. **12** to put on (a play). **13** (*coll.*) to rob, to burgle. **14** (*coll.*) to cheat, to swindle, to humbug. **15** (*coll.*) to convict. **16** (*coll.*) to injure, to kill. **17** (*coll.*) to spoil. **18** (*sl.*) to entertain, to feed. **19** (*coll.*) to serve (a period of time) in prison. **20** (*coll.*) to tire out, to fatigue, to exhaust. **21** (*coll.*) to visit and see the sights of. **22** (*taboo sl.*) to have sexual intercourse with. **23** (*sl.*) to take (a drug). ~*v.i.* **1** to act, to behave, to conduct oneself. **2** to perform deeds. **3** to finish, to make an end, to cease. **4** to fare, to get on (in an undertaking or in health etc.). **5** to serve, to suffice, to be enough, to answer the purpose. ~*v.aux.* **1** in neg. and interrog. sentences, as *I do not play*, *Do you play?*. **2** with any inflection for special emphasis, as *I do believe*, *They do love him*. **3** in the imper., as *Do give him my regards*, *Do not disturb*. **4** in inverted sentences, as *Seldom do I get so angry*. **5** also poetically, as *It did appear*. **6** as a substitute for a verb expressing any action, usu. to avoid repetition, as *I walked there in the same time as he did*; *You play whist as well as he does*; *Did he catch the train? I did*; *He often comes here*, *I seldom do*. ~*n.* (*pl.* **dos, do's**) **1** (*coll.*) a party, a celebration. **2** (*sl.*) a swindle, a fraud. **to be nothing to do with 1** to be no concern or business of. **2** not to be connected with. **to be to do with** to be connected with, to be about. **to do about** to do (something) to deal with. **to do away with** (*coll.*) to remove, to abolish. **to do by** to treat, to deal with (*hard done by*). **to do down 1** (*coll.*) to get the better of, to cheat. **2** (*coll.*) to humiliate. **to do for 1** to suit (*That dress does nothing for her*). **2** to put an end to; to ruin, to kill. **to do in 1** (*sl.*) to kill. **2** (*coll.*) to exhaust. **to do or die** to make a last, desperate attempt. **to do out** (*coll.*) to decorate (a room). **to do out of** (*coll.*) to deprive unfairly of (*I was done out of my chance to speak*). **to do over 1** (*sl.*) to attack, to beat. **2** (*sl.*) to decorate a room. **3** (*N Am.*) to perform a second time. **to do by** to do by. **to do up 1** to renovate, to decorate. **2** to dress up or make oneself up. **3** to fasten. **4** to pack in a parcel. **to do with 1** to need, to want (*I could do with a drink*). **2** to have business or connection with. **to do without** to dispense with. **to have (something) to do with** to have business or connection with. **doable** *a.* **doer** *n.* **do-gooder** *n.* a person who tries to help others, often in a meddlesome or ineffectual way. **do-it-yourself** *n.* decorating, household repairs and building as a hobby. **do-nothing** *n.* an idler. **do-or-die** *a.* denoting a reckless determination to succeed. **dos and don'ts** *n.pl.* rules.

do² DOH.

do. *abbr.* ditto.

DOA *abbr.* dead on arrival.

dobe (dō´bi) *n.* (*N Am., coll.*) an adobe.

Dobermann (dō´bəmən), **Dobermann pinscher** (pin´shə) *n.* a large breed of dog with a smooth black and tan coat, used as a guard dog.

doc (dok) *n.* (*coll.*) a doctor.

docile (dō´sīl) *a.* tractable; easily managed. **docilely** *adv.* **docility** (-sil´-) *n.*

dock¹ (dok) *n.* **1** an artificial basin in which ships are built or repaired. **2** (*often pl.*) an artificial basin for the reception of ships to load and unload; a dockyard. **3** (*N Am.*) a wharf. **4** a dry dock. **5** a scene dock. ~*v.t.* **1** to bring into dock. **2** to place in a dry dock. **3** to equip with docks. **4** to join (a spacecraft) with another. ~*v.i.* **1** to come into a dock. **2** (of a spacecraft) to join with another spacecraft. **dockage** *n.* **1** accommodation in docks. **2** dock-dues. **3** the practice of berthing ships. **dock-dues** *n.pl.* dues payable by ships using docks. **docker** *n.* a labourer at docks. **dockglass** *n.* a large glass, orig. used for sampling wine at the docks. **dockland** *n.* the land around docks. **dockside** *n.* the area beside a dock. **dockyard** *n.* a large enclosed area with wharves, docks etc. where vessels are built or repaired, usually in connection with the Navy.

dock² (dok) *n.* the enclosure for prisoners in a criminal court. **in the dock** charged with an offence.

dock³ (dok) *n.* a common name for various species of the genus *Rumex*, perennial herbs, most of them troublesome weeds, esp. the common dock, *R. obtusifolius.*

dock⁴ (dok) *v.t.* **1** to cut the tail off. **2** to cut short (an animal's tail). **3** to deduct a part from; to deprive a part of. ~*n.* **1** the solid bony part of an animal's tail. **2** the divided part of a crupper through which a horse's tail is put. **dock-tailed** *a.*

docket (dok´it) *n.* **1** a summary or digest. **2** (*Law*)

a register of judgements. **3** (*N Am.*) an alphabetical list of cases for trial. **4** (*N Am.*) a similar summary of business to be dealt with by a committee or assembly. **5** a ticket or label showing the address of a package etc.

Doc Martens® (dok mah´tinz) *n.pl.* DR MARTENS.

doctor (dok´tə) *n.* **1** a qualified practitioner of medicine or surgery. **2** (*N Am.*) a qualified dentist or veterinary surgeon. **3** a person who has been awarded the highest degree in a faculty at a university etc. either for proficiency or as a compliment. **4** a person who repairs things. **5** a name for various mechanical devices. **6** an artificial fly for salmon fishing. **7** a ship's cook. ~*v.t.* **1** to treat medically. **2** to confer the degree of doctor on. **3** to patch up, to mend. **4** to adulterate. **5** to falsify. **6** to castrate or spay (a dog or cat). ~*v.i.* to practise as a physician. **just what the doctor ordered** exactly what was needed. **doctoral** *a.* **doctorate** (-rət) *n.* the degree, rank or title of a doctor; doctorship. **doctorial** (-taw´ri-) *a.* **doctorly** *a.* **Doctor Martens** *n.pl.* DR MARTENS. **Doctor of Philosophy** *n.* **1** a person who holds the highest university degree in any faculty except medicine, law or theology. **2** the degree held by a Doctor of Philosophy. **doctorship** *n.*

doctrinaire (doktrinee´) *a.* visionary, theoretical, impractical. ~*n.* a person who theorizes in politics without regard to practical considerations; a theorizer, an ideologist. **doctrinairism** *n.* **doctrinarian** *n.*

doctrine (dok´trin) *n.* **1** what is taught. **2** the principles, tenets or dogmas of any church, sect, literary or scientific school, or party. **doctrinal** (-trī´-) *a.* **1** of or relating to doctrine. **2** of the nature of or containing a doctrine. **doctrinally** *adv.* **doctrinism** *n.* **doctrinist** *n.*

docudrama (dok´ūdrahmə) *n.* a television film of a dramatized version of a true story.

document¹ (dok´ūmənt) *n.* a written or printed paper containing information for the establishment of facts. **documental** (-men´-) *a.* **documentalist** (-men´-) *n.* a person whose work is documentation. **documentary** (-men´-) *n.* (*pl.* **documentaries**) a film which represents real events or phases of life. ~*a.* **1** relating to documents. **2** presenting facts or reality. **documentarian** (-teə´riən) *n.* **1** a documentary photographer or film-maker. **2** an analyst of historical documents. **documentarily** (-men´-) *adv.* **documentarist** (-men´-) *n.* a documentary film-maker.

document² (dok´ūment) *v.t.* **1** to furnish with the documents necessary to establish any fact. **2** to prove by means of documents. **3** to record in a document. **documentation** (-mentā´-) *n.* **1** the preparation or use of documents. **2** the documents or references given. **3** (*Comput.*) the written instructions etc. which are supplied with a program or a software system.

dodder (dod´ə) *v.i.* **1** to shake, to tremble, to

totter. **2** to be feeble and worn out. **dodderer** *n.*
doddery *a.* **dodderiness** *n.*

doddle (dod´əl) *n.* (*coll.*) something very easily
accomplished.

dodeca- (dōdek´ə) *pref.* twelve.

dodecagon (dōdek´əgon) *n.* (*pl.* **dodecagons**)
(*Geom.*) a plane figure of twelve equal angles and
sides.

dodecahedron (dōdekəhē´drən) *n.* (*pl.* **dodeca-
hedra, dodecahedrons**) (*Geom.*) a solid figure of
twelve equal sides, each of which is a regular
pentagon. **dodecahedral** *a.*

dodge (doj) *v.i.* **1** to move aside suddenly. **2** to
change place by a sudden movement. **3** to move
rapidly from place to place so as to elude pursuit
etc. ~*v.t.* **1** to escape from by quickly moving
aside. **2** to evade by cunning or deceit. **3** (*Austral.*, *sl.*) to obtain dishonestly. ~*n.* **1** a sudden
movement to one side. **2** a trick, an artifice. **3** an
evasion. **4** a skilful contrivance or expedient.
dodger *n.* **1** a person who dodges or evades. **2** a
trickster, a cheat. **3** a screen on the bridge of a
ship to protect against rough weather. **4** (*NAm.*)
an advertising leaflet. **5** (*sl.*) food, esp. bread.
dodgy *a.* (*comp.* **dodgier,** *superl.* **dodgiest**) (*coll.*)
1 full of dodges; crafty, artful, tricky. **2** uncertain,
risky.

Dodgem® (doj´əm) *n.* a bumper car in an amusement ground.

dodo (dō´dō) *n.* (*pl.* **dodos, dodoes**) **1** a large extinct bird, *Raphus cucullatus*, formerly found in
Mauritius. **2** a stupid person. **dead as a dodo**
completely obsolete or defunct.

doe (dō) *n.* **1** the female of the fallow deer. **2** the
female of the rabbit, hare etc. **doe-eyed** *a.* having
large, dark eyes, like a doe's. **doeskin** *n.* **1** the
skin of a doe. **2** leather made from doeskin. **3** an
untwilled fine woollen cloth resembling this.

doer, does DO¹.

doesn't (dŭz´ənt) *contr.* does not.

doff (dof) *v.t.* to take off (clothing, esp. one's hat).

dog (dog) *n.* **1** a domesticated mammal of numerous breeds classed together as *Canis familiaris*.
2 any wild animal of the genus *Canis*, which
includes wolves, jackals and coyotes, or of the
family Canidae, which includes foxes. **3** the
male of the dog, wolf or fox. **4** a surly fellow; a
contemptible person. **5** (*NAm.*, *Austral.*, *sl.*) an
informer. **6** a device with a tooth which pene-
trates or grips an object and detains it. **7** (*NAm.*,
sl.) something of poor quality. **8** an andiron or
firedog. **9** (*sl.*) a horse which is difficult to control. ~*v.t.* (*pres.p.* **dogging**, *past, p.p.* **dogged**) **1** to
follow like a dog; to track the footsteps of. **2** to
fasten or secure with a dog. **not a dog's chance**
not the slightest chance. **the dogs** (*coll.*) greyhound races. **to die like a dog** to die miserably or
shamefully. **to dog it** (*NAm.*, *coll.*) to be lazy, to
slack. **to go to the dogs** (*sl.*) to go to ruin. **to lead
a dog's life 1** to lead a life of continual wretchedness. **2** to be continually bickering. **to let sleeping dogs lie** to leave well alone. **to put on the dog**

(*NAm.*, *coll.*) to behave in a pretentious manner.
dogbiscuit *n.* a coarse biscuit for dogs. **dog box** *n.*
(*Austral.*, *sl.*) a compartment in a railway carriage which has no corridor. **dog cart** *n.* a light,
two-wheeled, double-seated, one-horse cart.
dog-clutch *n.* a clutch in which teeth in one part
fit into slots in another part. **dog collar** *n.* **1** a
leather or metal collar worn by dogs. **2** a clerical
collar. **3** a high, straight shirt collar. **dog days**
n.pl. the period in July and August during which
the dog-star rises and sets with the sun, a conjunction formerly supposed to account for the
high temperatures common at that season. **dog-
eared** *a.* (of a book) having the corners turned
down or torn. **dog-eat-dog** *a.* involving ruthless
pursuit of one's own interests. **dog-end** *n.* (*sl.*) a
cigarette end. **dogface** *n.* (*NAm.*, *sl.*) a US soldier.
dogfight *n.* **1** a fight between dogs. **2** a wrangle, a
struggle. **3** a duel in the air between two aircraft.
dogfighter *n.* **dogfighting** *n.* **dogfish** *n.* (*pl.* **dogfish, dogfishes**) any small shark of the families
Scylorhinidae and Squalidae, which follow their
prey in packs. **dogfox** *n.* a male fox. **doggie** *n.* a
dog (used by or to children). **doggish** *a.* **doggo** *a.*
hidden. **to lie doggo** (*coll.*) to wait silently and
motionlessly. **doggy** *n.* (*pl.* **doggies**) a dog (used
by or to children). ~*a.* (*comp.* **doggier,** *superl.*
doggiest) **1** of or relating to a dog. **2** fond of dogs.
3 flashy, raffish. **dogginess** *n.* **doggy bag** *n.* (*coll.*)
a bag for taking home uneaten food after a
restaurant meal. **doggy-paddle** *n.* the dog-paddle.
dog-handler *n.* a person, such as a police officer,
who works with a trained dog. **dog-handling** *n.*
doghouse, (*NAm.*) **doghutch** *n.* a dog-kennel. **in
the doghouse** (*sl.*) in disfavour. **dog in the
manger** *n.* a person who prevents other people
from enjoying what they cannot enjoy themselves; a churlish person. **dog-kennel** *n.* a house
or hut for a dog. **dog-leg** *n.* a sharp bend, like a
dog's hind leg. ~*a.* bent like a dog's hind leg. ~*v.i.*
(*pres.p.* **dog-legging,** *past, p.p.* **dog-legged**) to
bend sharply. **doglike** *a.* **dogman** (-mən) *n.* (*pl.*
dogmen) (*Austral.*) a person directing the operator of a crane while sitting on the load being
lifted by the crane. **dog-paddle** *n.* a simple swimming stroke in which the arms imitate the front
legs of a swimming dog. **dog rose** *n.* the wild
brier, *Rosa canina*. **dogsbody** *n.* (*pl.* **dogsbodies**)
1 (*coll.*) someone made use of by others; a useful
person treated as a drudge. **2** (*Naut.*, *sl.*) a junior
officer. **dog's breakfast** *n.* (*coll.*) a mess. **dog's
dinner** *n.* (*sl.*) a mess. **dressed up like a dog's
dinner** dressed too flamboyantly. **dog's disease**
n. (*Austral.*, *sl.*) influenza. **dogshore** *n.* either of
two struts that hold the cradle of a ship from
sliding on the slipways when the keel-blocks
are taken out. **dog sled** *n.* a sled pulled by a team
of dogs. **dog's mercury** *n.* a common poisonous
plant, *Mercurialis perennis*. **dogs of war** *n.pl.*
(*poet.*) the chaos or disorder which results from
war. **dog's-tail** *n.* a pasture-grass, *Cynosurus cristatus*. **dog-star** *n.* Sirius, the principal star in the

constellation Canis major. **dog's tooth** n. **1** any plant of the genus *Erythronium*, esp. *E. denscanis*, which has purple flowers. **2** a brokencheck pattern used in tweed. **dog's tooth violet** n. any plant of the genus *Erythronium*, esp. *E. denscanis*, which has purple flowers. **dog-tag** n. a metal disc attached to a dog's collar, showing the owner's address. **dog-tail** n. dog's-tail. **dog-tired** a. worn out. **dog-tooth** n. **1** (*Archit.*) a kind of ornament used in Early English mouldings. **2** a broken-check pattern used in tweed. **dog trials** n.pl. (*Austral., New Zeal.*) a competition to test the skills of sheepdogs. **dogtrot** n. a gentle, easy trot; a jog-trot. **dog-violet** n. the scentless wild violet, *Viola riviniana*. **dogwatch** n. (*Naut.*) either one of two watches of two hours each between 4 and 8 p.m.

dogberry (dog´bəri) n. (*pl.* **dogberries**) the fruit of the dogwood.

doge (dōj) n. (*Hist.*) the title of the chief magistrate of the republics of Venice and Genoa.

dogged (dog´id) a. stubborn, obstinate, persistent, tenacious. **doggedly** adv. **doggedness** n.

doggerel (dog´ərəl) n. verses written with little regard to rhythm or rhyme. ~a. of or relating to doggerel.

doggone (dog´on) a., adv. (*N Am., sl.*) damned. ~int. used to express annoyance.

dogie (dō´gi) n. (*N Am.*) a motherless calf.

dogma (dog´mə) n. (*pl.* **dogmas**) **1** an established principle, tenet or system of doctrines put forward to be received on authority, esp. that of a Church, as opposed to one deduced from experience or reasoning. **2** a positive, magisterial or arrogant expression of opinion. **dogmatic** (-mat´-), **dogmatical** a. **1** of or relating to dogma, doctrinal. **2** based on theory not induction. **3** asserted with authority, positive, authoritative. **4** magisterial, arrogant, dictatorial. **dogmatically** adv. **dogmaticalness** n. **dogmatics** n. **1** doctrinal theology, the science which deals with the statement and definition of Christian doctrine. **2** a system of dogma. **dogmatism** n. dogmaticalness; arrogance or undue positiveness in assertion. **dogmatist** n. **dogmatize, dogmatise** v.i. to make dogmatic assertions; to lay down principles with undue positiveness and confidence. ~v.t. to lay down as a dogma.

dogwood (dog´wud) n. **1** any shrub of the genus *Cornus*, esp. *C. sanguinea*, the wild cornel, with white flowers and purple berries. **2** any of various similar shrubs, esp. *Euonymus europaeus* or *Rhamnus frangula*. **3** the wood of the dogwood.

doh (dō), **do** n. (*pl.* **dohs, dos**) (*Mus.*) **1** the first note of a major scale in the tonic sol-fa system of notation. **2** the note C in the fixed-doh system.

doily (doi´li), **doyley** n. (*pl.* **doilies, doyleys**) a small ornamental mat or napkin on which to place cakes, sandwiches, bottles, glasses etc.

doing (doo´ing) n. **1** something done or performed; an event, transaction, proceeding, affair. **2** effort. **3** (*coll.*) a beating. **4** (*pl.*) objects whose

name one has forgotten or does not want to say. **5** (*pl.*) behaviour, conduct.

dol. abbr. dollar(s).

Dolby® (dol´bi) n. a system used to cut down interference on broadcast or recorded sound.

doldrums (dol´drəmz) n.pl. **1** low spirits, the dumps. **2** a state of inactivity. **3** that part of the ocean near the equator between the regions of the trade winds where calms and variable winds prevail.

dole[1] (dōl) n. **1** (*coll.*) unemployment benefit. **2** distribution, esp. in charity. **3** alms, money or food distributed in charity. ~v.t. to distribute. **on the dole** (*coll.*) receiving unemployment benefit. **to dole out** to distribute in small quantities.

dole[2] (dōl) n. (*poet.*) sorrow, lamentation. **doleful** a. **1** sorrowful, sad. **2** dismal, gloomy. **dolefully** adv. **dolefulness** n.

dolerite (dol´ərīt) n. a variety of trap-rock consisting of feldspar and pyroxene.

doll (dol) n. **1** a child's toy representing a human figure. **2** (*coll.*) a pretty but silly young woman. **3** (*esp. N Am., coll.*) a term of endearment to a woman. **to doll up** (*coll.*) to dress up, to make oneself look smart. **dollhouse** n. (*N Am.*) a doll's house. **dollish** a. **dollishly** adv. **dollishness** n. **doll's house** n. **1** a small toy house for dolls. **2** a very small house.

dollar (dol´ə) n. **1** the chief unit of currency of the US, Canada, Australia, New Zealand etc. **2** any of various coins of different values. **dollar area** n. the area in which currency is linked to the US dollar. **dollarization** (-īzā´-), **dollarisation** n. the domination of the US dollar over another country's economy. **dollar mark, dollar sign** n. the sign $, used to represent a dollar. **dollar spot** n. **1** a fungal disease of lawns. **2** a discoloured patch caused by dollar spots.

dollop (dol´əp) n. (*coll.*) **1** a shapeless lump. **2** a heap, quantity. ~v.t. (*pres.p.* **dolloping**, *past, p.p.* **dolloped**) to serve in dollops.

dolly (dol´i) n. (*pl.* **dollies**) **1** a doll (used by or to children). **2** (*coll.*) a simple catch in cricket. **3** a stick with which dirty clothes are agitated in a washtub. **4** a corn dolly. **5** (*coll.*) a dolly-bird. ~v.t. (*3rd pers. sing. pres.* **dollies**, *pres.p.* **dollying**, *past, p.p.* **dollied**) to dress up, to make (oneself) look smart. ~v.i. to move a dolly camera closer to or away from a subject. ~a. (*comp.* **dollier**, *superl.* **dolliest**) attractive, glamorous. **dolly-bird** n. (*coll.*) an attractive, glamorous young woman. **dolly camera** n. a cine-camera moving on a type of trolley. **dolly mixture** n. a mixture of tiny coloured sweets.

Dolly Varden (doli vah´dən) n. **1** a widebrimmed woman's hat with one side bent down. **2** a N American char, *Salvelinus malma*.

dolma (dol´mə) n. (*pl.* **dolmas, dolmades** (-mah´-dhez)) a vine leaf stuffed with rice and meat.

dolman (dol´mən) n. (*pl.* **dolmans**) **1** a long Turkish robe, open in front, and with narrow sleeves. **2** a woman's loose mantle with dolman sleeves. **3** a hussar's jacket or cape with the sleeves hanging loose. **dolman sleeve** *n.* a sleeve which tapers from a wide armhole to a tightly-fitting wrist.

dolmen (dol´mən) *n.* a cromlech; the megalithic framework of a chambered cairn, consisting usually of three or more upright stones supporting a roof-stone.

dolomite (dol´əmīt) *n.* a brittle, subtransparent or translucent mineral consisting of the carbonates of lime and magnesia. **dolomitic** (-mit´-) *a.*

dolorous (dol´ərəs) *a.* (*poet.*) **1** full of pain or grief. **2** causing or expressing pain or grief, doleful. **dolorously** *adv.* **dolorousness** *n.*

dolour (dol´ə), (*N Am.*) **dolor** *n.* pain, suffering, distress; grief, sorrow, lamentation.

dolphin (dol´fin) *n.* **1** any sea mammal of the family Delphinidae, having a beaklike snout. **2** the dorado, *Coryphaena hippuris.* **3** (*N Am.*) **a** a mooring-post. **b** an anchored spar with rings, serving as a mooring-buoy. **4** a protective structure on a bridge. **5** (*Her. etc.*) a conventional representation of a curved fish. **dolphinarium** (-eə´riəm) *n.* (*pl.* **dolphinariums**) an aquarium for dolphins, often one for public displays.

dolt (dōlt) *n.* a stupid person; a numskull. **doltish** *a.* **doltishly** *adv.* **doltishness** *n.*

Dom (dom) *n.* **1** in the Roman Catholic Church, a title given to members of the Benedictine and Carthusian orders. **2** the Portuguese equivalent of the Spanish *Don.*

-dom (dəm) *suf.* denoting power, jurisdiction, office or condition, a group of people, as in *earldom, kingdom, officialdom, freedom.*

domain (dəmān´) *n.* **1** territory, district or space over which authority, jurisdiction or control is or may be exercised. **2** one's landed property, estate. **3** (*fig.*) sphere, province, field of influence, thought or action. **4** (*Physics*) the part of a ferromagnetic solid where all the atoms are magnetically aligned. **5** (*Math.*) the aggregate to which a variable belongs. **domainal, domanial** (-mā´niəl) *a.*

dome (dōm) *n.* **1** a roof, usually central, the base of which is a circle, an ellipse or a polygon, and its vertical section a curved line, concave towards the interior; a cupola. **2** the revolving dome-shaped roof of an observatory, which can be opened up. **3** a natural vault, arching canopy or lofty covering. **4** a rounded hilltop. **5** (*poet.*) a mansion, temple or other building of a stately kind. **6** (*Geol.*) any dome-shaped object or structure. **7** (*sl.*) the head. ~*v.t.* to cover with or shape into a dome. ~*v.i.* to swell into a domelike shape. **domed** *a.* **1** furnished with a dome. **2** dome-shaped. **domelike** *a.*

domestic (dəmes´tik) *a.* **1** employed or kept at home. **2** fond of home. **3** tame, not wild. **4** relating to the internal affairs of a nation; not foreign. **5** made in one's own country. **6** of or relating to the home or household. ~*n.* a household servant.

domestically *adv.* **domesticate** *v.t.* **1** to naturalize (foreigners etc.). **2** to accustom to domestic life and the management of household affairs. **3** to tame. **4** to bring (a plant) into cultivation from a wild state. **domesticable** *a.* **domestication** (-ā´shən) *n.* **domestic science** *n.* the study of household skills, including cookery, needlework etc.

domesticity (domestis´iti, dō-) *n.* (*pl.* **domesticities**) **1** the state of being domestic. **2** domestic character, homeliness. **3** home life.

domicile (dom´isīl), **domicil** (-sil) *n.* **1** a house, a home. **2** (*Law*) **a** a place of permanent residence. **b** length of residence (differing in various countries) necessary to establish jurisdiction in civil actions. **3** the place at which a bill of exchange is made payable. ~*v.t.* **1** to establish in a place of residence. **2** to make payable at a certain place. **domiciled** *a.* **domiciliary** (-sil´-) *a.* of or relating to a domicile or residence.

dominant (dom´inənt) *a.* **1** predominant, ruling, governing. **2** overshadowing, prominent. **3** (of a gene) producing a particular feature even if inherited from only one parent, as distinct from *recessive.* ~*n.* **1** (*Mus.*) the fifth note of the scale of any key, counting upwards. **2** a prevalent species in a plant community. **dominance** *n.* **dominancy** *n.* **dominantly** *adv.*

dominate (dom´ināt) *v.t.* **1** to predominate over. **2** to overlook (as a hill). **3** to influence controllingly, to rule, govern. ~*v.i.* **1** to predominate, to prevail. **2** to be the most influential or the chief or most conspicuous. **domination** (-ā´shən) *n.* **1** the exercise of power or authority. **2** rule, sway, control, dominion. **3** (*pl.*) the fourth order of angels. **dominator** *n.* **dominatrix** (dominā´triks) *n.* (*pl.* **dominatrices** (-trisēz)) a dominant woman, esp. in a sadomasochistic relationship.

domineer (diminiə´) *v.i.* to exercise authority arrogantly and tyrannically; to assume superiority over others. **domineering** *a.* **domineeringly** *adv.*

dominical (dəmin´ikəl) *a.* among Christians, of or relating to the Lord or the Lord's Day.

Dominican (dəmin´ikən) *n.* **1** a member of an order of preaching friars, founded in 1216 by Domingo de Guzman (canonized as St Dominic); a Black Friar. **2** a nun in one of the orders founded by St Dominic. ~*a.* of or relating to the Dominicans.

dominion (dəmin´yən) *n.* **1** sovereign authority, lordship; control, rule, government. **2** (*Law*) uncontrolled right of possession or use. **3** a district, region or country under one government. **4** (*Hist.*) a self-governing country of the British Commonwealth, esp. Canada.

domino (dom´inō) *n.* (*pl.* **dominoes**) **1** any of 28 oblong dotted pieces, orig. of bone or ivory, used in playing dominoes. **2** a masquerade dress worn for disguise by both sexes, consisting of a loose black cloak or mantle with a small mask. **domino effect** *n.* the theory that a single event leads to many similar events elsewhere as a chain reaction, like the fall of a long row of dominoes, all standing on end, caused by pushing the first domino in the row. **dominoes** *n.* any of various games played with dominoes, often involving pairing up matching values. **domino theory** *n.* the domino effect.

Don (don) *n.* **1** a title formerly restricted to Spanish noblemen and gentlemen, now common to all men in Spain, Sir, Mr. **2** a Spanish gentleman. **3** a Spaniard. **4** (*NAm., sl.*) an important member of the Mafia.

don[1] (don) *n.* **1** a fellow or tutor of a college, esp. at Oxford or Cambridge. **2** (*Austral., New Zeal., sl.*) an adept, an expert. **donnish** *a.* **donnishly** *adv.* **donnishness** *n.*

don[2] (don) *v.t.* (*pres.p.* **donning**, *past, p.p.* **donned**) to put on (clothing).

donate (dōnāt´) *v.t.* to bestow as a gift, esp. on a considerable scale for public or religious purposes. **donator** *n.*

donation (dōnā´shən) *n.* **1** the act of giving. **2** something which is given, a gift, a presentation, a contribution, esp. to a public institution.

done (dŭn) *a.* **1** performed, executed. **2** socially acceptable (*not the done thing*). *~int.* accepted (used to express agreement to a proposal, as a wager, or a bargain). **to be done with** to have finished with. **to have done** to have finished. **to have done with** to have no further concern with. **done for** *a.* (*coll.*) ruined, killed, exhausted. **done in, done up** *a.* (*coll.*) worn out, exhausted.

doner kebab (don´ə) *n.* spit-roasted lamb served in pitta bread, usually with salad.

dong[1] (dong) *v.i.* to make the sound of a large bell. *~v.t.* (*Austral., New Zeal., coll.*) to punch hard. *~n.* **1** the sound of a large bell. **2** (*Austral., New Zeal., coll.*) a hard punch. **3** (*taboo sl.*) a penis.

dong[2] (dong) *n.* the standard unit of currency of Vietnam.

dongle (dong´gəl) *n.* (*Comput.*) an electronic device used to protect software from unauthorized use.

donjon (dŭn´jən) *n.* the grand central tower or keep of a castle, esp. a medieval Norman one, the lower storey generally used as a prison.

donkey (dong´ki) *n.* **1** a long-eared member of the horse family, an ass. **2** (*coll.*) a stupid person. **to talk the hind legs off a donkey** to talk a lot. **donkey derby** *n.* a race in which the competitors ride donkeys. **donkey engine** *n.* an auxiliary engine for light work on board steamships. **donkey jacket** *n.* a short, thick jacket worn by workmen. **donkey's years** *n.pl.* (*coll.*) a long time. **donkey work** *n.* drudgery, routine work.

donna (don´ə) *n.* **1** an Italian lady. **2** (**Donna**) an Italian title for, or form of address to, a lady, Madame, madam.

donor (dō´nə) *n.* **1** a giver. **2** a person who gives blood, semen or an organ for the medical treatment of another person. **3** (*Chem.*) an atom which supplies the electrons in a coordinate bond. **4** (*Physics*) an impurity in semiconductor material which contributes free electrons to increase its conductivity. **donor card** *n.* a card carried by a person willing to have parts of their body used for transplant after their death.

don't (dōnt) *contr.* do not. *~n.* a prohibition (*dos and don'ts*).

donut DOUGHNUT (under DOUGH).

doodah (doo´dah), (*N Am.*) **doodad** (-dad) *n.* (*coll.*) any small decorative article or gadget. **all of a doodah** flustered, in a state of confusion.

doodle (doo´dəl) *v.i.* to draw pictures or designs absent-mindedly while thinking or listening. *~n.* a picture drawn in this way. **doodler** *n.*

doodlebug (doo´dəlbŭg) *n.* **1** (*coll.*) the earliest type of flying bomb used by the Germans in the war of 1939–45, the V-1. **2** (*N Am.*) the larva of the ant-lion. **3** (*N Am.*) any scientific or unscientific instrument for locating minerals.

doodly-squat DIDDLY-SQUAT.

doohickey (doo´hiki), **doojigger** (doo´jigə) *n.* (*N Am., coll.*) any small mechanical device.

doom (doom) *n.* **1** fate or destiny (usu. in an evil sense). **2** ruin, destruction, perdition. **3** judgement; judicial decision or sentence. **4** condemnation, penalty. **5** the Day of Judgement. *~v.t.* **1** to condemn (to do something). **2** to predestine. **3** to consign to ruin or calamity. **doom-laden** *a.* suggesting disaster or tragedy. **doomsayer** *n.* a person who predicts disaster. **doomsaying** *n.* **doomsday** *n.* the Day of Judgement; the end of the world. **till doomsday** for ever. **doomster** *n.* a doomsayer. **doomwatch** *n.* observation of the environment to prevent its destruction by pollution etc. **doomwatcher** *n.*

door (daw) *n.* **1** a frame of wood or metal, usually on hinges, closing the entrance to a building, room, safe etc. **2** an opening for entrance and exit. **3** entrance, exit, access, means of approach. **4** a house, a room (*She lives two doors down from us*). **5** (*fig.*) the entrance or beginning; means of access (to). **out of doors** outside the house; in or into the open. **to lay at the door of** to blame. **to lie at the door of** to be the fault or responsibility of. **within doors** inside the house. **doorbell** *n.* a bell inside a building actuated by a button outside a door. **doorcase** *n.* the structure in which a door swings. **doored** *a.* **door head** *n.* the top of a doorcase. **doorkeeper** *n.* a doorman. **doorknob** *n.* a handle on a door. **doorknocker** *n.* a hinged device attached to a door, for knocking. **doorman** *n.* (*pl.* **doormen**) a porter, a person employed to open doors. **doormat** *n.* **1** a mat for removing dirt from the shoes, placed inside or outside a door. **2** (*coll.*) a submissive person, often imposed on by others. **doornail** *n.* a large nail formerly used for studding doors. **doorplate** *n.* a metal plate on a door bearing the name of the occupant. **doorpost** *n.* side-piece or jamb of a doorway. **doorstep** *n.* **1** a step leading up to an outer door. **2** (*sl.*) a thick slice of bread. *~v.i.* (*pres.p.* **doorstepping**, *past, p.p.* **doorstepped**) to go from door to door to canvass during a political campaign, or to try to sell goods, often intrusively. *~v.t.* **1** (of a journalist) to wait outside the house of (a person) to try to obtain a photograph or interview. **2** to leave in someone's care. **on one's doorstep** very close to one's home. **doorstop** *n.* a device which stops a door from moving. **door-to-door** *a.* **1** from one house to the next. **2** (of a journey) direct. **doorway** *n.* **1** an opening in a wall fitted with a door. **2** (*fig.*) a means of access (to).

X doormouse common misspelling of DOR-MOUSE.

dopamine (dō′pəmēn) *n.* a chemical found in the brain, acting as a neurotransmitter, a precursor of adrenalin.

dope (dōp) *n.* **1** a varnish used for waterproofing, protecting and strengthening the fabric parts of an aircraft. **2** any thick liquid or semi-fluid used for food or as a lubricant. **3** an antiknock compound added to petrol. **4** a drug given to a horse or greyhound, or taken by an athlete, to affect the outcome of a race; any illegal drug, esp. cannabis. **5** (*sl.*) a stupefying drug. **6** (*sl.*) a stupid person. **7** (*sl.*) **a** inside information, particulars. **b** misleading information. *~v.t.* **1** to drug, to stupefy with drugs. **2** to apply dope to, to smear. *~v.i.* to take illegal drugs. *~a.* (*sl.*) excellent. **to dope out** (*sl.*) to devise, to discover. **doper** *n.* **dopey** *a.* (*comp.* **dopier**, *superl.* **dopiest**) (*coll.*) **1** stupid. **2** drugged. **3** sleepy, sluggish. **dopy** *a.* dopey. **dopily** *adv.* **dopiness** *n.*

doppelgänger (dop′əlgengə, -gangə) *n.* the apparition of a living person; a wraith.

dorado (dərah′dō) *n.* (*pl.* **dorados**) **1** a fish, *Coryphaena hippurus*, of brilliant colouring. **2** a gold-coloured S American river fish.

Dorian (daw′riən) *n.* **1** an inhabitant of Doris, in ancient Greece. **2** a member of one of the four great ethnic divisions of the ancient Greeks. *~a.* of or relating to Doris or its inhabitants. **Doric** (dor′-) *n.* **1** (*Archit.*) the Doric order. **2** a broad, rustic dialect, esp. Scots. **Doric dialect** *n.* **1** the broad, rustic dialect of the natives of Doris. **2** any broad, rustic dialect, esp. Scots. **Doric order** *n.* the earliest, strongest and most simple of the three Grecian orders of architecture.

dork (dawk) *n.* (*sl.*) **1** a stupid or socially awkward person. **2** a penis. **dorkish** *a.* **dorky** *a.* (*comp.* **dorkier**, *superl.* **dorkiest**)

dorm (dawm) *n.* short for DORMITORY.

dormant (daw′mənt) *a.* **1** in a state resembling sleep, torpid, inactive. **2** undeveloped, inoperative. **3** not asserted or claimed. **4** in abeyance. **5** (of a plant) alive but not currently growing. **dormancy** *n.*

dormer (daw′mə) *n.* a dormer window. **dormer bungalow** *n.* a two-storeyed bungalow with dormer windows upstairs. **dormer window** *n.* a window piercing a sloping roof and having a vertical frame and a gable (orig. used in sleeping chambers).

dormitory (daw′mitri) *n.* (*pl.* **dormitories**) **1** a sleeping room, esp. in a school or public institution, containing a number of beds. **2** (*N Am.*) a students' hall of residence. **dormitory town, dormitory suburb** *n.* a town or suburb whose inhabitants work elsewhere, often in a nearby city.

dormouse (daw′mows) *n.* (*pl.* **dormice** (-mīs)) **1** a small British hibernating rodent, *Myoxus avellanarius*. **2** any of various other members of the family Gliridae, resembling both a mouse and a squirrel.

dormy (daw′mi), **dormie** *a.* in golf, of or relating to a player who is as many holes ahead of their opponent as there remain holes to play.

dorsal (daw′səl) *a.* **1** (*Anat.*) of or relating to the back. **2** situated on the back. **3** (*Bot.*) shaped like a ridge. **dorsally** *adv.*

dory[1] (daw′ri), **doree** *n.* (*pl.* **dories, dorees**) a golden-yellow sea fish of the family Zeidae, esp. the John Dory.

dory[2] (daw′ri) *n.* (*pl.* **dories**) (*N Am.*) a small, flat-bottomed boat.

dose (dōs) *n.* **1** the amount of any medicine which is taken or prescribed to be taken at one time. **2** (*fig.*) a quantity or amount of anything offered or given. **3** anything unpleasant which one has to take. **4** the amount of ionizing radiation absorbed by a person or thing. **5** (*sl.*) a venereal infection, esp. gonorrhoea. *~v.t.* **1** to administer doses to. **2** to adulterate, to mix (spirits with wine). **like a dose of salts** very quickly and thoroughly. **dosage** *n.* the process or method of dosing; the application of doses, for example of spirits to wine. **dosimeter** (-sim′itə), **dosemeter** (dōs′mētə) *n.* an instrument which measures radiation. **dosimetric** (-met′-) *a.* **dosimetry** (-sim′-) *n.*

do-se-do (dōsidō′, -zi-), **do-si-do** *n.* (*pl.* **do-se-dos, do-si-dos**) a square dance in which dancers pass each other back to back.

dosh (dosh) *n.* (*sl.*) money.

doss (dos) *v.i.* (*sl.*) **1** to sleep. **2** to sleep in a cheap lodging house. **3** to go to bed. **4** to spend time aimlessly. *~n.* a bed or a sleeping place in a cheap lodging house. **to doss down** to go to sleep in a makeshift bed. **dosser** *n.* **1** a person who sleeps in cheap lodging houses or hostels. **2** a doss-house. **doss-house** *n.* a cheap lodging house.

dossier (dos′iā, -iə) *n.* a collection of papers and other documents relating to a person, a thing or an event.

dot (dot) *n.* **1** a little mark, spot or speck made with a pen or pointed instrument. **2** a period mark, a full point, a point over *i* or *j*, or used as a diacritic. **3** (*Mus.*) a point used as a direction, in various senses. **4** the short element in Morse code. **5** a tiny thing. *~v.t.* (*pres.p.* **dotting**, *past, p.p.* **dotted**) **1** to mark with a dot or dots. **2** to mark or scatter with small detached objects like dots. **3** (*sl.*) to hit. *~v.i.* to make dots or spots. **on the dot (of)** (*coll.*) precisely (at). **to dot the i's**

and cross the t's 1 (*coll.*) to be precisely exact. 2 (*coll.*) to put the finishing touches to an undertaking. **dot matrix** *n.* (*Comput.*) a matrix consisting of lines of pins which are used selectively to create the characters. **dot matrix printer** *n.* (*Comput.*) a printer which operates by means of a dot matrix. **dotted line** *n.* a row of dots, esp. to indicate the place on a form where one should sign one's name. **dotter** *n.*

dotage (dō´tij) *n.* impairment of the intellect by age. **dotard** (-təd) *n.* 1 a person whose intellect is impaired by age. 2 a person who is foolishly and excessively fond of someone or something.

dote (dōt) *v.i.* to be silly or deranged, infatuated or feeble-minded. **to dote on** to be foolishly fond of. **doter** *n.* **dotingly** *adv.*

dotterel (dot´ərəl) *n.* a small migratory plover, *Endromias morinellus* (said to be so foolishly fond of imitation that it mimics the actions of the fowler, and so suffers itself to be taken).

dottle (dot´əl) *n.* a plug of tobacco left unsmoked in a pipe.

dotty (dot´i) *a.* (*comp.* **dottier,** *superl.* **dottiest**) 1 marked with dots, dotlike. 2 (*coll.*) a imbecile. b eccentric. c ridiculous. **dotty about/ on** (*coll.*) excessively or foolishly fond of. **dottily** *adv.* **dottiness** *n.*

double¹ (dŭb´əl) *a.* 1 composed of two, in a pair or in pairs. 2 forming a pair, twofold. 3 folded, bent back or forward. 4 twice as much, as great or as many. 5 of twice the strength or value. 6 designed for two people (*a double bed*). 7 (of a domino) having an equal number of spots on each half. 8 of two kinds, aspects or relations; ambiguous. 9 (*fig.*) hypocritical, treacherous, deceitful. 10 (*Mus.*) an octave lower in pitch. 11 (of a flower) having the stamens more or less petaloid. ~*adv.* 1 twice. 2 in two ways. 3 in twice the number, quantity, amount, strength etc. 4 two together. **bent double** stooping. **double acrostic** *n.* an acrostic in which the first and last letters of each line are used. **double act** *n.* two comedians or other entertainers who have a joint act. **double agent** *n.* a spy working for two opposing sides at the same time. **double-barrelled** *a.* 1 (of a gun) having two barrels. 2 (of a surname) having two parts joined by a hyphen. 3 producing a double effect, serving a double purpose. **double bass** *n.* the largest and lowest-toned of the stringed instruments, played with a bow. **double bassoon** *n.* the largest instrument in the oboe class, with the lowest pitch. **double bill** *n.* a theatre or cinema programme featuring two main items. **double bind** *n.* a dilemma. **double-blind** *a.* (of an experiment) having neither the tester nor the subject knowing details which could prejudice the results. ~*n.* a double-blind experiment. **double bluff** *n.* an attempt to deceive by making a true statement appear false. **double boiler** *n.* two saucepans, one fitting into the other, food being cooked gently in the inner pan by the heat of boiling water in the outer one. **double bond** *n.*

a pair of bonds linking two atoms in a molecule. **double-book** *v.t.* to make two reservations for (a room etc.) for the same time. **double-breasted** *a.* (of a jacket etc.) lapping over and buttoning on either side. **double-check** *v.t.* to check a second time. **double chin** *n.* a fold of fat below the chin. **double-chinned** *a.* **double coconut** *n.* the nut of the coco-de-mer. **double concerto** *n.* (*Mus.*) a concerto for two solo instruments. **double cream** *n.* thick cream, with a higher fat content than single cream. **double-cross** *v.t.* (*coll.*) to betray, to cheat. ~*n.* the act of double-crossing. **double-crosser** *n.* **double dagger** *n.* (*Print.*) a double obelus. **double-dealing** *n.* deceitful behaviour, esp. in business. ~*a.* deceitful, tricky. **double-dealer** *n.* **double-decker** *n.* 1 a bus with two decks. 2 anything with two layers. **double-declutch** *v.i.* to change to a different gear by moving into neutral and then into the desired gear. **double density** *a.* (*Comput.*) denoting a disk which has twice the basic storage capacity. **double dummy** *n.* in bridge, play in which two hands are revealed. **double Dutch** *n.* 1 gibberish, jargon; a language not understood by the hearer. 2 (*N Am.*) a skipping game in which one rope is turned clockwise and the other anticlockwise, the skipper jumping over each rope in turn. **double-dye** *v.t.* to dye with double intensity. **double-dyed** *a.* stained or tainted with infamy; doubly infamous. **double-edged** *a.* 1 having two cutting edges. 2 having two meanings or effects, one positive and one negative. **double entry** *n.* a method of bookkeeping in which every transaction is entered twice, once on the credit side of the account, and once on the debit side. **double exposure** *n.* 1 the recording of two superimposed images on a single piece of film. 2 the picture resulting from this. **double-faced** *a.* 1 double-dealing; insincere. 2 (of a textile) having a finished surface on each side; reversible. **double fault** *n.* in tennis, two faults in succession, resulting in the loss of a point. **double-fault** *v.i.* in tennis, to serve a double fault. **double feature** *n.* two full-length feature films shown in a single programme. **double figures** *n.pl.* a number greater than 9 but less than 100. **double first** *n.* 1 first-class honours in two subjects or examinations for a degree. 2 a person who achieves a double first. **double-fronted** *a.* (of a house) having main windows on each side of the front door. **double glazing** *n.* 1 the fitting of a double layer of glass in a window to act as a form of insulation. 2 the double layer of glass itself. **double-glaze** *v.t.* **double Gloucester** *n.* a rich hard cheese orig. made in Gloucestershire. **double-headed** *a.* 1 having two heads. 2 (of a train) drawn by two locomotives. 3 (*Bot.*) having flowers growing close to one another. **double header** *n.* 1 a train drawn by two locomotives. 2 (*N Am.*) two games played consecutively. 3 (*Austral.*) a coin with a head on each side. **double helix** *n.* two helices coiled round the same axis, the molecular structure of DNA. **double-jointedness** *n.* abnormal mobility of joints not associated with injury or disease, nor causing symptoms. **double knit** *n.* a fabric knitted on a double set of needles to give a double thickness. **double knitting** *n.* a knitting yarn of medium thickness. **double-lock** *v.t.* to fasten by turning the lock twice. **double negative** *n.* an ungrammatical sentence construction with two negatives where only one is needed, such as *I don't need nothing.* **doubleness** *n.* **double obelus, double obelisk** *n.* (*Print.*) a reference mark (‡). **double-park** *v.t.* to park (a vehicle) parallel with one already parked at the kerb. **double play** *n.* in baseball, a play in which two runners are put out. **double pneumonia** *n.* pneumonia affecting both lungs. **double quick** *adv.* very quickly. ~*a.* very quick. **double refraction** *n.* the formation of two unequally refracted rays of light from a single unpolarized ray. **double rhyme** *n.* a two-syllable rhyme. **double saucepan** *n.* a double boiler. **double-sided** *a.* able to be used on both sides. **double-space** *v.t.* to type with a line space between the lines. **doublespeak** *n.* talk that sounds sensible though it is actually a compound of sense and gibberish. **double standard** *n.* **1** a single moral principle applied in different ways to different groups of people and unfairly allowing different behaviour to the different groups. **2** bimetallism. **doublestar** *n.* two stars so near each other that they appear to be one when seen with the naked eye. **double-stop** *v.i.* (*pres.p.* **double-stopping,** *past, p.p.* **double-stopped**) (*Mus.*) to play chords on a violin on two stopped strings. **double stop** *n.* **double take** *n.* a delayed reaction. **double-talk** *n.* doublespeak. **doublethink** *n.* the holding of two contradictory beliefs at the same time. **double time** *n.* **1** pay at twice the usual rate, esp. for overtime. **2** (*Mil.*) a marching step at the rate of 165 steps to the minute, or (*US*) of 180 steps to the minute. **double top** *n.* a score of double twenty in darts. **double-u** *n.* W, the 23rd letter of the alphabet. **double whammy** *n.* (*coll.*) a twofold blow or misfortune. **doubly** *adv.*

double² (dŭb´əl) *n.* **1** twice as much or as many, a double quantity. **2** a drink of spirits which is twice the usual measure. **3** a bend or twist (in a road or river). **4** a wraith, a doppelgänger. **5** a person who almost exactly resembles someone else. **6** an understudy in a dramatic production. **7** a turn in running to escape pursuit. **8** (*fig.*) a trick, an artifice. **9** (*pl.*) in tennis etc., a game between two pairs. **10** in sport, two successive wins against the same team. **11** in bridge, the act of doubling an opponent's bid. **12** a bet on two races, the stake and winnings on the first being applied to the second race. **13** in darts, a throw between the two outer circles. ~*v.t.* **1** to increase by an equal quantity, amount, number, value etc., to multiply by two. **2** to fold down or over, to bend, to turn upon itself. **3** to be twice as

much as. **4** (*Mus.*) to add the upper or lower octave to. **5** to act two (parts) in the same play. **6** (*Naut.*) to sail round or by. **7** in bridge, to raise the scores at stake in. **8** to clench (one's fist). **9** in billiards, to cause to rebound. ~*v.i.* **1** to become twice as much or as great. **2** to be folded over. **3** to be an understudy. **4** to play a dual role. **5** to play more than one musical instrument. **6** in bridge, on the strength of one's own hand, to double the number of points an opponent may gain or lose. **7** to turn or wind to escape pursuit. **8** to run. **9** in billiards, to rebound. **at the double 1** very fast. **2** at twice the normal speed. **on the double** (*N Am.*) at the double. **to double back** to go back in the direction one has come from. **to double up 1** to bend one's body into a stooping or folded posture. **2** to collapse with pain or laughter. **3** to make (another person) double up. **4** to share a room or bed with someone. **5** to use the winnings from a bet to make another bet. **6** to clench. **7** to fold or become folded. **double or quits** *n.* a game such as pitch and toss to decide whether the person owing shall pay twice their debt or nothing. **doubler** *n.*

double-entendre (dooblätā´drə) *n.* **1** a word or phrase with two interpretations, one of which is usually indelicate. **2** a humour which relies on double entendres.

doublet (dŭb´lit) *n.* **1** either of a pair. **2** either of two words from the same root, but differing in meaning. **3** (*Physics*) a combination of two lenses. **4** (*pl.*) a pair of thrown dice showing the same number. **5** (*Physics*) a closely spaced pair of spectral lines. **6** (*Hist.*) a close-fitting garment covering the body from the neck to a little below the waist.

doubloon (dəbloon´) *n.* **1** (*Hist.*) a Spanish and S American gold coin (orig. the double of a pistole). **2** (*pl., sl.*) money.

doubt (dowt) *v.t.* **1** to hold or think questionable. **2** to hesitate to believe or assent to. ~*v.i.* to be in uncertainty about the truth, probability or propriety of anything. ~*n.* **1** uncertainty of mind upon any point, action or statement. **2** an unsettled state of opinion. **3** indecision, hesitation, suspense. **4** distrust, inclination to disbelieve. **5** a question, a problem, an objection. **beyond doubt** definitely true. **in doubt** uncertain. **no doubt** certainly, very unlikely, admittedly. **without (a) doubt** definitely. **doubtable** *a.* **doubter** *n.* **doubtful** *a.* **1** liable to doubt. **2** uncertain, admitting of doubt. **3** ambiguous, not clear in meaning. **4** uncertain, undecided, hesitating. **doubtfully** *adv.* **doubtfulness** *n.* **doubting** *n., a.* **doubtingly** *adv.* **Doubting Thomas** *n.* a person who persists in doubt until they have tangible evidence (from Thomas the apostle who would not believe in the Resurrection until he had seen Jesus (John, xx.24–25)). **doubtless** *a.* **doubtlessly** *adv.*

douche (doosh) *n.* **1** a jet of water or vapour directed upon some part of the body. **2** an instrument for applying this. ~*v.t.* to apply a douche to, esp. to flush out (the vagina or other cavity). ~*v.i.* to take a douche.

dough (dō) *n.* **1** the paste of bread etc. before baking; a mass of flour or meal moistened and kneaded. **2** anything resembling this in appearance or consistency. **3** (*sl.*) money. **doughboy** *n.* **1** a flour dumpling boiled in salt water. **2** (*NAm.*) a private soldier in the US Army. **doughnut,** (*N Am.*) **donut** *n.* **1** a cake, often ring shaped, made of sweetened dough and fried in fat. **2** any ring-shaped object. **doughnutting** *n.* (*coll.*) the practice of MPs sitting in the seats around a speaker during a televised debate to give the impression of a crowded house. **doughy** *a.* (*comp.* **doughier,** *superl.* **doughiest**) **1** like dough; soft. **2** pale, pasty. **doughiness** *n.*

†**doughty** (dow'ti) *a.* (*comp.* **doughtier,** *superl.* **doughtiest**) brave, valiant. **doughtily** *adv.* **doughtiness** *n.*

Douglas fir (dŭg'ləs), **Douglas pine, Douglas spruce** *n.* any tall American conifer of the genus *Pseudotsuga*, grown for ornament and timber.

dour (duə) *a.* (*Sc., North.*) hard, bold, sullen; stern, severe, obstinate. **dourly** *adv.* **dourness** *n.*

douse (dows), **dowse** *v.t.* **1** to plunge into water, to dip. **2** to throw water over, to drench. **3** (*Naut.*) **a** to strike or slacken (a sail) suddenly. **b** to close (a porthole). **4** to extinguish. ~*v.i.* to be plunged into water.

dove[1] (dŭv) *n.* **1** any bird of the family Columbidae, resembling a pigeon, but smaller and paler. **2** the symbol of the Holy Ghost. **3** in politics, an advocate of peaceable and conciliatory policies towards opponents, as distinct from *hawk.* **4** a gentle person (a term of endearment). **dove-coloured** *a.* grey with a tinge of pink. **dovecote, dovecot** (-kot) *n.* a small house or box for domestic pigeons. **dove grey** *n.* **dove-grey** *a.* **dovekie** (-ki) *n.* the little auk. **dovelike** *a.* **dove's-foot** *n.* one of the cranesbills, *Geranium molle.* **dove tree** *n.* a tree native to China, *Davidia involucrata*, which has white flowers resembling doves' wings.

dove[2] DIVE.

dovetail (dŭv'tāl) *n.* **1** a mode of fastening boards together by fitting tenons, shaped like a dove's tail spread out, into corresponding cavities. **2** a tenon or a joint of this kind. ~*v.t.* **1** to fit together by means of dovetails. **2** to fit exactly. ~*v.i.* to fit exactly.

dowager (dow'əjə) *n.* **1** a widow in possession of a dower or jointure. **2** a title given to a widow to distinguish her from the wife of her husband's heir. **3** (*sl.*) a dignified old lady.

dowdy (dow'di) *a.* (*comp.* **dowdier,** *superl.* **dowdiest**) dull, unfashionable. ~*n.* (*pl.* **dowdies**) a dull, unfashionably dressed woman. **dowdily** *adv.* **dowdiness** *n.*

dowel (dow'əl) *n.* a pin or peg for connecting two stones or pieces of wood, being sunk into the side of each. ~*v.t.* (*pres.p.* **dowelling,** (*N Am.*) **doweling,** *past, p.p.* **dowelled,** (*NAm.*) **doweled**)

to fasten by dowels. **dowelling,** (*N Am.*) **doweling** *n.* a long, thin rod of wood etc., for cutting into dowels.

dower (dow'ə) *n.* **1** the part of a husband's property which his widow enjoys during her life. **2** an endowment, a natural gift, a talent. ~*v.t.* to endow (with). **dower house** *n.* a house on an estate reserved for the widow of the late owner. **dowerless** *a.*

down[1] (down) *adv.* (*superl.* **downmost**) **1** towards the ground. **2** from a higher to a lower position. **3** on the ground. **4** below the horizon. **5** from former to later times. **6** from north to south. **7** away from the capital or a university. **8** (*Naut.*) **a** with a stream or current. **b** to leeward. **9** (of a crossword clue) to fit a word leading downwards in the grid. **10** into less bulk. **11** to finer consistency. **12** into quiescence (*Settle down!*). **13** in writing. **14** paid as a deposit. **15** to or in a state of subjection, disgrace or depression. **16** at a low level. **17** prostrate, in a fallen position or condition. **18** losing or beaten (*two goals down*). **19** temporarily out of action. **20** over one's throat. **21** downstairs, out of bed. **22** reduced in price. **23** in American football, out of play. ~*prep.* **1** along, through, or into, in a descending direction. **2** from the top or the upper part to the bottom or a lower part of. **3** at a lower part of. **4** along. ~*a.* (*superl.* **downmost**) **1** moving, sloping or directed towards a lower part or position. **2** of or relating to rail travel out of a city. **3** depressed, downcast. ~*v.t.* (*coll.*) **1** to put, strike or throw down, to overcome. **2** to eat or drink. ~*v.i.* to descend. ~*n.* **1** the act of putting down. **2** in American football, one of up to four chances to advance the ball for a score. **3** (*coll.*) a state of depression. **4** the act of playing the first piece in a game of dominoes. **5** (*esp. pl.*) a reverse. **6** (*coll.*) a grudge, dislike. **down with** abolish (*Down with the terrorists!*). **to be down on** to disapprove of, to be severe towards. **to down tools 1** to stop work. **2** to strike. **to have a down on** (*coll.*) to have a grudge against. **down!** *int.* (*ellipt.*) get, lie, put or throw down! **down and out** *a.* **1** utterly destitute and without resources. **2** in boxing, unable to continue the fight. **down-and-out** *n.* an utterly destitute person. **down at heel** *a.* **1** having worn heels. **2** shabby, disreputably dressed. **downbeat** *n.* (*Mus.*) **1** a downward movement of a conductor's baton. **2** an accented beat marked in this way. ~*a.* **1** depressed, pessimistic. **2** casual, relaxed. **downcast** *a.* **1** looking downward. **2** dejected, sad. ~*n.* a ventilating shaft. **down draught** *n.* a downward current of air. **downer** *n.* (*sl.*) **1** a tranquillizing drug, esp. a barbiturate. **2** a depressing experience. **3** a downturn. **downfall** *n.* **1** a sudden loss of prosperity, rank, reputation; ruin, overthrow. **2** a fall of rain, snow etc. **3** a cause of someone's downfall. **downfield** *adv.* UPFIELD (under UP- (+ C–H WORDS)). **downgrade**[1] (-grād') *v.t.* **1** to lower in status. **2** to disparage. **downgrade**[2] (down'-) *n.* **1** a downward gradient on a railway. **2** decadence. **3** an instance of lowering in rank. **on the downgrade** (*N Am.*) in decline. **downhearted** *a.* dispirited, dejected. **downheartedly** *adv.* **downheartedness** *n.* **downhill**[1] (downhil´) *adv.* **1** on a descending slope. **2** towards ruin or disgrace. **to go downhill** to deteriorate physically or morally. **downhill**[2] (down´hil) *a.* descending, sloping downwards, declining. ~*n.* **1** a declivity, a downward slope. **2** a decline. **3** a downhill race in skiing. **downhome** *a.* (*N Am.*) homely, rustic, unsophisticated. **down in the mouth** *a.* (*coll.*) unhappy, fed up. **download** *v.t.* (*Comput.*) to transfer (data) directly from one computer to another. ~*n.* an instance of downloading. **downmarket** *a.* of or relating to cheaply produced goods of poor quality. **down payment** *n.* a deposit paid on an article bought on hire purchase. **downpipe** *n.* a drainpipe which carries water from a roof to the ground. **downplay** *v.t.* to play down the importance of. **downpour** *n.* a heavy, persistent fall of rain. **downrate** *v.t.* to lower in value or importance. **downright** *a.* **1** directly to the point; plain, unequivocal; outspoken, artless, blunt. **2** complete, utter (*downright rudeness*). ~*adv.* thoroughly, absolutely. **downrightness** *n.* **downscale** *v.t.* (*N Am.*) to reduce in scale or size. ~*a.* inferior, esp. socially. **downshift** *n.* the act of changing to a lower gear when driving. ~*v.i.* to make a downshift. **downside** *n.* **1** a negative aspect of any situation; the negative side, adverse aspect; disadvantage. **2** a downward swing of share prices. **downsize** *v.t., v.i.* to reduce in size (esp. the workforce of a company). **downspout** *n.* (*N Am.*) a downpipe. **downstage** *a., adv.* at or to the front of the stage in a theatre. **downstair** *a.* downstairs. **downstairs** *adv.* **1** down the stairs. **2** on or to a lower floor. ~*a.* relating to a lower floor. ~*n.* the lower part of a building. **downstate** *a.* (*N Am.*) of or in a part of a state which is far from the large cities, esp. in the south of the state. ~*n.* a downstate part of a state. ~*adv.* in or to the downstate part of a state. **downstream** *a., adv.* in the direction of the current of a river. **downstroke** *n.* a downward stroke in handwriting. **downswing** *n.* **1** a downward trend in trade statistics etc. **2** the part of a swing in golf when the club is moving downwards towards the ground. **down time** *n.* the time during a normal working day when a computer, or other machinery, is inoperative. **down-to-earth** *a.* realistic, practical, sensible. **downtown** *n.* the business and commercial centre of a city. ~*a.* situated in (belonging to) this area. ~*adv.* in or towards this area. **downtrodden** *a.* **1** oppressed; tyrannized over. **2** trodden under foot. **downturn** *n.* a downward trend, esp. in business. **down under** *n., adv.* (*coll.*) (in or to) Australia or New Zealand. **downward** *a.* moving, directed or tending from higher, superior or earlier to lower, inferior or later. ~*adv.* downwards. **downwardly** *adv.* **downwards** *adv.* **1** from a higher to a lower position, level, condition or

character. **2** from earlier to later. **3** from superior to inferior. **downwind** *a., adv.* in the direction in which the wind is blowing.
down[2] (down) *n.* **1** the fine soft plumage of young birds or the plumage found under the feathers. **2** fine soft hair, esp. on the human face or on leaves, fruits etc. **3** any soft, fluffy substance. **downy** *a.* (*comp.* **downier**, *superl.* **downiest**) **1** covered with down. **2** made of down. **3** resembling down. **4** soft, placid, soothing. **5** (*sl.*) cunning, knowing, artful. **downily** *adv.* **downiness** *n.*
down[3] (down) *n.* **1** a tract of upland, esp. the chalk uplands of southern England, used for pasturing sheep. **2** a bank of sand etc. cast up by the sea. **downland** (-lənd) *n.*
Down's syndrome (downz) *n.* (*Med.*) a genetic disorder characterized by lower than average intelligence, short stature, sloping eyes and flattened facial features.
dowry (dow´ri) *n.* (*pl.* **dowries**) **1** the property which a wife brings to her husband. **2** an endowment, gift or talent.
dowse[1] (dows), **douse** *v.i.* to use a dowsing rod for the discovery of subterranean waters or minerals. **dowser** *n.* **dowsing rod** *n.* a forked twig or other stick used by dowsers to discover subterranean waters or minerals.
dowse[2] DOUSE.
doxology (doksol´əji) *n.* (*pl.* **doxologies**) a brief formula or hymn of praise to God. **doxological** (-soloj´-) *a.*
doyen (doi´en) *n.* the senior member of a body of people. **doyenne** (doi´en, -en´) *n.* a female doyen.
doyley DOILY.
doz. *abbr.* dozen.
doze (dōz) *v.i.* **1** to sleep lightly. **2** to be drowsy. ~*v.t.* to spend in drowsy inaction. ~*n.* a light sleep; a nap. **to doze off** to fall into a light sleep. **dozer** *n.* **dozy** *a.* (*comp.* **dozier**, *superl.* **doziest**). **dozily** *adv.* **doziness** *n.*
dozen (dŭz´ən) *n.* (*pl.* **dozen**, **dozens**) **1** an aggregate of twelve things or people. **2** about twelve, an indefinite number. **3** (*pl.*) a large number (of). ~*a.* twelve. **by the dozen** in large numbers. **the dozens** a game of exchanged verbal insults, indulged in by some African Americans. **to talk nineteen to the dozen** to talk incessantly. **dozenth** *a.*
DP *abbr.* **1** data processing. **2** displaced person.
D.Phil. *abbr.* Doctor of Philosophy.
Dr *abbr.* **1** Doctor. **2** Drive.
dr. *abbr.* **1** drachm(s). **2** drachma(s). **3** dram(s).
drab[1] (drab) *a.* (*comp.* **drabber**, *superl.* **drabbest**) **1** of a dull brown or dun colour. **2** dull, commonplace, monotonous. ~*n.* **1** drab colour. **2** monotony. **drably** *adv.* **drabness** *n.*
drab[2] (drab) *n.* a prostitute, a slut.
drab[3] DRIBS AND DRABS (under DRIB).
drachm (dram) *n.* **1** an apothecaries' weight of 60 grains (1/8 oz, 3.542 g). **2** an avoirdupois weight of 27 1/3 grains (1/16 oz, 1.771g). **drachma** (drak´mə) *n.* (*pl.* **drachmas**, **drachmae** (-mē))

1 the chief unit of currency of modern Greece.
2 the principal silver coin of the ancient Greeks,
worth six obols.

drack (drak) *a.* (*Austral.*, *sl.*) unattractive.

draconian (drəkō´niən), **draconic** (-kon´ik) *a.*
inflexible, severe, cruel.

draft (drahft) *n.* 1 the first outline of any writing
or document. 2 a rough copy. 3 a rough sketch of
work to be executed. 4 a written order for the
payment of money. 5 a cheque or bill drawn, esp.
by a department or a branch of a bank upon
another. 6 a demand (on). 7 a number of people
selected for some special purpose, a detachment,
a contingent. 8 the selection of people for some
special purpose. 9 (*N Am.*) conscription for
the army etc. 10 a reinforcement. 11 (*N Am.*) a
draught. ~*v.t.* 1 to draw up an outline of, to compose the first form of, make a rough copy of. 2 to
select (some of a larger number of people) for
some special purpose. 3 (*NAm.*) to conscript for
the army etc. **draft dodger** *n.* (*N Am.*) a person
who tries to avoid doing compulsory military
service. **draft dodging** *n.* **draftee** (drahftē´) *n.*
(*NAm.*) a conscript. **drafter** *n.* **drafting** *n.* **drafts-
man** *n.* (*pl.* **draftsmen**) 1 a person who draws up
documents. 2 a draughtsman. **drafty** *a.* (*comp.*
draftier, *superl.* **draftiest**).

drag (drag) *v.t.* (*pres.p.* **dragging**, *past*, *p.p.*
dragged) 1 to pull along the ground by main
force. 2 to draw by force; to haul. 3 to draw along
with difficulty. 4 to force (someone) to go somewhere. 5 to search (a river etc.) with a grapnel.
6 to perform too slowly. ~*v.i.* 1 (of a dress etc.) to
trail along the ground. 2 to search a river etc.
with a grapnel, nets etc. 3 to move slowly or
heavily. 4 (*coll.*) to draw on a cigarette. 5 to go on
at great length. ~*n.* 1 anything which retards
movement. 2 an iron shoe or skid fastened on
a wheel of a vehicle to check the speed. 3 (*Hist.*)
a kind of open four-horse coach. 4 a dredge. 5 a
four-clawed grapnel for dragging or dredging
under water. 6 a dragnet. 7 a draw on a cigarette.
8 the total resistance of an aeroplane along its
line of flight. 9 **a** in hunting, an artificial scent.
b a hunt in which a drag is used. 10 laborious
movement, slow process. 11 (*coll.*) something or
someone boring or irritating. 12 (*sl.*) **a** clothes
appropriate to the opposite sex, esp. women's
clothes worn by men. **b** a party where the people
wear drag. **c** clothes generally. 13 the act of
dragging. 14 (*sl.*) a motor car. 15 (*N Am.*, *sl.*)
influence. 16 (*sl.*) a road, a street (*the main drag*).
17 an impediment. **to drag in** to introduce (a
subject) gratuitously or irrelevantly. **to drag one's
feet/ heels** (*coll.*) to go slowly deliberately. **to
drag out** to make (something) last longer than
necessary. **to drag up 1** (*coll.*) to mention (an
unpleasant event or story). 2 (*coll.*) to bring up or
rear in a careless fashion. **drag-anchor** *n.* a sea
anchor. **draggy** *a.* (*comp.* **draggier**, *superl.* **drag-
giest**) (*coll.*) boring or unpleasant. **drag-hound** *n.*
a hound used in a drag hunt. **drag hunt** *n.* 1 a

hunt in which a drag is used. 2 a club devoted to
this kind of hunting. **dragnet** *n.* 1 a net dragged
along the bottom of a river etc. for catching fish.
2 a net drawn over a field to enclose game. 3 a
systematic police search of an area for criminals.
drag queen *n.* a man who wears women's
clothing, esp. as a theatrical act. **drag race** *n.* a
race in which specially modified cars race over a
timed course. **drag racing** *n.* **dragster** *n.* a car
modified for drag racing.

draggle (drag´əl) *v.t.* to make wet and dirty by
dragging on the ground. ~*v.i.* 1 to become dirty
by being trailed along the ground. 2 to trail along
the ground. 3 (*fig.*) to lag, to straggle.

dragoman (drag´əmən), **drogman** (drog´mən),
drogoman (-əmən) *n.* (*pl.* **dragomans, dragomen,
drogmans, drogmen, drogomans, drogomen**) a
person who acts as guide, interpreter and agent
for travellers in the Middle East.

dragon (drag´ən) *n.* 1 a fabulous monster found
in the mythology of nearly all nations, generally
as an enormous winged lizard with formidable
claws etc. 2 a flying lizard. 3 a violent, spiteful person, esp. a woman. **to chase the dragon**
(*sl.*) to smoke heroin. **dragonet** (-nit) *n.* any sea
fish of the family Callionymidae. **dragonfish** *n.*
(*pl.* **dragonfish**) any sea fish of the order
Stomiiformes, having a barbel on the chin.
dragonfly *n.* any insect of the order Odonata,
having a long brilliant body and two pairs of
large wings. **dragon's blood** *n.* a red resin exuding from various trees, much used for staining
and colouring. **dragon's teeth** *n.pl.* (*coll.*) concrete antitank obstacles which point upwards
from the ground. **dragon tree** *n.* a palmlike tree,
Dracaena draco, of W Africa and the adjacent
islands.

dragoon (drəgoon´) *n.* 1 a cavalry soldier, orig.
a mounted infantryman armed with a short
musket or carbine called a dragon. 2 a tough, belligerent man. 3 a kind of pigeon. ~*v.t.* 1 to subdue
by military force. 2 to compel by violent
measures.

drain (drān) *v.t.* 1 to draw off gradually. 2 to cause
to run off by tapping etc. 3 to empty by drawing
away moisture from. 4 to drink up. 5 to exhaust
or to deprive (of vitality, resources etc.). ~*v.i.* 1 to
flow off gradually. 2 to be emptied of moisture.
~*n.* 1 a strain, heavy demand. 2 a channel for
conveying water, sewage etc. 3 (*Med.*) a tube for
drawing off pus etc. **down the drain** (*coll.*)
wasted. **drainage** *n.* 1 the act, practice or science
of draining. 2 the natural or artificial system by
which land or a town is drained. 3 sewage etc.
which is carried away through drains. **drain-
board** *n.* (*NAm.*) a draining board. **draincock** *n.*
a tap for emptying a tank or other vessel. **drainer**
n. 1 a person who or something which drains.
2 a person who constructs drains. 3 a device on
which wet things are put to drain. **draining
board** *n.* a board beside a sink on which washed-
up crockery is put to dry. **drainpipe** *n.* 1 a pipe

for draining superfluous or waste water, particularly from a roof or gutter. **2** (*pl.*, *coll.*) trousers with very narrow legs. *~a.* (of trousers) having very narrow legs.

drake (drāk) *n.* the male of the duck.

Dralon® (drā´lon) *n.* an acrylic fibre, or a fabric made from it, usu. used in upholstery.

dram (dram) *n.* **1** a drachm in apothecaries' weight. **2** (*fig.*) a small quantity of spirits, as much as is drunk at once.

drama (drah´mə) *n.* **1** a play, usually intended for performance by living actors on the stage. **2** an exciting or distressing event. **3** dramatic art, the composition and presentation of plays. **4** dramatic aspect. **5** the dramatic literature or theatrical art of a particular country or period. **dramadocumentary** *n.* a film, play etc. composed of a mixture of fact and fiction. **dramatic** (drəmat´-), †**dramatical** *a.* **1** of, relating to or of the nature of drama. **2** of or relating to the stage, theatrical. **3** intended or suitable for representation on the stage. **4** striking, catastrophic, impressive. **5** over-emotional, flamboyant, meant for effect. **dramatically** *adv.* **dramatic irony** *n.* tragic irony. **dramatics** *n.pl.* **1** a display of exaggerated behaviour. **2** (*as sing.*) the producing or study of plays.

dramatis personae (dramətis pəsō´nī) *n.pl.* **1** the set of characters in a play. **2** a list of these.

dramatist (dram´ətist) *n.* a writer of plays.

dramatize (dram´ətīz), **dramatise** *v.t.* **1** to set forth in the form of a drama. **2** to describe dramatically. **3** to exaggerate. **4** to convert (a story, novel etc.) into a play. *~v.i.* (of a novel, story etc.) to be dramatized. **dramatizable** *a.* **dramatization** (-zā´shən) *n.*

drank DRINK.

drape (drāp) *v.t.* **1** to cover, clothe or decorate with cloth etc. **2** to adjust or arrange the folds of (a dress, curtains etc.). *~n.* **1** a hanging which drapes, a curtain. **2** the way that a garment hangs. **draper** *n.* a person who sells cloth and other fabrics. **drapery** *n.* (*pl.* **draperies**) **1** the trade of a draper. **2** cloth and other fabrics. **3** something with which an object is draped, hangings, tapestry etc. **4** a curtain. **5** the arrangement of dress in sculpture, painting etc. **draperied** *a.* draped.

drastic (dras´tik, drah´-) *a.* acting vigorously; effective, efficacious. **drastically** *adv.*

drat (drat) *int.* (*euphem.*) damn. **dratted** *a.*

draught (drahft), (*N Am.*) **draft** *n.* **1** a current of air. **2** the act of pulling. **3** the load being pulled. **4** the act of dragging with a net. **5** the quantity of fish taken in one sweep of a net. **6** the act of drinking. **7** the quantity of liquor drunk at once. **8** a dose of medicine. **9** (*Naut.*) the depth to which a ship sinks in water. **10** a draft, a preliminary drawing, design or plan for a work to be executed. **11** the drawing of beer from a cask. **12** (*pl.*) a game played by two persons on a

draughtboard with twelve round pieces of different colours on each side. *~v.t.* to draft. **on draught** (of beer) able to be obtained by drawing off from a cask. **to feel the draught** (*coll.*) to be aware of, or affected by, adverse (economic) conditions. **draught beer** *n.* beer drawn from the cask, as distinguished from bottled or canned beer. **draughtboard** *n.* a chequered board on which draughts is played. **draught horse** *n.* a horse used for pulling heavy loads. **draughtproof** *a.* proof against draughts. *~v.t.* to make proof against draughts.

draughtsman (drahfts´mən) *n.* (*pl.* **draughtsmen**) **1** a person who draws, designs or plans. **2** a person skilled in drawing. **3** a piece used in the game of draughts. **4** a person who draws up documents. **draughtsmanship** *n.* **draughtswoman** *n.* (*pl.* **draughtswomen**) a woman skilled in drawing.

draughty (drahf´ti), (*N Am.*) **drafty** *a.* (*comp.* **draughtier**, (*N Am.*) **draftier**, *superl.* **draughtiest**, (*N Am.*) **draftiest**) full of draughts or currents of air. **draughtily** *adv.* **draughtiness** *n.*

Dravidian (drəvid´iən) *n.* **1** a member of the people of S India and Sri Lanka speaking Tamil, Telugu, Canarese and Malayalam. **2** any of these languages. *~a.* of or relating to the Dravidians or any of their languages.

draw (draw) *v.t.* (*past* **drew** (droo), *p.p.* **drawn** (drawn)) **1** to draft, to picture, to portray. **2** to drag or pull. **3** to pull after one; to haul. **4** to pull out or up. **5** to extract or remove by pulling. **6** to cause to flow or come forth. **7** to elicit. **8** to induce to do something, esp. to reveal information. **9** in cards, to cause to be played. **10** to take, to receive, to derive. **11** to infer, to deduce. **12** to take in, to inhale. **13** to lengthen, to pull out, to stretch, to protract. **14** to extract. **15** to disembowel. **16** to take (tickets) out of a box or wheel. **17** to unsheathe (a sword). **18** to allure, attract, to cause to follow one. **19** to cause to come out. **20** in hunting, to search for game. **21** to write (a cheque etc.) for payment by (a bank). **22** to drag (an animal such as a badger) from a hole. **23** to compose (a document). **24** to note (a comparison). **25** to make (wire) by pulling a piece of metal through a series of small holes. **26** in golf, to drive to the left (or right if left handed). **27** in bowls, to bowl in a curve. **28** (*Naut.*) to need (a specified depth of water) to float. **29** to pull (curtains) open or shut. **30** to finish (a game) with equal scores. *~v.i.* **1** to practise the art of delineation. **2** to breathe in the smoke from a cigarette. **3** to pull, to haul. **4** (of a chimney, pipe etc.) to allow a free motion, current etc. **5** to unsheathe a sword or take a pistol from its holster. **6** to draw lots. **7** to make demands (on). **8** to move, to approach. **9** to finish a game with equal scores. **10** to write out a draft for payment. **11** (of a sail) to swell tightly. **12** (*Naut.*) to require a certain depth of water. *~n.* **1** the act or power of drawing. **2** a pull, a strain. **3** an attraction, a lure. **4** the act of drawing lots. **5** a lot or chance drawn. **6** a drawn game or contest. **7** a puff on a cigarette. **8** the act of pulling a gun quickly out of its holster to shoot. **9** (*N Am.*) the part of a drawbridge that can be moved. **to draw a blank** not to succeed in finding what one is looking for. **to draw back 1** to move back. **2** to withdraw; to be unwilling to fulfil a promise. **to draw breath 1** to pause, to have a break. **2** to breathe, to live. **to draw in 1** to contract. **2** to entice, to inveigle. **3** (of days) to close in, to shorten. **4** (of a train) to arrive at a station. **to draw near** to approach. **to draw off** to withdraw, to retire, to retreat. **to draw on 1** to lead to as a consequence. **2** to allure, attract, entice. **3** to approach. **4** to put on (clothes or shoes). **to draw out 1** to lengthen; to protract. **2** to set in order for battle. **3** to induce to talk, to elicit. **4** to write out. **5** (of days) to become longer. **6** (of a train) to leave the station. **to draw stumps** to stop playing cricket for the day. **to draw the line at** to refuse to go as far as. **to draw up 1** to compose. **2** to put into proper form. **3** to put (oneself) into a stiff erect attitude. **4** to come to a stop. **to draw up with** to overtake. **drawback** *n.* **1** a deduction, a rebate. **2** a disadvantage; an inconvenience; an obstacle. **drawbridge** *n.* a bridge that may be raised on hinges at one or both ends to allow ships to pass or to prevent passage across. **drawcord** *n.* a drawstring. **drawdown** *n.* the act of borrowing money. **draw-sheet** *n.* (*Med.*) an extra sheet doubled lengthwise and placed across the bed so that it may be pulled beneath the patient as required. **drawstring** *n.* a cord or thread, threaded through or otherwise attached to fabric, which can be pulled together in the fabric. **draw-well** *n.* a deep well from which water is drawn by means of a rope and bucket.

drawee (drawē´) *n.* the person on whom a bill of exchange or order for payment in money is drawn.

drawer[1] (draw) *n.* a sliding boxlike receptacle in a table etc. **drawerful** *n.* (*pl.* **drawerfuls**). **drawers** (drawz) *n.pl.* (*facet.*) an undergarment covering the lower body with holes for the legs.

drawer[2] (draw´ə) *n.* **1** a person who draws. **2** a person who draws a bill or order for the payment of money. **3** a person who or something which has the quality of attracting.

drawing (draw´ing) *n.* **1** the art of representing objects on a flat surface by means of lines drawn with a pencil, crayon etc. **2** a delineation of this kind. **3** a sketch in black and white, or monochrome. **4** the distribution of prizes in a lottery. **drawing board** *n.* a large rectangular frame for holding a sheet of paper while drawing. **back to the drawing board** back to start again after an unsuccessful attempt. **drawing paper** *n.* thick paper for drawing on. **drawing pin** *n.* a flat-headed tack for securing drawing paper to a board etc. **drawing room** *n.* **1** a room for the

reception of company. **2** (*N Am.*) a private compartment in a railway coach.

drawl (drawl) *v.t.* to utter in a slow, lengthened tone. ~*v.i.* to speak with a slow, prolonged utterance. ~*n.* a slow, lengthened manner of speaking. **drawler** *n.* **drawling** *a.* **drawlingly** *adv.*

drawn (drawn) *a.* **1** haggard. **2** (of butter) melted. **3** (of a position in chess) likely to result in a draw. **drawn out** *a.* long-drawn.

dray[1] (drā) *n.* **1** a low cart, generally of strong and heavy construction, used by brewers etc. **2** (*Austral., New Zeal.*) a cart with two wheels. **dray horse** *n.* a strong, heavy horse used for pulling a dray.

dray[2] DREY.

dread (dred) *v.t.* **1** to fear greatly. **2** to anticipate with terror and shrinking. **3** to be apprehensive or anxious about, to doubt. ~*n.* **1** great fear or terror. **2** apprehension of evil. **3** awe, reverence. **4** the person or thing dreaded. ~*a.* exciting great fear or terror, frightful. **dreaded** *a.* **1** greatly to be feared. **2** (*coll.*) annoying, inconvenient, unwelcome (*the dreaded hiccups*). **dreadful** *a.* **1** inspiring dread; terrible; awe-inspiring. **2** (*coll.*) annoying, disagreeable, troublesome, frightful, horrid. **3** (*coll.*) bad, extreme (*a dreadful mistake*). **dreadfully** *adv.* **dreadfulness** *n.* **dreadlocks** (dred´loks) *n.pl.* long hair worn in many tight plaits by Rastafarians. **dreadlocked** *a.*

dream (drēm) *n.* **1** a vision. **2** thoughts and images that pass through the mind of a sleeping person. **3** the state of mind in which these occur. **4** a visionary idea, a fancy, reverie. **5** someone or something beautiful or enticing. **6** the condition of being divorced from reality. ~*v.i.* (*past, p.p.* **dreamed, dreamt** (dremt)) **1** to have visions. **2** to think, to imagine as in a dream. **3** to conceive as possible. **4** to waste time in idle thoughts. **5** to indulge in a daydream. ~*v.t.* **1** to see, hear, feel etc. in a dream. **2** to imagine or conceive in a visionary fashion, to picture in hope or imagination. **like a dream** very smoothly; very successfully. **to dream away** to spend (time) idly. **to dream up** (*coll.*) to invent (an idea or excuse). **dreamboat** *n.* (*coll.*) **1** a very desirable person, esp. of the opposite sex. **2** a very desirable thing. **dreamer** *n.* **1** a person who dreams. **2** an impractical, unrealistic person. **dreamful** *a.* **dreamingly** *adv.* **dreamland** *n.* the region of fancy or imagination. **dreamless** *a.* **dreamlike** *a.* **dream ticket** *n.* two electoral candidates regarded as the ideal combination. **dream-world** *n.* a world of illusions. **dreamy** *a.* (*comp.* **dreamier,** *superl.* **dreamiest**) **1** habitually daydreaming. **2** visionary. **3** (*poet.*) full of or causing dreams. **4** dreamlike, soft and gentle. **5** (*coll.*) extremely attractive. **dreamily** *adv.* **dreaminess** *n.*

dreary (driə´ri) *a.* (*comp.* **drearier,** *superl.* **dreariest**) dismal, gloomy; cheerless, tiresome, dull. **drear** (driə) *a.* (*poet.*) dreary. **drearily** *adv.* **dreariness** *n.*

dredge[1] (drej) n. 1 an apparatus for dragging under water to bring up objects from the bottom for scientific purposes. 2 a bucket or scoop for scraping mud etc. from the bed of a pond etc. ~v.t. 1 to gather or bring up with a dredge. 2 to remove or clear away by means of a dredge. 3 to clean or deepen (a river or harbour) with a dredging-machine. ~v.i. to use a dredge. **to dredge up 1** to lift with a dredge. **2** to find (something) previously obscure or well hidden. **dredger**[1], **drudger** n. 1 a ship for dredging. 2 a dredging-machine.

dredge[2] (drej) v.t. 1 to sprinkle (flour etc.). 2 to sprinkle with flour etc. **dredger**[2] n. a box with a perforated lid for sprinkling.

dredger[1] DREDGE[1].

dredger[2] DREDGE[2].

dreg (dreg) n. (usu. pl.) 1 the sediment or lees of liquor. 2 worthless refuse. 3 the lowest class. 4 the most undesirable part. **to drain/ drink to the dregs** to enjoy to the full.

drench (drench) v.t. 1 to wet thoroughly. 2 to soak, to saturate. 3 to cause to swallow (esp. a medicinal draught). ~n. 1 a liquid medicine for horses or cattle. 2 a soaking, a flood. **drencher** n.

dress (dres) v.t. 1 to clothe, to attire. 2 to adorn, to decorate. 3 (Naut.) to decorate with flags etc. 4 to cleanse, trim, brush, comb etc. 5 to curry or rub down. 6 (Med.) to cleanse and treat (a wound). 7 to prepare for use, to cook. 8 to cover (a salad etc.) with dressing. 9 to make straight. 10 (Mil.) to form (ranks) into a straight line. 11 to order, arrange, array. 12 to prune, to cut. 13 to manure. 14 to square and give a smooth surface to (stone etc.). 15 to arrange goods attractively in (a shop window). 16 to smooth and give a nap to (cloth). ~v.i. 1 to clothe oneself. 2 to put on evening clothes. 3 to attire oneself elaborately. 4 (Mil.) to arrange oneself in proper position in a line. ~n. 1 that which is worn as clothes, esp. outer garments. 2 garments, apparel. 3 a lady's gown, a frock. 4 the art of adjusting dress. 5 an external covering, as plumage. 6 external appearance, outward form. **to dress down 1** (coll.) to chastise, to reprimand severely. **2** (coll.) to dress casually or informally. **to dress up 1** to clothe elaborately. **2** to invest with a fictitious appearance. **3** to wear fancy dress. **dress circle** n. the first tier of seats above the pit in a theatre. **dress coat** n. a man's coat with narrow pointed tails, worn as evening dress. **dress length** n. enough fabric to make a dress. **dressmaker** n. a person who makes women's dresses. **dressmaking** n. **dress rehearsal** n. the final rehearsal of a play etc., with costumes and effects. **dress sense** n. a knowledge of style in dress and the ability to pick clothes which suit one. **dress shirt** n. 1 a man's shirt worn with formal evening dress. 2 (N Am.) any long-sleeved shirt. **dress uniform** n. a full ceremonial military uniform. **dressy** a. (comp. **dressier**, superl. **dressiest**) 1 fond of

showy dress. 2 wearing rich or showy dress. 3 showy. 4 stylish, smart. **dressiness** n.

dressage (dres'ahzh) n. the training of a horse in deportment, obedience and response to signals given by the rider's body.

dresser[1] (dres'ə) n. 1 a kitchen sideboard with a set of shelves for displaying plates etc. 2 (N Am.) a chest of drawers.

dresser[2] (dres'ə) n. 1 a person who dresses another, esp. an actor for the stage. 2 a surgeon's assistant in operations etc. who dresses wounds etc. 3 a person who dresses in a specified manner (a smart dresser).

dressing (dres'ing) n. 1 the act of dressing. 2 gum, starch etc. used in sizing or stiffening fabrics. 3 sauce, salad dressing. 4 (N Am.) stuffing. 5 manure applied to soil. 6 ointment, liniment, a bandage etc. applied to a wound or sore. **dressing down** n. (coll.) a severe telling-off. **dressing gown** n. a loose robe worn over nightclothes. **dressing room** n. 1 a room next to a bedroom, for dressing in. 2 the room where actors put on costumes and stage make-up. **dressing station** n. a military, naval, or air-force first-aid post. **dressing table** n. a table fitted with drawers and a mirror, used while dressing, making up etc.

drew DRAW.

drey (drā), **dray** n. a squirrel's nest.

drib (drib) n. a driblet, a petty amount or quantity. **driblet** n. a small or petty portion or sum. **dribs and drabs** (drabz) n.pl. (coll.) small numbers at a time (They arrived in dribs and drabs).

dribble (drib'əl) v.i. 1 to fall in a quick succession of small drops. 2 to drip, to trickle. 3 to slaver, to drivel. 4 to manoeuvre a football in a forward direction by slight kicks from alternate sides. ~v.t. 1 to allow to drip. 2 to give out slowly by drops. 3 to move (a football) by dribbling. ~n. 1 a trickling stream. 2 saliva dribbling from the mouth. 3 in football, a piece of dribbling. **dribbler** n. **dribbly** a. (comp. **dribblier**, superl. **dribbliest**).

drier, **dried** DRY.

drift (drift) n. 1 something which is driven along by a wind or current. 2 a current, a driving or compelling force. 3 the course of drifting or movement. 4 meaning, aim, tenor (Do you catch my drift?). 5 a mass (of snow, leaves, sand etc.) driven together. 6 (Geol.) a loose accumulation of sand and debris deposited over the surface by the action of water or ice. 7 (Naut. etc.) deviation of a ship, aircraft or projectile from a direct course caused by a current or wind. 8 a mass of flowering plants. 9 (Mining) a horizontal passage following a lode or vein. 10 (S Afr.) a ford. 11 a gradual change in a supposedly constant piece of equipment. ~v.i. 1 to be driven into heaps. 2 to float or be carried along by or as if by a current. 3 to be carried along by circumstances. ~v.t. 1 to drive along or into heaps. 2 (of a current) to carry along. 3 to cover with drifts or driftage. **driftage**

n. **1** drifting or drifted substances. **2** the distance to which a ship drifts in bearing up against wind and currents. **drifter** *n.* **1** a trawler or fishing boat using a drift-net to fish, esp. for enemy mines. **2** a person who wanders aimlessly from place to place. **drift-net** *n.* a large fishing net. **drift-netter** *n.* **drift-netting** *n.* **driftwood** *n.* wood carried by water onto the shore.

drill[1] (dril) *n.* **1** a metal tool for boring holes in hard material. **2** constant practice or exercise in any art or business. **3** (*esp. Mil.*) **a** the act of drilling soldiers or sailors, the series of exercises by which they are rendered efficient. **b** rigorous training or discipline. **c** (*coll.*) correct procedure, the right way to do something. ~*v.t.* **1** to bore or pierce with a pointed tool, to perforate. **2** to make holes in, by this means. **3** to train by repeated exercise. **4** to train to the use of arms, to exercise in military exercises. **5** to shoot (someone). ~*v.i.* **1** to bore holes with a drill. **2** to go through a course of military exercise. **driller** *n.* **drill-sergeant** *n.* a non-commissioned officer who drills soldiers or school pupils. **drill stem** *n.* a rotating rod used in drilling.

drill[2] (dril) *n.* **1** a small trench or furrow, or a ridge with a trench along the top, for seeds or small plants. **2** a row of plants in such a furrow. **3** a machine for sowing grain in rows. ~*v.t.* to sow (seed) or plant in rows. ~*v.i.* to sow or plant in this manner.

drill[3] (dril) *n.* a baboon from W Africa, *Mandrillus leucophaeus.*

drill[4] (dril) *n.* a heavy cotton twilled cloth used for trousers etc.

drily (drī′li), **dryly** *adv.* **1** amusingly and cleverly. **2** in a dry manner.

drink (dringk) *v.t.* (*past* **drank** (drangk), *p.p.* **drunk** (drŭngk)) **1** to swallow (a liquid). **2** to imbibe, absorb, suck in. **3** to swallow up, to empty. **4** to take in by the senses. **5** to pledge, to toast. **6** to cause (oneself) to be in a particular condition by drinking too much alcohol (*He drank himself into oblivion*). **7** to waste (money, wages or property) on indulgence in alcohol. ~*v.i.* **1** to swallow a liquid. **2** to drink alcohol habitually, esp. to excess. ~*n.* **1** something to be drunk. **2** a draught, a potion. **3** intoxicating liquor. **4** an alcoholic drink. **5** excessive indulgence in intoxicating liquors, intemperance. **in drink** intoxicated. **the drink** (*coll.*) the sea. **to drink in** to absorb readily; to receive greedily, as with the senses; to gaze upon, listen to etc. with delight. **to drink off** to swallow at a single draught. **to drink to** to salute in drinking; to drink the health of. **to drink up** to swallow completely. **drinkable** *a.*, *n.* **drink-driving** *n.* the act of driving after drinking alcohol. **drink-driver** *n.* **drinker** *n.* **1** a person who drinks. **2** a person who habitually drinks alcohol, esp. to excess. **3** a large, brownish moth, *Euthrix potatoria*, whose caterpillar drinks dew. **drinking** *n.* **drinking song** *n.* a song in praise of drinking parties.

drinking-up time *n.* the time between the call for last orders and closing time, in which to finish drinks. **drinking water** *n.* water suitable for drinking.

Usage note In standard English, the past tense of the verb *drink* is *drank*, not *drunk*.

drip (drip) *v.i.* (*pres.p.* **dripping**, *past*, *p.p.* **dripped**) **1** to fall in drops. **2** to throw off moisture in drops. ~*v.t.* to let fall in drops. ~*n.* **1** the act of dripping, a falling in drops. **2** a drop of liquid. **3** a dripping sound. **4** (*coll.*) a stupid or insipid person. **5** (*Med.*) drip-feed. **drip-dry** *a.* (of clothing) made of such a material that, when hung up to drip, it dries quickly without wringing and needs no ironing. ~*v.i.*, *v.t.* (*3rd pers. sing. pres.* **drip-dries**, *pres.p.* **drip-drying**, *past*, *p.p.* **drip-dried**) to dry in this way. **drip-feed** *v.t.* (*past*, *p.p.* **drip-fed**) (*Med.*) to feed nutrients to (a patient) in liquid form, using a drip-feed. ~*n.* **1** the apparatus for the intravenous administration of some liquid, drop by drop. **2** the feeding of nutrients to a patient in this way. **3** the nutrients administered in this way. **dripless** *a.* **drip-mat** *n.* a small mat put under a glass to soak up drips. **drip-moulding** *n.* a corona or projecting tablet or moulding over the heads of doorways, windows etc. to throw off rain. **dripping** *n.* **1** the fat which falls from roasting meat. **2** (*pl.*) water, grease etc. falling or trickling from anything. **to be dripping with** to have a large number or amount of. **dripping wet** *a.* extremely wet. **drippy** *a.* (*comp.* **drippier**, *superl.* **drippiest**) **1** inclined to drip. **2** insipid, inane. **drippily** *adv.* **drippiness** *n.* **drip stone** *n.* a drip-moulding.

drive (drīv) *v.t.* (*pres.p.* **driving**, *past* **drove** (drōv), †**drave** (drāv), *p.p.* **driven** (driv′en)) **1** to push or urge by force. **2** to guide or direct (a vehicle or horse). **3** to convey in a vehicle. **4** to be licensed to drive. **5** to constrain, to compel. **6** to force into a particular state (*She drives me mad*). **7** (*Comput.*) to operate (a computer). **8** to prosecute, to carry on. **9** to chase, hunt, esp. to frighten (game) into an enclosure or towards guns. **10** to overwork. **11** to throw, to propel. **12** in golf, to propel (the ball) with the driver. **13** in cricket, to hit (the ball) to or past the bowler with a swift free stroke. **14** to force (a nail etc.) with blows. **15** to propel (machinery etc.). **16** (*Mining etc.*) to bore (a tunnel etc.). **17** to press (an argument). ~*v.i.* **1** to be urged forward by violence. **2** to dash, to rush violently, to hasten. **3** to drift, to be carried. **4** to travel in a vehicle, esp. under one's own direction or control. **5** to control or direct a vehicle, engine etc. **6** to hold a driving licence. **7** to aim a blow, to strike furiously. **8** to tend, to aim, to intend. **9** in golf, to hit the ball with the driver. ~*n.* **1** a ride in a vehicle. **2** a road for driving on, esp. a private carriageway to a house. **3** a forward stroke at cricket etc. **4** a concerted effort made for charity etc. **5** transmission of power to the wheels of a vehicle etc. **6** the position of the steering wheel in a vehicle (*left-hand drive*). **7** a driving of game, cattle, or of an enemy. **8** push, energy. **9** energy, motivation. **10** (*Comput.*) a disk drive. **11** a series of competitive games of whist, bridge etc. **12** (*Austral., New Zeal.*) a line of trees on a hillside, cut down when one falls on another. **to drive at** (*fig.*) to hint at. **to drive out 1** to expel; to oust. **2** to take the place of. **to drive up the wall** (*coll.*) to madden, to annoy greatly. **to let drive** to strike furiously, to aim a blow. **drivable, driveable** *a.* **drive-by** *a.* (of a crime, esp. a shooting) committed from a moving vehicle. **drive-in** *n.* a café, cinema etc. where customers are served or can watch a film without leaving their cars. ~*a.* denoting a drive-in café, cinema etc. **drive-on, drive-on/drive-off** *a.* (of a ship) able to be driven onto and off by motor vehicles. **driver** *n.* **1** a person who or something which drives. **2** a person who drives a vehicle or an engine. **3** an electronic device which provides power for output. **4** something which communicates motion to something else, as a wheel. **5** (*Comput.*) a program which controls a device. **6** a wooden-headed golf club used to propel the ball from the tee. **driverless** *a.* **driver's license** *n.* (*N Am.*) a driving licence. **driver's test** *n.* (*N Am.*) a driving test. **driveshaft** *n.* a shaft which transmits torque. **drive-through** *a.* **1** (*esp. N Am.*) denoting a restaurant etc. where customers are served at a window without leaving their cars. **2** (*esp. N Am.*) able to be driven through. **driveway** *n.* a path large enough for a car, from a road to a house. **driving** *a.* having great force (*driving rain*). **driving licence** *n.* a permit to drive, granted to a person who has passed a driving test. **driving mirror** *n.* the small mirror inside a car which enables a driver to see what is behind. **driving range** *n.* a place for practising driving golf balls. **driving seat** *n.* **1** the seat for the driver in a vehicle. **2** a position of authority or control. **driving-shaft** *n.* a shaft transmitting motion from the driving wheel. **driving test** *n.* an examination in the driving and handling of a motor vehicle. **driving wheel** *n.* **1** the wheel which communicates motion to other parts of the machinery. **2** a large wheel of a locomotive, a cycle-wheel or motor-wheel to which motive force is applied directly.

drivel (driv'əl) *n.* silly, nonsensical talk; twaddle. ~*v.i.* (*pres.p.* **drivelling**, (*N Am.*) **driveling**, *past* **drivelled**, (*N Am.*) **driveled**) **1** to slaver, to allow spittle to flow from the mouth, as a child, idiot or dotard. **2** to talk nonsense. ~*v.t.* to fritter (away). **driveller**, (*N Am.*) **driveler** *n.*

drizzle (driz'əl) *n.* **1** fine, small rain. **2** in cookery, small, fine drops of a liquid sprinkled over something. ~*v.i.* to rain slightly. ~*v.t.* **1** to shed in small, fine drops. **2** to sprinkle. **drizzly** *a.* (*comp.* **drizzlier**, *superl.* **drizzliest**).

Dr Martens® (doktə mah'tinz) *n.pl.* heavy lace-up boots with thick, cushioned soles.

drogue (drōg) *n.* **1** (*Naut.*) **a** a bag drawn behind a boat to prevent her broaching to. **b** a drag attached to a harpoon line to check the progress of a whale when struck. **2** a windsock. **3** a parachute which reduces the speed of a falling object or landing aircraft. **4** a target for firing practice, pulled along by an aircraft. **5** a cone-shaped device on the end of the refuelling hose of a tanker aircraft into which the probe of the receiving aircraft fits.

droll (drōl) *a.* odd, facetious, ludicrous, comical, laughable. **drollery** *n.* (*pl.* **drolleries**) **drollness** *n.* **drolly** (drōl'li) *adv.*

dromedary (drom'idəri) *n.* (*pl.* **dromedaries**) an Arabian camel.

drone (drōn) *n.* **1** the male of the bee, larger than the worker, which makes the honey. **2** an idler, a lazy person who lives on the industry of others. **3** a deep, humming sound. **4** the unchanging bass produced from the three lower pipes of a set of bagpipes. **5** any of these lower pipes. **6** a string which produces a droning sound on a stringed instrument. **7** a person with a low, monotonous speaking voice. **8** a monotonous speech. **9** a radio-controlled aircraft. ~*v.i.* **1** to make a monotonous, humming noise. **2** to talk in a monotonous tone. **3** to live in idleness. ~*v.t.* **1** to read or say in a monotonous tone. **2** to spend (time) idly.

drongo (drong'go) *n.* (*pl.* **drongos**) **1** any glossy, black, insect-eating bird of the family Dicruridae. **2** (*Austral., New Zeal., sl., derog.*) a slow-witted person.

drool (drool) *v.i.* **1** to drivel, to slaver. **2** to show excessive or lascivious pleasure in something. ~*n.* saliva trickling from the mouth.

droop (droop) *v.i.* **1** to hang, lean or bend down. **2** (of the eyes) to look downwards. **3** (*poet.*) (of the sun) to sink. **4** to fail, to flag, to languish, to decline; to be dejected, to despond, to lose heart. ~*v.t.* to let fall or hang down. ~*n.* **1** the act of drooping. **2** a drooping attitude. **3** loss of heart. **droop snoot** *n.* (*coll.*) an adjustable nose (of an aircraft). **droopy** *a.* (*comp.* **droopier**, *superl.* **droopiest**). **droopily** *adv.* **droopiness** *n.*

drop (drop) *n.* **1** a globule or small portion of liquid in a spherical form, which is falling, hanging or adhering to a surface. **2** a very small quantity of a fluid. **3** (*Med.*) the smallest separable quantity of a liquid. **4** (*pl.*) liquid medicine applied in such units with a dropper. **5** a minute quantity, an infinitesimal particle. **6** (*coll.*) a delivery. **7** (*sl.*) a cache, a hiding place. **8** (*sl.*) a bribe. **9** (*coll.*) a glass or drink of alcohol. **10** anything resembling a drop, or hanging as a drop, such as an earring, or other pendent ornament. **11** any of various sweetmeats (*chocolate drops*). **12** the act of dropping, a fall, a descent, a collapse. **13** a reduction, a lowering. **14** a thing that drops or is dropped. **15** the unloading of troops from an aircraft by parachute. **16** a painted curtain suspended on pulleys which is let down to conceal the stage in a theatre. **17** a falling trapdoor. **18** the part of a gallows contrived so as to fall from under the feet of persons to be hanged. **19** an abrupt fall in a surface. **20** the amount of this. **21** (*N Am.*) a slot in a receptacle through which things can be dropped. *~a.* lowered (*a drop waist*). *~v.t.* (*pres.p.* **dropping,** *past, p.p.* **dropped**) **1** to allow or cause to fall in drops, as a liquid. **2** to cause to fall, to fell. **3** to take off (one's trousers or underpants). **4** to lower, to let down. **5** to dismiss, to give up. **6** to set down (a passenger) from a vehicle. **7** to let fall, to utter casually, to mention casually. **8** to write to in an informal manner. **9** to bear (a foal, calf etc.). **10** to omit. **11** to stop (doing something), to have done with. **12** to let go. **13** to sprinkle with drops. **14** (*coll.*) to bring down, to kill. **15** (*coll.*) to lose. **16** to unload from an aircraft by parachute. **17 a** in rugby, to hit (a ball) by a drop kick. **b** to score (a goal) with a drop kick. **18** to stop seeing or associating with (someone). *~v.i.* **1** to fall in drops; to drip, to discharge itself in drops. **2** to fall. **3** to collapse suddenly, to sink as if exhausted, to faint. **4** to die. **5** to be uttered. **6** to cease, to lapse, to come to an end. **7** to fall (behind). **8** to jump down. **9** (of a card) to be played along with a card of a higher value. **at the drop of a hat** immediately. **to drop a curtsy** to curtsy. **to drop anchor** to let down the anchor. **to drop asleep** to fall asleep. **to drop away** to depart. **to drop back** to fall behind, to be overtaken. **to drop back into** to revert to (a former habit). **to drop behind** to drop back. **to drop by** to drop in. **to drop down 1** to descend a hill. **2** to sail down a river towards the sea. **to drop in 1** to make an informal visit. **2** to call unexpectedly. **to drop into 1** (*coll.*) to make an informal visit to (a place). **2** (*coll.*) to develop (a habit). **to drop off 1** to decrease, to become less. **2** (*coll.*) to fall gently asleep. **3** to set down (a passenger) from a vehicle. **to drop one's aitches/ h's** not to pronounce the *h*'s at the beginnings of words. **to drop out** (*coll.*) to refuse to follow a conventional lifestyle, esp. to leave school or college early. **to drop to** (*sl.*) to become aware of. **to drop to the rear** to drop back. **to let drop** to disclose, seemingly without any intention of so doing. **drop curtain** *n.* a drop scene. **drop-dead gorgeous** *a.* (*sl.*) stunningly attractive. **drop goal** *n.* a goal scored in rugby with a dropkick. **drophandlebars** *n.pl.* curving, lowered handlebars on a bicycle. **drophead** *n.* the folding roof of a convertible car. **drop-in centre** *n.* a day centre, usu. run by the social services, where clients may call informally for advice etc. **drop in the ocean, drop in a bucket** *n.* a proportionately tiny amount. **drop kick** *n.* in rugby, a kick made by letting the ball drop and kicking it on the rise. **drop-leaf** *a.* (of a table) having a hinged flap which can be lowered or raised. **droplet** *n.* **drop-off** *n.* **1** the act of dropping someone or something off. **2** a decrease. **3** (*N Am.*) a sheer cliff or slope. **drop-out** *n.* (*coll.*) a person who rejects

conventional society. **dropper** *n.* **1** a person who or something which drops. **2** a small glass tube with a rubber bulb at one end, for administering medicinal drops. **3** (*Austral., New Zeal., S Afr.*) a vertical stave in a fence. **droppings** *n.pl.* **1** something which falls or has fallen in drops. **2** the dung of animals or birds. **drop scene** *n.* a painted curtain suspended on pulleys which is let down to conceal the stage in a theatre. **drop scone** *n.* a small, thick pancake cooked on a hot griddle. **drop shot** *n.* a shot in tennis, squash or badminton which falls to the ground immediately after crossing the net or hitting the wall.

dropsy (drop´si) *n.* (*pl.* **dropsies**) **1** oedema. **2** (*sl.*) a tip, a bribe. **dropsical** *a.* **dropsically** *adv.*

drosophila (drosof´ilə) *n.* (*pl.* **drosophilas**) any of the small fruit flies of the genus *Drosophilia,* used in laboratory genetic experiments.

dross (dros) *n.* **1** the scum or useless matter left from the melting of metals. **2** anything utterly useless, refuse, rubbish. **3** anything impure. **drossy** *a.* (*comp.* **drossier,** *superl.* **drossiest**).

drought (drowt), (*Sc., Ir., N Am., poet.*) **†drouth** (drooth, drowth) *n.* **1** dryness, dry weather; long-continued rainless weather. **2** an absence of rain or moisture. **3** a protracted lack of something. **droughty** *a.* (*comp.* **droughtier,** *superl.* **droughtiest**).

drove[1] DRIVE.

drove[2] (drōv) *n.* **1** a collection of animals driven in a body. **2** a road for driving cattle on. **3** a shoal, a crowd, a mass of people, esp. when moving together. **drover** *n.* a person who drives cattle or sheep to market; a cattle-dealer.

drown (drown) *v.i.* **1** to be suffocated in water or other liquid. **2** to perish in this manner. *~v.t.* **1** to suffocate by submersion in water or other liquid. **2** to submerge, to drench, to overwhelm with water, to overflow, to deluge. **3** to overpower (by a volume of sound). **4** to overwhelm, to quench, to put an end to.

drowse (drowz) *v.i.* **1** to be sleepy or half asleep. **2** to doze. *~v.t.* **1** to make drowsy. **2** to spend (time) in an idle or sluggish way. *~n.* **1** the state of being half asleep. **2** drowsiness, heaviness. **drowsy** *a.* (*comp.* **drowsier,** *superl.* **drowsiest**) **1** inclined to sleep, sleepy. **2** disposing to sleep. **drowsiness** *n.*

drub (drŭb) *v.t.* (*pres.p.* **drubbing,** *past, p.p.* **drubbed**) **1** to beat with a stick; to cudgel. **2** to beat thoroughly in a fight or contest. **to drub into** to instil into.

drudge (drŭj) *n.* **1** a person employed in menial work. **2** a person who toils at uncongenial work and is ill-paid; a slave; a hack. *~v.i.* to perform menial work; to work hard with little reward; to slave. **drudger** *n.* a drudge. **drudgery** *n.* **drudgingly** *adv.*

drug (drŭg) *n.* **1** any substance, mineral, vegetable or animal, used as the basis or as an ingredient in medical preparations. **2** a narcotic causing addiction. *~v.t.* (*pres.p.* **drugging,** *past,* *p.p.* **drugged) 1** to mix drugs with, esp. to make narcotic. **2** to administer drugs, esp. narcotics, to. **3** to render insensible with drugs. **4** (*fig.*) to deaden. ~*v.i.* to take drugs, esp. narcotics. **drug addict, drug fiend** *n.* a person who is addicted to the use of narcotics. **druggist** *n.* (*N Am.*) a pharmaceutical chemist. **druggy, druggie** *n.* (*pl.* **druggies**) (*coll.*) a drug addict. ~*a.* of or relating to drugs, esp. narcotics. **drug pusher** *n.* a person who sells narcotic drugs illegally. **drug squad** *n.* a division of a police force which investigates drug-related crime. **drugstore** *n.* (*N Am.*) a chemist's shop where pharmaceuticals and other small articles are sold, often including refreshments.

drugget (drŭg´it) *n.* **1** a coarse woollen fabric, felted or woven, used as a covering or as a substitute for carpet. **2** a covering or carpet made of drugget.

Druid (droo´id) *n.* **1** one of the priests or teachers of the early Gauls and Britons or perh. of pre-Celtic peoples, who taught the transmigrating of souls, frequently celebrated their rites in oak groves, and are alleged to have offered human sacrifices. **2** an officer of the Welsh Gorsedd. **3** a member of any of several movements trying to revive Druidic practices. **Druidess** *n.* **Druidic** (-id´-), **Druidical** *a.* **Druidism** *n.*

drum¹ (drŭm) *n.* **1** a musical instrument made by stretching parchment over the head of a hollow cylinder or hemisphere. **2** (*often pl.*) a drummer or the percussion section of an orchestra. **3** the sound of a drum beating, or a sound resembling this. **4** (*Anat.*) the tympanum or hollow part of the middle ear. **5** the membrane across this. **6** anything drum-shaped, esp. a small cylindrical box for holding fruit, fish etc. **7** (*Archit.*) **a** the solid part of the Corinthian and the composite capitals. **b** the cylindrical block forming part of a column. **8** in machinery, a revolving cylinder over which a belt or band passes. **9** any sea fish of the family Sciaenidae, which emits a drumming or grunting noise. ~*v.i.* (*pres.p.* **drumming,** *past, p.p.* **drummed) 1** to beat or play a tune on a drum. **2** to beat rapidly or thump, on a table, the floor, a piano etc. **3** (of certain insects, birds etc.) to make a sound like the beating of a drum. **4** (*N Am.*) to tout for customers. ~*v.t.* **1** to perform on a drum. **2** to beat rapidly or thump one's fingers etc. on a table, the floor, a piano etc. **3** to summon. **to drum into** to instil into. **to drum out** (*Mil.*) to expel from a regiment with disgrace; to cashier. **to drum up** to canvass (aid or support). **drumbeat** *n.* the sound made by a beating drum. **drum brake** *n.* a type of brake with shoes which rub against a brake drum. **drumfire** *n.* **1** (*Mil.*) rapid, continuous gunfire. **2** a hail of criticism or complaints. **drumfish** *n.* any sea fish of the family Sciaenidae, which emits a drumming or grunting noise. **drumhead** *n.* **1** the membrane stretched at the top of a drum. **2** the membrane across the drum of the ear. **3** the top of the

capstan. **drum kit** *n.* a set of drums and cymbals. **drum machine** *n.* an electronic device programmed to reproduce the sound of drums and other percussion instruments. **drum major** *n.* a non-commissioned officer in charge of the drums of a regiment, or who leads the band on the march. **drum majorette** *n.* (*esp. N Am.*) a girl or young woman who marches in a procession dressed in a uniform and twirling a baton. **drummer** *n.* **1** a person who performs on a drum or a drum kit. **2** (*esp. N Am., coll.*) a commercial traveller. **3** (*sl.*) a thief. **4** the member of an orchestra in charge of the percussion instruments. **drumstick** *n.* **1** the stick with which a drum is beaten. **2** anything resembling such a stick, esp. the leg of a cooked fowl.

drum² (drŭm), **drumlin** (-lin) *n.* (*Geol.*) a long, narrow ridge of drift or alluvial formation. **drumlinoid** *n.*

drunk (drŭngk) *a.* **1** intoxicated, stupefied or overcome with alcoholic liquors. **2** inebriated, highly excited (with joy etc.). ~*n.* (*sl.*) **1** a habitually drunken person. **2** a period of drunkenness. **drunkard** (-kəd) *n.* a person who is habitually or frequently drunk. **drunken** *a.* **1** habitually intoxicated; given to drunkenness. **2** caused by drunkenness. **3** characterized by intoxication. **drunkenly** *adv.* **drunkenness** *n.*

drupe (droop) *n.* a fleshy fruit containing a stone with a kernel, such as the peach or plum. **drupaceous** (droopā´shəs) *a.* **drupel** (droo´pəl), **drupelet** (droop´lit) *n.* a succulent fruit formed by an aggregation of small drupes, for example the raspberry.

dry (drī) *a.* (*comp.* **drier,** *superl.* **driest) 1** devoid of moisture. **2** arid. **3** without sap or juice, not succulent. **4** lacking rain, having an insufficient rainfall. **5** thirsty. **6** dried up, removed by evaporation, draining or wiping. **7** not giving milk. **8** not yielding juice. **9** (of land, a shore etc.) not under water. **10** (of wine etc.) not sweet. **11** (of bread) without butter. **12** (of groceries etc.) not liquid. **13** prohibiting by law the sale of alcoholic liquors. **14** (esp. of an addict) not drinking alcohol or taking drugs. **15** (*fig.*) lifeless, insipid, lacking interest, dull. **16** meagre, bare, plain. **17** sarcastic, cynical, ironical, sly. **18** without sympathy or cordiality, cold, discouraging, harsh. ~*n.* (*pl.* **dries) 1** the act of drying. **2** a dry place (*the dry*). ~*v.t.* (*3rd pers. sing. pres.* **dries,** *pres.p.* **drying,** *past, p.p.* **dried) 1** to free from or deprive of water or moisture. **2** to deprive of juice, sap or succulence. **3** to drain, to wipe. **4** to cause to cease yielding milk. ~*v.i.* **1** to lose or be deprived of moisture. **2** to grow dry. **3** to cease yielding milk. **4** (of an actor) to forget one's lines. **to dry out 1** to become dry. **2** to undergo treatment for alcohol or drug abuse. **to dry up 1** to deprive totally of moisture. **2** to dry dishes after they have been washed. **3** (of moisture) to disappear. **4** to cease to flow, to cease to yield water. **5** (of an actor) to forget one's lines. **6** (*sl.*) to stop talking or doing something. **dry battery** *n.* a battery made up of dry cells. **dry cell** *n.* a battery cell in which the electrolyte is a paste and not a fluid. **dry-clean** *v.t.* to clean with a petrol-based solvent or other detergent. ~*v.i.* to be suitable for cleaning with a petrol-based solvent or other detergent. **dry-cleaner** *n.* **dry cough** *n.* a cough which does not produce phlegm. **dry dock** *n.* a dock which can be emptied of water for ship repairs. **dry-dock** *v.t.* to put in dry dock. **dryer, drier** *n.* 1 an apparatus for drying the hair, hands, clothes etc. after washing. 2 a clothes horse. 3 a material added to oil paints and printers' ink to make them dry. **dry-eyed** *a.* not shedding tears. **dry fly** *n.* an angler's fly which floats on the surface, as distinguished from one that is allowed to sink. **dry-goods** *n.pl.* 1 any non-liquid goods. 2 (*N Am.*) cloths, silks, drapery, haberdashery etc., as distinguished from groceries. **dry ice** *n.* solid carbon dioxide used in refrigeration. **dry-ish** *a.* **dry land** *n.* land, as distinguished from the sea. **dryly** DRILY. **dry measure** *n.* a measure for dry goods, for example a bushel. **dry milk** *n.* (*N Am.*) dried milk. **dryness** *n.* **dry-nurse** *n.* a nurse who rears a child without breastfeeding. **dry plate** *n.* a photographic plate with a hard, dry, sensitized film, adapted for storing and carrying about. **dry-point** *n.* 1 a needle for engraving on a copper plate without acid. 2 an engraving so produced. **dry rot** *n.* 1 decay in timber caused by fungi which reduce it to a dry brittle mass. 2 the fungi which cause dry rot. **dry run** *n.* (*coll.*) a practice run, a rehearsal. **dry-shod** *a., adv.* without wetting the feet. **dry slope** *n.* an artificial ski slope used for practising. **drystone** *a.* (of a wall) built without mortar. **drywall** *n.* (*esp. N Am.*) a plasterboard.

dryad (drī'əd) *n.* (*pl.* **dryads**) in mythology, a nymph of the woods.

DSC *abbr.* Distinguished Service Cross.

D.Sc. *abbr.* Doctor of Science.

DSM *abbr.* Distinguished Service Medal.

DSO *abbr.* Distinguished Service Order.

DT *abbr.* delirium tremens.

DTP *abbr.* desktop publishing.

DT's, DTs *abbr.* delirium tremens.

dual (dū'əl) *a.* 1 consisting of two. 2 twofold, binary, double. 3 (*Gram.*) expressing two (applied to an inflection of a verb, adjective, pronoun or noun, which, in certain languages, expresses two persons or things, as distinct from the plural which expresses more than two). ~*n.* (*Gram.*) a dual form. **dual carriageway** *n.* a road which has at least two lanes in each direction, with traffic travelling in opposite directions separated by a central reservation. **dual control** *a.* able to be operated by either of two people. **dual in-line package** *n.* DIP. **dualism** *n.* 1 duality, the state of being twofold. 2 (*Theol.*) a system or theory based on a radical duality of nature or animating principle, for example mind and matter, good and evil in the universe, divine and human personalities in

Christ, independence of the cerebral hemispheres. **dualist** *n.* **dualistic** (-lis'-) *a.* **dualistically** *adv.* **duality** (-al'-) *n.* (*pl.* **dualities**). **dualize, dualise** *v.t.* **dually** *adv.* **dual personality** *n.* a psychological condition in which a single person has two distinct characters. **dual-purpose** *a.* having, or intended for, two separate purposes.

dub[1] (dŭb) *v.t.* (*pres.p.* **dubbing**, *past, p.p.* **dubbed**) 1 to confer knighthood upon by a tap with a sword on the shoulder. 2 to confer any dignity, rank, character or nickname upon. 3 to dress or trim. 4 to smear (leather) with grease so as to soften.

dub[2] (dŭb) *v.t.* (*pres.p.* **dubbing**, *past, p.p.* **dubbed**) 1 to give a new soundtrack, esp. in a different language, to (a film). 2 to add (music etc.) to a film. 3 to combine (soundtracks). 4 to make a copy of (a recording). **dubbing**[1] *n.*

dubbin (dŭb'in) *n.* a preparation of grease for preserving and softening leather. ~*v.t.* to put dubbin on (boots and shoes). **dubbing**[2] *n.* dubbin.

dubious (dū'biəs) *a.* 1 undetermined; doubtful; wavering in mind. 2 of uncertain result or issue. 3 questionable. 4 open to suspicion. **dubiety** (-bī'ə-) *n.* (*pl.* **dubieties**). **dubiously** *adv.* **dubiousness** *n.*

dubitation (dūbitā'shən) *n.* doubt, hesitation, uncertainty. **dubitative** (dū'bitətiv) *a.* 1 tending to doubt. 2 expressing doubt. **dubitatively** *adv.*

Dublin Bay prawn (dŭb'lin) *n.* 1 a Norway lobster. 2 a large prawn, usu. cooked as scampi.

ducal (dū'kəl) *a.* of or relating to a duke or duchy. **ducally** *adv.*

ducat (dŭk'ət) *n.* (*Hist.*) a coin, of gold or silver, formerly current in several European countries.

duchess (dŭch'is) *n.* 1 the wife or widow of a duke. 2 a woman who holds a duchy in her own right. 3 (*coll.*) a woman of imposing appearance. **duchesse** (dooshes', dŭch'is) *n.* 1 a heavy satin. 2 a dressing table with a tilting mirror. **duchy** *n.* (*pl.* **duchies**) 1 the territory, jurisdiction or dominions of a duke. 2 the royal dukedom of Cornwall or Lancaster.

duck[1] (dŭk) *n.* (*pl.* **duck, ducks**) 1 a web-footed waterbird of the family Anatidae, esp. the domestic duck. 2 the female of this species, as distinct from a **drake**. 3 duck flesh, eaten as food. 4 (*coll.*) darling. 5 in cricket, a score of nothing. **like water off a duck's back** (*coll.*) completely without effect. **to play ducks and drakes with** to squander. **to take to (something) like a duck to water** to discover a natural aptitude for (something). **duckbill** *n.* a duck-billed platypus. **duck-billed** *a.* having a bill like a duck. **duck-billed platypus** *n.* PLATYPUS. **duck board** *n.* (*usu. pl.*) planking used to cover muddy roads or paths. **duckling** *n.* a young duck. **ducks** *n.* (*coll.*) a term of familiarity or endearment. **ducks and drakes** *n.* a game of making a flat stone skip along the surface of water. **duck soup** *n.* (*N Am.*) anything easy to do. **duckweed** *n.* any of several floating waterweeds of the genus *Lemna*, which are eaten by duck and geese. **ducky** *n.* (*pl.* **duckies**) (*coll.*) a term of familiarity or endearment. ~*a.* sweet, delightful.

duck² (dŭk) *v.i.* **1** to dive, dip or plunge under water. **2** to bob the head. **3** to bow. **4** in bridge, to lose a trick by deliberately playing a low card when holding a higher one. ~*v.t.* **1** to dip under water and suddenly withdraw. **2** to bob (the head). **3** (*coll.*) to avoid (a responsibility etc.). ~*n.* **1** a quick plunge or dip under water. **2** a bob or sudden lowering of the head. **to duck out of** (*coll.*) to dodge (a responsibility etc.). **ducker** *n.*

duck³ (dŭk) *n.* **1** a kind of untwilled linen or cotton fabric, lighter and finer than canvas, used for jackets, aprons etc. **2** (*pl.*) trousers or a suit made of this.

duct (dŭkt) *n.* **1** a tube, canal or passage by which a fluid is conveyed. **2** (*Anat.*) a tubular passage for conveying chyle, lymph and other fluids. **3** (*Bot.*) a canal or elongated cell holding water, air etc. ~*v.t.* to convey by means of a duct. **ducting** *n.* **1** a system of ducts. **2** material in the form of ducts. **ductless** *a.* **ductless gland** *n.* an endocrine gland.

ductile (dŭk´tīl) *a.* **1** able to be drawn out into threads or wire; malleable, not brittle. **2** capable of being moulded, plastic. **3** (*fig.*) pliant, tractable, yielding to persuasion or advice. **ductility** (-til´-), **ductileness** *n.*

dud (dŭd) *n.* **1** (*sl.*) a useless person or thing. **2** a counterfeit coin or cheque; a forgery. **3** a shell that has failed to explode. ~*a.* **1** useless, worthless. **2** counterfeit. **duds** *n.pl.* clothes.

dude (dūd) *n.* **1** a fop, an affected person; an aesthete. **2** (*NAm.*) a city-bred person, esp. one having a holiday on a dude ranch. **3** a man, a guy (*a cool dude*). **dude ranch** *n.* (*NAm.*) a ranch run as a pleasure resort by city people. **dudish** *a.*

dudgeon (dŭj´ən) *n.* anger, sullen resentment, indignation. **in high dudgeon** angry or resentful.

due (dū) *a.* **1** owed, owing, that ought to be paid, rendered or done to someone. **2** claimable, proper, suitable, appropriate. **3** expected, appointed to arrive, calculated to happen. **4** ascribable, that may be attributed (to). **5** planned or arranged. ~*adv.* exactly, directly. ~*n.* **1** what is owed or owing to one. **2** what one owes. **3** a debt, an obligation, tribute, toll, fee or other legal exaction. **due to** because of. **in due course** when the right time comes. **to become due** to fall due. **to fall due** to become payable; to mature as a bill. **to give someone their due** to be fair to someone. **due date** *n.* the date by which a payment must be made.

Usage note It is best to avoid the use of *due to* for 'because of' (as a compound preposition): *The delay was due to the weather* is generally acceptable, but *They were delayed due to the weather* is not.

duel (dū´əl) *n.* **1** (*Hist.*) a combat between two persons with deadly weapons to decide a private

quarrel, usu. an affair of honour. **2** any contest or struggle between two persons, parties, causes, animals etc. ~*v.i.* (*pres.p.* **duelling**, (*NAm.*) **dueling**, *past, p.p.* **duelled**, (*NAm.*) **dueled**) to fight in a duel; to contest. **dueller**, (*NAm.*) **dueler** *n.* **duellist**, (*NAm.*) **duelist** *n.*

✖ **duely** common misspelling of DULY.

duenna (dūen´ə) *n.* (*pl.* **duennas**) an elderly woman employed as companion and governess to young women, a chaperone.

duet (dūet´) *n.* **1** (*Mus.*) a composition for two performers, vocal or instrumental. **2** any performance by two people. **3** a dialogue. ~*v.i.* (*pres.p.* **duetting**, *past, p.p.* **duetted**) to perform a duet. **duettist** *n.*

duff¹ (dŭf) *n.* (*dial., coll.*) a stiff, flour pudding boiled in a bag.

duff² (dŭf) *v.t.* (*sl.*) **1** in golf, to bungle (a shot). **2** (*Austral.*) to steal (cattle) by altering the brands. ~*a.* useless, not working. **to duff up** to beat up.

duffel (dŭf´əl), **duffle** *n.* **1** a thick, coarse kind of woollen cloth, with a thick nap. **2** (*NAm.*) a camper's change of clothes, outfit, kit. **duffel bag** *n.* a cylindrical, canvas bag with a drawstring used to close it and carry it. **duffel coat** *n.* a three-quarter-length coat usu. made from duffel, hooded and fastened with toggles.

duffer (dŭf´ə) *n.* **1** (*sl.*) a stupid, awkward or useless person. **2** (*Austral., sl.*) a person who steals cattle. **3** (*Austral., sl.*) an unproductive mine.

dug¹ (dŭg) *a.* that has been dug. **dugout** *n.* **1** a canoe made of a single log hollowed out, or of parts of two logs thus hollowed out and afterwards joined together. **2** a cellar, cave or shelter used as a protection against enemy shelling. **3** the enclosure at a sports ground occupied by the manager, trainer and reserve players.

dug² (dŭg) *n.* **1** a teat, a nipple of an animal. **2** (*derog.*) a woman's breast.

dugong (doo´gong) *n.* (*pl.* **dugong, dugongs**) a large herbivorous aquatic mammal, *Dugong dugon*, with two forelimbs only, belonging to the Sirenia, and inhabiting the Indian seas.

duiker (dī´kə), **duyker** *n.* **1** any of several small African antelopes of the genus *Cephalophus*. **2** a southern African cormorant, *Phalacrocorax africanus*.

duke (dūk) *n.* **1** a noble holding the highest hereditary rank outside the royal family. **2** the sovereign prince of a duchy. **3** (*pl., sl.*) fists; hands. **4** a cross between the sweet cherry and the sour cherry. **dukedom** *n.* the territory, title or rank of a duke.

dulcet (dŭl´sit) *a.* sweet to the ear.

dulcimer (dŭl´simə) *n.* a musical instrument with strings of wire, which are struck with rods.

dull (dŭl) *a.* **1** slow of understanding; stupid, not quick in perception. **2** without sensibility. **3** blunt, obtuse. **4** not sharp or acute. **5** lacking keenness in any of the senses. **6** sluggish, inert, slow of movement. **7** not bright, dim, tarnished. **8** cloudy, overcast, gloomy, depressing. **9** uninteresting, tedious, wearisome. **10** hard of hearing, deaf. **11** not loud or clear. ~*v.t.***1** to make dull or stupid. **2** to stupefy. **3** to make blunt. **4** to render less acute, sensitive, interesting or effective. **5** to make heavy or sluggish, to deaden. **6** to tarnish, to dim. ~*v.i.* to become dull, blunt, stupid or inert. **dullard** (-ləd) *n.* a blockhead; a dunce. **dullish** *a.* **dullness, dulness** *n.* **dully** *adv.*

dulse (dŭls) *n.* an edible kind of seaweed, *Rhodymenia palmata.*

duly (dū′li) *adv.* **1** in a suitable manner; properly; becomingly; regularly. **2** punctually.

dumb (dŭm) *a.* **1** unable to utter articulate sounds. **2** unable to speak, esp. through deafness or some other physical cause. **3** silent, (temporarily) speechless. **4** refraining from speaking, reticent, taciturn. **5** soundless. **6** (*coll.*) stupid, unintelligent. **7** having no say. **8** (*Comput.*) able only to transmit or receive data, not able to be programmed, as distinct from *intelligent.* ~*v.t.* to make dumb; to silence. **to dumb down** (*N Am., sl.*) to bring or come down to a lower level of understanding. **dumb-bell** *n.* **1** one of a pair of weights connected by a short bar or handle, swung in the hand for exercise. **2** (*sl.*) a stupid person. **dumbly** *adv.* **dumbness** *n.* **dumbo** *n.* (*pl.* **dumbos**) (*sl.*) a stupid person. **dumbshow** *n.* **1** gestures without speech. **2** part of a play acted in pantomime. **dumbstruck** *a.* temporarily shocked into silence. **dumb waiter** *n.* **1** a movable framework for conveying food etc. from one room to another, a service lift. **2** a dining-room apparatus with revolving shelves for holding dishes etc.

Usage note Using *dumb* to refer to a person unable to speak through deafness etc. can give offence, and is best avoided.

dumbfound (dŭm′fownd), **dumfound** *v.t.* to strike dumb; to confound, to confuse, to perplex, to astound.

dumdum (dŭm′dŭm), **dumdum bullet** *n.* a soft-nosed expanding bullet that lacerates the flesh.

dummy (dŭm′i) *n.* (*pl.* **dummies**) **1** a ventriloquist's doll. **2** a figure for showing off clothes in a shop window. **3** a figure used as a target in shooting practice. **4** any sham article. **5** a prototype of a book. **6** a feigned pass in rugby or football. **7** (*coll.*) a stupid person. **8** (*derog., sl.*) a person who cannot speak. **9** a person who is a mere tool of another person. **10** a rubber teat for a baby to suck. **11** in bridge, the hand of the declarer's partner, exposed after the first lead, or the declarer's partner. **12** (*Mil.*) a blank round of ammunition, used for training. ~*a.* counterfeit, feigned. ~*v.t.* (*3rd pers. sing. pres.* **dummies**, *pres.p.* **dummying**, *past, p.p.* **dummied**) to pretend to pass (the ball) in rugby or football. ~*v.i.* to feign a pass in rugby or football. **to dummy up** (*N Am., sl.*) to say nothing. **to sell a dummy** to

feign a pass or move in rugby or football. **dummy run** *n.* a trial run, a rehearsal.

dump (dŭmp) *n.* **1** a pile of refuse. **2** a place for depositing rubbish. **3** (*coll.*) an unpleasant place, esp. a house. **4** an army storage depot. **5** a pile of earth or ore. **6** (*Comput.*) the act of dumping computer data. ~*v.t.* **1** to put down carelessly. **2** to unload. **3** to dispose of. **4** (*coll.*) to end a relationship with. **5** (*Mil.*) to leave (ammunition) in a dump. **6** to send (surplus produce, esp. manufactured goods that are unsaleable at home) to a foreign market for sale at a low price. **7** to get rid of (unwanted) things or people. **8** (*Comput.*) to record (the data on an internal computer memory) on an external storage device during a computer run. **to dump on** (*esp. N Am.*) to treat badly. **dumper** *n.* **1** a person who or something which dumps. **2** a vehicle which tips up at the back to dump its load. **3** (*Austral., New Zeal.*) a heavy wave dangerous to swimmers. **dumper truck, dump truck, dump wagon** *n.* a vehicle which tips up at the back to dump its load.

dumpling (dŭmp′ling) *n.* **1** a mass of dough or pudding, boiled or baked, often enclosing fruit etc. **2** a short, fat person.

dumps (dŭmps) *n.pl.* sadness, depression, melancholy. **in the dumps** low-spirited, depressed.

dumpy (dŭm′pi) *a.* (*comp.* **dumpier**, *superl.* **dumpiest**) short and thick; plump. **dumpily** *adv.* **dumpiness** *n.*

dun[1] (dŭn) *a.* (*comp.* **dunner**, *superl.* **dunnest**) **1** of a dull brown or brownish-grey colour. **2** (*poet.*) dark, gloomy. ~*n.* **1** a dun colour. **2** a dun horse.

dun[2] (dŭn) *v.t.* (*pres.p.* **dunning**, *past, p.p.* **dunned**) **1** to demand payment from with persistence. **2** to press, to plague, to pester. ~*n.* **1** a creditor who presses persistently for payment. **2** a debt-collector. **3** an importunate demand for the payment of a debt.

dunce (dŭns) *n.* a stupid person, a person who is slow in learning. **dunce's cap** *n.* a conical paper cap formerly worn by a school pupil to indicate slowness of learning.

dunderhead (dŭn′dəhed) *n.* a stupid person. **dunderheaded** *a.*

dune (dūn) *n.* a hill, mound or ridge of sand on the seashore. **dune buggy** *n.* a beach buggy.

dung (dŭng) *n.* **1** the excrement of animals; manure. **2** anything filthy. ~*v.t.* to manure or dress with dung. ~*v.i.* to void excrement. **dung-beetle** *n.* a beetle of the family Scarabaeidae, the larvae of which develop in dung. **dung-fly** *n.* a two-winged fly of the family Scatophagidae, which feeds upon dung. **dunghill, dungheap** *n.* **1** a heap of dung. **2** an accumulation of dung and refuse in a farmyard. **3** (*fig.*) a filthy place. **dungworm** *n.* a worm or larva found in dung and used as bait for fish.

dungaree (dŭng·gərē′) *n.* **1** a coarse kind of calico used for overalls. **2** (*pl.*) trousers with a bib.

dungeon (dŭn´jən) *n*. a prison or place of confinement, esp. one that is dark and underground.

dunk (dŭngk) *v.t.* **1** to dip (a cake or biscuit) in what one is drinking, e.g. tea or coffee. **2** to dip, to immerse.

dunlin (dŭn´lin) *n*. a small sandpiper, *Calidira alpina*, a common shorebird.

dunnage (dŭn´ij) *n*. **1** (*Naut*.) loose wood, faggots, boughs etc., laid in the hold to raise the cargo above the bilge-water, or wedged between the cargo to keep it from rolling when stowed. **2** (*coll*.) assorted luggage.

dunno (dənō´) *contr*. (*coll*.) (I) don't know.

dunnock (dŭn´ək) *n*. the hedge sparrow, *Prunella modularis* (from its colour).

duo (dū´ō) *n*. (*pl*. **duos**) **1** a pair of performers who work together. **2** (*Mus*.) a duet.

duodecimal (dūōdes´iməl) *a*. proceeding in computation by twelves (applied to a scale of notation in which the local value of the digits increases twelvefold as they proceed from right to left). ~*n*. **1** the duodecimal system. **2** duodecimal notation. **duodecimally** *adv*. **duodecimo** *n*. (*pl*. **duodecimos**) **1** a book consisting of sheets of twelve leaves or 24 pages. **2** the size of such a book (written 12mo and called 'twelvemo').

duodenary (dūōdē´nəri) *a*. **1** of or relating to the number twelve. **2** proceeding by twelves.

duodenum (dūōdē´nəm) *n*. (*pl*. **duodenums**) the first portion of the small intestine (so called from being about the length of twelve fingers' breadths). **duodenal** *a*. **duodenitis** (-ī´tis) *n*.

duologue (dū´əlog) *n*. **1** a dialogue for two persons. **2** a dramatic composition for two actors.

duopoly (dūop´əli) *n*. (*pl*. **duopolies**) an exclusive trading right enjoyed by two companies.

duotone (dū´ətōn) *n*. **1** an illustration in two tones or colours. **2** the process of producing a duotone. ~*a*. in two tones or colours.

dupe (dūp) *n*. a person who is easily deceived; a credulous person. ~*v.t.* to trick, to cheat, to make a dupe of. **dupable** *a*. **duper** *n*. **dupery** (-əri) *n*.

dupion (dū´piən) *n*. **1** a double cocoon formed by two or more silkworms. **2** silk made from such cocoons. **3** an imitation of this silk.

duple (dū´pəl) *a*. **1** double, twofold. **2** (*Mus*.) having two beats to the bar. **duple ratio** *n*. the ratio of two to one, six to three etc. **duplet** *n*. (*Mus*.) two equal notes played in the time of three. **duple time** *n*. musical time with two beats to the bar.

duplex (dū´pleks) *n*. (*NAm*.) a duplex apartment or house. ~*a*. double, twofold. **duplex apartment** *n*. (*NAm*.) a two-storey apartment. **duplex house** *n*. (*NAm*.) a house split into two dwellings.

duplicate[1] (dū´plikət) *a*. **1** double, twofold, existing in two parts exactly corresponding. **2** corresponding exactly with another. ~*n*. **1** one of two things exactly similar in material and form. **2** a reproduction, a replica, a copy. **3** (*Law*) a copy of an original legal document having equal binding

force. **4** a form of bridge or whist in which the players keep the hands that they are dealt and the same hands are played by different players in turn. **in duplicate** in the original plus a copy. **duplicate bridge** *n*. a form of bridge in which the players keep the hands they are dealt and the same hands are played by different players in turn. **duplicate ratio** *n*. the ratio of the squares of two numbers. **duplicate whist** *n*. a form of whist in which the players keep the hands they are dealt and the same hands are played by different players in turn.

duplicate[2] (dū´plikāt) *v.t.* **1** to make or be a reproduction of. **2** to double. **3** to make in duplicate. **4** to make copies of on a machine. **5** to do twice, esp. unnecessarily. **duplicable** (-plikəbəl) *a*. **duplication** (-ā´shən) *n*. **duplicator** *n*. a machine for duplicating typescript.

duplicity (dūplis´iti) *n*. double-dealing, dissimulation. **duplicitous** *a*.

dura DURRA.

durable (dūə´rəbəl) *a*. **1** having the quality of endurance or continuance. **2** lasting, permanent, firm, stable. **durability** (-bil´-) *n*. **durableness** *n*. **durably** *adv*.

dura mater (dūərə mā´tə) *n*. (*Anat*.) the first of three lining membranes of the brain and spinal cord.

duramen (dūrā´men) *n*. the heartwood or central wood in the trunk of exogenous trees.

duration (dūrā´shən) *n*. **1** continuance. **2** length of time of continuance. **3** power of continuance. **4** a specific length of time. **for the duration** (*sl*.) so long as a situation or war lasts.

durbar (dœ´bah) *n*. (*Hist*.) **1** an Indian ruler's court. **2** a state reception by an Indian ruler or by a British governor.

duress (dūres´) *n*. **1** constraint, compulsion, restraint of liberty, imprisonment. **2** (*Law*) restraint of liberty or threat of violence to compel a person to do some act of exculpation by one who has been so restrained or threatened.

Durex® (dūə´reks) *n*. a condom.

durian (dūə´riən) *n*. **1** a large tree, *Durio zibethinus*, grown in the Malay archipelago. **2** the globular pulpy fruit of this.

duricrust (dūə´rikrŭst) *n*. (*Geol*.) a hard, mineral crust found near the surface of soil in semi-arid regions.

during (dūə´ring) *prep*. **1** in or within the time of. **2** throughout the course or existence of.

durmast (dœ´mahst) *n*. a Eurasian oak, *Quercus petraea*.

durn DARN[2].

durned DARNED (under DARN[2]).

durra (dur´ə), **dari** (dah´ri), **dura, dhurra, doura** *n*. a kind of sorghum, *Sorghum bicolor*, cultivated for grain and fodder.

durrie (dŭr´i), **dhurrie** *n*. a coarse cotton fabric, made in squares, and used in the Indian subcontinent for carpets, curtains, coverings for furniture etc.

durum (dūə´rəm) *n.* a variety of spring wheat, *Triticum durum*, with a high gluten content, used mainly for the manufacture of pasta.

dusk (dŭsk) *n.* **1** shade, gloom. **2** partial darkness, twilight. **dusky** *a.* (*comp.* **duskier,** *superl.* **duskiest**) **1** dark. **2** shadowy. **duskily** *adv.* **duskiness** *n.*

dust (dŭst) *n.* **1** earth or other matter reduced to such small particles as to be easily raised and carried about by the air. **2** a stirring of such fine particles. **3** household refuse. **4** pollen. **5** the decomposed bodies of the dead. **6** the ground. **7** a low or despised condition. **8** turmoil, excitement, confusion, commotion, a row. ~*v.t.* **1** to brush or sweep away the dust from. **2** to sprinkle or cover with powdered chocolate, icing sugar etc. **3** to make dusty. **4** to clean by brushing or beating. ~*v.i.* to dust furniture or a room. **to bite the dust 1** to fail. **2** to die. **to dust down 1** to remove dust from. **2** (*coll.*) to scold, to reprimand. **3** to dust off. **to dust off 1** to remove dust from. **2** to reuse (an old idea or plan). **dust and ashes** *n.pl.* something disappointing. **dust-bath** *n.* the rubbing of dust into their feathers by birds, prob. to get rid of parasites. **dustbin** *n.* a receptacle for household refuse. **dust bowl** *n.* an area reduced to aridity by drought and overcropping. **dustcart** *n.* a vehicle for removing refuse from houses, streets etc. **dust cover** *n.* **1** a dust sheet. **2** a dust jacket. **duster** *n.* **1** a cloth used to remove dust. **2** a person who dusts. **dust jacket** *n.* a protective printed paper cover for a book. **dustless** *a.* **dustman** *n.* (*pl.* **dustmen**) **1** a person whose occupation is to remove refuse from dustbins. **2** a sandman. **dustpan** *n.* a small container into which dust is swept. **dust sheet** *n.* a sheet thrown over furniture while a room is being dusted or while it is unused. **dust storm** *n.* a windstorm which whips up clouds of dust as it travels through arid areas. **dust-trap** *n.* an object on which dust gathers. **dust-up** *n.* (*coll.*) a row, a heated quarrel, a fight. **dust-wrapper** *n.* a dust jacket. **dusty** *a.* (*comp.* **dustier,** *superl.* **dustiest**) **1** covered with or full of dust. **2** like dust. **3** dull, uninteresting. **4** (of a colour) dull. **not so dusty** (*sl.*) pretty good. **dustily** *adv.* **dustiness** *n.* **dusty answer** *n.* an unsatisfactory or bad-tempered response. **dusty miller** *n.* **1** any of various plants, esp. *Artemisia stelleriana*, whose leaves and flowers have a dusty appearance. **2** an artificial fly for fishing.

Dutch (dŭch) *a.* **1** of or relating to the Netherlands. **2** (*S Afr.*) of Dutch origin. **3** (*N Am., sl.*) of German extraction. ~*n.* **1** the language of the Netherlands. **2** (*S Afr., derog.*) Afrikaans. **3** (*as pl.*) **a** the people of the Netherlands. **b** (*S Afr.*) Afrikaans-speaking people. **to go Dutch** to share the cost of an outing. **Dutch auction** *n.* an auction sale in which the auctioneer keeps reducing prices until a buyer is found. **Dutch bargain** *n.* a bargain concluded over a glass of liquor. **Dutch barn** *n.* a barn for storage, with open sides and a steel frame supporting a curved roof. **Dutch cap** *n.* **1** a moulded rubber cap fitting over the cervix to act as a contraceptive barrier. **2** a woman's white lace cap, part of the Dutch national dress. **Dutch courage** *n.* false courage, inspired by stimulants. **Dutch doll** *n.* a wooden doll. **Dutch door** *n.* (*N Am.*) a stable door. **Dutch elm disease** *n.* a disease of elms caused by the fungus *Ceratocytis ulmi* and carried by beetles, causing withering and defoliation, and often fatal. **Dutch hoe** *n.* a garden hoe with a blade. **Dutchman** *n.* (*pl.* **Dutchmen**) **1** a male native inhabitant of the Netherlands, or a male descendant of one. **2** a Dutch ship. **3** (*N Am., sl.*) a German. **Dutchman's breeches** *n.* a N American plant, *Dicentra cucullaria*, with finely divided leaves and white or pink flowers. **Dutchman's pipe** *n.* a N American climbing plant, *Aristolochia durior*, with flowers shaped like a curved pipe. **Dutch metal** *n.* a highly malleable copper alloy with zinc, used instead of gold leaf. **Dutch oven** *n.* **1** a cooking chamber suspended in front of a fire so as to cook by radiation. **2** a heavy container with a lid, used for stewing, braising etc. **Dutch treat** *n.* (*coll.*) an outing with each person paying their own share. **Dutch uncle** *n.* a person who criticizes in a stern, blunt manner. **Dutchwoman** *n.* (*pl.* **Dutchwomen**) a female native or inhabitant of the Netherlands, or a female descendant of one.

dutch (dŭch) *n.* (*Cockney sl.*) a wife.

duty (dū´ti) *n.* (*pl.* **duties**) **1** something which is bound or ought to be paid, done or performed. **2** something which a particular person is bound morally or legally to do. **3** moral or legal obligation. **4** the course of conduct prescribed by ethics or religion, the binding force of the obligation to follow this course. **5** any service, business or office. **6** a toll, tax, impost or custom charged by a government on the importation, exportation, manufacture or sale of goods or on transfer of property etc. **7** office, function, occupation, work. **8** any of the various acts entailed in this. **9** the useful work done by an engine or motor, measured in units against units of fuel. **10** the performance of church services. **off duty** not engaged in one's appointed duties. **on duty** engaged in performing one's appointed duties. **to do duty for 1** to serve in lieu of someone or something else. **2** to serve as a makeshift for. **dutiable** *a.* liable to the imposition of a duty or custom. **dutiful** *a.* careful in performing the duties required by law, justice or propriety; reverential, deferential. **dutifully** *adv.* **dutifulness** *n.* **duty-bound** *a.* obliged by one's sense of duty (to do something). **duty-free** *a.* not liable to duty, tax or custom. **duty-free shop** *n.* a shop, usu. on a ship or at an airport, where duty-free goods are for sale. **duty officer** *n.* the officer on duty at any particular time. **duty-paid** *a.* on which duty has been paid. **duty visit** *n.* a visit paid out of a sense of duty rather than for pleasure.

duvet (doo´vā) *n.* a quilt stuffed with down or man-made fibres, used as a bed covering instead of blankets and a sheet.

duyker DUIKER.

DV *abbr.* God willing (L *Deo volente*).

Dvr. *abbr.* Driver.

dwale (dwāl) *n.* the deadly nightshade, *Atropa belladonna*.

dwarf (dwawf) *n.* (*pl.* **dwarfs, dwarves** (-vz)) **1** a human being, animal or plant much below the natural or ordinary size. **2** a supernatural being of small stature. **3** any relatively small star with high density and ordinary luminosity, e.g. the sun. ~*a.* **1** below the ordinary or natural size. **2** stunted, puny, tiny. ~*v.t.* **1** to stunt the growth of. **2** to cause to look small or insignificant by comparison. ~*v.i.* to become stunted in growth. **dwarfish** *a.* **dwarfism** *n.* (*Med.*) the condition of being a dwarf. **dwarf star** *n.* any relatively small star with high density and ordinary luminosity, e.g. the sun.

dweeb (dwēb) *n.* (*N Am., sl.*) a stupid or contemptibly weak man or boy.

dwell (dwel) *v.i.* (*past, p.p.* **dwelt** (-t), **dwelled**) **1** (*formal*) to reside, to abide (in a place); to live, to spend one's time. **2** to linger, pause, tarry. ~*n.* a pause; a slight regular stoppage of the movement of a machine while a certain operation is effected. **to dwell on/ upon 1** to think for a long time or continually about (something unpleasant). **2** to speak or write at length about. **3** to prolong (a sound). **dweller** *n.* (*formal*) **dwelling** *n.* (*formal*) a residence, an abode, a habitation. **dwelling house** *n.* a house for residence, as distinguished from a place of business, an office, a warehouse etc. **dwelling-place** *n.* (*formal*) a place of residence.

dwindle (dwin´dəl) *v.i.* **1** to shrink, to diminish, to become smaller; to waste away. **2** to degenerate, to decline.

d.w.t. *abbr.* dead-weight tonnage.

Dy *chem. symbol* dysprosium.

dyad (dī´ad), **duad** (dū´ad) *n.* (*Math.*) an operator which is two vectors combined. **dyadic** (-ad´-) *a.*

dyarchy DIARCHY.

dye (dī) *v.t.* (*pres.p.* **dyeing,** *past, p.p.* **dyed**) **1** to stain, to colour. **2** to impregnate with colouring matter. **3** to cause (a material) to take a certain colour. ~*v.i.* (of a material that is being dyed) to take a colour. ~*n.* **1** a substance used for dyeing, colouring-matter. **2** a colour, tinge or hue, produced by or as if by dyeing. **3** a substance which yields a dye. **dyeable** *a.* **dyed in the wool** *a.* fixed in one's opinions, uncompromising. **dye-line** *n.* a diazo print. **dyer** *n.* a person whose business is dyeing. **dyer's greenweed, dyer's broom** *n.* a small Eurasian shrub, *Genista tinctoria*, with yellow flowers formerly used to make a green dye. **dyer's oak** *n.* a Mediterranean oak, *Quercus infectoria*, with galls formerly used to make a yellow dye. **dyestuff** *n.* a substance which yields a dye.

dying (dī´ing) *a.* **1** about to die. **2** mortal, perishable. **3** done, given or uttered just before death. **4** associated with death. **5** drawing to an end, fading away. ~*n.* the act of dying, death. **to one's dying day** for the rest of one's life. **dying oath** *n.* an oath made on the point of death, or as seriously as if on the point of death.

dyke (dīk), **dike** *n.* **1** a wall built to protect lowlying lands from being flooded. **2** a ditch, a moat, a watercourse or channel, either natural or artificial. **3** a wall or fence of turf or stone without cement. **4** (*fig.*) a barrier, a defence. **5** (*Geol.*) a wall-like mass of cooled and hardened volcanic or igneous rock, occupying rents and fissures in sedimentary strata. **6** (*Austral., sl.*) a lavatory. **7** (*sl.*) a lesbian. ~*v.t.* to defend with dykes or embankments.

dyn *abbr.* dyne.

dynamic (dīnam´ik) *a.* **1** (*Physics*) of or relating to forces not in equilibrium, as distinct from *static.* **2** motive, active, energetic. **3** of or relating to dynamics. **4** (*Mus.*) of or relating to levels of loudness. ~*n.* **1** the motive force of any action. **2** (*Mus.*) dynamics. **dynamical** *a.* **1** dynamic. **2** (*Theol.*) inspiring or animating, not impelling mechanically. **dynamically** *adv.* **dynamic equilibrium** *n.* a balance between continuing processes. **dynamicist** (-nam´isist) *n.* **dynamics** *n.pl.* **1** (*as sing.*) **a** the branch of mechanics which deals with the behaviour of bodies under the action of forces which produce changes of motion in them. **b** the branch of any science which deals with forces or changes. **2** the opposing forces in any situation which cause it to change. **3** (*Mus.*) degrees of levels of loudness. **dynamic viscosity** *n.* a measurement of the force required to overcome internal friction.

dynamism (dī´nəmizm) *n.* **1** the restless energy of a forceful personality. **2** a system or theory explaining phenomena as the ultimate result of some immanent force, such as the doctrine of Leibnitz that all substance involves force. **dynamist** *n.*

dynamite (dī´nəmīt) *n.* **1** a powerful explosive compound, extremely local in its action, consisting of nitroglycerine mixed with an absorbent material. **2** an exciting or impressive person or thing. **3** (*sl.*) a narcotic, esp. heroin. ~*v.t.* to blow up with dynamite. **dynamiter** *n.*

dynamo (dī´nəmō) *n.* (*pl.* **dynamos**) **1** a machine for converting mechanical energy into electricity by means of electromagnetic induction. **2** (*coll.*) a very energetic person.

dynamometer (dīnəmom´itə) *n.* an instrument for the measurement of power, force or electricity.

dynast (din´əst, dī´nəst) *n.* **1** a ruler, a monarch. **2** a member or founder of a dynasty. **dynastic** (-nas´-) *a.* **dynastically** *adv.* **dynasty** (din´-) *n.* (*pl.* **dynasties**) **1** a line, race or succession of sovereigns of the same family. **2** a family with several generations dominant in any field of activity.

dynatron (dī´nətron) *n.* (*pl.* **dynatrons**) a four-electrode thermionic valve which generates continuous oscillation.

dyne (dīn) *n.* (*Physics*) a unit for measuring force, the amount that, acting upon a gram for a second, generates a velocity of one centimetre per second.

dys- (dis) *comb. form* (*esp. Med.*) diseased, difficult or bad.

dysentery (dis´əntri) *n.* an infectious tropical febrile disease, causing inflammation in the large intestines, and accompanied by mucous and bloody evacuations. **dysenteric** (-ter´-) *a.*

dysfunction (disfüngk´shən) *n.* impaired or abnormal functioning, esp. of any organ or part of the body. **dysfunctional** *a.*

dysgraphia (disgraf´iə) *n.* inability to write. **dysgraphic** *a.*

dyslexia (dislek´siə) *n.* an impaired ability in reading and spelling caused by a neurological disorder. **dyslexic** *a., n.*

dysmenorrhoea (dismenərē´ə), (*N Am.*) **dysmenorrhea** *n.* difficult or painful menstruation.

dyspepsia (dispep´siə), **dyspepsy** (-si) *n.* indigestion. **dyspeptic** (-tik) *a.* of, relating to, of the nature of, or suffering from dyspepsia. ~*n.* a person who is subject to dyspepsia.

dysphasia (disfā´ziə) *n.* (*Med.*) difficulty in speaking or understanding speech, caused by injury to or disease of the brain. **dysphasic** *a.*

dysphoria (disfaw´riə) *n.* a morbid uneasiness; feeling unwell. **dysphoric** (-for´ik) *a.*

dysplasia (displā´ziə) *n.* (*Med.*) abnormal growth of tissues. **dysplastic** (-plas´tik) *a.*

dyspnoea (dispnē´ə), (*N Am.*) **dyspnea** *n.* (*Med.*) difficulty of breathing. **dyspnoeal** *a.* **dyspnoeic** *a.*

dysprosium (disprō´ziəm) *n.* (*Chem.*) a rare silvery-white metallic element, at. no. 66, chem. symbol Dy, of the rare earth group, used in laser materials etc.

dystocia (distō´shə) *n.* (*Med.*) difficult childbirth.

dystopia (distō´piə) *n.* an imaginary wretched place, the opposite of a utopia. **dystopian** *a., n.*

dystrophy (dis´trəfi) *n.* (*Med.*) any of various disorders characterized by the wasting away of muscle tissue. **dystrophic** (-trof´-) *a.*

dysuria (disū´riə), **dysury** (dis´-) *n.* difficulty and pain in passing urine.

dzo (zhō, zō), **dzho, zho** *n.* (*pl.* **dzo, dzos, dzho, dzhos, zho, zhos**) a hybrid breed of Himalayan cattle developed from crossing the yak with common horned cattle.

E

E[1] (ē), **e** (*pl.* **Es, E's**) the fifth letter of the English and other versions of the Roman alphabet, corresponding to the Greek epsilon (ε, E). It has four principal sounds in stressed syllables: (1) high and long as in *me*, marked in this dictionary ē; (2) mid and short as in *men*, *set*, left unmarked, e; (3) central and long where historically an *r* followed as in *her*, marked œ; (4) front and diphthongized or long as in *there*, marked eə. In unstressed syllables it has two principal sounds: (1) reduced or indeterminate as in *camel*, *garment*, marked ə; (2) high and short as in *begin*, marked i. At the end of words it is usu. silent as in *mane*, *cave*, serving to indicate that the preceding syllable is long. After *c* and *g* it denotes that those letters are to be pronounced as soft, as *s* and *j* respectively. In conjunction with other vowels *e* also represents a variety of sounds, as in *death*, *ear*, *eerie*, *foetus*, *glue*, *health*, *pear*, *seize* etc. ~**symbol 1** the fifth of a series, the fifth highest in range, e.g. of marks, etc. **2** the fifth known quantity in an algebraic expression. **3** (*Mus.*) **a** the third note of the diatonic scale in C major. **b** the scale of composition in which the keynote is E. **4** (*Math.*) the basis of Naperian logarithms, approximately equalling 2.718.

E[2], **e** *abbr.* **1** East, Eastern. **2** Ecstasy (the drug). **3** Egyptian. **4** (*Physics*) energy ($E = mc^2$). **5** Europe, European. **E-layer, E-region** *n.* a region of the ionosphere which is able to reflect medium-frequency radio waves. **e-mail, email** *n.* electronic mail. ~*v.t.* **1** to send electronic mail to. **2** to send by electronic mail. **E number** *n.* a number preceded by the letter E denoting a certain food additive in accordance with EU regulations.

ea. *abbr.* each.

each (ēch) *a.*, *pron.* every one (of a limited number) considered separately. **each and every** *a.* all, every single. **each other** *pron.* one another, reciprocally (*They hate each other*). **each way** *adv.* in betting, for either a win or a place in the first three (*bet £5 each way*). **each-way** *a.*

eager (ē'gə) *a.* **1** excited by an ardent desire to attain, obtain or succeed (*eager to learn*; *eager for news*). **2** keen, enthusiastic. **3** (of a desire or wish) strong or impatient (*an eager wish*). **eager beaver** *n.* (*coll.*) a person who is always active or eager for work. **eagerly** *adv.* **eagerness** *n.*

eagle (ē'gəl) *n.* **1** any of various large birds of prey of the family Accipitridae, esp. of the genus *Aquila*, such as the golden eagle. **2** a figure or symbol representing an eagle. **3** a military standard carrying a figure of an eagle. **4** a US colonel's shoulder insignia. **5** a golf score of two strokes under par for a particular hole. ~*v.t.* to achieve a golf score of two strokes under par for (a particular hole). **eagle eye** *n.* sharp sight, watchfulness. **eagle-eyed** *a.* **eagle owl** *n.* any of various large European or Asian owls with large ear tufts, esp. the European *Bubo bubo*. **eagle ray** *n.* a large ray of the family Myliobatidae with long, narrow pectoral fins. **eaglet** *n.* a young eagle. **eaglewood** *n.*

eagre (ē'gə) *n.* a tidal wave or bore in an estuary.

-ean (ēən, iən), **-aean, -eian** *suf.* **1** belonging to, as in *European*. **2** like, as in *plebeian*.

ear[1] (iə) *n.* **1** the organ of hearing and balance, consisting of the external ear, middle ear and internal ear. **2** the external part of the ear; the pinna. **3** the sense of hearing. **4** a delicate perception of the differences of sounds and judgement of harmony (*He has an ear for languages*). **5** notice or attention (esp. favourable consideration). **6** a small earlike projection from a larger body, usu. for support or attachment, such as the handle of a jug. **all ears** (*coll.*) listening carefully and with great interest. **in one ear and out the other** heard but making no lasting impression. **out on one's ear** (*coll.*) sent away ignominiously. **to bring (down) about one's ears** to be responsible for causing oneself (trouble etc.). **to fall on deaf ears** (of a request etc.) to be ignored. **to give (an) ear** to listen (to). **to have/ keep one's ear to the ground** to be well informed about trends, rumours, opinions etc. **to have someone's ear** to be able to speak to and influence somebody. **to lend an ear** to listen (to). **up to one's ears** (*coll.*) completely, so as to be overwhelmed (*up to her ears in debt*). **with a flea in one's ear** (*coll.*) with a sharp or contemptuous rebuke (*She sent me away with a flea in my ear*). **earache** *n.* pain in the middle or internal ear. **earbash** *v.t.* (*Austral., New Zeal., sl.*) to talk excessively to; to harangue. ~*v.i.* to earbash someone. **earbasher** *n.* **earbashing** *n.* **eardrum** *n.* the tympanum or tympanic membrane. **eared** *a.* having ears (*a long-eared owl*). **earful** *n.* (*coll.*) **1** a severe and lengthy rebuke or reprimand (*to give somebody an earful*). **2** an excessively long conversation or talk. **earhole** *n.* the aperture of an ear. **earless** *a.* **ear lobe** *n.* the soft lower part of the external ear. **earmark** *n.* **1** a mark on the ear by which a sheep or other animal can be identified. **2** any distinctive mark or feature. ~*v.t.* **1** to mark (a sheep etc.) by cutting or slitting the ear. **2** to set a distinctive mark upon. **3** to set aside (funds etc.) for a particular purpose. **earphone** *n.* a part of a radio, telephone etc. which converts electrical signals into audible speech, worn or held close to the ear. **earpiece** *n.* the part of a telephone etc. that is held to the ear. **ear-piercing** *a.* painfully loud and shrill. ~*n.* the making of a small hole in the ear lobe from which an earring can be hung. **earplug** *n.* a piece of soft material placed in the ear to keep out sound, water etc. **earring** *n.* an ornament for the ear, usu. clipped onto or attached through the ear lobe. **earshot** *n.* hearing distance (*within earshot*; *out of earshot*). **ear-splitting** *a.* painfully loud. **ear-stopple** *n.* (*N Am.*) an earplug. **ear-trumpet** *n.* a trumpet-shaped tube to be held to the ear, formerly used as a hearing aid. **earwax** *n.* a waxlike substance secreted by the ear, cerumen.

ear² (iə) *n.* a seed-bearing head of corn (*an ear of wheat*). ~*v.i.* to form ears (of corn).

earl (œl) *n.* a British nobleman ranking next below a marquess and next above a viscount, equivalent to a COUNT². **earldom** *n.* the rank, title or position of an earl.

early (œ'li) *adv.* (*comp.* **earlier**, *superl.* **earliest**) **1** before the proper, expected or usual time (*The train arrived early*). **2** in good time (*Shop early for Christmas*). **3** soon after the beginning of a period (*Come early next week*). **4** quickly, promptly (*Reply early*). ~*a.* **1** before the proper, expected or usual time (*I was early for work*). **2** in good time (*We were early for the bus*). **3** soon after the beginning of a day, month etc. (*early evening*; *an early riser*). **4** happening or situated near the beginning of a period of development, existence etc. (*early settlers*; *at the earliest opportunity*). **5** primitive, in the distant past (*early man*). **6** quick, prompt (*early payment*). **7** occurring or relating to young childhood (*early learning*; *her early years*). **8** immature, of a person's younger years (*his early novels*). **9** ripening, flowering etc. before other similar plants (*early potatoes*). ~*n.* (*pl.* **earlies**) an early fruit or vegetable. **at the earliest** not before (*next week at the earliest*). **earliness** *n.* **early bird** *n.* (*coll.*) a person who gets up or arrives very early. **early days** *n.pl.* early in the course of something, before it is clear how it will progress. **early grave** *n.* a premature or untimely death (*He went to an early grave*). **early hours** *n.pl.* the very early morning. **early music** *n.* music from before the classical period, i.e. up to *c.*1750. **early musician** *n.* **early night** *n.* an occasion when a person goes to bed early. **early on** *adv.* at an early stage (*early on in history*). **earlier on** *adv.* before. **early retirement** *n.* retirement from work by choice before the statutory retirement age. **early warning** *n.* advance notice of a problem or military attack.

earn (œn) *v.t.* **1** to gain (money etc.) as the reward of labour. **2** (of an investment) to bring in (income) as interest or profit. **3** to merit, deserve or become entitled to as the result of any action or course of conduct (*You have earned a rest*; *He*

earned himself a name for duplicity). **earned income** *n.* income from paid employment. **earner** *n.* **1** a person who earns (*a wage earner*). **2** (*coll.*) a profitable job or business (*a nice little earner*). **earnings** *n.pl.* **1** money earned, wages. **2** profits from an investment. **earnings-related** *a.* (of a pension, benefit etc.) whose amount is based on present or past earnings.

Usage note In standard English, the past tense and participle of *earn* is *earned*, not *earnt*.

earnest¹ (œ'nist) *a.* **1** serious, grave (*an earnest expression*). **2** serious, not trifling or joking (*an earnest plea*). **3** ardent, eager or zealous in the performance of any act or the pursuit of any object (*an earnest student*; *earnest endeavour*). **4** heartfelt, sincere (*my earnest desire*). ~*n.* seriousness, reality, not a pretence. **in earnest 1** seriously, sincerely, not jokingly (*I say this in earnest*). **2** with determination (*get down to work in earnest*). **earnestly** *adv.* **earnestness** *n.*

earnest² (œ'nist) *n.* **1** earnest-money. **2** a pledge, an assurance or token of something to come (*in earnest of my intentions*). **earnest-money** *n.* an instalment paid to seal a contract or agreement.

earth (œth) *n.* **1** (*often* (**the**) **Earth**) the globe, the planet on which we live. **2** the ground, the visible surface of the globe (*to fall to earth*). **3** dry land, as opposed to the sea. **4** (*often* (**the**) **Earth**) this world, as opposed to other possible worlds such as heaven or hell. **5** the people of the world (*The whole earth rejoiced*). **6** soil; the soft material in which plants grow, composed of clay, mould etc. **7** dead, inert matter. **8** the human body, as opposed to the soul or spirit. **9** the hole of a fox, badger etc. **10 a** plates or wires of an electric circuit, aerial etc. connected to the ground, providing a point of zero voltage or an escape for electrical surges. **b** the part of the ground where such an electrical connection is made. **11** an earthlike metallic oxide, such as alumina (*rare earth*; *alkaline earth*). ~*v.t.* **1** to complete a circuit by connecting (an electrical device) to the earth. **2** (*usu. with up*) to cover (plants, roots etc.) with earth as protection against cold, light etc. **3** to drive (a fox etc.) to its earth. ~*v.i.* (of a fox) to go to its earth, to go to ground. **down to earth** realistic, practical, sensible. **gone to earth** in hiding. **on earth 1** (*coll.*) used as an intensifier after question words (*what on earth?*; *who on earth?*). **2** (*after superlatives, coll.*) in the world, of all (*the greatest show on earth*). **the earth** (*coll.*) an excessive amount, everything (*to want/cost the earth*). **to come back/down to earth** to come back to reality from daydreams or fantasy. **earthbound** *a.* **1** moving towards the earth. **2** restricted to the earth. **3** fixed or fastened in or to the earth. **4** (*fig.*) fixed on earthly objects; dull, lacking in imagination or refinement. **earthcloset** *n.* a lavatory in which earth is used to cover the excreta. **earthen** *a.* made of earth, baked clay or similar substance.

earthenware n. **1** coarse pottery made of baked clay (an earthenware jug). **2** vessels made of earthenware. **earthlike** a. **earthling** (-ling) n. (esp. in science fiction) an inhabitant of the earth, a human being. **earthly** a. (comp. **earthlier**, superl. **earthliest**) **1** of or relating to this world, terrestrial. **2** of or relating to this life, as opposed to heaven or a future life. **3** mortal, human (earthly remains). **4** carnal, material or materialistic, as opposed to spiritual. **5** (coll.) possible, conceivable (What earthly use is it?). **not an earthly** (coll.) not a chance. **earthliness** n. **earthly paradise** n. in the Bible, the Garden of Eden, the abode of Adam and Eve before the Fall. **earth mother** n. **1** in mythology, a female deity personifying the earth and viewed as the source of fertility. **2** a sensual and fertile woman. **earth mover** n. a large vehicle for digging and moving earth. **earth-moving** n. **earthnut** n. **1 a** a perennial umbelliferous plant of Europe and Asia, Canopodium majus, with edible dark-brown tubers, also called pignut. **b** the tuber of this plant. **2** any of various plants with roundish edible roots or tubers, such as the truffle. **3** a peanut. **earth-pig** n. AARDVARK. **earthquake** n. **1** a movement of a portion of the earth's crust produced by volcanic forces. **2** (fig.) a major social, political or other disturbance. **earth science** n. any science dealing with the earth or its atmosphere, e.g. geography, geology, meteorology. **earth-shaking** a. (coll.) momentous, of profound or devastating effect. **earth-shakingly** adv. **earth-shattering** a. (coll.) earth-shaking. **earth-shatteringly** adv. **earth tremor** n. a slight earthquake. **earthward** a., adv. moving towards the earth. **earthwards** adv. **earthwork** n. **1** mounds, ramparts etc. made of earth used for defensive purposes. **2** embankments, cuttings etc. in civil engineering. **earthworm** n. a burrowing annelid worm, esp. of the genus Lumbricus or Allolobophora. **earthy** a. (comp. **earthier**, superl. **earthiest**) **1** consisting of, composed of or resembling earth or soil. **2** talking about sex in a direct and rude way (earthy humour). **3** robust, lusty. **earthily** adv. **earthiness** n.

earwig (iə'wig) n. **1** any of various insects of the order Dermaptera, esp. Forficula auricularia, with curved forceps at its tail. **2** (N Am.) a small centipede. ~v.i. (pres.p. **earwigging**, past, p.p. **earwigged**) (coll.) to eavesdrop.

ease (ēz) n. **1** a state of freedom from labour, trouble or pain. **2** freedom from constraint or formality. **3** facility, readiness. **4** absence of effort. ~v.t. **1** to free from pain, anxiety, labour or trouble. **2** to relieve or free from a burden. **3** to make easier or lighter. **4** to assuage, to mitigate. **5** to render less difficult. **6** to make looser, to relax, to adjust. **7** (Naut.) to slacken (a rope, sail, speed etc.). ~v.i. to relax one's efforts or exertions. **at (one's) ease** in a state free from anything likely to disturb, annoy or cause anxiety. **to stand at ease** (Mil.) to stand with the legs apart

and hands behind the back. **easeful** a. promoting ease, quiet or repose; comfortable. **easement** n. (Law) a liberty, right or privilege, without profit, which one proprietor has in or through the estate of another, as a right of way, light, air etc. **easer** n.

easel (ē'zəl) n. a wooden frame used to support a picture, blackboard, open book etc.

east (ēst) a. **1** situated towards the point where the sun rises when in the equinoctial. **2** coming from this direction. ~n. **1** the point of the compass where the sun rises at the equinox; 90° to the right of north. **2** the eastern part of a country. **3** the countries to the east of Europe. **4** the east wind. **5** (East) in bridge, a player in a position to the left of 'North'. ~adv. towards, at or near the quarter of the rising sun. **eastbound** a. travelling eastwards. **easterly** a. **1** situated or in the direction of the east. **2** looking towards the east. **3** coming from the east, or parts lying towards the east; blowing from the east. ~adv. **1** towards the direction of the east. **2** in or from the east. ~n. (pl. **easterlies**) a wind from the east. **East Indies** n.pl. (Hist.) the countries of SE Asia; the islands of the Malay archipelago. **East Indian** a. **east-north-east** n. the point of the compass halfway between east and north-east. **east-south-east** n. the point of the compass halfway between east and south-east. **eastward** a., adv. towards the east. ~n. an eastward direction; the parts lying towards the east. **eastwardly** a., adv. **eastwards** adv.

Easter (ēs'tə) n. **1** the festival in commemoration of the resurrection of Christ, taking place on the Sunday after the full moon that falls on or next after 21 Mar. **2** the period around Easter. **Easter Day** n. Easter Sunday. **Easter egg** n. **1** an egg-shaped present, often made of chocolate, given at Easter. **2** an egg boiled hard and stained or gilded, to symbolize the resurrection. **Easter Sunday** n. the Sunday of the festival of Easter. **Easter week** n. the week beginning with Easter Sunday.

eastern (ēs'tən) a. **1** situated in the east. **2** of or relating to the east. **3** blowing from the east. **4** (Eastern) of or relating to the Far East, Middle East, or Near East. **easterner** n. an inhabitant of the eastern part of any country or region. **eastern hemisphere** n. the hemisphere of the earth containing Europe, Africa and Asia. **easternmost** a. **Eastern (Standard) Time** n. **1** the standard time established for the eastern US and parts of Canada. **2** the standard time established for eastern Australia.

easy (ē'zi) a. (comp. **easier**, superl. **easiest**) **1** not difficult, not requiring great labour, exertion or effort. **2** free from pain, trouble, care or discomfort. **3** in comfortable circumstances, well-to-do. **4** (Mil.) at ease. **5** not strict. **6** free from embarrassment, constraint or affectation. **7** written, spoken etc. in a natural, unforced way. **8** easily persuaded, compliant. **9** indulgent, not exacting.

10 (of money) not hard to get (as distinct from *tight*). ~*adv.* in an easy manner. **easy!** move or go gently. **easy as pie** (*coll.*) very easy. **easy of access** easy to get to or into. **easy on the ear** agreeable to listen to. **easy on the eye** agreeable to look at. **of easy virtue** (of a woman) promiscuous. **to go easy** to be careful, to slow down. **to go easy on/ with** to use only a little of. **to take it easy** to take one's time, to relax. **easily** *adv.* **easiness** *n.* **easy chair** *n.* an armchair stuffed and padded for resting or reclining in. **easygoing** *a.* **1** taking things in an easy manner. **2** indolent. **3** moving easily. **easy mark, easy meat, easy touch** *n.* (*coll.*) a gullible person. **easy money** *n.* (*coll.*) money acquired without much effort. **easy-peasy** *a.* (*coll.*) childishly easy or uncomplicated. **Easy Street** *n.* (*coll.*) a position of financial good fortune or security. **easy terms** *n.pl.* a hire purchase arrangement in which the payments are not too onerous.

eat (ēt) *v.t.* (*past* **ate** (āt, et), *p.p.* **eaten** (ē′tən)) **1** to chew and swallow as food. **2** to devour. **3** to destroy by eating. **4** (*fig.*) to corrode. **5** to consume. **6** to wear away, to waste. **7** (*coll.*) to vex. ~*v.i.* **1** to take food. **2** to be eaten. **3** to taste, to relish. **to eat away** to destroy, to rust, to corrode. **to eat into** to corrode. **to eat one's hat** (*coll.*) to admit that one's prediction has been mistaken. **to eat one's heart out** to pine away. **2** to be extremely envious. **to eat one's words** to retract what one has said. **to eat out of someone's hand** to be totally compliant or willing to obey a person. **to eat up 1** to eat completely, to finish. **2** to consume in (unnecessarily) large quantities. **3** to absorb. **eatable** *a.* fit to be eaten. ~*n.* **1** anything fit or proper for food. **2** (*pl.*) the solid materials of a meal. **eater** *n.* **1** a person who eats. **2** a fruit suitable for eating uncooked. **eatery** *n.* (*pl.* **eateries**) (*coll.*) a restaurant, café etc. **eating** *a.* **1** (esp. of apples) suitable for eating without being previously cooked. **2** of or relating to food or eating. **eats** *n.pl.* (*coll.*) food.

eau (ō) *n.* water (used in compounds to designate various spirituous waters and perfumes). **eau-de-Cologne** (dəkəlōn′) *n.* a scent consisting of a solution of volatile oils in alcohol, orig. made in Cologne. **eau de vie** (dəvē′) *n.* brandy.

eaves (ēvz) *n.pl.* the lower edge of the roof which projects beyond the wall, and serves to throw off the water which falls on the roof. **eavesdrop** *n.* an act of eavesdropping. ~*v.i.* (*pres.p.* **eavesdropping**, *past, p.p.* **eavesdropped**) to listen secretly so as to overhear confidences. **eavesdropper** *n.*

ebb (eb) *n.* **1** the flowing back or going out of the tide. **2** the draining away of flood water. ~*v.i.* **1** to flow back. **2** to recede, to decline, to decay. **at a low ebb** weak, in a state of decline. **ebb and flow** the continual improvement and deterioration of circumstances etc. **on the ebb 1** receding. **2** declining.

ebony (eb′əni) *n.* (*pl.* **ebonies**) **1** the wood of various species of *Diospyros*, noted for its solidity

and black colour, capable of a high polish, and largely used for mosaic work and inlaying. **2** a tree of the genus *Diospyros*. ~*a.* **1** made of ebony. **2** intensely black. **ebonite** (-nīt) *n.* vulcanite.

ebullient (ibŭl′yənt) *a.* **1** overflowing with high spirits or enthusiasm, exuberant. **2** (*Chem.*) boiling (over). **ebullience, ebulliency** *n.* **ebulliently** *adv.*

EC *abbr.* **1** East Central. **2** European Commission. **3** European Community. **4** executive committee.

ecad (ē′kad) *n.* in ecology, an organism which has been modified by the environment.

eccentric (iksen′trik) *a.* **1** peculiar or odd in manner or character. **2** erratic, irregular, anomalous. **3** departing from the usual practice or established forms or laws. **4** not placed centrally. **5** (*Geom.*) (of circles and spheres) not having the same centre, not concentric. ~*n.* **1** a person of odd or peculiar habits. **2** an oddity. **3** a mechanical contrivance for converting circular into reciprocating rectilinear motion, such as that operating the slide-valve of a steam engine or the cam in an internal-combustion engine. **eccentrically** *adv.* **eccentricity** (eksəntris′iti) *n.* (*pl.* **eccentricities**) **1** odd or whimsical conduct or character. **2** departure from what is usual, regular or established. **3** an oddity, a peculiarity. **4** the state of not being concentric. **5** deviation from a central position.

ecclesiastic (iklēzias′tik) *n.* a person in holy orders, a member of the clergy. ~*a.* ecclesiastical. **ecclesial** *a.* **ecclesiastical** *a.* of or relating to the Church or the clergy. **ecclesiastically** *adv.* **ecclesiasticism** (-sizm) *n.*

ecclesiology (iklēziol′əji) *n.* **1** the study of all matters connected with churches, esp. church architecture, decoration and antiquities. **2** theology in relation to the Church. **ecclesiological** (-loj′-) *a.* **ecclesiologist** *n.*

eccrine (ek′rin, -rīn) *a.* denoting a gland that secretes externally, esp. the sweat glands.

ECG *abbr.* electrocardiogram.

echelon (esh′əlon) *n.* **1** (a group of persons in) a level, stage or grade of an organization etc. **2** (*Mil.*) the arrangement of troops, ships, aircraft etc. as in the form of steps, with parallel divisions one in advance of another. ~*v.t.* to form in echelon.

echeveria (echiviə′riə) *n.* a succulent plant of the genus *Echeveria*, found in Central and S America.

echidna (ikid′nə) *n.* a mammal of the genus *Tachyglossus* or *Zaglossus*, popularly known as the spiny anteater, which lays eggs instead of giving birth to live young like other mammals.

echinoderm (ikī′nədœm) *n.* any individual of the Echinodermata, a phylum of animals containing the sea urchins, starfish and sea cucumbers.

echinus (ikī′nəs) *n.* (*pl.* **echini** (-nī), **echinuses**) **1** a sea urchin of the genus *Echinus*. **2** (*Archit.*)

the convex projecting moulding below the abacus of an Ionic column and in the cornices of Roman architecture. **echinoid** (-noid) *n.* a sea urchin.

echo (ek´ō) *n.* (*pl.* **echoes**) **1** the repetition of a sound caused by its being reflected from some obstacle. **2** a sound reflected from some obstacle; a reflected radio or radar beam. **3** a close imitation in words or sentiment; a hearty response. **4** a slavish imitator. **5** a reminder of something else. **6** (*Mus.*) a repetition of a phrase in a softer tone. **7** repetition of the last syllables of a verse in the next line, so as to give a continuous sense. **8** in whist etc., a response to a partner's call for trumps. ~*v.i.* (*3rd pers. sing. pres.* **echoes**, *pres.p.* **echoing**, *past, p.p.* **echoed**) **1** to give an echo; to resound. **2** to be sounded back. ~*v.t.* **1** to return or send back (as a sound). **2** to repeat with approval. **3** to imitate closely. **echocardiogram** *n.* the record produced by an echocardiograph. **echocardiograph** *n.* (*Med.*) a machine using ultrasound to investigate the heart for disease. **echocardiographer** *n.* **echocardiography** *n.* **echo chamber** *n.* a room whose walls echo sound for recording or radio effects or for measuring acoustics. **echoer** *n.* **echoey** (ek´ōi) *a.* **1** like an echo. **2** full of echoes. **echogram** *n.* a recording made by an echo sounder. **echograph** *n.* a machine which records echograms. **echoic** *a.* **1** of, relating to or like an echo. **2** imitative, onomatopoeic. **echoically** *adv.* **echoism** *n.* onomatopoeia. **echolalia** (-lā´liə) *n.* (*Psych.*) the automatic repetition of another person's utterances, a symptom of some forms of mental illness. **echoless** *a.* **echolocation** *n.* finding the position of objects by means of reflected sound waves. **echo sounder** *n.* (*Naut.*) an apparatus for sounding the depth of water beneath the keel of a ship. **echo-sounding** *n.* **echo verse** *n.* verse in which the last syllable of each line is repeated in the next.

echt (ekht) *a.* genuine, authentic.

eclair (iklee´) *n.* an iced, finger-shaped cream-filled pastry.

eclampsia (iklamp´siə) *n.* (*Med.*) convulsions or fits, particularly of the type that occur with acute toxaemia in pregnancy. **eclamptic** (-tik) *a.*

éclat (āklah´) *n.* **1** brilliant success. **2** acclamation, applause. **3** splendour, striking effect.

eclectic (iklek´tik) *a.* **1** broad, not exclusive. **2** selecting, choosing, picking out at will from the (best of) doctrines, teachings etc. of others. ~*n.* **1** a person who derives opinions, tastes or practical methods from various sources. **2** a philosopher who borrows doctrines from various schools. **eclectically** *adv.* **eclecticism** (-tisizm) *n.*

eclipse (iklips´) *n.* **1** the total or partial obscuration of the light from a heavenly body by the passage of another body between it and the eye or between it and the source of its light. **2** a temporary failure or obscuration. **3** a loss of brightness, glory, honour or reputation. **4** (*Zool.*) a

moulting phase during which a bird's distinctive markings are obscured. ~*v.t.* **1** to cause an eclipse of (a heavenly body) by passing between it and the spectator or between it and its source of light. **2** to intercept the light of, to obscure. **3** to outshine, surpass, excel. **in eclipse 1** having been outshone, in decline. **2** (of a bird) having lost its distinctive plumage. **ecliptic** (-tik) *a.* **1** of, constituting or relating to the sun's apparent path in the sky. **2** of or relating to an eclipse. ~*n.* **1** the apparent path of the sun round the earth. **2** the plane passing through the sun's centre which contains the orbit of the earth.

eclogue (ek´log) *n.* an idyll or pastoral poem, esp. one containing dialogue.

eco- (ē´kō, ek´ō) *comb. form* concerned with ecology, habitat or the environment.

ecocide (ē´kōsīd, ek´-) *n.* the destruction of an environment, or of aspects of an environment.

ecoclimate (ē´kōklīmət, ek´-) *n.* the climate of an area, perceived as of ecological importance.

eco-friendly (ē´kōfrendli, ek´-) *a.* not damaging to the environment.

ecolabel (ē´kōlābəl, ek´-) *n.* a label on a food or household product asserting that the product contains nothing damaging to the environment. **ecolabelling,** (*N Am.*) **ecolabeling** *n.*

E. coli (ē kō´lī) *abbr.* Escherichia coli, a bacterium causing food poisoning.

ecology (ikol´əji), **oecology** *n.* **1** the branch of biology dealing with the relations between organisms and their environment. **2** the study of the relations between people and their environment, human ecology. **ecological** (ēkəloj´-, ek´-) *a.* **ecologically** *adv.* **ecologist** *n.*

econometrics (ikonəmet´riks) *n.* statistical and mathematical analysis of economic theories. **econometric** *a.* **econometrical** *a.* **econometrician** (-mətrish´ən) *n.* **econometrist** (-nom´ə-) *n.*

economic (ēkənom´ik, ek-) *a.* **1** relating to the science of economics. **2** of or relating to industrial concerns or commerce. **3** maintained for the sake of profit or for the production of wealth. **4** capable of yielding a profit, financially viable. **5** frugal, thrifty, economical. **6** practical in application. **economical** *a.* **1** characterized by economic management; careful, frugal, thrifty. **2** cheap. **economically** *adv.* **economics** *n.* **1** the science of the production and distribution of wealth, political economy. **2** the financial aspects of an activity, business etc. **3** (*as pl.*) the condition of a country, community or individual, with regard to material prosperity.

Usage note The meanings of the adjectives *economic* and *economical* overlap, but in general *economic* refers to economics, and *economical* refers to thrift or frugality. The corresponding negatives in *un-* are similarly distinguished.

economy (ikon´əmi) *n.* (*pl.* **economies**) **1** the totality of goods and services produced and consumed by a community or state; the wealth or financial resources of a community etc. **2** an organized or formalized system for the production and consumption of wealth. **3** the management, regulation and government of an economy. **4** a frugal and judicious use or expenditure of money or resources; carefulness, frugality. **5** (*usu. pl.*) a saving or reduction of expense. **6** careful and judicious use of anything, as of time. **7** the disposition, arrangement or plan of any work. **economist** *n.* **1** a person skilled in the science of economics. **2** a person who manages with economy. **economize, economise** *v.i.* to manage domestic or financial affairs with economy. ~*v.t.* **1** to use, administer or expend with economy. **2** to use sparingly, to turn to the best account. **economization** (-zā´shən) *n.* **economizer** *n.* **economy class** *n.* the cheapest class of travel, with no luxuries. **economy-size** *a.* of a large size offering a proportionately lower cost.

ecosphere (ē´kōsfiə, ek´-) *n.* **1** the parts of the universe, esp. the earth, where life can exist. **2** the biosphere.

ecosystem (ē´kōsistəm, ek´-) *n.* a system consisting of a community of organisms and its environment.

ecoterrorism (ēkōter´ərizm, ek-) *n.* terrorist acts threatened or carried out in order to help environmentalist causes. **ecoterrorist** *n.*

ecotourism (ēkōtuə´rizm, ek-) *n.* tourism managed on a small scale and in environmentally friendly ways. **ecotourist** *n.*

ecru (ek´roo, ākrū´) *a.* of the colour of unbleached linen. ~*n.* this colour.

ecstasy (ek´stəsi) *n.* (*pl.* **ecstasies**) **1** a state of mental exaltation. **2** excessive emotion, rapture, excessive delight, or excessive grief, distress or pain. **3** prophetic or poetic frenzy. **4** a trance. **5** (**Ecstasy**) methylenedioxymethamphetamine (MDMA), a synthetic stimulant and hallucinogenic drug based on amphetamine. **6** (*Psych.*) a morbid state of the nervous system in which the mind is completely absorbed by one idea. **ecstasize, ecstasise** *v.t.* to fill with ecstasy, to enrapture. ~*v.i.* to go into ecstasies. **ecstatic** (-stat´-) *a.* **1** of, relating to or producing ecstasy; ravishing, entrancing, rapturous. **2** subject to ecstasy. **3** excited and extremely happy. **ecstatically** *adv.*

ECT *abbr.* electroconvulsive therapy.

ecto- (ek´tō) *comb. form* (*Biol.*) of or relating to the outside of something.

ectogenesis (ektōjen´əsis) *n.* (*Biol.*) the growth of an organism or part outside the body instead of inside. **ectogenetic** (-jənet´ik) *a.* **ectogenic** (-jen´ik) *a.* **ectogenous** (-toj´ənəs) *a.*

ectomorph (ek´təmawf) *n.* a person of slight or thin build. **ectomorphic** (-maw´-) *a.* **ectomorphy** *n.*

-ectomy (ek´təmi) *suf.* denoting the surgical removal of a part of the body, as *tonsillectomy*.

ectopia (ektō´piə) *n.* (*Med.*) congenital displacement of an organ or part. **ectopic** (-top´-) *a.* out of place. **ectopic pregnancy** *n.* (*Med.*) the abnormal development of a foetus outside the womb, usu. in a Fallopian tube.

ectoplasm (ek´təplazm) *n.* **1** the outer layer of protoplasm or sarcode of a cell. **2** a substance supposed to emanate from the body of a spiritualist medium during a trance. **ectoplasmic** (-plaz´-) *a.* **ectoplasmically** *adv.*

ecu (ek´ū, ā´kū), **ECU** *n.* (*pl.* **ecu, ecus, ECU, ECUs**) a currency unit used as a unit of account in the European Union, its value based on the value of several different European currencies.

ecumenical (ēkūmen´ikəl, ek-), **oecumenical** *a.* **1** belonging to the Christian Church or Christian world as a whole. **2** of or relating to the ecumenical movement. **ecumenically** *adv.* **ecumenical movement** *n.* a movement in the Christian Church encouraging and promoting unity on issues of belief, worship etc. **ecumenicism** (-sizm), **ecumenism** (ekū´-) *n.* the principles of the ecumenical movement.

eczema (ek´simə) *n.* an inflammatory disease of the skin, characterized by blisters and itching. **eczematous** (-sem´-) *a.*

ed. *abbr.* **1** edited. **2** edition. **3** editor. **4** educated. **5** education.

-ed (id, d) *suf.* **1** forming the past tense and participle of regular verbs (used also as participial adjectives). **2** forming adjectives from nouns or noun phrases, as in *cultured, good-natured, moneyed, talented*.

Edam (ē´dam) *n.* a kind of pressed, yellow cheese with a red outer skin of wax.

edaphic (idaf´ik) *a.* (*Bot.*) of or relating to the soil. **edaphically** *adv.*

eddy (ed´i) *n.* (*pl.* **eddies**) **1** a small whirlpool. **2** a current of air, fog, smoke etc. moving in a circle, whirling. ~*v.i.*, *v.t.* (*3rd pers. sing. pres.* **eddies**, *pres.p.* **eddying**, *past*, *p.p.* **eddied**) to whirl in an eddy. **eddy current** *n.* electrical current circulating in the mass of a conductor caused by a change in the magnetic field.

edelweiss (ā´dəlvīs) *n.* a small white composite plant, *Gnaphalium alpinum*, growing in rocky places in the Alps.

edema OEDEMA.

Eden (ē´dən) *n.* **1** a region or abode of perfect bliss. **2** a state of complete happiness.

edentate (ēden´tāt) *a.* (*Zool.*) **1** having no incisor teeth. **2** belonging to the Edentata, an order of mammals with no front teeth or no teeth whatsoever, containing the armadillos, sloths and anteaters. ~*n.* an edentate animal.

edge (ej) *n.* **1 a** the sharp or cutting part of an instrument, such as a sword. **b** the sharpness of this. **2** anything edge-shaped, the crest of a ridge, the line where two surfaces of a solid meet. **3** a boundary-line. **4** the brink, border, margin or extremity of anything. **5** penetrating power; sharpness, keenness. **6** acrimony, bitterness. ~*v.t.* **1** to sharpen, to put an edge on. **2** to make an edge or border to. **3** to be a border to. **4** to move or put forward little by little. ~*v.i.* **1** to move forward or away little by little. **2** to move sideways, to sidle (up). **on edge** irritable. **on the edge of** very nearly (doing or being involved in). **to have the edge on/over** to have an advantage over. **to set one's teeth on edge 1** to cause a tingling or grating sensation in the teeth. **2** to cause a feeling of irritation or revulsion. **to take the edge off** to weaken, to lessen the force of. **edgeless** *a.* **edger** *n.* **edge tool, edged tool** *n.* any of the heavier varieties of cutting tool. **edgeways, edgewise** *adv.* **1** with the edge turned up, or forward in the direction of the edge. **2** sideways. **to get a word in edgeways** to say something with difficulty because of someone else talking. **edging** *n.* **1** that which forms the border or edge of anything, such as lace, trimming etc. on a dress. **2** a border or row of small plants set along the edge of a bed. **edgy** *a.* (*comp.* **edgier,** *superl.* **edgiest**) **1** having or showing an edge. **2** irritable, nervy. **3** sharp in temper. **4** in art, too sharply defined. **edgily** *adv.* **edginess** *n.*

edible (ed´ibəl) *a.* fit for food, eatable. ~*n.* anything fit for food; an eatable. **edibility** (-bil´-) *n.*

edict (ē´dikt) *n.* a proclamation or decree issued by authority. **edictal** (idik´-) *a.*

edifice (ed´ifis) *n.* **1** a building, esp. one of some size and pretension. **2** a complicated organization or structure.

edify (ed´ifi) *v.t.* (*3rd pers. sing. pres.* **edifies,** *pres.p.* **edifying,** *past, p.p.* **edified**) **1** to instruct; to improve; to build up esp. morally and spiritually. **2** to enlighten. **edification** (-fikā´shən) *n.* **edifying** *a.* **edifyingly** *adv.*

edit (ed´it) *v.t.* (*pres.p.* **editing,** *past, p.p.* **edited**) **1** to prepare for publication or processing by compiling, selecting, revising etc. **2** to censor, to alter; to reword, to improve or correct. **3** to conduct or manage (a periodical etc.) by selecting and revising the literary matter. ~*n.* **1** an act or instance of editing. **2** something edited. **3** an editing facility. **to edit out** to remove during editing. **edition** (idish´ən) *n.* **1** the form in which a literary work is published. **2** the whole number of copies published at one time. **3** one particular broadcast forming part of a regular series. **4** a person or thing that closely resembles another except in one specified aspect (*a smaller edition of his brother*). **editor** *n.* **1** a person who prepares the work of others for publication or broadcasting. **2** a person who conducts or manages a newspaper or periodical or a section of one. **3** a person who cuts and makes up the shots for the final sequence of a film. **4** (*Comput.*) a program that facilitates the alteration of text already stored in a computer. **editorial** (-taw´-) *a.* **1** of or relating to an editor or editing. **2** written by or proceeding from an editor. ~*n.* an article written by or proceeding from an editor, a leading article. **editorialize, editorialise** *v.i.* to introduce personal opinions into reporting. **editorially** *adv.* **editorship** *n.*

-edly (idli) *suf.* forming adverbs from the p.p. of verbs, as *markedly, guardedly.*

EDP *abbr.* electronic data processing.

EDT *abbr.* Eastern Daylight Time.

EDTA *abbr.* (*Chem.*) ethylenediamine tetra-acetic acid, a chelating agent.

educate (ed´ūkāt) *v.t.* **1** to train and develop the intellectual and moral powers of. **2** to provide with schooling. **3** to train or develop (an organ or a faculty). **4** to train (an animal). **5** to bring up (a child or children). **educable** (-kəbəl) *a.* **educability** (-bil´-) *n.* **educatable** *a.* **educated** *a.* **1** having been educated to a high standard. **2** cultured. **3** informed (*an educated guess*). **education** (-kā´shən) *n.* **1** the process of educating, systematic training and development of the intellectual and moral faculties. **2** a type of educating or instruction. **3** a stage in the process of educating. **4** a course of instruction. **5** the result of a systematic course of training and instruction. **educational** *a.* **educationalist, educationist** *n.* **educationally** *adv.* **educative** (ed´ūkətiv) *a.* **educator** *n.*

educe (idūs´) *v.t.* **1** to bring out, evolve, develop. **2** to deduce, infer. **educible** *a.* **eduction** (idŭk´-) *n.* **eductive** *a.*

edutainment (edūtān´mənt) *n.* infotainment.

Edwardian (edwaw´diən) *a.* **1** of or relating to the periods of any of the kings of England named Edward, esp. that of Edward VII (1901–10). **2** characteristic of the manners, architecture etc. of the period of Edward VII. ~*n.* a person belonging to, or affecting the style of, this period.

-ee (ē) *suf.* **1** denoting the recipient, as in *grantee, legatee, payee, vendee.* **2** denoting the direct or indirect object, as in *addressee, employee.* **3** denoting something small in its class, as in *bootee.* **4** used arbitrarily, as in *bargee, devotee.*

EEG *abbr.* **1** electroencephalogram. **2** electroencephalograph.

eel (ēl) *n.* **1** a snakelike fish of the genus *Anguilla,* esp. the common European species, *A. anguilla.* **2** an eel-like fish. **3** a slippery or evasive person. **eelgrass** *n.* **1** GRASS-WRACK (under GRASS). **2** any plant of the genus *Vallisneria,* living submerged in fresh water. **eel-like** *a.* **eelpout** *n.* any fish of the family Zoarcidae. **eelworm** *n.* a minute eellike worm esp. of a kind found in vinegar or in plant roots. **eely** *a.*

-een (ēn) *suf.* forming feminine diminutive nouns, as in *colleen.*

-eer (iə) *suf.* **1** denoting an agent or a person concerned with or dealing in, as in *charioteer, musketeer, pamphleteer, sonneteer.* **2** forming verbs with the meaning 'to perform activities associated with', as in *electioneer, profiteer.*

eerie (iə´ri) *a.* (*comp.* **eerier,** *superl.* **eeriest**) **1** strange and frightening. **2** causing fear. **eerily** *adv.* **eeriness** *n.*

eff (ef) *v.i., v.t.* (*sl., euphem.*) a euphemism for FUCK. **effing and blinding** swearing copiously. **effing** *a.* **eff off!** *int.*

efface (ifās´) *v.t.* **1** to destroy or remove (something), so that it cannot be seen. **2** to cast into the shade. **3** to make not noticeable. **4** to render negligible. **effaceable** *a.* **effacement** *n.*

effect (ifekt´) *n.* **1** the result or product of a cause or operation, the consequence. **2** efficacy, power of producing a required result. **3** accomplishment, fulfilment. **4** purport, aim, purpose. **5** the impression created by a work of art etc. **6** a combination of colours, forms, sounds, rhythm etc., calculated to produce a definite impression. **7** (*pl.*) goods, movables, personal estate. **8** (*Physics*) a physical phenomenon. **9** the art of putting into operation. ~*v.t.* **1** to produce as a consequence or result. **2** to cause to happen. **for effect** in order to produce a striking impression. **in effect 1** in reality, substantially. **2** practically. **of no effect 1** without validity or force. **2** without result. **to bring/ carry into effect** to accomplish. **to give effect to 1** to carry out. **2** to make operative. **to no effect** in vain, uselessly. **to take effect 1** to operate. **2** to produce its effect. **to that effect** having that result. **to the effect that** such that. **with effect from** taking effect from (a specified date). **without effect** invalid, without result. **effective** *a.* **1** producing its proper effect. **2** producing a striking impression. **3** fit for duty or service. **4** real, actual. **5** starting officially. ~*n.* a person who is fit for duty. **effectively** *adv.* **effectiveness** *n.* **effectivity** (-tiv´iti) *n.* **effectless** *a.* **effector** *n.* (*Biol.*) an organ that effects response to stimulus, e.g. a muscle, gland. ~*a.* of or relating to such an organ. **effectual** (-chuəl) *a.* **1** productive of an intended effect. **2** adequate, efficacious. **3** valid. **effectuality** (-chual´-) *n.* **effectually** *adv.* **effectualness** *n.* **effectuate** *v.t.* to cause to happen. **effectuation** (-ā´shən) *n.*

Usage note The adjectives *effective* and *effectual* should not be confused: *effective* involves actual performance or achievement, and *effectual* only potential; unlike *effective*, *effectual* is not used of people (though *ineffectual* is). The meaning of *effectual* also overlaps with that of *efficacious*, but *efficacious* implies an established purpose and reliable performance. See also notes under AFFECT¹, EFFICIENT.

effeminate (ifem´inət) *a.* (of a man) womanish; unmanly, weak. **effeminacy** *n.* **effeminately** *adv.*
efferent (ef´ərənt) *a.* (*Med.*) conveying outwards.
effervesce (efəves´) *v.i.* **1** to bubble up, from the escape of gas, as fermenting liquors. **2** to escape in bubbles. **3** to boil over with excitement. **effervescence, effervescency** *n.* **effervescent** *a.*
effete (ifēt´) *a.* **1** decadent. **2** having lost all vigour and efficiency. **3** worn out or exhausted. **4** (of a man) womanish; unmanly, weak. **effeteness** *n.*
efficacious (efikā´shəs) *a.* producing or having power to produce the effect intended. **efficaciously** *adv.* **efficaciousness** *n.* **efficacy** (ef´ikəsi) *n.*
efficient (ifish´ənt) *a.* **1** causing or producing effects or results. **2** competent, capable. **efficiency** *n.* (*pl.* **efficiencies**) **1** the quality or state of being efficient. **2** power to produce a desired result.

3 (*Physics*) the ratio of the output of energy to the input of energy. **efficiently** *adv.*

Usage note The meanings of *efficient* overlap with those of *effective* and *efficacious*, but *efficient* implies skill or economy of effort.

effigy (ef´iji) *n.* (*pl.* **effigies**) a representation or likeness of a person, as on coins, medals etc. **to burn/ hang in effigy** to burn or hang an image of, to show hatred, dislike or contempt of.
effloresce (eflores´) *v.i.* **1** to burst into flower, to blossom. **2** (*Chem.*) **a** to crumble to powder through loss of water or crystallization on exposure to the air. **b** (of salts) to form crystals on the surface. **c** (of a surface) to become covered with saline particles. **3** to fulfil promise, to mature. **efflorescence** *n.* **efflorescent** *a.*
effluent (ef´luənt) *a.* flowing or issuing out; emanating. ~*n.* **1** the liquid that is discharged from a sewage tank. **2** a river or stream which flows out of another or out of a lake. **effluence** *n.* **1** the act or state of flowing out. **2** that which flows out, an emanation.
effluvium (ifloo´viəm) *n.* (*pl.* **effluvia** (-viə)) an emanation affecting the sense of smell, esp. a disagreeable smell and vapour as from putrefying substances etc.
efflux (ef´lŭks) *n.* **1** the act of flowing out or issuing. **2** outflow, effusion. **3** an emanation, that which flows out. **effluxion** (iflŭk´shən) *n.*
effort (ef´ət) *n.* **1** an exertion of physical or mental power, a strenuous attempt, an endeavour. **2** a display of power, an achievement. **3** (*coll.*) the result of an effort, something achieved. **effortful** *a.* **effortfully** *adv.* **effortless** *a.* **effortlessly** *adv.* **effortlessness** *n.*
effrontery (ifrŭn´təri) *n.* (*pl.* **effronteries**) **1** bold, shameless and rude behaviour. **2** an impudent speech or act.
effulgent (ifŭl´jənt) *a.* **1** shining brightly. **2** diffusing radiance. **effulgence** *n.* **effulgently** *adv.*
effuse¹ (ifūz´) *v.t.* **1** to pour out, to emit. **2** to diffuse. **effusion** (-zhən) *n.* **1** the act of pouring out. **2** that which is poured out. **3** a shedding, as of blood. **4** (*usu. derog. or facet.*) an outpouring of genius or emotion. **5** frank expression of feeling, effusiveness. **6** the escape of any fluid out of the proper part of the body into another. **effusive** (-siv) *a.* **1** showing strong feelings in an enthusiastic way. **2** (*Geol.*) (of rock) volcanic, poured out when molten and then solidifying. **effusively** *adv.* **effusiveness** *n.*
effuse² (ifūs´) *a.* **1** (*Bot.*) (of an inflorescence) spreading loosely. **2** (of a shell) having the lips separated by a groove.
EFL *abbr.* English as a foreign language.
eft (eft) *n.* the common newt.
EFTPOS, Eftpos (eft´pos), **Eftpos** *abbr.* electronic funds transfer at point of sale (a method of payment in which funds are transferred directly at the shop till through a computer network, using a debit or credit card).

e.g. *abbr.* for example.

Usage note The abbreviations *e.g.* and *i.e.* should not be confused: *e.g.* introduces an example, and *i.e.* an identification or paraphrase.

egalitarian (igalitee´riən) *a.* believing in the principle of human equality. ~*n.* a person who advocates equality for all humankind. **egalitarianism** *n.*

egg[1] (eg) *n.* **1** the ovum of birds, reptiles, fishes and many of the invertebrates, usu. enclosed in a spheroidal shell and containing the embryo of a new individual. **2** the egg of a bird, esp. of domestic poultry, largely used as food. **3** (*Biol.*) an ovum or germ-cell. **4** the early stage of anything; the germ, the origin. **5** something spheroidal. **6** (*coll.*) a person or thing (to be) dealt with. **as sure as eggs is eggs** (*coll.*) quite certainly. **to have egg on one's face** to be mistaken, to look foolish. **egg-beater** *n.* **1** a device for whisking eggs. **2** (*N Am., coll.*) a helicopter. **egg-cup** *n.* a cup-shaped vessel used to hold a boiled egg at table. **egg custard** *n.* a flavoured custard made with eggs. **egg-flip, egg-nog** *n.* a drink compounded of eggs beaten up, sugar, and beer, cider, wine or spirits. **egghead** *n.* (*coll.*) an intellectual. **eggless** *a.* **eggplant** *n.* (*N Am.*) the *Solanum esculentum*, or aubergine. **eggs-and-bacon** *n.* any of several plants with yellowish flowers. **eggshell** *n.* the calcareous envelope in which an egg is enclosed. **eggshell china** *n.* very thin porcelain. **eggshell paint** *n.* paint with a slightly glossy finish. **egg-spoon** *n.* a small spoon used for eating eggs. **egg-timer** *n.* a device for timing the boiling of an egg. **egg-tooth** *n.* a hard point or knob on the bill-sheath or snout of an embryo bird or reptile, for cracking the containing shell. **egg white** *n.* the albuminous part of an egg surrounding the yolk. **eggy** *a.* (*comp.* **eggier**, *superl.* **eggiest**).

egg[2] (eg) *v.t.* to incite, to urge (on).

egger-moth (eg´ə moth), **eggar-moth** *n.* any of various British moths of the family Lasiocampidae.

eglantine (eg´ləntīn, -tin) *n.* the sweet-brier.

ego (ē´gō, eg´ō) *n.* (*pl.* **egos**) **1** individuality, personality. **2** the self-conscious subject, as contrasted with the non-ego, or object. **3** (*Psych.*) the conscious self, which resists on the one hand the threats of the super-ego, and on the other the impulses of the id. **4** (*coll.*) self-confidence or self-conceit. **egocentric** (-sen´trik) *a.* self-centred. **egocentrically** *adv.* **egocentricity** (-tris´-) *n.* **egocentrism** *n.* **egoism** *n.* **1** egotism. **2** pure self-interest, systematic selfishness. **3** the theory that a person's chief good is the complete development and happiness of self, and that this is the proper basis of morality. **egoist** *n.* **egoistic** (-is´-), **egoistical** *a.* **egoistically** *adv.* **egomania** (-mā´niə) *n.* excessive or pathological egotism. **egomaniac** *n.* **egomaniacal** (-mənī´əkəl) *a.* **egotism** (-tizm) *n.* **1** the habit of too frequently using the word I in

writing or speaking. **2** a too frequent mention of oneself in writing or conversation. **3** an extreme sense of self-importance and obsession with oneself. **egotist** *n.* **egotistic** (-tis´-), **egotistical** *a.* **egotistically** *adv.* **egotize** (-tīz), **egotise** *v.i.* **ego trip** *n.* (*coll.*) an action or experience which adds to a person's self-important feelings.

egregious (igrē´jəs) *a.* **1** conspicuously bad, flagrant. **2** notable, notorious. **3** (*also facet.*) †extraordinary, out of the common, remarkable, exceptional. **egregiously** *adv.* **egregiousness** *n.*

egress (ē´gres) *n.* **1** departure. **2** a means or place of exit. **3** the act or power of going out. **4** (*Astron.*) the end of a transit or eclipse.

egret (ē´gret) *n.* a heron of those species that have long and loose plumage over the back, of the genus *Egretta* or *Bulbulcus*.

Egyptian (ijip´shən) *a.* of or relating to Egypt or the Egyptians. ~*n.* **1** a native or inhabitant of Egypt. **2** the language of ancient Egypt. **Egyptianize, Egyptianise** *v.t.* **Egyptianization** (-zā´shən) *n.* **Egyptology** (-tol´əji) *n.* the study of the antiquities, language etc. of ancient Egypt. **Egyptological** (-loj´-) *a.* **Egyptologist** (-tol´-) *n.*

eh (ā) *int.* used to express doubt, inquiry, surprise etc.

-cian (ēən) *suf.* forming adjectives and nouns from nouns ending in *-ey*, as *Harleian*, *Bodleian*.

Eid (ēd), **Id** *n.* a Muslim festival.

eider (ī´də) *n.* **1** a large Arctic duck, *Somateria mollissima*. **2** eiderdown. **eiderdown** *n.* **1** the soft and elastic down from the breast of this bird. **2** a quilt filled with eiderdown or similar material. **eider duck** *n.*

eight (āt) *n.* **1** the number or figure 8 or VIII. **2** the age of eight. **3** a set of eight things or people. **4** in rowing, a crew of eight in a boat. **5** in skating, a curved outline resembling the figure 8. **6** the size of an article of attire such as a shoe etc. denoted by the number 8. **7** a card with eight pips. **8** a score of eight points. **9** the eighth hour after midday or midnight. ~*a.* eight in number. **one over the eight** (*coll.*) slightly drunk. **eight-day** *a.* (of clocks) going for eight days. **eightfold** *a.* **eighth** (āthth) *n.* **1** any one of eight equal parts. **2** (*Mus.*) the interval of an octave. ~*n., a.* **1** (the) last of eight (people, things etc.). **2** the next after the seventh. **eighthly** *adv.* **eighth note** *n.* (*Mus., N Am.*) a quaver. **eightsome, eightsome reel** *n.* a form of Scottish reel for eight dancers.

eighteen (ātēn´) *n.* **1** the number or figure 18 or xviii. **2** the age of 18. ~*a.* **1** 18 in number. **2** aged 18. **eighteenmo** (-mō) *n.* (*pl.* **eighteenmos**) (*coll.*) an octodecimo, a book whose sheets are folded to form 18 leaves, written 18mo. **eighteenth** *n.* any one of 18 equal parts. ~*n., a.* **1** (the) last of 18 (people, things etc.). **2** (the) next after the 17th.

eighty (ā´ti) *n.* (*pl.* **eighties**) **1** the number or figure 80 or lxxx. **2** the age of 80. ~*a.* **1** 80 in number. **2** aged 80. **eighties** *n.pl.* **1** the period of time between a person's 80th and 90th birthdays. **2** the range of temperature between 80 and 90 degrees. **3** the period of time between the 80th and 90th years of a century. **eightieth** *n.* any one of 80 equal parts. ~*n.*, *a.* **1** (the) last of 80 equal parts. **2** the next after the 79th. **eightyfold** *a.*, *adv.* **eighty-one, eighty-two** etc. *n.*, *a.* the cardinal numbers between 80 and 90.

☒ **eigth** common misspelling of EIGHTH (under EIGHT).

einsteinium (īnstī´niəm) *n.* (*Chem.*) a radioactive element, at. no. 99, chem. symbol Es, artificially produced from plutonium.

eirenic IRENIC.

eisteddfod (īstedh´vod, -ted´fod) *n.* (*pl.* **eisteddfods, eisteddfodau** (-vodī)) a competitive congress of Welsh bards and musicians held annually to encourage native poetry and music. **eisteddfodic** *a.*

either (ī´dhə, ē´-) *a.*, *pron.* **1** one or the other of two. **2** each of two. ~*adv.*, *conj.* **1** in one or the other case (as a disjunctive correlative). **2** any more than the other (with neg. or interrog., as *If you don't I don't either*). **either-or** *a.* of or relating to a situation in which a choice must be made between two alternatives.

ejaculate[1] (ijak´ūlāt) *v.t.* **1** to utter suddenly and briefly; to exclaim. **2** to eject. ~*v.i.* **1** to utter ejaculations. **2** to emit semen. **ejaculation** (-lā´shən) *n.* **1** an abrupt exclamation. **2** the emission of seminal fluid. **ejaculative** *a.* **ejaculatory** *a.*

ejaculate[2] (ijak´ūlət) *n.* semen which has been ejaculated.

eject (ijekt´) *v.t.* **1** to cause to come out of e.g. a machine. **2** to force to leave. **3** (*Law*) to oust or dispossess. **4** to push out or remove forcefully. **ejecta** (-ə) *n.pl.* matter thrown out, esp. from a volcano. **ejection** (-shən) *n.* **ejective** *a.* **ejectment** *n.* **ejector** *n.* **ejector seat** *n.* a seat that can be shot clear of the vehicle in an emergency.

eke (ēk) *v.t.* **1** (*coll.*) to produce, support or maintain with difficulty. **2** to make up for or supply deficiencies in (with *out*).

el (el) *n.* (*US*) an elevated railway.

-el -LE[2].

elaborate[1] (ilab´ərət) *a.* **1** carefully or highly wrought. **2** highly finished. **elaborately** *adv.* **elaborateness** *n.*

elaborate[2] (ilab´ərāt) *v.t.* **1** to develop in detail. **2** to work up and produce from its original material (as the food of animals or plants, so to adapt it for nutrition). **3** to produce by labour. ~*v.i.* to go into more detail (on). **elaboration** (-ā´shən) *n.* **elaborative** *a.* **elaborator** *n.*

élan (ilan´, ālā´), **elan** *n.* energy and confidence.

eland (ē´lənd) *n.* a large oxlike antelope, *Tragelaphus derbianus*, from S Africa.

elapse (ilaps´) *v.i.* (esp. of time) to glide or pass away.

elasmosaurus (ilazməsaw´rəs) *n.* (*pl.* **elasmosauruses, elasmosauri** (-rī)) an extinct marine reptile with platelike gills and a tough skin.

elastane (ilas´tān) *n.* a polyurethane with elastic properties, used in the manufacture of close-fitting clothing.

elastic (ilas´tik) *a.* **1** having the quality of returning to that form or volume from which it has been compressed, expanded or distorted; springy, rebounding. **2** (e.g. of plans or ideas) that can be changed easily. **3** admitting of extension. **4** readily recovering from depression or exhaustion, buoyant. **5** (*Physics*) (of a collision) involving no reduction in kinetic energy. ~*n.* a strip of elastic substance, a string or cord woven with India rubber threads. **elastically** *adv.* **elasticate** *v.t.* to render elastic. **elasticated** *a.* **elastic band** *n.* a rubber band for holding things together. **elasticin** (-las´tisin), **elastin** *n.* (*Chem.*) the substance forming the fibres of elastic tissue. **elasticity** (ēlastis´iti) *n.* **elasticize** (-īz), **elasticise** *v.t.*

elastomer (ilas´tōmə) *n.* a synthetic rubberlike substance. **elastomeric** (-mer´ik) *a.*

Elastoplast® (ilas´təplahst) *n.* **1** a gauze surgical dressing on a backing of adhesive tape, suitable for small wounds, cuts and abrasions. **2** (**elastoplast**) a temporary measure used in an emergency etc.

elate (ilāt´) *v.t.* **1** to raise the spirits of, to stimulate. **2** to make exultant. ~*a.* lifted up, in high spirits, exultant. **elated** *a.* **elatedly** *adv.* **elatedness** *n.* **elation** (ilā´shən) *n.*

elbow (el´bō) *n.* **1** the joint uniting the forearm with the upper arm. **2** the part of a sleeve covering the elbow. **3** an elbow-shaped (usu. obtuse) angle, bend or corner. **4** an elbow-shaped piece of piping etc. ~*v.t.* **1** to push or thrust with the elbows, to jostle. **2** to force (a way or oneself into, out of etc.) by pushing with the elbows. **at one's elbow** near at hand. **out at (the) elbows 1** shabby in dress; in needy circumstances. **2** (of a coat etc.) worn through at the elbows, shabby. **to give someone the elbow** to dismiss or reject someone. **elbow grease** *n.* (*coll.*) hard and continued manual exercise. **elbow room** *n.* ample room for action.

elder[1] (el´də) *a.* **1** older. **2** senior in position. ~*n.* **1** a senior in years. **2** a person whose age entitles them to respect. **3** (*pl.*) persons of greater age. **4** a member of a senate, a counsellor. **5** an officer in the Jewish synagogue, in the early Christian, and in the Presbyterian and other churches. **elder hand** *n.* in cards, the person on the dealer's left, who has the right to play first. **elderly** *a.* old. **elderliness** *n.* **eldership** *n.* **elder statesman** *n.* a retired or experienced and respected politician or administrator. **eldest** *a.* **1** oldest. **2** first born of those surviving. **the eldest** the oldest person of the three or more in question. **eldest hand** *n.* ELDER HAND (under ELDER[1]).

elder[2] (el´də) *n.* a tree of the genus *Sambucus*, esp. *S. nigra*, a small tree bearing white flowers and dark purple berries. **elderberry** *n.* (*pl.* **elderberries**) **1** the elder tree. **2** the fruit of the elder tree. **elderflower** *n.* the flower of the elder tree.

El Dorado (el dərah´dō), **eldorado, Eldorado** *n.* **1** any place where money or profit is easily obtained. **2** an inexhaustible mine.

eldritch (el´drich) *a.* (*Sc., N Am.*) strange, weird, ghastly, frightful.

elecampane (elikampān´) *n.* a composite plant, *Inula helenium*, used in cooking and medicinally.

elect (ilekt´) *v.t.* **1** to choose for any office or employment. **2** to choose by vote. **3** to determine on any particular course of action. **4** (*Theol.*) to choose for everlasting life. ~*a.* **1** chosen, picked out. **2** (*placed after the noun*) designated to an office, but not yet in possession of it, as *president elect*. **3** (*Theol.*) chosen by God for everlasting life. **the elect 1** the people chosen by God etc. **2** highly select or self-satisfied people. **electable** *a.* **election** (ilek´shən) *n.* **1** the act of choosing from a number of people or things, esp. by vote. **2** the ceremony or process of electing. **3** power of choosing or selection. **electioneer** (-niə´) *v.i.* **1** to work at an election in the interests of some particular candidate. **2** (*derog.*) to say what one thinks voters want to hear to get elected. **electioneering** *n.* **elective** *a.* **1** appointed, filled up or bestowed by election. **2** of or relating to election or choice. **3** having or exercising the power of choice. **4** optional. **5** involving some not all, selective. ~*n.* (*N Am.*) an optional course of study. **electively** *adv.* **elector** *n.* **1** a person who has the right, power or privilege of electing. **2** (*Hist.*) (**Elector**) any one of the princes of Germany who were entitled to vote in the election of the Emperor. **electoral** *a.* **electoral college** *n.* **1** in the US, the body of people who elect the president and the vice-president, having been themselves elected by vote. **2** a body of electors. **electorally** *adv.* **electoral register, electoral roll** *n.* an official list of the people entitled to vote in a borough, district etc. **electorate** (-rət) *n.* **1** the whole body of electors. **2** (*Austral., New Zeal.*) the area represented by a Member of Parliament. **3** (*ist.*) the dignity or territory of an elector of the German Empire. **electorship** *n.* **Electress** *n.* (*Hist.*) the wife of a German Elector.

Electra complex (ilek´trə kompleks) *n.* (*Psych.*) attraction of a daughter to her father accompanied by hostility to her mother.

electric (ilek´trik) *a.* **1** containing, generating or operated by electricity. **2** (of a situation, atmosphere etc.) very exciting. **3** dramatic, highly charged with emotion etc. ~*n.* **1** a non-conductor, in which electricity can be excited by means of friction. **2** (*pl.*) electric circuits or equipment. **electrical** *a.* of or relating to electricity; electric. **electrically** *adv.* **electricals** *n.pl.* **1** shares in electricity companies. **2** electric circuits or equipment. **electric blanket** *n.* a blanket containing an electrically-heated element. **electric blue** *n.* a steely blue. ~*a.* of this colour. **electric chair** *n.* a chair in which persons condemned to death are electrocuted. **electric eel** *n.* a large S American

eel, *Electrophorus electricus*, able to give an electric shock. **electric eye** *n.* a photocell. **electric fence** *n.* a wire fence charged with electricity, used for purposes of security. **electric field** *n.* a region in which forces are exerted on any electric charge present there. **electric fire, electric heater, electric radiator** *n.* an apparatus which uses electricity to heat a room. **electric guitar** *n.* an electrically amplified guitar. **electric hare** *n.* an artificial hare made to run by electricity, used in greyhound racing. **electrician** (eliktrish´ən) *n.* **1** a person who installs or maintains electrical equipment. **2** a person skilled in the science and application of electricity. **electricity** (eliktris´iti) *n.* **1** a form of energy which makes its existence manifest by attractions and repulsions, by producing light and heat, chemical decomposition and other phenomena. **2** (*Physics*) the branch of physics dealing with the laws and phenomena of electricity. **3 a** an electric charge. **b** an electric current. **4** strong excitement or emotional tension. **electric organ** *n.* **1** (*Mus.*) an organ operated electrically. **2** (*Biol.*) in some fishes, an organ which can produce and discharge electricity. **electric ray** *n.* a flatfish of the genus *Torpedo* which can give an electric shock. **electric razor, electric shaver** *n.* an appliance for removing bristles, hair etc. by the rapid movement of a protected blade actuated by electricity. **electric shock** *n.* the sudden pain felt from the passing of an electric current through the body. **electric storm** *n.* a violent disturbance of electric conditions of the atmosphere. **electric torch** *n.* a small lamp carried in the hand, containing an electric battery and bulb. **electrify** (ilek´trifī) *v.t.* (*3rd pers. sing. pres.* **electrifies,** *pres.p.* **electrifying,** *past, p.p.* **electrified**) **1** to charge with electricity. **2** to thrill with joy, surprise or other exciting emotion. **3** to give an electric shock to. **electrification** (-fikā´shən) *n.* **1** the act or process of electrifying. **2** the state of being electrified. **3** conversion of a steam or other mechanical system into one worked by electricity. **electrifier** *n.*

electro- (ilektrō) *comb. form* **1** having electricity for its motive power. **2** of, relating to or resulting from electricity.

electrocardiograph (ilektrōkah´diəgrahf) *n.* an instrument which indicates and records the manner in which the heart muscle is contracting. **electrocardiogram** *n.* a record so produced.

electroconvulsive (ilektrōkənvŭl´siv) *a.* (of a therapy for mental or nervous disorders) using electric shocks to the brain.

electrocute (ilek´trəkūt) *v.t.* **1** to kill by an electric shock. **2** to carry out a judicial sentence of death by administering a powerful electric shock. **electrocution** (-kū´shən) *n.*

electrode (ilek´trōd) *n.* **1** any one of the poles of a galvanic battery or of an electrical device. **2** an anode, cathode, grid, collector, base etc.

electrodynamics (ilektrōdīnam´iks) *n.* the branch of mechanics concerned with electricity in motion. **electrodynamic** *a.*

electroencephalograph (ilektrōensef´ələgrahf, -kef´-) *n.* an instrument recording small electrical impulses produced by the brain. **electroencephalogram** *n.* the record produced by an electroencephalograph. **electroencephalography** (-log´rəfi) *n.*

electrolyse (ilek´trəlīz), (*N Am.*) **electrolyze** *v.t.* **1** to decompose by direct action of electricity. **2** to subject to electrolysis. **3** to remove (hair) by electrolysis. **electrolyser** *n.* **electrolysis** (-ol´isis) *n.* **1** (*Chem.*) the decomposition of chemical compounds by the passage of an electric current through them. **2** the removal of unwanted body hair by applying an electrically charged needle to the hair follicles. **electrolyte** (ilek´trəlīt) *n.* a compound which may be decomposed by an electric current. **electrolytic** (-lit´ik) *a.* **electrolytical** *a.* **electrolytically** *adv.*

electromagnet (ilektrōmag´nit) *n.* a bar of soft iron rendered magnetic by the passage of a current of electricity through a coil of wire surrounding it. **electromagnetic** (-net´ik) *a.* **electromagnetically** *adv.* **electromagnetic radiation** *n.* radiation with electric and magnetic fields at right angles to each other, visible light, radio waves, X-rays etc. **electromagnetic spectrum** *n.* the whole range of wave-lengths, from long radio waves to short gamma rays, over which electromagnetic radiation occurs. **electromagnetism** (-mag´-) *n.* **1** magnetism produced by an electric current. **2** the science which treats of the production of magnetism by electricity, and the relations between magnetism and electricity.

electromechanical (ilektrōmikan´ikəl) *a.* of or relating to the use of electricity in mechanical processes etc.

electrometer (eliktrom´itə) *n.* an instrument for measuring the amount of electrical force, or for indicating the presence of electricity. **electrometric** (ilektrōmet´-) *a.* **electrometry** (-trom´itri) *n.*

electromotion (ilektrōmō´shən) *n.* **1** the passage of an electric current in a circuit. **2** mechanical motion produced by means of electricity. **electromotive** *a.* **electromotive force** *n.* difference in potential giving rise to an electric current.

electron (ilek´tron) *n.* (*Physics*) a particle bearing a negative electric charge, the most numerous constituent of matter and probably the cause of all electrical phenomena. **electron beam** *n.* a stream of electrons in a gas etc. **electron diffraction** *n.* the study of crystal structures by the diffraction of an electron beam by the atoms or molecules of the crystal. **electron gun** *n.* a device for producing an electron beam from a cathode. **electron lens** *n.* a device for focusing an electron beam by means of electrodes etc. **electron microscope** *n.* a thermionic tube in which a stream of

electrons is focused on to a cathode and thence casts a magnified image of the cathode on to a screen, capable of very high magnification. **electron pair** *n.* **1** (*Chem.*) two electrons sharing the same orbit. **2** (*Physics*) an electron and a positron. **electron spin resonance** *n.* (*Physics*) a technique for finding electrons in a paramagnetic substance by the use of high-frequency radiation in a magnetic field. **electronvolt** *n.* a unit of energy in atomic physics, the increase in energy of an electron when its potential is raised by one volt.

electronic (ilektron´ik) *a.* **1** of or relating to electronics. **2** operated or produced by means of electronics. **electronically** *adv.* **electronic flash** *n.* a flash for high-speed photography produced from a gas-discharge tube. **electronic mail** *n.* messages sent from one computer or fax machine to another by means of linked terminals. **electronic publishing** *n.* publishing of books etc. by electronic means, i.e. on disk etc. rather than on paper. **electronics** (eliktron´iks) *n.* (*Physics*) the science of applied physics that deals with the conduction of electricity in a vacuum, or a semiconductor, and with other devices in which the movement of electrons is controlled. **electronic tagging** *n.* the tracking of people, goods etc. by attaching a tag with a transmitter.

electrophorus (ilektrof´ərəs) *n.* an instrument for generating static electricity by induction. **electrophoresis** (-fərē´sis) *n.* (*Chem., Physics*) the movement of charged particles under the influence of an electric field.

electroplate (ilek´trōplāt) *v.t.* to cover with a coating of silver or other metal by exposure in a solution of a metallic salt, which is decomposed by electrolysis. ~*n.* articles so produced. **electroplater** *n.*

electroporation (ilektrōpərā´shən) *n.* (*Biol.*) the introduction of DNA etc. into bacteria by opening the pores of the cell membranes with an electric pulse.

electroscope (ilek´trəskōp) *n.* an instrument for detecting the presence and the quality of electricity. **electroscopic** (-skop´ik) *a.*

electroshock (ilektrōshok´) *a.* (of medical treatment) using electric shocks.

electrostatic (ilektrōstat´ik) *a.* **1** of or relating to electrostatics. **2** produced by electricity at rest. **electrostatics** *n.* the science of static electricity. **electrostatic units** *n.pl.* a system of units based on the forces between static electric charges.

electrotechnology (ilektrōteknol´əji) *n.* the use of electricity in technology. **electrotechnic** *a.* **electrotechnical** *a.* **electrotechnics** *n.*

electrotherapeutics (ilektrōtherəpū´tiks), **electrotherapy** (-ther´əpi) *n.* (*Med.*) the use of electricity to treat paralysis etc. **electrotherapeutic** *a.* **electrotherapeutical** *a.* **electrotherapist** (-ther´əpist) *n.*

electrotype (ilek´trətīp) *n.* **1** the process of producing copies of medals, woodcuts, type etc., by the electric deposition of copper upon a mould. **2** the facsimile so produced. *~v.t.* to copy by this process. **electrotyper** *n.*

elegant (el'igənt) *a.* **1** pleasing to good taste. **2** graceful, well-proportioned, delicately finished, refined. **3** excellent, first-rate. **4** (of an apparatus, experiment etc.) simple and ingenious. **elegance** *n.* **elegantly** *adv.*

elegy (el'əji) *n.* (*pl.* **elegies**) **1** a lyrical poem or a song of lamentation. **2** a poem written in elegiac couplets. **3** a poem of a plaintive, meditative kind. **elegiac** (-jī'-) *a.* **1** mournful. **2** of, relating to or of the nature of elegies. **3** suited to elegy; used for elegies. **elegiacally** *adv.* **elegiac couplet** *n.* a couplet consisting of a hexameter and a pentameter. **elegiacs** *n.pl.* verse written in elegiac couplets, as were many of the elegies of the Greeks and Romans. **elegist** *n.* **elegize** (el'əjīz), **elegise** *v.t.* to compose an elegy upon. *~v.i.* **1** to compose an elegy. **2** to write in a plaintive strain.

element (el'əmənt) *n.* **1** any one of the fundamental parts of which anything is composed. **2** (*Chem.*) a substance which cannot be resolved by chemical analysis into simpler substances. **3** a contributory factor; an aspect of a whole. **4** (*pl.*) earth, air, fire and water, formerly considered as fundamental substances. **5** the natural habitat of any creature, as water of fish. **6** the proper or natural sphere of any person or thing. **7** (*pl.*) violent atmospheric agencies. **8** (*pl.*) the rudiments of any science or art. **9** the resistance wire of an electric heater. **10** (*Chem.*) any one of the electrodes of a primary or secondary cell. **11** (*pl.*) the bread and wine used in the Eucharist. **12** (*Math., Logic*) a sole member constituting a set. **elemental** (-men'-) *a.* **1** of or relating to the four elements of which the world was supposed to be formed. **2** of or relating to the primitive forces of nature; like the primitive forces of nature. **3** ultimate, simple, uncompounded. *~n.* an elemental spirit. **elementally** *adv.* **elemental spirit** *n.* any of those spirits identified with natural forces, such as salamanders, sylphs, gnomes and undines, said to inhabit respectively fire, air, earth and water. **elementary** (-men'-) *a.* **1** rudimentary, relating to first principles, introductory. **2** easy, simple. **3** (*Chem.*) consisting of one element; primary, uncompounded. **elementarily** *adv.* **elementariness** *n.* **elementary particle** *n.* any of several particles, such as electrons, protons or neutrons, which are less complex than atoms, so called because believed to be incapable of subdivision. **elementary school** *n.* **1** (*esp. Hist.*) a primary school. **2** (*N Am.*) a school attended by children for the first six to eight years of education.

elephant (el'ifənt) *n.* (*pl.* in general **elephant**, in particular **elephants**) a large pachydermatous animal, four-footed, with flexible proboscis and long curved tusks, of which two species now exist, *Elephas maximus* and *Loxodonta africana*, the former partially domesticated and used as a beast of draught and burden. **elephant-bird** *n.* an aepyornis. **elephant grass** *n.* any of several very tall tropical grasses, esp. *Pennisetum purpureum.* **elephantiasis** (elifəntī'əsis) *n.* a cutaneous disease occurring in tropical countries, in which the skin of the patient becomes hardened and the part affected greatly enlarged. **elephantine** (-fan'tīn) *a.* **1** of or relating to elephants. **2** resembling an elephant. **3** huge, immense. **4** unwieldy, clumsy. **elephantoid** (-fan'toid) *a.* **elephant seal** *n.* the sea elephant. **elephant shrew** *n.* a small African insectivorous mammal with a long snout, of the family Macroscelididae.

elevate (el'əvāt) *v.t.* **1** to lift up; to raise higher. **2** to raise from a lower to a higher place. **3** to exalt in position or dignity. **4** to make louder or higher. **5** to raise in character or intellectual capacity. **6** to refine, to improve. **elevated** *a.* **1** raised. **2** at or on a higher level. **3** (*coll.*) slightly intoxicated. **elevated railway** *n.* a city railway raised on pillars above the street-level. **elevation** (elivā'shən) *n.* **1** the act of elevating. **2** the state of being elevated. **3** an elevated position or ground. **4** height above sea level, or any other given level. **5** the height of a building. **6** a side or end view of an object or building drawn with or without reference to perspective. **7** (*Astron.*) the angular altitude of a heavenly body above the horizon. **8** in gunnery, the angle of the line of fire with the plane of the horizon. **9** (*fig.*) exaltation, grandeur, dignity. **10** in ballet, the ability to leap and seem to remain suspended in the air. **11** the tightening of elevators to raise the body. **elevator** *n.* **1** a person who or something which elevates. **2** a hinged flap on the tailplane to provide vertical control of an aircraft. **3** a muscle whose function it is to raise any part of the body. **4** a machine for hoisting, as to raise grain from a car or ship to a high level, whence it can be discharged into any other receptacle. **5** (*N Am.*) a lift for moving between floors or levels. **6** (*N Am.*) a place to which grain is lifted for storage. **elevatory** *a.*

eleven (ilev'ən) *n.* **1** the number or figure 11 or xi. **2** the age of 11. **3** a set of eleven things or people. **4** an article of attire, such as a shoe etc., denoted by the number 11. **5** a score of 11 points. **6** the 11th hour after midday or midnight. **7** in cricket or association football, the eleven people selected to play for a particular side. *~a.* **1** 11 in number. **2** aged 11. **elevenfold** *a., adv.* **elevenses** (-ziz) *n.pl.* (*coll.*) a snack taken in the middle of the morning. **eleventh** *n.* **1** any one of 11 equal parts. **2** (*Mus.*) the interval of an octave and a fourth. *~n., a.* **1** (the) last of 11 (people, things etc.). **2** (the) next after the 10th. **at the eleventh hour** at the last moment (in allusion to the parable of the labourers, Matthew xx).

elevon (el'ivon) *n.* a wing-flap on a delta wing aircraft.

elf (elf) *n.* (*pl.* **elves** (elvz)) **1** a tiny supernatural being supposed to inhabit groves and wild and desolate places and to exercise a mysterious power over human beings. **2** a mischievous person. **3** an imp. **4** a tiny creature, a dwarf. **elfin** *a*. very small and delicate, like an elf. ~*n*. **1** a little elf. **2** a sprite, an urchin. **elfish, elvish** *a*. **elf-lock** *n*. hair tangled in a knot, as if done by elves.

elicit (ilis´it) *v.t.* (*pres.p.* **eliciting,** *past, p.p.* **elicited**) **1** to draw out, evoke. **2** to obtain (information or a response), esp. when this is difficult. **elicitation** (-ā´shən) *n.* **elicitor** *n.*

Usage note The spellings of the verb *elicit* and the adjective *illicit* (pronounced the same) should not be confused.

---

elide (ilīd´) *v.t.* **1** to strike out, omit, delete. **2** esp. in grammar, to cut off (as the last syllable). **elision** (ilizh´ən) *n.* **1** the suppression of a letter or syllable for the sake of euphony, metre etc. **2** the suppression of a passage in a book or a discourse.

eligible (el´ijibəl) *a.* **1** fit or deserving to be chosen. **2** desirable, suitable. **3** fit or qualified to be chosen to any office or position. **4** desirable for marriage. **eligibility** (-bil´-) *n.* **eligibly** *adv.*

eliminate (ilim´ināt) *v.t.* **1** to cast out, expel. **2** to cast aside, remove, get rid of. **3** to exclude, to ignore (certain considerations). **4** to expel (waste matter) from the body. **5** (*sl.*) to murder. **6** (*Math.*) to cause to disappear from an equation. **eliminable** *a.* **elimination** (-ā´shən) *n.* **eliminator** *n.* **eliminatory** *a.*

ELINT (elint´), **Elint** *n.* gathering intelligence by electronic means.

elision ELIDE.

elite (ālēt´), **élite** *n.* the best part, the most powerful. **elitism** *n.* (*often derog.*) **1** the favouring of the creation of an elite. **2** a sense of pride or conceit at belonging to an elite. **elitist** *n., a.*

elixir (ilik´sə) *n.* **1** the alchemists' liquor for transmuting metal into gold. **2** a potion for prolonging life. **3** a cordial, a sovereign remedy. **elixir vitae** (vī´tē), **elixir of life** *n.* a potion which was supposed to prolong life.

Elizabethan (ilizəbē´thən) *a.* **1** of or relating to Queen Elizabeth I or Queen Elizabeth II or the time of either of these. **2** in the style characterizing the literature, architecture, dress etc. of the time of Elizabeth I. ~*n.* a personage or writer of the time of Elizabeth I or II.

elk (elk) *n.* (*pl. in general* **elk,** *in particular* **elks**) **1** the largest animal of the deer family, *Alces alces*, a native of northern Europe and of N America, where it is called the moose. **2** the wapiti. **elk-hound** *n.* **1** a large breed of hunting dog of the spitz type, orig. used for hunting elk. **2** a dog of this breed.

ell (el) *n.* (*Hist.*) a measure of length, varying in different countries, for measuring cloth: the English ell is 45 in. (114.3 cm).

ellipse (ilips´) *n.* a regular oval; a plane curve of such a form that the sum of two straight lines, drawn from any point in it to two given fixed

points called the foci, will always be the same. **ellipsis** (-sis) *n.* (*pl.* **ellipses** (-sēz)) **1** omission of one or more words necessary to the complete construction of a sentence. **2** (*Print.*) a set of three dots indicating omitted matter. **ellipsoid** (-soid) *n.* a solid figure of which every plane section through one axis is an ellipse and every other section an ellipse or a circle. **ellipsoidal** (elipsoi´-) *a.* **elliptic** (-tik), **elliptical** (-kəl) *a.* **1** of or relating to an ellipse. **2** of or relating to ellipsis. **elliptically** *adv.* **ellipticity** (eliptis´-) *n.*

elm (elm) *n.* **1** any tree of the genus *Ulmus.* **2** ENGLISH ELM (under ENGLISH). **3** the wood of the elm. **elm tree** *n.* **elmwood** *n.* **elmy** *a.*

elocution (eləkū´shən) *n.* **1** the art, style or manner of speaking or reading. **2** effective oral delivery. **3** a particular style of speaking. **elocutionary** *a.* **elocutionist** *n.*

elongate (ē´longgāt) *v.t.* **1** to extend. **2** to make longer. ~*v.i.* **1** to grow longer. **2** (*Bot.*) to increase in length, to taper. ~*a.* **1** lengthened, extended. **2** (*Zool., Bot.*) very slender in proportion to length. **elongated** *a.* slender in proportion to length. **elongation** (-gā´shən) *n.* **1** the act of lengthening or extending. **2** the state of being elongated. **3** a prolongation, an extension. **4** (*Astron.*) the angular distance of a planet from the sun or of a satellite from its primary.

elope (ilōp´) *v.i.* **1** to run away with a lover, with a view to a secret marriage, in defiance of social or moral restraint. **2** to run away in a secret manner, to abscond. **elopement** *n.* **eloper** *n.*

eloquence (el´əkwəns) *n.* **1** fluent, powerful and appropriate verbal expression, esp. of emotional ideas. **2** eloquent language. **3** rhetoric. **4** a way of expressing something clearly. **eloquent** *a.* **1** having the power of expression in fluent, vivid and appropriate language. **2** full of expression, feeling or interest. **eloquently** *adv.*

else (els) *adv.* **1** besides, in addition, other. **2** instead. **3** otherwise, in the other case, if not. **elsewhere** *adv.* in or to some other place.

ELT *abbr.* English language teaching.

elucidate (iloo´sidāt) *v.t.* **1** to make clear and easy to understand. **2** to render intelligible; to explain. **elucidation** (-ā´shən) *n.* **elucidative** (-loo´-) *a.* **elucidator** *n.* **elucidatory** *a.*

elude (ilood´) *v.t.* **1** to escape from by artifice or dexterity. **2** to evade, to dodge, to shirk. **3** to remain undiscovered or unexplained by. **4** to baffle (search or inquiry). **elusion** (-zhən) *n.* **elusive** (-siv) *a.* **1** difficult to catch or locate. **2** difficult to remember. **3** difficult to understand or describe. **elusively** *adv.* **elusiveness** *n.* **elusory** *a.*

Usage note The spellings of adjectives *elusive, elusory* (from *elude*) and *illusive* and *illusory* (deceptive, pronounced the same) should not be confused.

---

elute (iloot´) *v.t.* (*Chem.*) to wash out by the action of a solvent.

elver (el´və) *n.* a young eel, esp. a young conger.

elvish, elves ELF.

Elysium (iliz´iəm) *n.* a place or state of perfect happiness. **Elysian** *a.*

elytron (el´itron) *n.* (*pl.* **elytra** (-trə)) each of the horny sheaths which constitute the anterior wings of beetles.

em (em) *n.* **1** (*Print.*) the square of the body of any size of type, used as the unit of measurement for printed matter. **2** a printers' general measure of 12 points or ⅙ in. (0.42 cm). **em dash, em rule** *n.* a dash one em long (—), used in punctuation.

'em (əm) *pron.* (*coll.*) THEM.

emaciate (imā´siāt) *v.t.* **1** to cause to lose flesh or become lean. **2** to reduce to leanness, to impoverish (soil etc.). **emaciated** *a.* abnormally and unhealthily thin. **emaciation** (-ā´shən) *n.*

email E-MAIL (under E²).

emanate (em´ənāt) *v.i.* **1** to issue or flow as from a source, to originate. **2** to proceed (from). ~*v.t.* to emit, to send out. **emanation** (-ā´shən) *n.* **1** the act of emanating from something, as from a source. **2** that which emanates, an efflux, an effluence. **3** any product of a process of emanating. **emanative** *a.*

emancipate (iman´sipāt) *v.t.* **1** to release from bondage, slavery, oppression or legal, social or moral restraint. **2** to set free, to liberate. **emancipation** (-ā´shən) *n.* **emancipator** (-man´-) *n.* **emancipatory** *a.*

emasculate[1] (imas´kūlāt) *v.t.* **1** to castrate. **2** to deprive of masculine strength or vigour; to make effeminate, to weaken. **3** to deprive (as language) of force or energy. **4** to enfeeble (a literary work) by undue expurgation or excision. **emasculation** (-ā´shən) *n.* **emasculative** (-mas´-) *a.* **emasculator** *n.* **emasculatory** *a.*

emasculate[2] (imas´kūlət) *a.* **1** castrated. **2** enfeebled, effeminate, weak.

embalm (imbahm´) *v.t.* **1** to preserve (e.g. a body) from putrefaction by means of spices and aromatic drugs. **2** (*poet.*) to imbue with sweet scents. **3** (*fig.*) to preserve from oblivion. **embalmer** *n.* **embalmment** *n.*

embank (imbangk´) *v.t.* to confine or defend with a bank or banks, dykes, masonry etc. **embankment** *n.* **1** a bank or stone structure for confining a river etc. **2** a raised mound or bank for carrying a road etc.

❌ **embarass** common misspelling of EMBARRASS.

embargo (imbah´gō) *n.* (*pl.* **embargoes**) **1** a prohibition by authority upon the departure of vessels from ports under its jurisdiction. **2** a complete suspension of foreign commerce or of a particular branch of foreign trade. **3** a hindrance, check, impediment. **4** a prohibition or restraint, as on publication. ~*v.t.* (*3rd pers. sing. pres.* **embargoes**, *pres.p.* **embargoing**, *past, p.p.* **embargoed**) **1** to lay an embargo upon. **2** to seize for purposes of state. **3** to prohibit, to forbid.

embark (imbahk´) *v.t.* to put on board ship. ~*v.i.* **1** to go on board ship. **2** (*fig.*) to engage or enter (upon any undertaking). **3** to go on board a ship,

an aircraft etc. **embarkation** (embahkā´shən), **embarcation** *n.* **1** the act of putting or going on board a ship or vessel. **2** a cargo, anything that is embarked.

embarrass (imbar´əs) *v.t.* **1** to make (someone) feel ashamed or uncomfortable. **2** to encumber, hamper, entangle, impede, hinder. **3** to involve in pecuniary difficulties. **4** to complicate, render difficult. **embarrassed** *a.* **1** feeling ashamed or uncomfortable. **2** in financial difficulties. **embarrassedly** *adv.* **embarrassing** *a.* causing embarrassment. **embarrassingly** *adv.* **embarrassment** *n.*

embassy (em´bəsi) *n.* (*pl.* **embassies**) **1** the official residence or offices of an ambassador. **2** the body of persons sent as ambassadors; an ambassador and their suite. **3** the function, office or mission of an ambassador. **4** an official deputation or mission.

embattle (imbat´əl) *v.t.* **1** to array in order of battle. **2** to prepare for battle. **3** to fortify. **embattled** *a.* **1** prepared for battle. **2** involved in a battle or in conflict of another kind.

embed (imbed´), **imbed** *v.t.* (*pres.p.* **embedding, imbedding,** *past, p.p.* **embedded, imbedded**) **1** to lay as in a bed. **2** to set firmly in surrounding matter. **3** to enclose firmly (said of the surrounding matter). **embedment** *n.*

embellish (imbel´ish) *v.t.* **1** to decorate in order to make more attractive. **2** to add incidents or imaginary accompaniments so as to heighten (a narrative). **embellisher** *n.* **embellishment** *n.*

ember[1] (em´bə) *n.* **1** a smouldering piece of coal or wood. **2** (*often pl.*) smouldering remnants of a fire or of passion, love etc.

ember[2] (em´bə) *n.* an anniversary, a recurring time or season. **Ember days** *n.pl.* in the Christian Church, certain days set apart for fasting and prayer, the Wednesday, Friday and Saturday next following the first Sunday in Lent, Whit-Sunday, Holy Cross Day (14 Sept.), and St Lucy's Day (13 Dec.).

embezzle (imbez´əl) *v.t.* to take fraudulently (what is committed to one's care). ~*v.i.* to commit embezzlement. **embezzlement** *n.* **embezzler** *n.*

embitter (imbit´ə) *v.t.* **1** to cause (a person) to be bitterly resentful or hostile. **2** to make bitter, or more bitter. **3** to render harder or more distressing, to aggravate. **embitterment** *n.*

emblazon (imblā´zən) *v.t.* **1** to blazon; to adorn with heraldic figures or armorial designs. **2** to decorate; to make brilliant. **3** to celebrate, to make illustrious. **emblazonment** *n.*

emblem (em´bləm) *n.* **1** a symbolic figure; a picture, object or representation of an object symbolizing some other thing, class, action or quality, as a crown for royalty or a balance for justice. **2** a symbol, a type, a personification. **3** a heraldic device. **emblematic** (-mat´-), **emblematical** (-kəl) *a.* **emblematically** *adv.* **emblematize, emblematise** *v.t.* **1** to represent by or as an emblem. **2** to symbolize.

embody (imbod´i) *v.t.* (*3rd pers. sing. pres.* **embodies**, *pres.p.* **embodying**, *past, p.p.* **embodied**) **1** to incarnate or invest with a material body. **2** to express in a concrete form. **3** to be a concrete expression of, to form into a united whole. **4** to incorporate, to include. **embodier** *n.* **embodiment** *n.*

embolden (imbōl´dən) *v.t.* **1** to give boldness to. **2** to encourage.

embolism (em´bəlizm) *n.* (*Med.*) partial or total blocking-up of a blood vessel by a clot of blood, bubble of air etc. **embolus** (-ləs) *n.* (*pl.* **emboli** (-lī)) a clot which causes embolism.

emboss (imbos´) *v.t.* **1** to engrave or mould in relief. **2** to decorate with bosses or raised figures. **3** to cause to stand out in relief. **embossed** *a.* **embosser** *n.* **embossment** *n.*

embouchure (ābooshuə´) *n.* **1** (*Mus.*) **a** the shaping of the lips to the mouthpiece of a brass or wind instrument. **b** the mouthpiece of such an instrument. **2** the mouth of a river etc.

embowel (imbow´əl) *v.t.* (*pres.p.* **embowelling**, (*N Am.*) **emboweling**, *past, p.p.* **embowelled**, (*NAm.*) **emboweled**) to disembowel.

embrace (imbrās´) *v.t.* **1** to enfold in the arms. **2** to clasp and hold fondly. **3** to enclose, encircle, surround. **4** to include, contain, comprise. **5** to receive, adopt, accept eagerly. **6** to take in with the eye, to comprehend. *~v.i.* to join in an embrace. *~n.* a clasping in the arms. **embraceable** *a.* **embracement** *n.* **embracer** *n.*

embrasure (imbrā´zhə) *n.* **1** the inward enlargement, bevelling or splaying of the sides of a window or door. **2** an opening in a parapet or wall to fire guns through. **embrasured** *a.*

embrittle (imbrit´əl) *v.t.* to make brittle. **embrittlement** *n.*

embrocate (em´brəkāt) *v.t.* to moisten, bathe or foment (as a diseased part of the body). **embrocation** (-ā´shən) *n.* **1** a preparation for application by rubbing or fomenting. **2** the act of bathing or fomenting.

embroider (imbroi´də) *v.t.* **1** to ornament with figures or designs in needlework. **2** to variegate, to diversify. **3** to embellish with additions, esp. a narrative with exaggerations or fiction. *~v.i.* to do embroidery. **embroiderer** *n.* **embroidery** *n.* (*pl.* **embroideries**) **1** the act, process or art of embroidering. **2** ornamentation stitched with the needle. **3** the fabric ornamented. **4** additional embellishment. **5** exaggeration or fiction added to a narrative.

embroil (imbroil´) *v.t.* **1** to throw into confusion. **2** to entangle, to confuse. **3** to involve (someone) in a quarrel or contention (with another). **embroiler** *n.* **embroilment** *n.*

embryo (em´briō) *n.* (*pl.* **embryos**) **1** an unborn offspring. **2** the human offspring up to the end of the second month of development. **3** the rudimentary plant in the seed after fertilization. **4** the beginning or first stage of anything. **in embryo 1** in the first or earliest stage. **2** in a rudimentary

or undeveloped state. **embryoid** *a.* **embryonal** *a.* **embryonic** (-on´ik) *a.* **embryonically** *adv.*

embryo- (embriō), **embry-** *comb. form* of or relating to the embryo or embryos.

embryology (embriol´əji) *n.* the science of the embryo and the formation and development of organisms. **embryological** (-loj´-) *a.* **embryologically** *adv.* **embryologist** *n.*

emcee (emsē´) *n.* (*coll.*) a master of ceremonies. *~v.t., v.i.* (*3rd pers. sing. pres.* **emcees**, *pres.p.* **emceeing**, *past, p.p.* **emceed**) to act as emcee (for an occasion).

-eme (ēm) *suf.* in linguistics, forming nouns, meaning a smallest possible, indivisible unit, as *morpheme, phoneme*.

emend (imend´) *v.t.* **1** to correct, to remove faults from. **2** to improve (as the result of criticism). **emendable** *a.* **emendation** (ēmendā´shən) *n.* **emendator** (ē´men-) *n.* **emendatory** (imen´də-) *a.*

Usage note The meanings of the verbs *emend* and *amend* overlap, but *emend* is used mainly of corrections in texts being edited, and *amend* of correction and improvement more generally.

emerald (em´ərəld) *n.* **1** a variety of beryl, distinguished by its beautiful green colour. **2** the colour of this. *~a.* of a bright green colour. **emerald green** *n.* a bright green colour. **emeraldine** (-dīn, -din) *a.* **emerald moth** *n.* any of several green-coloured geometrid moths. *~*

emerge (iməj´) *v.i.* **1** to rise up out of anything in which a thing has been immersed or sunk. **2** to appear in sight (from below the horizon or from a place of concealment). **3** to appear, to come out (such as facts in an inquiry). **4** to become apparent. **5** to issue from a state of depression, suffering or obscurity. **emergence** *n.* **emergent** *a.* **1** coming into being, evolving. **2** arising or appearing unexpectedly. **3** (of a country etc.) having recently acquired independence.

emergency (imœ´jənsi) *n.* (*pl.* **emergencies**) **1** a sudden occurrence or situation demanding immediate action, a crisis. **2** a person requiring immediate medical attention. **3** (*Austral., New Zeal.*) a reserve player to substitute for an injured player in a team. **emergency exit** *n.* in a theatre or other public building, a door specially provided for exit in case of fire or other contingency.

emeritus (imer´itəs) *a.* (*placed after the noun*) having served one's term of office and retired with an honorary title (*professor emeritus*).

emery (em´əri) *n.* a coarse variety of corundum, of extreme hardness, and black or greyish-black colour, used for polishing hard substances. **emery board** *n.* a strip of card or wood, coated with crushed emery and used to file fingernails. **emery cloth, emery paper** *n.* cloth or paper brushed with liquid glue and dusted with powdered emery.

emetic (imet´ik) *a.* inducing vomiting. *~n.* a preparation for causing vomiting.

EMF *abbr.* **1** electromagnetic field. **2** (*often* **emf**) electromotive force.

-emia -AEMIA.

emigrate (em´igrāt) *v.i.* **1** to leave one's country in order to settle in another. **2** (*coll.*) to leave one's place of abode for another. ~*v.t.* to send (emigrants) out of the country. **emigrant** *a.* **1** emigrating. **2** of or relating to emigration. ~*n.* a person who emigrates. **emigration** (-rā´shən) *n.* **emigratory** *a.*

émigré (em´igrā), **emigre** *n.* an emigrant, esp. one of the royalists who left France at the time of the French Revolution.

éminence grise (eminās grēz´) *n.* (*pl.* **éminences grises** (eminās grēz´)) a man in the background exercising power unofficially.

eminent (em´inənt) *a.* **1** famous and respected. **2** (of services, qualities etc.) remarkable. **3** rising above others; high, lofty, prominent. **eminence**, **eminency** *n.* **1** loftiness, height. **2** a part rising above the rest, or projecting above the surface. **3** high rank, superiority. **4** the quality of being famous and respected. **5** (**Eminence**) a title of honour applied to cardinals. **eminent domain** *n.* the right of the state to confiscate private property for public use, payment usu. being made in compensation. **eminently** *adv.*

emir (imiə´) *n.* **1** in the Middle East and N Africa, a prince, chieftain, governor or commander. **2** a title given to the descendants of Muhammad through Fatima, his daughter. **emirate** (em´ərət) *n.* the jurisdiction, office or territory of an emir.

emissary (em´isəri) *n.* (*pl.* **emissaries**) a messenger or agent, esp. one sent on a secret, dangerous or unpleasant mission.

emission (imish´ən) *n.* **1** the act or process of emitting or being emitted. **2** the thing given off or out. **emission spectrum** *n.* ELECTROMAGNETIC SPECTRUM (under ELECTROMAGNET). **emissive** *a.* **emissivity** (emisiv´-) *n.*

emit (imit´) *v.t.* (*pres.p.* **emitting**, *past, p.p.* **emitted**) to give out, to give vent to, to issue, to discharge, to utter. **emitter** *n.* **1** somebody or something that emits. **2** an electrode of a transistor.

Emmental (em´əntahl), **Emmenthal** *n.* a type of Swiss cheese with holes in it.

emmer (em´ə) *n.* a variety of wheat, *Triticum dicoccum*, grown in Europe largely as livestock fodder.

emollient (imol´iənt) *a.* **1** softening, relaxing. **2** making soft or supple. ~*n.* **1** a substance which softens the part to which it is applied, and soothes and diminishes irritation. **2** anything intended to soothe or comfort. **emollience** *n.*

emolument (imol´ūmənt) *n.* **1** the profit arising from any office or employment. **2** remuneration.

emotion (imō´shən) *n.* **1** agitation of the mind. **2** a state of excited feeling of any kind, whether of pain or pleasure. **3** excitement. **emote** *v.i.* (*coll.*) to show or express exaggerated emotion as in acting. **emoter** *n.* **emotional** *a.* **1** of or relating to emotion. **2** easily affected with emotion. **3** arousing emotion. **4** based on emotion, using emotion rather than reason. **emotionalism** *n.* **emotionalist** *n.* **emotionality** (-nal´-) *n.* **emotionalize, emotionalise** *v.t.* **emotionally** (-mō´-) *adv.* **emotionless** *a.* **emotive** *a.* **1** of or relating to emotion. **2** tending to produce emotion. **emotively** *adv.* **emotiveness** *n.*

Usage note The uses of *emotional* and *emotive* overlap, but only *emotional* means easily affected with emotion, and *emotive* is more usual of arousing emotion.

empanel (impan´əl), **impanel** *v.t.* (*pres.p.* **empanelling, impanelling**, (*NAm.*) **empaneling, impaneling**, *past, p.p.* **empanelled, impanelled**, (*N Am.*) **empaneled, impaneled**) **1** to enter on the list of jurors. **2** to enrol as a jury. **empanelment** *n.*

empathy (em´pəthi) *n.* **1** (*Psych.*) the capacity for identifying with the experience of others, or appreciating things or emotions outside ourselves. **2** the losing of one's identity in, e.g. a work of art. **empathetic** (-thet´-) *a.* **empathetically** *adv.* **empathic** (-path´-) *a.* **empathically** *adv.* **empathist** *n.* **empathize, empathise** *v.t.*

emperor (em´pərə) *n.* **1** the sovereign of an empire. **2** the highest dignity (superior to king). **emperor moth** *n.* a large British moth, *Saturnia pavonia*. **emperor penguin** *n.* the largest type of penguin, *Aptenodytes forsteri*. **emperorship** *n.*

emphasis (em´fəsis) *n.* (*pl.* **emphases** (-sēz)) **1** a special prominence or significance put on an idea, policy etc. **2** a particular stress laid upon a word or words, to indicate special significance. **3** accent, stress on a word or syllable in speaking. **4** force or intensity of expression, language, feeling, gesture etc. **emphasize, emphasise** *v.t.* **1** to give special prominence to, to distinguish. **2** to pronounce (a word or syllable) with particular stress. **emphatic** (-fat´ik) *a.* **1** behaving or speaking in a forceful way. **2** (of words or syllables) carrying the accent. **3** using forceful language to show strong, certain feelings. **4** (e.g. of a victory) clear and undoubted. **emphatical** *a.* **emphatically** *adv.*

emphysema (emfisē´mə) *n.* **1** distension in the tissue of the lung, causing breathing difficulties. **2** the pressure of air causing distension in the cellular tissue.

empire (em´pīə) *n.* **1 a** the group of states or nations over which an emperor rules. **b** a state in which the sovereign is an emperor. **2 a** supreme and extensive dominion. **b** absolute power. **3** a large business conglomerate controlled by one person or company. **4** the period or duration of an empire. ~*a.* indicating the style of costume and furniture of the First or Second French Empire. **empire builder** *n.* a person who seeks added power and authority, esp. by increasing the number of their staff. **empire building** *n.*

empirical (impir'ikəl) *a.* **1** founded on experience or observation, not theory. **2** acting on this. **empiric** *a.* empirical. **empirical formula** *n.* (*Chem.*) a formula which gives the proportions of the atoms in a molecule, but not the exact numbers. **empirically** *adv.* **empiricism** (-sizm) *n.* **1** (*Philos.*) the theory that knowledge can only be derived from experience or observation. **2** the use of empirical methods. **empiricist** (-sist) *n.*, *a.*

emplacement (implās'mənt) *n.* **1** a setting in position. **2** a fortified platform for guns. **3** location, situation, position.

emplane (implān'), **enplane** (in-) *v.i.* to go on board an aeroplane. ~*v.t.* to place in an aeroplane.

employ (imploi') *v.t.* **1** to use, to exercise. **2** to set at work. **3** to keep in one's service, esp. for pay. **4** to spend or pass (time, oneself etc.) in any occupation. ~*n.* the state of being employed. **in the employ of** employed by. **employable** *a.* **employability** (-bil'-) *n.* **employee** (imploi'ē, emploiē'), (*N Am.*) **employe** *n.* a person who is employed regularly in some task or occupation for salary or wages. **employer** *n.* a person who employs people for salary or wages. **employment** *n.* **1** the act of employing. **2** the state of being employed. **3** regular occupation, trade or profession. **4** the act of using. **employment agency** *n.* (*pl.* **employment agencies**) a private agency used by people looking for work and by employers seeking employees. **employment office** *n.* a government office which advises the unemployed about job vacancies.

emporium (impaw'riəm) *n.* (*pl.* **emporiums**, **emporia** (-riə)) **1** a large shop where many kinds of goods are sold. **2** a commercial centre, a market.

empower (impow'ə) *v.t.* **1** to authorize. **2** to give power or self-determination to. **empowerment** *n.*

empress (em'pris) *n.* **1** the wife or widow of an emperor. **2** a female ruler of an empire.

empty (emp'ti) *a.* (*comp.* **emptier**, *superl.* **emptiest**) **1** void, containing nothing. **2** devoid (of). **3** vacant, unoccupied. **4** unloaded. **5** destitute, desolate. **6** meaningless, having no effect. **7** senseless, inane. **8** without intelligence, ignorant. **9** hungry, unsatisfied. ~*n.* (*pl.* **empties**) an empty packing-case, trunk, barrel, crate, bottle etc. ~*v.t.* (*3rd pers. sing. pres.* **empties**, *pres.p.* **emptying**, *past*, *p.p.* **emptied**) **1** to remove the contents from, to make vacant. **2** to deprive (of). **3** to remove from a receptacle (into another). **4** to pour out, discharge. ~*v.i.* **1** to become empty. **2** to discharge (as a river). **emptily** *adv.* **emptiness** *n.* **empty-handed** *a.* **1** bringing nothing. **2** carrying away nothing. **empty-headed** *a.* silly, witless. **empty-nester** *n.* a parent whose children have grown up and left home.

empurple (impœ'pəl) *v.t.* **1** to tinge or colour with purple. **2** to make angry.

empyrean (empirē'ən) *n.* **1** the highest and purest region of heaven, where the element of fire was supposed by the ancients to exist without any admixture of grosser matter. **2** (*poet.*) the upper sky. ~*a.* of or relating to the highest heaven or the upper sky. **empyreal** (-pir'i-) *a.*

emu[1] (ē'mū) *n.* (*pl.* **emus**) a large Australian cursorial bird of the genus *Dromaius*, esp. *D. Novaehollandiae*, resembling the cassowary but different in having no casque.

emu[2] *abbr.* electromagnetic unit.

emulate (em'ūlāt) *v.t.* **1** to try to equal or excel. **2** to imitate with intent to equal or excel. **3** to rival. **4** (*Comput.*) to imitate the functions of (another computer) so as to be able to use the same software etc. **emulation** (-lā'shən) *n.* **emulative** (-lətiv) *a.* **emulator** *n.*

emulous (em'ūləs) *a.* **1** desirous of equalling or excelling others. **2** engaged in rivalry or competition. **emulously** *adv.*

emulsion (imŭl'shən) *n.* **1** a colloidal suspension of one liquid in another. **2** a light-sensitive substance held in suspension in collodion or gelatine, used for coating plates or films. **3** emulsion paint. ~*v.t.* to apply emulsion paint to. **emulsify** (-mŭl'sifī) *v.t.* (*3rd pers. sing. pres.* **emulsifies**, *pres.p.* **emulsifying**, *past*, *p.p.* **emulsified**) to convert into an emulsion. **emulsification** (-fikā'shən) *n.* **emulsifier** *n.* something which emulsifies, esp. a food additive which prevents the ingredients of processed food from separating. **emulsionize, emulsionise** *v.t.* **emulsion paint** *n.* a water-thinnable paint made from an emulsion of a resin in water. **emulsive** *a.*

en (en) *n.* (*Print.*) the unit of measurement for casting-off copy, an en being the average width of a letter. **en dash, en rule** *n.* a dash one en long (–), used in punctuation.

en- (in, en, ən) *pref.* forming verbs with the meanings in, on, into, upon, as *enambush, encamp, encourage, engulf, enjewel, enslave, enlighten, encomium, energy, enthusiasm*.

-en[1] (ən) *suf.* forming diminutives of nouns, as *chicken, maiden*.

-en[2] (ən) *suf.* forming feminine nouns, as *vixen*.

-en[3] (ən) *suf.* forming adjectives from nouns, meaning pertaining to, made of, of the nature of, as *earthen, flaxen, golden, woollen*.

-en[4] (ən) *suf.* forming the pl. of nouns, as *oxen*.

-en[5] (ən) *suf.* forming verbs from adjectives or nouns, meaning to become or cause to become, as *deepen, fatten, heighten*.

-en[6] (ən) *suf.* forming the p.p. of strong verbs, as *broken, fallen, spoken*.

enable (inā'bəl) *v.t.* **1** to make able. **2** to authorize, to empower (to). **3** to supply with means (to do any act). **4** (*Comput.*) to render (a device) operational. **enablement** *n.* **enabler** *n.* **enabling act** *n.* legislation conferring specified powers on a person or organization.

enact (inakt') *v.t.* **1** to decree. **2** to pass, as a bill into a law. **3** to represent, act, play. **enactable** *a.*

enaction *n.* **enactive** *a.* **enactment** *n.* **1** the act or fact of enacting. **2** something enacted, as a law. **3** the performance of e.g. a play.

enamel (inam´əl) *n.* **1** a vitreous, opaque or semitransparent material with which metal, porcelain and other vessels, ornaments etc. are coated by fusion, for decorative or preservative purposes. **2** any smooth, hard, glossy coating. **3** a lacquer, a varnish, a paint, a cosmetic. **4** the ivory-like substance which covers the surface of the teeth. **5** a work of art made with enamel. **6** (*poet.*) a bright smooth surface. ~*v.t.* (*pres.p.* **enamelling**, (*N Am.*) **enameling**, *past, p.p.* **enamelled**, (*N Am.*) **enameled**) **1** to coat with enamel. **2** to paint, encrust or inlay with enamel. **3** to portray in enamel. **4** to form a smooth glossy surface upon. ~*v.i.* to practise the art of enamelling. **enameller**, (*N Am.*) **enameler** *n.* **enamelware** *n.* kitchen utensils coated with enamel.

enamour (inam´ə), (*N Am.*) **enamor** *v.t.* **1** to captivate, to charm. **2** to inflame with love. **to be enamoured 1** to be in love. **2** to be fond (of).

enantiomer (inan´tiōmə) *n.* (*Chem.*) a molecule which is the mirror image of another. **enantiomeric** (-mer´ik) *a.*

en bloc (ã blok´) *adv.* as one unit, all together.

enc. *abbr.* **1** enclosed. **2** enclosure.

encaenia (insē´niə) *n.pl.* a festival to commemorate the dedication of a church, the founding of a city etc.

encage (inkāj´) *v.t.* to shut in or as in a cage.

encamp (inkamp´) *v.i.* **1** to form an encampment. **2** to settle down temporarily in tents. ~*v.t.* **1** to settle (troops) in an encampment. **2** to lodge (troops) in tents. **encampment** *n.* **1** a camp. **2** the place where troops are encamped. **3** the act of encamping.

encapsulate (inkap´sūlāt) *v.t.* **1** to enclose in a capsule. **2** to capture the essence of. **3** to put in a shortened form. **4** to isolate. **encapsulation** (-ā´shən) *n.*

encase (inkās´), **incase** *v.t.* **1** to put into a case. **2** to enclose in a case. **3** to protect with a case. **encasement** *n.*

encash (inkash´) *v.t.* **1** to cash, to convert (bills etc.) into cash. **2** to realize, to obtain in the form of cash. **encashable** *a.* **encashment** *n.*

encaustic (inkaw´stik) *n.* **1** a mode of painting in which the colours are fixed by heat (now chiefly of painting on vitreous or ceramic ware in which the colours are burnt in). **2** a painting done by this method. ~*a.* of or relating to or executed by this method.

-ence (əns) *suf.* **1** forming abstract nouns meaning a state or quality, as *existence, corpulence*. **2** forming abstract nouns meaning an action, as *appearance, emergence.*

encephalin ENKEPHALIN.

encephalitis (insefəlī´tis, -kef-) *n.* inflammation of the brain. **encephalitic** (-lit´ik) *a.*

encephalo- (insef´əlō, -kef´-), **encephal-** *comb. form* brain.

encephalography (insefəlog´rəfi, -kef-) *n.* radiography of the brain. **encephalogram** (-sef´əlōgram, -kef-) *n.* an X-ray photograph of the brain. **encephalograph** (-grahf) *n.* an apparatus for making an X-ray photograph of the brain.

encephalon (insef´əlon, -kef´-) *n.* (*pl.* **encephala** (-lə)) (*Anat.*) the brain. **encephalic** (ensifal´ik, -ki-) *a.*

encephalopathy (insefəlop´əthi, -kef-) *n.* (*pl.* **encephalopathies**) any degenerative disease referable to a disorder of the brain.

enchain (inchān´) *v.t.* **1** to bind with chains. **2** to chain up. **3** to hold fast, to rivet (attention etc.). **enchainment** *n.*

enchant (inchahnt´) *v.t.* **1** to influence by magic, to bewitch. **2** to make (someone) feel interested and excited. **3** to delight in the highest degree. **enchanted** *a.* **enchantedly** *adv.* **enchanter** *n.* **1** a person who practises enchantment; a magician. **2** a person who delights or fascinates. **enchanter's nightshade**, (*N Am.*) **enchanter's nightshade** *n.* a woodland plant of the genus *Circaea*, esp. *C. lutetiana.* **enchanting** *a.* **enchantingly** *adv.* **enchantment** *n.* **enchantress** *n.* **1** a female magician. **2** a woman that men find very attractive and interesting.

enchilada (enchilah´də) *n.* a Mexican dish of a meat-filled tortilla served with chilli sauce.

encipher (insī´fə) *v.t.* to put (a message etc.) into cipher, to encode. **encipherment** *n.*

encircle (insœ´kəl) *v.t.* **1** to enclose or surround (with). **2** to take up a position round. **3** to embrace, to encompass.

encl. *abbr.* **1** enclosed. **2** enclosure.

enclasp (inklahsp´) *v.t.* to enfold in a clasp, to embrace.

enclave (en´klāv) *n.* **1** a territory completely surrounded by that of another state; an enclosure, as viewed from outside it. **2** a group of people whose behaviour and opinions differ from those of the people they live among.

enclitic (inklit´ik) *a.* (*Gram.*) of or relating to a word which cannot, as it were, stand by itself, but is pronounced as part of the preceding word, on which it throws its accent, e.g. *thee* in *prithee.* ~*n.* an enclitic word or particle. **enclitically** *adv.*

enclose (inklōz´), **inclose** *v.t.* **1 a** to shut in. **b** to surround or hem in on all sides. **2** to surround by a fence. **3** to put one thing inside another for transmission or carriage, esp. an extra sheet in a letter. **4** to contain. **5** (*Math.*) to surround on all sides. **enclosable** *a.* **encloser** *n.* **enclosure** (-zhə) *n.* **1** the act of enclosing an area of land, esp. to make common land private property. **2** a space of ground enclosed or fenced in. **3** that which encloses, as a fence. **4** anything enclosed in an envelope, wrapper etc.

encode (inkōd´) *v.t.* to translate a message into code. **encoder** *n.*

encomiast (inkō´miast) *n.* **1** a person who composes an encomium, a panegyrist. **2** a flatterer. **encomiastic** (-as´-) *a.*, †*n.*

encomium (inkō'miəm) *n.* (*pl.* **encomiums, encomia** (-miə)) **1** a formal eulogy or panegyric. **2** high commendation.

encompass (inkŭm'pəs) *v.t.* **1** to surround, to invest. **2** to go around or cover completely. **3** to include, to contain. **encompassment** *n.*

encore (ong'kaw) *int.* used as a call for a repetition at a concert, theatre etc. ~*n.* **1** a demand for a repetition of a song etc. **2** the repetition itself. ~*v.t.* **1** to call for a repetition of. **2** to call back (a performer).

encounter (inkown'tə) *v.t.* **1** to meet with, come across, esp. unexpectedly. **2** to meet in a hostile manner. ~*n.* **1** a hostile meeting, a skirmish, a battle. **2** an unplanned or unexpected meeting. **3** a meeting of an encounter group. **encounter group** *n.* a group of people who meet to develop self-awareness and understanding of others by frank exchange of feelings, opinions and contact.

encourage (inkŭr'ij) *v.t.* **1** to give courage or confidence to. **2** to animate, embolden. **3** to urge, to incite (to do). **4** to cause to happen, to increase or to foster (trade, opinion etc.). **encouragement** *n.* **encourager** *n.* **encouraging** *a.* **encouragingly** *adv.*

encroach (inkrōch') *v.i.* **1** to intrude (upon) what belongs to another. **2** to infringe (upon). **3** to get possession of anything gradually or by stealth. **encroacher** *n.* **encroachment** *n.*

encrust (inkrŭst'), **incrust** *v.t.* **1** to cover with a crust or hard coating. **2** to form a crust upon the surface of. **3** to apply a decorated layer or lining to the surface of. ~*v.i.* to form a crust. **encrustation** (enkrəstā'shən) *n.* **encrustment** *n.*

encrypt (inkript') *v.t.* **1** to put (information or a message) into code. **2** to conceal (information or a message) thus. **encryption** (-krip'shən) *n.*

encumber (inkŭm'bə) *v.t.* **1** to hamper, impede or embarrass by a weight, burden or difficulty; to burden. **2** to weigh down with debt. **3** to load or fill with rubbish or superfluous things. **encumberment** *n.* **encumbrance** *n.* **1** a hindrance to freedom of action or motion. **2** a burden, a hindrance, a clog. **3** (*Law*) a liability upon an estate, such as a mortgage, a claim etc.

-ency (ənsi) *suf.* forming abstract nouns meaning state or quality, as *efficiency, emergency, presidency.*

encyclical (insik'likəl, -sī'-), **encyclic** *n.* a circular letter, esp. a letter from the Pope to the bishops or to the Church at large. ~*a.* (of a letter) sent about to many persons or places.

encyclopedia (insīklōpē'diə), **encyclopaedia** *n.* a book containing information on all branches of knowledge, or on a particular branch, usu. arranged alphabetically. **encyclopedic** *a.* **1** of or relating to an encyclopedia. **2** (of knowledge) comprehensive; wide-ranging. **encyclopedism** *n.* **1** the compilation of an encyclopedia. **2** the possession of a large range of knowledge and information. **encyclopedist** *n.*

encyst (insist') *v.t.* (*Biol.*) to enclose in a cyst, bladder or vesicle. ~*v.i.* to become thus enclosed. **encystation** (ensistā'shən) *n.* **encystis** (-is) *n.* (*Med.*) an encysted tumour. **encystment** *n.*

end (end) *n.* **1** the extreme point or boundary of a line or of anything that has length. **2** the termination, limit or last portion. **3** the last part of a period. **4** the conclusion of a state or action. **5** a ceasing to exist. **6** the final lot or doom. **7** abolition. **8** death. **9** the cause of death. **10** a result, a natural consequence, a necessary outcome. **11** a purpose, an object, a designed result. **12** a reason for (a thing's) existence, a final cause. **13** the half of a sports court or pitch occupied by one player or team. **14** in bowls, the part of a game played from one of the ends of the green to the other. **15** in American football, a player on the wing. **16** (*usu. pl.*) a remnant. ~*v.i.* **1** to come to an end, to cease. **2** to result (in). ~*v.t.* **1** to bring to an end. **2** to put to an end, to destroy. **all ends up** completely. **at a loose end** (*coll.*) with nothing in particular to do. **at an end 1** finished, completed. **2** exhausted, used up. **at loose ends** (*N Am.*) at a loose end. **at the end of one's tether** at the limit of one's strength, endurance or patience. **end on** with the end pointing towards one. **end to end** with the ends touching, lengthwise. **in the end 1** finally. **2** after all. **no end** (*coll.*) plenty, much, many. **on end 1** upright, erect. **2** continuously. **the end** (*coll.*) something unendurably bad, the last straw. **to come to a bad end** to have an unpleasant or disgraceful future. **to come to an end** to end, to be finished, to be exhausted. **to end it all** to commit suicide. **to end up 1** to arrive at finally. **2** to become at last. **to keep one's end up** (*coll.*) to stand one's ground. **to make an end of** to bring to a close, to finish. **to make (both) ends meet** to keep expenditure within income. **to put an end to 1** to terminate, to stop. **2** to abolish. **to that end** for that purpose. **end-around** *n.* in American football, a play in which an end carries the ball around the opposite end. **endgame** *n.* the last part of a game of chess etc., when only a few pieces remain in play. **ending** *n.* **1** a conclusion, a termination. **2** the latter part of a story, an occurrence etc. **3** (*Gram.*) the terminating syllable of a word. **endless** *a.* **1** having no end. **2** seeming to continue for ever. **3** incessant. **4** innumerable. **endless band, endless cable, endless chain** *n.* a band with ends fastened together for conveying mechanical motion. **endlessly** *adv.* **endlessness** *n.* **endlong** *adv.* **1** lengthwise as distinguished from crosswise. **2** straight along. **endmost** *a.* the nearest to the end, the furthest. **endnote** *n.* a note at the end of a chapter or section of a book. **end of the line** *n.* the point at which something stops or beyond which it cannot continue. **end of the road** *n.* the point beyond which a person or thing can no longer go on or survive. **endpaper** *n.* any one of the blank pages placed between the cover and the body of a book. **end point** *n.* the point at which any process is seen as completed, esp. that where titration etc. shows an effect. **end product** n. the final product obtained after a series of processes. **end result** n. the final outcome. **end run** n. 1 (N Am.) an evasive tactic. 2 (in American football) a play in which the ball carrier runs round their own end. **end standard** n. a metal bar acting as a standard of length, of which the ends are the specified distance apart. **end-stopped** a. (of poetry) having a pause in sense at the end of a line. **end-user** n. the person, firm etc. in receipt of a manufactured product being sold. **endways** adv. 1 on end. 2 with the end foremost or uppermost. 3 end to end. 4 longthwise. **endwise** adv. **end zone** n. the rectangular area at the end of an American football pitch.

-end (ənd) suf. forming nouns meaning somebody or something to be perceived or treated in a particular way, as reverend.

endanger (indān´jə) v.t. to expose to danger. **endangered species** n. a species whose numbers are declining and which is at risk of extinction. **endangerment** n.

endear (indiə´) v.t. 1 to make dear (to). 2 to cause to be loved. **endearing** a. **endearingly** adv. **endearment** n. 1 the act of endearing. 2 the state of being endeared. 3 words or a gesture expressing affection.

endeavour (indev´ə), (N Am.) **endeavor** v.i. 1 to strive (after) a certain end. 2 to try, to make an effort (to). ~n. 1 an effort, an attempt. 2 exertion for the attainment of some object. **endeavourer** n.

endemic (indem´ik) a. peculiar to a particular locality or people. ~n. 1 an endemic disease. 2 an endemic plant. **endemically** adv. **endemicity** (endəmis´-) n. **endemism** n.

Usage note The adjectives endemic and epidemic should not be confused: an endemic disease is one common in a particular place or among a particular people, and an epidemic disease is one common at a particular time.

❌ endevour common misspelling of ENDEAVOUR.

endive (en´div, -dīv) n. 1 a kind of chicory, Cichorium endivia, much cultivated for use in salads, or C. intybus, the wild endive. 2 (N Am.) chicory in general.

endo- (en´dō) comb. form of or relating to the inside of anything.

endocardium (endōkah´diəm, endə-) n. (pl. **endocardia** (-diə)) a membrane lining the interior of the human heart. **endocardiac** (-ak) a. **endocarditis** (-dī´tis) n. inflammation of the endocardium. **endocarditic** (-dit´ik) a.

endocarp (en´dōkahp) n. (Bot.) the inner layer of a pericarp. **endocarpic** (-kah´pik) a.

endocrine (en´dōkrīn, -krin) a. (of a gland) having no duct and secreting directly into the bloodstream. **endocrinology** (-krinol´əji) n. the scientific study of the endocrine glands. **endocrinological** (-log´-) a. **endocrinologist** (-nol´-) n.

endoderm (en´dōdœm) n. 1 the inner layer of the blastoderm. 2 the membrane lining the internal cavity of certain organisms, esp. the Coelenterata. **endodermal** (-dœ´-) a.

endogamous (endog´əməs) a. necessarily marrying within the tribe. **endogamy** n. 1 the custom of taking a wife only within the tribe. 2 (Bot.) pollination between two flowers on the same plant.

endogen (en´dōjən) n. an endogenous plant. **endogenesis** (-jen´-) n. **endogenous** (-doj´-) a. growing from within. **endogeny** n.

endometrium (endōmē´triəm) n. (pl. **endometria** (-triə)) (Anat.) the membrane lining the cavity of the womb. **endometrial** a. **endometriosis** (-ō´sis) n. the presence of endometrial tissue outside the womb.

endomorph (en´dōmawf) n. 1 a person of plump, thick-set build. 2 a mineral enclosed inside another. **endomorphic** (-maw´-) a. **endomorphy** n.

endorphin (endaw´fin) n. any of a group of chemicals occurring naturally in the brain which have a similar effect to morphine.

endorse (indaws´), **indorse** v.t. 1 to write (one's name) on the back of (a cheque) to specify oneself as the payee. 2 to assign by writing on the back of (a negotiable document). 3 a to ratify, confirm, approve. b to declare one's approval of (a product), by way of advertising. 4 to record a conviction on (an offender's driving licence). **endorsable** a. **endorsee** (-sē´) n. the person to whom a negotiable document is assigned by endorsing. **endorsement** n. **endorser** n.

endoscope (en´dōskōp) n. an instrument for inspecting internal parts of the body. **endoscopic** (-skop´ik) a. **endoscopically** adv. **endoscopy** (endos´kəpi) n.

endoskeleton (endōskel´itən) n. the internal bony and cartilaginous framework of the vertebrates.

endosperm (en´dōspœm) n. the albumen of a seed.

endospore (en´dōspaw) n. 1 the inner layer of the wall of a spore. 2 a small spore produced by some algae and bacteria.

endotoxin (endōtok´sin) n. a toxin present within a bacterium and only released at death. **endotoxic** a.

endow (indow´) v.t. 1 to bestow a permanent income upon. 2 to invest (with talents, qualities etc.). 3 to invest with goods, estate, privileges etc. **endower** n. **endowment** n. 1 a the act of making permanent provision for the support of any person, institution etc. b the fund or property so appropriated. 2 (pl.) natural gifts, qualities or ability. **endowment mortgage** n. a form of mortgage in which the capital repayments go into a life assurance policy.

endue (indū´), **indue** v.t. (formal) 1 (usu. p.p.) to endow, to furnish. 2 to put on (as clothes). 3 to clothe, to invest (with).

endure

engineer

endure (indūə´) *v.t.* **1** to undergo, to suffer. **2** to tolerate (a person). **3** to bear, to stand (a test or strain). **4** to submit to. ~*v.i.* **1** to last, to continue to exist. **2** to stay in the same state. **3** to bear sufferings with patience and fortitude. **endurable** *a.* **endurability** (-bil´-) *n.* **endurableness** *n.* **endurance** *n.* **1** the act or state of enduring or suffering. **2** the capacity of bearing or suffering with patience. **3** continuance, duration. **endurer** *n.* **enduring** *a.* continuing to exist for a long time. **enduringly** *adv.*

ENE *abbr.* east-north-east.

-ene (ēn) *suf.* **1** (*Chem.*) denoting a hydrocarbon, such as *benzene, naphthalene.* **2** denoting an inhabitant of a place, as *Cairene.*

enema (en´əmə) *n.* (*pl.* **enemas, enemata** (-mətə)) **1** a fluid injected into the rectum. **2** an injection. **3** the apparatus with which an injection is made.

enemy (en´əmi) *n.* (*pl.* **enemies**) **1** someone hostile to another person, or to a cause etc. **2** an adversary, one opposed to any person, subject or cause. **3** a hostile army, military force or ship. **4** (a member of) a hostile force or nation.

energy (en´əji) *n.* (*pl.* **energies**) **1** internal or inherent power. **2** force, vigour. **3** capability of action or performing work by the use of physical or other resources, as *nuclear energy.* **4** active operation. **5** (*Physics*) a body's power of performing mechanical work. **energetic** (enəjet´ik) *a.* **1** active, vigorously operative. **2** forcible, powerful. **energetically** *adv.* **energize** (en´-), **energise** *v.t.* to give energy to. **energizer** *n.*

enervate (en´əvāt) *v.t.* to deprive of force or strength; to weaken. ~*a.* weakened; wanting in spirit, strength or vigour. **enervation** (enəvā´shən) *n.*

enfant terrible (āfā terēb´lə) *n.* (*pl.* **enfants terribles** (āfā terēb´lə)) a person who embarrasses people by behaving indiscreetly, unconventionally etc.

enfeeble (infē´bəl) *v.t.* to make feeble or weak. **enfeeblement** *n.*

enfetter (infet´ə) *v.t.* (*formal*) **1** to fetter. **2** to enslave (to).

enfilade (enfilād´) *n.* a fire that may rake a position, line of works or body of troops, from end to end. ~*v.t.* to pierce or rake with shot from end to end.

enfold (infōld´), **infold** *v.t.* **1** to wrap, cover or surround. **2** to hold close to oneself. **3** to arrange or shape in folds.

enforce (infaws´) *v.t.* **1** to compel obedience to (a law etc.). **2** to force or impose (loyalty, obedience, some form of activity etc.). **3** to bring into effect. **4** to press or urge forcibly (an argument etc.). **enforceable** *a.* **enforceability** (-bil´-) *n.* **enforced** *a.* forced, not voluntary. **enforcedly** (-sid-) *adv.* **enforcement** *n.* **enforcement notice** *n.* an official notice served on someone who has breached planning regulations. **enforcer** *n.*

enfranchise (infran´chīz) *v.t.* **1** to give (someone) the right to vote. **2** to give (a town, constituency etc.) full municipal or parliamentary rights and privileges. **3** to set free. **enfranchisement** (-chiz-) *n.*

ENG *abbr.* electronic news gathering.

engage (ingāj´) *v.t.* **1** to bind by a promise or contract, esp. by promise of marriage. **2** to hire, order, bespeak. **3** to employ, to occupy the time or attention of. **4** to attack, to come into conflict with. **5** to cause to interlock (parts of a gear etc.). ~*v.i.* **1** to promise (to do something). **2** to take part (in). **3** to enter into, embark (on). **4** to begin to fight, to enter into conflict (with). **5** to interlock (with). **engaged** *a.* **1** pledged to marry. **2** booked or occupied. **3** busy, employed. **4** (of a telephone line) already being used. **engaged column** *n.* (*Archit.*) a column fastened into a wall so that it is partly concealed. **engaged signal, engaged tone** *n.* a tone heard on a telephone line to indicate that it is already being used. **engagement** *n.* **1** the act of engaging. **2** an obligation, a contract. **3** a mutual promise of marriage. **4** employment or occupation of time or attention. **5** an appointment. **6** a hiring, a contract to employ. **7** the state of being hired. **8** an action or battle between armies or fleets. **engagement ring** *n.* a ring worn on the third finger of the left hand by a woman engaged to be married. **engaging** *a.* winning, pleasing, attractive (used of manners or address). **engagingly** *adv.* **engagingness** *n.*

engagé (āgazhā´, ong-gazh´ā) *a.* (of a writer, artist etc.) committed to a moral or political cause.

engender (injen´də) *v.t.* **1** to cause to happen. **2** (*formal*) to beget.

engine (en´jin) *n.* **1** an apparatus consisting of a number of parts for applying mechanical power, esp. one that converts energy into motion. **2** a machine or instrument used in war. **3** an instrument, a tool. **4** means to effect a purpose. **engine driver** *n.* a person who drives a locomotive. **engine house** *n.* a building containing an engine. **engine lathe** *n.* a lathe driven by machinery. **engine room** *n.* a room, esp. in a ship, where the engines are housed. **enginery** (-jin´ri) *n.* (*pl.* **engineries**) **1** engines. **2** apparatus, mechanism, machinery.

engineer (enjiniə´) *n.* **1** a person who is trained or qualified in a branch of engineering. **2** a person who designs or carries out construction work of mechanical, electrical or civic nature. **3** a person who maintains and repairs machinery, a mechanic. **4** (*N Am.*) someone who manages or attends to a locomotive, an engine driver. **5** a member of that part of an army which attends to engineering work. **6** (*fig.*) someone who carries through any undertaking skilfully or ingeniously. ~*v.t.* **1** to direct or carry out, as an engineer, the formation or execution of (as railways, canals etc.). **2** to contrive, to manage by tact or ingenuity. ~*v.i.* to act as an engineer. **engineering** *n.* **1** the skill or profession of an engineer. **2** the application of scientific principles to the design and construction of machinery, public works etc. **engineering science** n.

English (ing´glish) a. **1** of or relating to England or its inhabitants. **2** spoken or written in the English language. ~n. (pl. **English**) **1** the language of the British Isles, N America, Australasia, parts of Southern Africa, and other parts of the British Commonwealth. **2** (pl.) the people of England (sometimes of Britain). **3** (N Am.) a side spin on a billiard ball. ~v.t. **1** to translate into the English language. **2** to express in plain English. **English bond** n. bonding brickwork by means of alternate courses of headers and stretchers. **English elm** n. the elm Ulmus procera. **English horn** n. COR ANGLAIS (under COR²). **Englishman** n. (pl. **Englishmen**) a man who is a native or a naturalized inhabitant of England. **Englishness** n. **Englishwoman** n. (pl. **Englishwomen**) a woman who is a native or naturalized inhabitant of England.

engorge (ingawj´) v.t. **1** (Med.) to congest (with blood). **2** (in p.p.) to fill to excess. **3** to swallow up, to devour (food). **engorgement** n.

engraft (ingrahft´), **ingraft** v.t. **1** (Bot.) to graft upon, to insert (a scion of one tree) upon or into another. **2** to incorporate. **3** to implant, instil. **engraftment** n.

engrain INGRAIN¹.

engrave (ingrāv´) v.t. **1** to cut figures, letters etc. (on), with a chisel or graver. **2** to represent on wood, metal etc., by carving with a graver. **3** to inscribe or decorate (a surface) with figures etc. **4** to impress upon the mind deeply. ~v.i. to practise the art of engraving. **engraver** n. **engraving** n. **1** the act, process or art of cutting figures, letters etc. on wood, stone or metal. **2** that which is engraved. **3** an impression from an engraved plate, a print.

engross (ingrōs´) v.t. **1** to monopolize, to occupy the attention entirely, to absorb. **2** to write or type out formally, e.g. a legal document. **3** to write out in large, bold letters. **engrossed** a. absorbed (in, as in reading a book). **engrosser** n. **engrossing** a. absorbing, occupying the attention completely. **engrossment** n.

engulf (ingŭlf´), **ingulf**, †**engulph** v.t. **1** to cast, as into a gulf. **2** to swallow up, as in a gulf or whirlpool. **engulfment** n.

enhance (inhahns´) v.t. **1** to raise in importance, degree etc. **2** to improve. **3** to augment, to intensify. **enhancement** n. **enhancer** n. **enhancive** a.

enharmonic (enhahmon´ik) a. (Mus.) having intervals less than a semitone, as between G sharp and A flat. **enharmonically** adv.

enigma (inig´mə) n. **1** an inexplicable or mysterious proceeding, person or thing. **2** a saying in which the meaning is concealed under obscure language, a riddle. **enigmatic** (enigmat´-), **enigmatical** (-əl) a. **enigmatically** adv.

enjambment (injamb´mənt), **enjambement** n. the continuation of a sentence or clause, without a pause in sense, from one line of verse or couplet into the next.

enjoin (injoin´) v.t. **1** to direct, prescribe, impose (an act or conduct). **2** to direct or command (a person to do something). **3** to instruct (that). **4** (Law) to prohibit or restrain (a person) from doing something. **enjoinment** n.

enjoy (injoi´) v.t. **1** to take pleasure or delight in. **2** to have the use or benefit of. **3** to experience or have. **to enjoy oneself** (coll.) to experience pleasure or happiness. **enjoyable** a. **enjoyability** (-bil´-) n. **enjoyableness** n. **enjoyably** adv. **enjoyment** n.

enkephalin (enkef´əlin), **encephalin** (-sef´-, -kef´-) n. a chemical found in the brain, having a pain-killing effect similar to that of morphine.

enkindle (inkin´dəl) v.t. (formal) **1** to kindle, to set on fire. **2** to inflame, to rouse into passion, action etc.

enlace (inlās´) v.t. **1** to encircle tightly, to surround. **2** to embrace, enfold, entwine. **3** to entangle. **enlacement** n.

enlarge (inlahj´) v.t. **1** to make greater; to extend in dimensions, quantity or number. **2** to expand, to widen. **3** to make more comprehensive. **4** to reproduce (a photographic negative) on a larger scale. ~v.i. **1** to become bigger. **2** to expatiate (upon), to give more details about. **enlargeable** a. **enlargement** n. **1** the act or process of extending or increasing. **2** an increase in size or bulk. **3** something added on, an addition. **4** a photographic print or negative of a larger size taken from another. **enlarger** n. an apparatus for making enlargements of photographs.

enlighten (inlī´tən) v.t. **1** to give mental or spiritual light to, to instruct. **2** to release from ignorance, prejudice or superstition. **3** to give (someone) information (on). **4** (poet.) to shed light upon. **enlightened** a. **enlightener** n. **enlightenment** n. **1** the act of enlightening. **2** the state of having understanding and wisdom; freedom from ignorance or bias. **3** (Enlightenment) an 18th-cent. philosophical movement which stressed the importance of rationality and questioned tradition.

enlist (inlist´) v.t. **1** to enrol, esp. to engage for military service. **2** to gain the interest, assistance, participation or support of. ~v.i. to engage oneself for military service. **enlisted man** n. (pl. **enlisted men**) (US) a soldier or sailor who is not an officer. **enlister** n. **enlistment** n.

enliven (inlī´vən) v.t. **1** to give spirit or animation to. **2** to impart life to, to stimulate. **3** to brighten, render cheerful in appearance. **enlivener** n. **enlivenment** n.

en masse (ã mas´) adv. in a group, all together.

enmesh (inmesh´) v.t. to entangle or catch in or as if in a net. **enmeshment** n.

enmity (en´miti) n. (pl. **enmities**) **1** the state or quality of being an enemy. **2** hatred, hostility. **3** an instance of this.

ennoble (inō'bəl) *v.t.* **1** to make a noble of. **2** to make noble; to elevate in character or dignity. **ennoblement** *n.*

ennui (onwē') *n.* lack of interest in things, boredom.

eno- OENO-.

enormous (inaw'məs) *a.* **1** huge, immense. **2** exceedingly great in size, number or quantity. **enormity** *n.* (*pl.* **enormities**) **1** a monstrous crime, an outrage, an atrocity. **2** the state or quality of being excessively wicked. **3** enormousness. **enormously** *adv.* **enormousness** *n.*

Usage note The use of *enormity* of size (rather than *enormousness*) is sometimes disapproved of, though it is quite common.

---

enough (inŭf', †**enow** (inow') *a.* (*usu. placed after the noun*) sufficient or adequate for need or demand. *~pron.* **1** a sufficiency; a quantity or amount which satisfies a requirement or desire. **2** that which is equal to the powers or abilities. *~int.* used to denote sufficiency or satisfaction. *~adv.* sufficiently, tolerably, passably. **to have had enough of 1** to have had sufficient of. **2** to have had too much of, to be tired of.

en passant (ā pas'ā) *adv.* **1** by the way. **2** in chess, applied to the taking of a pawn that has moved two squares as if it has moved only one.

enplane EMPLANE.

enprint (en'print) *n.* an enlarged photographic print.

enquire INQUIRE.

enrage (inrāj') *v.t.* **1** to put in a rage. **2** to exasperate. **3** to provoke to fury. **enraged** *a.* **enragement** *n.*

enrapture (inrap'chə) *v.t.* to fill with rapture, to delight.

enrich (inrich') *v.t.* **1** to make rich or richer. **2** to add to the quality or value of. **3** to fertilize. **4** to add to the contents of. **5** (*Physics*) to increase the proportion of a particular isotope in (an element, esp. uranium). **enrichment** *n.*

enrobe (inrōb') *v.t.* **1** to put a robe upon, to attire. **2** to put a coating on.

enrol (inrōl'), (*N Am.*) **enroll** *v.t.* (*pres.p.* **enrolling**, *past, p.p.* **enrolled**) **1** to write down on or enter in a roll. **2** to record, to register, to celebrate. **3** to include as a member, to record the admission of. *~v.i.* to enrol oneself (as a member, student etc.). **enrollee** (-ē') *n.* **enrolment**, (*N Am.*) **enrollment** *n.* **1** the act of enrolling. **2** the state of being enrolled. **3** the total number of people enrolled.

en route (ā root') *adv.* on the way; on the road.

ensconce (inskons') *v.t.* **1** to settle (oneself) comfortably or securely. **2** to hide.

ensemble (āsā'blə, onsom'bəl) *n.* **1** all the parts of anything taken together. **2** the general effect of things taken together. **3** an outfit consisting of several (matching) garments. **4** (*Mus.*) the joint effort of all the performers. **5** (*Mus.*) a combination of two or more performers or players.

6 a group of supporting players or performers. **7** (*Math., Physics*) a set of systems having the same constitution but behaving in different ways. *~adv.* **1** all together. **2** all at once.

enshrine (inshrīn') *v.t.* **1** to place in or as if in a shrine. **2** to enclose and cherish (something) as if it is sacred. **3** to act as a shrine for. **enshrinement** *n.*

enshroud (inshrowd') *v.t.* (*formal*) **1** to cover with or as if with a shroud. **2** to conceal.

ensign (en'sīn, -sin) *n.* **1** a national banner, a standard, a regimental flag, the flag with distinguishing colours carried by ships. **2** a badge of rank or office. **3** (*Hist.*) the lowest rank of commissioned officers in an infantry regiment, by the senior of whom the colours were carried. **4** the lowest ranking commissioned officer in the US navy. **ensigncy, ensignship** *n.*

ensilage (en'silij, insī'lij) *n.* **1** a method of preserving forage crops whilst moist and succulent, without previously drying, by storing them en masse in pits or trenches. **2** fodder so preserved, silage. *~v.t.* to preserve by the process of ensilage. **ensile** (insīl') *v.t.* **1** to put into a silo for this purpose. **2** to ensilage.

enslave (inslāv') *v.t.* **1** to make a slave of, to reduce to bondage. **2** to bring under the domination of some influence, habit, vice etc. **enslavement** *n.* **enslaver** *n.*

ensnare (insnee') *v.t.* **1** to entrap. **2** to overcome by treachery. **ensnarement** *n.*

ensue (insū') *v.i.* (*3rd pers. sing. pres.* **ensues**, *pres.p.* **ensuing**, *past, p.p.* **ensued**) **1** to follow in course of time, to succeed. **2** to result (from).

en suite (ā swēt') *adv.* in succession, as part of a set. *~a.* forming a unit, as *en suite bathroom*.

ensure (inshooə') *v.t.* **1** to make certain (that). **2** to make safe (against or from any risk). **3** to assure or guarantee (something to or for). **ensurer** *n.*

enswathe (inswādh') *v.t.* to enwrap, to bandage. **enswathement** *n.*

ENT *abbr.* ear, nose and throat.

-ent (ənt) *suf.* **1** forming adjectives meaning causing or performing some action, or being in a condition, as *astringent, inherent*. **2** forming nouns denoting an agent, as *recipient, student*.

entablature (intab'lachə) *n.* (*Archit.*) the upper part of a classical building supported upon the columns, consisting in upward succession of the architrave, frieze and cornice.

entablement (intā'bəlmənt) *n.* **1** the platform or series of platforms supporting a statue, above the dado and base. **2** an entablature.

entail (intāl') *v.t.* **1** to involve, to necessitate. **2** (*Law*) **a** to bestow or settle (a possession) inalienably on a certain person and their heirs. **b** to restrict (an inheritance) to a particular class of heirs. *~n.* (*Law*) **1** an estate in fee limited in descent to a particular heir or heirs. **2** the limitation of inheritance in this way. **entailer** *n.* **entailment** *n.*

entangle (intang´gəl) *v.t.* **1** to ensnare, as in a net. **2** to involve in difficulties, obstacles, contradictions etc. **3** to twist together so that unravelling is difficult. **entanglement** *n.* **1** the act of entangling. **2** the state of being entangled. **3** a thing or set of circumstances that entangles. **4** an embarrassing or compromising relationship, esp. sexual. **5** (*Mil.*) an obstruction made using barbed wire etc. **entangler** *n.*

entellus (intel´əs) *n.* (*pl.* **entelluses**) (*Zool.*) an Indian monkey, the hanuman.

entente (ātänt´, ontont´) *n.* **1** a friendly understanding. **2** a group of states having such an understanding. **Entente Cordiale** (kawdiahl´) *n.* **1** the understanding between France and Britain reached in 1904. **2** (*also* **entente cordiale**) any such understanding between states or other powers.

enter (en´tə) *v.t.* **1** to go or come into. **2** to pierce, to penetrate. **3** to associate oneself with, become a member of. **4** to insert, to set down in writing, a list, a book etc. **5 a** to put down the name of as a competitor for a race etc. **b** to become a competitor in (a race etc.). **6** to initiate into a business etc. **7** to present or submit (a proposal, a protest etc.). **8** to join in, participate in. **9** to cause to be inscribed upon the records of a court or legislative body. **10** to admit into the regular pack (said of a young dog). **11** to admit as a pupil or member, to procure admission as such. **12** (*Law*) to take possession of. **13** to start doing something or being involved in something. ~*v.i.* **1** to go or come in. **2** to become a competitor. **3** (of an actor) to appear on stage. **to enter into 1** to form a part of. **2** to join. **3** to engage or take an interest in, to sympathize with. **4** to become a party to (an agreement, treaty, recognizances etc.). **to enter on** to begin, to set out upon. **to enter up 1** to set down in a regular series. **2** to complete a series of entries. **to enter upon 1** to begin, set out upon. **2** to begin to treat of (a subject etc.). **3** to take legal possession of.

enteric (inter´ik) *a.* of or relating to the intestines. ~*n.* enteric fever. **enteric fever** *n.* typhoid fever.

enteritis (entərī´tis) *n.* inflammation of the small intestine, usu. causing diarrhoea.

entero- (en´tərō), **enter-** *comb. form* of or relating to the intestines.

enterostomy (entəros´təmi) *n.* (*pl.* **enterostomies**) the surgical formation of an opening to the small intestine through the abdominal wall.

enterotomy (entərot´əmi) *n.* (*pl.* **enterotomies**) the surgical opening up of the intestines.

enterovirus (entərōvī´rəs) *n.* (*pl.* **enteroviruses**) a virus which enters the body through the intestinal tract.

enterprise (en´təprīz) *n.* **1** an undertaking, esp. a bold or difficult one. **2** spirit of adventure, boldness, readiness to attempt. **3** a business concern. **enterpriser** *n.* **enterprise zone** *n.* a depressed area given special government financial etc. backing to encourage commercial etc. improvement. **enterprising** *a.* **1** ready to undertake schemes involving difficulty or hazard. **2** energetic, adventurous. **3** full of enterprise. **enterprisingly** *adv.*

entertain (entətān´) *v.t.* **1** to receive and treat as a guest. **2** to occupy agreeably; to divert, to amuse. **3** to hold in mind, cherish. **4** to consider favourably. ~*v.i.* to exercise hospitality, to receive company. **entertainer** *n.* a person who entertains, esp. a person who performs amusingly at an entertainment. **entertaining** *a.* amusing. **entertainingly** *adv.* **entertainment** *n.* **1** the act of entertaining. **2** receiving guests with hospitality. **3** a public performance intended to amuse. **4** the art of entertaining, amusing or diverting. **5** the pleasure afforded to the mind by anything interesting, amusement. **6** hospitality.

enthalpy (en´thəlpi, -thalpi) *n.* (*Physics*) the heat content of a substance per unit mass.

enthral (inthrawl´), (*N Am.*) **enthrall, inthrall** *v.t.* (*3rd pers. sing. pres.* **enthrals,** (*N Am.*) **enthralls, inthralls,** *pres.p.* **enthralling,** (*N Am. also*) **inthralling,** *past, p.p.* **enthralled,** (*N Am. also*) **inthralled**) to enslave, to captivate. **enthralment,** (*N Am.*) **enthrallment, inthrallment** *n.*

enthrone (inthrōn´) *v.t.* **1** to place on a throne or place of dignity. **2** to invest with sovereign power. **3** to induct or install (as an archbishop or bishop) into the powers or privileges of a see. **enthronement** *n.*

enthusiasm (enthū´ziazm, -thoo´-) *n.* **1** intense and passionate zeal. **2** ardent admiration. **3** fervour. **4** an activity or subject that someone is very interested in. **enthuse** *v.i.* **1** (*coll.*) to manifest enthusiasm. **2** to speak gushingly. **enthusiast** *n.* **1** a person filled with or prone to enthusiasm. **2** a person whose mind is completely possessed by any subject. **3** a visionary. **enthusiastic** (-as´-) *a., n.* **enthusiastically** *adv.*

entice (intīs´) *v.t.* **1** to attract. **2** to tempt, seduce (from). **3** to try to persuade (someone) to do something by offering them something. **enticeable** *a.* **enticement** *n.* **enticer** *n.* **enticing** *a.* alluring, seductive. **enticingly** *adv.*

entire (intīə´) *a.* **1** whole, complete, perfect. **2** unbroken, undivided. **3** unmixed, pure. **4** unqualified, unreserved. **5** (of a horse) not castrated. **6** (*Bot.*) having the edges (as of a leaf) unbroken or unserrated. ~*n.* an uncastrated horse. **entirely** *adv.* **1** wholly, in every part; fully, completely. **2** exclusively. **entireness** *n.* **entirety** (-rəti) *n.* (*pl.* **entireties**) **1** entireness, completeness. **2** the entire amount, quantity or extent. **in its entirety** completely, as a whole.

entitle (intī´təl) *v.t.* **1** to give a right, title or claim to anything. **2** to give a certain name or title to, to designate. **3** to dignify (someone) by a title. **entitlement** *n.* **1** the state of being entitled (to). **2** something to which one is entitled.

entity (en'titi) *n.* (*pl.* **entities**) **1** anything that has real existence, a being. **2** the essential nature of a thing, that which constitutes its being. **entitative** *a.*

ento- (en'tō), **ent-** *comb. form* of or relating to the inside of anything.

entomb (intoom') *v.t.* **1** to place in a tomb, to bury. **2** to be a grave or tomb for. **entombment** *n.*

entomo- (en'təmō), **entom-** *comb. form* of or relating to insects.

entomology (entəmol'əji) *n.* the scientific study of insects. **entomologic** (-loj'-), **entomological** *a.* **entomologist** (-mol'-) *n.*

Usage note See note under ETYMOLOGY.

entourage (ātoorahzh', on-) *n.* **1** retinue, people following or attending on an important person. **2** surroundings, environment.

entr'acte (ātrakt') *n.* **1** the interval between the acts of a play. **2** music, dancing or other performance between the acts of a play.

entrails (en'trālz) *n.pl.* **1** the internal parts of animals; the intestines. **2** the internal parts (as of the earth).

entrammel (intram'əl) *v.t.* (*pres.p.* **entrammelling**, (*N Am.*) **entrammeling**, *past, p.p.* **entrammelled**, (*N Am.*) **entrammeled**) to entangle, hamper, fetter.

entrance[1] (en'trəns) *n.* **1** the act of entering, or an instance of entering. **2** the power, right or liberty of entering. **3** the passage or doorway by which a place is entered. **4** the means of entering into. **5** the act of coming on to the stage. **6** entering into or upon. **7** the right of admission. **8** entrance fee, or fee paid for admission, as to an entertainment, club, race etc. **9** (*Mus.*) an entry. **entrant** *n.* **1** a person who enters. **2** a person entering upon or into a new profession, sphere etc. **3** a person entering a competition, examination etc.

entrance[2] (intrahns') *v.t.* **1** to throw into a state of ecstasy. **2** to carry away, transport, enrapture. **3** to overwhelm (with some strong emotion). **entrancement** *n.* **entrancing** *a.*

entrap (intrap') *v.t.* (*pres.p.* **entrapping**, *past, p.p.* **entrapped**) **1** to catch in or as in a trap. **2** (*Law*) to lure into making a compromising statement or into committing a (criminal) offence. **3** to entangle in contradictions, difficulties etc. **entrapment** *n.* **entrapper** *n.*

entreat (intrēt') *v.t.* **1** to beseech, to ask earnestly. **2** to ask for (something) earnestly. ~*v.i.* to make entreaties. **entreatingly** *adv.* **entreaty** *n.* (*pl.* **entreaties**) **1** an urgent request. **2** importunity.

entrecôte (on'trəkōt, -kot) *n.* a beefsteak cut from between two ribs.

entrée (ā'trā, on-) *n.* **1** freedom or right of entrance. **2** (*orig. N Am.*) the main course of a meal. **3** a dish served between the fish and the meat courses.

entrench (intrench') , **intrench** *v.t.* **1** to put (oneself) in a defensible position, as if with trenches. **2** (*Mil.*) to surround with trenches. **3** to make furrows in. ~*v.i.* **1** to entrench oneself. **2** to trespass or encroach (upon). **entrenched** *a.* (of a person's attitude etc.) fixed, difficult to change by argument etc. **entrenchment** *n.*

entrepôt (ā'trəpō) *n.* **1** a warehouse for the temporary deposit of goods. **2** a commercial centre to which goods are sent for distribution.

entrepreneur (ātrəprənœ', on-) *n.* **1** a person who undertakes a (financial) enterprise, esp. one with an element of risk. **2** a contractor, or commercial intermediary. **3** an organizer of entertainments for the public. **entrepreneurial** (-nœ'riəl) *a.* **entrepreneurialism** *n.* **entrepreneurially** *adv.* **entrepreneurism** *n.* **entrepreneurship** *n.*

entrism ENTRYISM (under ENTRY).

entropy (en'trəpi) *n.* (*pl.* **entropies**) (*Physics*) the property of a substance, expressed quantitatively, which remains constant when the substance changes its volume or does work with no heat passing into or from it, thus forming an index of the availability of the thermal energy of a system for mechanical work. **entropic** (-trop'ik) *a.* **entropically** *adv.*

entrust (intrŭst'), **intrust** *v.t.* **1** to commit or confide (something or someone) to a person's care. **2** to charge with (a duty, care etc.). **entrustment** *n.*

entry (en'tri) *n.* (*pl.* **entries**) **1** the act of entering. **2** the passage, gate, opening or other way by which anything is entered. **3** the act of entering or inscribing in a book etc. **4** an item so entered. **5** (*Mus.*) **a** the coming in of an instrument or voice in ensemble music. **b** the point in a piece of ensemble music where this happens. **6 a** a person, animal or thing competing in a race or competition. **b** a list of competitors etc. **7** (*Law*) the act of taking possession by setting foot upon land or tenements. **8** the depositing of a document in the proper office. **9** the mouth of a river. **10** in bridge, (a card which provides) a chance to transfer the lead from oneself to one's partner or the dummy. **11** the right of admission. **entry form** *n.* an application form for a competition, a club etc. **entryism, entrism** *n.* the policy of joining a political party etc., in order to influence policy from within. **entryist** *n.*, *a.* **entry permit** *n.* a document authorizing a person to enter a building etc.

Entryphone® (en'trifon) *n.* a telephonic device at the entrance to a block of flats etc., which allows visitors to communicate with the flat occupier.

entwine (intwīn'), **intwine** *v.t.* **1** to twine or twist together. **2** (*fig.*) to interlace, to mingle together. **3** to embrace, clasp, enfold. **entwinement** *n.*

enumerate (inū'mərāt) *v.t.* **1** to reckon up one by one, to count. **2** to specify the items of. **enumerable** *a.* **enumeration** (-ā'shən) *n.* **enumerative** (-ətiv) *a.* **enumerator** *n.* **1** a person who enumerates. **2** a person who deals with population census forms.

enunciate (inŭn´siāt) *v.t.* **1** to pronounce distinctly, articulate clearly. **2** to express definitely, state or announce with formal precision. ~*v.i.* **1** to pronounce words or syllables. **2** to speak. **enunciable** *a.* **enunciation** (-ā´shən) *n.* **enunciative** *a.* **enunciator** *n.*

enure INURE.

enuresis (enūrē´sis) *n.* (*Med.*) involuntary urinating, incontinence of urine. **enuretic** (-ret´ik) *a.*

envelop (invel´əp) *v.t.* (*pres.p.* **enveloping**, *past*, *p.p.* **enveloped**) **1** to enwrap, to enclose, to surround so as to hide, to enshroud. **2** to wrap in or as in an envelope or covering. **3** (*Mil.*) to surround (an enemy) with troops or offensive works. **envelopment** *n.*

envelope (en´vəlōp, on´-) *n.* **1** a folded paper wrapper to contain a letter. **2** anything which wraps or envelops. **3** (*Astron.*) the nebulous covering of the head of a comet. **4** (*Bot.*) a whorl of altered leaves surrounding the organs of fructification. **5** the gas-bag of a balloon. **6** the outer glass covering of a light bulb, or the metal covering of a valve etc. **7** (*Math.*) a surface or curve which is tangential to each of a group of surfaces or curves.

envenom (inven´əm) *v.t.* **1** to make poisonous, to impregnate with poison. **2** (*fig.*) to make bitter or spiteful.

enviable, **envious** ENVY.

environ (invīə´rən) *v.t.* **1** to surround, to be or extend round, to encircle. **2** to surround so as to attend or protect, to beset. **3** to surround (with persons or things). **environs** *n.pl.* the parts or districts round any place.

environment (invīə´rənmənt) *n.* **1** the act of surrounding. **2** that which encompasses, surrounding objects, scenery, circumstances etc. **3** the sum of external influences affecting an organism. **4** living conditions. **5** (*usu.* **the environment**) the whole of the natural world inhabited by living organisms, esp. considered as vulnerable to pollution etc. **6** (*Comput.*) the whole operating system used by a computer for a particular application. **environmental** (-men´-) *a.* **environmentalism** *n.* **1** the belief that the environment is the main influence on people's behaviour and development. **2** concern for the environment and its preservation from pollution etc. **environmentalist** *n.* **environmentally** *adv.* **environment-friendly** *a.* not damaging to the environment.

envisage (inviz´ij) *v.t.* **1** to conceive of as a possibility. **2** to contemplate, esp. a particular aspect of. **envisagement** *n.*

envision (invizh´ən) *v.t.* to visualize, to envisage.

envoy (en´voi) *n.* **1** a diplomatic agent, next in rank below an ambassador, sent by one government to another on some special occasion. **2** a person sent as a messenger. **envoyship** *n.*

envy (en´vi) *n.* (*pl.* **envies**) **1** ill will at the superiority, success or good fortune of others, a grudging sense of another's superiority to oneself.

2 the object of this feeling. ~*v.t.* (*3rd pers. sing. pres.* **envies**, *pres.p.* **envying**, *past*, *p.p.* **envied**) **1** to regard with envy. **2** to covet. ~*v.i.* to have envious feelings. **enviable** *a.* **1** capable of exciting envy. **2** of a nature to be envied. **3** greatly to be desired. **enviably** *adv.* **envier** *n.* **envious** *a.* **1** feeling envy. **2** instigated by envy. **enviously** *adv.* **enviousness** *n.*

enwrap (inrap´), **inwrap** *v.t.* (*pres.p.* **enwrapping**, **inwrapping**, *past*, *p.p.* **enwrapped**, **inwrapped**) (*formal*) to wrap or enfold.

enwreathe (inrēth´), **inwreathe** *v.t.* (*formal*) to encircle with or as with a wreath.

enzyme (en´zīm) *n.* a protein produced by living cells which acts as a catalyst, esp. in the digestive system. **enzymic** (-zī´-, -zim´-), **enzymatic** (-mat´-) *a.* **enzymology** (-mol´-) *n.*

Eocene (ē´əsēn) *a.* (*Geol.*) of or relating to the lowest division of the Tertiary strata. ~*n.* **1** the Eocene period. **2** the Eocene strata.

Eolian AEOLIAN.

eolith (ē´əlith) *n.* a roughly-chipped flint dating from the very early palaeolithic age, found abundantly in parts of the North Downs, and originally thought to be artificial. **Eolithic** (-lith´-) *a.* of or relating to the early palaeolithic age.

eon AEON.

-eous (iəs) *suf.* forming adjectives meaning of the nature of, as *arboreous*, *ligneous*, *righteous*.

EP *abbr.* **1** electroplated. **2** extended play (record). **3** extreme pressure.

epaulette (ep´əlet), (*N Am.*) **epaulet** *n.* an ornamental badge worn on the shoulder in military, naval and certain civil full dress uniforms.

épée (ep´ā) *n.* **1** a duelling sword. **2** a fencing foil. **épéeist** *n.*

epeirogenesis (ipīrōjen´əsis), **epeirogeny** (-oj´əni) *n.* (*Geol.*) the making of a continent by the pushing up of parts of the earth's crust. **epeirogenetic** (-ənet´ik), **epeirogenic** (-jen´ik) *a.*

ephedra (ef´ədrə, efed´rə) *n.* any evergreen shrub of the genus *Ephedra*, growing in America and Eurasia. **ephedrine** *n.* an alkaloid drug obtained from some plants of the genus, used to treat asthma, hay fever etc.

ephemera (ifem´ərə) *n.* (*pl.* **ephemeras**, **ephemerae** (-rē)) **1** the mayfly. **2** (*pl. of* **ephemeron**) items, such as newspapers, packaging etc., of transient usefulness or interest. **ephemeral** *a.* **1** beginning and ending in a day. **2** short-lived, transient. **ephemerality** (-ral´-) *n.* **ephemerally** *adv.* **ephemeralness** *n.* **ephemerist** *n.* a collector of ephemera. **ephemeron** (-rən) *n.* **1** (*pl.* **ephemerons**) an insect of the *Ephemera*. **2** (*usu. in pl.* **ephemera** (-rə)) anything short-lived.

epi- (ep´i) *pref.* upon, at, to, besides, in addition, as *epigram*, *episode*.

epic (ep´ik) *a.* **1** narrating some heroic event in a lofty style. **2** large-scale. **3** impressive. ~*n.* **1** a long poem narrating the history, real or fictitious, of some notable action or series of actions, accomplished by a hero or heroes. **2** a work of art associated with some aspect of the epic poem, such as a long adventure novel, a long historical film. **epical** *a.* **epically** *adv.*

epicene (ep´isēn) *a.* **1** (*Gram.*) of common gender, having only one form for both sexes. **2** of or relating to both sexes. **3** hermaphrodite. **4** sexless. **5** effeminate. ~*n.* **1** (*Gram.*) a noun common to both genders, as *sheep*. **2** a person having the characteristics of both sexes.

epicentre (ep´isentə), (*N Am.*) **epicenter, epicentrum** (-sen´trəm) *n.* **1** (*Geol.*) the point on the earth's surface over the focus of an earthquake. **2** (*fig.*) the focus of a quarrel, a difficulty etc. **epicentral** (-sen´-) *a.*

epicure (ep´ikūə) *n.* **1** a person devoted to sensual pleasures, esp. those of food and drink. **2** †an Epicurean. **Epicurean** (-rē´ən) *a.* **1** of or relating to Epicurus or his system of philosophy, which taught that pleasure is the supreme good and the basis of morality. **2** (**epicurean**) devoted to pleasure, esp. the more refined varieties of sensuous enjoyment. ~*n.* **1** a follower of Epicurus. **2** (**epicurean**) a person devoted to pleasure. **3** a sensualist, a gourmet. **epicureanism** *n.*

epidemic (epidem´ik) *a.* affecting at once a large number in a community. ~*n.* **1** a disease attacking many persons at the same time, and spreading with great rapidity. **2** an outbreak of such a disease. **3** a widespread and rapid outbreak of an activity, type of behaviour etc. **epidemical** *a.* **epidemically** *adv.* **epidemiology** (-dēmiol´-) *n.* the study and treatment of epidemic diseases. **epidemiological** (-loj´-) *a.* **epidemiologist** *n.*

Usage note See note under ENDEMIC.

epidermis (epidœ´mis) *n.* **1** (*Zool.*) the cuticle or skin constituting the external layer in animals. **2** (*Bot.*) the exterior cellular coating of the leaf or stem of a plant. **epidermal, epidermic** *a.* of or relating to the epidermis. **epidermoid** (-moid), **epidermoidal** (-moi´-) *a.*

epidiascope (epidī´əskōp) *n.* an optical projector which may be used for opaque objects or transparencies.

epididymis (epidid´imis) *n.* (*pl.* **epididymides** (-didim´idēz)) (*Anat.*) a mass of sperm-carrying tubes at the back of the testes.

epidural (epidū´rəl) *a.* (*Anat.*) situated on, or administered outside, the lower portion of the spinal canal. ~*n.* the epidural injection of an anaesthetic, e.g. in childbirth.

epifauna (epifaw´nə) *n.* (*Zool.*) the animals which live on the surface of submerged ground, or attached to underwater objects etc. **epifaunal** *a.*

epigene (ep´ijēn) *a.* (*Geol.*) originating on the surface of the earth.

epigenesis (epijən´əsis) *n.* (*Biol.*) the theory that in reproduction the organism is brought into being by the union of the male and female elements. **epigenesist** *n.* **epigenetic** (-net´-) *a.* **1** of or

relating to epigenesis. **2** (of minerals) formed later than the surrounding rocks. **3** produced by external influences, not genetic.

epiglottis (epiglot´is) *n.* (*pl.* **epiglottises, epiglottides** (-dēz)) (*Anat.*) a leaflike cartilage at the base of the tongue which covers the glottis during the act of swallowing. **epiglottal** *a.* **epiglottic** *a.*

epigram (ep´igram) *n.* **1** a short poem or composition of a witty or pointed character. **2** a pithy or witty saying or phrase. **3** the use of such phrases. **epigrammatic** (-grəmat´-), **epigrammatical** *a.* **epigrammatically** *adv.* **epigrammatist** (-gram´-) *n.* **epigrammatize** (-gram´-), **epigrammatise** *v.t.* to write or express by way of epigrams.

epigraph (ep´igrahf) *n.* **1** a quotation, in verse or prose, placed at the beginning of a work, or of divisions in a work, as a motto. **2** an inscription placed on buildings, statues, tombs, coins and the like, denoting their use and appropriation. **epigraphic** (-graf´-), **epigraphical** *a.* **epigraphically** *adv.* **epigraphy** (ipig´-) *n.* the deciphering and explanation of inscriptions. **epigraphist** *n.*

epilate (ep´ilāt) *v.t.* (*Med.*) to remove hair by the roots, by any method. **epilation** (-ā´shən) *n.*

epilepsy (ep´ilepsi) *n.* a functional disorder of the brain which involves convulsions of varying intensity, with or without loss of consciousness. **epileptic** (-lep´-) *a.* **1** suffering from epilepsy. **2** of, relating to or indicating the presence of epilepsy. ~*n.* a person who has epilepsy. **epileptical** *a.*

epilimnion (epilim´niən) *n.* (*pl.* **epilimnia** (-iə)) the upper, warmer layer of water in a lake.

epilogue (ep´ilog), (*N Am.*) **epilog** *n.* **1** the concluding part of a book, essay or speech, a peroration. **2 a** a short speech or poem addressed to the spectators at the end of a play. **b** the actor who delivers this. **3** (*with* **the**) a short programme of a usu. religious nature, at the end of the day's broadcasting. **epilogist** (ipil´əjist) *n.*

epimer (ep´imə) *n.* (*Chem.*) either one of the two differing isomers which can form around asymmetric carbon atoms. **epimeric** (-mer´-) *a.* **epimerism** (epim´-) *n.* **epimerize** (epim´-), **epimerise** *v.t.* to convert from one epimer to the other.

epinasty (ep´inasti) *n.* (*pl.* **epinasties**) (*Bot.*) curving of an organ through more rapid growth of the upper surface.

epinephrine (epinef´rin, -rēn) *n.* (*N Am.*) adrenalin.

epiphany (ipif´əni) *n.* (*pl.* **epiphanies**) **1** (**Epiphany**) **a** the manifestation of Christ to the Magi at Bethlehem. **b** the annual festival, held on 6 January, the 12th day after Christmas, to commemorate this. **2** the appearance or manifestation of a divinity. **epiphanic** (epifan´ik) *a.*

epiphenomenon (epifinom´inən) *n.* (*pl.* **epiphenomena** (-nə)) (*Med.*) a phenomenon that is secondary and incidental, a mere concomitant of some effect, esp. a secondary symptom of a disease. **epiphenomenal** *a.*

epiphyte (ep´ifīt) *n.* a plant growing upon another, usu. not deriving its nourishment from this. **epiphytal** (-fī´-), **epiphytic** (-fit´-) *a.*

episcopacy (ipis´kəpəsi) *n.* (*pl.* **episcopacies**) **1** government of a Church by bishops, the accepted form in the Latin and Greek communions and the Church of England; prelacy. **2** (**the episcopacy**) the bishops taken collectively. **episcopal** *a.* **1** of or relating to a bishop or bishops. **2** (of a Church) constituted on the episcopal form of government. **Episcopal Church** *n.* the Anglican Church in Scotland or the United States. **episcopalian** (-pā´-) *n.* **1** (**Episcopalian**) a member of an Episcopal Church. **2** a supporter of episcopal Church government and discipline. ~*a.* **1** episcopal. **2** (**Episcopalian**) belonging to one of the Episcopal Churches. **episcopalianism** *n.* **episcopalism** *n.* **episcopally** *adv.* **episcopate** (-pət) *n.* **1** the office or see of a bishop. **2** the term during which any bishop holds office. **3** (**the episcopate**) bishops collectively.

episcope (ep´iskōp) *n.* an optical projector used for projecting an enlarged image of an opaque object onto a screen.

episematic (episimat´ik) *a.* (*Zool.*) (of coloration) serving to facilitate recognition by animals of the same species.

episiotomy (epēziot´əmi) *n.* (*pl.* **episiotomies**) the cutting of the perineum during childbirth in order to prevent its tearing.

episode (ep´isōd) *n.* **1** an incident or series of events in a story, separable though arising out of it. **2** an incident or closely connected series of events in real life. **3** one part of a series on radio or television. **4** (*Mus.*) a portion of a fugue deviating from the main theme. **episodic** (-sod´-), **episodical** *a.* **1** occurring as separate incidents. **2** irregular, sporadic. **episodically** *adv.*

epistaxis (epistak´sis) *n.* (*Med.*) bleeding from the nose.

epistemology (ipistəmol´əji) *n.* (*Philos.*) the science which deals with the origin and method of knowledge. **epistemic** (-stē´-, -stem´-) *a.* of or relating to knowledge or epistemology. **epistemically** *adv.* **epistemological** (-loj´-) *a.* **epistemologically** *adv.* **epistemologist** (-mol´-) *n.*

epistle (ipis´əl) *n.* **1** (*formal or facet.*) a written communication, a letter. **2** a literary work (usu. in verse) in the form of a letter. **3** (**Epistles**) letters written by Apostles to the Churches, now forming part of the New Testament. **4** a lesson in the Church service, so called as being taken from the apostolic epistles. **epistolary** (-tə-) *a.* **1** in the form or style of a letter or letters. **2** of or relating to or suitable for letters. **3** contained in or carried on by means of letters.

epistyle (ep´istīl) *n.* (*Archit.*) the architrave.

epitaph (ep´itahf) *n.* **1** a commemorative inscription in prose or verse, as for a tomb or monument. **2** an inscription on a tomb.

epitaxy (ep´itaksi) *n.* the growth of one layer of crystals on another so that they have the same structure. **epitaxial** (-tak´-) *a.*

epithelium (epithē´liəm) *n.* (*pl.* **epitheliums**, **epithelia** (-liə)) (*Anat.*) the cell tissues lining the alimentary canal and forming the outer layer of the mucous membranes. **epithelial** *a.*

epithet (ep´ithet) *n.* **1** an adjective or phrase denoting any quality or attribute. **2** a descriptive term. **3** (*coll.*) an abusive expression. **4** a nickname. **epithetic** (-thet´-), **epithetical** *a.* **epithetically** *adv.*

epitome (ipit´əmi) *n.* **1** a brief summary of a book, document etc. **2** a perfect example, a person or thing that embodies the characteristics of a group, class etc. **3** (*fig.*) a representation in miniature of something else. **epitomist** *n.* **epitomize, epitomise** *v.t.* **1** to make an abstract, summary or abridgement of. **2** to represent in miniature. **epitomization** (-zā´shən) *n.*

epizoon (epizō´on) *n.* (*pl.* **epizoa** (-zō´ə)) an animal parasitic upon the exterior surface of another.

EPNS *abbr.* electroplated nickel silver.

epoch (ē´pok) *n.* **1** a fixed point from which succeeding years are numbered, a memorable date. **2** a period in history or of a person's life characterized by momentous events, an era. **3** (*Geol.*) a subdivision of geological time, the period during which a set of strata is formed. **epochal** (ep´-, ē´-) *a.* **epoch-making** *a.* of such importance as to mark an epoch.

eponym (ep´ənim) *n.* **1 a** a name given to a people, place or institution, after some person. **b** the person (real or imaginary) whose name is used. **2** a character whose name is the title of a play or book. **eponymic** (-nim´-), **eponymous** (ipon´-) *a.*

EPOS *abbr.* electronic point-of-sale (a sales-recording system in which bar codes are read by a laser scanner).

epoxy (ipok´si) *a.* (*Chem.*) containing oxygen plus two other atoms, frequently carbon, themselves already attached. ~*n.* (*pl.* **epoxies**) any of a group of synthetic resins containing epoxy groups and used for coatings and adhesives. **epoxide** *n.* an epoxy compound. **epoxy resin** *n.*

EPROM (ē´prom) *n.* (*Comput.*) a kind of read-only memory which can be erased and reprogrammed.

eps *abbr.* earnings per share.

epsilon (ep´silon) *n.* the fifth letter of the Greek alphabet (ε, E).

Epsom salts (ep´səm) *n.pl.* sulphate of magnesia, a saline purgative.

equable (ek´wəbəl) *a.* **1** characterized by evenness or uniformity. **2** smooth, level, even. **3** not varying, not irregular. **4** not subject to irregularities or disturbance. **5** even-tempered. **equability** (-bil´-) *n.* **equableness** *n.* **equably** *adv.*

Usage note The adjectives *equable* and *equitable* should not be confused: *equable* means even or unvarying, and *equitable* fair or just.

equal (ē´kwəl) a. 1 the same in size, number, quality, degree etc. 2 even, uniform, not variable. 3 evenly balanced. 4 having the same status or rights. 5 fair, just, impartial. 6 having adequate power, ability or means (to). ~n. 1 a person or thing not inferior or superior to another. 2 a person of the same or similar age, rank, office, talents or the like. 3 a match. ~v.t. (pres.p. **equalling**, (N Am.) **equaling**, past, p.p. **equalled**, (N Am.) **equaled**) 1 to be equal to. 2 to become equal to, to match. 3 to return a full equivalent for. **to be equal to** to have the courage, intelligence etc. for. **to equal out** to become equal or balanced. **equalitarian** (-teə´riən) a., n. (an) egalitarian. **equalitarianism** n. **equality** (ikwol´-) n. (pl. **equalities**) the state of being equal. **on an equality with** on equal terms with. **equalize**, **equalise** v.t. to make equal (to, with). **equalization** (-zā´shən) n. **equalizer** n. 1 something that equalizes, esp. a score in a game. 2 (sl.) a gun. 3 a connection in an electric system which compensates for undesirable frequencies. **equally** adv. **equalness** n. **equal opportunity** n. (pl. **equal opportunities**) the right to equality (with those of different sex, race etc.) in obtaining employment and in treatment as an employee. ~a. (of an employer) not discriminating on grounds of sex, race etc. **equal-opportunities** a. **equal sign**, **equals sign** n. (Math.) the sign =, used to show that two quantities etc. are of equal value. **equal temperament** n. (Mus.) a system of tuning an instrument so that the octave is divided into twelve equal intervals or semitones.

Usage note It is best not to use equally as: preferred alternatives are equally with (a noun) and just as (an adjective).

equanimity (ekwənim´iti, ē-) n. evenness or composure of mind. **equanimous** (ikwan´-) a.
equate (ikwāt´) v.t. 1 to regard as equal (to). 2 to equalize. ~v.i. to be equal. **equatable** a.
equation (ikwā´shən) n. 1 the act of making equal. 2 equality. 3 (Math.) a statement consisting of two algebraic expressions equal to one another, and connected by the sign =. 4 (Chem.) a formula which expresses a chemical reaction and notes the proportions of the chemicals involved. **equational** a. **equation of the first order** n. an equation which involves the first derivative only. **equation of the second order** n. an equation which involves the second derivative only.
equator (ikwā´tə) n. 1 a great circle on the earth's surface, equidistant from its poles, and dividing it into the northern and southern hemispheres. 2 (Astron.) CELESTIAL EQUATOR (under CELESTIAL). **equatorial** (ekwətaw´-) a. 1 of or relating to the equator. 2 situated on or near the equator. **equatorially** adv. **equatorial mount**, **equatorial mounting** n. (Astron.) a mounting for an equatorial telescope. **equatorial telescope** n. a telescope mounted on an axis parallel to that of

the earth, used for noting the course of the stars as they move through the sky.
equerry (ek´wəri, ikwer´i) n. (pl. **equerries**) an officer of a royal household.
equestrian (ikwes´triən) a. 1 of or relating to horses or horsemanship. 2 mounted on horseback. ~n. 1 a rider on horseback. 2 a person who performs feats of horsemanship. 3 a circus-rider. **equestrianism** n. **equestrienne** (-en´) n. a female rider or performer on horseback.
equi- (ēk´wi, ek´wi) comb. form equal.
equiangular (ēkwiang´gūlə, ek-) a. (Math.) having or consisting of equal angles.
equidistant (ēkwidis´tənt, ek-) a. 1 equally distant from some point or place. 2 separated from each other by equal distances. **equidistance** n. **equidistantly** adv.
equilateral (ēkwilat´ərəl, ek-) a. having all the sides equal. **equilaterally** adv.
equilibrate (ēkwilī´brāt, ek-, ikwil´i-) v.t. 1 to balance (two things) exactly. 2 to counterpoise. ~v.i. 1 to balance (each other) exactly. 2 to be a counterpoise (to). **equilibration** (-rā´shən) n.
equilibrium (ēkwilib´riəm, ek-) n. (pl. **equilibriums**, **equilibria** (-riə)) 1 a state of equal balance, equipoise. 2 equality of weight or force. 3 mental or emotional balance or stability. 4 due proportion between parts. 5 (Physics) a state of rest or balance due to the action of forces which counteract each other. **equilibrist** (ikwil´-) n. a person who balances in unnatural positions, esp. a tight-rope walker, an acrobat.
equine (ek´wīn) a. 1 of or relating to a horse or horses. 2 resembling a horse.
equinox (ek´winoks, ē´-) n. 1 the moment at which the sun crosses the equator and renders day and night equal throughout the world, now occurring (vernal equinox) on 21 March and (autumnal equinox) on 23 September. 2 (Astron.) one of two points at which the sun in its annual course crosses the celestial equator. 3 †an equinoctial gale. **equinoctial** (-nok´shəl) a. 1 of or relating to the equinoxes, or the regions or climates near the terrestrial equator. 2 designating an equal length of day and night. 3 happening at or about the time of the equinoxes. ~n. the equinoctial line. **equinoctial line** n. (Astron.) the celestial equator. **equinoctial point** n. either of the two points wherein the equator and ecliptic intersect each other. **equinoctial year** n. an astronomical year.
equip (ikwip´) v.t. (pres.p. **equipping**, past, p.p. **equipped**) 1 to furnish, accoutre, esp. to supply with everything needed for some profession or activity. 2 to fit out (as a ship), to prepare for any particular duty. 3 to qualify. **equipage** (ek´wipij) n. 1 that with which a person is equipped. 2 a carriage with horses and attendants. 3 the outfit of a ship for a voyage. **equipment** n. 1 the act of equipping. 2 the state of being equipped. 3 that which is used in equipping or fitting out. 4 outfit, furniture, apparatus required for

work, intellectual and other qualifications. **equipper** *n.*

equipoise (ek´wipoiz) *n.* **1** a state of equality of weight or force, equilibrium. **2** that which counterbalances. ~*v.t.* to counterbalance.

equipollent (ēkwipol´ənt, ek-) *a.* **1** having equal force, power, significance etc. **2** equivalent. ~*n.* something that is equipollent. **equipollence, equipollency** *n.*

equipotential (ēkwipəten´shəl, ek-) *a.* (*Physics*) having the same, or being at the same, potential at all points (of a line, surface or region). ~*n.* an equipotential line, surface or region.

equiprobable (ēkwiprob´əbəl, ek-) *a.* (*Logic*) equally probable. **equiprobability** (-bil´-) *n.*

equisetum (ekwisē´təm) *n.* (*pl.* **equiseta** (-tə), **equisetums**) (*Bot.*) a plant of the genus of cryptogams *Equisetum*, containing the horsetails and constituting the order Equisetaceae.

equitable (ek´witəbəl) *a.* **1** acting or done with equity; fair, just. **2** (*Law*) of or relating to a court or the rules of equity. **equitableness** *n.* **equitably** *adv.*

Usage note See note under EQUABLE.

---

equitation (ekwitā´shən) *n.* **1** the act or art of riding on horseback. **2** horsemanship.

equity (ek´witi) *n.* (*pl.* **equities**) **1** justice, fairness. **2** the application of principles of justice to correct the deficiencies of law. **3** (*Law*) the system of law, collateral and supplemental to statute law, administered by courts of equity. **4** the net value of mortgaged property. **5 a** (*pl.*) stocks and shares not bearing a fixed rate of interest. **b** the value of all the shares in a company.

equivalent (ikwiv´ələnt) *a.* **1** of equal value, force or weight (to). **2** alike in meaning, significance or effect. **3** interchangeable, corresponding. **4** having the same result. **5** (*Chem.*) having the same combining power. ~*n.* **1** anything which is equal to something else in amount, weight, value, force etc. **2** (*Chem.*) (*also* **equivalent weight**) the weight of an element or compound which will combine with or displace one gram of hydrogen or eight grams of oxygen. **equivalence, equivalency** *n.* **equivalently** *adv.*

equivocal (ikwiv´əkəl) *a.* **1** doubtful of meaning, ambiguous, capable of a twofold interpretation. **2** of uncertain origin, character etc. **3** (of a person) open to doubt or suspicion. **equivocality** (-kal´-) *n.* **equivocally** *adv.* **equivocalness** *n.*

equivocate (ikwiv´əkāt) *v.i.* **1** to use words in an ambiguous manner. **2** to speak ambiguously so as to deceive. **equivocation** (-ā´shən) *n.* **equivocator** *n.* **equivocatory** *a.*

equivoque (ek´wivōk), **equivoke** *n.* **1** an ambiguous term or phrase, an equivocation. **2** a pun or other play upon words.

ER *abbr.* **1** Queen Elizabeth. **2** King Edward.

Er *chem. symbol* erbium.

er (œ) *int.* used to express a hesitation in speech.

-er[1] (ə) *suf.* **1 a** forming nouns, denoting an agent

or doer, as *hatter, player, singer.* **b** sometimes doubled, as *caterer, poulterer.* **2** forming nouns, denoting a resident or native of, as *Londoner, Lowlander.*

-er[2] (ə) *suf.* forming nouns, denoting a person or thing connected with, as *butler, officer, teenager.*

-er[3] (ə) *suf.* forming adjectives, denoting the comparative, as *richer, taller.*

-er[4] (ə) *suf.* forming nouns, denoting an action, as *disclaimer, user.*

-er[5] (ə) *suf.* forming verbs, with a frequentative meaning, as *chatter, slumber, twitter.*

-er[6] (ə) *suf.* forming nouns, with diminutive and colloquial meanings, as *soccer.*

era (iə´rə) *n.* **1** a historical period or system of chronology running from a fixed point of time marked by an important event such as the birth of Christ, the Hegira etc. **2** the date from which this is reckoned. **3** a long period of time having a unifying characteristic, as *Christian era.* **4** (*Geol.*) any one of the main divisions of geological time.

eradicate (irad´ikāt) *v.t.* **1** to root up. **2** to destroy or get rid of completely. **eradicable** *a.* **eradication** (-ā´shən) *n.* **eradicator** *n.*

erase (irāz´, irās´) *v.t.* **1** to rub out. **2** to obliterate, to expunge. **erasable** *a.* **eraser** *n.* **1** something that erases. **2** a piece of rubber etc. used to erase pencil or ink marks from paper. **erasure** (-zhə) *n.*

erbium (œ´biəm) *n.* (*Chem.*) a rare metallic element, at. no. 68, chem. symbol Er, forming a rose-coloured oxide.

ere (eə) *prep.* (*formal or poet.*) before, sooner than. ~*conj.* before that, sooner than.

erect (irekt´) *a.* **1** upright, vertical. **2** standing up straight. **3** not bending or stooping. **4** (of the penis, clitoris etc.) distended and stiff, as a result of sexual excitement. **5** (of hair) standing up from the skin, bristling. **6** attentive, alert. ~*v.t.* **1** to set upright; to raise. **2** to construct, to build. **3** (*fig.*) to elevate, to exalt. **4** to set up, to establish. **erectable** *a.* **erectile** (-tīl) *a.* susceptible of erection. **erection** *n.* **1** the act of setting upright, building, constructing, establishing etc. **2** the state of being erected. **3** a building, a structure. **4** the distension of a part consisting of erectile tissue, esp. the penis. **5** an instance of such distension. **erectly** *adv.* **erectness** *n.* **erector** *n.*

eremite (er´əmīt) *n.* a hermit or recluse. **eremitic** (-mit´-), **eremitical** *a.*

erg[1] (œg), **ergon** (-gon) *n.* (*Physics*) the unit of work done in moving a body through 1 cm of space against the resistance of 1 dyne.

erg[2] (œg) *n.* (*pl.* **ergs, areg** (ah´reg)) an area of shifting sand dunes, esp. in the Sahara.

ergative (œ´gətiv) *a.* (*Gram.*) **1** of or relating to a case in some languages used to denote the doer of an action as the object of the verb. **2** of or relating to a language which uses the ergative case. ~*n.* **1** the ergative case. **2** a noun in this case.

ergo (œ´gō) *adv.* (*formal*) **1** therefore. **2** consequently.

ergocalciferol (œgōkalsif´ərol) *n.* vitamin D₂, calciferol.

ergonomics (œgənom´iks) *n.* the scientific study of the relationship between workers, their environment and machinery. **ergonomic** *a.* **ergonomically** *adv.* **ergonomist** (-gon´əmist) *n.*

ergosterol (œgos´terol) *n.* a plant sterol which is converted to vitamin D₂ by ultraviolet radiation.

ergot (œ´gət) *n.* **1** a disease in various grains and grasses, esp. rye, caused by a fungus, *Claviceps purpurea*, whose presence can cause food poisoning. **2** this dried fungus, used medicinally. **3** a preparation of ergot of rye used in midwifery to produce contraction of the uterus. **4** a small horny bump on the back of a horse's fetlock. **ergotism** *n.* food poisoning produced by eating grain affected with ergot.

erica (er´ikə) *n.* a member of the genus *Erica* of shrubby plants forming the heath family. **ericaceous** (-kā´shəs) *a.* **1** of or relating to the Ericaceae family of plants, including heathers, azaleas etc. **2** (of compost) acidic, suitable for growing ericaceous plants.

erigeron (irij´ərən) *n.* a member of the genus *Erigeron* of plants resembling the aster.

eristic (iris´tik) *a.* **1** of or relating to controversy or disputation. **2** (of an argument) designed to win rather than to reach the truth. ~*n.* **1** a controversialist. **2** the art of disputation. **eristically** *adv.*

Eritrean (eritrā´ən) *a.* of or relating to Eritrea, a country in north-east Africa. ~*n.* a native or inhabitant of Eritrea.

erk (œk) *n.* (*sl.*) **1** a naval rating. **2** (*dated*) an aircraftman. **3** a despicable or disliked person.

ERM *abbr.* exchange rate mechanism.

ermine (œ´min) *n.* (*pl. in general* **ermine**, *in particular* **ermines**) **1** the stoat, *Mustela erminea*, hunted in winter for its fur, which then becomes snowy white, with the exception of the tip of the tail which is always black. **2** the fur of this used for the robes of judges, peers etc. **3** (*Her.*) a fur represented by triangular black spots on white. **ermined** *a.*

-ern (ən) *suf.* forming adjectives, as in *northern, southern.*

erne (œn), (*NAm.*) **ern** *n.* (*poet.*) an eagle, esp. the sea eagle.

erode (irōd´) *v.t.* **1** to eat into or away. **2** to corrode. **3** (*Geol.*) to wear away; to eat out (a channel etc.). **4** (*Med.*) (of an ulcer etc.) to destroy (tissue) gradually. ~*v.i.* to be worn away or gradually eaten away. **erodible** *a.* **erosion** (-zhən) *n.* **1** the act of eroding, or process of being eroded. **2** (*Geol.*) the wearing away of rock by water, wind or ice. **erosional** *a.* **erosive** (-siv) *a.*

erogenous (iroj´inəs) *a.* **1** sensitive to sexual stimulation. **2** producing sexual desire.

✕ eroneous common misspelling of ERRONEOUS.

erotic (irot´ik) *a.* of or relating to, caused by or causing sexual desire; amatory. ~*n.* **1** a person with strong sexual desires. **2** an amatory poem.

erotica *n.pl.* erotic art or literature. **erotically** *adv.* **eroticism** (-sizm) *n.* **1** erotic nature or quality. **2** the use in art or literature of erotic language or imagery. **eroticize, eroticise** *v.t.* **erotism** (er´ə-) *n.*

eroto- (irot´ō) *comb. form* erotic, eroticism.

erotogenic (irotōjen´ik), **erotogenous** (erətoj´-ənəs) *a.* erogenous.

erotology (erətol´əji) *n.* the study of eroticism or of sexual behaviour.

erotomania (irotōmā´niə) *n.* **1** abnormal or excessive sexual desire. **2** a preoccupation with sexual desire. **erotomaniac** *n.*, *a.*

err (œ) *v.i.* **1** to blunder, to miss the truth, right or accuracy; to be incorrect. **2** to deviate from duty. **3** to sin. **to err on the right side** to deviate from strict accuracy or the prescribed course of action so as to ensure a better outcome. **to err on the side of** to favour (a specified side, aspect etc.) in one's actions.

errand (er´ənd) *n.* **1** a short journey to carry a message or perform some other commission, esp. on another's behalf. **2** the object or purpose of such a journey. **errand of mercy** *n.* a charitable mission.

errant (er´ənt) *a.* **1** erring. **2** wandering, roving, rambling, esp. roaming in quest of adventure as a knight errant. **errancy, errantry** *n.* (*pl.* **errancies, errantries**).

erratic (irat´ik) *a.* **1** irregular in movement, eccentric, unpredictable. **2** irregular in behaviour. **3** (*Geol.*) (of boulders) transported by ice from their original situation. ~*n.* (*Geol.*) an erratic block, a boulder transported by ice. **erratically** *adv.* **erraticism** (-sizm) *n.*

erratum (irah´təm) *n.* (*pl.* **errata** (-tə)) **1** an error or mistake in printing or writing. **2** (*pl.*) a list of corrections appended to a book.

erroneous (irō´niəs) *a.* mistaken, incorrect. **erroneously** *adv.* **erroneousness** *n.*

error (er´ə) *n.* **1** a mistake in writing, printing etc. **2** a deviation from truth or accuracy. **3** a wrong opinion. **4** a false doctrine or teaching. **5** a transgression, a sin of a venial kind. **6** (*Astron.*) the difference between the positions of the heavenly bodies as determined by calculation and by observation. **7** in statistics, a measure of the difference between some quantity and an approximation of it, usu. expressed as a percentage. **errorless** *a.*

ersatz (œ´zats, eə´-) *a.* **1** imitation. **2** artificial. ~*n.* a substitute (in a pejorative sense).

†Erse (œs) *n.* the Gaelic dialect of Ireland or the Scottish Highlands. ~*a.* Irish or Scottish Gaelic.

erst (œst) *adv.* once, formerly, of yore. **erstwhile** *adv.* some while ago. ~*a.* previous, former.

eructation (ērŭktā´shən) *n.* the act or an instance of belching.

erudite (er´ədīt) *a.* **1** learned, well-read, well-informed. **2** (of a book etc.) displaying great scholarship. **eruditely** *adv.* **eruditeness** *n.* **erudition** (-dish´-) *n.*

erupt (irŭpt´) v.t. **1** to emit violently, as a volcano, geyser etc. **2** to force through (as teeth through the gums). ~v.i. **1** to burst out. **2** to break through (of teeth etc.). **3 a** (of pimples etc.) to appear (on the skin). **b** (of the skin) to produce pimples etc. **4** (of a volcano) to emit lava, gases etc. **eruption** n. **1** the act of bursting forth. **2** a sudden emission. **3** that which breaks out. **4** (Med.) the breaking out of vesicles, pimples, rash etc. upon the skin. **5** the breaking through of teeth. **6** an outburst of lava etc. from a volcano or other vent. **eruptive** a.

-ery (əri) suf. used with nouns and adjectives, and sometimes with verbs, to form nouns, generally abstract or collective, meaning a business, place of business, cultivation etc., conduct, things connected with or of the nature of etc.; orig. confined to Romance words, but now used with those of Germanic origin, e.g., foolery, grocery, pinery, rockery, tannery, witchery.

erysipelas (erisip´iləs) n. (Med.) a streptococcal infection of the skin in which the affected parts are of a deep red colour, with a diffused inflammation of the underlying cutaneous tissue and cellular membrane.

erythema (erithē´mə) n. a superficial redness of the skin, occurring in patches. **erythemal, erythematic** (-mat´-), **erythematous** a.

erythrism (irith´rizm) n. an abnormal red coloration, esp. of fur or plumage.

erythro- (irith´rō), **erythr-** comb. form red.

erythroblast (irith´rōblahst) n. a cell in the bone marrow that will develop into an erythrocyte.

erythrocyte (irith´rəsīt) n. a red blood cell in vertebrates. **erythrocytic** (-sit´ik) a.

erythroid (irith´roid) a. of or relating to erythrocytes.

Es chem. symbol einsteinium.

-es[1] (iz) suf. forming the plural of nouns that end in a sibilant sound, as kisses, witches, axes; also of some nouns that end in -o, as tomatoes.

-es[2] (iz) suf. forming the 3rd person singular present of verbs that end in a sibilant sound, as kisses, watches; also of some verbs that end in -o, as goes.

escadrille (eskədril´) n. a French squadron of aircraft.

escalade (eskəlād´) n. an attack on a fortified place in which ladders are used to mount the ramparts etc.

escalate (es´kəlāt) v.i. to increase (rapidly) in scale, intensity or magnitude. ~v.t. to cause to escalate. **escalation** (-ā´shən) n.

escalator (es´kəlātə) n. a conveyor for passengers consisting of a continuous series of steps on an endless chain, ascending or descending and arranged to give facilities for mounting or leaving at either end; a moving staircase.

escallonia (eskəlō´niə) n. an evergreen shrub of the S American flowering genus Escallonia, of the saxifrage family.

escallop (iskal´əp) n. **1** an escalope. **2** a scallop.

escalope (es´kəlop, iskal´əp) n. a thin boneless slice of meat, esp. veal or pork.

escapade (eskəpād´, es´-) n. an exciting or daring prank or adventure.

escape (iskāp´) v.t. **1** to get safely away from. **2** to flee so as to be free from. **3** to evade, to avoid (a thing or act). **4** to slip away from, elude attention or recollection of. **5** to find an issue from. **6** to slip from unawares or unintentionally. ~v.i. **1** to get free. **2** to get safely away. **3** to find an issue, to leak. **4** to evade punishment, capture, danger, annoyance etc. ~n. **1** the act or an instance of escaping. **2** the state of having escaped, a means of escaping. **3** a way of avoiding an unpleasant situation. **4** a means of escaping. **5** a leakage (from a gas or water pipe, electric main etc.). **6** a plant from a garden apparently growing wild. **7** (Comput.) a function key which can cancel a command, end the current operation etc. **escapable** a. **escape clause** n. a clause in a contract which specifies the circumstances which free one of the parties from any or all obligations. **escapee** (eskəpē´) n. a person who has escaped, esp. an escaped prisoner. **escapement** n. **1** a device in a clock or watch for checking and regulating the movement of the wheels. **2** (in a piano) the mechanism which removes the hammer from the string immediately after striking. **3** (in a typewriter) the mechanism which regulates the movement of the carriage. **escaper** n. **escape road** n. a short piece of roadway leading off a steep downward slope or a sharp bend to enable out-of-control vehicles to stop safely. **escape velocity** n. the minimum velocity needed to escape from a gravitational field. **escape wheel** n. a toothed wheel in the escapement of a watch or clock. **escapism** n. the shirking of unpleasant facts and realities by filling the mind with pleasing irrelevancies. **escapist** a., n. **escapologist** (eskəpol´əjist) n. a performer whose act is escaping from locked handcuffs, chains, boxes etc. **escapology** n.

escarp (iskahp´) n. **1** a steep slope below a plateau. **2** the slope on the inner side of a ditch, below the rampart and opposite the counterscarp. **escarpment** n. (Geol.) the precipitous face of a hill or ridge.

-esce (es) suf. forming inceptive verbs, as acquiesce, coalesce, effervesce.

-escence (es´əns) suf. forming abstract nouns from inceptive verbs, as acquiescence, coalescence, opalescence. **-escent** (es´ənt) suf. forming adjectives from inceptive verbs, as acquiescent, coalescent, iridescent, opalescent.

eschatology (eskətol´əji) n. the doctrine of the final issue of things, death, the last judgement, the future state etc. **eschatological** (-loj´-) a. **eschatologist** (-tol´-) n.

escheat (ischēt´) n. (Hist. or N Am.) **1** the reverting of property to the Crown or the state, on the death of the owner intestate without heirs. **2** the property so reverting. ~*v.t.* **1** to confiscate. **2** to forfeit (to). ~*v.i.* to revert by escheat.

eschew (ischoo´) *v.t.* (*formal*) **1** to avoid; to shun. **2** to abstain from. **eschewal** *n.*

eschscholtzia (esholt´siə) *n.* a member of the genus of flowering herbs, *Eschscholtzia*, comprising the California poppy.

escort[1] (es´kawt) *n.* **1** an armed guard attending persons, baggage etc. which are being conveyed from one place to another, as a protection against attack or for compulsion or surveillance. **2** a guard of honour. **3** a person or persons accompanying another for protection or guidance. **4** a person of the opposite sex who accompanies one on a social occasion.

escort[2] (iskawt´) *v.t.* **1** to act as escort to. **2** to attend upon.

escritoire (eskritwah´) *n.* a writing desk with drawers etc. for papers and stationery, a bureau.

escrow (eskrō´) *n.* (*Law*) a fully-executed deed or engagement to do or pay something, put into the custody of a third party until some condition is fulfilled. ~*v.t.* to place (a document) in escrow. **in escrow** (of a document) executed and placed in the custody of a third party.

escudo (eskū´dō) *n.* (*pl.* **escudos**) the standard unit of currency in Portugal.

esculent (es´kūlənt) *a.* (*formal*) **1** fit or good for food. **2** edible. ~*n.* a thing suitable for food.

escutcheon (iskŭch´ən) *n.* **1** a shield or shield-shaped surface charged with armorial bearings. **2** any similar surface or device. **3** a perforated plate to finish an opening, as a keyhole etc. **4** part of a ship's stern bearing her name. **escutcheoned** *a.*

ESE *abbr.* east-south-east.

-ese (ēz) *suf.* **1** forming adjectives and nouns, meaning belonging to a country etc. as inhabitant(s) or language, as *Maltese, Chinese.* **2** (*often derog.*) forming nouns, meaning the style, language, theme etc. of a particular writer, writing etc. as *Johnsonese, journalese.*

⊠ **esential** common misspelling of ESSENTIAL.

Eskimo (es´kimō), **Esquimau** *n.* (*pl.* **Eskimo, Eskimos, Esquimaux** (-mōz)) **1** a member of a group of peoples inhabiting Greenland and the adjacent parts of N America, the Aleutian Islands and Siberia. **2** any of the languages spoken by this group. ~*a.* of or relating to these peoples or their language or culture.

Usage note The word *Eskimo* can give offence, especially in Canada. *Inuit* is the preferred name for the Canadian group, and can also be used to refer to the people as a whole.

ESL *abbr.* English as a second language.

esoteric (esəter´ik, ē-) *a.* **1** of philosophical doctrines, religious rites etc., meant for or intelligible only to the initiated. **2** recondite, secret, confidential. **esoterical** *a.* **esoterically** *adv.* **esotericism** (-sizm) *n.* **esotericist** *n.*

ESP *abbr.* extrasensory perception.

esp. *abbr.* especially.

espadrille (espədril´) *n.* a rope-soled shoe with a cloth upper.

espalier (ispal´iə) *n.* **1** a lattice-work on which shrubs or fruit trees are trained flat against a wall. **2** a tree so trained. ~*v.t.* to train (a tree or shrub) in this way.

esparto (ispah´tō) *n.* (*pl.* **espartos**) a kind of coarse grass or rush, *Stipa tenacissima*, growing in the sandy regions of northern Africa and Spain, used largely for making paper, mats etc. **esparto grass** *n.*

especial (ispesh´əl) *a.* **1** distinguished in a certain class or kind. **2** pre-eminent, exceptional, particular. **3** of or relating to a particular case, not general or indefinite. **especially** *adv.*

Esperanto (espəran´tō) *n.* an international artificial language invented in 1887, based on the chief European languages. **Esperantist** *n.*

espial ESPY.

espionage (es´piənahzh) *n.* **1** the act or practice of spying. **2** the employment of spies.

esplanade (esplənād´, -nahd´) *n.* **1** a level space, esp. a level walk or drive by the seaside etc. **2** a clear space between the citadel and the houses of a fortified town.

espouse (ispowz´) *v.t.* **1** to adopt, to support, defend (a cause etc.). **2** (of a man) to marry. **3** to give in marriage (to). **espousal** *n.* **1** the adoption (of a cause etc.). **2** (*usu. in pl.*) the act or ceremony of contracting a man and woman to each other; betrothal, marriage. **espouser** *n.*

espresso (ispres´ō), **expresso** (iks-) *n.* (*pl.* **espressos, expressos**) **1** very strong black coffee made by a machine which uses steam pressure. **2** a coffee-making machine using steam pressure for high extraction.

esprit (isprē´, es-) *n.* **1** wit. **2** sprightliness. **esprit de corps** (də kaw´) *n.* the spirit of comradeship, loyalty and devotion to the body or association to which one belongs.

espy (ispī´) *v.t.* (*3rd pers. sing. pres.* **espies**, *pres.p.* **espying**, *past, p.p.* **espied**) (*formal*) **1** to catch sight of. **2** to detect, to discern. **espial** (ispī´əl) *n.* **1** the act or an instance of espying. **2** spying, observation. **espier** *n.*

Esq. *abbr.* Esquire.

-esque (esk) *suf.* forming adjectives, meaning like, in the manner or style of, as *arabesque, burlesque, Dantesque, picturesque.*

Esquimau, Esquimaux ESKIMO.

esquire (iskwīə´) *n.* **1** a title of respect, placed after a man's surname in the addresses of letters. **2** the armour-bearer or attendant on a knight, a squire. **3** a title of dignity next in degree below a knight. **4** (*US*) a title used after a lawyer's surname. ~*v.t.* to attend upon as an escort.

ESR *abbr.* (*Physics*) electron spin resonance.

-ess[1] (is) *suf.* forming nouns, denoting the feminine, as *empress, murderess, seamstress, songstress* (the last two are double feminines formed on the OE fem. *-ster*, as in *spinster*).

-ess² (es) *suf.* forming abstract nouns from adjectives, as *largess, duress.*

essay¹ (es´ā) *n.* **1** a short informal literary composition or disquisition, usu. in prose. **2** (*formal*) an attempt. **essayist** *n.*

essay² (esā´) *v.t.* (*formal*) to try, to attempt.

essence (es´əns) *n.* **1** the distinctive quality of a thing. **2** that which differentiates a thing from all other things, or one thing of a kind from others of the same kind. **3** a solution or extract obtained by distillation. **4** the essential oil or characteristic constituent of a volatile substance. **5** perfume, scent. **in essence** fundamentally. **of the essence** of the greatest importance.

essential (isen´shəl) *a.* **1** important in the highest degree. **2** necessary to the existence of a thing, indispensable (to). **3** real, actual, distinguished from accidental. **4** of or relating to the essence of a thing. **5** containing the essence or principle of a plant etc. **6** (*Med.*) idiopathic, not connected with another disease. **7** (of an amino or fatty acid) necessary for the normal growth of the body, but not synthesized by the body. **8** being a perfect example of a particular kind of person or thing. ~*n.* **1** that which is fundamental or characteristic. **2** an indispensable element. **3** a point of the highest importance. **essential element** *n.* any chemical element which is necessary for the normal growth of an organism. **essentiality** (-shial´-) *n.* **essentially** *adv.* **essentialness** *n.* **essential oil** *n.* a volatile oil containing the characteristic constituent or principle of a plant, usu. obtained by distillation with water.

EST *abbr.* **1** Eastern Standard Time. **2** electroshock treatment.

-est (ist) *suf.* forming the superlative degree of adjectives and adverbs, as *richest, tallest, liveliest.*

establish (istab´lish) *v.t.* **1** to set upon a firm foundation, to found, institute. **2** to settle or secure firmly (in office, opinion etc.). **3** to make firm or lasting (as a belief, custom, one's health etc.). **4 a** to ascertain. **b** to substantiate, verify, put beyond dispute. **5** to ordain officially and settle on a permanent basis (as a Church). **established Church** *n.* the Church established by law, the State Church. **establisher** *n.* **establishment** (-mənt) *n.* **1** the act of establishing. **2** the state of being established. **3** a permanent organization such as the army, navy or civil service, a staff of servants etc. **4** a public institution or business organization. **5** a private household. **6** (*often* **Establishment**) the group of people who are in positions of power and influence in society and the State, usu. perceived as being middle-aged and conservative. **establishmentarian** (-tee´ri-) *n.* an advocate or supporter of an established Church. ~*a.* advocating or supporting an established Church. **establishmentarianism** *n.*

estate (istāt´) *n.* **1** property, esp. a landed property. **2** (*Law*) a person's interest in lands and tenements (*real estate*) or movable property (*personal estate*). **3** a person's assets and liabilities taken collectively. **4** land built on either privately or by a local authority for housing (a *housing estate*) or for factories and businesses (an *industrial estate*). **5** a property given over to the growing of a particular crop, as *rubber estate*. **6** (*formal*) state, condition, circumstances, standing, rank. **7** a class or order invested with political rights (in the United Kingdom the three estates are the Lords spiritual, the Lords temporal and the Commons). **8** (*coll.*) an estate car. **estate agent** *n.* **1** an agent concerned with the renting or sale of real estate. **2** the manager of a landed property. **estate car** *n.* a car with a large open space behind the passenger seats, and a rear door. **estate of the realm** *n.* any of the social or political estates in a monarchy, esp. in the United Kingdom.

esteem (istēm´) *v.t.* **1** to hold in high estimation, to regard with respect; to prize. **2** (*formal*) to consider, to reckon. ~*n.* opinion or judgement as to merit or demerit, esp. a favourable opinion; respect, regard.

ester (es´tə) *n.* (*Chem.*) an organic compound derived by the replacement of hydrogen in an acid by an organic radical. **esterify** (-ter´ifī) *v.t.* (*3rd pers. sing. pres.* **esterifies**, *pres.p.* **esterifying**, *past, p.p.* **esterified**) to change into an ester.

esthete, esthetic AESTHETE.

estimable (es´timəbl) *a.* worthy of esteem or regard. **estimably** *adv.*

estimate¹ (es´timāt) *v.t.* **1** to compute the value of, to appraise. **2** to form an opinion about. **estimation** (-ā´shən) *n.* **1** the act of estimating. **2** opinion or judgement. **3** approval. **estimative** *a.* **estimator** *n.*

estimate² (es´timət) *n.* **1** an approximate calculation of the value, number, extent etc. of anything. **2** the result of this. **3** a contractor's statement of the sum for which he would undertake a piece of work. **4** (*pl.*) a statement of probable expenditure submitted to Parliament or other authoritative body. **5** a judgement respecting character, circumstances etc.

estival, estivate AESTIVAL.

Estonian (estō´niən, is-) *a.* of or relating to Estonia, its people or their language. ~*n.* **1** a native or inhabitant of Estonia. **2** the language of Estonia, related to Finnish and Hungarian.

estrange (istrānj´) *v.t.* **1** to alienate, to make indifferent or distant in feeling. **2** to cut off from friendship. **3** to make (oneself) a stranger to. **estranged** *a.* **1** having been estranged. **2** (of a husband or wife) no longer living with their spouse. **estrangement** *n.*

estrogen OESTROGEN.

estrus, estrum OESTRUS.

estuary (es´chuəri) *n.* (*pl.* **estuaries**) the mouth of a river etc. in which the tide meets the current; a firth. **estuarial** (-eə´riəl), **estuarian** *a.* **estuarine** (-rīn) *a.*

e.s.u. *abbr.* electrostatic unit.

-et[1] (it) *suf.* forming diminutive nouns, as *chaplet*, *circlet*, *coronet*, *dulcet*, *russet*, *violet*.

-et[2] (it), **-ete** (ēt) *suf.* forming nouns denoting a person involved in some activity as *poet*, *athlete*.

ETA *abbr.* estimated time of arrival.

eta (ē'tə, ā'-) *n.* the seventh letter of the Greek alphabet (η, H).

et al. (et al') *abbr.* and others.

etc. *abbr.* etcetera.

etcetera (itset'ərə), **et cetera** *adv.* and the rest, and so on. **etceteras** *n.pl.* **1** sundries, extras. **2** things unspecified.

Usage note Pronunciation as (ek-) is best avoided.

---

etch (ech) *v.t.* **1** to produce or reproduce (a picture) on a metal plate, for printing copies, by engraving with an acid through the lines previously drawn with a needle on a coated surface. **2** to engrave (a metal plate) in this way. **3** to corrode or eat away. **4** to impress on the mind. ~*v.i.* to practise this art. **etchant** *n.* an acid or other corrosive used in etching. **etcher** *n.* **etching** *n.* **1** the act of etching. **2** an impression taken from an etched plate.

ETD *abbr.* estimated time of departure.

eternal (itœ'nəl) *a.* **1** without beginning or end. **2** everlasting, perpetual. **3** unchanging. **4** (*coll.*) incessant, constant. **eternality** (-nal'iti) *n.* **eternalize, eternalise, eternize, eternise** *v.t.* **1** to make eternal. **2** to prolong indefinitely. **3** to immortalize. **eternally** *adv.* **eternalness** *n.* **eternal triangle** *n.* a sexual or emotional relationship involving three people, usu. two of one sex and one of the other, often resulting in tension or conflict.

eternity (itœ'niti) *n.* (*pl.* **eternities**) **1** eternal duration. **2** endless past or future time. **3** (*Theol.*) future life after death. **4** immortality of fame. **5** (*coll.*) a very long time. **6** (*pl.*) the eternal realities. **eternity ring** *n.* a ring set all round with stones, signifying continuity.

-eth -TH[1].

ethanal (eth'ənal) *n.* (*Chem.*) acetaldehyde.

ethane (ē'thān, eth'-) *n.* (*Chem.*) a colourless and odourless gaseous compound of the paraffin series. **ethanediol** (-dīol) *n.* ethylene glycol.

ethanoate (ēthan'ōāt) *n.* (*Chem.*) a salt or ester of acetic acid, acetate. **ethanoic acid** (ethənō'ik) *n.* acetic acid.

ethanol (eth'ənol) *n.* (*Chem.*) a colourless liquid produced by fermenting sugars and constituting the intoxicating agent in various drinks, alcohol.

ethene (ē'thə) *n.* (*Chem.*) ethylene.

ether (ē'thə) *n.* **1** (*Chem.*) a light, volatile and inflammable fluid, produced by the distillation of alcohol with an acid, esp. sulphuric acid, and used as an anaesthetic or a solvent. **2** any of a class of similar compounds, with an oxygen atom joined to two alkyl groups. **3** (*also* **aether**) a fluid of extreme subtlety and elasticity (formerly) assumed to exist throughout space and between the particles of all substances, forming

the medium of transmission of light and heat. **4** (*also* **aether**) the upper air, the higher regions of the sky, the clear sky. **ethereal** (ithiə'riəl), **etherial** *a.* **1** of the nature of ether. **2** resembling celestial ether, light, airy, tenuous, subtle, exquisite, impalpable, spiritual. **3** (*Chem.*) of or relating to ether. **ethereality** (-al'-) *n.* **ethereally** *adv.* **etheric** (ither'ik) *a.* **etherize, etherise** *v.t.* **1** (*Chem.*) to convert into ether. **2** (*Med.*) to anaesthetize with ether. **etherization** (-zā'shən) *n.*

Ethernet® (ē'thənet) *n.* (*Comput.*) a type of local area network.

ethic (eth'ik) *n.* a moral principle or a set of principles. ~*a.* ethical. **ethical** *a.* **1** treating of or relating to morals. **2** dealing with moral questions or theory. **3** conforming to a recognized standard. **4** (*Med.*) (of a drug) not advertised to the public and available only on prescription. **ethical investment** *n.* the practice of investing money only in those companies which are not involved in racial discrimination or in products causing potential harm to health, life or the environment, as cigarettes, nuclear weapons. **ethicality** (-kal'-) *n.* **ethically** *adv.* **ethicism** (-sizm) *n.* **ethicist** *n.* **ethics** *n.pl.* **1** the science of morals. **2** a system of principles and rules of conduct. **3** the whole field of moral science, including political and social science, law, jurisprudence etc.

Ethiopian (ēthiō'piən) *a.* **1** of or relating to Ethiopia, a country in north-eastern Africa, or its inhabitants. **2** (*Biol.*) of or relating to a biogeographical region consisting of Africa south of the Sahara. ~*n.* a native or inhabitant of Ethiopia. **Ethiopic** (-op'-) *n.* the liturgical language of the Church in Ethiopia.

ethnic (eth'nik) *a.* **1** of, relating to or characteristic of a race, people or culture. **2** of or relating to the culture or traditions of a particular people. **3** of or relating to a group within a community which has a racial or cultural identity different from that of the majority group. **4** of or relating to the food, clothing etc. used by such a group. **5** belonging to a nation by birth or origin rather than by acquired nationality. ~*n.* a member of an ethnic minority. **ethnical** *a.* of or relating to ethnology. **ethnically** *adv.* **ethnic cleansing** *n.* (*euphem.*) the systematic persecution of a distinct ethnic group within a community, members of which are killed, imprisoned, forced to move to another area etc. **ethnicity** *n.* **ethnic minority** *n.* (*pl.* **ethnic minorities**) a (relatively) small group within a community of different racial or cultural origin which remain unassimilated.

ethno- (eth'nō), **ethn-** *comb. form* ethnic, ethnological.

ethnobotany (ethnōbot'əni) *n.* (the study of) the knowledge and use of plants by traditional societies.

ethnocentrism (ethnōsen'trizm) *n.* the mental habit of viewing the world solely from the perspective of one's own culture. **ethnocentric** *a.* **ethnocentrically** *adv.* **ethnocentricity** (-tris'iti) *n.*

ethnography (ethnog´rəfi) *n.* the scientific study and description of different human societies. **ethnographer** *n.* **ethnographic** (-graf´-), **ethnographical** *a.*

ethnology (ethnol´əji) *n.* the science which treats of the varieties of the human race. **ethnologic** (-loj´-), **ethnological** *a.* **ethnologist** (-nol´-) *n.*

ethnomusicology (ethnōmūzikol´əji) *n.* the study of the music of different societies. **ethnomusicological** (-loj´-) *a.* **ethnomusicologist** (-kol´-) *n.*

ethology (ēthol´əji) *n.* **1** the science of animal behaviour. **2** the scientific study of the formation of patterns of human behaviour. **ethologic** (-loj´-), **ethological** *a.* **ethologist** *n.*

ethos (ē´thos) *n.* the characteristic spirit, character, disposition or genius of a people, community, institution, system etc.

ethoxyethane (ēthoksiē´thān) *n.* (*Chem.*) ether, as used as an anaesthetic.

ethyl (eth´il, ē´thīl) *n.* (*Chem.*) a monovalent fatty hydrocarbon radical of the paraffin series, forming the base of common alcohol and ether, acetic acid etc. **ethyl alcohol** *n.* the ordinary alcohol of commerce. **ethylene** (eth´ilēn) *n.* (*Chem.*) a hydrocarbon gas found in petroleum and natural gas, used in the manufacture of polythene etc. **ethylene glycol** *n.* a colourless soluble liquid used as an antifreeze and in the manufacture of polyesters. **ethylenic** (-lē´nik) *a.*

ethyne (ē´thīn, eth´-) *n.* (*Chem.*) acetylene.

-etic (et´ik) *suf.* forming nouns and adjectives, meaning (a person or thing) of the nature of or serving as, as *athletic, ascetic, prosthetic.*

etiolate (ē´tiəlāt) *v.t.* **1** to blanch (a plant) by keeping in the dark. **2** to make (a person) pale and unhealthy. **etiolation** (-ā´shən) *n.*

etiology AETIOLOGY.

etiquette (et´iket) *n.* **1** the conventional rules of behaviour in polite society. **2** the established rules of precedence and ceremonial in a court. **3** the codes of formal behaviour between members of a profession etc.

Etonian (itō´niən) *n.* a person educated or being educated at Eton College. *~a.* of or relating to Eton College. **Eton collar** (ē´tən) *n.* a wide, starched collar worn outside the jacket. **Eton jacket** *n.* a boy's untailed dress coat.

étrier (ā´triā) *n.* a small rope ladder used in mountaineering.

Etrurian (itroo´riən) *a.* of or relating to Etruria, an ancient country in central Italy. *~n.* a native or inhabitant of Etruria.

Etruscan (itrŭs´kən) *a.* Etrurian. *~n.* **1** an Etrurian. **2** the language of Etruria.

et seq., et seqq. *abbr.* and the following (passage(s), page(s) etc.).

-ette (et) *suf.* **1** forming nouns meaning diminutive, as *cigarette, kitchenette.* **2** forming female nouns, as *brunette,* often offensive, as *jockette.* **3** forming nouns meaning imitation, as *flannelette, leatherette.*

étude (ātüd´, -tüd´) *n.* (*Mus.*) a short composition written mainly to test or develop a player's technical skill.

-etum (ē´təm) *suf.* forming nouns meaning (a place or garden containing) a collection of plants, as *arboretum, pinetum.*

etymology (etimol´əji) *n.* (*pl.* **etymologies**) **1** the branch of linguistics that treats of the origin and history of words. **2** the history of the origin and modification of a particular word; derivation. **3** an account of the derivation of a word or words. **etymologic** (-loj´-), **etymological** *a.* **etymologically** *adv.* **etymologist** *n.* **etymologize, etymologise** *v.t.* to give or trace the etymology of. *~v.i.* to study etymology.

Usage note The subjects *etymology* and *entomology* should not be confused: *etymology* is concerned with words, and *entomology* with insects.

---

etymon (et´imon) *n.* (*pl.* **etymons, etyma** (-mə)) the primitive or root form of a word.

Eu *chem. symbol* europium.

eu- (ū) *comb. form* good, well, pleasant, as in *eulogy, euphony.*

eucalyptus (ūkəlip´təs) *n.* (*pl.* **eucalyptuses, eucalypti** (-tī)) **1** (*also* **eucalypt**) any evergreen myrtaceous tree belonging to the Australasian genus *Eucalyptus,* comprising the gum-trees. **2** eucalyptus oil. **eucalyptus oil** *n.* an aromatic oil obtained from eucalyptus leaves, used medicinally.

eucharis (ū´kəris) *n.* a bulbous plant from S America of the genus *Eucharis,* cultivated in hothouses for its pure white bell-shaped flowers.

Eucharist (ū´kərist) *n.* **1** the sacrament of the Lord's Supper. **2** the elements, bread and wine, given in this sacrament. **Eucharistic** (-ris´-), **Eucharistical** *a.*

euchre (ū´kə) *n.* an orig. American card game for several persons, usu. four, with a pack from which the cards from the twos to the nines have been excluded. *~v.t.* **1** to beat by taking three of the five tricks at euchre. **2** (*Austral., coll.*) to beat thoroughly, to ruin. **3** to outwit.

Euclidean (ūklid´iən) *a.* of or relating to Euclid or to the axioms and postulates of his geometry.

eugenic (ūjen´ik) *a.* of or relating to the development and improvement of offspring, esp. human offspring, through selective breeding. **eugenically** *adv.* **eugenics** *n.* the science or political beliefs relating to this. **eugenicist** *n.* **eugenist** *n.*

euglena (ūglē´nə) *n.* (*Biol.*) a single-celled aquatic animal of the genus *Euglena,* with a single flagellum.

eukaryon (ūkar´iən), **eucaryon** *n.* a highly organized cell nucleus, with DNA in the form of chromosomes, characteristic of higher organisms. **eukaryote** (-riōt) *n.* (*Biol.*) an organism which has such cell nuclei. **eukaryotic** (-iot´ik) *a.*

eulogy (ū´ləji) *n.* (*pl.* **eulogies**) **1** praise, encomium, panegyric. **2** a writing or speech in praise of a person. **3** (*NAm.*) a funeral oration. **eulogist** *n.* **eulogistic** (-jis´-), **eulogistical** *a.* **eulogistically** *adv.* **eulogium** (ūlō´jiəm) *n.* (*pl.* **eulogiums, eulogia** (-iə)) eulogy. **eulogize, eulogise** *v.t.* **1** to speak or write of in praise. **2** to commend, to extol.

eunuch (ū´nək) *n.* **1** a castrated man, esp. an attendant in a harem, or a state functionary in Oriental palaces and under the Roman emperors. **2** an ineffectual or powerless person.

euonymus (ūon´iməs) *n.* any tree or shrub of the genus *Euonymus*, containing the spindle tree.

eupeptic (ūpep´tik) *a.* **1** having a good digestion. **2** of or relating to or characteristic of good digestion.

euphemism (ū´fəmizm) *n.* **1** the use of a soft or pleasing term or phrase for one that is harsh or offensive. **2** such a term or phrase. **euphemist** *n.* **euphemistic** (-mis´-) *a.* **euphemistically** *adv.* **euphemize, euphemise** *v.t.* **1** to speak of euphemistically. **2** to express in euphemism. ~*v.i.* to speak in euphemism.

Usage note The linguistic practices of *euphemism* and *euphuism* should not be confused: *euphemism* is expressing something in alternative, more acceptable, terms, and *euphuism* using high-flown language.

euphonium (ūfō´niəm) *n.* (*pl.* **euphoniums**) (*Mus.*) a brass instrument related to the tuba.

euphony (ū´fəni) *n.* (*pl.* **euphonies**) **1** an agreeable sound. **2** smoothness or agreeableness of sound in words and phrases. **3** the tendency towards greater ease of pronunciation in phonetic change. **euphonic** (ūfon´-), **euphonical** *a.* **euphonious** (ūfō´-) *a.* **euphoniously** *adv.* **euphonize, euphonise** *v.t.*

euphorbia (ūfaw´biə) *n.* any plant of the genus *Euphorbia*, including the spurges, comprising about 700 species, many of which are poisonous while others have medicinal qualities.

euphoria (ūfaw´riə) *n.* a feeling of well-being, supreme content, esp. exaggerated or baseless. **euphoriant** *a.* inducing euphoria. ~*n.* a euphoriant drug. **euphoric** (-for´ik) *a.* **euphorically** *adv.*

euphuism (ū´fūizm) *n.* a pedantic affectation of elegant and high-flown language. **euphuist** *n.* **euphuistic** (-is´-) *a.* **euphuistically** *adv.*

Usage note See note under EUPHEMISM.

Eurasian (ūrā´zhən) *a.* **1** of mixed European and Asian descent; esp. formerly in British India etc., born of a European father and an Asian mother. **2** of or relating to both Europe and Asia. ~*n.* a person of European and Asian descent.

eureka (ūrē´kə) *int.* used to express exultation over a discovery. ~*n.* an exclamation of 'eureka'.

eurhythmics (ūridh´miks), (*NAm.*) **eurythmics** *n.* the scientific use or art of rhythmical movement, esp. as applied to dancing and gymnastic

exercises. **eurhythmic, eurhythmical** *a.* **1** of or relating to eurhythmics. **2** having a pleasing harmony or rhythm. **eurhythmy** (-mi) *n.*

Euro (ū´rō) *n.* (*pl.* **Euros**) **1** a European. **2** a Eurodollar. ~*a.* European.

Euro- (ū´rō), **Eur-** *comb. form* of or relating to Europe or Europeans, or the European Union.

euro[1] (ū´rō) *n.* (*pl.* **euros**) (*Austral.*) a wallaby of S and Central Australia, *Macropus robustus*.

euro[2] (ū´rō) *n.* (*pl.* **euros**) the European Union unit of currency.

Eurobond (ū´rōbond) *n.* a bond issued in a European country, but in one of the other European currencies.

Eurocentric (ūrōsen´trik) *a.* perceiving European culture, history etc. as of central importance in the world. **Eurocentrism** *n.*

Eurocheque (ū´rōchek) *n.* **1** a type of cheque able to draw on certain banks in other European countries on receipt of the appropriate card. **2** the banking system enabling the use of these cheques.

Eurocommunism (ūrōkom´ūnizm) *n.* the form of Communism followed by western European Communist parties, more pragmatic than, and independent of, the Soviet version. **Eurocommunist** *n., a.*

Eurocrat (ū´rəkrat) *n.* (*usu. derog.*) an official involved in the administration of any part of the European Union.

Euro-currency (ū´rōkūrənsi) *n.* (*pl.* **Euro-currencies**) currency of a country outside Europe held on deposit in a European bank.

Eurodollar (ū´rōdolə) *n.* a US dollar held in European banks to ease the financing of trade.

Euro-election (ū´rōilekshən) *n.* an election for the European Parliament.

Euromarket (ū´rōmahkit) *n.* **1** the money markets of the European Union collectively. **2** the market of any one of the Euro-currencies.

European (ūrəpē´ən) *a.* **1** of or relating to, happening in, or extending over, Europe. **2** native to Europe. **3** of or relating to, or concerning, Europe as a whole, rather than an individual country. **4** of or relating to the European Union. ~*n.* **1** a native or inhabitant of Europe. **2** a person of European descent. **3** a person who is interested in or supports the European Union. **Europeanism** *n.* **Europeanize, Europeanise** *v.t.* **Europeanization** (-zā´shən) *n.* **European plan** *n.* (*NAm.*) the system of charging for a hotel room without including meals.

Europhile (ū´rōfīl) *n.* (*coll.*) a person who is in favour of the European Union and its institutions. ~*a.* of or relating to the opinions and attitudes of a Europhile.

Europhobe (ū´rōfōb) *n.* (*coll.*) a person who dislikes the European Union and its institutions and who is against further links with Europe. ~*a.* of or relating to the opinions and attitudes of a Europhobe.

europium (ūrō´piəm) *n.* (*Chem.*) an extremely

rare metallic element, soft and silvery white, at. no. 63, chem. symbol Eu.

Euro-rebel (ū´rōrebəl) *n.* a politician who disagrees with their party's official line on the European Union.

Eurosceptic (ū´rōskeptik) *n.* a person who is sceptical about the benefits to the UK of membership of the European Union, and who is opposed to further integration into the Union. **Euroscepticism** (-tisizm) *n.*

eurythmics EURHYTHMICS.

Eustachian (ūstā´shən, -kiən) *a.* of or relating to Eustachius, an Italian physician of the 16th cent. **Eustachian tube** *n.* (*Anat.*) a duct leading to the cavity of the tympanum of the ear from the upper part of the pharynx.

eustasy (ūs´təsi) *n.* changes in the world shoreline level or sea level caused by melting ice, tectonic movements etc. **eustatic** (ūstat´-) *a.*

eutectic (ūtek´tik) *a.* (*Chem.*) of or relating to the mixture of two or more substances with a minimum melting point. ~*n.* a eutectic mixture. **eutectic point, eutectic temperature** *n.* the minimum melting point of a eutectic mixture.

euthanasia (ūthənā´ziə) *n.* **1** easy, painless death. **2** putting to death in this manner, esp. in cases of extreme or terminal human suffering.

eutherian (ūthiə´riən) *n.* (*Zool.*) a member of the subclass of mammals, Eutheria, which nourish their unborn young through a placenta. ~*a.* of or relating to this subclass, which includes most mammals.

eutrophic (ūtrof´ik, -trō´-) *a.* (of a body of water) rich in dissolved nutrients and supporting an abundance of plant life whose decomposition deoxygenates the water, harming the animal populations. **eutrophicate** *v.t.* **eutrophication** (-ā´shən) *n.* **eutrophy** (ū´trəfi) *n.*

eV *abbr.* electronvolt.

EVA *abbr.* extravehicular activity.

evacuate (ivak´ūāt) *v.t.* **1 a** to remove inhabitants from (a danger zone). **b** to remove (people) temporarily from a danger zone. **2** to withdraw from (esp. of troops). **3** to form a vacuum. **4** to make empty, esp. to eject from or to empty the excretory passages. **evacuant** *a.* purgative. ~*n.* a medicine producing this effect. **evacuation** (-ā´shən) *n.* **evacuative** *a.* **evacuator** *n.* **evacuee** (-ē´) *n.* a person, esp. a child, evacuated from a danger zone.

evade (ivād´) *v.t.* **1** to avoid or elude by artifice, stratagem or sophistry. **2** to avoid (doing something), to shirk. **3** to avoid answering (a question). **4** to avoid paying (taxes), e.g. by concealing income or falsifying accounts. **5** to defeat, baffle, foil. **evadable** *a.* **evader** *n.*

evaluate (ival´ūāt) *v.t.* **1** to determine the value or worth of, to appraise. **2** (*Math.*) to find a numerical expression for. **evaluation** (-ā´shən) *n.* **evaluative** (-val´-) *a.* **evaluator** *n.*

evanesce (evənes´) *v.i.* **1** to disappear, to vanish. **2** to fade away, as if in vapour. **evanescence** *n.*

evanescent *a.* **1** disappearing gradually. **2** fading, fleeting. **evanescently** *adv.*

evangelical (ēvənjel´ikəl) *a.* **1** of or relating to the Gospel. **2** according to the doctrine of the Gospel. **3** proclaiming or maintaining the truth taught in the Gospel. **4** of or relating to a tradition in the Protestant Churches which emphasizes the importance of the fundamental teaching of Scripture, the doctrines of the Fall, Christ's atonement, and salvation by faith not works. **5** belonging to an evangelical Church or party. **6** firmly believing in and actively promoting a cause. ~*n.* a member of the evangelical branch of Protestantism. **evangelic** *a.*, *n.* **evangelicalism** *n.* **evangelically** *adv.*

evangelism (ivan´jəlizm) *n.* **1** the preaching of the Gospel. **2** evangelicalism. **3** enthusiastic promotion of any cause. **evangelist** *n.* **1** (*also* **Evangelist**) any one of the four writers of the Gospels (Matthew, Mark, Luke and John). **2** a preacher of the Gospel. **3** a lay preacher. **4** a person who evangelizes or believes in evangelism. **5** an enthusiastic and active supporter of a cause. **evangelistic** (-lis´-) *a.* **1** of or relating to the four Evangelists. **2** of or relating to preaching of the Gospel. **3** evangelical. **evangelize, evangelise** *v.t.* **1** to preach the Gospel to. **2** to convert to Christianity. **3** to try to persuade (people) to join or support a cause. **evangelization** (-zā´shən) *n.* **evangelizer** *n.*

evaporate (ivap´ərāt) *v.t.* **1** to convert into vapour, to vaporize. **2** to drive off the moisture from by heating or drying. **3** to cause to vanish. ~*v.i.* **1** to become vapour. **2** to pass away in vapour. **3** to exhale moisture. **4** (*coll.*) to disappear, to vanish. **evaporable** *a.* **evaporated milk** *n.* unsweetened milk from which some of the water has been evaporated. **evaporation** (-ā´shən) *n.* **evaporative** (-ətiv) *a.* **evaporator** *n.*

evasion (ivā´zhən) *n.* **1** the act of evading or escaping (as from a question, argument or charge). **2** a subterfuge, an equivocation. **3** an evasive answer. **evasive** (-siv) *a.* **1** seeking to evade. **2** facilitating evasion or escape. **3** (of a person) not straightforward, devious. **evasively** *adv.* **evasiveness** *n.*

eve (ēv) *n.* **1** the evening before a holiday or other event or date. **2** the period immediately preceding some important event. **3** †evening.

even[1] (ē´vən) *n.* evening. **evensong** *n.* **1** a form of worship for the evening, esp. in Anglican churches. **2** the time for evening prayer. **eventide** *n.* (*poet.*) evening. **eventide home** *n.* a home for elderly people.

even[2] (ē´vən) *a.* **1** level, smooth, uniform. **2** on the same level, in the same plane (with). **3** parallel. **4** capable of being divided by the number 2 without any remainder, as opposed to *odd.* **5** (of numbers) round, not including fractions or remainders. **6** equal. **7** equally balanced, fair, impartial. **8** (of a competition) having competitors that are equally good. **9** uniform or unvarying in quality.

10 unvarying, equable, unruffled. **on an even keel 1** (*Naut.*) (of a ship) drawing the same water fore and aft. **2** (of a person) well-balanced, emotionally, mentally or financially. **to be/ get even with 1** to revenge oneself on. **2** to be quits with. **even break** *n.* an even chance. **even chance** *n.* an equal likelihood of success or failure. **evenhanded** *a.* impartial, equitable, fair. **evenhandedly** *adv.* **even-handedness** *n.* **evenly** *adv.* **even money** *n.* evens. **~a.** just as likely to be or happen as not. **evenness** *n.* **evens** *n.pl.* odds quoted on a racehorse etc. such that if it wins the person betting gains an amount equal to the stake. **even-tempered** *a.* not easily upset or angered, placid.

even[3] (ē´vən) *v.t.* **1** to make smooth or level. **2** to place on a level. **~v.i.** to be or become equal. **to even out** to make or become even or level. **to even up** to bring or come up to the same level. **evener** *n.*

even[4] (ē´vən) *adv.* **1** to a like degree, equally. **2** as much as, so much as (expressing unexpectedness, surprise, concession or emphasis, a comparison being implied). **3** evenly. **4** exactly, just, simply, neither more nor less than. **5** unexpectedly; in an extreme case. **even as** at the very same time that. **even now 1** at this very moment. **2** now and before. **even so 1** exactly; yes. **2** nevertheless. **3** in that case also. **even though** in spite of the fact that.

evening (ēv´ning) *n.* **1** the close or latter part of the day. **2** the period from sunset to dark, or from sunset to bed-time. **3** (*fig.*) the close or decline, as of life. **4** the latter part. **~a.** of, relating to or happening in the evening. **~int.** (*coll.*) GOOD EVENING (under GOOD). **evening dress** *n.* the dress prescribed by convention for wearing for a formal occasion in the evening. **evening primrose** *n.* any plant belonging to the genus *Oenothera*, the yellow flowers of which usu. open in the evening. **evenings** *adv.* (*coll.*) during most evenings. **evening star** *n.* Jupiter, Mercury or esp. Venus when visible in the west in the evening.

evens EVEN[2].

event (ivent´) *n.* **1** anything that happens, as distinguished from a thing that exists. **2** an occurrence, esp. one of great importance. **3 a** the fact of an occurrence. **b** the contingency or possibility of an occurrence. **4** the consequence of any action. **5** the issue or conclusion. **6** any of several possible occurrences regarded as having a probability of its own. **7** any item in a programme of games, contests etc., esp. one on which money is wagered. **8** (*Physics*) a single occurrence of a particular process. **~v.i.** to take part in one-day or three-day events. **at all events** in any case, whatever happens. **in any event** at all events. **in the event 1** as it turns out, or turned out. **2** if it should so turn out. **in the event of** if so, if it so happens. **in the event that** if it turns out that. **eventer** *n.* **1** a horse that takes part in one- or three-day events. **2** a person who takes part in

such events. **eventful** *a.* **1** full of events. **2** attended by important changes. **eventfully** *adv.* **eventfulness** *n.* **event horizon** *n.* (*Astron.*) the boundary of the gravitational field of a black hole, from which no electromagnetic radiation can escape. **eventing** *n.* taking part in one- or three-day events. **eventless** *a.* lacking (important) events.

eventide EVEN[1].

eventual (iven´chuəl) *a.* finally resulting, ultimate, final. **eventuality** (-al´-) *n.* (*pl.* **eventualities**) a possible event or result. **eventually** *adv.* **eventuate** *v.i.* (*formal*) **1** to happen, to come to pass, to result. **2** to turn out (well or ill). **eventuation** (-ā´shən) *n.*

ever (ev´ə) *adv.* **1** at all times; always. **2** continually. **3** at any time. **4** in any degree. **ever since** continually after a certain time. **ever so** to any degree or extent conceivable. **evergreen** *a.* **1** always green. **2** retaining its verdure throughout the year. **3** always young or fresh. **~n. 1** a plant which retains its verdure through the year. **2** a person, book, song etc. which stays fresh or popular for many years. **everlasting** *a.* **1** lasting for ever, eternal, perpetual. **2** continual, unintermittent. **3** interminable, tiresome. **4** of flowers, not changing colour when dried. **~n. 1** eternity. **2** IMMORTELLE. **everlastingly** *adv.* **everlastingness** *n.* **evermore** *adv.* always, eternally, continually.

every (ev´ri) *a.* **1** each of a group or collection, all separately. **2** each one at a specified interval from the one before, as *every fourth person*. **3** the greatest possible, as *every hope of succeeding*. **every bit 1** quite (as). **2** the whole. **every last** the total number of. **every now and again** from time to time. **every now and then** from time to time. **every one** each one. **every so often** intermittently. **every time 1** on each occasion, with no exception. **2** (*coll.*) yes, certainly. **every which way 1** (*N Am., coll.*) in all directions or ways. **2** (*N Am., coll.*) in a disorderly fashion. **everybody** *pron.* every person. **everyday** *a.* **1** met with or happening daily. **2** worn or used on ordinary occasions. **3** common, usual. **4** commonplace. **Everyman** *n.* (**everyman**) the person in the street, everyone. **everyone** *pron.* everybody. **every one** *n.* each person or thing, without exception. **everyplace** *adv.* (*N Am.*) everywhere. **everything** *pron.* **1** all things collectively. **2** all of the things making up a whole. **3** (*coll.*) a great deal. **4** (*fig.*) something of the highest importance. **to have everything** (*coll.*) to have every advantage, wealth, attractiveness etc. **everyway** *adv.* in every way, in every respect. **everywhere** *adv.* **1** in every place. **2** (*coll.*) in many places.

evict (ivikt´) *v.t.* to eject from lands, tenements or property by law. **eviction** *n.* **evictor** *n.*

evidence (ev´idəns) *n.* **1** anything that makes clear or obvious; grounds for knowledge, indication, testimony. **2** that which makes truth evident, or renders evident to the mind that it is truth. **3** (*Law*) information by which a fact is proved or sought to be proved, or an allegation proved or disproved. **4** such statements, proofs etc. as are legally admissible as testimony in a court of law. **5** obviousness. *~v.t.* to make evident; to be evidence of, to attest. **in evidence 1** received or offered as tending to establish a fact or allegation in a court of law. **2** (*coll.*) plainly visible, conspicuous. **evident** *a.* open or plain to the sight; manifest, obvious. **evidential** (-den´-) *a.* **1** of or relating to evidence. **2** affording evidence. **evidentially** *adv.* **evidentiary** (-den´shəri) *a.* of or relating to, or of the nature of evidence. **evidently** *adv.* **1** obviously. **2** apparently. **3** it is obvious that. **4** yes, it would appear so.

evil (ē´vəl) *a.* **1** bad, injurious, mischievous, worthless, morally bad, wicked. **2** calamitous, agitated, sorrowful. **3** unlucky, producing disastrous results. **4** malicious, slanderous. *~adv.* in an evil manner; badly, foully, as *evil-smelling.* *~n.* **1** an evil thing. **2** that which injures or displeases, calamity, harm. **3** sin, depravity, malignity. **to speak evil of** to slander, defame. **evildoer** *n.* a person who does evil, a wrong-doer, a malefactor. **evildoing** *n.* **evil eye** *n.* a supposed power of fascinating, bewitching or materially injuring by staring at. **evilly** *adv.* **evilness** *n.*

evince (ivins´) *v.t.* **1** to indicate, to make evident. **2** to demonstrate, to show possession of. **evincible** *a.* **evincive** *a.*

Usage note The verb *evince* is occasionally used as though it meant to attest (confused with the verb *evidence*) or to call up (*evoke*), but both are best avoided.

eviscerate (ivis´ərāt) *v.t.* (*formal*) **1** to disembowel. **2** to empty of all that is vital. **evisceration** (-ā´shən) *n.*

evoke (ivōk´) *v.t.* **1** to call up, to summon forth (a memory etc.) esp. from the past. **2** to elicit or provoke. **3** to cause (spirits) to appear. **evocation** (evəkā´shən) *n.* **evocative** (ivok´ətiv) *a.* tending to evoke, esp. feelings or memories. **evocatively** *adv.* **evocativeness** *n.* **evoker** *n.*

evolution (ēvəloo´shən, ev-) *n.* **1** the gradual cumulative change in the characteristics of organisms over many generations, which results in new species. **2** this process of gradual change, which accounts for the development from simpler to more complex forms. **3** any development from a simpler to a more complex or advanced form. **4** the act of unrolling, unfolding, opening or growing. **5** a series of things unrolled or unfolded. **6** development, as of an argument, plot, design, organism or political, social or planetary system etc. **7** (*Math.*) the opening or unfolding of a curve. **8** (*Math.*) the extraction of roots from any given power, the reverse of *involution.* **9** the evolving or giving off of gas, heat etc. **10** doubling of ranks or files, countermarching or other changes of position, by which the disposition of troops or ships is changed.

evolutional, evolutionary *a.* **evolutionally, evolutionarily** *adv.* **evolutionism** *n.* the theory or doctrine of evolution as the origin of species. **evolutionist** *n.* **evolutionistic** (-nis´-) *a.*

evolve (ivolv´) *v.t.* **1** to unfold, to expand. **2** to develop, to bring to maturity. **3** to give off (gas, heat etc.). **4** to bring forth, work out, set forth (an argument etc.) in an orderly manner. *~v.i.* **1** to open. **2** to develop. **evolvable** *a.* **evolvement** *n.*

ewe (ū) *n.* a female sheep.

ewer (ū´ə) *n.* a kind of pitcher or large jug for water with a wide mouth.

ex[1] (eks) *prep.* **1** from, out of, sold from. **2** without.

ex[2] (eks) *n.* (*pl.* **exes, ex's**) (*coll.*) a former spouse, boyfriend or girlfriend.

ex- (eks) *pref.* **1** out, forth, out of, as *exceed, exclude, exit, extend, extol.* **2** thoroughly, as *exacerbate, excruciate.* **3** without, -less, as *exonerate, expatriate, exalbuminous, exstipulate.* **4** formerly, previously occupying the position of, as *ex-chancellor, ex-president.*

exa- (ek´sə) *pref.* (*Math.*) a factor of 10^{18}.

exacerbate (igzas´əbāt, eksas´-) *v.t.* **1** to irritate, to exasperate, to embitter. **2** to aggravate, to increase the violence of (as a disease). **exacerbation** (-ā´shən) *n.*

exact[1] (igzakt´) *a.* **1** precisely agreeing in amount, number or degree. **2** accurate, strictly correct. **3** precise, strict, punctilious. **exactitude** (-titūd) *n.* **exactly** *adv.* **1** in an exact manner. **2** quite so, precisely, just so (in answer to a question or affirmation). **3** in express terms. **4** no more, no less or no different from w hat is stated. **not exactly 1** (*iron.*) not at all. **2** not precisely. **exactness** *n.* **exact sciences** *n.pl.* those in which mathematical accuracy is attainable.

exact[2] (igzakt´) *v.t.* **1** to compel (money etc.) to be paid or surrendered. **2** to demand as of right, to insist on, to require authoritatively. **exactable** *a.* **exacting** *a.* **1** severe or excessive in demanding. **2** requiring much effort or skill. **exactingly** *adv.* **exactingness** *n.* **exaction** *n.* **1** the act of exacting, or an instance of exacting. **2** a forcible, illegal or exorbitant demand, extortion. **3** that which is exacted. **4** a compulsory or oppressive impost or service. **exactor, exacter** *n.*

exaggerate (igzaj´ərāt) *v.t.* **1** to heighten, to overstate, to represent as greater than is in fact the case. **2** to increase, intensify, aggravate. **3** to represent (features, colours etc.) in a heightened manner. *~v.i.* to use or be given to exaggeration. **exaggerated** *a.* **exaggeratedly** *adv.* **exaggeratingly** *adv.* **exaggeration** (-ā´shən) *n.* **exaggerative** (-aj´-) *a.* **exaggeratively** *adv.* **exaggerator** *n.*

exalt (igzawlt´) *v.t.* **1** to raise in dignity, rank, power or position. **2** to elevate in character, spirits, diction or sentiment, to ennoble, to dignify. **3** to elate. **4** to praise, extol, glorify. **5** to increase in force, to intensify. **exaltation** (egzawltā´shən) *n.* **1** the act or instance of praising. **2** great happiness. **exalted** *a.* **1** lofty, noble. **2** very happy. **exaltedly** *adv.* **exaltedness** *n.*

exam (igzam´) n. (coll.) an examination.

examine (igzam´in) v.t. **1** to inquire into, to investigate, scrutinize. **2** to consider critically, to weigh and sift (as arguments for and against). **3** to inspect, to explore. **4** (Law) to question (e.g. the accused or a witness). **5** to test the capabilities, qualifications, knowledge of etc., by questions and problems. **6** to inspect ((a part of) a patient's body) with a view to diagnosing possible illness. ~v.i. to make inquiry or research. **examinable** a. **examination** (-ā´shən) n. **1 a** the act of examining, or an instance of examining. **b** the state of being examined. **2** careful inspection, scrutiny or inquiry. **3 a** the process of testing the capabilities or qualifications of a candidate for any post, or the progress, attainments or knowledge of a student. **b** a test of this kind. **4** the act or an instance of inspecting a patient's body to diagnose possible illness. **5** (Law) a careful inquiry into facts by taking evidence. **examinational** a. **examination paper** n. **1** a paper containing questions for candidates, pupils etc. **2** a series of answers to such questions by an examinee. **examinee** (-nē´) n. **examiner** n.

example (igzahm´pəl) n. **1** a sample, a specimen. **2** a copy, model or pattern. **3** any person, fact or thing illustrating a general rule. **4** a person, course of conduct etc. seen as worthy of imitation. **5** a person, a punishment, or the person punished serving as a warning. **6** a problem or exercise (in mathematics etc.) for the instruction of students. ~v.t. (usu. passive) **1** to exemplify. **2** to serve as an example to. **for example** as an illustration.

exasperate (igzas´pərāt) v.t. **1** to irritate to a high degree; to provoke. **2** to aggravate, to embitter. **exasperated** a. **exasperatedly** adv. **exasperating** a. **exasperatingly** adv. **exasperation** (-ā´shən) n.

☒ **exaust** common misspelling of EXHAUST.

ex cathedra (eks kəthē´drə) a. authoritative, to be obeyed. ~adv. authoritatively.

excavate (eks´kəvāt) v.t. **1** to hollow out. **2** to form by digging or hollowing out. **3** to remove (from the ground) by digging. **4** to uncover by digging, to dig out, esp. for archaeological research. **5** to investigate (an archaeological site) by digging. ~v.i. to conduct archaeological research by digging. **excavation** (-ā´shən) n. **excavator** n.

exceed (iksēd´) v.t. **1** to be more or greater than. **2** to do more than is warranted by. **3** to be or to do better than. **exceeding** a. **1** very great in amount, duration, extent or degree. **2** pre-eminent. **exceedingly** adv. **1** very much. **2** pre-eminently.

excel (iksel´) v.t. (pres.p. **excelling**, past, p.p. **excelled**) **1** to surpass in qualities. **2** to exceed, to outdo. ~v.i. to be superior, distinguished or pre-eminent (in or at). **to excel oneself** to do better than one (or others) had thought possible. **excellence** (ek´-) n. **1** the state of excelling. **2** superiority, pre-eminence. **3** surpassing virtue, goodness or merit. **4** that in which any person or thing

excels. **5** an excellent quality, feature or trait. **excellency** n. (pl. **excellencies**) **1** excellence. **2** (**Excellency**) a title of honour given to a governor, an ambassador, a commander-in-chief and certain other officers. **excellent** a. **1** surpassing others in some good quality. **2** of great virtue, worth etc. **3** superior or pre-eminent in bad or neutral qualities. **excellently** adv.

excentric (iksen´trik) a., n. ECCENTRIC (in technical uses).

except (iksept´) v.t. to leave out, to omit, to exclude. ~prep. not including, excluding, but. **excepting** prep. (usu. after not) omitting, with the exception of. **exception** n. **1 a** the act, or an instance, of excepting. **b** the state of being an exception. **2** that which is excepted. **3** an instance of that which is excluded from or is at variance with a rule, class or other generalization. **4** an objection, disapproval. **to take exception 1** to object, to find fault. **2** to express disapproval. **with the exception of** omitting; not including. **exceptionable** a. liable to objection. **exceptionably** adv. **exceptional** a. **1** forming an exception. **2** unusual, unprecedented. **3** extraordinarily good. **exceptionality** (-nal´-) n. **exceptionally** adv.

Usage note The adjectives exceptionable and exceptional should not be confused: exceptionable means objectionable, and exceptional outstanding. The corresponding negatives in un- are similarly distinguished.

excerpt¹ (iksœpt´) v.t. **1** to make an extract of or from. **2** to cite, to quote. **excerptible** a. **excerption** n.

excerpt² (ek´sœpt) n. (pl. **excerpts, excerpta** (-tə)) an extract or selection from a book, play, film etc.

excess (ikses´, ek´-) n. **1** that which exceeds what is usual or necessary. **2** an instance of exceeding. **3** the quality, state or fact of exceeding the ordinary measure, proportion or limit. **4** the amount by which one number or quantity exceeds another. **5** (usu. pl.) transgression of due limits. **6** over-indulgence, intemperance. **7** (pl.) outrageous behaviour. **8** a specified amount which must be paid by the policy-holder towards the amount of a claim. ~a. more than is usual or permitted. **in excess** to excess. **in excess of** more than. **to excess** more than is normal or proper. **excess baggage, excess luggage** n. a quantity above the weight allowed free carriage. **excessive** (-ses´-) a. **1** more than normal or proper. **2** too much. **excessively** adv. **excessiveness** n.

exchange (ikschānj´) v.t. **1** to give or receive in return for something else. **2** to hand over for an equivalent in kind. **3** to give and receive in turn, to interchange. **4** to give, resign or abandon (as one state or condition for another). ~v.i. to pass from one office or institution to another by taking the place of another person. ~n. **1** the act, or an instance, of exchanging; a parting with one article or commodity for an equivalent in kind.

2 the act of giving and receiving reciprocally, interchange. **3** the act of resigning one state for another. **4** something given or received in exchange. **5** a short argument or quarrel. **6** a short correspondence by letter. **7 a** the exchanging of money for its value in money of the same or another country. **b** the commission charged for such a transaction. **8** the system by which goods or property are exchanged and debts settled, esp. in different countries, without the transfer of money. **9** the place where merchants, brokers etc. meet to transact business. **10** a place where people are introduced to each other to exchange services or information, e.g. an employment exchange. **11** an apparatus or an office in which telephone lines are connected. **12** (in chess) the capture of a piece by each player in consecutive moves. **in exchange (for)** as something exchanged (for), in return (for). **exchangeable** *a.* **exchangeability** (-bil´-) *n.* **exchanger** *n.* **exchange rate** *n.* the ratio at which the currency of one country can be exchanged for that of another. **exchange student, exchange teacher** *n.* a student or teacher who exchanges posts with a corresponding person from another country.

exchequer (ikschek´ə) *n.* **1** a State treasury. **2** (*Hist.*) the Government department dealing with the public revenue. **3** finances or pecuniary resources. **4** the Court of Exchequer.

excise[1] (ek´siz, iksīz´) *n.* **1** a tax or duty on certain articles produced and consumed in a country. **2** a tax on licences to carry out certain activities. **3** the branch of the Civil Service which collects and manages the excise duties, called the Board of Customs and Excise. **excise officer, exciseman** *n.* (*pl.* **excise officers, excisemen**) (*Hist.*) an officer who collected the excise duties, and tried to prevent any evasion of the excise laws.

excise[2] (iksīz´) *v.t.* **1** to impose an excise duty on (goods). **2** to compel (a person) to pay excise duty.

excise[3] (iksīz´) *v.t.* to cut out (part of a book or of the body). **excision** (-sizh´ən) *n.*

excite (iksīt´) *v.t.* **1** to rouse, to stir into action, energy or agitation. **2** to stir up the feelings or emotions of (a person). **3** to arouse sexually. **4** to provoke, to bring about by stimulating. **5** (*Physics*) **a** to produce electrical activity in. **b** to supply electric current to the coils of (an electromagnet). **6** to supply a signal to (a transistor etc.). **7** (*Physics*) to raise (an atom) from its normal to a higher energy level. **8** to cause the emission of radiation from (a substance). **9** to cause a substance to emit (radiation). **excitable** *a.* **1** susceptible to stimulation. **2** characterized by excitability. **excitability** (-bil´-) *n.* **excitably** *adv.* **excitant** (ek´si-) *a.* **1** stimulating. **2** tending to excite. ~*n.* **1** that which excites increased action in an organism. **2** a stimulant. **excitation** (eksitā´shən) *n.* **1** the act, or an instance, of being excited. **2** the state of being excited. **excitative** *a.* **excitatory** *a.* **excited** *a.* **excitedly** *adv.* **excitedness**

n. **excitement** *n.* **exciter** *n.* **exciting** *a.* **1** stimulating. **2** producing excitement or enthusiasm. **excitingly** *adv.* **excitingness** *n.*

exclaim (iksklām´) *v.i.* to cry out abruptly or passionately. ~*v.t.* to utter in an abrupt or passionate manner. **exclaimer** *n.*

exclamation (ekskləmā´shən) *n.* **1** the act of exclaiming. **2** an expression of surprise, pain etc. **exclamation mark**, (*N Am.*) **exclamation point** *n.* a sign (!) indicating emotion etc. **exclamatory** (-klam´ə-) *a.* **1** containing or expressing exclamation. **2** using exclamation.

exclave (eks´klāv) *n.* part of a country disjoined from the main part and surrounded by foreign territory, where it is considered an enclave.

exclosure (iksklō´zhə) *n.* an area shut off from entry or intrusion, esp. a forested area fenced to keep out animals.

exclude (iksklood´) *v.t.* **1** to shut out, to prevent from coming in. **2** to prevent from participating. **3** to debar; to expel and keep out. **4** to reject, to except, to leave out. **5** to prevent the possibility of. **excludable** *a.* **exclusion** (-zhən) *n.* **1** the act, or an instance, of excluding. **2** the state of being excluded. **to the exclusion of** so as to exclude. **exclusionary** *a.* **exclusionist** *n.* a person who would exclude another from any privilege, position etc. ~*a.* favouring exclusion. **exclusionism** *n.* **exclusion order** *n.* an order preventing the entry into the United Kingdom of anyone known to be involved in terrorism. **exclusive** (-siv) *a.* **1** shutting out or tending to shut out. **2** desiring to shut out. **3** fastidious in the choice of associates, snobbish. **4** available only from a specified source, a shop etc. **5** serving, allowing entry to a few selected people. **6** not inclusive (of). **7** excluding all else. **8** excluding all that is not specified. ~*adv.* not taking into account or not inclusively (of). ~*n.* a story published only by one newspaper, radio station etc. **exclusively** *adv.* **exclusiveness** *n.* **exclusivism** *n.* **1** the act or practice of excluding. **2** systematic exclusiveness. **exclusivist** *n.* **exclusivity** (-siv´-) *n.*

excogitate (ekskoj´itāt) *v.t.* **1** to think out. **2** to devise by thinking. **excogitation** (-ā´shən) *n.*

excommunicate[1] (ekskəmū´nikāt) *v.t.* to exclude from the communion and privileges of the Church. **excommunication** (-ā´shən) *n.* **excommunicative** *a.* **excommunicator** *n.* **excommunicatory** *a.*

excommunicate[2] (ekskəmū´nikət) *a.* excommunicated. ~*n.* a person who has been excommunicated.

ex-con (ekskon´) *n.* (*coll.*) an ex-convict, a person who has served their sentence and been released from prison.

excoriate (ekskaw´riāt) *v.t.* **1** to strip the skin from. **2** to tear off (the skin) by abrasion. **3** to criticize severely. **excoriation** (-ā´shən) *n.*

excrement (eks´krəmənt) *n.* refuse matter discharged from the body after digestion, faeces. **excremental** (-men´-) *a.*

excrescence (ikskres´əns) *n.* **1** an abnormal, useless or disfiguring outgrowth. **2** an ugly and superfluous addition. **excrescent** *a.* **excrescential** (-en´shəl) *a.*

excrete (ikskrēt´) *v.t., v.i.* to separate and discharge (superfluous matter) from the organism. **excreta** (-tə) *n.pl.* matter discharged from the body, esp. faeces and urine. **excreter** *n.* **excretion** *n.* **excretive** *a.* **excretory** *a.*

excruciate (ikskroo´shiāt) *v.t.* to inflict severe pain or mental agony upon. **excruciating** *a.* **excruciatingly** *adv.* **excruciation** (-ā´shən) *n.*

exculpate (eks´kəlpāt, iks´kŭl-) *v.t. (formal)* **1** to clear from a charge. **2** to free from blame, exonerate. **exculpation** (ekskŭlpā´shən) *n.* **exculpatory** (ikskŭl´pə-) *a.*

excursion (ikskœ´shən) *n.* **1 a** a journey or ramble for health or pleasure. **b** a short tour, a trip by an individual or a body of persons. **2** a wandering from the subject, a digression. **3** (*Astron.*) a deviation from the fixed course. **excursional, excursionary** *a.* **excursionist** *n.*

excursive (ikskœ´siv) *a.* rambling, deviating, exploring. **excursively** *adv.* **excursiveness** *n.*

excuse[1] (ikskūz´) *v.t.* **1** to free from blame or guilt, to lessen the blame or guilt attaching to. **2** to pardon, to acquit (a person). **3** to ask pardon or indulgence for. **4** to serve as a vindication or apology for, to justify. **5** to relieve of or exempt from an obligation or duty. **6** to remit, not to exact (e.g. a debt). **7** to dispense with. **to excuse oneself 1** to (try to) justify one's actions. **2** to ask permission to leave. **excusable** *a.* **excusably** *adv.* **excusatory** *a.* **excuse-me** *n.* a dance during which partners may be changed on request. **excuser** *n.*

excuse[2] (ikskūs´) *n.* **1** a plea offered in extenuation of a fault or for release from an obligation, duty etc. **2** an apology, a justification. **3** a pretended reason. **excuse for** (*coll.*) a bad example of, a botched attempt at.

ex-directory (eksdirek´təri) *a.* **1** (of a telephone number) not listed in a telephone directory and not revealed to inquirers. **2** (of a person) having such a telephone number.

ex div. *abbr.* ex dividend.

ex dividend (eks div´idend) *a., adv.* not including the next dividend.

exec (egzek´) *n.* an executive.

execrate (ek´sikrāt) *v.t.* **1** to curse, to imprecate evil upon. **2** to detest. ~*v.i.* to utter curses. **execrable** *a.* **1** detestable, accursed. **2** abominable. **3** very bad, of very poor quality. **execrableness** *n.* **execrably** *adv.* **execration** (-ā´shən) *n.* **execrative** *a.* **execratory** *a.*

execute (ek´sikūt) *v.t.* **1** to carry into effect, to put in force. **2** to perform, to accomplish, complete. **3** to perform what is required to give validity to any legal instrument, as by signing and sealing. **4** to discharge (a duty, function, office etc.). **5** to play or perform (a piece of music, a part in a play). **6** to make or produce (a movement, drawing etc.). **7** to carry out a sentence of death on.

executable *a.* **executant** (igzek´ū-) *n.* (*formal*) **1** a person who performs or carries into effect. **2** (*Mus.*) a performer on any instrument. **execution** (-kū´shən) *n.* **1** the act, or an instance, of executing. **2** performance, accomplishment. **3** the carrying out of a death sentence. **4** the mode of performing a work of art, skill, dexterity. **5** the act of giving validity to a legal instrument, as by signing. **6** the carrying into effect of the judgement of a court. **7** a warrant empowering an officer to carry a judgement into effect, esp. one authorizing the seizure of a debtor's goods in default of payment. **executionary** *a.* **executioner** *n.* a person who carries out a death sentence. **executive** (igzek´ūtiv) *a.* **1** having the function or power of executing. **2** of or relating to performance or carrying into effect. **3** carrying laws, decrees etc. into effect. **4** of, relating to or suitable for the use of, a business executive. ~*n.* **1** the person or body of persons carrying laws, ordinances, sentences etc. into effect. **2** the administrative branch of a government or of a business. **3** in business, a senior manager or administrator. **executively** *adv.*

executor (igzek´ūtə) *n.* a person who executes, esp. one appointed by a testator to carry out the provisions of their will. **executorial** (-taw´ri-) *a.* **executorship** *n.* **executory** *a.* **executrix** (-triks) *n.* (*pl.* **executrixes, executrices** (-trī´sēz)) a woman executor.

exegesis (eksijē´sis) *n.* (*pl.* **exegeses** (-sēz)) exposition, interpretation, esp. of the Scriptures. **exegete** (ek´sijēt) *n.* **exegetic** (-jet´-) *a.* **exegetical** *a.* **exegetist** *n.*

exemplar (igzem´plə) *n.* **1** a pattern or model to be copied. **2** a typical example. **3** a parallel instance. **exemplary** *a.* **1** serving as a pattern or model. **2** worthy of imitation. **3** typical, serving to exemplify, illustrative. **4** serving as a warning. **exemplarily** *adv.* **exemplariness** *n.*

exemplify (igzem´plifī) *v.t.* (*3rd pers. sing. pres.* **exemplifies,** *pres.p.* **exemplifying,** *past, p.p.* **exemplified**) **1** to illustrate by example. **2** to be an example of. **3** (*Law*) to make an authenticated copy of (a document). **exemplifiable** *a.* **exemplification** (-fikā´shən) *n.*

exemplum (igzem´pləm) *n.* (*pl.* **exempla** (-plə)) **1** an example. **2** a short story or anecdote which illustrates a moral.

exempt (igzempt´) *a.* **1** free (from). **2** not liable or subject to (a tax, obligation etc.). ~*n.* **1** a person who is exempted or freed (from). **2** an exon. ~*v.t.* **1** to free or allow to be free. **2** to grant immunity (from). **exemption** *n.*

exequies (ek´sikwiz) *n.pl.* (*formal*) funeral rites; the ceremony of burial. **exequial** (-sē´-) *a.*

exercise (ek´səsīz) *n.* **1** systematic exertion of the body for the sake of health. **2** physical exertion for the training of the body. **3** (*often pl.*) drill, athletics. **4** mental practice designed to develop a faculty or skill. **5** a composition designed to improve the technique of a player or singer. **6** the act of using, employing or exerting (a skill, a right etc.). **7** practice (of a function, virtue, occupation, art etc.). **8** (*pl.*) military manoeuvres, simulated battles, for training purposes. **9** a course of action designed to demonstrate a specified fact or quality (*an exercise in diplomacy*). ~*v.t.* **1** to employ, to exert, to put in practice or operation. **2** to perform the duties of, to fulfil. **3** to train (a person). **4** to keep employed or busy. **5** to make anxious or solicitous, to perplex, worry. **6** to exert (muscles, brain, memory etc.) so as to develop their power. **7** to give (an animal) physical exercise. ~*v.i.* to take (regular) physical exercise; to do exercises. **exercisable** *a.* **exercise bicycle, exercise bike** *n.* an exercising machine, at a gymnasium etc., like a bicycle without wheels. **exercise book** *n.* **1** a book for writing notes etc. in. **2** a printed book containing exercises. **exerciser** *n.*

exergue (ek´sœg) *n.* **1** the small space beneath the base line of a subject engraved on a coin or medal. **2** the name, date or inscription placed there.

❌ **exerpt** common misspelling of EXCERPT¹.

exert (igzœt´) *v.t.* to apply or use (strength, power, ability etc.) with effort, to put in action or operation. **to exert oneself** to strive, to use effort. **exertion** (-shən) *n.*

exeunt (ek´siunt) *v.i.* they go off the stage, they retire (stage direction). **exeunt omnes** (om´nāz) they all go off the stage.

exfoliate (eksfō´liāt) *v.i.* **1** (of skin, rocks etc.) to shed or come off in flakes or scales. **2** to separate into flakes. **3** (of a tree) to shed its bark in layers. ~*v.t.* **1** to remove in flakes. **2** to cause to come off in flakes. **exfoliation** (-ā´shən) *n.* **exfoliative** *a.*

ex gratia (eks grā´sha) *a., adv.* as an act of favour, and with no acceptance of liability.

exhalation (eksəlā´shən) *n.* **1** the act or process of exhaling. **2** evaporation. **3 a** that which is exhaled. **b** a puff of breath. **4** vapour, mist. **5** effluvium, an emanation.

exhale (iks-hāl´, igzāl´) *v.t.* **1** to breathe out. **2** to emit, or cause to be emitted, in vapour. **3** to draw up in vapour. ~*v.i.* **1** to be given off as vapour. **2** to make an expiration, as distinct from *inhale*. **exhalable** *a.*

exhaust (igzawst´) *v.t.* **1** to use up the whole of, to consume. **2** to wear out by exertion. **3** to empty by drawing out the contents. **4** to drain of resources, strength or essential properties. **5** to study, discuss, treat the whole of (a subject). ~*n.* **1** the discharge of steam, gas, vapour etc. from an engine after it has performed its work. **2** the gases etc. so discharged. **3** the pipe or system which removes these gases. **4** an apparatus for withdrawing air by means of a partial vacuum. **5** the outward current of air so produced. **exhausted** *a.* **exhauster** *n.* **exhaustible** *a.* **exhaustibility** (-bil´-) *n.* **exhausting** *a.* **exhaustion** (-chən) *n.* **1** the act, or an instance, of exhausting. **2** the

state of being exhausted. **3** a complete loss of strength. **4** a method of proving a point by showing that all alternatives are absurd or impossible. **exhaustive** *a.* tending to exhaust (esp. a subject), comprehensive. **exhaustively** *adv.* **exhaustiveness** *n.*

exhibit (igzib´it) *v.t.* **1** to offer to public view. **2** to present for inspection. **3** to show, to display, to manifest. **4** to furnish an instance of. ~*n.* **1** anything exhibited. **2** an article or collection of articles sent to an exhibition. **3** a document or other item produced in court and used as evidence. **exhibiter** *n.* **exhibition** (eksibish´ən) *n.* **1** the act, or an instance, of exhibiting. **2** a display. **3** a public display of works of art or manufacture, natural products etc. **4** the act of allowing to be seen, as temper. **5** the production of documents etc. before any tribunal in proof of facts. **6** an allowance to a student in college, school etc., orig. maintenance, support, pecuniary assistance. **to make an exhibition of oneself** to behave so as to appear foolish or contemptible. **exhibitioner** *n.* a student who has obtained an exhibition at a college or school. **exhibitionism** *n.* **1** a tendency to show off, to attract attention to oneself. **2** (*Psych.*) a compulsive desire to exhibit one's genitals in public. **exhibitionist** *n.* **exhibitionistic** (-ist´ik) *a.* **exhibitionistically** *adv.* **exhibitor** (eksib´-) *n.*

exhilarate (igzil´ərāt) *v.t.* to gladden, to enliven, to animate. **exhilarant** *a., n.* **exhilarating** *a.* **exhilaratingly** *adv.* **exhilaration** (-ā´shən) *n.* **exhilarative** (-ətiv) *a.*

exhort (igzawt´) *v.t.* **1** to incite by words (to good deeds). **2** to urge, to advise or encourage by argument. ~*v.i.* to deliver an exhortation. **exhortation** (egzawtā´shən) *n.* **1** the act or practice of exhorting. **2** an admonition, earnest advice. **3** a formal address, esp. in church. **exhortative** (-awt´-) *a.* **exhortatory** *a.* **exhorter** *n.*

exhume (igzūm´, eks-hūm´) *v.t.* to dig out, esp. a corpse from its grave. **exhumation** (eks-hūmā´-shən, egzū-) *n.* **exhumer** *n.*

exigence (ek´sijəns, -sij´-), **exigency** (iksij´-, igzij´-) *n.* (*pl.* **exigences, exigencies**) **1** urgent need, demand, necessity. **2** a state of affairs demanding immediate action or remedy, an emergency.

exigent (ek´sijənt) *a.* **1** urgent, pressing. **2** demanding more than is reasonable, exacting. **exigently** *adv.*

exiguous (igzig´ūəs, iksig´-) *a.* small, slender, scanty. **exiguity** (eksigū´iti) *n.* **exiguously** *adv.* **exiguousness** *n.*

exile (eg´zīl, ek´sīl) *n.* **1** banishment, expatriation. **2** long absence from one's native country, whether voluntary or enforced. **3** a person who is banished, or has been long absent from their native country. ~*v.t.* to banish from one's native country, town etc. **exilian** (-il´-), **exilic** (-il´-) *a.* of or relating to exile or banishment, esp. to that of the Jews in Babylon.

exist (igzist´) *v.i.* **1** to be, to have actual being. **2** to live. **3** to continue to be. **4** to live or have being under specified conditions. **5** (of inanimate objects or circumstances) to be found, to occur. **6** to carry on living, after a fashion, in unfavourable circumstances. **existence** *n.* **1** the state of being or existing. **2** continuance of being. **3** life. **4** mode of existing. **5** a thing that exists; a being, an entity. **6** all that exists. **existent** *a.* having being or existence, existing, actual. **existential** (egzisten´shəl, eksi-) *a.* **1** of or relating to or consisting in existence. **2** (*Logic*) (of a proposition etc.) asserting the existence of something. **3** (*Philos.*) of or relating to human existence or to existentialism. **existentialism** *n.* a philosophical theory which considers human beings as morally free, and responsible for making their own system of values in an otherwise meaningless universe. **existentialist** *n., a.* **existentially** *adv.*

exit[1] (ek´sit, eg´zit) *n.* **1** a passage or door, a way out. **2** a going out. **3** freedom to go out. **4** a place where vehicles can enter or leave a motorway. **5** the departure of an actor from the stage. **6** departure, esp. from this life; death, decease. **exit permit** *n.* a written authorization to leave a country. **exit poll** *n.* an unofficial poll taken by asking people leaving a polling station how they have voted. **exit visa** *n.* an exit permit.

exit[2] (ek´sit) *v.i.* **1** to depart, to leave a place. **2** goes off the stage (stage direction). **3** (*formal*) to die. **4** (in bridge, whist etc.) to lose the lead deliberately. **5** (*Comput.*) to leave a subroutine, a program etc. ~*v.t.* (*N Am.*) to leave.

⊠ **exite** common misspelling of EXCITE.

⊠ **exma** common misspelling of ECZEMA.

exo- (ek´sō) *comb. form* of or relating to the outside of anything, external.

exocrine (ek´səkrīn, -krin) *a.* (of a gland) producing secretions that are released through a duct.

exoderm (eks´ədœm) *n.* (*Anat.*) the epidermis, the outer layer of the blastoderm.

exodus (eks´ədəs) *n.* **1** a departure, esp. of a large group of people. **2** (**Exodus**) the departure of the Israelites from Egypt under Moses.

ex officio (eks əfish´iō) *adv.* by virtue of one's office. ~*a.* official.

exogamy (eksog´əmi) *n.* **1** the custom of marrying outside one's own tribe. **2** (*Biol.*) the union of reproductive cells not related or only distantly related to each other. **exogamic** (-gam´-), **exogamous** (-og´-) *a.*

exogenous (eksoj´inəs) *a.* **1** developing externally. **2** having external origins (*exogenous depression*). **exogenously** *adv.*

exon[1] (ek´son) *n.* any one of the four officers of the Yeomen of the Guard ranking as corporals.

exon[2] (ek´son) *n.* (*Biol.*) any segment of a gene which consists of codons.

exonerate (igzon´ərāt) *v.t.* **1** to free from a charge or blame, to exculpate. **2** to relieve from a duty, obligation or liability. **exoneration** (-ā´shən) *n.* **exonerative** (-ətiv) *a.*

exoplasm (ek´səplazm) *n.* (*Biol.*) the denser outer layer of the cuticular protoplasm of certain protozoans, ectoplasm.

exorbitant (igzaw´bitənt) *a.* **1** out of all bounds, grossly excessive, inordinate, extravagant. **2** (of prices) unreasonably high. **exorbitance** *n.* **exorbitantly** *adv.*

exorcize (ek´sawsīz), **exorcise** *v.t.* **1** to expel (as an evil spirit) by prayers and ceremonies. **2** to free or purify from unclean spirits. **exorcist** *n.* **exorcism** *n.* **exorcization** (-zā´shən) *n.*

exordium (igzaw´diəm) *n.* (*pl.* **exordiums**, **exordia** (-diə)) the beginning of anything, esp. the introductory part of a literary work or discourse. **exordial** *a.*

exoskeleton (eksōskel´itən) *n.* an external skeleton, e.g. in arthropods, formed by a hardening of the integument. **exoskeletal** *a.*

exosphere (ek´sōsfiə) *n.* the outermost layer of the earth's atmosphere.

exoteric (eksəter´ik), **exoterical** *a.* **1** external, public, fit to be imparted to outsiders. **2** comprehensible to the general public, as distinct from *esoteric*. **3** ordinary, popular.

exothermic (eksōthœ´mik), **exothermal** (-məl) *a.* (*Chem.*) involving the evolution of heat. **exothermically**, **exothermally** *adv.*

exotic (igzot´ik) *a.* **1** introduced from a foreign country. **2** romantically strange, glamorous. **3** (*coll.*) unusual and different in an exciting way. **4** (of a fuel etc.) new and high-energy. ~*n.* **1** anything foreign. **2** anything introduced from a foreign country, as a plant. **exotica** (-kə) *n.pl.* rare or unusual objects, esp. when forming a collection. **exotically** *adv.* **exotic dancer** *n.* a striptease or belly dancer. **exoticism** (-sizm) *n.*

exotoxin (eksōtok´sin) *n.* a toxin released from within a living bacterium into the surrounding medium.

expand (ikspand´) *v.t.* **1** to open or spread out. **2** to distend, to cause to increase in bulk. **3** to widen, to extend, to enlarge. **4** to write out in full (what is condensed or abbreviated). ~*v.i.* **1** to become opened or spread out, distended or enlarged in bulk, not mass. **2** to become more relaxed, to talk more openly. **expandable** *a.* **expanded** *a.* **expanded metal** *n.* sheet metal cut and formed into a lattice, used for reinforcing concrete etc. **expander** *n.* **expansible** (-sibəl) *a.* **expansibility** (-bil´-) *n.* **expansile** (-sīl) *a.* **1** of or relating to expansion. **2** capable of expanding, expansible.

expanse (ikspans´) *n.* **1** a wide, open extent or area. **2** amount of expansion.

expansion (ikspan´shən) *n.* **1** the act, or an instance, of expanding. **2** the state of being expanded. **3** enlargement, extension, distension. **4** extension of business, increase of liabilities, extension of the currency or of territory. **5** increase of volume, as of fuel in a cylinder. **expansionary** *a.* **expansion card**, **expansion board** *n.* (*Comput.*) a printed circuit board that can be inserted in a computer to give extra facilities. **expansionist** n. a person who advocates territorial or economic expansion. **expansionism** n. **expansionistic** a. **expansion joint** n. a joint between metal rails, concrete pieces etc., which allows for expansion when heated. **expansion slot** n. (*Comput.*) a connector in a computer into which an expansion card can be fitted.

expansive (ikspan´siv) a. **1** having the power of expanding. **2** able or tending to expand. **3** extending widely, comprehensive. **4** frank, effusive. **expansively** adv. **expansiveness** n. **expansivity** (-iv´iti) n.

expat EXPATRIATE².

expatiate (ikspā´shiāt) v.i. to speak or write copiously (on a subject). **expatiation** (-ā´shən) n. **expatiatory** a.

expatriate¹ (ekspā´triāt) v.t. **1** to exile. **2** to drive into banishment. **3** to exile (oneself), or withdraw (oneself) from citizenship. **expatriation** (-ā´shən) n.

expatriate² (ekspā´triət), (*coll.*) **expat** (ekspat´) n. a person living away from their own country. ~a. **1** living abroad. **2** exiled.

expect (ikspekt´) v.t. **1** to look forward to. **2** to regard as certain or likely to happen, to anticipate. **3** to require as due. **4** (*coll.*) to think, to suppose (that). **expectable** a. **expectancy, expectance** n. (*pl.* **expectancies, expectances**) **1** the act or state of expecting, expectation. **2** prospect of possessing, enjoying etc. **3** a thing which is expected. **4** a feeling that something good or exciting is going to happen. **expectant** a. **1** expecting, waiting in expectation (of something). **2** anticipating, presumptive. **3** pregnant. ~n. a person who waits in expectation of something, as a candidate for an office etc. **expectantly** adv. **expectation** (ekspiktā´shən) n. **1** the act or state of expecting, anticipation. **2** a confident awaiting. **3** (*pl.*) prospects (of inheriting). **4** the probability of a future event. **5** something expected. **expecting** a. (*coll.*) pregnant. **expectingly** adv.

expectorate (ikspek´tərāt) v.t. to discharge from the lungs or throat by coughing, hawking or spitting. ~v.i. **1** to discharge matter from the lungs or throat by coughing etc. **2** to spit. **expectorant** a. having the quality of promoting expectoration. ~n. a medicine promoting expectoration. **expectoration** (-ā´shən) n. **expectorator** n.

expedient (ikspē´diənt) a. **1** promoting the object in view. **2** advantageous, convenient. **3** conducive to personal advantage. **4** appropriate, suitable. **5** politic as opposed to just. ~n. **1** that which promotes an object. **2** an advantageous way or means. **3** a shift, a contrivance. **expedience, expediency** n. **expediently** adv.

Usage note The adjectives *expedient* and *expeditious* should not be confused: *expedient* means advantageous or convenient, and *expeditious* speedy.

expedite (ek´spədīt) v.t. **1** to facilitate, to assist or accelerate the progress of. **2** to dispatch, accomplish quickly. **expediter** n. **expeditious** (-dish´əs) a. **1** speedy, ready, active. **2** done with efficiency and rapidity. **expeditiously** adv. **expeditiousness** n.

expedition (ekspədish´ən) n. **1** any journey or voyage by an organized body for some definite object. **2** the persons with their equipment engaged in this. **3** a march or voyage of an army or fleet to a distance with hostile intentions. **4** speed, promptness, dispatch. **expeditionary** a. relating to, constituting or used in an expedition. **expeditionist** n.

Usage note See note under EXPEDIENT.

expel (ikspel´) v.t. (*pres.p.* **expelling**, *past, p.p.* **expelled**) **1** to drive or force out. **2** to eject, to banish. **3** to turn out formally (as from a school, college, or society). **expellable** a. **expellant, expellent** a. **expellee** (-ē´) n. **expeller** n.

expend (ikspend´) v.t. **1** to spend, to lay out. **2** to consume, to use up. **expendable** a. **1** likely to be or intended to be wasted. **2** that can be sacrificed in order to attain some purpose. **3** unimportant, not worth saving. **4** that need not be reused. **expendability** (-bil´-) n. **expendably** adv. **expenditure** (-dichə) n. **1** the act of expending. **2** the amount expended. **3** the act of using energy, money etc.

expense (ikspens´) n. **1** cost, charge, outlay, price paid. **2** (*pl.*) outlay in performance of a duty or commission. **3** (*pl., coll.*) money reimbursed for this. **4** something on which money has to be spent. **at the expense of 1** at the cost of. **2** to the discredit or detriment of. **expense account** n. an account of expenses refunded to an employee by an employer. **expensive** a. **1** costly, causing or requiring a large expenditure. **2** extravagant, lavish. **expensively** adv. **expensiveness** n.

experience (ikspiə´riəns) n. **1** practical acquaintance with any matter. **2** knowledge gained by observation or trial. **3** a particular instance of such knowledge. **4** something undergone of an affecting or impressive nature. **5** the fact of being so affected or impressed. ~v.t. **1** to gain a practical knowledge of by trial or observation. **2** to undergo, to feel, to meet with. **experienceable** a. **experienced** a. **1** taught by experience. **2** practised, skilled.

experiential (ikspiəriən´shəl) a. of, relating to or derived from experience. **experientialism** n. (*Philos.*) experiential philosophy. **experientialist** a. **experientially** adv. **experiential philosophy** n. a philosophy which states that all knowledge and ideas are derived from experience.

experiment (iksper´imənt) n. **1** a trial, proof or test of anything. **2** an act, operation or process designed to discover some unknown truth, principle or effect, to test a hypothesis or to test a fact. ~v.i. to make an experiment or trial (on or with). **experimental** (-men´-) a. **1** pertaining to, derived from or founded upon experiment.

2 practising experiments. **3** empirical. **4** based on an (unfinished) experiment; provisional. **experimentalism** *n.* **experimentalist** *n.* **experimentalize, experimentalise** *v.i.* **experimentally** *adv.* **experimentation** (-tā´shən) *n.* the act or practice of making experiments. **experimenter** *n.*

expert (ek´spœt) *a.* **1** experienced, dexterous from use and experience. **2** practised, skilful (at or in). **3** based on, or resulting from, special skill or knowledge. ~*n.* **1** a person who has special skill or knowledge. **2** a scientific or professional witness. **expertise**[1] (-tēz´) *n.* expert skill, opinion or knowledge. **expertise**[2] EXPERTIZE (under EXPERT). **expertize** (eks´pœtīz), **expertise** *v.t., v.i.* to give an expert opinion (on). **expertly** *adv.* **expertness** *n.* **expert system** *n.* (*Comput.*) a computer system designed using expert knowledge and artificial intelligence techniques, so that it can solve problems and make intelligent decisions.

expiate (ek´spiāt) *v.t.* **1** to atone for. **2** to make reparation or amends for. **3** to pay the penalty of. **expiable** *a.* **expiation** (-ā´shən) *n.* **expiator** *n.* **expiatory** *a.*

expire (ikspīə´) *v.t.* **1** to breathe out from the lungs. **2** to send forth, to emit, to exhale. ~*v.i.* **1** to come to an end. **2** (of a guarantee, authorization etc.) to come to an end through passage of time, to lose validity. **3** to emit the last breath; to die. **4** to breathe out. **expiration** (ekspirā´shən) *n.* **1** the act of breathing out. **2** cessation, termination. **expiratory** (-spī´-) *a.* **expirer** *n.* **expiry** *n.* **1** expiration, termination. **2** death.

explain (iksplān´) *v.t.* **1** to make clear, plain or intelligible. **2** to expound and illustrate the meaning of. **3** to account for. **4** to state, as an explanation. ~*v.i.* to give explanations. **to explain away 1** to get rid of (difficulties) by explanation. **2** to modify or do away with (a charge etc.) by explanation. **to explain oneself 1** to make one's meaning clear. **2** to give an account of one's motives, intentions, conduct etc. **explainable** *a.* **explainer** *n.*

explanation (eksplənā´shən) *n.* **1** the act, or an instance, of explaining. **2** the sense or definition given by an interpreter or expounder. **3** the process of arriving at a mutual understanding or reconciliation. **4** that which accounts for anything. **explanatory** (-plan´-) *a.* **1** containing an explanation. **2** serving to explain. **explanatorily** *adv.*

explant[1] (eksplahnt´) *v.t.* (*Biol.*) to remove (living tissue) to a medium for tissue culture. **explantation** (-ā´shən) *n.*

explant[2] (eks´plahnt) *n.* a piece of living tissue removed for culture.

expletive (iksplē´tiv) *a.* **1** serving to fill out or complete. **2** introduced merely to fill a gap or vacancy. ~*n.* **1** a word, not necessary to the sense, introduced to fill up a line or a sentence. **2** an interjection or word added for emphasis, esp. a swear word.

explicate (eks´plikāt) *v.t.* **1** to unfold the meaning of. **2** to make clear, explain the difficulties of (a text etc.). **3** to develop (the contents of an idea, proposition etc.). **explicable** *a.* capable of being explained. **explication** (-ā´shən) *n.* **explicative, explicatory** *a.* **explicator** *n.*

explicit (iksplis´it) *a.* **1** plainly expressed, distinctly stated, as distinct from *implicit.* **2** definite. **3** (of a person) unreserved, outspoken. **4** showing or describing nudity or sexual activity quite plainly. **explicitly** *adv.* **explicitness** *n.*

explode (iksplōd´) *v.t.* **1** to cause to burst with a loud noise. **2** to refute, expose, discredit (a theory, fallacy etc.). ~*v.i.* **1** to burst with a loud noise. **2** to give vent suddenly to strong feelings, esp. anger. **3** (*fig.*) to come to an end as if by bursting, to collapse. **4** (of population) to increase suddenly and dramatically. **exploded** *a.* (of a drawing) depicting all the outer parts (of a machine, organism etc.) as lifted off the inner parts, so that all may be shown, with their relationships. **exploder** *n.*

exploit[1] (eks´sploit) *n.* **1** a feat, a great or noble achievement. **2** an adventure.

exploit[2] (eksploit´) *v.t.* **1** to make use of, derive benefit from. **2** (*usu. derog.*) to utilize, esp. to make use of or take advantage of for one's own profit. **exploitable** *a.* **exploitation** (-ā´shən) *n.* **exploitative** *a.* **exploiter** *n.* **exploitive** *a.*

explore (iksplaw´) *v.t.* **1** to search or inquire into. **2** to investigate, to examine. **3** to travel over (a country etc.) in order to examine or discover. **4** (*Med.*) to investigate (an organ etc.) in detail. **exploration** (eksplərā´shən) *n.* **explorational** *a.* **explorative** (-plor´-) *a.* **exploratory** *a.* **explorer** *n.* **1** a person who explores. **2** a traveller into unknown or little-known parts.

explosion (iksplō´zhən) *n.* **1** a bursting or exploding with a loud noise. **2** a sudden and violent noise. **3** a sudden and violent outbreak, as of physical forces, anger etc. **4** a sudden and very rapid increase or expansion. **explosive** (-siv) *a.* **1** bursting or driving out with great force and noise. **2** liable to explode or cause explosion. **3** (of a situation) tense, potentially violent. **4** (of consonants) plosive. ~*n.* an explosive agent or substance, as gunpowder, dynamite etc. **explosively** *adv.* **explosiveness** *n.*

Expo (eks´pō), **expo** *n.* (*pl.* **Expos, expos**) a large public exhibition.

exponent (ikspō´nənt) *a.* setting forth or explaining. ~*n.* **1** a person who sets forth or explains. **2** a person who or thing which advocates or promotes a party, principle or cause. **3** a type, a representative. **4** (*Math.*) a number or quantity written to the right of and above another number or quantity, to show how many times the latter is to be taken as a factor (thus, in the expression a^3, **3** is an exponent, and shows that *a* is to be taken three times as a factor thus, $a \times a \times a$). **5** a person who performs or interprets a play, dance etc. **exponential** (ekspənen´-) *a.* **1** (*Math.*) of or relating to an exponent or exponents. **2** involving variable exponents. **3** (*coll.*) very rapid. **exponential function** *n.* a function containing a quantity raised to an exponent. **exponential growth** *n.* growth at an ever-increasing rate as the total size or number increases. **exponentially** *adv.*

export[1] (iks'pawt) *v.t.* to carry or send (goods) to foreign countries. **exportable** (-spaw'-) *a.* **exportability** (-bil'-) *n.* **exportation** (ekspawtā'shən) *n.* **exporter** *n.*

export[2] (eks'pawt) *n.* **1** the act or process of exporting, exportation. **2** a commodity sent to a foreign country. **3** (*pl.*) the quantity or value of goods exported. **export reject** *n.* an item sold in its country of origin because it is not of high enough quality to export.

expose (ikspōz') *v.t.* **1** to leave unprotected or vulnerable. **2** to subject (to any influence or action). **3** to turn out and abandon (as a child). **4** to exhibit, to display, esp. for sale. **5** to disclose, reveal. **6** to unmask, reveal the identity of. **7** to subject (a photographic film in a camera) to light. **to expose oneself** to display one's genitals in public so as to shock or embarrass others. **exposé** (-zā) *n.* **1** a formal declaration or recital of facts. **2** a disclosure, an exposure (of damning or sensational information). **exposer** *n.* **exposition** (ekspəzi'shən) *n.* **1** the act of exposing. **2** an explanation, an account (of). **3** an explanation or interpretation of the meaning of an author or a work, a commentary. **4** a public exhibition. **5** (*Mus.*) the first statement of the themes in a sonata movement etc. **expositional** *a.* **expositive** (-spoz'-) *a.* **expositor** (-spoz'-) *n.* **1** a person who expounds or explains. **2** a commentator. **expository** (-spoz'-) *a.* **exposure** (ikspō'zhə) *n.* **1** the act of exposing. **2** the state of being exposed to view, inconvenience, danger etc. **3** the state of being unsheltered from cold, heat, sun etc. **4** physical illness resulting from prolonged coldness. **5** a disclosure, revelation, unmasking. **6** situation (of a property) with respect to the points of the compass, or free access of light and air; outlook, aspect. **7 a** the act of allowing light from an object to fall upon a sensitized photographic plate. **b** the duration of this exposure. **c** the piece of film thus exposed. **8** appearance in public, esp. on stage or television or in the press. **9** the direction in which a building etc. faces. **exposure meter** *n.* a device attached to a camera which measures the strength of the light so that the length of exposure etc. can be adjusted.

ex post facto (eks pōst fak'tō) *a., adv.* having retrospective force.

expostulate (ikspos'tūlāt) *v.i.* to reason earnestly (with a person), to remonstrate. **expostulation** (-ā'shən) *n.* **expostulatory** *a.*

expound (ikspownd') *v.t.* **1** to set out the meaning of in detail. **2** to explain, to interpret. **expounder** *n.*

express[1] (ikspres') *a.* **1** direct, explicit, definitely shown or stated, not merely implied. **2** intended, prepared, done, made, sent for a special purpose. **3** (of goods etc.) delivered by express messenger or post. **4** travelling quickly. *~adv.* **1** at high speed. **2** by express messenger, train or post. *~n.* **1** an express train. **2** an express messenger. **3** an express rifle. **4** (*NAm.*) a company which organizes express deliveries. *~v.t.* to send by express messenger or post. **expressly** *adv.* **express rifle** *n.* a sporting rifle with a high muzzle-velocity and low trajectory. **express train** *n.* a fast train with few intermediate stops. **expressway** *n.* (*Austral., NAm.*) a motorway.

express[2] (ikspres') *v.t.* **1** to set out, to represent, to put into words or symbolize by gestures etc. **2** (*Math.*) to represent (by symbols, in terms etc.). **3** to squeeze or press out; to emit, to exude. **to express oneself** to declare one's opinions or feelings in words (well, strongly etc.). **expresser** *n.* **expressible** *a.* **expression** (-shən) *n.* **1** the act, or an instance, of expressing. **2** that which is expressed, an utterance, saying, statement of a thought. **3** a word, a phrase. **4** (*Math.*) a combination of symbols representing a quantity or meaning. **5** mode of expression. **6** the aspect of the face as indicative of feeling and character, purpose etc. **7** intonation of voice. **8** the exhibition of character and feeling (in a picture, statue etc.). **9** (*Mus.*) the mode of execution that expresses the spirit and feeling of a passage. **expressional** *a.* **expressionism** *n.* a movement in literature and the visual arts in which artists express emotional experiences and reactions rather than representing external reality. **expressionist** *a.* of or relating to expressionism. *~n.* an artist who devotes themself to the expression of feeling, character etc. **expressionistic** *a.* **expressionistically** *adv.* **expressionless** *a.* **expressionlessly** *adv.* **expressionlessness** *n.* **expressive** *a.* **1** serving to express. **2** significant. **3** vividly indicating any expression or emotion. **expressively** *adv.* **expressiveness** *n.* **expressivity** (-siv'iti) *n.*

expresso ESPRESSO.

expropriate (iksprō'priāt) *v.t.* **1** (of the state) to take from an owner, esp. for public use. **2** to dispossess. **expropriation** (-ā'shən) *n.* **expropriator** (-prō'-) *n.*

expulsion (ikspŭl'shən) *n.* **1** the act, or an instance, of expelling. **2** the state of being expelled. **expulsive** *a., n.*

expunge (ikspŭnj') *v.t.* **1** to blot or rub out. **2** to efface, to erase. **expunction** (-pŭngk'-) *n.* **expunger** *n.*

expurgate (ek'spœgāt) *v.t.* **1** to free from anything offensive, obscene or noxious (used esp. of books). **2** to remove (such parts). **expurgation** (-ā'shən) *n.* **expurgator** *n.* **expurgatorial** (-pœgətaw'-) *a.* **expurgatory** (-pœ'-) *a.*

exquisite (ek'skwizit, ikskwiz'it) *a.* **1** fine, delicate, dainty. **2** delicately beautiful. **3** delicate or refined in perception, keenly sensitive, nice, fastidious. **4** (of pain or pleasure) very strong. ~*n.* a fop; a person who dresses or behaves finically. **exquisitely** *adv.* **exquisiteness** *n.*

exsert (iksœt´) *v.t.* (*Biol.*) to thrust out, protrude.

ex-service (eks·sœ´vis) *a.* **1** having formerly been a member of one of the armed forces. **2** of, relating to or serving, ex-servicemen or -women. **ex-serviceman** *n.* (*pl.* **ex-servicemen**). **ex-servicewomań** *n.* (*pl.* **ex-servicewomen**).

extant (ikstant´) *a.* **1** (of a species, document etc.) still existing. **2** surviving.

☒ **extasy** common misspelling of ECSTASY.

extemporaneous (ikstempərā´niəs) *a.* uttered, made, composed or done without preparation. **extemporaneously** *adv.* **extemporaneousness** *n.* **extemporary** (-tem´-) *a.* extemporaneous. **extemporarily** *adv.* **extemporariness** *n.*

extempore (ikstem´pəri) *adv.* without premeditation or preparation. ~*a.* unstudied, delivered without preparation. **extemporize, extemporise** *v.t.* to compose or produce without preparation. **extemporization** (-zā´shən) *n.*

extend (ikstend´) *v.t.* **1** to stretch out; to make larger in space, time or scope. **2** to prolong (as a line, a period etc.). **3** to amplify, to expand, to write out in full. **4** to cause to reach (to, over or across). **5** to hold out, offer, grant. **6** to stretch out, to unbend (of muscles). **7** to exert, to strain to the utmost. ~*v.i.* to stretch, to reach (in space, time or scope). **extendable** *a.* **extendability** (-bil´-) *n.* **extended** *a.* **1** spread out. **2** (of type) having a broad face. **3** made longer. **4** enlarged. **extended family** *n.* (*pl.* **extended families**) a social unit comprising more than a couple and their children, including e.g. grandparents, aunts, uncles etc. **extendedly** *adv.* **extended-play** *a.* (of a gramophone record) of the same size as a single, but playing for longer, typically two tracks per side instead of one. **extender** *n.* **1** a person or thing that extends. **2** a substance added to paint, ink etc. to give it extra bulk. **extendible, extensible** *a.* **extendibility** (-bil´-), **extensibility** *n.* **extensile** (-sīl) *a.* capable of being stretched out or protruded.

extension (əksten´shən) *n.* **1** the act or process of extending. **2** the state of being extended; prolongation, enlargement. **3** extent, range, space. **4** an increase of dimension, an addition, an additional part. **5** an additional wing or annexe of a house. **6 a** an additional telephone using the same line as the main one. **b** the number of this telephone. **7** an extra period of time allowed to complete some activity. **8** a variation to a licence allowing the sale of alcoholic drinks later than usual. **extensional** *a.*

extensive (iksten´siv) *a.* **1** widely spread or extended, large. **2** comprehensive. **3** depending on cultivation of a large area, as opposed to *intensive*. **extensively** *adv.* **extensiveness** *n.*

extensometer (ekstensom´itə), **extensimeter** (-im´-) *n.* **1** an instrument which measures small changes in length etc. of metal under stress. **2** an instrument which measures stresses and deformation in other materials.

extensor (iksten´sə) *n.* (*Anat.*) a muscle which serves to extend or straighten any part of the body. **extensor muscle** *n.*

extent (ikstent´) *n.* **1** the space, dimension or degree to which anything is extended. **2** size, width, compass, scope, comprehension, distribution, degree. **3** a large space.

extenuate (iksten´ūāt) *v.t.* **1** to lessen, to diminish the seriousness of, by showing mitigating circumstances. **2** to offer excuses for. **extenuation** (-ā´shən) *n.* **extenuator** (-ten´-) *n.* **extenuatory** *a.*

exterior (ikstiə´riə) *a.* **1** external, outer. **2** situated on the outside. **3** coming from without, extrinsic. **4** outward, visible. **5** (of a scene in a film or TV programme) filmed in the open air. ~*n.* **1** the outer surface. **2** the external features. **3** the outward or visible aspect, dress, conduct, deportment etc. **exterior angle** *n.* an angle between any side of a rectilinear figure and the adjacent side produced. **exteriority** (-rior´iti) *n.* **exteriorize, exteriorise** *v.t.* **exteriorly** *adv.*

exterminate (ikstœ´mināt) *v.t.* **1** to eradicate, to destroy utterly, esp. living creatures. **2** to get rid of, eliminate. **extermination** (-ā´shən) *n.* **exterminator** *n.* **exterminatory** *a.*

external (ikstœ´nəl) *a.* **1** situated on the outside. **2** of or relating to the outside, superficial. **3** derived from outside. **4** belonging to the world of phenomena as distinguished from the conscious mind, objective. **5** (*Med.*) applied to the outside of the body. **6** of or relating to relations with foreign countries. ~*n.* **1** an exterior or outer part. **2** (*pl.*) outward features, symbols, rites, circumstances. **3** (*pl.*) non-essentials. **external degree** *n.* a degree taken without actually attending the university that awards it, studying being done elsewhere. **external evidence** *n.* evidence which is independent of the matter under discussion. **externality** (ekstœnal´-) *n.* (*pl.* **externalities**). **externalize, externalise** *v.t.* **1** to give external shape or objective existence to. **2** to treat as consisting of externals. **externalization** (-ā´shən) *n.* **externally** *adv.* **external student** *n.* a student studying for an external degree.

exterritorial (eksteritaw´riəl) *a.* EXTRATERRITORIAL. **exterritoriality** (-al´-) *n.*

extinct (ikstingkt´) *a.* **1** extinguished, put out. **2** (of a volcano) that has permanently ceased eruption. **3** worn out, ended, finished. **4** come to an end, that has died out (as a family, species etc.). **5** (of an office, title etc.) obsolete.

extinction (ikstingk´shən) *n.* **1** the act of extinguishing or of making extinct. **2** the state of being extinguished or extinct. **3** extermination, destruction, annihilation. **4** the paying off of a debt, a mortgage etc. **5** (*Physics*) the absorption of light or other radiation by the earth's atmosphere. **extinctive** *a.*

extinguish (iksting´gwish) v.t. **1** to put out, to quench (as a light, hope, passion, life etc.). **2** to eclipse, to cloud, to obscure, to throw into the shade. **3** to destroy, to annihilate. **4** to suppress. **5** to pay off (a debt, mortgage etc.). **6** (*Law*) to render void. **extinguishable** a. **extinguisher** n. **1** a person or thing that extinguishes. **2** a device for putting out a fire. **extinguishment** n.

extirpate (ek´stəpāt) v.t. **1** to root out, to destroy utterly, to exterminate. **2** to cut out or off. **extirpation** (-ā´shən) n. **extirpator** n.

extol (ikstōl´, -tol´), (*N Am.*) **extoll** v.t. (*3rd pers. sing. pres.* **extols**, (*N Am.*) **extolls**, *pres.p.* **extolling**, *past, p.p.* **extolled**) to praise in the highest terms, to glorify. **extoller** n. **extolment** n.

extort (ikstawt´) v.t. to wrest or wring (from) by force, threats, importunity etc. **extorter** n. **extortion** n. **1** the act of extorting. **2** oppressive or illegal exaction. **3** something extorted. **4** a gross overcharge. **extortionate** (-ət) a. **1** (of prices) exorbitant. **2** characterized by extortion; oppressive. **extortionately** adv. **extortioner** n. **extortionist** n. **extortive** a.

extra (ek´strə) a. **1** beyond what is absolutely necessary. **2** larger or better than is usual; of superior quality. **3** supplementary, additional. ~adv. **1** over and above what is usual. **2** more than usually. **3** additionally. ~n. **1** something beyond what is absolutely necessary or usual, esp. something not covered by the ordinary fee. **2** an addition. **3** in cricket, a run scored otherwise than off the bat. **4** an actor temporarily engaged as one of a crowd etc. **5** a special edition of a newspaper containing late news. **extra cover** n. in cricket, a fielding position, or a fielder, between cover point and mid-off. **extra time** n. additional playing time allowed at the end of a sports match in the event of the scores being level.

extra- (ekstrə) comb. form **1** on the outside, without. **2** outside the bounds of. **3** beyond the scope of.

extracellular (ekstrəsel´ūlə) a. (*Biol.*) situated or occurring outside a cell or cells.

extract[1] (ikstrakt´) v.t. **1 a** to draw or pull out. **b** to draw out by mechanical or chemical means. **2** to select a part from, to copy out or quote (as a passage from a book etc.). **3 a** to obtain with difficulty. **b** (*coll.*) to extort. **4** to derive (from). **to extract the root of** (*Math.*) to find the root of (a number or quantity). **extractable** a. **extractability** (-bil´-) n. **extraction** n. **1** the act, or an instance, of extracting. **2** the process of being extracted. **3** descent, family, lineage, derivation. **4** the removal of a tooth. **extractive** a., n. **extractive industries** n.pl. those (e.g. mining, agriculture, fishing) concerned with obtaining natural resources. **extractor** n. **1** a person or thing that extracts. **2** an extractor fan. **extractor fan** n. an electric fan which extracts air, gas etc. from a room.

extract[2] (eks´trakt) n. **1** that which is extracted by distillation, solution etc. **2** a passage quoted from a book or writing. **3** a preparation containing the essence of a substance.

extra-curricular (ekstrəkərik´ūlə) a. (of an activity) outside or in addition to the normal course of study.

extradition (ekstrədish´ən) n. **1** the surrender of fugitives from justice by a government to the authorities of the country where the crime was committed. **2** (*Psych.*) in perception, the localizing of sensations at a distance from the centre of sensation. **extradite** (ek´-) v.t. **1** to surrender under a treaty of extradition. **2** to secure the extradition of. **extraditable** (-dī´-) a. subject to extradition, rendering one liable to extradition.

extragalactic (ekstrəgəlak´tik) a. being or occurring outside the Milky Way.

extrajudicial (ekstrəjoodish´əl) a. **1** taking place outside the court, not legally authorized. **2** outside the ordinary course of law or justice. **extrajudicially** adv.

extralinguistic (ekstrəling-gwis´tik) a. outside the area of language or of linguistics.

extramarital (ekstrəmar´itəl) a. (esp. of sexual relations) outside marriage. **extramaritally** adv.

extramundane (ekstrəmŭn´dān) a. of, relating to or existing in a region outside our world or outside the material universe.

extramural (ekstrəmū´rəl) a. **1** situated beyond or outside the walls or boundaries of a place. **2** (of a course or department) connected with a university or college, but additional to the usual courses. **3** taking place, or taught, off the premises of a college etc.

extraneous (ikstrā´niəs) a. **1** foreign, not belonging to a class, subject etc. **2** not intrinsic, external. **3** not essential. **extraneously** adv. **extraneousness** n.

extraordinary (ikstraw´dinəri, ekstrəaw´-) a. **1** beyond or out of the ordinary course, unusual. **2** of an uncommon degree or kind, remarkable, rare, exceptional, surprising. **3** sent, appointed, or convened for a special purpose or occasion. **extraordinarily** adv. **extraordinariness** n.

extrapolate (ikstrap´əlāt) v.t. **1** (*Math.*) to estimate (the value of a function etc.) beyond the known values by the extension of a curve. **2** to infer, conjecture from what is known. **extrapolation** (-ā´shən) n. **extrapolative** (-trap´-) a. **extrapolator** n.

extrasensory (ekstrəsen´səri) a. beyond the ordinary senses. **extrasensory perception** n. the supposed ability of some people to know things by means other than normal sense data.

extraterrestrial (ekstrətəres´triəl) a. **1** situated or occurring outside the earth or its atmosphere. **2** originating outside the earth, alien. ~n. in science fiction, a being from outer space.

extraterritorial (ekstrətəritaw´riəl) a. **1** beyond the jurisdiction of the laws of the country in which one is living. **2** situated, or valid, outside a country's territory. **extraterritoriality** (-al´-) n.

extravagant (ikstrav´əgənt) *a.* **1** exceeding due bounds, unrestrained by reason, immoderate. **2** visionary, fantastic, showy. **3** spending money immoderately or unrestrainedly, wasteful. **4** (of prices etc.) exorbitant. **extravagance** *n.* **1** the state or quality of being extravagant. **2** an extravagant act, statement or conduct. **3** excessive expenditure, prodigality. **extravagancy** *n.* (*pl.* **extravagancies**). **extravagantly** *adv.*

extravaganza (ekstravəgan´zə) *n.* **1** a fantastic composition in drama, fiction, poetry, music or other literary form. **2** an expensive and spectacular light entertainment production.

extravasate (ikstrav´əsāt) *v.t.* (*Med.*) to force or let out of the proper vessels (as blood). ~*v.i.* to flow out of the proper vessels. **extravasation** (-ā´shən) *n.*

extravehicular (ekstrəvēhik´ūlə) *a.* taking place outside a vehicle, esp. a spacecraft.

extravert EXTROVERT.

extreme (ikstrēm´) *a.* **1** of the highest degree, most intense. **2** beyond what is reasonable, immoderate. **3** outermost, farthest. **4** at the utmost limit, at either end. **5** last, final. **6** very strict or rigorous. **7** at the furthest right or left politically. ~*n.* **1** the utmost or farthest point or limit, the extremity. **2** the utmost or highest degree. **3** (*Math.*) the first or the last term of a ratio or series. **4** either one of two things or qualities as different or as far removed from each other as possible. **in the extreme 1** in the highest degree. **2** extremely. **to extremes** (resorting) to the most severe or drastic measures. **to the other extreme** to the opposite opinion, course of action etc. **extremely** *adv.* **extremeness** *n.* **extreme unction** *n.* in the Roman Catholic Church, the former name for the sacrament of Annointing the Sick. **extremist** *n.* **1** a person ready to go to extremes. **2** a person holding extreme opinions and ready to undertake extreme actions. ~*a.* of or relating to an extremist. **extremism** *n.* **extremity** (-strem´-) *n.* (*pl.* **extremities**) **1** the utmost point, side or limit. **2** the greatest degree. **3** the remotest part, the end. **4** a condition of the greatest difficulty, danger or distress. **5** (*pl.*) the hands and feet.

extricate (ek´strikāt) *v.t.* to disentangle, to set free from any perplexity, difficulty or embarrassment. **extricable** *a.* **extrication** (-ā´shən) *n.*

extrinsic (ikstrin´sik) *a.* **1** being outside or external. **2** proceeding or operating from the outside. **3** not inherent or contained in a body. **4** not essential. **extrinsicality** (-kal´-) *n.* **extrinsically** *adv.*

❌ **extrordinary** common misspelling of EXTRA-ORDINARY.

extrovert (ek´strəvœt), **extravert** *n.* **1** (*Psych.*) a person having a type of temperament which is predominantly engaged with the external world. **2** (*coll.*) a lively, sociable person. ~*a.* of or relating to (the personality of) such a person. **extroversion** *n.* **extroverted** *a.*

extrude (ikstrood´) *v.t.* **1** to thrust or push out or away. **2** to shape (metal or plastic) by melting and forcing through a die. ~*v.i.* to become pushed out. **extrusion** (-zhən) *n.* **extrusive** (-siv) *a.*

exuberant (igzū´bərənt) *a.* **1** overflowing with vitality, spirits or imagination. **2** effusive. **3** exceedingly fruitful; luxuriant in growth. **4** characterized by abundance or richness. **5** overflowing, copious, superabundant. **exuberance** *n.* **exuberantly** *adv.* **exuberate** *v.i.* **1** to abound, to overflow. **2** to indulge freely (in).

exude (igzūd´) *v.t.* **1** to emit or discharge through pores, as sweat, moisture or other liquid matter. **2** to give out slowly. **3** to show freely (a feeling, mood etc.). ~*v.i.* to ooze or flow out slowly through pores etc. **exudate** (eg´zūdāt) *n.* **exudation** (eksūdā´shən) *n.* **exudative** *a.*

exult (igzŭlt´) *v.i.* **1** to rejoice greatly. **2** to triumph (over). **exultant** *a.* **1** rejoicing, triumphing. **2** feeling or displaying exultation. **exultancy** *n.* **exultantly** *adv.* **exultation** (egzŭltā´shən) *n.* **exultingly** *adv.*

ex works (eks wœks´) *a., adv.* **1** direct from the factory. **2** (of a price) not including a delivery charge.

-ey -Y³.

eyas (ī´əs) *n.* **1** an unfledged hawk. **2** in falconry, a hawk taken from the nest for training or whose training is not complete.

eye¹ (ī) *n.* **1** the organ of vision. **2** the eyeball, iris or pupil. **3** the socket or part of the face containing this organ. **4 a** sight, ocular perception, view, public observation. **b** the power of seeing, discernment, acuteness of vision. **5** careful observation, oversight, care, attention. **6** look, mien, expression. **7** a mental perception, way of regarding. **8** consciousness, awareness. **9** (*coll.*) a private eye. **10** anything more or less eye-shaped. **11** the bud of a plant. **12** a spot on some feathers, as those of the peacock and argus pheasant. **13** the centre of a target, a bull's-eye. **14** the centre of some flowers. **15** a small opening or perforation. **16** the thread-hole of a needle. **17** the loop or catch in which the hook of a dress is fastened. **18** the hole in the head of an eye bolt. **19** the calm place at the very centre of a storm or hurricane. **an eye for an eye** strict retaliation. **before one's (very) eyes** right in front of one, in plain view. **in one's mind's eye** in one's imagination. **in the eye/ eyes of 1** in the regard, estimation or judgement of. **2** from the point of view of. **my eye!** (*sl.*) used to express astonishment. **to be all eyes** to watch intently. **to catch one's eye** to attract one's attention. **to close/ shut one's eyes to** to refuse to or pretend not to see. **to do someone in the eye** to defraud someone. **to get one's eye in** to gain skill or proficiency. **to have an eye for 1** to pay due regard to. **2** to appreciate. **3** to be on the lookout for. **to have an eye to** to regard, to have designs on. **to have eyes for** to be interested in. **to hit one between the eyes** to astonish or shock one. **to keep an eye on** to watch carefully or narrowly. **to keep an eye open/ out**

to keep a lookout (for). **to keep one's eye in** to retain skill or proficiency. **to keep one's eyes open/ peeled/ skinned** to watch carefully, to be careful. **to lower one's eyes** to look down towards the ground. **to make eyes at** to regard amorously. **to raise one's eyes 1** to look up from the ground. **2** to look upwards (to). **to see eye to eye** to be in complete agreement (with). **to set/ lay/ clap eyes on** to have sight of, to see. **to take one's eyes off** to look away from, to take one's attention off. **to wipe one's eyes** to stop weeping. **under the eye of** watched or supervised by. **up to the eyes** deeply (immersed, engaged, in debt etc.). **with one eye on** directing part of one's mind to. **with one eye shut** without needing to pay much attention. **with one's eyes open** aware of all the facts. **with one's eyes shut 1** not aware of all the facts. **2** very easily, without having to pay much attention. **eyeball** *n.* the globe of the eye. *~v.t.* (*esp. N Am.*, *sl.*) to stare at. *~v.i.* **to stare. eyeball to eyeball** (of discussions etc.) at close quarters, face to face. **(up) to the eyeballs** (*coll.*) completely immersed (in work etc.). **eyebath** *n.* a small vessel for bathing the eyes. **eye bolt** *n.* a bolt having an eye or loop at one end for the reception of a ring, hook etc. **eyebright** *n.* any plant of the genus *Euphrasia*, formerly much used as a remedy for diseases of the eye. **eyebrow** *n.* the fringe of hair above the orbit of the eyes. **to raise an eyebrow** to raise one's eyebrows to show surprise or disapproval. **eye-catching** *a.* striking. **eye contact** *n.* a direct look between people. **eyecup** *n.* (*N Am.*) an eyebath. **eyed** *a.* having eyes (*esp. in comb.* as *blue-eyed*). **eyedrop** *n.* **1** a tear. **2** (**eye drop**) a medication for the eye, administered as drops. **eyeful** *n.* (*pl.* **eyefuls**) **1** as much as the eye can take in at a look, long look. **2** (*sl.*) an attractive woman. **3** a foreign body in the eye. **eyeglass** *n.* **1** a lens to aid the sight. **2** (*pl.*) a pair of these fastened over the nose or held in the hand. **3** (*pl.*, *N Am.*) spectacles. **4** the lens nearest the eye in an optical instrument. **5** a glass for applying lotion to the eyes. **eyehole** *n.* a hole to look through. **eye language** *n.* communication by means of looks. **eyelash** *n.* **1** the row of hairs edging the eyelids. **2** a single hair from the edge of the eyelid. **by an eyelash** by a small margin. **eyeless** *a.* **eye level** *n.* the same height

above the ground as a person's eyes. **eyelid** *n.* a fold of skin above or below the eye that can be moved to open or close the eye. **eyeliner** *n.* a cosmetic used to draw a line along the edge of the eyelid. **eye mask** *n.* a covering for the eyes, esp. one soaked with a soothing lotion. **eye-opener** *n.* **1** something that furnishes enlightenment or astonishment. **2** (*N Am.*, *coll.*) an alcoholic drink taken in the early morning. **eye-opening** *a.* **eyepatch** *n.* a covering to protect an injured eye. **eyepiece** *n.* the lens or combination of lenses at the end nearest the eye in an optical instrument. **eye rhyme** *n.* similarity of words in spelling but not in sound. **eye-shade** *n.* a shade worn above the eyes to protect them from glare. **eyeshadow** *n.* a coloured cosmetic for the eyelids. **eyeshot** *n.* sight, range of vision, view. **eyesight** *n.* **1** vision, the ability to see. **2** view, observation. **eyesore** *n.* anything offensive to the sight. **eye-spot** *n.* **1** (*Biol.*) a light-sensitive spot on the body of some simple organisms. **2** a fungal disease of plants marked by eye-shaped spots. **eye-stalk** *n.* a movable stalk in crustaceans etc., bearing an eye. **eye strain** *n.* fatigue or irritation of the eyes. **eyetooth** *n.* (*pl.* **eye-teeth**) either one of the upper canine teeth of humans. **eyewash** *n.* **1** a lotion for the eyes. **2** (*coll.*) deception, humbug, a fraudulent pretence, a covering up of unpleasant facts. **eyewitness** *n.* a person who sees an event with their own eyes and is able to give evidence. **eyeworm** *n.* an African nematode worm, *Loa loa*, that infects the eye.

eye² (ī) *v.t.* (*pres.p.* **eyeing, eying,** *past,* *p.p.* **eyed**) to watch, to observe (fixedly, suspiciously, jealously etc.). **to eye askance** to look at with suspicion or distrust. **to eye up** (*coll.*) to assess visually, esp. admiringly.

eyelet (ī´lit) *n.* **1 a** a small hole or opening, an aperture like an eye, for a cord etc. to pass through. **b** a reinforcement for such a hole. **2** a loophole. **3** in embroidery, a small hole with stitched edges. **4** a small eye. *~v.t.* (*pres.p.* **eyeleting,** *past,* *p.p.* **eyeleted**) to provide with eyelets.

eyot AIT.

eyrie (īə´ri, iə´-), **aery** (eə´ri, iə´-), **aerie** (eə´ri) *n.* **1** the nest of any bird of prey, esp. of an eagle. **2** a human dwelling or retreat perched on a high and inaccessible place.

F

F¹ (ef), **f** (*pl.* **Fs, F's**) the sixth letter of the English and other versions of the Roman alphabet. It is pronounced as a voiceless labiodental fricative. ~*symbol* **1** the sixth of a series, the sixth highest in a range, e.g. of marks etc. **2** the sixth known quantity in an algebraic expression. **3** (*Mus.*) **a** the fourth note of the diatonic scale of C major. **b** the key of a composition in which the keynote is F. **F-layer** *n.* the highest layer of the ionosphere, having the greatest concentration of free electrons. **f-number** *n.* **1** the ratio of the focal length to the true diameter of a lens. **2** a number expressing the size of the aperture of a camera lens. **f-stop** *n.* in photography, a setting on a camera corresponding to a certain f-number. **F-word** *n.* a taboo word beginning with the letter *f*, usu. *fuck*.

F² *abbr.* **1** Fahrenheit. **2** fail, failure(s). **3** farad. **4** faraday. **5** (*Biol.*) filial generation. **6** force. **7** France.

F³ *chem. symbol* fluorine.

f *abbr.* **1** female. **2** feminine. **3** femto. **4** filly. **5** (of pencil lead) fine. **6** folio. **7** following. **8** (*Mus.*) forte. **9** frequency.

FA *abbr.* **1** Fanny Adams (euphem. for *fuck all*). **2** Football Association.

fa FAH.

fab (fab) *a.* (*coll.*) wonderful, very good.

fable (fā´bəl) *n.* **1** a story, esp. one in which animals are represented as endowed with speech in order to convey a moral lesson. **2** a legend, a myth. **3** a fabrication, a falsehood. ~*v.i.* **1** to write fables or fictitious tales. **2** to tell falsehoods. ~*v.t.* **1** to feign, to invent. **2** to describe or narrate fictitiously or falsely. **fabled** *a.* **1** celebrated in fable, mythical, fictitious. **2** legendary, famous. **fabler** *n.* a person who composes fables.

fabric (fab´rik) *n.* **1** woven, felted or knitted material. **2** the basic structure of a building, its stonework, timbers etc. **3** mode of construction or manufacture, workmanship, texture. **4** a building, an edifice. **5** the basic structure, a system of correlated parts (*the fabric of society*). **fabric conditioner** *n.* a liquid added when washing clothes to make them feel softer.

fabricate (fab´rikāt) *v.t.* **1** to build, to construct. **2** to form by art or manufacture. **3** to forge, to invent, to trump up. **fabrication** (-ā´shən) *n.* **fabricator** *n.*

fabulist (fab´ūlist) *n.* **1** a writer or inventor of fables. **2** a liar.

fabulous (fab´ūləs) *a.* **1** (*coll.*) wonderful, very

good, very enjoyable. **2** beyond belief, incredible. **3** feigned, fictitious, invented. **4** related or described in fables; mythical, legendary, unhistorical. **fabulosity** (-los´-), **fabulousness** *n.* **fabulously** *adv.*

facade (fəsahd´), **façade** *n.* **1** the front of a building, the principal face. **2** an outward appearance, esp. one put on for show or to deceive, a front.

face (fās) *n.* **1** the front part of the head, from the chin to the top of the forehead. **2** a facial expression, a look (*have a sad face*). **3** a grimace (*pull a face*). **4** a person, one communicating a quality (*nice to see some fresh faces*). **5** that part of anything which presents itself to the view, the front, the upper or main surface. **6** (*Geom.*) the plane surface of a solid. **7** an exposed surface of rock on a cliff or mountain, or in a mine or quarry. **8** the dial of a watch, clock etc. **9** the working side of a tool or instrument. **10** the printed surface of a playing card. **11** the printing surface of type. **12** a design or style of type. **13** the striking surface of a bat, racket or golf club. **14** the outward visible state of things, the appearance, aspect (*the unacceptable face of capitalism*). **15** dignity, reputation (*lose face*). **16** the obverse of a coin. **17** composure, coolness. **18** (*coll.*) impudence, effrontery, cheek. ~*v.t.* **1** to turn the face towards. **2** to confront boldly, to stand up to. **3** to acknowledge without evasion (*to face facts*). **4** to bring face to face with. **5** to stand opposite to. **6** to put a coating or covering on; to put facings on (a garment). **7** to cause to turn in any direction. ~*v.i.* **1** to look in a certain direction. **2** to be situated with a certain aspect. **3** to turn the face in a certain direction. **face down** with the face or front pointing downwards. **face downwards** face down. **face to face (with) 1** in someone's or each other's actual presence. **2** opposite; in confrontation. **3** clearly, without anything interposed. **face up** with the face or front pointing upwards. **face upwards** face up. **in (the) face of 1** in spite of. **2** when encountering. **on the face of it** to judge by appearances. **to face off 1** to drop the puck or ball to start or restart a game of ice hockey or lacrosse. **2** to have a confrontation. **to face out** to carry off by boldness or effrontery. **to face the music** to suffer unpleasant consequences of something, esp. punishment or criticism. **to face up to** to meet courageously. **to fly in the face of 1** to defy openly. **2** to act in direct opposition to. **to lose face 1** to be humiliated. **2** to suffer

loss of personal prestige. **to make/ pull a face
1** to distort the features. **2** to grimace. **to put a
bold/ brave/ good face on 1** to make the best of,
to pretend that one is not unduly upset by. **2** to
adopt a confident air. **to put a new face on** to
alter the appearance of. **to put one's face on**
(*coll.*) to put on make-up. **to save (one's) face** to
save oneself from disgrace or humiliation. **to set
one's face against** to oppose, to withstand firmly.
to show one's face to appear. **to shut one's face**
(*esp. imper., sl.*) to be quiet. **to someone's face
1** openly. **2** in plain words. **face card** *n.* a court
card. **face cloth, face flannel** *n.* a cloth used to
wash the face. **face cream** *n.* a cosmetic cream
that is rubbed into the face to moisturize the
skin. **faced** *a.* **faceless** *a.* **1** (of bureaucrats etc.)
remote from and unmoved by the concerns of
ordinary citizens. **2** anonymous. **3** without a
face. **facelessness** *n.* **facelift** *n.* **1** an operation to
remove wrinkles and make the face look younger
and smoother. **2** renovations, repairs carried
out to improve or modernize the appearance of
something. **face mask** *n.* **1** a mask covering part
of the face. **2** a face pack. **face-off** *n.* **1** the dropping of the puck or ball between two opposing
players to start or restart a game of ice hockey
or lacrosse. **2** a confrontation. **face pack** *n.* a
creamy cosmetic mixture applied to the face.
face paint *n.* paint that is applied to the face.
face-painting *n.* **face powder** *n.* cosmetic powder
for the face. **facer** *n.* **1** a blow in the face. **2** a
sudden difficulty, a dilemma. **face-saving** *a.* intended to prevent humiliation or loss of one's
prestige. **face-saver** *n.* **face-to-face** *a.* having the
people concerned talking to or looking at one
another. **face value** *n.* **1** the nominal value shown
on coins, banknotes etc. **2** the apparent value of
anything. **faceworker** *n.* a miner who works at
the coal face.
facet (fas´it) *n.* **1** an aspect or part of something.
2 a small face or surface. **3** any one of the small
planes which form the sides of a crystal, a cut
diamond or other gem. **4** a flat surface with a
definite boundary, as a segment of a compound
eye. **faceted,** (*NAm.*) **facetted** *a.*
facetious (fəsē´shəs) *a.* **1** given to or characterized by levity; flippant, waggish, jocular.
2 intended to be amusing. **facetiously** *adv.*
facetiousness *n.*
facia (fā´shə) *n.* **1** the instrument board of a car.
2 the nameboard above a shop.
facial (fā´shəl) *a.* of or relating to the face. **~n.** a
beauty treatment for the face. **facially** *adv.*
-facient *comb. form* added to the stems of Latin
and English verbs to give the sense of producing
the action expressed in the verb, as *calefacient,
liquefacient.*
facile (fas´īl) *a.* **1** easily done; easily surmountable. **2** (*usu. derog.*) **a** ready, fluent. **b**
glib, superficial, shallow. **facilely** *adv.* **facile-
ness** *n.*
facilitate (fəsil´itāt) *v.t.* **1** to make easy or less

difficult. **2** to further, to help forward. **facilitation**
(-ā´shən) *n.* **facilitative** (-tətiv) *a.* **facilitator** *n.*

Usage note *Facilitate* should not be used of
helping a person (with a person as its direct
object).

facility (fəsil´iti) *n.* (*pl.* **facilities**) **1** easiness in
performing or being performed; freedom from
difficulty. **2** ease, readiness, fluency (of speech
etc.). **3** quickness, dexterity, aptitude. **4** (*usu.
pl.*) means or equipment provided to facilitate
any activity (*recreational facilities*). **5** a service.
6 (*esp. NAm.*) a building or plant serving a particular purpose.
facing (fā´sing) *n.* **1** a covering in front for ornament, strength or other purposes. **2** a coating of a
different material, on a wall etc. **3** (*pl.*) the trimmings on the collar, cuffs etc. of a uniform, serving to distinguish one regiment from another.
facsimile (faksim´ili) *n.* **1** an exact copy of handwriting, printing, a picture etc. **2** the transmission
by electronic scanning and reproduction of written or pictorial material. **in facsimile** exactly like.
fact (fakt) *n.* **1** something that has really occurred
or been done; something known to be true or
existing, as distinct from an inference or conjecture. **2** (*usu. pl.*) a piece of information that can
be discovered. **3** reality, actuality, the concrete
basis of experience. **4** (*Law*) an act or deed. **after
the fact** after the actual committing of a crime. **as
a matter of fact** actually, in fact. **before the fact**
before the actual committing of a crime. **in (point
of) fact** in reality, actually, independently of
theory or argument. **fact sheet** *n.* a printed document containing information. **facts of life** *n.pl.*
1 the details of esp. human reproduction. **2** the
(often unpleasant) realities of a situation.
faction[1] (fak´shən) *n.* **1** a body of persons combined or acting in union, esp. a party within a
party combined to promote their own views or
purposes at the expense of order and the public
good. **2** partisanship, discord, dissension. **fac-
tional** *a.* **factionalism** *n.* **factionalize, faction-
alise** *v.t., v.i.* **factionally** *adv.* **factious** *a.* given to
faction or party; seditious, turbulent. **factiously**
adv. **factiousness** *n.*

Usage note The adjectives *factious* and *fractious* should not be confused: *factious* means
given to dissent, and *fractious* peevish.

faction[2] (fak´shən) *n.* literary etc. work which
blends factual events and characters with fiction.
-faction (fak´shən) *comb. form* denoting making,
turning or converting, as in *rarefaction, satisfaction, tumefaction.*
factitious (faktish´əs) *a.* **1** artificial, not natural.
2 affected; unreal, bogus. **factitiously** *adv.* **fac-
titiousness** *n.*

Usage note The adjectives *factitious* and *fictitious* should not be confused: *factitious* means
artificial, and *fictitious* imaginary.

factoid (fak´toid) *n.* **1** an item of information that is considered to be true because it is repeated frequently. **2** (*N Am.*) a piece of trivial information. ~*a.* relating to or of the nature of a factoid.

factor (fak´tə) *n.* **1** any circumstance, fact or influence which contributes to a result. **2** (*Math.*) each of the quantities that multiplied together make up a given number or expression. **3** an agent, a deputy. **4** (*Sc.*) a steward or agent of an estate. **5** a business that buys a manufacturer's invoices and collects payment from customers. **6** an agent employed to sell goods on commission. ~*v.t.* **1** to act as factor for or to look after (property). **2** (*Math.*) to factorize. **factorable** *a.* **factor analysis** *n.* (*Math.*) a statistical method of identifying a fewer number of underlying variables from a larger number of variables. **factorial** (-taw´-) *a.* **1** (*Math.*) of or relating to a series of mathematical factors. **2** of or relating to a factor or land agent. ~*n.* (*Math.*) **1** the product of a series of factors in arithmetical progression, as (*x*+2) (*x*+4) (*x*+6). **2** the product of an integer multiplied into all its lower integers, e.g. the factorial of 4 = 4 × 3 × 2 = 24. **factorially** *adv.* **factorize, factorise** *v.t.* (*Math.*) to express (a number) in terms of its factors. ~*v.i.* to be expressible in terms of its factors. **factorization** (-zā´shən) *n.*

factory (fak´təri, -tri) *n.* (*pl.* **factories**) **1** a building in which any manufacture is carried out, a works, a workshop, a mill. **2** a trading station established in a foreign place by a company of merchants. **factory farm** *n.* a farm practising factory farming. **factory farming** *n.* the intensive rearing of animals for milk, egg or meat production in a largely artificial environment. **factory floor** *n.* workers in a factory in contrast to the management. **factory ship** *n.* a vessel in a fishing fleet which processes the catches. **factory shop** *n.* an outlet in which manufactured goods that are surplus, slightly damaged etc. are sold to the public.

factotum (faktō´təm) *n.* (*pl.* **factotums**) a person employed to do all sorts of work, a handyman.

factual (fak´chuəl) *a.* concerned with or containing facts; actual or real. **factuality** (-al´iti) *n.* **factually** *adv.* **factualness** *n.*

faculty (fak´əlti) *n.* (*pl.* **faculties**) **1** a natural power of the mind, such as the will, reason, sense etc.; capacity for any natural action, such as seeing, feeling, speaking. **2** power or ability of any special kind. **3** the members collectively of any of the learned professions. **4** any one of the departments of instruction in a university. **5** the professors and lecturers in such a department. **6** an authorization or licence to perform certain functions, esp. ecclesiastical.

fad (fad) *n.* **1** a whim, a passing fancy, taste or fashion, a craze. **2** an idiosyncratic taste or distaste for something. **3** a hobby; a favourite theory or idea. **faddish** *a.* **faddishly** *adv.* **faddishness** *n.* **faddism** *n.* **faddist** *n.* **faddy** *a.* (*comp.* **faddier,**

superl. **faddiest**) fussy as regards likes and dislikes, esp. in food. **faddily** *adv.* **faddiness** *n.*

fade (fād) *v.i.* **1** to grow lighter in colour, pale, dim or indistinct. **2** to wither, as a plant; to lose freshness, brightness, vigour or beauty; to languish. **3** to disappear gradually. **4** (of a person) to grow weaker, to decline. **5** (of electronic signals) to decrease in strength or volume. **6** (of brakes) to lose their effectiveness gradually. **7** (of an athlete, team etc.) to perform less well, to cease to mount a serious challenge. **8** to perform a fade-in or fade-out. ~*v.t.* **1** to cause to grow lighter in colour. **2** to cause to wither or decay. **3** to cause to decrease in strength or volume. ~*n.* **1** an instance of fading in or out or both simultaneously. **2** a dimming of stage lighting. **to do a fade** (*sl.*) to go away, to leave. **to fade away 1** (*coll.*) to grow very thin. **to fade in** to cause (sound or a picture) to appear gradually. **to fade out** to cause (sound or a picture) to disappear gradually. **fade-in, fade-up** *n.* an act of fading sound or a picture in. **fadeless** *a.* unfading. **fade-out, fade-down** *n.* an act of fading sound or a picture out.

faeces (fē´sēz), (*esp. N Am.*) **feces** *n.pl.* excrement from the bowels. **faecal** (fē´kəl) *a.*

faff (faf) *v.i.* (*coll.*) to dither, to fuss (often with *about*). ~*n.* a fuss.

fag[1] (fag) *n.* **1** (*coll.*) a cigarette. **2** (*coll.*) a boring, tiresome or unwelcome task. **3** a junior at a public school who has to perform certain duties for a senior boy. ~*v.i.* (*pres.p.* **fagging**, *past, p.p.* **fagged**) **1** to toil wearily; to work till one is weary. **2** to act as a fag in a public school. ~*v.t.* **1** to tire, to exhaust, to weary (often with *out*). **2** to use as a fag or drudge in a public school. **fag end** *n.* **1** (*coll.*) a cigarette butt. **2** the unimportant or worthless remaining part of anything.

fag[2] (fag) *n.* (*esp. N Am., offensive*) a male homosexual.

faggot (fag´ət) *n.* **1** a cake or ball of chopped liver, herbs etc. **2** (*N Am.* **fagot**) **a** a bundle of sticks or small branches of trees, used for fuel, filling ditches, road-making etc. **b** a bundle of steel or wrought-iron rods. **c** a bundle of any material. **3** (*esp. N Am., offensive*) a male homosexual. ~*v.t.* (*pres.p.* **faggoting**, (*N Am.*) **fagoting**, *past, p.p.* **faggoted**, (*N Am.*) **fagoted**) **1** to bind or tie up in a faggot or bundle. **2** to join as in faggoting. **faggoting**, (*N Am.*) **fagoting** *n.* **1** a type of embroidery in which some horizontal threads are tied together in hourglass shapes. **2** the joining together of materials like this. **faggoty** *a.*

fah (fah), **fa** *n.* (*Mus.*) **1** the fourth note of a major scale in the tonic sol-fa system of notation. **2** the fixed F in the fixed-doh system.

Fahr. *abbr.* Fahrenheit.

Fahrenheit (far´ənhīt) *a.* of or relating to the temperature scale on which the freezing point of water is marked at 32° and the boiling point at 212°.

faience (fayās´) *n.* tin-glazed earthenware of a particular kind.

fail (fāl) *v.i.* **1** not to succeed (in). **2** not to succeed in the attainment (of). **3** not to pass an examination. **4** to be or become deficient or wanting; to run short; to come short of the due amount or measure. **5** to lose strength or spirit, to sink, to decline. **6** to die away. **7** to be or become ineffective or inoperative. ~*v.t.* **1** not to pass (an examination). **2** to cause not to pass. **3** to be insufficient for; to come short of. **4** to deceive, to disappoint, to desert. **5** to neglect or omit (to do something). ~*n.* **1** failure, default. **2** a failure grade in an examination. **3** a person who fails an examination. **without fail** certainly, assuredly, in spite of all hindrances. **failed** *a.* **1** unsuccessful. **2** deficient, worn-out. **failing** *n.* **1** a deficiency, shortcoming. **2** an imperfection, a weakness, a foible. ~*prep.* if not; in default of. **fail-safe** *a.* (of a mechanism) incorporated in a system to render it safe in the event of failure or malfunction. **failure** (-yə) *n.* **1** lack of success. **2** an unsuccessful person or thing. **3** an omission, non-performance, non-occurrence. **4** a failing or coming short. **5** decay, breaking down.

†fain (fān) *a.* **1** glad, well-pleased; desirous. **2** content or compelled (to) for lack of a better alternative. ~*adv.* gladly, readily.

faint (fānt) *a.* **1** (of sound or brightness) dim, indistinct, slight, feeble. **2** weak, frail. **3** giddy, inclined to faint. **4** slight, remote (*a faint chance*). **5** timid, fearful. **6** with light lines to guide writing. ~*v.i.* to lose consciousness because of hunger, shock etc. ~*n.* a fainting fit. **not to have the faintest (idea)** (*coll.*) not to know at all. **faint heart** *n.* a cowardly or timid nature. **faint-hearted** *a.* **faint-heartedly** *adv.* **faint-heartedness** *n.* **faintly** *adv.* **faintness** *n.*

fair¹ (feə) *a.* **1** just, reasonable, legitimate. **2** light in colour or complexion; blond. **3** passably good, not bad, of moderate quality; satisfactory. **4** beautiful, attractive, pleasing to the eye. **5** clear, pure, clean. **6** not effected by unlawful or underhand means, above board. **7** free from spot, blemish or cloud, serene. **8** (of the weather) fine and sunny, not raining. **9** favourable, auspicious, promising. **10** open, unobstructed. **11** civil, obliging, polite. **12** legible, plain. **13** specious. ~*adv.* **1** according to the rules, straight, clean. **2** completely, absolutely. **3** courteously, civilly, plausibly. **4** openly, honestly, justly. **5** on equal terms. **fair enough** (*coll.*) (indicating at least partial assent to a proposition, terms etc.) all right, OK. **fair's fair** (*coll.*) used as a protest or reminder that everyone is entitled to fair or equal treatment. **fair and square** *a.* honourable, straightforward, above board. ~*adv.* **1** fairly, honestly, without trickery or deceit. **2** exactly on target. **fair crack of the whip** *n.* a fair opportunity or chance. **fair dinkum** *a.* (*Austral., New Zeal., coll.*) fair, genuine. ~*n.* fair play. **fair dos** (dooz) *n.pl.* (*coll.*) fair play, equal shares etc., fair treatment. **fair game** *n.* a legitimate target for attack, criticism or ridicule. **fairing** *n.* **1** a structure to

provide streamlining of an aircraft, car etc. **2** the process of streamlining. **fairish** *a.* **fairlead** *n.* (*Naut.*) a device for guiding a rope etc., to keep it clear of obstructions, reduce chafing etc. **fairly** *adv.* **1** in a fair manner. **2** moderately, passably. **3** completely, absolutely, utterly. **fairly and squarely** fair and square. **fair-minded** *a.* honest, impartial, just. **fair-mindedly** *adv.* **fair-mindedness** *n.* **fairness** *n.* **fair play** *n.* reasonable behaviour; just or equal conditions for all. **fair rent** *n.* a rent set in accordance with official guidelines. **fair sex** *n.* women. **fairwater** *n.* a structure to assist a ship's smooth passage through water. **fairway** *n.* **1** the navigable part of a river, channel or harbour. **2** the smooth passage of turf between holes on a golf course. **fair-weather** *a.* appearing only in times of prosperity; not good in times of need (*a fair-weather friend*).

fair² (feə) *n.* **1** a funfair. **2** a market or gathering for trade in a particular town or place. **3** a trade show. **fairground** *n.* an open space where fairs, exhibitions etc. are held.

Usage note The pseudo-archaic spelling *fayre* is used especially of bazaars and trade shows.

Fair Isle (feə) *a.* applied to woollen articles knitted in coloured patterns typical of Fair Isle (one of the Shetland Islands).

fairy (feə´ri) *n.* (*pl.* **fairies**) **1** an imagined small supernatural being having magical powers, supposed to assume human form and to meddle for good or for evil in human affairs. **2** (*sl., offensive*) an effeminate man or homosexual. ~*a.* **1** of, relating to or connected with fairies; fairy-like; fanciful, imaginary. **2** small, delicate or dainty. **fairily** *adv.* **fairy cake** *n.* a small individual soft cake, esp. with icing. **fairy cycle** *n.* a child's small bicycle. **fairy godmother** *n.* a (usu. unexpected) benefactress. **fairyland** *n.* **1** the imaginary home of the fairies. **2** a region of enchantment. **fairy lights** *n.pl.* small lights of many colours used for decoration. **fairy-like** *a.* **fairy ring** *n.* a circular band of turf greener than the rest caused by the growth of fungi (formerly supposed to be caused by the dancing of fairies). **fairy story, fairy tale** *n.* **1** a tale about fairies. **2** a fanciful or highly improbable story.

fait accompli (fāt, fet əkom´plē) *n.* (*pl.* **faits accomplis** (fāt, fet əkom´plē)) an accomplished fact.

faith (fāth) *n.* **1** firm and earnest belief, conviction, complete confidence, reliance, trust. **2** the assent of the mind to what is stated or put forward by another. **3** a system of religious belief. **4** spiritual apprehension or voluntary acceptance of divine revelation apart from absolute proof. **5** active belief in the doctrines and moral principles forming a system of religion. **6** commitment to keep a promise etc., fidelity, constancy, loyalty. **7** credibility, reliability, trustworthiness. **8** a philosophical, scientific or political creed or system of doctrines. **faithful** *a.* **1** loyal to one's promises, duty or engagements; conscientious, trustworthy. **2** upright, honest. **3** truthful, worthy of belief. **4** exact, accurate. **the faithful** true believers in a particular creed or religious system. **faithfully** *adv.* in a faithful manner. **yours faithfully** a conventional way of ending a formal or business letter. **faithfulness** *n.* **faith healing** *n.* curing of disease by means of prayer and faith, without the use of drugs etc. **faith-healer** *n.* **faithless** *a.* **1** lacking faith, unbelieving. **2** disloyal, unfaithful, not true to promises or duty, unreliable. **faithlessly** *adv.* **faithlessness** *n.*

Usage note In closing letters, *Yours faithfully* is a formal style, and goes with an opening in which an unknown or unfamiliar person is addressed as 'Sir' or 'Madam' (*Dear Sirs, Dear Madam* etc.).

fajita (fəhē´tə) *n.* a kind of tortilla wrapped around meat, chillies, onions etc.
fake¹ (fāk) *v.t.* **1** to pretend, to simulate. **2** to do up, to cover up defects and faults so as to give a more valuable appearance to, to doctor; to contrive, to fabricate, to make up from defective material. *~n.* **1** a thing, e.g. a manufactured antique made to deceive, a sham. **2** a swindle, a dodge. *~a.* bogus, sham, counterfeit. **faker** *n.* **fakery** *n.*
fake² (fāk) *n.* (*Naut.*) one of the coils in a rope or cable when laid up. *~v.t.* to coil (a rope).
fakir (fā´kiə, fəkiə´), **faquir** *n.* **1** a Muslim religious mendicant. **2** a Hindu mendicant, ascetic or wonder-worker.
falafel FELAFEL.
falciform (fal´sifawm) *a.* (*Anat.*) having the form of a sickle.
falcon (fawl´kən, fal´-) *n.* **1** any diurnal bird of prey of the family *Falconidae* having pointed wings, esp. the peregrine falcon and others trained to hawk game. **2** a female falcon, esp. the peregrine (cp. TIERCEL). **falconer** *n.* **1** a person who keeps and trains hawks for hawking. **2** a person who hunts with hawks. **falconry** *n.* **1** the art of training falcons to pursue and attack game. **2** the sport of hawking.
fall (fawl) *v.i.* (*past* **fell** (fel), *p.p.* **fallen** (faw´lən)) **1** to descend from a higher to a lower place or position by the force of gravity. **2** to descend suddenly, to drop. **3** to sink, to flow down, to be poured down, to become lower in level of surface. **4** to hang down, to droop. **5** to come down, to become prostrate. **6** to be hit or wounded. **7** to be killed (esp. in battle). **8** to be overthrown, to lose power. **9** in cricket, to be taken by the bowling side. **10** to decrease in number, amount, value, weight, loudness etc. **11** to become lower in pitch. **12** to subside, to abate, to ebb, to languish, to die away. **13** to fail, to be degraded or disgraced. **14** to sink into sin, vice, error, to give away to temptation. **15** (of the face) to assume a despondent expression. **16** to become, to pass into a specified state, as in *fall asleep, fall ill.*

17 to be transferred by chance, lot, inheritance, or otherwise. **18** to turn out, to result, to happen. **19** to be uttered or dropped, as a chance remark. **20** to be born (said of certain animals). *~n.* **1** the act of falling. **2** a bout at wrestling or a throw in this. **3** a decrease in number, amount etc. **4** the degree of inclination, the gradient or slope. **5** a downward slope. **6** the amount of descent, the distance through which anything falls. **7** the discharging of a river. **8** (*esp. N Am.*) autumn. **9** (*usu. pl.*) a cataract, a cascade, a waterfall. **10** the amount of rain, snow etc. in a district. **11** downfall, degradation, declension from greatness or prosperity, ruin, disgrace. **12** death, destruction, overthrow. **13** the surrender or capture of a town. **14** the act of felling or cutting down. **15** the amount of timber cut down. **16** the number of certain animals, such as lambs, born. **17** a lapse from virtue; a yielding to temptation. **18** a long false hairpiece. **19** that part of the rope in hoisting-tackle to which the power is applied. **20** (*Mus.*) a cadence. **the Fall** the sin of disobedience of Adam, and through him, of all the human race. **to fall about** (*coll.*) to laugh hysterically. **to fall apart** to collapse, to become unstitched, unstuck etc., to go to pieces. **to fall away 1** to desert; to revolt; to apostatize; to fall into wickedness. **2** to extend or slope downwards, esp. suddenly. **to fall back** to recede, to give way, to retreat. **to fall back on/ upon** to have recourse to. **to fall behind 1** to be passed by, to lag behind. **2** to become in arrears with. **to fall between two stools 1** to fail through being unable to choose between two alternatives. **2** to be neither one thing or the other. **to fall down 1** to be thrown down, to drop. **2** to prostrate oneself. **3** to fail, to be inadequate. **to fall down on** to fail to carry out. **to fall for 1** (*coll.*) to be impressed by, to fall in love with. **2** to be fooled by. **to fall in 1** (*Mil.*) to take one's place in line. **2** to give way inwards. **to fall in with 1** to meet with accidentally. **2** to agree to, to concur in. **3** to coincide with. **to fall off 1** to decrease in quality, quantity or amount, to become depreciated. **2** to withdraw, to recede. **to fall on/ upon 1** (of the eyes, glance etc.) to alight on, to be directed towards. **2** to attack. **3** to meet or discover by chance, to come across. **to fall out 1** to happen, to come to pass, to turn out, to result. **2** to quarrel. **3** (of the hair etc.) to become separate from the body. **4** (*Mil.*) to leave the ranks. **to fall over 1** to tumble or be knocked down. **2** to trip or stumble over. **to fall over oneself 1** (*coll.*) to be eager, or overeager (to do something). **2** (*coll.*) to stumble clumsily. **to fall short 1** to be deficient. **2** to drop before reaching the mark or target. **to fall through** to fail, to miscarry, to come to nothing. **to fall to** to begin hastily or eagerly, to set to, e.g. to begin eating. **to fall to pieces** to fall apart, to go to pieces. **fall-back** *a.* **1** used as an alternative if plans fail or something unexpected happens. **2** (of a wage) being a minimum amount that is paid when no work is available. ~*n.* a reserve; a fall-back wage. **fallen** *a.* **1** killed, esp. in battle. **2** seduced; morally degraded. **3** overthrown. **fallenness** *n.* **faller** *n.* **1** a racehorse which falls during a race. **2** a share or stock which falls in value. **fallfish** *n.* (*pl. in general* **fallfish,** *in particular* **fallfishes**) a N American freshwater fish, *Semotilus corporalis*, similar to the chub. **fall guy** *n.* **1** a person who is easily duped. **2** a scapegoat, a cat's paw. **falling-out** *n.* a quarrel or disagreement. **falling star** *n.* a meteor appearing to fall rapidly to the earth. **fall-off** *n.* a decrease. **fallout** *n.* **1** the deposit of radioactive dust after a nuclear explosion. **2** secondary consequences, by-products. **fall-pipe** *n.* a downpipe.

fallacy (fal´əsi) *n.* (*pl.* **fallacies**) **1** a prevalent but mistaken belief, based on unsound reasoning or incorrect information. **2** (*Logic*) a delusive mode of reasoning, an example of such. **3** an error, a sophism; sophistry, delusiveness. **fallacious** (fəlā´shəs) *a.* **fallaciously** *adv.* **fallaciousness** *n.*

fallible (fal´ibəl) *a.* likely to make mistakes; liable to err. **fallibility** (-bil´-) *n.* **fallibly** *adv.*

Fallopian tube (fəlō´piən) *n.* (*Anat.*) either of two ducts or canals in female mammals by which ova are conveyed to the uterus.

fallow[1] (fal´ō) *a.* **1** (of land) ploughed and tilled but not sown; uncultivated. **2** unused, neglected. **3** (of a sow) not pregnant. ~*n.* land ploughed and harrowed but left unsown; land left uncultivated for a period. ~*v.t.* to plough and harrow and leave unsown. **fallowness** *n.*

fallow[2] (fal´ō) *a.* of a pale brownish or reddish-yellow colour. **fallow deer** *n.* a small species of deer, *Dama dama*, having a white-spotted fawn coat in summer.

false (fawls) *a.* **1** not true, contrary to truth, not conformable to fact; deceptive, misleading; erroneous, wrong, incorrect. **2** uttering untruth, lying, deceiving; deceitful, treacherous, faithless (to). **3** feigned, sham, spurious, counterfeit, not genuine. **4** forced, unconvincing. **5** artificial, man-made. **6** (esp. of plants) resembling a different species. ~*adv.* falsely; wrongly. **false alarm** *n.* a needless warning, a cause of unnecessary anxiety or excitement. **false bedding** *n.* (*Geol.*) strata in which the layers are not parallel through disturbance by currents whilst they were being laid down. **false colour** *n.* a colour used in the production of an image to help the interpretation of that image. **false colours** *n.pl.* **1** flags to which a ship has no right, raised to deceive an enemy. **2** misleading pretence or deceit. **false dawn** *n.* **1** light appearing just before sunrise. **2** a promising sign of change, progress etc. that in the end fails. **false gharial** *n.* an Indonesian and Malaysian crocodile, *Tomistoma schlegelii*. **falsehood** (-hud) *n.* **1** untruthfulness, falseness, lying, lies. **2** a lie, an untruth. **3** deceitfulness, unfaithfulness. **falsely** *adv.* **false move** *n.* an unwise or thoughtless action. **falseness** *n.* **false pretences** *n.pl.* (*Law*) misrepresentations

made with intent to deceive or defraud. **false rib** *n.* FLOATING RIB (under FLOAT). **false scent** *n.* **1** a series of scents left in order to mislead. **2** misleading clues etc. aimed at deceiving followers. **false scorpion** *n.* an arachnid of the order Pseudoscorpiones. **false start** *n.* **1** a disallowed start to a race, usu. caused by a competitor moving away too early. **2** an unsuccessful beginning to any activity. **false step** *n.* **1** a stumble or slip. **2** an imprudent action. **false topaz** *n.* CITRINE. **falsework** *n.* a temporary structure supporting actual construction work. **falsies** (-siz) *n.pl.* (*coll.*) pads used to improve the shape of the breasts. **falsity** *n.* (*pl.* **falsities**).

falsetto (fawlset´ō) *n.* (*pl.* **falsettos**) **1** a pitch or range of (usu. the male) voice higher than the natural register. **2** a singer using this range.

falsify (fawl´sifī) *v.t.* (*3rd pers. sing. pres.* **falsifies,** *pres.p.* **falsifying,** *past. p.p.* **falsified**) **1** to make false. **2** to give a false or spurious appearance to (a document, statement etc.). **3** to misrepresent. **4** to counterfeit, to forge. **5** to disappoint (expectations), to confute, to disprove. **falsifiable** *a.* **falsifiability** (-fīəbil´iti) *n.* **falsification** (-fikā´-shən) *n.*

falter (fawl´tə) *v.i.* **1** to stumble, to totter, to waver, to be unsteady. **2** to stammer, to stutter. **3** to hesitate in action; to act with irresolution. ~*v.t.* to utter with hesitation or stammering. **falterer** *n.* **falteringly** *adv.*

fame (fām) *n.* the state of being well-known, renown, celebrity. ~*v.t.* **1** to make famous or renowned. **2** to celebrate. **famed** *a.* much talked of; renowned, celebrated.

familiar (fəmil´yə) *a.* **1** of one's own acquaintance, well-known, intimate. **2** knowing or understanding a thing well; intimate (with). **3** easily understood, not obscure. **4** usual, common, ordinary, not novel. **5** sexually intimate. **6** too informal; presumptuous. **7** unconstrained, free, unceremonious. ~*n.* **1** an intimate or close friend or companion. **2** a familiar spirit. **familiarity** (-liar´-) *n.* (*pl.* **familiarities**) **1** the state of being familiar. **2** close friendship, intimacy. **3** (*sometimes pl.*) (an act of) sexual intimacy. **4** presumptuous behaviour. **familiarize** (fəmil´yəriz) **familiarise** *v.t.* **1** to make well acquainted (with), to accustom. **2** to make well-known. **familiarization** (-zā´shən) *n.* **familiarly** *adv.* **familiar spirit** *n.* a demon or spirit supposed to attend at call.

family (fam´ili) *n.* (*pl.* **families**) **1** a group of people related to one another, esp. parents and their children. **2** children, as distinguished from their parents. **3** those people who can trace their descent from a common ancestor; a house, kindred, lineage. **4** a race, a group of peoples from a common stock. **5** a group of persons or peoples united by bonds of civilization, religion etc. **6** a group of related things or beings having common characteristics. **7** a group of related languages. **8** (*Math.*) a group of curves or surfaces that differ only by one quality. **9** a group of genera. **10** (*Zool.*) a subdivision of an order. **11** (*Bot.*) an order. *~a.* **1** of, relating to or belonging to the family (*the family home*). **2** designed to be enjoyed or used by parents and (esp. young) children (*family viewing*). **3** providing for the needs of families (*a family butcher*). **in the family way** pregnant. **familial** (fəmil´iəl) *a.* characteristic of or relating to a family. **family credit** *n.* in Britain, a social security benefit paid to people in low-income work who have at least one child. **Family Division** *n.* a division of the High Court dealing with divorce, the custody of children etc. **family man** *n.* a man who has a wife and children, esp. a man who is fond of home life. **family name** *n.* a surname. **family planning** *n.* regulating the number of, and intervals between, children, usu. by means of contraceptives. **family tree** *n.* a genealogical chart.

famine (fam´in) *n.* **1** extreme shortage of food. **2** a period of this. **3** an extreme scarcity of anything.

famish (fam´ish) *v.i.* to suffer extreme hunger; to die of hunger. *~v.t.* to starve; to reduce to extreme hunger. **famished, famishing** *a.* (*coll.*) feeling extremely hungry.

famous (fā´məs) *a.* **1** very well-known; renowned, celebrated; illustrious; noted. **2** (*coll.*) first-rate, very good, excellent. **famously** *adv.* **1** (*coll.*) in a very friendly way (*get on famously*). **2** in a famous way. **famousness** *n.*

fan[1] (fan) *n.* **1** an apparatus with revolving blades to give a current of air for ventilation. **2** an instrument, usu. flat, with radiating sections opening out in a wedge-shape for agitating the air and cooling the face. **3** an implement, object or structure shaped like an open fan. **4** a bird's tail, a wing, a leaf shaped like a fan. **5** (*Geol.*) a fan-shaped deposit of alluvium. **6** a winnowing implement or machine. **7** a small sail or vane for keeping the sails of a windmill to the wind. *~v.t.* (*pres.p.* **fanning**, *past, p.p.* **fanned**) **1** to cool with a fan. **2** to move or stimulate with or as with a fan. **3** to spread like a fan. **4** to winnow; to winnow or sweep away (chaff). *~v.i.* **1** to move or blow gently. **2** to spread out like a fan. **to fan out** to radiate outwards in a fan-shape, to move off in divergent directions. **fan belt** *n.* a belt which drives the radiator cooling fan and generator in a car engine. **fan heater** *n.* an electric heater in which the heat from an element is dispersed by a fan. **fan-jet** *n.* TURBOFAN (under TURBO-). **fanlight** *n.* a small (originally semicircular) window above a door or another window. **fanlike** *a.* **fanner** *n.* **fan palm** *n.* any of various palm trees having fan-shaped leaves, such as *Chamaerops humilis*, esp. the genus *Corypha*, typified by the talipot, *C. umbraculifera*, from Sri Lanka and Malabar. **fantail** *n.* a variety of the domestic pigeon with a large tail. **fantailed** *a.* **fan vaulting** *n.* (*Archit.*) vaulting in which the tracery spreads out like a fan.

fan[2] (fan) *n.* an enthusiastic admirer; a devotee. **fandom** *n.* the world of enthusiastic devotees of a particular person or interest. **fan mail** *n.* letters to a famous person from admirers. **fanzine** (-zēn) *n.* a magazine for fans of a particular interest, activity or person, written by amateurs.

fanatic (fənat´ik) *a.* **1** enthusiastic in the extreme. **2** holding extravagant or extremely dogmatic or bigoted views. *~n.* a person who has an extreme enthusiasm for something. **fanatical** *a.* **fanatically** *adv.* **fanaticism** (-sizm) *n.* **fanaticize** (-sīz), **fanaticise** *v.t.* to make fanatical. *~v.i.* to become a fanatic.

fancy (fan´si) *v.t.* (*3rd pers. sing. pres.* **fancies**, *pres.p.* **fancying**, *past, p.p.* **fancied**) **1** (*coll.*) to want to have or do. **2** (*coll.*) to be attracted, esp. sexually, to. **3** (*coll.*) to have an excessively high opinion of (oneself etc.). **4** to like the idea of being or doing (*fancy yourself as the boss*). **5** to choose (a person, team etc.) as the probable winner. **6** to breed as a hobby or sport. *~n.* (*pl.* **fancies**) **1** a personal inclination, liking or attachment. **2** a liking that does not last long, a caprice, a whim. **3** an imaginary, unreal or improbable idea, a delusion. **4** something favoured. **5** the faculty or the act of forming images, esp. those of a playful, frivolous or capricious kind. **6** a mental image. *~a.* (*comp.* **fancier**, *superl.* **fanciest**) **1** elaborate, not plain; ornamental, decorative. **2** (*sometimes iron.*) extravagant or fine; expensive or impressive (*a fancy price*). **3** arising in or based on the imagination. **4** needing skill to be performed; complex. **5** (of flowers) particoloured. **6** (of animals) bred for particular qualities. **to take a fancy to** to develop a liking or an affection for, to desire. **to take someone's fancy** to attract someone. **to tickle someone's fancy** to attract someone. **fanciable** *a.* (*coll.*) (of a person) sexually attractive. **fancier** *n.* a connoisseur or follower of an activity (*usu. in comb.*, as *pigeon fancier*). **fanciful** *a.* **1** arising from the imagination; baseless, unreal, imaginary. **2** indulging in fancies; whimsical. **3** unusually elaborate and ornamented. **fancifully** *adv.* **fancifulness** *n.* **fancily** *adv.* **fanciness** *n.* **fancy dress** *n.* fanciful clothes worn at a party, representing a famous person from history, a story etc. **fancy-free** *a.* not in love, not involved in a relationship, and without responsibilities or commitments (*footloose and fancy-free*). **fancy goods** *n.pl.* articles of a showy rather than a useful kind; ornamental fabrics such as ribbons and coloured silks. **fancy man** *n.* (*sl.*, *derog.*) **1** a woman's lover. **2** a prostitute's pimp, a ponce. **fancy woman** *n.* (*sl.*, *derog.*) a mistress. **fancy-work** *n.* ornamental knitting, embroidery, crocheting etc.

fandango (fandang´gō) *n.* (*pl.* **fandangoes**, **fandangos**) **1** a lively Spanish dance in triple time, for two people who beat time with castanets. **2** the musical accompaniment of such a dance.

fanfare (fan´feə) *n.* **1** a short, loud sounding of trumpets, bugles etc. **2** fuss or publicity to accompany something such as an announcement or welcome.

fang (fang) n. **1** a large pointed tooth, esp. the canine tooth of a dog or wolf. **2** the long, hollow or grooved tooth of a poisonous snake through which it injects its venom. **3** the biting part of a spider. **4** the part of a tooth embedded in the gum. **5** (coll.) a person's tooth. **fanged** a. **fangless** a.

fanner FAN¹.

fanny (fan´i) n. (pl. **fannies**) **1** (taboo) the female genitals. **2** (N Am., sl.) the buttocks. **fanny pack** n. (N Am.) BUMBAG (under BUM¹).

Fanny Adams (ad´əmz), (usu.) **sweet Fanny Adams** n. (sl.) nothing at all (euphem. for fuck all).

fantasia (fantā´ziə, -təzē´ə) n. a musical or other composition that is not governed by traditional fixed form; a composition based on several popular tunes.

fantastic (fantas´tik) a. **1** (coll.) wonderful, very good, very enjoyable. **2** (coll.) very great; extravagant. **3** fanciful, strange or whimsical, capricious. **4** odd, grotesque. **fantastical** a. **fantasticality** (-kal´-) n. **fantastically** adv. **fantasticalness** n. **fantasticate** v.t. **fantastication** (-ā´shən) n.

fantasy (fan´təsi), **phantasy** n. (pl. **fantasies**, **phantasies**) **1** a fanciful mental image or daydream. **2** an extravagant, whimsical or bizarre fancy, image or idea. **3** the faculty of inventing or forming fanciful images. **4** a fanciful or whimsical invention or design. **5** a novel, drama, film etc. characterized by strange, unrealistic, alien or grotesque characters and settings; such works collectively. **6** (Mus.) a fantasia. ~v.t. (3rd pers. sing. pres. **fantasies**, pres.p. **fantasying**, past, p.p. **fantasied**) to fantasize. **fantasist** n. **fantasize**, **fantasise** v.i. **1** to conjure up and indulge in gratifying mental images. **2** to dream up fantastic (and usu. impracticable) schemes, ideas etc. ~v.t. to dream up fantastic ideas about. **fantasy football** n. a competition in which players make up their own teams from different players and score points according to how well their players perform in reality.

fanzine n. FAN².

faquir FAKIR.

far (fah) a. (comp. **farther**, **further**, superl. **farthest**, **furthest**) **1** distant, a long way off; separated by a wide space. **2** extending or reaching a long way. **3** more distant of two, other, opposite. **4** remote from or contrary to one's purpose, intention or wishes. ~adv. **1** at or to a great distance in space, time or proportion. **2** to a great degree or extent, very greatly, by a great deal. **3** by a great interval, widely. **as far as 1** to the distance of (a certain point). **2** to the extent that. **by far** in a very great measure; very greatly; exceedingly. **far and near** everywhere. **far and wide** over a large number of places; everywhere. **far be it from me** I would not even consider; I am very reluctant (to do something). **far from 1** anything but, not at all. **2** (followed by pres.p.) used to indicate that the speaker's actions or intentions are the opposite of those stated. **how far** to what extent, distance etc. **so far 1** up to a specified point. **2** up to now. **so far as** as far as. **to go far 1** to be successful (esp. in one's career). **2** (esp. in neg.) to be sufficient for. **to go too far** to exceed reasonable limits. **faraway** a. **1** remote in time, place or relationship; distant. **2** dreamy, absent-minded. **Far East** n. the region including China, Japan, North and South Korea and other countries in E Asia. **Far Eastern** a. **far-fetched** a. (of a story or explanation) improbable, unrealistic, unconvincing. **far-flung** a. extending to far-off places. **far gone** a. **1** in an advanced state (of exhaustion, illness, wear etc.). **2** (coll.) very drunk. **far-off** a. distant, remote. **far out** a. (sl.) **1** unconventional, eccentric, weird. **2** (also int.) wonderful, great. **far-reaching** a. having broad influence, effects or implications, extensive, thoroughgoing. **far-seeing** a. considering what will happen in the future and so making wise judgements. **far-sighted** a. **1** considering what will happen in the future and so making wise judgements. **2** (N Am.) LONG-SIGHTED (under LONG¹). **far-sightedly** adv. **far-sightedness** n.

Usage note See note under FURTHER¹.

farad (fa´rəd) n. the derived SI unit of capacitance, the capacity of a capacitor in which the electrical potential is raised one volt by the presence of one coulomb of charge on each plate. **faradaic** (farədā´ik), **faradic** (farad´-) a. (of an electric current) inductive.

farce (fahs) n. **1** a humorous play in which the actors are involved in ridiculously complex and improbable situations. **2** drama of this kind. **3** a ridiculously futile or disorganized situation or action; a pretence, mockery, hollow formality. **farcical** (-ikəl) a. **1** of or relating to farce; ludicrous, droll, comical. **2** ridiculous, absurd, contemptible. **farcicality** (-kal´-) n. **farcically** adv.

farceur (fahsœ´) n. **1** a joker, a jester, a wag. **2** a performer in or writer of farces.

farcical FARCE.

farcy (fah´si) n. a disease in horses, closely allied to glanders, in which the lymph vessels become inflamed.

fare (feə) n. **1** the sum of money to be paid by a passenger for a journey by bus, train etc. **2** a passenger who pays to travel in a taxi etc. **3** food provided in a restaurant or café. ~v.i. (formal) **1** to get on, progress. **2** to be in any state, to happen, to turn out (well or badly). **3** to go, to travel. **fare stage** n. **1** a section of a bus route for which a certain charge is made. **2** a bus stop marking this.

farewell (feəwel´) int. goodbye, adieu. ~n. **1** words said at another person's leave-taking. **2** departure; leave-taking. ~a. expressing leave-taking (a farewell speech).

farina (fərē´nə) *n.* **1** flour or meal of cereal; the powder obtained by grinding nuts, roots etc. **2** any powdery substance. **3** starch. **farinaceous** (farinā´-) *a.*

farl (fahl) *n.* a thin cake of oatmeal or flour, orig. a quarter of such a cake.

farm (fahm) *n.* **1** an area of land together with its buildings, used for growing crops or rearing animals. **2** a farmhouse. **3** an area of land or water where a particular kind of animal or fish is bred. **4** a place for storage. ~*v.t.* **1** to use (land) for growing crops or rearing animals. **2** to breed (animals or fish) on a farm. **3** to let out (labourers) on hire. **4** to contract for the feeding, lodging etc. of (children) at so much per head. **5** to lease or let out (taxes, offices etc.) at a fixed sum or rate per cent; to take the proceeds of (taxes, offices etc.) for such a fixed sum or rate. ~*v.i.* to be a farmer. **to farm out 1** to delegate, to contract out. **2** to put (esp. a child) into someone's care. **farmable** *a.* **farmer** *n.* a person who runs or owns a farm. **farmhand** *n.* an agricultural labourer employed on a farm. **farmhouse** *n.* a dwelling house attached to a farm. **farmhouse loaf** *n.* a large rectangular white loaf with a slightly curved top. **farming** *n.* the business of growing crops or rearing animals. **farmstead** (-sted) *n.* a farm with the dwelling and other buildings on it. **farmyard** *n.* a yard or open area surrounded by or adjacent to farm buildings. ~*a.* crude or vulgar.

faro (feə´rō) *n.* a game of cards in which players bet against the dealer.

farrago (fərah´gō) *n.* (*pl.* **farragos,** (*N Am.*) **farragoes**) a confused mixture, a medley. **farraginous** (-raj´i-) *a.*

farrier (far´iə) *n.* **1** a person who shoes horses. **2** a person who treats diseases and injuries in horses. **farriery** *n.* (*pl.* **farrieries**) **1** the occupation of a farrier. **2** a farrier's shop, a smithy.

farrow (far´ō) *n.* **1** a litter of pigs. **2** the act of giving birth to a litter of pigs. ~*v.t.* to give birth to (pigs). ~*v.i.* to farrow pigs.

Farsi (fah´sē) *n.* modern Persian, the Indo-European language of Iran.

fart (faht) *v.i.* (*taboo sl.*) to break wind through the anus. ~*n.* **1** (*taboo sl.*) a discharge of wind from the anus. **2** (*sl.*) an unpleasant, stupid or boring person. **to fart about** (*sl.*) to behave foolishly, to waste time.

farther FURTHER¹.

farthest FURTHEST (under FURTHER¹).

farthing (fah´dhing) *n.* **1** a quarter part of an old penny, the smallest British copper coin (withdrawn in 1961). **2** the smallest possible amount.

farthingale (fah´dhing-gāl) *n.* (esp. in the 16th cent.) a woman's hooped skirt used to extend the wide gown and petticoat.

fartlek (faht´lek) *n.* a method of athletic training, mixing fast and slow running.

fascia (fā´shə, fash´iə) *n.* (*pl.* **fasciae** (-shiē), **fascias**) **1** (*Archit.*) a flat surface in an entablature or elsewhere. **2** a band, stripe belt, sash, fillet. **3** (*Anat.*) a thin, tendon-like sheath surrounding the muscles and binding them in their places. **4** FACIA. **fascial** *a.* **fasciate** (fash´iāt), **fasciated** (-ātid) *a.* **1** (*Bot.*) flattened by the growing together of several parts. **2** striped. **fasciation** (-ā´shən) *n.*

fascicle (fas´ikəl) *n.* **1** any one of the parts of a book that is published in instalments. **2** a small bundle, cluster or group; a cluster of leaves, flowers etc., a tuft. **3** (*Anat.*) a bundle of fibres. **fascicled** *a.* **fascicular** (-sik´ū-) *a.* **fasciculate** (-sik´ūlət), **fasciculated** (-lātid) *a.* **fasciculation** (-lā´shən) *n.* **fascicule** (-kūl) *n.* a fascicle, esp. of a book.

fasciitis (fashiī´tis) *n.* (*Med.*) inflammation of the fascia of a muscle.

fascinate (fas´ināt) *v.t.* **1** to exercise an irresistible influence over; to captivate, to attract irresistibly, to enchant, to charm. **2** (of snakes) to make (prey) motionless by means of a look or presence. **fascinating** *a.* **fascinatingly** *adv.* **fascination** (-ā´shən) *n.* **fascinator** *n.*

Fascism (fash´izm) *n.* **1** the extreme right-wing theory of government introduced into Italy by Benito Mussolini in 1922, the object of which was to oppose socialism and communism by controlling every form of national activity. **2** (*usu.* **fascism**) any ideology or system regarded as brutal, repressive, excessively nationalistic or militaristic. **Fascist, fascist** *a., n.* **fascistic** (-shis´tik), **Fascistic** *a.*

fashion (fash´ən) *n.* **1** the activity or business concerned with the style of clothes. **2** the current popular style of clothes or way of behaving. **3** a way or style of doing something; manner, way, pattern. **4** the form, make, style or external appearance of any thing. **5** fashionable or genteel society. ~*v.t.* **1** to give shape and form to; to frame, to mould. **2** to fit, to adapt. **after a fashion** satisfactorily, but not very well. **in a fashion** after a fashion. **in fashion** popular and favoured at a particular time. **out of fashion** unpopular and disapproved of at a particular time. **fashionable** *a.* **1** popular and favoured at a particular time. **2** characteristic of, approved by, or patronized by people of fashion. **fashionability** (-bil´-), **fashionableness** *n.* **fashionably** *adv.* **fashioner** *n.* **fashion victim** *n.* a person who slavishly follows trends in fashion.

☒ **fasinate** common misspelling of FASCINATE.

fast¹ (fahst) *a.* **1** swift, rapid, moving quickly. **2** taking a short time. **3** intended for high speed (*a fast road*). **4** imparting quick motion, as a bowler, pitcher etc. **5** promoting quick motion, as a billiard table, cricket pitch etc. **6** (of a clock etc.) showing a time ahead of the correct time. **7** (of photographic film) needing only a short exposure time. **8** (of a camera shutter) permitting short exposure times. **9** firmly fixed, firm, tight. **10** firmly adhering, faithful, steady, close. **11** (of a colour) lasting, durable, permanent, unfading, not washing out. **12** (of a person) immoral, dissipated, pleasure-seeking, promiscuous. **13** acquired with little effort or by shady means. *~adv.* **1** quickly, swiftly, in rapid succession; without delay. **2** firmly, tightly, securely. **3** soundly, completely, thoroughly (*fast asleep*). **fast and furious** quickly, energetically; vigorous and eventful, noisy or heated. **to pull a fast one** (*coll.*) to trick, to deceive, to use underhand methods. **fastback** *n.* (a car with) a back which forms a continuous slope from roof to bumper. **fast breeder, fast breeder reactor** *n.* a nuclear reactor which produces at least as much fissionable material as it consumes. **fast buck** *n.* a lot of money easily earned. **fast food** *n.* food, e.g. burgers and chicken pieces, which can be prepared and served very quickly, esp. in certain types of restaurant. **fast forward** *n.* a control that enables video or recording tape to be wound on very rapidly. *~v.t.* to wind on by means of a fast-forward control. **fast-forward** *a.* relating to such a control. **fast lane** *n.* a part of the carriageway used by fast-moving traffic, esp. the outer lane of a motorway. **in the fast lane** (*coll.*) where the pace of life is particularly fast, exciting or risky. **fastness** *n.* **1** the quality or state of being fast or secure. **2** a fortress, a stronghold, esp. in a remote and inaccessible place. **fast reactor** *n.* a nuclear reactor using mostly fast neutrons. **fast-talk** *v.t.* (*esp. N Am., coll.*) to persuade by fast, clever, deceptive talk. **fast track** *n.* the quickest route to achieve a particular goal or position. **fast-wind** *v.t.* (*past, p.p.* **fast-wound**) to wind (video or recording tape) very rapidly.

fast² (fahst) *v.i.* to abstain from food, esp. as a religious observance for the mortification of the body or as a sign of grief, affliction or penitence. *~n.* a (period of) total or partial abstinence from or deprivation of food, esp. from religious motives.

fasten (fah´sən) *v.t.* **1** to fix firmly, to make secure, to attach. **2** to secure, as by a bolt, a lock, a tie, knot etc. **3** to fix or set firmly or earnestly. *~v.i.* **1** to become fast. **2** to seize, to lay hold (upon). **to fasten on 1** to lay hold on. **2** to become aware of and concentrate (one's attention) on (something). **3** to attach (blame, responsibility, a nickname etc.) to. **fastener** *n.* a device that fastens, makes fast or secures. **fastening** *n.* **1** the act of making fast or secure. **2** anything which makes fast or secure, such as a bolt, bar, strap or catch.

fastidious (fastid´iəs) *a.* **1** extremely careful, delicate, refined, esp. in matters of taste; fussy. **2** squeamish, easily disgusted. **fastidiously** *adv.* **fastidiousness** *n.*

fastigiate (fəstij´iət) *a.* (*Bot.*) tapering to a point like a pyramid.

fat (fat) *a.* (*comp.* **fatter**, *superl.* **fattest**) **1** having a lot of flesh and overweight; plump, fleshy, corpulent, full-fed. **2** (of animals) fed up for killing. **3** oily, greasy, unctuous; resinous. **4** fertile,

fruitful, rich. **5** (of a book) thick, substantial. **6** substantial, rewarding (*fat profits*). **7** (of coal) bituminous. **8** (of clay etc.) sticky, plastic. **9** (*coll., iron.*) very little (*a fat chance*). *~n.* **1** a natural substance of a more or less oily character that occurs esp. in animals. **2** that part of anything which is considered redundant or excessive. **3** (*Chem.*) an organic compound of glycerol with one of a group of acids. *~v.t.* (*pres.p.* **fatting**, *past, p.p.* **fatted**) **1** to make fat or plump. **2** to fatten. *~v.i.* to become fat, to gain flesh. **to live off/ on the fat of the land** to have the best of everything. **fat cat** *n.* (*esp. N Am., coll., derog.*) a very wealthy or influential person. **fat farm** *n.* (*N Am., sl.*) a health farm where people go to slim. **fat-head** *n.* (*coll.*) a stupid person. **fat-headed** *a.* **fat-headedness** *n.* **fat hen** *n.* the white goosefoot, *Chenopodium album.* **fatless** *a.* **fatly** *adv.* **fatness** *n.* **fatso** (-sō) *n.* (*pl.* **fatsoes**) (*sl., offensive*) a fat person. **fatstock** *n.* livestock fattened for slaughter. **fatten** *v.t.* **1** to make (esp. animals) fat, to feed for the table. **2** to make (ground) fruitful, to fertilize. *~v.i.* to grow or become fat, to gain flesh. **fattening** *a.* (of food) easily making people fat. **fattish** *a.* **fattism, fatism** *n.* discrimination against fat people. **fattist, fatist** *n., a.* **fatty** *a.* (*comp.* **fattier**, *superl.* **fattiest**) **1** consisting of or having the qualities of fat. **2** oily; greasy, unctuous. **3** of or relating to fat; adipose. *~n.* (*pl.* **fatties**) (*coll.*) a fat person. **fattiness** *n.* **fatty acid** *n.* any of a class of aliphatic, carboxylic acids, e.g. palmitic acid, acetic acid. **fatty oil** *n.* FIXED OIL (under FIX).

fatal (fā´təl) *a.* **1** causing death, destruction or ruin. **2** having very undesirable consequences **3** fateful, decisive. **4** decreed by fate, inevitable. **fatalism** *n.* **1** the belief that all events are predetermined and beyond human control. **2** submission to fate. **fatalist** *n.* **fatalistic** (-lis´-) *a.* **fatalistically** *adv.* **fatality** (fətal´-) *n.* (*pl.* **fatalities**) **1** a (person who suffers) death by accident or violence. **2** a fixed and unalterable course of things. **3** predetermination by fate esp. to death or disaster. **4** a fatal influence; deadliness. **fatally** *adv.*

fate (fāt) *n.* **1** a power considered to control and decide events unalterably. **2** destiny, lot, fortune; one's ultimate condition as brought about by circumstances and events; what is destined to happen. **3** death, destruction. **4** (*pl.*) (**the Fates**) three Greek goddesses supposed to preside over human birth, life and fortunes. *~v.t.* (*usu. pass.*) to decree by fate or destiny. **fated** *a.* **1** doomed to destruction. **2** decreed by fate, predetermined. **3** fatal, fateful. **fateful** *a.* **1** having momentous, often catastrophic, consequences. **2** bringing death or destruction. **fatefully** *adv.* **fatefulness** *n.*

father (fah´dhə) *n.* **1** a male parent. **2** a man who begets a child. **3** a man who exercises paternal care. **4** a stepfather. **5** a father-in-law. **6** any male animal considered as regards its offspring. **7** a male ancestor, a patriarch. **8** the first to practise

any art; an originator, author, contriver, an early leader. **9** a respectful mode of address to an old man or any man deserving great reverence. **10** a priest, a confessor, the superior of a convent, a religious teacher etc. **11** (*Theol.*) the first person of the Trinity. **12** the senior member of any profession or body. **13** (*pl.*) elders, senators, the leading men (of a city etc.). ~*v.t.* **1** to beget. **2** to be or act as father of. **3** to originate. **4** to adopt or assume as one's own child, work etc. **5** to accept responsibility for. **to father on/ upon** to suggest that (someone) is responsible for. **Father Christmas** *n.* SANTA CLAUS. **father figure** *n.* an older man whom one looks to for advice and support. **fatherhood** *n.* **father-in-law** *n.* (*pl.* **fathers-in-law**) the father of a person's husband or wife. **fatherland** *n.* a person's native country. **fatherless** *a.* **fatherlessness** *n.* **fatherlike** *a.* **fatherly** *a.* **1** like a father; kind, caring, loving. **2** proper to or becoming a father. **fatherliness** *n.* **Father's Day** *n.* a day (in Britain the third Sunday in June) observed as a day to honour fathers. **fathership** *n.*
fathom (fadh´əm) *n.* (*pl.* **fathoms,** (*esp. after a number*) **fathom**) **1** a measure of length, six ft. (1.8 m) used principally in nautical and mining measurements. **2** six ft. (1.8 m) square, as a measure of wood in cross-section independently of length. ~*v.t.* **1** (often with *out*) to penetrate, to comprehend, to get to the bottom of. **2** to measure the depth of. **fathomable** *a.* **fathometer** (-om´itə) *n.* an instrument for measuring the depth of the sea by sound waves. **fathomless** *a.* not to be fathomed.
fatigue (fətēg´) *n.* **1** weariness, exhaustion from bodily or mental exertion. **2** METAL FATIGUE (under METAL). **3** the reduction in response of a muscle, organ etc. as a result of overactivity. **4** exertion or an activity causing weariness or exhaustion. **5** labour not of a military nature performed by soldiers. **6** (*pl.*) military overalls. ~*v.t.* (*3rd pers. sing. pres.* **fatigues,** *pres.p.* **fatiguing,** *past, p.p.* **fatigued**) to tire, to weary; to exhaust the strength of by bodily or mental exertion. **fatiguable, fatigable** *a.* **fatiguability** (-gəbil´iti), **fatigability** *n.* **fatigueless** *a.*
fatuous (fat´ūəs) *a.* **1** idiotic, inane, silly. **2** stupid, imbecile, foolish. **fatuity** (fətū´iti) *n.* (*pl.* **fatuities**). **fatuitous** *a.* **fatuously** *adv.* **fatuousness** *n.*
fatwa (fat´wah) *n.* a religious edict issued by a Muslim leader.
fauces (faw´sēz) *n.pl.* (*Anat.*) the area from the cavity at the back of the mouth to the pharynx. **faucial** (-shəl), **faucal** (-kəl) *a.*
faucet (faw´sit) *n.* **1** (*esp. N Am.*) a tap. **2** the tap on a barrel.
fault (fawlt) *n.* **1** a defect, blemish, imperfection. **2** an error, failing, mistake or blunder. **3** a slight offence or deviation from right or propriety. **4** responsibility for a mistake or wrongdoing, blame. **5** an improper service at tennis. **6** a penalty point in showjumping. **7** (*Geol.*) a fracture in

the earth's surface, together with a break in the continuity of the strata. ~*v.t.* **1** to find a fault in, to criticize. **2** (*Geol.*) to cause to undergo a fault. ~*v.i.* **1** to commit a fault, to blunder. **2** (*Geol.*) to undergo a fault. **at fault** to blame, in error. **to a fault** excessively. **to find fault with** to complain of, to blame, to censure, esp. in a carping manner. **fault-finding** *n.* constant criticism; censoriousness. **fault-finder** *n.* **faultless** *a.* without fault; perfect, flawless. **faultlessly** *adv.* **faultlessness** *n.* **faulty** *a.* (*comp.* **faultier,** *superl.* **faultiest**) having faults; imperfect, defective, flawed. **faultily** *adv.* **faultiness** *n.*
faun (fawn) *n.* one of a kind of rural deities, with a human body and the horns and legs of a goat, bearing a strong resemblance to the satyrs, with whom they are generally identified.
fauna (faw´nə) *n.* (*pl.* **faunae** (-nē), **faunas**) **1** the animals found in or belonging to a certain region or time. **2** a treatise upon or list of these. **faunal** *a.* **faunist** *n.* **faunistic** (-nis´tik) *a.*
faute de mieux (fōt də mjœ´) *adv.* for lack of anything better.
faux (fō) *a.* imitation, false.
faux pas (fō pah´) *n.* (*pl.* **faux pas** (pahz´)) **1** a blunder, a slip. **2** a social indiscretion.
fave (fāv) *n., a.* (*sl.*) favourite.
favour (fā´və), (*N Am.*) **favor** *n.* **1** a kind or indulgent act. **2** friendly regard, kindness, goodwill; approval. **3** partiality, preference, excessive kindness or indulgence. **4** aid, support, furtherance, facility, convenience for doing something; behalf, advantage (of). ~*v.t.* **1** to regard or behave towards with kindness. **2** to approve, to prefer, to show partiality to. **3** to befriend, to support. **4** to facilitate. **5** to promote. **6** to oblige (with). **7** to be propitious or fortunate for. **8** to resemble in features. **in favour** approved. **in favour of 1** approving, on the side of. **2** to the advantage of. **out of favour** disapproved. **favourable** *a.* **1** approving, commending, consenting. **2** friendly, well-disposed, encouraging; propitious. **3** tending to promote or to encourage. **4** convenient, advantageous. **favourableness** *n.* **favourably** *adv.* **favoured** *a.*
favourite (fā´vərit), (*N Am.*) **favorite** *a.* preferred before all others. ~*n.* **1** a person or thing regarded with special affection, preference or partiality. **2** a person chosen as a companion and intimate by a superior and unduly favoured. **3** in sport, the competitor considered to have the best chance of winning. **favorite son** *n.* (*N Am.*) a person chosen as a candidate for presidency by the delegates from their home state. **favouritism** *n.* showing an unfair special preference for a person or group, partiality.
fawn[1] (fawn) *n.* **1** a young deer; a buck or doe in its first year. **2** the colour of a young deer, light yellowish brown. ~*a.* like a fawn in colour, light yellowish brown. ~*v.t.* (of deer) to bring forth. ~*v.i.* to bring forth a fawn. **in fawn** (of deer) pregnant.

fawn[2] (fawn) v.i. **1** (usu. with on or upon) to court in a servile manner, to grovel, to cringe. **2** (of animals, esp. dogs) to show affection by cringing, licking the hand etc. **fawner** n. **fawning** a., n. **fawningly** adv.

fax (faks) n. **1** a system for electronically scanning, transmitting and reproducing documents etc. via a telephone line. **2** a document etc. sent in this way. **3** (also **fax machine**) a machine for sending or receiving documents in this way. ~v.t. to send (a document) in this way.

fay (fā) n. a fairy.

faze (fāz) v.t. (coll.) to disconcert, to put off one's stroke. **fazed** a.

FBA abbr. Fellow of the British Academy.

FC abbr. Football Club.

FCO abbr. Foreign and Commonwealth Office.

Fe chem. symbol iron.

fealty (fē´alti) n. (pl. **fealties**) **1** fidelity of a vassal or feudal tenant to a lord. **2** fidelity, loyalty, allegiance.

fear (fiə) n. **1** an unpleasant feeling caused by impending danger, pain etc. **2** dread, a state of alarm. **3** a cause of fear. **4** anxiety, worry. **5** awe, reverence. **6** risk, possibility (of something unpleasant happening) (no fear of being misunderstood). ~v.t. **1** to be afraid of, to dread. **2** to suspect, to doubt. **3** to shrink from, to hesitate (to do). **4** to show reverence towards, to venerate. ~v.i. **1** to be afraid. **2** to feel anxiety or worry. **3** to doubt, to mistrust. **for fear 1** in order that not; lest. **2** in dread (that or lest). **never fear** there is no need to worry or be afraid. **no fear** (coll.) not likely; certainly not. **without fear or favour** showing no partiality. **fearful** a. **1** apprehensive, afraid (lest). **2** timid, timorous. **3** terrible, awful, frightful. **4** (coll.) extraordinary, unusual, annoying. **fearfully** adv. **fearfulness** n. **fearless** a. not afraid; courageous, intrepid. **fearlessly** adv. **fearlessness** n. **fearsome** a. fearful, terrible, alarming, formidable. **fearsomely** adv. **fearsomeness** n.

feasible (fē´zibəl) a. **1** that may or can be done, practicable, viable. **2** (coll.) manageable. **3** likely, plausible. **feasibility** (-bil´-) n. **feasibility study** n. a study of the practicability of a suggested scheme. †**feasibleness** n. **feasibly** adv.

Usage note The uses of feasible to mean likely, plausible or probable are sometimes disapproved of.

feast (fēst) n. **1** a large and sumptuous meal enjoyed by a great number of people; a banquet. **2** an anniversary or periodical celebration of some great event or person, esp. a religious anniversary. **3** anything giving great enjoyment to body or mind. ~v.t. **1** to entertain sumptuously. **2** to gratify or please greatly, as with something delicious. ~v.i. **1** to eat and drink sumptuously. **2** to be highly gratified or pleased. **to feast one's eyes on** to look at with great delight. **feast day** n. a day on which a feast, esp. a religious feast, is held; a festival.

feat (fēt) n. **1** a notable act or performance, esp. one displaying great strength, skill or daring. **2** an exploit, an accomplishment.

feather (fedh´ə) n. **1** a plume or quill, one of the appendages growing from a bird's skin, forming collectively the soft covering of a bird. **2** such a plume worn as an ornament, esp. in the hat. **3** something extremely light. **4** (pl.) plumage. **5** (collect.) game birds considered collectively. ~v.t. **1** to dress, cover or provide with feathers. **2** to decorate with or as with feathers. **3** to turn (an oar) so that the blade passes horizontally through the air. **4** (Naut. etc.) to change the angle or allow free rotation of (a propeller blade) to minimize wind resistance. ~v.i. to move as feathers. **in fine/ high feather** in high spirits, elated. **to feather one's nest 1** to accumulate wealth for oneself. **2** to make provision for oneself. **feather bed** n. a mattress stuffed with feathers. **feather-bed** v.t. (pres.p. **feather-bedding**, past, p.p. **feather-bedded**) **1** to pamper, to spoil. **2** to give financial assistance to (an industry). **feather-bedding** n. the practice of protecting jobs by allowing overmanning or inefficient or slow working. **feather-brain, feather-head, feather-pate** n. a silly, frivolous person. **feather-brained, feather-headed, feather-pated** a. **feathered** a. **feather edge** n. the thinner edge of a wedge-shaped board or plank. **feathering** n. **1** plumage. **2** the feathers on an arrow. **3** a feathery fringe or coat (of setters etc.). **4** (Archit.) an arrangement of small arcs or foils separated by projecting points or cusps. **feather in one's cap** n. an honour, a distinction that one can be proud of. **featherless** a. **feather-light** a. extremely light. **feather stitch** n. an embroidery stitch producing a zigzag line somewhat like feathers. **feather-stitch** v.t. to embroider with a feather stitch. **featherweight** n. **1** an extremely light person or thing. **2** a boxer, weightlifter etc. in the weight category intermediate between bantamweight and lightweight. **3** this weight category. **feathery** a. **featheriness** n.

feature (fē´chə) n. **1** a distinctive, characteristic or prominent part of anything. **2** (usu. pl.) a part of the face, such as the eyes, nose or mouth. **3** a special article in a newspaper or magazine on a particular topic. **4** (also **feature film**) a full-length film, esp. the main film in a programme. **5** (also **feature programme**) a radio or television documentary. ~v.t. **1** to give prominence to, to make a feature of. **2** to have as a characteristic. **3** to present in an important role or as an important subject. ~v.i. to be a characteristic, to figure prominently. **featured** a. **featureless** a.

Feb. abbr. February.

febrifuge (feb´rifūj) n. a medicine which has the property of dispelling or mitigating fever. **febrifugal** (-brif´ūgəl, -fū´gəl) a.

febrile (fē´brīl) a. of, relating to, proceeding from or indicating fever. **febrility** (fibril´iti) n.

February (feb´ruəri, feb´ūəri) n. (pl. **Februaries**) the second month of the year, containing in ordinary years 28 days, and in leap years 29.

Usage note The pronunciation with (ū) and only one (r) is sometimes disapproved of.

feces FAECES.

feckless (fek´lis) a. **1** weak, feeble, ineffective. **2** incompetent, irresponsible. **fecklessly** adv. **fecklessness** n.

feculent (fek´ūlənt) a. **1** filthy, foul. **2** full of dregs, lees or sediment. **3** muddy, turbid. **feculence, feculency** n.

fecund (fē´kənd, fek´-) a. (formal) fruitful, prolific, fertile, productive. **fecundability** (fikŭndəbil´iti) n. **fecundate** v.t. (formal) to make fruitful or prolific. **fecundation** (-dā´shən) n. **fecundity** (-kŭn´-) n. (formal).

Fed., fed. abbr. **1** Federal. **2** Federation.

fed[1] (fed) a. that has been fed. **fed up** a. (coll.) unhappy or bored (with). **to be fed up (to the back teeth) with** to have had more than enough of, to be sick of.

fed[2] (fed) n. (coll.) (in the US) a federal agent or official, esp. a member of the FBI.

fed[3] FEED.

fedayee (fedah´yē) n. (pl. **fedayeen** (-yēn)) a member of an Arab commando group, esp. fighting against Israel.

federal (fed´ərəl) a. **1** (also **Federal**) relating to, arising from or supporting a system of government formed by the union of several states. **2** relating to such a central government as distinguished from the government of the separate states. **3** (**Federal**) supporting the cause of the Union in the American Civil War. **4** of, relating to or based upon a treaty, league or contract. ~n. **1** a supporter of the principle of federation. **2** (**Federal**) a supporter of the American Union in the Civil War. **federacy** n. (pl. **federacies**) a federation of states. **federalism** n. **federalist** n. **federalize, federalise** v.t., v.i. **federalization** (-zā´shən) n. **federally** adv. **federate**[1] (-ərāt) v.t. **1** to organize as a federal group of states. **2** to bring together for a common object. ~v.i. to combine and form a federal group. **federate**[2] (-ərət) a. **1** united under a federal government or organization. **2** leagued together. **federation** (-ā´shən) n. **1** a federal government or group of states. **2** a confederated body. **3** the act of uniting in a confederacy. **federationist** n. **federative** a.

fedora (fidaw´rə) n. (N Am., coll.) a soft felt hat with a curled brim.

fee (fē) n. **1** payment or remuneration to a public officer, a professional person or an organization for the execution of official functions or for the performance of a professional service. **2** a charge paid for a privilege, such as admission to a society, public building etc. **3** (often pl.) charge, payment (school fees). **4** (Law) inherited ownership of land. ~v.t. (past, p.p. **fee'd, feed**) **1** to pay a fee or reward to. **2** to engage for a fee, to

hire. **to hold in fee** (Law) to own absolutely. **feeless** a.

feeble (fē´bəl) a. (comp. **feebler**, superl. **feeblest**) **1** weak, destitute of physical strength; infirm, debilitated. **2** lacking in force, vigour or energy. **3** lacking in moral or intellectual power. **4** dim, faint. **5** ineffective, pointless, insipid. **6** unconvincing, lame. **feeble-minded** a. **1** stupid, unintelligent. **2** mentally deficient, imbecile. **feeble-mindedly** adv. **feeble-mindedness** n. **feebleness** n. **feeblish** a. **feebly** adv.

feed v.t. (past, p.p. **fed** (fed)) **1** to give food to. **2** to put food into the mouth of. **3** to supply with that which is necessary to existence, continuance or development. **4** to cause (cattle) to graze. **5** to serve as food or nourishment for. **6** to nourish, to cause to grow or develop. **7** to cause (land) to be grazed. **8** to cause to pass (e.g. a rope or tape) through or into something. **9** to supply (a machine etc.) with material. **10** to supply a machine etc. with (the necessary material) for its operation. **11** to supply (a signal, power) to an electric circuit. **12** to cue in a response from (another performer). **13** to pass the ball or puck to (another player). **14** to provide (information) to. **15** to gratify. ~v.i. **1** to take food; to eat. **2** to subsist (on or upon). **3** (of a river etc.) to flow into a larger river etc. ~n. **1** food, fodder, pasturage. **2** the act of feeding or giving food. **3** an amount of food given to babies or provender given to horses, cattle etc. at a time. **4** (coll.) a meal, a feast. **5** the operation of supplying a machine with material, or of bringing a tool into operation. **6** the machinery for this. **7** the amount supplied. **8** the charge of a gun. **9** a performer who supplies cues, esp. a straight man. **to feed back** to produce or provide feedback. **to feed up 1** to give plenty to eat, to fatten. **2** to satiate. **feedback** n. **1** the return of part of the output of a system, circuit or mechanical process to the input. **2** (Biol.) the modification produced by the effects of a biological etc. process on another stage of the same pattern. **3** reactions and comments from customers, consumers, audience etc. **feeder** n. **1** a person who supplies food or nourishment. **2** a person who eats, esp. one who eats in a certain manner, as a quick feeder. **3** a feeding bottle. **4** a child's bib. **5** a tributary stream. **6** an artificial channel supplying a canal etc. **7** a railway, bus service etc. that links outlying areas to the main system. **8** a wire, usu. in pairs, carrying electricity to various points in a system. **9** the apparatus feeding a machine; a hopper. **feeding bottle** n. a bottle with a rubber teat for supplying liquid food to infants. **feedstock** n. raw material used in a manufacturing or industrial process. **feedstuff** n. fodder.

feel (fēl) v.t. (past, p.p. **felt** (felt)) **1** to perceive by touch. **2** to examine or explore by touch. **3** to touch, to handle, to try or find out by handling or groping. **4** to have a sensation of, otherwise than by the senses of sight, hearing, taste or smell.

5 to be conscious of. **6** to have the emotions stirred by. **7** to experience, to undergo. **8** to know in one's inner consciousness, to be convinced (that); think, consider. ~*v.i.* **1** to have perception by the sense or act of touching. **2** to be conscious of a certain sensation (as cold, wet, hungry or tired). **3** (*reflex.*) to be conscious of (oneself) as in a certain state (as afraid, anxious, busy etc.). **4** to be stirred in one's emotions. **5** to seem to the sense of touch, to produce a certain sensation (*the air feels cold*). ~*n.* **1** the sense of touch. **2** the characteristic sensation of something, esp. one related to that of touch; general impression. **3** perception, esp. of an emotional kind. **to feel free** not to hesitate (to do something). **to feel like** to wish to, to be in the mood for. **to feel one's way** to move ahead cautiously. **to feel out** to try to discover the opinions of, esp. indirectly; sound out. **to feel strange** to feel unwell. **to feel up** (*sl.*) to touch (someone) in such a way as to arouse oneself or the other person sexually. **to feel up to** (*coll.*) to feel able or strong enough to. **to get the feel of** to become familiar with. **to make one's presence/ influence felt** to do something that causes people to become aware of one's presence etc. **feeler** *n.* **1** an organ of touch in invertebrate animals. **2** a tentative enquiry (*to put out feelers*). **3** a person who or thing that feels. **feeler gauge** *n.* a thin metal strip of a known thickness used to measure a gap. **feeling** *n.* **1** the sense of touch; the sensation produced when a material body is touched. **2** a physical sensation of any kind. **3** an emotional state or reaction; emotion such as anger or joy. **4** (*pl.*) susceptibilities, sympathies. **5** sympathy or love. **6** an impression, a sense, an intuition. **7** a sentiment, belief or conviction (usu. non-rational). **8** the emotional content or mood of a work of art; the emotional response produced by such a work; emotional sensibilities shown in such a work. ~*a.* **1** perceiving by the touch. **2** easily affected or moved, sensitive, of great sensibility. **3** expressive of or manifesting great sensibility. **4** affecting. **feelingless** *a.* **feelingly** *adv.*

feet FOOT.

feign (fān) *v.t.* to invent, to pretend, to simulate, to counterfeit. ~*v.i.* to make pretences; to dissimulate.

feint[1] (fānt) *n.* **1** a pretence of aiming at one point while another is the real object. **2** a feigned or sham attack. **3** a pretence. ~*v.i.* to make a feint or pretended attack (upon, against or at).

feint[2] (fānt) *a.* (of ruled lines on paper) light, faint.

☒ **feirce** common misspelling of FIERCE.

feisty (fīs´ti) *a.* (*comp.* **feistier**, *superl.* **feistiest**) (*esp. N Am., coll.*) **1** spirited, tough. **2** irritable, touchy. **feistily** *adv.* **feistiness** *n.*

felafel (felah´fəl), **falafel** *n.* a spicy ball or cake of mashed chickpeas or beans.

feldspar (feld´spah), **felspar** (fel´spah) *n.* (*Mineral.*) any of a group of silicates of aluminium combined with a mineral, e.g. potassium, sodium or calcium, that are the most important group of rock-forming minerals and the major constituent of igneous rocks. **feldspathic** (-spath´-), **feldspathoid** (feld´spəthoid), **feldspathose** (feld´-spəthōs) *a.*

felicity (fəlis´iti) *n.* (*pl.* **felicities**) **1** happiness, blissfulness. **2** a source of happiness, a blessing. **3** appropriateness, neatness. **4** a happy turn or expression. **5** a happy way or faculty of expressing, behaving etc. **felicitate** (filis´itāt) *v.t.* to congratulate. **felicitation** (-ā´shən) *n.* (*usu. pl.*) congratulation. **felicitous** *a.* **1** well-suited, apt, well-expressed. **2** charming in manner, operation etc. **felicitously** *adv.* **felicitousness** *n.*

feline (fē´līn) *a.* **1** of or relating to cats, catlike; belonging to the Felidae, the cat family. **2** sly, stealthy. **3** graceful, sinuous. ~*n.* an animal of the cat family, the Felidae. **felinity** (-lin´-) *n.*

fell[1] FALL.

fell[2] (fel) *v.t.* **1** to hew or cut down. **2** to knock down; to bring to the ground. **3** to finish with a fell in sewing. ~*n.* **1** a quantity of timber felled. **2** a seam or hem in which one edge is folded over another and sewed down. **feller**[1] *n.*

fell[3] (fel) *n.* the hide or skin of an animal, esp. if covered with hair; a fleece.

fell[4] (fel) *n.* (*North.*) **1** a rocky hill. **2** a high stretch of barren moorland. **fell walking** *n.* the activity or recreation of walking on the fells. **fell walker** *n.*

fell[5] (fel) *a.* **1** (*poet.*) cruel, savage, fierce. **2** (*poet.*) destructive, terrible, deadly, dire. **at one fell swoop** in a single action, on a single occasion. **felly** *adv.*

fellatio (fəlā´shiō, -lah´t-) *n.* oral stimulation of the penis. **fellate** (filāt´) *v.t.* **fellator** *n.*

feller[1] FELL[2].

feller[2] (fel´ə) *n.* **1** (*coll.*) fellow, man. **2** (*dial.*) a male sweetheart.

felloe (fel´ō), **felly** (fel´i) *n.* (*pl.* **felloes**, **fellies**) **1** any one of the curved segments of a wheel, to which the spokes are attached. **2** the whole rim of a wheel.

fellow (fel´ō) *n.* **1** a man, a boy. **2** (*derog.*) a person considered as unimportant. **3** (*usu. pl.*) an associate, a comrade; a partner; a companion. **4** a contemporary. **5** one of the same kind or species. **6** an equal in rank, a peer, a compeer. **7** one of a pair. **8** a person or thing like or equal to another, a counterpart, a match. **9** a member of a learned or an incorporated society. **10** an incorporated member of a college. **11** the holder of a fellowship or stipendiary position endowed for purposes of research. **12** a member of a university governing body; one of the trustees of a college. ~*a.* (*attrib.*) associated with oneself or of the same class or relationship (*one's fellow workers*). ~*v.t.* to match, to pair with, to suit. **fellow feeling** *n.* sympathy esp. from sharing similar experiences; joint interest. **fellowship** *n.* **1** companionship, association, close friendship, friendliness, warmth of feeling, community of interest, participation. **2** a body of associates. **3** a brotherhood, a fraternity. **4** a company, a corporation, a guild. **5** the condition or state of being a fellow. **6** the position of fellow in a college or learned society. **7** an endowment for maintaining a graduate engaged in research; the status of such a graduate. **fellow-traveller** *n.* **1** a person who travels with another person on a journey. **2** (*usu. derog.*) a person who, without declaring themselves to be a member, sympathizes with the aims of the Communist Party or other similar organization.

felon (fel´ən) *n.* a person who has committed a felony. ~*a.* cruel, malignant, malicious; wicked, murderous. **felonious** (filō´-) *a.* **1** of the nature of a felony. **2** (*Law*) done with deliberate purpose to commit a crime. **3** (*Law*) that has committed felony. **feloniously** *adv.* **feloniousness** *n.* **felony** *n.* (*pl.* **felonies**) **1** in US law and in English law until 1967, an offence of graver character than a misdemeanour. **2** an offence of a very serious character, conviction for which formerly involved loss of lands and goods.

felspar FELDSPAR.

felt¹ FEEL.

felt² (felt) *n.* **1** a kind of cloth made of wool or wool and cotton compacted together by rolling, beating and pressing; similar cloth or material made from other fibres. **2** a piece of this material. ~*a.* made of this material (*a felt hat*). ~*v.t.* **1** to make into felt. **2** to cover with felt. **3** to press into a compact mass. ~*v.i.* to become matted together. **felt tip pen, felt-tipped pen, felt tip** *n.* a pen with a writing point made of pressed felt or similar fibres. **felty** *a.*

felucca (felŭk´ə) *n.* a small vessel used in the Mediterranean, propelled by oars or lateen sails or both.

felwort (fel´wœt) *n.* a gentian with purple flowers, *Gentianella amarella.*

female (fē´māl) *a.* **1** denoting the sex which gives birth to young or lays eggs from which new individuals are developed. **2** (*Bot.*) having a pistil, but no stamens, capable of being fertilized and producing fruit; bearing fruit. **3** of, relating to or characteristic of woman or womanhood or female animals and plants; womanly, feminine. **4** designed for receiving a correlative mechanical part designated male (*a female screw*). ~*n.* **1** (*sometimes derog.*) a woman or girl. **2** (*Zool.*) an individual of the female sex. **female condom** *n.* a contraceptive device worn in the vagina. **female impersonator** *n.* a male performer who dresses as and imitates a woman. **femaleness** *n.*

feminine (fem´inin) *a.* **1** of, relating to or characteristic of women or the female sex. **2** womanly; effeminate. **3** having qualities associated with women; gentle, tender, pretty. **4** (*Gram.*) belonging to the gender denoting or classified as females. **femininely** *adv.* **feminineness, feminity** (-min´-) *n.* **feminine rhyme** *n.* a rhyme on a word

ending with an unstressed syllable, e.g. *fable, table; notion, motion.* **femininity** (-nin´-) *n.* **feminism** *n.* **1** the advocacy of the rights of women to political, economic and social equality with men. **2** (*Med.*) the development of female characteristics in a male person. **feminist** *n., a.* **feministic** (-nis´-) *a.* **feminize, feminise** *v.t.* to make feminine. ~*v.i.* to become feminine.

femme fatale (fam fatahl´) *n.* (*pl.* **femmes fatales** (fam fatahl´)) a seductive woman, esp. one who lures men to their downfall.

femto- (fem´tō) *pref.* a thousand million millionth (10^{15}).

femur (fē´mə) *n.* (*pl.* **femurs, femora** (fem´ərə)) **1** (*Anat.*) the thigh bone. **2** (*Zool.*) the third joint of the leg in insects. **femoral** (fem´ərəl) *a., n.*

fen¹ (fen) *n.* low, flat and marshy land; a marsh, a bog. **fen-berry** *n.* (*pl.* **fen-berries**) the cranberry, *Vaccinium oxycoccos.* **fen-fire** *n.* the will-o'-thewisp. **fenland** *n.* a fen; fen country. **fenny** *a.*

fen² (fŭn, fen) *n.* (*pl.* **fen**) a Chinese monetary unit worth one-hundredth of a yuan; a coin of this value.

fence (fens) *n.* **1** a structure serving to enclose and protect a piece of ground, or to keep cattle from straying, e.g. a wall, a hedge or a line of rails or posts etc. **2** an obstacle in steeplechasing or showjumping. **3** a guardplate, guide or gauge of various kinds in machinery etc. **4** (*sl.*) a purchaser or receiver of stolen goods, or a place where such goods are purchased or deposited. **5** the art of fencing or swordplay. ~*v.t.* **1** to enclose, encircle or protect with or as with a fence. **2** to separate (off) with a fence. **3** to defend, shield or protect. **4** to parry, to ward off. **5** (*sl.*) to deal in (stolen goods). ~*v.i.* **1** to practise the art of swordplay. **2** to use a sword skilfully. **3** to defend oneself or repel attack skilfully. **4** (of a horse) to jump over fences. **5** to parry enquiries adroitly, to equivocate. **6** (*sl.*) to deal in stolen goods. **to mend fences** to restore good relations (with someone), to make up differences. **to sit on the fence** to remain neutral in respect to opposing policies. **fenceless** *a.* **fencer** *n.* **1** a person skilled in fencing. **2** a builder of fences. **3** a horse good at jumping over fences. **fencing** *n.* **1** the act of making fences. **2** a fence or fences, a railing or railings. **3** material for making fences. **4** the act or art of using a sword or foil in attack or defence.

fend (fend) *v.t.* (*Sc.*) to provide for, to support. ~*v.i.* (*Sc.*) to strive, to resist, to offer opposition. **to fend for** to provide or to get a living for. **to fend off** to keep off, ward off.

fender (fen´də) *n.* **1** a piece of furniture, usu. of iron or brass, placed on the hearth to keep in falling coals, ashes etc. **2** (*Naut.*) a piece of timber or plastic or mass of rope to protect the side of a vessel from injury by collision. **3** a person or thing that serves to defend, protect or ward off anything hurtful or dangerous. **4** (*N Am.*) **a** the wing or mudguard of a motor vehicle. **b** the bumper of a motor vehicle. **fender bender** *n.*

(*N Am., sl.*) a collision between motor vehicles, esp. one involving only minor damage.

fenestra (fines´trə) *n.* (*pl.* **fenestrae** (-trē)) **1** (*Anat.*) a window-like aperture in a bone. **2** a transparent spot or aperture in a wing, leaf etc. **3** a tiny hole in a surgical instrument. **4** a hole made by fenestration. **fenestrate** (-trət, fen´əs-) *a.* **1** (*Bot.*) (of leaves) having only a network of filamentous cells formed. **2** (*Zool.*) relating to the naked hyaline transparent spots on the wings of butterflies. **fenestrated** (-trātid, fen´is-) *a.* **1** furnished with windows. **2** (*Anat.*) having fenestrae. **3** perforated. **4** fenestrate. **fenestration** (-trā´shən) *n.* **1** (*Archit.*) the construction, arrangement or method of design of windows. **2** a surgical operation in which an artificial opening is made in the bony labyrinth of the inner ear, esp. to improve hearing. **3** the condition of having fenestrae.

fennec (fen´ek) *n.* a small fox, *Vulpes zerda*, common in Africa.

fennel (fen´əl) *n.* **1** a fragrant umbelliferous plant with yellow flowers, *Feniculum vulgare*, whose seeds and leaves are used as flavourings. **2** the seeds of this. **3** (*also* **Florence fennel, sweet fennel**) a variety of this with thickened stalks that are eaten as a vegetable.

fenugreek (fen´ūgrēk) *n.* a leguminous plant, *Trigonella foenum-graecum*, the seeds of which are used as a flavouring or in animal fodder.

feral (fiə´rəl, fer´-) *a.* **1** wild, savage, brutal. **2** changed from a domesticated into a wild state. **3** uncultivated.

ferial (fiə´riəl, fer´-) *a.* in the Church calendar, of or relating to ordinary weekdays as opposed to festival or fast days.

ferment[1] (fœ´ment) *n.* **1** commotion, tumult, agitation, excitement, uproar. **2** any substance, organic or inorganic, which causes fermentation. **3** fermentation; internal motion of the constituent parts of a fluid.

ferment[2] (fəment´) *v.t.* **1** to excite fermentation in, to subject to fermentation. **2** to rouse, to agitate, to excite. ~*v.i.* **1** to be in a state of fermentation, to effervesce. **2** to be agitated, as by violent emotions. **fermentable** (-men´-) *a.* **fermentation** (fœmentā´shən) *n.* **1** a process that takes place in certain substances or liquids through living organisms or chemical agents, with the production of heat, effervescence and chemical decomposition, esp. the change of sugar to ethyl alcohol. **2** commotion, agitation, excitement. **fermentative** (-tətiv) *a.* **fermenter** *n.*

fermi (fœ´mi) *n.* (*pl.* **fermis**) (*esp. Physics*) a unit of length equal to 10^{-15} metre. **fermion** (-ən) *n.* (*Physics*) any of a group of subatomic particles, e.g. a nucleon, that has half-integral spin and obeys the exclusion principle. **fermium** (-əm) *n.* (*Chem.*) an element, at. no. 100, chem. symbol Fm, artificially produced from plutonium.

fern (fœn) *n.* (*pl.* **fern, ferns**) a non-flowering plant springing from a rhizome, and having the reproductive organs on the lower surface of fronds or leaves, which are often divided in a graceful, feathery form. **fernery** *n.* (*pl.* **ferneries**) a place where ferns are grown. **ferny** *a.*

ferocious (fərō´shəs) *a.* **1** fierce, savage, cruel, barbarous. **2** (*esp. N Am., coll.*) intense, extreme. **ferociously** *adv.* **ferociousness** *n.* **ferocity** (-ros´-) *n.* (*pl.* **ferocities**) **1** the state or quality of being ferocious; savageness, fierceness, wildness, fury. **2** a ferocious act.

-ferous (fərəs), **-iferous** (if´ərəs) *suf.* bearing, producing, having, as in *auriferous, fossiliferous*. **-ferously** *suf.* **-ferousness** *suf.*

ferrel FERRULE.

ferret (fer´it) *n.* **1** a partially tamed variety of polecat, *Mustela putorius furo*, used for killing rats and driving rabbits out of their holes. **2** a sharp-eyed searcher or investigator. ~*v.t.* (*pres.p.* **ferreting**, *past, p.p.* **ferreted**) **1** to drive out of a hole or clear (ground) with ferrets. **2** to hunt or take with ferrets. **3** to search (out) by persevering investigation. ~*v.i.* **1** to hunt rabbits etc. with a ferret. **2** to search or rummage about (for). **ferreter** *n.* **ferrety** *a.*

ferri- (fer´i) *comb. form* (*Chem.*) denoting a compound of iron in the ferric state.

ferriage (fer´iij) *n.* **1** conveyance by a ferry. **2** the fare paid for this.

ferric (fer´ik) *a.* (*Chem.*) **1** of, relating to or extracted from iron. **2** containing trivalent iron.

ferrimagnetism (ferimag´nitizm) *n.* (*Physics*) the spontaneous magnetization of a substance in which one group of magnetic atoms is arranged in an opposite direction to the other. **ferrimagnetic** (-magnet´ik) *a.*

Ferris wheel (fer´is) *n.* a big, upright revolving fairground wheel with seats suspended from its rim.

ferrite (fer´īt) *n.* (*Chem.*) a sintered ceramic consisting of a mixture of ferric oxide and other metallic oxides, which possesses magnetic properties.

ferro- (fer´ō) *comb. form* **1** (*Mineral.*) denoting a substance containing iron. **2** (*Chem.*) denoting a compound of iron in the ferrous state.

ferroconcrete (ferōkong´krēt) *n.* concrete strengthened by incorporation of iron bars, strips etc.; reinforced concrete. ~*a.* made of reinforced concrete.

ferroelectric (ferōilek´trik) *a.* (*Physics*) (of materials) showing spontaneous electric polarization, but not conducting electric current. ~*n.* a ferroelectric material. **ferroelectricity** (-tris´iti) *n.*

ferromagnetism (ferōmag´nitizm) *n.* the magnetic properties of certain materials, e.g. iron and cobalt, that are easily magnetized, vary in their degree of magnetization depending on the strength of the applied magnetizing field, and in some cases retain their magnetization when that field is withdrawn. **ferromagnetic** (-magnet´ik) *a.*

ferrous (fer´əs) *a.* **1** containing iron. **2** (*Chem.*) of, relating to or containing divalent iron.

ferruginous (fəroo´jinəs) a. 1 containing iron or iron rust. 2 of the colour of iron rust. **ferruginous duck** n. a European duck, *Aythya nyroca*, with a reddish brown plumage.

ferrule (fer´ool, -əl), **ferrel** n. 1 a metallic ring or cap on the handle of a tool, the end of a stick, the joint of a fishing rod, a post etc. to strengthen it. 2 a short piece of pipe screwed into a main to form a connection with a service-pipe.

ferry (fer´i) v.t. (3rd pers. sing. pres. **ferries**, pres.p. **ferrying**, past, p.p. **ferried**) to transport over a river, strait or other narrow expanse of water, in a boat, barge etc. ~v.i. to go or pass across narrow water in a boat etc. ~n. (pl. **ferries**) 1 a boat, or occasionally an aeroplane etc., used for carrying passengers across a river, strait or other narrow expanse of water. 2 the provision of such a method of transport. 3 the passage where a ferry-boat plies. **ferryboat** n. a boat used as a ferry. **ferryman** n. (pl. **ferrymen**).

fertile (fœ´til) a. 1 able to support abundant growth. 2 able to bear offspring, fruitful. 3 capable of growing or developing. 4 productive, fruitful. 5 (of the mind) inventive, resourceful. 6 able to be transformed into fissionable material. **fertility** (-til´-) n. **fertilize** (-ti-), **fertilise** v.t. 1 to make fertile or productive. 2 (*Biol.*) to provide (an egg, a female animal or plant) with male reproductive material to form a new individual. 3 to make (esp. soil) rich. **fertilizable** a. **fertilization** (-zā´shən) n. **fertilizer** n. 1 a fertilizing agent. 2 a chemical applied to the soil to make it more fertile and modify its acidity or alkalinity.

ferule (fer´ool, -əl) n. a rod or cane formerly used to punish children in school. ~v.t. to punish with a ferule.

fervent (fœ´vənt) a. 1 ardent, earnest, zealous, vehement. 2 hot, boiling, glowing. **fervency** n. **fervently** adv. **fervid** (-vid) a. 1 ardent, impassioned. 2 (*poet.*) burning, very hot. **fervidly** adv. **fervidness** n. **fervour** (-və), (*N Am.*) **fervor** n. 1 ardour, intensity of feeling, vehemence; zeal. 2 heat, warmth.

fescue (fes´kū) n. a grass of the genus *Festuca*, important for pasture.

fess[1] (fes), **fesse** n. (*Her.*) a broad band of metal or colour crossing the shield horizontally, and occupying one-third of it. **in fess** arranged horizontally. **fess point** n. (*Her.*) the midpoint of a shield.

fess[2] (fes) v.i. (*coll.*) to confess.

festal (fes´təl) a. 1 festive, joyous, gay, merry. 2 actively involved in holiday pursuits. 3 of or relating to a feast or holiday. **festally** adv.

fester (fes´tə) v.i. 1 to become septic or infected. 2 to cause persistent annoyance or resentment; to rankle. 3 to become rotten; to decay. ~v.t. to make septic or infected.

festival (fes´tivəl) n. 1 a day or period of celebration or holiday, often with religious significance. 2 a series of concerts, plays etc., in a town. ~a. of, relating to or characterizing a festival or feast;

festal. **festival of lights** n. 1 Hanukkah. 2 Diwali.

festive a. 1 of, relating to or used for a feast or festival. 2 joyous, gay, celebratory. 3 (of a person) enjoying feasting. **festively** adv. **festiveness** n.

festivity (-tiv´-) n. (pl. **festivities**) 1 gaiety, mirth, joyfulness. 2 a feast, a festival, a joyous celebration or entertainment. 3 (pl.) celebrations; merrymaking.

festoon (festoon´) n. 1 a decorative chain or garland of flowers, foliage, drapery etc. suspended by the ends to hang as a curve. 2 a carved ornament in the form of a garland or wreath. ~v.t. to form into or adorn with or as with festoons; to decorate in a showy manner. **festoonery** n.

feta (fet´ə), **fetta** n. a firm white Greek cheese made from sheep's or goat's milk.

fetch[1] (fech) v.t. 1 to go for and bring back. 2 to cause to come. 3 to draw forth (breath), to heave (a sigh). 4 (*coll.*) to strike. 5 (*coll.*) to delight, to charm. 6 to bring in, to sell for (a price). 7 to derive, to elicit. 8 to bring to any state, condition or position. ~n. 1 an act of fetching. 2 a stratagem, a trick, a dodge. 3 (*Naut.*) the distance travelled, esp. by wind or waves, across open water without obstruction. **to fetch and carry** to go to and fro with things; to perform menial tasks. **to fetch out** to bring out, to cause to appear. **to fetch up 1** (*coll.*) to end up. 2 to vomit. 3 to recall, to bring to mind. 4 (*coll.*) to bring up, raise, rear (children). **fetcher** n. **fetching** a. (*coll.*) attractive, charming, taking. **fetchingly** adv.

fetch[2] (fech) n. a wraith or double.

fête (fāt, fet), **fete** n. 1 an outdoor event with stalls and entertainments, usu. locally organized to raise money for charity. 2 a festival, an entertainment. 3 the festival of the saint after whom a person is named. ~v.t. to entertain, to feast; to honour lavishly.

fetid (fet´id, fē´-), **foetid** a. having an offensive smell; stinking. **fetidly** adv. **fetidness** n. **fetor** (fē´tə) n. a strong or offensive smell; a stench.

fetish (fet´ish) n. 1 (*Psych.*) an object providing sexual gratification. 2 any material object supposed to be the vessel, vehicle or instrument of a supernatural being, the possession of which gives supposed special powers. 3 an object of devotion, an idol, a fixation. **fetishism** n. **fetishist** n. **fetishistic** (-shis´-) a. **fetishize, fetishise** v.t. **fetishization** (-zā´shən) n.

fetlock (fet´lok) n. 1 the back projecting part of a horse's leg, between the pastern and the cannon-bone. 2 the joint at this part of the leg. 3 the tuft of hair growing at this projection.

fetor FETID.

fetta FETA.

fetter (fet´ə) n. 1 a chain for the feet. 2 (usu. pl.) a shackle, a bond. 3 (pl.) captivity. 4 anything which restrains or confines. ~v.t. 1 to put fetters upon, to bind with fetters. 2 to confine, restrain; to hamper, impede. **fetterlock** n. 1 a shackle for a horse when turned out to grass. 2 (*Her.*) a figure of a shackle and padlock.

fettle (fet'əl) v.t. **1** to clean, trim or put right. **2** to remove (the rough edge of a metal casting etc.). **3** to line (a furnace). ~n. condition, order, trim. **fettler** n. **1** (Austral.) a person whose job is to maintain railway tracks. **2** a person who fettles.

fettuccine (fetuchē'ni), **fettucini** n. tagliatelle.

fetus FOETUS.

feu (fū) n. **1** (Sc. Law) a perpetual lease at a fixed rent. **2** the land, houses or other real estate so held. ~v.t. (3rd pers. sing. pres. **feus**, pres.p. **feuing**, past, p.p. **feued**) (Sc. Law) to give or take in feu.

feud[1] (fūd) n. **1** hostility between two tribes or families in revenge for an injury, often carried on for several generations. **2** a long and bitter dispute or quarrel. ~v.i. to carry on a feud.

feud[2] (fūd) n. land held on condition of performing certain services; a fief. **feudal** a. **1** according to or resembling the feudal system. **2** of, relating to, consisting of or founded upon a feud or fief. **3** old-fashioned. **feudality** (-dal'-) n. (pl. **feudalities**) **1** feudal principles; the feudal system. **2** the quality or state of being feudal. **3** a fief, a feudal holding. **feudalize, feudalise** v.t. **feudalization** (-zā'shən) n. **feudally** adv. **feudal system** n. the social system in Europe during the Middle Ages, by which the ownership of land was vested in the lord, with possession or tenancy being granted to the vassal in return for military service. **feudalism** n. the feudal system. **feudalist** n. **feudalistic** (-lis'-) a. **feudatory** a. **1** holding or held by feudal tenure. **2** subject to overlordship. ~n. (pl. **feudatories**) a person who holds lands of another by feudal tenure; a vassal.

fever (fē'və) n. **1** an abnormally high body temperature and quickened pulse, often accompanied by delirium. **2** any one of a group of diseases, e.g. scarlet fever or yellow fever, characterized by this. **3** a state of nervous excitement; agitation. ~v.t. to affect with or put into a fever. **fevered** a. **feverish** a. **1** suffering from or affected with fever. **2** indicating fever; resembling a fever. **3** excited, restless, hectic. **feverishly** adv. **feverishness** n. **feverous** a. **1** infested with fever. **2** causing a fever. **fever pitch** n. a state of extreme excitement or activity. **fever tree** n. **1** a tree that produces a febrifuge, esp. Pickneya pubens of the south-east USA. **2** a tall flowered swamp tree of southern Africa, Acacia xanthophloea.

feverfew (fē'vəfū) n. a bushy strong-scented plant, Tanacetum parthenium.

few (fū) a. **1** not many. **2** small, limited or restricted in number. ~pron. a small number (of). **a few** a small number (of). **a good few** (coll.) a considerable number (of). **every few** once in every series of a few (days, hours etc.). **few and far between** rare, occurring very infrequently. **no fewer than** as many as (a surprisingly large number). **not a few** a considerable number. **of few words** reserved, habitually saying little

(a woman of few words). **some few** not a great number.

Usage note See note on fewer under LESS.

fey (fā) a. **1** eccentric, odd in a whimsical, otherworldly way. **2** (chiefly Sc.) fated, doomed, on the verge of death (implying both the nearness of this event and the impossibility of avoiding it). **3** (chiefly Sc.) clairvoyant, psychic. **feyly** adv. **feyness** n.

fez (fez) n. (pl. **fezzes**) a flat-topped conical usu. red cap without a brim, fitting close to the head, with a tassel of silk, wool etc., worn by men in the Middle East.

ff abbr. **1** folios. **2** (and those e.g. pages) following. **3** (Mus.) fortissimo.

Fg. Off. abbr. Flying Officer.

fiancé (fiä'sā, -on'-) n. the man to whom a woman is engaged to be married. **fiancée** n. the woman to whom a man is engaged to be married.

fianchetto (fiənchet'ō, -ket'-) n. (pl. **fianchettoes**) in chess, the development of a bishop to a long diagonal of the board.

fiasco (fias'kō) n. (pl. **fiascos**) a complete and humiliating failure; a ridiculous breakdown; an ignominious result; a debacle.

fiat (fī'ət, -at) n. **1** an order, command, decree, esp. an arbitrary one. **2** (Law) the order or warrant of a judge or other constituted authority sanctioning or allowing certain processes; an authorization. **fiat money** n. (N Am.) paper currency made legal tender by a Government order, but not convertible into coins.

fib (fib) n. a harmless or venial lie; a white lie. ~v.i. (pres.p. **fibbing**, past, p.p. **fibbed**) to tell a fib. **fibber, fibster** n.

fiber FIBRE.

Fibonacci series (fēbanah'chi), **Fibonacci sequence** n. (Math.) a series of numbers, e.g. 1, 1, 2, 3, 5, in which each number is the sum of the preceding two numbers. **Fibonacci number** n. a number in the Fibonacci series.

fibre (fī'bə), (N Am.) **fiber** n. **1** a slender filament; a thread, string or filament, of which the tissues of animals and plants are made. **2** the substances composed of animal or vegetable tissue forming the raw material in textile manufacture. **3** a structure composed of filaments. **4** a piece of glass in the form of a filament. **5** DIETARY FIBRE (under DIET[1]). **6** essence, nature, material, character, nerve, strength (moral fibre). **fibreboard** n. a building material made of compressed wood or plant fibres. **fibred**, (N Am.) **fibered** a. **fibrefill** n. a synthetic material used as a filling for pillows, cushions etc. **fibreglass** n. **1** very fine filaments of molten glass worked into a synthetic fibre. **2** a plastic reinforced by glass fibres. **fibreless** a. **fibre optics** n. **1** (as sing.) a technology based on the transmission of light along bundles of very thin glass or plastic fibres, used esp. in telecommunications and exploratory medicine. **2** (as pl.) the fibres used in this technology. **fibriform**

(-brifawm) *a.* **fibrous** *a.* consisting of, containing or resembling fibres. **fibrously** *adv.* **fibrousness** *n.*

fibril (fī´bril), **fibrilla** (-bril´ə) *n.* (*pl.* **fibrils**, **fibrillae** (-lē)) a little fibre. **fibrillar** *a.* **fibrillary** *a.*

fibrillate (fī´brilāt, fib´-) *v.i.* **1** (of a fibre) to split into fibrils. **2** (of the muscle fibres in the heart) to undergo irregular contractions. ~*v.t.* to split (a fibre) into fibrils. **fibrillation** (-ā´shən) *n.*

fibrin (fī´brin, fib´-) *n.* a protein contained in the blood, causing it to clot. **fibrinogen** (-brin´əjən) *n.* a protein entering into the formation of fibrin and into coagulation.

fibro (fī´brō) *n.* (*pl.* **fibros**) (*Austral.*) **1** a cement mixed with asbestos fibre, used in sheets for building. **2** a house built mainly of this.

fibro- (fī´brō), **fibr-** *comb. form* denoting a substance consisting of or characterized by fibres.

fibroblast (fī´brōblahst) *n.* (*Anat.*) a cell that contributes to the formation of connective tissue fibres.

fibroid (fī´broid) *a.* of the nature or form of fibre or fibrous tissue. ~*n.* a benign tumour.

fibroin (fī´brōin) *n.* the protein that is the chief constituent of silk, cobwebs, the horny skeleton of sponges etc.

fibroma (fībrō´mə) *n.* (*pl.* **fibromas**, **fibromata** (-mətə)) a benign fibrous tumour.

fibrosis (fībrō´sis), **fibrositis** (-sī´tis) *n.* (*Med.*) muscular rheumatism. **fibrositic** (-sit´ik) *a.* **fibrotic** (-brot´ik) *a.*

fibrous FIBRE.

fibula (fib´ūlə) *n.* (*pl.* **fibulae** (-lē), **fibulas**) **1** (*Anat.*) the outer and smaller bone of the leg. **2** a clasp, buckle or brooch. **fibular** *a.*

-fic (fik) *suf.* forming adjectives from nouns, verbs etc., as *honorific, horrific, malefic.* **-fically** *suf.*

-fication (fikā´shən) *suf.* forming nouns from verbs in -FY, as *purification.*

fiche (fēsh) *n.* (*pl.* **fiche**, **fiches**) a microfiche.

fichu (fē´shoo) *n.* a light shawl or scarf worn by women over the neck and shoulders.

fickle (fik´əl) *a.* changeable, inconstant. **fickleness** *n.* **fickly** *adv.*

fictile (fik´tīl) *a.* **1** made of earth or clay. **2** manufactured by or suitable for the potter; of or relating to pottery.

fiction (fik´shən) *n.* **1** an invented statement or narrative; a story, a romance. **2** literature, esp. in prose, describing imaginary people and events. **3** a falsehood. **4** the act or art of feigning or inventing. **5** that which is feigned, imagined or invented. **6** any point or thing assumed for the purposes of justice or convenience (*legal fiction*). **fictional** *a.* **fictionality** (-nal´-) *n.* **fictionalize, fictionalise** *v.t.* **fictionalization** (-zā´shən) *n.* **fictionally** *adv.* **fictionist** *n.* **fictitious** (-tish´əs) *a.* **1** feigned, imaginary, counterfeit, false, assumed. **2** of or relating to novels. **3** having no real existence. **4** accepted by a conventional or legal fiction. **fictitiously** *adv.* **fictitiousness** *n.* **fictive** *a.*

1 imaginative, creative. **2** imaginary, fictitious, feigned, counterfeit.

Usage note See note on *fictitious* under FACTITIOUS.

ficus (fē´kəs, fī´-) *n.* any plant of the genus *Ficus*, including the fig tree and the rubber plant.

fiddle (fid´əl) *n.* **1** (*coll. or derog.*) a violin or stringed instrument with a bow. **2** (*coll.*) a swindle, a dishonest practice. **3** (*coll.*) an awkward or tricky operation. **4** (*Naut.*) a frame of bars and strings, to keep things from rolling off the cabin table in bad weather. ~*v.i.* **1** to make restless movements with the hands or fingers. **2** to move aimlessly; to waste time in aimless activity. **3** to play on a fiddle. **4** to tinker (with), to fuss (with), to tamper (with). ~*v.t.* **1** (*coll.*) to falsify (accounts etc.). **2** (*coll.*) to contrive to do or obtain (something) by underhand means. **3** to play (e.g. a tune) on a fiddle. **fit as a fiddle** in good condition, ready for anything. **on the fiddle** (*coll.*) cheating, being dishonest, falsifying accounts etc. for one's own advantage. **to play first fiddle** to take a leading part. **to play second fiddle** to take a subordinate part. **fiddle-back** *n.* **1** a fiddle-shaped back of a chair. **2** a chasuble with a fiddle-shaped front. **fiddle-de-dee** (-didē´) *n., int.* nonsense. **fiddle-faddle** (-fadəl) *n.* trifling talk; nonsense. ~*int.* nonsense. ~*a.* **1** trifling. **2** making a fuss about trifles. ~*v.i.* **1** to trifle. **2** to make a fuss about trifles. **fiddle-head** *n.* an ornamental scroll-like carving at the bows of a ship. **fiddle pattern** *n.* a fiddle-shaped pattern for the heads of spoons and forks. **fiddler** *n.* **1** a person who plays the fiddle. **2** (*coll.*) a cheat or swindler. **3** a small crab of the genus *Uca* having one large claw and one very small one. **fiddlestick** *n.* **1** a violin bow. **2** (*pl.*) rubbish, something absurd. ~*int.* (*pl.*) nonsense; rubbish. **fiddling** *a.* **1** trifling, fussy. **2** petty, contemptible. **3** fiddly. **fiddly** *a.* (*comp.* **fiddlier**, *superl.* **fiddliest**) **1** tricky, awkward. **2** small, difficult to manipulate. **3** fiddling.

fideism (fī´diizm) *n.* the religious doctrine that knowledge can be attained only by faith but by reason. **fideist** *n.* **fideistic** (fidiis´tik) *a.*

fidelity (fidel´iti) *n.* **1** careful and loyal observance of duty; faithful adherence to an agreement, a set of beliefs etc. **2** loyalty, faithfulness, esp. to one's husband or wife. **3** honesty, veracity, reliability. **4** accurate correspondence (of a copy, description, picture etc.) to the original. **5** exactness in sound reproduction (*high fidelity*). **fidelity insurance** *n.* insurance taken out by an employer to cover losses arising from an employee's dishonesty etc.

fidget (fij´it) *v.i.* (*pres.p.* **fidgeting**, *past, p.p.* **fidgeted**) **1** to move about restlessly. **2** to worry, to be uneasy. ~*v.t.* to worry or make (others) uncomfortable. ~*n.* **1** a state of nervous restlessness. **2** a person who fidgets. **3** a person who worries or makes others uncomfortable. **4** (*pl.*) restless movements. **fidgety** *a.* **fidgetiness** *n.*

fiducial (fidū´shǝl) a. (Astron. etc.) denoting a fixed point or line used as a basis for measurement or comparison. **fiduciary** a. **1** of or relating to a trust, trustee or trusteeship. **2** held or given in trust. **3** depending on public confidence for its value. ~n. (pl. **fiduciaries**) a trustee.

fie (fī) int. used to express contempt, irony, disgust, shame or impatience.

fief (fēf) n. **1** an estate held under the feudal system or in fee. **2** feudal tenure. **3** a person's realm of operations. **fiefdom** n. a fief.

field (fēld) n. **1** a piece of land, esp. one enclosed for crops or pasture. **2** a region that is rich in some natural product (such as an oilfield or coalfield). **3** the area of grass on which cricket, football or other games are played. **4** in cricket, the fielders collectively, especially with respect to their positions. **5** all the competitors in a race, or all except the favourite. **6** all the entrants, candidates etc. in a contest. **7** the open country. **8** a wide expanse, e.g. of sea or sky. **9** the place where a battle is fought. **10** the battle itself. **11** the scene of military operations. **12** the participants in a hunt. **13** a sphere of activity or knowledge; an interest or speciality. **14** the sphere of practical operations away from the office, laboratory etc. (a field naturalist). **15** the surface on which the figures in a picture are drawn. **16** a field of force; the force exerted in such an area. **17** the range of view or perception. **18** (Comput.) a set of characters comprising a unit of information as part of a record. **19** (Her.) the surface of a shield or one of its divisions. **20** (Math.) a set of mathematical elements subject to two binary operations, addition and multiplication, such that the set is a commutative group under addition and also under multiplication if zero is excluded. **21** each of two or more sets of scanning lines forming a television picture. ~v.t. **1** in cricket etc., to catch or stop (the ball) and return it. **2** to assemble (a team, an army) ready for action. **3** to deal with (questions etc.), esp. off the cuff. **4** to retrieve (something or someone liable to go astray). ~v.i. to act as a fielder in cricket and other games. **in the field 1** working away from the office, laboratory etc. **2** campaigning. **to hold the field 1** to maintain one's ground against all comers. **2** to surpass all competitors. **to keep the field** to continue a campaign. **to play the field** to diversify one's interests or activities, esp. not to commit oneself to a steady boyfriend or girlfriend. **to take the field 1** to commence active military operations. **2** to begin a campaign. **3** to go on to the field of play. **field-book** n. a book used by surveyors, engineers etc., in which the memoranda of surveys taken in the field are set down. **field day** n. **1** a day of unusual importance, excitement or display. **2** (Mil.) a day on which troops are exercised in manoeuvres, esp. in front of an audience. **3** a day spent working in the natural environment, away from the laboratory, office etc. **to have a field day** to take gleeful

advantage. **field-effect transistor** n. a semiconductor unipolar device in which the electric current flows through a narrow channel between two electrodes from one region to another. **fielder** n. a player who fields at cricket etc. **field events** n.pl. athletic events other than racing, e.g. discus-throwing and jumping etc. **field glasses** n.pl. binoculars. **field goal** n. **1** in American football, a score made by kicking the ball over the crossbar from ordinary play. **2** in basketball, a score made while the ball is in play. **field hockey** n. (N Am.) hockey played on grass. **field hospital** n. an ambulance or temporary hospital near a battlefield. **field marshal** n. an officer of the highest rank in the British army. **field mouse** n. any of several species of mice of the genus Apodemus living in fields etc. **field mushroom** n. the common edible mushroom, Agaricus campestrus. **field mustard** n. charlock. **field notes** n.pl. notes made on the spot during fieldwork. **field officer** n. (Mil.) an officer above the rank of captain, but below that of general (such as a major, a colonel etc.). **field of honour** n. the scene of a battle or duel. **field of view** n. the area in front of the eyes that can be seen without moving the eyes. **field of vision** n. field of view. **field rank** n. any army rank above that of captain but below that of general. **fieldsman** n. (pl. **fieldsmen**) a fielder. **field sport** n. an outdoor sport, such as hunting, shooting or coursing. **fieldstone** n. natural stone used in building. **field telegraph** n. a movable telegraph system for use on campaign, manoeuvres etc. **field trip** n. a visit undertaken by schoolchildren or students to study phenomena or collect information in situ. **fieldwork** n. **1** observations or operations carried out in situ by students, researchers, anthropologists, surveyors etc. **2** (pl.) temporary fortifications thrown up by besiegers or besieged. **fieldworker** n.

fieldfare (fēld´feǝ) n. a species of thrush, Turdus pilaris, a winter visitant in England.

fiend (fēnd) n. **1** a demon, a devil, an evil spirit. **2** a person of extreme wickedness or cruelty. **3** (coll.) an addict (a fresh-air fiend). **4** something disagreeable. **fiendish** a. **1** wicked, cruel or unpleasant. **2** very difficult; challenging. **fiendishly** adv. **fiendishness** n. **fiendlike** a.

fierce (fiǝs) a. (comp. **fiercer**, superl. **fiercest**) **1** savage, furiously hostile or aggressive; raging, violent. **2** vehement, ardent, eager, impetuous. **3** intense or strong in an unpleasant way. **4** (of a machine) not operating smoothly. **fiercely** adv. **fierceness** n.

fiery (fī´ri) a. (comp. **fierier**, superl. **fieriest**) **1** consisting of fire, on fire, flaming with fire. **2** hot, like fire; producing a burning sensation. **3** glowing or red, like fire. **4** (of skin or a sore) inflamed. **5** (of a mine etc.) highly inflammable, liable to explosions. **6** (of curry etc.) hot-tasting. **7** vehement, ardent, eager; passionate, hot-tempered, irascible. **8** pugnacious, mettlesome, untamed. **9** (of a cricket pitch) making the ball rise dangerously high. **fierily** *adv.* **fieriness** *n.* **fiery cross** *n.* **1** a wooden cross, the ends of which had been set on fire, formerly sent round the Scottish Highlands to summon a clan to war. **2** a flaming cross used as a symbol by the Ku Klux Klan.

fiesta (fies'tə) *n.* **1** a holiday or festivity. **2** (esp. in Spain and Latin America) a religious holiday or festival esp. on a saint's day.

fife (fif) *n.* **1** a small flutelike pipe, chiefly used in military music. **2** a player of this instrument. *~v.i.* to play upon a fife. *~v.t.* to play (tunes) on the fife. **fifer** *n.* **fife-rail** *n.* (*Naut.*) a rail on the quarter-deck and poop or around the mast of a vessel (perhaps so called because a fifer sat on this whilst the anchor was being weighed).

fifteen (fif'tēn, -tēn') *n.* **1** the number or figure 15 or xv. **2** the age of 15. **3** a team of 15 players, esp. in rugby football. **4** a set of 15 things. **5** a size measuring 15. **6** (of films) classified as suitable to be watched by people of 15 years and over. *~a.* **1** 15 in number. **2** aged 15. **fifteenth** *n.* **1** any one of 15 equal parts. **2** (*Mus.*) the interval of a double octave. **3** an organ stop sounding two octaves above the open diapason. *~a., n.* **1** (the) last of 15 (people, things etc.). **2** (the) next after the 14th.

fifth (fifth) *n.* **1** any one of five equal parts. **2** (*Mus.*) **a** a diatonic interval of five notes, equal to three tones and a semitone. **b** the resulting concord. **c** two notes separated by this interval sounded together. **3** (*NAm., coll.*) **a** a fifth part of a US gallon of liquor or spirits (about 750 ml). **b** a bottle containing this. *~a., n.* **1** (the) last of five (people, things etc.). **2** (the) next after the fourth. **fifth column** *n.* a group of people in a country who, whether as individuals or as members of an organization, are ready to give help to an enemy (from the reference of General Mola who, in the Spanish Civil War in 1936 said that he had four columns encircling Madrid and a fifth column in the city, being sympathizers ready to assist the attacking party). **fifth columnist** *n.* **fifth-generation** *a.* of or relating to a type of computer that uses artificial intelligence. **fifthly** *adv.* in the fifth place. **fifth wheel** *n.* **1** (*esp. NAm.*) a spare wheel. **2** a superfluous person or thing. **3** a horizontal steering bearing placed above the front axle of a carriage enabling it to turn freely.

fifty (fif'ti) *n.* (*pl.* **fifties**) **1** the number or figure 50 or l. **2** the age of 50. *~a.* **1** 50 in number. **2** aged 50. **fifties** *n.pl.* **1** the period of time between one's 50th and 60th birthdays. **2** the range of temperatures between 50 and 60 degrees. **3** the period of time between the 50th and 60th years of a century. **fiftieth** (-tiəth) *n.* any one of 50 equal parts. *~n., a.* **1** (the) last of 50 (people, things etc.). **2** (the) next after the 49th. **fifty-fifty** *adv.* in equal shares, half each. *~a.* **1** with equal shares, equal. **2** equally likely to happen or not to happen. **fifty-first, fifty-second etc.** *n., a.* the ordinal numbers corresponding to fifty-one etc. **fiftyfold** (-fōld) *a., adv.* **fifty-one, fifty-two etc.** *n., a.* the cardinal numbers between 50 and 60.

fig[1] (fig) *n.* **1** the pear-shaped fleshy fruit of the genus *Ficus*, esp. *F. carica*. **2** the tree bearing this, noted for its broad leaves. **3** other trees bearing similar fruit; the fruit of these. **4** anything valueless, a trifle. **5** a spongy excrescence on a horse's frog, consequent on a bruise. **not to care a fig** not to care at all. **fig leaf** *n.* **1** the leaf of a fig tree. **2** a flimsy covering to hide something (from Gen. iii.7 and the use made of the fig leaf in statues to cover genitals). **fig tree** *n.* **1** *Ficus carica*, a tropical tree or shrub which produces the edible fig. **2** any other tree bearing similar fruit. **figwort** *n.* any plant of the genus *Scrophularia*, esp. *S. aquatica* and *S. nodosa* (from their being popular remedies for piles).

fig[2] (fig) *v.t.* (*pres.p.* **figging**, *past, p.p.* **figged**) to dress, deck, rig (up or out). *~n.* dress, array, outfit, equipment. **in full fig** in full dress. **to fig out** to make (a horse) lively. **to fig up** to fig out.

fig. *abbr.* figure.

fight (fit) *v.i.* (*past, p.p.* **fought** (fawt)) **1** to contend in arms or in battle, or in single combat (with, against). **2** to strive for victory or superiority, to war. **3** to strive in a determined way to achieve something. **4** to oppose, to offer resistance. **5** (*esp. NAm.*) to quarrel, to disagree. *~v.t.* **1** to contend with, to struggle against (*to fight poverty*). **2** to engage in, to carry on or wage (a contest, battle, lawsuit, campaign etc.). **3** to maintain by conflict. **4** to contend over. **5** to gain or win by conflict. **6** to manage, lead or manoeuvre in battle. **7** to take part in (a boxing match). **8** to set on or cause (dogs or cocks) to fight. *~n.* **1** a struggle between individuals, armies or animals, to injure each other or obtain the mastery. **2** a battle, a combat. **3** a contest of any kind, contention. **4** a boxing match. **5** a determined effort to achieve something. **6** a quarrel, a row. **7** power of or inclination for fighting. **to fight back 1** to resist. **2** to counter-attack. **3** to hold back (tears, an emotion) with an effort. **to fight down** to hold back or suppress. **to fight for 1** to campaign or strive on behalf of. **2** to try with determination to gain or achieve. **to fight (it) out** to decide (a contest or wager) by fighting. **to fight off** to repel. **to fight shy of** to avoid from a feeling of mistrust, dislike or fear. **to put up a fight** to offer resistance. **fightback** *n.* a counter-attack; retaliation; recovery. **fighter** *n.* **1** a person or animal that fights. **2** a boxer. **3** a combative person, one who does not give in easily. **4** a fast military aircraft equipped to attack other aircraft. **fighter-bomber** *n.* a military aircraft designed to be both a fighter and a bomber. **fighting** *n.* **fighting chair** *n.* (*NAm.*) a chair mounted in a fixed position on a boat, used when catching a large fish. **fighting chance** *n.* a chance of success if every effort is made. **fighting-cock** *n.* a game cock. **fighting fish** *n.* SIAMESE FIGHTING FISH (under SIAMESE). **fighting fit** *a.* in peak condition. **fighting fund** *n.* money raised to support a campaign by, e.g. workers on strike. **fighting-top** *n.* one of the gun platforms on the mast of a sailing warship. **fighting words** *n.pl.* (*coll.*) words that show a readiness to engage in a fight.

figment (fig´mənt) *n.* a fiction, an invented statement, something that exists only in the imagination, a fabrication, a fable.

figure (fig´ə) *n.* **1** the external form or shape of a person or thing. **2** bodily shape, esp. from the point of view of its attractiveness. **3** an unidentified person seen in outline. **4** a personage, a character. **5** the mental impression that a person makes, appearance, distinction. **6** the representation of any form, as by carving, modelling, painting, drawing, embroidery, weaving or any other process. **7** a statue, an image, a likeness. **8** (*Geom.*) a combination of lines or surfaces enclosing a space, such as a triangle, sphere etc. **9** a diagram, an illustrative drawing, a pattern. **10** an emblem, a type, a simile. **11** a fancy, a creation of the imagination, an idea. **12** a symbol representing a number, esp. any one of the ten Arabic numerals; a number expressed in this way. **13** a sum, an amount. **14** a value, a price (*a high figure*). **15** (*pl.*) arithmetical calculations. **16** the several steps or movements which a dancer makes in accord with the music. **17** a certain movement or division in a set dance. **18** in skating, a movement or combination of movements beginning and ending at a fixed point. **19** any way of speaking or writing in which words are deflected from their literal or ordinary sense, such as metaphor, ellipsis, hyperbole. ~*v.t.* **1** to form an image, likeness or representation of. **2** to represent, to picture, to imagine. **3** to symbolize, to typify. **4** to cover, adorn or ornament a pattern with figures. **5** to work out in figures, to calculate, to reckon. **6** to mark with numbers or prices. **7** to express by a metaphor or image. **8** (*esp. N Am.*) to believe, to consider, to conclude. ~*v.i.* **1** to appear, to be conspicuous. **2** to do arithmetical calculations. **3** (*coll.*) to seem rational, to accord with expectation; to be likely. **to figure on** (*coll.*) to plan to; to base one's plans or calculations on; to bargain on. **to figure out 1** to ascertain by computation, to work out; to estimate. **2** to understand, to fathom out. **figural** *a.* **figuration** *n.* **1** the act of giving a certain determinate form to. **2** form, shape, conformation, outline. **3** a figurative representation. **4** ornamentation. **5** (*Mus.*) florid or figured counterpoint. **figurative** (fig´ərətiv, -ūə-) *a.* **1** representing something by a figure or type, typical. **2** emblematic, symbolic, metaphorical, not literal. **3** full of figures of speech. **4** flowery, ornate. **5** pictorial in representation. **figuratively** *adv.* **figurativeness** *n.* **figured bass** *n.* (*Mus.*) a bass having the accompanying chords indicated by numbers above or below the notes; continuo. **figurehead** *n.* **1** a nominal leader or head without real authority. **2** the ornamental bust or full-length carving on the prow of a ship. **figureless** *a.* **figure of eight** *n.* a shape or movement resembling the Arabic

numeral eight (8). **figure of fun** *n.* a person considered as being ridiculous. **figure of speech** *n.* a figurative use of language. **figure skating** *n.* skating in prescribed patterns. **figure skater** *n.* **figurine** (fig´ərēn, -ūə-) *n.* a statuette in clay or metal.

Fijian (fējē´ən) *n.* **1** a native or inhabitant of the Fiji islands. **2** the language of the Fijians. ~*a.* of or relating to Fiji, the Fijians or their language.

filagree FILIGREE.

filament (fil´əmənt) *n.* **1** a slender, threadlike process, a fibre or fibril, such as those of which animal and vegetable tissues are composed. **2** the thread of carbon or metal in an incandescent electric lamp. **3** the heater wire of a thermionic valve. **4** (*Bot.*) that part of the stamen which supports the anther. **filamentary** (-men´-) *a.* **filamented** *a.* furnished with filaments. **filamentose** (-men´-), **filamentous** (-men´-) *a.*

filaria (fileə´riə) *n.* (*pl.* **filariae** (-riē)) any of the genus of threadlike parasitic nematode worms producing live embryos which find their way into the bloodstream of the human host. **filarial** *a.* **filariasis** (fileəriā´sis, filərī´əsis) *n.* (*pl.* **filariases** (-riā´sez, -rī´əsēz)) a tropical disease caused by filarial infection, esp. in the lymph vessels.

filbert (fil´bət) *n.* **1** the nut of the cultivated hazel, *Corylus maxima*. **2** the shrub bearing these nuts. **3** (*also* **filbert brush**) an oval brush used in oil painting.

filch (filch) *v.t.* to steal, to pilfer. **filcher** *n.*

file[1] (fīl) *n.* **1** a box or folder, a string or wire, or similar devices in or on which documents are kept in order, for preservation and convenience of reference. **2** the set of papers kept in this way. **3** (*Comput.*) an organized collection of data with a unique name by means of which it can be accessed. **4** a set of periodicals arranged in order of publication. **5** a row of people or things arranged one behind the other from front to back. **6** a collection of papers arranged in order of date or subject for ready reference, esp. in a court of law in connection with a case. **7** in chess, a line of squares extending from player to player. ~*v.t.* **1** to place in or on a file. **2** to arrange in order and endorse. **3** (*Law*) to place on the records of a court, to initiate (charges, a lawsuit) (*to file a petition for divorce*). **4** to send in (a story) to a newspaper. ~*v.i.* **1** (*esp. Mil.*) to walk in file or line. **2** to place in file. **3** to initiate a lawsuit. **on file** preserved and catalogued for reference. **to file away 1** to preserve or catalogue in a file. **2** to make a mental note of. **filer**[1] *n.* **file server** *n.* (*Comput.*) a device that manages and controls access to stored files. **filing cabinet** *n.* a cabinet with drawers for storing files.

file[2] (fīl) *n.* **1** a steel instrument with a ridged surface, used for cutting and smoothing metals, ivory, wood, fingernails etc. **2** anything used to polish or refine. ~*v.t.* **1** to smooth or polish with a file. **2** to polish, to elaborate. **to file away** to remove (roughness etc.) from a surface by means of a file. **filefish** *n.* (*pl. in general* **filefish**,

in particular **filefishes**) any fish of the family Balistidae with a toothed dorsal spine. **filer**² *n.*
filer¹ FILE¹.
filer² FILE².
filet (fil´ā, fil´it) *n.* **1** a kind of net or lace having a square mesh. **2** a fillet of meat. **filet mignon** (fē´lā mē´nyŏ) *n.* a small, very tender steak cut from the tail end of a fillet of beef.
filial (fil´iəl) *a.* **1** of or relating to a son or daughter. **2** befitting a child in relation to parents. **3** (*Biol.*) bearing the relation of a son or daughter. **filially** *adv.* **filiation** (filiā´shən) *n.* **1** the relation of a child to its parents. **2** descent, transmission (from). **3** genealogical relation. **4** (*Law*) affiliation. **5** the development of offshoots. **6** a branch of something, e.g. a society.
filibeg (fil´ibeg), **fillibeg**, **philabeg** (-əbeg) *n.* a kilt.
filibuster (fil´ibŭstə) *n.* **1** (*esp. N Am.*) a parliamentary obstructionist, a person who seeks to hinder legislation by prolonged speeches. **2** an instance of obstructing a political process in this way. *~v.i.* to act as a filibuster. *~v.t.* to obstruct (a political process) in this way. **filibusterism** *n.* **filibusterous** *a.*
filigree (fil´igrē), **filagree** (-əgrē), †**filigrane** (-grān) *n.* **1** ornamental work, executed in fine gold or silver wire, plaited, and formed into delicate openwork or tracery. **2** any ornamental tracery or openwork. **3** anything delicate and fancy, showy and fragile. **filigreed** *a.*
filings (fī´lingz) *n.pl.* the fine particles cut or rubbed off with a file.
Filipino (filipē´nō) *n.* (*pl.* **Filipinos**) a native or inhabitant of the Philippine Islands. *~a.* of or relating to the Philippines or the Filipinos.
fill (fil) *v.t.* **1** to put or pour into until all the space is occupied, to make full (with). **2** to occupy the whole capacity or space of, to pervade, to spread over or throughout. **3** to block up (a crack with putty, a hollow tooth with stopping etc.). **4** to appoint a person to discharge the duties of. **5** to hold. **6** to discharge the duties of. **7** to occupy (time). **8** to satisfy, to glut. **9** to fulfil, to meet. **10** to stock or store abundantly. **11** to cause to be filled or crowded. **12** to trim (a sail) to catch the wind. *~v.i.* **1** to become or grow full. **2** (of a sail) to be distended. *~n.* **1** as much as will satisfy (*eat one's fill*). **2** a full supply. **3** as much as will fill. **4** material used for filling. **to fill in 1** to insert, so as to fill a vacancy. **2** to complete (anything that is unfinished, such as an outline or a form). **3** (*coll.*) to provide with necessary or up-to-date information. **4** to occupy (time). **5** to act as a temporary substitute (for). **6** to fill (a hole) completely. **7** (*sl.*) to beat up. **to fill out 1** to become bigger or fatter, to become distended. **2** to enlarge. **3** (*esp. N Am.*) to complete (a form etc.). **to fill up 1** to fill or occupy completely. **2** to complete (a form etc.). **3** to fill the petrol tank of (a car etc.). **4** to become full. **5** to make up the deficiencies in, to supply what is wanting in. **6** to

supply, to discharge; to fulfil, to satisfy. **7** to stop up by filling. **to have one's fill of** to have rather too much of. **filler** *n.* **1** material used to fill cracks and holes in plaster, woodwork etc. **2** an item used to fill a space between more important items (as in a newspaper, a TV programme, a schedule etc.). **3** the filling opening of a petrol tank, gearbox, crankcase etc. **4** a person or thing that fills. **filler cap** *n.* a cap closing the opening of a petrol tank on a car etc. **filling** *a.* **1** occupying the whole space or capacity. **2** (esp. of food) satisfying. *~n.* **1** anything serving to fill up. **2** gold or other material used to fill up a cavity in a tooth. **3** a substance used to fill up holes, cavities or defects. **4** a food mixture filling sandwiches, cakes etc. **5** (*esp. N Am.*) the weft of a woven fabric. **filling station** *n.* a roadside establishment supplying petrol, oil etc. to motorists. **fill-up** *n.* **1** a thing that fills up something. **2** an act of filling up the petrol tank of a car etc.
fillet (fil´it) *n.* **1** a fleshy portion or slice of meat. **2** the fleshy part of an animal from near its loin used for meat (*fillet steak*). **3** portions of meat or fish removed from the bone and served either flat or rolled together and tied round. **4** a band of metal, a string or ribbon for binding the hair or worn round the head. **5** a ribbon, a narrow band or strip. **6** a bandage. **7** a raised rim or moulding. **8 a** a plain liner band on the back of a book. **b** a tool used to impress this. **9** (*pl.*) the loins of a horse. **10** (*Archit.*) **a** a narrow, flat band between mouldings. **b** the projection between the flutes of a column. **11** (*Her.*) a small horizontal division of a shield. *~v.t.* (*res.p.* **filleting**, *past, p.p.* **filleted**) **1** to remove bones from (fish or meat); to make into fillets. **2** to bind with a fillet or bandage. **3** to adorn with a fillet or fillets. **filleter** *n.*
fillip (fil´ip) *n.* **1** a stimulus, an incentive, a boost. **2** a sharp, sudden blow with the finger jerked from under the thumb. *~v.t.* (*pres.p.* **filliping**, *past, p.p.* **filliped**) **1** to stimulate, incite, encourage. **2** to strike with the nail of the finger by a sudden jerk from under the thumb. **3** to propel with such a blow. *~v.i.* to make a fillip.
fillis (fil´is) *n.* a kind of loosely-twisted string used to tie up plants etc.
fillister (fil´istə) *n.* **1** the rabbet on the outer edge of a sash bar. **2** a plane for making a rabbet.
filly (fil´i) *n.* (*pl.* **fillies**) **1** a female foal. **2** (*dated*) a lively girl or young woman.
film (film) *n.* **1** a series of connected moving images projected on a screen; a story represented in this way. **2** in photography, a thin coating of sensitized material spread over a plate for receiving a negative or positive image. **3** a thin plate or strip of celluloid or other material supporting such a coating. **4** (*pl.*) the cinema industry generally. **5** a thin skin, coating or layer. **6** a fine thread or filament. **7** a thin, slight covering or veil. **8** a dimness or opaqueness affecting the eyes. **9** a thin sheet of plastic or similar material used for packaging. *~v.t.* **1** to record on a photographic

film. **2** to make a film of (a book etc.). **3** to cover with a film. ~*v.i.* **1** to make a photographic film of a book etc. **2** to be reproduced as a film in a certain way (*The story films well*). **3** to become covered with or as with a film. **film clip** *n.* a short extract from a film. **filmgoer** *n.* a person who often goes to the cinema. **film-going** *n.* **filmic** *a.* of or relating to films or the cinema. **film-maker** *n.* a person who makes films, esp. a director or producer. **film-making** *n.* **filmography** (-mog´-) *n.* (*pl.* **filmographies**) a list of films by a particular artist or director or on a particular subject. **filmset** *v.t.* (*pres.p.* **filmsetting**, *past*, *p.p.* **filmset**) to expose (type characters) on to photographic film from which printing plates are made. **filmsetter** *n.* **filmsetting** *n.* **film star** *n.* a leading cinema actor or actress. **filmstrip** *n.* a sequence of images on a strip of photographic film, projected as stills. **filmy** *a.* (*comp.* **filmier**, *superl.* **filmiest**) **1** thin and gauzy, transparent. **2** covered with or as if with film; misted, blurred. **filmily** *adv.* **filminess** *n.*

filo (fē´lō), **phyllo** *n.* a kind of flaky pastry, usually layered in thin leaves.

Filofax® (fī´lōfaks) *n.* a small ring-binder with a leather or similar cover into which the owner can insert sheets at will to make up e.g. a diary, an address list etc., intended as a personal, portable compendium of information.

filoselle (filəsel´, fil´əsel) *n.* floss silk.

fils (fils) *n.* (*pl.* **fils**) a monetary unit of Bahrain, Iraq, Jordan, Kuwait and Yemen.

filter (fil´tə) *n.* **1** an apparatus for straining liquids and freeing them from impurities, usu. by means of layers of sand, charcoal or other material through which they are passed. **2** the layer of porous material through which the liquids are passed. **3** an apparatus for purifying air or another gas by a similar process. **4** a filter tip. **5** a device for altering the relative intensity of the wavelengths in a beam of light, X-rays etc. **6** a circuit for altering the relative intensity of different frequencies of an alternating current. **7 a** an auxiliary traffic light at a road junction in the form of a green arrow, which permits a stream of traffic to turn left or right while the main stream is held up. **b** an arrangement or lane that has such a traffic light. ~*v.t.* **1** to pass (liquid etc.) through a filter. **2** to strain, to purify by passing through a filter. ~*v.i.* **1** to pass through a filter. **2** to pass gradually. **3** to percolate. **to filter out** to remove by filtering. **filterable, filtrable** (fi´ltrəbəl) *a.* **1** that can be filtered. **2** (*Med.*) (of a virus) capable of passing through the pores of a fine filter. **filter-bed** *n.* a reservoir with a layer of sand or other filtering material at the bottom through which water is allowed to flow. **filterfeeding** *n.* (*Zool.*) a method of feeding used by many aquatic invertebrates in which minute particles of food are filtered from the surrounding water. **filter-feeder** *n.* **filter-paper** *n.* a porous paper used for filtering liquids. **filter tip** *n.* (a

cigarette with) an attached tip made of a porous substance to trap impurities. **filter-tipped** *a.*

filth (filth) *n.* **1** anything dirty or foul; foulness, corruption, pollution. **2** anything that defiles morally. **3** foul language, obscenity. **the filth** (*sl.*, *offensive*) the police. **filthy** *a.* (*comp.* **filthier**, *superl.* **filthiest**) **1** dirty, foul, unclean. **2** morally impure; obscene. **3** (of weather) cold, wet and windy. **4** disgraceful, unpleasant. **filthily** *adv.* **filthiness** *n.* **filthy lucre** *n.* **1** gain obtained by dishonest methods. **2** (*facet.*) money.

filtrable FILTER.

filtrate (fil´trāt) *n.* any liquid that has passed through a filter. ~*v.t.*, *v.i.* to filter. **filtration** (-trā´shən) *n.*

fin (fin) *n.* **1** the organ by which fish propel, balance and steer themselves, consisting of a membrane supported by rays (*the anal fin*). **2** a part or appendage resembling a fin, such as the flipper of a seal. **3** a flat part that projects from an aircraft, rocket or motor vehicle to give stability. **4** a paddle-shaped device worn for underwater swimming. **5** a projecting rib that dissipates heat on a radiator, engine cylinder etc. **6** a sharp projection on a ploughshare. ~*v.t.* (*pres.p.* **finning**, *past*, *p.p.* **finned**) to provide with fins. ~*v.i.* to swim under water. **finless** *a.* **finlike** *a.* **finned** *a.* **finny** *a.* (*comp.* **finnier**, *superl.* **finniest**) **1** having fins. **2** like a fin. **3** (*poet.*) abounding in fish. **fin whale, fin-back, finner, finner-whale** *n.* a rorqual, *Balaenoptera physalus*, with a dorsal fin.

finable FINE².

finagle (finā´gəl) *v.i.* (*coll.*) to behave dishonestly. ~*v.t.* (*coll.*) to get or obtain dishonestly. **finagler** *n.*

final (fī´nəl) *a.* **1** of, occurring at or relating to the end or conclusion; ultimate, last. **2** that cannot be changed or questioned; conclusive, decisive. **3** concerned with the end or purpose. ~*n.* **1** the last game or contest in a series that decides the overall winner of a sports or other competition. **2** the edition of a newspaper that is published at the very latest time in a day. **3** (*usu. pl.*) the last series of examinations in a degree course. **4** (*N Am.*) an examination at the end of each university class. **5** (*Mus.*) the tonic note of a mode. **final cause** *n.* (*Philos.*) the end or aim, esp. the ultimate object of the creation of the universe. **final clause** *n.* (*Gram.*) a clause expressing the object or purpose. **finalism** *n.* (*Philos.*) the doctrine that everything exists or was created by a determinate cause. **finalistic** (-lis´tik) *a.* **finalist** *n.* a competitor in the finals of examinations, sports etc. **finality** (-nal´-) *n.* (*pl.* **finalities**) **1** the state or quality of being final. **2** the belief that something is final. **3** the state of being finally and completely settled. **4** the end of everything, completeness. **5** a final and decisive act, event, statement etc. **finalize, finalise** *v.t.* **1** to put in final form. **2** to complete; to settle. **3** to give approval to the final arrangements for or details of. **finalization** (-zā´shən) *n.* **finally** *adv.*

finale (finah´li) n. **1** the last section or movement of a musical composition. **2** the last part, piece, scene or action in any performance or exhibition. **3** the last piece in a programme. **4** the close, end, conclusion.

finance (finans´, fī´-) n. **1** the science or system of management of revenue and expenditure, esp. public revenue and expenditure. **2** (pl.) monetary affairs, the income of a state, sovereign, firm or individual. **3** obtaining money, esp. to fund purchases etc. **4** money. ~v.t. to provide with capital. **finance company, finance house** n. a company that specializes in making loans, esp. for hire purchase. **financial** (-nan´shəl) a. **1** of or relating to finance or revenue. **2** (Austral., New Zeal., sl.) having money. **financially** adv. **financial year** n. the period for which public or official accounts are made up, e.g. 6 April to 5 April for income-tax purposes in Britain; the tax year. **financier** (-nan´siə) n. a person engaged in large-scale monetary dealings. ~v.i. (usu. derog.) to manage financial affairs.

finch (finch) n. any songbird of the family Fringillidae, including the bullfinch, chaffinch and canary, with a short conical beak that is used to crack seeds.

find (fīnd) v.t. (past, p.p. **found** (fownd)) **1** to chance on, to meet with, to come across. **2** to discover, learn or acquire by search, study or other effort. **3** to rediscover (something lost). **4** to ascertain by experience or experiment. **5** to perceive, to recognize. **6** to consider, to be of the opinion that. **7** to reach, to arrive at. **8** to succeed in obtaining. **9** to reach the feelings of, to come home to. **10** to gain or regain the use of. **11** to summon up. **12** to supply, to furnish, to provide. **13** to discover to be present. **14** to maintain, to support. **15** (Law) to decide, to determine; to declare by verdict. **16** to invent. ~n. **1** the discovery of anything valuable. **2** the thing so found. **3** the finding of a fox. **all found** (of a worker's wages) with food and lodging included free. **to find against** (Law) to reach a verdict on (a person), judging them to be guilty or to have lost the case. **to find favour (in the eyes of)** to be considered acceptable (by). **to find for** (Law) to reach a verdict on (a person), judging them to be innocent or to have won the case. **to find it in one's heart** to be willing out of kindness (to do something). **to find oneself 1** to be or perceive oneself to be (in a certain situation). **2** to be or feel as regards health. **3** to provide oneself with the necessaries of life. **4** to realize one's own capabilities or vocation. **to find one's way 1** to succeed in reaching a place. **2** to come, esp. by chance. **to find out 1** to discover. **2** to get information. **3** to unravel, to solve. **4** to invent, to devise. **5** to detect, to discover the dishonesty of. **findable** a. **finder** n. **1** a person who finds. **2** a discoverer, an inventor. **3** a small telescope fixed to the tube and parallel to the axis of a larger one, for finding objects to be examined by the larger telescope. **4** the viewfinder of a camera. **finding** n. **1** a discovery. **2** the act of returning a verdict; a verdict. **3** (usu. pl.) the result of an investigation. **4** (pl.) tools and materials which some workers have to furnish at their own expense. **find-spot** n. the place where an archaeological object is found.

fine¹ (fīn) a. **1** excellent in quality, form or appearance. **2** good, satisfactory, enjoyable, pleasant. **3** well, in good health. **4** free from clouds or rain; bright, clear and sunny. **5** refined, pure, free from dross or extraneous matter. **6** (of silver or gold) containing a certain proportion of pure metal. **7** (of feelings, taste, differences, distinctions etc.) delicate, subtle, nice, fastidious, dainty. **8** in small grains or particles. **9** thin, small, slender, tenuous. **10** (of print) small. **11** keen, sharp. **12** of delicate texture or material. **13** finished, consummate, accomplished, brilliant. **14** handsome, beautiful. **15** showy, smart, decorative, pretentious. **16** well expressed. **17** dignified, impressive. **18** complimentary; euphemistic. **19** (iron.) unpleasant or unsatisfactory (We're in a fine mess). **20** in cricket, at or through a position close to the line of the stumps. ~adv. **1** finely. **2** (coll.) very well. ~v.t. **1** to refine, purify, clear from impurities. **2** to make finer, to sharpen, to taper. **3** to make less coarse. ~v.i. **1** to become finer, purer, clarified. **2** to taper, to dwindle (away). ~n. **1** fine weather (in rain or fine). **2** (Mining etc.) very fine or powdery particles in mining etc. ~int. good! all right! well done! **not to put too fine a point on it** speaking frankly. **to cut/ run it fine** to reduce to the minimum; to take a risk by allowing little margin. **to fine up** (Austral., coll.) (of the weather) to become fine. **fine arts** n.pl. the arts, such as poetry, music, painting, sculpture and architecture, that appeal to the mind or sense of beauty. **fine chemicals** n.pl. chemicals that have a high purity and are produced in small quantities. **fine-draw** v.t. (past **fine-drew**, p.p. **fine-drawn**) to draw together the edges of and mend (a tear) so that no trace remains visible. **fine-drawn** a. **1** drawn out finely or thinly. **2** excessively subtle. **3** (of features) slim, delicate. **fine-grained** a. having a fine grain; made up of small particles. **finely** adv. **fineness** n. **fine print** n. text typeset in small print, esp. the details of a contract. **fine-spun** a. **1** delicate, flimsy. **2** drawn or spun out to minuteness. **3** over-refined or elaborate. **4** unpractical. **fine-tooth comb, fine-toothed comb** n. a comb with thin teeth set very close together. **to go over with a fine-tooth comb** to examine minutely, to investigate very thoroughly. **fine-tune** v.t. to make delicate adjustments to. **fine-tuning** n.

fine² (fīn) n. **1** a sum of money imposed as a penalty for an offence. **2** a fee paid by an incoming tenant to the landlord. ~v.t. **1** to impose a financial penalty upon. **2** to punish by fine. **finable** a. deserving or liable to a fine.

finery (fī´nəri) n. fine clothes, showy decorations.

fines herbes (fēnz eəb´) *n.pl.* a mixture of finely chopped herbs used as flavouring.

finesse (fines´) *n.* **1** elegance, refinement. **2** artifice, stratagem or artful manipulation; a subtle contrivance to gain an end. **3** skill, dexterity, adroitness, esp. in handling difficult situations. **4** in whist etc., an attempt to take a trick with a lower card, so as to retain a higher one for later tricks. *~v.i.* **1** to use artifice to gain an end. **2** to try to win a trick with a lower card than a card possibly in one's opponent's hand, while one has a higher card in one's own. *~v.t.* **1** to play (a card) in this manner. **2** to manipulate, to manage by means of trickery or stratagem.

finger (fing´gə) *n.* **1** any of the five digits or parts at the end of the hand; any of the four longer digits as distinguished from the thumb. **2** the part of a glove that covers a finger. **3** anything resembling or serving the purpose of a finger, an index, a gripper, a catch, a guide shaped like a finger. **4** the width of a finger, a measure of length or of the quantity of liquid in a glass. **5** (*sl.*) **a** an informer. **b** a pickpocket. **c** a police officer. *~v.t.* **1** to touch with or turn about in the fingers. **2** to perform with the fingers. **3** to play (a musical instrument) with the fingers. **4** to mark (a piece of music) so as to indicate which fingers should be used. **5** (*sl.*) to identify (to the police). *~v.i.* to use the fingers esp. skilfully in playing an instrument. **all fingers and thumbs** clumsy or awkward. **not to lift a finger** to do nothing, to stand idly by. **to burn one's fingers** to hurt or bring trouble on oneself by meddling. **to get/ pull one's finger out** (*sl.*) to start making an effort, to get cracking. **to give someone the finger** to make an obscene gesture to someone, as a sign of contempt, by raising the middle finger. **to have a finger in** to be concerned in or mixed up with. **to have a finger in every pie** to be involved in everything. **to lay/ put a finger (up)on** to touch, to interfere with in the slightest. **to point the finger (at) 1** to accuse, to blame. **2** to censure. **to put one's finger (up)on** to detect or point out precisely (the cause, meaning etc.). **to put the finger on** (*sl.*) to identify or inform against. **finger alphabet** *n.* a form of sign language using signs made on the fingers for talking to the deaf. **fingerboard** *n.* the board at the neck of a stringed instrument, against which the fingers are pressed on the strings. **finger bowl, finger glass** *n.* a bowl or glass in which to rinse the fingers during a meal. **finger-dry** *v.t.* (*3rd pers. sing. pres.* **finger-dries,** *pres.p.* **finger-drying,** *past, p.p.* **finger-dried**) to dry and shape (the hair) by moving one's fingers through it. **fingered** *a.* **fingerer** *n.* **fingering** *n.* **1** the act of touching with the fingers. **2** (*Mus.*) a method of using the fingers in playing upon a keyed, stringed or holed instrument. **3** marks upon a piece of music to guide the fingers in playing. **finger language** *n.* a language that uses the finger alphabet. **fingerless** *a.* **fingermark** *n.* a dirty mark left by fingers. **fingernail** *n.*

the nail at the end of each finger. **finger-paint** *n.* thickish paint for applying with the fingers, hand etc., used esp. by children. *~v.i.* to apply finger-paint. **fingerpick** *n.* a plectrum that is worn on a finger. **finger-plate** *n.* a plate on the side of a door, near the handle, to preserve the paint from fingermarks. **finger-post** *n.* a signpost where roads cross or divide, pointing out directions. **fingerprint** *n.* **1** an impression of the whorls of lines on fingers, used for purposes of identification. **2** an identifying characteristic. *~v.t.* to take the fingerprints of. **finger-stall** *n.* a cover for protecting a finger during dissections, or when injured or diseased. **fingertip** *n.* the end or tip of a finger. **to have at one's fingertips** to know thoroughly, to be well versed in.

finial (fin´iəl, fī´-) *n.* (*Archit.*) **1** a terminal ornament on top of the apex of a gable, pediment, roof, canopy etc. **2** the highest part of a pinnacle.

finical (fin´ikəl) *a.* finicky. **finicality** (-kal´-) *n.* **finically** *adv.* **finicalness** *n.* **finicky** *a.* **1** affecting great nicety, precision or delicacy. **2** overnice, fussy, fastidious. **3** particular about details or trifles. **finickiness** *n.* **finicking** *a.*

finis (fin´is, fē´-) *n.* **1** the end, finish, conclusion (printed at the end of a book). **2** the end of all things, death.

finish (fin´ish) *v.t.* **1** to bring to an end. **2** to complete. **3** to arrive at the end of. **4** to perfect. **5** to give the final touches to, to treat the surface of, to trim, to polish. **6** to consume, to get through. **7** to kill, to defeat, to render powerless. **8** to complete the social education of (a girl). *~v.i.* **1** to come to the end, to reach the end, to cease, to expire. **2** to end up. **3** to leave off. *~n.* **1** the act of finishing. **2** the termination, the final stage; the end of a race when the competitors reach the winning post; the killing of the fox at the end of a hunt. **3** the last touches, what gives the effect of perfect completeness; the final stage of any work. **4** the appearance, texture etc. of the surface of wood, cloth etc. **5** grace, elegance, polish, refinement. **to fight to the finish** to continue fighting until one of the parties is killed or completely defeated. **to finish off 1** to complete. **2** to consume or use up the remainder of. **3** to kill or destroy (someone or something already wounded or facing defeat or ruin). **to finish up 1** to consume or use up entirely. **2** to arrive, come to rest or end up. **to finish with** to stop one's association with. **finisher** *n.* **1** a person or thing that finishes. **2** a worker or a machine that performs the final operation in a process of manufacture. **3** a crushing blow that settles a contest. **finishing** *n., a.* **finishing school** *n.* a private school where girls are taught social graces in preparation for entry into fashionable society. **finishing touch** *n.* (*usu. pl.*) the last detail that is necessary to complete something perfect.

finite (fī´nīt) *a.* **1** having limits or bounds, not infinite. **2** (*Gram.*) applied to those parts of a verb which are limited by number and person,

such as the indicative, subjunctive, imperative.
finitely *adv.* **finiteness, finitude** (fin´itūd) *n.*

fink (fingk) *n.* (*esp. N Am., sl.*) **1** an informer. **2** a
strike-breaker. **3** a contemptible person. *~v.t.*
(*chiefly N Am., sl.*) to inform on (someone) to the
police. **to fink out** (*chiefly N Am., sl.*) to go back
on (something); let (someone) down.

Finn (fin) *n.* a native inhabitant of Finland.
Finnic *a.* **1** belonging to the Finnish group of
peoples. **2** denoting the group of languages including Finnish and Estonian. **Finnish** *a.* of or
relating to Finland, the Finns or their language.
~n. the language of the Finns. **Finno-Ugric**
(finōoo´grik, -ū´grik), **Finno-Ugrian** (-oo´griən,
-ū´griən) *n.* the family of languages including
Hungarian, Lapp, Finnish and Estonian. *~a.* of or
relating to these languages.

finnan haddock (fin´ən), **finnan** *n.* a kind of
smoke-dried haddock.

finned FIN.

☒ **finnish** common misspelling of FINISH.

fino (fē´nō) *n.* (*pl.* **finos**) a light-coloured very dry
sherry.

fiord FJORD.

fipple (fip´əl) *n.* an arrangement of a block and a
sharp edge, the sound-producing mechanism in
e.g. a recorder. **fipple flute** *n.* an end-blown flute
with a fipple.

fir (fœ) *n.* **1** any coniferous tree of the genus *Abies*
with single needlelike leaves. **2** the wood of
these. **fir cone** *n.* the cone-shaped fruit of the fir.
firry *a.*

fire (fīə) *n.* **1** the production of heat and light by
combustion. **2** combustion, flame, incandescence. **3** fuel in a state of combustion, as in a
furnace or grate. **4** a radiant gas or electric heater.
5 anything burning. **6** a conflagration. **7** a light,
glow or luminosity resembling fire. **8** intense
heat, fever. **9** the discharge of firearms. **10** ardent
emotion, fervour. **11** liveliness of imagination,
vigour of fancy, poetic inspiration. *~v.t.* **1** to discharge, to cause to explode; to propel from a gun.
2 to set on fire, to kindle, to ignite. **3** (*coll.*) to
dismiss, to discharge from employment. **4** to
deliver in rapid succession. **5** to supply (e.g. a
furnace) with fuel. **6** to inflame, to irritate. **7** to
stimulate, to enthuse, to excite, to animate, to inspire. **8** to bake (pottery etc.). **9** to cure (tea or
tobacco). *~v.i.* **1** to catch fire, to be kindled. **2** (of
an internal-combustion engine) to be in opera-
tion. **3** to discharge firearms. **4** to shoot (at) with
firearms. *~int.* a word of command for soldiers to
discharge their firearms. **on fire 1** burning, in
flames. **2** excited, ardent, eager. **to catch fire 1** to
ignite. **2** to become excited. **to fire away** to begin,
to proceed. **to fire off 1** to discharge (a firearm).
2 to shoot (a round, a shell). **3** to utter in rapid
succession. **to fire out** to expel forcibly, to chuck
out. **to fire up 1** to start up (an engine etc.). **2** to
fill with enthusiasm. **3** to kindle a fire. **4** to be
inflamed with passion, to be irritated. **to go
through fire and water** to expose oneself to all

dangers. **to play with fire** to expose oneself to
risk. **to set fire to** to set on fire. **to set on fire 1** to
kindle. **2** to excite, to inflame. **to set the world/
Thames on fire** to do something remarkable or
striking. **to take fire** to catch fire. **under fire 1** exposed to the enemy's firearms. **2** exposed to one's
opponent's questions or criticism. **fire alarm**
n. an automatic apparatus for communicating
warning of a fire. **fire and brimstone** *n.* the torments of hell. **firearm** *n.* (*usu. pl.*) a weapon that
projects a missile by the explosive force of gunpowder etc., esp. a rifle or pistol. **fireback** *n.*
1 the rear wall of a furnace or fireplace. **2** an iron
slab for this. **3** any pheasant of the genus
Lophura of SE Asia. **fireball** *n.* **1** a large meteor or
shooting star. **2** the luminous cloud of hot gases
at the centre of a nuclear explosion. **3** an enthusiastic or energetic person. **4** globular lightning.
5 (*Mil.*) †a ball or sack filled with combustible
materials, a grenade. **fire blight, fire blast** *n.* a
disease of plants, esp. hops and fruit trees, giving
leaves and blossoms a scorched appearance. **firebomb** *n.* an incendiary bomb. *~v.t.* to attack with
a firebomb. **firebox** *n.* the chamber in which the
fuel is burned in a locomotive etc. **firebrand** *n.*
1 a piece of wood kindled or on fire. **2** a person
who causes trouble or inflames passions. **3** an
arsonist. **firebreak** *n.* a strip of land in a forest
etc. kept clear of trees or vegetation to stop the
spread of fire. **firebrick** *n.* a brick capable of
withstanding fire, used for fireplaces, furnaces
and all kinds of work exposed to intense heat.
fire brigade *n.* a body of people organized by a
public authority etc. for the extinguishing of
fires. **firebug** *n.* (*coll.*) an arsonist. **fireclay** *n.* a
kind of clay consisting of nearly pure silicate of
alumina, capable of standing intense heat, used
in the manufacture of firebricks. **fire-control** *n.*
the system of controlling gunfire from one spot.
firecracker *n.* (*esp. N Am.*) an explosive firework. **firecrest** *n.* a European warbler, *Regulus
ignicapillus*, with a red and orange crest. **firedamp** *n.* the explosive mixture of hydrocarbons,
esp. methanes, that accumulates in coal mines.
fire department *n.* (*N Am.*) a fire brigade. **firedog**
n. an andiron. **fire door** *n.* **1** a fire-resistant door
that has the aim of preventing a fire from spreading through a building. **2** an emergency exit. **fire
drill** *n.* a practice of the routine to be observed in
case of fire. **fire-eater** *n.* **1** a juggler who pretends
to swallow fire. **2** a belligerent person, a person
who is fond of fighting. **fire engine** *n.* a vehicle
equipped with fire-fighting equipment. **fire
escape** *n.* an emergency staircase or apparatus for
enabling people to escape from the upper parts
of buildings that are on fire. **fire extinguisher** *n.*
a portable apparatus for extinguishing fires by
spraying them with water or chemicals. **firefight**
n. an exchange of fire between military units.
firefighter *n.* a person who is employed to extinguish fires. **fire-fighting** *n.* **1** the extinguishing
of fires. **2** (*fig.*) dealing with emergencies or

unplanned critical situations. ~*a.* of or relating to fire-fighting. **firefly** *n.* (*pl.* **fireflies**) any small luminous winged insect of the family Lampyridae. **fireguard** *n.* **1** a wire frame placed before an open fire as a safeguard against accidental fire or injury to children etc. **2** (*N Am.*) **a** a fire-watcher. **b** a firebreak. **fire hose** *n.* a hosepipe used for extinguishing fires. **fire-irons** *n.pl.* the implements for tending a domestic fire, poker, tongs and shovel. **fireless** *a.* **firelight** *n.* the light from a fire in a fireplace. **firelighter** *n.* a flammable substance used to help start a fire in a grate, barbecue etc. **firelock** *n.* an old-fashioned musket or other gun having a lock with a flint and steel, by means of which the priming was ignited. **fireman** *n.* (*pl.* **firemen**) **1** a person who is employed to extinguish fires. **2** a stoker. **fire-opal** *n.* GIRASOL. **fireplace** *n.* (*Archit.*) **1** a place for a fire in a room, esp. the grate and the hearth. **2** the structure surrounding this. **3** the space around this. **firepower** *n.* **1** the effective capability of weaponry, missiles etc. **2** influence or strength from the point of view of something, e.g. finances or intelligence. **fire practice** *n.* a fire drill. **fireproof** *a.* capable of resisting fire; incombustible. ~*v.t.* to make fireproof. **firer** *n.* **fire-raising** *n.* **1** the act of setting on fire. **2** incendiarism, arson. **fire-raiser** *n.* **fire-resistant** *a.* tending not to catch fire and resistant to the effects of fire to a required degree. **fire screen** *n.* **1** a fireguard. **2** a screen placed between a person and the fire to keep off the direct rays. **3** a decorative screen placed in front of a fireplace. **fireside** *n.* **1** the space around a fireplace, the hearth. **2** a person's home or home life. **fireside chat** *n.* an informal talk. **fire station** *n.* a building from which fire engines and fire-fighters operate. **fire-step** FIRING-STEP (under FIRE). **fire-stone** *n.* a stone capable of bearing a high degree of heat, used in furnaces etc. **firestorm** *n.* a huge fire, esp. one started by bombing, which causes and is kept ablaze by violent inrushing winds. **firethorn** *n.* pyracantha. **firetrap** *n.* a building without adequate means of exit in case of fire. **fire-walking** *n.* the ritual of walking bare-foot over white-hot ashes, stones etc. **fire-walker** *n.* **fire warden** *n.* (*N Am.*) a person employed to prevent or control fires. **fire-watcher** *n.* a person who watches for the outbreak of fires, esp. during an air raid. **fire-watching** *n.* **firewater** *n.* (*coll.*) strong alcohol. **fireweed** *n.* any of several plants that spring up on burnt-over areas of land, esp. the rosebay willowherb. **firewood** *n.* wood for burning used as fuel. **firework** *n.* **1** a preparation of various kinds of combustible chemicals and explosives for producing a brilliant display for public entertainment, at times of public rejoicing etc. **2** similar preparations used for illumination, signalling, incendiary purposes or in war. **3** (*pl.*) a display of bad temper. **4** (*pl.*) a spectacular display of wit or virtuosity. **firing** *n.* **1** the act of discharging firearms. **2** material for a fire; fuel. **3** the baking of ceramic products in a kiln.

4 the ignition of an explosive mixture in an internal-combustion cylinder. **5** the adding of fuel to a boiler furnace. **firing line** *n.* a line of troops engaging the enemy with firearms. **to be in the firing line** to be at the forefront of any activity and exposed to greatest risk. **firing party** *n.* a detachment detailed to fire over a grave at a military funeral, or to shoot a condemned man. **firing squad** *n.* **1** a detachment which carries out executions by shooting. **2** a firing party. **firing-step, fire-step** *n.* a raised ledge inside a trench on which soldiers stand to fire.

firkin (fœ'kin) *n.* **1** a measure of capacity; one quarter of a barrel or nine gallons (about 41 l). **2** a small wooden cask used for butter, tallow etc., of no fixed capacity.

firm[1] (fœm) *a.* **1** fixed, stable, steady. **2** difficult to move or disturb; not shaking. **3** solid, compact, unyielding. **4** securely established, unchanging, definite, immutable. **5** steadfast, determined, constant. **6** staunch, enduring, resolute. **7** (of prices etc.) constant, unwavering, not changing in level. ~*adv.* firmly. ~*v.t.* **1** to fix firmly. **2** to make firm, to consolidate. **3** to fix firmly in the soil. ~*v.i.* to become firm. **firmly** *adv.* **firmness** *n.* **firmware** *n.* (*Comput.*) a computer program or data stored in a read-only memory.

firm[2] (fœm) *n.* **1** a business partnership. **2** the partners in such a business. **3** a group of doctors and assistants.

firmament (fœ'məmənt) *n.* (*poet.*) the sky regarded as an arch or vault. **firmamental** (-men'-) *a.* of or relating to the firmament; celestial; of the upper regions.

firry FIR.

first (fœst) *a.* **1** foremost in order, time, place, rank, importance or excellence. **2** earliest in occurrence. **3** nearest, coming next (to something specified or implied). **4** chief, highest, noblest. **5** basic, fundamental. **6** most willing (*be the first to admit the mistake*). **7** (*Mus.*) of the highest vocal part or principal player of a specified instrument. ~*adv.* **1** before all others in order, time, place, rank, importance or excellence. **2** before some time, act or event (specified or implied). **3** sooner, rather, in preference. **4** for the first time. **5** first-class (when travelling). ~*n.* **1** the person or thing that comes first. **2** the first mentioned. **3** the beginning; the first day of a month. **4** an important event that has not happened before. **5** a place in the first class of an examination list; a candidate winning this. **6** the first place in a race; the winner of this. **7** (*pl.*) the best quality of a commodity such as flour. **8** the upper part in a duet, trio etc. **9** first gear. **at first 1** at the beginning. **2** originally. **first and last** essentially; generally. **first off** (*coll.*) firstly, first of all. **first or last** sooner or later. **first up** (*esp. Austral.*) first of all. **from first to last 1** throughout. **2** altogether. **from the first** from the outset. **in the first place** as the first reason or point. **not to know the first thing about** to be entirely ignorant of. **first aid** *n.*

assistance rendered to an injured person before a doctor comes. **first aider** *n.* **first blood** *n.* **1** in boxing etc., the initial issue of blood. **2** the first point, goal etc. scored in a competition. **first-born** *a.* born first, eldest. ~*n.* the first in order of birth. **First Cause** *n.* the Creator of all things. **first-class** *a.* **1** first-rate, of the highest quality or degree. **2** of, belonging to or travelling by first class. **3** (of postage) charged at a higher rate for quicker delivery. ~*adv.* by first class. **first class** *n.* **1** the group of the best people or things. **2** first-class post. **3** the first or best class of railway carriage or other accommodation. **4 a** the highest division in an examination list. **b** a place in this. **first cousin** *n.* the child of an uncle or aunt. **first-degree** *a.* (*Med.*) of burns that affect only the surface of the skin, making it painful and red. **first finger** *n.* the finger next to the thumb. **first floor** *n.* **1** the floor or storey of a building next above the ground floor. **2** (*N Am.*) the ground floor. **first-foot** *n.* (*Sc.*) the first caller at a house on New Year's Day. ~*v.t.* to enter as first-foot. ~*v.i.* to be a first-foot. **first-fruits** *n.pl.* **1** the fruit or produce first gathered in any season, esp. as offered to God. **2** the first effects or results. **3** the first profits of any office, paid to a superior. **first gear** *n.* the lowest forward gear on a motor vehicle. **first-hand** *a.* **1** obtained directly from the first or original source. **2** direct. ~*adv.* directly. **at first hand** as the original purchaser, owner, hearer etc. **first intention** *n.* (*Med.*) the natural healing of a wound. **First Lady** *n.* (*pl.* **First Ladies**) the wife of or official hostess for the US president or a state governor. **first lieutenant** *n.* (*N Am.*) an officer in the army or air force that is next below a captain. **first light** *n.* the time when light first appears in the morning. **firstly** *adv.* in the first place, to begin with. **first mate** *n.* the chief officer of a merchant vessel, next in rank to the captain. **first name** *n.* a Christian name or first forename. **first night** *n.* the first public performance of a play etc. **first-nighter** *n.* **first offender** *n.* a person not previously convicted. **first officer** *n.* the chief officer of a merchant vessel, next in rank to the captain. **first past the post** *a.* **1** of an electoral system in which each voter casts a single vote and only the candidate who polls the highest number of votes is returned. **2** winning a race by being the first to reach the post. **first person** *n.* (*Gram.*) the form of a pronoun, verb etc. indicating or including the speaker. **first post** *n.* (*Mil.*) the first of two bugle calls announcing the time of retiring for the night. **first-rate** *a.* of the first or highest class or quality; of the highest excellence. ~*adv.* excellently, very well. **first reading** *n.* the introduction and presentation of a Bill in a legislative assembly. **first refusal** *n.* the choice or option of refusing something before it is offered to others. **first school** *n.* a primary school for children aged 5 to 8 or 9. **first sergeant** *n.* (*N Am.*) the highest-ranking non-commissioned officer in a military subdivision. **first strike** *n.* an initial, unprovoked

or pre-emptive attack with nuclear missiles. **first thing** *adv.* early, as the first action of the day; before doing other things. **first water** *n.* **1** the purest quality (of diamonds etc.). **2** the finest quality. **of the first water** of the purest or finest quality.

firth (fœth), **frith** (frith) *n.* (*Sc.*) an estuary, a narrow inlet of the sea.

fiscal (fis′kəl) *a.* of or relating to the public revenue or exchequer or to taxes, financial. ~*n.* **1** a public functionary with legal or financial duties in various foreign countries. **2** a procurator fiscal. **3** †a treasurer. **fiscality** (fiskal′iti) *n.* (*pl.* **fiscalities**) **1** (*pl.*) fiscal matters or arrangements. **2** undue concern for these. **fiscally** *adv.* **fiscal year** *n.* the financial year.

fish[1] (fish) *n.* (*pl. in general* **fish,** *in particular* **fishes**) **1** a cold-blooded vertebrate animal with gills and fins, living wholly in water. **2** an invertebrate creature, e.g. a jellyfish, living wholly in water. **3** the flesh of fish used as food. **4** (*coll.*) a certain kind of person, e.g. an *odd fish.* **5** (*Naut., sl.*) a torpedo or submarine. ~*v.i.* **1** to try to catch fish, esp. with a line or net. **2** to search for something under water. **3** to grope or feel around for. **4** to seek to learn or obtain anything by indirect means or finesse. ~*v.t.* **1** to attempt to catch (fish) in. **2** to lay hold of and retrieve or drag up from under water or from inside something. **3** to search (water etc.) by sweeping, dragging etc. **the Fish** the zodiacal sign or constellation Pisces. **the Fishes** the Fish, Pisces. **to drink like a fish** to drink to excess. **to fish for compliments** to lead people to pay compliments. **fish ball, fish cake** *n.* a fried cake of chopped fish and mashed potatoes. **fishbowl** *n.* a usu. spherical glass bowl in which fish are kept as pets. **fish eagle** *n.* any eagle, esp. of the genus *Haliaetus,* that catches and feeds on fish. **fisher** *n.* **1** †a person who is employed in fishing; a fisherman. **2** an animal that catches fish, esp. the pekan, a N American marten, *Martes pennanti,* having valuable fur. **fisherfolk** *n.pl.* people whose livelihood is fishing. **fisherman** *n.* (*pl.* **fishermen**) **1** a person whose job is to catch fish. **2** an angler. **3** a boat or vessel used in catching fish. **fishery** *n.* (*pl.* **fisheries**) **1** the business of catching or rearing fish. **2** any place where fishing is carried on. **fish-eye** *a.* of a wide-angle photographic lens with a convex front which covers up to 180°. **fish farm** *n.* an installation for the rearing of fish, usu. in ponds or tanks. **fish finger** *n.* a small bar-shaped portion of fish coated in breadcrumbs or batter. **fish-glue** *n.* **1** a glue made of the entrails and skin of fish. **2** isinglass. **fish-hawk** *n.* the osprey. **fish-hook** *n.* **1** a barbed hook for catching fish. **2** (*Naut.*) the hook in tackle for raising an anchor. **fishing** *n.* **1** the business of catching fish. **2** the sport or hobby of angling. **fishing boat** *n.* a boat used in catching fish. **fishing-fly** *n.* (*pl.* **fishing-flies**) a fly, either natural or synthetic, used as a bait in fishing. **fishing line** *n.* a line with a baited hook attached for catching fish.

fishing rod *n.* a long, slender, tapering rod, usu. in sections jointed together, for angling. **fish kettle** *n.* a long oval pan for boiling fish. **fish-knife** *n.* (*pl.* **fish-knives**) a broad-bladed knife for eating or serving fish with. **fish ladder** *n.* a series of pools arranged in steps to enable fish swimming upstream to bypass dams etc. **fishlike** *a.* **fishmeal** *n.* ground dried fish that is used as animal feed or as a fertilizer. **fishmonger** *n.* a retail dealer in fish. **fishnet** *n.* open mesh fabric resembling netting. **fish out of water** *n.* anyone out of their element, in a strange or bewildering situation. **fish pond** *n.* **1** a pond in which fish are kept. **2** (*facet.*) the sea. **fishpot** *n.* a trap made of wicker that is used to catch eels, lobsters etc. **fish slice** *n.* **1** a broad-bladed utensil used by cooks for turning fish or other fried foods or taking them out of the pan etc. **2** a broad-bladed knife, usually of silver, for serving fish at table. **fishtail** *n.* anything that is like a fish's tail in shape or movement. ~*v.i.* to move the rear part of a motor vehicle from side to side. **fishtail burner** *n.* a gas burner producing a jet of flame that broadens. **fishwife** *n.* (*pl.* **fishwives**) **1** a coarse, foul-mouthed woman. **2** a woman that sells fish. **fishy** *a.* (*comp.* **fishier**, *superl.* **fishiest**) **1** like, consisting of, relating to or suggestive of fish. **2** (*facet. or poet.*) inhabited by or abounding in fish. **3** (*coll.*) of a doubtful character, questionable, dubious. **fishily** *adv.* **fishiness** *n.*

fish² (fish) *n.* **1** a flat piece of wood or iron etc. used to strengthen a beam etc. **2** (*Naut.*) a strip of wood for mending or strengthening a spar. **3** a counter used in various games. ~*v.t.* **1** (*Naut.*) to mend or strengthen a spar with a fish. **2** to join with a fish-plate. **fish-bolt** *n.* a bolt that is used for fastening fish-plates to rails. **fish-plate** *n.* **1** a plate of iron etc. used to fasten rails end to end. **2** a flat piece of metal having ends that resemble a fish's tail, used in positioning masonry.

fissile (fisˊīl) *a.* **1** capable of undergoing nuclear fission. **2** that may be cleft or split, esp. in the direction of the grain, as wood, or along natural planes of cleavage, as rock. **fissility** (-silˊ-) *n.*

fission (fishˊən) *n.* **1** the act or process of cleaving, splitting or breaking up into parts. **2** (*Physics*) nuclear fission. **3** (*Biol.*) a form of asexual reproduction in certain simple organisms, the individual cell dividing into new cells. **fissionable** *a.* **fission bomb** *n.* atom bomb.

fissure (fishˊə) *n.* **1** a cleft or opening made by the splitting or parting of any substance. **2** (*Anat.*) a slit or narrow opening, such as the deep narrow depression between the anterior and middle lobes of the brain on each side. ~*v.t.* to cleave, to split. ~*v.i.* to become split or cleft.

fist (fist) *n.* **1** the clenched hand, esp. in readiness to strike a blow. **2** handwriting. **3** (*coll.*) blow. ~*v.t.* **1** to strike or grip with the fist. **2** (*Naut.*) to handle (ropes, sails etc.). **to make a good fist** (*coll.*) to make a good attempt (at). **to make a poor fist** (*coll.*) to make a poor attempt (at). **fisted**

a. **fist fight** *n.* a fight using one's bare fists. **fistful** *n.* (*pl.* **fistfuls**). **fistic, fistical** *a.* (*facet.*) of or relating to pugilism. **fisticuffs** (-tikŭfs) *n.pl.* **1** a fight in which the fists are used. **2** a boxing match.

fistula (fisˊtūlə) *n.* (*pl.* **fistulas, fistulae** (-lē)) **1** (*Med.*) an abnormal or surgically made opening between a hollow organ and the skin surface or between two hollow organs. **2** (*Zool.*) a narrow pipelike passage, duct or spout, in insects, whales etc. **fistular, fistulate** (-lət) *a.* **fistulose, fistulous** *a.*

fit¹ (fit) *a.* (*comp.* **fitter**, *superl.* **fittest**) **1** adapted, suitable, appropriate. **2** qualified, competent. **3** ready, prepared, in a suitable condition (to do or for). **4** in good physical condition. **5** (*coll.*) as if, in such an extreme mood or condition as (*fit to drop*). **6** becoming, proper, right. ~*v.t.* **1** to be of the right size, measure and shape for. **2** to adapt to any shape, size or measure. **3** to make suitable, to accommodate, to find room for. **4** to insert or fix. **5** to qualify, to prepare. **6** to be adapted, suitable or proper for. **7** to supply, to furnish, to equip. **8** to try on (a garment). **9** to be in harmony with. **10** to correspond to exactly. ~*v.i.* **1** to be adjusted or adapted to the right shape, measure, form etc. **2** to be proper, suitable, convenient or becoming. ~*n.* **1** exact adjustment, as of a dress to the body. **2** the manner in which anything fits, the style in which a garment fits. ~*adv.* as if in such an extreme condition, appropriately. **to fit in 1** to find room or time for. **2** to be esp. socially accommodating or suitable. **to fit on** to try on (a garment). **to fit out** to equip, to furnish with things that are necessary or suitable. **to fit up 1** to furnish with the things suitable or necessary. **2** (*sl.*) to frame. **to think fit to** to decide to (do something). **fitly** *adv.* **fitment** *n.* **1** a piece of furniture. **2** (*usu. pl.*) fittings. **fitness** *n.* **fitted** *a.* **1** adapted, suitable (for). **2** shaped or built to fit exactly into or over a certain space, and usu. permanently attached. **3** furnished with fitted, matching cupboards etc., built-in. **fitter** *n.* **1** a person or thing that fits. **2** a person who supervises the cutting, fitting etc. of garments. **3** a person who puts together the several parts of machinery. **4** a person who fits or repairs certain kinds of apparatus (*a gas-fitter*). **fitting** *a.* suitable, appropriate, right, proper. ~*n.* **1** preliminary trying on of a garment. **2** the act of making fit. **3** a small, removable part or attachment (*electric light fitting*). **4** (*pl.*) apparatus, furniture used in equipping a house, shop etc. **fittingly** *adv.* **fittingness** *n.* **fitting shop** *n.* a workshop in which machinery is fitted up. **fit-up** *n.* (*sl.*) **1** a temporary stage. **2** a travelling theatre company.

fit² (fit) *n.* **1** a sudden attack of epilepsy or other disease characterized by unconsciousness or convulsions. **2** a violent seizure or paroxysm. **3** a sudden transitory attack of illness. **4** a spasm, a seizure, a short burst. **5** a transient state of impulsive action, a mood, a caprice. **by/ in fits and starts** intermittently. **in fits** laughing uncontrollably. **to give someone a fit** (*coll.*) to surprise or shock a person. **to have a fit** (*coll.*) to be very angry or shocked. **fitful** *a.* **1** spasmodic, capricious, wavering. **2** acting by fits and starts. **fitfully** *adv.* **fitfulness** *n.*

five (fīv) *n.* **1** the number or figure 5 or v. **2** the age of five. **3** a set of five things; a team of five players. **4** the fifth hour after midnight or midday. **5** a card, counter etc. with five pips. **6** (in cricket etc.) a hit scoring five runs. **7** a size measuring five. ~*a.* **1** five in number. **2** aged five. **to take five** (*coll.*) to take a few minutes' break. **five-a-side** *a.* of a football game with five players in each team. ~*n.* a five-a-side football game. **five-corner, five-corners** *n.* (*Austral.*) a shrub of the genus *Styphelia* that produces a five-sided fruit; this fruit. **five-eighth** *n.* (*Austral.*) a player in rugby football posted between the half-backs and three-quarter backs. **fivefold** *a.*, *adv.* **1** five times as much or as many. **2** consisting of five parts. **five o'clock shadow** *n.* beard growth which becomes visible on a man's shaven face late in the day. **fivepence, fivepence piece, fivepenny piece** *n.* a coin worth five pence. **fiver** *n.* (*coll.*) **1** a five-pound note. **2** (*N Am.*) a five-dollar bill. **fives** *n.* a game in which a ball is struck against a wall by the open hand or a small wooden bat. **five senses** *n.pl.* the senses of sight, hearing, taste, smell and touch. **five-star** *a.* of the highest class, e.g. of hotels.

fix (fiks) *v.t.* **1** to make firm or stable; to fasten, attach, secure firmly. **2** to settle, to determine, to decide (on). **3** to establish, to implant. **4** to attract and hold (a person's eyes, attention etc.). **5** to direct steadily. **6** to mend or repair. **7** to adjust, to identify a definite position for. **8** (*coll.*) to adjust, to arrange properly, to set to rights. **9** (*esp. N Am.*) to prepare (food or drink). **10** (*usu. pass., coll.*) to provide with (*How are you fixed for money?*). **11** to make rigid. **12** to absorb (e.g. nitrogen) by forming a non-gaseous mixture. **13** to stop a change in. **14** to calculate the rate of occurrence in. **15** to deprive of volatility, to make permanent or stable (e.g. colours, a photographic image etc.). **16** to solidify. **17** (*sl.*) to punish, to get even with. **18** (*sl.*) to influence illicitly. **19** (*sl.*) to inject (esp. oneself) with a drug. **20** (*euphem.*) to spay or castrate (an animal). ~*v.i.* **1** to become fixed or rigid. **2** to lose volatility. **3** to become congealed. **4** (*esp. N Am., coll.*) to be about to, to be set to. **5** to settle down permanently. ~*n.* **1** an awkward predicament, a dilemma. **2** the position of a ship, aircraft etc. as determined by radar etc. **3** the determination of such a position. **4** (*sl.*) an injection of heroin or a similar drug. **5** (*sl.*) an act or instance of bribery. **to fix on/ upon** to determine on; to choose, to select. **to fix up 1** (*coll.*) to arrange, to organize; to settle. **2** to accommodate. **3** to assemble or construct. **4** to provide. **fixable** *a.* **fixed** *a.* **1** fast, firm. **2** established, settled, unalterable. **fixed assets, fixed capital** *n.* business assets of a relatively permanent nature, such as buildings or plant etc. **fixed-doh** *a.* (*Mus.*) of a notation used in sight-singing in which C is called 'doh', regardless of the key, as distinct from *movable-doh*. **fixed focus** *n.* a camera focus that cannot be altered. **fixed idea** *n.* a rooted idea, one tending to become a monomania, an idée fixe. **fixed income** *n.* income gained from a pension or investments yielding unchanging interest. **fixedly** (fik'sid-) *adv.* **fixedness** (fik'sid-) *n.* **fixed odds** *n.pl.* odds at the start of a race that are already determined. **fixed oil, fixed alkali** *n.* any oil or alkali that is not easily volatilized. **fixed point** *n.* (*Physics*) a reproducible unchanging temperature. **fixed star** *n.* a star which apparently maintains the same relative position to other stars in the sky, as distinct from planets. **fixer** *n.* **1** a person or thing that fixes. **2** a substance used to make a photographic image permanent. **3** (*coll.*) a person adept at finding esp. crafty or illicit solutions to problems. **fixing** *n.* a way or means of fixing. **fixings** *n.pl.* (*N Am.*) **1** equipment. **2** trimmings.

fixate (fik'sāt) *v.t.* **1** to fix the gaze upon. **2** (*Psych.*) to arrest the psychological development of at an immature stage. **3** (*usu. pass.*) to cause to be obsessed. **fixation** (fiksā'shən) *n.* **1** the act of fixing. **2** the act of fixating. **3** an obsession. **4** the process of making non-volatile, as causing a gas to combine with a solid. **5** the process of ceasing to be fluid and becoming firm. **6** (*Psych.*) an emotional arrest of development of the personality. **fixative** *a.* serving or tending to fix. ~*n.* **1** a substance used to make colours permanent or prevent crayon or pastel drawings from becoming blurred. **2** a substance used for holding e.g. hair or false teeth in place.

fixity (fiks'iti) *n.* **1** coherence of parts. **2** fixedness, stability, permanence.

fixture (fiks'chə) *n.* **1** anything fixed in a permanent position. **2** (*coll.*) a person or thing regarded as permanently established and immovable. **3** a sporting event arranged for a particular date; the date arranged for this. **4** (*Law*) articles attached to a house or land and regarded as part of it.

fizz (fiz) *v.i.* **1** to make a hissing or spluttering sound. **2** (of a drink) to effervesce. ~*n.* **1** a hissing, spluttering sound. **2** effervescence. **3** (*coll.*) champagne. **4** (*coll.*) gingerbeer, lemonade etc. **fizzy** *a.* (*comp.* **fizzier**, *superl.* **fizziest**) effervescent. **fizzily** *adv.* **fizziness** *n.*

fizzle (fiz'əl) *v.i.* to fizz. ~*n.* **1** the sound or action of fizzing or fizzling. **2** (*sl.*) a feeble ending. **to fizzle out** to end in a feeble or disappointing way.

fjord (fyawd), **fiord** *n.* a long, narrow inlet of the sea, bounded by high cliffs, as in Norway.

fl. *abbr.* **1** floor. **2** floruit. **3** flourished. **4** fluid.

flab FLABBY.

flabbergast (flab'əgahst) *v.t.* to overwhelm with wonder and amazement; to astound, to stagger with surprise. **flabbergasted** *a.*

flabby (flab´i) *a.* (*comp.* **flabbier,** *superl.* **flabbiest**) **1** hanging loosely; limp, flaccid. **2** lacking in fibre or nerve; languid, feeble, wasteful. **flab** *n.* (*coll.*) loose, hanging, fat body tissue, a sign of being overweight or out of condition. **flabbily** *adv.* **flabbiness** *n.*

flaccid (flak´sid, flas´id) *a.* **1** lacking firmness or vigour. **2** limp, flabby, drooping. **3** relaxed, feeble. **flaccidity** (-sid´-) *n.* **flaccidly** *adv.* **flaccidness** *n.*

flack[1] (flak) *n.* (*N Am., sl.*) a publicity agent.

flack[2] FLAK.

flag[1] (flag) *n.* **1** a piece of cloth, usu. square or oblong, and plain or bearing a design, attached by one edge to a staff or rope by which it can be hoisted on a pole or mast, and displayed as a banner, ensign or signal. **2** a child's toy or device similar to a flag. **3** an indicator that may be raised to show that a taxi is for hire. **4** (*Naut.*) a flag carried by a flagship to show that the admiral is in command. ~*v.t.* (*pres.p.* **flagging,** *past, p.p.* **flagged**) **1** to put a flag over. **2** to decorate with flags. **3** to mark out with or as if with flags. **4** to signal or communicate by means of a flag or flags. **5** to mark (a passage in a book or document etc.) for someone's attention. **6** to code (computer data) so as to make it easily retrievable. **to flag down** to signal to (a vehicle) to stop. **to keep the flag flying** to continue to represent or stand up for e.g. a country or principles. **to lower the flag** to strike the flag. **to put the flag out** to celebrate a triumph, success etc. **to show the flag 1** to send an official representative or military unit to a place as a courtesy or a means of asserting a claim etc. **2** (*coll.*) to put in an appearance. **flag-boat** *n.* a boat serving as a mark in sailing matches. **flag-captain** *n.* the commanding officer of a flagship. **flag day** *n.* a day on which street collections are made for a specific charity, a small flag being worn as a token of having given money. **flagger** *n.* **flag-lieutenant** *n.* an admiral's aide-de-camp. **flag-list** *n.* the roll or register of flag-officers. **flagman** *n.* (*pl.* **flagmen**) a person who makes signals with or as if with flags. **flag of convenience** *n.* a foreign flag under which a vessel is registered to escape taxation etc. in its real country of origin. **flag-officer** *n.* **1** a commander of a squadron. **2** a commodore, admiral, vice admiral or rear admiral. **flag of truce** *n.* a white flag indicating that the enemy has some peaceful communication to make. **flagpole** *n.* FLAGSTAFF (under FLAG[1]). **flagship** *n.* **1** the ship which carries the admiral, and on which his flag is displayed. **2** the most important of a group, esp. something regarded as embodying e.g. a company's prestige. **flagstaff** *n.* (*pl.* **flagstaffs**) the pole or staff on which a flag is displayed. **flag-station** *n.* a railway station at which trains stop only when signalled. **flag-wagging** *n.* **1** (*Mil., sl.*) signalling or signalling-drill with hand-held flags. **2** flag-waving. **flag-waving** *n.* showy expression of patriotic feeling. **flag-waver** *n.*

flag[2] (flag) *v.i.* (*pres.p.* **flagging,** *past, p.p.* **flagged**) **1** to lose strength or vigour. **2** to become spiritless or dejected; to lose interest. **3** to hang loosely, to droop. **4** to become limp.

flag[3] (flag) *n.* **1** a broad flat stone used for paving. **2** (*pl.*) a pavement made of such stones. ~*v.t.* (*pres.p.* **flagging,** *past, p.p.* **flagged**) to pave with flags. **flagstone** *n.* a flag. **flagstoned** *a.*

flag[4] (flag) *n.* **1** any of various herbaceous plants with long bladelike leaves growing in moist places, chiefly belonging to the genus *Iris.* **2** the long bladelike leaf of such a plant. **flaggy** *a.*

flag[5] (flag), **flag-feather** (flag´fedhə) *n.* a quill-feather of a bird's wing.

flagellate[1] (flaj´əlāt) *v.t.* to whip, to beat, to scourge. **flagellant** *n.* **1** a person who scourges themselves or others as part of a religious discipline. **2** a person who thrashes themselves or others for sexual gratification. ~*a.* of or relating to flagellation; given to scourging. **flagellation** (-ā´shən) *n.* a scourging or flogging; thrashing of oneself or others, esp. as part of a religious discipline or for sexual gratification. **flagellator** *n.* **flagellatory** *a.*

flagellate[2] (flaj´ələt, -lāt) *a.* having whiplike outgrowths or flagella. ~*n.* a flagellate protozoan. **flagellar** *a.* **flagelliform** (-jel´ifawm) *a.* whiplike in shape or form. **flagellum** (-jel´əm) *n.* (*pl.* **flagella** (-ə)) **1** (*Biol.*) a minute whiplike appendage. **2** (*Bot.*) a trailing shoot; a runner.

flageolet[1] (flajəlet´, flaj´-) *n.* **1** a small wind instrument blown from a mouthpiece at the end, with two thumb holes and producing a shrill sound similar to but softer than that of the piccolo. **2** an organ stop producing a similar sound.

flageolet[2] (flajəlet´, -lā´) *n.* a kind of French bean.

flagon (flag´ən) *n.* **1** a large squat bottle usually holding about 2 pints (1.13 litres), in which wine is sold. **2** a large vessel with a handle, narrow mouth or spout and a lid, used for liquors. **3** a similar vessel used to hold the wine in the Eucharist.

flagrant (flā´grənt) *a.* glaring, notorious, outrageous, scandalous. **flagrancy** *n.* **flagrantly** *adv.*

flail (flāl) *n.* a wooden instrument consisting of a short heavy bar hinged to a longer staff or handle, used for threshing grain by hand. ~*v.t.* to strike with or as if with a flail. ~*v.i.* to thresh around.

flair (fleə) *n.* **1** a natural aptitude or gift; talent. **2** stylishness; panache.

flak (flak), **flack** *n.* **1** fire from anti-aircraft guns. **2** adverse criticism, dissent. **flak jacket** *n.* a reinforced jacket worn by soldiers, police etc. as protection against gunshot etc.

flake[1] (flāk) *n.* **1** a loosely cohering mass, a fleecy particle (as of snow). **2** a thin piece peeled off. **3** a thin scalelike fragment. **4** in archaeology, a fragment of hard stone chipped off and used as a tool or weapon. **5** a natural part of the edible tissue of some fish. **6** dogfish etc. considered as food. **7** (*N Am., sl.*) an eccentric person. ~*v.t.* **1** to form into flakes or loose particles. **2** to chip flakes off, to chip off in flakes. **3** to sprinkle with flakes, to fleck. ~*v.i.* to peel or scale off in flakes. **to flake out** (*coll.*) to collapse or fall asleep from exhaustion. **flaky** *a.* (*comp.* **flakier,** *superl.* **flakiest**) **1** consisting of flakes. **2** liable to flake. **3** (*N Am., sl.*) unstable, unreliable. **4** (*N Am., sl.*) eccentric; crazy. **flakily** *adv.* **flakiness** *n.* **flaky pastry** *n.* pastry in the form of very thin light layers.

flake² (flāk) *n.* **1** a rack for drying fish. **2** a frame for storing provisions, esp. oatcake.

flambé (flãˊbā, flomˊ-) *v.t.* (*3rd pers. sing. pres.* **flambés,** *pres.p.* **flambéing,** *past, p.p.* **flambéed**) to sprinkle with brandy etc. and ignite. ~*a.* served in ignited brandy.

flambeau (flamˊbō) *n.* (*pl.* **flambeaus, flambeaux**) **1** a torch, esp. one made of thick wicks covered with wax or pitch. **2** a large ornamental candlestick.

flamboyant (flamboiˊənt) *a.* **1** exuberant, extravagant, showy. **2** florid, highly decorated. **3** gorgeously coloured. **4** (*Archit.*) of or relating to the decorated French Gothic style, having flamelike tracery. **flamboyance** *n.* **flamboyancy** *n.* **flamboyantly** *adv.*

flame (flām) *n.* **1** a mass or stream of vapour or gas in a state of combustion. **2** a blaze; fire. **3** a glow, a bright light. **4** a blaze of colour. **5** a strong reddish-orange colour. **6** ardour, excitement, passion. **7** (*coll.*) a boyfriend or girlfriend, a sweetheart. ~*v.t.* **1** to apply a flame to. **2** to send (a signal) with or as if with flame. ~*v.i.* **1** to burn with a flame. **2** to send out flame, to blaze, to burst into flames. **3** (*fig.*) to break (out) or blaze (up) in violent passion. **4** to shine, to glow, to flash. **5** (*poet.*) to move like flame. **to flame out 1** (of a jet engine) to lose power because of the extinction of the flame. **2** (*esp. N Am.*) to fail, esp. in an obvious way. **to go up in flames** to be destroyed by a fierce fire. **flame gun** *n.* a device that projects a stream of burning liquid to destroy garden weeds. **flameless** *a.* **flamelike** *a.* **flameout** *n.* **1** the extinction of the flame in a jet engine, causing loss of power. **2** (*esp. N Am.*) an utter or obvious failure. **flameproof** *a.* treated so as to withstand heat or fire without being damaged. ~*v.t.* to make flameproof. **flame-thrower, flame-projector** *n.* a weapon that projects a stream of burning liquid. **flaming** *a.* **1** burning, blazing. **2** intensely hot. **3** intensely bright. **4** inflaming, exciting, passionate. **5** vehement, violent. **6** (*sl.*) used to express annoyance; bloody. **flamy** *a.*

flamenco (fləmengˊkō) *n.* (*pl.* **flamencos**) **1** a kind of music played on the guitar or sung by gypsies. **2** a dance performed to such music.

flamingo (fləmingˊgō) *n.* (*pl.* **flamingos, flamingoes**) a long-necked web-footed wading bird, with a small body and very long legs, its feathers rose or scarlet in colour, belonging to the family Phoenicopteridae.

flammable (flamˊəbəl) *a.* that can catch fire and burn easily. **flammability** (-bilˊiti) *n.*

Usage note See note under INFLAMMABLE.

flan (flan) *n.* **1** an open pastry or sponge base with fruit or savoury filling. **2** a plain metal disc from which a coin is made.

flanch (flahnch), **flaunch** (flawnch) *v.i.* to slope inwards towards the top of a chimney. ~*v.t.* to cause to flanch. **flanching** *n.*

flange (flanj) *n.* a projecting rib or rim affixed to a wheel, tool, pipe etc., for strength, as a guide, or for attachment to something else. ~*v.t.* to supply with a flange. **flangeless** *a.*

flank (flangk) *n.* **1** the fleshy or muscular part of the side between the hips and the ribs. **2** the cut of meat from the flank of an animal. **3** either side of a building, mountain etc. **4** (*Mil.*) the side of an army or body of troops. ~*v.t.* **1** to stand or be at the flank or side of, to border. **2** (*Mil.*) **a** to attack, turn or threaten the flank of. **b** to direct sweeping gunfire at. **c** to secure or guard the flank of. **in flank** at the side. **flanker** *n.* **1** a person or thing that flanks, or is posted, stationed or placed on the flanks. **2** (*Mil.*) a fortification projecting so as to command the flank of an assailing body. **3** (*also* **flank forward**) in rugby, a wing forward. **4** in American football, an offensive back who lines up outside an end. **5** (*sl.*) a swindle or trick.

flannel (flanˊəl) *n.* **1** a soft woollen fabric, with a light nap. **2** (*pl.*) garments made of this material, esp. trousers. **3** a piece of flannel used for washing the face etc. **4** (*coll.*) flattery, soft soap. **5** (*coll.*) evasive waffling, nonsense. ~*v.t.* (*pres.p.* **flannelling,** (*N Am.*) **flanneling,** *past, p.p.* **flannelled,** (*N Am.*) **flanneled**) **1** to wrap in or rub with flannel or a flannel. **2** (*coll.*) to flatter. ~*v.i.* **1** to speak in a flattering way. **2** (*coll.*) to waffle on evasively. **flannelboard, flannelgraph** *n.* a piece of flannel attached to a piece of paper or board, on which pictures etc. can be stuck when pressed on, used as a toy or in teaching as a visual aid. **flannelette** (flanəletˊ) *n.* a cotton fabric made to imitate flannel. **flannelled,** (*N Am.*) **flanneled** *a.* wearing flannel trousers. **flannelmouth** *n.* (*N Am., sl.*) a braggart.

flap (flap) *v.t.* (*pres.p.* **flapping,** *past, p.p.* **flapped**) **1** to move (wings, one's arms etc.) rapidly up and down or to and fro. **2** to beat, strike or drive away with anything broad and flexible. ~*v.i.* **1** to be moved loosely to and fro, to flutter, swing about or oscillate. **2** to move the wings rapidly up and down or to and fro. **3** (*coll.*) to be in a state of anxiety or confusion. **4** (*coll.*) (of the ears) to listen eagerly. **5** to hang down, as the brim of a hat. **6** to strike a loose blow or blows. ~*n.* **1** anything broad and flexible, hanging loosely, or attached by one side only, usu. used to cover an opening. **2** the hinged leaf of a table or shutter. **3** the motion or act of flapping. **4** a light stroke or blow with something broad and loose. **5** a movable control surface on the wing of an aircraft to increase lift on take-off and drag on landing. **6** (*coll.*) a state of anxiety or confusion. **7** an open mushroom-top. **flapdoodle** *n.* rubbish, nonsense. **flapjack** *n.* **1** a biscuit made of oat flakes and syrup. **2** (*esp. N Am.*) a kind of pancake. **flapper** *n.* **1** a person or thing that flaps. **2** a device that is flapped, e.g. to kill flies. **3** (*sl.*) in the 1920s, a flighty young woman. **flappy** *a.*

flare (flee) *v.i.* **1** to open or spread outwards at one end. **2** to blaze, to flame up or to glow, esp. with an unsteady light. **3** to burst into anger. ~*v.t.* **1** to provide with a flare or flares (as a skirt or trousers). **2** to cause to flare up. **3** to burn off (excess gas or oil). ~*n.* **1** a large unsteady light, a glare. **2** a sudden outburst. **3** (a device producing) a blaze of light used for illumination, signalling or to attract attention. **4** a widening or spreading out. **5** (a thing with) a flared shape. **6** (*pl.*) wide-bottomed trousers. **7** (*Astron.*) a powerful eruption of radiation from a star. **8** the curving motion of a ship's bows, pushing water outwards. **9** unwanted light on a film as a result of reflections within the optical instrument. **to flare up 1** to blaze out. **2** to become angry suddenly. **flare-path** *n.* an area that is illuminated so that aircraft can land and take off. **flare-up** *n.* **1** a sudden outbreak into flame. **2** an outburst of anger, violence, hostilities etc.

flash (flash) *v.i.* **1** to send out a quick, sudden or regular gleam. **2** to appear with a sudden and transient gleam. **3** to reflect light, to glitter, to burst forth, appear or occur suddenly. **4** to burst suddenly into flame, light or perception. **5** to rush swiftly, to dash, break or splash, as water or waves. **6** to signal using e.g. a torch or the headlights of a car. **7** (*sl.*) to expose oneself indecently. ~*v.t.* **1** to emit or send forth in flashes or like flashes. **2** to cause to gleam. **3** to signal (a message) to (someone) using light. **4** (*often with out or up, coll.*) to display or expose suddenly and briefly. **5** to display ostentatiously. **6** to convey or transmit instantaneously (as news by radio). **7** to send swiftly along. **8** to send a rush of water down (a river, weir etc.). ~*n.* **1** a sudden and transitory blaze or gleam of bright light. **2** the space of time taken by this, an instant. **3** a sudden occurrence or display of feeling or understanding. **4** a sudden outburst, as of anger, wit, merriment etc. **5** in photography, flashlight, an apparatus for producing flashlight. **6** a newsflash. **7** an area of bright colour. **8** the momentary photographic exposure of a view. **9** vulgar show, ostentation. **10** a body of water driven along with violence. **11** a device such as a sluice for producing this. **12** (*Mil.*) a label with regimental name etc. sewn on the uniform shoulder. ~*a.* **1** gaudy, vulgarly showy. **2** counterfeit, forged. **3** occurring or carried out very quickly. **4** of or relating to thieves or vagabonds. **to flash over** to make an electric circuit by discharging over or across an insulator. **flashback** *n.* an interruption in the

narrative of e.g. a film or novel to show past events. **flash-board** *n.* a hatch for releasing water from a mill-dam. **flashbulb** *n.* a (usu. disposable) bulb used to produce flashlight. **flash burn** *n.* a burn suffered as the result of momentary exposure to intense heat. **flashcard** *n.* a card with e.g. words or numbers printed on it for children to look at briefly as an aid to learning. **flash-cube** *n.* a plastic cube containing four flashbulbs. **flasher** *n.* **1** (*sl.*) a man who exposes himself indecently. **2** a person or thing that flashes. **3** a device that causes a light to flash. **4** a vehicle indicator light. **flash flood** *n.* a sudden flood, caused by heavy local rainfall. **flashgun** *n.* a device which holds and fires a flashbulb. **flashing** *n.* a watertight joint used in roofing with sheet metal, a strip of lead carrying water into a gutter. **flashing point** *n.* FLASHPOINT (under FLASH). **flash in the pan** *n.* an abortive attempt (from a flash produced by the hammer of a gun on a flint which then fails to explode the powder). **flash lamp** *n.* a portable flashing electric torch. **flashlight** *n.* **1** a brilliant light for taking (usu. indoor) photographs. **2** an electric battery torch. **3** a flashing light. **flash memory** *n.* (*Comput.*) a kind of device in which data is kept even when the power supply fails. **flash-over** *n.* an instance of electricity flashing over. **flashpoint** *n.* **1** the degree of temperature at which the vapour from oil or spirit ignites. **2** the point at which tension erupts into violence. **3** a place or region where such eruptions are likely to occur. **flash unit** *n.* a flashgun. **flashy** *a.* (*comp.* **flashier**, *superl.* **flashiest**) **1** gaudy, tawdry, cheap and showy. **2** showy but empty, brilliant but shallow. **flashily** *adv.* **flashiness** *n.*

flask (flahsk) *n.* **1** a small bottle or similar vessel. **2** a flat bottle, usu. mounted in metal, for carrying spirits in the pocket. **3** a vacuum flask. **4** a thin, long-necked bottle, encased in wicker, for wine or oil. **5** a large reinforced metal container for transporting nuclear waste.

flat[1] (flat) *a.* (*comp.* **flatter**, *superl.* **flattest**) **1** having a level and even surface. **2** horizontal, level. **3** even, smooth, having few or no elevations or depressions. **4** having little depth or thickness. **5** level with the ground, lying prone, prostrate. **6** plain, positive, absolute, downright. **7** monotonous, dull, uninteresting, insipid, pointless, spiritless. **8** having lost sparkle or freshness. **9** depressed, dejected. **10** (of a tyre) deflated. **11** (of a battery) having little or no charge. **12** (of shoes) not having a raised heel. **13** (of feet) having little or no arch. **14** uniform, without variety of contrast, tint or shading. **15** (*Mus.*) **a** below the true pitch. **b** (of a key) containing a flat or flats. **c** being a semitone lower than the specified note. **d** minor (applied to intervals). **16** (*Archit.*) having only a small rise, as some arches. **17 a** (of prices) low. **b** (of a market) inactive. **18** (of a rate or price) fixed or standard. **19** in painting, wanting relief or prominence of the figures. **20** (of paint) not glossy; matt. **21** of or relating to flat racing. ~*adv.* **1** flatly, positively. **2** prostrate, level with the ground. **3** (*Mus.*) below the true pitch. **4** exactly, completely (*in ten seconds flat*). ~*n.* **1** a flat, plain surface. **2** a level plain or low tract of land. **3** a plot of ground laid down level. **4** a shallow, a low tract flooded at high tide. **5** a flat part of anything; anything that is flat. **6** a broad, flat-bottomed boat. **7** the palm of the hand. **8** in a theatre, scenery on a wooden frame pushed on to the stage from the sides. **9** (*NAm.*) a broad-brimmed straw hat. **10 a** a note that is a semitone lower than the one from which it is named. **b** the sign indicating this lowering of pitch. **11** a punctured tyre. **12** (*sl.*) a foolish person. ~*v.i.* (*pres.p.* **flatting**, *past, p.p.* **flatted**) **1** to flatten, to make flat and smooth. **2** (*Mus., N Am.*) to lower in pitch. **flat as a pancake** very flat. **flat out** at full speed, with maximum effort; using all one's resources. **the flat 1** the flat-racing season. **2** flat racing. **to fall flat** to be unsuccessful. **flat cap** *n.* a cap with a low, flat crown. **flatcar** *n.* a railway wagon that does not have raised sides. **flatchested** *a.* (of a woman) with small breasts. **flatfish** *n.* (*pl. in general* **flatfish**, *in particular* **flatfishes**) any fish (such as the sole, plaice, turbot etc.) of the Pleuronectidae, distinguished by their laterally highly compressed body, absence of coloration on the under side, and the position of both eyes on the upper side. **flatfoot** *n.* (*pl.* **flatfoots, flatfeet**) (*derog.*) a police officer. **flat-footed** *a.* **1** with the feet not arched. **2** awkward. **3** ponderous, unimaginative. **4** (*coll.*) off guard. **5** (*coll.*) downright, resolute, determined. **flat-footedly** *adv.* **flat-footedness** *n.* **flat iron** *n.* an instrument for smoothing clothes etc. **flatly** *adv.* **flatness** *n.* **flat-pack** *n.* an item of furniture designed for self-assembly at home, packed in a flat box to be transported relatively easily. ~*v.t.* to pack flat in a box. **flat-packed** *a.* **flat race** *n.* a horse race on level ground without obstacles. **flat racing** *n.* **flat rate** *n.* an invariable rate. **flat spin** *n.* **1** a spin in which the aircraft is almost horizontal. **2** (*coll.*) a confused and frantic state. **flatten** *v.t.* **1** to make flat, to level. **2** to knock down or out. **3** to defeat resoundingly. **4** (*Mus.*) to depress or lower in pitch. **5** to make vapid, dull or insipid. **6** to deject, to dispirit. ~*v.i.* **1** to become flat or level. **2** to lose force or interest, to pall. **3** to depress the voice, to fall in pitch. **to flatten out** (of an aircraft) to change from the gliding approach to the position to alight, when approaching to land. **flattener** *n.* **flattie** *n.* (*pl.* **flatties**) (*coll.*) **1** a shoe with a flat heel. **2** a flat boat. **3** a police officer. **flattish** *a.* **flat-top** *n.* **1** (*N Am., sl.*) an aircraft carrier. **2** (*sl.*) a man's short flat style of haircut. **flatworm** *n.* any worm of the phylum Platyhelminthes, including tapeworms and planarians, with a flattened body.

flat² (flat) *n.* a set of rooms on one floor forming a separate residence. ~*v.i.* (*pres.p.* **flatting**, *past, p.p.* **flatted**) (*Austral.*) to share a house (with).

flatlet *n.* **flatmate** *n.* a person with whom one shares a flat.

flatter (flat´ə) *v.t.* **1** to praise falsely or unduly. **2** to persuade (oneself concerning one's achievement or ability). **3** to display to advantage. **4** to represent too favourably. **5** to court, cajole or gratify by compliment, adulation or acclaim. **6** to raise false hopes in. ~*v.i.* to use flattery. **flatterer** *n.* **flattering** *a.* **flatteringly** *adv.* **flattery** *n.* (*pl.* **flatteries**) **1** the act or practice of flattering. **2** false or uncritical praise; adulation, cajolery.

flatulent (flach´ələnt) *a.* **1** affected with or troubled by wind or gases generated in the alimentary canal. **2** generating or likely to generate wind in the stomach. **3** pretentious, turgid. **4** inflated, empty, vain. **flatulence, flatulency** *n.* **flatulently** *adv.* **flatus** (flā´təs) *n.* wind in the stomach or bowels; flatulence.

flaunt (flawnt) *v.i.* **1** to make an ostentatious or gaudy show. **2** to wave or flutter in the wind. ~*v.t.* **1** to display ostentatiously or impudently; to parade, to show off. **2** to wave or flutter in the wind. ~*n.* **1** the act of flaunting; impudent parade. **2** a boasting or vaunting. **flaunter** *n.* **flaunty** *a.* flaunting, ostentatious.

Usage note The meanings of the verbs *flaunt* and *flout* should not be confused: *flaunt* means to display ostentatiously, and *flout* to disregard or defy. Rules are flouted, not flaunted.

flautist (flaw´tist) *n.* a player of the flute.

flavour (flā´və), (*N Am.*) **flavor** *n.* **1** that quality in any substance which affects the taste, or the taste and smell. **2** a characteristic or distinctive quality. **3** a faint mixture of a usu. unpleasant quality. **4** (*esp. N Am.*) flavouring. ~*v.t.* to impart a flavour to, to season. **flavorous, flavoursome** *a.* **flavourful** *a.* **flavouring** *n.* an (artificial) substance that gives flavour to food and drink. **flavourless** *a.* **flavour of the month, flavour of the week** *n.* (*often facet.*) a person or thing much in favour at a particular time.

flaw¹ (flaw) *n.* **1** a defect, an imperfection. **2** a crack, a slight fissure. **3** (*Law*) a defect in a document, evidence etc., rendering it invalid. ~*v.t.* **1** to break or crack. **2** to mar, to spoil. **3** to render invalid. ~*v.i.* to crack. **flawless** *a.* **flawlessly** *adv.* **flawlessness** *n.*

flaw² (flaw) *n.* **1** a sudden puff or gust. **2** a squall, a violent but brief storm.

flax (flaks) *n.* **1** a plant of the genus *Linum*, esp. *L. usitatissimum*, the common flax, the fibre of which is made into yarn, and woven into linen cloth. **2** the fibrous part of the plant prepared for manufacture. **3** any of various kinds of similar plants. **flaxen** *a.* **1** made of flax. **2** like flax in softness, silkiness or colour. **3** light yellow or straw-coloured. **flaxseed** *n.* linseed.

flay (flā) *v.t.* **1** to strip the skin from. **2** to peel, to pare. **3** to strip, to plunder.

flea (flē) *n.* **1** a small wingless blood-sucking insect belonging to the order Siphonaptera, parasitic on mammals and birds and noted for its leaping powers. **2** a flea beetle. **3** WATER FLEA (under WATER). **fleabag** *n*. (*sl.*) **1** a dirty or neglected person. **2** a shabby or dirty thing. **fleabane** *n*. any of various plants of the genus *Pulicaria* or *Inula*, supposed to drive away fleas. **flea beetle**, (*N Am.*) **flea-bug** *n*. a small leaping beetle of the family Halticidae, very destructive to hops and other plants. **flea bite** *n*. **1** the bite of a flea. **2** the red spot caused by the bite. **3** the smallest trifle, a trifling inconvenience. **flea-bitten** *a*. **1** bitten by a flea. **2** full of fleas. **3** dirty, shabby. **flea circus** *n*. a show of performing fleas. **flea collar** *n*. a collar for pets with a substance used for killing insects. **flea market** *n*. an open-air market selling usu. second-hand goods. **fleapit** *n*. (*coll., facet.*) a shabby cinema or theatre. **fleawort** (-wœt) *n*. a plant of the genus *Tephroseris*, supposed to drive away fleas.

fleck (flek) *n*. **1** a dot, stain or patch of colour or light. **2** a spot, a freckle, a stain, a speck. ~*v.t.* to spot, to streak, to dapple, to variegate with spots or flecks.

flection FLEXION (under FLEXIBLE).

fled FLEE.

fledge (flej) *v.t.* **1** to provide with feathers or plumage. **2** to rear (a young bird) until it can fly. **3** to feather (an arrow). ~*v.i.* to acquire feathers or plumage for flight. **fledged** *a*. **1** feathered. **2** able to fly. **3** mature, developed. **fledgeless** *a*. **fledgling, fledgeling** *n*. **1** a young bird just fledged. **2** a raw and inexperienced person. ~*a*. newly fledged.

flee (flē) *v.i.* (*past, p.p.* **fled** (fled)) **1** to run away, as from danger to a place of safety. **2** to vanish, to disappear. **3** to pass away. ~*v.t.* **1** to run away from. **2** to shun.

fleece (flēs) *n*. **1** the woolly covering of a sheep or similar animal. **2** the quantity of wool shorn from a sheep at one time. **3** anything resembling a fleece, such as a woolly head of hair, a fleecy cloud or fall of snow. **4** soft warm material with a pile, used as a hanging. ~*v.t.* **1** to rob, to plunder, to swindle, to overcharge. **2** to shear the wool from. **3** to cover with anything fleecy. **fleeceable** *a*. **fleeced** *a*. **fleece-picker** *n*. (*Austral., New Zeal.*) FLEECY². **fleecer** *n*.

fleecy¹ (flē´si) *a*. (*comp.* **fleecier**, *superl.* **fleeciest**) **1** woolly, wool-bearing. **2** resembling a fleece in appearance or qualities. **3** covered with fleece. **fleecily** *adv.* **fleeciness** *n*.

fleecy² (flē´si), **fleecie** *n*. (*pl.* **fleecies**) (*Austral., New Zeal.*) a person whose job is to pick up fleeces after shearing.

fleer (fliə) *v.i.* **1** to grin or laugh in contempt or scorn. **2** to gibe, to sneer. ~*v.t.* to laugh or sneer at. ~*n*. mockery or scorn expressed by words or looks. **fleeringly** *adv.*

fleet¹ (flēt) *n*. **1** a number of ships or smaller vessels with a common object, esp. a body of warships under one command. **2** the entire body of warships belonging to one government, a navy.

3 a collection of aircraft or road vehicles used for a common purpose and usu. under one ownership. **Fleet Admiral** *n*. (*N Am.*) Admiral of the Fleet. **Fleet Air Arm** *n*. the aviation branch of the Royal Navy.

fleet² (flēt) *a*. (*poet.*) swift of pace, nimble, rapid, speedy. ~*v.i.* **1** to move swiftly. **2** to pass swiftly. **3** (*fig.*) to glide away, to vanish. **fleet-footed** *a*. able to run with great speed. **fleeting** *a*. passing quickly, transient. **fleetingly** *adv.* **fleetly** *adv.* **fleetness** *n*.

Fleming (flem´ing) *n*. **1** a native of Flanders. **2** a member of a Flemish-speaking people of N and W Belgium. **Flemish** *a*. of or relating to Flanders. ~*n*. **1** the Flemish language. **2** (*as pl.*) Flemings. **Flemish bond** *n*. in brickwork, a bond that has alternating stretchers and headers in each course.

flesh (flesh) *n*. **1** the soft part of an animal body, esp. the muscular tissue, between the bones and the skin. **2** excess weight; fat. **3** †animal tissue used as food, as distinct from vegetable, fish, and sometimes from poultry. **4** the soft pulpy part of a fruit or plant. **5** the body, as distinguished from the soul, esp. when considered to be sinful. **6** flesh colour. ~*v.t.* **1** to embody in flesh. **2** to encourage by giving flesh to (hawks, dogs etc.). **3** to initiate. **4** to exercise or use for the first time. **5** to harden, to inure or accustom to any practice or habit. **in the flesh** in person; in bodily form. **to flesh out** to elaborate, to give more substance or detail to. **to lose flesh** to lose plumpness, to become thin. **to make someone's flesh creep** to arouse (a physical sense of) horror in someone. **to put on flesh** to grow fatter. **flesh and blood** *n*. **1** the body. **2** human nature, esp. as alive, not imaginary, or as liable to infirmities. **3** one's children or near relatives. **flesh colour** *n*. the colour of flesh; yellowish pink. **flesh-coloured** *a*. **fleshfly** *n*. (*pl.* **flesh-flies**) a carnivorous insect of the genus *Sarcophaga*, esp. *S. carnaria*, the larvae of which feed on decaying flesh. **fleshings** *n.pl.* light flesh-coloured tights to represent the skin, worn by actors, dancers etc. **fleshless** *a*. **fleshly** *a*. (*comp.* **fleshlier**, *superl.* **fleshliest**) **1** of or relating to the flesh, corporeal, sensual, lascivious. **2** human, as distinct from spiritual. **3** mortal, material; not divine or supernatural. **4** worldly. **fleshliness** *n*. **fleshpots** *n.pl.* **1** sumptuous living (Exod. xvi.3). **2** nightclubs etc. offering lavish or sexually titillating entertainment. **flesh side** *n*. the side of the hide next to the flesh. **flesh tints** *n.pl.* the colours which best represent the human skin. **flesh wound** *n*. a wound not reaching the bone or any vital organ. **fleshy** *a*. (*comp.* **fleshier**, *superl.* **fleshiest**) **1** like flesh. **2** fat, plump, corpulent. **3** (of flesh) without bone. **4** (of fruit etc.) pulpy. **fleshiness** *n*.

fleur-de-lis (flœdəlē´), **fleur-de-lys** *n*. (*pl.* **fleurs-de-lis** (flœdəlē´), **fleurs-de-lys**) **1** the iris flower. **2** (*Her.*) **a** a lily with three petals. **b** (*Hist.*) the royal arms of France.

flew FLY².

flex¹ (fleks) v.t. **1** to bend or cause to bend. **2** (*Geol.*) to subject (strata) to fracture or distortion. **3** in archaeology, to position (a dead body) with legs raised under chin. ~v.i. **1** to be bent. **2** (of a muscle) to contract. **to flex one's muscles 1** to contract the muscles, esp. of the arm, in order to display them or as a preliminary to a trial of strength. **2** (*fig.*) to put on a show of power or strength.

flex² (fleks) n. **1** flexible insulated wire. **2** a piece of this, used to connect an electrical appliance to the mains.

flexible (flek´sibəl) a. **1** pliant, easily bent. **2** tractable, easily persuaded, manageable. **3** variable, adaptable, versatile. **flexibility** (-bil´iti) n. **flexibly** adv. **flexion** (-shən), **flection** n. **1** the act or process of bending. **2** a condition of being bent. **3** a bending movement of a joint or limb. **4** a bend, a curve. **5** (*Math.*) flexure of a line. **flexional** a. **flexionless** a. **flexor, flexor muscle** n. a muscle that causes a limb or part to bend. **flexuose** (-ūōs) a. **1** winding, serpentine. **2** crooked, zigzag. **flexuosity** (-os´-) n. **flexuous** a. full of bends or turns, winding. **flexuously** adv. **flexure** (-shə) n. **1** the act, process or manner of bending. **2** the state of being bent. **3** a bend, a curve, a turn, curvature. **4** (*Math.*) curving of a line, surface or solid. **5** (*Geol.*) the bending or folding of strata under pressure. **flexural** a.

flexitime (flek´sitīm), (*N Am.*) **flextime** (fleks´-tīm) n. **1** a system of working which allows workers some freedom to choose the times when they arrive for and leave work, usu. so long as they are present during a stipulated period (core time). **2** the hours worked in this way.

flibbertigibbet (flib´ətijibit) n. **1** a chatterer. **2** a flighty, thoughtless person.

flick (flik) n. **1** a smart, light blow or flip, as with a whip. **2** the short sudden release of a bent finger or the wrist. **3** a short sudden movement. **4** a light sharp sound. **5** (*coll.*) a film, a movie. ~v.t. **1** to strike or move with a flick. **2** to jerk or flip (dust etc.) away. **3** to give a flick with. ~v.i. to make a flicking movement. **the flicks** (*coll.*) the cinema. **to flick through** to read through quickly or inattentively, to turn over (pages etc.) quickly. **flick knife** n. a knife with a blade that springs out when a button in the handle is pressed.

flicker¹ (flik´ə) v.i. **1** to shine unsteadily, to burn unsteadily, to waver. **2** to move quickly to and fro, to quiver, to flutter. **3** (of hope etc.) to appear faintly and briefly. ~n. **1** the act of flickering. **2** an unsteady or dying light. **3** a brief and faint feeling etc. **to flicker out** to die away after an unsteady brightness. **flickeringly** adv.

flicker² (flik´ə) n. any N American woodpecker of the genus *Colaptes*.

flier FLYER¹.

flight¹ (flīt) n. **1** the act, manner or power of flying through the air. **2** an air or space journey, esp. a scheduled trip made by a commercial airline. **3** the basic tactical unit of an airforce. **4** swift movement or passage, such as the motion of a projectile or the passing of time. **5** a trajectory. **6** a soaring, a sally, an excursion, a sustained effort (*a flight of fancy*). **7** the distance to which anything can fly. **8** a number of birds or insects moving together. **9** a migration. **10** a volley (of arrows, spears etc.). **11** a series of steps mounting in one direction. **12** a line of hurdles on a course. **13** in angling, a device for causing the bait to spin rapidly. **14** the pursuit of game by a hawk. **15** a feather or vane attached to the tail of an arrow or dart. ~v.t. **1** to give a high, slow trajectory to (a ball etc.). **2** to put a feather or vane on (an arrow or dart). **in the first/ top flight** taking a leading position; outstanding. **to take/ wing one's flight** to fly. **flight attendant** n. a steward or stewardess who looks after passengers on an aircraft. **flight bag** n. a small zipped shoulder bag carried by travellers in an aeroplane. **flight control** n. a system that controls the movement of an aeroplane. **flight deck** n. **1** an aircraft carrier's deck on which aircraft take off and land. **2** the compartment at the front of a large aircraft housing the controls, navigation equipment etc. **flight feather** n. any of the large feathers that cover the wings of a bird and provide lift and control in flying. **flightless** a. unable to fly. **flight lieutenant** n. a commissioned rank in the RAF next below squadron leader. **flight path** n. the planned course of an aircraft or spacecraft. **flight plan** n. the proposed route and schedule of an aircraft flight. **flight recorder** n. an instrument which records details of an aircraft's performance in flight, used to provide evidence in the event of an accident. **flight sergeant** n. a noncommissioned rank in the RAF, ranking above chief technician. **flight-test** v.t. to test (an aircraft, spacecraft etc.) during a flight. **flighty** a. (*comp.* **flightier**, *superl.* **flightiest**) **1** capricious, volatile, frivolous, fickle. **2** mentally unstable; crazy. **flightily** adv. **flightiness** n.

flight² (flīt) n. **1** the act of fleeing or running away. **2** a hasty departure, retreat or evasion. **to put to flight** to cause to run away or disappear. **to take (to) flight** to run away, to flee.

flimflam (flim´flam) n. **1** nonsense, rubbish. **2** humbug, deception. **3** a piece of deception. ~v.t. (*pres.p.* **flimflamming**, *past, p.p.* **flimflammed**) to deceive, to swindle. **flimflammer** n. **flimflammery** n. (*pl.* **flimflammeries**).

flimsy (flim´zi) a. (*comp.* **flimsier**, *superl.* **flimsiest**) **1** without strength or solidity; insubstantial. **2** easily torn or damaged. **3** (of an excuse etc.) weak, ineffective, unconvincing. **4** thin, slight, frail. **5** frivolous, trivial, superficial, paltry. ~n. (*pl.* **flimsies**) **1** very thin paper. **2** a copy made on this. **flimsily** adv. **flimsiness** n.

flinch (flinch) v.i. **1** to shrink from (an undertaking, suffering etc.). **2** to wince, to give way, to fail. ~n. an act or instance of flinching. **flincher** n. **flinchingly** adv.

fling (fling) *v.t.* (*past, p.p.* **flung** (flŭng)) **1** to cast or throw with sudden force; to hurl. **2** to move (part of one's body) forcefully. **3** to send or put suddenly and unceremoniously. **4** to utter hastily or violently. **5** to throw to the ground, to defeat. ~*v.i.* **1** to rush violently, to flounce. **2** (of horses) to kick, struggle, plunge (out). ~*n.* **1** a cast or throw from the hand. **2** a period of unrestrained behaviour or enjoyment. **3** a lively Scottish, esp. Highland dance. **to fling away** to discard, to reject. **to fling oneself into 1** to rush into. **2** to undertake (an activity) enthusiastically. **to have a fling at 1** to make a passing attempt at. **2** to gibe or scoff at. **to have one's fling 1** to give oneself up to unrestrained behaviour or enjoyment. **2** to have one's own way. **flinger** *n.*

flint (flint) *n.* **1** a variety of quartz, usu. grey, smoke-brown or brownish-black and encrusted with white, easily chipped into a sharp cutting edge. **2** a nodule of flint, a flint pebble. **3** a piece of flint shaped for use in a gun, a tinderbox, lighter or a primitive tool or weapon. **4** a piece of iron alloy used to make a spark in a cigarette lighter. **5** anything extremely hard. **6** extreme hardness. **flint corn** *n.* a kind of maize with hard translucent grains. **flint glass** *n.* a very pure and lustrous kind of glass, orig. made with calcined flints. **flintlock** *n.* **1** a lock for an obsolete kind of gun in which the cock holds a piece of flint, and comes down upon the steel cap of the pan containing the priming, which is ignited by the spark so caused. **2** a gun having such a lock. **flinty** *a.* (*comp.* **flintier,** *superl.* **flintiest**). **flintiness** *n.*

flip (flip) *v.t.* (*pres.p.* **flipping,** *past, p.p.* **flipped**) **1** to flick, jerk or toss (e.g. a coin) quickly to make it spin in the air. **2** to strike lightly. **3** to move (about or away) with a light blow. **4** to turn over. ~*v.i.* **1** to strike lightly, to flap or flick (at). **2** to make a flicking noise. **3** to move with a sudden jerky motion. **4** (*sl.*) to lose control of oneself, to become very angry. **5** (*sl.*) to become wildly enthusiastic. ~*n.* **1** a quick, light blow. **2** an act of flipping, a somersault. **3** a short trip in an aeroplane. **4** a short quick tour. **5** a mixed alcoholic drink containing beaten egg. **6** a drink of heated beer and spirit. ~*a.* (*coll.*) **1** flippant. **2** impertinent. **to flip one's lid** (*coll.*) to lose self-control. **to flip over** to (cause to) turn over. **to flip through** to read through quickly or carelessly. **flip chart** *n.* a large blank pad placed on a stand and bound at the top so that one page can be turned over to show the next page in the sequence of information. **flip-flop** *n.* **1** a kind of sandal consisting simply of a sole and a strap held between the toes. **2** (*N Am.*) a backward handspring. **3** (*esp. N Am.*) a complete reversal (of opinion etc.). **4** an electronic device or circuit capable of assuming either of two stable states. ~*v.i.* (*pres.p.* **flip-flopping,** *past, p.p.* **flip-flopped**) to move about with a flapping noise. **flipper** *n.* **1** the broad fin of a fish. **2** the flat broad limb

or paddle of a turtle, penguin etc. **3** a paddle-shaped shoe worn for esp. underwater swimming. **flipping** *a., adv.* (*sl., euphem.*) used to express annoyance; bloody. **flipside** *n.* **1** the less important side of a popular single record on which material additional to the title number is recorded. **2** the opposite or less familiar side of a person or thing.

flippant (flip´ənt) *a.* **1** trifling, lacking in seriousness. **2** impertinent, disrespectful. **flippancy** *n.* **flippantly** *adv.*

flirt (flœt) *v.i.* **1** to make sexual advances for amusement or self-gratification. **2** to move with jerks, short flights or springs. ~*v.t.* **1** to jerk (away). **2** to wave or jerk (a fan etc.) to and fro rapidly. ~*n.* **1** a person who flirts a lot. **2** a flirting motion, a jerk, a fling. **to flirt with 1** to treat lightly, to risk carelessly. **2** to entertain thoughts of superficially, to toy with. **flirtation** (-tā´shən) *n.* **flirtatious** (-tā´-) *a.* **flirtatiously** *adv.* **flirtatiousness** *n.* **flirtingly** *adv.* **flirty** *a.* (*comp.* **flirtier,** *superl.* **flirtiest**).

flit (flit) *v.i.* (*pres.p.* **flitting,** *past, p.p.* **flitted**) **1** to move, to pass from place to place. **2** to fly about lightly and rapidly. **3** to depart. **4** to leave one's house, usu. secretly to escape one's creditors or responsibilities. **5** (*Sc., North.*) to move from one place of abode to another. ~*n.* **1** the act of flitting. **2** a stealthy departure. **flitter** *n.*

flitch (flich) *n.* **1** a side of pork salted and cured. **2** a board or plank from a tree trunk, usu. from the outside. **3** (*also* **flitch-plate**) a strengthening plate in a beam. **flitch beam** *n.* a beam made up of an iron plate between two pieces of wood.

flitter (flit´ə) *v.i.* **1** to flit about. **2** to flutter.

flixweed (fliks´wēd) *n.* a plant *Descurainia sophia*, formerly supposed to cure dysentery.

float (flōt) *v.i.* **1** to be supported on the surface of or in a fluid. **2** to swim or get afloat on water. **3** to hover in the air. **4** to move or glide without effort. **5** to move in a fluid or gas, to drift. **6** to move aimlessly, e.g. in the mind. **7** (of a currency) to be free to find its own level on foreign exchange markets. **8** to circulate. ~*v.t.* **1** to support on the surface of or in a fluid. **2** (of water) to bear up or bear along. **3** to convey, to carry on or as if on water. **4** to set afloat, to launch. **5** to flood with a liquid. **6** to waft through the air. **7** to put into circulation. **8** to make financially current. **9** to form into a limited company with a view to making a public issue of shares. **10** to offer for sale on the Stock Exchange. **11** to cause (a currency) to float. **12** to suggest (an idea etc.) for consideration. ~*n.* **1** anything buoyed up on the surface of a liquid. **2** a·buoyant device designed to keep a person afloat. **3** the cork or quill on a fishing line. **4** a cork on a fishing net. **5** the bladder supporting fish, animals etc. in the water. **6** a floating mechanism in a ballcock etc. regulating a supply-tap. **7** a timber raft, a floating wharf. **8** the gear of an aircraft for alighting on water. **9** a small delivery vehicle with a flat platform for goods. **10** (a vehicle carrying) a tableau or exhibit in a parade. **11** (*usu. pl.*) the footlights of a theatre. **12** a kind of trowel for smoothing the plastering on walls. **13** a drink with a lump of ice cream floating in it. **14** a small sum of money used to provide change at the start of business. **15** a small sum of money for expenditure on minor items. **16** an act of floating. **floatable** *a.* **floatability** *n.* **floatage, flotage** *n.* **1** anything found floating, flotsam. **2** the right to appropriate flotsam. **3** floating power, buoyancy. **4** ships and other vessels on a river. **5** the part of a ship above the waterline. **floatation** FLOTATION. **float-board** *n.* one of the boards of an undershot waterwheel or a paddle wheel. **floater** *n.* **1** a person or thing that floats. **2** a person who frequently changes jobs. **3** (*sl.*) a mistake. **floating** *a.* **1** resting on the surface of a fluid. **2** unattached, free, disconnected. **3** circulating, not fixed or invested. **4** fluctuating, variable, of uncertain amount. **floating anchor** *n.* a sea anchor. **floating bridge** *n.* **1** a bridge of rafts and timber floating on the surface of the water. **2** a ferry that uses chains. **floating debt** *n.* the portion of the national debt repayable at a stated time or on demand. **floating dock** *n.* a large iron or wooden structure into which a vessel can be floated, the internal water then being pumped out to result in a floating dry dock. **floating kidney** *n.* **1** a condition in which the kidney is unusually mobile. **2** such a kidney. **floating light** *n.* **1** a lightship. **2** a lifebuoy to which a light is attached, to attract attention to a person in the water, and to direct the boat's crew coming to the rescue. **floatingly** *adv.* **floating point** *n.* (*Comput.*) a decimal point that does not hold a fixed position in a mathematical rotation. **floating rib** *n.* either of the lowest two pairs of ribs, which are not attached to the breastbone. **floating voter** *n.* a person of no fixed party-political allegiance. **float-stone** *n.* a spongy variety of opal light enough to float on the surface of water. **floaty** *a.* (*comp.* **floatier**, *superl.* **floatiest**) (of material or clothes) light and airy.

floatel (flōtel´), **flotel** *n.* a boat or platform providing accommodation for offshore oil-rig workers.

floccus (flok´əs) *n.* (*pl.* **flocci** (flok´si)) **1** a tuft of woolly hair. **2** the down of unfledged birds. **flocculate** (-ūlāt) *v.t., v.i.* to form into a flocculent mass. **flocculation** (-lā´shən) *n.* **floccule** (-ūl) *n.* **1** a loose tuft. **2** a small woolly or tuftlike portion. **flocculent** *a.* **1** in small flakes, woolly, tufted. **2** (*Chem.*) (of precipitates) loosely aggregated in cloudlike masses. **flocculence** *n.* **flocculus** (-ləs) *n.* (*pl.* **flocculi** (-lī)) **1** a floccule. **2** (*Anat.*) a lobe on the undersurface of the human cerebellum. **3** (*Astron.*) a cloudy marking on the surface of the sun.

flock[1] (flok) *n.* **1** a company or collection of animals, esp. sheep, goats or birds. **2** a crowd, a large body. **3** a congregation, considered in relation to their minister. **4** a group of children or

pupils. *~v.i.* **1** to come together in a flock, to congregate, to assemble. **2** to move or go in crowds. *~v.t.* **1** to crowd. **2** to press by crowding.

flock[2] (flok) *n.* **1** a lock or tuft of wool, cotton, hair etc. **2** (*usu. pl.*) wool-dust used in coating certain portions of the patterns in some wallpapers. **3** fibrous material, made by tearing up woollen rags by machinery, used to stuff upholstery, mattresses etc. **flock paper**, **flock wallpaper** *n.* wallpaper, to which flock is attached with size. **flocky** *a.*

floe (flō) *n.* a large sheet of floating ice.

flog (flog) *v.t.* (*pres.p.* **flogging**, *past, p.p.* **flogged**) **1** to beat with a whip or stick as punishment. **2** to urge or drive by beating. **3** to repeat or labour to the point of tedium. **4** (*sl.*) to sell. *~v.i.* to make progress by forceful or painful means. **to flog a dead horse 1** to try to revive interest in something stale. **2** to pursue a hopeless task. **to flog to death** (*coll.*) to talk about to the point of tedium. **flogger, flogster** *n.*

flood (flŭd) *n.* **1** an abundant flow of water. **2** a body of water rising and overflowing land not usually covered with water, an inundation. **3** the inflow of the tide. **4** a downpour, a torrent. **5** (*poet.*) a river, the sea. **6** an overflowing abundance. **7** (*coll.*) a floodlight. *~v.t.* **1** to overflow, to inundate, to deluge. **2** to supply copiously (with). **3** to irrigate. **4** to supply too much petrol to (the carburettor). *~v.i.* **1** (of the sea) to be at its highest. **2** to rise and overflow. **3** to arrive in large numbers (*enquiries flooded in*). **4** to have uterine haemorrhage. **the Flood** the flood recorded in Genesis. **to flood out** to drive from one's home etc. because of a flood. **flood and field** *n.* (*poet.*) sea and land. **floodgate** *n.* **1** a gate in a waterway arranged to open when the water attains a certain height, and so allow it to escape freely to prevent floods, a sluice. **2** the lower gate of a lock. **3** a restraint against an esp. emotional outburst. **floodlight** *n.* **1** a powerful beam of artificial light used esp. in the theatre, in sports stadiums or to illuminate buildings. **2** a lamp producing such light. *~v.t.* (*pres.p.* **floodlighting**, *past, p.p.* **floodlit**) to illuminate with floodlight. **flood tide** *n.* the rising tide. **flood water** *n.* water left by flooding.

floor (flaw) *n.* **1** the bottom surface of a room, on which people walk and which supports the furniture. **2** the boards or other material of which this is made. **3** the bottom of the sea, a cave etc. **4** a storey in a building. **5** the part of the house assigned to members of a legislative assembly. **6** the trading hall of a stock exchange. **7** the (area occupied by) people attending a meeting or debate as the audience. **8** the right to address a meeting, assembly etc. **9** any level area corresponding to the floor of a room. **10** the lowest limit of prices, wages etc. *~v.t.* **1** to furnish with a floor. **2** to be or serve as a floor (to). **3** to knock down. **4** (*coll.*) to baffle or confound, to put to silence (as in argument). **5** (*coll.*) to get the better of, to defeat. **to cross the floor** (of an MP etc.) to change party-political allegiance. **to have the floor** to be given the right to address a meeting, assembly etc. **to take the floor 1** to rise to speak, to take part in a debate. **2** to get up to dance. **to wipe the floor with someone** (*coll.*) to defeat someone completely. **floorboard** *n.* any of the planks making up a floor. **floorcloth** *n.* a piece of soft fabric used for washing floors. **floor exercises** *n.pl.* gymnastic exercises that do not require equipment. **flooring** *n.* **1** material for floors. **2** a floor, a platform. **floor lamp** *n.* (*NAm.*) a lamp, usu. portable, that stands on the floor. **floor-length** *a.* (of garments) that reach to the floor. **floorless** *a.* **floor manager** *n.* **1** the stage manager of a television programme. **2** the manager of a floor in a large store. **floor polish** *n.* a manufactured substance used for polishing floors. **floor show** *n.* a performance on the floor of a restaurant, nightclub etc. **floorwalker** *n.* (*NAm.*) a shopwalker.

floozie (floo´zi), **floozy** *n.* (*pl.* **floozies**) (*derog.*) a woman who is attractive in a common sort of way and thought to be free with her company and favours.

flop (flop) *v.i.* (*pres.p.* **flopping**, *past, p.p.* **flopped**) **1** to tumble about or fall loosely and heavily. **2** to sway about heavily, to flap. **3** to make a dull sound as of a soft body flapping. **4** to move or walk about (in an ungainly manner). **5** to move or sit suddenly. **6** (*coll.*) to fail dismally. **7** (*sl.*) to go to bed. ~*n.* **1** the act or motion of flopping. **2** the noise of a soft outspread body falling suddenly to the ground. **3** (*coll.*) a complete failure. **4** (*esp. NAm., sl.*) a place to sleep. ~*adv.* with a flop. **flophouse** *n.* (*esp. NAm., sl.*) a doss-house, a cheap lodging house. **floppy** *a.* (*comp.* **floppier**, *superl.* **floppiest**) soft and flexible, limp. ~*n.* (*pl.* **floppies**) (*Comput.*) a floppy disk. **floppily** *adv.* **floppiness** *n.* **floppy disk** *n.* (*Comput.*) a flexible magnetic disk for data storage.

-flop (flop) *comb. form* (*Comput.*) floating-point operations per second, as in *megaflop*.

floptical (flop´tikəl) *a.* (*Comput.*) of, relating to or designed for a kind of floppy disk drive that uses a laser to set the read-write head.

flor. *abbr.* floruit.

flora (flaw´rə) *n.* (*pl.* **floras, florae** (-rē)) **1** the whole vegetation of a country, district or geological period. **2** a book dealing with the vegetation of a country or district. **floral** *a.* **1** of or relating to flowers. **2** of or relating to floras. **3** consisting of, or decorated with, flowers. **florally** *adv.*

Florentine (flo´rəntīn) *a.* **1** of or relating to Florence. **2** (**florentine** (-tēn)) served or prepared with spinach. ~*n.* **1** a native or inhabitant of Florence. **2** a biscuit containing nuts and dried fruit, coated on one side with chocolate.

florescence (flawres´əns) *n.* **1** the flowering of a plant. **2** the season when a plant flowers.

floret (flor´it, flaw´-) *n.* (*Bot.*) **1** a small flower.

2 a small flower forming part of a composite one. **3** any one of the flowering stems on the head of a cauliflower etc.

floriate (flaw´riāt) *v.t.* to adorn with floral ornaments or designs.

floribunda (floribŭn´də, flaw-) *n.* a plant, esp. a rose, whose flowers grow in dense clusters.

floriculture (flo´rikŭlchə, flaw´-) *n.* the cultivation of flowers or flowering plants. **floricultural** (-kŭl´-) *a.* **floriculturist** (-kŭl´-) *n.*

florid (flor´id) *a.* **1** flushed with red, ruddy. **2** flowery, highly embellished, elaborately ornate. **3** covered with or abounding in flowers; showy. **floridity** (-rid´iti) *n.* **floridly** *adv.* **floridness** *n.*

floriferous (florif´ərəs, flaw-) *a.* bearing many flowers.

florin (flor´in) *n.* **1** a former British coin, orig. silver, worth the equivalent of 10p, a two-shilling piece. **2** a foreign gold or silver coin, of various values according to country and period. **3** an English gold coin of Edward III, worth 6s. 8d. (33p).

florist (flor´ist) *n.* **1** a person who sells flowers. **2** a person skilled in growing flowers; a cultivator of flowers. **floristic** (-ris´-) *a.* of or relating to flowers or their distribution. **floristically** *adv.* **floristics** *n.* **floristry** *n.*

floruit (flor´uit, flaw´-) *v.i.* (he or she) was alive and actively working; flourished, used to express the period during which a person, e.g. a painter or writer, was most active (in the absence of exact dates of birth and death). ~*n.* the period during which a person was alive and actively working.

floss (flos) *n.* **1** the exterior rough silk envelope of a silkworm's cocoon. **2** dental floss. **3** untwisted silk thread used in embroidery. ~*v.t., v.i.* to use dental floss (on). **floss silk** *n.* untwisted filaments of the finest silk, used in embroidery etc. **flossy** *a.* (*comp.* **flossier**, *superl.* **flossiest**) **1** of, resembling or relating to floss. **2** (*coll.*) showily stylish; fancy.

flotation (flōtā´shən), **floatation** *n.* **1** the floating of a company on the Stock Exchange. **2** the separation of the particulars of a material, e.g. powdered ore, by their relative capacities to float.

flotilla (flətil´ə) *n.* **1** a small fleet. **2** a fleet of small vessels.

flotsam (flot´səm) *n.* goods lost in shipwreck and found floating. **flotsam and jetsam** *n.* **1** wreckage or any property found floating or washed ashore. **2** odds and ends. **3** vagrants etc.

flounce[1] (flowns) *v.i.* **1** to move abruptly or violently. **2** to exaggerate one's movements as a means of calling attention to oneself or one's impatience etc. ~*n.* a flouncing movement.

flounce[2] (flowns) *n.* a gathered or pleated strip of cloth sewed to a petticoat, dress etc., with the lower border hanging loose. ~*v.t.* to deck or trim with flounces.

flounder[1] (flown´də) *n.* **1** a flatfish, *Pleuronectes flesus*, resembling the plaice, but with paler

spots. **2** any small flatfish of the family Pleuronectidae or Bothidae.

flounder[2] (flown´də) *v.i.* **1** to struggle or stumble
about violently, as when stuck in mud. **2** to
struggle along with difficulty. **3** to blunder along,
to do things badly. ~*n.* the motion or act of
floundering. **flounderer** *n.*

flour (flow´ə) *n.* **1** the finer part of meal, esp. of
wheatmeal. **2** fine soft powder of any substance.
~*v.t.* **1** to sprinkle flour upon. **2** (*N.Am.*) to grind
into flour. **floury** *a.* (*comp.* **flourier,** *superl.*
flouriest) **1** covered with flour. **2** like flour.
flouriness *n.*

flourish (flŭr´ish) *v.i.* **1** to grow in a strong and
healthy way. **2** to thrive, to prosper, to increase
in wealth, honour or happiness. **3** to be in good
health. **4** to be in a state of complete development. **5** to be alive or at work (at or about a certain date). ~*v.t.* **1** to brandish, fling or wave
about. **2** to flaunt, to show ostentatiously. ~*n.* **1** a
brandishing or waving of a weapon or other
thing. **2** a figure formed by strokes or lines fancifully drawn. **3** rhetorical display, a florid expression. **4** (*Mus.*) **a** a passage played for display. **b** a
fanfare of trumpets etc. **c** an improvised prelude
or other addition. **flourisher** *n.*

flout (flowt) *v.t.* **1** to mock, to insult. **2** to treat
with contempt, to disregard, to defy. ~*v.i.* to behave with contempt or mockery. ~*n.* a word or
act of contempt. **flouter** *n.* **floutingly** *adv.*

Usage note See note under FLAUNT.

flow (flō) *v.i.* **1** (of a fluid) to move, run or spread.
2 (of blood etc.) to circulate. **3** (of the tide) to rise.
4 to issue, to spring, to gush out. **5** to sway, glide,
hang or float, to move easily or freely, to undulate. **6** to be poured out abundantly, to abound, to
come or go in abundance or great numbers. **7** to
result, to issue, to be descended (from). **8** (of talk
etc.) to proceed smoothly without hesitation.
9 (of a rock) to yield to pressure without breaking
so that the shape is changed. ~*n.* **1** the act, state,
manner or motion of flowing. **2** the quantity that
flows. **3** a flowing liquid, a stream. **4** a copious
stream, abundance, a plentiful supply. **5** the rise
of the tide. **6** the change in shape of a rock under
pressure. **7** (*Sc.*) a wet or marshy tract. **8** undulation (of drapery etc.). **to go with the flow** to do
the same as others, not trying to do something
different. **flow chart, flow diagram, flowsheet** *n.*
a diagram showing the sequence of operations in
a complex process or computer program. **flowing**
a. **1** moving as a stream. **2** copious, fluent, easy.
3 smooth, unbroken, not abrupt or stiff. **4** hanging loose and waving. **flowingly** *adv.* **flowing
sheet** *n.* (*Naut.*) a sheet that is slackened to allow
it greater movement in the wind. **flowmeter** *n.* a
device that measures the rate of flow of a liquid
or gas in a pipe. **flow-on** *n.* (*Austral.*) an adjustment to wages or salary, given as a result of
one already made to another group of workers
undertaking similar work. **flowstone** *n.* rock that

has been deposited in a thin sheet by flowing
water.

flower (flow´ə) *n.* **1** (*Bot.*) **a** the organ or growth
comprising the organs of reproduction in a plant.
b a flowering plant. **c** the blossom, the bloom.
2 the finest, choicest or best individual, part,
period etc. **3** the prime; the period of youthful
vigour. **4** (*pl.*) decorative phrases; figures of
speech. **5** (*pl., Chem.*) substances of a powdery
consistency or form, esp. if produced by sublimation. ~*v.i.* **1** to produce flowers, to bloom, to
blossom. **2** to be in the prime. ~*v.t.* **1** to embellish
with flowers. **2** to cause to blossom. **in flower**
with the flowers appeared and opened. **flower
bed** *n.* a plot of ground in a garden or park in
which flowers are grown. **flowered** *a.* **flowerer** *n.*
a plant that flowers at a particular time or in a
particular way (*spring flowerer*). **floweret** *n.* a
little flower. **flower girl** *n.* a girl or woman selling flowers, esp. in the street. **flower-head** *n.*
CAPITULUM. **flowering** *a.* **1** that flowers. **2** flowery,
in bloom. **flowering plant** *n.* an angiosperm.
flowerless *a.* **flower-like** *a.* **flowerpot** *n.* an
earthenware pot to hold plants. **flowers of sulphur** *n.pl.* (*Chem.*) a form of sulphur obtained by
distillation from other forms. **flowers of zinc**
n.pl. (*Chem.*) zinc oxide. **flowery** *a.* **1** abounding
in or full of flowers or blossoms. **2** highly figurative or decorative, florid.

flown FLY[2].

fl. oz. *abbr.* fluid ounce.

Flt. Lt. *abbr.* Flight Lieutenant.

flu (floo) *n.* (*coll.*) a highly contagious viral disease marked by fever, aches and catarrhal inflammation of the respiratory passages.

fluctuate (flŭk´chūāt) *v.i.* **1** to vary, to change
irregularly in degree, to be unsettled. **2** to rise
and fall like waves. **fluctuation** (-ā´shən) *n.*

flue (floo) *n.* a passage or tube by which smoke
can escape or hot air be conveyed. **flue pipe** *n.* an
organ pipe in which the sound is produced by
air passing through a fissure and striking an edge
above.

fluence (floo´əns) *n.* (*coll.*) influence. **to put the
fluence on** to hypnotize.

fluent (floo´ənt) *a.* **1** able to speak a foreign language easily, accurately and without hesitation
(*fluent in Spanish*). **2** ready and natural in the
use of words. **3** moving or curving smoothly,
graceful. **fluency** *n.* **1** fluent command of a
foreign language. **2** readiness and easy flow (of
words or ideas). **3** the quality of being fluent.
fluently *adv.*

fluff (flŭf) *n.* **1** light down or fur. **2** flocculent
matter. **3** (*sl.*) a mistake made esp. in delivering
lines, reading a text or playing a game or a piece
of music. **4** something insubstantial. ~*v.t.* **1** to
cover with fluff or give a fluffy surface to. **2** to
shake or spread (feathers out, as a bird). **3** (*coll.*)
to bungle. ~*v.i.* **1** to become a soft mass. **2** (*coll.*)
to make a mistake in performing. **fluffy** *a.* (*comp.*
fluffier, *superl.* **fluffiest**) **1** of, like or relating to

fluff. **2** covered with fluff. **fluffily** *adv.* **fluffiness** *n.*

flugelhorn (floo´gəlhawn) *n.* a valved brass instrument resembling, but slightly larger than, a cornet.

fluid (floo´id) *n.* **1** a liquid or gas, not a solid. **2** a substance whose particles readily move and change their relative positions. *~a.* **1** capable of flowing, as water. **2** composed of particles that move freely in relation to each other. **3** liquid, gaseous. **4** not rigid or stable. **5** smooth and graceful. **6** using liquid for the transmission of power. **fluid drachm** *n.* one-eighth of a fluid ounce. **fluidics** *n.* the study and use of fluids flowing in channels simulating the flow of electricity in conductors, used in applications usu. performed by electronic devices. **fluidic** *a.* **fluidify** (-id´-) *v.t.* (*3rd pers. sing. pres.* **fluidifies**, *pres.p.* **fluidifying**, *past, p.p.* **fluidified**). **fluidity** (-id´-) *n.* **fluidize, fluidise** *v.t.* to make (a solid) a fluid by pulverizing it and moving it in a rapidly flowing upward stream of gas. **fluidization** (-zā´shən) *n.* **fluidized bed** *n.* a layer of fluidized solids, used as a medium in a heat exchanger. **fluidly** *adv.* **fluid mechanics** *n.* the study of forces and flow within liquids. **fluidness** *n.* **fluid ounce** *n.* **1** a British unit of liquid capacity equal to ¹/₂₀ of an imperial pint (28.4 ml). **2** (*also* **fluidounce**) a unit equal to ¹/₁₆ of a US pint (29.5 ml). **fluidram** *n.* (*N Am.*) a fluid drachm.

fluke¹ (flook) *n.* **1** an accidentally successful stroke; any lucky chance. **2** a chance breeze. *~v.i.* to score by luck. *~v.t.* to hit or obtain in this way. **fluky** *a.* (*comp.* **flukier**, *superl.* **flukiest**) obtained by chance, not skill. **flukily** *adv.* **flukiness** *n.*

fluke² (flook) *n.* **1** a parasitic worm belonging to the Trematoda, found chiefly in the livers of sheep. **2** a flounder or other flatfish.

fluke³ (flook) *n.* **1** (*Naut.*) the broad holding portion of an anchor. **2** either of the flat lobes of a whale's tail. **3** a barb of a lance, harpoon etc.

flume (floom) *n.* **1** an artificial channel for conveying water to a mill or for some other industrial use. **2** a deep ravine traversed by a torrent. **3** a water chute or water slide at a swimming pool or amusement park. *~v.t.* to carry down a flume. *~v.i.* to make flumes.

flummery (flŭm´əri) *n.* (*pl.* **flummeries**) **1** nonsense, humbug. **2** empty compliments. **3** a kind of blancmange.

flummox (flŭm´əks) *v.t.* (*coll.*) to perplex, confound.

flump (flŭmp) *v.i.* **1** to fall down heavily. **2** to sit down with a flop. *~v.t.* to throw down with a dull, heavy noise. *~n.* **1** a dull, heavy noise, as of something let fall. **2** the action of flumping.

flung FLING.

flunk (flŭngk) *v.t.* (*esp. N Am., coll.*) to (cause to) fail (a subject, course etc.). *~v.i.* to fail, esp. in an examination or course. *~n.* an instance of flunking. **to flunk out** (*esp. N Am., coll.*) to be expelled for failure.

flunkey (flŭng´ki), **flunky** *n.* (*pl.* **flunkeys**, **flunkies**) (*usu. derog.*) **1** a servant in livery, a footman. **2** a toady; a snob. **3** (*N Am.*) a person who does menial work. **flunkeyism** *n.*

fluor (floo´aw), **fluorspar** (fluə´spah, flaw´-), **fluorite** (fluə´rīt) *n.* an isometric, transparent or subtranslucent brittle mineral, having many shades of colour, composed of calcium fluoride.

fluorescence (fluəres´əns, flaw-) *n.* **1** a quality existing in certain substances of giving out light of a different colour from their own or that of the light falling upon them. **2** the coloured luminosity thus produced, esp. the visible light produced by the action of ultraviolet rays. **fluoresce** *v.i.* **1** to be or become fluorescent. **2** to exhibit fluorescence. **fluorescein** (-sēn, -sin) *n.* (*Chem.*) an orange dye with a greenish-yellow fluorescence. **fluorescent** *a.* having the quality of fluorescence. **fluorescent lamp, fluorescent bulb** *n.* a lamp consisting of a glass tube with a fluorescent coating of phosphor inside, which emits light on the passage through the tube of an electric current. **fluorescent screen** *n.* a screen coated on one side with a phosphor that fluoresces when exposed to X-rays etc.

fluorine (fluə´rēn, flaw´-) *n.* (*Chem.*) a nonmetallic gaseous element, at. no. 9, chem. symbol F, forming with chlorine, bromine and iodine the halogen group. **fluoride** (-rīd) *n.* a compound of fluorine with an element or radical. **fluoridate** (-ri-) *v.t.* to add traces of fluoride to (water) to prevent or reduce tooth decay. **fluoridation** (-dā´shən), **fluoridization** (-zā´shən), **fluoridisation** *n.*

fluorite FLUOR.

fluoro- (fluə´rō, flaw´rə), **fluor-** *comb. form* **1** fluorine. **2** fluorescence.

fluorocarbon (fluərōkah´bən, flaw-) *n.* any of a series of compounds of fluorine and carbon, which are chemically inert and highly resistant to heat.

fluoroscope (fluə´rəskōp, flaw-) *n.* an apparatus consisting of a lightproof box with a fluorescent screen, for observing the effects of X-rays.

fluorosis (fluərō´sis, flaw-) *n.* poisoning by fluorine or its compounds.

flurry (flŭr´i) *n.* (*pl.* **flurries**) **1** a squall. **2** a sudden and violent shower of rain, snow etc. **3** a short and intense period of activity. **4** commotion, agitation, bustle, confusion. **5** nervous excitement. *~v.t.* (*3rd pers. sing. pres.* **flurries**, *pres.p.* **flurrying**, *past, p.p.* **flurried**) to agitate, to fluster, to upset, to bewilder with noise or excitement.

flush¹ (flŭsh) *v.i.* to colour as if with a rush of blood, to redden up, to blush, to glow. *~v.t.* **1** to cause to colour or become red. **2** to inflame. **3** to encourage, to excite, as with passion. *~n.* **1** a sudden flow or rush of blood to the face causing a redness. **2** any warm colouring or glow. **3** a sudden rush of emotion, elation, excitement. **4 a** (*also* **hot flush**) a sudden feeling of heat during the menopause. **b** a hot fit in fever. **5** vigour. **6** bloom, blossoming. **flushed** a.

flush[2] (flŭsh) v.i. **1** to flow swiftly. **2** to rush. **3** to become filled (as pipes) with a sudden rush of water. **4** to become suffused. **5** (of a plant) to grow fresh shoots. ~v.t. **1** to cleanse by a rush of water. **2** to remove (an object). **3** to flood. ~n. **1** a sudden flow of water. **2** the cleansing of a drain, lavatory etc. with a rush of water. **flusher** n.

flush[3] (flŭsh) a. **1** level, even, on the same plane. **2** plentifully supplied, esp. with money. **3** abundant; filled up. **4** full to overflowing. **5** copious, abounding. ~v.t. **1** to make even. **2** to level (up). **3** to fill in (a joint) so as to make even with the surface. **flushness** n.

flush[4] (flŭsh) n. a hand of cards all of one suit.

flush[5] (flŭsh) v.i. **1** to take wing. **2** (of game birds) to start up suddenly. ~v.t. to cause to take wing; to put up. **to flush out** to find and force to come out.

fluster (flŭs′tə) v.t. **1** to flurry or confuse. **2** to agitate, to make nervous. **3** to befuddle, to make tipsy, to intoxicate. ~v.i. to be in an agitated or confused state. ~n. confusion of mind, agitation.

flute (floot) n. **1** a tubular wind instrument with a blowhole near the end and holes stopped by the fingers or with keys for producing variations of tone, esp. a transverse flute. **2** an organ stop with a similar tone. **3** a flute-player. **4** (Archit.) a long vertical groove, semicircular in section, esp. in the shaft of a column. **5** a similar groove or corrugation in a dress etc. **6** a long thin French roll of bread. **7** a tall, narrow wine glass. ~v.i. **1** to play a flute. **2** to whistle or sing with a flutelike sound. ~v.t. **1** to play, sing or utter with flutelike tones. **2** to play (a tune etc.) on a flute. **3** to form flutes or grooves in. **flutelike** a. **fluting** n. **1** a groove, a channel. **2** fluted work in pillars etc. **flutist** n. a person who plays the flute, a flautist. **fluty** a. resembling a flute in tone.

flutter (flŭt′ə) v.i. **1** to flap the wings rapidly. **2** to hover, flit or move about in a fitful, restless way. **3** to move with quick, irregular motions. **4** to quiver, to vibrate. **5** (of the pulse etc.) to beat spasmodically. **6** to be agitated or uncertain. ~v.t. **1** to cause to move about with quick vibrations. **2** to vibrate, to cause to quiver or flap about rapidly. **3** to agitate or alarm. ~n. **1** the act of fluttering. **2** quick, short and irregular vibration. **3** a state of excitement, anxiety, or agitation. **4** (coll.) a gamble, a bet. **5** a spasmodic beating of the heart etc. **6** (Mus.) a quick movement of the tongue when playing the flute or other wind instrument. **7** a variation or distortion in pitch occurring at higher frequencies in sound reproduction. **8** potentially dangerous oscillation set up in something, e.g. part of an aircraft, by natural forces. **flutterer** n. **flutteringly** adv. **fluttery** a.

fluvial (floo′viəl), **fluviatic** (-at′-), **fluviatile** (-tīl, -til) a. **1** of or belonging to a river. **2** (Geol.) caused by a river. **3** living in rivers.

fluvio- (floo′viō) comb. form relating to a river or rivers.

flux (flŭks) n. **1** the act or state of flowing. **2** the motion of a fluid. **3** a state of movement or continual change. **4** an issue or flowing out, a discharge. **5** (Physics) **a** the rate of flow of a fluid etc. across a given surface. **b** the amount of fluid crossing a surface at a given time. **6** an abnormal discharge of fluid matter from the body. **7** any substance which assists the fusion of minerals or metals. **8** fusion. **9** the amount of radiation or particles falling on an area. **10** the strength of a magnetic field. ~v.t. **1** to melt, to fuse. **2** to facilitate fusion with a flux. ~v.i. to melt. **fluxion** (-shən) n. (Math.) the rate of variation of a variable quantity.

fly[1] (flī) n. (pl. **flies**) **1** a two-winged insect of the order Diptera, esp. the housefly Musca domestica. **2** any other winged insect. **3** a disease in turnips, hops etc. caused by various flies. **4** an artificial fly used as bait in fishing. **like flies** in vast numbers and offering no resistance. **there are no flies on (a person)** the specified person is no fool. **fly agaric** n. a poisonous scarlet mushroom, Amanita muscaria, growing in woods. **flyblown** a. **1** tainted by flies or maggots. **2** impure, corrupt, tainted. **flycatcher** n. any of various passerine birds that catch flying insects, esp. of the family Muscicapidae or Tyrannidae. **flyfish** v.i. to angle with natural or artificial flies for bait. **fly-fisher** n. **fly in the ointment** n. a slight flaw, or minor disadvantage, that spoils the quality of something. **fly on the wall** n. an intimate, but unnoticed, observer of events. **fly-paper** n. paper prepared to catch or poison flies. **flytrap** n. any of various plants that catch flies, esp. the Venus flytrap. **flyweight** n. **1** a boxer, wrestler, weightlifter etc. in the weight category below bantam weight. **2** this weight category.

fly[2] (flī) v.i. (3rd pers. sing. pres. **flies**, pres.p. **flying**, past **flew** (floo), p.p. **flown** (flōn)) **1** to move through the air with wings. **2** to pilot or ride in an aircraft. **3** to flutter or wave in the air. **4** to pass or be driven through the air with great speed or violence. **5** (of time) to pass very swiftly. **6** to depart in haste. **7** to flee, to run away, to try to escape. **8** to burst or break violently (in pieces). **9** to start, to pass suddenly or violently, to spring, to hasten, to burst (as to arms or into a rage) (to fly into a temper). ~v.t. **1** to cause to fly or float in the air. **2** to pilot (an aircraft). **3** to travel over by air. **4** to transport by air. **5** to use (e.g. an airline) for air travel. **6** to flee from, to avoid, to quit by flight. **7** to hunt with a hawk. **8** to make (a hawk, pigeon etc.) fly. **9** to set or keep (a flag) flying. ~n. (pl. **flies**) **1** the act or state of flying. **2** the distance that something flies. **3** (usu. pl.) a a flap covering buttonholes. **b** the fastening in such a flap. **4** a loose flap for covering the entrance to a tent. **5** (pl.) a gallery over the proscenium in a theatre where the curtains or scenes are controlled. **6** (pl. usu. **flys**) a one-horse carriage, a hackney coach. **7** a flywheel or a regulating device acting on the same principle. **on the fly** in baseball, in the air, without bouncing. **to fly high 1** to be ambitious. **2** to succeed, to excel. **flyable** *a.* **fly-away** *a.* **1** streaming, loose. **2** (of hair) tending not to stay in place. **3** flighty, volatile. **fly boy** *n.* (*N Am., sl.*) a member of the US Air Force, esp. a pilot. **fly-by** (-bī) *n.* (*pl.* **fly-bys**) an observation flight, esp. by a spacecraft, past a target at close range. **fly-by-night** *a.* unreliable, untrustworthy. ~*n.* an unreliable or untrustworthy person. **fly-by-wire** *n.* a system of aircraft control that uses electronic rather than mechanical connections between the controls and the aircraft parts. **fly-drive** *a.* of or relating to a holiday that includes the cost of the flight and also car rental. ~*v.i.* (*past* **fly-drove**, *p.p.* **fly-driven**) to go on such a holiday. **flyer, flier** *n.* **1** a pilot or aviator. **2** (*in comb.*) a person or thing that flies in a particular way, as a *high-flyer*. **3** an animal, vehicle, train etc. that goes with exceptional speed. **4** a small handbill. **5** a flying jump. **6** (*coll.*) a flying start. **7** a speculative attempt or venture. **fly-half** *n.* (*pl.* **fly-halves**) in rugby, a stand-off half. **flyleaf** *n.* (*pl.* **flyleaves**) a blank leaf at the beginning or end of a book. **flyover** *n.* **1** an intersection, esp. of two roads or railways at which one is carried over the other on a bridge. **2** (*N Am.*) a fly-past. **fly-past** *n.* a ceremonial flight by aircraft over a certain point. **fly-pitcher** *n.* (*sl.*) a street trader. **fly-pitching** *n.* **fly-posting** *n.* unauthorized affixing of posters. **flysheet** *n.* **1** a two- or four-page tract. **2** a handbill; a prospectus. **3** an extra sheet of canvas that can be fitted over the roof of a tent. **flywheel** *n.* a heavy-rimmed wheel attached to a machine for regulating the speed by its inertia.

fly³ (flī) *a.* (*comp.* **flyer**, *superl.* **flyest**) (*sl.*) **1** clever, sharp, wide-awake. **2** (*N Am.*) stylish, fine. **flyness** *n.*

flying (flī´ing) *a.* **1** fluttering in the air, streaming, loose. **2** brief, hurried. **3** moving with or as if with wings. **4** moving or adapted to move swiftly. **flying boat** *n.* a large seaplane with a buoyant fuselage. **flying bomb** *n.* a jet-propelled, pilotless aeroplane with a charge of explosive in the head which is detonated when the plane falls. **flying buttress** *n.* (*Archit.*) an arched or slanting structure springing from solid masonry and serving to support another part of a structure. **flying doctor** *n.* a doctor in remote areas who uses an aircraft to answer calls. **flying dragon** *n.* a flying lizard. **flying fish** *n.* a marine fish esp. of the family Exocoetidae with enlarged winglike pectoral fins used for gliding through the air. **flying fox** *n.* **1** a large fruit bat, esp. belonging to the genus *Pteropus*, having a foxlike head. **2** (*Austral.*) a conveyor on a suspended wire. **flying lemur** *n.* either of two mammals of the genus *Cynocephalus* of SE Asia, whose fore and hind limbs are connected by a fold of skin enabling the animal to take flying leaps from tree to tree.

flying lizard *n.* any lizard of the SE Asian genus *Draco*, which can make gliding leaps. **flying officer** *n.* a junior commissioned rank in the RAF next below flight lieutenant. **flying phalanger** *n.* any of various Australian marsupials of the genus *Petaurus* or *Petauroides* whose fore and hind limbs are connected by a fold of skin enabling the animal to move with gliding leaps. **flying picket** *n.* (a member of) a mobile band of pickets who reinforce local pickets during a strike. **flying saucer** *n.* an unidentified flying object, esp. in the shape of a large disc. **flying squad** *n.* a mobile detachment of police. **flying squirrel** *n.* a squirrel of the subfamily Pteromyinae with a patagium or fold of skin like that of the flying lemurs, by which it makes flying leaps. **flying start** *n.* **1** the start of a race etc. in which the competitors are already travelling at speed as they pass the starting point. **2** a promising strong start giving initial advantage. **flying suit** *n.* a one-piece garment worn by aircrew.

FM *abbr.* **1** Field Marshal. **2** frequency modulation.

Fm *chem. symbol* fermium.

fm., fm *abbr.* fathom(s).

FO *abbr.* **1** Field Officer. **2** Flying Officer.

fo. *abbr.* folio.

foal (fōl) *n.* the young of a horse or related animal; a colt, a filly. ~*v.i.* (of a mare) to give birth to young. ~*v.t.* to give birth to (a foal). **with foal** (of a mare etc.) pregnant.

foam (fōm) *n.* **1** a mass of bubbles produced in liquids by violent agitation or fermentation. **2** the similar formation produced by saliva in an animal's mouth. **3** froth, spume. **4** chemical froth used in fire-fighting. **5** a light, cellular solid, produced by aerating and then solidifying a liquid. ~*v.i.* **1** to gather, produce or emit foam. **2** to be covered or filled with foam. **to foam at the mouth** to be very angry. **foamless** *a.* **foam plastic** *n.* plastic of foamlike consistency. **foam rubber** *n.* rubber of foamlike consistency largely used in upholstery etc. **foamy** *a.* (*comp.* **foamier**, *superl.* **foamiest**).

fob¹ (fob) *n.* **1** (*also* **fob chain**) a chain by which a pocket watch is carried in a waistband pocket. **2** a small pocket for carrying a watch. **3** a tab on a keyring. ~*v.t.* (*pres.p.* **fobbing**, *past*, *p.p.* **fobbed**) to put into one's pocket.

fob² (fob) *v.t.* (*pres.p.* **fobbing**, *past*, *p.p.* **fobbed**) to cheat, to impose upon. **to fob off** to put off with lies or excuses. **to fob off with** to delude into accepting by a trick.

f.o.b. *abbr.* free on board.

focaccia (fəkach´ə) *n.* (*pl.* **focaccias**) **1** a kind of Italian bread sprinkled before baking with olive oil, salt and often herbs. **2** a loaf of this.

fo'c'sle FORECASTLE.

focus (fō´kəs) *n.* (*pl.* **focuses, foci** (fō´sī)) **1** (*Physics*) a point at which rays of light, heat, electrons etc. meet after reflection, deflection or refraction, or from which they appear to diverge. **2** the relation between the eye or lens and the object necessary to produce a clear image. **3** a state of clear definition. **4** (*Med. etc.*) the point from which any activity (such as a disease or an earthquake wave) originates. **5** the point on which attention or activity is concentrated. **6** (*Geom.*) one of two points having a definite relation to an ellipse or other curve. ~*v.t.* (*pres.p.* **focusing, focussing,** *past, p.p.* **focused, focussed**) **1** to bring (rays) to a focus or point. **2** to adjust (eye or instrument) so as to be at the right focus. **3** to bring into focus. **4** to concentrate. **5** to cause to converge to a focus. ~*v.i.* **1** to concentrate. **2** to converge to a focus. **in focus 1** adjusted so as to obtain a clear image. **2** clearly perceived or defined. **focal** *a.* of, relating to or situated at a focus. **focal length, focal distance** *n.* the distance between the centre of a lens and the point where initially parallel rays converge. **focal point** *n.* **1** the focus of reflected rays of lights etc. **2** the focus of attention or activity.

fodder (fod´ə) *n.* food such as straw or hay fed to cattle. ~*v.t.* to feed or supply with fodder.

foe (fō) *n.* (*esp. formal or poet.*) **1** a personal enemy; an opponent, an adversary. **2** an enemy in war.

foetid FETID.

foetus (fē´təs), (*esp. N Am.*) **fetus** *n.* (*pl.* **foetuses,** (*esp. N Am.*) **fetuses**) the young of animals in the womb, of vertebrates in the egg, after the parts are distinctly formed, esp. an unborn human more than eight weeks after conception. **foetal** *a.* **foeticide** (-tisīd) *n.*

fog (fog) *n.* **1** a dense watery vapour rising from land or water and suspended near the surface of land or sea, reducing or obscuring visibility. **2** a dense cloud of smoke with similar effect. **3** a cloudiness on a photographic negative. **4** a state of confusion, uncertainty or perplexity. ~*v.t.* (*pres.p.* **fogging,** *past, p.p.* **fogged**) **1** to surround or cover with or as if with a fog. **2** to perplex, to bewilder. **3** to make (a photographic negative) cloudy. ~*v.i.* **1** to become foggy. **2** in photography, to become cloudy. **in a fog** confused, in a state of uncertainty. **fog bank** *n.* a dense mass of fog at sea. **fogbound** *a.* **1** immobilized by fog. **2** covered in fog. **fog-bow** *n.* a faint bow, resembling a rainbow, produced by light on a fog. **foggy** *a.* **1** thick, murky. **2** full of or subject to fog. **3** of, relating to or resembling fog. **4** confused, vague, obscure, perplexed, indistinct. **not to have the foggiest** (*coll.*) not to have the slightest notion. **foggily** *adv.* **fogginess** *n.* **foghorn** *n.* **1** an instrument to give warning to ships in a fog. **2** (*coll.*) a loud deep resounding voice. **fog lamp, foglight** *n.* a strong light fitted to a vehicle to facilitate driving in fog. **fog signal** *n.* a detonator placed on a railway for the guidance of engine drivers.

fogey (fō´gi), **fogy** *n.* (*pl.* **fogeys, fogies**) an old-fashioned eccentric person. **fogeydom** (-dəm) *n.* **fogeyish** *a.*

foible (foi´bəl) *n.* **1** a weak point in a person's

character. **2** the part of a sword blade between the middle and point.

foie gras (fwah grah´) *n.* PÂTÉ DE FOIE GRAS (under PÂTÉ).

foil¹ (foil) *n.* **1** very thin sheet metal. **2** an amalgam of quicksilver and tin at the back of a mirror. **3** a thin leaf of metal put under gems to increase their lustre or brighten or alter their colour. **4** something that serves to set off something else to advantage. **5** a rounded leaflike space or arc in window tracery.

foil² (foil) *v.t.* **1** to baffle, to frustrate. **2** to throw off the scent, to spoil or obliterate (the scent of a hunted animal) by crossing. **3** to defeat, to repulse, to parry. ~*v.i.* (of an animal) to spoil the scent of a hunted animal. ~*n.* the trail of hunted game.

foil³ (foil) *n.* a straight thin sword, blunted by means of a button on the point, used in fencing. **foilist** *n.*

foil⁴ (foil) *n.* HYDROFOIL.

foist (foist) *v.t.* **1** to impose (an unwelcome thing or person) (on). **2** to palm off (on or upon) as genuine. **3** to introduce surreptitiously or wrongfully. **foister** *n.*

fol. *abbr.* folio.

folacin FOLIC ACID.

fold¹ (fōld) *n.* **1** a pen or enclosure for sheep. **2** a flock of sheep. **3** a group of believers or members of a Church. ~*v.t.* to put or enclose in or as if in a fold.

fold² (fōld) *v.t.* **1** to double or lay one part of (a flexible thing) over another. **2** to bring together and entwine (e.g. arms, legs). **3** (*poet.*) **a** to clasp (arms etc.) round. **b** to embrace. **4** to enfold, to envelop. **5** to make compact by folding. **6** to close (e.g. wings, petals). ~*v.i.* **1** to become folded or doubled. **2** to shut in folds. **3** to fail, to cease operations, to go bankrupt. ~*n.* **1** the act or an instance of folding. **2** a part doubled or laid on another. **3** a line made by folding. **4** a bend or doubling, a pleat. **5** a hollow between two parts (as of a fabric). **6** a coil, a folding, an embrace. **7** (*Geol.*) a flexure in strata. **to fold in** in cookery, to mix in gradually and carefully. **foldable** *a.* **foldaway** *a.* designed to be folded away when not in use. **folding** *n., a.* **folding door** *n.* a door with vertical jointed sections that can be folded against one another. **folding money** *n.* (*esp. N Am., coll.*) banknotes. **fold-out** *n.* an oversize page in a book or magazine that is folded out by the reader.

-fold (fōld) *suf.* forming adjectives and adverbs denoting multiplication, as *fourfold, manifold,* or composition of a number of parts, as *sixfold.*

folder (fōl´də) *n.* **1** a person who or thing that folds. **2** a holder for loose papers. **3** a folded leaflet.

foliage (fō´liij) *n.* **1** leaves in the aggregate. **2** in art, architecture etc. the representation of leaves or clusters of leaves, as ornament. **foliage leaf** *n.* (*pl.* **foliage leaves**) a leaf excluding petals, modified leaves etc. **foliar** *a.* of, consisting of or relating to leaves.

foliate[1] (fō´liāt) *v.i.* to split or disintegrate into thin laminae. ~*v.t.* **1** to decorate with leaf-patterns, foils, leaflike tracery etc. **2** to number the leaves of (a manuscript, book etc.). **foliation** (-ā´shən) *n.* **1** foliating. **2** (*Archit.*) ornamentation by trefoil, quatrefoil, cinquefoil, and similar tracery based on the form of a leaf.

foliate[2] (fō´liət, -iāt) *a.* **1** leaflike, leaf-shaped. **2** furnished with leaves. **3** having a particular number of leaves.

folic acid (fō´lik, fol´-), **folacin** (fō´ləsin) *n.* a vitamin of the vitamin B complex found esp. in green vegetables and liver and used in the treatment of anaemia.

folio (fō´liō) *n.* (*pl.* **folios**) **1** a leaf of paper or other material for writing etc., numbered on the front. **2** a page of manuscript. **3** a sheet of paper folded once. **4 a** a book of the largest size, whose sheets are folded once. **b** any large volume or work. **5** the number of a page. ~*a.* (of a book) of, relating to or having the format of a folio. **in folio** made or composed of folios.

foliole (fō´liōl) *n.* a leaflet, one of the separate parts of a compound leaf.

folk (fōk) *n.* (*pl.* **folk, folks**) **1** (*pl. in constr.*) people, people collectively. **2** (*pl. in constr.*) a particular class of people, as *old folk*. **3** (*usu.* **folks**) members of one's own family; also used as a familiar form of address to a group of assembled people. **4** a people, nation or ethnic group. **5** folk music. **6** (*in comb.*) people of a specified kind, as *menfolk*, *kinsfolk*. ~*a.* **1** originating among the common people. **2** based on or employing traditional or popular motifs. **folk dance** *n.* **1** a traditional dance of countryfolk. **2** the music for such a dance. **folk etymology** *n.* (*pl.* **folk etymologies**) a popular but often erroneous derivation of a word. **folkish** *a.* traditional, popular. **folklore** *n.* **1** popular beliefs, tales, traditions or legends. **2** the systematic study of such beliefs etc. **folkloric** *a.* **folklorism** *n.* **folklorist** *n.* **folkloristic** (-ris´tik) *a.* **folk memory** *n.* (*pl.* **folk memories**) a memory of a distant event passed down through several generations of a community. **folk music** *n.* **1** the traditional popular music of the common people. **2** modern popular music in the style of this. **folk singer** *n.* a person who sings folk songs. **folk song** *n.* **1** a song or ballad, supposed to have originated among the people and to have been handed down by tradition. **2** a modern song in this style. **folksy** *a.* (*comp.* **folksier**, *superl.* **folksiest**) **1** (*esp. N Am.*, *coll.*) informal, casual, sociable, friendly. **2** (affectedly) traditional in style. **folksiness** *n.* **folk tale** *n.* a traditional or popular legend or story. **folkways** *n.pl.* traditional social customs. **folkweave** *n.* a loosely woven fabric. **folky** *a.* (*comp.* **folkier**, *superl.* **folkiest**) traditional or popular in style. **folkiness** *n.*

follicle (fol´ikəl) *n.* (*Anat.*) a small cavity, sac or gland. **follicular** (-lik´ū-), **folliculate** (-lik´ū-), **folliculated** (-lik´ū-) *a.*

follow (fol´ō) *v.t.* **1** to go or come after. **2** to move behind. **3** to pursue (e.g. an enemy). **4** to go along (a path, road etc.). **5** to come or happen after in point of time, order, rank or importance. **6** to imitate, to pattern oneself upon. **7** to go after as an admirer or disciple. **8** to engage in, to practise (as a profession). **9** to conform, to act upon (a rule, policy etc.). **10** to watch the course of. **11** to keep the mind or attention fixed on. **12** to understand, to grasp the meaning of. **13** to result, to be the consequence of. **14** to seek after, to try to attain. **15** to provide (with a successor). **16** to accompany, to attend upon, to serve. **17** to adhere to, to side with, to support the cause of. ~*v.i.* **1** to come or go after another person or thing. **2** to pursue. **3** to be the next thing to be done or said. **4** to be a natural consequence, to ensue. **5** to be the logical consequence, to be deducible. **as follows** used as an introductory formula to a statement, list etc. **to follow on 1** to continue without a break. **2** to continue from where somebody else left off. **3** in cricket, to bat again immediately after completing one's first innings because one is more than a certain number of runs behind. **to follow out** to implement (an idea, instructions etc.). **to follow through 1** in golf, cricket etc., to continue the swing after hitting the ball. **2** to take further action consequent upon an initial act. **3** to follow to a conclusion. **to follow up 1** to pursue an advantage. **2** to make further efforts to the same end. **3** to take appropriate action about. **follower** *n.* **1** a person who follows. **2** a devotee, a disciple, an imitator or adherent. **3** a machine part that is driven by another part. **following** *a.* **1** coming next after, succeeding, now to be mentioned. **2** (of wind) blowing in the direction one is travelling. ~*prep.* after. ~*n.* a body of followers or adherents. **the following** the person(s) or thing(s) now to be mentioned. **follow-on** *n.* an act of following on. **follow-the-leader, follow-my-leader** *n.* a game in which those behind must follow the steps and imitate the actions of the leader. **follow-through** *n.* the act of following through. **follow-up** *n.* **1** a reminding circular sent by an advertiser. **2** a further or consequent action.

folly (fol´i) *n.* (*pl.* **follies**) **1** foolishness, lack of understanding or judgement, senselessness. **2** a foolish act, idea or conduct. **3 a** a structure built for picturesque effect or to gratify the builder's whim. **b** (*derog.*) any building which seems more grand, elaborate or expensive than its purpose warrants. **4 a** a revue in which the performers wear elaborate costumes. **b** the performers in such a revue.

foment (fəment´) *v.t.* **1** to cause (trouble or a riot) to develop. **2** to nourish, to foster, to encourage, to promote. **3** to apply warm or medicated lotions to. **fomentation** (fōmentā´shən) *n.* **1** the act of fomenting. **2** the lotion, poultice, warm cloths etc. applied. **fomenter** *n.*

fond (fond) *a.* **1** doting on, delighting in (*fond of children*). **2** tender or loving, affectionate. **3** foolishly naive. **fondly** *adv.* **fondness** *n.*

fondant (fon´dənt) *n.* a sweet paste made of sugar and water. **fondant icing** *n.* icing made of this paste.

fondle (fon´dəl) *v.t.* to caress. **fondler** *n.*

fondue (fon´doo, -dū) *n.* a dish consisting of a hot sauce (usu. of cheese and white wine) into which pieces of bread etc. are dipped, or of cubes of meat which are cooked by dipping into hot oil at table and eaten with a variety of spicy sauces.

font[1] (font) *n.* **1** the vessel or basin to contain water for baptism. **2** the oil reservoir for a lamp. **fontal** *a.*

font[2] (font), **fount** (fownt) *n.* a set of type of one face and size.

fontanelle (fontənel´), (*N Am.*) **fontanel** *n.* an interval between the bones of the infant cranium.

food (food) *n.* **1** any substance, esp. solid in form, which, taken into the body, assists in sustaining or nourishing the living being. **2** victuals, provisions; aliment, nutriment. **3** nutriment for plants. **4** anything that provides stimulus for thinking (*food for thought*). **food additive** *n.* a substance used to preserve food or to enhance its colour, flavour etc. **food chain** *n.* a community of organisms thought of as a hierarchy in which each eats the one below and is eaten by the one above. **foodie, foody** *n.* (*pl.* **foodies**) (*coll.*) a person with an intense interest in (esp. more exotic kinds of) food. **foodless** *a.* **food poisoning** *n.* a severe gastrointestinal condition caused by eating food which is naturally poisonous or has been contaminated. **food processor** *n.* an electrical appliance which chops, shreds or blends etc. food. **foodstuff** *n.* any thing or material used for food. **food value** *n.* a measure of the nourishment of a food, measured in calories, vitamins or minerals.

fool[1] (fool) *n.* **1** a person without common sense or judgement; a silly person. **2** a dupe. **3** (*Hist.*) a jester, a buffoon. ~*a.* (*esp. N Am., coll.*) foolish, silly. ~*v.t.* **1** to make a fool of. **2** to dupe, to cheat, to impose upon, to play tricks upon, to trick. **3** to waste (time away). ~*v.i.* **1** to play the fool. **2** to trifle, to idle. **to act the fool** to behave in a foolish, playful way. **to fool around/ about 1** to behave foolishly or irresponsibly. **2** to waste time. **3** to trifle (with). **to fool with** to meddle with in a careless and risky manner. **to make a fool of 1** to cause to appear ridiculous. **2** to deceive, to disappoint. **to play the fool** to act the fool. **foolery** *n.* (*pl.* **fooleries**) **1** the act of playing the fool. **2** folly, absurdity. **foolish** *a.* **1** silly, not sensible, not wise. **2** absurd or ridiculous. **foolishly** *adv.* **foolishness** *n.* **foolproof** *a., adv.* secure against any ignorant mishandling. **fool's errand** *n.* an absurd or fruitless errand or quest; the pursuit of what cannot be found. **fool's gold** *n.* iron pyrites. **fool's mate** *n.* the simplest mate in chess. **fool's paradise** *n.* a state of unreal or deceptive joy or good fortune.

fool[2] (fool) *n.* a dish made of fruit, esp. gooseberries, stewed and crushed with cream etc.

foolhardy (fool´hahdi) *a.* (*comp.* **foolhardier**, *superl.* **foolhardiest**) daring without sense or judgement, foolishly bold; rash, reckless. **foolhardihood, foolhardiness** *n.* **foolhardily** *adv.*

foolscap (foolz´kap) *n.* a size of writing paper 17 × 13½ in. (43.2 × 34.3 cm) or of printing paper, folio, 13½ × 8½ in. (34.3 × 21.6 cm), quarto, 8½ × 6¾ in. (21.6 × 17.1 cm), octavo, 6¾ × 4¼ in. (17.1 × 10.8 cm).

foot (fut) *n.* (*pl.* **feet** (fēt)) **1** the part of the leg which treads on the ground in standing or walking, and on which the body is supported; the part below the ankle. **2** that which serves to support a body. **3** that part of an article of dress which receives the foot. **4** a pace or step. **5** (*pl.* **feet, foot**) a measure of 12 in. (30.5 cm), named as being roughly the length of a man's foot. **6** the lowest part, the base, the lower end of e.g. a table, chair or bed; the bottom. **7** foot soldiers, infantry. **8** in prosody, a set of syllables forming the rhythmical unit in verse, speech etc. **9** an attachment on a sewing machine that holds the material in position. **10** (*Zool.*) the locomotive organ of invertebrate animals, the tube-foot of an echinoderm. **11** (*Bot.*) the part by which a petal is attached. ~*v.i.* **1** to walk, to dance. **2** to pace. **3** to go or travel on foot. ~*v.t.* to travel over by walking. **at the feet of 1** humbly adoring or supplicating. **2** submissive to. **3** as a disciple or student of. **my foot!** used to express disbelief, contradiction etc. **not to put a foot wrong** to not make a mistake. **on foot** walking. **on one's feet 1** standing up. **2** in good health. **3** thriving, getting on well. **to catch on the wrong foot** to take unprepared or at a disadvantage. **to fall on one's feet** to emerge safely or successfully. **to find one's feet** to become accustomed to, and able to function effectively in, new circumstances. **to foot a bill** (*coll.*) to pay a bill. **to foot it 1** to go on foot. **2** to dance. **to get off on the wrong foot** to make a bad start, esp. in personal relations with someone. **to have one foot in the grave** to be near death, very old or moribund. **to have one's/ both feet on the ground** to be realistic, sensible or practical. **to keep one's feet** not to fall. **to put one's best foot forward 1** to step out briskly. **2** to try to show oneself at one's best. **to put one's feet up** (*coll.*) to rest. **to put one's foot down 1** to be firm, determined. **2** to go faster in a car etc. **to put one's foot in it** to blunder, to get into a scrape. **to set foot on/ in** to go into, to enter. **to sweep off one's feet** to enrapture, to make a complete and sudden conquest of. **to think on one's feet** to react to situations as they arise. **under foot** on the ground. **under one's feet** in the way. **feet of clay** *n.pl.* serious weakness in a person who is admired. **footage** *n.* **1** length or distance measured in feet. **2** the length of a film (in feet). **foot-and-mouth disease** *n.* a contagious eczematous viral disease chiefly affecting cattle. **footboard** *n.* **1** a board to support the feet. **2** a board at the foot of a bed. **footbrake** *n.* a brake operated by the foot in a motor vehicle. **footbridge** *n.* a narrow bridge for foot passengers. **footed** *a.* **footer** (fut´ə) *n.* **1** (*in comb.*) **a** a person or thing of a particular number of feet in length or height (*a six-footer*). **b** a particular kind of kick of a football (*a right-footer*). **2** a line of text printed at the foot of a page. **3** (*coll.*) the game of football. **footfall** *n.* the sound of a footstep. **foot-fault** *n.* in tennis etc. the act of overstepping the baseline when serving. ~*v.i.* to make a foot-fault. ~*v.t.* to award a foot-fault against. **foothill** *n.* a hill lying at the base of a range of mountains. **foothold** *n.* **1** something which sustains the foot. **2** a basis of operations; a secure position from which further progress can be made. **footie** FOOTY (under FOOT). **foot in both camps** *n.* a connection with both of two mutually antagonistic groups. **foot in the door** *n.* **1** a first step towards a desired end. **2** a favourable position from which to advance. **footless** *a.* **footlights** *n.pl.* a row of lights, screened from the audience, in front of the stage of a theatre. **footloose** *a.* free, unbound by ties (*footloose and fancy free*). **footman** *n.* (*pl.* **footmen**) **1** a male domestic servant in livery. **2** (*Hist.*) a foot soldier. **footmark** *n.* a footprint. **footnote** *n.* a note at the bottom of the page of a book. ~*v.t.* to provide with footnotes. **footpad** *n.* (*Hist.*) a highwayman who robs on foot. **foot passenger** *n.* a person who travels on e.g. a ferry on foot, a pedestrian. **footpath, footway** *n.* a narrow path or way for pedestrians only. **footplate** *n.* a platform for the driver and fireman on a locomotive. **foot-pound** *n.* (*pl.* **foot-pounds**) a unit of energy, the amount that will raise one pound avoirdupois one foot. **footprint** *n.* **1** the mark or print of a foot or shoe. **2** any sign of the presence of a person. **3** the area of the earth's surface within which the signal of a geostationary communications satellite can be received. **4** (*Comput.*) the space on a desktop occupied by a computer. **footrest** *n.* a support for a foot or the feet. **foot-rot** *n.* a disease in the feet of sheep and cattle, characterized by an abnormal growth. **foot-rule** *n.* a ruler 12 in. (30.5 cm) long. **foots** *n.pl.* **1** sediment, dregs, oil refuse etc. **2** coarse sugar. **footsie** (-si) *n.* (*coll.*) amorous or flirtatious touching with the feet. **footslog** *v.i.* (*pres.p.* **footslogging**, *past*, *p.p.* **footslogged**) to march or tramp, esp. laboriously. ~*n.* a laborious march or walk. **footslogger** *n.* **foot soldier** *n.* an infantry soldier. **footsore** *a.* having the feet sore or tender. **footstalk** *n.* **1** (*Bot.*) **a** the petiole of a leaf. **b** the peduncle of a flower. **2** (*Zool.*) the attachment of a crinoid etc. **footstep** *n.* **1** the act of stepping or treading with the feet; tread. **2** a footprint. **3** the sound of the step of a foot. **4** (*pl.*) traces of a course pursued or actions done (*She followed in her father's footsteps and became a butcher*). **footstool** *n.* a stool for resting the feet. **footwear** *n.* shoes, boots, socks etc. **footwell** *n.* a space for the feet in front of the front seats of a car. **footwork**

n. **1** skilful use of the feet in boxing, dancing etc. **2** clever manoeuvring, esp. of an evasive kind. **footy, footie** *n.* (*coll.*) the game of football.

football (fut´bawl) *n.* **1** any of several games played between two teams with a ball that is kicked, or handled and kicked, to score goals or points. **2** a large ball used in the game of football. **3** a contentious issue, esp. one which is bandied about between opposing groups. **footballer** *n.* **football hooligan** *n.* a hooligan at a football match or one travelling to or from a football match. **football pools** *n.pl.* a form of gambling based on forecasting the results of football matches.

footing (fut´ing) *n.* **1** a place for standing or putting the feet on. **2** foothold. **3** a firm or secure position. **4** relative position, status or condition; relationship. **5** (*Archit.*) a course at the base or foundation of a wall.

footle (foo´təl) *v.i.* (*coll.*) to trifle; to potter about aimlessly. **footling** *a.* trivial; silly.

fop (fop) *n.* a man overfond of dress; a dandy, a coxcomb. **foppery** *n.* (*pl.* **fopperies**). **foppish** *a.* **foppishly** *adv.* **foppishness** *n.*

for (faw, fə) *prep.* **1** in the place of, instead of. **2** in exchange against, as the equivalent of. **3** as the price or requital or payment of. **4** in consideration of, by reason of. **5** because of, on account of, in favour of, on the side of. **6** in order to, with a view to. **7** appropriate or suitable to. **8** toward, tending toward, conducive to. **9** to fetch, to get, to save. **10** to attain, to reach, to arrive at. **11** (*sl.*) against. **12** on behalf of, for the sake of. **13** with regard to, in relation to. **14** as regards. **15** so far as. **16** as, as being, in the character of. **17** to the amount or extent of. **18** at the cost of. **19** in spite of, notwithstanding. **20** in comparison of, contrast with. **21** during. **22** to prevent. **23** because of. **24** so as to start promptly at. ~*conj.* **1** since, because. **2** seeing that. **3** in view of the reason that. **for all that 1** nevertheless. **2** in spite of all that. **o/ oh for** used to express a desire for something. **to be for it** (*coll.*) to be marked for reprimand or punishment.

f.o.r. *abbr.* free on rail.

for- (faw) *pref.* **1** away, off, as *forget, forgive*. **2** negative, prohibitive or privative, as *forbear, forbid, forsake*. **3** amiss, badly, as *fordo*. **4** intensive, as *forlorn*.

forage (for´ij) *n.* **1** food for horses and cattle. **2** the act of foraging. ~*v.i.* **1** to seek for or to collect forage. **2** to hunt for supplies. **3** to rummage (about). ~*v.t.* **1** to obtain for forage. **2** to supply with forage or food. **forage cap** *n.* a military undress cap. **forager** *n.*

foramen (fərā´men) *n.* (*pl.* **foramina** (-ram´inə)) a small natural opening, passage or perforation in parts of plants and animals.

†**forasmuch as** (forəzmŭch´ az) *conj.* seeing that; since; in consideration that.

foray (for´ā) *n.* a sudden attacking expedition, a raid. ~*v.i.* to go foraging or pillaging.

forbade, forbad FORBID.
forbear[1] (fawbeə´) v.t. (past **forbore** (-baw´), p.p. **forborne** (-bawn´)) to refrain or abstain from. ~v.i. to refrain or abstain (from). **forbearance** n. patience, self-control.

Usage note The spellings of the verb forbear (to refrain) and the noun forebear (an ancestor) should not be confused.

forbear[2] FOREBEAR.
forbid (fəbid´) v.t. (pres.p. **forbidding,** past **forbade** (-bad´, -bād´), forbad (-bad), p.p. **forbidden** (-bid´ən)) **1** to order not to do. **2** to interdict, to prohibit. **3** to exclude, to oppose. **forbidden** a. **forbidden fruit** n. anything desired but pronounced unlawful (from the fruit of the tree of the knowledge of good and evil, which Adam was commanded not to eat (Gen. ii.17)). **forbidder** n. **forbidding** a. **1** repulsive, disagreeable. **2** threatening, formidable. **forbiddingly** adv. **forbiddingness** n.
forbore, forborne FORBEAR[1].
force (faws) n. **1** strength, energy, active power. **2** military or naval strength. **3** violence, coercion, compulsion. **4** unlawful violence. **5** an organized body of e.g. soldiers, police officers or workers; an army or part of an army. **6** (pl.) troops. **7** efficacy, validity. **8** significance, weight, import, full meaning. **9** persuasive or convincing power; a person or thing considered as having this. **10** energy, vigour, animation, vividness. **11** power exerted on a person or object. **12** (Physics) **a** that which produces or tends to produce a change of velocity in a body at rest or in motion. **b** a measure of the intensity of this. ~v.t. **1** to constrain (a person) by force or against their will; to compel. **2** to use violence to. **3** to strain, to distort. **4** to impose or impress (upon) with force. **5** to bring about, to accomplish, or to make a way by force. **6** to drive or push violently or against resistance. **7** to stimulate artificially. **8** to cause to grow or ripen by artificial heat. **9** to cause to ripen prematurely. **10** in card playing, to compel (a player) to play in a certain way, to compel (a certain card) to be played. **by force of** by means of. **in force 1** in operation, valid, enforced. **2** in large numbers, in great strength. **to force one's way** to push through obstacles by force. **to join forces** to work together in a combined manner. **forceable** a. **forced** a. **1** constrained, affected. **2** brought about by force. **3** unnatural. **forced labour,** (N Am.) **forced labor** n. involuntary labour. **forced landing** n. an unavoidable landing of an aircraft in an emergency, e.g. because of mechanical failure. **forced march** n. a march in which the physical capacity of troops is exerted to the utmost. **force-feed** v.t. (past, p.p. **force-fed**) to feed forcibly. **force field** n. an invisible barrier created by a force. **forceful** a. **1** full of or possessing force, forcible, strong, powerful. **2** impelled with force. **forcefully** adv. **forcefulness** n. **force-land** v.t., v.i. to make a forced landing

(with). **forceless** a. **force-pump, forcing-pump** n. a pump which delivers water under pressure, so as to raise it to an elevation above that attainable by atmospheric pressure. **forcer** n. **forcible** a. **1** done or brought about by force. **2** having force, powerful, efficacious, impressive. **forcibleness** n. **forcibly** adv.
force majeure (faws mazhœ´) n. **1** superior power. **2** circumstances not under a person's control, so excusing them from fulfilling a contract.
forceps (faw´səps, -sips) n. (pl. **forceps**) **1** a surgical instrument in the form of a pair of tongs, pincers or pliers for holding or extracting anything. **2** (Anat., Zool.) an organ shaped like a pair of forceps.
ford (fawd) n. a shallow part of a river where it may be crossed by wading or in a vehicle. ~v.t. to cross (water) at a ford. **fordable** a. **fordless** a.
fore (faw) a. being in front. ~n. **1** the front part. **2** (Naut.) the bow. ~int. in golf, before, beware in front (warning to persons standing in the direction of a drive). **to come to the fore** to become important or popular. **to the fore** to the front, prominent, conspicuous. **fore and aft** adv. at, along or over the whole length of a ship. **fore-and-aft** a. at, along or over the whole length of a ship from stem to stern. **fore-and-aft rigged** a. having sails set lengthwise to the ship, as opposed to square sails set on yards.
fore- (faw) pref. **1** before, in front, beforehand, chiefly with verbs, as in foreordain. **2** in front, the front or front part, as in forecourt, forerunner. **3** (Naut.) of, near or at the bow or the foremast.
forearm[1] (fawrahm´) v.t. to prepare beforehand for attack or defence.
forearm[2] (faw´rahm) n. **1** the anterior part of the arm, between the wrist and elbow. **2** the equivalent part in a foreleg or a wing.
forebear (faw´beə), **forbear** n. an ancestor.

Usage note See note under FORBEAR[1].

forebode (fawbōd´) v.t. **1** to foretell, predict. **2** to be an advance warning of, to foreshadow. **3** to feel a presentiment of something, esp. evil. **forebodingly** adv.
forebrain (faw´brān) n. (Anat.) the front part of the brain, including the cerebrum, thalamus and hypothalamus.
forecast (faw´kahst) v.t. (past, p.p. **forecast, forecasted**) **1** to foresee, to predict. **2** to be an early sign of. **3** to calculate beforehand. ~n. a statement or calculation of probable events, esp. regarding future weather. **forecaster** n.
forecastle (fōk´səl, faw´kahsəl), **fo'c'sle** n. (Naut.) **1** in merchant ships, a forward space below deck where the crew live. **2** (also **forecastle deck**) a short upper deck forward, formerly raised to command the enemy's decks.
foreclose (fawklōz´), **forclose** v.t. **1** to shut out, exclude or bar. **2** to preclude. ~v.i. to foreclose a mortgage. **to foreclose a mortgage** to deprive the

mortgager of equity of redemption on failure to pay money due on a mortgage. **foreclosure** (-zhə) *n.*

forecourt (faw´kawt) *n.* **1** an open or paved area in front of a building, esp. a filling station. **2** the first or outer court, that immediately inside the entrance to the precincts of a building. **3** (in tennis etc.) the part of the court between the service line and the net.

foredeck (faw´dek) *n.* **1** the forepart of a deck. **2** the deck in the forepart of a ship.

foredoom (fawdoom´) *v.t.* to doom beforehand.

forefather (faw´fahdhə) *n.* **1** an ancestor. **2** a member of a previous generation of a people or family.

forefinger (faw´fing-gə) *n.* the finger next to the thumb.

forefoot (faw´fut) *n.* (*pl.* **forefeet**) **1** either of the front feet of a four-footed animal. **2** (*Naut.*) the forward end of a vessel's keel.

forefront (faw´frŭnt) *n.* **1** the extreme front. **2** a leading or influential part or position.

foregather (fawga´dhə), **forgather** *v.i.* **1** to meet together, to assemble. **2** to meet or associate (with).

forego[1] (fawgō´) *v.t., v.i.* (*3rd pers. sing. pres.* **foregoes** (-gōz´), *pres.p.* **foregoing** (-gō´ing), *past* **forewent** (-went´), *p.p.* **foregone** (-gon´)) to go before, to precede in time, order or place. **foregoer** *n.* **foregoing** *a.* preceding, previously mentioned. **foregone** *a.* **1** past, preceding. **2** determined before. **foregone conclusion** *n.* **1** a conclusion determined beforehand or arrived at in advance of evidence or reasoning. **2** a result that might be foreseen.

Usage note The spellings of the verbs *forego* (to precede) and *forgo* (to go without) should not be confused.

forego[2] FORGO.

foreground (faw´grownd) *n.* **1** the nearest part of a view. **2** the part of a picture which seems to lie nearest the spectator. **3** the most prominent position. ~*v.t.* **1** to put in the foreground. **2** to make prominent.

forehand (faw´hand) *n.* **1** a forehand stroke. **2** the side on which such strokes are made. **3** that part of a horse in front of the rider. ~*a.* (in tennis etc.) of, relating to or being a stroke made with the palm of the hand facing in the direction of the stroke. **forehanded** *a.* in tennis etc., forehand.

forehead (for´id, faw´hed) *n.* the part of the face which reaches from the eyebrows upwards to the hair.

forehock (faw´hok) *n.* a foreleg cut of pork or bacon.

foreign (for´ən) *a.* **1** belonging to, connected with or derived from a country or nation other than one's own. **2** dealing with other countries. **3** introduced from outside. **4** unfamiliar, strange, extraneous, dissimilar, not belonging (to). **foreign body** *n.* (*pl.* **foreign bodies**) a substance

occurring in an organism or tissue where it is not normally found. **foreign correspondent** *n.* a representative of a newspaper sent to a foreign country to report on its politics etc. **foreigner** *n.* **1** a person born or belonging to a foreign country or speaking a foreign language. **2** a foreign ship, an import or product from a foreign country. **3** (*esp. dial.*) a stranger, an outsider. **foreign exchange** *n.* (trading in) foreign currencies. **foreign legion** *n.* a unit of foreign volunteers serving within a national regular army, esp. the French. **foreign minister** *n.* a foreign secretary. **foreignness** *n.* **foreign secretary** *n.* (*pl.* **foreign secretaries**) a cabinet minister in charge of relations with foreign countries. **foreign service** *n.* (*esp.* N Am.) DIPLOMATIC SERVICE (under DIPLOMACY).

forejudge (fawjŭj´) *v.t.* to judge before trial or decide before hearing the evidence.

foreknow (fawnō´) *v.t.* (*pres.p.* **foreknowing**, *past* **foreknew** (-nū´), *p.p.* **foreknown** (-nōn´)) to know beforehand. **foreknowledge** (-nol´ij) *n.*

forelady (faw´lādi) *n.* (*pl.* **foreladies**) (N Am.) a forewoman.

foreland (faw´lənd) *n.* **1** a point of land extending into the sea, a promontory. **2** a strip of land outside of or in front of an embankment etc.

foreleg (faw´leg) *n.* a front leg of an animal, chair etc.

forelock (faw´lok) *n.* a lock of hair growing over the forehead. **to take time by the forelock** to grasp an opportunity. **to touch/tug one's forelock** to raise one's hand to one's forehead as a sign of deference to a person of a higher social class.

foreman (faw´mən) *n.* (*pl.* **foremen**) **1** a worker supervising others. **2** the person who acts as chairperson and spokesperson for a jury.

foremast (faw´mahst) *n.* the mast nearest the bow of a vessel.

foremost (faw´mōst) *a.* **1** first in time, place, order, rank or importance. **2** chief, most notable. ~*adv.* **1** in the first place. **2** first, before anything else.

foremother (faw´mŭdhə) *n.* a female ancestor or predecessor.

forename (faw´nām) *n.* a name preceding the surname, a Christian name.

forenoon (fawnoon´) *n.* (*esp.* Sc.) the early part of the day, from morning to noon.

forensic (fəren´sik) *a.* **1** of or relating to courts of law, crime detection or to public debate. **2** of, used in or relating to forensic science. **3** used in debates or legal proceedings. ~*n.* (*usu. pl.*, *coll.*) forensic science. **forensically** *adv.* **forensic medicine** *n.* the science of medicine in its relation to law, medical jurisprudence. **forensic science** *n.* the application of scientific techniques to the investigation and detection of crimes.

foreordain (fawrawdān´) *v.t.* to ordain beforehand, to predestinate. **foreordination** (-dinā´-shən) *n.*

forepaw (faw´paw) *n.* either of the front paws of a four-footed animal.

forepeak (faw´pēk) *n.* (*Naut.*) the part of a vessel's hold in the angle of the bow.

foreplay (faw´plā) *n.* sexual stimulation preceding intercourse.

forequarter (faw´kwawtə) *n.* **1** the front half of the side of a carcass, as of beef. **2** (*pl.*) the forelegs, shoulders and chest of a horse or similar quadruped.

forerun (fawrŭn´) *v.t.* (*pres.p.* **forerunning**, *past* **foreran** (-ran´), *p.p.* **forerun**) **1** to precede, to go before. **2** to betoken, to usher in. **forerunner** (faw´-) *n.* **1** a predecessor, an ancestor. **2** a precursor, herald. **3** a messenger sent before.

foresail (faw´sāl, -səl) *n.* (*Naut.*) the principal sail on the foremast.

foresee (fawsē´) *v.t.* (*pres.p.* **foreseeing**, *past* **foresaw** (-saw´), *p.p.* **foreseen** (-sēn´)) **1** to see beforehand. **2** to know beforehand, to have prescience of. **foreseeable** *a.* **foreseeability** (-bil´iti) *n.* **foreseeably** *adv.* **foreseer** *n.*

foreshadow (fawshad´ō) *v.t.* **1** to show or be a sign or warning of beforehand. **2** to typify beforehand, to prefigure.

foresheet (faw´shēt) *n.* (*Naut.*) **1** the rope holding the lee corner of a foresail. **2** (*pl.*) the space in a boat forward of the foremost thwart, usu. covered with a grating.

foreshock (faw´shok) *n.* a comparatively small earthquake that precedes a much larger earthquake.

foreshore (faw´shaw) *n.* **1** the part of the shore lying between high- and low-water marks. **2** the ground between the sea and land that is cultivated or built upon.

foreshorten (fawshaw´tən) *v.t.* in drawing or painting, to represent (figures or parts of figures that project towards the spectator) so as to give a correct impression of form and proportions.

foreshow (fawshō´) *v.t.* (*past* **foreshowed**, *p.p.* **foreshown** (-shōn´)) **1** to predict, to represent beforehand. **2** to foreshadow.

foresight (faw´sīt) *n.* **1** consideration beforehand, forethought. **2** provident care for the future, prudence, precaution. **3** the front sight of a gun. **foresighted** (fawsī´tīd) *a.* **foresightedly** *adv.* **foresightedness** *n.*

foreskin (faw´skin) *n.* the prepuce, the loose skin covering the end of the penis.

forest (for´ist) *n.* **1** an extensive wood or area of wooded country. **2** the trees growing in such an area. **3** something resembling a forest, because having a dense mass of tall vertical objects. *~v.t.* **1** to plant with trees. **2** to convert into a forest. **forestation** (foristā´shən) *n.* the planting of a forest. **forester** *n.* **1** a person who is in charge of a forest. **2** an inhabitant of a forest. **3** a bird, beast or tree of a forest. **4** a person who looks after the trees on an estate. **forestry** *n.* **1** the science of cultivating trees and managing forests. **2** the management of growing timber. **3** (*poet.*) woodland, a multitude of trees. **forest tree** *n.* a large tree that is suitable to be grown in a forest.

forestall (fawstawl´) *v.t.* **1** to hinder by anticipation; to act beforehand in order to prevent. **2** to anticipate. **3** to deal beforehand with. **4** to buy up (commodities) beforehand so as to control the sale. **forestaller** *n.*

forestay (faw´stā) *n.* (*Naut.*) a strong rope, reaching from the foremast head to the bowsprit end, to support the mast.

foretaste[1] (faw´tāst) *n.* **1** experience or enjoyment (of) beforehand. **2** anticipation.

foretaste[2] (fawtāst´) *v.t.* **1** to taste beforehand. **2** to anticipate enjoyment (of).

foretell (fawtel´) *v.t.* (*past, p.p.* **foretold** (-tōld´)) to predict, to prophesy. **foreteller** *n.*

forethought (faw´thawt) *n.* **1** consideration beforehand. **2** deliberate intention beforehand. **3** foresight, provident care.

foretoken[1] (fawtō´kən) *v.t.* to foreshadow, to prognosticate.

foretoken[2] (faw´tōkən) *n.* a token beforehand, an omen.

foretop (faw´top, -təp) *n.* (*Naut.*) the top or platform at the head of the foremast. **fore-topgallant-mast** *n.* (*Naut.*) the mast above the fore-topmast. **fore-topgallant-sail** *n.* (*Naut.*) the sail above the fore-topsail. **fore-topmast** *n.* (*Naut.*) the mast at the head of the foremast. **fore-topsail** *n.* (*Naut.*) the sail above the foresail.

forever (fəre´və) *adv.* **1** (**for ever**) for all future time, eternally. **2** continually, persistently. **forevermore** (-maw´) *adv.* (*N Am.*) used to add more emphasis than *forever* or *for ever*.

forewarn (faw·wawn´) *v.t.* to warn or caution beforehand. **forewarner** *n.*

forewent FOREGO[1].

forewoman (faw´wumən) *n.* (*pl.* **forewomen** (-wimin)) **1** a woman who supervises other workers. **2** the woman who acts as a chairperson and spokesperson for a jury.

foreword (faw´wœd) *n.* a short introduction at the beginning of a book, often written by someone other than the author.

foreyard (faw´yahd) *n.* (*Naut.*) the lowest yard on a foremast.

forfeit (faw´fit) *n.* **1** a penalty, a fine, esp. a stipulated sum to be paid in case of breach of contract. **2** something which is lost through fault, crime, omission or neglect. **3** (*pl.*) a game in which for every breach of the rules the players have to give up some article or perform a playful task or ceremony. **4** the article given up or task etc. performed in this way. **5** the process of forfeiting. *~a.* lost or surrendered through fault or crime. *~v.t.* (*pres.p.* **forfeiting**, *past, p.p.* **forfeited**) to lose the right to or possession of by fault, crime, omission or neglect. **forfeitable** *a.* **forfeiter** *n.* **forfeiture** (-chə) *n.*

forfend (fawfend´), **forefend** *v.t.* **1** †to avert, to ward off. **2** (*N Am.*) to secure or protect.

❌ **forfit** common misspelling of FORFEIT.

forgather FOREGATHER.

forgave FORGIVE.

forge[1] (fawj) *v.t.* **1** to make, invent, or imitate fraudulently, to counterfeit (*to forge money*). **2** to fabricate, esp. to counterfeit or alter a signature or document with intent to defraud. **3** to make or construct. **4** to form or fabricate by heating and hammering. ~*n.* **1** the workshop of a smith. **2** a blacksmith's open fireplace or hearth where iron is heated by forced draught. **3** a furnace or hearth for making wrought iron. **forgeable** *a.* **forger** *n.* **forgery** (-jə-) *n.* (*pl.* **forgeries**) **1** the act of forging, counterfeiting or falsifying. **2** a fraudulent imitation.

forge[2] (fawj) *v.i.* **1** to move steadily (forward or ahead). **2** to move at an increased speed (forward or ahead).

forget (fəget´) *v.t., v.i.* (*pres.p.* **forgetting**, *past* **forgot** (-got´), *p.p.* **forgotten** (-got´ən), (*N Am.*) **forgot**) **1** to lose remembrance of. **2** to fail to remember or bring through inadvertence. **3** to neglect (to do something). **4** to put out of mind purposely. **to forget oneself 1** to lose one's self-control, to behave unbecomingly. **2** to act unselfishly. **forgetful** *a.* **1** tending to be absent-minded. **2** neglectful, forgetting. **forgetfully** *adv.* **forgetfulness** *n.* **forget-me-not** (fəget´minot) *n.* a small plant of the genus *Myosotis*, esp. *M. scorpoides*, with small bright blue flowers. **forgettable** *a.* **forgetter** *n.*

forgive (fəgiv´) *v.t.* (*pres.p.* **forgiving**, *past* **forgave** (-gāv´), *p.p.* **forgiven** (-giv´ən)) **1** to cease to feel anger or resentment towards. **2** to pardon, not to punish (a person or offence). **3** not to exact the penalty for. ~*v.i.* to show forgiveness. **forgivable** *a.* **forgivably** *adv.* **forgiveness** *n.* **1** the act of forgiving. **2** the tendency to forgive. **3** the state of being forgiven. **forgiver** *n.* **forgiving** *a.* inclined to forgive; merciful, gracious. **forgivingly** *adv.*

forgo (fawgō´, fə-), **forego** *v.t.* (*3rd pers. sing. pres.* **forgoes**, **foregoes**, *pres.p.* **forgoing**, **foregoing**, *past* **forwent** (-went´), **forewent**, *p.p.* **forgone** (-gon´), **foregone**) **1** to go without, to refrain from. **2** to give up, deny oneself, renounce, relinquish, decline; to quit.

Usage note See note under FOREGO[1].

forgone FORGO.

forgot, forgotten FORGET.

☒ **foriegn** common misspelling of FOREIGN.

forint (for´int) *n.* the monetary unit of Hungary since 1946, equivalent to 100 fillér.

fork (fawk) *n.* **1** an instrument with two or more prongs, used in eating or cooking. **2** an agricultural implement terminating in two or more prongs, used for digging, impaling, lifting, carrying or throwing. **3** anything of a similar form (*a tuning fork*). **4** a forking or bifurcation. **5** a diverging branch. **6** a confluent, a tributary. **7** a point where a road divides into two. **8** a forked support into which a bicycle wheel fits. **9** the crutch, the bifurcation of the human body. **10** in chess or draughts, a simultaneous attack on two pieces. **11** a flash of forked lightning. ~*v.t.* **1** to raise or pitch with a fork. **2** to dig or break up (ground) with a fork. **3** to make sharp or pointed. **4** in chess or draughts, to attack two pieces so that only one can escape. ~*v.i.* **1** to divide into two. **2** to send out branches. **3** to take one or other branch at a fork in the road etc. **to fork out/ up** (*coll.*) to hand over or pay (money), esp. unwillingly. **to fork over 1** to turn over (soil) using a fork. **2** (*coll.*) to hand over (money), esp. unwillingly. **forked** *a.* **1** dividing into branches, branching, cleft, bifurcated. **2** terminating in points or prongs. **3** having a certain number of prongs (*two-forked*). **forked lightning** *n.* lightning in the form of a jagged or branching line. **fork-lift truck** *n.* a vehicle which raises and transports by means of two power-driven horizontal steel prongs. **forklike** *a.* **fork lunch, fork supper** *n.* a buffet at which food is eaten using a fork.

forlorn (fəlawn´) *a.* **1** lonely and sad. **2** deserted, abandoned, uncared-for. **3** helpless, wretched, hopeless. **forlornly** *adv.* **forlornness** *n.*

forlorn hope (fəlawn hōp´) *n.* **1** a bold, desperate enterprise. **2** a faint hope.

form (fawm) *n.* **1** the shape or external appearance of anything apart from its colour. **2** configuration, figure, outline, esp. of the human body. **3** particular arrangement, disposition, organization or constitution. **4** a document with blanks to be filled in. **5** a document that is regularly drawn. **6** established practice or method. **7** a rule of procedure, ceremony or ritual. **8** the mode in which anything is perceptible to the senses or intellect. **9** kind, specific state, species, variety, variation. **10** a specific shape of a word as regards inflection, spelling or pronunciation. **11** the outward aspects of words, in contrast to their meaning. **12** a shape, mould or model upon which a thing is fashioned. **13** a customary method or formula. **14** a fixed order of words. **15** artistic style or mode of expression, as opposed to content or subject matter. **16** orderly arrangement of parts, order, symmetry. **17** behaviour according to accepted rules or conventions. **18** good physical condition or fitness, a good state of health or training; general state or inclination. **19** in sport, the performance of a person or animal over a period of time. **20** (*sl.*) a criminal record. **21** a long seat without a back. **22** a class in a school considered as an administrative unit, all the pupils in a particular year or a subdivision of a year group. **23** the seat or bed of a hare. **24** (*esp. N Am.*) FORME. **25** (*also* **formwork**) a temporary mould that is used to hold concrete while setting. **26** that which differentiates matter and generates species. **27** (*Philos.*) the essential nature of something. ~*v.t.* **1** to give form or shape to. **2** to arrange in any particular manner. **3** to make, construct or create. **4** to train, to instruct, to mould or shape by discipline. **5** to develop, conceive, devise, construct (ideas etc.). **6** to be the material for. **7** to be or constitute (a part or one of). **8** to organize or embody. **9** to articulate. **10** (*Mil.*) to combine into (a certain order). **11** (*Gram.*) to make by derivation or by affixes or prefixes. ~*v.i.* **1** to assume a form. **2** (*Mil.*) to combine (into a certain order). **in/ on form** showing one's talent to advantage, playing, running or performing well. **off form** playing or performing below one's usual standard. **out of form** not playing, running or performing well. **formless** *a.* **1** without form, shapeless. **2** having no regular form. **formlessly** *adv.* **formlessness** *n.* **form letter** *n.* (a copy of) a standard letter sent to many different people, often with relevant individual details added.

-form (fawm), **-iform** (ifawm) *suf.* **1** like, having the shape of, as *cruciform, dendriform.* **2** having a certain number of forms, as *multiform, uniform.*

formal (faw´məl) *a.* **1** made, performed, held or done according to established forms. **2** observant of established form, ceremonious, serious, punctilious, precise. **3** conventional, perfunctory. **4** explicit, definite. **5** orderly, regular. **6** in a set form. **7** of or relating to the outward form as opposed to reality, content or subject matter, outward. ~*n.* (*N Am.*) **1** a social occasion at which formal dress is worn. **2** an evening gown. **formalism** *n.* **1** (*esp. derog.*) the quality of being formal, esp. without consideration of the inner reality or content. **2** formality, esp. in religion. **3** (*Math.*) **a** the notation or structure in which information is expressed. **b** a mathematical description of a physical situation. **4** a stylistic method of theatrical production. **formalist** *n.* **formalistic** (-lis´-) *a.* **formality** (-mal´-) *n.* (*pl.* **formalities**) **1** conventionality, mere form. **2** an established order or method, an observance required by custom or etiquette, esp. without having any real effect. **3** conformity to custom, rule or established method. **4** the condition or quality of being formal. **5** artistic precision, observance of rule as opposed to originality. **formalize, formalise** *v.t.* **1** to make or render formal. **2** to give legal formality to, to formulate. **formalization** (-zā´shən) *n.* **formally** *adv.*

formaldehyde (fawmal´dihīd) *n.* (*Chem.*) formic aldehyde, a colourless gas generated by the partial oxidation of methyl alcohol, and used as an antiseptic and disinfectant.

formalin (fawm´əlin) *n.* a solution of formaldehyde used as an antiseptic, for the destruction of disease germs, and as a food preservative.

format (faw´mat) *n.* **1** the external form and size of a book, magazine etc. **2** the general plan, arrangement and style of e.g. a television programme. **3** (*Comput.*) the arrangement of data on a disk etc. ~*v.t.* (*pres.p.* **formatting**, *past, p.p.* **formatted**) **1** to arrange in a specific format. **2** (*Comput.*) to prepare (a disk etc.) for the reception of data.

formate FORMIC.

formation (fawmā´shən) *n.* **1** the act or process of forming or creating. **2** the state of being formed

or created. **3** the manner in which anything is formed. **4** conformation, arrangement, disposition of parts, structure. **5** a thing formed, regarded in relation to form or structure. **6** (*Geol.*) a group of rocks or strata of common origin, structure or physical character. **7** an arrangement of troops, aircraft, ships etc. (*formation flying*). **formational** *a.* **formative** (faw´mə-) *a.* **1** having the power of giving form, shaping. **2** of or relating to formation, growth or development. **3** (*Gram.*) (of combining forms, prefixes etc.) serving to form words. ~*n.* (*Gram.*) a formative combining form, prefix etc. **formatively** *adv.*

forme (fawm) *n.* (*Print.*) **1** a body of type composed and locked in a chase for printing. **2** a quantity of film arranged for making a plate.

former[1] (faw´mə) *a.* **1** preceding in time. **2** mentioned before something else, the first-mentioned (of two). **3** past, earlier, ancient, bygone. **formerly** *adv.* **1** in former times. **2** of the past or earlier times.

Usage note *The former* should not be used to mean the first-mentioned of more than two (*the first*).

---

former[2] (faw´mə) *n.* **1** a person or thing that forms. **2** in electrical engineering, a frame or core on which a coil can be wound. **3** a structural part of an aircraft that helps to maintain the shape of the fuselage, a wing etc. **4** (*in comb.*) a member of a certain school form (*a sixth-former*).

formic (faw´mik) *a.* (*Chem.*) of, relating to or produced by ants. **formate** (-māt) *n.* (*Chem.*) a salt or ester of formic acid. **formic acid** *n.* an acid found in the fluid emitted by ants, in stinging nettles etc., and now obtained from oxalic acid distilled with glycerine.

Formica® (fawmī´kə) *n.* a hard, long-lasting laminated plastic used for surfacing materials and other purposes.

formidable (faw´midəbəl, -mid´-) *a.* **1** tending to excite fear or respect. **2** to be feared. **3** dangerous to encounter. **4** difficult to resist, overcome or accomplish. **formidability** (-bil´-) *n.* **formidableness** *n.* **formidably** *adv.*

Usage note The pronunciation (-mid´-), with stress on the second syllable, is sometimes disapproved of.

---

formula (faw´mūlə) *n.* (*pl.* **formulas, formulae** (-lē)) **1** (*Chem.*) (*pl.* **formulae**) an expression by means of symbols of the elements of a compound. **2** (*Math.*) (*pl.* **formulae**) the expression of a rule or principle in algebraic symbols. **3** a prescribed form of words. **4** a fixed rule, a set form, a conventional usage. **5** a formal enunciation of faith, doctrine, principle etc. **6** a compromise solution to a dispute, an agreed form of words. **7** a prescription, a recipe. **8** a milk mixture or substitute used as baby food. **9** a technical specification which determines the class in which a racing car competes. **formulaic** (-lā´ik) *a.* **formularize, formularise** *v.t.* to formulate. **formulary** *a.* **1** stated, prescribed. **2** of the nature of a formula; using formulae. *~n.* (*pl.* **formularies**) **1** a book containing stated and prescribed forms, esp. relating to religious belief or ritual. **2** a collection of formulae used in preparation of medicinal drugs. **formulate** *v.t.* **1** to express in a formula. **2** to set forth in a precise and systematic form. **formulation** (-lā´shən) *n.* **formulator** *n.* **formulism** *n.* strict observance of or dependence upon formulas. **formulist** *n.* **formulistic** (-lis´-) *a.* **formulize, formulise** *v.t.* to formulate. **formulization** (-zā´shən) *n.*

fornicate (faw´nikāt) *v.i.* (*formal or facet.*) to commit fornication. **fornication** (-kā´shən) *n.* voluntary sexual intercourse between two unmarried people or between people not married to each other. **fornicator** *n.*

forsake (fəsāk´) *v.t.* (*pres.p.* **forsaking**, *past* **forsook** (-suk´), *p.p.* **forsaken** (-sā´kən)) **1** to leave, to abandon, to withdraw from. **2** to renounce, to cast off, to reject, to give up. **forsaker** *n.*

forsooth (fəsooth´) *adv.* (*esp. iron.*) in truth, certainly, doubtless.

forswear (fəswea´) *v.t.* (*past* **foreswore** (-swaw´), *p.p.* **foresworn** (-swawn´)) to abjure, to renounce upon oath or with protestations. **to forswear oneself** to perjure oneself.

forsythia (fawsī´thiə) *n.* any oleaceous shrub of the genus *Forsythia* bearing numerous yellow flowers in early spring before the leaves.

fort (fawt) *n.* a fortified place, esp. a detached outwork or an independent fortified work of moderate extent.

forte¹ (faw´tā, faw´ti, fawt) *n.* **1** a person's strong point. **2** that in which a person excels. **3** the strong part of a sword blade, i.e. from the hilt to the middle.

forte² (faw´ti) *adv.* (*Mus.*) with loudness or force. *~a.* performed with loudness or force. *~n.* a passage to be performed with loudness or force. **fortepiano** *n.* (*pl.* **fortepianos**) an early form of piano. **forte piano** *adv.* (*Mus.*) loudly, then softly. *~a.* loud, then soft.

forth (fawth) *adv.* **1** forward. **2** out. **3** out into view. **4** out from home or another starting point. **5** out of doors. **6** forwards in place, time or order. **back and forth** to and fro. **forthcoming** *a.* **1** coming forth, ready to appear or to be produced, published etc. **2** approaching, soon to take place. **3** available. **4** (of a person) communicative, responsive. **forthcomingness** *n.* **forthright** *a.* outspoken, direct, to the point. *~adv.* in a direct or outspoken manner. **forthrightly** *adv.* **forthrightness** *n.* **forthwith** (-with´, -widh´) *adv.* immediately, without delay.

forties, fortieth FORTY.

fortify (faw´tifī) *v.t.* (*3rd pers. sing. pres.* **fortifies**, *pres.p.* **fortifying**, *past, p.p.* **fortified**) **1** to strengthen or secure by forts, ramparts etc. **2** to make strong, to give power or strength to, to invigorate, to encourage. **3** to strengthen the structure of.

4 to add alcoholic strength to. **5** to enrich (a food) by adding vitamins etc. **6** to confirm, to corroborate. *~v.i.* to raise fortifications. **fortifiable** *a.* **fortification** (-fikā´shən) *n.* **1** (*Mil.*) **a** the act, process, art or science of fortifying a place or position against the attacks of an enemy. **b** a defensive work, a fort. **2** increasing the strength of wine with alcohol. **fortifier** *n.*

fortissimo (fawtis´imō) *adv.* (*Mus.*) very loudly. *~a.* performed very loudly. *~n.* (*pl.* **fortissimos**, **fortissimi** (-mē)) a passage that is to be performed very loudly.

fortitude (faw´titūd) *n.* strength, esp. that strength of mind which enables one to meet danger or endure pain with calmness.

fortnight (fawt´nīt) *n.* **1** a period of two weeks or 14 days. **2** two weeks from a certain day (*on Thursday fortnight*). **fortnightly** *a.* happening or produced once a fortnight. *~adv.* **1** once a fortnight. **2** every fortnight. *~n.* (*pl.* **fortnightlies**) a fortnightly publication.

fortress (faw´tris) *n.* a fortified place, esp. a strongly fortified town accommodating a large garrison and forming a permanent stronghold.

fortuitous (fawtū´itəs) *a.* happening by chance; casual, accidental. **fortuitously** *adv.* **fortuitousness** *n.* **fortuity** *n.* (*pl.* **fortuities**) **1** a chance occurrence; an accident. **2** fortuitousness.

Usage note *Fortuitous* is sometimes used as though it meant fortunate or opportune, but this is best avoided.

fortunate (faw´chənət) *a.* **1** lucky, prosperous. **2** happening by good luck. **3** bringing or indicating good fortune, auspicious. **fortunately** *adv.* **1** luckily. **2** it is fortunate that.

fortune (faw´choon, -chən) *n.* **1** wealth. **2** a large property or sum of money. **3** chance, luck, that which happens as if by chance. **4** that which brings good or ill, a personification of this, a supernatural power supposed to control one's lot and to bestow good or evil (*Fortune smiled on them*). **5** good luck, prosperity. **6** a person's future destiny. **7** (*pl.*) the progress or history of a person or thing. **to make a/ one's fortune** to gain great wealth. **to tell a person's fortune** to make predictions about a person's future, by looking e.g. at the lines on their hand. **fortune cookie** *n.* (*N Am.*) a biscuit with a slip of paper inside it, which has a prediction, proverb, joke etc. written on it. **fortune hunter** *n.* (*coll.*) a person who seeks to gain wealth, esp. through marriage. **fortune-hunting** *n., a.* **fortune-teller** *n.* a person who makes predictions about a person's future. **fortune-telling** *n.*

forty (faw´ti) *n.* (*pl.* **forties**) **1** the number or figure 40 or xl. **2** the age of 40. **3** a set of 40 people or things. *~a.* **1** 40 in number. **2** aged 40. **forties** (faw´tiz) *n.pl.* **1** the period of time between one's 40th and 50th birthdays. **2** the range of temperature between 40 and 50 degrees. **3** the period of time between the 40th and 50th years of a

forum

foundation

century. **fortieth** (faw´tiəth) *n.* any one of 40 equal parts. ~*n., a.* **1** (the) last of 40 (people, things etc.). **2** the next after the 39th. **forty-first, forty-second etc.** *n., a.* the ordinal numbers corresponding to forty-one etc. **fortyfold** *a., adv.* **forty-one, forty-two etc.** *n.* the cardinal numbers between forty and fifty. **forty winks** *n.pl.* a nap.

forum (faw´rəm) *n.* (*pl.* **forums, fora** (-rə)) **1** a place of assembly for public discussion or judicial purposes. **2** a meeting to discuss matters of public interest. **3** a medium, e.g. a magazine, for open discussion. **4** a tribunal, a court of law.

forward (faw´wəd) *a.* **1** at or near the forepart of anything. **2** in front. **3** towards the front. **4** onward. **5** in advance, advancing or advanced. **6** well advanced, progressing, early, premature, precocious. **7** eager, prompt. **8** pert, presumptuous. **9** of or relating to future commercial dealings, products etc. ~*n.* a mainly attacking player at football etc. stationed at the front of a formation. ~*v.t.* **1** to help onward, to promote. **2** to send on or ahead, to send to a further destination. **3** to send. ~*adv.* **1** (*also* **forwards**) **a** towards the front. **b** onward in place or time. **c** onward so as to make progress. **d** towards the future. **e** ahead, in advance. **f** to the front, to a prominent position. **2** (*Naut. etc.*) towards, at or in the forepart of a vessel or aircraft. **forwarder** *n.* **forward-looking** *a.* **1** progressive. **2** looking to, or planning for, the future. **forwardly** *adv.* **forwardness** *n.*

forwent FORGO.

fosse (fos) *n.* a ditch, a trench, esp. around a fortification, commonly filled with water.

fossil (fos´əl) *n.* **1** the hardened remains of a prehistoric animal or plant found inside a rock etc. **2** (*coll.*) an antiquated, out-of-date or inflexible person or thing. **3** a word or phrase once current but now found only in a few special contexts. ~*a.* **1** preserved in the strata of the earth's crust, esp. if mineralized. **2** of, like or relating to fossils. **3** antiquated. **fossil fuel** *n.* a naturally-occurring fuel formed by the decomposition of prehistoric organisms. **fossiliferous** (-lif´-) *a.* **fossilize, fossilise** *v.t.* **1** to convert into a fossil. **2** to render antiquated or inflexible. ~*v.i.* **1** to be converted into a fossil. **2** to become antiquated or inflexible. **fossilization** (-zā´shən) *n.*

foster (fos´tə) *v.t.* **1** to nourish, to support, to encourage, to promote the growth of. **2** to bring up or nurse (esp. a child not one's own). **3** to place in the charge of foster parents. **4** (of circumstances) to be favourable to. **5** to harbour (an ill feeling). ~*a.* of or relating to fostering (*a foster home*). **fosterage** *n.* **fosterer** *n.*

fouetté (fwet´ā) *n.* a step in ballet in which the dancer stands on one foot and makes a whiplike movement with the other.

fought, †foughten FIGHT.

foul (fowl) *a.* **1** dirty, filthy, unclean. **2** loathsome, offensive to the senses. **3 a** covered or filled with noxious matter. **b** overgrown with weeds,

clogged, choked. **4** (*coll.*) disgusting, revolting. **5** morally offensive, obscene, disgusting. **6** polluted. **7** unfair, unlawful, dishonest, against the rules. **8** stormy, cloudy, rainy. **9** (of a rope) entangled. **10** (of the bottom of a vessel) covered with barnacles, weeds etc. **11** (of a proof) full of printer's errors, dirty, inaccurate. ~*adv.* irregularly, against the rules. ~*n.* **1** in sport, a foul stroke, any breach of the rules of a game or contest. **2** an entanglement, blockage or collision, e.g. in sailing, riding or fishing. **3** a foul thing. ~*v.t.* **1** to make foul or dirty. **2** in sport, to commit a foul against. **3** to come into collision with, to impede, block or entangle. ~*v.i.* **1** to become foul or dirty. **2** to come into collision. **3** to become clogged or entangled. **4** in sport, to commit a foul. **to fall foul of 1** to come or run against with force. **2** to come into collision, entanglement or conflict with. **3** to quarrel with. **4** to be contrary to, to go against. **to foul up 1** to make dirty, to pollute. **2** to block, to entangle. **3** to become blocked or entangled. **4** (*coll.*) to blunder. **foully** *adv.* **foul mouth** *n.* a person who uses offensive language. **foul-mouthed, foul-spoken, foul-tongued** *a.* **foulness** *n.* **foul play** *n.* **1** unfair behaviour in a game or contest, a breach of the rules. **2** dishonest or treacherous conduct. **3** violence, murder. **foul-up** *n.* a bungled or blundered situation.

foulard (foolah´, -lahd´) *n.* **1** a soft, thin material of silk or silk mixed with cotton. **2** something made of this, e.g. a silk handkerchief.

found¹ FIND.

found² (fownd) *v.t.* **1** to set up or establish (an institution, organization etc.) by providing the necessary money, to endow. **2** to lay the foundation or basis of. **3** to begin to erect or build. **4** to originate, to give origin to. **5** to construct or base (upon). ~*v.i.* to rest (upon) as a foundation or basis. **founder¹** *n.* a person who founds or originates anything, esp. one who endows a permanent fund for the support of an institution. **founding** *n., a.* **founding father** *n.* **1** a member of the American Constitutional Convention of 1787. **2** a person who establishes or institutes something.

found³ (fownd) *v.t.* **1** to cast by melting (metal) or fusing (material for glass) and pouring it into a mould. **2** to make of molten metal or glass. **founder²** *n.* **foundry** *n.* (*pl.* **foundries**) **1** a building where metals are cast. **2** the act or art of casting metals.

foundation (fowndā´shən) *n.* **1** the natural or artificial base of a structure. **2** (*pl.*) the part of a structure below the surface of the ground. **3** the grounds, principles or basis on which anything stands. **4** the reasons on which an opinion etc. is founded. **5** the act of founding or establishing. **6** that on which anything is established or by which it is sustained. **7** an endowed institution. **8** (*also* **foundation garment**) a woman's undergarment that supports the figure, e.g. a corset. **9** a cosmetic used as a base for other facial make-up. **foundational** *a.* **foundation course** *n.* a basic, general course, taught e.g. in the first year at some universities and colleges. **foundation cream** *n.* a cream over which cosmetics are applied. **foundation stone** *n.* **1** a stone laid with ceremony to commemorate the founding of a building. **2** the basis of something on which future success depends.

founder¹ FOUND².

founder² FOUND³.

founder³ (fown´də) *v.i.* **1** (of a ship) to fill with water and sink. **2** to fail, to break down. **3** to be ruined. **4** to fall in, to give way. **5** (of a horse) to fall lame. ~*v.t.* **1** to sink (a ship) by making it fill with water. **2** to lame by causing soreness or inflammation in the feet of (a horse).

foundling (fownd´ling) *n.* a deserted child of unknown parents.

foundry FOUND³.

fount¹ (fownt) *n.* (*poet.*) **1** a spring, a fountain, a well. **2** a source.

fount² FONT².

fountain (fown´tin) *n.* **1** an ornamental jet of water driven high into the air by pressure. **2** the structure for producing such a jet. **3** a public structure with a drinking supply. **4** a spring of water, natural or artificial. **5** a source, a first principle. **6** a reservoir to contain a liquid, as in a lamp, printing press, fountain pen etc. **7** a soda fountain. **fountained** *a.* **fountainhead** *n.* an original source or spring. **fountain pen** *n.* a pen with a reservoir or cartridge containing ink.

four (faw) *n.* **1** the number or figure 4 or iv. **2** the age of four. **3** the fourth hour after midnight or midday. **4** a set of four persons or things, a team of four horses, a four-oared boat or its crew. **5** a card or domino with four spots. **6** in cricket, (a score of four runs from) a shot which crosses the boundary after hitting the ground. **7** a size measuring four. ~*a.* four in number, aged four. **on all fours 1** crawling on the hands and feet or knees. **2** agreeing precisely (with). **four-eyes** *n.* (*sl.*) a person wearing glasses. **four-flush** *n.* a worthless poker hand in which only four of the five cards are of the same suit. **four-flusher** *n.* (*N Am., sl.*) a bluffer. **fourfold** *a.* **1** four times as many or as much, quadruple. **2** consisting of four parts. ~*adv.* in fourfold measure. **four-in-hand** *a.* drawn by four horses. ~*adv.* with four horses driven by one driver. ~*n.* **1** a vehicle so drawn and driven. **2** (*N Am.*) a long necktie tied in a skip-knot with the ends left dangling. **four-leaf, four-leaved** *a.* (of a clover leaf) with four leaflets instead of three, supposed to bring good luck. **four-letter word** *n.* any of a number of short English words referring to the body, sex or excrement and considered vulgar or obscene. **four o'clock** *n.* the marvel of Peru, *Mirabilis jalapa*, so named from its flowers opening at four o'clock in the afternoon. **fourpence** (faw´pəns) *n.* the sum of four pence. **fourpenny** *a.* worth fourpence, costing fourpence. **four-poster** *n.* a (usu. large) bedstead with a canopy and curtains.

†**fourscore** *a.* **1** 4 times 20, 80. **2** 80 years old. ~*n.* the number of 4 times 20. **foursome** *n.* **1** a group of four people. **2** a game of golf between two pairs, the partners playing their ball alternately. **four-square** *a.* **1** having four sides and angles equal. **2** square-shaped. **3** firmly established. **4** immovable, resolute, forthright. ~*adv.* resolutely. **four-stroke** *a.* **1** (of an internal-combustion engine) firing once every four strokes of movement of the piston. **2** (of a vehicle) having a four-stroke engine. ~*n.* a four-stroke engine or vehicle. **four-wheel drive** *n.* a system whereby power is transmitted to all four wheels of a motor vehicle.

fourteen (faw´tēn, -tēn´) *n.* **1** the number or figure 14 or xiv. **2** the age of 14. **3** a size measuring 14. ~*a.* **1** 14 in number. **2** aged 14. **fourteenth** *n.* any one of 14 equal parts. ~*n., a.* **1** (the) last of 14 (people, things etc.). **2** (the) next after the 13th.

fourth (fawth) *n.* **1** any one of four equal parts, a quarter. **2** the person or thing in fourth position. **3** the fourth forward gear of a motor vehicle. **4** (*Mus.*) **a** an interval of four diatonic notes, comprising two whole tones and a semitone. **b** two notes separated by this interval sounded together. ~*n., a.* **1** (the) last of four (people, things etc.). **2** (the) next after the third. **fourth dimension** *n.* the extra coordinate (time) needed to locate a point in space. **fourth estate** *n.* (*facet.*) the newspaper press; journalism or journalists collectively. **fourthly** *adv.* in the fourth place.

X **fourty** common misspelling of FORTY.

fovea (fō´viə) *n.* (*pl.* **foveae** (-viē)) **1** (*Anat.*) a small pit or depression. **2** a small depression in the back of the retina of the eye, for sharpest vision. **foveal** *a.* **foveate** (-āt) *a.*

fowl (fowl) *n.* (*pl. in general* **fowl**, *in particular* **fowls**) **1** a cock or hen of the domestic or poultry kind, kept mainly for its eggs and flesh. **2** any other domesticated bird e.g. the turkey or duck, kept for its eggs and flesh. **3** their flesh used as food. **4** a bird. **5** birds collectively. ~*v.i.* to hunt, catch or kill wild birds for sport. **fowler** *n.* **fowling** *n.* **fowl pest** *n.* a contagious virus disease of fowls.

fox (foks) *n.* **1** any of various doglike mammals of the genus *Vulpes* or a related genus with a pointed snout, erect ears and a straight bushy tail, esp. the reddish brown *V. vulpes*. **2** the fur of a fox. **3** a sly, cunning person. **4** (*esp. N Am., sl.*) a physically attractive woman. ~*v.t.* **1** to baffle, to perplex. **2** to trick, to outwit. **3** (*esp. p.p.*) to discolour (pages of a book etc.). ~*v.i.* **1** to be crafty. **2** (of paper etc.) to become discoloured, esp. to turn reddish. **foxed** *a.* stained with spots, as a book or print. **foxglove** *n.* any tall plant of the genus *Digitalis*, esp. *D. purpurea*, with purple flowers resembling the fingers of a glove, the leaves of which are used as a sedative. **foxhole** *n.* **1** (*Mil.*) a small trench. **2** a place of refuge or hiding. **foxhound** *n.* a hound bred and trained to hunt foxes. **fox-hunt** *n.* **1** the hunting of a fox with hounds. **2** a group of people involved with this. ~*v.i.* to hunt foxes with hounds. **fox-hunter** *n.* **fox-hunting** *a.* of, relating to, or fond of hunting foxes. ~*n.* the act or practice of hunting foxes with a pack of hounds. **foxlike** *a.* **foxtail** *n.* any of several grasses of the genus *Alopecurus*, with soft cylindrical spikes of flowers, esp. *Alopecurus pratensis.* **fox terrier** *n.* a short-haired breed of dog, orig. employed to unearth foxes, now chiefly as a pet. **foxtrot** *n.* **1** a ballroom dance with a combination of slow and quick steps. **2** the music for this dance. ~*v.i.* (*pres.p.* **foxtrotting**, *past, p.p.* **foxtrotted**) to perform this dance. **foxy** *a.* (*comp.* **foxier**, *superl.* **foxiest**) **1** foxlike, tricky, crafty. **2** foxed. **3** (*esp. N Am.*) physically attractive. **4** reddish-brown in colour. **foxily** *adv.* **foxiness** *n.*

foyer (fo´yā, -yə) *n.* the entrance hall or other large public area where people meet or wait in a hotel, theatre etc.

fp *abbr.* **1** fortepiano. **2** (*also* **FP**) freezing point.

FPS *abbr.* Fellow of the Pharmaceutical Society.

fps, **f.p.s.** *abbr.* **1** feet per second. **2** foot-pound-second.

Fr *chem. symbol* francium.

Fr. *abbr.* Father.

fr. *abbr.* franc(s).

fracas (frak´ah) *n.* (*pl.* **fracas** (-ahz)) a disturbance, a row, an uproar, a noisy quarrel.

fraction (frak´shən) *n.* **1** a number that is not a whole number, e.g. ¼, 0.7. **2** a very small amount or portion. **3** a component of a mixture separated by a fractional process such as fractional distillation. **4** an organized dissenting political group. **5** the rite of breaking the bread in the Eucharist. **fractional, fractionary** *a.* **1** of or relating to fractions. **2** constituting a fraction. **3** forming but a small part, insignificant. **fractional distillation** *n.* (*Chem.*) the separation of liquids having different boiling points. **fractionalize, fractionalise** *v.t.* **fractionally** *adv.* **fractionate** (-nāt) *v.t.* to separate (a mixture) into portions having different properties, by distillation or analogous process. **fractionation** (-ā´shən) *n.* **fractionize, fractionise** *v.t.* to break up into fractions or divisions.

fractious (frak´shəs) *a.* **1** apt to quarrel. **2** snappish, cross, fretful, peevish. **3** unruly. **fractiously** *adv.* **fractiousness** *n.*

Usage note See note under FACTION[1].

fracture (frak´chə) *n.* **1** the act of breaking by violence. **2** a break, a breakage. **3** the result of breaking. **4** (*Med.*) the breakage of a bone or cartilage. ~*v.t.* **1** to break across. **2** to separate the continuity of the parts of. ~*v.i.* to break or crack.

fragile (fraj´īl) *a.* **1** brittle, easily broken. **2** weak, frail, delicate. **fragilely** *adv.* **fragility** (-jil´-) *n.*

fragment[1] (frag´mənt) *n.* **1** a piece broken off. **2** a small detached portion. **3** an incomplete or unfinished portion. **4** the surviving portion of a whole work of art etc. that has been destroyed.

fragmental (-men´-) *a.* **fragmentally, fragmentarily** *adv.* **fragmentary** *a.* **fragmentariness** *n.* **fragmentary rocks** *n.pl.* (*Geol.*) rocks made up of fragments, as breccias, conglomerates etc. **fragmentize, fragmentise** *v.t.*

fragment[2] (fragment´) *v.t., v.i.* (to cause) to break into fragments. **fragmentation** (-tā´shən) *n.* **fragmentation bomb** *n.* a bomb whose casing is designed to shatter in small, deadly fragments on explosion. **fragmented** *a.*

fragrant (frā´grənt) *a.* emitting a pleasant perfume, sweet-smelling, odorous. **fragrance** *n.* **1** a sweet smell. **2** the particular scent of a perfume, toilet water etc. **fragranced** *a.* **fragrancy** *n.* (*pl.* **fragrancies**) a fragrance. **fragrantly** *adv.*

frail (frāl) *a.* **1** fragile, delicate. **2** infirm, in weak health. **3** weak in character or resolution, liable to be led astray. **4** perishable, insubstantial. ~*n.* (*N Am., sl.*) a woman. **frailly** *adv.* **frailness** *n.* **frailty** *n.* (*pl.* **frailties**) **1** the condition of being frail. **2** a weakness or fault. **3** a liability to be led astray.

framboesia (frambē´ziə), (*N Am.*) **frambesia** *n.* (*Med.*) the yaws, a contagious eruption characterized by swellings like raspberries.

frame (frām) *n.* **1** a case or border to enclose or surround a picture, a pane of glass etc. **2** a structure that gives strength and shape to something. **3** a fabric or structure composed of parts fitted together. **4** the structure of a human body. **5** the rigid part of a bicycle. **6** the construction, constitution or build of anything. **7** (*pl.*) the structure of a pair of glasses, holding the lenses. **8** the established order or system (of society or the body politic). **9** disposition of mind (*a frame of mind*). **10** any of various machines in the form of framework used in manufacturing, mining, building, printing etc. **11** a single exposure on a film. **12** a single, complete television picture. **13 a** a triangular structure used to set up the balls for a break in snooker etc. **b** the balls so arranged. **c** a single round of a game of snooker etc. **14** a glazed portable structure for protecting plants from frost. **15** one of the sections of which a beehive is composed, esp. one for a honeycomb. **16** (*N Am., sl.*) a frame-up. ~*v.t.* **1** to surround with a frame; to serve as a frame to. **2** to form or construct by fitting parts together. **3** to fit, adapt or adjust. **4** to contrive. **5** to devise, to invent. **6** to compose, to express. **7** to plan, to arrange. **8** to form in the mind, to conceive, imagine. **9** to articulate, to form with the lips. **10** (*coll.*) to (conspire to) incriminate. **framable** *a.* **frame house** *n.* a house with a wooden framework covered with boards. **frameless** *a.* **frame of reference** *n.* **1** a set or system of standards, derived from an individual's experience, to which they refer when making judgements etc. **2** (*Geom.*) a set of axes used to describe the location of a point. **framer** *n.* **frame-saw** *n.* a flexible saw blade stretched in a frame to stiffen it. **frame-up** *n.* (*coll.*) an attempt to incriminate, a false criminal charge. **framework** *n.* **1** the frame of a structure. **2** the fabric for enclosing or supporting anything, or forming the substructure to a more complete fabric. **3** (*fig.*) structure, arrangement (of society etc.). **framing** *n.* **1** a frame, framework. **2** a setting.

franc (frangk) *n.* the standard unit of currency in France, Belgium, Switzerland and various other countries.

franchise (fran´chīz) *n.* **1** the right to vote. **2** the qualification for this. **3** citizenship. **4** a licence to market a company's goods or services in a specified area. **5** a right, privilege, immunity or exemption granted to an individual or to a body. **6** the district or territory to which a certain privilege or licence extends. ~*v.t.* to grant a franchise to. **franchisee** (-zē´) *n.* **franchisor, franchiser** *n.*

Franciscan (fransis´kən) *a.* of or relating to St Francis of Assisi, or the order of mendicant friars founded by him in 1209. ~*n.* a member of the Franciscan order, a grey friar.

francium (fran´siəm) *n.* (*Chem.*) a radioactive chemical element of the alkali metal group, at. no. 87, chem. symbol Fr.

Franco- (frang´kō), **franco-** *comb. form* of or relating to France or the French, as in *Franco-German, Franco-Russian.*

Francophile (frang´kōfīl) *n.* an admirer of France or the French.

Francophone (frang´kōfōn) *a.* French-speaking, having French as the native or an official language. ~*n.* a Francophone person.

frangible (fran´jibəl) *a.* that may be easily broken.

frangipane (fran´jipān) *n.* **1** a kind of pastry made with cream, almonds and sugar; a flan filled with this. **2** frangipani.

frangipani (franjipah´ni) *n.* (*pl.* **frangipanis**) **1** a shrub or tree of the tropical American genus *Plumeria* with clusters of fragrant white or pink flowers. **2** the perfume prepared from this plant.

franglais (frã´glā) *n.* an informal version of French which contains a high proportion of English words.

Frank (frangk) *n.* a member of the ancient Germanic peoples or tribes who conquered France in the 6th cent. **Frankish** *a., n.*

frank (frangk) *a.* **1** open, ingenuous, sincere, candid. **2** generous, liberal, profuse, free, unrestrained. **3** (*Med.*) unmistakable. ~*v.t.* to mark (a letter etc.) in such a way as to indicate that postage has been paid. ~*n.* a signature authorizing a letter to go through the post free of charge. **frankable** *a.* **franker** *n.* **franking machine** *n.* a machine that franks letters etc. **frankly** *adv.* **1** in a frank manner. **2** to be frank. **frankness** *n.*

Frankenstein (frang´kənstīn), **Frankenstein's monster** *n.* a work that brings disaster to its creator.

frankfurter (frangk´fœtə) *n.* a small, smoked sausage of beef and pork.

frankincense (frang´kinsens) *n.* a gum or resin

burning with a fragrant smell, used as incense, obtained from trees of the genus *Boswellia.*

frantic (fran´tik) *a.* **1** mad, distracted; wildly excited or desperately worried. **2** marked by extreme haste, agitation or desperation. **3** (*coll.*) intense, very great. **frantically, franticly** *adv.* **franticness** *n.*

frappé (frap´ā) *a.* iced. ~*n.* **1** an iced drink. **2** a soft water ice.

fraternal (frətœ´nəl) *a.* **1** brotherly. **2** of, relating to or suitable for brothers. **3** existing between brothers. **4** (of twins) from two separate ova. **5** (*N Am.*) of or relating to a fraternity. **fraternally** *adv.* **fraternity** *n.* (*pl.* **fraternities**) **1** a brotherhood, a group of men associated for a common interest or for religious purposes. **2** a group of men associated or linked together by similarity of rank, profession, interests etc. **3** (*N Am.*) a college association of male students. **4** the state of being a brother; brotherliness. **fraternize** (frat´-), **fraternise** *v.i.* **1** to associate or hold fellowship with others of like occupation or tastes. **2** to associate (with members of a hostile group) on friendly terms. **fraternization** (-zā´shən) *n.* **fraternizer** *n.*

fratricide (frat´risīd) *n.* **1** the murder of a brother or sister. **2** a person who murders their brother or sister. **fratricidal** *a.*

Frau (frow) *n.* (*pl.* **Frauen** (frow´ən)) a German woman, wife or widow; Mrs. **Fräulein** (froi´līn, frow´-, frow´-) *n.* (*pl.* **Fräulein**) (*often offensive*) a young lady, a German spinster; Miss.

fraud (frawd) *n.* **1** an act or course of deception deliberately practised to gain unlawful or unfair advantage. **2** (*Law*) such deception directed to the detriment of another. **3** a deception, a trick, trickery. **4** (*coll.*) a deceitful person or thing. **fraudful** *a.* **fraudster** *n.* a person who commits fraud. **fraudulence** *n.* **fraudulent** (-ūlənt) *a.* **1** practising fraud. **2** characterized by or containing fraud. **3** intended to defraud, deceitful. **fraudulently** *adv.*

fraught (frawt) *a.* **1** involving, entailing, attended by, filled (with). **2** tense, characterized by or inducing anxiety or stress. **3** freighted, laden, stored (with).

Fräulein FRAU.

fraxinella (fraksinel´ə) *n.* a kind of rue or dittany, esp. *Dictamnus albus*, cultivated for its leaves and flowers which give off an inflammable vapour.

fray[1] (frā) *v.t.* **1** to wear away by rubbing. **2** to fret, to chafe. **3** to make strained or irritated. ~*v.i.* (of a garment, cloth etc.) to become rubbed or worn, esp. so as to become unravelled or ragged at the edges.

fray[2] (frā) *n.* **1** an affray; fighting. **2** a noisy quarrel, a brawl, a riot. **3** a combat, a contest.

frazzle (fraz´əl) *v.t.* **1** to reduce to a state of physical or nervous exhaustion. **2** to burn thoroughly, to char. **3** to fray at the edge, to unravel. ~*n.* an exhausted or charred state (*worn/burnt to a frazzle*).

freak (frēk) *n.* **1** an abnormal or deformed person or thing (*a freak of nature*). **2** (*coll.*) an unconventional or eccentric person. **3** (*coll.*) an unrestrained enthusiast for a certain thing (*a computer freak*). **4** a highly unusual or abnormal occurrence. **5** (*coll.*) a person who has hallucinations from the use of or addiction to drugs. **6** a sudden wanton whim or caprice; a humour, a vagary. *~a.* highly unusual, abnormal, esp. in magnitude or intensity. *~v.t.* **1** (*coll.*) to freak out. **2** (*usu. p.p.*) to variegate, to streak. *~v.i.* (*coll.*) to freak out. **to freak out 1** (*coll.*) (to cause) to hallucinate. **2** (*coll.*) (to cause) to be in a highly emotional, excited or angry state. **3** to assume a strikingly unconventional lifestyle. **freakish** *a.* **1** eccentric, unconventional. **2** abnormal. **3** whimsical. **freakishly** *adv.* **freakishness** *n.* **freak-out** *n.* (*coll.*) **1** an act or instance of freaking out. **2** a highly emotional or hallucinatory experience. **freak show** *n.* a sideshow at a fair where people with physical abnormalities can be seen. **freaky** *a.* (*comp.* **freakier**, *superl.* **freakiest**) (*coll.*) freakish. **freakily** *adv.* **freakiness** *n.*

freckle (frek´əl) *n.* **1** (*usu. pl.*) a yellowish or light-brown spot on the skin, caused by sunburn or other causes. **2** any small spot or discoloration. *~v.t.* (*usu. p.p.*) to mark with freckles. *~v.i.* to become marked with freckles. **freckle-faced** *a.* with a freckled face. **freckly** *a.*

free[1] (frē) *a.* (*comp.* **freer** (frē´ə), *superl.* **freest** (frē´ist)) **1** at liberty; not in bondage or under restraint. **2** living under a government based on the consent of the citizens. **3** (of a government) not arbitrary or despotic. **4** (of a state) not under foreign domination. **5** released from authority or control. **6** not confined, restricted, checked or impeded. **7** at liberty to choose or act, permitted (to do). **8** independent, unattached, unconnected with the State. **9** available without payment or charge, costing nothing. **10** not subject to (charges, duties, fees etc.). **11** without restriction, open, gratuitous. **12** liberal, generous. **13** released, clear, exempt (from). **14** unconstrained, not bound or limited (by rules, conventions etc.). **15** not containing a certain thing. **16** spontaneous, unforced. **17** unoccupied, vacant. **18** clear, unobstructed. **19** not busy, having no obligations or commitments. **20** not fixed or joined. **21** (of a translation) not literal. **22** unconventional, unceremonious, careless, reckless. **23** forward, impudent. **24** indelicate, broad. **25** unreserved, frank, ingenuous. **26** admitted to or invested with certain privileges (of). **27** (*Physics*) **a** not charged by an external force. **b** not bound in an atom or molecule. **28** (of energy) available. **29** (*Chem.*) not combined with another body. *~adv.* **1** freely. **2** without cost or charge. **3** (*Naut.*) not close-hauled. **for free** (*coll.*) gratis, for nothing. **free alongside ship** delivered free on the dock or wharf. **free on board** (of goods) delivered on board or into conveyance free of charge. **free on rail** (of goods) delivered free to a

railway wagon. **-free** *comb. form* free from, not containing. **free agent** *n.* a person who is free to act according to their own opinions and wishes. **free and easy** *a.* unconstrained, unceremonious, informal. **free association** *n.* (*Psych.*) the bringing to consciousness of unconscious processes through words and ideas which the subject spontaneously associates with keywords provided by a psychoanalyst. **freebase** *v.t., v.i.* (*sl.*) **1** to purify (cocaine). **2** to smoke (cocaine) so purified. *~n.* purified cocaine produced by freebasing. **freeboard** *n.* the space between the water-line on a vessel and the upper side of the deck, or the uppermost full deck. **free-born** *a.* inheriting the right and liberty of a citizen. **Free Church** *n.* a Protestant Church dissenting or seceding from an established Church, a Nonconformist Church. **free enterprise** *n.* an economic system in which commercial companies compete for profit, largely without state interference or control. **free fall** *n.* **1** the motion of an unrestrained or unpropelled body in a gravitational field. **2** the part of a parachute jump before the parachute opens. **3** the movement of a spacecraft in space, without power from the engines. **4** a state of fast, esp. uncontrollable, falling (*prices going into free fall*). **free-fall** *v.i.* (*past* **free-fell**, *p.p.* **free-fallen**) to move into a free fall. **free fight** *n.* a fight in which anyone can join. **Freefone, Freephone, freefone, freephone** *n.* a telephone service in which callers can telephone a company free of charge, with the company paying the cost of the calls. **free-for-all** *n.* a free fight, a disorganized brawl or argument. **free-form** *a.* having an irregular shape or structure. **free hand** *n.* complete freedom to act as one wishes. **free-hand** *a.* (of a drawing etc.) executed by the hand without the aid of instruments. *~adv.* in a free-hand manner. **free-handed** *a.* generous, liberal. **free-handedly** *adv.* **free-handedness** *n.* **free house** *n.* a public house that is free to buy beer or liquor from any supplier. **free kick** *n.* in football, a kick with which an opponent may not interfere, awarded for a foul or infringement by the other side. **freelance** *n.* (*also* **freelancer**) a self-employed person hired by others for specific (usu. short-term) assignments. *~a., adv.* not bound to a particular employer. *~v.i.* to work freelance. **free-liver** *n.* **1** a person who indulges their appetites, esp. at table. **2** (*Biol.*) an organism which is neither parasitic nor symbiotic. **free-living** *n., a.* **freeload** *v.i.* (*coll.*) to sponge, to live at another's expense. **freeloader** *n.* **free love** *n.* sexual intercourse without marriage or without formal or legal commitments. **free lover** *n.* a person who advocates or practises free love. **freely** *adv.* **free market** *n.* an economic market in which prices are regulated by supply and demand. **freeness** *n.* **free pardon** *n.* a complete or partial remission of the legal consequences of crime. **free pass** *n.* an official authorization, entitling the holder to travel or to enter an exhibition, theatre etc. without having to pay. **free port** *n.* **1** a port or section of a port where goods are received and shipped free of duty. **2** a port where ships of all nations may load or unload free of duty. **Freepost** *n.* a postal service in which letters etc. can be sent to a company free of charge, with the company paying the postage. **free radical** *n.* an atom, or group of atoms, containing at least one unpaired electron. **free-range** *a* kept or produced in natural conditions. **free sheet** *n.* a newspaper distributed free. **free skating** *n.* that part of a figure-skating competition in which the competitors have partial or complete freedom to organize their programmes. **free speech** *n.* the right to express one's opinions publicly. **free spirit** *n.* an independent or unconventional person. **free-spoken** *a.* **1** speaking without reserve. **2** blunt, candid, frank. **free-standing** *a.* not attached to, supported by or integrated with other objects. **freestone** *n.* **1** a stone which can be cut freely in any direction. **2** a kind of peach or other fruit easily freed from its stone when ripe. **freestyle** *n.* **1** a race, in swimming, skiing etc. in which each competitor can choose which style to use. **2** all-in wrestling. ~*a.* of or relating to such a race or style of wrestling. **freestyler** *n.* **free-thinker** *n.* **1** a rationalist, sceptic or agnostic. **2** a person who rejects authority in religious belief. **free-thinking** *a.*, *n.* **free throw** *n.* **1** an unimpeded throw awarded because of a foul by an opponent. **2** in basketball, an unimpeded shot at the basket from a marked line. **free trade** *n.* international trade, free interchange of commodities without protection by customs duties. **free verse** *n.* unrhymed verse with no set metrical pattern. **free vote** *n.* a parliamentary vote left to the individual's choice, free from party discipline. **freeway** *n.* (*N Am.*) **1** a motorway. **2** a toll-free highway. **free wheel** *n.* **1** a driving wheel on a bicycle that can be disconnected from the driving gear and allowed to revolve while the pedals are at rest. **2** a bicycle with such a wheel. **freewheel** *v.i.* **1** to run down a hill (on a bicycle or in a motor car) without using engine power or brakes. **2** to move or live in an unconstrained or irresponsible fashion. **free will** *n.* **1** the power of directing one's own actions without constraint by any external influence. **2** voluntariness, spontaneity.

free[2] (frē) *v.t.* (*3rd pers. sing. pres.* **frees**, *pres.p.* **freeing**, *past*, *p.p.* **freed**) **1** to set at liberty, to emancipate. **2** to rid or relieve (of or from). **3** to extricate, to clear, to disentangle. **to free up 1** (*coll.*) to make available. **2** (*coll.*) to cause to operate with fewer restrictions. **freedman** *n.* (*pl.* **freedmen**) an emancipated slave.

freebie (frē´bi) *n.* (*coll.*) something given for which a person does not have to pay.

freebooter (frē´boota) *n.* a pirate or buccaneer, an adventurer who makes a business of plundering. **freeboot** *v.i.* **freebooting** *a.*

freedom (frē´dəm) *n.* **1** the state of being free,

liberty, independence. **2** personal liberty, nonslavery, civil liberty. **3** liberty of action, free will. **4** exemption, immunity (from). **5** lack of conventionality, frankness, excessive familiarity. **6** violation of the rules of good breeding, a liberty. **7** ease or facility in doing anything. **8** participation in certain privileges, exemptions, and immunities of or relating to citizenship of a city or membership of a company. **9** free use (of). **10** boldness in form. **freedom fighter** *n.* a person who fights (esp. as an irregular soldier) for the liberation of a nation etc. from foreign rule or a tyrannical regime.

freehold (frē´hōld) *n.* **1** an estate held in fee simple, fee tail or for life. **2** the tenure by which such an estate is held. ~*a.* of, being or related to the nature of a freehold. **freeholder** *n.*

freeman (frē´mən) *n.* (*pl.* **freemen**) **1** a person who is not a slave or serf. **2** a person who holds the franchise of a citizen or a particular privilege, esp. the freedom of a city, company etc.

Freemason (frē´māsən) *n.* a member of an association of 'Free and Accepted Masons', a secret order or fraternity (probably originating as a fraternity of skilled masons, with right of free movement, about the 14th cent.). **Freemasonry** *n.* **1** the system, rites and principles of Freemasons. **2** (*usu.* **freemasonry**) a secret understanding, community of interests, or instinctive sympathy among a number of people.

freesia (frē´ziə, -zhə) *n.* any of a S African genus of bulbous flowering plants allied to the iris.

freeze (frēz) *v.i.* (*pres.p.* **freezing**, *past* **froze** (frōz), *p.p.* **frozen** (frō´zən)) **1** to be turned from a fluid to a solid state by cold. **2** (*impers.*) to be at that degree of cold at which water turns to ice or becomes covered with ice. **3** to become covered or clogged by ice. **4** to become attached (to) or fastened (together) by frost. **5** to feel very cold. **6** to die of cold. **7** to become motionless or paralysed. **8** to respond with sudden detachment. ~*v.t.* **1** to congeal by cold. **2** to form ice upon or convert into ice. **3** to injure, overpower or kill with cold. **4** to preserve (food) by freezing and storing at a temperature below freezing point. **5** to chill with fear. **6** to anaesthetize (as if) by cold. **7** to render motionless or paralysed. **8** to cause to respond with sudden detachment. **9** to stop at a particular stage or state. **10** to stop (a moving film) at a particular frame. **11** in finance, to prohibit the use of or dealings in. **12** to fix or stabilize (prices etc.). ~*n.* **1** the act or state of freezing. **2** a frost. **to freeze out** (*coll.*) to compel the retirement of from business, competition, society etc., by boycotting, contemptuous treatment or similar methods. **to freeze up** to (cause to) be obstructed by the formation of ice. **freezable** *a.* **freeze-dry** *v.t.* (*3rd pers. sing. pres.* **freeze-dries**, *pres.p.* **freeze-drying**, *past*, *p.p.* **freeze-dried**) to dehydrate while in a frozen state in a vacuum, esp. for preservation. **freeze-frame** *n.* **1** a single frame of a film repeated to give the effect of a still photograph. **2** a single frame of a video recording viewed as a still. **3** the facility to produce a freeze-frame. ~*v.t.* to use freeze-frame on. **freezer** *n.* an apparatus for freezing food etc., a room or cabinet, or a compartment in a refrigerator for the long-term storage of perishable foodstuffs. **freezing** *a.* **1** (*also* **freezing cold**) very cold. **2** distant, chilling. **freezingly** *adv.* **freezing point** *n.* **1** the point at which water freezes, marked 32° on the Fahrenheit scale, and 0° on the Celsius and Réaumur scales. **2** the temperature at which a substance freezes.

freight (frāt) *n.* **1** the transportation of goods by road, railway, sea or air. **2** goods transported, a cargo. **3** the money due or paid for the transportation of goods, esp. for water. **4** ordinary transportation, as distinct from express. **5** the hire of a ship, aircraft etc. for transporting goods. **6** a burden or load. ~*v.t.* **1** to transport (goods) as freight. **2** to load with goods for transportation. **3** to hire or charter for this purpose. **4** to load, to fill. **freightage** *n.* **1** the transporting of goods. **2** money paid for the hire of a ship or the transportation of goods. **3** freight. **freight car** *n.* (*N Am.*) a railway wagon for goods. **freighter** *n.* **1** a ship or aircraft designed for transporting goods. **2** a person who hires or loads a ship. **3** a person who contracts to receive and forward goods. **freight ton** *n.* a unit of weight or volume of cargo equivalent to a metric ton (2, 205 lb., 1000 kg) or 40 cu. ft. **freight train** *n.* (*N Am.*) a goods train.

☒ **freind** common misspelling of FRIEND.

French (french) *a.* **1** of or relating to France, its inhabitants or language. **2** belonging to or native to France. ~*n.* **1** the language spoken by the people of France, also an official language in Belgium, Switzerland, Canada and other countries. **2** (*as pl.*) the people of France. **3** (*coll.*) dry vermouth. **French bean** *n.* **1** the kidney or haricot bean, *Phaseolus vulgaris*. **2** the pod or seed of this used as food. **French bread** *n.* crusty white bread in a thin, long loaf. **French Canadian** *n.* a Canadian whose main language is French. **French-Canadian** *a.* of or relating to the French-speaking part of Canada or its people. **French chalk** *n.* a variety of talc, steatite or soapstone used for marking cloth, and in powder as a dry lubricant for tight boots etc. **French cricket** *n.* a children's version of cricket in which the legs of the person who is batting serve as the wicket. **French door** *n.* FRENCH WINDOW (under FRENCH). **French dressing** *n.* **1** a salad dressing made of oil and vinegar or lemon juice with seasoning. **2** a creamy, often sweet, salad dressing. **French fries, French fried potatoes** *n.pl.* (potato) chips. **French horn** *n.* a metal wind instrument of circular shape with a gradual taper from the mouthpiece to a large flaring bell. **Frenchify** *v.t.* (*3rd pers. sing. pres.* **Frenchifies,** *pres.p.* **Frenchifying,** *past, p.p.* **Frenchified**) **1** to make French. **2** to influence with French tastes or manners. **French**

kiss *n.* a kiss in which one partner's tongue is inserted into the other partner's mouth. **French knickers** *n.pl.* wide-legged knickers. **French leave** *n.* absence without permission. **French letter** *n.* (*coll.*) a contraceptive sheath, a condom. **French loaf** *n.* (*pl.* **French loaves**) a loaf of French bread. **Frenchman** *n.* (*pl.* **Frenchmen**) a male native or inhabitant of France. **French mustard** *n.* a type of mustard mixed with vinegar etc. **Frenchness** *n.* **French polish** *n.* **1** a solution of resin or gum resin in alcohol or wood naphtha, for polishing wood. **2** the polish produced. ~*v.t.* to polish with this. **French polisher** *n.* **French roll** *n.* a light kind of fancy bread. **French roof** *n.* (*pl.* **French roofs**) a mansard roof or one having portions of two different pitches. **French seam** *n.* a double seam, stitched first on the wrong, then on the right side, so that the edges are invisible. **French toast** *n.* **1** bread toasted one side only. **2** bread dipped in beaten egg and lightly fried. **French vermouth** *n.* dry vermouth. **French window** *n.* (*usu. pl.*) a pair of doors with full-length glazing, opening onto a garden, balcony etc. **Frenchwoman** *n.* (*pl.* **Frenchwomen**) a female native or inhabitant of France.

frenetic (frənet´ik), †**phrenetic** *a.* **1** frantic, frenzied. **2** fanatic. **frenetically** *adv.*

frenzy (fren´zi) *n.* (*pl.* **frenzies**) **1** a violent bout of wild or unnatural excitement, agitation or fury. **2** delirium, madness. **3** temporary mental derangement. ~*v.t.* (*3rd pers. sing. pres.* **frenzies,** *pres.p.* **frenzying,** *past, p.p.* **frenzied**) **1** (*usu. p.p.*) to drive to madness. **2** to infuriate. **frenzied** *a.* **frenziedly** *adv.*

frequency (frē´kwənsi), **frequence** (-ns) *n.* (*pl.* **frequencies, frequences**) **1** the quality of occurring frequently. **2** common occurrence. **3** repetition at short intervals. **4** rate of occurrence. **5** in statistics, the number or proportion of individuals or things in a single class. **6** in electricity, a term referring to the speed of variations of alternating currents, alternating electromotive forces, and electromagnetic waves. **7** (*Physics*) rate of repetition or recurrence. **frequency band** *n.* a range of frequencies or wavelengths in the radio spectrum. **frequency modulation** *n.* **1** in electronics, the varying of the frequency of the carrier wave in accordance with the frequency of speech or music, for example. **2** the broadcasting system using this.

frequent[1] (frē´kwənt) *a.* **1** occurring often, common. **2** repeated at short intervals. **3** occurring near together, abundant. **4** constant, habitual. **frequentative** (-kwen´-) *n., a.* (*Gram.*) (a verb or verbal form) expressing frequent repetition or intensity of an action. **frequently** *adv.* **frequentness** *n.*

frequent[2] (frikwent´) *v.t.* to visit or resort to often or habitually. **frequentation** (-tā´shən) *n.* **frequenter** *n.*

fresco (fres´kō) *n.* (*pl.* **frescos, frescoes**) a kind of watercolour painting on fresh plaster or on a wall covered with mortar not quite dry. **frescoed** a.

fresh (fresh) a. **1** new. **2** not known, met with or used previously, recent. **3** other, different, additional. **4** newly produced, not withered or faded, not stale, decayed or tainted. **5** pure, not salt, drinkable. **6** not preserved with salt, or by pickling, tinning, freezing etc. **7** raw, inexperienced. **8** just arrived (from). **9** looking young or healthy. **10** bright and clean in appearance. **11** vividly and distinctly retained in the mind. **12** refreshed, reinvigorated. **13** (of a horse) frisky. **14** brisk, active, vigorous, fit. **15** (of air, a breeze etc.) refreshing, reviving, cool. **16** (coll.) cheeky, impertinent, amorously impudent. ~adv. **1** (esp. in comb.) freshly, as fresh-cut. **2** recently. ~n. (ellipt.) the fresh part (of the day, season etc.). **freshen** v.t. **1** to make fresh. **2** to enliven, to revive. ~v.i. to become fresh. **to freshen up 1** to refresh oneself, to have a wash or shower, change one's clothes etc. **2** to revive, to give a fresher, more attractive appearance to. **3** to replenish (a drink). **fresher** n. (coll.) a freshman. **freshet** n. **1** a sudden flood caused by heavy rains or melted snow. **2** a freshwater stream. **fresh-faced** a. having a clean, young-looking complexion. **freshly** adv. **freshman** n. (pl. **freshmen**) a novice, a beginner, esp. a student in the first year at a university or college. **freshness** n. **freshwater** a. **1** of or relating to, found in or produced by fresh water. **2** (N Am.) (esp. of a college) small or little known. **freshwater flea** n. any of several waterfleas of the genus Daphnia, having a transparent shell and prominent eyes.

fret[1] (fret) v.i. (pres.p. **fretting**, past, p.p. **fretted**) **1** to be worried, irritated, vexed or troubled. **2** to be in a state of agitation or commotion. **3** to grieve, to be discontented. **4** to be worn or eaten away. **5** to flow in little waves or ripples. ~v.t. **1** to irritate, vex, annoy. **2** to make uneasy or distressed. **3** to eat away, to corrode. **4** to wear away, to rub or chafe. **5** to make (a way or passage) by rubbing. ~n. a state of irritation or vexation. **fretful** a. **1** worried, distressed; angry, irritable. **2** captious. **fretfully** adv. **fretfulness** n.

fret[2] (fret) v.t. (pres.p. **fretting**, past, p.p. **fretted**) **1** to ornament, to decorate. **2** to ornament (esp. a ceiling) with carved work. **3** to variegate. ~n. an ornament formed by small bands or fillets intersecting each other at right angles, used in classical architecture. **fretsaw** n. a small saw with a long thin narrow blade on a frame, used in cutting fretwork. **fretted**[1] a. **fretwork** n. **1** carved or open woodwork in ornamental patterns and devices. **2** a variegated pattern composed of interlacing lines of various patterns.

fret[3] (fret) n. any of several small pieces of metal, wood, or ivory placed upon the fingerboard of certain stringed instruments to regulate the pitch of the notes. **fretboard** n. a fingerboard with frets. **fretless** a. **fretted**[2] a.

Freudian (froi´dien) a. (Psych.) of or relating to the psychological theories of Freud. ~n. a follower of Freud or his methods. **Freudianism** n. **Freudian slip** n. an unintentional action, such as a slip of the tongue, held to betray an unconscious thought.

Fri. abbr. Friday.

friable (frī´əbəl) a. readily crumbled. **friability** (-bil´-), **friableness** n.

friar (frī´ə) n. a member of a monastic order, esp. one of the four mendicant orders, Augustinians or Austin Friars, Franciscans or Grey Friars, Dominicans or Black Friars, and Carmelites or White Friars. **friarlike, friarly** a. **friar's balsam, friars' balsam** n. a tincture of benzoin used esp. as an inhalant. **friary** n. (pl. **friaries**) a monastery of a mendicant order.

fricassee (frik´əsē, -sē´) n. small pieces of meat, esp. chicken or veal, fried, stewed and served in a usu. white sauce. ~v.t. (3rd pers. sing. pres. **fricassees**, pres.p. **fricasseeing**, past, p.p. **fricasseed**) to cook as a fricassee.

fricative (frik´ətiv) n. a consonant, such as f, sh, th, produced by the friction of the breath issuing through a narrow opening. ~a. produced by such friction.

friction (frik´shən) n. **1** the act of two bodies rubbing together. **2** (Physics) resistance which any body meets with in moving over another body. **3** conflict, disagreement, lack of harmony. **4** (in comb.) of devices that transmit motion by friction between surfaces (friction clutch; friction gear). **5** chafing or rubbing a part of the body to promote circulation. **frictional** a. **frictionally** adv. **frictionless** a.

Friday (frī´di) n. the sixth day of the week, following Thursday. ~adv. (coll.) on Friday. **Fridays** adv. (coll.) on Fridays, each Friday.

fridge (frij), **frig** n. short for REFRIGERATOR (under REFRIGERATE). **fridge-freezer** n. an upright kitchen unit consisting of a refrigerator and a freezer.

friend (frend) n. **1** a person known well to another and regarded with affection, usually excluding sexual or familial relationships. **2** an acquaintance. **3** a person of the same nation or party, one who is not an enemy. **4** a person on the same side, an adherent, a sympathizer, a patron or promoter (of a cause, institution etc.). **5** (Friend) a member of the Society of Friends. **6** anything that helps one, esp. in an emergency. **my honourable friend** used in the House of Commons to refer to another member of one's own party. **my learned friend** used in a court of law by one lawyer to refer to another lawyer. **my noble friend** used in the House of Lords to refer to another member of one's own party. **to be/ keep friends with** to be friendly with. **to make friends** to become intimate or reconciled (with). **friended** a. **friendless** a. **friendlessness** n. **friendly** a. (comp. **friendlier**, superl. **friendliest**) **1** having the disposition of a friend, good-natured. **2** acting as a friend. **3** characteristic of friends or of kindly feeling. **4** amicable, not hostile. **5** favourable, propitious. **6** played for amusement or entertainment, not as part of a competition. **7** useful, convenient, opportune. **8** user-friendly. *~adv.* in the manner of a friend. *~n.* (*pl.* **friendlies**) a game played for entertainment or practice, not a league or competition fixture. **friendlily** *adv.* **friendliness** *n.* **-friendly** *comb. form* **1** helpful to (*reader-friendly*). **2** favouring, protecting. **friendly fire** *n.* (*Mil.*) gunfire from one's own side that accidentally causes casualties or damage to one's own forces. **friendly match** *n.* a match played for entertainment or practice, a friendly. **Friendly Society** *n.* (*pl.* **Friendly Societies**) a society for the purpose of mutual assurance against sickness, old age etc. **friendship** *n.* **1** a relationship between friends. **2** the state of being friends. **3** an act of personal kindness or goodwill.

frier FRYER (under FRY¹).

Friesian (frē´zhən) *n.* **1** any of a breed of large black and white dairy cattle originally from Friesland. **2** this breed of cattle. **3** Frisian. **4** a Frisian. *~a.* of or relating to Friesians.

frieze¹ (frēz) *n.* (*Archit.*) **1** the middle division of an entablature, between the architrave and the cornice, usu. enriched by sculpture. **2** the band of sculpture occupying this. **3** a horizontal band or strip, either plain or decorated, elsewhere in a wall.

frieze² (frēz) *n.* a coarse woollen cloth, with a rough nap on one side.

frig¹ (frig) *v.t., v.i.* (*pres.p.* **frigging**, *past, p.p.* **frigged**) (*taboo sl.*) **1** to masturbate. **2** to have sexual intercourse (with). *~n.* an act of sexual intercourse. **frigging** *a.* used as an intensive to express one's annoyance (with something). *~adv.* very, extremely.

frig² FRIDGE.

frigate (frig´ət) *n.* **1** a naval escort vessel between a corvette and a destroyer in size. **2** (*N Am.*) a similar vessel between a destroyer and cruiser in size. **3** (*Hist.*) a warship next in size below a ship of the line. **frigate bird** *n.* a large tropical bird of the family Fregitidae with a long bill, a wide wingspan and a forked tail.

fright (frīt) *n.* **1** sudden and violent fear or alarm; an instance of this. **2** a state of terror. **3** a person who or thing that presents a ridiculous or grotesque appearance in person or dress. *~v.t.* (*poet.*) to frighten. **to take fright** to become frightened. **frighten** *v.t.* **1** to alarm, terrify, scare; to throw into a state of fright. **2** to drive (away, out of, or into) by fright. *~v.i.* to become frightened. **frightener** *n.* (*sl.*) someone or something intended to frighten a person, esp. for criminal purposes. **to put the frighteners on** to (attempt to) coerce or deter someone with threats (of violence). **frightful** *a.* **1** dreadful, fearful, shocking. **2** horrible, hideous, very disagreeable. **3** causing fright. **4** (*coll.*) awful, extreme, extraordinary. **frightfully** *adv.* **frightfulness** *n.*

frigid (frij´id) *a.* **1** lacking warmth or feeling or ardour. **2** stiff, formal, forbidding. **3** without animation or spirit, dull, flat. **4** (esp. of a woman) sexually unresponsive. **5** cold, lacking heat or warmth. **frigidity** (-jid´-) *n.* **frigidly** *adv.* **frigidness** *n.* **frigid zone** *n.* either of the two parts of the earth between the Arctic Circle and the North Pole or between the Antarctic Circle and the South Pole.

frijol (frīhōl´) *n.* (*pl.* **frijoles** (-hō´les)) a bean resembling the kidney bean, used in Mexican cookery.

frill (fril) *n.* **1** a pleated or fluted strip of cloth sewn upon one edge only. **2** a ruff or frill-like fringe of hair, feather etc. on an animal, bird or plant. **3** a similar paper decoration on a chop or other cut of meat. **4** (*pl., coll.*) finery, frippery, decorative non-essentials. **5** (*pl., coll.*) airs, affectations. *~v.t.* **1** to furnish with a frill, to form into a frill. **2** to serve as a frill to. **with no frills** plain, unornamented, no-nonsense. **without frills** with no frills. **frilled** *a.* **frillies** *n.pl.* (*coll.*) women's underwear. **frilling** *n.* **1** material for frills. **2** a group or set of frills. **frill lizard, frilled lizard, frill-necked lizard** *n.* a large Australian lizard, *Chlamydosaurus kingli*, with an erectile fold of skin around its neck. **frilly** *a.* (*comp.* **frillier**, *superl.* **frilliest**) **1** having many frills. **2** resembling a frill. **frilliness** *n.*

fringe (frinj) *n.* **1** an ornamental border to dress or furniture, consisting of loose threads or tassels. **2** a border, an edging, a margin. **3** the front hair cut short with a straight edge along the forehead. **4** (*Bot.*) a row of long filiform processes. **5** (*Zool.*) a border of hairs or other processes. **6** (*Physics*) **a** any of the alternating light or dark bands produced by the interference or diffraction of light. **b** a strip of false colour in an image. **7** something marginal or additional. **8** a group with marginal or extreme views. **9** (*N Am.*) a fringe benefit. *~v.t.* **1** to border with or as if with a fringe. **2** to serve as a fringe to. *~a.* **1** existing alongside mainstream or conventional forms, institutions etc. **2** marginal, secondary, peripheral. **fringe benefit** *n.* something additional to wages or salary regularly received as part of an employee's remuneration from an employer. **fringeless** *a.* **fringelike** *a.* **fringe medicine** *n.* the treatment of illnesses by methods that are considered to be unconventional by the medical profession. **fringing** *n.* material for a fringe. **fringing reef** *n.* a coral reef fringing the shore. **fringy** *a.*

frippery (frip´əri) *n.* (*pl.* **fripperies**) **1** worthless, needless or showy adornments. **2** tawdry finery. **3** mere display. **4** **a** knick-knacks, gewgaws. **b** knick-knack. *~a.* **1** tawdry, trifling. **2** contemptible.

Frisbee® (friz´bi) *n.* a plastic disc, used in throwing and catching games.

frisée (frē´zā) *n.* ENDIVE.

Frisian (friz´iən) *a.* of or relating to Friesland. *~n.*

1 the language of Friesland. **2** a native or inhabitant of Friesland.

frisk (frisk) *v.i.* to leap, skip or gambol about, to frolic. ~*v.t.* (*coll.*) to search (a person) for firearms etc. ~*n.* a gambol, a frolic. **frisker** *n.* **frisky** *a.* (*comp.* **friskier**, *superl.* **friskiest**) playful, lively. **friskily** *adv.* **friskiness** *n.*

frisson (frē´sō) *n.* a shudder, a thrill.

frit[1] (frit) *n.* **1** a calcined mixture of sand and fluxes ready to be melted in a crucible to form glass. **2** a vitreous composition used in the manufacture of porcelain, enamel etc. ~*v.t.* (*pres.p.* **fritting**, *past, p.p.* **fritted**) to expose to dull red heat so as to decompose and fuse.

frit[2] (frit) *a.* (*dial., coll.*) frightened.

frith FIRTH.

fritillary (fritil´əri) *n.* (*pl.* **fritillaries**) **1** any plant of the liliaceous genus *Fritillaria*, esp. snake's head (*F. meleagris*), with drooping bell-like flowers speckled with dull purple. **2** any of various butterflies of the genus *Argynnis*, with brownish wings chequered with black and silver.

fritter[1] (frit´ə) *n.* a piece of fruit, meat etc. dipped in a light batter and fried.

fritter[2] (frit´ə) *n.* (*pl.*) fragments, bits, shreds. ~†*v.t.* to break into small pieces. **to fritter away** to waste (esp. time or money).

frivolous (friv´ələs) *a.* **1** trifling, trumpery, of little or no importance or significance. **2** lacking seriousness, inclined to trifling or silly behaviour. **frivol** *v.i.* (*pres.p.* **frivolling**, (*N Am.*) **frivoling**, *past, p.p.* **frivolled**, (*N Am.*) **frivoled**) to trifle. ~*v.t.* to trifle (away); to spend foolishly. **frivolity** (-vol´-) *n.* (*pl.* **frivolities**). **frivolously** *adv.* **frivolousness** *n.*

frizz (friz) *v.t.* **1** to form (the hair) into a mass of small tight curls. **2** to raise a nap on (cloth). **3** to treat (chamois leathers) with pumice etc. ~*v.i.* (of hair) to form into small tight curls. ~*n.* **1** frizzed hair, a mass or row of curls. **2** a frizzed state. **frizzy** *a.* (*comp.* **frizzier**, *superl.* **frizziest**) in a mass of small tight curls. **frizziness** *n.*

frizzle[1] (friz´əl) *v.t., v.i.* to form (into) crisp, tight curls. ~*n.* frizzed hair.

frizzle[2] (friz´əl) *v.t.* to fry (bacon etc.) with a hissing noise. ~*v.i.* to make a hissing noise while being fried. **to frizzle up** to burn or shrivel.

fro (frō) *adv.* away, backwards (only as below). **to and fro 1** forwards and backwards. **2** repeatedly from one place to another and back again.

frock (frok) *n.* **1** a woman's or girl's dress. **2** the long upper garment with loose sleeves worn by monks. **3** the office of a priest. **4** a frock coat. **5** a military coat of similar shape. **6** a smock. **7** a woven woollen tunic worn by sailors. ~*v.t.* to invest with priestly status or office. **frock coat** *n.* a close-fitting coat, with long broad skirts of the same length in front and behind.

frog[1] (frog) *n.* **1** a squat, smooth-skinned, tailless amphibian of the order Anura with the back legs developed for jumping. **2** (*offensive*) (*often* **Frog**) a French person. **3** a grooved piece of iron or steel to guide train wheels over an intersection in the track. **4** the hollow in one or both faces of a brick. **5** the block by which the hair is attached to the heel of a violin etc. bow. **frog in one's/ the throat** (*coll.*) phlegm on the vocal chords impeding speech. **frogbit** *n.* a small aquatic plant, *Hydrocharis morsusranae*. **frogfish** *n.* (*pl. in general* **frogfish**, *in particular* **frogfishes**) an angler fish, esp. of the family Antennariidae. **froggy** *a.* **1** abounding with frogs. **2** of, like or relating to frogs. **3** (*offensive*) French. **Froggy** *n.* (*pl.* **Froggies**) (*derog.*) a French person. **froghopper** *n.* a genus of small insects of the family Cercopidae remarkable for their leaping powers, and whose larvae secrete a protective spittle-like substance. **frogman** *n.* (*pl.* **frogmen**) an underwater swimmer equipped with rubber suit, flippers, face mask etc. and an oxygen supply. **frogmarch** *v.t.* **1** to carry face downwards between four people each holding a limb. **2** to move (a person) by force, usu. by seizing from behind and propelling forwards while the arms are pinioned, or by dragging backwards between two people each grasping an arm. ~*n.* the act of frogmarching a person. **frogspawn** *n.* a gelatinous mass of frogs' eggs.

frog[2] (frog) *n.* **1** a spindle-shaped button or toggle used for fastening military cloaks and coats. **2** the loop of a scabbard. **frogged** *a.* **frogging** *n.*

frog[3] (frog) *n.* a tender horny substance in the middle of the sole of a horse's foot.

frolic (frol´ik) *v.i.* (*pres.p.* **frolicking**, *past, p.p.* **frolicked**) **1** to play pranks. **2** to frisk. **3** to indulge in merrymaking. ~*n.* **1** a wild prank. **2** an outburst of gaiety and mirth. **3** a merrymaking. **4** a light-hearted entertainment. **frolicker** *n.* **frolicsome** *a.* **frolicsomely** *adv.* **frolicsomeness** *n.*

from (from) *prep.* **1** away, out of (expressing separation, departure, point of view, distinction or variation). **2** beginning with, after (expressing the starting point or lower limit in time or space). **3** arriving, coming, deriving (indicating the original location, source or model). **4** by means of, because of, by reason of (expressing instrumentality, cause, reason or motive). **from a child** from childhood. **from day to day** as the days pass; daily. **from hour to hour** as the hours pass; hourly. **from now on** from this time onwards. **from out** out from, forth from. **from time to time** at intervals, now and then. **from year to year** as the years pass; yearly.

fromage frais (fromahzh-frā´) *n.* a kind of smooth low-fat soft cheese with a light texture.

frond (frond) *n.* **1** (*Bot.*) a leaflike expansion in which the functions of stem and foliage are not entirely differentiated, often bearing the organs of fructification, as in many cryptogams, esp. the ferns. **2** the leaflike thallus of some algae. **3** (*Zool.*) a leaflike expansion, as in many zoophytes. **frondage** *n.* **frondose** *a.*

front (frŭnt) *n.* **1** the forward part or side of anything. **2** the most conspicuous part. **3** the beginning, the first part. **4** the part of a garment covering the chest. **5** a face of a building, esp. the principal face. **6** a frontage. **7** a seaside promenade. **8** a position directly ahead, or in the foremost part of something. **9** the position of leadership. **10** (*Mil.*) **a** the vanguard. **b** the main forward positions of an army etc. **c** the lateral space occupied by a military unit. **d** the direction in which a line of troops faces. **e** a line of battle. **f** the place where a battle is fought. **11** a particular sphere of activity. **12** a group of people or organizations who make common cause together. **13** the line of separation between air masses of different density and temperature. **14** the auditorium in a theatre. **15** outward appearance or bearing. **16** impudence, boldness. **17** something which serves as a cover or disguise for secret or illegal activities. **18** a frontman. **19** (*poet.*) the forehead. **20** the face. ~*a.* **1** relating to or situated in or at the front. **2** articulated at or towards the front of the mouth. ~*v.t.* **1** to stand or be situated opposite to. **2** to face, to look (to or towards). **3** to furnish with a front. **4** to be the leader or head of. **5** to be the presenter of (a TV programme etc.). ~*v.i.* **1** to face, to look, to be situated with the front (towards). **2** (*coll.*) to act as a front or cover (for). **in front 1** in an advanced or the leading position. **2** facing or ahead of one. **in front of 1** before. **2** in advance of; ahead of. **3** in the presence of. **frontage** *n.* **1 a** the front part of a building. **b** the extent of this. **c** land between this and a road. **2** land facing a road or water. **3** the direction in which anything faces, an outlook. **frontager** *n.* **1** the owner of a frontage. **2** a person who lives on the frontier. **frontage road** *n.* (*N Am.*) a service road. **frontal** *a.* **1** situated on, of or relating to the front. **2** belonging to the forehead. ~*n.* **1** an ornamental hanging or panel in front of an altar. **2** the façade of a building. **frontal lobe** *n.* the front lobe of either side of the brain. **frontally** *adv.* **front bench** *n.* the foremost bench in the House of Commons, assigned to leaders of the government or opposition. **frontbencher** *n.* **front door** *n.* **1** the principal entrance to a building. **2** the main means of access to a situation etc. **frontless** *a.* **front line** *n.* **1** the positions closest to the enemy in a battle. **2** the most advanced and active, or most exposed and dangerous positions in any field of activity. **frontman** *n.* (*pl.* **frontmen**) **1** a nominal leader or figurehead. **2** the leader of a group of musicians etc. **3** the presenter of a TV programme. **4** a person with the role of covering for illegal activities. **front matter** *n.* the preliminary pages of a book, consisting of the title-page, table of contents etc. before the main part of the book. **front office** *n.* a main office, e.g. a headquarters of the police. **front page** *n.* the first page of a newspaper, containing important or noteworthy news. **front passage** *n.* (*coll.*) the vagina. **front room** *n.* a room in the front of a house, esp. a living room. **front runner** *n.* **1** the leader or most favoured contestant in a race, election etc. **2** a person or horse that runs or performs best when in the lead. **frontward** *a.*, *adv.* **frontwards** *adv.* **front-wheel drive** *n.* transmission of power to the front wheels of a motor vehicle.

frontier (frŭn´tiə, -tiə´) *n.* **1 a** that part of a country which fronts or borders upon another. **b** the line marking a boundary between states or areas. **2** (*esp. N Am.*) the margins of settled and unsettled territory. **3** (*often pl.*) the current limit of knowledge or attainment in a particular sphere. ~*a.* of, relating to or situated on the frontier. **frontierless** *a.* **frontiersman** *n.* (*pl.* **frontiersmen**) a person living in the margins of settled and unsettled territory. **frontierswoman** *n.* (*pl.* **frontierswomen**) a female frontiersman.

frontispiece (frŭn´tispēs) *n.* **1** a picture facing the title-page of a book. **2** (*Archit.*) **a** a façade, a decorated front or chief entrance. **b** a pediment above a door, window etc.

frost (frost) *n.* **1** minute crystals of frozen dew or vapour, rime or hoar frost, esp. covering the ground at night. **2** the act or state of freezing, the congelation of fluids by the abstraction of heat. **3** temperature below freezing point. **4** the state of the atmosphere that produces freezing. **5** frosty weather. **6** coldness of manner or attitude. **7** (*sl.*) a disappointment, a fiasco, a failure. ~*v.i.* to become covered with frost. ~*v.t.* **1** to cover with or as if with frost. **2** to injure by frost. **3** to give a fine-grained, slightly roughened appearance to (glass, metal etc.). **4** (*esp. N Am.*) to ice (a cake). **frostbite** *n.* inflammation often resulting in gangrene, usu. of the fingers or toes, caused by exposure to extreme cold. **frostbitten** *a.* **frosted** *a.* **frosting** *n.* **1** (*esp. N Am.*) icing. **2** a rough, granulated surface produced on glass, metal etc. in imitation of frost. **frostless** *a.* **frost-work** *n.* the figures formed by frost on glass etc. **frosty** *a.* (*comp.* **frostier**, *superl.* **frostiest**) **1** producing frost. **2** excessively cold. **3** affected or injured by frost. **4** covered with or as if with frost. **5** cool, unfriendly, unenthusiastic. **frostily** *adv.* **frostiness** *n.*

froth (froth) *n.* **1** foam, spume, the mass of small bubbles caused in liquors by shaking or fermentation. **2** foamy excretion, scum. **3** empty display of ideas or talk. **4** light, insubstantial matter. ~*v.t.* **1** to cause to foam. **2** to cover with froth. ~*v.i.* to form or emit froth. **frothless** *a.* **frothy** *a.* (*comp.* **frothier**, *superl.* **frothiest**). **frothily** *adv.* **frothiness** *n.*

frou-frou (froo´froo) *n.* **1** a rustling, as of a silk dress. **2** elaborate dress, frills.

frown (frown) *v.i.* **1** to express displeasure, worry or seriousness by contracting the brows. **2** to look gloomy, threatening or with disfavour. **3** to scowl, to lour. **4** to express displeasure (at or upon). ~*v.t.* **1** to repress, repel or rebuke with a

frown. 2 to express with a frown. ~n. a knitting of the brows in displeasure, worry or mental absorption. **frowner** n. **frowningly** adv.

frowst (frowst) n. (coll.) stuffiness. **frowsty** a. (comp. **frowstier**, superl. **frowstiest**). **frowstiness** n.

frowzy (frow´zi), **frowsy** a. (comp. **frowzier**, **frowsier**, superl. **frowziest**, **frowsiest**) **1** musty, fusty, close. **2** slovenly, unkempt, dirty. **frowziness** n.

froze FREEZE.

frozen (frō´zən) a. **1** preserved by freezing. **2** very cold. **3** fixed, immobilized. **4** (of prices etc.) pegged at a certain level. **5** (of assets etc.) not convertible. **6** frigid, aloof, disdainful. **frozenly** adv. **frozen mitt** n. (coll.) hostility, rejection. **frozenness** n. **frozen shoulder** n. (Med.) painful stiffness in the shoulder joint.

FRS abbr. Fellow of the Royal Society.

fructify (frŭk´tifī) v.t. (3rd pers. sing. pres. **fructifies**, pres.p. **fructifying**, past, p.p. **fructified**) **1** to make fruitful or productive. **2** to fertilize. ~v.i. to bear fruit. **fructiferous** (-tif´-) a. bearing fruit. **fructification** (-fikā´shən) n. (Bot.) **1** the act or process of fructifying. **2** any spore-bearing structure in ferns, mosses, fungi etc. **fructose** (-tōz, -tōs) n. (Chem.) the very sweet soluble form of sugar that occurs esp. in fruit juices and honey.

frugal (froo´gəl) a. **1** thrifty, sparing. **2** not profuse or lavish. **3** economical in the use or expenditure of food, money etc. **frugality** (-gal´-) n. **frugally** adv. **frugalness** n.

frugiferous (froojif´ərəs) a. bearing fruit, fruitful. **frugivorous** (-jiv´-) a. feeding on fruit.

fruit (froot) n. **1 a** the edible succulent product of a plant or tree in which the seeds are enclosed. **b** (collect. sing.) these in quantity. **2** (Bot.) the matured ovary or seed vessel with other parts adhering thereto. **3** the spores of cryptogams. **4** (pl.) the vegetable products yielded by the earth, serving for food to humans and animals. **5** (Bible) offspring. **6** product, result or consequence. **7** (usu pl.) benefit, profit. **8** (esp. N Am., sl., offensive) a male homosexual. ~v.i. to bear fruit. ~v.t. to cause to produce fruit. **fruitage** n. **fruitarian** (-tea´ri-) n. a person who eats only fruit. **fruit bar** n. a piece of dried pressed fruit. **fruitbat** n. any large Old World fruit-eating bat of the suborder Megachiroptera found in tropical and subtropical regions. **fruit-body** n. (pl. **fruit-bodies**) FRUITING BODY (under FRUIT). **fruitcake** n. (sl.) an eccentric or insane person. **fruit cake** n. a cake containing currants and other dried fruit. **fruit cocktail** n. a fruit salad, esp. one of small finely chopped fruit. **fruited** a. **fruiter** n. **1** a tree that bears fruit, esp. considered with reference to its quality. **2** a ship that carries fruit. **3** a fruit-grower. **fruiterer** n. a person who deals in fruits. **fruit fly** n. (pl. **fruit flies**) any of various flies, esp. of the genus Drosophila, with larvae which feed on fruit. **fruitful** a. **1** producing fruit in abundance.

2 successful, productive, fertile. **3** bearing children, prolific. **fruitfully** adv. **fruitfulness** n. **fruiting** a. bearing fruit. **fruiting body** n. (pl. **fruiting bodies**) the part of a fungus that bears spores. **fruitless** a. **1** not bearing fruit, unproductive. **2** unsuccessful, unprofitable, useless, vain, idle. **fruitlessly** adv. **fruitlessness** n. **fruitlet** n. a drupel. **fruit machine** n. a coin-in-the-slot gambling machine which spins symbols (as of fruit) and pays out if certain combinations are visible when it stops. **fruit salad** n. **1** a mixture of fruits cut up and sweetened. **2** (sl.) a displayed arrangement of medals etc. **fruit sugar** n. fructose. **fruit tree** n. a tree cultivated for its fruit. **fruitwood** n. the wood of a fruit tree, esp. when used in making furniture. **fruity** a. (comp. **fruitier**, superl. **fruitiest**) **1** of or like fruit, in taste, smell etc. **2** (of wine) tasting of the grape. **3** (of a voice) round, mellow and rich. **4** salacious, risqué. **fruitily** adv. **fruitiness** n.

fruition (frooish´ən) n. **1** the bearing of fruit. **2** attainment, fulfilment. **3** pleasure or satisfaction derived from attainment of a desire.

frump (frŭmp) n. an old-fashioned, unattractive or dowdy-looking woman. **frumpish** a. **frumpishly** adv. **frumpy** a. (comp. **frumpier**, superl. **frumpiest**) old-fashioned, unattractive or dowdy. **frumpily** adv. **frumpiness** n.

frustrate (frŭstrāt´) v.t. **1** to make ineffective. **2** to prevent from succeeding, to defeat, to thwart, to baulk. **3** to nullify, to disappoint. **4** to cause feelings of dissatisfaction or discouragement. **frustrated** a. **1** thwarted. **2** dissatisfied, discouraged. **3** sexually unfulfilled. **frustratedly** adv. **frustrater** n. **frustrating** a. **frustratingly** adv. **frustration** (-strā´shən) n.

fry[1] (frī) v.t. (3rd pers. sing. pres. **fries**, pres.p. **frying**, past, p.p. **fried**) **1** to cook with hot fat or oil in a pan. **2** to burn or overheat. **3** (sl.) to electrocute. ~v.i. **1** to be cooked with hot fat or oil in a pan. **2** to be burnt or overheated. **3** (sl.) to be electrocuted. ~n. (pl. **fries**) **1** a dish of anything fried. **2** the liver, lights, heart etc. of pigs, sheep, calves or oxen. **3** (pl.) potato chips. **4** (N Am.) a social gathering at which the main food is fried. **to fry up** to heat or reheat in a frying pan. **fried** a. (sl.) drunk. **fryer**, **frier** n. **1** a vessel or pan for frying. **2** a person who fries. **3** (N Am.) a young chicken suitable for frying. **frying pan**, (N Am.) **frypan** n. a shallow metal pan with a long handle, in which food is fried. **fry-up** n. (coll.) a dish of various fried food.

fry[2] (frī) n.pl. **1** young fish, esp. those fresh from the spawn, also yearling salmon. **2** the young of certain other creatures, e.g. frogs. **3** a swarm of children.

FS abbr. Flight Sergeant.

FSH abbr. follicle-stimulating hormone.

ft. abbr. **1** foot, feet. **2** fort.

FTP abbr. (Comput.) file-transfer protocol.

fubsy (fŭb´zi), **fubby** (-i) a. (comp. **fubsier**, **fubbier**, superl. **fubsiest**, **fubbiest**) fat, squat.

fuchsia (fū´shə) n. any garden plant of the genus Fuchsia, with hanging purple, red or white funnel-shaped flowers.

fuck (fŭk) v.i., v.t. (taboo. sl.) to have sexual intercourse (with). ~n. 1 an act of sexual intercourse. 2 a partner in sexual intercourse. ~int. used to express violent displeasure or one's disregard or defiance of someone. **fuck all** nothing at all. **not to give a fuck** not to care in the least. **to fuck about/ around** 1 to waste time, to mess around. 2 to treat inconsiderately. **to fuck off** to go away. **to fuck up** 1 to botch, to damage. 2 to make a mess of. 3 to disturb emotionally. **fucked** a. 1 broken, damaged, kaput. 2 exhausted. **fucker** n. a (stupid) person, fellow. **fucking** n. sexual intercourse. ~a. used as an expletive to express one's annoyance with something. ~adv. very, extremely. **fuck-up** n. a muddle or mess.

fucus (fū´kəs) n. (pl. **fuci** (fū´sī)) 1 a genus of algae, containing some of the commonest seaweeds. 2 any species of this genus. **fucoid** a., n.

fuddle (fŭd´əl) v.t. 1 to make stupid with drink, to intoxicate. 2 to confuse. ~n. 1 a drinking bout. 2 intoxication. 3 the state of being muddled.

fuddy-duddy (fŭd´idŭdi) a. (coll.) 1 old-fogeyish, old-fashioned. 2 stuffy, pompous. 3 fussy, prim, censorious. ~n. (pl. **fuddy-duddies**) a fuddy-duddy person.

fudge[1] (fŭj) n. 1 a soft sweet of chocolate, candy etc. 2 a made-up or nonsensical story. 3 nonsense. ~int. used to express mild annoyance.

fudge[2] (fŭj) v.t. 1 to deal with in a makeshift, careless way. 2 to falsify, to fake, to make imprecise, esp. as a means of covering up unpalatable facts. 3 to patch or make up, to fake. ~v.i. 1 to do things in a makeshift way. 2 to be evasive and imprecise. 3 to cheat. ~n. 1 a makeshift compromise. 2 an evasion. 3 an item of late news inserted into a newspaper. **fudgy** a.

fuehrer FÜHRER.

fuel (fū´əl) n. 1 combustible matter, such as wood, coal or peat burnt to provide heat or power. 2 fissile material for use in a nuclear reactor. 3 food considered as a source of energy. 4 anything which serves to feed or increase passion or excitement. ~v.t. (pres.p. **fuelling**, (N Am.) **fueling**, past, p.p. **fuelled**, (NAm.) **fueled**) 1 to supply or store with fuel. 2 to feed, increase or sustain. ~v.i. to get or receive fuel. **fuel cell** n. a cell in which chemical energy is continuously converted into electrical energy. **fuel element** n. a can containing nuclear fuel for use in a reactor. **fuel injection** n. a system whereby fuel is introduced directly into the combustion chamber of an internal-combustion engine, without the need for a carburettor. **fuel-injected** a. **fuelless** a. **fuel oil** n. an oil that is used for fuel, esp. in engines and furnaces. **fuel rod** n. a rod-shaped fuel element in a nuclear reactor.

fug (fŭg) n. (coll.) the close atmosphere of an unventilated room. ~v.i. (pres.p. **fugging**, past, p.p. **fugged**) to remain in or enjoy a fug. **fuggy** a.

fugal, fugato FUGUE.

-fuge (fūj) comb. form expelling, driving out, as in febrifuge.

fugitive (fū´jitiv) a. 1 fleeing, running away, having taken flight, runaway. 2 transient, not stable or durable, volatile, easily wafted or carried away. 3 fleeting, evanescent, ephemeral, of only passing interest. ~n. a person who flees from danger, pursuit, justice, bondage or duty. **fugitively** adv.

fugue (fūg) n. 1 (Mus.) a musical composition on one or more short subjects, which are repeated by successively entering voices and developed contrapuntally. 2 (Psych.) loss of memory coupled with disappearance from one's usual environments. ~v.i. (3rd pers. sing. pres. **fugues**, pres.p. **fuguing**, past, p.p. **fugued**) (Mus.) to compose or play a fugue. **fugal** a. in the style or nature of a fugue. **fugally** adv. **fugued** a. in the style of a fugue. **fuguist** n.

führer (fū´rə, fü´-), **fuehrer** n. a leader, esp. one who exerts tyrannical authority.

-ful (ful, fəl) suf. 1 full of, abounding in, having, able to, as in artful, beautiful, sinful, mournful, wilful. 2 (pl. **-fuls**) the quantity or number required to fill, as in cupful, handful, houseful.

fulcrum (ful´krəm, fŭl´-) n. (pl. **fulcra** (-krə), **fulcrums**) 1 the fixed point on which the bar of a lever rests or about which it turns. 2 a means of making any kind of force or influence effective.

fulfil (fulfil´), (N Am.) **fulfill** v.t. (pres.p. **fulfilling**, past, p.p. **fulfilled**) 1 to accomplish, to carry out, to execute, to perform. 2 to satisfy, to correspond to, to comply with. 3 to finish, to complete (a term of office etc.). 4 (also reflex.) to realize the potential of. **fulfillable** a. **fulfilled** a. happy and satisfied. **fulfiller** n. **fulfilment, fulfilling** n.

full[1] (ful) a. (comp. **fuller**, superl. **fullest**) 1 filled up, replete. 2 having no space empty, containing as much as the limits will allow. 3 well supplied, having abundance (of). 4 filled to repletion, satisfied with. 5 charged or overflowing (with feeling etc.). 6 preoccupied or engrossed with. 7 plentiful, copious, ample. 8 complete, perfect, at the height of development. 9 ample or intense in volume or extent, swelling, plump. 10 strong, sonorous. 11 (of clothes etc.) made of a large amount of material. 12 visible in its entire dimensions. 13 (of the moon) having the whole disc illuminated. 14 (of the tide) high. ~adv. 1 quite, equally. 2 completely, exactly, directly. 3 very. 4 more than adequately. ~n. 1 complete measure or degree. 2 the utmost or fullest extent. 3 the highest state or point. 4 a state of satiety. 5 the state or time of a full moon. **full of oneself** having an exaggerated view of one's own importance. **full speed/ steam ahead** used as an order to go or work as fast as possible. **in full** completely, without abridgement, abatement or deduction. **in full face** with all the face visible towards the spectator. **in full view** completely visible. **to the full** to the utmost extent. **full age** n. the status of being an adult, with responsibilities and rights. **full-back** *n.* in football, hockey etc., a defensive player, usu. the rearmost in any on-field formation. **full beam** *n.* the brightest setting of the headlights of a car or other motor vehicle. **full-blooded** *a.* **1** vigorous. **2** sensual. **3** of pure blood, not hybrid. **full-bloodedly** *adv.* **full-bloodedness** *n.* **full-blown** *a.* **1** fully expanded, as a flower. **2** mature, perfect, fully developed. **full board** *n.* tho provision by a hotel etc. of accommodation and all meals. **full-bodied** *a.* having a full, rich flavour or quality. **full-bottomed** *a.* (of a wig) long at the back. **full brother** *n.* a brother having both parents in common. **full colour,** (*N Am.*) **full color** *n.* the complete range of colours. **full-colour, full-coloured** *a.* **full-cream** *a.* (of milk) not skimmed. **full dress** *n.* **1** formal dress worn on ceremonial occasions. **2** evening dress. **full-dress** *a.* at which full dress is to be worn. **full-dress debate** *n.* a debate previously arranged on some important question, in contrast to one arising casually. **full face** *adv.* with all the face visible towards the spectator. **full-frontal** *a.* **1** (of a nude) with the genitals fully revealed. **2** unrestrained, omitting no detail. **full-grown** *a.* mature, fully developed. **full hand** FULL HOUSE (under FULL¹). **full-hearted** *a.* **1** brave, confident, courageous. **2** full of feeling, deeply stirred. **full-heartedly** *adv.* **full-heartedness** *n.* **full house** *n.* **1** (*also* **full hand**) (in poker) three of a kind and a pair. **2** in bingo etc., the set of numbers needed to win. **3** an auditorium filled to capacity. **fullish** *a.* **full-length** *a.* **1** of or showing the entire figure. **2** of the standard or greatest length. ~*n.* a full-length portrait. ~*adv.* stretched to the full extent. **full lock** *n.* **1** maximum turn imparted to the front wheels of a vehicle. **2** the full extent to which the front wheels will turn. **full marks** *n.pl.* the highest score in a test, examination or other assessment. **full moon** *n.* **1** the moon with its whole disc illuminated. **2** the time at which this occurs. **fullness, fulness** *n.* **1** the state or quality of being full. **2** completeness, satiety. **3** largeness, richness, volume, force. **4** everything contained in (the earth etc.). **in the fullness of time** at the eventual time. **the fullness of the heart** full, true feelings. **full out** *adv.* **1** at full power. **2** fully, completely. **3** (*Print.*) adjoining the margin, not indented. **full pitch** *n.*, *adv.* FULL TOSS (under FULL¹). **full point** FULL STOP (under FULL¹). **full professor** *n.* a professor of the highest academic grade at a university etc. **full-scale** *a.* **1** of the same size as the original. **2** using all available resources. **full sister** *n.* a sister having both parents in common. **full stop** *n.* **1** (*also* **full point**) a punctuation mark (.), used at the end of a sentence or an abbreviation. **2** an abrupt finish. **full term** *n.* the normal or expected end date for a pregnancy. **full-term** *a.* **full-throated** *a.* with the full power of the voice. **full time** *n.* **1** the end of play in a sports match. **2** the total usual duration of work. **full-time** *adv.* for the whole of the

(standard) working week. ~*a.* working or using the whole of the (standard) working week. **full-timer** *n.* **full toss** *n.* in cricket, a delivery which reaches the batsman without touching the ground. **full up** *adv.* completely full, with no room for more. **fully** *adv.* **1** completely, entirely, quite. **2** not less than. **-fully** (fuli, fəli) *suf.* forming adverbs, as in *dreadfully*. **fully-fashioned, full-fashioned** *a.* shaped to the lines of the body. **fully-fledged, full-fledged** *a.* **1** (of a bird) having all its feathers. **2** fully qualified, having full status as. **3** fully developed, mature.

full² (ful) *v.t.* to cleanse and thicken (cloth). **fuller** *n.* a person whose occupation is to full cloth. **fuller's earth** *n.* a kind of clay that absorbs grease, esp. used in fulling cloth.

fullerene (ful'ərēn) *n.* (*Chem.*) a molecule consisting of 60 carbon atoms arranged in spherical shape, with possible uses as a lubricant, superconductor etc., also called a *Buckyball*.

⊠ **fullfil** common misspelling of FULFIL.

fulmar (ful'mə) *n.* a seabird of the genus *Fulmaris glacialis*, allied to the petrels, abundant in the Arctic seas.

fulminate¹ (ful'mināt, ful'-) *v.i.* **1** to lighten or thunder. **2** to explode with a loud noise or report, to detonate. **3** to express denunciations very loudly. **4** (of a disease) to develop suddenly. **fulminant** *a.* **1** fulminating. **2** (*Med.*) (of diseases) developing suddenly. **fulminating** *a.* thundering, explosive. **fulmination** (-ā'shən) *n.* **fulminatory** *a.*

fulminate² (ful'minət) *n.* **1** (*Chem.*) a salt of fulminic acid. **2** an explosive containing this. **fulminic** (-min'-) *a.* of, relating to or capable of detonation. **fulminic acid** *n.* (*Chem.*) an unisolated acid that unites with certain metals to form explosive fulminates.

fulness FULLNESS (under FULL¹).

fulsome (ful'səm) *a.* **1** (esp. of compliments, flattery etc.) disgusting by excess or grossness, coarse, excessive, satiating. **2** abundant, copious. **fulsomely** *adv.* **fulsomeness** *n.*

Usage note The use of *fulsome* in a favourable sense is now widely disapproved of, though in fact it is the oldest use of the word.

fulvous (ful'vəs) *a.* tawny, reddish yellow. **fulvescent** (-ves'-) *a.*

fumarole (fū'mərōl) *n.* a hole in the ground in a volcanic region forming an exit for subterranean vapours. **fumarolic** (-rol'-) *a.*

fumble (fŭm'bəl) *v.i.* **1** to grope about. **2** to act, esp. to use one's hands, in an uncertain, aimless or awkward manner. **3** to bungle in any business. ~*v.t.* **1** to handle or manage awkwardly. **2** to fail to catch or hold. **3** to deal with in an uncertain or hesitating manner. ~*n.* an act or instance of fumbling. **fumbler** *n.* **fumblingly** *adv.*

fume (fūm) *n.* **1** (*usu. pl.*) a smoke, vapour or gas, esp. an unpleasant or toxic one. **2** mental agitation, esp. an angry mood. **3** anything empty, fleeting or unsubstantial. ~*v.i.* **1** to emit smoke or vapour. **2** to pass off in smoke or vapour. **3** to show irritation, to fret, to chafe. ~*v.t.* **1** to dry, perfume, stain or cure with smoke, esp. to darken (oak, photographic plates etc.) with chemical fumes, as of ammonia. **2** to dissipate in vapour. **3** to flatter. **4** to perfume. **5** to fumigate. **fumeless** *a.* **fumingly** *adv.* **fumy** *a.* **1** full or composed of fumes. **2** causing fumes.

fumigate (fū´migāt) *v.t.* to subject to the action of smoke or vapour, esp. for the purpose of disinfection. **fumigant** *n.* **fumigation** (-gā´shən) *n.* **fumigator** *n.*

fumitory (fū´mitəri) *n.* (*pl.* **fumitories**) a herb belonging to the genus *Fumaria*, esp. *F. officinalis*, formerly used for skin diseases.

fun (fŭn) *n.* **1** (a source of) amusement, enjoyment, pleasure. **2** hectic activity or argument. ~*a.* (*coll.*) **1** enjoyable. **2** amusing, entertaining. **for fun** for pleasure simply. **in fun** as a joke. **like fun 1** (*coll.*) energetically. **2** (*coll.*) thoroughly. **3** (*coll., iron.*) not at all. **to be great/ good fun** to be very enjoyable or amusing. **to have fun** to enjoy oneself. **to make fun of 1** to hold up to or turn into ridicule, to mock. **2** to banter. **to poke fun at** to make fun of. **fun and games** *n.* (*iron.*) frivolous activity, trouble. **funboard** *n.* in windsurfing, a kind of board that is less steady but faster than a normal board. **funfair** *n.* a usu. outdoor show with rides, sideshows, games of skill and other amusements. **fun run** *n.* (*coll.*) a long-distance run organized not as a competition but for enjoyment, to raise money for charity etc. **funster** (fŭn´stə) *n.* a person who makes fun; a teaser or joker.

funambulist (fūnam´būlist) *n.* a rope-walker or rope-dancer; a performer on the tight or slack rope.

function (fŭngk´shən) *n.* **1** the specific activity, operation or power belonging to an agent. **2** duty, occupation, office. **3** a public or official ceremony. **4** a social entertainment of some importance. **5** the specific purpose of any animal or plant organ. **6** (*Comput.*) a part of a program corresponding to a single value. **7** (*Math.*) a quantity dependent for its value on another or other quantities so that a change in the second correspondingly affects the first. ~*v.i.* **1** to perform a function or duty. **2** to operate. **functional** *a.* **1** of or relating to some office or function; official. **2** formal. **3** practical, utilitarian, avoiding ornament. **4** able to perform (its function), working. **5** of, relating to or affecting the action or functions of an organ, not its substance or structure. **6** (of a mental disorder) not having a direct organic cause. **7** (*Math.*) relating to or depending on a function. **functional food** *n.* a food that contains additives which contribute to good health. **functional group** *n.* (*Chem.*) the group of atoms in a compound that determines the chemical behaviour of the compound. **functionalism** *n.* emphasis on the practical usefulness of a thing. **functionalist**

n. **functionality** (-al´-) *n.* **functionally** *adv.* **functionary** *n.* (*pl.* **functionaries**) a person who holds any office or trust; an official. **function key** *n.* (*Comput.*) a key that generates special instructions. **functionless** *a.*

fund (fŭnd) *n.* **1** a sum of money or stock of anything available for use or enjoyment. **2** (*pl.*) assets, capital. **3** a sum of money set apart for a specific purpose, permanent or temporary. **4** (*pl.*) **a** money lent to a government and constituting a national debt. **b** the stock of a national debt regarded as an investment. **c** (*coll.*) money, finances, financial resources. ~*v.t.* **1** to provide money for. **2** to amass, collect, store. **3** to place in a fund. **4** to convert into a single fund or debt, esp. to consolidate into stock or securities bearing interest at a fixed rate. **in funds** (*coll.*) provided with cash, flush with money. **fundable** *a.* **fundholder** *n.* **1** a person who has property invested in the public funds. **2** a general practitioner who is provided with and controls their own budget. **fundholding** *n.*, *a.* **fundless** *a.* **fundraiser** *n.* a person who raises money for an (often charitable) organization, project etc. **fundraising** *n.*, *a.*

fundament (fŭn´dəmənt) *n.* (*facet.*) **1** the lower part of the body, the buttocks. **2** the anus.

fundamental (fŭndəmen´təl) *a.* **1** of, relating to or serving as a foundation or base. **2** basic, essential, primary, original, indispensable. ~*n.* **1** (*usu. pl.*) a principle, rule or article forming the basis or groundwork. **2** (*Mus.*) the lowest note of a chord. **fundamentalism** *n.* **1** in Christianity, strict belief in the literal truth of the Bible. **2** in Islam, strict observance of the teachings of the Koran and of Islamic law. **3** strict adherence to the fundamental principles of any religion. **fundamentalist** *n.*, *a.* **fundamentality** (-tal´-) *n.* **fundamentally** *adv.* **fundamental note** *n.* (*Mus.*) the lowest note of a chord. **fundamental particle** *n.* a subatomic particle. **fundamental tone** *n.* (*Mus.*) the tone produced by the vibration of the whole of a string etc.

funeral (fū´nərəl) *n.* **1** the ceremony held at the burial or cremation of a dead person. **2** a procession of people at a funeral. **3** (*coll.*) someone's concern or affair in which they alone will be (adversely) affected (*that's your funeral!*). ~*a.* of, relating to or connected with the committal of the dead. **funeral director** *n.* an undertaker. **funeral home** *n.* (*N Am.*) a funeral parlour. **funeral parlour**, (*N Am.*) **funeral parlor** *n.* a place where the dead are prepared for burial or cremation and funerals may be held. **funeral pile, funeral pyre** *n.* a pile of wood etc. on which a dead body is burnt. **funeral urn** *n.* an urn that holds the ashes of a cremated corpse. **funerary** *a.* of, used at or relating to funerals. **funereal** (-niə´ri-) *a.* **1** of, relating to or suitable for a funeral. **2** dismal, sad, mournful. **3** gloomy, dark. **funereally** *adv.*

fungus (fŭng´gəs) *n.* (*pl.* **fungi** (-gī, -jī), **funguses**) **1** a mushroom, toadstool, mould, mildew, or other cryptogamous plant, without chlorophyll and feeding on organic matter. **2** (*Med.*) a morbid growth or excrescence of a spongy nature. **3** something of rapid or parasitic growth. **4** (*sl.*) a beard. **fungal** *a.*, *n.* **fungicide** (-jisīd) *n.* anything that destroys fungi or their spores. **fungicidal** (-sī´-) *a.* **fungistatic** (-jistat´ik) *a.* slowing down the growth of fungi. **fungistatically** *adv.* **fungoid** (-goid) *a.* of the nature of or like a fungus. ~*n.* a fungoid plant. **fungous** *a.* **1** like or of the nature of a fungus. **2** excrescent, springing up suddenly, ephemeral.

funicular (fūnik´ūlə, fən-) *a.* **1** of, relating to, consisting of, or depending on a rope or cable. **2** (of a mountain railway) operated by means of a cable. ~*n.* a railway worked by means of a cable, usu. a mountain railway.

funk[1] (fŭngk) *n.* (*sl.*) **1** a state of fear or panic. **2** a coward. ~*v.i.* **1** to be in a state of terror. **2** to flinch, to shrink in fear or cowardice. ~*v.t.* **1** to be afraid of. **2** to shirk, to try to evade through fear or cowardice. **3** (*usu. p.p.*) to frighten, to scare. **in a funk** (*N Am.*) in a state of despondency or depression. **funker** *n.* **funky**[1] *a.* (*comp.* **funkier**, *superl.* **funkiest**) **1** very fearful, terrified. **2** cowardly.

funk[2] (fŭngk) *n.* **1** (*N Am.*, *sl.*) a stink. **2** funky music. **funky**[2] *a.* (*comp.* **funkier**, *superl.* **funkiest**) **1** (of jazz, pop etc.) having a strong rhythmical beat, earthy, unsophisticated, soulful, like early blues. **2** fashionable. **3** unconventional, odd, quaint. **4** smelly, stinking. **funkily** *adv.* **funkiness** *n.*

funkia (fŭng´kiə) *n.* HOSTA.

funky[1] FUNK[1].

funky[2] FUNK[2].

funnel (fŭn´əl) *n.* **1** a conical vessel usu. terminating below in a tube, for pouring liquids etc. into vessels with a small opening. **2** a tube or shaft for ventilation, lighting etc. **3** something resembling a funnel in shape or function. **4** the chimney of a steamship or steam-engine. **5** the inside of a chimney, a flue. ~*v.t.* (*pres.p.* **funnelling**, (*N Am.*) **funneling**, *past, p.p.* **funnelled**, (*N Am.*) **funneled**) to pour or pass (as if) through a funnel. ~*v.i.* to move (as if) through a funnel. **funnel-like** *a.*

funny (fŭn´i) *a.* (*comp.* **funnier**, *superl.* **funniest**) **1** amusing, causing mirth or laughter. **2** droll, comical, laughable. **3** strange, curious, odd, puzzling. **4** suspicious; underhand, involving trickery. **5** (*coll.*) slightly unwell. ~*n.* (*pl.* **funnies**) (*coll.*) **1** a joke. **2** (*pl.*) comic strips or the comics section of a newspaper. **funnily** *adv.* **funniness** *n.* **funniosity** (-os´-) *n.* (*pl.* **funniosities**) (*facet.*) **1** a comical thing. **2** comicality. **funny bone** *n.* the lower part of the elbow over which the ulnar nerve passes, a blow on which causes a curious tingling sensation. **funny business** *n.* **1** (*coll.*) dubious or suspicious goings-on; trickery. **2** jokes, drollery. **funny-face** *n.* (*coll.*, *facet.*) used as an affectionate form of address. **funny farm**

n. (*sl.*) a mental hospital. **funny-ha-ha** *a.* (*coll.*) funny in its amusing or comical sense. **funnyism** *n.* **funny man** *n.* (*pl.* **funny men**) **1** a clown. **2** a buffoon or wag. **funny money** *n.* (*coll.*) counterfeit or inflated money. **funny paper** *n.* a newspaper or magazine that contains comical matter. **funny-peculiar** *a.* (*coll.*) funny in its strange or odd sense.

funster FUN.

fur (fœ) *n.* **1** the soft fine hair growing thickly upon certain animals, distinct from ordinarily longer hair. **2** (*pl.*) the skins, esp. dressed skins, of such animals. **3** the skin of such animals used for lining or trimming garments. **4** a lining, trimming or garment made of fur. **5** (*as pl.*) fur-bearing animals. **6** the downy covering on the skin of a peach. **7** a coat or crust deposited by a liquid. **8** a coat of morbid matter collected on the tongue. **9** a crust deposited on the interior of kettles etc. by hard water. ~*v.t.* (*pres.p.* **furring**, *past, p.p.* **furred**) **1** to cover, provide, line or trim with fur. **2** to cover or coat with morbid matter. **3** to nail pieces of timber to (as joists or rafters) in order to bring them into a level. ~*v.i.* to become encrusted with fur or scale, as the inside of a boiler. **fur and feather** *n.pl.* fur-bearing animals and game birds. **furless** *a.* **furred** *a.* **1** lined or ornamented with fur. **2** coated with fur or scale. **furrier** (fŭr´iə) *n.* **1** a dealer in furs. **2** a person who prepares and sells furs. **furriery** *n.* the work of a furrier. **furry** *a.* (*comp.* **furrier**, *superl.* **furriest**) **1** covered in fur, wearing fur. **2** made of fur. **3** of or resembling fur. **furriness** *n.* **fur seal** *n.* a seal yielding a fur valuable commercially.

fur. *abbr.* furlong(s).

furbelow (fœ´bilō) *n.* **1** a piece of material, plaited and puckered, used as trimming on skirts and petticoats, a flounce. **2** (*pl.*, *derog.*) finery (*frills and furbelows*). ~*v.t.* to furnish or trim with furbelows.

furbish (fœ´bish) *v.t.* **1** to rub so as to brighten, to polish up. **2** to renovate, to restore the newness or brightness of. **furbisher** *n.*

furcate[1] (fœ´kāt, -kət) *a.* forked, dividing into branches like the prongs of a fork.

furcate[2] (fœ´kāt, fœkāt´) *v.i.* to fork, to divide into branches. **furcation** (-kā´shən) *n.*

furcula (fœ´kūlə) *n.* (*pl.* **furculae** (-lē)) (*Zool.*, *Anat.*) the two clavicles of birds joined together so as to form one V-shaped bone, the wishbone. **furcular** *a.*

furious (fū´riəs) *a.* **1** extremely angry; full of fury, raging, violent, frantic. **2** rushing with vehemence or impetuosity, tempestuous. **3** vehement, eager. **furiously** *adv.* **furiousness** *n.*

furl (fœl) *v.t.* **1** to roll up (a sail) and wrap about a yard, mast or stay. **2** to roll, wrap, fold or close (up). **3** to give up (hopes). ~*v.i.* to become rolled or folded up. **furlable** *a.*

furlong (fœ´long) *n.* a measure of length, the eighth part of a mile, 220 yd. (201 m).

furlough (fœ'lō) *n.* leave of absence, esp. from military duty or from missionary service. ~*v.t.* (*NAm.*) to grant leave of absence to. ~*v.i.* (*NAm.*) to spend furlough.

furnace (fœ'nis) *n.* **1** a chamber or structure containing a chamber in which fuel is burned for the production of intense heat, esp. for melting ores, metals etc. **2** a closed fireplace for heating a boiler, hot water or hot-air pipes etc. **3** a very hot place. **4** a time, place or occasion of severe trial or torture.

furnish (fœ'nish) *v.t.* **1** to equip, to fit up, esp. (a house or room) with movable furniture. **2** to provide or supply (with). **3** to supply, to afford, to yield. **furnished** *a.* (of a house, flat etc.) rented or let with furniture. **furnisher** *n.* **1** a dealer in furniture. **2** a person who furnishes. **furnishings** *n.pl.* furniture, carpets, curtains etc.

furniture (fœ'nichə) *n.* **1** movable articles, e.g. beds, chairs, tables etc. with which a house or room is furnished. **2** equipment, equipage, outfit. **3** (*Naut.*) the masts and rigging of a ship. **4** an ornamental addition. **5** locks, door and window trimmings etc. **furniture beetle** *n.* a beetle, *Anobium puncatatum*, the larvae of which bore into wood. **furniture van** *n.* a large high-sided van for transporting furniture, esp. when moving house.

furor (fū'raw) *n.* (*NAm.*) FURORE.

furore (fūraw'ri, fū'raw) *n.* **1** an uproar, an outburst of public indignation. **2** a craze, a rage.

furrier FUR.

furrow (fŭr'ō) *n.* **1** a trench in the earth made by a plough. **2** a narrow trench, groove or hollow. **3** a rut. **4** the track of a ship. **5** a wrinkle on the face. ~*v.t.* **1** to plough. **2** to make grooves, furrows or wrinkles in. **3** to mark (the face) with deep wrinkles. ~*v.i.* to become furrowed. **furrowless** *a.* **furrowy** *a.*

furry FUR.

further[1] (fœ'dhə), **farther** (fah'-) *a.* **1** more remote. **2** more advanced. **3** going or extended beyond that already existing or stated, additional. ~*adv.* **1** at or to a greater distance, degree or extent. **2** at or to a more advanced point. **3** moreover, in addition, also. **further to** (*formal*) with reference to (an earlier letter etc.). **till further notice** to continue until clearly changed. **further education** *n.* formal, post-school education usu. below degree level. **furthermore** *adv.* moreover, besides. **furthermost** *a.* furthest, most remote. **furthest** *a.* most remote in time or place. ~*adv.* at or to the greatest distance or extent. **at (the) furthest** at the greatest distance; at most.

Usage note The forms *farther* and *farthest*, rather than *further* and *furthest*, are now used only occasionally and restricted to physical distance.

further[2] (fœ'dhə) *v.t.* to help forward, to advance, to promote. **furtherance** *n.* **furtherer** *n.*

furtive (fœ'tiv) *a.* **1** stealthy, sly. **2** secret, surreptitious, designed to escape attention. **3** obtained by or as if by theft. **furtively** *adv.* **furtiveness** *n.*

fury (fū'ri) *n.* (*pl.* **furies**) **1** vehement, uncontrollable anger, rage. **2** a fit of rage. **3** impetuosity, uncontrolled violence. **4** intense, ecstatic passion, inspiration, enthusiasm. **5** (**Fury**) each of the three avenging goddesses of classical mythology. **6** an avenging spirit. **7** a furious woman, a virago. **like fury** (*coll.*) with furious energy. **furylike** *a.* raging, frenzied.

furze (fœz) *n.* gorse. **furzy** *a.*

fuscous (fŭs'kəs) *a.* brown tinged with grey or black; dingy.

fuse[1] (fūz) *v.t.* **1** to reduce to a liquid or fluid state by heat. **2** to unite by or as if by melting together. **3** to provide with a fuse. **4** to cause to fail by blowing a fuse. ~*v.i.* **1** to become fluid. **2** to become united by or as if by melting together. **3** to fail because of a blown fuse. ~*n.* **1** (a device containing) a strip of fusible wire or metal which melts if the current in an electric circuit exceeds a certain value. **2** the melting of wire etc. caused by a short circuit. **to blow a fuse** to lose one's temper. **fuse box** *n.* a box containing one or more fuses. **fuse wire** *n.* the wire used in a fuse. **fusible** *a.* capable of being easily fused or melted. **fusibility** (-bil'-) *n.* **fusion** (-zhən) *n.* **1** the act of melting or rendering liquid by heat. **2** the state of being so melted or liquefied. **3** union by or as if by melting together, blending. **4** a product of such melting or blending; a fused mass. **5** (*Physics*) the combination at very high temperature of atomic nuclei of hydrogen or deuterium to form helium nuclei and liberate nuclear energy (*nuclear fusion*). **fusional** *a.* **fusion bomb** *n.* a bomb, e.g. the hydrogen bomb, whose energy results from nuclear fusion.

fuse[2] (fūz), **fuze** *n.* **1** a tube, cord or casing filled or saturated with combustible material, and used for igniting a charge in a mine or projectile. **2** a detonating device in a bomb or shell. ~*v.t.* to provide with a fuse or fuses. **fuseless** *a.*

fusee (fūzē'), (*NAm.*) **fuzee** *n.* **1** the cone round which the chain is wound in a clock or watch. **2** a match with a mass of inflammable material at its head, used for lighting pipes etc. in a wind. **3** (*NAm.*) a railway red flare light, used as a warning signal.

fuselage (fū'zəlahzh) *n.* the main body of an aeroplane.

fusible FUSE[1].

fusil (fū'zil), †**fusee** (-zē') *n.* an obsolete firelock, lighter than a musket. **fusilier** (-liə'), (*also*, *NAm.*) **fusileer** *n.* **1** (*Hist.*) a soldier armed with a fusil. **2** a soldier in any of several regiments formerly armed with fusils. **fusillade** (-lād') *n.* **1** a continuous, rapid discharge of firearms. **2** a rapid succession of blows, critical comments etc.

fusilli (fuzil'i) *n.pl.* pasta in the form of short, thick spirals.

fusion FUSE[1].

fuss (fŭs) n. 1 excessive activity, labour or trouble, taken or exhibited. 2 unnecessary bustle or commotion, too much ado. 3 undue importance given to trifles or petty details. 4 a quarrel, dispute or protest. 5 a person who fusses. ~v.i. 1 to make a fuss. 2 to be very busy with trifles or petty details. 3 to move fussily. 4 to worry, to be nervous or restless. ~v.t. to worry, to agitate. **to make a fuss** to cause a commotion, esp. by complaining. **to make a fuss of** to lavish attention on as a sign of affection. **fusser** n. **fusspot, fussbudget** n. (coll.) a person who fusses. **fussy** a. (comp. **fussier,** superl. **fussiest**) 1 nervous, excitable, esp. over small details. 2 finicky, fastidious. 3 over-elaborate, over-ornate. **fussily** adv. **fussiness** n.

fustian (fŭs′chən) n. 1 a coarse twilled cotton or cotton and linen cloth, with short velvety pile. 2 inflated or pompous writing or speaking; bombast; claptrap, mere verbiage. ~a. 1 made of fustian. 2 bombastic, pompous, pretentious, inflated. 3 using bombastic language. 4 worthless.

fustic (fŭs′tik) n. a yellow wood used in dyeing, from either of two kinds of tree, esp. old fustic.

fusty (fŭs′ti) a. (comp. **fustier,** superl. **fustiest**) 1 mouldy, musty. 2 rank, smelling unpleasant. 3 close, stuffy. 4 old-fashioned. **fustily** adv. **fustiness** n.

futile (fū′tīl) a. 1 useless, of no effect. 2 trifling, worthless, frivolous. **futilely** adv. **futility** (-til′-) n.

futon (foo′ton) n. 1 a Japanese floor-mattress used as a bed. 2 a kind of low wooden sofa bed with such a mattress.

futtock (fŭt′ək) n. (Naut.) any of the timbers in the compound rib of a vessel.

future (fū′chə) a. 1 that will be. 2 that is to come or happen after the present. 3 that is to come or happen after death. 4 (Gram.) expressing action yet to happen. 5 that will be something specified (our future king). ~n. 1 time to come. 2 what will be or will happen in the future. 3 prospective condition, state, career, etc. 4 likelihood of success. 5 (Gram.) the future tense. 6 (pl.) **a** goods, stocks etc., bought or sold for future delivery. **b** contracts for these. **for the future** from now onwards. **in the future** from now onwards. **futureless** a. **future perfect** n., a. (Gram.)

(the tense) expressing an action as completed in the future, as it will have been. **future shock** n. a state of stress, disorientation and inability to cope caused by an excess of significant and rapid change in society. **futurism** n. an early 20th-cent. movement in painting, poetry, sculpture, music and literature, aiming at expressing the movement and development of objects, instead of the picture they present at a given moment. **futurist** n. 1 a follower of futurism. 2 a student of the future. 3 a believer in human progress. 4 (Theol.) a person who holds that a great part of Scripture prophecy (esp. of the book of Revelation) is still to be fulfilled. **futuristic** (-ris′-) a. 1 of the future or futurism. 2 (of design, architecture etc.) ultramodern, apparently anticipating styles of the future. **futuristically** adv. **futurity** (-tūə′-) n. (pl. **futurities**) 1 the state of being future. 2 future time, esp. eternity. 3 (often pl.) future events, things to come. **futurology** (-rol′-) n. the prediction of future developments from current, esp. sociological and technological, trends. **futurological** (-loj′-) a. **futurologist** (-rol′-) n.

fuze FUSE[2].

fuzee FUSEE.

fuzz (fŭz) v.i. 1 to fly off in minute particles. 2 to become fluffy. ~v.t. to make fluffy. ~n. 1 minute light fibres or particles of down or similar matter, fluff. 2 fluffy or frizzled hair. 3 fuzziness. **the fuzz** 1 (sl.) the police. 2 (sl.) a police officer. **fuzz-ball** n. a puffball. **fuzzbox** n. an electronic device that breaks up the sound, esp. of guitars, that passes through it, esp. by adding a buzzing. **fuzzy** a. (comp. **fuzzier,** superl. **fuzziest**) 1 covered with fuzz, fluffy. 2 having many small, tight curls. 3 blurred, indistinct. 4 (Math., Logic) of or relating to a form of set theory in which membership of the set depends on probability functions (fuzzy logic). **fuzzily** adv. **fuzziness** n. **fuzzy-wuzzy** (-wŭzi) n. (pl. **fuzzy-wuzzies**) (sl., offensive) 1 a black person, esp. one with tightly curled hair. 2 (Hist.) a Sudanese, a Sudanese fighter.

fwd abbr. 1 front-wheel drive. 2 four-wheel drive.

-fy (fī) suf. forming verbs, meaning to bring into a certain state, to make, to produce, as in beautify, deify, horrify, petrify, sanctify, terrify, speechify.

G

G¹ (jē), **g** (pl. **Gs, G's**) the seventh letter of the English and other versions of the Roman alphabet, corresponding to the Greek gamma (γ, Γ). It has two sounds: (1) hard, a voiced velar plosive, before *a, o, u*, as in *gate, god, gun* (except in *gaol*), and when initial, always before *e* and *i* in words of English origin, as in *get, give*, and when final as in *bag*; also before the consonants *l* and *r*, as in *glove, grove*; (2) soft, a voiced palatal affricate, like that of *j*, in words of Greek or Latin origin before *e* or *i*. ~*symbol* **1** the seventh of a series, the seventh highest in a range, e.g. of marks, etc. **2** (*Mus.*) **a** a fifth note of the diatonic scale of C major. **b** the scale of composition in which the keynote is G. **G-string** *n.* a garment consisting of a small piece of cloth covering the pubic area and attached front and back to a waistband, worn e.g. by an entertainer when performing striptease.

G² *abbr.* **1** gauss. **2** giga-. **3** grand, i.e. a thousand dollars or pounds. **4** gravitational constant.

G-man *n.* (*pl.* **G-men**) (*US, sl.*) a Government man, a member of the Federal Bureau of Investigation specially selected for intrepidity as a criminal-hunter.

g *abbr.* **1** gas. **2** gelding. **3** gram(s). **4** gravity; acceleration due to this.

Ga *chem. symbol* gallium.

gab (gab) *n.* idle talk, chatter. ~*v.i.* (*pres.p.* **gabbing**, *past, p.p.* **gabbed**) to talk glibly, to chatter, to prate. **the gift of the gab** (*coll.*) a talent for speaking, fluency. **gabby** *a.* (*comp.* **gabbier**, *superl.* **gabbiest**) (*coll.*) talkative, loquacious.

gabardine (gab´əden, -dēn´), **gaberdine** *n.* **1** a cloth with a corded effect, used largely for raincoats. **2** a raincoat made of this.

gabble (gab´əl) *v.i.* **1** to utter inarticulate sounds rapidly. **2** to talk rapidly and incoherently. ~*v.t.* to utter noisily or inarticulately. ~*n.* rapid, incoherent or inarticulate talk. **gabbler** *n.*

gaberdine GABARDINE.

gable (gā´bəl) *n.* **1** the triangular upper portion of the end of a building, between the sloping sides of the roof. **2** a wall with the upper part shaped like this. **3** a canopy or other architectural member with this shape. **gabled** *a.* **gable end** *n.* the end wall of a building with a gabled upper part.

gad (gad) *v.i.* (*pres.p.* **gadding**, *past, p.p.* **gadded**) to rove or wander idly (about, out etc.). ~*n.* gadding or roaming about. **gadabout** *n.* a person who gads about habitually.

gadfly (gad´flī) *n.* (*pl.* **gadflies**) **1** a bloodsucking insect of the genus *Tobanidae* or *Oestrus*, which

bites cattle and other animals, a horsefly. **2** a person, thing or impulse that irritates or torments.

gadget (gaj´it) *n.* **1** a small tool, an appliance. **2** an ingenious device for making a job easier. **gadgeteer** (-iə´) *n.* **gadgetry** *n.* **gadgety** *a.*

gadoid (gā´doid) *n.* any fish of the cod family Gadidae. ~*a.* of or belonging to the cod family Gadidae.

gadolinite (gad´əlinīt) *n.* a black, vitreous silicate of yttrium, beryllium and iron, formed in crystals. **gadolinium** (gadəlin´iəm) *n.* (*Chem.*) a soft metallic element, at. no. 64, chem. symbol Gd, of the rare-earth group.

gadwall (gad´wawl) *n.* a large freshwater duck, *Anas strepera*, of N Europe and America.

Gael (gāl) *n.* **1** a Scottish Celt. **2** (*less commonly*) an Irish Celt. **Gaelic** (gā´lik, gal´ik) *a.* of or relating to the Gaels or their language. ~*n.* the language spoken by the Gaels. **Gaeltacht** (gāl´təkht) *n.* any of the regions in Ireland where Irish Gaelic is the vernacular language.

gaff¹ (gaf) *n.* (*Naut.*) **1** a stick with a metal hook at the end, used by anglers to land heavy fish. **2** on a sailing boat, the spar which extends the upper edge of fore-and-aft sails not set on stays. ~*v.t.* to seize or land with a gaff.

gaff² (gaf) *n.* (*sl.*) foolish talk, nonsense, outcry. **to blow the gaff** to let out the secret, to give information.

gaffe (gaf) *n.* a social blunder, esp. a tactless comment.

gaffer (gaf´ə) *n.* **1** (*coll.*) a foreman, an overseer. **2** the chief lighting electrician on a television or film set. **3** an old fellow, esp. an aged rustic (formerly a term of respect, now of familiarity).

gag (gag) *v.t.* (*pres.p.* **gagging**, *past, p.p.* **gagged**) **1** to stop the mouth of (a person) by thrusting something into it or tying something round it, so as to prevent speech. **2** to silence, esp. to deprive of freedom of speech. **3** to apply the gag-bit to a horse. **4** to cause to choke or retch. ~*v.i.* to struggle for breath, choke, retch. ~*n.* **1** something thrust into the mouth to prevent one from speaking. **2** a joke, esp. a rehearsed one. **3** an interpolation introduced by an actor into their part. **4** (*sl.*) an imposture, a lie. **gag-bit** *n.* a very powerful bit used in horse-breaking. **gagman** *n.* (*pl.* **gagmen**) **1** a person who writes jokes. **2** a comedian. **gagster** *n.* GAGMAN (under GAG).

gaga (gah´gah) *a.* (*coll., derog.*) foolish, senile, fatuous.

gage¹ (gāj) *n.* **1** something laid down as security, to be forfeited in case of non-performance of some act; a pledge, a pawn. **2** (*Hist.*) a glove or other symbol thrown down as a challenge to combat. ~*v.t.* to deposit as a pledge or security for some act.

gage² (gāj) *n.* a greengage.

gage³ GAUGE.

❌ **gaget** common misspelling of GADGET.

gaggle (gag´əl) *v.i.* to make a noise like a goose. ~*n.* **1** a collection of geese on land. **2** (*coll.*) a group of people, usu. disorganized or animated.

Gaia (gī´ə) *n.* the earth as a self-regulating organism.

gaiety (gā´əti) *n.* (*pl.* **gaieties**) **1** mirth, merriment. **2** a state of lively happiness. **3** a gay appearance, a brave show. **4** brilliance in appearance; showiness.

gaillardia (gəlah´diə) *n.* any plant of the genus *Gaillardia*, the daisy family.

gaily GAY.

gain (gān) *n.* **1** anything obtained as an advantage or in return for labour. **2** profit. **3** increase, growth, accession. **4** amount of increase, growth. **5** (*pl.*) profits, emoluments (*ill-gotten gains*). **6** the acquisition of wealth. **7** the ratio of the output power of an amplifier to the input power usu. measured in decibels, volume. ~*v.t.* **1** to obtain through effort. **2** to earn, to win, to acquire. **3** to progress, to advance, to get more of. **4** to reach, to attain to. **5** to win (over). **6** to obtain as a result, to incur, e.g. a penalty. **7** (of a clock etc.) to become fast to the extent of. ~*v.i.* **1** to advance in interest, possessions or happiness. **2** to gain ground, to encroach (upon). **3** to get the advantage (on or upon). **4** (of a clock etc.) to become fast. **to gain ground 1** to advance in any undertaking. **2** to make progress. **to gain time** to obtain delay for any purpose. **gainable** *a.* **gainer** *n.* **gainful** *a.* **1** profitable, advantageous, remunerative. **2** devoted to gain. **gainfully** *adv.* **gainfulness** *n.* **gainings** *n.pl.* profits, gains.

gainsay (gānsā´) *v.t.* (*past, p.p.* **gainsaid** (-sed´)) to contradict, to deny. **gainsayer** *n.*

gait (gāt) *n.* a manner of walking or going, carriage. **gaited** *a.*

gaiter (gā´tə) *n.* a covering for the ankle or the leg below the knee, usu. fitting down upon the shoe. **gaitered** *a.* **gaiterless** *a.*

❌ **gaity** common misspelling of GAIETY.

gal¹ (gal) *n.* (*coll., N Am.*) a girl.

gal² (gal) *n.* (*Physics*) a unit of acceleration equal to 1 cm per second per second.

gal. *abbr.* gallons.

gala (gah´lə, gā´-) *n.* **1** a festivity, a fête. **2** a sporting occasion involving several events (*swimming gala*). ~*a.* festive.

galactic (gəlak´tik) *a.* (*Astron.*) of or relating to a galaxy, esp. the Milky Way.

galactose (gəlak´tōs) *n.* a sweet crystalline glucose obtained from milk-sugar by treatment with dilute acid.

galago (gəlā´gō) *n.* (*pl.* **galagos**) the bushbaby, one of an African genus of lemurs.

galah (gəlah´) *n.* (*Austral.*) **1** the grey, rose-breasted cockatoo, *Eulophus roseicapillus*. **2** (*coll.*) a silly person, a simpleton.

galantine (gal´əntēn) *n.* a dish of white meat, freed from bone, tied up, sliced, boiled, covered with jelly and served cold.

galaxy (gal´əksi) *n.* (*pl.* **galaxies**) **1** a star system held together in a symmetrical or asymmetrical shape by gravitational attraction. **2** a brilliant assemblage of persons or things. **3** (**Galaxy**) the disc-shaped system of stars that contains our solar system; it is known as the Milky Way from its appearance as a luminous band consisting of innumerable stars indistinguishable to the naked eye, stretching across the sky.

galbanum (gal´bənəm) *n.* a bitter, odorous gum resin obtained from Persian species of *Ferula*, esp. *F. galbaniflua*, an ingredient in the anointing-oil used by Jewish people.

gale¹ (gāl) *n.* **1** a wind stronger than a breeze but less violent than a storm. **2** a wind with a velocity of 40 m.p.h. (64 k.p.h.) or over, registering force eight on the Beaufort scale. **3** an outburst (*gales of laughter*).

gale² (gāl) *n.* the bog myrtle, *Myrica gale*, a twiggy shrub growing on marshy ground, sweet-gale.

Galen (gā´lən) *n.* a physician. **Galenic** (gəlen´ik), **Galenical** *a.* of or according to Galen, esp. applied to medicines prepared from vegetable substances by infusion or decoction, as opposed to chemical remedies. ~*n.* a medicine prepared in this manner.

galena (gəlē´nə) *n.* (*Chem.*) native sulphide of lead or lead-ore.

galia melon (gah´liə) *n.* a small round melon with orange flesh and rough skin.

Galilean¹ (galilē´ən) *a.* of or according to Galileo, esp. applied to the simple telescope developed and used by him.

Galilean² GALILEE.

Galilee (gal´ilē) *n.* a porch or chapel at the entrance of a church. **Galilean**² (-lē´-) *a.* of or relating to Galilee. ~*n.* **1** a native or inhabitant of Galilee. **2** a Christian (applied contemptuously by pagans at the time of Christ).

galingale (gal´ing-gāl), **galangal** (-əng-gal) *n.* the aromatic rootstock of certain E Asian plants of the ginger family and of the genus *Alpinia* and *Kaempferia*, used for culinary purposes.

galium (gal´iəm) *n.* bedstraw, a genus of slender herbaceous plants, containing goosegrass, lady's bedstraw etc.

gall¹ (gawl) *n.* **1** self-assurance, cheek, impudence. **2** bile, the bitter, yellowish fluid secreted by the liver. **3** anything exceedingly bitter. **4** rancour, malignity, bitterness of mind. **5** the gall bladder. **gall bladder** *n.* a pear-shaped membraneous sac, lodged on the undersurface of the liver, which receives the bile. **gall stone** *n.* an abnormal calcareous concretion formed in the gall bladder.

gall[2] (gawl) *n.* an abnormal growth on plants, esp. the oak, caused by the action of some insect. **gall-fly, gall-insect, gall-louse, gall-wasp** *n.* an insect, chiefly belonging to the genus *Cynips,* that causes the production of galls. **gallnut, gall apple** *n.* a gall produced on the oak, esp. by the puncture by *C. gallae tinctoria* of the leaf-buds of the gall-oak, used (esp. formerly) in the making of ink and for other purposes. **gall-oak** *n.* the oak, *Quercus infectoria.*

gall[3] (gawl) *n.* **1** a sore, swelling, or blister, esp. one produced by friction or chafing on a horse. **2** soreness, irritation. **3** someone who or something that causes soreness or irritation. ~*v.t.* **1** to annoy, to harass, to vex. **2** to chafe, hurt or injure by rubbing. **galling** *a.* vexing, irritating, chafing. **gallingly** *adv.*

gall. *abbr.* gallon(s).

gallant[1] (gal'ənt) *a.* **1** brave, high-spirited, courageous, chivalrous. **2** fine, stately. **3** showy, well-dressed. **gallantly** *adv.* **gallantry**[1] *n.* courage of a bold, dashing, magnanimous kind.

gallant[2] (gal'ənt, gəlant') *n.* **1** a man of fashion, a beau. **2** a man who is attentive and polite to women. **3** a lover, a wooer; a paramour. ~*a.* specially attentive to women. **gallantry**[2] *n.* (*pl.* **gallantries**) **1** politeness and deference to women, with or without evil intent. **2** a polite or deferential act. **3** amorous intrigue.

gallantry[1] GALLANT[1].

gallantry[2] GALLANT[2].

galleon (gal'iən) *n.* a large ship, with three or four decks, much used in 15th–17th cents., esp. by the Spaniards in trade with their American possessions.

galleria (galərē'ə) *n.* a number of small independent shops in one building, on one floor or arranged in galleries on several floors.

gallery (gal'əri) *n.* (*pl.* **galleries**) **1** an elevated floor or platform projecting from the wall toward the interior of a church, hall, theatre, or other large building, commonly used for musicians, singers or part of the congregation or audience. **2** a corridor, a passage, a long and narrow room. **3** a room or building used for the exhibition of pictures and other works of art; a collection of works of art. **4** a passage open at one side, usu. projecting from the wall of a building and supported on corbels or pillars. **5** the highest and cheapest tier of seats in a theatre, concert hall etc. **6** a body of spectators. **7** (*derog.*) an unrefined section of an audience. **8** a portico or colonnade, a balcony, a veranda. **9** (*Mil.*) a covered passage in a fortification, either for defence or communication. **10** (*Mining*) an adit, drift, or heading, within a mine. **to play to the gallery** to court popular applause. **galleried** *a.* **galleryite** (-īt) *n.* a regular playgoer, a member of the audience in the gallery.

galley[1] (gal'i) *n.* **1** the cook-house on board a ship, boat or aircraft. **2** (*Hist.*) a low, flat vessel, with one deck, navigated with sails and oars, that were usu. worked by slaves or convicts. **3** an ancient Greek or Roman war-vessel of this type with one or more tiers of oars. **galley slave** *n.* **1** in ancient times, a criminal condemned to the galleys. **2** a drudge.

galley[2] (gal'i) *n.* **1** in the traditional method of printing by hot-metal composition, an oblong tray on which compositors placed type as it was set up. **2** a galley-proof. **galley-proof** *n.* a proof taken from type in a galley, usu. in one column on a long strip of paper as distinct from that arranged in pages.

galliard (gal'yəd) *n.* **1** a lively dance, common in the 16th and 17th cents. **2** the music to this.

Gallic (gal'ik) *a.* **1** French; characteristic of the French. **2** of or relating to ancient Gaul. **gallice** (-isi) *adv.* in French. **Gallicism** (-sizm) *n.* a French expression or idiom. **Gallicize** (-sīz) **Gallicise** *v.t., v.i.* to make or become French in style, attitude, language etc.

gallimaufry (galimaw'fri) *n.* (*pl.* **gallimaufries**) **1** a hash, a hotchpotch. **2** an inconsistent or ridiculous medley.

gallinaceous (galinā'shəs) *a.* of or relating to the order Galliformes of birds, containing pheasants, partridges, grouse, turkeys, domestic fowls, and allied forms.

gallium (gal'iəm) *n.* (*Chem.*) a soft, grey metallic element of extreme fusibility, at. no. 31, chem. symbol Ga, used in semiconductors.

gallivant (galivant') *v.i.* **1** to gad about, to go around seeking pleasure. **2** to flirt.

Gallo- (gal'ō) *comb. form* **1** French. **2** Gaulish.

gallon (gal'ən) *n.* **1** a British liquid measure of capacity equal to eight pints (4.55 l). **2** a British dry measure equal to one-eighth of a bushel (4.55 l). **3** a US liquid measure of capacity equal to 3.79 l. **4** (*pl.*) a large quantity. **gallonage** *n.*

gallop (gal'əp) *v.i.* (*pres.p.* **galloping**, *past, p.p.* **galloped**) **1** to run in a series of springs, as a horse at its fastest pace. **2** to ride at a gallop. **3** to go or do anything at a very rapid pace. ~*v.t.* to make (a horse) gallop. ~*n.* **1** the motion of a horse at its fastest speed, with all the feet off the ground at one point in the progressive movement of the four limbs. **2** the act of riding or a ride at this pace. **3** an area set aside for this. **4** a galop. **galloper** *n.* **galloping** *a.* progressing rapidly, out of control (*galloping inflation*; *galloping consumption*).

galloway (gal'əwā) *n.* a black breed of cattle, orig. bred in Galloway.

gallows (gal'ōz) *n.sing.* **1** a framework, usu. consisting of timber uprights and a crosspiece, on which criminals are executed by hanging. **2** execution by hanging. **gallows humour** *n.* macabre, ironic humour.

Gallup poll (gal'əp) *n.* **1** a method of ascertaining the trend of public opinion by questioning a representative cross-section of the population. **2** a poll according to this method.

galluses (gal´əsiz), †**gallowses** *n.pl.* (*N Am., Sc., coll.*) braces for trousers.

galoot (gəloot´) *n.* (*coll.*) an awkward, uncouth person.

galop (gal´əp, gəlop´) *n.* **1** a lively dance in 2/4 time. **2** the music to the dance. *~v.i.* (*pres.p.* **galoping**, *past, p.p.* **galoped**) to dance this.

galore (gəlaw´) *adv.* in plenty, abundantly (*There was food galore at the feast*).

galoshes (gəlosh´əz) *n.pl.* a pair of waterproof overshoes, usu. of vulcanized rubber, for protecting a person's boots or shoes in wet weather.

galumph (gəlŭmf´) *v.i.* **1** to move noisily and clumsily. **2** to prance exultantly.

galvanism (gal´vənizm) *n.* electricity produced by chemical action, esp. that of acids on metals. **galvanic** (galvan´ik) *a.* **1** of, relating to or produced by galvanism. **2** (of movements, expression etc.) forced and spasmodic, as if caused by the action of an electric current. **galvanically** *adv.* **galvanist** *n.*

galvanize (gal´vənīz), **galvanise** *v.t.* **1** to rouse into life or activity as by a galvanic shock. **2** to apply galvanism to, esp. to stimulate muscular action etc. by galvanism. **3** to plate with gold or other metal by galvanism. **galvanization** (-zā´shən) *n.* **galvanizer** *n.*

galvanometer (galvənom´itə) *n.* a delicate apparatus for determining the existence, direction, and intensity of electric currents. **galvanometric** (-met´rik), **galvanometrical** *a.*

Gambian (gam´biən) *a.* of or relating to The Gambia in W Africa. *~n.* a native or inhabitant of The Gambia.

gambit (gam´bit) *n.* **1** an opening in chess, in which a pawn is sacrificed in order to obtain a favourable position for attack (*King's gambit; Queen's gambit; Steinitz gambit*). **2** an opening move or manoeuvre in any strategy, campaign, battle of wits etc.

gamble (gam´bəl) *v.i.* **1** to play, esp. a game of chance, for money. **2** to risk large sums or other possessions on some contingency. **3** to speculate financially. **4** to knowingly take any sort of serious risk. *~v.t.* to bet (a sum etc.) in gambling. *~n.* **1** gambling. **2** a gambling venture or speculation. **to gamble away** to squander or lose in gambling. **gambler** *n.*

gamboge (gambōj´, -boozh´) *n.* a gum resin, from E Asia, used as a yellow pigment and in medicine.

gambol (gam´bəl) *v.i.* (*pres.p.* **gambolling**, (*N Am.*) **gamboling**, *past, p.p.* **gambolled**, (*N Am.*) **gamboled**) to frisk or skip about; to frolic. *~n.* a frolic; a skipping or playing about.

game[1] (gām) *n.* **1** an exercise for diversion, usu. with other players, a pastime. **2** a contest played according to specified rules and decided by chance, strength, skill or a combination of these. **3** (*pl.*) athletic contests, esp. such as are held at periodical dates, as the Olympic Games etc.

4 (*pl.*) athletics and sports on a school curriculum. **5** (*N Am.*) a match, e.g. baseball. **6** a single round in a sporting or other contest. **7** the number of points required to win a game. **8** the score in a game. **9** a project, plan, or scheme designed to defeat others. **10** a success in a game or contest. **11** (*coll.*) **a** (*pl.*) tricks, dodges, subterfuges. **b** a lark, an amusing incident. **12** sport, merriment, diversion. **13** jest, as opposed to being serious. **14** wild animals or birds pursued or shot in field sports, as hares, grouse, partridges, pheasants. **15** the flesh of animals or birds pursued or shot in field sports. **16** an object of pursuit. **17** a flock of swans that are not wild. **18** an occupation or business. *~a.* **1** of or relating to game. **2** plucky, spirited. **3** ready, willing (to do etc.). *~v.i.* **1** to play at games of chance. **2** to play for a stake. **3** to gamble. **game, set and match** (*coll.*) a final and convincing victory. **off one's game** off form. **on one's game** on form. **the game** (*coll.*) prostitution. **to give the game away 1** to reveal a secret or strategy. **2** (*coll.*) to reject or abandon a competition etc. **to make (a) game of** to turn into ridicule. **to play the game 1** to abide by the rules. **2** to act in an honourable way. **game bird** *n.* **1** a bird hunted for sport or food. **2** a bird of the order of Galliformes, which includes many of those hunted for sport. **gamecock** *n.* a cock bred and trained for fighting. **game-egg** *n.* an egg from which game birds are bred. **game fish** *n.* a large fish that is caught for sport. **gamekeeper** *n.* a person employed to look after game, coverts etc., and to prevent poaching on a private estate or game reserve. **gamekeeping** *n.* **gamely** *adv.* **gameness** *n.* **game of chance** *n.* a game depending on luck rather than skill. **game plan** *n.* **1** the tactics etc. of a football team, prearranged before a match. **2** any carefully planned strategy. **game point** *n.* a situation in a game of tennis etc. when one point is enough to determine the game. **gamer** *n.* a person who plays a game, esp. a role-playing game or a computer game. **game show** *n.* a television programme, esp. a quiz show, in which selected contestants compete for prizes. **gamesman** *n.* (*pl.* **gamesmen**) a person who practises gamesmanship. **gamesmanship** *n.* the art or practice of winning games by disconcerting the opponent (by talking etc.) but without actually cheating. **gamesome** *a.* **1** inclined to play. **2** merry, gay. **gamesomely** *adv.* **gamesomeness** *n.* **gamester** *n.* a person who is addicted to gaming, a gambler. **game theory, games theory** *n.* the analysis of all choices and strategies available by means of a game or military, social etc. conflict in order to choose the best possible course of action. **game warden** *n.* a person employed to look after game, esp. on a game reserve. **gaming** *n.* gambling. **gaming house** *n.* **1** a house where gambling is carried on. **2** a house of ill-repute, a brothel. **gaming table** *n.* a table for gambling games. **gamy** *a.* (*comp.* **gamier**, *superl.* **gamiest**) **1** having the flavour or odour of game, high. **2** abounding in game. **3** plucky, spirited, game. **4** (*N Am.*) suggestive of scandal. **gamily** *adv.*

game[2] (gām) *a.* **1** lame, crippled. **2** (of the arm or leg) crooked. **gammy** (gam´i) *a.* (*comp.* **gammier,** *superl.* **gammiest**) (*coll.*) **1** crippled, crooked (*gammy leg*). **2** wrong, spurious.

gamelan (gam´əlan) *n.* **1** a SE Asian percussion instrument similar to a xylophone. **2** an orchestra made up of a number of gamelans or similar instruments.

gamete (gam´ēt, -mēt´) *n.* (*Biol.*) a sexual reproductive cell, either of the two germ cells that unite to form a new organism – in the male, a spermatozoon, in the female an ovum. **gametal** (gam´ətəl, -ē´-), **gametic** (-et´-, -ē´-) *a.*

gameto- (game´tō), **gamet-** *comb. form* (*Biol.*) gamete.

gametocyte (game´tōsīt) *n.* (*Biol.*) a cell that breaks up into gametes.

gametogenesis (gamētōjen´əsis) *n.* (*Biol.*) the formation of gametes.

gametophyte (game´tōfīt) *n.* a plant of the generation that produces gametes in plant species which show alternation of generations. **gametophytic** (-fit´ik) *a.*

gamin (gam´in, -mā´) *n.* **1** a homeless child, an urchin. **2** a cheeky child.

gamine (gam´ēn, -ēn´) *n.* **1** a small boylike girl or woman. **2** a female gamin.

gamma (gam´ə) *n.* **1** the third letter of the Greek alphabet (γ, Γ). **2** a third-class mark given for a student's work. **gamma globulin** *n.* any of a group of proteins that are carried in blood and serum and include most known antibodies. **gamma radiation, gamma rays** *n.* shortwavelength, penetrating electromagnetic rays emitted by radioactive substances, used in the treatment of cancer and in radiography of metals.

gammon (gam´ən) *n.* **1** the buttock or thigh of a hog salted and dried. **2** a cured ham. *~v.t.* to make into bacon.

gammy GAME[2].

gamp (gamp) *n.* (*coll.*) an umbrella, esp. a large and clumsy one.

gamut (gam´ət) *n.* **1** the whole range, compass or extent. **2** (*Mus.*) **a** the whole series of notes recognized by musicians. **b** a major diatonic scale. **to run the gamut of** to go through the complete range of.

gamy GAME[1].

gander (gan´də) *n.* **1** the male of the goose. **2** a simpleton, a noodle. **3** (*coll.*) a quick look. *~v.i.* to look quickly.

g and t *abbr.* gin and tonic.

gang[1] (gang) *n.* **1** a number of persons associated for a particular purpose (often in a bad sense). **2** a number of manual workers under a supervisor, or of slaves or convicts. **3** a set of tools operating together. *~v.i.* to act in concert with. **to gang up** to join with others (in doing something).

to gang up on to join with others to make an attack on (someone). **gang-bang** *n.* (*sl.*) an occasion on which a number of males have successive sexual intercourse with one female. **ganger** *n.* the overseer or foreman of a gang of labourers. **gangland** *n.* the world of organized crime. **gang rape** *n.* successive rapes by a number of people committed on one victim on one occasion. **gang-rape** *v.t.* **gang show** *n.* a variety entertainment performed by members of the Scout Association and Guide Association. **gangsta** (-stə) *n.* **1** (*sl.*) a gangster. **2** (*also* **gangsta rap**) a type of rap music with lyrics often inspired by gangsters. **gangster** (-stə) *n.* a member of a criminal gang.

gang[2] (gang) *v.i.* (*Sc.*) to go. **gangplank** *n.* a plank, usu. with cleats, used for boarding or landing from a vessel. **gangway** *n.* **1** an opening in the bulwarks affording entrance to or exit from a vessel. **2** a temporary bridge affording means of passage from a ship to the shore. **3** a passage into or out of a building or between rows of seats. **4** a passage connecting different parts of a vessel. **5** in a mine, a main level. *~int.* clear the way!

gangling (gang´gling) *a.* loosely built, lanky, awkward. **gangle** *v.i.* to move awkwardly. **gangly** *a.* (*comp.* **ganglier,** *superl.* **gangliest**).

ganglion (gang´gliən) *n.* (*pl.* **ganglia** (-ə)) (*Med.*) **1** in pathology, a globular growth in the sheath of a tendon. **2** an enlargement in the course of a nerve forming a local centre for nervous action. **3** an aggregation of nerve cells forming a nucleus in the central nervous system. **gangliac** (-ak), **gangliar, ganglionic** (-on´-) *a.* **gangliated** (-ātid), **gangliform** (-fawm), **ganglionary** (-əri), **ganglionated** *a.*

gangrene (gang´grēn) *n.* **1** (*Med.*) death or decay in a part of the body, the first stage of mortification, as a result of poor blood supply to the part. **2** moral corruption, social decay. *~v.t.* **1** (*Med.*) to cause gangrene in. **2** to infect with decay or vice; to corrupt. *~v.i.* (*Med.*) to become gangrenous. **gangrenous** (-grə-) *a.*

gangsta, gangster GANG[1].

gangue (gang), **gang** *n.* the earthy matter or matrix in which ores are embedded.

gangway GANG[2].

ganja (gan´jə) *n.* marijuana, a dried preparation of *Cannabis sativa* or Indian hemp, smoked as an intoxicant and narcotic.

gannet (gan´it) *n.* **1** a seabird, *Sula bassana,* also called *solan goose.* **2** (*coll.*) a greedy person. **gannetry** *n.* (*pl.* **gannetries**) a gannet colony.

gantry (gan´tri), **gauntry** (gawn´-) *n.* (*pl.* **gantries, gauntries**) **1** (*only* **gantry**) a structure surrounding a rocket on the launch pad, for carrying railway signals, a travelling crane etc. **2** a wooden frame for standing a barrel upon.

gaol JAIL.

gap (gap) *n.* **1** an opening, a breach, as in a hedge, a fence etc. **2** a chasm, a break in a mountain ridge. **3** a breach of continuity, a blank, hiatus, interruption. **4** a deficiency. **5** a wide divergence.

gapped *a.* **gappy** *a.* **gap-toothed** *a.* having spaces between the teeth.

gape (gāp) *v.i.* **1** to stare with open mouth in wonder, surprise or perplexity. **2** to open the mouth wide. **3** to yawn. **4** to open in a fissure or chasm, to split or stand open. ~*n.* **1** the act of gaping; a fit of staring open-mouthed. **2** a stare with open mouth. **3** (*facet.*) a yawn; a fit of yawning. **4** the width of the mouth when opened, as of birds etc. **5** the part of a beak that opens. **6** (*pl.*) a disease in young poultry caused by the gape-worm and characterized by much gaping. **gaper** *n.* someone who or something which gapes, esp. various kinds of birds, fish and molluscs. **gape-worm** *n.* a nematode worm of the family Syngamidae, that causes gapes in poultry. **gapingly** *adv.*

gar (gah), **garfish** *n.* (*pl. in general* **gar, garfish**, *in particular* **gars, garfishes**) **1** any fish of the family Belonidae with a long pointed snout, esp. *Belone belone.* **2** (*N Am.*) a garpike. **garpike** *n.* (*N Am.*) any fish of the American genus *Lepisosteus.*

garage (gar´ahzh, -ij) *n.* **1** a building for housing or repairing motor vehicles. **2** an establishment where this is done as a business or where motor fuels etc. are sold. **3 a** GARAGE ROCK (under GARAGE). **b** a type of house music. ~*v.t.* to put or keep in a garage. **garage rock** *n.* a type of unsophisticated rock music.

garam masala (gŭrəm məsah´lə) *n.* a mixture of spices often used in Indian cookery.

❌ **garantee** common misspelling of GUARANTEE.

garb (gahb) *n.* **1** dress, costume. **2** distinctive style of dress. **3** outward appearance. ~*v.t.* **1** to put garments upon. **2** to put in a distinctive dress.

garbage (gah´bij) *n.* **1** kitchen waste. **2** anything worthless or offensive, sordid rubbish. **3** nonsense. **4** irrelevant or invalid data. **garbage bin** *n.* (*esp. Austral.*) a dustbin. **garbage can** *n.* (*N Am.*) a dustbin.

garble (gah´bəl) *v.t.* **1** to jumble, give a confused version of (a story, quotation etc.). **2** to distort or mutilate (an account, story etc.) deliberately, in such a way as to convey a false impression. **3** to pervert, to falsify. **garbler** *n.*

Garda (gah´də) *n.* the police force of the Irish Republic. **garda** *n.* (*pl.* **gardai** (-dē)) a member of the Irish police force.

garden (gah´dən) *n.* **1** an enclosed piece of ground appropriated to the cultivation of fruit, flowers or vegetables, often with a lawn. **2** (*pl.*) a public pleasure-ground adorned with trees, flower-beds etc. **3** (*US*) a hall for public assemblies. ~*a.* **1** of or relating to a garden. **2** cultivated, not wild. ~*v.i.* **1** to cultivate a garden. **2** (*coll.*) in cricket, to smooth out bumps etc. in the pitch with the bat, often as a delaying tactic. **common or garden** (*coll.*) the ordinary (sort). **garden centre** *n.* a place where plants, fertilizers and garden tools and equipment are sold. **garden city, garden suburb, garden village** *n.* a planned town or suburb in rural surroundings. **garden cress** *n.* a pepperwort, *Lepidium sativum.* **gardener** *n.* a person who gardens, esp. one whose occupation is to attend to or to manage gardens. **gardening** *n.* **1** horticulture. **2** work in a garden. **garden party** *n.* a social meeting or a company entertained on a lawn or in a garden. **garden warbler** *n.* a European woodland bird, *Sylvia borin.*

gardenia (gahdē´niə) *n.* any shrub or tree of the tropical genus *Gardenia,* usu. cultivated in greenhouses for its large fragrant flowers.

❌ **gardian** common misspelling of GUARDIAN.

garganey (gah´gəni) *n.* (*pl.* **garganeys**) a small duck of Europe and Asia, *Anas querquedula,* the male of which has a white stripe over each eye.

gargantuan (gahgan´tūən) *a.* immense, enormous, incredibly big.

gargle (gah´gəl) *v.t.* to rinse (the mouth or throat) with some medicated liquid, which is prevented from passing down the throat by the breath. ~*v.i.* **1** to rinse the mouth or throat in this way. **2** to make a sound like that in gargling. ~*n.* **1** a liquid used for washing the mouth or throat. **2** (*sl.*) an alcoholic drink.

gargoyle (gah´goil), **gurgoyle** (gœ´-) *n.* a grotesque spout, usu. carved to represent a human or animal figure, projecting from Gothic buildings, esp. churches, to throw rainwater clear of the wall.

garibaldi (garibawl´di) *n.* (*pl.* **garibaldis**) **1** a loose kind of blouse worn by women or children and popular in the 1860s, like the red shirts worn by Garibaldi and his men. **2** a garibaldi biscuit. **3** a small red fish, *Hypsypops rubicundus,* of California. **garibaldi biscuit** *n.* a sandwich-type biscuit with a layer of currants.

garish (geə´rish) *a.* **1** gaudy, showy, flashy. **2** excessively or extravagantly decorated. **3** dazzling, glaring. **garishly** *adv.* **garishness** *n.*

garland (gah´lənd) *n.* **1** a wreath or festoon of flowers, leaves etc. worn round the neck or hung up. **2** a festoon of metal, stone, ribbons or other material used for decoration etc. **3** the prize, the chief honour. **4** a collection of choice pieces, esp. of poems. ~*v.t.* to deck with a garland.

garlic (gah´lik) *n.* any of various bulbous-rooted plants of the genus *Allium,* esp. *A. sativum,* with a strong odour and a pungent taste, used in cookery. **garlicky** *a.*

garment (gah´mənt) *n.* **1** an article of clothing, esp. one of the larger articles, such as a coat or gown. **2** (*pl.*) clothes. **3** a visible covering. ~*v.t.* (*usu. p.p., poet.*) to attire with or as with a garment.

garner (gah´nə) *v.t.* to store in or as in a granary, to gather. ~*n.* **1** a place for storing grain, a granary. **2** a store, a repository.

garnet (gah´nit) *n.* a vitreous mineral of varying composition, colour and quality, the deep red, transparent kinds of which are prized as gems.

garnish (gah´nish) *v.t.* **1** to adorn; to embellish (as a dish of food) with something laid round it. **2** to supply, to furnish. **3** (*Law*) **a** to warn to appear in court. **b** to give notice to, not to pay money to a defendant. *~n.* an ornament, a decoration, especially things put round a dish of food as embellishment. **garnishee** (-shē´) *n.* a person who has received notice not to pay any money which they owe to a third person, who is indebted to the person giving notice. *~v.t.* (*p.p.* **garnisheed**) (*Law*) **1** to garnish. **2** to attach (money etc.) to prevent payment to a defendant. **garnisher** *n.* **garnishing** *n.* **1** the act of ornamenting. **2** things used for decoration, esp. of dishes of food. **garnishment** *n.*

garniture (gah´nichə) *n.* **1** ornamental appendages, trimmings, ornament, embellishment. **2** furniture, appurtenances.

garotte GARROTTE.

garret (gar´it) *n.* an upper room or storey immediately under the roof, an attic.

garrison (gar´isən) *n.* **1** a body of troops stationed in a fort or fortified place. **2** a fortified place manned with soldiers, guns, etc., a stronghold. *~v.t.* **1** to furnish (a fortress) with soldiers. **2** to occupy as a garrison. **3** to place on duty defending a garrison.

garrotte (gərot´), **garotte,** (*N Am.*) **garrote** *n.* **1** (*Hist.*) a method of execution in which the victim was fastened by an iron collar to an upright post, and a knob operated by a screw or lever dislocated the spinal column, or a small blade severed the spinal cord at the base of the brain (orig. the method was strangulation by a cord twisted with a stick). **2** killing with a length of wire around the throat. *~v.t.* to execute or kill by this means. **garrotter** *n.*

garrulous (gar´ələs) *a.* **1** talkative, loquacious, chattering. **2** wordy. **garrulity** (-roo´-) *n.* **garrulously** *adv.* **garrulousness** *n.*

garter (gah´tə) *n.* **1** a band round the leg for holding a stocking up. **2** (*N Am.*) a suspender for a stocking or sock. *~v.t.* **1** to fasten (a stocking etc.) with a garter. **2** to put a garter upon. **garter belt** *n.* (*N Am.*) a suspender belt. **garter snake** *n.* a harmless American snake belonging to the genus *Thamnophis.* **garter stitch** *n.* plain knitting.

garth (gahth) *n.* the grass plot surrounded by the cloisters of a cathedral, monastery etc.

gas (gas) *n.* (*pl.* **gases,** (*esp. N Am.*) **gasses**) **1** a substance in the form of air, possessing the condition of perfect fluid elasticity. **2** a gaseous substance used for lighting and heating, esp. that obtained from gas-bearing rock structures or from coal. **3** (*esp. N Am., coll.*) gasoline, petrol. **4** in coal-mining, an explosive mixture of firedamp and air. **5** a gas used as an anaesthetic. **6** empty talk, frothy eloquence. **7** boasting, bragging. **8** (*dated coll. or dial.*) something great or wonderful (*It's a gas!*). *~v.i.* (*pres.p.* **gassing,** *past, p.p.* **gassed**) **1** to indulge in empty talk. **2** to boast. *~v.t.* **1** to attack, to stupefy or kill by means

of poison gas. **2** to supply gas to, to treat or inflate with gas. **to step on the gas 1** to accelerate a motor vehicle. **2** to hurry. **gasbag** *n.* **1** a bag for holding gas or stopping an escape from a gas main. **2** (*coll.*) a talkative person. **gas burner** *n.* the tube or jet at which the gas issues and is ignited. **gas chamber, gas oven** *n.* an airtight place designed for killing animals or humans by means of a poisonous gas. **gas-cooled** *a.* cooled by a flow of gas. **gaseous** (gā´siəs, gas´-) *a.* **1** in the form of gas. **2** like gas. **gaseousness** *n.* **gas field** *n.* a region in which natural gas occurs. **gas fire** *n.* a device for heating a room etc. by burning gas. **gas-fired** *a.* fuelled by a gas or gases. **gas-fitter** *n.* a person employed to lay pipes and put up fixtures for gas. **gas gangrene** *n.* a gangrenous infection in deep wounds caused by bacteria which produce gases in the surrounding tissues. **gas-guzzler** *n.* (*N Am., coll.*) a (usu. large) car that uses a lot of petrol. **gasholder** *n.* a large structure for storing gas. **gasify** *v.t.* (*3rd pers. sing. pres.* **gasifies,** *pres.p.* **gasifying,** *past, p.p.* **gasified**) to convert into gas. **gasifiable** *a.* **gasification** (-fikā´shən) *n.* **gas jet** *n.* **1** a gas burner. **2** a jet of flame from it. **gaslight** *n.* **1** the light produced by the combustion of coal gas. **2** a gas jet. **gaslit** *a.* **gasman** *n.* (*pl.* **gasmen**) **1** a person employed to read household gas meters. **2** a gas-fitter. **gas mask** *n.* a mask with a chemical filter to protect the wearer against poisonous gases and fumes. **gas meter** *n.* a machine for measuring and recording the quantity of gas consumed. **gasohol** *n.* a fuel made by mixing petrol and ethyl alcohol. **gas oil** *n.* an oil distilled from crude petroleum used as a fuel for heating etc. **gas-permeable** *a.* allowing gases to pass, esp. to the cornea of the eye. **gas plant** *n.* fraxinella. **gas ring** *n.* a circular hollow pipe with perforations that serve as gas jets, used for cooking. **gasser** *n.* **1** (*coll.*) a person who talks a lot, a gossip. **2** (*sl.*) an attractive or impressive person or thing. **gas station** *n.* (*N Am., coll.*) a filling station, petrol station. **gassy** *a.* (*comp.* **gassier,** *superl.* **gassiest**) **1** (of carbonated drinks etc.) very effervescent. **2** like gas. **3** gaseous. **4** full of empty talk. **gassiness** *n.* **gas-tight** *a.* (of pipes etc.) not allowing gas to escape, not leaky. **gas turbine** *n.* an internal-combustion engine in which air is heated under pressure; the hot, expanding gas drives a turbine, which in turn powers the compressor. **gasworks** *n.* an industrial plant where gas, esp. coal gas, is produced.

Gascon (gas´kən) *n.* a native of Gascony, France.

gash[1] (gash) *n.* **1** a long, deep, open cut, esp. in flesh; a flesh wound. **2** a cleft. **3** an act of gashing someone or something. *~v.t.* to make a long, deep, gaping cut in.

gash[2] (gash) *a.* (*sl.*) spare, extra, surplus to requirements. *~n.* rubbish, surplus material.

gasket (gas´kit) *n.* **1** a strip of tough but flexible material for packing or caulking joints in pipes, engines etc. to make them airtight or watertight. **2** (*Naut.*) a plaited cord by which the sails, when furled, are bound close to the yards or gaffs. **to blow a gasket** (*coll.*) to lose one's temper.

gaskin (gas´kin) *n.* the part of a horse's hind leg between the stifle and the hock, lower thigh.

gasoline (gas´əlēn), **gasolene** *n.* **1** a volatile inflammable product of the distillation of petroleum, used for heating and lighting. **2** (*N Am.*) petrol.

gasometer (gəsom´itə) *n.* **1** (*Chem.*) an apparatus for measuring, collecting, preserving or mixing different gases. **2** (*coll.*) a gasholder.

gasp (gahsp) *v.i.* to breathe in a convulsive manner, as from exhaustion or astonishment. ~*v.t.* to emit or utter with gasps. ~*n.* **1** a short painful catching of the breath. **2** an utterance gasped out. **at the last gasp 1** at the last extremity. **2** at the point of death. **gasper** *n.* **1** a person who gasps. **2** (*dated sl.*) a cigarette.

gasteropod GASTROPOD.

❌ **gastly** common misspelling of GHASTLY.

gastrectomy (gastrek´təmi) *n.* (*pl.* **gastrectomies**) the surgical removal of (part of) the stomach.

gastric (gas´trik) *a.* of or relating to the stomach. **gastric flu** *n.* (*coll.*) any of several types of stomach disorder, with symptoms including nausea, diarrhoea, abdominal cramps and high temperature. **gastric juice** *n.* a clear, colourless acid secreted by the stomach, one of the principal agents in digestion. **gastritis** (-trī´tis) *n.* inflammation of the stomach.

gastro- (gas´trō), **gastr-** *comb. form* stomach.

gastroenteric (gastrōenter´ik) *a.* of or relating to the stomach and the intestines. **gastroenteritis** (-teri´tis) *n.* inflammation of the stomach and of the intestines. **gastroenterology** (-tərol´əji) *n.* the study of diseases of the stomach and the intestines. **gastroenterological** (-loj´-) *a.* **gastroenterologist** *n.*

gastrointestinal (gastrōintestī´nəl) *a.* of or relating to the stomach or the intestines.

gastronomy (gastron´əmi) *n.* the art or science of good eating, epicurism. **gastronome** (gas´trənōm) *n.* a lover and connoisseur of good food and drink, a gourmet. **gastronomic** (-nom´-), **gastronomical** *a.* of or relating to eating and drinking. **gastronomically** *adv.*

gastropod (gas´trəpod), **gasteropod** (-tər-) *n.* an individual of the Gastropoda, a class of molluscs usu. inhabiting a univalve shell (as the snails), of which the general characteristic is a broad muscular ventral foot. ~*a.* gastropodous. **gastropodous** (-trop´-) *a.* belonging to or characteristic of the Gastropoda.

gastroscope (gas´trəskōp) *n.* a medical instrument for examining the interior of the stomach.

gate (gāt) *n.* **1** a movable barrier, consisting of a frame of wood or iron, swinging on hinges or sliding, to close a passage or opening, usu. distinguished from a door by openwork instead of solid panels. **2** an opening in a wall or fence affording entrance and exit to an enclosure, a

gateway. **3** an entrance, an opening, an opportunity. **4** in an airport, any one of the designated points for boarding or disembarking from aircraft, usu. numbered. **5** a natural opening, as a strait, a mountain pass etc. **6** a sluice admitting water to or shutting it off from a lock or dock. **7** a part of a gearbox, having slots into which the gear lever is moved to engage a particular gear. **8** in a film projector, the mechanism to guide and gain access to the film as it passes the light source. **9** the number of people attending a racemeeting, football match etc. **10** the amount of money taken at the gates, gate money. **11** (*coll.*) the starting moments of a race (*to get a good gate*). **12** an electronic circuit (in a computer) that controls the passage of information signals when permitted by another independent source of similar signals. **13** (*sl.*) the mouth. ~*v.t.* **1** to furnish with a gate. **2** to confine (a student) to the grounds of a school or college. **to get/ be given the gate** (*N Am.*, *sl.*) to be dismissed. **gatecrash** *v.t.*, *v.i.* to attend a function or entertainment without an invitation. **gatecrasher** *n.* **gatefold** *n.* a folded insert in a book or magazine that exceeds the size of the other pages; fold-out. **gatehouse** *n.* **1** a lodge, house or defensive structure at or over a gate. **2** a toll gate cottage. **gatekeeper** *n.* **1** a person in charge of a gate. **2** a brown butterfly, *Pyronia tythonus*. **gateleg** *a.*, *n.* (a folding table) with legs that swing in to permit the leaves to be shut down. **gatelegged** *a.* **gateman** *n.* (*pl.* **gatemen**) a person in charge of a gate. **gate money** *n.* entrance money taken at a sports ground etc. **gatepost** *n.* a post on which a gate is hung or against which it shuts. **gate valve** *n.* a sliding valve which opens the full area of a pipe. **gateway** *n.* **1** an opening or passage that may be closed by a gate. **2** an entrance, a means of ingress or egress. **3** a location through which one has access to an area (*Carlisle, gateway to Scotland*). **4** (*Comput.*) a device connecting two different computer networks.

-gate (gāt) *comb. form* added to the name of a place or person to denote a scandal connected with that place or person, as *Billygate, Irangate*.

gateau (gat´ō) *n.* (*pl.* **gateaus** (-ōz), **gateaux** (-ō, -ōz)) a rich cake filled with cream and decorated with icing etc.

gather (gadh´ə) *v.t.* **1** to bring together, to collect, to cause to assemble. **2** to accumulate, to acquire. **3** to cull, to pluck. **4** to pick (up). **5** to get in, as harvest. **6** to deduce, to infer, to conclude. **7** to draw together, to contract, to pucker, to draw into folds or pleats. **8** to summon (up). **9** to take (someone) into one's arms in an embrace. ~*v.i.* **1** to come together, to assemble, to congregate, to unite. **2** to grow by addition, to increase. **3** to concentrate, to generate pus or matter. ~*n.* a pleat or fold of cloth, made by drawing together. **to gather way** (of a vessel) to begin to move, to gain impetus, so as to answer to the helm. **gatherable** *a.* **gathered** *a.* (*euphem.*) dead. **gatherer** *n.*

gathering n. **1** the act of collecting or assembling together. **2** people collected together; a meeting. **3** an abscess, a boil. **4** a group of leaves bound together in a book.

gator (gā'tə) n. (N Am.) an alligator.

gauche (gōsh) a. **1** awkward, clumsy. **2** tactless, uncouth, boorish. **gaucherie** (-əri, -ərē') n. **1** awkwardness. **2** a blunder, esp. a social mistake or awkwardness. **3** awkward manners.

gaucho (gow'chō) n. (pl. **gauchos**) a cowboy of the pampas of Uruguay and Argentina, noted for their horse-riding skills.

gaudy¹ (gaw'di) a. (comp. **gaudier**, superl. **gaudiest**) vulgarly and tastelessly brilliant and ornate, garish, flashy. **gaud** n. **1** a showy ornament or trinket, finery. **2** (pl.) †showy ceremonies, festivities. **gaudily** adv. **gaudiness** n.

gaudy² (gaw'di) n. (pl. **gaudies**) a grand festival or entertainment, esp. one held annually at an English college in commemoration of some event.

gauge (gāj), (Naut., N Am.) **gage** v.t. **1** to ascertain the dimensions, quantity, content, capacity or power of. **2** to test the content or capacity of (casks etc.) for excise purposes. **3** to estimate or appraise (abilities, character etc.), judge. **4** to reduce to a standard size. **5** in dressmaking, to gather into a uniform series of puckers. ~n. **1** a standard of measurement. **2** an instrument for regulating or determining dimensions, amount, capacity etc. according to a fixed standard. **3** a graduated instrument showing the height of a stream, quantity of rainfall, force of the wind, steam-pressure in a boiler etc. **4** the distance between the two rails of a railway track. **5** the diameter of the barrel of a gun. **6** the thickness of a sheet of plastic, film, metal etc. **7** the diameter of wire, screws, needles etc. **8** the position of a ship with reference to another and the wind. **9** extent, capacity, scope. **10** a criterion. **to take the gauge of** to estimate. **gaugeable** a. **gauge pressure** n. the amount by which the pressure within a fluid exceeds that of the surrounding atmosphere. **gauger** n.

Gaul (gawl) n. a native or inhabitant of the ancient Roman province of Gaul (at the centre of which was France). **Gaulish** a. of or relating to Gaul. ~n. the language of ancient Gaul.

gauleiter (gow'lītə) n. **1** the chief official of a district in Germany under the Nazi regime. **2** (coll.) someone in a position of petty authority who behaves in an overbearing and excessively authoritarian manner.

gault (gawlt) n. (Geol.) **1** a series of geological beds of stiff dark-coloured clay and marl between the upper and lower greensand. **2** clay or marl from these beds.

gaunt (gawnt) a. thin, emaciated, haggard, pinched, attenuated. **gauntly** adv. **gauntness** n.

gauntlet¹ (gawnt'lit) n. **1** a long stout glove covering the wrists. **2** a long glove covered with plate-metal, worn with armour. **3** the part of a glove covering the wrists. **to take up the gauntlet**

to accept a challenge. **to throw down the gauntlet** to challenge, to defy.

gauntlet² (gawnt'lit), (US) **gantlet** (gant'-) n. a military (and sometimes a naval) punishment, in which a prisoner had to run between two files of men armed with sticks, knotted cords or the like, with which they struck him as he passed. **to run the gauntlet 1** to suffer this punishment. **2** to be exposed to an ordeal, severe criticism etc.

gauntry GANTRY.

gaur (gow'ə) n. a large fierce Indian ox, Bos gaurus.

gauss (gows) n. (pl. **gauss, gausses**) the cgs unit of magnetic flux density.

gauze (gawz) n. **1** a surgical dressing of an open-work mesh such as muslin. **2** a light, transparent silk or cotton fabric. **3** a thin veil or haze. **gauzy** a. (comp. **gauzier**, superl. **gauziest**). **gauzily** adv. **gauziness** n.

gave GIVE.

gavel (gav'əl) n. a small mallet, esp. one used by a chairman for demanding attention or by an auctioneer. ~v.i. (pres.p. **gavelling**, (N Am.) **gaveling**, past, p.p. **gavelled**, (N Am.) **gaveled**) to use a gavel. ~v.t. to use a gavel to end or dismiss.

gavial GHARIAL.

gavotte (gəvot') n. **1** a dance of a lively yet dignified character resembling the minuet. **2** the music for this. **3** a dance-tune in common time and in two parts, each repeated.

Gawd (gawd) n., int. (sl.) God.

gawk (gawk) n. a clumsy, awkward, shy person. ~v.i. to stare (at or about) stupidly. **gawkish** a.

gawky (gaw'ki) a. (comp. **gawkier**, superl. **gawkiest**) awkward, clownish. **gawkily** adv. **gawkiness** n.

gawp (gawp), **gaup** v.i. to gape, esp. in astonishment. **gawper** n.

gay (gā) a. (comp. **gayer**, superl. **gayest**) **1** full of mirth; light-hearted, cheerful, merry. **2** given over to pleasure or cheerfulness. **3** showy, brilliant in appearance, dressed in bright colours. **4** (of an occasion) very entertaining and enjoyable. **5** (coll.) homosexual. **6** (coll.) of, relating to or frequented by homosexuals. **7** (coll.) licentious, immoral. ~n. a homosexual, esp. a male. **gaily** adv. **gayness** n. **gay plague** n. (coll., offensive) the illness Aids. **gay rights** n.pl. legal and social rights for homosexuals, esp. to achieve equal treatment with heterosexuals.

gazania (gəzā'niə) n. any plant of the S African genus Gazania, with bright yellow or orange flowers that close up in the afternoon.

gaze (gāz) v.i. to fix the eye intently (at or upon). ~n. a fixed look. **gazer** n.

gazebo (gəzē'bō) n. (pl. **gazebos, gazeboes**) **1** an ornamental turret, lantern or summer house with a wide prospect, often erected in a garden. **2** a belvedere.

gazelle (gəzel') n. a swift and very graceful antelope of Africa and Asia, esp. Gazella dorcas, noted for its large, soft black eyes.

gazette (gəzet´) *n.* **1** an official journal containing lists of appointments to any public office or commission, legal notices, lists of bankrupts etc. **2** a newspaper. *~v.t.* to publish in a gazette, esp. to announce the appointment or bankruptcy of (*usu. in p.p.*). **gazetteer** (gazətiə´) *n.* a dictionary of place names, a geographical index.

gazpacho (gaspach´ō) *n.* (*pl.* **gazpachos**) a spicy Spanish soup made with tomatoes, chopped onion, cucumber, green peppers, garlic etc. and usu. served cold.

gazump (gəzŭmp´) *v.t., v.i.* (*coll.*) **1** to raise the price of a property etc. after accepting an offer from (a buyer) but before contracts have been signed, usu. because other parties have made a subsequent higher offer. **2** to swindle. **gazumper** *n.*

gazunder (gəzŭn´də) *v.t., v.i.* (*coll.*) to lower the sum offered to (a seller) on a property etc. just before the contracts are signed.

GBH, gbh *abbr.* grievous bodily harm.

GC *abbr.* George Cross.

GCB *abbr.* (Knight or Dame) Grand Cross of the Bath.

GCMG *abbr.* (Knight or Dame) Grand Cross of the Order of St Michael and St George.

GCSE *abbr.* the General Certificate of Secondary Education in England, Wales and N Ireland, designed to suit a range of academic abilities and based on both coursework and examinations.

GCVO *abbr.* (Knight or Dame) Grand Cross of the Royal Victorian Order.

Gd *chem. symbol* gadolinium.

Gdn. *abbr.* Garden.

Gdns. *abbr.* Gardens.

GDP *abbr.* gross domestic product.

Ge *chem. symbol* germanium.

gean (gēn) *n.* **1** the wild cherry, *Prunus avium.* **2** the fruit of this.

gear (giə) *n.* **1** apparatus, tools, mechanical appliances, harness, tackle, equipment, dress. **2** a set of cog-wheels, links, levers etc. **3** a connection by which an engine, motor etc. is brought into work. **4** the arrangement by which the driving-wheel of a cycle, motor vehicle etc. performs more or fewer revolutions relatively to the pedals, piston etc. **5** the gear ratio in use (*Engage low gear*). **6** on a vessel, the ropes, blocks etc. belonging to any particular sail or spar. **7** (*coll.*) clothes. **8** goods, movables. **9** (*coll.*) illegal drugs, esp. marijuana. *~v.t.* **1** to harness, to put gear on. **2** to put (a machine or motor vehicle) into gear. **3** to furnish with gearing. *~v.i.* **1** to come or be in gear (with). **2** to fit (into) exactly (as a cog-wheel). **in gear** (of a machine or motor vehicle) connected up and ready for work. **out of gear 1** (of gearing or couplings) disconnected. **2** out of working order. **3** disturbed, upset. **to change gear 1** to engage a different gear in a motor vehicle. **2** to change pace. **to gear up** to increase activity, facilities etc., usu. industrial, in response to a change in situation. **gearbox** *n.* **1** the casing in which gears are enclosed in a motor vehicle. **2** a set of gears and its casing. **gear case** *n.* the casing in which gears are enclosed on a bicycle etc. **gear change** *n.* **1** an act of changing gear, usu. in a motor vehicle. **2** (*N Am.*) a gear lever. **geared-up** *a.* fully equipped and ready. **gearing** *n.* **1** gear, working parts. **2** the ratios of a particular system of gears in comparison with other systems. **3** in company finance, the ratio of the amount a company has borrowed to its share capital, usu. expressed as a percentage. **gear lever,** (*esp. N Am.*) **gear shift, gearstick** *n.* in a motor vehicle, a device for selecting or connecting gears. **gearwheel** *n.* a wheel with cogs, esp. the wheel transmitting motion in a cycle.

gecko (gek´ō) *n.* (*pl.* **geckos, geckoes**) any of various lizards with adhesive toes, by which means they can walk on a wall or ceiling.

gee¹ (jē), **gee-up** (jēŭp´) *int.* go on, move faster (a command to a horse etc.). *~v.t.* (*past, p.p.* **geed**) **1** to command (a horse etc.) to move faster. **2** to encourage, hearten. **gee-gee** *n.* a horse (used by or to children).

gee² (jē) *n.* (*pl.* **gees**) (*usu. pl., US, sl.*) a thousand dollars.

gee³ (jē), **gee-whizz** (jēwiz´) *int.* (*coll.*) an exclamation expressing surprise, delight etc.

geek (gēk) *n.* **1** (*sl.*) an odd or eccentric person, a misfit, an inept person. **2** (*Austral., sl.*) a look. **geeky** *a.*

geese GOOSE.

geezer (gē´zə) *n.* (*coll.*) **1** a man. **2** an old man or woman.

Geiger counter (gī´gə) *n.* a device for the detection and counting of particles from radioactive materials.

geisha (gā´shə) *n.* (*pl.* **geisha, geishas**) **1** a Japanese girl or woman trained in the art of being a hostess for men, with skills in conversation, dancing, music. **2** a Japanese prostitute. **geisha girl** *n.*

gel (jel) *n.* the jelly-like material formed when a colloidal solution is left standing. *~v.i.* (*pres.p.* **gelling,** *past, p.p.* **gelled**) **1** to become a gel. **2** (*coll.*) to form a friendship or satisfactory working relationship with someone. **3** (*coll.*) (of a situation, relationship etc.) to begin to function co-operatively and satisfactorily. *~v.t.* to make into a gel, to cause to gel.

gelada (jəlah´də) *n.* (*pl.* **gelada, geladas**) a baboon from NE Africa, *Theropithecus gelada*, with long mane, bare red chest and ridged muzzle.

gelatin (jel´ətin), **gelatine** (-tēn) *n.* a transparent substance forming a jelly in water, obtained from connective animal tissue, such as skin, tendons, bones, horns etc. **gelatinize** (-lat´-), **gelatinise** *v.i.* to be converted into jelly, or a substance like jelly. *~v.t.* to convert into a substance like jelly. **gelatinization** (-zā´shən) *n.* **gelatinous** (-lat´-) *a.* of the nature of or consisting of gelatin, jelly-like. **gelatin paper** *n.* photographic paper coated with sensitized gelatin.

geld (geld) *v.t.* (*past, p.p.* **gelded, gelt** (gelt)) to castrate (esp. a horse), to emasculate, to spay. **gelding** *n.* a castrated animal, esp. a castrated horse.

gelid (jel´id) *a.* **1** extremely cold. **2** icy.

gelignite (jel´ignīt) *n.* an explosive containing nitroglycerin. **gelly** *n.* (*coll.*) gelignite.

gelsemium (jelsē´miəm) *n.* (*pl.* **gelsemiums**) any plant of the genus of climbing shrubs *Gelsemium*, which contains three species, of which the best known is the American yellow jasmine, *Gelsemium sempervirens*, the poisonous root of which yields a medicinal substance.

gem (jem) *n.* **1** a precious stone, such as the diamond, ruby, emerald etc. **2** a person or object of great rarity, beauty or value. **3** a treasure, the most prized or the choicest part. ~*v.t.* (*pres.p.* **gemming**, *past, p.p.* **gemmed**) to adorn with or as with gems. ~*v.i.* to bud. **gemlike** *a.* **gemmy** *a.* **gemstone** *n.* a precious stone cut or polished for ornamental purposes.

geminate[1] (jem´inət) *a.* united or arranged in pairs.

geminate[2] (jem´ināt) *v.t.* to double, to arrange in pairs. ~*v.i.* to occur in pairs. **gemination** (-ā´shən) *n.*

Gemini (jem´inī) *n.* (*pl.* **Gemini, Geminis**) **1** (*as pl., Astron.*) a constellation, the Twins, containing the two conspicuous stars, Castor and Pollux. **2** (*Astrol.*) **a** the third sign of the zodiac. **b** a person born under Gemini.

gemma (jem´ə) *n.* (*pl.* **gemmae** (-ē)) (*Zool.*) a budlike outgrowth in polyps, ascidians etc., which separates from the parent organism and develops into an individual.

gemmate (jem´āt) *a.* (*Zool.*) reproducing by gemmation. ~*v.i.* to reproduce by gemmation. **gemmation** (-ā´shən) *n.* **gemmative** *a.*

gemmule (jem´ūl) *n.* any one of the small reproductive bodies thrown off by sponges.

gemsbok (gemz´bok), **gemsbuck** (-bŭk) *n.* a large antelope of W and E Africa, *Oryx gazella*, with long straight horns.

gemütlich (gəmoo´tlikh) *a.* **1** comfortable, cosy. **2** friendly, genial.

Gen. *abbr.* General.

gen (jen) *n.* (*coll.*) full particulars (of), information (about). ~*v.i.* (*pres.p.* **genning**, *past, p.p.* **genned**) to read up about (*I'm genning up on the subject*). **genned-up** *a.* (*coll.*) well informed, armed with the right information.

-gen (jən) *comb. form* **1** (*Chem.*) producing (*antigen*). **2** produced (*oxygen*). **3** (*Bot.*) growth (*endogen*).

genco (jen´kō) *n.* (*pl.* **gencos**) a company generating and selling power, esp. electricity.

gendarme (zhã´dahm) *n.* **1** an armed policeman, in France and some other Continental countries. **2** a pinnacle of rock blocking a mountain ridge. **gendarmerie** (-mərē´), **gendarmery** (-dah´-) *n.* (*pl.* **gendarmeries**) **1** a body of gendarmes. **2** the headquarters of a body of gendarmes.

gender (jen´də) *n.* **1** (*Gram.*) any one of the classes (usually *masculine, feminine* and *common* or *neuter*) into which words referring to people or things are divided, often coinciding with their sex or sexlessness. **2** classification of words into genders according to their forms etc. **3** (*loosely, esp. euphem.*) sex (*an issue of gender; the male gender*). **gendered** *a.* GENDER-SPECIFIC (under GENDER). **gender-specific** *a.* belonging to or limited to either one sex or the other.

gene (jēn) *n.* the unit of heredity, one of the units of DNA occupying a fixed linear position on the chromosome. **gene pool** *n.* the entire stock of different genes in an interbreeding population. **gene therapy** *n.* (*Med.*) the treatment of certain diseases by the insertion of new genes into nonreproductive cells in a patient (such new genes not being inherited by the patient's offspring). **genic** (jen´-) *a.*

genealogy (jēnial´əji) *n.* (*pl.* **genealogies**) **1** the history or investigation of the descent of families. **2** a record or exhibition of a person's or family's descent in the natural order of succession. **3** pedigree, lineage. **4** the course of a plant's or an animal's development from earlier forms. **genealogical** (-niəloj´-) *a.* **1** of or relating to genealogy. **2** exhibiting the successive stages of family descent. **genealogically** *adv.* **genealogical tree** *n.* the genealogy of a family or species drawn out in an inverted figure resembling a tree, with a root, branches etc. **genealogist** *n.* **genealogize, genealogise** *v.i.* to investigate descent, to prepare genealogies. ~*v.t.* **1** to investigate the descent of, to trace a pedigree. **2** to prepare a genealogy of.

genera GENUS.

general (jen´ərəl) *a.* **1** common, universal. **2** ordinary, usual, widespread, prevalent. **3** not special, particular, partial or local. **4** (*Biol.*) relating to a whole genus, kind, class or order. **5** not limited in scope or application. **6** indefinite, vague. **7** not specialized or restricted. **8** taken or viewed as a whole. **9** added to words expressive of rank or office, indicating that the office holder is chief or supreme within a certain sphere (*director-general, postmaster-general*). ~*n.* **1** an officer ranking next below a field marshal, usu. extended to lieutenant generals and major generals. **2** the commander of an army. **3** a strategist (*a midfield general*). **4** in the Roman Catholic Church, the chief of a religious order, or of all the houses or congregations having the same rule. **5** the chief part, the majority. **6** (*pl.*) general facts or principles. **as a general rule** in most cases or in all ordinary cases. **in general 1** in the main, generally. **2** in most cases or in all ordinary cases, for the most part. **General American** *n.* American English of a form that is not distinctively regional or local. **general anaesthetic**, (*N Am.*) **general anesthetic** *n.* a drug which anaesthetizes the whole body, with loss of consciousness. **general delivery** *n.* (*N Am.*) the equivalent of poste restante. **general election** *n.* an election for representatives for all constituencies in a state. **general headquarters** *n.* the headquarters of a military commander. **generalist** *n.* a person knowledgeable in many fields as distinct from a specialist. **generality** (jenəral´əti) *n.* (*pl.* **generalities**) **1** the state of being general, as opposed to specific. **2** a general statement or principle. **3** a vague statement. **4** the main body, the majority. **5** vagueness. **generalize** (jen´ərəlīz), **generalise** *v,i.* **1** to draw goncral inferences. **2** to speak vaguely, to employ generalities. **3** to form general ideas. **4** to reason inductively. **5** in paintings, to represent typical not particular features. **generalizable** *a.* **generalizability** (-bil´-) *n.* **generalization** (-zā´shən) *n.* **1** a general statement or inference. **2** the act or process of generalizing. **generalizer, generaliser** *n.* **generally** *adv.* **1** for the most part, in most cases. **2** ordinarily, commonly, usually. **3** without minute detail, without specifying. **general meeting** *n.* a meeting open to all members of an institution, society etc. **generalness** *n.* **general practice** *n.* **1** the state of being a general practitioner. **2** the surgery, patients, staff etc. of a general practitioner. **general practitioner** *n.* a physician or surgeon treating all kinds of cases, a GP. **general-purpose** *a.* useful for several different functions. **generalship** *n.* **1** the office or rank of a general. **2** skill in the management of troops and the conduct of war, strategy. **3** skilful leadership, management or organization. **general staff** *n.* in the army, officers assigned to advise senior officers on operations and policy. **general strike** *n.* a strike by all or most workers in most parts of a city, province or country. **general theory of relativity** *n.* an extension of the special theory of relativity to consider the effects of acceleration and gravitation.

generalissimo (jenərəlis´imō) *n.* (*pl.* **generalissimos**) the chief commander of a force furnished by several powers, or military and naval in combination.

generate (jen´ərāt) *v.t.* **1** to produce or bring into existence; to cause to be. **2** to produce, to evolve, to originate. **3** to beget, to procreate. **4** to produce by rule from a given set. **5** (*Math.*) to trace out or form by the motion of a point or a magnitude of inferior order. **generation** (-ā´shən) *n.* **1** a single succession or step in natural descent or in development. **2** the people of the same period or age. **3** an age or period between one succession and another; a stage in development. **4** the average time in which the child takes the place of the parent (usu. estimated at about one third of a century). **5** the act of generating. **6** production, creation, bringing into existence. **7** propagation of the species. **8** reproduction, propagation. **generation gap** *n.* the difference in opinions and understanding between members of different generations. **generative** (-ərətiv) *a.* **1** having the power of generating. **2** of or relating to

generation or production. **3** productive, fruitful. **generator** *n.* **1** an apparatus for producing electrical energy from mechanical energy. **2** someone who or something which generates or produces. **3** any apparatus for the production of gas, steam, electricity etc.

generic (jəner´ik), **generical** (-əl) *a.* **1** of or relating to a class or kind, as opposed to specific. **2** (*Biol.*) of or relating to a genus. **3** comprehensive, applied to large classes of goods or drugs, identified by the product itself and not by a brand name, not having a trademark. **generically** *adv.*

generous (jen´ərəs) *a.* **1** open-handed, bountiful, liberal, munificent. **2** magnanimous, high-spirited. **3** overflowing, abundant, fertile. **4** strong, stimulating (as wine). **generosity** (-ros´-) *n.* **generously** *adv.* **generousness** *n.*

genesis (jen´əsis) *n.* (*pl.* **geneses** (-sēz)) **1** the act of begetting, producing or giving origin to. **2** creation, beginning, origination, mode of production or formation.

genet (jen´it), **genette** (jinet´) *n.* **1** a small mammal, *Genetta vulgaris*, related to the civet. **2** its fur, or cat-skin dressed in imitation of this fur.

genetic (jənet´ik) *a.* **1** of or relating to genes or genetics. **2** of or relating to the origin, generation or creation of a thing. **genetically** *adv.* **genetic code** *n.* the system, based on the molecular arrangement of the chromosomes, that ensures the transmission of hereditary characteristics. **genetic engineering** *n.* the artificial alteration of the genes of an organism in order to control the transmission of certain hereditary characteristics. **genetic fingerprint** *n.* the particular DNA pattern that is unique to an individual and can be used to identify that individual or their offspring. **genetic fingerprinting, genetic profiling** *n.* the act or process of taking a genetic fingerprint from an individual's saliva, blood or sperm, used in forensic science etc. **geneticist** (-sist) *n.* a student of genetics. **genetics** *n.* **1** the study of heredity and variation in organisms. **2** the inherited characteristics of an organism, species or group.

Usage note See note under CONGENITAL.

genial (jē´niəl) *a.* **1** of a cheerful and kindly disposition, cordial, sympathetic, enlivening. **2** conducive to life and growth, soft, mild. **geniality** (-al´-) *n.* **genially** *adv.* **genialness** *n.*

genic GENE.

-genic (jen´ik) *comb. form* **1** of or relating to generation, as in *antigenic*. **2** suited for, as in *photogenic*. **-genically** *comb. form* forming adverbs.

genie (jē´ni) *n.* **1** in fairy stories etc., a magical being who appears suddenly to carry out a person's wishes. **2** JINNEE.

genii GENIUS.

genital (jen´ital) *a.* of or relating to the reproductive organs. **genitals, genitalia** (-tā´liə) *n.pl.* the external reproductive organ(s).

genitive (jen'itiv) *a.* (*Gram.*) denoting a grammatical case indicating origin, possession or the like, applied to a case in inflected languages and also to the Eng. possessive. ~*n.* **1** the genitive case. **2** a word or form in the genitive case. **genitival** (-tī'-) *a.* **genitivally** *adv.*

genito- (jen'itō) *comb. form* genital.

genito-urinary (jenitōū'rinəri) *a.* of or relating to the genital and urinary organs.

genius (jē'niəs) *n.* (*pl.* **geniuses, genii** (-niī)) **1** a person of extraordinary intellectual, imaginative, expressive or inventive ability. **2** an extraordinary endowment of ability. **3** the dominant character, spirit or sentiment (of). **4** natural bent or inclination of the mind. **5** a person who exercises powerful influence over another for good or ill. **6** in mythology, a guardian deity or spirit, supposed to preside over the destinies of an individual, place, nation etc.

genoa (jen'ōə), **genoa jib** *n.* in yachting, a large triangular jib sail. **Genoa cake** *n.* a rich fruit cake with almonds on the top.

genocide (jen'əsīd) *n.* the (attempted) intentional and systematic destruction of a national, ethnic or religious group, e.g. the Jews by the Nazi Germans during World War II. **genocidal** (-sī'-) *a.*

genome (jē'nōm) *n.* the complete set of chromosomes that is contained in any single cell.

genotype (jen'ətīp) *n.* (*Biol.*) the basic genetic structure of an organism. **genotypic** (-tip'-), **genotypical** *a.*

-genous (jinəs) *comb. form* **1** born (*indigenous*). **2** bearing, producing (*endogenous*).

genre (zhā'rə, zhon'rə) *n.* **1** a kind, sort, class, particularly in the field of the arts. **2** a style, manner, esp. artistic. **3** a type of painting, the subject of which is some scene in everyday life. **genre painting** *n.* the painting of scenes from everyday life.

gent (jent) *n.* **1** (*coll.*) a gentleman. **2** (*pl.*) men (in trade descriptions of goods). **the gents/ gents'** a public lavatory for males.

genteel (jentēl') *a.* **1** (*now coll. or facet.*) gentlemanly or ladylike. **2** elegant in appearance, manners or dress, stylish. **3** well-bred, refined, free from vulgarity. **genteelism** *n.* a word or phrase used in place of another word that is perceived to be coarse or vulgar. **genteelly** *adv.* **genteelness** *n.*

gentian (jen'shən) *n.* **1** any plant of the genus *Gentiana* or *Gentianella* of bitter herbs, usu. having blue flowers, common in mountain regions. **2** gentian bitter. **gentian bitter** *n.* a liquor made from gentian roots. **gentian violet** *n.* a greenish crystalline substance that forms a violet solution in water and is used in the treatment of burns and boils, as an antiseptic and as a biological stain.

gentile (jen'tīl) *a.* **1** Christian, as opposed to Jewish. **2** non-Jewish. **3** heathen, pagan. **4** not of one's religious faith, esp. not Mormon. **5** of or

relating to a people or tribe. ~*n.* **1** a Christian, as opposed to a Jew. **2** a non-Jewish person. **3** a heathen, a pagan. **4** a person who is not a Mormon.

gentility (jentil'əti) *n.* **1** social superiority, polite good breeding. **2** respectable manners and habits associated with good society. **3** people of noble birth.

gentle (jen'təl) *a.* (*comp.* **gentler,** *superl.* **gentlest**) **1** mild, tender, kindly. **2** not rough, coarse, violent or stern. **3** moderate, not severe, not energetic. **4** not steep (*a gentle slope*). ~*n.* the larva of the meat-fly or bluebottle, used as bait in angling. ~*v.t.* **1** to handle gently but firmly. **2** to make gentle, amiable or kind. **of gentle birth** of honourable birth, belonging to the gentry, having good breeding. **gentlefolk, gentlefolks** *n.pl.* (*poet.*) people of good position, of gentle birth. **gentleness** *n.* **gently** *adv.*

gentleman (jen'təlmən) *n.* (*pl.* **gentlemen**) **1** a man of good breeding, kindly feelings and high principles, a man of honour. **2** (*pl.*) men, esp. the male members of an audience. **3** a man who by education, occupation or income holds a good social position. **4** a man of respectable position who follows no occupation. **5** a man entitled to bear arms. **6** (*coll.*) the personal attendant of a man of rank. **gentleman-at-arms** *n.* (*pl.* **gentlemen-at-arms**) a member of a company forming a bodyguard to the sovereign on state occasions. **gentleman farmer** *n.* (*pl.* **gentlemen farmers**) a man of property who occupies his own farm. **gentlemanly** *a.* **1** like a gentleman in appearance, feeling or behaviour. **2** of or relating to or becoming a gentleman. **gentlemanliness** *n.* **gentleman's agreement, gentlemen's agreement** *n.* an agreement binding in honour but not legally.

gentlewoman (jen'təlwumən) *n.* (*pl.* **gentlewomen** (-wimən)) **1** a woman of good birth or breeding. **2** a woman who waits upon a lady of high rank.

gentoo (jen'too) *n.* (*pl.* **gentoos**) a penguin, *Pygoscelis papua*, found esp. in the Falkland Islands.

gentry (jen'tri) *n.* **1** people of high birth and social standing. **2** the social class immediately below the nobility in position and birth. **3** (*coll.*, *derog.*) people, folks. **gentrification** (-fikā'shən) *n.* the process by which the character of an esp. inner urban area formerly lived in by working-class people is changed by an influx of middle-class people, with a consequent increase in property values. **gentrify** (-fī) *v.t.* (*3rd pers. sing. pres.* **gentrifies,** *pres.p.* **gentrifying,** *past, p.p.* **gentrified**) to change by gentrification. **gentrifier** *n.*

genuflect (jen'ūflekt) *v.i.* to bend the knee, esp. in worship. **genuflection** (-flek'shən), **genuflexion** *n.* **genuflector** *n.*

genuine (jen'ūin) *a.* **1** natural, belonging to or coming from the true source. **2** not counterfeit, false, spurious or adulterated. **3** sincere, honest. **4** (*Zool.*) true to type, not aberrant. **genuinely** *adv.* **genuineness** *n.*

genus (jē´nəs) *n.* (*pl.* **genera** (jen´ərə)) **1** (*Biol.*) a class or kind of objects containing several subordinate classes or species. **2** a group or class of plants or animals differentiated from all others by certain common characteristics and comprising one or more species. **3** a kind, group, class, order, family.

-geny (jəni) *comb. form* production or mode of production, as *ontogeny, philogeny.*

geo- (jē´ō) *comb. form* of or relating to the earth.

geocentric (jēōsen´trik), **geocentrical** (-kəl) *a.* **1** having the earth as centre. **2** viewed from the earth as centre. **geocentrically** *adv.* **geocentric latitude** *n.* the latitude at which a planet would appear if viewed from the centre of the earth.

geochemistry (jēōkem´istri) *n.* the study of the chemical composition of the crust of the earth. **geochemical** *a.* **geochemist** *n.*

geochronology (jēōkrənol´əji) *n.* the measuring of geological time. **geochronological** (-kronəloj´-) *a.* **geochronologist** *n.*

geode (jē´ōd) *n.* **1** a hollow nodule of any mineral substance, often lined with crystals. **2** the cavity in such a nodule. **geodic** (-od´-) *a.*

geodesy (jēod´əsi), **geodetics** (-det´-) *n.* the science or art of measuring the earth's surface or large portions of it, as distinguished from surveying, which deals only with limited tracts. **geodesic** (-dē´-, -des´-), **geodetic** (-det´-) *a.* **1** of or relating to geodesy. **2** carried out or determined by means of geodesy. **geodesic dome** *n.* a light, strong dome built from a latticework of polygons so that the pressure load is evenly distributed throughout the structure. **geodesic line, geodetic line** *n.* the shortest line between two points on the earth's surface or that of a geometrical solid. **geodesist** *n.*

geography (jēog´rəfi) *n.* **1** the science of the surface of the earth, its physical features, natural productions, inhabitants, political divisions, commerce etc. **2** the layout and locations of a limited area (*the geography of a building*). **geographer** *n.* **geographic** (-graf´-) *a.* of or relating to geography. **geographical** *a.* geographic. **geographical latitude** *n.* the angle between the plane of the equator and a perpendicular to the surface of the earth at a given point. **geographically** *adv.* **geographical mile** *n.* one minute of longitude measured at the equator, also called a nautical mile.

geology (jēol´əji) *n.* **1** the science of the earth's crust, its composition, its structure, and the history of its development. **2** the geological structure of a particular area. **geologic** (jēəloj´-) *a.* **geological** *a.* **geologically** *adv.* **geologist** *n.* **geologize, geologise** *v.i.* **1** to study geology. **2** to make geological investigations, esp. in a particular district. ~*v.t.* to study the geology of.

geomagnetism (jēōmag´nətizm) *n.* the study of the earth's magnetism. **geomagnetic** (-net´-) *a.* **geomagnetically** *adv.* **geomagnetist** *n.*

geometer (jēom´itə) *n.* **1** a geometrician. **2** a geometrid. **geometer moth** *n.* a geometrid moth. **geometrid** (-trid) *n.* a moth or its caterpillar belonging to the family called Geometridae on account of their seeming to measure the ground as they move along, a looper. ~*a.* of or relating to the Geometridae.

geometry (jiom´ətri) *n.* **1** the branch of mathematics concerned with the properties and relationships of points, lines, curves, surfaces and solids. **2** the relative arrangement of points, lines etc. **geometric** (jēəmet´-) *a.* **1** of or relating to geometry. **2** (of architecture, design etc.) composed of or decorated by regular lines or shapes such as circles, triangles or rectangles. **geometrical** *a.* geometric. **geometrically** *adv.* **geometrical progression** *n.* a progression in which the terms increase or decrease by a common ratio, as 1, 3, 9, 27; 144, 72, 36, 18. **geometrical series** *n.* a series in geometrical progression. **geometrician** (jēəmətrish´ən), **geometrist** *n.* **geometric mean, geometrical mean** *n.* the central number of a geometrical progression, which can be calculated, where there are *n* numbers, as the *n*th root of their product. **geometric tracery, geometrical tracery** *n.* window tracery of which the openings are simple geometrical patterns.

geomorphology (jēōmawfol´əji) *n.* the study of the origin, development and characteristics of land forms. **geomorphologic** (-fələj´-), **geomorphological** *a.* **geomorphologically** *adv.* **geomorphologist** *n.*

geophysics (jēōfiz´iks) *n.* (*Physics*) the science that deals with the physical characteristics of the earth. **geophysical** *a.* **geophysicist** (-sist) *n.*

geopolitics (jēōpol´itiks) *n.* **1** the study of how the political views and aims of a nation are affected by its geographical position. **2** (*as pl.*) the combination of the geographical and political factors that affect a country or area. **geopolitical** (-lit´-) *a.* **geopolitician** (-tish´ən) *n.*

Geordie (jaw´di) *n.* **1** (*coll.*) a native of Tyneside, NE England. **2** (*coll.*) the dialect spoken by the people of NE England. ~*a.* of or relating to Tyneside, its people, dialect, culture etc.

George (jawj) *n.* (*coll.*) an automatic aircraft pilot. **by George!** used to express surprise mixed with admiration.

georgette (jawjet´) *n.* a plain semi-transparent dress material usually of silk or crêpe.

Georgian[1] (jaw´jən) *a.* **1** relating to the period of George I–IV in Great Britain, 1714–1830. **2** relating to the reign of George V, 1910–36.

Georgian[2] (jaw´jən) *a.* **1** of or relating to Georgia, a republic of SE Europe. **2** of or relating to Georgia, one of the southern states of the US. ~*n.* a native or inhabitant of either Georgia.

geoscience (jēōsī´əns) *n.* **1** any of the sciences that are concerned with the earth, e.g. geology, geophysics or geodesy. **2** earth sciences collectively. **geoscientist** *n.*

geosphere (jē´əsfiə) *n.* **1** the solid part of the earth, the lithosphere. **2** any one of the concentric regions of the earth and its atmosphere.

geostationary (jēōstā´shənəri) *a.* (of a satellite) orbiting the earth at the same speed as the earth rotates so remaining above the same spot on the earth's surface.

geosynchronous (jēōsing´krənəs) *a.* GEO-STATIONARY.

geothermal (jēōthœ´məl) *a.* of or relating to the internal heat of the earth.

geotropism (jēot´rəpizm) *n.* the tendency exhibited by the organs of a plant to turn towards the centre of the earth. **geotropic** (-trop´-) *a.* **geotropically** *adv.*

geranium (jərā´niəm) *n.* **1** any hardy herbaceous plant or shrub of the genus *Geranium*, natives of all temperate regions, such as the cranesbill. **2** a cultivated plant of the allied genus *Pelargonium*.

gerbera (gœ´bərə, j-) *n.* any plant of the genus *Gerbera*, esp. *G. jamesonii*, the Transvaal daisy from S Africa.

gerbil (jœ´bil) *n.* any of numerous small, burrowing, mouselike rodents of the subfamily Gerbillinae, from desert regions of Asia and Africa, often kept as pets.

gerfalcon GYRFALCON.

geriatrics (jeriat´riks) *n.* the branch of medicine dealing with old age and its diseases. **geriatric** *a.* **1** of or relating to geriatrics or to elderly people. **2** (*coll., derog.*) old, senile, worn out, useless. **geriatrician** (-riətrish´ən) *n.*

germ (jœm) *n.* **1** a micro-organism, esp. the type that is supposed to cause disease, a microbe. **2** (*Biol.*) **a** the portion of living matter from which an organism develops. **b** the embryo of an animal or plant. **c** a partially-developed organism. **3** the origin, source or elementary principle (*the germ of an idea*). **in germ** existing in an undeveloped state. **germ cell** *n.* the parent cell from which a new individual develops, usu. distinguished as the female element in reproduction from the sperm cell or male element. **germicide** (-misīd) *n.* a substance used for destroying germs. **germicidal** (-sī´dəl) *a.* **germ layer** *n.* (*Biol.*) any of the three layers of cells (ectoderm, mesoderm, endoderm) formed in an embryo. **germless** *a.* **germ line** *n.* (*Biol.*) a series of germ cells continuing through successive generations of an organism. **germ plasm** *n.* the part of the protoplasm in which the power of reproduction is supposed to reside and which is transmitted from one generation to its offspring. **germ warfare** *n.* the use of bacterial weapons to cause disease in enemy troops and population. **germy** *a.*

German (jœ´mən) *a.* of or relating to Germany or its inhabitants. ~*n.* **1** a native or inhabitant of Germany. **2** the language of Germany, spoken also in Austria and parts of Switzerland. **Germanic** (jəman´-) *a.* **1** characteristic of Germans or

Germany. **2** of or relating to the peoples originating in the area which became Germany (Anglo-Saxons, Scandinavians and Germans). **3** of or relating to the branch of Indo-European languages including German, Dutch, English and the Scandinavian languages. ~*n.* **1** the Germanic branch of Indo-European languages. **2** the unrecorded ancestor of this branch. **Germanize, Germanise** *v.t.* to assimilate or make to conform to German ideas, customs, idioms etc. ~*v.i.* to conform to these. **Germanization** (-zā´shən) *n.* **Germanizer** *n.* **German measles** *n.* rubella, a mild infectious disorder resembling measles which if contracted by a pregnant woman may cause birth deformities in her unborn child. **German shepherd (dog)** *n.* an Alsatian dog. **German silver** *n.* a white alloy of nickel, copper and zinc, used for mathematical instruments, tableware etc.

german (jœ´mən) *a.* **1** having both parents the same (*brother german*). **2** having both grandparents the same on one side (*cousin german*).

germander (jœman´də) *n.* any plant of the genus *Teucrium*. **germander speedwell** *n.* an English wild plant with blue flowers, *Veronica chamaedrys*.

germane (jœmān´) *a.* relevant (to), appropriate.

germanium (jəmā´niəm) *n.* (*Chem.*) a metallic element of a greyish-white colour, at. no. 32, chem. symbol Ge, used in the construction of transistors because of its electrical properties. **germanic** (-man´-) *a.* (*Chem.*) containing germanium, esp. in the tetravalent state. **germanous** (jœ´mənəs) *a.* containing germanium in the divalent state.

Germano- (jœman´ō) *comb. form* German.

germen (jœ´men) *n.* (*pl.* **germens, germina** (jœ´minə)) (*Biol.*) the ovary or rudimentary seed-vessel of a plant. **germinal** (-mi-) *a.* **1** relating to or of the nature of a germ. **2** germinative. **3** in the earliest stage of development, embryonic. **4** productive of new ideas. **germinally** *adv.*

germicide GERM.

germinate (jœ´mināt) *v.i.* **1** to sprout, to shoot, to bud. **2** to develop. ~*v.t.* to cause to sprout or bud. **germination** (-ā´shən) *n.* **germinative** (-nətiv) *a.* **germinator** *n.*

gerontocracy (jerəntok´rəsi) *n.* (*pl.* **gerontocracies**) **1** government by old men or old people. **2** a government of old men or old people. **3** a state so governed. **gerontocrat** (jəron´-) *n.* **gerontocratic** (-krat´-) *a.*

gerontology (jerəntol´əji) *n.* the science dealing with old age, the ageing process and the problems special to old people. **gerontological** (-loj´-) *a.* **gerontologist** *n.*

-gerous (jərəs) *comb. form* bearing, having, as in *armigerous*.

gerrymander (jer´imandə) *v.t.* **1** to tamper with the boundaries of (an electoral district or constituency) so as to secure unfair advantages for a particular candidate, party or class. **2** to tamper with or manipulate to secure advantage. ~*n.* an unfair rearrangement of a constituency in this manner; an act of gerrymandering. **gerrymanderer** *n.*

gerund (jer´ənd) *n.* (*Gram.*) a form of a verb acting as a noun: in English a form ending in -*ing*, in Latin, a part of the verb used as a noun instead of the infinitive in cases other than the nominative. **gerundial** (-rŭn´-) *a.* **gerundive** (-rŭn´div) *n.* in Latin, a form of a verb acting as an adjective, ending in -*ndus* and declinable, giving the sense of *must* and *should* (be done). **gerundival** (-dī´-) *a.*

gesso (jes´ō) *n.* (*pl.* **gessoes**) **1** plaster of Paris used for painting, sometimes for sculpture. **2** a ground made of this.

gestalt (gəstalt´) *n.* (*Psych.*) an organized whole in which each part affects every other part. **gestaltism** *n.* **gestaltist** *n.* **gestalt psychology** *n.* a system of thought maintaining that all perceptions, reactions etc. are gestalts or organized wholes.

Gestapo (gəstah´pō) *n.* **1** the body of secret police formed to secure strict obedience to the government of Nazi Germany. **2** (*derog.*) any similar organization.

gestation (jestā´shən) *n.* **1** the process of being carried in the uterus from the time of conception to that of birth. **2** the period between conception and birth. **3** the process of being developed or elaborated in private thought. **4** the period during which a plan, idea, etc. is conceived and developed. **gestate** *v.t.* **1** to carry (a foetus) in gestation. **2** to develop (an idea, plan etc.) usu. privately.

gesticulate (jestik´ūlāt) *v.i.* to make expressive gestures or motions, as in speaking or instead of speaking. ~*v.t.* to express or represent by gestures. **gesticulation** (-lā´shən) *n.* **gesticulative** (-lətiv), **gesticulatory** *a.* of, relating to or represented by gesticulation. **gesticulator** *n.*

gesture (jes´chə) *n.* **1** a motion of the face, body or limbs, used to express emotion or to illustrate or enforce something that is said. **2** a significant move or act, usu. of a friendly nature. **3** the art of using gesture for rhetorical or dramatic purposes. ~*v.i.* to gesticulate. ~*v.t.* to accompany or represent with gestures or action. **gestural** *a.* **gesturer** *n.*

get (get) *v.t.* (*pres.p.* **getting**, *past* **got** (got), †**gat** (gat), *p.p.* **got**, (*esp. N Am.*) **gotten** (got´ən)) **1** to procure, to obtain, to gain possession of by any means, to acquire (*to get a new car*). **2** to earn, to win (*to get first prize*). **3** to receive, to obtain (*to get a letter*). **4** to receive as one's portion or penalty, to suffer (*to get a £20 fine*). **5** to understand, learn, commit to memory (*Do you get what I mean?*). **6** (*coll., in p.p.*) to have, to possess (*I have got a car*). **7** (*coll.*) to be obliged to (*You have got to do it*). **8** to beget, to procreate (*She has got three children*). **9** to succeed in obtaining, bringing, putting etc. (*to get a train*). **10** to induce,

to persuade (to) (*Get him to accept*). **11** to betake (oneself) (*I got myself to the doctor's*). **12** (*coll.*) to catch, to outwit, to nonplus (*I got him with a slower ball*). **13** to become infected with (an illness). **14** to establish communication with. **15** to fetch. **16** to arrest, to catch. **17** to affect emotionally. **18** to prepare. **19** to annoy, to irritate. ~*v.i.* **1** to arrive at any place (*to get there*). **2** to go, to depart (*Go away! get!*). **3** (*coll.*) to succeed, to find the way or opportunity (to) (*I got to be manager*). **4** to be a gainer, to profit (*to give as good as you get*). **5** to become. **6** to start doing something. **get along!** used to express mild disbelief. **get away!** used to express mild disbelief. **get on!** used to express mild disbelief. **to be getting on for** to approach in time or age. **to get about 1** to be able to move or walk about (after an illness). **2** to become known, to be reported abroad. **3** to travel from place to place. **to get across 1** to communicate, to make oneself understood. **2** to be communicated. **to get ahead 1** to prosper. **2** to come in advance (of). **to get along 1** to proceed, to advance. **2** to succeed, to fare, to manage (well or badly). **3** (*coll.*) to go away. **4** (*coll.*) to have a friendly relationship. **to get around** to get about. **to get around to** to get round to. **to get at 1** to be able to reach. **2** to ascertain (*to get at the truth*). **3** (*sl.*) to criticize repeatedly esp. in an annoying way. **4** to influence, corrupt, bribe (a jockey etc.). **5** to drug or illegally tamper with (a racehorse). **6** to imply, to hint at. **to get away 1** to escape. **2** to disengage oneself (from). **to get away with 1** to make off with. **2** to escape discovery in connection with (something wrong or illegal). **to get back 1** to receive back, to recover. **2** to return, to come back. **3** to contact again. **to get back at** to retaliate against. **to get by 1** (*coll.*) to have only enough money for the things one needs, to survive. **2** to elude. **3** to be good enough. **to get down 1** to alight, to descend. **2** to swallow. **3** (*coll.*) to make unhappy, to depress. **4** to write down. **to get down to** to concentrate upon. **2** to start work on. **to get even 1** to revenge oneself. **2** to equalize (with). **to get going 1** to begin. **2** to make haste. **to get in 1** to enter. **2** to collect and place under cover (as crops). **3** to make room for. **4** to be elected. **5** to arrive home. **to get into 1** to put on (as clothes etc.). **2** (*coll.*) to become involved in. **3** to possess, dominate or take over (a person's mood, personality etc.). **to get it** (*sl.*) to be in trouble, to be punished. **to get it into one's head** to become convinced (that). **to get it together** to become well organized, to take control. **to get off 1** to dismount, to alight (from). **2** to escape, to be released (from). **3** to be acquitted, to be let off (with or for). **4** to start. **5** to go to sleep. **6** to take off, to remove. **7** to procure the acquittal of. **8** to cause to go to sleep. **to get off on 1** (*coll.*) to be impressed by. **2** (*coll.*) to enjoy. **to get off with 1** (*coll.*) to behave flirtatiously with. **2** (*coll.*) to begin or have a sexual relationship with. **3** (*coll.*) to escape blame or punishment for. **to get**

on 1 to put or pull on. **2** to move on. **3** to advance. **4** to succeed or prosper. **5** to grow late. **6** to grow old. **7** to have a friendly relationship. **8** to do, fare or manage (with or without). **9** to mount. **to get on to 1** to make contact with. **2** to become aware of, discover. **to get out 1** to pull out, to extract. **2** to escape from any place of confinement or restraint. **3** to be divulged. **4** to publish or say finally, after difficulties. **5** to complete the solution of. **to get out of 1** to avoid (doing something). **2** to obtain (something) from, with some difficulty. **to get outside (of)** (*sl.*) to eat or drink, to ingest. **to get over 1** to surmount, overcome (a difficulty etc.). **2** to recover from (illness, surprise, disappointment etc.). **3** to make intelligible. **4** (*coll.*) to persuade. **5** to finish (a task etc.) with relief. **to get over with** to finish (a task etc.) with relief. **to get round to** to deal with in due course. **to get there 1** (*coll.*) to succeed. **2** (*coll.*) to understand. **to get through 1** to reach a point beyond, to reach one's destination. **2** to succeed in doing, to complete, to finish (with). **3** to pass (an examination). **4** (of a bill) to be passed. **5** to use up. **6** to make a telephone connection. **to get through to 1** to make a telephone connection with. **2** (*coll.*) to make understand or pay attention. **to get to 1** to reach, to arrive at. **2** to begin (a task etc.). **3** (*coll.*) to annoy or irritate. **4** (*coll.*) to affect emotionally. **to get together 1** to meet, to assemble. **2** to bring together, to amass. **to get under way** to cause to begin. **to get up 1** to rise (as from a bed etc.). **2** to mount. **3** to dress up, to disguise. **4** to begin to rage or be violent (as the wind, waves etc.). **5** to prepare, to get ready. **6** to learn, to work up. **7** to invent, to devise. **to get up to** (*coll.*) to be doing, to be involved in, esp. wrongly. **to have got it bad/ badly** (*sl.*) to be infatuated or obsessed. **get-at-able** *a.* accessible. **getaway** *n.* (*coll.*) an escape, esp. from the scene of a crime. ~*a.* used in a getaway. **get-out** *n.* a means of avoiding something. **get-rich-quick** *a.* with the purpose of making a lot of money in a short time (*a get-rich-quick scheme*). **gettable** *a.* obtainable. **getter** *n.* **1** a person or thing that gets. **2** (*Physics*) a substance for removing residual gas from a vacuum tube etc. ~*v.t.* (*Physics*) **1** to remove with a getter. **2** to remove from with a getter. **getting on** *a.* (*coll.*) growing old, advanced in years. **get-together** *n.* (*coll.*) an informal gathering. **get-up** *n.* **1** a person's dress and other accessories. **2** the manner in which anything is presented, as on the stage. **3** the style or format (of a book). **get-up-and-go** *n.* **1** energy and enthusiasm. **2** ambition.

gewgaw (gū´gaw) *n.* a showy trifle; a toy, a bauble.

geyser (gē´zə) *n.* **1** a hot spring throwing up a column of water at intervals (as in SW Iceland, the Yellowstone region in N America, and New Zealand). **2** an apparatus for heating a stream of water supplying a bath etc.

Ghanaian (gahnā´ən) *n.* a native or inhabitant of Ghana in W Africa. ~*a.* of or relating to Ghana.

gharial (gar´iahl), **gavial** (gā´viəl) *n.* a large Indian crocodile, *Gavialis gangeticus*, with a long, slender muzzle.

ghastly (gahst´li) *a.* (*comp.* **ghastlier**, *superl.* **ghastliest**) **1** horrible, frightful, shocking. **2** (*coll.*) awful, unpleasant (*a ghastly mistake*). **3** pale, deathlike, haggard. **4** very ill. ~*adv.* in a ghastly manner. **ghastlily** *adv.* **ghastliness** *n.*

ghat (gaht, gawt), **ghaut** (gawt) *n.* (*Ind.*) **1** a flight of steps descending to a river, a landing-place. **2** a range of mountains (*Eastern and Western Ghats*). **3** a mountain pass.

ghee (gē), **ghi** *n.* butter, usu. prepared from buffalo-milk, clarified into an oil, which can be kept for a long time.

gherkin (gœ´kin) *n.* a young and green small variety of cucumber, used for pickling.

ghetto (get´ō) *n.* (*pl.* **ghettos**, **ghettoes**) **1** a poor, densely populated area of a city, esp. inhabited by an ethnic minority. **2** the quarter of a town formerly inhabited by Jews. **3** a segregated area, a place apart. **4** a group confined to such an area. ~*v.t.* (*3rd pers. sing. pres.* **ghettoes**, *pres.p.* **ghettoing**, *past, p.p.* **ghettoed**) to confine to a ghetto. **ghetto-blaster** *n.* a large portable stereo radio-cassette or CD player. **ghettoize**, **ghettoise** *v.t.* to make into a ghetto. **ghettoization** (-zā´shən) *n.*

ghi GHEE.

ghillie GILLIE.

ghost (gōst) *n.* **1** the spirit or soul of a dead person appearing to the living, an apparition. **2** the soul of a dead person in the other world. **3** the soul or spirit, the vital principle. **4** a mere shadow or semblance. **5** the remotest likelihood (*a ghost of a chance*). **6** a person who does literary or artistic work for which another takes the credit. **7** in optics, a spot, gleam or secondary image caused by a defect in a lens. **8** in television reception, a duplicated image. ~*v.i.* to be a ghost writer. ~*v.t.* to ghost-write (a book etc.). **to give up the ghost** to die, to expire. **ghostbuster** *n.* (*coll.*) a person supposed to banish ghosts etc. **ghosting** *n.* the phenomenon of duplicated images in television reception. **ghostlike** *a.* **ghostly** *a.* (*comp.* **ghostlier**, *superl.* **ghostliest**) of or relating to ghosts or apparitions. **ghostliness** *n.* **ghost town** *n.* a deserted or semi-deserted town, such as a formerly flourishing mining town. **ghost train** *n.* a fairground miniature railway in a dark space, where the rider is confronted by ghostly apparitions. **ghost-write** *v.t., v.i.* to write (a speech, autobiography etc.) for another person. **ghost writer** *n.* a person who writes (speeches, books etc.) for someone else who is presumed to be the author.

ghoul (gool) *n.* **1** an evil spirit supposed, in Eastern tales, to devour human corpses. **2** a person interested in morbid things. **ghoulish** *a.* **ghoulishly** *adv.* **ghoulishness** *n.*

GHQ *abbr.* General Headquarters.

ghyll GILL².

GI (jēī´) n. (pl. **GIs, GI's**) (N Am., coll.) a soldier in the US Army, esp. a private. ~a. of or relating to US servicemen.

giant (jī´ent) n. **1** a mythical being of human form but superhuman size. **2** a man of extraordinary size. **3** any person, animal, plant etc. of abnormal size. **4** a person of extraordinary powers, ability etc. (a literary giant). **5** GIANT STAR (under GIANT). ~a. **1** gigantic. **2** very large of its class, type, species etc. **3** like a giant. **giantism** n. abnormal development in size esp. as caused by dysfunction of the pituitary gland. **giant-killer** n. **1** in folklore, a person who overcomes giants. **2** in sport, a lowly person or team that beats a bigger one. **giant-killing** a., n. **giant-like** a. **giant panda** n. a large, black-and-white, bearlike mammal, Ailuropoda melanoleuca, from China and Tibet. **giant sequoia** n. the sequoia Sequoiadendron giganteum. **giant slalom** n. a slalom of greater distance and with more widely spaced obstacles than the standard. **giant star** n. a star of great brightness and a very low mean density.

gib (gib) n. a metal wedge, pin or bolt to hold a machine part etc. in place.

gibber (jib´e), **jibber** v.i. to jabber, to talk rapidly and inarticulately. ~n. talk or noise of this kind. **gibberish** n. **1** inarticulate sounds. **2** unmeaning or unintelligible language, jargon.

gibbet (jib´it) n. **1** an upright post with a crosspiece from which the bodies of executed criminals were formerly hung on display. **2** a gallows. **3** the gallows, death by hanging. ~v.t. (pres.p. **gibbeting**, past, p.p. **gibbeted**) **1** to execute by hanging. **2** to hang or expose on or as on a gibbet. **3** to expose to public contempt and derision.

gibbon (gib´en) n. any individual of the genus Hylobates, long-armed anthropoid apes from E Asia.

gibbous (gib´es), **gibbose** (-ōs) a. **1** protuberant, convex, swelling into inequalities. **2** (of the illuminated portion of the moon or of a planet) exceeding a semicircle but falling short of a circle. **3** hunch-backed, humped, crook-backed. **gibbosity** (-bos´-) n. **gibbously** adv. **gibbousness** n.

gibe (jīb), **jibe** v.i. **1** to use sneering or taunting expressions. **2** to jeer, to scoff (at), to rail, to flout. ~n. a sneer, a scoff, a taunt. **giber** n. **gibingly** adv.

giblets (jib´lits) n.pl. the feet, neck, and internal eatable parts of a fowl, such as the heart, liver, gizzard etc., which are removed before cooking.

giddy (gid´i) a. (comp. **giddier**, superl. **giddiest**) **1** having a whirling, swimming or dizziness in the head. **2** reeling, tending to stagger or fall. **3** causing the sensation of giddiness (as a precipice, a dance, success etc.). **4** inconstant, changeable, fickle, flighty. **5** elated, excited, rash. ~v.t. (3rd pers. sing. pres. **giddies**, pres.p. **giddying**, past, p.p. **giddied**) to make giddy. ~v.i. to become giddy. **giddily** adv. **giddiness** n.

giddy-up (gidiŭp´) int. used as a command to a horse to make it start moving or go faster.

gift (gift) n. **1** a thing given, a present, a contribution. **2** a natural quality, talent or endowment. **3** the act, right, or power of giving. **4** (Law) the voluntary bestowal of property without consideration. ~v.t. to give as a gift. **to look a gift horse in the mouth** to find fault with what cost one nothing. **gifted** a. **1** given, bestowed. **2** largely endowed with intellect, talented. **giftedly** adv. **giftedness** n. **gift of tongues** n. the power of speaking in unknown tongues, esp. as conferred on the Apostles at Pentecost. **gift token, gift voucher** n. a voucher worth a specified amount, given as a gift, which can be exchanged for goods etc. by the recipient. **giftware** n. goods suitable as gifts. **gift-wrap** v.t. (pres.p. **gift-wrapping**, past, p.p. **gift-wrapped**) to wrap (a gift) in attractive paper. **giftwrap** n. paper for wrapping gifts.

gig¹ (gig) n. **1** a light two-wheeled vehicle drawn by one horse. **2** a light clinker-built boat, 20–28 ft. (6–9 m) long, rowed by 4, 6 or 8 alternate oars.

gig² (gig) n. (coll.) a job, esp. a booking for a musician to perform. ~v.i. (pres.p. **gigging**, past, p.p. **gigged**) to perform at a gig.

giga- (gig´e, gī´ge) comb. form denoting 10⁹, as gigawatt, or 2³⁰, as gigabyte.

gigabyte (gig´ebīt) n. a unit of computer memory capacity equal to 1,024 megabytes.

gigaflop (gig´eflop, gī´-) n. (Comput.) a unit of computer processing speed equal to 1,000 million floating-point operations per second.

gigantic (jīgan´tik) a. **1** huge, enormous, giant-like; immense, extraordinary. **2** suitable for a giant. **gigantesque** (-tesk´) a. **gigantically** adv. **gigantism** (jī´-) n. **1** abnormal largeness. **2** (Med.) GIANTISM (under GIANT). **3** (Bot.) abnormal largeness due to polyploidy.

gigawatt (gig´awot, gī´-) n. a unit of power equal to 10⁹ watts.

giggle (gig´el) v.i. **1** to laugh in a silly or affected manner, to titter. **2** to laugh in a nervous, catchy way, with attempts to restrain oneself. ~n. a silly or nervous laugh. **giggler** n. **giggly** a. (comp. **gigglier**, superl. **giggliest**) given to giggling, inclined to giggle.

gigolo (zhig´elō) n. (pl. **gigolos**) **1** a young man paid by an older woman to be a sexual partner or escort. **2** a professional dance-partner or escort.

gigot (jig´et) n. a leg of mutton or lamb. **gigot sleeve** n. a leg-of-mutton sleeve.

gild (gild) v.t. (past, p.p. **gilded, gilt** (gilt)) **1** to coat, overlay or wash thinly with gold. **2** to impart a golden colour or appearance to. **3** to make brilliant, to brighten. **4** to give a specious or agreeable appearance to, to gloss over. **to gild the lily** to spoil beauty by overembellishing. **gilded** a. **gilded cage** n. an environment of wealth and luxury in which a person is obliged by others or by circumstance to spend a restricted life. **gilded youth** n. young people of wealth and fashion. **gilder** n. **gilding** n. **1** the act, process or art of overlaying with gold. **2** gilding-metal in leaf, powder, or liquid, for application to any surface.

Usage note The spellings of the verb *gild* (with gold) and the noun *guild* (a society) should not be confused.

gilet (jilā´) *n.* **1** a woman's light sleeveless top resembling a waistcoat. **2** a sleeveless padded jacket.

gill¹ (gil) *n.* (*usu. pl.*) **1** each of the organs of respiration, or branchiae, of fishes and some amphibia. **2** in fish or other aquatic creatures, a double row of long slender lamellae, extending, like the teeth of a comb, from the convex side of a branchial arch, and supported by a delicate membrane. **3** each of the vertical lamellae under the cap of mushrooms and other fungi. **4** each of the loose fleshy appendages, or wattles, at a fowl's throat. **5** (*pl., facet.*) the flesh about a person's jaws and chin. **gill cover** *n.* the external bony covering of a fish's gills. **gilled** *a.* **gill-net** *n.* a net, usu. set vertically, for entangling fish by the gills.

gill² (gil), **ghyll** *n.* **1** a deep and narrow ravine, often wooded. **2** a gully or stream bed on a precipitous hillside.

gill³ (jil) *n.* a liquid measure, usu. one quarter of a pint (about 140 cl).

gillie (gil´i), **ghillie** *n.* a man or boy who attends a person fishing or hunting, esp. in the Scottish highlands.

gillyflower (jil´iflowə) *n.* **1** the clove-scented pink, *Dianthus caryophyllus.* **2** any of various flowers with a similar scent, esp. the white stock and the wallflower.

gilt¹ (gilt) *a.* **1** gilded. **2** adorned with something resembling gold, gold-coloured. ~*n.* **1** gold laid over the surface of a thing, gilding. **2** (*pl.*) gilt-edged securities. **gilt-edged** *a.* having the edges gilded. **gilt-edged securities** *n.pl.* investments of the most reliable character.

gilt² (gilt) *n.* a young sow.

gimbals (jim´bəlz, gim´-) *n.pl.* forms of universal joint for securing free motion in suspension, or for suspending anything, such as a lamp, a compass, a chronometer etc., so that it retains a horizontal or other required position, or is in equilibrium.

gimcrack (jim´krak), **jimcrack** *n.* **1** a pretty but useless or flimsy article, a worthless knick-knack. **2** †a showy person, a dandy, a fop. ~*a.* showy but flimsy and worthless. **gimcrackery** *n.* **gimcracky** *a.*

gimlet (gim´lit) *n.* **1** a small boring-tool with a worm or screw for penetrating wood, and a wooden crosspiece for a handle. **2** a cocktail of gin and lime juice. **gimlet eye** *n.* a piercing eye.

gimmick (gim´ik) *n.* a trick, device or oddity of behaviour used to attract extra interest, attention or publicity. **gimmickry** *n.* **gimmicky** *a.*

gimp¹ (gimp), **guimp, gymp** *n.* **1** silk, wool, or cotton twist interlaced with wire or coarse cord.

2 a silk fishing line whipped with thin wire to protect it against injury from the teeth of large fish.

gimp² (gimp) *n.* (*esp. N Am., sl.*) **1** a lame or crippled person, esp. an old one. **2** an awkward, clumsy or ineffectual person.

gin¹ (jin) *n.* an alcoholic drink, distilled usu. from grain, and flavoured with juniper berries. **gin rummy** *n.* a form of the card game rummy.

gin² (jin) *n.* **1** a trap, a snare for small mammals and birds. **2** a machine for separating cotton-fibre from the seeds, a cotton gin. **3** a portable hoisting-machine usu. having a tripod frame, one leg being movable. ~*v.t.* (*pres.p.* **ginning**, *past, p.p.* **ginned**) **1** to clean (as cotton) of the seeds by means of a gin. **2** to snare, to entrap. **ginner** *n.*

ginger (jin´jə) *n.* **1** the hot spicy root of the ginger plant used, either whole or powdered, in cookery, as a preserved sweet, in drinks or in medicine. **2** a plant, *Zingiber officinale,* with a pungent, spicy rootstock. **3** the light reddish colour of powdered ginger. **4** (*coll.*) a red-haired person. **5** mettle, dash, go. **6** stimulation. ~*v.t.* **1** to liven (up), to stimulate, to put on one's mettle. **2** to flavour with ginger. **ginger ale** *n.* a carbonated drink, prepared by dissolving sugar in water, flavouring with ginger or essence of ginger, and colouring with a solution of caramel. **ginger beer** *n.* a fermented, carbonated soft drink prepared from ginger, white sugar, water and yeast. **ginger group** *n.* a group of people within an organization such as a political party who share a specialized interest or viewpoint and who seek to influence the main body of the organization through their enthusiasm. **ginger nut** *n.* a ginger-flavoured biscuit. **ginger snap** *n.* a crisp thin ginger-flavoured biscuit; a brandy snap. **ginger wine** *n.* a wine made by the fermentation of sugar, water and ginger. **gingery** *a.*

gingerbread (jin´jəbred) *n.* a dark-coloured cake or biscuit made of flour, treacle or molasses, ground ginger and other spices. ~*a.* **1** made of gingerbread. **2** showy, tawdry, flimsy and fantastic (in allusion to the fanciful shapes, often gilded, in which gingerbread used to be moulded). **to take the gilt off the gingerbread** to reveal the unattractive reality behind something which appears to be glamorous.

gingerly (jin´jəli) *adv.* daintily, fastidiously, cautiously, so as to move without noise or risk of hurting oneself or anything trodden upon. ~*a.* dainty, fastidious, cautious. **gingerliness** *n.*

gingham (ging´əm) *n.* a kind of linen or cotton fabric woven of dyed yarn, usu. in stripes or checks.

gingival (jinjī´vəl) *a.* (*Med.*) of or relating to the gums. **gingivitis** (-jivī´təs) *n.* inflammation of the gums.

ginkgo (gingk´gō), **gingko** (ging´kō), **jingko** *n.* (*pl.* **ginkgos, ginkgoes, gingkos, gingkoes**) a Japanese tree, *Ginkgo biloba*, with fan-shaped leaves, also called *maidenhair tree*.

ginormous (jīnaw´məs) *a.* (*coll.*) huge, enormous.

ginseng (jin´seng) *n.* **1** any of several herbs belonging to the genus *Panax*, esp. *P. schinseng* of China and *P. quinquefolius* of N America, the root of which has a sharp, aromatic taste, and is highly esteemed as a medicine or tonic by the Chinese and others. **2** this root.

gippy tummy (jip´i), **gyppy tummy** *n.* (*coll.*) an upset stomach, diarrhoea etc.

gipsy GYPSY.

giraffe (jirahf´, -raf´) *n.* (*pl.* **giraffe, giraffes**) an African ruminant, *Giraffa camelopardalis*, with an extremely long neck, and two bony excrescences on the head, light fawn in colour with darker spots.

girasol (jir´əsol), **girasole** (-sōl) *n.* a variety of opal with reddish refractions, also called *fireopal*.

gird (gœd) *v.t.* (*past, p.p.* **girded, girt** (gœt)) **1** to bind round (usu. the waist) with some flexible band, esp. in order to secure or confine the clothes. **2** to secure (one's clothes) with a girdle, belt etc. **3** to fasten (a sword on or to) with a girdle or belt. **4** to invest or equip (with). **5** to surround or encircle with or as with a girdle, to encompass, to besiege. **to gird (up) one's loins 1** to get ready to do something. **2** to prepare oneself for (vigorous) action.

girder (gœ´də) *n.* a principal beam, esp. a compound structure of iron, steel, wood or metal, spanning the distance from wall to wall, or pier to pier, used to support joints, walls, roof, roadway, or other similar load.

girdle[1] (gœ´dəl) *n.* **1** a lightweight elasticated undergarment worn by women about the hips and thighs. **2** a belt, zone or cord for securing a loose garment round or encircling the waist. **3** anything that encircles as a belt or zone. **4** the bones by which the limbs are united to the trunk in vertebrate animals. **5** the line of greatest marginal circumference of a gemstone, at which it is grasped by the setting. **6** (*Bot.*) a zonelike ring on a stem etc. ~*v.t.* **1** to gird or surround with or as with a girdle. **2** to make a cut round (the trunk of a tree) through the bark, in order to kill it or in some cases to make it fruit better.

girdle[2] (gœ´dəl) *n.* (*Sc., North*) a round flat plate of iron for baking cakes etc. (*girdle scones*).

girl (gœl) *n.* **1** a female child, a young and unmarried woman. **2** a female waitress or servant. **3** a girlfriend. **girl Friday** *n.* a female secretary and general assistant in an office. **girlfriend** *n.* **1** a regular female companion, esp. one with whom there is a romantic relationship. **2** a female friend. **Girl Guide** *n.* a member of the Guides Association, an international organization founded with the aim of developing health, character and practical skills. **girlhood** *n.* **girlie, girly** *n.* (*pl.* **girlies**) a girl (esp. as a term of endearment). ~*a.*

1 (*derog.*) girlish. **2** denoting or relating to magazines containing pictures of women in erotic poses. **girlish** *a.* **girlishly** *adv.* **girlishness** *n.* **Girl Scout** *n.* a girl belonging to the Scout Association.

girn GURN.

giro (jī´rō) *n.* (*pl.* **giros**) **1** in the UK, a system operated by banks and post offices whereby, when the required instructions have been issued, payments can be made by transfers from one account to another. **2** a giro cheque. ~*v.t.* (*3rd pers. sing. pres.* **giroes,** *pres.p.* **giroing,** *past, p.p.* **giroed**) to pay by giro.

❌ **girrafe** common misspelling of GIRAFFE.

girt (gœt) *a.* **1** girded, bound. **2** (of a vessel) moored so taut by cables fixed in opposite directions as to prevent her swinging.

girth (gœth), †**girt** (gœt) *n.* **1** the measurement round anything, the circumference e.g. of one's waist, of a tree. **2** the band by which a saddle or burden is made fast and kept secure on a horse's back by passing round its belly. ~*v.t.* **1** to secure on (a horse) with a girth. **2** to fit with a girth. **3** to measure (a certain amount) in girth. **4** to surround, to encompass.

gismo GIZMO.

gist (jist) *n.* **1** the essence or main point of a question. **2** (*Law*) the real ground of an action.

git (git) *n.* (*sl.*) an unpleasant or worthless person; a bastard.

gîte (zhēt) *n.* in France, a privately-owned, self-contained, self-catering apartment or cottage available for holiday lets.

give (giv) *v.t.* (*past* **gave** (gāv), *p.p.* **given** (giv´ən)) **1** to hand over or transfer the possession of or right to without price or compensation. **2** to bestow, to confer, to present. **3** to grant, to concede, to allow, to put in one's power. **4** to hand over, to deliver. **5** to commit, to consign, to put in someone's keeping. **6** to transfer as price or in exchange, to pay, to sell. **7** to return, to render as due. **8** to surrender, to relinquish. **9** to yield up, to devote. **10** to yield as product. **11** to communicate, to impart. **12** to be the source or author of. **13** to occasion, to cause. **14** to offer, to hold out, to show or exhibit. **15** to care to the extent of (*I don't give a damn*). **16** to assign, to suppose, to assume (as conditions or circumstances). **17** to utter, to emit. **18** to perform. **19** to organize (a party). ~*v.i.* **1** to part with freely and gratuitously. **2** to yield to pressure, to collapse. **3** to move back, to recede. **4** to make way or room. **5** to lead, to open (upon). **6** (*coll.*) to be forthcoming. ~*n.* **1** the state of yielding or giving away. **2** elasticity. **3** adaptability, compliance. **give me** I prefer (*Give me radio, any day!*). **give or take** (*coll.*) if you add or subtract (an amount or number) in making an estimate. **to be given to** to have a habit of, to be fond of. **to give and take 1** to be fair, to act fairly. **2** to exchange. **to give as good as one gets** to be a match for an opponent throughout a contest, argument etc. **to give away 1** to make over as a gift, to transfer. **2** to hand over in marriage to a bridegroom during the wedding ceremony. **3** to let out or divulge inadvertently. **4** to give or concede to an opposing player or side by mistake. **5** (*Austral.*) to abandon, to lose interest in. **to give back** to restore, return something to someone. **to give birth (to)** to bring forth, to have a baby, young etc. **to give chase to** to pursue. **to give down** (of a cow) to give milk. **to give forth** to emit. **to give in 1** to yield. **2** to hand in. **to give in marriage** to permit the marriage of (a daughter). **to give into** to afford a prospect into, to face. **to give it to** (*coll.*) to scold, punish severely, beat. **to give of** to contribute. **to give off** to emit. **to give oneself** (of a woman) to yield to sexual intercourse. **to give oneself up to** to abandon or addict oneself to. **to give on to** to afford a prospect on or into, to face. **to give out 1** to emit. **2** to publish, to proclaim. **3** to distribute. **4** (*coll.*) to show, to profess. **5** to break down. **6** to run short. **7** in cricket (of an umpire) to indicate that a batsman is out. **to give over 1** to hand over, to transfer. **2** to abandon, to despair of. **3** (*in p.p.*) to devote or addict (*given over to gambling*). **4** to cease (from), to desist (*Give over!*). **5** to yield. **to give to understand** to inform authoritatively; to lead to believe. **to give up 1** to surrender. **2** to resign. **3** to commit. **4** to despair of. **5** to stop doing. **to give way 1** to yield, to fail to resist. **2** to make concessions. **3** to make room for. **4** to be superseded. **5** to break down, to collapse. **6** to abandon (oneself to). **7** to be depreciated in value. **8** to begin to row. **9** to row with increased energy. **give and take** *n.* **1** mutual concession or forbearance. **2** fair measure on either side. **give-away** *n.* **1** (*coll.*) an unintentional revelation. **2** something given free. **given** *a.* **1** that has been given. **2** assumed or specified. **3** (*Law*) signed and dated. ~*n.* a known fact, a thing to be assumed. **given that** granted that. **given name** *n.* a forename, a baptismal name. **giver** *n.*

gizmo (giz´mō), **gismo** *n.* (*pl.* **gizmos, gismos**) (*coll.*) a gadget.

gizzard (giz´əd) *n.* **1** a strong muscular division of the stomach, esp. the second stomach in birds. **2** a thickened muscular stomach in certain fish, insects and molluscs. **to stick in one's gizzard** (*coll.*) to be very disagreeable to one.

glacé (glas´ā) *a.* **1** (of fruit etc.) preserved in sugar, candied (and usu. glossy). **2** (of leather goods etc.) polished, smooth. **glacé icing** *n.* icing that sets with a shiny surface.

glacial (glā´shəl, glā´siəl) *a.* **1** (*Geol.*) (of geological formations) due to or characterized by glaciers, ice sheets or floating ice. **2** due to or like ice, icy. **3** of or relating to ice. **4** (*Chem.*) crystallizing at ordinary temperatures. **glacially** *adv.* **glacial period, glacial epoch, glacial era** *n.* a period during which a large part of the northern hemisphere was covered with an ice sheet, an ice age. **glaciate** (glā´siāt) *v.t.* **1** to scratch, polish or wear down by means of ice. **2** to cover with

ice in the form of sheets or glaciers. **glaciated** *a.* **glaciation** (-ā´shən) *n.*

glacier (glas´iə, glā´-) *n.* a streamlike mass of ice, formed by consolidated accumulations of snow at high altitudes, slowly descending to lower regions.

glaciology (glāsiol´əji, glas-) *n.* the study of glacial action and its geological effects. **glaciologic** (-loj´-), **glaciological** *a.* **glaciologist** *n.*

glad (glad) *a.* (*comp.* **gladder,** *superl.* **gladdest**) **1** pleased, gratified. **2** indicating pleasure or satisfaction. **3** affording pleasure, joy or satisfaction (*glad tidings*). **4** bright, cheerful (*glad expression*). **5** willing and eager. **gladden** *v.t.* **1** to make glad or joyful. **2** to cheer up. **glad eye** *n.* (*coll.*) ogling (*to give someone the glad eye*). **glad hand** *n.* (*coll.*) a welcome, esp. a fulsome one. ~*v.t.* (**glad-hand**) to welcome, esp. by shaking hands. **glad-hander** *n.* a person keen to win many people over by greeting them effusively, e.g. a vote-seeking politician. **gladly** *adv.* **gladness** *n.* **glad rags** *n.pl.* (*coll.*) **1** one's best or smartest clothes. **2** evening dress.

glade (glād) *n.* an open space in a wood or forest.

gladiator (glad´iātə) *n.* **1** in Roman times, a man employed to fight in the amphitheatre. **2** a political combatant. **3** a controversialist. **gladiatorial** (-iətaw´riəl) *a.*

gladiolus (gladiō´ləs) *n.* (*pl.* **gladioli** (-lī), **gladioluses**) any iridaceous plant of the genus *Gladiolus*, with a fleshy bulb, sword-shaped leaves and spikes of bright-coloured flowers.

Gladstone (glad´stən), **Gladstone bag** *n.* a light leather bag with flexible sides, opening along the middle and secured with a clasp and straps.

glair (gleə), **glaire** *n.* **1** white of egg, or a preparation made with this, used as size or varnish. **2** any similar viscous, transparent substance. **glairy** *a.*

glam (glam) *a.* (*coll.*) glamorous. ~*v.t.* (*pres.p.* **glamming,** *past, p.p.* **glammed**) to glamorize. **glam rock** *n.* (*coll.*) a type of pop or rock music distinguished by performers in showy, glamorous clothes, hairstyles etc.

glamour (glam´ə), (*esp. N Am.*) **glamor** *n.* fascinating attractiveness due largely to grooming, expensive clothes or other artifice, or to unfamiliarity. **to cast a glamour over** to bewitch, enchant. **glamorize, glamorise** *v.t.* to make glamorous. **glamorization** (-zā´shən) *n.* **glamorous** *a.* **glamorously** *adv.* **glamorousness** *n.* **glamour boy, glamour girl** *n.* a young man or woman with a glamorous appearance or lifestyle.

glance (glahns) *v.i.* **1** to give a quick or cursory look (at). **2** to glide off or from (as a blow). **3** to dart or flash a gleam of light or brightness. **4** to touch, to allude, to hint (at). **5** to move about rapidly. **6** to give only cursory consideration (to). ~*v.t.* **1** to strike obliquely. **2** to direct (a look or the eye) rapidly or cursorily. ~*n.* **1** a quick or transient look, a hurried glimpse (at). **2** in cricket, a hit with the bat turned obliquely to the ball. **3** an oblique impact of an object on another causing it to be deflected. **4** a flash, a gleam. **at a glance** immediately, at a first look. **glancing** *a.* **glancingly** *adv.*

gland (gland) *n.* **1** an organ secreting certain constituents of the blood, either for extraction and specific use or for elimination as waste products. **2** (*Bot.*) a cellular organ in plants, usu. secreting oil or aroma. **3** a sleeve employed to press packing tight on or around a piston-rod etc. **glandular** *a.* **1** characterized by the presence of a gland or glands. **2** consisting or of the nature of a gland or glands; affecting the glands. **glandular fever** *n.* an infectious disease characterized by the swelling of the lymph nodes.

glanders (glan´dəz) *n.pl.* a very dangerous and contagious disease in horses, characterized by a running discharge from the nostrils, and enlargement and hardening of the glands of the lower jaw. **glandered** *a.* **glanderous** *a.*

glans (glanz) *n.* (*pl.* **glandes** (glan´dēz)) **1** a structure of a similar shape to an acorn, such as the extremity of the penis. **2** a cushion-like swelling.

glare (gleə) *v.i.* **1** to shine with a dazzling or overpowering light. **2** to look with fierce, piercing eyes, to stare. **3** to be obtrusively overdressed or gaudy. **4** to be very conspicuous. ~*v.t.* to send out or express with a glare. ~*n.* **1** an intense, fierce look or stare. **2** a fierce overpowering light, disagreeable brightness. **3** exposure to attention. **4** tawdry splendour. **glaring** *a.* **1** shining with dazzling brightness. **2** staring. **3** too conspicuous or overcoloured. **4** notorious, barefaced, infamous. **glaringly** *adv.* **glaringness** *n.* **glary** *a.*

glasnost (glaz´nost) *n.* esp. of the USSR government of the later 1980s, a willingness to be more open and accountable.

glass (glahs) *n.* (*pl.* **glasses**) **1** a hard, brittle, transparent substance, formed by fusing together mixtures of the silicates of potash, soda, lime, magnesia, alumina and lead in various proportions, according to the quality or kind required. **2** a substance of vitreous structure or composition. **3** a drinking vessel of glass. **4** the quantity which a drinking glass will hold. **5** an instrument for indicating atmospheric changes, a barometer. **6** a mirror, a looking-glass. **7** a lens. **8** an optical instrument composed partly of glass, an eyeglass, a telescope. **9** a sand-glass, an hourglass. **10** a thermometer. **11** a window pane. **12** (*pl.*) spectacles, also called *pair of glasses*. **13** (*collect.*) ornaments or utensils made of glass; greenhouses; windows. ~*v.t.* **1** to fit or cover with or as with glass, to glaze. **2** (*poet.*) to mirror, to reflect (oneself or itself) in or as in a glass. **people who live in glass houses** critical people susceptible to criticism through their own pursuits or opinions. **glass-blowing** *n.* the art or process of shaping molten or softened glass into vessels. **glass-blower** *n.* **glass case** *n.* a case or shallow box having a glass lid or sides to show the contents. **glass ceiling** *n.* a situation in an organization where promotion appears to be possible but is prevented by discrimination etc. **glass cloth** *n.* **1** a cloth for wiping and cleaning glasses. **2** cloth covered with powdered glass, like sandpaper. **3** a fabric woven of fine-spun glass threads. **glass-cutting** *n.* the art or process of cutting, grinding and polishing glassware. **glass-cutter** *n.* a worker or a tool that cuts glass. **glass eye** *n.* an artificial eye of glass. **glass fibre** *n.* FIBREGLASS (under FIBRE). **glassful** *n.* as much as a drinking glass will hold. **glass-gall** *n.* SANDIVER. **glasshouse** *n.* **1** a greenhouse or conservatory. **2** (*sl.*) a military prison. **3** (*esp. N Am.*) a house or building where glass is made. **glassless** *a.* **glasslike** *a.* **glass-making** *n.* the manufacture of glass. **glass-maker** *n.* **glasspaper** *n.* paper covered with finely-powdered glass used for rubbing down and smoothing rough surfaces of wood etc. **glass snake** *n.* an American lizard without limbs, *Ophisaurus ventralis.* **glassware** *n.* (*collect.*) articles made of glass. **glass wool** *n.* fine fibres of glass used for packing and insulation. **glasswort** *n.* any of various maritime herbs of the genus *Salicornia* or *Salsola*, containing alkali formerly used in glass-making, marsh samphire. **glassy** *a.* (*comp.* **glassier**, *superl.* **glassiest**) **1** hard, dull, lacking fire, fixed (of the eye). **2** like glass, vitreous. **3** lustrous, smooth, mirror-like (of water). **glassily** *adv.* **glassiness** *n.*

Glaswegian (glāzwē´jən, glas-) *n.* a native or inhabitant of Glasgow in Scotland. ~*a.* of or relating to Glasgow.

glaucoma (glawkō´mə) *n.* a disease of the eye in which the pressure within the eyeball causes dimness and ultimately loss of vision. **glaucomatous** *a.*

glaucous (glaw´kəs) *a.* **1** sea-green, pale greyish-blue. **2** (*Bot.*) covered with a bloom or down of this tinge (as with grapes). **glaucous gull** *n.* a large grey and white gull, *Larus hyperboreus*, found in N and Arctic regions.

glaze (glāz) *v.t.* **1** to furnish, fit or cover with glass. **2** to fit with a sheet or panes of glass. **3** to furnish with windows. **4** to overlay (pottery) with a vitreous substance. **5** to cover (a surface) with a thin glossy coating. **6** to make smooth and glossy. ~*v.i.* to become glassy (as the eyes). ~*n.* **1** a smooth, lustrous coating. **2** a coating, formed of various substances, used to glaze earthenware, pictures, paper, confectionery etc. **3** a glazed surface. **4** (*US*) a thin sheet of ice. **glazed** *a.* **1** having been glazed. **2** (esp. of a person's expression) vacant, bored. **glazed frost** *n.* a coating of ice caused by the freezing of rain or by refreezing after thawing. **glazer** *n.* **glazier** (-ziə, -zhə) *n.* a person whose business it is to set glass in windows etc. **glaziery** *n.* **glazing** *n.* **1** the act or process of setting glass in window frames, picture frames etc. **2** covering with a glaze, or giving a glazed or glossy surface to pottery and other articles. **3** the glaze or other material used to give something a glazed finish. **4** glasswork. **5** glazed windows. **glazy** *a.*

gleam (glēm) *n.* a flash, a beam, a ray, esp. one of a faint or transient kind. ~*v.i.* **1** to send out rays of a quick and transient kind. **2** to shine, to glitter. **gleamingly** *adv.* **gleamy** *a.*

glean (glēn) *v.t.* **1** to collect bit by bit, to pick up here and there (*to glean information*). **2** to gather (ears of corn which have been passed over) from a cornfield. **3** to gather ears of corn from. **gleaner** *n.* **gleanings** *n.pl.* **1** snippets of information etc. collected here and there. **2** the useful remnants of a crop gathered up after harvest.

glebe (glēb) *n.* the land furnishing part of the revenue of an ecclesiastical benefice.

glee (glē) *n.* **1** joy, mirth, gladness, delight. **2** a musical composition for several voices in harmony, consisting usu. of two or more contrasted movements and without instrumental accompaniment. **glee club** *n.* a club or society devoted to singing glees and other choral music. **gleeful** *a.* merry, joyous. **gleefully** *adv.*

glen (glen) *n.* a narrow valley, esp. in Scotland, a dale.

glengarry (glengar´i), **glengarry bonnet** *n.* (*pl.* **glengarries**, **glengarry bonnets**) a woollen cap, high in front with ribbons hanging down behind, worn by some Highland regiments.

glib (glib) *a.* voluble, fluent, not very weighty or sincere. **glibly** *adv.* **glibness** *n.*

glide (glīd) *v.i.* **1** to move smoothly and gently. **2** to slip or slide along, as on a smooth surface. **3** to pass rapidly, smoothly and easily. **4** to pass imperceptibly (away) (*Time glided away*). **5** (*Mus.*) to pass from tone to tone without a perceptible break. **6** to fly an engineless heavier-than-air aeroplane which is catapulted or launched from a height, and makes use of rising air currents. ~*v.t.* to cause something to glide. ~*n.* **1** the act of gliding. **2** (*Mus.*) a passage from one tone to another without a break. **3** in phonetics, a continuous sound produced in passing from one position of the organs of speech to another. **4** in cricket, a hit with the bat turned obliquely to the ball, a glance. **glide path** *n.* the path followed by an aircraft as it descends to a landing. **glider** *n.* **1** a heavier-than-air flying-machine with no motive power. **2** someone or something that glides. **gliding** *n.* the sport of piloting a glider.

glimmer (glim´ə) *v.i.* **1** to emit a faint or feeble light. **2** to shine faintly. ~*n.* **1** a faint, uncertain or unsteady light. **2** a faint vestige, an uncertain sign (*a glimmer of hope, intelligence, sense*). **3** a glimpse. **glimmeringly** *adv.*

glimpse (glimps) *n.* **1** a momentary look, a rapid and imperfect view (of). **2** a passing gleam, a faint and transient appearance. ~*v.t.* **1** to catch a glimpse of. **2** to see for an instant. ~*v.i.* **1** to appear for an instant. **2** to glance (at). **3** (*poet.*) to appear faintly, to glimmer.

glint (glint) *v.i.* **1** to gleam, to flash. **2** to glitter, to

sparkle. ~*v.t.* to reflect, to flash back. ~*n.* a gleam, a flash, a sparkle.

glissade (glisahd´, -sād´) *n.* **1** a method of sliding down a steep snow slope, usu. with an ice axe or alpenstock held as rudder and support. **2** a gliding step in ballet. ~*v.i.* to slide down a steep snow slope using an ice axe etc. for support.

glissando (glisan´dō) *a.*, *n.* (*pl.* **glissandos**, **glissandi** (-dē)) (*Mus.*) (of) an esp. rapid sliding up and down the musical scale.

glisten (glis´ən) *v.i.* to gleam, to sparkle, usu. by reflection. ~*n.* a glitter or sparkle, esp. by reflection.

†**glister** (glis´tə) *v.i.* to glitter, to sparkle. ~*n.* glitter, lustre, brightness. **glisteringly** *adv.*

glitch (glich) *n.* (*sl.*) an unexpected problem, malfunction etc., technical hitch, hiccup.

glitter (glit´ə) *v.i.* **1** to gleam, to sparkle. **2** to shine with a succession of brilliant gleams or flashes. **3** to be brilliant, showy or specious. ~*n.* **1** a bright sparkling light. **2** brilliancy, splendour. **3** speciousness, attractiveness. **4** tiny glittering particles used for decoration. **glitteringly** *adv.* **glittery** *a.*

glitterati (glitərah´ti) *n.pl.* (*sl.*) fashionable people, such as media personalities, artists, jet-setters etc., as a social group.

glitz (glits) *n.* (*coll.*) ostentation, conspicuous showiness. **glitzy** (glit´si) *a.* (*comp.* **glitzier**, *superl.* **glitziest**). **glitzily** *adv.* **glitziness** *n.*

gloaming (glō´ming) *n.* (*poet.*) evening twilight.

gloat (glōt) *v.i.* to look or dwell (on or over) with exultant feelings of malignity, lust, greed etc. ~*n.* **1** the act of gloating. **2** an unpleasant look of triumphant satisfaction. **gloater** *n.* **gloatingly** *adv.*

glob (glob) *n.* a rounded lump of something soft, a dollop.

globe (glōb) *n.* **1** a ball, a sphere, a round or spherical body. **2** the earth. **3** a sphere on which are represented the land and sea, and usu. the political divisions of the world. **4** anything of a globular or nearly globular shape. **5** an orb borne as emblem of sovereignty. **6** an almost spherical vessel, such as an aquarium, lampshade etc. **7** the eyeball. ~*v.t.* to form into a globe. ~*v.i.* to become globular. **global** (glō´bəl) *a.* **1** worldwide. **2** relating to the globe as an entirety. **3** taking in entire groups or classes (*global search-and-replace*). **globalize, globalise** *v.t.* to make global in scope or application. **globalization** (-zā´shən) *n.* **globally** *adv.* **global village** *n.* the world viewed as an integrated system, esp. as linked by means of instant (mass) communication. **global warming** *n.* the potential increase in the temperature of the earth's atmosphere caused by pollution, the greenhouse effect. **globe artichoke** *n.* a type of artichoke, *Cynara scolymus*, cultivated for food. **globe-fish** *n.* any tropical fish of the family *Tetradontidae*, one having the power of inflating its skin till it becomes nearly globular. **globe flower** *n.* any plant of the ranunculaceous genus *Trollius*, esp. the British *T. europaeus*, with yellow, almost spherical flowers. **globe lightning** n. BALL LIGHTNING (under BALL[1]). **globe-like** a. **globe-trotter** n. a traveller who hurries from place to place sight-seeing or who visits many foreign countries. **globe-trotting** a., n. **globose** a. spherical, globular.

globule (glob´ūl) n. **1** a particle of matter in the form of a small globe. **2** a minute drop or pill. **globular** a. **1** having the shape of a small globe or sphere. **2** composed of globules. **globular cluster** n. (Astron.) a spherical cluster of stars usu. in the outer regions of a galaxy. **globularity** (-lar´-) n. **globularly** adv. **globularness** n. **globulin** (-lin) n. any of a group of single proteins obtained from animals and plants, esp. forming a large part of blood serum protein, usu. insoluble in water but soluble in salt solution. **globulous** a.

glockenspiel (glok´ənshpēl) n. a musical instrument consisting of hanging metal bars or tubes, to be struck with a hammer.

gloom (gloom) n. **1** obscurity, partial darkness. **2** depression, dejection, melancholy. **3** circumstances that occasion melancholy or despondency. ~v.i. **1** to appear obscurely or dimly. **2** to look dismal, sullen or frowning. **3** to lour, to be or become cloudy or dark. ~v.t. **1** to fill or cover with darkness or obscurity. **2** to render dark, sullen, or dismal. **gloomful** a. **gloomfully** adv. **gloomy** a. (comp. **gloomier**, superl. **gloomiest**) **1** dark, obscure. **2** sad, melancholy, dispiriting, louring. **3** sullen, morose. **gloomily** adv. **gloominess** n.

gloop (gloop) n. (coll.) a thick, sticky liquid.

glop (glop) n. (NAm., sl.) a soft, gooey mush, esp. unpalatable food of this consistency.

glorify (glaw´rifī) v.t. (3rd pers. sing. pres. **glorifies**, pres.p. **glorifying**, past, p.p. **glorified**) **1** to make glorious, to pay honour and glory to in worship, to praise, to extol (God). **2** to exalt to celestial glory. **3** to make splendid, to beautify. **4** to magnify, to make glorious, to praise. **glorification** (-fikā´shən) n. **glorified** a. (coll.) seeming to be more splendid than it really is (This room is just a glorified cupboard). **glorifier** n.

glory (glaw´ri) n. (pl. **glories**) **1** high honour, honourable distinction. **2** fame, renown. **3** an occasion of praise, a subject for pride or boasting. **4** illustriousness, splendour of estate, magnificence, grandeur. **5** brilliance, effulgence, splendour. **6** a state of exaltation. **7** adoration or praise ascribed in worship. **8** the felicity of heaven. **9** a combination of the nimbus and aureola. **10** a halo. ~v.i. (3rd pers. sing. pres. **glories**, pres.p. **glorying**, past, p.p. **gloried**) to boast, to feel pride, to exult. **to glory in** to be proud of. **to go to glory** (sl.) to die, disintegrate, go wrong etc. (That shot has gone to glory!). **glorious** (glaw´riəs) a. **1** full of glory, illustrious. **2** worthy of admiration or praise. **3** entitling one to fame or honour. **4** splendid, magnificent. **gloriously** adv. **gloriousness** n. **glory be!** int. used to express surprise. **glory box** n. (Austral.) a box, chest etc. in which a young

woman stores her trousseau etc., bottom drawer. **glory hole** n. (coll.) a room, cupboard etc. where rubbish and odds and ends have been stowed away anyhow. **glory-of-the-snow** n. the liliaceous plant Chionodoxa luciliae, native to W Asia and cultivated for its blue flowers.

gloss[1] (glos) n. **1** the brightness or lustre from a polished surface. **2** polish, sheen. **3** a specious or deceptive outward appearance. ~v.t. **1** to make glossy or lustrous. **2** to render specious or plausible. **to gloss over** to seek to avoid drawing attention to by mentioning only briefly or misleadingly. **glosser** n. **gloss paint** n. paint containing a varnish that gives it a shiny finish. **glossy** a. (comp. **glossier**, superl. **glossiest**) having a smooth, lustrous surface. **glossily** adv. **glossiness** n. **glossy magazine** n. a magazine printed on glossy paper with many colour illustrations.

gloss[2] (glos) n. **1** an explanatory word or note in the margin or between the lines of a book, as an explanation of a foreign or strange word. **2** a comment, interpretation or explanation. **3** a superficial or misleading interpretation etc. **4** a glossary, translation, or commentary. ~v.t. **1** to explain by note or comment. **2** to annotate. **3** to comment upon, esp. in a censorious way. ~v.i. to make comments, to annotate, to write glosses. **glossator** (-sā´-), **†glossatist** n. a writer of glosses.

glossary (glos´əri) n. (pl. **glossaries**) **1** a list, vocabulary or dictionary of explanations of technical, obsolete, rare or dialectal words or forms. **2** a collection of glosses or notes. **glossarial** (-seə´ri-) a. **glossarist** n.

glossolalia (glosəlā´liə) n. speech in an unknown language, occurring in religious ecstasy, trances etc.

glottis (glot´is) n. (pl. **glottises**, **glottides** (-dēz)) the mouth of the windpipe forming a narrow aperture covered by the epiglottis when one holds the breath or swallows, contributing, by its dilatation and contraction, to the modulation of the voice. **glottal** a. **glottal stop** n. a speech sound produced by closing and suddenly opening the glottis. **glottic** a.

glove (glŭv) n. **1** a covering for the hand, usu. with a separate division for each finger. **2** a boxing glove. ~v.t. to cover with or as with a glove. **to fight with the gloves off** to fight or contend in earnest, to show no mercy. **to fit like a glove** to fit perfectly in size and shape. **glove box** n. **1** a glove compartment in a car. **2** a sealed glass box for handling radioactive materials using built-in gloves. **glove compartment** n. a small storage compartment in a car, usu. set into the dashboard. **gloveless** a. **glove puppet** n. a puppet that fits on to the hand. **glover** n. a person who makes or sells gloves.

glow (glō) v.i. **1** to radiate light and heat, esp. without flame. **2** to be incandescent. **3** to be bright or red with heat, to show a warm colour. **4** to feel great bodily heat. **5** to be warm or flushed with passion or fervour. **6** to be ardent.

~*n*. **1** incandescence, red or white heat. **2** brightness, redness, warmth of colour. **3** vehemence, ardour. **4** heat produced by exercise. **5** a strong feeling of satisfaction or pleasure. **glow-worm** *n*. a beetle, *Lampyris noctiluca* or *L. splendidula*, the female of which is phosphorescent.

glower (glow´ə) *v.i.* to scowl, to stare fiercely or angrily. ~*n*. a savage stare, a scowl. **gloweringly** *adv.*

gloxinia (gloksin´iə) *n*. any tropical plant of the genus *Gloxinia*, with large bell-shaped flowers, from tropical America.

gloze (glōz) *v.t.* to explain away, to palliate, to extenuate. ~*n*. **1** flattery, wheedling. **2** specious show.

glucose (gloo´kōs) *n*. (*Chem.*) **1** a fermentable sugar, less sweet than cane sugar, obtained from dried grapes and other fruits, dextrin etc. and occurring in the urine of persons suffering from glucosuria. **2** any of the group of sweet compounds including dextrose, laevulose etc. **glucoside** (-sīd) *n*. a vegetable substance yielding glucose when decomposed. **glucosidic** (-sid´ik) *a*.

glue (gloo) *n*. **1** an adhesive or sticky substance. **2** an impure gelatin made of the chippings of hides, horns and hoofs, boiled to a jelly, cooled in moulds, and used hot as a cement. ~*v.t.* (*3rd pers. sing. pres.* **glues**, *pres.p.* **gluing, glueing,** *past, p.p.* **glued**) **1** to join or fasten with glue. **2** to unite, to attach firmly. **glue ear** *n*. (*Med.*) a blocking of the Eustachian tube by mucus, caused by infection and perh. resulting in deafness. **gluepot** *n*. a vessel for heating glue, with an outer vessel to hold water and prevent burning. **gluer** *n*. **glue-sniffing** *n*. the inhalation of the fumes of certain glues for their narcotic effects. **gluesniffer** *n*. **gluey** *a*. (*comp.* **gluier,** *superl.* **gluiest**). **glueyness** *n*.

glug (glŭg) *n*. (*coll.*) the sound of liquid being poured, esp. out of or into a narrow opening.

glum (glŭm) *a*. sullen, moody, dejected, dissatisfied. **glumly** *adv.* **glumness** *n*.

glut (glŭt) *n*. **1** an oversupply of a market. **2** a surfeit. **3** a superabundance. ~*v.t.* (*pres.p.* **glutting,** *past, p.p.* **glutted**) **1** to fill to excess, to stuff, to gorge, to sate. **2** to fill with an oversupply (as a market). **3** to swallow, to swallow down.

glutamate (gloo´təmāt) *n*. a salt or ester of glutamic acid, esp. a sodium salt used as a flavour enhancer in some foods.

glutamic acid (glootam´ik) *n*. an amino acid occurring in proteins which plays an important part in the nitrogen metabolism of plants and animals.

glutamine (gloo´təmēn) *n*. an amino acid present in many proteins.

gluten (gloo´tən) *n*. a yellowish-grey, elastic albuminous substance, left in wheat flour which has been washed in water.

gluteus (gloo´tiəs) *n*. (*pl.* **glutei** (-tiī)) each of the three large muscles forming the buttock. **gluteal** *a*.

glutinous (gloo´tinəs) *a*. **1** viscous, gluey, sticky. **2** covered with a sticky exudation. **glutinously** *adv.*

glutton (glŭt´ən) *n*. **1** a person who eats to excess. **2** a person who indulges in anything to excess, as a voracious reader, worker etc. **3** a carnivorous animal of the weasel tribe, the wolverine, formerly supposed to be a voracious feeder. **glutton for punishment** *n*. a person eager to take on hard or unpleasant tasks. **gluttonize, gluttonise** *v.i.* to eat to excess, to gorge. **gluttonous** *a*. **gluttonously** *adv.* **gluttony** *n*.

glycerol (glis´ərol) *n*. (*Chem.*) a sticky, sweet, colourless liquid obtained from animal and vegetable fats and oils, used in the manufacture of soaps, medicines, confectionery, antifreeze etc. **glyceride** (-rīd) *n*. any fatty acid ester of glycerol. **glycerine** (-rin, -rēn), **glycerin** (-rin) *n*. glycerol.

glyco- (glī´kō), **glyc-** *comb. form* containing glycerol or compounds producing sugars.

glycogen (glī´kəjən) *n*. a white insoluble, starch-like compound occurring in animal tissues such as the liver and convertible into dextrose. **glycogenesis** (-jen´-) *n*. the formation of glycogen from sugar. **glycogenic** (-jen´-) *a*.

glycol (glī´kōl) *n*. (*Chem.*) a diatomic alcohol of the fatty group typified by ethyl glycol, used as an antifreeze in car engines and for de-icing aircraft wings. **glycolic** (-kol´-), **glycollic** *a*.

glycolysis (glīkol´isis) *n*. the breakdown of glucose by enzymes into acids, with the release of energy.

glycoprotein (glīkōprō´tēn) *n*. any of a group of complex proteins containing a carbohydrate mixed with a simple protein.

glyph (glif) *n*. **1** in a computer or word processor, a character or symbol beyond the normal range of characters. **2** a hieroglyph. **3** (*Archit.*) a fluting or channel, usu. vertical. **glyphic** *a*. carved, sculptured. ~*n*. a hieroglyph.

GMT *abbr.* Greenwich Mean Time.

gnamma (nam´ə), **namma** *n*. a waterhole in a rock.

gnarled (nahld) *a*. rugged, lined, weather-beaten, twisted. **gnarl** *n*. a protuberance, a twisted growth or contorted knot, in a tree. **gnarly** *a*. full of knots or gnarls.

gnash (nash) *v.t.* to strike or grind (the teeth) together. **gnashers** *n.pl.* (*sl.*) teeth, esp. false teeth.

gnat (nat) *n*. any small two-winged fly of the genus *Culex*, the females of which have a blood-sucking proboscis, esp. *C. pipiens*, the common gnat.

gnaw (naw) *v.t.* (*p.p.* **gnawed, gnawn** (nawn)) **1** to bite or eat away by degrees. **2** to bite repeatedly or persistently. **3** to bite in agony, rage or despair. **4** to corrode. **5** to consume or wear away by degrees (*gnawed by indecision*). **6** to cause persistent distress to. ~*v.i.* **1** to use the teeth in biting repeatedly or persistently (at or into). **2** to cause corrosion or wearing away. **gnawer** *n*. **gnawingly** *adv.*

gneiss (nīs) *n.* a laminated metamorphic rock consisting of feldspar, quartz and mica. **gneissic** *a.* **gneissoid** *a.* **gneissose** *a.*

gnocchi (nok´i, nyok´i) *n.* an Italian dish consisting of small potato or semolina dumplings, served with a sauce or used to garnish soup etc.

gnome¹ (nōm) *n.* **1** an imaginary being, a kind of misshapen sprite, dwarf, goblin, supposed to inhabit the interior of the earth, and to be the guardian of mines, quarries etc. **2** an ornamental garden figure in the supposed shape of a gnome. **gnomish** *a.*

gnome² (nōm) *n.* a pithy saying expressing a general truth, a maxim, an aphorism. **gnomic** *a.* dealing in maxims, sententious, didactic.

gnomon (nō´mon) *n.* **1** a rod, pillar, pin or plate on a sundial, indicating the time of day by its shadow. **2** (*Astron.*) a vertical pillar used in an analogous way for determining the altitude of the sun. **3** (*Geom.*) the figure remaining when a parallelogram has been removed from the corner of a larger one of the same form. **gnomonic** (-mon´-), **gnomonical** *a.*

gnosis (nō´sis) *n.* (*pl.* **gnoses** (-sēz)) knowledge, esp. of mysteries.

gnostic (nos´tik) *a.* **1** relating to knowledge or cognition, intellectual. **2** having esoteric knowledge. **3** of or belonging to the Gnostics or Gnosticism. ~*n.* an adherent of Gnosticism. **gnostically** *adv.* **Gnosticism** (-sizm) *n.* a system of religious philosophy flourishing in the first six centuries of the Church, that combined ideas from Greek and Oriental philosophy with Christianity, which it professed to expound as a mystical philosophy or gnosis. **gnosticize** (-sīz), **gnosticise** *v.t., v.i.*

GNP *abbr.* Gross National Product.

Gnr. *abbr.* Gunner.

gnu (noo) *n.* (*pl.* **gnus, gnu**) any large-horned antelope of the genus *Connochaetes,* native to S Africa, also called *wildebeest.*

GNVQ *abbr.* General National Vocational Qualification, a qualification designed to fit students for training or advanced study in a specific field.

go¹ (gō) *v.i.* (*2nd pers. sing. pres.* †**goest** (-ist), *3rd pers. sing. pres.* **goes** (gōz), *pres.p.* **going**, *past* **went** (went), *p.p.* **gone** (gon)) **1** to move, to move from one place, condition, or station to another. **2** to begin to move, to start to move from a place, to depart, to pass away, as opposed to come (*I am going now*). **3** to keep up a movement, to be moving, to be acting, operating, or working (*Is the clock going?*). **4** to travel (*We are going to Australia*). **5** to proceed, to advance (*to go for goal*). **6** to end, to come out, to succeed, to turn out (well or ill) (*How did it go?*). **7** to take a certain course (*The verdict went for him*). **8** to be habitually (*to go hungry*; *to go barefoot*). **9** to be used, said etc., habitually, to pass, to be circulated or current (*the going rate of exchange*). **10** to average. **11** to extend, to reach, to point in a certain direction (*The road goes west from here*). **12** to tend, to conduce (*It all goes to show...*). **13** to run, to have a certain tenor (*The song goes like this*). **14** to be applicable, to fit, to suit (with) (*The bag goes with your hat*). **15** to be harmonious (with a tune etc.). **16** to be released, to get away (*You may go*). **17** to be given up, to be abandoned, abolished, or lost (*My watch has gone*). **18** to fail, to give way, break down (*That roof is going!*). **19** (*usu. in. p.p.*) to die. **20** to pass into a certain state, to become (*to go wild*; *to go mad*). **21** to be sold (*Going at £30!*). **22** to be spent (*His wages had gone on drink*). **23** (*as aux. verb*) to be about (to do), to intend (*She is going to get up shortly*). **24** to make a certain noise (*go 'bang'*). **25** to belong. **26** (of time) to lapse or pass. **go ahead** start, proceed without hesitation. **go on** used to express mild disbelief, come now, come come! **to go** (*coll.*) (of food) for taking away from the restaurant. **to go about 1** to get to work at. **2** to go from place to place. **3** to take a circuitous course. **4** (*Naut.*) (of a vessel) to tack, to change course. **to go against** to be in opposition to. **to go ahead 1** to proceed in advance. **2** to make rapid progress. **3** to start. **to go at 1** to attack. **2** to work at vigorously. **to go away** to depart. **to go back on** to fail to keep (one's word). **to go behind 1** to call in question. **2** to look beyond (the apparent facts etc.). **to go between** to mediate between. **to go by 1** to pass by or near to. **2** to pass by. **3** to pass unnoticed or disregarded. **4** to take as a criterion. **to go down 1** to descend. **2** to fall, become lower. **3** to set. **4** to founder (as a ship). **5** to fall (before a conqueror). **6** to be beaten in a sports match. **7** to be set down in writing. **8** esp. in the UK, to leave university. **9** to be swallowed, to be palatable or acceptable. **to go down (with)** to fall ill (with). **to go for 1** to go somewhere to obtain something. **2** to attack. **3** to be true for, include (*and that goes for her as well*). **4** to be attracted by. **5** to be sold for. **to go in 1** to enter. **2** (of the sun) to go behind clouds. **3** in cricket, to have an innings. **to go in for 1** to be in favour of. **2** to follow as a pursuit or occupation. **3** to enter or take part in (an examination or competition). **to go into 1** to enter. **2** to frequent. **3** to take part in. **4** to investigate or discuss. **to go it 1** to carry on. **2** to keep a thing up. **3** to conduct oneself recklessly or outrageously. **to go it alone** to carry on single-handedly. **to go off 1** to depart. **2** to be fired, explode (as a gun, firework etc.). **3** to rot, perish, putrefy. **4** to fall away. **5** to become unconscious. **6** to die. **7** to cease to be perceptible. **8** to fare, to succeed (well or badly). **to go on 1** to proceed, to continue, to persevere. **2** to grumble, to complain. **3** to talk at length. **4** (*int., coll.*) rubbish, nonsense. **5** (*coll.*) to behave (badly etc.). **6** to appear on the stage. **7** to happen. **8** at cricket, to begin a spell of bowling. **to go out 1** to depart, to leave (a room etc.). **2** to be extinguished. **3** to vacate office. **4** to leave home and enter employment. **5** to go into society. **6** to go on strike.

7 to lose consciousness. **8** to have a romantic or sexual relationship. **to go out with** to have a romantic or sexual relationship with. **to go over 1** to cross, to pass over. **2** to rat, to change one's party or opinions. **3** to read, to examine. **4** to rehearse. **5** to retouch. **to go round 1** to pay a number of visits. **2** to encompass or be enough to encompass, to be enough for (the whole party etc.). **to go steady** to go about regularly with the same boyfriend or girlfriend. **to go through 1** to pass through. **2** to undergo. **3** to suffer. **4** to examine. **5** (*coll.*) to overhaul, to ransack, to strip. **6** to discuss thoroughly. **7** to perform (a duty, ceremony etc.). **8** to be completed. **9** to use or consume. **to go through with** to perform thoroughly, perh. despite reluctance, to complete. **to go together 1** to harmonize, to be suitable to or match each other. **2** to have a romantic or sexual relationship. **to go under 1** to be known as (a title or a name). **2** to sink. **3** to be submerged or ruined. **4** to perish. **to go up 1** to climb, pass upwards. **2** to rise, increase. **3** to be constructed. **4** to be destroyed, as by fire or explosion. **to go upon** to act upon as a principle. **to go with 1** to accompany. **2** to follow the meaning of, to understand. **3** to be with (child). **4** to side or agree with. **5** to suit, to match. **6** to have a romantic or sexual relationship with. **to go without** to be or manage without, to put up with the want of. **go-ahead** *a.* characterized by energy and enterprise. ~*n.* permission to go ahead. **go-as-you-please** *a.* unceremonious, untroubled by rules etc. **go-between** *n.* a person who acts as an intermediary between two parties. **go-by** *n.* **1** the act of passing without notice. **2** intentional failure to notice. **go-cart** *n.* **1** a small handcart. **2** a child's toy wagon. **3** GO-KART (under GO¹). **go-devil** *n.* (*N Am.*) a jointed instrument used to clean the inside of pipes, pipelines etc. **go-getter** *n.* a bustling, pushing person. **go-kart** *n.* a small light racing car with a low-powered engine. **go-off** *n.* (*coll.*) the start. **go-slow** *n.* a deliberate curtailment of the rate of production by organized labour in an industrial dispute.

go² (gō) *n.* (*pl.* **goes**) **1** a turn, a bout (of doing something). **2** one's turn in a game. **3** a try, an attempt. **4** rush, energy, enterprise. **5** spirit, life, animation. **6** the act of going. **7** (*coll.*) a fix, a scrape, an awkward turn of affairs. **8** (*coll.*) fashion, the mode. **9** a spree. **all the go** entirely in the fashion. **from the word go** (*coll.*) from the very beginning. **on the go 1** vigorously in motion. **2** on the move. **to have a go** (*coll.*) to make an attempt. **to have a go at someone** (*coll.*) to attack someone, physically or verbally.

go³ (gō) *n.* a Japanese board game for two people, its aim being to capture one's opponent's counters (or stones) in order to occupy a greater amount of the board.

goad (gōd) *n.* **1** a pointed instrument to urge oxen to move faster. **2** (*fig.*) anything that stings, spurs or incites. ~*v.t.* **1** to prick, drive or urge on with a

goad. **2** to stimulate, to incite. **3** to drive (on, to, into etc.).

goal (gōl) *n.* **1** in football, hockey etc., the posts connected by a crossbar between which the ball must be driven to win a point. **2** the act of kicking the ball between such posts or over such a bar. **3** destination, purpose, aim. **4** the ultimate aim of a person's ambition. **5** the winning post or mark indicating the end of a race. **goal average** *n.* in sport, the ratio of the number of goals scored for a team to those scored against. **goalball** *n.* a ball game played between teams of visually handicapped people. **goal difference** *n.* in sport, the difference between the number of goals scored for and against a team. **goalie** *n.* (*coll.*) a goalkeeper. **goalkeeper** *n.* in sport, esp. football, a player stationed near to guard the goal. **goal kick** *n.* in football, a free kick from the goal area taken by the defence side after the ball has been put out of play over the goal line by a member of the attacking side. **goal kicker** *n.* in rugby football, a player assigned to kick for goal when penalties or conversions arise. **goal kicking** *n.* **goal line** *n.* a line drawn through the goalposts to form the boundary at each end of the field of play in football. **goalmouth** *n.* in sport, the area immediately in front of a goal. **goalpost** *n.* in football etc., either of the two upright posts marking the goal. **to move the goalposts** (*coll.*) to change the conditions, regulations, limits etc. applying to a particular matter or action. **goalscorer** *n.* in sport, a player who scores a goal. **goaltender, goalminder** *n.* (*N Am.*) in sport, esp. ice hockey, a player stationed near to guard the goal.

goanna (gōan´ə) *n.* (*Austral.*) a large monitor lizard.

goat (gōt) *n.* **1** a hairy, horned and bearded domesticated ruminant belonging to the genus *Capra*, esp. *C. hircus*, of which there are many varieties. **2** a bad or inferior person or thing. **3** a fool. **4** a lascivious person, a lecher. **the Goat** the sign of the zodiac Capricorn. **to get one's goat** to make one angry. **goat antelope** *n.* a ruminant mammal of the subfamily *Rupicaprini*, including the chamois, goral and Rocky Mountain goat. **goatherd** *n.* a person who tends goats. **goatish** *a.* **goat moth** *n.* any large moth of the family *Cossidae*, esp. *Cossus cossus* and *C. ligniperda*. **goat's-beard** *n.* **1** a meadow plant with large yellow flowers, *Tragopogou pratensis*. **2** a white-flowered herbaceous plant of the rose family, *Aruncus dioicus*. **goatskin** *n.* the skin of a goat. ~*a.* made of goatskin. **goatsucker** *n.* the nightjar, any bird of the genus *Caprimulgus*, chiefly nocturnal and insectivorous, once falsely thought to milk goats, esp. *C. europaeus*, a British summer visitant. **goaty** *a.*

goatee (gōtē´) *n.* **goatee beard** *n.* a small beard like a goat's on the point of the chin.

gob (gob) *n.* **1** the mouth. **2** a mouthful. **3** a clot of something slimy, such as saliva. ~*v.i.* (*pres.p.*

gobbing, *past, p.p.* gobbed) to spit. **gobsmacked,
gobstruck** *a.* (*sl.*) amazed, dumbfounded. **gob-
stopper** *n.* a large boiled sweet.

gobbet (gob´it) *n.* **1** a mouthful, a lump, a piece,
esp. of meat. **2** an extract from a text, esp. one
used for educational purposes.

gobble (gob´əl) *v.t.* to swallow down hastily and
greedily or noisily. ~*v.i.* **1** to swallow food in this
manner. **2** to make a noise in the throat as a
turkeycock. ~*n.* a noise made in the throat like
that of a turkeycock. **gobbler** *n.* a turkeycock.

gobbledegook (gob´əldigook), **gobbledygook** *n.*
(*coll.*) pretentious, esp. unintelligible, language
characterized by jargon and circumlocution.

goblet (gob´lit) *n.* **1** a drinking vessel, usu. of
glass, with a stem, a foot and without a handle.
2 a drinking cup, usu. bowl-shaped and of glass
or metal.

goblin (gob´lin) *n.* a mischievous spirit of ugly or
grotesque shape; an elf, a gnome.

goby (gō´bi) *n.* (*pl.* **gobies**) a small fish belonging
to the genus *Gobius*, characterized by the union
of the ventral fins into a disc or sucker.

god (god) *n.* **1** a superhuman or supernatural
being regarded as controlling natural forces and
human destinies and worshipped or propitiated
by humans. **2** (*Theol.*) (**God**) in monotheistic
religions, the Supreme Being, the self-existent
and eternal creator and ruler of the universe. **3** a
personification of any of the forces of nature.
4 a person formally recognized as divine and
entitled to worship. **5** an image, animal etc., worshipped as an embodiment or symbol of supernatural power, an idol. **6** a person or thing greatly
idolized. **7** (*pl.*) the upper gallery in a theatre.
God almighty! used to express surprise or anger.
God forbid used to express the hope that a certain event etc. will not happen. **God help you/
her/** etc. **1** used to express sympathy, concern
etc. **2** (*iron.*) used to imply that a person's situation is not to be envied. **God knows 1** a mild
oath expressing apathy or annoyance. **2** God is
my (etc.) witness that. **God willing** if circumstances permit. **to god it** to behave as if one were
godlike. **god-awful** *a.* (*coll.*) terrible, dreadful.
godchild *n.* (*pl.* **godchildren**) someone for whom
a person stands sponsor at baptism. **goddam,
goddamn, goddamned** *a.* **1** damned. **2** hateful.
goddaughter *n.* a female godchild. **goddess** *n.*
1 a female deity. **2** a woman of pre-eminent
beauty, goodness or charm. **godfather** *n.* **1** a
male godparent. **2** the head of a Mafia family or
other criminal organization. **God-fearing** *a.* worshipping or reverencing God, moral, upright.
God-forsaken *a.* **1** (of a place) forlorn, deserted,
unwelcoming. **2** (of a person) wretched, miserable, depraved. **God-given** *a.* **1** received from
God. **2** possessed from birth or by divine authority. **Godhead** *n.* **1** a deity. **2** divine nature or
essence. **the Godhead** God. **godless** *a.* **1** acknowledging no god. **2** without God. **3** impious,
irreligious. **4** wicked. **godlessly** *adv.* **godlessness**

n. **godlike** *a.* **godly** *a.* (*comp.* **godlier,** *superl.*
godliest) God-fearing, pious, devout. **godliness** *n.*
godmother *n.* a female godparent. **godparent** *n.* a
person who is a sponsor for a child at a baptism.
godsend *n.* an unlooked-for acquisition or gain, a
piece of good fortune. **God's gift** *n.* (*iron.*) a person of utmost importance (to). **godship** *n.* **godson**
n. a male godchild. **God squad** *n.* (*sl.*) a religious
group or organization, usu. evangelical in its outlook and behaviour. **God's truth** *int.* STREWTH.
godward *adv.*, *a.* **godwards** *adv.*

godetia (gədē´shə) *n.* any plant of the genus
Godetia, a flowering herb allied to the evening
primroses.

godown (gōdown´, gō´-) *n.* an E Asian or Indian
warehouse.

godwit (god´wit) *n.* a marsh or shore bird of the
genus *Limosa*, resembling the curlew but having
a slightly upturned bill.

goer (gō´ə) *n.* **1** a person who attends regularly
(*usu. in comb.* as in *churchgoer*). **2** (*Austral.,
coll.*) a person or thing that is likely to succeed,
a proposal etc. that is acceptable. **3** (*coll.*) a lively
dynamic person. **4** (*coll.*) a sexually promiscuous
person, usu. female. **5** someone who or something which goes (*usu. in comb.* as in *fast-goer*).

gofer (gō´fə), **gopher** *n.* (*coll.*) a person employed
to run errands, give general assistance etc.

goffer (gō´fə, gof´ə), **gauffer** (gōf´ə) *v.t.* **1** to plait,
to crimp (edges of lace etc.) with a heated iron.
2 to raise in relief, to emboss (edges of books).
~*n.* **1** a plaiting, fluting, or ruffle. **2** a tool for
goffering.

goggle (gog´əl) *v.i.* **1** to strain or roll the eyes. **2** to
stare. **3** (of the eyes) to protrude, to bulge. ~*v.t.* to
roll (the eyes) about, to turn (the eyes) sideways.
~*a.* **1** prominent, staring, full (*goggle eyes*). **2** rolling from side to side. ~*n.* a strained or staring
rolling of the eyes. **goggle-box** *n.* (*coll.*) a television set. **goggle-dive** *n.* an underwater dive,
using goggles. **goggle-eyed** *a.* **goggles** *n.pl.* **1** protective spectacles, as those worn in swimming,
welding etc. **2** (*sl.*) spectacles worn to correct
defective eyesight. **3** (*sl.*) the eyes. **4** blinkers for
horses that are apt to take fright. **5** a disease of
sheep, staggers. **goggly** *a.*

go-go (gō´gō), **gogo** *a.* (*coll.*) **1** active, lively.
2 alert to opportunities. **go-go dancer** *n.* (*dated*)
a (scantily clad) dancer who performs gyrating,
usu. erotic routines in nightclubs etc.

going (gō´ing) *n.* **1** the act of moving or walking.
2 departure. **3** the condition of ground, roads,
racecourse, track etc., as regards walking, riding,
etc. (*also in comb.* as in *slow-going, rough-going*).
~*a.* **1** working, in actual operation. **2** existing, to
be had (*the best that are going*). **going on** (esp. of
the time, one's age etc.) almost, nearly (*I am 16,
going on 17*). **to go while the going's good** to seize
the chance of getting away, to put into action.
going away *n.*, *a.* (for) leaving, departure, esp. on
honeymoon (*going away outfit*). **going concern** *n.*
a business etc., in actual operation. **going-over** *n.*

(*pl.* **goings-over**) (*coll.*) **1** a thorough inspection, overhaul etc. **2** a beating, mugging, thrashing. **3** (*N Am.*) a scolding, telling-off. **goings-on** *n.pl.* behaviour, conduct (usu. in a bad sense).

goitre (goi´tə), (*N Am.*) **goiter** *n.* (*Med.*) a morbid enlargement of the thyroid gland, causing an unsightly deformity of the neck. **goitred** *a.* **goitrous** *a.*

gold (gōld) *n.* **1** (*Chem.*) a precious metallic element, at. no. 79, chem. symbol Au, of a bright yellow colour, the most ductile, malleable, and one of the heaviest of metals, much used for coins, jewellery etc. **2** the metal gold in the form of coin, money. **3** wealth, riches. **4** anything very precious or valuable and genuine or pure. **5** the metal gold used as a coating or wash, gilding. **6** the colour of gold. **7** a gold medal. **8** the centre of an archery target. ~*a.* **1** made of gold, consisting of gold. **2** coloured like gold. **gold amalgam** *n.* gold combined with mercury in a soft plastic state. **gold-beater** *n.* a person who beats out gold for gilding. **gold-beater's skin** *n.* a prepared membrane of the caecum of the ox, used for separating the leaves of gold under the hammer, and also as an application to cuts. **gold bloc** *n.* in economics, a group of countries having a gold standard. **gold brick** *n.* **1** something with a bogus display of value, a fraud. **2** a lazy person. **gold card** *n.* a credit card issued only to people with a high credit rating, offering superior benefits. **gold-digger** *n.* **1** (*sl.*) a person who forms an intimate relationship only for material gain. **2** a person who mines for gold. **gold-digging** *n.* **gold disc** *n.* an award given to a recording artist, group etc. for the high sales of a particular record, CD etc., often presented in the form of a golden replica disc. **gold dust** *n.* gold in very fine particles. **goldfield** *n.* a district where gold is found. **goldfinch** *n.* any songbird of the genus *Carduelis*, esp. the European *C. carduelis* which has a yellow band across the wings. **goldfish** *n.* (*pl.* in general **goldfish**, in particular **goldfishes**) a golden-red carp, *Carassius auratus*, kept in ponds, aquariums etc. **goldfish-bowl** *n.* **1** a fishbowl. **2** (*coll.*) a state or situation of exposure to public curiosity, a place lacking in privacy. **gold foil** *n.* a thicker kind of gold leaf. **gold leaf** *n.* gold beaten into a very thin sheet. **gold medal** *n.* an award for first place in a race or competition, esp. in the Olympic Games (as distinct from *silver medal* or *bronze medal*). **gold mine** *n.* **1** a place where gold is mined. **2** (*coll.*) a source of wealth or profit. **gold of pleasure** *n.* a yellow-flowered plant, *Camelina sativa*. **gold plate** *n.* vessels, dishes etc. of gold. **gold record** *n.* GOLD DISC (under GOLD). **gold reserve** *n.* the total amount of gold held by a central bank to make national and international payments and to protect the value of currency. **gold rush** *n.* a rush to a place where gold has been discovered. **goldsmith** *n.* a worker in gold. **gold standard** *n.* a system which defines the currency of a nation in

terms of its value in gold. **gold thread** *n.* **1** a flattened silver-gilt wire, laid over a thread of silk. **2** a bitter plant, *Coptis trifolia*.

golden (gōl´dən) *a.* **1** of the colour or lustre of gold. **2** made or consisting of gold. **3** bright, shining, resplendent. **4** excellent, precious, most valuable (*a golden moment*). **5** most favourable (*a golden opportunity*). **golden age** *n.* **1** a fabled primeval period of perfect human happiness and innocence, in which the earth yielded her fruits without toil, and all creatures lived in peace. **2** the most illustrious period of a nation's literature or prosperity, esp. the first part of the Classical age of Latin literature. **golden ager** *n.* (*N Am.*) an old person. **golden balls** *n.pl.* the three balls displayed as the emblem of a pawnbroker. **golden boy, golden girl** *n.* a popular or successful person in a particular field. **golden calf** *n.* (*fig.*) money as an aim in itself (Ex. xxxii.4). **golden chain** *n.* the laburnum. **golden delicious** *n.* a variety of sweet, green-skinned apple. **golden eagle** *n.* a large eagle, *Aquila chrysaetos*, found in the mountainous parts of Britain, esp. Scotland. **golden-eye** *n.* any marine duck of the genus *Bucephala*. **golden girl** GOLDEN BOY (under GOLDEN). **golden goose** *n.* a reliable and continuing source of wealth and profit. **golden hamster** *n.* the hamster *Mesocricetus auratus*, kept as a pet. **golden handshake** *n.* (*coll.*) a payment or benefit given to an employee when leaving a job, esp. on retirement. **golden hello** *n.* (*coll.*) a payment or benefit given to an employee on joining a company. **golden jubilee** *n.* the 50th anniversary of an event of public importance. **golden mean** *n.* **1** the principle of neither too much nor too little, moderation. **2** GOLDEN SECTION (under GOLDEN). **golden number** *n.* the number denoting the year's place in a Metonic lunar cycle of 19 years, used in calculating the movable feasts, such as Easter. **golden oldie** *n.* (*coll.*) **1** an old recording or film that is still popular. **2** an old person who is still popular, successful, sprightly etc. **golden opinions** *n.pl.* high regard. **golden orfe** *n.* a yellow aquarium variety of the orfe fish. **golden oriole** *n.* a European bird, *Oriolus oriolus*, the male of which has yellow and black, the female green plumage. **golden parachute** *n.* (*coll.*) a clause in the contract of a company executive guaranteeing financial recompense in the event of redundancy following a merger, takeover etc. **golden perch** *n.* CALLOP. **golden retriever** *n.* a retriever with a golden-coloured or dark cream coat. **golden rod** *n.* a tall yellow-flowered plant of the genus *Solidago*, esp. *S. virgaurea*. **golden rule** *n.* **1** any important rule or principle. **2** the rule that we should do as we would be done by (Matt. vii.12). **golden section** *n.* in fine arts, the division of a line, plane figure etc. into two sections where the proportion of the smaller to the larger section is the same as that of the larger section to the whole. **golden share** *n.* a controlling share (block), esp. as held by the government in a privatized company, that can be used to prevent a takeover by an unacceptable party. **golden syrup** *n.* a pale-coloured treacle. **golden wedding** *n.* the 50th anniversary of a marriage.

golf (golf) *n.* a game played by two persons or couples with clubs and small hard balls on commons, moorlands, fields or links with short grass, consisting of hitting the balls into a series of small holes in the ground in as few strokes as possible. ~*v.i.* to play golf. **golf bag** *n.* a tall, cylindrical bag used for carrying clubs, balls etc. **golf ball** *n.* **1** a small, hard, white ball used in playing golf. **2** (an electric typewriter that has) a small metal ball bearing the type that moves to press them onto the paper (as distinct from *daisy-wheel*). **golf cart** *n.* **1** a motorized cart for carrying golfers and equipment. **2** a hand-pulled trolley used for carrying golf equipment. **golf club** *n.* **1** any of the clubs used in playing golf. **2** a golfing establishment usu. with a golf course and a clubhouse, which golfers join as members. **golf course** *n.* the course of 9 or 18 holes on which golf is played. **golfer** *n.* a person who plays golf. **golf links** *n.pl.* a golf course set in undulating rough country by the sea.

golliwog (gol´iwog) *n.* a black-faced doll with fuzzy hair and bright clothes.

golly[1] (gol´i) *int.* used to express surprise.

golly[2] (gol´i) *n.* (*pl.* **gollies**) (*coll.*) a gollywog.

-gon (gən) *comb. form* used to form nouns denoting a figure with a number of angles, as in *hexagon, octagon, pentagon.*

gonads (gō´nadz, gon´-) *n.pl.* undifferentiated sex glands, the embryonic sexual apparatus, with rudiments of both sexes which later develop into either ovaries or testes. **gonadal** (-nad´-), **gonadic** *a.* **gonadotrophic** (-dətrō´fik), **gonadotropic** (-pik) *a.* stimulating the gonads. **gonadotrophin, gonadotrophic hormone** *n.* the hormone that stimulates the gonads.

gondola (gon´dələ) *n.* **1** a long, narrow Venetian boat with peaked ends, propelled by one oar. **2** the car of an airship, balloon, ski lift etc. **3** a free-standing block of shelves used to display goods in a supermarket etc. **4** (*N Am.*) **a** a large, light, flat-bottomed freight-boat. **b** (*also* **gondola car**) a flat railway wagon. **gondolier** (-liə´) *n.* a person who rows a gondola.

gone (gon) *a.* **1** past (*It is gone eight*). **2** dead. **3** (*sl.*) enthralled, entranced, usu. on music, drugs etc. **4** (*coll.*) pregnant (*six months gone*). **5** lost, beyond hope. **6** ruined, undone. **gone on** (*sl.*) infatuated with. **goner** *n.* (*coll.*) a person who or something that is ruined or ill beyond recovery.

gong (gong) *n.* **1** a tambourine-shaped metal instrument which when struck with a padded stick emits a loud sonorous note, used as a signal for meals etc. **2** a flattish bell struck with a hammer. **3** (*sl.*) a medal. ~*v.t.* (*coll.*) to stop a person or activity by sounding a gong.

gonna (gon´ə) *contr.* (*coll.*) going to (*I'm gonna be strong*).

gonorrhoea (gonərē´ə), (*N Am.*) **gonorrhea** *n.* a venereal disease affecting the urethra and other mucous surfaces, accompanied by inflammation and purulent discharge. **gonorrhoeal** (-əl) *a.*

gonzo (gon´zō) *a.* (*N Am., coll.*) bizarre, crazy, esp. of exaggerated journalistic writing style.

goo (goo) *n.* (*coll.*) sticky matter. **gooey** *a.* (*comp.* **gooier,** *superl.* **gooiest**) **gooeyness, gooiness** *n.*

good (gud) *a.* (*comp.* **better,** *superl.* **best**) **1** having such qualities as are useful, proper, and satisfactory. **2** fit, proper, suitable, expedient (*a good match of colours*). **3** conducive to the end desired, profitable, serviceable (*The car has good brakes*). **4** adequate, satisfactory, competent (*a good worker; good at spelling*). **5** advantageous, beneficial (*good value*). **6** genuine, sound, valid (*You need a good meal; The ticket is good for three games*). **7** perfect, complete, thorough (*a good clean*). **8** reliable, safe, sure (*a good driver*). **9** sound financially (*a good investment*). **10** ample, considerable (*a good way away*). **11** possessed of moral excellence, righteous, virtuous (*a good deed; a good person*). **12** kind, benevolent, friendly, amiable, courteous (*That was good of you*). **13** pleasant, acceptable, palatable (*good food; a good time*). **14** well-behaved (*a good child*). **15** beneficial to one's health, wholesome. **16** (of weather) dry and sunny. ~*n.* **1** that which contributes to happiness, advantage etc. **2** that which is right, useful etc. **3** welfare. **4** prosperity. **5** benefit, advantage. **6** goodness, good qualities, virtuous and charitable deeds. **7** (*pl., Law*) movable property, chattels, effects. **8** wares, merchandise. **as good as** not less than, the same as, practically, virtually. **as good as one's word 1** fulfilling one's promises. **2** trustworthy. **for good (and all)** finally, definitely, completely. **good as gold** (esp. of children) very well behaved. **good for you!** used to express approval, encouragement etc. **good on you!** good for you! **to be good for** to be relied on to pay or bring in (a stated amount). **to come good 1** (*coll.*) esp. after a setback, to succeed or improve. **2** to recover one's health after illness etc. **to make good 1** to perform, to fulfil, to become successful. **2** to supply a deficiency. **3** to replace. **4** to compensate (for). **5** to confirm. **6** to prosper, to be successful. **to take in good part** not to take offence. **to the good** extra, over and above, as a balance or profit (*We are £5 to the good*). **good afternoon** *n., int.* a form of salutation at meeting or parting in the afternoon. **Good Book** *n.* the Bible. **good breeding** *n.* courteous manners formed by nurture and education. **good company** *n.* **1** a pleasant companion. **2** a pleasant group of friends. **good day** *n., int.* a form of salutation at meeting or parting. **good evening, good even, †good e'en** *n., int.* a form of salutation at meeting or parting in the evening. **good faith** *n.* honest intentions. **good form** *n.* **1** good manners. **2** breeding.

good-for-nothing, †good-for-nought *a.* of no value, worthless. *~n.* an idle person, a vagabond. **good-hearted** *a.* kind, well-meaning. **good heavens!** *int.* used to express surprise, dismay, irritation etc. **good humour,** (*N Am.*) **good humor** *n.* a cheerful temper, amiability. **good-humoured** *a.* **good-humouredly** *adv.* **goodie** GOODY. **goodish** *a.* **good job** *n.* (*coll.*) a satisfactory turn of affairs. **Good King Henry** *n.* a weed of the goosefoot family, *Chenopodium bonus-henricus,* found in the northern hemisphere. **good-looking** *a.* handsome, attractive. **good-looker** *n.* **good luck** *n.* good fortune, prosperity. *~int.* may good luck befall you. **goodly** *a.* (*comp.* **goodlier,** *superl.* **goodliest**) **1** handsome, comely, graceful, kind. **2** large, considerable. **goodliness** *n.* **good money** *n.* **1** real money, money that might have been spent elsewhere (*to throw good money after bad*). **2** (*coll.*) high earnings. **good morning, †good morrow** *n., int.* a form of salutation at meeting or parting in the morning. **good nature** *n.* **1** kindness of disposition. **2** freedom from selfishness. **good-natured** *a.* **good-naturedly** *adv.* **goodness** *n.* **1** the quality or state of being good. **2** that which is good. **3** moral excellence, virtue. **4** kindness, good nature, generosity. **5** the virtue or essence of anything. **6** the nutritious or wholesome part of something. **goodness gracious!** used to express surprise etc. **goodness knows!** used to express lack of knowledge etc. **good night** *n., int.* a form of salutation on parting at night or at bedtime. **goodo** (gud´ō) *a.* (*Austral., New Zeal., coll.*) good. **good-oh** (gudō´) *int.* used to express enthusiasm. **good riddance** *n., int.* a welcome relief from someone or something undesirable. **goods** *n.pl.* **1** merchandise. **2** possessions that can be moved. **the goods 1** (*sl.*) just what is wanted. **2** (*esp. N Am., coll.*) evidence (against someone). **goods and chattels** *n.pl.* personal belongings of all kinds. **goods train** *n.* a train carrying merchandise only, a freight train. **good temper** *n.* freedom from irritability. **good-tempered** *a.* good-humoured. **good-temperedly** *adv.* **good-time girl** *n.* **1** a woman who recklessly pursues pleasure. **2** (*euphem.*) a prostitute. **good times** *n.pl.* a period of prosperity, happiness etc. **goodwill** *n.* **1** kindly feeling or disposition. **2** benevolence, favour. **3** acquiescence, ready consent. **4** the established popularity or custom of a business sold with the business itself. **good word** *n.* a recommendation or endorsement (*to put in a good word for*). **good works** *n.pl.* acts of charity. **goody¹** *int.* (*coll.*) used, esp. by children, to express delight. **goody², goodie** *n.* (*pl.* **goodies**) (*coll.*) **1** a person on the side of what is right and truthful, esp. a good character in fiction, cinema, television or radio. **2** (*usu. in pl.*) an object, gift etc. which is especially desirable. **3** a goody-goody. **goody-goody** *n.* (*pl.* **goody-goodies**) (*coll., usu. derog.*) a priggishly good person. *~a.* priggishly good.
goodbye (gudbī´), (*N Am.*) **goodby** *int.* (*pl.* **goodbyes,** (*N Am.*) **goodbys**) farewell. *~n.* a farewell.

goof (goof) *n.* (*coll.*) **1** a foolish mistake, a blunder. **2** a stupid person. *~v.i., v.t.* to blunder. **goofy** *a.* (*comp.* **goofier,** *superl.* **goofiest**) (*coll.*) **1** silly. **2** (of front teeth) protruding. **3** infatuated. **goofily** *adv.* **goofiness** *n.*
googly (goo´gli) *n.* (*pl.* **googlies**) in cricket, a ball bowled in a disguised manner to break a different way from that expected, an off-break ball bowled with a leg-break action.
goolie (goo´li), **gooly** *n.* (*pl.* **goolies**) (*sl.*) **1** (*usu. pl.*) a testicle. **2** (*Austral.*) a stone, pebble.
goon (goon) *n.* **1** a stupid person. **2** a thug hired to terrorize others, esp. in an industrial or political context.
goop¹ (goop) *n.* (*sl.*) a rude or foolish person. **goopy** *a.* (*comp.* **goopier,** *superl.* **goopiest**) **goopiness** *n.*
goop² (goop) *n.* a thick, sticky liquid, gloop.
goosander (goosan´də) *n.* a large diving duck, *Mergus merganser.*
goose (goos) *n.* (*pl.* **geese** (gēs)) **1** a web-footed bird intermediate in size between the duck and the swan, belonging to the family Anatidae. **2** the female of this, as distinct from gander. **3** a silly person, a simpleton. **4** (*pl.* **gooses**) a tailor's smoothing iron. **5** (*sl.*) a prod between the buttocks. *~v.t.* (*sl.*) to prod between the buttocks. **goose-flesh,** (*N Am., Sc.*) **goose bumps, goose pimples, goose-skin** *n.* a peculiar roughness of the human skin produced by cold, fear etc. **goosefoot** *n.* (*pl.* **goosefoots**) any herb of the genus *Chenopodium* with leaves shaped like a goose's foot. **goosegrass** *n.* **1** the Eurasian plant cleavers, *Galium aparine.* **2** the plant silverweed, *Potentilla anserina.* **goose-step** *n.* a marching step in which the legs are raised almost parallel with the ground without bending the knees.
gooseberry (guz´bəri, goos´-) *n.* (*pl.* **gooseberries**) **1** the thorny shrub *Ribes grossularia.* **2** the fruit of this shrub. **to play gooseberry** to act as an unwanted third party to a pair of lovers.
gopher (gō´fə) *n.* any of various American burrowing animals of the family Geomyidae.
goral (gaw´rəl) *n.* a Himalayan goatlike antelope, *Nemorhedus goral.*
Gordian (gaw´diən) *a.* intricate, complicated. **Gordian knot** *n.* any apparently inextricable difficulty or deadlock. **to cut the Gordian knot** to remove a difficulty by drastic measures.
gore¹ (gaw) *n.* blood from a wound, esp. thick, clotted blood. **gory** *a.* (*comp.* **gorier,** *superl.* **goriest**) **1** covered with gore. **2** bloody, involving bloodshed and killing. **gorily** *adv.* **goriness** *n.*
gore² (gaw) *v.t.* to pierce with a horn, point etc.
gore³ (gaw) *n.* a triangular piece in a dress, sail, balloon, umbrella etc. *~v.t.* to make into or shape as a gore.
gorge (gawj) *n.* **1** a narrow pass between cliffs or hills. **2** (*dated*) the throat, gullet. **3** the contents of the stomach. **4** a heavy meal, a surfeit. **5** in a fortification, the narrow entrance into a bastion

or other outwork. ~*v.t.* **1** to swallow, to devour greedily. **2** to glut, to satiate, to choke up. ~*v.i.* to feed greedily. **one's gorge rises at** one is nauseated or disgusted by. **gorger** *n.*

gorgeous (gaw´jəs) *a.* **1** splendid, richly decorated, magnificent. **2** ornate. **3** (*coll.*) very fine, beautiful etc. **gorgeously** *adv.* **gorgeousness** *n.*

gorget (gaw´jit) *n.* **1** a piece of armour for defending the throat or neck. **2** a ruff or wimple formerly worn by women. **3** a necklace.

gorgon (gaw´gən) *n.* **1** in Greek mythology, any one of three snake-haired female monsters so terrible in appearance that the sight of them was fabled to turn beholders to stone. **2** a person of frightening appearance, esp. a repulsive-looking woman.

Gorgonzola (gawgənzō´lə) *n.* a soft blue-veined Italian cheese.

gorilla (gəril´ə) *n.* **1** a large vegetarian African anthropoid ape, *Gorilla gorilla*, growing to about 5½ ft. (1.6 m) in height. **2** (*coll.*) a threateningly large man.

gormless (gawm´lis), **gaumless** *a.* witless, clumsy, stupid. **gormlessly** *adv.* **gormlessness** *n.*

☒ gorrila common misspelling of GORILLA.

gorse (gaws) *n.* any yellow-flowered, prickly shrub of the genus *Ulex*, furze, whin. **gorsy** *a.*

Gorsedd (gaw´sedh) *n.* a meeting of bards and Druids in Wales, esp. associated with the eisteddfod.

gory GORE¹.

gosh (gosh) *int.* used to express surprise.

goshawk (gos´hawk) *n.* a large, short-winged hawk, *Accipiter gentilis*.

gosling (goz´ling) *n.* a young goose.

gospel (gos´pəl) *n.* **1** the teaching or revelation of Jesus Christ. **2** the doctrine preached by Christ and the Apostles. **3** (**Gospel**) **a** any one of the canonical books ascribed respectively to Matthew, Mark, Luke and John. **b** a selection from these books read in the Church service. **4** anything accepted as infallibly true. **5** the principle that one adopts as a guide to life or action. **gospeller,** (*N Am.*) **gospeler** *n.* a person who reads the Gospel in the Communion service. **gospel music** *n.* black religious vocal music, orig. from the southern US. **gospel truth** *n.* the absolute truth, something completely true.

gossamer (gos´əmə) *n.* **1** the slender cobweb-like threads floating in the air in calm weather, produced by small spiders. **2** thin, filmy gauze. **3** anything exceedingly flimsy or unsubstantial. **gossamered** *a.* **gossamery** *a.*

gossip (gos´ip) *n.* **1** idle talk, tittle-tattle. **2** mere rumour. **3** informal chat or writing, esp. about persons or incidents of the day. **4** a person who regularly indulges in tittle-tattle. ~*v.i.* (*pres.p.* **gossiping,** *past, p.p.* **gossiped**) **1** to tattle, to chat. **2** to talk or write in an informal easy-going way. **gossip column** *n.* a section of a newspaper devoted to information and rumour about well-known personalities. **gossip columnist** *n.*

gossiper *n.* **gossipmonger** *n.* a spreader of gossip. **gossipy** *a.*

got (got), **got-up** *a.* dressed up, disguised, prepared for effect or to take in.

Goth (goth) *n.* **1** a member of an ancient Germanic tribe which invaded southern Europe in the 3rd–5th cents., establishing kingdoms in Italy, southern France and Spain. **2** a rude, ignorant person. **3** (**goth**) a member of a subculture identified by black clothing, striking black and white make-up, metallic jewellery and a preference for a particular form of rock music. **Gothish** *a.*

Gothic (goth´ik) *a.* **1** in the style of architecture characterized by pointed arches, clustered columns etc. **2** (of a novel, film etc.) in a style characterized by gloomy, menacing surroundings in which supernatural or horrifying events take place. **3** of or relating to the Goths or their language. **4** rude, barbarous. ~*n.* **1** the Gothic style of architecture. **2** the language of the Goths. **3** (*Print.*) a heavy black-letter typeface, old-fashioned German or sans serif. **Gothically** *adv.* **Gothicism** (-sizm) *n.* **Gothicist** (-sist) *n.* **Gothicize** (-sīz), **Gothicise** *v.t.* **1** to make Gothic. **2** to bring back to barbarism. ~*v.i.* to go back to barbarism.

gotta (got´ə) *contr.* (*coll.*) **1** have got to (*I gotta go*). **2** have got a (*I gotta horse*).

gotten GET.

gouache (gooahsh´) *n.* a method of painting with opaque colours mixed with water, honey and gum.

Gouda (gow´də) *n.* a round mild cheese originally made at Gouda, in the Netherlands.

gouge (gowj) *n.* **1** a chisel with a concave blade, used to cut holes or grooves. **2** a groove, cut etc. made with this tool. ~*v.t.* **1** to cut, force or scoop (out) with or as with a gouge. **2** (*N Am.*) to cheat. **gouger** *n.*

goujon (goo´zhon) *n.* a small strip of chicken or fish, usu. deep-fried in a coating of breadcrumbs etc.

goulash (goo´lash) *n.* a stew of meat and vegetables highly seasoned with paprika.

gourami (goo´rəmi), **goramy** (gaw´-) *n.* (*pl.* **gouramis, goramies**) a nest-building Oriental fish, *Osphrenemus goramy*, much valued for food.

gourd (guəd) *n.* **1** a large fleshy fruit of climbing or trailing plants belonging to the Cucurbitaceae, the hard outer coat of which can serve as a container for water, wine etc. **2** a bottle, cup etc. made from a gourd. **gourdful** *n.*

gourmand (guə´mənd) *n.* a glutton. ~*a.* gluttonous, fond of eating. **gourmandism, gourmandise** (-ēz) *n.* gluttony, the habits of a gourmand.

Usage note The nouns *gourmand* and *gourmet* should not be confused: a *gourmand* is a glutton, and a *gourmet* a connoisseur.

gourmet (guə´mā) *n.* a connoisseur of good food, an epicure. ~*a.* **1** of or relating to a gourmet. **2** of a standard considered appropriate to a gourmet (*a gourmet meal*).

Usage note See note under GOURMAND.

gout (gowt) *n.* **1** a disease affecting the joints, esp. the big toe and foot, with inflammation, pain and irritability being the leading symptoms. **2** †a drop, a clot, esp. of blood. **gouty** *a.* (*comp.* **goutier,** *superl.* **goutiest**) **goutiness** *n.*

govern (gŭv'ən) *v.t.* **1** to direct and control. **2** to rule with authority, esp. to administer the affairs of a state. **3** to exercise military command over. **4** to regulate, to sway, to influence, to determine. **5** to conduct (oneself) in a specific way. **6** to restrain, to curb. **7** (*Gram.*) (of a verb or preposition) to require a particular case in (a word following it), to have (a noun or case) dependent upon it. ~*v.i.* **1** to exercise authority. **2** to administer the law. **3** to have the control (over). **governable** *a.* **governability** (-bil'-) *n.* **governance** (-əns) *n.* **1** the action, manner or system of governing. **2** government, authority, control. **governing body** *n.* a board, committee etc. of people who collectively oversee an institution.

governess (gŭv'ənis) *n.* a woman employed to teach children in a private household. **governessy** *a.*

government (gŭv'ənmənt, gŭv'əmənt) *n.* **1** control, direction, regulation, exercise of authority, esp. authoritative administration of public affairs. **2** the form or system of such administration. **3** the body of persons in charge of the government of a state at any particular time, an administration, a ministry. **4** self-control, manageableness. **5** the power of controlling. **6** the right of governing. **7** (*Gram.*) the influence of a word in determining the case or mood of another. **governmental** (-men'-) *a.* **governmentally** *adv.* **government issue** *a.* (*esp. US*) supplied by the government. **government pension** *n.* (*N Am.*) a state pension. **government surplus** *n.* unused government equipment for disposal by sale.

Usage note The pronunciation with the first *n* silent is sometimes disapproved of.

governor (gŭv'ənə) *n.* **1** a person who governs, esp. someone invested with authority to execute the laws and administer the affairs of a state, province etc. **2** a ruler, a head of the executive. **3** the Crown representative in a colony or dependency. **4** (*US*) the elective chief magistrate of a state. **5** the commander in a fortress or garrison. **6** (*sl.*) a term used by a person to refer to their employer, father etc. **7** an unceremonious mode of address (*Look here, governor!*). **8** a device for limiting the speed of an engine, motor etc., or the flow or pressure of a fluid or gas. **governor-general** *n.* (*pl.* **governors-general**) a chief of the executive in a large dependency, having subordinate deputy governors. **governor-generalship** *n.* **governorship, governorate** (-rət) *n.*

Govt. *abbr.* Government.

gown (gown) *n.* **1** a woman's loose, long, outer garment, a dress, esp. a handsome or stylish one. **2** a long, loose robe worn by members of the clergy, judges, lawyers, university graduates etc. **3** a protective garment as worn by surgeons during an operation. **town and gown** the townspeople and the university staff and students in a university town, as opposed to or contrasted with each other. **gowned** *a.*

goy (goi) *n.* (*pl.* **goyim** (-im), **goys**) (*sl., offensive*) among Jews, a name for a non-Jewish person.

GP *abbr.* **1** General Practitioner. **2** Grand Prix.

Gp. Capt. *abbr.* Group Captain (in the RAF).

GPO *abbr.* **1** General Post Office. **2** (*US*) Government Printing Office.

gr. *abbr.* **1** grain(s). **2** gram(s). **3** gross.

grab (grab) *v.t.* (*pres.p.* **grabbing,** *past, p.p.* **grabbed**) **1** to seize, snatch or grasp suddenly. **2** to take possession of violently or lawlessly. **3** (*coll.*) to capture, to arrest. **4** (*coll.*) to interest (*How does that grab you?*). ~*v.i.* to grasp, snatch, or clutch (at). ~*n.* **1** a sudden snatch, grasping or seizing (at). **2** an implement for clutching, a grip. **3** rapacious or dishonest acquisition, esp. in commerce or the foreign policy of a government. **up for grabs 1** (*coll.*) on offer. **2** for sale. **3** ready for the taking. **grab bag** *n.* (*N Am.*) a lucky dip. **grabber** *n.* **grabby** *a.* (*coll.*) greedy, grasping, eager to grab. **grab handle, grab rail** *n.* a handle, rail etc. to steady passengers in a moving vehicle.

grace (grās) *n.* **1** the quality which makes form, movement, expression or manner elegant, harmonious, refined and charming. **2** a natural gift or endowment. **3** an acquired accomplishment, charm or attraction. **4** a courteous or affable demeanour. **5** free, unmerited favour or goodwill. **6** clemency, mercy. **7** a boon, a benefaction. **8** (*Theol.*) the free, unmerited favour of God. **9** a short prayer before a meal invoking a blessing or expressing thanks. **10** a privilege or indulgence, esp. an extension of time legally allowed after a payment falls due. **11** (**Grace**) used as part of a formula for addressing or referring to a duke, duchess or archbishop (*Your Grace*). ~*v.t.* **1** to lend grace to, to dignify. **2** to give honour to, to give dignity to. **her grace** a courteous phrase adopted in speaking of a duchess and formerly of a female sovereign. **his grace** a courteous phrase adopted in speaking of an archbishop or duke, and formerly of a male sovereign. **the Graces** in Greek mythology, three goddesses embodying and conferring beauty and charm. **to be in the good graces of** to enjoy the favour of. **with a bad grace** reluctantly. **with a good grace** willingly. **your grace** a courteous phrase adopted in speaking to an archbishop, duke or duchess, and formerly to a sovereign. **grace-and-favour** *a.* (of a house, flat etc.) granted free of rent by the sovereign as a mark of gratitude. **graceful** *a.* full of grace, elegance or beauty, esp. of form or movement. **gracefully** *adv.* **gracefulness** *n.* **graceless** *a.*

lacking in grace, elegance etc., ungraceful. **gracelessly** *adv.* **gracelessness** *n.* **grace note** *n.* (*Mus.*) an extra note introduced for embellishment.

gracile (gras´ĭl) *a.* slender, lean, thin, esp. in an anthropological sense. **gracility** (grəsil´-) *n.* **1** slenderness. **2** unadorned simplicity.

gracious (grā´shəs) *a.* **1** exhibiting grace, favour or kindness. **2** graceful, pleasing, bland. **3** proceeding from divine grace. **4** benignant, merciful. **gracious living** *n.* an elegant way of life. **graciously** *adv.* **gracious me!** *int.* used to express surprise or protest. **graciousness, graciosity** (-os´-) *n.*

grackle (grak´əl), **grakle** *n.* **1** any American oriole of the genus *Quiscalus*, also called *blackbird* in N America. **2** any mynah bird of the genus *Gracula*, allied to the starlings.

gradation (grədā´shən) *n.* **1** an orderly arrangement, succession or progression step by step. **2** (*usu. in pl.*) a step, stage or degree in order, rank, quality, merit etc. **3** in art, the gradual blending of one tint, tone etc. with another. **4** (*Mus.*) an ascending or descending succession of chords. **5** in philology, ablaut. **gradate** *v.t.* to arrange or blend (colours etc.) by imperceptible gradation. ~*v.i.* to pass from one tint to another by such gradations. **gradational** *a.* **gradationally** *adv.*

grade (grād) *n.* **1** a degree or step in rank, quality, value, order etc. **2** a class of people of similar rank, ability, proficiency etc. **3** a mark given to a student's work as an indication of its quality. **4** class (at school). **5** an animal or class of animals (such as cattle or sheep) produced by crossing a common stock with some better breed. **6** (*Zool.*) a group supposed to have branched off from a parent stem at a certain stage of development. **7** gradient, the degree of slope in a road. **8** a sloping road, track etc. **9** in philology, the position of a vowel or root in an ablaut series. ~*v.t.* **1** to arrange in grades. **2** to gradate. **3** to adjust the rate of slope in, as a road. **4** (of cattle) to cross (a stock) with a better breed. **at-grade** (*N Am.*) at the same level (as of a place where two roads cross each other). **to make the grade** to succeed. **gradable** *a.* **grade crossing** *n.* (*N Am.*) a level crossing. **grader** *n.* **1** a person who or thing which grades. **2** a motor-driven vehicle with a blade for pushing earth, rubble etc., used in road construction etc. **3** (*NAm.*) a pupil at a particular grade (*in comb.*, as *seventh grader*). **grade school** *n.* (*N Am.*) primary school.

gradient (grā´diənt) *n.* **1** the rate of ascent or descent in a railway or road, degree of slope, inclination. **2** a stretch of sloping road, railway etc. **3** rate of variation or increase or decrease in height of thermometer or barometer over a large area or the diagrammatic line denoting such variation.

gradual (grad´ūəl, graj´əl) *a.* **1** regular and slow, as opposed to abrupt, steep, rapid. **2** proceeding by steps or degrees. ~*n.* **1** in church music, an antiphon sung between the reading of the Epistle and the Gospel. **2** a book containing such antiphons or the music for them. **gradualism** *n.* esp. regarding political policy, the principle of making change slowly and gradually rather than quickly or by violent means. **gradualist** *n.* **gradually** *adv.* **gradualness** *n.*

graduate¹ (grad´ūāt, graj´-) *v.i.* **1** to be awarded a first degree from a university. **2** to alter, change or pass by degrees. ~*v.t.* **1** to mark with degrees. **2** to divide into or arrange by gradations. **3** to apportion (a tax etc.) according to a scale of grades. **4** to temper or modify by degrees. **5** (*N Am.*) to confer an academic degree upon. **graduand** (-and) *n.* a person who is about to graduate from a university. **graduated pension** *n.* a system of pension contributions deducted from an employee's salary in proportion to their earnings. **graduation** (-ā´shən) *n.* **1** regular progression by successive degrees. **2** a division into degrees or parts. **3** the conferring or receiving of academical degrees. **graduator** *n.* an instrument for dividing lines into minute equal parts.

graduate² (grad´ūət, graj´-) *n.* a person who has received a degree from a university. **graduate school** *n.* a university department for advanced work by graduates.

Graeco- (grē´ko, grī´-), **Greco-** (grē´kō) *comb. form* Greek.

graffiti (grəfē´ti) *n.pl.* (*sing.* **graffito** (-tō)) **1** (*pl.*) drawings or words, sometimes obscene, sometimes political, painted or written on walls etc. in public view. **2** (*pl.*) drawings or inscriptions scratched on an ancient wall or other surface. **3** a piece of graffiti. **4** SGRAFFITO.

Usage note As a mass or collective noun *graffiti* can be either singular or plural (*Graffiti cover(s) the walls*), though the singular construction is less widely acceptable. As a countable noun it should always be a plural, however, with *graffito* as the singular.

graft¹ (grahft) *n.* **1** (*Bot.*) a small shoot of a tree or plant inserted into another tree of a different stock which supplies the sap to nourish it. **2** living tissue from a person or animal transplanted to another. **3** incorporation with a foreign stock. **4** (*coll.*) hard work, unremitting labour. ~*v.t.* **1** (*Bot.*) to insert (a shoot or scion) in or upon another plant or tree. **2** to insert grafts upon. **3** (*Bot.*) to plant (a tree or stock) thus with another variety. **4** to transplant (as living animal tissue). **5** to insert or implant (upon) so as to form a vital union. ~*v.i.* **1** (*Bot.*) to insert grafts or scions in or on other stocks. **2** (*coll.*) to work hard. **grafter**¹ *n.* **grafting clay, grafting wax** *n.* a composition used for covering grafted parts of plants and trees to exclude air.

graft² (grahft) *n.* **1** acquisition of money etc. by taking advantage of an official position. **2** manipulation of state or municipal business in order to secure illicit profits or influence. **3** illicit gains so obtained. **grafter**² *n.*

grafter[1] GRAFT[1].
grafter[2] GRAFT[2].
Grail (grāl) n. 1 a dish or cup said to have been used by Christ at the Last Supper, and employed by Joseph of Arimathea to collect Christ's blood while on the cross. 2 the object of a quest.
grain (grān) n. 1 a single seed of a plant, particularly of food plants. 2 corn in general, the fruit of cereal plants, such as wheat, barley, rye etc. 3 (N Am.) wheat. 4 (pl.) the husks or refuse of malt after brewing or of any grain after distillation. 5 any small, hard particle. 6 the smallest particle or amount. 7 the smallest unit of weight in the troy and avoirdupois system, approx. equivalent to 0.0648 grams. 8 in photography, any one of the particles in a photographic emulsion of a film or plate the size of which limits the extent to which the projected image can be enlarged. 9 granular texture, degree of roughness or smoothness of surface. 10 the lines of fibre in wood or, in stone, of cleavage planes, forming a pattern. 11 temper, disposition, natural tendency. ~v.t. 1 to form into grains, to granulate. 2 to treat so as to bring out the natural grain. 3 to paint or stain in imitation of this. 4 to give a granular surface to. 5 to scrape the hair off (hides) with a grainer. ~v.i. to form grains, to become granulated. **against the grain** contrary to inclination, reluctantly, with aversion. **in grain** downright, thorough, absolute, inveterate. **grained** a. **grainer** n. 1 a person who paints or stains in imitation of the grain of wood. 2 the brush that a grainer uses. 3 a tanner's knife. **grain leather** n. leather dressed with the grain side outwards. **grainless** a. **grain side** n. the side (of leather) from which the hair has been removed. **grains of Paradise** n.pl. the seeds of Aframomum melegueta, a tropical W African spice, used in stimulants, diuretics and spirituous liquors. **grain whisky** n. a whisky made using other cereals in addition to malted barley, as distinct from malt whisky. **grainy** a. (comp. **grainier**, superl. **grainiest**) 1 granular in composition or appearance, esp. in a photographic image or television picture. 2 resembling the grain of wood. **graininess** n.
grallatorial (gralətaw´riəl) a. (Zool.) of or relating to long-legged wading birds such as storks, flamingoes etc.
gram (gram), **gramme** n. the standard unit of mass in the metric system, defined as the mass of one cubic centimetre of distilled water at its maximum density weight equalling a thousandth of a kilogram (about 0.04 oz.). **gram-equivalent** n. (Chem.) the amount of a substance equal to its atomic or molecular weight in grams.
-gram (gram) comb. form forming compounds with prepositional prefixes, numerals etc., to denote something written, as in epigram, monogram, anagram.
graminaceous (graminā´shəs), **gramineous** (-min´-) a. of or relating to grass or the tribe of grasses. **graminivorous** (graminiv´ərəs) a. feeding on grass.
grammar (gram´ə) n. 1 a system of principles and rules for speaking and writing a language. 2 a person's manner of applying these rules, or speech or writing considered with regard to its correctness (His grammar is awful!). 3 the study of the way a language shows the relationship between words, including its inflectional systems, syntax and phonology. 4 a book containing the principles and rules of grammar. 5 the elements of an art or science, a treatise on these. **grammarian** (-meə´ri-) n. an expert in grammar, esp. one who writes about or teaches grammar. **grammarless** a. **grammar school** n. a selective secondary school with a mainly academic curriculum. **grammatical** (-mat´ikəl), †**grammatic** a. 1 of or relating to grammar. 2 according to the rules of grammar. **grammatically** adv. **grammaticalness** n.
gramme GRAM.
gramophone (gram´əfōn) n. (dated) a recordplayer.
grampus (gram´pəs) n. (pl. **grampuses**) 1 the dolphin Grampus griseus, characterized by a blunt snout and pointed black flippers. 2 the killer whale. 3 (coll.) a person who breathes heavily and loudly.
gran (gran) n. (coll.) grandmother.
granadilla GRENADILLA.
granary (gran´əri) n. (pl. **granaries**) 1 a storehouse for grain. 2 a country or district producing and exporting an abundance of corn. **granary bread** n. brown bread containing whole grains of wheat.
grand (grand) a. 1 great or imposing in size, character or appearance. 2 magnificent, fine, splendid. 3 dignified, lofty, noble. 4 (coll.) highly satisfactory, excellent. 5 morally impressive, inspiring (a grand gesture). 6 (Mus.) great, of full compass, for full orchestra, or with all accessory parts and movements. 7 (coll.) distinguished, fashionable or aristocratic (society). 8 pre-eminent in rank etc., chief (Grand Master). 9 (Law) principal, as opposed to petty, common etc. (grand larceny). 10 main, comprehensive, complete, final (grand total). 11 in the second degree (of relationships) (grandmother, grandchild). ~n. (sl.) 1,000 dollars or pounds. **grand-dad** (gran´dad), **granddad, grandaddy** n. (coll.) grandfather. **grandchild** (gran´chīld) n. (pl. **grandchildren**) the child of a son or daughter. **granddaughter** (gran´daw-) n. the daughter of a son or daughter. **grand duke, grand duchess** n. a sovereign of lower rank than a king, the ruler in certain European states. **grand ducal** a. **grand duchy** n. a state, province etc. ruled by a grand duke or duchess. **grandfather** n. the father of a parent. **grandfather clock** n. an old-fashioned clock worked by weights, in a tall wooden case. **grandfatherly** a. **grand jury** n. (Law) a jury whose duty is to enquire if there is sufficient ground

for a prisoner to be tried by a petty or ordinary jury. **grandly** *adv.* **grandma** (gran´mah), (*dated*) **grandmama** (-məmah) *n.* (*coll.*) grandmother. **grand master** *n.* **1** in chess or bridge, an outstanding player, winner of many international tournaments, competitions etc. **2** the head of a military order of knighthood, the head of the Freemasons, Good Templars etc. **grandmother** *n.* the mother of a parent. **to teach one's grandmother to suck eggs** to seek presumptuously to advise a more experienced or knowledgeable person. **grandmother clock** *n.* a clock similar to but slightly smaller than a grandfather clock. **grandmotherly** *a.* **grandness** *n.* **grand opera** *n.* an opera with a serious plot that is sung throughout, as opposed to comic opera. **grandpa** (gram´pah, gran´-), (*dated*) **grandpapa** (-pəpah), **grandpappy** (-papi) *n.* (*coll.*) grandfather. **grandparent** *n.* a grandfather or grandmother. **grand piano** *n.* a large piano with horizontal framing. **grandsire** *n.* **1** a grandfather. **2** an animal's sire's sire. **3** a male ancestor. **4** in bell-ringing, a method of change-ringing. **grand slam** *n.* **1** in auction bridge, the winning of 13 tricks by a side. **2** in contract bridge, a fulfilled contract to take all 13 tricks. **3** in tennis, golf etc., the winning of all the major competitions in a season. **4** in baseball, a home run hit when all three bases are occupied by members of the batting team allowing all of them to score. **grandson** *n.* the son of a son or daughter. **grandstand** *n.* the principal stand for spectators on a racecourse etc. **grandstand finish** *n.* a close and exciting finish in a sporting contest. **grand total** *n.* the total of all subordinate sums. **grand tour** *n.* **1** a tour through the countries of continental Europe, esp. as formerly undertaken as an essential part of the education of young people of wealthy families. **2** any extended esp. educational sightseeing tour. **grand unified theory** *n.* (*Physics*) any of several theories attempting to give a single mathematical formalism to the electromagnetic, strong and weak interactions of elementary particles.

grandee (grandē´) *n.* **1** a Spanish or Portuguese nobleman of the highest rank. **2** a person of high rank or power.

grandeur (gran´dyə) *n.* **1** the quality of being grand. **2** greatness, nobility, impressiveness, sublimity, majesty. **3** splendour, magnificence, dignity, splendid or magnificent appearance or effect.

grandiflora (grandiflaw´rə) *a.* (of a plant etc.) bearing large flowers.

grandiloquent (grandil´əkwənt) *a.* **1** using lofty or pompous language. **2** bombastic. **grandiloquence** *n.* **grandiloquently** *adv.*

grandiose (gran´diōs) *a.* **1** imposing, impressive, producing the effect of grandeur. **2** intended to produce the effect of grandeur, affecting impressiveness, pompous. **3** great in style or scale. **grandiosely** *adv.* **grandiosity** (-os´-) *n.*

grand mal (grã mal´) *n.* a major epileptic attack, as opposed to *petit mal.*

Grand Prix (grã prē´) *n.* (*pl.* **Grands Prix** (grã prē´)) **1** any of several international motor or motorcycle races taking place annually in locations round the world. **2** any of various other major international competitive events, e.g. in horse racing.

grange (grānj) *n.* a farmhouse with the outbuildings etc., esp. if occupied as a country residence.

graniferous (grənif´ərəs) *a.* bearing grain or seed of grainlike form. **graniform** (gran´ifawm) *a.* **granivorous** (-niv´-) *a.* feeding on grain.

granite (gran´it) *n.* **1** a granular, igneous rock consisting of feldspar, quartz and mica, confusedly crystallized. **2** the personal quality of endurance, determination, toughness etc. **granite ware** *n.* an enamelled ironware or hard pottery with speckled surface resembling granite. **granitic** (-nit´-), **granitoid** *a.*

granny (gran´i), **grannie** *n.* (*pl.* **grannies**) a grandmother. **granny flat, granny annexe** *n.* a self-contained flat added to or part of a house, designed to accommodate an elderly relative. **granny-knot, granny's bend** *n.* a badly-tied reefknot having the tie crossed the wrong way. **Granny Smith** *n.* a green-skinned apple suitable for cooking or eating.

grant (grahnt) *v.t.* **1** to bestow, concede or give, esp. in answer to a request. **2** to allow as a favour or indulgence. **3** (*Law*) to transfer the title to, to confer or bestow (a privilege, charter etc.). **4** to admit as true, to concede or allow (as premises to an argument). ~*n.* **1** a sum of money bestowed or allowed. **2** a gift, an assignment, a formal bestowal. **3** the act of granting. **4** the thing granted. **5** a concession or admission of something as true. **6** (*Law*) a conveyance in writing. **7** the thing conveyed. **to take for granted 1** to assume as admitted basis of an argument. **2** to cease to show appreciation for another's help, work etc. due to familiarity. **grantable** *a.* **grant aid, grant-in-aid** *n.* a central government grant to a local government authority or to an institution. **grant-aid** *v.t.* **grantee** (-tē´) *n.* (*Law*) the person to whom a grant or conveyance is made. **granter** *n.* a person who grants (a wish etc.). **grant-maintained** *a.* (of a school) self-governing and funded by central government as opposed to local authority. **grantor** *n.* (*Law*) a person who makes a conveyance.

granule (gran´ūl) *n.* **1** a little grain. **2** a small particle. **granular** *a.* composed of or resembling granules. **granularity** (-lar´-) *n.* **granularly** *adv.* **granulate** (-lāt) *v.t.* **1** to form into granules or small particles. **2** to make rough on the surface. ~*v.i.* to collect or be formed into grains. **granulation** (-ā´shən) *n.* **granulator** *n.*

grape (grāp) *n.* **1** a berry, the fruit of the vine. **2** grapeshot. **3** (*pl.*) a tumour shaped like a bunch of grapes, on the legs of horses. **the grape** (*coll.*) wine. **grapefruit** *n.* (*pl.* **grapefruit**) **1** a large

graph 552 **grasshopper**

round yellow citrus fruit, growing in bunches. **2** the tree, *Citrus paradisi*, which bears this fruit. **grape hyacinth** *n.* a bulbous plant belonging to the genus *Muscari* with usu. blue flowers. **grapeseed** *n.* the seed of the vine. **grapeseed oil** *n.* the oil pressed from grapeseeds, used in cooking. **grapeshot** *n.* (*Hist.*) small balls for a cannon, loaded in tiers so as to scatter when fired. **grapestone** *n.* a pip or seed of the grape. **grape-sugar** *n.* dextrose. **grapevine** *n.* **1** any vine of the genus *Vitis*, esp. *V. vinifera.* **2** (*coll.*) ill-defined unofficial sources of intelligence by which news, rumour etc. is conveyed. **grapey, grapy** *a.* made of or like grapes.

graph (grahf, graf) *n.* (*Math.*) a diagram representing a mathematical or chemical relationship and based on two graduated scales. ~*v.t.* to plot on a graph. **graphical** (-ikəl) *a.* **1** in the form of a graph or graphs. **2** indicating by means of diagrams etc. instead of numbers, statistics etc. **3** graphic. **graph paper** *n.* squared paper used for drawing graphs, diagrams etc.

-graph (grahf, graf) *comb. form* written, writing, writer, as in *autograph, lithograph, seismograph, tachograph.* **-grapher** (grəfə) *comb. form* a person versed in a particular science, technique etc.

graphic (graf'ik) *a.* **1** of or relating to the art of writing, delineating, engraving, painting etc. **2** well delineated (*graphic art*). **3** vividly or forcibly descriptive (*graphic detail*). **4** having the faculty of vivid description. ~*n.* **1** a product of delineating etc. **2** (*pl.*) the art of drawing, esp. in mathematics, engineering etc. **3** (*pl.*) the production of designs and images by computer. **4** (*pl.*) designs produced in this way. **-graphic, -graphical** *comb. form* forming adjectives. **graphically** *adv.* **graphicalness, graphicness** *n.* **graphic arts** *n.pl.* the visual and technical arts, such as drawing, printing, design etc. **graphic artist** *n.* **graphic equalizer** *n.* an electronic device for adjusting the output of various sound frequencies from a tape player, CD or similar source. **graphic novel** *n.* an adult novel presented in comic strip format.

graphite (graf'īt) *n.* a form of carbon used in pencils, as a lubricant and in nuclear reactors, blacklead, plumbago. **graphitic** (-fit'-) *a.*

graphology (grəfol'əji) *n.* **1** the study of handwriting. **2** the art of inferring character from handwriting. **3** graphic formulae or notation. **graphologic** (grafəloj'-), **graphological** *a.* **graphologist** *n.*

-graphy (grəfi) *comb. form* **1** denoting a particular style of writing, drawing etc., as in *lithography.* **2** denoting a particular area of study, writing etc., as in *geography.*

grapnel (grap'nəl) *n.* **1** an instrument with several flukes or claws for seizing, grasping or lifting. **2** an anchor with flukes for mooring boats, balloons etc.

grapple (grap'əl) *v.i.* **1** to contend or struggle (with or together) in close fight. **2** to get to close quarters (with a task, subject etc.) and strive to accomplish etc. ~*v.t.* **1** to lay fast hold of, to seize, to clutch. **2** to come to close quarters with. ~*n.* **1** a grappling iron. **2** a grapnel or similar clutching device. **3** a close hold or grip in wrestling or other contest. **4** a close struggle. **grappler** *n.* **grappling iron, grappling hook** *n.* an iron instrument with claws or hooks for seizing and holding fast.

grasp (grahsp) *v.t.* **1** to seize and hold fast. **2** to lay hold of and keep possession of, esp. with eagerness or greed. **3** to comprehend with the mind. ~*v.i.* **1** to clutch (at). **2** to attempt to lay hold. ~*n.* **1** a fast grip, clutch or hold. **2** ability to seize and hold. **3** forcible possession, mastery. **4** intellectual comprehension. **graspable** *a.* **grasper** *n.* **grasping** *a.* greedy. **graspingly** *adv.* **graspingness** *n.*

grass (grahs) *n.* **1** the green-bladed herbage on which cattle, sheep etc. feed. **2** any plant of the family Gramineae, distinguished by simple, sheathing leaves, a stem usu. jointed and tubular, and flowers enclosed in glumes, including the cereals, reeds and bamboos, as well as the plants pop. known as grasses. **3** pasture, grazing. **4** (*coll.*) marijuana. **5** (*sl.*) an informer. **6** (*Mining*) the surface of the ground. **7** (*pl.*) heads or spires of grass flowers gathered. ~*v.t.* **1** to cover with grass or turf. **2** to bring to grass, to land (as a fish). **3** (*sl.*) to fall, to knock down. **4** to discharge. ~*v.i.* (*sl.*) to inform against. **to go out to grass 1** to go out to pasture. **2** to go out from work, on a holiday, into retirement etc. **to let the grass grow under one's feet** to waste time and so lose an opportunity. **to put out to grass** to send out to grass. **to send out to grass 1** to send out to pasture. **2** to send out from work, on a holiday, into retirement etc. **to turn out to grass** to send out to grass. **grass box** *n.* a container attached to a lawnmower to catch grass cuttings. **grasscloth** *n.* a fine soft Eastern fabric made from the fibres of the inner bark of *Boehmeria nivea.* **grass court** *n.* a tennis court with a surface of closely mown grass. **grassless** *a.* **grasslike** *a.* **grass parakeet** *n.* an Australian parakeet, esp. of the genus *Neophema*, commonly found in grassland. **grass roots** *n.pl.* **1** the ordinary people. **2** the basic essentials, foundation, origin. **grass skirt** *n.* a skirt made of long grass fastened to a waistband. **grass skis** *n.pl.* short skis with wheels or rollers for skiing on grassy slopes. **grass skiing** *n.* **grass snake** *n.* a harmless Eurasian snake, *Natrix natrix.* **grass widow, grass widower** *n.* a person whose husband or wife is away for a lengthy period. **grass-wrack** *n.* a seaweed belonging to the genus *Zostera*, also called *eelgrass.* **grassy** *a.* (*comp.* **grassier**, *superl.* **grassiest**) **1** covered with grass. **2** like grass. **3** green. **grassiness** *n.*

grasshopper (grahs'hopə) *n.* a grass-eating, chirping insect of the order Orthoptera, with hind legs formed for leaping. ~*a.* (of a person's mind etc.) constantly moving from subject to subject.

grate[1] (grāt) *n.* **1** a frame of iron bars for holding fuel for a fire. **2** the recess of a fireplace, boiler etc. **3** a grating.

grate[2] (grāt) *v.t.* **1** to rub against a rough surface so as to reduce to small particles. **2** to rub, as one thing against another, so as to cause a harsh sound. **3** to grind down. **4** to produce (as a hard, discordant sound) by the collision or friction of rough bodies. **5** to irritate, to vex, to offend (one's nerves). ~*v.i.* **1** to rub (upon) so as to emit a harsh, discordant noise. **2** to have an irritating effect (upon). **grater** *n.* a kitchen utensil with a rough surface for reducing a substance to small particles. **grating**[1] *a.* harsh, discordant, irritating. **gratingly** *adv.*

grateful (grāt´fəl) *a.* **1** thankful, marked by or indicative of gratitude. **2** pleasing, agreeable, acceptable, refreshing. **gratefully** *adv.* **gratefulness** *n.*

graticule (grat´ikūl) *n.* **1** a grid of intersecting lines in a telescope or other optical instrument to aid viewfinding or to measure the scale of the object viewed. **2** a grid of intersecting lines on which a map is drawn.

gratify (grat´ifī) *v.t.* (*3rd pers. sing. pres.* **gratifies,** *pres.p.* **gratifying,** *past, p.p.* **gratified**) **1** to please, to delight. **2** to humour, to satisfy the desire of. **3** to indulge, to give free rein to. **gratification** (-fikā´shən) *n.* **gratifier** *n.* **gratifying** *a.* **gratifyingly** *adv.*

gratin (grat´ĭ) *n.* **1** in cookery, a light crust on a dish, usu. made by browning breadcrumbs and cheese. **2** a dish prepared in this way with breadcrumbs and grated cheese.

grating[1] GRATE[2].

grating[2] (grā´ting) *n.* **1** an open framework or lattice of metal bars or wooden slats, parallel or crossed. **2** a series of parallel wires or lines ruled on glass or the like for producing spectra by diffraction.

gratis (grat´is) *adv., a.* for nothing, without charge, free.

gratitude (grat´itūd) *n.* thankfulness, appreciation of kindness.

gratuitous (grətū´itəs) *a.* **1** uncalled for, unnecessary. **2** without cause, motive or warrant. **3** granted without claim or charge. **4** free, voluntary. **gratuitously** *adv.* **gratuitousness** *n.*

gratuity (grətū´iti) *n.* (*pl.* **gratuities**) a gift, a present voluntarily given in return for a service, a tip.

graunch (grawnch) *v.i.* (*coll.*) to make a crunching, grating or grinding sound. ~*v.t.* to cause (something) to make this sound.

gravadlax GRAVLAX.

gravamen (grəvā´men) *n.* (*pl.* **gravamens, gravamina** (-minə) the most serious part of a charge.

grave[1] (grāv) *n.* **1** a hole in the earth for burying a dead body in. **2** a place of burial, a sepulchre. **3** a monument over this, a tomb. **4** mortality, death, destruction. **5** a place of destruction,

extinction, or abandonment. ~*v.t.* to form or shape by cutting or carving into a surface, to engrave. **to turn in one's grave** (of a dead person) to be (thought to be) shocked or distressed by some modern event. **gravedigger** *n.* **1** a person who digs graves. **2** an insect that buries dead insects etc., to feed its larvae. **graven** *a.* carved or inscribed. **graven image** *n.* an idol. **graver** *n.* an engraving tool, a burin. **gravestone** *n.* a stone, usu. inscribed, set over or at the head or foot of a grave. **graveyard** *n.* a burial ground.

grave[2] (grāv) *a.* **1** important, serious, momentous. **2** sedate, solemn, dignified. **3** sombre, plain, not gaudy. **grave accent** (grahv) *n.* a mark (`) placed over a vowel in some languages to indicate a change in pronunciation from that of the normal letter, originally to a lower pitch. **gravely** *adv.*

grave[3] (grāv) *v.t.* to clean (a ship's bottom) by scraping or burning, and (formerly) by covering it with pitch and tallow. **graving dock** *n.* a dry dock into which vessels are floated for this purpose.

gravel (grav´əl) *n.* **1** small water-worn stones or pebbles mixed with sand etc. **2** (*Geol.*) fragments of water-worn rock larger than sand, a stratum of this. **3** a bed of such material bearing gold. **4** (*Med.*) a disease characterized by the presence of minute concretions in the urine. ~*v.t.* (*pres.p.* **gravelling,** (*N Am.*) **graveling,** *past, p.p.* **gravelled,** (*N Am.*) **graveled**) **1** to cover, lay or strew with gravel. **2** to embarrass, to confound, to perplex. **gravelly** *a.* **1** of or like gravel. **2** (of a voice) deep and rough in sound.

gravid (grav´id) *a.* **1** (*Zool., formal*) pregnant. **2** (*Zool.*) containing a foetus.

gravimeter (grəvim´itə) *n.* an instrument for determining variations in gravity at different points of the earth's surface. **gravimetric** (-met´-) *a.* **gravimetrically** *adv.* **gravimetry** *n.*

gravitate (grav´itāt) *v.i.* **1** to be powerfully drawn (towards). **2** to be attracted, to tend (towards). **3** to be acted on by gravity. **4** to tend downwards, to sink, to settle down. **gravitation** (-tā´shən) *n.* **1** the act or process of gravitating. **2** the force of gravity. **gravitational** *a.* **gravitational constant** *n.* in Newton's law of gravitation, the factor (*G*) relating force to mass and distance. **gravitational field** *n.* the region around a body in space within which it exerts a gravitational pull. **gravitationally** *adv.*

gravity (grav´iti) *n.* **1** (*Physics*) the force causing bodies to tend towards the centre of the earth. **2** the degree of intensity of this force. **3** the similar tendency towards the centre of other bodies. **4** importance, seriousness, enormity. **5** solemnity, sedateness, sobriety, grave demeanour. **6** weight, heaviness. **gravity feed** *n.* a feed or supply in which the material (oil, grain etc.) runs downhill.

gravlax (grav´laks), **gravadlax** (grav´ədlaks) *n.* dry-cured salmon marinated in salt, sugar, herbs and spices, originally from Scandinavia.

gravure (grəvūə´) *n.* **1** (short for) photogravure. **2** an engraving.

gravy (grā´vi) *n.* **1** the fat and juice from meat during and after cooking. **2** a sauce made with this or other ingredients. **3** (*sl.*) money acquired with little effort. **gravy boat** *n.* a boat-shaped bowl or dish for holding gravy. **gravy train** *n.* (*sl.*) a job, course of action etc. requiring little effort in return for easy money, benefits etc.

gray GREY.

grayling (grā´ling) *n.* **1** any freshwater fish of the genus *Thymallus* with a large dorsal and an adipose fin. **2** any butterfly of the genus *Hipparchia*, esp. *H. semele*, which has grey or grey-brown wings.

graze¹ (grāz) *v.i.* **1** to eat growing grass. **2** (of land, fields etc.) to supply grass for grazing. **3** to feed, to browse. **4** to move along devouring. **5** (*coll.*) to eat snacks etc. standing up or moving around (as at a party, gathering etc.) rather than sitting down to a meal. ~*v.t.* **1** to feed (cattle, etc.) on growing grass. **2** to supply with pasturage. **3** to tend (cattle etc.) at pasture. **4** to pasture. **5** to feed on, to eat. **grazer** *n.* **grazing** *n.* **1** the act of pasturing or feeding on grass. **2** a pasture.

graze² (grāz) *v.t.* **1** to touch, rub or brush slightly in passing. **2** to scrape or abrade in rubbing past. ~*v.i.* to pass (along, by, past etc.) in light or momentary contact. ~*n.* **1** a slight abrasion. **2** a slight touch or rub in passing.

grazier (grā´ziə) *n.* **1** a person who pastures cattle, and rears and fattens them for market. **2** (*Austral.*) a large-scale cattle or sheep farmer. **graziery** *n.*

grease¹ (grēs) *n.* **1** oily or fatty matter of any kind. **2** animal fat in a melted or soft state. **grease gun** *n.* a syringe for injecting grease or oil into machinery. **greasepaint** *n.* a paste used for painting the face in theatrical make-up. **greaseproof paper** *n.* paper which will not allow grease to penetrate, used for wrapping food, lining tins etc. **greaser** *n.* **1** someone who or something that greases, a mechanic. **2** (*N Am., offensive*) a Mexican or Spanish-American.

grease² (grēs, -z) *v.t.* **1** to smear, lubricate or soil with grease. **2** to cause to go smoothly. **like greased lightning** (*coll.*) very quickly. **to grease someone's palm** (*coll.*) to bribe someone.

greasy (grē´zi, -si) *a.* (*comp.* **greasier**, *superl.* **greasiest**) **1** smeared, saturated or soiled with grease. **2** made of or like grease. **3** unctuous, oily, exuding grease. **4** slimy or slippery with something having the effect of grease. **5** gross, unpleasantly unctuous. **greasily** *adv.* **greasiness** *n.* **greasy pole** *n.* (*coll.*) a difficult route to success, with many potential pitfalls.

great (grāt) *a.* (*comp.* **greater**, *superl.* **greatest**) **1** large in bulk, number, amount, extent or degree. **2** very large, big, vast. **3** beyond the ordinary, extreme. **4** important, weighty, momentous, critical. **5** of the highest importance, capital (of letters), pre-eminent, the chief. **6** of exceptional ability, highly gifted, possessing genius. **7** (*coll.*) very skilful, experienced or knowing (at). **8** having lofty moral qualities, magnanimous, noble. **9** grand, majestic, sublime. **10** pregnant. **11** excessive, grievous, burdensome. **12** notorious. **13** denoting a step of ascending or descending consanguinity (*great-grandfather*). ~*n.* (*collect.*) great people (*the great*). **the great and the good** (*often iron.*) worthy and distinguished people. **to be great at** to be skilful at. **great ape** *n.* any of the larger apes, such as the gorilla, chimpanzee etc. **great auk** *n.* a flightless bird, *Alca impennis*, now extinct. **great-aunt** *n.* the sister of a grandfather or grandmother. **Great Bear** *n.* (*Astron.*) the constellation Ursa Major. **great circle** *n.* a circle on a sphere (such as the earth) formed by a plane passing through the centre of the sphere, representing the shortest distance between two points on the sphere. **great coat** *n.* an overcoat. **great crested grebe** *n.* a large Eurasian diving bird, *Podiceps cristatus*. **Great Dane** *n.* **1** a breed of large short-haired dog. **2** any dog of this breed. **Greater**, **greater** *a.* (of a city) used to describe the whole city including outer suburbs and adjacent urban areas. **Greater Bairam** *n.* the four-day Muslim festival which falls at the end of the Islamic year. **great-grandchild** *n.* (*pl.* **great-grandchildren**) a grandchild's son or daughter. **great-granddaughter** *n.* a grandchild's daughter. **great-grandfather** *n.* a grandparent's father. **great-grandmother** *n.* a grandparent's mother. **great-grandparent** *n.* a grandparent's parent. **great-grandson** *n.* a grandchild's son. **great-hearted** *a.* **1** high-spirited, magnanimous. **2** brave. **greatly** *adv.* **1** to a great degree, much, exceedingly. **2** nobly, magnanimously. **great majority** *n.* (*euphem.*) the dead. **great-nephew** *n.* the grandson of a brother or sister. **greatness** *n.* **great-niece** *n.* the granddaughter of a brother or sister. **great northern diver** *n.* a seabird, *Gavia immer*, of the northern hemisphere. **great organ** *n.* the principal manual of a large organ with its pipes and mechanism. **Great Russian** *n.* the Russian language. ~*a.* of or relating to the Russian people or their language. **great tit** *n.* a Eurasian bird, *Parus major*, with a black-and-white head and yellow underparts. **great toe** *n.* the big toe. **great-uncle** *n.* the brother of a grandfather or grandmother.

❌ **greatful** common misspelling of GRATEFUL.

greave (grēv) *n.* (*usu. pl.*) armour for the legs.

grebe (grēb) *n.* a diving bird of the family Podicipedidae with lobed feet and no tail.

Grecian (grē´shən) *a.* **1** of or relating to Greece. **2** in the Greek style, esp. in being classically simple in appearance. **Grecian nose** *n.* a straight nose continuing the line of the forehead.

Greco- GRAECO-.

greed (grēd) *n.* **1** avarice, insatiable desire or covetousness. **2** an inordinate desire for food or drink. **greedy** *a.* (*comp.* **greedier**, *superl.* **greediest**) **1** having an inordinate desire for food or drink, voracious, gluttonous. **2** eager to obtain, covetous, desirous (of). **greedily** *adv.* **greediness** *n.*

Greek (grēk) *n.* **1** a native or inhabitant of Greece. **2** a person of Greek descent. **3** the language of Greece. **4** something one does not understand (*It's all Greek to me*). *~a.* of or relating to Greece or its people. **Greek cross** *n.* an upright beam with a transverse beam of the same length, the shape of a + sign. **greeking** *n.* in desktop publishing, advertising etc., the representation of text by roughly drawn characters that have no meaning in themselves.

green (grēn) *a.* **1** having a colour like growing herbage, of the colour in the spectrum between blue and yellow. **2** unripe, immature. **3** undeveloped, inexperienced, easily imposed on. **4** fresh, not withered, not dried, seasoned, cured, dressed or tanned. **5** pale, sickly. *~n.* **1** the colour of growing herbage. **2** a colour composed of blue and yellow. **3** a green pigment or dye. **4** a grassy plot or piece of land (*village green*). **5** (*coll.*) a person who is concerned about environmental issues. **6** (*pl.*) fresh leaves or branches of trees. **7** (*pl.*) the young leaves and stems of plants of the cabbage kind, used for food. **8** vigour, youth, prime. *~v.i.* to become or grow green. *~v.t.* **1** to make green. **2** to make (urban areas) more attractive by the addition of trees, gardens and parks. **3** (*sl.*) to hoax. **green in one's eye** a sign that one is gullible. **greenback** *n.* **1** (*coll.*) a legal-tender banknote first issued by the US in 1862, the back being printed in green. **2** a note issued by any national bank in the US. **green belt** *n.* an area around a city in which building is restricted. **Green Beret** *n.* a commando, esp. in the US. **greenbottle** *n.* any fly of the genus *Lucilia*, esp. *L. sericata* which lays eggs on the skin of sheep. **green card** *n.* **1** an international car insurance document. **2** (*US*) a permit allowing foreign nationals to live and work in the US. **green cheese** *n.* **1** unripened cheese, whey cheese. **2** cheese coloured with sage. **green crop** *n.* a crop of fodder used in the green state. **green drake** *n.* the common mayfly. **green earth** *n.* a hydrous silicate of potassium, iron and other metals, glauconite. **greenery** *n.* green plants and trees, fresh green growth. **green-eyed** *a.* **1** having green eyes. **2** seeing things with jealous eyes. **the green-eyed monster** jealousy. **green fat** *n.* the green gelatinous part of the turtle, much esteemed by gourmets. **green fee**, (*N Am.*) **greens fee** *n.* the fee paid to play a round of golf, esp. by non-members of a golf club. **greenfeed** *n.* (*Austral., New Zeal.*) crop grown to be fed fresh to livestock, green crop. **greenfield** *a.* (of a building site, development area etc.) previously unbuilt, undeveloped. **greenfinch** *n.* a common British songbird, *Carduelis chloris*, with green and gold plumage. **green fingers** *n.pl.* skill at growing plants. **green-fingered** *a.* **greenfly** *n.* (*pl.* **greenfly, greenflies**) any of several small green

insects that are destructive to plants, esp. the green aphid. **greengrocer** *n.* a retailer of vegetables, fruit etc. **greengrocery** *n.* (*pl.* **greengroceries**). **greenhead** *n.* **1** any biting fly of the genus *Chrysops*. **2** an Australian stinging ant, *Chalcoponera metallica*. **greenheart** *n.* **1** a hardtimbered W Indian tree, *Ocotea rodiaei*. **2** the wood of this, used for dock gates, shipbuilding, fishing rods etc. **greenhorn** *n.* an inexperienced or foolish person. **greenhouse** *n.* a glasshouse for cultivating and preserving tender plants. **greenhouse effect** *n.* the increased temperature of the earth caused by its atmosphere acting as the glass of a greenhouse does due to high levels of carbon dioxide, ozone etc. **greenhouse gas** *n.* any of the gases, esp. carbon dioxide, whose emission causes the greenhouse effect. **greenie** (-ni) *n.* (*coll.*) a conservationist. **greening** *n.* **1** the act of becoming green. **2** greenness. **3** the planting of greenery in urban or desert areas. **4** a kind of apple which is green when ripe. **greenish** *a.* **greenishness** *n.* **greenkeeper**, (*N Am.*) **greenskeeper** *n.* the person in charge of a golf course. **green leek** *n.* any of several Australian parrots, green or mainly green in colour. **greenlet** *n.* the vireo, a small American songbird. **green light** *n.* a signal to proceed. **green linnet** *n.* GREENFINCH (under GREEN). **greenly** *adv.* **greenmail** *n.* a business tactic whereby a company buys a large number of shares in another company with the threat of a takeover, thereby forcing the threatened company to repurchase the shares at a higher price. **greenmailer** *n.* **green manuring** *n.* the cultivation and ploughing-in of a crop of vetch, rape etc. **green manure** *n.* **greenness** *n.* **Green Paper** *n.* a set of policy proposals issued by the government. **green pepper** *n.* the green unripe fruit of the sweet pepper, *Capsicum annuum*, eaten raw or cooked. **green plover** *n.* a lapwing. **green pound** *n.* an agreed exchange rate for certain agricultural produce within the European Union. **green revolution** *n.* **1** agricultural advances in developing countries based on fertilizers, pesticides etc. **2** the rise in concern for the environment in industrialized countries. **green room** *n.* a room in which actors or musicians wait before or during the performance. **greensand** *n.* two series of beds of sandstone (largely consisting of green earth or glauconite) called the Upper and Lower greensand, in the Cretaceous series. **greenshank** *n.* a large sandpiper, *Tringa nebularia*, breeding in northern Eurasia. **green shoots** *n.pl.* evidence of growth or renewal, used esp. in describing economic recovery. **greensickness** *n.* chlorosis, severe anaemia. **greensick** *a.* **greenskeeper** GREENKEEPER (under GREEN). **green-stick fracture** *n.* a form of fracture to which children are very liable, in which one side of the bone is broken and the other merely bent. **greenstone** *n.* **1** a greenish igneous rock consisting of a crystalline granular mixture of feldspar and hornblende. **2** a kind of jade. **greenstuff** n. green vegetables for culinary use. **greensward** n. (formal) turf covered with grass. **green tea** n. tea prepared by drying leaves with steam, as opposed to fermenting them. **green thumb** n. GREEN FINGERS (under GREEN). **greenweed** n. DYER'S GREENWEED (under DYE). **greenwood** n. a wood in summer. ~a. of or relating to a greenwood. **green woodpecker** n. the green and yellow European woodpecker *Picus viridis*, with a red crown. **greeny** a. (comp. **greenier**, superl. **greeniest**).

greengage (grēn´gāj) n. a green, sweet variety of plum, *Prunus domestica italica*.

Greenwich Mean Time (grin´ij, gren´ich) n. mean time for the meridian of Greenwich, adopted as the standard time in Great Britain and several other countries.

greet¹ (grēt) v.t. **1** to address with a salutation at meeting. **2** to receive at meeting or on arrival (with speech, gesture etc.). **3** to receive (*The news was greeted with applause*). ~v.i. to exchange greetings. **greeting** n. **1** the act of saluting or welcoming. **2** a salutation, a welcome. **greetings card**, **greeting card** n. a decorative card conveying congratulations, good wishes etc.

greet² (grēt) v.i. (chiefly Sc.) to weep, to cry, to lament.

gregarious (grigeə´riəs) a. **1** tending to associate with others, sociable. **2** living or going in flocks, herds etc. **3** growing in clusters or in association with others. **gregariously** adv. **gregariousness** n.

Gregorian (grigaw´riən) a. of, relating to, produced or established by Gregory. **Gregorian calendar** n. the reformed calendar introduced by Pope Gregory XIII in 1582. **Gregorian chant** n. plainsong, choral music arranged by Gregory I, Pope 590–604.

☒ **greive** common misspelling of GRIEVE.

gremlin (grem´lin) n. **1** (sl.) an imaginary mischievous sprite, jokingly held to be responsible for problems in mechanical, electronic equipment, systems etc. **2** any source of mischief.

grenade (grənād´) n. **1** a small explosive shell thrown by hand (also known as a *hand grenade*) or fired from a rifle. **2** a glass shell containing chemicals for extinguishing fires, discovering leakages in drains etc.

grenadier (grenədiə´) n. **1** (pl.) (**Grenadiers**) the Grenadier Guards, the first regiment of the royal household infantry. **2** any deep-sea fish of the family Macrouridae, with a large head and body and a long tapering tail. **3** †a foot soldier armed with grenades.

grenadilla (grenədil´ə), **granadilla** (gran-) n. **1** any of various species of passion flower, *Passiflora*. **2** its edible fruit.

grew GROW.

grey (grā), (N Am.) **gray** a. **1** of a colour between white and black, ash-coloured. **2** dull, clouded, dim. **3** dark, dismal, depressing. **4** having grey hair. **5** old, aged, of or relating to old age, ancient. **6** (coll.) nondescript, lacking in charisma. ~n. **1** a grey colour, grey pigment. **2** grey light, twilight, cold, sunless light. **3** grey clothes. **4** a grey or white animal, esp. a horse. ~v.t. to make grey. ~v.i. to become grey. **grey area** n. an issue or situation that is not clear-cut. **greybeard** n. **1** an old man. **2** a large earthen jar for spirit. ~a. having a grey beard. **grey-bearded** a. **grey eminence** n. ÉMINENCE GRISE. **Grey Friar** n. a Franciscan friar. **grey goose** n. (pl. **grey geese**) any grey-coloured goose of the genus *Anser*, esp. the greylag. **greyhen** n. the female of the black grouse. **greyish** a. **greylag** n. the European wild goose, *Anser anser*, the original of the domestic goose. **greyly** adv. **grey market** n. the unofficial, but not necessarily illegal, selling of products, alongside selling on the official market. **grey matter** n. **1** (coll.) intellect, intelligence. **2** the greyish tissue of the brain and spinal cord containing the nerve cells. **grey mullet** n. any food fish of the family Mugilidae, found near coasts. **greyness** n. **grey seal** n. the large N Atlantic seal, *Halichoerus grypus*. **grey squirrel** n. the squirrel *Sciurus carolinensis*, introduced to Europe from N America in the 19th cent.

greyhound (grā´hownd) n. a variety of dog characterized by its tall slender form, keen sight, and swiftness. **greyhound racing** n. the sport of racing greyhounds on an oval track in pursuit of an electrically-propelled dummy hare.

grid (grid) n. **1** a grating of parallel bars. **2** a system of intersecting horizontal and vertical lines on a map, plan etc., used to identify locations. **3** a system of principal routes for the transmission of power, supply of gas etc. **4** an electrode placed in a thermionic tube between two other electrodes for the purpose of controlling the flow of current between them. **5** in motor racing, a system of markings on the track to indicate starting positions. **grid bias** n. voltage applied to the grid of a valve.

griddle (grid´əl) n. **1** a heated metal plate for cooking, usu. commercially, eggs, burgers etc. **2** a circular iron plate for baking cakes. **3** (*Mining*) a wire-bottomed sieve or screen. ~v.t. (*Mining*) to screen with a griddle.

gridiron (grid´īən) n. **1** a grated iron utensil for broiling fish, meat etc. **2** a framework of parallel timbers or iron beams for supporting a ship in dry dock. **3** in a theatre, a framework above the stage for supporting the apparatus for drop-scenes etc. **4** (*N Am.*) an American football field.

gridlock (grid´lok) n. a large-scale traffic jam where a whole area of intersecting roads is at a standstill. **gridlocked** a.

grief (grēf) n. **1** deep sorrow or mental distress due to loss, disaster or disappointment. **2** regret, sadness. **3** something which causes sorrow or sadness. **to come to grief 1** to meet with disaster. **2** to fail. **3** to come to ruin. **griefless** a. **grieflessness** n. **grief-stricken** a. suffering great sorrow.

grievance (grē´vəns) n. **1** a cause for complaint. **2** a wrong, an injustice.

grieve (grēv) *v.t.* **1** to lament, to sorrow over. **2** to cause pain or sorrow to. **3** to annoy. ~*v.i.* to feel grief, to mourn, to sorrow. **grievingly** *adv.* **grievous** *a.* **1** causing grief or pain, hurtful, injurious. **2** hard to be borne, distressing, oppressive. **3** flagrant, atrocious, heinous. **grievous bodily harm** *n.* (*Law*) a serious injury to one person caused by another. **grievously** *adv.* **grievousness** *n.*

Usage note The word *grievous* is sometimes heard pronounced (grē´viəs), as though it were *grievious*, but this is best avoided.

griffin (grif´in), **griffon** (-ən), **gryphon** *n.* a fabulous creature, with the body and legs of a lion, the head and wings of an eagle and listening ears, emblematic of strength, agility and watchfulness. **griffin-like** *a.*

griffon[1] (grif´ən) *n.* a variety of dog like a terrier, with short, coarse hair.

griffon[2] (grif´ən), **griffon vulture** *n.* a vulture, *Gyps fulvus*, of Eurasia and N Africa.

grig (grig) *n.* **1** a sand eel or a young eel. **2** a cricket or grasshopper. **3** a lively or merry person.

grill[1] (gril) *v.t.* **1** to cook under a grill, broil on a gridiron. **2** (*coll.*) to interrogate severely. **3** to subject to extreme heat. ~*n.* **1** a device on a cooker which radiates heat. **2** a gridiron. **3** meat etc. grilled. **griller** *n.* **grill room** *n.* a room in a restaurant where meat etc. is grilled and served.

grill[2] GRILLE.

grille (gril), **grill** *n.* **1** an open grating, railing or screen of lattice-work, to enclose or shut a sacred or private place, or to fill an opening in a door etc. **2** a metal grid etc. allowing ventilation (*radiator grille*).

grilse (grils) *n.* a young salmon when it first returns from the sea, usu. in its second year.

grim (grim) *a.* (*comp.* **grimmer**, *superl.* **grimmest**) **1** stern, relentless, severe, unyielding. **2** of a forbidding aspect. **3** savage, cruel. **4** hideous, ghastly. **like grim death** tenaciously. **grimly** *adv.* **grimness** *n.*

grimace (grimās´, grim´əs) *n.* a distortion of the features, a wry face, expressing disgust, contempt, affectation etc. ~*v.i.* to make grimaces. **grimacer** *n.*

grime (grīm) *n.* **1** dirt, smut. **2** dirt deeply engrained. ~*v.t.* to dirty, to begrime. **grimy** *a.* (*comp.* **grimier**, *superl.* **grimiest**). **grimily** *adv.* **griminess** *n.*

grin (grin) *v.i.* (*pres.p.* **grinning**, *past*, *p.p.* **grinned**) **1** to show the teeth as in laughter, derision or pain. **2** to smile in a malicious, sickly or affected manner. ~*v.t.* to express by grinning. ~*n.* **1** the act of grinning. **2** a smile with the teeth showing. **to grin and bear it** to endure pain etc. with stoicism. **grinningly** *adv.*

grind (grīnd) *v.t.* (*past*, *p.p.* **ground** (grownd)) **1** to reduce to powder or fine particles by crushing and friction. **2** to produce (flour etc.) by this process. **3** to wear down, sharpen, smooth or polish by friction, esp. on a grindstone. **4** to grate. **5** to oppress with laws, taxes etc. **6** to work (a mill). **7** to turn the handle of (various appliances). **8** to study laboriously. ~*v.i.* **1** to perform the act of grinding. **2** to be rubbed together. **3** to be ground. **4** to grate, to rub gratingly. **5** to toil hard and distastefully. **6** to study laboriously. ~*n.* **1** the act or process of grinding. **2** hard and monotonous work (*the daily grind*). **3** hard study, esp. for an examination. **4** a turn at the handle of a machine or instrument. **to grind to a halt** to stop gradually, esp. because of a breakdown, failure etc. **grinder** *n.* **1** a person who or something that grinds. **2** a grinding machine. **3** a molar tooth, a tooth generally. **grindingly** *adv.* **grindstone** *n.* a flat circular stone, used for grinding tools. **to keep one's nose to the grindstone** to stick to one's work.

gringo (gring´gō) *n.* (*pl.* **gringos**) (*esp. N Am.*, *derog.*) an English-speaking foreigner.

grip (grip) *v.t.* (*pres.p.* **gripping**, *past*, *p.p.* **gripped**) **1** to seize hold of. **2** to grasp or hold tightly. **3** to hold the attention of. ~*v.i.* to take firm hold. ~*n.* **1** the act of seizing or holding firmly. **2** a firm grasp, a clutch. **3** the power of grasping. **4** a particular mode of clasping hands, holding a bat, club etc. **5** the part of a weapon, instrument etc. that is held in the hand. **6** a grasping or clutching part of a machine, a clutch. **7** a tool for gripping. **8** (*pl.*) on a film set or in the theatre, a person employed to carry equipment, shift scenery, props etc. **9** the power of holding the attention. **10** a suitcase, a hold-all, handgrip. **in the grip of** dominated by, affected by, esp. in a negative way. **to come to grips with** to deal with, tackle (a problem etc.). **to get a grip on oneself** to bring oneself under control, to discipline oneself. **to get to grips with** to come to grips with. **gripper** *n.* **gripping** *a.* having the power of holding the attention, absorbing, compelling. **grippy** *a.*

gripe (grīp) *v.i.* **1** to complain, esp. in a persistent, peevish way. **2** (of the stomach etc.) to be painful with colic. **3** (*Naut.*) (of a vessel) to come up too close to the wind against the helm as in sailing close-hauled. ~*v.t.* **1** to affect with severe spasmodic gastric or intestinal pain. **2** to seize and hold firmly. **3** to clutch, to pinch. ~*n.* **1** a complaint, esp. of a minor nature. **2** the act of complaining. **3** (*pl.*) severe, sporadic pains in the abdomen. **4** a grasp, a firm hold with the hands, a pinch, a squeeze. **5** (*Naut.*) a series of ropes, dead-eyes and hooks, fastened to ring-bolts in the deck, for securing boats. **griper** *n.* **gripe water** *n.* a solution given to a baby to ease the pain of colic. **gripingly** *adv.*

grisaille (grizāl´, -zī´) *n.* a style of painting or staining in grey monochrome, esp. on stained glass, representing solid bodies in relief, such as ornament of cornices etc.

grisly (griz´li) *a.* (*comp.* **grislier**, *superl.* **grisliest**) horrible, terrible, fearful, grim. **grisliness** *n.*

grist (grist) *n.* **1** corn to be ground. **2** malt for brewing or distilling. **grist to the mill** *n.* something advantageous or profitable.

gristle (gris'əl) *n.* cartilage, esp. when found in meat. **gristly** *a.*

grit (grit) *n.* **1** coarse rough particles such as sand or gravel. **2** gritstone, a compact sandstone of sharp siliceous grain. **3** (*coll.*) firmness, determination, pluck. *~v.i.* (*pres.p.* **gritting**, *past, p.p.* **gritted**) **1** to be ground together. **2** to give out a grating sound. *~v.t.* **1** to grind or grate (as the teeth). **2** to apply salt, grit etc. to (an icy road etc.). **gritstone** *n.* a coarse-grained sandstone. **gritter** *n.* a person who or machine which applies grit etc. to icy roads. **gritty** *a.* (*comp.* **grittier**, *superl.* **grittiest**). **grittily** *adv.* **grittiness** *n.*

grits (grits) *n.pl.* **1** (*NAm.*) coarsely-ground grain, esp. corn. **2** husked and granulated but unground meal, esp. coarse oatmeal.

grizzle[1] (griz'əl) *v.i.* (usu. of a child) to cry, complain etc. in a fretful way.

grizzle[2] (griz'əl) *n.* **1** a grey colour. **2** grey hair. **grizzled** *a.* **1** grey, grey-haired. **2** interspersed with grey. **grizzly** *a.* grey, greyish. *~n.* (*pl.* **grizzlies**) a grizzly bear. **grizzly bear** *n.* a N American bear, *Ursus horribilis*, of great size and strength.

groan (grōn) *v.i.* **1** to utter a deep moaning sound, as in pain or grief. **2** to be burdened. **3** to suffer hardship. *~v.t.* to utter with groans. *~n.* **1** a low moaning sound, as of someone in pain or sorrow. **2** such a sound simulated in derision or disapproval. **to groan inwardly** to feel disappointment etc. without expressing it. **groaner** *n.* **groaningly** *adv.*

groat (grōt) *n.* (*Hist.*) a small silver coin worth four old pence.

groats (grōts) *n.pl.* husked oats or wheat.

grocer (grō'sə) *n.* a dealer in food and miscellaneous household supplies. **grocery** *n.* (*pl.* **groceries**) **1** (*usu. pl.*) the food, provisions etc. sold by a grocer. **2** the grocer's trade or shop.

grockle (grok'əl) *n.* (*dial., coll., often derog.*) a tourist (as described by a resident of the host region).

grog (grog) *n.* **1** a mixture of rum and cold water, orig. issued in the Royal Navy. **2** (*Austral., coll.*) any esp. cheap alcoholic drink. **groggy** *a.* (*comp.* **groggier**, *superl.* **groggiest**) dazed, unsteady through illness, exhaustion, drink etc. **groggily** *adv.* **grogginess** *n.*

groin[1] (groin) *n.* **1** the hollow in the human body where the thigh and the trunk unite. **2** (*Archit.*) the edge formed by an intersection of vaults. **3** the fillet or moulding covering this. *~v.t.* **1** to form (a roof) into groins. **2** to furnish with groins.

groin[2] GROYNE.

grommet (grom'it), **grummet** (grŭm'-) *n.* **1** a ring or eyelet of metal, rubber or plastic designed to strengthen or protect the opening of a hole. **2** (*Med.*) a tube inserted in the ear to allow air to enter the middle ear.

groom (groom) *n.* **1** a person in charge of horses or a stable. **2** a bridegroom. **3** (*Mil.*) any of several officers in the royal household (*groom-in-waiting*). *~v.t.* **1** to tend or care for, esp. in a very careful way. **2** to prepare and train (a person).

groove (groov) *n.* **1** a channel, furrow or long hollow, esp. cut with a tool for something to fit into or work in. **2** natural course or events of one's life, a rut. **3** (*dated sl.*) an exalted state (*It's a groove!*). *~v.t.* to cut or form a groove or grooves in. *~v.i.* (*dated sl.*) to be delighted, pleased, satisfied etc. **groovy** *a.* (*comp.* **groovier**, *superl.* **grooviest**) **1** of a groove. **2** (*dated or facet., sl.*) up to date, excellent, very good, pleasant. **grooviness** *n.*

grope (grōp) *v.i.* **1** to search (after) something as in the dark, by feeling about with the hands. **2** to feel about with the hands. **3** to feel one's way. **4** to seek blindly. *~v.t.* **1** (*sl.*) to fondle for sexual gratification. **2** to seek out by feeling with the hands in the dark, or as a blind person. **groper**[1] *n.* **gropingly** *adv.*

groper[1] GROPE.

groper[2] GROUPER.

grosbeak (grōs'bēk) *n.* any of several finches and cardinals having thick bills and bright plumage.

grosgrain (grō'grān) *n.* a heavy ribbed silk, rayon etc. fabric or ribbon.

gros point (grō pwī') *n.* a stitch in embroidery covering two horizontal and two vertical threads, as distinct from *petit point*.

gross (grōs) *a.* **1** big, rank. **2** fat, bloated, overfed. **3** flagrant, glaring (*gross misconduct*). **4** total, not net (*gross income*). **5** coarse, indelicate, obscene. **6** lacking fineness, dense, thick, material. **7** dull, unrefined. **8** general, not specific. *~n.* **1** 12 dozen. **2** the sum total. **3** the main body, the mass. *~v.t.* to receive or produce as gross income etc. **by the gross** in gross. **in gross 1** in bulk, wholesale. **2** in a general way, on the whole. **to gross up** to convert (a net figure) to a gross figure (as net income to its pre-tax value). **gross domestic product** *n.* the total annual value of all goods and services produced domestically in a country. **grossly** *adv.* **gross national product** *n.* the total annual value of all goods and services produced in a country, including net investment incomes from foreign nations. **grossness** *n.* **gross ton** *n.* a unit measuring gross internal capacity, equivalent to 100 cu. ft. (2.83 m³). **gross weight** *n.* the weight of goods with their container included.

grot (grot) *n.* (*coll.*) rubbish, junk, dirt, filth. *~a.* dirty.

grotesque (grōtesk') *a.* **1** distorted, irregular, extravagant or fantastic in appearance. **2** ludicrous through these qualities, absurd, bizarre. *~n.* **1** a grotesque person or thing. **2** whimsically designed ornamentation consisting of figures of plants and animals of fanciful invention. **grotesquely** *adv.* **grotesqueness** *n.* **grotesquerie** (-kəri) *n.*

grotto (grot´ō) *n.* (*pl.* **grottoes, grottos**) **1** a small cave, esp. one that is picturesque. **2** an artificial cave or cave-like room decorated with rocks, shells and the like. **grottoed** *a.*

grotty (grot´i) *a.* (*comp.* **grottier,** *superl.* **grottiest**) (*coll.*) **1** unattractive. **2** dirty, filthy. **3** inferior, substandard. **grottily** *adv.* **grottiness** *n.*

grouch (growch) *v.i.* to grumble, to grouse. ~*n.* **1** a discontented mood. **2** an irritable and complaining person, a grumbler. **grouchy** *a.* (*comp.* **grouchier,** *superl.* **grouchiest**). **grouchily** *adv.* **grouchiness** *n.*

ground[1] (grownd) *n.* **1** the surface of the earth as distinct from the air or the heavens. **2** a floor, pavement or other supporting surface. **3** a region or tract of land. **4** (*pl.*) private enclosed land attached to a house. **5** an area of land designated for a special purpose (*sports ground, showground*). **6** the firm, solid earth. **7** the bottom of the sea. **8** the substratum, the base or foundation. **9** the background, the surface on which a picture or design is laid, the prevailing colour or tone. **10** the reason, motive, origin, cause. **11** (*pl.*) basis, valid reason, pretext, the first or fundamental principles. **12** the extent of an inquiry or survey, area, scope. **13** (*pl.*) sediment, dregs, esp. of coffee. **14** (*Geol.*) strata containing a mineral lode or coal-seam. ~*v.t.* **1** to set or place upon or in the ground. **2** to base or establish (on). **3** to instruct thoroughly (in) the elementary principles of. **4** to run (a ship) aground. **5** to prevent (an aeroplane) from taking to the air. **6** to withhold permission for (a person, esp. a young one) to go out socially, usu. as a punishment. ~*v.i.* (of a vessel) to strike the ground. **down to the ground 1** (*coll.*) thoroughly. **2** (*coll.*) in every respect. **on one's own ground** in familiar and comfortable circumstances, on one's own subject or terms. **on the ground** in practical conditions, the place of operations as distinct from a place where related administrative decisions are made. **to cut the ground from under someone/ someone's feet** (*coll.*) to anticipate someone's arguments or actions etc., and thereby render them meaningless or ineffective. **to gain ground** to advance, to meet with success, to prevail. **to get off the ground** (*coll.*) to make a start, esp. one that is successful. **to give ground** to give way, to retire, to yield. **to lose ground 1** to be driven back, to give way. **2** to lose advantage or credit. **3** to decline, to fall off. **groundage** *n.* dues paid for space occupied by a ship on a beach or in port. **ground ash** *n.* an ash sapling. **groundbait** *n.* bait thrown into the water to attract fish. **ground bass** *n.* (*Mus.*) a bass passage of a few bars constantly repeated, with a varied melody and harmony. **ground control** *n.* control of landing an aircraft or spacecraft by information transmitted from the ground. **ground cover** *n.* **1** low-growing plants and shrubs, esp. as used to cover a whole area. **2** air support for ground troops. **ground crew** *n.* the people who supervise an aircraft's

progress etc. from the ground. **grounded** *a.* **1** that has been grounded. **2** having a solid foundation to one's life, having strong roots. **grounder** *n.* (*esp. N Am.*) in sport, a ball that is hit or passed along the ground. **ground floor** *n.* the storey or rooms level with the exterior ground (in the US called the first floor). **ground frost** *n.* a ground temperature on grass of 0°C (32°F) or under. **groundhog** *n.* the American marmot, *Marmota monax*, the woodchuck. **grounding** *n.* instruction in the elements of a subject. **ground ivy** *n.* a labiate creeping plant, *Glechoma hederacea*, with purple-blue flowers. **groundless** *a.* without foundation, reason or warrant, baseless. **groundlessly** *adv.* **groundlessness** *n.* **groundling** *n.* **1** a creeping plant. **2** a fish that keeps at the bottom, esp. the loach and the gudgeon. **3** (*Hist.*) a spectator who stood on the floor of a theatre; one of the common people. **groundnut** *n.* **1** the peanut. **2** the American wild bean, *Apios tuberosa*, having an edible tuber. **3** the edible tuber of this. **ground plan** *n.* **1** a horizontal plan of a building at the ground level. **2** an outline or general plan of anything. **ground rent** *n.* rent paid by a leaseholder to the owner of the land built on. **ground rule** *n.* (*often pl.*) a basic rule of a game, procedure etc. **groundsheet** *n.* a waterproof sheet spread on the ground to give protection against dampness, esp. inside a tent. **groundskeeper** *n.* (*N Am.*) a groundsman. **groundsman** *n.* (*pl.* **groundsmen**) a person employed to look after a sports ground. **ground speed** *n.* the speed of an aircraft relative to the earth's surface. **ground squirrel** *n.* any burrowing rodent resembling a squirrel, esp. one of the genus *Spermophilus*. **ground staff** *n.* **1** the non-flying staff of an airport or airbase. **2** the people employed to maintain a sports ground. **ground state** *n.* (*Physics*) the lowest (or normal) energy state of an atom etc. **ground stroke** *n.* a stroke (as in tennis) made by hitting a ball that has bounced up off the ground. **groundswell** *n.* **1** a long, deep swell or rolling of the sea, caused by a past or distant storm or earthquake. **2** the increasingly apparent presence of an intangible phenomenon such as a public feeling or opinion. **groundwater** *n.* underground water consisting mainly of surface water that has seeped down. **groundwork** *n.* **1** preliminary work necessary before further work can be undertaken, a foundation or basis. **2** a fundamental principle. **ground zero** *n.* the point on the ground directly below a nuclear explosion in the air.

ground[2] (grownd) *a.* having been ground. **ground glass** *n.* glass with the surface ground to make it obscure.

ground[3] GRIND.

groundsel (grownd´səl) *n.* any plant of the genus *Senecio* with pinnatifid leaves and small yellow flowers, esp. the common weed, *S. vulgaris*, which is used for feeding cage birds.

group (groop) *n.* **1** the combination of several

figures or objects to form a single mass. **2** a number of persons or things stationed near each other, a cluster, an assemblage. **3** a number of persons or things classed together on account of certain resemblances. **4** (*Chem.*) a series of minerals agreeing essentially in chemical composition. **5** (*Geol.*) a series of rocks or strata deposited about the same period. **6** in the RAF, the highest subdivision of a command. ~*v.t.* **1** to form into or place in a group. **2** to put (an object) in close relation or contact (with). **3** to bring together so as to produce a harmonious whole or effect. ~*v.i.* to form or fall into a group. **groupage** *n.* **group captain** *n.* a commissioned rank in the RAF equivalent to that of colonel in the army. **group dynamics** *n.* (*Psych.*) **1** (*sing.*) the field of psychology concerned with the development and interaction of human groups. **2** (*pl.*) the interaction of people in groups. **groupie** *n.* (*sl.*) **1** a (usu. female) fan who travels with and is sexually available to the members of a pop group. **2** an enthusiast, follower etc. of a particular sport or activity. **group practice** *n.* a medical practice run by a partnership of general practitioners. **group therapy** *n.* in psychiatry, the treatment of a group of patients in regular sessions where problems are shared in group discussion. **groupware** *n.* (*Comput.*) computer software that enables collective working by several different users.

grouper (groo´pə), (*esp. Austral., New Zeal.*) **groper** (grō´-) *n.* any marine fish of the family Serranidae, characterized by heavy body, big head and large mouth.

grouse[1] (grows) *n.* (*pl.* **grouse**) **1** any gallinaceous game bird of the family Tetraonidae with a plump body and feet more or less feathered, esp. *Lagopus scoticus*, the red grouse, moor fowl or moor game, *Lyrurus tetrix*, the black game or heath fowl, *Tetrao urogallus*, the capercaillie, wood or great grouse, and *Lagopus mutus*, the ptarmigan or rock grouse. **2** the flesh of these, esp. of the red grouse.

grouse[2] (grows) *v.i.* to grumble. ~*n.* a grievance. **grouser** *n.*

grout (growt) *n.* a thin, coarse mortar to run into the joints of masonry and brickwork. ~*v.t.* to fill up with grout.

grove (grōv) *n.* **1** a small wood. **2** a cluster of trees shading an avenue or walk. **groves of Academe** *n.pl.* a university environment. **grovy** *a.*

grovel (grov´əl) *v.i.* (*pres.p.* **grovelling**, (*N Am.*) **groveling**, *past*, *p.p.* **grovelled**, (*N Am.*) **groveled**) **1** to make an abject apology. **2** to behave in an obsequious manner. **3** to lie or move with the body prostrate on the earth. **groveller** *n.* **grovellingly** *adv.*

grow (grō) *v.i.* (*past* **grew** (groo), *p.p.* **grown** (grōn)) **1** to increase in bulk by the assimilation of new matter into the living organism. **2** to develop. **3** to increase in number, degree, power etc. **4** to exist as a living thing. **5** to spring up, to be produced, to arise. **6** to pass into a certain

state. **7** to adhere. **8** to become rooted. ~*v.t.* to cultivate, to raise by cultivation, to produce. **to grow on one** to increase in one's estimation, to impress one more and more. **to grow out of 1** to issue from. **2** to develop or result from. **3** to become too big or mature for, outgrow. **to grow together** to become closely united, to become incorporated in each other. **to grow up 1** to arrive at manhood or womanhood. **2** to advance to full maturity. **3** to arise, to become prevalent or common. **4** to begin to behave sensibly. **Gro-bag**®, **growbag, growing bag** *n.* a large plastic bag, containing a growing medium (such as compost) in which seeds can be germinated and plants grown to full size. **growable** *a.* **grower** *n.* **1** a person who or something that grows. **2** a cultivator. **growing** *n.*, *a.* **growingly** *adv.* **growing pains** *n.pl.* **1** neuralgic pains in the limbs felt by young children (not in fact caused by growing). **2** (*coll.*) difficulties experienced in the early stages of a project, business etc. **grown** *a.* **grown-up** *a.* adult. ~*n.* an adult. **growth** (grōth) *n.* **1** the act or process of growing. **2** increase, development, in number, extent, bulk, stature etc. **3** cultivation of vegetable produce. **4** something which grows or is grown. **5** (*Med.*) an abnormal formation, such as a tumour. **6** a product, a result. **growth hormone** *n.* a substance which stimulates growth in plants, animals and human beings. **growth industry** *n.* a commercial activity that is growing rapidly. **growth ring** *n.* a concentric layer of new growth, esp. on a tree, representing a year's development. **growth stock** *n.* stock that is invested in for capital value rather than high income yield.

growl (growl) *v.i.* **1** to make a deep guttural sound as of anger. **2** to murmur. **3** to grumble. **4** to speak angrily or gruffly. **5** to rumble. ~*v.t.* to utter or express by a growl. ~*n.* **1** a deep guttural sound like that made by an angry dog. **2** a grumbling. **3** a complaint. **growler** *n.* **1** a person or animal that growls. **2** a grumbler. **3** a small iceberg. **growlery** *n.* (*pl.* **growleries**) a place to grumble in, a person's private room or den. **growlingly** *adv.*

groyne (groin), **groin** *n.* a structure of piles, concrete etc., acting as a breakwater on a foreshore, and causing sand and shingle to be retained.

grub (grŭb) *v.i.* (*pres.p.* **grubbing**, *past*, *p.p.* **grubbed**) **1** to dig by scratching or tearing up the ground superficially. **2** to search, to rummage. **3** to drudge, to toil, to do manual work. ~*v.t.* **1** to dig (up or out). **2** to clear (ground) of roots etc. **3** to find by searching. **4** (*sl.*) to provide with food. ~*n.* **1** the larva of an insect, esp. of bees and wasps, with a distinct head but no legs. **2** (*sl.*) food. **to grub along** (*coll.*) to plod or drudge along. **to grub up** to dig up by the roots. **grubber** *n.* **1** (*derog.*) a person who is excessively and demeaningly devoted to amassing wealth, votes etc. (*money-grubber*). **2** an instrument for stirring up the soil and clearing out weeds. **3** a machine to pull up stumps and roots. **grubbing** *a.*, *n.*

grubby a. (comp. **grubbier**, superl. **grubbiest**) 1 dirty, grimy. 2 full of grubs. **grubbily** adv. **grubbiness** n. **grub-screw** n. a small headless screw. **grubstake** n. provisions etc., given to a prospector in return for a share of the finds. ~v.i. (sl.) to supply food in return for a share of profit.

grudge (grŭj) v.t. 1 to feel discontent or envy at. 2 to give or take unwillingly or reluctantly. ~v.i. to be unwilling or reluctant. ~n. ill-will, a feeling of malice or malevolence. **grudger** n. **grudging** a. **grudgingly** adv.

gruel (groo´əl) n. semi-liquid food made by boiling oatmeal or other meal in water or milk. **gruelling**, (N Am.) **grueling** a. arduous, demanding, requiring fortitude. ~n. severe or harsh treatment or experience. **gruellingly** adv.

gruesome (groo´səm) a. frightful, horrible, repulsive. **gruesomely** adv. **gruesomeness** n.

gruff (grŭf) a. 1 of a rough, surly or harsh aspect. 2 sour, rough, harsh, hoarse-voiced. **gruffly** adv. **gruffness** n.

grumble (grŭm´bəl) v.i. 1 to murmur with discontent. 2 to complain in a surly or muttering tone. 3 to growl, to mutter, to rumble. ~v.t. to express or utter in a complaining manner. ~n. 1 the act of grumbling. 2 a complaint. **grumbler** n. **grumbling** a. causing intermittent discomfort or discontent (a grumbling appendix). **grumblingly** adv. **grumbly** a.

grumpy (grŭm´pi) a. (comp. **grumpier**, superl. **grumpiest**) surly, cross, peevish, ill-tempered. **grump** n. 1 a bad-tempered person. 2 (pl.) a fit of bad temper or sulkiness. **grumpily** adv. **grumpiness** n. **grumpish** a. **grumpishly** adv.

grunge (grŭnj) n. (orig. N Am., sl.) a style of rock music, fashion etc. emphasizing discordant, often ugly elements, the music being characterized by raucous, distorted guitar, the fashion by loose-fitting uncoordinated outfits. **grungy** (grŭn´ji) a. squalid, seedy.

grunt (grŭnt) v.i. 1 to make a deep guttural noise like a pig. 2 to grumble, to growl, to complain. ~v.t. to express or utter in a grunting manner. ~n. a deep guttural sound, as of a hog. **grunter** n. 1 a person or animal that grunts. 2 a hog. 3 any of several fishes that grunt when caught.

Gruyère (groo´yeə, grē´-) n. a Swiss or French cheese made from cows' milk, pale-coloured, firm and full of cavities.

gryphon GRIFFIN.

GT abbr. gran turismo, a touring car, usu. a fast sports car.

Gt abbr. Great.

GTi abbr. gran turismo injection, a GT car with fuel injection.

guacamole (gwahkəmō´li) n. a Mexican dish of mashed avocado, citrus juice and seasonings.

X **guage** common misspelling of GAUGE.

guanaco (gwənah´kō) n. (pl. **guanacos**) a wild mammal, Lama guanicoe, related to the llama and inhabiting the chain of the Andes to their most southerly point.

guano (gwah´nō) n. (pl. **guanos**) 1 a valuable manure, composed chiefly of the excrement of seabirds found esp. on islands off S America and in the Pacific. 2 an artificial manure, esp. fish manure. ~v.t. (3rd pers. sing. pres. **guanoes**, pres.p. **guanoing**, past, p.p. **guanoed**) to manure or fertilize with guano. **guanine** (-nēn) n. a white amorphous substance found in guano and in the liver and pancreas of animals.

Guarani (gwərah´nē) n. (pl. **Guarani, Guaranis**) 1 a member of a S American Indian people of Paraguay, S Brazil and Bolivia. 2 the language of this people. 3 (**guarani**) the chief monetary unit of Paraguay. ~a. of or relating to the Guarani or their language.

guarantee (garəntē´) n. 1 a formal promise to see an agreement, duty or liability fulfilled, esp. with regard to the quality etc. of a bought product. 2 any security, warranty or surety given. 3 guaranty. 4 a person who becomes surety for the performance of certain acts by another. ~v.t. 1 to undertake responsibility for the fulfilment of a promise, contract etc. 2 to pledge oneself or engage (that). 3 to become guarantor or surety for. 4 to assure the continuance or permanence of. 5 to undertake to secure (to another). 6 to assure or secure against or from risk or damage. **guarantor** n. a person who gives a guarantee or guaranty.

guaranty (gar´ənti) n. (pl. **guaranties**) 1 the act of guaranteeing, esp. an undertaking to be responsible for a debt or obligation of another person. 2 that which guarantees, that on which a guarantee or security is based.

guard (gahd) v.t. 1 to watch over, to protect, to defend (from or against). 2 to stand guard over, to prevent the escape of. 3 to secure the safety of. 4 to secure (against criticism etc.). ~v.i. to be cautious or take precautions (against). ~n. 1 defence, protection, a state of vigilance, watch against attack, surprise etc. 2 a person or body of people on guard. 3 a screen to prevent accident placed in front of a fireplace etc. 4 a contrivance to prevent injury, accident or loss. 5 a sentry, an escort. 6 a person in charge of a railway train or a coach. 7 a state, posture or act of defence, esp. in boxing, fencing, cricket etc. 8 (N Am.) a prison warder. 9 the part of a sword-hilt which protects the hand. **off guard** off one's guard. **off one's guard** unprepared for attack, surprise etc. **on guard** on one's guard. **on one's guard** prepared for attack, surprise etc. **to guard against** to take precautionary action to try to prevent (something happening). **to raise one's guard** to become vigilant against danger. **to stand guard** (of a sentry) to keep watch. **guard cell** n. (Bot.) either of the two cells that border the pore of a stoma and cause it to open and close. **guarded** a. (of a comment, remark etc.) cautious, avoiding commitment. **guardedly** adv. **guardedness** n. **guarder** n. **guardhouse, guardroom** n. a house or room for those on guard or for prisoners. **guardless** a.

guard rail *n.* **1** a rail to protect against falling off a deck etc. **2** a rail fixed inside the inner rail at curves, points etc., to prevent derailment. **guard ring** *n.* **1** a ring-shaped electrode used to counteract distortion of electric fields at the edges of other electrodes, esp. in a capacitor. **2** a ring that keeps another ring from slipping off the finger. **Guards** *n.pl.* household troops responsible for ceremonial duties and guarding the head of state. **Guardsman** *n.* (*pl.* **Guardsmen**) an officer or private in the Guards. **guard's van** *n.* a compartment or carriage usu. at the rear of a train for the use of the guard, caboose.

guardian (gah´diən) *n.* **1** a person who has the charge, care or custody of any person or thing. **2** a protector. **3** the superior of a Franciscan convent. **4** (*Law*) a person who has the charge, custody and supervision of a person not legally capable of managing their own affairs. *~a.* **1** guarding. **2** acting as a guardian or protector. **guardian angel** *n.* an angel or spirit supposed to be assigned to a person as guardian and protector. **guardianship** *n.*

guava (gwah´və) *n.* **1** the luscious fruit of various species of the tropical American myrtaceous genus *Psidium*, esp. *P. guajava*. **2** any of the trees on which they grow.

gubbins (gŭb´inz) *n.* (*coll.*) **1** a small device, gadget etc. **2** paraphernalia, odds and ends. **3** something of little value.

gubernatorial (gūbənətaw´riəl) *a.* of or relating to a governor, esp. of a US state.

gudgeon[1] (gŭj´ən) *n.* **1** a small freshwater fish, *Gobio gobio*, easily caught and largely used as bait. **2** a person who is easily taken in.

gudgeon[2] (gŭj´ən) *n.* **1** any of several types of pivot at the centre of a wheel, bell mechanism etc. **2** the tubular 'sleeve' part of a hinge into which a pin fits. **3** an eye or socket in which a rudder turns. **gudgeon pin** *n.* a metal pin that links the piston of an internal combustion engine to the little-end bearing of the connecting rod.

guelder rose (gel´də) *n.* a shrubby plant, *Viburnum opulus*, bearing ball-shaped bunches of white flowers, also called the *snowball tree*.

Guernsey (gœn´zi) *n.* (*pl.* **Guernseys**) **1** a Guernsey cow. **2** a close-fitting knitted or woven woollen sweater, usu. blue, originally worn by seamen. **3** (*Austral.*) a similar garment, sometimes sleeveless, worn by football players. **to get a guernsey 1** (*Austral.*) to be selected for a football team. **2** (*Austral., coll.*) to win approval, succeed. **Guernsey cow** *n.* a breed of dairy cattle originating from Guernsey.

guerrilla (gəril´ə), **guerilla** *n.* a member of a small independent fighting band carrying out irregular warfare, esp. against an army, and usu. politically motivated.

guess (ges) *v.t.* **1** to judge or estimate on imperfect grounds, to conjecture. **2** to imagine, to suppose on probable grounds, to divine (one to be). **3** to conjecture rightly. **4** (*N Am., coll.*) to suppose. **5** to believe. *~v.i.* **1** to form a conjecture, to judge at random. **2** to hazard a supposition (that). *~n.* **1** a conjecture. **2** an opinion, estimate or supposition based on imperfect grounds. **anybody's guess** anyone's guess. **anyone's guess** something that is difficult to determine or predict. **I guess** (*N Am., coll.*) I suppose so, I think it likely. **guessable** *a.* **guesser** *n.* **guessingly** *adv.* **guess-rope** *n.* GUEST-ROPE. **guesstimate**[1] (-timət), **guestimate** *n.* (*coll.*) an estimate made by guessing. **guesstimate**[2] (-āt), **guestimate** *v.t.* to estimate by guessing. **guesswork** *n.* **1** action or calculation based on guess. **2** procedure by guessing.

guest (gest) *n.* **1** a person invited by another to a meal, party etc. or to stay at their house. **2** a person who stays temporarily at a hotel, guest house etc. **3** an entertainer, actor etc. invited to perform in the show, film etc. of other people. **4** a parasitic animal or vegetable. *~v.i.* **1** to appear as a guest on a television or radio show etc. **2** to be a guest. **be my guest 1** please make use of the facilities available. **2** do whatever you wish. **guest house** *n.* a boarding house, a small hotel. **guest night** *n.* a night when visitors are entertained by a club etc. **guest of honour** *n.* the most important guest at a function.

guest-rope (gest´rōp), **guess-rope** (ges´-) *n.* **1** a hawser carried by a boat to a distant object for warping a vessel towards this. **2** a rope for making fast a boat to a ship.

guff (gŭf) *n.* (*coll.*) nonsense, humbug.

guffaw (gəfaw´) *n.* a burst of loud or coarse laughter. *~v.i.* to laugh loud or coarsely. *~v.t.* to say with such a laugh.

guide (gīd) *v.t.* **1** to direct, lead or conduct. **2** to rule, to regulate, to govern. **3** to direct the course of. **4** to be the object, motive or criterion of (action, opinion etc.). *~n.* **1** a person who leads another or points the way. **2** a leader, a conductor, esp. a person employed to conduct a party of tourists etc. **3** an adviser. **4** (**Guide**) a Girl Guide. **5** anything adopted as a sign or mark of direction or criterion of accuracy. **6** a guidebook. **7** a soldier acting as a pivot to regulate an evolution or alignment in a manoeuvre. **8** a ship by which a squadron or fleet regulate their movements. **9** a bar, rod, bearing surface or other device acting as indicator or regulating motion. **guidable** *a.* **guidance** *n.* **1** the act of guiding. **2** direction. **3** government. **guidebook** *n.* a book for tourists, describing places of interest, means of transit etc. **guided missile** *n.* a rocket- or jet-propelled projectile with a warhead, electronically guided to its target by remote control. **guide dog** *n.* a dog trained to lead a blind person. **Guide Guider** *n.* the adult leader of a company of Guides. **guideless** *a.* **guideline** *n.* **1** a statement setting out future policy, courses of action etc. **2** a line drawn as a guide for further drawing or writing. **guide-post** *n.* a finger-post to show the way, a signpost. **guider** *n.* **guide-rope** *n.* GUY[2].

guideway *n.* on a machine, a groove, track or frame directing the motion of a part.

guild (gild) *n.* a society or corporation belonging to the same class, trade or pursuit, combined for mutual aid and protection of interests. **guildhall** *n.* **1** a hall where a guild or corporation meets. **2** a town hall. **3** the hall where the corporation of a city meets. **guildsman** *n.* (*pl.* **guildsmen**). **guildswoman** *n.* (*pl.* **guildswomen**).

Usage note See note under GILD.

guilder (gil´də) *n.* the chief monetary unit of the Netherlands.

guile (gīl) *n.* deceit, craft, cunning. **guileful** *a.* **guilefully** *adv.* **guileless** *a.* **guilelessly** *adv.* **guilelessness** *n.*

guillemot (gil´imot) *n.* any swimming seabird of the genus *Uria* or *Cepphus*, with a short tail and pointed wings.

guillotine (gil´ətēn) *n.* **1** an apparatus for beheading a person at a stroke, consisting of an upright frame, down which a weighted blade slides in grooves. **2** a machine for cutting thicknesses of paper etc. **3** a surgical instrument for cutting tonsils etc. **4** in Parliament, the curtailment of debate by fixing beforehand the hours when parts of a bill must be voted on. ~*v.t.* **1** to execute by guillotine. **2** to cut with a guillotine.

guilt (gilt) *n.* **1** the state of having committed a crime or offence. **2** criminality, culpability. **3** the feeling that one is to blame. **guilt complex** *n.* a (real or imagined) obsessive feeling of guilt or responsibility. **guiltless** *a.* **1** free from guilt. **2** innocent. **3** having no knowledge (of), inexperienced. **guiltlessly** *adv.* **guiltlessness** *n.* **guilty** *a.* (*comp.* **guiltier**, *superl.* **guiltiest**) **1** (*Law*) having committed a crime. **2** criminal, culpable (of). **3** characterized by guilt (*a guilty expression*). **guiltily** *adv.* **guiltiness** *n.*

guimp GIMP¹.

guinea (gin´i) *n.* **1** (*Hist.*) a gold coin formerly current in Great Britain, coined 1663–1813, orig. of gold from Guinea, with the nominal value of 20s. (£1) until 1717, when this was fixed at 21s. **2** a sum of money equivalent to a guinea, £1.05. **guinea fowl, guinea hen** *n.* a gallinaceous bird of the family Numididae, esp. *Numida meleagris*, something like the turkey, of a dark grey colour with white spots, orig. from Africa. **guinea pig** *n.* **1** a small domesticated cavy, *Cavia porcellus*, native to Brazil. **2** a person or thing used as a subject for a medical or other experiment. **Guinea worm** *n.* a whitish or dark brown nematode worm, *Dracunculus medinensis*, parasitic in the skin of the human feet etc.

guipure (gipūə´) *n.* a lace without a ground or mesh, the pattern being held in place by threads.

guise (gīz) *n.* **1** external appearance. **2** semblance, pretence. **3** manner, way, fashion.

guitar (gitah´) *n.* a (usu. six-)stringed instrument, somewhat like the violin in shape, but larger, with frets stopped by one hand, the strings being plucked with the fingers of the other or with a plectrum. **guitarist** *n.*

Gujarati (goojərah´ti), **Gujerati** *n.* **1** the language of Gujarat in W India. **2** a native or inhabitant of Gujarat. ~*a.* of or relating to Gujarat or its language.

gulch (gŭlch) *n.* a deep ravine caused by the action of water. ~†*v.t.* to swallow greedily.

gulf (gŭlf) *n.* **1** an inlet of the sea, deeper and narrower proportionately than a bay. **2** a deep hollow, chasm or abyss. **3** a whirlpool, anything that swallows or engulfs. **4** a profound depth, as of the ocean. **5** an impassable difference between two opinions, negotiating positions etc. **gulfweed** *n.* SARGASSO.

gull (gŭl) *n.* **1** any long-winged, web-footed bird of the family Laridae, mostly marine in habitat. **2** a simpleton, a dupe. ~*v.t.* **1** to fool, to trick. **2** to impose upon. **gullery** *n.* (*pl.* **gulleries**) a breeding place for gulls.

gullet (gŭl´it) *n.* **1** the throat. **2** the oesophagus.

gullible (gŭl´ibəl) *a.* credulous, easily deceived. **gullibility** (-bil´-) *n.* **gullibly** *adv.*

gully (gŭl´i), **gulley** *n.* (*pl.* **gullies, gulleys**) **1** a channel or ravine worn by water. **2** a ditch, drain or gutter. **3** a gully-hole. **4** in cricket, (a fielder in) the position between slips and point. ~*v.t.* (*3rd pers. sing. pres.* **gullies**, *pres.p.* **gullying**, *past, p.p.* **gullied**) to wear a channel by water action. **gully-hole** *n.* **1** an opening into a drain at the side of a street. **2** a manhole.

gulp (gŭlp) *v.t.* to swallow (down) eagerly or in large draughts. ~*v.i.* to make a noise in swallowing or trying to swallow, to gasp or choke. ~*n.* **1** the act of gulping. **2** a large mouthful. **3** an effort to swallow, a catching or choking in the throat. **to gulp back** to keep back or suppress (esp. tears). **gulper** *n.* **gulpy** *a.*

gum¹ (gŭm) *n.* the fleshy tissue around the roots of the teeth. **gumboil** *n.* a boil or small abscess on the gums. **gummy¹** *a.* (*comp.* **gummier**, *superl.* **gummiest**) toothless. ~*n.* (*pl.* **gummies**) **1** (*Austral.*) a sheep that has lost its teeth. **2** a small shark, *Mustelus antarcticus*, found off coasts of Tasmania and Victoria. **gummily** *adv.* **gumshield** *n.* a pad worn by boxers etc. to protect the gum and teeth.

gum² (gŭm) *n.* **1** a sticky substance which exudes from certain trees, and hardens, but is more or less soluble in water, used for sticking things together. **2** a gum tree or other plant or tree exuding this. **3** (*coll.*) chewing gum. ~*v.t.* (*pres.p.* **gumming**, *past, p.p.* **gummed**) **1** to cover or stiffen with gum. **2** to fasten or stick (down, in, together, up) with or as with gum. ~*v.i.* **1** to exude gum. **2** (of an axle etc.) to become sticky or clogged with disuse, dirt etc. **to gum up the works** (*coll.*) to interfere with, spoil or delay something. **gum benjamin** *n.* BENZOIN. **gumboot** *n.* a rubber boot, either of a pair of wellingtons. **gumdrop** *n.* a gelatinous sweet containing gelatine or gum arabic. **gum-juniper** *n.* sandarac.

gummy[2] *a.* (*comp.* **gummier,** *superl.* **gummiest**) **1** sticky, viscous, adhesive. **2** productive of or covered with gum. **gumminess** *n.* **gum resin** *n.* a vegetable secretion consisting of a gum and a resin, e.g. gamboge. **gumshoe** *n.* **1** (*esp. N Am.*) a rubber overshoe, either of a pair of galoshes. **2** (*N Am.*, *coll.*) a policeman or detective. **gum tree** *n.* (*Austral.*) any of several species of eucalyptus. **to be up a gum tree** (*coll.*) to be cornered, in a fix, brought to bay. **gum turpentine** *n.* an oleoresin exuding naturally or from incisions in several coniferous trees, esp. the terebinth.

gumbo (gŭm′bō) *n.* (*pl.* **gumbos**) **1** the okra, *Abelmoschus esculentus.* **2** a soup or a dish made of young capsules of this, seasoned, stewed and served with melted butter.

gumma (gŭm′ə) *n.* (*pl.* **gummas, gummata** (-ətə)) (*Med.*) a tumour with gummy contents, usu. due to syphilis. **gummatous** *a.*

gummy[1] GUM[1].

gummy[2] GUM[2].

gumption (gŭmp′shən) *n.* common sense, practical shrewdness, acuteness, tact, capacity for getting on. **gumptious** *a.*

gun (gŭn) *n.* **1** a tubular weapon from which projectiles are shot by means of gunpowder or other explosive force, a cannon, musket, rifle or carbine. **2** a person with a gun, a member of a shooting party. ~*v.t.* (*pres.p.* **gunning,** *past, p.p.* **gunned**) to accelerate a vehicle rapidly. **to go great guns** to make vigorous and successful progress. **to gun for 1** (*coll.*) to seek to kill, harm or destroy. **2** to strive to obtain. **to jump the gun 1** to begin (a race) before the starting pistol has fired, to make a false start. **2** (*coll.*) to begin prematurely. **to stick to one's guns** to maintain an opinion in the face of opposition. **gunboat** *n.* (*Naut.*) a warship of small size carrying heavy guns, formerly armed with a single heavy gun. **gunboat diplomacy** *n.* the use of naval or military threats as part of international negotiations. **gun carriage** *n.* the apparatus upon which a cannon is mounted for service. **gun cotton** *n.* a highly explosive substance made by soaking cotton in nitric and sulphuric acids, and then carefully drying. **gun dog** *n.* a dog which is trained to locate and retrieve game. **gunfight** *n.* a fight using firearms. **gunfighter, gunslinger** *n.* (*esp. Hist.*, *N Am.*) a person known for their skill in fighting with firearms. **gunfire** *n.* the repeated firing of guns. **gunless** *a.* **gunlock** *n.* the mechanism by which the charge in a gun is exploded. **gunman** *n.* (*pl.* **gunmen**) an armed gangster. **gunmetal** *n.* **1** a dull blue-grey colour. **2** an alloy of copper and tin or zinc from which cannon were formerly cast. **gunner** *n.* **1** (*Mil.*) in the army, an artillery soldier, esp. a private. **2** (*Naut.*) in the navy, a warrant officer in charge of ordnance or ordnance stores. **3** in an aircraft crew, a member who operates a gun. **4** a person shooting game. **gunnery** *n.* **1** the art of managing heavy guns. **2** the firing of heavy guns. **gunplay** *n.* the use of

guns. **gunpoint** *n.* the muzzle of a gun. **at gunpoint** being under the threat of being shot. **gunpowder** *n.* **1** a mixture of saltpetre, carbon and sulphur, reduced to a fine powder, then granulated and dried, used as an explosive. **2** gunpowder tea. **gunpowder tea** *n.* a fine kind of green tea, each leaf of which is rolled up. **gunpower** *n.* the strength or number of available guns. **gunroom** *n.* **1** a room on one of the lower decks of a warship to accommodate junior officers. **2** a room where guns are stored. **gun-runner** *n.* a person who smuggles any kind of firearms into a country. **gun-running** *n.* **gunshot** *n.* **1** a shot fired from a gun. **2** the range of a gun (*within gunshot*). **gun-shy** *a.* (of a dog, horse etc.) frightened at the sound of firearms. **gun-site** *n.* a gun emplacement, usu. fortified. **gunslinger** *n.* GUNFIGHTER (under GUN). **gunsmith** *n.* a person who makes or repairs small firearms. **gunstock** *n.* the shaped block of wood to which the barrel of a gun is fixed.

gunge (gŭnj) *n.* (*coll.*) an unpleasant sticky substance, a dirty encrustation. **gungy** *a.*

gung-ho (gŭnghō′) *a.* **1** uninhibited, over-eager. **2** enthusiastic.

gunk (gŭngk) *n.* (*coll.*) an unpleasant sticky or slimy substance, gunge.

gunnel GUNWALE.

gunny (gŭn′i) *n.* (*pl.* **gunnies**) **1** a heavy coarse sackcloth, usu. of jute or hemp, of which bags etc. are made. **2** a bag made of this.

gunwale (gŭn′əl), **gunnel** *n.* the upper edge of a ship's side next to the bulwarks.

guppy (gŭp′i) *n.* (*pl.* **guppies**) a small brightly-coloured W Indian freshwater fish, now a common aquarium fish.

gurdwara (guə′dwahrə, gœdwah′rə) *n.* a Sikh temple.

gurgle (gœ′gəl) *v.i.* **1** to make a bubbling sound, as water poured from a bottle or running over a stony stream bottom. **2** to run or flow with such a sound. ~*v.t.* to utter with such a sound. ~*n.* a gurgling sound.

Gurkha (gœ′kə) *n.* **1** a member of the dominant ethnic group in Nepal, of Hindu descent, expelled from Rajputana by the Muslim invasion. **2** (*pl.*) Indian soldiers of this ethnic group serving in the British army.

gurn (gœn), **girn** *v.i.* (*esp. dial.*) **1** to pull a face. **2** to pull as ugly a face as possible, esp. in a competition.

gurnard (gœ′nəd), **gurnet** (gœ′nət) *n.* any sea fish of the family Triglidae, characterized by a large angular head, covered with bony plates, and three free pectoral rays.

guru (gur′oo) *n.* **1** a Hindu spiritual teacher or guide. **2** a mentor with particular expertise or knowledge.

gush (gŭsh) *v.i.* **1** to flow or rush out copiously or with violence. **2** to be effusive or affectedly sentimental. ~*v.t.* to pour (out) rapidly or copiously. ~*n.* **1** a violent and copious issue of a fluid. **2** the fluid thus emitted. **3** an outburst. **4** extravagant affectation of sentiment. **gusher** *n.* **1** an oil well that discharges with great force or without requiring pumps. **2** a person who or something that gushes. **gushing** *n.*, *a.* **gushingly** *adv.* **gushy** *a.* (*comp.* **gushier**, *superl.* **gushiest**) effusive or affectedly sentimental. **gushily** *adv.* **gushiness** *n.*

gusset (gŭs´it) *n.* **1** a small triangular piece of cloth inserted in a dress to enlarge or strengthen some part. **2** an angle-iron or bracket for stiffening an angle in construction work. **gusseted** *a.*

gust (gŭst) *n.* **1** a short but violent rush of wind, a squall. **2** an outburst of passion. **gusty** *a.* (*comp.* **gustier**, *superl.* **gustiest**). **gustily** *adv.* **gustiness** *n.*

gustation (gŭstā´shən) *n.* **1** the act of tasting. **2** the sense of taste. **gustative** (gŭs´tətiv) *a.* **gustatory** *a.*

gusto (gŭs´tō) *n.* zest, enjoyment, pleasure (*to eat with gusto*).

gut (gŭt) *n.* **1** the intestinal canal. **2** (*pl.*) the intestines. **3** an intestine or a part of the alimentary canal. **4** the belly or the stomach as a symbol of gluttony. **5** (*pl.*) the core or essential part of something. **6** (*pl.*, *coll.*) stamina, courage, persistence. **7** catgut, the prepared intestines of animals used for the strings of musical instruments. **8** fibre drawn from a silkworm before it spins its cocoon, used for fishing lines. **9** a narrow passage of water, esp. a sound or strait. ~*v.t.* (*pres.p.* **gutting**, *past*, *p.p.* **gutted**) **1** to eviscerate, to draw the entrails out of. **2** (of fire etc.) to plunder, to remove or destroy the contents of. ~*a.* of or relating to instinctive feelings, intuition (*a gut feeling*). **to hate someone's guts** (*coll.*) to dislike someone intensely. **to work/ slog one's guts out** (*coll.*) to work extremely hard. **gutless** *a.* cowardly. **gutlessly** *adv.* **gutlessness** *n.* **gut-rot** *n.* (*sl.*) **1** a stomach upset. **2** cheap, harmful liquor, rot-gut. **gutsy** *a.* (*comp.* **gutsier**, *superl.* **gutsiest**) **1** greedy. **2** plucky. **gutsily** *adv.* **gutsiness** *n.* **gutted** *a.* (*sl.*) fed up, disappointed.

gutta-percha (gŭtəpœ´chə) *n.* a tough, waterproof rubber substance obtained from the latex of various Malaysian trees.

gutter (gŭt´ə) *n.* **1** a channel at the side of a street or a trough below eaves for carrying away water. **2** a channel worn by water. **3** a trench, conduit etc. for the passage of water or other fluid. ~*v.t.* **1** to form channels or gutters in. **2** to provide with gutters. ~*v.i.* **1** to become channelled or worn with hollows, as a burning candle. **2** to stream (down). **guttering** *n.* **1** material for gutters. **2** a gutter or arrangement of gutters. **3** the act of forming gutters. **gutter press** *n.* cheap and sensationalist newspapers. **guttersnipe** *n.* a street urchin.

guttural (gŭt´ərəl) *a.* **1** (of a sound, voice etc.) throaty, harsh, raucous. **2** produced or formed in the throat. **3** of or relating to the throat. ~*n.* a sound or combination of sounds produced in the throat or the back part of the mouth, such as *k*, *q*,

hard *c* and *g*, *ng* and the German *ch*. **gutturally** *adv.*

guv (gŭv) *n.* (*coll.*, *esp. dial.*) used as a term of address to a man (usu. in authority).

guy[1] (gī) *n.* **1** (*coll.*) a man, a fellow, a person. **2** an effigy of Guy Fawkes burnt on 5 Nov. in memory of the Gunpowder Plot. **3** (*coll.*) a ridiculously dressed person. ~*v.t.* **1** to ridicule. **2** to display in effigy.

guy[2] (gī) *n.* a rope, chain etc., to steady a load in hoisting or to act as a stay. ~*v.t.* to guide or steady by means of a guy or guys. **guy-rope** *n.*

guzzle (gŭz´əl) *v.i.* to drink or eat greedily. ~*v.t.* to drink or eat (something) greedily. **guzzler** *n.*

gybe (jīb), (*N Am.*) **jibe** *v.i.* (*Naut.*) **1** to take the wind on the other quarter (of a sailing boat). **2** to swing from one side of the mast to the other (of a fore-and-aft sail). ~*v.t.* **1** to make (a vessel) take the wind on the opposite quarter. **2** to shift (a sail) in this way. ~*n.* the act or process of gybing.

gym (jim) *n.* **1** short for GYMNASIUM. **2** short for GYMNASTICS. **gym shoe** *n.* a plimsoll. **gymslip** *n.* a tunic worn by schoolgirls as part of a school uniform.

gymkhana (jimkah´nə) *n.* a meeting for equestrian sports and games, orig. a place for athletic sports.

gymnasium (jimnā´ziəm) *n.* (*pl.* **gymnasiums**, **gymnasia** (-ə)) a building or room where gymnastics, indoor sports etc. are done. **gymnasial** *a.*

gymnastics (jimnas´tiks) *n.* **1** (*as sing. or pl.*) a course of instruction, discipline or exercise for the development of body or mind. **2** (*as pl.*) exercises for the development of bodily strength and agility. **gymnast** (jim´-) *n.* a person skilled in gymnastics. **gymnastic** *a.* **1** of or relating to exercises for the development of the body. **2** involving athletic effort. **3** involving great mental effort or discipline. **gymnastically** *adv.*

gymnosperm (jim´nōspœm) *n.* any one of a class of plants having naked seeds, such as the pine. **gymnospermous** (-spœ´məs) *a.*

gymp GIMP[1].

gynaeco- (gī´nikō, jī´-), (*N Am.*) **gyneco-** *comb. form* of or relating to women.

gynaecology (gīnikol´əji), (*N Am.*) **gynecology** *n.* the science dealing with the functions and diseases of women and girls. **gynaecological** (-kəloj´-) *a.* **gynaecologist** *n.*

-gynous (jinəs) *comb. form* **1** of or relating to women, as in *androgynous*, *misogynous*. **2** (*Bot.*) (of a plant) having female organs or pistils.

gyp[1] (jip) *v.t.* (*pres.p.* **gypping**, *past*, *p.p.* **gypped**) (*coll.*) to cheat, swindle. ~*n.* a swindle.

gyp[2] (jip), **gip** *n.* (*coll.*) pain. **to give someone gyp** to cause someone pain.

gyppy tummy GIPPY TUMMY.

gypsophila (jipsof´ilə) *n.* any plant of the genus *Gypsophila*, a hardy perennial with small white and pink flowers, related to the pinks.

gypsum (jip´səm) *n.* a mineral consisting of hydrous sulphate of lime, used to make plaster, paint, glass, fertilizer etc. ~*v.t.* to manure with gypsum. **gypseous** *a.* **gypsiferous** (-sif´-) *a.*

gypsy (jip´si), **gipsy** *n.* (*pl.* **gypsies, gipsies**) **1** a member of a nomad people (calling themselves Romany), prob. of Hindu extraction, dark in complexion and hair, and speaking a language descended from Sanskrit. **2** a person resembling a gypsy, esp. in dark complexion. **3** an itinerant traveller, wanderer. **gypsyish** *a.* **gypsy moth** *n.* a moth, *Lymatria dispar*, whose hairy caterpillar is destructive of trees.

gyrate (jīrāt´) *v.i.* to rotate, revolve, whirl, in either a circle or a spiral. ~*a.* (*Bot.*) arranged in rings, curved in a coil. **gyration** (-ā´shən) *n.* **gyrational** *a.* **gyratory** (jī´rətəri) *a.* **gyre** *n.* (*esp. poet.*) a gyration, a revolution. ~*v.i.* to turn or move in a circle.

gyrfalcon (jœ´fawlkən), **gerfalcon, jerfalcon** *n.* a large and powerful falcon of northern regions, *Falco rusticolus.*

gyro (jī´rō) *n.* (*pl.* **gyros**) (*coll.*) **1** a gyroscope. **2** a gyrocompass.

gyro- (jī´rō) *comb. form* **1** round, curved. **2** relating to revolutions.

gyrocompass (jī´rōkŭmpəs) *n.* a navigating compass consisting of an electrically driven gyroscope, the axle of which orientates the sensitive element.

gyroscope (jī´rəskōp) *n.* a heavy flywheel rotated (usu. electrically) at very high speed and supported on an axis at right angles to the plane of the wheel, used as a controlling or stabilizing device or as a compass in ships, aeroplanes etc. **gyroscopic** (-skop´-) *a.* **gyroscopically** *adv.*

H

H¹ (āch), **h** (*pl.* **Hs, H's**) the eighth letter of the English and other versions of the Roman alphabet. It is pronounced mostly as a simple breathing at the beginning of a word or syllable, as in *help, hard, hope* etc., but is also commonly joined to other consonants to form digraphs, as *ch* in *child, chill, sh* in *shin, th* in *this, that, think.* Joined with *p*, and sometimes with *g*, it gives the sound of *f*, as in *philosophy, enough*; sometimes the latter digraph is silent, as in *bough, plough. Ch* is common in words derived from Greek, and in such cases is usu. pronounced as *k* in *chemistry, chyle* etc.; the Scottish and German *ch*, marked in this dictionary kh, is a velar fricative corresponding to the Greek χ, as in *clachan, Reichstag.* ~*symbol* **1** magnetic field strength. **2** (h) Planck's constant. **H-girder** *n.* a girder having a crosspiece, in the shape of a capital letter H.

H² *chem. symbol* hydrogen. **H-bomb** *n.* a hydrogen bomb.

H³ *abbr.* **1** (of a pencil lead) hard. **2** henry(s). **3** (*sl.*) heroin. **4** hospital (on signs). **5** hydrant. **H-hour** *n.* the hour at which a military operation etc. is scheduled to begin (H for *hour*).

h *abbr.* **1** hecto-. **2** height. **3** high. **4** horse. **5** hot. **6** hour(s). **7** husband.

Ha. *chem. symbol* hahnium.

ha¹ (ha, hah), **hah** *int.* **1** used to express surprise, joy, suspicion or other sudden emotion. **2** an inarticulate sound expressive of hesitation. ~*v.i.* **1** to express surprise, wonder etc. **2** to hesitate. **ha ha! 1** used to express the sound of laughter. **2** used to express surprise, joy, suspicion or other sudden emotion.

ha² *abbr.* hectare(s).

habeas corpus (hābiəs kaw'pəs) *n.* a writ to produce a prisoner before a court, with details of the day and cause of the arrest and detention, in order that the justice of this may be determined.

haberdasher (hab'ədashə) *n.* **1** a seller of small articles of apparel, as ribbons, laces, silks etc. **2** (*N Am.*) a person who sells men's clothing. **haberdashery** *n.* (*pl.* **haberdasheries**).

habiliment (həbil'imənt) *n.* (*usu. pl.*) an item of clothing.

habit (hab'it) *n.* **1** a permanent tendency to perform certain actions. **2** a settled inclination, disposition or trend of mind. **3** a manner, practice, use or custom, acquired by frequent repetition. **4** an addiction. **5** (*Zool., Bot.*) a characteristic manner of growth. **6** physical constitution. **7** garb, dress or costume, esp. one of a distinctive kind, as of a religious order. **8** RIDING HABIT (under RIDE). ~*v.t.* to dress, to clothe. **to be in the habit of** to do (something) usually or regularly. **to make a habit of** to do (something) usually or regularly. **habited** *a.* clothed, dressed. **habit-forming** *a.* tending to become a habit or an addiction.

habitable (hab'itəbəl) *a.* that may be lived in or inhabited. **habitability** (-bil'-), **habitableness** *n.* **habitably** *adv.* **habitant** *n.* **1** an inhabitant of Lower Canada of French origin. **2** an inhabitant. **habitation** (-ā'shən) *n.* **1** the act of inhabiting. **2** the state of being inhabited. **3** a place of abode.

habitat (hab'itat) *n.* **1** the natural home or locality of an animal or plant. **2** the place where a person or group is at home or usually found.

habitual (habit'ūəl) *a.* **1** formed or acquired by habit. **2** according to habit, usual. **3** customary, constant. **4** given to a specified habit. **habitually** *adv.* **habitualness** *n.* **habituate** *v.t.* to accustom (to). **habituation** (-ā'shən) *n.* **habitude** (hab'itūd) *n.* **1** a customary manner or mode, habit, aptitude, tendency, propensity. **2** customary relation, familiarity.

habitué (həbit'ūā) *n.* a person who habitually frequents a place, esp. a place of amusement.

háček (hah'chek) *n.* a diacritical mark (ˇ) placed above a letter to modify its pronunciation, esp. in Slavonic languages.

hachure (hashooə') *n.* (*usu. pl.*) any one of a series of short lines employed to represent halftints and shadows, and on maps to denote hill slopes. ~*v.t.* to cover or mark with hachures.

hacienda (hasien'də) *n.* **1** in Spain, Latin America etc., an estate, a farm or plantation, an establishment in the country for stock-raising etc., esp. with a residence for the proprietor. **2** a (Spanish or Latin American) factory.

hack¹ (hak) *v.t.* **1** to cut irregularly or into small pieces. **2** to chop, to notch. **3** to cut unskilfully. **4** to kick (a player's shins) at football. **5** (*sl.*) to tolerate. **6** (*sl.*) to cope with. **7** to gain access to (a computer system or data) illegally. ~*v.i.* **1** to cut or chop away at anything. **2** to use computers as a hobby, esp. in order to manipulate another computer system illegally. ~*n.* **1** an irregular cut, a gash, a notch, a dent. **2** a kick (on the shins etc.). **3** the result of this. **4** a mattock or large pick. **hacker** *n.* **1** a person who writes computer programs as a hobby. **2** a person who uses a computer to gain access to another computer system, often for illegal purposes. **hacking** *a.* **1** slashing, chopping, mangling. **2** (of a cough) short, dry and intermittent. **hacksaw** *n.* a handsaw used for cutting metal. ~*v.t.* (*past, p.p.* **hacksawed, hack-sawn**) to cut with a hacksaw.

hack[2] (hak) *n.* **1** a hackney, a horse for hire. **2** a horse for general purposes, esp. as distinct from a hunter or racer. **3** an inferior or worn-out horse. **4** (*N Am.*) a hackney carriage. **5** a person who earns money from routine literary or journalistic work. ~*v.t.* **1** to ride (a horse) for pleasure. **2** to make common or hackneyed. ~*v.i.* to go riding for pleasure. **hackette** (haket´) *n.* (*derog.*) a female journalist. **hackwork** *n.* work done by a literary or journalistic hack.

hackle (hak´əl) *n.* **1** a long shining feather on or from a cock's neck. **2** a fly for angling, dressed with this. **3** a feather in a Highland soldier's bonnet. **4** the hairs on a cat's or dog's neck. **5** an instrument with sharp steel spikes for dressing or combing (flax etc.). ~*v.t.* to dress or comb (flax or hemp) with a hackle. **to make someone's hackles rise** to make someone angry.

hackney (hak´ni) *n.* (*pl.* **hackneys**) **1** a horse kept for riding or driving. **2** a hackney carriage. **hackney carriage, hackney coach** *n.* a passenger road vehicle licensed for hire. **hackneyed** *a.* (of a phrase) used so often that it has become stale, trite and ineffective.

had HAVE.

haddock (had´ək) *n.* (*pl. in general* **haddock**, *in particular* **haddocks**) a sea fish, *Melanogrammus aeglefinus*, allied to the cod and fished for food.

hadji (haj´i), **hajji, haji** *n.* (*pl.* **hadjis, hajjis, hajis**) (a title conferred on) a Muslim who has performed the pilgrimage to Mecca. **hadj, hajj, haj** *n.* (*pl.* **hadjes, hajjes, hajes**) a pilgrimage to Mecca.

hadn't (had´ənt) *contr.* had not.

hadron (had´ron) *n.* (*Physics*) an elementary particle taking part in strong nuclear interactions. **hadronic** (-ron´-) *a.*

haema- (hē´mə), (*N Am.*) **hema-** *comb. form* blood.

haemal (hē´məl), (*NAm.*) **hemal** *a.* (*Anat.*) **1** of or relating to the blood. **2** on, of or relating to the side of the body containing the heart and great blood vessels.

haematite (hē´mətīt), **hematite** *n.* a native sesquioxide of iron, occurring in two forms, red and brown, a valuable iron ore.

haemato- (hē´mətō), (*N Am.*) **hemato-** *comb. form* blood. **haematocele** (hē´mətəsēl, hem-) *n.* (*Med.*) a cavity containing blood. **haematology** (hēmətol´əji, hem-) *n.* (*Med.*) the branch of physiology dealing with blood. **haematologic** (-loj´ik), **haematological** *a.* **haematologist** *n.* **haematoma** (hēmətō´mə, hem-) *n.* (*pl.* **haematomas, haematomata** (-mətə)) (*Med.*) a lump of clotted blood. **haematophagous** (hēmətof´əgəs) *a.* that feeds on blood.

-haemia -AEMIA.

haemo- (hē´mō, hem´ō), (*N Am.*) **hemo-** *comb. form* short form of HAEMATO-. **haemocoel** (-sēl) *n.* (*Zool.*) the main body cavity of many invertebrate creatures. **haemocyanin** (-sī´ənin) *n.*

an oxygen-bearing substance containing copper, found in arthropods and molluscs. **haemodialysis** (hēmōdīal´əsis, hem´-) *n.* dialysis (of blood). **haemoglobin** (hēməglō´bin) *n.* the colouring matter of the red corpuscles of the blood. **haemolymph** (hē´mōlimf, hem´-) *n.* the fluid in invertebrate creatures having a similar function to that of blood. **haemolysis** (hēmol´isis, hem-) *n.* the release of haemoglobin from red blood cells. **haemolytic** (-lit´-) *a.* **haemophilia** (hēməfil´iə, hem-) *n.* (*Med.*) a constitutional tendency to bleed heavily because the clotting mechanism does not function normally. **haemophiliac** (-ak) *n.* a person suffering from this. ~*a.* suffering from haemophilia. **haemophilic** *a.* **haemostatic** (hēməstat´ik, hem-) *a.* serving to stop bleeding. **haemostasis** (hēmōstā´sis, hem-), **haemostasia** (-stā´ziə) *n.*

haemorrhage (hem´ərij), (*N Am.*) **hemorrhage** *n.* **1** an abnormal discharge of blood from the heart, arteries, veins or capillaries. **2** an extensive loss of people, resources etc. ~*v.i.* **1** to have a haemorrhage of blood. **2** to lose people, resources etc. extensively. **3** to be lost extensively. ~*v.t.* to lose in large numbers or quantities. **haemorrhagic** (-raj´-) *a.*

haemorrhoids (hem´əroidz), (*N Am.*) **hemorrhoids** *n.pl.* (*Med.*) swollen veins around the anus. **haemorrhoidal** (-roi´-) *a.*

haeremai (hī´rəmī), **haere mai** *int.* (*New Zeal.*) welcome!

hafiz (hah´fiz) *n.* (a Muslim title for) a person knowing the Koran by heart.

hafnium (haf´niəm) *n.* (*Chem.*) a metallic element occurring in zirconium ores, symbol Hf, at. no. 72.

haft (hahft) *n.* a handle, esp. of a dagger, knife or tool. ~*v.t.* to set in or fit with a handle.

hag (hag) *n.* **1** a witch. **2** a fury. **3** an ugly old woman. **4** a hagfish. **hagfish** *n.* (*pl. in general* **hagfish**, *in particular* **hagfishes**) an eel-like fish, of the family Myxinidae, that feeds on the bodies or remains of other fish. **haggish** *a.* **hag-ridden** *a.* suffering from nightmares.

haggard (hag´əd) *a.* **1** anxious, careworn or gaunt from fatigue, trouble etc. **2** wild-looking. **3** (of a hawk) caught wild. ~*n.* a wild or untrained hawk. **haggardly** *adv.* **haggardness** *n.*

haggis (hag´is) *n.* a Scottish dish traditionally made of liver, lights, heart etc. minced with onions, suet, oatmeal etc., enclosed in a sheep's stomach.

haggle (hag´əl) *v.i.* to wrangle, esp. over a bargain. ~*n.* a wrangle about terms. **haggler** *n.*

hagio- (hag´iō) *comb. form* of or relating to saints or to holy things.

hagiography (hagiog´rəfi) *n.* (*pl.* **hagiographies**) **1** the writing of the biography of saints. **2** a series of lives of saints. **3** any biography that treats its subject as excessively good, noble etc. **hagiographer** *n.* **hagiographic** (-graf´-), **hagiographical** *a.*

hagiolatry (hagiol´ətri) *n.* the worship of saints.
hagiology (hagiol´əji) *n.* (*pl.* **hagiologies**) literature relating to the lives and legends of saints. **hagiologic** (-loj´-), **hagiological** *a.* **hagiologist** *n.*
hah HA¹.
ha-ha (hah´hah), **haw-haw** (haw´haw) *n.* (*pl.* **ha-has, haw-haws**) a hedge, fence or wall sunk between slopes.
hahnium (hah´niəm) *n.* (*Chem.*) a radioactive element, chem. symbol Ha, at. no. 105, produced artificially from californium.
haiku (hī´koo) *n.* (*pl.* **haiku**) **1** a Japanese verse of 17 syllables, in 3 parts. **2** an imitation of this in English etc.
hail¹ (hāl) *n.* **1** frozen rain or particles of frozen vapour falling in showers. **2** (*fig.*) a great number of violent or abusive words etc. ~*v.i.* **1** (*impers.*) to pour down hail. **2** to come down with swiftness or violence. ~*v.t.* to pour down or out (abuse, blows etc.), as hail. **hailstone** *n.* a single pellet of hail. **hailstorm** *n.* **haily** *a.*
hail² (hāl) *v.t.* **1** to call or signal to (a person, taxi etc.) from a distance. **2** to designate or acclaim (as). **3** to welcome, to salute. ~*v.i.* to come (from a particular place) originally or as one's home (*She hails from Manchester*). ~*n.* **1** a salutation. **2** a shout to attract attention. **within hail** within hailing distance. **hailer** *n.* **hail-fellow-well-met** *a.* on easy, familiar terms. **Hail Mary** *n.* (*pl.* **Hail Marys**) AVE MARIA (under AVE).
hair (heə) *n.* **1** a filament composed of a tube of horny, fibrous substance, with a central medulla enclosing pigment cells, growing from the skin of an animal. **2** (*collect.*) the mass of filaments forming a covering for the human head. **3** hairlike cellular processes on the surface of plants. **4** a hairlike strand in a hairbrush etc. **5** the mass of such objects. **6** (*fig.*) something very small or fine; a very minute distance. **keep your hair on!** (*coll.*) don't lose your temper. **not to turn a hair** not to show any sign of fatigue or alarm. **to get in one's hair** to become a nuisance, to make one irritated. **to let one's hair down 1** (*coll.*) to talk without restraint. **2** (*coll.*) to forget ceremony, to behave uninhibitedly. **to make someone's hair curl** (*coll.*) to shock or scandalize someone greatly. **to make someone's hair stand on end** to make someone very frightened or horrified. **to split hairs** to quibble about trifles, to be overnice. **hairbreadth, hair's breadth** *n.* **1** the breadth of a hair. **2** a very minute distance. **hairbrush** *n.* a brush for the hair. **haircare** *n.* the process of keeping hair clean and in good condition. **haircloth** *n.* cloth made wholly or in part of hair. **haircut** *n.* **1** the act of cutting a person's hair. **2** the style in which a person's hair is cut. **hairdo** *n.* (*pl.* **hairdos**) (*coll.*) **1** a (woman's) hairstyle when it has been curled or put up. **2** an act or process of so styling hair. **hairdresser** *n.* **1** a person who styles and cuts hair. **2** a hairdresser's shop or business. **hairdressing** *n.* **hairdryer, hairdrier** *n.* an electric device for drying the hair,

either a hand-held one that blows warm air, or a hood that covers the head. **haired** *a.* **hair-grass** *n.* any tall, tufted grass of the genera *Aira*, *Deschampsia*, *Corynephous* etc. **hairgrip** *n.* a narrow hairpin with ends that spring tightly together. **hair lacquer** *n.* a chemical substance used to keep a hairstyle in place. **hairless** *a.* **hairlike** *a.* **hairline** *n.* **1** the edge of the hair on a person's head, esp. the forehead. **2** (*usu. attrib.*) a very thin crack or narrow line. **hairnet** *n.* a net, sometimes almost invisible, to keep the hair in place. **hair of the dog** *n.* (*coll.*) a small amount of what has proved harmful, esp. of alcohol during a hangover. **hairpiece** *n.* a piece of artificial hair worn to change the style of the natural hair. **hairpin** *n.* a pin for fastening the hair. **hairpin bend** *n.* a sharp V-shaped turn in a road. **hair-raising** *a.* very frightening. **hair's breadth** HAIRBREADTH (under HAIR). **hair shirt** *n.* a shirt made of horsehair, worn as a penance. **hairslide** *n.* a decorative clip for holding hair in place. **hair-splitting** *n.* the practice of making distinctions that are too minute to be significant. ~*a.* quibbling. **hairsplitter** *n.* **hairspray** *n.* lacquer for the hair sprayed from an aerosol can. **hairspring** *n.* the fine steel spring regulating the balance wheel in a watch. **hairstreak** *n.* any butterfly marked with fine streaks, belonging to the genera *Callophrys*, *Strymonidia* etc. **hairstyle** *n.* a particular way of arranging the hair. **hairstyling** *n.* **hairstylist** *n.* **hair-trigger** *n.* a secondary trigger for releasing a main trigger by very slight pressure. **hairy** *a.* (*comp.* **hairier,** *superl.* **hairiest**) **1** covered with hair. **2** consisting of or resembling hair. **3** (*coll.*) difficult, exciting or dangerous. **4** (*sl.*) clumsy. **hairily** *adv.* **hairiness** *n.*
haji, hajji HADJI.
haka (hah´kə) *n.* **1** a ceremonial Maori dance. **2** a similar display by a New Zealand rugby team before a match.
hake (hāk) *n.* (*pl. in general* **hake,** *in particular* **hakes**) a fish belonging to the genus *Merlucius*, allied to the cod.
halal (həlahl´) *n.* meat which is prepared in accordance with Muslim law. ~*v.t.* (*pres.p.* **halalling,** *past, p.p.* **halalled**) to prepare (meat) in this way. ~*a.* (of meat) prepared in this way.
halberd (hal´bəd), **halbert** (hal´bət) *n.* a weapon consisting of a combination of spear and battleaxe, mounted on a pole 5 to 7 ft. (1.5 to 2m) in length. **halberdier** (-diə´) *n.* a person armed with a halberd.
halcyon (hal´siən) *n.* **1** a tropical (esp. Australasian) kingfisher of the genus *Halcyon*. **2** a bird, supposed by the ancients to make a floating nest at the winter solstice, and to have the power of calming the sea while it was breeding. ~*a.* **1** peaceful, calm. **2** happy, pleasant, prosperous.
hale¹ (hāl) *a.* (esp. of an elderly man) sound and vigorous, robust (*hale and hearty*). **haleness** *n.*
hale² (hāl) *v.t.* to drag, to draw violently.

haler (hah'lə) *n.* (*pl.* **haler, halers, haleru** (hah'-ləroo)) a unit of currency of the Czech Republic.

half (hahf) *n.* (*pl.* **halves** (hahvz)) **1** either of two equal parts into which a thing or quantity is or may be divided. **2** a half part or share. **3** (*coll.*) a half-pint. **4** HALF-BACK (under HALF). **5** a half-price travel ticket. **6** a score for a golfer that is the same as their opponent's. ~*a.* **1** consisting of or forming a half. **2** partial. ~*adv.* **1** to the extent or degree of a half. **2** to a certain extent or degree. **3** partially, imperfectly (*often in comb.*). **4** (*coll.*) half past (*It's half three*). **by half** to a considerable degree. **by halves** badly, imperfectly. **half a** one half of a; roughly one half of a. **half past** half an hour past, as in *half past three*. **half the time** (*coll.*) as often as not. **not half 1** (*iron.*) rather. **2** (*sl.*) not at all. **to go halves** to share equally (with another or in). **too clever by half** far too clever. **too cocky by half** far too cocky. **half a chance** *n.* (*coll.*) even the slightest chance or opportunity. **half-and-half** *n.* **1** a mixture of equal parts of two drinks, esp. beer and stout or bitter and mild. **2** (*N Am.*) a mixture of milk and cream for tea or coffee. ~*a.* languid, spiritless. ~*adv.* using two equal parts. **half an eye** *n.* **1** some part of one's attention or perceptiveness. **2** a modicum of perceptiveness or intelligence. **half-back** *n.* **1** in football, hockey etc., a position behind the forwards. **2** a person who plays in this position. **half-baked** *a.* **1** not thorough. **2** (*sl.*) half-witted, silly. **3** inexperienced. **4** not quite baked. **half-blood** *n.* **1** the relationship between two people who have only one parent in common. **2** a person so related. **3** a person with parents of different racial origins. **half-blooded** *a.* born of parents of different racial origins. **half board** *n.* in hotels etc., the provision of bed, breakfast and one main meal per day. **half-boot** *n.* a boot reaching high up the ankle. **half-bottle** *n.* **1** a bottle that is half the full standard size. **2** a quantity equal to the contents of this. **half-breed** *n.* (*offensive*) an offspring of parents of different racial origins. ~*a.* half-blooded. **half-brother** *n.* a brother by one parent only. **half-caste** *n.* (*offensive*) a person with parents of different racial origins, esp. with one parent from the Indian subcontinent and one from Europe. **half-century** *n.* (*pl.* **half-centuries**) **1** fifty years. **2** a score of fifty in cricket. **half-cock** *n.* the position of the cock of a firearm when retained by the first notch, so that it cannot be moved by the trigger. **to go off at half-cock** to fail as a result of being too impetuous. **half-crown, half a crown** *n.* a former British silver coin, value two shillings and sixpence (approx. 12p). **half-cut** *a.* (*sl.*) quite drunk. **half-dozen, half a dozen** *n.*, *a.* six or slightly more. **half-duplex** *a.* allowing a communication signal to be sent in only one direction at a time. **half-hardy** *a.* (of a plant) able to survive outside except in severe frosts. **half-hear** *v.t.* (*past, p.p.* **half-heard**) to hear indistinctly. **half-hearted** *a.* **1** lukewarm, indifferent.

2 poor-spirited, weak. **half-heartedly** *adv.* **half-heartedness** *n.* **half-hitch** *n.* a knot made by passing the end of a rope over a higher part of it and up through the resulting loop. **half holiday** *n.* **1** the latter half of a working day taken as a holiday. **2** a day on which this is allowed. **half-hose** *n.* socks. **half-hour, half an hour** *n.* thirty minutes. **on the half-hour** at half past each hour, at 30 minutes past the hour. **half-hourly** *adv.*, *a.* **half-hunter** *n.* a watch that has a hinged cover with a hole allowing you to see part of the face and the approximate time. **half-inch** *n.* a unit of length equal to half an inch. **half-landing** *n.* a landing halfway up a flight of stairs. **half-length** *n.* a portrait showing only the upper half of the body. **half-life** *n.* the time taken for the radiation from a radioactive substance to decay to half its initial value. **half-light** *n.* a dim light as at dawn or dusk. **half-marathon** *n.* a running race of 13 miles 352 yards (21.243 km). **half mast** *n.* the middle of or halfway up the mast, the position of a flag denoting respect for a dead person. **at half mast** (*coll., often facet.*) (of trousers etc.) around the knees, having slipped down. **half measures** *n.pl.* methods of dealing with a problem that are not satisfactory or effective. **half-moon** *n.* **1** the moon when only half of its surface can be seen from earth. **2** the time when a half-moon is visible. **3** something in the shape of a half-moon. **half note** *n.* (*Mus.*) a minim. **half pay** *n.* a reduced salary esp. because of sickness or retirement. **half-pay** *a.* entitled to half pay, on half pay. **halfpenny** (hāp'ni), **ha'penny** *n.* (*pl.* **halfpennies, halfpence, ha'pennies, ha'pence**) a former British copper coin, half the value of a penny. **halfpennyworth, ha'p'orth** (hā'pəth) *n.* **1** as much as can be bought for a halfpenny. **2** a very small amount. **half-plate** *n.* a photographic plate 16.5 cm by 10.8 cm in size. **half-relief** *n.* **1** relief in moulding or carving etc. in which the design stands out half as much as the true proportion of the objects depicted. **2** a sculpture, carving etc. in this. **half-sister** *n.* a sister by one parent only. **half-step** *n.* (*Mus.*) a semitone. **half term** *n.* a short holiday halfway through a school term. **half the battle** *n.* an immense advantage. **half-timbered** *a.* (*Archit.*) having the foundations and principal supports of timber, and the spaces filled with plaster or brickwork to form the walls. **half-time** *n.* **1** the time at which the first half of a game is completed. **2** an interval in play at this time. **half-title** *n.* **1** a short title of a book, printed on the recto preceding the title page. **2** a title printed on the recto preceding a separate section of a book. **half-tone** *a.* of or relating to a process by which printing blocks are made with the shaded portions in small dots, by photographing on to a prepared plate through a finely ruled screen or grating. ~*n.* **1** a reproduction made by this process. **2** (*Mus., US*) a semitone. **half-track** *n.* **1** a vehicle running on one pair of wheels and one pair of Caterpillar tracks or

similar. **2** this type of propulsion mechanism.
half-truth n. a statement suppressing part of the
truth. **half-volley** n. (pl. **half-volleys**) a stroke in
tennis in which a ball is hit immediately after it
bounces. **halfway** adv. **1** in the middle. **2** at half
the distance. **3** more or less. ~a. situated in the
middle or at half the distance; equidistant from
two extremes. **halfway house** n. **1** a compromise.
2 a place providing short-term accommodation
for people leaving institutions such as prisons or
mental hospitals to provide rehabilitation before
going back into the community. **3** the midpoint
in a progression. **4** an inn halfway between two
towns etc. **halfwit** n. **1** a silly person. **2** (often
offensive) a mentally handicapped person. **half-
witted** a. **half-wittedly** adv. **half-wittedness** n.
half-yearly a. happening every six months. ~adv.
once in every six months.

Usage note Use of a half a(n), with an extra
indefinite article (as in a half an hour) is best
avoided.

halibut (hal´ibət) n. (pl. in general **halibut**, in particular **halibuts**) a large flat fish of the N Atlantic,
Hippoglossus hippoglossus, sometimes weighing
from 300 to 400 lb. (135–180 kg), used for food.
halide (hā´lid, hal´-) n. (Chem.) a binary salt of
halogen.
haliotis (haliō´tis) n. any gastropod belonging to
the genus Haliotis, having a shell lined with
mother-of-pearl.
halite (hā´līt) n. rock salt.
halitosis (halitō´sis) n. offensive breath.
hall (hawl) n. **1** a large room, esp. one in which
public meetings or concerts are held, the large
public room in a palace, castle etc. **2** a large
building in which public business is transacted.
3 a room or passage forming the entry area of a
house. **4** (N Am.) a connecting passage between
rooms, a landing. **5** a residential building for
undergraduates or other students. **6 a** a large
room in which members of a college etc. dine
in common. **b** dinner in such a room. **7** a manor
house or mansion. **8** the building occupied by a
guild etc. **Hall of Fame** n. (esp. N Am.) **1** a building containing memorials to famous people. **2** a
group of people who are famed for a particular
reason. **hall of residence** n. a residential building
for students. **hall porter** n. a person who carries
bags for guests in a hotel. **hall stand,** (N Am.)
hall tree n. a piece of furniture with pegs for
coats and a place for umbrellas, sometimes with
a mirror. **hallway** n. an entrance hall.
hallelujah ALLELUIA.
hallmark (hawl´mahk) n. **1** an official stamp
stamped by the Goldsmiths' Company and Government assay offices on gold and silver articles
to guarantee the standard. **2** any mark of genuineness. **3** a distinctive feature. ~v.t. **1** to stamp
with a hallmark. **2** to mark or label as genuine or
excellent.
hallo HELLO.

halloo (həloo´), **hallo** (həlō´), **halloa** v.i. (past,
p.p. **hallooed, halloed, halloaed**) **1** to cry, to call
attention. **2** to cheer dogs on with cries. ~v.t. **1** to
shout loudly to. **2** to cheer or urge on. **3** to chase
with shouts. ~n., int. a call to cheer on dogs.
hallow (hal´ō) v.t. **1** to make sacred or worthy of
reverence. **2** to revere. **3** to consecrate, to sanctify. **Hallowe'en** (-ēn´) n. 31 October, the eve of
All Saints' Day.
hallucinate (həloo´sināt) v.i. to have hallucinations. ~v.t. to affect with hallucinations. **halluci-
nant** a., n. **hallucination** (-ā´shən) n. an apparent
sense perception or appearance of an external
object that is not present in reality, an illusion.
hallucinator n. **hallucinatory** a. **hallucinogen**
(-əjən) n. a drug etc. that induces hallucinations.
hallucinogenic (-jen´-) a.
halm HAULM.
halo (hā´lō) n. (pl. **haloes, halos**) **1** a luminous
circle round the sun or moon caused by the
refraction of light through mist. **2** a nimbus or
bright disc surrounding the heads of saints etc.
3 a concept of glory associated with an object.
~v.t. (3rd pers. sing. pres. **haloes,** pres.p. **haloing,**
past, p.p. **haloed**) to surround with or as with a
halo.
halogen (hal´əjən) n. (Chem.) an element or
other radical which by combination with a metal
forms a salt (fluorine, chlorine, bromine, iodine
and astatine). **halogenate** (haloj´-) v.t. to combine
or treat with halogen. **halogenated** a. **halogena-
tion** (-ā´shən) n. **halogenic** (-jen´-) a. **halogen
lamp** n. a lamp with a filament surrounded by
halogen.
halon (hā´lon) n. (Chem.) any of various halo-
gens, used in fire extinguishers.
halophyte (hal´əfīt, hā´-) n. a plant suited to
growing in salty conditions.
halt¹ (hawlt) n. **1** a stop or interruption in activity
or motion. **2** a minor stopping-place on a railway
line. ~v.i. **1** to come to a stop. **2** to stop an activity. ~v.t. to cause to stop. **to call a halt (to)** to
bring some activity to an end.
halt² (hawlt) v.i. **1** to limp, to be lame. **2** to doubt,
to hesitate. **3** to be faulty in measure or rhyme.
halting a. **haltingly** adv.
halter (hawl´tə) n. **1** a headstall and strap or rope
by which an animal is fastened. **2** a rope to hang
criminals. **3** death by hanging. **4** the strap of a
halter-neck top. ~v.t. **1** to put a halter on. **2** to tie
up with a halter. **3** to hang with a halter. **halter-
break** v.t. to train (a horse) to submit to the halter.
halter-neck n., a. (a style of neckline, bodice or
top) with a piece of fabric around the neck,
leaving the back and shoulders bare.
halva (hal´və, -vah), **halvah** n. a sweet made from
sesame seeds and honey, typically from the
Eastern Mediterranean.
halve (hahv) v.t. **1** to divide into two equal parts.
2 to share equally. **3** to lessen by half, to reduce
to half. **4** to join (timbers) together by chopping
away half the thickness of each. **5** in golf, to win

the same number of holes, or to reach a hole in the same number of strokes, as the other side.

halves HALF.

halyard (hal´yəd), **halliard** n. (*Naut.*) a rope or tackle for hoisting or lowering yards, sails or flags.

ham (ham) n. **1** the hind part of the thigh. **2** (*usu. in pl.*) the thigh and buttock. **3** the thigh of an animal, esp. of a hog, salted and dried in smoke, or otherwise cured. **4** an amateur radio operator, a radio ham. **5** a ham actor. **6** the acting of a ham actor. ~v.t., v.i. (*pres.p.* **hamming**, *past, p.p.* **hammed**) (*sl.*) to act in a clumsy or exaggerated way. **to ham up** (*sl.*) to overact. **ham actor** n. **1** a bad, inexperienced actor. **2** an amateur actor. **ham-fisted** a. (*coll.*) **1** clumsy. **2** inept. **ham-fistedly** adv. **ham-fistedness** n. **ham-handed** a. HAM-FISTED (under HAM). **ham-handedly** adv. **ham-handedness** n. **hammy** a. (*comp.* **hammier**, *superl.* **hammiest**) **1** of or relating to ham. **2** like ham. **3** (*sl.*) like a ham actor, over-theatrical.

hamadryas (hamədrī´əs, -as) n. (*pl.* **hamadryases**) an Arabian and NE African baboon, *Papio hamadryas*.

hamamelis (haməmēˊlis) n. (*pl.* **hamamelises**) a shrub, such as the witch hazel, belonging to the genus *Hamamelis*.

hamburger (ham´bœgə) n. a flat cake of minced beef, fried or grilled and often served in a bun.

Hamite (ham´īt) n. a member of a group of peoples in Egypt and N Africa, supposedly descended from Noah's son Ham. **Hamitic** (-mit´-) a. **1** of or relating to a group of N African languages including ancient Egyptian and Berber. **2** of or relating to the Hamites. ~n. the Hamitic group of languages.

hamlet (ham´lit) n. a small village, a little cluster of houses in the country.

hammer (ham´ə) n. **1** a tool for driving nails, beating metals etc., consisting of a head, usu. of steel, fixed at right angles on a handle. **2** a machine, part of a machine or other appliance, performing similar functions, as a steam-hammer or the block striking the strings of a piano. **3** the part of a gunlock for exploding the charge. **4** the striker of a bell etc. **5** an auctioneer's mallet. **6** a metal ball, approx. 16 lb. (7.3 kg) in weight, attached to a handle by a long wire and thrown in an athletics contest. **7** the contest in which this is thrown. **8** MALLEUS. ~v.t. **1** to strike, beat or drive with or as with a hammer. **2** to forge or form with a hammer. **3** to work hard or persistently. **4** (*coll.*) to defeat easily. **5** in the Stock Exchange, to declare a defaulter. ~v.i. **1** to work or beat with or as with a hammer. **2** to make a noise like a hammer. **3** to work hard (at). **hammer and tongs 1** with great noise and vigour. **2** violently. **to come under the hammer** to be sold by auction. **to hammer out 1** to flatten with a hammer. **2** to produce (an agreement) after a lot of discussion and disagreement. **3** to play (a tune) heavy-handedly. **hammer and sickle** n.

the emblem symbolic of worker and peasant adopted on the flag etc. of the former USSR. **hammerbeam** n. (*Archit.*) a short beam projecting horizontally from a wall, in place of a tie-beam, to support the timbers of a roof. **hammer drill** n. an electric drill in which the bit moves backwards and forwards as well as rotating, used for drilling masonry. **hammerer** n. **hammerhead** n. **1** the head of a hammer. **2** a S African marsh bird, *Scopus umbretta*. **3** (*also* **hammerhead shark**) a shark of the family Sphyrnidae, with a head like a hammer. **hammer-headed** a. **hammerless** a. **hammerlock** n. a grip in wrestling in which one person's arm is held twisted and bent behind their back by their opponent. **hammertoe** n. a malformation of the foot consisting of permanent angular fixing of one or more toes.

hammock (ham´ək) n. a swinging or suspended bed made of canvas or netting, and hung by hooks from a roof, ceiling, tree etc.

hammy HAM.

hamper[1] (ham´pə) n. **1** a large wickerwork basket, with a cover. **2** this and its contents, usu. food for a picnic. **3** a package of groceries etc. put together for a special occasion. **4** (*N Am.*) a laundry basket.

hamper[2] (ham´pə) v.t. **1** to impede the movement or free action of. **2** to obstruct or impede (movement etc.). **3** to hinder, to shackle, to fetter.

hamsin KHAMSIN.

hamster (ham´stə) n. a ratlike rodent of the subfamily Cricetinae, with large cheek pouches in which it carries grain for food during hibernation.

hamstring (ham´string) n. **1** (*Anat.*) any of the tendons of the thigh muscle behind the knee. **2** (in quadrupeds) the large tendon at the back of the hock in the hind leg. ~v.t. (*past, p.p.* **hamstrung** (-strŭng), **hamstringed**) **1** to lame or disable by cutting or severing the hamstring. **2** to prevent (someone) from carrying out their plan.

hand (hand) n. **1** the part of the body used for grasping and holding, consisting of the palm and fingers, at the extremity of the human arm. **2** a similar body part of monkeys and other primates. **3** the end of a limb, esp. a forelimb, in other animals, when serving as a prehensile organ. **4** a direction to one side (right or left). **5** the power of execution, skill, performance, handiwork. **6** a person having skill. **7** a pledge of marriage. **8** (*often in pl.*) possession, control, authority, power. **9** a source, a person giving information etc. **10** (*pl.*) operatives, labourers, the crew of a ship, players, people engaged in a game etc. **11** a part, a share, a turn, an innings. **12** an act of helping. **13** a game at cards. **14** the cards held by a player. **15** a part in a game of cards. **16** one of the players in a game of cards. **17** a player's turn to serve the ball at tennis, rackets etc. **18** a style of handwriting. **19** a signature. **20** a lineal measure of 4 ins. (10 cm), a palm (for measuring horses). **21** a handful. **22** a handle.

23 the pointer or index finger of a watch, clock or counter. **24** five of any articles for sale. **25** a bunch of bananas. **26** a bundle of tobacco leaves. **27** a shoulder (of pork). **28** a round of applause. ~*v.t.* **1** to give, deliver or transmit with the hand. **2** to assist or conduct with the hand (into, out of etc.). **3** to deliver verbally. **4** (*coll.*) to deliver readily or inappropriately. **at hand 1** close by. **2** available. **3** about to happen. **at/ on all hands 1** by all parties. **2** from all quarters. **at the hands/ hand of 1** from or through (a person). **2** by the means or instrumentality of. **by hand 1** by a person, with the hands (as distinct from with instruments or machines). **2** by messenger or agent. **3** by artificial rearing (of children or the young of animals). **from hand to hand** from one person to another, bandied about. **from hand to mouth** without provision for the future. **hand and foot** completely, attending to every need (*She waits on him hand and foot*). **hand in glove** on most intimate terms (with). **hand in hand 1** holding hands (with each other). **2** in union, unitedly. **hand over fist** (*coll.*) with rapid, unchecked progress. **hand to hand 1** at close quarters. **2** in close fight. **in hand 1** in a state of preparation or execution. **2** in possession. **3** under control. **not to do a hand's turn** (*coll.*) to do no work at all. **off one's hands 1** finished with. **2** no longer one's responsibility. **on all hands** everywhere, on all sides. **on every hand** everywhere, on all sides. **on one's hands 1** (left) to one's responsibility. **2** (left) unsold. **on the one hand...on the other** from this point of view...from that point of view. **out of hand 1** without further consideration; at once, directly, extempore. **2** out of control. **to bear a hand** to lend assistance. **to force someone's hand** to make someone take action against their will. **to give a hand** to help, to lend a hand. **to hand 1** near. **2** available. **to hand down 1** to transmit, to give in succession. **2** to bequeath. **3** to pass on after use. **4** (*N Am.*) to express authoritatively in court. **to hand in** to deliver to an office etc. **to hand it to** to give credit to, to acknowledge the superiority, victory etc. of. **to hand off 1** to push off with the hand. **2** in American football, to pass the ball by hand. **to hand on** to transmit, to give in succession. **to hand out 1** to distribute. **2** to allocate. **to hand over** to deliver (to a person). **to hand round/ around** to distribute. **to have a hand in 1** to have a share in. **2** to be mixed up with. **to have one's hands full** to be fully occupied. **to have one's hands tied** to have no freedom of action. **to hold someone's hand** to make something easier for someone by helping and supporting them, showing them how to do something etc. **to keep one's hand in** to keep oneself in practice. **to lay hands on 1** to touch. **2** to assault. **3** to seize. **4** to lay the hands on the head of (in ordination, confirmation etc.). **to lay one's hands on 1** to get, to acquire, to seize. **2** to find. **to lend a hand** to help, to give assistance. **to shake hands** to clasp each other's right hand in

token of friendship etc. **to show one's hand** to disclose one's designs (orig. of cards). **to take in hand 1** to undertake, attempt. **2** to deal with, to manage. **3** to discipline. **to tie someone's hands** to prevent someone from taking action. **to win hands down** to win without an effort, easily. **under one's hand** with one's proper signature. **handbag** *n.* a small bag for carrying money and personal things. ~*v.t.* (*pres.p.* **handbagging**, *past*, *p.p.* **handbagged**) (of a woman) to abuse or reprimand publicly, to treat insensitively. **handbagging** *n.* **handball** *n.* **1** in football, a ball illegally played with the hand. **2** a game similar to football, played by throwing the ball between the goals. **3** a game played in a walled court, hitting the ball against the wall with the hand. **handbasin** *n.* a basin for washing the hands in a bathroom. **handbell** *n.* a small bell rung with the hand, esp. one of a series played musically. **handbill** *n.* a small printed sheet for circulating information. **handbook** *n.* a small book or treatise on any subject, a compendium, a manual. **handbrake** *n.* a brake worked by a hand lever, esp. on a motor vehicle. **hand-breadth** HAND'S-BREADTH (under hand). **handcart** *n.* a two-wheeled vehicle for carrying parcels or goods, pushed or drawn by hand. **handclap** *n.* an act of clapping. **hand cream** *n.* cream for moisturizing the hands. **handcuff** *n.* (*usu. pl.*) a manacle for the wrists, consisting of a chain and locking-rings. ~*v.t.* to secure with handcuffs. **-handed** *comb. form* **1** having a hand of a certain kind. **2** involving the number of hands specified (*a one-handed vault*). **3** using or made for the hand specified (*left-handed scissors*). **-handedly** *adv.* **-handedness** *n.* **-hander** *n.* (*in comb.*) a blow, stroke etc. using the stated hand, part of the hand or number of hands. **handful** *n.* (*pl.* **handfuls**) **1** as much or as many as can be held in the hand. **2** a small number or quantity. **3** (*coll.*) a troublesome person or task. **handglass** *n.* **1** a small mirror with a handle. **2** a magnifying glass for holding in the hand. **hand grenade** *n.* a grenade for throwing by hand. **handgrip** *n.* **1** a grasp or seizure with the hands. **2** a convenient handle. **3** (*esp. N Am.*) a suitcase, a large bag for holding luggage, equipment etc. **handgun** *n.* a gun that can be held and fired in one hand. **hand-held** *a.* held in the hands when in use. ~*n.* a hand-held computer. **handhold** *n.* something for the hand to hold on by (in climbing etc.). **hand-hot** *a.* (of water etc.) of a degree of heat that the hands can still be put into. **handless** *a.* **handlist** *n.* a brief list for reference. **handmade** *a.* produced by hand, not by machinery. †**handmaid**, **handmaiden** *n.* a female servant or attendant. **hand-me-downs** *n.pl.* (*coll.*) second-hand clothes. **handout** *n.* **1** a short informal document given to students, an audience etc. to help them understand a particular lesson, lecture etc. **2** a statement handed out to the press. **3** a gift of money etc. esp. to the poor. **handover** *n.* an act of handing over, a transfer. **hand-pick** *v.t.* to choose carefully. **hand-picked** *a.* **hand press** *n.* a press, esp. for printing, worked by the hand, as distinct from one worked by steam, water etc. **handpump** *n.* a pump worked by the hand. **handrail** *n.* a rail alongside stairs, landings etc. **handsaw** *n.* a saw riveted at one end to a handle, and designed to be used by one hand. **hand's-breadth, hand-breadth** *n.* a linear measurement equal to the breadth of the hand. **handset** *n.* the receiver of a telephone. **handshake** *n.* a shake of another's hand as a greeting. **hands-on** *a.* **1** having or through practical experience. **2** requiring practical involvement. **handspring** *n.* a somersault done by springing first onto the hands, then over on to the feet. **handstand** *n.* the act of balancing upright on one's hands. **hand-to-hand** *a.* (of fighting) at close quarters, using swords, fists etc. **hand tool** *n.* a tool worked with the hand, without electricity etc. **handwork** *n.* work done with the hands, as distinct from that done by machinery etc. **handworked** *a.* **handwriting** *n.* **1** writing done by hand. **2** the style of writing peculiar to a person. **handwritten** *a.*

h & c *abbr.* hot and cold (water).

handicap (han´dikap) *n.* **1** any physical or mental disability. **2** a disadvantage. **3** a race or contest in which an allowance of time, distance or weight is made to the inferior competitors. **4** the more difficult conditions imposed on a superior competitor. **5** a golfer's average number of strokes above par. ~*v.t.* (*pres.p.* **handicapping**, *past, p.p.* **handicapped**) **1** to impose heavier weight or other disadvantageous conditions on (a competitor). **2** to put at a disadvantage. **handicapped** *a.* having a physical or mental disability. **handicapper** *n.*

handicraft (han´dikrahft) *n.* a manual occupation or trade requiring both skill and art. ~*a.* of or relating to manual skills or labour.

handiwork (han´diwœk), **handywork** *n.* **1** work done by the hands. **2** the product of one's hands, labour or effort.

handkerchief (hang´kəchif) *n.* (*pl.* **handkerchiefs, handkerchieves** (-chēvz)) a piece of cloth, silk, linen or cotton, carried for wiping the nose, face etc.

Usage note The plural *handkerchiefs* is preferred to *handkerchieves*.

---

handle (han´dəl) *v.t.* **1** to touch, to feel with, to wield or use with the hands. **2** to treat (well etc.). **3** to deal with, to manage. **4** to deal in. **5** to treat of. **6** to be in charge of. **7** to operate or control. ~*v.i.* (of a vehicle) to respond in a specified way to control by a driver. ~*n.* **1** that part of a vessel, tool or instrument, by which it is grasped and held in the hand. **2** an instrument or means by which anything is done. **3** the quality of fabric in respect of how it feels and how easy it is to work with. **4** (*sl.*) a name, title, a call sign. **to fly off the handle** (*coll.*) to become angry suddenly, to go

into a rage. **to get a handle on** (*coll.*) to find a means of understanding etc. **handleable** *a.* **handleability** (-bil´-) *n.* **handlebar** *n.* a horizontal bar with grips at each end for steering a bicycle, motorcycle etc. **handlebar moustache** *n.* a thick, wide moustache that curls upwards at each end. **handled** *a.* **handler** *n.* **1** a person who handles or deals in something. **2** a person who trains and controls an animal, as a police dog. **handling** *n.*

handsome (han´səm) *a.* (*comp.* **handsomer**, *superl.* **handsomest**) **1** good-looking, well formed, finely featured. **2** liberal, generous. **3** ample, large. **4** (*N Am.*) showing skill and cleverness, adroit. **5** noble. **handsomely** *adv.* **1** in a handsome manner. **2** (*Naut.*) carefully. **handsomeness** *n.*

handy (han´di) *a.* (*comp.* **handier**, *superl.* **handiest**) **1** useful and easy to use. **2** close at hand, near, convenient. **3** dexterous, skilful with the hands. **handily** *adv.* **handiness** *n.* **handyman** *n.* (*pl.* **handymen**) **1** a person who does odd jobs. **2** a person who is good at DIY.

hang (hang) *v.t.* (*past, p.p.* **hung** (hŭng)) **1** to attach to a point of support higher than its own height. **2** to attach loosely to a point of support above the centre of gravity. **3** to fasten so as to leave movable (as a bell, gate, the body of a coach etc.). **4** (*past, p.p.* **hanged**) to suspend by the neck on a gallows as capital punishment. **5** to place (a painting etc.) on view on a wall. **6** to attach (wallpaper) in vertical strips to a wall. **7** to suspend (game) from a hook to mature. **8** to cover or decorate with anything suspended. **9** to attach, to fasten. **10** (*coll.*) to attach the blame for. **11** to cause to droop (*hung her head*). ~*v.i.* **1** to be hung or suspended. **2** to dangle. **3** (of clothing) to drape or fall. **4** to be immobile in the air. **5** to be executed by hanging. **6** to droop, to bend forwards. **7** to be fixed or suspended with attention. **8** to depend on future events. **9** to be in suspense; to be stuck. ~*n.* **1** a slope, a declivity. **2** the way that something hangs. **3** a general tendency, drift or bent. **not to care/ give a hang** (*coll.*) to be totally unconcerned. **to get the hang of 1** to understand the drift or connection of. **2** to get the knack of. **to go hang** (*coll.*) to do one's worst without anyone caring. **to hang about/ around 1** to loiter, to loaf. **2** to stay near, to frequent. **3** to wait. **4** to associate (with). **to hang back 1** to act reluctantly, to hesitate. **2** to stay behind. **to hang down** to droop. **to hang fire** to hesitate. **to hang heavy/ heavily** (of time) to go slowly. **to hang in 1** (*esp. N Am., coll.*) to persist. **2** (*esp. N Am., coll.*) to linger. **to hang on 1** to grasp or hold. **2** to persist. **3** to depend on. **4** (*coll.*) to wait. **to hang on to 1** to keep holding. **2** to retain. **to hang on/ upon 1** to be dependent on. **2** to listen closely to. **3** to adhere closely to. **4** to be a weight or drag on. **5** to rest, to dwell upon. **to hang out 1** to suspend from a window etc. **2** (of a tongue) to protrude loosely. **3** (*sl.*) to live (in a particular place); to spend a lot of time (somewhere). **to hang over** to be oppressively present to. **to hang together 1** to be consistent, to make sense. **2** to be closely united. **to hang up 1** to suspend. **2** to replace a telephone receiver and so end the call. **3** to put aside, to leave undecided. **4** (*sl.*) to cause neurosis or anxiety in. **to let it all hang out** (*sl.*) to be completely relaxed, to abandon inhibition. **hangdog** *a.* sullen, guilty-looking. **hanger** *n.* **1** a person who hangs or causes to be hanged. **2** that on which a thing is hung or suspended. **3** a coathanger. **4** a sloping wood or grove (largely in place-names). **hanger-on** *n.* (*pl.* **hangers-on**) a person who hangs on or sticks to a person, place etc., a dependant, a parasite. **hang-glider** *n.* **1** a type of large kite controlled by a person suspended beneath it in a harness. **2** a person who flies a hang-glider. **hang-glide** *v.i.* **hang-gliding** *n.* **hanging** *n.* **1** the act of suspending etc. **2** an execution by the gallows. **3** (*pl.*) fabrics hung up to cover or drape a room. ~*a.* **1** suspended, dangling. **2** steep, inclined. **3** punishable by hanging. **hanging valley** *n.* a valley that joins another at a higher level. **hanging committee** *n.* a committee appointed to choose and arrange pictures in an exhibition. **hangman** *n.* (*pl.* **hangmen**) **1** a public executioner who hangs people. **2** a guessing-game in which suggestions of letters not in the word to be guessed are recorded by drawing the lines of a gallows and hanged person. **hangnail** *n.* an agnail. **hang-out** *n.* (*coll.*) a haunt. **hangover** *n.* **1** the after-effects of drinking too much alcohol. **2** a survival from an earlier time. **hang-up** *n.* (*coll.*) **1** a neurosis or anxiety. **2** the source of this.

hangar (hang´ə) *n.* a large shed, esp. for aircraft. **hangarage** *n.*

hank (hangk) *n.* a coil or skein.

hanker (hang´kə) *v.i.* to have strong desire or longing (after). **hankerer** *n.* **hankering** *n.*

❌ **hankerchief** common misspelling of HANDKERCHIEF.

hanky (hang´ki), **hankie** *n.* (*pl.* **hankies**) (*coll.*) a handkerchief. **hanky-panky** (hangkipang´ki) *n.* (*coll.*) **1** improper activity esp. of a sexual kind. **2** jugglery, trickery, fraud.

Hanoverian (hanəviə´riən, -veə´-) *a.* of or relating to Hanover or the Hanoverians. ~*n.* **1** a native or inhabitant of Hanover. **2** an adherent of the House of Hanover, the dynasty holding the throne of Great Britain and Ireland from 1714–1901.

Hansen's disease (han´sənz) *n.* leprosy.

hansom (han´səm), **hansom cab** *n.* a two-wheeled horse-drawn cab in which the driver's seat is behind the body, the reins passing over the hooded top.

Hants (hants) *abbr.* Hampshire.

Hanukkah (han´əkə, -nukə), **Chanukah, Chanukkah** *n.* the Jewish festival of lights in commemoration of the rededication of the temple (165 BC).

hanuman (han´uman) *n.* a lemur, *Presbytis entellus*, sacred to Hindus.

†**hap** (hap) *n.* chance, luck.

ha'penny HALFPENNY (under HALF).

haphazard (haphaz´əd) *a.* **1** happening by chance. **2** random. ~*adv.* at random. **haphazardly** *adv.* **haphazardness** *n.*

hapless (hap´lis) *a.* unhappy, unfortunate, luckless. **haplessly** *adv.* **haplessness** *n.*

haploid (hap´loid) *a.* **1** having half the usual number. **2** (*Biol.*) **a** having a single set of unpaired chromosomes. **b** composed of haploid cells. ~*n.* (*Biol.*) a haploid cell or organism.

ha'p'orth HALFPENNY (under HALF).

happen (hap´ən) *v.i.* **1** to occur. **2** to befall, to occur by chance. **3** to chance (to). **4** to light (upon). **as it happens** actually, in fact. **happening** *n.* **1** (*usu. in pl.*) something that happens, a chance occurrence. **2** (*coll.*) a spontaneous event, performance etc. ~*a.* (*esp. N Am., sl.*) trendy, modern. **happenstance** (-stans) *n.* (*esp. N Am.*) something that happens by chance.

happy (hap´i) *a.* (*comp.* **happier**, *superl.* **happiest**) **1** enjoying pleasure from something good. **2** contented, satisfied. **3** lucky, fortunate. **4** prosperous, successful. **5** apt, felicitous. **6** favourable. **7** willing. **8** (*coll.*) slightly drunk. **9** (*in comb.*) in a dazed state. **happily** *adv.* **happiness** *n.* **happy event** *n.* (*coll.*) the birth of a baby. **happy families** *n.* a card game with a pack having representatives of family members instead of suits. **happy-go-lucky** *a.* careless, thoughtless, improvident. **happy hour** *n.* a period when a bar etc. sells drinks at reduced prices to attract customers. **happy hunting ground** *n.* (*coll.*) an area of activity offering easy rewards. **happy medium** *n.* a compromise; a state of affairs avoiding extremes.

haptic (hap´tik) *a.* relating to the sense of touch.

hara-kiri (harəkē´ri, -kir´-), **hari-kari** (harikar´i) *n.* a Japanese method of suicide by disembowelling.

Usage note The spelling *hari-kari* and pronunciation (harikar´i) are best avoided.

harangue (hərang´) *n.* **1** a declamatory address to a large assembly. **2** a noisy and vehement speech, a tirade. ~*v.t.* (*pres.p.* **haranguing**, *past, p.p.* **harangued**) to address in an angry, vehement way. **haranguer** *n.*

harass (har´əs, həras´) *v.t.* **1** to torment. **2** to molest. **3** to tire out with care or worry. **4** (*Mil.*) to worry by repeated attacks. **harassed** *a.* **harasser** *n.* **harassingly** *adv.* **harassment** *n.*

Usage note The pronunciation (-ras´), with the stress on the second syllable, is sometimes disapproved of.

harbinger (hah´binjə) *n.* **1** a person who announces the approach of another. **2** a person who or thing which foretells what is coming. **3** a precursor.

harbour (hah´bə), (*N Am.*) **harbor** *n*. **1** a refuge, esp. a refuge or shelter for ships. **2** a port or haven. ~*v.t.* **1** to shelter. **2** to keep in mind, esp. secretly. ~*v.i.* to come to anchor in a harbour. **harbourage** (-rij) *n*. a shelter, harbour, refuge. **harbourer** *n*. **harbourless** *a*. **harbour master** *n*. an official having charge of the berthing and mooring of ships in a harbour. **harbour seal** *n*. (*N Am.*) the common greyish-black seal, *Phoca vitulina*.

hard (hahd) *a*. **1** firm, solid, compact. **2** not yielding to pressure. **3** difficult to accomplish, understand or explain. **4** laborious, fatiguing, strenuous. **5** intolerable, full of problems. **6** intricate, perplexing. **7** harsh, severe; galling, inflexible, cruel, unfeeling. **8** hostile, resentful. **9** ideologically rigid. **10** not open to dispute, definite. **11** difficult to bear, oppressive, unjust. **12** high in alcohol. **13** (of a drug) highly addictive and harmful. **14** using force. **15** coarse, unpalatable. **16** rough and harsh to the palate, the touch etc. **17** (of water) containing mineral salts making it difficult to use for washing. **18** in phonetics, sounded gutturally (as *c* and *g* when not pronounced like *s* and *j*); aspirated (as *k*, *t*, *p*, compared with *g*, *d*, *b*). **19** (of stocks and shares) stable in value. ~*adv*. **1** forcibly, violently. **2** strenuously, using a lot of effort. **3** severely, with hardship or pain. **4** with effort or difficulty. **5** close, near. **6** so as to be firm or solid. **7** as hard or as far as possible, to the utmost limit. **8** closely, carefully. **9** (of rain) falling very heavily. ~*n*. **1** a firm landing place, jetty or roadway. **2** (*coll.*) hard cash. **3** (*sl.*) hard labour. **4** something that is hard. **hard by 1** close by. **2** close at hand. **hard on 1** difficult for. **2** unkind to, unpleasant to. **3** critical of. **4** close behind. **hard put to** unlikely to find it easy to. **hard put to it** in difficulties. **hard upon** close behind. **to go hard with** to cause problems or difficulties for someone. **to put the hard word on** (*Austral., New Zeal., sl.*) to ask or pressurize (someone) to do something. **hard and fast** *a*. strict; that must be strictly adhered to. **hardback** *n*. a book with a stiff binding. ~*a*. having a stiff binding. **hardbacked** *a*. **hardball** *n*. (*N Am.*) **1** a baseball. **2** (*sl.*) severe or uncompromising tactics. ~*v.t.* (*sl.*) to put pressure on (a person). **hardbitten** *a*. tough and not easily shocked. **hardboard** *n*. thin board made of compressed woodchips bound together with resin. **hard-boiled** *a*. **1** boiled until hard. **2** (*coll.*) hard-headed, unemotional, callous, shrewd. **hard cash** *n*. actual coin; ready money. **hard cheese** *n*., *int*. (*coll.*) hard luck. **hard coal** *n*. anthracite, non-bituminous coal. **hard copy** *n*. printout, or a paper version, of a computer document. **hard core** *n*. **1** a group within a larger group, devoted to their beliefs and resistant to change. **2** an irreducible central core. **hard-core** *a*. **1** loyal to beliefs and resistant to change. **2** (of pornography) sexually explicit. **hardcover** *n*., *a*. (*esp. N Am.*) HARDBACK (under HARD). **hard disk** *n*.

(*Comput.*) a rigid magnetizable disk for computer storage. **hard doer** *n*. (*Austral.*) a smart Alec, a tough nut. **hard-done-by** *a*. treated unfairly or badly. **hard-earned** *a*. earned or acquired with difficulty. **hard error** *n*. (*Comput.*) an irreversible error. **hard feelings** *n.pl.* feelings of bitterness and resentment. **hard hat** *n*. **1** a protective helmet of a type worn on construction sites. **2** a reactionary. **hardhead** *n*. **1** a hard-headed person. **2** HARDHEADS (under HARD). **hard-headed** *a*. practical, not sentimental, matter-of-fact. **hard-headedly** *adv*. **hard-headedness** *n*. **hardheads** *n*. a knapweed, *Centaurea nigra*, with purple flower heads. **hard-hearted** *a*. cruel, unfeeling, pitiless. **hard-heartedly** *adv*. **hard-heartedness** *n*. **hard hit** *a*. seriously damaged or affected, esp. by monetary losses. **hard-hitting** *a*. forceful, effective, outspoken. **hardish** *a*. **hard labour**, (*N Am.*) **hard labor** *n*. enforced labour, esp. when added to imprisonment. **hard landing** *n*. **1** an awkward, bumpy aircraft landing. **2** a spacecraft landing which destroys the vehicle. **hard line** *n*. an approach that is without compromise; an unyielding attitude. **hardline** *a*. (of a policy) uncompromising, extreme. **hardliner** *n*. **hard lines** *n.pl., int*. (*coll.*) hard luck. **hard luck** *n*. misfortune, undeserved lack of success. ~*int*. used to express commiseration. **hardness** *n*. **hard-nosed** *a*. (*coll.*) unsentimental, tough, realistic. **hard nut** *n*. (*sl.*) an aggressive person. **hard nut to crack** *n*. **1** a problem that is difficult to solve. **2** something that is difficult to understand. **3** a person who is not easily convinced. **hard-on** *n*. (*taboo sl.*) an erect penis, an erection. **hard pad** *n*. a form of distemper in dogs. **hard palate** *n*. the front part of the palate. **hardpan** *n*. (*Geol.*) a layer of hard clay below the soil. **hard-paste** *a*. denoting, of or relating to porcelain made from clay and stone and fired at a high temperature. **hard porn, hard pornography** *n*. sexually explicit pornography. **hard-pressed** *a*. **1** closely pursued. **2** having difficulties or problems; under strain. **hard radiation** *n*. highly penetrating radiation. **hard rock** *n*. (*coll.*) rock music with an aggressive style and heavy beat. **hard roe** *n*. the roe of a female fish. **hard sauce** *n*. a firm mixture of butter and sugar, often flavoured with rum, brandy etc. **hard sell** *n*. (*coll.*) **1** aggressive selling, advertising etc. **2** an instance of this. **hardshell** *a*. **1** (of a crab etc.) having a hard shell. **2** rigid, unyielding, uncompromising. **hard shoulder** *n*. an extra lane beside the nearside lane of a motorway etc. used for stopping in emergencies. **hardstanding** *n*. a hard surface of tarmac etc. on which a vehicle may stand when not in use. **hard stuff** *n*. (*coll.*) the strongest alcoholic drink, spirits, esp. whisky. **hard tack** *n*. coarse ship's biscuit. **hard top** *n*. a car with a roof of metal or other rigid material, esp. when this is detachable. **hard up** *a*. in need, esp. of money, very poor. **hard up for** in need of, short of. **hardware** *n*. **1** items of metal, ironmongery etc. **2** items of machinery, heavy weaponry etc. **3** the physical apparatus of a computer system. **hard-wearing** *a.* durable. **hard wheat** *n.* a type of wheat with hard kernels that are high in gluten, used for making bread and pasta. **hard-wired** *a.* (of an electronic circuit) involving a permanent connection, and having a specific function. **hardwood** *n.* close-grained wood from deciduous trees, as distinct from that from pines etc. **hard-working** *a.* given to working hard and diligently.

harden (hah´dən) *v.t.* **1** to make hard or harder. **2** to confirm (in effrontery, wickedness, obstinacy etc.). **3** to make insensible, unfeeling or callous. ~*v.i.* **1** to become hard or harder. **2** to become unfeeling or callous. **3** to become confirmed (in vice). **4** (of prices) to become stable. **to harden off** to make (a plant) more able to withstand cold conditions by increasing periods of exposure. **hardener** *n.* **hardening** *n.* **hardening of the arteries** *n.* (*Med.*) ARTERIOSCLEROSIS (under ARTERY).

hardihood, hardiness etc. HARDY.

hardly (hahd´li) *adv.* **1** scarcely, not quite. **2** harshly, rigorously. **3** unfavourably. **4** with difficulty. **hardly any** very few, very little. **hardly ever** very seldom.

Usage note (1) A clause with the word *hardly* is a negative one, and so should not contain another negative word: *They couldn't hardly think* and *without hardly a thought* are not standard English. (2) When *hardly* refers to time ('only just'), a following *when* is preferable to *than* (so *She hardly got in when the phone rang*).

hardship (hahd´ship) *n.* **1** that which is hard to bear, as privation, suffering, toil, fatigue, oppression, injury, injustice. **2** the conditions or occasion causing this.

hardy (hah´di) *a.* (*comp.* **hardier,** *superl.* **hardiest**) **1** unaffected by fatigue; robust. **2** (of plants) capable of bearing exposure to winter weather. **hardihood** *n.* boldness, daring. **hardily** *adv.* **hardiness** *n.* **hardy annual** *n.* **1** an annual plant that may be sown in the open. **2** (*facet.*) a question that crops up annually or periodically.

hare (heə) *n.* **1** a long-eared short-tailed mammal of the genus *Lepus,* similar to but larger than the rabbit and with longer hind legs. **2** ELECTRIC HARE (under ELECTRIC). **3** the flesh of the mammal as food. ~*v.i.* to run swiftly. **to run with the hare and hunt with the hounds** to keep in with both sides. **to start a hare** to raise a topic of conversation. **hare and hounds** *n.* a paperchase. **harebell** *n.* the bluebell of Scotland, *Campanula rotundifolia.* **hare-brained** *a.* **1** (*coll.*) (of a plan) very silly; unlikely to be successful. **2** giddy, flighty. **harelip** *n.* (*perh. offensive*) a congenital fissure of the upper lip, a cleft lip. **hare-lipped** *a.* **hare's-foot, hare's-foot clover** *n.* a species of clover, *Trifolium arvense.*

Usage note Using *harelip* can give offence: the term *cleft lip* is preferred.

harem (heə´rəm, hah´rēm, -rēm´), **hareem** (hah´-rēm, -rēm´) *n.* **1** the apartments reserved for the women in a Muslim household. **2** the occupants of these. **3** a group of female animals that share the same mate.

harewood (heə´wud) *n.* stained sycamore, used for furniture.

haricot (har´ikō), **haricot bean** *n.* the kidney or French bean, often dried.

hark (hahk) †*v.i.* to listen (*usu. in imper.*). **to hark back to** to return to (some point or matter from which a temporary digression has been made).

harken HEARKEN.

harlequin (hah´likwin) *n.* **1** (*also* **Harlequin**) a leading character in a pantomime or harlequinade, dressed in a mask and parti-coloured and spangled clothes. **2** the harlequin duck. ~*a.* parti-coloured, variegated. **harlequinade** (-nād´) *n.* **1** that part of a pantomime in which the harlequin and clown play the principal parts. **2** an extravaganza. **3** a piece of fantastic conduct. **harlequin duck** *n.* a sea duck with variegated plumage, *Histronicus histronicus,* of the northern hemisphere.

†**harlot** (hah´lət) *n.* a prostitute; a promiscuous woman. **harlotry** *n.*

harm (hahm) *n.* **1** hurt, injury, damage. **2** evil. ~*v.t.* to injure, hurt or damage. **out of harm's way** safe. **harmful** *a.* hurtful, injurious, detrimental. **harmfully** *adv.* **harmfulness** *n.* **harmless** *a.* **1** not hurtful or injurious. **2** inoffensive. **harmlessly** *adv.* **harmlessness** *n.*

harmonic (hahmon´ik) *a.* (*Mus.*) **1** of or relating to harmony or music. **2** concordant, harmonious. ~*n.* (*usu. in pl.*) **1** (*Mus.*) a harmonic tone. **2** a radio frequency which is a multiple of a main frequency. **harmonica** (hahmon´ikə) *n.* a mouth organ. **harmonical** *a.* **harmonically** *adv.* **harmonic motion** *n.* a type of symmetrical oscillatory motion. **harmonic progression** *n.* (*Math.*) a series of numbers whose reciprocals are in arithmetical progression, as $\frac{1}{5}$, $\frac{1}{7}$, $\frac{1}{9}$. **harmonic series** *n.* HARMONIC PROGRESSION (under HARMONIC). **harmonic tone** *n.* (*usu. in. pl.*) an overtone accompanying a fundamental note at a fixed interval.

harmonium (hahmō´niəm) *n.* a keyed musical wind instrument whose tones are produced by the forcing of air through free reeds.

harmony (hah´məni) *n.* (*pl.* **harmonies**) **1** the adaptation of parts to each other, so as to form a complete, symmetrical or pleasing whole. **2** the agreeable combination of simultaneous sounds, the production of musical chords or chord progressions. **3** the science dealing with the musical combination of sounds. **4** concord or agreement in views, sentiments etc. **in harmony 1** producing musical chords or chord progressions. **2** in agreement. **harmonious** (-mō´-) *a.* **1** equal, tuneful. **2** concordant, having harmony. **3** having parts adapted and proportioned to each other, symmetrical. **4** without discord or dissension.

harmoniously *adv.* **harmoniousness** *n.* **harmonist** *n.* a person skilled in harmony or harmonizing. **harmonistic** (-nis´-) *a.* **harmonize, harmonise** *v.t.* **1** to make harmonious. **2** to arrange in musical concord, to add the proper accompaniment to. **3** to adjust in proper proportions. **4** to cause to agree (with). ~*v.i.* **1** to agree in sound or effect. **2** to live in peace and concord. **3** to correspond, to be congruous (with). **harmonization** (-ā´shən) *n.* **harmonizer** *n.*

harness (hah´nis) *n.* **1** the working gear of a horse or other draught animal. **2** an arrangement of straps etc. to hold a person or thing safely, e.g. in a pram, hang-glider etc. ~*v.t.* **1** to put a harness on (a horse etc.). **2** to utilize (natural forces, e.g. water) for motive power. **3** to attach by a harness (to). **in harness** at one's work. **harnesser** *n.*

harp (hahp) *n.* a musical instrument of triangular shape, with strings which are plucked by the fingers with the frame upright. ~*v.i.* **1** to play on a harp. **2** to dwell incessantly (on) (*Stop harping on about it!*). **harper, harpist** *n.* a player on the harp. **harp seal** *n.* an Arctic seal, *Phoca groenlandica*, with dark bands on its back suggestive of the shape of a harp. **harp-shell** *n.* a mollusc of the tropical genus *Harpa*.

harpoon (hahpoon´) *n.* a barbed, spearlike missile weapon with a line attached, used for striking and killing whales etc. ~*v.t.* to strike, catch or kill with a harpoon. **harpooneer** (-niə´), **harpooner** *n.* **harpoon gun** *n.* a gun for firing a harpoon.

harpsichord (hahp´sikawd) *n.* a stringed instrument with a keyboard moving quills that pluck instead of hammers that strike, similar in form to the pianoforte.

harpy (hah´pi) *n.* (*pl.* **harpies**) **1** in Greek and Roman mythology, a monster represented with the face of a woman, the body of a vulture and fingers armed with sharp claws. **2** an extortioner, a rapacious person or animal. **harpy eagle** *n.* a crested eagle, *Harpia harpyja*, from S America.

harquebus (hah´kwibəs), **arquebus** (ah´-) *n.* (*pl.* **harquebuses, arquebuses**) an old kind of musket fired from a forked hand rest or tripod.

☒ **harrass** common misspelling of HARASS.

harridan (har´idən) *n.* an ill-tempered or bullying (old) woman.

harrier[1] (har´iə) *n.* **1** a variety of dog, smaller than the foxhound, orig. used for hare-hunting. **2** (*pl.*) a pack of such hounds with huntsmen. **3** a member of a club of cross-country or hare-and-hounds runners.

harrier[2] (har´iə) *n.* **1** a person who harries or plunders. **2** a bird of prey of the genus *Circus*.

harrow (har´ō) *n.* a large rake or frame with teeth, drawn over ground to level it, stir the soil, destroy weeds or cover seed. ~*v.t.* **1** to draw a harrow over. **2** to torment, to cause anguish or suffering to. **under the harrow** in distress or tribulation. **harrower** *n.* **harrowing** *a.* causing anguish or torment. **harrowingly** *adv.*

harrumph (hərŭmf´) *v.i.* to make a sound as if clearing one's throat, often to indicate disapproval. ~*v.t.* to say in such a manner.

harry (har´i) *v.t.* (*3rd pers. sing. pres.* **harries,** *pres.p.* **harrying,** *past, p.p.* **harried**) **1** to plunder, to pillage, to lay waste. **2** to harass.

harsh (hahsh) *a.* **1** rough to the touch or other senses. **2** discordant, irritating. **3** austere, morose, severe. **4** rigorous, inclement. **5** unfeeling. **6** unpleasantly loud or bright. **harshen** *v.t.* to make harsh or harsher. ~*v.i.* to become harsh or harsher. **harshly** *adv.* **harshness** *n.*

harslet HASLET.

hart (haht) *n.* a stag, esp. a male red deer, from its fifth year onwards. **hart's tongue** *n.* a fern, *Phyllitis scolopendrium*, with tongue-shaped leaves.

hartebeest (hah´tibēst) *n.* a large African antelope of the genus *Alcephalus*, with horns that bend at the tips.

harum-scarum (heərəmskeə´rəm) *a.* giddy, hare-brained, reckless. ~*n.* a giddy, hare-brained or reckless person.

harvest (hah´vist) *n.* **1** the process of reaping and gathering crops, esp. of corn. **2** the season for this. **3** ripe corn or other agricultural products gathered and stored. **4** the yield of any natural product for the season. **5** the product or result of any labour or effort. ~*v.t.* **1** to reap and gather in (corn, grain etc.). **2** to receive as payment, penalty etc. **harvestable** *a.* **harvester** *n.* **1** a reaper. **2** a reaping and binding machine. **3** a harvest mite. **harvest festival** *n.* a religious service of thanksgiving for the harvest. **harvest home** *n.* **1** the close of harvesting. **2** a merrymaking in celebration of this. **harvestless** *a.* **harvestman** *n.* (*pl.* **harvestmen**) an arachnid with long slender legs. **harvest mite, harvest bug, harvest louse, harvest tick** *n.* a minute tick, mite or acaridan which burrows in or attaches itself to the skin during late summer and autumn, setting up an irritating itch. **harvest moon** *n.* the moon at its full about the time of the autumnal equinox. **harvest mouse** *n.* a very small fieldmouse, *Micromys minutus*, which makes a nest usu. among wheat stalks.

has HAVE.

has-been (haz´bēn) *n.* (*coll.*) a person or idea that is no longer important, influential or useful.

hash[1] (hash) *n.* **1** a dish of meat that has already been cooked, cut into small pieces and recooked, often mixed with vegetables etc. **2** (*coll.*) a mess, a muddle. **3** a second preparation of old matter. **4** reused material. **5** (*in full* **hash sign**) the # symbol. ~*v.t.* **1** to cut or chop up in small pieces. **2** to mince. **to make a hash of** (*coll.*) to make a mess of. **to settle someone's hash** (*coll.*) to defeat a person completely. **hash browns** *n.pl.* a fried mixture of chopped potatoes and onion.

hash[2] (hash) *n.* (*coll.*) hashish.

hashish (hash´ēsh), **hasheesh** *n.* the tender tops and sprouts of Indian hemp, *Cannabis indica*, used as a narcotic for smoking, chewing etc.

Hasid (has´id) *n.* (*pl.* **Hasidim** (-im)) a member of any of several mystical Jewish sects. **Hasidic** (-sid´-) *a.*

haslet (haz´lit), **harslet** (hah´-) *n.* mixed pieces of the entrails, liver, heart etc. of an animal, usu. a hog, cooked and pressed into a loaf.

hasn't (haz´ənt) *contr.* has not.

hasp (hahsp) *n.* a fastening, esp. a clamp or bar hinged at one end, the other end passing over a staple, where it is secured by a pin, key or padlock. ~*v.t.* to fasten, shut or secure with a hasp.

hassle (has´əl) *n.* (*coll.*) **1** something causing difficulty or problems. **2** an argument. ~*v.t.* **1** to cause difficulty or problems for. **2** to harass. ~*v.i.* to argue.

hassock (has´ək) *n.* **1** a small stuffed footstool or cushion for kneeling on in church. **2** a matted tuft of rank grass, a tussock.

haste (hāst) *n.* **1** hurry, speed of movement or action; urgency, precipitance. **2** excessive speed. **in haste** speedily, precipitately. **to make haste** to be quick. **hasten** (hā´sən) *v.i.* to move with haste or speed. ~*v.t.* **1** to cause to hurry. **2** to expedite. **hastener** *n.* **hasty** *a.* (*comp.* **hastier**, *superl.* **hastiest**) **1** hurried, quick. **2** eager, precipitate. **3** rash, inconsiderate. **4** irritable. **hastily** *adv.* **hastiness** *n.*

hat (hat) *n.* **1** a covering for the head, usu. having a crown or top and a continuous brim. **2** a specified function or occupation (*wearing my teacher's hat, I would say yes, but as a parent, no*). ~*v.t.* (*pres.p.* **hatting**, *past, p.p.* **hatted**) to provide, fit or cover with a hat. **hats off to** used to express admiration for or approval of. **out of a hat 1** (selected) at random. **2** as if by a clever trick or magic. **to hang up one's hat** to make oneself at home (in another house). **to keep under one's hat** (*coll.*) to keep secret. **to pass (round) the hat** to ask for contributions of money, donations etc. **to take off one's hat to** (*coll.*) to express admiration for or approval of. **to talk through one's hat** to talk about something one does not understand. **to throw one's hat into the ring** to enter a contest, election etc. **hatband** *n.* a ribbon or band of fabric round a hat. **hatbox** *n.* a box for carrying or storing a hat in. **hatful** *n.* (*pl.* **hatfuls**). **hatless** *a.* **hatpin** *n.* a long pin, often with a decorative head, used to hold a hat in place by pinning it to the hair. **hat stand** *n.* a set of hooks or a piece of furniture for hanging hats on. **hatter** *n.* a person who makes or sells hats. **hat-trick** *n.* **1** the feat at cricket of taking three wickets with consecutive balls (from its being held to entitle the bowler to the reward of a new hat). **2** the feat of one player scoring three goals etc. in one match. **3** three successes in any area of activity.

hatch[1] (hach) *n.* **1** an opening in a wall between two rooms. **2** a small door in a spacecraft, aircraft etc. **3** an opening in a roof for access to the outside. **4** (*Naut.*) a hatchway, or a trapdoor or shutter to cover this. **5** a floodgate or a grated opening in a weir used as a fish trap. **down the**

hatch! (*coll.*) drink up! (as a toast). **under hatches 1** (*Naut.*) confined below; out of sight. **2** dead. **hatchback** *n.* a car with a door at the back that opens upwards. **hatchway** *n.* a large opening in the deck of a ship for lowering cargo etc.

hatch[2] (hach) *v.t.* **1** to produce (young) from eggs by incubation or artificial heat. **2** to produce young from (eggs). **3** to evolve, to contrive, to devise (a plan, plot etc.). ~*v.i.* **1** to come out of the egg. **2** (of eggs) to produce young. ~*n.* **1** the act of hatching. **2** a brood hatched. **hatchery** *n.* (*pl.* **hatcheries**) a place where eggs are hatched artificially, esp. those of fish or poultry. **hatchling** *n.* a young bird, fish or reptile that has just hatched.

hatch[3] (hach) *v.t.* **1** to mark with fine lines, parallel or crossing each other. **2** to inlay with thin strips of another material. **hatching** *n.* lines crossing each other at more or less acute angles, esp. as shading on a drawing, or as road markings.

hatchet (hach´it) *n.* a small axe with a short handle for use with one hand. **to bury the hatchet** to forgive and forget, to effect a reconciliation (in allusion to an American Indian custom of burying a tomahawk on the conclusion of peace). **hatchet-faced** *a.* having a narrow face with sharp, prominent features. **hatchet job** *n.* (*coll.*) a fiercely critical speech or piece of writing. **hatchet man** *n.* (*pl.* **hatchet men**) **1** a person hired to carry out violent or illegal tasks. **2** a person appointed to sack people in an organization.

hatchment (hach´mənt) *n.* a funeral escutcheon or panel bearing the coat of arms of a deceased person placed on the front of the person's house, in a church etc.

hate (hāt) *n.* **1** extreme dislike or aversion, hatred. **2** (*coll.*) a hated thing or person (*a pet hate*). ~*v.t.* **1** to dislike exceedingly; to abhor, to detest. **2** (*coll.*) to dislike. **3** to be unwilling or reluctant (to do something). **hatable, hateable** *a.* **hateful** *a.* causing hate; odious, detestable. **hatefully** *adv.* **hatefulness** *n.* **hate mail** *n.* a series of unpleasant or aggressive letters, usu. from an anonymous writer. **hater** *n.* **hatred** (-rid) *n.* **1** great dislike or aversion. **2** active malevolence, animosity, enmity.

hatha yoga (hathə yō´gə) *n.* a form of yoga involving physical exercises and breathing control.

hatter, hat-trick HAT.

haughty (haw´ti) *a.* (*comp.* **haughtier**, *superl.* **haughtiest**) proud, arrogant, disdainful, supercilious. **haughtily** *adv.* **haughtiness** *n.*

haul (hawl) *v.t.* **1** to pull or drag with force. **2** to transport by dragging or in a lorry etc. **3** to bring unceremoniously or forcibly (*hauled before the judge*). ~*v.i.* **1** to alter the course of a ship. **2** to pull or drag (at or upon) with force. ~*n.* **1** a hauling, a pull. **2** the drawing of a net. **3** an amount that is taken or stolen at once. **4** a distance travelled. **to haul up** (*coll.*) to bring for trial in a court of law. **haulage** (-ij) *n.* **1** transporting of goods. **2** the charge for this. **hauler** *n.* **1** a person who or thing which hauls. **2** HAULIER (under HAUL). **haulier** *n.* **1** a person or business that transports goods by lorry. **2** a worker who hauls trucks to the bottom of the shaft in a coal mine.

haulm (hawm), **halm** *n.* **1** a stem, a stalk. **2** (*collect.*) the stems or stalks of peas, beans, potatoes etc.

haunch (hawnch) *n.* **1** that part of the body between the ribs and the thigh; the buttock, the basal joint. **2** the leg and loin of an animal used as meat. **3** (*Archit.*) the shoulder of an arch.

haunt (hawnt) *v.t.* **1** to visit (a place or person) frequently as a ghost or spirit. **2** to frequent, to resort to often; to frequent the company of. **3** to recur to the mind of (a person) frequently in an irritating way. ~*v.i.* to stay or be frequently (about, in etc.). ~*n.* **1** a place which one often visits or frequents. **2** a den, a feeding place for animals etc. **haunted** *a.* **haunter** *n.* **haunting** *a.* having a lasting effect on the emotions; poignant. **hauntingly** *adv.*

haute couture (ōt kutūə´, -tuə´) *n.* **1** the designing and making of exclusive trend-setting fashions. **2** the designers and houses creating such fashions.

haute cuisine (ōt kwizēn´) *n.* cooking of a very high standard.

hauteur (ōtœ´) *n.* haughtiness, lofty manners or demeanour.

have (hav) *v.t.* (*3rd pers. sing. pres.* **has** (haz), †**hath** (hath), *pres.p.* **having**, *past, p.p.* **had** (had), *2nd pers. sing. pres.* †**hast** (hast), *past* †**hadst** (hadst)) **1** to possess, to hold as owner. **2** to hold at one's disposal. **3** to enjoy, to suffer, to experience. **4** to engage in. **5** to give birth to; to have given birth to. **6** to receive, to get, to obtain. **7** to take for consumption; to eat or drink. **8** to require, to claim. **9** to hold mentally, to retain. **10** to feel as an emotion. **11** to show as an action. **12** (*usu. neg.*) to tolerate, to entertain. **13** to maintain. **14** to hold as part, appurtenance, quality etc., to contain, to comprise. **15** to know, to understand, to be engaged in. **16** to know as a language. **17** to vanquish, to hold at one's mercy. **18** (*coll.*) to circumvent, to cheat, to bring forth, to bear. **19** (*taboo sl.*) to engage in sexual intercourse with. ~*v.i.* (*usu. in imper.*) to go, to get (at, after, with etc.). ~*v.aux.* **1** used with past participles to denote the completed action of verbs. **2** used with past participles in conditional clauses (*had I known*; *if I had known*). ~*n.* **1** (*usu. in pl., coll.*) a wealthy person. **2** (*sl.*) a deception, a swindle. **to be had** to be taken in. **to have got to** (*coll.*) to have to. **to have had it 1** (*coll.*) to have let one's opportunity or moment go by. **2** (*coll.*) to have done something that will have serious consequences for one. **3** (*coll.*) to have been killed or overcome. **4** (*coll.*) to be too old. **to have it 1** to have found the solution. **2** to win a vote etc. **to have it in for** to want to harm. **to have it in one** to be capable, to have the ability. **to have it off/**

away (*taboo sl.*) to have sexual intercourse. **to have it out** to settle a quarrel or dispute by fighting, debate etc. **to have it that** to maintain or argue that. **to have nothing on someone 1** to have no evidence that a person has done something wrong. **2** to have no advantage over another person. **to have on 1** to be wearing (something). **2** to have (something) planned. **3** to deceive (someone), to trick (someone). **to have out** to have (a tooth etc.) removed or extracted. **to have something on someone 1** to have evidence that a person has done something wrong. **2** to have an advantage over another person. **to have to** to be obliged to. **to have up** (*coll.*) to cause to be prosecuted in court. **have-not** *n.* (*usu. pl., coll.*) a poor person.

Usage note It is incorrect to write *of* for *have* in *could have, should have* etc. (informal *could've, should've*).

haven (hā´vən) *n.* **1** a port, a harbour. **2** a station or refuge for ships. **3** a refuge, an asylum.

haven't (hav´ənt) *contr.* have not.

haver (hā´və) *v.i.* **1** to talk nonsense. **2** to hesitate, to dither. **haverer** *n.*

haversack (hav´əsak) *n.* a strong bag carried over the shoulder or on the back to hold provisions etc. when walking.

havoc (hav´ək) *n.* **1** widespread destruction; devastation, waste. **2** chaos. ~*v.t.* (*pres.p.* **havocking**, *past, p.p.* **havocked**) to lay waste; to devastate. **to play havoc with 1** to damage. **2** to upset.

haw[1] (haw) *n.* **1** the berry or fruit of the hawthorn. **2** the hawthorn itself.

haw[2] (haw) *int., n.* a sound expressive of hesitation in speaking. ~*v.i.* to utter this sound, to speak with hesitation (*hum and haw*).

Hawaiian (həwī´ən) *a.* of or relating to Hawaii, its people or their language. ~*n.* **1** a native or inhabitant of Hawaii. **2** the Austronesian language of Hawaii.

hawfinch (haw´finch) *n.* a large European finch, *Coccothraustes coccothraustes*, with a sturdy beak.

hawk[1] (hawk) *n.* **1** a bird of prey belonging to the family Accipitridae, having a long tail, short rounded wings and a curved beak. **2** a rapacious or aggressive person. **3** an advocate of an aggressive foreign policy. ~*v.i.* **1** to hunt birds etc. by means of trained hawks or falcons. **2** to attack on the wing, to soar (at). ~*v.t.* to pursue or attack on the wing. **hawkbit** *n.* a plant with yellow daisy-like flowers, of the genus *Leontodon*. **hawk-eyed** *a.* having sharp sight. **hawkish** *a.* **hawkishness** *n.* **hawklike** *a.* **hawkmoth** *n.* a moth of the family Sphingidae, the flight of which is not unlike that of a hawk in quest of prey. **hawk-nosed** *a.* having a hooked nose. **hawksbill, hawksbill turtle** *n.* a small turtle, *Eretmochelys imbricata*, living in tropical climates and having curved beaklike jaws. **hawkweed** *n.* any daisy of the composite genus *Hieracium*.

hawk² (hawk) v.i. to clear or try to clear the throat in a noisy manner. ~v.t. to force (up) phlegm from the throat.

hawk³ (hawk) v.t. **1** to carry about for sale, to try to sell. **2** to carry or spread about.

hawker¹ (haw´kə) n. **1** a person who practises the sport of hawking. **2** a falconer.

hawker² (haw´kə) n. a person who travels around selling goods in the street or from house to house.

hawse (hawz) n. (Naut.) **1** that part of the bow in which the hawse-holes are situated. **2** the distance between a ship's head and the anchors by which she rides. **3** the situation of the cables when a ship is moored from the bows with two anchors. **hawse-hole** n. a hole in each bow through which a cable or hawser can be passed.

hawser (haw´zə), **halser** n. (Naut.) a cable, used in towing and mooring.

hawthorn (haw´thawn) n. a thorny, rosaceous shrub or tree belonging to the genus Crataegus, bearing white or pink flowers which develop into haws.

hay¹ (hā) n. grass cut and dried for fodder. **to hit the hay** (coll.) to go to bed, to sleep. **to make hay while the sun shines** to take advantage of every favourable opportunity. **haybox** n. an airtight box, with a thick layer of hay, used for keeping food hot, and for continuing the process of slow cooking after the food has been removed from the fire. **haycock** n. a conical heap of hay. **hay fever** n. a severe catarrh with asthmatic symptoms, frequent in summer and caused by a reaction to pollen, dust etc. **haymaker** n. **1** a person employed in making hay. **2** a machine for tossing hay. **3** (coll.) a swinging punch. **haymaking** n. **haymow** n. **1** a hayrick. **2** a mass of hay laid up in a barn. **hayrick** n. HAYSTACK (under HAY¹). **hayseed** n. **1** grass seed from hay. **2** (N Am., Austral., New Zeal.) a yokel, a rustic. **haystack** n. a pile of hay in the open air, built with a conical or ridged top, traditionally thatched to keep it dry. **haywire** a. (coll.) **1** crazy, mad. **2** chaotic, disordered.

hay² (hā), **hey** n. **1** a country dance with a winding movement. **2** a dance figure following a weaving pattern.

hazard (haz´əd) n. **1** a danger, a risk. **2** chance. **3** a game at dice; the stake in gaming. **4** a difficulty, obstacle, bunker etc. on a golf course. ~v.t. **1** to risk; to expose to chance or danger. **2** to run the risk of. **3** to venture (an act, statement etc.). **hazard light, hazard warning light** n. a flashing light on a vehicle indicating that it has stopped in an emergency or is doing something unexpected. **hazardous** a. **1** full of hazard, danger, or risk. **2** depending on chance. **hazardously** adv. **hazardousness** n.

haze¹ (hāz) n. **1** lack of transparency in the air, a very thin mist or vapour, usu. due to heat. **2** obscurity or indistinctness of perception, understanding etc. **hazy** a. (comp. **hazier**, superl.

haziest) **1** misty; thick with haze. **2** dim, vague, indistinct, obscure. **3** muddled. **hazily** adv. **haziness** n.

haze² (hāz) v.t. **1** (Naut.) to harass or punish with overwork. **2** (N Am.) to bully, to tease.

hazel (hā´zəl) n. **1** a shrub or small tree of the genus Corylus, esp. the European C. avellana, bearing the hazelnut. **2** the wood of this tree. **3** a reddish-brown or greenish-brown colour, esp. of eyes. ~a. (esp. of eyes) reddish-brown or greenish-brown. **hazelnut** n. the fruit of the hazel, the cobnut, a round nut with a reddish-brown shell.

HB abbr. hard and black (of pencil lead).

Hb abbr. haemoglobin.

HBM abbr. Her (or His) Brittanic Majesty.

h.c. abbr. honoris causa.

HCF abbr. highest common factor.

HCFC abbr. hydrochlorofluorocarbon.

HDTV abbr. high-definition television.

HE abbr. **1** Her Excellency, His Excellency. **2** His Eminence. **3** high explosive.

He chem. symbol helium.

he (hē) pron. (obj. **him**, poss. **his**) **1** the male person or animal referred to. **2** the person of unknown or unspecified sex, esp. referred to in an antecedent indefinite pronoun or noun (If anyone insults you, punch him). ~n. **1** a male person. **2** a children's game of chasing to touch another player. **3** the chaser in this game. **he-cat, he-goat** etc. n. a male cat, goat, etc. **he-man** n. (**he-men**) (coll.) a virile man.

Usage note He is sometimes used as an objective pronoun (after a verb or preposition), especially when joined by and to a personal name or pronoun, he and X, but this is best avoided. See also note under THEY.

head¹ (hed) n. **1** the foremost part of the body of an animal, the uppermost in a human, consisting of the skull, with the brain and the special sense organs. **2** any part, organ or thing of an analogous kind. **3** a measure of length equal to a head, esp. in a horse race. **4** the upper part of anything, the top. **5** the upper end of a valley, lake, gulf etc. **6** the front part of a ship, plough, procession, column of troops etc. **7** the first or most honourable place, the forefront, the place of command. **8** a chief, a ruler, a principal or leader. **9** a head teacher of a school. **10** the more honourable end of a table etc. **11** the part of a bed where the head rests. **12** the obverse of a coin or medal. **13** the knobbed end of a nail etc. **14** the striking part of a tool. **15** the globular cluster of flowers or leaves at the top of a stem. **16** the ripened part of an ulcer or boil. **17** froth on liquor. **18** the part of a machine tool etc. that holds a drill or cutter. **19** the device on a tape recorder that can record sound, or play back or erase recorded sound. **20** a promontory. **21** the capital of a pillar etc. **22** a person, an individual, esp. as counted. **23** a single one (as of cattle). **24** a main division, a topic, a category. **25** a culmination, a crisis, a pitch. **26** pressure of water available for driving mills; available steam-pressure. **27** liberty, licence, freedom from restraint. **28** an aptitude for something specified. **29** the mind, the understanding, the intellect, esp. as distinguished from the feelings. **30** (*sl.*) an addict, a devotee, a fan. **31** (*coll.*) a headache. **32** (*sl.*) a headline. ~*a.* (*attrib.*) chief, principal. **a head for** an ability to understand or tolerate. **head and shoulders 1** by the height of the head and shoulders. **2** by a great margin. **head over heels 1** turning upside down. **2** completely (in love). **in one's head 1** by thinking only, without physical aids. **2** in one's mind. **off one's head 1** out of one's mind. **2** wildly excited, demented. **on one's (own) head** being one's own responsibility; at one's own risk. **out of one's head 1** off one's head. **2** out of one's own head. **out of one's own head 1** by one's own invention. **2** of one's own accord. **over someone's head 1** beyond someone's understanding. **2** appealing to a higher authority than someone. **3** without regard for one's higher status. **to be unable to make head or tail of** to be unable to understand at all. **to bite someone's head off** (*coll.*) to snap at someone; to be irritable. **to come into one's head** to enter one's head. **to come to a head 1** to reach a crisis or culminating point. **2** (of an ulcer or boil) to suppurate. **3** to ripen. **to enter one's head** to occur as a thought in one's mind. **to get one's head together** to collect one's thoughts, to achieve a more balanced state of mind. **to give someone their head** to give liberty or licence to. **to go to one's head 1** (of alcoholic drink) to make one slightly drunk. **2** (of success etc.) to make one vain, arrogant etc. **to have one's head screwed on the right way** to be sensible or well-balanced. **to keep one's head** to remain calm. **to keep one's head down** (*coll.*) to avoid being noticed when there are problems. **to let someone have their head** to give someone their head. **to lose one's head 1** to be carried away by excitement. **2** to lose one's presence of mind. **3** to be decapitated. **to make head or tail of** to have the slightest understanding of (usu. in neg. and interrog. contexts). **to put one's heads together** to consider (a problem) together. **to take it into one's head 1** to fix on the idea or belief (that), esp. with no supporting evidence. **2** to resolve (to do something). **to turn someone's head** to cause someone to be vain or infatuated. **with one's head in the clouds** being unrealistic; daydreaming. **headache** *n.* **1** a neuralgic or other persistent pain in the head. **2** (*coll.*) a source of worry. **headachy** *a.* **headband** *n.* **1** a band for the hair. **2** a band at the top and bottom inside the back of a book. **headbanger** *n.* (*sl.*) **1** a person who makes violent head movements in time to pop music. **2** a stupid, crazy or violent person. **headbanging** *n.* (*sl.*) **1** the making of violent head movements in time to pop music. **2** forcing people to cooperate. **headboard** *n.* a panel at the

head of a bed. **head-butt** *n.* a forceful attack made by thrusting the top of the head at another person. ~*v.t.* to strike (a person) using a head-butt. **head case** *n.* (*coll.*) a mad or foolish person. **headcount** *n.* a count of all the people etc. present, employed etc. **headdress** *n.* a covering or decoration for the head. **headed** *a.* **head first, head foremost** *adv.* **1** with the head in front (of a plunge). **2** precipitately. **headgear** *n.* what is worn on the head; covering or ornaments for the head. **headhunt** *v.t.* to seek and recruit for a vacancy as a business executive etc. ~*v.i.* to engage in headhunting. **headhunter** *n.* **1** a person or agency that specializes in seeking and recruiting business executives etc. **2** a member of a people, notably the Dyaks of Borneo and Celebes, who make or made hostile raids in order to secure human heads as trophies. **headhunting** *n.* **headlamp** *n.* HEADLIGHT (under HEAD¹). **headland** *n.* a point of land projecting into the sea, a cape, a promontory. **headless** *a.* **headlight** *n.* **1** a lamp at the front of a vehicle, locomotive etc. **2** a beam of light from this. **headlike** *a.* **headline** *n.* **1** the line at the head of a page or paragraph giving the title etc. **2** (*pl.*) news set out in large, heavy type. **3** (*pl.*) the main news summarized in a broadcast news bulletin. ~*v.t.* to give a headline to, to include among the headlines. ~*v.i.* to appear as the main act or performer, to star. **headlock** *n.* a wrestling hold with an arm locked around the opponent's head. **headlong** *adv.* **1** head first. **2** violently, hastily, rashly. ~*a.* **1** steep, precipitous. **2** violent, precipitate. **3** rash, thoughtless. **headman** *n.* (*pl.* **headmen**) a chief, a leader, a head worker. **headmaster** *n.* a male head teacher. **headmasterly** *a.* **headmistress** *n.* a female head teacher. **headmost** *a.* most forward, most advanced. **head of state** *n.* (*pl.* **heads of state**) the leader of a government, or a monarch. **head-on** *a., adv.* **1** (of a collision) with the front of one vehicle hitting that of another. **2** head-to-head. **headphones** *n.pl.* a set of earphones for listening to music etc. **headpiece** *n.* **1** an ornamental engraving at the head of a chapter etc. **2** armour for the head, a helmet. **headrest** *n.* a padded support for the head, esp. at the top of a seat in a vehicle. **head restraint** *n.* an extension of or addition to the top of a seat in a vehicle, to prevent the head from jolting backwards. **headroom** *n.* room or space for the head in a low tunnel etc.; the amount of space above a vehicle passing under a bridge etc. **headsail** *n.* a sail on the foremast or forward of this. **headscarf** *n.* (*pl.* **headscarves, headscarfs**) a scarf worn over the head. **headset** *n.* a set of earphones joined by a band over the head. **headship** *n.* the office of head teacher, a post as a head teacher. **headshrinker** *n.* (*sl.*) a psychiatrist. **headsquare** *n.* a headscarf. **headstall** *n.* the bridle without the bit and reins. **head start** *n.* **1** an advantage given or taken at the beginning of a race etc. **2** an advantageous beginning to any enterprise. **headstone** *n.* a stone at the head of a grave. **headstrong** a. ungovernable, obstinate, intractable, self-willed. **head teacher** n. the principal teacher at a school. **head-to-head** n. a direct debate or contest between two people or teams. ~adv. directly confronting the opposition. ~a. involving direct confrontation. **headward** a., adv. **headwater** n. (usu. pl.) the upper part of a stream near its source. **headway** n. 1 motion ahead, rate of progress. 2 headroom. **to make headway** to advance, to make progress. **headwind** n. a contrary wind. **headword** n. a word constituting a heading, esp. in a dictionary. **headwork** n. mental work. **heady** a. (comp. **headier**, superl. **headiest**) 1 headstrong, precipitate. 2 violent, impetuous, intoxicating, inflaming, exhilarating. 3 headachy.

head[2] (hed) v.t. 1 to lead, to be the leader to, to direct. 2 to move or travel in (a specified direction). 3 to be or form a head to. 4 to provide with a head. 5 to put or to be a heading to a chapter, etc. 6 to oppose, to check. 7 to strike (a ball) with the head. ~v.i. 1 to go or tend in a direction. 2 to form a head. **to head back** 1 to intercept, to get ahead of and turn back or aside. 2 to return to one's starting point. **to head off** 1 to intercept, to get ahead of and turn back or aside. 2 to leave, to set off. 3 to forestall. **to head up** to be in charge of (a team of people etc.).

-head (hed) suf. denoting state or quality, as in godhead, maidenhead.

header (hed´ə) n. 1 (coll.) an act of heading a ball. 2 a plunge or dive head first. 3 a brick or stone laid with its end in the face of the wall. 4 a running title or rubric. 5 a header tank. **header tank** n. a water tank that feeds or maintains pressure in a plumbing system.

heading (hed´ing) n. 1 an inscription at the head of an article, chapter etc. 2 a running title. 3 a division of the topics of a discourse. 4 the band of fabric at the top of a curtain onto which tape for the hooks is sewn. 5 (Mining) the end or the beginning of a drift or gallery in a mine; a gallery, drift or adit.

headquarters (hedkwaw´təz) n. (in constr. sing. or pl.) 1 the residence of the commander-in-chief of an army. 2 the main office of an organization. 3 the centre of authority.

heal (hēl) v.t. 1 to make sound or whole again, to restore to health; to cure of (disease etc.). 2 to cause to skin over. 3 to reconcile (differences etc.). 4 to end the suffering caused by. ~v.i. 1 to grow or become sound or whole again. 2 to skin over. **healable** a. **heal-all** n. 1 a universal remedy. 2 any of various medicinal herbs. **healer** n.

health (helth) n. 1 a state of bodily or organic soundness, freedom from bodily or mental disease or decay. 2 physical condition (good, bad etc.). 3 the condition with respect to finances, morals etc. 4 a toast wishing that someone may be well, prosperous etc. **health centre** n. a building where several doctors see patients, and where other health services are available. **health**

farm n. an establishment, often in the country, where clients can diet, exercise, relax etc. **health food** n. types of food, e.g. organically grown or with no synthetic ingredients, regarded as promoting health. **healthful** a. 1 promoting health, either physical or spiritual. 2 healthy, salubrious. **healthfully** adv. **healthfulness** n. **health service** n. a medical service provided by the State. **health visitor** n. a nurse specializing in preventive medicine, who visits people in their own homes. **healthy** a. (comp. **healthier**, superl. **healthiest**) 1 enjoying good health. 2 promoting health, salubrious, salutary. 3 ample. **healthily** adv. **healthiness** n.

heap (hēp) n. 1 a pile or accumulation of many things placed or thrown one on another. 2 (esp. in pl., coll.) a large number, a lot, a crowd, a good many times, a good deal. 3 an old thing in very bad condition; a wreck. ~v.t. 1 to throw (together) or pile (up) in a heap. 2 to load or overload (with). 3 to pile (upon). **heaped** a. (of a spoonful etc.) with more above the brim than in the bowl.

hear (hiə) v.t. (past, p.p. **heard** (hœd)) 1 to perceive by the ear, to perceive the sound of. 2 to listen to, to attend to. 3 to listen to as a judge etc. 4 to understand by listening. 5 to be a hearer of. 6 to pay regard to, to heed, to obey. 7 to be informed of by report. 8 to receive a communication (from). ~v.i. 1 to have the sense of hearing. 2 to be told, to be informed (of, about etc.). **hear!** **hear!** used to express agreement or approval. **to hear someone out** to listen to what a person has to say without interrupting. **to hear tell/ say** to have been told (of something). **will not hear of** will not consider allowing or agreeing. **hearable** a. **hearer** n. 1 a person who hears. 2 a member of an audience. **hearing** n. 1 the act of perceiving sound. 2 the sense by which sound is perceived. 3 audience, attention. 4 (Law) a judicial trial or investigation. 5 earshot (within hearing). **hearing aid** n. a device for assisting a person with a hearing problem to hear. **hearing-impaired** a. having defective hearing.

†**hearken** (hah´kən), **harken** v.i. to listen attentively (to). ~v.t. to hear, to regard. **hearkener** n.

hearsay (hiə´sā) n. common talk, report or gossip. **hearsay evidence** n. evidence given in a court of law based on what was reported to the witness.

hearse (hœs) n. a vehicle in which the dead are taken to the place of burial or cremation.

heart (haht) n. 1 the muscular central organ of the circulation of the blood, which keeps going by its rhythmical contraction and dilation. 2 the breast, the position of the heart. 3 capacity for feeling; the emotions or affections, esp. the passion of love. 4 sensibility, tenderness. 5 zeal, ardour, courage, spirit. 6 the central or innermost part. 7 the essential or most important part. 8 the round head of a cabbage etc. 9 strength, efficacy, fertility. 10 a conventional representation of a heart, as on a valentine. 11 anything heart-shaped. **12 a** (*pl.*) a suit of cards marked with figures like hearts. **b** a card of this suit. **c** (*pl.*) a card game involving the taking of tricks, those of hearts being disadvantageous. **after one's own heart** exactly as one desires; as one feels or thinks oneself. **at heart 1** in reality, truly, at bottom. **2** in one's inmost feelings. **by heart** by rote, by or from memory. **from (the bottom of) one's heart 1** with absolute sincerity. **2** fervently. **have a heart!** be more considerate; do not be so harsh. **heart and soul** with full commitment, devotedly. **in (good) heart** in good spirits. **in one's heart** inwardly, secretly. **to break someone's heart** to cause someone overwhelming grief. **to cross one's heart** to promise or aver something solemnly. **to have one's heart in** (*usu. neg.*) to be fully committed or devoted to. **to have one's heart in one's mouth** to be violently frightened or startled. **to have one's heart in the right place** to have a kind nature; to have good intentions. **to have the heart to** (*usu. neg.*) to be able or have the courage to (do something unkind or unpleasant). **to lose heart** to become discouraged. **to one's heart's content** as much as one likes. **to put one's heart into** to become fully committed or devoted to, to do whole-heartedly. **to set one's heart on** to want very much. **to take heart** to pluck up courage. **to take to heart** to be greatly affected by. **to wear one's heart on one's sleeve 1** to be excessively frank and unreserved. **2** to reveal one's inmost feelings and thoughts. **with all one's heart 1** very willingly. **2** completely, utterly. **heartache** *n.* anguish of mind. **heart attack** *n.* an acute loss of normal function in the heart, a coronary thrombosis. **heartbeat** *n.* a pulsation of the heart. **heartbreak** *n.* overpowering sorrow. **heartbreaker** *n.* a person who or thing which breaks the heart. **heartbreaking** *a.* **heartbreakingly** *adv.* **heartbroken** *a.* **heartburn** *n.* a burning pain in the stomach arising from indigestion. **hearted** *a.* **heart failure** *n.* a condition in which the heart fails to function normally, often leading to death. **heartfelt** *a.* deeply felt, sincere. **heartland** *n.* (*often pl.*) the central or most important part of a country etc. **heartless** *a.* having or showing no feeling or affection; insensible, pitiless, cruel. **heartlessly** *adv.* **heartlessness** *n.* **heart-lung machine** *n.* a machine that adopts the function of a patient's heart and lungs during heart surgery. **heart-rending** *a.* heartbreaking, intensely afflictive. **heart-rendingly** *adv.* **heart's-blood** *n.* the lifeblood. **heart-searching** *n.* an anguished examination of one's feelings etc. **heartsick** *a.* **1** pained in mind. **2** deeply afflicted. **heartsickness** *n.* **heartstrings** *n.pl.* **1** the sensibilities; pity, compassion. **2** one's deepest affections. **heart-throb** *n.* **1** the beating of the heart. **2** a person, e.g. a film star, adulated by many. **heart-to-heart** *n.*, *a.* (a conversation) of a searching and intimate nature. **heart-warming** *a.* inspiring emotional approval. **heartwood** *n.* the hardest, inner section of a tree trunk; duramen.

hearten (hah´tən) *v.t.* to encourage, to inspire, to stir up. **heartener** *n.* **heartening** *a.* **hearteningly** *adv.*

hearth (hahth) *n.* **1** the floor of a fireplace; the area around a fireplace. **2** the fireside as a symbol of the domestic circle, the home. **3** that part of a reverberatory furnace in which the ore is laid, or in a blast furnace the lowest part through which the metal flows. **hearthrug** *n.* a rug placed in front of a fireplace. **hearthstone** *n.* **1** a stone forming a hearth. **2** a soft kind of stone for whitening hearths etc.

heartsease (hahts´ēz), **heart's-ease** *n.* **1** the wild pansy, *Viola tricolor.* **2** peace of mind.

hearty (hah´ti) *a.* (*comp.* **heartier,** *superl.* **heartiest**) **1** proceeding from the heart, sincere. **2** cordial, good-natured, kindly. **3** healthy (*hale and hearty*). **4** of keen appetite. **5** full, abundant, satisfying. **6** boisterous. **~n.** **1** a brave, hearty person, esp. a sailor; a fellow sailor. **2** an extrovert person, esp. a sporty one. **heartily** *adv.* **heartiness** *n.*

heat (hēt) *n.* **1** (*Physics*) a form of energy capable of melting and decomposing matter, and transmissible by means of radiation, conduction or convection. **2** hotness, the sensation produced by a hot body. **3** hot weather. **4** an inflamed condition of the skin, flesh etc. **5** hotness or pungency of flavour. **6** violence, vehemence, fury; anger. **7** intense excitement. **8** warmth of temperament; animation, fire. **9** sexual receptiveness in animals, esp. in female mammals. **10** any one of a series of courses in a race or other contest. **11** (*sl.*) coercive pressure. **12** (*sl.*) searches etc. by police after a crime. **~v.t.** **1** to make hot. **2** to inflame, to cause to ferment; to excite. **~v.i.** **1** to become hot. **2** to become inflamed or excited. **in the heat of the moment** without thinking; without prior consideration (because of the pressure of events). **on heat** (of a female mammal) ready for mating. **to take the heat out of** to make (a situation) less emotional or tense. **to turn the heat on** (*coll.*) to put (a person) under pressure; to direct criticism at (a person). **heated** *a.* **1** passionate, angry. **2** made hot. **heatedly** *adv.* **heater** *n.* **1** a device that heats. **2** (*sl.*) a pistol. **heat-exchanger** *n.* a device that transfers heat from one fluid to another. **heating** *n.* **1** the action of making hot. **2** the means of provision of heat to a building etc. **heatproof** *a.* designed to be able to resist heat. **~v.t.** to make heatproof. **heat-resistant** *a.* heatproof. **heat-seeking** *a.* (of a missile) guided by an infra-red detector. **heatspot** *n.* an urticarious pimple attributed to heat. **heatstroke** *n.* a condition characterized by a high temperature, faintness etc., caused by exposure to excessive heat. **heatwave** *n.* an unbroken spell of hot weather.

heath (hēth) *n.* **1** an open space of country, esp. one covered with shrubs and coarse herbage. **2** (*Bot.*) an area with many ericaceous shrubs. **3** any plant belonging to the genus *Erica*, or the allied genus *Calluna*, consisting of narrow-leaved evergreen shrubs with wiry stems and red or reddish flowers. **heathland** *n.* an area of heath. **heathy** *a.*

heathen (hē´dhən) *n.* **1** a person who is not Christian, Jewish or Muslim. **2** a non-believer, a pagan, an idolater. **3** an unenlightened or barbarous person. ~*a.* **1** that is a heathen. **2** of or relating to heathens. **the heathen** (*collect.*) heathen people. **heathendom** *n.* **heathenism, heathenry** *n.*

heather (hedh´ə) *n.* **1** a low-growing ericaceous plant, *Calluna vulgaris*, with narrow leaves, wiry stems and purple, pink or white flowers. **2** any of various similar plants. **heather mixture** *n.* **1** a fabric of a speckled colour supposed to resemble heather. **2** the speckled colour of this. **heathery** *a.*

Heath Robinson (hēth rob´insən) *a.* (of a device) ingenious and extremely complex.

heave (hēv) *v.t.* (*past, p.p.* **heaved**, (*esp. Naut.*) **hove** (hōv)) **1** to lift, to raise, with effort. **2** to utter or force from the breast (*heave a sigh*). **3** (*coll.*) to throw, to cast (something heavy). **4** (*Naut.*) to hoist (as the anchor), to haul. ~*v.i.* **1** to rise and fall with alternate or successive motions. **2** to pant. **3** to retch, to vomit. ~*n.* **1** an upward motion or swelling. **2** the act of heaving. **3** a sigh. **4** an effort to vomit. **5** the amount of displacement of a vein or stratum, esp. measured in a horizontal direction. **to heave in/ into sight** to come into sight. **to heave to 1** (*Naut.*) to bring a ship to a standstill. **2** (*Naut.*) to bring the head (of a ship) to the wind and so stop its motion. **heave-ho** *int.* used by sailors in hauling up the anchor. ~*n.* **1** a cry of 'heave-ho'. **2** dismissal, removal. **heaver** *n.*

heaven (hev´ən) *n.* **1** (*often in pl.*) the sky, the firmament; the atmosphere enveloping the earth regarded as the region in which the clouds float, the winds blow etc. **2** (*also* **Heaven**) the abode of God or the gods and the blessed. **3** (*usu.* **Heaven**) God, providence. **4** any place or state of extreme joy or pleasure. **5** (*coll.*) something extremely pleasing. ~*int.* (*sing. or pl.*) used to express surprise, irritation etc. **heavens above!** used to express surprise, dismay, irritation etc. **heavenly** *a.* **1** of or relating to the heavens, celestial. **2** inhabiting heaven; divine. **3** situated in the heavens (as the planets, stars etc.). **4** supremely blessed or excellent. **5** (*coll.*) highly pleasing, delicious. **heavenliness** *n.* **heavenly body** *n.* a sun, star, planet or other mass of matter, as distinct from the earth. **heavenly host** *n.* the host of heaven. **heaven-sent** *a.* (of an opportunity etc.) coming at an opportune moment. **heavenward** *a., adv.* **heavenwards** *adv.*

heavy (hev´i) *a.* (*comp.* **heavier**, *superl.* **heaviest**) **1** having great weight, weighty, ponderous. **2** of great density or specific gravity, dense. **3** (*Physics, Mil.*) of a larger and weightier kind than the usual or standard (as metal, artillery etc.). **4** great, powerful, forcible, violent. **5** concerned with large amounts or dealings. **6** requiring great effort. **7** unwieldy, clumsy. **8** plentiful, abundant; large in amount. **9** hard to digest. **10** weighed down, loaded (with). **11** not easily borne. **12** oppressive, grievous, severe; burdensome, obstructive, clogging; difficult. **13** stern, strict. **14** drowsy, dull, sluggish, stupid. **15** tedious. **16** doleful, depressing, depressed. **17** excessively serious, sombre. **18** (of the ground) soft and wet. **19** (of the sky, clouds etc.) threatening, louring. **20** (of bread, cakes etc.) not properly raised. **21** (of wine etc.) of full body. **22** armed with heavy weapons. ~*n.* (*pl.* **heavies**) **1** (*coll.*) a thug, a villain. **2** a villainous or tragic role in a play. **3** (*usu. in pl., coll.*) a serious, broadsheet newspaper, rather than a popular tabloid. **4** anything large or weighty of its kind. ~*adv.* heavily, with great weight. **heavy on 1** using a lot of. **2** unduly strict with or harsh to. **3** giving hard wear to. **heavily** *adv.* **heaviness** *n.* **heavy breather** *n.* **1** a person who breathes audibly. **2** a person who makes obscene telephone calls, panting audibly while doing so. **heavy breathing** *n.* **heavy chemicals** *n.pl.* chemicals produced in bulk for agriculture and industry. **heavy-duty** *a.* **1** designed to sustain more than usual wear. **2** (*N Am., coll.*) larger than usual in size, amount etc. **heavy-footed** *a.* walking heavily or clumsily, ponderous. **heavy going** *pred.a.* difficult to get through, laborious. **heavy-handed** *a.* **1** clumsy, awkward. **2** oppressive. **heavy-handedly** *adv.* **heavy-handedness** *n.* **heavy-headed** *a.* headachy, stupid, drowsy. **heavy-hearted** *a.* dejected. **heavy hydrogen** *n.* deuterium. **heavy industry** *n.* industry involved in the manufacturing of large machinery, vehicles etc., or the extraction and processing of raw materials. **heavyish** *a.* **heavy metal** *n.* **1** a metal with a high specific gravity. **2** a type of loud rock music with a strong beat. **3** heavy artillery. **heavy petting** *n.* close sexual contact without intercourse. **heavy sleeper** *n.* a person who sleeps very deeply and is not easy to wake. **heavy water** *n.* deuterium oxide, a liquid similar to ordinary water, with density about 10% greater. **heavyweight** *n.* **1** a person or animal of more than average weight. **2** a boxer, wrestler, weightlifter etc. in the highest main weight category. **3** this weight category. **4** a jockey above the average weight. **5** (*coll.*) a person of great power, influence or intellect.

hebe (hē´bi) *n.* an evergreen shrub of the genus *Hebe*, with spikes of purple or white flowers.

Hebraic (hibrā´ik) *a.* **1** of or relating to the Hebrews. **2** of or relating to Hebrew. **Hebraically** *adv.* **Hebraism** (hē´-) *n.* **1** the thought or religion of the Hebrews. **2** a Hebrew characteristic. **3** a Hebrew idiom or expression. **Hebraist** *n.* a person learned in Hebrew language and literature.

Hebrew (hē´broo) *n.* **1** the Semitic language of the ancient Jews and, in a modern form, of the State of Israel. **2** an Israelite. **3** (*often offensive*) a

Jew. ~a. **1** of or relating to Hebrew. **2** of or relating to the Israelites or Jews.

heck (hek) *int.* (*coll.*) used to express irritation, dismay etc. ~*n.* hell (*What the heck do you think you're up to?*).

heckle (hek´əl) *v.t.* **1** to interrupt and worry (a public speaker) by deliberately inconvenient questions, taunts etc. **2** to hackle. ~*n.* an act of heckling a speaker. **heckler** *n.*

hectare (hek´teə, -tah) *n.* a measure of area equal to 10,000 sq. metres or 2.471 acres. **hectarage** *n.*

hectic (hek´tik) *a.* full of excitement, exciting, wild; very busy. **hectically** *adv.*

hecto- (hek´tō) *comb. form* a hundred. **hectogram** (hek´təgram), **hectogramme** *n.* a weight of 100 grams or 3.52 oz. **hectograph** (hek´təgrahf) *n.* a machine for multiplying copies of writings or drawings. **hectolitre** (hek´təlētə), (*N Am.*) **hectoliter** *n.* a liquid measure 100 litres or 3.531 cu. ft. **hectometre** (hek´təmētə), (*N Am.*) **hectometer** *n.* a measure of length equal to 100 metres or 109.3633 yds.

hector (hek´tə) *v.t.* to bully, to treat with insolence. ~*n.* a bully, a blusterer. **hectorer** *n.* **hectoringly** *adv.*

he'd (hēd) *contr.* **1** he had. **2** he would.

heddle (hed´əl) *n.* one of the sets of parallel cords or wires forming loops for the warp threads of a loom.

hedge (hej) *n.* **1** a fence of bushes or small trees. **2** a barrier of any kind. **3** a means of securing oneself against loss. **4** a shifty or non-committal statement. ~*v.t.* **1** to fence (in) with or separate (off) by a hedge. **2** to surround or enclose with or as with a hedge. **3** to secure oneself against loss (on a speculation etc.) by transactions that would provide some compensation. ~*v.i.* **1** to plant or repair hedges. **2** to act in a shifty way, to avoid making a decisive statement. **hedge-hop** *v.i.* (*pres.p.* **hedge-hopping**, *past, p.p.* **hedge-hopped**) to fly very low over fields etc. **hedgeless** *a.* **hedger** *n.* **hedgerow** *n.* a row of shrubs planted as a hedge. **hedge sparrow** *n.* a common European bird, *Prunella modularis*, one of the warblers; the dunnock. **hedge trimmer** *n.* a power tool with a cutter for trimming hedges.

hedgehog (hej´hog) *n.* **1** a small insectivorous mammal, *Erinaceus europaeus*, covered above with spines, and able to roll itself up into a ball. **2** any other animal covered with spines, such as the porcupine.

hedonism (hē´dənizm, hed´-) *n.* **1** the doctrine or belief that pleasure is the chief good. **2** behaviour motivated by this. **hedonist** *n.* **hedonistic** (-nis´-) *a.* **hedonistically** *adv.*

-hedron (hē´drən, hed´-) *comb. form* (*pl.* **-hedra** (-drə), **-hedrons**) a solid figure having the specified number of sides. **-hedral** *comb. form* having the specified number of sides.

heebie-jeebies (hēbijē´biz) *n.pl.* (*coll.*) nervous anxiety, apprehension (*suffering from the heebie-jeebies*).

heed (hēd) *v.t.* to pay attention to, to take notice of. ~*n.* **1** care, attention. **2** careful consideration. **heedful** *a.* **1** attentive, regardful (of). **2** circumspect, wary. **heedfully** *adv.* **heedfulness** *n.* **heedless** *a.* **1** careless. **2** thoughtless. **3** negligent (of). **heedlessly** *adv.* **heedlessness** *n.*

hee-haw (hē´haw) *v.i.* to bray like a donkey. ~*n.* **1** a donkey's bray. **2** a loud and foolish laugh.

heel¹ (hēl) *n.* **1** the rounded hinder part of the human foot. **2** the corresponding part of the hind limb in quadrupeds, often above the foot. **3** the part of a shoe, stocking etc. covering the heel. **4** a block built up of pieces of leather to raise the hinder part of a boot or shoe from the ground. **5** a heel-like protuberance, knob or part, such as the lower end of a mast, the hindermost part of a ship's keel, the cusp of a molar tooth, the crook in the head of a golf club. **6** the crusty end of a loaf of bread. **7** the rind of a cheese. **8** the latter part, the tail-end of anything. **9** (*coll.*) a contemptible person. ~*v.t.* **1** to add a heel to; to repair a heel of. **2** in rugby, to pass (the ball) with the heels. **3** in golf, to hit (the ball) with the heel of a club. ~*int.* used to instruct a dog to walk close behind. **at heel** (of a dog) close behind. **at the heels of** close behind. **on the heels of** following closely after. **to dig one's heels in** to be obstinate. **to heel 1** (of a dog) close behind. **2** (of a person) under control. **to show a clean pair of heels (to)** to run away (from). **to take to one's heels** to run away. **to turn on one's heel** to turn round sharply. **heelball** *n.* a composition of hard wax and lampblack, used to give a smooth surface to heels, and for taking rubbings of inscriptions etc. **-heeled** *a.* **heelless** *a.*

heel² (hēl) *v.i.* of a ship, to incline or cant over to one side. ~*v.t.* to make (a ship) do this. ~*n.* an inclination to one side (of a ship, etc.).

heel³ (hēl) *v.t.* to plant in the ground and cover the roots.

heft (heft) *v.t.* to try the weight of by lifting. ~*n.* (*dial., N Am.*) weight, heaviness.

hefty (hef´ti) *a.* (*comp.* **heftier**, *superl.* **heftiest**) **1** strong, muscular, powerful. **2** big. **heftily** *adv.* **heftiness** *n.*

hegemony (higem´əni, -jem´-) *n.* leadership, predominance, esp. applied to the relation of one state to another or to a confederation. **hegemonic** (hegəmon´-, hej-) *a.*

Hegira (hej´irə), **Hejira, Hijra** (hij´rə) *n.* **1** the flight of Muhammad from Mecca to Medina, in AD 622, from which the Muslim era is computed. **2** a hurried escape from a dangerous situation.

heifer (hef´ə) *n.* **1** a young cow that has not yet calved. **2** (*sl., offensive*) a woman.

heigh (hā) *int.* used to call attention or express enquiry or encouragement. **heigh-ho** (-hō´) *int.* used to express disappointment, weariness or regret.

height (hīt) *n.* **1** the distance of the top above the foot, basis or foundation. **2** altitude above the ground, sea level or other recognized level. **3** the quality or state of being high. **4** an elevated position. **5** an eminence, a summit. **6** stature. **7** elevation in rank, office, society etc. **8** the fullest extent or degree. **heighten** v.t. **1** to make high or higher, to raise, to elevate. **2** to increase, to enhance, to intensify, to accentuate, to emphasize. ~v.i. **1** to rise. **2** to increase, to augment. **3** to intensify.

heinous (hā′nəs, hē′-) a. abominable, flagrant, atrocious; wicked in the highest degree. **heinously** adv. **heinousness** n.

heir (eə) n. **1** a person who by law succeeds or is entitled to succeed another in the possession of property or rank. **2** a person who succeeds to any gift, quality etc. **heir apparent** n. (pl. **heirs apparent**) the heir who will succeed on the death of the present possessor and whose right to succeed cannot be challenged. **heir-at-law** n. (pl. **heirs-at-law**) a person who inherits property by right of descent. **heirdom** n. **heiress** n. a female heir. **heirless** a. **heirloom** n. **1** an item of property which descends with an estate to an heir. **2** any possession that has remained in a family for several generations. **heir presumptive** n. (pl. **heirs presumptive**) an heir whose actual succession may be prevented by the birth of someone else. **heirship** n.

heist (hīst) n. (N Am., sl.) a burglary, a robbery. ~v.t. to rob, to steal.

Hejira HEGIRA.

held HOLD¹.

helenium (helē′niəm) n. any plant belonging to the genus Helenium, having daisy-like flowers and often growing up to 5 ft (1.6 m) tall.

heli- (hel′i) comb. form helicopter.

heliacal (hilī′əkəl) a. (Astron.) **1** closely connected with the sun. **2** rising just before the sun. **heliacal rising, heliacal setting** n. (Astron.) the apparent rising or setting of a star when it first becomes perceptible or invisible in the rays of the sun.

helianthemum (hēlian′thiməm) n. any low-growing evergreen plant of the genus Helianthemum, having yellow or orange saucer-shaped flowers.

helianthus (hēlian′thəs) n. any plant, such as the sunflower, belonging to the genus Helianthus, typically having large daisy-like flowers.

helical (hel′ikəl) a. like a helix; spiral. **helically** adv. **helicoid** (-koid) a.

helices HELIX.

helichrysum (helikrī′səm) n. any plant of the genus Helichrysum, having daisy-like flowers with papery petals.

helicopter (hel′ikoptə) n. an aircraft with one or more power-driven airscrews mounted on vertical axes with the aid of which it can take off and land vertically. ~v.t. to transport by helicopter. ~v.i. to fly in a helicopter. **helicopter pad** n. an area, e.g. on the roof of a building, where helicopters can take off and land.

helio- (hē′liō) comb. form **1** of or relating to the sun. **2** produced by the rays of the sun.

heliocentric (hēliōsen′trik) a. **1** having reference to the sun as centre. **2** regarded from the point of view of the sun. **heliocentrically** adv.

heliograph (hē′liəgrahf) n. **1** an apparatus for signalling by reflecting flashes of sunlight. **2** a heliogram. **3** an instrument for obtaining photographs of the sun. **4** an engraving obtained by a process in which a prepared plate is exposed to the light. ~v.i., v.t. to signal with a heliograph; to photograph by a heliographic process. **heliogram** (-gram) n. a message transmitted by heliograph. **heliography** (-og′rə-) n. (pl. **heliographies**).

heliogravure (hēliōgrəvūə′) n. photogravure.

heliolatry (hēliol′ətri) n. sun-worship. **heliolater** n. **heliolatrous** a.

heliolithic (hēliōlith′ik) a. of or relating to a civilization known for sun-worship and the erection of megaliths.

heliometer (hēliom′itə) n. an instrument for measuring small angles in the heavens, such as the angular distance between stars, the diameter of stars etc. (orig. for measuring the diameter of the sun).

heliostat (hē′liəstat) n. an instrument, comprising a mirror turned by clockwork, by which the rays of the sun are continuously reflected in a fixed direction. **heliostatic** (-stat′ik) a.

heliotherapy (hēliəther′əpi) n. curative treatment by exposing the body to the rays of the sun.

heliotrope (hē′liətrōp) n. **1** any plant of the borage family belonging to the genus Heliotropium, having scented purple flowers. **2** any of various plants whose flowers turn with the sun. **3** a purple colour characteristic of heliotrope flowers. **4** a red-spotted variety of quartz, bloodstone. ~a. of the purple colour of heliotrope flowers. **heliotropic** (-trop′-), **heliotropical** a. of, relating to or manifesting heliotropism. **heliotropism** (-ot′rə-), **heliotropy** (-ot′rəpi) n. movement of leaves or flowers towards the sun.

heliotype (hē′liətīp) n. a picture obtained by printing from a gelatin surface in the same way as from a lithographic stone.

helipad (hel′ipad) n. a helicopter pad.

heliport (hel′ipawt) n. an airport for the landing and departure of helicopters.

heli-skiing (hel′iskēing) n. skiing from a starting point reached by helicopter.

helium (hē′liəm) n. (Chem.) a gaseous inert element, chem. symbol He, at. no. 2.

helix (hē′liks) n. (pl. **helices** -lisēz) **1** a spiral or coiled curve, as of wire or rope. **2** (Geom.) a curve cutting a line at a constant angle with the axis of a cylinder or solid cone. **3** (Anat.) the rim or fold of the external ear. **4** (Archit.) a small volute under the abacus of a Corinthian column, and other spiral ornaments. **5** a gastropod of the genus Helix, containing the common snails.

hell (hel) *n*. **1** the place of punishment for the wicked after death in Christianity, Judaism and Islam; the place or state of the dead. **2** a place of extreme misery, pain or suffering; torment, torture. *~int*. used to express anger, annoyance etc. **a hell of a/ helluva** (*coll*.) a very good, bad, remarkable etc. (thing of its kind). **come hell or high water** (*coll*.) whatever may happen. **for the hell of it** for amusement, just for fun. **hell for leather** (*coll*.) very fast. **hell to pay** very unpleasant consequences. **like hell 1** (*coll*.) very hard, much etc. **2** (*coll*.) used to deny a statement made by another. **not to have a hope in hell** not to have any chance at all. **to beat/ scare etc. the hell out of** to beat, scare etc. severely. **to give someone hell 1** to scold someone severely. **2** to make life very difficult for someone. **to play (merry) hell with 1** (*coll*.) to harm or damage. **2** (*coll*.) to scold. **what the hell?** what does it matter? **hellbender** *n*. a salamander, *Cryptobranchus alleganiensis*, of N America. **hell-bent** *a*. recklessly intent (on). **hell-cat** *n*. a witch, a hag; a vicious woman. **hellfire** *n*. the torments of hell. **hell-hole** *n*. a terrible place. **hell-hound** *n*. a fiend of hell. **hellish** *a*. **1** of or relating to hell. **2** detestable. **3** atrociously wicked. *~adv*. (*coll*.) very; terribly (*hellish difficult*). **hellishly** *adv*. **hellishness** *n*. **hell-like** *a*. **hellraiser** *n*. a troublemaker. **hellraising** *a*., *n*. **Hell's Angel** *n*. a member of a gang wearing leather and riding motorcycles, often with a reputation for causing trouble. **hellward** *a*., *adv*.

hellebore (hel´ibaw) *n*. **1** any plant of the ranunculaceous genus *Helleborus*, containing *H. niger*, the Christmas rose, and the hellebore of the ancients, *H. officinalis*. **2** a lily, *Veratrum alba*. **helleborine** (-rēn, -rīn) *n*. any temperate orchid of the genus *Epipactis* or *Cephalanthera*.

Hellene (hel´ēn) *n*. (*pl*. **Hellenes**) **1** an ancient Greek, a person of Greek descent whether inhabiting Europe or Asia Minor. **2** a citizen of modern Greece. **Hellenic** (-len´-, -lē´-), **†Hellenian** (-lē´-) *a*. **Hellenism** (hel´ə-) *n*. **1** Greek civilization or culture. **2** cultivation of Greek ideas, language, style etc. **Hellenist** *n*. a person who is learned in Greek language and literature. **Hellenistic** (-nis´-) *a*.

hello (həlō´), **hallo, hullo** *int*. **1** an informal greeting. **2** a preliminary summons and answer when telephoning. **3** an exclamation of surprise. **4** a call for attention. *~n*. (*pl*. **hellos, hallos, hullos**) a cry of 'hello'. *~v.i.* (*3rd pers. sing. pres.* **helloes, halloes, hulloes**, *past*, *p.p.* **helloed, halloed, hulloed**) to cry 'hello'.

helm (helm) *n*. **1** the instrument or apparatus by which a vessel is steered; the rudder and its operative parts, such as the tiller or wheel; the tiller. **2** turning of the helm. *~v.t.* **1** to guide, to steer. **2** to manage. **at the helm** steering, in control, at the head. **helmsman** *n*. (*pl*. **helmsmen**) person who steers a vessel.

...et (hel´mit) *n*. **1** a piece of defensive armour for the head. **2** a protective covering for the head worn by police officers, cyclists etc. **3** (*Bot*.) the hooded upper lip of some flowers. **4** a helmet shell. **helmeted** *a*. **helmet shell** *n*. a tropical mollusc belonging to the genus *Cassis*.

helot (hel´ət) *n*. a slave or serf. **helotism** *n*. **helotry** *n*.

help (help) *v.t.* (*past* **helped**, **†holp** (holp), *p.p.* **helped**, **†holpen** (hol´pən)) **1** to provide with something needed or wanted to achieve an end; to assist, to aid. **2** to contribute to. **3** to improve (a situation etc.). **4** to supply succour or relief to in an emergency. **5** to remedy, to prevent. *~v.i.* **1** to lend aid or assistance. **2** to be of use. **3** to be an improvement. *~n.* **1** aid, assistance, the act of helping; the fact of being helped. **2** a person or thing that helps. **3 a** a person hired for a job, esp. a farm worker or domestic servant. **b** several employees collectively. **4** an escape, a remedy. **so help me (God)** a strong oath or asseveration. **to help oneself** to refrain from acting (*He tried not to laugh, but couldn't help himself*). **to help oneself to** to take for oneself without waiting for offer or permission. **to help out** to help to complete or to get out of a difficulty. **helpdesk** *n*. an information point or telephone line offering technical support etc. within an organization. **helper** *n*. **helpful** *a*. **1** giving help, useful. **2** obliging. **helpfully** *adv*. **helpfulness** *n*. **helping** *a*. giving help or support. *~n.* a portion of food given at table. **helping hand** *n*. an act of assisting. **helpless** *a*. **1** lacking power to help oneself. **2** without help. **3** made powerless or weak. **helplessly** *adv*. **helplessness** *n*. **helpline** *n*. **1** a telephone line operated by a charity etc. for people in distress. **2** a telephone line operated by a commercial organization to provide assistance or information.

helpmate (help´māt) *n*. a partner or helpful companion, esp. a spouse.

helter-skelter (heltəskel´tə) *adv*. in great hurry and confusion. *~a.* hurried and confused. *~n.* **1** hurry or confusion. **2** a funfair amusement consisting of a tower with a spiral slide.

helve (helv) *n*. the handle of a weapon or tool.

hem[1] (hem) *n*. the edge or border of a garment or piece of cloth, esp. when doubled and sewn in to strengthen it. *~v.t.* (*pres.p.* **hemming**, *past*, *p.p.* **hemmed**) **1** to double over and sew in the border of. **2** to enclose or shut (in, about or round). **hemline** *n*. the hemmed bottom edge of a skirt or dress etc. **hemstitch** *n*. an ornamental stitch made by drawing out parallel threads and fastening the cross threads. *~v.t.* to hem with this stitch.

hem[2] (hem) *int*., *n*. a voluntary short cough, uttered by way of warning, encouragement etc. *~v.i.* (*pres.p.* **hemming**, *past*, *p.p.* **hemmed**) **1** to utter this sound. **2** to hesitate in speech. **to hem and haw** to hum and haw.

hema- HAEMA-.

hemerocallis (hemərōkal´is) *n*. (*pl*. **hemerocallises**) the day lily.

hemi- (hem´i) *comb. form* **1** half, halved. **2** of or relating to one half.

-hemia -AEMIA.

hemidemisemiquaver (hem´idemisemi- kwāvə) *n.* (*Mus.*) a musical note equal in time to half a demisemiquaver.

hemiplegia (hemiplē´jə) *n.* (*Med.*) paralysis of one side of the body. **hemiplegic** (-plej´-, -plē´-) *a., n.*

hemipterous (hemip´tərəs) *a.* of or belonging to the order Hemiptera of insects with piercing or sucking mouthparts, and usu. having four wings, the upper pair partly horny and partly mem- branous, comprising bugs, lice etc.

hemisphere (hem´isfiə) *n.* the half of a sphere or globe, divided by a plane passing through its centre. **hemispheric** (-sfer´-), **hemispherical** *a.*

hemlock (hem´lok) *n.* **1** any poisonous umbel- liferous plant of the genus *Conium*, esp. *C. macu- latum*, having finely divided leaves, spotted stems and small white flowers. **2** a poison derived from this. **3** HEMLOCK SPRUCE (under HEM- LOCK). **hemlock spruce, hemlock fir** *n.* **1** any coniferous tree of the genus *Tsuga*, having short flat needles. **2** the wood of any of these trees.

hemo- HAEMO-.

hemp (hemp) *n.* **1** an Asian herbaceous plant, *Cannabis sativa.* **2** the fibre of this, used for making ropes, coarse fabrics etc. **3** any of several narcotic drugs derived from the hemp plant, esp. cannabis or marijuana. **4** any of various other vegetable fibres used for cloth or cordage. **hemp agrimony** *n.* a composite plant, *Eupatorium cannabinum*, having small clusters of reddish flowers. **hempen** *a.* made of or resembling hemp. **hemp-nettle** *n.* a coarse plant of the labiate genus *Galeopsis.*

hen (hen) *n.* **1** the female of any bird, esp. the domestic fowl. **2** a female of certain other animals such as the lobster, crab or salmon. **hen and chickens** *n.* (*pl.* **hens and chickens**) (*sing. or pl. in constr.*) any of several plants, such as the houseleek or ground ivy, that produce many off- shoots or runners. **henbane** *n.* **1** a poisonous plant, *Hyoscyamus niger*, having sticky hairy leaves and an unpleasant smell. **2** a narcotic drug obtained from this. **hen-coop** *n.* a coop or cage for fowls. **hen harrier, +hen-driver** *n.* the com- mon harrier, *Circus cyaneus.* **hen house** *n.* a small shed for fowls to roost in. **hen-party** *n.* (*coll., sometimes derog.*) a gathering for women only. **henpeck** *v.t.* (of a woman) to harass (a man, esp. her husband) by constant nagging. **hen- pecked** *a.* **hen-roost** *n.* a place for fowls to roost in. **hen-run** *n.* an enclosure for fowls, esp. one made of chicken wire. **hen-toed** *a.* having the toes turned in.

hence (hens) *adv.* **1** from this time. **2** in con- sequence of this, consequently, therefore. **hence- forth, henceforward, henceforwards** *adv.* from this time on.

henchman (hench´mən) *n.* (*pl.* **henchmen**) (*often. derog.*) a faithful follower or supporter.

hendeca- (hen´dekə, hendek´ə) *comb. form* eleven.

hendecagon (hendek´əgon) *n.* a plane figure of eleven sides and angles.

henge (henj) *n.* a circle of stones or staves of prehistoric date.

henna (hen´ə) *n.* **1** a tropical shrub, *Lawsonia inermis*, having white or red fragrant flowers. **2** a dye from this plant used for dyeing hair and, in the East, parts of the body. ~*v.t.* (*3rd pers. sing. pres.* **hennas**, *pres.p.* **hennaing**, *past, p.p.* **hennaed**) to dye with henna.

henry (hen´ri) *n.* (*pl.* **henries, henrys**) a unit of inductance of a circuit in which a change of current of 1 ampere per second induces an emf of 1 volt.

hep[1] (hep) *a.* (*comp.* **hepper**, *superl.* **heppest**) (*sl.*) HIP[4]. **hepcat** *n.* a stylish or fashionable person, esp. as regards jazz.

hep[2] HIP[2].

heparin (hep´ərin) *n.* a polysaccharide, con- taining sulphate groups, present in most body tissues; an anticoagulant used in the treatment of thrombosis. **heparinize, heparinise** *v.t.*

hepatic (hipat´ik) *a.* **1** of or relating to the liver. **2** resembling the liver in colour or form. **hepatica** (-kə) *n.* any plant of the genus *Hepatica*, the members of which have lobed leaves.

hepatitis (hepətī´tis) *n.* inflammation or con- gestion of the liver. **hepatitis A** *n.* a form of viral hepatitis transmitted in contaminated food or drink. **hepatitis B** *n.* a form of viral hepatitis transmitted by infected blood transfusions or contaminated hypodermic needles.

hepta- (hep´tə) *comb. form* consisting of seven.

heptad (hep´tad) *n.* a sum or group of seven.

heptagon (hep´təgən) *n.* a plane figure having seven sides and seven angles. **heptagonal** (-tag´- ənəl) *a.*

heptahedron (heptəhē´drən) *n.* (*pl.* **heptahedra** (-drə), **heptahedrons**) a solid figure having seven sides. **heptahedral** *a.*

heptameter (heptam´itə) *n.* a line or verse of seven metrical feet.

heptathlon (heptath´lon) *n.* an athletic contest in which competitors take part in seven events. **heptathlete** *n.*

heptavalent (heptəvā´lənt) *a.* (*Chem.*) having a valency of seven.

her (hœ) *pron.* **1** objective (accusative and dative) of SHE. **2** (*dial.*) HERSELF. ~*a.* possessive of SHE. **her indoors** *n.* (*coll.*) one's wife.

Usage note Use of *her* in a subject, as in *Her and her brother were late*, is best avoided. See also notes under AS, BE, THAN.

---

herald (her´əld) *n.* **1** a messenger. **2** a harbinger, a precursor. **3** (*Hist.*) a person who had charge of the etiquette of chivalry and whose duties in- cluded blazoning the arms of the nobility etc.; an official at a tournament. **4** a member of the College of Arms. ~*v.t.* **1** to announce publicly. **2** to introduce, to usher in. **heraldry** (-ri) *n.* **1** the art and study of armorial bearings etc. **2** pomp, ceremony etc. **3** armorial bearings, emblazonment. **heraldic** (-ral´-) *a.* **heraldically** *adv.* **heraldist** *n.* a student of heraldry.

herb (hœb) *n.* **1** a plant producing shoots of only annual duration. **2** herbage, grass and other green food for cattle. **3** a plant having medicinal, culinary or aromatic properties. **herbaceous** (-bā´shəs) *a.* **1** of or relating to herbs. **2** that is a herb. **herbaceous border** *n.* a flower border with mainly perennial plants. **herbaceous perennial** *n.* a plant producing shoots of only annual duration but whose roots survive. **herbage** (-ij) *n.* **1** herbs collectively. **2** grass, pasture. **3** (*Law*) the right of pasture on another's land. **herbal** *a.* of or relating to herbs in medicine, cooking or perfumery. ~*n.* a book containing the names of plants, with a description of their properties, medicinal and other virtues etc. **herbalist** *n.* **1** a person skilled in the knowledge of herbs and their qualities. **2** a dealer in medicinal herbs. **3** a collector of plants. **herbarium** (-beə´riəm) *n.* (*pl.* **herbaria** (-riə), **herbariums**) **1** a systematic collection of dried plants. **2** a case, room or building for these. **herb beer** *n.* a soft drink made from herbs. **herb bennet** *n.* a common yellow-flowered plant, *Geum urbanum.* **herb Christopher** *n.* (*pl.* **herbs Christopher**) a baneberry, *Actaea spicata,* with white flowers. **herb Gerard** *n.* (*pl.* **herbs Gerard**) ground elder. **herbicide** *n.* a chemical that destroys vegetation, used to control weeds. **herbicidal** (-sī´-) *a.* **herbiferous** (-bif´ərəs) *a.* **herblike** *a.* **herb Paris** *n.* (*pl.* **herbs Paris**) a herb, *Paris quadrifolia,* growing in woods, with four leaves in the form of a cross and a terminal green flower. **herb Robert** *n.* (*pl.* **herbs Robert**) a cranesbill, *Geranium robertianum.* **herb tea** *n.* a drink made by infusing herbs. **herb tobacco** *n.* a mixture of herbs prepared for smoking. **herby** *a.* (*comp.* **herbier,** *superl.* **herbiest**) **1** of the nature of or like herbs. **2** abounding in herbs.

herbivore (hœ´bivaw) *n.* an animal, esp. a mammal, that feeds on grass or plants. **herbivorous** (-biv´-) *a.*

Hercules (hœ´kūlēz) *n.* a man of enormous strength. **Herculean** (-lē´ən) *a.* **1** exceedingly great, difficult or dangerous (as the labours of Hercules). **2** exceedingly strong or powerful. **Hercules beetle** *n.* a Brazilian arboreal beetle, *Dynastes hercules,* 5–6in. (12–15 cm) long, with hornlike projections on the head and thorax.

herd (hœd) *n.* **1** a number of beasts or cattle feeding, kept or driven together. **2** a crowd of people, a rabble. **3** (*usu. in comb.*) a keeper of a herd (*cowherd*; *goatherd*). ~*v.i.* to go in herds or companies. ~*v.t.* **1** to tend or watch (cattle etc.). **2** to form or bring into a herd. **3** to drive in a herd. **to ride herd on** (*N Am.*) to guard, to watch over. **herd book** *n.* a book containing the pedigrees of

high-bred cattle or pigs. **herd instinct** *n.* the impulse that urges people and animals to associate and act together and to do what others do. **herdsman,** †**herdman** *n.* (*pl.* **herdsmen,** †**herdmen**) a person who tends domestic animals, esp. cattle.

here (hiə) *adv.* **1** in or at this place or position. **2** to this place or position, hither, in this direction. **3** in the present life or state. **4** at this point. **5** on this occasion. ~*n.* this place, point or time. **here and now** right now, the present. **here and there 1** in this place and that. **2** hither and thither. **here goes!** said by a speaker who is about to do something. **here's to** let us drink a toast to. **here we go again!** said when the same unpleasant, predictable etc. thing seems to be about to happen again. **neither here nor there** unimportant, irrelevant. **hereabouts, hereabout** *adv.* somewhere about or near this place. **hereafter** *adv.* **1** for the future. **2** in a future state. ~*n.* **1** a future state. **2** the future life. **hereby** *adv.* by this means, by virtue of this. **herein** *adv.* (*formal*) in this document etc. **hereinafter** *adv.* (*formal*) **1** from this point or time onwards. **2** later or below in this document etc. **hereinbefore** *adv.* (*formal*) earlier or above in this document etc. **hereof** *adv.* (*formal*) of this; concerning this. **hereto** *adv.* (*formal*) **1** (attached) to this. **2** up to this place, point or time. **heretofore** *adv.* (*formal*) **1** below in this (document etc.). **2** before this time. **hereunder** *adv.* (*formal*) below in this document etc. **hereupon** *adv.* upon this, after this, at this, in consequence of this. **herewith** *adv.* with this (esp. of an enclosure in a letter etc.).

hereditable (hired´itəbəl) *a.* that may be inherited. **hereditability** (-bil´-) *n.* **hereditably** *adv.*

hereditament (herədit´əmənt) *n.* (*Law*) **1** any property that may be inherited. **2** inheritance.

hereditary (hired´itəri) *a.* **1** descending or passing by inheritance. **2** transmitted by descent from generation to generation. **3** holding or deriving by inheritance. **4** of or relating to inheritance. **hereditarily** *adv.* **hereditariness** *n.*

heredity (hired´iti) *n.* **1** the tendency to transmit individual characteristics to one's offspring. **2** genetically transmitted characteristics. **3** genetic constitution.

Hereford (her´ifəd) *n.* a breed of red and white beef cattle.

heresy (her´əsi) *n.* (*pl.* **heresies**) **1** departure from what is held to be true doctrine, esp. when such opinions lead to division in the Christian Church. **2** opinion that is contrary to what is normally accepted. **3** an instance of heresy; an unacceptable doctrine or opinion.

heretic (her´ətik) *n.* a person who holds unorthodox opinions, esp. in religious matters. **heretical** (-ret´-) *a.* **heretically** *adv.*

heritable (her´itəbəl) *a.* **1** (*esp. Biol.*) capable of being inherited. **2** (*Law*) passing by inheritance, esp. of lands and appurtenances as distinct from movable property. **3** capable of inheriting. **heritability** (-bil´-) *n.* **heritably** *adv.* by inheritance.

heritage (her´itij) *n.* **1** land or other property that passes by descent or course of law to an heir. **2** a share, portion, lot. **3** anything passed from one generation to another. **heritage centre** *n.* a local museum focusing on the cultural heritage of a specific area.

hermaphrodite (hœmaf´rədīt) *n.* **1** (*Biol.*) a human being or an animal abnormally combining in itself both male and female reproductive organs. **2** (*Zool.*) an animal in which the organs of both sexes are normally combined in the same individual. **3** (*Bot.*) a plant having the stamens and pistils in the same flower. **4** a person or thing in which opposite qualities are embodied. ~*a.* having the characteristics of a hermaphrodite. **hermaphroditic** (-dit´-), **hermaphroditical** *a.* **hermaphroditism** (-dit-) *n.*

hermeneutic (hœmənū´tik), **hermeneutical** *a.* interpreting, explaining, explanatory. **hermeneutically** *adv.* **hermeneutics** *n.* the art or science of interpretation, esp. of Scripture.

hermetic (hœmet´ik), **hermetical** (-ikəl) *a.* **1** having an airtight closure. **2** protected from outside forces. **3** of or belonging to alchemy. **4** esoteric, abstruse. **hermetically** *adv.* **hermetic seal** *n.* an airtight seal.

hermit (hœ´mit) *n.* **1** an early Christian recluse. **2** any person living in solitary contemplation. **hermitage** (-ij) *n.* **1** the cell or habitation of a hermit. **2** a monastery. **hermit crab, hermit lobster** *n.* a crab of the family Paguridae (so called because they live in abandoned mollusc shells). **hermitic** (-mit´-), **hermitical** *a.* **hermit thrush** *n.* a migratory N American thrush *Catharus guttatus.*

hernia (hœ´niə) *n.* (*pl.* **hernias, herniae** (-niē)) the protrusion of any organ, or part of an organ, from its natural place; a rupture. **hernial, herniary, herniated** *a.*

hero (hiə´rō) *n.* (*pl.* **heroes**) **1** a person of extraordinary valour, fortitude or enterprise. **2** the principal male character in a novel, play, poem etc. **heroi-comic** (hirōikom´-), **heroi-comical** *a.* **1** combining the heroic and the comic. **2** mockheroic, burlesque. **heroine** (her´ōin) *n.* **1** a heroic woman. **2** the principal female character in a novel, play, poem etc. **heroism** (her´-) *n.* **1** the quality, character or conduct of a hero. **2** extreme bravery. **heroize** (her´-), **heroise** *v.t.* to regard or treat as a hero, to make heroic. ~*v.i.* to show oneself off as a hero. **hero's welcome** *n.* a rapturous welcome, as given to a successful warrior. **hero-worship** *n.* **1** the deification of a hero. **2** excessive devotion shown to a person who is regarded as a hero. ~*v.t.* (*pres.p.* **hero-worshipping**, (*N Am.*) **hero-worshiping**, *past, p.p.* **hero-worshipped**, (*N Am.*) **hero-worshiped**) to worship as a hero. **hero-worshipper** *n.*

heroic (hirō´ik) *a.* **1** of, relating to or becoming a hero. **2** having the qualities or attributes of a hero. **3** relating to or describing the deeds of heroes. **4** bold, vigorous, attempting extreme deeds or methods. **5** (of art) large in scale or

subject. **6** (of language) high-flown or bombastic. **heroically** *adv.* **heroic couplet** *n.* a rhyming couplet in iambic pentameters. **heroics** *n.pl.* **1** heroic verses. **2** high-flown or bombastic language or sentiments. **3** heroic behaviour. **heroic verse** *n.* the metre of heroic or epic poetry, in English, German and Italian poetry, the iambic pentameter, in French, the alexandrine, and in Latin and Greek the hexameter.

heroin (her´oin) *n.* a derivative of morphine, used in medicine and by drug addicts.

heroine HERO.

heron (her´ən), †**hern** (hœn) *n.* a long-legged, long-necked wading bird of the family Ardeidae, esp. *Ardea cinerea*, the common European heron. **heronry** *n.* (*pl.* **heronries**) a place where herons breed.

herpes (hœ´pēz) *n.* a viral infection producing vesicles grouped on an inflamed skin surface such as the lip. **herpes simplex** (sim´pleks) *n.* infection with a herpes virus producing cold sores, genital inflammation or conjunctivitis. **herpes virus** *n.* any one of a family of viruses that cause herpes or other diseases. **herpes zoster** (zos´tə) *n.* SHINGLES. **herpetic** (-pet´-) *a., n.*

herpetology (hœpitol´əji) *n.* the study of reptiles and amphibians. **herpetologic** (-əloj´-), **herpetological** *a.* **herpetologist** *n.*

Herr (hea) *n.* (*pl.* **Herren** (her´ən)) **1** the German title corresponding to the English Mr. **2** a German man.

herring (her´ing) *n.* a soft-finned marine fish, *Clupea harengus*, of the N Atlantic, moving in large shoals and spawning near the coast. **herringbone** *n.* **1** a pattern used in textiles etc. resembling the spine and bones of a herring. **2** a kind of masonry in which the stones etc. are set obliquely in alternate rows. ~*v.t.* **1** to sew or stitch with herringbone stitch. **2** to give a herringbone pattern to. **herringbone stitch** *n.* a kind of cross stitch used in mending sails and for ornamental purposes. **herring gull** *n.* a large seagull, *Larus argentatus*, which feeds on herrings.

hers (hœz) *pron.* something which belongs to or is associated with her. **of hers** belonging or relating to her.

herself (həself´) *pron.* **1** SHE or HER (objective), used to give emphasis (usu. in apposition). **2** the reflexive form of HER. **3** her normal or usual self. **by herself** alone, unaided. **to be herself** to act in her normal manner.

Herts. (hahts) *abbr.* Hertfordshire.

hertz (hœts) *n.* (*pl.* **hertz**) a standard unit of frequency equal to one cycle per second.

he's (hēz) *contr.* **1** he is. **2** he has.

hesitate (hez´itāt) *v.i.* **1** to stop or pause in action. **2** to be doubtful or undecided. **3** to be reluctant (to). **4** to stammer. **hesitant** *a.* hesitating, dubious, vacillating, undecided. **hesitance, hesitancy** *n.* **hesitantly** *adv.* **hesitatingly** *adv.* **hesitation** (-ā´shən) *n.* **hesitative** *a.* **hesitator** *n.*

hesperidium (hesperid´iəm) *n.* (*pl.* **hesperidia** (-iə)) a citrus fruit, e.g. the orange, with a tough rind and a pulp divided into sections.

Hessian (hes´iən) *n.* **1** a native or inhabitant of Hesse. **2** (**hessian**) a coarse cloth made of hemp and jute. *~a.* **1** of or belonging to Hesse. **2** (**hessian**) made of hessian. **Hessian boot** *n.* a high boot with tassels, fashionable early in the 19th cent. **Hessian fly** *n.* (*pl.* **Hessian flies**) a small fly or midge, *Mayetiola destructor*, the larva of which attacks wheat in the US (believed to have been introduced to America by Hessian soldiers).

hetero (het´ərō) *n.* (*pl.* **heteros**) (*coll.*) a heterosexual person.

hetero- (het´ərō) *comb. form* **1** different, dissimilar. **2** irregular, abnormal.

heterochromatic (hetərōkrōmat´ik), **heterochromous** (-krō´məs) *a.* of different colours.

heterocyclic (hetərōsī´klik) *a.* (*Chem.*) (of an organic chemical compound) having a ring structure of atoms of different kinds in the molecules.

heterodox (het´ərədoks) *a.* contrary to received or established doctrines, principles or standards; heretical, not orthodox. **heterodoxy** *n.*

heterodyne (het´ərədīn) *a.* of or relating to a beat frequency caused in a radio receiver by the interplay of two alternating currents of similar frequencies. *~v.i.* to produce a lower frequency in this way.

heterogamous (hetərog´əməs) *a.* **1** (*Bot.*) having flowers or florets sexually different, as in certain Compositae, where the disc florets are male and the ray florets neuter or female. **2** characterized by alternation of generations. **3** (*Biol.*) characterized by reproduction by fusion of gametes differing in size and form. **heterogamy** *n.*

heterogeneous (hetərəjē´niəs), **heterogenous** (-oj´i-) *a.* **1** diverse in character or structure. **2** varied in content. **3** (*Math.*) of different kinds, dimensions or degree. **heterogeneity** (-nē´-) *n.* **heterogeneously** *adv.* **heterogeneousness** *n.*

heterogenesis (hetərəjen´əsis) *n.* **1** the production of offspring differing in kind from the parent. **2** spontaneous generation from inorganic matter. **heterogenetic** (-jinet´-) *a.*

heterogonous (hetərog´ənəs) *a.* (of certain flowers) having stamens and styles or pistils on different plants of the species differing in length so as to promote cross-fertilization. **heterogony** *n.* **1** the condition of being heterogonous. **2** alternation of generations, esp. sexual and hermaphroditic.

heterograft (het´ərəgrahft) *n.* a tissue graft obtained from a member of one species for a member of another.

heterologous (hetərol´əgəs) *a.* not homologous. **heterology** (-ji) *n.*

heteromerous (hetərom´ərəs) *a.* differing in number, form or character of parts; not isomerous.

heteromorphic (hetərōmaw´fik), **heteromorphous** (-fəs) *a.* **1** differing from the normal form. **2** having dissimilar forms. **3** (*Biol.*) (of insects) having different forms at different stages of development. **heteromorphism, heteromorphy** *n.*

heteronomous (hetəron´əməs) *a.* **1** subject to the law or rule of another, not autonomous. **2** (*Biol.*) having different laws of growth, diverging from the type. **heteronomy** *n.*

heteropathic (hetərəpath´ik) *a.* **1** allopathic. **2** having different effects. **heteropathy** (-rop´-) *n.*

heterophyllous (hetərəfil´əs) *a.* having leaves of different form on the same plant. **heterophylly** (-of´-) *n.*

heteropolar (hetərōpō´lə) *a.* having dissimilar (magnetic) poles.

heteropteran (hetərop´tərən) *n.* an insect of the suborder Heteroptera, including bugs in which the wings are of dissimilar parts. **heteropterous** *a.*

heterosexual (hetərəsek´sūəl, -shəl) *a.* **1** feeling sexual attraction to the opposite sex. **2** of or relating to heterosexuals or heterosexuality. *~n.* a heterosexual person. **heterosexism** *n.* discrimination by heterosexuals against homosexuals. **heterosexist** *a.*, *n.* **heterosexuality** (-al´-) *n.*

heterosis (hetərō´sis) *n.* abnormal vigour or strength typical of a hybrid plant or animal.

heterotaxy (het´ərətaksi) *n.* deviation of organs or parts from ordinary arrangement.

heterotrophic (hetərōtrō´fik) *a.* (*Biol.*) obtaining nourishment from organic compounds.

het up (het) *a.* (*coll.*) excited, agitated, annoyed.

heuchera (hū´kərə) *n.* a herbaceous plant of the genus *Heuchera* of the saxifrage family, with roundish leaves and stalks of red, white or green flowers rising directly from the rootstock.

heuristic (hūris´tik) *a.* **1** serving or tending to find out; not correct or provable, but aiding the discovery of truth. **2** (*Comput.*) proceeding by trial and error. *~n.* **1** the science of heuristic procedure. **2** a heuristic procedure or method. **heuristically** *adv.* **heuristic method** *n.* in education, a system where pupils are trained to find out things for themselves. **heuristics** *n.* (*Comput.*) the study and use of heuristic techniques.

hevea (hē´viə) *n.* any tree of the South American genus *Hevea*, having a milky sap which provides rubber.

hew (hū) *v.t.* (*p.p.* **hewed, hewn** (hūn)) **1** to cut (down, away, off etc.) with an axe etc. **2** to hack, to chop. **3** to make or fashion with toil and exertion. *~v.i.* **1** to strike cutting blows (at etc.). **2** (*N Am.*) to conform (to a code etc.). **to hew one's way** to make a passage etc. for oneself by hewing. **hewer** *n.* **1** a person who hews. **2** a person who cuts coal from a seam.

hex¹ (heks) *v.i.* to practise witchcraft. *~v.t.* **1** to cast a spell on. **2** to jinx. *~n.* **1** a magic spell; a curse. **2** a person who practises witchcraft.

hex² (heks) *n.* (*Comput.*) the hexadecimal number system; hexadecimal notation.

hexa- (hek´sə), **hex-** comb. form six.
hexachord (hek´səkawd) n. (Mus.) 1 a scale or diatonic series of six notes with a semitone between the third and the fourth. 2 an interval of four tones and a semitone.
hexad (hek´sad) n. a group of six.
hexadecimal (heksədes´iməl) a. (esp. Comput.) (of a number system) having 16 as its base. ~n. the hexadecimal number system; hexadecimal notation. **hexadecimally** adv.
hexagon (hek´səgən) n. a plane figure having six sides. **hexagonal** (-sag´-) a.
hexagram (hek´səgram) n. 1 a figure formed by two equilateral triangles whose points coincide with those of a regular hexagon. 2 a six-sided figure.
hexahedron (heksəhē´drən) n. (pl. **hexahedrons**, **hexahedra** (-drə)) a solid body of six sides, esp. a regular cube. **hexahedral** a.
hexameter (heksam´itə) n. a line or verse consisting of six metrical feet. **hexametric** (-met´-), **hexametrical** a. **hexametrist** n.
hexane (hek´sān) n. (Chem.) a liquid hydrocarbon of the alkane series.
hexavalent (heksəvā´lənt) a. having a valency of six.
hexose (hek´sōz) n. a monosaccharide, such as glucose, that contains six carbon atoms per molecule.
hey[1] (hā) int. 1 used to express joy, surprise, interrogation, encouragement etc. 2 (esp. N Am.) used to attract someone's attention, often used meaninglessly.
hey[2] HAY[2].
heyday (hā´dā) n. the time of unexhausted spirits, vigour, prosperity etc.
HF abbr. high frequency.
Hf chem. symbol hafnium.
hf. abbr. half.
HG abbr. His or Her Grace.
Hg chem. symbol mercury.
hg abbr. hectogram(s).
HH abbr. 1 His or Her Highness. 2 His Holiness (the Pope). 3 extra hard (of a pencil lead).
hh. abbr. hands (as a unit of measurement).
hi (hī) int. 1 used as a greeting or to call attention. 2 used to express surprise, derision etc.
hiatus (hīā´təs) n. (pl. **hiatuses**) 1 a gap, a break, a lacuna in a manuscript, connected series etc. 2 (Gram.) the coming together of two vowels in successive syllables or words. **hiatal** a. **hiatus hernia** n. (Med.) a hernia in which part of the stomach protrudes through the oesophageal opening in the diaphragm.
Hib (hib) n. (Med.) a bacterium, Haemophilus influenzae type B, causing meningitis in children.
hibernate (hī´bənāt) v.i. 1 (of some animals) to pass the winter in sleep or torpor. 2 to live in seclusion or remain inactive at a time of stress. **hibernation** (-ā´shən) n. **hibernator** n.
Hibernian (hībœ´niən) a. (poet.) of or relating to Ireland. ~n. a native or inhabitant of Ireland.

Hiberno- (hībœ´nō) comb. form of or relating to Ireland, Irish.
hibiscus (hibis´kəs) n. (pl. **hibiscuses**) a mallow of the mostly tropical genus Hibiscus with large brightly coloured flowers.
hic (hik) int. used to represent a sound like a hiccup, denoting interruption, as in the speech of a drunken person.
hiccup (hik´ŭp), **hiccough** n. 1 a short, audible catching of the breath due to spasmodic contraction of the diaphragm and the glottis. 2 (pl.) a spasm of hiccuping. 3 (coll.) a temporary or minor difficulty, problem etc. ~v.i. (pres.p. **hiccuping**, **hiccoughing**, past, p.p. **hiccuped**, **hiccoughed**) to have or utter a hiccup or series of hiccups. ~v.t. to utter with a hiccup. **hiccupy** a.
hick (hik) n. (coll.) a country bumpkin, a farmer, a yokel; an unsophisticated person. ~a. rustic, rural.
hickory (hik´əri) n. (pl. **hickories**) 1 any of several N American trees of the genus Carya, allied to the walnuts, esp. C. alba, the timber of which is tough and elastic. 2 the wood of a hickory. 3 a stick made from hickory wood.
hide[1] (hīd) v.t. (past **hid** (hid), p.p. **hidden** (hid´ən), †**hid**) 1 to put out of or withhold from sight or observation. 2 to obscure from view, to cover up. 3 to keep secret, to withhold from knowledge. 4 to suppress. ~v.i. to lie concealed, to conceal oneself. ~n. a place of concealment for observing wildlife. **to hide one's head** to keep or remain out of sight, esp. from shame. **hidden** a. **hidden agenda** n. a concealed or ulterior motive behind one's actions, statements etc. **hidden economy** n. economic activity involving payment in cash or kind not declared for tax purposes. **hiddenly** adv. **hiddenness** n. **hidden reserves** n.pl. extra resources etc. kept concealed. **hide-and-seek**, (N Am.) **hide-and-go-seek** n. 1 a children's game in which players hide and others try to find them. 2 searching and evasion. **hideaway** n. a concealed or secluded place. **hideout** n. a place where someone can hide or take refuge. **hider** n. **hidey-hole**, **hidy-hole** n. (coll.) a hiding place. **hiding**[1] n. 1 the act of concealing. 2 a state of concealment. **hiding place** n. a place of concealment, a place where someone can hide or take refuge.
hide[2] (hīd) n. 1 the skin of an animal, esp. when dressed. 2 (coll., facet.) the human skin. ~v.t. (pres.p. **hiding**, past, p.p. **hided**) (coll.) to flog. **hidebound** a. 1 narrow-minded, bigoted, obstinate. 2 (of the law etc.) constricted by tradition. 3 (of an animal) difficult to skin because the hide adheres closely to the ribs and back, esp. because of poor feeding. **hiding**[2] n. (coll.) a thrashing, a flogging. **on a hiding to nothing** unable to succeed, no matter what happens.
hideous (hid´iəs) a. 1 exceedingly ugly, repulsive. 2 horrible, frightful, shocking. 3 (coll.) nasty, unpleasant. **hideosity** (-os´-) n. (pl. **hideosities**). **hideously** adv. **hideousness** n.

hiding[1] HIDE[1].

hiding[2] HIDE[2].

†hie (hī) v.i., v.refl. (3rd pers. sing. pres. **hies**, pres.p. **hieing, hying,** past, p.p. **hied**) (also poet.) to hasten, to hurry.

hierarchy (hīə´rahki) n. (pl. **hierarchies**) **1** a system of persons or things arranged in a graded order. **2** the collective body of those organized in a graded order. **3** organization in grades or orders, esp. of a priesthood. **4** (Theol.) **a** any one of three orders of angels. **b** the angels collectively. **hierarch** n. **1** the chief of a sacred order, a person who has authority in sacred things, a chief priest. **2** a prelate or archbishop. **hierarchic** (-ah´-), **hierarchical** a.

hieratic (hīərat´ik) a. **1** of or relating to the priesthood, priestly. **2** denoting, of or related to the form of hieroglyphics employed in early Egyptian records written by priests. **3** of or relating to early styles in Egyptian and Greek art. **hieratically** adv.

hiero- (hīə´rō), **hier-** comb. form sacred; of or relating to sacred things.

hieroglyph (hīə´rəglif) n. **1** the figure of an animate or inanimate object used in writing to represent a word, sound etc., as practised by the ancient Egyptians, the Aztecs and others. **2** a piece of writing consisting of such characters. **3** a character or symbol employed to convey a secret meaning. **4** (usu. in pl., facet.) illegible writing. **hieroglyphic** (-glif´-) a. **1** written in or covered with hieroglyphs. **2** written in characters difficult to decipher. **3** mysterious, emblematic, esoteric. **hieroglyphical** a. **hieroglyphically** adv. **hieroglyphics** n. hieroglyphic writing; hieroglyphs.

hi-fi (hī´fī) n. (pl. **hi-fis**) (coll.) any equipment for high-quality sound reproduction. ~a. high-fidelity.

higgledy-piggledy (higəldipig´əldi) adv. (coll.) in confusion, topsy-turvy. ~a. confused, jumbled about anyhow. ~n. a jumble.

high (hī) a. **1** rising or extending upwards for or to a great extent. **2** rising or extending upwards for or to a specified extent. **3** situated at a great elevation. **4** upper, inland. **5** extending above the normal or average level (trousers with a high waistband). **6** involving a great elevation; taking place from a great elevation (high diving). **7** exalted in rank, position or office. **8** of noble character or purpose; exalted in quality (high principles; high art). **9** proud, lofty in tone or temper, arrogant. **10** great, extreme, intense. **11** full, complete, consummate. **12** (of a period, age etc.) far advanced (high summer). **13** expensive, costly (in price). **14** boisterous, violent. **15** (of a sound) of a high frequency, sharp, acute in pitch. **16** (esp. of meat) tainted, approaching putrefaction. **17** chief, principal. **18** (coll.) intoxicated by alcohol or drugs. **19** (coll.) in an animated or hysterical state. **20** (of latitude) near either of the poles. **21** (of a vowel) articulated with the tongue

raised close to the palate. ~adv. **1** to a great altitude, aloft. **2** in or to a high degree. **3** at a high price. **4** eminently, greatly, powerfully. **5** at or to a high pitch (She sings high). ~n. **1** a high level, a high point. **2** the highest level, the highest point. **3** an anticyclone (with high barometric pressure). **4** (sl.) a state of euphoria, esp. one due to intoxication with drugs. **5** a motor vehicle's top gear. **6** (NAm., coll.) a high school. **from on high** from aloft, from heaven. **on high 1** aloft. **2** to or in heaven. **on one's high horse** (coll.) behaving arrogantly or affecting superiority. **riding high** in a state of good fortune or prosperity. **to play high 1** to play or gamble for heavy amounts. **2** to play a high card. **to run high 1** (of the sea) to have a strong current with high tide. **2** (of emotions) to be strongly felt. **with a high hand** in an arrogant or arbitrary manner. **High Admiral** n. a chief officer ranking as an admiral. **high altar** n. the principal altar of a church. **high and dry** adv. **1** left behind, stranded without resources. **2** (Naut.) out of the water, aground. **high and low** adv. everywhere (They searched high and low for the mouse). **high and mighty** a. (coll.) arrogant. **highball** n. **1** a drink of spirits and soda served in a tall glass. **2** (orig. on a railway) a signal to proceed. **highbinder** n. (NAm., sl.) **1** a thug, a hired killer. **2** a cheat, a swindler. **high-born** a. of noble birth. **highboy** n. (NAm.) a tall chest of drawers with legs. **highbrow** n. (coll., often derog.) an intellectual or cultural person. ~a. intellectual, cultural. **high camp** n., a. (of or displaying) sophisticated camp style, behaviour, etc. **high card** n. a card, such as an ace or court card, which outranks others. **high chair** n. a baby's chair with a tray, raised on long legs to table height. **High Church** n. one of the main traditions in the Anglican Church, distinguished by its maintenance of sacerdotal claims and assertion of the efficacy of the sacraments. **high-class** a. of high quality, refined. **high colour,** (NAm.) **high color** n. a flushed complexion. **high command** n. **1** an army commander-in-chief and senior staff. **2** the supreme headquarters of the armed forces. **High Commission** n. an embassy of one Commonwealth country in another. **High Commissioner** n. **High Court, high court** n. a supreme court of justice. **High Court of Justice** n. in England, the supreme court of civil jurisdiction. **High Court of Justiciary** n. the supreme court of civil jurisdiction in Scotland. **high day** n. a feast, a festival. **high-definition television** n. a television offering a picture with superior definition, using over 1000 scanning lines. **high enema** n. an enema administered into the colon. **high-energy** a. concerning elementary particles accelerated in a particle accelerator. **higher** a. **Higher** n. in Scotland, an examination leading to the SCE (Scottish Certificate of Education) Higher Grade. **higher animal** n. an animal manifesting relatively advanced characteristics. **higher education** n. education after secondary schools, e.g. at a college or university. **higher mathematics** n. advanced mathematics taught at colleges, universities etc. **higher plant** n. a plant manifesting relatively advanced characteristics. **higher-up** n. (pl. **higher-ups**) (coll.) a person in a position of greater authority or higher rank. **highest** a. **highest common factor** n. the highest number that can be divided exactly into each of a group of numbers. **high explosive** n. an explosive of extreme rapidity and great destructive energy. **highfalutin** (-fəloo´tin), **highfaluting** a. (coll.) bombastic, affected. ~n. bombast. **high fashion** n. HAUTE COUTURE. **high fidelity** n. the reproduction of sound with very little distortion. **high finance** n. transactions involving large amounts of money. **high-five** n. (esp. N Am., sl.) a gesture of victory, greeting etc. in which two people slap the palms of their hands together above their heads. ~v.t. to greet with a high-five. **high-five sign** n. **high-flown** a. (of language, style etc.) turgid, bombastic. **high-flyer, high-flier** n. **1** a person with high qualifications, or who aims to achieve high position. **2** a thing likely to be commercially successful. **high-flying** a. **high frequency** n. (pl. **high frequencies**) a radio-frequency band or radio frequency between 3–30 megahertz. **high gear** n. on cycles, motor vehicles etc., the apparatus for transmitting high speed to the driving-wheel relatively to the motion of pedals, engine etc. **High German** n. the form of German spoken in central and southern Germany, regarded as standard speech. **high-grade** a. of high quality. **high ground** n. the morally or intellectually superior position in a debate, argument etc. **high-handed** a. overbearing, domineering, arbitrary. **high-handedly** adv. **high-handedness** n. **high hat** n. **1** a tall hat, a top hat. **2** (coll.) a snobbish or overbearing person. **3** a pair of cymbals operated with the foot. **high-hat** a. snobbish, arrogant. **high heels** n.pl. shoes with high heels, esp. for women. **high-heeled** a. **high jinks** n.pl. high festivities or lively enjoyment. **high jump** n. an athletic event where competitors jump over a high bar. **to be for the high jump** (coll.) to be liable to receive some form of severe punishment etc. **high-jumper** n. **high-jumping** n. **high-key** a. (of a photograph etc.) having mostly light-grey tones or light colours. **high kick** n. a dancer's or athlete's kick high in the air. **high-kicking** a. **high latitudes** n.pl. regions near the poles. **high-level** a. **1** (of gatherings etc.) involving important people. **2** having a high rank. **high-level language** n. (Comput.) a language in which each word is equal to several machine instructions, making it closer to human language. **high life** n. the style of living or the manners of the fashionable world. **highlight** n. **1** the most brilliantly lit spot in a photograph or picture. **2** a moment or event of particular importance or interest. **3** (pl.) streaks of artificial light colour in dark hair. ~v.t. (past, p.p. **highlighted**) **1** to put emphasis on. **2** to put highlights in (hair). **3** to

mark with a highlighter. **highlighter** n. a marker pen used to overlay colour on a document etc. to emphasize certain details etc. **high living** n. living in extravagance and luxury. **highly** adv. **1** in a high degree, extremely, intensely. **2** honourably, favourably. **highly strung** a. of a nervous and tense disposition. **High Mass** n. a Mass in which the celebrant is attended by deacon and subdeacon, usu., but not necessarily, sung at the high altar. **high-minded** a. magnanimous, having high moral principles. **high-mindedly** adv. **high-mindedness** n. **highness** n. **1** the quality or state of being high. **2** (**Highness**) a title of honour given to princes and others of royal rank (used with a possessive pronoun) (Her Royal Highness). **3** height. **high-octane** a. (of petrol) having a high octane number. **high-pitched** a. **1** (of sound) high. **2** (of style etc.) aspiring, haughty. **3** (of roofs) steeply sloping. **high places** n.pl. the upper ranks of an organization etc. **high point** n. a moment or occasion of great intensity, interest etc. **high-powered** a. **1** having great power, energy etc. **2** important, dynamic or influential. **high pressure** n. **1** a pressure above the norm. **2** a condition of the atmosphere where the pressure is above the average. **3** great activity or effort. **high priest** n. **1** a chief priest, esp. the head of the Jewish hierarchy. **2** the head of any cult, sect etc. **high priestess** n. a chief priestess. **high profile** n. a high degree of exposure to attention or publicity esp. in the media. **high relief** n. ALTO-RELIEVO. **high-rise** a. (of a building) having many storeys. ~n. such a building. **high-risk** a. involving danger, exposed to danger (high-risk categories; high-risk sports). **high road** n. **1** a main road, a highway. **2** a direct route (to). **high roller** n. (N Am., sl.) a person who spends money extravagantly or gambles recklessly. **high school** n. a secondary school. **high sea, high seas** n. the open sea or ocean. **high season** n. the most popular time of year at a holiday resort etc. **high-security** a. **1** (of a prison etc.) extremely secure. **2** (of a prisoner) kept in such a prison. **High Sheriff** n. the chief Crown officer of a county or shire charged with the keeping of the peace, the execution of writs, sentences etc., the conduct of elections etc. **high sign** n. (N Am., coll.) a surreptitious gesture etc. to show that all is well. **high-sounding** a. pompous, ostentatious. **high-speed** a. **1** moving or operating at a high speed. **2** (of photographic film) requiring brief exposure. **3** (of steel) suitable for tools, cutting extremely rapidly. **high-spirited** a. **1** full of high spirits. **2** having a lofty or courageous spirit; bold, daring. **high spirits** n.pl. **1** cheerfulness, liveliness, vivacity. **2** lively enjoyment. **in high spirits** in a vivacious, cheerful or lively mood. **high spot** n. (coll.) a moment or event of particular importance or interest. **high street** n. the principal street of a town etc. (often used as the proper name of a street). **high table** n. the main table at a public dinner, raised on a platform;

the table for the fellows of a college etc. **hightail** *v.i.* (*N Am.*, *coll.*) to move quickly. **to hightail it** to run away. **high tea** *n.* a main evening meal taken relatively early and at which tea and bread and butter may be served. **high tech** (tek) *n.* **1** advanced technology, high technology. **2** a style of interior design using features of industrial equipment. **high-tech** *a.* **high technology** *n.* highly sophisticated, often electronic, techniques used in manufacturing etc. **high-tensile** *a.* (of metal) having great tensile strength. **high tide** *n.* **1** the tide at its highest and fullest level. **2** the time of this. **high time** *n.* (*coll.*) **1** the latest possible time, almost too late. **2** an enjoyable and exciting time. **high-toned** *a.* **1** high in pitch. **2** strong in sound. **3** morally or culturally elevated. **high treason** *n.* a violation of allegiance by a subject against the sovereign or government, esp. an overt attempt to subvert the government. **high-up** *n.* (*coll.*) a person of high rank or authority. **high voltage** *n.* a voltage great enough to cause damage or injury. **high water** *n.* HIGH TIDE (under HIGH). **high water mark** *n.* **1** the level reached by the water at high tide. **2** the highest recorded value, the highest point of achievement. **high wire** *n.* a tightrope high above the ground. **high words** *n.pl.* angry talk.

highland (hī´lənd) *n.* high or mountainous ground. **the Highlands** the northern mountainous parts of Scotland. **Highland** *a.* of or relating to the Highlands of Scotland. **Highland cattle** *n.* a breed of cattle with shaggy hair, usu. of a reddish-brown colour, and long horns. **Highland dress** *n.* **1** the historical costume, incl. the kilt, bonnet etc. as worn by Highlanders. **2** a modern version of this worn at formal occasions. **Highlander** *n.* **1** a native or inhabitant of the Highlands of Scotland. **2** (**highlander**) a native or inhabitant of a highland. **Highland fling** *n.* a whirling Scottish Highland dance. **Highlandman** *n.* (*pl.* **Highlandmen**).

highway (hī´wā) *n.* **1** a public road open to all passengers. **2** a main route for any form of transport. **3** (*esp. N Am.*) a main road, esp. one that connects towns, cities. **4** a direct path or course. **Highway Code** *n.* the official guide and instructions for proper behaviour on the road in the UK. **highwayman** *n.* (*pl.* **highwaymen**) (*Hist.*) a robber, usu. on horseback, who held up travellers on the highway. **highwaywoman** *n.* (*pl.* **highwaywomen**) (*Hist.*) a female robber holding up travellers on the highway.

HIH *abbr.* His or Her Imperial Highness.

hijack (hī´jak), **highjack** *v.t.* **1** to take over (a vehicle, aircraft etc.) by force, esp. to divert it from its route. **2** to steal (goods) in transit. **3** to take over or change the direction of (a project etc.). ~*n.* an act of hijacking. **hijacker** *n.*

Hijra HEGIRA.

hike (hīk) *n.* **1** a ramble, a long country walk. **2** (*coll.*) an increase, e.g. in prices. ~*v.i.* **1** to go for a hike. **2** to become hoisted or hitched up. ~*v.t.*

1 to hoist or lift; to hitch up. **2** (*coll.*) to increase (prices etc.). **hiker** *n.*

hila HILUM.

hilarious (hileə´riəs) *a.* **1** extremely funny. **2** cheerful, mirthful, merry. **hilariously** *adv.* **hilariousness, hilarity** (-lar´-) *n.*

hill (hil) *n.* **1** a noticeable natural elevation on the surface of the earth, less high and abrupt than a mountain. **2** a heap, a mound. **3** a sloping stretch of road, an incline. ~*v.t.* **1** to form into hills, heaps or mounds. **2** to heap (up) earth around the roots of. **over the hill 1** (*coll.*) beyond one's prime. **2** (*coll.*) beyond the crisis. **hillbilly** *n.* (*pl.* **hillbillies**) (*N Am.*) **1** (*usu. derog.*) a person from the mountain country regarded as unsophisticated; a hick. **2** country music of a traditional variety. **hill climb** *n.* a competition in which competitors race up a hill in vehicles. **hill fort** *n.* a fort on a hill, a fortified hilltop. **hill man** *n.* (*pl.* **hill men**) a person from a hilly region. **hillock** (-ək) *n.* a little hill or mound. **hillocky** *a.* **hillside** *n.* the sloping side of a hill. **hilltop** *n.* the summit of a hill. **hillwalking** *n.* walking over hilly countryside for recreation and exercise. **hillwalker** *n.* **hilly** *a.* (*comp.* **hillier**, *superl.* **hilliest**). **hilliness** *n.*

hilt (hilt) *n.* **1** the handle of a sword, dagger etc. **2** the handle of a tool. ~*v.t.* to provide with a hilt. **up to the hilt** to the fullest extent. **hilted** *a.*

hilum (hī´ləm) *n.* (*pl.* **hila** (-lə)) **1** (*Bot.*) the spot on a seed where it was attached to the seed vessel. **2** (*Anat.*) a small aperture or a small depression in a bodily organ.

HIM *abbr.* His or Her Imperial Majesty.

him (him) *pron.* **1** objective (accusative and dative) of HE. **2** (*dial.*) HIMSELF.

Usage note Use of *him* in a subject, as in *Him and his sister were late*, is best avoided. See also notes under AS, BE, THAN.

himself (himself´) *pron.* **1** HE or HIM (objective), used to give emphasis (usu. in apposition). **2** the reflexive form of HIM. **3** his normal or usual self. **4** (*esp. Ir.*) the important male person being referred to. **by himself** alone, unaided. **to be himself** to act in his normal manner.

hind[1] (hīnd), **hinder** *a.* of, relating to or situated at the back or rear. **hindbrain** *n.* (*Anat.*) the lower part of the brainstem, the cerebellum, pons and medulla oblongata considered together. **hindermost, hindmost** *a.* **1** last in position, furthest back. **2** that is or comes last of all. **hindquarters** *n.pl.* the hind legs and rump of a quadruped. **hindsight** *n.* wisdom after the event, the reverse of foresight.

hind[2] (hīnd) *n.* the female of the deer, esp. the red deer.

hinder[1] (hin´də) *v.t.* to obstruct, to impede, to prevent from proceeding or moving. ~*v.i.* to cause a hindrance; to interpose obstacles or impediments. **hinderer** *n.* **hindrance** *n.* **1** the act of

hindering. **2** that which hinders; an impediment, an obstacle.
hinder² HIND¹.
Hindi (hin´di) *n.* **1** the group of Indo-European languages spoken in northern India. **2** the literary or official form of this. ~*a.* of or relating to Hindi.
Hindu (hindoo´, hin´-), †**Hindoo** *n.* (*pl.* **Hindus,** †**Hindoos**) a follower of Hinduism. ~*a.* of or relating to Hindus or Hinduism. **Hinduism** (hin´-) *n.* the dominant religion of India, comprising the Hindu polytheistic system of Brahminism modified by Buddhism and other accretions. **Hinduize** (hin´-), **Hinduise** *v.t.* **Hindustani** (-stah´ni) *n.* **1** all spoken forms of Hindi and Urdu considered together. **2** the dialect of Hindi spoken in Delhi, used as a lingua franca throughout the Indian subcontinent. ~*a.* of or relating to Hindustani or Hindustan.
hinge (hinj) *n.* **1** the joint or mechanical device on which a door or lid turns. **2** (*Biol.*) a natural articulation fulfilling similar functions. **3** the point on which anything depends or turns. ~*v.t.* (*pres.p.* **hingeing, hinging**) to furnish with or as with a hinge. ~*v.i.* **1** to turn on or as on a hinge. **2** to depend (upon). **hinged** *a.* **hingeless** *a.* **hingewise** *adv.*
hinny (hin´i) *n.* (*pl.* **hinnies**) the offspring of a male horse and female donkey.
hint (hint) *n.* **1** a slight or distant allusion. **2** a small piece of helpful or practical information. **3** a small amount (of); a trace. ~*v.t.* to mention indirectly, to suggest, to allude to. ~*v.i.* to make remote allusion. **to hint at** to mention indirectly. **hinter** *n.* **hintingly** *adv.*
hinterland (hin´tɘland) *n.* **1** the region situated behind something, esp. a coast or the shore of a river. **2** the remote or underdeveloped areas of a country. **3** an area located near and dependent on a large city, esp. a port.
hip¹ (hip) *n.* **1** the projection of the articulation of the femur and the thigh bone; the projecting fleshy part covering a hip joint. **2** the human body as seen or measured surrounding the hip joints (*usu. in pl.*). **3** (*Archit.*) the external angle formed by the meeting sides of a roof. **hip bath** *n.* a bath in which the body can be immersed to the hips. **hip bone** *n.* a bone forming the hip. **hip flask** *n.* a flask, usu. containing spirits, carried in a pocket at the hip. **hip hop** *n.* a dance culture and form of music originating among US black and Hispanic youths in the late 1970s. **hip joint** *n.* the articulation of the femur and the thighbone. **hip-length** *a.* (of a garment) reaching down to the hips. **hipped**¹ *a.* **hipped roof** *n.* HIP ROOF (under HIP¹). **hippy**¹ *a.* (*coll.*) having large hips. **hip roof** *n.* a roof rising directly from the walls on every side and consequently having no gable. **hipsters** (-stɘz) *n.pl.* (*coll.*) trousers that start at the hips, not the waist. **hipster**¹ *a.* (*coll.*) (of trousers) starting at the hips, not the waist.

hip² (hip), **hep** (hep) *n.* the fruit of a rose plant.
hip³ (hip) *int.* used to introduce cheers (*hip, hip, hurrah*).
hip⁴ (hip) *a.* (*comp.* **hipper,** *superl.* **hippest**) (*esp. N Am.* (*dated*) *sl.*) aware, in the know. **hipped**² *a.* infatuated, very keen (on). **hipster**² *n.* a person who knows what's what; a person in the know. **hipsterism** *n.*
☒ **hipocrisy** common misspelling of HYPOCRISY.
hipped¹ HIP¹.
hipped² HIP⁴.
hippie HIPPY².
hippo (hip´ō) *n.* (*pl.* **hippos**) (*coll.*) short for HIPPOPOTAMUS.
hippo- (hip´ō), **hipp-** *comb. form* of, relating to or resembling a horse.
hippocampus (hipōkam´pɘs) *n.* (*pl.* **hippocampi** (-pī)) **1** a sea horse of the genus *Hippocampus.* **2** (*Anat.*) either of two eminences on the floor of the lateral ventricle of the brain.
Hippocratic (hipɘkrat´ik), **Hippocratian** (-krat´iɘn), **Hippocratical** (-kɘl) *a.* of or relating to Hippocrates. **Hippocratic oath** *n.* (*esp. Hist.*) an oath taken by physicians binding them to observe the code of medical practice derived from that of Hippocrates.
hippodrome (hip´ɘdrōm) *n.* **1** a music hall, variety theatre or circus. **2** in ancient Greece and Rome, a circus for equestrian games and chariot races.
hippopotamus (hipɘpot´ɘmɘs) *n.* (*pl.* **hippopotamuses, hippopotami** (-mī)) **1** a massive African thick-skinned quadruped, *Hippopotamus amphibius,* of amphibious habits, with a heavy body, short, blunt muzzle and short limbs and tail. **2** a related but smaller animal, *Choeropsis liberiensis,* the pygmy hippopotamus.
hippy¹ HIP¹.
hippy² (hip´i), **hippie** *n.* (*pl.* **hippies**) a member of the youth culture of the 1960s, which stressed universal love and brotherhood, rejection of middle-class values, the wearing of long hair and colourful clothes, and the use of drugs.
hipster¹ HIP¹.
hipster² HIP⁴.
hire (hīɘ) *n.* **1** the act of hiring or the state of being hired. **2** the price paid for labour or services or the use of things. **3** (*N Am.*) a person recently hired. ~*v.t.* **1** to procure the temporary use of for an agreed payment. **2** to employ (a person) for a stipulated payment. **on/ for hire** available for service or temporary use in exchange for a fee. **to hire oneself out** to make oneself available for employment. **to hire out** to pay independent contractors for (work to be done). **hireable,** (*esp. N Am.*) **hirable** *a.* **hire car** *n.* a car hired or available for hire, usu. for a short period. **hired girl, hired man** *n.* (*N Am.*) a domestic servant, esp. on a farm. **hireling** *n.* (*usu. derog.*) a person who works for hire. **hire purchase** *n.* a method by which payments for hire are accepted as instalments of the price and the article eventually

becomes the property of the hirer. **hirer** *n.* a person who hires or lets on hire.

hirsute (hœ´sūt) *a.* **1** rough or hairy. **2** having uncut hair. **hirsuteness** *n.* **hirsutism** *n.* the condition of having excessive facial or bodily hair.

his (hiz) *a.* possessive of HE. *~pron.* something which belongs to or is associated with him. **his and hers** (*esp. facet.*) (of paired objects) for husband and wife, or a man and a woman. **his 'n' hers** his and hers. **of his** belonging or relating to him.

Hispanic (hispan´ik) *a.* **1** of or relating to Spain or Spain and Portugal. **2** of Spain and other Spanish-speaking countries or regions. *~n.* a Spanish-speaking person, esp. of Central or South American descent, living in the US. **Hispanicize, Hispanicise** *v.t.* **Hispano-** *comb. form* Spain and Spanish. **Hispanophile** (-fîl) *n., a.* (a person who is) fond of Spain.

hiss (his) *v.i.* **1** (of a person, snake, goose etc.) to make a sound like that of the letter *s*, to make a sibilant sound. **2** (esp. of a crowd or audience) to express disapprobation by making such a sound. *~v.t.* **1** to utter with a hissing sound. **2** to condemn or drive away by hissing. *~n.* **1** a hissing sound. **2** an expression of derision or disapprobation. **3** continuous audible interference in sound reproduction. **hissingly** *adv.*

histamine (his´təmēn) *n.* an amine formed from histidine and released by the body tissues in allergic reactions.

histidine (his´tidēn) *n.* an amino acid derived from proteins.

histo- (his´tō), **hist-** *comb. form* (*Biol.*) of or relating to organic tissues.

histogram (his´təgram) *n.* a pictorial method of showing the distribution of various quantities, e.g. rainfall month by month.

histology (histol´əji), **histiology** (-tiol´-) *n.* the (microscopic) study of the tissues of plants or animals. **histologic** (-loj´-), **histological** *a.* **histologist** *n.*

historian (histaw´riən) *n.* **1** a writer of history, esp. one who is an authority on it. **2** a person studying or versed in history.

historiated (histaw´riātid) *a.* ornamented with figures (as illuminated capitals etc.).

historic (histor´ik) *a.* **1** celebrated in history, associated with historical events. **2** potentially important, momentous. **3** (*Gram.*) used in past narration. **historical** *a.* **1** of or relating to history. **2** of the nature of history; not legendary, fictitious etc. **3** involving analysis of change over time. **4** belonging to the past; dealing with the past. **historically** *adv.* **historicism** (-sizm) *n.* **1** the theory that all political and social events are historically determined. **2** the theory that history is governed by laws. **3** emphasis on historical development. **4** undue regard for the past. **historicist** *n.* **historicity** (-ris´-) *n.* historical existence; the historical genuineness of an event.

historic present *n.* the present tense used in a past sense.

Usage note The adjectives *historic* and *historical* should not be confused: *historic* is relatively limited in scope, and means celebrated in history, important, while *historical* is used of more general connections with history.

historiographer (histawriog´rəfə) *n.* **1** a writer of history, esp. an official historian. **2** a student of the writing of history. **historiographic** (-əgraf´-), **historiographical** *a.* **historiography** *n.*

history (his´təri) *n.* (*pl.* **histories**) **1** a systematic record of past events, esp. those of public importance. **2** the study of past events in human affairs. **3** a study of or a book dealing with the past of any country, people, science, art etc. **4** past events, esp. regarded as material for such a study. **5** an eventful past, an interesting career. **6** a historical play, a story. **7** a record, e.g. of someone's past medical treatment. **to make history 1** to do something momentous. **2** to influence the course of history.

histrionic (histrion´ik) *a.* **1** of or relating to actors or acting. **2** (of behaviour) theatrical, stagey, affected, unreal. *~n.* **1** (*in pl.*) an ostentatious display of usu. false emotion. **2** (*in pl.*) theatricals. **3** (*in pl.*) the art of theatrical representation. **histrionically** *adv.*

hit (hit) *v.t.* (*pres.p.* **hitting**, *past, p.p.* **hit**) **1** to strike or touch with a blow or missile, esp. after taking aim. **2** to collide with. **3** to affect suddenly or adversely, to wound. **4** to attain to, to light upon, to arrive at; to guess. **5** (*esp. N Am., sl.*) to kill. **6** (*coll.*) to encounter, meet. **7** in various sports and games, to propel (a ball etc.) with a bat etc. to score runs, points etc. **8** to score (runs etc.) in this way. **9** to strike a ball delivered by (a bowler etc.). *~v.i.* **1** to direct a blow or missile (at, against etc.). **2** to come into collision (against). **3** to agree, to suit, to fall in with. *~n.* **1** a blow, a stroke; a collision. **2** a touch with the sword or stick in fencing. **3** a shot etc. that hits the intended target. **4** a lucky chance. **5** a felicitous expression or turn of thought. **6** a successful effort. **7** (*coll.*) a best-selling book, record etc. **8** a stroke of sarcasm, wit etc. **9** (*sl.*) an injection of a drug. **10** (*sl.*) a murder, a violent attack etc. **to hit back** to retaliate. **to hit for six** to defeat in argument. **to hit it off together** to get along well (with), to agree. **to hit it off with** to get along well together, to agree. **to hit off** to represent or describe rapidly or cleverly. **to hit on/ upon 1** to light or chance on. **2** to discover by luck. **to hit out** to strike out straight from the shoulder. **to hit the ground running** (*N Am., coll.*) to proceed in an enthusiastic way. **to make a hit (with)** to be a sudden success, to become popular. **hit-and-miss** *a.* succeeding and failing in a haphazard way. **hit-and-run** *a.* **1** (of a driver) causing an accident and not stopping to help or report the incident. **2** (of an accident) involving a hit-and-run driver. **hitlist** *n.*

(*coll.*) **1** a list of people to be killed, punished etc. **2** in business, commerce etc., a list of clients, companies etc. to be contacted. **hitman** *n.* (*pl.* **hitmen**) (*coll.*) a hired professional killer. **hit-or-miss** *a.* HIT-AND-MISS (under HIT). **hit parade** *n.* a list of the currently most popular recordings of pop music. **hitter** *n.* **hitwoman** *n.* (*pl.* **hitwomen**) (*sl.*) a female hired professional killer.

hitch (hich) *v.t.* **1** to fasten with a hook or knot, esp. temporarily. **2** to pull up with a jerk. **3** to drag (in). **4** (*coll.*) to obtain (a lift) by hitch-hiking. *~v.i.* **1** to become entangled or caught. **2** (*coll.*) to hitch-hike. *~n.* **1** an impediment, a temporary difficulty. **2** an abrupt pull or jerk up. **3** a catch, noose or knot. **4** the act of catching, as on a rope. **5** any of various types of knot by which a rope is bent to a spar or to another rope. **6** (*coll.*) a free ride in a vehicle. **7** (*N Am., sl.*) a period of service. **to get hitched** (*sl.*) to get married. **to hitch one's wagon to a star** to rely on powers higher than one's own. **to hitch up** to lift (esp. clothing) with a jerk. **hitcher** *n.* **hitch-hike** *v.i.* to travel by obtaining free lifts from passing motorists. *~n.* a journey made in this way. **hitch-hiker** *n.* **hitch-hiking** *n.*

hi-tech (hītek´) *a.* HIGH-TECH (under HIGH).

hither (hidh´ə) *adv.* (*usu. formal*) **1** to this place, end or point. **2** in this direction. *~a.* **1** situated on this side. **2** the nearer (of two objects) to the speaker. **hither and thither 1** to this place and that. **2** here and there. **hither and yon 1** to this place and that. **2** here and there. **hitherto** (-too´) *adv.* up to this place, limit or time.

Hitler (hit´lə) *n.* a person resembling the Nazi dictator Adolf Hitler, 1889–1945. **Hitlerism** *n.* the ideology of National Socialism as propounded by Adolf Hitler. **Hitlerite** (-īt) *n.*

Hittite (hit´īt) *a.* of or relating to the Hittites, a people of uncertain origin inhabiting parts of Asia Minor and Syria before 1000 BC. *~n.* the language of the Hittites.

HIV *abbr.* human immunodeficiency virus, the retrovirus which causes Aids. **HIV-positive** *a.* carrying the virus.

hive (hīv) *n.* **1** an artificial structure for housing bees, a beehive. **2** the bees inhabiting a hive. **3** a place swarming with busy occupants. *~v.t.* **1** to put into or secure in a hive. **2** to house as in a hive. **3** to store up for future use. *~v.i.* **1** to enter or live in a hive. **2** to take shelter or swarm together, as bees do. **to hive off 1** to assign part of a firm's work to a subsidiary company. **2** to transfer (assets) from one concern to another such as in privatization. **3** to separate from a larger group. **to hive up** to hoard.

hives (hīvz) *n.pl.* **1** nettle-rash or a similar inflammation of the skin. **2** laryngitis.

hiya (hī´yə) *int.* (*coll.*) used as a greeting.

hl *abbr.* hectolitre(s).

HM *abbr.* **1** His or Her Majesty. **2** (*Mus.*) heavy metal.

HMG *abbr.* His or Her Majesty's Government.

HMI *abbr.* His or Her Majesty's Inspector or Inspectorate (of schools).

HMS *abbr.* His or Her Majesty's Ship or Service.

HMSO *abbr.* His or Her Majesty's Stationery Office.

HNC *abbr.* Higher National Certificate.

HND *abbr.* Higher National Diploma.

Ho *chem. symbol* holmium.

ho (hō) *int.* used to call attention, or to express exultation, surprise etc. **eastward ho!** used to announce or encourage eastward travel. **westward ho!** used to announce or encourage westward travel. **ho! ho!** *int.* expressing amusement, derision etc.

ho. *abbr.* house.

hoar (haw) *a.* **1** grey with age. **2** ancient. **3** white, grey or greyish-white. *~n.* **1** hoariness. **2** hoar frost. **hoar frost** *n.* frozen dew, white frost.

hoard (hawd) *n.* **1** an accumulated store (often of valuables) hidden away for future use. **2** an accumulation of knowledge etc. *~v.t.* to collect and put away, to store. *~v.i.* to amass and store up anything of value. **hoarder** *n.*

Usage note The spellings of the nouns *hoard* (a stock or store) and *horde* (a large group) should not be confused.

hoarding (haw´ding) *n.* **1** a large screen for posting bills on. **2** a temporary screen of boards round or in front of a building where erections or repairs are in progress.

hoarhound HOREHOUND.

hoarse (haws) *a.* **1** (of the voice) harsh, rough or husky. **2** having such a voice, as from a cold. **hoarsely** *adv.* **hoarsen** *v.t., v.i.* **hoarseness** *n.*

hoary (haw´ri) *a.* (*comp.* **hoarier**, *superl.* **hoariest**) **1** white or whitish-grey as with age. **2** white- or grey-headed. **3** of great antiquity, venerable. **4** old and trite (*a hoary joke*). **5** (*Bot., Zool.*) covered with very short dense hairs, which give an appearance of whiteness to the surface. **hoarily** *adv.* **hoariness** *n.*

hoax (hōks) *n.* a deception meant as a practical joke. *~v.t.* to play a practical joke upon, to take in for sport. **hoaxer** *n.*

hob (hob) *n.* **1** the flat top part of a cooking stove containing hotplates or burners. **2** the projecting side of a grate, or the top of this, on which things are placed to be kept warm. **3** a hardened, threaded spindle by which a comb or chasing tool may be cut.

hobbit (hob´it) *n.* a member of a fictional race of small people living in holes.

hobble (hob´əl) *v.i.* **1** to walk lamely or awkwardly. **2** to move in a halting or irregular way. *~v.t.* **1** to cause (a person etc.) to hobble. **2** to tie the legs of (horses etc.) to prevent straying. *~n.* **1** a rope, shackle, clog etc. for hobbling an animal. **2** an awkward, uneven or limping gait. **hobbler** *n.* **hobble skirt** *n.* a skirt fitting so closely round the legs and ankles that it impedes walking. **hobblingly** *adv.*

hobbledehoy (hob´əldihoi) *n.* (*dial.*) a clumsy, awkward youth.

hobby¹ (hob´i) *n.* (*pl.* **hobbies**) **1** any recreation or pursuit. **2** a hobbyhorse. **hobbyhorse** *n.* **1** a child's simple toy of a horse's head on a stick. **2** a preoccupation, a favourite subject of conversation. **3** a simple figure or model imitating a horse used in morris dances, pantomime etc. **4** a horse on a merry-go-round. **5** a rocking horse. **hobbyism** *n.* **hobbyist** *n.* **hobbyless** *a.*

hobby² (hob´i) *n.* (*pl.* **hobbies**) a small species of falcon, *Falco subbuteo.*

hobgoblin (hobgob´lin) *n.* a kind of goblin, elf or fairy, esp. one of a frightful appearance.

hobnail (hob´nāl) *n.* a short thick nail with a large head, used for heavy boots. **hobnailed** *a.*

hobnob (hob´nob) *v.i.* (*pres.p.* **hobnobbing**, *past*, *p.p.* **hobnobbed**) **1** to associate familiarly (with). **2** to drink familiarly.

hobo (hō´bō) *n.* (*pl.* **hobos**, **hoboes**) (*esp. N Am.*) a wandering worker, vagrant or tramp.

Hobson's choice (hobsənz chois´) *n.* no alternative.

hock¹ (hok), **hough** *n.* **1** the joint between the knee and the fetlock in the hind leg of quadrupeds. **2** the lower joint of ham or pork. ~*v.t.* to hamstring.

hock² (hok) *n.* any white wine of the Rhine region.

hock³ (hok) *v.t.* (*N Am.*, *sl.*) to pawn. ~*n.* **1** the state of being pawned or pledged. **2** prison. **in hock** in pawn, debt or prison.

hockey¹ (hok´i) *n.* **1** a team ball game played with a club having a curved end. **2** (*N Am.*) ICE HOCKEY (under ICE).

hockey² OCHE.

hocus (hō´kəs) *v.t.* (*3rd pers. sing. pres.* **hocusses**, (*N Am. also*) **hocuses**, *pres.p.* **hocussing**, (*N Am. also*) **hocusing**, *past*, *p.p.* **hocussed**, (*N Am. also*) **hocused**) **1** to take in, to hoax. **2** to stupefy (a person) with drugs. **3** to put a drug into (liquor). **hocus-pocus** (-pō´kəs) *n.* **1** trickery, fraud. **2** an expression used by jugglers in playing tricks. **3** jargon, mumbo-jumbo. **4** a juggler's trick, a fraud, a hoax. ~*v.i.* (*3rd pers. sing. pres.* **hocus-pocusses**, (*N Am. also*) **hocus-pocuses**, *pres.p.* **hocus-pocussing**, (*N Am. also*) **hocus-pocusing**, *past*, *p.p.* **hocus-pocussed**, (*N Am. also*) **hocus-pocused**) to juggle, to conjure. ~*v.t.* to cheat, to trick.

hod (hod) *n.* **1** a wooden holder shaped like a trough and fixed on a long handle, for carrying mortar or bricks on the shoulder. **2** a coal scuttle. **hod-carrier**, **hodman** *n.* (*pl.* **hod-carriers**, **hodmen**) **1** a labourer who carries a hod for bricklayers etc. **2** a drudge, a hack.

hodgepodge (hoj´poj) *n.* **1** a dish of mixed ingredients. **2** a mixture or medley; a confused jumble.

Hodgkin's disease (hoj´kinz) *n.* a malignant disease characterized by progressive anaemia and enlargement of the liver, lymph glands etc.

hodometer ODOMETER.

hoe (hō) *n.* a tool used to scrape or stir up earth around plants, cut weeds up from the ground etc. ~*v.t.* (*3rd pers. sing. pres.* **hoes**, *pres.p.* **hoeing**, *past*, *p.p.* **hoed**) to scrape or loosen (ground), cut (weeds), or dig (up) with a hoe. ~*v.i.* to use a hoe. **to hoe in** (*Austral.*, *New Zeal.*, *sl.*) to eat heartily. **to hoe into** (*Austral.*, *New Zeal.*, *sl.*) to attack vigorously. **hoe-cake** *n.* (*N Am.*) a maize cake, orig. cooked on a hoe. **hoedown** *n.* (*esp. N Am.*) **1** a type of energetic folk dance. **2** music for this. **3** a lively social gathering for dancing the hoedown. **hoer** *n.*

hog (hog) *n.* **1** a swine, esp. a castrated boar meant for killing. **2** (*N Am.*) any kind of pig. **3** (*dial. also* **hogg**) a young sheep or bullock, usu. a year old. **4** a dirty, filthy or low person. **b** (*sl.*) a greedy person. ~*v.t.* (*pres.p.* **hogging**, *past*, *p.p.* **hogged**) **1** (*sl.*) to keep greedily to oneself. **2** to cause (a ship, keel etc.) to rise in the middle and droop at the ends. ~*v.i.* **1** to droop at both ends. **2** (of animals) to carry the head down and back up. **to go the whole hog** (*coll.*) to do a job completely, making no compromise or reservations. **hogback**, **hog's back** *n.* a long ridged hill. **hoggish** *a.* **hoggishly** *adv.* **hoglike** *a.* **hogwash** *n.* **1** the refuse of a kitchen or brewery, used for feeding hogs. **2** (*sl.*) anything worthless. **hogweed** *n.* any of numerous coarse plants, esp. the cow parsnip.

hogmanay (hogmənā´) *n.* **1** in Scotland, the last day of the year, New Year's Eve. **2** an entertainment or a present given on that day.

hogshead (hogz´hed) *n.* **1** a large cask. **2** a measure of capacity containing about 52 imperial gal. (238.7 l). **3** a butt.

ho-hum (hōhŭm´) *int.* used to express a feeling of tedium, lack of interest, resignation etc.

hoick (hoik) *v.t.* **1** (*coll.*) to pull up or out of something, esp. abruptly. **2** to force (an aeroplane) upwards.

hoi polloi (hoi pəloi´) *n.* (*often derog.*) **1** the common herd, the masses. **2** the majority.

hoist (hoist) *v.t.* **1** to raise up. **2** to lift by means of tackle. ~*n.* **1** the act of lifting or hoisting up. **2** an apparatus for hoisting or raising. **3** a lift or elevator. **4** (*Naut.*) the vertical height of a yard, sail or flag. **hoister** *n.*

hoity-toity (hoititoi´ti) *int.* used to express astonishment mixed with disapproval and contempt. ~*a.* **1** haughty and petulant. **2** snobbish.

hokey (hō´ki), **hoky** *a.* (*comp.* **hokier**, *superl.* **hokiest**) (*N Am.*, *sl.*) sentimental, corny or phoney. **hokeyness**, **hokiness** *n.*

hokey-cokey (hōkikō´ki) *n.* a dance in which a group forms a circle and moves and shakes arms and legs in accordance with the song to which it is danced.

hoki (hō´ki) *n.* an edible fish of New Zealand coasts, *Macruronus novaezelandiae*, related to the hake.

hokum (hō′kəm) n. (esp. N Am., coll., sl.) **1** bunkum. **2** foolish stage or book plotting. **3** counterfeit culture.

hoky HOKEY.

Holarctic (hōlahk′tik), **holarctic** a. of or relating to the entire northern region of the globe. ~n. the Holarctic region.

hold[1] (hōld) v.t. (past, p.p. **held** (held), p.p. †**holden**) **1** to grasp and retain. **2** to keep in, to confine. **3** to enclose, to contain. **4** to be able to contain, to keep from running or flowing out. **5** to set aside or reserve (tickets etc.). **6** to keep back, to restrain. **7** to keep in a certain manner or position. **8** to retain possession or control of. **9** to occupy, to possess (a house, qualifications etc.). **10** to regard, to believe (He holds that the theory is correct). **11** to maintain (that). **12** to judge, to lay down or decide; to assert (that). **13** to carry on (a meeting etc.). **14** to celebrate, to conduct (a festival, meeting etc.). **15** to use, to employ (a language etc.). **16** (coll.) to wager, to accept as a bet or wager. **17** (Comput.) to retain (data) in a storage device after copying it into another storage device. **18** (Mus.) to sustain (a note). ~v.i. **1** to maintain a grasp or attachment. **2** to continue firm, not to break. **3** to adhere (to). **4** (of weather) to remain dry and bright. **5** to keep the attention of (an audience etc.). **6** to maintain a course. **7** to be valid or true, to stand. **8** to be fit or consistent. **9** (usu. in imper.) to stop, to stay, to refrain. **hold everything!** stop doing anything! **hold hard!** (coll.) stop! **hold it!** stop! **to hold aloof** to avoid communication with others. **to hold (a thing) against someone** to be resentful towards another because of (a past action etc.), to regard (something) as discreditable to them. **to hold back 1** to restrain, to prevent (something or someone) from progressing. **2** to retain in one's possession. **3** to keep oneself in check. **to hold by** to hold to, to adhere to. **to hold cheap** not to value highly. **to hold court** to preside over one's admirers, entertaining or conversing etc. **to hold dear** to regard with affection. **to hold down 1** to repress, to restrain. **2** (coll.) to be good enough at (one's job etc.) to retain it. **to hold forth 1** to stretch or put forward. **2** (esp. sometimes derog.) to speak in public or for a long time. **3** to propose, to offer. **to hold good 1** to remain valid. **2** to apply, to be relevant. **to hold in 1** to restrain, to restrain oneself. **2** to keep quiet, to keep silent. **to hold in esteem** to regard with esteem. **to hold it good** to think it sensible (to do). **to hold off 1** to keep (someone or something) at a distance. **2** to remain at a distance. **3** to delay. **4** to refrain from. **to hold on 1** to continue without interruption, to persist. **2** (coll.) to stop. **3** to wait a moment. **4** not to end a telephone connection. **to hold one's own** to maintain one's position. **to hold out 1** to hold forward, to stretch out. **2** to offer. **3** to bear, to endure, not to yield. **4** to persist, to last. **to hold out for** to continue demanding in spite of alternative offers. **to hold out on** (coll.) to refuse or

delay in telling etc. something to (a person). **to hold over 1** to keep back or reserve, to defer. **2** (Law) to keep possession of after the expiration of one's term. **3** to threaten (someone) with. **to hold the fort** to cope temporarily. **to hold the line 1** not to give in. **2** not to end a telephone connection. **to hold to 1** to bind to (bail, one's statement etc.). **2** to adhere to. **to hold together 1** to cohere or cause to cohere. **2** to continue united. **to hold true 1** to remain valid. **2** to apply, to be relevant. **to hold under** to derive title from. **to hold up 1** to raise or lift up. **2** to support, to encourage. **3** to sustain. **4** to show forth, to exhibit (to ridicule etc.). **5** to stop and rob by violence or threats. **6** to arrest the progress of, to obstruct. **7** (of the weather) to remain fine. **8** to continue at the same speed. **to hold with** to approve of, to side with. **holdable** a. **holdall** n. a bag or case for carrying clothes etc. **holdback** n. a restraint, a check, a hindrance. **holder** (hōl′də) n. **1** a device or implement for holding something. **2** a tenant, occupier or owner. **3** a person who holds a title etc. **4** the payee of a bill of exchange or promissory note. **5** a smallholder. **holdfast** n. **1** a means by which something is clamped to another. **2** any device used to secure an object. **3** the organ of attachment of a seaweed or related plant. **holdout** n. **1** an act of holding out against something. **2** a refusal to take part in some activity. **3** a person who does this. **hold-over** n. (N Am.) a relic. **hold-up** n. **1** a robbery, esp. an armed one. **2** a delay, stoppage. **3** (N Am.) an excessive charge, extortion. **4** either of a pair of stockings held up by elasticated tops.

hold[2] (hōld) n. **1** the act of seizing or grasping in the hands. **2** a grasp, a clutch. **3** mental grasp. **4** a support, anything to hold by or support oneself by. **5** moral influence. **6** custody, possession. **7** a manner of seizing or grasping an opponent in wrestling etc. **no holds barred** observing no rules. **on hold 1** (of a telephone call or caller) waiting to be connected. **2** deferred until later. **to get hold of 1** to grasp. **2** to get in contact with. **to take hold 1** to take a grip (of). **2** to become established. **to take hold of** to seize.

hold[3] (hōld) n. a cavity in the lower part of a ship or aircraft, in which the cargo is stowed.

holding (hōl′ding) n. **1** tenure or occupation. **2** that which is held, esp. land, property, stocks or shares. **holding company** n. a company formed to acquire the majority of shares in one or more subsidiary companies. **holding operation** n. a manoeuvre designed to maintain things as they are.

hole (hōl) n. **1** a hollow place or cavity. **2** an aperture, an orifice, a perforation. **3** a wild animal's burrow. **4** a small pit or hollow into which the ball has to be driven in various games. **5** in golf, one of the points made by the player who drives the ball from one hole to another with the fewest strokes; the distance between the tee and a hole. **6** (coll.) an awkward situation. **7** (coll.) a dingy, disreputable place. **8** a vacancy due to absence of an electron, esp. one acting as a mobile positive particle in a semiconductor. ~*v.t.* **1** to make a hole or holes in. **2** to put or drive into a hole. **3** to pierce the side of (a ship). ~*v.i.* **1** to go into a hole. **2** to hibernate. **3** in golf, to send one's ball into a hole. **in holes** (of materials etc.) worn so much that holes have formed. **to hole out 1** in golf, to play the ball into the hole. **2** (of a batsman in cricket) to be caught out. **to hole up** (*N Am., coll.*) to go into hiding. **to make a hole in** to take or consume a large part of. **to pick holes in** to find fault with. **hole-and-corner** *a.* secret, clandestine. **hole-in-one** *n.* (*pl.* **holes-in-one**) (in golf) a shot entering the hole from the tee. **hole in the heart** *n.* a defect of the heart where there is an abnormal opening in any of the walls dividing the four chambers of the heart. **hole-in-the-wall** *n.* (*coll.*) **1** a small dingy place, esp. one that is hard to find. **2** an automatic cash dispenser situated in the outside wall of a bank etc. **holey** *a.*

holiday (hol'idā) *n.* **1** (*often in pl.*) a period away from work, school or one's usual duties; an extended period spent away from home for recreation. **2** a day of exemption from work by law or custom (a religious festival, bank holiday etc.). ~*a.* of or relating to a holiday (*holiday money*). ~*v.i.* to spend a holiday. **on holiday 1** having a break from work. **2** during one's holidays. **on one's holidays 1** during one's holidays. **2** having a break from work. **holiday camp** *n.* an enclosed area with accommodation, entertainment facilities etc. for holidaymakers. **holidaymaker** *n.* a person taking a holiday away from home. **holiday village** *n.* a modern holiday camp.

holier-than-thou, **holily** etc. HOLY.

holism (hō'lizm), **wholism** *n.* **1** (*Philos.*) the tendency in nature to evolve wholes that are more than the sum of the parts. **2** (*Med.*) the treating of the whole person including mental factors etc. rather than just the symptoms of a disease. **holist** *a., n.* **holistic** (-is'-) *a.* **holistically** *adv.*

holland (hol'ənd) *n.* coarse unbleached linen with a glazed surface, first made in Holland.

hollandaise sauce (holəndāz') *n.* a sauce made with butter, egg yolk and lemon juice etc. often served with fish.

holler (hol'ə) *v.i.* (*esp. N Am., coll. or dial.*) to shout loudly, to cry out. ~*v.t.* to communicate in a shout. ~*n.* a loud shout or cry.

hollo (hol'ō), **holloa** (həlō') *int.* used to call attention. ~*n.* (*pl.* **hollos, holloas**) a call of 'hollo!'. ~*v.i.* (*3rd pers. sing. pres.* **holloes, holloas, hollows,** *pres.p.* **holloing, holloaing, hollowing,** *past, p.p.* **holloed, holloaed, holloa'd, hollowed**) (*also* **hollow**) to shout to call attention. ~*v.t.* to call to (hounds).

hollow (hol'ō) *a.* **1** containing a cavity or empty space. **2** not solid. **3** excavated, sunken, concave. **4** empty, vacant. **5** without significance, meaningless. **6** (of sounds) deep, low. **7** insincere, not genuine. ~*n.* **1** a depression or unoccupied space.

2 a cavity, a hole, a basin. **3** a valley. ~*v.t.* to make hollow, to excavate. **hollow-cheeked** *a.* with sunken cheeks. **hollow-eyed** *a.* having sunken eyes. **hollow-hearted** *a.* insincere, false. **hollowly** *adv.* **hollowness** *n.* **hollow square** *n.* a body of troops drawn up in the form of a square with a vacant space in the middle. **hollowware** *n.* hollow vessels, such as pots, kettles etc. made of metal, china etc.

holly (hol'i) *n.* (*pl.* **hollies**) **1** a shrub or tree of the genus *Ilex*, esp. *I. aquifolium*, a tree with glossy, prickly leaves and scarlet or, more rarely, yellow berries. **2** branches of these trees used as Christmas decorations. **holly oak** *n.* HOLM².

hollyhock (hol'ihok) *n.* a tall garden plant, *Althaea rosea*, with red, pink and yellow flowers.

holm¹ (hōm), **holme** *n.* **1** flat ground, liable to flooding, along the side of a river. **2** an island in a river or estuary.

holm² (hōm), **holm-oak** *n.* an evergreen oak, *Quercus ilex*.

holmium (hōl'miəm) *n.* (*Chem.*) a metallic element of the rare-earth group, chem. symbol Ho, at. no. 67.

holo- (hol'ō), **hol-** *comb. form* complete or completely.

holocaust (hol'əkawst) *n.* **1** a wholesale sacrifice of life, or general destruction, esp. by fire or nuclear weapons. **2** (**the Holocaust**) the wholesale slaughter of Jews in Europe by the Nazis in the 1940s.

Holocene (hol'əsēn) *n.* (*Geol.*) the most recent period of geological time. ~*a.* of or concerning this period.

hologram (hol'əgram) *n.* (*Physics*) **1** (a photographic reproduction of) a pattern produced by the interference between a beam of coherent light (e.g. from a laser) and a direct beam of such light reflected off an object. **2** a three-dimensional image produced by illuminating such a reproduction.

holograph (hol'əgrahf) *a.* wholly in the handwriting of the author or signatory. ~*n.* a document, letter etc. so written. **holographic** (-graf'-) *a.* **holographically** *adv.* **holography** (-log'rə-) *n.* (*Physics*) the technique of making or using a hologram.

holophyte (hol'əfīt) *n.* a plant that obtains food like a green plant, esp. by photosynthesis. **holophytic** (-fit'-) *a.*

holothurian (holəthū'riən) *a.* belonging to the Holothuroidea, a class of echinoderms comprising the sea slugs. ~*n.* an animal of this class.

holotype (hol'ətīp) *n.* the original specimen from which a new species is derived or described.

hols (holz) *n.pl.* (*coll.*) holidays.

holster (hōl'stə) *n.* a leather case, usu. on a belt or attached to a saddle bow, to hold a pistol or revolver. **holstered** *a.*

holt (hōlt) *n.* the burrow of an animal, esp. an otter.

holy (hōˊli) a. (comp. **holier**, superl. **holiest**) **1** of high spiritual excellence. **2** associated with God or a deity. **3** sacred, consecrated. **4** morally pure, free from sin. **5** used in mild or trivial exclamations (holy cow!; holy smoke!). **holier-than-thou** a. (coll.) convinced of one's moral superiority, sanctimonious. **holily** adv. **holiness** n. **His Holiness** a title of the Pope, given formerly to the Greek emperors and other sacred and ecclesiastical dignitaries. **Holy Communion** n. the administration of the Eucharist. **holy day** n. a day commemorating some religious event. **Holy Family** n. the infant Jesus with Joseph and Mary. **Holy Father** n. the Pope. **Holy Ghost** n. (Theol.) the third person of the Trinity. **Holy Grail** n. GRAIL. **Holy Land** n. **1** Palestine. **2** a region that is revered in non-Christian religions. **Holy Name** n. in the Roman Catholic Church, the name of Jesus as an object of formal devotion. **Holy Office** n. the Inquisition. **holy of holies** n. **1** the innermost and most sacred apartment of the Jewish Tabernacle and the Temple, where the ark was kept. **2** an innermost shrine. **3** something regarded as most sacred. **holy orders** n.pl. **1** the different ranks of the Christian ministry. **2** the clerical office. **holy roller** n. (derog.) a member of a sect that expresses religious fervour in an ecstatic or frenzied way. **Holy Sacrament** n. **1** the Eucharist. **2** the consecrated elements of the Eucharist, esp. the bread. **Holy Saturday** n. the Saturday before Easter. **Holy Scripture** n. the Bible. **Holy See** n. the bishopric of Rome, the Pope's see. **Holy Spirit** n. the third person of the Trinity. **holy terror** n. (coll.) **1** a formidable person, a troublesome person or thing. **2** the use of organized intimidation. **Holy Trinity** n. the union of three persons (the Father, the Son, and the Holy Ghost) in one godhead. **holy war** n. a war waged on behalf of a religion. **holy water** n. water blessed by a priest or used for holy purposes. **Holy Week** n. the week from Palm Sunday to Holy Saturday inclusive. **Holy Writ** n. sacred scriptures, esp. the Bible. **Holy Year** n. in the Roman Catholic Church, a period of remission from sin, esp. one granted every 25 years.

homage (homˊij) n. **1** a public show of respect or honour to someone or something. **2** deference, obeisance, reverence, worship. **3** (in feudal society) the service paid and fealty professed to a sovereign etc.

hombre (omˊbrā) n. (N Am., sl.) man.

Homburg (homˊbœg) n. a man's hat of soft felt with a dented crown and a depression in the top.

home[1] (hōm) n. **1** the place where one lives. **2** the residence of one's family. **3** the members of a family collectively. **4** one's own country or that of one's ancestors. **5** one's family background. **6** the place of constant residence, of commonest occurrence, or where anything is indigenous. **7** a place or state of rest or comfort. **8** a charitable institution of rest or refuge for orphans, the destitute or the afflicted. **9** the environment or habitat of a person or animal. **10** in various games, the goal, den or finishing point. **11** in sport, one's own ground (The match was at home). **12** in football pools, a match won by a team playing on their own ground. **13** in lacrosse, a position of play nearest the opponent's goal. **14** the home base, the home plate. ~a. **1** connected with, carried on or produced at home or in one's native country. **2** domestic, as opposed to foreign. **3** in sport, relating to one's own ground. **4** in the neighbourhood of home. **5** (N Am.) central, principal. ~adv. **1** to one's home or country. **2** arrived at, returned home. **3** (N Am.) at home. **4** to the point, pointedly, closely, intimately. **5** to the fullest extent. **at home 1** in one's own house, area or country. **2** at ease, comfortable. **3** conversant (with). **4** accessible to visitors. **home and dry** safe after having successfully come through an experience. **near home** concerning one deeply. **nothing/ not much to write home about** (coll.) not very impressive, great etc. **home base, home plate** n. in baseball, the rubber plate on which the batter stands. **home-bird** n. (coll.) a homebody. **homebody** n. (pl. **homebodies**) a person who likes to stay at home, whose interests are in the home. **homeboy** n. (esp. N Am., sl.) a person from one's home town or neighbourhood. **home-brew** n. an alcoholic beverage brewed at home. **home-brewed** a., n. **homecoming** n. a return to, or arrival at home. ~a. returning home. **Home Counties** n.pl. the counties nearest London: Middlesex, Surrey, Kent, Essex, Herts., Bucks., Berks. **home farm** n. a farm belonging to and providing food for the owner of a country estate. **home from home** n. a place other than one's own home where one can be at ease. **home-grown** a. (esp. of fruit and vegetables) grown in one's own garden, area, country etc. **Home Guard** n. **1** the citizen army formed in Britain in May 1940, under the title of Local Defence Volunteers. **2** a member of this. **home help** n. a person employed, often by a local authority, to do domestic work for persons unable to look after themselves sufficiently. **homeland** n. **1** one's native land. **2** (Hist.) in S Africa, a semi-autonomous state reserved for a black African people. **3** any similar semi-autonomous area. **homeless** a. without a home. ~n.pl. homeless people as a class. **homelessness** n. **homelike** a. **home loan** n. a loan made to a person to assist in buying a home. **homely** a. (comp. **homelier**, superl. **homeliest**) **1** plain, without affectation, unpretending. **2** unadorned, unvarnished. **3 a** (of a person) warm and domesticated in manner, looks etc. **b** (N Am.) (of a person) plain or ugly in manner, looks etc. **4** good at housekeeping. **homeliness** n. **home-made** a. made at home. **homemaker** n. a person who manages or creates a home. **home-making** n. **home movie** n. a film, usu. by an amateur, depicting home life, one's interests etc. **homeowner** n. a person who owns their own home. **home perm** n. a permanent wave that a person does or has done at home. **home port** *n.* the port from where a ship originates. **home rule** *n.* the government of a country, esp. Ireland, by a separate parliament. **home run** *n.* in baseball, a hit that allows the batter to make a complete circuit and score a run. **Home Secretary** *n.* in British government, the Secretary of State for the Home Department who is in charge of the Home Office. **home shopping** *n.* shopping done from home through catalogues, satellite television, the Internet etc. **homesick** *a.* depressed at being away from one's home, family etc. **homesickness** *n.* **home signal** *n.* a railway signal that must not be passed if it is against a train, distinguished from distance signal. **homespun** *a.* **1** plain, unaffected, unsophisticated. **2** (of cloth or yarn) spun or wrought at home. *~n.* **1** cloth spun at home. **2** anything plain or unsophisticated. **homestead** (-sted) *n.* **1** a house, esp. a farmhouse, with the buildings attached. **2** (*N Am.*) a lot granted for the residence and maintenance of a family, under the Homestead Act of 1862. **3** (*Austral., New Zeal.*) the owner's house on a sheep station. **homesteader** *n.* **homesteading** *n.* **home straight, home stretch** *n.* **1** the last section of a racecourse. **2** the last phase of any enterprise. **homestyle** *a.* (*N Am.*) (usu. of food) home-made in style; homely. **home town** *n.* the town where one's home is or was. **home trade** *n.* trade conducted within a country. **home truth** *n.* an unwelcome truth expressed in a pointed way. **homeward** *adv.* towards home. *~a.* being or going in the direction of home. **homeward-bound** *a.* returning home from abroad. **homewards** *adv.* **homework** *n.* **1** work to be done at home, esp. for school. **2** any preparatory work or study. **3** work done at home for pay. **homeworker** *n.* **homy, homey** *a.* (*comp.* homier, *superl.* homiest). **hominess, homeyness** *n.*

home² (hōm) *v.i.* **1** (of birds, esp. pigeons and other animals) to reach home accurately from a distance. **2** to be directed on to a target, e.g. with a navigational device. **3** to go home. **4** to dwell. *~v.t.* **1** to send or guide (pigeons etc.) home. **2** to provide with a home. **3** to direct on to a target, e.g. with a navigational device. **homer** *n.* **1** a homing pigeon. **2** in baseball, a home run. **homing** *a.* **1** (*Zool.*) having or relating to the ability to return home accurately from a great distance (*homing instinct; homing pigeon*). **2** (of a navigational device etc.) guiding itself on to a target etc. **3** returning home.

homeopathy HOMOEOPATHY.

homeotherm (hō´miəthœm), **homoeotherm, homoiotherm** *n.* **1** an organism that maintains the same body temperature. **2** a warm-blooded organism. **homeothermal** (-thœ´məl), **homeothermic** (-thœ´mik) *a.* **homeothermy** *n.*

Homeric (hōmer´ik) *a.* **1** of, relating to, or resembling Homer or his poems. **2** epic, large-scale or heroic. **3** of Bronze Age Greece as depicted in Homer's poems.

homicide (hom´isīd) *n.* **1** the act of killing a human being. **2** a person who kills another. **homicidal** (-sī´-) *a.*

homiletic (homilet´ik) *a.* of or relating to homilies. **homiletics** *n.pl.* the art of preaching; the art or method of presenting religious doctrine to an audience in the most effective form.

homily (hom´ili) *n.* (*pl.* **homilies**) **1** a discourse or sermon on a moral or religious topic. **2** a tedious moral exhortation. **homiliary** (hōmil´iəri) *n.* (*pl.* **homiliaries**) a book of homilies. **homilist** *n.*

hominid (hom´inid) *n.* a creature of the family Hominidae, comprising humans and their precursors. *~a.* of or relating to the Hominidae.

hominoid (hom´inoid) *a.* **1** of or like man. **2** of, relating to, or belonging to the superfamily Hominoidea, comprising humans and their ancestors. **3** hominid or pongid. *~n.* a hominid animal.

hominy (hom´ini) *n.* (*esp. N Am.*) maize hulled and coarsely ground, boiled with water or milk for food.

Homo (hō´mō) *n.* (*pl.* **Homines** (hom´ināz)) any primate of the genus *Homo*, of which man is the only living species.

homo (hō´mō) *n.* (*pl.* **homos**) (*coll., usu. derog.*) short for HOMOSEXUAL.

homo- (hō´mō, hom´ō), **hom-** *comb. form* alike, similar, identical.

homoeopathy (hōmiop´əthi, hom-), (*esp. NAm.*) **homeopathy** *n.* the system which aims at curing diseases by administering in small doses medicines which would produce in healthy persons symptoms similar to those they are designed to remove. **homoeopath** (hō´-, hom´-) *n.* a homoeopathist. **homoeopathic** (-path´-) *a.* **homoeopathically** *adv.* **homoeopathist** *n.* a person who practises or believes in homoeopathy.

homoerotic (hōmōirot´ik) *a.* of or concerning sexual attraction to the same sex. **homoeroticism** (-sizm) *n.*

homogeneous (homəjē´niəs) *a.* **1** composed of the same or similar parts or elements. **2** of the same kind or nature throughout. **3** (*Math.*) having all its terms of the same degree. **homogeneity** (-jinē´iti, -nā´-) *n.* **homogeneously** *adv.* **homogeneousness** *n.* **homogenize** (-moj´-), **homogenise** *v.t.* **1** to make homogeneous. **2** to process (milk or cream) so that the fat globules are emulsified. *~v.i.* to become homogeneous. **homogenization** (-zā´shən) *n.* **homogenizer** *n.* **homogenous** (-moj´-) *a.* **1** HOMOGENEOUS. **homogeny** (-moj´-) *n.*

Usage note The use of *homogenous* to mean *homogeneous* is sometimes disapproved of.

homograph (hom´əgrahf) *n.* a word having the same spelling as another, but differing in pronunciation, origin or meaning.

homolog HOMOLOGUE

homologous (həmol´əgəs) *a.* **1** having the same relative position, proportion, value, structure etc. **2** corresponding. **3** (of chromosomes) pairing at meiosis where one member of each pair is carried by every gamete. **4** (*Biol.*) (of organs etc.) of the same evolutionary origin but having different functions. **5** (*Chem.*) (of a series of organic compounds) having similar characteristics and structure but differing in composition by a number of atoms. **homologic** (homəloj´-), **homological** *a.* **homologize** (-jīz), **homologise** *v.i.* to be homologous; to correspond. *~v.t.* to make homologous. **homologue** (hom´əlog), (*N Am.*) **homolog** *n.* something that is homologous. **homology** *n.*

homomorphic (homəmaw´fik), **homomorphous** (-fəs) *a.* analogous, identical or closely similar in form. **homomorphically** *adv.* **homomorphism** *n.* **homomorphy** *n.*

homonym (hom´ənim) *n.* **1** a word having the same sound or spelling as another, but differing in meaning; a homograph or homophone. **2** a person with the same name as another. **homonymic** (-nim´-), **homonymous** (-mon´-) *a.* **homonymously** *adv.* **homonymy** (-mon´əmi) *n.*

homophobia (homəfō´biə, hō-) *n.* a hatred or fear of homosexuals or homosexuality. **homophobe** (hom´-, hō´-) *n.* **homophobic** *a.*

homophone (hom´əfōn) *n.* **1** a word having the same sound as another, but differing in meaning or spelling, as *heir* and *air.* **2** a symbol indicating the same sound as another. **homophonic** (-fon´-) *a.* (*Mus.*) **1** having the same pitch. **2** in unison, as opposed to polyphonic. **homophonically** *adv.* **homophonous** (həmof´-) *a.* **1** having the same sound. **2** (*Mus.*) homophonic. **homophony** (həmof´-) *n.* **1** identity of sound. **2** (*Mus.*) unison.

homopteran (həmop´tərən) *n.* any insect of the suborder Homoptera having wings of a uniform texture. **homopterous** *a.*

homosexual (homəsek´sūəl, hō´-, -shəl) *a.* **1** feeling sexual attraction to one's own sex. **2** of or relating to homosexuals or homosexuality. **3** of or relating to the same sex. *~n.* a homosexual person. **homosexuality** (-shual´-) *n.* **homosexually** *adv.*

homunculus (həmŭng´kūləs), **homuncule** (-kūl) *n.* (*pl.* **homunculi** (-lī), **homuncules**) a little man; a dwarf; a manikin. **homuncular** *a.*

Hon. *abbr.* **1** Honorary. **2** Honourable.

hon HONEY.

honcho (hon´chō) *n.* (*pl.* **honchos**) (*N Am., sl.*) **1** a boss, leader or manager. **2** an important or able man.

hone (hōn) *n.* **1** a whetstone esp. for sharpening razors. **2** any of several stones used for this purpose. *~v.t.* to sharpen on a hone.

honest (on´ist) *a.* **1** upright, fair, truthful, trustworthy in dealings, business or conduct. **2** open, frank, candid, sincere, honourable. **3** just, equitable. **4** (of an act, feeling etc.) characterized by fairness or sincerity (often used patronizingly). **5** (of money, gain etc.) legitimate, fair (*an honest day's work*). **6** worthy or respectable. **7** unimpeached, unstained. *~adv.* (*coll.*) genuinely, truly. **to make an honest woman of** (*coll. or facet.*) to marry (esp. a pregnant woman). **to make/ earn/**

turn an honest penny (*coll.*) to earn money legitimately or fairly. **honest broker** *n.* an impartial mediator in international, industrial etc. disputes. **honest Injun** *adv.* (*coll.*) genuinely, really. **honestly** *adv.* **1** in an honest way. **2** really. *~int.* used to express disgust, disbelief etc. **honest-to-God, honest-to-goodness** *a.* genuine, outright. *~adv.* genuinely, really, completely. **honesty** *n.* (*pl.* **honesties**) **1** the quality or state of being honest. **2** truthfulness. **3** a cruciferous garden plant, *Lunaria biennis*, bearing flat, round, semitransparent seed pods.

honey (hŭn´i) *n.* (*pl.* **honeys**) **1** a sweet viscid product collected from plants by bees, and largely used as food. **2** the colour of this; golden brown. **3** sweetness. **4** the nectar of flowers. **5** (*esp. N Am.*) (*also* **hon**) used as a term of endearment. **6** a person, thing etc. considered to be excellent of its kind. **honey badger** *n.* a ratel. **honey bee** *n.* a bee that produces honey. **honeybun** *n.* honeybunch. **honeybunch** *n.* (*esp. N Am., coll.*) used as a term of endearment. **honeybuzzard** *n.* any bird of prey of the genus *Pernis* which feeds on the larvae and honey of bees and wasps. **honeycomb** *n.* **1** a waxy substance formed in hexagonal cells by the honey bee, for the reception of honey and for the eggs and larvae. **2** anything similarly structured or perforated, esp. flaws in a metal casting. **3** (*Zool.*) the reticulum. *~v.t.* **1** to fill with holes or cavities. **2** to mark with a honeycomb-like pattern. **honeycreeper** *n.* **1** any bird of the family Drepanidiae of Hawaii. **2** any of several kinds of small S American birds, such as the tanager, which feeds on nectar. **honeydew** *n.* **1** a saccharine substance excreted by aphids and found on the leaves of plants. **2** a honeydew melon. **3** something extremely sweet, nectar. **honeydew melon** *n.* a type of melon with sweet flesh and a yellow rind. **honeyeater** *n.* any bird of the Australasian family Meliphagidae with a long tongue for extracting nectar from flowers. **honeyed, honied** *a.* **1** of, containing or resembling honey. **2** (of words etc.) ingratiating, sweet-sounding. **honey fungus** *n.* an edible fungus, *Armillaria mellea*, parasitic on the roots of woody plants. **honeyguide** *n.* **1** any small bird of the family Indicatoridae which feeds on beeswax, honey and insects and whose cry guides people to the nests of bees. **2** a marking on a flower said to guide bees to nectar. **honey pot** *n.* **1** a container for honey. **2** a posture with the hands clasped under the hams. **3** (*pl.*) a children's game involving this posture. **4** something very attractive or irresistible. **honeysuckle** *n.* any climbing shrub of the genus *Lonicera*, with sweet-scented white, yellow or pink tubular flowers. **honey-sweet** *a.* **1** much loved. **2** sweet as honey.

honeymoon (hŭn´imoon) *n.* **1** a holiday taken by a newly married couple. **2** HONEYMOON PERIOD (under HONEYMOON). *~v.i.* to spend a honeymoon (in, at etc.). **honeymooner** *n.* **honeymoon period**

n. a period of goodwill and harmony at the start of a new business appointment, relationship etc.

honk (hongk) *n.* **1** the cry of the wild goose. **2** any similar cry or noise, esp. that of a vehicle's horn. *~v.i.* to make a honk. *~v.t.* to cause to make a honk. **honker** *n.* **honking** *a.*

honky (hong'ki), **honkie** *n.* (*pl.* **honkies**) (*NAm.*, *offensive*, *sl.*) **1** a white person. **2** white people collectively.

honky-tonk (hong'kitongk) *n.* **1** (*NAm.*, *sl.*) a disreputable nightclub, bar etc. **2** a type of ragtime piano-playing, esp. on a cheap upright piano.

honor HONOUR.

honorable HONOURABLE.

honorand (on'ərand) *n.* a person receiving an honour such as an honorary degree.

honorarium (onərəə'riəm) *n.* (*pl.* **honorariums**, **honoraria** (-riə)) a fee or payment for the services of a professional person.

honorary (on'ərəri) *a.* **1** done, made or conferred as a mark of honour. **2** holding a title or an office without payment or without undertaking the duties. **3** (of duties or obligations) depending on honour, not enforceable by law.

honorific (onərif'ik) *a.* **1** conferring or showing honour. **2** in oriental languages, applied to phrases, words etc. to imply respect. *~n.* **1** an honorific title etc. **2** an honorific word, phrase etc. **honorifically** *adv.*

honour (on'ə), (*NAm.*) **honor** *n.* **1** respect, esteem, reverence. **2** reputation, glory, integrity. **3** conformity to the accepted code of social conduct. **4** nobleness of mind, probity, uprightness. **5** something conferred as a mark or token of distinction for bravery, achievement etc. **6** high rank; exalted position. **7** (*pl.*) a distinction awarded for meritorious or advanced university work. **8** (*pl.*) a degree course that is above the level of an ordinary degree. **9** a person or thing that confers honour, position etc. **10** (*poet.*) an ornament or decoration. **11** a title of address given to certain officers, as a county court judge etc. **12** in golf, the right of driving off first. **13** (*pl.*) **a** in bridge etc., any of the top five cards in a suit (esp. of trumps) or the four aces at no trumps. **b** in whist, the four highest trump cards. *~v.t.* **1** to treat with reverence or respect. **2** to confer honour upon. **3** to accept or pay (a bill or cheque) when due. **4** to acknowledge. **5** to dignify, to glorify, to exalt. **in honour of** out of respect for; as a celebration of. **on/ upon one's honour** used to pledge one's honour or reputation on the accuracy or good faith of a statement. **to do the honours 1** to perform the duties of a host or hostess to guests. **2** (*coll.*) to perform a social task, courtesy etc., such as serving food, proposing a toast etc. **honourer** *n.* **honours list** *n.* a list of people awarded honours, e.g. knighthoods etc., from the sovereign. **honour-trick** *n.* QUICK TRICK (under QUICK).

honourable (on'ərəbəl), (*NAm.*) **honorable** *a.* **1** worthy of honour. **2** conferring honour. **3** illustrious, of distinguished rank, noble. **4** actuated by principles of honour, upright; not base. **5** consistent with honour or reputation. **6** accompanied or performed with or as with marks of honour. **7** proceeding from a laudable cause (*honourable intentions*). **8** (**Honourable**) a title of respect or distinction borne by the children of peers below the rank of marquess, maids of honour, Justices of the High Court etc. **honourable mention** *n.* a distinction sometimes awarded to a competitor who has just failed to win a prize. **honourableness** *n.* **honourably** *adv.*

hooch (hooch), **hootch** *n.* (*NAm.*, *coll.*) crude alcoholic liquor.

hood[1] (hud) *n.* **1** a loose covering for the head and back of the neck, separate, or part of a cloak etc. **2** an appendage to an academic gown marking a degree. **3** anything hoodlike, as the blinding cap on a hawk, a carriage top, a paper cornet etc. **4** the folding roof or top of a car or pram etc. **5** (*NAm.*) the bonnet of a motor car etc. **6** an overhanging or protective canopy, cover etc. **7** (*Biol.*) a hoodlike structure or marking such as the expansion of a cobra. *~v.t.* to dress or cover in a hood. **hooded** *a.* covered with a hood; blinded. **hooded crow** *n.* a subspecies of the carrion crow having a grey body with black head, wings and tail. **hoodless** *a.* **hoodlike** *a.* **hoodwink** *v.t.* to deceive, to take in. **hoodwinker** *n.*

hood[2] (hud) *n.* (*sl.*) a hoodlum, a gangster.

-hood (hud) *suf.* **1** denoting a state or quality, as in *childhood*, *parenthood*. **2** indicating a group etc., as in *sisterhood*, *brotherhood*, *neighbourhood*.

hoodlum (hood'ləm) *n.* (*NAm.*, *sl.*) **1** a street rowdy, a hooligan, orig. esp. one of a gang of street ruffians who flourished in San Francisco during the 1870s and 1880s. **2** a gangster. **hoodlumism** *n.*

hoodoo (hoo'doo) *n.* (*pl.* **hoodoos**) (*esp. NAm.*, *coll.*) **1** bad luck. **2** the cause of bad luck, a Jonah. **3** voodoo. *~v.t.* (*3rd pers. sing. pres.* **hoodoos**, *pres.p.* **hoodooing**, *past*, *p.p.* **hoodooed**) **1** to bring bad luck to. **2** to bewitch. **hoodooism** *n.*

hooey (hoo'i) *n.*, *int.* (*sl.*) rubbish, nonsense.

hoof (hoof) *n.* (*pl.* **hooves** (hoovz), **hoofs**) the horny sheath covering the feet of horses, oxen etc. *~v.t.* **1** to strike or attack with the hoof. **2** (*sl.*) to kick. *~v.i.* (*sl.*) to kick (out). **on the hoof 1** (of livestock) alive; not yet slaughtered. **2** (*coll.*) while standing up or moving around. **to hoof it 1** (*sl.*) to walk, to go on foot. **2** (*sl.*) to dance. **hoofed** *a.* **hoofer** *n.* (*NAm.*, *sl.*) a dancer.

hooh-ha (hoo'hah), **hoo-ha** *n.* (*coll.*) fuss, noisy commotion or excitement.

hook (huk) *n.* **1** a curved piece of metal or other material by which an object is caught or suspended. **2** FISH-HOOK (under FISH[1]). **3** a curved instrument for cutting grass or corn, a sickle. **4 a** a sharp bend. **b** a sharply curved spit of land.

5 a cape, a headland. **6** a trap, a snare. **7** in boxing, a short swinging blow made with the elbow bent. **8** in cricket, a shot in which the ball is hit square on the leg side with an upward stroke. **9** in golf, a shot in which the ball goes towards the player's left. **10** a curved stroke in writing, printing etc. **11** (*Mus.*) one of the lines at the end of a quaver. **12** (*sl.*) a repetitive catchy musical phrase. **13** (*pl., sl.*) fingers. ~*v.t.* **1** to catch, grasp or hold with or as with a hook. **2** to fasten with a hook or hooks. **3** (*esp. passive, coll.*) to attract or cause to become addicted. **4** (*sl.*) to snatch, to steal, to pilfer. **5** in boxing, to hit (one's opponent) with a hook. **6** in cricket, to play (a ball) with a hook. **7** in golf, to drive (the ball) widely to the left. **8** in rugby, to secure and pass (the ball) backwards from a scrum using the feet. **9** in football, to pull (the ball) in with the foot in a certain manner. ~*v.i.* to fit or fasten (on) with or as with hooks. **by hook or by crook** by fair means or foul. **hook, line and sinker** completely. **off the hook 1** (*coll.*) no longer in danger or difficulty. **2** (of a telephone receiver) not on its rest. **to sling/ take one's hook 1** (*sl.*) to decamp. **2** (*sl.*) to run away. **hook and eye** *n.* a metal hook and corresponding loop for fastening a dress. **hooked** *a.* **1** bent; hook-shaped. **2** furnished with hooks. **3** (of a rug etc.) created by pulling yarn through canvas etc. with a hook. **hooked on** (*coll.*) addicted to. **hookless** *a.* **hooklet** *n.* **hooklike** *a.* **hook-nose** *n.* an aquiline nose. **hook-nosed** *a.* **hook-up** *n.* a radio network, a series of connected stations. **hookworm** *n.* **1** any of various parasitic nematode worms having hooked mouthparts for feeding, which infest humans and animals. **2** the disease caused by such worms.

hookah (huk´ə), **hooka** *n.* a tobacco pipe in which the smoke passes through water.

hooker (huk´ə) *n.* **1** a person or thing that hooks. **2** (*sl.*) a prostitute. **3** in rugby, the central forward in the front row of the scrum who tries to hook the ball.

hookey (huk´i), **hooky** *n.* (*NAm., coll.*) truant (*to play hookey*).

hooligan (hoo´ligən) *n.* any of a gang of street ruffians given to violent attacks on people. **hooliganism** *n.*

hoop[1] (hoop) *n.* **1** a strip of wood or metal bent into a band or ring to hold the staves of casks etc. together or for forming part of a framework. **2** a large iron or wooden ring for a child to trundle or whirl around the body. **3** a large ring through which circus performers or animals jump. **4** a circular strip of whalebone etc. formerly used to expand the skirts of women's dresses. **5** in croquet, a small iron arch through which the ball is driven. **6** HOOP-PETTICOAT (under HOOP[1]). **7** in basketball, the round metal frame to which the net is attached. **8** an earring consisting of one or more circles of metal etc. **9** a colour-contrasting band on a sports shirt etc. **10** (*Austral., coll.*) a jockey. ~*v.t.* **1** to bind or fasten with hoops. **2** to

encircle. **to be put through hoops/ the hoop** to be put through an ordeal. **hoopla** (-lah) *n.* **1** a game of winning prizes by throwing rings over them. **2** (*coll.*) a disturbance or commotion. **3** (*coll.*) gratuitous activity; nonsense. **hoop-petticoat, hoop-skirt** *n.* a woman's dress expanded by means of a hoop.

hoop[2] WHOOP.

hoopoe (hoo´poo, -pō) *n.* a bird, *Upupa epops*, a rare British visitor with large crest and fine plumage.

hoorah (hurah´) *int.* HURRAH.

hooray (hurā´) *int.* **1** HURRAH. **2** (*Austral., New Zeal.*) goodbye. **Hooray Henry** (hoorā hen´ri) *n.* (*pl.* **Hooray Henries, Hooray Henrys**) (*coll.*) a young upper-class man, often with affected manners, who is extroverted and ostentatious.

hoot (hoot) *v.i.* **1** (of an owl) to utter its hollow cry. **2** to cry as an owl; to make a sound like this. **3** to shout or make loud cries in contempt or dissatisfaction, or in amusement. ~*v.t.* **1** to shout at in contempt or dissatisfaction. **2** to send (away, out etc.) with contemptuous hoots. **3** to express by hooting. **4** to sound (a motor horn, siren etc.) ~*n.* **1** the cry of an owl. **2** a cry like that of an owl, esp. that of a motor horn. **3** an inarticulate shout in contempt or dissatisfaction. **4** an outburst of laughter. **5** (*coll.*) an extremely funny or enjoyable person or event. **6** (*coll.*) anything at all (*I don't give a hoot*; *it doesn't matter two hoots*). **hooter** *n.* **1** a person, animal or object that hoots. **2** a steam whistle or siren, esp. one used to signal the beginning or end of work time. **3** (*sl.*) a nose. **4** (*pl., NAm., taboo sl.*) a woman's breasts.

hootch HOOCH.

hoots (hoots), **hoot** *int.* (*Sc., North.*) used to express disgust, impatience etc.

Hoover® (hoo´və) *n.* a type of vacuum cleaner. **hoover** *v.t., v.i.* to clean with a vacuum cleaner. **to hoover up** to clean with or suck up etc. as if with a vacuum cleaner.

hooves HOOF.

hop[1] (hop) *v.i.* (*pres.p.* **hopping**, *past, p.p.* **hopped**) **1** to spring, leap or skip on one foot. **2** to skip with both feet (as birds) or with all four feet (as quadrupeds). **3** to move or go quickly. **4** (*coll.*) to make a quick trip. **5** (*coll.*) to make a quick change of location etc. **6** to limp. ~*v.t.* **1** to jump lightly or skip over. **2** (*coll.*) to jump into (a bus etc.). ~*n.* **1** a jump, spring or light leap on one foot or (of animals etc.) on both or all feet. **2** (*coll.*) a dance. **3** a short trip by aircraft, a short run, a quick passage. **4** a distance easily covered in a few paces. **on the hop 1** (*coll.*) unawares; unprepared. **2** (*coll.*) active. **to hop in** (*coll.*) to get into a vehicle. **to hop it** (*coll.*) to go away. **to hop off 1** (*coll.*) to get down or off lightly. **2** (*coll.*) to go away. **to hop out** (*coll.*) to get out of a vehicle. **hopper**[1] *n.* **1** a person or thing that hops. **2** a hopping insect, a flea, the larva of a cheese-fly etc. **3** a funnel through which something is conveyed or fed such as fuel etc. to a furnace etc.

4 a railway truck able to discharge loose minerals etc. through underside doors. **hopping** a. (*N Am., coll.*) very busy or active; lively. **hopping mad** a. (*coll.*) very angry. **hop, skip and jump, hop, step and jump** n. **1** the triple jump. **2** a short distance.

hop² (hop) n. **1** a perennial climbing plant, *Humulus lupulus*, the mature cones of which are used in brewing. **2** (*pl.*) the dried flowers of this plant used to give a bitter flavour to beer. **3** (*Austral., New Zeal., coll.*) beer. **4** (*N Am., sl.*) opium or any other narcotic. ~*v.t.* (*pres.p.* **hopping**, *past, p.p.* **hopped**) to impregnate with hops. ~*v.i.* to pick hops. **hop-bind, hop-bine** n. the stem of the hop. **hophead** n. **1** (*esp. N Am., sl.*) a heroin or opium addict. **2** (*Austral., New Zeal., sl.*) a drunkard. **hopped up** a. (*N Am., sl.*) **1** intoxicated or drugged. **2** excited; agitated. **hopper**² n. a hop-picker. **hop-picker** n. **1** a person who gathers hops. **2** a machine for this purpose. **hoppy** a. tasting of hops. **hopsack** n. **1** a coarse fabric made from hemp etc. **2** (*also* **hopsacking**) sacking for hops made from this. **3** a rough woven fabric of wool etc. used for clothing.

hope (hōp) n. **1** an expectant desire; confidence in a future event (*Her hopes were justified*). **2** a ground for such expectation, trust or confidence (*There is still room for hope*). **3** a person or thing that is the cause for hope. **4** that which is hoped for. ~*v.i.* **1** to feel hope (*We hope for a victory*). **2** to have confidence; to be hopeful. ~*v.t.* **1** to expect with desire. **2** to look forward to with confidence. **to hope against hope** to cling to a slight chance. **hope chest** n. (*N Am.*) a woman's bottom drawer. **hopeful** a. **1** feeling hope. **2** giving rise to hope. **3** promising. ~n. (*sometimes iron.*) a person poised for success (used ironically where a person is not likely to succeed). **hopefully** adv. **1** in a hopeful way. **2** (*coll.*) it is hoped (*Hopefully, he'll pay*). **hopefulness** n. **hopeless** a. **1** destitute of hope, despairing. **2** affording no hope, desperate. **3** incompetent or showing incompetence. **hopelessly** adv. **hopelessness** n.

Usage note The use of *hopefully* to express a general hope (as a sentence adverb) is quite widely disapproved of, though it is very common.

hopper¹ HOP¹.

hopper² HOP².

hopscotch (hop´skoch) n. a children's game in which a stone is driven by the foot of a player hopping from one compartment to another of a figure traced on the ground.

horde (hawd) n. **1** (*usu. derog.*) a gang, a multitude. **2** a nomadic tribe or clan esp. a Central Asian group. **3** a large moving mass of animals or insects.

Usage note See note under HOARD.

horehound (haw´hownd), **hoarhound** n. **1** a labiate herb, *Marrubium vulgare*, with woolly stem and leaves and aromatic juice, used as a tonic and a remedy for colds etc.; white horehound. **2** a labiate herb, *Ballota nigra*, with an unpleasant aroma; black horehound. **3** any of various allied herbs.

horizon (hərī´zən) n. **1** the circular line where the sky and the earth seem to meet, the sensible horizon. **2** the great circle parallel to it, the centre of which is the centre of the earth, the celestial horizon. **3** the boundary of one's mental vision, experience etc. **4** in archaeology, the level at which a particular set of remains or artefacts is found. **5** (*Geol.*) a layer of rock within a stratum etc. that has particular characteristics. **on the horizon 1** (of an event etc.) imminent; likely to appear or happen soon. **2** visible. **horizonless** a.

horizontal (horizon´təl) a. **1** of or relating to the horizon. **2** parallel to the plane of the horizon, at right angles to the vertical. **3** applied uniformly to all members of a group. **4** in economics, relating to companies etc. engaged in identical stages of production etc. (*horizontal integration*). ~n. a horizontal line, plane, bar etc. **horizontality** (-tal´-) n. **horizontally** adv.

hormone (haw´mōn) n. **1** a secretion from an internal gland having the property of stimulating vital and functional physiological activity. **2** in plants, an organically produced compound that is essential for growth. **3** any synthetic substance with similar effects or properties. **hormonal** (-mō´-) a. **hormonally** adv. **hormone replacement therapy** n. treatment involving replacement of deficient hormones to counteract conditions associated with the menopause.

horn (hawn) n. **1** a projecting bony growth, usu. pointed and in pairs on the heads of certain animals. **2** the substance, usu. keratin, of which such growths are composed. **3** an organ or growth resembling horns, as the feeler of a snail etc. **4** anything made of or like a horn in shape, as a powder flask or a drinking vessel. **5** a metal wind instrument, orig. of horn. **6** FRENCH HORN (under FRENCH). **7** (*Mus.*) a horn player. **8** a device for sounding a warning or other signal (*foghorn*). **9** an extremity of a curved object, as of the moon when on the wane or waxing. **10** (*N Am., sl.*) the telephone. **11** (*Geol.*) a pyramid-shaped peak formed by glacial action. **12** (*taboo sl.*) an erection of the penis. **13** a wing of an army. **14** one of the alternatives of a dilemma. ~*v.t.* **1** to provide with horns. **2** to gore. **on the horns of a dilemma** in a situation involving a choice between two equally undesirable alternatives. **to horn in** (*sl.*) to push in, to intrude (on). **hornbeam** n. any tree of the genus *Carpinus*, having smooth bark and yielding tough timber. **hornbill** n. any bird of the family Bucerotidae, having a large bone-crested bill. **horned** a. **1** having a horn or horns. **2** having projections or extremities like horns. **3** curved like a horn (*horned moon*). **horned owl, horn owl** n. any owl of the genus *Bubo*, having large ear tufts. **horned toad** n. a small

American toad-like lizard, *Phrynosoma cornu-tum*, covered with spines. **hornless** *a.* **hornlike** *a.* **horn of plenty** *n.* CORNUCOPIA. **hornpipe** *n.* **1** a lively dance, usu. for one person, popular among sailors. **2** the music for such a dance. **horn-rimmed** *a.* (esp. of spectacles) having rims made of (a material resembling) horn. **hornwort** *n.* any aquatic plant of the genus *Ceratophyllum*, with submerged branching leaves. **horny** *a.* (*comp.* **hornier**, *superl.* **horniest**) **1** of or like horn. **2** callous (*horny-handed*). **3** having or abounding in horns. **4** (*sl.*) sexually excited; lustful. **hornily** *adv.* **horniness** *n.*

hornblende (hawn′blend) *n.* a dark-coloured mineral consisting of silica, magnesia, lime and iron.

hornet (haw′nit) *n.* a large social wasp, *Vespa crabro*, with a severe sting. **to stir up a hornet's nest** to stir up trouble or excite the animosity of other people.

†**horologe** (hor′əloj) *n.* a timepiece. **horologer** (-rol′-), **horologist** (-rol′-) *n.* **1** a person skilled in horology. **2** a person who makes horologes. **horo-logic** (-loj′-), **horological** *a.* **horology** (-rol′əji) *n.* **1** the art of measuring time, or of construct-ing instruments to indicate time. **2** the study of this.

horoscope (hor′əskōp) *n.* (*Astrol.*) **1** the predic-tion of a person's future based on a map showing the relative position of the stars and planets at that person's birth. **2** such a map. **3** an observa-tion of the sky and the configuration of the planets at a particular time, esp. at the moment of a person's birth, in order to foretell that per-son's future. **horoscopic** (-skop′-), **horoscopical** *a.* **horoscopy** (-os′-) *n.* (*pl.* **horoscopies**).

horrendous (həren′dəs) *a.* awful; horrifying. **horrendously** *adv.* **horrendousness** *n.*

horrible (hor′ibəl) *a.* **1** causing or tending to cause horror; dreadful, shocking, harrowing. **2** (*coll.*) unpleasant, excessive. **horribleness** *n.* **horribly** *adv.*

horrid (hor′id) *a.* **1** horrible, repellent. **2** (*coll.*) nasty, unpleasant, frightful. **horridly** *adv.* **horrid-ness** *n.*

horrify (hor′ifī) *v.t.* (*3rd pers. sing. pres.* **horrifies**, *pres.p.* **horrifying**, *past, p.p.* **horrified**) **1** to strike with horror. **2** to scandalize. **horrific** (-if′-) *a.* **horrifically** *adv.* **horrifiedly** *adv.* **horrifying** *a.* **horrifyingly** *adv.*

horripilation (horipilā′shən) *n.* (*formal*) goose-flesh, a sensation of a creeping or motion of the hair of the body, caused by disease, terror etc. **horripilate** (-ip′-) *v.t., v.i.*

horror (hor′ə) *n.* **1** dread or terror. **2** intense loathing; hatred. **3** (*coll.*) intense dismay. **4** that which excites terror or repulsion. **5** (*coll.*) a bad, ugly or mischievous person or thing (*He's a little horror*). **6** a shaking, shuddering or shivering. ~*a.* (of novels, films etc.) depicting gruesome, fright-ening, often paranormal events. **the horrors 1** a fit of horror or depression; the blues. **2** delirium

tremens. **horror-stricken, horror-struck** *a.* over-whelmed with horror; shocked.

hors (aw) *prep.* out of, beyond. **hors de combat** (də kō′bah) *a.* out of the battle or the running. **hors d'œuvre** (dœ′vrə) *n.* (*pl.* **hors d'œuvres** (dœ′vrə, dœ′vrəz)) a dish not forming part of the main meal, served as an appetizer before or sometimes during a meal.

horse (haws) *n.* **1** a solid-hoofed quadruped, *Equus caballus*, with mane and tail of long coarse hair, domesticated and employed as a beast of draught and burden. **2** the adult male of the species; a stallion or gelding. **3** any other quadruped of the genus *Equus*, such as asses, zebras etc. **4** (*collect.*) cavalry. **5** a frame or other device used as a support. **6** VAULTING HORSE (under VAULT²). **7** SAWHORSE (under SAW¹). **8** CLOTHES HORSE (under CLOTHE). **9** (*coll.*) a unit of horsepower. **10** (*Mining*) a mass of rock, clay etc., forming an obstruction. **11** (*Naut.*) any of various ropes, bars etc. **12** (*sl.*) heroin. ~*v.t.* to provide with a horse or horses. ~*v.i.* **1** to fool about. **2** to mount or ride on horseback. **horses for courses** the matching of tasks to talents, skills etc. **the horse's mouth** (of information etc.) the most reli-able source. **to change horses in midstream** to alter plans, views etc. in the middle of a project. **to eat like a horse** (*coll.*) to eat a lot. **to get on one's high horse** (*coll.*) to be arrogant or dis-dainfully aloof. **to hold one's horses 1** (*coll.*) to stop. **2** (*coll.*) to hesitate; refrain from acting. **horse-and-buggy** *a.* (*N Am.*) belonging or appro-priate to an earlier period. **horseback** *n.* the back of a horse. **on horseback** mounted on a horse. **horse-block** *n.* a block or stage to assist a person in mounting on horseback. **horsebox** *n.* a closed van, car or trailer for transporting horses. **horse brass** *n.* a brass decoration of a type originally hung on a horse's harness. **horsebreaker** *n.* a per-son who breaks in or trains horses. **horse chest-nut** *n.* **1** (*also* **horse chestnut tree**) a large tree of the genus *Aesculus*, with coarse, bitter fruit. **2** the nut of this tree, a conker. **horse-cloth** *n.* a rug to cover a horse. **horse-doctor** *n.* a veterinary surgeon. **horse-drawn** *a.* (of a vehicle) pulled by a horse or horses. **horseflesh** *n.* **1** the flesh of a horse, used as food. **2** (*collect.*) horses. **horsefly** *n.* (*pl.* **horseflies**) any of the insects of the family Tabanidae that irritate horses. **horsehair** *n.* the long hair of the mane and tail of horses, used for padding etc. **horse latitudes** *n.pl.* the region of calms on the northern edge of the north-east trade winds (said to be so called because early navigators frequently threw overboard there any horses they were carrying to America and the W Indies). **horseleech** *n.* **1** a large freshwater leech of the genus *Haemopis*, which feeds by swal-lowing. **2** (*fig.*) a rapacious person, a bloodsucker (in allusion to Prov. xxx.15). **horseless** *a.* **horse-like** *a.* **horse mackerel** *n.* any large mackerel-type fish such as the scad, tuna etc. **horseman** *n.* (*pl.* **horsemen**) **1** a rider on horseback. **2** a person skilled in riding or managing horses. **3** a mounted soldier. **horsemanship** *n.* the art of riding, managing etc. horses; skill in doing this. **horse mushroom** *n.* a large coarse edible mushroom, *Agaricus arvensis.* **horse opera** *n.* (*N Am., sl.*) a western film. **horseplay** *n.* rough, boisterous play. **horsepower** *n.* **1** an imperial unit of power equivalent to 550 foot-pounds (745.7 watts) per second. **2** mechanical power expressed in such units. **horse race** *n.* a race between horses with riders. **horse racing** *n.* **horse radish** *n.* **1** a plant, *Armoracia rusticana*, with long leaves and a pungent, acrid root, used as a condiment. **2** the root of this. **horse-rider** *n.* a person riding a horse. **horse-riding** *n.* **horse sense** *n.* (*coll.*) common sense. **horseshoe** *n.* **1** a shoe for horses. **2** anything resembling this in shape. **horseshoe bat** *n.* any bat of the Old World family Rhinolophidae, having a horseshoe-shaped growth round the nostrils. **horseshoe crab** *n.* a large marine anthropod, *Xiphosura polyphemus*, having a heavily armoured crescent-shaped body. **horse's neck** *n.* (*sl.*) a drink of ginger ale usu. with spirits. **horse-soldier** *n.* a horse-mounted soldier. **horsetail** *n.* **1** the tail of a horse. **2** a plant of the cryptogamous genus *Equisetum*, with whorls of branches like the hairs in a horse's tail. **3** PONYTAIL (under PONY). **horse-trading** *n.* **1** hard bargaining. **2** (*N Am.*) dealing in horses. **horsewhip** *n.* a whip for driving horses. ~*v.t.* (*pres.p.* **horsewhipping**, *past, p.p* **horsewhipped**) to flog with a horsewhip; to thrash. **horsewoman** *n.* (*pl.* **horsewomen**) **1** a woman who rides on horseback. **2** a woman skilled in riding and managing horses. **horsey, horsy** *a.* (*comp.* **horsier**, *superl.* **horsiest**) **1** of or like a horse. **2** of, relating to or fond of horses or horse racing. **3** (esp. of a woman) affecting upper-class speech or manner. **horsily** *adv.* **horsiness** *n.*

hortative (haw´tətiv), **hortatory** (haw´tətəri) *a.* giving or containing advice or encouragement. **hortation** (-ā´shən) *n.*

horticulture (haw´tikŭlchə) *n.* the art of cultivating or managing gardens. **horticultural** (-kŭl´-) *a.* **horticulturalist, horticulturist** *n.*

hosanna (hōzan´ə) *n., int.* **1** an acclamatory prayer for blessing. **2** a shout of praise and adoration.

hose (hōz) *n.* **1** (a piece of) flexible tubing for water or other fluid, as that used by firefighters. **2** (*pl.*) (*also* †**hosen**) stockings, socks etc. collectively. **3** (*Hist.*) close-fitting breeches or trousers reaching to the knees. ~*v.t.* **1** to water or drench with a hose. **2** to provide with hose. **hosepipe** *n.* a length of hose for water etc. **hosier** (-ziə) *n.* a person who deals in hosiery. **hosiery** *n.* (*pl.* **hosieries**) **1** stockings and socks. **2** knitted or woven underclothing.

hospice (hos´pis) *n.* **1** a nursing home or hospital for the terminally ill, needy or afflicted. **2** a convent or other place for the reception

and entertainment of travellers on some difficult or dangerous road or pass, as among the Alps.

hospitable (hos´pitəbəl, -pit´-) *a.* entertaining or disposed to entertain strangers or guests with kindness. **hospitableness** *n.* **hospitably** *adv.* **hospitality** (-tal´-) *n.* liberal entertainment of strangers or guests.

hospital (hos´pitəl) *n.* **1** an institution for the reception and treatment of the sick or injured. **2** †a place of shelter or entertainment, a hospice; one of the establishments of the Knights Hospitallers. **hospitalize, hospitalise** *v.t.* **1** to send to hospital. **2** to admit for hospital treatment. **hospitalization** (-ā´shən) *n.* **hospital ship** *n.* a ship equipped for the specific task of treating and transporting sick etc. soldiers. **hospital trust** *n.* a trust consisting of a National Health Service hospital which is run independent of the local authority.

hospitality HOSPITABLE.

hospitaller (hos´pitələ), (*N Am.*) **hospitaler** *n.* **1** (*Hist.*) one of a religious brotherhood whose office was to relieve the poor, strangers and the sick. **2** a chaplain residing in a hospital for the reception of the poor or strangers.

host[1] (hōst) *n.* **1** a person who entertains another. **2** the landlord of an inn or hotel. **3** the compère of a TV or radio show. **4** (*Biol.*) an animal or plant on which another is parasitic. **5** an organism into which an organ or tissue is grafted or transplanted. ~*v.t.* **1** (of a person) to act as host at (a social event, occasion etc.). **2** to receive and entertain as one's guest. **3** to be the compère of (a show etc.). **hostess** *n.* **1** a woman who receives or entertains guests. **2** a woman paid to entertain customers in a bar, nightclub etc. **3** a woman employed to attend to the comfort of travellers on passenger planes, ships etc. **4** the landlady of an inn or hotel.

host[2] (hōst) *n.* a great number, a multitude. **a host in oneself** a person of extraordinary skills, resources etc. **host of heaven** *n.* **1** the stars, planets etc. **2** the angels and archangels.

host[3] (hōst) *n.* the consecrated bread or wafer used in the Eucharist.

hosta (hos´tə) *n.* any plant of the genus *Hosta* having green decorative leaves and blue, lilac and white flowers.

hostage (hos´tij) *n.* **1** a person given or seized in pledge for the performance of certain conditions or for the safety of others. **2** the state of being so held. **3** any security or pledge. **hostageship** *n.* **hostage to fortune** *n.* **1** an acquisition or undertaking etc. considered as endangered by misfortune, unforeseen events etc. **2** (*pl.*) the people and things a person most values.

hostel (hos´təl) *n.* **1** a house or extra-collegiate hall for the residence of students etc. **2** a place of residence not run commercially, esp. for the homeless. **3** a youth hostel. **hosteller**, (*N Am.*) **hosteler** *n.* a student in a hostel. **hostelling**,

(*N Am.*) **hosteling** *n.* the practice of staying at youth hostels when travelling. **hostelry** *n.* (*pl.* **hostelries**) (*facet.*) an inn, a pub.

hostess HOST[1].

hostile (hos´til) *a.* **1** of or relating to an enemy. **2** showing enmity; unfriendly. **3** (of a place, situation etc.) inhospitable, harsh. **4** resistant (*He is hostile to change*). **hostilely** *adv.* **hostility** (-til´-) *n.* (*pl.* **hostilities**) **1** enmity; antagonism. **2** state of war. **3** (*pl.*) acts of war. **4** opposition (in thought etc.) or resistance (to change etc.).

hot (hot) *a.* (*comp.* **hotter,** *superl.* **hottest**) **1** having a high temperature. **2** (of food) made by heating and served before cooling. **3** producing a sensation of heat. **4** (of spices etc.) acrid, pungent. **5** ardent, impetuous; passionate, fierce. **6** (*coll.*) knowledgeable (*hot on sports cars*). **7** eager, enthusiastic. **8** (*coll.*) strict or severe. **9** angry or upset. **10** (*coll.*) exciting, excited, arduous. **11** sexually excited. **12** (of the scent in hunting) fresh and strong. **13** (of a player) very skilful. **14** much favoured (*He's the hot favourite to win*). **15** (of news) fresh, recent. **16** (*coll.*) (of Treasury bills) newly issued. **17** (*sl.*) (of stolen goods) easily identifiable. **18** (*sl.*) wanted by the police. **19** (*coll.*) very good. **20** (*sl.*) radioactive. **21** (of the ball in ball games) thrown or struck in such a way that the opponent has difficulty in returning it. **22** (of jazz) arousing excitement or emotion (by improvisation etc.). **23** (*coll.*) (of information) very reliable. ~*adv.* **1** hotly. **2** fiercely, angrily. **3** ardently, eagerly. ~*v.t., v.i.* (*pres.p.* **hotting,** *past, p.p.* **hotted**) **1** to make or become hot. **2** to make or become active, intense or exciting. **hot under the collar 1** indignant, angry. **2** embarrassed. **the hots** (*sl.*) strong sexual desire. **to go hot and cold** to feel alternately hot and cold (owing to fear etc.). **to hot up** to become more intense, exciting etc. **to make it/ things hot for someone** to make a situation unpleasant for someone. **to sell/ go like hot cakes** to be sold (or go) quickly. **hot air** *n.* (*coll.*) boastful, empty talk. **hot-air balloon** *n.* a balloon containing air which is heated by a flame causing it to rise. **hotbed** *n.* **1** a bed of earth heated by means of ferment-ing manure, used for raising early and tender plants. **2** any place which favours rapid growth of disease, vice etc. **hot-blooded** *a.* excitable, irritable, passionate. **hot cathode** *n.* a cathode heated to emit electrons. **hot cross bun** *n.* a spicy yeast bun with a cross marked on the top, eaten esp. on Good Friday. **hot dog** *n.* a hot sausage sandwiched in a roll. **hot favourite,** (*N Am.*) **hot favorite** *n.* the horse, runner etc. most likely to win in a race etc. **hot flush** *n.* a sudden feeling of warmth accompanied by blushing, esp. during the menopause. **hotfoot** *adv.* very hastily, swiftly. ~*a.* acting quickly. **to hotfoot it** (*sl.*) to run or go quickly. **hot gospeller,** (*N Am.*) **hot gospeler** *n.* **1** a revivalist preacher with a loud, enthusiastic style of addressing an audience. **2** a fanatical propagandist. **hothead** *n.*

a fiery or impetuous person. **hot-headed** *a.* fiery, impetuous, passionate. **hot-headedly** *adv.* **hot-headedness** *n.* **hothouse** *n.* **1** a plant house where a relatively high artificial temperature is maintained to facilitate growth. **2** any environment encouraging the rapid growth (of skills etc.). ~*v.t.* **1** to raise etc. in or as if in a hothouse. **2** to encourage or force the development of (skills etc.). **hotline** *n.* a telephone line for swift communication, esp. in emergencies. **hotly** *adv.* **hot metal** *n.* (*Print.*) (of machines, methods etc.) using type made from molten metal. **hot money** *n.* capital transferred from one financial institution to another at frequent intervals. **hotness** *n.* **hot pants** *n.pl.* very brief skin-tight women's shorts, often with a bib. **hotplate** *n.* **1** a round plate, electrically heated, on top of a cooker. **2** a portable heatable plate for keeping food warm. **hotpot** *n.* a dish of meat cooked with potatoes and other vegetables in a closed pot in an oven. **hot potato** *n.* (*pl.* **hot potatoes**) a controversial issue, something difficult or dangerous to deal with. **hot rod** *n.* a car with an engine considerably modified to increase its performance greatly. **hot-rodder** *n.* **hot seat** *n.* (*sl.*) **1** an awkward, difficult or dangerous position. **2** the electric chair. **hot shoe** *n.* in photography, a socket on a camera through which electrical contact is made to an electronic flash. **hot-short** *a.* (of iron) brittle when hot. **hotshot** *n.* (*esp. N Am., coll.*) **1** an important, often ostentatious person. **2** a prolific goal-scorer or point-scorer in football, basketball etc. ~*a.* **1** important, ostentatious. **2** accurate, expert. **3** high-profile. **hot spot** *n.* **1** a warm, sunny place, esp. a holiday resort. **2** a place of potential trouble. **3** a point in an engine etc. with an (excessively) high temperature. **4** (*coll.*) a lively nightclub etc. **hot spring** *n.* a spring of mineral water which has been heated underground. **hotspur** *n.* a rash or sometimes violent person. **hot stuff** *n.* (*coll.*) **1** an impressive or excellent thing or person. **2** a very attractive person. **3** a spirited, vigorous or passionate person. **4** pornographic or erotic literature, film etc. **hot-tempered** *a.* quick to anger; irascible. **hottie, hotty** *n.* (*pl.* **hotties**) (*coll.*) a hot-water bottle. **hotting** *n.* (*sl.*) driving fast in a stolen vehicle. **hottish** *a.* **hot tub** *n.* a bath resembling a Jacuzzi. **hot war** *n.* real war. **hot water** *n.* (*coll.*) a state of trouble or disgrace. **hot-water bottle,** (*N Am.*) **hot-water bag** *n.* a usu. rubber container filled with hot water, used for warming a bed. **hot-wire** *v.t.* (*N Am., sl.*) to start the engine of (a car etc.) without the ignition key.

hotchpotch (hoch´poch) *n.* **1** a confused mixture, a jumble. **2** a dish composed of various ingredients, esp. thick broth made with mutton or other meat and vegetables.

hotel (hōtel´) *n.* **1** a commercial establishment providing accommodation, meals etc. **2** (*Austral., New Zeal.*) a public house. **hotelier** (-iə) *n.* a hotel-keeper.

Hottentot (hot´əntot) *n.* (*pl.* **Hottentot, Hottentots**) (*offensive*) NAMA.

Usage note The use of *Hottentot* gives offence: the preferred term is *Nama*.

hough HOCK[1].

hoummos HUMMUS.

hound (hownd) *n.* **1** a dog used in hunting (*bloodhound, deerhound, foxhound*). **2** a runner who chases the hares in hare and hounds. **3** (*coll.*) a mean, contemptible man. *~v.t.* **1** to hunt or chase with or as with hounds. **2** to set a dog, person etc. in pursuit. **3** to urge or cheer (on), to nag. **hound's tongue** *n.* a coarse, hairy plant, *Cynoglossum officinale*, of the borage family, with dull red flowers. **houndstooth** *n.* a pattern in material of broken checks resembling dogs' teeth.

hour (owə) *n.* **1** the 24th part of a natural day, the space of 60 minutes. **2** the point of time indicated by a clock etc. **3** (*pl.*) a particular time after midnight in the 24-hour clock. **4** a time allocated to some purpose (*lunch hour, happy hour*). **5** (*Astron.*) 15° of longitude. **6** (*pl.*) times appointed for work, attendance at office etc. **7** in the Roman Catholic Church, certain prayers to be said at fixed times of the day. **8** the distance travelled in an hour. **after hours** after closing time. **at all hours** at all times. **on the hour** at exactly one, two etc. o'clock. **the hour 1** the present time. **2** the time to act. **hourglass** *n.* a glass having two bulbs and a connecting opening through which the sand in one bulb runs into the other, used for measuring small periods of time. *~a.* (of a woman's figure) having a narrow waist and large bust and hips. **hour hand** *n.* that hand which shows the hour on a clock or watch, distinct from minute hand. **hour-long** *a.* lasting for an hour. *~adv.* for an hour. **hourly** *a.* **1** happening or done every hour. **2** continual. *~adv.* **1** hour by hour. **2** frequently.

houri (hoo´ri) *n.* (*pl.* **houris**) **1** a nymph of the Muslim paradise. **2** a beautiful woman.

house[1] (hows) *n.* (*pl.* **houses** (how´ziz)) **1** a building for shelter or residence, a dwelling, a place of abode. **2** a building used for a specified purpose (*bakehouse, coffee house, farmhouse, hen house, public house, warehouse*). **3 a** the abode of a religious order, a monastery. **b** the order itself. **4** a household. **5** a family or stock, esp. a noble family. **6 a** an assembly, esp. one of the legislative assemblies of a country. **b** a quorum of a legislative body. **7 a** a residential section of a boarding school. **b** the pupils within that section. **c** a division of a day school comprising pupils of all ages. **8** the audience at a place of entertainment. **9** a commercial establishment. **10** the game of bingo. **11** (*Astron.*) the station of a planet in the heavens. **12** (*Astrol.*) a twelfth part of the heavens. **13** house music. **like a house on fire** very quickly and successfully. **on the house** (esp. of alcoholic drinks) given for no payment. **to**

play house to play at being members of a family in their home. **to put/ set one's house in order** to settle one's affairs. **to set up house** to move into a separate dwelling. **house agent** *n.* a person who sells and lets houses, collects rents etc. **house and home** *n.* (an emphatic expression for) home. **house arrest** *n.* detention in one's own home under guard. **houseboat** *n.* a boat or barge with a cabin or house for living in. **housebound** *a.* unable to leave one's house, e.g. because of a disability. **houseboy** *n.* a male servant in a house, esp. in N Africa or India. **housebreaker** *n.* **1** (*Hist., Law*) a person who breaks into and robs houses, ·esp. in the daytime. **2** a worker employed to pull down houses. **housebreaking** *n.* **house-broken** *a.* HOUSE-TRAINED (under HOUSE[1]). **housecoat** *n.* a woman's long overgarment, worn in the house. **housecraft** *n.* the skills of managing a household. **house-father** *n.* a man in charge of children in a children's home etc. **housefly** *n.* (*pl.* **houseflies**) any fly of the family Muscidae, esp. the common fly, *Musca domestica*. **houseful** *n.* (*pl.* **housefuls**). **house guest** *n.* a guest in a private house. **house-hunting** *n.* the activity of seeking a house in which to live. **house-hunt** *v.i.* **househunter** *n.* **house-husband** *n.* a married man who stays at home to run a household while his wife has a paid job. **housekeeper** *n.* **1** a woman employed to manage the affairs of a household. **2** a person in charge of a house, place of business etc. **housekeeping** *n.* **1** the care of a household. **2** the money allotted for this. **3** routine maintenance and organizational work in a business or computer context. **houseleek** *n.* a plant with thick, fleshy leaves, *Sempervivum tectorum*, growing on the tops of walls and houses in Britain. **houseless** *a.* **house lights** *n.pl.* the lights in the auditorium of a theatre, cinema etc. **house magazine** *n.* a magazine published by a company etc. largely concerning its own personnel, activities etc. **housemaid** *n.* a female servant employed to keep a house clean etc., esp. one in charge of reception rooms and bedrooms. **housemaid's knee** *n.* inflammation of the kneecap, often due to excessive kneeling. **houseman** *n.* (*pl.* **housemen**) a junior doctor resident at a hospital. **house martin** *n.* a black and white bird, *Delichon urbica*, with a forked tail, resembling a swallow. **housemaster, housemistress** *n.* a teacher in charge of a house of residence at a boarding school. **house-mother** *n.* a woman in charge of children in a children's home etc. **house mouse** *n.* any greyish mouse of the genus *Mus*, esp. *M. musculus*, a household pest also bred as a pet and for experimental purposes. **house music** *n.* a type of dance music characterized by electronically synthesized effects and a heavy beat. **house of cards** *n.* **1** a structure built of playing cards. **2** any scheme or enterprise of an insecure or precarious kind. **house officer** *n.* a junior hospital doctor. **house of God** *n.* a church, a place of worship. **house of ill repute, house of ill fame** *n.*

a brothel. **house-parent** *n.* a house-father or house-mother. **house party** *n.* (*pl.* **house parties**) a party of guests at a country house. **house plant** *n.* a plant for growing indoors. **house-proud** *a.* taking a pride in the care and decoration of a home. **houseroom** *n.* space or accommodation in a house. **house-sitter** *n.* a person who stays in a house to look after it while the occupier is away. **house-sit** *v.i.* (*pres.p.* **house-sitting**, *past*, *p.p.* **house-sat**). **house sparrow** *n.* the common sparrow, *Passer domesticus.* **house style** *n.* an individual printer's or publisher's preferred method of presentation, writing etc. **house-to-house** *a.* (of an enquiry etc.) performed at every house. **housetop** *n.* the top or roof of a house. **to shout/ proclaim from the housetops** to announce very publicly. **house-trained** *a.* **1** (of an animal) trained not to foul places indoors. **2** (of a person) well-mannered. **house-train** *v.t.* **house-warming** *n.* a party to celebrate moving into a new house etc. **housework** *n.* physical work connected with housekeeping.

house[2] (howz) *v.t.* **1** to place or store in a building. **2** to lodge, contain. **3** to shelter. **4** (*Naut.*) to put (a gun) in a secure state or position.

household (hows'hōld) *n.* **1** those who live together under the same roof and compose a domestic unit. **2** a domestic establishment. **householder** *n.* the head of a household, the occupier of a house. **household name**, **household word** *n.* a familiar name or word. **household troops** *n.pl.* troops specially employed to guard the person of the sovereign.

housewife (hows'wīf) *n.* (*pl.* **housewives** (-wīvz)) **1** a married woman who stays at home to run a household rather than having a full-time paid job. **2** a case for holding pins, needles etc. **housewifely** *a.*, *adv.* **housewifery** (-wifri) *n.* female management of domestic affairs, housekeeping, housecraft.

Usage note As a case for holding pins, needles etc. pronounced (hŭz'if)

housey-housey (howsihow'si), **housie housie** *n.* the game of bingo.

housing (how'zing) *n.* **1** lodging, shelter, accommodation. **2** a protective case for machinery. **3** a hole etc. cut in one piece of wood to receive the end of another. **housing estate** *n.* a planned residential area.

hove HEAVE.

hovel (hov'əl, hŭv'əl) *n.* **1** a miserable dwelling. **2** a conical building enclosing a kiln. **3** a shed or outhouse open at the sides.

hover (hov'ə) *v.i.* **1** to hang or remain (over or about) fluttering in the air or on the wing. **2** to loiter (about). **3** to be irresolute, to waver. **hovercraft** *n.* (*pl.* **hovercraft**) a craft supported above land or water on a cushion of air which it generates itself. **hoverer** *n.* **hoverfly** *n.* (*pl.* **hoverflies**) any brightly coloured fly of the family Syrphidae, which hover and dart. **hoverport** *n.* a

place where passengers enter and leave hovercraft.

how[1] (how) *adv.* **1** in what way or manner. **2** by what means. **3** to what extent, degree etc. **4** in what proportion. **5** in what condition. **6** by what name. **7** at what price. ~*n.* the way, manner, means (of becoming, happening, doing etc.). **how are you? 1** what is your state of health, wellbeing etc.? **2** how do you do? **how come?** (*coll.*) how does it, did that etc. happen? **how do you do?** used as a conventional form of greeting. **how many** what number. **how much 1** what price. **2** what amount. **how's that? 1** what is your opinion, explanation etc.? **2** howzat. **how-d'ye-do** *n.* (*pl.* **how-d'ye-dos**) (*coll.*) an awkward situation. **however**, (*poet.*) **howe'er** *adv.* **1** in whatever manner or degree. **2** nevertheless, notwithstanding. **howsoever**, (*poet.*) **howsoe'er** *adv.* **1** in whatsoever manner. **2** however. **3** to what extent or degree soever. **how's your father** *n.* (*coll.*, *facet.*) illicit goings-on, esp. of a sexual nature. **howzat** (-zat´) *int.* used in cricket to ask for the batsman to be given out.

how[2] (how) *int.* used as a N American Indian greeting.

howdah (how'də), **houdah** *n.* a seat, usu. canopied, carried on an elephant's back.

howdy (how'di) *int.* (*esp. N Am.*) hello.

howitzer (how'itsə) *n.* a short, light or heavy field gun with a high trajectory and low muzzle velocity.

howl (howl) *v.i.* **1** to utter a protracted hollow cry, as a dog or wolf. **2** to wail. **3** to make a wailing sound like the wind. ~*v.t.* to utter in wailing or mournful tones. ~*n.* **1** the cry of a wolf or dog. **2** a protracted, hollow cry, esp. one of anguish, distress or derision. **to howl down** to prevent (a speaker) from being heard by derisive shouting, laughter etc. **howler** *n.* **1** (*coll.*) a ludicrous blunder. **2** a S American monkey of the genus *Alouatta.* **3** a person who howls. **howling** *a.* **1** (*sl.*) extreme, glaring. **2** that howls. **howling dervish** *n.* a member of a Muslim ascetic order whose observances include howling or wailing.

hoy (hoi) *int.* **1** used to draw attention etc. **2** (*Naut.*) used to hail aloft.

hoyden (hoi'dən) *n.* a boisterous girl, a tomboy. **hoydenish** *a.*

HP, **h.p.** *abbr.* **1** high pressure. **2** hire purchase. **3** horsepower.

HQ *abbr.* headquarters.

hr. *abbr.* hour.

HRH *abbr.* His or Her Royal Highness.

hrs. *abbr.* hours.

HRT *abbr.* hormone replacement therapy.

HSH *abbr.* His or Her Serene Highness.

HT *abbr.* high tension.

hub (hŭb) *n.* **1** the central part of a wheel from which the spokes radiate. **2** a place of central importance. **hubcap** *n.* a (decorative) plate or disc covering the hub of a wheel.

hubble-bubble (hŭbəlbŭb´əl) n. 1 a type of pipe in which the smoke is drawn through water, making a bubbling noise, a kind of hookah. 2 a bubbling noise. 3 a jabbering or chattering.

hubbub (hŭb´ŭb) n. 1 a confused noise. 2 a noisy disturbance. 3 a tumult, an uproar.

hubby (hŭb´i) n. (pl. **hubbies**) (coll.) husband.

hubris (hū´bris) n. insolent pride or security, arrogance. **hubristic** (-bris´-) a.

huckleberry (hŭk´əlbəri) n. (pl. **huckleberries**) 1 any low shrub of the genus Gaylussacia of N America. 2 the edible fruit of this shrub. 3 the fruit of the blueberry and other plants of the allied genus Vaccinium.

huckster (hŭk´stə) n. 1 a retailer of small goods, a pedlar, a hawker. 2 a mean, crafty, mercenary person. 3 (N Am.) a person who produces advertising material for radio or TV. ~v.i. 1 to deal in petty goods. 2 to bargain, to haggle. **huckster-ism** n.

huddle (hŭd´əl) v.t. 1 to throw or crowd (together, up etc.) closely. 2 to coil (oneself up) into a small space. ~v.i. to gather or crowd (up or together) closely. ~n. 1 (coll.) a secretive discussion between a group of people. 2 a confused crowd. 3 disorder, confusion. **to go into a huddle** to have a secretive discussion.

hue (hū) n. 1 colour, tint. 2 a compound colour, esp. one in which a primary predominates. **-hued** a. **hueless** a.

hue and cry (hū ənd krī´) n. 1 a clamour or outcry (against). 2 a great stir or alarm.

huff (hŭf) v.t. 1 to blow or puff (up). 2 to bully, to hector. 3 in draughts, to remove (one's opponent's piece) from the board when they omit to capture with it. 4 (usu. p.p.) to offend. ~v.i. to take offence. ~n. 1 a sudden fit of anger or petulance. 2 in draughts, the act of huffing. **in a huff** annoyed, offended, in a mood. **huffish** a. **huffy** a. (comp. **huffier**, superl. **huffiest**). **huffily** adv. **huffiness** n.

hug (hŭg) v.t. (pres.p. **hugging**, past, p.p. **hugged**) 1 to embrace closely. 2 to clasp or squeeze tightly. 3 to hold fast or cling to, to cherish. 4 to keep close to (The cyclist hugged the kerb). ~v.i. to embrace each other. ~n. 1 a close embrace. 2 a grip in wrestling involving squeezing one's opponent. **to hug oneself** to congratulate oneself complacently. **huggable** a.

huge (hūj) a. very large, enormous, immense. **hugely** adv. 1 in a huge manner. 2 (coll.) exceedingly, extremely. **hugeness** n.

hugger-mugger (hŭg´əmŭgə) n. 1 secrecy, privacy. 2 disorder, confusion. ~a. 1 clandestine. 2 confused, slovenly. ~adv. 1 secretly, clandestinely. 2 in a confused way. ~v.i. 1 to act clandestinely. 2 to muddle.

huh (hŭ, hə) int. used to express surprise, contempt, disbelief etc.

hula (hoo´lə), **hula-hula** n. a Hawaiian dance performed by women. **hula hoop** n. a light hoop kept in motion by swinging round the waist. **hula skirt** n. a grass skirt worn by hula dancers.

hulk (hŭlk) n. 1 the hull or body of a ship, esp. an unseaworthy one. 2 an old ship used as a store, (formerly) as a prison, or for other purposes. 3 a bulky and unwieldy ship. 4 (coll.) any unwieldy object or person. **hulking** a. (coll.) bulky, unwieldy, awkward.

hull¹ (hŭl) n. the body of a ship. ~v.t. to pierce the hull of with a cannonball, gunshot etc.

hull² (hŭl) n. 1 the outer covering of a nut or seed, the pod, shell or husk. 2 any outer covering. ~v.t. to strip the hull or husk off.

hullabaloo (hŭləbəloo´) n. (pl. **hullabaloos**) an uproar.

hullo HELLO.

hum¹ (hŭm) v.i. (pres.p. **humming**, past, p.p. **hummed**) 1 to make a prolonged murmuring sound like a bee. 2 to sing with the lips closed. 3 to make an inarticulate sound in speaking, from embarrassment or hesitation. 4 (sl.) to smell unpleasant. ~v.t. to utter in a low murmuring voice. ~n. 1 a low droning or murmuring sound. 2 the act of humming. 3 an inarticulate expression of hesitation, disapproval etc. **to hum and haw/ ha** 1 to hesitate in speaking. 2 to refrain from giving a decisive answer. **hummable** a. **hummer** n. **hummingbird** n. any small, mostly tropical bird of the family Trochilidae, of brilliant plumage and very rapid flight. **humming-top** n. a child's toy, being a hollow top with a hole in the side, which emits a humming noise in spinning.

hum² (hŭm) int. used to express hesitation, disapproval etc.

human (hū´mən) a. 1 of or relating to people or humankind; of or relating to the genus Homo. 2 having the nature, qualities or characteristics of people or humankind. 3 of or relating to humankind as distinct from God or gods, animals or machines. ~n. a human being. **human being** n. a member of the species Homo sapiens, a person. **human chain** n. a line of people formed up to pass things along from hand to hand, esp. in an emergency. **human ecology** n. the study of the relations between people and their environment. **human engineering** n. 1 the management of labour in industry, esp. regarding the relationships between humans and machines. 2 the study of this. **human geography** n. the branch of geography studying the interaction between human beings and the earth's surface. **human interest** n. (in a newspaper article etc.) reference to issues of personal experience, emotions that most people can identify with. **humanize**, **humanise** v.t. 1 to make human. 2 to give human character or expression to. 3 to make humane. **humanization** (-zā´shən) n. **humankind** n. the members of the species Homo sapiens collectively. **humanly** adv. 1 in the manner of human beings. 2 according to the knowledge or capacity of human beings. 3 from the human point of view. **human nature** *n.* all those characteristics considered typical of human beings, esp. the weaknesses. **humanness** *n.* **humanoid** *a.* like a human in form or attributes. ~*n.* a humanoid animal or object. **human race** *n.* the species *Homo sapiens*. **human rights** *n.pl.* the rights of an individual to freedom of speech, freedom of movement, justice etc. **human shield** *n.* a person or group of people placed so as to protect a potential target from attack.

humane (hūmān´) *a.* **1** having the feelings proper to humans. **2** tender, compassionate, kind, gentle. **3** elevating, refining. **4** polite, elegant. **5** relieving distress, aiding those in danger etc. **humane killer** *n.* an instrument for slaughtering animals painlessly. **humanely** *adv.* **humaneness** *n.*

humanism (hū´mənizm) *n.* **1** a moral or intellectual system that regards the interests of humankind as of supreme importance, as distinct from individualism or theism. **2** humanitarianism. **3** devotion to humanity or human interests. **4** (**Humanism**) culture derived from literature, esp. the Greek and Latin classics. **humanist** *n.* **1** an adherent of humanism. **2** a person versed in the humanities, esp. one of the classical scholars of Renaissance times. **humanistic** (-is´-) *a.* **humanistically** *adv.*

humanitarian (hūmaniteə´riən) *a.* **1** humane. **2** of or relating to the humanitarians. ~*n.* **1** a person who attempts to improve human welfare. **2** a philanthropist. **humanitarianism** *n.*

Usage note The adjective *humanitarian* is sometimes used as though it meant simply *human*, but this is best avoided.

humanity (hūman´iti) *n.* (*pl.* **humanities**) **1** human nature. **2** (*collect.*) humankind, people. **3** kindness, benevolence, humaneness. **the humanities** the study of literature, music, history etc. as distinct from social or natural sciences.

humble (hŭm´bəl) *a.* (*comp.* **humbler**, *superl.* **humblest**) **1** having or showing a sense of lowliness or inferiority, modest. **2** of lowly condition, kind, dimensions etc. **3** submissive, deferential. ~*v.t.* **1** to bring low, to abase. **2** to bring to a state of subjection or inferiority. **3** to lower the rank or status of (a person). **humbleness** *n.* **humble pie** *n.* a pie made of the umbles or entrails of the deer. **to eat humble pie 1** to apologize humbly (said to have arisen from the fact that at hunting-feasts humble pie was given to the menials). **2** to submit oneself to humiliation or insult. **humbly** *adv.*

humble-bee (hŭm´bəlbē) *n.* a bumble-bee.

humbug (hŭm´bŭg) *n.* **1** a boiled sweet highly flavoured with peppermint. **2** nonsense, rubbish. **3** a spirit of deception or trickery, sham. **4** an impostor. ~*v.t.* (*pres.p.* **humbugging**, *past, p.p.* **humbugged**) **1** to hoax, to take in. **2** to cajole (into, out of etc.). ~*v.i.* to behave in a fraudulent or misleading manner. **humbuggery** *n.*

humdinger (hŭmding´ə) *n.* (*coll.*) an excellent person or thing.

humdrum (hŭm´drŭm) *a.* dull, commonplace, tedious. ~*n.* **1** dull, tedious talk. **2** dullness.

humerus (hū´mərəs) *n.* (*pl.* **humeri** (-rī)) **1** the long bone of the upper arm, articulating above with the scapula and below with the radius and the ulna. **2** the corresponding bone in the foreleg of quadrupeds. **humeral** *a.* of or relating to the shoulder.

humid (hū´mid) *a.* moist, damp. **humidify** (-mid´-) *v.t.* (*3rd pers. sing. pres.* **humidifies**, *pres.p.* **humidifying**, *past, p.p.* **humidified**) to make humid. **humidification** (-fikā´shən) *n.* **humidifier** *n.* a device for making or keeping the air in a room moist. **humidity** (-mid´-) *n.* (*pl.* **humidities**) **1** the state of being humid. **2** a measure of the amount of moisture in the atmosphere. **humidly** *adv.* **humidor** (-daw) *n.* a container constructed to keep its contents in a moist state.

humiliate (hūmil´iāt) *v.t.* **1** to lower in self-esteem, to mortify. **2** to humble, to lower in condition, to abase. **humiliating** *a.* **humiliatingly** *adv.* **humiliation** (-ā´shən) *n.* **humiliator** *n.*

humility (hūmil´iti) *n.* **1** the state of being humble. **2** modesty, a sense of unworthiness. **3** self-abasement.

hummock (hŭm´ək) *n.* **1** a mound or hillock, a protuberance formed by pressure in an ice field. **2** (*NAm.*) an elevation in a swamp or bog, esp. if wooded. **hummocky** *a.*

hummus (hŭm´əs, hum´əs), **hoummos** *n.* a kind of Middle Eastern hors d'œuvre consisting of puréed chickpeas, sesame oil, garlic and lemon.

humongous (hūmŭng´gəs), **humungous** *a.* (*sl.*) huge, enormous.

humor HUMOUR.

humoresque (hūməresk´) *n.* (*Mus.*) a composition of a humorous or capricious character.

humorist (hū´mərist) *n.* **1** a person who displays humour in their conversation, writings etc. **2** a facetious person, a wag. **humoristic** (-ris´-) *a.*

humorous (hū´mərəs) *a.* **1** full of humour. **2** tending to excite laughter. **3** jocular. **humorously** *adv.* **humorousness** *n.*

humour (hū´mə), (*NAm.*) **humor** *n.* **1** the quality of being amusing, comical, witty etc. **2** playful yet sympathetic imagination or mode of regarding things, delighting in the absurdity of incongruities. **3** mental disposition, frame of mind, mood. **4** bias, caprice, whim. **5** (*Hist.*) each of the four bodily fluids (blood, phlegm, yellow bile, black bile) supposed to produce diversity of temperament. ~*v.t.* **1** to indulge, to give way to, to make concessions to. **2** to fall in with the humour of. **out of humour** in a bad mood, displeased. **-humoured** *a.* **humourless** *a.* **humourlessly** *adv.* **humourlessness** *n.* **humoursome** *a.* led by caprice or fancy, whimsical.

❌ **humourous** common misspelling of HUMOROUS.

hump (hŭmp) *n.* **1** a swelling or protuberance, esp. on the back. **2** a rounded hillock. **3** (*coll.*) a fit of annoyance, ill-temper or the blues. *~v.t.* **1** to make (the back) hump-shaped. **2** (*coll.*) to carry on the back. **3** (*taboo sl.*) to have sexual intercourse with. *~v.i.* (*taboo sl.*) to have sexual intercourse. **over the hump** past the difficult or critical stage of something. **humpback** *n.* **1** a crooked back. **2** a person having a humpback. **3** (*also* **humpbacked whale**) an American whale, *Megaptera nodosa*. **humpback bridge** *n.* a small, narrow bridge with steep inclines on either side leading to its centre. **humpbacked** *a.* **humped** *a.* **humpless** *a.* **humpy** *a.* (*comp.* **humpier,** *superl.* **humpiest**) **1** having many humps. **2** (*coll.*) irritable, sulky.

humph (hŭmf) *int.* used to express doubt, disapproval etc.

humus (hū´məs) *n.* soil or mould, esp. that largely composed of decayed vegetation. **humic** *a.*

Hun (hŭn) *n.* **1** a member of an ancient Tartar people from Asia that overran Europe in the 4th and 5th cents. and gave their name to Hungary. **2** (*coll., offensive*) a German. **3** a barbarian, a destroyer, a savage. **Hunnish** *a.*

hunch (hŭnch) *n.* **1** an intuitive feeling or premonition. **2** a hump. **3** a lump, a thick piece. *~v.t.* **1** to crook, to arch (esp. the back). **2** to bend or thrust out into a hump. **hunchback** *n.* a person with a humped back. **hunchbacked** *a.*

hundred (hŭn´drid) *n.* (*pl.* **hundred, hundreds**) **1** the cardinal number representing 10 times 10, the product of 10 multiplied by 10. **2** (*coll.*) a hundred pounds (money). **3** (*Hist.*) an administrative division of a county in England, supposed to have originally contained 100 families or freemen. *~a.* **1** amounting to a hundred. **2** used to express whole hours in the 24-hour clock (*three hundred hours (03:00)*). **(one) hundred per cent** entire(ly), total(ly), complete(ly). **hundredfold** *n.* **hundreds and thousands** *n.pl.* tiny strips or balls of sugar coated with different colours, used esp. for cake decoration. **hundredth** *a.* the ordinal of a hundred. *~n.* **1** one of a hundred equal parts. **2** the one after the ninety-ninth in a series. **hundredweight** *n.* (*pl.* **hundredweight, hundredweights**) a weight of 112 lbs. (50.8 kg), a long hundredweight.

hung (hŭng) *a.* **1** (of an election) not resulting in a clear majority for any party. **2** (of a Parliament) produced by such an election. **3** (of a jury) unable to reach a verdict. **hung-over** *a.* suffering from a hangover. **hung up** *a.* (*sl.*) nervous, tense, obsessed. **hung up on** neurotic about, obsessed by.

Hungarian (hŭng-gea´riən) *a.* of or relating to Hungary. *~n.* **1** a native or inhabitant of Hungary. **2** the Hungarian language.

hunger (hŭng´gə) *n.* **1** a craving for food. **2** a painful sensation or weakened condition caused by lack of food. **3** any strong desire. *~v.i.* **1** to feel the pain or sensation of hunger, to crave for food. **2** to desire or long eagerly (for). **hunger strike** *n.* a refusal to take food, usu. as a protest. **hunger striker** *n.*

hungry (hŭng´gri) *a.* (*comp.* **hungrier,** *superl.* **hungriest**) **1** feeling a sensation of hunger. **2** having a keen appetite. **3** showing hunger, emaciated, thin. **4** longing or craving eagerly. **5** (of soil) barren, poor. **hungrily** *adv.* **hungriness** *n.*

hunk (hŭngk) *n.* (*coll.*) **1** a large piece. **2** a big, strong, sexually attractive man. **hunky** *a.* (*comp.* **hunkier,** *superl.* **hunkiest**).

hunker (hŭng´kə) *v.i.* (*Sc., NAm.*) to squat on the calves or heels. *~n.pl.* the haunches.

hunky-dory (hŭngkidaw´ri) *a.* (*esp. NAm., coll.*) satisfactory, fine.

hunt (hŭnt) *v.t.* **1** to search for, to seek after. **2** to pursue or chase in or over (a district etc.). **3** to chase (as wild animals) for the purpose of catching and killing. **4** to employ (horses, dogs etc.) in hunting. *~v.i.* **1** to search (after or for). **2** to pursue game or wild animals. **3** to follow the chase. **4** (of a machine etc.) to vary in speed of operation as if to stop. *~n.* **1** hunting, the chase. **2** a pack of hounds. **3** a group of people who regularly go hunting together. **4** a district hunted by a pack of hounds. **to hunt down 1** to track, pursue and capture. **2** to destroy by persecution or violence. **to hunt out** to track out, to find by searching. **hunter** *n.* **1** a person or animal that hunts. **2** a horse trained for hunting. **3** a person who searches or seeks for anything (*usu. in comb.* as *fortune-hunter*). **4** a hunting watch. **huntergatherer** *n.* a member of a society who live by hunting animals and gathering plants etc. **hunter's moon** *n.* the next full moon after the harvest moon. **hunting** *n.* the practice of pursuing wild animals to kill them. **hunting crop** *n.* a riding crop with a loop at the end for attaching a thong. **hunting ground** *n.* **1** a likely place for finding anything. **2** ground or region where hunting takes place. **hunting horn** *n.* a bugle or horn used in hunting. **hunting pink** *n.* the scarlet coat worn by people at a hunt. **hunting watch** *n.* a watch with a metal cover over the face. **huntress** *n.* a woman who goes hunting. **hunt saboteur** *n.* a person who is opposed to hunting and who actively tries to disrupt it. **huntsman** *n.* (*pl.* **huntsmen**) **1** a person who hunts. **2** a person employed to manage hunting hounds.

Huntington's chorea (hŭn´tingtənz) *n.* (*Med.*) a rare hereditary type of chorea accompanied by progressive dementia.

hurdle (hœ´dəl) *n.* **1** a movable framework of withes or split timber serving for gates, enclosures etc. **2** a barrier for jumping over in racing. **3** a barrier or obstacle. *~v.t.* **1** to leap over. **2** to surmount. **3** to enclose, hedge or barricade with hurdles. **hurdler** *n.* **1** a person who runs in hurdle-races. **2** a hurdle-maker. **hurdle-race** *n.* a race over hurdles or fences, esp. in horse racing.

hurdy-gurdy (hœdigœ´di) n. (pl. **hurdy-gurdies**) a barrel organ, or other similar instrument which is played with a handle.

hurl (hœl) v.t. **1** to throw with violence. **2** to drive or fling with great force. **3** to utter or emit with vehemence. ~v.i. to play the game of hurley. ~n. the act of throwing with great force. **hurling** n. the game of hurley.

hurley (hœ´li) n. (pl. **hurleys**) **1** an Irish game resembling hockey in which two teams of 15 players each equipped with sticks try to score goals. **2** a stick used in this.

hurly-burly (hœlibœ´li) n. commotion, uproar, boisterous activity.

hurrah (hərah´), **hurray** (-rā´) int. used to express joy, welcome, applause etc. ~v.i. to shout hurrahs. ~n. a shout of hurrahs.

hurricane (hŭr´ikən) n. **1** a storm with a violent wind of force 12, i.e. having a mean velocity of over 75 mph (120 kph). **2** an extremely violent gale, orig. a W Indian cyclone. **3** anything that sweeps along violently. **hurricane-bird** n. a frigate bird. **hurricane deck** n. **1** the upper deck above the cabins of a river steamer. **2** a raised deck on an ocean-going vessel. **hurricane lamp** n. a lamp designed to keep alight in a strong wind.

hurry (hŭr´i) v.i. (3rd pers. sing. pres. **hurries**, pres.p. **hurrying**, past, p.p. **hurried**) **1** to hasten. **2** to move or act with excessive haste. ~v.t. **1** to impel to greater speed, to accelerate. **2** to push forward. **3** to drive or cause to act or do carelessly or precipitately. ~n. **1** the act of hurrying. **2** urgency, bustle, precipitation. **3** eagerness (to do etc.). **4** (coll.) need for haste. **in a hurry** hurrying, in a rush. **not in a hurry** not soon, not easily. **to hurry along** to hurry up. **to hurry up 1** to make haste. **2** to cause or cajole (someone) to make haste. **hurried** a. **hurriedly** adv. **hurriedness** n. **hurryingly** adv. **hurry-scurry** a., adv. **1** in a hurry or bustle. **2** confusedly. ~n. a confused bustle.

hurt (hœt) v.t. (past, p.p. **hurt**) **1** to cause pain, injury, loss or detriment to. **2** to damage. **3** to grieve or distress (e.g. the feelings). ~v.i. (usu. impers.) to be painful, to cause pain. ~n. **1** anything that causes pain, injury or detriment. **2** an injury, damage, harm. **3** a wound. **hurtful** a. **1** causing hurt, esp. to the feelings. **2** mischievous, noxious. **hurtfully** adv. **hurtfulness** n.

hurtle (hœ´təl) v.i. **1** to rush with great force and noise. **2** to make a crashing noise. ~v.t. **1** to strike or dash against with violence. **2** to move or whirl with great force.

husband (hŭz´bənd) n. a married man in relation to his wife. ~v.t. to manage (resources) carefully, to economize. **husbander** n. **husbandless** a.

husbandry (hŭz´bəndri) n. **1** the business of a farmer, agriculture. **2** economy, esp. domestic. **3** frugality, careful management. †**husbandman** n. (pl. **husbandmen**) a farmer, a tiller of the soil.

hush (hŭsh) v.t. to make silent, to repress the noise of. ~v.i. to be still or silent. ~n. silence, stillness. ~int. silence! be still! **to hush up** to keep concealed, to suppress. **hushaby** (-əbī) **hushabye** int. used in lulling a child to sleep. **hushed** a. **hush-hush** a. (coll.) very secret. **hush money** n. a bribe paid to secure silence (about a scandal etc.). **hush puppy** n. (pl. **hush puppies**) (N Am.) a ball of maize bread or dough, quickly fried.

husk (hŭsk) n. **1** the dry external covering of certain fruits or seeds. **2** a mere frame, shell or worthless part. ~v.t. to strip the husk from. **husked** a. **husky**[1] a. (comp. **huskier**, superl. **huskiest**) **1** dry, hoarse, rough and harsh in sound (a husky voice). **2** abounding in husks. **3** consisting of or resembling husks. **4** rough. **5** (esp. N Am., coll.) strong, stalwart. **huskily** adv. **huskiness** n.

husky[1] (hŭs´ki) n. (pl. **huskies**) a powerful breed of Arctic sledge dog with a thick coat and a curled tail.

husky[2] HUSK.

huss (hŭs) n. the flesh of various kinds of dogfish.

hussar (huzah´) n. **1** a soldier of a light cavalry regiment in European armies. **2** (Hist.) a light horseman of the Hungarian cavalry in the 19th cent.

hussy (hŭs´i) n. (pl. **hussies**) **1** (derog.) a pert, forward girl. **2** (derog.) an immoral woman.

hustings (hŭs´tingz) n. proceedings at a parliamentary election.

hustle (hŭs´əl) v.t. **1** to hurry or cause to move quickly. **2** to jostle, to push violently, to shake together in confusion. **3** (sl.) to acquire (something) by aggressive or dishonest means. ~v.i. **1** to push one's way in an unceremonious or unscrupulous way. **2** (sl.) to make a living by aggressive or dishonest means. **3** (esp. N Am., sl.) to engage in prostitution. ~n. **1** hustling. **2** (coll.) a fraud or swindle. **hustler** n.

hut (hŭt) n. **1** a small, simple house. **2** a cabin, a shelter. **3** (Mil.) a small temporary house for troops in a camp. ~v.t. (pres.p. **hutting**, past, p.p. **hutted**) (Mil.) to place (troops) in huts. ~v.i. to lodge in huts. **hutlike** a. **hutment** n. (Mil.) a camp of huts.

hutch (hŭch) n. **1** a coop or boxlike pen for small animals. **2** (derog.) a small house. ~v.t. to store, as in a hutch.

Hutu (hoo´too) n. (pl. **Hutus, Bahutu** (bəhoo´too)) **1** a member of a people of Rwanda and Burundi. **2** their language, one of the Bantu group of languages. ~a. of or relating to this people or their language.

HWM abbr. high water mark.

hyacinth (hī´əsinth) n. **1** any plant of the genus Hyacinthus, esp. H. orientalis, a bulbous-rooted flowering plant of the order Lilaceae. **2** the grape hyacinth. **3** a brownish, orange or reddish variety of zircon. **4** a colour ranging from purplish-blue to violet. **hyacinthine** (-sin´thin, -thīn) a.

hyaena HYENA.

hyaline (hī´əlīn, -lin) a. 1 glassy, transparent, crystalline. 2 vitreous. **hyalite** (-līt) n. a glassy variety of opal.

hybrid (hī´brid) a. 1 (Biol.) produced by the union of two distinct species, varieties etc. 2 heterogeneous. 3 derived from incongruous sources. ~n. 1 an animal or plant produced by the union of two distinct species, varieties etc. 2 anything composed of heterogeneous parts or elements. 3 (offensive) a person of mixed racial origin. **hybridism** n. **hybridity** (-brid´-) n. **hybridize, hybridise** v.t. 1 to produce by the union of different species or varieties. 2 to produce by cross-fertilization or interbreeding. ~v.i. to produce hybrids, to be capable of cross-fertilization or interbreeding. **hybridizable** a. **hybridization** (-ā´shən) n. **hybridizer** n. **hybrid vigour** n. (Biol.) the increased size, strength etc. of a hybrid in comparison with its parents, heterosis.

hydra (hī´drə) n. (pl. **hydras, hydrae** (-drē)) 1 any freshwater polyp of the genus Hydra, with a slender body and tentacles round the mouth, which multiplies when divided. 2 any water snake. 3 an evil or calamity difficult to extinguish. **hydroid** (-droid) n. (Zool.) any colonial hydrozoan coelenterate of the order Hydroida in which the polyp phase is dominant, as the hydras, sea anemones and corals. ~a. of or relating to the Hydroida.

hydrangea (hīdrān´jə) n. any flowering shrub of the genus Hydrangea, from Asia and America.

hydrant (hī´drənt) n. a spout or discharge pipe, usu. with a nozzle for attaching a hose, connected with a water main for drawing water, esp. in emergencies.

hydrate (hī´drāt) n. (Chem.) a compound of water with an element or another compound. ~v.t. to combine with water to form a hydrate. **hydratable** a. **hydrated** a. **hydration** (-drā´shən) n. **hydrator** n.

hydraulic (hīdrol´ik) a. 1 of or relating to fluids in motion, or to the power exerted by water conveyed through pipes or channels. 2 operating or operated by such power. **hydraulically** adv. **hydraulicity** (-lis´iti) n. **hydraulic press** n. a heavy pressing machine worked by water-power. **hydraulic ram** n. a machine by which the fall of a column of water supplies power to elevate a portion of the water to a greater height than that at the source. **hydraulics** n. the science of water or other liquids both at rest and in motion, esp. the conveyance of water through pipes etc., and the practical application of water-power.

hydrazine (hī´drəzēn, -zin) n. (Chem.) a colourless corrosive liquid that is a strong reducing agent, used esp. in rocket fuel.

hydric (hī´drik) a. of or containing hydrogen in chemical combination. **hydride** (-drīd) n. (Chem.) a compound of hydrogen with another element or radical. **hydriodic** (-driod´-) a. (Chem.) of or containing hydrogen and iodine in chemical

combination. **hydriodic acid** n. a colourless or pale yellow solution of the gas hydrogen iodide in water.

hydro (hī´drō) n. (pl. **hydros**) (coll.) an establishment such as a hotel or clinic orig. offering hydropathic treatment.

hydro- (hī´drō), **hydr-** comb. form 1 of, relating to or connected with water (hydroponic). 2 (Chem.) containing hydrogen in chemical combination (hydrochloric). 3 (of a mineral) containing water as a constituent. 4 (Med.) affected with an accumulation of watery fluid, oedematous (hydrocephalic). 5 belonging to the genus Hydra or the class Hydrozoa.

hydrobromic (hīdrōbrō´mik) a. (Chem.) composed of hydrogen and bromine. **hydrobromic acid** n. a colourless or pale yellow solution of the gas hydrogen bromide in water.

hydrocarbon (hīdrōkah´bən) n. (Chem.) a compound of carbon and hydrogen.

hydrocele (hī´drəsēl) n. (Med.) an accumulation of fluid, often swollen and painful, in a saclike cavity, esp. in the scrotum.

hydrocephalus (hīdrəsef´ələs, -kef´-), **hydrocephaly** (-li) n. (Med.) an accumulation of water on the brain, resulting in an enlargement of the head and possible brain damage. **hydrocephalic** (-fal´-), **hydrocephaloid** (-loid), **hydrocephalous** a.

hydrochloric acid (hīdrəklaw´rik) n. (Chem.) a solution of hydrogen chloride in water, a strong corrosive acid.

hydrochloride (hīdrəklaw´rīd) n. (Chem.) a compound of hydrochloric acid, esp. with an organic base.

hydrocortisone (hīdrəkaw´tizōn) n. (Med.) the steroid hormone naturally secreted by the adrenal cortex, synthesized to treat inflammatory conditions.

hydrocyanic acid (hīdrōsīan´ik) n. (Chem.) a poisonous volatile liquid formed by the combination of hydrogen and cyanogen in aqueous solution, having a faint odour of bitter almonds; also called prussic acid, hydrogen cyanide.

hydrodynamics (hīdrōdīnam´iks) n. the science which deals with water and other liquids in motion, hydromechanics. **hydrodynamic, hydrodynamical** a. **hydrodynamicist** (-sist) n.

hydroelectric (hīdroilek´trik) a. of or relating to electricity generated from water-power. **hydroelectrically** adv. **hydroelectricity** (-tris´-) n.

hydrofluoric acid (hīdrōfluə´rik) n. (Chem.) a colourless solution of hydrogen fluoride in water.

hydrofoil (hī´drəfoil) n. 1 a fast vessel with one or more pairs of vanes attached to its hull which lift it out of the water at speed. 2 such a vane.

hydrogel (hī´drəjel) n. protoplasm comprising gelatine or albumen in a jelly-like state with water filling the interstices.

hydrogen (hī´drəjən) n. (Chem.) an invisible, flammable, gaseous element, the lightest of all known elements, which in combination with oxygen produces water. **hydrogenase** (-droj´-) n. any enzyme serving as a catalyst for the reduction of a substrate by hydrogen, as in certain micro-organisms. **hydrogenate** (hīdroj´-, hī´drə-) v.t. **1** to cause to combine with hydrogen. **2** to charge with hydrogen. **hydrogenation** (-ā´shən) n. **hydrogen bomb** n. an exceedingly powerful nuclear bomb in which an immense release of energy is obtained by the conversion by fusion of hydrogen nuclei into -helium nuclei. **hydrogen bond** n. (Chem.) a weak chemical bond between an electronegative atom, e.g. fluorine or oxygen, and a hydrogen atom bonded to another electronegative atom. **hydrogenous** (-droj´-) a. **hydrogen peroxide** n. a bleaching compound, used mainly for lightening the hair and as an antiseptic. **hydrogen sulphide** n. a colourless poisonous gas smelling of rotten eggs, formed by decaying animal matter.

hydrogeology (hīdrōjēol´əji) n. the branch of geology concerned with the geological effects of underground and surface water. **hydrogeological** (-jiəloj´-) a. **hydrogeologist** n.

hydrography (hīdrog´rəfi) n. the science and art of studying, surveying and mapping seas, lakes, rivers and other waters, and their physical features, tides, currents etc. **hydrographer** n. **hydrographic** (-graf´-), **hydrographical** a. **hydrographically** adv.

hydroid HYDRA.

hydrolase (hī´drəlāz) n. any enzyme serving as a catalyst in the hydrolysis of a substrate.

hydrology (hīdrol´əji) n. the science of water, its properties, phenomena, laws and distribution. **hydrologic** (-drəloj´-), **hydrological** a. **hydrologically** adv. **hydrologist** n.

hydrolysis (hīdrol´isis) n. (Chem.) the formation of an acid and a base from a salt by the action of water. **hydrolyse** (hī´drə-), **hydrolyze** v.t. to subject to hydrolysis. **hydrolytic** (-lit´-) a. **hydrolytically** adv.

hydromagnetic (hīdrōmagnet´ik) a. relating to the behaviour of fluids within magnetic fields.

hydromania (hīdrōmā´niə) n. morbid craving for water.

hydromechanics (hīdrōmikan´iks) n. the mechanics of liquids, hydrodynamics.

hydrometer (hīdrom´itə) n. an instrument for determining the specific gravity of liquids or solids by means of flotation. **hydrometric** (-drəmet´-), **hydrometrical** a. **hydrometry** n. the art or process of measuring the specific gravity of fluids etc.

hydropathy (hīdrop´əthi) n. (Med.) the treatment of disease by the internal and external application of water. **hydropathic** (-drəpath´-) a., n. **hydropathically** adv. **hydropathist** n.

hydrophilic (hīdrōfil´ik), **hydrophil** (hī´drōfil), **hydrophile** (-fīl) a. **1** having a great affinity for water. **2** (Chem.) readily mixed or wetted with water.

hydrophobia (hīdrəfō´biə) n. **1** an unnatural dread of water, esp. as a symptom of rabies resulting from the bite of a rabid animal. **2** rabies. **hydrophobic** a. **1** of or concerning hydrophobia. **2** (Chem.) tending not to mix, dissolve in or be wetted by water.

hydrophone (hī´drəfōn) n. an instrument for detecting sound by water, used to locate submarines etc.

hydrophyte (hī´drəfīt) n. (Bot.) an aquatic plant or one which grows in very moist conditions.

hydroplane (hī´drəplān) n. **1** a light motor boat capable of rising partially above the surface of water. **2** a flat fin for governing the vertical direction of a submarine. ~v.i. (of a boat) to move across the water like a hydroplane.

hydroponics (hīdrōpon´iks) n. the cultivation of plants without soil in water containing chemicals. **hydroponic** a. **hydroponically** adv.

hydroquinone (hīdrōkwin´ōn) n. a compound derived from benzoquinone, employed in the development of photographs.

hydrosphere (hī´drəsfiə) n. the watery part of the surface of the earth, the sea and oceans.

hydrostatics (hīdrəstat´iks) n. the science concerned with the pressure and equilibrium of liquids at rest. **hydrostatic, hydrostatical** a. **1** relating to hydrostatics. **2** of or relating to the pressure and equilibrium of liquids at rest. **hydrostatically** adv. **hydrostatic press** n. a hydraulic press.

hydrotherapy (hīdrōther´əpi) n. (Med.) the therapeutic application of water, usu. the use of swimming pools etc. for the treatment of muscular conditions, arthritis etc. **hydrotherapist** n.

hydrothermal (hīdrōthœ´məl) a. relating to the action of heated water, esp. on the materials of the earth's crust. **hydrothermally** adv.

hydrothorax (hīdrōthaw´raks) n. (Med.) an abnormal accumulation of fluid in the chest.

hydrotropism (hīdrot´rəpizm) n. (Bot.) the tendency in the growing parts of plants to turn towards or away from moisture.

hydrous (hī´drəs) a. (Chem., Mineral.) containing water.

hydroxide (hīdrok´sīd) n. (Chem.) a compound formed by the union of a basic oxide with the molecules of water.

hydroxy- (hīdrok´si) comb. form (Chem.) containing the radical hydroxyl.

hydroxyl (hīdrok´sil) n. (Chem.) the monad radical formed by the combination of one atom of hydrogen and one of water occurring in many chemical compounds.

hydrozoan (hīdrəzō´ən) n. any aquatic coelenterate of the class Hydrozoa, including the hydra, medusa, jellyfish etc. ~a. of or relating to this class.

hyena (hīē´nə), **hyaena** n. any carnivorous quadruped of the family Hyaenidae, allied to the dog, with three modern species, the striped *Hyena striata*, the spotted *H. crocuta*, and the brown hyena, *H. brunnea* (the first is also called the laughing hyena).

hygiene (hī'jēn) *n.* **1** the science of the prevention of disease. **2** the art of preserving health, esp. of the community at large. **3** practices that promote health. **hygienic** (-jē'-) *a.* **hygienically** *adv.* **hygienics** *n.* the study and principles of hygiene. **hygienist** (-jē'-) *n.* a specialist in the promotion and practice of hygiene.

hygro- (hī'grō), **hygr-** *comb. form* of, relating to or denoting the presence of moisture.

hygrology (hīgrol'əji) *n.* the branch of physics relating to humidity, esp. of the atmosphere.

hygrometer (hīgrom'itə) *n.* an instrument for measuring the moisture of the air etc. **hygrometric** (-met'-), **hygrometrical** *a.* **hygrometry** *n.*

hygrophilous (hīgrof'iləs) *a.* (*Bot.*) (of a plant) living or growing in moist places.

hygrophyte (hī'grəfīt) *n.* a hydrophyte.

hygroscope (hī'grəskōp) *n.* an instrument for indicating the degree of moisture in the atmosphere. **hygroscopic** (-skop'-), **hygroscopical** *a.* **1** (of bodies) imbibing moisture from the atmosphere. **2** of, relating to or indicated by the hygroscope. **hygroscopically** *adv.*

hying HIE.

hylic (hī'lik) *a.* of or relating to matter, material.

hylo- (hī'lō) *comb. form* of matter, as opposed to spirit.

hymen (hī'mən) *n.* (*Anat.*) a membrane stretched across the vaginal entrance. **hymenal** *a.*

hymeneal (hīmənē'əl) *a.* (*poet.*) of or relating to marriage. *~n.* a wedding hymn or poem.

hymenium (hīmē'niəm) *n.* (*pl.* **hymenia** (-niə), **hymeniums**) (*Bot.*) the spore-bearing stratum or surface in fungi.

hymenopteran (hīmənop'tərən) *n.* any insect of the order Hymenoptera, having four membranous wings, such as the bee, wasp, ant etc. **hymenopterous** *a.*

hymn (him) *n.* **1** a song or ode in praise or adoration of God, esp. in Christian worship. **2** a solemn song or ode to a god or a revered person or thing. *~v.t.* to praise or worship in hymns. *~v.i.* to sing hymns. **hymnal** (him'nəl) *n.* a collection of hymns, esp. for public worship. **hymnary** (-nə-) *n.* (*pl.* **hymnaries**) a hymnal. **hymn book** *n.* a book of hymns. **hymnody** (him'nədi) *n.* (*pl.* **hymnodies**) **1** the singing of hymns. **2** the composition of hymns. **3** hymns collectively. **4** a hymnology. **hymnodist** *n.* **hymnographer** (-nog'-) *n.* a writer of hymns. **hymnography** *n.* **hymnology** (-nol'-) *n.* (*pl.* **hymnologies**) **1** the composition or the study of hymns. **2** hymns collectively. **hymnologist** *n.*

hyoid (hī'oid) *a.* **1** U-shaped. **2** (*Anat.*) of or relating to the hyoid bone. *~n.* (*Anat.*) the hyoid bone. **hyoid bone** *n.* the bone supporting the tongue.

hyoscyamine (hīəsī'əmēn, -mīn) *n.* a white crystalline alkaloid obtained from the seeds of henbane, *Hyoscyamus niger*, highly poisonous, used as a sedative. **hyoscine** (hī'əsēn, -sīn) *n.* a

strong narcotic drug, scopolamine, used as an antiemetic and prior to eye examination.

hype[1] (hīp) *n.* (*coll.*) **1** exaggerated or false publicity used to sell or promote. **2** a deception, a swindle. *~v.t.* to sell or promote (something or someone) by using exaggerated or false publicity.

hype[2] (hīp) *n.* (*coll.*) **1** a drug addict. **2** a hypodermic needle. **hyped up** *a.* (*sl.*) full of nervous excitement.

hyper- (hī'pə) *comb. form* **1** above, beyond. **2** excessive, beyond measure.

hyperactive (hīpərak'tiv) *a.* abnormally active. **hyperactivity** (-tiv'-) *n.*

hyperaesthesia (hīpərēsthē'ziə), (*N Am.*) **hyperesthesia** *n.* (*Med.*) excessive sensibility to stimuli, esp. of the nerves and the skin. **hyperaesthetic** (-thet'-) *a.*

hyperbaric (hīpəbar'ik) *a.* (esp. of oxygen) at higher than normal pressure. **hyperbarically** *adv.*

hyperbola (hīpœ'bələ) *n.* (*pl.* **hyperbolas**, **hyperbolae** (-ē)) (*Geom.*) a plane curve formed by cutting a cone when the intersecting plane makes a greater angle with the base than the side of the cone makes. **hyperboloid** *n.* a solid formed by the revolution of a hyperbola about its axis. **hyperboloidal** (-oi'dəl) *a.*

hyperbole (hīpœ'bəli) *n.* a figure of speech expressing much more than the truth, rhetorical exaggeration. **hyperbolic** (hīpəbol'ik) *a.* **1** of, relating to, or of the nature of a hyperbola. **2** hyperbolical. **hyperbolical** *a.* of the nature of hyperbole. **hyperbolically** *adv.* **hyperbolic function** *n.* any of a set of functions of an angle related algebraically to a rectangular hyperbola in the same way as a trigonometric function is related to a circle. **hyperbolism** *n.*

hyperconscious (hīpəkon'shəs) *a.* acutely or excessively aware (of).

hypercritical (hīpəkrit'ikəl) *a.* **1** unreasonably critical. **2** captiously censorious, overnice. **hypercritically** *adv.*

hyperesthesia HYPERAESTHESIA.

hyperfocal distance (hīpəfō'kəl) *n.* the distance beyond which objects appear sharply defined through a lens focused at infinity.

hyperglycaemia (hīpəglīsē'miə), (*N Am.*) **hyperglycemia** *n.* (*Med.*) an excessive level of sugar in the blood. **hyperglycaemic** *a.*

hypergolic (hīpəgol'ik) *a.* (of a rocket fuel) able to ignite spontaneously on contact with an oxidizer.

hypericum (hīper'ikəm) *n.* any herbaceous plant or shrub of the genus *Hypericum* typified by the St John's wort.

hyperinflation (hīpərinflā'shən) *n.* a very high level of inflation in an economy.

hyperkinesis (hīpəkinē'sis), **hyperkinesia** (-ziə) *n.* (*Med.*) **1** excessive movement, as in a muscle spasm. **2** a disorder resulting in hyperactivity and a very short attention span. **hyperkinetic** (-et'ik) *a.*

hypermarket (hī´pəmahkit) n. a very large self-service store selling a wide range of household and other goods, usu. on the outskirts of a town or city.

hypermedia (hīpəmē´diə) n. multimedia.

hypermetrical (hīpəmet´rikəl) a. (of a line of verse) having an extra syllable or extra syllables.

hypermetropia (hīpəmitrō´piə), **hyperopia** (-pərō´-) n. (Med.) an abnormal state of the eye characterized by long-sightedness, as opposed to myopia. **hypermetropic** (-trop´-), **hyperopic** (-pərop´-) a.

hypernym (hī´pənim) n. a word representing a general class or family which is applicable to more specific related words (e.g. tree is a hypernym for ash and beech).

hyperopia, hyperopic HYPERMETROPIA.

hyperphysical (hīpəfiz´ikəl) a. supernatural. **hyperphysically** adv.

hypersensitive (hīpəsen´sitiv) a. excessively sensitive. **hypersensitiveness** n. **hypersensitivity** (-tiv´-) n.

hypersonic (hīpəson´ik) a. (of speeds) higher than Mach 5. **hypersonically** adv.

hyperspace (hī´pəspās) n. space that has more than three dimensions.

hypersthene (hī´pəsthēn) n. (Mineral.) an orthorhombic, foliated, brittle mineral, magnesium iron silicate, allied to hornblende, with a beautiful pearly lustre.

hypertension (hīpəten´shən) n. 1 abnormally high blood pressure. 2 a state of excessive emotional tension. **hypertensive** a. suffering from hypertension.

hypertext (hī´pətekst) n. (Comput.) a system of hardware and software that allows easy movement between related text, sound and graphics.

hyperthermia (hīpəthœ´miə) n.(Med.) abnormally high body temperature. **hyperthermic** a.

hyperthyroidism (hīpəthī´roidizm) n. (Med.) excessive activity of the thyroid gland, causing an accelerated metabolic rate, rapid heartbeat, nervousness etc. **hyperthyroid** a. **hyperthyroidic** (-roi´-) a.

hypertonic (hīpəton´ik) a. 1 (Med.) (of muscles) being excessively tense. 2 (Chem.) (of a solution) more concentrated than a surrounding medium or than another liquid. **hypertonia** (-tō´-) n. excessive muscle tension. **hypertonicity** (-tənis´iti) n.

hypertrophy (hīpœ´trəfi) n. (Med.) excessive development or enlargement of an organ or tissue. **hypertrophic** (hīpətrof´-), **hypertrophous**, **hypertrophical**, **hypertrophied** a.

hyperventilation (hīpəventilā´shən) n. excessive breathing, causing excessive loss of carbon dioxide in the blood. **hyperventilate** (-ven´-) v.i.

hypha (hī´fə) n. (pl. **hyphae** (-fē)) any of the filaments in the mycelium of a fungus. **hyphal** a.

hyphen (hī´fən) n. a short stroke (-) joining two words or parts of words. ~v.t. to join by a hyphen. **hyphenate** v.t. **hyphenation** (-ā´shən) n.

hypno- (hip´nō) comb. form relating to sleep or hypnosis.

hypnogenesis (hipnəjen´əsis) n. inducement of hypnotic sleep. **hypnogenetic** (-net´-) a.

hypnology (hipnol´əji) n. the study of the phenomena of sleep. **hypnologist** n.

hypnopaedia (hipnōpē´diə), (N Am.) **hypnopedia** n. learning by hearing during sleep.

hypnosis (hipnō´sis) n. (pl. **hypnoses** (-sēz)) 1 a state resembling sleep in which the subconscious mind responds to external suggestions and forgotten memories are recovered. 2 the inducement of this state, hypnotism. 3 artificially induced sleep.

hypnotherapy (hipnōther´əpi) n. treatment by hypnotism. **hypnotherapist** n.

hypnotic (hipnot´ik) a. 1 of, relating to or inducing hypnotism. 2 causing sleep. 3 (of a drug) soporific. ~n. a drug that produces sleep. **hypnotically** adv.

hypnotism (hip´nətizm) n. the practice of inducing hypnosis. **hypnotist** n. **hypnotize, hypnotise** v.t. 1 to affect with hypnosis. 2 to capture the attention of completely. **hypnotizable** a. **hypnotizability** (-bil´-) n. **hypnotizer** n.

hypo[1] (hī´pō) n. sodium thiosulphate, the normal fixing solution in photography.

hypo[2] (hī´pō) n. (pl. **hypos**) (coll.) a hypodermic needle.

hypo[3] (hī´pō) n. (pl. **hypos**) (coll.) an attack of hypoglycaemia.

hypo- (hī´pō), **hyp-** comb. form 1 under, below. 2 less than. 3 (Chem.) denoting compounds having a lower degree of oxidation in a series.

hypo-allergenic (hīpōaləjen´ik) a. not likely to cause an allergic reaction.

hypocaust (hī´pəkawst) n. in ancient Roman buildings, a space or series of channels under the floor by which heat was conducted from a furnace to heat a building, room, bath etc.

hypochlorite (hīpəklaw´rīt) n.(Chem.) a salt or ester of hypochlorous acid. **hypochlorous acid** n.(Chem.) an unstable acid formed when chlorine dissolves in water, used as a bleach, disinfectant etc.

hypochondria (hīpəkon´driə) n. 1 a condition characterized by excessive anxiety with regard to one's health. 2 (Med.) chronic depression without apparent cause. **hypochondriac** (-ak) n. a person affected with hypochondria. ~a. 1 produced or characterized by hypochondria. 2 having a disordered mind. **hypochondriacal** (-drī´-) a.

hypocorism (hīpok´ərizm) n. (Gram.) a pet name. **hypocoristic** (-pəkəris´-) a.

hypocrisy (hipok´rəsi) n. (pl. **hypocrisies**) 1 dissimulation, pretence, a feigning to be what one is not. 2 a pretence to virtue or goodness. **hypocrite** (hip´əkrit) n. a person who practises hypocrisy, a dissembler. **hypocritical** (hipəkrit´-) a. **hypocritically** adv.

hypodermic (hīpədœ´mik) a. (Med.) 1 of or

relating to the layers beneath the skin. **2** (of a drug etc.) injected subcutaneously by means of a hypodermic syringe etc. ~*n.* **1** a hypodermic syringe. **2** (a drug introduced into the system by) an injection beneath the skin. **hypodermically** *adv.* **hypodermic injection** *n.* an injection (of narcotics, antitoxins etc.) beneath the skin. **hypodermic needle** *n.* (the hollow needle of) a hypodermic syringe. **hypodermic syringe** *n.* a small syringe with a hollow needle for giving hypodermic injections.

hypoglycaemia (hīpōglīsē´miə), (*N Am.*) **hypoglycemia** *n.* (*Med.*) an abnormally low level of sugar in the blood. **hypoglycaemic** *a.*

hypomania (hīpəmā´niə) *n.* (*Psych.*) the mental state of overexcitability. **hypomanic** (-man´-) *a.*

hyponym (hī´pənim) *n.* a word with a more specific meaning that is included in the scope of another word (e.g. *ash* is a hyponym of *tree*). **hyponymy** (-pon´-) *n.*

hypophysis (hīpof´isis) *n.* (*pl.* **hypophyses** (-sēz)) (*Anat.*) the pituitary gland. **hypophyseal** (-fiz´-iəl), **hypophysial** *a.*

hypostasis (hīpos´təsis) *n.* (*pl.* **hypostases** (-sēz)) **1** that which forms the basis of anything. **2** in metaphysics, that by which a thing subsists, substance as distinct from attributes. **3** the essence or essential principle. **4** the personal subsistence as distinct from substance. **5** (*Theol.*) **a** one of the persons of the Trinity. **b** the person of Christ. **6** (*Med.*) the accumulation and congestion of blood in the lower parts of the body due to the effects of gravity in circumstances of poor circulation. **hypostasize, hypostasise** *v.t.* **1** to embody, to personify. **2** to treat as or make into a substance or concrete reality. **hypostatic** (-pəstat´-), **hypostatical** *a.* in Christian theology, relating to the three persons of the Trinity. **hypostatically** *adv.* **hypostatic union** *n.* the union between divinity and humanity represented in Christ. **hypostatize** *v.t.* (*N Am.*) to hypostasize.

hypostyle (hī´pəstīl) *a.* (*Archit.*) having the roof supported by pillars.

hypotension (hīpōten´shən) *n.* abnormally low blood pressure. **hypotensive** *a.*

hypotenuse (hīpot´ənūz) *n.* the side of a right-angled triangle opposite to the right angle.

hypothalamus (hīpōthal´əməs) *n.* (*pl.* **hypothalami** (-mī)) (*Anat.*) a region at the base of the brain controlling autonomic functions, e.g. hunger and thirst.

hypothermia (hīpōthœ´miə) *n.* (*Med.*) subnormal body temperature, esp. when induced for surgical purposes.

hypothesis (hīpoth´əsis) *n.* (*pl.* **hypotheses** (-sēz)) **1** a proposition assumed for the purpose of an argument. **2** a theory assumed to account for something not understood. **3** a mere supposition or assumption. **hypothesist** *n.* **hypothesize, hypothesise** *v.i.* to form hypotheses. ~*v.t.* to assume. **hypothesizer** *n.* **hypothetic** (-thet´-), **hypothetical** *a.* **1** founded on or of the nature of a hypothesis. **2** conjectural, conditional. **hypothetically** *adv.*

hypothyroidism (hīpəthī´roidizm) *n.* underactivity of the thyroid gland. **hypothyroid** *n.*, *a.* **hypothyroidic** (-roi´-) *a.*

hypoventilation (hīpōventilā´shən) *n.* abnormally slow breathing, causing an excessive amount of carbon dioxide in the blood.

hypoxia (hīpok´siə) *n.* (*Med.*) a deficiency of oxygen reaching the body tissues. **hypoxaemia** (-ē´miə), (*N Am.*) **hypoxemia** *n.* (*Med.*) deficiency of oxygenation of the blood.

hypso- (hip´sō), **hyps-** *comb. form* height.

hyrax (hī´raks) *n.* (*pl.* **hyraxes, hyraces** (-rəsēz)) any small harelike quadruped of the order Hyracoidea, including the Syrian rock rabbit (the dassie) and the S African rock badger.

hyssop (his´əp) *n.* **1** any small labiate aromatic herb of the genus *Hyssopus*, esp. *H. officinalis*, with blue flowers. **2** (*Bible*) an unidentified plant the twigs of which were used for sprinkling in Jewish rites of purification.

hysterectomy (histərek´təmi) *n.* (*pl.* **hysterectomies**) the removal of the womb by surgery. **hysterectomize, hysterectomise** *v.t.*

hysteresis (histərē´sis) *n.* (*Physics*) the tendency of a magnetic substance to remain in a certain magnetic condition, the lag of magnetic effects behind their causes.

hysteria (histiə´riə) *n.* **1** an outbreak of frenzied uncontrollable emotion. **2** (*Psych.*) a nervous disorder, occurring in paroxysms, and often simulating other diseases. **hysteric** (-ter´-) *n.* a person subject to hysteria. ~*a.* hysterical. **hysterical** *a.* **1** (*Psych.*) of, relating to or affected with hysteria. **2** neurotically emotional or excitable. **3** (*coll.*) very funny. **hysterically** *adv.* **hysterics** *n.pl.* **1** a hysterical fit. **2** (*coll.*) a fit of uncontrollable laughter.

Hz. *abbr.* hertz.

I

I¹ (ī), **i** (*pl.* **Is, I's**) the ninth letter of the English and other versions of the Roman alphabet, corresponding to the Greek iota (ι, I). It has two principal sounds: (1) long and diphthongal as in *bind*, *find*, marked in this dictionary ī; (2) short as in *fin*, *bin*, *win*, left unmarked, i. It also has three minor sounds: (1) long, central and unrounded as in *dirk*, marked œ; (2) long and monophthongal as in *intrigue*, marked ē; (3) the consonantal sound of *y*, as in *behaviour*, *onion*, marked y. In conjunction with other vowels *i* also represents a variety of sounds, as in *hair*, *seize*, *boil*, *fruit* etc. **~symbol 1** one in Roman numerals. **2** (*Math.*) the square root of minus one. **3** electric current. **I-beam** *n.* a girder with an I-shaped cross-section.

I² (ī) *pron.* (*obj.* **me**, *poss.* **my, mine**) in speaking or writing denotes oneself. **~n.** the self-conscious subject, the ego.

Usage note The use of *I* as an objective pronoun, quite commonly heard in *between you and I* and in objects ending *and I* after verbs and other prepositions, is best avoided.

I³ *abbr.* Island(s), Isle(s).

I⁴ *chem. symbol* iodine.

-i¹ (ī) *suf.* forming the plural of L nouns in *-us*, as in *fungi*, *hippopotami*.

-i² (ē, i) *suf.* forming the plural of It. nouns in *-o* or *-e*, as in *banditti*, *timpani*.

-i³ (i) *suf.* forming adjectives and nouns from names of Eastern countries or regions, as in *Bangladeshi*, *Yemeni*.

-ia (iə) *suf.* **1** forming abstract nouns, as in *mania*, *militia*. **2** forming names of countries etc., as in *Australia*, *Bulgaria*, *Helvetia*. **3** (*Bot.*) forming names of (members of) botanical genera etc., as in *begonia*, *Saponaria*. **4** (*Med.*) forming names of diseases and medical conditions, as in *hysteria*, *malaria*, *neuralgia*. **5** forming names of alkaloids, as in *morphia*. **6** (*esp. Zool.*) forming plurals of L nouns in *-ium* and Gr. nouns in *-ion*, as in *bacteria*, *regalia*, including zoological groups, as in *Reptilia*.

IAA *abbr.* indoleacetic acid.

-ial (iəl) *suf.* forming adjectives, as in *celestial*, *terrestrial*.

iambus (īam'bəs), **iamb** (ī'amb) *n.* (*pl.* **iambuses**, **iambi** (-bī), **iambs**) a poetic foot of one short and one long, or one unaccented and one accented syllable. **iambic** *a.* **1** of or relating to the iambus. **2** composed of iambics. **~n.** **1** an iambic foot. **2** (*usu. in pl.*) iambic verse.

-ian (iən) *suf.* forming nouns or adjectives, as *Athenian*, *Baconian*, *Cantabrigian*.

-iasis (ī'əsis) *comb. form* indicating a disease, as *elephantiasis*, *psoriasis*.

ib. *abbr.* ibidem.

Iberian (ībiə'riən) *a.* **1** of or relating to ancient Iberia in SW Europe, comprising modern Spain and Portugal. **2** of or relating to Spain and Portugal. **~n.** **1** a native or inhabitant of ancient Iberia in Europe. **2** the language of ancient Iberia in Europe.

Ibero- (ībiə'rō) *comb. form* Iberian.

ibex (ī'beks) *n.* (*pl. in general* **ibex**, *in particular* **ibexes**) a wild goat of any of several species inhabiting the mountain regions of Europe, N Africa and Asia, of which the best known is *Capra ibex*.

ibid. *abbr.* ibidem.

ibidem (ib'idem) *adv.* in the same place (when referring to a book, page etc. already cited).

ibis (ī'bis) *n.* (*pl. in general* **ibis**, *in particular* **ibises**) any of the heron-like wading birds belonging to the family Threskiornithidae, esp. *Threskiornis aethiopica*, the sacred ibis, which was venerated by the ancient Egyptians.

-ible (ibəl) *suf.* forming adjectives, able to be, that may, as in *forcible*, *terrible*. **-ibility** (-bil'-) *suf.* forming nouns. **-ibly** *suf.* forming adverbs from adjectives in *-ible*, as *forcibly*.

ibuprofen (ībūprō'fən) *n.* a drug used esp. for relieving arthritic pain and reducing inflammation.

i/c *abbr.* in charge; in command.

-ic (ik), **†-ick**, **†-ique** (ēk) *suf.* **1** forming adjectives, of or relating to, like, as in *alcoholic*, *algebraic*, *domestic*, *Miltonic*, *plutonic*. **2** (*Chem.*) denoting a higher state of oxidation or valence than the suffix *-ous*. **3** forming names of sciences, arts etc., as in *arithmetic*, *logic*, *music*, some of which have alternative forms ending in -ICS, as *aesthetic*, *metaphysic* etc. **-ical** (ikəl) *suf.* forming adjectives, as *algebraical*, *comical*, *historical*, *political*. **-ically** *suf.* forming adverbs, as *historically*, *politically*.

ice (īs) *n.* **1** frozen water. **2** an ice cream. **3** a confection of sugar etc. used for coating cakes etc. **4** (*sl.*) diamonds. **5** (*sl.*) a very addictive synthetic form of crystallized metamphetamine. **~v.t.** (*pres.p.* **icing**, *past*, *p.p.* **iced**) **1** to cool with ice (*iced lemonade*). **2** to freeze (up, over). **3** to coat (a cake) with icing. **4** (*NAm.*, *sl.*) to kill. **5** (*NAm.*, *sl.*) to achieve (victory) conclusively. **~v.i.** **1** to freeze. **2** to become covered with ice. **on ice 1** in abeyance. **2** performed by ice-skaters. **to cut no ice** (*coll.*) to fail to make an impression, to be unimportant. **ice age** *n.* a glacial period. **ice axe,** (*N Am.*) **ice ax** *n.* an axe shaped like a pickaxe, used by mountain climbers for cutting steps on glaciers etc. **ice-bag** *n.* a bag filled with ice used to reduce swelling or ease pain. **iceblink** *n.* a luminous reflection over the horizon from snowfields or ice fields. **iceblock** *n.* (*Austral., New Zeal.*) ICE LOLLY (under ICE). **ice blue** *n.* a pale blue colour. ~*a.* of this colour. **iceboat** *n.* **1** (*also* **ice yacht**) a boat with runners for travelling on ice. **2** a heavily-built boat for breaking a passage through ice. **icebound** *a.* **1** completely surrounded with ice. **2** unable to get out because of ice. **icebox** *n.* the freezing compartment of a refrigerator. **ice-breaker** *n.* **1** a ship with a re-inforced hull for forcing a channel through ice. **2** (*coll.*) something that encourages a relaxed atmosphere among a group of people meeting for the first time. **ice bucket, ice pail** *n.* a bucket containing ice, for keeping mine etc. cool. **ice cap** *n.* a mass of ice and snow permanently covering an area. **ice-cold** *a.* very cold, like ice. **ice cream** *n.* a creamy confection flavoured and frozen. **ice cube** *n.* a small block of ice for cooling drinks. **ice dancing** *n.* ice-skating based on ballroom dancing and performed in pairs. **ice field** *n.* a large expanse of ice, esp. such as exist in the polar regions. **ice floe** *n.* a sheet of floating ice. **ice hockey** *n.* a type of hockey played on ice by teams of skaters. **ice lolly, iced lolly** *n.* a flavoured piece of ice or ice cream on a stick. **iceman** *n.* (*pl.* **icemen**) **1** (*esp. N Am.*) a man who delivers or sells ice. **2** a man who is skilled in traversing or navigating through ice. **ice pack** *n.* **1** floating ice packed together. **2** a bag etc. containing ice applied to a part of the body to reduce swelling or ease pain. **ice pick** *n.* a pointed tool for splitting ice. **ice rink** *n.* a rink for ice-skating. **ice sheet** *n.* a thick layer of ice covering a very large area of land, as in the last ice age. **ice-skate** *n.* a boot with a blade attached for skating on ice. ~*v.i.* to skate on ice. **ice-skater** *n.* **ice-skating** *n.* **ice station** *n.* a research centre in polar regions, where meteorological conditions are monitored. **ice storm** *n.* a storm in which rain freezes and leaves deposits of ice. **ice water** *n.* **1** water from melted ice. **2** (*also* **iced water**) water cooled by ice. **icing** *n.* **1** a coating of concreted sugar. **2** the formation of ice over a surface. **3** in ice hockey, a shot from one's own team's end of the rink but not at goal, incurring a penalty. **icing on the cake** *n.* an additional extra that is not necessary but is very pleasant or attractive. **icing sugar** *n.* powdered sugar used for icing cakes etc. **icy** *a.* (*comp.* **icier,** *superl.* **iciest**) **1** of, relating to or consisting of ice. **2** like ice, frozen. **3** (*fig.*) (of a tone, look) cold and unfriendly. **icily** *adv.* **iciness** *n.*

iceberg (īs´bœg) *n.* **1** a large mass of ice floating in the sea, usu. formed by detachment from a

glacier. **2** a cold and unresponsive person. **iceberg lettuce** *n.* a type of lettuce with crisp tightly-packed leaves.

Icelander (īs´ləndə) *n.* a native or inhabitant of Iceland, an island in the N Atlantic between Scandinavia and Greenland. **Icelandic** (-lan´-) *a.* of or relating to Iceland. ~*n.* the language of Iceland.

ichneumon (iknū´mən) *n.* **1** a small carnivorous animal, *Herpestes ichneumon*, related to the mongoose, found in Egypt, where it was formerly held sacred on account of its devouring crocodiles' eggs. **2** (*also* **ichneumon fly**) a hymenopterous insect of the family Ichneumonidae, which lays its eggs in or upon the larvae of other insects, upon which its larvae will feed.

ichthyo- (ik´thiō), **ichthy-** *comb. form* **1** of or relating to fish. **2** having the characteristics of a fish.

ichthyology (ikthiol´əji) *n.* the study of fishes. **ichthyologic** (-loj´-), **ichthyological** *a.* **ichthyologist** *n.*

ichthyosaurus (ikthiəsaw´rəs), **ichthyosaur** (ik´-) *n.* (*pl.* **ichthyosauruses, ichthyosauri** (-rī), **ichthyosaurs**) any extinct marine reptile of the order Ichthyosauria, shaped like a fish, with flippers and a long head.

-ician (ish´ən) *suf.* indicating a specialist in a subject, as in *beautician*.

icicle (ī´sikəl) *n.* a hanging conical point of ice, formed when dripping water freezes.

icily, icing etc. ICE.

-icist (isist) *suf.* forming nouns indicating a specialist in a subject from adjectives in -*ic* or nouns in -*ics,* as in *classicist.*

-icity (is´iti) *suf.* forming abstract nouns from adjectives in -*ic* etc., as in *publicity.*

icky (ik´i), **ikky** *a.* (*coll.*) **1** cloying; over-sentimental. **2** unpleasant.

-icle (ikəl) *suf.* forming diminutive nouns, as in *particle, versicle.*

icon (ī´kon), **ikon** *n.* **1** (*also* **eikon**) in the Eastern Church, a sacred image, picture, mosaic, or monumental figure of a holy personage. **2** a symbol. **3** a hero figure, esp. one who represents a particular movement or belief (*a pop icon*). **4** (*Comput.*) a pictorial representation of a facility available to the user of a computer system. **5** a linguistic sign that shares something with or suggests what it signifies. **iconic** (-kon´-) *a.* **1** of, relating to or being an icon. **2** of, relating to or consisting of figures or pictures. **3** (of art) following a conventional pattern or type, such as busts, memorial effigies etc.

icono- (ī´kənō, īkon´ō) *comb. form* of or relating to images or idols.

iconoclasm (īkon´əklazm) *n.* **1** active hostility towards or disregard of established opinions, practices etc. **2** the breaking of idols. **iconoclast** (-klast) *n.* **1** a person who attacks or despises established opinions, practices etc. **2** a breaker of images, esp. one of the religious zealots in the

Eastern Empire in the 8th and 9th cents. who destroyed icons and religious images. **icono-clastic** (-klas´-) *a.* **iconoclastically** *adv.*

iconography (īkənog´rəfi) *n.* (*pl.* **iconographies**) **1** the study of portraits, pictures, statues, symbolism etc. **2** the illustration of a subject by means of figures etc. **3** a treatise on pictures, statues, etc. **4** a book or other collection of figures, drawings etc. **5** pictorial matter relating to a subject. **iconographer** *n.* **iconographic** (-graf´-), **iconographical** *a.* **iconographically** *adv.*

iconolatry (īkənol´ətri) *n.* the adoration of images.

iconology (īkənol´əji) *n.* **1** the study of images, pictures etc. **2** symbolism.

iconostasis (īkənos´təsis) *n.* (*pl.* **iconostases** (-sēz)) in the Eastern Church, a screen on which icons are placed, separating the sanctuary from the rest of the church.

icosahedron (īkosəhē´drən) *n.* (*pl.* **icosahedra** (-drə), **icosahedrons**) a solid figure having 20 plane sides. **icosahedral** *a.*

-ics (iks) *suf.* **1** indicating a science or art, as *linguistics.* **2** indicating specified activities, as *acrobatics.* **3** indicating matters etc. relating to, as *mechanics.*

icterus (ik´tərəs) *n.* (*pl.* **icteruses**) (*Med.*) jaundice. **icteric** (-ter´-) *a., n.*

ictus (ik´təs) *n.* (*pl.* **ictuses, ictus**) **1** the stress, or rhythmical accent on a syllable in a line of verse. **2** (*Med.*) a stroke; a fit.

icy ICE.

ID *abbr.* identification (*an ID card*).

Id EID.

I'd (īd) *contr.* **1** I had. **2** I should; I would.

id (id) *n.* (*Psych.*) the instinctive impulses in the unconscious mind of the individual.

i.d. *abbr.* inner diameter.

id. *abbr.* idem.

-id (id) *suf.* **1** forming adjectives denoting the quality orig. expressed by a L verb, as in *acid, frigid, morbid, tepid.* **2** (*Bot.*) forming nouns denoting a member of a family in *-idaceae*, as in *amaryllid, orchid.* **3** (*Zool.*) forming nouns denoting a member of a family in *-idae* or class *-ida*, as in *arachnid.* **4** (*Astron.*) forming nouns denoting a member of a group, category, or class with a classical proper name, as in *cepheid* (a star), *Leonid* (a meteor).

ide (īd) *n.* a northern European fish, *Leuciscus idus*, of the carp family.

-ide (īd) *suf.* (*Chem.*) indicating chemical compounds of an element with another element or a radical, as *chloride, fluoride, oxide.*

idea (īdē´ə) *n.* **1** a mental image, form, or representation of anything. **2** a conception, a plan (*I've just had an idea*). **3** a more or less vague belief, or fancy (*I had an idea you were divorced*). **4** an intention or design (*The idea is to raise public awareness*). **5** a view, a way of thinking or conceiving (something) (*She has her own ideas on how it should be done*). **6** an archetype or pattern

as distinct from an instantiation or example of it. **7** (*Philos.*) **a** in Platonism, the archetype or perfect and eternal pattern of which actual things are imperfect copies. **b** a concept of pure reason transcending mere experience. **not one's idea of** not what one considers to be (*It's not my idea of fun*). **to get ideas 1** (*coll.*) to become overambitious. **2** (*coll.*) to develop the wrong expectations or impressions. **to have no idea 1** to be unaware of what is going on. **2** (*coll.*) to be innocent or stupid. **ideate** *v.t.* to form an idea of, to imagine. **ideation** (-ā´shən) *n.* **ideational** *a.* **ideationally** *adv.*

ideal (īdē´əl) *a.* **1** reaching one's standard of perfection; perfect. **2** visionary, fanciful. **3** consisting of, existing in, or of or relating to ideas, mental. **4** (*Philos.*) of or relating to idealism or the Platonic ideas. ~*n.* **1** an imaginary standard of perfection. **2** an actual thing realizing this. **ideal gas** *n.* a hypothetical gas made up of molecules of negligible size and exerting no forces on each other, thereby obeying physical laws under all conditions. **idealism** *n.* **1** the practice of forming ideals. **2** the quest for an ideal. **3** the representation of things in conformity with an ideal standard of perfection. **4** (*Philos.*) the doctrine that in external perceptions the objects immediately known are ideas. **idealist** *n.* **idealistic** (-lis´-) *a.* **idealistically** *adv.* **ideality** (-al´-) *n.* (*pl.* **idealities**) **1** the quality of being ideal. **2** an ideal state or thing. **idealize, idealise** *v.t.* **1** to make ideal. **2** to portray in conformity with an ideal. **3** to think of as ideal, to regard as perfect. ~*v.i.* to form ideals. **idealization** (-zā´shən) *n.* **idealizer** *n.* **ideally** *adv.* **1** in an ideal state or manner. **2** intellectually, mentally. **idealness** *n.*

idée fixe (ēdā fēks´) *n.* (*pl.* **idées fixes** (ēdā fēks´)) a fixed idea, an obsession.

idem (id´em) *n.* the same (word, author, book etc.). ~*adv.* in the same author, book etc.

identical (īden´tikəl) *a.* **1** (of one thing viewed or found under different conditions) absolutely the same, not different. **2** (of different things) exactly alike. **3** (*Logic, Math.*) expressing identity. **identically** *adv.* **identicalness** *n.* **identical twins** *n.pl.* twins developed from the fertilization of a single ovum.

identify (īden´tifī) *v.t.* (*3rd pers. sing. pres.* **identifies**, *pres.p.* **identifying**, *past, p.p.* **identified**) **1** to determine or prove the identity of. **2** to establish, to pinpoint (a problem). **3** to unite or associate closely (with a party, interests etc.). **4** to consider or represent as precisely the same (with). **5** to treat as identical (with). ~*v.i.* **1** to associate oneself (with). **2** to consider oneself to be at one (with). **identifiable** *a.* **identifiably** *adv.* **identification** (-fikā´shən) *n.* **1** the act of identifying. **2** the state of being identified. **3** a proof of identity. **identification parade** *n.* a number of persons assembled by the police, among whom a witness is invited to identify a suspect. **identifier** *n.* **1** a person who or thing that identifies.

2 (*Comput.*) a name or label used to identify a set of data.

Identikit® (īden'tikit), **identikit** *n.* **1** a set of facial features on transparent slips, used to compose a likeness, esp. of a criminal suspect. **2** a portrait built up in this way.

identity (īden'titi) *n.* (*pl.* **identities**) **1** the condition of being a particular person or thing (*The police are unable to reveal his identity*). **2** one's individuality (*a loss of identity*). **3** the state of being identical; absolute sameness (*identity of opinion*). **4** identification. **5** (*Math.*) **a** absolute equality between two expressions. **b** an equation expressing such equality. **c** a transformation that does not change the object. **identity crisis** *n.* a state of psychological confusion resulting from a failure to reconcile discordant elements in one's personality. **identity element** *n.* a mathematical element belonging to a set and which leaves any other member of that set unchanged when combining with it. **identity parade** *n.* IDENTIFICATION PARADE (under IDENTIFY).

ideograph (id'iəgrahf), **ideogram** (-gram) *n.* a symbol, figure etc., suggesting or conveying the idea of an object, without expressing its name. **ideographic** (-graf'-), **ideographical** *a.* **ideographically** *adv.* **ideography** (-og'-) *n.* (*pl.* **ideographies**)

ideology (īdiol'əji) *n.* (*pl.* **ideologies**) **1** the political or social philosophy of a nation, movement, group etc. **2** abstract or fanciful theorizing. **ideological** (-loj'-) *a.* **ideologically** *adv.* **ideologist** *n.*

ides (īdz) *n.pl.* in the ancient Roman calendar, the 15th of March, May, July, October, and 13th of the other months.

idiocy IDIOT.

idiolect (id'iəlekt) *n.* a form of speech or language peculiar to an individual.

idiom (id'iəm) *n.* **1** a phrase etc. whose meaning cannot be deduced simply from the meaning of each of its words. **2** a mode of expression peculiar to a particular language. **3** a peculiarity of expression or phraseology. **4** a dialect or language of a country. **5** the unique character of a language. **6** a mode of artistic expression characteristic of a particular person or school. **idiomatic** (-mat'-), **idiomatical** *a.* **1** of or relating to an idiom; expressed in idioms. **2** peculiar to or characteristic of a particular language. **idiomatically** *adv.*

idiosyncrasy (idiəsing'krəsi) *n.* (*pl.* **idiosyncrasies**) **1** a characteristic, habit or attitude peculiar to an individual. **2** anything that is highly eccentric. **3** a mode of expression that is peculiar to a particular author. **4** (*Med.*) individual temperament or constitution. **idiosyncratic** (-krat'-) *a.* **idiosyncratically** *adv.*

idiot (id'iət) *n.* **1** a stupid, silly person. **2** a person of very low intelligence. **idiocy** (-si) *n.* (*pl.* **idiocies**). **idiot board, idiot card** *n.* (*coll.*) an autocue. **idiot box** *n.* (*sl.*) a television set. **idiotic** (-ot'-), **idiotical** *a.* **idiotically** *adv.*

idle (ī'dəl) *a.* (*comp.* **idler**, *superl.* **idlest**) **1** averse to work, lazy. **2** doing nothing, inactive. **3** not occupied, free (*in an idle moment*). **4** (of a machine) not in use. **5** (of a threat) useless, vain, ineffectual. **6** (of a rumour) trifling, without foundation. ~*v.i.* **1** to spend time in idleness. **2** (of an engine) to run slowly without the transmission being engaged. ~*v.t.* **1** to pass (time) without doing anything very useful (*She idled the morning away*). **2** to cause (an engine) to idle. **idleness** *n.* **idler** *n.* **1** a person who spends their time in idleness. **2** IDLE WHEEL (under IDLE). **idle wheel** *n.* a cogged wheel between two others for transmitting motion. **idly** *adv.*

Usage note The spellings of the words *idle* (inactive) and *idol* (a false god) should not be confused.

idol (ī'dəl) *n.* **1** an image, esp. one worshipped as a god. **2** (*Bible*) a false god. **3** a person or thing loved or honoured excessively. **idolater** (idol'-ətə) *n.* **1** a person who worships idols. **2** an adorer, an extravagant admirer. **idolatress** (-tris) *n.* a female idolater. **idolatrous** *a.* **idolatry** *n.* **1** the worship of idols. **2** excessive adoration of a person or thing. **idolize, idolise** **1** to love or venerate to excess. **2** to make an idol of. **idolization** (-zā'shən) *n.* **idolizer** *n.*

Usage note See note under IDLE.

idyll (id'əl), **idyl** *n.* **1** a brief, artistic, and picturesque narrative or description of rustic life, either in verse or prose. **2** a work of art, esp. a musical piece, of a similar character. **3** a scene, episode, or situation suitable for the tone of such a composition. **idyllic** (idil'-) *a.* **1** perfect, esp. because peaceful and beautiful. **2** of, relating to or suitable for an idyll. **idyllically** *adv.*

i.e. *abbr.* id est, that is to say.

Usage note See note under E.G.

-ie -Y³.

-ier (iə) *suf.* denoting occupation, profession etc., as in *bombardier, brigadier, chevalier, financier.*

IF *abbr.* intermediate frequency.

if (if) *conj.* **1** providing that; in the case that (*We'll have a picnic outside if the weather stays fine*; *If he rings, let me know*; *If I'd left any later I would have missed my train*). **2** on the supposition that (*If I were you I'd tell her the truth*). **3** although (*She was polite, if a little distant*). **4** whenever (*I always pop in to see them if I'm in the area*). **5** whether (*He asked me if I played tennis*). **6 a** used to express a wish or a surprise (*If you could see him now!*; *If it isn't Bob!*). **b** used to introduce a request (*If you wouldn't mind signing this form*). **7** used to modify a statement (*many, if not most; rarely if ever*). ~*n.* **1** (*coll.*) an uncertain or doubtful factor (*It's a big if*). **2** a condition. **as if** as it would be if. **if anything** possibly even (*If anything, it's too short*). **if only 1** if for no other reason than (*It's worth going, if only for the* music). **2** used to express a desire or wish (*If only I'd been there*). **ifs and buts** objections. **if so** if that is the case.

-iferous -FEROUS.

iffy (if´i) *a.* (*comp.* **iffier,** *superl.* **iffiest**) (*coll.*) **1** doubtful, uncertain. **2** risky.

-ific -FIC.

-ification -FICATION.

-iform -FORM.

igloo (ig´loo) *n.* an Eskimo (Inuit) hut, often built of snow.

igneous (ig´niəs) *a.* **1** of or like fire. **2** (*Geol.*) (of rocks) produced by volcanic action.

ignis fatuus (ignis fat´ūəs) *n.* (*pl.* **ignes fatui** (ignēz fat´ūī)) **1** an apparent flame, probably due to the spontaneous combustion of inflammable gas, floating above the ground in marshes etc. **2** a delusive object or aim.

ignite (ignīt´) *v.t.* **1** to set on fire. **2** (*Chem.*) to heat to the temperature at which combustion occurs. **3** to arouse or excite (interest, controversy). ~*v.i.* to catch fire. **ignitable, ignitible** *a.* **ignitability** (-bil´-), **ignitibility** *n.* **igniter** *n.* **1** a person who, or a thing that, ignites, esp. a contrivance for igniting powder in an explosive, firing the gases in an internal-combustion engine etc. **2** an electrode used in an ignitron to cause an electric arc. **ignition** (-nish´-) *n.* **1** the act of igniting; the state of being ignited. **2** a mechanism for igniting the explosive mixture in an internal-combustion engine. **ignition key** *n.* a key that operates the ignition system in a motor vehicle.

ignoble (ignō´bəl) *a.* (*comp.* **ignobler,** *superl.* **ignoblest**) **1** mean, base, dishonourable. **2** of humble or low birth. **ignobility** (-bil´-), **ignobleness** *n.* **ignobly** *adv.*

ignominy (ig´nəmini) *n.* (*pl.* **ignominies**) public disgrace or shame; dishonour. **ignominious** (-min´-) *a.* **1** disgraceful. **2** humiliating. **ignominiously** *adv.* **ignominiousness** *n.*

ignoramus (ignərā´məs) *n.* (*pl.* **ignoramuses**) an ignorant person.

ignorance (ig´nərəns) *n.* the state of being ignorant, lack of knowledge (of). **ignorant** *a.* **1** lacking knowledge. **2** unaware (of a fact etc.). **3** (*coll.*) showing a lack of politeness and good manners. **ignorantly** *adv.*

Usage note The constructions *ignorant of* and *ignorant in* are preferred to *ignorant about*.

ignore (ignaw´) *v.t.* **1** to pass over without notice, to disregard. **2** to deliberately pay no attention to. **ignorable** *a.* **ignorer** *n.*

iguana (igwah´nə) *n.* any large lizard of the American genus *Iguana,* esp. *I. tuberculata,* of S and Central America and the W Indies.

iguanodon (igwah´nədon) *n.* a large, bipedal, herbivorous dinosaur of the Cretaceous period.

i.h.p. *abbr.* indicated horsepower.

ikebana (ikibah´nə) *n.* the Japanese art of arranging flowers.

ikky ICKY.

ikon ICON.

-il (əl, il), **-ile** (īl) *suf.* that may be, capable of being, of or relating to etc., as in *civil, fossil, docile, fragile, Gentile, puerile, senile.*

ilang-ilang YLANG-YLANG.

☒ **illegal** common misspelling of ILLEGAL.

ileum (il´iəm) *n.* (*pl.* **ilea** (-iə)) (*Anat.*) the portion of the small intestine communicating with the larger intestine. **ileitis** *n.* (*Med.*) inflammation of the ileum. **ileostomy** *n.* (*pl.* **ileostomies**) a surgical operation in which a permanent opening is made through the abdominal wall into the ileum.

ilex (ī´leks) *n.* (*pl.* **ilexes**) **1** the holm-oak. **2** any tree or shrub of the genus *Ilex* with coriaceous leaves, esp. the holly.

☒ **iliterate** common misspelling of ILLITERATE.

ilium (il´iəm) *n.* (*pl.* **ilia** (-iə)) the upper part of the hip bone. **iliac** (il´iak) *a.*

ilk (ilk) *n.* (*coll., usu. derog.*) a class, sort or kind (*people of that ilk*). **of that ilk** (*Sc.*) of the same name (used when the surname of a person is the same as the name of their estate).

I'll (īl) *contr.* I shall; I will.

ill (il) *a.* (*comp.* **worse,** *superl.* **worst**) **1** unwell, sick, diseased (*She's ill in hospital*). **2** malevolent, hostile, adverse (*ill feelings*). **3** noxious, mischievous, harmful (*the ill effects of alcohol*). **4** unfavourable, unlucky (*ill fortune*). **5** morally bad, evil (*ill deeds*). **6** faulty, incorrect, improper (*ill manners*). **7** unskilful (*ill discipline*). ~*adv.* (*comp.* **worse,** *superl.* **worst**) **1** not well, badly (*conduct ill befitting a man of his standing*). **2** not rightly (*Their success was ill-deserved*). **3** not easily (*We can ill afford another scandal*). **4** imperfectly (*ill-supplied*). **5** unfavourably (*He was warned that it would go ill with him if he refused*). ~*n.* **1** evil. **2** injury, harm (*I wish you no ill*). **3** (*pl.*) troubles, problems (*social ills*). **to be taken ill** to fall sick. **to speak ill** to speak unfavourably (of or about). **ill-advised** *a.* **1** imprudent. **2** (of a plan) not well thought out. **ill-advisedly** *adv.* **ill-assorted** *a.* poorly matched; not compatible. **ill-behaved** *a.* lacking good manners. **ill-bred** *a.* brought up badly; rude and lacking good manners. **ill-conceived** *a.* not well planned. **ill-considered** *a.* done without careful thought. **ill-defined** *a.* poorly defined; lacking a clear outline. **ill-disposed** *a.* **1** unfavourably inclined (towards). **2** wickedly or maliciously inclined. **ill-equipped** *a.* inadequately qualified, equipped etc. (to do something). **ill fame** *n.* disrepute. **ill-fated** *a.* destined to end badly or in failure. **ill-favoured** (*N Am.*) **ill-favored** *a.* ugly, unattractive. **ill feeling** *n.* resentment, enmity. **ill-fitting** *a.* not fitting well. **ill-founded** *a.* lacking any foundation in fact, not substantiated. **ill-gotten** *a.* obtained in an improper way. **ill health** *n.* poor health. **ill humour** *n.* bad temper. **ill-humoured** *a.* **ill-informed** *a.* not very knowledgeable (about). **ill-judged** *a.* not well-judged; injudicious, unwise. **ill-mannered** *a.* rude, boorish.

ill-matched *a.* not well-matched or suited. **ill nature** *n.* lack of kindness or good feeling; churlishness. **ill-natured** *a.* **ill-naturedly** *adv.* **ill-naturedness** *n.* **ill-omened** *a.* unlucky, inauspicious. **ill-prepared** *a.* not well or adequately prepared. **ill-starred** *a.* unlucky; ill-fated. **ill-suited** *a.* not suited (to something). **ill-tempered** *a.* having a bad temper, sour, peevish. **ill temper** *n.* **ill-timed** *a.* done or said at an unsuitable time. **ill-treat** *v.t.* to treat badly or cruelly. **ill treatment** *n.* **ill will** *n.* malevolence; enmity. **ill wind** *n.* an unfavourable situation that must bring advantage (from the proverb *It's an ill wind that blows nobody any good*).

illegal (ilē´gəl) *a.* **1** not according to law. **2** contrary to law, unlawful. **illegality** (-gal´-) *n.* (*pl.* illegalities). **illegally** *adv.*

illegible (ilej´ibəl) *a.* that cannot be read or deciphered. **illegibility** (-bil´-), **illegibleness** *n.* **illegibly** *adv.*

illegitimate[1] (iləjit´imət) *a.* **1** born of parents not married to each other. **2** contrary to law or recognized usage. **3** irregular, improper. **4** illogical, contrary to logical rules, unsound. *~n.* **1** an illegitimate child, a bastard. **2** a person of illegitimate status. **illegitimacy** (-əsi) *n.* **illegitimately** *adv.*

illegitimate[2] (iləjit´imāt) *v.t.* to render or declare illegitimate.

illiberal (ilib´ərəl) *a.* **1** narrow-minded. **2** not characterized by wide views or by culture. **3** not generous; niggardly. **illiberality** (-ral´-) *n.* (*pl.* illiberalities). **illiberally** *adv.*

illicit (ilis´it) *a.* **1** not allowed or permitted. **2** unlawful. **illicitly** *adv.* **illicitness** *n.*

Usage note See note under ELICIT.

illimitable (ilim´itəbəl) *a.* boundless, limitless. **illimitability** (-bil´-), **illimitableness** *n.* **illimitably** *adv.*

illiterate (ilit´ərət) *a.* **1** unable to read or write. **2** ignorant in a specific subject (*technologically illiterate*). **3** ignorant, uncultivated. *~n.* an ignorant or uneducated person, esp. one unable to read. **illiteracy** (-əsi), **illiterateness** *n.* **illiterately** *adv.*

illness (il´nəs) *n.* **1** the state of being ill. **2** sickness, a disease or ailment.

illogical (iloj´ikəl) *a.* **1** contrary to reason. **2** ignorant or careless of the rules of logic. **illogicality** (-kal´-) *n.* (*pl.* illogicalities). **illogically** *adv.*

illuminate[1] (iloo´mināt) *v.t.* **1** to light up. **2** to throw light upon (a subject, problem). **3** to decorate (buildings, streets etc.) with festive light. **4** to decorate (a manuscript etc.) with coloured pictures, letters etc. **5** to enlighten mentally or spiritually. **6** to make illustrious. **illuminant** *a.* illuminating. *~n.* something which illuminates. **illuminating** *a.* **1** that lights up. **2** enlightening. **illuminatingly** *adv.* **illumination** (-ā´shən) *n.* **1** the act of lighting up or state of being lit up. **2** enlightenment. **3** a source of light. **4** (*often pl.*)

a display of ornamental lights. **5** the decoration of manuscripts etc. with ornamental coloured letters and pictures. **6** clarification. **illuminative** (-ātiv, -nətiv) *a.* **illuminator** *n.*

illuminate[2] (iloo´mināt, -it) *n.* a person who claims to possess special enlightenment.

illusion (iloo´zhən) *n.* **1** deception. **2** a mistaken belief or false perception. **3** a deceptive appearance or impression. **4** an unreal image presented to the vision. **5** (*Psych.*) a wrong interpretation of what is perceived through the senses. **to be under the illusion** to believe mistakenly (that). **illusional** *a.* **illusionism** *n.* the artistic practice of giving an illusion of reality, e.g. through the use of perspective. **illusionist** *n.* a conjurer. **illusionistic** *a.* **illusive** (-siv) *a.* illusory. **illusively** *adv.* **illusory** (-zəri) *a.* delusive, deceptive. **illusorily** *adv.* **illusoriness** *n.*

Usage note The nouns *illusion* and *allusion* should not be confused: an *illusion* is a deception, and an *allusion* an indirect reference. See also note under ELUDE.

illustrate (il´əstrāt) *v.t.* **1** to embellish (a book, etc.) with pictures. **2** to make clear or explain by means of examples, figures etc. **illustration** (-trā´shən) *n.* **1** an engraving or drawing illustrating a book or article in a periodical. **2** something which illustrates, an example, a typical instance. **3** the act of illustrating; the state of being illustrated. **illustrational** *a.* **illustrative** *a.* serving as an illustration or example. **illustratively** *adv.* **illustrator** *n.*

illustrious (ilŭs´triəs) *a.* distinguished, famous. **illustriously** *adv.* **illustriousness** *n.*

☒ **iluminate** common misspelling of ILLUMINATE.

I'm (īm) *contr.* I am.

image (im´ij) *n.* **1** a visible representation or likeness of a person or thing, esp. in sculpture. **2** the impression given to others of a person's character etc. (*Involvement in charities is good for a company's image*). **3** a copy, a counterpart. **4** the living embodiment of a particular quality (*the image of fairness and decency*). **5 a** an idea, a conception. **b** a mental picture. **6** an expanded metaphor or simile. **7** the figure of an object formed (through the medium of a mirror, lens etc.) by rays of light. **8** a mental representation of a sense impression. **9** (*Math.*) a set mapped from another set. *~v.t.* **1** to make an image of; to portray. **2** to mirror. **3** to represent mentally; to conceive in the mind. **4** to typify, to symbolize. **imageable** *a.* **image intensifier** *n.* any of various electronic devices for intensifying an optical image. **imageless** *a.* **image-maker** *n.* a public relations expert employed to improve the impression that someone, e.g. a politician, makes on the general public. **image processing** *n.* (*Comput.*) the filtering, storing and retrieving of images. **image processor** *n.* **imagery** (-əri) *n.* **1** figurative description, esp. in poetry. **2** (*collect.*) images; statues. **3** mental pictures. **imagism** *n.* an early

20th-cent. poetic movement that aimed at clear and simple language and precise images. **imagist** *n.* **imagistic** (-jis´-) *a.*

imagine (imaj´in) *v.t.* **1** to form an image of in the mind, to conceive, to form an idea of. **2** to suppose, to think (*I imagine she'll come by car*). **3** to believe without any justification (*You're imagining things*). **4** to conjecture, to guess (*I can't imagine what he was thinking of*). *~v.i.* to form images or ideas in the mind (*Can you imagine!*). **imaginable** *a.* **imaginably** *adv.* **imaginal¹** *a.* of or relating to images. **imaginary** *a.* **1** existing only in imagination or fancy. **2** (*Math.*) (of a mathematical quantity or value) assumed as real for the purposes of an equation etc. **imaginarily** *adv.* **imaginariness** *n.* **imaginary number** *n.* (*Math.*) a number involving the square root of a negative number. **imagination** (-ā´shən) *n.* **1** the mental faculty that forms ideal images or combinations of images from the impressions left by sensuous experience. **2** the constructive or creative faculty of the mind. **3** the act or process of imagining. **4** fancy, fantasy. **imaginative** *a.* **1** endowed with imagination. **2** produced or characterized by imagination. **imaginatively** *adv.* **imaginativeness** *n.* **imaginer** *n.* **imaginings** *n.pl.* things that exist only in the mind.

imago (imā´gō) *n.* (*pl.* **imagoes, imagines** (-jinēz)) **1** (*Zool.*) the adult, fully-developed insect after its metamorphoses. **2** (*Psych.*) an idealized image of a parent or other person that exercises a persistent influence in the unconscious. **imaginal²** (-maj´-) *a.* (*Zool.*) of or relating to a fully-developed insect.

imam (imahm´) *n.* **1** a person who leads congregational prayer in a mosque. **2** the title of various Muslim rulers and founders. **imamate** (-āt), **imamship** *n.*

imbalance (imbal´əns) *n.* a lack of balance or proportion.

imbecile (im´bəsēl) *a.* **1** mentally weak, half-witted. **2** stupid, fatuous. *~n.* **1** a person of abnormally low intelligence. **2** (*coll.*) a stupid or foolish person. **imbecilic** (-sil´ik) *a.* **imbecility** (-sil´-) *n.* (*pl.* **imbecilities**).

imbed EMBED.

imbibe (imbīb´) *v.t.* (*formal*) **1** to drink. **2** to absorb (liquid etc.). **3** to assimilate (ideas etc.). **4** to draw in (air). *~v.i.* (*facet.*) to drink. **imbiber** *n.* **imbibition** (-bibish´ən) *n.*

imbroglio (imbrō´liō), **embroglio** *n.* (*pl.* **imbroglios, embroglios**) **1** a perplexing or confused state of affairs. **2** a disorderly heap.

imbue (imbū´) *v.t.* (*3rd pers. sing. pres.* **imbues**, *pres.p.* **imbuing**, *past*, *p.p.* **imbued**) **1** to inspire, to impregnate (with). **2** to saturate (with). **3** to dye (with).

❌ **imediate** common misspelling of IMMEDIATE.
❌ **imense** common misspelling of IMMENSE.

imitate (im´itāt) *v.t.* **1** to follow the example of; to copy. **2** to mimic, to ape. **3** to produce a likeness or copy of. **4** to be like; to resemble. **imitable** *a.*

imitability (-bil´-) *n.* **imitation** (-ā´shən) *n.* **1** the act of imitating; an instance of this. **2** a copy or likeness. **3** (*often attrib.*) something that is not genuine (*imitation jewellery*). **imitative** (-tətiv) *a.* **1** given to or aiming at imitation. **2** done in imitation (of). **3** counterfeit. **4** (of words) onomatopoeic. **imitatively** *adv.* **imitativeness** *n.* **imitator** *n.*

immaculate (imak´ūlət) *a.* **1** spotlessly clean or tidy. **2** pure; free from blemish. **3** (of a performance etc.) absolutely faultless. **4** (*Biol.*) not spotted. **immaculacy** (-si), **immaculateness** *n.* **Immaculate Conception** *n.* in the Roman Catholic Church, the doctrine (made an article of faith in 1854) that the Virgin Mary was conceived and born free from original sin. **immaculately** *adv.*

immanent (im´ənənt) *a.* **1** remaining within, inherent; indwelling. **2** (*Theol.*) present throughout the universe as an essential sustaining spirit. **immanence, immanency** *n.* **immanently** *adv.*

Usage note The adjectives *immanent* and *imminent* should not be confused: *immanent* means indwelling, and *imminent* impending.

immaterial (imətiə´riəl) *a.* **1** irrelevant, unimportant. **2** not consisting of matter; incorporeal. **3** spiritual. **immaterialism** *n.* the doctrine that there is no material substance, and that all being may be reduced to mind and ideas in the mind. **immaterialist** *n.* **immateriality** (-al´-) *n.* **immaterialize, immaterialise** *v.t.* **immaterially** *adv.*

immature (imətūə´) *a.* **1** not fully developed. **2** lacking the appropriate maturity of character etc. **3** not ripe. **immaturely** *adv.* **immatureness, immaturity** *n.*

immeasurable (imezh´ərəbəl) *a.* **1** that cannot be measured. **2** immense. **immeasurability** (-bil´-), **immeasurableness** *n.* **immeasurably** *adv.*

immediate (imē´diət) *a.* **1** done or occurring at once, instant (*an immediate response*). **2** situated in the closest relation; nearest (*her immediate family*). **3** nearest in time (*in the immediate future*). **4** acting or acted upon by direct agency, direct (*the immediate cause of the conflict*). **5** present; of most concern (*our immediate needs*). **6** (of knowledge, concepts) that is directly known; intuitive. **immediacy** (-si), **immediateness** *n.* **immediately** *adv.* **1** without delay, at once. **2** closely or directly. **3** just close by. *~conj.* as soon as.

immemorial (imimaw´riəl) *a.* **1** beyond memory or record. **2** ancient. **immemorially** *adv.*

immense (imens´) *a.* **1** huge, vast, immeasurable. **2** very great, very large. **3** (*coll.*) very good, excellent. **immensely** *adv.* **immenseness, immensity** *n.*

immerse (imœs´) *v.t.* **1** to plunge, to dip (into or under water or other fluid). **2** (*usu. reflex. or pass.*) to involve or absorb deeply (in difficulty, debt, study, etc.). **3** to bury (in). **immersion** (-shən) *n.* **1** the act of immersing; the state of being immersed. **2** baptism by plunging completely under water. **3** the state of being deeply involved (in thought etc.). **4** (*Astron.*) the disappearance of a celestial body behind or into the shadow of another. **immersion heater** *n.* an electric heater designed to heat liquid by being directly immersed in it, esp. as a fixture in a hot-water tank.

immigrate (im´igrāt) *v.i.* to enter a foreign country for settlement there. ~*v.t.* to bring (a person) into a foreign country for settlement. **immigrant** *n.* a person who immigrates. ~*a.* of or relating to immigrants (*the immigrant population*). **immigration** (-rā´shən) *n.* **immigratory** *a.*

imminent (im´inənt) *a.* impending; close at hand. **imminence** *n.* **imminently** *adv.*

Usage note See note under IMMANENT.

immiscible (imis´ibəl) *a.* not capable of being mixed (with). **immiscibility** (-bil´-) *n.* **immiscibly** *adv.*

immobile (imō´bīl) *a.* **1** not moving. **2** not mobile, immovable. **immobility** (-bil´-) *n.* **immobilize** (-bil-), **immobilise** *v.t.* **1** to render (a vehicle, an attacker etc.) immobile. **2** to restrict the movement of (a limb etc.) for healing purposes. **3** to withdraw (coins) from circulation. **immobilization** (-zā´shən) *n.* **immobilizer** *n.*

immoderate (imod´ərət) *a.* **1** excessive. **2** unreasonable. **immoderately** *adv.* **immoderation** (-ā´shən), **immoderateness** *n.*

immodest (imod´ist) *a.* **1** not modest, forward. **2** improper, indecent. **immodestly** *adv.* **immodesty** *n.*

immolate (im´əlāt) *v.t.* **1** to kill or offer up in sacrifice. **2** to sacrifice (a highly valued thing). **immolation** (-ā´shən) *n.* **immolator** *n.*

immoral (imor´əl) *a.* **1** not moral. **2** inconsistent with or contrary to (esp. sexual) morality. **3** licentious, vicious. **immorality** (-ral´-) *n.* (*pl.* **immoralities**). **immorally** *adv.*

Usage note See note under AMORAL.

immortal (imaw´təl) *a.* **1** not mortal, not subject to death. **2** imperishable. **3** relating to immortality. **4** eternally famous. ~*n.* **1** a person who is immortal, esp. one of the ancient gods. **2** a person, esp. an author, who is enduringly famous. **immortality** (-tal´-) *n.* **immortalize, immortalise** *v.t.* **1** to make immortal. **2** to perpetuate the memory of. **immortalization** (-zā´shən) *n.* **immortally** *adv.*

immortelle (imawtel´) *n.* an everlasting flower, esp. a helichrysum.

immovable (imoo´vəbəl), **immoveable** *a.* **1** that cannot be moved. **2** firmly fixed. **3** steadfast. **4** unchanging, unalterable. **5** unfeeling. **6** (*Law*) not liable to be removed. **immovability** (-bil´-), **immovableness** *n.* **immovably** *adv.*

immune (imūn´) *a.* **1** (*Biol.*) protected against a particular disease, infection etc. owing to inoculation or the body's natural resistance (*immune*

to *typhoid*). **2** of or relating to immunity (*the immune system*). **3** unaffected; free or exempt (from) (*immune to criticism*). **immune response** *n.* (*Biol.*) the response of the body to the introduction of an antigen. **immunity** *n.* (*pl.* **immunities**) **1** (*Biol.*) freedom from liability to infection. **2** freedom or exemption from an obligation, duty or penalty. **immunize** (im´-), **immunise** *v.t.* to give protection against a disease to, usu. by inoculation. **immunization** (-zā´shən) *n.*

immuno- (im´ūnō, imū´nō) *comb. form* **1** immunity. **2** immune.

immunodeficiency (imūnōdifish´ənsi) *n.* (*Med.*) a deficiency in a person's immune response.

immunogenic (imūnōjen´ik) *a.* (*Med.*) causing or able to produce an immune response.

immunoglobulin (imūnōglob´ūlin) *n.* (*Med.*) any one of five classes of proteins showing antibody activity.

immunology (imūnol´əji) *n.* (*Med.*) the scientific study of immunity. **immunologic** (-loj´-), **immunological** *a.* **immunologically** *adv.* **immunologist** *n.*

immunosuppressive (imūnōsəpres´iv) *a.* (*Med.*) (of a drug) that minimizes the body's natural reactions to a foreign substance, e.g. a transplanted organ. ~*n.* an immunosuppressive drug. **immunosuppressant** *n.*, *a.* **immunosuppressed** *a.* (of a person) whose immune response has been partially or completely suppressed. **immunosuppression** *n.*

immure (imūə´) *v.t.* **1** to surround as with a wall; to confine. **2** to shut (oneself) away.

immutable (imū´təbəl) *a.* **1** unchangeable. **2** not susceptible to change or variation, invariable. **immutability** (-bil´-), **immutableness** *n.* **immutably** *adv.*

❌ **imortal** common misspelling of IMMORTAL.

imp (imp) *n.* **1** a mischievous child. **2** a little devil or malignant spirit. **impish** *a.* **impishly** *adv.* **impishness** *n.*

impact[1] (im´pakt) *n.* **1** a forcible striking (upon or against), a collision. **2** an effect or influence (on).

impact[2] (impakt´) *v.t.* **1** to press or drive firmly together, to pack firmly in. **2** to have an effect on. ~*v.i.* to have an effect (on). **impacted** (-pak´-) *a.* **1** (of a tooth) wedged in such a way as to be unable to come through the gum. **2** (of a fracture) having jagged ends that are wedged into each other. **3** (of faeces) lodged in the intestines. **impaction** (-pak´-) *n.*

impair (impeə´) *v.t.* to damage or weaken in quality, strength etc. (*impaired vision*). **impairment** *n.*

impala (impah´lə) *n.* (*pl.* **impala, impalas**) an antelope, *Aepyceros melampus*, of southern and eastern Africa, that has lyre-shaped horns and is able to move with long high leaps.

impale (impāl´) *v.t.* to transfix, esp. to put to death by transfixing with a sharp stake. **impalement** *n.*

impalpable (impal´pəbəl) *a.* **1** not able to be readily apprehended by the mind; intangible. **2** not perceptible to the touch. **3** (of powder) not coarse. **impalpability** (-bil´-) *n.* **impalpably** *adv.*

impanel EMPANEL.

impart (impaht´) *v.t.* **1** to communicate (knowledge, information). **2** to give, to bestow (a quality, feeling). **impartation** (-tā´shən), **impartment** *n.* **imparter** *n.*

impartial (impah´shəl) *a.* not partial; not favouring one party or one side more than another. **impartiality** (-al´-), **impartialness** *n.* **impartially** *adv.*

impassable (impah´səbəl) *a.* that cannot be passed or travelled through. **impassability** (-bil´-), **impassableness** *n.* **impassably** *adv.*

Usage note The adjectives *impassable* and *impassible* should not be confused: *impassable* means unable to be passed, and *impassible* impassive or insensible.

impasse (am´pas, im´-) *n.* a blind alley; an insurmountable obstacle; deadlock.

impassible (impas´ibəl) *a.* **1** impassive. **2** insensible to pain or suffering. **3** incapable of being injured. **impassibility** (-bil´-), **impassibleness** *n.* **impassibly** *adv.*

Usage note See note under IMPASSABLE.

impassion (impash´ən) *v.t.* to rouse the deepest feelings of, to stir to ardour or passion. **impassioned** *a.* charged with passion.

impassive (impas´iv) *a.* **1** not showing or affected by pain, feeling or passion. **2** unmoved, serene. **3** having no sensation. **impassively** *adv.* **impassiveness, impassivity** (-siv´-) *n.*

impaste (impāst´) *v.t.* in painting, to lay colours thickly and boldly on. **impasto** (-pas´tō) *n.* **1** the application of a thick layer of paint, to give relief etc. **2** paint applied in this way.

impatiens (impā´shienz) *n.* (*pl.* **impatiens**) any plant of the genus *Impatiens*, including the busy Lizzie and balsam.

impatient (impā´shənt) *a.* **1** not able to wait or to endure. **2** eager (for or to). **3** not patient or tolerant (of). **impatience** *n.* **impatiently** *adv.*

impeach (impēch´) *v.t.* **1** to charge with a crime, esp. treason. **2** (*esp. N Am.*) to charge with misconduct while holding office. **3** to call in question (a person's honesty etc.). **impeachable** *a.* **impeacher** *n.*

impeccable (impek´əbəl) *a.* **1** (of manners, behaviour etc.) faultless. **2** not liable to fall into sin. **impeccability** (-bil´-) *n.* **impeccably** *adv.*

impecunious (impikū´niəs) *a.* **1** having no money. **2** short of money. **impecuniosity** (-os´-), **impecuniousness** *n.*

impede (impēd´) *v.t.* to hinder, to obstruct. **impedance** *n.* **1** resistance to alternating current, esp. due to inductance or capacitance together with ohmic resistance. **2** a similar resistance

caused by applied forces (*mechanical impedances*). **impediment** (-ped´-) *n.* **1** something which impedes; a hindrance or obstruction. **2** a speech defect. **impedimenta** (-men´tə) *n.pl.* **1** things that impede progress. **2** baggage, esp. supplies for an army on the march. **impedimental** *a.*

impel (impel´) *v.t.* (*pres.p.* **impelling**, *past, p.p.* **impelled**) **1** to drive or urge (to an action or to do). **2** to drive or push forward. **impellent** *a., n.* **impeller** *n.*

impend (impend´) *v.i.* **1** to threaten, to be imminent. **2** to hang (over), to be suspended (over). **impending** *a.*

impenetrable (impen´itrəbəl) *a.* **1** that cannot be penetrated or pierced. **2** inscrutable, incomprehensible. **3** impervious to ideas, influences etc. **impenetrability** (-bil´-), **impenetrableness** *n.* **impenetrably** *adv.*

impenitent (impen´itənt) *a.* not penitent, not contrite. **impenitence, impenitency** *n.* **impenitently** *adv.*

imperative (imper´ətiv) *a.* **1** urgent. **2** obligatory. **3** authoritative, peremptory. **4** (*Gram.*) (of a mood of verbs) expressing command. ~*n.* **1** the mood of the verb used to express command, entreaty or exhortation. **2** a command. **3** something absolutely essential or very urgent. **imperatival** (-tī´-) *a.* **imperatively** *adv.* **imperativeness** *n.*

imperceptible (impəsep´tibəl) *a.* **1** not able to be perceived. **2** extremely slight, small, or gradual. **imperceptibility** (-bil´-), **imperceptibleness** *n.* **imperceptibly** *adv.*

impercipient (impəsip´iənt) *a.* not perceiving; not having power to perceive. **impercipience** *n.*

imperf. *abbr.* imperfect.

imperfect (impœ´fikt) *a.* **1** not perfect, defective. **2** incomplete, not fully made, done etc. **3** (*Gram.*) (of a tense or aspect) expressing action as continuous and not completed, usu. in the past. **4** (*Mus.*) **a** diminished. **b** less than a semitone. **c** (of a cadence) passing to a dominant chord from another, esp. a tonic, chord. ~*n.* **1** the imperfect tense. **2** a verb in this tense. **imperfection** (-fek´-) *n.* **1** the condition of being imperfect. **2** a defect. **3** deficiency. **imperfective** (-fek´-) *a.* (*Gram.*) (of a verb aspect) showing that the action is in progress. ~*n.* **1** the imperfective aspect of a verb. **2** a verb in this aspect. **imperfectively** *adv.* **imperfectly** *adv.* **imperfectness** *n.*

imperial (impiə´riəl) *a.* **1** of or relating to an empire, an emperor, or other supreme ruler. **2** suitable to or like an emperor; sovereign; supreme; lordly, majestic. **3** (of weights and measures) conforming to official British nonmetric standards. **4** (of commodities and products) of a superior size, quality etc. **imperialism** *n.* **1 a** the policy of extending the authority of a nation by means of colonies or dependencies. **b** (*often derog.*) the extension of influence or authority by a country, institution etc. (*dollar imperialism*). **2** government by an emperor. **3** the spirit, state, authority etc. of an empire. **imperialist** *n.* a supporter or advocate of imperialism. *~a.* of or relating to imperialism. **imperialistic** (-is´-) *a.* **imperialistically** *adv.* **imperially** *adv.*

imperil (imper´il) *v.t.* (*pres.p.* **imperilling**, (*NAm.*) **imperiling**, *past, p.p.* **imperilled**, (*NAm.*) **imperiled**) to endanger.

imperious (impiə´riəs) *a.* 1 dictatorial, overbearing. 2 urgent, pressing. **imperiously** *adv.* **imperiousness** *n.*

imperishable (imper´ishəbəl) *a.* 1 enduring permanently. 2 not subject to decay. **imperishability** (-bil´-), **imperishableness** *n.* **imperishably** *adv.*

impermanent (impœ´mənənt) *a.* not permanent. **impermanence, impermanency** *n.* **impermanently** *adv.*

impermeable (impœ´miəbəl) *a.* not allowing passage, esp. of a fluid; impervious. **impermeability** (-bil´-), **impermeableness** *n.*

impermissible (impəmis´ibəl) *a.* not permissible. **impermissibility** (-bil´-) *n.*

impersonal (impœ´sənəl) *a.* 1 without personality. 2 not relating to any particular person or thing. 3 lacking in human warmth. 4 (*Gram.*) (of a verb) used only in the third person singular in modern English with the neuter pronoun *it* as subject. **impersonality** (-nal´-) *n.* **impersonally** *adv.*

impersonate (impœ´sənāt) *v.t.* 1 to pretend to be (someone) in order to entertain or deceive. 2 to play the part of (a character). **impersonation** (-ā´shən) *n.* **impersonator** *n.*

impertinent (impœ´tinənt) *a.* 1 impudent, insolent. 2 inappropriate. **impertinence, impertinency** *n.* **impertinently** *adv.*

imperturbable (impœtœ´bəbəl) *a.* not easily disturbed or excited; calm, cool. **imperturbability** (-bil´-), **imperturbableness, imperturbation** (-pœtəbā´shən) *n.* **imperturbably** *adv.*

impervious (impœ´viəs) *a.* 1 not receptive or open (to). 2 not allowing passage of a liquid. **imperviously** *adv.* **imperviousness** *n.*

impetigo (impətī´gō) *n.* (*pl.* **impetigos, impetigines** (-tij´inēz)) a contagious bacterial skin infection marked by the formation of pustules and yellow crusty sores.

impetuous (impet´ūəs) *a.* 1 acting hastily or suddenly; impulsive. 2 moving with violence or great speed. **impetuosity** (-os´-), **impetuousness** *n.* **impetuously** *adv.*

impetus (im´pitəs) *n.* (*pl.* **impetuses**) 1 an impulse or driving force; stimulus. 2 the force with which a body moves or is impelled.

impiety (impī´əti) *n.* (*pl.* **impieties**) 1 the quality of being impious. 2 an impious act.

impinge (impinj´) *v.i.* (*pres.p.* **impinging**) 1 to have an effect (on). 2 to encroach (on). **impingement** *n.* **impinger** *n.*

impious (im´piəs, impī´əs) *a.* 1 lacking piety or reverence, esp. towards God. 2 irreverent, lacking respect. **impiously** *adv.* **impiousness** *n.*

implacable (implak´əbəl) *a.* 1 not to be appeased. 2 inexorable, unrelenting. **implacability** (-bil´-), **implacableness** *n.* **implacably** *adv.*

implant[1] (implahnt´) *v.t.* 1 to plant for the purpose of growth. 2 to set or fix (in). 3 (*Med.*) **a** to insert (tissue, an electrode etc.) into the body. **b** (*pass.*) (of a fertilized ovum) to become attached to the lining of the uterus. 4 to inculcate, to instil (ideas etc.). **implantation** (-tā´shən) *n.*

implant[2] (im´plahnt) *n.* something implanted, esp. something grafted or inserted into the body.

implausible (implaw´zibəl) *a.* not having an appearance of truth and credibility. **implausibility** (-bil´-), **implausibleness** *n.* **implausibly** *adv.*

implement (im´plimənt) *n.* 1 a tool, a utensil. 2 (*pl.*) things that serve for equipment, furniture, etc. 3 (*fig.*) an agent, an instrument. 4 (*Sc. Law*) the fulfilment of an obligation. *~v.t.* 1 to carry (a policy, law etc.) into effect. 2 to fulfil. 3 to complete. 4 to supplement. **implementation** (-tā´shən) *n.* **implementer** *n.*

implicate (im´plikāt) *v.t.* 1 to show (a person) to be involved (in). 2 to involve. 3 to imply. **implication** (-ā´shən) *n.* 1 something that is implied or suggested. 2 the act of implicating; the state of being implicated. **by implication** by indirect suggestion. **implicative** (-plik´ətiv) *a.* **implicatively** *adv.*

implicit (implis´it) *a.* 1 implied rather than directly stated. 2 tacitly contained (in) but not expressed. 3 unquestioning, unreserved (*implicit trust*). **implicitly** *adv.* **implicitness** *n.*

implode (implōd´) *v.i.* to burst inwards. *~v.t.* 1 to cause to burst inwards. 2 to pronounce (a consonant) by implosion. **implosion** (-zhən) *n.* **implosive** *a., n.*

implore (implaw´) *v.t.* 1 to supplicate or beg (someone to do something). 2 to ask for earnestly. *~v.i.* to entreat, to beg, to supplicate. **imploringly** *adv.*

imply (implī´) *v.t.* (*3rd pers. sing. pres.* **implies**, *pres.p.* **implying**, *past, p.p.* **implied**) 1 to indicate strongly the truth or existence of (something) in an indirect way. 2 to mean indirectly, to hint (*Are you implying I did it on purpose?*). 3 to signify. **implied** *a.* **impliedly** (-plī´əd-) *adv.*

Usage note See note under INFER.

impolite (impəlīt´) *a.* not polite, ill-mannered. **impolitely** *adv.* **impoliteness** *n.*

impolitic (impol´itik) *a.* not politic, injudicious, inexpedient. **impoliticly** *adv.*

imponderable (impon´dərəbəl) *a.* 1 incalculable. 2 very light. 3 (*Physics*) not having sensible weight. *~n.* (*usu. pl.*) an element or factor whose importance cannot be assessed or evaluated. **imponderability** (-bil´-), **imponderableness** *n.*

import[1] (impawt´) *v.t.* 1 to bring (goods) from a foreign country (into). 2 to introduce (ideas, words etc.) from elsewhere. 3 to imply, to signify, to mean. 4 (*Comput.*) to transfer (data) from one software package to another. **importable** *a.* **importation** (-tā´shən) *n.* **importer** *n.*

import² (im´pawt) *n.* **1** something which is imported from abroad. **2** the act or process of importing. **3** something which is signified or implied. **4** importance.

importance (impaw´təns) *n.* **1** the quality of being important. **2** weight, authority, consequence. **3** personal consideration, self-esteem. **important** (-paw´-) *a.* **1** of great moment or consequence, weighty. **2** notable, eminent. **3** pretentious. **4** significant (*She's talented, and more important, committed*). **importantly** *adv.*

importunate (impaw´tūnət) *a.* **1** unreasonably insistent or demanding. **2** urgent. **3** troublesome. **importunacy, importunateness, importunity** (-tū´-) *n.* **importunately** *adv.*

importune (impaw´tūn) *v.t.* **1** to solicit insistently or urgently. **2** to solicit for immoral purposes.

impose (impōz´) *v.t.* **1** to lay (e.g. a burden, tax, toll etc.) upon. **2** to force (one's beliefs, views etc.) upon. **3** to palm off (upon). **4** to arrange (pages of type) in a forme for printing. ~*v.i.* **1** to cause inconvenience. **2** to take advantage of someone's good nature or kindness. **imposer** *n.* **imposing** *a.* commanding; impressive. **imposingly** *adv.* **imposingness** *n.*

imposition (impəzish´ən) *n.* **1** the act of imposing or placing upon. **2** an unfair and excessive burden. **3** a duty or tax. **4** an exercise enjoined as a punishment in schools etc.

impossible (impos´ibəl) *a.* **1** not possible. **2** (*loosely*) impracticable, not feasible. **3** that cannot be done, thought, endured etc. **4** (*coll.*) outrageous. **impossibility** (-bil´-) *n.* (*pl.* **impossibilities**) **1** the state of being impossible. **2** something impossible. **impossibly** *adv.*

impost¹ (im´pōst) *n.* **1** something which is imposed or levied as a tax, tribute or duty (esp. on imported goods). **2** a weight carried by a horse in a handicap race.

impost² (im´pōst) *n.* the upper member of a pillar or entablature on which an arch rests.

impostor (impos´tə), **imposter** *n.* **1** a person who falsely assumes a character. **2** a deceiver by false pretences. **imposture** (-chə) *n.*

impotent (im´pətənt) *a.* **1** powerless; helpless. **2** (of a male) unable to have sexual intercourse because of an inability to achieve an erection. **impotence, impotency** *n.* **impotently** *adv.*

impound (impownd´) *v.t.* **1** to take possession of or confiscate (a document etc.). **2** to confine. **3** to shut up (animals) in a pound. **4** to collect and confine or retain (water) in a reservoir, dam etc. **impoundable** *a.* **impounder** *n.* **impoundment** *n.*

impoverish (impov´ərish), †**empoverish** *v.t.* **1** to make poor. **2** to exhaust the strength, fertility or resources of. **impoverishment** *n.*

impracticable (imprak´tikəbəl) *a.* **1** not able to be carried out in practice; not feasible. **2** unsuitable for a particular purpose. **3** (of a road)

impassable. **4** intractable, stubborn. **impracticability** (-bil´-), **impracticableness** *n.* **impracticably** *adv.*

Usage note The meanings of the adjectives *impracticable* and *impractical* overlap (especially in North America), but *impracticable* usually means not possible, and *impractical* not realistic.

impractical (imprak´tikəl) *a.* **1** not practical. **2** (*esp. N Am.*) not possible in practice. **impracticality** (-kal´-), **impracticalness** *n.* **impractically** *adv.*

imprecate (im´prikāt) *v.t.* **1** to invoke (as an evil on). **2** to put a curse on. ~*v.i.* to curse. **imprecation** (-ā´shən) *n.* **1** the act of imprecating. **2** a prayer for evil to fall on someone; a curse. **imprecatory** *a.* involving a curse.

imprecise (imprisīs´) *a.* not precise. **imprecisely** *adv.* **impreciseness, imprecision** (-izh´ən) *n.*

impregnable (impreg´nəbəl) *a.* **1** (of a castle, defences) that cannot be stormed or taken by assault. **2** able to resist all attacks. **impregnability** (-bil´-) *n.* **impregnably** *adv.*

impregnate (im´pregnāt) *v.t.* **1** to make pregnant. **2** (*Biol.*) to fertilize (an ovum). **3** to saturate (with). **4** to imbue, to inspire (with). ~*a.* **1** impregnated, pregnant. **2** imbued (with). **impregnation** (-nā´shən) *n.*

impresario (imprizah´riō) *n.* (*pl.* **impresarios**) **1** a person who organizes musical or theatrical performances. **2** a director of an opera company, a ballet company etc.

impress¹ (impres´) *v.t.* **1** to produce a favourable effect on (*I'm impressed with your efficiency*). **2** to affect strongly. **3** to press or stamp (a mark etc., in or upon). **4** to make a mark etc. on (something) with a stamp or seal. **to impress on/upon** to emphasize to (someone) (*He impressed on us the need for discretion*). **impressible** *a.* **impressive** *a.* **1** adapted to make an impression on the mind; commanding; inspiring. **2** leaving a deep impression. **impressively** *adv.* **impressiveness** *n.*

impress² (im´pres) *n.* **1** the act of marking by pressure or with a stamp, seal etc. **2** a stamp, an impression. **3** a characteristic mark. **4** an effect produced by the senses, feelings etc.

impress³ (impres´) *v.t.* (*Hist.*) **1** to compel (men) to enter government service. **2** to seize or set apart (goods, property etc.) for the public service. **impressment** *n.*

impression (impresh´ən) *n.* **1** an effect produced upon the senses, feelings etc. **2** a strong, esp. favourable, effect (*She made quite an impression on me*). **3** a vague notion or belief (*My impression is they're worried*). **4** an imitation or impersonation. **5 a** the act of impressing a mark. **b** the mark made by impressing. **6** a copy taken from type, an engraved plate etc. **7** a reprint from standing type, as distinct from an edition. **8 a** the total number of copies of a book printed at one time. **b** the act of printing these. **9** in dentistry, an imprint of the teeth and gums obtained by pressing them into a soft substance such as wax. **impressionable** *a.* easily impressed. **impressionability** (-bil´-) *n.* **impressionably** *adv.* **impressional** *a.* **impressionism** *n.* **1** an artistic movement that began in France and was based on the principle that the hand should paint what the eye sees, thus ruling out established conventions of lighting and composition. **2** a style of writing or music that seeks to suggest a mood or feeling rather than to give a precise description. **impressionist** *n.* **1** an entertainer who impersonates well-known people. **2** an exponent of impressionism. ~*a.* of or relating to impressionism. **impressionistic** (-nis´-) *a.* **1** in an impressionist style. **2** not systematic. **impressionistically** *adv.*

imprimatur (imprimā´tə, -ah´tə) *n.* **1** a licence to print a book, granted by the Roman Catholic Church. **2** official sanction or approval.

imprint[1] (imprint´) *v.t.* **1** to impress, to stamp. **2** to print. **3** to establish firmly or impress (on the mind). **4** (*Biol.*) to cause (a young animal) to undergo the process of imprinting. **imprinting** *n.* (*Biol.*) the process by which young animals develop the tendency to recognize and be attracted to members of their own species.

imprint[2] (im´print) *n.* **1** a mark, stamp or impression. **2** the name of the printer or publisher of a book, periodical etc., with the place and usu. the date of publication (on the title-page or at the end of a book).

imprison (impriz´ən) *v.t.* **1** to put into prison. **2** to confine, to hold in custody or captivity. **imprisonment** *n.*

impro (im´prō) *n.* (*pl.* **impros**) (*coll.*) **1** improvisation. **2** an instance of improvising.

improbable (improb´əbəl) *a.* **1** not likely to be true. **2** not likely to happen. **improbability** (-bil´-) *n.* **improbably** *adv.*

improbity (imprō´biti) *n.* (*pl.* **improbities**) **1** lack of probity; wickedness. **2** dishonesty. **3** a dishonest or wicked act.

impromptu (impromp´tū) *adv.* off-hand, without previous study. ~*a.* done or said off-hand, extempore. ~*n.* (*pl.* **impromptus**) **1** an extempore speech, performance, act etc. **2** a short piece of music, often for the piano, and sometimes having the character of an improvisation.

improper (improp´ə) *a.* **1** unbecoming, indecent. **2** unsuitable. **3** not accurate, wrong. **improper fraction** *n.* a fraction in which the numerator is equal to or greater than the denominator. **improperly** *adv.*

impropriety (impreprī´əti) *n.* (*pl.* **improprieties**) **1** the quality of being improper, indecency. **2** an unbecoming act, expression etc. **3** incorrectness. **4** unfitness.

improve (improov´) *v.t.* **1** to make better. **2** to increase the value of (land etc.) by cultivating or building. ~*v.i.* **1** to become better. **2** to increase in value. **to improve on/ upon** to achieve something better than. **improvement** *n.* **1 a** the act of

improving or the state of being improved. **b** an instance of improving or being improved. **2** something which is added or done to something in order to improve it. **3** a beneficial or valuable addition or substitute. **4** something which has been improved. **improver** *n.* **improving** *a.* tending to improve and edify.

improvident (improv´idənt) *a.* **1** neglecting to make provision for the future. **2** thriftless. **3** careless, heedless. **improvidence** *n.* **improvidently** *adv.*

improvise (im´prəvīz) *v.t.*, *v.i.* **1** to play, sing or perform, composing as one goes along. **2** to do or make without prior preparation, using the materials to hand. **improvisation** (-zā´shən) *n.* **improvisational** *a.* **improvisator** (-prov´izātə) *n.* **improvisatorial** (-vizətaw´-), **improvisatory** (-viz´ətəri) *a.* **improviser** *n.*

imprudent (improo´dənt) *a.* rash, incautious, indiscreet. **imprudence** *n.* **imprudently** *adv.*

impudent (im´pūdənt) *a.* **1** rude and disrespectful. **2** lacking in shame or modesty. **impudence** *n.* **impudently** *adv.* **impudicity** (-dis´-) *n.* immodesty, shamelessness.

impugn (impūn´) *v.t.* to call in question, to contradict, to gainsay. **impugnable** *a.* **impugner** *n.* **impugnment** *n.*

impulse (im´pŭls) *n.* **1** a sudden desire or whim (*I bought it on impulse*). **2** an influence acting suddenly on the mind tending to produce action. **3** the application or effect of an impelling force. **4** a stimulus, an inspiration. **5** (*Physics*) **a** a large force acting for an extremely short time. **b** the momentum due to such a force. **6** a disturbance passing along a nerve or muscle. **impulse buying** *n.* the act of buying something on a sudden whim. **impulsion** (-pŭl´shən) *n.* **1** the act of impelling or the state of being impelled. **2** impetus. **3** a compulsion. **impulsive** (-pŭl´-) *a.* **1** resulting from or liable to be actuated by impulse rather than reflection. **2** communicating impulse, urging forward. **3** (*Physics*) acting momentarily, not continuous. **impulsively** *adv.* **impulsiveness** *n.*

impunity (impū´niti) *n.* exemption from punishment or the unpleasant consequences of an action. **with impunity** without having to suffer unpleasant consequences.

impure (impūə´) *a.* **1** not pure; mixed with other substances, adulterated. **2** defiled, unclean. **3** unchaste. **4** mixed with other colours. **impurely** *adv.* **impureness** *n.* **impurity** *n.* (*pl.* **impurities**) **1** the state or quality of being impure. **2** something that is impure. **3** a small amount of foreign matter added to a semiconductor.

impute (impūt´) *v.t.* **1** to ascribe or attribute (esp. something dishonourable) to a person. **2** (*Theol.*) to ascribe (righteousness, guilt etc.) on account of another. **imputable** *a.* **imputation** (-tā´shən) *n.* **1** the act of imputing. **2** something which is imputed as a charge or fault. **3** reproach, censure. **4** (*Theol.*) the attributing of righteousness or personal guilt and its consequences to a person or persons, on account of another. **imputative** *a.* **imputatively** *adv.* **imputer** *n.*

In *chem. symbol* indium.

in (in) *prep.* **1** denoting presence or situation within the limits of time, place, circumstance etc. (*in Europe*; *in prison*; *in my pocket*). **2** during (*in 1996*; *in the afternoon*). **3** within a certain period of time (*The cafe closes in 20 minutes*). **4** working in the field of (*in advertising*). **5** wearing (*in a suit*; *in red*). **6** taking part in (*in a play*). **7** with respect to (*cloudy in places*; *shot in the arm*). **8** as a proportion to (*one in five*). **9** arranged as (*in a line/circle*). **10** having the condition of; suffering from (*in danger*; *in poverty*). **11** as regards the content (*There's nothing in these rumours*). **12 a** using a particular way of talking (*in a loud voice*; *They spoke in Dutch*). **b** (of music) having as its key (*quartet in D major*). **13** using a particular material (*drawn in ink*). **14** within the capabilities of (*He doesn't have it in him*). **15** (of a word) having as its beginning or ending (*nouns in -um*). **16** in the person of (*You have a loyal friend in Sue*). **17** (of an animal) pregnant with (*in foal*). **18** used with verbs to express motion or change (*Divide it in two*; *Put it in the oven*). **19** used to introduce an indirect object after a verb (*believe in*; *confide in*). **20** forming adverbial and prepositional phrases (*in favour of*; *in fact*). ~*adv.* **1** within or inside some place (*I went in*; *We were shut in*). **2** indoors, at home (*Are you in this evening?*). **3** inwards (*Massage it in*). **4** in office. **5** in favour (*Our luck is in*). **6** in fashion (*Miniskirts are in*). **7** (of fruit etc.) in season. **8** in a book, newspaper etc. (*The article is in tomorrow*). **9** (of a ball, serve etc.) within the playing area. **10** in cricket, at the wicket. **11** (of a train, boat etc.) having arrived (*Her flight's not in yet*). **12** sent in (*Applications must be in by Friday*). **13** (of a fire) burning. **14** (of the tide) at its highest point. ~*a.* **1** directed inwards. **2** internal, living inside (*in-patients*). **3** fashionable (*It's the in thing at the moment*). **4** understood by a select group only. **in absentia** (*coll.*) in (his, her etc.) absence. **in as far as** in so far as. **in as much as** inasmuch as. **in at** present at (*in at the start*). **ins and outs** the intricacies or details (of). **in so far as** in such measure as. **in that 1** seeing that; since. **2** in so far as. **to be in for 1** to be about to experience (esp. something unpleasant) (*You're in for a disappointment*). **2** to be committed to or involved in. **3** to be entered for (a race etc.). **in-between** *a.* (*coll.*) intermediate. **in-car** *a.* happening or situated in a car. **in-depth** *a.* detailed, thorough, comprehensive. **in-flight** *a.* available or occurring during an aeroplane flight. **in-house** *a.* of or relating to, or employed within, a particular organization, company etc. ~*adv.* within a particular organization, company etc. **in-joke** *n.* a joke only understood by a select group. **in-line** *a.* **1** forming a part of a sequence of processes or operations. **2** (of an engine) having its cylinders

arranged in a line. **in-line skate** *n.* a type of roller skate with a single row of small wheels fitted to the side of the boot. **in-patient** *n.* a person in hospital receiving regular treatment. **in-service** *a.* (of training) given to employees to improve their skills. **in-store** *a.*, *adv.* inside a store. **in-tray** *n.* a tray holding letters and documents to be dealt with. **in-your-face, in your face** *a.* (*sl.*) offering a direct challenge, aggressively provocative.

in. *abbr.* inch, inches.

in-[1] (in) *pref.* in, into, within, on, against, towards, as in *indicate*, *induce*.

in-[2] (in) *pref.* not, without, as in *incomprehensible*, *inequality*.

-in[1] (in) *suf.* (*Chem.*) **1** denoting neutral compounds, and usu. distinct from alkaloids and basic compounds in -INE, e.g. *albumin*, *casein*. **2** denoting certain enzymes, as in *pepsin*. **3** denoting pharmaceutical products, as in *aspirin*.

-in[2] (in) *comb. form* indicating a gathering for common activity (*sit-in*; *work-in*).

inability (inəbil′iti) *n.* **1** the state of being unable (to do, understand etc.). **2** lack of power or means.

inaccessible (inəkses′ibəl) *a.* **1** that cannot be reached, attained, or approached. **2** (of a person) not affable, not encouraging advances. **inaccessibility** (-bil′-), **inaccessibleness** *n.* **inaccessibly** *adv.*

inaccurate (inak′ūrət) *a.* not accurate. **inaccuracy** *n.* (*pl.* **inaccuracies**) **inaccurately** *adv.*

inaction (inak′shən) *n.* **1** inactivity; a lack of action. **2** sluggishness. **inactivate** *v.t.* to make inactive. **inactivation** (-ā′shən) *n.* **inactive** *a.* **1** not active. **2** sluggish, inert. **3** idle, indolent. **inactively** *adv.* **inactivity** (-tiv′-) *n.*

inadequate (inad′ikwət) *a.* **1** not adequate; insufficient. **2** unable to cope. **inadequacy** *n.* (*pl.* **inadequacies**). **inadequately** *adv.*

inadmissible (inədmis′ibəl) *a.* (of evidence) that cannot be admitted, allowed or received. **inadmissibility** (-bil′-) *n.* **inadmissibly** *adv.*

inadvertent (inədvœ′tənt) *a.* **1** (of an action) unintentional, accidental. **2** not paying attention. **3** heedless, careless, negligent. **inadvertence, inadvertency** *n.* **inadvertently** *adv.*

inadvisable (inədvī′zəbəl) *a.* not advisable. **inadvisability** (-bil′-) *n.*

inalienable (inā′liənəbəl) *a.* that cannot be alienated or transferred. **inalienability** (-bil′-) *n.* **inalienably** *adv.*

inalterable (inawl′tərəbəl) *a.* incapable of alteration. **inalterability** (-bil′-) *n.* **inalterably** *adv.*

inane (inān′) *a.* **1** silly, fatuous. **2** empty, void. **inanely** *adv.* **inaneness** *n.* **inanition** (inənish′ən) *n.* **1** exhaustion from lack of food or nourishment. **2** emptiness, voidness. **inanity** (inan′-) *n.* (*pl.* **inanities**).

inanimate (inan′imət) *a.* **1** not living; lacking any sign of life. **2** not endowed with life; not animate. **3** void of animation, dull, lifeless. **inanimately** *adv.* **inanimation** (-ā´shən) *n.*

inapplicable (inap´likəbəl, -əplik´-) *a.* **1** not applicable. **2** irrelevant. **inapplicability** (-bil´-), **inapplicableness** *n.* **inapplicably** *adv.*

inapposite (inap´əzit) *a.* not apposite; not pertinent. **inappositely** *adv.* **inappositeness** *n.*

inappropriate (inəprō´priət) *a.* not appropriate, unsuitable. **inappropriately** *adv.* **inappropriateness** *n.*

inapt (inapt´) *a.* **1** not apt; unsuitable. **2** not skilful. **inaptitude, inaptness** *n.* **inaptly** *adv.*

Usage note See note under INEPT.

inarch (inahch´) *v.t.* to graft (a plant) by inserting a scion, without separating it from the parent tree, into a stock.

inarguable (inah´gūəbəl) *a.* that cannot be disputed. **inarguably** *adv.*

inarticulate (inahtik´ūlət) *a.* **1** unable to express oneself clearly. **2** not uttered with distinct articulation, indistinct. **3** dumb. **4** (*Biol.*) not articulated, not jointed. **inarticulacy** (-si), **inarticulateness** *n.* **inarticulately** *adv.*

inartistic (inahtis´tik) *a.* **1** not designed, done etc., according to the principles of art. **2** not having artistic taste or ability. **inartistically** *adv.*

inasmuch (inəzmŭch´) *adv.* (*followed by as*) seeing that; since; in so far as.

inattention (inəten´shən) *n.* **1** lack of attention; heedlessness; negligence. **2** disregard of courtesy. **inattentive** *a.* **inattentively** *adv.* **inattentiveness** *n.*

inaudible (inaw´dibəl) *a.* not audible, that cannot be heard. **inaudibility** (-bil´-) *n.* **inaudibly** *adv.*

inaugurate (inaw´gūrāt) *v.t.* **1** to install or induct into office solemnly or with appropriate ceremonies. **2** to commence, introduce, or celebrate the opening of with some degree of formality, solemnity, pomp or dignity. **inaugural** *a.* of, relating to or performed at an inauguration. ~*n.* an inaugural address. **inauguration** (-rā´shən) *n.* **inaugurator** *n.* **inauguratory** *a.*

inauspicious (inawspish´əs) *a.* **1** unlucky, unfortunate. **2** ill-omened, unfavourable. **inauspiciously** *adv.* **inauspiciousness** *n.*

inauthentic (inawthen´tik) *a.* not authentic. **inauthenticity** (-tis´iti) *n.*

inboard (in´bawd) *adv.* within the sides or towards the middle of a ship, aircraft or vehicle. ~*a.* situated thus (*inboard motor*). ~*prep.* inside, within (a ship etc.).

inborn (in´bawn) *a.* innate, naturally inherent.

inbreathe (inbrēdh´) *v.t.* **1** to draw in (breath). **2** to inspire.

inbred (inbred´, in´bred) *a.* **1** innate, inborn, natural. **2** produced as a result of inbreeding.

inbreed (inbrēd´) *v.t.* (*past, p.p.* **inbred** (-bred´)) to breed from closely related individuals. **inbreeding** *n.*

inbuilt (in´bilt) *a.* that is included as a part of something.

Inc. (ingk) *abbr.* Incorporated.

Inca (ing´kə) *n.* a member of a South American Indian people in Peru until the Spanish conquest in 1531. **Incaic** (-kā´ik), **Incan** *a.*

incalculable (inkal´kūləbəl) *a.* **1** that cannot be reckoned or estimated in advance. **2** too vast or numerous to be calculated. **3** not to be reckoned upon, uncertain. **incalculability** (-bil´-), **incalculableness** *n.* **incalculably** *adv.*

in camera CAMERA.

incandesce (inkandes´) *v.i.* to glow with heat. ~*v.t.* to cause to glow with heat. **incandescence** *n.* **incandescent** *a.* **1** glowing with heat. **2** strikingly radiant or bright. **incandescently** *adv.*

incantation (inkantā´shən) *n.* **1** a formula, said or sung, supposed to add force to magical ceremonies; a charm. **2** the recitation of such formulas. **incantational** *a.* **incantatory** (-kan´tə-) *a.*

incapable (inkā´pəbəl) *a.* **1** not physically, intellectually, or morally capable (of). **2** lacking power, ability, or fitness (of doing, committing etc.). **3** not susceptible (of). **4** unable to take care of oneself, esp. as a result of being incapacitated by drink. **incapability** (-bil´-), †**incapableness** *n.* **incapably** *adv.*

incapacitate (inkəpas´itāt) *v.t.* **1** to render incapable; to disable. **2** to render unfit; to disqualify. **incapacitant** *n.* **incapacitated** *a.* **incapacitation** (-ā´shən) *n.*

incapacity (inkəpas´iti) *n.* (*pl.* **incapacities**) **1** a lack of power or capacity; inability. **2** legal disqualification. **3** an instance of incapacity.

incarcerate (inkah´sərāt) *v.t.* to imprison; to shut up or confine. **incarceration** (-ā´shən) *n.* **incarcerator** *n.*

incarnate[1] (inkah´nət) *a.* **1** invested or clothed with flesh, embodied in flesh, esp. in human form. **2** typified, personified.

incarnate[2] (in´kahnāt, inkah´nāt) *v.t.* **1** to embody in flesh. **2** to embody (an idea) in a living form. **3** to be the embodiment of. **incarnation** (-nā´shən) *n.* **1** the act of assuming flesh. **2** embodiment, esp. in human form. **3** (**Incarnation**) Christ's assumption of human nature. **4** a vivid exemplification or personification (of).

incase ENCASE.

incautious (inkaw´shəs) *a.* lacking in caution; rash, unwary. **incaution** *n.* **incautiously** *adv.* **incautiousness** *n.*

incendiary (insen´diəri) *a.* **1** of or relating to the malicious burning of property. **2** exciting or tending to excite factions, seditions or quarrels; inflammatory. **3** (of a device, substance) capable of causing fires or igniting readily. ~*n.* (*pl.* **incendiaries**) **1** a person who maliciously sets fire to property etc. **2** an incendiary bomb. **3** a person who excites factions, seditions etc. **incendiarism** *n.*

incense[1] (in´sens) *n.* **1** a mixture of fragrant gums, spices etc. used for producing perfumes when burnt, esp. in religious rites. **2** the smoke of this. **3** any agreeable perfume. **4** flattery; adulation. *~v.t.* **1** to perfume with or as with incense. **2** to offer incense to.

incense² (insens´) *v.t.* to inflame, to enrage.

incentive (insen´tiv) *n.* **1** something which acts as a motive, incitement or spur (to action). **2** a payment or benefit offered to workers to encourage greater output. *~a.* inciting, urging. **incentivize, incentivise** *v.t.* to stimulate to further activity by offering incentives.

inception (insep´shən) *n.* a beginning. **inceptive** *a.* **1 a** beginning, commencing. **b** initial. **2** (*Gram.*) denoting the beginning of an action. *~n.* a verb that denotes the beginning of an action.

incertitude (insœ´titūd) *n.* uncertainty.

incessant (inses´ənt) *a.* unceasing, continual. **incessancy** *n.* **incessantly** *adv.* **incessantness** *n.*

incest (in´sest) *n.* sexual intercourse between persons who are considered to be too closely related to marry. **incestuous** (-tūəs) *a.* **1** guilty of or involving incest. **2** (of a group etc.) inward-looking, closed to external influences etc. **incestuously** *adv.* **incestuousness** *n.*

inch (inch) *n.* **1** the 12th part of a linear foot (2.54 cm). **2** (as a unit of measurement) the quantity of rainfall that would cover the surface of the ground to the depth of one inch. **3** an amount of pressure, atmospheric or other, equivalent to the weight of a column of mercury one inch high in a barometer. **4** a small amount or degree (*He would not give an inch; Give someone an inch and they'll take a mile*). **5** (*pl.*) stature. *~v.t.* to drive by inches or small degrees. *~v.i.* to move in this way. **every inch 1** entirely, from head to foot (*He was every inch a gentleman*). **2** the whole area (*She knows every inch of the city*). **inch by inch** bit by bit; gradually; by very small degrees. **within an inch of** very close to. **inchworm** *n.* MEASURING WORM¹.

-in-chief (inchēf´) *comb. form* leading, most important, as *commander-in-chief.*

inchoate (inkō´āt, in´-, -ət) *a.* **1** only begun, commenced. **2** incomplete, undeveloped, rudimentary. **inchoative** *a.* incipient; indicating the beginning of an action.

Usage note The adjectives *inchoate* and *incoherent* should not be confused: *inchoate* means just begun, and *incoherent* lacking intelligibility or consistency.

---

incident (in´sidənt) *n.* **1** an event or occurrence, esp. one of a picturesque or striking nature. **2** a relatively minor event that might lead to a more serious dispute between two countries (*a frontier/ diplomatic incident*). **3** a distinct episode in a narrative. **4** (*Law*) a privilege, burden etc. legally attaching to property etc. *~a.* **1** likely to happen. **2** naturally appertaining or belonging (to). **3** consequent (on). **4** falling or striking (on or upon). **incidence** *n.* **1** the fact, manner or

frequency of occurrence. **2** the scope, bearing or range of influence of something. **3** the act or state of falling on or upon. **4** (*Physics*) the direction in which a body, a ray of light, heat etc. falls upon any surface. **incidental** (-den´təl) *a.* **1** happening in connection with something that is more important; casual; fortuitous. **2** concomitant, naturally connected with or related to. **3** liable to occur. *~n.* **1** something that is incidental. **2** (*pl.*) casual expenses. **incidentally** *adv.* **1** by the way. **2** in an incidental way. **incidental music** *n.* music used to accompany the action of a film, play etc.

incinerate (insin´ərāt) *v.t.* to burn completely; to reduce to ashes. **incineration** (-ā´shən) *n.* **incinerator** *n.* a furnace or receptacle in which refuse etc. is burned.

incipient (insip´iənt) *a.* beginning; in the first stages. **incipience, incipiency** *n.* **incipiently** *adv.*

incise (insīz´) *v.t.* **1** to cut into. **2** to engrave. **incision** (-sizh´ən) *n.* **1** the act of incising. **2** a cut; a gash; a notch. **incisive** (-siv) *a.* **1** sharp, acute. **2** trenchant, penetrating. **3** clear and direct. **4** having a sharp cutting edge. **incisively** *adv.* **incisiveness** *n.*

incisor (insī´zə) *n.* a pointed tooth at the front of the mouth, adapted for cutting or dividing food.

incite (insīt´) *v.t.* to stir up; to prompt (to action). **incitation** (insitā´shən) *n.* **1** the act of inciting. **2** something which incites. **3** an incitement. **incitement** *n.* **inciter** *n.* **incitingly** *adv.*

incl. *abbr.* including.

inclement (inklem´ənt) *a.* rough, severe, stormy. **inclemency** (-si) *n.* (*pl.* **inclemencies**). **inclemently** *adv.*

incline¹ (inklīn´) *v.i.* **1** to be disposed (to). **2** to have a tendency (to) (*I incline to agree*). **3** to deviate from any direction that is regarded as the normal one. **4** to bend down or forwards. *~v.t.* **1** (*usu. pass.*) to give an inclination, leaning or tendency to (*I'm inclined to believe her*). **2** to cause (the head or body) to bend down, to bow. **3** to cause to deviate from a line or direction. **inclination** (-klinā´shən) *n.* **1** a disposition or tendency (to, towards). **2** a liking or preference (for). **3** the act of inclining or bending. **4** a deviation from any direction regarded as the normal one. **5** (*Geom.*) the angle that a plane makes with another, esp. a horizontal or vertical plane. **6** the angle that the earth's magnetic field makes with the horizontal. **inclinational** *a.* **inclined** *a.* **inclined plane** *n.* one of the mechanical powers, consisting of a plane set at an acute angle to the horizon. **incliner** *n.*

incline² (in´klīn) *n.* an inclined plane; a slope, a gradient.

include (inklood´) *v.t.* **1** to contain or to comprise as a part, member etc. **2** to put in or classify as part of a set etc. **3** to enclose, to confine (within). **to include out** (*coll. or facet.*) to exclude. **included** *a.* **1** enclosed. **2** contained, comprised.

inclusion (inkloo´zhən) *n.* **inclusive** (inkloo´siv) *a.* **1** including, containing (*prices inclusive of VAT*). **2** including everything (*The rent is £400 a month inclusive*). **3** including the limits specified (*from the 1st to the 8th inclusive*). **4 a** not restricted to certain sections of society. **b** (of language) that includes rather than excludes particular members of society, esp. women, e.g. by avoiding the use of the masculine pronoun to refer to both men and women. **inclusively** *adv.* **inclusiveness** *n.*

incog (inkog´) *a., adv., n.* (*coll.*) INCOGNITO.

incognito (inkognē´tō, inkog´nitō) *a., adv.* with one's real name or identity disguised or kept secret. ~*n.* (*pl.* **incognitos**) **1** a person who is incognito. **2** an assumed identity.

incoherent (inkəhiə´rənt) *a.* **1** inarticulate, unable to express oneself intelligibly. **2** lacking cohesion; disconnected; inconsistent. **3** (*Physics*) (of waves) not having the same phase. **incoherence** *n.* **incoherency** *n.* (*pl.* **incoherencies**). **incoherently** *adv.*

Usage note See note under INCHOATE.

incombustible (inkəmbŭs´tibəl) *a.* incapable of being burnt or consumed by fire. **incombustibility** (-bil´-) *n.*

income (in´kəm) *n.* the amount of money (usu. annual) accruing as payment, profit, interest etc. from labour, business, profession or property. **income group** *n.* a section of the population receiving incomes within a certain range. **income support** *n.* in Britain, a social security payment made to the unemployed or people on low incomes, such as part-time workers. **income tax** *n.* a tax levied for state purposes on incomes above a certain amount.

incomer (in´kŭmə) *n.* **1** a person who comes in. **2** an immigrant. **3** an intruder. **4** a person who succeeds another. **incoming** *a.* **1** coming in. **2** entering; immigrant. **3** succeeding. **4** accruing. ~*n.* **1** an entrance or arrival. **2** (*usu. pl.*) income, gain, revenue.

incommensurable (inkəmen´shərəbəl) *a.* **1** having no common standard and not able to be compared. **2** not fit or worthy to be compared (with). **3** (*Math.*) having no common factor (with another integral or fractional number or quantity). ~*n.* (*usu. pl.*) something that is incommensurable. **incommensurability** (-bil´-) *n.* **incommensurably** *adv.* **incommensurate** (-rət) *a.* **1** not commensurate or proportionate (to or with); inadequate. **2** incommensurable. **incommensurately** *adv.* **incommensurateness** *n.*

incommode (inkəmōd´) *v.t.* to cause trouble or inconvenience to. **incommodious** *a.* **1** cramped, too small. **2** inconvenient. **incommodiously** *adv.* **incommodiousness** *n.*

incommunicable (inkəmū´nikəbəl) *a.* **1** that cannot be communicated to or shared with another. **2** not communicative. **incommunicability** (-bil´-), **incommunicableness** *n.* **incommunicably**

adv. **incommunicative** *a.* **incommunicatively** *adv.* **incommunicativeness** *n.*

incommunicado (inkəmūnikah´dō) *a.* **1** with no means of communication with the outside world. **2** in solitary confinement.

incomparable (inkom´pərəbəl) *a.* **1** not to be compared (to or with). **2** unequalled, peerless. **incomparability** (-bil´-), **incomparableness** *n.* **incomparably** *adv.*

Usage note Pronunciation of *incomparable* as (-par´-), with stress on the third syllable, is best avoided.

incompatible (inkəmpat´ibəl) *a.* **1** opposed in nature or quality; discordant. **2** inconsistent (with). **3** (of two people) unable to cooperate, live or work together. **4** (of drugs, blood groups) not suited for use together because of harmful effects. **5** (of machines etc.) incapable of being used together. ~*n.* (*often pl.*) an incompatible person or thing. **incompatibility** (-bil´-), **incompatibleness** *n.* **incompatibly** *adv.*

incompetent (inkom´pitənt) *a.* **1** lacking in ability or fitness for a task (*an incompetent manager*). **2** showing a lack of skill or ability (*incompetent handling of the dispute*). **3** (*Law*) (of a witness) lacking legal fitness or qualification. ~*n.* an incompetent person. **incompetence, incompetency** *n.* **incompetently** *adv.*

incomplete (inkəmplēt´) *a.* not complete; not perfect. **incompletely** *adv.* **incompleteness, incompletion** *n.*

incomprehensible (inkomprihen´sibəl) *a.* that cannot be conceived or understood. **incomprehensibility** (-bil´-), **incomprehensibleness** *n.* **incomprehensibly** *adv.* **incomprehension** (-shən) *n.* a failure to understand.

inconceivable (inkənsē´vəbəl) *a.* **1** not conceivable; incomprehensible. **2** (*coll.*) incredible, most extraordinary. **inconceivability** (-bil´-), **inconceivableness** *n.* **inconceivably** *adv.*

inconclusive (inkənkloo´siv) *a.* (of evidence, a discussion etc.) not conclusive or decisive. **inconclusively** *adv.* **inconclusiveness** *n.*

incondensable (inkənden´səbəl) *a.* not condensable; not reducible to a liquid or solid condition.

incongruous (inkong´gruəs) *a.* **1** not fitting, improper, out of place. **2** not congruous, not agreeing or harmonizing (with). **incongruent** *a.* **incongruity** (-groo´-) *n.* (*pl.* **incongruities**). **incongruously** *adv.* **incongruousness** *n.*

inconsequent (inkon´sikwənt) *a.* **1** irrelevant. **2** illogical. **3** disconnected. **inconsequence** *n.* **inconsequential** (-kwen´-) *a.* **1** of no consequence, trivial. **2** not consequential, inconsequent. **inconsequentiality** (-kwenshial´-) *n.* (*pl.* **inconsequentialities**). **inconsequentially** *adv.* **inconsequentialness** *n.* **inconsequently** *adv.*

inconsiderable (inkənsid´ərəbəl) *a.* **1** small. **2** not deserving consideration; insignificant. **inconsiderableness** *n.* **inconsiderably** *adv.*

inconsiderate (inkənsid´ərət) *a.* **1** hasty, incautious. **2** having no consideration for the feelings of others. **inconsiderately** *adv.* **inconsiderateness** *n.* **inconsideration** (-ā´shən) *n.*

inconsistent (inkənsis´tənt) *a.* **1** not in keeping; incompatible (with). **2** (of behaviour etc.) not uniform, changeable. **3** self-contradictory, not agreeing with itself or oneself. **inconsistency** *n.* (*pl.* **inconsistencies**). **inconsistently** *adv.*

inconsolable (inkənsō´ləbəl) *a.* (of a person, grief etc.) not to be consoled. **inconsolability** (-bil´-), **inconsolableness** *n.* **inconsolably** *adv.*

inconsonant (inkon´sənənt) *a.* not consonant, discordant (with). **inconsonance** *n.* **inconsonantly** *adv.*

inconspicuous (inkənspik´ūəs) *a.* not conspicuous; not easy to see. **inconspicuously** *adv.* **inconspicuousness** *n.*

inconstant (inkon´stənt) *a.* **1** not constant, changeable, fickle. **2** variable, unsteady, irregular. **inconstancy** *n.* (*pl.* **inconstancies**). **inconstantly** *adv.*

incontestable (inkəntes´təbəl) *a.* indisputable, undeniable, unquestionable. **incontestability** (-bil´-) *n.* **incontestably** *adv.*

incontinent (inkon´tinənt) *a.* **1** unable to restrain one's desires, esp. sexual desires. **2** (*Med.*) not able to control the passing of waste from the body. **3** lacking control (of). **incontinence, incontinency** *n.* **incontinently** *adv.*

incontrovertible (inkontrəvœ´tibəl) *a.* incontestable, indisputable. **incontrovertibility** (-bil´-), **incontrovertibleness** *n.* **incontrovertibly** *adv.*

inconvenience (inkənvēn´yəns) *n.* **1** the quality or state of being inconvenient. **2** something which inconveniences, a cause of difficulty. ~*v.t.* to put to inconvenience; to trouble. **inconvenient** *a.* **1** not convenient. **2** causing or tending to cause trouble, awkward. **inconveniently** *adv.*

incorporate (inkaw´pərāt) *v.t.* **1** to unite or combine into one body (with). **2** to combine (ingredients) into one mass. **3** to form into a legal corporation. **4** to receive into a corporation. ~*v.i.* to become united or incorporated (with another substance, society etc.) so as to form one body or whole. **incorporated** *a.* forming a legal corporation. **incorporation** (-ā´shən) *n.* **incorporator** *n.*

incorporeal (inkawpaw´riəl) *a.* **1** not having a body or material form. **2** spiritual or metaphysical. **incorporeality** (-al´-), **incorporeity** (-rē´-, -rā´-) *n.* **incorporeally** *adv.*

incorrect (inkərekt´) *a.* **1** wrong, inaccurate, inexact. **2** improper, unbecoming. **incorrectly** *adv.* **incorrectness** *n.*

incorrigible (inkor´ijibəl) *a.* **1** bad beyond hope of amendment. **2** not easily improved. **incorrigibility** (-bil´-), **incorrigibleness** *n.* **incorrigibly** *adv.*

incorrupt (inkərŭpt´) *a.* **1** not corrupt; pure. **2** not decayed, marred or impaired. **incorruptible** *a.* **1** not to be bribed; high-principled. **2** incapable of corruption, decay or dissolution;

eternal. **incorruptibility** (-bil´-) *n.* **incorruptibly** *adv.*

increase[1] (inkrēs´) *v.i.* to become greater in quantity, number, value, degree etc. ~*v.t.* to make greater in number, quantity, value etc. **increasable** *a.* **increasingly** *adv.*

increase[2] (in´krēs) *n.* **1** the act, state or process of increasing; growth, multiplication. **2** the amount by which something increases. **on the increase** increasing.

incredible (inkred´ibəl) *a.* **1** not credible; difficult to believe. **2** (*coll.*) very great, amazing. **incredibility** (-bil´-), **incredibleness** *n.* **incredibly** *adv.*

incredulous (inkred´ūləs) *a.* indisposed to believe, sceptical (of). **incredulity** (-dū´-), **incredulousness** *n.* **incredulously** *adv.*

increment (in´krimənt) *n.* **1** an increase, esp. one of a series. **2** the amount of increase. **3** the act or process of increasing. **incremental** (-men´-) *a.* **incrementally** *adv.*

incriminate (inkrim´ināt) *v.i.* **1** to make seem guilty (*incriminating evidence*). **2** to charge with a crime. **3** to involve (a person) in a charge. **incrimination** (-ā´shən) *n.* **incriminatory** *a.*

incrustation (inkrŭstā´shən) *n.* **1** the act or process of encrusting. **2** a crust or hard coating on a surface etc. **3** a facing or lining of marble, stone etc. on masonry. **incrust** ENCRUST.

incubate (ing´kūbāt) *v.t.* **1** to sit on or artificially heat (eggs) until the young birds etc. emerge. **2** to cause (bacteria etc.) to develop. **3** to evolve (a plan etc.) by meditation. ~*v.i.* **1** to sit on eggs for hatching, to brood. **2** to undergo incubation. **3** to evolve slowly. **incubation** (-bā´shən) *n.* **1** the act or process of incubating or hatching. **2** brooding, as of a hen upon eggs. **3** meditation on a scheme etc.; brooding. **4** (*Med.*) (*also* **incubation period**) the period between infection and the development of symptoms of a disease. **incubative, incubatory** *a.* **incubator** *n.* an apparatus for hatching eggs by artificial heat, for developing bacteria etc., or rearing a child prematurely born.

incubus (ing´kūbəs) *n.* (*pl.* **incubi** (-bī)) **1** a demon supposed to have sexual intercourse with women at night. **2** a nightmare. **3** any person, thing or influence that oppresses or disturbs.

inculcate (in´kəlkāt) *v.t.* to impress upon the mind by emphasis or frequent repetition. **inculcation** (-kā´shən) *n.* **inculcator** *n.*

inculpate (in´kəlpāt) *v.t.* **1** to charge with participation in a crime. **2** to blame. **inculpation** (-pā´shən) *n.* **inculpative** (-kŭl´-), **inculpatory** *a.*

incumbent (inkŭm´bənt) *a.* **1** imposed (upon) as a duty or obligation. **2** currently holding a post or office. **3** lying or resting (on); pressing or weighing (upon). ~*n.* a person in possession of an office etc., esp. one of the clergy. **incumbency** (-si) *n.* (*pl.* **incumbencies**).

incunabulum (inkūnab´ūləm) *n.* (*pl.* **incunabula** (-lə)) an early printed book, esp. one printed before AD 1500.

incur (inkœ´) *v.t.* (*pres.p.* **incurring**, *past, p.p.* **incurred**) to render oneself liable to or bring upon oneself (risk, injury, punishment etc.). **incurable** *a.*

incurable (inkūə´rəbəl) *a.* that cannot be cured or healed. ~*n.* a person suffering from an incurable disease. **incurability** (-bil´-), **incurableness** *n.* **incurably** *adv.*

incurious (inkūə´riəs) *a.* **1** not curious or inquisitive. **2** indifferent, heedless. **incuriosity** (-os´-), **incuriousness** *n.* **incuriously** *adv.*

incursion (inkœ´shən) *n.* **1** a sudden raid. **2** an irruption. **incursive** *a.*

incurvate (inkœ´vāt) *v.t.* to cause to curve inwards. **incurvation** (-vā´shən) *n.*

incurve (inkœv´) *v.t.* INCURVATE.

incus (ing´kəs) *n.* (*pl.* **incudes** (ingkū´dēz, ing´-)) one of the small bones of the ear, shaped rather like an anvil and connected to the malleus and stapes.

Ind. *abbr.* **1** Independent. **2** India. **3** Indian.

indebted (indet´id) *a.* **1** being under a debt or obligation (to or for). **2** owing money (to). **indebtedness** *n.*

☒ **indecate** common misspelling of INDICATE.

indecent (indē´sənt) *a.* **1** unbecoming, unseemly. **2** offensive to modesty or propriety. **indecency** (-si) *n.* (*pl.* **indecencies**). **indecent assault** *n.* a sexual assault that does not involve rape. **indecent exposure** *n.* the offence of publicly exposing a part of the body, esp. the genitals, in breach of accepted standards of decency. **indecently** *adv.*

indecision (indisizh´ən) *n.* lack of decision; irresolution. **indecisive** (-sī´-) *a.* **1** not decisive, final, or conclusive. **2** irresolute, vacillating, hesitating. **indecisively** *adv.* **indecisiveness** *n.*

indeclinable (indiklī´nəbəl) *a.* **1** (*Gram.*) having no inflections. **2** that cannot be declined. **indeclinably** *adv.*

indecorous (indek´ərəs) *a.* violating propriety, decorum or good manners; improper. **indecorously** *adv.* **indecorousness** *n.*

indeed (indēd´) *adv.* **1** in reality, in truth (*It is, indeed, an extraordinary claim*). **2** used to express emphasis (*It's very unusual indeed*). **3** used to express concession (*There are indeed some disadvantages*). **4** in point of fact (*if indeed you can call it that*). **5** used to express disbelief, surprise, or annoyance (*'Paul said so.' - 'Did he indeed?'*). ~*int.* used to express surprise, irony, interrogation etc.

indefatigable (indifat´igəbəl) *a.* not yielding to fatigue or exertion; unwearied, unremitting. **indefatigability** (-bil´-), **indefatigableness** *n.* **indefatigably** *adv.*

indefensible (indifen´sibəl) *a.* incapable of being defended, excused or justified. **indefensibility** (-bil´-) *n.* **indefensibly** *adv.*

indefinable (indifī´nəbəl) *a.* that cannot be defined. **indefinably** *adv.*

indefinite (indef´init) *a.* **1** not limited or defined, not determinate. **2** vague, uncertain.

3 (*Gram.*) (of certain adjectives, adverbs and pronouns) not defining or determining the persons, things etc. **indefinite article** *n.* (*Gram.*) a word (*a* or *an* in English) used before a noun and indicating lack of specificity. **indefinitely** *adv.* **indefiniteness** *n.*

indehiscent (indihis´ənt) *a.* (*Bot.*) (of fruits) not opening to set free the seeds.

indelible (indel´ibəl) *a.* **1** that cannot be blotted out or effaced. **2** (of ink) that makes indelible marks. **indelibility** (-bil´-), **indelibleness** *n.* **indelibly** *adv.*

indelicate (indel´ikət) *a.* **1** lacking delicacy or tact. **2** coarse, unrefined. **3** offensive to modesty or propriety. **indelicacy** *n.* (*pl.* **indelicacies**). **indelicately** *adv.*

indemnify (indem´nifī) *v.t.* (*3rd pers. sing. pres.* **indemnifies**, *pres.p.* **indemnifying**, *past, p.p.* **indemnified**) **1** to secure from damage, loss, penalty or responsibility (*The insurance indemnifies the house against fire*). **2** to compensate (a person) for loss, damage etc. **indemnification** (-fikā´shən) *n.*

indemnity (indem´niti) *n.* (*pl.* **indemnities**) **1** security against damage, loss or penalty. **2** compensation for damage, loss or penalties incurred. **3** a sum paid as such compensation, esp. by a defeated state to the victor as a condition of peace. **4** legal exemption from liabilities or penalties incurred.

indent[1] (indent´) *v.t.* **1** (*Print.*) to set (a line of text) further in from the margin than the rest of the paragraph. **2** to order (goods), esp. from abroad. **3** to notch or cut into as with teeth. **4** to make recesses in (a coastline etc.). ~*v.i.* to make an official requisition (upon). **indentation** (-tā´shən) *n.* **1** the act or process of indenting. **2** a notch, dent or incision, esp. in a margin. **3** a deep recess, esp. in a coastline. **indenter**, **indentor** *n.* **indention** *n.* **1** (*Print.*) the setting in of a line of print farther from the margin; indentation. **2** an instance of this.

indent[2] (in´dent) *n.* **1** an indented line of text. **2** an indentation or recess. **3** an official order for stores. **4** an order for goods, esp. one from abroad.

indent[3] (indent´) *v.t.* **1** to dent; to make a dent in. **2** to impress (a mark, dent etc.).

indenture (inden´chə) *n.* **1** an agreement or contract under seal, esp. one binding an apprentice to a master. **2** an official voucher, certificate, register etc. **3** an indentation. ~*v.t.* (*Hist.*) to bind (esp. an apprentice) by an indenture. **indentureship** *n.*

independence (indipen´dəns) *n.* the quality or state of being independent (from, of). **independent** *a.* **1 a** not dependent upon or subject to the control, power or authority of another. **b** free to manage one's own affairs without the interference of others. **2 a** able to support oneself financially. **b** making it possible to live comfortably without having to work (*an independent* *income*). **3** confident and capable of acting by oneself. **4** unwilling to accept help from others. **5** not affiliated with or part of a larger organization. **6** not depending on anything for its value, cogency etc. **7** not funded by the state (*an independent school*). ~*n.* a person who exercises their judgement and choice of action without dependence on any person, party etc. **independently** *adv.*

indescribable (indiskrī´bəbəl) *a.* **1** too fine, bad etc. to be described. **2** vague, imprecise. **indescribability** (-bil´-) *n.* **indescribably** *adv.*

❌ **indespensable** common misspelling of INDISPENSABLE.

indestructible (indistrŭk´tibəl) *a.* incapable of being destroyed. **indestructibility** (-bil´-) *n.* **indestructibly** *adv.*

indeterminable (inditœ´minəbəl) *a.* **1** that cannot be determined or defined. **2** (of a dispute etc.) that cannot be terminated. **indeterminably** *adv.*

indeterminate (inditœ´minət) *a.* **1** not fixed or limited in scope, nature etc. **2** indefinite, not precise. **3** (*Math.*) having no fixed value. **indeterminacy** (-si), **indeterminateness** *n.* **indeterminately** *adv.* **indeterminate vowel** *n.* a vowel with an obscure or slurred sound, such as the *a* in *advice*; a schwa.

indetermination (inditœminā´shən) *n.* **1** lack of determination, vacillation. **2** the state of being indeterminate.

index (in´deks) *n.* (*pl.* **indexes, indices** (-disēz) **1** a list of names, subjects, places etc. in alphabetical order, with page references, usu. at the back of a book. **2** CARD INDEX (under CARD¹). **3** THUMB INDEX (under THUMB). **4** a numerical scale indicating variations in the cost of living, wages etc., by reference to a given base level. **5** (*Math.*) an exponent (indicating powers of multiplication). **6** (*Med., Physics*) a number expressing a ratio or property (*cranial, refractive index*). **7** a pointer on a dial, watch etc. **8** a sign, token or indicator. **9** (*Comput.*) a value that identifies an element in a set of data. **10** a printed symbol in the shape of a pointing hand, used to point to a note, paragraph etc. ~*v.t.* **1** to provide (a book) with an index. **2** to enter (a word etc.) in an index. **3** to relate (interest rates, wages etc.) to an index. **indexation** (-sā´shən) *n.* **indexer** *n.* **index finger** *n.* the forefinger. **indexical** (-dek´-) *a.* **index-linked** *a.* (of wages, pensions etc.) increasing or decreasing in direct relation to changes in an index, esp. the cost of living index. **index-linking** *n.*

Indian (in´diən) *a.* **1** of or relating to India or the Indian subcontinent (India, Pakistan and Bangladesh). **2** of or relating to the aboriginal inhabitants of America. ~*n.* **1** a native or inhabitant of India. **2** an American Indian. **3** any of the languages spoken by the aboriginal peoples of America. **Indian club** *n.* either of two bottle-shaped clubs used in gymnastic exercises to develop the arm muscles. **Indian corn** *n.* maize. **Indian elephant** *n.* the elephant, *Elephas maximus*, that lives in India and SE Asia and is smaller than the African elephant. **Indian file** *n.* single file. **Indian hemp** *n.* the plant *Cannabis sativa*. **Indian ink** *n.* **1** a black pigment, composed of lamp black and animal glue, orig. made in China and Japan. **2** a black liquid ink made from this. **Indian summer** *n.* **1** summer-like weather, occurring in late autumn. **2** a time of calm or of renewed success or activity towards the end of a particular period, e.g. the end of a person's life. **India paper** *n.* **1** a fine paper, originally imported from China, used by engravers for taking proofs. **2** a very thin tough opaque paper, used esp. for printing Bibles. **India rubber** *n.* a soft, elastic substance obtained from the coagulated juice of certain tropical plants; rubber.

Usage note See note on *Native American* under AMERICAN.

Indic (in´dik) *a.* of or relating to the Indian branch of the Indo-European languages.

indicate (in´dikāt) *v.t.* **1** to show, to point out. **2** to be a sign or token of. **3** (*usu. pass.*) to require; to call for. **4** to state briefly, to suggest. **5** (of an instrument) to show a reading of. ~*v.i.* to show which way one is going to turn using an indicator. **indication** (-ā´shən) *n.* **1** the act of indicating. **2** something which indicates or suggests. **3** something that is indicated as advisable or suitable. **4** a reading shown by a gauge etc. **indicative** (-dik´ə-) *a.* **1** serving as a sign or indication (of); suggestive (of). **2** (*Gram.*) (of a mood of verbs) expressing fact. ~*n.* **1** the indicative mood. **2** a verb in this mood. **indicatively** *adv.* **indicator** *n.* **1** a person who or something which indicates. **2** a device for indicating the times of departure etc. of trains. **3** a device, esp. a flashing light, on a vehicle to show an intention to change direction. **indicatory** (indik´ətəri, in´dikātəri) *a.*

indices INDEX.

indict (indīt´) *v.t.* to charge (a person) with a crime or misdemeanour, esp. by means of an indictment. **indictable** *a.* **1** (of a person) liable to be indicted. **2** (of an offence) forming a ground of indictment. **indictee** (-tē´) *n.* a person indicted. **indicter** *n.* **indictment** *n.* **1** the act of indicting. **2** a formal accusation of a crime or misdemeanour, presented upon oath by the grand jury to a court. **3** the document embodying this. **4** something that provides a reason for condemnation (*a damning indictment of government policy*).

indie (in´di) *a.* (*coll.*) (of pop music) produced by a small independent record company. ~*n.* **1** an independent record company. **2** an independent film company.

indifferent (indif´rənt) *a.* **1** unconcerned, apathetic (*They were indifferent to our plight*). **2** having no inclination or disinclination (to); impartial. **3** neither good nor bad. **4** of no importance, of little moment (to). **5** of a barely passable quality, not good. **6** chemically neutral, not active. **indifference** *n.* **1** lack of interest or attention (to or towards). **2** impartiality, neutrality. **3** unimportance, insignificance. **indifferently** *adv.*

indigenous (indij´ənəs) *a.* **1 a** (of plants and animals) naturally existing in a region, not exotic. **b** (of people) not immigrant or descended from immigrants, native. **2** natural, innate (to). **indigenize** (indij´ənīz), **indigenise** *v.t.* **1** to expose to native influence; to make indigenous. **2** to subject to an increase in the number of indigenous people in administration etc. **indigenization** (-zā´shən) *n.* **indigenously** *adv.*

indigent (in´dijənt) *a.* in want, poor, needy. **indigence** *n.* **indigently** *adv.*

indigest (indijest´) *a.* shapeless. **indigested** *a.* **1** not well formed or ordered. **2** shapeless. **3** not digested. **indigestible** *a.* **1** not easily digested. **2** hard to understand or to follow. **indigestibility** (-bil´-) *n.* **indigestibly** *adv.* **indigestion** (-chən) *n.* **1** difficulty in digesting food, dyspepsia. **2** pain and belching caused by this. **indigestive** *a.*

indignant (indig´nənt) *a.* feeling or showing indignation, esp. at meanness, injustice etc. **indignantly** *adv.* **indignation** (-nā´shən) *n.* a feeling of anger and scorn provoked by supposed injustice or unfairness.

indignity (indig´niti) *n.* (*pl.* **indignities**) **1** undeserved contemptuous treatment; humiliation. **2** a slight, an insult.

indigo (in´digō) *n.* (*pl.* **indigos, indigoes**) **1 a** a violet-blue dye obtained from the indigo plant. **b** a dye of this colour produced synthetically. **2** a plant of the genus *Indigofera*, esp. *I. tinctoria*. **3** (*also* **indigo blue**) a violet-blue colour. ~*a.* (*also* **indigo blue**) of a violet-blue colour.

indirect (indirekt´, -dī-) *a.* **1** not direct, deviating from a direct line. **2** not resulting directly or immediately from a cause (*an indirect consequence*). **3** avoiding direct reference to something. **4** not open or straightforward. **indirectly** *adv.* **indirectness** *n.* **indirect object** *n.* (*Gram.*) a person or thing indirectly affected by an action, e.g. *them* in *She bought them some flowers.* **indirect question** *n.* (*Gram.*) a question that is reported rather than expressed in direct speech, as in *She asked me where I lived.* **indirect speech** *n.* the reporting of spoken or written discourse by indicating what was meant rather than by repetition of the exact words, as in *He said he would be late.* **indirect tax** *n.* a tax levied on goods and services rather than on a person's income or a company's profits.

indiscernible (indisœ´nibəl) *a.* not discernible, not distinguishable. **indiscernibility** (-bil´-), **indiscernibleness** *n.* **indiscernibly** *adv.*

indiscipline (indis´iplin) *n.* lack of discipline.

indiscreet (indiskrēt´) *a.* **1** not discreet. **2** injudicious, incautious, rash. **indiscreetly** *adv.*

indiscretion (-kresh´ən) *n.* **1** lack of discretion. **2** imprudence, rashness. **3** an indiscreet act.

Usage note The spellings of the adjectives *indiscreet* (not circumspect) and *indiscrete* (not distinct) should not be confused.

indiscrete (indiskrēt´) *a.* not discrete or separated.

Usage note See note under INDISCREET.

indiscriminate (indiskrim´inət) *a.* **1** not discriminating or making distinctions. **2** confused, promiscuous. **indiscriminately** *adv.* **indiscriminateness, indiscrimination** (-ā´shən) *n.* **indiscriminative** *a.*

indispensable (indispen´səbəl) *a.* **1** that cannot be dispensed with; absolutely necessary or requisite. **2** (of a law, duty etc.) that cannot be disregarded or set aside. **indispensability** (-bil´-), **indispensableness** *n.* **indispensably** *adv.*

indispose (indispōz´) *v.t.* **1** to make disinclined or unfavourable (to or towards). **2** to render unfit or unable (for or to). **indisposed** *a.* **1** disinclined, unwilling. **2** slightly ill. **indisposition** (-pəzish´ən) *n.* **1** disinclination. **2** aversion. **3** a slight illness.

indisputable (indispū´təbəl) *a.* **1** that cannot be disputed or doubted. **2** not open to question. **indisputability** (-bil´-), **indisputableness** *n.* **indisputably** *adv.*

indissoluble (indisol´ūbəl) *a.* **1** that cannot be dissolved or disintegrated. **2** (of a bond etc.) stable and binding. **indissolubility** (-bil´-), **indissolubleness** *n.* **indissolubly** *adv.*

indistinct (indistingkt´) *a.* **1** not distinct, obscure. **2** confused, faint. **indistinctive** *a.* not distinctive. **indistinctively** *adv.* **indistinctiveness** *n.* **indistinctly** *adv.* **indistinctness** *n.*

indistinguishable (indisting´gwishəbəl) *a.* not distinguishable (from). **indistinguishableness** *n.* **indistinguishably** *adv.*

indite (indīt´) *v.t.* **1** (*formal or facet.*) to put into words, to compose. **2** (*formal or facet.*) to write. **inditement** *n.* **inditer** *n.*

indium (in´diəm) *n.* (*Chem.*) a soft, silver-white metallic element, at. no. 49, chem. symbol In, occurring in minute quantities in zinc ores.

individual (individ´ūəl) *a.* **1** subsisting as a single indivisible entity. **2** single, particular as opposed to general. **3** separate or distinct. **4** characteristic of a particular person or thing, distinctive. **5** designed for one person. ~*n.* **1** a single person, esp. when regarded as distinct or separate from a group. **2** a single member of a species, class etc. **3** (*coll.*) a person. **individualism** *n.* **1** conduct or feeling centred in self, egoism. **2** an attitude, tendency or system in which each individual works for their own ends. **individualist** *n.* **individualistic** (-is´-) *a.* **individualistically** *adv.* **individuality** (-al´-) *n.* (*pl.* **individualities**) **1** separate or distinct existence. **2** distinctive character. **individualize, individualise** *v.t.* **1** to mark out or distinguish from other individuals. **2** to specify. **3** to package separately. **4** to make so as to suit the needs of a particular person. **individualization** (-zā´shən) n. **individually** adv. **1** separately. **2** in an individual capacity. **3** in an individual manner. **individuate** (individ´ūāt) v.t. **1** to give individuality to. **2** to make an individual or a distinct entity. **individuation** (-ā´shən) n.

indivisible (indiviz´ibəl) a. not divisible. **indivisibility** (-bil´-) n. **indivisibly** adv.

Indo- (in´dō) comb. form Indian.

indoctrinate (indok´trināt) v.t. **1** to teach (someone) to accept, esp. without questioning, a set of beliefs. **2** to instruct. **indoctrination** (-ā´shən) n. **indoctrinator** n.

Indo-European (indōūrəpē´ən), †**Indo-Germanic** a. **1** of or relating to the family of languages spoken over most of Europe and over Asia as far as northern India. **2** of or relating to the hypothetical language from which this family originates. ~n. **1** the Indo-European language family. **2** the hypothetical language from which the languages of this family originate.

indolent (in´dələnt) a. habitually idle or lazy. **indolence** n. **indolently** adv.

indomitable (indom´itəbəl) a. **1** untamable, unconquerable. **2** stubbornly determined. **indomitability** (-bil´-), **indomitableness** n. **indomitably** adv.

Indonesian (indənē´zhən) a. of or relating to Indonesia, its people or language. ~n. a native or inhabitant of Indonesia.

indoor (in´daw) a. being or done inside a building or under cover. **indoors** (-dawz´) adv. into or within a house or other building.

indorse ENDORSE.

indrawn (in´drawn) a. **1** drawn in. **2** detached and aloof.

indubitable (indū´bitəbəl) a. that cannot be doubted or questioned. **indubitably** adv.

induce (indūs´) v.t. **1** to lead by persuasion or reasoning, to prevail on (to do something). **2** to bring about, to cause. **3** (Med.) to bring on or speed up (labour) by artificial means, as by the use of drugs. **4** to produce (an electric current) by induction. **5** (Physics) to produce (radioactivity) by bombardment with neutrons or high-energy particles. **6** (Logic) to derive as a deduction, to infer. **inducement** n. **1** the act of inducing. **2** something which induces. **inducer** n. **inducible** a.

induct (indŭkt´) v.t. **1** to put in possession of an ecclesiastical benefice or of any office, with the customary forms and ceremonies. **2** to initiate (into). **3** (N Am.) to enlist for military service. **inductance** n. the property of an electric circuit that causes an electromotive force to be generated by a change in the current passing through it. **inductee** (-tē´) n. (N Am.) a military conscript. **induction** (indŭk´shən) n. **1** (Logic) **a** the process of inferring a law or general principle from

particular instances, as distinct from deduction. **b** a general statement or conclusion attained by this kind of reasoning. **2** (Math.) the proving of the universal truth of a theorem by showing it to be true of any case in a series or of a particular case. **3 a** the production of an electric or magnetic state by the proximity or movement of an electric or magnetized body. **b** the production of an electric current in a conductor by changes in the magnetic field. **4** a formal introduction to or instalment in an office or position (an induction course). **5** (N Am.) enlistment for military training. **inductional** a. **induction coil** n. an apparatus for producing a high voltage from a low voltage. **induction heating** n. the heating of a conductive material as a result of an induced electric current passing through it. **induction loop** n. a sound system in which a wire looped around an area in a theatre, cinema etc. emits electromagnetic signals which can be picked up by hearing aids for the partially deaf. **inductive** a. **1** (Logic) proceeding or characterized by induction. **2** of or relating to electric or magnetic induction. **inductively** adv. **inductiveness** n. **inductor** (indŭk´tə) n. **1** any part of an electrical apparatus acting inductively. **2** a person who inducts a member of the clergy into office.

indue ENDUE.

indulge (indŭlj´) v.t. **1** to yield to (a desire, whim etc.). **2** to favour; to gratify the wishes, whims etc. of. ~v.i. **1** to yield to one's desires (in). **2** (coll.) to take alcoholic drink, esp. in excess. **indulgence** (indŭl´jəns) n. **1** the act or practice of indulging, yielding or complying to a desire etc. **2** an indulgent act, a favour or privilege granted. **3** a pleasurable thing or habit indulged in. **4** in the Roman Catholic Church, a remission of the temporal punishment still due for sin after sacramental absolution. **indulgent** a. indulging or disposed to indulge the wishes, whims or caprices of others. **indulgently** adv.

industry (in´dəstri) n. (pl. **industries**) **1** useful work, esp. mechanical and manufacturing pursuits as distinct from agriculture and commerce. **2** any branch of these. **3** diligence, steady application to any business or pursuit. **4** the employment of labour in production. **5** any field of activity as organized for economic gain. **industrial** (indŭs´triəl) a. **1** of or relating to industry. **2** (of a country) characterized by advanced and sophisticated industries. **3** used in industry (industrial detergents). **industrial action** n. action, esp. a strike or go-slow, taken by employees as a protest. **industrial archaeology** n. the study of the remains of past industrial activity. **industrial espionage** n. attempting to obtain trade secrets by dishonest means. **industrial estate** n. an industrial area specially planned to provide employment in factories of different kinds. **industrialism** n. an economic or social system based on industry. **industrialist** n. a person engaged in management or ownership of industry. **industrialize, industrialise** v.t. to introduce industry to (a country or region). ~v.i. to develop industries. **industrialization** (-zā´shən) n. **industrially** adv. **industrial relations** n.pl. the relations between employer and employees in industries. **industrial-strength** a. (often facet.) strong. **industrial tribunal** n. a tribunal which makes judgements on disputes between employers and employees regarding unfair dismissal, discrimination etc. **industrious** (indŭs´triəs) a. diligent and assiduous. **industriously** adv. **industriousness** n.

Indy (in´di) n. a kind of motor racing, practised chiefly in the US, in which cars race at very high speeds around oval circuits. **Indycar** n. a car used in Indy racing.

-ine (īn, in, ēn) suf. 1 forming adjectives meaning of or relating to or of the nature of, as *crystalline, divine, equine, hyacinthine, marine*. 2 forming feminine nouns, as *heroine, landgravine*, and abstract nouns, as *discipline, medicine*. 3 (Chem.) forming names of alkaloids and basic substances, as *cocaine, morphine*.

inebriate¹ (inē´briāt) v.t. 1 to make drunk. 2 to intoxicate or exhilarate. **inebriation** (-ā´shən) n. **inebriety** (-brī´-) n.

inebriate² (inē´briət) a. intoxicated, drunk. ~n. a habitual drunkard.

inedible (ined´ibəl) a. not edible; not suitable for eating. **inedibility** (-bil´-) n.

ineducable (ined´ūkəbəl) a. incapable of being educated, esp. because of mental handicap. **ineducability** (-bil´-) n.

ineffable (inef´əbəl) a. 1 unutterable, beyond expression. 2 too sacred to be spoken. **ineffability** (-bil´-), **ineffableness** n. **ineffably** adv.

ineffaceable (inifā´səbəl) a. that cannot be rubbed out or obliterated. **ineffaceability** (-bil´-) n. **ineffaceably** adv.

ineffective (inifek´tiv) a. 1 not having an effect. 2 (of a person) inefficient. 3 not having artistic effect. **ineffectively** adv. **ineffectiveness** n.

ineffectual (inifek´chuəl) a. 1 not producing any effect or the desired effect; powerless. 2 (of a person) not able to achieve results, ineffective. **ineffectuality** (-al´-), **ineffectualness** n. **ineffectually** adv.

inefficacious (inefikā´shəs) a. not efficacious; producing no result or effect. **inefficaciously** adv. **inefficaciousness** n. **inefficacy** (-ef´-) n.

inefficient (inifish´ənt) a. 1 not efficient. 2 (of a person) lacking in ability or capacity. **inefficiency** n. **inefficiently** adv.

inelastic (inilas´tik) a. 1 not elastic. 2 inflexible. **inelastically** adv. **inelasticity** (-ēlastis´-) n.

inelegant (inel´igənt) a. not elegant; wanting in grace, polish, refinement etc. **inelegance, inelegancy** n. **inelegantly** adv.

ineligible (inel´ijibəl) a. 1 not eligible. 2 not suitable. **ineligibility** (-bil´-) n. **ineligibly** adv.

ineluctable (inilŭk´təbəl) a. 1 that cannot be escaped. 2 that cannot be overcome by struggling.

inept (inept´) a. 1 clumsy, incompetent. 2 silly, absurd. 3 not apt, fit or suitable. **ineptitude** (-titūd), **ineptness** n. **ineptly** adv.

Usage note The meanings of the adjectives *inept* and *inapt* overlap: both can mean unsuitable, but the more common sense of *inept* is clumsy, and it is best to restrict it to that use.

inequable (inek´wəbəl) a. 1 unfair. 2 not uniform.

inequality (inikwol´iti) n. (pl. **inequalities**) 1 a lack of equality. 2 variability. 3 irregularity, unevenness.

inequitable (inek´witəbəl) a. not equitable, not fair or just. **inequitably** adv. **inequity** n. (pl. **inequities**) 1 lack of equity, unfairness; injustice. 2 an instance of this.

ineradicable (inirad´ikəbəl) a. that cannot be eradicated. **ineradicably** adv.

inert (inœt´) a. 1 lacking inherent power of motion or active resistance to motive power applied. 2 slow, sluggish. 3 (Chem.) not chemically reactive. **inert gas** n. any of a group of gaseous elements that react very little with other elements. **inertia** (-shə) n. 1 reluctance to move or act. 2 a tendency to continue unchanged. 3 (Physics) a property of matter by which it persists in an existing state of rest or of uniform motion in a straight line, unless an external force changes that state. **inertial** a. **inertia-reel seat belt** n. a type of vehicle seat belt in which the belt unwinds freely except when violent deceleration of the vehicle causes it to lock. **inertia selling** n. the practice of sending unsolicited goods to householders and requesting payment if the goods are not returned. **inertly** adv. **inertness** n.

inescapable (iniskā´pəbəl) a. inevitable, that cannot be escaped or avoided.

inessential (inisen´shəl) a. 1 not essential or necessary. 2 dispensable. ~n. (often pl.) something that is inessential.

inestimable (ines´timəbəl) a. too valuable, great, excellent etc. to be estimated. **inestimably** adv.

inevitable (inev´itəbəl) a. 1 that cannot be avoided or prevented. 2 that is sure to happen or predictable (the inevitable car-chase scene). 3 (coll.) customary. **inevitability** (-bil´-), **inevitableness** n. **inevitably** adv.

inexact (inigzakt´) a. not exact, not precisely accurate. **inexactitude** (-titūd), **inexactness** n. **inexactly** adv.

inexcusable (inikskū´zəbəl) a. that cannot be excused or justified. **inexcusably** adv.

inexhaustible (inigzaws´tibəl) a. 1 that cannot be exhausted. 2 unfailing, unceasing. **inexhaustibility** (-bil´-), **inexhaustibleness** n. **inexhaustibly** adv.

inexorable (inek´sərəbəl) a. 1 relentless. 2 incapable of being persuaded or moved by entreaty or prayer. **inexorability** (-bil´-) n. **inexorably** adv.

inexpedient (inikspē´diənt) a. not expedient;

inadvisable, disadvantageous. **inexpedience, in-expediency** n.

inexpensive (inikspen´siv) a. not expensive, cheap. **inexpensively** adv. **inexpensiveness** n.

inexperience (inikspiə´riəns) n. lack of experience or of knowledge gained by experience. **inexperienced** a.

inexpert (inek´spœt) a. not expert, unskilful. **inexpertly** adv. **inexpertness** n.

inexplicable (iniksplik´əbəl, -ek´-) a. that cannot be explained. **inexplicability** (-bil´-), **inexplicableness** n. **inexplicably** adv.

inexplicit (inikspslis´it) a. not definitely or clearly stated.

inexpressible (inikspres´ibəl) a. incapable of being expressed or described. **inexpressibly** adv. **inexpressive** a. not expressive. **inexpressively** adv. **inexpressiveness** n.

inextinguishable (iniksting´gwishəbəl) a. incapable of being extinguished, quenched or repressed. **inextinguishably** adv.

in extremis (in ikstrē´mis) a. 1 in desperate circumstances, in extremity. 2 at the point of death.

inextricable (inek´strikəbəl, -strik´-) a. 1 that cannot be disentangled or solved. 2 inescapable. 3 intricately involved. **inextricability** (-bil´-) n. **inextricably** adv.

infallible (infal´ibəl) a. 1 exempt from liability to error or to failure. 2 (of a test, method etc.) certain not to fail. **infallibility** (-bil´-) n. **infallibleness** n. **infallibly** adv.

infamous (in´fəməs) a. 1 having a very bad reputation. 2 detestable, scandalous. **infamously** adv. **infamy** n. (pl. **infamies**) 1 total loss of reputation or character. 2 an infamous act.

infant (in´fənt) n. 1 a child during the earliest years of its life. 2 a schoolchild less than seven years old. 3 (Law) a minor. **infancy** (-si) n. (pl. **infancies**) 1 babyhood or early childhood. 2 an early stage in the development of something. 3 (Law) the state of being a minor. **infantile** (-tīl) a. 1 of or relating to infants or infancy. 2 characteristic of infancy, childish. 3 in its early stages of development. **infantile paralysis** n. poliomyelitis. **infant mortality** n. death before the age of one.

infanticide (infan´tisīd) n. 1 murder of a newborn infant. 2 the practice of killing newborn children. 3 the murderer of an infant. **infanticidal** (-sī´-) a.

infantry (in´fəntri) n. (pl. **infantries**) footsoldiers, usu. armed with small arms or rifle and bayonet; a branch of an army made up of such soldiers. **infantryman** n. (pl. **infantrymen**).

infarct (infahkt´, in´-) n. (Med.) an area of tissue that is dying from lack of blood supply. **infarction** n.

infatuate (infat´ūāt) v.t. 1 to inspire with an extravagant and usu. transitory passion. 2 to affect with folly or extravagance. **infatuated** a. **infatuation** (-ā´shən) n.

infect (infekt´) v.t. 1 to contaminate (water, food

etc.) with a bacterium, virus etc., and so cause disease. 2 to affect (a person) with the germs of disease. 3 (of a feeling, mood) to affect and spread to. 4 to imbue with noxious opinions etc. 5 (Comput.) to affect with a computer virus. **infection** n. 1 the act or process of infecting, esp. the communication of disease by means of water, the atmosphere etc., as distinct from contagion. 2 an infectious disease. 3 moral contamination. 4 (Comput.) the act of infecting with a computer virus. **infectious** a. 1 infecting or capable of infecting. 2 (of a disease) liable to be communicated by the atmosphere, water etc. 3 (of feelings etc.) apt to spread, catching. **infectiously** adv. **infectiousness** n. **infective** a. infectious. **infectiveness** (-tiv´-) n. **infector** n.

infelicitous (infilis´itəs) a. 1 not felicitous; unfortunate. 2 inappropriate, inept. **infelicitously** adv. **infelicity** n. (pl. **infelicities**) 1 unhappiness, misery. 2 misfortune. 3 inappropriateness, ineptness. 4 an inappropriate or inept remark, expression etc.

infer (infœ´) v.t. (pres.p. **inferring**, past, p.p. **inferred**) 1 to deduce as a fact, consequence or result; to conclude. 2 to imply. ~v.i. to draw inferences. **inferable, inferrable** a. **inference** (in´-) n. 1 the act of inferring. 2 (Logic) something which is inferred from premisses, a conclusion or deduction. **inferential** (-ren´-) a. **inferentially** adv.

Usage note It is best to avoid the use of infer to mean imply or suggest: although it has a long history, it is still widely disapproved of.

inferior (infiə´riə) a. 1 lower in place, rank, value, ability etc. 2 of mediocre or poor quality. 3 (of a printed character) set below ordinary letters or below the line, as the figures in H_2SO_4, subscript. ~n. 1 a person who is inferior to another in ability, rank etc. 2 an inferior figure or letter. **inferiority** (-or´-) n. **inferiority complex** n. a suppressed sense of inferiority which is sometimes compensated for by aggressive behaviour. **inferiorly** adv.

Usage note Inferior does not function as a true comparative in English, and should not be followed by than (the correct form is inferior to).

infernal (infœ´nəl) a. 1 of or relating to hell or the lower regions. 2 worthy of hell, hellish; diabolic. 3 (coll.) abominable, detestable. **infernally** adv. **inferno** (-nō) n. (pl. **infernos**) 1 hell, esp. as conceived by Dante. 2 any place or state of horror and confusion. 3 a blaze or conflagration.

infertile (infœ´tīl) a. not fertile; unfruitful. **infertility** (-til´-) n.

infest (infest´) v.t. (of vermin, parasites) to overrun, to swarm over in large numbers. **infestation** (-tā´shən) n. **infester** n.

infidel (in´fidel) a. disbelieving in religion or a

particular religion. ~*n.* a person who rejects religion or a particular religion. **infidelity** *n.* (*pl.* **infidelities**) **1** breach of trust, disloyalty, esp. unfaithfulness to the marriage vow. **2** an instance of this.

infield (in´fēld) *n.* **1 a** in cricket, the part of the field close to the wicket. **b** the cricketers fielding in this area. **2 a** in baseball, the ground within the base lines. **b** the players, other than the pitcher and catcher, who play in this area. **c** the positions of these players. **infielder** *n.*

infighting (in´fīting) *n.* **1** behind-the-scenes squabbling or jockeying for power within a group or organization. **2** fighting or boxing at close quarters, so that blows from the shoulder are impossible. **infighter** *n.*

infill (in´fil) *v.t.* to fill in. ~*n.* **1** (*also* **infilling**) closing up gaps, esp. between houses. **2** material for filling in holes etc.

infiltrate (in´filtrāt), **infilter** (-fil´-) *v.t.* **1** to secretly gain or cause to gain access or entrance to. **2 a** to cause (a fluid) to pass into the pores or interstices of a solid. **b** to permeate (a solid) in this way. ~*v.i.* **1** to secretly gain or cause someone to gain access or entrance to an enemy organization etc. **2** to permeate by infiltration. **infiltration** (-trā´shən) *n.* **infiltrator** *n.*

infinite (in´finit) *a.* **1** having no bounds or limits, endless. **2** very great (*infinite patience*). **3** numerous, very many. **4** (*Gram.*) (of a verb part) not limited by person or number. ~*n.* **1** (**the Infinite**) God. **2** (**the infinite**) infinite space. **infinitely** *adv.* **infiniteness** *n.* **infinitesimal** (-tes´iməl) *a.* infinitely or extremely small. ~*n.* an infinitesimal quantity. **infinitesimal calculus** *n.* differential and integral calculus. **infinitesimally** *adv.* **infinitude** (infin´itūd) *n.* **infinity** (infin´iti) *n.* (*pl.* **infinities**) **1** the state of being infinite. **2** an infinite amount or distance. **3** (*Math.*) an indefinite number of.

infinitive (infin´itiv) *a.* (*Gram.*) (of a verb) which expresses action without regard to person, tense etc., as *go* in *let me go* and *it's time to go.* ~*n.* **1** the infinitive form. **2** a verb in this form. **infinitival** (-tī´-) *a.* **infinitively, infinitively** *adv.*

infirm (infœm´) *a.* **1** lacking bodily strength or health, esp. through age or disease. **2** weakminded, irresolute. **infirmary** (infœ´məri) *n.* (*pl.* **infirmaries**) a hospital or place for the sick or injured. **infirmity** *n.* (*pl.* **infirmities**). **infirmly** *adv.*

infix (infiks´) *v.t.* **1** to fasten or fix in. **2** to implant firmly (in the mind).

in flagrante (in fləgran´ti), **in flagrante delicto** (dilik´tō) *adv.* whilst actually committing the misdeed.

inflame (inflām´) *v.t.* **1** to excite, to stir up strong feelings in (someone). **2** (*Med.*) to cause inflammation in; to make hot by exciting excessive action in the blood vessels and tissues. **3** to intensify, to aggravate. **4** to cause to blaze, to kindle. ~*v.i.* **1** to become excited or angry.

2 (*Med.*) to become inflamed. **3** to burst into a blaze.

inflammable (inflam´əbəl) *a.* **1** that may be easily set on fire. **2** easily excited. ~*n.* (*usu. pl.*) something that catches fire easily. **inflammability** (-bil´-), **inflammableness** *n.* **inflammably** *adv.*

Usage note It is safer to use *flammable*, which avoids possible misunderstanding of *inflammable* as its exact opposite, not easily set on fire. The corresponding negative is *non-flammable*.

inflammation (infləmā´shən) *n.* **1** (*Med.*) an abnormal physical condition characterized by heat, redness, swelling, pain and loss of function in the part affected. **2** the act of inflaming or the state of being inflamed. **inflammatory** (-flam´-) *a.* **1** exciting or arousing passions. **2** of or characterized by inflammation of the body.

inflate (inflāt´) *v.t.* **1** to cause (a balloon, mattress etc.) to expand by filling with air. **2** to make greater than normal or appropriate. **3** to raise (prices, reputation etc.) artificially or excessively. **inflatable** *a.* that can be inflated. ~*n.* **1** an inflatable toy, esp. an imitation castle etc. for children to jump or climb on. **2** anything inflatable. **inflated** *a.* **1** distended with air. **2** bombastic, turgid. **3** greater than normal or appropriate, exaggerated (*an inflated idea of one's own importance*). **inflation** *n.* **1** the act of inflating, the state of being inflated. **2** a systematic increase in prices over time. **3** an increase in the money supply, regarded as causing this. **inflationary** *a.* **inflationism** *n.* **inflationist** *n., a.*

inflect (inflekt´) *v.t.* **1** to modulate (the voice). **2** (*Gram.*) to change the form, esp. the ending of a word in order to express gender, tense, mood etc. **3** to bend, to curve. **inflection** (inflek´shən), **inflexion** *n.* **1** the act of inflecting or the state of being inflected; an instance of this. **2** modulation of the voice. **3** (*Gram.*) **a** the variation of the forms of nouns etc. in declension, and of verbs in conjugation. **b** an inflected form. **c** a suffix etc. added to a word to produce an inflected form, e.g. *s* or *ing*. **inflectional** *a.* **inflectionally** *adv.* **inflectionless** *a.* **inflective** *a.*

inflexible (inflek´sibəl) *a.* **1** incapable of being bent or curved. **2** firm; obstinate. **inflexibility** (-bil´-) *n.* **inflexibly** *adv.*

inflict (inflikt´) *v.t.* **1** (*sometimes facet.*) to impose (suffering, a penalty, oneself) on. **2** to deal out (defeat, a blow, wound etc.). **inflictable** *a.* **inflicter, inflictor** *n.* **infliction** *n.* **1** the act of inflicting. **2** a punishment inflicted. **3** a trouble, an annoyance. **inflictive** *a.*

Usage note See note under AFFLICT.

inflorescence (infləres´əns) *n.* (*Bot.*) **1** the flower head of a plant. **2** the arrangement of flowers upon a branch or stem. **3** the act or process of flowering.

inflow (in'flō) *n.* **1** a flowing in; an influx. **2** something that flows in. **inflowing** *n., a.*

influence (in'fluəns) *n.* **1** power to move, direct or control, ascendancy (over). **2** the effect of such power. **3** a person or thing exercising such power (on). ~*v.t.* **1** to exercise influence upon; to affect. **2** to bias, to sway. **under the influence** (*coll.*) drunk. **influencer** *n.* **influential** (-en'-) *a.* having great influence. **influentially** *adv.*

influent (in'fluənt) *a.* flowing in. ~*n.* a tributary.

influenza (influen'zə) *n.* a highly contagious virus infection, often occurring in epidemics, often characterized by muscular aches and pains, catarrh and fever. **influenzal** *a.*

influx (in'flŭks) *n.* **1** the arrival of a large number of people or things. **2** a flowing in of a stream, river (into).

info (in'fō) *n.* (*coll.*) information.

infomercial (infəmœ'shəl), **informercial** *n.* (*esp. NAm.*) a short film advertising something.

inform (infawm') *v.t.* **1** to communicate knowledge to, to tell (of, about). **2** to animate, to inspire (with feeling, vitality etc.). **3** to impart some essential quality to. ~*v.i.* to disclose facts about someone; to make an accusation (against) (*He threatened to inform on them*). **informant** *n.* **information** (infəma'shən) *n.* **1** something communicated; knowledge. **2** news (on, about) (*the latest information on the hijacking*). **3** (*Law*) a complaint or accusation presented to a court or magistrate. **4** (*Comput.*) data. **informational** *a.* **informationally** *adv.* **information retrieval** *n.* the storage, classification and recovery of esp. computerized information. **information science** *n.* the computerized processing and communication of data; the study of this. **information superhighway** *n.* a network of computer links, enabling users to communicate with each other internationally. **information technology** *n.* the gathering, processing and communication of information using computers, telecommunications etc. **informative** (-faw'-) *a.* conveying information; instructive. **informatively** *adv.* **informativeness** *n.* **informed** *a.* **1** having information. **2** based on knowledge of the facts (*an informed decision/judgement*). **3** educated (*an informed public*). **informer** *n.* **1** a person who informs against someone else. **2** a person who provides information or advice.

informal (infaw'məl) *a.* **1** without formality; relaxed (*an informal get-together*). **2** ordinary; everyday (*informal clothes*). **3** (of writing, language) containing everyday conventional vocabulary. **informality** (-mal'-) *n.* (*pl.* **informalities**). **informally** *adv.*

infotainment (infōtān'mənt) *n.* the presentation of news and current affairs as entertainment.

infra- (in'frə) *pref.* below, beneath, as *inframarginal, infraorbital.*

infraction (infrak'shən) *n.* (*Law*) a violation, an infringement. **infractor** *n.*

infra dig (infrə dig') *a.* (*coll.*) beneath one's dignity.

infra-red (infrəred'), **infrared** *a.* of, relating to or using electromagnetic radiation having a wavelength longer than that of the red end of the visible spectrum but shorter than that of microwaves. ~*n.* infra-red radiation.

infrastructure (in'frəstrŭkchə) *n.* **1** an underlying structure or basic framework. **2** roads, transport, schools etc. regarded as the basis of a country's economy. **3** a network of communications etc. essential for military operations etc. **infrastructural** *a.*

infrequent (infrē'kwənt) *a.* rare, uncommon, unusual. **infrequency, infrequence** *n.* **infrequently** *adv.*

infringe (infrinj') *v.t.* to break or violate (a law, contract etc.). ~*v.i.* to encroach, to intrude (on, upon). **infringement** *n.* **infringer** *n.*

infuriate (infū'riāt) *v.t.* to provoke to fury. **infuriating** *a.* **infuriatingly** *adv.*

infuse (infūz') *v.t.* **1** to pervade or fill (with) (*infused with optimism*). **2** to inculcate, to instil (vitality, life etc. into something). **3** to steep (tea, herbs) in liquid so as to extract the flavour. **4** to pour (into). ~*v.i.* (of tea, herbs) to be steeped in liquid so that the flavour is extracted. **infusable** *a.* **infuser** *n.* **infusion** (infū'zhən) *n.* **1** the liquid extract obtained by steeping any substance. **2** something which is instilled, an admixture. **3** the act of infusing. **4** (*Med.*) the introduction into the body of a fluid, e.g. via a drip. **infusive** (-siv) *a.* having the power of infusing.

Usage note The adjectives *infusable* and *infusible* should not be confused: *infusable* means able to be infused, and *infusible* unable to be fused.

infusible (infū'zibəl) *a.* that cannot be fused or melted. **infusibility** (-bil'-) *n.*

Usage note See note on INFUSABLE (under INFUSE).

-ing¹ (ing) *suf.* **1** forming verbal nouns denoting an action or its result, as *cleansing, hunting, painting, washing.* **2** forming nouns denoting an occupation or event, as *bricklaying, lumbering, soldiering, wedding.* **3** forming nouns denoting the material used in making something, as *roofing, scaffolding.*

-ing² (ing) *suf.* **1** forming the present participle of verbs, as *standing, talking.* **2** forming participial adjectives, as *charming, fleeting, horrifying.* **3** forming adjectives from nouns, as *hulking, whopping.* **-ingly** *suf.* forming adverbs, esp. denoting manner of action, as *fleetingly, unknowingly.*

-ing³ (ing) *suf.* forming nouns with the sense of belonging to or having the quality of, as *sweeting, shilling, atheling.*

ingenious (injēn'yəs) *a.* **1** skilful, clever, esp. at inventing or contriving. **2** cleverly designed or contrived. **ingeniously** *adv.* **ingeniousness** *n.* **ingenuity** (-jənū´-) *n.*

Usage note The adjectives *ingenious* and *ingenuous* should not be confused: *ingenious* means clever or inventive, and *ingenuous* candid or frank.

ingénue (īzhānū´) *n.* an ingenuous or naive girl, esp. such a character on the stage.

ingenuous (injen´ūəs) *a.* **1** innocent or artless. **2** open, candid, frank. **ingenuously** *adv.* **ingenuousness** *n.*

Usage note See note under INGENIOUS.

ingest (injest´) *v.t.* **1** to take (food) into the stomach. **2** to take in (facts, knowledge etc.). **ingestible** *a.* **ingestion** (-chən) *n.* **ingestive** *a.*

ingle (ing´gəl) *n.* **1** a fire on the hearth. **2** a fireplace. **inglenook** *n.* a chimney corner, an alcove by the side of a large fireplace.

inglorious (inglaw´riəs) *a.* **1** shameful, ignominious. **2** unknown, not famous. **ingloriously** *adv.* **ingloriousness** *n.*

ingoing (in´gōing) *a.* going in, entering.

ingot (ing´gət) *n.* a mass of metal, esp. steel, gold or silver, cast in a mould.

ingraft ENGRAFT.

ingrain¹ (ingrān´), **engrain** *v.t.* to cause (a dye etc.) to permeate something. **ingrained** *a.* **1** (of a habit, belief etc.) deeply imprinted. **2** (of dirt etc.) worked into the fibres, pores etc.

ingrain² (in´grān) *a.* **1** dyed in the grain or yarn before manufacture. **2** thoroughly imbued, inherent. ~*n.* a yarn or fabric dyed with fast colours before manufacture.

ingratiate (ingrā´shiāt) *v.t.* to insinuate (oneself) into goodwill or favour (with) another. **ingratiating** *a.* **ingratiatingly** *adv.* **ingratiation** (-ā´shən) *n.*

ingratitude (ingrat´itūd) *n.* lack of gratitude.

ingredient (ingrē´diənt) *n.* an element or a component part in a compound, recipe, mixture etc.

ingress (in´gres) *n.* **1** the act of entering, entrance. **2** power, right or permission to enter. **3** (*Astron.*) the start of an eclipse or occultation. **ingression** (-shən) *n.*

ingrowing (in´grōing) *a.* **1** growing inwards. **2** (of a toenail) growing abnormally into the flesh. **ingrown** *a.* **ingrowth** *n.*

inguinal (ing´gwinəl) *a.* of, relating to or situated near the groin.

inhabit (inhab´it) *v.t.* (*pres.p.* **inhabiting**, *past*, *p.p.* **inhabited**) to live or dwell in (a house, town etc.); to occupy. **inhabitable** *a.* **inhabitant** *n.* **inhabitation** (-ā´shən) *n.*

inhale (inhāl´) *v.t.* to breathe in, to draw into the lungs. ~*v.i.* to breathe in. **inhalant** *n.* **1** a medicinal preparation designed to be inhaled. **2** a substance inhaled by drug-abusers. ~*a.* **1** inhaling. **2** of or relating to inhalants. **inhalation** (-həlā´shən) *n.* **inhaler** *n.* **1** a person who inhales. **2** a respirator. **3** a device for inhaling vapours etc., esp. one for relieving nasal congestion.

inharmonious (inhahmō´niəs) *a.* (*Mus.*) not harmonious; unmusical. **inharmonic** (-mon´-) *a.* not harmonic. **inharmoniously** *adv.*

inhere (inhiə´) *v.i.* (*formal*) **1** to be an essential or necessary part (in). **2** to be vested (in). **inherent** (inher´ənt, -hiə´-) *a.* **1** inseparable from and permanently existing (in). **2** innate, inborn. **inherently** *adv.*

inherit (inher´it) *v.t.* (*pres.p.* **inheriting**, *past, p.p.* **inherited**) **1** to receive (property, a title etc.) by legal succession as the representative of a former possessor. **2** to derive (a characteristic etc.) from one's ancestors by genetic transmission. **3** to take over (a position etc.) from a predecessor. ~*v.i.* to take or come into possession as an heir. **inheritable** *a.* **inheritability** (-bil´-) *n.* **inheritance** *n.* **1** the act of inheriting. **2** something which is inherited. **3** hereditary succession to an estate etc. **inheritor** *n.* **inheritress** (-tris), **inheritrix** (-triks) *n.* a female inheritor.

inhibit (inhib´it) *v.t.* (*pres.p.* **inhibiting**, *past, p.p.* **inhibited**) **1** to restrain, to hinder, to put a stop to (an action, process etc.). **2** to prohibit, to forbid (from doing something). **inhibited** *a.* having inhibitions. **inhibition** (inibish´ən) *n.* **1** (*Psych.*) the unconscious restraining of an impulse or instinct. **2** (*coll.*) an inability to express a thought, action etc. because of feelings of embarrassment, shyness etc. (*He has no inhibitions about getting up on stage*). **3** the act of inhibiting; the state of being inhibited. **inhibitor** *n.* **inhibitory**, **inhibitive** (-hib´-) *a.*

inhospitable (inhəspit´əbəl, inhos´pit-) *a.* **1** not inclined to show hospitality to strangers. **2** (of a landscape, region etc.) affording no shelter, desolate. **inhospitableness** *n.* **inhospitably** *adv.*

inhuman (inhū´mən) *a.* **1** brutal; savage; unfeeling. **2** not human. **inhumanity** (-man´-) *n.* (*pl.* **inhumanities**) **1** brutality; savagery; barbarousness. **2** a barbarous act. **inhumanly** *adv.*

inhumane (inhūmān´) *a.* lacking in humanity. **inhumanely** *adv.*

inimical (inim´ikəl) *a.* **1** hostile. **2** adverse, unfavourable (to). **inimicality** (-kal´-), **inimicalness** *n.* **inimically** *adv.*

inimitable (inim´itəbəl) *a.* **1** that cannot be imitated; unique. **2** superb. **inimitability** (-bil´-), **inimitableness** *n.* **inimitably** *adv.*

iniquity (inik´witi) *n.* (*pl.* **iniquities**) **1** a lack of equity, gross injustice. **2** unrighteousness, wickedness. **iniquitous** *a.* **iniquitously** *adv.* **iniquitousness** *n.*

initial (inish´əl) *a.* placed at, or of or relating to, the beginning. ~*n.* **1** the first letter of a word. **2** (*pl.*) the first letters of a forename and surname. ~*v.t.* (*pres.p.* **initialling**, (*N Am.*) **initialing**, *past, p.p.* **initialled**, (*N Am.*) **initialed**) to mark with one's initials, as a guarantee of correctness, a sign of ownership etc. **initialism** *n.* **1** an abbreviation consisting of the initial letters of a series of words, each pronounced separately, e.g. DOE. **2** (*N Am.*) an acronym. **initialize, initialise** *v.t.*

(*Comput.*) **1** to run (a floppy disk) through a special program so as to make it ready for use. **2** to define the various settings of (a printer) so as to make it ready for use. **initial letter**, **initial consonant** *n.* a letter or consonant at the beginning of a word. **initially** *adv.*

initiate (inish´iāt) *v.t.* **1** to begin or originate. **2** to instruct (a person) in the rudiments or principles of something. **3** to admit (a person) into a society, association, secret etc., usu. with ceremonial rites. **initiation** (-ā´shən) *n.* **initiative** *a.* serving to begin or initiate. *~n.* **1** the energy and resourcefulness typical of those able to initiate new projects etc. (*We are looking for someone with flair and initiative*). **2** a first step. **3** the power or right to take the lead or originate (esp. legislation). **on one's own initiative** without being prompted by others. **to have the initiative** to have the advantage. **to take the initiative** to take action before others. **initiator** *n.* **initiatory** *a., n.*

inject (injekt´) *v.t.* **1** (*Med.*) to introduce (a fluid) into the body by or as if by a syringe. **2** to introduce or insert (*I tried to inject some humour into the discussion*). **3** to interject (a comment etc.). **injection** *n.* **1** the act of injecting. **2** something which is injected, esp. a fluid injected into the body. **3** the spraying of oil fuel into the cylinder of a compression-ignition engine. **injection moulding** *n.* the manufacture of rubber or plastic items by the injection of heated material into a mould. **injection-moulded** *a.* **injector** *n.*

injudicious (injudish´əs) *a.* done without judgement, unwise. **injudiciously** *adv.* **injudiciousness** *n.*

injunction (injŭngk´shən) *n.* **1** (*Law*) a writ or process whereby a party is required to do or (more usually) to refrain from doing certain acts. **2** an admonition, direction or order. **injunctive** *a.*

injure (in´jə) *v.t.* **1** to hurt, to damage (*Two people were badly injured in the accident*). **2** to do wrong or harm to. **3** to impair or diminish (*This may have injured their chances of winning*). **injured** *a.* **1** hurt (*her injured leg*). **2** offended (*an injured look*). **injurer** *n.* **injurious** (-joo´ri-) *a.* **1** wrongful. **2** hurtful; detrimental (to). **3** insulting, abusive. **injuriously** *adv.* **injuriousness** *n.*

injury (in´jəri) *n.* (*pl.* **injuries**) **1** damage, hurt, harm. **2** a wrong. **injury time** *n.* time added on to normal playing time in soccer, rugby etc. to compensate for interruptions to play on account of injuries.

injustice (injŭs´tis) *n.* **1** the quality of being unjust; unfairness. **2** a violation of justice, a wrong. **to do someone an injustice** to judge someone unfairly.

ink (ingk) *n.* **1** a coloured liquid or viscous material used in writing or printing. **2** (*Zool.*) the dark fluid exuded by a cuttlefish or octopus to cover its escape. *~v.t.* **1** to mark (in or over) with ink. **2** to cover (type) with ink before printing. **3** to blacken, daub or colour with ink. **to ink out** to blot out with ink. **ink-blot** *n.* (*Psych.*) a

standardized blot of ink used in the Rorschach test. **ink-blot test** *n.* RORSCHACH TEST. **ink-cap** *n.* any of several fungi of the genus *Coprinus*. **inker** *n.* **ink-jet printer** *n.* (*Comput.*) a computer printer that produces characters by sending tiny jets of electrically charged ink onto the paper. **ink-pad** *n.* a small pad, used for putting ink on a rubber stamp. **inkwell** *n.* a container for ink often fitted into a hole in a desk. **inky** *a.* (*comp.* **inkier**, *superl.* **inkiest**) **1** of the nature of or resembling ink. **2** discoloured with ink. **3** black as ink. **inkiness** *n.*

inkling (ing´kling) *n.* a hint; a slight suspicion or intimation (of).

inland (in´lənd, -land) *a.* **1** situated in the interior of a country away from the sea. **2** carried on within a country; domestic, not foreign. *~adv.* in or towards the interior of a country. *~n.* the interior of a country. **inland duty** *n.* a tax levied on domestic trade. **inland navigation** *n.* the passage of boats on rivers and canals.

in-law (in´law) *n.* (*pl.* **in-laws**) (*coll.*) a relation by marriage.

inlay[1] (inlā´) *v.t.* (*past, p.p.* **inlaid** (-lād´)) **1** to lay or insert in. **2** to decorate by inserting different materials such as wood or metal into a groundwork, leaving the surfaces even. **3** to insert (a print, picture etc.) into a space in a page. **inlaid** *a.* (of a piece of furniture etc.) decorated by inlaying. **inlayer** (in´-) *n.*

inlay[2] (in´lā) *n.* **1** material inlaid or prepared for inlaying. **2** inlaid work.

inlet (in´lət) *n.* **1** a small arm of the sea; a creek. **2** something inserted, e.g. in dressmaking. **3** a passage allowing fuel etc. into a machine. **4** a means of entrance.

in loco parentis (in lōkō pərən´tis) *adv.* in the place of a parent (used esp. of a teacher).

inmate (in´māt) *n.* a resident or occupant, esp. of a prison or institution.

in memoriam (in mimaw´riam) *prep.* in memory of. *~n.* an obituary.

inmost (in´mōst) *a.* **1** remotest from the surface; most inward. **2** deepest, most heartfelt, most secret.

inn (in) *n.* **1** a public house providing alcoholic drink and sometimes food and lodging. **2** a lodging house, esp. for travellers. **innkeeper**, †**innholder** *n.* a person who keeps an inn. **Inns of Court** *n.pl.* (*Law*) **1** the four corporate societies in London (*Inner Temple, Middle Temple, Lincoln's Inn, Gray's Inn*) which have the exclusive right of admitting persons to practise at the bar. **2** the buildings belonging to these societies.

⊠ **innaccurate** common misspelling of INACCURATE.

innards (in´ədz) *n.pl.* **1** (*coll.*) entrails. **2** (*coll.*) the components of a machine etc.

innate (ināt´, in´āt) *a.* inborn, natural. **innately** *adv.* **innateness** *n.*

inner (in´ə) *a.* **1** interior; farther inward or nearer the centre. **2** spiritual; relating to the mind, soul etc. ~*n.* **1** that part of a target immediately outside the bull's eye. **2** a shot striking that part. **inner bar** *n.* (*Law*) Queen's or King's Counsel collectively. **inner circle** *n.* an exclusive group within a larger group. **inner city** *n.* the central part of a city, esp. when associated with poor housing, social problems etc. (*inner-city schools*). **inner ear** *n.* the part of the ear consisting of the vestibule, semicircular canals and cochlea. **innerly** *adv.* inwardly. **inner man, inner woman** *n.* **1** the inner or spiritual part of a person. **2** (*facet.*) the stomach. **innermost** *a.* INMOST. **innerness** *n.* **inner tube** *n.* an inflatable tube inside a tyre.

innervate (in' œvāt) *v.t.* to supply (an organ) with nerves or nerve filaments. **innervation** (-vā'shən) *n.*

innings (in'ingz) *n.* (*pl.* **innings**, (*coll.*) **inningses**) **1 a** in cricket, the time or turn for batting of a player or a side. **b** the runs scored by a player during a turn at batting. **2** the time during which a party or person is in office, in power etc. **3 a** a period during which things can be achieved. **b** (*coll.*) the lifespan of a person (*She had a good innings*). **inning** (in'ing) *n.* (*N Am.*) each of the playing periods in a game of baseball during which both sides have a turn at batting.

innocent (in'əsənt) *a.* **1** free from moral guilt; blameless; sinless. **2** guiltless (of a crime etc.). **3** guileless; naive or credulous. **4** lacking, devoid (of). **5** harmless. ~*n.* **1** an innocent person, esp. a child. **2** a person caught up by chance in a war, crime etc. **innocence, †innocency** *n.* **innocently** *adv.*

☒ **innoculate** common misspelling of INOCULATE.

innocuous (inok'ūəs) *a.* having no injurious qualities, harmless. **innocuously** *adv.* **innocuousness** *n.*

innovate (in'əvāt) *v.i.* **1** to introduce alterations (in). **2** to introduce new ideas or ways of doing things. ~*v.t.* to begin to introduce (methods, ideas etc.). **innovation** (-ā'shən) *n.* **innovational** *a.* **innovative, innovatory** (-ā'təri) *a.* **innovator** *n.*

innuendo (inūen'dō) *n.* (*pl.* **innuendos, innuendoes**) **1** an indirect or oblique hint, esp. one that is disparaging or disapproving. **2** a suggestive remark.

Innuit INUIT.

innumerable (inū'mərəbəl) *a.* countless, numberless. **innumerability** (-bil'-), **innumerableness** *n.* **innumerably** *adv.*

innumerate (inū'mərət) *a.* ignorant of or unskilled in mathematics or science.

innutrition (inūtrish'ən) *n.* lack of nutrition or nourishment. **innutritious** *a.*

inobservant (inəbzœ'vənt) *a.* **1** not observant. **2** heedless. **inobservance** *n.* lack of observance (of a law etc.).

☒ **inocent** common misspelling of INNOCENT.

inoculate (inok'ūlāt) *v.t.* **1** to inject (a person or animal) with a mild form of a disease in order to induce immunity against the disease. **2** to introduce (bacteria, a virus) into an organism. **3** to

introduce (organisms) into a culture medium. **4** (*fig.*) to imbue (a person) with ideas etc. **inoculable** *a.* **inoculation** (-lā'shən) *n.* **inoculative** *a.* **inoculator** *n.*

inoffensive (inəfen'siv) *a.* giving no offence; harmless. **inoffensively** *adv.* **inoffensiveness** *n.*

inoperable (inop'ərəbəl) *a.* **1** that cannot be operated on. **2** unworkable. **3** that cannot be operated. **inoperability** (-bil'-), **inoperableness** *n.* **inoperably** *adv.*

inoperative (inop'ərətiv) *a.* **1** not in operation. **2** producing no result; ineffective.

inopportune (inop'ətūn, -tūn') *a.* not opportune; unseasonable. **inopportunely** *adv.* **inopportuneness** (-tū'-), **inopportunity** (-tūn'-) *n.*

inordinate (inaw'dinət) *a.* **1** excessive, immoderate, passing all bounds. **2** unrestrained. **3** irregular, disorderly. **inordinately** *adv.*

inorganic (inawgan'ik) *a.* **1** not organic, not having the organs or characteristics of living organisms. **2** (*Chem.*) of or relating to chemical compounds not containing carbon. **3** not having an ordered physical structure. **4** not resulting from natural growth. **inorganically** *adv.* **inorganic chemistry** *n.* the branch of chemistry concerning mineral substances.

input (in'put) *n.* **1** something that is put into a machine, the body etc. **2 a** a place where energy, information etc. goes into an electrical system. **b** a signal or current fed into a system or device. **3** (*Comput.*) **a** data fed into a computer. **b** the process of entering such data. **4** a contribution. ~*v.t.* (*pres.p.* **inputting**, *past, p.p.* **inputted, input**) **1** to put in. **2** (*Comput.*) to enter (data) into a computer.

inquest (in'kwest) *n.* **1** (*Law*) **a** a judicial inquiry or investigation, esp. a coroner's inquest, usu. held before a jury. **b** the jury at such an inquiry. **2** any inquiry or investigation.

inquietude (inkwī'ətūd) *n.* restlessness, uneasiness.

inquire (inkwīə') , **enquire** *v.i.* **1** to ask questions (of). **2** to seek information by asking questions (about or after). **3** to investigate (into). ~*v.t.* to ask (what, whether, how etc.) (*She inquired my date of birth*). **inquirer** *n.* **inquiring** *a.* given to inquiry; inquisitive. **inquiringly** *adv.* **inquiry** (inkwī'ri) *n.* (*pl.* **inquiries**) **1** an official investigation. **2** the act of inquiring. **3** a question. **4** a searching for truth, information or knowledge. **5** examination of facts or principles.

Usage note It is conventional to use *enquire*, *enquiry* of simple asking, and *inquire*, *inquiry* of investigating.

inquisition (inkwizish'ən) *n.* **1** (*esp. derog.*) a thorough search or investigation. **2** a judicial inquiry, an inquest. **3** (*Hist.*) (**Inquisition**) a tribunal in the Roman Catholic Church for inquiring into offences against the canon law, aimed especially at the suppression of heresy. **inquisitional** *a.* **inquisitive** (inkwiz'itiv) *a.* **1** unduly given to asking questions; prying, curious. **2** eager for knowledge. **inquisitively** *adv.* **inquisitiveness** *n.* **inquisitor** (inkwiz´itə) *n.* **1** a person who inquires. **2** a person who carries out an official investigation. **3** (*Hist.*) a functionary of the Inquisition. **inquisitorial** (-taw´-) *a.* **1** of, relating to or like an inquisitor. **2** prying, searching. **3** (*Law*) (of criminal proceedings) in which the judge is also prosecutor. **inquisitorially** *adv.*

inquorate (inkwaw´rāt) *a.* not having enough people to constitute a quorum.

in re (in rē´, rā´) *prep.* RE¹.

inroad (in´rōd) *n.* **1** (*often pl.*) an encroachment (on). **2** a hostile incursion.

inrush (in´rŭsh) *n.* a sudden rush in; an influx.

ins. *abbr.* inches.

insalubrious (insəloo´briəs) *a.* not salubrious, unhealthy. **insalubrity** *n.*

insane (insān´) *a.* **1** deranged in mind; mad. **2** (*coll.*) exceedingly rash or foolish. **insanely** *adv.* **insanity** (-san´-) *n.* (*pl.* **insanities**).

insanitary (insan´itəri) *a.* not sanitary.

insatiable (insā´shəbəl) *a.* **1** that cannot be satisfied or appeased. **2** very greedy (of). **insatiability** (-bil´-), **insatiableness** *n.* **insatiably** *adv.* **insatiate** (-ət) *a.* never satisfied.

inscribe (inskrīb´) *v.t.* **1 a** to write, carve or engrave (words, a design etc.) on a stone, paper or some other surface. **b** to mark (a stone etc.) with writing or letters. **2** to address or dedicate (a book to someone). **3** to enter (a name) in or on a book, list etc. **4** to issue (stock etc.) to registered shareholders. **5** (*Geom.*) to draw (a figure) within another so that it touches the boundary surfaces of the latter. **inscribable** *a.* **inscriber** *n.*

inscription (inskrip´shən) *n.* **1** the art or act of inscribing. **2** something which is inscribed, e.g. a dedicatory address, the words on the reverse of some coins and medals, or the titular line or lines of an illustration. **inscriptional, inscriptive** *a.*

inscrutable (inskroo´təbəl) *a.* unfathomable, mysterious. **inscrutability** (-bil´-), **inscrutableness** *n.* **inscrutably** *adv.*

insect (in´sekt) *n.* **1** a member of the Insecta, a class of articulate, usu. winged animals, with three pairs of legs, and divided into three distinct segments, the head, thorax and abdomen. **2** any other articulated animal resembling these, e.g. a spider or centipede. **3** a small or contemptible person or creature. **insecticide** (-sek´tisīd) *n.* a preparation for killing insects. **insecticidal** (-sī´-) *a.*

insectivore (insek´tivaw) *n.* **1** any mammal of the order Insectivora, including moles, shrews and hedgehogs. **2** any animal or plant that feeds on insects. **insectivorous** (-tiv´-) *a.*

insecure (insikūə´) *a.* **1** lacking in self-confidence; apprehensive; uncertain. **2** not secure or safe; not strongly fixed or supported. **3** not effectually guarded. **insecurely** *adv.* **insecurity** *n.*

inseminate (insem´ināt) *v.t.* **1** to impregnate, esp. by artificial means. **2** to sow (in the soil). **3** to implant (in the mind etc.). **insemination** (-ā´shən) *n.*

insensate (insen´sət, -sāt) *a.* **1** lacking sensation; inanimate or unconscious. **2** lacking in sensibility; unfeeling. **3** foolish, mad. **insensately** *adv.*

insensible (insen´sibəl) *a.* **1** not having the power of feeling or perceiving, unconscious. **2** unaware (of); indifferent (to). **3** not susceptible of feeling, emotion or passion; callous. **4** that cannot be perceived or felt; imperceptible. **insensibility** (-bil´-) *n.* **1** lack of feeling, emotion or passion. **2** unconsciousness. **3** insusceptibility or indifference (to). **insensibly** *adv.*

insensitive (insen´sitiv) *a.* **1** unfeeling, unsympathetic (to). **2** not sensitive (to). **insensitively** *adv.* **insensitiveness, insensitivity** (-tiv´-) *n.*

insentient (insen´shiənt) *a.* not sentient, inanimate. **insentience** *n.*

inseparable (insep´ərəbəl) *a.* incapable of being separated. **inseparability** (-bil´-), **inseparableness** *n.* **inseparably** *adv.*

insert (insœt´) *v.t.* **1** to set or place (a thing) into another. **2** to introduce (text, an article, an advertisement etc.) into something, such as a newspaper. ~*n.* **1** something inserted. **2** a printed sheet etc. placed inside the leaves of a newspaper, periodical etc. **inserter** *n.* **insertion** (insœ´shən) *n.* **1** the act of inserting. **2** something which is inserted, an intercalation, a passage etc. introduced (in or into). **3** a band of lace or embroidery inserted in a dress, handkerchief etc.

inset¹ (in´set) *n.* **1** a piece let into a dress etc. **2** a small map or diagram set within a larger one. **3** a page or number of pages inserted in a book, newspaper etc.

inset² (inset´) *v.t.* (*pres.p.* **insetting**, *past*, *p.p.* **inset, insetted**) **1** to set or fix (in), to insert (in). **2** to decorate with an inset. **insetter** *n.*

inset³ (in´set) *abbr.* in-service education and training (for teachers).

inshore (inshaw´) *a.*, *adv.* on, near or towards the shore. **inshore of** closer to the shore than.

inside¹ (in´sīd) *a.* **1** situated within; interior, internal, inner. **2** in hockey and football, near the centre of the field (*inside forward*). ~*n.* **1** the inner or interior part. **2** the inner side or surface (of). **3** the side of a path away from the road. **4** (*coll.*) a position from which inside information can be obtained. **5** (*Print.*) the side of a sheet containing the second page. **6** (*pl.*, *coll.*) the bowels. **inside information** *n.* confidential knowledge not generally accessible. **inside job** *n.* (*coll.*) a crime committed with the help of someone trusted or employed by the victim. **inside out** *adv.* having the inner side turned out and vice versa. **to know inside out** to have thorough knowledge of. **to turn inside out 1** to turn the inner side of (something) outwards. **2** (*coll.*) to cause chaos or a mess in. **inside-out** *a.* **insider** (-sī´-) *n.* **1** a person who belongs to a society, clique etc. **2** a person who has inside information. **insider dealing, insider trading** n. the criminal practice of conducting share deals on the basis of inside information. **inside track** n. **1** the inner and therefore shorter track. **2** a position of advantage.

inside² (insīd´) adv. **1** in or into the interior, within; indoors. **2** (sl.) in or into prison. ~prep. **1** within, on the inner side of, into. **2** in less than (inside a week). **inside of a mile/ an hour** etc. (coll.) within or in less than a mile/an hour etc.

insidious (insid´iəs) a. **1** treacherous, sly. **2** developing gradually or subtly but dangerously (an insidious influence). **insidiously** adv. **insidiousness** n.

insight (in´sīt) n. **1** the capacity to observe or discern the real character of things. **2** a clear and often sudden understanding of something. **insightful** a. **insightfully** adv.

insignia (insig´niə) n.pl. **1** (often sing. in constr., NAm.) badges of office or honour. **2** distinguishing marks or signs (of).

Usage note Insignia is sometimes used as a countable noun (an insignia, insignias), but this is best avoided.

insignificant (insignif´ikənt) a. **1** unimportant, trivial. **2** (of a person) of a little distinction. **3** small. **4** without meaning. **insignificance, insignificancy** n. **insignificantly** adv.

insincere (insinsiə´) a. not sincere; false. **insincerely** adv. **insincerity** (-ser´-) n. (pl. insincerities).

insinuate (insin´ūāt) v.t. **1** to indicate indirectly or obliquely; to hint. **2** to introduce (oneself, a person etc.) into favour, office, a place etc. by gradual and artful means. **insinuatingly** adv. **insinuation** (-ā´shən) n. **insinuative** a. **insinuator** n.

insipid (insip´id) a. **1** tasteless, savourless. **2** lacking in life or animation; dull; vapid. **insipidity** (-pid´-), **insipidness** n. **insipidly** adv.

insist (insist´) v.i. to be emphatic, positive, urgent or persistent (on or upon). ~v.t. **1** to maintain emphatically. **2** to demand strongly or without accepting any refusal. **to insist on 1** to demand emphatically. **2** to assert positively. **insistent** a. **1** insisting; demanding strongly and continually. **2** obtrusive and hard to ignore (the insistent creaking of the gate). **insistence, insistency** n. **insistently** adv.

in situ (in sit´ū) adv. **1** in its place. **2** in the original position.

insobriety (insəbrī´əti) n. lack of sobriety; intemperance (usu. in drinking).

insofar (insōfah´) adv. in so far (as).

insolate (in´səlāt) v.t. to expose to the sun's rays, e.g. for bleaching, or as a form of medical treatment. **insolation** (-ā´shən) n.

insole (in´sōl) n. **1** the inner sole of a boot or shoe. **2** a strip of waterproof or other material placed inside a boot or shoe for warmth, comfort etc.

insolent (in´sələnt) a. **1** showing overbearing contempt; impudent. **2** insulting. **insolence** n. **insolently** adv.

insoluble (insol´ūbəl) a. **1** that cannot be solved. **2** that cannot be dissolved. **insolubility** (-bil´-), **insolubleness** n. **insolubilize, insolubilise** v.t. **insoluble soap** n. a compound of a fatty and another metallic base. **insolubly** adv.

insolvable (insol´vəbəl) a. **1** that cannot be solved, insoluble. **2** that cannot be dissolved.

insolvent (insol´vənt) a. **1** not able to discharge all debts or liabilities. **2** of or relating to insolvents. ~n. a debtor unable to pay their debts. **insolvency** n.

insomnia (insom´niə) n. sleeplessness; chronic inability to sleep or sleep well. **insomniac** (-ak) n., a.

insomuch (insōmŭch´) adv. **1** to such a degree (that). **2** inasmuch (as).

insouciant (insoo´siənt) a. carefree or unconcerned. **insouciance** n. **insouciantly** adv.

inspect (inspekt´) v.t. **1** to look closely into or at; to scrutinize carefully. **2** to view and examine officially. **inspection** (inspek´shən) n. **1** the act of inspecting. **2** a careful, narrow or critical examination or survey. **3** an official examination. **inspector** (inspek´tə) n. **1** a person who inspects. **2** an overseer, a superintendent. **3** a police officer usu. ranking below a superintendent. **inspectorate** (-ət) n. **inspectorial** (-taw´ri-) a. **inspectorship** n.

inspire (inspīə´) v.t. **1** to stimulate (a person) to some activity, esp. creative activity (What inspired you to paint?). **2** to imbue or animate (a person with a feeling). **3** to infuse or instil (an emotion in or into). **4** to be the source of motivation for something (a film inspired by real events). **5** to breathe or take (air) into the lungs etc. ~v.i. to take air into the lungs. **inspirable** a. **inspiration** (inspirā´shən) n. **1** an act of inspiring, breathing in or infusing feelings, ideas etc. **2** a person, idea etc. that inspires others. **3** feelings, ideas, creativity etc. imparted by or as by divine agency. **4** a sudden and brilliant idea. **5** the act of drawing air into the lungs. **inspirational** a. **inspirationally** adv. **inspiratory** (-spir´ətəri) a. **inspired** a. **1** (of a poem, piece of music etc.) imparted by or as by supernatural agency. **2** (of a guess) accurate but based on intuition rather than knowledge. **inspiredly** (-ridli) adv. **inspirer** n. **inspiring** a. **inspiringly** adv.

inspirit (inspir´it) v.t. (pres.p. **inspiriting**, past, p.p. **inspirited**) **1** to infuse spirit, life or animation into. **2** to inspire, to encourage (to action or to do). **inspiriting** a. **inspiritingly** adv.

inspissate (inspis´āt) v.t. to thicken by boiling or evaporation. **inspissation** (-ā´shən) n. **inspissator** n.

inst. (inst) abbr. **1** instant (this month). **2** institute. **3** institution.

instability (instəbil´iti) n. (pl. **instabilities**) **1** lack of stability or firmness. **2** (Psych.) lack of mental or emotional consistency. **3** an instance of this.

install (instawl´), **instal** v.t. (pres.p. **installing**, past, p.p. **installed**) **1** to put (apparatus, equipment etc.) in position for use. **2** to settle or establish (a person, oneself) somewhere (She installed herself by the fire). **3** to place (a person) in an official position with customary ceremonies (He was installed as bishop). **installation** (-stəlā´shən) n. **1** the act of installing or the process of being installed. **2** a piece of machinery, equipment etc. installed for use. **3** a military base etc.

instalment (instawl´mənt), (N Am.) **installment** n. **1** each one of the parts into which a sum of money owed is divided, each part being paid at intervals over an agreed period of time. **2** each one of several parts of a serial story etc. shown on television, published in a magazine etc.

instance (in´stəns) n. **1** an example, illustrative case or precedent (There have been several instances of mismanagement). **2** a particular situation or case (The rules don't apply in this instance). **3** (Law) a process or suit. ~v.t. to bring forward as an instance or example. **at the instance of** at the suggestion or desire of. **for instance** for example.

instant (in´stənt) a. **1** immediate (an instant success). **2** (esp. of food) processed so as to be quickly and easily prepared. **3** pressing; urgent. **4** of the current month (used in commercial correspondence). ~n. **1** a particular point of time (Do it this instant; I phoned the instant I knew). **2** a moment, a very brief space of time. **instantaneous** (instəntā´niəs) a. **1** happening or done in an instant or immediately. **2** (Physics) relating to a particular instant. **instantaneity** (-nē´i-), **instantaneousness** n. **instantaneously** adv. **instantiate** (instan´shiāt) v.t. to represent by an instance. **instantiation** (-ā´shən) n. **instantly** adv. immediately; without delay.

instead (insted´) adv. **1** in the place (of) (Could I have cheese instead of ham?). **2** as an alternative or substitute (We went to a restaurant instead).

instep (in´step) n. **1** the arched upper side of the human foot, near the ankle. **2** the part of a shoe etc., corresponding to this.

instigate (in´stigāt) v.t. **1** to provoke or bring about (an action). **2** to incite, to urge on (to an action esp. of an evil kind). **instigation** (-ā´shən) n. **instigator** n.

instil (instil´), (N Am.) **instill** v.t. (pres.p. **instilling**, past, p.p. **instilled**) **1** to introduce slowly and gradually (into the mind of a person). **2** to pour by drops (into). **instillation** (-ā´shən) n. **instilment** n.

instinct[1] (in´stingkt) n. **1** a natural impulse present in most animals, leading them without reasoning or conscious design to perform certain actions. **2** a similar innate or intuitive impulse in human beings. **3** intuition; unreasoning

perception of rightness, beauty etc. **instinctive** (-stingk´-) a. **1** prompted by instinct. **2** spontaneous, impulsive. **instinctively** adv. **instinctual** (-stingk´-) a. of or relating to instinct. **instinctually** adv.

instinct[2] (instingkt´) a. **1** animated or impelled from within. **2** imbued (with).

institute (in´stitūt) v.t. **1** to set up, to establish. **2** to start, to begin. **3** to nominate, to appoint (to or into), esp. to appoint to an ecclesiastical benefice. ~n. **1** a society established for the promotion or furtherance of science, literature etc. **2** the building in which such a society meets. **3** an established law, precept or principle. **institution** (institū´shən) n. **1** the act of instituting. **2** a society or association established esp. for charitable, social or educational purposes. **3** the building used by such a society. **4** an established order, law, regulation or custom. **5** (coll.) a familiar custom, person etc. **6** the act or ceremony of investing a member of the clergy with the spiritual part of a benefice. **institutional** a. **1** of or relating to an institution. **2** typical of institutions, e.g. in being routine or unimaginative. **institutionalism** n. **institutionalize, institutionalise** v.t. **1** to make an institution of. **2** to confine to an institution. **institutionalization** (-zā´shən) n. **institutionalized** a. **1** (of a long-term patient etc.) made dependent and apathetic, bored etc. by a long stay in an institution. **2** that has become established or accepted. **institutionally** adv. **institutional religion** n. religion that expresses itself through ritual and church services.

instruct (instrŭkt´) v.t. **1** to teach, to educate (in a subject). **2** to order or direct (someone to do something). **3** to inform (someone of, that). **4** to supply (a solicitor, counsel etc.) with information relating to a case. **5** to authorize (a barrister or solicitor) to act for one. **instruction** (-shən) n. **1** (often pl.) a direction or order. **2** the act of instructing; teaching, education. **3** (pl., Law) directions to a solicitor, counsel etc. **4** (Comput.) a code directing a computer to perform a certain operation. **instructional** a. **instructive** a. conveying instruction. **instructively** adv. **instructor** n. **1** a person who instructs. **2** (N Am.) a college teacher having a rank inferior to professor. **instructress** n. a female instructor.

instrument (in´strəmənt) n. **1** a tool, a mechanical implement, esp. one for scientific or delicate operations. **2** MUSICAL INSTRUMENT (under MUSIC). **3** something by means of which work is done or any object or purpose effected. **4** an agent, a person used as a means by another. **5** a measuring device, e.g. in a car or an aircraft, for measuring pressure, speed etc. **6** (Law) a document giving formal expression to an act. ~v.t. **1** (Mus.) to arrange (music) for instruments. **2** to equip with instruments. **instrumental** (instrəmen´təl) a. **1** serving as an instrument or means (to some end or in some act). **2** (of errors, etc.) due to the instrument used. **3** (of music) for instruments, not for voices. **4** (*Gram.*) (of a case of nouns etc. in some languages) denoting the means or instrument. ~*n*. **1** (*Gram.*) the instrumental case. **2** a piece of music for instruments as opposed to voices. **instrumentalist** *n*. a person who plays an instrument. **instrumentality** (-tal´-) *n*. **instrumentally** *adv*. **instrumentation** (-tā´shən) *n*. **1** the arrangement of music for several instruments in combination. **2** the instruments used in a piece of music. **3** the art or manner of using an instrument or instruments. **4** instrumentality. **5** the use, design etc. of instruments or tools. **6** such instruments or tools collectively. **instrument panel, instrument board** *n*. a panel, esp. in a car or aircraft, containing instruments for measuring speed etc.

insubordinate (insəbaw´dinət) *a*. not submissive to authority; disobedient, disorderly. **insubordinately** *adv*. **insubordination** (-ā´shən) *n*.

insubstantial (insəbstan´shəl) *a*. **1** unreal. **2** flimsy or slight. **insubstantiality** (-al´-) *n*. **insubstantially** *adv*.

insufferable (insŭf´ərəbəl) *a*. not able to be borne or endured; detestable; intolerable. **insufferableness** *n*. **insufferably** *adv*.

insufficient (insəfish´ənt) *a*. not sufficient; deficient; inadequate. **insufficiency** *n*. **insufficiently** *adv*.

insular (in´sülə) *a*. **1** of or relating to an island. **2** of the nature of an island; remote. **3** narrow, contracted (in outlook). **insularism** *n*. **insularity** (-lar´-) *n*. **insularly** *adv*.

insulate (in´sülāt) *v.t.* **1** to separate from other bodies by a non-conductor, so as to prevent the passage of electricity or heat. **2** to place in a detached situation or position. **insulation** *n*. **insulator** *n*.

insulin (in´sülin) *n*. a protein hormone produced in the pancreas which regulates the metabolism of sugar and fat, and the lack of which causes diabetes.

insult¹ (insŭlt´) *v.t.* **1** to treat or speak to rudely or contemptuously. **2** to offend. **insulter** *n*. **insulting** *a*. **insultingly** *adv*.

insult² (in´sŭlt) *n*. **1** an insulting act or remark. **2** an affront; something that is offensive (*an insult to one's intelligence*).

insuperable (insoo´pərəbəl, -sü´-) *a*. insurmountable; impossible to overcome. **insuperability** (-bil´-) *n*. **insuperably** *adv*.

insupportable (insəpaw´təbəl) *a*. **1** insufferable, intolerable. **2** incapable of being sustained or defended; indefensible. **insupportableness** *n*. **insupportably** *adv*.

insure (inshuə´) *v.t.* **1** to secure compensation, whole or partial, in the event of loss or injury to (property, life etc.) by paying a periodical premium (*Our household goods are insured against theft*). **2** (of the owner or the insurance company) to secure the payment of (a specified sum) in the event of loss, injury etc. **3** to provide (a person) with an insurance policy. **4** (*N Am.*)

ENSURE. ~*v.i.* **1** to take out an insurance policy. **2** to make provision for a possible contingency (*It's impossible to insure against every eventuality*). **insurable** *a*. **insurance** (inshuə´rəns, -shaw´-) *n*. **1** the act of insuring against damage or loss. **2** an insurance policy. **3** a sum insured. **4 a** a sum of money paid regularly to an insurance company; a premium. **b** a means of providing for a possible contingency. **insurance policy** *n*. **1** a contract of insurance. **2** a document detailing such a contract. **insured** *a*. covered by insurance. **the insured 1** the person to whom compensation for fire, damage etc. will be paid. **2** the person whose life is insured. **insurer** *n*. **1** a person or company providing insurance policies for premiums. **2** a person who insures.

insurgent (insœ´jənt) *a*. rising up in revolt; rebellious. ~*n*. a person who rises up against established government or authority; a rebel. **insurgence, insurgency** *n*.

insurmountable (insəmown´təbəl) *a*. that cannot be surmounted, passed over or overcome. **insurmountably** *adv*.

insurrection (insərek´shən) *n*. the act of rising in open opposition to established authority; an uprising. **insurrectional, insurrectionary** *a*. **insurrectionist** *n*.

insusceptible (insəsep´tibəl) *a*. not susceptible (of, to); incapable of being moved by any feeling or impression.

intact (intakt´) *a*. **1** untouched. **2** unimpaired; uninjured. **3** entire. **intactness** *n*.

intaglio (intah´lyō) *n*. (*pl.* **intaglios**) **1** a figure cut or engraved in a hard substance. **2** the act or process of producing this. **3** a gem with a figure cut or engraved into it, as distinct from a *cameo*. **4** a method of printing from an etched or engraved design.

intake (in´tāk) *n*. **1** the act of taking in. **2** something which is taken in. **3** a number or amount taken in or received (*They've increased their intake of students*). **4** the people or things taken in or received. **5** a place where water is taken in, an inlet.

intangible (intan´jibəl) *a*. **1** not tangible; imperceptible to the touch. **2** not able to be grasped mentally. ~*n*. something intangible. **intangibility** (-bil´-) *n*. **intangibly** *adv*.

integer (in´tijə) *n*. **1** a whole number as distinguished from a fraction. **2** anything that is whole.

integral (in´tigrəl, -teg´-) *a*. **1** whole, entire, complete. **2** necessary to completeness, forming an essential part of a whole. **3** forming a whole. **4** (*Math.*) of, relating to or constituting an integer. **5** of, relating to or produced by integration. ~*n*. **1** (*Math.*) the limit of the sum of a series of values of a differential *f* (*x*) *dx* when *x* varies by indefinitely small increments from one given value to another. **2** a whole, a total, an integer. **integral calculus** *n*. a method of summing up differential quantities. **integrality** (-ral´-) *n.* **integrally** *adv.*

Usage note The pronunciation (-teg´-), with stress on the second syllable, is sometimes disapproved of.

integrate (in´tigrāt) *v.t.* **1** to make into a whole, to complete by adding parts. **2** to combine into a whole. **3** to bring (a person, group) into equal participation in and full acceptance by society, an organization etc. **4** to end the racial segregation of. **5** (*Math.*) to find the integral of. ~*v.i.* to become integrated into society, an organization etc. **integrable** (in´tigrəbəl) *a.* **integrated** *a.* **integrated circuit** *n.* a minute electronic circuit consisting of an assembly of elements made from a chip of semiconductor material. **integration** (-rā´shən) *n.* **1** the making into a whole. **2** the act of integrating people into society, an organization etc. **3** the amalgamation of a previously segregated group with an existing community. **4** (*Math.*) the act or process of integrating. **integrationist** *n.* **integrator** *n.*

integrity (integ´riti) *n.* **1** probity; honesty; high principle. **2** entireness, completeness. **3** soundness.

integument (integ´ūmənt) *n.* a covering, esp. a natural one, such as a skin, husk, rind or shell. **integumentary** (-men´-), **integumental** *a.*

intellect (in´tilekt) *n.* **1** the faculty of understanding, thinking and reasoning, as distinguished from the faculty of feeling or wishing. **2** the understanding; intelligence (*a man of great intellect*). **3** an intelligent or clever person. **4** intellectual people collectively; the intelligentsia. **intellectual** (intilek´chuəl) *a.* **1** possessing intellect in a high degree. **2** of, relating to or performed by the intellect. **3** appealing to or perceived by the intellect. ~*n.* an intellectual person. **intellectualism** *n.* the cultivation of the intellect, esp. at the expense of feelings. **intellectuality** (-al´-) *n.* **intellectualize, intellectualise** *v.t.* **1** to make intellectual. **2** to treat intellectually; to give an intellectual character or significance to. ~*v.i.* **1** to become intellectual. **2** to employ the intellect. **intellectualization** (-zā´shən) *n.* **intellectually** *adv.*

intelligence (intel´ijəns) *n.* **1** the exercise of the understanding; intellectual power. **2** acquired knowledge. **3** quickness or sharpness of intellect. **4** a department concerned with gathering secret or little-known information esp. of importance for military activity. **5** such information. **6** the activity of gathering such information. **7** an intelligent being, esp. an incorporeal or spiritual being regarded as pure intellect. **intelligence quotient** *n.* a number denoting a person's intelligence, traditionally arrived at by dividing the mental age by the age in years and multiplying the result by 100. **intelligence test** *n.* a psychological test to determine a person's relative mental capacity.

intelligent (intel´ijənt) *a.* **1** endowed with understanding. **2** clever, quick. **3** (of a machine etc.) able to adapt in response to varying circumstances and requirements. **4** (of a computer terminal) within which a certain amount of computing can be done without contacting a central computer. **intelligently** *adv.* **intelligentsia** (-jent´-siə) *n.* **1** the class of people who are considered to be cultured, educated and politically aware. **2** intellectuals.

intelligible (intel´ijibəl) *a.* capable of being understood, comprehensible. **intelligibility** (-bil´-), **intelligibleness** *n.* **intelligibly** *adv.*

intemperate (intem´pərət) *a.* **1** not exercising due moderation or self-restraint; immoderate. **2** indulging any appetite or passion in excess. **3** addicted to excessive indulgence in alcoholic drink. **4** (of a climate etc.) extreme; inclement. **intemperance** *n.* **intemperately** *adv.* **intemperateness** *n.*

intend (intend´) *v.t.* **1** to propose, to plan (*I intend to continue*; *We intend coming*). **2** to mean, to have in mind (*It was intended as a compliment*). **3** to design (for) (*It's intended for beginners*). **4** to destine (for) (*He was intended for a career in the army*). **5** to signify or mean to express. **intended** *a.* **1** done deliberately or on purpose. **2** designed. ~*n.* (*dated or facet.*) a person whom one is expecting to marry.

intense (intens´) *a.* (*comp.* **intenser,** *superl.* **intensest**) **1** extreme in degree (*intense feelings*; *intense heat*). **2** strongly or deeply emotional. **3** (of an activity, effort etc.) very concentrated (*intense concentration*). **intensely** *adv.* **intenseness** *n.* **intensify** (-fī) *v.t.* (*3rd pers. sing. pres.* **intensifies,** *pres.p.* **intensifying,** *past, p.p.* **intensified**) to render more intense. ~*v.i.* to become more intense. **intensification** (-fikā´shən) *n.* **intensifier** *n.* **1** a person who or a thing which intensifies. **2** (*Gram.*) a word that gives force or emphasis to the word that it modifies. **intensity** *n.* (*pl.* **intensities**) **1** the condition or quality of being intense. **2** an extreme degree of force or strength. **3** (*esp. Physics*) the measurable amount of something, e.g. sound, radiation etc.

intensive (inten´siv) *a.* **1** concentrated, thorough. **2** unremitting. **3** characterized by intensity. **4** (*chiefly in comb.*) utilizing one specified element of production proportionately more than others (*capital-intensive*). **5** conducive to high productivity within a narrow area (*intensive farming*). **6** (*Gram.*) serving to intensify, or to add force or emphasis. ~*n.* (*Gram.*) an intensive particle, word or phrase. **intensive care** *n.* **1** continuous care and close monitoring of a person who is dangerously ill in hospital. **2** a unit in a hospital that is specially designed for this. **intensively** *adv.* **intensiveness** *n.*

intent (intent´) *n.* **1** design, purpose, intention (*with intent to inflict injury*; *That wasn't my intent*). **2** meaning, drift. ~*a.* **1** bent or determined (on) (*intent on winning*). **2** giving complete attention to something (*She was intent on her books*). **3** fixed; earnest (*an intent stare*). **to all intents and purposes** practically, really, in reality. **intently** *adv.* **intentness** *n.*

intention (inten´shən) *n.* **1** purpose, design, intent (*He has no intention of giving up; It wasn't my intention to cause offence*). **2** determination to act in some particular manner. **3** (*pl., coll.*) designs with regard to marriage. **intentional** *a.* done with design or purpose. **intentionality** (-al´-) *n.* **intentionally** *adv.* **intentioned** *a.*

inter (intœ´) *v.t.* (*pres.p.* **interring**, *past, p.p.* **interred**) to bury; to place in a grave or tomb. **interment** *n.*

Usage note The nouns *interment* and *internment* should not be confused: *interment* refers to burial, and *internment* to confinement.

---

inter- (in´tə) *pref.* **1** among or between, as *interstate*. **2** mutually or reciprocally, as *interplay, interdepend*.

interact (intərakt´) *v.i.* to act reciprocally; to act on each other. **interaction** (-rak´shən) *n.* **interactional** *a.* **interactive** *a.* **1** capable of mutual action. **2** (*Comput.*) permitting continuous mutual communication between computer and user (*interactive multimedia*).

inter alia (intər ah´liə, ā´liə) *adv.* among other things.

interbreed (intəbrēd´) *v.i.* to breed with members of a different species, race etc. *~v.t.* to cause to breed in this way.

intercalary (intœ´kələri, intəkal´-), **intercalar** (-lə) *a.* **1** (of a day, month) inserted in the calendar to make it correspond with the solar year. **2** (of a year) containing such an addition. **3** inserted, interpolated. **intercalate** (intœ´-) *v.t.* **1** to insert between or amongst others (esp. a day or month into a calendar). **2** to interpolate; to insert in an unusual or irregular way. **intercalated** *a.* interposed; inserted. **intercalation** (-ā´shən) *n.*

intercede (intəsēd´) *v.i.* **1** to plead (with someone) in favour of another. **2** to mediate. **interceder** *n.*

intercellular (intəsel´ūlə) *a.* occurring or situated between or among cells.

intercept (intəsept´) *v.t.* **1** to stop, take or seize on the way from one place to another. **2** to obstruct; to stop; to shut off. **interception** *n.* **interceptive** *a.* **interceptor** (in´-) *n.* **1** a person who or thing which intercepts. **2** a swift aeroplane used to pursue and intercept enemy aircraft.

intercession (intəsesh´ən) *n.* **1** the act of interceding. **2** a prayer offered for others. **intercessional** *a.* **intercessor** (-ses´ə) *n.* **intercessorial** (-saw´ri-), **intercessory** *a.*

interchange¹ (intəchānj´) *v.t.* **1** (of two people) to exchange with each other. **2** to put each (of two things) in the place of the other, to alternate. *~v.i.* to alternate. **interchangeable** *a.* **interchangeability** (-bil´-), **interchangeableness** *n.* **interchangeably** *adv.*

interchange² (in´təchānj) *n.* **1** reciprocal exchange. **2** alternate succession, alternation. **3** a junction of two or more roads designed to prevent traffic streams crossing one another.

intercity (intəsit´i) *a.* existing, carried on or travelling between different cities. *~n.* (*pl.* **intercities**) a fast train travelling between cities.

intercom (in´təkom) *n.* (*coll.*) **1** a system of intercommunication by telephone in aircraft, within a building etc. **2** a device used for this.

intercommunicate (intəkəmū´nikāt) *v.i.* **1** to hold or enjoy mutual communication. **2** (of rooms) to have free passage to and from each other. **intercommunicable** *a.* **intercommunication** (-ā´shən) *n.* **intercommunion** (-yən) *n.* **1** fellowship between members of different Christian denominations. **2** mutual action or communion.

interconnect (intəkənekt´) *v.i., v.t.* to connect with each other. **interconnectedness** *n.* **interconnection** *n.*

intercontinental (intəkontinen´təl) *a.* existing or travelling between or connecting different continents.

interconvert (intəkənvœt´) *v.t., v.i.* to convert into each other. **interconversion** *n.* **interconvertible** *a.*

intercooler (in´təkoolə) *n.* a heat exchanger used e.g. in a supercharged internal-combustion engine to cool gas between successive compressions. **intercool** *v.t.*

intercorrelate (intəkor´əlāt) *v.i.* to correlate with each other. *~v.t.* to cause to intercorrelate. **intercorrelation** (-ā´shən) *n.*

intercostal (intəkos´təl) *a.* **1** situated between the ribs. **2** between the framework of the keel of a ship. **intercostally** *adv.*

intercourse (in´təkaws) *n.* **1** reciprocal dealings, association, communication etc., between people, nations etc. **2** sexual intercourse.

intercrop (intəkrop´) *n.* a crop raised between the rows of another crop. *~v.t.* (*pres.p.* **intercropping**, *past, p.p.* **intercropped**) to raise (a crop) in this way. *~v.i.* to plant intercrops. **intercropping** *n.*

intercut (intəkŭt´) *v.t.* (*pres.p.* **intercutting**, *past, p.p.* **intercut**) to alternate (contrasting camera shots) by cutting.

interdenominational (intədinominā´shənəl) *a.* existing or carried on between different religious denominations. **interdenominationally** *adv.*

interdepartmental (intədēpahtmen´təl) *a.* involving more than one department. **interdepartmentally** *adv.*

interdepend (intədipend´) *v.i.* to depend upon each other. **interdependence, interdependency** *n.* **interdependent** *a.* **interdependently** *adv.*

interdict¹ (in´tədikt) *n.* **1** an official prohibition. **2** in the Roman Catholic Church, a sentence by which places or persons are debarred from ecclesiastical functions and privileges. **interdictory** (-dik´-) *a.*

interdict · 657 · **interline**

interdict² (intədikt´) v.t. **1** to forbid; to prohibit. **2** to restrain (from). **3** to lay under an interdict. **4** (N Am.) to stop or intercept. **interdiction** (-dik´shən) n.

interdisciplinary (intədisiplin´əri) a. involving two or more disciplines or fields of study.

interest¹ (in´trist) n. **1** lively, sympathetic or curious attention; concern (She didn't show much interest). **2** the power of eliciting attention or concern (The subject holds little interest for me). **3** something, such as a hobby or subject, in which one has a personal concern (What are your interests?). **4** participation in advantages, benefits or profits. **5** (often pl.) benefit, advantage (It's not in your interest). **6** proprietary right or concern; a share, a portion or stake (in). **7** (collect.) those having a concern in a particular business etc. (the shipping interest). **8** a business etc. in which a group or party has a concern. **9** payment for the use of borrowed money or on a debt. **10** selfish concern for one's own welfare. **at interest** (of money borrowed) on which interest is payable. **in the interest/ interests of** as a way of furthering or ensuring (in the interests of hygiene). **with interest 1** with interest added. **2** with added force etc. (He hit him back with interest).

interest² (in´trist) v.t. **1** to arouse or hold the attention or curiosity of (Might this book interest you?). **2** to cause to participate (in) (Can I interest you in a game of tennis?). **interested** a. **1** having one's interest excited. **2** having an interest, concern or share in. **3** liable to be biased through personal interest, not disinterested. **interestedly** adv. **interesting** a. arousing interest, attention or curiosity. **interestingly** adv. **interestingness** n.

interface (in´təfās) n. **1** (esp. Physics) a surface lying between two spaces. **2** the point at which independent systems, processes etc. meet and act on each other. **3** (Comput.) an electrical circuit linking two computers or other devices. ~v.t. (Comput.) to connect (a device) with another device by an interface. ~v.i. **1** to be connected with another device in this way. **2** to interact (with). **interfacing** n. stiffening material inserted between layers of fabric.

interfaith (in´təfāth) a. of, relating to or occurring between different religious faiths or their representatives.

interfere (intəfiə´) v.i. **1** to hinder or obstruct a process, activity etc. **2** to meddle (with). **3** (euphem.) to assault sexually. **4** to intervene or get involved (in), esp. when this is unnecessary or unwanted. **5** (Physics) (of light or other waves) to act reciprocally, to modify each other. **interference** n. **1** the act of interfering. **2** an instance of this. **3** the spoiling of radio reception by atmospherics or by other signals. **4** (Physics) the effect of combining two or more waves of the same frequency. **interferential** (-fəren´shəl) a. **interferer** n. **interfering** a., n. **interferingly** adv.

interferon (intəfiə´ron) n. an antiviral protein substance produced in living cells in humans and other creatures in response to infection from a virus.

interfile (intəfīl´) v.t. **1** to file (two sets of items) together. **2** to file (one or more items) into an existing arrangement of items.

interfuse (intəfūz´) v.t. **1** to intersperse (with). **2** to blend together, to cause to flow into each other. ~v.i. to blend into each other. **interfusion** (-zhən) n.

intergalactic (intəgəlak´tik) a. between galaxies. **intergalactically** adv.

interglacial (intəglā´shəl, -siəl) a. occurring or formed between two of the glacial periods. ~n. a period between two of the glacial periods.

intergovernmental (intəgŭvənmen´təl) a. involving or concerning two or more governments.

interim (in´tərim) n. the meantime; the intervening time or period (in the interim). ~a. temporary, provisional (an interim measure).

interior (intiə´riə) a. **1** internal, inner. **2** inland; remote from the coast, frontier or exterior. **3** domestic, as distinct from foreign. **4** of or relating to the inner consciousness, the soul or spiritual matters. **5** within a building. **6** coming from within. ~n. **1** the internal part of anything; the inside. **2** the central or inland part of a country. **3** the inside of a building or room, esp. as portrayed in a picture, photograph etc. **4** the domestic affairs of a country. **5** the government department dealing with these. **interior angle** n. the angle between two sides of a polygon. **interior decoration, interior design** n. the design and decoration of the interior of a house, room etc. **interiorize, interiorise** v.t. interior **monologue** n. in a novel, the representation of a character's train of thought. **interior-sprung** a. (of a mattress etc.) having springs.

interject (intəjekt´) v.t. **1** to insert (a remark etc.) abruptly. **2** to interrupt with. **interjection** n. **1** the act of interjecting. **2** a word which expresses sudden feeling, and which is differentiated as a separate part of speech; an exclamation. **interjectional, interjectory, interjectural** a.

interlace (intəlās´) v.t. **1** to lace or weave together; to interweave. **2** to intersperse (with). ~v.i. to be interwoven (with each other); to intersect in a complicated fashion. **interlacement** n.

interlard (intəlahd´) v.t. to diversify (a conversation, passage in a book etc.) with unusual phrases etc.

interleaf (in´təlēf) n. (pl. **interleaves** (-lēvz)) a leaf, usu. blank, inserted between the leaves of a book, e.g. in order to protect an illustration. **interleave** (-lēv´) v.t. to insert blank leaves between the leaves of (a book).

interleukin (intəlū´kin) n. any of a number of proteins that are produced by white blood cells and stimulate activity against infection.

interlibrary (intəli´brəri) a. between libraries.

interline¹ (intəlīn´) v.t. **1** to write or print between the lines of. **2** to insert (words) between lines. **interlineal** (-lin´iəl), **interlinear** (-lin´iə) a.

written between lines of text. **interlineation** (-ā´shən) n.

interline[2] (intəlīn´) v.t. to insert an extra lining between the outer fabric and the lining of (a garment). **interlining** n. the material used to interline a garment.

interlink (intəlingk´) v.t., v.i. to link together.

interlock[1] (intəlok´) v.t. to connect firmly together by reciprocal engagement of parts; to link or lock together. ~v.i. to engage with each other by reciprocal connections.

interlock[2] (in´təlok) a. (of a fabric) closely knitted. ~n. 1 the state of being interlocked. 2 a device in a logic circuit preventing the initiation of an activity in the absence of certain preceding events.

interlocution (intələkū´shən) n. conversation, dialogue, discussion. **interlocutor** (-lok´-) n. a person who takes part in a conversation. **interlocutory** a. 1 consisting of dialogue. 2 (Law) intermediate, not final. **interlocutress** (-tris), **interlocutrice** (-trēs), **interlocutrix** (-triks) n. a female interlocutor.

interloper (in´təlōpə) n. 1 an intruder. 2 a person who interferes in someone else's affairs. **interlope** v.i.

interlude (in´təlood) n. 1 a pause or a short entertainment between the acts of a play. 2 an intervening period or event that contrasts with what comes before and after. 3 an incident, esp. an amusing one, coming between graver events. 4 a piece of instrumental music played between the acts of a drama, between the verses of a hymn, portions of a church service etc.

intermarriage (intəmar´ij) n. 1 marriage between people of different families, tribes, castes or nations. 2 marriage between people closely related. **intermarry** v.i. (3rd pers. sing. pres. **intermarries**, pres.p. **intermarrying**, past, p.p. **intermarried**) 1 (of different races, tribes etc.) to become connected by marriage. 2 to marry within one's family, group etc.

intermediary (intəmē´diəri) a. being, coming or acting between; intermediate. ~n. (pl. **intermediaries**) an intermediate agent, a go-between. **intermediacy** (-si) n.

intermediate[1] (intəmē´diət) a. coming between two things, extremes, places etc. ~n. 1 something that is intermediate. 2 a chemical compound produced by a reaction and used as a starting point for the synthesis of some other product. **intermediately** adv. **intermediateness** n. **intermediate technology** n. technology as adapted for the conditions and requirements of developing nations.

intermediate[2] (intəmē´diāt) v.i. to act as intermediary; to mediate (between). **intermediation** (-ā´shən) n. **intermediator** n.

interment INTER.

intermesh (intəmesh´) v.i. to become meshed together. ~v.t. to cause (things) to become intermeshed.

intermezzo (intəmet´sō) n. (pl. **intermezzi** (-si), **intermezzos**) 1 a short movement connecting the main divisions of an opera or a large musical composition. 2 a piece of this kind performed independently. 3 a short piece of music for a solo instrument. 4 a short dramatic or other entertainment between the acts of a play.

interminable (intœ´minəbəl) a. 1 endless or seeming to have no end. 2 tediously protracted. **interminableness** n. **interminably** adv.

intermingle (intəming´gəl) v.t. to mingle together, to intermix. ~v.i. to be mingled (with).

intermit (intəmit´) v.t. (pres.p. **intermitting**, past, p.p. **intermitted**) to cause to cease for a time; to suspend. **intermission** (-shən) n. 1 a pause or temporary cessation. 2 an interval between acts of a play, parts of a concert etc. **intermittent** a. occurring at intervals. **intermittence**, **intermittency** n. **intermittently** adv.

intermix (intəmiks´) v.t., v.i. to mix together. **intermixable** a. **intermixture** (-chə) n.

intermolecular (intəmlek´ūlə) a. between molecules.

intern[1] (intœn´) v.t. to confine (aliens, political opponents etc.), esp. during wartime. **internee** (-nē´) n. a person who is interned. **internment** n.

Usage note See note on INTERMENT (under INTER).

intern[2] (in´tœn), **interne** n. (esp. N Am.) an assistant surgeon or physician resident in a hospital. ~v.i. to serve as an intern. **internship** n.

internal (intœ´nəl) a. 1 of or relating to or situated in the inside. 2 domestic as opposed to foreign. 3 relating to or affecting the inside of the body. 4 (of a student) at a university and sitting its examinations. 5 occurring or applying within an organization. 6 inherent, intrinsic. 7 of or relating to the inner being, inward. ~n.pl. intrinsic or essential qualities. **internal-combustion engine** n. an engine in which mechanical energy is produced by the combustion or explosion of a mixture of air and gas in its cylinder. **internal exile** n. banishment from one's city or province, but not from one's country. **internality** (-nal´-) n. **internalize**, **internalise** v.t. 1 to assimilate (an idea etc.) into one's outlook. 2 (Psych.) to contain (an emotion) within oneself instead of expressing it. **internalization** (-zā´shən) n. **internally** adv. **internal market** n. 1 SINGLE MARKET (under SINGLE). 2 in the National Health Service, a decentralized system of funding whereby health authorities purchase health care for their local residents through arranging contracts with hospitals.

international (intənash´ənəl) a. 1 of or relating to, subsisting or carried on between, different nations. 2 recognised or used by many countries. ~n. 1 a match between two national teams. 2 a person who takes part in such a match. 3 (**International**) any of the four associations set up between 1864 and 1936 to promote socialist or communist action throughout the world. **International Date Line** *n.* a line roughly along the 180th meridian, east and west of which the date is one day different. **internationalism** *n.* the promotion of a community of interests between nations. **internationalist** *n.* **internationality** (-nal´-) *n.* **internationalize, internationalise** *v.t.* **1** to make international. **2** to bring under the joint protection or control of different nations. **internationalization** (-zā´shən) *n.* **international law** *n.* an accepted system of laws regulating intercourse between nations. **internationally** *adv.* **International Phonetic Alphabet** *n.* an internationally recognised series of phonetic symbols intended to give an accurate representation of human speech sounds. **international system of units** *n.* SI units.

interne INTERN².

internecine (intənē´sīn) *a.* mutually destructive.

Internet (in´tənet) *n.* an international computer network via which business, academic and private users can exchange information and communicate.

internist (intœ´nist) *n.* (*Med.*, *esp. N Am.*) a specialist in internal medicine.

internode (in´tənōd) *n.* **1** (*Anat.*) a part between two nodes or joints. **2** (*Bot.*) a part of a stem between two nodes. **internodal** (-nō´-) *a.*

internuclear (intənū´kliə) *a.* between nuclei.

interoceanic (intərōshian´ik) *a.* situated between or connecting two oceans.

interoceptive (intərōsep´tiv) *a.* (*Biol.*) of or relating to stimuli developing inside the viscera.

interoperable (intərop´ərəbəl) *a.* able to operate jointly. **interoperability** (-bil´-) *n.*

interosseal (intəros´iəl), **interosseous** (-iəs) *a.* situated between bones.

interpellate (intœ´pəlāt) *v.t.* to interrogate, esp. to interrupt discussion in a parliament in order to demand a statement or explanation from (a minister). **interpellation** (-ā´shən) *n.* **interpellator** *n.*

interpenetrate (intəpen´itrāt) *v.t.* **1** to penetrate thoroughly, to permeate. **2** to penetrate (each other). ~*v.i.* to penetrate each other. **interpenetration** (-rā´shən) *n.* **interpenetrative** (-rətiv) *a.*

interpersonal (intəpœ´sənəl) *a.* involving communication between people (*interpersonal skills*). **interpersonally** *adv.*

interphase (in´təfāz) *n.* (*Biol.*) the period between one division of a cell and the next.

interplait (intəplat´) *v.i.*, *v.t.* to plait together.

interplanetary (intəplan´itəri) *a.* **1** of or relating to travel between the planets. **2** between planets.

interplay (in´təplā) *n.* reciprocal action between parts or things.

interpolate (intœ´pəlāt) *v.t.* **1** to insert (esp. a spurious word or passage) in (a book or document). **2** to interject. **3** (*Math.*) to introduce (intermediate terms) in a series. ~*v.i.* to make

interpolations. **interpolation** (-ā´shən) *n.* **interpolative** *a.* **interpolator** *n.*

interpose (intəpōz´) *v.t.* **1** to place between or among. **2** to put forward (an objection, veto, obstruction etc.) by way of intervention or interference. ~*v.i.* **1** to intervene; to intercede; to mediate (between). **2** to remark by way of interruption, to interrupt. **interposition** (intəpəzish´ən) *n.* **1** the act of interposing; intervention; mediation. **2** that which is interposed. **3** an interference.

interpret (intœ´prit) *v.t.* (*pres.p.* **interpreting**, *past*, *p.p.* **interpreted**) **1** to explain the meaning of. **2** to find out the meaning of, to construe or understand in a particular way. **3** to represent the meaning of or one's idea of artistically. ~*v.i.* to act as an interpreter. **interpretable** *a.* **interpretability** (-bil´-) *n.* **interpretation** (-ā´shən) *n.* **interpretational** *a.* **interpretative** (-prətətiv) *a.* **interpretatively** *adv.* **interpreter** *n.* **1** a person who interprets, esp. one employed to translate orally to persons speaking a foreign language. **2** (*Comput.*) a program that translates and executes a second program line by line. **interpretive** *a.* **interpretively** *adv.*

interprovincial (intəprəvin´shəl) *a.* existing, carried on etc. between different provinces.

interracial (intərā´shəl) *a.* existing, carried on etc. between different races. **interracially** *adv.*

interregnum (intəreg´nəm) *n.* (*pl.* **interregnums, interregna** (-nə)) **1** the period between two reigns, ministries or governments. **2** a suspension or interruption of normal authority, succession etc. **3** an interval, a pause. **interregnal** *a.*

interrelate (intərilāt´) *v.t.* to relate (things) to each other. ~*v.i.* to be interrelated. **interrelation** (-ā´shən) *n.* **interrelationship** *n.*

interrogate (inter´əgāt) *v.t.* to put questions to, esp. in a formal or thorough way. ~*v.i.* to ask questions. **interrogation** (-ā´shən) *n.* **interrogational** *a.* **interrogative** (-rog´-) *a.* **1** denoting a question. **2** expressed in the form or having the character of a question. ~*n.* (*Gram.*) a word used in asking questions, e.g. *what?*, *who?* **interrogatively** *adv.* **interrogator** *n.* **interrogatory** (-rog´-) *a.* interrogative.

interrupt (intərŭpt´) *v.t.* **1** to stop or obstruct by breaking in upon. **2** to break the continuity of. **3** to obstruct (a view etc.). **4** to disturb. ~*v.i.* to make an interruption. **interruptedly** *adv.* **interrupter, interruptor** *n.* **interruptible** *a.* **interruption** *n.* **interruptive, interruptory** *a.* **interruptively** *adv.*

intersect (intəsekt´) *v.t.* to divide by cutting or passing across. ~*v.i.* to cut or cross each other. **intersection** *n.* **1** the act of intersecting. **2** a crossroads. **3** (*Geom.*) the point or line on which lines or planes cut each other. **intersectional** *a.*

intersex (in´təseks) *n.* **1** (*Zool.*) an individual developing characteristics of both sexes. **2** the condition of being intersexual. **intersexual** (-sek´-) *a.* **1** intermediate in sexual characteristics between male and female. **2** between the sexes. **intersexuality** (-al´-) *n.* **intersexually** *adv.*

interspace[1] (in´təspās) *n.* **1** intervening space. **2** an interval between two things or occurrences. **interspatial** (-spā´shəl) *a.*

interspace[2] (intəspās´) *v.t.* **1** to put a space or spaces between. **2** to fill the intervals between.

interspecific (intəspisif´ik) *a.* subsisting between different species.

intersperse (intəspœs´) *v.t.* **1** to scatter here and there (among etc.). **2** to diversify or variegate (with scattered objects, colours etc.). **interspersion** (-shən) *n.*

interstate (in´təstāt) *a.* subsisting, maintained or carried on between states, esp. the states of the US. ~*n.* (*US*) a motorway going from one state to another.

interstellar (intəstel´ə) *a.* situated between or passing through the regions between the stars.

interstice (intœ´stis) *n.* a space, opening, crevice etc. between things near together or between the component parts of a body. **interstitial** (-stish´əl) *a.* of, relating to, occupying or forming interstices. **interstitially** *adv.*

intertidal (intətī´dəl) *a.* of or relating to the area between the low-water and high-water marks.

intertribal (intətrī´bəl) *a.* occurring or carried on between different tribes.

intertwine (intətwīn´) *v.t.* to entwine or twist together. ~*v.i.* to be twisted together. **intertwinement** *n.* **intertwiningly** *adv.*

intertwist (intətwist´) *v.t.* to twist together.

☒ **interupt** common misspelling of INTERRUPT.

interval (in´təvəl) *n.* **1** an intervening space, distance or time. **2** a break, gap or pause. **3** the extent of difference between two things, persons etc. **4** the difference in pitch between two sounds. **5** the break between scenes or acts of a play etc. **at intervals 1** from time to time. **2** with spaces in between. **intervallic** (-val´-) *a.*

intervene (intəvēn´) *v.i.* **1** to happen or break in so as to interrupt or disturb; to interfere. **2** to occur between points of time or events. **3** to come or be situated between. **4** to come in as an extraneous feature or thing. **intervener, intervenor** *n.* **intervenient** *a.* **intervention** (-ven´-) *n.* **1** the act of intervening. **2** violating a sovereign state's independence by interfering in its domestic or external affairs. **3** mediation. **interventionist** *n.* a person who favours intervention, esp. in the economy or in the affairs of a foreign country. **interventionism** *n.*

intervertebral (intəvœ´tibrəl) *a.* situated between vertebrae.

interview (in´təvū) *n.* **1** a meeting in which an employer questions a candidate for a job, college place etc. in order to test the candidate's suitability. **2** a meeting between a person of public interest and a press representative employed to obtain information or opinions for publication. **3** the article describing this or recording the result. **4** a meeting between two persons face to face. **5** a session of questioning by the police etc.

~*v.t.* to hold an interview with, esp. in order to obtain matter for publication or to test a candidate's suitability for a post. ~*v.i.* to take part in an interview; to perform in a particular way at interview (*She interviewed well*). **interviewee** (-ē´) *n.* **interviewer** *n.*

inter-war (intəwaw´) *a.* occurring in the period between two wars, esp. World Wars I and II.

interweave (intəwēv´) *v.t.* (*past* **interwove** (-wōv´), *p.p.* **interwoven** (-wō´vən)) **1** to weave together (with). **2** to blend or mingle closely together.

interwind (intəwīnd´) *v.t., v.i.* (*past, p.p.* **interwound** (-wownd´)) to wind together.

interwork (intəwœk´) *v.t.* (*past, p.p.* **interwrought** (-rawt´), **interworked**) to work (things) together or into each other. ~*v.i.* to work together; to interact.

intestate (intes´tāt) *a.* **1** dying without having made a will. **2** (of property) not disposed of by will. ~*n.* an intestate person. **intestacy** *n.*

intestine (intes´tin) *n.* **1** (*usu. pl.*) the part of the alimentary canal from the stomach to the anus. **2** (*Zool.*) the whole of the alimentary canal. **intestinal** (-tī´-, -tes´-) *a.* **intestinal flora** *n.pl.* harmless bacteria inhabiting the intestinal tract. **intestinally** *adv.*

inthrall ENTHRALL.

intifada (intifah´də) *n.* the Palestinian uprising in the Israeli-occupied West Bank and Gaza Strip, that began in 1987.

intimate[1] (in´timət) *a.* **1** close in friendship; familiar (*an intimate friend*). **2** private, personal. **3** having an atmosphere conducive to close personal relationships. **4** thorough (*an intimate knowledge*). **5** of or relating to one's inner being. **6** close (*an intimate connection/link*). **7** having sexual relations (with). ~*n.* a close friend. **intimacy** (-si) *n.* (*pl.* **intimacies**) **1** closeness; close friendship. **2** sexual intercourse. **3** a warm intimate atmosphere. **4** (*often pl.*) an intimate remark. **intimately** *adv.*

intimate[2] (in´timāt) *v.t.* **1** to make known, to announce. **2** to indicate, to hint. **intimation** (-ā´shən) *n.*

intimidate (intim´idāt) *v.t.* to frighten or to influence with threats or aggressive behaviour. **intimidating** *a.* **intimidation** (-ā´shən) *n.* **intimidator** *n.* **intimidatory** (-ā´təri) *a.*

into (in´tu) *prep.* **1** expressing motion or direction within or against (*She got into the car; I bumped into him*). **2** expressing investigation, inquiry etc. (*I'll look into the matter*). **3** expressing a change from one state to another (*translated into French*). **4** after a particular period of time (*one week into the course*). **5** (*coll.*) very keen on or enthusiastic about (*She's really into aromatherapy*). **6** indicating the dividend in division.

intolerable (intol´ərəbəl) *a.* not tolerable, unendurable. **intolerableness** *n.* **intolerably** *adv.*

intolerant (intol´ərənt) *a.* not tolerant (of); not enduring or allowing difference of opinion, teaching, worship etc. **intolerance** *n.* **intolerantly** *adv.*

intone (intōn´) *v.i.* **1** to recite or chant prayers etc., esp. in a monotone. **2** to speak with a particular tone. ~*v.t.* **1** to recite or chant in a monotone. **2** to utter with a particular tone. **intonation** (intənā´shən) *n.* **1** modulation of the voice; accent. **2** intoning. **3** accuracy of pitch when playing an instrument or singing. **intoner** *n.*

in toto (in tō´tō) *adv.* completely.

intoxicate (intok´sikāt) *v.t.* **1** to make drunk. **2** to excite; to make delirious, as with joy. **intoxicant** *a.* that intoxicates. ~*n.* any intoxicating substance. **intoxicating** *a.* **intoxicatingly** *adv.* **intoxication** (-ā´shən) *n.*

intra- (in´trə) *pref.* within or inside, as *intrauterine*.

intracellular (intrəsel´ūlə) *a.* (*Biol.*) in a cell or cells.

intracranial (intrəkrā´niəl) *a.* within the skull. **intracranially** *adv.*

intractable (intrak´təbəl) *a.* **1** unmanageable. **2** difficult, obstinate. **intractability** (-bil´-), **intractableness** *n.* **intractably** *adv.*

intramolecular (intrəmolek´ūlə) *a.* within a molecule.

intramural (intrəmū´rəl) *a.* **1** situated or happening within walls or boundaries. **2** taking place within or involving those in an institution, esp. a university or college.

intranet (in´trənet) *n.* a computer networking link restricted to a specific group of users.

intransigent (intran´sijənt) *a.* uncompromising, obdurate, inflexible. ~*n.* an intransigent person. **intransigence** *n.* **intransigently** *adv.*

intransitive (intran´sitiv) *a.* (*Gram.*) (of a verb) denoting action confined to the agent and so not requiring a direct object. **intransitively** *adv.* **intransitiveness, intransitivity** (-tiv´-) *n.*

intrapreneur (intrəprənœ´) *n.* a person who initiates or manages a new business or division within an existing firm.

intrauterine (intrəū´terīn) *a.* situated or occurring inside the womb. **intrauterine device** *n.* a metal or plastic coil, loop or ring, placed in the womb to prevent conception.

intravenous (intrəvē´nəs) *a.* into a vein or veins. **intravenously** *adv.*

intrench ENTRENCH.

intrepid (intrep´id) *a.* fearless, brave, bold. **intrepidity** (-pid´-) *n.* **intrepidly** *adv.*

intricate (in´trikət) *a.* entangled, involved, complicated. **intricacy** (-si) *n.* (*pl.* **intricacies**). **intricately** *adv.*

intrigue¹ (intrēg´) *v.i.* (*3rd pers. sing. pres.* **intriguing**, *past, p.p.* **intrigued**) to carry on a plot or scheme to effect some object by underhand means. ~*v.t.* to make curious or to fascinate. **intriguer** *n.* **intriguing** *a.* **intriguingly** *adv.*

intrigue² (in´trēg, intrēg´) *n.* **1** the act of intriguing. **2** a plot to effect some object by underhand means.

intrinsic (intrin´sik), †**intrinsical** *a.* inherent, essential; belonging to the nature of a thing. **intrinsically** *adv.*

intro (in´trō) *n.* (*pl.* **intros**) (*coll.*) an introduction.

intro- (intrō) *comb. form* in, into, as *introspection*.

introduce (intrədūs´) *v.t.* **1** to make (a person, oneself) known in a formal way to another. **2** to bring into use or notice. **3** to present (a programme etc.) to an audience. **4** to cause (a person) to discover. **5** to bring (a bill etc.) before Parliament. **6** to bring or lead in; to usher in. **7** to insert. **8** to bring before the public. **9** to preface. **introducer** *n.* **introduction** (intrədŭk´shən) *n.* **1** the act of introducing. **2** a formal presentation of a person to another. **3** a preface or preliminary discourse in a book etc. **4** an opening section in a piece of music. **5** an elementary treatise. **6** something that is introduced. **introductory** *a.* serving as an introduction; preliminary. **introductorily** *adv.*

introit (in´troit) *n.* a psalm or antiphon sung or recited as the priest approaches the altar to begin the Mass or Eucharist.

introject (intrəjekt´) *v.t.* to assimilate unconsciously into one's personality. **introjection** *n.*

introspection (intrəspek´shən) *n.* the analysis and observation of the workings of one's own mind. **introspective** *a.* **introspectively** *adv.* **introspectiveness** *n.*

introvert¹ (in´trəvœt) *n.* **1** (*Psych.*) a person who is interested chiefly in their own feelings and mental processes rather than in the outside world. **2** a shy, reflective person.

introvert² (intrəvoet´) *v.t.* (*Psych.*) to turn (one's mind or thoughts) inwards. **2** (*Zool.*) to turn (an organ or a part) in upon itself. **introversion** *n.* **introversive, introvertive** *a.* **introverted** *a.*

intrude (introod´) *v.t.* to thrust or force (on to, into). ~*v.i.* **1** to thrust oneself or force one's way (into). **2** to force oneself upon others; to enter without invitation. **intruder** *n.*

intrusion (intrū´zhən) *n.* **1** the act of intruding. **2** an unwelcome visit, interruption etc. **3** (*Geol.*) the penetration of volcanic rocks into sedimentary strata.

intrusive (intrū´siv) *a.* **1** tending to intrude or characterized by intrusion. **2** entering without invitation or welcome. **3** (of a speech sound) inserted into a word or between words to make pronunciation easier, e.g. the *r* in *draw a picture*. **intrusively** *adv.* **intrusiveness** *n.*

intrust ENTRUST.

intubate (in´tūbāt) *v.t.* (*Med.*) to insert a tube into (the larynx), as in a case of diphtheria. **intubation** (-bā´shən) *n.*

intuition (intūish´ən) *n.* **1** immediate perception by the mind without reasoning. **2** the power of the mind for such perception. **3** instinctive knowledge. **intuit** (-tū´it) *v.t.* to know by intuition. ~*v.i.* to acquire knowledge by means of intuition. **intuitable** *a.* **intuitional** *a.* **intuitive** (-tū´-)

a. **1** perceived by intuition. **2** perceiving by intuition. **3** seeing immediately and clearly. **intuitively** *adv.* **intuitiveness** *n.*

intumesce (intūmes´) *v.i.* to swell up. **intumescence** *n.* **intumescent** *a.*

intwine ENTWINE.

Inuit (in´ūit), **Innuit** *n.* (*pl* **Inuit, Inuits, Innuit, Innuits**) **1** a Canadian Eskimo. **2** a member of any of the Eskimo peoples inhabiting N America and Greenland. **3** any Eskimo. **4** any of the languages of the Inuit or Eskimos. *~a.* of or relating to the Inuit or Eskimos, or any of their languages.

inundate (in´əndāt) *v.t.* **1** to overflow, to flood. **2** to deluge; to overwhelm. **inundation** (-dā´shən) *n.*

inure (inūə´), **enure** *v.t.* to accustom, to habituate, to harden (to). *~v.i.* (*Law*) to come into operation; to take or have effect. **inurement** *n.*

in utero (in ū´tərō) *adv.* in the womb.

invade (invād´) *v.t.* **1** to enter (a country) by force, as an enemy. **2** to overrun (*Tourists invade the island every year*). **3** (of bacteria etc.) to assail (a body etc.). **4** to encroach on, to violate (someone's privacy, rights etc.). *~v.i.* to make an invasion. **invader** *n.*

invaginate (invaj´ināt) *v.t.* **1** to put into or as into a sheath. **2** to introvert or turn (a tubular sheath) upon itself. **invagination** (-ā´shən) *n.*

invalid[1] (inval´id) *a.* having no force, weight or cogency; null. **invalidate** *v.t.* to weaken or destroy the validity of, to render not valid. **invalidation** (-ā´shən) *n.* **invalidator** *n.* **invalidly** *adv.* **invalidness** *n.*

invalid[2] (in´vəlid, -ēd) *a.* infirm or disabled through ill health or injury. *~n.* an infirm or disabled person. *~v.t.* (*pres.p.* **invaliding**, *past, p.p.* **invalided**) **1** (*usu. pass.*) to disable by illness or injury. **2** to register or discharge as unfit for military or naval duty on account of illness etc. (*He was invalided out*). *~v.i.* to become an invalid. **invalidism** *n.*

invalidity (invəlid´iti) *n.* **1** the fact or condition of being without validity. **2** the fact or condition of being infirm or disabled.

invaluable (inval´ūəbəl) *a.* precious above estimation; priceless. **invaluableness** *n.* **invaluably** *adv.*

invariable (invēə´riəbəl) *a.* **1** not variable, uniform; not liable to change. **2** (*Math.*) fixed, constant. **invariability** (-bil´-), **invariableness** *n.* **invariably** *adv.* **invariant** *a.* not varying or subject to variation. *~n.* (*Math.*) a function which remains fixed and unchanged though its constituents may vary. **invariance** *n.*

invasion (invā´zhən) *n.* **1** the act of invading. **2** a hostile attack upon or entrance into the territory of others. **invasive** (-siv) *a.* **1** tending to spread. **2** (of surgery) involving making a relatively large incision in the body. **3** tending to infringe on another's rights, privacy etc.

invective (invek´tiv) *n.* a violent expression of censure or abuse; vituperation.

inveigh (invā´) *v.i.* to utter or make use of invectives; to speak censoriously and abusively (against). **inveigher** *n.*

inveigle (invē´gəl, -vā´-), **enveigle** *v.t.* to entice, to wheedle; to entrap (into). **inveiglement** *n.*

invent (invent´) *v.t.* **1** to devise or contrive (a new means, instrument etc.). **2** to concoct, to fabricate. **invention** *n.* **1** the act of inventing. **2** the production of something new. **3** the faculty or power of inventing, inventiveness. **4** something which is invented; a contrivance. **5** a fabrication, a fiction. **inventive** *a.* **1** able to invent. **2** ingenious; imaginative. **3** characterized by creative skill. **inventively** *adv.* **inventiveness** *n.* **inventor** *n.* a person who invents things, esp. as an occupation.

inventory (in´vəntəri) *n.* (*pl.* **inventories**) **1** a detailed list or catalogue of goods, possessions etc. **2** the articles enumerated in such a list. **3** (*esp.* N Am.) the quantity or value of a firm's current assets in terms of raw materials and stock. *~v.t.* (*3rd pers. sing. pres.* **inventories**, *pres.p.* **inventorying**, *past, p.p.* **inventoried**) **1** to enter in an inventory. **2** to make a list or catalogue of. **inventorial** (-taw´ri-) *a.* **inventorially** *adv.*

inverse (invœs´, in´-) *a.* **1** opposite in order or relation; contrary. **2** inverted. *~n.* **1** the state of being inverted. **2** the direct opposite (of). **inversely** *adv.* **inverse proportion, inverse ratio** *n.* a relation between two quantities in which an increase in one results in a proportional decrease in the other.

inversion (invœ´shən) *n.* **1** the act of inverting. **2** a reversal of order, place or relation. **3** the result of inverting. **4** TEMPERATURE INVERSION (under TEMPERATURE). **inversion layer** *n.* in meteorology, a layer of air in which temperature increases with altitude. **inversive** *a.*

invert[1] (invœt´) *v.t.* **1** to turn upside down. **2** to place in a contrary position or order; to reverse. **3** (*Mus.*) to change (a chord, interval etc.) by placing the lowest note higher. **invertase** (-tāz) *n.* an enzyme able to convert sucrose into invert sugar. **inverted** *a.* **inverted comma** *n.* QUOTATION MARK (under QUOTE). **inverted snob** *n.* a person who admires those things that a snob might be expected to disapprove of. **inverter, invertor** *n.* **invertible** (-vœ´-) *a.* **invertibility** (-bil´-) *n.*

invert[2] (in´vœt) *n.* **1** an inverted arch, esp. such as forms the bottom of a sewer etc. **2** a homosexual. **invert sugar** *n.* a mixture of sugar and fructose obtained by the hydrolysis of cane sugar.

invertebrate (invœ´tibrət) *a.* **1** (of an animal) not having a backbone or vertebral column. **2** (of a person) lacking strength or firmness. *~n.* **1** an invertebrate animal. **2** an irresolute person. **invertebral** *a.*

invest (invest´) *v.t.* **1** to employ (money) in remunerative property, business, stocks etc. **2** to devote (effort, time etc.) to a project etc. for future rewards. **3** to provide or endue (with office, authority, dignity etc.). **4** to attribute (qualities, characteristics etc.) to someone. **5** to cover (with or as with a garment). **6** to besiege. ~*v.i.* **1** to make an investment (in). **2** (*coll.*) to buy (*Isn't it time you invested in a new coat?*). **investable**, **investible** *a.* **investment** *n.* **1** the act of investing money. **2** money invested. **3** something in which money is invested. **4** the act of surrounding or besieging. **investment trust** *n.* a financial enterprise which invests its subscribers' capital in securities and distributes the net return among them. **investor** *n.*

investigate (inves´tigāt) *v.t.* to examine or inquire into closely. ~*v.i.* to carry out a thorough search or inquiry. **investigable** *a.* **investigation** (-ā´shən) *n.* **1** the act or an instance of investigation. **2** a formal and careful examination. **investigational** *a.* **investigative**, **investigatory** *a.* **investigator** *n.*

investiture (invest´ichə) *n.* **1** the act of investing, esp. the ceremony of investing with office, rank etc. **2** the state of being invested.

inveterate (invet´ərət) *a.* **1** determinedly settled in a habit. **2** long-established, deeply-rooted. **3** habitual. **inveteracy** (-si), **inveterateness** *n.* **inveterately** *adv.*

invidious (invid´iəs) *a.* **1** tending to incur or provoke envy, ill will or indignation. **2** offending through real or apparent unfairness or injustice. **invidiously** *adv.* **invidiousness** *n.*

invigilate (invij´ilāt) *v.i.* to supervise students during an examination. ~*v.t.* to supervise. **invigilation** (-ā´shən) *n.* **invigilator** *n.*

invigorate (invig´ərāt) *v.t.* to give vigour or strength to. **invigorating** *a.* **invigoratingly** *adv.* **invigoration** (-ā´shən) *n.* **invigorative** *a.* **invigorator** *n.*

invincible (invin´sibəl) *a.* that cannot be conquered. **invincibility** (-bil´-), **invincibleness** *n.* **invincibly** *adv.*

inviolable (invī´ələbəl) *a.* not to be violated, profaned or dishonoured. **inviolability** (-bil´-), **inviolableness** *n.* **inviolably** *adv.* **inviolate** (-lət) *a.* **1** not violated or profaned. **2** safe from violation, injury etc. **inviolately** *adv.*

invisible (inviz´ibəl) *a.* **1** not visible; imperceptible to the eye. **2** too small, distant, misty etc. to be seen. **3** cleverly hidden or concealed. **4** not recorded in published accounts. **5** of or relating to services as opposed to goods (*invisible earnings*). ~*n.* **1** an invisible person or thing. **2** (*pl.*) invisible exports and imports. **invisibility** (-bil´-), **invisibleness** *n.* **invisible exports**, **invisible imports** *n.pl.* invisible items of trade, esp. services. **invisibly** *adv.*

invite[1] (invīt´) *v.t.* **1** to ask (someone) courteously to do something, come to an event etc. (*I've been invited to dinner*). **2** to request formally and courteously (*The speaker invited questions*). **3** to allure, to attract. **4** to draw upon one, esp. unintentionally (*You're inviting trouble*). ~*v.i.* to allure; to tempt. **invitation** (-vitā´shən) *n.* **1** the act of inviting or the fact of being invited. **2** a card,

letter etc. inviting someone. **3** allurement; attraction. **invitee** (-tē´) *n.* a person invited. **inviter** *n.* **inviting** *a.* **1** attractive. **2** seductive; enticing. **invitingly** *adv.*

invite[2] (in´vīt) *n.* (*coll.*) an invitation.

in vitro (in vē´trō) *a.*, *adv.* (*Biol.*) (of biological processes etc.) taking place outside a living organism, e.g. in a test tube.

in vivo (in vē´vō) *a.*, *adv.* (*Biol.*) (of biological processes) occurring within a living organism.

invocation (invəkā´shən) *n.* **1** the act of invoking. **2** a supplication or call to God, esp. as part of a religious service. **3** a petition addressed to a muse, saint etc., for help or inspiration. **4** the calling up of a spirit by incantation. **invocatory** (-vok´-) *a.*

invoice (in´vois) *n.* a list of goods dispatched, with particulars of quantity and price, sent to a consignee. ~*v.t.* **1** to enter (goods) in an invoice. **2** to send an invoice to.

invoke (invōk´) *v.t.* **1** to address in prayer. **2** to solicit earnestly for (assistance, protection etc.). **3** to call upon solemnly. **4** to call on as a witness; to appeal to as an authority. **5** to summon by magical means. **6** (*Comput.*) to cause (a subroutine etc.) to be carried out. **invocable** *a.* **invoker** *n.*

involucre (in´vəlookə) *n.* **1** (*Bot.*) a whorl of bracts surrounding the flowers of certain plants. **2** (*Anat.*) a membranous envelope or cover of certain parts and organs. **3** a covering or envelope. **involucral** (-loo´krəl), **involucrate** (-loo´-krət) *a.*

involuntary (invol´əntəri) *a.* **1** done unintentionally, not from choice. **2** (of a movement) performed independently of will or volition. **involuntarily** *adv.* **involuntariness** *n.*

involute (in´vəloot) *a.* **1** complicated, involved. **2** (*Bot.*) (of leaves, petals) rolled inwards at the margins. **3** closely coiled. **involuted** *a.*

involution (invəloo´shən) *n.* **1** the act of involving. **2** the state of being involved. **3** a complication; an entanglement. **4** intricacy. **5** a rolling up or curling of parts. **6** anything folding up or curling inwards.

involve (involv´) *v.t.* **1** to cause to take part (in); to include (in). **2** to comprise as a logical or necessary consequence; to imply, to entail. **3** to implicate (in a crime etc.). **4** to have an effect on. **5** to enwrap, to enfold (in). **involved** *a.* **1** concerned or associated. **2** (of a story, explanation etc.) complicated. **3** having a romantic or sexual relationship (with). **involvement** *n.*

invulnerable (invŭl´nərəbəl) *a.* incapable of being wounded or injured. **invulnerability** (-bil´-), **invulnerableness** *n.* **invulnerably** *adv.*

inward (in´wəd) *a.* **1** internal; situated or being within. **2** towards the interior. **3** connected with the mind or soul. ~*adv.* **inwards. inward investment** *n.* investment in a country, esp. by foreign investors. **inward-looking** *a.* self-absorbed. **inwardly** *adv.* **1** internally, within. **2** in one's thoughts and feelings, secretly. **3** not aloud (*She sighed inwardly*). **inwardness** *n.* **inwards** *adv.* **1** towards the interior, internal parts or centre. **2** in the mind or soul.

inwrap ENWRAP.

inwreathe ENWREATHE.

inwrought (in´rawt, -rawt´) *a.* **1** (of a pattern etc.) wrought or worked in. **2** (of a fabric) adorned with work or figures. **3** closely blended.

inyala (inyah´lə) *n.* NYALA.

iodine (ī´ədēn, -dīn) *n.* **1** (*Chem.*) a non-metallic bluish-black element, at. no. 53, chem. symbol I, yielding violet fumes when heated, and resembling bromine and chlorine in chemical properties, used in medicine and photography. **2** a solution of this in alcohol used as an antiseptic. **iodide** (-dīd) *n.* a compound of iodine with an element or radical. **iodize** (ī´ədīz), **iodise** *v.t.* **1** to treat with iodine. **2** to prepare with iodine. **iodization** (-zā´shən) *n.* **iodoform** (īod´əfawm) *n.* an iodine compound resembling chloroform in its antiseptic effects.

ion (ī´ən) *n.* an electrically charged atom or group of atoms formed by the loss or gain of electrons. **ion exchange** *n.* a process by which ions are exchanged between a solution and a solid or another liquid, as used in the softening of water etc. **ion-exchanger** *n.* **ionic** (īon´-) *a.* **ionically** *adv.* **ionize** *v.t.* to convert into an ion or ions. **ionizable** *a.* **ionization** (-zā´shən) *n.* **ionizer** *n.* something which produces ionization. **ionizing radiation** *n.* radiation that can cause ionization.

-ion (ən, iən, yən) *suf.* forming nouns indicating an action, process or resulting state or product, as *distribution, celebration, aspiration.*

Ionian (īō´niən) *a.* of or relating to Ionia, a district of Asia Minor, or to the Ionians. ~*n.* a member of a Hellenic people living in ancient Ionia. **Ionic** (īon´-) *a.* Ionian. ~*n.* the Ionic dialect. **Ionic order** *n.* one of the five classical orders of architecture, the distinguishing characteristic of which is the volute on both sides of the capital.

ionosphere (īon´əsfiə) *n.* the region surrounding the earth at a height of approx. 60–1000 km, in which ionized layers of gas occur. **ionospheric** (-fer´-) *a.*

iota (īō´tə) *n.* **1** the ninth of the Greek alphabet (ι, I). **2** (*usu. with neg.*) a jot, a very small quantity.

IOU (ī ō ū´) *n.* a formal acknowledgement of debt, bearing these letters, the sum involved and the debtor's signature.

-iour (iə, yə), (*esp. N Am.*) **-ior** *suf.* forming nouns, as in *behaviour, saviour, warrior.*

-ious (iəs, əs) *suf.* characterized by, full of, as in *ambitious, cautious, suspicious.*

IPA *abbr.* International Phonetic Alphabet (or Association).

ipecacuanha (ipikakūan´ə) *n.* the dried root of *Cephaelis ipecacuanha*, a cinchonaceous plant from Brazil, used in medicine as an emetic and purgative. **ipecac** (ip´-) *n., a.*

ipomoea (ipəmē´ə) *n.* any twining plant of the genus *Ipomoea*, including the morning glory and jalap.

ipso facto (ipsō fak´tō) *adv.* **1** by that very fact. **2** thereby.

IQ *abbr.* Intelligence Quotient.

Ir *chem. symbol* iridium.

IRA *abbr.* Irish Republican Army.

Iranian (irā´niən) *a.* **1** of or belonging to Iran in SW Asia, formerly Persia. **2** of or relating to the Iranian branch of Indo-European. ~*n.* **1** a native or inhabitant of Iran. **2** a branch of the Indo-European family of languages including Persian, Kurdish and Avestan. **3** the modern Persian language.

Iraqi (irah´ki) *a.* of or relating to Iraq. ~*n.* (*pl.* **Iraqis**) a native or inhabitant of Iraq.

irascible (iras´ibəl) *a.* easily excited to anger; irritable. **irascibility** (-bil´-), **irascibleness** *n.* **irascibly** *adv.*

irate (īrāt´) *a.* angry, enraged. **irately** *adv.* **irateness** *n.*

❌ **irational** common misspelling of IRRATIONAL.

ire (īə) *n.* (*poet.*) anger. **ireful** *a.*

❌ **iregular** common misspelling of IRREGULAR.

❌ **irelevant** common misspelling of IRRELEVANT.

irenic (īrē´nik, -ren´-), **eirenic**, **irenical** (-əl), **eirenical** *a.* pacific; promoting peace.

❌ **iresistible** common misspelling of IRRESISTIBLE.

iridacious (iridā´shəs, ī-) *a.* (*Bot.*) of or relating to the Iridaceae family of plants which grow from bulbs, corms or rhizomes and include the iris.

iridescent (irides´ənt) *a.* **1** exhibiting a spectrum of luminous or shimmering colours. **2** changing colour as the observer's position changes. **iridescence** *n.* **iridescently** *adv.*

iridium (irid´iəm) *n.* (*Chem.*) a shining white metallic element belonging to the platinum group, at. no. 77, chem. symbol Ir.

iridology (iridol´əji) *n.* a diagnostic technique in alternative medicine involving studying the iris of the eye. **iridologist** *n.*

iris (ī´ris) *n.* (*pl.* **irises, irides** (ī´ridēz, ir´-)) **1** the flat circular coloured membrane surrounding the pupil of the eye. **2** any plant of the genus *Iris* of the family Iridaceae, with tuberous roots, sword-shaped leaves, and large variously-coloured flowers. **3** a rock crystal with iridescent properties. **4** IRIS DIAPHRAGM (under IRIS). **iris diaphragm** *n.* an adjustable diaphragm regulating the entry of light into an optical instrument.

Irish (ī´rish) *a.* of or relating to Ireland or its inhabitants or Celtic language. ~*n.* **1** a native or inhabitant of Ireland. **2** (*as pl.*) the people of Ireland. **3** the Celtic language of Ireland. **Irish bull** *n.* a ludicrous contradiction in terms, supposed to be characteristic of the Irish. **Irishman** *n.* (*pl.* **Irishmen**) a man who is a native or inhabitant of Ireland, or a man of Irish descent. **Irish moss** *n.* CARRAGEEN. **Irishness** *n.* **Irish stew** *n.* a stew of vegetables and meat boiled together.

Irish wolfhound *n.* a large breed of dog with a long, usually grey, coat. **Irishwoman** *n.* (*pl.* **Irishwomen**) a woman who is a native or inhabitant of Ireland, or a woman of Irish descent.

☒ **iritate** common misspelling of IRRITATE.

irk (œk) *v.t.* to bore, annoy or irritate. **irksome** *a.* wearisome, tedious, tiring. **irksomely** *adv.* **irksomeness** *n.*

iroko (irō´kō) *n.* **1** either of two African trees of the genus *Chlorophora*. **2** the hard light-coloured wood of these trees.

iron (ī´ən) *n.* **1** (*Chem.*) a malleable ductile metallic element, at. no. 26, chem. symbol Fe, widely used for tools etc. **2** an article, tool, utensil etc., made of iron (*a soldering iron*). **3** a usu. electrical implement for smoothing clothes. **4** great firmness and resolve (*a will of iron*). **5** a metal-headed golf club used for lofting. **6** (*pl.*) fetters. **7** (*usu. pl.*) a stirrup. **8** a preparation of iron for medicinal purposes. ~*a.* **1** made or composed of iron. **2** robust, strong. **3** inflexible, unyielding or merciless. ~*v.t.* **1** to smooth (clothes) with an iron. **2** to fetter with irons. **3** to furnish or cover with iron. **in irons** in fetters. **to have several irons in the fire 1** to be engaged in several projects at the same time. **2** to have several expedients. **to iron out 1** to correct (defects etc.). **2** to find a solution to (problems etc.). **Iron Age** *n.* the late prehistoric age, following the Bronze Age, when weapons and many implements began to be made of iron. **ironbark** *n.* any of several Australian eucalyptus trees, esp. *Eucalyptus paniculata* and *E. sideroxylon*, with a hard, firm bark. **ironclad** *n.* (*Hist.*) a warship having the parts above water plated with iron. ~*a.* **1** covered or protected with iron. **2** impregnable, inflexible. **Iron Curtain** *n.* **1** (*Hist.*) the imperceptible barrier to communication between the former USSR with its satellites and the West. **2** (**iron curtain**) any similar barrier to communication. **ironer** *n.* **iron-grey** *n.* a grey colour like that of iron freshly broken. ~*a.* of iron-grey. **iron hand** *n.* strict control, often tyranny. **ironing** *n.* **1** the act of ironing clothes. **2** clothes that have just been ironed or that are about to be ironed. **ironing board** *n.* a board, usu. on legs of adjustable height, used for ironing clothes etc. on. **ironless** *a.* **iron-like** *a.* **iron lung** *n.* a mechanical device employed for maintaining or assisting respiration. **ironmonger** *n.* a person who deals in ironware or hardware. **ironmongery** *n.* (*pl.* **ironmongeries**) **1** ironware, hardware. **2** an ironmonger's shop or business. **iron-mould**, (*NAm.*) **iron-mold** *n.* a spot on cloth etc. caused by ink or rust. **iron-on** *a.* that can be fixed to a fabric by ironing. **iron pyrites** *n.* a yellow native sulphide of iron, one of two common sulphides, also called *fool's good*. **iron rations** *n.pl.* complete emergency rations packed in a sealed case. **ironstone** *n.* **1** an iron ore containing oxygen and silica. **2** a kind of hard durable china. **ironware** *n.* goods made of iron, hardware. **ironwood** *n.* any of several very hard

and heavy woods. **ironwork** *n.* **1** things made of iron. **2** work, esp. decorative work, done in iron. ~*n.pl.* (*often sing. in constr.*) an establishment where iron is manufactured.

irony (ī´rəni) *n.* (*pl.* **ironies**) **1** an expression, often humorous or slightly sarcastic, intended to convey the opposite of its usual meaning. **2** the use of such expressions. **3** incongruity between what is expected and what happens; a result showing such incongruity. **4** TRAGIC IRONY (under TRAGIC). **ironic** (īron´-), **ironical** *a.* **ironically** *adv.* **ironist** *n.* a person who uses irony. **ironize**, **ironise** *v.i.*

Iroquois (ir´əkwoi, -koi) *n.* (*pl.* **Iroquois**) **1** the American Indian confederacy of the Mohawk, Oneida, Seneca, Onondaga, Cayuga and Tuscarora. **2** a member of any of these peoples. **3** any of the Iroquoian languages. **Iroquoian** *a.* of or relating to the Iroquois or their languages. ~*n.* **1** a North American Indian family of languages including Cherokee and Seneca. **2** a member of the Iroquois.

irradiate (irā´diāt) *v.t.* **1** to subject to sunlight or ultraviolet rays. **2** to make bright or brilliant; to light up. **3** to shed light upon (a subject etc.). **4** to expose (food) to low levels of gamma radiation in order to sterilize and preserve it. **irradiance** *n.* **irradiant** *a.* **irradiation** (-ā´shən) *n.* **irradiative** *a.*

irrational (irash´ənəl) *a.* **1** without reason or understanding. **2** illogical, contrary to reason, absurd. **3** (*Math.*) not expressible by a whole number or common fraction, not commensurable with a finite number. ~*n.* an irrational number. **irrationality** (-nal´-) *n.* **irrationalize**, **irrationalise** *v.t.* **irrationally** *adv.*

irreclaimable (irəklā´məbəl) *a.* incapable of being reclaimed; obstinate; inveterate. **irreclaimably** *adv.*

irreconcilable (irekənsī´ləbəl) *a.* **1** incapable of being reconciled; implacably hostile. **2** incompatible. ~*n.* **1** a person who cannot be reconciled, appeased or satisfied; an intransigent. **2** (*usu. pl.*) each of two or more opinions, principles etc. that cannot be reconciled. **irreconcilability** (-bil´-), **irreconcilableness** *n.* **irreconcilably** *adv.*

irrecoverable (irikŭv´ərəbəl) *a.* that cannot be recovered; irreparable. **irrecoverably** *adv.*

irredeemable (iridē´məbəl) *a.* **1** not redeemable. **2** beyond redemption, offering no scope for salvage or rectification. **irredeemability** (-bil´-), **irredeemableness** *n.* **irredeemably** *adv.*

irredentist (iriden´tist) *n.* a person who advocates the reclaiming of territory that once belonged to their country. **irredentism** *n.*

irreducible (iridū´sibəl) *a.* **1** not reducible; not to be lessened or lowered. **2** not to be brought to a required condition etc. **irreducibility** (-bil´-), **irreducibleness** *n.* **irreducibly** *adv.*

irrefutable (irifū´təbəl) *a.* incapable of being refuted. **irrefutability** (-bil´-) *n.* **irrefutably** *adv.*

irregular (ireg´ülə) *a.* **1** not according to rule or established principles or custom. **2** not uniform or even; asymmetrical. **3** not occurring at regular times. **4** (*Gram.*) deviating from the common form in inflection. **5** not belonging to the regular army. **6** (of a flower) not having petals etc. of the same size or shape. ~*n.* (*pl.*) irregular troops. **irregularity** (-lar´-) *n.* (*pl.* **irregularities**). **irregularly** *adv.*

irrelevant (irel´əvənt) *a.* not applicable or pertinent; having no application (to the matter in hand). **irrelevance** *n.* **irrelevancy** *n.* (*pl.* **irrelevancies**). **irrelevantly** *adv.*

irreligion (irilij´ən) *n.* indifference or hostility to religion. **irreligionist** *n.* **irreligious** *a.* **1** hostile or indifferent to religion. **2** not having a religion. **irreligiously** *adv.* **irreligiousness** *n.*

irremediable (irəmē´diəbəl) *a.* incapable of being remedied or corrected. **irremediableness** *n.* **irremediably** *adv.*

irremissible (irəmis´ibəl) *a.* **1** that cannot be remitted or pardoned. **2** obligatory. **irremissibility** (-bil´-) *n.* **irremissibly** *adv.*

irremovable (irimoo´vəbəl) *a.* that cannot be removed or displaced. **irremovability** (-bil´-) *n.* **irremovably** *adv.*

irreparable (irep´ərəbəl) *a.* incapable of being repaired, remedied or restored. **irreparably** *adv.*

irreplaceable (iriplā´səbəl) *a.* **1** that cannot be replaced. **2** not to be made good in case of loss.

irrepressible (iripres´ibəl) *a.* that cannot be repressed. **irrepressibility** (-bil´-), **irrepressibleness** *n.* **irrepressibly** *adv.*

irreproachable (iriprō´chəbəl) *a.* blameless, faultless. **irreproachably** *adv.*

irresistible (irizis´tibəl) *a.* **1** that cannot be resisted or withstood. **2** extremely attractive or alluring. **irresistibility** (-bil´-), **irresistibleness** *n.* **irresistibly** *adv.*

irresolute (irez´əloot) *a.* **1** not resolute. **2** undecided, hesitating. **irresolutely** *adv.* **irresoluteness, irresolution** (-oo´shən) *n.*

irresolvable (irizol´vəbəl) *a.* **1** incapable of being resolved, insoluble. **2** that cannot be analysed or separated into its parts.

irrespective (irispek´tiv) *a.* (*followed by of*) regardless of, without reference to.

irresponsible (irispon´sibəl) *a.* **1** performed or acting without a proper sense of responsibility. **2** lacking the capacity to bear responsibility. **irresponsibility** (-bil´-) *n.* **irresponsibly** *adv.*

irresponsive (irispon´siv) *a.* not responsive (to). **irresponsiveness** *n.*

irretrievable (iritrē´vəbəl) *a.* not to be retrieved; irreparable. **irretrievability** (-bil´-) *n.* **irretrievably** *adv.*

irreverent (irev´ərənt) *a.* lacking in reverence; disrespectful. **irreverence** *n.* **irreverential** (-ren´shəl) *a.* **irreverently** *adv.*

irreversible (irivœ´sibəl) *a.* not reversible; irrevocable. **irreversibility** (-bil´-), **irreversibleness** *n.* **irreversibly** *adv.*

irrevocable (irev´əkəbəl) *a.* incapable of being

revoked or altered, unalterable. **irrevocability** (-bil´-), **irrevocableness** *n.* **irrevocably** *adv.*

irrigate (ir´igāt) *v.t.* **1** to water (land) by causing a stream to flow over it. **2** (of streams etc.) to supply (land) with water. **3** (*Med.*) to moisten (a wound etc.) with a continuous jet or stream of antiseptic fluid. **irrigable** *a.* **irrigation** (-ā´shən) *n.* **irrigative** *a.* **irrigator** *n.*

irritate (ir´itāt) *v.t.* **1** to excite to impatience or ill-temper; to annoy; to exasperate. **2** to cause discomfort in (the skin, an organ etc.). **3** (*Biol.*) to stimulate (an organ) artificially. **irritable** *a.* **1** easily provoked or angered. **2** easily inflamed or made painful, highly sensitive. **irritability** (-bil´-), **irritableness** *n.* **irritable bowel syndrome** *n.* a condition which is marked by abdominal pain and constipation or diarrhoea and which is often associated with stress etc. **irritably** *adv.* **irritant** *n.* something that irritates. ~*a.* causing irritation. **irritancy** *n.* **irritatedly** *adv.* **irritating** *a.* **irritatingly** *adv.* **irritation** (-ā´shən) *n.* **irritative** *a.* **irritator** *n.*

irruption (irŭp´shən) *n.* **1** a bursting in. **2** a sudden invasion or incursion. **3** a sudden temporary increase in the local population of an animal or plant.

is BE.

isagogic (īsəgoj´ik) *a.* introductory. **isagogics** *n.* an introductory study, esp. of the literary history, authorship etc. of the Bible.

ISBN *abbr.* International Standard Book Number.

ischaemia (iskē´miə), (*esp. N Am.*) **ischemia** *n.* (*Med.*) a shortage of blood in part of the body. **ischaemic** *a.*

ischium (is´kiəm) *n.* (*pl.* **ischia** (-ə)) either of the posterior bones of the pelvic girdle. **ischial** *a.*

ISDN *abbr.* integrated services digital network.

-ise[1] (īz, ēz) *suf.* forming abstract nouns, as *franchise, merchandise.*

-ise[2] (īz) *suf.* forming verbs, as *advertise.*

Usage note See note under -IZE.

-ise[3] -IZE.

-ish[1] (ish) *suf.* **1** of the nature of, of or relating to, as *childish.* **2** rather, somewhat, as *reddish.* **3** of the nationality of, as *English.* **4** (*coll.*) indicating approximate age, time etc., as *thirtyish, twoish.*

-ish[2] (ish) *suf.* forming verbs, as *cherish, finish, punish.*

isinglass (ī´zing-glahs) *n.* **1** a gelatinous substance prepared from the swimming-bladders of the sturgeon, cod, and other fish, used for making jellies, glue etc. **2** mica.

Islam (iz´lahm) *n.* **1** the Muslim religion, that teaches that there is only one God and that Muhammad is his prophet. **2** the Muslim world. **Islamic** (-lah´mik) *a.* **Islamism** *n.* **Islamist** *n.* **Islamize, Islamise** *v.t.* to convert to Islam. **Islamization** (-zā´shən) *n.*

island (ī´lənd) *n.* **1** a piece of land surrounded by water. **2** anything isolated or resembling an island. **3** an area in the middle of a road which divides the traffic and affords a refuge for the pedestrian. **4** a cluster of cells, mass of tissue etc., different in formation from those surrounding it. **5** (*Naut.*) the superstructure on a ship. **islander** *n.* a native or inhabitant of an island. **island-hop** *v.i.* (*pres.p.* **island-hopping**, *past, p.p.* **island-hopped**) to travel from one island to another, esp. as a tourist. **isle** (īl) *n.* (*esp. poet.*) an island, esp. a small island. **islet** (-lit) *n.* **1** a little island. **2** (*Anat.*) a portion of tissue different in formation from tissues surrounding it. **3** an isolated place.

ism (iz´m) *n.* (*usu. derog.*) a doctrine or system of a distinctive kind.

-ism (izm) *suf.* **1** forming abstract nouns denoting a doctrine, theory or system, as *Conservatism*, *Socialism*. **2** forming nouns denoting an action, process or result, as *plagiarism*, *exorcism*. **3** forming nouns denoting a condition or quality, as *altruism*, *fanaticism*. **4** forming nouns denoting prejudice or discrimination on a particular basis, as *sexism*, *ageism*. **5** forming nouns denoting a particular linguistic feature or usage, as *Gallicism*, *regionalism*. **6** forming nouns denoting a pathological condition, as *rheumatism*.

isn't (iz´ənt) *contr.* is not.

iso- (ī´sō), **is-** (īs) *comb. form* **1** equal, having the same number of parts, as *isodynamic*. **2** (*Chem.*) indicating an isomeric substance, as *isocyanide*.

isobar (ī´sōbah) *n.* **1** a line on a map connecting places having the same mean barometric pressure, or the same pressure at a given time. **2** (*Chem.*) a curve relating qualities measured at the same pressure. **3** (*Physics*) any of two or more isotopes of different elements that have the same atomic weight. **isobaric** (-bar´-) *a.*

isocheim (ī´sōkīm) *n.* a line on a map connecting places having the same mean winter temperature.

isochromatic (īsōkrəmat´ik) *a.* of the same colour.

isochronal (isok´rənəl), **isochronous** (-əs) *a.* **1** denoting or occupying equal spaces of time. **2** occurring at equal intervals of time. **isochronously** *adv.*

isoclinal (īsōklī´nəl), **isoclinic** (-klin´-) *a.* **1** having the same magnetic dip. **2** (*Geol.*) (of folds) in which the limbs are parallel to each other.

isodynamic (īsōdīnam´ik) *a.* having equal force, esp. magnetic force.

isoelectric (īsōilek´trik) *a.* having identical electric potential.

isoenzyme (ī´sōenzīm) *n.* (*Biol.*) any of two or more enzymes with identical activities but different structure.

isogamy (īsog´əmi) *n.* (*Biol.*) the sexual fusion of two gametes of similar size and form.

isogeotherm (īsōjē´əthœm) *n.* an imaginary line below the surface of the earth connecting places having the same mean temperature. **isogeothermal** (-thœ´-), **isogeothermic** *a.*

isogloss (ī´sōglos) *n.* a line on a map separating off a region that has a specific dialectal feature.

isogon (ī´sōgon) *n.* a geometrical figure in which all the angles are equal. **isogonic** (-gon´-) *a.* connecting points (on the earth's surface) having the same magnetic declination or variation from true north.

isohel (ī´sōhel) *n.* a line on a map connecting places having equal amounts of sunshine.

isohyet (īsōhī´it) *n.* a line on a map connecting places having equal amounts of rainfall.

isokinetic (īsōkinet´ik) *a.* **1** not involving any change in speed. **2** of or relating to muscle action that has a constant rate of movement.

isolate (ī´səlāt) *v.t.* **1** to place apart; to detach. **2** to quarantine (a person thought to be contagious). **3** to separate (a problem, idea etc.) in order to examine or deal with it. **4** to insulate (electrical equipment). **5** (*Chem.*) to obtain in an uncombined form. **isolable** *a.* **isolation** (-ā´shən) *n.* in **isolation** considered separately and not in relation to anything else. **isolationism** *n.* a policy of holding aloof from international affairs. **isolationist** *n.* **isolator** *n.*

isomer (ī´sōmə) *n.* **1** (*Chem.*) any of two or more compounds with the same molecular composition but a different structure and different properties. **2** (*Physics*) any of two or more atomic nuclei which have the same atomic number and the same mass number, but have different energy states. **isomeric** (īsəmer´ik), **isomerical** *a.* **isomerism** (īsom´-) *n.* **isomerize**, **isomerise** *v.i., v.t.* **isomerous** (īsom´-) *a.* (*Zool., Bot.*) having the same number of parts or segments.

isometric (īsōmet´rik), **isometrical** (-əl) *a.* **1** of equal measure. **2** (of muscle action) producing tension but not producing any contraction of the muscle. **3** (*Math.*) (of a transformation) with distance remaining unaltered. **isometrically** *adv.* **isometrics** *n.pl.* a system of exercises in which the muscles are strengthened as one muscle is opposed to another or to a resistant object. **isometry** (īsom´itri) *n.*

isomorph (ī´sōmawf) *n.* an organism or substance exhibiting isomorphism. **isomorphic**, **isomorphous** *a.* **isomorphism** (-maw´-) *n.* **1** similarity of form. **2** the property of crystallizing in identical or nearly identical forms. **3** (*Math.*) identity of form and construction between two or more groups.

isopleth (ī´sōpleth) *n.* a line on a map connecting points at which a variable such as humidity has a constant value.

isopod (ī´sōpod) *n.* any of the Isopoda or sessile-eyed crustaceans characterized by seven pairs of thoracic legs almost of the same length, including woodlice and many aquatic species.

isosceles (īsos´əlēz) *a.* (of a triangle) having two sides equal.

isoseismal (īsōsīz´məl), **isoseismic** (-mik) *a.* connecting points at which an earthquake has been of the same intensity. *~n.* an isoseismal line.

isostatic (īsōstat´ik) *a.* (*Geol.*) in equilibrium

owing to equality of pressure on every side, as that normally prevailing in the crust of the earth.

isothere (ī′sōthiə) *n.* a line on a map connecting points having the same mean summer temperature.

isotherm (ī′sōthœm) *n.* **1** a line on a globe or map passing over places having the same mean temperature. **2** (*Physics*) a curve on a graph relating quantities of equal temperature. **isothermal** (-thœ′-) *a.*, *n.* **isothermally** *adv.*

isotonic (īsōton′ik) *a.* **1** (of muscles) having equal tension or tonicity. **2** (of the corpuscles of the blood) having the same osmotic pressure. **isotonically** *adv.* **isotonicity** (-nis′i-) *n.*

isotope (ī′sətōp) *n.* (*Chem.*) each of two or more atoms of a chemical element having the same atomic number but differing in atomic mass. **isotopic** (-top′-) *a.* **isotopically** *adv.* **isotopy** (īsot′-) *n.*

isotropic (īsōtrop′ik) *a.* manifesting the same physical properties in every direction. **isotropically** *adv.* **isotropy** *n.*

I spy (ī spī′) *n.* **1** a children's game in which one player specifies the initial letter of a visible object, which the other players then try to guess. **2** hide-and-seek.

Israeli (izrā′li) *a.* of or relating to the modern state of Israel. ~*n.* (*pl.* **Israelis**) a native or inhabitant of Israel. **Israelite** (iz′rəlīt) *n.* a member of the ancient Hebrew people, esp. an inhabitant of the kingdom of Israel (922–721 BC). ~*a.* of or relating to the Israelites.

issue (ish′oo, is′ū) *n.* **1** the act of sending, giving out or putting into circulation. **2** something that is given out or put into circulation. **3** something which is published at a particular time as part of a regular series (*the March issue*). **4** the whole quantity or number of stamps, coins, copies of a newspaper etc. sent out or put on sale at one time. **5** the act of passing or flowing out. **6** an outgoing, outflow. **7** an outlet, e.g. the mouth of a river. **8** something which passes or flows out. **9** (*Law*) progeny, offspring. **10** the produce of the earth; profits from land or other property. **11** a result; a consequence. **12** an important point or subject of debate. **13** (*Law*) a matter of dispute between contending parties. ~*v.i.* (*3rd pers. sing. pres.* **issues**, *pres.p.* **issuing**, *past*, *p.p.* **issued**) **1** to go or come out. **2** to emerge (from). **3** to proceed, to be derived (from). **4** to end or result (in). ~*v.t.* **1** to send out; to publish; to put into circulation. **2** to provide or supply officially (with) (*We were issued with uniforms*). **3** to announce officially (a warning etc.). **at issue 1** in dispute. **2** at variance. **to join issue with** to take issue with. **to make an issue of** to make a fuss about (something) that one disagrees with. **to take issue with** to argue against or disagree with. **issuable** *a.* **issuance** *n.* **issueless** *a.* **issuer** *n.*

-ist (ist) *suf.* **1** forming nouns and corresponding adjectives denoting an adherent or follower, as *Baptist, fatalist, Socialist*. **2** denoting a person who practises a particular profession or is involved in a particular field, as *botanist, herbalist*. **3** denoting a person who uses or performs something, as *flautist, motorist, exorcist*. **4** denoting a person characterized by a particular attribute, as *optimist*. **5** forming nouns and corresponding adjectives denoting a person with a particular prejudice, as *ageist, sexist*.

isthmus (is′məs) *n.* **1** (*pl.* **isthmuses**) a neck of land connecting two larger portions of land. **2** (*Anat.*) (*pl.* **isthmi** (-mī)) a narrow passage or part between two larger cavities or parts. **isthmian** *a.*

istle (ist′li) *n.* a species of Mexican agave, or the tough wiry fibre of its leaves, used for cord, nets etc.

IT *abbr.* information technology.

it (it) *pron.* (*poss.* **its**) **1** the thing, or sometimes the animal or small child, mentioned or referred to (*She unlocked the case and opened it*). **2** the person present, speaking etc. (*It is I*). **3** used as the subject of impersonal verbs (*It's snowing; It's half past six*). **4** used to stand in for a deferred object or subject (*It's a good thing you arrived when you did; It's a waste of time, all this hanging around*). **5** used as an indefinite object (*to rough it; to fight it out*). **6** used as the antecedent of a following clause (*It's one of the best plays (that) I've ever seen*). **7** the ultimate point or extreme limit. **8** something that corresponds exactly to what one is looking for. **9** the player in a children's game chosen to oppose the others. **10** (*coll.*) sexual intercourse; sex appeal. **that's it 1** that is what is wanted. **2** that is enough. **3** that is the difficulty or problem. **this is it 1** this is the moment when something that has been expected is about to actually happen. **2** this is the problem.

i.t.a., ITA *abbr.* initial teaching alphabet.

ital. *abbr.* italic.

Italian (ital′yən) *a.* of or relating to Italy, its people or language. ~*n.* **1** a native or inhabitant of Italy. **2** the Italian language. **Italianate** *a.* Italian in style.

italic (ital′ik) *a.* **1** applied to a sloping type (*thus*), often used for emphasis or for foreign words. **2** (of handwriting) that slants to the right. **3** (**Italic**) of or relating to ancient Italy, its peoples or their languages, esp. as distinguished from Roman. ~*n.pl.* italic letters or type. **italicize** (-sīz), **italicise** *v.t.* to print in italics. **italicization** (-zā′shən) *n.*

Italo- (ital′ō, it′əlō) *comb. form* Italian, as *Italophile*.

itch (ich) *v.i.* **1** to have an uncomfortable and irritating sensation in the skin causing a desire to scratch. **2** to feel a constant teasing desire (to do something). ~*n.* **1** a sensation of uneasiness in the skin causing a desire to scratch. **2** an impatient desire or craving. **itching** *n.*, *a.* **itching powder** *n.* a powder that makes the skin itch, used esp. as a practical joke. **itchy** *a.* (*comp.* **itchier**, *superl.* **itchiest**) having or causing an itch. **to have itchy feet 1** to want to travel. **2** to be restless. **itchiness** *n.*

it'd (it´əd) *contr.* (*coll.*) **1** it had. **2** it would.

-ite[1] (īt) *suf.* **1** (*sometimes derog.*) denoting a follower of, as *Pre-Raphaelite, Hitlerite.* **2** denoting a fossil, mineral, as *belemnite, ichnite, dolomite.* **3** denoting a native or inhabitant of a country, as *Hittite.* **4** denoting a part of a body or organ, as *somite.* **5** denoting an explosive, as *gelignite.* **6** denoting a commercial product, as *vulcanite.* **7** denoting a salt of an acid ending with the suffix *-ous,* as *sulphite.*

-ite[2] (īt, it) *suf.* **1** forming nouns, as *infinite.* **2** forming adjectives, as *recondite.* **3** forming verbs, as *ignite.*

item (ī´təm) *n.* **1** any of a series of things listed or enumerated. **2** an individual entry in an account, schedule etc. **3** a piece of news in a newspaper, television programme etc. **4** an article, esp. one of a number. **5** (*coll.*) two people who are in a romantic or sexual relationship. **itemize, itemise** *v.t.* to list. **itemization** (-zā´shən) *n.* **itemizer** *n.*

iterate (it´ərāt) *v.t.* to repeat; to say over and over again. **iteration** (-ā´shən) *n.* **iterative** *a.* **1** repetitious. **2** (*Gram.*) FREQUENTATIVE (under FREQUENT[1]). **iteratively** *adv.*

-itic (it´ik) *suf.* forming adjectives from nouns ending in *-ite, -itis* etc., as *arthritic.*

itinerant (itin´ərənt) *a.* **1** passing or moving from place to place. **2** (of a judge, worker etc.) working for a short time in one place after another. ~*n.* a person who journeys from place to place. **itineracy, itinerancy** *n.* **itinerantly** *adv.*

itinerary (ītin´ərəri) *n.* (*pl.* **itineraries**) **1** a route taken or to be taken. **2** an account of places and their distances on a road; a guidebook. **3** an account of travels. ~*a.* of or relating to roads or to travel.

-ition (ish´ən) *suf.* forming nouns, as *proposition, contrition.*

-itious[1] (ish´əs) *suf.* forming adjectives that correspond to nouns ending in *-ition,* as *ambitious, nutritious.*

-itious[2] (ish´əs) *suf.* having the nature of, as *adventitious, factitious.*

-itis (ī´tis) *suf.* **1** denoting inflammation, as *gastritis, peritonitis.* **2** (*coll., facet.*) denoting a condition that is like a disease, as *examitis.*

it'll (it´əl) *contr.* (*coll.*) it will, it shall.

its (its) *a.* possessive of IT. ~*pron.* something which belongs to or is associated with it.

Usage note The spellings of the pronoun *its* and the contraction *it's* should not be confused: the possessive pronoun does not have an apostrophe, but should always be an apostrophe for 'it is' or 'it has'.

it's (its) *contr.* **1** it is. **2** it has.

Usage note See note under ITS.

itself (itself´) *pron.* **1** IT, used to give emphasis (usu. in apposition). **2** the reflexive of IT. **by itself** alone; separately. **in itself** independently of other things; in its essential qualities.

itsy-bitsy (itsibit´si), **itty-bitty** (itibit´i) *a.* (*coll., usu. derog.*) tiny.

-ity (iti) *suf.* **1** denoting a state or condition, as *equality, fragility.* **2** denoting an instance of this, as *calamity.*

IU *abbr.* international unit.

IUD *abbr.* **1** intrauterine device. **2** intrauterine death (of a foetus).

-ium (iəm) *suf.* **1** (*also* -**um**) used to form names of metals, as *aluminium, lithium, sodium.* **2** used to form names of parts of the body, as *myocardium.* **3** used to form names of biological structures, as *prothallium.*

IV *abbr.* intravenous.

I've (īv) *contr.* I have.

-ive (iv) *suf.* **1** disposed, serving or tending; of the nature or quality of, as *active, massive, pensive, restive, talkative.* **2** forming corresponding nouns, as *captive, detective.* **-ively** *suf.* forming adverbs. **-iveness** *suf.* forming nouns.

IVF *abbr.* in vitro fertilization.

ivied IVY.

ivory (ī´vəri) *n.* (*pl.* **ivories**) **1** the hard white substance composing the tusks of the elephant, the narwhal etc. **2** the colour of ivory. **3** an ornament etc. made of ivory. **4** (*pl., sl.*) things resembling or made of ivory, e.g. teeth, billiard balls, dice, keys of a piano. ~*a.* **1** consisting of, made of or resembling ivory. **2** of the colour of ivory. **ivory tower** *n.* a shelter from the realities of everyday life.

IVR *abbr.* International Vehicle Registration.

ivy (ī´vi) *n.* (*pl.* **ivies**) **1** an evergreen climbing plant, *Hedera helix,* usu. having five-angled leaves, and adhering by aerial rootlets. **2** any of various other climbing plants, such as the poison ivy. **ivied** *a.* covered with ivy. **Ivy League** *n.* a group of eight long-established and prestigious US universities.

izard (iz´əd) *n.* a kind of antelope related to the chamois, inhabiting the Pyrenees.

-ize (īz), **-ise** *suf.* **1** forming verbs meaning to follow or practise some principle, policy etc., as *economize.* **2** to come to resemble; to come into a specified state, as *crystallize.* **3** to cause to resemble or come into such a specified state, as *Anglicize, sterilize.* **4** to treat in a specified way, as *vulcanize.* **5** to feel a specified thing, as *empathize.* **6** to subject to, as *memorize, hypnotize.* **7** to provide with, as *motorize.* **-ization** (īzā´shən) *suf.* forming corresponding nouns. **-izer** *suf.*

Usage note This dictionary uses the spelling *-ize.* The alternative *-ise,* which is common especially in Britain, is listed for the first relevant word in each entry. (The ending *-ise* is also found in words where it does not represent this suffix, as in *advertise.*) American spelling also prefers *-ize.*

J

J[1] (jā), **j** (*pl.* **Js, J's**) the tenth letter of the English and other versions of the Roman alphabet. It is pronounced as a voiced affricate, the sound of *g* in *gem*, except in a few words adopted from German etc., where it has the sound of *y*. ~*symbol* **1** current density. **2** one in Roman numerals, as a variant of *i* in final position, as in *vj*.

J[2] *abbr.* joule(s).

jab (jab) *v.t.* (*pres.p.* **jabbing**, *past, p.p.* **jabbed**) **1** to poke violently. **2** to stab. **3** to thrust (something) roughly (into). ~*n.* **1** a sharp poke, a stab, a thrust. **2** (*coll.*) a vaccination or injection.

jabber (jab´ə) *v.i.* **1** to talk volubly and incoherently. **2** to chatter. ~*v.t.* to utter rapidly and indistinctly. ~*n.* rapid, indistinct or nonsensical talk. **jabberer** *n.*

jabiru (jab´iroo) *n.* a bird of the genus *Ephippiorhynchus*, esp. *E. mycteria*, S American storklike wading birds.

jabot (zhab´ō) *n.* **1** a lace frill worn at the neck of a woman's bodice. **2** a ruffle on a shirt front.

jacana (jak´ənə), **jaçana** (jasənah´) *n.* any bird of the family Jacanidae, from the warmer parts of N and S America.

jacaranda (jakəran´də) *n.* a tropical American tree, esp. of the genus *Jacaranda*, yielding fragrant and ornamental wood.

jacinth (jas´inth, jā´-) *n.* a variety of zircon.

jack (jak) *n.* **1** a contrivance for lifting heavy weights. **2** a device for lifting the axle of a vehicle off the ground so that a wheel etc. can be changed. **3** the knave of cards. **4** a small flag. **5** a socket for a jack plug, a jack socket. **6** in bowls, a small white ball at which bowlers aim. **7** a stone or small piece of metal etc. used in tossing games, a jackstone. **8** (*pl.*) a game played esp. by children, in which small pieces of metal etc. are tossed and caught, jackstones. **9** the figure of a man striking a bell on a clock. **10** (*sl.*) a detective or police officer. **11** (*N Am., coll.*) a lumberjack. **12** a steeplejack. **13** a sailor. **14** (**Jack**) a fellow, one of the common people. **15** any of various perch-like fish of the family Carangidae. **16** a pike, esp. a young or small one. **17** a species or variety of animal smaller than other kinds. **18** the male of some animals. **19** a lever or other part in various machines. **20** a contrivance for turning a spit. **21** a device for plucking a string or moving a hammer in some instruments. **22** a wooden frame on which wood or timber is sawn. **23** (*N Am., sl.*) money. ~*v.t.* **1** to lift, hoist or move with a jack. **2** (*sl.*) to resign, to give (up). **3** (*coll.*) to raise (prices etc.). **every man jack** every individual. **to jack in** (*sl.*) to abandon. **to jack off** (*taboo sl.*) to masturbate. **to jack up** to abandon.

jackboot *n.* **1** a large boot with a front piece coming above the knee. **2** (*fig.*) unintelligent and inhuman behaviour in dictatorial rule (from the high boots worn by German soldiers). **jackbooted** *a.* **Jack-by-the-hedge** *n.* a cruciferous plant, *Alliaria petiolata*, with white flowers. **Jack Frost** *n.* frost personified. **jackhammer** *n.* a hand-held compressed-air hammer used for drilling rock. **jack-in-the-box** *n.* a grotesque figure that springs out of a box when the lid is raised. **jackknife** *n.* (*pl.* **jackknives**) **1** a large clasp-knife, esp. orig. one with a horn handle, carried by seamen. **2** a dive in which the diver doubles up and then straightens out again. ~*v.i.* (*pres.p.* **jackknifing**, *past, p.p.* **jackknifed**) **1** to double up like a jackknife. **2** (of an articulated vehicle) to turn or rise and form an angle of 90° or less when out of control. **3** to perform a jackknife dive. ~*v.t.* to double up like a jackknife. **jack of all trades** *n.* a person who can turn their hand to any business, activity etc. **jack-o'-lantern** *n.* **1** a will-o'-the wisp. **2** a lantern made from a hollowed-out pumpkin etc. **jack plane** *n.* the first and coarsest of the joiner's bench planes. **jack plug** *n.* a one-pronged plug used esp. in sound equipment. **jackpot** *n.* **1** the money pool in card games and competitions. **2** a fund of prize money. **to hit the jackpot 1** (*coll.*) to win a large prize. **2** (*coll.*) to have a big success. **jackrabbit** *n.* any of the various large prairie hares of N America, of the genus *Lepus*. **Jack Russell (terrier)** *n.* **1** a breed of small terrier introduced by John Russell in the 19th cent. **2** a dog of this breed. **jack socket** *n.* a socket for a jack plug; also called *jack.* **jackstaff** *n.* (*Naut.*) a flagstaff on the bowsprit cap for flying the jack. **jackstone** *n.* **1** a small piece of metal etc. used in tossing games; also called *jack.* **2** (*pl.*) the children's game of jacks. **Jack tar** *n.* a sailor. **Jack the Lad** *n.* (*coll.*) an adventurous, stylish young man.

jackal (jak´əl, -awl) *n.* **1** a gregarious animal, *Canis aureus*, closely allied to the dog. **2** (*coll.*) a person who does dirty work or drudgery for another (from the belief that the jackal hunts up prey for the lion).

jackaroo (jakəroo´), **jackeroo** *n.* (*pl.* **jackaroos, jackeroos**) (*Austral., coll.*) a newcomer, a novice.

jackass (jak´as) *n.* **1** a male ass. **2** a stupid ignorant person.

jackdaw (jak´daw) *n.* the smallest of the British crows, *Corvus monedula*.

jacket (jak´it) *n.* **1** a short coat or sleeved outer garment for men or women. **2** something that resembles this, worn for protection or support. **3** the coat of an animal. **4** a wrapper, a cover. **5** an outer covering of paper put on a book bound in cloth or leather. **6** the skin of a potato. **7** an exterior covering or casing esp. a covering round a boiler, steam pipe, cylinder of an internal-combustion engine etc., to prevent radiation of heat. *~v.t.* (*pres.p.* **jacketing**, *past, p.p.* **jacketed**) to envelop in a jacket. **jacket potato** *n.* a baked potato in its skin.

Jacobean (jakəbē´ən) *a.* **1** belonging to the reign of James I. **2** (of furniture) in the style of this time, esp. of dark oak. *~n.* a person of the time of James I.

Jacobite (jak´əbīt) *n.* (*Hist.*) a partisan of James II after his abdication, or of the Stuart pretenders to the throne. *~a.* of, relating to or holding the opinions of the Jacobites. **Jacobitism** *n.*

Jacob's ladder (jā´kəbz) *n.* **1** a garden plant, *Polemonium caeruleum*, with closely pinnate leaves. **2** a rope ladder with wooden rungs.

jacquard (jak´ahd, -əd) *n.* **1** an apparatus with perforated cards used to weave intricate designs. **2** fabric so woven. **jacquard loom** *n.* a loom for weaving figured fabrics.

Jacuzzi® (jəkoo´zi) *n.* (*pl.* **Jacuzzis**) **1** a type of bath or small pool with a mechanism which makes the water swirl round. **2** a bathe in such a bath.

jade¹ (jād) *n.* **1** a broken-down, worthless horse. **2** (*derog.*) an old woman; a wench, a young woman. *~v.t.* **1** to overdrive. **2** (*usu. in p.p.*) to tire out. **jaded** *a.* **jadedly** *adv.* **jadedness** *n.*

jade² (jād) *n.* **1** a green, massive, sometimes crypto-crystalline, silicate of lime and magnesia, used for ornamental purposes. **2** the green colour of jade. **jadeite** *n.* a sodium aluminium silicate form of jade.

jaeger (yā´gə) *n.* (*N Am.*) a seabird of the skua family esp. of the genus *Stercoraria*.

jag¹ (jag) *n.* **1** a notch. **2** a ragged piece, tooth or point. **3** a stab, a prick. *~v.t.* (*pres. p.* **jagging**, *past, p.p.* **jagged**) **1** to cut or tear raggedly. **2** to cut into notches, to form denticulations in. **jagged** (jag´id) *a.* **1** having notches. **2** ragged, sharply uneven. **jaggedly** *adv.* **jaggedness** *n.* **jagger** *n.* **jaggy** *a.* (*comp.* **jaggier**, *superl.* **jaggiest**) **1** jagged. **2** (*Sc.*) (*also* **jaggie**) prickly.

jag² (jag) *n.* **1** (*sl.*) a bout of drinking or drug-taking. **2** (*coll.*) a bout of indulgence. **3** a bundle or load of hay etc.

jaguar (jag´ūə) *n.* a S American feline animal, *Panthera onca*, resembling the leopard.

jaguarundi (jagwərŭn´di) *n.* (*pl.* **jaguarundis**) a wild cat, *Felis yaguarondi*, of Central and S America.

jai alai (hīəlī´) *n.* a game played by two or four players on a court, who wear woven baskets tied to their wrists and using these hurl a ball at the walls.

jail (jāl), **gaol** *n.* **1** a prison, a public place of confinement for persons charged with or convicted of crime. **2** confinement in a jail. *~v.t.* to put in jail. **jailbait** *n.* (*sl.*) a girl who is below the legal age of consent. **jailbird** *n.* **1** a person who has been to prison. **2** an inveterate criminal. **jailbreak** *n.* an escape from jail. **jailer** *n.* the keeper of a prison. **jailhouse** *n.* (*esp. N Am.*) a prison.

Jain (jīn, jān), **Jaina** (-nə) *n.* an adherent of a non-Brahminical Indian religion. *~a.* of or belonging to the Jains or Jainism. **Jainism** *n.* **Jainist** *n.*

jake (jāk) *a.* (*coll.*) (*Austral., New Zeal.*) all right, very good.

jalap (jal´əp, jol´əp) *n.* the dried tubercles of *Exogonium purga*, used as a purgative.

jalapeño (haləpān´yō, -pē´nō) *n.* (*pl.* **jalapeños**) (*also* **jalapeño pepper**) a very hot green chilli pepper.

jalopy (jəlop´i) *n.* (*pl.* **jalopies**) (*coll.*) a much-worn motor vehicle.

jalousie (zhal´uzi) *n.* a louvre blind, a Venetian shutter. **jalousied** *a.*

jam¹ (jam) *v.t.* (*pres.p.* **jamming**, *past, p.p.* **jammed**) **1** to wedge or squeeze (in or into). **2** to squeeze, to compress between two surfaces. **3** to squeeze together. **4** to block up by crowding into. **5** to make (a machine etc.) immovable or unworkable by forcible handling. **6** to prevent clear radio reception of (a signal) by transmitting an interfering signal on the same wavelength. *~v.i.* **1** to become wedged. **2** (of a machine etc.) to become immovable or unworkable by rough handling. **3** to push or crowd. **4** (*coll.*) (of a musician) to improvise freely. **5** (*coll.*) to take part in a jam session. *~n.* **1** a crush, a squeeze. **2** a stoppage in a machine due to jamming. **3** a crowd, a press. **4** congestion (*a traffic jam*). **5** (*coll.*) a jam session. **to be in a jam** to be in a predicament. **jammer** *n.* **jam-packed** *a.* **1** very crowded. **2** filled to capacity. **jam session** *n.* (*coll.*) an improvised session of playing by jazz, rock etc. musicians.

jam² (jam) *n.* **1** a conserve of fruit made by boiling with sugar. **2** (*coll.*) something easy or desirable. *~v.t.* (*pres.p.* **jamming**, *past, p.p.* **jammed**) **1** to spread jam on. **2** to make into jam. **jam tomorrow** better things promised but usu. never forthcoming. **jammy** *a.* (*comp.* **jammier**, *superl.* **jammiest**) (*coll.*) **1** sticky (with jam). **2** lucky. **3** desirable.

Jamaican (jəmā´kən) *a.* of or relating to Jamaica, in the West Indies. *~n.* a native or inhabitant of Jamaica. **Jamaica satinwood** *n.* WEST INDIAN SATINWOOD (under WEST).

jamb (jam) *n.* (*Archit.*) any one of the upright sides of a doorway, window, or fireplace.

jambalaya (jambəlī´ə) *n.* a Southern US dish consisting of meat, seafood, rice, onions etc.

jamboree (jambərē´) *n.* **1** a Scout rally. **2** a frolic.

Jan. *abbr.* January.

jane (jān) *n.* (*N Am., Austral., sl.*) a woman.

jangle (jăng´gəl) *v.i.* to sound harshly or discordantly. *~v.t.* **1** to cause to sound discordantly.

2 to irritate, upset. ~*n*. discordant sound, as of bells out of tune. **jangler** *n*. a wrangler.

janitor (jan´itə) *n*. **1** a doorkeeper. **2** a caretaker, porter. **janitorial** (-taw´ri-) *a*.

janizary (jan´izəri), **janissary** (-səri) *n*. (*pl*. **janizaries, janissaries**) **1** (*Hist*.) a soldier of the old Turkish infantry forming the Sultan's bodyguard (orig. young prisoners trained to arms), disbanded in 1826. **2** a follower, supporter.

January (jan´ūəri) *n*. (*pl*. **Januaries**) the first month of the year.

Jap (jap) *a*., *n*. (*derog. or offensive*) JAPANESE.

japan (jəpan´) *n*. **1** an intensely hard varnish, or varnishing liquid, made from linseed oil, resin, shellac etc. **2** a hard, black varnish obtained from *Stagmaria verniciflua*. **3** work varnished and figured in the Japanese style. ~*v.t*. (*pres. p*. **japanning**, *past*, *p.p*. **japanned**) to cover with or as with japan. **Japan earth** *n*. catechu.

Japanese (japənēz´) *a*. of or relating to Japan or its inhabitants. ~*n*. (*pl*. **Japanese**) **1** a native or inhabitant of Japan. **2** (*as pl*.) the people of Japan. **3** the language of Japan. **Japanese cedar** *n*. a tall Japanese conifer, *Cryptomeria japonica*. **Japanese print** *n*. a colour print from woodblocks. **Japanese quince** *n*. japonica.

jape (jāp) *v.i*. to jest, to play tricks. ~*n*. a jest, a trick, a joke. **japer** *n*. **japery** *n*.

Japlish (jap´lish) *n*. a blend of Japanese and English.

japonica (jəpon´ikə) *n*. any flowering shrub of the genus *Chaenomeles*, esp. *C. speciosa*, the Japanese quince.

jar¹ (jah) *v.i*. (*pres.p*. **jarring**, *past*, *p.p*. **jarred**) **1** to emit a harsh or discordant sound. **2** to vibrate harshly. **3** to be discordant, disagreeable, or offensive. **4** to disagree, to clash, to be inconsistent (with). ~*v.t*. **1** to cause to shake or tremble. **2** to give a shock to. ~*n*. **1** a harsh vibration as from a shock. **2** a harsh discordant sound. **3** a shock. **4** a disagreement, a conflict of opinions or interests. **jarring** *a*. **jarringly** *adv*.

jar² (jah) *n*. **1** a vessel of glass or earthenware of various shapes and sizes, used for various domestic purposes. **2** the contents of this. **3** (*coll*.) (a glass of) alcoholic drink. **jarful** *n*. (*pl*. **jarfuls**).

jardinière (zhahdinyeə´) *n*. **1** an ornamental pot or stand for growing flowers in a room etc. **2** a dish of mixed cooked vegetables.

jargon (jah´gən) *n*. **1** any professional, technical or specialized language. **2** debased or illiterate speech or language. **3** unintelligible talk, gibberish, gabble. **jargonesque** (-nesk´), **jargonic** (-gon´-), **jargonistic** (-nis´tik) *a*. **jargonize, jargonise** *v.i*. **jargonization** (-zā´shən) *n*.

jarrah (jar´ə) *n*. **1** the W Australian mahogany gum tree, *Eucalyptus marginata*. **2** the timber of this.

jasmine (jaz´min), **jasmin, jessamin** (jes´əmin), **jessamine** *n*. any plant of the genus *Jasminum*, many of which are climbers with sweet-scented white or yellow flowers, esp. the common white *J. officinale*. **jasmine tea** *n*. tea perfumed with jasmine blossom.

jasper (jas´pə) *n*. an impure variety of quartz, of many colours and shades, opaque even in thin splinters.

jato (jā´tō) *n*. (*pl*. **jatos**) **1** jet assisted take-off. **2** a power unit which provides extra thrust at take-off.

jaundice (jawn´dis) *n*. **1** (*Med*.) a condition due to obstruction of the bile or absorption of the colouring matter into the blood, characterized by yellowness of the skin, diarrhoea and general debility. **2** a mental attitude or condition, such as that caused by jealousy, prejudice etc., which warps the vision. ~*v.t*. **1** to affect with or as with jaundice. **2** to poison the mind with jealousy, prejudice etc. **jaundiced** *a*.

jaunt (jawnt) *n*. a ramble, an excursion, a short journey, a trip. ~*v.i*. to take a short excursion. **jaunting car** *n*. (*Hist*.) an Irish horse-drawn vehicle having two seats, back to back, over the wheels, and a seat for the driver in front.

jaunty (jawn´ti) *a*. (*comp*. **jauntier**, *superl*. **jauntiest**) **1** sprightly, airy, self-satisfied, perky. **2** smart. **jauntily** *adv*. **jauntiness** *n*.

Javanese (jahvənēz´) *a*. of or relating to Java. ~*n*. (*pl*. **Javanese**) **1** a native or inhabitant of Java. **2** (*as pl*.) the people of Java. **3** the language of Java. **Java man** *n*. a fossil human of the species *Homo erectus*. **Javan** *n*., *a*. **Java sparrow** *n*. a waxbill, *Padda oryzivora*, often kept in aviaries.

javelin (jav´əlin) *n*. **1** a light spear thrown by the hand, used as a weapon or in field events. **2** the competitive sport of javelin-throwing.

jaw (jaw) *n*. **1** either of two bones or bony structures in which the teeth are fixed, forming the framework of the mouth. **2** (*pl*.) the mouth. **3** (*pl*.) the narrow opening of a gorge, narrow valley etc. **4** either of two opposing members of a vice or similar implement or machine. **5** (*pl*.) a narrow opening or entrance. **6** (*coll*.) abuse, wrangling, long-winded talk. **7** a lecture. ~*v.i*. (*coll*.) to talk lengthily. ~*v.t*. **1** to abuse. **2** to lecture. **3** to persuade by talking. **jawbone** *n*. either of the pair of bones forming the lower jaw. **jaw-breaker** *n*. (*coll*.) an unpronounceable word. **jawed** *a*. **jaw-jaw** *n*. talking, esp. pointless discussion. ~*v.i*. to talk, esp. pointlessly or at length. **jawless** *a*. **jaw-line** *n*. the outline of the jaw. **jaw-tooth** *n*. (*pl*. **jaw-teeth**) a molar.

jay (jā) *n*. **1** a chattering bird, *Garrulus glandarius*, with brilliant plumage. **2** any other bird of the subfamily Garrulinae. **3** an impudent chatterer. **jaywalker** *n*. (*coll*.) a pedestrian who crosses the street heedless of the traffic. **jaywalk** *v.i*.

jazz (jaz) *n*. **1** syncopated music of African-American origin. **2** (*coll*.) insincere talk. ~*v.i*. to play or dance to jazz. **to jazz up 1** to quicken the tempo of (a piece of music). **2** to make more attractive, livelier, colourful etc. **jazzer** *n*. **jazzman** *n*. (*pl*. **jazzmen**) a jazz musician. **jazzy** *a*.

(*comp.* **jazzier**, *superl.* **jazziest**) **1** of or like jazz. **2** vivid or flashy. **jazzily** *adv.* **jazziness** *n.*

JCB® (jäsēbē´) *n.* a type of construction machine with a hydraulically operated shovel at the front and an excavator at the back.

JCL *abbr.* (*Comput.*) job-control language.

J cloth® (jā´kloth), **J-cloth** *n.* a type of cloth used esp. for cleaning, wiping work surfaces etc.

jealous (jel´əs) *a.* **1** suspicious or apprehensive of being supplanted in the love or favour (of a wife, husband, lover or friend). **2** suspicious or apprehensive (of a rival). **3** solicitous or anxiously watchful (of one's honour, rights etc.). **4** envious (of another or another's advantages etc.). **5** (*Bible*) requiring exclusive devotion (of God). **jealously** *adv.* **jealousness** *n.* **jealousy** *n.* (*pl.* **jealousies**).

jeans (jēnz) *n.pl.* close-fitting casual trousers usu. made of denim or other cotton fabric.

Jeep® (jēp) *n.* **1** (*US*) a fast, light car for military use. **2** a utility motor van.

jeepers (jē´pəz), **jeepers creepers** (krē´pəz) *int.* (*N Am.*, *sl.*) used to express surprise etc.

jeer (jiə) *v.i.* to scoff, to mock (at). *~v.t.* to scoff at, to make a mock of, to deride. *~n.* a scoff, a gibe, a taunt, mockery. **jeerer** *n.* **jeeringly** *adv.*

Jeez (jēz) *int.* (*sl.*) used to express surprise etc.

~~**jehad** JIHAD.~~

Jehovah (jihō´və) *n.* the most sacred name given in the Old Testament to God, esp. regarded as the God of the Jewish people. **Jehovah's Witness** *n.* a member of the millenarian sect, the International Bible Students' Association, founded by the American Pastor C. T. Russell, 1852–1916.

jejune (jijoon´) *a.* **1** bare, meagre, scanty. **2** wanting in substance. **3** devoid of interest or life. **4** poor, barren. **5** puerile, childish, naive. **jejunely** *adv.* **jejuneness** *n.*

Usage note Use in the sense 'puerile, childish' is sometimes disapproved of.

jejunum (jijoo´nəm) *n.* (*Anat.*) the second portion of the small intestine between the duodenum and the ileum.

Jekyll and Hyde (jek´əl ənd hīd´, jē´-) *n.* a person with a split personality, one side evil, the other good.

jell (jel), **gell** *v.i.* (*coll.*) **1** to turn into jelly. **2** (of ideas etc.) to come together. **3** (of people) to co-operate, to get on well. **jellify** *v.t.*, *v.i.* (*3rd pers. sing. pres.* **jellifies**, *pres.p.* **jellifying**, *past, p.p.* **jellified**) to make or become like jelly. **jellification** (-fikā´shən) *n.*

jellaba DJELLABA.

jelly (jel´i) *n.* (*pl.* **jellies**) **1** any gelatinous substance, esp. that obtained by decoction from animal matter. **2** a conserve made of the inspissated juice of fruit boiled with sugar. **3** (*sl.*) gelignite. *~v.i.* (*3rd pers. sing. pres.* **jellies**, *pres.p.* **jellying**, *past, p.p.* **jellied**) to turn into jelly. *~v.t.* to convert into jelly. **Jell-O**® (jel´ō), **jello** *n.* (*pl.* **Jell-Os**, **jellos**) (*esp. N Am.*) a fruit-flavoured jelly-like dessert. **jelly baby** *n.* (*pl.* **jelly babies**) a sweet

made of jelly and shaped like a baby. **jelly bag**, **jelly cloth** *n.* a bag or cloth used for straining jelly. **jelly bean** *n.* a sugar-coated, bean-shaped sweet filled with jelly. **jellyfish** *n.* (*pl. in general* **jellyfish**, *in particular* **jellyfishes**) **1** a marine coelenterate with a jelly-like body and stinging tentacles, of the class Scyphozoa. **2** (*coll.*) a feeble person. **jelly-like** *a.* **jelly roll** *n.* (*N Am.*) a Swiss roll.

jemmy (jem´i) *n.* (*pl.* **jemmies**) a short, stout crowbar, used by burglars. *~v.t.* (*3rd pers. sing. pres.* **jemmies**, *pres.p.* **jemmying**, *past, p.p.* **jemmied**) to force open with a jemmy.

je ne sais quoi (zhə nə sä kwa´) *n.* an indefinable something.

jennet (jen´it) *n.* a small Spanish horse.

jenny (jen´i) *n.* (*pl.* **jennies**) **1** a female ass, animal, bird etc. **2** (*Hist.*) a spinning jenny. **3** a travelling crane. **jenny-wren** *n.* a wren.

jeopardy (jep´ədi) *n.* **1** exposure to danger, loss or injury. **2** risk, hazard, danger, peril. **3** (*Law*) danger faced by an accused person in a criminal case. **jeopardize**, **jeopardise** *v.t.* **1** to put in jeopardy. **2** to risk.

jerboa (jœbō´ə) *n.* a small mouselike rodent of the family Dipodidae, with long hind legs adapted for leaping.

jeremiad (jerəmī´əd) *n.* a lamentation, esp. over modern degeneracy, in the style of the prophet Jeremiah.

Jeremiah (jerəmī´ə) *n.* **1** a prophet of doom. **2** a pessimistic person.

jerk¹ (jœk) *v.t.* **1** to pull, push, or thrust sharply. **2** to throw with a sharp, suddenly arrested action. **3** in weightlifting, to raise (a weight) from shoulder level to above the head. *~v.i.* to move with jerks. *~n.* **1** a sharp, sudden push or tug. **2** a twitch, a spasmodic movement due to involuntary contraction of a muscle. **3** (*sl.*) a stupid, ignorant or contemptible person. **4** a quick sudden movement, jolt. **5** (*pl.*) violent twitches or spasmodic movements of the face or members, often due to religious excitement. **6** (*pl.*, *coll.*) exercises. **7** in weightlifting, the raising of a weight from shoulder level to above the head. **to jerk off** (*taboo sl.*) to masturbate. **jerker** *n.* **jerky** *a.* (*comp.* **jerkier**, *superl.* **jerkiest**) **jerkily** *adv.* **jerkiness** *n.*

jerk² (jœk) *v.t.* to cure (beef) by cutting it into long pieces and drying it in the sun.

jerkin (jœ´kin) *n.* **1** a short coat or jacket, formerly often made of leather. **2** a close waistcoat.

jeroboam (jerəbō´əm) *n.* a wine bottle holding 10–12 quarts (about 12 l).

Jerry (jer´i) *n.* (*pl.* **Jerries**) (*sl., often derog.*) **1** a German soldier. **2** the Germans collectively.

jerry (jer´i) *a.* cheaply and badly built, flimsy. *~n.* (*pl.* **jerries**) (*sl.*) a chamber pot. **jerry-builder** *n.* a speculative builder of cheap and inferior houses. **jerry-building** *n.* **jerry-built** *a.*

jerrycan (jer´ikan), **jerrican** *n.* a can for petrol, water etc., orig. German.

jerrymander GERRYMANDER.

jersey (jœ´zi) *n.* (*pl.* **jerseys**) **1** a knitted garment, as a pullover, worn on the upper part of the body. **2** fine wool yarn; a plain-knitted (orig. woollen) fabric. **3** a close-fitting woollen knitted tunic worn in sports and athletics. **4** (**Jersey**) a Jersey cow. **Jersey cow** *n.* a breed of dairy cattle originating from Jersey.

Jerusalem artichoke (jəroo´sələm) *n.* **1** a species of sunflower, *Helianthus tuberosus*, the tuberous roots of which are edible. **2** the tuber of it eaten as a vegetable.

jess (jes) *n.* in falconry, a short leather or silk ribbon for tying round each leg of a hawk, to which the leash may be attached. *~v.t.* to put jesses on.

jessamin, jessamine JASMINE.

jest (jest) *n.* **1** a joke, something ludicrous said or done to provoke mirth. **2** a jeer, a taunt. **3** a laughing stock. *~v.i.* **1** to joke. **2** to provoke mirth by ludicrous actions or words. **3** to ridicule, to jeer (at). **in jest** not seriously or in earnest. **jester** *n.* **1** a person who jests or jokes. **2** a buffoon, esp. one formerly retained by persons of high rank to make sport. **jestingly** *adv.*

Jesuit (jez´ūit) *n.* a member of the Society of Jesus, a Roman Catholic order founded in 1534 by Ignatius Loyola. **Jesuitic** (-it´-), **Jesuitical** *a.* **1** of or relating to the Jesuits. **2** (*offensive*) crafty, cunning, designing. **Jesuitically** *adv.*

jet¹ (jet) *n.* **1** a black compact variety of lignite capable of being brilliantly polished, formerly much used for articles of personal ornament. **2** the colour of jet. *~a.* of this colour. **jet black** *n.* a glossy black colour.

jet² (jet) *v.i.* (*pres.p.* **jetting**, *past, p.p.* **jetted**) **1** to spurt or shoot out, to come out in a jet or jets. **2** to travel by jet plane. *~v.t.* **1** to send out in a jet or jets. **2** to send in a jet plane. *~n.* **1** a sudden spurt or shooting out of water or flame, esp. from a small orifice. **2** a spout or nozzle for the discharge of water etc. **3** a jet-propelled plane. **4** a jet engine. **jet engine** *n.* an engine using jet propulsion, esp. one fitted to an aircraft. **jetfoil** *n.* a hydrofoil powered by a jet of water. **jet lag** *n.* the exhaustion caused by the body's inability to adjust to the time-zone changes involved in long-distance air travel. **jet-lagged** *a.* **jet plane** *n.* a jet-propelled plane. **jet-propelled** *a.* **1** (of an aircraft or vehicle) propelled by heating and expanding air which is directed in a jet from the rear of the plane. **2** very fast. **jet propulsion** *n.* **jet set** *n.* the group of fashionable people who can afford constant travel by jet plane. **jet-setter** *n.* **jet-setting** *n.* **jet ski** *n.* a small powered water vehicle with a flat keel shaped like a water-ski. **jet-ski** *v.i.* (*3rd pers. sing. pres.* **jet-skies**, *pres.p.* **jet-skiing**, *past, p.p.* **jet-skied**). **jet-skiing** *n.* **jet stream** *n.* **1** a belt of winds 12,000 m above the earth. **2** the exhaust from a jet engine.

jeté (zhet´ā, -tā´) *n.* a leap from one foot to another in ballet.

jetsam (jet´səm) *n.* goods, cargo etc., thrown

overboard in order to lighten a ship in distress, and subsequently washed ashore.

jettison (jet´isən) *n.* the casting of goods overboard to lighten a vessel in distress. *~v.t.* **1** to throw (goods) overboard in order to lighten a vessel. **2** to drop (anything unwanted) from an aircraft or spacecraft in flight. **3** to cast aside; to rid oneself of.

jetton (jet´ən) *n.* a stamped or engraved counter used in card-playing, or as a coin in a machine.

jetty (jet´i) *n.* (*pl.* **jetties**) **1** a structure of stone or timber projecting into water and serving as a mole, pier, or wharf. **2** a landing pier.

Jew (joo) *n.* a person of Hebrew descent or whose religion is Judaism. **jew** *v.t.* (*offensive*) to drive a hard bargain, to cheat. **Jewess** *n.* (*sometimes offensive*) a female Jew. **jewfish** *n.* (*pl. in general* **jewfish**, *in particular* **jewfishes**) **1** a grouper, *Epinephelus itajara*. **2** any of several large Australian fish, esp. the mulloway. **Jewish** *a.* of or relating to Jews or Judaism. **Jewishly** *adv.* **Jewishness** *n.* **Jew's-ear** *n.* a tough edible fungus, *Auricularia auricula-judae*, growing on elder and elm trees. **jew's harp** *n.* a musical instrument held between the teeth, the sound produced by the vibrations of a metal tongue set in motion by the forefinger.

jewel (joo´əl) *n.* **1** a precious stone, a gem. **2** a personal ornament containing a precious stone or stones. **3** a person or thing of very great value or excellence. **4** the best or most valuable part of something. *~v.t.* (*pres.p.* **jewelling**, (*N Am.*) **jeweling**, *past, p.p.* **jewelled**, (*N Am.*) **jeweled**) **1** to adorn with or as with jewels. **2** to fit (a watch) with jewels in the pivot-holes. **jewel-fish** *n.* (*pl. in general* **jewel-fish**, *in particular* **jewel-fishes**) a brightly-coloured tropical fish, *Hemichromis bimaculatus*. **jeweller**, (*N Am.*) **jeweler** *n.* a maker of or dealer in jewels. **jeweller's rouge** *n.* finely ground rouge used for polishing metal. **jewellery** (-əlri), **jewelry** *n.* **1** (*collect.*) jewels in general. **2** the art or trade of a jeweller. **jewel-like** *a.* **jewelly** *a.*

Usage note Pronunciation of *jewellery* as (joo´ləri) is best avoided.

Jewry (joo´ri) *n.* (*pl.* **Jewries**) **1** (*collect.*) the Jews or the land where they dwell or dwelt. **2** (*Hist.*) the Jews' quarter in a town or country.

Jezebel (jez´əbel) *n.* a wicked, bold, or vicious woman, esp. a woman who paints her face.

jib¹ (jib) *n.* **1** a large triangular sail set on a stay between the fore-topmast-head and bowsprit or jib-boom in large vessels and between the masthead and the bowsprit in smaller ones. **2** the extended arm of a crane or derrick. **the cut of one's jib** (*orig. Naut., sl.*) one's physical appearance. **jib-boom** *n.* a movable spar running out beyond the bowsprit.

jib² (jib) *v.t.* (*pres.p.* **jibbing**, *past, p.p.* **jibbed**) to shift (a boom, yard or sail) from one side of a vessel to the other. ~*v.i.* to swing round (of a sail etc.).

jib³ (jib) *v.i.* (*pres.p.* **jibbing**, *past, p.p.* **jibbed**) **1** (of a horse etc.) to move restively sideways or backwards. **2** to make difficulties (at some task, course, person etc.). **3** (of a horse etc.) to stop short and refuse to move forwards. **to jib at 1** (of a person) to refuse to do (something). **2** to show aversion to (a person or thing). **jibber** *n.*

jibba (jib´ə), **jibbah, djibba, djibbah** *n.* a long, loose coat worn by Muslims.

jibe¹ (jīb) *v.i.* (*N Am., coll.*) to agree, accord (with).

jibe² GIBE.

jibe³ GYBE.

jiff (jif), **jiffy** (-i) *n.* (*pl.* **jiffs, jiffies**) (*coll.*) a moment, an instant, an extremely short time.

Jiffy bag® (jif´i) *n.* a padded envelope.

jig (jig) *n.* **1** a lively dance for one or more performers. **2** the music for such a dance. **3** a fishhook with a weighted shank, used for snatching at fish. **4** a device for holding an object and guiding a cutting-tool in a machine for the manufacture of standard parts. ~*v.i.* (*pres.p.* **jigging**, *past, p.p.* **jigged**) **1** to dance a jig. **2** to skip about. **3** to move up and down rapidly or jerkily. **4** to fish (for) or catch with a jig. ~*v.t.* **1** to jerk up and down rapidly. **2** to work on or equip with a jig. **3** to fish for or catch with a jig. **to jig about** to fidget. **jigsaw** *n.* **1** a vertically-reciprocating saw moved by a vibrating lever or crank-rod, used for cutting scrolls, fretwork etc. **2** a jigsaw puzzle. **jigsaw puzzle** *n.* a puzzle to put together a picture cut into irregularly shaped pieces.

jigger¹ (jig´ə) *n.* **1** (*Naut.*) a small tackle used for holding on to the cable as it is heaved in, and similar work. **2** a small sail, usu. set on a jiggermast. **3** a small smack carrying this. **4** (*sl.*) any kind of mechanical contrivance, implement etc. **5** in golf, an iron club with a narrow face, used for lofting and for medium distance shots. **6** (*coll.*) a rest for a billiard cue. **7** a small measure of spirits. **8** a small glass for this. **9** a person who or thing which jigs. **jigger-mast** *n.* a small mast at the stern of a yawl, a small mizzen-mast.

jigger² (jig´ə) *n.* the flea *Tunga penetrans*, a chigger.

jiggered (jig´əd) *a.* (*coll.*) very surprised, confounded. **I'll be jiggered** used to express surprise etc.

jiggery-pokery (jigəripō´kəri) *n.* (*coll.*) underhand goings-on.

jiggle (jig´əl) *v.t.* to jerk or rock lightly to and fro. ~*v.i.* to fidget. ~*n.* a jiggling movement. **jiggly** *a.*

jihad (jihad´, -hahd´), **jehad** *n.* a holy war proclaimed by Muslims against unbelievers or the enemies of Islam.

jilt (jilt) *v.t.* to throw over or discard (one's lover). ~*n.* a person, esp. a woman who jilts a lover.

Jim Crow (jim krō´) *n.* **1** (*N Am., offensive*) a black person. **2** the policy of segregating blacks. **3** an implement for bending or straightening rails. **Jim Crowism** *n.*

jim-jams (jim´jamz) *n.pl.* (*coll.*) pyjamas.

jimmy (jim´i) *n.* (*pl.* **jimmies**) (*N Am.*) a short crowbar, a jemmy.

jimson (jim´sən), **jimson weed** *n.* (*N Am.*) a poisonous weed, *Datura stramonium*, the thorn apple.

jingle (jing´gəl) *v.i.* **1** to make a clinking or tinkling sound like that of small bells, bits of metal etc. **2** to correspond tritely or annoyingly in sound, rhyme etc. ~*v.t.* to cause to make a clinking or tinkling sound. ~*n.* **1** a tinkling metallic sound. **2** a correspondence or repetition of sounds in words, esp. of a catchy inartistic kind. **3** doggerel. **4** a simply rhythmical verse, esp. one used in advertising. **jingly** *a.*

jingo (jing´gō) *n.* (*pl.* **jingoes**) a person given to (excessive) belligerent patriotism. **by jingo 1** used to express surprise etc. **2** used to emphasize a statement of intention etc. **jingoism** *n.* **jingoist** *n.* **jingoistic** (-is´-) *a.*

jink (jingk) *v.i.* (*Sc.*) **1** to move nimbly. **2** to dodge. ~*v.t.* to dodge. ~*n.* a slip, an evasion, a dodging · turn, a dodge.

jinnee (jinē´), **jinn** (jin), **djinn** *n.* (*pl.* **jinn, djinn**) any of a race of spirits or demons in Muslim mythology supposed to have the power of assuming human or animal forms.

jinx (jingks) *n.* (*coll.*) a person or thing that brings ill luck. ~*v.t.* to subject to bad luck, put a spell on.

JIT *abbr.* just-in-time.

jitter (jit´ə) *v.i.* to be nervous, behave in a nervous way. **jitterbug** *n.* **1** a person who spreads alarm. **2** (*Hist.*) a fast dance performed to swing music. **3** (*Hist.*) a dancer who greatly exaggerates swing dancing. ~*v.i.* (*pres.p.* **jitterbugging**, *past, p.p.* **jitterbugged**) to dance the jitterbug. **jitters** *n.pl.* (*sl.*) nervous apprehension. **jittery** *a.* **jitteriness** *n.*

jiu-jitsu JU-JITSU.

jive (jīv) *n.* **1** a style of lively, jazz-style music. **2** dancing to such music. ~*v.i.* **1** to dance to jive music. **2** to play jive music. **jiver** *n.*

jizz (jiz) *n.* the characteristic features, appearance, behaviour etc. which distinguish a bird or other animal or plant from other species.

Jnr *abbr.* Junior.

Job (jōb) *n.* an uncomplaining sufferer or victim. **Job's comforter** *n.* a false friend who lacerates one's feelings whilst pretending to sympathize. **Job's tears** *n.pl.* the seeds of a grass, *Coix lacryma-jobi*, used as beads.

job (job) *n.* **1** a piece of work, esp. one done for a stated price. **2** an occupation. **3** a responsibility or duty. **4** (*coll.*) a difficult task. **5** a piece of work or business yielding unfair profit or advantage, esp. one in which public interests are sacrificed to personal gain. **6** (*coll.*) a situation. **7** (*sl.*) a crime, esp. a robbery. **8** a specified operation, esp. one involving plastic surgery (*a nose job*). **9** (*sl.*) an example of a particular product. **10** a situation in paid employment. ~*a.* **1** applied to collections of things sold together. **2** let on hire. ~*v.t.* (*pres.p.* **jobbing**, *past, p.p.* **jobbed**) **1** to buy up in miscellaneous lots and retail. **2** to deal in (stocks). **3** to deal with in an underhand way for one's private benefit. **4** (*N Am., sl.*) to swindle. ~*v.i.* **1** to buy and sell as a broker. **2** to do job-work. **3** to make profit corruptly out of a position of trust, esp. at public expense. **just the job** (*coll.*) exactly what is wanted. **on the job 1** (*coll.*) at work, in activity. **2** (*coll., euphem.*) engaged in sexual activity. **out of a job** unemployed. **to make a (good) job of** to do thoroughly or successfully. **job analysis** *n.* the analysis of the contents of a job for the purpose of providing a job description etc. **job analyst** *n.* **jobber** *n.* **1** a person who deals in stocks and shares on the Stock Exchange. **2** (*N Am.*) a wholesaler. **3** a person who does small jobs. **4** (*derog.*) a person who uses a position of trust, esp. a public office, commission etc., to private advantage. **jobbery** *n.* **1** jobbing. **2** corrupt dealing. **jobbing** *n.* working by the job. ~*a.* of or relating to a person who works by the job. **jobcentre** *n.* a government-run centre where information about available jobs is displayed. **job-control language** *n.* (*Comput.*) a language which allows the user to control the tasks undertaken by the operating system. **job-hunt** *v.i.* (*coll.*) to look for work. **jobless** *a.* **joblessness** *n.* **job lot** *n.* a miscellaneous lot of goods bought cheap in the expectation of random profit. **jobs for the boys** *n.pl.* (*coll.*) jobs given to someone's supporters or favourites. **job-sharing** *n.* the division of one job by two or more people who work hours complementary to each other. **job-share** *n.*, *v.i.* **jobsheet** *n.* a sheet on which details of a job are recorded. **jobsworth** *n.* (*coll.*) a minor functionary who is quite inflexible in their interpretation of the law and is very unhelpful to the public (from the phrase 'it's more than my *job's worth*'). **jobwork** *n.* work done or paid for by the job.

Jock (jok) *n.* (*coll.*) (*often offensive*) a Scotsman.

jock[1] (jok) *n.* (*coll.*) **1** a jockey. **2** a disc jockey.

jock[2] (jok) *n.* (*sl., orig. N Am.*) **1** an athlete. **2** a jockstrap.

jockey (jok´i) *n.* (*pl.* **jockeys**) a professional rider in horse races. ~*v.t.* (*3rd pers. sing. pres.* **jockeys**, *pres.p.* **jockeying**, *past, p.p.* **jockeyed**) **1** to deceive in a bargain. **2** to employ sharp practices against. **3** to outwit, outmanoeuvre etc. **4** to cheat. ~*v.i.* to play a tricky game. **to jockey for position 1** to try by skill to get an advantageous position. **2** to gain an unfair advantage. **jockey cap** *n.* a cap with a long peak, worn by jockeys. **jockeydom, jockeyism, jockeyship** *n.*

jockstrap (jok´strap) *n.* **1** a support for the genitals worn by men engaged in athletic or sporting activity. **2** (*N Am., coll.*) an athletic person, esp. a student.

jocose (jəkōs´) *a.* **1** humorous, facetious. **2** given to jokes or jesting. **3** containing jokes, amusing.

jocosely *adv.* **jocoseness** *n.* **jocosity** (-kos´-) *n.* (*pl.* **jocosities**).

jocular (jok´ūlə) *a.* **1** addicted to jesting. **2** merry, facetious, amusing. **jocularity** (-lar´-) *n.* (*pl.* **jocularities**). **jocularly** *adv.*

jocund (jok´ənd) *a.* **1** sportive, merry. **2** inspiring mirth. **jocundity** (-kŭn´-) *n.* (*pl.* **jocundities**). **jocundly** *adv.*

jodhpurs (jod´pəz) *n.pl.* long riding-breeches fitting closely from the knee to the ankle.

Joe Bloggs (jō blogz´), (*N Am.*) **Joe Blow** (blō´) *n.* (*coll.*) a typical or ordinary person. **Joe Public** *n.* (*coll.*) the general public.

joey (jō´i) *n.* (*pl.* **joeys**) (*Austral.*) **1** a young kangaroo. **2** a young animal.

jog (jog) *v.t.* (*pres.p.* **jogging**, *past, p.p.* **jogged**) **1** to push or jerk lightly, usu. with the hand or elbow. **2** to nudge, esp. to excite attention. **3** to stimulate (one's memory or attention). ~*v.i.* **1** to run at a steady, slow pace for exercise. **2** to move with an up-and-down leisurely pace. **3** to walk or trudge idly, heavily, or slowly (on, along etc.). **4** to go, to depart, to be off. ~*n.* **1** a light push or nudge to arouse attention. **2** a leisurely trotting or jogging motion. **to jog on** to get along (somehow or in some specified manner). **jogger** *n.* a person who jogs (for exercise). **jogtrot** *n.* **1** a slow, easy, monotonous trot. **2** humdrum progress. **3** slow routine. ~*a.* monotonous.

joggle (jog´əl) *v.t.* **1** to shake, push, nudge or jerk slightly. **2** in building, to unite by means of joggles, to prevent sliding. ~*v.i.* to shake slightly, to totter. ~*n.* **1** a joint in stone or other material to prevent sliding of one piece over another. **2** a notch, projection, dowel etc., used to form such joints.

john (jon) *n.* (*sl.*) **1** a lavatory. **2** a prostitute's client. **John Bull** *n.* **1** the English people personified. **2** an Englishman. **John Doe** *n.* (*N Am.*) **1** (*Law*) the fictitious plaintiff in an (obsolete) action for ejectment, the defendant being called Richard Roe. **2** (*coll.*) JOE BLOGGS. **John Dory** *n.* (*pl.* **John Dories**) a European marine fish, *Zeus faber*, which has spiny dorsal fins and a black spot on each side.

johnny (jon´i) *n.* (*pl.* **johnnies**) **1** (*sl.*) a condom **2** (*coll.*) a fellow, a chap. **johnny-come-lately** *n.* (*pl.* **johnny-come-latelies, johnnies-come-lately**) (*coll.*) a newcomer.

joie de vivre (zhwa də vē´vrə) *n.* joy of living; exuberance.

join (join) *v.t.* **1** to connect, to fasten together, to unite. **2** to couple, to associate. **3** to unite (two persons, or a person or persons with or to) in marriage etc. **4** to begin, to engage in (battle etc.). **5** to become a member of (a club etc.). ~*v.i.* **1** to be contiguous or in contact. **2** to become associated or combined (with etc.) in views, partnership, action etc. **3** to become a member (of a society etc.). ~*n.* **1** a joint. **2** a point, line, or mark of junction. **to join hands 1** to clasp hands (with). **2** to come to an understanding or combine (with). **to join in** to take part. **to join up 1** to enlist. **2** to connect. **joinable** *a*. **joinder** (-də) *n*. (*Law*) **1** the act of joining. **2** conjunction. **joiner** *n*. **1** a carpenter who makes articles of furniture, finishes woodwork etc. **2** (*coll*.) a person who likes joining clubs etc. **3** a person who joins. **joinery** *n*.

joint (joint) *n*. **1** a junction or mode of joining parts together. **2** the place where two things are joined together. **3** the union of two bones in an animal body. **4** an analogous point or mechanical device connecting parts of any structure, whether fixed or movable. **5** any of the pieces into which a butcher cuts up a carcass. **6** a node. **7** an internode. **8** (*Geol*.) a natural fissure or line of parting traversing rocks in a straight and well-determined line. **9** (*sl*.) a marijuana cigarette. **10** (*sl*.) a low and usu. illicit opium or gambling den. **11** (*sl*., *often derog*.) a place, building etc. **12** (*sl*.) a bar or nightclub. **13** (*N Am*., *sl*.) an eating house. ~*a*. **1** of, belonging to, performed or produced by different persons in conjunction. **2** sharing or participating (with others). ~*v.t.* **1** to form with joints or articulations. **2** to connect by joints. **3** to plane and prepare (boards etc.) for joining. **4** to point (masonry). **5** to divide or cut (meat) into joints, to disjoint. **out of joint 1** dislocated. **2** out of order. **to put someone's nose out of joint** to upset, disconcert or supplant a person. **joint account** *n*. a bank account held by more than one person. **joint and several** *a*. (ofan obligation etc.) undertaken by two or more people. **jointed** *a*. **jointer** *n*. **1** a person who or thing which joints. **2** in carpentry, a long plane used to true the edges of boards to be joined. **3** a pointing tool used by masons and bricklayers. **jointless** *a*. **jointly** *adv*. **jointress** (-tris), **jointuress** (-tūris) *n*. a woman who has a jointure. **joint stock** *n*. stock or capital divided into shares and held jointly by several persons. **joint-stock company** *n*. **jointure** (-tūə) *n*. an estate in lands or tenements, settled upon a woman in consideration on marriage, which she is to enjoy after her husband's decease. ~*v.t.* to settle a jointure upon.

joist (joist) *n*. any of a series of parallel horizontal timbers to which floorboards or the laths of a ceiling are nailed. **joisted** *a*.

jojoba (həhō′bə, hō-) *n*. a desert shrub, *Simmondsia chinensis*, native to Arizona, Mexico and California, whose edible seeds provide waxy oil similar to spermaceti, used in cosmetics, toiletries etc.

joke (jōk) *n*. **1** something said or done to excite laughter or merriment. **2** a jest. **3** a ridiculous incident, circumstance, person etc. ~*v.i.* to make jokes, to jest. ~*v.t.* **1** to crack jokes about. **2** to rally, to banter. **joker** *n*. **1** a person who jokes, a jester. **2** (*sl*.) a fellow. **3** an extra card (often printed with a comic device) used with various values in some card games. **4** (*N Am*.) a clause in a bill or document which looks innocent but

effectively makes it inoperative. **5** an unforeseen factor. **joker in the pack** *n*. a person who or thing which is unpredictable. **jokingly** *adv*. **joky, jokey** *a*. (*comp*. **jokier**, *superl*. **jokiest**). **jokily** *adv*. **jokiness** *n*.

jolly[1] (jol′i) *a*. (*comp*. **jollier**, *superl*. **jolliest**) **1** happy and cheerful. **2** jovial, festive. **3** inspiring or expressing mirth. **4** slightly drunk. **5** (*coll*.) pleasant, agreeable, charming. **6** remarkable, extraordinary. **7** (*iron*.) nice, precious. ~*adv*. (*coll*.) very, exceedingly. ~*v.t.* **1** to banter, to joke, to rally. **2** (*coll*.) to treat agreeably so as to keep in good humour or secure a favour (usu. with *along*). ~*n*. (*pl*. **jollies**) (*coll*.) a celebration. **jollify** (-fī) *v.i.* (*3rd pers. sing. pres.* **jollifies**, *pres.p.* **jollifying**, *past, p.p.* **jollified**) **1** to make merry. **2** to tipple. ~*v.t.* to make (a person) merry, esp. with drink. **jollification** (-fikā′shən) *n*. **jollily** *adv*. **jolliness** *n*. **jollity** *n*. (*pl*. **jollities**). **Jolly Roger** *n*. a pirate's flag with skull and crossbones.

jolly[2] (jol′i), **jolly boat** *n*. (*pl*. **jollies, jolly boats**) a small boat for the general work of a ship.

jolt (jōlt, jolt) *v.t.* **1** to shake with sharp, sudden jerks, as in a vehicle along a rough road. **2** to disturb, to shock. ~*v.i.* (of a vehicle) to move with sharp, sudden jerks. ~*n*. **1** a sudden shock or jerk, esp. physical. **2** sudden, unexpected shock, esp. from information received. **jolty** *a*.

Jonah (jō′nə) *n*. a bringer of bad luck.

jonquil (jong′kwil, jŭng′-) *n*. a narcissus, *Narcissus jonquilla*, with two to six yellow or white flowers on a stem.

Jordanian (jawdā′niən) *n*. **1** a native or inhabitant of Jordan. **2** a person of Jordanian descent. ~*a*. of or relating to the kingdom of Jordan.

josh (josh) *v.t.* to make fun of, to ridicule. ~*v.i.* to indulge in ridicule. ~*n*. (*coll*.) a friendly joke. **josher** *n*.

Joshua tree (josh′ūə) *n*. a yucca, *Yucca brevifolia*, with sword-shaped leaves and greenish-white flowers, of the south-western US.

joss (jos) *n*. a Chinese idol. **josser** *n*. (*sl*.) **1** a fellow. **2** a fool. **3** (*Austral*.) a clergyman. **joss stick** *n*. a stick of perfumed material burnt as incense, orig. in China.

jostle (jos′əl), **justle** (jŭs′əl) *v.t.* **1** to push against, to hustle. **2** to elbow. ~*v.i.* **1** to push (against, along etc.). **2** to hustle, to crowd. ~*n*. **1** a hustling. **2** a collision, a conflict.

jot (jot) *n*. a tittle, an iota. ~*v.t.* (*pres.p.* **jotting**, *past, p.p.* **jotted**) to write (down a brief note or memorandum of). **jotter** *n*. a pad or exercise book for taking notes etc. **jotting** *n*. a note or memorandum.

joule (jool) *n*. the SI unit of work and energy, equal to the work done when a force of 1 newton advances its point of application 1 metre.

jounce (jowns) *v.t.*, *v.i.* to jolt or shake.

journal (jœ′nəl) *n*. **1** a record of events or news; any newspaper or other periodical published at regular intervals. **2** a daily record of events, a diary. **3** (*Naut.*) a logbook or daily register of a ship's course and distance etc. **4** an account of daily transactions. **5** in bookkeeping, the book from which daily entries are posted up in the ledger. **6** the part of a shaft that rests on the bearings. **journalese** (-lēz´) *n.* (*derog.*) a superficial style of writing full of clichés etc., regarded as being typical of writing in newspapers etc. **journalist** *n.* **1** an editor of or contributor to a newspaper or other journal. **2** a reporter for radio or television. **3** a person who keeps a diary. **journalism** *n.* **journalistic** (-lis´-) *a.* **journalistically** *adv.* **journalize, journalise** *v.t.* to enter in a diary. **journo** *n.* (*pl.* **journos**) (*sl.*) a journalist.

journey (jœ´ni) *n.* (*pl.* **journeys**) **1** passage or travel from one place to another, esp. by land or at a long distance. **2** the distance travelled in a given time. **3** the travelling of a vehicle along a route at a stated time. ~*v.i.* (*3rd pers. sing. pres.* **journeys**, *pres.p.* **journeying**, *past, p.p.* **journeyed**) **1** to travel. **2** to make a journey. **journeyer** *n.* **journeyman** *n.* (*pl.* **journeymen**) **1** a mechanic or artisan who has served an apprenticeship and works for an employer. **2** (*sometimes derog.*) a mere drudge, hack or hireling.

joust (jowst), **just** (jŭst) *v.i.* (*Hist.*) to tilt, to encounter on horseback with lances. ~*n.* **1** a tilting match. **2** a combat between knights or men-at-arms on horseback. **jouster** *n.*

Jove (jōv) *n.* Jupiter, the chief of the Roman divinities. **by Jove!** used to express surprise or approval. **Jovian** *a.* **1** of, relating to or like Jupiter, chief of the Roman divinities. **2** of or relating to the planet Jupiter.

jovial (jō´viəl) *a.* mirthful, merry, cheerful. **joviality** (-al´-), **jovialness** *n.* **jovially** *adv.*

jowar (jowah´) *n.* DURRA.

jowl (jowl), **†jole** (jōl), **joll** *n.* **1** the (lower) jaw. **2** (*often pl.*) the cheek. **3** the throat or neck, esp. of a double-chinned person. **4** the dewlap. **5** the crop or wattle of a fowl. **jowled** *a.* **jowly** *a.*

joy (joi) *n.* **1** the emotion produced by gratified desire, success, happy fortune etc.; gladness, happiness, delight. **2** a cause of joy or happiness. **3** success or satisfaction. ~*v.i.* (*esp. poet.*) to rejoice. ~*v.t.* (*esp. poet.*) to gladden. **to have no joy** (*coll.*) to be unsuccessful in a task etc. **to wish a person joy of** (*iron.*) to be gladly rid of (what that person has). **joyful** *a.* **joyfully** *adv.* **joyfulness** *n.* **joyless** *a.* **joylessly** *adv.* **joyous** *a.* **1** joyful. **2** causing joy. **joyously** *adv.* **joyousness** *n.* **joyride** *n.* (*coll.*) a ride in a car for pleasure, esp. when unauthorized. ~*v.i.* (*past* **joyrode**, *p.p.* **joyridden**) to go for a joyride. **joyrider** *n.* **joystick** *n.* **1** (*coll.*) the control lever of an aeroplane. **2** a lever for controlling the movement of a cursor on a computer screen.

JP *abbr.* Justice of the Peace.

Jr., jr. *abbr.* junior.

jube (joob) *n.* (*Austral., New Zeal.*) a jujube.

jubilant (joo´bilənt) *a.* exultant, rejoicing, shouting for joy. **jubilance** *n.* **jubilantly** *adv.*

jubilate (joo´bilāt) *v.i.* **1** to exult. **2** to express intense joy. **jubilation** (-ā´shən) *n.*

jubilee (joo´bilē) *n.* **1** a season of great public rejoicing or festivity. **2** the anniversary of an event of public interest, esp. the 25th or 50th. **3** an outburst of joy. **Jubilee clip®** *n.* an adjustable metal band placed around a tube, hose etc. to form a watertight connection.

Judaeo- (judē´ō), (*N Am.*) **Judeo-** *comb. form* of or relating to the Jews or Judaism.

Judaic (joodā´ik), **Judaical** *a.* of or relating to the Jews, Jewish. **Judaism** (joo´-) *n.* **1** the religious doctrines and rites of the Jews, according to the law of Moses. **2** conformity to such doctrines and rites. **Judaist** *n.* **Judaize, Judaise** *v.t., v.i.* **Judaization** (-zā´shən) *n.*

Judas (joo´dəs) *n.* **1** a traitor. **2** (**judas**) a Judas hole. **Judas hole, Judas window** *n.* a small hole cut in a door etc. to enable a person to pry into a room. **Judas tree** *n.* the leguminous tree, *Cercis siliquastrum*, which flowers before the leaves appear (trad. the tree on which Judas hanged himself).

judder (jŭd´ə) *v.i.* **1** to wobble. **2** to vibrate. **3** in singing, to make rapid changes in intensity during the emission of a note. ~*n.* **1** a wobble. **2** the vibration of an aircraft.

judge (jŭj) *n.* **1** a civil officer invested with power to hear and determine causes in a court of justice. **2** a person authorized to decide a dispute or contest. **3** a person skilled in deciding on relative merits, a connoisseur. ~*v.t.* **1** to decide (a question). **2** to hear or try (a cause). **3** to pass sentence upon. **4** to examine and form an opinion upon. **5** to criticize. **6** (*coll.*) to consider, to estimate, to decide. **7** to decide the winner in a competition, dispute etc. ~*v.i.* **1** to hear and determine a case. **2** to give sentence. **3** to form or give an opinion. **4** to come to a conclusion. **5** to criticize, to be censorious. **6** to sit in judgement. **judgement, judgment** *n.* **1** the act of judging. **2** a judicial decision, a sentence of a court of justice. **3** discernment, discrimination. **4** the capacity for arriving at reasonable conclusions leading to well-adapted behaviour, esp. as indicated by conduct in the practical affairs of life. **5** criticism. **6** the critical faculty. **7** opinion, estimate. **8** a misfortune regarded as sent by God. **against one's better judgement** contrary to one's preferred course of action. **judgemental** (-men´-) *a.* **1** involving judgement. **2** (over-) critical. **judgementally** *adv.* **Judgement Day** *n.* the end of the world. **judgement-seat** *n.* **1** the seat or bench on which judges sit. **2** a court, a tribunal. **judger** *n.* **judgeship** *n.* **judge's marshal** *n.* an official who accompanies a judge on circuit.

judicature (joo´dikəchə) *n.* **1** the administration of justice by trial and judgement. **2** the authority of a judge. **3** a court of justice. **4** the jurisdiction of a court. **5** judges collectively.

judicial (joodish´əl) *a.* **1** of, relating to or proper to courts of law or the administration of justice.

2 proceeding from a court of justice. **3** showing judgement. **4** critical, discriminating. **5** impartial. **judicially** *adv.* **judicial separation** *n.* separation of married persons by court decree. **judiciary** *n.* (*pl.* **judiciaries**) a judicature. **judicious** *a.* **1** sagacious, clear-headed, discerning. **2** wise, prudent. **3** done with reason or judgement. **judiciously** *adv.* **judiciousness** *n.*

Usage note The adjectives *judicial* and *judicious* should not be confused: *judicial* relates to law and legal judgements, and *judicious* to discernment or intellectual judgement.

judo (joo´dō) *n.* a modern sport derived from a form of ju-jitsu. **judoist** *n.* **judoka** (joo´dōkə) *n.* a person who is an expert in, or practises judo.

jug (jŭg) *n.* **1** a vessel, usu. with a swelling body, narrow neck, and handle, for holding liquids. **2** the contents of this. **3** (*sl.*) a prison, a lock-up. **4** (*pl., taboo sl.*) a woman's breasts. ~*v.t.* (*pres.p.* **jugging**, *past, p.p.* **jugged**) **1** (*usu. p.p.*) to stew (a hare) in a covered vessel, orig. in a jug or jar. **2** (*sl.*) to imprison. **jugful** *n.* (*pl.* **jugfuls**).

juggernaut (jŭg´ənawt) *n.* **1** a very large articulated lorry (causing damage to the environment). **2** a relentless destroying force or object. **3** (**Juggernaut**) a belief, institution etc., to which one is ruthlessly sacrificed or by which one is ruthlessly destroyed.

juggle (jŭg´əl) *v.i.* **1** to play tricks by sleight of hand, to conjure. **2** to throw in the air and catch several objects, such as balls, continuously so that some are in the air all the time. **3** to practise artifice or imposture (with). ~*v.t.* **1** to deceive by trickery. **2** to obtain, convey etc. (away, out of etc.) by trickery. **3** to manipulate (facts, figures etc.) in order to deceive. **4** to try to keep several things (such as jobs etc.) going at the same time. ~*n.* **1** a trick by sleight of hand. **2** an imposture. **juggler** *n.* **jugglery** *n.*

Jugoslav YUGOSLAV.

jugular (jŭg´ūlə) *a.* **1** belonging to the neck or throat. **2** (of fish) having the ventral fins anterior to the pectoral. ~*n.* a jugular vein. **jugular vein** *n.* any of several large veins of the neck which return the blood from the head.

juice (joos) *n.* **1** the watery part of fruits etc. or the fluid part of animal bodies. **2** a bodily secretion. **3** (*coll.*) electricity, electric current, petrol. **4** the essence or characteristic element of anything. **juiceless** *a.* **juicy** *a.* (*comp.* **juicier**, *superl.* **juiciest**) **1** abounding in juice, succulent. **2** (*coll.*) interesting esp. in a titillating or scandalous way. **3** (*coll.*) profitable. **juicily** *adv.* **juiciness** *n.*

ju-jitsu (joojit´soo), **jiu-jitsu, ju-jutsu** *n.* the Japanese art of wrestling, based on the principle of making one's opponent exert their strength to their own disadvantage.

ju-ju (joo´joo) *n.* **1** a fetish, an idol credited with supernatural power. **2** the ban or taboo worked by this.

jujube (joo´joob) *n.* **1** the berry-like fruit of *Zizyphus vulgaris* or *Z. jujuba*, spiny shrubs of the buckthorn family, dried as a sweetmeat. **2** a lozenge of sweetened gum arabic or gelatin flavoured with or imitating this. **3** any plant of the genus *Zizyphus*.

jukebox (jook´boks) *n.* an automatic record or disc player, usu. in a public place, in which coins are inserted and buttons pressed to select the relevant tunes.

Jul. *abbr.* July.

julep (joo´lep) *n.* **1** a sweet drink, esp. a preparation with some liquid used as a vehicle for medicine. **2** (*N Am.*) a drink of spirits, sugar, ice and mint.

Julian (joo´liən) *a.* of, relating to or originated by Julius Caesar. **Julian calendar** *n.* the calendar instituted by him in 46 BC.

julienne (joolien´) *n.* any foodstuff, esp. vegetables, cut into short thin strips.

Juliet cap (joo´liet) *n.* a small close-fitting cap worn esp. by brides.

July (jəlī´) *n.* (*pl.* **Julys**) the seventh month of the year.

jumble (jŭm´bəl) *v.t.* **1** to mix confusedly. **2** to throw or put together without order. ~*v.i.* to move (about, along etc.) confusedly. ~*n.* **1** a confused mixture. **2** a muddle, disorder, confusion. **3** articles donated to, or suitable for, a jumble sale. **jumble sale** *n.* a sale of miscellaneous articles at a bazaar etc. **jumbly** *a.*

jumbo (jŭm´bō) *n.* (*pl.* **jumbos**) **1** a huge, unwieldy person, animal or thing, esp. a large elephant. **2** a jumbo jet. **3** an oversized object. ~*a.* huge, unwieldy or oversized. **jumbo jet** *n.* a very large jet-propelled aircraft.

jumbuck (jŭm´bŭk) *n.* (*Austral., coll.*) a sheep.

jump (jŭmp) *v.i.* **1** to throw oneself from the ground by a sudden movement of the muscles of the legs and feet. **2** to spring, to leap, to bound. **3** to move suddenly (along, up, out) with such springs or bounds. **4** to start or rise (up) abruptly. **5** to change or move suddenly from one topic to another. **6** to agree, to tally (with or together). **7** to rise or increase suddenly by a significant amount. ~*v.t.* **1** to pass over or cross by leaping. **2** to cause to leap over. **3** to skip (a chapter, pages etc.). **4** to get on or off (a train etc.) illegally. **5** to pounce on or attack. **6** to take or appropriate (land etc.). **7** to start (a car) using jump leads. **8** (of a train) to come off (a track). **9** to pass through (a red traffic light). **10** (*sl.*) (of a man) to have sexual intercourse with. ~*n.* **1** the act of jumping. **2** a leap, a spring, a bound. **3** a start, an involuntary nervous movement. **4** (*pl.*) convulsive twitching as in delirium tremens. **5** (*pl.*) nervousness or anxiety. **6** a sudden rise (in price, value etc.). **7** an obstacle to be jumped. **8** a break, a gap. **9** (*Geol.*) a fault. **one jump ahead** one stage further than someone else. **on the jump** (*coll.*) in a hurry. **to get/ have the jump on** (*coll.*) to get or have an advantage over (a person). **to**

jump at 1 to accept eagerly. **2** to reach hastily (as a conclusion). **to jump down someone's throat** (*coll.*) to answer or interrupt violently. **to jump on/ upon 1** to reprimand, abuse, or assail violently. **2** to pounce upon. **to jump out of one's skin** (*coll.*) to be startled. **to jump ship** (of a sailor etc.) to leave a ship without permission, to desert. **to jump the queue** to get ahead of one's turn. **to jump to it** (*coll.*) to act swiftly. **jumpable** *a.* **jumped-up** *a.* (*coll.*) upstart. **jumping** *n.*, *a.* **jumping bean, jumping seed** *n.* the seed of various plants belonging to the Euphorbiaceae, which jump about through the movements of larvae inside them. **jumping jack** *n.* **1** a toy figure whose limbs move when a string is pulled. **2** a small firework which jumps along the ground with small explosions. **jumping-off place, jumping-off point** *n.* a starting point. **jump jet** *n.* a jet aircraft that can take off and land vertically. **jump lead** *n.* each of a pair of cables for supplying power to start a vehicle from another battery. **jump-off** *n.* an extra, deciding round in a showjumping contest. **jump rope** *n.* (*N Am.*) a skipping rope. **jump seat** *n.* a movable seat. **jump-start** *v.t.* to start (a car) by pushing it and then engaging gear. ~*n.* the act of jump-starting (a car). **jumpsuit** *n.* a one-piece garment consisting of combined trousers and top. **jumpy** *a.* (*comp.* **jumpier**, *superl.* **jumpiest**) **1** moving or proceeding with jumps and jerks. **2** (*coll.*) nervous, easily startled. **jumpily** *adv.* **jumpiness** *n.*

jumper¹ (jŭm´pə) *n.* **1** a knitted or crocheted woollen upper garment. **2** a loose, coarse outer jacket worn by sailors, labourers etc. **3** (*N Am.*) a pinafore dress.

jumper² (jŭm´pə) *n.* **1** a person who, or animal or thing which jumps or leaps. **2** a tool or implement worked with a jumping motion. **3** a short wire used to shorten a circuit, bypass a component etc. **jumper cable** *n.* (*esp. N Am.*) a jump lead.

Jun. *abbr.* **1** June. **2** Junior.

junco (jŭng´kō) *n.* (*pl.* **juncos, juncoes**) any small American bunting of the genus *Junco*, which has a greyish plumage.

junction (jŭngk´shən) *n.* **1** the act of joining or the state of being joined, a combination. **2** the point where roads or railway lines meet. **3** a joint, a point or place of union. **4** in electronics, a region between regions of differing electrical properties in a semiconductor. **junction box** *n.* an earthed box in which wires and cables can be safely connected.

Usage note The meanings of the nouns *junction* and *juncture* overlap, but in general *junction* refers to a place, and *juncture* to a point in time.

juncture (jŭngk´chə) *n.* **1** a junction, a union. **2** the place, line, or point at which two things are joined, a joint, an articulation. **3** a point of

time marked by the occurrence of critical events or circumstances.

Usage note See note under JUNCTION.

June (joon) *n.* the sixth month of the year. **June bug** *n.* (*esp. N Am.*) an insect or beetle that appears about June.

Jungian (yoong´iən) *a.* of or relating to the psychoanalytical system of Carl Jung, 1875–1961. ~*n.* an adherent of Jungian psychoanalysis.

jungle (jŭng´gəl) *n.* **1** land covered with forest trees or dense, matted vegetation. **2** a place of ruthless competition. **3** anything difficult to negotiate, understand etc. **4** a confusing mass. **5** (*also* **jungle music**) a type of fast dance music influenced by reggae and soul. **jungled** *a.* **jungle fever** *n.* a remittent tropical fever, a form of malaria. **jungly** *a.*

junior (joo´nyə) *a.* **1** the younger (esp. as distinguishing a son from his father of the same name, or two of the same surname). **2** lower in standing. ~*n.* **1** a person younger or of lower standing than another. **2** (*N Am.*) a son. **junior college** *n.* (*N Am.*) a college providing a two-year course esp. as the first part of a four-year course. **junior high school** *n.* (*N Am.*) a school between elementary school and high school. **juniority** (-nior´-) *n.* **junior lightweight** *n.* **1** a professional boxer in the lower weight range of the lightweight category. **2** this weight category. **junior management** *n.* **1** the lowest level of management in an organization. **2** the managers at this level. **junior middleweight** *n.* **1** a professional boxer in the lower weight range of the middleweight category. **2** this weight category. **junior school** *n.* (in England and Wales), a school for pupils aged about 7 to 11. **junior technician** *n.* a person next above senior aircraftman or aircraftwoman in the RAF. **junior welterweight** *n.* **1** a professional boxer in the lower weight range of the welterweight category. **2** this weight category.

Usage note An implicit double comparative *more junior* is occasionally encountered, but it is best avoided: *junior* already includes the notion of 'more'. However *junior* does not function as a true comparative in English, and should not be followed by *than* (the correct form is *junior to*).

juniper (joo´nipə) *n.* any evergreen shrub or tree of the genus *Juniperus*, esp. *J. communis*, the berries of which are used to flavour gin.

junk¹ (jŭngk) *n.* **1** rubbish, valueless odds and ends. **2** (*sl.*) narcotic drugs, esp. heroin. **3** pieces of old cable and rope cut into lengths for making mats, swabs, gaskets, fenders, oakum etc. **4** (*Naut.*) salt beef supplied to ships bound on long voyages, from its being as tough as old rope. **5** a lump of fibrous tissue in a sperm whale's head, containing spermaceti. ~*v.t.* **1** to discard, abandon. **2** to cut into junks. **junk bond** *n.* a bond giving a high yield but low security. **junk food** *n.* food of little nutritional value, quick to prepare. **junkie, junky** *n.* (*pl.* **junkies**) (*sl.*) a drug addict. **junk mail** *n.* unsolicited mail, usu. advertising material. **junk shop** *n.* a shop where second-hand goods of all kinds are sold. **junkyard** *n.* a scrapyard.

junk² (jŭngk) *n.* a flat-bottomed vessel with lugsails, used in the Chinese seas.

junket (jŭng'kit) *n.* **1** a dish of curds sweetened and flavoured, and served with cream. **2** a sweetmeat, delicacy, a confection. **3** a feast, a banquet, an entertainment. **4** a supposed business trip (at public expense) which is really for pleasure. ~*v.i.* (*pres.p.* **junketing**, *past, p.p.* **junketed**) to feast, to picnic, to make good cheer. ~*v.t.* to regale at a feast. **junketer** *n.* **junketing** *n.*

junta (jŭn'tə, hun'-) *n.* **1** a group, esp. of military officers who take control of a country e.g. after a coup. **2** a cabal. **3** a legislative or administrative council, esp. in Spain, Portugal, and S America.

jural (joo'rəl) *a.* of or relating to law or jurisprudence, esp. with regard to rights and obligations.

Jurassic (jooras'ik) *a.* (*Geol.*) belonging to the second period of the Mesozoic era. ~*n.* the Jurassic system or period, coming between the Triassic and the Cretaceous.

juridical (joorid'ikəl) *a.* of or relating to the administration of justice, to courts of justice, or to jurisprudence. **juridically** *adv.*

juried JURY.

jurisconsult (jooriskənsŭlt') *n.* a person learned in law, esp. civil or international law.

jurisdiction (joorisdik'shən) *n.* **1** the legal power or right of administering justice, making and enforcing laws, or exercising other authority. **2** the district or extent within which such power may be exercised. **jurisdictional** *a.*

jurisprudence (joorisprooʹdəns) *n.* **1** the science or philosophy of law. **2** the science of human laws, constitutions, and rights. **3** skill in law. **jurisprudent** *n.,* a. **jurisprudential** (-den'-) *a.*

jurist (joo'rist) *n.* **1** a person learned in the law. **2** a writer on legal subjects. **3** (*N Am.*) a lawyer. **4** (*N Am.*) a judge. **juristic** (-ris'-), **juristical** (-ris'tikəl) *a.*

juror (joo'rə) *n.* **1** a person who serves on a jury. **2** a person who takes an oath.

jury (joo'ri) *n.* (*pl.* **juries**) **1** (*Law*) a body of persons selected according to law and sworn to try, and give a true verdict upon, questions put before them. **2** a body of persons selected to award prizes at public shows, exhibitions etc. **the jury is (still) out** a decision has not yet been reached. **juried** *a.* (*N Am.*) judged or selected by a jury. **jury box** *n.* the enclosure in a court where the jury sit. **juryman** *n.* (*pl.* **jurymen**). **jurywoman** *n.* (*pl.* **jurywomen**).

jury- (joo'ri) *comb. form* makeshift, temporary. **jury-rigged** *a.* **1** (*Naut.*) having makeshift rigging. **2** makeshift.

jussive (jŭs'iv) *a.* (*Gram.*) expressing command.

just (jŭst) *a.* **1** acting according to what is right and fair. **2** exact, accurate, precise. **3** fit, proper, suitable. **4** merited, deserved. **5** righteous. **6** lawful, legal. ~*adv.* **1** exactly, precisely. **2** barely, only, with nothing to spare. **3** precisely at the moment. **4** only a moment ago, a very little time ago. **5** (*coll.*) perfectly, quite. **6** (*coll.*) simply, merely. **7** (*coll.*) really, indeed. **just about 1** (*coll.*) nearly. **2** (*coll.*) more or less. **just in case** as a precaution. **just now 1** a very little time since, but a moment ago. **2** at this instant. **just so 1** exactly. **2** that is right. **3** with great precision. **just-in-time** *a.* of or relating to an industrial method in which components etc. are produced as needed, eliminating waste and the need for storage. **justly** *adv.* **justness** *n.*

justice (jŭs'tis) *n.* **1** the quality of being just. **2** fairness in dealing with others. **3** uprightness, rectitude, honesty. **4** just requital of deserts. **5** the authoritative administration or maintenance of law and right. **6** a magistrate. **7** a judge, esp. of the Supreme Court of Judicature in England or of the US Supreme Court or a state Supreme Court. **8** judicial proceedings. **9** lawfulness, legality. **in justice to** out of fairness to. **to do justice to 1** to treat fairly. **2** to treat appreciatively. **to do oneself justice** to acquit oneself worthily of one's ability. **with justice** with good reason. **Justice of the Peace** *n.* a local magistrate commissioned to keep the peace and try cases of felony and other misdemeanours. **justiceship** *n.* **justiciable** (-tish'i-) *a.* liable to be tried in a court of justice. **justiciary** (-əri) *n.* (*pl.* **justiciaries**) an administrator of justice. ~*a.* of or relating to the administration of justice.

justify (jŭs'tifī) *v.t.* (*3rd pers. sing. pres.* **justifies**, *pres.p.* **justifying**, *past, p.p.* **justified**) **1** to prove or show to be just or right. **2** to vindicate, to make good, to show grounds for. **3** to exonerate. **4** (*Theol.*) to declare free from the penalty of sin. **5** to adjust and make (lines of type) even in length. **justifiable** *a.* **justifiability** (-bil'-), **justifiableness** *n.* **justifiable homicide** *n.* the killing of a person in a lawful fashion, esp. in self-defence or in carrying out a death sentence. **justifiably** *adv.* **justification** (-fikā'shən) *n.* **justificative** (jŭs'-), **justificatory** *a.* **justificator**, **justifier** *n.*

jut (jŭt) *v.i.* (*pres.p.* **jutting**, *past, p.p.* **jutted**) to project, to protrude, to stick (out). ~*n.* a projection, a protruding point or part.

Jute (joot) *n.* a member of a Germanic people orig. from Jutland, who settled in Britain in the 5th 6th cents. **Jutish** *a.*

jute (joot) *n.* the fibre from the inner bark of two Asian plants, *Corchorus capsularis* and *C. olitorius*, from which fabrics, paper and cordage are prepared.

juvenescent (joovənes´ənt) *a.* growing or being young. **juvenescence** *n.*

juvenile (joo´vənīl) *a.* **1** young, youthful. **2** befitting or characteristic of youth. **3** (*often derog.*) immature. ~*n.* **1** a young person. **2** a book for children. **3** an actor who usu. performs the part of a young person. **juvenile court** *n.* a court for young people under 17 or (in the US) 18 years of age. **juvenile delinquent** *n.* an offender under 17 years of age. **juvenile delinquency** *n.* **juvenilely** *adv.* **juvenileness** *n.* **juvenilia** (-nil´iə) *n.pl.* writings etc., produced in youth. **juvenility** (-nil´-) *n.*

juxtapose (jŭkstəpōz´) *v.t.* **1** to place (things) side by side. **2** to place (a thing) next to another. **juxtaposition** (-zish´ən) *n.* **juxtapositional** *a.*

K¹ (kā), **k** (*pl.* **Ks, K's**) the 11th letter of the English and other versions of the Roman alphabet, corresponding to the Greek kappa (κ, K). It is pronounced as a voiceless velar plosive. ~*symbol* the solar constant.

K² *abbr.* **1** Kelvin(s). **2** King, King's. **3** Knight. **4** Köchel (catalogue of Mozart's work). **5** (*Comput.*) 1024 words, bytes or bits (from *kilo-*). **6** one thousand (from *kilo-*).

K³ *chem. symbol* potassium.

k *abbr.* **1** kilo, kilo-. **2** (*Math.*) a constant.

kabuki (kəbooˊki) *n.* a highly-stylized, traditional and popular form of Japanese drama, based on legend and acted only by men, in elaborate costumes.

Kaddish (kadˊish), **Qaddish** *n.* a form of thanksgiving and prayer used by the Jews, esp. in mourning.

kadi CADI.

Kaffir (kafˊə), **Kafir** *n.* (*offensive*) **1** a member of the S African Xhosa-speaking people. **2** their language, Xhosa. **3** (*S Afr.*) any black African.

kaffiyeh KEFFIYEH.

Kafkaesque (kafkæeskˊ) *a.* of or like the ideas and work of the Czech novelist Franz Kafka, 1883–1924, esp. his ideas on the alienation of man.

kaftan (kafˊtan, -tən), **caftan** *n.* **1** a long belted tunic worn in the East. **2** a woman's long loose dress with wide sleeves.

❌ **kahki** common misspelling of KHAKI.

kail KALE.

kaiser (kīˊzə) *n.* **1** an emperor. **2** (*Hist.*) the Emperor of Germany or Austria. **kaisership** *n.*

kalanchoe (kalənkōˊi) *n.* a succulent plant of the genus *Kalanchoe*, often grown indoors or in a greenhouse, with pink, red or yellow flowers.

Kalashnikov (kalashˊnikof) *n.* a type of submachine gun made in Russia.

kale (kāl), **kail** *n.* **1** a variety of cabbage with crinkled leaves. **2** (*N Am., sl.*) money. **kaleyard** *n.* (*Sc.*) a kitchen garden.

kaleidoscope (kəlīˊdəskōp) *n.* **1** an instrument showing by means of bits of coloured glass, paper etc. and a series of reflecting surfaces, an endless variety of symmetrical forms. **2** any complex, changing pattern. **kaleidoscopic** (-skopˊ-), **kaleidoscopical** *a.* **kaleidoscopically** *adv.*

kalends CALENDS.

kameez (kəmēzˊ) *n.* a type of loose tunic with tight sleeves worn esp. by Muslim women in the Indian subcontinent and S Asia.

kamikaze (kamikahˊzi) *n.* a Japanese airman or plane performing a suicidal mission in World War II. ~*a.* **1** of or relating to a kamikaze. **2** (*coll.*) suicidal, self-destructive.

Kampuchean (kampuchēˊən) *n.* a native or inhabitant of Kampuchea, a Cambodian. ~*a.* of or relating to Kampuchea, Cambodian.

Kanarese (kanərēzˊ), **Canarese** *n.* (*pl.* **Kanarese, Canarese**) **1** a member of the Dravidian people living largely in Kanara in southern India. **2** the language of this people. ~*a.* of or relating to Kanara or the Kanarese.

kangaroo (kang·gəroo´) *n.* any of several marsupial quadrupeds of the genus *Macropus*, native to Australia, Tasmania, New Guinea and adjacent islands, distinguished by their large hind limbs, used for leaping, and short front limbs. **kangaroo closure** *n.* the parliamentary procedure whereby the chairman or speaker decides what shall be discussed (e.g. which amendments to a bill) and what passed over. **kangaroo court** *n.* an irregular court, set up by e.g. the mob, prisoners, or strikers. **kangaroo mouse** *n.* any small American rodent of the genus *Microdipodops*, inhabiting deserts. **kangaroo paw** *n.* any of several Australian plants of the genus *Anigozanthus* or *Macropidia* with green and red flowers. **kangaroo rat** *n.* any small rodent of the genus *Dipodamys*. **kangaroo vine** *n.* an evergreen climbing plant, *Cissus antarctica*, grown as a house plant.

kaolin (kāˊəlin) *n.* a porcelain clay (also used medicinally as a poultice or internally) derived principally from the decomposition of feldspar, China clay. **kaolinic** (-linˊ-) *a.* **kaolinize, kaolinise** *v.t.* to convert into kaolin. **koalinization** (-zāˊshən) *n.*

kapellmeister (kəpelˊmīstə), **capellmeister** *n.* (*pl.* **kapellmeister, capellmeister**) the musical director of a choir, band or orchestra, esp. a German one.

kapok (kāˊpok) *n.* a fine woolly or silky fibre enveloping the seeds of a tropical tree, *Ceiba pentandra*, used for stuffing cushions etc.

Kaposi's sarcoma (kəpōˊsiz) *n.* (*Med.*) a type of skin cancer often found in people with Aids.

kappa (kapˊə) *n.* the tenth letter of the Greek alphabet (κ, K).

kaput (kəputˊ) *a.* (*coll.*) finished, done for, smashed up.

karabiner (karəbēˊnə) *n.* a metal clip with a spring inside it, for attaching to a piton, used in mountaineering.

karakul (karˊəkul), **caracul** *n.* **1** a breed of sheep from the Bukhara district of Central Asia. **2** the fleece prepared as fur from the lambs of these sheep.

karaoke (karəō´ki, kari-) *n.* a leisure activity in which members of an audience can sing solo with pre-recorded backing music.

karat CARAT.

karate (kərah´ti) *n.* a traditional Japanese martial art, based on blows and kicks. **karate chop** *n.* a downward blow with the side of the hand.

karma (kah´mə) *n.* **1** in Buddhism and Hinduism, the results of action, ethical causation as determining future existence, esp. the cumulative consequence of a person's acts in one stage of existence as controlling their destiny in the next. **2** destiny. **karmic** *a.*

karst (kahst) *n.* the characteristic scenery of a limestone region with underground streams, caverns and potholes forming a drainage system.

kart (kaht) *n.* a go-kart. **karting** *n.* go-kart racing.

karyo- (kar´iō), **caryo-** *comb. form* (*Biol.*) relating to the nucleus of an animal or vegetable cell.

kasbah (kaz´bah), **casbah** *n.* **1** the castle or fortress in a N African city. **2** the area around this.

Kashmiri (kashmiə´ri) *n.* (*pl.* **Kashmiris**) **1** a native or inhabitant of Kashmir. **2** the language of Kashmir. ~*a.* of or relating to Kashmir.

katabolism CATABOLISM.

kathode CATHODE.

kation CATION.

katydid (kā´tidid) *n.* any of various large green grasshoppers of the genus *Microcentrum* and related genera, common in N America.

kauri (kow´ri) *n.* (*pl.* **kauris**) a New Zealand coniferous forest tree, *Agathis australis*. **kauri gum** *n.* a resinous gum from the kauri.

kayak (ki´ak), **kaiak** *n.* **1** the Eskimo (Inuit) and Alaskan canoe, made of sealskins stretched on a light wooden framework. **2** a small covered canoe resembling this. ~*v.i.* (*pres.p.* **kayaking**, *past, p.p.* **kayaked**) to travel in a kayak, to paddle a kayak.

kayo (kāō´) *n.* (*pl.* **kayos**) a knockout. ~*v.t.* (*3rd pers. sing. pres.* **kayoes**, *pres.p.* **kayoing**, *past, p.p.* **kayoed**) to knock someone out.

kazoo (kəzoo´) *n.* (*pl.* **kazoos**) a tube of metal or plastic with a membrane covering a hole in the side, through which a player sings or hums to produce sound.

KB *abbr.* **1** kilobyte(s). **2** King's Bench.

KBE *abbr.* Knight Commander of the Order of the British Empire.

kbyte *abbr.* kilobyte(s).

KC *abbr.* King's Counsel.

kc *abbr.* kilocycle(s).

kcal *abbr.* kilocalorie(s).

KCB *abbr.* Knight Commander of the Order of the Bath.

KCMG *abbr.* Knight Commander of the Order of St Michael and St George.

kc/s *abbr.* kilocycles per second.

KCVO *abbr.* Knight Commander of the Royal Victorian Order.

KE *abbr.* kinetic energy.

kea (kā´ə) *n.* a brownish green mountain parrot, *Nestor notabilis*, of New Zealand whose diet includes carrion.

kebab (kibab´), **cabob** (kəbob´) *n.* small pieces of meat, vegetables etc. cooked on skewers.

kedge (kej) *n.* (*Naut.*) a small portable anchor, used in warping. ~*v.t.* to move (a ship) by a light cable attached to a kedge. ~*v.i.* (of a ship) to move in this way. **kedge anchor, kedger** *n.* a kedge.

kedgeree (kej´ərē) *n.* **1** a stew of rice, pulse, onions, eggs etc., a common Indian dish. **2** a dish of fish, rice, hard-boiled eggs etc.

keek (kēk) *v.i.* (*Sc., North.*) to peep, to pry. ~*n.* a peep.

keel (kēl) *n.* **1** the principal timber or steel structure of a ship, extending from bow to stern and supporting the whole structure. **2** (*poet.*) a ship. **3** a projecting ridge or longitudinal process. **4** (*Bot.*) the two lower petals of a papilionaceous corolla. ~*v.i.* **1** (of a ship) to roll on its keel. **2** to turn (over), to careen. ~*v.t.* to turn up the keel of, to turn over or keel upwards. **to keel over 1** to capsize, to turn over. **2** (*coll.*) to fall over. **keelboat** *n.* **1** a yacht with a permanent keel. **2** (*N Am.*) a large covered riverboat without sails. **keelhaul** *v.t.* **1** to punish by dragging under water on one side of the ship and up again on the other. **2** to berate. **keelless** *a.*

keelson (kēl´sən), **kelson** (kel´-) *n.* a longitudinal piece placed along the floor-timbers of a ship binding them to the keel.

keen[1] (kēn) *a.* **1** enthusiastic, eager, ardent. **2** sensitive, acute, penetrating. **3** having a sharp edge or point. **4** (of an edge) sharp. **5** (of cold etc.) biting, piercing, intense. **6** bitter, acrimonious. **7** (of a price) low, competitive. **8** (*coll.*) excellent. **9** strong, intense. **10** clever, quick to understand. **keen on** enthusiastic about, interested in. **keenly** *adv.* **keenness** *n.*

keen[2] (kēn) *n.* a wailing lamentation over the body of a dead person. ~*v.i.* to wail for the dead. ~*v.t.* **1** to mourn by keening. **2** to utter with keening. **keener** *n.*

keep[1] (kēp) *v.t.* (*past, p.p.* **kept** (kept)) **1** to hold for a significant length of time, to retain. **2** to have in one's continuous charge. **3** to guard, preserve, protect. **4** to maintain in a given state, position etc. **5** to place or store regularly. **6** to conduct as a business on one's own account. **7** to supply with the necessaries of life. **8** to own and tend, to look after out of interest or for profit. **9** to have in one's pay. **10** to observe, to pay proper regard to. **11** to fulfil. **12** to have regularly on sale; to stock. **13** to write regular entries in. **14** to restrain (from), to cause to abstain (from). **15** to detain (in custody etc.), to cause to wait or be late. **16** to reserve (for). **17** to refrain from divulging. **18** to preserve. **19** to adhere to, to continue to follow. **20** to remain in. **21** to reside in college etc.

during (a term). **22** to associate with. *~v.i.* **1** to continue or retain one's place (in, on etc.), to remain. **2** to continue to be (in a specified condition etc.). **3** to continue (doing). **4** to remain unspoiled, untainted etc. **5** to be able to be withheld without loss of significance etc. **6** to adhere (to). **7** to restrict oneself (to). **8** to lodge, to reside. **how are you keeping?** how are you? **to keep at 1** to persist with. **2** to cause to persist with. **to keep away** to prevent from approaching. **to keep away from** not to approach, to avoid contact with. **to keep back 1** to restrain, to hold back. **2** to reserve, to withhold. **3** to keep secret. **4** to remain at a distance. **to keep down 1** to repress, to subdue. **2** to keep (expenses etc.) low. **3** to digest (food) without vomiting. **to keep from 1** to abstain or refrain from. **2** not to tell (someone about something). **3** to stop or prevent. **4** to protect or preserve. **to keep off 1** to hinder from approach. **2** to avert. **3** to remain at a distance. **4** to abstain from. **5** to avoid mentioning or discussing. **to keep on 1** to continue to employ etc. **2** to continue (doing etc.), to persist. **3** to talk continuously, esp. in an annoying way; to nag. **to keep on at** to nag at, to pester. **to keep oneself to oneself** to avoid other people. **to keep out** to hinder from entering or taking possession (of). **to keep to 1** to adhere strictly to. **2** not to stray from. **to keep together** to remain or cause to remain together or in harmony. **to keep to oneself 1** to avoid other people. **2** to tell no one else about. **to keep under** to hold down, to repress. **to keep up 1** to maintain. **2** to keep in repair or good condition. **3** to prevent from falling or diminishing. **4** to carry on. **5** to cause to stay up at night. **6** to bear up. **7** to go on at the same pace (with). **to keep up with the Joneses** (*coll.*) to keep on the same social level as one's friends and neighbours. **keeper** (kē′pə) *n.* **1** a person who keeps something. **2** a person who has the charge, care or superintendence of anything, esp. of a park, art gallery etc. **3** a person who retains others in custody or charge. **4** a gamekeeper. **5** a position in some games, a wicketkeeper or goalkeeper. **6** a perishable article that keeps well. **7** a ring worn to protect another, esp. a wedding ring. **8** an earring worn to keep the hole in a pierced ear open, a sleeper. **9** a bar of soft iron used to prevent permanent magnets from losing magnetism. **keep fit** *n.* physical exercises to keep one fit and healthy. **keeping** (kē′ping) *n.* **1** the action of holding, guarding, preserving etc. **2** charge, custody, guardianship. **3** harmony, accord. **4** consistency, congruity. *~a.* (of fruit etc.) that can be kept. **keepnet** *n.* a net kept in the water by anglers, where they put the fish they have caught to keep them alive. **keepsake** (kēp′sāk) *n.* anything kept or given to be kept for the sake of or as a reminder of the giver.

keep² (kēp) *n.* **1** subsistence, maintenance. **2** food required for subsistence. **3** control, charge. **4** a donjon, the main tower or stronghold of a medieval castle. **for keeps** permanently.

keeshond (kās′hond, kēs′-) *n.* a Dutch breed of dog, with a heavy coat, pointed muzzle, and erect ears.

keffiyeh (kefē′yə), **kaffiyeh** (kafē′yə) *n.* a Bedouin Arab's kerchief headdress.

keg (keg) *n.* a small cask or barrel. **keg beer** *n.* any beer kept in pressurized kegs.

kelp (kelp) *n.* **1** any large, coarse seaweed. **2** the calcined ashes of seaweed, from which carbonate of soda was obtained for glass and soap making, now chiefly used for obtaining iodine.

kelpie (kel′pi) *n.* **1** (*Sc.*) a water-spirit usu. in the form of a horse, supposed to haunt fords, and to rejoice in the drowning of wayfarers. **2** (*Austral.*) a smooth-haired variety of sheepdog.

kelson KEELSON.

kelt (kelt) *n.* (*Sc.*) a salmon or sea trout after spawning.

kelter KILTER.

kelvin (kel′vin) *n.* the basic SI unit of temperature. **Kelvin scale** *n.* a thermometer scale in which zero is absolute zero.

kemp (kemp) *n.* the coarse rough hairs of wool. **kempy** *a.*

kempt (kempt) *a.* (of hair) combed, neat.

ken (ken) *n.* **1** range of sight or knowledge, apprehension. **2** view, sight. *~v.t.* (*pres.p.* **kenning**, *past, p.p.* **kenned, kent** (kent)) (*esp. Sc.*) **1** to be acquainted with. **2** to know. **beyond one's ken** beyond the limits of one's knowledge or experience.

kendo (ken′dō) *n.* the Japanese martial art of fencing, usu. with pliable bamboo staves, occasionally with swords.

kennel (ken′əl) *n.* **1** a house or shelter for a dog or hounds. **2** (*as pl.*) a place where dogs are bred or boarded. **3** a hovel, a wretched haunt or den. *~v.i.* (*pres.p.* **kennelling**, (*N Am.*) **kenneling**, *past, p.p.* **kennelled**, (*N Am.*) **kenneled**) to lie or lodge in or as in a kennel. *~v.t.* to confine in or as in a kennel.

kent KEN.

Kentish (ken′tish) *a.* of or relating to the English county of Kent. **Kentish fire** *n.* rhythmical volleys of applause showing disapproval.

Kenyan (ke′nyən) *n.* a native or inhabitant of Kenya in E Africa. *~a.* of or relating to Kenya.

kepi (kā′pē, kep′ē) *n.* (*pl.* **kepis**) a French flat-topped military hat with a horizontal peak.

kept KEEP¹.

keratin (ker′ətin) *n.* a nitrogenous substance, the chief constituent of hair, feathers, claws and horns. **keratinize, keratinise** *v.i., v.t.* to become covered or to cover with keratin. **keratinization** (-zā′shən) *n.* **keratitis** (kerətī′tis) *n.* (*Med.*) inflammation of the cornea of the eye. **keratose** (ker′ətōs, -tōz) *n.* the substance of the skeleton of horny sponges. *~a.* (of sponge) horny. **keratotomy** (-tot′əmi) *n.* (*pl.* **keratotomies**) (*Med.*) a surgical incision into the cornea.

kerb (kœb) *n.* a row of stones set as edging to a pavement etc. **kerb-crawling** *n.* the act of driving along slowly with the intention of enticing someone into the car for sexual purposes. **kerb-crawler** *n.* **kerb-drill** *n.* a pedestrian's procedure, such as looking to the left and right, for crossing a road in safety, esp. as taught to and used by children. **kerbside** *n.* the side of a pavement etc., nearer the kerb. **kerbstone** *n.* each of the stones edging a pavement etc.

kerchief (kœ´chif) *n.* (*pl.* **kerchiefs**) **1** a cloth to cover the head. **2** (*poet.*) a handkerchief, a napkin. **kerchiefed** *a.*

kerfuffle (kəfŭf´əl), **carfuffle** *n.* a commotion, a fuss.

kermes (kœ´mēz) *n.* **1** the dried bodies of the females of an insect, *Kermes ilicis*, yielding a red or scarlet dye. **2** dye from this source. **kermes mineral** *n.* a bright red mineral, hydrous trisulphide of antimony. **kermes oak** *n.* a shrubby, dwarf Mediterranean oak, *Quercus coccifera*.

kern (kœn) *n.* **1** the part of a letter which overhangs the main body of type. **2** (*Print.*) the projecting part of a piece of metal type. ~*v.t.* **1** to provide with kerns. **2** to place so as to overlap. **3** to adjust the spacing between. **kerned** *a.* **kerning** *n.*

kernel (kœ´nəl) *n.* **1** the substance, usu. edible, contained in the shell of a nut or the stone of a fruit. **2** that which is enclosed in a shell, husk, integument etc. **3** the nucleus, core, gist or essence.

kerosene (ker´əsēn), **kerosine** *n.* an oil distilled from petroleum, coal or bituminous shale, used for burning in jet engines and oil lamps.

kersey (kœ´zi) *n.* (*pl.* **kerseys**) a coarse woollen cloth, usu. ribbed.

kerseymere (kœ´zimiə) *n.* a fine twilled woollen cloth used esp. for suits.

keskidee KISKADEE.

kestrel (kes´trəl) *n.* a small species of hawk, *Falco tinnunculus*.

ketamine (ket´əmēn) *n.* an anaesthetic drug, also used as a hallucinogenic recreational drug.

ketch (kech) *n.* a fore-and-aft rigged two-masted sailing boat.

ketchup (kech´ŭp), **catchup** (kach´-), (*N Am.*) **catsup** (kat´səp) *n.* a sauce, usu. prepared from mushrooms, tomatoes etc., used as a condiment.

ketone (kē´tōn) *n.* (*Chem.*) any of a class of organic compounds, usu. formed by oxidation of a secondary alcohol. **ketone body** *n.* a compound produced in the liver from fatty acids, found in the blood and urine in abnormal amounts in people unable to use glucose, such as diabetics. **ketonic** (kiton´-) *a.* **ketonuria** (-ūə´riə) *n.* the presence of large amounts of ketone bodies in the urine. **ketosis** (-tō´sis) *n.* (*Med.*) the excessive formation of ketone bodies, as in diabetes.

kettle (ket´əl) *n.* a vessel, usu. of metal and with a lid, handle and spout, for heating water or other liquid. **a different kettle of fish** a matter to be considered separately. **a fine kettle of fish** a pretty kettle of fish. **a pretty kettle of fish** a mess, a muddle, a troublesome state of affairs. **kettledrum** *n.* a drum made of a thin hemispherical shell of copper or brass etc., with a parchment or plastic head. **kettledrummer** *n.* **kettle hole** *n.* a hollow on the ground caused by the melting of trapped glacial ice.

keV *abbr.* kilo-electronvolt.

Kevlar® (kev´lah) *n.* a strong synthetic fibre, used in the manufacture of tyres.

Kewpie doll® (kū´pi), **kewpie** *n.* a plump baby doll with hair in a topknot.

key[1] (kē) *n.* **1** a portable instrument, usu. of metal, for working the bolt of a lock to and fro. **2** a tool or instrument by which something is screwed up or turned. **3** a small lever actuated by the fingers in playing certain musical instruments, operating certain machines etc. **4** any of the buttons depressed by the fingers in operating a typewriter, entering data at a computer terminal etc. **5** a means of access to or opportunity for something. **6** that which explains anything difficult, a solution, an explanation. **7** a translation. **8** a series of solutions of problems etc. **9** the first move in the solution to a chess problem. **10** one of several systems of musical notes having definite tonic relations among themselves and to one fundamental note called the keynote. **11** the general tone or style (of a picture, literary composition, speech etc.). **12** a place whose military occupation gives control over a region of land or sea. **13** a piece of wood or metal let transversely into the back of a board to prevent warping. **14** a keystone. **15** the roughness of a surface for plastering. **16** the first coat of plaster on a wall or ceiling. **17** the winged seed of a sycamore etc. ~*a.* (*attrib.*) leading, essential. ~*v.t.* **1** to fasten (on, in etc.) with a key, bolt, wedge etc. **2** to enter (data) into a computer using a keyboard. **3** (*Mus.*) to tune, to regulate. **4** to align or link (to). **5** to vary the wording (of an advertisement) so that the source prompting each response can be identified. **6** to roughen (a surface) for plastering. **7** to stir (up) to an action etc. **to key in** to enter (data) into a computer using a keyboard. **to key up** to brace up, to incite, to encourage. **keyboard** *n.* **1** the range of keys on a piano, organ, typewriter, computer etc. **2** an electronic instrument with keys resembling those on a piano. ~*v.t.* to set (text) in type using a keyboard, to key in. **keyboarder** *n.* a person who enters data into a computer using a keyboard. **keyboardist** *n.* a player of a keyboard. **keyer** *n.* **keyholder** *n.* a person who keeps a key to give access to an office etc. **keyhole** *n.* the hole in a lock, door, cover etc., by which a key is inserted. **keyhole surgery** *n.* surgery performed through very small incisions. **key industry** *n.* an industry upon which the other interests and the economic welfare of a country depend. **keyless** *a.* **key map** *n.* a simple map with plain outlines. **key money**

n. a premium demanded, in addition to rent, for the granting or renewal of a tenancy. **keynote** *n.* **1** (*Mus.*) the fundamental note of a key. **2** the general tone or spirit (of a picture, poem etc.). ~*a.* (*attrib.*) setting the tone or agenda (*a keynote speech*). **keypad** *n.* a small device with a push-button keyboard for operating, for example, a television or teletext system. **keypunch** *n.* a keyboard operated manually and used to put data onto punched cards. ~*v.t.* to transfer (data) in this way. **keypuncher** *n.* **keyring** *n.* a ring for carrying keys on. **key signature** *n.* (*Mus.*) the sharps and flats on a musical staff, showing the key of a piece of music. **keystone** *n.* **1** the central stone of an arch locking the others together. **2** the fundamental element, principle etc. **keystroke** *n.* the operation of a key on a keyboard-operated machine. **keyway** *n.* a slot into which a machined key is inserted. **keyword** *n.* **1** the key to a code. **2** an important word, e.g. describing the contents of a document.

key² (kē) *n.* a low island, esp. of coral, such as off the coast of Florida.

Keynesian (kā´nziǝn) *a.* of or relating to the philosophy that governments should control the economy through monetary and fiscal policies. ~*n.* a believer in Keynesian economics. **Keynesianism** *n.*

KG *abbr.* Knight of the Order of the Garter.

kg *abbr.* kilogram(s).

khaki (kah´ki) *a.* dust-coloured, dull brownish yellow. ~*n.* (*pl.* **khakis**) **1** a dull brownish yellow colour. **2** a twilled cloth of this colour, used for army uniforms.

khamsin (kam´sin), **hamsin** (ham´sin) *n.* a hot southerly wind blowing in Egypt for some 50 days in March to May.

khan (kahn, kan) *n.* a title given to officials and rulers in Central Asia etc., equivalent to 'esquire'. **khanate** (-āt) *n.*

khat (kat, kaht), **kat** *n.* **1** an evergreen shrub, *Catha edulis*, grown in Africa and Arabia. **2** the leaves of this shrub, chewed as a narcotic.

Khmer (kmeǝ, kmœ) *n.* **1** a member of a people inhabiting Cambodia. **2** the language of this people. ~*a.* of or relating to this people or their language.

khus-khus (kŭs´kŭs), **cuscus** *n.* the fibrous, aromatic root of an Indian grass, used for making fans, baskets etc.

kHz *abbr.* kilohertz.

kibble¹ (kib´ǝl) *n.* a strong iron (formerly wooden) bucket for raising ore from a mine.

kibble² (kib´ǝl) *v.t.* to grind (grain, beans etc.) coarsely. ~*n.* (*N Am.*) ground meal made into pellets.

kibbutz (kibuts´) *n.* (*pl.* **kibbutzim** (-im)) a communal agricultural settlement in Israel. **kibbutznik** (-nik) *n.* a person who lives and works on a kibbutz.

kibitzer (kib´itsǝ) *n.* (*N Am.*, *coll.*) **1** an interfering looker-on, esp. at a card game. **2** a meddler, an offerer of unwanted advice. **kibitz** *v.i.*

kiblah (kib´lǝ), **qibla** *n.* **1** the direction of the Kaaba at Mecca, to which Muslims turn during prayer. **2** a mihrab.

kibosh (kī´bosh), **kybosh** *n.* (*sl.*) bosh, humbug. **to put the kibosh on 1** to checkmate, to do for. **2** to put an end to.

kick (kik) *v.t.* **1** to strike with the foot or hoof etc. **2** to push, move, or drive, by or as by kicking. **3** to strike in recoil. **4** in football, to score (a goal) with a kick. **5** to abandon, give up, esp. an addiction. ~*v.i.* **1** to strike out with the foot or feet, or with the hoof etc. **2** to recoil, as a gun. **3** to show opposition, dislike etc. (against, at etc.). **4** to be alive and well. **5** to make a sudden violent movement. **6** (of a ball in cricket etc.) to rise sharply from the pitch. ~*n.* **1** the act of kicking. **2** a blow with the foot or hoof etc. **3** a recoil (of a gun). **4** a stimulating reaction to alcohol or pungent seasoning. **5** a sudden thrill of excitement. **6** an enthusiastic, short-lived interest. **7** energy, resilience. **8** a kicker of a ball (of a given ability). **9** the erratic course of an arrow owing to wrong handling of the bow. **10** a transient high-voltage discharge in an inductive electric current. **11** energy, strong effect. **for kicks** for pleasure. **to get a kick out of** to get enjoyment from. **to kick about/ around 1** (*coll.*) to go from place to place aimlessly. **2** to be discarded and left lying about or forgotten. **3** to treat harshly. **4** to discuss informally, to raise but not consider seriously. **to kick in 1** to break open (a door) by kicking. **2** to begin to function, to be activated. **3** (*N Am.*, *Austral.*, *sl.*) to pay one's share. **to kick off 1** to remove or discard by kicking. **2** in football, to give the ball the first kick, to start play. **3** to begin. **to kick oneself** to be angry with oneself. **to kick one's heels** to stand idly waiting. **to kick out** to eject or dismiss unceremoniously or with violence. **to kick over the traces** to throw off any means of restraint or control. **to kick (some) ass** (*N Am.*, *sl.*) to behave forcefully or aggressively. **to kick up one's heels** to enjoy oneself with no inhibitions. **kickable** *a.* **kickabout** *n.* an informal football game. **kick-ass** *a.* (*N Am.*, *sl.*) forceful, aggressive. **kickback** *n.* **1** a strong reaction to something. **2** a sum paid to another person, confidentially, for favours past or future. **kick-boxing** *n.* a martial art that allows punching and kicking. **kickdown** *n.* a way of changing gear in an automatic car, by pressing the accelerator pedal right down. **kicker** *n.* **kick in the teeth, kick in the pants** *n.* (*coll.*) a humiliating rejection, an unexpected personal attack. **kick-off** *n.* **1** in football, the first kick to start play. **2** a start. **for a kick-off** (*coll.*) for a start. **kicksorter** *n.* a device for sorting and counting electrical pulses according to amplitude. **kickstand** *n.* a bicycle or motorcycle stand that can be kicked into position. **kick-start** *n.* **1** an act of starting an engine by kicking down a pedal. **2** an act of giving extra impetus at the beginning of a project etc. **3** a kick-starter. *~v.t.* to start (an engine) by kicking down a pedal. **kickstarter** *n.* a pedal for kick-starting e.g. a motorcycle. **kick-turn** *n.* in skiing, a standing turn.

kid[1] (kid) *n.* **1 a** the young of the goat. **b** leather from the skin of this. **c** (*pl.*) gloves of this leather. **2** (*coll.*) a child, a young person. *~v.i.* (*pres.p.* **kidding**, *past, p.p.* **kidded**) to give birth to a kid or kids. **kid brother** *n.* (*coll.*) a younger brother. **kiddie, kiddy** *n.* (*pl.* **kiddies**) (*coll.*) a little child. **kiddo** *n.* (*pl.* **kiddos**) (*coll.*) (used as a form of address) a child or young person. **kid glove** *n.* a glove made of kid. **with kid gloves** very carefully or tactfully. **kid-glove** *a.* **1** characterized by care and tact. **2** too fastidious for common tasks etc. **kid sister** *n.* (*coll.*) a younger sister. **kidskin** *n.* a smooth, soft leather from a young goat. **kidvid** *n.* (*sl.*) **1** children's television. **2** a children's television programme or video.

kid[2] (kid) *v.t.* (*pres.p.* **kidding**, *past, p.p.* **kidded**) (*coll.*) **1** to humbug, to hoax, to pretend. **2** to deceive for fun, to tease. *~v.i.* to joke, to deceive someone for fun. **no kid** (*sl.*) no kidding, honestly. **no kidding** (*sl.*) really, honestly. **kidder** *n.* **kiddingly** *adv.* **kidology** (-ol'-) *n.* (*coll.*) the art or practice of kidding, bluffing.

kiddie KID[1].

kiddo, kiddy KID[1].

kidnap (kid'nap) *v.t.* (*pres.p.* **kidnapping**, (*N Am.*) **kidnaping**, *past, p.p.* **kidnapped**, (*N Am.*) **kidnaped**) to carry off (a person) by force or illegally, to abduct. **kidnapper**, (*NAm.*) **kidnaper** *n.*

kidney (kid'ni) *n.* (*pl.* **kidneys**) **1** (*Anat.*) an oblong flattened glandular organ embedded in fatty tissue in the lumbar region on each side of the spine, and serving to secrete urine and remove nitrogenous matter from the blood. **2** an animal's kidney used as food. **3** anything resembling a kidney. **4** temperament, kind, fashion. **kidney bean** *n.* a kidney-shaped bean, esp. the dwarf French bean and the scarlet runner. **kidney dish** *n.* a kidney-shaped container used in surgery. **kidney machine** *n.* a machine used to carry out blood dialysis in cases of kidney failure. **kidney-shaped, kidney-form** *a.* shaped like a kidney, having one concave and one convex side. **kidney vetch** *n.* a leguminous plant, *Anthyllis vulneraria*, lady's finger.

kidology KID[2].

kiekie (kē'kē) *n.* a New Zealand climber, *Freycinetia banksii*, the berries of which are eaten and the leaves used for baskets etc.

kieselguhr (kē'zəlguə) *n.* a type of diatomite.

Kikuyu (kikoo'ū) *n.* (*pl.* **Kikuyu, Kikuyus**) **1** a member of a Bantu-speaking people of Kenya. **2** their language. *~a.* of or relating to the Kikuyu or their language.

kilim (kil'im, kē'lim) *n.* a pileless woven carpet made in the Middle East.

kill (kil) *v.t.* **1** to deprive of life, to put to death. **2** to put an end to, to destroy, to quell. **3** to deaden, to still (pain etc.). **4** to neutralize (effects of colour etc.). **5** (*coll.*) to cause pain or discomfort to. **6** (*coll.*) to cause great amusement to. **7** (*coll.*) to overwhelm with admiration, astonishment, personal charms etc. **8** to pass or consume (time) idly. **9** to discard, to cancel. **10** to mark a paragraph or article not to be used. **11** (*coll.*) to delete (text) from a computer file. **12** to prevent the passing of (a bill) in Parliament. **13** in tennis etc., to strike (the ball) so forcibly that it cannot be returned. **14** in football etc., to stop the momentum of (the ball). **15** (*coll.*) to switch off (an engine, light etc.). **16** (*coll.*) to drink or eat the whole of. *~v.i.* **1** to cause death. **2** to engage in slaughter, esp. in sport. *~n.* **1** the act of killing. **2** an animal or number of animals killed, esp. in sport. **3** (*coll.*) the destruction of an enemy aircraft, tank etc. **dressed to kill** dressed to be as attractive as possible. **in at the kill** present at the end or conclusion of something. **to kill off** **1** to get rid of by killing. **2** to destroy completely. **3** to remove from a story by writing in the death of (a fictional character). **to kill oneself 1** to commit suicide. **2** (*coll.*) to overexert oneself. **3** (*coll.*) to laugh uncontrollably. **to kill two birds with one stone** to achieve two things with a single action. **to kill with kindness** to be too gentle or indulgent. **killer** *n.* **1** something that kills. **2** (*coll.*) a very impressive or difficult person, thing or action. **3** (*coll.*) a very funny joke. **killer bee** *n.* an Africanized honey bee which is very aggressive when disturbed. **killer cell** *n.* a white blood cell that destroys other cells. **killer instinct** *n.* **1** a tendency to kill. **2** in business, sport etc., the ability to be merciless. **killer whale** *n.* a black-and-white toothed whale, *Orcinus orca*, found in most seas. **killing** *a.* **1** that kills. **2** fascinating, irresistibly charming. **3** (*coll.*) excruciatingly funny. *~n.* **1** the act of causing death or a death, slaughter. **2** (*coll.*) a spectacular gain or success. **3** the number of animals killed by sportsmen. **to make a killing** to make a large profit. **killing bottle** *n.* a bottle containing poisonous gas, used for killing insects. **killingly** *adv.* **killjoy** *n.* a person who sheds a general depression on company, a wet blanket. **kill or cure** *a.* drastic in its effects.

killifish (kil'ifish) *n.* (*pl. in general* **killifish**, *in particular* **killifishes**) any minnow-like fish of the genus *Fundulus* and related genera, used as bait and to control mosquitoes.

kiln (kiln) *n.* a furnace, oven or stove for calcining, drying, hardening etc., esp. one for calcining lime or firing pottery etc. *~v.t.* to dry or bake in a kiln.

kilo (kē'lō) *n.* (*pl.* **kilos**) **1** a kilogram. **2** a kilometre.

kilo- (kil'ō, kē'lō) *comb. form* denoting a factor of one thousand, esp. in the metric system.

kilobyte (kil´əbīt) n. (Comput.) a unit of computer storage equal to 1024 bytes.

kilocalorie n. a unit of heat equalling 1000 (small) calories, used in measuring the energy content of food.

kilocycle (kil´əsīkəl) n. (Hist.) a unit for measuring the frequency of alternating current, equal to 1000 cycles per second.

kilogram (kil´əgram), **kilogramme** n. a measure of weight, 1000 grams or 2.2046 lb. av., the SI base unit of mass.

kilohertz (kil´əhœts) n. a unit used to measure the frequency of radio waves, equal to 1000 hertz.

kilojoule (kil´əjool) n. a unit of energy equal to 1000 joules.

kilolitre (kil´əlētə), (N Am.) **kiloliter** n. a liquid measure, 1000 litres.

kilometre (kil´əmētə, kilom´ itə) n. a measure of distance, equal to 1000 metres or 0.621 miles. **kilometrical** (-met´-) a.

Usage note The pronunciation of kilometre as (kilom´-), with stress on the second syllable, is sometimes disapproved of (other similar metric units have initial stress), though it is very common.

kiloton (kil´ətŭn), **kilotonne** n. a measure of explosive power, equal to 1000 tons of TNT.

kilovolt (kil´əvolt) n. a unit of electromotive force equal to 1000 volts.

kilowatt (kil´əwot) n. a unit of measurement of electrical energy, equal to 1000 watts. **kilowatt-hour** n. a unit of energy or work equal to that performed by 1 kilowatt acting for 1 hour.

kilt (kilt) n. a kind of short skirt usu. of tartan cloth gathered in vertical pleats, worn as part of male dress by the highlanders of Scotland. **kilted** a. 1 wearing a kilt. 2 gathered into vertical pleats.

kilter (kil´tə), **kelter** (kel´-) n. (coll.) good condition, fitness, form.

kimberlite (kim´bəlīt) n. a diamond-bearing claylike bluish rock, found in S Africa and Siberia.

kimono (kimō´nō) n. (pl. **kimonos**) 1 a loose robe fastened with a sash, the principal outer garment of Japanese costume. 2 a dressing gown resembling this.

kin (kin) n. 1 one's blood relations or family connections collectively, kindred. 2 a relation, a family connection. ~a. of the same family, nature or kind, akin. **kinless** a. **kinsfolk**, (N Am.) **kinfolk** n.pl. family relations, kindred. **kinship** n. 1 relationship by blood. 2 affinity. **kinsman** n. (pl. **kinsmen**). **kinswoman** n. (pl. **kinswomen**).

-kin (kin) suf. forming diminutive nouns (manikin).

kina (kē´nə) n. the standard monetary unit of Papua New Guinea.

kinaesthesia (kinəsthē´ziə, kī-), (esp. N Am.) **kinesthesia**, **kinaesthesis** (-thē´sis), (esp. N Am.) **kinesthesis** n. (Med.) the brain's sense of the body's positioning, the perception of muscular movement. **kinaesthetic** (-thet´-) a.

kincob (king´kob) n. a rich Indian fabric interwoven with gold or silver thread.

kind (kīnd) n. 1 a genus, a species, a natural group. 2 sort, class, variety. 3 manner, fashion, way. 4 each Eucharistic element. 5 essential nature. ~a. 1 disposed to do good to others. 2 sympathetic, benevolent, tender. 3 proceeding from or characterized by goodness of heart. **a kind of** 1 a sort of. 2 roughly or approximately of the description or class expressed. **in kind** 1 (of payment, wages etc.) in produce or commodities. 2 in the same way or manner. **nothing of the kind** 1 something quite different. 2 not at all (as a rejoinder). **of a kind** 1 (derog.) that is not a good example of its type. 2 of the same type (two of a kind). **something of the kind** something similar. **kinda** (-də) adv. (coll.) kind of, rather. **kind-hearted** a. of a sympathetic or generous disposition. **kind-heartedly** adv. **kind-heartedness** n. **kindly** a. (comp. **kindlier**, superl. **kindliest**) 1 kind, good-natured, benevolent. 2 favourable, auspicious. ~adv. 1 in a considerate or tolerant way. 2 (iron.) as an act of kindness. **to look kindly on** to be favourably disposed towards. **to take kindly to** to react favourably to. **to take something kindly** to react favourably to (something). **to thank kindly** to thank sincerely. **kindlily** adv. **kindliness** n. **kindness** n. 1 the fact or condition of being kind, kind behaviour. 2 a kind act. **kind of** adv. (coll.) rather.

Usage note Kind of should not be used as a plural (as in those kind of dictionaries), or followed by the indefinite article a, an (as in this kind of a dictionary).

kindergarten (kin´dəgahtən) n. a school for infants and children below official school age, in which knowledge is imparted chiefly by simple object lessons, by toys, games, singing and work.

kindle (kin´dəl) v.t. 1 to set fire to, to light. 2 to inflame, to inspire (the passions etc.). 3 to excite, to stir up (to action or feeling). 4 to light up or illumine. ~v.i. 1 to catch fire, to begin to burn or flame. 2 to become inflamed or excited. 3 to react or respond (to). 4 to become illumined. **kindler** n. **kindling** n. wood, shavings etc., for lighting fires, firewood.

kindred (kin´drid) n. 1 (collect.) relatives, kin. 2 relationship by blood or marriage. 3 affinity or likeness of character. ~a. 1 related by blood or marriage. 2 of like nature or qualities, congenial, sympathetic. **kindred spirit** n. a person with the same interests and attitudes as one's own.

kinematics (kīnəmat´iks, kin-) n. the science of pure motion, admitting conceptions of time and velocity but excluding that of force. **kinematic** a. **kinematically** adv.

kinematograph CINEMATOGRAPH.

kinesi- (kinē´si) comb. form movement.

kinesis (kinē´sis) n. 1 movement. 2 (Biol.)

movement under stimulus. **3** (*Zool.*) movement of the bones of the skull. **kinesics** *n.* **1** the study of body movements as non-verbal communication. **2** (*as pl.*) body movements as communicating information.

kinesthesia, kinesthesis KINAESTHESIA.

kinetic (kinet´ik) *a.* **1** of or producing motion. **2** due to or depending upon motion. **kinetically** *adv.* **kinetic art** *n.* art, e.g. sculpture, which has moving parts. **kinetic energy** *n.* the energy of a body in actual motion (measured by the product of half the mass and the square of the velocity). **kinetics** *n.* **1** the branch of dynamics which deals with forces imparting motion to or influencing motion already imparted to bodies. **2** the study and measuring of the rates of chemical or biochemical reactions. **kinetic theory** *n.* (*Chem.*) a theory which accounts for the behaviour of gases, vapours, liquids etc. in terms of the motions of molecules or atoms comprising them.

kinetin (ki´nitin) *n.* a synthetic kinin used to promote cell division in plants.

king (king) *n.* **1** the male sovereign of a nation, esp. a hereditary sovereign of an independent state. **2** a person who or thing which is preeminent in any sphere. **3** a playing card bearing a representation of a king, usu. ranking next to the ace and before the queen. **4** in chess, a piece which has to be protected from checkmate. **5** in draughts, a piece which has been crowned and is entitled to move in any direction. ~*v.t.* **1** to make a king of. **2** to raise to a throne. ~*v.i.* to act as king, to govern. **king high** in a card game, having the king as the top-ranking card. **to king it** (*coll.*) to behave as if one is superior to others. **king bird** *n.* any American flycatcher of the genus *Tyrannus*. **kingbolt** *n.* a main or central pin, bolt or pivot. **King Charles spaniel** *n.* a small breed of spaniel. **king cobra** *n.* a large, venomous cobra, *Ophiophagus hannah*. **king crab** *n.* **1** a horseshoe crab. **2** (*N Am.*) a large edible spider crab. **kingcup** *n.* the marsh marigold, *Caltha palustris*. **kingdom** *n.* **1** the territory under the rule of a king or queen. **2** a people ruled by a king (or queen). **3** a domain, a territory. **4** each of the three highest and most comprehensive of the divisions into which natural objects may be arranged. **5** (*Biol.*) the highest taxonomic classification. **6** (*Theol.*) the spiritual reign or realm of God. **to come into/ to one's kingdom** to reach one's desired status. **kingdom come** *n.* (*coll.*) the world to come, eternity. **till kingdom come** for ever. **kingfish** *n.* any of several types of large food and game fish. **kingfisher** *n.* any bird of the family Alcedinidae which dive for fish in rivers etc., esp. *Alcedo atthis*, a small European bird with brilliant blue and green plumage. **kingless** *a.* **kinglet** *n.* **1** a petty king. **2** any of several small warblers of the genus *Regulus*. **kinglike** *a.* **kingly** *a.*, *adv.* **kingmaker** *n.* (*Hist.*) a person who sets up kings, esp. Richard Neville,

Earl of Warwick, who supported the Houses of York and Lancaster alternately in the Wars of the Roses. **king of beasts** *n.* the lion. **king of birds** *n.* the eagle. **King of Kings** *n.* **1** God. **2** the title of various oriental monarchs. **king of metals** *n.* gold. **King of the Castle** *n.* **1** a children's game in which a player stands on a mound and others try to displace him or her. **2** the most important person in a group. **kingpin** *n.* **1** a main or central pin, bolt or pivot. **2** (*coll.*) the most important person or thing in an organization or structure. **king post** *n.* the middle post of a roof, reaching from the ridge to the tie-beam. **king prawn** *n.* a large prawn of the genus *Penaeus*. **king's bishop** *n.* in chess, the bishop on the king's side of the board at the start of play. **King's Counsel** *n.* counsel to the Crown, an honorary title which gives precedence over ordinary barristers, during the reign of a king. **King's English** *n.* correct English as spoken by educated people, during the reign of a king. **King's evidence** *n.* (*Law*) evidence given against one's accomplice in return for a free pardon, during the reign of a king. **King's Guide** *n.* a Guide who has reached the highest level of proficiency, during the reign of a king. **King's highway** *n.* a public road, a right-of-way. **kingship** *n.* **king-size, king-sized** *a.* (of beds etc.) larger than is usual. **king's knight** *n.* in chess, the knight on the king's side of the board at the start of play. **king's pawn** *n.* in chess, the pawn in front of the king at the start of play. **king's ransom** *n.* a large sum of money. **king's rook** *n.* in chess, the rook on the king's side of the board at the start of play. **King's Scout** *n.* a Scout who has reached the highest level of proficiency, during the reign of a king. **King's Speech** *n.* during the reign of a king, an address by the sovereign to Parliament at the beginning of every session, outlining the government's proposed legislation.

kinin (ki´nin) *n.* **1** any of a group of polyptetides formed in the body which cause dilation of the blood vessels. **2** a plant hormone which promotes cell division and slows down the ageing process in plants.

kink (kingk) *n.* **1** a twist or abrupt bend in a rope, thread, wire etc. **2** a prejudice, a whim. **3** an imperfection. **4** a cramp in part of the body. ~*v.i.* to twist or run into kinks. ~*v.t.* to cause to kink. **kinky** *a.* (*comp.* **kinkier**, *superl.* **kinkiest**) **1** (*coll.*) given to abnormal sexual practices. **2** (*coll.*) (sexually) provocative. **3** eccentric, odd. **4** twisted, curly. **kinkily** *adv.* **kinkiness** *n.*

kinkajou (king´kejoo) *n.* (*pl.* **kinkajous**) an arboreal fruit-eating quadruped, *Potos flavus*, of S and Central America, allied to the raccoon, with long body and prehensile tail.

-kins (kinz) *suf.* added to nouns to show affection, as in *mummykins*, *daddykins* etc.

kinsfolk, kinsman etc. KIN.

kiosk (ke´osk) *n.* **1** an open-fronted structure for the sale of newspapers etc. **2** a public telephone booth. **3** (*Austral.*) a café in the grounds of a park, zoo etc.

kip[1] (kip) *n.* (*sl.*) **1** a sleep. **2** a cheap lodging-house. **3** a bed. *~v.i.* (*pres.p.* **kipping**, *past, p.p.* **kipped**) to go to sleep. **to kip down** to lie down and go to sleep.

kip[2] (kip) *n.* (*pl.* **kip**, **kips**) the standard monetary unit of Laos.

kip[3] (kip) *n.* (*Austral., sl.*) a wooden bat for tossing coins in the game of two-up.

kipper (kip´ə) *n.* **1** a salmon or herring split open, salted and dried in smoke or the open air. **2** a male salmon during the spawning season. *~v.t.* to cure and preserve (salmon, herrings etc.) by rubbing with salt and drying in smoke or in the open air. **kipperer** *n.* **kipper tie** *n.* a very wide tie.

kipsie (kip´si), **kipsy** *n.* (*pl.* **kipsies**) (*Austral., sl.*) a home, house or shelter.

Kir® (kiə), **kir** *n.* a drink made from white wine and cassis.

kirby grip (koeˊbigrip), **Kirbigrip**® *n.* a type of hairgrip.

Kirghiz, **Kirgiz** KYRGYZ.

kirk (kœk) *n.* (*Sc., North.*) **1** a church. **2** (**Kirk**) the established (Presbyterian) Church of Scotland, esp. in contradistinction to the Church of England or the Scottish Episcopal Church. **Kirk-session** *n.* the lowest court in the Church of Scotland.

kirsch (kiəsh), **kirschwasser** (kiəsh´vasə) *n.* an alcoholic liqueur distilled from the fermented juice of the black cherry.

kiskadee (kiskədē´), **keskidee** (kes-) *n.* a South and Central American flycatcher, *Pitangus sulphuratus*.

kismet (kiz´mət, kis´-) *n.* fate, destiny.

kiss (kis) *n.* **1** a touch with the lips, esp. in affection or as a salutation. **2** in snooker, billiards etc., a mere touch of the moving balls. **3** a confection of sugar, white of eggs etc. *~v.t.* **1** to press or touch with the lips, esp. in affection or as a salutation. **2** (of a ball or balls) in snooker, billiards etc., to touch lightly in passing. *~v.i.* **1** to join lips in affection or respect. **2** (of moving balls) in snooker, billiards etc. to come in contact. **to kiss away** to wipe away by kissing. **to kiss goodbye to 1** to give a kiss to on parting. **2** (*coll.*) to accept the loss of. **to kiss off 1** (*N Am., sl.*) to get rid of (someone) rudely. **2** (*N Am., sl.*) to die, to go away. **to kiss someone's arse** (*taboo sl.*) to be obsequious. **to kiss the dust 1** to be conquered, to yield. **2** to die, to be slain. **to kiss the rod** to submit tamely to punishment. **kissable** *a.* **Kissagram**® (-əgram), **kissogram** *n.* a congratulatory message delivered by an agency with a kiss. **kiss and tell** *n.* the practice of selling stories of one's sexual relationships to the press. **kiss-curl** *n.* a curl hanging over the forehead, in front of the ear or at the nape of the neck. **kisser** *n.* **1** a person who kisses. **2** (*sl.*) the mouth, the face. **kissing** *n., a.* **kissing cousin**, **kissing kin**, **kissing kind** *n.* a relation familiar enough to be kissed on

meeting. **kissing gate** *n.* a gate hung in a U or V-shaped enclosure. **kiss of death** *n.* something which will inevitably lead to failure. **kiss-off** *n.* (*N Am., sl.*) a dismissal, the sack. **kiss of life** *n.* mouth-to-mouth resuscitation. **kiss of peace** *n.* a ceremonial kiss among Christians, esp. during the Eucharist. **kissy** *a.* (*coll.*) affectionate, liking to kiss.

Kiswahili (kēswəhēˊli) *n.* a widely-spoken Bantu language, Swahili.

kit[1] (kit) *n.* **1** the equipment needed for a particular job, sport etc. **2** the clothes needed for a particular activity, e.g. playing football. **3** pieces of equipment, sold as a set, and ready for assembly. **4** a container for the necessaries, tools etc. for a particular job. **5** a kitbag. *~v.t.* (*pres.p.* **kitting**, *past, p.p.* **kitted**) (*usu. with out, up*) to fit out with the necessary clothes or equipment. **the whole kit (and caboodle)** (*coll.*) the whole lot. **kitbag** *n.* a strong bag for holding a person's clothes and equipment, esp. that of a member of the service.

kit[2] (kit) *n.* **1** a kitten. **2** a young fox or badger. **kit-fox** *n.* either of two North American foxes, *Vulpes velox* and *Vulpes macrotis*.

kitchen (kich´ən) *n.* **1** a room or area in a house etc. where food is cooked. **2** a set of units and fitments for a kitchen. **3** (*sl.*) the percussion section of an orchestra. **kitchen cabinet** *n.* a political leader's unofficial advisers esp. when considered too influential. **kitchenette** (-netˊ) *n.* a small kitchen. **kitchen garden** *n.* a garden in which herbs and vegetables etc. are cultivated for the table. **kitchen-midden** *n.* a prehistoric refuse heap or shell-mound indicating an ancient settlement (first noticed on the coast of Denmark, and since found in the British Isles etc.). **kitchen roll** *n.* a roll of absorbent paper used for wiping, cleaning etc. **kitchen-sink** *a.* (of drama etc.) depicting the reality and often the sordid quality of everyday life. **kitchen tea** *n.* (*Austral., New Zeal.*) a party held before a wedding to which the guests bring gifts of kitchenware. **kitchenware** *n.* the pots, pans, china and other utensils used in the kitchen.

kite (kīt) *n.* **1** a device consisting of a light frame of wood covered with fabric or paper, constructed to fly in the air by means of a string. **2** any of various medium-sized birds of prey of the genus *Milvus*, esp. the European kite, *M. milvus*. **3** (*sl.*) an aircraft. **4** (*pl.*) light sails, set only in very light winds, above the other sails. **5** (*Geom.*) a four-sided figure that is symmetrical on each side of one diagonal. *~v.i.* to fly like a kite. **to fly a kite** to try out an idea, to find out about a situation, public opinion etc. **kite balloon** *n.* a captive balloon for scientific or military observations etc. **kite-flying** *n.* **1** flying and controlling a kite. **2** the circulation of rumours to test public opinion. **kite-flyer** *n.* **Kitemark** *n.* a kite-shaped mark indicating that goods conform in all particulars with the specifications of the British Standards Institution.

kith (kith) *n.* kindred. **kith and kin** close friends and relations.

kitsch (kich) *n.* art or literature that is inferior or in bad taste, esp. that designed to appeal to popular sentimentality. **kitschy** *a.* (*comp.* **kitschier,** *superl.* **kitschiest**). **kitschiness** *n.*

kitten (kit´ən) *n.* **1** the young of the cat. **2** a young ferret, fox etc. **3** a playful girl. ~*v.i.,* *v.t.* to give birth to (kittens). **to have kittens** (*coll.*) to be overexcited, very annoyed etc. **kittenish** *a.* **1** like a kitten. **2** (of a girl) playful in a sexy way. **kittenishly** *adv.* **kittenishness** *n.* **kitty**[1] *n.* (*pl.* **kitties**) (*coll.*) (a pet name for) a kitten.

kittiwake (kit´iwāk) *n.* a seagull of the genus *Rissa,* esp. *R. tridactyla,* common on the British coasts.

kitty[1] KITTEN.

kitty[2] (kit´i) *n.* (*pl.* **kitties**) **1** the pool into which each player puts a stake in poker, and other games. **2** a common fund of money. **3** the jack in bowls.

kitty-cornered CATER-CORNERED (under CATER[2]).

kiwi (kē´wē) *n.* (*pl.* **kiwis**) **1** a New Zealand wingless bird of the genus *Apteryx.* **2** (*coll.*) (**Kiwi**) a New Zealander. **kiwi fruit** *n.* the edible green fruit of a climbing plant, *Actinidia chinensis,* also called *Chinese gooseberry.*

kJ *abbr.* kilojoule(s).

kl. *abbr.* kilolitre(s).

Klan (klan) *n.* the Ku Klux Klan. **Klansman, Klanswoman** *n.* (*pl.* **Klansmen, Klanswomen**) a member of the Ku Klux Klan.

Klaxon® (klak´sən), **klaxon** *n.* a loud horn or hooter, formerly used on cars.

Kleenex® (klē´neks) *n.* (*pl.* **Kleenex, Kleenexes**) a soft paper tissue used as a handkerchief etc.

kleptomania (kleptōmā´niə) *n.* a form of mental illness displaying itself in an irresistible urge to steal. **kleptomaniac** (-ak) *n., a.*

klieg (klēg), **klieg light** *n.* a powerful arc lamp used as floodlighting in a film studio.

klipspringer (klip´springə) *n.* a small S African antelope, *Oreotragus oreotragus.*

Klondike (klon´dīk), **Klondyke** *n.* a source of wealth.

kludge (klŭj) *n.* **1** (*sl.*) an untidy mixture of things. **2** (*Comput.*) an unreliable system or program.

klutz (klŭts) *n.* (*N Am., sl.*) a clumsy or foolish person. **klutzy** *a.*

klystron (klī´stron) *n.* an electron tube used to amplify or generate microwaves.

km *abbr.* kilometre(s).

kn. *abbr.* (*Naut.*) knot(s).

knack (nak) *n.* **1** a trick or adroit way of doing a thing. **2** dexterity, adroitness. **3** a habit, a mannerism. **knacky** *a.* **knackiness** *n.*

knacker (nak´ə) *n.* **1** a buyer of worn-out horses, cattle etc. for slaughter; a horse-slaughterer. **2** a dealer in second-hand goods, houses, ships etc.

~*v.t.* **1** (*coll.*) to break, ruin or kill. **2** to wear out, exhaust. **knackered** *a.* (*coll.*) exhausted, tired out. **knackery** *n.* (*pl.* **knackeries**) a knacker's business, a knacker's yard.

knap[1] (nap) *n.* (*dial.*) a hill crest, rising ground.

knap[2] (nap) *v.t.* (*pres.p.* **knapping,** *past, p.p.* **knapped**) to break into pieces, esp. with a sharp snapping noise, to break, flake, or chip (flint). **knapper** *n.*

knapsack (nap´sak) *n.* a case or bag for clothes, food etc., carried on the back by soldiers on a march or by hikers etc.

knapweed (nap´wēd) *n.* any of various composite plants with purple globular flowers, of the genus *Centaurea,* esp. *C. nigra,* and *C. scabiosa.*

knar (nah), **gnar** *n.* a knot in wood, a protuberance on the trunk or branch of a tree.

knave (nāv) *n.* **1** a deceitful, cunning person, a rogue. **2** a court card with a representation of a soldier or servant, the jack. **knavery** (-vəri) *n.* (*pl.* **knaveries**) **1** dishonesty. **2** a dishonest act. **knavish** *a.* **knavishly** *adv.* **knavishness** *n.*

knawel (naw´əl) *n.* any of several short plants of the genus *Scleranthus.*

knead (nēd) *v.t.* **1** to work up (flour, clay etc.) into a plastic mass by pressing and folding it with the hands. **2** to shape, make, mingle or blend by this method. **3** to blend together. **4** to pummel and press with the heel of the hand in massage. **kneadable** *a.* **kneader** *n.*

knee (nē) *n.* (*pl.* **knees**) **1** the joint of the thigh or femur with the lower leg. **2** a joint roughly corresponding to this in other animals. **3** the upper part of a person's thighs, when sitting. **4** the part of a garment covering the knee. **5** a piece of timber or metal cut or cast with an angle like that of the knee to connect beams etc. **6** anything resembling a knee in shape or function. ~*v.t.* (*3rd pers. sing. pres.* **knees,** *pres.p.* **kneeing,** *past, p.p.* **kneed**) **1** to touch or strike with the knee. **2** to fasten or strengthen (beams etc.) with knees. **3** (*coll.*) to cause (trousers) to bag at the knees. **to bend/ bow the knee 1** to kneel in submission. **2** to submit. **to bring to one's knees** to reduce to submission. **knee-breeches** *n.pl.* breeches reaching just below the knee. **kneecap** *n.* **1** the heart-shaped sesamoid bone in front of the knee joint, the patella. **2** a padded cover for the knee. ~*v.t.* (*pres.p.* **kneecapping,** *past, p.p.* **kneecapped**) to shoot or injure (esp. an informer) in the knee. **kneecapping** *n.* **knee-deep** *a.* **1** (of a person or animal) sunk in as far as the knees. **2** (of liquid) deep enough to reach the knees. **3** deeply involved. **knee-high** *a.* coming up to the knee. **kneehole** *n.* a space for the knees between the pedestals of a writing table or desk. **knee-jerk** *n.* **1** a reflex kick of the lower part of the leg. **2** (*coll.*) a reflex, an automatic reaction. **knee joint** *n.* **1** (*Anat.*) the articulation of the femur with the tibia. **2** a joint between two pieces hinged together. **knee-length** *a.* reaching down to, or up to, the knee. **knees-up** *n.* (*coll.*) a party, a celebration. **knee-trembler** *n.* (*sl.*) an act of sexual intercourse standing up.

kneel (nēl) *v.i.* (*past, p.p.* **knelt** (nelt), (*N Am.*) **kneeled** (nēld)) **1** to bend or incline the knees. **2** to fall on the knees. **3** to support the body on the knees. **kneeler** *n.* **1** a stool or cushion for kneeling on. **2** a person who kneels.

knell (nel) *v.i.* **1** to ring, to toll, as for a death or funeral. **2** to sound in a mournful or ominous manner. ~*v.t.* to proclaim or summon by or as by a knell. ~*n.* **1** the sound of a bell when struck, esp. for a death or funeral. **2** an evil omen, a death blow.

knelt KNEEL.

knew KNOW.

knickerbocker (nik´əbokə) *n.* **1** (*pl.*) loose breeches gathered in below the knee. **2** (**Knickerbocker**) a New Yorker esp. one of original Dutch descent. **Knickerbocker Glory** *n.* a large ice cream sundae, with fruit and jelly.

knickers (nik´əz) *n.pl.* **1** women's underpants; also called *pair of knickers.* **2** (*N Am.*) knicker-bockers. **3** (*N Am.*) short trousers. ~*int.* (*sl.*) used to express disagreement or contempt.

knick-knack (nik´nak), **nick-nack** *n.* **1** any little ornamental article. **2** a showy trifle. **knick-knackery** *n.* **knick-knackish** *a.*

knife (nīf) *n.* (*pl.* **knives**) **1** a blade with one edge sharpened, usu. set in a handle. **2** a cutting blade forming part of a machine. ~*v.t.* **1** to stab or cut with a knife. **2** (*coll.*) to betray, to defeat or injure deceitfully. ~*v.i.* to cut (through) like a knife. **that one could cut like a knife 1** (*coll.*) (of an accent) thick, very marked. **2** (*coll.*) (of an atmosphere etc.) very tense, oppressive. **the knife** (*coll.*) surgical operations. **to get/ have one's knife in someone** to be vindictive towards someone. **knife-edge** *n.* **1** the edge of a knife. **2** a hard steel edge used as fulcrum for a balance, pendulum etc. **3** a difficult situation where things could go either right or wrong. **4** a sharp mountain ridge. **knife-grinder** *n.* a person who sharpens knives, esp. an itinerant knife-sharpener. **knifelike** *a.* **knife-pleat** *n.* a narrow flat pleat turned in a single direction. **knifepoint** *n.* the pointed end of a knife. **at knifepoint** threatened by someone with a knife. **knifer** *n.*

knight (nīt) *n.* **1** a man who holds a non-hereditary dignity conferred by the sovereign or their representative, and entitling the possessor to the title of 'Sir' prefixed to his name. **2** (*Hist.*) a man of gentle birth, usu. one who had served as page and esquire, admitted to an honourable degree of military rank, with ceremonies or religious rites. **3** (*Hist.*) a champion to a lady in war or at a tournament. **4** a chess piece, usu. shaped like a horse's head, entitled to move two squares straight and one at right-angles. ~*v.t.* to create or dub (a person) a knight. **knightage** (-ij) *n.* **1** knights collectively. **2** a list of knights. **knight**

bachelor *n.* (*pl.* **knights bachelor**) **1** a knight of the oldest order of knighthood. **2** one knighted but not belonging to any of the special orders. **knight commander** *n.* a member of one of the higher grades in some orders of knighthood. **knight errant** *n.* **1** a medieval knight who wandered about in quest of adventures to show his prowess and generosity. **2** a chivalrous or quixotic person. **knight-errantry** *n.* **knighthood** *n.* (*pl.* **Knights Hospitallers**) a member of a military order of monks founded in the crusades. **knight in shining armour** *n.* (*coll.*) a man who helps a woman in difficulty. **knightlike** *a.* **knightly** *a., adv.* (*poet.*). **knightliness** *n.* **knight of the road** *n.* (*coll.*) **1** a footpad, a highwayman. **2** a tramp. **3** a commercial traveller. **4** a lorry driver or taxi driver. **Knight Templar** *n.* (*pl.* **Knights Templars**) (*Hist.*) a member of a religious and military order founded in the 12th cent., for the protection of pilgrims to the Holy Land.

kniphofia (nifō´fiə) *n.* any of various tall plants of the genus *Kniphofia*, native to S and E Africa and having spikes of red, orange or yellow flowers, esp. the red-hot poker.

knit (nit) *v.t.* (*pres.p.* **knitting**, *past, p.p.* **knit**, **knitted**) **1** to form into a fabric or form (a fabric, garment etc.) by looping or knotting a continuous yarn or thread, by hand with knitting needles or on a knitting machine. **2** to join closely together, to unite. **3** to make close or compact. **4** to contract into folds or wrinkles. **5** to make (a plain stitch) by the simplest form of loop in knitting. ~*v.i.* **1** to make a textile fabric by interweaving yarn or thread. **2** to grow together in healing etc. **3** to become closely united. **4** (of the brows) to contract into a frowning or puzzled expression. ~*n.* **1** style of knitting, knitted texture. **2** a knitted garment, knitted fabric. **to knit up 1** to repair by knitting. **2** to conclude, to wind up (a speech, argument etc.). **knitter** *n.* **knitting** *n.* **1** a piece of knitted work in the process of being made. **2** the making of a textile fabric by interweaving yarn or thread. **3** contracting, growing together etc. **knitting machine** *n.* an apparatus for mechanically knitting jerseys etc. **knitting needle** *n.* a long eyeless rod of metal, wood, plastic etc., used to hold and make stitches in knitting. **knitwear** *n.* knitted clothes, usu. sweaters.

knives KNIFE.

knob (nob) *n.* **1** a rounded protuberance, usu. at the end of something. **2** a rounded handle of a door, lock, drawer etc. **3** (*N Am.*) a rounded hill, a knoll. **4** an ornamental terminal boss. **5** a lump (of coal, sugar etc.). **6** (*taboo sl.*) the penis. ~*v.t.* (*pres.* **knobbing**, *past, p.p.* **knobbed**) to furnish with a knob or knobs. ~*v.i.* **1** to become knobby. **2** to bulge or bunch (out). **with knobs on** (*sl.*) even more so. **knobbed** *a.* **knobble** (nob´əl) *n.* a small knob. **knobbly** *a.* (*comp.* **knobblier**, *superl.* **knobbliest**). **knobby** *a.* **knobbiness** *n.*

knoblike *a.* knobstick *n.* a knobbed stick used as a weapon.

knobkerrie (nob´keri), knopkierie (knop´kiəri) *n.* the round-headed club used as a weapon by S African tribesmen.

knock (nok) *v.t.* 1 to strike so as to make a sound, to hit, to give a hard blow to. 2 to drive or force by striking. 3 to make by knocking. 4 to cause to strike together. 5 (*coll.*) to criticize. 6 (*sl.*) to amaze. 7 (*taboo sl., offensive*) to have sex with. ~*v.i.* 1 to strike hard or smartly (at, against, together etc.). 2 to rap on a door for admitting or attention. 3 to collide (with). 4 (of an engine) to make knocking sounds. ~*n.* 1 a blow. 2 a rap, esp. on a door for admittance or attention. 3 the sound of knocking in an engine. 4 an act of knocking. 5 an unpleasant experience, a setback. **to knock about/ around** 1 to strike with repeated blows. 2 to handle violently. 3 (*coll.*) to wander about, to lead an irregular life. 4 to keep company (with). 5 to be somewhere for no particular reason. **to knock against** 1 to collide with. 2 to encounter casually. **to knock back** 1 (*coll.*) to drink quickly, to eat up. 2 (*coll.*) to cost (a person). 3 (*coll.*) to shock. 4 (*Austral., New Zeal., coll.*) to reject, to rebuff. **to knock down** 1 to fell with a blow. 2 to demolish. 3 to prostrate (with astonishment etc.). 4 to sell (with a blow of the hammer) to a bidder at an auction. 5 (*coll.*) to lower in price, quality etc. 6 to dismantle (furniture etc.). 7 (*N Am., sl.*) to earn. **to knock off** 1 to strike off, with a blow. 2 to dispatch, to do or finish quickly. 3 to cease work. 4 to leave off (work). 5 to deduct (from a price etc.). 6 (*sl.*) to steal. 7 (*sl.*) to kill. 8 (*taboo sl., offensive*) to have sex with. **to knock on** in rugby, to play (the ball) with the hand or arm and in the direction of the opponents' goal line. **to knock oneself out** (*coll.*) to exhaust oneself. **to knock on the head** 1 to stun or kill with a blow on the head. 2 to frustrate, to spoil, to defeat. **to knock on wood** (*N Am.*) to touch wood (for luck etc.). **to knock out** 1 to make unconscious by a blow to the head. 2 to force out with a blow. 3 to defeat (a boxer) by knocking down for a count of ten. 4 to eliminate from a contest by defeating. 5 (*coll.*) to astonish or impress. 6 (*coll.*) to do or make quickly. 7 (*sl.*) to earn. 8 to empty tobacco from (a pipe) by tapping. **to knock sideways** to knock off course, to destroy the composure of. **to knock together** to put hastily or roughly into shape. **to knock up** 1 to strike or force upwards. 2 to arouse by knocking. 3 to fatigue, to wear out, to exhaust. 4 to put together or make up hastily. 5 to score (runs) quickly at cricket. 6 (*sl.*) to make (someone) pregnant. 7 to practise before starting to play a ball game. **to knock wood** (*N Am.*) to touch wood (for luck etc.). knockabout *a.* 1 noisy, rough, violent, slapstick. 2 (of clothes etc.) suitable for rough usage. 3 irregular, bohemian. ~*n.* 1 a knockabout performance or performer. 2 (*Austral.*) a farm or station handyman. 3 a light,

partly-decked yacht or sailing boat. **knock-back** *n.* (*Austral., New Zeal., coll.*) a rejection, a setback. **knock-down** *a.* 1 (of a blow) that knocks an opponent down. 2 (of an event etc.) overwhelmingly bad, decisive. 3 **a** (of a price at auction) reserve or minimum. **b** (of a sale price) very low. 4 (of furniture) easy to dismantle and reassemble. 5 (of insecticide) that acts quickly. ~*n.* (*Austral., New Zeal., sl.*) an introduction to someone. knocker *n.* 1 a hammer-like attachment to an outer door to give notice that someone desires admittance or attention. 2 a person or thing that knocks. 3 (*pl., taboo sl.*) a woman's breasts. 4 an itinerant salesperson. **on the knocker** 1 (*coll.*) door-to-door. 2 on credit. 3 (*Austral., New Zeal.*) promptly, at once. **knock-for-knock** *a.* denoting an agreement between vehicle insurance companies by which each company pays for the damage sustained to a vehicle insured by them irrespective of legal liability. knocking *n.* explosions in the cylinder of an internal combustion engine due to over-compression of the mixture of air and petrol vapour before sparking. **knocking shop** *n.* (*sl.*) a brothel. **knock knees** *n.pl.* knees that touch when the feet are still apart. **knock-kneed** *a.* knock-off *n.* (*coll.*) an imitation of a competitor's idea. **knock-on** *n.* in rugby, an act of playing the ball with the hand or arm in the direction of the opponents' goal line. **knock-on effect** *n.* an indirect result of an action. knockout *a.* 1 (of a blow etc.) disabling, causing unconsciousness. 2 (of a competition) in which the loser is eliminated in each round. ~*n.* 1 the act of knocking a person out with a blow. 2 a blow that knocks the opponent out. 3 (*sl.*) a marvel, a wonder. 4 a knockout competition. **knockout drops** *n.pl.* (*sl.*) a drug put into someone's drink secretly. **knock-up** *n.* a practice session before the start of a racket game.

knoll (nōl) *n.* a rounded hill, a mound, a hillock. knolly *a.*

knot¹ (not) *n.* 1 the interlacement or intertwining of a rope or ropes, cords etc., so as to fasten one part to another part of the rope etc. or to another object. 2 a particular method of tying a knot, a type of knot. 3 an ornamental bow or interlacement of a ribbon etc. on a dress. 4 an irregular or twisted portion in a tree caused by branches, buds etc. 5 a hard cross-grained part in a piece of wood, caused by interlacing fibres. 6 a tangle in hair etc. 7 anything resembling a knot. 8 a union or bond, esp. marriage. 9 a group, a cluster. 10 a difficulty, a perplexity, a problem. 11 the gist or kernel of a matter. 12 a nautical mile per hour as a unit of speed. 13 (*coll.*) a nautical mile. 14 a division of the log-line marked off by knots, used as a unit for measuring speed. 15 a node or joint in a stem. 16 a hard hump in the body of a person or animal. 17 a protuberance or excrescence. 18 a flower bud. ~*v.t.* (*pres.p.* knotting, *past, p.p.* knotted) 1 to tie in a knot or knots. 2 to fasten with a knot. **3** to intertwine. **4** to make (a fringe) by means of knots. **5** to knit (the brows). **6** to join together closely or intricately. **7** to entangle, to perplex. ~*v.i.* **1** (of plants) to form knots. **2** to make knots for fringing. **at a rate of knots** (*coll.*) very quickly. **get knotted!** (*sl.*) an expression of anger, exasperation etc. **to tie in knots** (*coll.*) to baffle (a person) completely, to confuse. **knot-garden** *n.* an intricate formal garden. **knotgrass** *n.* a creeping plant, *Polygonum aviculare*, with internodes and white, pink, crimson or green inconspicuous flowers. **knot-hole** *n.* a hole in wood where a knot used to be. **knotless** *a.* **knotter** *n.* **knotting** *n.* **1** fancy knotted work. **2** the removal of knots from textile fabrics. **knotty** *a.* (*comp.* **knottier,** *superl.* **knottiest**) **1** full of knots. **2** rugged, rough. **3** intricate. **4** perplexing, difficult to solve. **knottily** *adv.* **knottiness** *n.* **knotweed** *n.* any of several plants of the genus *Polygonum*, esp. *Fallopia japonica*. **knotwork** *n.* **1** an ornamental fringe made by knotting cords together. **2** a representation of this in painting or carving. **3** a kind of ornamental needlework.

knot² (not) *n.* a small sandpiper, *Calidris canutus*.

know (nō) *v.t.* (*past* **knew** (nū), *p.p.* **known** (nōn)) **1** to have a clear and certain perception of. **2** to recognize from memory or description, to identify. **3** to be convinced of the truth or reality of. **4** to be acquainted with. **5** to have personal experience of. **6** to be subject to. **7** to be familiar with. **8** to be on intimate terms with. **9** to be aware of. **10** to understand from learning or study. **11** to be informed of. ~*v.i.* to have knowledge. ~*n.* knowledge, knowing. **before one knows where one is** surprisingly quickly. **don't I know it!** (*coll.*) used to express ironic agreement. **don't you know** (*coll. or facet.*) used to express emphasis. **for all I know** as far as I am aware. **in the know 1** in the secret. **2** acquainted with what is going on. **not to know someone from Adam** to have no idea at all who someone is. **not to know what hit one** to be suddenly taken by surprise. **to have been known to** to have done in the past. **to know a thing or two** (*coll.*) to have considerable experience, to be worldly-wise. **to know best** to be the most informed person, in the best position for making decisions etc. **to know better than to** to have enough the intelligence, common sense or courtesy not to. **to know by name 1** to have heard mentioned. **2** to be able to provide the name of. **to know by sight** to be familiar enough to recognize (but not to speak to). **to know how** to know the way to accomplish something. **to know of** to be informed of, to have heard of. **to know one's own mind** to be decisive. **to know one's stuff** (*coll.*) to be competent in one's chosen field, to know what one needs to know. **to know the ropes** (*coll.*) to be acquainted with the particular conditions of any affair or proceeding. **to know the score** (*coll.*) to know the facts of the situation. **to know what's what 1** (*coll.*) to be experienced, to know the ways of the world. **2** to

appreciate a good thing. **to know which side one's bread is buttered (on)** to appreciate what is in one's best interests. **to know who's who** (*coll.*) to be able to name or identify everybody. **what do you know (about that)?** an expression of incredulity. **you know 1** (*coll.*) used as a meaningless filler in conversation. **2** used as a reminder that the person addressed is familiar with who or what is mentioned. **you know something?/ what?** (*coll.*) used to introduce information regarded as new. **you never know** things are never certain. **knowable** *a.* **know-all** *n.* (*derog.*) someone who thinks they know everything. **knower** *n.* **know-how** *n.* **1** (*coll.*) specialized skill, expertise. **2** natural skill. **knowing** *a.* **1** conscious, deliberate. **2** skilful, experienced. **3** (*usu. derog.*) sharp, cunning, sly. **4** showing that one understands something. ~*n.* awareness, possession of information. **there is no knowing** one can never tell. **knowingly** *adv.* **1** consciously, deliberately. **2** in a knowing manner. **knowingness** *n.* **know-it-all** *n.* (*esp. N Am., derog.*) a know-all. **know-nothing** *n.* **1** an ignorant person. **2** an agnostic.

knowledge (nol´ij) *n.* **1** familiarity or understanding gained by experience or study or from instruction; an instance of this. **2** a person's range or scope of information. **3** learning, science, the sum of what is known, instruction, wisdom, schooling. **4** (*Philos.*) certain or clear apprehension of truth or fact. **5** information, notice. **6** cognition, the process of knowing. **knowledgeable, knowledgable** *a.* **1** sharp, intelligent; well informed. **2** having knowledge of. **knowledgeability** (-bil´-), **knowledgeableness** *n.* **knowledgeably** *adv.*

Knt. *abbr.* knight.

knuckle (nŭk´əl) *n.* **1** the bone at each one of the joints of a finger, esp. at the base. **2** the middle or tarsal joint of a quadruped. **3** a joint of meat comprising this and adjoining parts. **4** a knuckle-shaped joint or part in a structure, machinery etc. ~*v.t.* to hit with the knuckles. ~*v.i.* (*with down or under*) to submit, to yield. **to knuckle down** to get down to some hard work. **to knuckle under** to bow to the pressure of authority. **knuckle-bone** *n.* **1** a bone forming a knuckle. **2 a** a bone forming the knuckle of a sheep or other animal. **b** a joint of meat including this. **3** (*pl.*) the game of jacks played with animal knuckle-bones. **knuckleduster** *n.* a metal guard worn to protect the knuckles, and to add force to a blow. **knucklehead** *n.* (*coll.*) an idiot. **knuckle sand-wich** *n.* (*sl.*) a punch. **knuckly** *a.*

knurl (nœl) *n.* **1** a knot, a lump, an excrescence. **2** a bead or ridge produced on a metal surface as a kind of ornamentation. **knurled** *a.* **knurly** *a.*

KO *abbr.* **1** kick-off. **2** knockout.

koa (kō´ə) *n.* **1** a Hawaiian acacia, *Acacia koa*. **2** the wood of this, used for cabinet work and building.

koala (kōah´lə) *n.* an Australian marsupial,

Phascolarctos cinereus, not unlike a small bear, with dense fur, which feeds on eucalyptus leaves.

kob (kob) *n.* (*pl.* **kob**) an African antelope, *Kobus kob.* **kob antelope** *n.*

KO'd (kāōd´) *a.* knocked out.

Kodiak (kō´diak), **Kodiak bear** *n.* a brown bear, *Ursus arctos*, found in Alaska and the neighbouring Aleutian Islands, esp. Kodiak Island.

koel (kō´əl) *n.* any of several SE Asian and Australasian cuckoos of the genus *Eudynamys*, esp. *E. scolopacea*.

kofta (kof´tə, kō´-) *n.* in Indian cookery, a spiced ball of meat, vegetables etc.

kohl (kōl) *n.* fine black powder, usu. of antimony or lead sulphide used to darken the eyelids.

kohlrabi (kōlrah´bi) *n.* (*pl.* **kohlrabies**) a variety of cabbage, *Brassica oleracea caulorapa*, with an edible swollen stem resembling a turnip.

koi (koi), **koi carp** *n.* (*pl.* **koi, koi carp**) a large Japanese variety of carp.

kola COLA.

kolinsky (kəlin´ski) *n.* (*pl.* **kolinskies**) 1 a type of Asian mink, *Mustela sibirica.* 2 the fur from this mink.

Komodo dragon (kəmō´dō), **Komodo monitor** *n.* the largest known lizard, *Veranus komodoensis*, from Indonesia.

koodoo KUDU.

kook (kook) *n.* (*esp. N Am., coll.*) an eccentric, mad or foolish person. *~a.* eccentric, mad, foolish. **kooky** (-i), **kookie** *a.* (*comp.* **kookier**, *superl.* **kookiest**).

kookaburra (kuk´əbŭrə) *n.* any large Australian kingfisher of the genus *Dacelo*, also called the laughing jackass.

kopeck, kopek COPECK.

kopi (kō´pi) *n.* (*Austral.*) powdered gypsum.

kopje (kop´i), **koppie** *n.* (*S Afr.*) a small hill.

koradji (kor´əji, kəraj´i) *n.* (*Austral.*) an Aboriginal medicine man.

Koran (kərahn´), **Quran, Qur'an** *n.* the Muslim sacred scriptures consisting of the revelations delivered orally by Muhammad and collected after his death. **Koranic** *a.*

Korean (kərē´ən) *a.* of or relating to Korea, its people or its language. *~n.* 1 a native or inhabitant of Korea. 2 the language spoken in N or S Korea.

korfball (kawf´bawl) *n.* a game not unlike basketball, with teams each consisting of six men and six women.

korma (kaw´mə) *n.* an Indian dish composed of braised meat or vegetables cooked in spices and a yoghurt or cream sauce.

koruna (koroo´nə) *n.* the standard monetary unit of the Czech Republic and Slovakia, equal to 100 haleru.

kosher (kō´shə) *a.* 1 (of food or a shop where it is sold) fulfilling the requirements of the Jewish law. 2 (*coll.*) genuine, above board. 3 permitted, right. *~n.* 1 kosher food. 2 a kosher shop.

kotow KOWTOW.

koumiss KUMISS.

kowhai (kō´wī, kaw´fī) *n.* (*pl.* **kowhais**) a small shrub with clusters of golden flowers, *Sophora tetraptera*, found in Australasia and Chile.

kowtow (kowtow´), **kotow** (kōtow´) *n.* the ancient Chinese method of obeisance by kneeling or prostrating oneself, and touching the ground with the forehead. *~v.i.* 1 to act obsequiously. 2 (*Hist.*) to perform the kowtow.

k.p.h. *abbr.* kilometres per hour.

Kr *chem. symbol* krypton.

kraal (krahl) *n.* (*S Afr.*) 1 a S African village or group of huts enclosed by a palisade. 2 an enclosure for cattle or sheep.

kraft (krahft), **kraft paper** *n.* strong, brown, wrapping paper.

kraken (krah´kən) *n.* a fabulous sea monster, said to have been seen at different times off the coast of Norway.

Kraut (krowt) *n.* (*sl., offensive*) a German.

kremlin (krem´lin) *n.* the citadel of a Russian town. **the Kremlin** 1 the citadel of Moscow enclosing the old imperial palace, now government buildings etc. 2 the Russian Government.

krill (kril) *n.* (*collect.*) tiny shrimplike crustaceans, the main food of whales.

kromesky (krəmes´ki) *n.* (*pl.* **kromeskies**) a roll or ball of minced meat or fish wrapped in bacon, then fried.

krona (krō´nə) *n.* 1 (*pl.* **kronor**) the basic monetary unit of Sweden. 2 (*pl.* **kronur**) the basic monetary unit of Iceland.

krone (krō´nə) *n.* (*pl.* **kroner**) the monetary unit of Denmark and Norway.

krugerrand (kroo´gərand) *n.* a coin minted in S Africa containing 1 troy oz. of gold.

krummhorn (krum´hawn, krŭm´-), **crumhorn** *n.* 1 a medieval wind instrument with a curved tube and a tone like that of a clarinet. 2 an organ stop consisting of reed pipes, with a similar tone.

krypton (krip´tən) *n.* (*Chem.*) an inert gaseous element, at no. 38, chem. symbol Kr, discovered by Ramsay in 1898 as a constituent of the atmosphere.

Kshatriya (kshat´riyə) *n.* a member of the warrior caste in the Hindu caste system.

KT *abbr.* 1 Knight of the Order of the Thistle. 2 Knight Templar.

Kt. *abbr.* Knight.

kt *abbr.* 1 karat. 2 (*also* **kt.**) knot.

Ku *chem. symbol* kurchatovium.

kudos (kū´dos) *n.* 1 glory, fame, credit. 2 (*N Am.*) praise, acclaim.

Usage note *Kudos* is an uncountable noun. A singular *kudo* is sometimes encountered, as is *kudos* treated or pronounced as a plural, but both uses are best avoided.

kudu (koo´doo), **koodoo** *n.* (*pl.* **kudu, kudus, koodoo, koodoos**) either of two southern African antelopes, *Tragelaphus stepsericos* or *T. imberbis*, with white stripes.

Kufic (koo´fik, kū´-), **Cufic** *n.* an early form of the Arabic alphabet. ~*a.* of or relating to this script.

Ku Klux Klan (koo klŭks klan´) *n.* a secret society in the Southern States of the US, aiming to repress the black population, orig. formed after the American Civil War of 1861–65 and though suppressed by the US government in 1871 since revived with the aim of preserving white supremacy. **Ku Klux Klanner** (klan´ə) *n.*

kukri (kuk´ri) *n.* (*pl.* **kukris**) a curved knife broadening at the end, used by the Gurkhas.

kumara (koo´mərə), **kumera** *n.* (*New Zeal.*) the sweet potato.

kumiss (koo´mis), **koomis, koumiss, kumis** *n.* a spirituous liquor made by Tartars from fermented mare's milk.

kümmel (kum´əl) *n.* a liqueur flavoured with caraway seeds made in Germany and Russia.

kumquat (kŭm´kwot), **cumquat** *n.* **1** a small orangelike fruit with acid pulp and a sweet rind. **2** a shrub or tree of the genus *Fortunella* yielding this fruit.

kung fu (kŭng foo´, kung) *n.* a Chinese martial art resembling karate.

kurchatovium (kœchətō´viəm) *n.* (*Chem.*) an artificial chemical element, at. no. 104, chem. symbol Ku, whose discovery was claimed by the Soviets in 1966; also called *rutherfordium*.

Kurd (kœd) *n.* a native or inhabitant of Kurdistan. **Kurdish** *a.* of or relating to the Kurds or Kurdistan. ~*n.* the language of the Kurds.

kurrajong (kŭr´əjong), **currajong** *n.* (*Austral.*) any of several trees and shrubs with fibrous bark, esp. *Brachychitou populeum*.

kurta (kuə´tə), **kurtha** *n.* a loose tunic worn by Hindus.

kurtosis (kœtō´sis) *n.* in statistics, the distribution and density of points around the mean.

kuru (koo´roo) *n.* (*Med.*) a disease, usu. fatal, of the nervous system occurring in the inhabitants of eastern New Guinea.

kV *abbr.* kilovolt(s).

kvetch (kvech) *v.i.* (*esp. N Am., sl.*) to whine, to complain. **kvetcher** *n.*

kW *abbr.* kilowatt(s).

Kwa (kwah) *n.* (*pl.* **Kwa**) **1** a group of languages spoken in West Africa from the Ivory Coast to Nigeria. **2** a member of a Kwa-speaking people. ~*a.* of or relating to this group of languages.

kwacha (kwah´chə) *n.* the standard monetary unit in Zambia and Malawi.

kwanza (kwan´zə) *n.* (*pl.* **kwanza, kwanzas**) the standard monetary unit of Angola.

kWh *abbr.* kilowatt-hour(s).

kyanite (sī´ənīt), **cyanite** *n.* (*Geol.*) a hard, translucent mineral, often blue, occurring in flattened prisms in gneiss and mica-schist. **kyanitic** (-nit´-) *a.*

kyanize (kī´ənīz), **kyanise** *v.t.* to impregnate (wood) with a solution of mercuric chloride (corrosive sublimate) to prevent dry rot.

kyat (kyaht) *n.* (*pl.* **kyat, kyats**) the basic monetary unit of Burma (Myanmar).

kybosh KIBOSH.

kyle (kīl) *n.* a narrow channel in Scotland, between an island and another island or the mainland.

kylie (kī´li), **kiley** *n.* (*Austral.*) a boomerang.

Kyrgyz (kœ´giz), **Kirghiz, Kirgiz** *n.* **1** a member of a Mongolian people inhabiting central Asia, mainly Kyrgyzstan. **2** the language of this people. ~*a.* of or relating to this people or their language.

L

L¹ (el), **l** (*pl.* **Ls, L's**) the 12th letter of the English and other versions of the Roman alphabet, corresponding to the Greek lambda (λ, Λ). It is pronounced as a voiced alveolar continuant, a lateral or liquid. ~*symbol* **1** (*Chem.*) Avogadro's constant. **2** 50 in Roman numerals. ~*n.* **1** an L-shaped thing, part or building. **2** a rectangular joint.

L², **L.** *abbr.* **1** laevorotatory. **2** Lake. **3** Learner (driver). **4** Liberal. **5** (*Biol.*) Linnaeus. **6** Lire. **L-dopa** *n.* the laevorotatory form of dopa which is used in the treatment of Parkinson's disease. **L-driver** *n.* a learner driver. **L-plate** *n.* a sign, in the form of a red L on a white background, which must by law in the UK be attached to the front and rear of any vehicle driven by a learner driver.

l, l. *abbr.* **1** left. **2** length. **3** line. **4** liquid. **5** litre(s).

La *chem. symbol* lanthanum.

la LAH.

laager (lah´gə) *n.* **1** (*Hist.*) in S Africa, a defensive encampment, esp. one formed by wagons drawn into a circle. **2** (*Mil.*) a park for armoured vehicles etc. ~*v.t.* **1** to form into a laager. **2** to encamp (a body of people) in a laager. ~*v.i.* to encamp.

Lab. (lab) *abbr.* **1** Labour. **2** Labrador.

lab (lab) *n.* (*coll.*) short for LABORATORY.

label (lā´bəl) *n.* **1** a piece of cloth, paper, plastic or other material attached to an object to indicate contents, destination, ownership or other particulars. **2** a descriptive phrase associated with a person, group etc. **3** a firm's tradename or logo (esp. that of a fashion designer or of a record company). **4** a piece of paper attached to the centre of a gramophone record giving information about its contents. **5** a recording company or a section of one with its own trademark. **6** an adhesive stamp. **7** (*Archit.*) a moulding over a doorway or window, a drip-stone. **8** in dictionaries, a word or abbreviation, usu. preceding a definition, that indicates its geographical provenance or area of usage, its register, the subject area to which it applies etc. **9** (*Biol., Chem.*) a radioactive isotope or fluorescent dye used to make a substance traceable. ~*v.t.* (*pres.p.* **labelling**, (*N Am.*) **labeling**, *past*, *p.p.* **labelled**, (*N Am.*) **labeled**) **1** to affix a label to. **2** to describe, to categorize. **3** (*Biol.*, *Chem.*) to render (a substance) traceable by replacing an atom in its molecule with a radioactive isotope by marking it with fluorescent dye. **labeller**, (*N Am.*) **labeler** *n.*

labellum (ləbel´əm) *n.* (*pl.* **labella** (-lə)) **1** (*Bot.*) the lower lip-shaped part of the corolla in an orchidaceous flower. **2** (*Zool.*) a lobe at the top of the proboscis of certain insects.

labia LABIUM.

labial (lā´biəl) *a.* **1** of or relating to the lips or the labium. **2** (*Zool.*) serving as or resembling a lip. **3** (of the surface of a tooth) adjacent to the lips. **4** formed or modified in sound by the lips. ~*n.* a sound, or a letter representing a sound, formed with the lips, such as *b, f, v, p, m,* or *w.* **labialize, labialise** *v.t.* to pronounce with rounded lips like the sound *oo.* **labially** *adv.* **labial pipe** *n.* a fluepipe of an organ. **labiate** (-ət) *a.* **1** (*Bot.*) having lips or parts like lips, esp. having a corolla with an upper and lower part like a pair of lips. **2** belonging to the order Labiatae, the mint family. ~*n.* any plant of the Labiatae family, e.g. mint, rosemary.

labile (lā´bīl) *a.* (*Chem.*) unstable, liable to chemical or other change. **lability** (ləbil´iti) *n.*

labio- (lā´biō) *comb. form* labial.

labiodental (lābiōden´təl) *a.* produced by the agency of the lips and teeth. ~*n.* a sound so produced, as *f* or *v.*

labium (lā´biəm) *n.* (*pl.* **labia** (-biə)) **1** a lip or liplike structure or part. **2** (*Anat.*) each of the four liplike folds enclosing the vulva. **3** the lower part of the mouth in insects, crustaceans etc. **4** the lower lip of a labiate corolla.

labor LABOUR.

laboratory (ləbor´ətri, lab´rətəri) *n.* (*pl.* **laboratories**) **1** a room or building in which scientific experiments and research are conducted. **2** a place where drugs, medicines and other chemical products etc. are manufactured.

labour (lā´bə), (*N Am., Austral.*) **labor** *n.* **1** physical or mental exertion, esp. to obtain the means of subsistence, the performance of work, toil. **2** workers, esp. manual workers, considered as a class or category, usu. as opposed to *capital, management.* **3** the element contributed by workers to production, esp. as opposed to *capital.* **4** a task, esp. a task requiring great effort. **5** the process of childbirth from the start of frequent uterine contractions to delivery. **6** (**Labour**) the Labour Party. ~*v.i.* **1** to work hard, to exert oneself. **2** to strive, to work (for, to do). **3** to move or proceed with difficulty. **4** to be burdened or handicapped (*labour under a delusion*). **5** (of ships) to move heavily and slowly or to pitch or roll heavily. ~*v.t.* to overelaborate, to deal with in too much detail or at too great length. **laborious** (ləbaw´riəs) *a.* **1** difficult, hard, arduous, fatiguing. **2** betraying marks of labour, laboured. **3** industrious, assiduous. **laboriously** *adv.* **laboriousness** *n.* **labour camp** *n.* a penal establishment where prisoners are forced to labour. **laboured** *a.* **1** showing signs of strain, effort or contrivance, not spontaneous or fluent. **2** (of breathing) performed with difficulty. **labourer** *n.* a person who labours, esp. someone who performs work requiring manual labour but little skill. **Labour Exchange** *n.* (*Hist.*) an employment office or jobcentre. **labour force** *n.* the workers collectively, esp. those employed at a single plant. **labour-intensive** *a.* (of a production process) requiring a large labour force or a great deal of work in relation to output. **labourism** *n.* support for working people and their rights. **labourist** *n.* **Labourite** *n.* a follower or member of the Labour Party. **labour market** *n.* the supply of unemployed labour in relation to the demand. **labour of Hercules** *n.* a task requiring an enormous effort. **labour of love** *n.* work done without expectation of payment. **Labour Party** *n.* **1** a British political party established to represent workers. **2** a similarly constituted party in another country. **labour-saving** *a.* intended to reduce or eliminate the work involved in performing a task. **labour union** *n.* (*N Am.*) a trade union.

Labrador (lab´rədaw) *n.* a Labrador retriever. **Labrador retriever, Labrador dog** *n.* **1** a breed of large, short-haired retriever dog with a coat of either a golden or black colour. **2** a dog of this breed.

laburnum (ləbœ´nəm) *n.* a poisonous tree or shrub of the genus *Laburnum*, that has racemes of yellow flowers.

labyrinth (lab´irinth) *n.* **1** a structure composed of intricate winding passages, paths, tunnels etc. rendering it difficult to penetrate to the interior and equally difficult to return, a maze. **2** an intricate combination, arrangement etc. **3** (*Anat.*) the internal portion of the ear. **labyrinth fish** *n.* a tropical fish with bright coloration and spiny fins, also called *gourami*. **labyrinthine** (-rin´thīn), †**labyrinthian** (-rin´-), **labyrinthic** (-rin´-) *a.*

LAC *abbr.* Leading Aircraftman.

lac¹ (lak) *n.* a resinous incrustation secreted, chiefly on the banyan tree, by parasitic lac insects and used in the making of shellac. **lac insect** *n.* any of various insects of the family Lacciferidae, esp. *Laccifer lacca* that secretes lac. **lac**² LAKH.

lace (lās) *n.* **1** a kind of ornamental network of threads of linen, cotton, silk, gold or silver wire or other suitable material, forming a fabric of open texture. **2** a cord or string used to bind or fasten, esp. by interweaving between eyelets or hooks as a shoelace etc. **3** an ornamental braid or edging for uniforms etc. ~*v.t.* **1** to fasten by

means of a lace or string through eyelet-holes etc. **2** to compress or tighten by lacing. **3** to add a small quantity of spirits, a drug, poison to. **4** to introduce into or intermingle with. **5** to embellish with or as with stripes. **6** to intertwist or interweave (with thread etc.). **7** to trim or adorn with lace. **8** (*coll.*) to beat, to thrash. ~*v.i.* **1** (of boots etc.) to fasten with laces. **2** to compress the waist by tightening laces. **to lace into** to attack vigorously. **lace-glass** *n.* Venetian glass decorated with lacelike patterns. **lacelike** *a.* **lacemaker** *n.* **lacemaking** *n.* **lace-pillow** *n.* a cushion on which various kinds of lace are made. **lace-up** *a.* (of shoes) fastened with a lace or laces. ~*n.* a shoe or boot fastened by a lace or laces. **lacewing, lacewing fly** *n.* any of various flying insects with veiny wings, esp. any of the families Chrysopidae and Hemerobiidae. **lacewood** *n.* timber from the plane tree. **lacework** *n.* articles made of lace. **lacing** *n.* **1** a fastening by a cord passing through holes etc. **2** a lace or cord for fastening. **3** lace trimming, esp. on a uniform. **4** anything added to or intermingled with something else, esp. a dose of spirit added to a liquor to strengthen or flavour it. **5** (*coll.*) a thrashing. **6** (*also* **lacing course**) a strengthening course of brick, stone etc. built into an arch or wall. **lacy** *a.* (*comp.* **lacier**, *superl.* **laciest**) made of or like lace. **lacily** *adv.* **laciness** *n.*

lacerate (las´ərāt) *v.t.* **1** to tear, to mangle. **2** to distress or afflict severely, to harrow, to wound. **lacerable** *a.* **laceration** (-ā´shən) *n.*

lachrymal (lak´riməl), **lacrimal, lacrymal** *a.* **1** (*formal*) of or relating to tears. **2** (*Anat.*) (of glands, ducts etc.) secreting or conveying tears. ~*n.* (*pl.*, *Anat.*) the lachrymal organs. **lachrymation** (-ā´shən) *n.* **lachrymator** *n.* a substance that causes or increases the flowing of tears. **lachrymatory** *a.* of, relating to or causing tears. **lachrymose** (-mōs) *a.* **1** excessively doleful; characterized by much shedding of tears. **2** (*formal*) given to shedding tears, weepy. **3** (*formal*) sad, mournful, tearful. **lachrymosely** *adv.*

Usage note The adjectives *lachrymal* and *lachrymose* should not be confused: *lachrymal* means relating to tears, and *lachrymose* tearful.

---

lacing LACE.

lack (lak) *n.* **1** deficiency, want, need (of). **2** something that is absent or that is needed. ~*v.t.* **1** to be in need of, to be deficient in. **2** to be without. **for lack of** because of an absence or insufficiency of. **to be lacking 1** to be absent; to be in short supply. **2** to be deficient (in). **3** (*coll.*) (of a person) to be mentally deficient. **to lack for** (*usu. neg.*) to be without, to lack. **lackland** *n.* having no property or estate. ~*n.* a person who owns no land. **lacklustre** (lak´lŭstə), (*N Am.*) **lackluster** *a.* **1** dull, without brightness or vivacity. **2** mediocre.

lackadaisical (lakədã´zikəl) *a*. **1** careless, slipshod, inattentive. **2** listless, absent-minded. **3** affectedly pensive, languishing or sentimental. **lackadaisically** *adv*. **lackadaisicalness** *n*.

lacker LACQUER.

lackey (lak´i), **lacquey** *n*. (*pl*. **lackeys, lacqueys**) **1** (*derog*.) a servile political follower or hanger-on. **2** a footman; a menial attendant. ~*v.t.*, *v.i.* (*3rd pers. sing. pres.* **lackeys**, *pres.p.* **lackeying**, *past, p.p.* **lackeyed**) **1** (*derog*.) to act or attend servilely. **2** to follow or attend as a servant.

laconic (ləkon´ik), **laconical** *a*. using few words, brief, pithy, concise. **laconically** *adv*. **laconicism** (-sizm), **laconism** (lak´-) *n*. **1** a concise, pithy or sententious style. **2** a laconic saying.

lacquer (lak´ə), **lacker** *n*. **1** a varnish composed of shellac dissolved in alcohol and often coloured with gold, gamboge, saffron etc., that dries hard and is used to coat articles of metal or wood. **2** a similar substance used to keep a hairstyle in place, hair lacquer. **3** a hard glossy varnish made from black resin. **4** decorative objects coated with such varnish and often inlaid. **lacquerer** *n*. **lacquer tree** *n*. an E Asian tree, *Rhus verniciflua*, which produces the resin used to make black lacquer varnish. **lacquerware** *n*. decorative articles coated with lacquer.

lacquey LACKEY.

lacrimal LACHRYMAL.

lacrosse (ləkros´) *n*. a ball game of N American Indian origin resembling hockey, but played with a crosse or stringed bat with which the players throw and catch the ball.

lacrymal LACHRYMAL.

lactase (lak´tāz) *n*. an enzyme that acts on lactose to produce glucose and galactose.

lactate[1] (laktāt´) *v.i.* to secrete or produce milk. **lactation** (-tā´shən) *n*. **1** the secretion and excretion of milk from the mammary glands. **2** the act or process of breastfeeding an infant.

lactate[2] (lak´tāt) *n*. (*Chem*.) a salt of lactic acid.

lacteal (lak´tiəl) *a*. **1** of or relating to milk; milky. **2** (*Anat*.) conveying chyle. **lacteals** *n.pl.* the lymphatic vessels which convey chyle from the lymphatic small intestine to the thoracic duct.

lactescent (laktes´ənt) *a*. **1** having a milky appearance or consistency. **2** yielding milky juice. **3** turning to milk.

lactic (lak´tik) *a*. (*Chem*.) of, relating to or derived from milk. **lactic acid** *n*. a colourless liquid acid produced in tissue by the anaerobic breakdown of carbohydrates and also formed during the souring of milk.

lacto- (lak´tō), **lact-** *comb. form* of or relating to milk.

lactobacillus (laktōbəsil´əs) *n*. (*pl*. **lactobacilli** (-lī)) (*Biol*.) any rod-shaped bacterium of the family Lactobacillaceae which ferments carbohydrates to produce lactic acid.

lactose (lak´tōs) *n*. (*Chem*.) the form in which sugar occurs in milk, a glucose and a galactose monomer.

lacuna (ləkū´nə) *n*. (*pl*. **lacunas, lacunae** (-nē)) **1** a gap, blank or hiatus, esp. in a manuscript or text. **2** (*Anat*.) a cavity, small pit or depression, e.g. in a bone. **lacunal, lacunary, lacunose** *a*. of, relating to or containing lacunae. **lacunar** *a*. lacunal.

lacustrine (ləkŭs´trīn) *a*. (*Biol*., *also formal*) of, relating to or living on or in a lake. **lacustral** *a*.

LACW *abbr*. Leading Aircraftwoman.

lacy LACE.

lad (lad) *n*. **1** a boy, a youth. **2** a (young) son. **3** (*coll*.) a man; a fellow, a companion, a mate. **4** (*coll*.) an extrovert, audacious or roguish man (*a bit of a lad*). **5** a person (of either sex) who looks after horses. **laddie** (-i) *n*. (*coll*.) a boy, a lad.

laddish *a*. exuberant, hearty or rumbustious, esp. as a result of being one of a group of (young) men out to have a good time. **laddishness** *n*.

ladder (lad´ə) *n*. **1** a device of wood, iron, rope etc. for going up or down by, often portable and consisting of two long uprights, connected by rungs or cross-pieces, which form steps. **2** a vertical rent in a stocking or tights. **3** anything serving as a means of ascent. **4** a hierarchical structure. ~*v.t.* to cause a ladder in (stockings). ~*v.i.* (of stockings, tights, knitted fabrics etc.) to form a rent through the snapping of a longitudinal thread. **ladder-back** *n*. (a chair with) a back consisting of several horizontal struts between two uprights. **ladder-stitch** *n*. a crossbar stitch used in embroidery and fancy-work. **ladder tournament** *n*. a competition in which the contestants' names are listed in descending order and the aim is to ascend the list by defeating and replacing the contestant ranked above one.

lade (lād) *v.t.* (*p.p.* **laden** (-dən)) **1** to put a cargo or freight on board. **2** to ship (goods) as cargo. **3** (*esp. in p.p.*) to load, to weigh down. ~*v.i.* (of a ship) to take on cargo. **laden** *a*. **1** weighed down, loaded; encumbered. **2** burdened, painfully aware of. **lading** *n*. **1** cargo. **2** the act or process of loading cargo.

la-di-da (lahdidah´), **lah-di-dah** *a*. (*coll*.) affectedly genteel, pretentious and precious in speech or manners. ~*n*. **1** a la-di-da person. **2** la-di-da speech or manner.

ladies, ladify LADY.

ladle (lā´dəl) *n*. **1** a large spoon, usu. with a deep bowl at right angles to a long handle, with which liquids are lifted out or served from a vessel. **2** a bucket-shaped container or pan with a long handle to hold molten metal. ~*v.t.* to serve out or transfer with a ladle. **to ladle out** to give or hand out freely; to distribute liberally. **ladleful** *n*. **ladler** *n*.

lady (lā´di) *n*. (*pl*. **ladies**) **1** a woman regarded as being of refinement or social standing. **2** a polite term for a woman (*often used attrib*., as *lady doctor*). **3** (*coll*.) a wife; a girlfriend. **4** (*Hist*.) an object of romantic love, a mistress, sweetheart. **5** a woman who has authority or control, esp. the mistress of a house or family. **6** (**Lady**) a title prefixed to the surname or territorial title of a peeress or the wife of a knight or peer, or to the Christian name of the daughter of an earl, marquess or duke, or to the Christian name of a woman's husband if he is the son of a marquess or duke. **7** a respectful addition to the title of an office or position held by a woman (*lady wife*; *lady mayor*). **8** (*pl.*) the ladies' room, a public lavatory for women. **my lady** a form of address for a person holding the title of 'lady'. **ladies' fingers** *n.pl.* LADY'S FINGER (under LADY). **ladies' man, lady's man** *n.* a man who enjoys the company of women or is particularly attentive to them or successful in attracting or seducing them. **ladies' room** *n.* a women's lavatory in a large building such as a store, office etc. **ladify** LADYFY (under LADY). **ladybird,** (*esp. N Am. or dial.*) **ladybug** *n.* a small coleopterous insect, of the family Coccinellidae, with red or reddish-brown wing cases with black spots. **Lady Bountiful** *n.* a wealthy woman charitable in her neighbourhood. **Lady chapel** *n.* a chapel dedicated to the Virgin Mary (usu. in a cathedral or large church). **lady-fern** *n.* a tall slender fern, *Athyrium filix-femina.* **ladyfy** (-fī), **ladify** *v.t.* **1** to make a lady of. **2** to treat as a lady; to give the title 'lady' to. **ladified** *a.* affecting the manners and air of a fine lady. **ladyhood** *n.* **lady-in-waiting** *n.* a lady attending on a queen or princess. **lady-killer** *n.* **1** a man who devotes himself to seducing women. **2** a man who is irresistibly fascinating to women. **ladylike** *a.* refined, graceful. **lady-love** *n.* a female sweetheart. **lady mayoress** *n.* the wife of a lord mayor. **Lady Muck** *n.* (*sl., derog.*) a woman with social pretensions. **lady of the bedchamber** *n.* (*pl.* **ladies of the bedchamber**) a lady-in-waiting. **lady of the night** *n.* a prostitute. **lady's bedstraw** *n.* a herbaceous plant, *Galium verum.* **lady's finger** *n.* **1** the kidney vetch. **2** okra. **ladyship** *n.* the position or status of a lady. **her ladyship** the equivalent of 'your ladyship' in speaking of someone. **your ladyship 1** a formula used in speaking deferentially to a lady. **2** (*iron.*) a formula used in speaking to a woman or girl who adopts an arrogant manner. **lady's maid** *n.* a female attendant on a lady. **lady's man** LADIES' MAN (under LADY). **lady's mantle** *n.* any of various rosaceous herbs of the genus *Alchemilla*, having clustered yellowish-green leaves and flowers resembling drapery. **lady's slipper** *n.* an orchid of the genus *Cypripedium.* **lady's smock** *n.* the cuckoo flower, *Cardamine pratensis.*

laevo- (lē'vō), **levo-** *comb. form* **1** left, as opposed to right. **2** noting the turning of a ray of polarized light to the left, as opposed to *dextro-.*

laevorotatory (lēvōrō'tətəri), (*N Am.*) **levorotatory** *a.* (*Chem.*) turning the plane of polarization to the left.

laevulose (lē'vūlōs), (*N Am.*) **levulose** *n.* a sugar or glucose distinguished from dextrose by its turning the plane of polarization to the left, fructose.

lag¹ (lag) *v.i.* (*pres.p.* **lagging,** *past, p.p.* **lagged**) to fall behind. *~n.* **1** a delay in response. **2** the interval between two events, esp. between an action and the reaction. **3** (*Physics*) retardation of current or movement. **laggard** (-əd) *a.* slow, sluggish, lagging behind. *~n.* **1** a slow, sluggish person. **2** a loiterer. **laggardly** *a., adv.* **laggardness** *n.* **lagger** *n.*

lag² (lag) *n.* **1** a convict. **2** a long-term prisoner. *~v.t.* (*pres.p.* **lagging,** *past, p.p.* **lagged**) **1** to send to prison. **2** (*sl.*) to arrest.

lag³ (lag) *n.* **1** the non-heat-conducting jacket of a boiler or cylinder. **2** a stave, lath or strip of wood, felt etc. *~v.t.* (*pres.p.* **lagging,** *past, p.p.* **lagged**) to cover or encase with a lag or lagging, esp. to preserve against freezing. **lagging** *n.* insulating material wrapped esp. around water pipes or tanks to prevent freezing or heat loss.

lager (lah'gə) *n.* a light beer, blond in colour and effervescent, the ordinary beer of Germany. **lager lout** *n.* (*sl.*) a youth who behaves like a hooligan, esp. when having drunk too much alcohol, esp. lager or beer.

lagoon (ləgoon') *n.* **1** a shallow lake near a river or the sea, due to the infiltration or overflow of water from the larger body. **2** the water enclosed by an atoll or coral island. **3** an artificial pool for the storage or treatment of effluent, slurry etc. or of the overflow from surface drains after heavy rainfall. **lagoonal** *a.*

lah (lah), **la** *n.* (*Mus.*) **1** the sixth note of a major scale in the tonic sol-fa system of notation. **2** the note A in the fixed-doh system.

laid (lād) *a.* **1** lying down. **2** placed or pressed down. **3** set out. **4** flattened by wind and rain. **laid-back** *a.* (*coll.*) relaxed, casual. **laid paper** *n.* paper made with a ribbed surface, marked by the wires on which the pulp is laid, as opposed to *wove paper.* **laid up** *a.* ill; confined to bed or the house.

lain LIE².

lair¹ (leə) *n.* **1** the den or retreat of a wild animal. **2** (*usu. facet.*) a person's private room or place, a den. **3** a pen or shed for cattle on the way to slaughter or the market. *~v.i.* **1** to go to or lie in a lair. **2** to make one's lair (in). *~v.t.* to place in a lair. **lairage** (-rij) *n.*

lair² (leə) *n.* (*Austral., coll.*) an over-dressed man; a show-off. **laired up** *a.* dressed in a flashy manner. **lairy** *a.*

laird (leəd) *n.* (*Sc.*) the owner of a landed estate. **lairdship** *n.*

laissez-faire (lesāfeə'), **laisser-faire** *n.* the principle of non-interference, esp. by the Government in industrial and commercial affairs. *~a.* operating on this principle.

laity LAY².

lake¹ (lāk) *n.* **1** a large sheet of water entirely surrounded by land. **2** a large amount of wine, milk etc., a commodity surplus. **lakeless** *a.*

lakelet *n.* **lakelike** *a.* **lakeside** *a.* situated, growing etc. beside a lake.

lake[2] (lāk) *n.* **1** a crimson pigment, orig. derived from lac or cochineal. **2** an insoluble coloured pigment formed by a soluble dye mixed with a mordant. **3** the colour of these, carmine.

lakh (lahk), **lac** *n.* in the Indian subcontinent, the number 100,000 (usu. of a sum of rupees).

Lallans (lal'ənz), **Lallan** *n.* the Lowland Scots dialect, esp. in its modern literary use. **Lallan** *a.* of or relating to the Lowlands of Scotland.

lam (lam) *v.t.* (*pres.p.* **lamming**, *past*, *p.p.* **lammed**) (*coll.*) to thrash, to wallop. **to lam into** to hit hard; to thrash. **lamming** *n.* a beating.

lama (lah'mə) *n.* a Tibetan or Mongolian Buddhist priest or monk. **lamaism** *n.* **lamaist** *a.*, *n.* **lamasery** *n.* (*pl.* **lamaseries**) a lamaist monastery.

lamb (lam) *n.* **1** the young of a sheep. **2** the flesh of this used for food. **3** a person, esp. a child, who is as innocent and gentle as a lamb. **~v.i.** to bring forth lambs. **~v.t.** to tend (ewes) at lambing. **like a lamb** without fuss or protest. **like a lamb to the slaughter** defenceless, innocent, unresisting. **the Lamb** Christ. **the Lamb of God** Christ. **lambhood** *n.* **lambkin** *n.* **lamblike** *a.* **lamb's ears** *n.* a perennial herb, *Stachys byzantina*, grown as a garden plant for its white downy foliage. **lamb's fry** *n.* **1** the offal, esp. the testicles, of a lamb as food. **2** (*Austral.*, *New Zeal.*) lamb's liver as food. **lambskin** *n.* the skin of a lamb dressed as a leather with the fleece on. **lamb's lettuce** *n.* a plant, *Valerianella locusta*, used in salads. **lamb's-tails** *n.pl.* catkins of hazel and filbert. **lambswool**, **lamb's-wool** *n.* fine wool from lambs, esp. at the first shearing, used for knitted garments. **~a.** made of lambswool.

lambada (lambah'də) *n.* **1** an erotic Brazilian dance performed by couples in close contact with one another who gyrate their hips in synchronized movements. **2** the music to accompany this dance.

lambast (lambast'), **lambaste** (-bāst') *v.t.* **1** to beat. **2** to give a verbal thrashing to.

lambda (lam'də) *n.* **1** the 11th letter of the Greek alphabet (λ, Λ) transliterated as Roman *l*. **2** a symbol denoting wavelength. **3** a symbol denoting celestial longitude.

lambent (lam'bənt) *a.* **1** (of flame or light) playing or moving about, touching slightly without burning. **2** softly radiant. **3** (of wit) light, sparkling. **lambency** *n.* **lambently** *adv.*

lame (lām) *a.* **1** disabled in one or more of the limbs, esp. the foot or leg. **2** limping, halting. **3** (of an excuse, argument, ending) unsatisfactory, implausible, unconvincing. **4** (of verse) not running smoothly or evenly. **5** (*N Am.*, *sl.*) conventional, square. **~v.t.** **1** to make lame. **2** to cripple, to disable. **lamebrain** *n.* (*N Am.*, *coll.*) a stupid person. **lame duck** *n.* **1** a weak, ineffective or disabled person. **2** a defaulter on the Stock Exchange. **3** a company in financial difficulties, esp. one requiring government assistance. **4** (*N*

Am.) an elected official (esp. the President) whose term of office is about to expire and whose successor has already been chosen. **lamely** *adv.* **lameness** *n.* **lamish** *a.*

lamé (lah'mā) *n.* a fabric containing metallic, usu. gold or silver threads. **~a.** made of such a fabric.

lamella (ləmel'ə) *n.* (*pl.* **lamellae** (-lē)) **1** a thin plate, layer, scale or membrane, esp. in bone tissue. **2** (*Bot.*) a membranous fold in a chloroplast. **lamellar**, **lamellate** (-ət), **lamellose** (-ōs) *a.*

lament (ləment') *v.i.* **1** to mourn, to wail. **2** to feel or express sorrow. **~v.t.** **1** to bewail, to mourn over. **2** to deplore, to express regret or remorse for. **~n.** **1** a passionate expression of sorrow in cries or complaints. **2** an elegy, a dirge. **3** a mournful song or melody. **lamentable** (lam'-) *a.* **1** very unfortunate, deplorable. **2** wretched. **lamentably** *adv.* **lamentation** (ləməntā'shən) *n.* **1** the act of lamenting. **2** an audible expression of grief. **3** a wail. **lamented** *a.* **1** mourned for. **2** deceased, late. **lamenter** *n.* **lamenting** *n.*, *a.* **lamentingly** *adv.*

lamina (lam'inə) *n.* (*pl.* **laminae** (-nē)) a thin layer, plate, flake esp. of mineral or bone. **laminar**, **laminose** *a.* made up of laminae. **laminar flow** *n.* a smooth liquid flow following the shape of a streamlined surface. **laminate**[1] (-nāt) *v.t.* **1** to beat, press or roll (metal) into thin plates. **2** to overlay or cover with a thin sheet of material, e.g. plastic. **3** to produce by bonding successive layers or sheets. **4** to cut or split into thin layers or sheets. **~v.i.** to split into thin sheets. **laminate**[2] (-nət) *a.* consisting of laminae, laminated. **~n.** a laminated material. **laminated** *a.* **lamination** (-ā'shən) *n.* **laminator** *n.* **laminitis** (-ī'tis) *n.* inflammation of the lamina of the hoof.

lamish (lā'mish) *a.* LAME.

Lammas (lam'əs), **Lammas Day** *n.* **1** 1 Aug., the day on which first-fruits were offered in Anglo-Saxon times. **2** the Roman Catholic feast of St Peter celebrated on the same day.

lammergeier (lam'əgīə), **lammergeyer** *n.* the great bearded vulture, *Gypaetus barbatus*, an inhabitant of the high mountains of S Europe, Asia and N Africa.

lamp (lamp) *n.* **1** a device for the production of artificial light, which may be fixed or portable and usu. has a glassed container enclosing the light source which may be an electric bulb, gas-jet or wick. **2** any of various usu. movable holders with fittings for one or more electric light bulbs, such as a *table lamp, standard lamp.* **3** an electric device which emits esp. infrared or ultraviolet light waves, such as a *sun lamp.* **4** (*poet.*) any source of light, such as the sun, moon etc. **lampblack** *n.* amorphous carbon, obtained by the imperfect combustion of oil or resin, used as a pigment or filler. **lamplight** *n.* the light from a lamp or lamps. **lamplighter** *n.* **1** (*Hist.*) a person employed to light the public lamps. **2** (*N Am.*) a spill for lighting lamps. **lamplit** *a.* **lamp-post** *n.* a

post or column supporting a street lamp.
lampshade n. a cover for a lamp which softens or directs the light emitted by the electric bulb.
lamp standard n. a lamp-post, esp. a tall one made of concrete or metal.
lampoon (lampoon´) n. a satire, often a scurrilous personal one. ~v.t. to write lampoons about; to satirize. **lampooner, lampoonist** n. **lampoonery** n.
lamprey (lam´pri) n. (pl. **lampreys**) a bloodsucking eel-like fish belonging to the family Petromyzonidae, with a suctorial mouth with which it clings to its prey or to rocks.
LAN abbr. (Comput.) local area network.
Lancastrian (langkas´trien) a. 1 of or relating to Lancashire or Lancaster. 2 of or relating to the family descended from John of Gaunt, Duke of Lancaster. ~n. 1 a native or inhabitant of Lancashire. 2 an adherent of the House of Lancaster, one of the Red Rose party in the Wars of the Roses.
lance (lahns) n. 1 a thrusting weapon consisting of a long shaft with a sharp point, formerly the weapon of knights, later used by some regiments of cavalry. 2 a similar weapon used for killing a harpooned whale, for spearing fish etc. 3 a lancet. 4 a metal-cutting tool that uses a very hot flame. ~v.t. 1 (Med.) to pierce or open with a lancet. 2 to pierce with or as with a lance. **lance bombardier** n. a rank in the Royal Artillery equivalent to lance corporal. **lance corporal** n. the lowest rank for a non-commissioned officer in the British army. **lance-jack** n. (sl.) a lance corporal. **lancer** n. 1 a cavalry soldier armed with a lance. 2 (pl.) **a** a set of quadrilles for eight or sixteen couples. **b** the music for this. **lance-sergeant** n. a corporal acting as a sergeant. **lance-snake** n. the fer-de-lance. **lancewood** n. the tough, elastic wood of Oxandra lanceolata and other W Indian, Australian and New Zealand trees, used in making carriage shafts, fishing rods etc.
lanceolate (lahn´sielet, -āt) a. tapering to a point at each end.
lancet (lahn´sit) n. a sharp surgical instrument with a two-edged blade, used in making incisions, opening abscesses etc. **lancet arch** n. an arch with a sharply pointed top. **lancet window** n. a high narrow window with a sharply pointed arch.
Lancs. abbr. Lancashire.
Land (lant, land) n. (pl. **Länder** (len´də) a federal state in Germany; a province in Austria.
land (land) n. 1 the solid portion of the earth's surface, as distinct from the oceans and seas. 2 this solid surface considered as a usable commodity, ground. 3 a country, nation or state. 4 a district, a region. 5 landed property, real estate. 6 (pl.) estates. ~v.t. 1 to bring to or set on shore. 2 to bring (an aircraft) back to the ground after a flight. 3 to set down from a vehicle. 4 to bring (a fish) to land. 5 to bring to or place in a

certain location, position, predicament etc. 6 to hit something or somebody with (a blow). 7 (coll.) to win, attain, capture or secure (a prize, business deal). ~v.i. 1 to come or go on shore. 2 to disembark from a ship. 3 to return to the ground after a flight, leap etc. 4 to find oneself in a certain location, position, predicament etc. **how the land lies** how matters stand, the state of play in a situation. **the land 1** agricultural or rural areas as opposed to towns. **2** agriculture as a profession or way of life. **to land on one's feet** to end up, by chance, in an advantageous situation. **to land up** to end up. **to land with** to burden with. **land agent** n. 1 a person employed to manage land for the proprietor, a steward. 2 an agent for the sale of land. **land breeze** n. a wind blowing seawards off the land. **land bridge** n. a connecting piece of land between two large land masses, esp. one that allowed the migration of humans and animal species from one continent to the other in prehistoric times. **land-crab** n. a crab of the family Gecarcinidae, which lives mainly on land, visiting the sea chiefly for breeding. **land drain** n. a drain for subsoil drainage consisting of porous or perforated pipe laid in a gravel-filled trench. **land drainage** n. **landed** a. 1 having an estate in land. 2 consisting of real estate. **lander** n. a spacecraft designed to land on the surface of the moon or a planet. **landfall** n. 1 an approach to land after a voyage. 2 the first land sighted after a voyage. **landfill** n. 1 the practice of burying rubbish under layers of earth. 2 a rubbish dump where refuse is buried. 3 the rubbish so buried. **landfilling** n. **land force** n. a military force employed on land. **landform** n. a natural feature of the earth's surface. **land girl** n. (Hist.) a girl or woman employed in farm work during the two World Wars. **landholder** n. a person who owns or (usu.) rents land. **landholding** n., a. **landing** n. 1 the act or an instance of returning to earth after a flight, leap etc. 2 the act or an instance of going or setting on land from a vessel. 3 a pier, wharf, jetty or other place for disembarking or alighting. 4 a level space at the top of a flight of stairs or between flights. 5 a passage leading to rooms on an upper floor. **landing craft** n. a small naval vessel for making shore landings (with troops, equipment etc.). **landing gear** n. the undercarriage of an aircraft. **landing net** n. a bag-net used to take fish from the water when hooked. **landing pad** n. a small area designed for helicopters to land on. **landing stage** n. a platform, fixed or floating, on which passengers and goods are disembarked. **landing strip** n. a strip of ground for aircraft landings and take-offs; an airstrip. **landlady** n. (pl. **landladies**) 1 a woman who lets land, a building, lodgings etc. to a tenant. 2 a woman who keeps a public house or a boarding or lodging house. **landless** a. **landline** n. an overland telecommunications cable or wire. **landlocked** a. enclosed by land. **landlord** n. 1 a man who lets land, a building, lodgings etc. to a tenant. **2** a man who keeps a public house or a boarding or lodging house. **landlubber** *n.* (*derog.*) a landsman, a person unused to the sea or ships. **landmark** *n.* **1** a prominent object on land serving as a guide. **2** a conspicuous object in a place or district. **3** an important event in history etc. **4** anything set up to mark the boundaries of land. *~a.* constituting or manifesting an important change or development. **landmass** *n.* a large area of land uninterrupted by the sea. **landmine** *n.* **1** a mine set in the ground to explode under advancing troops etc. **2** (in World War II) a large bomb dropped by parachute. **land office** *n.* (*N Am.*) an office that administers and registers the sale of public land. **land-office business** *n.* (*N Am.*) extensive and rapid business; a roaring trade. **land of Nod** *n.* the state of being asleep. **land of the living** *n.* (*facet.*) the state of being alive or being awake. **landowner** *n.* a person who owns land. **landownership** *n.* **landowning** *a.* **landrail** *n.* the corncrake. **landside** *n.* the part of an airport complex to which the non-travelling public has access (cp. AIRSIDE (under AIR)). **landslide** *n.* **1** a landslip. **2** an overwhelming victory or overwhelming majority in an election. **landslip** *n.* **1** the sliding down of a considerable portion of ground from a higher to a lower level. **2** the ground thus slipping. **landsman** *n.* (*pl.* **landsmen**) a person unused to the sea and its ways. **land-tie** *n.* a structural member, such as a beam, buttress etc. that supports a wall or structure by connecting it to the ground. **landward** (-wəd) *a., adv.* **landwards** *adv.* **land-wind** *n.* a wind blowing off the land. **land yacht** *n.* a wheeled vehicle with a sail, usu. for recreational use on a beach.

landau (lan´daw, -dow) *n.* a four-wheeled horse-drawn carriage with folding hoods at the front and back which can be raised to cover the occupants. **landaulet** (-let´), **landaulette** *n.* **1** a small landau. **2** an early motor car with a covering or hood over the rear seats.

landscape (land´skāp) *n.* **1** an extensive area of ground, esp. in the country, regarded as a setting or scenery, as a visual whole, or in relation to its particular topography. **2** a picture representing country scenery. **3** the genre to which such pictures belong. **4** a graphic format in which the width of the illustration is greater than its height (cp. *portrait*). *~a.* **1** of, relating to or producing landscapes or landscaping. **2** (*Print.*) **a** (of a format, illustration) having the width greater than the height. **b** (of a page) containing an illustration or table printed at right angles to the text on the standard pages. *~v.t.* to develop the natural beauty of (an area) by landscape gardening. *~v.i.* to work as a landscape gardener. **landscape architecture** *n.* the art or practice of designing and constructing buildings, roads etc. so that they form a pleasant environment or harmonize with the existing landscape. **land-**

scape architect *n.* **landscape gardening** *n.* the art of laying out grounds in such a way as to create a natural-seeming but particularly harmonious and interesting landscape. **landscape gardener** *n.* **landscape-marble** *n.* a variety of marble with dendriform markings. **landscape painter** *n.* a painter of landscapes. **landscapist** *n.*

lane (lān) *n.* **1** a narrow road, way or passage, esp. between hedges. **2** a narrow street. **3** a division of a road for a single stream of traffic. **4** a prescribed route, as for sea or air traffic. **5** a marked out strip of a track, swimming pool etc. for an individual competitor in a race. **6** a passage through a crowd of people or objects.

langlauf (lang´lowf) *n.* cross-country skiing; a cross-country skiing race. **langlaufer** *n.*

langouste (lāgoost´) *n.* the spiny lobster. **langoustine** (-tēn´) *n.* the smaller Norway lobster.

language (lang´gwij) *n.* **1** the communication of ideas by articulate sounds or words of agreed meaning. **2** the human faculty which permits the creation and use of such systems of communication. **3** the vocabulary peculiar to a nation, tribe or people. **4** the vocabulary appropriate to a particular science, profession etc. **5** the phrases and manner of expression peculiar to an individual. **6** literary style. **7** the phraseology or wording (of a book, passage, speech etc.). **8** any formal or informal method of communicating information by symbols, gestures etc. **to speak the same language** to have a similar background, outlook, habits of mind, tastes etc. **language laboratory** *n.* a place where foreign languages are taught with the aid of tape recorders, headphones etc.

languid (lang´gwid) *a.* **1** lacking energy; indisposed to exertion. **2** limp, slack; weak. **3** lacking animation, slow-moving; dull. **4** (of trade) sluggish. **languidly** *adv.* **languidness** *n.*

languish (lang´gwish) *v.i.* **1** to become weak, feeble or sluggish; to lose vitality, energy or animation. **2** to suffer hardship or deprivation. **3** to fall off, to fade, to grow slack. **4** to droop, to pine (for). **5** to put on a languid expression, to affect a tender, wistful or sentimental air. **languisher** *n.* **languishingly** *adv.* **languishment** *n.*

languor (lang´gə) *n.* **1** languidness, lassitude, faintness, lack of energy. **2** debility, faintness, weakness. **3** a pleasantly relaxed or sleepy state. **4** oppressive stillness (of the air etc.). **5** softness, tenderness of mood or expression. **languorous** *a.* **languorously** *adv.* **languorousness** *n.*

langur (lŭng·guə´) *n.* any of several Asian monkeys, esp. of the genus *Presbytis*, having long tails and a circle of long hair around the face.

lank (langk) *a.* **1** lean, long and thin, shrunken-looking. **2** (of hair) long, straight and falling limply. **lankly** *adv.* **lankness** *n.* **lanky** *a.* (*comp.* **lankier**, *superl.* **lankiest**) (of a person, limb) tall or long, thin, loose-joined and rather ungainly. **lankily** *adv.* **lankiness** *n.*

lanolin (lan´əlin), **lanoline** n. an oily, viscous substance forming the basis of ointments etc., extracted from wool.

lantern (lan´tən) n. **1** a light enclosed in a case with transparent sides or panes. **2** such a case. **3** a glazed structure on the top of a dome or roof, for the admission of light and air. **4** the upper chamber of a lighthouse containing the light. **5** MAGIC LANTERN (under MAGIC). **lantern fish** n. any small deep-sea fish of the family Myctophidae with light organs on its head and body. **lantern-jawed** a. having a long, thin, hollow-looking face. **lantern jaws** n.pl. **lantern slide** n. the glass slide holding the image projected by a magic lantern.

lanthanum (lan´thənəm) n. (*Chem.*) a metallic divalent element, at. no. 57, chem. symbol La, usu. occurring with didymium and cerium in cerite and used in the making of alloys and electronic devices. **lanthanide** (-nīd), **lanthanoid** (-noid), **lanthanon** (-non) n. any of a group of rare metallic elements, at. nos. 58–71, a rare earth.

lanyard (lan´yəd), **laniard** n. **1** cord, esp. one worn round the neck, to which a whistle or knife is attached. **2** cord for firing a large gun. **3** (*Naut.*) a short cord, line or gasket for seizing or lashing.

Lao (low) n. (pl. **Laos, Lao**) **1** a member of a Buddhist people of Laos and NE Thailand. **2** the language of this people, which is closely related to Thai. ~a. of or relating to this people, their language or Laos. **Laotian** (lāō´shən, low´-) n. a native or inhabitant of Laos. ~a. of or relating to Laos or its people.

Laodicean (lāōdisē´ən) a. lukewarm or half-hearted in religion, politics etc. ~n. a person of this character.

lap[1] (lap) n. **1** the part of the body from the waist to the knees in a sitting position, esp. as a place for holding an object, a child etc. **2** the part of a skirt, dress or other garment that covers this; the front part of a dress or skirt held out to catch or carry something. **3** a place where anything rests or lies securely. **4** a loose hanging part of a garment or other object. **5** a hollow or sunken area, esp. among hills. **in the lap of the gods** outside human control, up to chance. **to drop in someone's lap** to give someone responsibility for something, a situation etc. **lapdog** n. a small pet dog. **lapful** n. **lapheld** a., n. LAPTOP (under LAP[1]). **lap of luxury** n. a state of wealth and ease. **laptop** a. (of a portable computer etc.) small enough to be held and operated on a person's lap. ~n. a laptop computer.

lap[2] (lap) n. **1** one circuit of a racecourse, running track etc. **2** a stage of a journey or similar undertaking. **3** the part of anything that extends over something else, the overlap. **4** the amount of overlap. **5** the length of rope, cord, thread etc. making one turn round a wheel, roller etc. **6** a continuous band or sheet of cotton or other fibres wound on a roller ready for further processing. **7** a wheel, disc or piece of leather made

to rotate, for polishing gems, metal articles etc. ~v.t. (*pres.p.* **lapping**, *past, p.p.* **lapped**) **1** to overtake a competitor in a race so as to lead them by one or more laps. **2** to wrap, to twist, to roll (around, about etc.). **3** to enfold, to enwrap, to swathe. **4** to surround or envelop protectively or luxuriously. **5** to lay (one thing) partly over another. **6** to cause to overlap. **7** to polish with a lap. ~v.i. **1** to be turned over. **2** to lie partly over something else, to overlap. **lap joint** n. a joint in which one part laps over the other. **lap-jointed** a. **lap of honour** n. a victory circuit made by a winning contestant (e.g. around a racing track). **lapper** n.

lap[3] (lap) v.i. (*pres.p.* **lapping**, *past, p.p.* **lapped**) **1** to drink by lifting with the tongue. **2** to beat gently (as waves on the shore) with a sound as of lapping. ~v.t. **1** to lick or take up with the tongue. **2** (of water) to strike against (the shore, the side of a boat) with a rippling or gently slapping sound. ~n. **1** the act of lapping; the sound of water lapping. **2** a lick. **3** the amount taken up by this. **4** food or drink that can be lapped up, esp. liquid food for animals. **5** a weak kind of drink. **to lap up 1** to eat or drink, esp. eagerly or greedily. **2** to take great and often vain or self-indulgent delight in. **3** to accept or believe uncritically.

laparoscope (lap´ərəskōp) n. a fibre-optical instrument for the internal examination of the abdominal organs after insertion in the wall of the abdomen. **laparoscopy** (-ros´kəpi) n. (pl. **laparoscopies**) an internal examination using a laparoscope.

laparotomy (lapərot´əmi) n. (pl. **laparotomies**) incision into the cavity of the abdomen for examination or diagnosis.

lapel (ləpel´) n. that part of a garment made to lap or fold over, esp. the fold on the front of a coat or jacket below the collar. **lapelled** a.

lapidary (lap´idəri) n. (pl. **lapidaries**) a person who cuts, polishes or engraves gems. ~a. **1** of or relating to the art of cutting, engraving or polishing gems. **2** inscribed on or suitable for inscription on stones. **3** formal or monumental in style.

lapis lazuli (lapis laz´ūlĭ) n. **1** a rich blue mineral, used as a gemstone, containing sodium aluminium silicate and sulphur. **2** a pigment made from this. **3** its colour.

Lapp (lap) n. **1** a member of a nomadic tribe inhabiting the region of Lapland in the far north of Europe. **2** the Finno-Ugric language spoken by this people. ~a. of or relating to this people or their language. **Laplander** (lap´landə) n. a Lapp. **Lappish** a., n.

lappet (lap´it) n. **1** a little lap, fold or loose part of a garment or headdress; a flap. **2** a loose, fleshy process, a lobe, a wattle. **lappeted** a. **lappet-moth** n. a large brown velvety Eurasian moth, *Gastropacha quercifilia*, which has grey furry caterpillars with lappets on their sides.

lapse (laps) *v.i.* **1** to slide, to glide, to pass insensibly or by degrees. **2** to decline into or revert to a worse or inferior state. **3** to fall into disuse, usu. through negligence. **4** to discontinue one's adherence to, membership of or support for an organization. **5** to make a slip or fault. **6** to become void. ~*n.* **1** a mistake, a slip, an error, a fault, deviation from what is right. **2** a falling into disuse, neglect, decay or ruin. **3** an interval of time, esp. a break in the occurrence of something; the imperceptible passage of time. **4** (*Law*) the termination of a right or privilege through desuetude. **lapsed** *a.* (of a person) no longer maintaining a former belief, adherence, membership etc. **lapse rate** *n.* the rate of change of atmospheric factors (e.g. temperature, humidity) with changing altitude.

lapwing (lap´wing) *n.* a bird of the genus *Vanellus*, of the plover family, esp. *V. vanellus*, a British bird with black and white plumage, a backward-pointing crest and a shrill cry; the peewit.

larboard (lah´bəd) *n.* (*Naut., Hist.*) the port or left side of a vessel to a person standing on deck and facing the bow. ~*a.* of or relating to the left side of a vessel.

larceny (lah´səni) *n.* (*pl.* **larcenies**) (*Hist., Law*) the unlawful taking away of another's personal goods with intent to convert them for one's own use; theft. **larcener, larcenist** *n.* **larcenous** *a.* **larcenously** *adv.*

larch (lahch) *n.* **1** a tree of the coniferous genus *Larix*, having deciduous bright-green foliage and tough, durable timber and yielding Venetian turpentine. **2** (*also* **larchwood**) the wood of this.

lard (lahd) *n.* the rendered fat of pigs, esp. in solid white form for use in cooking. ~*v.t.* **1** to insert strips of fat or bacon in (meat) before roasting. **2** to cover or smear with lard. **3** to intermix or garnish (writing, talk etc.) with foreign phrases, flowery speech etc. **lardon** (-dən), **lardoon** (-doon´) *n.* a strip of bacon or fat for larding meat. **lardy** *a.* **lardy-cake** *n.* a rich cake made from yeast, lard, flour, dried fruits etc.

larder (lah´də) *n.* **1** a room where meat and other provisions are kept, a pantry. **2** a store of food kept by a wild animal, esp. for consumption in winter.

large (lahj) *a.* **1** great in size, number, quantity, extent or capacity. **2** big, bulky. **3** wide, extensive. **4** abundant, ample, copious. **5** (of two or more similar objects) the bigger or biggest. **6** wide in range or scope, comprehensive, far-reaching. **7** operating on a large scale. **8** having breadth of understanding or sympathy. **9** liberal, generous, lavish, prodigal. ~*adv.* prominently, importantly (*loom large*). **at large 1** (esp. of a criminal) at liberty, free; roaming without constraint. **2** as a whole, in general. **3** diffusely, with ample detail. **4** freely, without restraint; without a particular target. **5** (of a political representative in the US) representing a whole

area, not a subdivision of it. **large as life** unmistakably present or real. **larger than life** remarkably vivid or eye-catching. **large calorie** *n.* a unit of heat equalling 1000 (small) calories, used in measuring the energy content of food. **large intestine** *n.* in the digestive system, that part of the intestine comprising the caecum, colon and rectum. **largely** *adv.* to a large extent. **large-minded** *a.* having liberal and tolerant views. **largeness** *n.* **large-scale** *a.* **1** extensive. **2** detailed. **largish** *a.*

largesse (lahjes´), **largess** *n.* **1** a present, a reward, a generous bounty (usu. from a superior to inferiors). **2** liberality, esp. in giving.

largo (lah´gō) *adv.* (*Mus.*) slowly, broadly, in an ample, dignified style. ~*n.* (*pl.* **largos**) a piece of music played in this manner. **larghetto** (-get´ō) *adv.* (*Mus.*) somewhat slow.

lariat (lar´iət) *n.* **1** a lasso. **2** a rope for picketing horses in camp.

lark[1] (lahk) *n.* **1** any bird of the family Alaudidae, with five British species, esp. the skylark, *Alauda arvensis*. **2** any of various similar birds such as a meadowlark. **larkspur** *n.* **1** a plant with spur-shaped calyx belonging to the genus *Consolida*, the buttercup family. **2** a plant of the genus *Delphinium*, esp. *D. ajacis*.

lark[2] (lahk) *n.* **1** a prank, a frolic, a spree. **2** (*coll.*) any activity or undertaking (*don't fancy this mind-reading lark*). ~*v.i.* to behave in a carefree or mischievous way, to frolic. **larkish, larky** *a.*

larva (lah´və) *n.* (*pl.* **larvae** (-vē)) **1** the first condition of an insect on its issuing from the egg, when it is usu. in the form of a grub, caterpillar or maggot. **2** the half-developed state of other invertebrates that undergo metamorphosis. **larval** *a.* **larvicide** (lah´-) *n.*

laryngeal (larin´jiəl), **laryngal** (-gəl) *a.* **1** of or relating to the larynx. **2** in phonetics, produced in the larynx by partial closure and vibration of the vocal cords.

laryngitis (larinjī´tis) *n.* inflammation of the larynx. **laryngitic** (-rinjit´-) *a.*

larynx (lar´ingks) *n.* (*pl.* **larynges** (lərin´jēz), **larynxes**) a hollow muscular organ, situated in the upper part of the windpipe and containing the vocal cords in humans and higher vertebrates, the voice box.

lasagne (ləsan´yə, -zan´-, -sahn´-), **lasagna** *n.* **1** pasta in the form of wide flat strips. **2** a baked dish consisting of this pasta, esp. layered with bolognese and béchamel sauces.

Lascar (las´kə) *n.* a sailor from SE Asia or India.

lascivious (ləsiv´iəs) *a.* **1** lewd, wanton, lustful. **2** exciting or provoking lust. **lasciviously** *adv.* **lasciviousness** *n.*

laser (lā´zə) *n.* an instrument which amplifies light waves by stimulation to produce a powerful, coherent beam of monochromatic light, an optical maser. **lase** *v.i.* **1** to function or be capable of functioning as a laser. **2** to undergo the physical processes employed in a laser. **laser**

disc *n.* a disc on which signals and data are recorded for reproduction by a laser beam directed on to its surface. **laser printer** *n.* a high-performance computer printer incorporating a laser which forms a pattern of dots on a photosensitive drum corresponding to the matter to be printed. **LaserVision®** *n.* a video disc system, incorporating a laser, for reproducing digitally recorded audio-visual material via a television set or hi-fi.

lash (lash) *n.* **1** a stroke with a whip. **2** the thong or flexible part of a whip. **3** a whip, a scourge. **4** an eyelash. **5** sarcasm, satire, vituperation. *~v.t.* **1** to whisk or flick (e.g. a tail) suddenly or with a jerk in a menacing fashion. **2** to strike or flog with anything pliant and tough, to whip. **3** to drive with or as with a whip. **4** to assail fiercely with satire, reproach etc. **5** (of wind, rain, waves) to beat or dash against. **6** to fasten or bind with a rope or cord. *~v.i.* **1** to make a whiplike movement. **2** (of rain, wind) to fall, blow, strike with great force. **3** to strike or kick violently (at, out etc.). **4** to make satirical, sarcastic etc. attacks. **5** to use a whip. **the lash** punishment by flogging. **to lash out 1** to make a strong, usu. sudden physical or verbal attack. **2** to be extravagant with money. **lasher** *n.* **lashing** *n.* **1** a rope or gasket by which anything is secured. **2** a whipping, a flogging. **lashings** *n.pl.* (*coll.*) plenty, lots, an abundance. **lashless** *a.* **lash-up** *n.* something improvised or makeshift, esp. an improvised or temporary connection.

lass (las) *n.* (*esp. Sc., North. or poet.*) a young woman, a girl. **lassie** (-i) *n.*

Lassa fever (las´ə) *n.* an often fatal tropical viral disease symptomized by fever and muscle pain and transmitted by rats etc.

lassitude (las´itūd) *n.* **1** weariness. **2** lack of energy or animation, languor.

lasso (lasoo´) *n.* (*pl.* **lassoes, lassos**) a rope, esp. of untanned hide, with a running noose, used for catching cattle, horses etc. *~v.t.* (*3rd pers. sing. pres.* **lassoes, lassos**, *pres.p.* **lassoing**, *past, p.p.* **lassoed**) to catch with a lasso. **lassoer** *n.*

last[1] (lahst) *a.* **1** coming after all others or at the end, closing, final. **2** conclusive, definitive. **3** utmost, extreme. **4** next before the present, most recent. **5** only remaining. **6** lowest, in rank or position. **7** furthest from the thoughts, least suitable, least likely etc. **8** of or relating to the end, esp. of life or of the world. *~n.* **1** (*ellipt.*) the thing most recently done, mentioned etc., or the most recent doing, mention etc. of something. **2** the end, the conclusion. **3** the last moment, hour, day etc. **4** death. *~adv.* **1** after all the others. **2** most recently, on the last time or occasion. **3** for the last time. **at last** after a long time or interval, esp. after a long period of waiting; after too long a time. **at long last** after a very long delay or period of waiting. **on its last legs** (of a machine, utensil etc.) near the end of its useful life, nearly worn-out. **on one's last legs 1** in an extreme stage

of exhaustion. **2** near to death, ruin etc. **the last lap** the beginning of the end, the closing stages. **to the last 1** to the end. **2** till death. **last ditch** *n.* a last resort; the place for a final desperate struggle or defence. **last-ditch** *a.* **Last Judgement** *n.* the judgement of humankind by God at the end of the world. **lastly** *adv.* finally, to conclude. **last minute, last moment** *n.* the latest possible time. **last name** *n.* a surname. **last offices** *n.pl.* rites due to the dead. **last post** *n.* **1** (*Mil.*) the bugle-call signalling the time of going to bed. **2** a bugle-salute at military funerals. **last rites** *n.pl.* religious rites for the dying. **last sleep** *n.* death. **last straw** *n.* the thing that finally takes one past the limit of endurance or patience. **Last Supper** *n.* the supper shared by Christ and his disciples the evening before his crucifixion. **last thing** *n.* late in the evening; just before going to bed. **last word** *n.* **1** a concluding statement. **2** a final decision. **3** the latest improvement, most up-to-date model.

last[2] (lahst) *v.i.* **1** to continue in existence, to go on. **2** to hold out, to continue unexhausted or unimpaired, to endure. **3** to be enough for (a person over a specified period of time). **to last out 1** to endure to the end, to persevere, to survive. **2** to be enough to meet one's requirements till the end of (a period of time). **lasting** *a.* **1** continuing in existence. **2** enduring, permanent, durable. **lastingly** *adv.* **lastingness** *n.*

last[3] (lahst) *n.* a shaped wooden block on which boots and shoes are fashioned or repaired. **to stick to one's last** to concern oneself with what one knows about and is skilled in (and not meddle with other matters).

lat. *abbr.* latitude.

latch (lach) *n.* **1** a fastening for a door, gate etc., consisting of a bolt and catch. **2** a spring-lock that fastens with the shutting of a door and is opened with a key. *~v.t., v.i.* to fasten with a latch. **on the latch** fastened by the latch only, not locked. **to latch on to 1** (*coll.*) to understand the meaning of. **2** to attach oneself to. **latchkey** *n.* a key to the latch on a front door. **latchkey child** *n.* a child who lets themselves into the house after school, usu. one with working parents.

late (lāt) *a.* **1** coming after the proper, usual or agreed time. **2** slow, tardy, backward, long delayed. **3** far on into the evening or night. **4** far on in any period. **5** far advanced, far on in development. **6** existing at a previous time but now gone or ceased. **7** deceased, departed (esp. recently). **8** former; recently in office etc. **9** recent in date. *~adv.* **1** after the proper or usual time. **2** at or till a late hour, season, stage etc. **at the latest** no later than. **late in the day 1** at an advanced stage in proceedings. **2** too late. **later on** at some unspecified later or future time. **of late 1** a short time ago, lately, recently. **2** latterly, formerly. **the late 1** the recently deceased, resigned etc. **2** the recent. **the latest** (*coll.*) the most recent news. **latecomer** *n.* a person or thing that arrives late. **lately** *adv.* a short time ago, recently; in recent times. **lateness** *n.* **later** *adv.* **latish** *a.*, *adv.*

lateen (lətēn´) *a.* a term applied to a triangular sail, inclined at an angle of about 45°, used principally in the Mediterranean. ~*n.* (*also* **lateen sail**) such a sail.

latent (lā´tənt) *a.* **1** hidden or concealed. **2** not seen, not apparent. **3** dormant, not active, potential. **latency** *n.* **latent heat** *n.* (*Physics*) the heat required to turn a solid into a liquid, or a liquid into a gas, at constant temperature. **latent image** *n.* a photographic image not yet made visible by developing. **latently** *adv.*

-later (lətə) *comb. form* a person who worships a particular thing, as *idolater.*

lateral (lat´ərəl) *a.* **1** of or relating to, at, from or towards the side. **2** descended from a brother or sister of a person in the direct line. **3** (of a speech sound) pronounced with the tip of the tongue touching the alveolar ridge so that air can pass to one or both sides of it. ~*n.* **1** a part, member, process, shoot etc., situated or developing at the side. **2** a lateral consonant. **lateral line** *n.* (*Zool.*) a sensory organ on the side of fish for detecting movement or changes in water pressure through vibrations. **laterally** *adv.* **lateral thinking** *n.* a way of thinking which seeks to solve problems by finding new perspectives rather than following conventional or strictly logical lines of thought.

laterite (lat´ərīt) *n.* a red porous rock, composed of silicate of alumina and oxide of iron, found in extensive beds in India and SW Asia. **lateritic** (-rit´-) *a.*

latex (lā´teks) *n.* (*pl.* **latexes, latices** (-tisēz)) **1** the juice of milky plants, esp. rubber trees. **2** a similar emulsion of a polymer in a watery liquid.

lath (lahth, lath) *n.* (*pl.* **laths** (lahdhz, lahths, laths)) **1** a thin strip of wood, esp. one nailed to rafters to support tiles or to the studs of partitions to support plastering. **2** anything of similar dimensions or used for the same purposes. ~*v.t.* to cover or line with laths.

lathe (lādh) *n.* a machine for cutting, shaping and polishing wood, ivory, metal etc. by rotating it against a fixed tool.

lather (lah´dhə, ladh´ə) *n.* **1** froth or foam made by soap moistened with water or caused by profuse sweating. **2** (*coll.*) a flustered or excited state. ~*v.i.* **1** to form a lather, e.g. by using soap and water. **2** (of soap) to form lather. **3** (of a horse) to become covered with lather. ~*v.t.* **1** to cover with lather. **2** (*coll.*) to thrash, to flog. **lathery** *a.*

latices, laticifer etc. LATEX.

Latin (lat´in) *a.* **1** of, relating to or expressed in the language of the ancient Romans. **2** of or relating to one or any of the (Romance) languages derived from this or the peoples who speak them. **3** of or relating to ancient Latium, its inhabitants or their language. **4** of or relating to the

Roman Catholic Church. ~*n.* **1** the language of ancient Rome, originally the language of Latium. **2** an inhabitant of ancient Latium. **3** a person belonging to a people whose language derives from Latin. **4** (*N Am.*) a Latin American. **5** a Roman Catholic. **Latina** (lətē´nə) *n.* a female inhabitant of the United States of Latin American origin. **Latin America** *n.* the parts of America where the official language is derived from Latin (e.g. Spanish, Portuguese). **Latin American** *a.* of or relating to the states of Latin America. ~*n.* a native or inhabitant of Latin America. **Latinate** (-nāt) *a.* imitating or derived from Latin. **Latin cross** *n.* a cross with a long upright below the crosspiece. **Latinism** *n.* **Latinist** *n.* **Latinize, Latinise** *v.t.* **1** to give a Latin form to (a word, phrase etc.). **2** to translate into Latin. **3** to bring into conformity with the ideas, customs, forms etc., of the Romans, the Latin peoples or the Roman Catholic Church. ~*v.i.* to use Latin words, idioms or phrases. **Latinization** (-zā´shən) *n.* **Latinizer** *n.* **Latino** (lətē´nō) *n.* (*pl.* **Latinos**) an inhabitant of the United States of Latin American origin. ~*a.* of or relating to the Latinos.

latish LATE.

latitude (lat´itūd) *n.* **1** angular distance on a meridian, angular distance of a place north or south of the equator. **2** (*pl.*) regions, climates, esp. with reference to distance from the equator or the tropics. **3** freedom of action; freedom to deviate from a standard or rule. **4** absence of strictness, tolerance, breadth; laxity. **5** looseness of application or meaning. **6** (*Astron.*) the angular distance of a celestial body from the ecliptic. **latitudinal** (-tū´-) *a.* **latitudinally** *adv.* **latitudinarian** (-nea´ri-) *n.* a person who does not attach great importance to dogmas. ~*a.* **1** liberal, tolerant of diversity of opinion, esp. in religion. **2** not confined within narrow or dogmatic limits. **latitudinarianism** *n.*

latrine (lətrēn´) *n.* a lavatory, a toilet, esp. in a camp or barracks.

-latry (lətri) *comb. form* worship or excessive devotion, as in *bibliolatry, idolatry, zoolatry.*

latter (lat´ə) *a.* **1** (of two) second, second-mentioned. **2** (*coll.*) (of more than two) last-mentioned. **3** coming or happening after something else, later. **4** recent, modern, present. **5** of or relating to the end of a period, life, the world etc. **latter-day** *a.* modern, recent. **Latter-day Saints** *n.pl.* the Mormons. **latterly** *adv.* **1** recently. **2** towards the end of a period.

Usage note The use of *the latter* to mean the last-mentioned of more than two (*the last*) is often disapproved of.

lattice (lat´is) *n.* **1** a structure of laths or strips of metal or wood crossing and forming openwork. **2** in a crystal, the geometric pattern of molecules, atoms or ions, or of the points around which they vibrate. **latticed** *a.* **lattice girder, lattice frame** *n.* a beam or girder consisting of bars connected together by iron lattice-work. **lattice window** *n.* a window consisting of small (usu. diamond-shaped) panes set in strips of lead. **lattice-work** *n.* the arrangement of laths etc., forming a lattice. **latticing** *n.*

Latvian (lat´viən) *n.* **1** a native or inhabitant of Latvia, a Lett. **2** the language of Latvians, Lettish. ~*a.* of or relating to Latvia, its people or its language, Lettish.

laud (lawd) *v.t.* to praise, to celebrate, to extol. ~*n.* **1** (*poet.*) praise; thankful adoration; worship consisting of praise. **2** a song of praise, a hymn. **3** (*pl.*) the office of the first canonical hour of prayer in the Western Church, now usu. said with matins. **laudable** *a.* praiseworthy, commendable. **laudableness, laudability** (-bil´-) *n.* **laudably** *adv.* **laudation** (-dā´shən) *n.* (*formal*) **laudatory** (law´dətəri), **laudative** (-dətiv) *a.* **lauder** *n.*

laudanum (law´dənəm) *n.* opium prepared in alcohol, tincture of opium, formerly used as a painkiller.

laugh (lahf) *v.i.* **1** to express amusement, scorn or exultation by inarticulate sounds and the convulsive movements of the face and body which are the involuntary effects of such emotions. **2** to deride, jeer or scoff (at). ~*v.t.* **1** to express by laughing. **2** to utter with laughter. **3** to move or influence by ridicule or laughter. ~*n.* **1** the action of laughing. **2** an act or explosion of laughter. **3** a person's manner of laughing. **4** (*coll.*) something or someone that causes laughter; a bit of fun. **a laugh a minute** very funny or amusing. **to be laughing** (*coll.*) to have no further problems; to be in an advantageous position. **to have the last laugh** to be ultimately triumphant after a former setback. **to laugh in someone's face** to show someone open contempt or ridicule. **to laugh off** to treat as of trifling importance. **to laugh on the other side of one's face** to feel vexation or disappointment after amusement or satisfaction. **to laugh to scorn** to treat with the utmost contempt. **to laugh up/ in one's sleeve** to be inwardly amused while one's expression remains serious or demure. **laughable** *a.* **1** ludicrous, ridiculous; derisory. **2** exciting laughter, comical. **laughableness** *n.* **laughably** *adv.* **laugher** *n.* **laughing** *n.*, *a.* **no laughing matter** something serious, not a proper subject for levity. **laughing gas** *n.* nitrous oxide, used as an anaesthetic (so-called because when inhaled it produces violent exhilaration). **laughing hyena** *n.* a striped dog of the species *Hyena striata*. **laughing jackass** *n.* a kookaburra. **laughingly** *adv.* **laughing stock** *n.* an object of ridicule. **laughter** *n.* the act or sound of laughing.

launch[1] (lawnch) *v.t.* **1** to cause to glide into the water (e.g. a vessel), or take off from land (e.g. a space rocket). **2** to put (a vessel) into the water for the first time. **3** to throw, to hurl, to propel. **4** to start or set (a person etc.) going. **5** to introduce a new product or publication onto the market,

usu. with a publicity campaign. ~*v.i.* (of a ship, rocket etc.) to be launched; to put to sea. ~*n.* the act or occasion of launching a ship, rocket, product etc. **to launch into 1** to propel oneself into a new activity, career etc. with vigour and enthusiasm. **2** to embark on a long speech, story or explanation. **to launch out 1** to enter on a new and usu. more ambitious sphere of activity. **2** (*coll.*) to spend money freely. **launcher** *n.* the apparatus for launching a rocket, vessel etc. **launch pad, launching pad** *n.* **1** a platform from which a rocket is launched. **2** the initiating event or starting place or point which propels a new activity or from which it gets underway.

launch[2] (lawnch) *n.* **1** a large open pleasure-boat propelled by steam, electricity or internal-combustion engine. **2** (*Hist.*) the largest boat belonging to a man-of-war.

launder (lawn´də) *v.t.* **1** to wash and iron (clothing, linen etc.). **2** (*coll.*) to legitimize illegally acquired money by transferring it through banks, foreign institutions etc. ~*v.i.* **1** to wash and iron clothing, linen etc. **2** to become clean and ready for use by washing and ironing. ~*n.* a trough or gutter for carrying water. **launderer** *n.* **launderette** (-dəret´, -dret´), **laundrette** *n.* an establishment containing coin-operated washing-machines etc., for public use. **laundress** (-dris) *n.* a woman who washes and irons (clothes, linen etc.). **Laundromat**® (-drəmat) *n.* a launderette. **laundry** (-dri) *n.* (*pl.* **laundries**) **1** a room or establishment where clothes are washed and ironed. **2** the batch of clothes sent to or received from a laundry. **3** the act of laundering. **laundryman, laundrywoman** *n.* (*pl.* **laundrymen, laundrywomen**) a person who is employed in a laundry or who collects and delivers washing.

lauraceous (lawrā´shəs) *a.* of or relating to the family Lauraceae which includes the laurels and avocado.

laureate (law´riət, lor´-) *a.* **1** crowned or decked with laurel. **2** worthy of laurels, eminent, distinguished, esp. as a poet. **3** consisting or made of laurels. ~*n.* **1** a person who has received a particular award or honour. **2** a Poet Laureate. **3** a person who has been crowned with laurel. **laureateship** *n.*

laurel (lor´əl) *n.* **1** a glossy-leaved evergreen shrub, *Laurus nobilis*, also called the *bay tree*. **2** (*sing. or pl.*) the foliage of this, esp. in the form of a wreath, conferred as a distinction on victorious competitors in the ancient classical games, on heroes, poets etc. **3** (*sing. or pl.*) the honours conferred by this. **4** any of various trees and shrubs resembling the laurel, e.g. the cherry laurel, spurge laurel. **to look to one's laurels** to guard against rivalry, to take care not to lose one's pre-eminence. **to rest on one's laurels** to be satisfied with what one has achieved and not to strive for further success. **laurelled,** (*N Am.*) **laureled** *a.* crowned with laurel.

lav (lav) *n.* (*coll.*) short for LAVATORY.
lava (lah´və) *n.* (*pl.* **lavas**) **1** molten matter flowing in streams from volcanic vents. **2** the solidified rock formed from the same matter by cooling.
lavatory (lav´ətri) *n.* (*pl.* **lavatories**) **1** a receptacle for urinating or defecating into, usu. connected by pipes to a sewer and flushed with water; a toilet. **2** a room with a toilet and usu. a washhand basin. **3** a room or place for washing, esp. in a monastery. **lavatorial** (-taw´-) *a.* **1** of, relating to or resembling a lavatory, esp. a public lavatory. **2** (of humour) heavily reliant on references to faeces, excretion, lavatories etc. **lavatory paper** *n.* toilet paper.
lavender (lav´əndə) *n.* **1** a sweet-scented flowering shrub, *Lavandula vera*, cultivated for its scent, its mauve or blue flowers, and its oil which is used in perfumery. **2** the flower and stalks or the oil used for perfuming linen etc. **3** the colour of the flowers, a pale lilac. ~*a.* of the colour of lavender blossoms, pale lilac. ~*v.t.* to perfume or sprinkle with lavender. **lavender-water** *n.* a liquid perfume, consisting of essential oil of lavender, ambergris, and alcohol.
laver (lā´və, lah´-) *n.* any of various types of seaweed, esp. *Porphyra umbilicaulis, P. vulgaris* and other edible species. **laver bread** *n.* a Welsh dish of boiled laver coated in oatmeal and fried.
lavish (lav´ish) *a.* **1** spending or giving with profusion. **2** prodigal, spendthrift, unrestrained. **3** existing or produced in profusion. **4** excessive, superabundant. ~*v.t.* **1** to expend or bestow profusely. **2** to be excessively free or liberal with, to squander. **lavisher** *n.* **lavishly** *adv.* **lavishness** *n.*
law (law) *n.* **1** a rule of conduct imposed by authority or accepted by the community as binding. **2** a system of such rules regulating the intercourse of mankind, of individuals within a state, or of states with one another. **3** the controlling influence of this. **4** the condition of order and stability it secures. **5** the practical application of these rules, esp. by trial in courts of justice; litigation, judicial process. **6** the interpretation of these rules, the science of legal principles and enactments, jurisprudence. **7** legal knowledge. **8** common and statute law (as opposed to *equity*). **9** one of a set of rules governing the conduct of a profession, art, association, sport, game or other activity or department of life. **10** the orderly recurrence of natural phenomena as the uniform results of corresponding conditions. **11** a generalized statement of such conditions and their consequences. **12** a theoretical principle drawn from experience or observation. **at law** according to the law. **in law** according to the law. **the law 1** the legal profession. **2** (*coll.*) the police; a police officer. **to be a law unto oneself** to act in accordance with one's principles, wishes etc. in defiance of customs, rules etc. **to go to law** to take legal proceedings. **to lay down the law** to talk or direct in a dictatorial manner. **to take the law into one's own hands** to try to secure satisfaction or retaliation by one's own methods or actions. **law-abiding** *a.* obedient to the law. **law-abidingness** *n.* **law agent** *n.* (*Sc.*) a solicitor. **lawbreaker** *n.* a person who violates the law. **lawbreaking** *n., a.* **law centre** *n.* a publicly-funded office where free legal advice can be obtained. **law court** *n.* a court of law. **lawful** *a.* **1** conformable with law. **2** allowed by law. **3** legitimate, valid, rightful. **lawfully** *adv.* **lawfulness** *n.* **lawgiver** *n.* a person who makes or enacts laws, a legislator. **lawgiving** *a.* **lawless** *a.* **1** not subject to or governed by law. **2** regardless of or unrestrained by the law. **3** unbridled, licentious. **lawlessly** *adv.* **lawlessness** *n.* **Law Lord** *n.* a member of the House of Lords qualified to deal with the judicial business of the House. **lawmaker** *n.* a legislator. **law-making** *n., a.* **lawman** *n.* (*pl.* **lawmen**) (*N Am.*) a law enforcement officer. **law of averages** *n.* the principle that extremes cancel one another out thereby reaching a balance. **lawsuit** *n.* an action in a court of law. **law term** *n.* any one of the periods appointed for the sitting of the Law Courts. **lawyer** (-yə) *n.* a person who practises law, esp. an attorney or solicitor. **lawyer-like, lawyerly** *a.*
lawn¹ (lawn) *n.* a grassy space kept smooth and closely mown in a garden, park etc. **lawnmower** *n.* a machine for mowing a lawn. **lawn tennis** *n.* the former name for the game of tennis, orig. played on a lawn but now frequently on a hard court.
lawn² (lawn) *n.* a cotton or linen fabric, finer than cambric (e.g. used for the sleeves of an Anglican bishop's rochet). **lawny** *a.*
lawrencium (lawren´siəm) *n.* (*Chem.*) a radioactive element, at. no. 103, chem. symbol Lr, with a short half-life, orig. produced in America.
lawyer LAW.
lax (laks) *a.* **1** not exact, not strict; negligent, careless. **2** porous. **3** slack, loose, not tight, firm or compact. **4** (of a speech sound) pronounced with relaxed vocal muscles and therefore not precisely articulated and short in duration. **laxative** *a.* opening or loosening the bowels. ~*n.* a laxative medicine. **laxity, laxness** *n.* **laxly** *adv.*
lay¹ (lā) *v.t.* (*past, p.p.* **laid** (lād)) **1** to cause to lie, to place in a horizontal, prostrate or recumbent position. **2** to put or bring into a certain state or position (*laid my hand on his arm*). **3** to dispose regularly, to put in proper position (*lay a carpet*). **4** to put down, to place, to deposit; to establish as a base or basis (*lay the foundations*). **5** (of a bird) to produce (eggs). **6** to spread on a surface, to apply. **7** to cause to lie flat or smooth. **8** to cause to settle (as dust). **9** to cause to be still, to allay, to calm. **10** to exorcize. **11** to put forward, to present. **12** to attribute, to impute. **13** to impose, to enjoin, to inflict. **14** to stake, to wager. **15** to think out, to devise, to plan, to prepare. **16** to bring down (a weapon, blows etc., on). **17** to

beat down, to prostrate. **18** to locate (a scene, story etc.). **19** (*Mil.*) to aim and set (a gun) prior to firing. **20** in horticulture, to propagate by layers. **21** (*taboo sl., offensive*) to have sexual intercourse with. *~v.i.* **1** to drop or deposit eggs. **2** (*Naut., coll., dial.*) to lie. *~n.* **1** the way, direction or position in which a region or object is situated. **2** (*taboo sl., offensive*) **a** an act of sexual intercourse. **b** a sexual partner. **3** the direction the strands of a rope are twisted. **in lay** (of hens) laying eggs. **to lay about one 1** to hit out on all sides; to fight vigorously. **2** to issue criticism, reprimands etc. indiscriminately. **to lay a charge** to make an accusation. **to lay aside 1** to put to one side. **2** to give up, to abandon; to reject. **3** to store for future use. **to lay back** to place or construct sloping back from the vertical. **to lay bare 1** to reveal. **2** to strip. **to lay before 1** to exhibit to. **2** to bring to the notice of. **to lay by 1** to save. **2** to reserve for a future occasion. **to lay down 1** to put down. **2** to resign, to surrender. **3** to declare, to affirm, to assert; to stipulate. **4** to formulate, to draw up. **5** to put down the main structural parts of. **6** to record on paper. **7** to sacrifice. **8** to store (wine etc.). **9** (*coll.*) to wager. **10** to pay. **11** to convert (land) to pasture. **12** to record (tracks of an album). **to lay hold of** to grasp or seize. **to lay in** to acquire a store of, to stock up with. **to lay into** (*coll.*) to assault physically or verbally. **to lay it on 1** to speak or flatter extravagantly. **2** to charge exorbitantly. **3** to strike or beat hard. **4** to criticize severely. **to lay low 1** to fell or destroy. **2** to cause to become weak or ill. **to lay off 1** to suspend from employment. **2** to discharge (workers) permanently, to make redundant. **3** to desist. **4** to avoid. **to lay on 1** (*coll.*) to provide (facility, entertainment). **2** to install and supply (water, gas). **3** to impose, to inflict. **4** to deal (blows etc.). **5** to apply, to spread on. **to lay oneself open to** to expose oneself to (criticism, attack etc.). **to lay oneself out** (*coll.*) to busy or exert oneself to do something. **to lay open 1** to cut so as to expose the interior of. **2** to expose, to reveal. **3** to explain. **to lay out 1** to arrange according to a plan. **2** to spread out. **3** to expound, to explain. **4** to expend. **5** to dress in grave-clothes and prepare for burial. **6** (*coll.*) to knock to the ground or render unconscious. **to lay over 1** to spread over, to overlay. **2** (*N Am.*) to stop over during a journey. **3** (*N Am.*) to postpone. **to lay the table** to set a table with cutlery, crockery etc. for a forthcoming meal. **to lay to rest 1** to bury. **2** to prevent from causing further trouble or dispute. **3** to calm, to assuage. **to lay up 1** to store, to treasure, to save. **2** (of illness) to confine (someone) to their bed or room. **3** to decommission a ship or take out of service. **layabout** *n.* an idle person, a lounger. **lay-by** *n.* (*pl.* **lay-bys**) **1** a widening of a road to enable vehicles to stop without holding up traffic. **2** a similar passing point on a railway or canal. **3** (*Austral., New*

Zeal.) a system whereby payment of a deposit reserves an article for future purchase; an article reserved in this way. **lay-off** *n.* **1** an act of suspending workers from employment. **2** a period when workers are suspended from employment. **3** redundancy. **layout** *n.* **1** a planned arrangement of buildings etc. **2** the way in which text, illustrations, drawings etc. are arranged on a printed page. **3** something which is set out or displayed in a particular way.

Usage note *Lay* should not be used instead of *lie* as an intransitive verb.

lay² (lā) *a.* **1** of or relating to the people as distinct from the *clergy*. **2** non-professional, lacking specialized knowledge. **laity** (lā´iti) *n.* **1** (*collect.*) the people, as distinct from the clergy. **2** laymen and laywomen, those not belonging to a particular profession. **lay brother, lay sister** *n.* a brother or sister in a monastery, under vows and wearing the habit of the order but not ordained, engaged chiefly in manual labour and exempt from other duties. **layman, laywoman** *n.* (*pl.* **laymen, laywomen**) **1** a member of the people, as distinct from the clergy. **2** a non-professional, a person who is not an expert. **lay reader** *n.* a member of the Church of England laity authorized to conduct certain religious services. **lay vicar** *n.* in the Church of England, a lay person acting as vicar choral.

lay³ (lā) *n.* **1** a lyric song or ballad. **2** a short narrative poem for singing or recitation.

lay⁴ LIE².

layer (lā´ə) *n.* **1** a thickness or anything spread out (usu. one of several), a stratum, a bed. **2** a person who or something which lays, esp. a hen. **3** a shoot laid with part of its length on or beneath the surface of the ground in order that it may take root. *~v.t.* **1** to place, cut or form in layers. **2** to propagate by layers. **layer cake** *n.* a cake made in layers with a filling in between. **layer-out** *n.* a person who prepares a body for burial.

layette (lāet´) *n.* the outfit for a newborn infant.

lay figure (lā) *n.* **1** a jointed figure of the human body used by artists for hanging drapery on etc. **2** a puppet, a nonentity. **3** an unreal character in a story etc.

lazy (lā´zi) *a.* (*comp.* **lazier**, *superl.* **laziest**) **1** idle, indolent, slothful, disinclined to labour or exertion. **2** conducive to or characterized by idleness or sloth. **3** (of movement) slow; languorous. **laze** *v.i.* **1** to be lazy. **2** to live in idleness. *~v.t.* to waste or spend in idleness. *~n.* a time or spell of idleness. **lazily** *adv.* **laziness** *n.* **lazybones** *n.* (*pl.* **lazybones**) (*coll.*) a lazy person, an idler. **lazy Susan** *n.* a revolving tray for a dining table with compartments for various condiments.

lb *abbr.* **1** (*also* **l.b.**) in cricket, leg bye. **2** (*also* **lb.**) pound(s).

L/Bdr *abbr.* Lance Bombardier.

LBO *abbr.* leveraged buy-out.

LBV *abbr.* Late Bottled Vintage (of port wine that has been matured in casks for six years before bottling).

l.b.w. *abbr.* in cricket, leg before wicket.

lc *abbr.* **1** letter of credit. **2** *loco citato*, in the place cited. **3** lower case (type).

lcd, LCD *abbr.* **1** Liquid Crystal Display. **2** lowest common denominator.

lcm, LCM *abbr.* least or lowest common multiple.

L/Cpl *abbr.* Lance Corporal.

LD *abbr.* lethal dosage (usu. with a subscript number appended to show the percentage of animals or organisms killed by the dose).

Ld. *abbr.* Lord.

Ldg. *abbr.* Leading (Seaman etc.).

LDL *abbr.* low-density lipoprotein.

LDS *abbr.* **1** Latter-day Saints. **2** Licentiate in Dental Surgery.

-le[1] (əl) *suf.* forming nouns esp. denoting appliances or instruments as *handle*, *thimble* or animals and plants, *beetle*, *thistle*.

-le[2] (əl), **-el** *suf.* forming nouns which orig. had a diminutive sense, e.g. *angle*, *castle*, *puddle*, *novel*, *tunnel*.

-le[3] (əl) *suf.* forming adjectives, often with, or orig. with, the sense 'likely or liable to', e.g. *brittle*, *fickle*, *little*.

-le[4] (əl) *suf.* forming verbs, esp. expressing repeated action or having a diminutive sense, e.g. *crackle*, *tickle*, *wriggle*.

LEA *abbr.* Local Education Authority.

lea (lē) *n.* (*poet.*) **1** a meadow. **2** grassland. **3** open country.

leach (lēch) *v.t.* **1** to wash out or separate (a soluble constituent) by percolation. **2** to strain or drain (liquid) from some material (*usu.* out or away). **3** to wash or wet by letting liquid percolate through. ~*v.i.* (of liquid in any material) to drain out. ~*n.* the solution obtained by leaching.

lead[1] (lēd) *v.t.* (*past, p.p.* **led** (led)) **1** to conduct, to guide by taking by the hand or halter or by showing the way. **2** to direct the actions, movements, opinions etc. of. **3** to be in command of. **4** to direct or induce by persuasion, instruction or advice. **5** to be at the head of (a procession, march etc.). **6** to be ahead of in a race, competition etc. **7** to take first place or be pre-eminent among. **8** (of a path, road, route) to provide with a means of reaching a place; (of a door, room) to give access to. **9** to live or cause to live (a certain kind of life). **10** to be the person who initiates and oversees (a discussion). **11** to direct by example (*lead the fashion*). **12** to be the principal player in (an orchestra) or the conductor of (a band). **13** to begin a round of cards with. **14** to conduct (a wire, rope etc.) along a particular course, esp. along a channel of some kind. **15** to phrase a question to (a witness) in such a way as to suggest the answer desired. **16** to be the main feature of (a newspaper or part of a newspaper). **17** to aim in front of (a moving target). ~*v.i.* **1** to go ahead, esp. to act as conductor or guide. **2** to be ahead of all the other competitors. **3** to be the commander, head or foremost person in any undertaking etc. **4** to go towards, to extend, to reach (to). **5** to tend (to) as a result. **6** (of a newspaper, news report) to have as its principal item. **7** in boxing, to make an attack (with); to use as one's habitual attacking hand. **8** to guide the movements of one's partner in a dance. **9** to be the first player in a game of cards to put down a card. ~*n.* **1** guidance, direction, esp. by going in front. **2** precedence, command, leadership. **3** a position ahead of all the others. **4** the distance or amount by which one is ahead. **5** a cord or strap for leading a dog. **6** an example for others to follow. **7** a clue. **8** the principal role in a play, film etc.; the person playing this role. **9** a principal conductor for distribution of current in an electrical installation. **10** in cards, the first play or the right to this. **11** the main story in a newspaper or news broadcast. **12** a way, passage, channel, esp. through ice. **13** an artificial watercourse, esp. a mill-race. **14** the direction in which a rope runs. **15** the distance advanced by a screw in one turn. **16** a boxer's habitual attacking punch. ~*a.* principal, chief, main, leading. **to lead astray** to lead into error, misbehaviour, crime or sin. **to lead by the nose** to cause to follow unthinkingly; to deceive. **to lead off 1** to make a start. **2** (*coll.*) to lose one's temper. **to lead on 1** to entice, to draw further towards some end. **2** to fool or trick. **to lead the way 1** to go first so as to point the way. **2** to take the precedence. **to lead up the garden path** (*coll.*) to mislead; to trick, to deceive. **to lead up to 1** to conduct conversation towards (some particular subject). **2** to conduct towards. **3** to pave the way for. **leadable** *a.* **leadin** *n.* **1** an introduction to a topic. **2** the electric conductor connecting a radio transmitter or receiver with an outside aerial or transmission cable. **lead-off** *n.* a start, a beginning. **lead time** *n.* the interval between the design and manufacture of a product. **led** *a.* under another's influence or leading.

Usage note The past tense *led* should not be spelt like the chemical element *lead* (pronounced the same).

lead[2] (led) *n.* **1** (*Chem.*) a soft malleable and ductile, bluish-grey, toxic heavy metal, at. no. 82, chem. symbol Pb, occurring naturally in galena and used in building, in alloys and paints and as a shield against radiation. **2** (*Chem.*) graphite, as used in lead pencils; a thin stick of this as the core of a pencil. **3** a plummet, usu. consisting of a mass of lead, used for sounding. **4** (*pl.*) strips of lead used for covering a roof. **5** (*pl.*) a roof, esp. a flat roof, or part of a roof, covered with lead. **6** (*pl.*) the metal strips or cames holding the glass in diamond-paned windows. **7** (*Print.*) a thin plate of type-metal used to separate lines; a space made by this means. ~*a.* **1**

of, relating to or containing lead. **2** consisting more or less of lead. ~*v.t.* **1** to cover, fasten, weight, frame or fit with lead. **2** to space out (as lines of type) by inserting leads. **3** to add a lead compound to. **like a lead balloon** utterly useless, a complete failure. **leaded** *a.* **leaden** *a.* **1** made of lead. **2** of the colour of lead, dark. **3** heavy as lead. **4** heavy, slow, burdensome. **leadenly** *adv.* **leadenness** *n.* **leaden seal** *n.* a stamped piece of lead. **lead-free** *a.* (of petrol) unleaded; not containing tetraethyl lead. **leading**[1] *n.* **1** strips of lead inserted between lines of print, leads. **2** the space introduced between lines of type by inserting leads. **3** the lead strips framing panes of glass or covering a roof. **leadless** *a.* **lead pencil** *n.* a pencil containing a strip of graphite. **lead poisoning** *n.* poisoning caused by the prolonged absorption of lead into the system. **lead shot** *n.* small pellets of lead used in quantity in the cartridge of a shotgun. **lead wool** *n.* a fibrous form of lead used in jointing water pipes. **leady** *a.*

leader (lē'də) *n.* **1** a person who or something which leads. **2** a chief, a commander. **3** (*Mus.*) the principal player or conductor of a band or group; the principal first violin of an orchestra; a conductor of an orchestra. **4** a chief editorial article in a newspaper. **5** a blank strip of film or tape preceding or following the recorded material. **6** (*pl.*, *Print.*) a row of dots to lead the eye across a page or column. **7** the terminal bud or shoot at the apex of a stem or branch. **8** the foremost horse, or one of the foremost horses abreast, in a team. **leader board** *n.* a scoreboard, esp. at a golf course, showing the names, positions etc. of the leading players in a tournament. **leaderene** (-rēn') *n.* (*facet.*) a female leader, esp. an autocratic one. **leaderless** *a.* **Leader of the House** *n.* in the House of Commons or House of Lords, a member of the government who has the responsibility for initiating legislative business. **leadership** *n.*

leading[1] LEAD[2].

leading[2] (lē'ding) *a.* **1** chief, main, principal. **2** in first position. **3** guiding, influential. ~*n.* guidance, influence. **leading aircraftman** *n.* a rank in the British Air Force below senior aircraftman. **leading aircraftwoman** *n.* a rank in the British Air Force below senior aircraftwoman. **leading article** *n.* a leader in a newspaper. **leading counsel** *n.* the senior of two or more barristers conducting a case. **leading edge** *n.* **1** on an aircraft, the foremost edge of an aerofoil (e.g. of a wing). **2** the forefront of something, esp. of technological advance. **3** the part of a pulse signal in which the amplitude increases. **leading-edge** *a.* **leading lady** *n.* the actress taking the chief role in a play, film etc. **leading light** *n.* **1** an expert in a particular field. **2** an influential or prominent member of a movement, group etc. **leading man** *n.* (*pl.* **leading men**) the actor taking the chief role in a play, film etc. **leading note** *n.* (*Mus.*) the seventh note of the major and minor

scales. **leading question** *n.* a question (esp. in cross-examination) that suggests a certain answer. **leading-rein** *n.* a rein for leading a horse by. **leading seaman** *n.* the most senior rank below that of a non-commissioned officer in the British navy.

leaf (lēf) *n.* (*pl.* **leaves** (lēvz)) **1** any of the usu. flat, green, lateral organs of plants which aid in the assimilation of food-materials and the transpiration and absorption of carbon dioxide from the atmosphere. **2** anything resembling this, esp. any similar plant structure, a petal, scale or sepal. **3** foliage. **4** a sheet of paper in a book or manuscript, usu. comprising two pages. **5** a thin sheet of metal or other material. **6** a hinged, sliding or detachable part of a bridge, door, table, shutter, screen etc. **7** a crop that is harvested in the form of leaves, esp. the leaves of tea or tobacco. **8** a foil or strip of metal forming part of a laminated material or structure. ~*v.i.* to shoot out or produce leaves or foliage. **in leaf** with its leaves out. **to leaf through** to turn the pages of a book, magazine etc., in a casual way, to browse through. **to take a leaf out of someone's book** to follow the example of, to imitate. **to turn over a new leaf** to change one's mode of life or conduct for the better. **leafage** *n.* foliage. **leafcutter** *n.* any of various insects (such as a bee or ant) which cut out sections of leaves. **leafed, leaved** *a.* **leaf green** *n.* the colour of green leaves, a light bright green. **leaf-green** *a.* **leafhopper** *n.* any of various jumping insects belonging to the superfamily Cicadelloidea that suck plant juices. **leaf insect** *n.* an insect having camouflaged wing covers resembling leaves. **leafless** *a.* **leaflessness** *n.* **leaflike** *a.* **leaf monkey** *n.* the langur. **leaf mould, leaf mold,** (*N Am.*) *n.* decayed leaves reduced to mould, forming a constituent of soil or used as compost. **leaf spring** *n.* a spring consisting of several broad, flat pieces of metal. **leaf-stalk** *n.* a petiole supporting a leaf. **leafy** *a.* **1** having, or covered with, leaves. **2** (of a place) pleasantly covered or shaded with or abounding in foliage. **3** like a leaf. **leafiness** *n.*

leaflet (lēf'lit) *n.* **1** a one-page handbill, circular etc.; a pamphlet. **2** a small leaf. **3** (*Bot.*) any of the primary divisions of a compound leaf. ~*v.i.* (*pres.p.* **leafleting,** *past*, *p.p.* **leafleted**) to distribute leaflets. **leafleter** *n.*

league[1] (lēg) *n.* **1** a combination or union for mutual help or protection or the pursuit of common interests. **2** a treaty or compact of alliance or confederation. **3** a category, class or group. **4** an association of clubs that play matches against one another. ~*v.i.* (*3rd pers. sing. pres.* **leagues,** *pres.p.* **leaguing,** *past*, *p.p.* **leagued**) to join in a league, to confederate, to combine together (with). **in league with** having formed an alliance with, usu. for a dubious purpose. **league football** *n.* (*Austral.*) Rugby League or Australian Rules football played in leagues. **leaguer** *n.* (*N Am.*) a league member. **league table** *n.* **1** a table of competitors in a league listed in order of performance. **2** a list showing the order of achievement, merit, performance etc.

league² (lēg) *n.* an old measure of distance, varying in different countries (in England usu. about three land or nautical miles, about 4.8 km).

leak (lēk) *v.i.* **1** to let liquid, gas etc. pass in or out through a hole, crevice or fissure. **2** (of a liquid, gas etc.) to pass in or out through a hole, crevice or fissure. **3** (of confidential information) to become known. ~*v.t.* **1** to cause or allow to enter or pass out. **2** to divulge (confidential information). ~*n.* **1** a crack, hole, puncture etc. which accidentally lets water, liquid, gas etc. in or out. **2** the oozing of water, fluid, gas etc. through such an opening. **3** a disclosure of confidential information. **4** a loss of electric current from a conductor; the current lost. **5** (*sl.*) an act of urinating. **to leak out** to become gradually known or public, esp. in an underhand manner. **leakage** *n.* **1** a leak. **2** the substance or quantity that escapes or enters by a leak. **leaker** *n.* **leaky** *a.* (*comp.* **leakier**, *superl.* **leakiest**) **1** having a leak or leaks. **2** apt to divulge confidential information. **leakiness** *n.*

lean¹ (lēn) *v.i.* (*past, p.p.* **leaned, leant** (lent)) **1** to incline one's body from an erect attitude. **2** to incline one's body so as to rest (against or upon). **3** to deviate from a straight or perpendicular line or direction. **4** to depend (upon) as for support. **5** to have a tendency or propensity (to or towards). ~*v.t.* **1** to cause to incline. **2** to support, to rest (upon or against). ~*n.* a leaning, inclination, slope or deviation. **to lean on** (*coll.*) to coerce, threaten (someone). **leaning** *n.* inclination, partiality, propensity (towards or to). **lean-to** *n.* (*pl.* **lean-tos**) a building with a roof supported by another building or wall.

lean² (lēn) *a.* **1** thin, without surplus fat or flesh, sinewy. **2** (of meat) not fat, consisting of muscular tissue. **3** meagre, of poor quality. **4** unproductive, unrewarding, unremunerative. **5** (of a fuel mixture) having a high or too high air content. **6** (of a mixture, compound) containing less of a major constituent than usual. ~*n.* the part of meat that consists of muscular tissue without fat. **lean-burn** *a.* (of an internal-combustion engine) designed to run on a lean mixture so as to reduce fuel consumption and exhaust emissions. **leanly** *adv.* **leanness** *n.*

leap (lēp) *v.i.* (*past, p.p.* **leapt** (lept), **leaped** (lept, lēpt)) **1** to jump, to spring upwards or forwards. **2** to act or react swiftly; to rush, to fly, to dart. **3** (of prices) to increase suddenly by a large amount. **4** to make a sudden transition. **5** to pass over an interval, esp. in music. ~*v.t.* **1** to jump or spring over or across. **2** to cause to jump or spring. **3** (*Mus.*) to pass from one note to another by an interval which is greater than a degree of the scale. **4** (of male animals) to copulate with. ~*n.* **1** the act of leaping, a jump, a spring, a

bound. **2** the space passed over by leaping. **3** a space or interval. **4** a sudden transition. **5** an increase. **to leap to the eye** to be very prominent or noticeable. **leaper** *n.* **leapfrog** *n.* **1** a game in which one person stoops down and another vaults over their back. **2** a form of movement or progression in which two or more people or things overtake each other in turns. ~*v.i.* (*pres.p.* **leapfrogging**, *past, p.p.* **leapfrogged**) **1** to vault in this way. **2** to progress. **leaping** *n.* **leapingly** *adv.* **leap in the dark** *n.* a hazardous step or action, one whose consequences cannot be foreseen. **leap year** *n.* an intercalary year of 366 days, which adds one day to February every four years (leap year is every year the number of which is a multiple of four, except those divisible by 100 and not by 400).

learn (lœn) *v.t.* (*past, p.p.* **learnt** (lœnt), **learned** (lœnt, lœnd)) **1** to acquire knowledge of or skill in by study, experience or instruction. **2** to fix in the memory. **3** to find out, to be informed of, to ascertain. ~*v.i.* **1** to acquire knowledge or skill. **2** to receive instruction. **to learn of** to find out, to ascertain, to be informed of. **learnable** *a.* **learned** (-nid) *a.* **1** having acquired learning by study, erudite. **2** skilled, skilful (in). **3** characterized by great learning or scholarship. **4** (of a word, journal etc.) chiefly used, read etc. by learned people. **5** used in courteous references to lawyers (*my learned friend; the learned judge*). **learnedly** *adv.* **learnedness** *n.* **learner** *n.* **learning** *n.* **1** the act of learning. **2** knowledge acquired by study, erudition, scholarship. **learning curve** *n.* **1** a person's rate of progress in acquiring knowledge or skill. **2** a graphic representation of this.

lease (lēs) *n.* **1** a letting or renting of land, houses, offices etc. for a specified period. **2** the written contract for, the term of or the rights of tenure under such letting. ~*v.t.* to grant or to take or hold under lease. **leasable** *a.* **leaseback** *n.* an arrangement whereby the seller of a property leases it back from the buyer. **leasehold** *n.* **1** tenure by lease. **2** property held by lease. ~*a.* held thus. **leaseholder** *n.*

leash (lēsh) *n.* a lead for a dog or other animal. ~*v.t.* to bind, hold or fasten (as) by a leash. **straining at the leash** anxious or impatient to begin.

least (lēst) *a.* **1** smallest, slightest. **2** less than all others in size, amount, degree, quantity, value, importance etc. ~*adv.* in the smallest or slightest degree. ~*n.* the smallest amount, degree etc. **at least 1** at any rate, whatever else may be said on the subject. **2** if nothing else. **3** at the minimum. **at the least** at the minimum. **in the least** in the slightest degree, at all. **to say the least** not to put in stronger terms; without any exaggeration. **least common denominator** *n.* LOWEST COMMON DENOMINATOR (under LOW¹). **least common multiple** *n.* LOWEST COMMON MULTIPLE (under LOW¹). **leastways** *adv.* **1** at least. **2** or rather.

Usage note *The least* should not be used in comparisons of two: the correct form for two is *the less.*

leather (ledh´ə) *n.* **1** the tanned or dressed skin or hide of an animal. **2** dressed hides collectively. **3** an article or part made of leather (*often in comb.*, as *stirrup-leather*); a piece of leather used for polishing. **4** (*pl.*) leather clothes, esp. for wearing on a motorcycle, or a pair of leather breeches or leggings. **5** (*sl.*) a cricket ball or football. ~*a.* made of leather. ~*v.t.* **1** to cover or furnish with leather. **2** to polish with a leather. **3** to thrash, as with a leather strap. **leatherback** *n.* a leathery, soft-shelled turtle, *Dermochelys coriacea.* **leatherette** (-ret´) *n.* a kind of imitation leather. **leatherjacket** *n.* **1** the tough-skinned larva of a crane-fly. **2** any of various marine fishes of the families Carangidae and Balistidae which have tough skins. **leathery** *a.* **1** like leather. **2** (esp. of meat) tough. **leatheriness** *n.*

leave[1] (lēv) *v.t.* (*past, p.p.* **left** (left)) **1** to go or depart from, to quit. **2** to allow to remain when one departs, to go without taking, often accidentally. **3** to cease to live or work at or belong to. **4** to withdraw from, to forsake, to abandon. **5** to bequeath. **6** to be survived by. **7** to refrain from removing, consuming or interfering with. **8** to desist from, to cease, to discontinue. **9** to commit, to entrust, to refer for consideration, approval etc. **10** to depute (a person) to carry out a task. **11** to deposit (an object, message) to be collected, delivered, dealt with. **12** to deposit or allow to remain in a particular state (*left a trail of mud*). **13** to cause to be or remain in a particular state (*left the door ajar*). **14** to move on beyond (a landmark) in a particular direction relative to its position (*leave the town hall on your right*). **15** to have as a remainder (after subtraction, division). ~*v.i.* **1** to depart, to go away. **2** (esp. as a command to a dog) to cease, to discontinue. **to leave alone 1** not to interfere with. **2** to have no dealings with. **to leave be** to avoid disturbing or interfering with. **to leave behind 1** to go away without. **2** to outstrip. **3** to leave as a record, mark, consequence etc. **to leave go** to let go. **to leave it at that** not to do or say any more. **to leave off 1** to stop, to cease. **2** to desist from, to discontinue. **3** to cease to wear. **to leave out** to omit. **to leave over** to leave for future consideration etc. **to leave someone to themselves** to refrain strictly from interfering with, approaching, becoming involved with etc. **leaver** *n.* **leaving** *n.* **1** the act of departing. **2** (*pl.*) residue, remnant, refuse, offal.

leave[2] (lēv) *n.* **1** permission. **2** (*also* **leave of absence**) permission to be absent from duty. **3** the period of this. **4** the act of departing, a formal parting, a farewell, an adieu. **5** a holiday. **by/ with your leave** (*often iron.*) with your permission. **on leave 1** absent from duty by permission. **2** on holiday. **to take leave of one's senses**

to think or act contrary to reason. **to take leave to** (*formal*) to venture to, to be so bold as to. **to take (one's) leave 1** to say goodbye. **2** to depart. **leave-taking** *n.* **1** a parting. **2** a farewell.

leaven (lev´ən) *n.* **1** fermenting dough or any other substance (e.g. yeast) mixed with other dough, a batter etc. in order to cause fermentation and make it lighter. **2** any influence tending to cause a general change. **3** a tincture or admixture (of). ~*v.t.* **1** to raise and make light (as) with leaven. **2** to imbue, to pervade with an influence causing change. **3** to temper (with). **leavening** *n.* **leaven.**

leaves LEAF.

Lebanese (lebənēz´) *a.* of, relating or belonging to the Mediterranean country of Lebanon. ~*n.* (*pl.* **Lebanese**) **1** a native or inhabitant of Lebanon. **2** (*as pl.*) the people of the Lebanon.

lech LECHER.

lecher (lech´ə) *n.* a man who continually lusts after or seduces women. **lech, letch** *v.i.* (*sl.*) **1** to lust (after). **2** to act lecherously. ~*n.* **1** a lecher. **2** a strong desire, esp. a sexual one. **lecherous** *a.* feeling or motivated by strong sexual desire. **lecherously** *adv.* **lecherousness** *n.* **lechery** *n.* promiscuous and unrestrained sexual desire or activity.

lecithin (les´ithin) *n.* a nitrogenous fatty substance containing phosphorus found in the cellular tissue of animal and vegetable bodies.

lectern (lek´tən) *n.* **1** a reading desk or stand for a book from which parts of a church service, esp. the lessons, are said or sung. **2** any similar reading desk.

lectin (lek´tin) *n.* any of various usu. plant-derived proteins that bind to specific carbohydrate groups and cause agglutination of specific cell types.

lector (lek´tə) *n.* **1** a person whose duty it is to read the lessons in church services. **2** a university teacher, esp. one employed in a foreign university to give tuition in their native language. **lectrice** (-trēs´) *n.* a female lector at a university.

lecture (lek´chə) *n.* **1** a formal expository or instructive discourse on any subject, before an audience or a class. **2** a reproof, a reprimand. ~*v.i.* **1** to deliver a lecture or lectures. **2** to give instruction by means of lectures. ~*v.t.* **1** to reprimand, to talk seriously to. **2** to instruct by lectures. **lecturer** *n.* a person who gives lectures, esp. at a university. **lectureship** *n.* the academic office of a lecturer.

LED *abbr.* light-emitting diode. **LED display** *n.* a flat screen display, as in pocket calculators, digital clocks and watches etc., that uses light-emitting diodes.

led LEAD[1].

ledge (lej) *n.* **1** a shelf or shelflike projection. **2** a shelf-like ridge or outcrop of rock on a cliff or mountain. **ledged** *a.* **ledgy** *a.*

ledger (lej´ə) *n.* the principal book in a set of

account-books, in which a record of all trade transactions is entered. **ledger line** *n.* **1** (*Mus.*) (*also* **leger line**) in musical notation, an additional short line above or below the stave to express ascending or descending notes. **2** a fishing line with ledger tackle. **ledger tackle** *n.* a type of fishing tackle in which a lead weight keeps the bait on the bottom.

lee (lē) *n.* **1** shelter, protection. **2** the side or quarter opposite to that against which the wind blows. **3** the sheltered side (cp. *windward side*, *weather side*). **lee-board** *n.* a board let down on the lee side of a flat-bottomed vessel to prevent a leeward drift. **lee shore** *n.* the shore on the lee side of a vessel. **lee side** *n.* the lee of a vessel. **leeward** (-wəd, loo´əd) *a.* relating to, in or facing the lee side. **~***adv.* towards the lee side. **~***n.* the lee side or direction. **leeway** *n.* **1** the leeward drift of a vessel. **2** allowable scope, toleration inside defined limits. **3** a safety margin. **to make up leeway** to recover lost ground or time.

leech (lēch) *n.* **1** an aquatic annelid worm of the suctorial order Hirudinea, employed for the local extraction of blood. **2** someone who clings tenaciously to someone else. **3** someone who abstracts or absorbs the gains of others. **like a leech** persistently, tenaciously.

leek (lēk) *n.* a culinary vegetable, *Allium porrum*, allied to the onion, with a straight green stem that unfurls as overlapping leaves and a small, white cylindrical bulb, the national emblem of Wales.

leer (liə) *n.* **1** an oblique, sly or arch look. **2** a look expressing a feeling of malice, lasciviousness or triumph. **~***v.i.* to look with a leer. **leering** *n.*, *a.* **leeringly** *adv.* **leery** *a.* (*comp.* **leerier**, *superl.* **leeriest**) knowing, sly. **to be leery of** to be wary of. **leeriness** *n.*

lees (lēz) *n.pl.* **1** the sediment of liquor which settles to the bottom. **2** dregs, refuse.

left¹ (left) *a.* **1** of, relating to or situated on the side that is to the west when a person faces south, as opposed to *right*. **2** correspondingly situated in relation to the front or the direction of anything. **3** (*also* **Left**) radical, politically innovative. **4** (*also* **Left**) of or relating to socialism or communism. **~***adv.* on or towards the left. **~***n.* **1** the side opposite to the right. **2** the left hand. **3** a left-handed blow. **4** the left foot. **5** the left wing of an army. **6** (*also* **Left**) the progressive, democratic or socialist party, wing or faction (which originally sat on the left of the president in a legislative assembly). **left-back** *n.* in football, hockey etc., a defender who plays primarily on the left side of the pitch. **left field** *n.* in baseball, the third of the outfield to the left and in front of a batter facing the pitcher; the position of a fielder defending this area. **left-footed** *a.* **1** using the left foot by preference (e.g. for kicking). **2** made with the left foot. **left hand** *n.* the left side, direction or region. **left-hand** *a.* **1** situated on or relating to the left side. **2** executed by the left

hand. **3** twisted or turning anticlockwise. **left-handed** *a.* **1** using the left hand more readily than the right. **2** designed or made for the left hand. **3** performed with the left hand; (of a blow) delivered with the left hand. **4** turning from right to left; turning anticlockwise. **5** awkward, clumsy, stupid. **6** insincere, malicious, sinister. **7** ambiguous, equivocal. **left-handedly** *adv.* **left-handedness** *n.* **left-hander** *n.* a left-handed person or a left-handed blow. **leftism** *n.* the policies and principles of the political left. **leftist** *n.*, *a.* **leftmost** *a.* situated furthest to the left. **leftward** *adv.*, *a.* **leftwards** *adv.* **left wing** *n.* **1** the more radical or liberal wing of a political party. **2** the left side of a sports pitch; (the position of) an attacking player. **3** the part of an army massed on the left side of a battle position. **left-wing** *a.* **left-winger** *n.* **lefty, leftie** *n.* (*derog.*) a left-winger, a leftist. **~***a.* left-wing.

left² (left) *a.* that has been discarded or laid aside. **to be left at the post** to be left far behind at the beginning of a race, contest; to be beaten by a wide margin. **to be left for dead** to be assumed to be dead and consequently abandoned. **to be left with 1** to retain (an impression, feeling) as a result of usu. lengthy exposure to something. **2** to have to deal with after an event. **left luggage** *n.* **1** luggage deposited temporarily, esp. at a railway station etc. **2** a left-luggage office. **left-luggage office** *n.* a place where luggage can be temporarily deposited for a small charge. **leftover** *n.* (*usu. pl.*) a remainder, esp. of uneaten food. **~***a.* surplus, unused.

left³ LEAVE¹.

leg (leg) *n.* **1** each of the limbs by which humans and other mammals walk, esp. the part from the knee to the ankle. **2** the analogous member in other species. **3** an animal's hind leg (esp. the upper portion) which is eaten as meat. **4** the part of a garment that covers the leg. **5** anything resembling a leg in form or function. **6** each of a set of posts or rods supporting a table, bed, chair etc. **7** a branch of a forked object, a limb of a pair of compasses etc. **8** a stage in a long-distance flight, journey, race etc. **9** in a contest, one of two or more events, games, rounds etc. **10** the distance run by any one of the runners in a relay race. **11** a single game in darts. **12** (*Naut.*) the course and distance run by a vessel on one tack. **13** in cricket, the leg side, esp. the part on a level with and behind the batsman's stumps. **~***a.* in cricket, fielding on or struck towards the leg side. **leg before** (*coll.*) leg before wicket. **leg before wicket** a grounds for dismissal in cricket, stoppage by the batsman's leg of a ball when it would have hit the wicket. **not to have a leg to stand on** to have no support or basis for one's position (e.g. in a controversy). **on one's (hind) legs** standing up, esp. in order to make a speech. **to get one's leg over** (*sl.*) (of a man) to have sexual intercourse. **to leg it 1** (*coll.*) to run away. **2** (*coll.*) to run, hurry. **3** (*coll.*) to go on foot. **to pull**

someone's leg 1 to hoax, to make a fool of. **2** to tease. **to shake a leg** (*often int.*) to hurry up. **to show a leg 1** to get out of bed. **2** to make an appearance. **to stretch one's legs/ a leg** to take exercise, esp. after inactivity. **leg-break** *n.* in cricket, a ball which breaks from the leg side towards the off. **leg-bye** *n.* in cricket, a run scored for a ball that touches the batsman anywhere on the body except the hand and does not touch the bat. **legged** *a.* **legging** *n.* **1** (*pl.*) thick footless tights or close-fitting trousers for women and children. **2** an additional outer covering, often of leather, for the legs. **leggy** *a.* (*comp.* **leggier,** *superl.* **leggiest**) **1** (*coll.*) having long legs. **2** (of a woman) having long, shapely legs. **3** (of plants) spindly. **legginess** *n.* **leg-iron** *n.* a fetter for the leg. **legless** (-lis) *a.* **1** without legs. **2** (*coll.*) very drunk. **legman, legwoman** *n.* (*pl.* **legmen, legwomen**) **1** (*N Am.*) a reporter who visits the scene of a news story, interviews people involved etc. **2** a person who is employed to do jobs such as running errands and gathering information, away from their employer's offices. **leg-of-mutton** *a.* (of a sleeve etc.) shaped like a leg of mutton, wider or fuller at the top and narrow or close-fitting at the bottom. **leg-of-mutton sail** *n.* a triangular mainsail. **leg-over** *n.* (*taboo sl.*) an act of sexual intercourse (of a man, with a woman). **leg-pull** *n.* a hoax. **leg-pulling** *n.* **legroom** *n.* space for the legs (e.g. in a car). **leg side** *n.* in cricket, that half of the field, divided by a line running between the wickets, which a batsman's body is facing away from in the usual sideways-on stance. **leg spin** *n.* in cricket, spin applied by the bowler to make the ball turn from the leg side towards the off. **leg-spinner** *n.* **1** in cricket, a bowler who uses leg spin. **2** a ball bowled with leg spin. **leg-up** *n.* **1** assistance, usu. a hand under the foot, in mounting a horse, climbing onto something etc. **2** a boost; a piece of practical assistance. **legwarmers** *n.pl.* long footless stockings usu. worn to cover the lower leg, rolled down over other garments. **legwork** *n.* **1** work involving much travel on foot. **2** groundwork.

☒ **legable** common misspelling of LEGIBLE.

legacy (leg′əsi) *n.* (*pl.* **legacies**) **1** a bequest, money or property bequeathed by will. **2** anything left or handed on by a predecessor. **legatee** (-te′) *n.* a person to whom a legacy is bequeathed. **legator** (-gā′-) *n.* a person who leaves a legacy.

legal (lē′gəl) *a.* **1** of, relating to, or according to law. **2** lawful, legitimate, recognized or sanctioned by the law. **3** appointed or laid down by the law. **4** concerned with the law; characteristic of lawyers. **5** recognized, enforceable or having a remedy in law rather than equity. **legal aid** *n.* financial assistance for legal proceedings granted by the state to those with low incomes. **legalese** *n.* the (obscure or convoluted) language of legal documents. **legal fiction** *n.* a fact or point of law that is probably no

longer true or valid but is assumed to be so to serve some useful, esp. legal purpose. **legalism** *n.* **1** strict adherence to law and formulas. **2** respect for the letter rather than the spirit of religious or ethical laws. **legalist** *n.* **legalistic** (-lis′-) *a.* **legalistically** *adv.* **legality** (ligal′-) *n.* (*pl.* **legalities**) **1** lawfulness. **2** legalism. **3** (*pl.*) obligations under the law. **legalize, legalise** *v.t.* **1** to make lawful. **2** to bring into harmony with the law. **legalization** (-zā′shən) *n.* **legally** *adv.* **legal proceedings** *n.* steps in the prosecution of an action at law. **legal tender** *n.* money which a creditor is bound to accept in discharge of a debt.

legate (leg′ət) *n.* **1** a papal emissary. **2** a lieutenant or deputy attached to a Roman general or governor. **legateship** *n.* **legatine** (-tīn) *a.* **legation** (ligā′shən) *n.* **1** a diplomatic mission headed by a minister. **2** the official residence or office of a diplomatic minister. **3** a body of delegates. **4** the act of sending someone as legate or deputy. **5** a legateship.

legatee LEGACY.

legato (ligah′tō) *adv., a.* (*Mus.*) in an even gliding manner without a break. ~*n.* (*pl.* **legatos**) **1** this style of playing. **2** a legato passage.

legator LEGACY.

legend (lej′ənd) *n.* **1** a traditional story, esp. one popularly accepted as true. **2** a myth, a fable. **3** traditional or non-historical storytelling or literature. **4** a person who is renowned for outstanding deeds or qualities, whether real or fictitious etc. **5** an inscription on a coat of arms or round the field of a medal or coin. **6** a caption to an illustration; a key to a map, table etc. **legendary** *a.* **1** of or relating to legend. **2** celebrated in legend. **3** famous or notorious enough to be a subject of legend. **legendry** *n.*

legerdemain (lejədimān′) *n.* **1** sleight of hand, a trick in which the eye is deceived by the quickness of the hand, conjuring. **2** jugglery, sophistry.

leger line LEDGER LINE (under LEDGER).

legging, leggy LEG.

legible (lej′ibəl) *a.* **1** clear enough to be read. **2** easily decipherable. **legibleness, legibility** (-bil′-) *n.* **legibly** *adv.*

legion (lē′jən) *n.* **1** a division of the ancient Roman army, varying, at different periods, from 3000 to 6000 men. **2** a military force, esp. in France and other foreign countries. **3** a host, a vast army or multitude. **legionary** *a.* of or relating to a legion or legions. ~*n.* (*pl.* **legionaries**) a soldier of a legion. **legionnaire** (-neə′) *n.* **1** a member of a foreign legion. **2** a member of the British or American Legions. **legionnaire's disease** *n.* a serious, sometimes fatal, bacterial disease resembling pneumonia, caused by *Legionella pneumophila* (so named because of its occurrence at an American Legion convention in 1976).

legislate (lej′islāt) *v.i.* **1** to make or enact a law or laws. **2** to make allowance or provision (for).

legislation (-lā´shən) n. 1 the act or process of making laws. 2 laws or prospective laws. **legislative** (lej´islətiv, -lātiv) a. 1 enacting laws. 2 having power to legislate. 3 enacted by or relating to legislation. **legislatively** adv. **legislator** n. 1 a lawgiver. 2 a member of a legislative assembly. **legislature** (-ləchə) n. a body of people in which is vested the power or right to enact, alter, repeal or suspend laws.

legit (lijit´) a. (coll.) short for LEGITIMATE¹. ~n. 1 the legitimate theatre. 2 an actor in the legitimate theatre.

legitimate¹ (lijit´imət) a. 1 lawful, legal, properly authorized. 2 born to parents who are lawfully married. 3 (of descent) through a legitimate person. 4 (of a title to sovereignty) derived from strict hereditary right. 5 proper, regular, natural. 6 conformable to accepted standards or usage. 7 following by logical sequence. 8 of or relating to formal or serious theatre rather than television, cinema, variety etc. **legitimacy** n. **legitimately** adv. **legitimation** (-ā´shən) n. **legitimatize**, **legitimatise** v.t. to legitimize. **legitimatization** (-zā´shən) n. **legitimism** n. 1 support for the principle of hereditary monarchical government. 2 support for a monarch or pretender (esp. formerly in France and Spain) whose claim is based on hereditary descent or primogeniture. **legitimist** n., a. **legitimize**, **legitimise** v.t. to render legitimate. **legitimization** (-zā´shən) n.

legitimate² (lijit´imāt) v.t. 1 to make, pronounce or prove legitimate or legitimately born. 2 to justify, to serve as justification for.

Lego® (leg´ō) n. a building toy mainly consisting of connecting plastic bricks.

legume (leg´ūm) n. 1 the fruit or pod of a leguminous plant, usu. dehiscent along its face and back, and bearing its seeds on either margin of the ventral suture (as the pod of the pea). 2 a leguminous plant. **leguminous** (-gū´-) a. of or relating to the Leguminosae, an order of herbs, shrubs and trees, including the peas and beans, that produce seed in pods.

lei¹ (lā´i) n. a garland or necklace of flowers.

lei² LEU.

Leicester (les´tə) n. a type of usu. orange-coloured cheese resembling cheddar.

leisure (lezh´ə) n. 1 freedom from business, occupation or hurry. 2 time at one's own disposal, unoccupied time. 3 opportunity, convenience. ~a. unoccupied, free, idle. **at leisure** 1 not busy or occupied. 2 without hurry. 3 deliberately. **at one's leisure** when one has the time, at one's convenience. **leisure centre**, (N Am.) **leisure center** n. a complex containing facilities for sports, entertainments, meetings etc. **leisured** a. having a great deal of leisure. **leisureless** a. **leisurely** a. done at a slow, unhurried pace; relaxed. ~adv. without haste. **leisureliness** n. **leisurewear** n. casual clothing.

leitmotiv (līt´mōtēf), **leitmotif** n. (Mus.) a leading, representative or recurring theme in a

composition, orig. a musical theme invariably associated with a certain person, situation or idea throughout an opera etc.

lek¹ (lek) n. the chief currency of Albania.

lek² (lek) n. an area where certain species of birds (esp. black grouse) assemble for sexual display and courtship.

LEM abbr. lunar excursion module.

lemming (lem´ing) n. 1 a small Arctic volelike rodent of the genus Lemmus and related genera, esp. the Scandinavian variety L. lemmus which migrates in very large numbers when its population reaches a peak, often attempts to cross large areas of water and is popularly supposed to be prone to mass suicide. 2 someone who joins a mass movement or dashes headlong into situations without forethought.

lemon (lem´ən) n. 1 the oval, acid, yellow-skinned fruit of the lemon tree. 2 (also **lemon tree**) the small Asian evergreen tree, Citrus limon, bearing this. 3 the pale yellow colour of a lemon. 4 (sl.) a person who or something which is disappointing, unpleasant, useless. ~a. 1 of or relating to the lemon. 2 of the colour of a lemon. 3 lemon-flavoured. **lemonade** (-nād´) n. lemon juice or flavouring mixed with still or aerated water and sweetened. **lemon balm** n. a common bushy plant, Melissa officinalis, whose leaves smell and taste of lemon. **lemon cheese**, **lemon curd** n. a spread made from lemon, butter, eggs and sugar. **lemon drop** n. a lemon-flavoured hard sweet. **lemon geranium** n. a pelargonium, Pelargonium crispum, with lemon-scented leaves. **lemon grass** n. a lemon-scented hardy grass of the tropical genus Cymbopogon which yields an essential oil. **lemon plant** n. LEMON VERBENA (under LEMON). **lemon squash** n. a sweet concentrated lemon drink. **lemon squeezer** n. a device for extracting juice from lemons. **lemon thyme** n. Thymus citriodorus which has lemon-scented leaves. **lemon verbena** n. a S American shrub, Aloysia triphylla, cultivated for its lemon-scented foliage. **lemony** a.

lemon sole (lem´ən), **lemon dab** n. a flatfish, Microstomus kitt, with brown markings, valued as a food.

lempira (lempiə´rə) n. the standard monetary unit of Honduras, equivalent to 100 centavos.

lemur (lē´mə) n. (pl. lemurs) any member of a genus of arboreal nocturnal animals allied to the monkeys, having pointed snouts, long tails and occurring naturally only in Madagascar.

lend (lend) v.t. (past, p.p. lent (lent)) 1 to grant for temporary use. 2 to grant the use of on condition of repayment or compensation. 3 to let out (money) at interest. 4 to furnish, to contribute, esp. for temporary service. ~v.i. to make loans. **to lend itself to** to have the right qualities for, to be appropriate for using as. **to lend oneself to** to give support to. **lendable** a. **lender** n. **lending** n. **lending library** n. a library from which books can be borrowed freely or for a subscription.

length (length) *n.* **1** measure or extent from end to end, as distinct from breadth or thickness. **2** the longest line that can be drawn from one extremity of anything to the other. **3** extent of time, duration, long continuance. **4** the extent from beginning to end of something, such as a book. **5** the distance anything extends. **6** a definite portion of the linear extent of anything, such as a piece of cloth, pipe or timber. **7** (*usu. pl.*) extent or degree of action, thoroughness etc. **8** in prosody, the quantity of a vowel or syllable. **9** in cricket, the distance traversed by a bowled ball before it strikes the ground; the most desirable or effective distance for this. **10** in racing, the linear measure of the body of a horse, boat etc. **11** the length of a swimming pool as a distance swum. **12** the extent of a piece of clothing measured vertically. **13** the full extent of a person's body. **at length 1** to the full extent, in full detail. **2** at last. **to go to any length/ lengths 1** to stop at no obstacle. **2** to be restrained by no scruples. **to go to great lengths** to take great care, to go to a great deal of trouble. **lengthen** *v.t.* to make long or longer. ~*v.i.* to grow longer. **lengthener** *n.* **lengthways, lengthwise** *adv., a.* along or in the direction of its length. **lengthy** *a.* (*comp.* **lengthier,** *superl.* **lengthiest**) long and usu. tedious. **lengthily** *adv.* **lengthiness** *n.*

Usage note Pronunciation as (lenth) is best avoided.

lenient (lē´niənt) *a.* **1** merciful, tending not to be strict or punish severely. **2** (of a punishment) mild, gentle. **lenience, leniency** *n.* **leniently** *adv.* **lenitive** (len´-) *a.* **1** (*Med.*) soothing, palliative. **2** having the power or quality of softening or mitigating. ~*n.* (*Med.*) a lenitive medicine or application. **lenity** (len´-) *n.* (*pl.* **lenities**) **1** the fact of being lenient. **2** (*formal*) a merciful act.

Leninism (len´inizm) *n.* the political and economic theories of Lenin; Marxism as modified by Lenin. **Leninist, Leninite** *a., n.*

lenitive, lenity LENIENT.

lens (lenz) *n.* (*pl.* **lenses**) **1** (*Physics*) **a** a piece of transparent substance, usu. glass, with one or both surfaces curved so as to change the direction of rays of light, and diminish or increase the apparent size of objects viewed through it. **b** a device for converging beams of electrons and other charged particles. **c** a device for directing sound waves. **2** a combination of lenses used to focus a beam of light or form an image. **3** a contact lens. **4** (*Anat.*) the crystalline body in the eye through which rays of light are focused on the retina. **lensed** *a.* **lens hood** *n.* a projecting device that shields the lens of a camera from direct sunlight. **lensless** *a.* **lensman** *n.* (*pl.* **lensmen**) a cameraman.

Lent (lent) *n.* a period of 40 days (excluding Sundays) from Ash Wednesday to Easter Eve, observed in the Christian Church as a season of penitence and fasting in commemoration of Christ's fasting in the wilderness. **lenten** *a.* of, relating to or used in Lent. **Lenten fare** *n.* a meatless diet. **Lent lily** *n.* the daffodil.

lent LEND.

-lent (lənt) *suf.* forming adjectives, such as *violent, redolent.*

lenticel (len´tisel) *n.* (*Bot.*) a lens-shaped mass of cells in the bark of a plant, through which respiration takes place.

lenticular (lentik´ūlə) *a.* **1** resembling in shape a lentil or doubly convex lens. **2** of or relating to the lens of the eye.

lentil (len´təl) *n.* **1** a small branching leguminous plant, *Lens culinaris.* **2** any of the seeds of this plant, largely used for food.

lento (len´tō) *a., adv.* (*Mus.*) (to be played) slowly.

Leo (lē´ō) *n.* **1** (*Astron.*) one of the 12 zodiacal constellations, the Lion. **2** (*Astrol.*) **a** the fifth sign of the zodiac, which the sun passes through between approx. 23 July and 22 August. **b** a person born under this sign. **Leonid** (-nid) *n.* any of the meteors that appear in numbers radiating from the constellation Leo. **leonine** (-nīn) *a.* **1** of, relating to or like a lion. **2** majestic, undaunted. **3** (*also* **Leonine**) of or relating to one of the Popes Leo, esp. Leo I.

leone (lēō´ni) *n.* the standard monetary unit of Sierra Leone, equivalent to 100 cents.

leopard (lep´əd) *n.* **1** a large mammal, *Panthera pardus,* of the cat family from Africa and S Asia, having a pale fawn to tan coat with dark spots; the panther. **2** a leopard-like animal, such as the jaguar, the cheetah, or the ounce. **leopardess** *n.* a female leopard. **leopard's bane** *n.* a plant of the composite genus *Doronicum* with large yellow flowers.

leotard (lē´ətahd) *n.* a close-fitting garment resembling a swimsuit, though sometimes having legs and sleeves, worn during exercise, dance practice etc.

leper (lep´ə) *n.* **1** a person affected with leprosy. **2** a person who is deliberately avoided by others. **leprosarium** (-prəseə´riəm) *n.* (*pl.* **leprosaria** (-riə)) a leper hospital. **leprosy** (-rəsi) *n.* **1** a chronic contagious bacterial disease, usu. characterized by the formation of tubercles or of painful inflamed nodules beneath the skin, thickening of the skin, loss of feeling, and ulceration and necrosis of the affected parts. **2** moral corruption. **leprous** *a.* **1** suffering from leprosy. **2** resembling leprosy.

lepidopteran (lepidop´tərən) *n.* any member of an order of insects, Lepidoptera, characterized by having four wings clothed with minute powder-like scales, containing the butterflies and moths. ~*a.* of, relating or belonging to this order. **lepidopterist** *n.* **lepidopterous** *a.*

leprechaun (lep´rəkawn) *n.* in Irish folklore, a brownie or dwarfish sprite who performs domestic tasks, mends shoes etc.

lepton[1] (lep´ton) *n.* (*pl.* **lepta** (-tə)) a modern

Greek coin and monetary unit worth one-hundredth of a drachma.

lepton² (lep'ton) *n.* (*pl.* **leptons**) (*Physics*) any of various elementary particles (e.g. electron, muon) that participate only in weak interaction.

lesbian (lez'biən) *n.* a female homosexual. ~*a.* of or relating to lesbians or homosexuality in women. **lesbianism** *n.*

lese-majesty (lēzmaj'əsti), **lèse-majesté** (lāzmazh'əstā) *n.* **1** an offence against the sovereign power or its representative, high treason. **2** an insult to a ruler or authority. **3** presumption.

lesion (lē'zhən) *n.* **1** (*Med.*) physical change in a tissue or organ due to injury. **2** a hurt, an injury. **3** damage.

less (les) *a.* **1** not so much. **2** of smaller size, extent, amount, degree, importance, rank etc. **3** (*coll.*) fewer. ~*prep.* minus, with deduction of. ~*adv.* **1** in a smaller or lower degree. **2** not so much. ~*n.* **1** a smaller part, quantity or number. **2** the smaller, the inferior, the junior etc., of things compared. **3** (*coll.*) enough. **in less than no time** (*facet.*) very quickly; very soon. **less and less** gradually diminishing. **much less** used to introduce an alternative which is even less the case (*I've never met him, much less gone out with him*). **still less** used to introduce an alternative, much less. **lessen** *v.t.* to make less in size, extent, number, quantity or degree. ~*v.i.* to become less in size, extent, number, degree or quantity. **lesser** *a.* **1** less, smaller. **2** inferior. **Lesser Bairam** *n.* the three-day Muslim festival which falls at the end of Ramadan. **lesser-known** *a.* not so well-known as others of the type.

Usage note The use of *less* rather than *fewer* with countable nouns is sometimes disapproved of. Strictly you should have *less trouble* or *fewer troubles*, and buy *six items or fewer*, rather than *six items or less*.

-less (lis) *suf.* devoid of, free from, as in *fearless, godless, sinless, tireless.*

lessee (lesē') *n.* a person to whom a lease is granted. **lesseeship** *n.*

lesson (les'ən) *n.* **1** the amount or duration of instruction given to a pupil or pupils at one time. **2** the time allocated for a period of instruction in a timetable. **3** (*pl.*) a course of instruction (in any subject). **4** an assignment or exercise set for a pupil by a teacher, esp. a portion of a book to be read or studied. **5** an occurrence or example taken as a warning or caution. **6** knowledge gained from such examples or from experience. **7** a portion of Scripture read in divine service. **to learn one's lesson** to gain wisdom or learn prudence as a result of usu. bitter experience. **to teach someone a lesson** to show someone, esp. by punishing them, that something is unwise, wrong etc.

lessor (les'ə) *n.* a person who grants a lease.

lest (lest) *conj.* **1** for fear that, in case, so that (one

may) not. **2** (after words expressing alarm, anxiety etc.) that.

let¹ (let) *v.t.* (*pres.p.* **letting**, *past, p.p.* **let**) **1** to permit, to allow, to suffer (to be or do). **2** to give leave to. **3** to cause to. **4** to grant the use, occupation or possession of for a stipulated sum, to lease. **5** to give out on contract. **6** to allow or cause (gas or liquid) to escape from. ~*v.aux.* used in the imperative mood, with the force of prayer, exhortation, assumption, permission or command. ~*v.i.* to be let or leased for rent. ~*n.* a letting. **let alone 1** not to mention. **2** much less. **to let available** for renting. **to let alone 1** not to interfere with. **2** not to do or deal with. **3** not to mention. **to let be** not to interfere with. **to let down 1** to allow to sink or fall. **2** to fail or disappoint (someone). **3** to make (a garment) longer by lowering the hem. **4** to deflate. **5** to untie (hair) and allow to hang loose. **to let down gently** to avoid humiliating or causing too great distress or disappointment to. **to let drop/ fall 1** to drop. **2** to mention by accident, or as if by accident. **to let go 1** to release. **2** to relinquish hold of. **3** to cease to retain. **4** to dismiss from the mind. **to let in 1** to allow to enter. **2** to insert. **3** to inlay. **to let in for** to involve (someone) in something unpleasant, difficult etc. **to let in on** to allow to be involved in or to profit from. **to let into 1** to allow to enter. **2** to allow to have knowledge of. **3** to set within another surface. **to let loose 1** to free from restraint, to release. **2** to utter abruptly and violently. **3** to discharge, to fire off, to unleash abruptly. **to let off 1** to refrain from punishing or to punish lightly. **2** to excuse or dispense from. **3** to discharge, to fire off (an arrow, gun etc.); to detonate (a bomb, firework). **4** to allow to alight or disembark. **5** to allow or cause (air, liquid) to escape from. **6** to rent out (part of a building). **to let on 1** to divulge, to let out. **2** to pretend. **to let oneself go 1** to give way to any impulse. **2** to lose interest in maintaining one's appearance. **to let oneself in** to use one's own key to enter a building. **to let out 1** to open the door for. **2** to allow to go out. **3** to free from restraint. **4** to divulge. **5** to utter, emit, give vent to. **6** to enlarge or make less tight-fitting. **7** to lease or let on hire. **8** to allow (air, liquid) to escape. **9** to exculpate. **to let slip 1** to allow to escape. **2** to lose, to miss. **3** to reveal inadvertently. **to let through 1** to allow to pass. **2** to overlook, to fail to correct, emend etc. **to let up** to become less (severe), to abate. **to let up on** to treat less harshly; to stop harassing, pressing etc. **let-down** *n.* **1** a disappointment. **2** the release of milk from a cow's udder or a mammary gland. **let-off** *n.* (*coll.*) an instance of escaping from a threatening danger or punishment. **let-out** *n.* (*coll.*) an opportunity to escape or avoid something. **letting** *n.* a property that is to let or that has been let. **let-up** *n.* (*coll.*) **1** an abatement, a lessening of intensity. **2** a reduction in effort.

let² (let) *n.* **1** in tennis etc., a stoppage, hindrance etc., requiring the ball to be served again. **2** a rally or service affected by this. **3** †a hindrance, an obstacle.

-let (lit) *suf.* forming nouns, usu. diminutives, as *cutlet*, *tartlet*, or items of dress or ornament, as *anklet*.

lethal (lē´thəl) *a.* deadly, fatal, mortal. **lethal chamber** *n.* a chamber in which animals are killed painlessly with gas. **lethal dose** *n.* the amount of any toxic agent that will cause death if administered to a human, animal or any other organism. **lethality** (-thal´-) *n.* **lethally** *adv.*

lethargy (leth´əji) *n.* **1** a state of torpor, apathy, dullness or inactivity. **2** (*Med.*) morbid drowsiness, unnatural sleepiness. **lethargic** (-thah´-), **lethargical** *a.* **lethargically** *adv.*

let's (lets) *contr.* let us.

†**Lett** (let) *n.* a member of a people largely inhabiting Latvia (Lettland), a Latvian. **Lettish** *a.*, *n.* Latvian.

letter (let´ə) *n.* **1** a mark or character employed to represent a sound in speech. **2** any of the characters in the alphabet. **3** a written, typed or printed message or communication usually sent by post. **4** the literal or precise meaning of a term or terms, as distinct from the spirit. **5** characters used in printing, type; font of type. **6** (*pl.*) literature; literary culture. **7** (*pl.*) learning, erudition. **8** (*pl.*) a university degree, membership, title etc. abbreviated after a surname. **9** (*pl.*) a formal or legal document for any of a variety of purposes addressed to a particular recipient. **10** (*pl.*, *N Am.*) the initials of a school or university as a mark of proficiency in sport. *~v.t.* **1** to impress, mark or stamp with letters. **2** to classify by means of letters. **the letter of the law** literal or precise definition of the law. **letter bomb** *n.* an explosive device contained in an envelope, which detonates when opened. **letter box** *n.* a box or slot for the reception of letters. **letter-card** *n.* a folded card with gummed edges for sending by post as a letter. **letter-carrier** *n.* (*N Am.*) a postman or postwoman. **lettered** *a.* learned, erudite. **letterhead** *n.* **1** notepaper with a printed heading. **2** (*also* **letter-heading**) the heading on such notepaper. **lettering** *n.* **1** the act or technique of impressing or marking with letters. **2** an inscription, a title. **letter of comfort** *n.* an assurance given by a third party to a bank in respect of a debt, not amounting to a legal guarantee. **letter of credit** *n.* an order authorizing a person to draw money from an agent. **letter of marque, letter of marque and reprisal** *n.* a privateer's licence to seize and plunder merchant ships of a hostile state. **letter-perfect** *a.* (of actors etc.) having learnt one's part thoroughly, word-perfect. **letterpress** *n.* **1** printing from raised type with ink; matter printed by this method. **2** printed matter other than illustrations. **letter-quality** *a.* **1** (of the output of a computer printer) of sufficient sharpness, neatness etc. to be used for communications. **2** (of a computer printer)

producing output of this quality. **letters of administration** *n.pl.* a document issued by a court authorizing a person to administer an intestate estate. **letters patent** *n.pl.* an open document from the sovereign or an officer of the Crown conferring a title, right, privilege etc., esp. the exclusive right to make or sell a new invention. **letter-writer** *n.* a person who (commonly) writes letters.

letting LET¹.

lettuce (let´is) *n.* **1** a crisp-leaved garden plant of the genus *Lactuca*, esp. *L. sativa*, much used for salad. **2** the leaves of this plant used as food. **3** any of various plants resembling lettuce.

leu (lā´oo) *n.* (*pl.* **lei** (lā)) the basic monetary unit of Romania, equal to 100 bani.

leucin (loo´sin), **leucine** *n.* an essential amino acid present in many proteins.

leuco- (loo´kō), **leuc-, leuko-, leuk-** *comb. form* white, pale.

leucocyte (loo´kōsīt), **leukocyte** *n.* a white corpuscle or blood cell. **leucocytic** (-sit´-) *a.*

leucoma (lookō´mə) *n.* a white opaque spot in the cornea, due to a wound, inflammation etc.

leucorrhoea (lookərē´ə), (*N Am.*) **leucorrhea** *n.* a mucous discharge from the vagina, commonly called whites. **leucorrhoeal** *a.*

leucotomy (lookot´əmi) *n.* (*pl.* **leucotomies**) a surgical operation to cut white nerve fibres within the brain, esp. a prefrontal lobotomy.

leukaemia (lookē´miə), (*N Am.*) **leukemia** *n.* (*Med.*) any of various acute and often fatal diseases of the bone marrow in which leucocytes multiply inordinately causing loss of red corpuscles, hypertrophy of the spleen etc.

leukocyte LEUCOCYTE.

❎ **leutenant** common misspelling of LIEUTENANT.

lev (lef) *n.* (*pl.* **leva** (lev´ə)) the basic monetary unit of Bulgaria, equal to 100 stotinki.

levant (livant´) *v.i.* to abscond, to run away, esp. with gambling liabilities undischarged.

levator (livā´tə) *n.* a muscle that raises some part of the body.

levee¹ (lev´i, lev´ā) *n.* **1** (*N Am.*) a general reception or assembly of visitors. **2** (*Hist.*) in Britain, an early afternoon reception held by a sovereign or person of high rank for men only. **3** (*Hist.*) a reception held on getting out of bed.

levee² (lev´i) *n.* **1** an artificial bank to prevent overflow and flooding. **2** the natural bank of a river formed by the deposition of silt. **3** a quay, a landing place on a river.

level (lev´əl) *n.* **1** a horizontal line or plane or plane surface; a line or plane at all points at right angles to the vertical. **2** the altitude of any point or surface. **3** a position on a scale of values. **4** a stage or degree of progress or rank. **5** an instrument for determining whether a surface or a series of objects is horizontal. **6** a surveying instrument incorporating a telescope for measuring relative heights of land. **7** level country. **8** a surface that is more or less level. *~a.*

1 horizontal. **2** even, not higher or lower at any part, flat. **3** at the same height as or horizontal with something else. **4** (of runners, competitors) equal in position, score etc. having no advantage or disadvantage relative to one another. **5** equal in rank or degree. **6** equable, uniform, well-balanced. **7** (of a spoonful) filled so that the contents are even with the rim. ~*v.t.* (*pres.p.* **levelling,** (*N*Am.) **leveling,** *past, p.p.* **levelled,** (*N* Am.) **leveled**) **1** to make horizontal. **2** to make smooth or even. **3** to bring (up or down) to the same level. **4** to raze, to overthrow, to make level (with the ground etc.), to knock down. **5** to point (a gun) in taking aim. **6** to aim, to direct (an attack, satire etc.). **7** to bring to an equality of state, rank, condition or degree. **8** in surveying, to use a level to ascertain the elevation of (a piece of land). ~*v.i.* to aim or point a gun (at). **on the level** honest, genuine. **to do one's level best** to do the best one can. **to find its (own) level 1** (of liquids) to reach the same height in a number of interconnecting vessels or chambers. **2** to reach a stable level, usu. with respect to something else. **to level down** to bring down to the level or standard of something or someone else. **to level off 1** to make flat. **2** to reach and stay in a state of equilibrium. **3** (of an aircraft) to return to horizontal flight after a dive. **to level out 1** to make level. **2** to remove differences between. **3** (of an aircraft) to return to the horizontal flight after a dive. **to level up** to bring up to the level or standard of something or someone else. **to level with** (*sl.*) to be honest with, to come clean. **level crossing** *n.* a level place where a road crosses a railway line. **level-headed** *a.* sensible, shrewd, untemperamental. **level-headedly** *adv.* **level-headedness** *n.* **leveller,** (*N*Am.) **leveler** *n.* **1** a person who or something which levels. **2** a person who wishes to destroy all social distinctions. **3** (**Leveller**) a member of a radical republican and egalitarian group during the English Civil War. **levelling** *n.* **levelling screw** *n.* a screw that adjusts the level of an instrument. **levelly** *adv.* **levelness** *n.* **level pegging** *a.* equal. ~*n.* (of contestants etc.) the state of being at the same level or at the same place in a race etc.

lever (lē´və) *n.* **1** a bar of wood, metal, or other rigid substance resting on a fixed point of support (or fulcrum), used to overcome a certain resistance or lift a certain weight. **2** a part of a machine, instrument etc., acting on the same principle. **3** a projecting handle that can be moved to operate a machine. **4** anything that brings power or influence to bear. ~*v.t.* to move or lift with or as with a lever. ~*v.i.* to use a lever. **leverage** *n.* **1** the action of a lever. **2** the mechanical power or advantage gained by the use of a lever. **3** means of accomplishing, influencing etc. **4** an arrangement of levers. **5** (*N* Am.) the ratio between the amount of a company's borrowings and that of its share

capital. **leveraged buyout** *n.* a buyout made with the assistance of third-party capital.

leveret (lev´ərit) *n.* a young hare, esp. one in its first year.

leviable LEVY.

leviathan (livī´əthən) *n.* **1** a huge aquatic monster (perh. the Nilotic crocodile) described in the Book of Job; a huge sea monster. **2** anything huge or monstrous, esp. a huge ship, a whale, the state.

levigate (lev´igāt) *v.t.* **1** to grind or rub down to a fine powder. **2** to make into a smooth paste. **levigation** (-ā´shən) *n.*

Levis® (lē´vīz) *n.pl.* a type of (blue) denim jeans.

levitate (lev´itāt) *v.t., v.i.* to (cause to) rise or float in the air, esp. a body through supernatural causes. **levitation** (-ā´shən) *n.* **levitational** *a.* **levitator** *n.*

levity (lev´iti) *n.* **1** lack of seriousness or earnestness, inappropriate humour, frivolity. **2** fickleness, inconstancy.

levo- LAEVO-.

levodopa (lēvōdō´pə) *n.* L-dopa, the laevorotatory form of dopa.

levulose LAEVULOSE.

levy (lev´i) *n.* (*pl.* **levies**) **1** the act of raising or collecting (e.g. a tax, a fine, a fee). **2** something which is so raised or collected. **3** the calling out of troops for military service. **4** a body of troops called out for military service. **5** the number of troops called out. ~*v.t.* (*3rd pers. sing. pres.* **levies,** *pres.p.* **levying,** *past, p.p.* **levied**) **1** to impose and collect (as a tax or forced contribution). **2** to raise, to collect together, to enlist (as an army). **3** to seize (property) by a judicial writ etc.; to raise (money) by such seizure. **4** to begin to wage (war). **leviable** *a.*

lewd (lood, lūd) *a.* lascivious, unchaste; indecent. **lewdly** *adv.* **lewdness** *n.*

lewis (loo´is), **lewisson** (-sən) *n.* a hoisting device for heavy stone blocks employing metal, usu. curved pieces which fit into and grasp the stone.

lewisite (loo´isīt) *n.* a poisonous liquid used in chemical warfare obtained from arsenic and acetylene.

lexicon (lek´sikən) *n.* **1** a dictionary (usu. applied to Greek, Hebrew, Arabic or Syriac). **2** the vocabulary of a language, an individual, an area of study etc. **lexical** (-kəl) *a.* **1** of or relating to the words of a language, as opposed to grammar. **2** of or relating to a lexicon or lexicography. **lexically** *adv.* **lexicography** (leksikog´rəfi) *n.* the art or process of compiling lexicons or dictionaries. **lexicographer** *n.* **lexicographic** (-graf´-), **lexicographical** *a.* **lexicographically** (-graf´-) *adv.* **lexicology** (-kol´-) *n.* that branch of learning concerned with the derivation, signification and application of words. **lexicologist** *n.* **lexigraphy** (-sig´rəfi) *n.* a system of writing in which each word is represented by a distinct character. **lexis** *n.* the complete vocabulary of a language, individual or subject.

ley (lā) *n.* **1** arable land laid down (temporarily) to grass. **2** a ley line. **ley farming** *n.* a type of farming in which land is alternately tilled and used for pasture over periods of several years. **ley line** *n.* a straight line across the landscape joining two landmarks, supposed to be of pre-historic origin.

Leyden jar (lī´dən) *n.* a glass bottle or jar coated inside and out with tinfoil used as an electrical condenser.

LF *abbr.* low frequency.

LH *abbr.* **1** (*also* **l.h.**) left hand. **2** luteinizing hormone.

Li *chem. symbol* lithium.

liable (lī´əbəl) *a.* **1** tending, apt or likely (to). **2** bound or obliged in law or equity. **3** responsible (for). **4** subject (to). **5** exposed or open (to). **liability** (-bil´-) *n.* (*pl.* **liabilities**) **1** the state of being liable. **2** something for which one is liable. **3** (*pl.*) debts, pecuniary obligations. **4** a person or thing that hinders, disadvantages or causes trouble.

liaison (liā´zon) *n.* **1** communication and contact between units, groups etc., esp. between military units. **2** an illicit intimacy between a man and woman. **3** in cooking, a thickening for a sauce or soup usu. made of yolk of egg. **liaise** *v.i.* **1** to maintain communication and contact. **2** to form a liaison. **liaison officer** *n.* **1** an officer acting as go-between for forces or bodies of men under different commands. **2** a person in charge of communication between units, groups etc.

liana (liah´nə), **liane** (-ahn´) *n.* any of the climbing and twining plants common in the forests of tropical America.

liar (lī´ə) *n.* a person who knowingly utters a falsehood, esp. someone addicted to lying. **liar dice** *n.* a game played using poker dice in which the result of a throw may be announced falsely.

Lias (lī´əs) *n.* **1** (*Geol.*) the lowest series of rock strata of the Jurassic system. **2** (**lias**) a blue limestone rock found in SW England. **Liassic** (-as´-) *a.*

❌ **liason** common misspelling of LIAISON.

Lib. *abbr.* Liberal.

lib (lib) *n.* (*coll.*) short for LIBERATION (under LIBERATE).

libation (lībā´shən) *n.* **1** a sacrificial offering to a deity involving the pouring of oil or wine. **2** the liquid poured. **3** (*usu. facet.*) an (alcoholic) drink. **libational** *a.* **libatory** (lī´bə-) *a.*

libber (lib´ə) *n.* (*coll.*) short for LIBERATIONIST (under LIBERATE).

Lib. Dem. *abbr.* Liberal Democrat.

libel (lī´bəl) *n.* **1** a publication of any kind containing false statements or representations tending to bring any person into ridicule, contempt or disrepute. **2** the act or crime of publishing a libel. **3** an unfair representation or defamatory statement. **4** in civil and ecclesiastical law, the written statement containing a plaintiff's allegations. **5** (*Sc. Law*) the statement of the grounds of the charge. ~*v.t.* (*pres.p.* **libelling**, (*N Am.*) **libeling**, *past, p.p.* **libelled**, (*N Am.*) **libeled**) **1** to make or publish a defamatory statement about. **2** to defame, to misrepresent. **3** to bring a suit against by means of a written complaint. ~*v.i.* to spread libels or defamatory statements. **libeller, libelist** *n.* **libellous** *a.* being or containing a libel. **libellously** *adv.*

liberal (lib´ərəl) *a.* **1** favourable to individual freedom, democratic government, progress and moderate reform. **2** ample, abundant, profuse. **3** generous, open-handed, bountiful, munificent. **4** broad-minded, unprejudiced. **5** not strict, narrow or literal. **6** (**Liberal**) of or relating to a Liberal Party. **7** (esp. of education) not technical, tending to free mental development. **8** (*Theol.*) in religion and theology, progressive, re-evaluating or discarding traditional beliefs and dogmas in the light of modern thought. **9** free, open, candid. ~*n.* **1** a person who advocates progress and reform, esp. in the direction of conferring greater power upon the people. **2** (**Liberal**) a member or supporter of a Liberal Party. **liberal arts** *n.pl.* non-technical or non-professional studies including the fine arts, history, languages, literature, philosophy etc., the arts. **Liberal Democrat** *n.* in the UK, a member of a political party founded in 1988 by the merging of the Liberal Party and the bulk of the Social Democratic Party. **liberalism** *n.* **liberalist** *n.* **liberalistic** (-lis´-) *a.* **liberality** (-ral´-) *n.* **1** the quality of being liberal. **2** bounty, munificence, generosity. **3** largeness or breadth of views, catholicity. **4** freedom from prejudice. **liberalize, liberalise** *v.t.* to make more liberal. **liberalization** (-zā´shən) *n.* **liberally** *adv.* **liberalness** *n.* **Liberal Party** *n.* a party having liberal policies.

liberate (lib´ərāt) *v.t.* **1** to set at liberty. **2** to release from domination, injustice, restraint or confinement. **3** to release from occupation by or subjugation to a foreign power. **4** (*Chem.*) to set free from chemical combination. **5** (*euphem. or facet.*) to steal. **liberated** *a.* **1** freed, having liberty. **2** freed from foreign occupation or domination. **3** no longer subject to traditional constraints, sexual and social roles etc. **liberation** (-ā´shən) *n.* **1** the act of setting free. **2** the process of becoming liberated. **liberationism** *n.* **liberationist** *n.* a person who supports the cause of equality, freedom or liberty (e.g. *women's liberationist, gay liberationist*). **liberation theology** *n.* the theory (orig. amongst the Roman Catholic clergy of Latin America) that political involvement to effect social equality and justice is a necessary part of Christianity. **liberator** *n.*

libertine (lib´ətēn) *n.* a licentious or dissolute person, a debauchee, a profligate. ~*a.* loose, licentious, dissolute. **libertinage** (-nij), **libertinism** *n.* licentiousness.

liberty (lib´əti) *n.* (*pl.* **liberties**) **1** the quality or state of being free from captivity, bondage, subjection or despotic control. **2** freedom of choice, opinion or action. **3** an action which seems socially presumptuous or improper, a breach of decorum. **4** any instance of a person treating someone or something with too little respect. **5** (*pl.*) rights, privileges or exemptions, enjoyed by grant or prescription. **6** (*Naut.*) leave of absence for sailors. **at liberty 1** free. **2** having the right (to do etc.). **3** disengaged, not occupied. **to take liberties (with) 1** to be unduly familiar or presumptuous (with). **2** to transgress rules or usages. **3** to falsify. **to take the liberty 1** to venture. **2** to do something without permission. **libertarian** (-teə´ri-) *a.* **1** advocating the widest possible extension of liberty. **2** believing in free will. ~*n.* **1** an advocate of liberty. **2** a believer in the doctrine of free will. **libertarianism** *n.* **liberty boat** *n.* (*Naut.*) a boat taking sailors ashore on leave. **liberty bodice** *n.* a sleeveless bodice worn as an undergarment, esp. by children. **liberty hall** *n.* a place where one may do as one pleases. **liberty horse** *n.* a riderless circus horse.

libidinous (libid´inəs) *a.* characterized by lewdness or lust, lustful. **libidinously** *adv.* **libidinousness** *n.*

libido (libe´dō) *n.* (*pl.* **libidos**) (*Psych.*) **1** the sexual drive. **2** in psychoanalysis, the life force deriving from biological impulses. **libidinal** (-bid´inəl) *a.*

Lib-Lab (liblab´) *a.* in the UK, involving or uniting the Liberal or Liberal Democrat and Labour Parties.

Libra (lē´brə) *n.* **1** (*Astron.*) one of the 12 zodiacal constellations, the Scales and Balance. **2** (*Astrol.*) **a** the seventh sign of the zodiac which the sun passes through between approx. 23 September and 22 October. **b** a person born under this sign. **Libran** *a., n.*

library (lī´brəri) *n.* (*pl.* **libraries**) **1** a collection of books, esp. one that is classified and catalogued, or otherwise organized, to facilitate its use either by the public or by private persons. **2** a building, room, or series of rooms containing such a collection. **3** an institution established for the formation or maintenance of such a collection. **4** a series of books similar in subject, literary form etc., issued (usu. in similar format) by a publisher. **5** a collection of computer software, films, records, tapes etc. **librarian** (-breə´ri-) *n.* a person who has charge of a library or one of their assistants. **librarianship** *n.* the professional care, organization and administration of a collection of books.

librate (lī´brāt) *v.i.* to move like a balance, to oscillate, to swing or sway. **libration** (-brā´shən) *n.* oscillation.

libretto (libret´ō) *n.* (*pl.* **libretti** (-ti), **librettos**) **1** the words of an opera, oratorio etc. **2** a book containing such words. **librettist** *n.*

Librium® (lib´riəm) *n.* a tranquillizing drug containing chlordiazepoxide.

Libyan (lib´iən) *a.* of or relating to the N African country of Libya, its language or its people. ~*n.* **1**

a native or inhabitant of Libya. **2** the Hamitic language of ancient Libya, now extinct.

lice LOUSE.

licence[1] (lī´səns), (*N Am.*) **license** *n.* **1** a document certifying consent or permission granted by a constituted authority (to marry, drive a motor vehicle, possess a firearm, carry on a business etc.). **2** authority, leave, permission. **3** permitted freedom of thought or action. **4** unrestrained liberty of action, disregard of law or propriety. **5** abuse of freedom, licentiousness. **6** in literature or art, deviation from the ordinary rules or mode of treatment. **7** a certificate of competence in a university faculty.

licence[2] LICENSE[1].

license[1] (lī´səns), **licence** *v.t.* **1** to authorize by a legal permit. **2** to allow, to permit, esp. to allow entire freedom of action, comment etc. **licensable** *a.* **licensed** *a.* **licensed victualler** *n.* a person who holds a licence to sell spirits, wines, beer etc. **licensee** (-sē´) *n.* a person who holds a licence (esp. a publican). **license plate** *n.* (*esp. N Am.*) the number plate on a vehicle. **licenser, licensor** *n.* **licentiate** (-sen´shiət) *n.* **1** a person who holds a certificate of competence in some profession from a university or other collegiate body. **2** in the Presbyterian Church, a person who has a licence to preach.

license[2] LICENCE[1].

licentious (līsen´shəs) *a.* lascivious, dissolute, profligate, loose. **licentiously** *adv.* **licentiousness** *n.*

lichee LYCHEE.

lichen (lī´kən) *n.* **1** a cryptogamic thallophytic plant of the order Lichenaceae, parasitic fungi on algal cells covering rocks, tree trunks etc., with variously coloured crusts. **2** a papular inflammatory eruption of the skin. **lichened** *a.* **lichenology** (-ol´-) *n.* that branch of botany which deals with lichens.

lich-gate (lich´gāt), **lych-gate** *n.* a churchyard gate with a roof, under which a coffin used to be placed while the introductory portion of the burial service was read.

licit (lis´it) *a.* lawful, allowed. **licitly** *adv.*

lick (lik) *v.t.* **1** to draw or pass the tongue over. **2** to take in or lap (up) with the tongue. **3** (of flames etc.) to stroke or pass lightly over. **4** (*coll.*) to overcome, to defeat; to be beyond, to surpass. **5** (*coll.*) to thrash. ~*v.i.* (of flames etc.) to flicker or move with a lapping or stroking motion. ~*n.* **1** the act of licking. **2** a slight smear or coat (as of paint); a small amount. **3** SALT LICK (under SALT). **4** (*coll.*) a smart blow or slap. **5** (*coll.*) great exertion, effort or pace. **a lick and a promise** (*coll.*) something done very quickly, esp. a quick or superficial wash. **to lick into shape** to bring into a satisfactory condition or shape (from the notion that young bears are born shapeless, and are licked into shape by their dam). **to lick one's lips/chops** to anticipate or remember something with pleasure. **to lick one's wounds** to withdraw after a defeat to recuperate physically or mentally. **to lick someone's boots/ shoes** to be servile towards. **licker** *n.* **licking** *n.* (*coll.*) a beating, a defeat. **lickspittle** *n.* an abject parasite or toady.

lickety-split (likətisplit´) *adv.* (*esp. N Am., coll.*) very quickly.

licorice LIQUORICE.

lid (lid) *n.* **1** a hinged or detachable cover or cap, usu. for shutting a vessel, container or aperture. **2** an eyelid. **3** (*Bot.*) an operculum. **4** (*sl.*) a hat. **to blow/ lift/ take the lid off** (*coll.*) to reveal, uncover (esp. something clandestine or corrupt). **to flip one's lid** (*sl.*) to go berserk, to become mad. **to put the (tin) lid on it 1** (*coll.*) to be a final blow, misfortune etc. **2** (*coll.*) to curb, to put an end to. **lidded** *a.* **lidless** *a.*

lido (lē´dō) *n.* (*pl.* **lidos**) a bathing beach, an outdoor swimming pool.

lie¹ (lī) *v.i.* (*3rd pers. sing. pres.* **lies**, *pres.p.* **lying**, *past, p.p.* **lied**) **1** to say or write anything with the deliberate intention of deceiving. **2** to convey a false impression, to deceive. *~v.t.* to take (away) or get (oneself into or out of) by lying. *~n.* **1** a false statement deliberately made for the purpose of deception. **2** an intentional violation of the truth. **3** a deception, an imposture. **to give the lie to** to show to be false; to disprove. **lie detector** *n.* a device for monitoring physiological changes taken as evidence of mental stress accompanying the telling of lies; a polygraph. **lying**¹ *a.* telling lies; false, deceitful. **lyingly** *adv.*

lie² (lī) *v.i.* (*3rd pers. sing. pres.* **lies**, *pres.p.* **lying**, *past* **lay** (lā), *p.p.* **lain** (lān)) **1** to rest or place oneself in a reclining or horizontal posture. **2** to rest on or over a horizontal surface. **3** to be situated in a specified location or direction. **4** to stretch or extend. **5** to exist, to be, to reside, in a specified state, position, relation etc. **6** to remain undisturbed (*let things lie*). **7** to be buried. **8** to seem to weigh heavily on (*the food lies on my stomach*). **9** (*Law*) (of an action, objection etc.) to be sustainable. **10** (of a game bird) not to rise. *~n.* **1** position, arrangement, direction, manner of lying. **2** the retiring-place or lair (of an animal). **3** in golf, the position of the ball when about to be struck. **to let lie** not to bring forward for discussion (because likely to cause controversy). **to lie about/ around** to be left scattered randomly over an area. **to lie ahead** to be in prospect or in store. **to lie back** to rest in a comfortable reclining position. **to lie behind** to be the cause of or explanation for. **to lie down 1** to take up a lying position. **2** to take a short rest. **3** to submit tamely. **to lie hard/ heavy on** to oppress, to be a weight upon. **to lie in** to remain in bed later than normal. **to lie in wait** (for) **1** to wait in ambush or concealment (in order to waylay). **2** to be in store (for). **to lie low 1** to remain in hiding. **2** to conceal one's knowledge or intentions in order to outwit, forestall etc. **to lie off** (*Naut.*) (of a ship) to stay at a distance from the shore or another ship. **to lie over** to be deferred. **to lie to**

(*Naut.*) (of a ship) to be checked or stopped with its head to the wind. **to lie under** to be subject to or oppressed by. **to lie up 1** to rest, to stay in bed or in one's room to recuperate. **2** (of a ship) to go into dock. **to lie with** to be the responsibility or duty of. **to take lying down** to accept (an insult, rebuff) without retaliation, resistance or complaint. **lie-down** *n.* a short rest. **lie-in** *n.* a longer than normal stay in bed. **lie of the land** *n.* **1** the topography of a place. **2** the nature of the situation as it stands and as it is likely to develop. **lying**² *n.* a place to lie in.

Usage note *Lie* should not be used instead of *lay* as a transitive verb: *Lay your head on my shoulder,* not *lie your head.*

---

lied (lēd, -t) *n.* (*pl.* **lieder** (-də)) a type of German song, often a poem set to music and usu. for solo voice with piano accompaniment.

liege (lēj) *a.* **1** bound by some feudal tenure, either as a vassal or as a lord. **2** of or relating to such tenure. *~n.* **1** a feudal superior, a lord, a sovereign. **2** a vassal bound to do service to his lord. **liegeman** *n.* (*pl.* **liegemen**) **1** a liege vassal. **2** a faithful supporter or follower.

lien (lē´ən) *n.* (*Law*) a right to detain the goods of another until some claim has been satisfied.

☒ **liesure** common misspelling of LEISURE.

lieu (lū, loo) *n.* place, stead. **in lieu** instead, as a substitute. **in lieu of** instead of.

lieutenant (leften´ənt) *n.* **1** an officer acting as deputy or substitute to a superior. **2** an army officer ranking next below a captain. **3** a naval officer ranking next below a lieutenant-commander. **4** in the US, a police officer ranking next below a captain. **lieutenancy** *n.* (*pl.* **lieutenancies**) **lieutenant colonel** *n.* an officer next in rank below a colonel, in actual command of a battalion. **lieutenant commander** *n.* a naval officer ranking between a lieutenant and a commander. **lieutenant general** *n.* an army officer next in rank below a general and above a major general. **lieutenant-governor** *n.* **1** a deputy governor. **2** the acting governor in subordination to a governor general.

Usage note The usual N Am. pronunciation is (looten´ənt).

---

life (līf) *n.* (*pl.* **lives** (līvz)) **1** the state or condition which distinguishes animate beings from dead ones and from inorganic matter and involves the ability to grow, change, respond to stimuli, reproduce etc. **2** the period from birth to death. **3** the period from birth to the present time. **4** the period from the present to death. **5** any other specified period of a person's existence. **6** the period of time for which an object functions or operates. **7** living things collectively, animated existence. **8** human presence or activity. **9** a person's individual existence (*saved her life*). **10** a person's mode, manner or course of living; any particular aspect of this, such as one's professional or sex life. **11** human affairs. **12** a particular area of human activity or affairs. **13** animation, vivacity, spirit. **14** a person who or something which imparts spirit or animation. **15** the animating principle, the essential or inspiring idea (of a movement etc.). **16** someone or something that one devotes all or most of one's energy, attention or devotion to. **17** in art, the living form, esp. a nude model. **18** a person considered as the object of a policy of assurance. **19** the average period which a person of a given age may expect to live. **20** a narrative of one's existence, a biography. **21** (*coll.*) a life sentence. **22** each one of the points or chances to which each player is entitled in a game that are lost in certain contingencies. ~*a.* **1** for the duration or remainder of one's life. **2** in drawing, sculpture etc., taken from life. **a matter of life and death** a matter of utmost urgency. **for dear life** with extreme vigour, in order to escape death. **for the life of me** even if my life depended upon it (used to indicate one's utter inability to do something). **not on your life** under no circumstances. **the life and soul of** a person who is the chief source of amusement or interest, esp. at a party. **the life of Riley** (*coll.*) an easy, carefree existence. **the time of one's life** an experience of unequalled pleasure. **to bring to life** to give animation to, to enliven, to make interesting or exciting. **to come to life 1** to emerge from unconsciousness, inactivity, torpor etc. **2** (of an inanimate object) to become animate. **3** (of a machine, engine) to start operating. **to give one's life 1** to die in a self-sacrificial way. **2** to devote all one's time, energy and care. **to save one's life** under any circumstances at all (used to indicate one's utter inability to do something) (*can't speak a word of French to save his life*). **to save someone's life 1** to prevent someone from dying. **2** (*coll.*) to help someone who is in serious difficulty. **to the life 1** (of the way in which a likeness has been made) with great fidelity to the original. **2** (of a likeness) as if the original stood before one. **upon my life** a mild oath. **with life and limb** without serious injury. **life assurance, life insurance** *n.* insurance providing for the payment of a specified sum to a beneficiary on the policyholder's death, or to the policyholder on reaching a certain age. **lifebelt** *n.* a belt of buoyant or inflated material for supporting a person in the water. **lifeblood** *n.* **1** the blood necessary to life. **2** something which is essential to existence, success or strength. **lifeboat** *n.* **1** a boat specially constructed for saving life in storms and heavy seas. **2** a small boat carried by a ship for use in an emergency, esp. if the ship has to be abandoned. **lifeboatman** *n.* (*pl.* **lifeboatmen**) a member of the crew of a lifeboat. **lifebuoy** *n.* a buoyant device to support a person in the water. **life cycle** *n.* the series of changes in the form and function of an organism etc. during its lifetime. **life expectancy** *n.* the average number of years that a person of a

certain age or in a certain category can expect to live. **life-force** *n.* **1** animating principle, driving force. **2** a vital urge supposed to be inherent in living organisms. **life form** *n.* any living creature. **life-giving** *a.* uplifting, invigorating, animating. **lifeguard** *n.* a trained attendant at a bathing beach or pool who helps swimmers in difficulties. **Life Guards** *n.pl.* a regiment of cavalry forming part of the bodyguard of the British sovereign. **life history** *n.* (*pl.* **life histories**) **1** the events, achievements etc. that make up a person's life. **2** an account of these, often a tediously long one. **life imprisonment** *n.* in the UK, imprisonment for an indefinite length of time, usu. about 15 years, the mandatory sentence after a conviction for murder. **life insurance** LIFE ASSURANCE (under LIFE). **life jacket** *n.* a sleeveless inflatable or buoyant jacket used as a lifebelt. **lifeless** *a.* **1** destitute or deprived of life; dead, inanimate, inorganic, inert. **2** unconscious. **3** lacking vitality or interest, dull, heavy, spiritless, vapid. **4** deprived of physical energy. **lifelessly** *adv.* **lifelessness** *n.* **lifelike** *a.* **1** (of a portrait) like the original. **2** like a living being. **lifeline** *n.* **1** a rope used for saving life, esp. at sea. **2** a rope used as an additional safeguard. **3** a vital line of communication. **4** the line by which a deep-sea diver is raised and lowered or communicates with the surface. **5** in palmistry, a linear crease in the palm of the hand supposed to indicate the length of one's life. **6** an emergency telephone counselling service. **lifelong** *a.* (lasting) for the whole of one's life. **life member** *n.* a person who is entitled to membership of an organization for the rest of their life. **life membership** *n.* **life peer** *n.* a peer whose title lapses at death. **life peerage** *n.* **life-preserver** *n.* **1** (*NAm.*) a lifebelt, life jacket etc. **2** a loaded stick or cane for defending one's life. **lifer** *n.* a person sentenced to imprisonment for life. **life raft** *n.* a raft kept on board ships etc. for use in emergencies. **life-saver** *n.* **1** a person who saves a person's life. **2** a person trained to rescue swimmers or bathers from drowning. **3** (*coll.*) a person who or something which provides help in distress. **life-saving** *a.*, *n.* **life science** *n.* a science that deals with the structure and function of living organisms, such as biology, medicine, anthropology or zoology. **life sentence** *n.* **1** a sentence of life imprisonment. **2** something that will affect, confine or threaten one for the whole of one's life. **life-size, life-sized** *a.* representing the actual size of an object. **lifespan** *n.* the length of time during which an organism lives or a machine etc. remains functional. **lifestyle** *n.* the attitudes, behaviour, surroundings etc. characteristic of an individual or group. **life-support** *a.* (*Med.*) of or relating to a device or system which maintains a person's life, e.g. during a serious illness. **life-support machine** *n.* a respirator or ventilator. **life-threatening** *a.* that may cause death. **lifetime** *n.* **1** the duration of one's life. **2** the length of time something functions.

lift (lift) *v.t.* **1** to raise to a higher position, to elevate, to hold or support on high. **2** to raise or take up from the ground, to pick up. **3** to take hold of in order to move or remove, e.g. from a hook or shelf. **4** to move or direct upwards. **5** to raise, rescind or remove (a restriction, ban). **6** to give one's confidence or spirits a boost. **7** to raise to a higher spiritual, intellectual etc. plane. **8** to improve the quality of, esp. to make more interesting and lively. **9** to make audible; to make louder; to raise the pitch of. **10** (*coll.*) to carry off, to steal, to appropriate, to plagiarize. **11** to transport, esp. by air. **12** to dig up (root vegetables) to harvest them. **13** to hit, kick etc. (a ball) into the air. **14** to perform cosmetic surgery on to prevent wrinkling, sagging etc. ~*v.i.* **1** to rise, to move upwards. **2** to perform or attempt to perform the act of raising something. **3** to rise and disperse, as a mist. **4** (of a floor) to swell and bulge upwards. ~*n.* **1** an act of lifting. **2** a compartment or platform for people or goods travelling up and down a shaft between different floors of a building, levels in a mine etc. **3** any of various devices for transporting up mountain slopes. **4** a ride in a vehicle as a passenger for part or all of a journey. **5** the component of the aerodynamic force on an aircraft or aerofoil acting upwards at right angles to the airflow and opposing the pull of gravity. **6** a rise in spirits, morale. **7** a rise in condition, status etc. **8** a helping hand. **9** a layer of material inserted in the heel of a shoe, esp. to increase the height of the wearer. **10** a rise in the height of the ground. **11** the height to which anything is lifted; e.g. the distance water rises in a canal lock. **to lift down** to pick up and move to a lower position. **to lift off 1** (of a spacecraft, rocket) to take off vertically from a launching pad. **2** to remove or detach by raising slightly. **3** to be removable by lifting; to come away easily from a surface to which it adheres. **to lift up one's voice** (to begin) to sing out loud. **lift-off** *n.* **1** the take-off of a rocket or missile. **2** the instant at which this occurs.

ligament (lig´əmənt) *n.* (*Anat.*) **1** a short band of fibrous tissue by which bones are bound together. **2** any tough bands or tissues holding parts together. **ligamental** (-men´-), **ligamentary**, **ligamentous** *a.*

ligand (lī´gənd, lig´-) *n.* (*Chem.*) a single atom, molecule, radical or ion attached to a central atom to form a coordination complex.

ligate (lī´gāt) *v.t.* to tie with a ligature. **ligation** (-ā´shən) *n.* **ligative** (lig´ətiv) *a.* **ligature** (lig´əchə) *n.* **1** something which binds, esp. a thread or cord to tie arteries or veins to stop bleeding or a wire used in removing tumours. **2** (*Mus.*) a tie connecting notes, a slur. **3** (*Print.*) two or more letters joined or cast on one shank, as œ, ffi. **4** anything that unites, a bond. **5** the act of binding or tying. ~*v.t.* to bind with a ligature.

liger (lī´gə) *n.* a cross between a lion and a tigress.

light[1] (līt) *n.* **1** electromagnetic radiation which, by acting on the retina, stimulates the sense of sight. **2** the sensation produced by the stimulation of the visual organs. **3** the state or condition in which things are visible, opposed to *darkness.* **4** the amount of illumination in a place or required by a person. **5** a source of light, a lamp, a candle, the sun etc. **6** daylight. **7** a traffic light. **8** (*pl.*) illuminations. **9** something by which light is admitted into a place, a window, a division of a window, esp. a perpendicular division in a mullioned window, a pane or glazed compartment in a greenhouse. **10** something that kindles or ignites, e.g. a spark or flame; a device which produces this. **11** exposure, publicity, general knowledge. **12** point of view, aspect. **13** mental illumination, elucidation, enlightenment. **14** brightness on the face or in the eyes. **15** (*pl.*) one's intellectual powers or capacity. **16** a person who or something which enlightens, a model, an example. **17** the manner in which the light appears to fall on the objects in a picture. **18** a part of a picture which is illuminated or highlighted. **19** the answer to a clue in a crossword. **20** (*often pl., Law*) the light falling on a window which a neighbour is prohibited from obstructing. ~*a.* **1** (of a room, space) well provided with (natural) light, bright. **2** (of colours) reflecting a lot of light, pale. **3** (of hair, complexion) pale-coloured, fair. ~*v.t.* (*past, p.p.* **lit** (lit), **lighted**) **1** to kindle, to set fire to. **2** to give light to. **3** to fill (up) with light. **4** to conduct with a light. **5** to brighten. ~*v.i.* **1** to take fire, to begin to burn. **2** to be illuminated. **3** to brighten (up). **according to one's lights** according to one's information or knowledge of a situation. **in a bad/ poor light** in such a way as to reflect discredit on. **in a good/ favourable light** in such a way as to reflect credit on. **in the light of** considering, allowing for. **out like a light** deeply asleep or unconscious. **the light of one's life** (*usu. facet.*) a much loved person or thing. **to bring to light** to discover, to detect, to disclose. **to come to light** to become known. **to light up 1** (*coll.*) to light a cigarette, pipe etc. **2** to illuminate. **3** to switch on (car) lights. **4** to become cheerful or animated suddenly. **to shed/ throw light on/ upon** to elucidate, to explain. **light bulb** *n.* a glass bulb filled with a low density gas and containing a metal filament which glows when an electric current is passed through it. **light-emitting diode** *n.* a semiconductor junction which emits light when an electric current passes through it, used in indicators and the displays of calculators, watches etc. **lightfast** *a.* (of dye, pigments) not affected by exposure to light. **lightfastness** *n.* **lighthouse** *n.* a tower or other structure which supports a powerful light for the warning and guidance of ships at sea. **lighting** *n.* **1** the act of providing light or illumination to something. **2**

the equipment used to provide artificial light to an area, esp. to a stage, film set, photographic studio etc. **3** the effect or effects produced by the use of such equipment or by natural light. **lighting-up time** *n.* the time of day when vehicles are required by law to show their lights. **lightish**[1] *a.* **lightless** *a.* **light meter** *n.* EXPOSURE METER (under EXPOSE). **lightness**[1] *n.* **light of day** *n.* **1** daylight. **2** public awareness, general notice. **light-pen** *n.* **1** a pen-shaped photoelectric device which when pointed at a visual display unit senses whether a spot is illuminated, used for creating or entering information on a computer esp. in graphics and design. **2** a pen-shaped light-emitting device used to read bar codes. **light pollution** *n.* excessive brightness in the night sky caused by street lamps etc. **lightship** *n.* a moored vessel carrying a light to give warning or guidance to ships. **lights out** *n.* **1** the time when residents in an institution (e.g. a boarding school) are expected to retire for the night. **2** a signal indicating when lights are to be put out. **light year** *n.* **1** (*Astron.*) the distance (about 6,000,000,000,000 miles or 9460 × 10⁹ km) travelled by light in one year. **2** (*pl.*, *coll.*) a long way away from. **lit-up** *a.* (*coll.*) slightly drunk.

light[2] (līt) *a.* **1** of small weight, not heavy; easy to be lifted, carried, moved, handled etc. **2** having relatively low density (*light metal*). **3** short in weight, below the standard weight. **4** not great in degree, number, intensity etc. (*light traffic*). **5** (of a task, duties etc.) easy to perform, not requiring great effort. **6** (of equipment) employed in or adapted for easy work. **7** (of a type of vehicle) adapted for small loads. **8** (of a ship or vehicle) unladen or not heavily laden. **9** (of troops) lightly armed and equipped (*light infantry*). **10** (of a meal) small in quantity and consisting of easily digestible food. **11** (of food) not rich, low in fat, sugar etc. easily digested. **12** (of wine, beer) not strong, low in alcohol and easily digested. **13** (of bread, sponge) not dense, well risen and aerated. **14** (of reading, entertainment) intended for amusement, not serious, profound or deeply moving. **15** (of a remark) of little consequence, unimportant, trivial. **16** (of movement) nimble, active, quick. **17** (of a building or structure) not massive, not heavy in construction or appearance. **18** (of fabrics) thin, delicate. **19** (of a blow, impact) not forcible, gentle, slight. **20** (of a mood) cheerful, merry. **21** dizzy, giddy; delirious. **22** (of soil) loose, porous, sandy. **23** (of type) not bold, thick or heavy. ~*adv.* **1** lightly. **2** with little baggage or a small load. **light on** (*coll.*) short of, having insufficient. **to make light of 1** to treat as insignificant. **2** to treat as pardonable or excusable. **light air** *n.* a very gentle movement of the air, force one on the Beaufort scale. **lighter-than-air** *a.* (of an aircraft) buoyant in air, weighing less than the air it displaces. **light-fingered** *a.* **1** given to thieving. **2** having nimble fingers. **light**

flyweight *n.* **1** an amateur boxer in the lower part of the flyweight category, weighing not more than 106 lb. (48 kg). **2** this weight category. **light-footed** *a.* nimble, active. **light-headed** *a.* **1** delirious. **2** giddy. **3** frivolous, thoughtless. **light-headedness** *n.* **light-hearted** *a.* **1** free from care or anxiety, merry, cheerful. **2** casual, not or insufficiently serious. **light-heartedly** *adv.* **light-heartedness** *n.* **light heavyweight** *n.* **1** a boxer or wrestler in the weight category intermediate between middleweight and heavyweight. **2** this weight category. **light horse** *n.* lightly armed and very mobile cavalry. **light industry** *n.* industry that produces smaller and lighter goods. **lightish**[2] *a.* **lightly** *adv.* **light middleweight** *n.* **1** an amateur boxer weighing 148–157 lb. (67–71 kg). **2** this weight category. **lightness**[2] *n.* **light opera** *n.* **1** an operetta or opera with a light, comic theme. **2** the genre to which such works belong. **light railway** *n.* a railway, usu. less than the standard gauge, adapted for light traffic. **light touch** *n.* the ability to handle people or affairs delicately or tactfully. **light-weight** *n.* **1** an animal or person below average weight. **2** a boxer, wrestler, weightlifter etc. in the weight category intermediate between featherweight and welterweight. **3** this weight category. **4** (*coll.*) a person of small importance or ability. ~*a.* **1** light in weight. **2** trivial. **light welterweight** *n.* **1** an amateur boxer weighing 132–140 lb. (60–63.5 kg). **2** this weight category.

light[3] (līt) *v.i.* (*past, p.p.* **lit** (lit), **lighted**) (of a bird) to descend as from flight, to settle. ~*v.t.* (*Naut.*) to lift or help to move (along etc.). **to light into** (*sl.*) to attack physically or verbally. **to light on/ upon** to happen on, to find by chance. **to light out** (*sl.*) to leave in a hurry.

lighten[1] (līˊtən) *v.i.* **1** to become light, to brighten. **2** to emit lightning, to flash. **3** to shine out. ~*v.t.* to illuminate, to enlighten.

Usage note See note under LIGHTNING.

lighten[2] (līˊtən) *v.t.* **1** to reduce in weight. **2** to reduce the weight or load of. **3** to relieve, to mitigate, to alleviate. **4** to cheer. ~*v.i.* **1** to be lightened, to grow lighter. **2** to become less burdensome.

Usage note See note under LIGHTNING.

lighter[1] (līˊtə) *n.* **1** a pocket appliance for lighting cigarettes, a pipe etc. **2** a person who or something which ignites.

lighter[2] (līˊtə) *n.* a large, open, usu. flat-bottomed boat, used in loading and unloading ships. **lighterage** *n.* **lighterman** *n.* (*pl.* **lightermen**) a person who works on a lighter.

lightning (lītˊning) *n.* the dazzling flash caused by the discharge of electricity between clouds or from a cloud to the earth. ~*a.* very fast or sudden. **lightning conductor, [*N Am.*] lightning rod** *n.* a wire or rod for carrying the electric discharge to earth and protecting a building, mast etc., against damage.

Usage note The spellings of the nouns *lightning* and *lightening* should not be confused: *lightning* is a flash of light, and *lightening* means making or becoming light (part of the verbs LIGHTEN[1] and LIGHTEN[2]).

lights (līts) *n.pl.* the lungs of animals, esp. as food for cats etc.

ligneous (lig´niəs) *a.* 1 made or consisting of wood. 2 resembling wood, woody.

lignin (lig´nin) *n.* (*Bot.*) a complex organic material which forms the woody cell walls of certain plants.

lignite (lig´nīt) *n.* a partially carbonized coal showing fibrous woody structure, usu. of Cretaceous or Tertiary age. **lignitic** (-nit´-) *a.*

lignocaine (lig´nōkān) *n.* a local anaesthetic, usu. administered by injection.

like[1] (līk) *prep.* 1 similar to, resembling (*a voice like a foghorn*). 2 characteristic of (*it's not like her to forget*). 3 in the manner of, to the same extent or degree as. 4 such as, for example. ~*a.* similar, alike, having all or many of the same qualities as. ~*adv.* 1 (*coll., dial.*) likely (*as like as not*). 2 (*coll.*) as it were, so to speak. ~*conj.* (*coll.*) 1 in the same manner as. 2 as if. ~*n.* 1 a counterpart. 2 a similar or equal thing, person or event. **and the like** and other similar things, etcetera. **as like as not** very probably. **like as not** very probably. **like so** in this way, thus. **more like it** nearer or more closely resembling what is desired. **nothing like 1** in no way similar to or comparable with. **2** far short of (what is required). **of like mind** holding a similar or identical opinion. **the likes of** (*coll., usu. derog.*) people such as. **to look like 1** to resemble in appearance. 2 to have the appearance of. 3 to seem likely. **what is he/ she/ it like?** what are his/ her/ its main characteristics? **likely** *a.* (*comp.* **likelier**, *superl.* **likeliest**) 1 probable, credible, plausible. 2 liable, to be expected (to). 3 promising, suitable, well-adapted. ~*adv.* probably. **likelihood, likeliness** *n.* **like-minded** *a.* having similar disposition, opinions, purpose etc. **liken** *v.t.* to compare, to represent as similar (to). **likeness** *n.* 1 similarity, resemblance. 2 a picture or other representation of a person or thing. 3 form, appearance, guise. **likewise** *adv.* 1 also, moreover, too. 2 in like manner.

Usage note (1) The use of *like* as a conjunction is sometimes disapproved of, though it is common. In formal contexts it is safer to use *as* or *as if* instead. (2) In standard British English, *likely* as an adverb is always preceded by *very*, *more* or *most*.

like[2] (līk) *v.t.* 1 to find pleasure or satisfaction in, to enjoy. 2 to be pleased with. 3 to be inclined towards or attracted by. 4 to be fond of. 5 wish, prefer (*would like her to be there*). 6 to feel about (*How do you like your new job?*). ~*n.* (*pl.*) things

that one likes. **I like that!** (*iron.*) a reaction to a piece of brazen effrontery. **like it or not** (*coll.*) whether one is pleased or not. **likeable, likable** *a.* pleasant, amiable, easy to like. **likeability** (-bil´-), **likeableness** *n.* **liking** *n.* 1 inclination, fondness, fancy (for). 2 taste, satisfaction. **to one's liking** to one's taste.

-like (līk) *suf.* 1 forming adjectives, as in *warlike*. 2 forming adverbs, as in *childlike* (*she replied*).

lilac (lī´lək) *n.* 1 a shrub of the genus *Syringa*, esp. *S. vulgaris*, with very fragrant pale violet or purple flowers, white in cultivated varieties. 2 a pale violet or purple colour. ~*a.* of the colour of lilac.

liliaceous LILY.

Lilliputian (lilipū´shən) *a.* tiny, diminutive. ~*n.* a very small person or thing.

Lilo® (lī´lō), **Li-lo** *n.* (*pl.* **Lilos, Li-los**) a type of inflatable mattress used in camping etc.

lilt (lilt) *n.* 1 a jaunty, springing rhythm or movement. 2 a lively song or tune. 3 the cadence or accent of an individual voice, esp. a pleasant and musical one. ~*v.i.* 1 to sing, speak, sound out with a lilt. 2 to walk or move jauntily.

lily (lil´i) *n.* (*pl.* **lilies**) 1 a flower or plant of the bulbous genus *Lilium*, producing white or coloured trumpet-shaped flowers of great beauty, esp. the Madonna lily, *L. candidum*. 2 any of various similar plants, such as the Lent lily or daffodil, the water lily etc. 3 (*Her.*) the fleur-de-lis. **to gild/ paint the lily** to try to improve what is already perfect. **liliaceous** (-ā´shəs) *a.* of or relating to lilies, or the Liliaceae, a family of plants with elongated leaves growing from bulbs, corms or rhizomes. **lily-livered** *a.* cowardly. **lily of the valley** *n.* (*pl.* **lilies of the valley**) a fragrant spring-flowering plant of the genus *Canvallaria*, with a scape of white hanging cuplike flowers. **lily pad** *n.* the broad floating leaf of the water lily. **lily white** *n.* a pure white colour. **lily-white** *a.* 1 pure white. 2 (*coll.*) irreproachable.

lima bean (lē´mə) *n.* 1 a tropical American climbing bean plant, *Phaseolus lunatus*. 2 the flat white edible seed of this; a butter bean.

limb[1] (lim) *n.* 1 each of the articulated extremities of an animal, an arm, leg or wing. 2 a main branch of a tree. 3 a projecting part. 4 a member, branch or arm of a larger group or institution. **out on a limb 1** in a precarious or exposed position. 2 isolated. **to tear limb from limb** to dismember savagely. **limbed** *a.* **limbless** *a.*

limb[2] (lim) *n.* 1 the outermost edge of the sun, moon etc. 2 the graduated arc of a sextant etc. 3 (*Bot.*) the expanded portion of a gamosepalous corolla, petal etc.

limber[1] (lim´bə) *a.* 1 lithe, agile. 2 flexible. **to limber up 1** to stretch and flex the muscles in preparation for physical exercise. 2 to make (something) flexible, to loosen up.

limber[2] (lim´bə) *n.* the detachable part of a gun carriage consisting of two wheels and ammunition box. ~*v.t.* to attach the limber to the gun (usu. with *up*). ~*v.i.* to fasten (up) the limber and gun.

limbo[1] (lim´bō) *n.* (*pl.* **limbos**) **1** the edge or uttermost limit of hell, the abode of those who died unbaptized through no fault of their own, such as the just before Christ and infants. **2** an uncertain or transitional state. **3** a place of neglect or oblivion. **4** prison, confinement.

limbo[2] (lim´bō) *n.* (*pl.* **limbos**) a West Indian dance in which the participants bend backwards and pass under a bar.

lime[1] (līm) *n.* **1** a white caustic alkaline substance, calcium oxide, obtained by burning calcium carbonate (usu. in limestone form), used in building and agriculture; quicklime. **2** calcium hydroxide, a white powder obtained by the action of water on quicklime; slaked lime. **3** any of various calcium compounds used to improve lime-deficient soil. ~*v.t.* **1** to manure with lime; to spread lime over (land). **2** to dress (hides) in lime and water. **3** to smear with birdlime. **limekiln** *n.* a kiln in which limestone is calcined and reduced to lime. **limelight** *n.* **1** a form of lighting, formerly used in theatres, produced by projecting a jet of ignited hydrogen and oxygen upon a ball of lime, making it incandescent. **2** the glare of publicity. **limestone** *n.* (*Geol.*) any rock the basis of which is calcium carbonate, esp. mountain limestone, the principal rock of the Carboniferous series, used as building material and in the manufacture of cement. **limy** *a.* **liminess** *n.*

lime[2] (līm) *n.* (*also* **lime tree**) any tree of the genus *Tilia*, esp. *T. europaea*, with soft timber, heart-shaped leaves, and small clusters of delicately-scented flowers.

lime[3] (līm) *n.* **1** (*also* **lime tree**) a small tropical citrus tree, *Citrus aurantifolia*. **2** the greenish-yellow fruit of this tree with acid flesh. **3** lime juice or a squash or cordial made from it. **lime green** *n.* a bright yellowish-green colour. ~*a.* (*also* **lime-green**) of this colour. **Limey** *n.* (*pl.* **Limeys**) (*N Am., sl., offensive*) **1** a British sailor (from the former use of lime juice on British ships to prevent scurvy). **2** any British person.

limerick (lim´ərik) *n.* a nonsense verse, usu. of five lines, the first, second and fifth having three feet and rhyming together, and the third and fourth having two feet and a different rhyme.

limit (lim´it) *n.* **1** a boundary, a line, point or edge marking termination or utmost extent. **2** (*pl.*) the boundary of an area, district. **3** the maximum or minimum amount permissible or possible. **4** a restraint, a check. **5** (*Math.*) a value, position, quantity etc. which a function or the sum of a series can approach indefinitely. ~*v.t.* (*pres.p.* **limiting**, *past, p.p.* **limited**) **1** to set a limit or boundary to. **2** to confine within certain bounds. **3** to restrict (to). **4** to serve as boundary or restriction to. **off limits** out of bounds, esp. to

military personnel. **to be the limit** to be unacceptable, intolerable or extremely annoying. **within limits** to a certain degree or extent. **limitable** *a.* **limitation** (-ā´shən) *n.* **1** the act of limiting; the state of being limited. **2** (*usu. pl.*) something which limits a person's achievements, competence etc. **3** a restriction. **4** (*Law*) the period within which an action must be brought and beyond which it may not lie. **limitative** (-ətiv) *a.* **limited** *a.* **1** not universal or general, confined within limits. **2** restricted, narrow. **3** few, sparse, scanty. **4** (*coll.*) not very clever or well-read. **5** (after the name of a company) whose shareholders have limited liability. ~*n.* a limited company. **limited company** *n.* a company whose shareholders have limited liability. **limited edition** *n.* an edition of a book, print etc. of which only a small number is issued. **limited liability** *n.* responsibility for the debts of a company only to a specified amount, which is proportionate to the amount of stock held. **limited liability company** *n.* a limited company. **limitedly** *adv.* **limitedness** *n.* **limiter** *n.* **limitless** *a.*

limnology (limnol´əji) *n.* the study of the physical, biological, geographical etc. features of lakes, ponds and other freshwater bodies. **limnological** (-loj´-) *a.* **limnologist** *n.*

limo (lim´ō) *n.* (*pl.* **limos**) (*coll.*) short for LIMOUSINE.

limonite (lī´mənīt) *n.* a common mineral consisting of hydrated ferric oxides, a source of iron.

limousine (lim´əzēn) *n.* a large opulent car (orig. having a closed body with a separate driver's seat), esp. one with a glass partition dividing the driver from the passengers.

limp[1] (limp) *v.i.* **1** to walk lamely, esp. dragging one injured leg. **2** to proceed slowly and with difficulty. **3** (of verse, logic etc.) to be irregular. ~*n.* a limping step or walk. **limpingly** *adv.*

limp[2] (limp) *a.* **1** wanting in stiffness, flaccid, flexible, pliable. **2** lacking in energy or impact. **3** (of book covers) not stiffened by boards. **limply** *adv.* **limpness** *n.* **limp-wristed** *a.* **1** (of a man) effeminate. **2** effete, ineffectual.

limpet (lim´pit) *n.* **1** any individual of the genus of gastropods *Patella*, having an open conical shell, found adhering firmly to rocks. **2** a tenacious person or thing. **limpet mine** *n.* an explosive device which clings to a ship's hull, tank etc. by magnetic or adhesive means.

limpid (lim´pid) *a.* **1** clear, pellucid, transparent. **2** lucid, perspicuous. **limpidity** (-pid´-) *n.* **limpidly** *adv.*

linage (lī´nij) *n.* **1** amount of printed matter reckoned by lines. **2** payment by the line.

Usage note The nouns *linage* and *lineage* should not be confused: *linage* refers to printed matter, and *lineage* to ancestry.

linchpin (linch´pin), **lynchpin** *n.* **1** a pin serving

to hold a wheel on the axle. **2** a person or thing essential to an organization etc.
Lincs. *abbr.* Lincolnshire.
linctus (lingk´təs) *n.* (*pl.* **linctuses**) a syrupy cough medicine.
linden (lin´dən) *n.* a tree of the genus *Tilia*, a lime tree.
line[1] (līn) *n.* **1** a threadlike mark; such a mark drawn by a pencil, pen, graver or other instrument. **2** a streak, narrow band, seam, furrow, wrinkle etc. resembling this. **3** (*Math.*) something which has length without breadth or thickness. **4** the track of a moving point. **5** the curve connecting a series of points. **6** the edge or contour of a shape, outline, lineament. **7** such outlines collectively as a feature of art or of an artist's style. **8** (*pl.*) the general appearance or outline of a thing. **9** a limit, a boundary. **10** in sport, a line delimiting the playing area or part of it; the starting or finishing point for a race. **11** a row or continuous series of letters, words, people or other objects. **12** a short letter, a note. **13** a single verse of poetry. **14** (*pl.*) a piece of poetry. **15** (*pl.*) the words of an actor's part. **16** (*pl.*) a specified quantity of verse or prose for a school student to copy out as an imposition. **17** (*pl.*) a certificate of marriage. **18** a length of rope, cord, wire or string. **19** a rope, cord, string, wire etc. used for a specific purpose, such as a fishing line, a plumb line, a clothes line etc. **20** a wire or cable for telegraph or telephone. **21** a connection by means of this. **22** a course or channel for communication of any kind. **23** the course or direction taken by a moving object. **24** a railway track. **25** a particular railway route or link. **26** a railway system under one management. **27** a series of ships or public conveyances plying between certain places or under one management. **28** a company operating these. **29** a series of persons related in direct descent or succession, family, lineage. **30** a branch of business, field of activity, particular interest. **31** a certain class of goods. **32** mode of procedure, conduct, thought. **33** policy. **34** a series of trenches, ramparts etc. **35** a row of men, ships etc. ranged as in order of battle. **36** the aggregate of troops in an army apart from support units etc. **37** any one of the horizontal lines on a television screen, traced by a scanning electron beam, which creates the picture. **38** a narrow band in a spectrum that appears noticeably lighter or darker than adjacent areas. **39** (*Mus.*) each one of the five horizontal marks forming a stave; a series of notes or tones forming a part or melody. **40** (*coll.*) pertinent facts; a useful hint or tip. **41** (*sl.*) a piece of smooth talk; a false or exaggerated account. **42** the base of most letters in printing or writing. **43** the twelfth part of an inch. ~*v.t.* **1** to draw lines upon, to cover with lines. **2** to mark (in, off etc.) with lines. **3** to spread out, extend or post (troops etc.) in line. **all along the line** at every point, throughout. **in line for** likely to

receive; a candidate for. **in line with 1** in accordance with. **2** in alignment with. **in the line of** during or as part of the normal course of (esp. duty). **on the line 1** available to be communicated with, esp. by telephone. **2** (*esp. N Am.*) at risk. **out of line** (*esp. N Am.*) (of a person) acting in an inappropriate, improper or unruly manner. **out of line with 1** not in accordance with. **2** out of alignment with. **the line/ Line** the equator. **to bring into line** to cause to conform (with). **to come into line** to conform. **to get a line on** (*coll.*) to learn or discover useful information about. **to lay it on the line** to speak out frankly or uncompromisingly. **to lay/ put on the line** to put at risk. **to line up 1** to arrange in a line or lines. **2** to align. **3** to queue. **4** to secure or arrange for the appearance of (a speaker, celebrity). **5** to prepare. **6** to take a stand for or against. **linebacker** *n.* in American football, a defensive player whose position is just behind the line of scrimmage. **lined** *a.* **line dance** *n.* a dance in which the dancers perform synchronized movements while standing in a line. **line dancing** *n.* **line drawing** *n.* a drawing with pen or pencil using lines only. **linefeed** *n.* **1** on a printer, the ability to advance the paper by the space of one line at a time. **2** a similar facility on a VDU screen. **lineman** *n.* (*pl.* **linemen**) **1** a person employed in the maintenance and repair of a line of railway, telegraph etc. **2** in surveying, a person who carries the line or chain. **line of country** *n.* one's special field of interest. **line of credit** *n.* the maximum amount of credit allowed to a borrower. **line of fire** *n.* the expected path of a bullet, shell etc. fired from a gun aimed in a particular direction. **line of sight** *n.* a straight line along which an observer's vision is unobstructed. **line of vision** *n.* the straight line along which an observer looks. **line-out** *n.* a method of restarting a match in Rugby Union when the ball has gone out of play, by throwing it in between the forwards of each team lined up facing the touchline. **line printer** *n.* a high-speed output device, used esp. in conjunction with a computer, which prints copy a whole line at a time. **-liner** (līnə) *comb. form* (usu. preceded by a numeral) a thing with (the specified number of) lines. **linesman** *n.* (*pl.* **linesmen**) **1** in tennis etc., an official who has to note when and where a ball crosses a line. **2** a lineman. **line-up** *n.* **1** a row or group of persons assembled for a particular purpose, such as the members of a team, the people appearing in a show. **2** (*esp. N Am.*) a queue. **liny** *a.* (*comp.* **linier**, *superl.* **liniest**) **1** marked with lines. **2** wrinkly.
line[2] (līn) *v.t.* **1** to put a covering of different material on the inside of (a garment, box etc.). **2** to serve as such a covering for. **3** to fill the inside of. **liner**[1] *n.* **1** a removable thing that fits inside something else. **2** material used as lining. **lining** *n.* **1** a covering for the inside of anything; the act of fitting such a

covering. **2** an interior surface or layer (e.g. of an organ).

lineage (lin´iij) *n.* descendants in a direct line from a common progenitor, ancestry, pedigree.

Usage note See note under LINAGE.

lineal (lin´iəl) *a.* **1** ascending or descending in the direct line of ancestry, as opposed to *collateral.* **2** linear. **lineality** (-al´-) *n.* **lineally** *adv.*

lineament (lin´iəmənt) *n.* **1** (*usu. pl.*) characteristic lines or features. **2** outline, contour.

Usage note The nouns *lineament* and *liniment* should not be confused: a *lineament* is an outline or feature, and *liniment* an embrocation.

linear (lin´iə) *a.* **1** composed of or having the form of lines. **2** having a straight or lengthwise direction. **3** narrow, slender with parallel sides. **4** of one dimension. **5** (of mathematical functions, expressions etc.) containing only first degree terms, and able to be represented on a graph as a straight line. **linearly** *adv.* **linear measure** *n.* a system of units for measuring length. **linear programming** *n.* a method of solving practical problems in economics etc., using mathematical models involving complex interactions of linear equations.

linen (lin´in) *n.* **1** a cloth made of flax. **2** (*collect.*) articles chiefly made of linen, esp. underclothing, sheets, table cloths etc. ~*a.* made of linen or flax. **to wash one's dirty linen in public** to expose one's private scandals, quarrels etc. to public attention. **linen basket** *n.* a basket for dirty laundry.

liner¹ LINE².

liner² (lī´nə) *n.* **1** each of a regular line of passenger ships or aircraft. **2** colouring material for pencilling the eyebrows. **liner train** *n.* a fast goods train with permanently-coupled wagons for transporting containers.

ling¹ (ling) *n.* a long slender food fish, *Molva molva,* found in the northern seas.

ling² (ling) *n.* heather or heath, *Calluna vulgaris.*

-ling¹ (ling) *suf.* forming nouns denoting a person or thing, as in *grayling, sibling.*

-ling² (-ling) *suf.* forming adverbs and adjectives, as in *darkling.*

linger (ling´gə) *v.i.* **1** to delay going, to be slow or reluctant to leave. **2** to remain in or around a place. **3** not to dissipate or disappear, to persist. **4** to remain alive, though slowly dying. **5** to loiter; to be slow in doing something. **lingerer** *n.* **lingering** *a.* **lingeringly** *adv.*

lingerie (lă´zhəri) *n.* women's underwear and nightclothes.

lingo (ling´gō) *n.* (*pl.* **lingos, lingoes**) (*coll.*) a foreign language, peculiar dialect or technical phraseology.

lingua franca (ling-gwə frang´kə) *n.* (*pl.* **lingua francas**) a language serving as a medium of communication between different peoples.

lingual (ling´gwəl) *a.* **1** of or relating to the tongue. **2** in phonetics, formed by the tongue. **3** (*formal*) of or relating to languages. **lingually** *adv.* **linguiform** (-gwifawm) *a.* having the shape of a tongue.

linguine (lingwē´ni) *n.pl.* pasta in the form of long flat ribbons.

linguist (ling´gwist) *n.* **1** a person who is skilled in languages. **2** a person who studies languages. **linguistic** (-gwis´-) *a.* of or relating to languages or the study of languages. **linguistically** *adv.* **linguistics** *n.* the scientific study of languages.

liniment (lin´imənt) *n.* a liquid preparation, usu. with oil, for rubbing on bruised or inflamed parts, an embrocation.

Usage note See note under LINEAMENT.

lining LINE².

link (lingk) *n.* **1** a ring or loop of a chain. **2** a connecting part in machinery etc. or in a series, sequence, argument etc. **3** a means of contact between two points in a communications system. **4** a means of transport between two places. **5** a cuff link. **6** one-hundredth of a surveyor's chain equal to 7.92 in. (about 20 cm). ~*v.t.* **1** to connect or attach (to, together, up etc.) by or as by a link or links. **2** to connect by association. **3** to clasp (hands) or intertwine (arms). ~*v.i.* to be connected. **linkage** *n.* **1** the act or manner of linking or being linked. **2** a system of links. **3** the occurrence of two genes on the same chromosome so that they tend to be inherited together. **linkman** *n.* (*pl.* **linkmen**) **1** a television or radio presenter who provides continuity between separate items (e.g. of news, sport) in a broadcast. **2** in football, a player with an intermediate role between two main groups, as between the midfield and the strikers. **link-up** *n.* **1** a connection. **2** an association or union. **3** the act of linking.

links (lingks) *n.pl.* (*sometimes treated as sing.*) a golf course.

Linnaean (linē´ən, -nā´-), **Linnean** *a.* of or relating to Linnaeus or his system of classification and naming of plants and animals. ~*n.* a follower of Linnaeus.

linnet (lin´it) *n.* a finch, *Acanthis cannabina,* with brownish plumage.

lino (lī´nō) *n.* (*pl.* **linos**) short for LINOLEUM.

linocut *n.* an engraving on linoleum in the manner of a woodcut.

linoleic acid (linōlē´ik) *n.* (*Chem.*) a colourless oily polyunsaturated fatty acid occurring as a glyceride in linseed and other natural oils, used in making soaps and emulsifiers and essential to the human diet.

linolenic acid (linōlen´ik) *n.* (*Chem.*) a fatty acid similar in its properties and provenance to linoleic acid but with one more double bond.

linoleum (linō´liəm) *n.* a preparation of oxidized linseed oil mixed with ground cork and laid upon fabric, used as a floor covering.

linseed (lin´sēd) *n.* the seed of the flax plant.

linseed cake *n.* the solid mass left after the oil has been pressed out of flax seed. **linseed oil** *n.* the oil expressed from linseed, used in paints, printer's ink, linoleum etc.

linsey-woolsey (linziwul´zi) *n.* a coarse fabric of linen or cotton warp with wool filling.

lint (lint) *n.* **1** absorbent cotton cloth with the nap raised on one side, used for dressing wounds etc. **2** fluff or down from cloth.

lintel (lin´təl) *n.* (*Archit.*) the horizontal beam or stone over a door or window. **lintelled,** (*N Am.*) **linteled** *a.*

liny LINE¹.

lion (lī´ən) *n.* **1** a large and powerful carnivorous quadruped, *Panthera leo,* usu. brown or tawny, with tufted tail and (in the adult male) a long mane, inhabiting southern Asia and Africa. **2** a courageous person. **3** an eminent celebrity, an object of general attention. **the lion's mouth** a dangerous place. **the lion's share** the largest part or the whole. **lioness** *n.* a female lion. **lion-heart** *n.* a very courageous person. **lion-hearted** *a.* **lionize, lionise** *v.t.* to treat as an object of interest or curiosity. **lionization** (-zā´shən) *n.* **lionizer** *n.* **lionlike** *a.* **lion tamer** *n.* a circus performer who trains lions and performs tricks with them in the ring.

lip (lip) *n.* **1** either of the two fleshy parts enclosing the opening of the mouth. **2** anything resembling a lip, such as the projecting lobe of a bilabiate corolla; a labium. **3** the edge or rim of an orifice, chasm, container etc. **4** (*sl.*) impudence, cheek. **5** (*pl.*) the mouth, as organ of speech. ~*v.t.* (*pres.p.* **lipping,** *past, p.p.* **lipped**) **1** to touch with the lips. **2** to kiss. **3** to touch gently; (of water) to lap against. **to bite one's lip** to express vexation, to repress anger, laughter or other emotion. **to curl one's lip** to express scorn or contempt. **to hang on someone's lips** to listen eagerly for every word spoken. **to keep a stiff upper lip** to be self-reliant, inflexible, unflinching. **to pass one's lips** to be eaten, drunk or spoken. **to smack one's lips** to part one's lips making a loud smacking noise as a sign of appetite, gleeful anticipation etc. **lip-gloss** *n.* a cosmetic which makes the lips glossy. **lipless** *a.* **lipped** *a.* **lippy** *a.* (*comp.* **lippier,** *superl.* **lippiest**) cheeky, insolent. **lip-read** *v.t., v.i.* (*past, p.p.* **lip-read**) to follow what a person says by observing the movement of their lips. **lip-reader** *n.* **lip-reading** *n.* **lipsalve** *n.* **1** ointment for the lips. **2** compliments, flattery. **lip-service** *n.* flattery, servile agreement with a sentiment etc. expressed but not put into practice. **lipstick** *n.* a stick of cosmetic for colouring the lips. **lip-sync, lip-synch** *v.t.* to synchronize the movement of the lips with a prerecorded soundtrack (of words, music etc.) on film or television.

lipase (lip´āz) *n.* any enzyme which decomposes fats.

lipid (lip´id) *n.* (*Chem.*) any of various organic compounds which are esters of fatty acids, insoluble in water but soluble in other substances, and important structural components of living cells. **lipidic** *a.* **lipidosis** (lipidō´sis) *n.* (*pl.* **lipidoses** (-sēz)) any lipidic disorder.

lipo- (lip´ō), **lip-** *comb. form* fat, fatty.

lipoprotein (lipōprō´tēn) *n.* a soluble protein which carries lipids in the bloodstream.

liposome (lip´əsōm) *n.* a minute synthetic sac made of a lipid substance containing an aqueous droplet, used to convey drugs to specific tissues.

liposuction (lip´ōsŭkshən) *n.* a surgical process for the cosmetic removal of excess fat from beneath the skin by suction.

lippy LIP.

liquefy (lik´wifī), **liquify** *v.t.* (*3rd pers. sing. pres.* **liquefies, liquifies,** *pres.p.* **liquefying, liquifying,** *past, p.p.* **liquefied, liquified**) (*Chem.*) to convert from a solid (or gaseous) to a liquid form. ~*v.i.* to become liquid. **liquefacient** (-fā´shənt) *n.* a substance which liquefies or causes liquefaction. ~*a.* serving to liquefy. **liquefaction** (-fak´-) *n.* **liquefactive** (-fak´-) *a.* **liquefiable** *a.* **liquefier** *n.* **liquescence** (-kwes´-), **liquescency** *n.* the process of becoming or tending to become liquid. **liquescent** (-kwes´-) *a.*

liqueur (likūə´) *n.* an alcoholic cordial sweetened or flavoured with an aromatic substance and drunk in small quantities, usu. after a meal.

liquid (lik´wid) *a.* **1** flowing or capable of flowing, like water or oil. **2** (of a gas) able to flow after being subject to intense cold. **3** transparent, limpid, clear. **4** (of sounds) not guttural, fluent, smooth, easily pronounced. **5** (of assets) readily convertible into cash; (of a person, company) having cash or liquid assets. **6** (of principles etc.) unstable, changeable. ~*n.* **1** a substance that is able to flow; a substance whose molecules are incompressible and inelastic, but, though moving freely among themselves, cannot escape as in a gaseous state. **2** a letter pronounced with a slight contact of the organs of articulation, as *l, r,* and sometimes *m.* **liquidate** *v.t.* **1** to pay off (a debt etc.). **2** to wind up (a bankrupt estate etc.). **3** to convert (assets) into cash. **4** to assassinate; to destroy. ~*v.i.* (of a company) to have its debts, liabilities and assets liquidated. **liquidation** (-ā´shən) *n.* **liquidator** *n.* the person officially appointed to effect a liquidation. **liquid crystal** *n.* a liquid with physical, esp. optical, properties analogous to crystals. **liquid crystal display** *n.* a display, esp. in electronic calculators, using liquid crystal cells which change their reflectivity in an electric field. **liquidity** (-kwid´-) *n.* (*pl.* **liquidities**) **1** the state of being liquid. **2** the possession of sufficient liquid assets to discharge current liabilities. **3** (*pl.*) liquid assets. **liquidize, liquidise** *v.t.* **1** to reduce to liquid, to liquefy. **2** to purée (food) into a liquid. **liquidizer** *n.* a kitchen appliance with blades and various attachments for chopping or puréeing vegetables, blending soup etc. **liquidly** *adv.* **liquid measure** *n.* a unit or system of units used to measure liquids.

liquidness *n.* **liquid paraffin** *n.* an oily liquid obtained from petroleum distillation and used as a laxative. **liquid storax** *n.* a balsam obtained from *Liquidambar orientalis.*

liquidambar (likwidam´bə) *n.* **1** any tropical tree of the genus *Liquidambar,* several species of which yield a fragrant resin or balsam called storax. **2** the resin so produced.

liquify LIQUEFY.

liquor (lik´ə) *n.* **1** an alcoholic drink, usu. not including wine or beer; such drinks collectively. **2** a liquid or fluid substance, esp. the liquid part of anything, e.g. a solution, a secretion, food or the water used for cooking. **3** the water used in brewing beer. **4** an aqueous solution of a drug.

liquorice (lik´əris), (*N Am.*) **licorice** *n.* **1** a black extract from the root of the leguminous plant *Glycyrrhiza glabra,* used in medicine and confectionery. **2** this plant.

lira (liə´rə) *n.* (*pl.* **lire** (liə´rə, -rā, -ri), **liras**) **1** the standard monetary unit of Italy. **2** the standard monetary unit of Turkey.

lisle (līl) *n.* a fine, strong cotton thread, esp. for stockings.

lisp (lisp) *v.i.* **1** to pronounce *s* and *z* with the sound of *th* or *dh.* **2** to speak affectedly; to speak imperfectly, as a child. *~v.t.* to pronounce with a lisp. *~n.* **1** the act or habit of lisping. **2** the speech defect which causes one to lisp. **3** (*poet.*) a rustling or rippling sound. **lisper** *n.* **lispingly** *adv.*

lissom (lis´əm), **lissome** *a.* lithe, supple, nimble. **lissomly** *adv.* **lissomness** *n.*

list[1] (list) *n.* **1** a record or catalogue of items, names etc. which are related in some way or to be used for some specific purpose, usu. entered one below the other. **2** (*Comput.*) a data structure in linear order. *~v.t.* **1** to make a list of. **2** to enter (an item, name) on a list. **3** to approve for dealings on the Stock Exchange. **4** in the UK, to declare to be a listed building. **listed** *a.* **listed building** *n.* in the UK, a building officially listed as being of particular architectural or historical interest which may not be altered or demolished without special consent. **listing** *n.* **1** a list. **2** an entry on a list. **3** the act of making a list. **4** placement on a list, esp. on the official List of Securities of the London Stock Exchange. **5** (*pl.*) lists printed in newspapers, magazines etc. showing the dates and times of concerts, plays, films and similar events. **list price** *n.* the price of an article as given in the manufacturer's catalogue or advertisement.

list[2] (list) *n.* **1** the border, edge or selvage of cloth. **2** a strip of this used as material. **3** (*pl., Hist.*) the palisades enclosing a piece of ground for a tournament; the ground so enclosed. **4** a ridge in ploughed land thrown up between two furrows. **to enter the lists** to enter into a contest.

list[3] (list) *n.* the fact of leaning over to one side (of a ship, building etc.). *~v.i.* to lean over, to careen.

listen (lis´ən) *v.i.* **1** to make an effort to hear. **2** to pay attention (to). **3** to heed, to obey, to follow. **4** to wait in the hope or expectation of hearing. *~n.* an act of listening. **to listen in 1** to be present at, but not contribute to, a conversation, discussion etc. **2** to eavesdrop; to intercept and listen to a telephone or radio communication. **3** to listen to a radio broadcast. **to listen out** to wait in the hope or expectation of hearing. **to listen up** (*N Am., coll.*) to pay attention. **listenable** *a.* pleasant to listen to. **listener** *n.* a person who listens, esp. to radio broadcasting. **listening** *a.* **listening post** *n.* **1** a position where people are posted to overhear what the enemy is saying or planning. **2** a place where electronic communications are intercepted. **3** any place for gathering useful information about the affairs of another country, area, organization etc.

listeria (listiə´riə) *n.* any bacterium of a genus, *Listeria,* found in certain foods, esp. poultry and soft cheese, and capable of affecting the central nervous system and causing meningitis, encephalitis or miscarriage if not killed by cooking. **listeriosis** (-ō´sis) *n.* serious food-poisoning caused by the presence of *Listeria monocytogenes.*

listless (list´lis) *a.* lacking the will or energy to do anything; bored and languid but uneasy or querulous at the same time. **listlessly** *adv.* **listlessness** *n.*

lit[1] LIGHT[1].

lit[2] LIGHT[3].

litany (lit´əni) *n.* (*pl.* **litanies**) **1** a solemn form of supplicatory prayer, used in public worship, consisting of a series of short invocations followed by fixed responses. **2** a long, usu. boring, list or catalogue. **the Litany** the supplicatory prayer in this form found in the Book of Common Prayer.

litchi LYCHEE.

lit crit *abbr.* literary criticism.

-lite (līt) *suf.* forming names of minerals and fossils such as *aerolite, coprolite, radiolite.*

liter LITRE.

literacy LITERATE.

literal (lit´ərəl) *a.* **1** according or limited to the primary or explicit meaning, not figurative or metaphorical. **2** following the exact words (as a translation). **3** unimaginative, prosaic, matter-of-fact. **4** without exaggeration; so called without exaggeration. **5** used with the meaning 'without exaggeration' but applied to an often exaggerated metaphor as in *a literal deluge of offers.* **6** consisting of or expressed by letters. *~n.* a misprint or misspelling of a word. **literalism** *n.* **1** the interpretation or understanding of words and statements in a literal sense. **2** realistic or unimaginative portrayal in art or literature. **literalist** *n.* **literalistic** *a.* **literality** (-ral´-), **literalness** *n.* **literally** *adv.* **1** in a literal manner. **2** without exaggeration (often used with considerable exaggeration to reinforce a metaphor as in *I literally jumped out of my skin*).

Usage note *Literal* and *literally* as emphasizers (implying some figurative use or exaggeration) reverse the usual meanings of the words, and so are often disapproved of.

literary (lit´ərəri) *a.* **1** of or relating to literature or writing. **2** versed or engaged in literature. **3** well-read. **4** consisting of written or printed compositions. **5** (of language) derived from or used in literature, formal not colloquial in style. **literary criticism** *n.* (the art of making) evaluative and interpretative judgements on literary works. **literary critic** *n.* **literary executor** *n.* a person appointed to deal with the copyrights and unpublished works of a deceased author.

literate (lit´ərət) *a.* **1** able to read and write. **2** educated. **3** (*as comb. form*) having knowledge or competence in (*computer-literate*). ~*n.* **1** a person who is able to read and write. **2** an educated person. **literacy** *n.* **literati** (-rah´ti) *n.pl.* **1** men and women of letters. **2** the learned. **literature** (lit´rəchə) *n.* **1** (*collect.*) the written or printed productions of a country or period or those relating to a particular subject. **2** the class of writings distinguished for beauty of form or expression, as poetry, novels, essays etc. **3** printed matter, usu. of an informative kind. **4** the production of literary works. **5** the literary profession.

-lith (lith) *suf.* denoting a type of stone, as in *monolith.*

litharge (lith´ahj) *n.* a red or yellow mineral form of lead monoxide.

lithe (līdh) *a.* flexible, limber, supple. **lithely** *adv.* **litheness** *n.* **lithesome** *a.*

lithium (lith´iəm) *n.* (*Chem.*) a soft, silver-white element, the lightest metallic element, at. no. 3, chem. symbol Li, a member of the alkali series, used, esp. in alloys and batteries.

litho (lī´thō, lith´ō) *n.* (*pl.* **lithos**) **1** short for LITHOGRAPH. **2** short for LITHOGRAPHY (under LITHOGRAPH).

litho- (lith´ō) **lith-** *comb. form* of or relating to stone.

lithograph (lith´əgrahf) *v.t.* to print by lithography. ~*n.* **1** a print made by lithography. **2** an impression from a drawing on stone or metal. **lithographer** (-thog´-) *n.* **lithographic** (-graf´-), **lithographical** *a.* **lithographically** *adv.* **lithography** (-thog´-) *n.* the art or process of printing from a stone or plate which is treated so that it is ink-receptive in some parts and ink-repellent in others.

lithosphere (lith´əsfiə) *n.* (*Geol.*) the outer, rocky shell of the earth, the crust of the earth. **lithospheric** (-sfer´ik) *a.*

Lithuanian (lithūā´niən) *a.* of or relating to Lithuania, an independent republic (formerly part of the USSR) on the Baltic Sea. ~*n.* **1** a native or inhabitant of Lithuania. **2** the language of Lithuania.

litigate (lit´igāt) *v.t.* to contest in a court of law.

~*v.i.* **1** to go to law. **2** to carry on a lawsuit. **litigable** *a.* **litigant** *a.* engaged in a lawsuit. ~*n.* a party to a lawsuit. **litigation** (-ā´shən) *n.* **litigious** (-tij´əs) *a.* **1** fond of litigation. **2** quarrelsome, contentious. **3** subject or open to legal dispute. **4** of or relating to litigation. **litigiosity** (-ios´-), **litigiousness** *n.* **litigiously** *adv.*

litmus (lit´məs) *n.* a substance obtained from *Roccella tinctoria* or other lichens, that is turned red by acids or blue by alkalis. **litmus paper** *n.* unsized paper stained with litmus, used to test the acidity or the alkaline nature of a solution. **litmus test** *n.* **1** a test using litmus paper. **2** any test that indicates the fundamental nature of something.

litotes (lītō´tēz) *n.* an understatement by which an affirmative is expressed by negation of its contrary, as in 'not a little' for 'very' or a weaker expression used to suggest a stronger one.

❌ **litrature** common misspelling of LITERATURE (under LITERATE).

litre (lē´tə), (*esp. N Am.*) **liter** *n.* the unit of capacity in the metric system, equal to a cubic decimetre, or about 1.75 pints.

Litt. B, Lit. B *abbr.* Bachelor of Letters, Bachelor of Literature.

Litt. D., Lit. D. *abbr.* Doctor of Letters, Doctor of Literature.

litter (lit´ə) *n.* **1** refuse, rubbish, esp. waste paper, scattered about in a public place. **2** a scattered, disorderly collection of odds and ends. **3** a state of disorder or untidiness. **4** the young brought forth by a sow, bitch, cat etc. at one birth. **5** a couch in which a person may be carried by animals or on people's shoulders. **6** a stretcher used for transporting the sick or wounded. **7** straw, hay or other soft material used as a bed for horses, cattle etc. or as a covering for plants. **8** cat litter. ~*v.t.* **1** to scatter (things) about carelessly. **2** to make (a place) untidy with articles scattered about. **3** to bring forth (said esp. of the sow, dog, cat etc., applied derogatively to human beings). **4** to supply (beasts) with litter. **5** to spread bedding for. ~*v.i.* to bring forth a litter of young. **litterbug, litter lout** *n.* (*coll.*) a person who drops rubbish in public places. **littery** *a.*

little (lit´əl) *a.* (*comp.* **less, lesser**, (*coll.*) **littler**, *superl.* **least**, (*coll.*) **littlest**) **1** small, not great in size, amount or quantity. **2** not tall, short in stature. **3** short in duration or distance. **4** slight, inconsiderable, trifling, petty. **5** young or younger. **6** small in comparison to others of the same name or description. **7** resembling something else, but on a small scale. **8** used to reinforce a sense of the endearing qualities of something (*a sweet little house*). **9** used to reinforce an expression of contempt (*you rotten little liar*). ~*adv.* (*comp.* **less**, *superl.* **least**) **1** to only a small extent, not much (*has improved little since my last visit*). **2** not at all (*they little expected*). ~*n.* **1** a small amount, quantity, space, distance, time etc. **2** not much. **a little** to a small extent, slightly (*feeling a little better*). **in little** in miniature. **little by little** by small degrees, (very) gradually. **little or nothing** scarcely anything. **no little** considerable; a fair amount of. **not a little 1** very, greatly, extremely. **2** a great deal. **little auk** *n.* a small Arctic auk, *Plautus alle*. **Little Bear** *n.* (*Astron.*) the constellation Ursa Minor. **little end** *n.* the smaller end of a connecting rod in an internal-combustion engine. **little finger** *n.* the smallest of the fingers. **little grebe** *n.* a small brownish European diving bird, *Podiceps ruficolis*, of the grebe family. **little green men** *n.pl.* (*coll.*) beings from outer space. **little man** *n.* 1 the ordinary man in the street without special power or status. **2** (*esp. facet.*) (as a form of address) a boy. **littleness** *n.* **little ones** *n.pl.* children or young animals. **little owl** *n.* a small owl, *Athene noctua*, of Eurasia and Africa, which has speckled brown plumage and a flattish head. **little people** *n.pl.* the fairies. **Little Russian** *a.* (*Hist.*) Ukrainian. **little woman** *n.* (*often derog. or facet.*) one's wife.

littoral (lit´ərəl) *a.* of or relating to the shore, esp. the zone between high- and low-water marks. ~*n.* a coastal region.

liturgy (lit´əji) *n.* (*pl.* **liturgies**) **1** a form of public worship laid down by a Church. **2** a Church's entire ritual for public worship or the set of formularies in which this is set forth. **3** (**Liturgy**) the Communion office of the Orthodox Church. **the Liturgy** (in the Anglican Church) the Book of Common Prayer. **liturgic** (-tœ´-), **liturgical** *a.* **liturgically** *adv.* **liturgist** *n.*

live[1] (liv) *v.i.* **1** to have life, to be alive, to be capable of performing animal or vegetable functions. **2** to reside, to dwell (at, in etc.). **3** to be nourished, to subsist (upon). **4** to depend for subsistence (upon). **5** to receive or gain a livelihood (by). **6** to pass or conduct one's life in a particular condition, manner etc. **7** to live strenuously, to enjoy life intensely. **8** to continue alive, to survive. **9** to remain in operation or as an active principle. ~*v.t.* **1** to pass, to spend (a specified kind of life). **2** to manifest, express or effect, by living. **long live** an expression of loyal good wishes to a particular person, institution etc. **to live and let live** to be tolerant of the deficiencies of others in return for indulgence of one's own. **to live down** to efface the recollection of (former mistakes, scandal etc.) by one's conduct. **to live in 1** (of an employee) to reside at one's place of work. **2** (of a student) to reside on the campus. **to live it up** (*coll.*) to enjoy oneself without restraint, to go on the spree. **to live off 1** to be dependent on financially, for one's livelihood. **2** to feed oneself (exclusively) on. **to live on 1** to continue to exist, to endure, to survive. **2** to support oneself on (a specific amount of money). **3** to feed oneself (exclusively) on. **to live out 1** to spend the whole or the remainder of (one's life, days). **2** to express, manifest or fulfil in one's life and conduct. **3** (of an employee) to

reside away from one's place of work. **4** (of a student) not to reside on campus. **to live through** to experience and survive (an unpleasant experience). **to live together** to cohabit. **to live up to** to be worthy of, to conform to a prescribed standard. **to live with 1** to cohabit with. **2** to accept or tolerate. **liveable, livable** *a.* **1** (of life) worth living. **2** (of a house, accommodation) fit to live in. **3** (*also* **liveable with**) (of a person) fit to live with. **liveableness, liveability** (-bil´-) *n.* **lived** *a.* **lived-in** *a.* **1** (of a room) showing signs of habitation; homely, comfortable, reassuring. **2** (of a face) bearing the marks of experience. **live-in** *a.* **1** (of a lover) cohabiting. **2** (of an employee) resident on the premises. **liver**[1] *n.* a person who spends their life in a specified way (as a *good liver*).

live[2] (līv) *a.* **1** alive, living. **2** charged with energy, esp. with electrical energy; having the potential to function or discharge immediately; not exhausted or spent. **3** (of coals) burning, ignited. **4** (of a shell, bomb) unexploded. **5** (of a volcano) still active. **6** (of a radio, television broadcast) transmitted or transmitting at the actual time of an event, not a recording. **7** (of a performance of a play, concert etc.) given in front of an audience which sees or hears the event taking place. **8** (of a recording) made at a live performance; recorded at a single take without subsequent overdubbing. **9** (of an issue) of current interest and concern. **10** (of a wheel, axle etc.) able to transmit power; moving with a driving member. ~*adv.* at the actual time of the event; before an actual audience. **to go live** (*Comput.*) (of a system) to become operational. **liven** *v.t.* to make lively, to enliven. ~*v.i.* to cheer (up). **live oak** *n.* a N American evergreen tree, esp. *Quercus virginianus*, valuable for shipbuilding. **livestock** *n.* animals kept for farming or domestic purposes. **liveware** *n.* (*Comput.*) the staff operating and working with computer systems. **live wire** *n.* **1** a wire through which an electric current is flowing. **2** (*coll.*) an energetic person.

livelihood (līv´lihud) *n.* means of subsistence; occupation.

livelong (liv´long) *a.* (*poet.*) the whole, entire, the whole length of.

lively (līv´li) *a.* (*comp.* **livelier,** *superl.* **liveliest**) **1** full of life, brisk, active, vigorous. **2** vivacious, cheerful, sociable. **3** animated, stimulating. **4** (of a description) lifelike, actual, vivid. **5** (of an impression) striking, forcible. **6** (of a colour) bright, vivid. **7** (of pace) brisk, fast. **8** (of a bouncing ball, boat etc.) moving in a springy, jerky or unpredictable fashion. **look lively** hurry up, make haste. **livelily** *adv.* **liveliness** *n.*

liver[1] LIVE[1].

liver[2] (liv´ə) *n.* **1** a glandular organ in the abdominal cavity of vertebrates which secretes bile and purifies the blood. **2** the flesh of this from a sheep, calf etc., used as food. ~*a.* liver-coloured. **liver chestnut** *n.* a horse of a dark chestnut colour. **liver colour,** (*N Am.*) **liver color** *n.* the colour of the liver, a reddish-brown. **liver-coloured** *a.* **liver fluke** *n.* any of various parasitic worms, esp. *Fasciola hepatica*, that infect the bile ducts of sheep, cattle etc. **liverish** *a.* 1 having a disordered liver. 2 irritable. **liverishly** *adv.* **liverishness** *n.* **liver salts** *n.pl.* a preparation of mineral salts used to relieve indigestion. **liver sausage, liverwurst** *n.* sausage made from liver. **liverwort** *n.* any plant of the Hepaticae family, cryptogamic plants similar to mosses, that grow in damp places and some of which have liver-shaped leaves. **livery**[1] *a.* 1 resembling liver. 2 (of soil) heavy, tenacious. 3 (*coll.*) liverish.

Liverpudlian (livəpŭd′liən) *n.* a native or inhabitant of Liverpool.

livery[1] LIVER[2].

livery[2] (liv′əri) *n.* (*pl.* **liveries**) 1 a distinctive dress worn by the servants of a particular person or the members of a city company. 2 a distinctive colour scheme used on the vehicles, trains, aircraft etc. of a particular company or line. 3 any distinctive dress, guise or outward appearance. 4 the privileges of a city company or guild. 5 (*N Am.*) a livery stable. **at livery** kept at a stable for the owner at a fixed charge. **liveried** *a.* wearing a livery. **livery company** *n.* any of the guilds or companies of the City of London that formerly had a distinctive costume. **livery stable** *n.* a stable where horses are kept at livery or hired.

lives LIFE.

livid (liv′id) *a.* 1 (*coll.*) furious, very angry. 2 of a leaden colour. 3 black and blue, discoloured (as by a bruise). **lividity** (-vid′-), **lividness** *n.* **lividly** *adv.*

living (liv′ing) *a.* 1 alive, having life. 2 alive now, existing, contemporary. 3 (of a language) in current use. 4 (of a portrait) true to life, exact. 5 flowing, running. ~*n.* 1 the state of being alive, existence. 2 livelihood, means of subsistence; occupation. 3 the benefice of a clergyman. 4 manner of life. 5 (of an area, room) for everyday general use. **within living memory** within the memory of people still alive. **living death** *n.* a life of unmitigated suffering. **living room** *n.* a family sitting room. **living wage** *n.* the wage on which it is possible to maintain oneself and one's family adequately. **living will** *n.* a document without legal force, stating a person's desire not to be kept alive by artificial means in case of terminal illness, serious accident etc.

lizard (liz′əd) *n.* any member of the reptilian order Lacertilia, esp. of the typical genus *Lacerta*, having a long, scaly body and tail, and four limbs, each with five toes of unequal length.

LJ *abbr.* Lord Justice.

LL *abbr.* Lord-Lieutenant.

ll. *abbr.* lines (of written matter).

'll (əl) *contr.* (*coll.*) will, shall.

llama (lah′mə) *n.* 1 a domesticated Peruvian wool-bearing animal, *Lama glama*, resembling a camel, but humpless and smaller, used as a beast

of burden. 2 its wool, material made from this.

LL B *abbr.* Bachelor of Laws.

LL D *abbr.* Doctor of Laws.

LL M *abbr.* Master of Laws.

LM *abbr.* 1 long metre. 2 lunar module.

lm *abbr.* lumen.

LNB *abbr.* low noise blocker (on a satellite dish).

lo (lō) *int.* see! behold! look! **lo and behold** (*esp. facet.*) used to introduce a startling fact or revelation.

loach (lōch) *n.* any of the Cobitidae, a group of the carp family, esp. *Nemachilus barbatulus*, a small British river fish.

load (lōd) *n.* 1 a burden. 2 something which is laid on or put in anything for conveyance. 3 as much as can be carried at a time. 4 a measure of weight varying according to the material carried. 5 something which is borne with difficulty; a mental burden, a commitment. 6 (*pl.*, *coll.*) heaps, lots, any amount. 7 something which presses upon, obstructs or resists. 8 the downward pressure of a superstructure. 9 the resistance to an engine or motor apart from friction. 10 the power output of a machine, circuit etc. 11 a device which receives power. ~*v.t.* 1 to put a load upon or in. 2 to put (a load or cargo) on or in a ship, vehicle etc. 3 to add weight to, to make heavy or heavier, to weight. 4 to weigh down, to encumber, to oppress. 5 to charge (a gun etc.). 6 to put a film, cartridge, cassette etc. in a camera, video machine etc. 7 (*Comput.*) to transfer (a program) into the memory, usu. from tape or disk. 8 to fill to overflowing. 9 to cover, to heap or overwhelm (with abuse, honours etc.). 10 to bias, esp. with something to increase strength or weight. 11 to make (a question, statement) biased or tendentious. 12 to add charges to (an insurance premium). 13 to draw power from (an electrical device or circuit). ~*v.i.* 1 to take in a load or cargo (usu. with *up*). 2 to charge a firearm. **a load of** (*coll.*) used for emphasis when dismissing something as merely or completely rubbish, nonsense etc. **to get a load of** (*sl.*) listen to, pay attention to. **load-displacement, load draught** *n.* a ship's displacement when fully loaded. **loaded** *a.* 1 carrying a (heavy) load. 2 (of a gun) charged with ammunition. 3 (*coll.*) wealthy. 4 (*sl.*) drunk or drugged. 5 biased, weighted in a certain direction. 6 likely to cause argument. **loader** *n.* 1 a person who or something which loads; a loading-machine. 2 (*in comb.*) a gun that is loaded in a particular way, as *breech-* or *muzzle-loader.* 3 a person employed to load a sportsman's gun. **loading** *n.* 1 the maximum amount of current or power taken by an appliance. 2 an addition to an insurance premium to cover increased risk. 3 (*Austral., New Zeal.*) an addition to a basic wage for special skills etc. **load line** *n.* a Plimsoll line.

loadstar LODESTAR (under LODE).

loadstone LODESTONE (under LODE).

loaf (lōf) n. (pl. **loaves** (lōvz)) **1** a shaped mass of bread, esp. of a standard size or weight. **2** a moulded mass of any material, esp. a conical mass of refined sugar. **3** (sl.) the head or brains. **loaf sugar** n. sugar in the form of a loaf or in sections, cubes etc. from a loaf.

loaf² (lōf) v.i. **1** to lounge or idle about. **2** to saunter. ~v.t. to spend or pass (time away) idly. ~n. a saunter, an idle time, a loafing. **loafer** n. **1** a person who loafs, an idler. **2** a low leather shoe similar to a moccasin.

loam (lōm) n. **1** soil consisting of sand and clay loosely coherent, with admixture of organic matter or humus. **2** in brickmaking etc., a mixture of sand and clay with chopped straw, used for making moulds. ~v.t. to cover with loam. **loamy** a. **loaminess** n.

loan (lōn) n. **1** something which is lent, esp. a sum of money lent at interest. **2** the act of lending; the state of being lent. **3** funds acquired by the state from individuals and regarded as a debt. **4** a word, myth, custom etc., adopted from another people. ~v.t. to grant the loan of. **on loan** given or taken as a loan. **loanable** a. **loanee** (-nē´) n. **loaner** n. **loan holder** n. **1** a person who holds securities for a loan. **2** a mortgage. **loan shark** n. (coll.) a person who lends money at excessive or illegal interest rates. **loan sharking** n. **loan-translation** n. a compound word or phrase which is a literal translation of the corresponding elements of a foreign expression (e.g. Superman from G Übermensch), also called a calque. **loanword** n. a word borrowed from another language.

loath (lōth), **loth** a. unwilling, averse, reluctant.

Usage note The spellings and pronunciations of the adjective loath and the verb loathe should not be confused: loath (-th) means averse, and loathe (-dh) to detest.

loathe (lōdh) v.t. **1** to feel disgust at. **2** to abhor, to detest. **loather** n. **loathing** a., n. **loathsome** a. causing loathing or disgust, odious, detestable. **loathsomely** adv. **loathsomeness** n.

Usage note See note under LOATH.

loaves LOAF¹.

lob (lob) n. **1** in tennis, a ball struck in a high arc, usu. over one's opponent's head; a stroke that sends the ball on this trajectory. **2** in cricket, a slow underarm ball. ~v.t. (pres.p. **lobbing**, past, p.p. **lobbed**) **1** to hit or throw (a ball) in a high arc. **2** to send (an opponent) a lobbed ball. ~v.i. to make a lob.

lobby (lob´i) n. (pl. **lobbies**) **1** a passage, corridor or vestibule, usu. opening into several apartments. **2** a small hall or ante-room. **3** that part of a hall of a legislative assembly to which the public are admitted. **4** a group of people who try to influence legislators on behalf of special interests. **5** an organized attempt by members of the public to influence legislators. **6** the lobby system; journalists who work in the lobby

system. ~v.i. (3rd pers. sing. pres. **lobbies**, pres.p. **lobbying**, past, p.p. **lobbied**) **1** to seek to gain support, esp. from legislators, (for). **2** to frequent a parliamentary lobby, to act as a lobbyist. ~v.t. **1** to attempt to influence or persuade (legislators) to support something. **2** to attempt to gain (support), to attempt to gain the support of (a person). **3** to secure the passage of (a bill) by lobbying. **lobbyist** n. **lobby system** n. the system which allows correspondents access to political information on condition that the source remains anonymous.

lobe (lōb) n. **1** any rounded and projecting or hanging part. **2** the soft lower part of the ear. **lobar** a. **lobate** (-āt), **lobated** (-ā´tid) a. (Biol.) having or resembling lobes. **lobectomy** (ləbek´təmi) n. (pl. **lobectomies**) the surgical removal of a lobe from an organ or gland. **lobed** a.

lobelia (ləbē´lyə) n. any of a genus, Lobelia, of herbaceous and brilliant flowering plants.

lobotomy (ləbot´əmi) n. (pl. **lobotomies**) (Med.) a surgical incision into the lobe of an organ or gland. **lobotomize, lobotomise** v.t.

lobscouse (lob´skows) n. (Naut.) a hash of meat with vegetables of various kinds and ship's biscuit.

lobster (lob´stə) n. **1** a large marine long-tailed and stalk-eyed decapod crustacean with large pincers, of the genus Homarus. **2** the flesh of this as food. **lobster pot** n. a wickerwork trap for lobsters.

lobule (lob´ūl) n. (Anat.) (a subdivision of) a small lobe. **lobular, lobulated** (-lātid) a.

lobworm (lob´wœm) n. **1** a large earthworm, used as bait by anglers. **2** a lugworm.

local (lō´kəl) a. **1** existing in or peculiar to a particular place or places. **2** of or relating to a neighbourhood. **3** of or relating to a part, not the whole (as a disease etc.). **4** (of a bus, train) serving a particular area; stopping at all stations or stops. **5** of or relating to place. ~n. **1** an inhabitant of a particular place. **2** a train or bus serving a particular district. **3** a public house in one's neighbourhood. **4** a local anaesthetic. **5** locale. **local anaesthesia,** (N Am.) **local anesthesia** n. anaesthesia affecting only a particular area of the body and not involving general unconsciousness. **local anaesthetic** n. **local area network** n. a network of computers in close proximity to one another so that a high rate of data transfer is possible. **local authority** n. the elected body which administers a particular district. **local bus** n. **1** a bus or bus service operating in a particular district. **2** (Comput.) a connection from a microprocessor to an adjacent peripheral device allowing rapid transfer of data. **local call** n. a telephone call to a number on the same or a neighbouring exchange, usu. charged at a cheaper rate. **local derby** n. (pl. **local derbies**) a game between two teams from the same district. **local government** n. **1** administration of towns, districts etc. by elective councils. **2** (N Am.) a local authority. **localism** *n*. **locality** (-kal´-) *n*. (*pl.* **localities**) **1** a particular place, area or neighbourhood. **2** the site or scene of something. **3** existence in a certain portion of space. **localize** (lō´kəlīz), **localise** *v.t.* **1** to make local; to identify with a place. **2** to ascertain or indicate the exact place or locality of. **3** to restrict to a particular place. **4** to decentralize. **localizable** *a*. **localization** (-zā´shən) *n*. **locally** *adv*. **local time** *n*. time calculated on the noon of the meridian of a place, as distinct from standard time.

locale (lōkahl´) *n*. a place, site, esp. with reference to an event taking place there.

locate (ləkāt´) *v.t.* **1** to discover or determine the site of. **2** to set or place in a particular locality. **3** to state the location of. **4** (*in p.p.*) to situate. ~*v.i.* to settle, to take up residence. **location** *n*. **1** situation or position. **2** the act of locating. **3** a site outside the studio grounds where a scene for a film is shot. **4** (*Comput.*) a specific area in memory capable of holding a unit of information, e.g. a word. **on location** (of filming etc.) outside the studio. **locative** (lok´ətiv) *a*. (*Gram.*) denoting place. ~*n*. a case denoting place.

Usage note *Locate* should not be used as though it meant simply to find.

loc. cit. (lok sit´) *adv*. in the place cited.

loch (lokh) *n*. a lake or a narrow or land-locked arm of the sea in Scotland.

loci LOCUS.

lock[1] (lok) *n*. **1** a device for fastening doors etc., usu. having a bolt moved by a key of a particular shape. **2** a mechanical device for checking or preventing movement, as of a wheel. **3** an enclosure in a canal, between gates, for raising and lowering vessels by letting water in or out. **4** a degree of turn imparted to the front wheels of a vehicle; the full extent to which the front wheels will turn. **5** a fastening together or interlocking. **6** a hug or grapple in wrestling that prevents an opponent from moving a limb. **7** in rugby, a lock forward. **8** the firing apparatus of a gun. **9** an airtight antechamber to a caisson or tunnel. **10** an air bubble blocking the flow of gas or liquid through a pipe. ~*v.t.* **1** to fasten (a door, window etc.) by means of a lock. **2** to secure (a building, car etc.) by locking its doors etc. **3** to fix together (a coupling, interlocking parts) so as to make secure or immovable. **4** to cause (a mechanism) to jam. **5** to hold closely and firmly (in an embrace). **6** (*usu. in pass.*) to engage in a contest, struggle, state etc. **7** (*usu. in pass.*) (of land, hills) to hem, to enclose. ~*v.i.* **1** to be able to be fastened by a lock. **2** (of a coupling, interlocking parts) to become fixed together securely or immovably. **3** to become jammed. **lock, stock and barrel** the whole lot. **to lock away 1** to hide, keep in a secure place. **2** to imprison. **3** to make unavailable or inaccessible. **to lock in** to keep in, confine or imprison by locking doors etc. **to lock on (to)** to track automatically (an object) by

means of a radar beam or sensor. **to lock out 1** to prevent from entering by locking doors etc. **2** to prevent (workers) from working during an industrial dispute usu. by closing premises. **to lock up 1** to close, fasten or secure with lock and key. **2** to close and lock all the doors and windows of (a building). **3** to hide, keep in a secure place. **4** to imprison. **5** to make unavailable or inaccessible. **under lock and key** securely locked up. **lock forward** *n*. in rugby, either of the two inside players in the second row of the scrum. **lockjaw** *n*. **1** a symptom of tetanus in which the muscles of the jaw are violently contracted and its motion suspended; trismus. **2** tetanus. **lock-keeper** *n*. a person who attends to a lock on a river or canal. **lock-knit** *a.*, *n.* (a fabric) knitted with an interlocking stitch. **lockout** *n.* the temporary exclusion of workers from their workplace by an employer as a means of bringing pressure to bear on them during an industrial dispute. **locksmith** *n.* a maker and repairer of locks. **lock stitch** *n.* a sewing-machine stitch which locks two threads together. **lock-up** *n.* **1** a place where prisoners are temporarily confined. **2** the act of or time for locking up premises for the night. **3** a small garage. **4** a lock-up shop. ~*a.* that may be locked. **lock-up shop** *n.* a small shop having access only from the street, with no connection with the rest of the building.

lock[2] (lok) *n.* **1** a number of strands of hair curled or hanging together, a tress, a ringlet. **2** (*pl.*) a person's hair. **3** a tuft of wool or similar substance.

locker (lok´ə) *n.* **1** a cupboard, chest or other closed receptacle, with lock and key, esp. one of a number for public use e.g. at a swimming pool or railway station. **2** (*Naut.*) a chest or compartment on a ship for locking up stores etc. **3** a person who or something which locks. **locker room** *n.* a room with lockers for storing clothes and other belongings, also usu. used for changing for sport etc.

locket (lok´it) *n.* a small gold or silver case, worn as an ornament and adapted to contain hair, a miniature etc.

loco[1] (lō´kō) *n.* (*pl.* **locos, locoes**) short for LOCOMOTIVE (under LOCOMOTION).

loco[2] (lō´kō) *a.* (*esp N Am., sl.*) insane, mad.

locomotion (lōkəmō´shən) *n.* **1** the act or power of moving from place to place. **2** moving about, travel, travelling. **locomotive** *a.* **1** of or relating to locomotion. **2** moving from place to place, not stationary. **3** having the power of locomotion, or causing locomotion. ~*n.* (*also* **locomotive engine**) an engine powered by electricity, diesel fuel or steam that runs on railway tracks and is used for hauling trains. **locomotor** *a.* of or relating to locomotion. **locomotory** *a.*

locum (lō´kəm), **locum tenens** (tē´nenz, ten´-) *n.* (*pl.* **locums, locum tenentes** (tinen´tēz)) a deputy or substitute, esp. one acting in the place of a doctor or member of the clergy. **locum tenency** (ten´ənsi) *n.*

locus (lō´kəs) *n.* (*pl.* **loci** (lō´sī, -kī, -kē)) **1** the exact place, the locality (of). **2** (*Math.*) the line generated by a point, or the surface generated by a line, moving according to specified conditions. **3** (*Biol.*) the location of a particular gene on a chromosome. **locus classicus** (klas´ikəs) *n.* (*pl.* **loci classici** (lōsī klas´isī, lōkē klas´ikē)) the best or most authoritative passage that can be quoted as an instance or illustration.

locust (lō´kəst) *n.* **1** a winged insect of various species allied to the grasshopper, which migrates in vast swarms and is very destructive to vegetation. **2** a locust tree. **locust bean** *n.* the sweet pod of the carob. **locust-bird, locust-eater** *n.* any of various species of birds that feed on locusts. **locust tree** *n.* **1** the carob. **2** the N American false acacia, *Robinia pseudacacia.* **3** the kowhai.

locution (ləkū´shən) *n.* **1** a phrase or expression considered with regard to style or idiom. **2** style of speech, mode of delivery.

lode (lōd) *n.* a vein in rock bearing precious ore. **lodestar, loadstar** *n.* **1** a guiding star or one that a ship is steered by, usu. the pole star. **2** one's aim, ambition or guiding principle. **lodestone, loadstone** *n.* **1** magnetic oxide of iron; a natural magnet. **2** something that attracts.

loden (lō´dən) *n.* a thick soft waterproof woollen cloth used for making coats.

lodge (loj) *n.* **1** a small house at the entrance to or in a park, esp. for a gatekeeper or gardener. **2** a cottage, a hut, a cabin for seasonal use; a hunting lodge. **3** a large house or hotel (esp. in the name of such). **4** a room or apartment for a porter in a college, chambers etc. **5** a local branch or place of meeting of certain societies, such as the Freemasons. **6** the local branch of a trade union. **7** a N American Indian wigwam; the family that lives in it. **8** a beaver's or otter's lair. *~v.t.* **1** to supply with temporary quarters, esp. for sleeping. **2** to receive as an inmate, usu. for a fixed charge. **3** to find accommodation for. **4** to deposit (a complaint, information) in court or with a prosecuting officer. **5** to deposit, to leave for security (in, with etc.). **6** to implant, to fix. **7** to place (power, authority) in the hands of. *~v.i.* **1** to reside temporarily, esp. to have sleeping quarters. **2** to reside as an inmate at a fixed charge. **3** to stay or become fixed (in). **lodgement, lodgment** *n.* **1** the act of lodging, the state of being lodged. **2** the depositing or a deposit of money. **3** an accumulation of matter that remains at rest, a deposit. **lodger** *n.* a person who rents and occupies furnished rooms. **lodging** *n.* **1** a temporary residence. **2** (*usu. in pl.*) a room or rooms hired in another's house. **3** (*formal*) a dwelling place. **lodging house** *n.* a private home that provides accommodation for rent.

loess (lō´is, lœs) *n.* a wind-borne deposit of clay, loam, sand etc., in the Rhine, Mississippi and other river valleys.

loft (loft) *n.* **1** the room or air space under a roof. **2** an elevated gallery in a church or hall. **3** a room over a barn or stable. **4** a pigeon-house; a flock of pigeons. **5** in golf, a backward inclination of the face of a club; a lofting stroke. *~v.t.* to strike (the ball) so that it rises high in the air. **lofter** *n.* a golf club for lofting. **lofty** *a.* (*comp.* **loftier**, *superl.* **loftiest**) **1** (*poet.*) very high, towering, of imposing height. **2** elevated in character, sentiment, style etc., sublime. **3** high-flown, grandiose. **4** haughty, arrogant. **loftily** *adv.* **loftiness** *n.*

log[1] (log) *n.* **1** a bulky piece of unhewn timber. **2** a block. **3** a device (orig. a piece of wood with a line attached) used for ascertaining the rate of a ship's motion. **4** a detailed record of the voyage of a ship or flight of an aircraft. **5** a logbook. **6** any record of events, performance, transmissions made etc. or of the work done by a computer. *~v.t.* (*pres.p.* **logging**, *past, p.p.* **logged**) **1** to enter in the logbook or other regular record. **2** (of a ship) to make (a specified distance) by the log. **3** to log up. **4** to fell (trees) for timber. **5** to cut into logs. *~v.i.* to fell trees. **to log in/ on 1** to begin to use a computer system. **2** to gain access to a computer system (by means of a code, password). **to log off/ out** to exit from or conclude the use of a computer system. **to log up** to spend (a specified amount of time) working, flying etc. as recorded in a logbook or other record. **to sleep like a log** to be in a deep sleep. **logbook** *n.* **1** a book in which an official diary of events occurring in a ship's voyage or aircraft's flight is kept. **2** any book containing a detailed record of work done, performance etc. **3** the registration document of a motor vehicle. **log cabin** *n.* a cabin built of logs. **logger** *n.* a lumberjack. **logging** *n.* the work of felling, cutting up and preparing forest timber. **logjam** *n.* **1** a blockage in a river caused by floating logs. **2** a deadlock, a standstill. **log-line** *n.* a knotted line, fastened to the ship's log for finding the speed of the vessel. **logrolling** *n.* **1** (*N Am.*) mutual political assistance in carrying legislative measures. **2** a sport in which two opponents attempt to spin each other off a floating log on which both are standing. **logroller** *n.*

log[2] (log) *n.* short for LOGARITHM.

-log -LOGUE.

logan (log´ən), **logan-stone** *n.* a rocking-stone.

loganberry (lō´gənbəri) *n.* (*pl.* **loganberries**) **1** a permanent hybrid plant obtained by crossing the raspberry and a species of blackberry. **2** the fruit of this.

logarithm (log´əridhm) *n.* the exponent of the power to which a fixed number, called the base, must be raised to produce a given number (tabulated and used as a means of simplifying arithmetical processes by enabling addition and subtraction to be substituted for multiplication and division). **logarithmic** (-ridh´-) *a.* **logarithmically** *adv.*

loggerhead (log´əhed) *n.* 1 (*also* **loggerhead turtle**) a large marine turtle, *Caretta caretta.* 2 a tool consisting of a long handle with a bulbous iron head for heating liquids, melting tar etc. **at loggerheads** in conflict, locked in dispute.

logic (loj´ik) *n.* 1 the science of reasoning, correct thinking, proving and deducing. 2 a treatise on this. 3 a particular mode, system or chain of reasoning. 4 reasoning, argument etc. considered with regard to correctness or incorrectness. 5 reasoned argument. 6 the necessary consequences of an argument, a situation etc. 7 force of circumstances, situation etc. 8 (*Comput.*) the elementary principles for performing arithmetical and logical operations in a computer; logical operations collectively. **logical** *a.* 1 of or relating to, used in or according to the rules of logic, consistent or accurate in reasoning. 2 reasonable. 3 versed or skilled in accurate reasoning. **logicality** (-kal´-), **logicalness** *n.* **logically** *adv.* **logical positivism, logical empiricism** *n.* a philosophical school based on linguistic analysis which demands that meaningful statements must be empirically verifiable, so rejecting metaphysics etc. as nonsense. **logic bomb** *n.* (*Comput.*) an instruction programmed (usu. secretly) into a computer that will trigger a breakdown if a specified set of circumstances occurs. **logician** (-jish´ən) *n.* a person skilled in logic.

-logic (loj´ik), **-logical** (-kəl) *comb. form* forming adjectives from nouns ending in *-logy.*

-logist (ləjist), **-loger** (ləjə) *comb. form* forming nouns meaning a person versed in or working in, as *anthropologist, astrologer.*

logistics (ləjis´tiks) *n.pl.* 1 the branch of strategy concerned with the moving and supply of troops. 2 the planning and organization of any complex enterprise. **logistic, logistical** *a.*

logo (log´ō, lō´-) *n.* (*pl.* **logos**) a symbol or simple design used to identify a company, organization etc.

logogram (log´əgram) *n.* a sign representing a word, esp. in shorthand.

logorrhoea (logərē´ə), (*N Am.*) **logorrhea** *n.* excessive or uncontrollable talkativeness.

logotype (log´ətīp) *n.* 1 (*Print.*) a type having two or more letters cast in one piece, but not as a ligature, as *are, was* etc. 2 a logo. 3 a piece of type that prints a logo.

-logue (log), (*N Am.*) **-log** *comb. form* 1 forming nouns relating to discourse, as in *epilogue, prologue.* 2 equivalent to *-logist,* as in *ideologue.*

-logy (ləji), **-ology** (ol´əji) *comb. form* forming names of sciences and departments of knowledge, and nouns denoting modes of speaking or discourses, as *astrology, eulogy, tautology.*

loin (loin) *n.* 1 the part of the body of a human being or quadruped lying between the lower ribs and the hip joint. 2 a joint of meat from this part. 3 (*pl.*) the genitals and the surrounding area.

loincloth *n.* a cloth worn round the loins as an elementary kind of garment.

loiter (loi´tə) *v.i.* 1 to linger, to dawdle. 2 to move or travel with frequent halts. *~v.t.* to waste or consume (time) in trifles, to idle (time) away. **loiterer** *n.* **loiteringly** *adv.*

loll (lol) *v.i.* 1 to stand, sit or lie in a lazy attitude, to lounge. 2 (of the tongue) to hang from the mouth. *~v.t.* to let (one's head or limbs) hang or recline lazily (on or against). **loller** *n.* **lollingly** *adv.*

Lollard (lol´əd) *n.* any one of a sect of English religious reformers in the 14th and 15th cents., followers of John Wyclif (?1330–84). **Lollardism, Lollardy** *n.*

lollipop (lol´ipop) *n.* 1 a flat or round boiled sweet on the end of a stick. 2 an ice lollipop. 3 a piece of popular classical music. **lollipop man, lollipop lady, lollipop woman** *n.* (*pl.* **lollipop men, lollipop ladies, lollipop women**) (*coll.*) a person who conducts children safely across roads by controlling traffic using a pole with a disc on the top.

lollop (lol´əp) *v.i.* (*pres.p.* **lolloping,** *past, p.p.* **lolloped**) 1 to move with an ungainly bouncing gait. 2 to roll or flop about heavily.

lolly (lol´i) *n.* (*pl.* **lollies**) 1 a lollipop, a sweet on a stick. 2 an ice lolly. 3 (*sl.*) money.

Lombard (lom´bəd, -bahd) *n.* 1 any of a Germanic people who conquered Italy in the 6th cent. 2 a native or inhabitant of Lombardy. *~a.* of or relating to the Lombards or Lombardy. **Lombardic** (-bah´-) *a.* **Lombardy poplar** (-bədi) *n.* a variety of poplar tree with erect branches.

lone (lōn) *a.* 1 single, solitary, without company or a comrade. 2 unmarried, widowed. 3 (*esp. poet. or formal*) solitary, retired, uninhabited, lonely, deserted. **lone hand** *n.* 1 in euchre, quadrille, a hand played without help from one's partner's cards. 2 any action taken by a person without assistance or allies. **loneness** *n.* **loner** *n.* a person or animal that avoids the company of others. **lonesome** *a.* 1 lonely, companionless. 2 (of a place) unfrequented; arousing feelings of loneliness. **on one's lonesome** alone. **lonesomely** *adv.* **lonesomeness** *n.* **lone wolf** *n.* a person who prefers to be or to operate alone.

lonely (lōn´li) *a.* (*comp.* **lonelier,** *superl.* **loneliest**) 1 sad through lacking company or companionship. 2 solitary, companionless. 3 (of a place) unfrequented, sequestered; causing feelings of loneliness. **loneliness** *n.* **lonely heart** *n.* a lonely person, esp. one seeking friendship or marriage.

long[1] (long) *a.* (*comp.* **longer** (long´gə), *superl.* **longest** (long´gist)) 1 of considerable or relatively great linear extent. 2 of great or relatively great extent in time. 3 of a specified linear extent or duration in time. 4 having or consisting of a large number of items or parts. 5 turning more than the average or usual quantity, extent or duration. 6 seeming to be of greater duration than it actually is. 7 lengthy, verbose, tedious. 8 far-reaching; involving a long interval. **9** (of a person's memory) retaining things over a long period of time. **10** protracted in sound, not short. **11** (of odds) representing only a small chance of success. **12** (of a garment) ankle-length. **13** (of a drink) large; containing a large quantity of non-alcoholic beverage. **14** (*coll.*) (of a person) tall. ~*adv.* **1** over a great extent in distance or time. **2** for a long time. **3** by a long time. **4** throughout a specified period. **as long as 1** provided that, only if. **2** for the whole of the time that. **before long** soon, shortly. **in the long run 1** in the end, eventually. **2** over a long period of time. **long on** well supplied with, strong in. **no longer** formerly but not now. **so long as** as long as. **the long and the short of it 1** the whole matter in a few words. **2** the eventual outcome. **to be long** to take a long time. **to go a long way 1** to make a substantial contribution (towards). **2** (of food, money etc.) to last for a long time, to provide material or the means to do many things. **3** to be successful. **long ago** *adv.* in the distant past. **long-ago** *a.* **long-awaited** *a.* waited for (usu. with pleasant anticipation) for a long time. **longboard** *n.* a type of surfboard. **longboat** *n.* the largest boat on a sailing vessel. **longbow** *n.* a long powerful bow drawn by hand, used as a weapon in medieval England. **long-case clock** *n.* a grandfather clock. **long-dated** *a.* (of securities) not due for redemption in less than 15 years. **long-dead** *a.* who or which died a long time ago. **long-distance** *a.* **1** covering, extending over a long distance or long distances. **2** (of a telephone call) between places that are far apart. **3** (of a race) over a distance of 6 miles (or 10,000 metres) or further; (of a runner) competing at such distances. ~*adv.* using a long-distance telephone line or service. **long division** *n.* (*Math.*) the process of dividing a number by another number greater than 12, the stages being fully set out. **long dozen** *n.* thirteen. **long-drawn-out** *a.* prolonged, extended to great length. **long face** *n.* a gloomy or dejected expression. **long field** *n.* in cricket, the part of the outfield behind the wicket at the bowler's end. **long figure** *n.* a high price. **longhand** *a.* ordinary writing, as opposed to *shorthand.* **long haul** *n.* **1** a journey (esp. the transport of goods) over a great distance. **2** a difficult or extended period of time. **long-haul** *a.* **long-headed** *a.* **1** shrewd, sensible, far-sighted. **2** dolichocephalous. **longhorn** *n.* **1** any of several breeds of cattle with long horns. **2** a beetle with long antennae. **long hundredweight** *n.* the standard British hundredweight of 112 lb. (about 50.8 kg). **longish** *a.* **long johns** *n.pl.* underpants with long legs. **long jump** *n.* an athletic event involving a horizontal jump for distance from a running start. **long-lasting** *a.* that lasts or has lasted for a long time; durable. **long leg** *n.* in cricket, a fielder or fielding position close to the boundary on the leg side behind the batsman. **long-life** *a.* (of foodstuffs) specially treated to

resist decay and preserve freshness. **long-lived** *a.* living or having lived, existed, been current etc. for a long time. **long-lost** *a.* that has been lost or not seen or heard from for a long time. **long off** *n.* in cricket, a fielder or fielding position close to the boundary on the offside behind the bowler. **long on** *n.* in cricket, a fielder or fielding position close to the boundary on the onside behind the bowler. **long-playing** *a.* (of a gramophone record) fine-grooved and with a playing time of approx. 30 minutes per side. **long-player** *n.* **long-range** *a.* **1** designed to operate at long distances from a base; often without refuelling. **2** (of a missile) intended for a distant target. **3** (of a forecast) covering a period of time into the relatively distant future. **long-running** *a.* **1** (of a play) that has been continuously in performance over a long period of time. **2** (of a dispute etc.) that has been going on for a long time. **longship** *n.* a long open sturdy vessel with oars and a square sail used esp. by the Vikings for carrying warriors. **long shot** *n.* **1** a camera shot from a long distance. **2** a random guess, a remote possibility. **3** a bet at long odds. **(not) by a long shot** (not) by any means. **long sight** *n.* a condition in which one can see distant objects clearly but not those close to. **long-sighted** *a.* **1** having long sight. **2** shrewd, far-sighted. **long-sleeved** *a.* having sleeves that reach the whole length of the arm. **long-standing** *a.* of long duration. **long-stay** *a.* staying, or for people who are staying, a long time. **long stop** *n.* **1** in cricket, a fielder positioned to stop balls which pass the wicketkeeper. **2** any person or thing that acts as a final safeguard. **long-suffering** *a.* patient, enduring. **long suit** *n.* **1** the most numerous suit in a hand of cards. **2** a person's strong point or special interest or skill. **long-term** *a.* (of a policy) looking to the future rather than the immediate present; extending over a long period of time. **long-time** *a.* long-standing. **long ton** *n.* an imperial ton of 2,240 lb. (1016.05 kg). **long vacation** *n.* the long summer holidays of universities, schools etc. **long waist** *n.* **1** (of a garment) a deep or dropped waist. **2** (of a person) a greater than average distance from armpits to hips. **long-waisted** *a.* **long wave** *n.* a radio wave with a wavelength of 1000 m or more. **longways**, **longwise** *adv.* lengthways. **long weekend** *n.* a holiday which extends over several days including a weekend. **long-winded** *a.* wordy, tiresome. **long-windedly** *adv.* **long-windedness** *n.*

long² (long) *v.i.* **1** to have an earnest desire (for). **2** to yearn (to or for). **longing** *n.* an intense desire (for). **longingly** *adv.*

long. *abbr.* longitude.

longe LUNGE².

longeron (lon´jəron) *n.* a longitudinal spar of an aeroplane's fuselage.

longevity (lonjev´iti) *n.* great length of life.

longitude (long´gitūd, lon´ji-) *n.* **1** angular distance of a place E or W of a given meridian, usu. that of Greenwich. **2** (*Astron.*) distance in degrees on the ecliptic from the vernal equinox to the foot of a perpendicular from, or circle of latitude of, a heavenly body. **longitudinal** (-tū´-) *a*. **1** of or relating to longitude or length. **2** running lengthwise. **longitudinally** *adv*.

Usage note Pronunciation as (long´titūd), as though the word were *longtitude* (after *latitude*), is best avoided.

longshore (long´shaw) *a*. **1** of or belonging to, existing or working on the shore. **2** directed along the shore. **longshoreman** *n*. (*pl*. **longshoremen**) **1** a person who works in or about boats along the shore or in fishing from the shore. **2** (*N Am.*) a docker.

lonicera (lonis´ərə) *n*. **1** a dense evergreen shrub of the genus, *Lonicera*, used for hedging. **2** honeysuckle.

loo[1] (loo) *n*. (*pl*. **loos**) (*coll.*) a lavatory.

loo[2] (loo) *n*. **1** a round game at cards. **2** the pool in this game into which penalties are paid. **3** the penalty.

loof LUFF.

loofah (loo´fə), (*N Am. also*) **luffa** (luf´ə) *n*. **1** a tropical gourdlike climbing plant, *Luffa cylindrica*, with an edible fruit. **2** the fibrous interior of the fruit of this plant used as a bath sponge, back-scrubber etc.

look (luk) *v.i.* **1** to direct the eyes (towards, at etc.) in order to see an object. **2** to watch. **3** to gaze, to stare. **4** to direct the mind or understanding, to give consideration. **5** to face, to front, to be turned or have a particular direction (towards, to, into etc.). **6** to seem, to appear. **7** to make a physical or mental search. **8** to take care. ~*v.t.* **1** to view, to inspect, to examine. **2** to express or show by one's expression. **3** to ascertain, to determine. **4** to expect, to hope (to do something). ~*n.* **1** the act of looking or seeing, a glance. **2** (*pl.*) personal appearance, esp. of the face, attractiveness, beauty. **3** facial expression. **4** (*often pl.*) general appearance. **5** style, line, fashion (for clothes or general design). ~*int.* **1** a request or demand for someone to turn their eyes in a particular direction. **2** (*also* **look here**) used to demand attention at the beginning of a statement or to express mild annoyance or protest. **to be looking at** (*coll.*) to have at a rough estimate, to expect to pay, spend etc. **to look after 1** to take care of. **2** to attend to. **3** to follow (a departing person, thing) with one's eyes. **to look around** to look round. **to look as if** to seem or suggest from the available evidence that. **to look back 1** to turn and look in the direction from which one has come. **2** to refer back (to). **3** to review or return to (a period, event, experience in the past) in one's mind. **4** (*usu. neg.*) to cease to make progress (*never looked back after that*). **5** to pay another short visit. **to look down one's nose at** to look down on. **to look down on/ upon 1** to despise. **2** to assume superiority over. **to look for 1** to seek. **2** to hope for. **3** to expect,

anticipate, be on the watch for. **to look forward to** to anticipate or hope for with pleasure. **to look in** to call, to pay a brief visit. **to look into 1** to inspect carefully, to investigate. **2** to examine the inside of. **to look like 1** to resemble; to have the appearance of. **2** to seem to be going to. **3** to threaten or promise (e.g. rain). **4** to suggest the presence of. **to look on 1** to be a mere spectator. **2** to regard, to consider (as, with etc.). **to look oneself** to look healthy; to have one's customary air and appearance. **to look out 1** to be on the watch, to be prepared (for). **2** to put one's head out of a window etc. **3** to search for or select and give to. **4** to have a view or outlook (over). **to look over 1** to inspect by making a tour of. **2** to read or examine cursorily. **to look round 1** to look behind one, or in another direction than in front. **2** to make a tour of and inspect. **3** to examine various options, possible purchases etc. before coming to a decision. **to look sharp** to be quick, make haste. **to look someone in the eye/ eyes/ face** to look at someone steadily, unflinchingly and without shame. **to look through 1** to see or direct the eyes through. **2** to penetrate with one's sight or insight. **3** to examine the contents of. **4** to ignore, or seem to ignore, the presence of (another person). **to look to/ unto 1** to direct one's eyes or thoughts towards. **2** to take heed for, to be careful about, to keep a watch over. **3** to rely upon (for). **to look up 1** to search for, esp. in a book. **2** to pay a visit to. **3** to improve, to become more prosperous. **to look up and down** to examine (a person) from head to foot attentively or with disdain or contempt. **to look upon** to regard (as or with). **to look up to to** admire and respect. **lookalike** *n*. a person or thing that closely resembles another; a double. **looker** *n*. **1** an observer. **2** (*coll.*) an attractive person, esp. a woman. **looker-on** *n*. a (mere) spectator. **look-in** *n*. (*coll.*) **1** a call, a short visit. **2** a chance, as of winning in a game. **looking-glass** *n*. a mirror. ~*a*. in which ordinary reality is reversed or distorted in some way. **lookout** *n*. **1** a watch. **2** a person engaged in watching or looking out. **3** a place from which watch or observation is kept. **4** a view, a prospect. **5** future prospect. **6** (*coll.*) a person's personal affair or concern. **look-see** *n*. (*coll.*) an inspection.

loom[1] (loom) *n*. a machine in which yarn or thread is woven into a fabric.

loom[2] (loom) *v.i.* **1** to appear indistinctly or faintly in the distance. **2** to appear larger than the real size, as in a mist, and often threatening. **3** (of an event) to be imminent, esp. ominously so. ~*n*. the first indistinct appearance, as of land at sea.

loon (loon) *n*. (*N Am.*) a diver, any bird of the Gaviidae family.

loony (loo´ni) *n*. (*pl.* **loonies**) (*sl.*) a lunatic; a foolish person. ~*a*. (*comp.* **loonier**, *superl.* **looniest**) crazy; foolish. **loony-bin** *n*. (*sl., offensive*) a mental hospital.

loop (loop) *n.* **1** a folding or doubling of a string, rope, thread etc. across itself to form a curve or eye; a noose, a bight. **2** anything resembling this, e.g. a pattern in a finger print. **3** a ring, eye or curved piece by which anything is hung up, fastened, held etc. **4** a loop-shaped intrauterine contraceptive device. **5** a loop line. **6** a flight manoeuvre comprising a complete revolution in flight in a vertical plane, the upper surface of the aircraft being on the inside of the circle. **7** in skating, a curve performed on one edge and crossing itself. **8** a length of film or tape joined end to end to form a continuous strip. **9** (*Comput.*) a set of instructions repeated in a program until a specific condition is met. **10** a closed circuit around which a signal can pass. ~*v.t.* **1** to form into a loop or loops. **2** to encircle with a loop. **3** to fasten or secure with loops. ~*v.i.* **1** to form a loop. **2** to follow a looplike path; to loop the loop. **3** to travel by curling itself in loops and uncurling again. **to loop the loop** to travel round in a vertical loop in an aeroplane etc. **looped** *a.* **loop line** *n.* a railway, telegraph line etc. diverging from the main line and joining it again. **loop-the-loop** *n.* the manoeuvre of looping the loop in an aircraft. **loopy** *a.* (*comp.* **loopier,** *superl.* **loopiest**) (*coll.*) slightly mad.

loophole (loop´hōl) *n.* **1** an aperture in a wall for shooting or looking through or for admission of light. **2** an outlet, a means of evasion or escape, esp. a means of evading the consequences or penalties of a law or regulation.

loose (loos) *a.* **1** not tied, fastened or confined. **2** unfastened; detachable; hanging partly free. **3** not fixed or tight. **4** not specially packaged or in units or a container. **5** not crowded together, not compact or dense. **6** relaxed, slack. **7** careless, slovenly. **8** not strict; vague, indefinite. **9** incorrect; ungrammatical. **10** dissolute, wanton. **11** lax in the bowels, as opposed to *costive*. **12** (of the ball in ball games) not in any player's possession. **13** (of play) not involving a set formation or strategy. **14** (of bowling in cricket) inaccurate. ~*v.t.* **1** to release, to set at liberty, to unbind. **2** to undo, to untie, to unfasten. **3** to free from obligation or burden. **4** to relax. **5** to discharge (a projectile, volley etc.). **on the loose 1** no longer in captivity. **2** on the spree. **the loose** in rugby, play when the ball is loose and the forwards close round it or try to obtain and keep possession of it. **to cut loose 1** to escape or get away (from). **2** to begin to act without restraint. **to give loose to** to give free vent to (one's tongue, feelings etc.). **to hang loose** (*N Am.*, *coll.*) to behave in a relaxed and informal manner. **loose box** *n.* a compartment for an animal in a stable or vehicle in which it can move about. **loose cannon** *n.* a person or thing that causes danger or damage because they are uncontrolled. **loose change** *n.* coins kept for small items of expenditure. **loose cover** *n.* an easily removable cloth cover for a chair, sofa etc. **loose-leaf** *a.*

bound so that pages may be inserted or removed. ~*n.* a folder, notebook etc. bound in this way. **loose-limbed** *a.* having flexible or supple limbs. **loosely** *adv.* **loosen** *v.t.* **1** to make less tight, firm, fixed etc. **2** to make less strict or severe. **3** to free, to set loose. **4** to release (the bowels) from constipation. **5** to relieve the dryness of (a cough). ~*v.i.* to become loose, to become less tight, firm, fixed etc. **to loosen a person's tongue** to make a person talk more freely, often indiscreetly. **to loosen up 1** to limber up. **2** to relax, to become less shy or restrained. **loosener** *n.* **looseness** *n.* **loosish** *a.*

loosestrife (loos´strīf) *n.* **1** any of a genus of plants of the primrose family, esp. *Lysimachia vulgaris* with yellow flowers; yellow loosestrife. **2** a waterside plant, *Lythrum salicaria*, with red or purple flowers; purple loosestrife.

loot (loot) *n.* **1** booty, plunder, esp. from a conquered city. **2** stolen money, jewellery etc. **3** (*coll.*) money. ~*v.t.* **1** to steal (unprotected goods) or to steal from (unprotected premises), e.g. during a riot. **2** to plunder, to pillage, esp. a city. **3** to carry off as plunder. ~*v.i.* to plunder. **looter** *n.*

lop[1] (lop) *v.t.* (*pres.p.* **lopping,** *past, p.p.* **lopped**) **1** to cut off the top or extremities of (a tree, body etc.). **2** to trim (trees, shrubs etc.) by cutting. **3** to omit or remove as superfluous. **lopper** *n.*

lop[2] (lop) *v.i.* (*pres.p.* **lopping,** *past, p.p.* **lopped**) to hang down limply, to flop, to droop. ~*v.t.* **1** to allow to hang down. **2** to let fall. **lopsided** *a.* **1** heavier on one side than the other. **2** not symmetrical. **3** ill-balanced. **lopsidedly** *adv.* **lopsidedness** *n.*

lope (lōp) *v.i.* to gallop, swing or move (along) with long strides or leaps. ~*n.* motion of this kind. **loper** *n.*

loquacious (lōkwā´shəs) *a.* talkative, garrulous, chattering. **loquaciously** *adv.* **loquacity** (-kwas´-), **loquaciousness** *n.*

loquat (lō´kwot) *n.* **1** a Chinese and Japanese tree, *Eriobotrya japonica*. **2** its yellow edible fruit.

lor (law) *int.* (*coll.*) Lord.

loran (lō´rən, lor´-) *n.* a system of navigation in which position is determined by the intervals between pulses received from widely spaced radio transmitters.

lord (lawd) *n.* **1** a ruler, a master; a man possessing supreme power, a sovereign. **2** (**Lord**) God. **3** (**Lord**) Jesus Christ. **4** a nobleman, a peer of the realm. **5** a courtesy title given to the son of a duke or marquis, or the son of an earl holding a barony. **6** a title of honour conferred on certain official personages, as Lord Chief Justice, Lord Commissioner, Lord Mayor, Lord Rector etc. **7** (*Hist.*) a feudal superior, the holder of a manor. **8** (*Astrol.*) the ruling planet (of a sign, house, chart). ~*int.* (*coll.*) (*also* **Lord, lordy**) an exclamation of surprise or dismay. **my lord** a formula for addressing a nobleman (not a duke), bishop, lord mayor or judge of the Supreme Court. **the Lords 1** the House of Lords. **2** the members of the House of Lords. **Lord Advocate** *n.* (*Sc. Law*) the chief law officer of the Crown in Scotland, in charge of the administration of criminal justice. **Lord Chamberlain (of the Household)** *n.* a British officer of state having control of the royal household and formerly licensing plays for performance. **Lord Chancellor, Lord High Chancellor** *n.* the highest officer of the British Crown, keeper of the Great Seal, speaker of the House of Lords, head of the judiciary in England and Wales. **Lord Chief Justice** *n.* in the UK, the president of the Queen's Bench of the High Court of Justice. **Lord Lieutenant** *n.* an official representing the sovereign, and the chief executive authority and head of the magistracy in a county. **lordlike** *a.*, *adv.* **lordly** *a.* (*comp.* **lordlier**, *superl.* **lordliest**) **1** lofty, proud, haughty, insolent. **2** becoming or befitting a lord, noble, grand, magnificent. **lordliness** *n.* **Lord Mayor** *n.* the chief magistrate of London, York and certain other large towns. **Lord President of the Council** *n.* a member of the House of Lords who acts as president of the Privy Council. **Lord Privy Seal** *n.* the officer of State entrusted with the Privy Seal. **Lord Provost** *n.* the head of the municipal corporation of Edinburgh, Glasgow, Aberdeen, Perth or Dundee. **lords and ladies** *n.* the wild arum lily, *Arum maculatum.* **Lord's day** *n.* Sunday. **lordship** *n.* **1** control, rule (over). **2** the position or status of a lord. **his lordship** the equivalent of 'your lordship' in speaking of someone. **your lordship 1** a formula used in speaking deferentially to a lord. **2** (*iron.*) a formula used in speaking to someone who adopts a lordly or arrogant manner. **Lord's Prayer** *n.* the prayer taught by Jesus Christ to his disciples (Math. vi.9–13, Luke xi:2–4). **Lords spiritual** *n.pl.* the archbishops and bishops who have seats in the House of Lords. **Lord's Supper** *n.* the Eucharist. **Lords temporal** *n.pl.* lay peers who have seats in the House of Lords.

lordosis (lawdō´sis) *n.* (*Med.*) curvature of a bone, esp. of the spine, forward. **lordotic** (-dot´-) *a.*

lore (law) *n.* the collective traditions and knowledge relating to a given subject.

lorgnette (lawnyet´) *n.* a pair of eyeglasses or opera glasses with a long handle.

lorikeet (lor´ikēt) *n.* any of various brightly-coloured parrots of the subfamily Lorunae, belonging to Australasia and SE Asia.

loris (law´ris) *n.* **1** a slow-moving, nocturnal primate with small ears and a short tail, of S India and Sri Lanka, *Nycitebus coucang.* **2** a similar creature of SE Asia, *Loris tardigradus.*

lorry (lor´i) *n.* (*pl.* **lorries**) a large motor vehicle for carrying heavy loads.

lory (law´ri) *n.* (*pl.* **lories**) a brilliantly coloured parrot-like bird of various genera of Loriinae, found in SE Asia and Australia.

lose (looz) *v.t.* (*past*, *p.p.* **lost** (lost)) **1** to be deprived of. **2** to mislay, to be unable to find; to miss, to stray from. **3** to fail to gain, win, obtain or enjoy. **4** to fail to keep possession of, to fail to hold or grasp. **5** to be freed from. **6** to part with accidentally or as a forfeit, penalty etc. **7** to fail to hear or understand. **8** to spend uselessly, to waste. **9** to be deprived of (a parent, friend) by death. **10** to fail to give birth to, esp. by miscarriage. **11** (of a doctor) to be unable to keep (a patient) alive. **12** to cause someone the loss of. **13** (of a watch, clock) to become slow (by a specified amount of time). **14** (*in pass.*) to disappear, to die, to perish. **15** (*coll.*) to get rid of, to discard. **16** (*coll.*) to elude, to outdistance (a pursuer). ~*v.i.* **1** to fail to be successful, to be beaten. **2** to suffer loss. **3** to be worse off (by). **4** to decrease or depreciate in value or effectiveness. **5** (of a clock etc.) to run slow. **to lose oneself 1** to lose one's way. **2** to become bewildered. **3** to become rapt or engrossed (in). **to lose one's/ the way** to become lost, to take a false direction, to go astray. **to lose out 1** (*coll.*) to make a loss, to be at a disadvantage. **2** to fail to obtain or take advantage of. **to lose out to** to be defeated by (a competitor). **losable** *a.* **loser** *n.* **1** a person who loses, esp. a person, horse, boat etc. failing to win a race. **2** (*pl.*) the beaten party in a game, battle etc. **3** (*coll.*) a failure, a person who seems destined to be unfortunate or to lose. **losing** *a.* **losing battle** *n.* a struggle, contest etc. in which one seems doomed to failure. **lost** *a.* **1** unable to find the way or determine one's position or whereabouts. **2** missing, unable to be found. **3** confused, bewildered. **4** ruined, destroyed. **5** no longer possessed or known. **6** engrossed. **7** morally fallen or corrupted. **8** damned. **to be lost in 1** to be engrossed in. **2** to merge or be obscured in. **to be lost on** to make no impression on, to be wasted on. **to be lost to 1** (of a valuable thing or person) to be no longer available or accessible to. **2** (of a person) to be impervious or unresponsive to. **to be lost without** to be dependent on. **lost cause** *n.* **1** a futile endeavour. **2** a person whom one can no longer influence or help. **lost soul** *n.* **1** a person who is damned or beyond redemption. **2** a person who seems bewildered by, and unable to cope with, the demands of everyday life. **lost wax** *n.* CIRE PERDUE.

loss (los) *n.* **1** the act of losing or the state of being deprived of. **2** failure to win or gain. **3** something which is lost or the amount of this. **4** (*pl.*) casualties and those taken prisoner in war. **5** detriment, disadvantage. **6** wasted expenditure, effort etc. **at a loss** for less than the buying price; with costs, expenditure etc. exceeding income. **to be at a loss 1** to be embarrassed or puzzled. **2** (*followed by for*) to be rendered helpless for lack of. **to cut one's losses** to write off as lost, to abandon a speculation. **loss adjuster** *n.* a person who assesses losses through fire, theft etc. for an insurance company. **loss-leader** *n.* an article sold at a loss to attract customers. **loss-making** *a.* that makes or causes a financial loss. **loss-maker** *n.*

lost LOSE.

lot (lot) *n.* **1** (*often in pl.*) a considerable quantity or amount, a great deal. **2** anything, such as a dice, paper or other object, used in reaching a decision by random selection. **3** choice or decision by this method. **4** the chance, share or fortune falling to anyone. **5** one's fortune, destiny or condition in life. **6** a distinct portion, collection or parcel of things offered for sale, esp. at auction. **7** a number or quantity of things or persons. **8** (*esp. N Am.*) a plot of land. ~*v.t.* (*pres.p.* **lotting**, *past, p.p.* **lotted**) **1** to divide into lots. **2** to apportion. **a lot** (*coll.*) much. **a whole lot** (*coll.*) very much. **the lot** the whole quantity. **the whole lot** all, everything. **to cast lots** to determine by the throw of a dice or other contrivance. **to draw lots** to determine by drawing one name etc. from a number. **to throw/ cast in one's lot with** to join with or make common cause with and share the fortunes of. **lots** *n.* (*coll.*) a large number, a great deal (of). ~*adv.* very much.
loth LOATH.
lotion (lō´shən) *n.* a medicinal or cosmetic liquid application for external use.
lottery (lot´əri) *n.* (*pl.* **lotteries**) **1** a method of allotting valuable prizes by chance or lot among purchasers of tickets. **2** an activity in which success is dependent on mere chance. **lotto** (-ō) *n.* (*pl.* **lottos**) **1** a game of chance, played with discs placed on cards divided into numbered squares. **2** (*N Am.*) a lottery.
lotus (lō´təs) *n.* (*pl.* **lotuses**) **1** in Greek legend, any of several plants the fruit of which was said to induce a dreamy languor in those who ate it. **2** the Indian water lily, *Nelumbo nucifera*, with large pink flowers. **3** this used as a sacred symbol, an architectural ornament etc. **4** the Egyptian water lily, *Nymphaea lotus*, with white flowers. **lotus-eater** *n.* a person who wants nothing more from life than dreamy ease. **lotus-eating** *a., n.* **lotus position** *n.* a position used in yoga in which one sits cross-legged with each foot nestled against or on top of the opposite thigh.
louche (loosh) *a.* **1** morally suspect. **2** seedy. **3** sinister.
loud (lowd) *a.* **1** powerful in sound, sonorous. **2** noisy, clamorous. **3** (of attire, manners etc.) conspicuous, ostentatious, flashy. **4** (of behaviour) bumptious, aggressive. **out loud 1** aloud. **2** loudly. **louden** *v.t., v.i.* **loud hailer** *n.* a megaphone with a built-in amplifier and microphone. **loudish** *a.* **loudly** *adv.* **loudmouth** *n.* (*coll.*) someone who brags or talks offensively in a loud voice. **loudmouthed** *a.* **loudness** *n.* **loudspeaker** *n.* an electromechanical device which converts electrical signals into audible sound.
lough (lokh) *n.* a lake, an arm of the sea in Ireland.
lounge (lownj) *v.i.* **1** to loll or recline. **2** to move lazily, to saunter. **3** to idle about. ~*n.* **1** a place for lounging. **2** the sitting room in a house. **3** a public room with comfortable seating for waiting

or relaxing in. **4** (*also* **lounge bar**) a more comfortable and expensive section of a public house or hotel. **5** the act of lounging. **lounge lizard** *n.* a person who spends a lot of time idly at social gatherings, esp. in the company of rich or famous people. **lounger** *n.* **1** a person who lounges. **2** a comfortable sofa or extending chair for relaxing on. **3** a loose-fitting garment. **lounge suit** *n.* a man's suit for daily wear.
lour (lowə), **lower** *v.i.* **1** (of clouds, weather etc.) to look threatening, to appear dark or gloomy. **2** to frown, to scowl. ~*n.* **1** a scowl. **2** sullenness. **3** gloominess (of weather etc.). **louring, loury** *a.* **louringly** *adv.*
louse (lows) *n.* (*pl.* **lice** (līs)) **1** a blood-sucking insect of the genus *Pediculus*, three species of which are parasitic on man. **2** any of various other parasites infesting animals, birds, fish and plants. **3** (*coll.*) (*pl.* **louses**) a mean, contemptible person. ~*v.t.* to remove lice from. **to louse up** to spoil, to make a mess of. **lousy** (-zi) *a.* (*comp.* **lousier,** *superl.* **lousiest**) **1** infested with lice. **2** (*coll.*) bad, inferior, disgusting. **lousy with** swarming with, excessively supplied with. **lousily** *adv.* **lousiness** *n.*
lout (lowt) *n.* a rough, crude, ill-mannered person, an oaf. **loutish** *a.* **loutishly** *adv.* **loutishness** *n.*
louvre (loo´və), (*N Am.*) **louver** *n.* **1** a louvre-board. **2** (*also pl.*) a set of louvre boards and the frame in which they are set. **3** an opening in a chimney pot etc. to let out smoke. **louvre-board** *n.* each of a set of sloping overlapping boards across a window, door etc. to exclude rain but allow the passage of air. **louvred** *a.*
lovage (lŭv´ij) *n.* **1** a European umbelliferous herb, used in salads and for flavouring food, *Levisticum officinale*. **2** a related white-flowered plant of N Europe, *Ligusticum scoticum*.
lovat (lŭv´ət), **lovat green** *n.* a muted blueish-grey green colour, usu. found in tweed or woollen cloth. ~*a.* of this colour.
love (lŭv) *n.* **1** a feeling of deep regard, fondness and devotion (for, towards etc.). **2** deep affection, usu. accompanied by yearning or desire for. **3** sexual desire or passion. **4** (*also* **Love**) a personification of this or of Cupid, usu. in the form of a naked winged boy. **5** sexual relations. **6** a beloved one, a sweetheart (as a term of endearment). **7** (*coll.*) a delightful person; a charming thing. **8** affectionate greetings, a formula for ending an affectionate letter. **9** in games, no points scored, nil. ~*v.t.* **1** to have strong affection for, to be fond of. **2** to desire passionately, to be in love with. **3** to like greatly, to delight in, to have a strong partiality or predilection for. ~*v.i.* to be in love. **for love** for pleasure or out of benevolence, affection etc., not for payment. **for the love of** for the sake of (esp. in adjuration). **in love** feeling a strong desire and attachment (for another person, for each other). **(not) for love or money** by no means, in no

circumstances. **out of love** no longer in love. **to fall in love** to begin to feel love. **to give/ send one's love** to give, send an affectionate message. **to make love to** to have sexual intercourse with. **lovable, loveable** *a.* **1** worthy of love. **2** amiable. **lovableness** *n.* **lovably** *adv.* **love affair** *n.* **1** a romantic or sexual attachment between two people, often temporary in nature. **2** an enthusiasm for or fascination with (an object, activity etc.). **lovebird** *n.* **1** a short-tailed parrot of the African genus *Agapornis*, from the attachment they show to their mates. **2** (*pl., coll.*) a very fond or demonstratively affectionate couple. **lovebite** *n.* a temporary red or purple mark on the skin caused by a partner biting or sucking it during lovemaking. **love child** *n.* an illegitimate child. **love game** *n.* a game in tennis etc., in which the loser has not scored. **love-hate relationship** *n.* a relationship characterized by powerful but contradictory feelings of attraction and repulsion. **love-in-a-mist** *n.* a plant, *Nigella damascena*, with blue flowers and many green bracts. **loveless** *a.* **1** destitute of love. **2** not loving. **3** not loved. **lovelessly** *adv.* **lovelessness** *n.* **love letter** *n.* a letter between lovers or professing love. **love life** *n.* a person's romantic or sexual experiences and attachments. **lovelock** *n.* a curl or tress hanging at the ear or on the forehead. **lovelorn** *a.* pining away for love. **lovely** *a.* (*comp.* **lovelier**, *superl.* **loveliest**) **1** beautiful and attractive. **2** delightful, pleasant, enjoyable. *~n.* (*pl.* **lovelies**) (*coll.*) a beautiful woman. **lovelily** *adv.* **loveliness** *n.* **lovemaking** *n.* sexual play or intercourse between partners. **love match** *n.* a marriage for love, not for other considerations. **love nest** *n.* a secret place where lovers meet, esp. for illicit sexual relations. **lover** *n.* **1** a person with whom one is having a sexual relationship. **2** (*pl.*) a couple who are having a love affair. **3** a person, esp. a man, who is in love. **4** a person who is fond of anything. **loverless** *a.* **love seat** *n.* a small sofa or double chair for two people. **lovesick** *a.* languishing with love. **lovesickness** *n.* **lovey** (-i) *n.* (*pl.* **loveys**) (*coll.*) a person who is loved, a term of endearment. **lovey-dovey** (-dŭv´i) *a.* (*coll.*) demonstratively loving, affectionate. **loving** *a.* feeling or showing affection. *~n.* affection, love. **loving cup** *n.* a large two- or three-handled drinking-vessel passed round with wine at a banquet. **lovingly** *adv.* **lovingness** *n.*

low[1] (lō) *a.* (*comp.* **lower**, *superl.* **lowest**) **1** not reaching or situated far up. **2** not high or tall, below the usual or normal height. **3** below or little above a given surface or level, not elevated. **4** (of the sun, moon etc.) near the horizon. **5** (of latitude) near the equator. **6** small or below the norm in amount, extent, intensity etc. **7** reduced in amount, scanty, nearly exhausted. **8** humble in rank or position. **9** dejected, depressed. **10** lacking in vigour, weak, feeble. **11** (of sounds) not raised in pitch, deep, produced by slow vibrations, not loud or intense, soft. **12** not

sublime, not exalted, commonplace. **13** coarse, vulgar. **14** base, dishonourable. **15** (of a vowel sound) open. *~adv.* **1** in or to a low position. **2** at a low price. **3** in a humble rank or position. **4** with a subdued voice, in low tones; softly, quietly. **5** at a deep pitch. **6** of humble birth. *~n.* **1** a low position or level. **2** an area of low atmospheric pressure. **to bring low** to reduce in wealth, position, health etc. **low birth** *n.* humble parentage. **low-born** *a.* **lowbrow** *n.* a person making no claims to culture or intellectuality. *~a.* **1** unintellectual. **2** assuming no airs of intellectual superiority. **lowbrowed** *a.* **Low Church** *n.* the evangelical party in the Church of England. **low-class** *a.* of poor quality or of low social class. **low-cut** *a.* (of a dress etc.) cut low at the neck, exposing part of the shoulders and breasts. **low-density lipoprotein** *n.* the form of lipoprotein in which cholesterol is transported in the bloodstream. **low-down** *a.* degraded, mean, abject. *~n.* (*coll.*) the inner history, real facts. **lowest** *a.* (the) most low. **lowest common denominator** *n.* **1** (*Math.*) the smallest number or quantity that is exactly divisible by each denominator of a set of fractions. **2** the least desirable or edifying feature common to all members of a group. **lowest common multiple** *n.* the smallest number or quantity that is exactly divisible by each of the set of numbers or quantities. **low frequency** *n.* a radio frequency lying between 30 and 300 kHz. **low gear** *n.* on cycles, motor vehicles etc., apparatus for transmitting low speed to the driving-wheel relatively to the motion of pedals, engine etc. **Low German** *n.* the dialect of German, closely related to Dutch, spoken esp. in the rural areas of N Germany. **low-grade** *a.* of low quality or strength. **lowish** *a.* **low-key, low-keyed** *a.* **1** of low intensity. **2** undramatic. **3** restrained. **lowland** *n.* low-lying or level country. *~a.* of or relating to a lowland or the Lowlands. **Lowlander** *n.* **Lowlands** *n.pl.* the eastern and southern or less mountainous parts of Scotland. **low-level language** *n.* (*Comput.*) a computer programming language that corresponds more to machine code than to human language. **low life** *n.* life in the criminal underworld or in the lowest social strata. **lowlife** *n.* (*pl.* **lowlifes**) **1** a member of the criminal underworld. **2** criminals and the degenerate members of a society collectively. **lowlight** *n.* **1** (*facet.*) a particularly dull, inglorious or unsuccessful moment or period in the course or history of something. **2** (*usu. pl.*) a portion of hair dyed to a colour darker than the natural one. **low-loader** *n.* a road or rail vehicle with a low platform for heavy loads. **lowly** *a.* (*comp.* **lowlier**, *superl.* **lowliest**) **1** humble, modest, unpretentious. **2** low in size, rank or condition. **3** low, mean, inferior. **4** comparatively undeveloped or unevolved. **lowlily** *adv.* **lowliness** *n.* **low-lying** *a.* situated at a low level with respect to the surrounding countryside and to rivers or bodies of water. **low Mass** *n.* Mass said without music and without elaborate ritual. **lowness** *n.* **low-pitched** *a.* **1** having a low tone or key. **2** (of a roof) having a low angular elevation. **low-pressure** *a.* **1** having, using or exerting a lower pressure than the norm. **2** having low barometric pressure. **3** relaxed, calm; undemanding. **low profile** *n.* a reserved or inconspicuous attitude or manner to avoid attention or publicity. **low-profile** *a.* **1** deliberately avoiding prominence or publicity. **2** (of a motor vehicle tyre) having greater than usual width in relation to its height. **low relief** *n.* basrelief. **low-rise** *a.* (of buildings) having only one or two storeys. **low season** *n.* the season during which there is least demand, traffic etc. **low-spirited** *a.* dejected, depressed. **low technology, low tech** *n.* simple unsophisticated machinery, implements and techniques as used for centuries for the production of basic necessities. **low-technology, low-tech** *a.* **low tide** *n.* **1** the lowest point of the ebb tide; the level of the sea at ebb tide. **2** the time of this. **low water** *n.* low tide. **low-water mark** *n.* **1** the point reached by the sea at low tide or something marking this. **2** the lowest level or value; the nadir.

low² (lō) *v.i.* to utter the moo of cow. ~*n.* the moo of a cow. **lowing** *n.*

lower¹ (lō´ə) *a.* **1** situated at a less high level than, or below, another thing. **2** smaller in quantity, number etc. **3** (often **Lower**) a situated on a lower terrain. **b** situated to the south. **4** (*Geol.*) (often **Lower**) relating to an older period and therefore usu. to deeper strata. ~*adv.* in or to a lower position, status etc. ~*v.t.* **1** to bring down in height, force, pitch, intensity, amount, price, estimation etc. **2** to haul or let down. **3** to degrade, to demean. **4** to diminish. ~*v.i.* **1** to become lower or less. **2** to sink, to fall. **to lower the tone** to make a conversation, social gathering etc., less refined, prestigious or edifying. **lower case** *n.* (*Print.*) small letters; a case containing the small letters. **lower-case** *a.* **lower class** *n.* (often *pl.*) the working classes. **lower-class** *a.* **Lower House** *n.* **1** the larger, usu. popularly elected house of a bicameral legislative assembly. **2** in the UK, the House of Commons. **lowermost** *a.* **lower regions** *n.pl.* hell; the realm of the dead. **lower world** *n.* **1** the earth, as opposed to heaven. **2** the lower regions.

lower² LOUR.

lox¹ (loks) *n.* a kind of smoked salmon.

lox² (loks) *n.* liquid oxygen, used in rocket fuels.

loyal (loi´əl) *a.* **1** faithful, true, constant, in a trust or obligation (to). **2** faithful to one's sovereign, government or country. **loyalist** *n.* **1** a patriotic supporter of sovereign or government. **2** (**Loyalist**) in Northern Ireland, a Protestant who supports Ulster's union with Britain. **loyalism** *n.* **loyally** *adv.* **loyal toast** *n.* a toast to the sovereign. **loyalty** *n.* (*pl.* **loyalties**).

lozenge (loz´inj) *n.* **1** a rhombus or oblique-angled parallelogram. **2** a confection or medi-

cated sweet etc. in a tablet of this shape. **3** a small rhombus-shaped pane of glass. **4** (*Her.*) a diamond-shaped bearing, appropriated to the arms of spinsters and widows. **5** a rhombus-shaped facet in a cut gem. **lozenged** *a.* **lozengy** *a.*

LP¹ (elpē´) *n.* a long-playing record, usu. 12 in. (30 cm) in diameter and designed to rotate at 33.3 revolutions per minute.

LP² *abbr.* low pressure.

LPG *abbr.* liquefied petroleum gas.

Lr *chem. symbol* lawrencium.

LSD (elesdē´) *n.* lysergic acid diethylamide, a hallucinogenic drug.

L.S.D., l.s.d, £.s.d *abbr.* librae, solidi, denarii, pounds, shillings and pence.

Lt. *abbr.* **1** Lieutenant. **2** light.

Ltd. *abbr.* limited liability.

Lu *chem. symbol* lutetium.

lubber (lŭb´ə) *n.* (*dial.*) a lazy, clumsy person, an awkward lout. **lubberly** *a., adv.*

lubricate (loo´brikāt) *v.t.* **1** to cover or treat with grease, oil or similar substance, in order to reduce friction. **2** to make smooth or slippery. **lubricant** (-brikənt) *n.* a substance used to lubricate. ~*a.* that lubricates. **lubrication** (-ā´shən) *n.* **lubricator** *n.*

lubricious (loobrish´əs), **lubricous** (loo´brikəs) *a.* **1** (*formal*) lewd, lascivious. **2** †slippery. **lubricity** (-bris´-) *n.*

luce (loos) *n.* a pike (the fish), esp. when full-grown.

lucent (loo´sənt) *a.* (*poet.*) **1** shining, bright, luminous, resplendent. **2** translucent. **lucency** *n.*

lucerne (loosœn´), **lucern** *n.* alfalfa.

lucid (loo´sid) *a.* **1** clear, transparent, perspicuous, easily understood. **2** sane; denoting an interval of sanity occurring during insanity or dementia. **3** (*Bot.*) having a smooth, shiny surface. **4** (*poet.*) bright, shining, radiant. **lucidity** (-sid´-) *n.* **lucidly** *adv.* **lucidness** *n.*

luck (lŭk) *n.* **1** chance, accident, as bringer of fortune, whether good or bad. **2** what happens to one, fortune, hap. **3** good fortune, success. **4** a person or thing that is supposed to bring good fortune. **for luck** in the hope of gaining good fortune. **no such luck** unfortunately not. **to luck into** (*sl.*) to acquire or achieve by good fortune or chance. **to luck out** (*N Am., sl.*) to be successful or fortunate, esp. by chance. **to try one's luck** to attempt something. **with luck** if everything goes well. **worse luck** unfortunately. **luckless** *a.* unfortunate. **lucklessly** *adv.* **lucky** *a.* (*comp.* **luckier,** *superl.* **luckiest**) **1** characterized or usu. attended by good luck, favoured by fortune. **2** successful, esp. by a fluke or more than is deserved. **3** bringing luck, auspicious. **luckily** *adv.* fortunately (for). **luckiness** *n.* **lucky dip** *n.* a receptacle containing an assortment of articles, for one of which people dip blindly. **lucky dog** *n.* (*coll.*) a lucky fellow.

lucrative (loo´krətiv) *a.* producing gain, profitable, bringing in money. **lucratively** *adv.*

lucre (loo´kə) *n.* (*derog. or facet.*) pecuniary gain or advantage, usu. as an object of greed.

lud (lŭd) *n.* lord, as in *m'lud*, *my lud*, phrases used to address a judge in court.

Luddite (lŭd´īt) *n.* **1** a member of a band of workmen who organized riots, 1811–16, for the destruction of machinery as a protest against unemployment. **2** any opponent of technological change. **Luddism** *n.*

ludicrous (loo´dikrəs) *a.* liable to excite laughter or derision; comical, ridiculous. **ludicrously** *adv.* **ludicrousness** *n.*

ludo (loo´dō) *n.* a game played with counters on a specially chequered board.

luff (lŭf), **loof** (loof) *n.* (*Naut.*) **1** the weather edge of a fore-and-aft sail. **2** that part of a ship's bows where the timbers begin to curve in towards the stem. ~*v.i.* to bring a ship's head or to steer nearer the wind. ~*v.t.* **1** to bring (a ship's head) or the head of (a ship) nearer the wind. **2** to turn (the helm) so as to do this. **3** to obstruct (an opponent) in yacht racing by sailing closer to the wind. **4** to raise or lower (the jib of a crane or derrick).

luffa LOOFAH.

lug[1] (lŭg) *v.t.* (*pres.p.* **lugging**, *past, p.p.* **lugged**) **1** to drag, to pull, esp. roughly or with exertion. **2** to carry with effort and difficulty. **3** to drag in, to insert unnecessarily. ~*v.i.* to drag or pull (at). ~*n.* a drag or tug.

lug[2] (lŭg) *n.* **1** a projecting part, esp. a projecting part of a machine made to hold or grip another part. **2** (*coll. or Sc.*) the ear. **3** (*N Am.*) a stupid or awkward person; an oaf. **lughole** *n.* (*coll.*) earhole.

luge (loozh) *n.* a small toboggan for one or two people. ~*v.i.* to toboggan in one of these.

luggage (lŭg´ij) *n.* a traveller's suitcases, trunks etc. **luggage van** *n.* a railway carriage for luggage, bicycles etc.

lugger (lŭg´ə) *n.* a small vessel with two or three masts, a running bowsprit and lugsails.

lugsail (lŭg´səl), **lug** *n.* (*Naut.*) a four-cornered sail bent to a yard lashed obliquely to the mast.

lugubrious (logoo´briəs) *a.* mournful, dismal, funereal. **lugubriously** *adv.* **lugubriousness** *n.*

lugworm (lŭg´wœm), **lug** *n.* any large marine worm of the genus *Arenicola*, burrowing in the sand, used for bait.

lukewarm (look´wawm, -wawm´) *a.* **1** moderately warm. **2** indifferent, cool, lacking enthusiasm or conviction. **lukewarmly** *adv.* **lukewarmness** *n.*

lull (lŭl) *v.t.* **1** to soothe to sleep, to calm, to quiet. **2** to allay the fears, anxieties etc. of, usu. in order to deceive. ~*v.i.* to subside, to become quiet. ~*n.* **1** a temporary calm. **2** an intermission or abatement. **lullaby** (-əbī) *n.* (*pl.* **lullabies**) a refrain or song for lulling a child to sleep. ~*v.t.* (*3rd pers. sing. pres.* **lullabies**, *pres.p.* **lullabying**, *past, p.p.* **lullabied**) to sing to sleep. **lullingly** *adv.*

lumbago (lŭmbā´gō) *n.* rheumatism in the lumbar region.

lumbar (lŭm´bə) *a.* (*Anat.*) of or relating to the portion of the body between the lower ribs and the upper part of the hip bone. ~*n.* a lumbar nerve, vertebra, artery etc. **lumbar puncture** *n.* the insertion of a needle between two lumbar vertebrae to withdraw cerebrospinal fluid.

lumber[1] (lŭm´bə) *v.i.* to move heavily, cumbrously or clumsily. **lumbering** *a.* **lumberingly** *adv.* **lumbersome** *a.*

lumber[2] (lŭm´bə) *n.* **1** discarded articles of furniture and other rubbish taking up room. **2** useless and cumbersome things. **3** (*N Am.*) timber sawn into marketable shape. ~*v.t.* **1** to burden (with), to leave to deal with (something unwanted or unpleasant). **2** to fill with lumber. **3** to encumber, to obstruct. **4** to heap up in a disorderly way. **5** (*N Am.*) to cut and prepare (timber) for the market. ~*v.i.* to fell and prepare timber, to work as a lumberjack. **lumberjack**, **lumberman** *n.* (*pl.* **lumberjacks, lumbermen**) a person who is employed in felling, preparing and transporting forest timber. **lumber-jacket** *n.* **1** a man's loose-fitting jacket in a heavy, usu. chequered material that fastens up to the neck. **2** a woman's cardigan similarly fastened. **lumberroom** *n.* a room for the storage of lumber, trunks etc.

lumen (loo´mən) *n.* (*pl.* **lumens, lumina** (-minə)) **1** (*Physics*) the SI unit of luminous flux, being the quantity of light emitted per second in a solid angle of one steradian by a uniform pointsource having an intensity of one candela. **2** (*Anat.*) the cavity of a tubular organ. **3** a cavity within a plant cell wall. **luminance** *n.* (*Physics*) a measure, in candela/cm², of the luminous intensity of any surface in a given direction per unit of projected area.

luminaire (loominee´) *n.* a light fitting.

luminary (loo´minəri) *n.* (*pl.* **luminaries**) **1** a famous person. **2** a person who enlightens mankind or is a brilliant exponent of a subject. **3** (*formal*) any body yielding light, esp. a heavenly body.

luminesce (loomines´) *v.i.* to exhibit luminescence. **luminescence** *n.* the emission of light at low temperatures by processes other than incandescence, e.g. by chemical action. **luminescent** *a.*

luminiferous (loominif´ərəs) *a.* giving, yielding or transmitting light.

luminous (loo´minəs) *a.* **1** emitting light. **2** shining brightly, brilliant. **3** visible in darkness; phosphorescent. **4** lucid, perspicuous; shedding light (on a subject etc.). **5** relating to visible radiation. **luminosity** (-nos´-) *n.* (*pl.* **luminosities**). **luminously** *adv.* **luminousness** *n.*

lump[1] (lŭmp) *n.* **1** a small mass of matter of no definite shape. **2** a mass, a quantity, a heap, a lot. **3** a swelling, a protuberance; a tumour. **4** a heavy, stupid person. ~*v.t.* **1** to put together in a lump, to form into a mass. **2** to take collectively, to treat as all alike. ~*v.i.* **1** to form or collect into lumps. **2** to move (about) heavily or clumsily. **the lump** the collective group of self-employed workers in the building trade. **lumpectomy** (-ek'təmi) *n.* (*pl.* **lumpectomies**) the removal by surgery of a cancerous lump in the breast. **lumper** *n.* **lumping** *a.* **1** large, heavy. **2** big, bulky, plentiful. **lump in the throat** *n.* a feeling of constriction in the throat caused by emotion. **lumpish** *a.* **1** like a lump. **2** heavy. **3** lazy, inert. **4** stupid. **lumpishly** *adv.* **lumpishness** *n.* **lump sugar** *n.* cube sugar; loaf sugar broken into small lumps. **lump sum** *n.* the whole amount of money taken together, as opposed to instalments. **lumpy** *a.* (*comp.* **lumpier,** *superl.* **lumpiest**) **1** full of lumps. **2** (*Naut.*) running in short waves that do not break. **lumpily** *adv.* **lumpiness** *n.*

lump² (lŭmp) *v.t.* (*coll.*) to put up with. **like it or lump it** put up with it as there is no alternative.

lumpfish (lŭmp'fish) *n.* (*pl. in general* **lumpfish,** *in particular* **lumpfishes**) a suctorial fish, *Cyclopterus lumpus,* of northern seas, with a globular body covered in tubercles and pelvic fins modified as a sucker.

lunacy (loo'nəsi) *n.* (*pl.* **lunacies**) **1** unsoundness of mind, insanity, formerly supposed to be caused by the moon. **2** gross folly, senseless conduct; a senseless action.

luna moth (loo'nə) *n.* a large N American moth, *Actias luna,* with crescent-shaped markings on its forewings.

lunar (loo'nə) *a.* **1** of or relating to, caused or influenced by the moon. **2** resembling the moon, crescent-shaped. **3** (of light) pale, weak. **lunar cycle** *n.* a Metonic cycle. **lunar distance** *n.* the angular distance of the moon from the sun, a planet or a star, used at sea in finding longitude. **lunar module, lunar excursion module** *n.* a small spacecraft used in the Apollo missions to transfer astronauts from an orbiting spacecraft to the moon's surface. **lunar month** *n.* **1** the period of a complete revolution of the moon, 29½ days. **2** (in general use) four weeks. **lunar node** *n.* either of the two points at which the moon's orbit intersects the ecliptic. **lunar orbit** *n.* **1** the moon's orbit around the earth. **2** an orbit around the moon. **lunar year** *n.* a period of twelve lunar months. **lunate** (-nāt) *n.* (*also* **lunate bone**) a crescent-shaped bone in the wrist. ~*a.* (*also* **lunated** (-nātid)) crescent-shaped. **lunation** (-nā'shən) *n.* the period between two returns of the moon, a lunar month.

lunatic (loo'nətik) *a.* **1** insane. **2** mad, frantic, crazy, extremely foolish. ~*n.* an insane person. **lunatic asylum** *n.* (*offensive*) formerly the name for a hospital for the care and treatment of the mentally ill. **lunatic fringe** *n.* members of society or of a group regarded as holding extreme or fanatical views.

lunch (lŭnch) *n.* **1** a midday meal. **2** the food eaten at such a meal. **3** lunch hour. **4** a light meal or snack eaten at any time. ~*v.i.* to take lunch. ~*v.t.* to provide lunch for. **lunch box** *n.* a container for carrrying food to eat. **luncheon** (-chən) *n.* (*formal*) lunch. **luncheonette** (-chənet') *n.* (*esp. N Am.*) a restaurant serving light lunches. **luncheon meat** *n.* a type of pre-cooked meat, usu. pork minced with cereal, served cold. **luncheon voucher** *n.* a voucher given to employees which can be used to pay for take-away food or a meal in a restaurant. **lunch hour** *n.* time allowed off work to eat lunch. **lunchtime** *n.* the time at which lunch is usually eaten.

lunette (loonet') *n.* **1** a semicircular aperture in a concave ceiling. **2** a crescent-shaped or semicircular space or panel for a picture or decorative painting. **3** a flattened watch-glass. **4** a ring on a vehicle to enable it to be towed by a towing hook. **5** a temporary fortification which has two faces and two flanks.

lung (lŭng) *n.* **1** either of the two organs of respiration in vertebrates, situated on each side of the chest. **2** an analogous organ in invertebrates. **lunged** *a.* **lungfish** *n.* (*pl. in general* **lungfish,** *in particular* **lungfishes**) a dipnoan, having lungs as well as gills. **lungless** *a.* **lung-power** *n.* strength of voice. **lungworm** *n.* a parasitic nematode worm infecting the lungs of mammals, esp. pigs. **lungwort** *n.* **1** any plant of the genus *Pulmonaria,* of the borage family, formerly held to be good for pulmonary diseases. **2** a lichen, *Lobaria pulmonacea,* growing on the trunks of trees, also used as a domestic remedy for lung disease.

lunge¹ (lŭnj) *n.* **1** a sudden thrust with a sword etc., esp. an attacking move in fencing in which the front foot is thrust forward and the back leg straightened as the sword arm is extended. **2** a sudden forward movement, a plunge. ~*v.i.* **1** to make a lunge. **2** in boxing, to deliver a blow from the shoulder. ~*v.t.* to thrust (a weapon) forward.

lunge² (lŭnj), **longe** *n.* a long rope or rein used in training horses. ~*v.t.* to drive (a horse) round in a circle at the end of a lunge.

lunisolar (loonisō'lə) *a.* of, relating to, or compounded of the revolutions of, the sun and the moon.

lunula (loo'nūlə), **lunule** *n.* (*pl.* **lunulae** (-lē), **lunules**) a crescent-shaped mark, spot or part, esp. at the base of a fingernail.

lupin (loo'pin), (*N Am.*) **lupine** *n.* **1** a leguminous plant of the genus *Lupinus,* with spikes of white or coloured flowers, grown in flower-gardens and for fodder. **2** (*pl.*) the seeds of this plant.

lupine (loo'pīn) *a.* **1** of or relating to wolves. **2** like a wolf.

lupus (loo'pəs) *n.* a spreading tuberculous or ulcerous inflammation of the skin, esp. lupus vulgaris. **lupoid** (-poid), **lupous** *a.* **lupus vulgaris** (vŭlgah'ris) *n.* tuberculosis of the skin, esp. of the face, causing dark red patches.

lurch[1] (lœch) *v.i.* **1** (of a ship) to roll suddenly to one side. **2** to stagger. ~*n.* **1** a sudden roll sideways, as of a ship. **2** a stagger.

lurch[2] (lœch) *n.* a losing position in the game of cribbage and some other games. **to leave in the lurch** to leave in difficulties.

lurcher (lœ´chə) *n.* a dog, usu. a cross between a retriever or collie and a greyhound.

lure (luə) *n.* **1** an enticement, an allurement. **2** the alluring qualities (of). **3** an object resembling a fowl, used to recall a hawk. ~*v.t.* **1** to attract or bring back by a lure. **2** to entice. ~*v.i.* to call or tempt an animal, esp. a hawk.

Lurex® (lū´reks, loo´-) *n.* (a fabric made from) a thin plastic-coated metallic thread.

lurgy (lœ´gi) *n.* (*pl.* **lurgies**) (*facet.*) an unspecified (horrible) illness, usu. in *the dreaded lurgy.*

lurid (lū´rid, luə´-) *a.* **1** shockingly or glaringly bright. **2** gaudy, showy, in bright colours. **3** (of a story etc.) sensational, shocking, horrifying. **4** ghastly, unearthly. **5** of a pale yellow colour, wan. **luridly** *adv.* **luridness** *n.*

lurk (lœk) *v.i.* **1** to move about furtively. **2** to wait concealed, esp. with a sinister purpose. **3** to lie in wait. **4** to be latent, to exist unperceived. **lurker** *n.* **lurking** *a.*

luscious (lŭsh´əs) *a.* **1** very sweet, delicious. **2** extremely attractive, voluptuous. **3** (of music, poetry etc.) cloying, fulsome, over-rich in imagery, sensuousness etc. **lusciously** *adv.* **lusciousness** *n.*

lush[1] (lŭsh) *a.* **1** luxuriant in growth. **2** succulent, juicy. **3** (of sound, colour) rich and voluptuous. **4** luxurious. **lushness** *n.*

lush[2] (lŭsh) *n.* (*sl.*) **1** a heavy drinker, an alcoholic. **2** (*N Am.*) alcohol. ~*v.i.* to drink. ~*v.t.* to ply with liquor.

lust (lŭst) *n.* **1** a powerful desire for sexual pleasure, concupiscence, lasciviousness. **2** sensual appetite. **3** passionate desire (for). **4** passionate enjoyment, relish. ~*v.i.* to have powerful or inordinate desire (for or after). **lustful** *a.* **lustfully** *adv.* **lustfulness** *n.* **lusty** *a.* (*comp.* **lustier,** *superl.* **lustiest**) full of health and vigour. **lustily** *adv.* **lustiness** *n.*

lustre (lŭs´tə), (*N Am.*) **luster** *n.* **1** gloss, sheen, bright light, reflected light. **2** a shiny or reflective surface. **3** radiant or brilliant light. **4** splendour, illustriousness, glory (of an achievement etc.). **5** a chandelier ornamented with pendants of cut glass. **6** a glass pendant on such a chandelier. **7** a cotton, woollen or other fabric with a glossy surface. **8** a glossy enamel on pottery etc. **9** lustreware. ~*v.t.* to put lustre on (pottery, cloth). **lustreless** *a.* **lustreware** *n.* ceramics with an iridescent glaze. **lustrous** (-trəs) *a.* **lustrously** *adv.*

lute[1] (lūt, loot) *n.* a stringed instrument with a pear-shaped body and a long fretted fingerboard. **lutenist** (-tənist), **lutanist** *n.* a lute-player.

lute[2] (lūt, loot) *n.* **1** (*also* **luting**) a composition of clay or cement used to secure the joints of

vessels and tubes, or as a covering to protect crucibles etc. from fire. **2** a rubber washer. ~*v.t.* to seal up or coat with lute.

luteal (lū´tiəl, loo´-) *a.* of or relating to the corpus luteum. **lutein** (lū´tiin) *n.* a deep yellow pigment found in egg yolk etc. **luteinize** (-tiə-), **luteinise** *v.t.*, *v.i.* to produce or form corpora lutea. **luteinizing hormone** *n.* a hormone secreted from the front lobe of the pituitary gland which stimulates, in females, ovulation and the development of corpora lutea and, in males, maturation of the interstitial cells of the testes and androgen production.

lutetium (lootē´shiəm), **lutecium** (-si-) *n.* (*Chem.*) an extremely rare metallic element, at. no. 71, chem. symbol Lu, one of the lanthanides, discovered in 1907 by Georges Urbain, 1872–1938, a French chemist.

Lutheran (loo´thərən) *a.* of or belonging to Luther or his doctrines. ~*n.* **1** a follower of Luther. **2** a member of the Church based on Luther's religious doctrines. **Lutheranism, Lutherism** *n.*

luthier (lū´tiə, loo´-) *n.* a maker of lutes, guitars and other stringed instruments.

lutz (luts) *n.* in figure-skating, a jump from one skate with one, two or three rotations and a return to the other skate.

luvvy (lŭv´i), **luvvie** *n.* (*pl.* **luvvies**) (*coll.*) **1** a member of the acting profession, esp. one given to sentiment, effusiveness or camp. **2** a lovey.

lux (lŭks) *n.* (*pl.* **lux, luxes**) (*Physics*) the SI unit of illumination equal to one lumen per square metre.

luxe (luks) *n.* luxury, sumptuousness, superfine elegance.

Luxembourger (lŭk´səmbœgə) *n.* a native or inhabitant of Luxembourg.

luxury (lŭk´shəri) *n.* (*pl.* **luxuries**) **1** great comfort with abundant provision of pleasant and delightful things. **2** something which is not a necessity, esp. something particularly delightful and expensive that one indulges in only occasionally. **3** luxuriousness. ~*a.* **1** designed to provide luxury, extremely comfortable. **2** nonessential, constituting an expensive indulgence. **3** providing a high level of comfort, service etc. **luxuriant** (lŭgzū´riənt) *a.* **1** (of vegetation) abundant in growth, lush, rank. **2** fertile, prolific, profuse, exuberant. **3** (of style) ornate, florid, extravagant, sumptuous. **luxuriance, luxuriancy** *n.* **luxuriantly** *adv.* **luxuriate** *v.i.* **1** to revel, to indulge oneself voluptuously. **2** to grow abundantly or profusely. **luxurious** *a.* **1** characterized by luxury, provided with an ample supply of comforts and pleasures. **2** extremely comfortable. **3** self-indulgent. **luxuriously** *adv.* **luxuriousness** *n.*

LV *abbr.* luncheon voucher.

LWM *abbr.* low water mark.

lx *abbr.* lux.

-ly[1] (li) *suf.* forming adjectives, esp. meaning

having the qualities of, e.g. *godly, manly* or at intervals of, e.g. *hourly, weekly*.

-ly² (li) *suf.* forming adverbs from adjectives, e.g. *badly, heavily, mightily*.

lycanthropy (līkan´thrəpi) *n.* **1** insanity in which patients believe themselves to be a wolf or some other animal, whose instincts and habits they assume. **2** a form of witchcraft by which men or women transform themselves into wolves. **lycanthrope** (lī´kənthrōp) *n.* **1** a werewolf. **2** a person suffering from lycanthropy.

lychee (lī´chē, lich´-), **lichee, litchi** *n.* **1** the fruit of the Chinese tree, *Nephelium litchi*, which has a hard, scaly skin and a soft white pulp. **2** this tree.

lych-gate LICH-GATE.

lychnis (lik´nis) *n.* any of a genus of plants, *Lychnis*, belonging to the family Silenaceae, comprising the campions.

lycopod (lī´kəpod) *n.* a clubmoss, a member of the genus *Lycopodium*, or the order Lycopodiaceae. **lycopodium** (-pō´diəm) *n.* **1** a clubmoss of the genus *Lycopodium*. **2** an inflammable yellow powder in the spore-cases of some species, used for making fireworks and as an absorbent in surgery.

Lycra® (lī´krə) *n.* a synthetic elastic fibre and material used in swimwear and other tight-fitting garments.

lye (lī) *n.* **1** an alkaline solution leached from wood ashes or other alkaline substance. **2** any strong alkaline solution used for washing or cleansing, esp. potassium hydroxide.

lying¹ LIE¹.

lying² LIE².

lymph (limf) *n.* **1** the comparatively transparent, colourless, alkaline fluid in the tissues and organs of the body, consisting mainly of white blood corpuscles. **2** lymphatic fluid containing the virus of a disease, obtained from a diseased body or by culture, and used in vaccination. **3** exudation from a sore etc. **4** (*poet.*) water or any clear transparent fluid. **lymphatic** (-fat´-) *a.* **1** of or relating to, containing, secreting or conveying lymph. **2** pale, flabby. **3** (of temperament) sluggish, lacking vigour. ~*n.* a vessel that conveys lymph. **lymphatic system** *n.* the network of capillary vessels that conveys lymph to the venous system. **lymph gland, lymph node** *n.* any of the small localized masses of tissue distributed along the lymphatic vessels that produce lymphocytes. **lymphocyte** (-fəsīt) *n.* a type of white blood cell formed in the lymph nodes, which forms part of the body's immunological defence against infection. **lymphoid** (-foid) *a.* **lymphoma** (-fō´mə) *n.* (*pl.* **lymphomas, lymphomata** (-mətə) a tumour of lymphoid tissue.

lyncean LYNX.

lynch (linch) *v.t.* (of a mob) to execute, esp. by hanging, without a trial or after mock trial. **lynch law** *n.* summary punishment without trial or upon trial by a self-appointed court.

lynchpin LINCHPIN.

lynx (lingks) *n.* (*pl.* **lynx, lynxes**) **1** a feline mammal of Europe and North America, *Felis lynx*, characterized by tufted ear-tips, short tail and extremely sharp sight. **2** its fur. **lyncean** (linse´ən) *a.* **1** of or relating to the lynx. **2** lynx-eyed, sharp-sighted. **lynx-eyed** *a.* having sharp sight.

lyre (līə) *n.* an ancient Greek stringed instrument like a small harp, consisting of a resonating box with a pair of curved arms above it connected by a crossbar. **lyrate** (-rət), **lyrated** (-rātid) *a.* (*Biol.*) shaped like a lyre. **lyre-bird** *n.* an insectivorous Australian bird, *Menura superba*, having the 16 tail feathers of the male disposed in the form of a lyre. **lyre-flower** *n.* the bleeding heart.

lyric (lir´ik) *a.* **1** (of a poem) expressing the individual emotions of the poet. **2** (of a poet) writing poetry of this kind. **3** intended to be sung or fitted for expression in song. **4** relating to or suited for the lyre. **5** (of singing) having a light quality and tone. ~*n.* **1** a lyric poem. **2** (*often pl.*) the words of a popular song. **3** a song. **lyrical** *a.* **1** lyric. **2** using language suitable for lyric poetry. **3** extremely enthusiastic and effusive (*wax lyrical*). **lyrically** *adv.* **lyricism** (-sizm) *n.* **1** a lyrical quality or style. **2** a lyrical expression. **3** emotional or enthusiastic effusions. **lyricist** *n.* a writer of song lyrics.

lysergic acid (līsœ´jik) *n.* a crystalline compound derived from ergot. **lysergic acid diethylamide** (dīəthī´ləmīd, dīēthīlam´īd) *n.* a powerful hallucinogenic drug better known as LSD.

lysis (lī´sis) *n.* (*pl.* **lyses** (lī´sēz)) (*Biol.*) the destruction of cells by the action of a lysin. **lyse** (līz) *v.t., v.i.* (*Biol.*) (to cause) to undergo lysis. **lysin** (-sin) *n.* (*Biol.*) a substance, esp. an antibody, which causes the disintegration of cells. **lysine** (-sīn, -sēn) *n.* (*Biol.*) an amino acid obtained from dietary sources which is essential to nutrition in humans. **-lysis** (lisis) *comb. form* denoting a breaking down, loosening or disintegration. **lysosome** (-səsōm) *n.* (*Biol.*) any of numerous small particles, present in the cytoplasm of most cells, that contain degradative enzymes. **lysozyme** (-səzīm) *n.* an enzyme found in tears and egg white that destroys certain bacteria by hydrolysing polysaccharides in their cell walls. **lytic** (lit´ik) *a.* of, relating to or causing lysis. **-lytic** (lit´ik), **-lytical** *comb. form* of or producing decomposition.

M

M¹ (em), **m** (*pl.* **Ms, M's**) the 13th letter of the English and other versions of the Roman alphabet. It is pronounced as a bilabial nasal continuant. ~*symbol* 100 in Roman numerals.

M² *abbr.* **1** mega. **2** (*Chem.*) molar. **3** Monsieur. **4** Motorway (*M4*).

m *abbr.* **1** maiden over. **2** male. **3** mare. **4** married. **5** masculine. **6** (*Physics*) mass. **7** metre(s). **8** mile(s). **9** milli-. **10** minute(s).

m' (m) *a.* my (*m'lud*).

'm (m) *contr.* (*coll.*) **1** am (*I'm*). **2** madam (*Yes'm*).

MA *abbr.* Master of Arts.

ma (mah) *n.* (*coll.*) mother.

ma'am (mam, mahm, məm) *n.* madam (used esp. in addressing a queen or a royal princess).

Mac (mak) *n.* (*coll.*) **1** a Scotsman. **2** (*N Am.*) used in addressing a stranger (*You got a light, Mac?*).

mac (mak), **mack** *n.* a mackintosh, a raincoat.

macabre (məkahˊbrə) *a.* gruesome.

macadam (məkadˊəm) *n.* broken stone for road-making. **macadamize, macadamise** *v.t.*

macadamia (makədāˊmiə) *n.* any evergreen tree of the genus *Macadamia* of Australia, esp. *M. integrifolia* and *M. tetraphylla.* **macadamia nut** *n.* the edible nutlike seed of the macadamia.

macaque (məkahkˊ) *n.* any monkey of the genus *Macaca,* including the rhesus monkey and the Barbary ape.

macaroni (makərōˊni) *n.* (*pl.* **macaronies, macaronis**) an Italian pasta made of fine wheat flour formed into long slender tubes.

macaronic (makəronˊik) *a.* consisting of a jumble of incongruous words, as of different languages, or of modern words Latinized or Latin words modernized, in burlesque poetry. ~*n.* (*pl.*) macaronic verse.

macaroon (makəroonˊ) *n.* a small sweet cake or biscuit made of flour, almonds, sugar etc.

Macassar (məkasˊə), **Macassar oil** *n.* an oil formerly used on the hair to make it shiny, orig. brought from Macassar in Indonesia.

macaw (məkawˊ) *n.* any S and Central American parrot, of the genus *Ara* or *Anodorhynchus,* distinguished by their large size and bright, beautiful plumage.

Mace® (mās) *n.* a liquid causing the eyes to run and a feeling of nausea, used in self-defence, riot control etc. ~*v.t.* (*also* **mace**) to spray Mace at.

mace¹ (mās) *n.* **1** an ornamented staff of office. **2** a medieval weapon shaped like a club with a heavy metal head, usu. spiked. **3** a mace-bearer. **mace-bearer** *n.* a person who carries the mace before a judge etc. **macer** *n.* **1** a mace-bearer. **2** (*Sc.*) an officer who keeps order in courts of law.

mace² (mās) *n.* a spice made from the dried covering of the nutmeg.

macédoine (masədwanˊ) *n.* **1** a dish of mixed vegetables. **2** a medley.

macerate (masˊərāt) *v.t.* **1** to soften by steeping. **2** to make lean, to cause to waste away. ~*v.i.* to undergo maceration. **maceration** (-āˊshən) *n.* **macerator** *n.*

Mach (mak, mahkh, mahk), **Mach number** *n.* a number representing the ratio of the velocity of a body in a certain medium to the velocity of sound in the same medium, used as an indicator of air speed (*Mach 1, 2 etc.*). **Machmeter** *n.* an instrument showing air speed as a Mach number.

machete (məshetˊi, -shaˊti), **matchet** (machˊit) *n.* a broad knife or cutlass used in tropical America as a weapon, to cut down sugar canes etc.

machiavellian (makiəvelˊiən) *a.* unscrupulous, scheming, cunning. **Machiavellianism, Machiavellism** *n.*

machinate (makˊināt, mash´-) *v.i.* to contrive, to plot, to intrigue. **machination** (-āˊshən) *n.* **machinator** *n.*

machine (məshēnˊ) *n.* **1** a mechanical apparatus by which motive power is applied. **2** any mechanism, simple (as a lever or tool) or compound, for applying or directing force. **3** any organization of a complex character designed to apply power of any kind. **4** any vehicle, esp. a bicycle or motorcycle, or aircraft. **5** a person who acts mechanically and without intelligence. **6** any intricate structure or system of control (*the party machine*). ~*v.t.* **1** to produce by means of machinery. **2** to sew with a sewing machine. **3** to print by machinery. **machinable** *a.* **machinability** (-bilˊ-) *n.* **machine code, machine language** *n.* a set of instructions for coding information in a form usable by a computer. **machine-gun** *n.* a light gun loaded and fired automatically. ~*v.t.* (*pres.p.* **machine-gunning,** *past, p.p.* **machine-gunned**) to fire a machine-gun at. **machine-gunner** *n.* **machine-minder** *n.* a person whose job is to look after a machine, usu. in a factory. **machine-readable** *a.* (of data) in a form usable by a computer. **machinery** (-nəri) *n.* (*pl.* **machineries**) **1** machines collectively. **2** the parts or mechanism of a machine. **3** any combination to keep anything in action or to effect a purpose. **machine tool** *n.* a power-driven machine such as a lathe, router etc. for working on wood, metal etc. **machine translation** *n.*

translation done by a computer. **machine-washable** *a.* able to be washed in a washing machine without damage. **machinist** *n.* **1** a person who works or tends a machine, esp. a sewing machine. **2** a person who constructs machines.

macho (mach'ō) *a.* masculine, virile, esp. in an ostentatious or exaggerated way. ~*n.* (*pl.* **machos**) **1** a macho man. **2** machismo. **machismo** (məkiz'mo, -chiz'-) *n.* aggressive arrogant assertiveness, often associated with masculinity.

macintosh MACKINTOSH.

mack MAC.

mackerel (mak'ərəl) *n.* (*pl. in general* **mackerel**, *in particular* **mackerels**) a marine fish, *Scomber scombrus*, moving in shoals in the N Atlantic and coming inshore in summer to spawn, valuable as a food. **mackerel shark** *n.* the porbeagle. **mackerel sky** *n.* a sky with small roundish masses of cirrocumulus, frequent in summer.

mackintosh (mak'intosh), **macintosh** *n.* **1** a raincoat. **2** a waterproof material made of rubber and cloth.

macramé (məkrah'mā) *n.* **1** a fringe or trimming of knotted thread or cord. **2** knotted work. **3** the art of making knotted work.

macro (mak'rō) *n.* (*pl.* **macros**) (*Comput.*) a single computer instruction that represents a sequence of instructions in performing a task. **macro instruction** *n.* a macro.

macro- (mak'rō), **macr-** *comb. form* great, large (as distinct from small).

macrobiotic (makrōbīot'ik) *a.* **1** (of a diet) consisting chiefly of whole grains or of vegetables grown without chemical additives. **2** of or relating to such a diet. **macrobiotics** *n.* the principles of such a macrobiotic diet.

macrocarpa (makrōkah'pə) *n.* a large coniferous tree, *Cupressus macrocarpa*, often cultivated for hedges, shelter belts etc.

macrocosm (mak'rəkozm) *n.* **1** the world, the universe, as distinct from *microcosm*. **2** the whole of any body etc., esp. as imagined on a small scale by a part. **macrocosmic** (-koz'-) *a.* **macrocosmically** *adv.*

macroeconomics (makrōēkənom'iks, -ek-) *n.* the study of economics on a large scale, e.g. of national economies. **macroeconomic** *a.*

macromolecule (mak'rōmolikūl) *n.* a large complex molecule formed from a number of simple molecules. **macromolecular** (-lek'-) *a.*

macron (mak'ron) *n.* a short horizontal line put over a vowel (as ē) to show that it is pronounced with a long sound or with stress.

macronutrient (makrōnū'triənt) *n.* any substance that is required in large amounts for the growth and development of organisms, such as carbon, hydrogen, oxygen.

macrophage (mak'rəfāj) *n.* a large phagocytic white blood cell found in connective tissue.

macrophotography (makrōfōtog'rəfi) *n.* close-up photography producing an image as large as or larger than the object.

macroscopic (makrəskop'ik) *a.* large enough to be visible with the naked eye, as distinct from *microscopic*. **macroscopically** *adv.*

macula (mak'ūlə) *n.* (*pl.* **maculae** (-lē)) a spot, as on the skin, the surface of the sun etc. **macula lutea** (loo'tiə) *n.* a small yellowish spot near the centre of the retina of the eye, where vision is especially acute. **macular** *a.*

mad (mad) *a.* (*comp.* **madder**, *superl.* **maddest**) **1** disordered in mind, lunatic, insane, crazy. **2** furious, frantic, wildly excited. **3** (of an animal) rabid. **4** extravagant, infatuated, inflamed, wild, frolicsome. **5** exceedingly foolish, very unwise. **6** (*coll.*) enraged, annoyed, vexed. **like mad** (*coll.*) violently, wildly, excitedly. **madcap** *a.* mad, eccentric. ~*n.* a person of wild and eccentric habits. **mad cow disease** *n.* (*coll.*) bovine spongiform encephalopathy, BSE. **madden** *v.t.*, *v.i.* **maddening** *a.* **maddeningly** *adv.* **madhouse** *n.* **1** a scene of confusion or uproar. **2** (*Hist.*) a mental hospital. **madly** *adv.* **1** in an insane manner. **2** (*coll.*) extremely (*madly in love*). **madman** *n.* (*pl.* **madmen**). **madness** *n.* **madwoman** *n.* (*pl.* **madwomen**).

madam (mad'əm) *n.* **1** a polite form of address to a woman. **2** (*coll.*) a female brothel-keeper. **3** (*coll.*) an impertinent girl (*You little madam!*).

Madame (mədahm') *n.* (*pl.* **Mesdames** (mādahmz')) the French title for married women and polite form of address to a woman.

madder (mad'ə) *n.* **1** a shrubby climbing-plant, *Rubia tinctorum*, the root of which is used in dyeing. **2** the dye obtained from this plant.

made (mād) *a.* that has been made. **made for** perfectly suited to. **made dish** *n.* a dish made up of various ingredients. **made man, made woman** *n.* (*pl.* **made men, made women**) a person whose success is assured. **made of money** *a.* (*coll.*) very wealthy. **made road** *n.* a road surfaced with tarmac, concrete etc. **made-to-measure** *a.* made according to the customer's measurements. **made-to-order** *a.* **1** manufactured according to a customer's individual requirements. **2** just as wanted. **made-up** *a.* **1** (of complexion etc.) artificial; wearing make-up. **2** (of a story etc.) invented, coined. **3** ready prepared. **4** surfaced with tarmac, concrete etc.

Madeira (mədiə'rə) *n.* a fortified white wine made in Madeira. **madeira cake** *n.* a light, spongy cake without fruit. **Madeiran** *a.*, *n.*

madeleine (mad'əlin) *n.* a small sponge cake, often coated with jam and coconut.

Mademoiselle (madəmwəzel') *n.* (*pl.* **Mesdemoiselles** (mādəmwəzel')) **1** the French title for unmarried women or girls and polite form of address to an unmarried woman or a girl. **2** (**mademoiselle**) a young Frenchwoman. **3** (**mademoiselle**) a French governess or teacher.

Madonna (mədon'a) *n.* **1** the Virgin Mary. **2** (*usu.* **madonna**) a picture or statue of the Virgin

Mary. **madonna lily** *n.* the white lily, *Lilium candidum.*

madras (mədras´) *n.* **1** a fine cotton or silk fabric. **2** a large bright-coloured handkerchief worn on the head by Afro-Caribbeans. **3** (**Madras**) a style of curry, medium hot and usu. with chicken or meat.

madrigal (mad´rigəl) *n.* **1** an unaccompanied vocal composition in five or six parts. **2** a short amorous poem. **madrigalian** (-āl´iən) *a.* **madrigalist** *n.*

maelstrom (māl´strəm, -om) *n.* **1** a dangerous whirlpool, dangerously swirling water. **2** a turmoil, an overwhelming situation.

maenad (mē´nəd) *n.* a frenzied woman. **maenadic** (-nad´-) *a.*

maestoso (mīstō´sō) *a., adv.* (*Mus.*) with dignity, grandeur and strength. *~n.* (*pl.* **maestosos**) a piece of music to be played this way.

maestro (mīs´trō) *n.* (*pl.* **maestros, maestri** (-ē)) **1** a master in any art, esp. in music. **2** a great composer or conductor.

Mae West (mā west´) *n.* an inflatable life jacket.

Mafia (maf´iə) *n.* **1** a secret criminal society based on active hostility to the law and its agents, engaged in international organized crime, esp. in Sicily and the US. **2** any group of people considered to be using power for their own ends. **Mafioso** (-ō´so, -zō) *n.* (*pl.* **Mafiosi** (-sē, -zē)) **1** a member of the Mafia. **2** a member of a group who in some way resemble the Mafia.

mag (mag) *n.* (*coll.*) **1** short for MAGAZINE. **2** short for MAGNETO.

magazine (magəzēn´, mag´-) *n.* **1** a periodical publication or broadcast containing miscellaneous articles by different people. **2** a storeroom for explosives etc. aboard ship. **3** the chamber holding cartridges in certain types of automatic gun. **4** a building or apartment for military stores, esp. ammunition. **5** a light-tight receptacle or enclosure for holding exposed or unexposed films or plates.

magenta (məjen´tə) *n.* **1** a brilliant crimson colour. **2** an aniline dye of this colour.

maggot (mag´ət) *n.* **1** a grub, a worm, esp. the larva of the cheese-fly or flesh-fly. **2** a whimsical fancy. **maggoty** *a.*

magi, magian MAGUS.

magic (maj´ik) *n.* **1** the supposed art of employing supernatural power to influence or control events. **2** sorcery, witchcraft. **3** any agency, power or action that has astonishing results. *~a.* **1** of or relating to or used in magic. **2** using magic. **3** exercising supernatural powers. **4** produced by magic. **5** (*coll.*) excellent, wonderful. *~v.t.* (*pres.p.* **magicking,** *past, p.p.* **magicked**) to affect or move (away) by magic. **magical** *a.* **magically** *adv.* **magic bullet** *n.* (*coll.*) a drug etc. that is very specific in its effect on a tumour, disease etc. **magic carpet** *n.* a carpet in fairy stories capable of transporting people through the air. **magic circle** *n.* a circle possessing

properties analogous to those of the magic square. **magic eye** *n.* **1** a photo-electric cell operating a door, security camera etc. **2** a small cathode ray tube that indicates when a radio etc. is correctly tuned. **magician** (-jish´ən) *n.* **1** a person supposedly employing magic. **2** a conjuror. **3** a person who produces astonishing results. **magic lantern** *n.* an apparatus with a lens through which a magnified image from a glass slide is projected on a screen by a powerful light. **magic mushroom** *n.* a type of fungus containing a hallucinogenic substance. **magic square** *n.* a series of numbers so disposed in a square that the totals, taken perpendicularly, horizontally or diagonally, are equal.

magisterial (majistē´riəl) *a.* **1** authoritative, commanding. **2** of or relating to a magistrate or master. **3** dictatorial, domineering. **magisterially** *adv.* **magisterium** *n.* the teaching authority of the Roman Catholic Church. **magistral** (maj´istrəl, məjis´trəl) *a.* **1** of or like a master, magisterial. **2** (of a medicine) specially prescribed or devised, not in the ordinary pharmacopoeia.

magistrate (maj´istrāt, -strət) *n.* a public officer commissioned to administer the law, a Justice of the Peace. **magistracy, magistrateship, magistrature** *n.* **magistrates' court** *n.* a court of summary jurisdiction for minor offences and preliminary hearings.

maglev (mag´lev) *n.* a rapid transport system in which trains glide along a continuous magnetic field, supported by magnetic repulsion.

magma (mag´mə) *n.* (*pl.* **magmas, magmata** (-tə)) **1** the molten semi-fluid matter below the earth's crust. **2** a crude mixture of mineral or organic matter in a thin paste.

magnanimous (magnan´iməs) *a.* great-minded, not petty in conduct or feelings, generous. **magnanimity** (-nim´-) *n.* **magnanimously** *adv.*

magnate (mag´nāt) *n.* a person of great wealth and influence, esp. in business.

magnesia (magnē´shə, -zhə) *n.* (*Chem.*) **1** magnesium oxide, a white alkaline antacid earth. **2** hydrated magnesium carbonate, used as an antacid and laxative. **magnesian** *a.* **magnesite** (mag´nəsīt) *n.* naturally occurring magnesium carbonate.

magnesium (magnē´ziəm, -zhəm, -shəm) *n.* (*Chem.*) a divalent metallic element, at. no.12, chem. symbol Mg, the base of magnesia, used in alloys and burned as a source of bright light.

magnet (mag´nit) *n.* **1** a piece of iron or steel etc. having the properties of attracting iron and pointing to the poles. **2** a lodestone. **3** a thing or person exercising a powerful attractive influence. **magnetic** (-net´-) *a.* **1** of or relating to a magnet or magnetism. **2** having the properties of a magnet. **3** attractive, mesmeric. **magnetically** *adv.* **magnetic compass** *n.* a compass showing the direction of magnetic north and bearings in relation to it. **magnetic disk** *n.* (*Comput.*) a small, circular piece of plastic in a rigid case, coated with a magnetic oxide substance, used for storing information and software. **magnetic equator** *n.* an imaginary line round the globe where the magnetic needle has no dip. **magnetic field** *n.* the area within which the force of a magnet etc. is effective. **magnetic inclination** *n.* dip of the needle. **magnetic mine** *n.* a mine detonated by the passing over it of a metal ship. **magnetic moment** *n.* a measure of the strength of a magnet etc. when interacting with an applied field to produce a mechanical moment. **magnetic needle** *n.* a slender poised bar of magnetized steel, as in the mariner's compass, pointing north and south. **magnetic north** *n.* the direction indicated by the north end of a compass needle. **magnetic pole** *n.* **1** either of the two points on the earth's surface towards which a compass needle points, and where a magnetic needle dips vertically. **2** either of the regions in a magnet from which its magnetic force appears to originate. **magnetic resonance** *n.* the vibration of electrons, atoms, molecules or nuclei in a magnetic field in response to various radiation frequencies. **magnetic resonance imaging** *n.* a medical scanning technique using the magnetic resonance of protons in the body. **magnetic storm** *n.* a disturbance of the earth's magnetism setting up an oscillation of the magnetic needle, caused by charged particles from the sun. **magnetic tape** *n.* a tape coated or impregnated with a magnetic powder used for the recording and reproduction of sound, video pictures and computer data. **magnetism** (mag′nitizm) *n.* **1** the property whereby certain bodies, esp. iron and its compounds, attract or repel each other according to certain laws. **2** the attractive power itself. **3** personal attractiveness, charm. **magnetist** *n.* a person who is skilled in the science of magnetism or in animal magnetism. **magnetite** (mag′nitīt) *n.* magnetic iron oxide. **magnetize, magnetise** *v.t.* **1** to communicate magnetic properties to. **2** to attract as with a magnet. **3** to mesmerize. **magnetizable** *a.* **magnetization** (-zā′shən) *n.* **magnetizer** *n.*

magneto (magnē′tō) *n.* (*pl.* **magnetos**) a magneto-electric machine (esp. the igniting apparatus of an internal-combustion engine).

magneto- (magnē′tō) *comb. form* of a magnet or magnetism.

magnetometer (magnitom′itə) *n.* a device for measuring the intensity or direction of a magnetic field, esp. of the earth. **magnetometry** *n.*

magnetomotive (magnē′tōmōtiv) *a.* (of a force) being the sum of magnetic forces along an electric circuit.

magnetosphere (magnē′təsfiə) *n.* the region surrounding the earth or other planet, star etc. in which its magnetic field has effect.

magnetron (mag′nitron) *n.* a thermionic tube for generating very high frequency microwave oscillations.

magnificent (magnif′isənt) *a.* **1** grand in appear-ance, majestic, splendid. **2** characterized by sumptuousness, luxury, splendour or generous profusion. **3** (*coll.*) first-rate, excellent. **magnificence** *n.* **magnificently** *adv.*

magnify (mag′nifī) *v.t.* (*3rd pers. sing. pres.* **magnifies**, *pres.p.* **magnifying**, *past, p.p.* **magnified**) **1** to increase the apparent size of (an object) with an optical instrument. **2** to make greater, to increase. **3** to exaggerate. *~v.i.* to increase the apparent size of objects. **magnifiable** *a.* **magnification** (-fikā′shən) *n.* **magnifier** *n.* **magnifying glass** *n.* an optical lens for magnifying objects.

magniloquent (magnil′əkwənt) *a.* using high-flown, pompous or bombastic language. **magniloquence** *n.* **magniloquently** *adv.*

magnitude (mag′nitūd) *n.* **1** size, bulk, extent, quantity, amount. **2** anything that can be measured. **3** importance. **4** the degree of brightness of a star etc. **5** a class of stars arranged according to their brightness.

magnolia (magnō′liə) *n.* **1** any flowering tree or shrub of the genus *Magnolia*, chiefly N American. **2** a pale pinkish-white or pinkish-cream colour.

magnox (mag′noks) *n.* any one of several magnesium-based alloys containing aluminium, used in nuclear reactors to enclose the uranium fuel elements.

magnum (mag′nəm) *n.* (*pl.* **magnums**) **1** a wine bottle containing the equivalent of two normal bottles (about 1½ litres). **2** a large-calibre pistol. **3** a particularly powerful cartridge or shell.

magnum opus (magnəm ō′pəs, op′-) *n.* (*pl.* **magnum opuses, magna opera** (magnə ō′pərə, op′-)) the greatest work of a writer, painter etc.

magpie (mag′pī) *n.* **1** a chattering bird of the crow family, *Pica pica*, with black and white plumage. **2** a chatterer. **3** (*coll.*) a person who collects and hoards small objects. **4** any of several Australian black and white birds, esp. *Gymnorhina tibicen*. **5** in rifle-shooting, the outermost division but one of the target. **6** a shot that hits this. **magpie lark** *n.* any of several Australian birds of the family Grallinidae, esp. *Grallinidae cyanoleuca*, the Australian peewee. **magpie moth** *n.* a white geometrid moth, *Abraxas grossulariata*, patterned with black and yellow spots.

maguey (mag′wā) *n.* a type of agave plant whose leaves yield fibre used to make an alcoholic drink.

magus (mā′gəs) *n.* (*pl.* **magi** (-jī)) **1** a member of the priestly caste among the Medes and Persians. **2** a magician, a sorcerer. **the Magi** the three 'wise men' of the East who brought presents to the infant Christ. **magian** (-jiən) *n., a.* **magianism** *n.*

Magyar (mag′yah) *n.* **1** a member of the Ural-Altaic people (entering Europe in 884), predominant in Hungary. **2** the language of this people, Hungarian.

maharaja (mah·hərah′jə), **maharajah** *n.* a title assumed by some Indian princes. **maharani**

(-ni), **maharanee** n. **1** the wife or widow of a maharaja. **2** an Indian princess.

maharishi (mah·hərish′i, -rē′shi) n. a Hindu religious teacher.

mahatma (məhat′mə) n. **1** in the Indian subcontinent, a much revered person. **2** an adept or sage of the highest order in some Indian and Tibetan religious thinking.

Mahayana (mah·əyah′nə) n. the most widespread tradition of Buddhism, practised esp. in China, Japan and Tibet.

mah-jong (mahjong′), **mah-jongg** n. a Chinese table game played with 136 or 144 pieces called tiles.

mahlstick MAULSTICK.

mahogany (məhog′əni) n. **1** the hard, fine-grained wood of *Swietenia mahogani*, a tree of tropical America, largely used in making furniture. **2** the tree itself. **3** any other tree of the genus *Swietenia* yielding similar wood. ~a. of the colour of mahogany, reddish-brown.

mahonia (məhō′niə) n. any evergreen shrub of the genus *Mahonia*, with small yellow flowers and spiny leaves.

mahout (məhowt′) n. an elephant driver or keeper.

maid (mād) n. **1** a female servant. **2** (*also poet.*) †a girl, a young unmarried woman, a virgin. **maidhood** n. MAIDENHEAD (under MAIDEN). **maidish** a. **maidishness** n. **maid of honour** n. **1** an unmarried lady attending a royal person. **2** (*esp. N Am.*) an unmarried attendant of a bride. **3** a variety of custard tart. **maidservant** n. a female servant.

maiden (mā′dən) n. **1** (*also poet.*) †a girl, an unmarried woman. **2** in cricket, a maiden over. **3** a racehorse that has never won a prize. ~a. **1** of or relating to a maid. **2** unmarried (*a maiden aunt*). **3** (of a female animal) unmated. **4** (of a racehorse) never having won a prize. **5** (of a race) open to such horses. **6** first, new; unused, untried (*maiden flight*). **maidenhead** n. **1** the state of being a virgin, virginity. **2** the hymen. **maidenhood** n. the state of being a virgin. **maidenish** a. **maidenlike** a. **maidenly** a., adv. **maidenliness** n. **maiden name** n. the surname of a woman before marriage. **maiden over** n. in cricket, an over in which no runs are scored.

maidenhair (mā′dənheə), **maidenhair fern** n. a fern with delicate fronds, esp. *Adiantum capillus-veneris*. **maidenhair tree** n. a ginkgo.

mail[1] (māl) n. **1** the letters etc. conveyed by the post. **2** the system of conveying letters etc., the postal system. **3** a delivery or collection of letters etc. **4** electronic mail, e-mail. **5** a train, ship etc. carrying mail. ~v.t. to send by mail, to post. **mailable** a. **mailbag** n. a bag or sack for carrying letters etc. **mailbox** n. a letter box. **mail carrier** n. (*N Am.*) a postman or postwoman. **mail drop** n. (*N Am.*) a box etc. for receiving mail. **mailing** n. **1** the process of sending something by mail. **2** a batch of letters etc. sent by mail. **mailing list** n. a

list of names and addresses of people to whom letters, advertising material etc. are to be posted. **mailman** n. (*pl.* **mailmen**) (*N Am.*) a postman. **mail order** n. the ordering of goods to be sent by post. **mailshot** n. **1** a batch of advertising material etc. sent by mail to a number of addresses. **2** an item of unsolicited mail, usu. an advertisement.

mail[2] (māl) n. **1** defensive armour for the body, formed of rings, chains or scales. **2** any defensive covering. ~v.t. (*poet.*) to clothe with or as with mail. **mailed** a. clad in mail. **mailed fist** n. the application of physical force.

maim (mām) v.t. **1** to deprive of the use of a limb. **2** to cripple, to mutilate. **3** to damage emotionally etc.

main[1] (mān) a. **1** principal, chief, most important. **2** (of force) concentrated or fully exerted. **main brace** n. (*Naut.*) a brace attached to the main yard of a sailing ship. **main chance** n. **1** an opportunity for personal gain. **2** self-interest. **main clause** n. (*Gram.*) a clause that is able to stand on its own as a complete sentence, as distinct from *subordinate clause*. **main course** n. the most substantial course of a meal. **maincrop** a. (of a vegetable) from the main crop of the season. **main drag** n. (*N Am., coll.*) the main street of a town. **mainframe** n. **1** a large, powerful computer. **2** the central processing and storage unit of a computer. **mainland** n. the principal body of land as opposed to islands etc. **mainlander** n. **main line** n. **1** a primary railway route. **2** (*sl.*) a principal vein, when used as a site for injecting drugs. **mainline** v.t., v.i. (*sl.*) to inject (a narcotic drug etc.) into a vein. **mainliner** n. **mainly** adv. **1** principally, chiefly, in the main. **2** greatly, strongly. **mainmast** n. (*Naut.*) the principal mast of a ship. **mainplane** n. any one of the principal supporting surfaces of an aircraft, esp. either or both of the wings. **mainsail** (-sāl, -səl) n. (*Naut.*) **1** a sail bent to the mainyard of a square-rigged ship. **2** the sail set on the after part of the mainmast of a fore-and-aft rigged vessel. **mainsheet** n. (*Naut.*) the rope that extends and fastens the mainsail. **mainspring** n. **1** the chief spring of a watch etc. **2** the chief driving force. **mainstay** n. **1** the chief support. **2** (*Naut.*) the stay from the maintop to the foot of the foremast. **main street** n. the principal street of a town or city. **maintop** n. (*Naut.*) a platform above the head of the lower mainmast. **maintopmast** n. (*Naut.*) a mast above the head of the lower main mast. **main yard** n. (*Naut.*) the yard on which the mainsail is extended.

main[2] (mān) n. **1** a chief sewer, conduit, conductor, electric cable etc. **2** (*also poet.*) †the main or high sea, the ocean. **3** †strength, force, violent effort. **in the main** for the most part. **the mains 1** the electricity supply from a central distributor. **2** the distribution of electricity, water etc. from a central source. **with might and main** with all one's strength.

mainstream (mān′strēm) n. **1** the most

prevalent or widely accepted aspects of a culture, society etc. **2** mainstream jazz. **3** the main current of a river. ~*a*. **1** of or relating to the mainstream of society. **2** (of jazz music) of the type prevalent between early and modern jazz, based on swing.

maintain (māntān´) *v.t.* **1** to keep in order, proper condition or repair. **2** to support, to provide with the means of living. **3** to sustain, to keep up. **4** to hold, preserve or carry on in any state. **5** to assert, to affirm, to support by reasoning, argument etc. **maintainable** *a*. **maintainability** (-bil´-) *n*. **maintained school** *n*. a school receiving financial support from the state or from a local authority. **maintainer** *n*. **maintenance** (mān´tənəns) *n*. **1** the act of maintaining or the state of being maintained. **2** means of support.

maiolica (məyol´ikə), **majolica** (-jol´-) *n*. tinglazed earthenware having metallic colours on a white ground (orig. from Italy).

maisonette (māzənet´, -sə-), **maisonnette** *n*. **1** part of a house or block of flats let separately, usu. having two floors and with a separate entrance. **2** a small house.

maitre d'hôtel (metrə dōtel´) *n*. (*pl.* **maitres d'hôtel** (metrə dōtel´)) **1** the manager, chief steward etc. of a hotel. **2** a head waiter.

maize (māz) *n*. **1** a cereal plant from N America, *Zea mays*, also called Indian corn. **2** the cobs or grains yielded by this.

Maj. *abbr.* Major.

majesty (maj´əsti) *n*. (*pl.* **majesties**) **1** the quality of inspiring awe or reverence. **2** impressive dignity, grandeur, stateliness. **3** sovereign power and dignity. **4** (**Majesty**) used as part of a title or formula for addressing or referring to a king, queen or emperor (*His Majesty*). **majestic** (-jes´-), **majestical** *a*.

majolica MAIOLICA.

major (mā´jə) *a*. **1** of considerable importance. **2** serious. **3** main, principal. **4 a** (*Mus*.) (of a scale) having the intervals tone, tone, semitone, tone, tone, tone, tone, semitone. **b** (of a key) based on a major scale. **c** (of an interval) that is a semitone greater than the minor interval of the same denomination. **5** greater in number, quantity, extent or importance. **6** of full legal age (in the UK now 18 years). ~*n*. **1** (*Mil*.) an army officer next above captain and below lieutenant colonel. **2** (*NAm*.) **a** a subject of specialization at a college or university. **b** a person specializing in a particular subject. **3** a person of full legal age. **4** an officer in charge of a section of a military band. **5** (*Mus*.) a major scale, key or interval. **major-domo** (-dō´mō) *n*. (*pl.* **major-domos**) **1** the chief officer of a royal or princely household, in Italy or Spain. **2** a person who takes charge of a household, a butler or steward. **majorette** (-ret´) *n*. a member of a group of girls, who march in parades twirling batons, playing instruments etc., a drum majorette. **major general** *n*. an

officer ranking next below lieutenant general. **majority** (-jor´-) *n*. (*pl.* **majorities**) **1** the greater part, more than half. **2** the amount of the difference between the greater and the lesser number, esp. of votes in an election. **3** the greater number. **4** full legal age. **5** the rank or position of a major. **6** a party with an electoral majority. **in the majority** belonging to the party etc. that has the greatest number of members. **majority rule** *n*. the principle that those who are greater in number should exercise greater power. **majority verdict** *n*. a verdict reached by a majority of a jury as distinct from a unanimous one. **major league** *n*. a league of the highest classification in US sport, esp. baseball. **major part** *n*. the majority (of). **majorship** *n*.

Usage note *Majority* should not be used with uncountable nouns (so not *the majority of the time*).

majuscule (maj´əskūl) *n*. **1** a capital or large letter, as in Latin manuscripts, before the introduction of minuscules. **2** large lettering. ~*a*. of or relating to majuscules; written in majuscules. **majuscular** (məjŭs´-) *a*.

make (māk) *v.t.* (*pres.p.* **making**, *past, p.p.* **made** (mād)) **1** to frame, construct, produce. **2** to bring into existence, to create. **3** to give rise to, to effect, to bring about. **4** to execute, to perform, to accomplish (with nouns expressing action). **5** to result in, to cause to be or become. **6** to compose (a book, verses etc.). **7** to prepare for use. **8** to prepare for consumption; to infuse (tea). **9** to establish, to enact. **10** to raise or appoint to a rank or dignity. **11** to constitute, to form, to become, to turn out to be. **12** to gain, to acquire, to achieve. **13** to move or proceed (towards etc.). **14** in a card game, to win (a trick) or cause (a card) to win; to shuffle. **15** to score. **16** to cause, to compel (to do). **17** to cause to appear, to represent to be. **18** to reckon, to calculate or decide to be. **19** to conclude, to think. **20** to reach the end of. **21** to amount to, to serve for. **22** to travel over (a distance etc.). **23** to be sold for, to fetch, as a price. **24** (*Naut*.) to come near. **25** to arrive at. **26** to arrive in time for. **27** (*sl*.) to succeed in seducing. ~*v.i.* **1** to go, move, tend or lie (in a specified direction). **2** to contribute, to have effect (for or to). **3** (of the tide) to ebb or flow. **4** (*usu. with adjective*) to do, to act in a specified way (*make so bold as to*). ~*n*. **1** the brand, type etc. of manufacture. **2** form, shape. **3** arrangement of parts. **4** making. **5** style. **6** disposition, mental or moral constitution. **7** making of electrical contact, completion of a circuit. **on the make 1** (*coll*.) intent on personal profit, after the main chance. **2** (*coll*.) seeking sexual partners. **to make a day of it** to spend a day in enjoyment or festivity. **to make a night of it** to spend an evening or night in enjoyment or festivity. **to make as if** to pretend (to), to feint. **to make as though** to make as if. **to make away to**

hurry away. **to make away with 1** to get rid of, to kill. **2** to waste, to squander. **to make conversation** to engage in polite talk. **to make do** to cope or be satisfied (with) though the resources etc. are not completely adequate. **to make for 1** to conduce to. **2** to corroborate. **3** to move toward. **4** to attack. **to make free** to venture (to). **to make free with** to treat without ceremony. **to make it 1** (*coll.*) to reach an objective. **2** (*coll.*) to succeed. **3** (*sl.*) to have sexual intercourse (with). **to make it up 1** to be reconciled, to stop quarrelling. **2** to compensate for something missing. **to make it up to** to compensate for an insult or injury to. **to make like 1** (*esp. N Am.*) to pretend. **2** (*esp. N Am.*) to imitate. **to make little of 1** to have a low opinion of. **2** to have little benefit from. **to make merry** to feast, to be jovial. **to make money** to obtain an income, to acquire wealth. **to make much of 1** (*usu. with neg.*) to treat with fondness or favour. **2** to treat as of great importance. **3** to derive much benefit from. **to make no doubt** to be sure. **to make of 1** to understand, interpret. **2** to attach a specified degree of importance to. **3** to construct from. **to make off** to hurry away. **to make off with** to take away wrongfully. **to make one's way** to proceed. **to make or break** to be crucial to the success or failure of. **to make or mar** to make or break. **to make out 1** to identify or distinguish with the eyes or ears. **2** to understand, to decipher. **3** to prove, to establish. **4** to claim or allege. **5** to draw up, to write out. **6** (*coll.*) to be successful, to get on. **7** (*N Am., coll.*) **a** to engage in necking or petting. **b** to have sexual intercourse. **to make over 1** to transfer. **2** to redesign, reshape etc., to give a new look to. **to make place** to move so as to leave space (for). **to make room** to move so as to leave space (for). **to make up 1** to compose. **2** to compound. **3** to collect together. **4** to compile. **5** to fabricate, to concoct. **6** to complete, to supply (what is wanting). **7** to compensate. **8** to be reconciled, to stop quarrelling. **9** to settle, to adjust, to arrange. **10** (of an actor) to dress up, to prepare the face to represent a character. **11** to prepare (a bed etc.) for use. **12** to repair. **13** to apply cosmetics to the face. **14** to apply cosmetics to the face of. **15** to arrange (type etc.) in columns or pages. **to make up one's mind** to decide, to resolve. **to make up to** to make advances to. **to make water 1** to urinate. **2** (*Naut.*) to leak. **to make way 1** to make room, to open a passage. **2** to progress. **to make with 1** (*N Am., coll.*) to happen or proceed with. **2** (*N Am., coll.*) to show, to produce. **makable** *a.* **make-believe, make-belief** *n.* pretending, a pretence, a sham. ~*a.* **1** unreal. **2** counterfeit. ~*v.t.*, *v.i.* to pretend (that). **make-or-break** *a.* crucial to success or failure. **make-over** *n.* a complete redesign or reshaping, a transformation in look. **maker** *n.* a person who makes something. **one's Maker** God. **the Maker** God. **makeshift** *n.* a temporary expedient. ~*a.* used as a

makeshift. **make-up** *n.* **1** cosmetics for use on the face. **2** the manner in which a person's face is made up, esp. how an actor's face is made to represent a character. **3** a person's character or temperament. **4** a thing's composition or constitution. **5** (*dated*) the arrangement of type into columns or pages; the type so arranged. **make-weight** *n.* **1** something, usu. small, that is added to make up the weight of a product, commodity etc. **2** an unimportant additional element. **making** *n.* **1** the act of constructing, producing, causing etc. **2** possibility or opportunity of success or full development. **3** (*pl.*) composition, essential qualities. **4** (*pl.*) profits, earnings. **5** (*pl.*) materials for rolling a cigarette. **in the making** gradually developing or being made. **to be the making of** to play a crucial part in the successful development, outcome etc. of.

mako (mah´kō) *n.* (*pl.* **makos**) a large shark of the genus *Isurus*.

mal- (mal), **male-** (mal´i) *comb. form* **1** bad(ly). **2** evil. **3** faulty. **4** abnormal.

malacca (məlak´ə), **malacca cane** *n.* the stem of a palm tree used as a walking stick.

malachite (mal´əkīt) *n.* a bright green monoclinic carbonate of copper, often polished for ornamental use.

maladjusted (maləjŭs´tid) *a.* **1** imperfectly adjusted. **2** unable to adjust oneself to the physical or social environment. **maladjustment** *n.*

maladministration (malədministrā´shən) *n.* defective or dishonest management, esp. of public affairs. **maladminister** (-min´-) *v.t.*

maladroit (malədroit´) *a.* awkward, clumsy. **maladroitly** *adv.* **maladroitness** *n.*

malady (mal´ədi) *n.* (*pl.* **maladies**) **1** a disease, an ailment, esp. a lingering or deep-seated disorder. **2** a moral defect or disorder.

Malaga (mal´əgə) *n.* sweet, fortified white wine imported from Málaga.

malaise (malāz´) *n.* **1** a feeling of uneasiness, esp. as premonition of a serious malady. **2** a mild feeling of sickness or depression.

malamute (mal´əmūt), **malemute** *n.* a powerful dog used to pull sledges in Arctic regions.

malapropism (mal´əpropizm), **malaprop** *n.* **1** grotesque misapplication of words. **2** a misapplied word.

malapropos (maləprəpō´) *adv.* unseasonably, unsuitably, out of place. ~*a.* unseasonable etc. ~*n.* an unseasonable or inopportune thing, remark, event etc.

malaria (məlea´riə) *n.* a fever of an intermittent and remittent nature caused by a parasite of the genus *Plasmodium* introduced by the bite of mosquitoes. **malarial, malarian, malarious** *a.*

malarkey (məlah´ki), **malarky** *n.* (*coll.*) foolish or insincere talk, nonsense.

malathion (maləthī´ən) *n.* an insecticide used for houseflies and garden pests.

Malay (məlā´) *a.* of or relating to a people of Malaysia and Indonesia. ~*n.* **1** a member of this people. **2** their language, the official language of Malaysia. **Malayan** *n.*, *a.* **Malayo-** *comb. form* Malayan and, as in *Malayo-Polynesian*.

Malaysian (məlā´ziən, -zhən) *n.* a native or inhabitant of Malaysia in SE Asia. *~a.* of or relating to Malaysia.

malcontent (mal´kəntent) *n.* a person who is discontented, esp. with the government, a rebel. *~a.* discontented, esp. with the government or its administration.

male (māl) *a.* **1** of or relating to the sex that begets young or has organs for impregnating ova. **2** (of organs) adapted for fertilization. **3** (*Bot.*) having stamens but no pistil. **4** of, relating to or characteristic of men or manhood or male animals or plants; masculine, virile. **5** designed for entering a correlative mechanical part designated female (*a male bolt*). *~n.* **1** an individual of the male sex. **2** a plant, or part of a plant, that bears the fertilizing organs. **male chauvinist (pig)** *n.* a man with an arrogant belief in the superiority of the male sex. **male fern** *n.* a fern, *Dryopleris filixmas*, with the fronds clustered in a crown. **male menopause** *n.* a (supposed) period in a man's middle life when he experiences an emotional crisis focused on diminishing sexual prowess. **maleness** *n.*

malediction (malədik´shən) *n.* a curse, an imprecation. **maledictive** *a.* **maledictory** *a.*

malefactor (mal´əfaktə) *n.* an evildoer, a criminal. **malefaction** (-fak´shən) *n.*

malefic (məlef´ik) *a.* mischief-making, harmful, hateful. **maleficent** (məlef´isənt) *a.* **maleficence** *n.*

maleic acid (məlē´ik) *n.* a colourless, crystalline acid used in making synthetic compounds.

malevolent (məlev´ələnt) *a.* wishing evil or injury to others. **malevolence** *n.* **malevolently** *adv.*

malfeasance (malfē´zəns) *n.* (*Law*) evildoing, esp. illegal conduct by a public official. **malfeasant** *n.*, *a.*

malformation (malfəmā´shən) *n.* **1** faulty formation. **2** a faulty structure or irregularity of form. **malformed** (-fawmd´) *a.*

malfunction (malfŭngk´shən) *n.* **1** a failure to function. **2** defective function or operation. *~v.i.* to operate defectively.

malic acid (mā´lik) *n.* an organic acid derived from unripe apples and other fruit.

malice (mal´is) *n.* **1** a disposition to injure others, active malevolence. **2** (*Law*) a premeditated design to do evil or injure another. **malice aforethought, malice prepense** *n.* (*Law*) a premeditated desire to commit an illegal act, esp. murder. **malicious** (məlish´əs) *a.* characterized by malice, full of malice. **maliciously** *adv.* **maliciousness** *n.*

malign (məlīn´) *a.* **1** unfavourable, pernicious, malignant, hurtful. **2** malevolent. *~v.t.* to speak evil of, to slander. **maligner** *n.* **malignly** *adv.*

malignant (məlig´nənt) *a.* **1** (of a disease,

tumour etc.) resisting treatment and threatening life. **2** exercising a pernicious influence, virulent. **3** motivated by extreme enmity or malice. **malignancy** *n.* **malignantly** *adv.* **malignity** *n.* (*pl.* **malignities**).

malinger (məling´gə) *v.i.* to exaggerate or pretend illness in order to avoid work or other responsibility. **malingerer** *n.*

mall (mawl, mal) *n.* **1** an enclosed street or area of shops reserved for pedestrians. **2** a sheltered public walk, promenade.

mallard (mal´əd, -lahd) *n.* (*pl.* **mallard, mallards**) a wild duck or drake.

malleable (mal´iəbəl) *a.* **1** capable of being rolled out or shaped by hammering without being broken. **2** easily influenced by outside forces, pliant. **malleability** (-bil´-), **malleableness** *n.* **malleably** *adv.*

mallee (mal´i) *n.* **1** any of various dwarf species of eucalyptus growing in the deserts of Victoria and S Australia. **2** an area of scrub dominated by these trees. **mallee bird, mallee fowl, mallee hen** *n.* an Australian megapode, *Leipoa ocellata*, similar to a turkey.

malleolus (məlē´ələs) *n.* (*pl.* **malleoli** (-lī)) (*Anat.*) either of two hammer-shaped bony projections extending either side of the ankle.

mallet (mal´it) *n.* **1** a light hammer, usu. of wood. **2** a long-handled wooden hammer for striking the ball in croquet or polo.

malleus (mal´iəs) *n.* (*pl.* **mallei** (-iī)) (*Anat.*) one of the small bones of the middle ear or tympanum.

mallow (mal´ō) *n.* **1** a plant of various species belonging to the genus *Malva*, usu. with pink or mauve flowers and hairy stems and foliage, and having emollient properties (from which perh. it derives its name). **2** any of various other plants of the same family (Malvaceae).

malmsey (mahm´zi) *n.* a strong sweet white wine now chiefly made in Madeira.

malnourished (malnŭr´isht) *a.* suffering from malnutrition. **malnourishment** *n.*

malnutrition (malnūtrish´ən) *n.* insufficient or defective nutrition.

malodorous (malō´dərəs) *a.* having an unpleasant smell. **malodour** *n.* an offensive odour.

malpractice (malprak´tis) *n.* illegal or immoral conduct, esp. improper treatment of a case by a physician, lawyer etc.

malt (mawlt) *n.* **1** grain, usu. barley, steeped in water and fermented, then dried in a kiln, usu. used for brewing and distilling. **2** (*coll.*) (a) malt whisky, malt liquor. **3** (*N Am.*) malted milk. *~v.t.* **1** to convert into malt. **2** to treat with malt. *~v.i.* to be converted into malt. **malted** *a.* mixed with malt or malt extract. *~n.* (*N Am.*) malted milk. **malted milk** *n.* a hot drink made from dried milk and a powdered preparation of malt. **malt extract** *n.* a thick, sticky liquid made from malt, taken as a health food. **malthouse** *n.* a building where malt is prepared and stored. **malting** *n.* **1**

brewing or distilling with malt. **2** (*also pl.*) MALTHOUSE (under MALT). **malt liquor** *n.* liquor made from malt by fermentation, such as beer, stout etc. **maltster** *n.* a person whose occupation is to make malt. **malt whisky** *n.* whisky distilled from malted barley as distinct from grain whisky or blended whisky. **malty** *a.* (*comp.* **maltier,** *superl.* **maltiest**). **maltiness** *n.*

Maltese (mawltēz´) *a.* of or relating to Malta or its inhabitants. ~*n.* (*pl.* **Maltese**) **1** a native or inhabitant of Malta. **2** (*as pl.*) the Maltese people. **3** the Maltese language. **Maltese cross** *n.* a cross with arms of equal size widening from the point of junction towards the extremities, and usu. with each arm split so as to form two points.

Malthusian (malthū´ziən) *a.* of or relating to or supporting the teachings of Malthus. ~*n.* a follower of Malthus, i.e. a person who believes that some check is necessary to prevent over-population. **Malthusianism** *n.*

maltose (mawl´tōs) *n.* (*Chem.*) a sugar obtained by the action of malt or diastase on starch paste.

maltreat (maltrēt´) *v.t.* to ill-treat, to abuse. **maltreater** *n.* **maltreatment** *n.*

malvaceous (malvā´shəs) *a.* (*Bot.*) belonging to or resembling the genus *Malva* or the family Malvaceae, including the mallows.

malversation (malvəsā´shən) *n.* (*formal*) fraudulent conduct or corruption in a position of trust, esp. corrupt administration of public funds.

mam (mam) *n.* (*coll.*) mother.

mama MAMMA¹.

mamba (mam´bə) *n.* any of various African poisonous snakes of the genus *Dendroaspis*.

mambo (mam´bō) *n.* (*pl.* **mambos**) a W Indian syncopated dance or dance tune, like the rumba.

mamilla (məmil´ə), (*N Am.*) **mammilla** *n.* (*pl.* **mamillae, mammillae** (-ē)) **1** a nipple or teat. **2** a nipple-shaped organ or part. **mamillary** (mam´-), **mamillate** (mam´ilət), **mamillated** (mam´-), **mamilliform** *a.*

mamma¹ (məmah´, mam´ə), **mama** *n.* mother (used by or to children). **mammy** (mam´i) *n.* (*pl.* **mammies**) **1** mother (used by or to children). **2** (*N Am.*, *offensive*) a black woman working as a children's nurse in a white family.

mamma² (mam´ə) *n.* (*pl.* **mammae** (-ē)) the milk-secreting organ in female mammals. **mammary** *a.* of or concerning the mammae. **mammary gland** *n.* a mamma. **mammogram** *n.* (*Med.*) an image obtained by the process of mammography. **mammography** (-mog´-) *n.* (*Med.*) examination of the breasts by X-ray.

mammal (mam´əl) *n.* (*Zool.*) any vertebrate of the class Mammalia, having milk-secreting organs for suckling their young, the highest division of vertebrates. **mammalian** (-mā´-) *a.* **mammaliferous** (-lif´-) *a.* (*Geol.*) (of rocks) containing mammalian remains. **mammalogy** (-mal´-) *n.* **mammalogist** *n.*

mammee (məmē´) *n.* a tropical American tree,

Mammea americana, bearing edible pulpy fruit.

Mammon (mam´ən) *n.* riches personified as an idol or an evil influence.

mammoth (mam´əth) *n.* a large extinct species of elephant of the genus *Mammuthus*. ~*a.* gigantic, huge.

mammy MAMMA¹.

man (man) *n.* (*pl.* **men** (men)) **1** an adult male of the human race. **2** a human being, a person **3** anyone. **4** (*collect.*) humankind, the human race. **5** a person with manly qualities. **6** (*dial.*, *coll.*) a husband, a male lover. **7** a manservant, a valet, a workman. **8** (*pl.*) soldiers, esp. privates. **9** a person under one's control. **10** (*in comb.*) a prehistoric human (*Neanderthal man*). **11** (*pl.*) pieces used in playing chess or draughts. **12** (*in comb.*) a ship, as *man-of-war*, *merchantman* etc. ~*v.t.* (*pres.p.* **manning,** *past, p.p.* **manned**) **1** to furnish with (a person or persons), esp. for defence, a period of duty etc. **2** to fortify the courage of (esp. oneself). **as one man** all together, in unison. **man and boy** from boyhood upwards. **man to man 1** as between individual people, one with or against the other. **2** with complete frankness. **my (good) man** used as a patronizing form of address to a man. **one's man** the person needed or suitable (for). **the Man** (*N Am.*, *sl.*, *derog.*) the white people in authority, e.g. the police. **the man for** the person needed or suitable for. **to a man** without exception. **to be one's own man** to be of independent mind. **to separate/ sort out the men from the boys** (*coll.*) to reveal those who are really tough or capable. **man about town** *n.* a fashionable man of leisure. **man-at-arms** *n.* (*pl.* **men-at-arms**) a heavily-armed mounted soldier, esp. in the Middle Ages. **man-day** *n.* the amount of work done by one person in one day. **Man Friday** *n.* a personal servant, factotum. **manful** *a.* brave, courageous, resolute, manly. **manfully** *adv.* **manfulness** *n.* **manhandle** *v.t.* **1** to move by manpower alone. **2** (*coll.*) to handle roughly, to maltreat. **manhole** *n.* a hole in a floor, drain or parts of machinery etc., to allow entrance for cleansing and repairs. **manhood** *n.* **1** the state of being a man. **2** the state of being a male person of full age. **3** manliness, courage, resolution. **4** (*euphem.*) the penis. **5** the men of a country or place collectively. **6** the state of being a human. **man-hour** *n.* the amount of work done by one person in one hour. **manhunt** *n.* a large-scale search for a person, e.g. an escaped prisoner. **man in the moon** *n.* the personage attributed to the semblance of a face on the surface of the moon as seen from earth. **man in the street,** (*N Am.*) **man on the street** *n.* an ordinary person. **mankind** *n.* **1** the human species. **2** male people as distinct from females. **manless** *a.* **manlike** *a.* **1** manly. **2** mannish. **3** resembling a man or a human. **manly** *a.* (*comp.* **manlier,** *superl.* **manliest**) **1** befitting a man. **2** having qualities such as courage, resoluteness, magnanimity. **3** mannish. **manliness** *n*. **man-made** *a*. made by humans, not natural, artificial. **manned** *a*. **1** having a crew, workers etc. **2** (of a spacecraft) having a human pilot or crew. **mannish** *a*. (*esp. derog.*) (esp. of a woman) masculine, characteristic of a man. **mannishly** *adv*. **mannishness** *n*. **man of God** *n*. **1** a clergyman. **2** a male saint. **man of honour** *n*. a man who can be trusted. **man of letters** *n*. a writer, literary critic etc. **man of straw** *n*. **1** a man of no substance. **2** a false argument or adversary put forward for the sake of being refuted. **man of the cloth** *n*. a clergyman. **man of the house** *n*. the male head of a household. **man of the match** *n*. the outstanding player in a sports match. **man of the moment** *n*. a man who is important, in the news etc. at a particular time. **man of the world** *n*. an experienced person, sophisticated and urbane. **man-of-war, man-o'-war** *n*. (*pl*. **men-of-war, men-o'-war**) (*Hist.*) a warship belonging to a navy. **manpower** *n*. the amount of workpeople etc. available for any purpose. **manservant** *n*. (*pl*. **menservants**) a male servant. **man-size, man-sized** *a*. **1** (*coll.*) large. **2** of a suitable size for a man. **manslaughter** *n*. **1** (*Law*) the killing of a person unlawfully but without prior intent. **2** the killing of a human being or beings. **mantrap** *n*. a trap set for poachers etc. **men's (room)** *n*. a lavatory for men.

Usage note The word *humankind* is sometimes preferred to *man* or *mankind* to refer to the human species, to avoid charges of sexism.

manacle (man´əkəl) *n*. (*usu. pl.*) a handcuff, fetter, shackle. *~v.t.* to put manacles on, to fetter.

manage (man´ij) *v.t.* **1** to direct, to carry on, to control, to conduct. **2** to conduct the affairs of. **3** to handle, to wield. **4** to bring or keep under control. **5** to lead or guide by flattery etc. **6** to break in, to train (as a horse). **7** to deal with, to make use of. **8** to make or keep an appointment for (a certain time etc.). *~v.i.* **1** to direct affairs. **2** to contrive (to do etc.). **3** to get on (with or without). **4** to succeed (with). **manageable** *a*. **manageability** (-bil´-), **manageableness** *n*. **manageably** *adv*. **management** *n*. **1** the act of managing. **2** conduct, administration. **3** those who manage, a board of directors etc. **4** skilful employment of means. **management buyout** *n*. the purchase of the control of a company by its directors. **manager** *n*. **1** a person who manages, esp. a business, institution etc. **2** (*usu. with good, bad* etc.) a person skilled in economical management. **3** (*pl.*) a committee appointed by either House of Parliament to perform a duty concerning both Houses. **manageress** (-es´) *n*. a female manager, esp. of a retail shop, canteen, restaurant etc. **managerial** (-jē´-) *a*. **managerially** *adv*. **managership** *n*. **managing** *a*. having the management or control of a business, department etc.

mañana (mənyah´nə) *n., adv.* **1** tomorrow. **2** presently, later on, in the indefinite future.

manatee (man´ətē) *n*. a large herbivorous aquatic mammal of the genus *Trichechus*, a sea cow.

Mancunian (mankū´niən, mang-) *n*. a native or inhabitant of Manchester. *~a.* of or relating to Manchester.

-mancy (mansi) *comb. form* divination by, as in *necromancy, pyromancy*. **-mantic** *comb. form* forming adjectives.

mandala (man´dələ, -dah´-) *n*. **1** any of various symbols used to represent the universe in Buddhism or Hinduism, used as an aid to meditation. **2** (*Psych.*) a circular symbol seen in dreams, supposed to represent personal wholeness.

mandamus (mandā´məs) *n*. (*pl*. **mandamuses**) (*Law*) a writ or (now) order issued from a higher court directed to a person, corporation or inferior court, requiring them to do a particular thing relating to their office or duty.

mandarin (man´dərin) *n*. **1** (*also* **mandarine**) a mandarin orange. **2** a high-ranking public servant. **3** a Chinese official. **4** an influential, esp. reactionary (literary) figure. **5** a mandarin duck. **6** a grotesque ornament or statuette in Chinese costume. **7** (**Mandarin**) the chief dialect of the Chinese language. **mandarinate** *n*. **mandarin collar** *n*. a stiff, narrow stand-up collar. **mandarin duck** *n*. a brightly-coloured Asiatic duck, *Aix galericulata*. **mandarin orange** *n*. **1** a small flattish sweet Chinese orange of a dark-yellow colour, a tangerine. **2** the tree bearing mandarins, *Citrus reticulata*. **mandarin sleeve** *n*. a wide loose sleeve.

mandate (man´dāt) *n*. **1** an authoritative charge, order or command. **2** a direction from electors to a representative or a representative body to undertake certain legislation etc. **3** (*Law*) a judicial command to an officer or a subordinate court. **mandatory** *a*. **1** obligatory, compulsory. **2** containing, or of the nature of a mandate. **3** bestowing a mandate. **mandatorily** *adv*.

Usage note The spellings of the noun *mandatary* (a person or state mandated) and the adjective *mandatory* (compulsory) should not be confused.

mandible (man´dibəl) *n*. the jaw, the lower jaw in vertebrates, the upper or lower in birds, and the pair in insects. **mandibular** (-dib´-), **mandibulate** (-lət), **mandibulated** (-lātid) *a*.

mandolin (man´dəlin), **mandoline** *n*. **1** a musical instrument with a deep almond-shaped body and two or three pairs of metal strings. **2** a kitchen utensil with metal strings or blades, for slicing vegetables. **mandolinist** *n*.

mandrake (man´drāk) *n*. the poisonous plant *Mandragora officinarum*, having emetic and narcotic properties, the root of which was anciently believed to be like the human form and to shriek when pulled up.

mandrel (man´drəl) *n.*´ **1** an arbor or axis of a lathe on which work is fixed for turning. **2** a cylindrical rod or core round which metal or other material is forged or shaped. **3** the revolving spindle of a circular saw. **4** a miner's pick.

mandrill (man´dril) *n.* a W African baboon, *Mandrillus sphinx*, which has a brightly-coloured face and blue hindquarters.

mane (mān) *n.* **1** the long hair on the neck of some animals, such as the horse or (male) lion. **2** long, thick hair on a person's head. **maned** *a.* **maneless** *a.*

manège (manāzh´, -nezh´), **manege** *n.* **1** a school for training horses or teaching horsemanship. **2** the movements of a trained horse. **3** horsemanship.

maneuver MANOEUVRE.

manganese (mang´gənēz, -nēz´) *n.* (*Chem.*) a metallic element, at. no. 25, chem. symbol Mn, of a greyish-white colour. **manganous, manganesian** (-ē´-), **manganesic, manganic** (-gan´-) *a.*

mange (mānj) *n.* a skin disease caused by a mite, occurring in cattle, dogs etc. **mangy** *a.* (*comp.* **mangier,** *superl.* **mangiest**) **1** infected with mange. **2** shabby, squalid. **mangily** *adv.* **manginess** *n.*

mangel-wurzel (mang-gəlwœ´zəl), **mangold-wurzel** (-gəld-), **mangel** (mang´-), **mangold** *n.* a large-rooted variety of the common beet, *Beta vulgaris*, cultivated as fodder for cattle.

manger (mān´jə) *n.* a trough for horses or cattle to eat out of.

mangetout (māzh´too, māzhtoo´) *n.* (*pl.* **mangetout, mangetouts** (māzh´too, māzhtoo´)) a type of pea which is eaten complete with the pod.

mangle¹ (mang´gəl) *v.t.* **1** to lacerate, to mutilate, to disfigure by hacking. **2** to mar, to ruin, to destroy the symmetry or completeness of, by blundering etc. **mangler** *n.*

mangle² (mang´gəl) *n.* **1** (*Hist.*) a rolling machine for pressing water out of washing, damp sheets etc. **2** (*N.Am.*) a large rolling machine for ironing. ~*v.t.* to press or smooth in a mangle.

mango (mang´gō) *n.* (*pl.* **mangoes**) **1** the fruit of an Indian tree, *Mangifera indica*. **2** (*also* **mango tree**) the tree bearing this.

mangold-wurzel MANGEL-WURZEL.

mangrove (mang´grōv) *n.* any tropical tree of the genus *Rhizophora*, growing in muddy places by the coast, the bark of which is used for medicine and in tanning.

mangy MANGE.

mania (mā´niə) *n.* **1** (*Psych.*) a form of mental disorder characterized by hallucination, emotional excitement and violence. **2** (*coll.*) an infatuation, a craze. **maniac** (-ak) *n.* **1** (*coll.*) a person exhibiting symptoms of wild, uncontrolled behaviour. **2** a person who suffers from mania. **3** (*coll.*) a person with an obsessive enthusiasm for a hobby, craze etc. ~*a.* affected with mania, insane, raving. **maniacal** (mənī´əkəl) *a.* **maniacally** *adv.* **manic** (man´ik) *a.* **1** of or affected by mania. **2** (*coll.*) overexcited, wildly energetic. **manic-depressive** *a.* (*Psych.*) suffering from or characterized by alternating bouts of mania and depression. ~*n.* a person with a manic-depressive illness. **manic depression** *n.* **-mania** (mā´niə) *comb. form* (*esp. Psych.*) denoting special kinds of derangement, hallucination, infatuation or excessive enthusiasm, as in *erotomania, kleptomania, megalomania, monomania*. **-maniac** *comb. form* forming nouns and adjectives.

manicure (man´ikūə) *n.* **1** the care of the hands, fingernails etc. **2** a cosmetic treatment of the hands and fingernails. ~*v.t.* to give a manicure to. **manicurist** *n.* a person who undertakes the treatment of the hands and fingernails as a business.

manifest¹ (man´ifest) *a.* not concealed, plainly apparent, clear, obvious. ~*v.t.* **1** to make manifest, to show clearly. **2** to display, to exhibit, to evince. **3** to be evidence of. **4** to reveal or exhibit (itself). ~*v.i.* **1** (of a spirit) to reveal its presence. **2** to make a public demonstration of opinion. **manifestable** *a.* **manifestation** (-tā´shən) *n.* **manifestly** *adv.*

manifest² (man´ifest) *n.* **1** a list of a ship's cargo for the use of customs officers. **2** a list of passengers on an aircraft. **3** a list of railway trucks, containers etc. or their cargo.

manifesto (manifes´tō) *n.* (*pl.* **manifestos**) a public declaration, esp. by a political party, government, sovereign or other authoritative body, of opinions, motives or intentions.

manifold (man´ifōld) *a.* **1** of various forms or kinds. **2** many and various, abundant. **3** shown, applied or acting in various ways. ~*n.* **1** something which has many forms, parts etc. **2** a tube or system of tubes for conveying exhaust gases etc., in an engine, motor etc. **manifoldly** *adv.* **manifoldness** *n.*

manikin (man´ikin), **mannikin** *n.* **1** a little man or a dwarf. **2** an anatomical model exhibiting the parts, organs and structure of the human body. **3** an artist's lay figure. **4** (*usu.* **mannikin**) an African and Australian bird of the genus *Lonchura*.

Manila (mənil´ə), **Manilla** *n.* **1** Manila hemp. **2** a rope of this. **3** (*also* **manila**) Manila paper. **Manila hemp** *n.* hemp made from the fibre of *Musa textilis*, used for making rope. **Manila paper** *n.* a strong brown paper, orig. made from Manila hemp.

manioc (man´iok) *n.* **1** the cassava, *Manihot esculenta*, *M. dulcis* etc. **2** flour made from the root of this.

manipulate (mənip´ūlāt) *v.t.* **1** to operate on with the hands, to handle. **2** to treat manually, esp. skilfully or dexterously. **3** to manage, influence or tamper with by artful or sly means. **4** (*Comput.*) to edit or move (data etc.). **5** to stimulate sexually by hand. ~*v.i.* to use the hands skilfully, as in scientific experiments etc. **manipulable** *a.* **manipulability** (-bil´-) *n.* **manipulatable** *a.* **manipulation** (-lā´shən) *n.* **manipulative, manipulatory** *a.* **1** of or relating to manipulation. **2** given to artful or sly managing or influencing for one's own ends. **manipulatively** *adv.* **manipulativeness** *n.* **manipulator** *n.*

manky (mang´ki) *a.* (*comp.* **mankier,** *superl.* **mankiest**) (*coll.*) **1** dirty, unpleasant, bad. **2** inferior, worthless.

manna (man´ə) *n.* **1** the food miraculously supplied to the Israelites in the wilderness. **2** divine food, spiritual nourishment, esp. the Eucharist. **3** a sweetish exudation, of a slightly laxative nature, from certain species of ash, esp. the manna-ash. **manna-ash** *n.* a S European ash tree, *Fraxinus ornus.*

mannequin (man´ikin, -kwin) *n.* **1** a woman employed to wear and display clothes. **2** a window dummy.

manner (man´ə) *n.* **1** the mode in which anything is done or happens. **2** method, style, mannerism. **3** practice, habit, use, custom. **4** demeanour, bearing, address. **5** (*pl.*) conduct in social interaction, behaviour, deportment. **6** (*pl.*) politeness, habits showing good breeding. **7** (*pl.*) general modes of life, social conditions. **all manner of** all kinds of. **in a manner of speaking** in a certain way, somewhat, so to speak. **to the manner born** (as if) accustomed to something from birth. **mannered** *a.* **1** betraying mannerisms, affected. **2** (*usu. in comb.*) having a certain type of manners (*ill-mannered*). **mannerism** *n.* **1** an idiosyncrasy, the excessive adherence to the same manner or peculiarity. **2** peculiarity of style in art and architecture. **mannerist** *n.* **manneristic** (-is´-), **manneristical** *a.* **manneristically** *adv.* **mannerless** *a.* devoid of manners or breeding. **mannerly** *a.* well-mannered, polite. ~*adv.* politely. **mannerliness** *n.*

mannikin MANIKIN.

mannish MAN.

manoeuvre (mənoo´və), (*N Am.*) **maneuver** *n.* **1** a tactical movement or change of position by troops or warships. **2** (*pl.*) tactical exercises in imitation of war. **3** a contrived plan or action, a trick, a stratagem. ~*v.i.* **1** to perform manoeuvres. **2** to manage with skill. **3** to employ stratagem. ~*v.t.* **1** to move, drive or effect by means of strategy or skilful management. **2** to cause (troops) to perform manoeuvres. **3** to manipulate. **manoeuvrable** *a.* **manoeuvrability** (-bil´-) *n.* **manoeuvrer** *n.*

manometer (mənom´itə) *n.* an instrument for measuring the pressure of a gas or liquid. **manometric** (manəmet´-) *a.* **manometry** (-nom´-) *n.*

manor (man´ə) *n.* **1** a large country house, usu. with an estate. **2** a landed estate consisting of a demesne and certain rights over lands held by freehold tenants etc., orig. a barony held by a

lord and subject to the jurisdiction of his court-baron. **3** (*sl.*) a police district. **manor house** *n.* **manorial** (-naw´riəl) *a.*

manqué (mã´kā) *a.* having the potential to be, but not actually being, something specified (*actor manqué*).

mansard roof (man´sahd) *n.* a roof with four sloping sides, the lower sections of which slope more steeply, giving space for attics.

manse (mans) *n.* the residence of a clergyman, esp. a Presbyterian minister.

-manship (mənship) *comb. form* used to form nouns indicating skill, expertise or daring in a particular field, as in *penmanship, brinkmanship.*

mansion (man´shən) *n.* **1** a residence of considerable size and pretensions. **2** (*pl.*) a large building or set of buildings divided into residential flats.

manta (man´tə), **manta ray** *n.* any of various very large fish of the family Mobulidae, esp. *Manta birostris,* with wide, winglike fins and feeding on plankton.

mantel (man´təl) *n.* **1** the ornamental facing round a fireplace with the shelf above it. **2** a mantelpiece. **3** a mantelshelf. **mantelpiece** *n.* a structure above and sometimes around a fireplace. **mantelshelf** *n.* (*pl.* **mantelshelves**) a shelf above a fireplace.

-mantic -MANCY.

mantilla (mantil´ə) *n.* a veil for the head and shoulders, worn in Spain and Italy.

mantis (man´tis) *n.* (*pl.* **mantis, mantises**) any carnivorous orthopterous insect of the family Mantidae, esp. *Mantis religiosa,* which holds its forelegs as if in prayer lying in wait for other insects as prey.

mantissa (mantis´ə) *n.* the decimal or fractional part of a logarithm.

mantle (man´təl) *n.* **1** a sleeveless cloak or loose outer garment. **2** a covering. **3** a conical or tubular network coated with refractory earth placed round a gas jet to give an incandescent light. **4** a covering or concealing skin, part or organ, such as the fold enclosing the viscera in molluscs. **5** the back and scapular feathers and coverts of a bird. **6** the layer of the earth between the crust and the core. **7** leadership, power or authority, esp. as handed on. ~*v.t.* **1** to clothe in or as a mantle. **2** to cover, to envelop, to conceal. ~*v.i.* **1** to be overspread or suffused (as with a blush). **2** (of a blush) to suffuse the cheeks. **3** (of liquids) to become covered or coated.

mantra (man´trə) *n.* **1** a word or phrase chanted inwardly in meditation, orig. a Hindu formula or charm. **2** a Vedic hymn of praise.

manual (man´ūəl) *a.* **1** of or performed with the hands. **2** involving physical exertion (*manual labour*). **3** not mechanical or automatic (*manual gearbox*). ~*n.* **1** a book of instructions, a handbook. **2** any small book. **3** an organ keyboard played by the hands. **4** (*coll.*) a motor vehicle with a manual gearbox. **5** (*Mil.*) a manual exercise. **manual alphabet** *n.* FINGER ALPHABET (under FINGER). **manual exercise** *n.* the drill by which soldiers are taught to handle their rifles etc. properly. **manually** *adv.*

manufacture (manūfak´chə) *n.* **1** the making of articles by means of labour or machinery, esp. on a large scale, industrial production. **2** any particular branch of this. **3** (*pl.*) the products of industry or any particular industry. **4** (*derog.*) the production of anything without much thought or imagination. ~*v.t.* **1** to produce or fashion by labour or machinery, esp. on a large scale. **2** to make or work up into suitable forms for use. **3** to fabricate, to invent (a story, evidence etc.). **4** to produce (pictures, literature etc.) in a mechanical way. ~*v.i.* to be occupied in manufacture. **manufactory** *n.* (*pl.* **manufactories**) a factory. **manufacturable** *a.* **manufacturability** (-bil´-) *n.* **manufacturer** *n.* **manufacturing** *n.*

manumit (manūmit´) *v.t.* (*pres.p.* **manumitting**, *past, p.p.* **manumitted**) (*Hist.*) to release from slavery. **manumission** *n.*

manure (mənūə´) *n.* **1** animal dung, esp. that of horses, used to fertilize land for cultivation. **2** any substance, including compost or chemical preparations, used to fertilize land. ~*v.t.* to enrich (a soil) with fertilizing substances. **manurer** *n.*

manuscript (man´ūskript) *n.* **1** a book or document written by hand, not printed. **2** an author's text in its original state, as submitted for publication. **3** handwritten copy or form. ~*a.* written by hand. **manuscript paper** *n.* paper for writing music on, printed with staves.

✖ **manuver** common misspelling of MANOEUVRE.

Manx (mangks) *a.* of or relating to the Isle of Man, its inhabitants or its language. ~*n.* **1** (*pl.*) the people of the Isle of Man. **2** the Celtic language formerly spoken by natives of the Isle of Man. **Manx cat** *n.* a tailless variety of domestic cat. **Manxman** *n.* (*pl.* **Manxmen**). **Manx shearwater** *n.* a long-winged black and white shearwater, *Puffinus puffinus*, of the N Atlantic. **Manxwoman** *n.* (*pl.* **Manxwomen**).

many (men´i) *a.* numerous, comprising a great number. ~*n.* **1** a multitude. **2** a great number. **a good many** a large number. **a great many** a very great number. **as many** the same number of (*six ambulances and as many police cars*). **as many again** the same number in addition (*ten there and as many again here*). **many a one** many individuals. **many a time** often, many times. **many's the time** often. **the many 1** the majority. **2** the multitude, the common crowd. **too many** to have one too many to become drunk. **too many 1** superfluous, not wanted, in the way. **2** (*coll.*) too clever, too able or skilful (for). **manyfold** *adv.* by many times (*The investment increased manyfold in value*). **many-sided** *a.* **1** having many sides, aspects etc. **2** widely sympathetic, versatile, liberal. **many-sidedness** *n.*

manzanilla (manzənil´ə, -thənē´lyə) *n.* a very dry sherry.

Maoism (mow´izm) *n.* (*Hist.*) the political thought expounded by the Chinese communist leader Mao Zedong, 1893–1976. **Maoist** *n., a.*

Maori (mow´ri) *n.* (*pl.* **Maori, Maoris**) **1** any of the Polynesian original inhabitants of New Zealand. **2** their language. ~*a.* of or relating to the Maoris or their language.

map (map) *n.* **1** a representation of a portion of the earth's surface or the heavens or the surface of a planet etc. on a two-dimensional surface. **2** any delineation or diagram of a route etc. **3** (*Biol.*) a diagram of the genes on a chromosome or the bases in a molecule. **4** (*sl.*) the face. ~*v.t.* (*pres.p.* **mapping**, *past, p.p.* **mapped**) **1** to represent or set down in a map. **2** to plan (out) in exact detail. **3** (*Math.*) to assign (each of the elements of a set) to each of the elements in a different set. **off the map 1** (*coll.*) of no account, not worth consideration, remote. **2** out of the way. **on the map** important, well-known. **to map out** to plan in detail, to lay out a plan of. **mapless** *a.* **maplike** *a.* **map-maker** *n.* a person who makes maps. **map-making** *n.* **mappable** *a.* **mapper** *n.* **map-read** *v.i.* to look at and interpret a map. **map-reader** *n.* **map-reading** *n.* **map reference** *n.* a set of co-ordinates giving a location on a particular map.

maple (mā´pəl) *n.* **1** (*also* **maple tree**) a tree or shrub of the genus *Acer*. **2** the wood of this. **maple leaf** *n.* the leaf of the maple, used as an emblem of Canada. **maple sugar** *n.* a coarse sugar obtained from the sugar maple *Acer saccharum* and other maples. **maple syrup** *n.* a syrup produced from the sap of the sugar maple and other maples.

maquette (maket´) *n.* **1** a sculptor's preliminary model in clay, wax etc. **2** a preliminary sketch.

Maquis (makē´) *n.* (*pl.* **Maquis**) **1** those surreptitiously resisting the German invaders of France etc., in 1940–45. **2** a member of the French resistance. **3** (**maquis**) scrub or bush in Corsica and other Mediterranean coastal regions.

Mar. *abbr.* March.

mar (mah) *v.t.* (*pres.p.* **marring**, *past, p.p.* **marred**) to spoil, to impair; to disfigure.

marabou (mar´əboo), **marabout** *n.* **1** a W African stork, *Leptoptilos crumeniferus*, the downy feathers from under the wings and tail of which are used for trimming hats etc. **2** a tuft of feathers used in this way.

maraca (mərak´ə) *n.* a hollow gourd or shell containing beads, shot etc. shaken, usu. in a pair, as a percussive accompaniment to music, esp. in Latin America.

maraschino (marəskē´nō, -shē´-) *n.* (*pl.* **maraschinos**) a cordial or liqueur distilled from bitter cherries grown in Dalmatia. **maraschino cherry** *n.* a cherry preserved in maraschino etc., used in cocktails.

marathon (mar´əthən) *n.* **1** a long-distance race,

usu. a running race, of 26 miles 385 yards (42.195 km). **2** any task or contest requiring great endurance. **marathoner** *n.*

maraud (mərawd´) *v.i.* **1** to make a plundering raid (on). **2** to rove in quest of plunder. ~*v.t.* to plunder. **marauder** *n.*

marble (mah´bəl) *n.* **1** a fine-grained or crystalline limestone often polished for decorative use in sculpture or building. **2** (*usu. pl.*) a piece of sculpture in this material. **3** a type of smoothness, hardness or inflexibility. **4** a small ball of marble, glass or other hard substance used in a game, played esp. by children. **5** (*pl.*) a game which involves rolling a marble along the ground in order to hit another and so win it. **6** (*pl.*, *coll.*) sanity, wits (*to lose one's marbles*). ~*v.t.* to stain or vein (end-papers of books etc.) to look like marble. ~*a.* **1** composed of marble. **2** veined like marble. **3** hard, unfeeling. **marble cake** *n.* a cake made with light and dark sponge to have a mottled appearance. **marbled** *a.* **1** (of a book, soap etc.) stained to look like marble. **2** (of meat) streaked with veins of fat amongst lean. **marbled white** *n.* a butterfly, *Melanargia galathea*, with whitish wings and black markings. **marbling** *n.* **1** the veined or speckled appearance of marble. **2** the presence of veins of fat amongst lean meat. **marbly** *a.*

marc (mahk) *n.* **1** the compressed residue of grapes left after pressing, in the making of wine or oil. **2** brandy made from this.

marcasite (mah´kəsīt) *n.* pyrites, esp. a white orthorhombic form of iron pyrites, used for making ornaments.

March (mahch) *n.* the third month of the year. **March hare** *n.* a hare during its breeding season in March, characterized by leaping, gambolling and otherwise strange behaviour.

march[1] (mahch) *v.i.* **1** to move with regular steps like a soldier. **2** to walk in a grave, deliberate or determined manner. **3** to continue steadily (*The years marched by*). **4** to participate in a protest march. ~*v.t.* to cause to move (on, off etc.) in a military order or manner. ~*n.* **1** the act of marching. **2** a stately, deliberate or measured movement, esp. of soldiers. **3** the distance marched or walked in a particular period of time. **4** progress, advance. **5** (*Mus.*) a composition for accompanying a march or one in a similar style. **on the march 1** advancing steadily. **2** making progress. **to steal a march on 1** to get to an objective before, to start in advance of. **2** to gain an advantage over. **marcher** *n.* **marching order** *n.* (*Mil.*) the formation or equipment for a march. **marching orders** *n.pl.* **1** (*Mil.*) instructions for service personnel to proceed to war. **2** (*coll.*) instructions by which a worker, lodger etc. is required to leave their job, lodging etc., a dismissal. **march past** *n.* a marching of troops in a review past a superior officer etc.

march[2] (mahch) *n.* **1** (*pl.*) the frontier or boundary of a territory. **2** (*often pl.*) a borderland

or debatable land between two countries, as the border country of England and Wales (*the Welsh Marches*).

marchioness (mah´shənes) *n.* **1** the wife or widow of a marquess. **2** a woman holding this rank in her own right.

Mardi Gras (mahdi grah´) *n.* **1** Shrove Tuesday. **2** the carnival celebrated at this time.

mare[1] (mee) *n.* **1** the female of the horse or other equine animal. **2** (*sl.*, *offensive*) a woman. **mare's-nest** *n.* **1** a discovery that turns out a hoax or a delusion. **2** a complex state of affairs. **mare's-tail** *n.* **1** an aquatic plant, *Hippuris vulgaris*. **2** (*pl.*) long fibrous cirrus clouds, similar in appearance to horses' tails.

mare[2] (mah´rā, -ri) *n.* (*pl.* **maria** (mah´riə), **mares**) any of the darkish areas on the moon or other planets etc.

margarine (mahjərēn´, -gər-, mah´-) *n.* an emulsion of edible oils and fat with water, skimmed milk or other substances with or without the addition of colouring matter, used for the same purposes as butter.

margay (mah´gā) *n.* a Brazilian wildcat, *Felis wiedi.*

marge (mahj) *n.* (*coll.*) short for MARGARINE.

margin (mah´jin) *n.* **1** an edge, a border, a brink. **2** the blank space round the printed matter on a page. **3** a line drawn in an exercise book etc. to mark off a margin. **4** the space of time or the range of conditions within which a thing is just possible. **5** an allowance of time, money, space etc. for contingencies, growth etc. **6** the difference between cost and selling price. **7** a sum deposited with a broker as protection against loss. **8** the lowest amount of profit allowing an industry etc. to continue. **9** (*Austral.*) a differential paid for skill etc. **margin of error** *n.* in assessing the feasibility, time, cost etc. of an action, project etc., the amount of latitude allowed for possible miscalculation, changing circumstances etc.

marginal (mah´jinəl) *a.* **1** of or relating to or at the margin. **2** near the limit. **3** written or printed on the margin. **4** (*coll.*) small, slight (*a marginal chance*). **5** (of land) difficult to cultivate. **6** (of the sea) next to the shore in territorial waters. ~*n.* a marginal constituency or parliamentary seat. **marginal constituency** *n.* a parliamentary constituency where there is only a small difference between the totals of votes cast for the parties of the leading candidates. **marginal cost** *n.* the additional cost of making one more of a particular product. **marginalia** (-ā´liə) *n.pl.* marginal notes. **marginality** (-nal´-) *n.* **marginalize**, **marginalise** *v.t.* **1** to reduce in influence, power, importance etc. **2** to cause to seem irrelevant. **marginalization** (-zā´shən) *n.* **marginally** *adv.*

marguerite (mahgərēt´) *n.* the ox-eye daisy and other wild or cultivated varieties of chrysanthemum.

maria MARE².

Marian (meə´riən) a. of or relating to the Virgin Mary.

marigold (mar´igōld) n. any plant of the genus *Calendula* or *Tagetes*, usu. bearing bright yellow or orange flowers.

marijuana (mariwah´nə), **marihuana** n. 1 dried leaves, flowering tops and stems of Indian hemp, usu. used to make cigarettes smoked as a narcotic. 2 Indian hemp.

marimba (mərim´bə) n. a musical instrument similar to a xylophone.

marina (mərē´nə) n. a system of sheltered moorings designed mainly for pleasure boats.

marinade (marinād´) n. 1 a mixture of vinegar, oil etc. flavoured with wine, spices etc. for soaking fish or meat prior to cooking. 2 fish or meat soaked in this. ~v.t. to marinate. **marinate** (mar´ināt) v.t. to soak (meat, fish etc.) in a marinade. **marination** (-ā´shən) n.

marine (mərēn´) a. 1 of or relating to, found in or produced by the sea. 2 used at sea or in navigation, nautical, naval. 3 serving on board ship. ~n. 1 the shipping, fleet or navy of a country (*merchant marine*). 2 a member of a body of troops for service on board warships. 3 a member of the Royal Marines, the US Marine Corps etc., a specialist in amphibious military operations. 4 a seascape. **tell that to the marines** an expression of incredulity and derision (from the sailor's contempt for landsmen).

mariner (mar´inə) n. a seaman, a sailor. **mariner's compass** n. a magnetic compass indicating bearings from true or magnetic north.

marionette (mariənet´) n. a puppet moved by strings.

marital (mar´itəl) a. 1 of or relating to marriage. 2 of or relating to a husband. **maritally** adv.

maritime (mar´itīm) a. 1 of or relating to, connected with or bordering on the sea. 2 (of countries, cities etc.) having a navy or commerce by sea.

marjoram (mah´jərəm) n. an aromatic herb of the mint family, esp. wild or sweet marjoram.

mark¹ (mahk) n. 1 a visible sign or impression, such as a stroke, cut, dot etc. 2 an indication, symbol, character, device or token. 3 a model, brand or type (*Jaguar Mark X*). 4 a number or sign indicating merit in an examination. 5 a distinguishing feature, a characteristic, a symptom. 6 a limit, a standard. 7 a starting line in a race. 8 the point to be reached. 9 a distinguishing sign, a seal etc. 10 a character made by a person who cannot write, a signature. 11 a target, an object to aim at. 12 (*coll.*) a victim, esp. of fraud. 13 a in rugby, an indentation made in the ground by the heel of a player who has secured a fair catch. b in Australian Rules football, a fair catch of a ball kicked at least ten metres; the place from which the next kick is taken. 14 a boundary, frontier or limit. 15 in

boxing, the pit of the stomach. ~v.t. 1 to make a mark on. 2 to distinguish or designate or indicate, by a mark or marks. 3 to award marks to (a student's work etc.). 4 to indicate or serve as a mark to. 5 to characterize, to be a feature of. 6 to express or produce by marks. 7 to record as a score (points in games). 8 to select, to single out. 9 to pay heed to. 10 in football, hockey etc., to keep close to (an opponent) so as to make it difficult for them to receive the ball. 11 in Australian Rules football, to catch (the ball). 12 (*Austral., New Zeal.*) to castrate (a lamb). ~v.i. to observe something critically, to take note. **below the mark** not of the desired standard, unsatisfactory. **beside the mark** wide of the mark. **mark you** (*coll.*) please note (*Mark you, it will soon be raining*). **not up to the mark** below the mark. **off the mark 1** making a start. 2 wide of the mark. **of mark** noteworthy. **on the mark** accurate, straight. **on your marks** an order from the starter in a race for runners to take their position on the starting line. **to make one's mark** to do something that brings fame, recognition etc. **to mark down 1** to lower the price of. 2 to make a note of. 3 to decide to victimize. 4 to award a lower mark to. **to mark off** to separate (one thing from another), to set boundaries. **to mark out 1** to set out (boundaries and levels) for a proposed building. 2 to set out (lines and marks) on material as a guide for cutting, drilling or other operations. 3 to set out plans for. 4 to destine. **to mark time 1** (*Mil.*) to move the feet alternately as in marching, without changing position. 2 to pause until further progress can be made. 3 to do something just to pass time. **to mark up 1** to raise the price of. 2 to write alterations or instructions on for keying etc. **up to the mark** up to standard, satisfactory. **wide of the mark** not hitting the target. 2 not to the point, irrelevant. **markdown** n. the amount by which a price is reduced. **marked** a. 1 noticeable, definite (*a marked improvement*). 2 (of a person) destined to suffer misfortune, attack, suspicion etc. 3 having a visible or distinctive mark. 4 having natural markings of a specified kind. **markedly** (-kid-) adv. **marked man** n. 1 a person whose conduct is being scrutinized, esp. with suspicion or hostility. 2 a person apparently destined to succeed, because of recognition by superiors. **markedness** (-kid-) n. **marker** n. 1 a person who marks. 2 an object placed to mark a position, distance etc. 3 a felt-tipped pen used for labelling etc. 4 a person who notes the score at billiards, snooker etc. 5 a counter used in card-playing. 6 a bookmark. 7 a source of light identifying the target of a bomb etc. 8 (*N Am.*) an IOU. **marking** n. 1 (*often in pl.*) a mark or pattern of colouring, esp. on an animal or natural object. 2 the activity of assessing the work of pupils, students etc. 3 the making of a mark or marks. **mark-up** n. the amount by which a cost price is increased to cover overheads, profit etc.

mark² (mahk) *n.* a German unit of currency, the Deutschmark or (formerly) Ostmark.

market (mah'kit) *n.* **1** an open space or large building in which cattle, provisions or other commodities are offered for sale. **2** demand for a commodity; value as determined by this. **3** a geographical or commercial area regarded as suitable for buying and selling commodities in general or a particular form of merchandise. **4** a meeting for buying and selling. **5** a stock market. ~*v.i.* (*pres.p.* **marketing**, *past, p.p.* **marketed**) to buy or sell in a market. ~*v.t.* **1** to sell or attempt to sell (a product). **2** to sell in a market. **to be in the market for** to be ready to purchase or acquire (a particular item, commodity etc.). **to come into the market** to be offered for sale. **to make a market** to cause active dealing in a stock or shares. **to put on the market** to offer for sale. **marketable** *a.* **marketability** (-bil'-), **marketableness** *n.* **marketably** *adv.* **market cross** *n.* a cross or other stone structure set up in a market place. **marketeer** (-iə') *n.* a supporter of Britain's membership of the EU. **marketer** *n.* **market garden** *n.* a plot of land on which vegetables and fruit are raised for market. **market gardener** *n.* **marketing** *n.* the processes involved in selling goods, e.g. promotion, distribution etc. **market maker** *n.* a dealer in securities on the Stock Exchange who combines the roles of stockbroker and stockjobber. **market place** *n.* **1** an open space where a public market is held. **2** the sphere of commercial trading. **market price, market rate** *n.* the current price or rate in dealings. **market research** *n.* research into public demand, need etc. for particular commercial goods. **market researcher** *n.* **market town** *n.* a town which holds a regular public market. **market value** *n.* the price that something would fetch if it were offered for sale.

markka (mah'kə) *n.* the standard unit of currency in Finland.

marksman (mahks'mən) *n.* (*pl.* **marksmen**) a person who shoots well. **marksmanship** *n.* **markswoman** *n.* (*pl.* **markswomen**)

marl (mahl) *n.* soil containing clay and lime, much used as a fertilizer. ~*v.t.* to manure with marl. **marlite** (mah'līt) *n.* a variety of marl that remains solid after exposure to the air. **marly** *a.*

marlin (mah'lin) *n.* any of various large oceanic fishes of the genera *Makaira* and *Tetrapterus*, with a long upper jaw. **marlinspike, marlinespike** *n.* a pointed iron pin for opening the strands of rope in splicing.

marmalade (mah'məlād) *n.* a jam or preserve prepared from fruit, esp. oranges or lemons, boiled with the sliced rind. **marmalade cat** *n.* a cat having streaks of orange and brown in its fur.

Marmite® (mah'mīt) *n.* a savoury yeast extract used as a spread or for flavouring.

marmoreal (mahmaw'riəl), **marmorean** (-ən) *a.* **1** made of marble. **2** (*poet.*) like marble, esp. cold,

smooth or polished, pure white. **marmoreally** *adv.*

marmoset (mah'məzet) *n.* a small tropical American monkey of various species belonging to the family Callithricidae, called squirrelmonkeys from their bushy tails.

marmot (mah'mət) *n.* any burrowing squirrellike rodent of the genus *Marmota*, in N America the woodchuck.

marocain (mar'əkān) *n.* a cloth similar in structure to crêpe de Chine, but made from coarser yarns.

Maronite (mar'ənīt) *n.* a member of a Christian sect whose home is the Lebanon region.

maroon¹ (məroon') *a.* of a brownish-crimson colour. ~*n.* **1** this colour. **2** a detonating explosive device, often used as a warning signal.

maroon² (məroon') *v.t.* **1** to put ashore and abandon on a desolate island. **2** to leave isolated or unable to leave.

marque¹ (mahk) *n.* a brand, esp. a make of motor car as distinct from a specific model of car.

marque² (mahk) *n.* (*Hist.*) reprisals.

marquee (mahkē') *n.* **1** a large tent used for social or commercial purposes. **2** (*N Am.*) an awning over the entrance to a hotel, theatre etc.

marquess (mah'kwis) *n.* a title or rank of nobility in England, ranking next below a duke and above an earl. **marquessate** (-sət) *n.*

marquetry (mah'kətri), **marqueterie** *n.* work inlaid with different pieces of fine wood, ivory, plates of metal, steel etc.

marquis (mah'kwis) *n.* a foreign title or rank of nobility between a duke and a count. **marquisate** (-sət) *n.* **marquise** (mahkēz') *n.* **1** the wife or widow of a marquis. **2** a woman holding this rank in her own right.

marram (mar'əm) *n.* a seaside grass, *Ammophila arenaria*, frequently used to stabilize sand dunes.

marriage (mar'ij) *n.* **1** the legal union of a man and woman, wedlock. **2** the act or ceremony of marrying, a wedding, a nuptial celebration. **3** one particular such union (*her fifth marriage*). **4** close conjunction or union (*a marriage of interests*). **5** in cards, the union of a king and queen of the same suit. **by marriage** as a result of a marriage (*nephew by marriage*). **in marriage** as a husband or wife (*given in marriage; taken in marriage*). **marriageable** *a.* **1** fit or of age for marriage. **2** desirable as a partner in marriage. **marriageability** (-bil'-) *n.* **marriage bureau** *n.* an agency arranging introductions between single people with a view to marriage. **marriage certificate** *n.* an official document certifying that a marriage ceremony has been conducted. **marriage guidance** *n.* counselling and advice given to couples with marital problems. **marriage licence** *n.* a licence for the solemnization of a marriage without the proclamation of banns. **marriage lines** *n.pl.* (*coll.*) a marriage certificate. **marriage of convenience** *n.* **1** a marriage contracted for practical advantage rather than for love. **2** any union that is made to secure an advantage. **marriage settlement** *n.* an arrangement about property made before marriage, usu. securing a provision for the wife and sometimes for future children.

marron glacé (marō glas´ā) *n.* (*pl.* **marrons glacés** (marō glas´ā)) a preserved chestnut coated with sugar.

marrow (ma´rō) *n.* **1** a large edible gourd with white flesh from the plant *Cucurbita pepo.* **2** a fatty substance contained in the cavities of bones. **3** the essence, the pith. **to the marrow** right through, completely (*chilled to the marrow*). **marrowbone** *n.* a bone containing marrow. **marrowfat** *n.* a large variety of pea. **marrowless** *a.* **marrowy** *a.*

marry (mar´i) *v.t.* (*3rd pers. sing. pres.* **marries**, *pres.p.* **marrying**, *past, p.p.* **married**) **1** to take for one's husband or wife. **2** to officiate at the marriage of, to unite as man and wife. **3** to join closely together, to unite intimately. **4** (*Naut.*) to splice together. **5** to give in marriage. *~v.i.* to enter into the state of wedlock. **to marry off** to find a husband or wife for (a daughter or son). **to marry up** to link or join (with). **married** *a.* **1** united in marriage. **2** of or relating to married persons, conjugal. *~n.* a married person.

Marsala (mahsah´lə) *n.* a sweet white fortified dessert wine.

marsh (mahsh) *n.* a tract of low land covered wholly or partially with water. **marsh gas** *n.* methane, evolved from stagnant water. **marsh harrier** *n.* a European harrier hawk, *Circus aeruginosus.* **marsh hawk** *n.* HEN HARRIER (under HEN). **marshland** *n.* **marsh mallow** *n.* a shrubby herb, *Althaea officinalis,* growing near salt marshes. **marshmallow** *n.* a spongy sweet made of sugar, egg white, gelatin etc. **marsh marigold** *n.* a plant, *Caltha palustris,* of the buttercup family with bright yellow flowers, growing in marshy places, a kingcup. **marshy** *a.* (*comp.* **marshier**, *superl.* **marshiest**). **marshiness** *n.*

marshal (mah´shəl) *n.* **1** an officer regulating ceremonies and directing processions, races etc. **2** an officer of state with functions varying by country and period. **3** a military officer of the highest rank in some countries. **4** (*N Am.*) a civil officer responsible for keeping the peace. **5** (*N Am.*) the head of a fire department. *~v.t.* (*pres.p.* **marshalling**, (*N Am.*) **marshaling**, *past, p.p.* **marshalled**, (*N Am.*) **marshaled**) **1** to arrange or rank in order. **2** to conduct in a ceremonious manner. *~v.i.* (of armies, processions etc.) to assemble, to take up a position. **marshaller**, (*N Am.*) **marshaler** *n.* **marshalling yard**, (*N Am.*) **marshaling yard** *n.* a place where goods trucks, containers etc. are sorted according to their destination, and goods trains etc. made up. **Marshal of the Royal Air Force** *n.* the highest rank in the RAF, corresponding in rank to Field Marshal in the Army. **marshalship** *n.*

marsupial (mahsū´piəl, -soo´-) *n.* any individual of the order Marsupialia, mammals carrying the young in a pouch, such as the kangaroos and opossums. *~a.* belonging to the order Marsupialia.

mart (maht) *n.* **1** a trade centre, market, market place etc. **2** a saleroom.

Martello (mahtel´ō), **Martello tower** *n.* (*pl.* **Martellos, Martello towers**) a circular, isolated tower of masonry, erected on the coast to oppose the landing of invaders.

marten (mah´tin) *n.* a small carnivorous mammal, of the genus *Martes,* allied to the weasel, with a valuable fur.

martial (mah´shəl) *a.* **1** of or suited to war, military. **2** warlike, courageous, bellicose. **martial arts** *n.pl.* the various forms of single combat pursued as a sport, e.g. judo, karate. **martial law** *n.* military law abrogating ordinary law for the time being, proclaimed in time of war, insurrection or similar emergency. **martially** *adv.*

Martian (mah´shən) *n.* a supposed inhabitant of the planet Mars. *~a.* of the planet or god Mars.

martin (mah´tin) *n.* any swallow of the family Hirundinidae, esp. the house martin or sand martin.

martinet (mahtinet´) *n.* a strict disciplinarian. **martinettish, martinetish** *a.*

martingale (mah´ting·gāl) *n.* a strap or straps fastened to a horse's girth to keep the head down.

martyr (mah´tə) *n.* **1** a person who suffers death or persecution in defence of their faith or principles, esp. one of the early Christians who suffered death for their religion. **2** a person who feigns or advertises their suffering in order to gain sympathy. *~v.t.* **1** to put (someone) to death for their adherence to religion or principles. **2** to persecute, to torture. **a martyr to** a continual sufferer from. **martyrdom** *n.* **martyrology** (-ol´-) *n.* (*pl.* **martyrologies**) a list or history of martyrs. **martyrological** (-oj´-) *a.* **martyrologist** *n.*

marvel (mah´vəl) *n.* **1** a wonderful or astonishing thing. **2** a prodigy. *~v.i.* (*pres.p.* **marvelling**, (*N Am.*) **marveling**, *past, p.p.* **marvelled**, (*N Am.*) **marveled**) **1** to be astonished (at or that). **2** to be curious to know (why etc.). **marvellous**, (*N Am.*) **marvelous** *a.* **1** astonishing, prodigious. **2** excellent. **3** very unlikely. *~adv.* (*coll.*) marvellously. **marvellously** *adv.* **marvellousness** *n.*

Marxism (mahk´sizm) *n.* the theory that human and political motives are at root economic, and that class struggle explains the events of history and will inevitably lead to the overthrow of capitalism. **Marxism-Leninism** *n.* the political ideology developed by Lenin from the theories of Marx. **Marxist-Leninist** *n., a.* **Marxist, Marxian** *a.* of or relating to Karl Marx or his theories. *~n.* a believer in Marxism.

marzipan (mah´zipan, -pan´), †**marchpane** (mahch´pān) *n.* a confection of ground almonds, sugar and white of egg. *~v.t.* (*pres.p.* **marzi-**

panning, *past, p.p.* **marzipanned**) to cover with marzipan.

masala (məsah′lə) *n.* 1 any of several spice mixtures used in Indian cookery. 2 a dish prepared with such a mixture.

mascara (maskah′rə) *n.* a dark cosmetic for eyelashes.

mascarpone (maskəpō′ni) *n.* a soft mild cream cheese made in Italy.

mascot (mas′kot) *n.* an object or person that acts as a talisman and is thought to bring luck.

masculine (mas′kūlin) *a.* 1 belonging to or having the characteristic qualities of the male sex. 2 strong, robust, vigorous. 3 manly, spirited. 4 mannish. 5 (*Gram.*) denoting or relating to the gender based on words classed as male. ~*n.* 1 the masculine gender. 2 a masculine word. **masculinely** *adv.* **masculine rhyme** *n.* a rhyme on a word ending with a stressed syllable, e.g. true/new, contend/defend. **masculinist** (-ist), **masculist** *n.* a person advocating the rights of men. ~*a.* advocating the rights of men. **masculinity** (-lin′-) *n.* **masculinize, masculinise** *v.t.*

maser (mā′zə) *n.* a device similar to a laser used for amplifying microwave radiation.

mash (mash) *n.* 1 a mass of ingredients crushed and mixed into a pulp. 2 a mixture of bran and hot water for horses etc. 3 crushed or ground grain or malt steeped in hot water to form wort. 4 (*coll.*) mashed potatoes. ~*v.t.* 1 to crush into a pulpy mass. 2 to make an infusion of (malt) in hot water. **masher** *n.*

mask (mahsk) *n.* 1 a covering for the face, for protection or to conceal one's identity. 2 a disguise, a pretence, a subterfuge. 3 an impression of a face in plastic material. 4 a reproduction of a face used as a gargoyle or part of a moulding. 5 a model of a human head worn in ancient classical drama. 6 a face pack. 7 in photography, a shield of paper etc. used in printing to cover part of the unexposed film. 8 the head of a fox. ~*v.t.* 1 to cover with a mask. 2 to hide, conceal or disguise. 3 to screen during a process. 4 (*Mil.*) to hinder the effective action of (a force) by watching or by standing in the line of fire. **masked** *a.* 1 that has been covered with a mask. 2 disguised with a mask. **masked ball** *n.* a ball attended by guests wearing masks. †**masker** *n.* **masking tape** *n.* adhesive tape used in painting, car spraying etc. to protect areas where paint is not required.

masochism (mas′əkizm) *n.* 1 a variety of sexual perversion in which a person takes delight in being dominated or cruelly maltreated by another. 2 (*coll.*) enjoyment of something unpleasant or boring. **masochist** *n.* **masochistic** (-kis′-) *a.* **masochistically** *adv.*

mason (mā′sən) *n.* 1 a craftsman who works in stone. 2 (**Mason**) a Freemason. ~*v.t.* (*pres.p.* **masoning**, *past, p.p.* **masoned**) to build with masonry. **Masonic** (məsən′-) *a.* of or relating to Freemasonry. **masonry** *n.* 1 stonework. 2 the art

or occupation of a mason. 3 (**Masonry**) Freemasonry. **mason's mark** *n.* a mark cut in the stone of a building to identify the mason who dressed it.

masque (mahsk) *n.* (*Hist.*) a play or dramatic entertainment, usu. presented by amateurs at court or in noblemen's houses, the performers wearing masks, orig. in dumb show, later with dialogue, poetical and musical accompaniments. **masquer** *n.*

masquerade (maskərād′, mahs-) *n.* 1 a ball or assembly at which people wear masks. 2 a disguise, a pretence. ~*v.i.* to wear a mask or disguise, to pass oneself off in a false guise. **masquerader** *n.*

Mass (mas), **mass** *n.* 1 (the celebration of) the Eucharist, esp. in the Roman Catholic Church. 2 the liturgy for this. 3 a setting of certain portions of this to music.

mass (mas) *n.* 1 a body of matter collected, concreted or formed into a coherent whole of indefinite shape. 2 a compact aggregation of things. 3 a great quantity or amount. 4 the greater proportion, the principal part or the majority (of). 5 volume, bulk, magnitude. 6 (*Physics*) the quantity of matter which a body contains. ~*v.t.* 1 to form or gather into a mass. 2 (*Mil.*) to concentrate (as troops). ~*v.i.* to gather into a mass. **in the mass** in the aggregate. **the masses** the ordinary people, the populace. **to be a mass of** to be covered with, to have many. **mass defect** *n.* the difference in mass between a nucleus and its constituent particles. **mass energy** *n.* the ability of a body to do work in direct proportion to its mass, as indicated by the theory of relativity. **massless** *a.* **mass market** *n.* a very wide area of sales for a mass-produced product. **mass-market** *v.t.* **mass media** *n.pl.* the means of communication with large numbers of people, the media. **mass noun** *n.* (*Gram.*) a noun referring to something that cannot be counted and usu. has no plural or accompanying indefinite article, e.g. woodwork, sadness, artistry. **mass number** *n.* (*Physics*) the atomic weight of an isotope, the total number of protons and neutrons in a nucleus. **mass production** *n.* the production of standardized articles in large quantities in which the processes are reduced to simple, usually mechanical, operations performed along a conveyor belt, production line etc. **mass-produce** *v.t.* **mass-producer** *n.* **mass spectrograph** *n.* an instrument for separating charged particles into a ray spectrum according to their mass and for detecting them photographically. **mass spectrometer** *n.* an instrument like a mass spectrograph which detects particles photographically or electrically. **mass spectrum** *n.* a record produced by a mass spectrometer of the types and amounts of ions present in a sample.

massacre (mas′əkə) *n.* 1 indiscriminate slaughter, carnage, wholesale murder. 2 (*coll.*) an emphatic defeat in a competition, match etc.

~v.t. **1** to kill or slaughter indiscriminately. **2** (*coll.*) to defeat emphatically.

massage (mas´ahzh, -ahj, -sahzh´) n. **1** treatment by rubbing or kneading the muscles and body, usu. with the hands. **2** an instance of this. ~v.t. **1** to subject to massage. **2** to manipulate or misrepresent (esp. statistics). **3** to flatter. **massage parlour**, (*N Am.*) **massage parlor** n. **1** a place where massages are administered. **2** (*euphem.*, *coll.*) a kind of brothel. **massager** n. **masseur** (masœ´), **massagist** (-jist) n. a person skilled in massage. **masseuse** (masœz´) n. a female masseur.

massif (mas´ēf, masēf´) n. the main or central mass of a mountain or range.

massive (mas´iv) a. **1** heavy, weighty, ponderous, bulky. **2** (*coll.*) very large. **3** substantial, solid. **4** serious in effect, of large magnitude (*a massive heart attack*). **5** (*Geol.*) without defined strata. **6** (*Mineral.*) without definite crystalline form. **massively** adv. **massiveness** n.

mast[1] (mahst) n. **1** a long pole of timber, or a metal tube, placed upright in a ship to support the yards, sails etc. **2** a tall, slender structure carrying telecommunications aerials, dishes etc. **3** a flagpole. **4** MOORING-MAST (under MOOR[1]). **masted** a. **-master** comb. form a ship with the specified number or kind or masts. **masthead** n. **1** the top of a mast, usu. of the lower mast as a place for a lookout etc., or of the topmast. **2** the name of a newspaper or periodical as printed at the top of the front page. **3** (*N Am.*) a list of details about a newspaper printed in its pages. **mastless** a.

mast[2] (mahst) n. the fruit of the oak, beech or other forest trees. **mast cell** n. a cell in connective tissue that releases histamine, serotonin etc. during inflammations and allergic reactions.

mastectomy (məstek´təmi) n. (*pl.* **mastectomies**) surgical removal of the breast.

master (mahs´tə) n. **1** a person thoroughly acquainted with or skilled in an art, craft etc., an expert, a great artist. **2** a person who has secured the control or upper hand (*master of the situation*). **3** a person who has control or authority over others. **4** the owner of a dog, horse, slave etc. **5** a schoolmaster, a teacher, a tutor. **6** a holder of a degree ranking next above bachelor. **7** (*Naut.*) **a** the captain of a merchant vessel. **b** an officer who navigates a ship of war under the direction of the captain. **8** a chess player of international standard. **9** the person in charge of a pack of hounds. **10** an original or definitive version of a recording, typescript etc. from which copies can be taken. **11** a machine, device etc. which controls subsidiary machines or devices, cp. SLAVE. **12** a title of certain judicial officers. **13** (*formal*) a title prefixed to the names of boys. **14** the head of a household. **15** the head of certain colleges, corporations etc. **16** (*dated*) an employer. ~a. **1** having control or authority. **2** overall, subsuming others. **3** principal, largest.

~v.t. **1** to become thoroughly conversant with or skilled in using. **2** to become the master of. **3** to overpower, to defeat. **4** to subdue, to bring under control. **5** to be the master of, to rule as a master. **to be one's own master** to be free to do as one likes. **Master Aircrew** n. an RAF warrant rank, equal to but before a warrant officer. **master-at-arms** n. (*pl.* **masters-at-arms**) a first-class petty officer acting as head of the ship's police. **master bedroom** n. the principal bedroom in a house. **masterclass** n. a lesson, esp. in music, given by a leading expert to gifted students. **masterdom** n. **masterful** a. **1** expressing mastery, masterly. **2** domineering, self-willed. **masterfully** adv. **masterfulness** n. **master hand** n. **1** an expert. **2** the performance or skill of an expert. **masterhood** n. **master key** n. a key which opens all the locks of a set, normally each opened by a separate key. **masterless** a. **masterly** a. (of a performance, display etc.) showing the skill of a master. **masterliness** n. **master mariner** n. **1** the captain of a merchant ship. **2** a person qualified to be captain of a ship. **master mason** n. **1** a highly-skilled and qualified mason. **2** a Freemason who has attained the third degree. **mastermind** n. **1** a person who has conceived and is in charge of a project etc. **2** a person of great intellect. **3** the ruling mind or intellect. ~v.t. to conceive and direct, to plan. **Master of Ceremonies** n. **1** a person who introduces speakers, announces toasts etc. on formal occasions. **2** a person in charge of procedure at ceremonies, state occasions etc. **Master of the Rolls** n. a judge who presides over the Court of Appeal in England and Wales. **masterpiece** n. **1** a performance superior to anything of the same kind. **2** an achievement showing surpassing skill. **mastership** n. **master stroke** n. an instance of great skill, mastery etc. **master switch** n. a single switch controlling the supply of electricity to an entire system. **masterwork** n. a masterpiece. **mastery** n. **1** control, authority. **2** the skill of a master. **3** complete competence, thorough knowledge (of).

mastic (mas´tik) n. **1** a putty-like preparation used for bedding window frames etc. in buildings. **2** a gum or resin exuding from a Mediterranean evergreen tree, *Pistacia lentiscus*, chiefly used for varnish. **mastic tree** n. the tree that exudes mastic.

masticate (mas´tikāt) v.t. to grind and crush with the jaw, to chew. **mastication** (-ā´shən) n. **masticator** n. **masticatory** a.

mastiff (mas´tif) n. a breed of large dog of great strength and courage, characterized by drooping ears, often used as a watchdog.

mastitis (mastī´tis) n. inflammation of the breast or udder.

mastodon (mas´tədon) n. an extinct mammal of the genus *Mammut*, closely allied to the elephant, with nipple-shaped crests on the molar teeth. **mastodontic** (-don´-) a.

mastoid (mas'toid) *n.* 1 (*Anat.*) a conical prominence of bone behind the ear. 2 (*coll.*) mastoiditis. **mastoiditis** (-dī'tis) *n.* inflammation of the mastoid. **mastoid process** *n.* (*Med.*) a mastoid.

masturbate (mas'təbāt) *v.i.* to excite one's genitals, usu. with the hand, to obtain sexual pleasure. ~*v.t.* to do this for (oneself or another). **masturbation** (-ā'shən) *n.* **masturbator** *n.* **masturbatory** *a.*

mat¹ (mat) *n.* 1 a piece of coarse fabric of fibre, rushes, hemp, wire etc. or of perforated rubber etc., used as a carpet, to wipe shoes on, for packing etc. 2 a flat piece of cork, wood, plastic etc. placed under a dish or similar object to protect a surface from heat or moisture etc. 3 a piece of padded material to cushion landings in gymnastics. wrestling etc. 4 a small rug. ~*v.t.* (*pres.p.* **matting**, *past, p.p.* **matted**) 1 to cover or lay with mats. 2 to twist or twine together, to tangle. ~*v.i.* (of hair etc.) to become twisted into a tangled mass. **on the mat** on the carpet, being reprimanded. **matting** *n.* 1 mats collectively. 2 material for mats. 3 the making of mats.

mat² (mat) *n.* (*coll.*) a matrix, a mould.

matador (mat'ədaw) *n.* in Spanish bullfights, the person who has to kill the bull.

match¹ (mach) *n.* 1 a person or thing, equal, like, or corresponding to another. 2 a counterpart, a facsimile. 3 a person able to cope with another. 4 a contest of skill, strength etc. 5 a pairing or alliance by marriage. 6 a person eligible for marrying. ~*v.t.* 1 to be a match for, to compare as equal. 2 to find a match for. 3 to oppose as equal. 4 to oppose (against or with) as a rival, opponent etc. 5 to be the equal of, to correspond to. 6 in electronics, to adjust for maximum power. ~*v.i.* (of different things or persons) to agree, to be equal, to tally, to correspond. **to match** matching, appropriate (*a shirt with tie to match*). **to match up** to form a whole (with). **to match up to** to be equal to or as good as. **matchable** *a.* **matchboard** *n.* a board having a tongue along one edge and a corresponding groove on the other for fitting into similar boards. **matcher** *n.* **matching** *a.* **matchless** *a.* without equal, incomparable. **matchlessly** *adv.* **matchlessness** *n.* **matchmaker** *n.* 1 a person fond of planning and bringing about marriages. 2 a person who arranges introductions with a view to marriage. **matchmaking** *n., a.* **matchplay** *n.* in golf, a match or competition decided by the number of holes won as distinct from *stroke play.* **match point** *n.* 1 the point that needs to be won in order for a match to be won in tennis, squash etc. 2 a unit of scoring in bridge competitions.

match² (mach) *n.* 1 a small strip of wood or taper tipped with combustible material for producing or communicating fire. 2 a fuse burning at a uniform rate for firing charges. **matchbox** *n.* a box for holding matches. **matchlock** *n.* 1 a

musket fired by means of a lighted match placed in its lock. 2 the lock of such a musket. **matchstick** *n.* the wooden part of a match. **matchwood** *n.* 1 wood reduced to small splinters. 2 wood suitable for making matches.

matchet MACHETE.

mate¹ (māt) *n.* 1 a companion, a comrade, a fellow-worker, an equal, a match. 2 either of a pair of the lower animals, esp. birds, associated for breeding. 3 a suitable partner, esp. in marriage, a spouse. 4 (*Naut.*) **a** an officer in a merchant ship ranking below the captain. **b** an assistant to the surgeon, cook etc. 5 an assistant to a plumber etc. ~*v.t.* 1 to pair (birds, animals etc.) for breeding. 2 to match, to couple. 3 to join together in marriage. ~*v.i.* 1 to pair for breeding. 2 (of mechanical parts) to fit well. **mateless** *a.* **mateship** *n.* **matey, maty** *a.* (*comp.* **matier,** *superl.* **matiest**) (*coll.*) friendly. ~*n.* (*pl.* **mateys**) friend, companion (used as a form of address). **mateyness, matiness** *n.* **matily** *adv.*

mate² (māt) *v.t.* 1 to checkmate. 2 to confound, to paralyse. ~*a.* confounded, paralysed. ~*n.* a checkmate.

maté (mat'ā) *n.* **mate** *n.* 1 an infusion of the leaves of *Ilex paraguayensis,* a Brazilian holly. 2 this shrub. 3 the leaves of this shrub. 4 the vessel in which the infusion is made.

matelot (mat'lō), **matlo, matlow** *n.* (*coll.*) a sailor.

mater (mā'tə) *n.* (*pl.* **matres** (-trēz)) (*sl.*) a mother (see also DURA MATER, PIA MATER).

material (mətiə'riəl) *n.* 1 the substance or matter from which anything is made. 2 stuff, fabric. 3 elements or component parts (of). 4 notes, ideas etc. for a written or oral composition. 5 a person or persons suitable to fulfil a specified function after training etc. ~*a.* 1 of, relating to or consisting of matter. 2 corporeal, substantial. 3 of, relating to or concerning the human physical nature or needs (*material well-being*). 4 sensual, unspiritual, of or relating to the matter or essence of a thing, not to the form. 5 important, momentous, essential (*a material witness*). **materialism** *n.* (excessive) devotion to the pursuit of material wealth and physical wellbeing. **materialist** *n.* **materialistic** (-lis'-) *a.* **materialistically** *adv.* **materiality** (-al'-) *n.* **materialize, materialise** *v.i.* 1 to become actual fact. 2 (of a spirit) to appear. 3 (*coll.*) to arrive on the scene. ~*v.t.* 1 to make material, to invest with matter or corporeity. 2 to cause (a spirit) to become material or to appear. 3 to make materialistic. **materialization** (-zā'shən) *n.* **materially** *adv.* 1 in a material way. 2 to a significant extent.

materiel (mətiəriel') *n.* the material, supplies, machinery or instruments, as distinct from the personnel, employed in an art, business, military or naval activity etc.

maternal (mətœ'nəl) *a.* 1 motherly. 2 of or relating to a mother or to maternity. 3 connected or

related on the mother's side. **maternally** *adv.*
maternity *n.* **1** motherhood. **2** motherliness.
matey MATE[1].
math (math) *n.* (*N Am., coll.*) short for MATHE-
MATICS.
mathematical (mathəmat´ikəl) *a.* **1** of or
relating to mathematics. **2** rigidly precise or
accurate. **mathematically** *adv.* **mathematical
tables** *n.pl.* tables of logarithms, trigonometrical
values etc. **mathematician** (-tīsh´-) *n.*
mathematics (mathəmat´iks) *n.* **1** the science of
quantity or magnitude as expressed by numbers.
2 the mathematical calculations involved in a
particular problem, area of study etc.
maths (maths) *n.* (*coll.*) short for MATHEMATICS.
matinée (mat´inā), **matinee** *n.* an afternoon
performance of a play, film etc. **matinée coat,
matinée jacket** *n.* an infant's top short coat of
wool etc. **matinée idol** *n.* a handsome film star
etc., esp. popular with women.
matins (mat´inz), **mattins** *n.pl.* **1** the daily office
of morning prayer in the Anglican Church. **2** one
of the canonical hours of prayer, properly recited
at midnight but also at daybreak.
matlow, matlo MATELOT.
❌ **matress** common misspelling of MATTRESS.
matriarch (mā´triahk) *n.* **1** the female head of a
family, tribe etc. **2** a venerable or imposing lady.
matriarchal (-ah´-) *a.* **matriarchy** *n.* (*pl.* **mat-
riarchies**) **1** a social system in which the mother
is head of the family, or in which descent is
reckoned through the female line. **2** a society
having such a system.
matrices MATRIX.
matricide (mā´trisīd, mat´-) *n.* **1** the murder of
one's mother. **2** a person who murders their
mother. **matricidal** (-sī´-) *a.*
matriculate (mətrik´ūlāt) *v.i.* to be admitted as a
member or student at a university, college etc.
~*v.t.* to admit to membership of a body or society,
esp. a university, college etc. **matriculation**
(-lā´shən) *n.* **matriculatory** *a.*
matrimony (mat´riməni) *n.* (*pl.* **matrimonies**) **1**
the act of marrying. **2** the state of being married,
marriage, wedlock. **matrimonial** (-mō´niəl) *a.*
matrimonially *adv.*
matrix (mā´triks) *n.* (*pl.* **matrices** (-sez), **matrixes**)
1 a mould in which anything is cast or shaped. **2**
a place where anything is generated or
developed. **3** (*Biol.*) the formative part from
which a structure is produced, intercellular substance. **4** the concave bed into which a stamp or
die fits. **5** a mass of rock in which a mineral or
fossil is embedded. **6** the impression left by a
fossil, crystal etc. after its removal from rock.
7 (*Math.*) a rectangular table of elements in
rows and columns, used to simplify problem
solving, communication of information etc.
matrix printer *n.* DOT MATRIX PRINTER (under DOT).
matron (mā´trən) *n.* **1** a married woman, esp. an
elderly one. **2** the head of the nursing staff in a
hospital. **3** a female superintendent within an
institution (*a school matron*). **matronhood,
matronship** *n.* **matronly** *a., adv.* **matron of
honour** *n.* a bride's principal married attendant
at a wedding.
matt (mat), **mat, matte** *a.* dull, lustreless, not
glossy. ~*n.* **1** a dull, lustreless surface, groundwork, border etc., esp. in unburnished gold or in
roughened metal or frosted glass. **2** matt paint.
~*v.t.* **1** to dull. **2** to give a wet surface or appearance to. **3** to frost (glass). **matt paint** *n.* paint that
produces a matt finish when dry.
matte[1] (mat) *n.* an impure metallic product
containing sulphur, from the smelting of ore,
esp. copper.
matte[2] (mat) *n.* in film-making etc., a mask used
to obscure part of an image to allow the superimposition of another image.
matter (mat´ə) *n.* **1** that which constitutes the
substance of physical things, as distinguished
from thought, mind, spirit etc. **2** that which has
weight or mass, occupies space and is perceptible by the senses. **3** a physical substance. **4** a
subject for thought or feeling. **5** an object of or for
attention. **6** meaning, sense or substance (of a
book, discourse etc.). **7** an affair, a business. **8** the
cause or occasion of or for difficulty, regret etc. **9**
importance, moment. **10** (*Logic*) content as
opposed to form. **11** (*Law*) a statement or fact
forming the ground of an action etc. **12** purulent
substance in an abscess, pus. ~*v.i.* **1** to be of
moment, to signify. **2** to discharge pus. **a matter
of** approximately (*a matter of £500*). **as a matter
of fact** in reality, in fact. **for that matter 1** so far
as that is concerned. **2** as an additional point. **in
the matter of** as regards. **no matter 1** it does not
matter. **2** regardless of. **what is the matter?** what
is wrong (with)? **matter of course** *n.* what may be
expected in the natural course of events. **matter
of fact** *n.* (*Law*) the part of a judicial inquiry
concerned with establishing the truth or otherwise of allegations. **matter-of-fact** *a.* **1** treating of
or adhering to facts or realities. **2** not fanciful or
imaginary. **3** commonplace, prosaic, plain,
ordinary. **matter-of-factly** *adv.* **matter-of-factness**
n. **matter of form** *n.* **1** an issue of etiquette or
convention. **2** a purely routine matter. **matter of
life and death** *n.* something of vital importance.
matter of opinion *n.* a matter open to debate or
question. **matter of record** *n.* something established as a fact by being recorded.
matting MAT[1].
mattins MATINS.
mattock (mat´ək) *n.* a kind of pick with one
broad adze-edged end, for loosening ground,
severing roots etc.
mattress (mat´ris) *n.* **1** a case, usu. of padding,
springs etc., used for the bottom of a bed. **2** any
case of coarse material used to lie on.
maturation (matūrā´shən) *n.* **1** the attainment of
maturity or ripeness, the completion of growth. **2**
(*Med.*) the formation of pus, the bringing about
of suppuration. **maturational** *a.*

mature (mətūə´) *a.* **1** ripe, ripened. **2** completely developed, fully grown. **3** fully elaborated, considered etc. **4** (of a bill etc.) become payable. **5** (*Med.*) beginning to suppurate. ~*v.t.* **1** to bring to a state of ripeness or complete development. **2** (*Med.*) to bring to a state of suppuration. ~*v.i.* **1** to become ripened or fully developed. **2** (of a bill, insurance policy etc.) to become payable. **maturely** *adv.* **mature student** *n.* an adult student, i.e. one beyond the normal age of formal education. **maturity, matureness** *n.*

matutinal (matūtī´nəl), **matutine** (mat´ūtīn) *a.* **1** of, relating to or occurring in the morning. **2** early.

maty MATE¹.

matzo (mat´sō) *n.* (*pl.* **matzoth** (-ōt), **matzos**) (a thin wafer of) unleavened bread, eaten esp. at the Passover.

maudlin (mawd´lin) *a.* **1** characterized by sickly sentimentality, mawkish. **2** tearfully or pathetically sentimental, esp. when drunk.

maul (mawl) *v.t.* **1** to handle roughly. **2** to beat, to bruise (as with a maul). **3** to damage. **4** (of an animal) to paw and mutilate. ~*n.* **1** a tussle, a struggle. **2** a loose scrum in rugby. **3** a heavy wooden hammer, a beetle. **mauler** *n.*

maulstick (mawl´stik), **mahlstick** *n.* a light stick with a round pad at the end used as a rest for the right hand by painters, signwriters etc.

maunder (mawn´də) *v.i.* **1** to talk incoherently, to ramble. **2** to act or move about aimlessly. **maunderer** *n.*

Maundy (mawn´di) *n.* **1** the ceremony of washing the feet of poor people on the Thursday before Easter, in commemoration of Christ's performing this office for his disciples. **2** a distribution of alms following this. **Maundy money** *n.* silver money specially struck and distributed by the sovereign on Maundy Thursday. **Maundy Thursday** *n.* the Thursday before Easter.

mausoleum (mawsəlē´əm) *n.* (*pl.* **mausolea** (-ə), **mausoleums**) a sepulchral monument of considerable size or architectural pretensions.

mauve (mōv) *n.* a pale purple colour. ~*a.* of this colour. **mauvish** *a.*

maverick (mav´ərik) *n.* **1** an individualist, a determined non-conformer. **2** (*N Am.*) an unbranded beast.

maw (maw) *n.* **1** the stomach of lower animals, esp. the fourth stomach of ruminants. **2** the crop of birds. **3** (*facet.*) the human stomach, esp. that of a greedy person.

mawkish (maw´kish) *a.* **1** falsely or feebly sentimental. **2** nauseating or insipid in flavour, smell etc. **mawkishly** *adv.* **mawkishness** *n.*

max (maks) *n.* (*N Am.*, *coll.*) maximum (*pushed it to the max*). ~*a.* maximum, maximal (*max revs*). ~*adv.* to the utmost degree, maximally. ~*v.i.* to

perform to the limit of one's ability (*The car maxed out at 130 m.p.h.*). **maxed out** *a.* completely exhausted after total exertion.

max. *abbr.* maximum.

maxi (mak´si) *n.* (*pl.* **maxis**) something which is large or long esp. an ankle-length skirt, a coat etc.

maxi- (mak´si) *comb. form* very large or long.

maxilla (maksil´ə) *n.* (*pl.* **maxillae** (-ē)) **1** a jawbone, esp. the upper jaw in mammals. **2** the mouthpart for chewing in some arthropods. **maxillary** *a.*, *n.*

maxim (mak´sim) *n.* **1** a general principle of a practical kind. **2** a rule derived from experience.

maxima MAXIMUM.

maximal (mak´siməl) *a.* **1** of the greatest, largest etc. size, rate etc. **2** of an upper limit. **maximalist** *n.* a person who refuses to compromise, expecting a full accedance to (esp. political) demands. **maximally** *adv.*

maximum (mak´siməm) *n.* (*pl.* **maximums**, **maxima** (-mə)) the greatest quantity or degree attainable in any given case. ~*a.* greatest. **maximize, maximise** *v.t.* to raise to a maximum, to increase to the utmost extent. **maximization** (-zā´shən) *n.* **maximizer** *n.*

maxwell (maks´wəl) *n.* a unit of magnetic flux in the cgs system.

May (mā) *n.* **1** the fifth month of the year. **2** (**may**) hawthorn or hawthorn blossom (from its appearing in May). **3** (*poet.*) the springtime of life, youth. **may apple** *n.* a N American herb, *Podophyllum peltatum*, with a single white flower and an edible egg-shaped fruit. **May-bug** *n.* the cockchafer. **May Day** *n.* the first of May as a spring festival or, in some countries, as a public holiday in honour of workers. **mayflower** *n.* any of several flowers blooming in May, such as the cowslip, lady's smock or hawthorn, but esp. the trailing arbutus, *Epigaea repens*. **mayfly** *n.* (*pl.* **mayflies**) **1** any insect of the order Ephemeroptera. **2** an angler's fly made in imitation of this. **maying** *n.*, *a.* taking part in May Day festivities. **maypole** *n.* a pole decorated with garlands etc., round which people dance, esp. on May Day. **May queen** *n.* a young girl chosen to act as queen of the festivities on May Day.

may¹ (mā) *v.aux.* (*2nd pers. sing. pres.* †**mayest** (mā´əst), †**mayst**, *3rd pers. sing. pres.* **may**, *past* **might** (mīt)) expressing possibility, ability, permission, desire, obligation, contingency or uncertainty. **may as well** might as well. **might as well** would be as desirable or sensible as not to (*I might as well go home*). **that is as may be** that may or may not be the case (implying that there are further factors to consider). **maybe** *adv.* perhaps, possibly. **mayn't** (mānt) *contr.* may not. **might-have-been** *n.* (*coll.*) **1** a state of affairs that could once have obtained but is no longer possible. **2** a person who could have been more successful than they are. **mightn't** (mī´tənt) *contr.* might not.

Usage note It is best to use *may* rather than *can* to express permission in very formal contexts or where *can* could be misunderstood as meaning 'to be able to'.

may² MAY.

Maya (mī´ə) *n.* (*pl.* **Maya, Mayas**) **1** a member of an ancient Indian people of Yucatan, Honduras and other parts of central America. **2** the language of this people. ~*a.* of or relating to the Maya or their language. **Mayan** *a., n.*

mayday (mā´dā) *n.* an international distress signal used by ships and aircraft.

mayhem (mā´hem) *n.* **1** a state of disorder or confusion. **2** wilful damage.

mayonnaise (māənāz´) *n.* **1** a thick sauce or salad dressing made of egg yolk, vinegar etc. **2** a dish with this as a dressing (*egg mayonnaise*).

mayor (meə) *n.* the chief officer of a city or borough, or a district council with the same status. **mayoral** *a.* **mayoralty** *n.* (*pl.* **mayoralties**) **1** the office of mayor. **2** the period of office of a mayor. **mayoress** *n.* **1** a female mayor. **2** the wife of a mayor, or a woman who accompanies a mayor on ceremonial duties. **mayorship** *n.*

mayweed (mā´wēd) *n.* a wild camomile of Eurasia, often found as a weed.

maze (māz) *n.* **1** a network of paths and hedges etc. designed as a puzzle or challenge. **2** a labyrinth, a confusing network of winding and turning passages. **3** a state of bewilderment, uncertainty, perplexity. **mazed** *a.* bewildered, confused, giddy, dizzy. **mazeful** *a.* **mazy** *a.* (*comp.* **mazier**, *superl.* **maziest**) involved, winding, perplexing, intricate. **mazily** *adv.* **maziness** *n.*

mazuma (məzoo´mə) *n.* (*sl.*) money, cash.

mazurka (məzœ´kə) *n.* **1** a lively Polish dance like the polka. **2** the music for this.

MB *abbr.* Bachelor of Medicine.

Mb *abbr.* (*Comput.*) megabyte.

MBA *abbr.* Master of Business Administration.

MBE *abbr.* Member of the Order of the British Empire.

MBO *abbr.* management buyout.

MC¹ *abbr.* **1** Master of Ceremonies. **2** Member of Congress. **3** Military Cross. **4** music cassette.

MC² (emsē´) *n.* the lead vocalist in a rap-music group.

Mc *abbr.* megacycle(s).

McCarthyism (məkah´thiizm) *n.* **1** the hunting down of suspected Communists and their dismissal from public employment. **2** intolerance of liberalism.

McCoy REAL¹.

M.Ch., M.Chir. *abbr.* Master of Surgery.

mCi *abbr.* millicurie(s).

MCP *abbr.* (*coll.*) male chauvinist pig.

Mc/s *abbr.* megacycles per second.

MD *abbr.* **1** Managing Director. **2** Doctor of Medicine. **3** Musical Director.

Md *chem. symbol* mendelevium.

MDMA *abbr.* methylenedioxymethamphetamine, the hallucinatory drug Ecstasy.

ME *abbr.* myalgic encephalomyelitis.

me¹ (mē, mi) *pron.* **1** objective (accusative and dative) of I². **2** (*dial.*) MYSELF. **me and mine** me and my family.

Usage note Use of *me* in a subject, as in *Me and Joe will come*, is best avoided. See also notes under AS, BE, THAN.

me² (mē), **mi** *n.* (*Mus.*) **1** the third note of a major scale in the tonic sol-fa system of notation. **2** the note E in the fixed-doh system.

mead (mēd) *n.* a fermented liquor made from honey, water and spices.

meadow (med´ō) *n.* **1** a tract of land under grass, esp. if grown for hay. **2** low, rich, moist ground, esp. near a river. **meadowland** *n.* land used for grass cultivation. **meadow saffron** *n.* a plant of the genus *Colchicum*, esp. *C. autumnale*, the autumn crocus. **meadowsweet** *n.* **1** a rosaceous plant, *Alipendula ulmaria*, with white, plumy, fragrant flowers. **2** any N American rosaceous plant of the genus *Spiraea*. **meadowy** *a.*

meagre (mē´gə), (*N Am.*) **meager** *a.* **1** lean, thin, lacking flesh. **2** destitute of richness, fertility or productiveness. **3** poor, scanty. **meagrely** *adv.* **meagreness** *n.*

meal¹ (mēl) *n.* **1** food taken at one of the customary times of eating, a repast. **2** the occasion or usual time of this. **to make a meal of 1** to exaggerate the importance, difficulty etc. of. **2** to eat as a meal. **meals on wheels** *n.* a scheme by which pre-cooked meals are delivered by vehicles to the housebound, needy etc. **meal ticket** *n.* **1** a ticket given in exchange for a meal, often at a subsidized price. **2** (*coll., often derog.*) a person upon whom one can depend for financial support. **mealtime** *n.*

meal² (mēl) *n.* **1** the edible portion of grain or pulse ground into flour. **2** (*Sc.*) oatmeal. **3** (*N Am.*) cornflour. **4** any powder produced by grinding. **meal-beetle** *n.* a beetle of the genus *Tenebrio*, esp. *T. molitor*, feeding on meal, flour etc. **mealworm** *n.* the larva of the meal-beetle. **mealy** *a.* (*comp.* **mealier**, *superl.* **mealiest**) **1** of, containing or resembling meal. **2** besprinkled with or as with meal, spotty. **3** (of the complexion) pale. **4** mealy-mouthed. **mealiness** *n.* **mealy-mouthed** *a.* unwilling to speak plainly and honestly, hypocritical.

mean¹ (mēn) *v.t.* (*past, p.p.* **meant** (ment)) **1** to intend, to purpose, to have in the mind. **2** to denote, to signify. **3** to entail, to involve. **4** (of a word) to have as an explanation or equivalent. **5** to intend to convey or to indicate. **6** to design, to destine (for). ~*v.i.* **1** to have a specified intention or disposition. **2** to have a specified degree of importance (to). **to mean it** to be serious, not joking about something. **to mean well** to have good intentions. **meaning** *n.* that which is meant, significance, import. ~*a.* significant, expressive (*a meaning look*). **meaningful** *a.* **1** significant. **2** (*Logic*) able to be interpreted. **meaningfully** *adv.* **meaningfulness** *n.* **meaningless** *a.* **meaninglessly** *adv.* **meaninglessness** *n.* **meaningly** *adv.*

mean² (mēn) *a.* **1** equidistant from two extremes. **2** (*Math.*) **a** intermediate in value between the first and last quantities of a progression. **b** average. ~*n.* **1** the middle point, state, course, quality or degree between two extremes. **2** (*Math.*) **a** a quantity intermediate between the first and last quantities of a progression. **b** an average. **mean sea level** *n.* the sea level at the midpoint between high and low water. **meantime, meanwhile** *adv.* **1** in the intervening time. **2** while this was happening etc. ~*n.* the interval between two given times (*in the meantime, in the meanwhile*).

mean³ (mēn) *a.* **1** low in quality, capacity, value, rank etc. **2** inferior, poor, inefficient. **3** low-minded, petty, stingy, miserly. **4** shabby, lowly. **5** ignoble, disreputable, despicable. **6** (*esp. N Am.*) bad-tempered, vicious, aggressive. **7** (*coll.*) having or showing great skill, excellent. **no mean** good, not to be underestimated (*no mean cricketer*). **meanie, meany** *n.* (*pl.* **meanies**) (*coll.*) a petty-minded or miserly person. **meanly** *adv.* **meanness** *n.*

meander (mian′də) *v.i.* to wander, wind or flow in a tortuous course. ~*n.* **1** (*usu. pl.*) a tortuous or intricate course or bend. **2** (*usu. pl.*) a winding, a circuitous path or movement, a deviation. **meandering** *a.*

means (mēnz) *n.pl.* **1** (*also as sing.*) that by which anything is done or a result attained. **2** available resources, income, wealth. **by all manner of means** certainly, by all means. **by all means** certainly, undoubtedly. **by any means 1** in any way possible, somehow. **2** at all. **by means of** by the agency or instrumentality of. **by no manner of means** certainly not, by no means. **by no means** certainly not, on no account whatever. **means test** *n.* the official investigation into the means of a person applying for pension, unemployment benefit etc. **means-test** *v.t.*

meant MEAN¹.

measles (mē′zəlz) *n.pl.* **1** a contagious viral disease, indicated by red spots on the skin, usu. attacking children. **2** the spots of this disease. **3** a disease caused by the larvae of a tapeworm in pigs, cattle etc. **measly** *a.* **1** (*coll.*) worthless, paltry, meagre. **2** infected with measles. **3** (of pork etc.) infected with tapeworm larvae.

measure (mezh′ə) *n.* **1** the extent or dimensions of a thing as determined by measuring. **2** an instrument for measuring, as a rod, tape etc., or a vessel of standard capacity. **3** a standard of measurement. **4** a definite unit of capacity or extent. **5** the measurements necessary to make an article of dress. **6** a system of measuring. **7** the act of measuring, measurement. **8** a quantity measured out, taken as a rule or standard. **9** a prescribed or allotted extent, length or quantity. **10** limit, moderation, just degree or amount. **11**

metre, poetical rhythm. **12** an action to achieve a purpose (*emergency measures*). **13** a law, a statute, an Act of Parliament. **14** (*pl.*) a series of beds, strata. **15** (*Mus.*) time, pace, the contents of a bar. ~*v.t.* **1** to determine the extent or quantity of by comparison with a definite unit or standard. **2** to take the dimensions of. **3** to weigh, to judge, to value or estimate by comparison with a rule or standard. **4** to serve as the measure of. **5** to allot or apportion by measure. ~*v.i.* **1** to take measurements. **2** to be in extent, to show by measurement. **beyond measure** exceedingly, excessively. **for good measure** as an additional amount, over and above that required. **in some measure** to some extent, to a certain degree. **to measure up 1** to measure with a view to fitting something. **2** to take complete measurements. **3** to be good enough. **to measure up to** to be adequate for. **to take measures** to adopt means, to take steps (to). **within measure** in moderation. **without measure** immoderately. **measurable** *a.* **measurability** (-bil′-) *n.* **measurably** *adv.* **measured** *a.* **1** well-considered, carefully weighed. **2** of definite measure. **3** deliberate and uniform. **4** rhythmical. **measuredly** *adv.* **measureless** *a.* **measurelessly** *adv.* **measurement** *n.* **1** the act of measuring. **2** an extent or dimension determined by measurement. **3** (*pl.*) detailed dimensions; vital statistics. **measure of capacity** *n.* a measure for vessels, liquids, grain etc. **measurer** *n.*

meat (mēt) *n.* **1** the flesh of animals, usu. excluding fish and fowl, used as food. **2** the substance of something, the pith. **3** the edible part of a nut, egg, shellfish etc. **4** †the partaking of food, a meal. **after meat** immediately after a meal. **before meat** immediately before a meal. **meat and drink** something readily acceptable (to), a source of pleasure (to). **meatball** *n.* a ball of minced meat, eaten e.g. with a sauce and spaghetti. **meat-fly** *n.* (*pl.* **meat-flies**) a fly that breeds in meat, a blowfly. **meatless** *a.* **meat loaf** *n.* a loaf-shaped mass of minced or chopped meat, cooked and often eaten cold. **meat safe** *n.* a cupboard, usu. of wire gauze or perforated zinc, for storing meat. **meaty** *a.* (*comp.* **meatier**, *superl.* **meatiest**) **1** containing much meat. **2** of or like meat. **3** substantial, pithy. **meatily** *adv.* **meatiness** *n.*

Mecca (mek′ə) *n.* **1** a place frequently visited (*a tourist Mecca*). **2** a holy place. **3** the object of a person's aspirations.

mechanic (mikan′ik) *n.* **1** a person who is employed or skilled in repairing or maintaining machines. **2** a skilled workman. **3** (*pl.*) the practical details of an operation, project etc. **mechanician** (mekənish′ən) *n.* a person skilled in contructing machines, tools etc. **mechanics** *n.* **1** the branch of physics treating of the motion and equilibrium of material bodies. **2** the science of machinery.

mechanical (mikan′ikəl) *a.* **1** of or relating to machinery or mechanisms. **2** working with tools or machinery. **3** of or relating to mechanics. **4** a machine-like, automatic, done from force of habit. **b** slavish, unoriginal. **5** in accordance with physical laws. **6** acting or affected by physical power without chemical change. **7** produced by machinery. ~*n.* (*pl.*) the mechanical parts of something. **mechanical advantage** *n.* the ratio of personal force exerted to the force actually applied by a machine. **mechanical drawing** *n.* a precise scale drawing of a piece of machinery etc. from which measurements can be taken. **mechanical engineer** *n.* an engineer dealing with the design and construction of machinery. **mechanical engineering** *n.* **mechanical excavator** *n.* a machine to excavate soil by means of a scoop suspended from a crane jib and dragged along the ground. **mechanicalist** *n.* **1** a mechanician. **2** a believer in philosophical mechanism. **mechanicalism** *n.* **mechanically** *adv.* **mechanicalness** *n.*

mechanism (mek′ənizm) *n.* **1** the structure or correlation of parts of a machine. **2** a piece of machinery. **3** a system of correlated parts working reciprocally together, as a machine. **4** a means. **5** in art, mechanical execution as distinguished from style etc., technique. **6** (*Philos.*) the doctrine that phenomena can be explained purely in terms of mechanical or biological interactions. **mechanist** *n.* **mechanistic** (-nis′-) *a.* **mechanistically** *adv.*

mechanize (mek′ənīz), **mechanise** *v.t.* **1** to make mechanical. **2** to introduce machines in or to do. **3** (*Mil.*) to equip (troops) with mechanical transport. **mechanization** (-zā′shən) *n.* **mechanizer** *n.*

M.Ed. *abbr.* Master of Education.

med. *abbr.* medium.

medal (med′əl) *n.* a piece of metal, often in the form of a coin, stamped with a figure and inscription to commemorate some illustrious person, event or achievement. **medalled,** (*N Am.*) **medaled** *a.* **medallic** (midal′-) *a.* **medallion** (midal′yən) *n.* **1** a large medal. **2** (*Archit.*) a tablet or panel, usually round or oval, containing painted or sculptured figures, decorations etc. **medallist,** (*N Am.*) **medalist** *n.* **1** a person who has gained a medal. **2** a person who designs or engraves medals. **medal play** *n.* in golf, scoring by strokes, not by holes, stroke play.

meddle (med′əl) *v.i.* **1** to interfere (in) officiously. **2** to concern or busy oneself (with) unnecessarily. **meddler** *n.* **meddlesome** *a.* **meddlesomely** *adv.* **meddlesomeness** *n.*

☒ **medecine** common misspelling of MEDICINE.

media¹ (mē′diə) *n.pl.* the means of communication with large numbers of people, i.e. radio, TV, Internet, newspapers etc. **media event** *n.* an event arranged primarily to gain publicity, rather than being of intrinsic interest.

Usage note *Media* is sometimes used as a singular noun (a *media*), and a plural *medias* may also be encountered, but both these uses are best avoided.

media² MEDIUM.

mediaeval MEDIEVAL.

medial (mē′diəl) *a.* **1** of, relating to or situated in the middle, intermediate. **2** mean or average. ~*n.* a medial letter. **medially** *adv.*

median (mē′diən) *a.* **1** (*Anat.*) situated in the middle, esp. in the plane dividing the body longitudinally into two equal halves. **2** intermediate, as a line or zone between the extreme limits of winds, calm belts etc. ~*n.* **1** (*Geom.*) a straight line joining the vertex of a triangle to the midpoint of the opposite side. **2** (*Math.*) in statistics, a number in the middle position within a series of numbers. **3** (*Anat.*) a median artery etc. **medianly** *adv.*

mediate (mē′diāt) *v.t.* **1** to interpose between (parties) in order to reconcile them. **2** to effect by means of intervention. **3** to serve as a connecting link or medium between. ~*v.i.* **1** to interpose (between) in order to reconcile parties etc. **2** to serve as a connecting link or medium (between). **mediation** (-ā′shən) *n.* **mediator** *n.* **mediatorial** (-taw′-) *a.* **mediatorially** (-taw′-) *adv.* **mediatory** (mē′-) *a., n.*

medic (med′ik) *n.* (*coll.*) **1** a medical student. **2** a physician, a doctor.

medical (med′ikəl) *a.* **1** of or relating to medicine. **2** curative, healing, medicinal. **3** of or relating to medicine as opposed to surgery etc. (*a medical ward*). ~*n.* an examination to ascertain a person's state of physical fitness. **medicable** *a.* able to be treated or cured. **medical certificate** *n.* a document issued by a doctor stating that a person is unfit for work etc. **medical examination** *n.* an examination by a doctor to ascertain a person's physical fitness. **medical jurisprudence** *n.* FORENSIC MEDICINE (under FORENSIC). **medically** *adv.* **medical officer** *n.* a doctor in charge of health services in a local authority, institution etc. **medical practitioner** *n.* a physician or surgeon, a doctor. **medicament** (medik′ə-, med′-) *n.* a healing substance or application. **medicate** *v.t.* **1** to treat medically. **2** to impregnate with anything medicinal. **medication** (-ā′shən) *n.* **1** treatment with medicine or drugs. **2** a medicine or drug. **medicative** (-kə-) *a.*

medicine (med′sin, -isin) *n.* **1** a substance, usu. taken internally, used for the alleviation or removal of disease. **2** the art or science of preserving health and curing or alleviating disease, esp. as distinct from surgery and obstetrics. **3** among N American Indians, anything supposed to possess supernatural powers or influence, a charm, a fetish. **a taste of one's own medicine** unpleasant treatment in retaliation for the same. **to take one's medicine** to accept stoically an unpleasant ordeal, duty, undertaking etc. **medicinal** (-dis′-) *a.* **medicinally** *adv.* **medicine ball** *n.* a very heavy ball thrown from one person to another as physical exercise. **medicine chest** *n.* a box, cupboard etc. containing medicine, bandages etc. **medicine man** *n.* **1** a witch doctor.

2 a person believed to have magical powers of healing, esp. among N American Indians.

medico (med´ikō) n. (pl. **medicos**) (coll.) **1** a physician, a doctor. **2** a medical student.

medieval (mediē´vəl), **mediaeval** a. of or relating to, or characteristic of the Middle Ages. **medieval history** n. history from the fall of Rome (AD 476) until the Renaissance (15th cent.). **medievalism** n. **medievalist** n. **medieval Latin** n. the Latin language as used in Europe in the Middle Ages AD 600–1500. **medievally** adv.

mediocre (mēdiō´kə) a. **1** of middling quality. **2** indifferently good or bad, average, commonplace. **mediocrity** (-ok´-) n. (pl. **mediocrities**) **1** the state of being mediocre. **2** a mediocre person.

meditate (med´itāt) v.i. **1** to engage in contemplation, esp. on religious or spiritual matters. **2** to enter into a state of relaxation and unconscious thought by means of mental exercise. **3** to ponder, to engage in thought (upon), to muse, to cogitate. ~v.t. **1** to dwell upon mentally. **2** to plan, to design, to intend. **meditation** (-ā´shən) n. **meditative** (-tə-) a. **meditatively** adv. **meditativeness** n. **meditator** n.

Mediterranean (meditərā´niən) a. **1** denoting, of or relating to the sea between Europe and Africa or the countries surrounding it. **2** having a warm climate similar to that of the Mediterranean countries.

medium (mē´diəm, mē´dyəm) n. (pl. **media** (-diə), **mediums**) **1** anything serving as an intermediary, agent or instrument. **2** a means of communication. **3** an intervening substance or element, such as the air or ether, through which forces act, impressions are conveyed etc. **4** (Biol.) a substance in which germs are developed. **5** an instrument of exchange, such as money. **6** a middle or intermediate object, quality, degree etc. **7** any material used in a work of art. **8** (pl. **mediums**) a person claiming to receive communications from the spirit world. ~a. **1** intermediate in quantity, quality or degree. **2** average, moderate, middling, mediocre. **medium bowler** n. in cricket, a bowler who bowls at medium pace. **medium dry, medium sweet** a. (of a wine etc.) having a flavour between dry and sweet. **medium frequency** n. the frequency of radio waves between 300 kHz and 3 MHz. **mediumistic** (-mis´-) a. of or relating to a spiritualistic medium. **medium-range** a. (of a missile) having a range between 300 and 3100 miles (about 500 to 5000 km). **mediumship** n. the fact of supposedly being a spiritualistic medium. **medium-sized** a. of average size. **medium wave** n. the medium frequency; a radio wave in the medium frequency.

medlar (med´lə) n. **1** a rosaceous tree, Mespilus germanica. **2** the fruit of this tree, which is eaten when beginning to decay.

medley (med´li) n. (pl. **medleys**) **1** a musical or literary miscellany. **2** a mixed or confused mass, esp. of incongruous objects, persons, materials

etc. **medley relay** n. a relay race in which each swimmer uses a different stroke.

medulla (midŭl´ə) n. (pl. **medullas, medullae** (-lē)) **1** (Anat.) the inner part of certain organs, as the kidneys. **2** (Bot.) the internal tissue or pith of plants. **medulla oblongata** (oblong-gah´tə) n. the elongated medulla or continuation of the spinal cord forming the hindmost segment of the brain. **medullary, medullar** a.

medusa (midū´zə, -sə) n. (pl. **medusae** (-zē, -sē), **medusas**) (Zool.) **1** a jellyfish. **2** a coelenterate in its jelly-like form. **medusan, medusoid** n., a.

meek (mēk) a. mild, submissive, humble, tame, gentle, forbearing. **meeken** v.t. **meekly** adv. **meekness** n.

meerkat (miə´kat) n. a small, carnivorous mongoose of southern Africa, esp. the grey meerkat.

meerschaum (miə´shəm) n. **1** a white compact hydrous magnesium silicate, used for tobacco pipes. **2** a pipe made of this.

meet (mēt) v.t. (past, p.p. **met** (met)) **1** to come face to face with. **2** to go to a place in order to join or receive (someone). **3** to be introduced to (another person). **4** (of a road, railway, etc.) to reach and touch or unite with. **5** to encounter, to confront, to oppose. **6** to experience. **7** to refute. **8** to answer, to satisfy. **9** to pay, to discharge. ~v.i. **1** to come face to face. **2** to assemble. **3** to be introduced, to become acquainted. **4** to come into contact. **5** to be united. ~n. **1** a meeting of people, usu. for a hunt or sports activities involving cyclists, athletes etc. **2** the persons assembled or the place appointed for a meet. **3** (Austral.) an appointment. **more than meets the eye** complexities or problems that are not apparent at first. **to meet halfway** to compromise with. **to meet someone's eye** to exchange glances, usu. in a knowing way. **to meet the ear** to be heard. **to meet the eye** to be seen. **to meet up** to make contact (with), esp. by chance. **to meet with 1** to come across. **2** to have a meeting with. **3** to experience, to encounter, to engage, to receive (to meet with problems; to meet with approval). **meeting** n. **1** an assembly. **2** the persons assembled. **3** a coming together, a union (a meeting of minds). **4** a race meeting. **5** a confluence, intersection. **meeting house** n. a place of worship, esp. of Quakers.

mega (meg´ə) a. (coll.) **1** very large in number. **2** excellent, brilliant.

mega- (meg´ə) comb. form **1** great, large. **2** one million.

megabuck (meg´əbŭk) n. (coll.) **1** a million dollars. **2** (pl.) a large amount of money.

megabyte (meg´əbīt) n. (Comput.) **1** one million bytes. **2** 2^{20} bytes.

megadeath (meg´ədeth) n. one million deaths, esp. in nuclear war.

megaflop (meg´əflop) n. **1** (Comput.) a measure of processing speed equal to one million floating-point operations per second. **2** (sl.) a huge failure.

megahertz (meg´əhœts) *n.* (*pl.* **megahertz**) a unit of frequency equal to one million hertz.

megalith (meg´əlith) *n.* **1** a great stone. **2** a monument made of large stones, such as a cromlech, stone circle etc. **megalithic** (-lith´-) *a.*

megalo- (meg´əlō), **megal-** *comb. form* great.

megalomania (megələmā´niə) *n.* **1** a form of mental disorder characterized by delusions of grandeur or power. **2** a craze for overstatement etc. **megalomaniac** (-ak) *n., a.* **megalomaniacal** (-mənī´əkəl) *a.* **megalomanic** (-man´-) *a.*

megalopolis (megəlop´əlis) *n.* (*pl.* **megalopolises**) a large, densely-populated urban area. **megalopolitan** (-ləpol´itən) *a.*

megalosaurus (megələsaw´rəs), **megalosaur** *n.* an extinct carnivorous lizard of the genus *Megalosaurus.*

megaphone (meg´əfōn) *n.* **1** a hand-held apparatus for amplifying the voice. **2** a large speaking-trumpet.

megapode (meg´əpōd), **megapod** (-pod) *n.* an Australian or Malaysian bird of the family Megapolidae, which builds mounds to incubate its eggs in.

megaspore (meg´əspaw) *n.* any one of the larger kind of spores in some cryptogams, from which female gametophytes develop.

megastar (meg´əstah) *n.* a very popular, internationally-known star of the cinema, theatre etc. **megastardom** *n.*

megastore (meg´əstaw) *n.* a large usu. out-of-town store selling many different products.

megaton (meg´ətun), **megatonne** *n.* **1** one million tons. **2** a unit of explosive power in nuclear weapons, equal to a million tons of TNT.

megavolt (meg´əvōlt) *n.* one million volts.

megawatt (meg´əwot) *n.* one million watts.

megohm (meg´ōm) *n.* one million ohms.

megrim (mē´grim) *n.* either of two deep-water flatfishes *Lepidorhombus whiffiagonis* and *Arnoglossus laterna*, the sail-fluke.

meiosis (mīō´sis, mi-) *n.* (*pl.* **meioses** (-sēz)) **1** (*Biol.*) the diminution of the number of chromosomes in the cell nucleus. **2** (*Gram.*) litotes, depreciative hyperbole. **meiotic** (-ot´ik) *a.* **meiotically** *adv.*

melamine (mel´əmēn) *n.* **1** a white crystalline compound used for making synthetic resins. **2** (*also* **melamine resin**) a resin made from this, used in moulded products, adhesives, coatings etc.

melancholia (melənkō´liə) *n.* a mental disorder, often preceding mania, characterized by depression, frequently with suicidal tendencies (formerly supposed to be due to excess of black bile).

melancholy (mel´ənkəli) *n.* (*pl.* **melancholies**) **1** (*Med.*) a gloomy, dejected state of mind, sadness, gloom, depression, despondency, melancholia. **2** (*poet.*) pensive contemplation. *~a.* **1** sad, gloomy, depressed in spirits. **2** mournful, saddening. **3**

pensive. **melancholic** (-kol´-) *a.* **melancholically** *adv.*

Melanesian (melənē´zhən) *a.* **1** of or relating to Melanesia, the group of islands in the Pacific Ocean lying to the east of New Guinea. **2** of or relating to the language of Melanesia. *~n.* **1** a native or inhabitant of Melanesia, esp. one of the dominant ethnic group. **2** the group of languages spoken by the dominant Melanesians.

mélange (mālãzh´) *n.* a mixture, medley or miscellany.

melanin (mel´anin) *n.* a black or dark brown pigment occurring in the hair, skin and iris of the eye. **melanoma** (-nō´mə) *n.* a malignant tumour with dark pigmentation, esp. on the skin. **melanosis** (-ō´sis), **melanism** *n.* **1** (*Med.*) excess of colouring-matter in the skin, hair and tissues. **2** (*Bot.*) a disease producing blackness in plants. **melanotic** (-ot´ik), **melanistic** (-is´tik) *a.*

Melba toast (mel´bə) *n.* very thin crisp toast. **Melba sauce** *n.* a sauce for puddings made from raspberries and icing sugar.

meld[1] (meld) *v.t., v.i.* in the card games, rummy, canasta etc., to declare (one's cards) for a score. *~n.* a set or run of cards in the same games.

meld[2] (meld) *v.t., v.i.* to mix, blend, combine.

mêlée (mel´ā), (*N Am.*) **melee** *n.* **1** a confused hand-to-hand fight, an affray. **2** a muddle.

melilot (mel´ilot) *n.* a plant of the leguminous genus *Melilotus.*

mellifluous (melif´luəs) *a.* flowing smoothly and sweetly, pleasant, musical (usu. of a voice, words etc.). **mellifluence** *n.* **mellifluent** *a.* **mellifluously** *adv.* **mellifluousness** *n.*

mellow (mel´ō) *a.* **1** fully ripe, pulpy, sweet. **2** ripened or softened by age and experience, genial, kindly. **3** (*coll.*) jolly, half tipsy. **4** (of earth) rich, friable. **5** (of tones and colours) soft and rich. *~v.i.* to become ripe, mature or softened, by age etc. *~v.t.* to ripen, mature, soften. **mellowly** *adv.* **mellowness** *n.*

melodeon (məlō´diən), **melodion** *n.* **1** a small German accordion. **2** an instrument similar to a harmonium with a row of reeds and a keyboard.

melodic, melodious etc. MELODY.

melodrama (mel´ədrahmə) *n.* **1** a sensational play, film, novel etc. with a plot characterized by startling situations, crude sentimentality and a happy ending. **2** sensational and extravagant events, behaviour or speech. **melodramatic** (-drəmat´-) *a.* **melodramatically** *adv.* **melodramatics** *n.* melodramatic behaviour. **melodramatist** (-dram´-) *n.* **melodramatize** (-dram´-), **melodramatise** *v.t.* to make (a situation etc.) melodramatic.

melody (mel´ədi) *n.* (*pl.* **melodies**) **1** an agreeable succession of sounds, esp. of simple tones in the same key, a tune. **2** a simple setting of words to music. **3** the chief part in harmonic music, the air. **4** music. **melodic** (-lod´-) *a.* **1** of, characterized by or producing melody. **2** musical, sounding sweetly. **melodically** *adv.* **melodic**

minor n. a minor scale with a sharpened sixth or seventh when ascending which are played at the original pitch when descending. **melodious** (-lō´-) a. agreeably tuneful, melodic. **melodiously** adv. **melodiousness** n. **melodist** (mel´ədist) n. a composer of melodies. **melodize, melodise** v.t. to make a musical phrase, song etc. melodious. ~v.i. to compose or play sweet music. **melodizer** n.

melon (mel´ən) n. **1** the edible fruit of various plants of the gourd family, usu. large and round with pulpy flesh and many seeds. **2** the plant that produces this. **3** (Zool.) a waxy mass in the head of some whales.

melt (melt) v.i. (p.p. melted, †molten (mōl´tən)) **1** to pass from a solid to a liquid state by heat. **2** to dissolve. **3** to be dissipated, to disappear, to vanish (away). **4** to be softened to kindly influences, to give way. **5** to dissolve in tears. **6** to merge or blend (into). **7** (coll.) to perspire with heat, to be uncomfortably hot. ~v.t. **1** to make liquid by heat. **2** to dissolve. **3** to soften to tenderness. **4** to dissipate. ~n. **1** molten material. **2** a period of melting, a thaw. **3** a quantity melted together. **to melt away** to (make) disappear, esp. by liquefaction. **to melt down 1** to reduce (esp. metal articles) to a molten state by heat. **2** to become liquid or molten. **to melt in the mouth** (of food) to be light and tasty. **meltable** a. **meltdown** n. **1** the melting of fuel rods in a nuclear reactor, often causing the escape of radiation into the environment. **2** an economic collapse. **melter** n. **melting** a. **1** that melts. **2** (of sound etc.) gentle and moving, tender. **meltingly** adv. **melting point** n. the temperature at which a solid begins to melt. **melting pot** n. **1** a crucible. **2** a situation or place where there is a mixture of ethnic groups, cultures, ideas etc. **melt water** n. water produced by melting snow or ice, esp. from a glacier.

member (mem´bə) n. **1** a person belonging to a society or body. **2** (**Member**) a member of Parliament or a similar body. **3** a branch or division of a society or organization. **4** a component part or element of an organism or complex whole. **5** a limb, a part or organ of the body. **6** the penis. **7** a set of figures or symbols forming part of a mathematical expression. **8** (in titles) a person admitted to a particular grade of honour. ~a. (attrib.) that is a member (a member state). **membered** a. **memberless** a. **membership** n. **1** the state of being a member. **2** (a number of) members. **3** the whole body of members.

membrane (mem´brān) n. **1** a thin sheet of tissue lining or covering parts of an organism. **2** a thin sheet of plastic, rubber etc. acting as a lining, barrier etc. (damp-proof membrane). **membranaceous** (-brənā´-), **membraneous** (-brā´-), **membraniform** (-brā´-), **membranous** (-brə-) a.

memento (mimen´tō) n. (pl. mementos, mementoes) a memorial, a souvenir, a reminder. **memento mori** (maw´ri) n. an emblem of mortality, esp. a skull.

memo (mem´ō) n. (pl. memos) short for MEMORANDUM.

memoir (mem´wah) n. **1** (usu. pl.) an account of events or transactions in which the narrator took part. **2** an autobiography or a biography. **3** a communication to some learned society on a special subject. **4** (pl.) the published proceedings of a learned society. **memoirist** n.

memorabilia (memərəbil´iə) n.pl. souvenirs of past events, people etc.

memorable (mem´ərəbəl) a. **1** worthy to be remembered. **2** notable, remarkable. **memorability** (-bil´-) n. **memorably** adv.

memorandum (memərən´dəm) n. (pl. memoranda, memoranda (-də)) **1** a note to help the memory. **2** a short informal letter, usu. unsigned, with the sender's name etc. printed at the head, often sent internally within a company etc. **3** a brief record or note. **4** (Law) a summary, outline or draft of an agreement etc.

Usage note Memoranda is sometimes used as a singular noun (a memoranda), and a plural memorandas may also be encountered, but both these uses are best avoided.

---

memorial (məmaw´riəl) a. intended to preserve the memory of a past event, person etc., commemorative. ~n. **1** a monument, festival etc. commemorating a person, event etc. **2** (Hist.) a written statement of facts, esp. of the nature of a petition, remonstrance etc. **memorialist** n. **memorialize, memorialise** v.t. to honour, commemorate etc.

memorize (mem´ərīz), **memorise** v.t. to commit to memory, to learn by heart. **memorizable** a. **memorization** (-zā´shən) n. **memorizer** n.

memory (mem´əri) n. (pl. memories) **1** the mental faculty that retains and recalls previous ideas and impressions. **2** the exercise of this faculty, remembrance, recollection. **3** something that is remembered. **4** the state of being remembered. **5** posthumous reputation. **6** the period during which anything is remembered. **7** (Comput.) **a** a device for storing data in a computer. **b** the storage capacity of a computer. **8** the capacity of a material to return to its former condition after distortion. **from memory** as far as one can remember without proper verification. **in memory of** commemorating. **memory bank** n. **1** the memory of a computer etc. **2** the collective memories of a group or individual. **memory board, memory card** n. a detachable piece of electronics providing a computer with additional memory. **memory lane** n. an imaginary route to nostalgic remembrance of the past (a stroll down memory lane).

memsahib (mem´sahb) n. (Hist.) a term of address formerly applied by Indians in speaking to or of European married women living in the Indian subcontinent.

men MAN.

menace (men´əs) n. **1** a threat. **2** (coll.) a

nuisance (*Dennis the Menace*). ~*v.t.* to threaten. **menacer** *n.* **menacing** *a.* **menacingly** *adv.*

ménage (mānahzh´) *n.* a household. **ménage à trois** (a trwah´) *n.* (*pl.* **ménages à trois** (mānahzh a trwah´)) a household of three adults living together, usu. a married couple and the lover of one of them.

menagerie (mənaj´əri) *n.* **1** a collection of wild animals. **2** a place or enclosure where wild animals are kept.

menaquinone (menəkwin´ōn) *n.* one of the K vitamins, produced by bacteria of the intestine and essential for blood-clotting, vitamin K$_2$.

menarche (mənah´ki) *n.* the first onset of menstruation. **menarcheal** *a.*

mend (mend) *v.t.* **1** to repair, to restore, to make good. **2** to improve, to make better. **3** to correct, to amend. **4** to add fuel to (a fire). ~*v.i.* **1** to grow better, to improve. **2** to recover health. ~*n.* **1** the act or process of mending. **2** improvement. **3** a repaired part (in a garment etc.). **on the mend** improving, recuperating. **to mend one's ways** to reform, to improve one's behaviour, habits etc. **mendable** *a.* **mender** *n.* **mending** *n.* **1** the act of repairing, improving etc. **2** articles, esp. clothes, to be mended.

mendacious (mendā´shəs) *a.* given to lying, untruthful. **mendaciously** *adv.* **mendacity** (-das´-) *n.*

Usage note The nouns *mendacity* and *mendicity* should not be confused: *mendacity* means lying or deceiving, and *mendicity* begging.

mendelevium (mendəlē´viəm) *n.* (*Chem.*) an artificially-produced transuranic element, at. no. 101, chem. symbol Md.

Mendelism (men´dəlizm) *n.* a theory of heredity based on the observation that the characters of the parents of cross-bred offspring reappear by certain proportions in successive generations according to definite laws. **Mendelian** (-dē´-) *a.*, *n.*

mendicant (men´dikənt) *n.* **1** a beggar. **2** (*Hist.*) a member of a mendicant order. ~*a.* begging, reduced to beggary. **mendicancy** *n.* **mendicant order** *n.* (*Hist.*) a monastic order of friars subsisting on alms. **mendicity** (-dis´-) *n.*

Usage note See note on *mendicity* under MENDACIOUS.

menfolk (men´fōk) *n.pl.* the men, esp. of a particular family or community.

menhir (men´hiə) *n.* a prehistoric monument consisting of a tall upright stone.

menial (mē´niəl) *a.* **1** servile, low, degrading (a *menial task*). **2** (*derog.*) of or relating to a servant. ~*n.* **1** a person doing servile work. **2** a servile person. **menially** *adv.*

meningitis (meninjī´tis) *n.* (*Med.*) inflammation of the meninges owing to infection.

meninx (me´ningks) *n.* (*pl.* **meninges** (-in´jēz)) (*Anat.*) each of the three membranes that envelop the brain and spinal cord. **meningeal** (-in´jiəl) *a.* **meningococcus** (-kok´əs) *n.* (*pl.* **meningococci** (-kok´ī, -kok´sī)) a bacterium causing some forms of meningitis and cerebro-spinal infection.

meniscus (mənis´kəs) *n.* (*pl.* **menisci** (-is´ī), **meniscuses**) **1** (*Physics*) the top of a liquid column made convex or concave by capillarity (as mercury in a barometer). **2** a lens convex on one side and concave on the other. **3** (*Anat.*) a thin crescent-shaped cartilage between the surfaces of some joints such as the knee. **4** (*Math.*) a crescent-shaped figure.

Mennonite (men´ənīt) *n.* a member of a Protestant sect originating in Friesland in the 16th cent., with principles similar to those of the Anabaptists.

menopause (men´əpawz) *n.* **1** final cessation of menstruation, the change of life. **2** the period of a woman's life when this occurs. **menopausal** (-paw´-) *a.*

menorah (minaw´rə) *n.* a candelabrum with several branches, used in Jewish worship.

menses (men´sēz) *n.pl.* **1** the flow of blood etc. from the uterus of women at menstruation, the period. **2** the time of this. **3** the blood etc. discharged at menstruation. **menstrual, menstruous** *a.* **1** monthly. **2** of or relating to menstruation. **menstrual cycle** *n.* the continuing process of ovulation and menstruation in females. **menstruate** *v.i.* to undergo menstruation. **menstruation** (-ā´shən) *n.* the process of discharging blood and other uterine material, usu. occurring once every lunar month in non-pregnant adult females before the menopause.

mensuration (mensūrā´shən) *n.* **1** the act or practice of measuring. **2** (*Math.*) the branch of mathematics concerned with the determination of lengths, areas and volumes.

menswear (menz´weə) *n.* clothing for men.

-ment (mənt) *suf.* forming nouns denoting result, state, action etc., as in *agreement*, *bereavement*, *enticement*, *impediment*, *ornament*.

mental (men´təl) *a.* **1** of or relating to the mind. **2** due to or done by the mind. **3** of or concerning psychiatric illness. **4** (*coll.*) slightly deranged in mind. **5** (*coll.*) very enthusiastic, fanatical. **mental age** *n.* the intellectual maturity of an individual expressed in terms of the age of the average person attaining a similar level of intellectual maturity. **mental arithmetic** *n.* arithmetic done in the head, without writing it down or using a calculator. **mental block** *n.* a temporary interruption to the thought processes due to subconscious emotional factors. **mental defective** *n.* (*now offensive*) a mentally-handicapped person. **mental deficiency** *n.* (*now offensive*) the condition of being mentally handicapped. **mentally deficient** *a.* **mental handicap** *n.* a state of permanent intellectual disability such as to prevent normal functioning in society. **mentally handicapped** *a.* **mental illness** *n.* a disorder of the mind causing abnormality in a person's behaviour or affecting their ability to think. **mentality** (-tal´-) *n.* (*pl.* **mentalities**) **1** mental attitude or disposition. **2** intelligence. **3** the contents or functioning of the mind. **mentally** *adv.* **mental patient** *n.* PSYCHIATRIC PATIENT (under PSYCHIATRY). **mental reservation** *n.* an unspoken note of caution or qualification within the mind of a speaker or listener.

Usage note In the context of illness or disability, *mental* is now often felt to be derogatory or dismissive, and compounds such as *psychiatric hospital* and *psychiatric patient* are preferred to *mental hospital* and *mental patient*.

menthol (men´thol) *n.* a waxy crystalline substance obtained from oil of peppermint, used as a flavouring and as a local anaesthetic for neuralgia etc. **mentholated** *a.* (esp. of cigarettes) treated with menthol.

mention (men´shən) *n.* **1** a concise notice (of), an allusion. **2** a referring to by name. **3** the military honour of being mentioned in dispatches. *~v.t.* **1** to refer to, to allude to. **2** to indicate by naming without describing. **3** to reveal by speaking of. **not to mention** to say nothing of. **mentionable** *a.*

mentor (men´taw) *n.* an experienced adviser.

menu (men´ū) *n.* (*pl.* **menus**) **1** a list of dishes available at a restaurant etc. **2** a list of dishes to be served at a meal. **3** (*Comput.*) a list of alternative operations, topics etc., usu. displayed on-screen, which the user can choose from. **menu-driven** *a.* (*Comput.*) presenting a menu, operated through a menu.

meow MIAOW.

MEP *abbr.* Member of the European Parliament.

meperidine (meper´idēn) *n.* the drug pethidine.

mephitis (məfī´tis) *n.* a foul, offensive or poisonous stench. **mephitic** (-fit´-), **mephitical** *a.*

-mer (mə) *comb. form* (*Chem.*) a substance of a specified type as in *polymer*, *elastomer*.

⊠ merangue common misspelling of MERINGUE.

mercantile (mœ´kəntīl) *a.* **1** commercial, or of relating to buying and selling. **2** mercenary.

Mercator projection (mœkā´tə), **Mercator's projection** *n.* a projection of a map of the surface of the earth on to a plane so that the lines of latitude are represented by horizontal lines and the meridians by parallel lines at right angles to them.

mercenary (mœ´sənəri, -sənri) *a.* **1** done from or actuated by motives of gain. **2** hired or serving for money. **3** venal. *~n.* (*pl.* **mercenaries**) a person who is hired, esp. a soldier hired in foreign service. **mercenarily** *adv.* **mercenariness** *n.*

mercer (mœ´sə) *n.* a person who deals in silk, cotton, woollen and linen goods.

mercerise (mœ´sərīz), **mercerise** *v.t.* to treat (cotton fabrics) with an alkaline solution before dyeing, to impart strength and lustre. **mercerization** (-zā´shən) *n.*

merchandise (mœ´chəndīz) *n.* goods for sale

and purchase. *~v.i.* to trade, to barter. *~v.t.* **1** to trade in (a commodity). **2** to put (a product) on the market. **3** to promote, advertise etc. **merchandisable** *a.* **merchandiser** *n.*

merchant (mœ´chənt) *n.* **1** a person who carries on trade on a large scale, esp. with foreign countries. **2** (*esp. N Am., Sc.*) a retailer, a shopkeeper, a tradesman. **3** (*coll., usu. derog.*) a person with a particular inclination, habit etc. (*speed merchant*). **merchantable** *a.* saleable, of a quality to be marketed. **merchant bank** *n.* a private bank whose business chiefly involves dealing in bills of exchange and underwriting new security issues for commercial and financial institutions. **merchant banker** *n.* **merchantlike** *a.* **merchantman** *n.* (*pl.* **merchantmen**) a merchant ship. **merchant navy**, **merchant marine** *n.* a nation's commercial ships collectively. **merchant prince** *n.* a wealthy merchant. **merchant ship** *n.* a ship for conveying merchandise, a merchantman.

mercury (mœ´kūri) *n.* **1** (*Chem.*) a liquid, silvery, toxic, metallic element, at. no. 80, chem. symbol Hg. **2** any plant of the genus *Mercurialis*, esp. *M. perenne* or dog's mercury. **3** †a messenger. **mercurial** (mœkū´riəl) *a.* **1** flighty, volatile, fickle. **2** of, relating to, consisting of or caused by mercury. *~n.* a preparation containing mercury, used as a drug. **mercurially** *adv.* **mercuric** *a.* containing mercury in the divalent state. **mercurous** (-kū´rəs) *a.* containing mercury in the monovalent state.

mercy (mœ´si) *n.* (*pl.* **mercies**) **1** a disposition to temper justice with mildness. **2** forbearance, clemency, compassion. **3** an act of clemency, pity or compassion. **4** pardon, forgiveness. **5** control, discretion, liberty to punish or spare. **6** (*coll.*) something to be thankful for. **at the mercy of** wholly in the power of. **to have mercy on/ upon** to show mercy to. **merciful** *a.* **mercifully** *adv.* **mercifulness** *n.* **merciless** *a.* **mercilessly** *adv.* **mercilessness** *n.*

†mere[1] (miə) *n.* (*also poet.*) a lake, a pool.

mere[2] (miə) *a.* such and no more (*a mere youth; a mere trifle; no mere fluke*). **merely** *adv.* **merest** *a.*

mere[3] (mer´i), **meri** *n.* a short flat Maori war club, esp. one made of greenstone.

-mere (miə) *comb. form* part, segment as in *blastomere*.

meretricious (meritrish´əs) *a.* **1** alluring by false or empty show, unreal, tawdry. **2** of or relating to or befitting a prostitute. **meretriciously** *adv.* **meretriciousness** *n.*

Usage note The adjectives *meretricious* and *meritorious* should not be confused: *meretricious* means tawdry, and *meritorious* praiseworthy.

merganser (mœgan´sə) *n.* any diving or fish-eating duck belonging to the genus *Mergus*, the sawbill.

merge (mœj) *v.i.* **1** to be absorbed or swallowed

up (with). **2** to lose individuality or identity (in). ~*v.t.* to cause to be swallowed up or absorbed, to sink (in a larger estate, title etc.). **mergence** *n.* **merger** *n.* **1** the merging of an estate, limited company etc. into another. **2** absorption.

meridian (mərid´iən) *a.* **1** of or relating to midday. **2** of or relating to a geographical or astronomical meridian. **3** of or relating to the point or period of highest splendour or vigour. ~*n.* **1** a great circle drawn through the poles and the zenith of any given place on the earth's surface. **2** the line in which the plane of this circle intersects the earth's surface. **3** the time when the sun or other heavenly body crosses this. **4** culmination, zenith, point of highest splendour or vigour. **meridional** *a.* **1** of or relating to a meridian. **2** of or relating to the south, esp. of Europe.

meringue (mərang´) *n.* **1** a baked confection of white of eggs, sugar etc. **2** a cake made of this, usu. filled with cream etc.

merino (mərē´nō) *n.* (*pl.* **merinos**) **1** a breed of sheep valuable for their fine wool. **2** a fine woollen dress fabric, orig. of this wool. **3** a fine woollen yarn used for hosiery.

merit (mer´it) *n.* **1** the quality of deserving, desert. **2** excellence deserving honour or reward, worth, worthiness. **3** a reward or recompense, a mark or award of merit. **4** (*pl., Law*) the essential rights and wrongs of a case. ~*v.t.* (*pres.p.* **meriting,** *past, p.p.* **merited**) **1** to deserve, to earn. **2** to be entitled to receive as a reward. **3** to have a just title to. **on its merits** on its intrinsic qualities, virtues etc. **to make a merit of** to think or try to show that (one's conduct, action etc.) deserves praise. **merited** *a.* **meritocracy** (-tok´-) *n.* (*pl.* **meritocracies**) **1** (a society ruled by) those who have gained their positions through talent, intellect or industriousness, not through their family background, inherited wealth etc. **2** the rule of such people. **meritocrat** *n.* **meritocratic** (-krat´-) *a.* **meritorious** (-taw´riəs) *a.* **1** deserving reward. **2** praiseworthy. **meritoriously** *adv.* **meritoriousness** *n.*

Usage note See note on *meritorious* under MERETRICIOUS.

---

merlin (mœ´lin) *n.* the smallest of the European falcons, *Falco columbarius.*

mermaid (mœ´mād) *n.* an imaginary marine creature, having the upper half like a woman and the lower like a fish. **mermaid's purse** *n.* SEA PURSE (under SEA). **merman** *n.* (*pl.* **mermen**) an imaginary creature like a mermaid but male.

-merous (mərəs) *comb. form* (*Biol., Bot.*) having so many parts, as in *dimerous.*

merry (mer´i) *a.* (*comp.* **merrier,** *superl.* **merriest**) **1** cheerful, happy, jovial, mirthful. **2** causing merriment. **3** (*coll.*) slightly tipsy. **the more the merrier** the pleasure will be greater, the more people are involved. **merrily** *adv.* **merriment,** **merriness** *n.* **merry-go-round** *n.* **1** a revolving

frame with seats or wooden horses on which people ride at fairs etc. **2** an endless round of activity. **merrymaking** *n.* **1** merriment. **2** a festivity. ~*a.* making merry, jovial. **merrymaker** *n.*

mesa (mā´sə) *n.* a plateau with steep sides, a tableland.

mésalliance (māzaliãs´, -zal´-) *n.* marriage with a person of inferior social position.

mescal (meskal´) *n.* **1** a small globular cactus, *Lophophora williamsii,* the peyote, of the southern US and Mexico, the tubercles of which are chewed for their hallucinogenic effects. **2** an alcoholic liquor distilled from this. **mescal button** *n.* the tubercle of the mescal cactus. **mescaline** (mes´kalin), **mescalin** *n.* a hallucinogenic substance derived from mescal buttons.

Mesdames MADAME.

Mesdemoiselles MADEMOISELLE.

mesembryanthemum (mizembrian´thiməm) *n.* any succulent plant of the genus *Mesembryanthemum,* with thick, fleshy leaves and brilliant flowers, including the ice plant.

mesencephalon (mesensef´əlon, -kef´-) *n.* (*Anat.*) the midbrain. **mesencephalic** (-fal´-) *a.*

mesentery (mes´əntəri, mez´-) *n.* (*pl.* **mesenteries**) (*Anat.*) a fold of the peritoneum supporting the small intestines and connecting them with the wall of the abdomen. **mesenteric** (-ter´-) *a.* **mesenteritis** (-ī´tis) *n.*

mesh (mesh) *n.* **1** a fabric or structure of network. **2** (*pl.*) a network. **3** the space or interstice between the threads of a net. **4** an interlacing structure. **5** the engagement of gear teeth etc. **6** (*pl.*) a trap, a snare. ~*v.t.* **1** to cause to engage (gear teeth etc.). **2** to catch in a net, to ensnare. ~*v.i.* **1** to coordinate (with). **2** (of gear teeth etc.) to engage (with). **in mesh** (of cogs) engaged. **mesh-work** *n.* **meshy** *a.*

mesmerism (mez´mərizm) *n.* **1** (*Psych.*) **a** the art or power of inducing an abnormal state of the nervous system, in which the will of the patient is controlled by that of the agent. **b** the hypnotic state so induced. **2** fascination. **mesmeric** (-mer´-) *a.* **mesmerically** *adv.* **mesmerist** *n.* **mesmerize,** **mesmerise** *v.t.* **1** to hypnotize. **2** to occupy (someone's attention) totally. **mesmerization** (-zā´shən) *n.* **mesmerizer** *n.*

meso- (mē´sō), **mes-** *comb. form* **1** intermediate, in the middle. **2** of or relating to the middle.

mesolithic (mēsōlith´ik, -z-) *a.* of or relating to the phase of the Stone Age between the Neolithic and Palaeolithic phases. ~*n.* this period.

mesomorphic (mēsōmaw´fik, -z-) *a.* having a compact muscular physique. **mesomorph** (mē´-) *n.* **mesomorphy** (mē´-) *n.*

meson (mē´zon) *n.* (*Physics*) a particle intermediate in mass between a proton and an electron. **mesic** *a.* **mesonic** (-zon´-) *a.*

mesosphere (mē´səsfiə, -z-) *n.* the region of the earth's atmosphere extending for about 80 km above the stratosphere.

Mesozoic (mēsōzō´ik, mēz-) *a.* (*Geol.*) belonging

to the second great geological epoch, Secondary. ~*n.* this epoch.

mesquite (meskēt´, mes´kēt), **mesquit** *n.* (*Bot.*) any leguminous shrub or tree of the genus *Prosopis* growing in the SW United States and as far south as Peru, yielding the pods used for fodder. **mesquite-bean** *n.*

mess (mes) *n.* **1** a state of dirt and disorder. **2** a muddle, a difficulty. **3** officers' living quarters. **4** a number of persons who sit down to table together (used esp. of soldiers and sailors). **5** a communal meal. **6** a dish or a portion of food sent to table at one time. **7** liquid or semi-liquid food, esp. for animals. **8** a quantity of such food. **9** (*coll.*) the excreta of a pet animal. ~*v.i.* **1** to muddle or potter (about). **2** (esp. of soldiers etc.) to take a meal or meals in company. **3** (*coll.*) to defecate. ~*v.t.* **1** to mix together, to muddle, to jumble. **2** to dirty, to soil. **to make a mess** to make a bad job (of), to bungle. **to mess about 1** to tumble or fool about. **2** to treat roughly. **3** to treat improperly or inconsiderately. **4** to potter about. **to mess around** to mess about. **to mess up** to ruin, spoil. **to mess with** to interfere with. **mess hall** *n.* (*Mil.*) a dining area for service personnel. **mess kit** *n.* (*Mil.*) a soldier's eating utensils for use in the field. **messmate** *n.* (*Mil.*) a member of the same mess. **mess of pottage** *n.* a material gain for which something of a higher value is sacrificed. **mess tin** *n.* (*Mil.*) a small tin for cooking or eating in the field, part of the mess kit. **messy** *a.* (*comp.* **messier**, *superl.* **messiest**) **1** dirty, muddled. **2** complicated and difficult to handle. **messily** *adv.* **messiness** *n.* a state of dirt or disorder.

message (mes´ij) *n.* **1** a communication, oral or written, from one person to another. **2** the chief theme of a play, novel etc. **3** the truths, ideas or opinions of a writer or inspired person. **4** an errand, a mission. **to get the message** to understand what another person is trying to communicate.

Messeigneurs MONSEIGNEUR.

messenger (mes´injə) *n.* a person who carries a message or messages or goes on an errand or errands. **messenger RNA** *n.* a type of RNA that carries genetic information from DNA to the ribosomes for the synthesis of protein, mRNA.

Messiah (misī´ə) *n.* **1** an expected saviour or deliverer. **2** the anointed one, Christ, as the promised deliverer of the Jews. **Messiahship** *n.* **Messianic** (mesian´ik) *a.* **1** of, or inspired by the hope of, a Messiah. **2** marked by great zeal in support of a cause. **Messianism** (mes´iənizm) *n.*

Messieurs (mesyœ´), **Messrs** (mes´əz) *n.pl.* sirs, gentlemen.

messuage (mes´wij) *n.* (*Law*) a dwelling house with the adjacent buildings and land for the use of the household.

met[1] (met) *a.* **1** meteorological. **2** metropolitan.

met[2] MEET.

met- (met), **meta-** (met´ə), **meth-** (meth) *comb.*

form **1** beyond, above, as in *metamathematics*. **2** behind, between, as in *metacarpus*. **3** after (implying change or transposition), as in *metabolism*. **4** (*Chem.*) derivative, as in *metaldehyde*.

metabolism (mitab´əlizm) *n.* the continuous chemical change going on in living matter. **metabolic** (metəbol´-) *a.* **metabolically** *adv.* **metabolite** *n.* a substance involved in or produced by metabolism. **metabolize, metabolise** *v.t.* **metabolizable** *a.*

metacarpus (metəkah´pəs) *n.* (*pl.* **metacarpi** (-pī)) **1** the part of the hand between the wrist and the fingers. **2** the set of bones connecting the wrist and the fingers. **metacarpal** *a.*

metal (met´əl) *n.* **1** any of a class of elementary substances which usu. present in various degrees certain physical characters, such as lustre, malleability and ductility, possessed by the six metals known to the ancients, viz. gold, silver, copper, iron, lead and tin. **2** material of this kind. **3** a compound of the elementary metals, an alloy. **4** broken stone for road-making etc. **5** molten glass ready for blowing or casting. **6** (*pl.*) the rails of a railway etc. ~*v.t.* (*pres.p.* **metalling,** (*N Am.*) **metaling,** *past*, *p.p.* **metalled,** (*N Am.*) **metaled**) **1** to furnish or fit with metal. **2** to cover or repair (a road) with metal. **metal detector** *n.* an electronic instrument which gives an audible signal when metal is present. **metal fatigue** *n.* a weakening in metals due to prolonged stress or repeated blows. **metallic** (mital´-) *a.* **1** having the characteristics or properties of a metal. **2** made or consisting of metal. **3** (of a sound) sharp and reverberant, like a metal when struck. **4** lustrous like a metal. **metallically** *adv.* **metalliferous** (-lif´-) *a.* bearing or yielding metal. **metallize** (met´əlīz), **metallise** *v.t.* **1** to coat with a metal. **2** to give metallic properties to. **metallization** (-zā´shən) *n.* **metalloid** *a.* resembling a metal in form or appearance. ~*n.* an element having some of the properties of metals and some of non-metals. **metalwork** *n.* **1** the craft of working in metal. **2** metal objects collectively. **metalworker** *n.* **metalworking** *n.*

Usage note The spellings of the nouns *metal* (a substance) and *mettle* (spirit, courage) should not be confused.

metalanguage (met´əlang·gwij) *n.* **1** a language or system of symbols used to speak about another language. **2** a system of propositions used to speak about other propositions.

metallography (metəlog´rəfi) *n.* the science of metals, esp. the microscopic study of their internal structure. **metallographic** (-lōgraf´ik), **metallographical** *a.* **metallographically** *adv.*

metallurgy (mital´əji, met´əlœji) *n.* **1** the science of metals. **2** the art of separating metals from ores. **metallurgic** (metəlœ´-), **metallurgical** *a.* **metallurgically** *adv.* **metallurgist** *n.*

metamere (met´əmiə) *n.* (*Zool.*) each of a series

of similar parts of a body. **metameric** (-mer´-) *a.* **1** (*Chem.*) having the same composition and molecular weight, isomeric but different in chemical properties. **2** (*Zool.*) of or relating to metameres. **metamerism** (-tam´ə-) *n.*

metamorphose (metəmaw´fōz) *v.t.* **1** to change into a different form. **2** to transmute (into, to). **metamorphic** (-maw´fik) *a.* **1** causing or showing the results of metamorphosis, transforming or transformed. **2** (*Geol.*) changed in structure by a natural agency, such as heat or pressure. **metamorphism** *n.* **metamorphosis** (-fəsis, -mawfō´sis) *n.* (*pl.* **metamorphoses** (-sēz)) **1** a change of form. **2** the result of such a change. **3** (*Zool.*) transformation, such as that of a chrysalis into a winged insect. **4** a complete change of character, purpose etc.

metaphor (met´əfə, -faw) *n.* **1** a figure of speech by which a word is transferred in application from one object to another, so as to imply comparison. **2** an instance of this. **3** a symbol (for). **metaphoric** (-for´-), **metaphorical** *a.* **metaphorically** *adv.*

metaphysics (metəfiz´iks) *n.* **1** the philosophy of being and knowing. **2** the philosophy of mind. **3** anything vague, abstract and abstruse. **metaphysic** *n.* a system of metaphysics. **metaphysical** *a.* **1** of or relating to metaphysics. **2** transcendental, dealing with abstractions. **3** abstruse, oversubtle. **4** imaginary, fantastic. **5** (*also* **Metaphysical**) belonging to the group of 17th-cent. poets noted for their intellectual tone and ingenious imagery. ~*n.* (*also* **Metaphysical**) a metaphysical poet. **metaphysically** *adv.* **metaphysician** (-zish´-) *n.*

metapsychology (metəsīkol´əji) *n.* **1** the body of theory on psychological matters. **2** studies, theories etc. of psychology that are beyond the limits of experimentation. **metapsychological** (-kəloj´-) *a.*

metastable (metəstā´bəl) *a.* **1** seeming stable because passing slowly from one state to another. **2** stable under small disturbances only. **metastability** (-stəbil´-) *n.*

metastasis (mitəs´təsis) *n.* (*pl.* **metastases** (-sēz)) (*Med.*) **1** a change in the seat of a disease, esp. cancer, from one organ to another. **2** a secondary tumour. **metastasize, metastasise** *v.i.* **metastatic** (metəstat´ik) *a.*

metatarsus (metətah´səs) *n.* (*pl.* **metatarsi** (-sī)) **1** that part of the foot between the tarsus and the toes, in humans consisting of five long bones. **2** the set of bones linking the tarsus and the toes. **metatarsal** *a.*

metathesis (mitath´əsis) *n.* (*pl.* **metatheses** (-əsēz)) **1** (*Gram.*) the transposition of sounds or letters in a word. **2** (*Chem.*) interchange of radicals or groups of atoms in a compound with others. **metathetic** (metəthet´ik), **metathetical** *a.*

mete[1] (mēt) *v.t.* **1** to allot, to apportion (out). **2** (*poet., dial.*) to measure.

mete[2] (mēt) *n.* a limit, a boundary, a boundary stone.

meteor (mē´tiə) *n.* **1** a luminous body appearing for a few moments in the sky and then disappearing, a shooting star. **2** anything which transiently dazzles or strikes with wonder. **meteoric** (-or´-) *a.* **1** of or relating to meteors. **2** rapid, like a meteor (*meteoric rise to fame*). **3** brilliant but fading quickly, dazzling. **4** (of a plant) affected by atmospheric conditions. **meteorically** *adv.* **meteoric stone** *n.* a meteorite. **meteorite** *n.* a fallen meteor, a stone, metal or a compound of earth and metal, that has fallen upon the earth from space. **meteoritic** (-it´ik) *a.* **meteoroid** *n.* a body that becomes visible as a meteor. **meteoroidal** (-oi´-) *a.*

meteorology (mētiərol´əji) *n.* **1** the science of the atmosphere and its phenomena, esp. for the purpose of forecasting the weather. **2** the general character of the weather in a particular place. **meteorologic** (-loj´-) *a.* **meteorological** *a.* **meteorologically** *adv.* **meteorologist** *n.*

meter[1] (mē´tə) *n.* **1** a person who or something which measures, esp. an instrument for registering the quantity of gas, water, electric energy etc. supplied. **2** a parking meter. ~*v.t.* to measure by means of a meter. **meterage** *n.*

Usage note The British spellings of the nouns *meter* (an instrument) and *metre* (of verse, or as a metric unit) should not be confused.

meter[2] METRE[1].

meter[3] METRE[2].

-meter (mitə) *comb. form* **1** a measuring instrument, as in *barometer, thermometer*. **2** a verse metre with a specified number of feet, as in *pentameter*.

methadone (meth´ədōn) *n.* a synthetic drug similar to morphine, often used in the treatment of addiction.

methamphetamine (methamfet´əmēn, -min) *n.* a variety of amphetamine used as a stimulant.

methanal (meth´ənal) *n.* (*Chem.*) formaldehyde.

methane (mē´thān) *n.* (*Chem.*) a light, colourless gas produced by the decomposition or dry distillation of vegetable matter, one of the chief constituents of coal gas, and also of firedamp and marsh gas. **methanometer** (-nom´itə) *n.*

methanoic acid (methənō´ik) *n.* (*Chem.*) formic acid.

methanol (meth´ənol) *n.* (*Chem.*) a colourless, volatile liquid used as a solvent or as fuel, methyl alcohol.

Methedrine® (meth´ədrēn) *n.* METHAMPHETAMINE.

methinks (mithingks´) *v.i.* (*past* **methought** (-thawt´)) it seems to me, I think.

method (meth´əd) *n.* **1** a mode of procedure, way or order of doing. **2** an orderly, systematic or logical arrangement. **3** orderliness, system. **4** a system or the basis of a system of classification. **method in one's madness** careful thought underlying a seemingly careless action. **method acting** *n*. an acting technique based on the actor's identification of themselves with the part. **methodical** (mithod´-), **methodic** *a*. **1** done according to a method. **2** habitually proceeding in a systematic way. **methodically** *adv*. **methodize, methodise** *v.t*. **1** to arrange systematically. **2** to reduce to order. **methodizer** *n*. **methodology** (-dol´-) *n*. **1** the branch of logic dealing with the methods of accurate thinking. **2** the methods used in a particular project, discipline etc. **methodological** (-loj´-) *a*. **methodologically** *adv*. **methodologist** (-dol´-) *n*.

Methodist (meth´ədist) *n*. **1** a member of any of the religious bodies that have grown out of the evangelical movement begun in the middle of the 18th cent. by John Wesley, 1703–91, his brother Charles, and George Whitefield, 1714–70. **2** (**methodist**) a strict observer of method in philosophical inquiry or medical practice. **Methodism** *n*. **Methodistic** (-dis´-), **Methodistical** *a*. **Methodistically** *adv*.

meths (meths) *n.pl*. (*coll*.) methylated spirits.

Methuselah (mithū´zələ, -oo´-) *n*. **1** a very old person; a very old thing. **2** (*also* **methuselah**) a large wine bottle, about 8 times the usual size.

methyl (meth´əl, mē´thīl) *n*. (*Chem*.) the hypothetical radical of wood spirit, formic acid and many other organic compounds. **methyl alcohol** *n*. methanol. **methylate** (meth´ilāt) *v.t*. **1** to mix or saturate with methyl alcohol. **2** to introduce a methyl group into. **methylated spirit, methylated spirits** *n*. spirit of wine, mixed with 10% of methyl alcohol so as to be rendered unfit to drink and accordingly not subject to duty. **methylation** (-ā´shən) *n*. **methylbenzene** (-ben´-) *n*. toluene. **methylic** (mithil´ik) *a*.

meticulous (mitik´ūləs) *a*. **1** very careful. **2** cautious or overscrupulous about trivial details, finicky. **meticulously** *adv*. **meticulousness** *n*.

métier (met´iā, mā´-) *n*. **1** trade, profession. **2** an area of activity in which one is skilled, feels comfortable etc., one's forte.

Metonic cycle (miton´ik) *n*. the cycle of 19 Julian years at the end of which the new and full moons recur on the same dates.

metonymy (miton´imi) *n*. (*pl*. **metonymies**) a figure of speech in which one word is used for another with which it is associated, as the effect for the cause, the material for the thing made etc., e.g. 'bench' for 'magistrates'. **metonym** (met´ənim) *n*. a word used metonymically. **metonymic** (-nim´-), **metonymical** *a*. **metonymically** *adv*.

metre[1] (mē´tə), (*esp. N Am*.) **meter** *n*. the standard measure of length in the metric system, orig. the ten-millionth part of the quadrant of a meridian, 39.37 in., now defined as the distance travelled by light in a vacuum in 1/299,792,458 of a second. **metreage** (-tərij) *n*. **metre-kilogram-second** *a*. denoting the metric system of units based on the metre, the kilogram and the second as units of length, mass and time.

Usage note See note under METER[1].

metre[2] (mē´tə), (*esp. N Am*.) **meter** *n*. **1** the rhythmical arrangement of syllables in verse. **2** verse. **3** any particular form of poetic rhythm. **4** the basic rhythm of a piece of music.

Usage note See note under METER[1].

metric (met´rik) *a*. **1** of or relating to the metre as a unit of measurement or the metric system. **2** metrical. ~*n*. **1** a system or basis of measurement. **2** (*Math*.) a function based on distances. **3** (*usu. pl*.) the science or art of metre, prosody. **metrical** *a*. **1** of or relating to or composed in metre. **2** of or relating to measurement. **metrically** *adv*. **metricate** *v.t*. to convert to the metric system. **metrication** (-ā´shən) *n*. **metric hundredweight** *n*. a unit of weight equal to 50 kg. **metricize** (-isīz), **metricise** *v.t*. **metric system** *n*. a system of weights and measures in which units are multiples of ten times the basic units and in which ascending units carry Greek prefixes and descending units Latin prefixes. **metric ton, metric tonne** *n*. a unit of weight equal to 1,000 kg (2,205 lb.).

-metric (met´rik), **-metrical** (-əl) *comb. form* forming adjectives denoting measurement, as in *geometric*. **-metrically** *comb. form* forming adverbs denoting measurement, as in *isometrically*.

metro (met´rō) *n*. (*pl*. **metros**) an underground railway network in a city.

metronome (met´rənōm) *n*. (*Mus*.) an instrument for indicating and marking time in music by means of a pendulum. **metronomic** (-nom´-) *a*.

metropolis (mitrop´əlis) *n*. (*pl*. **metropolises**) **1** the chief town or capital of a country. **2** the seat or see of a metropolitan bishop. **3** a large town or city.

metropolitan (metrəpol´itən) *a*. **1** of or relating to a capital or large city. **2** of or relating to an archbishopric or (ecclesiastical) metropolis. **3** forming part of a sovereign state as distinct from its colonies. ~*n*. **1** an inhabitant of a metropolis. **2** a bishop having authority over other bishops in a province, in the Western Church an archbishop, in the ancient and the modern Greek Church ranking above an archbishop and next to a patriarch. **metropolitan bishop** *n*. **metropolitanism** *n*. **metropolitan magistrate** *n*. a stipendiary magistrate in London.

-metry (mitri) *comb. form* science of measuring, as in *geometry, trigonometry*.

mettle (met´əl) *n*. **1** quality of temperament or disposition. **2** constitutional ardour. **3** spirit, courage. **to put on one's mettle** to test one's courage, determination etc. **mettled,**

mettlesome *a.* high-spirited, fiery, ardent. **mettlesomeness** *n.*

Usage note See note under METAL.

meunière (mœnyeə´) *a.* (of fish) cooked or served in butter with lemon juice and herbs, esp. parsley.

MeV *abbr.* mega-electronvolt.

mew¹ (mū) *v.i.* to make a characteristic high-pitched cry, as a cat or seagull. ~*n.* the cry of the cat or seagull.

mew² (mū), **mew gull** *n.* a kind of seagull, esp. *Larus canus.*

mew³ (mū) *n.* a cage for hawks, esp. whilst moulting. ~*v.t.* 1 to put (a hawk) in a mew or cage. 2 to shut (up), to confine.

mewl (mūl), **mule** *v.i.* 1 to cry, whine or whimper, as a child. 2 to mew, as a cat. **mewler** *n.*

mews (mūz) *n.* 1 stabling, orig. for carriage-horses etc. 2 a row of dwellings, garages etc. converted from such stables; a row of houses built in a similar style.

Mexican (mek´sikən) *a.* of or relating to Mexico. ~*n.* 1 a native or inhabitant of Mexico. 2 Nahuatl, or any other indigenous language of Mexico. **Mexican wave** *n.* an apparent rippling effect passing round a crowd at a sports event etc. caused by people standing up and sitting down in sequence (first observed as a phenomenon at the soccer World Cup finals of 1986 at Mexico City).

mezzanine (mez´ənēn, met´sə-) *n.* 1 a storey intermediate in level between two main storeys, usu. between the ground and first floors. 2 a floor beneath the stage of a theatre from which the traps etc. are worked. 3 (*N Am.*) the dress circle in a theatre. ~*a.* of or relating to unsecured high-interest loans of intermediate status between secured loans and equities.

mezza voce (metsə vō´chi) *a., adv.* (*Mus.*) 1 (singing or sung) softly. 2 quiet(ly).

mezzo (met´sō) *a.* half or medium. ~*n.* (*pl.* mezzos) (*Mus.*) a mezzo-soprano. **mezzo forte** *a., adv.* (*Mus.*) moderately loud(ly). **mezzo piano** *a., adv.* (*Mus.*) moderately soft(ly). **mezzo-relievo** (metsōrəlyä´vō), **mezzo-rilievo** *n.* (*pl.* mezzo-relievos, mezzo-rilievos) half-relief; a sculpture in which the figures stand out from the background to a half of their proportions. **mezzo-soprano** *n.* 1 a female singing voice lower than a soprano and higher than a contralto. 2 a singer with such a voice. 3 a part written for such a voice.

mezzotint (met´sōtint) *n.* 1 a process of engraving in which a copper plate is uniformly roughened so as to print a deep black, tones and half-tones being then produced by scraping away the burr. 2 a print from this. ~*v.t.* to engrave in mezzotint. **mezzotinter** *n.*

MF *abbr.* medium frequency.

mf *abbr.* mezzo forte.

Mg *chem. symbol* magnesium.

mg *abbr.* milligrams.

Mgr. *abbr.* 1 manager. 2 Monseigneur. 3 Monsignor.

MHz *abbr.* megahertz.

MI *abbr.* Military Intelligence.

mi ME².

mi. *abbr.* mile(s).

miaow (miow´), **meow** *n.* the cry of a cat. ~*v.i.* (of a cat) to cry 'miaow'.

miasma (miaz´mə) *n.* (*pl.* miasmata (-tə), miasmas) 1 an infectious or poisonous vapour. 2 an unwholesome atmosphere. **miasmal, miasmatic** (miəzmat´-), **miasmatical, miasmic** *a.* **miasmically** *adv.*

miaul (miowl´) *v.i.* (of a cat) to cry 'miaow'.

mica (mī´kə) *n.* any of a group of silicates having a perfect basal cleavage into thin, tough and shining plates, formerly used instead of glass. **micaceous** (-kā´-) *a.*

mice MOUSE¹.

Michaelmas (mik´əlməs) *n.* the feast of St Michael the Archangel, 29 Sept. **Michaelmas daisy** *n.* any plant of the genus *Aster*, which flowers in the autumn.

mick (mik) *n.* (*sl., often offensive*) 1 an Irishman. 2 a Roman Catholic. **to take the mick** (*coll.*) to tease, to take the mickey out of someone.

mickey (mik´i), **micky** *n.* (*pl.* mickeys, mickies) 1 (*N Am., sl.*) an Irish lad. 2 (*Austral., sl.*) a young wild bull. **to take the mickey out of** to tease, mock, debunk. **mickey-taking** *n.*

Mickey Finn (miki fin´) *n.* (*esp. N Am.*) 1 a doped drink. 2 a narcotic or laxative used in this.

Mickey Mouse (mik´i) *a.* (*coll.*) 1 of poor quality, suitable for play only, as distinct from the real thing. 2 trivial, ridiculous.

mickle (mik´əl), **muckle** (mŭk´əl) *a.* (*chiefly Sc.*) much, great. ~*n.* a large amount.

micro (mī´krō) *n.* (*pl.* micros) 1 (*coll.*) short for MICROCOMPUTER. 2 (*coll.*) short for MICROPROCESSOR.

micro- (mī´krō), **micr-** *comb. form* 1 of or relating to small things (as opposed to large ones). 2 indicating smallness.

microanalysis (mīkrōənal´isis) *n.* (*pl.* microanalyses (-sēz)) the chemical analysis of substances using a very small sample.

microbe (mī´krōb) *n.* any minute organism, esp. a bacterium or microzyme causing disease or fermentation. **microbial** (mīkrō´biəl), **microbian** (-biən), **microbic** (-bik) *a.* **microbiology** (-bīol´-) *n.* **microbiological** (-əloj´-) *a.* **microbiologically** *adv.* **microbiologist** *n.*

microburst (mī´krəbœst) *n.* a particularly strong downward movement of turbulent air, esp. during a thunderstorm.

microchip (mī´krəchip) *n.* a chip of silicon etc. bearing many integrated circuits.

microcircuit (mī´krəsœkit) *n.* a very small integrated circuit on a semiconductor. **microcircuitry** *n.*

microclimate (mī´krəklīmət) *n.* the climate of a

very small area, as distinct from that of the area around. **microclimatic** (-mat´-) a.

microcode (mī´krəkōd) n. 1 a microinstruction. 2 a sequence of microinstructions.

microcomputer (mī´krəkəmpūtə) n. a small computer with one or more microprocessors.

microcosm (mī´krəkozm) n. 1 a representation (of) in miniature form. 2 the universe on a small scale. 3 humankind as an epitome of the macrocosm or universe. 4 a little community. **microcosmic** (-koz´-) a. **microcosmically** adv.

microdot (mī´krədot) n. a photographic image reduced to the size of a dot, e.g. for espionage purposes.

microeconomics (mīkrōēkənom´iks, -ek-) n. the branch of economics concerned with individual commodities, firms etc. and the economic relationships between them. **microeconomic** a.

microelectronics (mīkrōilektron´iks) n. electronics as applied to microcircuits. **microelectronic** a.

microfiche (mī´krəfēsh) n. (pl. **microfiche**, **microfiches**) a sheet of film bearing miniature photographs of documents etc.

microfilm (mī´krəfilm) n. a strip of film on which successive pages of a document or book are photographed for purposes of record. ~v.t. to photograph using microfilm.

microform (mī´krəfawm) n. a method of storing symbolic information using microphotographic techniques.

microgram (mī´krəgram) n. one-millionth of a gram.

micrograph (mī´krəgrahf) n. a very small picture, photograph etc. taken by using a microscope.

microgravity (mī´krəgraviti) n. 1 a state of weak or no gravity. 2 gravitational effects operating in a localized area, e.g. a spacecraft in orbit.

microinstruction (mī´krōinstrŭkshən) n. a computer instruction that activates a particular circuit to execute part of an operation specified by a machine instruction.

microlight (mī´krəlīt) n. a very small light aircraft, usu. for one person.

micromesh (mī´krəmesh) n., a. (material) made of a fine mesh, esp. nylon.

micrometer (mīkrom´itə) n. an instrument used to measure small distances or objects. **micrometry** n.

micrometre (mī´krəmētə), (N Am.) **micrometer** n. one-millionth of a metre, a micron.

microminiaturization (mīkrōminəchərīzā´-shən), **microminiaturisation** n. the production of very small electronic components and circuitry by using integrated circuits.

micron (mī´kron) n. one-millionth of a metre, the unit of length in microscopic research.

Micronesian (mīkrənē´ziən) a. of or relating to Micronesia, a group of small islands in the W Pacific. ~n. 1 a native or inhabitant of Micronesia. 2 the languages spoken in Micronesia.

micronutrient (mīkrōnū´triənt) n. a substance, chemical element etc. required in very small amounts for the survival and development of living organisms.

micro-organism (mīkrōaw´gənizm) n. an organism of microscopic size.

microphone (mī´krəfōn) n. an instrument for converting sound into electrical waves. **microphonic** (-fon´-) a.

microphotography (mīkrōfatog´rəfi) n. the production of microscopic photographs. **microphotograph** (-fō´təgrahf) n.

microprocessor (mīkrōprō´sesə) n. an integrated circuit operating as the central processing unit of a microcomputer.

microprogram (mī´krōprōgram) n. (Comput.) a sequence of microinstructions controlling the central processing unit of a computer.

microscope (mī´krəskōp) n. an optical instrument by which objects are so magnified that details invisible to the naked eye are clearly seen. **microscopic** (-skop´-) a. 1 too small to be visible except by the aid of a microscope. 2 very small. 3 viewed in terms of very small units. 4 microscopical. **microscopical** a. of or relating to the microscope. **microscopically** adv. **microscopy** (-kros´-) n. the use of the microscope. **microscopist** n.

microsecond (mī´krəsekənd) n. one-millionth of a second.

microstructure (mīkrōstrŭk´chə) n. the arrangement of crystals etc. esp. within metals and alloys, as made visible by a microscope.

microsurgery (mī´krəsœjəri) n. surgery performed using a microscope and special small instruments. **microsurgical** a.

microswitch (mī´krəswich) n. a very small electronic switch, operated by very slight movement or pressure.

microtome (mī´krətōm) n. an instrument for cutting thin sections of tissue etc. for microscopic examination.

microtone (mī´krətōn) n. (Mus.) any interval smaller than a semitone.

microtubule (mīkrōtū´būl) n. (Biol.) a very small rigid structure of protein occurring in the cytoplasm of many plants and animal cells.

microwave (mī´krəwāv) n. 1 (coll.) a microwave oven. 2 an electromagnetic wave with a wavelength between 30 cm and 1 mm. ~v.t. to cook in a microwave oven. **microwaveable** (-wā´-), **microwavable** a. **microwave oven** n. an oven that cooks food with microwaves.

micturition (miktürish´ən) n. 1 (Med.) a frequent desire to urinate. 2 the act of urinating. **micturate** (mik´-) v.i. (Med., also formal) to urinate.

mid[1] (mid) prep. (poet.) amid.

mid[2] (mid) a. (superl. **midmost**) middle.

mid- (mid) comb. form 1 middle, medium. 2 that is in the middle of, as in mid-June, mid-calf. **midbrain** (mid´-) n. (Anat.) the central part of the brainstem, the mesencephalon. **midday** *n*. noon, the middle of the day. *~a*. of or relating to noon. **midfield** (mid´fēld, midfēld´) *n*. **1** the central area of a sports pitch, esp. a football pitch. **2** the players with positions between the attackers and defenders, esp. in football. **midfielder** *n*. **midiron** (mid´-) *n*. an iron golf club with a moderate amount of loft. **mid-life** *n*. middle age. **mid-life crisis** *n*. a feeling of panic, loss of self-confidence etc. often experienced at the onset of middle age. **midline** (mid´-) *n*. (*Geom.*) a median line forming the axis of bilateral symmetry. **mid-off** *n*. in cricket, the fieldsman to the left of the bowler (when the batsman is right-handed). **mid-on** *n*. in cricket, the fieldsman to the right of the bowler (when the batsman is right-handed). **midrib** (mid´-) *n*. the central vein of a leaf. **midship** (mid´-) *n*. the middle part of a ship or boat. *~a*. situated in or belonging to this. **midshipman** *n*. (*pl*. **midshipmen**) (*Hist*.) a naval officer ranking between a cadet and a sub lieutenant, a young officer under instruction on a ship. **midships** *adv*. AMIDSHIPS (under AMID). **midstream** *adv*. **1** in the middle of a stream. **2** in the middle of an action or process. *~n*. the middle of a stream. **midsummer** *n*. the middle of summer, esp. the period of the summer solstice, about 21 June. **Midsummer Day, Midsummer's Day** *n*. 24 June. **midsummer madness** *n*. foolish behaviour, esp. associated with summer. **midway** (mid´wā, midwā´) *a*. situated in the middle or the middle of the way. *~adv*. **1** in the middle. **2** halfway. *~n*. (*N Am*.) a fair, a place in a carnival etc. where sideshows are located. **midweek** *n*., *a*., *adv*. (occurring in) the middle of the week, i.e. Tuesday, Wednesday, Thursday. **Midwest** *n*. the N central part of the USA, from Ohio west to the Rocky Mountains. **Midwestern** *a*. **midwicket** *n*. **1** in cricket, a fielding position on the leg side opposite the middle of the playing strip. **2** a person at that position. **midwinter** *n*. the middle of winter, esp. the winter solstice, 21 Dec.

midden (mid´ən) *n*. **1** a dunghill. **2** a refuse tip near a house.

middle (mid´əl) *a*. (*superl*. **middlemost**) **1** placed equally distant from the extremes. **2** intervening, intermediate. **3** average. **4** (of a language) of the period between old and modern. **5** (*Gram*.) (esp. of verbs in Greek) between active and passive, reflexive. *~n*. **1** the point or place equally distant from the extremes. **2** the waist. **3** the midst, the centre. **4** (*Gram*.) the middle voice, a middle verb. *~v.t*. **1** to place in the middle. **2** (*Naut*.) to fold or double in the middle. **3** in football, to pass or return (the ball) to midfield from one of the wings. **4** in cricket, to hit (the ball) with the middle of the bat. **in the middle of** during, while. **middle age** *n*. the period of life between youth and old age (about 45–60), or about the middle of the ordinary human life. **middle-aged** *a*. **middle-age spread, middle-aged spread** *n*. the increased amount of fat at the waist often associated with

middle age. **Middle Ages** *n.pl*. the period from the 5th-15th cents. inclusive in Europe. **Middle America** *n*. **1** the midwestern region of the US. **2** the middle class of the US. **3** Mexico and Central America. **middlebrow** *a*. (*coll*., *derog*.) of moderate intellect and conventional tastes. *~n*. a person with these characteristics. **middle C** *n*. (*Mus*.) on a keyboard, the note C at the centre, between the treble and bass staves. **middle class** *n*. the class between the upper and lower classes, largely consisting of business and professional people and their families. **middle-class** *a*. **middle course** *n*. an action or decision that represents a compromise between possible extremes. **middle distance** *n*. **1** the central portion of a picture between the foreground and the distance. **2** in athletics, a race measuring 800m or 1,500m. **middle ear** *n*. the cavity of the ear behind the drum, containing the malleus, incus and stapes. **Middle East** *n*. the geographical area including SW Asia as far as Afghanistan and parts of N Africa. **Middle Eastern** *a*. **Middle English** *n*. the English language in use from about 1150–1500. **middle finger** *n*. the second finger (third from the little finger inclusive). **middle game** *n*. in chess, the central phase of the game when strategies are developed, as distinct from the opening and the endgame. **middle ground** *n*. **1** in a given issue, the point of view tending to moderation and compromise as opposed to extreme opinions. **2** the people holding this point of view. **middle-income** *a*. **1** of or relating to those people earning average salaries. **2** of or relating to countries with an average national income. **middleman** *n*. (*pl*. **middlemen**) **1** a person through whose hands a commodity passes between the producer and the consumer. **2** an agent, an intermediary. **middle management** *n*. **1** those people responsible for the day-to-day running of a company, organization etc. **2** this level of responsibility. **middle manager** *n*. **middle name** *n*. **1** any name between a person's first given name and their family name. **2** (*coll*.) a person's most typical quality (*Punctuality is his middle name!*). **middle-of-the-road** *a*. **1** moderate, not extreme in political views, tastes etc. **2** (of music) intended to appeal to the widest range of tastes, undemanding to listen to. **middle school** *n*. a school for children between 8 or 9 years of age and 12 or 13 years of age. **middle-sized** *a*. of medium size. **middle way** *n*. a middle course. **middleweight** *n*. **1** a boxer, wrestler, weightlifter etc. in the weight category intermediate between welterweight and (light) heavyweight. **2** this weight category. **Middle West** *n*. the Midwest. **middling** *a*. **1** of middle size, quality or condition. **2** moderately good. **3** mediocre, second-rate. **4** (*coll*.) in moderately good health. *~adv*. moderately, tolerably. **middlingly** *adv*.

Middx. *abbr*. Middlesex.

midge (mij) *n*. **1** a gnat or other minute fly, esp. of the families Chironomidae and Ceratopogonidae. **2** a tiny person. **midget** (-it) *n.* a very small person. *~a.* very small.

MIDI (mid´ĩ) *n.* an electronic system to link musical instruments with computer technology for composition and performance.

midi- (mid´ĩ) *comb. form* **1** of middle size. **2** (of a skirt etc.) reaching to the mid-calf. **midi** (mid´ĩ) *n.* (*pl.* **midis**) a midi-skirt, midi-dress etc. **midi system** *n.* a compact stacking set of hi-fi equipment.

midland (mid´lənd) *a.* **1** situated in the middle or interior of a country. **2** surrounded by land. **3** (**Midland**) of or relating to the central counties of England. *~n.* **1** the interior of a country. **2** (**Midlands**) the midland counties of England.

midnight (mid´nīt) *n.* **1** the middle of the night, twelve o'clock at night. **2** intense darkness. **midnight blue** *a.* very dark blue. *~n.* this colour. **midnight sun** *n.* the sun visible around midnight in summer in the polar regions.

midriff (mid´rif) *n.* **1** the middle part of the front of the body, between waist and chest. **2** the diaphragm. **3** the part of a garment covering the abdomen.

midst (midst) *n.* the middle (now only in idioms below). *~prep.* (*poet.*) in the middle of, amidst. **in our/ your/ their midst** among us, you etc. **in the midst of** among, surrounded by or involved in.

midwife (mid´wīf) *n.* (*pl.* **midwives** (-wīvz)) **1** a person who assists at childbirth. **2** any person who helps to bring about a significant development. **midwifery** (-wifəri) *n.* **midwife toad** *n.* the toad *Alytes obstetricans*, the male of which carries the developing eggs on his hind legs until they hatch.

mien (mēn) *n.* air or manner, appearance, deportment, demeanour, bearing, carriage.

miff (mif) *n.* (*coll.*) **1** a petty quarrel. **2** a huff. *~v.t.* (*usu. in pass.*) to vex, to annoy slightly, to offend (*I was miffed that she ignored me*). **miffy** (-i) *a.* easily upset or annoyed.

might¹ (mīt) *n.* **1** strength, force. **2** power, esp. to enforce will or arbitrary authority. **mighty** *a.* (*comp.* **mightier,** *superl.* **mightiest**) **1** strong, powerful. **2** very great, huge, immense. **3** (*coll.*) great, considerable. *~adv.* (*coll.*) exceedingly, very (*mighty glad to see you*). **mightily** *adv.* **mightiness** *n.*

might² MAY¹.

mignonette (minyənet´) *n.* **1** any annual plant of the genus *Reseda*, esp. *R. odorata*, which has fragrant greenish flowers. **2** the greenish colour of its flowers. **3** a type of fine narrow pillowlace.

migraine (mē´grān, mĩ´-) *n.* a recurrent severe headache, esp. on one side of the head only, often accompanied by nausea and visual disturbances. **migrainous** *a.*

migrate (mīgrāt´) *v.i.* **1** to move permanently from one country, place or habitation to another. **2** (of birds, fishes etc.) to pass from one region to another according to the season. **3** to pass from one part of the body to another. **migrant** (mĩ´-) *n.*,

a. **migration** (-grā´shən) *n.* **migrational** *a.* **migrator** *n.* **migratory** (mĩ´grətəri) *a.*

mihrab (mē´rahb) *n.* a niche etc. in a mosque indicating the direction of Mecca.

mikado (mikah´dō) *n.* (*pl.* **mikados**) (*Hist.*) the emperor of Japan.

mike (mīk) *n.* (*coll.*) short for MICROPHONE.

mil (mil) *n.* **1** a unit of length, a thousandth part of an inch (0.0254 mm), in measuring wire. **2** in pharmacy, a millilitre.

milage MILEAGE (under MILE).

Milanese (milənēz´) *a.* of or relating to Milan. *~n.* (*pl.* **Milanese**) a native or inhabitant of Milan.

milch (milch) *a.* (of a farm animal) giving milk. **milch cow** *n.* **1** a cow kept for milk. **2** a person from whom money is easily obtained.

mild (mīld) *a.* **1** gentle in manners or disposition. **2** tender, pacific, clement, placid, bland, pleasant. **3** (of fruit, liquor etc.) soft, not harsh, sharp or strong. **4** (of beer) not bitter, not strongly flavoured with hops. **5** moderate, not extreme, tame. **6** moderate in degree. **7** (of medicines) operating gently. *~n.* mild beer. **milden** *v.t., v.i.* **mildish** *a.* **mildly** *adv.* **to put it mildly** with understatement. **mild-mannered** *a.* of a gentle disposition. **mildness** *n.* **mild steel** *n.* a tough steel containing a low proportion of carbon.

mildew (mil´dū) *n.* a harmful fungoid growth on plants, cloth, paper, food etc. after exposure to damp. *~v.t.* to taint with mildew. *~v.i.* to be tainted with mildew. **mildewy** *a.*

mile (mīl) *n.* **1** a measure of length or distance, 1760 yds. (1.609 km). **2** a Roman measure of 1000 paces, about 1620 yds. (1.481 km). **3** (*pl., coll.*) a great distance, a large amount. **4** a race over a course one mile long. **mileage** (mĩ´lij), **milage** *n.* **1** the number of miles concerned. **2** an allowance paid for the number of miles travelled. **3** the distance travelled by a vehicle on one gallon or litre of petrol. **4** the benefit to be derived from something. **milepost** *n.* **1** in a race, a post set one mile from the finish. **2** (*N Am., Austral.*) a milestone. **miler** *n.* a person, animal or thing qualified to run or travel a mile, or (*in comb.*) a specified number of miles (as *tenmiler*). **miles** *adv.* (*coll.*) considerably, very much. **miles away** *adv.* lost in thought, daydreaming, preoccupied. **milestone** *n.* **1** a stone set up by a road marking the distance to relevant places. **2** an important point in the life or development of a person, historical phenomenon, project etc. **milometer** (-lom´-), **mileometer** *n.* a device for recording the number of miles travelled by a vehicle.

☒ **milennium** common misspelling of MILLENNIUM.

milfoil (mil´foil) *n.* **1** the yarrow, *Achillea millefolium*, named because the leaves are finely divided. **2** any aquatic plant of the genus *Myriophyllum*, water milfoil.

milieu (mēlyœ´, mē´-) *n.* (*pl.* **milieux**, **milieus** (-yœz)) environment, surroundings, setting.

militant (mil´itənt) *a.* **1** combative, warlike, aggressive. **2** actively engaged in fighting. ~*n.* a militant person. **militancy** *n.* **militantly** *adv.*

military (mil´itəri) *a.* **1** of or relating to soldiers, arms or warfare. **2** soldierly, warlike, martial. **3** engaged in war. ~*n.* **1** (*collect.*) soldiers generally. **2** the army. **militaria** (-teə´riə) *n.pl.* military uniforms, medals etc. of the past that are of interest to collectors. **militarily** *adv.* **militariness** *n.* **militarism** *n.* **1** domination by the spirit of aggression. **2** military or warlike policy. **3** military spirit. **militarist** *n.* **militaristic** (-is´tik) *a.* **militaristically** *adv.* **militarize, militarise** *v.t.* **1** to provide with military equipment. **2** to make military or militaristic. **militarization** (-zā´shən) *n.* **Military Cross, Military Medal** *n.* a British army decoration awarded for conspicuous courage under fire. **military honours** *n.pl.* courtesies paid to a soldier or person of high rank at their funeral, wedding etc. **military police** *n.pl.* a police force for enforcing discipline in the army. **military policeman** *n.* (*pl.* **military policemen**).

militate (mil´itāt) *v.i.* to have weight or influence, to tell (against).

***

Usage note The verbs *militate* and *mitigate* should not be confused: *militate* means to have weight or influence, and *mitigate* to moderate or alleviate. You cannot *mitigate against* anything.

***

militia (milish´ə) *n.* a supplementary military force consisting of the body of citizens not enrolled in the regular army. **militiaman** *n.* (*pl.* **militiamen**).

milk (milk) *n.* **1** the whitish fluid secreted by female mammals for the nourishment of their young. **2** that of the cow, goat or sheep, used as food for humans. **3** the white juice of certain plants or fruits. **4** an emulsion made from herbs, drugs etc. (*milk of magnesia*). ~*v.t.* **1** to draw milk from. **2** to exploit or get money out of (a person) in an underhand or disreputable way. **3** to exploit to the full. **4** to extract venom from. **milk and honey** *n.* prosperity, abundance. **milk and water** *n.* namby-pamby or mawkish talk, sentiment etc. **milk-and-water** *a.* namby-pamby, weak, twaddling. **milk bar** *n.* a snack bar selling milk drinks etc. **milk chocolate** *n.* chocolate made with milk. **milker** *n.* **milk fever** *n.* **1** an illness of female farm animals etc. that have just given birth to young, caused by calcium deficiency. **2** (*Med.*) a fever of women caused by infection after childbirth (formerly thought to be connected with the first secretion of milk). **milk float** *n.* a usu. electrically-propelled vehicle for delivering milk to houses. **milk-loaf** *n.* a loaf of bread made using milk. **milkmaid** *n.* a woman employed in dairy work. **milkman** *n.* (*pl.* **milkmen**) a person who sells milk, usu. by delivering door-to-door. **Milk of Magnesia®** *n.* an antacid stomach medicine consisting of a suspension of hydrated magnesium carbonate. **milk powder** *n.* dehydrated milk in powder

form. **milk pudding** *n.* a pudding made by boiling or baking milk with rice, semolina etc. **milk round** *n.* **1** the route and the delivery points along it for a milkman etc. delivering door-to-door. **2** a regular trip from place to place for selling etc. **milk run** *n.* **1** a routine trip, flight etc. **2** a regular journey to deliver milk. **milk shake** *n.* a drink of milk, flavouring and ice cream, shaken up in a machine. **milksop** *n.* a feeble, spiritless person, usu. a man or youth. **milk sugar** *n.* lactose. **milk tooth** *n.* any of the temporary teeth in young mammals. **milk train** *n.* an early morning train for transporting milk. **milk white** *n.* a white colour similar to that of milk. **milk-white** *a.* **milky** *a.* (*comp.* **milkier,** *superl.* **milkiest**) **1** consisting of, mixed with or resembling milk. **2** (of liquids) white, opaque, clouded. **3** mild, effeminate. **4** timid. **milkily** *adv.* **milkiness** *n.* **Milky Way** *n.* a luminous zone of innumerable stars, stretching across the heavens, being the galaxy of which our solar system is a part.

mill (mil) *n.* **1** a machine for grinding corn to a fine powder. **2** a building with machinery for this purpose. **3** a machine for reducing solid substances of any kind to a finer consistency. **4** a building fitted up with machinery for any industrial purpose, a factory. ~*v.t.* **1** to grind (as corn) in a mill. **2** to produce (flour) by grinding. **3** to serrate the edge of (a coin). '**4** to cut with a rotating tool. **5** to full (cloth). **6** to beat to a froth. ~*v.i.* to move slowly (around). **to go through the mill** to undergo a harrowing, exhausting etc. experience. **to put through the mill** to subject to a harrowing, exhausting etc. experience. **millable** *a.* **millboard** *n.* thick pasteboard used by bookbinders for book covers. **mill-dam** *n.* a wall or dam built across a stream to divert it to a mill. **miller** *n.* **1** a person who keeps or works in a flour mill. **2** a person who mills anything. **3** any of various moths and other insects with white or powdery wings etc., esp. *Apatele leporina.* **miller's thumb** *n.* a small freshwater fish, *Cottus gobio,* the bullhead. **millhand** *n.* a factory worker. **millpond** *n.* a pool of water behind a mill-dam. **like a millpond** (of water) very smooth and still. **mill-race** *n.* **1** the current of water for driving a mill-wheel. **2** the channel that provides this water. **millstone** *n.* **1** either of a pair of circular stones for grinding corn. **2** a very burdensome person or thing. **millstream** *n.* MILL-RACE (under MILL). **mill-wheel** *n.* a large wheel moved by water, flowing over or under it, for driving the machinery in a mill. **millworker** *n.* a factory worker. **millwright** *n.* a person who constructs or repairs the machinery of mills.

millefeuille (mēlfœy´) *n.* a cake of puff pastry filled with jam and cream.

millennium (milen´iəm) *n.* (*pl.* **millenniums, millennia** (-iə)) **1** a period of 1000 years. **2** (*Theol.*) the 1000-year reign of Christ (prophesied in Rev. xx.1–5). **3** a period of general happiness and prosperity. **4** the festival of a thousandth anniversary. **millenarian** (milən-eə´riən) *a.* **1** consisting of 1000 years. **2** of or relating to the millennium. **3** believing in the millennium. ~*n.* a person who believes in the millennium. **millenarianism** *n.* **millenary** *n.* (*pl.* **millenaries**) **1** a period of 1000 years. **2** a festival of a thousandth anniversary. **3** a millenarian. ~*a.* of or relating to a millenary. **millennial** *a.* of or relating to the millennium. ~*n.* a thousandth anniversary. **millennialism** *n.* **millennialist** *n.*

millepede MILLIPEDE.

miller MILL.

millesimal (miles´iməl) *a.* **1** consisting of thousandth parts. **2** of or relating to thousandths. ~*n.* one-thousandth. **millesimally** *adv.*

millet (mil´it) *n.* **1** the cereal plant *Panicum miliaceum.* **2** the nutritive seeds of this plant. **3** any of various other similar species of grasses bearing edible seeds. **millet-grass** *n.* a tall N American grass, *Milium effusum.*

milli- (mil´i) *comb. form* one-thousandth.

milliampere (miliam´peə), **milliamp** (mil´-) *n.* a unit of electrical current equal to one-thousandth of an ampere.

milliard (mil´iahd) *n.* one thousand million.

millibar (mil´ibah) *n.* a unit of atmospheric pressure, one-thousandth of a bar, equivalent to 100 pascals, the pressure exerted by a column of mercury about 0.03 in. (0.762 mm) high.

milligram (mil´igram), **milligramme** *n.* one-thousandth of a gram, 0.0154 of an English grain.

millilitre (mil´ilētə), (*N Am.*) **milliliter** *n.* one-thousandth of a litre, 0.06103 cu. in.

millimetre (mil´imētə), (*N Am.*) **millimeter** *n.* one-thousandth of a metre, 0.03937 in.

milliner (mil´inə) *n.* a person who makes and sells hats for women. **millinery** *n.*

million (mil´yən) *n.* (*pl.* **million, millions**) **1** one thousand thousand. **2** (*pl.* **millions**) an indefinitely great number. **3** a million pounds, dollars etc. ~*a.* amounting to a million. **millionaire** (-neə´) *n.* **1** a person who has a million pounds, francs or dollars. **2** a very rich person. **millionairess** (-neə´res) *n.* **millionfold** *a., adv.* **millionth** *n., a.*

millipede (mil´ipēd), **millepede** *n.* any arthropod of the class Diplopoda, having a cylindrical body made up of many segments, each with two pairs of legs.

millisecond (mil´isekənd) *n.* one-thousandth of a second.

millivolt (mil´ivōlt) *n.* one-thousandth of a volt.

milometer MILE.

milt (milt) *n.* **1** the spleen in mammals. **2** the spermatic organ of a male fish. **3** the soft roe of fishes. **milter** *n.* a male fish that is ready to breed.

mimbar (mim´bah), **minbar** (min´-) *n.* the pulpit of a mosque.

mime (mīm) *n.* **1** communication through facial expression, gesture etc. and without words. **2** a theatrical performance involving this. **3** an actor in mime. **4** a mimic, a clown or buffoon. ~*v.i.* **1** to communicate through facial expression, gesture etc. and without words. **2** to act in mime. ~*v.t.* to mimic. **mime artist** *n.* **mimer** *n.*

mimeograph (mim´iəgrahf) *n.* a duplicating apparatus in which a paraffin-coated sheet is used as a stencil for reproducing written or type-written matter. ~*v.t.* to reproduce by means of this.

mimesis (mimē´sis) *n.* (*Biol.*) mimicry, imitation of or close natural resemblance to the appearance of another animal or of a natural object. **mimetic** (-met´-) *a.* **mimetically** *adv.*

mimic (mim´ik) *n.* a person who mimics. ~*a.* **1** having an aptitude for imitation. **2** imitative. **3** counterfeit. ~*v.t.* (*pres.p.* **mimicking**, *past, p.p.* **mimicked**) **1** to imitate, esp. in order to ridicule. **2** to ape, to copy. **3** (of animals, plants etc.) to resemble closely. **mimicker** *n.* **mimicry** *n.* (*pl.* **mimicries**) **1** mimicking. **2** a thing that mimics another. **3** (*Biol.*) close resemblance (in animals, plants etc.).

mimosa (mimō´sə) *n.* **1** any leguminous shrub of the genus *Mimosa,* including the sensitive plant, *M. pudica.* **2** any of various acacias with yellow flowers.

Min. *abbr.* **1** Minister. **2** Ministry.

min. *abbr.* **1** minim (liquid measure). **2** minimum. **3** minute(s).

mina MYNAH.

minaret (minəret´, min´-) *n.* a lofty slender turret on a mosque, from which the muezzin summons the people to prayers. **minareted** *a.*

minatory (min´ətəri) *a.* threatening, menacing.

minbar MIMBAR.

mince (mins) *v.t.* **1** to cut or chop into very small pieces. **2** to restrain (one's words) for politeness' sake. **3** to utter or pronounce with affected delicacy. ~*v.i.* **1** to walk in a prim and affected manner. **2** to talk with affected elegance. ~*n.* **1** minced meat. **2** mincemeat. **not to mince matters** to speak plainly. **mincemeat** *n.* a filling for pies etc. composed of suet, raisins, currants, candied peel etc. chopped fine. **to make mincemeat of** to crush or destroy completely. **mince pie** *n.* a small pie filled with mincemeat. **mincer** *n.* **mincing** *a.* affectedly elegant. **mincingly** *adv.*

mind (mīnd) *n.* **1** the intellectual powers of a human being, the understanding, the intellect. **2** one's candid opinion (*to speak one's mind*). **3** the soul. **4** recollection, memory (*always on my mind*). **5** sanity (*to lose one's mind*). **6** disposition, liking, way of feeling or thinking. **7** intention, purpose, desire, inclination. **8** mental concentration. **9** a person regarded as an intellect. ~*v.t.* **1** to heed, to regard. **2** to pay attention to, to apply oneself to. **3** to object to (*Do you mind if I smoke?*). **4** to look after (*to mind the shop*). **5** (*Sc., dial.*) to remember. **6** (*N Am., Ir.*) to obey. ~*v.i.* to take care, to be on the watch. **don't mind me** (*usu. iron.*) do as you please, irrespective of my feelings, opinions etc. **do you mind?** used to express irritation at a person's inconsiderate behaviour. **in two minds** unable to choose between alternatives, undecided. **mind out** watch out (for), be careful. **mind you** (*coll.*) used to qualify a previous statement (*I finished work early*; *mind you, I had done twice the usual amount*). **never mind** used to console someone. **never you mind** used to rebut a prying question. **to bring/ call to mind** to recall. **to close one's mind** to refuse to consider something, often unreasonably. **to come into someone's mind 1** to be remembered. **2** to form as an idea. **to come to mind** to occur to one, to suggest itself. **to have a good mind** to be inclined (to). **to have (half) a mind** to be inclined (to). **to have in mind** to intend. **to one's mind** in one's opinion. **to open one's mind** to give thought (to something previously unconsidered or rejected). **to put in mind** to remind (of). **to put out of one's mind** to stop thinking about. **to put/ set someone's mind at rest** to reassure (someone). **to set one's mind on** to be determined to have or do. **to shut one's mind to** to refuse to or pretend not to think about. **to spring to mind** to come suddenly to mind. **mind-bending** *a.* altering one's state of mind (esp. of drugs). **mind-blowing** *a.* **1** confusing, amazing. **2** of or inducing a state like that produced by psychedelic drugs. **mind-boggling** *a.* (*coll.*) amazing, astonishing. **minded** *a.* (*usu. in comb.*) of a certain disposition or way of thinking (*evil-minded*). **minder** *n.* **1** a person whose job is to look after something or somebody. **2** (*coll.*) a bodyguard. **mind-expanding** *a.* producing a sense of heightened or broader perception, psychedelic. **mindful** *a.* attentive, heedful (of). **mindfully** *adv.* **mindfulness** *n.* **mindless** *a.* **1** done for no reason. **2** done without need for thought. **3** heedless, regardless, stupid. **mindlessly** *adv.* **mindlessness** *n.* **mind-numbing** *a.* (*coll.*) causing extreme boredom. **mind-numbingly** *adv.* **mind of one's own** *n.* an ability to think independently, an inclination to take a different course from the usual. **mind-reader** *n.* a person who claims to know what others are thinking. **mind-read** *v.t.* **mind-reading** *n.* **mindset** *n.* a fixed attitude of mind.

mine[1] (mīn) *pron.* something which belongs to or is associated with me. ~**†a.** my (used before vowels and sometimes *h*) (*mine host*). **of mine** belonging or relating to me.

mine[2] (mīn) *v.t.* **1** to dig into or burrow in. **2** to obtain by excavating in the earth. **3** to make by digging. **4** to undermine, to sap. **5** to set with (explosive) mines. ~*v.i.* to dig a mine, to engage in digging for ore etc. ~*n.* **1** an excavation in the earth for the purpose of obtaining minerals. **2** a receptacle filled with explosive, floating in the sea or buried in the ground, which is exploded by contact. **3** a rich source of wealth, or of information etc. **4** an excavation under an enemy's works for blowing them up, formerly to form a means of entering or to cause a collapse of the wall etc. **5** a rich deposit of minerals suitable for

mining. **mine-detector** *n.* an instrument for detecting explosive mines. **minefield** *n.* **1** an area of ground in which large quantities of landmines are set. **2** an area of concern where mistakes are easily made, a potentially dangerous situation. **miner** *n.* **1** a person who digs for minerals. **2** a person who works in mines. **3** a soldier employed to lay mines. **4** a burrowing larva or insect. **mine shaft** *n.* a shaft (usu. vertical) giving access to a mine. **minesweeper** *n.* a vessel employed to clear mines laid by the enemy. **mineworker** *n.* a person who works in a mine, esp. a coal miner. **mining** *n.*

mineral (min´ərəl) *n.* **1** an inorganic body, homogeneous in structure, with a definite chemical composition, found in the earth. **2** any inorganic substance found in the ground. **3** mineral water, lemonade etc. ~*a.* **1** of, relating to or consisting of minerals. **2** impregnated with mineral matter. **mineralogy** (-al´əji) *n.* the science of minerals, their nature and properties. **mineralogical** (-əloj´-) *a.* **mineralogically** *adv.* **mineralogist** *n.* **mineral oil** *n.* **1** any oil derived from minerals. **2** (*NAm.*) liquid paraffin. **mineral water** *n.* **1** water naturally impregnated with mineral matter. **2** an artificial imitation of this, esp. soda water. **3** any effervescent soft drink. **mineral wax** *n.* ozocerite. **mineral wool** *n.* a fibrous packing material made from inorganic substances.

minestrone (ministrō´ni) *n.* a thick soup of mixed vegetables with pasta or rice.

mingle (ming´gəl) *v.t.* **1** to mix up together. **2** to come into close association (with). ~*v.i.* to be mixed, blended or united (with). **to mingle with** to go among (a group of people). **mingler** *n.* **minglingly** *adv.*

mingy (min´ji) *a.* (*comp.* **mingier**, *superl.* **mingiest**) (*coll.*) mean, stingy. **mingily** *adv.* **minginess** *n.*

mini (min´i) *n.* (*pl.* **minis**) **1** (*coll.*) a miniskirt. **2** (**Mini**) a small car.

mini- (min´i) *comb. form* smaller than the usual size.

miniature (min´əchə) *n.* **1** a small-sized painting, esp. a portrait on ivory, vellum etc., orig. a small picture in an illuminated manuscript. **2** anything smaller than the normal size. **3** the art of painting on a small scale. ~*a.* **1** smaller than the norm. **2** represented on a very small scale. **in miniature** on a small scale. **miniaturist** *n.* **miniaturize, miniaturise** *v.t.* **miniaturization** (-zā´shən) *n.*

minibar (min´ibah) *n.* a selection of drinks placed in a hotel room for guests' possible use.

minibus (min´ibŭs) *n.* (*pl.* **minibuses**, (*N Am.*) **minibusses**) a small bus for 12 passengers.

minicab (min´ikab) *n.* a taxi that can be ordered by telephone, but may not cruise in search of passengers.

minicomputer (min´ikəmpūtə) *n.* a computer of medium capacity and power.

minigolf (min´igolf) *n.* a small version of the game of golf, played on a lawn etc.

minim (min´im) *n.* **1** (*Mus.*) a note of the value of two crotchets or half a semibreve. **2** a fluid measure, one sixtieth of a drachm (0.059 g), about equal to one drop. **3** a downstroke in writing.

minimal (min´iməl) *a.* **1** least possible. **2** smallest, very small. **3** of, relating to or being a minimum. **minimalism** *n.* music, art, design etc. using a few simple elements to achieve maximum effect. **minimalist** *n.* **1** a person who practises minimalism. **2** a person ready to accept the minimal course of action, policy etc. ~*a.* of or relating to minimalism or minimalists. **minimally** *adv.*

minimize (min´imīz), **minimise** *v.t.* **1** to reduce to the smallest possible amount or degree. **2** to belittle, to underestimate, to downplay. **minimization** (-zā´shən) *n.* **minimizer** *n.*

minimum (min´iməm) *n.* (*pl.* **minimums**, **minima** (-mə)) the smallest amount or degree possible or usual. ~*a.* least possible. **minimum wage** *n.* the rate of wages established by law or collective bargaining below which workers cannot be employed.

minion (min´yən) *n.* (*derog.*) a servile dependant.

minipill (min´ipil) *n.* a low-dose oral contraceptive pill without oestrogen.

miniscule MINUSCULE.

miniseries (min´isiəriz) *n.* (*pl.* **miniseries**) a short series of television programmes.

miniskirt (min´iskœt) *n.* a skirt with the hem far above the knees.

minister (min´istə) *n.* **1** (*also* **Minister**) a person entrusted with the direction of a state department. **2** the pastor of a church, esp. a Nonconformist one. **3** a person representing their government with another state, an ambassador. **4** a person charged with the performance of a duty, or the execution of a will etc. ~*v.i.* **1** to render aid, service or attendance. **2** to contribute, to be conducive (to). **3** to serve as minister. **ministerial** (-tiə´-) *a.* **1** of or relating to a minister of state or of religion. **2** of or relating to a ministry. **3** subsidiary, instrumental. **ministerially** *adv.* **Minister of State** *n.* a junior minister in a government department. **Minister of the Crown** *n.* a government minister of Cabinet status. **ministership** *n.* **Minister without Portfolio** *n.* a government minister of Cabinet status, but without specific departmental responsibilities. **ministrable** *a.* **ministrant** *n.*, *a.* **ministration** (-trā´shən) *n.* **1** (*usu. in pl.*) an act of assistance or service. **2** the action of ministering. **ministrative** (min´istrətiv) *a.* **ministry** *n.* (*pl.* **ministries**) **1** (*also* **Ministry**) **a** a government department. **b** the building or offices of a government department. **2** the ministers of state or of religion collectively. **3** the occupation or calling of a minister of religion. **4** the period of tenure of a minister. **5** the act of ministering, administration.

✗ miniture common misspelling of MINIATURE.

mink (mingk) *n.* **1** either of two amphibious stoatlike animals of the genus *Mustela*, esteemed for their fur. **2** their fur. **3** a coat or jacket made of this. ~*a.* of this fur.

minke (ming´kə, -ki) *n.* a small whale, *Balaenoptera acutorostrata*.

minnow (min´ō) *n.* **1** a small fish of the carp family common all over Europe, *Phoxinus phoxinus*. **2** any tiny fish. **3** an insignificant person or thing.

Minoan (minō´ən) *a.* of or relating to ancient Crete or its people or the Bronze Age civilization of which it was the centre. ~*n.* **1** an inhabitant of ancient Crete or the Minoan world. **2** the language of the Minoans.

minor (mī´nə) *a.* **1** less, smaller (not used with *than*). **2** petty, comparatively unimportant. **3** (*Mus.*) **a** less by a semitone than the major. **b** (of a scale) having a semitone above the second, fifth and seventh note. **c** (of a key) based on a minor scale. **4** denoting the younger of two brothers in a (public) school. **5** under age. ~*n.* **1** a person under legal age. **2** (*Mus.*) a minor key or a composition or strain in this. **3** (*N Am.*) a subsidiary subject or course of study. ~*v.i.* (*N Am.*) to pursue study (in) as a subsidiary subject. **in a minor key** conducted or passed quietly or uneventfully. **minor canon** *n.* a cleric, not a member of the chapter, assisting in the daily service at a cathedral. **minority** (-nor´-) *n.* (*pl.* **minorities**) **1** the smaller number, esp. the smaller of a group or party voting together in an election, on a bill etc. **2** the number of votes constituting this. **3** a distinct cultural etc. group within a larger society. **4** the state of being under legal age. **5** the period of this. **in the minority** in the state of being outnumbered. **minor league** *n.* (*N Am.*) a league of professional baseball or football clubs other than a major league. **minor term** *n.* (*Logic*) the subject of the conclusion of a categorical syllogism.

minster (min´stə) *n.* **1** a cathedral or other large and important church. **2** the church of a monastery.

minstrel (min´strəl) *n.* **1** any of a class of men in the Middle Ages who lived by singing and reciting, a travelling gleeman, musician, performer or entertainer. **2** any of a troupe of entertainers with blackened faces. **minstrelsy** *n.* (*pl.* **minstrelsies**)

mint¹ (mint) *n.* **1** a place where money is coined, usu. under state authority. **2** a source of invention or fabrication. **3** a great quantity, supply or amount. ~*v.t.* **1** to make (coin by stamping metal). **2** to invent, to coin (a phrase etc.). ~*a.* (of a book, coin etc.) in its unused state, as new. **in mint condition** as perfect as when first produced. **minter** *n.*

mint² (mint) *n.* **1** any plant of the aromatic genus *Mentha*, many of which are used for flavouring, esp. spearmint, *M. spicata*. **2** a sweet or lozenge with a peppermint flavour. **mint julep** *n.* a sweet alcoholic drink of bourbon, sugar and pounded ice flavoured with mint. **mint sauce** *n.* mint chopped up with vinegar and sugar, used as a sauce with roast lamb. **minty** *a.* (*comp.* **mintier**, *superl.* **mintiest**).

minuet (minūet´) *n.* **1** a slow stately dance in triple time. **2** (*Mus.*) music for this or in the same time or style. *~v.i.* (*pres.p.* **minueting**, *past*, *p.p.* **minueted**) to dance a minuet.

minus (mī´nəs) *a.*, *prep.* **1** less by, with the deduction of. **2** (*coll.*) short of, lacking. **3** (*Math.*) negative. **4** (*Physics*) having a negative electrical charge. *~n.* (*pl.* **minuses**) **1** a minus sign. **2** a negative quantity. **3** a deficit, a disadvantage. **minus sign** *n.* the sign of subtraction (-).

minuscule (min´əskūl), **miniscule** *a.* **1** very small. **2** of or relating to a cursive script of the 7th 9th cents. **3** lower case. *~n.* **1** a cursive script of the 7th 9th cents. **2** a small or lower-case letter. **3** anything very small. **minuscular** (minŭs´-) *a.*

minute¹ (min´it) *n.* **1** the 60th part of an hour. **2** a very small portion of time, an instant (*I will only be a minute*). **3** an exact point of time (*timed to the minute*). **4** (*coll.*) the present time. **5** the 60th part of a degree of angular distance. **6** (*pl.*) official records of proceedings of a committee etc. **7** an official memorandum of a court or other authority. *~v.t.* **1** to take a note of. **2** to write minutes of. **3** to send minutes to. **4** to time to the exact minute. **just a minute 1** (*coll.*) used to ask someone to wait for a short time. **2** (*coll.*) used as a prelude to a query or objection. **up to the minute** very modern. **wait a minute** (*coll.*) just a minute. **minute-gun** *n.* a gun fired at intervals of one minute as a signal of distress or mourning. **minute hand** *n.* the hand pointing to minutes on a clock or watch. **minute steak** *n.* a thin steak that can be cooked quickly.

minute² (mīnūt´) *a.* (*superl.* **minutest**) **1** very small. **2** petty, trifling. **3** particular, exact, precise. **minutely** *adv.* **minuteness** *n.*

minutia (minū´shiə, mī-) *n.* (*pl.* **minutiae** (-iē)) (*usu. in pl.*) a small and precise or trivial particular.

minx (mingks) *n.* a flirtatious, pert or scheming young woman.

Miocene (mī´əsēn) *a.* (*Geol.*) denoting the middle division of the Tertiary strata or period. *~n.* this division.

MIPS (mips) *n.* (*Comput.*) a unit of computing speed, equal to a million instructions per second.

mirabelle (mirəbel´) *n.* **1** a European plum tree, *Prunus institia*, bearing small firm yellow fruit. **2** the fruit of this tree. **3** a liqueur made from this fruit.

miracle (mir´əkəl) *n.* **1** a marvellous event or act attributed to a supernatural agency. **2** an extraordinary occurrence. **3** an extraordinary example (of). **miracle play** *n.* a medieval dramatic representation, usu. dealing with historical or traditional events in the life of Christ or of the Saints. **miraculous** (-rak´ū-) *a.* **miraculously** *adv.* **miraculousness** *n.*

mirage (mirahzh´) *n.* **1** an optical illusion by which images of distant objects are seen as if inverted, esp. in a desert where the inverted sky appears as a sheet of water. **2** an illusory thing, a delusion.

MIRAS (mī´ras), **Miras** *abbr.* mortgage interest relief at source.

mire (mīə) *n.* **1** an extent of wet, clayey soil, swampy ground, a bog. **2** mud, dirt. *~v.t.* **1** to plunge in a mire. **2** to involve in difficulties. *~v.i.* to sink in a mire.

mirk MURK.

mirror (mir´ə) *n.* **1** an appliance with a polished surface for reflecting images. **2** a looking-glass. **3** anything that reflects objects. **4** an exemplar, a pattern, a model. *~v.t.* to reflect in or as in a mirror. **mirror finish** *n.* a shiny, reflective surface. **mirror image** *n.* **1** an image as observed in a mirror. **2** an object that corresponds to another in this way. **mirror writing** *n.* handwriting from right to left, as if reflected in a mirror.

mirth (mœth) *n.* merriment, jollity, gaiety, hilarity. **mirthful** *a.* **mirthfully** *adv.* **mirthfulness** *n.* **mirthless** *a.* **mirthlessly** *adv.* **mirthlessness** *n.*

MIS *abbr.* (*Comput.*) management information systems.

mis-¹ (mis) *pref.* wrongly, badly, amiss, unfavourably.

mis-² (mis), **miso-** (mi´sō, mī´-) *comb. form* dislike, hatred.

misaddress (misədres´) *v.t.* **1** to direct (a letter etc.) to the wrong address. **2** to address (a person) incorrectly.

misadventure (misədven´chə) *n.* **1** an unlucky chance or accident. **2** bad luck.

misalign (misəlīn´) *v.t.* to align wrongly. **misalignment** *n.*

misalliance (misəlī´əns) *n.* an improper alliance, esp. by marriage. **misally** *v.t.* (*3rd pers. sing. pres.* **misallies**, *pres.p.* **misallying**, *past*, *p.p.* **misallied**)

misandry (mis´əndri) *n.* a hatred of men.

misanthrope (mis´ənthrōp, miz´-) *n.* **1** a hater of humankind. **2** a person who avoids fellow human beings. **misanthropic** (-throp´-), **misanthropical** *a.* **misanthropist** (-an´-) *n.* **misanthropy** (-an´-) *n.*

misapply (misəplī´) *v.t.* (*3rd pers. sing. pres.* **misapplies**, *pres.p.* **misapplying**, *past*, *p.p.* **misapplied**) to apply wrongly. **misapplication** (-aplikā´shən) *n.*

misapprehend (misaprihend´) *v.t.* to misunderstand. **misapprehension** *n.* **misapprehensive** *a.*

misappropriate (misəprō´priāt) *v.t.* to apply to a wrong use or purpose (esp. funds to one's own use). **misappropriation** (-ā´shən) *n.*

misbegotten (misbigot´ən) *a.* **1** illegitimate. **2** badly planned, designed etc. **3** disreputable.

misbehave (misbihāv´) *v.i.* to behave badly or improperly. **misbehaviour** (-yə) *n.*

miscalculate (miskal´kūlāt) *v.t.* to calculate wrongly. **miscalculation** (-lā´shən) *n.*

miscall (miskawl´) *v.t.* to call by a wrong or unsuitable name.

miscarry (miskar´i) *v.i.* (*3rd pers. sing. pres.* **miscarries**, *pres.p.* **miscarrying**, *past, p.p.* **miscarried**) 1 to have a miscarriage. 2 to fail, to be unsuccessful. 3 to be carried to the wrong place. **miscarriage** (miskar´ij, mis´-) *n.* the spontaneous premature expulsion of a foetus before it can survive outside the womb. **miscarriage of justice** *n.* a mistake or wrong committed by a court of justice.

miscast (miskahst´) *v.t.* (*past, p.p.* **miscast**) to cast (a play or an actor) inappropriately.

miscegenation (misijinā´shən) *n.* intermarriage or interbreeding between people of different races.

miscellaneous (misələ´niəs) *a.* 1 consisting of several kinds, mixed, multifarious, diversified. 2 various, many-sided. **miscellaneously** *adv.* **miscellaneousness** *n.* **miscellany** (-sel´əni) *n.* (*pl.* **miscellanies**) a mixture of various kinds, a medley, a number of compositions on various subjects in one volume.

mischance (mischahns´) *n.* misfortune, bad luck.

mischief (mis´chif) *n.* 1 irritating action or conduct that is non-malicious, esp. pranks, practical jokes etc. 2 harm, injury, damage. 3 a person who is mischievous. **to do someone a mischief** to wound or kill a person. **to get up to mischief** to make mischief. **to make mischief** to cause trouble or ill-feeling. **mischief-maker** *n.* a person who stirs up trouble, ill-feeling etc. esp. by gossip. **mischief-making** *n.*, *a.* **mischievous** (mis´chivəs) *a.* 1 (of a child) full of pranks, continually in mischief. 2 making mischief, causing or intending to cause harm. 3 slightly malicious. **mischievously** *adv.* **mischievousness** *n.*

Usage note *Mischievous* should not be spelt or pronounced as *mischievious*.

miscible (mis´ibəl) *a.* capable of being mixed (with). **miscibility** (-bil´-) *n.*

misconceive (miskənsēv´) *v.t.* to have a wrong idea of, to misapprehend. **misconceived** *a.* **misconceiver** *n.* **misconception** (-sep´-) *n.*

misconduct (miskon´dŭkt) *n.* 1 improper conduct, esp. adultery. 2 mismanagement.

misconstrue (miskənstroo´) *v.t.* (*3rd pers. sing. pres.* **misconstrues**, *pres.p.* **misconstruing**, *past, p.p.* **misconstrued**) 1 to put a wrong interpretation or construction upon. 2 to mistake the meaning of. **misconstruction** (-strŭk´-) *n.*

miscopy (miskop´i) *v.t.* (*3rd pers. sing. pres.* **miscopies**, *pres.p.* **miscopying**, *past, p.p.* **miscopied**) to copy incorrectly.

miscount[1] (miskownt´) *v.t.* 1 to count wrongly. 2 to estimate or regard wrongly.

miscount[2] (mis´kownt) *n.* a mistake in counting, esp. of votes.

miscreant (mis´kriənt) *n.* a vile wretch, a scoundrel. ~*a.* depraved, vile, villainous. **miscreance, †miscreancy** *n.*

miscue (miskū´) *n.* in billiards, snooker etc., failure to strike a ball properly with the cue. ~*v.i.* (*3rd pers. sing. pres.* **miscues**, *pres.p.* **miscuing**, *past, p.p.* **miscued**) to make a miscue.

misdate (misdāt´) *v.t.* to date wrongly.

misdeal (misdēl´) *v.t.* (*past, p.p.* **misdealt** (-delt´)) to deal wrongly (as cards). ~*v.i.* to make a misdeal. ~*n.* a wrong or false deal.

misdeed (misdēd´) *n.* an evil deed, a crime.

misdemeanour (misdimē´nə), (*N Am.*) **misdemeanor** *n.* 1 misbehaviour, misconduct. 2 (*Law*) an indictable offence of less gravity than a felony. **misdemeanant** *n.*

misdescribe (misdiskrīb´) *v.t.* to describe wrongly. **misdescription** (-skrip´shən) *n.*

misdiagnose (misdī´əgnōz) *v.t.* to diagnose incorrectly. **misdiagnosis** (-nō´sis) *n.*

misdial (misdī´əl) *v.t., v.i.* (*pres.p.* **misdialling**, (*N Am.*) **misdialing**, *past, p.p.* **misdialled**, (*N Am.*) **misdialed**) to dial (a telephone number) incorrectly.

misdirect (misdirekt´, -dī-) *v.t.* 1 to direct (a person, letter etc.) wrongly. 2 to instruct wrongly (as a judge etc.). **misdirection** *n.*

misdivision (misdivizh´ən) *n.* wrong or erroneous division.

misdoing (misdoo´ing) *n.* a misdeed, a wrong action.

miser (mī´zə) *n.* 1 a person who denies themselves the comforts of life for the sake of hoarding. 2 an avaricious person. **miserly** *a.* **miserliness** *n.*

miserable (miz´ərəbəl) *a.* 1 very wretched or unhappy, distressed. 2 causing misery, distressing. 3 sorry, despicable, worthless. 4 very poor or mean. 5 (*Sc., Austral., New Zeal.*) stingy, mean. **miserableness** *n.* **miserably** *adv.*

miserere (mizəree´ri) *n.* 1 a prayer or cry for mercy. 2 a misericord.

misericord (mizer´ikawd) *n.* a bracketed projection on the underside of the seat of a choir stall, to allow a person standing to rest.

misery (miz´əri) *n.* (*pl.* **miseries**) 1 great unhappiness or wretchedness of mind or body. 2 affliction, poverty. 3 (*coll.*) an ill-tempered, gloomy person. 4 a cause of misery. **to put out of one's misery** 1 to release (an animal etc.) from suffering, esp. by killing. 2 to release (someone) from the suspense of waiting.

misfeasance (misfē´zəns) *n.* (*Law*) a trespass, a wrong, esp. negligent or improper performance of a lawful act.

misfield[1] (misfēld´) *v.t.* to field (a cricket ball, baseball etc.) badly.

misfield[2] (mis´fēld) *n.* an act of misfielding a cricket ball, baseball etc.

misfire (misfīə´) *n.* 1 failure to go off or explode

(of a gun, charge etc.). **2** in a motor vehicle engine, failure to fire in the correct ignition sequence. ~*v.i.* **1** to fail to go off. **2** to fail to achieve the intended effect. **3** (of a motor vehicle engine) to fail to fire correctly.

misfit (mis´fit) *n.* **1** a bad fit. **2** a garment that does not fit properly. **3** an awkward person.

misfortune (misfaw´chən) *n.* **1** bad luck, calamity. **2** a mishap, a disaster.

misgive (misgiv´) *v.t.* (*past* **misgave** (-gāv´), *p.p.* **misgiven** (-giv´ən)) (*impers.*) to fill (one's mind) with doubt or suspicion. **misgiving** *n.* a doubt, a suspicion.

misgovern (misgŭv´ən) *v.t.* **1** to govern badly. **2** to administer unfaithfully. **misgovernment** *n.*

misguided (misgī´did) *a.* mistaken in thought, foolish. **misguidance** *n.* **misguide** *v.t.* **1** to guide wrongly. **2** to lead astray. **misguidedly** *adv.* **misguidedness** *n.*

mishandle (mis·han´dəl) *v.t.* **1** to deal with (a matter etc.) ineffectively or incorrectly. **2** to handle roughly, to ill-treat.

mishap (mis´hap) *n.* **1** an unfortunate accident, a mischance. **2** bad luck.

❌ **mishape** common misspelling of MISSHAPE.

mishear (mis·hiə´) *v.t.* (*past, p.p.* **misheard** (-hœd´)) to hear incorrectly.

mishit[1] (mis·hit´) *v.t.* (*pres.p.* **mishitting**, *past, p.p.* **mishit**) to hit wrongly.

mishit[2] (mis´hit) *n.* an instance of hitting wrongly.

mishmash (mish´mash) *n.* a hotchpotch, a jumble.

misidentify (misīden´tifī) *v.t.* (*3rd pers. sing. pres.* **misidentifies**, *pres.p.* **misidentifying**, *past, p.p.* **misidentified**) to identify wrongly. **misidentification** (-fikā´shən) *n.*

misinform (misinfawm´) *v.t.* to give erroneous information to. **misinformation** (-ā´shən) *n.*

misinterpret (misintœ´prit) *v.t.* (*pres.p.* **misinterpreting**, *past, p.p.* **misinterpreted**) **1** to interpret wrongly. **2** to draw a wrong conclusion from. **misinterpretation** (-ā´shən) *n.* **misinterpreter** *n.*

misjudge (misjŭj´) *v.t.* **1** to form an erroneous opinion of. **2** to judge erroneously. **misjudgement, misjudgment** *n.*

miskey (miskē´) *v.t.* (*3rd pers. sing. pres.* **miskeys**, *pres.p.* **miskeying**, *past, p.p.* **miskeyed**) to enter (data) wrongly from a keyboard.

miskick[1] (miskik´) *v.t.* to kick (a ball) badly.

miskick[2] (mis´kik) *n.* an instance of miskicking a ball.

mislay (mislā´) *v.t.* (*past, p.p.* **mislaid**) **1** to put in a wrong place or in a place that cannot be remembered. **2** (*euphem.*) to lose.

mislead (mislēd´) *v.t.* (*past, p.p.* **misled** (-led´)) **1** to deceive, to delude. **2** to cause to go wrong, esp. in conduct. **misleader** *n.* **misleading** *a.* **misleadingly** *adv.* **misleadingness** *n.*

mismanage (misman´ij) *v.t., v.i.* to manage badly or wrongly. **mismanagement** *n.*

mismatch[1] (mismach´) *v.t.* to match unsuitably.

mismatch[2] (mis´mach) *n.* an unsuitable match.

mismeasure (mismezh´ə) *v.t.* **1** to measure wrongly. **2** to estimate wrongly. **mismeasurement** *n.*

misname (misnām´) *v.t.* to call by a wrong or unsuitable name.

misnomer (misnō´mə) *n.* **1** a mistaken or misapplied name or designation. **2** an incorrect term.

miso (mē´sō) *n.* a food paste made from soya beans fermented in brine, used for flavouring.

miso- MIS-[2].

misogamy (misog´əmi, mī-) *n.* hatred of marriage. **misogamist** *n.*

misogyny (misoj´əni, mī-) *n.* hatred of women. **misogynist** *n.* **misogynistic** (-ist´ik) *a.* **misogynous** *a.*

❌ **mispell** common misspelling of MISSPELL.

mispickel (mis´pikəl) *n.* a mineral composed of iron, arsenic and sulphur, arsenical pyrites.

misplace (misplās´) *v.t.* **1** to mislay. **2** to set on or devote to an undeserving object (*misplaced affection*). **misplacement** *n.*

misplay (misplā´) *v.t.* to play (a card, ball etc.) wrongly or ineffectively. ~*n.* wrong or foul play.

misprint[1] (misprint´) *v.t.* to print incorrectly.

misprint[2] (mis´print) *n.* a mistake in printing.

misprision (misprizh´ən) *n.* **1** (*Law*) an offence involving the concealment or neglect of one's knowledge of a crime. **2** a wrong act. **misprision of treason, misprision of a felony** *n.* concealment of treason or felony without actual participation.

mispronounce (misprənowns´) *v.t.* to pronounce wrongly. **mispronunciation** (-nŭnsiā´shən) *n.*

mispunctuate (mispŭngk´chuāt) *v.t., v.i.* to punctuate wrongly. **mispunctuation** (-ā´shən) *n.*

misquote (miskwōt´) *v.t.* to quote erroneously. **misquotation** (-tā´shən) *n.*

misread (misrēd´) *v.t.* (*past, p.p.* **misread** (-red´)) **1** to read incorrectly. **2** to misinterpret.

misremember (misrimem´bə) *v.t.* to remember imperfectly.

misreport (misripawt´) *v.t.* to report wrongly. ~*n.* a false report.

misrepresent (misreprizent´) *v.t.* to represent falsely or incorrectly. **misrepresentation** (-tā´shən) *n.* **misrepresentative** *n., a.*

misrule (misrool´) *n.* **1** bad government. **2** disorder, confusion, tumult, riot. ~*v.t.* to rule incompetently, misgovern.

miss[1] (mis) *v.t.* **1** to fail to reach, hit, meet, perceive, find, or obtain. **2** to fall short of, to let slip, to overlook. **3** to fail to understand. **4** to omit. **5** to escape, to dispense with. **6** to feel or perceive the lack or absence of. ~*v.i.* **1** to fail to hit the mark. **2** to misfire. **3** to be unsuccessful. ~*n.* **1** a failure to hit, reach, obtain etc. **2** (*coll.*) a miscarriage (of a foetus). **not to miss a trick** to be alert, esp. to any possible opportunity, advantage etc. **not to miss much** to be alert and astute. **to be**

missing to lack (something, esp. an integral part). **to give a miss** not to take an opportunity to see, visit, enjoy etc. (something). **to go missing** to disappear or be lost. **to miss out 1** to omit. **2** to fail to receive or enjoy. **to miss the boat** to miss an opportunity, to be too late. **missable** *a.* **missing** *a.* **missing link** *n.* **1** something required to complete a series. **2** a hypothetical form connecting types that are probably related, as humans and the anthropoid apes.

miss² (mis) *n.* (*pl.* **misses**) **1** a title of address for an unmarried woman or girl. **2** (*coll., usu. derog. or facet.*) a girl. **3** used before the name of a place, activity etc. to refer to a young woman who represents that place, activity etc., often in beauty contests. **missy** *n.* (*coll.*) a form of address to a young woman or little girl, usu. affectionately or scathingly.

missal (mis'əl) *n.* **1** in the Roman Catholic Church, the book containing the service of the Mass for the whole year. **2** a medieval illuminated manuscript book of prayers.

missel thrush MISTLE THRUSH.

misshape (mis-shāp') *v.t.* (*p.p.* **misshapen** (-shā'pən)) **1** to give a bad shape to. **2** to deform. **misshapen** *a.* **misshapenly** *adv.* **misshapenness** *n.*

missile (mis'īl) *n.* a weapon or other object projected or propelled through the air, esp. a rocket-propelled weapon, often with a nuclear warhead. **missilery** (-ri), **missilry** *n.*

mission (mish'ən) *n.* **1** the commission, charge or office of a messenger, agent etc. **2** a person's appointed or chosen end, a vocation. **3** a body of persons sent on a diplomatic errand, an embassy or legation. **4** a task, goal etc. assigned to a person, group etc. **5** a body of missionaries established in a district at home or sent to a foreign country to spread religious teaching. **6** their field of work. **7** a missionary station. **8** a series of special services for rousing spiritual interest. **missionary** (-əri) *a.* of or relating to missions, esp. those of a religious nature. ~*n.* (*pl.* **missionaries**) a person sent to carry on such work. **missionary position** *n.* (*coll.*) the conventional position for sexual intercourse, lying down with the woman on her back and the man on top of her. **missioner** *n.* **mission statement** *n.* a concise statement of the aims and principles of a company, corporation etc. distributed or otherwise made known to all connected with that organization.

missis (mis'iz), **missus** *n.* (*sl., often facet.*) **1** a wife. **2** used as a form of address to a woman. **the missis** used by men to refer to their own or someone else's wife.

missive (mis'iv) *n.* (*often facet.*) a message, a letter. ~*a.* sent or for sending.

misspell (mis-spel') *v.t.* (*past, p.p.* **misspelt** (-spelt'), **misspelled**) to spell incorrectly. **misspelling** *n.*

misspend (mis-spend') *v.t.* (*past, p.p.* **misspent**

(-spent')) **1** to spend wastefully or inadvisedly. **2** to waste. **misspent** *a.*

misstate (mis-stāt') *v.t.* to state wrongly. **misstatement** *n.*

mist (mist) *n.* **1** visible water vapour in the atmosphere at or near the surface of the earth. **2** a watery condensation dimming a surface. **3** a watery film before the eyes. **4** anything which dims, obscures or darkens. ~*v.t.* to cover as with mist. ~*v.i.* to be misty. **mistful** *a.* **mistlike** *a., adv.* **misty** *a.* (*comp.* **mistier**, *superl.* **mistiest**) **1** characterized by or overspread with mist. **2** vague, dim, indistinct, obscure. **mistily** *adv.* **mistiness** *n.*

mistake (mis-tāk') *v.t.* (*past* **mistook** (-tuk'), *p.p.* **mistaken** (-tā'kən)) **1** to understand wrongly, to take in a wrong sense. **2** to take (one person or thing) for another. ~*n.* **1** an error of judgement or opinion. **2** a misunderstanding. **3** a thing done incorrectly, a blunder. **by mistake** accidentally, due to error. **make no mistake** without doubt, certainly. **there is no mistaking** one is certain to recognize (someone or something). **mistakable** *a.* **mistakably** *adv.* **mistaken** *a.* wrong in judgement, opinion etc. **mistakenly** *adv.* **mistakenness** *n.*

misteach (mis-tēch') *v.t.* (*past, p.p.* **mistaught** (-tawt')) to teach wrongly or incorrectly.

mister (mis'tə) *n.* **1** (**Mister**) the common form of address prefixed to untitled men's names or certain official titles (abbr. in writing to Mr). **2** an untitled man. **3** (*sl. or facet.*) used as a form of address to a man.

mistime (mis-tīm') *v.t.* to say or do at an inappropriate time.

mistle thrush (mis'əl thrŭsh), **missel thrush** *n.* the largest of the European thrushes, *Turdus viscivorus*, that feeds on mistletoe berries.

mistletoe (mis'əltō) *n.* **1** a plant, *Viscum album*, parasitic on the apple and other trees, bearing white glutinous berries. **2** a related N American plant of the genus *Phoradendron*.

mistook MISTAKE.

mistral (mistrahl') *n.* a cold dry NW wind of S France.

mistranslate (mistranslāt', -tranz-) *v.t.* to translate wrongly. **mistranslation** (-lā'shən) *n.*

mistreat (mistrēt') *v.t.* to ill-treat. **mistreatment** *n.*

mistress (mis'tris) *n.* **1** a woman with whom a man has a long-term extramarital relationship. **2** a female teacher. **3** a woman who has authority or control. **4** the female head of a family, school etc. **5** the female owner of a pet animal. **6** a woman having the control or disposal (of). **7** a woman who has mastery (of a subject etc.).

mistrial (mistrī'əl, mis'-) *n.* an abortive or inconclusive trial.

mistrust (mistrŭst') *v.t.* to regard with doubt or suspicion. ~*n.* distrust, suspicion. **mistrustful** *a.* **mistrustfully** *adv.* **mistrustfulness** *n.*

mistype (mistīp´) v.t. to type (a character, number etc.) incorrectly.

misunderstand (misŭndəstand´) v.t. (past, p.p. misunderstood (-stud´)) to mistake the meaning or sense of, to misconceive, to misapprehend. **misunderstanding** n. 1 a failure of understanding. 2 a slight disagreement or argument. **misunderstood** a.

misuse[1] (misūz´) v.t. 1 to use or treat improperly. 2 to apply to a wrong purpose. 3 to ill-treat. **misusage** (-ū´sij) n. **misuser** n.

misuse[2] (misūs´) n. 1 improper use. 2 abuse.

mite[1] (mīt) n. any minute arachnid of the order Acarida occurring in terrestrial or aquatic habitats.

mite[2] (mīt) n. 1 a very small coin, orig. Flemish. 2 any very small coin. 3 a small contribution, a minute amount. 4 a tiny thing, esp. a child.

miter MITRE.

mitigate (mit´igāt) v.t. 1 to make less rigorous or harsh, to relax (severity). 2 to alleviate (pain, violence etc.). 3 to soften, to diminish, to moderate. **mitigable** a. **mitigating circumstances** n.pl. (Law) in a trial, circumstances which are conducive to greater leniency in verdict, sentence etc. **mitigation** (-ā´shən) n. **mitigator** n. **mitigatory** a.

Usage note See note under MILITATE.

mitosis (mītō´sis) n. (pl. **mitoses** (-sēz)) (Biol.) indirect cell division. **mitotic** (-tot´-) a.

mitre (mī´tə), (NAm.) **miter** n. 1 a tall ornamental cap shaped like a cleft cone rising into two peaks, worn as a symbol of office by bishops and abbots. 2 the dignity of a bishop or abbot. 3 a joint at an angle (usu. of 90°), as the corner of a picture frame, each jointing surface being cut at an angle of 45° to the piece on which it is formed. 4 a diagonal join where two edges of a folded piece of fabric meet at a corner. ~v.t. 1 to join with a mitre. 2 to shape off at an angle of 45°. 3 to confer a mitre upon. ~v.i. to join with a mitre. **mitre block, mitre bound, mitre box** n. a block or box used to guide the saw in cutting mitres. **mitred** a. **mitre joint** n. **mitre wheel** n. a bevelled cogwheel engaged with another at an angle of 45°.

mitt (mit) n. 1 a mitten. 2 a kind of glove or covering for the wrist and palm (but not the fingers and thumb). 3 a thick glove worn by the catcher in baseball. 4 (sl.) a hand, a fist.

mitten (mit´ən) n. 1 a glove with a thumb but no fingers. 2 (sl.) a boxing glove. **mittened** a.

mix (miks) v.t. 1 to put together or blend into one mass or compound. 2 to mingle or incorporate (several substances, quantities or groups) so that the particles of each are indiscriminately associated. 3 to compound by mingling various ingredients. 4 to combine in a single action or on a single occasion. 5 to combine into a single sound signal. 6 (Mus.) to produce by combining different recordings or soundtracks. 7 to cross in

breeding. ~v.i. 1 to become united. 2 to be mingled (with or together). 3 to be compatible. 4 to be sociable. 5 to be associated or be regularly sociable (with). ~n. 1 mixed ingredients for a cake, mortar etc. 2 a mixture, a combination. 3 an act or process of mixing. 4 the merging of sound or pictures by means of a mixer. **to be mixed up in** to be involved in (esp. something dubious). **to be mixed up with** to be involved with (esp. someone undesirable). **to mix and match** to choose from a range of combinations, e.g. of fabrics, wallpaper etc. **to mix in** to be sociable, to get on well with others. **to mix it** to start a fight. **to mix it up** (NAm.) to mix it. **to mix up 1** to mix thoroughly. 2 to confuse, to bewilder. 3 to involve (in an (esp. dubious) undertaking or with an (esp. undesirable) person). **mixable** a. **mixed** (mikst) a. 1 consisting of various kinds or constituents. 2 consisting of various different types of people. 3 for or involving both sexes. 4 not wholly good or bad, not of consistent quality. **mixed bag, mixed bunch** n. a diverse mixture of people or things, often in terms of quality. **mixed blessing** n. something that has advantages and disadvantages. **mixed doubles** n.pl. in tennis, badminton etc., matches with a man and woman player as partners on each side. **mixed economy** n. an economy containing both private enterprise and state-controlled industries etc. **mixed farm** n. a farm combining arable and livestock production. **mixed feelings** n.pl. a mixture of pleasure and sadness with regard to a single event etc. **mixed grill** n. a dish of various grilled meats, often served with fried egg, mushrooms and tomatoes. **mixed marriage** n. a marriage in which the contracting parties are of different creeds or races. **mixed media** n. the use of different media in a work of art, presentation, entertainment etc. **mixed-media** a. **mixed metaphor** n. a metaphor that brings together incongruous concepts. **mixedness** n. **mixed-up** a. 1 confused, chaotic, muddled. 2 in emotional turmoil. **mixer** n. 1 a person or thing that causes mixing, that mixes. 2 a kitchen appliance for mixing food ingredients. 3 a non-alcoholic drink suitable for mixing with alcoholic drinks. 4 a person with social tact, a person who gets on well with all sorts of people. 5 (coll.) a person who stirs up trouble. 6 a device for combining sound or pictures into a single output. 7 a person who uses this. **mixer tap** n. a tap that combines hot and cold water in a single outlet.

mixture (miks´chə) n. 1 something which is being or has been mixed. 2 (Chem.) a combination of substances without any chemical reaction between them. 3 a combination of different qualities and characteristics. 4 gas or vaporized oil mixed with air to form the explosive charge in an internal-combustion engine. 5 the process of mixing.

mizzen (miz´ən), **mizzen-sail** n. (Naut.) a fore-and-aft sail set on the mizzen-mast of a sailing ship. **mizzen-mast** *n.* the aftermost mast of a three-masted sailing ship.

ml *abbr.* **1** mile(s). **2** millilitre(s).

MLD *abbr.* minimum lethal dose.

M.Litt. *abbr.* Master of Letters.

Mlle *abbr.* Mademoiselle.

Mlles *abbr.* Mesdemoiselles.

MM *abbr.* **1** Messieurs. **2** Military Medal.

mm *abbr.* millimetre(s).

Mme *abbr.* Madame.

Mmes *abbr.* Mesdames.

Mn *chem. symbol* manganese.

mnemonic (nimon´ik) *n.* an aid to memory. ~*a.* of, relating to or aiding the memory. **mnemonically** *adv.*

MO *abbr.* **1** Medical Officer. **2** money order.

Mo *chem. symbol* molybdenum.

mo (mō) *n.* (*pl.* **mos**) (*coll.*) moment (*just a mo*; *half a mo*).

moa (mō´ə) *n.* (*pl.* **moas**) an extinct, flightless bird of the genus *Dinornis*.

moan (mōn) *n.* **1** a low prolonged sound expressing pain or sorrow. **2** a complaint. ~*v.i.* **1** to utter a moan or moans. **2** to complain, grumble. **moaner** *n.*

moat (mōt) *n.* a ditch round a castle, fort etc., usu. filled with water. ~*v.t.* to surround with or as with a moat.

mob (mob) *n.* **1** a gang of criminals engaged in organized crime. **2** a disorderly or riotous crowd, a rabble. **3** (*coll.*, *derog.*) a group or class (of people of a specified kind). **4** (*derog.*) the masses. ~*v.t.* (*pres.p.* **mobbing**, *past, p.p.* **mobbed**) **1** to attack in a mob. **2** to crowd roughly round and annoy. ~*v.i.* to gather together in a mob. **the Mob 1** (*esp. N Am.*) the Mafia. **2** organized crime. **mobber** *n.* **mob rule, mob law** *n.* **1** the rule of the mob. **2** lynch law. **mobster** *n.* a member of a criminal mob.

mob cap (mob) *n.* (*Hist.*) a plain indoor cap or headdress for women, usu. tied under the chin.

mobile (mō´bīl) *a.* **1** movable, free to move. **2** easily moved. **3** easily changing (as an expression). **4** able to be moved from place to place. **5** able to move in social status. ~*n.* an artistic concoction of items suspended in balance from wires etc. **mobile home** *n.* a caravan or larger movable building used as a permanent dwelling. **mobile phone, mobile telephone** *n.* a small portable radio telephone. **mobility** (-bil´-) *n.* **mobilize** (-bil-), **mobilise** *v.t.* **1** to make mobile. **2** to put (troops, a fleet etc.) in a state of readiness for active service. ~*v.i.* to be put in a state of readiness for active service. **mobilizable** *a.* **mobilization** (-zā´shən) *n.*

Möbius strip (mœ´biəs) *n.* (*Math.*) a long, rectangular strip of paper twisted through 180° and joined at the ends, to form a one-sided surface bounded by one continuous curve.

moccasin (mok´əsin) *n.* **1** a bedroom slipper of soft leather made of one piece. **2** a foot-covering, usu. of deerskin or soft leather in one piece,

worn by N American Indians. **3** the water moccasin and other snakes of the genus *Agkistrodon*.

mocha (mok´ə) *n.* **1** a choice quality of coffee, orig. from Mocha. **2** a drink made with this and often also chocolate.

mock (mok) *v.t.* **1** to deride, to laugh at. **2** to mimic, esp. in derision. **3** to defy contemptuously. **4** to delude, to take in. ~*v.i.* to express ridicule, derision or contempt. ~*a.* **1** sham, false, counterfeit. **2** imitating reality. ~*n.* **1** something which is derided or deserves derision. **2** (*usu. in pl.*) an examination taken as practice prior to an official one. **3** an imitation. **4** a derisive action, a sneer. **to make (a) mock of** to ridicule, to sneer at. **mockable** *a.* **mocker** *n.* **to put the mockers on 1** (*sl.*) to cause to fail. **2** (*sl.*) to make impossible. **mockery** *n.* (*pl.* **mockeries**) **1** the act of mocking, ridicule, derision. **2** a delusive imitation. **3** a futile effort. **4** a subject of ridicule. **mocking** *n.*, *a.* **mockingbird** *n.* any American songbird of the family Mimidae, esp. *Mimus polyglottos*, with great powers of mimicry. **mockingly** *adv.* **mock orange** *n.* the common syringa, *Philadelphus coronarius*, the flowers of which smell like orange blossoms. **mock turtle soup** *n.* a soup prepared from calf's head, veal etc. to imitate turtle soup. **mock-up** *n.* **1** an experimental dummy model or replica, usu. full-size. **2** an unprinted model of a book.

mod (mod) *a.* modern. ~*n.* a member of a youth subculture of the 1960s, who wore smart casual clothes, rode motor scooters and were often involved in fights with gangs of rockers, a rival subculture.

modal (mō´dəl) *a.* **1** of or relating to mode, form or manner, as opposed to substance. **2** (*Gram.*) (of a verb) of or relating to mood or denoting manner. **3** in statistics, of or relating to a mode. **4** (*Mus.*) using a particular mode. **5** (*Logic*) affirming with or expressing qualification. ~*n.* a modal proposition or verb. **modality** (-dal´-) *n.* (*pl.* **modalities**). **modally** *adv.*

mod cons (mod konz´) *n.pl.* (*coll.*) modern devices or appliances that give comfort, convenience etc.

mode (mōd) *n.* **1** manner, method, way of doing, existing etc. **2** style. **3** common fashion, prevailing custom. **4** (*Math.*) in statistics, the value occurring most frequently in a set of data. **5** an operational state. **6** (*Mus.*) any of the systems of dividing the octave, the form of the scale.

model (mod´əl) *n.* **1** a representation or pattern in miniature, in three dimensions, of something made on a larger scale. **2** a person employed to wear clothes, make-up etc. to display their effect. **3** a particular style or type, e.g. of a car or a garment. **4** a person employed to pose as subject to an artist. **5** a standard, an example to be imitated or emulated. **6** a description or representation of something that cannot be observed directly (*computer model*). **7** a figure in clay, plaster etc. for execution in durable material. **8** a set of postulates, mathematical equations etc. used e.g. to predict developments in the economy. ~*a*. **1** serving as a model or example. **2** worthy of imitation, perfect. ~*v.t.* (*pres.p.* **modelling**, (*N Am.*) **modeling**, *past, p.p.* **modelled**, (*N Am.*) **modeled**) **1** to display (clothes) by wearing them. **2** to shape, mould or fashion in clay etc. **3** to form after or upon a model. **4** to give a plan or shape to (a document, book etc.). **5** to give a three-dimensional appearance to. ~*v.i.* **1** to act as a mannequin. **2** to make a model or models. **modeller**, (*N Am.*) **modeler** *n*. a person who makes models.

modem (mō´dem) *n*. a device used to transmit and receive data, esp. between computers over a telephone line.

moderate[1] (mod´ərət) *a*. **1** temperate, reasonable, mild, keeping within bounds. **2** not extreme or excessive. **3** of medium quantity or quality. ~*n*. a person of moderate views in politics, religion etc. **moderately** *adv*.

moderate[2] (mod´ərāt) *v.t.* **1** to reduce to a calmer, less violent, energetic or intense condition. **2** to restrain from excess. **3** to temper, to mitigate. **4** to assess (examination papers etc.) in order to achieve consistency in marking. ~*v.i.* **1** to become less violent. **2** to quieten or settle down. **3** to preside as a moderator. **4** (*Physics*) to retard with a moderator. **moderation** (-ā´shən) *n*. **in moderation** not to excess, in a moderate manner or degree. **moderator** *n*. **1** a person who or something that moderates. **2** a person who presides at a meeting, esp. the presiding officer at a court of the Presbyterian Church. **3** (*Physics*) a substance used to retard neutrons.

modern (mod´ən) *a*. **1** of or relating to the present or recent time. **2** not ancient, old-fashioned or obsolete. **3** being or concerning the present or most recent form of a language. ~*n*. a person of modern times. **modern English** *n*. the English language as used since *c*.1500. **modernism** *n*. **1** a modern mode of expression or thought. **2** a modern term or idiom. **3** in art and literature, the conscious rejection of traditional forms and use of new forms of expression. **4** a tendency towards freedom of thought and the acceptance of the results of modern criticism and research in religious matters. **modernist** *n*. **modernistic** (-nis´-) *a*. **modernistically** *adv*. **modernity** (-dœ´-) *n*. **modernize, modernise** *v.t.*, *v.i.* **modernization** (-zā´shən) *n*. **modernizer** *n*. **modern Latin** *n*. Latin as used since *c*.1500. **modernly** *adv*. **modernness** *n*. **modern pentathlon** *n*. a sports contest involving swimming, cross-country running, fencing, equestrian steeplechasing and shooting.

modest (mod´ist) *a*. **1** humble, unassuming or diffident in regard to one's merits or importance. **2** not presumptuous, forward or arrogant. **3** bashful, retiring. **4** restrained by a sense of propriety. **5** moderate, not extreme or excessive.

modestly *adv*. **modesty** *n*. the quality of being modest.

modicum (mod´ikəm) *n*. a little, a small amount, a scanty allowance.

modify (mod´ifī) *v.t.* (*3rd pers. sing. pres.* **modifies**, *pres.p.* **modifying**, *past, p.p.* **modified**) **1** to alter, to make different. **2** to reduce in degree or extent, to moderate, to tone down. **3** (*Gram.*) to qualify the sense of. **modifiable** *a*. **modification** (-fikā´shən) *n*. **modificatory** (-fi-) *a*. **modifier** *n*. **1** (*Gram.*) a word or phrase that modifies another. **2** any person or thing that modifies.

modish (mō´dish) *a*. fashionable, stylish. **modishly** *adv*. **modishness** *n*.

modiste (modēst´) *n*. **1** a milliner. **2** a dressmaker.

modular (mod´ūlə) *a*. **1** of or relating to a module, consisting of modules. **2** of or relating to a modulus, consisting of moduli. **modularity** (-lar´-) *n*.

modulate (mod´ūlāt) *v.t.* **1** to adjust, to regulate. **2** to vary or inflect the sound or tone of. **3** (*Mus.*) to change the key of. ~*v.i.* (*Mus.*) to pass from one key to another. **modulation** (-lā´shən) *n*. **modulator** *n*.

module (mod´ūl) *n*. **1** any element or unit that forms part of a larger system, e.g. of a spacecraft, an educational course. **2** a measure or unit of proportion. **3** (*Archit.*) the semidiameter or other unit taken as a standard for regulating the proportions of a column.

modulus (mod´ūləs) *n*. (*pl.* **moduli** (-lī)) (*Math.*) **1** a constant number or coefficient expressing a force, effect, function, etc. **2** a constant multiplier in a function of a variable. **3** the absolute value of a complex number.

modus operandi (mōdəs operan´dī) *n*. (*pl.* **modi operandi** (mōdī)) **1** a method of working. **2** the way something operates.

modus vivendi (mōdəs yiven´dī) *n*. (*pl.* **modi vivendi** (mōdī)) **1** a way of living, or life. **2** an arrangement by means of which people who are in dispute carry on in a situation pending a settlement.

mog (mog), **moggie** (-i) *n*. (*coll.*) a cat.

Mogadon® (mog´adon) *n*. a drug used to treat insomnia.

mogul[1] (mō´gəl) *n*. **1** a powerful and influential entrepreneur. **2** (**Mogul**) a Mongolian, a Mughal.

mogul[2] (mō´gəl) *n*. a mound of packed snow on a ski slope.

MOH *abbr.* Medical Officer of Health.

mohair (mō´heə) *n*. **1** the hair of the angora goat. **2** a fabric made from it. **3** an imitation of this fabric in cotton and wool.

Mohammedan MUHAMMADAN.

Mohawk (mō´hawk) *n*. (*pl.* **Mohawks, Mohawk**) **1** a member of a N American Indian people. **2** their language. **3** in skating, a stroke from either edge to the same edge on the other foot, but in the opposite direction. ~*a*. of or relating to the Mohawks or their language.

Mohican (mōhē´kən) *n*. **1** a member of a

N American Indian people living in the Hudson river valley. **2** the language of the Mohicans. **3** (*also* **mohican**) a hairstyle in which the head is shaved apart from a narrow central strip of erect hair from front to rear, often brightly coloured. ~*a.* **1** of or relating to the Mohicans or their language. **2** (of a hairstyle) cut into a Mohican.

moiety (moi´əti) *n.* (*pl.* **moieties**) **1** (*Law*) a half. **2** a part or share.

moire (mwah), **moire antique** *n.* **1** watered silk. **2** a watered appearance on textile fabrics or metals. **moiré** (-rā) *a.* watered (of silk, surfaces of metal etc.). ~*n.* a surface or finish like watered silk.

moist (moist) *a.* moderately wet, damp, humid. **moisten** (-sən) *v.t., v.i.* **moistly** *adv.* **moistness** *n.* **moisture** *n.* liquid throughout or on the surface of something, or in a vapour. **moistureless** *a.* **moisturize, moisturise** *v.t.* to add moisture to. **moisturizer** *n.* anything which moisturizes, esp. a cosmetic cream or lotion.

mol *abbr.* MOLE⁴.

molar (mō´lə) *n.* any of the back or grinding teeth. ~*a.* **1** having power to grind. **2** grinding.

molasses (məlas´iz) *n.* **1** the sticky, dark-brown uncrystallizable syrup drained from sugar during the refining process. **2** treacle.

mold MOULD¹.

mole¹ (mōl) *n.* a spot on the human skin, usu. dark-coloured and sometimes covered with hair.

mole² (mōl) *n.* **1** a small soft-furred burrowing mammal of the family Talpidae, esp. *Talpa europaea.* **2** a spy or subversive person working within an organization on behalf of a rival organization, enemy etc. **mole cricket** *n.* a burrowing cricket of the family Gryllotalpidae. **molehill** *n.* **1** a hillock thrown up by a mole burrowing underground. **2** an unimportant or very small matter, problem etc. **mole-rat** *n.* any of various mouselike burrowing rodents, esp. of the family Bathyergidae of Africa. **moleskin** *n.* **1** the skin of the mole used as fur. **2** a kind of fustian, dyed after the surface has been shaved. **3** (*pl.*) clothes, esp. trousers, of this material.

mole³ (mōl) *n.* **1** a pile of masonry, such as a breakwater, pier or jetty before a port. **2** an artificial harbour.

mole⁴ (mōl) *n.* (*Chem.*) the basic SI unit of substance, being the amount of substance of a system which contains as many specified elementary entities as there are atoms in 0.012 kg of carbon-12.

molecule (mol´ikūl) *n.* **1** (*Chem.*) any of the structural units of which matter is built up, the smallest quantity of substance capable of separate existence without losing its chemical identity with that substance. **2** a particle. **molecular** (məlek´-) *a.* **molecular biology** *n.* the study of the structure and chemical organization of living matter, esp. of nucleic acids and protein synthesis. **molecularity** (-lar´-) *n.* **molecular**

weight *n.* (*Chem.*) RELATIVE MOLECULAR MASS (under RELATIVE).

molest (məlest´) *v.t.* **1** to trouble, to disturb, to harm. **2** to assault or attack, esp. for sexual purposes. **molestation** (molestā´shən, mō-) *n.* **molester** *n.*

moll (mol) *n.* (*sl.*) **1** a gangster's girlfriend. **2** a wench, a prostitute.

mollify (mol´ifī) *v.t.* (*3rd pers. sing. pres.* **mollifies**, *pres.p.* **mollifying**, *past, p.p.* **mollified**) **1** to soften, to assuage. **2** to pacify, to appease. **mollient** *a.* **mollifiable** *a.* **mollification** (-fikā´-shən) *n.* **mollifier** *n.*

mollusc (mol´əsk), (*N Am.*) **mollusk** *n.* any invertebrate of the Mollusca. **molluscan** (-lŭs´-), **molluscoid** (-lŭs´-) *n., a.* **molluscous** (-lŭs´-) *a.*

molly (mol´i) *n.* (*pl.* **mollies**) an effeminate man or boy, a person who likes to be coddled, a milksop. **mollycoddle** *v.t.* to coddle. ~*n.* a milksop.

Molotov cocktail (mol´ətof) *n.* a home-made incendiary device consisting of a bottle containing an inflammable liquid, with a rag for a wick.

molt MOULT.

molten (mōl´tən) *a.* **1** made of melted metal. **2** melted by heat. **moltenly** *adv.*

molto (mol´tō) *adv.* (*Mus.*) much, very.

molybdenum (məlib´dənəm) *n.* (*Chem.*) a rare metallic element, at. no. 42, chem. symbol Mo, found in combination as molybdenite. **molybdenite** *n.* molybdenum disulphide.

mom (mom) *n.* (*N Am., coll.*) mother.

moment (mō´mənt) *n.* **1** a minute portion of time, an instant. **2** a short period of time. **3** a particular point in time. **4** importance, consequence. **5** (*Physics*) the measure of a force by its power to cause rotation. **at the moment** at the present, just now. **in a moment 1** in a short while (*I'll do it in a moment*). **2** instantly (*In a moment, she was gone*). **this moment** at once. **to have one's moments** to be successful, impressive, happy etc. on occasions. **momentary** *a.* **1** lasting only for a moment. **2** done or past in a moment. **3** transient, ephemeral. **momentarily** *adv.* **1** for a moment. **2** (*N Am.*) immediately. **momentariness** *n.* **momentous** (-men´-) *a.* weighty, important. **momentously** *adv.* **momentousness** *n.*

momentum (məmen´təm) *n.* (*pl.* **momenta** (-tə)) (*Physics*) **1** impetus, power of overcoming resistance to motion. **2** the quantity of motion in a body, the product of the mass and the velocity.

momma (mom´ə) *n.* (*N Am., coll.*) mother.

mommy (mom´i) *n.* (*pl.* **mommies**) (*N Am., coll.*) mummy, mother.

Mon. *abbr.* Monday.

monad (mon´ad, mō´-) *n.* **1** a simple, indivisible unit. **2** (*Philos.*) one of the primary elements of being, esp. according to the philosophy of Leibnitz. **3** (*Biol.*) an elementary, single-celled organism. **monadic** (-nad´-) *a.* **monadism** *n.*

monadelphous (monədel´fəs) *a.* (*Bot.*) **1** having

the stamens united by their filaments. **2** (of stamens) having the filaments united.
monarch (mon´ək) *n*. **1** a sole ruler. **2** a hereditary sovereign, such as emperor, empress, king or queen. **3** the chief of its class. **monarchal** (-ah´-) *a*. **monarch butterfly** *n*. a large orange and black butterfly, *Danais plexippus*. **monarch flycatcher** *n*. a flycatcher of the Old World family Monarchidae. **monarchic** (-ah´-), **monarchical** (-ah´-) *a*. **monarchically** *adv*. **monarchism** *n*. **1** belief in or advocacy of monarchy. **2** the monarchic principle. **monarchist** *n*. **monarchy** *n*. (*pl*. **monarchies**) **1** government in which the supreme power is vested in a monarch. **2** a state under this system, a kingdom. **3** supreme control. **monarchial** *a*.
monastery (mon´əstəri) *n*. (*pl*. **monasteries**) a residence for a community, esp. of monks, living under religious vows of seclusion. **monasterial** (-stiə´-) *a*. **monastic** (-nas´-) *a*. **1** of or relating to monks or monasteries. **2** resembling the way of life of a monastic community, reclusive, austere, celibate. **monastically** *adv*. **monasticism** (-nas´tisizm) *n*. the theory and system of the monastic life. **monasticize** (-nas´-), **monasticise** *v.t.*
monatomic (monətom´ik) *a*. (*Chem*.) having one atom in the molecule, monovalent.
monaural (monaw´rəl) *a*. **1** (of recorded sound) monophonic as distinct from stereophonic. **2** having or using one ear. **monaurally** *adv*.
monazite (mon´əzīt) *n*. a mineral consisting of a phosphate of thorium, cerium and lanthanum.
Monday (mun´dā, -di) *n*. the second day of the week, following Sunday. *~adv*. (*coll*.) on Monday. **Mondayish** *a*. miserable, reluctant to start the week's work. **Mondays** *adv*. (*coll*.) on Mondays, each Monday.
monetary (mun´itəri) *a*. of or relating to money or coinage. **monetarily** *adv*. **monetarism** *n*. the economic theory that advocates strict control of the money supply as the best method of regulating the economy. **monetarist** *n.*, *a*. **monetize, monetise** *v.t.* **1** to give a standard value to (a metal) as currency. **2** to form into coin. **monetization** (-zā´shən) *n*.
money (mun´i) *n*. (*pl*. **moneys, monies**) **1** coin or other material used as medium of exchange. **2** banknotes, bills, notes of hand and other documents representing coin. **3** wealth, property, regarded as convertible into coin. **4** (*with pl*.) coins of a particular country or denomination. **5** (*pl*.) sums of money, receipts or payments. **for my money** in my opinion. **in the money** having or having won a lot of money. **money for old rope** (*coll*.) money made with little effort. **money to burn** more money than one needs. **to put money into** to invest in. **moneybags** *n*. (*derog*.) a rich or miserly person. **money box** *n*. a box with a slit through which savings or contributions are put in. **moneyed** *a*. **1** rich. **2** consisting of money. **money-grubber** *n*. a person

who greedily saves or amasses money. **money-grubbing** *n*. **moneylender** *n*. a person whose business is to lend money at interest. **moneylending** *n.*, *a*. **moneyless** *a*. **moneymaking** *n.*, *a*. highly profitable (business). **moneymaker** *n*. **1** a person who earns a lot of money. **2** a project, idea etc. that makes a lot of money. **money market** *n*. the field of operation of dealers in stocks etc., the financial world. **money of account** *n*. a denomination not actually coined, but used for convenience in keeping accounts, e.g. the guinea. **money order** *n*. an order for money, granted at one post office and payable at another. **money spider** *n*. a small spider, esp. of the family Linyphiidae, supposed to bring financial luck. **money-spinner** *n*. a thing that makes a good profit. **money supply** *n*. the total amount of money in a country's economy at a given time. **money's-worth** *n*. full value, an equivalent for money paid. **moneywort** *n*. a trailing plant, *Lysimachia nummularia*, with broad glossy leaves.
monger (mŭng´gə) *n*. (*often derog*.) a trader, a dealer (now only in comb., as *ironmonger*, *scandalmonger*).
Mongol (mong´gəl) *n*. **1** a member of an Asian people now inhabiting Mongolia. **2** (*offensive*) (**mongol**) a person with Down's syndrome. *~a*. **1** of or relating to the Mongols. **2** (*offensive*) (**mongol**) of, relating to or having Down's syndrome. **Mongolian** (-gō´-) *a*. of or relating to Mongolia or the Mongols. *~n*. **1** a native or inhabitant of Mongolia. **2** the language of the Mongols or of Mongolia. **mongolism** *n*. (*offensive*) Down's syndrome. **Mongoloid, mongoloid** *a*. **1** characteristic of or resembling the Mongolians, esp. in broad facial features and yellowish complexion. **2** (*offensive*) (**mongoloid**) having Down's syndrome. *~n*. **1** a Mongoloid person. **2** (*offensive*) (**mongoloid**) a person with Down's syndrome.

Usage note The use of *mongol, mongolism* etc. with reference to Down's syndrome gives offence, and is best avoided.

mongoose (mong´goos) *n*. (*pl*. **mongooses**) any of various small civet-like mammals of the family Viverridae, esp. of the genus *Herpestes*, found in Africa, S Europe and SE Asia, which feed on venomous snakes.
mongrel (mŭng´grəl) *n*. anything, esp. a dog, of mixed breed. *~a*. **1** of mixed breed, arising from the crossing of two varieties. **2** of mixed nature or character. **mongrelism** *n*. **mongrelize, mongrelise** *v.t.* **mongrelization** (-zā´shən) *n*.
monial (mō´niəl) *n*. (*Archit*.) a mullion.
monies MONEY.
moniker (mon´ikə), **monicker, monniker** *n*. (*sl*.) a name.
moniliform (mənil´ifawm) *a*. (*Anat*., *Zool*.) shaped like a necklace or string of beads.
monism (mon´izm) *n*. (*Philos*., *Theol*.) **1** the

doctrine that all existing things and activities are forms or manifestations of one ultimate principle or substance. **2** any philosophic theory such as idealism, pantheism or materialism, opposed to dualism. **monist** *n*. **monistic** (-nis´-) *a*.

monitor (mon´itə) *n*. **1** a television screen used e.g. in a studio or with a computer for displaying and checking pictures or information. **2** a pupil given a particular area of responsibility within a class. **3** a person who warns or admonishes. **4** a person whose duty it is to listen to foreign or other broadcasts. **5** (*Zool*.) any large tropical lizard of the genus *Varanus* found in Asia, Africa and Australia. **6** a detector for radioactivity. ~*v.t.*, *v.i.* **1** to maintain regular surveillance on (a situation). **2** to listen to (radio broadcasts) in order to glean information. **monitorial** (-taw´-) *a*. **monitorially** *adv*. **monitorship** *n*. **monitory** *a*. giving warning or admonition.

monk (mŭngk) *n*. a member of a religious community of men, living apart under vows of poverty, chastity and obedience. **monkfish** *n*. **1** any of various angler fish of the genus *Lophius*, esp. *L. piscatorius*. **2** the angel-shark, *Squatina squatina*. **monkish** *a*. **monkshood** *n*. a plant of the genus *Aconitum*, esp. *A. napellus* (from its hooded sepals).

monkey (mŭng´ki) *n*. (*pl*. **monkeys**) **1** a long-tailed quadrumanous mammal of various species and families ranging from the anthropoid apes to the lemurs. **2** (*coll*.) a rogue, an imp, a mischievous child. **3** an ape, a mimic. **4** a monkey engine. **5** (*sl*.) a sum of £500 or $500. ~*v.i.* (*3rd pers. sing. pres.* **monkeys**, *pres.p.* **monkeying**, *past, p.p.* **monkeyed**) **1** to meddle or interfere (with). **2** to play foolish or mischievous tricks. ~*v.t.* to mimic, to ape. **to have a monkey on one's back** to be a drug addict. **to make a monkey of** to cause to seem foolish. **monkey bars** *n.pl.* a children's climbing frame. **monkey bread** *n*. the fruit of the baobab tree, *Adansonia digitata*. **monkey business** *n*. (*coll*.) **1** devious or underhand behaviour. **2** mischievous behaviour. **monkey engine** *n*. a pile-driving machine. **monkey flower** *n*. a plant of the genus *Mimulus*, esp. *M. cardinalis*. **monkeyish** *a*. **monkey-jacket** *n*. a short, close-fitting jacket worn by sailors etc. **monkey-nut** *n*. a peanut. **monkey-puzzle**, **monkey-puzzle tree** *n*. the Chile pine, *Araucaria araucana*, having spiny leaves and branches. **monkeyshines** *n.pl.* (*N Am*.) monkey tricks. **monkey suit** *n*. a dinner suit, evening dress. **monkey tricks** *n.pl.* mischievous pranks etc. **monkey wrench** *n*. a spanner with a movable jaw. **monkeywrench** *v.t.* to sabotage, esp. as a protest. **monkeywrenching** *n*.

mono (mon´ō) *n*., *a*. monophonic (sound).

mono- (mon´ō), **mon-** (mon) *comb. form* alone, single, as in *monograph*, *monosyllable*.

monoacid (monōas´id), **monacid** (monas´id) *a*. (*Chem*.) capable of saturating one molecule of

monobasic acid, having only one hydroxide ion per molecule.

monobasic (monōbā´sik) *a*. (*Chem*.) (of an acid) with one base or replaceable atom.

monocarpic (monōkah´pik), **monocarpous** (-pəs) *a*. (*Bot*.) bearing fruit only once, and dying after fructification.

monocausal (monōkaw´zəl) *a*. attributing or assuming a single cause.

monocephalous (monōsef´ələs, -kef´-) *a*. (*Bot*.) having a single head of flowers.

monochord (mon´əkawd) *n*. (*Mus*.) a musical instrument with one string for determining the ratios of musical intervals.

monochromatic (monōkrəmat´ik) *a*. **1** (*Physics*) (of light) presenting rays of one colour only. **2** painted etc. in monochrome. **monochromatically** *adv*. **monochromatism** *n*. **monochrome** (mon´əkrōm) *n*. **1** a painting in tints of one colour only. **2** any representation in one colour. ~*a*. monochromic. **monochromic** *a*. executed in one colour. **monochromy** (mon´-) *n*.

monocle (mon´əkəl) *n*. an eyeglass for one eye.

monoclinal (monōklī´nəl) *a*. (*Geol*.) (of strata) dipping continuously in one direction. **monocline** *n*. a monoclinal fold, a hogback. **monoclinic** (-klin´-), **monoclinate** (-nət) *a*. (of a crystal) having two oblique axes and a third at right angles to these.

monocoque (mon´əkok) *n*. **1** in an aircraft, a form of streamlined fuselage shaped like an elongated egg. **2** an aeroplane with such a fuselage. **3** a car or vehicle with a body and chassis manufactured as an integrated structure.

monocotyledon (monōkotilē´dən), **monocot** (mon´-) *n*. (*Bot*.) a plant having a single cotyledon. **monocotyledonous** *a*.

monocracy (monok´rəsi) *n*. government by a single person. **monocratic** (-krat´-) *a*.

monocular (monok´ūlə) *a*. **1** one-eyed. **2** for use with one eye only. **monocularly** *adv*.

monoculture (mon´əkŭlchə) *n*. **1** the cultivation of a single type of crop. **2** an area where a single type of crop is grown.

monocycle (mon´əsīkəl) *n*. a unicycle.

monocyte (mon´əsīt) *n*. (*Biol*.) the largest white blood cell in vertebrate blood.

monodactylous (monōdak´tiləs) *a*. having one finger, toe or claw.

monodrama (mon´ədrahmə) *n*. a dramatic piece for one performer only. **monodramatic** (-drəmat´-) *a*.

monody (mon´ədi) *n*. (*pl*. **monodies**) **1** (*Mus*.) a song for one voice, or a musical composition in which one voice predominates. **2** a mournful or plaintive song or poetical composition, a threnody. **monodic** (mənod´-) *a*. **monodist** *n*.

monoecious (mənē´shəs) *a*. **1** having separate male and female flowers on the same plant. **2** (*Zool*.) hermaphrodite.

monogamy (mənog´əmi) *n*. **1** marriage to one wife or husband only at a time. **2** (*Zool*.) the habit of pairing with a single mate. **monogamist** *n.* **monogamous** *a.* **monogamously** *adv.*

monoglot (mon´əglot) *a.* speaking only one language. ~*n.* a monoglot person.

monogram (mon´əgram) *n.* a character composed of two or more letters interwoven. **monogrammatic** (-mat´-) *a.* **monogrammed** *a.*

monograph (mon´əgrahf) *n.* a treatise on a single thing or class of things. **monographer** (-nog´-), **monographist** *n.* **monographic** (-graf´-) *a.*

monogynous (monoj´inəs), **monogynian** (-ōjin´-iən) *a.* (*Bot.*) (of plants) having flowers with one pistil. **monogyny** (-noj´-) *n.* the custom of having only one wife at a time.

monohull (mon´əhŭl) *n.* (*Naut.*) a vessel with a single hull as distinct from a catamaran, trimaran etc.

monohybrid (monōhī´brid) *n.* (*Biol.*) the offspring of two parents that differs with respect to the alleles of one gene.

monohydric (monōhī´drik) *a.* (*Chem.*) containing one hydroxyl group per molecule.

monokini (mon´əkēni) *n.* a one-piece beach garment for a woman, usu. similar to the bottom half of a bikini.

monolayer (mon´əlāə) *n.* **1** (*Chem.*) a single layer of atoms or molecules adsorbed on a surface. **2** (*Biol., Med.*) a tissue culture in a layer one cell thick.

monolingual (monōling´gwəl) *a.* using or expressed in only one language.

monolith (mon´əlith) *n.* a monument or other structure formed of a single stone. **monolithic** (-lith´-) *a.* **1** of or like a monolith. **2** consisting of a large and undifferentiated whole, often entailing inflexibility.

monologue (mon´əlog) *n.* **1** a dramatic scene in which a person speaks by themselves, a soliloquy. **2** a dramatic piece for one actor. **3** a long speech in conversation. **monologic** (-loj´-), **monological** *a.* **monologist** (-nol´əjist), **monologuist** (-gist) *n.* **monologize** (-nol´əjīz, -gīz), **monologise** *v.i.*

monomania (monōmā´niə) *n.* an obsession of the mind on one subject only. **monomaniac** (-ak) *n., a.* **monomaniacal** (-mənī´əkəl) *a.*

monomer (mon´əmə) *n.* (*Chem.*) a compound that can undergo polymerization. **monomeric** (-mer´-) *a.*

monomial (mənō´miəl) *n.* a mathematical expression consisting of a single term. ~*a.* (*Math.*) consisting of a single term.

monomolecular (monōmələk´ūlə) *a.* (*Chem.*) only one molecule in thickness.

monomorphic (monōmaw´fik), **monomorphous** (-fəs) *a.* having the same structure or morphological character, esp. throughout successive stages of development. **monomorphism** *n.*

mononucleosis (monōnūkliō´sis) *n.* (*Biol.*) the presence of an abnormally large number of monocytes in the blood.

monopetalous (monōpet´ələs) *a.* (*Bot.*) having the petals coherent in a single corolla.

monophonic (monōfon´ik) *a.* (of sound) reproduced through only one electronic channel, monaural. **monophonically** *adv.*

monophthong (mo´nəfthong) *n.* a simple or single vowel sound. **monophthongal** (-thong´gəl) *a.*

monophyletic (monōfīlet´ik) *a.* (*Biol.*) of or relating to a single family or race or descended from one parental form.

monoplane (mon´əplān) *n.* an aircraft with one set of wings.

monopod (mon´əpod) *n.* a structure with only one foot, e.g. a shooting stick.

monopole (mon´əpōl) *n.* **1** (*Physics*) a single electrical charge or a magnetic pole considered in isolation. **2** a radio aerial consisting of one, usu. straight, element.

monopoly (mənop´əli) *n.* (*pl.* **monopolies**) **1** an exclusive trading right in a certain commodity or class of commerce or business. **2** this as conferred by government. **3** a company or combination enjoying this. **4** the subject of such a right. **5** exclusive possession, control or enjoyment (of). **monopolist** *n.* **monopolistic** (-lis´-) *a.* **monopolize, monopolise** *v.t.* **1** to obtain or possess a monopoly of. **2** to engross the whole of (attention, conversation etc.). **monopolization** (-zā´shən) *n.*

monorail (mon´ərāl) *n.* a railway, usu. elevated, with a track consisting of a single rail.

monosaccharide (monōsak´ərīd) *n.* (*Chem.*) a sugar that cannot be hydrolysed to form simpler sugars.

monosodium glutamate (monōsōdiəm gloo´təmāt) *n.* (*Chem.*) a salt of glutamic acid used as a flavour-enhancing food additive.

monospermous (monōspœ´məs) *a.* (*Bot.*) having only one seed. **monospermal** *a.*

monosyllable (mon´əsiləbəl) *n.* a word of one syllable. **in monosyllables** in simple direct words. **monosyllabic** (-lab´-) *a.* **1** (of a word) having one syllable. **2** speaking in words of a single syllable. **monosyllabically** *adv.*

monotheism (mon´əthēizm) *n.* the doctrine that there is only one God. **monotheist** *n.* **monotheistic** (-is´-) *a.* **monotheistically** *adv.*

monotint (mon´ətint) *n.* a picture or other representation in one colour.

monotone (mon´ətōn) *n.* **1** continuance of or repetition in the same tone. **2** a succession of sounds of the same pitch. ~*a.* monotonous. **monotonic** (-ton´-) *a.* **monotonically** *adv.* **monotonize** (-not´-), **monotonise** *v.t.* **monotonous** (mənot´-) *a.* **1** wearisome through sameness, tedious. **2** unvarying in pitch. **monotonously** *adv.* **monotony, monotonousness** *n.*

monotreme (mon´ətrēm) *n.* any mammal of the sub-class Monotremata, having only one aperture or vent for the genital organs and the excretions.

monotype (mon´ətīp) *n.* an impression on paper produced by inking glass or metal. **Monotype**® *n.* a typesetting machine that casts and sets single printing-types.

monotypic (monōtip´ik) *a.* (of a genus etc.) having only one type of animal or plant.

monounsaturated (monōŭnsach´ərātid) *a.* (*Chem.*) (of a compound, esp. oils, fats etc.) saturated except for one multiple bond.

monovalent (monōvā´lənt) *a.* UNIVALENT.

monoxide (mənok´sīd) *n.* (*Chem.*) an oxide containing one atom of oxygen in combination with a radical.

Monseigneur (monsenyœ´, mō-) *n.* (*pl.* **Messeigneurs** (māsenyœ´)) a French title of honour given to high dignitaries, esp. in the Church.

Monsieur (məsyœ´, mis-) *n.* (*pl.* **Messieurs**) **1** the French title of address, Mr or Sir. **2** a Frenchman.

Monsignor (monsē´nyə) *n.* (*pl.* **Monsignori** (-yaw´ri)) a title given to Roman Catholic prelates, officers of the Pope's court and others.

monsoon (monsoon´) *n.* **1** a wind in SW Asia and the Indian Ocean. **2** any of various other periodical winds. **monsoonal** *a.*

monster (mon´stə) *n.* **1** something misshapen, abnormal, out of the ordinary course of nature, a deformed creature. **2** an imaginary animal, usually compounded of incongruous parts, such as a centaur, griffin, mermaid, gorgon etc. **3** an abominably cruel or depraved person. **4** a person, animal or thing of extraordinary size. ~*a.* of extraordinary size, huge.

monstera (monstē´rə) *n.* any climbing plant of the genus *Monstera*, esp. *M. deliciosa*, the Swiss cheese plant.

monstrance (mon´strəns) *n.* an open or transparent vessel in which the Host is carried in procession or exposed for adoration, esp. in a Roman Catholic church.

monstrous (mon´strəs) *a.* **1** unnatural in form. **2** out of the ordinary course of nature. **3** enormous, huge. **4** shocking, atrocious, outrageous. **monstrosity** (-stros´-) *n.* (*pl.* **monstrosities**) **1** a monster. **2** a deformity, a distortion. **3** the quality of being monstrous. **monstrously** *adv.* **monstrousness** *n.*

montage (montahzh´) *n.* **1** the cutting and assembling of shots taken when making a film, video etc. **2** a sequence of such shots. **3** an artistic, literary or musical work consisting of heterogeneous elements in juxtaposition.

montane (mon´tān) *a.* of or relating to mountainous regions.

Montezuma's revenge (montizoo´məz) *n.* (*sl., facet.*) acute diarrhoea, esp. as suffered by travellers in Mexico.

month (mŭnth) *n.* **1** each of the twelve parts into which the year is divided, orig. the period of one revolution of the moon round the earth, a calendar month. **2** a period of four weeks. **monthly** *a.* **1** done in or continuing for a month. **2** happening or payable once a month. ~*adv.*

once a month. ~*n.* (*pl.* **monthlies**) **1** a periodical published every month. **2** (*pl.*) menstruation. **month of Sundays** *n.* an indefinitely long period.

monument (mon´ūmənt) *n.* **1** anything by which the memory of persons or things is preserved, esp. a building or permanent structure. **2** anything that serves as a memorial of a person, event or of past times. **3** a document, a record. **monumental** (-men´-) *a.* **1** of or serving as a monument. **2** stupendous, colossal. **3** lasting. **monumentalism** *n.* **1** the style of monuments. **2** building on a massive scale. **monumentality** (-tal´-) *n.* **monumentalize** (-men´-), **monumentalise** *v.t.* to commemorate with a monument. **monumentally** *adv.* **monumental mason** *n.* a stonemason who engraves and erects tombstones etc.

-mony (məni) *suf.* forming nouns, esp. denoting abstract concepts, as in *ceremony, matrimony, parsimony.*

moo (moo) *v.i.* (*3rd pers. sing. pres.* **moos**, *pres.p.* **mooing**, *past, p.p.* **mooed**) to make the vocal noise of cattle, to make a noise like a cow. ~*n.* the sound 'moo'. **moo cow** *n.* a cow (used by or to children).

mooch (mooch) *v.i.* (*coll.*) to wander aimlessly, amble. ~*v.t.* **1** to cadge. **2** to steal. **moocher** *n.*

mood[1] (mood) *n.* **1** a state of mind, disposition, humour. **2** the expression of mood in art, literature etc. ~*a.* expressing a mood. **in a mood** experiencing a period of sulkiness, gloom, withdrawal etc. **in the mood** inclined (to or for), in a positive state of mind. **moody** *a.* (*comp.* **moodier**, *superl.* **moodiest**) **1** indulging in unpredictable moods, temperamental. **2** peevish, sullen, out of temper. ~*n.* (*pl., coll.*) a bad mood, temper tantrum etc. **moodily** *adv.* **moodiness** *n.*

mood[2] (mood) *n.* **1** (*Gram.*) a verb form expressing the manner in which the act, event or fact is conceived, whether as actual, contingent, possible, desirable etc. **2** (*Logic*) the form of a syllogism with regard to the quantity and quality of the propositions.

Moog® (moog, mōg), **Moog synthesizer**, **Moog synthesiser** *n.* an electronic keyboard instrument producing a variety of sounds.

moolah (moo´lə) *n.* (*sl.*) money.

mooli (moo´li) *n.* (*pl.* **moolis**) a large white root vegetable like a radish.

moon (moon) *n.* **1** the earth's satellite revolving round it monthly. **2** the satellite of any planet. **3** anything shaped like a moon or crescent. **4** (*poet.*) a lunar month. ~*v.i.* **1** to wander (about) or stare in a listless manner. **2** (*sl.*) to expose one's buttocks to others. ~*v.t.* to pass (time) in a listless manner. **many moons ago** a long time ago. **over the moon** very pleased or happy. **moonbeam** *n.* a ray of light reflected from the moon. **moon boot** *n.* a tall thickly-padded boot for wearing in low temperatures. **mooncalf** *n.* (*pl.* **mooncalves**) a blockhead, a born fool. **moon-faced** *a.* having a round face. **moonfish** *n.* (*pl.* **moonfish**) any fish that is silvery and disc-shaped, e.g. the opah or the platy. **moonless** a. **moonlight** n. the light of the moon. ~a. moonlit. ~v.i. (past, p.p. **moonlighted**) to have a part-time job in the evening as well as full-time work during the day. **moonlighter** n. **moonlight flit** n. a removal of household furniture after dark to escape paying rent etc. **moonlit** a. **moonquake** n. a light tremor detected on the surface of the moon. **moonrise** n. 1 the rising of the moon. 2 the time of this. **moonscape** n. 1 the surface or landscape of the moon. 2 a desolate landscape similar to this. **moonset** n. 1 the setting of the moon. 2 the time of this. **moonshine** n. 1 moonlight. 2 unreality, visionary ideas, nonsense. 3 smuggled or illicitly-distilled spirits. **moonshiner** n. 1 an illicit distiller. 2 a smuggler, esp. of spirits. **moonshot** n. the launching of a spacecraft to the moon. **moonstone** n. a variety of feldspar with whitish or opalescent reflections. **moonstruck, moonstricken** a. 1 mentally deranged. 2 fanciful, sentimental. **moony** a. (comp. **moonier,** superl. **mooniest**) 1 like the moon. 2 moonstruck, listless, dreamy, silly. 3 (sl.) tipsy. **moonily** adv. **mooniness** n.

Moonie (moo'ni) n. (coll., offensive) a member of the Unification Church, whose followers give all their possessions to it and live in communes.

Moor (maw, muə) n. a member of a mixed Berber and Arab people inhabiting Morocco and the adjoining parts of NW Africa. **Moorish** a. **Moorish idol** n. a brightly-coloured tropical fish, Zanclus canescens, common in the Pacific esp. around coral reefs.

moor¹ (maw, muə) v.t. to secure (a ship, boat etc.) with chains, ropes or cable and anchor. ~v.i. 1 to secure a ship in this way, to anchor. 2 to lie at anchor or secured by cables etc. **moorage** n. **mooring** n. 1 (usu. pl.) the place where a ship is moored. 2 anchors, chains etc. by which a ship is moored. **mooring-mast** n. a tower for mooring an airship to.

moor² (maw, muə) n. a tract of wild open land, esp. if overgrown with heather. **moorcock** n. the male of the red grouse. **moorfowl** n. the red grouse Lagopus scoticus. **moorhen** n. 1 a small water bird, Gallinula chloropus, with black plumage and a red bill. 2 the female of the moorfowl. **moorish** a. **moorland** n. an expanse of moor. **moory** a. (comp. **moorier,** superl. **mooriest**).

moose (moos) n. (pl. **moose**) the elk, Alces alces, inhabiting the colder parts of N America.

moot (moot) v.t. to raise for discussion, to suggest. ~a. open to discussion or argument. ~n. 1 (Hist.) an assembly of freemen in a township, tithing etc. 2 (Law) a law students' debate on a supposed case. **moot point, moot case** n. 1 a debatable point or case. 2 an open question.

mop (mop) n. 1 a bundle of rags, yarn etc. or a pad of synthetic material fastened to a long handle, and used for cleaning floors etc. 2 a thick mass,

as of hair. ~v.t. (pres.p. **mopping,** past, p.p. **mopped**) to wipe or soak up moisture from with a mop etc. **to mop up 1** to wipe up with or as with a mop. **2** (Mil.) to clear (a place) of enemy troops etc. **3** (sl.) to seize, to appropriate, to get hold of. **4** to dispatch, to finish off. **mophead** n. 1 a thick head of hair. 2 a person with such a head. 3 the head of a mop. **moppy** a. (comp. **moppier,** superl. **moppiest**).

mope (mōp) v.i. to be dull or dispirited. ~n. 1 a person who mopes. 2 (pl.) ennui, the blues. **moper** n. **mopy** a. (comp. **mopier,** superl. **mopiest**). **mopily** adv. **mopiness** n.

moped (mō'ped) n. a motorized pedal cycle, of less than 50cc.

moppet (mop'it) n. a pet, a darling (applied to children, young girls etc.).

moquette (moket') n. a woven fabric of wool and hemp or linen with a velvety pile, used for carpets and upholstery.

mor (maw) n. (Geol.) acidic humus formed where decomposition is slow.

moraine (mərān') n. the debris of rocks brought down by glaciers. **morainal, morainic** a.

moral (mor'əl) a. 1 of or relating to character and conduct in terms of the distinction between right and wrong. 2 conforming to or regulated by what is right, good, virtuous, esp. in sexual relations. 3 subject to the rules of morality, distinguishing between right and wrong. 4 based on morality. 5 concerned with or treating of conduct or morality. 6 conveying a moral. 7 practical, virtual, in spirit (a moral victory). 8 (esp. of support) psychological rather than practical. ~n. 1 the moral lesson taught by a story, incident etc. 2 (pl.) moral habits, conduct, behaviour, esp. in sexual relations. 3 (pl.) ethics, moral science. **moral certainty** n. probability that leaves little doubt. **moralism** n. morality distinguished from religion or divested of religious teaching. **moralist** n. 1 a person who teaches morality. 2 a person who behaves in accordance with moral rules. **moralistic** (-lis'-) a. **moralistically** adv. **morality** (-ral'-) n. (pl. **moralities**) 1 the doctrine, principles or practice of moral duties, moral science, ethics. 2 morals, moral conduct, esp. in sexual relations. 3 a morality play. **morality play** n. (Hist.) a kind of drama (popular in the 16th cent.) in which the characters represent virtues, vices etc. **moralize, moralise** v.i. to make moral reflections (on). ~v.t. 1 to provide with moral lessons. 2 to interpret or apply in a moral sense. 3 to render moral. **moralization** (-zā'shən) n. **moralizer** n. **moralizingly** adv. **moral law** n. the rules of right and wrong which any right course of action must satisfy. **morally** adv. **moral majority** n. (esp. N Am.) the majority of the country's population, regarded as acting on and favouring adherence to strict moral principles. **moral philosophy** n. ethics. **moral pressure** n. an attempt to persuade by appealing to a person's sense of morality. **Moral Rearmament** n. 1 the principles of the Oxford Group. **2** the movement to promote these. **moral science** *n.* a systematic study and knowledge of moral issues. **moral sense** *n.* the ability to judge what is right and wrong in one's conduct.

morale (mərahl´) *n.* **1** mental or moral condition. **2** courage and endurance in supporting fatigue, danger or other threats to one's mental well-being.

morass (məras´) *n.* **1** anything that is confused or complicated, esp. when it impedes progress. **2** a swamp, a bog.

moratorium (morətaw´riəm) *n.* (*pl.* **moratoriums, moratoria** (-riə)) **1** a deferment, delay or temporary suspension. **2** a legal act authorizing a debtor or bank to defer or suspend payment for a time. **3** the period of such a suspension.

Moravian (mərā´viən) *a.* of or relating to Moravia, the Moravians or their dialect of Czech. *~n.* a native or inhabitant of Moravia.

moray (mor´ā) *n.* any brightly-patterned coastal eel of the family Muraenidae, esp. *Muraena helena.*

morbid (maw´bid) *a.* **1** unhealthily preoccupied with unpleasant matters, esp. with death. **2** (*Med.*) sickly, unhealthy, diseased. **3** pathological. **morbid anatomy** *n.* the anatomy of diseased organs, tissues etc. **morbidity** (-bid´-) *n.* **morbidly** *adv.* **morbidness** *n.* **morbific** (-bif´-) *a.* producing disease.

mordant (maw´dənt) *a.* **1** biting, caustic, pungent. **2** causing pain or smarting. **3** serving to fix colours etc. *~n.* **1** a substance for fixing colouring matter in dyeing. **2** an adhesive substance used in applying gold leaf. **3** acid or other corrosive used by etchers. **mordancy** *n.* **mordantly** *adv.*

mordent (maw´dənt) *n.* **1** (*Mus.*) a rapid alternation of a note with the one immediately below it, a kind of trill. **2** the character indicating this.

more (maw) *a.* **1** greater in quantity, extent, degree, number, importance etc. **2** additional, extra. *~adv.* **1** in or to a greater degree, extent, or quantity (used to form comp. of most adjectives and adverbs of more than one syllable). **2** further, besides, again. *~n.* **1** a greater quantity, amount, number or degree. **2** an additional quantity. **more and more** with continual increase. **more of** to a greater extent (*more of a director than an actor*). **more or less 1** about. **2** thereabouts. **3** to a greater or less extent. **more so** to a greater extent or degree. **more than** very. **moreish, morish** *a.* (*coll.*) (of food) causing one to want more, delicious.

morel (mərel´) *n.* an edible fungus, *Morchella esculenta,* and other species of *Morchella.*

morello (mərel´ō) *n.* (*pl.* **morellos**) a bitter dark-red cherry.

moreover (mawrō´və) *adv.* besides, in addition, further.

mores (maw´rāz) *n.pl.* the customs and conduct

which embody the fundamental values of a social group.

✖ **morgage** common misspelling of MORTGAGE.

morganatic (mawgənat´ik) *a.* of or relating to a marriage between a person of high rank and one of lower rank, by virtue of which the latter does not acquire the spouse's rank and, along with any children of the marriage, is not entitled to inherit the spouse's title or possessions. **morganatically** *adv.*

morgue (mawg) *n.* **1** a mortuary. **2** a stock of files, clippings etc., esp. future obituaries, kept by a newspaper for reference.

moribund (mor´ibŭnd) *a.* **1** in a dying state. **2** lacking vitality and energy. **moribundity** (-bŭn´-) *n.*

morish MORE.

Mormon (maw´mən) *n.* a member of an American religious body, founded by Joseph Smith in 1830, now calling themselves the Latter-Day Saints, who claim continuous divine revelation through their priesthood, and formerly practised polygamy. **Mormonism** *n.*

morn (mawn) *n.* (*poet.*) morning.

mornay (maw´nā) *a.* served with a cheese sauce (*salmon mornay*).

morning (maw´ning) *n.* **1** the first part of the day, beginning at twelve o'clock at night and extending to twelve noon, or from dawn to midday. **2** the early part of a period or epoch. **3** (*poet.*) dawn. *~int.* (*coll.*) good morning. *~a.* of, relating to or meant to be taken or worn in the morning. **in the morning** tomorrow morning. **morning after** *n.* **1** a time of physical and mental discomfort following the activity of the previous night. **2** a hangover. **morning-after pill** *n.* a contraceptive pill effective when taken within a specified time after intercourse. **morning coat** *n.* a coat with tails and a cutaway front. **morning dress** *n.* men's clothes worn on formal occasions during the day, esp. for weddings etc. **morning glory** *n.* (*pl.* **morning glories**) any of various climbing or twining plants of the genus *Ipomoea.* **morning room** *n.* a sitting room used in the morning. **morning sickness** *n.* nausea and vomiting frequently accompanying early pregnancy. **morning star** *n.* the planet Venus when visible in the east at dawn.

Moroccan (mərok´ən) *a.* of or relating to Morocco or its inhabitants. *~n.* a native or inhabitant of Morocco. **morocco** (-ō) *n.* (*pl.* **moroccos**) a fine leather from goatskin, tanned with sumach and dyed (formerly made in Morocco).

moron (maw´ron) *n.* **1** (*coll.*) a very stupid or foolish person. **2** (*Psych.*) an adult with the mental age of between eight and twelve years. **moronic** (məron´-) *a.* **moronically** *adv.* **moronism** *n.*

morose (mərōs´) *a.* peevish, sullen, gloomy, churlish, given to morbid brooding. **morosely** *adv.* **moroseness** *n.*

morpheme (maw´fēm) n. a linguistic element that can carry meaning and cannot be divided into smaller elements of this kind. **morphemic** (-fē´-) a. **morphemically** adv. **morphemics** n. the study of the composition of words.

morphine (maw´fēn), **morphia** (-fiə) n. the alkaloid derived from opium, used in medicine as a sedative and analgesic.

morphing (maw´fing) n. in a film, video etc. the transformation of one image to another by means of computer technology.

morphology (mawfol´əji) n. 1 (Biol.) the branch of biology dealing with the form of organisms. 2 the study of the forms of words. **morphologic** (-əloj´-), **morphological** a. **morphologically** adv. **morphologist** n.

morris dance (mor´is) n. a style of folk dance performed by groups in colourful rustic costume, often using bells, sticks, handkerchiefs etc. and accompanied by the concertina or fiddle. **morris dancer** n. **morris dancing** n.

morrow (mor´ō) n. 1 (poet.) the day next after the present, the following day. 2 (poet.) the succeeding period.

Morse (maws), **Morse code** n. a system of sending messages by telegraph in which letters are represented by combinations of dots and dashes.

morsel (maw´səl) n. 1 a mouthful, a bite, a small piece of food. 2 a small quantity, a piece.

mortadella (mawtədel´ə) n. (pl. **mortadelle** (-i)) a type of large spicy pork sausage, sold ready to eat.

mortal (maw´təl) a. 1 liable to death; human. 2 causing death, deadly, fatal. 3 inveterate, implacable (mortal foe). 4 involving physical or spiritual death. 5 of or relating to death. 6 (coll.) extreme, excessive. 7 (coll.) long and tedious. 8 (coll.) imaginable. ~n. 1 a being subject to death; a human being. 2 (facet.) a person. **mortality** (-tal´-) n. (pl. **mortalities**) 1 the quality of being mortal. 2 human nature. 3 (collect.) human beings. 4 loss of life, esp. on a large scale. 5 (in full **mortality rate**) the number of deaths in a given period, the death rate. **mortally** adv. **mortal sin** n. (Theol.) a grave sin regarded as involving the total loss of grace.

mortar (maw´tə) n. 1 a cement, made of lime, sand and water, for joining bricks etc. in building. 2 a short large-bore cannon used for throwing missiles at a high angle. 3 a vessel in which substances are pounded with a pestle. 4 a device for firing fireworks, lifelines etc. ~v.t. 1 to join, plaster or close up with mortar. 2 to fire mortars at. **mortarboard** n. 1 a square-topped academic cap. 2 a square board for holding mortar. **mortarless** a. **mortary** a.

mortgage (maw´gij) n. 1 the conditional conveyance of a house, estate or other property into the ownership of a building society etc. as security for the repayment of a loan, to be voided on the discharge of the debt or loan. 2 the loan

thus made; the debt thus secured. 3 a deed effecting this. ~v.t. 1 to grant or make over (property) by mortgage. 2 to pledge, to plight (oneself etc. to or for). **mortgageable** a. **mortgagee** (-jē´) n. the party who makes the loan in a mortgage arrangement. **mortgager** (-jə), **mortgagor** (-jaw´) n. a person who mortgages their property. **mortgage rate** n. the rate of interest charged by building societies, banks etc. for mortgage loans.

Usage note MortgagEr is the form of the agent noun in everyday use; mortgagOr is usual in legal contexts.

mortice MORTISE.

mortician (mawtish´ən) n. (N Am.) an undertaker.

mortify (maw´tifī) v.t. (3rd pers. sing. pres. **mortifies**, pres.p. **mortifying**, past, p.p. **mortified**) 1 to humiliate, to wound. 2 to subdue (the passions etc.) by abstinence or self-discipline. ~v.i. to lose vitality, to decay, to go gangrenous. **mortification** (-fikā´shən) n. **mortifying** a. **mortifyingly** adv.

mortise (maw´tis), **mortice** n. a hole cut in timber etc. to receive the end of another part, esp. a tenon. ~v.t. 1 to cut a mortise in. 2 to join by means of mortise and tenon. **mortise lock** n. a lock set into a mortise in the edge of a door, so that the lock mechanism is enclosed by the door.

mortuary (maw´chuəri, -chəri) n. (pl. **mortuaries**) a building for the temporary reception of the dead. ~a. of or relating to death or the burial of the dead.

Mosaic (məzā´ik) a. of or relating to Moses or to the law given through him. **Mosaic law** n. the laws of the Hebrews attributed to Moses and contained in the Pentateuch.

mosaic (məzā´ik) n. 1 a pattern, picture etc. produced by the arrangement of small pieces of coloured marble, glass or stone. 2 the art of producing such patterns etc. 3 a diverse or composite thing. 4 (Biol.) an organism, or part of one, consisting of tissues with different genetic constitutions, a chimera. 5 a composite photosensitive surface in a television camera tube. ~v.t. (pres.p. **mosaicking**, past, p.p. **mosaicked**) 1 to decorate with mosaic. 2 to combine into a mosaic. **mosaically** adv. **mosaic disease** n. a viral disease of plants in which the leaves display a mottled yellowing. **mosaic gold** n. 1 tin disulphide. 2 an alloy of copper and zinc used in gilding cheap jewellery etc. **mosaicist** (-sist) n.

moschatel (moskətel´) n. a small perennial herb, Adoxa moschatellina, with yellowish-green flowers and a musky scent.

mosey (mō´zi) v.i. (3rd pers. sing. pres. **moseys**, pres.p. **moseying**, past, p.p. **moseyed**) (esp. N Am., coll.) to walk, amble.

Moslem MUSLIM.

mosque (mosk) n. a Muslim place of worship.

mosquito (məskē´tō) n. (pl. **mosquitoes**) an insect of the family Culicidae, esp. of the genera

Culex, Anopheles or *Aedes*, with a proboscis for piercing the skin of animals and sucking their blood. **mosquito-boat** *n.* (*N Am.*) a motor torpedo boat. **mosquito net** *n.* a fine-mesh netting round a bed, over windows etc. to ward off mosquitoes.

moss (mos) *n.* **1** a low, tufted, herbaceous plant of the cryptogamous class Musci, usually growing on damp soil or the surface of stones, trees etc. **2** a bog, a peatbog, wet spongy land. **moss agate** *n.* agate with dendritic markings similar to moss. **mosslike** *a.* **moss stitch** *n.* a stitch in knitting consisting of alternating plain and purl stitches. **mossy** *a.* (*comp.* **mossier,** *superl.* **mossiest**) **1** overgrown with moss. **2** mosslike. **3** (*N Am., coll.*) old-fashioned, conservative. **mossiness** *n.*

most (mōst) *a.* greatest in amount, number, extent, quality, degree etc. ~*adv.* **1** in the greatest or highest degree (forming the superl. of most adjectives and adverbs of more than one syllable). **2** (*coll.*) very. ~*n.* **1** the greatest number, quantity, amount etc. **2** the best, the worst etc. **3** the majority. **at most 1** at the utmost extent. **2** no more than. **at the most 1** as the greatest amount. **2** not more than. **for the most part** in the main, usually. **to make the most of** to use to the best advantage. **Most High** *n.* the Supreme Being, God. **mostly** *adv.* **1** chiefly, mainly. **2** on most occasions, usually. **Most Reverend** *n.* a title given to an Archbishop or an Irish Roman Catholic bishop.

Usage note The use of *most* (rather than *more*) when comparing only two is best avoided.

-most (mōst) *suf.* forming superlatives of adjectives and adverbs denoting position, order etc., as in *hindmost, inmost, utmost.*

MOT (emōtē´) *abbr.* (*Hist.*) Ministry of Transport. ~*n.* (*pl.* **MOTs**) (*coll.*) an MOT test. **MOT test** *n.* a test of the roadworthiness of a motor vehicle more than three years old.

mot (mō) *n.* (*pl.* **mots** (mō)) a witty or pithy saying. **mot juste** (zhoost´) *n.* the appropriate or felicitous word or phrase.

mote (mōt) *n.* **1** a particle of dust, a speck, a spot. **2** anything proverbially small.

motel (mōtel´) *n.* a roadside hotel or furnished cabins providing accommodation for motorists.

motet (mōtet´) *n.* (*Mus.*) a vocal composition in harmony, of a sacred character.

moth (moth) *n.* any of a group of nocturnal or crepuscular insects of the order Lepidoptera, distinct from butterflies by not having knotted antennae and folding the wings flat when at rest. **mothball** *n.* a ball of naphthalene or similar substance that keeps away clothes-moths. ~*v.t.* **1** to lay up in mothballs. **2** to lay up for later use. **in mothballs** in long-term storage pending possible future use. **moth-eaten** *a.* **1** eaten into holes by moths. **2** ragged, decayed, time-worn, outdated. **mothproof** *a.* (of clothes etc.) treated so as to repel moths. ~*v.t.* to treat in this way. **mothy**

a. (*comp.* **mothier,** *superl.* **mothiest**) full of moths.

mother (mŭdh´ə) *n.* **1** a female parent. **2** a woman performing the function of a mother in continuously caring for a child. **3** the source or origin of anything. **4** the head of a religious community, a Mother Superior. **5** (*N Am., taboo sl.*) short for MOTHERFUCKER (under MOTHER). ~*v.t.* **1** to act as mother towards. **2** to give birth to. **3** to give rise to. **4** to acknowledge that one is or claim to be mother or originator of. **motherboard** *n.* (*Comput.*) the principal printed circuit in a microcomputer etc. through which all other systems are routed. **Mother Carey's chicken** *n.* the storm petrel. **mother-cell** *n.* (*Biol.*) a cell that produces other cells by division. **mother country** *n.* **1** one's native country. **2** a country in relation to its colonies. **mothercraft** *n.* expertise, knowledge etc. in rearing children as a mother. **mother figure** *n.* an older woman whom one looks to for advice and support. **motherfucker** *n.* (*N Am., taboo sl.*) an offensive or unpleasant person or thing. **motherfucking** *a.* **Mother Goose rhyme** *n.* (*N Am.*) a nursery rhyme. **motherhood** *n.* **Mothering Sunday** *n.* the fourth Sunday in Lent, when mothers traditionally receive presents from their children. **mother-in-law** *n.* (*pl.* **mothers-in-law**) the mother of a person's wife or husband. **mother-in-law's tongue** *n.* a herbaceous perennial plant, *Sansevieria trifasciata,* with long pointed leaves. **motherland** *n.* a person's native country. **motherless** *a.* **motherlike** *a., adv.* **mother lode** *n.* (*Mining*) the main vein of a system. **motherly** *a.* **1** like a mother; nurturing, loving. **2** proper to or becoming a mother. **motherliness** *n.* **mother-naked** *a.* completely naked. **mother-of-pearl** *n.* the iridescent pearly substance forming the internal layer of many shells. **Mother's Day** *n.* **1** Mothering Sunday. **2** (*N Am.*) the second Sunday in May, similarly set apart for the honouring of one's mother. **mother's ruin** *n.* (*coll.*) gin. **mother's son** *n.* (*coll.*) a man. **every mother's son** all without exception. **Mother Superior** *n.* a woman having charge of a community of women in religious orders. **mother-to-be** *n.* (*pl.* **mothers-to-be**) a pregnant woman. **mother tongue** *n.* **1** a person's native language. **2** a language from which others have sprung. **mother wit** *n.* natural sagacity, common sense.

motif (mōtēf´) *n.* **1** the dominant feature or idea in a literary, musical or other artistic composition. **2** an ornamental piece of lace etc. sewn on a dress.

motile (mō´tīl) *a.* (*Zool., Bot.*) capable of motion. **motility** (-til´-) *n.*

motion (mō´shən) *n.* **1** the act, process or state of moving. **2** passage of a body from place to place. **3** change of posture. **4** a gesture. **5** an evacuation of the bowels. **6** a combination of moving parts in a machine etc. **7** a proposal, esp. in a deliberative assembly. **8** (*Law*) an application to a court for a rule or order. **9** impulse, instigation. ~*v.t.* to direct by a gesture. ~*v.i.* to make significant gestures. **to go through the motions** to do something without enthusiasm or conviction. **to put/ set in motion** to set going or in operation. **motional** *a.* **motionless** *a.* **motionlessly** *adv.* **motion picture** *n.* a cinematograph film. **motion sickness** *n.* nausea induced by travelling in a car, ship, aircraft etc.

motive (mō´tiv) *n.* **1** that which incites to action, or determines the will; a cause, ground, incentive. **2** in art, the predominant idea, feeling etc., motif. ~*a.* **1** causing or initiating motion. **2** of or relating to movement. **3** of or relating to a motive or motives. ~*v.t.* to motivate. **motivate** *v.t.* **1** to provide an incentive or motive to. **2** to instigate. **3** to rouse to interest or effort. **motivation** (-ā´shən) *n.* **motivational** *a.* **motivationally** *adv.* **motiveless** *a.* **motivelessly** *adv.* **motivelessness** *n.* **motive power** *n.* **1** the power by which mechanical motion is imparted. **2** any impelling force. **motivity** (-tiv´-) *n.*

motley (mot´li) *a.* (*comp.* **motlier,** *superl.* **motliest**) **1** of varied character, heterogeneous. **2** variegated in colour. **3** dressed in multicoloured clothes. ~*n.* **1** a heterogeneous mixture. **2** the multicoloured quartered dress of fools or jesters. **to wear motley** to play the fool.

motmot (mot´mot) *n.* a S American and Mexican bird of the family Momotidae allied to the kingfishers.

motocross (mō´təkros) *n.* the sport of racing on motorcycles over rough ground.

motor (mō´tə) *n.* **1** something that imparts motive power, esp. a machine imparting motion to a vehicle or vessel (usu. excluding steam engines). **2** a device that converts electrical energy into mechanical energy. **3** (*coll.*) a car. **4** (*Anat.*) **a** a muscle for moving some part of the body. **b** a nerve exciting muscular action. ~*a.* causing or imparting motion. ~*v.i.* to drive or ride in a car. ~*v.t.* to convey in a car. **motorable** *a.* (of a road) able to be used by motor vehicles. **motor area** *n.* part of the frontal lobe of the brain which initiates the action of muscles. **motorbike** *n.* (*coll.*) a motorcycle. **motor boat** *n.* a boat propelled by a motor. **motorcade** (-kād) *n.* a procession of motor vehicles. **motor caravan** *n.* a motor vehicle fitted with sleeping accommodation, cooking facilities etc. **motorcycle** *n.* a two-wheeled motor vehicle without any form of pedal propulsion. **motorcycling** *n.* **motorcyclist** *n.* **motorhome** *n.* a large motor caravan. **motorist** *n.* a driver of a car. **motorize, motorise** *v.t.* **1** to convert to being motor-driven. **2** to equip (troops) with motor vehicles. **motorization** (-zā´shən) *n.* **motorman** *n.* (*pl.* **motormen**) a man in charge of a motor, esp. of an electric tram or train. **motormouth** *n.* (*sl.*) someone who talks incessantly and trivially. **motor nerve** *n.* an efferent nerve that excites muscular activity. **motor neurone disease** *n.* (*Med.*) a disease

involving progressive degeneration of the motor neurones leading to wasting of the muscles. **motor racing** *n.* the sport of racing in motor vehicles, usu. on a track. **motor scooter** *n.* a small motorcycle, usu. with a fairing reaching from below the handlebars in a curve to under the rider's feet. **motor sport** *n.* a sport involving racing in motor vehicles. **motor vehicle** *n.* a road vehicle driven by a motor or engine, esp. by an internal-combustion engine. **motorway** *n.* a road for fast motor traffic, usu. with a relatively high speed limit. **motory** *a.* **motor yacht** *n.* a motor-driven yacht.

motte (mot) *n.* a mound on which a castle, camp etc. is situated.

mottle (mot´əl) *v.t.* to blotch, to variegate with spots of different colours or shades of colour. ~*n.* **1** a blotch or patch of colour. **2** a spotted, blotched or variegated appearance on a surface. **mottled** *a.*

motto (mot´ō) *n.* (*pl.* **mottoes**) **1** (*pl.*) a short pithy sentence or phrase expressing a sentiment or maxim. **2** a principle or maxim adopted as a rule of conduct. **3** a joke, verse or maxim contained in a paper cracker. **mottoed** *a.*

mouflon (moo´flon), **moufflon** *n.* a wild sheep, *Ovis orientalis,* of Sardinia and Corsica.

mould[1] (mōld), (*N Am.*) **mold** *n.* **1** a hollow shape into which molten metal etc. is poured in a fluid state to cool into a permanent shape. **2** a template used by plasterers for shaping cornices etc. **3** any of various analogous appliances used in trades and manufactures. **4** a hollow vessel for shaping puddings etc. **5** (*Archit.*) a moulding or group of mouldings. **6** a pudding etc. shaped in a mould. **7** physical form, shape, build. **8** character, nature. ~*v.t.* **1** to form into a particular shape. **2** to fashion, to make, to produce. **3** to give a particular character to. **4** to fit closely to. **moulder**[1] *n.* **moulding** *n.* **1** an ornamental part of a cornice, capital, arch, woodwork etc., usu. in the form of continuous grooves and projections, showing in profile a complex series of curves. **2** a strip of wood, stone etc. for use as a moulding. **3** anything formed in or as in a mould. **4** the act or process of shaping anything in or as in a mould.

mould[2] (mōld), (*N Am.*) **mold** *n.* a minute fungoid growth forming a woolly or furry coating on matter left in the damp. **mouldy** *a.* (*comp.* **mouldier,** *superl.* **mouldiest**) **1** covered with mould. **2** (*coll.*) bad, poor, nasty. **mouldiness** *n.*

mould[3] (mōld), (*N Am.*) **mold** *n.* **1** fine soft earth, easily pulverized, suitable for cultivation. **2** the earth, the ground.

moulder[1] MOULD[1].

moulder[2] (mōl´də), (*N Am.*) **molder** *v.i.* **1** to turn to dust by natural decay. **2** to crumble. **3** to waste away gradually.

moult (mōlt), (*N Am.*) **molt** *v.i.* to shed the feathers, hair, skin, horns etc. (of certain birds and animals). ~*v.t.* to shed or cast. ~*n.* the act of moulting.

mound (mownd) *n.* **1** an artificial elevation of earth, stones etc. **2** a hillock, a knoll. **3** a barrow, a tumulus. **4** in baseball, a slight elevation on which the pitcher stands to pitch. ~*v.t.* **1** to heap up in a mound or mounds. **2** to furnish, enclose or protect with a mound.

mount¹ (mownt) *v.t.* **1** to ascend, to climb. **2** to ascend upon, to get up on to. **3** to form a path up. **4** to copulate with. **5** to place on a raised support, to raise. **6** to prepare for use. **7** to put (a picture etc.) on a mount. **8** to affix (a stamp, photograph etc.) with mounts. **9** to place for microscopic examination on. **10** to stage (a play etc.); to present (an exhibition etc.) for public view. **11** to put (someone) on a horse. **12** to provide with a horse or horses. ~*v.i.* **1** to rise, to ascend. **2** to get on horseback. **3** to rise in amount. **4** to soar. **5** (of blood) to flush the cheeks. ~*n.* **1** something on which anything is mounted. **2** an adhesive hinge for affixing stamps, photographs etc. to a page. **3** a piece of cardboard etc. upon which a drawing is placed. **4** a slide on which something is placed for microscopic examination. **5** the margin around a picture. **6** the parts by which various objects are prepared for use, strengthened or ornamented. **7** a horse with the appurtenances necessary for riding. **mountable** *a.* **mounted** *a.* **1** on horseback. **2** placed on a mount. **mounter** *n.* **Mountie, Mounty** *n.* (*pl.* **Mounties**) (*coll.*) a member of the Royal Canadian Mounted Police. **mounting** *n.* **mounting block** *n.* a horse-block.

mount² (mownt) *n.* a high hill, a mountain (in poetry, or as first part of a proper name).

mountain (mown´tin) *n.* **1** a natural elevation of the earth's surface rising high above the surrounding land. **2** ha large heap or pile. **3** something of very great bulk. **4** a commodity surplus, esp. of an agricultural product. **to make a mountain out of a molehill** to make far more of an issue, task etc. than is justified or reasonable. **to move mountains** to achieve what was seemingly impossible by effort, persistence etc. **mountain ash** *n.* **1** the rowan, *Sorbus aucuparia.* **2** (*Austral.*) any of various kinds of eucalyptus. **mountain avens** *n.* a trailing evergreen alpine plant, *Dryas octopetala,* of the rose family, having white flowers. **mountain bike** *n.* a sturdy bicycle with many gears and thick tyres for use on steep or rugged terrain. **mountain chain** *n.* a range or series of mountains. **mountaineer** (-niə´) *n.* **1** a person who climbs mountains as a hobby or occupation. **2** a person who lives among mountains. **mountaineering** *n.* **mountain goat** *n.* **1** any wild goat living in mountainous areas, often associated with being agile. **2** the Rocky Mountain goat, *Oreamnos americanus,* of western N America. **mountain laurel** *n.* an ericaceous shrub, *Kalmia latifolia,* of N America. **mountain lion** *n.* a puma. **mountainous** *a.* **1** full of mountains. **2** exceedingly large.

mountainously *adv.* **mountainousness** *n.* **mountain panther** *n.* the Asian wild cat, the ounce. **mountain range** *n.* an area or line of mountains of similar origin. **mountain sickness** *n.* a feeling of indisposition, varying in different people, brought on by ascending into rarefied mountain air. **mountainside** *n.* **mountainy** *a.*

mountebank (mown´tibangk) *n.* a swindler, a boastful pretender, a charlatan. **mountebankery, mountebankism** *n.*

mourn (mawn) *v.i.* **1** to express or feel sorrow or grief. **2** to observe the mourning customs, dress etc. ~*v.t.* to grieve or sorrow for. **mourner** *n.* **mournful** *a.* **mournfully** *adv.* **mournfulness** *n.* **mourning** *a.* **1** grieving, sorrowing. **2** expressive of grief or sorrow. ~*n.* **1** grief, sorrow, lamentation. **2** the customary dress, usu. black, worn by mourners. **in mourning** wearing mourning. **mourning cloak** *n.* a large butterfly, the Camberwell Beauty. **mourning dove** *n.* an American dove, *Zenaida macroura,* so called from its plaintive note. **mourningly** *adv.*

mousaka MOUSSAKA.

mouse¹ (mows) *n.* (*pl.* **mice** (mīs)) **1** a small rodent quadruped of various species belonging to the family Muridae. **2** any of various similar animals, such as the shrews, voles etc. **3** (*Comput.*) (*pl.* **mouses**) a device that allows manual control of the cursor and selection of computer functions without use of the keyboard. **4** (*coll.*) a shy or inconspicuous person. **5** (*sl.*) a black eye. **mouse-colour, mouse-coloured,** (*N Am.*) **mouse-color, mouse-colored** *a.* darkish grey with a tinge of brown. **mouse deer** *n.* a chevrotain. **mouse hare** *n.* a pika. **mouselike** *a.* **mousetrap** *n.* **1** a trap for catching mice. **2** (*coll.*) low-quality cheese. **mousy, mousey** *a.* (*comp.* **mousier,** *superl.* **mousiest**) **1** of a drab grey or brown colour. **2** (*coll.*) shy, timid or inconspicuous. **mousily** *adv.* **mousiness** *n.*

mouse² (mows, mowz) *v.i.* **1** to hunt for or catch mice. **2** to hunt, to watch craftily, to prowl (about). **mouser** *n.* a cat good at catching mice.

moussaka (moosah´kə), **mousaka** *n.* a Greek dish of minced meat, aubergines and tomatoes, topped with a cheese sauce.

mousse (moos) *n.* **1** a dish of flavoured cream whipped and frozen. **2** any of various light, stiff liquid preparations, e.g. used for hairstyling or cosmetic purposes. **3** oil and sea water forming a froth after a spillage of oil.

mousseline (mooslēn´) *n.* **1** fine French muslin. **2** a light sauce made by whipping cream with hollandaise sauce.

moustache (məstahsh´), (*N Am.*) **mustache** *n.* **1** the hair on the upper lip, esp. the hair of men when left to grow. **2** a growth of hair round the mouth on various animals. **moustache cup** *n.* a drinking-cup with a guard to keep liquid from wetting the moustache. **moustached** *a.*

mousy MOUSE¹.

mouth¹ (mowth) *n.* (*pl.* **mouths** (mowdhz)) **1** the opening through which food is taken into the body. **2** the cavity behind this, containing the organs of mastication, salivation and vocalization. **3** anything analogous to a mouth, the opening of a vessel, pit, cave or the like. **4** a person regarded as needing to be fed. **5** the outfall of a river. **6** (*coll.*) **a** talkativeness. **b** impudent talk, cheek. **7** a horse's responsiveness to the bit. **to give mouth** (of a dog) to bark or bay. **to keep one's mouth shut** (*coll.*) not to speak, esp. not to reveal secrets. **to put words into a person's mouth** to represent, perh. incorrectly, what one assumes another person means. **to stop the mouth of** to put to silence. **to take words out of a person's mouth** to say what another person was about to say. **mouthbrooder** *n.* any fish that carries its eggs and young around in the mouth. **mouthed** (-dhd) *a.* **mouthful** *n.* (*pl.* **mouthfuls**) **1** an amount that fills the mouth. **2** a small quantity of food etc. **3** (*coll.*) a word or phrase that is pompous or difficult to say. **4** (*coll.*) an abusive tirade. **5** (*N Am.*) an important statement. **mouthless** *a.* **mouth organ** *n.* a small musical instrument, played by blowing on metallic reeds, a harmonica. **mouthpart** *n.* any of the usu. paired appendages around the mouth of an insect, arthropod etc. and adapted for feeling. **mouthpiece** *n.* **1** that part of a musical instrument put between the lips. **2** that party of a telephone spoken into. **3** a tube by which a cigar or cigarette is held in the mouth. **4** a spokesman for others. **5** (*coll.*) a lawyer. **6** an attached outlet. **mouth-to-mouth** *a.* (of resuscitation) carried out by breathing air into someone's mouth directly. **mouthwash** *n.* **1** an antiseptic liquid used to cleanse the mouth. **2** (*coll.*) nonsense. **mouthwatering** *a.* (appearing to be) delicious. **mouthy** (-dhi) *a.* (*comp.* **mouthier**, *superl.* **mouthiest**) **1** (*coll.*) impudent, cheeky. **2** ranting, bombastic, aggressively loud.

mouth[2] (mowdh) *v.t.* **1** to utter pompously or in an elaborate or constrained manner, to declaim. **2** to utter in exaggerated manner to help communication. **3** to say (words) silently moving the lips. **4** to take up or seize with the mouth. **5** to chew or roll with the mouth. ~*v.i.* **1** to talk pompously or affectedly. **2** to communicate by forming words silently with the lips. **3** to make grimaces. †**mouther** *n.*

move (moov) *v.t.* **1** to cause to change position or posture. **2** to carry, lift, draw or push from one place to another. **3** to put in motion, to stir. **4** to cause (the bowels) to act. **5** to incite, to incline, to prompt, to rouse (to action). **6** to excite, to provoke (laughter etc.). **7** to prevail upon. **8** to affect with feelings, usu. of tenderness, to touch. **9** to propose, to submit for discussion. ~*v.i.* **1** to change place or posture. **2** to go from one place to another. **3** to advance, to progress. **4** to change one's place of residence. **5** to change the position of a piece at chess etc. **6** to make an application, appeal etc. **7** to begin to act. **8** to take action, to

proceed. **9** to be moved, to have an evacuation (of the bowels). **10** to live, to exercise one's activities (in or among). ~*n.* **1** the act of moving. **2** the right to move (in chess etc.). **3** proceeding, action, line of conduct. **4** a step, a device to obtain an object. **5** a change of abode. **on the move 1** stirring. **2** moving from place to place, travelling about. **to get a move on** (*coll.*) to hurry. **to make a move 1** to start. **2** to begin to go. **3** to move a piece at chess etc. **to move away** to go to live elsewhere, esp. at some distance. **to move in 1** to move into a new house etc. **2** to take up a position of power, influence, advantage etc. **to move in with** to start to share accommodation with (an established resident). **to move on/ along** to change one's position, esp. to avoid crowding or to accommodate others. **to move out** to go to live elsewhere. **to move over/ up** to adjust one's position to accommodate others. **movable**, **moveable** *a.* **1** capable of being moved. **2** occurring at varying times (as a festival). ~*n.* **1** anything that can be moved or removed, esp. a movable or portable piece of furniture etc. that is not a fixture. **2** (*pl.*) goods, furniture, chattels etc., as distinct from houses and lands, personal as distinct from real property. **movability** (-bil´-), **movableness** *n.* **movable-doh** *a.* (*Mus.*) denoting a notation used in sight-singing in which 'doh' is adjusted to become the key note of the scale being used, as distinct from *fixed-doh*. **movable feast** *n.* **1** a festival the date of which varies. **2** (*facet.*) a meal taken at irregular times. **movably** *adv.* **movement** *n.* **1** the act or process of changing position, place or posture. **2** manner or style of moving. **3** the working mechanism of a watch, clock, machine etc., or a connected group of parts of this. **4** a connected series of impulses, efforts and actions, directed to a special end. **5** a tendency in art, politics, literature etc., either actively promoted or occurring spontaneously. **6** the people involved in this. **7** an activity in a market, esp. change of value. **8** (*Mus.*) the mode or rate of a piece of music, also a section of a large work having the same general measure or time. **mover** *n.* **1** someone who or something which moves. **2** a cause or source of motive power. **3** a proposer (of a resolution etc.). **4** a person who originates or instigates. **mover and shaker** *n.* (*usu. in pl.*, *coll.*) a person with power and influence in politics, business etc. **moving** *a.* **1** causing motion. **2** in motion. **3** impelling, persuading. **4** pathetic, affecting. **movingly** *adv.* **moving pavement** *n.* a type of conveyor belt for pedestrians, a travolator. **moving picture** *n.* the photographic record of a series of events in the form of shots taken at very short intervals and projected in sequence. **moving staircase** *n.* an escalator.

movie (moo´vi) *n.* (*coll.*) **1** (*esp. N Am.*) a cinema film. **2** (*US*) a cinema. **movie theatre**, **movie house** *n.* a cinema.

mow[1] (mō) *v.t.* (*past* **mowed**, *p.p.* **mown** (mōn), mowed) **1** to cut down (grass, corn etc.) with a mower, scythe etc. **2** to cut the grass off (a lawn etc.). **to mow down 1** to kill in great numbers. **2** to destroy indiscriminately. **mower** n.

mow² (mō) n. (dial. or N Am.) **1** a heap or pile of hay, corn or other field produce, a stack. **2** a place in a barn etc. for storing heaps of hay etc.

moxa (mok´sə) n. a downy material obtained from the dried leaves of Crossostrephium artemisioides, burnt on the skin in oriental medical treatments such as acupuncture, or as a counterirritant. **moxibustion** (-bŭs´-) n. the burning of moxa on or near the skin.

moxie (mok´si) n. (N Am., sl.) vigour, courage, force of character, wit.

mozzarella (motsərel´ə) n. a soft white unsalted Italian curd cheese.

MP abbr. **1** Member of Parliament. **2** Military Police.

mp abbr. **1** melting point. **2** (Mus.) mezzo piano.

m.p.g. abbr. miles per gallon.

m.p.h. abbr. miles per hour.

M.Phil. abbr. Master of Philosophy.

Mr (mis´tə) (pl. **Messrs**) mister. **Mr Right** n. (facet.) the ideal marriage partner for a woman.

MRBM abbr. medium-range ballistic missile.

MRCA abbr. multi-role combat aircraft.

mRNA abbr. (Biol.) messenger RNA.

Mrs (mis´iz) n. (pl. **Mrs**) the title of a married woman.

MS abbr. **1** manuscript. **2** motor ship. **3** multiple sclerosis.

Ms (miz) n. the title of a woman of unknown or undisclosed marital status.

M.Sc abbr. Master of Science.

Msgr abbr. (N Am.) **1** Monseigneur. **2** Monsignor.

MSS abbr. manuscripts.

Mt abbr. Mount.

mu (mū) n. (pl. **mus**) the twelfth letter of the Greek alphabet (μ, M).

much (mŭch) a. (comp. **more**, superl. **most**) **1** great in quantity or amount. **2** long in duration. ~adv. **1** in or to a great degree or extent. **2** almost, nearly, about. ~n. **1** a great quantity, a great deal. **2** something uncommon. **a bit much** (coll.) rather excessive, unreasonable etc. **as much** an equal quantity. **much as** even though (Much as I had hoped to...). **not much** (sl., sometimes iron.) certainly not, not likely. **not much in it** little difference between things being compared. **not up to much** (coll.) not very good, of poor quality. **too much** more than enough. **too much for 1** superior in a contest etc., more than a match for. **2** beyond what is acceptable, endurable etc. **muchly** adv. (sl., facet.) very much. **muchness** n. **much of a muchness** practically the same, very nearly alike.

mucilage (mū´silij) n. **1** a sticky or viscous substance from the seeds, bark or roots of various plants. **2** adhesive prepared for use. **3** a viscous lubricating secretion in animal bodies. **mucilaginous** (-laj´-) a.

muck (mŭk) n. **1** dung or manure. **2** refuse, filth. **3** anything filthy, disgusting or nasty. ~v.t. **1** to make dirty or untidy. **2** to bungle, to make a mess of. **3** to manure. **to make a muck of** to bungle, to make a mess of. **to muck about/ around 1** to fool around, to mess around. **2** to potter, to mess about. **to muck in** (coll.) to help others to do something. **to muck out** to clean muck from (esp. a stable). **to muck up 1** to make dirty or untidy. **2** to bungle, to make a mess of. **mucker** n. **1** (coll.) a friend. **2** (sl.) a bad fall, esp. in the mud. **muckrake** v.i. to stir up scandal. **muckraker** n. **muckraking** n. **muck-spreader** n. a machine for spreading manure. **muck-spreading** n. **muck sweat** n. (coll.) a state of profuse sweating. **mucky** a. (comp. **muckier**, superl. **muckiest**) **muckiness** n.

muckle MICKLE.

mucus (mū´kəs) n. **1** the slimy secretion of the mucous membrane. **2** applied to other slimy secretions in animals and fishes. **3** gummy matter found in all plants, soluble in water but not in alcohol. **mucoid** a. **mucosa** (-kō´-) n. (pl. **mucosae** (-sē)) a mucous membrane. **mucous** (-kəs) a. **1** of or relating to, like or covered with mucus. **2** secreting mucus. **3** slimy, sticky. **mucosity** (-kos´-) n. **mucous membrane** the membraneous lining of the cavities and canals of the body.

Usage note The spellings of the adjective mucous and the noun mucus (pronounced the same) should not be confused.

mud (mŭd) n. **1** moist, soft earth, or earthy matter. **2** anything that is worthless or defiling. **mud in your eye!** used as a drinking toast. **one's name is mud** one is in disgrace, unpopular etc. **to drag through the mud** to disgrace publicly, to denigrate. **to sling/ fling/ throw mud** to make disgraceful imputations. **mudbank** n. a bank of mud on the bed of a river, the floor of the sea. **mudbath** n. **1** (coll.) a very muddy area, sports pitch, event etc. **2** a bath of mineral water and mud in which patients are immersed for medicinal purposes. **mudbrick** n. a brick made of baked mud. **muddy** a. (comp. **muddier**, superl. **muddiest**) **1** covered with mud. **2** of the colour of mud. **3** resembling mud. **4** turbid, cloudy. **5** confused, muddled, obscure. ~v.t. (3rd pers. sing. pres. **muddies**, pres.p. **muddying**, past, p.p. **muddied**) **1** to make muddy or foul. **2** to confuse. **muddily** adv. **muddiness** n. **mudfish** n. a New Zealand fish that burrows in the mud at a distance from water. **mudflap** n. a flap hanging behind the road-wheel of a vehicle to prevent mud etc. being thrown behind. **mudflat** n. a flat expanse of mud revealed by the ebb tide. **mudflow** n. a flow of soil mixed with water down a slope. **mudguard** n. a board or strip of metal fastened over a wheel of a bicycle, motorcycle etc. to protect persons riding from mud. **mudhole** n. a place full of mud. **mud pack**

n. a cosmetic containing fuller's earth, applied in paste form to the face. **mud pie** *n.* a heap of mud shaped by a child to resemble a pie. **mudskipper** *n.* any small goby of the family Periophthalmidae, able to move over mud by means of its strong pectoral fins. **mud-slinger** *n.* a person given to making malicious remarks about others. **mud-slinging** *n.* **mudstone** *n.* a dark grey clay rock. **mud volcano** *n.* (*pl.* **mud volcanoes**) a cone-shaped mound formed from mud discharge from hot springs, geysers etc.

muddle (mŭd´əl) *v.t.* **1** to confuse, to bewilder. **2** to mix (up), to jumble (together) confusedly. **3** to make a mess of, to bungle, to waste, to squander. ~*v.i.* to act or proceed in a confused or bungling way. ~*n.* **1** a mess. **2** a state of confusion or bewilderment. **to make a muddle of 1** to reduce to disorder. **2** to bungle. **to muddle along** to get along somehow. **to muddle on** to keep going somehow. **to muddle through** to attain a desired result without any efficiency or organization. **to muddle up** to confuse (two or more things). **muddle-headed** *a.* **muddle-headedness** *n.* **muddler** *n.* **muddlingly** *adv.*

muesli (mūz´li) *n.* (*pl.* **mueslis**) a dish of crushed cereals, dried fruit and nuts, usu. eaten as a breakfast cereal.

muezzin (mooez´in) *n.* a Muslim crier of the hour of prayer.

muff (mŭf) *n.* a covering, usu. cylindrical, of fur or other material, in which the hands are placed to keep them warm.

muff (mŭf) *v.t.* **1** to bungle or fail in. **2** to miss (a catch) or to fail to catch (the ball) at cricket etc. ~*n.* **1** a bungling action, esp. failure to catch the ball at cricket etc. **2** an awkward or stupid fellow.

muffin (mŭf´in) *n.* **1** a plain, round cake made with yeast dough, usu. toasted and eaten hot with butter. **2** (*N Am.*) a small sponge cake.

muffle (mŭf´əl) *v.t.* **1** to wrap or cover (up) closely and warmly. **2** to wrap up the head of so as to silence. **3** to wrap up (oars, bells etc.) so as to deaden the sound. **4** to dull, to deaden. ~*n.* **1** anything employed to deaden sound. **2** an oven or receptacle placed in a furnace used in operations in which the pottery etc. is not in direct contact with the products of combustion. **muffler** *n.* **1** a wrapper or scarf for the throat. **2** a pad or other contrivance for deadening sound, as in a piano. **3** (*N Am.*) the silencer on a motor vehicle.

mufti (mŭf´ti) *n.* **1** civilian dress worn by members of the armed service off duty. **2** ordinary dress as distinct from that worn on state or ceremonial occasions.

mug (mŭg) *n.* **1** a drinking vessel, usu. cylindrical without a lip, used without a saucer. **2** the contents of this. **3** (*coll.*) a dupe, a gullible person. **4** (*sl.*) the face or mouth. **5** a beerglass with a handle. ~*v.i.* (*pres.p.* **mugging**, *past, p.p.* **mugged**) to make faces, to grimace. **mugful** *n.* (*pl.*

mugfuls). **mugshot** *n.* (*sl.*) a photograph of the face, esp. for official purposes.

mug (mŭg) *v.t.* (*pres.p.* **mugging**, *past, p.p.* **mugged**) to rob (someone) violently or by threatening violence, esp. in the street. **mugger** *n.* **mugging** *n.*

mug (mŭg) *v.i.* (*pres.p.* **mugging**, *past, p.p.* **mugged**) (*coll.*) to study hard, to grind. ~*v.t.* to work or get up (a subject). **to mug up** to work hard (on) learning a subject, esp. in a rapid, superficial way.

muggins (mŭg´inz) *n.* (*pl.* **muggins, mugginses**) (*sl.*) a fool, a simpleton, used esp. of oneself (*I suppose muggins will have to do it*).

muggy (mŭg´i) *a.* (*comp.* **muggier**, *superl.* **muggiest**) damp and close, sultry. **mugginess** *n.*

Mughal (moo´gahl) *n.* **1** a Mongolian. **2** used to refer to the Muslim dynasty in India in the 16th–19th cents.

mugwort (mŭg´wœt) *n.* any of several herbs of the genus *Artemisia*, esp. *A. vulgaris*, the motherwort.

Muhammadan (mŭham´ədən), **Mohammedan** *a.* of or relating to Muhammad or Islam. ~*n.* a follower of Muhammad, a Muslim; an adherent of Islam. **Muhammadanism**, †**Muhammadism** *n.* the Muslim religion founded by Muhammad (*c.*570–632). **Muhammadanize, Muhammadanise**, †**Muhammadize**, †**Muhammadise** *v.t.*

Usage note This series of words can give offence to Muslims: it is best to use *Muslim* or *Islam* or some associated word or phrase instead.

mujahedin (mŭjah·hidēn´), **mujahideen**, **mujahidin** *n.pl.* fundamentalist Muslim guerrilla fighters.

mulatto (mŭlat´ō) *n.* (*pl.* **mulattos, mulattoes**) the offspring of a white person and a black person. ~*a.* of the skin colour of a mulatto, tawny, esp. when intermediate in colour between the parents.

mulberry (mŭl´bəri) *n.* (*pl.* **mulberries**) **1** any tree of the genus *Morus*, bearing a collective fruit like a large blackberry. **2** its fruit. **3** the colour of this. **mulberry tree, mulberry bush** *n.*

mulch (mŭlch) *n.* a surface layer of dead vegetable matter, manure etc. to keep the ground or the roots of plants moist. ~*v.t.* to cover with mulch.

mulct (mŭlkt) *n.* a fine, esp. for an offence or misdemeanour. ~*v.t.* **1** to deprive (a person) (of). **2** to swindle. **3** to punish with a fine or forfeiture.

mule (mūl) *n.* **1** the offspring of a male donkey and a female horse. **2** a hinny, the offspring of a male horse and a female donkey. **3** a stupidly stubborn or obstinate person. **4** a hybrid between different animals or plants. **5** a spinning mule. **mule deer** *n.* the N American black-tailed deer, *Odocoileus hemionus*. **muleteer** (-litiə´) *n.* a mule driver. **mulish** *a.* **1** like a mule. **2** obstinate, sullen. **mulishly** *adv.* **mulishness** *n.*

mule (mūl) *n.* a backless shoe or slipper.

mule[3] MEWL.

mulga (mŭl′gə) *n.* **1** (*Austral.*) the tree *Acacia aneura.* **2** the wood of this tree. **3** the outback, the bush.

mull[1] (mŭl) *v.t.* (*usu. followed by* over) to ponder, consider.

mull[2] (mŭl) *v.t.* to warm (wine, beer etc.), sweeten and flavour with spices. **mulled** *a.*

mull[3] (mŭl) *n.* a layer of humus formed rapidly in non-acid conditions.

mull[4] (mŭl) *n.* (*Sc.*) a promontory.

mull[5] (mŭl) *n.* a thin soft muslin.

mullah (mŭl′ə), **mollah** (mol′ə) *n.* an honorary title among Muslims for persons learned in theology and sacred law, and for Muslim ecclesiastical and civil dignitaries.

mullein (mŭl′in) *n.* any herbaceous plant of the genus *Verbascum*, such as *V. thapsus*, having woolly leaves and tall spikes of yellow flowers, sometimes called Aaron's rod.

muller (mŭl′ə) *n.* a stone with a flat surface, used to grind and mix pigment etc. on a slab.

mullet (mŭl′it) *n.* a fish living near coasts and ascending rivers, belonging either to the genus *Mullus* and family Mullidae (red mullet) or the genus *Mugil* and the family Mugilidae (grey mullet).

mulligatawny (mŭligətaw′ni) *n.* a highly-flavoured curry soup.

mullion (mŭl′yən), **munnion** (mŭn′-) *n.* a vertical bar separating the compartments of a window. **mullioned** *a.*

mulloway (mŭl′əwā) *n.* a large edible Australian seafish, *Argyrosomos hololepidotus.*

multangular (mŭltang′gūlə) *a.* having many angles.

multi- (mŭl′ti), **mult-** *comb. form* many, several.

multi-access (mŭltiak′ses) *n.* (*Comput.*) a system in which several users have simultaneous connection to the same computer.

multiaxial (mŭltiak′siəl) *a.* having many axes or lines of growth.

multichannel (mŭltichan′əl) *a.* having or using many communication or television channels.

multicolour (mŭl′tikŭlə), (*N Am.*) **multicolor** *a.* of or in many colours, many-coloured. **multicoloured** *a.*

multicultural (mŭltikŭl′chərəl) *a.* **1** (of a society) made up of many cultural and ethnic groups. **2** relating to, or designed for, such a society. **multiculturalism** *n.* **multiculturalist** *n.* **multiculturally** *adv.*

multidimensional (mŭltidimen′shənəl, -dī-) *a.* having more than three dimensions. **multidimensionality** *n.* **multidimensionally** *adv.*

multidirectional (mŭltidirek′shənəl, -dī-) *a.* extending in several directions.

multi-ethnic (mŭltieth′nik) *a.* composed of, or relating to several ethnic groups.

multifaceted (mŭltifas′itid) *a.* **1** (of a gem) having many facets. **2** having many aspects or factors.

multifarious (mŭltifeə′riəs) *a.* having great multiplicity, variety or diversity (*multifarious interests*). **multifariously** *adv.* **multifariousness** *n.*

multifid (mŭl′tifid), **multifidous** (mŭltif′idəs) *a.* (*Biol.*) having many divisions, cleft into parts, lobes, segments etc.

multiform (mŭl′tifawm) *a.* having many forms. **multiformity** (-faw′-) *n.*

multifunctional (mŭltifŭngk′shənəl), **multifunction** *a.* having many functions.

multigrade (mŭl′tigrād) *a., n.* (of) an engine oil with a viscosity that matches several standard grades.

multigym (mŭl′tijim) *n.* **1** a single piece of apparatus with weights, levers etc. for improving muscular fitness in a variety of ways. **2** a room containing similar apparatus.

multihull (mŭl′tihŭl) *n.* a vessel with more than one hull.

multilateral (mŭltilat′ərəl) *a.* **1** of an agreement or treaty in which more than two states participate. **2** many-sided. **multilateralism** *n.* **multilateralist** *n.* **multilaterally** *adv.*

multilingual (mŭltiling′gwəl) *a.* **1** able to speak, or speaking, several languages. **2** in many languages. **multilingualism** *n.* **multilingually** *adv.*

multimedia (mŭl′timēdiə) *a.* using different media. ~*n.pl.* systems of access by computer to text, sound and graphics for information, education, entertainment etc.

multimillionaire (mŭltimilyəneə′) *n.* a person who possesses several million pounds, dollars etc. **multimillion** (mŭl′-) *a.* costing or involving several million pounds, dollars etc.

multinational (mŭltinash′ənəl) *n., a.* (a company) operating in several countries. **multinationally** *adv.*

multinomial (mŭltinō′miəl) *a.* (*Math.*) having many terms, polynomial. ~*n.* a quantity of more than two terms, connected by the plus or minus signs.

multiparous (mŭltip′ərəs) *a.* **1** giving birth to many at one time. **2** bearing or having borne more than one child.

multipartite (mŭltipah′tīt) *a.* divided into many parts.

multi-party (mŭl′tipahti) *a.* (of a state etc.) having several political parties.

multiphase (mŭl′tifāz) *a.* (of an electrical device etc.) polyphase.

multiple (mŭl′tipəl) *a.* **1** having many parts, components or relations. **2** numerous and multifarious, manifold. ~*n.* **1** a quantity that contains another a number of times without a remainder. **2** (*coll.*) a multiple store. **multiple-choice** *a.* (of an examination question etc.) giving a number of different answers, from which the candidate must choose the correct one. **multiple fruit** *n.* (*Bot.*) a single fruit formed by the aggregation of numerous flowers, as in the mulberry, pineapple etc. **multiple sclerosis** *n.* a progressive disease causing paralysis, speech and visual defects etc., caused by the loss of myelin sheath from nerve tissue in the brain and spinal cord. **multiple star** *n*. three or more stars in close proximity to each other due to their gravitational force. **multiple store, multiple shop** *n*. a number of retail stores under the same ownership. **multiplicity** (-plis´-) *n*. (*pl*. **multiplicities**) 1 many of the same kind. 2 the quality of being many or manifold.

multiplex (mŭl´tipleks) *a*. 1 multiple, manifold. 2 (of a channel, cable etc.) allowing more than one signal to be transmitted simultaneously. 3 (of a cinema) having several screens within one building. ~*n*. 1 a multiplex system or electronic signal. 2 a cinema having several screens. ~*v.t.* to incorporate into a multiplex system or signal. **multiplexer, multiplexor** *n*. **multiplexing** *n*.

multiply (mŭl´tiplī) *v.t.* (*3rd pers. sing. pres.* **multiplies**, *pres.p.* **multiplying**, *past, p.p.* **multiplied**) 1 to add (a quantity called the multiplicand) to itself a certain number of times (called the multiplier) so as to produce a quantity called the product. 2 to make more numerous, to increase in number or quantity. ~*v.i.* 1 to increase in number or extent. 2 to increase by propagation. **multiplicable** (-plik-), **multipliable** (-plī-) *a*. **multiplicand** (-plikand´) *n*. the quantity to be multiplied. **multiplication** (-plikā´shən) *n*. **multiplication sign** *n*. the sign × indicating multiplication. **multiplication table** *n*. a table exhibiting the products of quantities taken in pairs, usually to 12 times 12. **multiplicative** (-plikə-, -tip´-) *a*. **multiplier** *n*. 1 a quantity by which a number is multiplied. 2 the ratio of an increase in income to the resulting increase in savings and investment. 3 (*Physics*) an instrument for increasing the intensity of a current, force etc.

multipolar (mŭltipō´lə) *a*. having more than two poles.

multiprocessing (multiprō´sesing) *n*. (*Comput.*) processing by a number of central processing units working together in parallel. **multiprocessor** *n*. a computer capable of this.

multiprogramming (mŭltiprō´graming) *n*. (*Comput.*) the handling of several computer programs simultaneously by interleaving them in a single system.

multi-purpose (mŭltipœ´pəs) *a*. serving several purposes.

multiracial (mŭltirā´shəl) *a*. relating to or incorporating several racial groups. **multiracially** *adv*.

multiskill (mŭl´tiskil) *v.t.* to train in a range of skills, esp. relating to the same manufacturing process. **multiskilling** *n*.

multi-storey (mŭltistaw´ri), (*NAm.*) **multi-story** *a*. (esp. of a car park) having several storeys. ~*n*. (*pl*. **multi-storeys**, (*NAm.*) **multi-stories**) a multi-storey car park.

multitasking (mŭltitahsk´ing) *n*. (*Comput.*) the

carrying out by a computer or system of several tasks simultaneously.

multi-track (mŭl´titrak) *a*. (of a sound recording) using several different tracks blended to produce the final sound. **multi-tracking** *n*.

multitude (mŭl´titūd) *n*. 1 a great number. 2 a very large crowd or throng of people. **the multitude** the common people. **multitudinous** (-tū´-) *a*. 1 very numerous. 2 made up of many constituent parts. 3 vast. **multitudinously** *adv*. **multitudinousness** *n*.

multi-user (mŭltiū´zə) *a*. (*Comput.*) (of a computer system) designed for use by several people simultaneously.

multivalent (mŭltivā´lənt) *a*. (*Chem.*) 1 having several degrees of valency. 2 having a valency greater than two. **multivalence, multivalency** *n*.

multivariate (mŭltivee´riət) *a*. having two or more variable quantities.

multivitamin (mŭltivit´əmin) *n*. a pill etc. containing doses of several vitamins.

multivocal (mŭltiv´əkəl) *a*. having several possible interpretations, ambiguous.

mum[1] (mŭm) *n*. (*coll.*) MOTHER.

mum[2] (mŭm) *a*. silent. ~*v.i.* (*pres.p.* **mumming**, *past, p.p.* **mummed**) to play as a mummer. **mum's the word** a phrase used to ask for silence or discretion.

mumble (mŭm´bəl) *v.i.* to speak indistinctly, to mutter. ~*v.t.* 1 to mutter indistinctly or inarticulately. 2 to chew or mouth gently. ~*n*. 1 an indistinct utterance. 2 a mutter. **mumbler** *n*. **mumbling** *a.*, *n*. **mumblingly** *adv*.

mumbo-jumbo (mŭmbōjŭm´bō) *n*. (*pl*. **mumbo-jumbos**) 1 (*coll.*) incomprehensible or nonsensical language. 2 an absurd object of popular veneration.

mummer (mŭm´ə) *n*. an actor in a mime, esp. one of a number of people who formerly went from house to house at Christmas in fantastic disguises performing a folk play. **mummery** *n*. (*pl*. **mummeries**) 1 the act or performance of mumming. 2 tomfoolery, hypocritical parade of ritual etc.

mummy[1] (mŭm´i) *n*. (*pl*. **mummies**) 1 a body of a person or animal preserved from decay by embalming, esp. after the manner of the ancient Egyptians. 2 a bituminous pigment giving a rich brown tint. 3 a pulpy mass. **mummify** *v.t.* (*3rd pers. sing. pres.* **mummifies**, *pres.p.* **mummifying**, *past, p.p.* **mummified**). **mummification** (-fikā´shən) *n*.

mummy[2] (mŭm´i) *n*. (*pl*. **mummies**) (*coll.*) MOTHER.

mump (mŭmp) *v.i.* (*dial.*) 1 to sulk, to mope. 2 to mumble, to munch. 3 to grimace. ~*v.t.* to munch.

mumps (mŭmps) *n*. 1 a contagious disease characterized by a swelling and inflammation in the parotid and salivary glands. 2 the sulks. **mumpish** *a.* sulky.

mumsy (mŭm´zi) *a.* (*comp.* **mumsier**, *superl.*

mumsiest) maternal, drab, homely, unfashionable. ~*n.* (*facet.*) mummy.

munch (mŭnsh, mŭnch) *v.t.* to chew audibly, to eat with much movement of the jaws. **muncher** *n.*

Münchausen's syndrome (munsh´howzənz, münsh-) *n.* (*Med.*) a syndrome in which the patient repeatedly simulates illness in order to obtain hospital treatment.

mundane (mŭndān´) *a.* **1** prosaic, everyday, banal. **2** belonging to this world, earthly, worldly. **mundanely** *adv.* **mundaneness** *n.* **mundanity** (-dan´-) *n.* (*pl.* **mundanities**).

mung (mŭng), **mung bean** *n.* (the seed of) an E Asian bean plant of the genus *Vigna*, used as a forage plant and as the main source of beansprouts.

municipal (mūnis´ipəl) *a.* of or relating to the government of a town or city or to local government in general. **municipality** (-pal´-) *n.* (*pl.* **municipalities**) **1** a town, city or district having a charter of incorporation or enjoying local self-government. **2** the local government of such an area. **municipalize, municipalise** *v.t.* **municipalization** (-zā´shən) *n.* **municipally** *adv.*

munificent (mūnif´isənt) *a.* liberal, generous, bountiful, characterized by splendid liberality. **munificence** *n.* **munificently** *adv.*

muniment (mū´nimənt) *n.* **1** a title deed, charter or record kept as evidence or defence of a title. **2** an archive.

munition (mūnish´ən) *n.* **1** (*usu. pl.*) military ammunition and stores of all kinds. **2** anything required for an undertaking. ~*v.t.* to supply with munitions. **munitioner** *n.*

munnion MULLION.

muntjac (mŭnt´jak), **muntjak** *n.* a small SE Asian deer of the genus *Muntiacus*.

muon (mū´on) *n.* (*Physics*) a subatomic particle, an unstable lepton with a mass approx. 207 times that of the electron.

mural (mū´rəl) *n.* a large painting, mosaic etc. on a wall. ~*a.* of or relating to, on or like a wall. **muralist** *n.* a painter of murals.

murder (mœ´də), †**murther** (-dhə) *n.* **1** (*Law*) homicide with malice aforethought, a premeditated killing of another person. **2** (*coll.*) an extremely unpleasant or dangerous experience. ~*v.t.* **1** (*Law*) to kill (a human being) with malice aforethought. **2** to slay barbarously. **3** to spoil, to mar, by blundering or clumsiness. **to cry/scream bloody murder** (*N Am.*, *sl.*) to cry blue murder. **to cry/scream blue murder** (*sl.*) to make a terrible din or commotion. **to get away with murder** (*coll.*) to do something criminal, outrageous etc. without being punished. **murderer** *n.* **murderess** *n.* **murderous** *a.* **1** of or relating to murder. **2** (apparently) intent on murder. **3** (*coll.*) extremely unpleasant or difficult. **murderously** *adv.* **murderousness** *n.*

murex (mūə´reks) *n.* (*pl.* **murices** (-risēz),

murexes) any marine gastropod mollusc of the genus *Murex*, used as a source of a purple dye.

murk (mœk), **mirk** *n.* **1** darkness. **2** fog, mist, poor seeing conditions. **murky** *a.* (*comp.* **murkier**, *superl.* **murkiest**) **1** dark, gloomy. **2** unclear, hazy. **3** turbid, muddy. **4** dubiously respectable. **murkily** *adv.* **murkiness** *n.*

murmur (mœ´mə) *n.* **1** a low, confused, continuous or repeated sound, as of running water. **2** a half-suppressed protest or complaint, a grumble. **3** a subdued speech. **4** (*Med.*) an abnormal sound heard on listening with a stethoscope to the heart, lungs or arteries. ~*v.i.* **1** to make a low continued noise, like that of running water. **2** to mutter in discontent. **3** to find fault. ~*v.t.* to utter in a low voice. **murmurer** *n.* **murmuringly** *adv.* **murmurous** *a.*

murphy (mœ´fi) *n.* (*pl.* **murphies**) (*sl.*) a potato.

Murphy's Law (mœ´fiz) *n.* (*facet.*) the maxim that if something can go wrong, it *will* go wrong.

murrain (mŭr´ən) *n.* an infectious disease among cattle.

Mus.B., Mus.Bac. *abbr.* Bachelor of Music.

muscatel (mŭskətel´), **muscadel** (-del´), **muscat** (mŭs´kat) *n.* **1** a kind of rich wine made from muscadine grapes. **2** the grapes from which such wine is made. **3** a sweet fragrant pear. **muscadine** (mŭs´kədīn, -din) *n.* any of several varieties of grape with a musky flavour or odour.

muscle (mŭs´əl) *n.* **1** an organ consisting of a band or bundle of contractile fibrous tissue serving to move or hold in place some part of an animal body. **2** the tissue of which this is composed. **3** muscular strength. **4** power or influence. **not to move a muscle** to keep absolutely still. **to muscle in 1** to force one's way in. **2** to interfere. **muscle-bound** *a.* stiff and inflexible as a result of over-developed muscles. **muscled** *a.* **muscleless** *a.* **muscle-man** *n.* (*pl.* **muscle-men**) a man with very developed muscles, often used to intimidate. **muscly** *a.*

muscovado (mŭskəvah´dō) *n.* (*pl.* **muscovados**) a moist, dark-coloured, unrefined sugar left after evaporation from the juice of sugar cane and the draining off from the molasses.

Muscovite (mŭs´kəvīt) *n.* **1** a native or inhabitant of Moscow. **2** †a native of Muscovy (Russia). ~*a.* of Muscovy or Moscow. **Muscovy duck** (-vi) *n.* the tropical American duck, *Cairina moschata*.

muscovite (mŭs´kəvīt) *n.* a silver-grey form of mica, used for electrical insulation.

muscular (mŭs´kūlə) *a.* **1** of or relating to the muscles. **2** having well-developed muscles, strong, brawny. **muscular dystrophy** *n.* a genetic disease causing progressive deterioration of the muscles. **muscularity** (-lar´-) *n.* **muscularly** *adv.* **muscular rheumatism** *n.* myalgia. **muscular stomach** *n.* any organ using muscles to digest food by grinding or squeezing. **musculature** (-ləchə) *n.* the arrangement or disposition of the muscles in the body or an organ. **musculo-** *comb. form* **musculoskeletal** *a.* of or relating to the musculature and skeleton together.

Mus.D., Mus.Doc. *abbr.* Doctor of Music.

muse[1] (mūz) *n.* 1 (**Muse**) in Greek mythology, each of nine goddesses, daughters of Zeus and Mnemosyne, who presided over the liberal arts. 2 the inspiring power of poetry, poetical genius. 3 a person, esp. a woman, who inspires or influences a poet or poem.

muse[2] (mūz) *v.i.* 1 to ponder, to meditate (upon). 2 to study or reflect (upon) in silence. 3 to dream, to engage in reverie. ~*v.t.* 1 to meditate on. 2 to think or say meditatively. **muser** *n.* **musingly** *adv.*

museum (mūzē´əm) *n.* a room or building for the preservation or exhibition of objects illustrating antiquities, art, natural science etc. **museology** (-ol´-) *n.* the study or practice of organizing and managing museums. **museologist** *n.* **museum-piece** *n.* an object so splendid or old-fashioned that it should be on display in a museum.

mush[1] (mŭsh) *n.* 1 a mash, a soft pulp, pulpy mass. 2 (*sl.*) sentimental nonsense. 3 (*N Am.*) porridge made of maize meal boiled. **mushy** *a.* (*comp.* **mushier**, *superl.* **mushiest**). **mushily** *adv.* **mushiness** *n.*

mush[2] (mŭsh) *v.i.* 1 (*in imper.*) a command to a team of sled dogs to move forward. 2 to go on a journey by dog sled. ~*n.* a journey by dog sled.

mushroom (mŭsh´room, -rum) *n.* 1 a quick-growing edible fungus, esp. *Agaricus campestris*, the field mushroom. 2 the pale brownish colour of this. 3 an object shaped like a mushroom. 4 an upstart. ~*a.* 1 of, relating to or made from mushrooms. 2 similar to a mushroom in colour. 3 ephemeral, upstart. ~*v.i.* 1 to grow or increase quickly. 2 to gather mushrooms. 3 (of bullets) to expand and flatten out. **mushroom cloud** *n.* a cloud shaped like a mushroom produced by a nuclear explosion. **mushroom growth** *n.* 1 a sudden large increase, development, expansion etc. 2 anything undergoing this. **mushroomy** *a.*

music (mū´zik) *n.* 1 the art of combining vocal and instrumental tones in a rhythmic form for the expression of emotion and pleasing of the aesthetic sense. 2 such an artistic combination of tones, musical compositions. 3 any pleasant combination of sounds. 4 melody, harmony. 5 musical taste. 6 a musical score. **musical** *a.* 1 of or relating to music. 2 fond of or skilled in music. 3 harmonious, melodious. 4 set to or accompanied by music. ~*n.* a stage show, film etc. with much singing and dancing. **musical box**, (*N Am.*) **music box** *n.* a box with a barrel-organ mechanism for playing different tunes. **musical bumps** *n.* a party game similar to musical chairs where players sit on the floor when the music stops. **musical chairs** *n.* 1 a party game in which players strive to sit on a decreasing number of chairs when music stops

playing. 2 (*derog.*) any series of changes, manoeuvres etc. taking place within politics, organizations etc. **musical comedy** *n.* (*pl.* **musical comedies**) 1 a light, romantic play or film with singing and dancing. 2 such plays or films collectively. **musical director** *n.* the person in charge of music within a stage or film production. **musicale** (-kahl´) *n.* (*N Am.*) a musical party. **musical film** *n.* a film in which singing and dancing play an important part. **musical glasses** *n.pl.* a musical instrument consisting of a series of glass vessels or tubes of varying pitch. **musical instrument** *n.* a device for producing music by vibrations, air, percussion etc. **musicality** (-kal´-), **musicalness** *n.* **musicalize, musicalise** *v.t.* **musically** *adv.* **musical saw** *n.* a bent saw played with a violin bow. **musical sound** *n.* vibrations of a regular and continuous nature as opposed to noise. **music centre**, (*N Am.*) **music center** *n.* a unit incorporating several devices for sound reproduction, e.g. a turntable, tape deck. **music drama** *n.* an opera where music and drama are of equal importance, having no formal arias. **music hall** *n.* 1 (*Hist.*) a theatre devoted to variety entertainments. 2 a variety entertainment in the style of the old music halls. **musician** (-zish´ən) *n.* a person skilled in music, esp. in playing an instrument. **musicianly** *a.* **musicianship** *n.* **music of the spheres** *n.* in Pythagorean theory, the natural harmonies said to be produced by the movement of the celestial spheres or of the heavenly bodies set in them. **musicology** (-kol´-) *n.* the science of musical lore and history. **musicological** (-loj´-) *a.* **musicologist** *n.* **music paper** *n.* manuscript paper. **music stand** *n.* a light frame for supporting a sheet of music. **music stool** *n.* a stool with a revolving adjustable seat, usu. for a pianist. **music to one's ears** *n.* something that one is pleased to hear.

musk (mŭsk) *n.* 1 an odoriferous, resinous substance obtained from a sac in the male musk deer. 2 the odour of this. 3 any similar perfume. 4 the plant *Mimulus moschatus* (which originally had the smell of musk). **musk deer** *n.* a small hornless deer, *Moschus moschiferus*, of Central Asia, from which musk is obtained. **musk melon** *n.* the melon, *Cucumis melo*. **musk ox** *n.* an Arctic-American bovine ruminant, *Ovibos moschatus*, the male of which emits a strong smell during rutting. **muskrat** *n.* 1 any of several rodents emitting a musky odour, esp. *Ondatra zibethicus*. 2 the fur of this. **musk-rose** *n.* a rambling rose, *Rosa moschata*, with large white flowers and a musky odour. **musky** *a.* (*comp.* **muskier**, *superl.* **muskiest**). **muskiness** *n.*

musket (mŭs´kit) *n.* (*Hist.*) 1 the old firearm of the infantry superseded by the rifle. 2 any old-fashioned smooth-bore gun. **musketeer** (-tiə´) *n.* a soldier armed with a musket. **musketry** *n.* 1 muskets or musketeers collectively. 2 the art of using the musket.

Muslim (muz´lim, mŭz´-), **Moslem** (moz´ləm) *n.*

muslin

820 muslin mutter

a person of the Islamic faith. *~a.* of or relating to the Islamic faith, culture etc.

muslin (mŭz´lin) *n.* **1** a fine, thin, cotton fabric used for dresses, curtains etc. **2** (*N Am.*) calico. **muslined** *a.*

muso (mū´zō) *n.* (*pl.* **musos**) (*sl.*) a musician.

musquash (mŭs´kwosh) *n.* MUSKRAT (under MUSK).

muss (mŭs) *n.* (*N Am.*) a state of confusion or disorder, a mess. *~v.t.* to disarrange, to throw into disorder. **mussy** *a.*

mussel (mŭs´əl) *n.* **1** any mollusc of the bivalve genus *Mytilus*, esp. the edible *M. edulis.* **2** any similar freshwater, pearl-forming mollusc of the genera *Margaritifer* and *Anodonta.*

must¹ (mŭst) *v.aux.* (*3rd pers. sing. pres.* **must**, *past in indirect speech* **must**) **1** to be obliged to, to be under a necessity to. **2** to be required or recommended to. **3** to be requisite to. **4** to be virtually or logically necessary to, to be certain to. **5** (as a sort of historic present) to be fated to (*What must they go and do but invade the pitch*). *~n.* a thing that must not be missed, an essential thing. **must not 1** to be forbidden to. **2** ought not, need not. **3** to be essential that not.

Usage note In direct speech the past is expressed by *had to.*

must² (mŭst) *n.* mustiness, mould.

must³ (mŭst) *n.* new wine, the expressed juice of the grape before fermentation.

mustache MOUSTACHE.

mustachio (məstah´shiō) *n.* (*pl.* **mustachios**) a moustache, esp. a large one. **mustachioed** *a.*

mustang (mŭs´tang) *n.* the wild horse of the American prairies.

mustard (mŭs´təd) *n.* **1** the seeds of *Sinapis alba* ground and used esp. as a condiment. **2** any plant of the genus *Brassica*, with yellow flowers and slender pods, esp. *B. nigra.* **3** a brownish-yellow colour. **4** (*coll.*) zest. *~a.* brownish-yellow. **to cut the mustard** (*N Am., sl.*) to be up to the required standard. **mustard and cress** *n.* white mustard and cress used in the seed-leaf as salad herbs. **mustard gas** *n.* an irritant poison gas. **mustard seed** *n.* **1** the seed of the mustard plant. **2** a small thing from which something bigger may develop.

mustelid (mŭs´təlid, mŭstel´id) *n.* a small mammal of the family Mustelidae which contains the weasels, martens, skunks, badgers etc. *~a.* of or relating to this family.

muster (mŭs´tə) *v.t.* **1** to summon (up) (strength, courage etc.). **2** to bring together. **3** to collect or assemble for review, roll-call etc. **4** (*Austral.*) to round up (livestock). *~v.i.* to meet in one place. *~n.* **1** the assembling of troops for parade or review. **2** a register of forces mustered. **3** a collection, a gathering. **4** (*Austral.*) a round-up of livestock. **to muster in** (*N Am.*) to enrol (a recruit) in the forces. **to muster out** (*N Am.*) to discharge (a soldier) from the army. **to pass**

muster 1 to be accepted as satisfactory. **2** to pass inspection without censure. **muster-book** *n.* a book in which military forces are registered. **musterer** *n.* **muster-roll** *n.* a roll or register of troops, a ship's company etc.

musty (mŭs´ti) *a.* (*comp.* **mustier**, *superl.* **mustiest**) **1** mouldy. **2** sour, stale. **3** vapid, antiquated, spiritless. **mustily** *adv.* **mustiness** *n.*

mutable (mū´təbəl) *a.* **1** liable to change. **2** inconstant, fickle, unstable. **mutability** (-bil´-), †**mutableness** *n.*

mutagen (mū´təjən) *n.* something that causes or assists genetic mutation. **mutagenesis** (-jen´ə-) *n.* **mutagenic** *a.*

mutant (mū´tənt) *n.* an organism that has undergone mutation. *~a.* resulting from mutation.

mutate (mūtāt´) *v.i.* **1** to change. **2** to be transmuted. **3** (*Biol.*) to develop into a new species, to sport. *~v.t.* to change or modify (a sound), esp. by umlaut. **mutation** *n.* **1** the act or process of changing. **2** a permanent variation in organisms giving rise to a new species. **3** a species so produced. **mutational** *a.* **mutationally** *adv.* **mutative** (-tə-), **mutatory** *a.*

mutatis mutandis (mūtahtis mūtan´dis) *adv.* the necessary alterations having been made.

mute (mūt) *a.* **1** silent, uttering no sound, speechless. **2** not having the power of speech, dumb. **3** (of hounds) not giving tongue. **4** not spoken. **5** not sounded, unpronounced. **6** (of a consonant) plosive. *~n.* **1** a dumb person. **2** (*Mus.*) a contrivance for deadening sound (as in a trumpet). **3** a person who is silent or speechless. **4** an actor in mime or whose part is speechless. **5** a letter of a word which is not pronounced. **6** a plosive consonant. **7** a hired attendant at a funeral. *~v.t.* **1** to deaden or muffle the sound of. **2** to make more subdued. **to stand mute 1** to refuse or be unable to speak. **2** (*Law*) to refuse to plead (usu. from malice). **muted** *a.* unassertive, subdued. **mutely** *adv.* **muteness** *n.* **mute swan** *n.* a Eurasian swan, *Cygnus olor*, with white plumage and an orange bill. **mutism** *n.* muteness; silence; inability to hear and speak, dumbness.

mutilate (mū´tilāt) *v.t.* **1** to maim, to mangle. **2** to disfigure. **3** to cut off a limb or an essential part of. **4** to damage (literary and other work) by excision. **mutilation** (-ā´shən) *n.* **mutilator** *n.*

mutineer (mūtiniə´) *n.* a person who mutinies. **mutinous** (mū´-) *a.* ready or inclined to mutiny; rebellious. **mutinously** *adv.* **mutinousness** *n.* **mutiny** (mū´tini) *n.* (*pl.* **mutinies**) (an instance of) open resistance to or a revolt against constituted authority, esp. by sailors or soldiers against their officers. *~v.i.* (*3rd pers. sing. pres.* **mutinies**, *pres.p.* **mutinying**, *past, p.p.* **mutinied**) to rise or rebel against authority (esp. in the army or navy).

mutism MUTE.

mutt (mŭt) *n.* **1** (*sl.*) a fool, a stupid or inept person. **2** (*derog. or facet.*) a dog, esp. a mongrel.

mutter (mŭt´ə) *v.i.* **1** to speak, in a low voice or

with compressed lips. **2** to grumble, to murmur (at or against). **3** to make a low rumbling noise. ~*v.t.* **1** to utter in a low or indistinct voice. **2** to say in secret. ~*n.* **1** a low or indistinct utterance. **2** a low rumbling sound. **3** a murmur, a grumble. **mutterer** *n.* **mutteringly** *adv.*

mutton (mŭ´tən) *n.* **1** the flesh of sheep used as food. **2** (*facet.*) a sheep. **mutton-bird** *n.* **1** any Pacific bird of the genus *Puffinus*, esp. the sooty shearwater, *P. griseus* of New Zealand, and the short-tailed shearwater, *P. tenuirostris* of Australia. **2** any of various petrels. **mutton dressed as lamb** *n.* (*coll., derog.*) an older woman dressed or made up to look younger. **mutton-headed** *a.*

mutual (mū´chuəl) *a.* **1** reciprocal, reciprocally given and received. **2** possessed, done, felt etc. by each of two persons, parties etc., to or towards the other. **3** shared by or common to two or more persons (*mutual friend*). **mutual fund** *n.* (*N Am.*) a unit trust. **mutual insurance** *n.* insurance under a company granting a certain share of the profits to policyholders. **mutualism** *n.* **1** the doctrine that true welfare is based on mutual dependence. **2** symbiosis in which organisms are associated without detriment to either. **mutualist** *n.* **mutualistic** *a.* **mutualistically** *adv.* **mutuality** (-al´-) *n.* **mutually** *adv.*

Usage note The use of *mutual* to mean shared or common is still sometimes disapproved of, though it has been recorded for 400 years.

muu-muu (moo´moo) *n.* a loose brightly-coloured dress worn by women in Hawaii.

Muzak® (mū´zak), **muzak** *n.* **1** recorded background music played in shops, restaurants etc. **2** a system for this.

muzzle (mŭz´əl) *n.* **1** the projecting mouth and nose of an animal, as of a horse, dog etc., the snout. **2** a guard put over an animal's muzzle to prevent biting or feeding. **3** the mouth of a gun or cannon. ~*v.t.* **1** to put a muzzle on. **2** to silence. **muzzle-loader** *n.* a gun loaded at the muzzle, as distinct from *breech-loader*. **muzzle velocity** *n.* the velocity of a projectile as it leaves the muzzle of a gun etc.

muzzy (mŭz´i) *a.* (*comp.* **muzzier**, *superl.* **muzziest**) **1** muddled, dazed. **2** fuddled, tipsy. **3** blurred. **muzzily** *adv.* **muzziness** *n.*

MV *abbr.* megavolt.

MW *abbr.* **1** medium wave. **2** megawatt.

mW *abbr.* milliwatt(s).

Mx *chem. symbol* maxwell.

my (mī) *a.* **1** possessive of I². **2** used in some forms of address, as *my boy, my dear.* **3** used in some expressions of surprise, admiration etc., as *my goodness!, my word!* ~*int.* used to express mild surprise.

myalgia (mīal´jiə) *n.* (*Med.*) a morbid state of the muscles characterized by pain and cramp, muscular rheumatism. **myalgic** *a.* **myalgic encephalomyelitis** *n.* (*Med.*) a condition of

excessive fatigue, general malaise, lack of coordination, depression etc., often following a viral infection.

myall (mī´əl) *n.* **1** any tree of the genus *Acacia*, esp. *A. pendula*, yielding scented wood used in making tobacco pipes. **2** an Australian Aborigine leading a traditional way of life.

Myanman (mī´anman) *a.* of or relating to Myanmar (Burma) in SE Asia. ~*n.* a native or inhabitant of Myanmar.

myasthenia (mīəsthē´niə) *n.* (*Med.*) a condition causing loss of muscle power. **myasthenic** (-then´-) *a.*

mycelium (mīsē´liəm) *n.* (*pl.* **mycelia** (-liə)) (*Bot.*) the vegetative parts of fungi, mushroom spawn. **mycelial** *a.*

Mycenaean (mīsinē´ən) *a.* of or relating to the late Bronze Age civilization of Mycenae, an ancient city of Argolis, Greece. ~*n.* an inhabitant of Mycenae or the area influenced by its culture.

myceto- (mīsē´tō), **myco-** (mī´kō) *comb. form* used to form words denoting a connection with fungi, as in *mycetophagous, mycobacterium*.

-mycin (mī´sin) *comb. form* used to form the names of antibiotic compounds developed from fungi, as in *streptomycin*.

myco- MYCETO-.

mycology (mīkol´əji) *n.* **1** the study of fungi. **2** the fungi of a particular area. **mycological** (-loj´-) *a.* **mycologically** *adv.* **mycologist** *n.*

mycoprotein (mī´kəprōtēn) *n.* protein obtained from fungi, esp. that produced for human consumption.

myelin (mī´əlin) *n.* (*Anat.*) a soft, white, fatty tissue forming a sheath round certain nerve fibres. **myelination** (-ā´shən) *n.*

myelitis (mīəlī´tis) *n.* (*Med.*) inflammation of the spinal cord.

myelo- (mī´əlō), **myel-** *comb. form* of or relating to the spinal cord.

myeloid (mī´əloid) *a.* of or relating to the spinal cord.

myeloma (mīəlō´mə) *n.* (*pl.* **myelomas**, **myelomata** (-mətə)) a usu. malignant tumour of the bone marrow.

mylodon (mī´lədon) *n.* a gigantic Pleistocene slothlike edentate of the genus *Mylodon*.

mynah (mī´nə), **mina, myna** *n.* any of various SE Asian passerine birds, esp. *Gracula religiosa*, known particularly for its ability to imitate the human voice.

myo- (mī´ō), **my-** *comb. form* of or relating to muscles.

myocardium (mīōkah´diəm) *n.* (*pl.* **myocardia** (-diə)) the muscular substance of the heart. **myocardial** *a.* **myocarditis** (-dī´tis) *n.*

myopia (mīō´piə) *n.* **1** short-sightedness. **2** lack of imagination, foresight etc. **myope** (mī´ōp) *n.* a short-sighted person. **myopic** (-op´-) *a.* **myopically** *adv.*

myosin (mī´əsin) *n.* (*Anat.*) a protein in the contractile muscular tissue.

myosotis (mīəsō´tis), **myosote** (mī´əsōt) *n.* any hardy plant of the genus *Myosotis*, esp. the forget-me-not.

myriad (mir´iəd) *a.* innumerable, countless. ~*n.* (*poet.*) **1** ten thousand. **2** a very great number.

myriapod (mir´iəpod) *n.* any terrestrial arthropod of the class Myriapoda, including the centipedes and millipedes and characterized by a very large indeterminate number of jointed feet. ~*a.* having numerous legs.

myrmidon (mœ´midən) *n.* a faithful follower, esp. an unscrupulous underling, a hired ruffian.

myrobalan (mīrob´ələn), **myrobalan plum** *n.* the cherry plum.

myrrh[1] (mœ) *n.* a gum resin from trees of the genus *Commiphora* or other trees growing in the Near East, used in the manufacture of incense, perfumes etc. **myrrhic** (mœ´rik-, mir´-), **myrrhy** *a.*

myrrh[2] (mœ) *n.* an umbelliferous plant, *Myrrhis odorata*, also called *sweet cicely.*

myrtle (mœ´təl) *n.* **1** a tree or shrub of the genus *Myrtus*, esp. *M. communis*, a tall shrub with glossy evergreen leaves and sweet-scented white or rose-coloured flowers, anciently sacred to Venus. **2** (*N Am.*) the periwinkle. **myrtaceous** (-tā´-) *a.* of or relating to the plant family Myrtaceae.

myself (mīself´) *pron.* **1** I[2] or ME[1] (objective) used to give emphasis (usu. in apposition). **2** the reflexive form of ME[1]. **3** my normal or usual self. **by myself** alone, unaided. **I myself** I, for my part. **to be myself** to act in my normal manner.

mystery (mis´təri) *n.* (*pl.* **mysteries**) **1** a secret or obscure matter. **2** something beyond human comprehension. **3** secrecy, obscurity. **4** a divine truth partially revealed. **5** (*pl.*) secret rites and ceremonies known to and practised only by the initiated. **6** a mystery story. **to make a mystery of** to treat something with exaggerated secrecy. **mysterious** (-tia´ri-) *a.* **1** secret, incomprehensible, not easily understood. **2** obscure, mystic, occult. **3** fond of mystery. **mysteriously** *adv.* **mysteriousness** *n.* **mystery play** *n.* a form of medieval drama the characters and events of which are drawn from sacred history. **mystery story** *n.* (*pl.* **mystery stories**) a fictional work that involves the reader in a puzzling event. **mystery tour** *n.* an excursion to a destination that is kept secret until it is reached.

mystic (mis´tik) *a.* **1** of or relating to mystery or

mysticism. **2** occult, esoteric. ~*n.* **1** a person who practises mysticism. **2** a supporter of the doctrine of mysticism. **mystical** *a.* **mystically** *adv.* **mysticalness** *n.* **mysticism** (-sizm) *n.* **1** the doctrine that self-surrender and spiritual understanding can lead to direct communion with and absorption in God, or that truth may be apprehended directly by the soul without the intervention of the senses and intellect. **2** the pursuit of these ends.

mystify (mis´tifī) *v.t.* (*3rd pers. sing. pres.* **mystifies**, *pres.p.* **mystifying**, *past, p.p.* **mystified**) **1** to bewilder, to puzzle, to hoax. **2** to involve in mystery. **mystification** (-fikā´shən) *n.* **mystifying** *a.* **mystifyingly** *adv.*

mystique (mistēk´) *n.* **1** professional skill or technique that impresses the layperson. **2** the mystery surrounding some creeds, professions etc. **3** any mysterious aura surrounding a person or thing.

myth (mith) *n.* **1** a fictitious legend or tradition, accepted as historical, usu. embodying the beliefs of a people on the creation, the gods, the universe etc. **2** the body of such legends or traditions. **3** a parable, an allegorical story. **4** a fictitious event, person, thing etc. **5** a thing widely believed in but not true. **mythic**, **mythical** *a.* **mythically** *adv.*

mytho- (mith´ō) *comb. form* of or relating to myth.

mythogenesis (mithōjen´əsis) *n.* the creation or production of myths.

mythography (mithog´rəfi) *n.* the writing or narration of myths, fables etc. **mythographer** *n.*

mythology (mithol´əji) *n.* (*pl.* **mythologies**) **1** a system of myths in which are embodied the beliefs of a people concerning their origin, deities, heroes etc. **2** the study of myths. **mythologer**, **mythologist** *n.* **mythologic** (-loj´-), **mythological** *a.* **mythologically** *adv.* **mythologize**, **mythologise** *v.i.* **1** to invent myths. **2** to study or interpret myths. ~*v.t.* to make (an event, person, story etc.) the basis of a myth. **mythologizer** *n.*

mythomania (mithōmā´niə) *n.* an abnormal tendency to lie or exaggerate. **mythomaniac** *n.*

mythos (mī´thos, mith´-) *n.* (*pl.* **mythoi** (-oi)) **1** (*poet.*) myth. **2** the mythology, beliefs, attitudes etc. of a society. **3** a narrative theme, a scheme of events.

myxomatosis (miksəmətō´sis) *n.* a contagious and fatal virus disease in rabbits.

N

N¹ (en), **n** (*pl.* **Ns, N's**) the 14th letter of the English and other versions of the Roman alphabet, corresponding to the Greek nu (ν, Ν). It is pronounced as a dentilingual or alveolar nasal continuant. ~*symbol* **1** (*Math.*) an indefinite number. **2** a printed dash the width of a letter n, an en. **to the nth (degree) 1** (*Math.*) to any power. **2** to the utmost.

N², **N.** *abbr.* **1** knight (in chess). **2** New. **3** newton(s). **4** North; Northern. **5** nuclear.

N³ *chem. symbol* nitrogen.

n, n. *abbr.* **1** name. **2** nano-. **3** neuter. **4** noon. **5** note.

'n (ən), **'n'** *conj.* (*coll.*) and.

Na *chem. symbol* sodium.

n/a *abbr.* **1** not applicable. **2** not available.

NAAFI (naf´i), **Naffy** *n.* **1** an organization running canteens for the Services. **2** a canteen run by this organization.

naan NAN².

nab (nab) *v.t.* (*pres.p.* **nabbing**, *past, p.p.* **nabbed**) (*sl.*) to catch, to seize, to apprehend.

nabob (nā´bob) *n.* **1** (*Hist.*) a deputy-governor or prince under the Mughal empire in India. **2** a very rich person, esp. one who amassed wealth in India.

nacho (nah´chō) *n.* (*pl.* **nachos**) a crisp corn chip used as an appetizer in Mexican cuisine, often served with melted cheese, a chilli dip etc.

nacre (nā´kə) *n.* mother-of-pearl. **nacreous** (nā´kriəs), **nacrous** (nā´krəs) *a.*

nadir (nā´diə) *n.* **1** the point of the heavens directly opposite to the zenith or directly under our feet. **2** the lowest point or stage (of decline, degradation etc.).

naevus (nē´vəs), (*N Am.*) **nevus** *n.* (*pl.* **naevi** (-vī), (*N Am.*) **nevi**) a congenital discoloration of the skin, a birthmark or mole.

naff¹ (naf) *a.* (*sl.*) unfashionable, lacking in taste, style or credibility.

naff² (naf) *v.i.* (*sl.*) to go away (*Naff off!*). **naffing** *a.* (*sl., euphem.*) bloody.

Naffy NAAFI.

nag¹ (nag) *v.i.* (*pres.p.* **nagging**, *past, p.p.* **nagged**) **1** to be continually finding fault. **2** to scold (at). **3** to cause pain or discomfort. **4** to worry (at). ~*v.t.* **1** to find fault with or scold continually. **2** to be continually pestering with complaints or fault-finding. **3** to cause pain, discomfort or worry to. ~*n.* a person who continually nags. **nagger** *n.* **nagging** *a.* **naggingly** *adv.*

nag² (nag) *n.* **1** a small horse or pony for riding. **2** (*coll.*) a horse.

naiad (nī´ad) *n.* (*pl.* **naiads, naiades** (-ədēz)) **1** a water nymph. **2** the larva of a dragonfly. **3** any aquatic plant of the genus *Najas*, having narrow leaves and small flowers.

naïf (nīēf´) *a.* NAIVE. ~*n.* a naive person.

nail (nāl) *n.* **1** a small, pointed spike, usu. of metal, with a head, for hammering into wood or other material to fasten things together, or for use as a peg etc. **2** the horny substance at the tip of human fingers and toes. **3** a claw, a talon. **4** a horny plate on the soft bill of certain birds. ~*v.t.* **1** to fasten or secure with nails. **2** to stud with nails. **3** to hold, to fix. **4** to seize, to catch. **5** to engage (attention). **6** to expose (a lie). **nail in the coffin of** something likely to cause the ruin of. **on the nail** on the spot; at once. **to hit the nail on the head 1** to hit upon the true facts of a case. **2** to do exactly the right thing. **to nail down 1** to extract a promise from. **2** to determine, to find out the identity or meaning of. **3** to fix with nails. **to nail one's colours to the mast** to persist in one's support of something. **to nail up 1** to close or fasten up by nailing. **2** to fix at a height with nails. **nail-biting** *a.* (of an event or experience) creating tension. **nail brush** *n.* a small brush for cleaning the fingernails. **nailed** *a.* (*usu. in comb.*) as in *long-nailed, nailed-on*. **nail enamel** *n.* (*N Am.*) nail polish. **nailer** *n.* a maker of nails. **nailery** *n.* **nail file** *n.* a small file for trimming fingernails. **nail-headed** *a.* **nailless** *a.* **nail polish** *n.* a type of varnish, often coloured, for putting on fingernails or toenails. **nail punch** *n.* a punch for driving a nail down so that the head is flush with the surface. **nail scissors** *n.pl.* small scissors for cutting the fingernails and toenails. **nail set** *n.* a nail punch. **nail varnish** *n.* nail polish.

naira (nī´rə) *n.* the standard monetary unit of Nigeria.

naive (nīēv´), **naïve** *a.* **1** artless, ingenuous, simple, unaffected. **2** gullible, credulous. **3** (of art) deliberately unsophisticated and childlike. **naively** *adv.* **naiveness** *n.* **naivety, naïvety, naïveté** (-tā) *n.* (*pl.* **naiveties, naïveties, naïvetés**) **1** the state of being naive. **2** a naive act or deed. **3** unaffected simplicity, artlessness. **4** gullibility, inexperience.

naked (nā´kid) *a.* **1** without clothing, uncovered, nude. **2** without natural covering, as leaves, hair, shell etc. **3** not sheathed. **4** exposed, unsheltered, defenceless, unarmed. **5** stripped, destitute or devoid (of). **6** having no trees. **7** unfurnished; not ornamented. **8** bare, plain, undisguised (*naked greed*). **9** unsupported, uncorroborated, unconfirmed. **the naked eye** the eye unassisted by any optical instrument. **nakedly** *adv.* **nakedness** *n.*

Nama (nah´mə) *n.* (*pl.* **Nama, Namas**) **1** a member of a people of South Africa and Namibia. **2** the language of the Nama. *~a.* of or relating to the Nama.

namby-pamby (nambipam´bi) *a.* **1** weakly and insipidly sentimental. **2** affectedly pretty or simple. **3** lacking strength or vigour. *~n.* (*pl.* **namby-pambies**) **1** namby-pamby talk or writing. **2** a namby-pamby person.

name (nām) *n.* **1** a word denoting any object of thought, esp. one by which a person, animal, place or thing is known, spoken of or addressed. **2** a mere term, as distinct from substance; sound or appearance, as opposed to reality. **3** a famous person. **4** reputation, honourable character, fame, glory. **5** a race, a family. **6** an underwriter of a Lloyd's syndicate. *~v.t.* **1** to give a name to, to call, to style. **2** to call by name. **3** to nominate, to appoint. **4** to mention, to specify, to cite. **by name** called (*Mary Smith by name*). **by the name of** called (*a writer by the name of John Truten*). **in all but name** virtually, practically. **in name only** officially but not genuinely (*a marriage in name only*). **in one's own name** by one's own authority. **in the name of 1** for the sake of. **2** with the authority of. **the name of the game** (*coll.*) the central or important thing; what something is all about. **to call names** to abuse verbally. **to have to one's name** to own, to possess. **to make a name for oneself** to become well known. **to name after** to call (a child) by the same name as (*I am named after my grandmother*). **to name for** (*N Am.*) to name after. **to name names** to mention people by name usu. in order to accuse or blame them. **to put one's name down for 1** to apply for. **2** to promise to give. **you name it** (*coll.*) whatever you want or think of (*There was smoked salmon, caviar, you name it*). **nameable** *a.* **name-calling** *n.* verbal abuse. **name-dropper** *n.* a person who tries to impress by mentioning the names of important or famous people as if they were close friends. **name-drop** *v.i.* (*pres.p.* **name-dropping**, *past, p.p.* **name-dropped**). **nameless** *a.* **1** having no name. **2** anonymous. **3** unknown, obscure, inglorious. **4** inexpressible, indefinable. **5** unfit to be named, abominable, detestable. **namelessly** *adv.* **namelessness** *n.* **namely** *adv.* that is to say. **nameplate** *n.* a sign showing the name of the occupant of a room or building. **namesake** *n.* a person or thing having the same name as or named after another. **name-tape** *n.* a tape attached to a garment or other object showing the owner's name.

Namibian (nəmib´iən) *n.* a native or inhabitant of Namibia. *~a.* of or relating to Namibia.

namma GNAMMA.

nan[1] (nan) *n.* (*dial.*) a grandmother.

nan[2] (nahn), **naan** *n.* in Indian cookery, a type of slightly leavened bread.

nana[1] (nah´nə) *n.* (*sl.*) a fool.

nana[2] (nan´ə), **nanna** *n.* (*coll.*) a grandmother.

nancy (nan´si), **nance** (nans) *n.* (*pl.* **nancies, nances**) (*offensive, sl.*) **1** an effeminate young man. **2** a homosexual. *~a.* effeminate. **nancy boy** *n.* a nancy.

nanny (nan´i) *n.* (*pl.* **nannies**) **1** a children's nurse. **2** an overprotective person, government etc. **3** NAN[1]. *~v.t.* (*3rd pers. sing. pres.* **nannies**, *pres.p.* **nannying**, *past, p.p.* **nannied**) to treat in an overprotective manner. **nanny goat** *n.* a female goat.

nano- (nan´ō) *comb. form* one thousand-millionth.

nanometre (nan´ōmētə), (*N Am.*) **nanometer** *n.* one thousand-millionth of a metre.

nanosecond (nan´ōsekənd) *n.* one thousand-millionth of a second.

nanotechnology (nanōteknol´əji) *n.* the branch of technology which deals with measuring, making or manipulating extremely small objects. **nanotechnological** (-loj´-) *a.* **nanotechnologist** *n.*

nap[1] (nap) *v.i.* (*pres.p.* **napping**, *past, p.p.* **napped**) to sleep lightly or briefly, to doze. *~n.* a short sleep, a doze, esp. in the daytime. **to catch napping 1** to find asleep. **2** to take unawares; to catch unprepared or at a disadvantage.

nap[2] (nap) *n.* **1** the smooth and even surface produced on cloth or other fabric by cutting and smoothing the fibre or pile. **2** a smooth, woolly, downy or hairy growth on a surface. **3** (*Austral., coll.*) bedding, blankets. *~v.t.* (*pres.p.* **napping**, *past, p.p.* **napped**) to put a nap on. **napless** *a.*

nap[3] (nap) *n.* **1** a card-game in which five cards are dealt to each player, the one engaging to take the highest number of tricks playing against the others. **2 a** the act of betting all one's money on one horse etc. **b** a tip claimed to be a certainty. *~v.t.* (*pres.p.* **napping**, *past, p.p.* **napped**) to name as a likely winner. **to go nap 1** in nap, to offer to take all five tricks. **2** to risk everything on one venture.

napalm (nā´pahm) *n.* **1** a thickening agent which is produced from naphthenic acid, other acids and aluminium. **2** a highly inflammable petroleum jelly which is produced from naphthalene and coconut-palm oil, largely used for bombs. *~v.t.* to attack with napalm bombs.

nape (nāp) *n.* the back of the neck.

naphtha (naf´thə) *n.* (*Chem.*) an inflammable oil produced by dry distillation of organic substances, such as bituminous shale or coal. **naphthalene** (-lēn) *n.* a white crystalline product of the dry distillation of coal tar, used as a disinfectant and in the manufacture of dyes and explosives. **naphthalic** (-thal´-) *a.*

napkin (nap´kin) *n.* **1** a small square of linen or paper, esp. one used at table to wipe the hands, protect the clothes, or serve fish etc., on; a serviette. **2** a baby's nappy. **3** a small towel. **4** (*N Am.*) a sanitary towel. **napkin ring** *n.* a ring used to hold a table napkin and indicate the owner.

napoleon (nəpō′liən) *n.* **1** the card game, nap. **2** (*N Am.*) a millefeuille.

Napoleonic (nəpōlion′ik) *a.* **1** of or relating to Napoleon I or his times. **2** resembling Napoleon I; dominating, masterful; spectacular.

nappy (nap′i) *n.* (*pl.* **nappies**) a piece of soft absorbent material fastened round a baby's bottom to absorb urine and faeces. **nappy rash** *n.* a rash on a baby's body caused by prolonged contact with a wet nappy.

narcissism (nah′sisizm) *n.* (*Psych.*) a state of self-love. **narcissist** *n.* **narcissistic** (-sis′tik) *a.* **narcissistically** *adv.*

narcissus (nahsis′əs) *n.* (*pl.* **narcissi** (-ī), **narcissuses**) any bulbous plant of the genus *Narcissus*, containing the daffodils and jonquils, esp. the white *N. poeticus.*

narcolepsy (nah′kəlepsi) *n.* (*Med.*) a nervous disease characterized by fits of irresistible drowsiness. **narcoleptic** (-lep′tik) *a.*, *n.*

narcosis (nahkō′sis) *n.* **1** (*Med.*) narcotic poisoning, the effect of continuous use of narcotics. **2** a state of stupor.

narcoterrorism (nahkōter′ərizm) *n.* terrorism involving illegal drugs. **narcoterrorist** *n.*

narcotic (nahkot′ik) *a.* **1** allaying pain and causing sleep or dullness. **2** producing torpor or coma. ~*n.* **1** a substance that allays pain by inducing sleep or torpor. **2** any of a group of addictive drugs, such as opium and morphine, which induce numbness and stupor. **narcotically** *adv.* **narcotism** (nah′kə-) *n.* **narcotize** (nah′kə-), **narcotise** *v.t.* **narcotization** (-zā′shən) *n.*

nark (nahk) *n.* (*sl.*) **1** a police spy, a decoy. **2** (*Austral.*) an annoying person or thing. **narked** *a.* (*sl.*) annoyed. **narky** *a.* (*comp.* **narkier,** *superl.* **narkiest**) (*sl.*) irritable, complaining.

narrate (nərāt′) *v.t.* to tell, to relate, to give an account of the successive particulars of in speech or writing. **narratable** *a.* **narration** (-ā′shən) *n.* **narrative** (nar′ə-) *n.* **1** a recital of a series of events; a tale, a story. **2** the art of narrating. ~*a.* **1** in the form of narration. **2** relating to an event or story. **narratively** *adv.* **narrator** *n.*

narrow (na′rō) *a.* (*comp.* **narrower,** *superl.* **narrowest**) **1** of little breadth or extent from side to side. **2** restricted, of limited scope. **3** constricted, limited. **4** illiberal in views or sentiments; prejudiced, bigoted. **5** close, near, within a small distance, with little margin. **6** (of a vowel) tense. ~*v.i.* to become narrow or narrower. ~*v.t.* **1** to make narrow or narrower. **2** to contract in range, views or sentiments. **3** to confine, to limit, to restrict. ~*n.* (*usu. pl.*) **1** a strait. **2** a narrow mountain pass. **narrow boat** *n.* a long, narrow canal boat. **narrowcast** *v.t., v.i.* (*past, p.p.* **narrowcast, narrowcasted**) (*esp. N Am.*) to transmit (television programmes) by cable to a small area. ~*n.* **1** the practice of narrowcasting. **2** a narrowcast programme or transmission.

narrowcaster *n.* **narrowcasting** *n.* **narrow gauge** *n.* a railway gauge of less than 4 ft. 8½ in. (1.43 m). **narrowish** *a.* **narrowly** *adv.* **narrow-minded** *a.* illiberal, bigoted. **narrow-mindedly** *adv.* **narrow-mindedness** *n.* **narrowness** *n.* **narrow squeak** *n.* (*coll.*) a narrow escape or margin, a close shave.

narwhal (nah′wəl) *n.* an Arctic delphinoid cetacean, *Monodon monoceros*, with a long tusk or tusks developed from one or both of its teeth.

nary (neə′ri) *a.* (*coll., dial.*) not one single (*nary a one*).

nasal (nā′zəl) *a.* **1** of or relating to the nose. **2** sounded or produced with the nasal passage open. **3** pronounced through or as if through the nose. ~*n.* a letter or sound produced with the nasal passage open. **nasality** (-zal′-) *n.* **nasalize**, **nasalise** *v.i., v.t.* **nasalization** (-zā′shən) *n.* **nasally** *adv.*

nascent (nas′ənt, nā′-) *a.* **1** coming into being; beginning to develop; immature. **2** (*Chem.*) having a higher reactivity than usual because just being formed. **nascency** *n.*

naso- (nā′zō) *comb. form* of or relating to the nose.

nasturtium (nəstœ′shəm) *n.* (*pl.* **nasturtiums**) **1** a trailing plant, *Tropaeolum majus*, with vivid orange flowers. **2** any cruciferous plant of the genus *Nasturtium*, containing the watercress.

nasty (nahs′ti) *a.* (*comp.* **nastier,** *superl.* **nastiest**) **1** extremely unpleasant. **2** objectionable, annoying, vexatious. **3** awkward, trying. **4** spiteful, odious, vicious. **5** dirty, foul, filthy to a repulsive degree. **6** indecent, obscene. **7** repellent to taste, smell etc., nauseous. **8** (of weather) unpleasantly wet. ~*n.* (*pl.* **nasties**) **1** a nasty person. **2** a video nasty. **nastily** *adv.* **nastiness** *n.* **nasty piece of work** *n.* (*coll.*) a nasty person.

Nat. *abbr.* **1** National. **2** Nationalist. **3** Natural.

natal (nā′təl) *a.* of, from or relating to one's birth. **natality** (-tal′-) *n.* (*pl.* **natalities**) birth rate.

natch (nach) *int.* (*sl.*) of course.

nation (nā′shən) *n.* **1** a people under the same government and inhabiting the same country. **2** a people belonging to the same ethnological family and speaking the same language. **3** a federation of N American Indian tribes. **nationhood** (-hud) *n.* **nation state** *n.* a state which is entirely inhabited by a single nation. **nationwide** *a., adv.* covering the whole nation.

national (nash′ənəl) *a.* **1** of or relating to the nation, esp. to the whole nation. **2** peculiar to a nation. ~*n.* **1** a member or subject of a particular nation. **2** one's fellow countryman. **national anthem** *n.* a hymn or song embodying the patriotic sentiments of a nation, such as the British 'God Save the Queen' or the French 'La Marseillaise'. **national bank** *n.* (*US*) a commercial bank chartered under the federal government. **national curriculum** *n.* a standardized curriculum for all schools in England and Wales, specifying the subjects which all pupils must study and the required levels of attainment at various stages. **national debt** *n.* the debt of a nation in its corporate capacity. **national grid** *n.* **1** a country-wide network of high-voltage electric power lines linking major power stations. **2** the coordinate system in Ordnance Survey maps. **National Guard** *n.* organized militia of individual states in the US. **National Health (Service)** *n.* in Britain, the system of state-provided medical service, established in 1948. **National Insurance** *n.* a system of compulsory insurance paid for by employers and employees and yielding benefits to the sick, retired and unemployed. **nationalism** *n.* **1** extreme devotion to one's nation. **2** the policy of national independence. **nationalist** *n.*, *a.* **nationalistic** (-lis´tik) *a.* **nationalistically** *adv.* **nationality** (-nal´-) *n.* (*pl.* **nationalities**). **nationalize, nationalise** *v.t.* **1** to make national. **2** to naturalize. **3** to bring (an industry etc.) under State control. **nationalization** (-zā´shən) *n.* **nationally** *adv.* **national park** *n.* an area owned by the nation and set aside to preserve beauty, wildlife etc. **national service** *n.* (*Hist.*) compulsory service in the armed forces. **National Socialism** *n.* (*Hist.*) the political doctrine of the National Socialist German Workers' Party, which came into power in Germany under Adolf Hitler in 1933, with prominent among its teachings the superiority of the German race, hatred of Jews and a need for world expansion. **National Socialist** *n.* **National Vocational Qualification** *n.* a qualification in any of a variety of vocational subjects, set at various levels.

native (nā´tiv) *n.* **1** a person born in a specified place. **2** a local resident. **3** a plant or animal indigenous to a district or country. **4** (*offensive*) a member of a non-white indigenous people of a country. ~*a.* **1** of or relating to a place or country by birth, indigenous, not exotic. **2** belonging to a person, animal or thing, by nature; inborn, innate, natural, not acquired. **3** of or relating to the time or place of one's birth. **4** (*Geol.*) (of metals) occurring in a pure or uncombined state. **5** of or relating to the natives of a place or region. **6** (*Austral.*) resembling an animal or plant from another country (*native bear*). **to go native** (of a settler) to live and dress like local inhabitants. **Native American** *n.* an American Indian from the US. **native bear** *n.* (*Austral.*) a koala. **natively** *adv.* **nativeness** *n.* **native rock** *n.* a rock found in its original place. **native speaker** *n.* a person who speaks a particular language as their first language. **nativism** *n.* (*Philos.*) the doctrine of innate ideas. **nativist** *n.*

Usage note Because of associations with racism and imperialist domination, the use of *native* of the original inhabitants of formerly (or still) colonized countries has come to be considered offensive, and is best avoided. See also, however, the note on *Native American* under AMERICAN.

nativity (nətiv´iti) *n.* (*pl.* **nativities**) **1** birth, esp. that of Jesus Christ, the Virgin Mary or St John the Baptist. **2** a festival in commemoration of this. **3** a picture of the birth of Jesus Christ. **4** a horoscope. **nativity play** *n.* a play about the birth of Jesus Christ performed by children at Christmas.

natter (nat´ə) *v.i.* **1** to chatter idly; to chat, exchange gossip. **2** to find fault, to be peevish. ~*n.* **1** idle chatter. **2** a chat, gossip. **3** grumbling. **natterer** *n.*

natterjack (nat´əjak) *n.* a European toad, *Bufo calamita*, with a yellow stripe down the back.

natty (nat´i) *a.* (*comp.* **nattier,** *superl.* **nattiest**) (*coll.*) neat, tidy, spruce. **nattily** *adv.* **nattiness** *n.*

natural (nach´ərəl) *a.* **1** of, relating to, produced by or constituted by nature. **2** not artificial; (of food) with nothing added, not having been processed. **3** inborn, instinctive. **4** in conformity with the ordinary course of nature, normal, not irregular, exceptional or supernatural. **5** of or relating to physical things, animal, not spiritual. **6** true to life. **7** unaffected, not forced or exaggerated. **8** undisguised. **9** ordinary, to be expected, not surprising. **10** coming by nature, easy (to). **11** related by nature only. **12** illegitimate. **13** (*Mus.*) **a** (of a note) not sharp or flat. **b** denoting the diatonic scale of C. **c** (of a key) having no sharps or flats. **14** (of a fabric) unbleached; cream or beige. ~*n.* **1** a certainty, something by its very nature certain, esp. a person who is naturally good at something. **2** (*Mus.*) **a** a sign cancelling the effect of a preceding sharp or flat. **b** a natural note. **natural-born** *a.* having a quality or position by birth (a *natural-born winner*). **natural childbirth** *n.* (*Med.*) a method of childbirth involving breathing and relaxation exercise with no anaesthetic. **natural classification** *n.* classification according to natural features. **natural death** *n.* death owing to disease or old age, not violence or accident. **natural food** *n.* food with no added preservatives. **natural gas** *n.* gas from the earth's crust, specifically a combination of methane and other hydrocarbons, used mainly as a fuel and as raw material in industry. **natural history** *n.* **1** the science or study of animal life, zoology. **2** a description of all the flora and fauna of a particular place. **natural historian** *n.* **naturalism** *n.* **1** strict adherence to nature in literature and art, realism. **2** a philosophical or theological system that explains the universe as being produced and governed entirely by physical laws. **3** condition or action based on natural instincts. **naturalist** (nach´ərəlist) *n.* **1** a person who is versed in natural history. **2** a believer in naturalism. **3** a realist, as distinct from an idealist. ~*a.* naturalistic. **naturalistic** (-lis´-) *a.* **1** in accordance with nature. **2** realistic, not conventional or ideal. **3** of or relating to natural history. **naturalistically** *adv.* **naturalize, naturalise** *v.t.* **1** to make natural. **2** to adopt (a foreign expression or custom). **3** to acclimatize. **4** to confer the rights and privileges of a natural-born subject on. **5** to cause to look natural. ~*v.i.* **1** to become naturalized. **2** to study natural history. **naturalization** (-zā´shən) *n.* **natural language** *n.* a language which has evolved naturally.· **natural law** *n.* **1** the sense of right and wrong implanted by nature. **2** a law governing the operations of physical life etc. **natural life** *n.* one's lifetime. **naturally** *adv.* **1** according to nature. **2** spontaneously. **3** as might be expected, of course. **naturalness** *n.* **natural note** *n.* (*Mus.*) a note which is not sharp or flat. **natural numbers** *n.pl.* the whole numbers starting from one upwards. **natural order** *n.* (*Bot.*) an order of plants in a system of classification based on the nature of their sexual organs or their natural affinities. **natural resources** *n.pl.* features or properties of the land, such as minerals, water, timber etc., which occur naturally and can be exploited by people. **natural science** *n.* the science of physical things, as distinguished from mental and moral science; natural history. **natural selection** *n.* the process by which plants and animals best fitted for the conditions in which they are placed survive and reproduce, while the less fitted leave fewer or no descendants. **natural uranium** *n.* unenriched uranium. **natural wastage** *n.* the reduction of staff through retirements and resignations, rather than sackings or redundancies. **natural year** *n.* the time it takes for the earth to revolve round the sun, 365 days, 5 hours and 48 minutes.

Usage note The nouns *naturalist* and *naturist* should not be confused: a *naturalist* studies natural history, a *naturist* is a nudist.

nature (nā´chə) *n.* **1** the essential qualities of anything. **2** the physical or psychical constitution of a person or animal. **3** natural character or disposition. **4** kind, sort, class. **5** the whole sum of things, forces, activities and laws constituting the physical universe. **6** the physical power that produces the phenomena of the material world. **7** this personified. **8** the sum of physical things and forces regarded as distinct from human beings. **9** the natural condition of human beings preceding social organization. **10** the undomesticated condition of animals or plants. **11** picturesque countryside. **against nature 1** unnatural. **2** miraculous; miraculously. **by nature** innately. **contrary to nature** miraculous; miraculously. **from nature** in art, directly from the living model or natural landscape. **in a state of nature 1** in an uncultivated state. **2** completely naked. **3** in an unregenerate state. **in nature 1** in actual existence. **2** anywhere; at all. **in the nature of** rather like, more or less. **in the nature of things** to be expected. **to get back to nature** to return to a simple way of life. **natured** *a.* **nature reserve** *n.* an area of land which is protected in order to preserve its flora, fauna and

other natural features. **nature study** *n.* the study of plant and animal life at a basic level. **nature trail** *n.* a route through the countryside which is signposted to highlight the natural features. **naturism** *n.* **1** nature-worship. **2** naturalism in religion. **3** nudism. **naturist** *n.*, *a.* **naturistic** (-ris´-) *a.* **naturopathy** (-rop´əthi) *n.* a method of treating or preventing disease without drugs, but with diet, exercise, fresh air etc. **naturopath** (-path) *n.* **naturopathic** (-path´ik) *a.*

Usage note See note on *naturist* under NATURALIST (under NATURAL).

naught (nawt) *n.* **1** †nothing. **2** (*N Am.*) zero, nought. **to bring to naught** to thwart, frustrate, defeat; to ruin. **to come to naught** to be unsuccessful. **to set at naught** to disregard.

naughty (naw´ti) *a.* (*comp.* **naughtier**, *superl.* **naughtiest**) **1** perverse, mischievous; disobedient, badly behaved. **2** (*coll., facet.*) mildly indecent. **naughtily** *adv.* **naughtiness** *n.*

nausea (naw´ziə) *n.* **1** a feeling of sickness, with a propensity to vomit. **2** loathing. **nauseate** *v.t.* **1** to cause to feel nausea. **2** to fill with loathing. ~*v.i.* **1** to feel nausea. **2** to turn away in disgust (at). **nauseating** *a.* **nauseatingly** *adv.* **nauseous** *a.* **1** feeling sick. **2** causing nausea. **3** disgusting, distasteful. **nauseously** *adv.* **nauseousness** *n.*

nautical (naw´tikəl) *a.* of or relating to ships, navigation or sailors; naval. **nautically** *adv.* **nautical mile** *n.* a unit of measurement equal to 6080 ft., or 2026 2 3 yards (1.853 km).

nautilus (naw´tiləs) *n.* (*pl.* **nautiluses**, **nautili** (-lī)) **1** any cephalopod of the genus *Nautilus*, esp. the pearly nautilus. **2** the paper nautilus or argonaut. **nautiloid** (-loid) *n.*

NAV *abbr.* net asset value.

naval (nā´vəl) *a.* **1** consisting of or relating to ships or a navy. **2** fought or won by warships or navies. **naval academy** *n.* a training college for naval officers. **naval architecture** *n.* the process of designing ships. **naval architect** *n.* **navally** *adv.* **naval officer** *n.* an officer in a navy. **naval stores** *n.pl.* materials used in shipping.

navarin (nav´ərin) *n.* a lamb casserole with vegetables.

nave[1] (nāv) *n.* the body of a church, extending from the main doorway to the choir or chancel, distinct, and usually separated by pillars, from the aisles.

nave[2] (nāv) *n.* the central block of a wheel in which the axle and spokes are inserted, the hub.

navel (nā´vəl) *n.* **1** the scar of the umbilical cord, forming a depression on the surface of the abdomen. **2** a central point. **navel-gazing** *n.* vague, introspective meditation. **navel orange** *n.* a variety of orange with a navel-like depression and a smaller orange enclosed. **navelwort** (-wœt) *n.* a pennywort.

navigate (nav´igāt) *v.i.* **1** to sail, to pass from place to place by water or air. **2** to direct and plot the route or position of a ship, aircraft etc. **3** to manage a ship. **4** to be in charge of plotting and pointing out a route to the driver of a car. ~*v.t.* **1** to pass over or across, in a ship etc. **2** to manage the course, to conduct (a ship, aircraft etc.). **3** (*coll.*) to make (one's way) through a crowd. **navigable** *a.* **navigability** (-bil´-) *n.* **navigation** (-ā´shən) *n.* **1** the act, art or science of navigating. **2** a voyage. **navigational** *a.* **navigator** *n.* **1** a person who navigates. **2** a person who is skilled in navigation. **3** an explorer by sea.

navvy (nav´i) *n.* (*pl.* **navvies**) a labourer in any kind of excavating work, esp. construction of railways etc.

navy (nā´vi) *n.* (*pl.* **navies**) **1** the warships of a nation. **2** their officers, men, dockyards etc. **3** navy blue. **4** (*poet.*) a fleet. ~*a.* navy-blue. **navy bean** *n.* a haricot bean. **navy blue** *n.* the dark-blue colour used for naval uniforms. **navy-blue** *a.*

nawab (nəwahb´) *n.* **1** in Pakistan, a distinguished Muslim. **2** (*Hist.*) an Indian governor or nobleman; a nabob.

nay (nā) *adv.* **1** not only so, not this alone, more than that, and even. **2** no; a word expressing negation or refusal. ~*n.* **1** the word 'nay'; a denial, a refusal. **2** a vote against. **naysay** (nā´sā) *v.i.* (*past, p.p.* **naysaid**) (*esp. N Am.*) to make a refusal or denial. ~*v.t.* to refuse, to contradict. **naysayer** *n.*

Nazarene (naz´ərēn) *n.* **1** a native or inhabitant of Nazareth. **2** (*derog.*) an early Christian. ~*a.* of or relating to Nazareth.

Nazi (naht´si) *n.* (*pl.* **Nazis**) **1** (*Hist.*) a member of the German National Socialist Party. **2** (*derog.*) a racist, extremist or authoritarian person. **3** a person who belongs to any extreme right-wing organization. ~*a.* of or relating to the Nazis. **Nazidom** (-dəm) *n.* **Nazify** (-fī) *v.t.* (*3rd pers. sing. pres.* **Nazifies**, *pres.p.* **Nazifying**, *past, p.p.* **Nazified**). **Naziism, Nazism** *n.*

NB *abbr.* note well.

Nb *chem. symbol* niobium.

NCO *abbr.* non-commissioned officer.

Nd *chem. symbol* neodymium.

n.d. *abbr.* no date.

NE *abbr.* **1** north-east. **2** north-eastern.

Ne *chem. symbol* neon.

Neanderthal (nian´dətahl) *a.* **1** of or relating to a Palaeolithic species of man whose remains were first found in the Neanderthal valley. **2** (*coll.*) extremely old-fashioned, reactionary. **3** (*coll.*) boorish. **Neanderthal man** *n.*

neap (nēp) *a.* low or lowest (applied to the tides which happen in the middle of the second and fourth quarters of the moon, when the rise and fall are least). ~*n.* a neap tide.

Neapolitan (nēəpol´itən) *a.* of or relating to Naples. ~*n.* a native or inhabitant of Naples, Italy. **Neapolitan ice cream** *n.* ice cream made of different ices in distinct layers. **Neapolitan violet** *n.* a double, sweet-scented viola.

near (niə) *adv.* **1** at or to a short distance, at hand; not far off, not remote in place or time or degree. **2** closely. ~*prep.* close to in place, time, condition etc. ~*a.* **1** nigh, close at hand, not distant in place or degree. **2** close in time, imminent. **3** closely resembling, almost. **4** closely related. **5** familiar, intimate. **6** close, narrow. **7** (of a road etc.) direct, short, straight. **8** (of a horse, part or side of a vehicle etc.) on the left, as distinct from *off.* **9** (*coll.*) parsimonious, niggardly. ~*v.t.* to approach, to draw near to. ~*v.i.* to draw near. **near as dammit** (*coll.*) very nearly. **near at hand** close in distance or time. **to come near** almost to (do something) (*I came near to losing my temper*). **to go near** to only just fail (to do something). **near-death experience** *n.* an experience of being outside one's body and observing the scene, reported by some people who have come very close to death. **Near East** *n.* **1** the Middle East. **2** eastern Europe. **Near Eastern** *a.* **nearest and dearest** *n.pl.* one's close relatives and friends. **near go** *n.* (*coll.*) a narrow squeak, a close shave. **nearish** *a.* **nearly** *adv.* **1** almost. **2** intimately, closely. **3** in a parsimonious manner. **not nearly** nowhere near, far from (*not nearly as good*). **near miss** *n.* a miss that is almost a hit, such as a bomb which narrowly misses its target. **nearness** *n.* **nearside** *n., a.* **1** (of) the left side of a horse etc., as distinct from *offside.* **2** (of) the side of a vehicle nearer the kerb, as distinct from *offside.* **near sight** *n.* (*N Am.*) short sight. **near-sighted** *a.* **near-sightedly** *adv.* **near-sightedness** *n.* **near thing** *n.* a situation in which danger or trouble is only just avoided.

near- (niə) *comb. form* **1** almost, as *near-fatal.* **2** being a substitute for, as *near-beer.*

nearby[1] (niə´bī) *a.* situated close at hand.

nearby[2] (niəbī´), **near by** *adv.* close at hand.

neat (nēt) *a.* **1** tidy, trim. **2** simply but becomingly ordered. **3** nicely proportioned, well made. **4** elegantly and concisely phrased. **5** adroit, dexterous, clever. **6** (of an alcoholic drink) undiluted, pure. **7** (*N Am., sl.*) excellent, admirable. **neaten** *v.t.* to make neat or tidy. **neatly** *adv.* **neatness** *n.*

neath (nēth) *prep.* (*poet.*) beneath.

NEB *abbr.* New English Bible.

nebbish (neb´ish) *n.* (*coll.*) a timid person. ~*a.* timid, submissive.

Nebuchadnezzar (nebūkədnez´ə) *n.* a large wine bottle which holds 20 times as much as a standard bottle.

nebula (neb´ūlə) *n.* (*pl.* **nebulae** (-lē), **nebulas**) **1** (*Astron.*) a cloudy patch of light in the heavens produced by groups of stars or by a mass of gaseous or stellar matter. **2** (*Med.*) a speck on the cornea causing defective vision. **nebular** *a.* **nebulizer, nebuliser** *n.* a device which produces a fine spray. **nebulize** *v.t.* **nebulous** *a.* **1** cloudy. **2** turbid; hazy, vague, indistinct, obscure, uncertain. **3** muddled, bewildered. **4** (*Astron.*) belonging to or resembling a nebula. **nebulosity** (-los´-) *n.* **nebulously** *adv.* **nebulousness** *n.* **nebulous star** *n.* (*Astron.*) a hazy single star or a cluster of small indistinct stars appearing as a cloudy patch of light.

necessary (nes´isəri) *a.* **1** needful, requisite, indispensable, requiring to be done. **2** such as cannot be avoided, inevitable. **3** resulting from external causes or determinism. **4** determined by natural laws. **5** not voluntary, not of free will, compulsory. ~*n.* (*pl.* **necessaries**) **1** what is indispensably requisite. **2** (*pl.*) things that are essentially requisite, esp. to life. **the necessary 1** (*coll.*) money. **2** (*coll.*) anything which is essential for some purpose. **necessarily** (nes´-. -ser´ə-) *adv.* **1** automatically. **2** of necessity; inevitably. **necessitarian** (nisesiteə´ri-) *n.* (*Philos.*) a person who believes in the doctrine that the human will is not free, but that actions and volitions are determined by antecedent causes. ~*a.* of or relating to necessitarianism. **necessitarianism** *n.* **necessitate** (nises´itāt) *v.t.* **1** to make necessary or unavoidable. **2** to constrain, to compel. **3** to entail as an unavoidable condition, result etc. **necessitation** (-ā´shən) *n.* **necessitous** (nises´-) *a.* needy, destitute, in poverty. **necessity** (nises´-) *n.* (*pl.* **necessities**) **1** (*often in pl.*) something which is necessary, an essential requisite. **2** the quality of being necessary; inevitableness. **3** absolute need, indispensability. **4** constraint, compulsion. **5** the compelling force of circumstances, the external conditions that compel one to act in a certain way. **6** want, poverty. **7** basic things that are necessary. **of necessity** unavoidably, necessarily.

Usage note (1) The pronunciation of *necessarily* with stress on the third syllable is sometimes disapproved of. (2) The uses of *necessaries* and *necessities* overlap, though *necessities* is now more usual for the essentials of life.

neck (nek) *n.* **1** the narrow portion of the body connecting the trunk with the head. **2** this part of an animal, used for food. **3** anything resembling this, such as an isthmus, a narrow passage or strait. **4** the slender part of a bottle near the mouth. **5** the long, slender part of a guitar, violin etc. **6** the length of a horse's head and neck, used to measure its lead in a race. **7** (*Geol.*) a solid block of lava in an old volcano crater. **8** (*Archit.*) the lower part of a capital. **9** the part of a garment that is close to the neck. **10** (*coll.*) impudence, cheek. ~*v.i.* **1** (*coll.*) to kiss and hug passionately. **2** to become narrow. ~*v.t.* to make narrow. **neck and neck** equal, very close (in a race or contest). **neck or nothing** at all risks; desperately. **one's neck of the woods** the part of the country to which one belongs. **to get it in the neck 1** (*coll.*) to be reprimanded severely. **2** (*coll.*) to be hit hard. **up to one's neck** deeply involved (in). **neckband** *n.* a part of a garment fitting round the neck. **necked** *a.* **neckerchief** (-əchif) *n.* (*pl.* **neckerchiefs**) a kerchief worn round the neck. **neckless** *a.* **necklet** (-lit) *n.* **1** a small necklace. **2** a small fur boa for the neck. **neckline** *n.* the edge of a garment which goes round the neck. **necktie** *n.* (*esp. N Am.*) a tie for wearing round the neck. **neckwear** *n.* garments worn round the neck, such as ties and scarves.

necklace (nek´ləs) *n.* **1** a string of beads or gems worn round the neck. **2** (*S Afr.*) a tyre soaked in petrol, put round a person's neck and set alight, in order to kill by burning. ~*v.t.* (*S Afr.*) to kill (a person) by means of a burning necklace. **necklacing** *n.*

necro- (nek´rō) *comb. form* of or relating to dead bodies or the dead.

necromancy (nek´rəmansi) *n.* **1** the supposed art of revealing future events by communication with the dead. **2** enchantment, magic. **necromancer** *n.* **necromantic** (-man´-) *a.*

necrophilia (nekrəfil´iə) *n.* an obsession with, and usu. an erotic interest in, corpses. **necrophile** (nek´rəfīl) *n.* **necrophiliac** (-ak) *n.* **necrophilic** (-fīl´-) *a.* **necrophilism** (-krof´-) *n.* **necrophilist** (-krof´-) *n.*

necropolis (nekrop´əlis) *n.* (*pl.* **necropolises**) a cemetery, esp. one on a large scale.

necrosis (nekrō´sis) *n.* (*Med.*) the mortification of part of the body, esp. of bone. **necrotic** (-krot´-) *a.* **necrotize** (nek´rə-), **necrotise** *v.i.*

nectar (nek´tə) *n.* **1** in Greek and Roman mythology, the drink of the gods. **2** any delicious drink. **3** the honey or sweet fluid secretion of plants. **nectarean** (-teə´ri-) *a.* **nectareous** (-teə´ri-), **nectarous** *a.* **nectariferous** (-rif´-) *a.* **nectary** *n.* (*pl.* **nectaries**) the organ or part of a plant or flower secreting honey.

nectarine (nek´tərēn) *n.* **1** a smooth-skinned, firm variety of peach. **2** a tree on which nectarines grow.

neddy (ned´i) *n.* (*pl.* **neddies**) **1** a donkey (used by or to children). **2** (*coll.*) a fool.

née (nā), (*N Am.*) **nee** *a.* born (used with the maiden name of a married woman), as in *Joan Murphy née Smith*.

need (nēd) *v.t.* (*3rd pers. sing. pres.* **needs, need**) **1** to be in want of, to require. **2** to be necessary, to require, to be bound, to be under necessity or obligation (to do something). ~*n.* **1** a state of urgently requiring something; lack of something. **2** something which is wanted, a requirement. **3** a state requiring relief, urgent want. **4** indigence, destitution. **5** a difficult, critical or perilous situation; an emergency. **at need** at a time of need. **in need** poor or in distress. **in need of** requiring, needing. **need not have** did not need to (*I need not have worried*). **to have need of** to require, to need. **needful** *n.* **the needful** (*coll.*) something which is required, esp. money. **needfully** *adv.* **needfulness** *n.* **needless** *a.* **1** unnecessary, not required. **2** useless, superfluous. **needless to say** obviously, of course. **needlessly** *adv.* **needlessness** *n.* †**needs** *adv.* of necessity, necessarily, indispensably (*usu. with* must). **needy** *a.* (*comp.* **needier,** *superl.* **neediest**) **1** in need. **2** necessitous, indigent. **needily** *adv.*

needle (nē´dəl) *n*. **1** a small, thin, rod-shaped, pointed steel instrument with an eye for carrying a thread, used in sewing. **2** any of various analogous instruments of plastic, metal, bone, wood etc., used in knitting, crocheting etc. **3** a piece of magnetized steel used as an indicator in a mariner's compass, a telegraphic receiver etc. **4** any of various pointed instruments used in surgery, assaying, etching etc., and in machinery, firearms etc. **5** a pointed peak or pinnacle of rock. **6** an obelisk. **7** a needle-like leaf of a pine tree. **8** a needle-shaped crystal. **9** a pointed piece of metal, fibre etc., used to receive or transmit the vibrations in the groove of a revolving gramophone record. ~*v.t.* **1** (*coll.*) to irritate; to force into action. **2** to work upon with a needle. **to get the needle** (*sl.*) to become irritated or bad-tempered. **to look for a needle in a haystack** to engage in a hopeless search. **needlecord** *n*. a cotton material with closer ribs and flatter pile than corduroy. **needlecraft** *n*. the art of needlework. **needle exchange** *n*. a place where drug addicts may exchange their used hypodermic needles for new ones. **needlefish** *n*. (*pl. in general* **needlefish**, *in particular* **needlefishes**) a garfish. **needleful** *n*. (*pl.* **needlefuls**). **needle game** *n*. a game which is intensified because it involves a personal grudge. **needle-lace** *n*. lace made with needles, not with bobbins. **needle match** *n*. a needle game. **needlepoint** *n*. **1** any fine sharp point. **2** needle-lace. **3** gros point or petit point. **needle's eye** *n*. the smallest opening possible. **needle time** *n*. the time allocated by a radio station for the playing of music. **needle valve** *n*. a valve which is closed by a needle-like part. **needlewoman** *n*. (*pl.* **needlewomen**) a seamstress. **needlework** *n*. sewing, embroidery etc.

needn't (nē´dənt) *contr.* need not.

neep (nēp) *n*. (*Sc.*) a turnip, a swede.

ne'er (neə) *adv*. (*poet.*) never. **ne'er-do-well** *n*. a lazy, useless person. ~*a*. lazy, useless.

nefarious (nifeə´riəs) *a*. wicked, abominable, infamous. **nefariously** *adv*. **nefariousness** *n*.

neg (neg) *n*. (*coll.*) a photographic negative.

neg. *abbr.* negative.

negate (nigāt´) *v.t.* **1** to render negative, to nullify. **2** to be the negation of. **3** to deny, to affirm the non-existence of. **negation** (-ā´shən) *n*. **1** denial. **2** a declaration of falsity. **3** the act of cancelling or nullifying. **4** the absence or the opposite of certain qualities. **5** nullity, voidness. **6** (*Logic*) negative statement, affirmation of absence or exclusion. **negative** (neg´ə-) *a*. **1** containing, declaring or implying negation. **2** denying, contradicting, prohibiting, refusing. **3** lacking positive qualities such as optimism or enthusiasm. **4** characterized by the absence of a quality (*negative results*). **5** (of a word etc.) indicating negation. **6** (*Logic*) denoting difference or discrepancy. **7** denoting the opposite to positive, denoting what is to be subtracted (expressed by the minus sign -). **8** denoting the

kind of electricity produced by friction on resin, as opposed to positive, produced on glass. **9** showing the lights dark and the shadows light. ~*n*. **1** a proposition, reply, word etc., expressing negation. **2** an image or plate bearing an image in which the lights and shades of the object are reversed. **3** (*Gram.*) a negator. **4** the side of a question that denies. **5** a negative quality, lack or absence of something. **6** (*Logic*) a negation. **7** negative electricity, or the negative plates in a voltaic cell. **8** a negative or minus sign or quantity. ~*v.t.* **1** to veto, to reject, to refuse to accept, sanction or enact. **2** to disprove. **3** to contradict. **4** to neutralize. **in the negative** indicating dissent or refusal. **negative equity** *n*. the state of owing more in mortgage repayments on a property than the market value of the property. **negative feedback** *n*. **1** the interconnection of input and output terminals of an amplifier in such a manner that the output opposes the input, thereby decreasing the gain but increasing the stability and the fidelity of the amplifier. **2** (*Biol.*) the lessening of an effect by its own influence on the process from which it originated. **3** a negative result or response. **negative geotropism** *n*. the tendency of plant stems to grow upwards irrespective of the position in which they are placed. **negatively** *adv*. **negativeness** *n*. **negative pole** *n*. the pole of a freely swinging magnet that swings to the south. **negative prescription** *n*. the time limit for making a claim. **negative sign** *n*. a symbol (-) used to indicate subtraction or a negative number. **negativism** *n*. the quality of being negative. **negativist** *n*. **negativistic** (-is´tik) *a*. **negativity** (-tiv´-) *n*. **negator** *n*. **1** a person who denies something. **2** (*Gram.*) a word or suffix used to express the negative, such as *not*.

neglect (niglekt´) *v.t.* **1** to treat carelessly. **2** to slight, to disregard. **3** to pass over. **4** to leave undone. **5** to omit (to do or doing). ~*n*. **1** disregard (of). **2** omission to do anything that should be done. **3** carelessness, negligence. **4** the state of being neglected. **neglectful** *a*. **neglectfully** *adv*. **neglectfulness** *n*.

negligée (neg´lizhā), **negligee**, **négligé** *n*. **1** a woman's loose dressing gown of flimsy material. **2** a state of undress or free-and-easy attire.

negligence (neg´lijəns) *n*. **1** disregard of appearances, conventions etc., in conduct, literature etc. **2** a negligent act or deed. **3** (*Law*) contributory negligence. **4** failure to exercise the proper care. **negligent** *a*. careless, neglectful. **negligently** *adv*. **negligible** *a*. able to be ignored, so small or unimportant that it is not worth considering.

negotiate (nigō´shiāt) *v.i.* to discuss a matter with other people in order to make a bargain, agreement, compromise etc. ~*v.t.* **1** to arrange, bring about or procure by negotiating. **2** to carry on negotiations concerning. **3** to transfer (a bill, note etc.) for value received. **4** to obtain or give value for. **5** to accomplish, to get over successfully. **negotiable** (-shəbəl) *a*. **negotiability**

(-bil´-) *n.* **negotiant** *n.* **negotiation** (-ā´shən) *n.* **negotiator** *n.*

Negress NEGRO.

Negritude (neg´ritūd) *n.* **1** the state of belonging to a black race. **2** awareness and promotion of black culture.

Negro (nē´grō) *n.* (*pl.* **Negroes**) (*offensive*) a person belonging to, or descended from, one of the dark-skinned African peoples. *~a.* of or relating to these peoples. **Negress** (-gris) *n.* (*offensive*) a female black. **Negroid** (-groid) *a.* **1** of or relating to blacks. **2** having the physical characteristics associated with black peoples of or originating in Africa. *~n.* a Negroid person. **Negro spiritual** *n.* a type of religious song which originated among the black slaves in the southern US.

Usage note The terms *Negro* and *Negress* give offence: it is better to use *black* instead.

negro (nē´grō) *a.* (*Zool.*) black, dark.

❌ neice common misspelling of NIECE.

neigh (nā) *v.i.* to utter the cry of a horse; to whinny. *~v.t.* to utter with a neighlike sound. *~n.* **1** the cry of a horse. **2** a neighlike laugh or other sound. **neighlike** *a.*

neighbour (nā´bə), (*N Am.*) **neighbor** *n.* **1** a person who lives near, a person living in the same street, village, community etc. **2** a person or thing standing or happening to be next to or near another. **3** a person having the claims of a fellow man etc., such as friendship. *~v.t.* **1** to adjoin. **2** to lie near to. *~v.i.* to border (upon). **neighbourhood** (-hud) *n.* **1** the locality round or near; the vicinity. **2** (*collect.*) those who live near, neighbours. **3** neighbourliness. **4** the state of being neighbours. **5** nearness. **6** the part of a town etc. in which people live. **in the neighbourhood of** approximately. **neighbourhood watch** *n.* a crime-prevention scheme organized by the residents of a street or area, who keep watch on each other's property. **neighbouring** *a.* situated or living near. **neighbourless** *a.* **neighbourly** *a.* friendly and helpful. **neighbourliness** *n.* **neighbourship** *n.*

neither (nī´dhə, nē´-) *a.* not either. *~pron.* not the one nor the other. *~conj.* **1** not either, not on the one hand (usu. preceding one of two alternatives and correlative with *nor* preceding the other). **2** nor, nor yet. *~adv.* (*at end of sentence, coll.*) either, any more than another person or thing.

Usage note A following verb should be in the singular (as also after *neither…nor*), though the plural is common.

nelly (nel´i), **nellie** *n.* (*pl.* **nellies**) a foolish or weak person. **not on your nelly** (*sl.*) certainly not.

nelson (nel´sən) *n.* a wrestling hold in which one or both arms are passed under the opponent's arm or arms from behind, and the hands joined so that pressure can be exerted with the palms on the back of the opponent's neck.

nematode (nem´ətōd) *n.* a worm of the phylum Nematoda, which includes the parasitic roundworm and the threadworm. *~a.* of or relating to nematodes.

nem. con. (nem kon´) *adv.* with no one dissenting.

nemesis (nem´əsis) *n.* (*pl.* **nemeses** (-sēz)) **1** retributive justice. **2** an instance or agent of this.

neo- (nē´o) *comb. form* new, recent, modern, later, revived.

neoclassical (nēōklas´ikəl), **neoclassic** *a.* of or relating to the 18th-cent. revival of classicism. **neoclassicism** (-sizm) *n.* **neo-classicist** (-sist) *n.*

neocolonialism (nēōkəlō´niəlizm) *n.* the policy of a strong nation gaining control over a weaker one through economic pressure etc. **neocolonialist** *n., a.*

Neo-Darwinism (nēōdah´winizm) *n.* Darwinism as modified by later investigators, esp. to take account of the findings of genetics. **Neo-Darwinian** (-win´-) *a., n.* **Neo-Darwinist** *n.*

neodymium (nēōdim´iəm) *n.* (*Chem.*) a silvergrey metallic element, at. no. 60, chem. symbol Nd, of the cerium group of rare earth elements.

neo-fascism (nēōfash´izm) *n.* a movement attempting to reinstate the policies of fascism. **neo-fascist** *n., a.*

neolithic (nēəlith´ik) *a.* of or relating to the later Stone Age, characterized by ground and polished implements and the introduction of agriculture. *~n.* the neolithic period.

neologism (niol´əjizm) *n.* **1** a new word or phrase, or a new sense for an old one. **2** the use of new words. **neologist** *n.* **neologize, neologise** *v.i.*

neomycin (nēōmī´sin) *n.* an antibiotic effective against some infections that resist ordinary antibiotics.

neon (nē´on) *n.* (*Chem.*) a colourless gaseous element, at. no. 10, chem. symbol Ne, existing in minute quantities in the air, isolated from argon in 1898.

neonatal (nēōnā´təl) *a.* of or relating to the first few weeks after birth in human babies. **neonate** (nē´-) *n.* a baby at this stage in its development.

neo-Nazi (nēōnah´tsi) *n.* (*pl.* **neo-Nazis**) a person belonging to an organization attempting to reinstate the policies of Naziism. *~a.* of or relating to neo-Nazis. **neo-Nazism** *n.*

neophobia (nēōfō´biə) *n.* a fear of anything new.

neophyte (nē´əfīt) *n.* **1** a person who is newly converted or newly baptized. **2** a person who is newly admitted to a monastery or to the priesthood. **3** a beginner, a novice. **neophytic** (-fit´-) *a.*

neoplasm (nē´əplazm) *n.* an abnormal growth of new tissue in some part of the body, a cancer. **neoplastic** (-plas´-) *a.*

neoprene (nē´əprēn) *n.* a synthetic rubber-like polymer, used in waterproof products.

neotropical (nēōtrop´ikəl) *a.* of, relating to or characteristic of tropical and S America.

Nepali (nipaw'li), **Nepalese** (nepəlēz') *n.* (*pl.* **Nepali, Nepalis, Nepalese**) **1** a native or inhabitant of Nepal, or a descendant of one. **2** the language of Nepal. *~a.* of or relating to Nepal.

nepenthes (nipen'thēz) *n.* (*pl.* **nepenthes**) **1** (*poet.*) (*also* **nepenthe** (-thi)) a drug or potion that drives away sorrow or grief. **2** any pitcher plant of the genus *Nepenthes*.

nephew (nef'ū) *n.* **1** the son of a brother or sister. **2** the son of a brother-in-law or sister-in-law.

nephrite (nef'rīt) *n.* jade, formerly believed to cure kidney disease.

nephritic (nefrit'ik) *a.* **1** of or relating to the kidneys. **2** suffering from kidney disease. **nephritis** (nifrī'tis) *n.* a disease or disorder of the kidneys.

nephro- (nef'rō), **nephr-** *comb. form* of or relating to the kidneys.

ne plus ultra (nā plus ul'trə) *n.* the most perfect or uttermost point.

nepotism (nep'ətizm) *n.* favouritism towards one's relations, for example in business. **nepotist** *n.* **nepotistic** (-tis'-) *a.*

neptunium (neptū'niəm) *n.* (*Chem.*) a radioactive metallic element, at. no. 93, chem. symbol Np, obtained by the bombardment of uranium with neutrons.

nerd (nœd), **nurd** *n.* (*sl.*) an ineffectual or socially awkward person, a fool. **nerdish** *a.* **nerdy** *a.* (*comp.* **nerdier**, *superl.* **nerdiest**).

nereid (niə'riid) *n.* (*pl.* **nereids**) **1** a sea nymph. **2** (*Zool.*) a sea worm or marine centipede of the family Nereidae.

nerve (nœv) *n.* **1** any of the fibres or bundles of fibres conveying sensations and impulses to and from the brain or other organs. **2** the tissue constituting these fibres. **3** strength, coolness, resolution, pluck. **4** any of the ribs or fibrovascular bundles in a leaf. **5** (*pl.*) the nervous system, esp. as regards its state of health or the state of interaction between it and the other parts of the organism. **6** (*pl.*) an excited or disordered condition of the nerves, nervousness. **7** (*coll.*) impudence, cheek, audacity. *~v.t.* **1** to prepare (oneself) for something which requires courage. **2** to give strength or firmness to. **to get on someone's nerves** (*coll.*) to irritate someone. **to lose one's nerve** to lose confidence; to become afraid. **to touch a nerve** to upset someone by mentioning a sensitive subject. **nerve cell** *n.* any cell forming part of the nervous system. **nerve centre**, (*N Am.*) **nerve center** *n.* **1** an aggregation of nerve cells from which nerves branch out. **2** the central or most important part of a business, organization etc. **nerved** *a.* **nerve gas** *n.* any one of a number of gases which have a paralysing and potentially fatal effect on the nervous system, used in warfare etc. **nerveless** (-lis) *a.* **1** destitute of strength, energy or vigour. **2** calm and confident. **3** (*Anat.*, *Zool.*) without nerves. **4** without nervures. **5** feeble, flabby. **nervelessly** *adv.* **nervelessness** *n.* **nerve-racking** *a.* tense, frightening, worrying. **nervine** (nœ'vīn) *a.* (of a

medicine) capable of acting upon the nerves. *~n.* a medicine that acts on the nerves. **nervo-** (nœ'vō), **nerv-** *comb. form* a nerve or nerves. **nervous** *a.* **1** having weak or sensitive nerves, excitable, highly strung, timid. **2** abounding in nervous energy. **3** affecting the nerves. **4** apprehensive (of). **5** of, relating to or composed of nerves. **nervous breakdown** *n.* an attack or period of mental illness which prevents a person from functioning normally, often characterized by depression, agitation or excessive anxiety. **nervously** *adv.* **nervousness** *n.* **nervous system** *n.* a network of nerve cells, including the spinal cord and brain, which collectively controls the body. **nervous wreck** *n.* (*coll.*) an extremely nervous or worried person. **nervure** (-vūe) *n.* **1** the principal vein of a leaf. **2** any of the ribs supporting the membranous wings of insects. **nervy** *a.* (*comp.* **nervier**, *superl.* **nerviest**) **1** nervous, jerky, jumpy. **2** (*N Am.*) full of nerve, cool, confident. **nervily** *adv.* **nerviness** *n.*

nescient (nes'iənt) *a.* (*formal*) ignorant, having no knowledge (of). **nescience** *n.*

ness (nes) *n.* a promontory, a cape.

-ness (nəs, nis) *suf.* forming nouns denoting state, condition, as *happiness*.

nest (nest) *n.* **1** the bed or shelter constructed or prepared by a bird for laying its eggs and rearing its young. **2** any place used by animals or insects for similar purposes. **3** a snug place of abode, shelter or retreat. **4** a haunt (of robbers etc.). **5** a brood, a swarm. **6** a series or set, esp. a number of small tables each fitting inside the next larger. *~v.t.* to put, lodge or establish in or as if in a nest. *~v.i.* **1** to build and occupy a nest. **2** to hunt for or take birds' nests or eggs. **3** to pack one inside another. **nest box** *n.* a box provided for a domestic chicken or other bird to lay eggs in. **nest egg** *n.* **1** a sum of money laid by as savings for the future. **2** a real or artificial egg left in a nest to encourage hens to lay eggs there. **nestful** *n.* (*pl.* **nestfuls**). **nestlike** *a.* **nestling** *n.* a bird too young to leave the nest.

nestle (nes'əl) *v.i.* **1** to settle oneself (down, in etc.). **2** to press closely up to someone. **3** to lie half concealed. **4** to be close or snug. *~v.t.* **1** to put or shelter in or as if in a nest. **2** to settle down snugly. **nestler** *n.*

net[1] (net) *n.* **1** a fabric of twine, cord etc., knotted into meshes, for catching fish, birds, or other animals, or for covering, protecting, carrying etc. **2** a snare. **3** a piece of netting used in various sports, often as a goal. **4** a network of spies, interconnected computers etc. *~v.t.* (*pres.p.* **netting**, *past, p.p.* **netted**) **1** to make or form in a network. **2** to make network of, to reticulate. **3** to cover, hold or confine with a net. **4** to catch in a net. **5** to fish with nets or set nets in (a stream, pond etc.). **6** to catch as if in a net, to ensnare. **7** to score (a goal). **8** to make into a net or netting. *~v.i.* to make netting or network. **the net** (*Comput.*) the Internet. **netball** *n.* a team game in which a ball has to be thrown into a suspended net. **netful** n. (pl. **netfuls**). **network** n. **1** an open-work fabric, netting. **2** a system of intersecting lines, a reticulation. **3** a system of stations for simultaneous broadcasting. **4** any system of lines, roads etc., resembling network. **5** (Comput.) a system of communication between different computers, terminals, circuits etc. **6** a system of interconnected electrical conductors. **7** a system of units related in some way, e.g. part of a business organization. **8** a group of people who are useful to each other because of the similarity of their aims, background etc., as in old boy network. ~v.t. **1** to connect. **2** to broadcast (a television or radio programme) throughout the country rather than in one region. **3** (Comput.) to create or use a system of communication between computers, circuits etc. ~v.i. **1** to form or be part of a network, e.g. through business contacts. **2** to establish professional contacts through social meetings. **networker** n. **networking** n.

net² (net), **nett** n. a. **1** free from all deductions. **2** obtained or left after all deductions. **3** not subject to discount. **4** (of a weight) minus packaging. **5** (of a result etc.) final, ultimate. ~v.t. (pres.p. **netting**, past, p.p. **netted**) to yield or realize as clear profit. **net profit** n. profit after expenses have been deducted. **net ton** n. a unit measuring net internal capacity, equivalent to 100 cu. ft. (2.83 m³).

†**nether** (nedh´ə) a. lower. **nethermost** a. **nether regions** n.pl. hell. **nether world** n. the nether regions.

netsuke (net´suki) n. (pl. **netsuke, netsukes**) a small piece of carved wood or ivory worn or attached to various articles, as a toggle or button, by the Japanese.

nettle (net´əl) n. **1** any plant of the genus Urtica, with two European species, the great or common and the small nettle, with inconspicuous flowers and minute stinging hairs. **2** any of various plants bearing some resemblance to these. ~v.t. **1** to irritate, to provoke. **2** to sting. **to grasp the nettle** to take decisive or bold action. **nettle-rash** n. (Med.) an eruption on the skin resembling the sting of a nettle.

network NET¹.

🗵 **neumonia** common misspelling of PNEUMONIA.

neural (nū´rəl) a. of or relating to the nerves or the nervous system. **neurally** adv. **neural network, neural net** n. (Comput.) a system with interconnected processors working simultaneously and sharing information, and capable of learning from experience.

neuralgia (nūral´jə) n. an acute pain in a nerve or series of nerves, esp. in the head or face. **neuralgic** a.

neurasthenia (nūrəsthē´niə) n. weakness of the nervous system, nervous debility. **neurasthenic** (-then´-) a., n.

neuritis (nūrī´tis) n. inflammation of a nerve. **neuritic** (-rit´-) a.

neuro- (nū´rō), **neur-** comb. form **1** of or relating to a nerve cell. **2** of or relating to nerves. **3** of or relating to the nervous system.

neuroanatomy (nūrōənat´əmi) n. the anatomy of the nervous system. **neuroanatomical** (-anətom´-) a. **neuroanatomist** n.

neurobiology (nūrōbīol´əji) n. the biology of the nervous system. **neurobiological** (-bīəloj´-) a. **neurobiologist** n.

neurocomputer (nūrōkəmpū´tə) n. a computer using a neural network.

neurology (nūrol´əji) n. the scientific study of the anatomy, physiology and pathology of nerves. **neurological** (-loj´-) a. **neurologically** adv. **neurologist** n.

neuromuscular (nūrōmŭs´kūlə) a. of or relating to nerves and muscles.

neurone (nū´rōn), **neuron** (-ron) n. a nerve cell with its processes and ramifications, one of the structural units of the nervous system. **neuronal** (-rō´nəl) a. **neuronic** (-ron´ik) a.

neuropath (nū´rəpath) n. a person suffering from a nervous disorder or having abnormal nervous sensibility. **neuropathic** (-path´-) a. **neuropathist** (-rop´-) n. **neuropathology** (-thol´-) n. the pathology of the nervous system. **neuropathologist** n. **neuropathy** (-rop´əthi) n. any nervous disease.

neurophysiology (nūrōfiziol´əji) n. the physiology of the nervous system. **neurophysiological** (-loj´-) a. **neurophysiologist** n.

neuropteran (nūrop´tərən) n. any insect of the order Neuroptera, having four reticulated membranous wings. **neuropterous, neuropteral, neuropteroid** a.

neurosis (nūrō´sis) n. (pl. **neuroses** (-sēz)) **1** functional disorder of the nervous system. **2** a mild mental disorder, usu. with symptoms of anxiety. **neurotic** (-rot´-) a. **1** of or relating to neurosis. **2** suffering from neurosis. **3** (coll.) unreasonably anxious, oversensitive. ~n. a neurotic person. **neurotically** adv. **neuroticism** (-sizm) n.

neurosurgery (nūrōsœ´jəri) n. the branch of surgery dealing with the nervous system. **neurosurgeon** n. **neurosurgical** a.

neurotomy (nūrot´əmi) n. (pl. **neurotomies**) an incision in a nerve, usu. to produce sensory paralysis.

neurotoxin (nūrōtok´sin) n. any poison which acts on the nervous system.

neurotransmitter (nūrōtranzmit´ə) n. a chemical substance by means of which nerve cells communicate with each other.

neuter (nū´tə) a. **1** (Gram.) neither masculine nor feminine. **2** (of a plant) neither male nor female, without pistil or stamen. **3** (of an animal, esp. an insect) undeveloped sexually, sterile. ~n. **1** a neuter word. **2** a sterile female insect, such as a working bee. **3** a castrated animal. ~v.t. to remove the reproductive organs of (an animal).

neutral (nū´trəl) a. **1** taking no part with either

side, esp. not assisting either of two belligerents.
2 belonging to a state that takes no part in
hostilities. **3** indifferent, impartial. **4** having no
distinct or determinate character, colour etc. **5**
neither good nor bad, indefinite, indeterminate.
6 denoting the position of parts in a gear mechanism when no power is transmitted. **7** (*Chem.*)
neither acid nor alkaline. **8** (*Physics*) neither
positive nor negative. **9** (*Biol.*) neuter, asexual. **10**
having a pale or light colour, e.g. grey or light
brown. *~n.***1** a neutral state. **2** a subject of a neutral state. **3** a neutral gear. **neutralism** *n.* the
policy of remaining neutral. **neutralist** *n.*
neutrality (-tral´-) *n.* **neutralize, neutralise** *v.t.* **1**
to render neutral. **2** to render inoperative or ineffective, to counteract. **3** to declare (a state or
territory) neutral, either permanently or during
hostilities. **4** (*euphem.*) to make harmless, to kill.
neutralization (-zā´shən) *n.* **neutralizer** *n.*
neutrally *adv.*
neutrino (nūtrē´nō) *n.* (*pl.* **neutrinos**) any of a
class of subatomic particles with almost zero
mass and zero charge but specified spin.
neutron (nū´tron) *n.* (*Physics*) a particle that is
neutral electrically with approximately the same
mass as a proton. **neutron bomb** *n.* a bomb which
produces neutrons without a huge blast, designed to destroy all life in the area hit without
causing much damage to property. **neutron star**
n. a very dense star composed of neutrons.
never (nev´ə) *adv.* **1** not ever, at no time. **2** on no
occasion. **3** not at all. *~int.* surely not! **never a
one** not a single person etc., none. **well I never!**
(*coll.*) used to express surprise. **nevermore**
(-maw´) *adv.* at no future time; never again.
never-never *n.* (*coll.*) the hire-purchase system.
never-never land *n.* an imaginary place with
conditions too ideal to exist in real life.
nevertheless *conj.* but for all that; notwithstanding; all the same.
nevus NAEVUS.
new (nū) *a.* **1** not formerly in existence. **2** lately
made, invented or introduced. **3** not before
known. **4** recently entered upon or begun. **5**
never before used, not worn or exhausted. **6**
renewed; reinvigorated. **7** replacing something (*a
new job*). **8** in addition to others of the same kind
(*a new cinema*). **9** fresh, unfamiliar, unaccustomed. **10** fresh (from), not yet accustomed (to).
11 (*often derog.*) modern, newfangled. **12**
advanced. *~adv.* **1** newly, recently (*usu. in comb.*,
as *new-born*). **2** anew, afresh. **New Age** *n.* a cultural movement which emphasizes the spiritual
and mystical aspects of western society, incorporating elements of eastern religion, astrology,
alternative medicine and ecology. *~a.* of or
relating to the New Age movement or New Age
music. **New Age music** *n.* a type of gentle,
melodic popular music played mainly on
synthesizer and acoustic instruments. **new
arrival** *n.* (*coll.*) a newborn baby. **new birth** *n.*
(*Theol.*) spiritual regeneration. **newborn** *a.* **1** just

born. **2** reborn, regenerated. **new broom** *n.* a
recently appointed person who is expected to
make many changes. **newcomer** *n.* **1** a person
who has recently arrived in a place. **2** a person
who has just begun to take part in something.
newish *a.* **new-laid** *a.* (of an egg) freshly laid.
newly *adv.* **1** recently. **2** anew. **3** differently.
newly-wed *n.* a recently married person. **new
man** *n.* (*pl.* **new men**) a man who supports
women's liberation and who undertakes tasks
traditionally associated with women, such as
housework. **new mathematics, new maths** *n.* a
system of teaching mathematics with a strong
emphasis on investigation and set theory. **new
moon** *n.* the moon at the beginning of its course
with its face invisible or partially illuminated.
newness *n.* **new potatoes** *n.pl.* potatoes which
have been harvested early. **Newspeak** *n.* a form
of language, often used by officials and bureaucrats, which is ambiguous, misleading and verbose (coined by George Orwell in his novel *Nineteen Eighty-Four*). **new star** *n.* a nova. **New Style**
- *n.* the method of reckoning dates which is currently used, based on the Gregorian calendar.
new-style *a.* in a new style (*a new-style passport*).
New Testament *n.* the part of the Christian Bible
dealing with the Christian dispensation composed after the birth of Christ. **new town** *n.* a
town planned by the government to relieve
housing problems in nearby large cities, stimulate development etc. **new wave** *n.* **1** the nouvelle vague. **2** a style of rock music of the late
1970s, developing from punk. **New World** *n.* the
American continent. **new year** *n.* **1** the beginning
of a new calendar year. **2** the first few days or
weeks of a year. **New Year's Day** *n.* the first day
of the year. **New Year's Eve** *n.* the last day of the
year.
newel (nū´əl) *n.* **1** the central column from which
the steps of a winding stair radiate. **2** an upright
post at the top or bottom of a stair supporting the
handrail.
newfangled (nūfang´gəld) *a.* (*derog.*) newfashioned; different from the accepted fashion.
Newfoundlander (nū´fəndləndə, nūfəndlan´də) *n.* a native or inhabitant of Newfoundland, Canada.
Newmarket (nū´mahkit) *n.* a gambling card
game in which players try to match cards with
cards laid out.
news (nūz) *n.* **1** recent or fresh information. **2** a
regular radio or television broadcast of up-to-date information on current affairs. **3** (*coll.*)
information previously unknown (to) (*that's
news to me*). **news agency** *n.* an organization for
supplying information to newspapers etc.
newsagent *n.* a dealer in newspapers, magazines
etc. **newsboy** *n.* a boy who delivers or sells newspapers in the street. **news bulletin** *n.* a collection
of news items for broadcasting. **newscast** *n.* a
radio or television news programme. **newscaster**
n. a newsreader. **news conference** *n.* a press

conference. **newsflash** *n.* a short important news item, esp. one which interrupts a television or radio programme. **news-gatherer** *n.* a person who researches news items for broadcast or publication. **newsgirl** *n.* a girl who delivers or sells newspapers in the street. **news hound** *n.* (*coll.*) a reporter in search of news. **newsless** *a.* **newsletter** *n.* a printed report of news sent out regularly to a particular group. **newsman** *n.* (*pl.* **newsmen**) a news reporter. **newsmonger** *n.* a person who makes it their business to spread news, usu. false; a busybody in news. **newspaper** *n.* a printed publication, usu. issued daily or weekly, containing news. **newspaperman**, **newspaperwoman** *n.* (*pl.* **newspapermen, newspaperwomen**) a journalist working for a newspaper. **newsprint** *n.* the cheap-quality paper upon which newspapers are printed. **newsreader** *n.* a person who reads the news on radio or television. **newsreel** *n.* a short film giving the day's news. **newsroom** *n.* **1** a room where news is edited for broadcasting or publication. **2** a room in a library for reading newspapers etc. **newssheet** *n.* a printed sheet of news, an early form of newspaper. **news-stand** *n.* a newspaper kiosk. **news-vendor** *n.* a seller of newspapers. **newsworthy** *a.* interesting enough to be reported as news. **newsworthiness** *n.* **newsy** *a.* (*comp.* **newsier,** *superl.* **newsiest**). **newsiness** *n.*

newt (nūt) *n.* a small, tailed amphibian of the genus *Tritunus*, like the salamander.

newton (nū´tən) *n.* (*Physics*) a unit of force equal to 100,000 dynes.

Newtonian (nūtō´niən) *a.* **1** of or relating to Sir Isaac Newton or his theories. **2** discovered or invented by Newton.

New Yorker (nū yaw´kə) *n.* a native or inhabitant of New York, USA.

New Zealander (nū zē´ləndə) *n.* a native or inhabitant of New Zealand, or a descendant of one.

next (nekst) *a.* **1** nearest in place, time or degree. **2** nearest in order or succession, immediately following. ~*adv.* **1** nearest or immediately after. **2** in the next place or degree. ~*n.* the next person or thing. ~*prep.* (*coll.*) nearest to. **next to** almost; all but. **next to nothing** scarcely anything. **next-best** *a.* second best. **next but one** *n.* the one immediately after the one following. **next door** *adv., n.* (in, at or to) the adjoining house or room. **next door to 1** in or at the house adjoining. **2** almost, near to. **next-door** *a.* of or relating to the adjoining house or room, living next door. **next of kin** *n.* the nearest blood relation. **next world** *n.* life after death.

nexus (nek´səs) *n.* (*pl.* **nexuses**) **1** a connected group. **2** a link, a connection.

ngaio (nī´ō) *n.* (*pl.* **ngaios**) a New Zealand tree, *Myoporum laetum*, noted for its fine white wood.

NGO *abbr.* non-governmental organization.

ngultrum (neg·gul´trəm) *n.* (*pl.* **ngultrums**) the chief monetary unit of Bhutan, central Asia.

NHS *abbr.* National Health Service.

NI *abbr.* **1** National Insurance. **2** Northern Ireland.

Ni *chem. symbol* nickel.

niacin (nī´əsin) *n.* nicotinic acid.

nib (nib) *n.* **1** the point of a pen. **2** the point of a tool etc. **3** the beak of a bird. **4** (*pl.*) crushed cocoa beans. ~*v.t.* (*pres.p.* **nibbing,** *past, p.p.* **nibbed**) **1** to put a nib into (a pen). **2** to sharpen the nib of (a quill pen). **3** to nibble. ~*v.i.* to nibble. **his nibs** (*coll., facet.*) an important or self-important person.

nibble (nib´əl) *v.t.* **1** to bite little by little. **2** to bite little bits off. **3** to bite at cautiously. ~*v.i.* **1** to take small bites or to bite cautiously (at). **2** to take a cautious interest (in). ~*n.* **1** the act of nibbling. **2** (*pl.*) party snacks, such as crisps, nuts and biscuits. **3** a little bite. **4** a bit which is nibbled off. **5** (*Comput.*) half a byte. **nibbler** *n.*

niblet (nib´lit) *n.* a small piece (of food).

niblick (nib´lik) *n.* a golf club with a small cup-shaped iron head.

nicad (nī´kad), **nicad battery** *n.* a battery which has a nickel anode and a cadmium cathode.

Nicam (nī´kam) *n.* a sound system in which audio signals are converted into digital form and transmitted along with a standard television signal.

Nicaraguan (nikərag´ūən, -wən) *n.* a native or inhabitant of Nicaragua, Central America. ~*a.* of or relating to Nicaragua.

nice (nīs) *a.* **1** pleasing or agreeable. **2** delightful, attractive, friendly, kind. **3** (*iron.*) terrible (*a nice mess*). **4** fastidious, overparticular, hard to please, dainty, punctilious, scrupulous. **5** acute, discerning, discriminating, sensitive to minute differences. **6** requiring delicate discrimination or tact, delicate, subtle, minute. **7** (of weather) warm and pleasant. **nicely** *adv.* **niceness** *n.* **nice one** *int.* (*coll.*) used to express approval or pleasure. **nicety** (nī´siti) *n.* (*pl.* **niceties**) **1** exactness, precision. **2** a minute point, a delicate distinction. **3** a small detail. **4** (*pl.*) refinements, delicacy. **to a nicety** exactly, with precision. **nice work** *int.* used to express approval. **nicish** (nī´sish), **niceish** *a.*

niche (nich, nēsh) *n.* **1** a recess in a wall for a statue, vase etc. **2** one's proper place or natural position. **3** in business, a small, specialized, but profitable area of the market. ~*v.t.* **1** to put in a niche. **2** to settle (oneself) in a comfortable place.

Nichrome® (nī´krōm) *n.* a nickel-chromium alloy with high electrical resistance and an ability to withstand high temperature.

nick¹ (nik) *n.* **1** a small notch, cut or dent, esp. used as a guide or a tally or score for keeping account. **2** (*sl.*) a prison, a police station. **3** (*coll.*) condition (of a given description) (*in good nick*). **4** in a squash court, the junction between the floor and the walls. ~*v.t.* **1** to cut or make a nick or nicks in. **2** (*sl.*) to steal. **3** (*sl.*) to arrest. **in the nick of time** only just in time.

nick² (nik) *v.i.* (*sl.*) to go quickly or furtively.

nickel (nik´əl) *n.* **1** (*Chem.*) a lustrous silvery-white ductile metallic element, at. no. 28, chem. symbol Ni, usu. found in association with cobalt, used in the manufacture of German silver and in other alloys. **2** (*N Am.*) a 5-cent piece. ~*v.t.* (*pres.p.* **nickelling**, (*N Am.*) **nickeling**, *past*, *p.p.* **nickelled**, (*N Am.*) **nickeled**) to coat with nickel. **nickel brass** *n.* an alloy of copper, zinc and nickel. **nickelic** *a.* **nickelous** *a.* **nickel-plate** *v.t.* to cover with nickel. **nickel-plating** *n.* **nickel silver** *n.* German silver. **nickel steel** *n.* an alloy of nickel and steel.

nickelodeon (nikəlōˊdiən) *n.* (*pl.* **nickelodeons**) (*N Am.*) **1** (*coll.*) an early form of jukebox, esp. one operated by a 5-cent piece. **2** (*Hist.*) a cinema whose admission fee was one nickel.

nicker (nikˊə) *n.* (*pl.* **nicker**) (*sl.*) a pound (money).

nick-nack KNICK-KNACK.

nickname (nikˊnām) *n.* a name given in derision or familiarity. ~*v.t.* **1** to give a nickname to. **2** to call by a nickname.

nicol (nikˊəl), **nicol prism** *n.* a crystal of calcium carbonate so cut and cemented as to transmit only the extraordinary ray, used for polarizing light.

nicotine (nikˊətēn) *n.* an acrid, poisonous alkaloid contained in tobacco. **nicotinamide** (-tinˊəmīd) *n.* the amide of nicotinic acid, essential for the prevention of pellagra. **nicotinic acid** (-tinˊik) *n.* a vitamin of the B complex, a deficiency of which causes pellagra. **nicotinism** *n.* **nicotinize**, **nicotinise** *v.t.*

nictitate (nikˊtitāt), **nictate** (nikˊtāt) *v.i.* (*Zool.*) to wink, esp. to open and shut the eyes rapidly. **nictitating membrane** *n.* a third or inner eyelid possessed by birds, fishes and many animals. **nictitation** (-āˊshən) *n.*

niece (nēs) *n.* the daughter of one's brother or sister, or one's brother-in-law or sister-in-law.

niello (nielˊō) *n.* (*pl.* **nielli** (-lē), **niellos**) **1** a black alloy used to fill the lines of incised designs on metal plates. **2** an example of this work. **nielloed** *a.*

niff (nif) *n.* (*coll.*) a stink, a bad smell. ~*v.i.* to stink, to smell bad. **niffy** *a.* (*comp.* **niffier**, *superl.* **niffiest**).

nifty (nifˊti) *a.* (*comp.* **niftier**, *superl.* **niftiest**) (*coll.*) **1** quick, slick. **2** smart, stylish. **niftily** *adv.* **niftiness** *n.*

nigella (nījelˊə) *n.* a plant of the genus *Nigella*, of ranunculaceous plants comprising love-in-a-mist.

Nigerian (nījiəˊriən) *n.* a native or inhabitant of Nigeria, Africa. ~*a.* of or relating to Nigeria.

niggard (nigˊəd) *n.* a stingy person, a miser; a person who is grudging. **niggardly** *a.* **1** miserly, mean, parsimonious. **2** worth very little. ~*adv.* in a miserly manner. **niggardliness** *n.*

nigger (nigˊə) *n.* **1** (*offensive*) a black person. **2** (*offensive*) any dark-skinned person. **to work like a nigger** (*offensive*) to work hard. **nigger in**

the woodpile *n.* (*offensive*) a person who or something which spoils something good.

niggle (nigˊəl) *v.i.* **1** to busy oneself with petty details. **2** to find fault constantly. ~*v.t.* to worry, to annoy. ~*n.* a minor criticism or worry. **niggler** *n.* **niggling** *a.*, *n.* **nigglingly** *adv.*

†**nigh** (nī) *adv.* (*also dial.*) **1** near. **2** almost. ~*a.* near. ~*prep.* near, close to.

night (nīt) *a.* **1** the time of darkness from sunset to sunrise. **2** the darkness of this period. **3** the end of daylight, nightfall. **4** a period or state of darkness. **5** an evening set aside for a particular activity. ~*int.* (*coll.*) goodnight. **nightbird** *n.* (*coll.*) a person who habitually stays up late. **night-blindness** *n.* nyctalopia. **nightcap** *n.* **1** (*Hist.*) a cap worn in bed. **2** a hot drink or an alcoholic drink taken at bedtime. **nightclothes** *n.pl.* clothes worn in bed. **nightclub** *n.* a club open late at night, providing refreshments, dancing and entertainment. **nightdress** *n.* a woman's or child's loose dress-shaped garment worn in bed. **nightfall** *n.* the beginning of night, the coming of darkness; dusk. **night fighter** *n.* an aircraft used for intercepting at night. **nightgown** *n.* **1** nightdress. **2** (*Hist.*) a dressing gown. **nighthawk** *n.* **1** a person, esp. a thief, who prowls about at night. **2** an American nightjar of the genus *Chordeiles*. **nightie** *n.* (*coll.*) a nightdress. **nightjar** *n.* any nocturnal bird of the family Caprimulgidae, having grey-brown plumage. **nightless** *a.* **nightlife** *n.* late evening entertainment or social life. **night light** *n.* a low light kept alight at night. **night-long** *a.* lasting through a night.~*adv.* all night. **nightly** *a.*, *adv.* **nightmare** (-meə) *n.* **1** a terrifying dream. **2** a haunting sense of dread. **3** (*coll.*) anything inspiring such a feeling; a terrifying experience. **nightmarish** *a.* **nightmarishly** *adv.* **night nurse** *n.* a nurse who is on duty during the night. **night owl** *n.* (*coll.*) a person who habitually stays up late. **night safe** *n.* a safe built into the outer wall of a bank where customers can deposit money when the bank is closed. **night school** *n.* an evening school for those at work during the day. **night shift** *n.* **1** work during the night, as distinct from *day shift* and *back shift*. **2** the group of workers undertaking such work. **nightshirt** *n.* a long shirt worn in bed. **night-soil** *n.* (*Hist.*) the contents of lavatories and cesspools removed at night. **nightspot** *n.* (*coll.*) a nightclub. **nightstick** *n.* (*N Am.*) a truncheon. **night terrors** *n.pl.* great fear felt esp. by children on waking suddenly during the night, not remembered next morning. **nighttime** *n.* **night-watch** *n.* a watch or guard on duty at night. **nightwatchman** *n.* (*pl.* **nightwatchmen**) **1** a person who keeps watch on a public building, factory etc. at night, a night security guard. **2** in cricket, a batsman sent in towards the close of a day's play, esp. in place of a higher order batsman. **nightwear** *n.* clothes worn in bed. **nighty** *n.* (*pl.* **nighties**) (*coll.*) a nightdress.

nightingale (nīˊting-gāl) *n.* a small, brownish

migratory bird, *Luscinia megarhynchos*, singing at night as well as by day.

nightshade (nīt´shăd) *n*. **1** any of several plants of the genus *Solanum*, esp. the black nightshade or woody nightshade. **2** DEADLY NIGHTSHADE (under DEADLY).

nigrescent (nīgres´ənt) *a*. blackish. **nigrescence** *n*.

nigritude (nig´ritūd) *n*. blackness.

nihil (nī´hil) *n*. nothing. **nihilism** (nī´ilizm) *n*. **1** any theological, philosophical or political doctrine of a negative kind. **2** (*Philos*.) denial of all existence, or of the knowledge of all existence. **nihilist** *n*. **nihilistic** (-lis´-) *a*. **nihility** (nihil´-) *n*. (*pl*. **nihilities**) **1** the state of being nothing or of nothingness. **2** a mere nothing.

-nik (nik) *comb. form* a person who practises something, e.g. *beatnik, kibbutznik, peacenik*.

nil (nil) *n*. nothing; zero.

Nile (nīl) *n*. (*also* **Nile blue, Nile green**) a pale greenish-blue or pale green. ~*a*. (*also* **Nile-blue, Nile-green**) pale greenish-blue or pale green.

nilgai (nil´gī), **nilghau** (nil´gaw), **nylghau** *n*. (*pl*. **nilgais, nilghaus, nylghaus**) a large Indian antelope, *Boselaphus tragocamelus*.

nimble (nim´bəl) *a*. **1** light and quick in motion; agile, swift, dexterous. **2** alert, clever, brisk, lively, versatile. **nimbleness** *n*. **nimbly** *adv*.

nimbostratus (nimbōstrah´təs) *n*. (*pl*. **nimbostrati** (-tī)) a dense, grey, rain- or snow-bearing cloud.

nimbus (nim´bəs) *n*. (*pl*. **nimbi** (-bī), **nimbuses**) **1** a halo or glory surrounding the heads of divine or sacred personages in paintings etc. **2** a rain cloud, a dark mass of cloud, usu. with ragged edges, from which rain is falling or likely to fall. **nimbused** *a*.

Nimby (nim´bi) *a*. supporting the dumping of nuclear waste, the construction of ugly buildings etc., as long as one's own property is not affected. ~*n*. (*pl*. **Nimbies**) a person who takes this attitude. **nimbyism** *n*.

niminy-piminy (niminipim´ini) *a*. affecting niceness or delicacy; mincing; affected.

nincompoop (ning´kəmpoop) *n*. an idiot, a fool.

nine (nīn) *n*. **1** the number or figure 9 or IX. **2** the age of 9. **3** a set of nine things; a team of nine players. **4** the ninth hour after midnight or midday. **5** a card, counter etc. with nine pips. **6** a size measuring nine. ~*a*. nine in number. **dressed (up) to the nines** (*coll*.) very smartly or glamorously dressed. **nine times out of ten** usually, generally. **nine to five** normal office working hours. **nine days' wonder** *n*. an event, person or thing that is a novelty for the moment but is soon forgotten. **ninefold** *a*., *adv*. **1** nine times as much or as many. **2** consisting of nine parts. **ninepin** *n*. **1** a skittle. **2** (*pl*.) a game with nine skittles set up to be bowled at. **to go down like ninepins** to become ill or fail in large numbers. **nineteen** (-tēn´) *n*. **1** the number or figure 19 or XIX. **2** the age of 19. **3** a set of 19 things; a group of 19

people. ~*a*. **1** 19 in number. **2** aged 19. **nineteenth** (-th) *n*. any one of 19 equal parts. ~*n*., *a*. **1** (the) last of nineteen (people, things etc.). **2** (the) next after the 18th. **nineteenth hole** *n*. (*sl*.) the clubhouse bar at a golf club. **nine-tenths** *n*. (*coll*.) nearly all (of). **ninetieth** (-tiəth) *n*. any one of 90 equal parts. ~*n*., *a*. **1** (the) last of ninety (people, things etc.). **2** (the) next after the 89th. **ninety** *n*. (*pl*. **nineties**) **1** the number or figure 90 or XC. **2** the age of 90. ~*a*. **1** 90 in number. **2** aged 90. **nineties** *n.pl*. **1** the period of time between one's 90th and 100th birthdays. **2** the range of temperature between 90 and 100 degrees. **3** the period of time between the 90th and final year of a century. **ninety-first, ninety-second** etc. *n*., *a*. the ordinal numbers corresponding to ninety-one etc. **ninetyfold** *a*., *adv*. **1** ninety times as much or as many. **2** made up of ninety parts. **ninety-one, ninety-two** etc. *n*., *a*. the cardinal numbers between 90 and 100.

ninja (nin´jə) *n*. (*pl*. **ninjas**) a person who is skilled in ninjutsu.

ninjutsu (ninjŭt´soo) *n*. a Japanese martial art involving stealth and camouflage.

ninny (nin´i) *n*. (*pl*. **ninnies**) (*coll*.) a fool, a simpleton.

ninth (nīnth) *n*. **1** any one of nine equal parts. **2** (*Mus*.) **a** a diatonic interval of an octave and a second. **b** two notes separated by this interval sounded together. ~*n*., *a*. **1** (the) last of nine (people, things etc.). **2** (the) next after the eighth. **ninthly** *adv*.

niobium (nīō´biəm) *n*. (*Chem*.) a grey-blue metallic element, at. no. 41, chem. symbol Nb, occurring in tantalite etc. **niobic** *a*. **niobous** *a*.

nip[1] (nip) *v.t.* (*pres.p.* **nipping**, *past*, *p.p.* **nipped**) **1** to pinch, to squeeze or compress sharply. **2** to cut or pinch off the end or point of. **3** to bite. **4** to sting, to pain. **5** (of cold or frost) to check the growth of. **6** (*N Am*., *sl*.) to steal. ~*v.i.* **1** (*coll*.) to move, go, or step quickly (in, out, etc.). **2** to cause pain. ~*n*. **1** a pinch, a sharp squeeze or compression. **2** a bite. **3** bitter cold. **4** a check to vegetation, esp. by frost. **nip and tuck** *n*. (*coll*.) a surgical operation performed for cosmetic reasons. ~*adv*. (*N Am*.) neck and neck. **nipper** *n*. **1** a person who or something which nips. **2** the claw of a crab or other crustacean. **3** (*sl*.) a boy, a lad. **4** (*pl*.) a pair of pincers, forceps or pliers. **5** (*Austral*.) a prawn of the order Thalassinidea, used as fishing bait. **nippy** *a*. (*comp*. **nippier**, *superl*. **nippiest**) (*coll*.) **1** cold. **2** active; agile. **3** quick, alert. **nippily** *adv*.

nip[2] (nip) *n*. a small drink of spirits.

nipa (nē´pə, nī´-) *n*. **1** a palm tree of tropical SE Asia and the islands of the Indian Ocean, *Nipa fruticans*, with feathery leaves used in thatching, basket-weaving etc., and for packing bunches of fruit. **2** an alcoholic drink made from the sap of the nipa.

nipple (nip´əl) *n*. **1** the small prominence in the breast of female mammals, by which milk is sucked or drawn. **2** a similar structure in male mammals. **3** a similar contrivance attached to a baby's feeding bottle. **4** a nipple-shaped perforated projection, as on a gun-breach for holding a percussion-cap. **5** a nipple-shaped prominence on the surface of metal or glass. **6** (*N Am.*) a section of pipe with a screw-thread at each end. **nipplewort** *n.* a slender weed, *Lapsana communis*, with small yellow flowers.

Nipponese (nipənēz´) *n.* (*pl.* **Nipponese**) a Japanese person. ~*a.* Japanese.

nippy NIP¹.

nirvana (niəvah´nə) *n.* **1** absorption of individuality into the divine spirit with extinction of personal desires and passions, the Buddhist state of beatitude. **2** (*coll.*) bliss, heaven.

nisei (nē´sā, -sā´), **Nisei** *n.* a person of Japanese descent born in the US.

Nissen hut (nis´ən) *n.* a long hut of corrugated iron with a semicircular roof.

nit¹ (nit) *n.* the egg of a louse or other small, esp. parasitic, insect. **nit-picking** *n.* (*coll.*) petty criticism of minor details. ~*a.* criticizing minor details. **nit-pick** *v.i.* **nit-picker** *n.* **nitty** *a.* (*comp.* **nittier,** *superl.* **nittiest**).

nit² (nit) *int.* (*Austral., sl.*) used to express warning of someone's approach. **to keep nit** to keep a lookout.

nit³ (nit) *n.* (*coll.*) a fool.

niter NITRE.

nitinol (nit´inol) *n.* an alloy of nickel and titanium.

nitrate¹ (nī´trāt) *n.* (*Chem.*) **1** a salt of nitric acid. **2** sodium or potassium nitrate.

nitrate² (nītrāt´) *v.t.* to treat or combine with nitric acid. **nitration** (-ā´shən) *n.*

nitre (nī´tə), (*N Am.*) **niter** *n.* saltpetre, potassium nitrate, occurring as an orthorhombic mineral. **nitrify** (-fī) *v.t.* (*3rd pers. sing. pres.* **nitrifies,** *pres.p.* **nitrifying,** *past, p.p.* **nitrified**) **1** to turn into nitre. **2** to make nitrous. **nitrification** (-ā´shən) *n.* **nitrite** (-trīt) *n.* any salt or ester of nitrous acid.

nitric (nī´trik) *a.* (*Chem.*) of or relating to nitre. **nitric acid** *n.* a colourless, corrosive acid liquid based on the ingredients of nitre. **nitric oxide** *n.* a colourless gas, nitrogen monoxide, involved in physiological processes in minute quantities.

nitride (nī´trīd) *n.* (*Chem.*) a compound of nitrogen with phosphorus, boron, silicon etc.

nitrile (nī´trīl) *n.* (*Chem.*) any organic compound consisting of an alkyl radical bound to a cyanide radical.

nitrite NITRE.

nitro- (nī´trō) *comb. form* nitric.

nitrobenzene (nītrōben´zēn) *n.* an oily compound of benzene with nitric acid, having an odour of oil of bitter almonds, used for flavouring perfumes and confectionery.

nitrocellulose (nītrōsel´ūlōz, -lōs) *n.* an extremely flammable material made by treating cellulose with nitric acid, used to make explosives and celluloid.

nitrogen (nī´trəjən) *n.* (*Chem.*) a colourless, tasteless, gaseous element, at. no. 7, chem. symbol N, forming 80% of the atmosphere, the basis of nitre and nitric acid. **nitrogen cycle** *n.* the cycle of processes by which nitrogen is absorbed from the atmosphere and returned to it by biological systems. **nitrogen dioxide** *n.* a reddish-brown poisonous gas. **nitrogenous** (-troj´-), **nitrogenic** (-trōjen´-) *a.*

nitroglycerine (nītrōglis´ərēn, -rin), **nitroglycerin** *n.* a highly explosive colourless oil, obtained by adding glycerine to a mixture of nitric and sulphuric acids.

nitrous (nī´trəs) *a.* (*Chem.*) obtained from, impregnated with, or resembling nitre. **nitrous acid** *n.* a weak acid which exists only in solution and in the gaseous state. **nitrous oxide** *n.* dinitrogen oxide used as an anaesthetic, laughing gas.

nitty-gritty (nitigrit´i) *n.* the basic facts, the realities of a situation.

nitwit (nit´wit) *n.* (*coll.*) a foolish or stupid person. **nitwitted** *a.* stupid. **nitwittedness** *n.* **nitwittery** (-wit´əri) *n.*

nix¹ (niks) *n.* (*sl.*) **1** nothing, nobody. **2** a rejection, a denial. ~*v.t.* (*sl.*) **1** to cancel. **2** to reject.

nix² (niks), **nixie** *n.* a water sprite.

nix³ (niks) *int.* look out! **to keep nix** to keep watch.

nm *abbr.* **1** nanometre(s). **2** nautical mile(s).

NMR, nmr *abbr.* nuclear magnetic resonance.

NNE *abbr.* north-north-east.

NNW *abbr.* north-north-west.

No¹ *chem. symbol* nobelium.

No² NOH.

No. *abbr.* **1** (*N Am.*) North. **2** (*also* **no.**) number.

no¹ (nō) *a.* **1** not any. **2** not one, not a. **3** quite other than, quite the opposite or reverse of. **4** hardly any. **5** expressing opposition, objection, or rejection (as *no popery*). **no man** no one, no person, nobody. **no way** (*coll.*) definitely not, under no circumstances. **... or no ...** in spite of, regardless of (*Husband or no husband, you must turn him in*). **there is no ...ing** it is impossible to ... (*There is no getting out of this visit*). **no-account** *a.* good-for-nothing, worthless. **no-ball** *n.* in cricket, a ball not delivered according to the rules, counting for one to the other side. ~*v.t.* to declare (a bowler) to have bowled this. **no-claims bonus, no-claim bonus** *n.* a reduction in the price of an insurance policy because no claims have been made on it. **no-claims discount, no-claim discount** *n.* no-claims bonus. **no-fault compensation** *n.* a system of compensation for accidental injury which does not depend on proving someone guilty of misconduct, negligence etc. **no-fly zone** *n.* a zone in which aircraft are not permitted to fly. **no-frills** *a.* basic, having no unnecessary extra features. **no go** *n.* a complete failure. **no-go** *a.* **1** of no use. **2** not to be done. **no-go area** *n.* an area which unauthorized people are not permitted to enter. **no good** n. mischief, trouble (up to no good). ~a. useless, vain, pointless. **no-good** a. (coll.) worthless. ~n. (coll.) a bad or worthless person or thing. **no-hitter** n. in baseball, a match in which a team concedes no hits. **no-hoper** n. (sl.) an ineffectual or worthless person. **nohow** adv. (N Am.) in no way, not by any means. **no man's land** n. 1 (Mil.) the contested land between two opposing forces. 2 waste or unclaimed land. **no-nonsense** a. efficient and sensible. **no one** pron. nobody, no person. **no place** adv., pron. nowhere. **no-score draw** n. in football, a draw in which no goals are scored. **no-see-em** (nōsē'əm), **no-see-um** n. (N Am.) a small, bloodsucking insect. **no-show** n. a person who does not take up something reserved and does not cancel in advance. **no side** n. in rugby, the end of a game, as announced by the referee. **no trump** n. no-trumps. **no-trumper** n. a hand on which a no-trump bid can be made. **no trumps** n. in bridge, a call for the playing of a hand without any trump suit. **no-vote** n. a vote against a motion. **noway,** (N Am., dial.) **noways** adv. nowise. **no-win situation** n. a situation in which it is impossible to succeed. **nowise** adv. in no way, not at all.

no² (nō) adv. 1 a word of denial or refusal, the categorical negative. 2 not. 3 (with comp.) not at all, by no amount. ~n. (pl. noes) 1 the word 'no'. 2 a negative reply, a denial, a refusal. 3 (pl.) voters against a motion. **no better than one should be** having dubious morals. **no can do** (coll.) I cannot do that. **no less** 1 as much. 2 as important or special. 3 no fewer. **no, no** (emphat.) no. **not to take no for an answer** not to be deterred by refusal or rejection. **no more** n. nothing more. ~a. not any more. ~adv. 1 not any more. 2 nothing further. 3 no longer. 4 dead, gone. 5 never again. 6 just as little. **no-no** n. (pl. no-nos) (coll.) something which is forbidden or unacceptable.

n.o. abbr. in cricket, not out.

nob¹ (nob) n. (sl.) a person of rank or distinction.

nob² (nob) n. (sl.) the head.

nobble (nob'əl) v.t. (sl.) 1 to dose, lame or otherwise tamper with (a horse) to prevent its winning a race. 2 to persuade or win over by dishonest means, to influence (a member of a jury etc.) esp. by bribery or threats. 3 to catch, to nab. 4 to steal. **nobbler** n.

Nobelist (nōbel'ist) n. (N Am.) a Nobel prize-winner.

nobelium (nōbē'liəm) n. (Chem.) an artificially produced, radioactive element, at. no. 102, chem. symbol No.

Nobel Prize (nōbel') n. any of six prizes awarded annually by the will of Alfred Nobel for excellence in various branches of learning and the furtherance of universal peace. **Nobel prize-winner** n.

nobility (nōbil'iti) n. (pl. **nobilities**) 1 the quality of being noble. 2 magnanimity, greatness,

dignity. 3 nobleness of birth or family. 4 nobles, the peerage.

noble (nō'bəl) a. (comp. **nobler**, superl. **noblest**) 1 lofty or illustrious in character, worth or dignity; magnanimous, high-minded, morally elevated. 2 of high rank, of ancient or illustrious lineage; belonging to the nobility. 3 magnificent, grand, stately, splendid, imposing. 4 excellent, fine, admirable. 5 (Chem.) (of a metal) valuable, pure. ~n. 1 a nobleman or noblewoman, a peer. 2 an obsolete gold coin. **noble art of self-defence** n. boxing. **noble gas** n. any member of a group of gaseous elements which do not combine with other elements. **nobleman** n. (pl. **noblemen**) a peer. **noble metal** n. a metal such as gold, silver or platinum, which is not affected by air or water, and not easily attacked by acids. **nobleness** n. **noble rot** n. a type of fungi which causes over-ripe grapes to rot, producing the characteristic richness of wines such as Sauterne and Tokay. **noble savage** n. in Romantic literature, an idealized view of primitive man. **noble science** n. boxing. **noblewoman** n. (pl. **noblewomen**) a peeress. **nobly** adv.

noblesse (nōbles') n. the nobility (of a foreign country). **noblesse oblige** (əblēzh') n. the idea that privileged people are obliged to behave honourably and to help less privileged people.

nobody (nō'bədi) pron. no one, no person. ~n. (pl. **nobodies**) a person of no importance. **like nobody's business** (coll.) very energetically or intensively. **nobody's fool** n. a sensible or wise person.

nock (nok) n. 1 the notched tip at each end of a bow. 2 a notched tip of horn etc. at the butt-end of an arrow. 3 the notch in this. 4 the upper fore corner of a sail. ~v.t. to fit (an arrow) to the bow-string.

noctambulism (noktam'būlizm) n. somnambulism. **noctambulist** n.

noctuid (nok'tūid) n. any nocturnal moth of the family Noctuidae. ~a. of or relating to the Noctuidae.

noctule (nok'tūl) n. a large European bat, Nyctalus noctula.

nocturn (nok'tœn) n. in the Roman Catholic Church, one of the divisions of matins, usually said at night.

nocturnal (noktœ'nəl) a. relating to or occurring in-the night, performed, or active by night. **nocturnal emission** n. an involuntary emission of semen while asleep. **nocturnally** adv.

nocturne (nok'tœn) n. 1 (Mus.) a dreamy piece of music suited to the night or evening. 2 a painting or drawing of a night scene.

nocuous (nok'ūəs) a. (formal) hurtful, noxious. **nocuously** adv.

nod (nod) v.i. (pres.p. **nodding**, past, p.p. **nodded**) 1 to incline the head with a slight, quick motion in token of assent. 2 to incline the head with a slight, quick motion in token of salutation. 3 to incline the head with a slight, quick motion in token of command or indication. **4** to let the head fall forward; to be drowsy, to sleep. **5** (of a flower) to bend over and sway. **6** to make a careless mistake. ~*v.t.* **1** to bend or incline (the head). **2** to signify by a nod. ~*n.* **1** a quick bend of the head. **2** a bending downwards. **on the nod 1** (*coll.*) without question or argument. **2** (*coll.*) on credit. **to get the nod** (*N Am.*) to be given approval or permission. **to nod off** (*coll.*) to fall asleep. **to nod through 1** to pass (a motion etc.) without formal discussion, voting etc. **2** in Parliament, to allow to vote by proxy. **nodder** *n.* **nodding** *n.*, *a.* **nodding acquaintance** *n.* a slight acquaintance.

noddle[1] (nod'əl) *n.* (*coll.*) the head.

noddle[2] (nod'əl) *v.t.* to nod, to wag.

noddy (nod'i) *n.* (*pl.* **noddies**) **1** a simpleton, a fool. **2** any tropical seabird of the genus *Anous stolida* or *Procelsterna*.

node (nōd) *n.* **1** a knot, a knob. **2** (*Bot.*) the point of a stem from which leaves arise. **3** (*Anat.*) **a** a thickening or swelling e.g. of a joint of the body. **b** an interruption of the myelin sheath of a nerve. **4** (*Astron.*) the point at which the orbit of a planet intersects the ecliptic, or in which two great circles of the celestial sphere intersect. **5** (*Math.*) **a** the point at which a curve crosses itself and at which more than one tangent can be drawn or a similar point on a surface. **b** a vertex in a graph. **6** (*Physics*) a point of rest in a vibrating body. **7** (*Comput.*) a network component. **nodal** *a.* **nodical** *a.* **nodule** (nod'ūl) *n.* **1** a small knot, node or lump; a rounded lump or mass of irregularly rounded shape. **2** a small tumour. **nodular, nodulated, noduled, nodulose** (-lōs), **nodulous** *a.* **nodulation** (-ā'shən) *n.* **nodus** (nō'dəs) *n.* (*pl.* **nodi** (-dī)) **1** a knotty point, a complication, a difficulty. **2** a node.

Noel (nōel'), **Noël**, †**Nowel**, †**Nowell** *n.* Christmas.

nog (nog) *n.* **1** a pin, treenail or peg. **2** a wooden block shaped like a brick, built into a wall to take nails. **3** a snag or stump. **4** nogging.

noggin (nog'in) *n.* **1** a small mug. **2** a measure of spirits, usu. a gill (125 ml). **3** (*coll.*) the head.

nogging (nog'ing) *n.* a timber frame filled with bricks.

Noh (nō), **No** *n.* the Japanese drama developed out of religious dance.

nohow NO[1].

noil (noil) *n.* (*often pl.*) tangles and knots of wool removed by a comb.

noise (noiz) *n.* **1** a sound of any kind, esp. a loud, discordant, harsh or disagreeable one. **2** clamour, din, loud or continuous talk. **3** any unwanted electrical disturbance in a circuit. **4** (*pl.*) vague remarks of an appropriate kind (*She made encouraging noises*). ~*v.t.* to make public, to spread about. **to make a noise** to become well known or notorious. **to make a noise about** to complain about. **noiseless** *a.* **noiselessly** *adv.* **noiselessness** *n.* **noises off** *n.pl.* offstage sounds intended to be heard by the audience of a play. **noisy** *a.* (*comp.*

noisier, *superl.* **noisiest**) **1** causing noise. **2** making a lot of noise. **3** full of loud noise. **4** (of a colour, dress, style etc.) glaring, violent, loud. **noisily** *adv.* **noisiness** *n.*

noisette (nwazet') *n.* **1** a small round piece of mutton, veal, etc. **2** a chocolate made with chopped hazelnuts.

noisome (noi'səm) *a.* (*formal*) **1** hurtful, noxious. **2** (esp. of a smell) unwholesome, offensive, disgusting. **noisomeness** *n.*

nomad (nō'mad) *n.* **1** a member of a people that wanders about seeking pasture for their flocks. **2** a wanderer. ~*a.* **1** being a nomad. **2** wandering. **nomadic** (-mad'-) *a.* **nomadically** *adv.* **nomadism** *n.* **nomadize, nomadise** *v.i.*

nom de guerre (nom də geə') *n.* (*pl.* **noms de guerre** (nom)) an assumed name, a pseudonym.

nom de plume (nom də ploom') *n.* (*pl.* **noms de plume** (nom)) a pen-name.

nomenclature (nōmeng'kləchə) *n.* **1** a system of names for the objects of study in any branch of science. **2** a system of terminology. **3** a catalogue, a register. **nomenclatural** (-klach'-) *a.*

nominal (nom'inəl) *a.* **1** existing in name only, as distinct from *real.* **2** trivial, inconsiderable. **3** of, relating to or consisting of a name or names. **4** containing names. **5** of or relating to a noun. **nominalism** *n.* (*Philos.*) the doctrine that general or abstract concepts have no existence but as names or words, as distinct from *realism.* **nominalist** *n.* **nominalistic** (-lis'tik) *a.* **nominalize, nominalise** *v.t.* to form a noun from (a verb, adjective etc.). **nominalization** (-ā'shən) *n.* **nominally** *adv.* in name only. **nominal value** *n.* the face value of coins, shares etc.

nominate (nom'ināt) *v.t.* **1** to propose as a candidate. **2** to appoint to an office or duty. **3** to name, to designate. **4** to mention by name. **5** to call, to denominate. **nomination** (-ā'shən) *n.* **nominator** *n.* **nominee** (-nē') *n.* **1** a person named or appointed by name. **2** a person in whose name a stock is registered.

nominative[1] (nom'inətiv) *n.* (*Gram.*) **1** the case of the subject of a verb. **2** a word in this case. ~*a.* of or relating to this case. **nominatival** (-tī'-) *a.*

nominative[2] (nom'inātiv) *a.* appointed by nomination, rather than by election.

nomogram (nom'əgram), **nomograph** (-grahf) *n.* a chart with scales of quantities arranged side by side, which can be used to carry out rapid calculations. **nomographer** (-mog'-) *n.* **nomographic** (-graf'-) *a.* **nomographically** *adv.* **nomography** (-mog'-) *n.*

-nomy (nəmi) *comb. form* an area of knowledge (*astronomy*).

non- (non) *pref.* not.

non- (+ a- words) non-abstainer *n.* a person who is not a total abstainer from alcoholic drink. **non-acceptance** *n.* **non-access** *n.* a lack of access. **non-addictive** *a.* not causing addiction. **non-aggression** *n.* restraint from aggression. **non-alcoholic** *a.* not containing alcohol. **non-aligned**

a. not taking any side in international politics, esp. (formerly) not belonging to the Warsaw Pact or NATO. **non-alignment** *n.* **non-allergic** *a.* not causing or suffering from allergy. **non-ambiguous** *a.* **non-appearance** *n.* default of appearance, esp. in court. **non-art** *n.* something which does not conform to the accepted forms of art. **non-attached** *a.* not being attached. **non-attendance** *n.* **non-attributable** *a.* not able to be attributed to any particular source. **non-attributably** *adv.* **non-availability** *n.* the state of not being available.

nona- (non´ə, nō´nə) *comb. form* nine.

nonage (nō´nij) *n.* **1** (*Hist.*) the state of being under age; minority. **2** a period of immaturity.

nonagenarian (nonəjinee´riən) *n.* a person aged between 90 and 100. ~*a.* a person aged between 90 and 100.

nonagon (non´əgon) *n.* a figure having nine sides and nine angles.

nonary (nō´nəri) *a.* (*Math.*) (of a scale of notation) based on the number nine. ~*n.* (*pl.* **nonaries**) a group of nine.

non- (+ **b**– **words**) **non-believer** *n.* a person who does not believe, esp. in God. **non-belligerent** *a.* not involved in hostilities. ~*n.* a neutral. **non-belligerency** *n.* **non-biological** *a.* **1** not relating to biology. **2** (of washing powder etc.) containing no enzymes. **non-black** *a.* **1** not belonging to a dark-skinned race. **2** of or relating to non-blacks. ~*n.* a non-black person. **non-breakable** *a.*

non- (+ **c**– **words**) **non-capital** *a.* not punishable by death. **non-Catholic** *a.* not Roman Catholic. ~*n.* a non-Catholic person. **non-Christian** *a.*, *n.* **non-citizen** *n.* a person who is not a citizen of a particular town etc. **non-classified** *a.* (of information) not classified. **non-clerical** *a.* not involving clerical work. **non-collegiate** *a.* **1** (of a student) not belonging to a college. **2** (of a university) not having colleges. **non-com** (non´kom) *n.* (*sl.*) a non-commissioned officer. **non-combatant** *n.* a civilian, esp. a surgeon, chaplain etc. attached to troops. **non-commissioned** *a.* (of a military officer) not holding a commission. **non-committal** *a.* not committing oneself, impartial. **non-committally** *adv.* **non-communicant** *n.* a person who does not attend Holy Communion. **non-communicating** *a.* **non-communist, non-Communist** *a.* not practising communism. ~*n.* a non-communist person. **non-compliance** *n.* (*Law*) failure to comply. **non-conducting** *a.* not conducting heat or electricity. **non-conductor** *n.* a substance or medium that offers resistance to heat or electricity. **non-confidential** *a.* **nonconformist** *n.* a person who does not conform to usual or normal ways of behaving or thinking. ~*a.* of or relating to non-conformists or nonconformism. **nonconformism** *n.* **nonconformity** *n.* **non-contagious** *a.* not contagious. **non-content** *n.* in the House of Lords, a person who votes in the negative. **non-contentious** *a.* **non-contributory** *a.* (of a pension scheme etc.) not requiring employees to pay contributions. **non-controversial** *a.* **non-cooperation** *n.* refusal to cooperate.

nonce (nons) *n.* the present time, occasion, purpose etc. **for the nonce** for the time being. **nonce-word** *n.* a word coined for the occasion.

nonchalant (non´shələnt) *a.* careless, cool, unmoved, indifferent. **nonchalance** *n.* **nonchalantly** *adv.*

Usage note Pronunciation with (ch) rather than (sh) is best avoided.

non compos mentis (non kompos men´tis), **non compos** (non kom´pos) *a.* not in one's right mind.

non- (+ **d**– **words**) **non-delivery** *n.* **non-denominational** *a.* not restricted to a particular religious denomination. **non-destructive** *a.* not causing destruction. **non-drinker** *n.* a person who does not drink alcohol. **non-driver** *n.* a person who does not drive a car. **non-durable** *a.*

nondescript (non´diskript) *a.* not easily described or classified; neither one thing nor another. ~*n.* a nondescript person or thing. **nondescriptly** *adv.* **nondescriptness** *n.*

none (nŭn) *pron.* **1** no one, no person. **2** (*coll.*) no persons. **3** not any, not any portion. ~*a.* **1** no, not any. **2** not to be included in a specified category. ~*adv.* **1** by no amount. **2** in no respect; not at all (*none too clever*). **none other than** exactly, precisely (the person or thing specified). **none the less** nonetheless. **nonetheless** *adv.* nevertheless.

non- (+ **e**– **words**) **non-earning** *a.* not earning. **non-effective** *a.* not having an effect. **non-ego** *n.* (*Philos.*) the external or objective in perception or thought. **non-essential** *a.* not essential. ~*n.* something non-essential. **non-Euclidean** *a.* (*Geom.*) denying Euclidean principles. **non-European** *a.* not European. ~*n.* a non-European person. **non-event** *n.* a disappointing or unexciting occurrence. **non-existence** *n.* **non-existent** *a.* **non-explosive** *a.*

nonentity (nonen´titi) *n.* (*pl.* **nonentities**) **1** an unimportant person or thing. **2** non-existence. **3** a thing not existing, a mere figment, an imaginary thing.

nonesuch NONSUCH.

non- (+ **f**– **words**) **non-fattening** *a.* **non-ferrous** *a.* containing no iron. **non-fiction** *n.* literary work, containing no deliberate fictitious element. **non-fictional** *a.* **non-flam** *a.* non-flammable. **non-flammable** *a.* not capable of supporting flame, though combustible, difficult or impossible to set alight. **non-fulfilment** *n.* **non-functional** *a.* not having a function.

non- (+ **g**–**h words**) **non-governmental** *a.* not belonging to or associated with a government. **non-human** *a.* not belonging to the human race. ~*n.* a non-human being.

non- (+ **i**–**k words**) **non-infectious** *a.* **non-inflammable** *a.* **non-inflected** *a.* (of a language) without inflections. **non-interference** *n.* a lack of interference. **non-intersecting** *a.* **non-intervention** *n.* the principle or policy of not becoming involved in the disputes of other nations. **non-interventionist** *a.*, *n.* **non-intoxicating** *a.* **non-invasive** *a.* (*Med.*) **1** not involving surgery. **2** not tending to spread. **non-iron** *a.* (of a fabric) not requiring ironing. **nonjuror** *n.* a person who refuses to take an oath. **non-jury** *a.* without a jury.

non- (+ l–n words) **non-linear** *a.* not progressing smoothly from one stage to the next. **non-literary** *a.* **non-logical** *a.* **non-magnetic** *a.* **non-member** *n.* a person who is not a member of a club etc. **non-membership** *n.* **non-metal** *a.* not made of metal. **non-metallic** *a.* **non-militant** *a.* **non-military** *a.* **non-ministerial** *a.* **non-moral** *a.* not involving ethical considerations. **non-natural** *a.* not natural (in a simply descriptive sense). **non-negotiable** *a.* **non-nuclear** *a.* not having, or using, nuclear power or weapons.

non- (+ o–p words) **non-objective** *a.* in art, abstract, non-representational. **non-observance** *n.* **non-occurrence** *n.* **non-operational** *a.* **1** not operating. **2** out of order. **non-organic** *a.* **non-participating** *a.* **non-partisan** *a.* **non-party** *a.* not concerned with questions of political party. **non-payment** *n.* **non-penetrative** *a.* (of sexual activity) not involving penetration. **non-performance** *n.* **non-person** *n.* an insignificant person. **non-personal** *a.* **non-physical** *a.* **non-physically** *adv.* **non-playing** *a.* not playing, not taking part in a game. **non-poisonous** *a.* **non-political** *a.* **non-porous** *a.* **non-professional** *a.* **1** not professional, amateur. **2** unskilled. **non-profit, non-profit-making** *a.* **non-proliferation** *n.* the limiting of the production of nuclear or chemical weapons etc.

nonpareil (nonpərā´) *a.* having no equal; peerless, unrivalled, unique. ~*n.* a paragon or a thing of unequalled excellence.

nonplus (nonplŭs´) *v.t.* (*3rd pers. sing. pres.* **nonplusses**, (*N Am.*) **nonpluses**, *pres.p.* **nonplussing**, (*N Am.*) **nonplusing**, *past*, *p.p.* **nonplussed**, (*N Am.*) **nonplused**) to puzzle, to confound, to bewilder.

non- (+ r– words) **non-racial** *a.* **non-reader** *n.* a person who cannot read. **non-residence** *n.* **non-resident** *a.* **1** not residing in a place. **2** (of a post) not requiring the holder to reside at the place of work. ~*n.* a non-resident person. **non-residential** *a.* **non-resistance** *n.* passive obedience or submission, even to power unjustly exercised. **non-returnable** *a.* **non-rigid** *a.*

non- (+ s– words) **non-scientific** *a.* **non-scientist** *n.* **non-sectarian** *a.* **non-sexist** *a.* **non-sexual** *a.* not involving sex. **non-sexually** *adv.* **non-skid** *a.* (of a tyre) designed to prevent skidding. **non-slip** *a.* designed to prevent slipping. **non-smoker** *n.* **1** someone who does not smoke. **2** a part of a train etc. in which it is not permitted to smoke. **non-smoking** *a.*, *n.* **non-soluble** *a.* **non-specialist** *n.* **non-specific** *a.* **non-specific**

urethritis *n.* (*Med.*) inflammation of the urethra caused by an unspecified infection. **non-standard** *a.* **non-starter** *n.* **1** in a race, a person or animal that is entered but does not start. **2** (*coll.*) an idea or person with no chance whatsoever of success. **non-stick** *a.* (of a cooking pan) treated so that food will not stick to it. **non-stop** *a.* **1** not stopping at intermediate stations. **2** without a pause. ~*adv.* without a pause. **non-subscriber** *n.* **non-swimmer** *n.* a person who cannot swim.

nonsense (non´səns) *n.* **1** unmeaning words, ideas etc. **2** foolery, absurdity. **3** rubbish, worthless stuff, trifles. **nonsense verse** *n.* **1** verse which is intentionally absurd, written to amuse. **2** verse which has no meaning, used for mnemonic purposes. **nonsensical** (-sen´sikəl) *a.* **nonsensicality** (-kal´-), **nonsensicalness** *n.* **nonsensically** *adv.*

non sequitur (non sek´witə) *n.* an inference not warrantable from the premisses.

nonsuch (non´sŭch), **nonesuch** (nŭn´-) *n.* **1** a person who or something which is without an equal, a paragon, a nonpareil. **2** a leguminous plant, *Mendicago lupilina*, which has black pods.

non- (+ t–u words) **non-technical** *a.* **1** not technical. **2** having no technical knowledge or skill. **non-toxic** *a.* **non-transferable** *a.* **non-U** *a.* (*coll.*) not characteristic of the upper class. **non-uniform** *a.* **non-union** *a.* not connected with a trade union. **non-usage** *n.* non-use. **non-use** *n.* failure to use something. **non-user** *n.*

non- (+ v–w words) **non-verbal** *a.* without using words or speech. **non-verbally** *adv.* **non-vintage** *a.* **non-violence** *n.* the practice of refraining from violence on principle. **non-violent** *a.* **non-volatile** *a.* **non-voter** *n.* **non-voting** *a.* **non-white** *a.* **1** not belonging to a light-skinned race. **2** of or relating to non-whites. ~*n.* a non-white person. **non-word** *n.* a word which has never been recorded.

noodle[1] (noo´dəl) *n.* a strip or ring of pasta.

noodle[2] (noo´dəl) *n.* **1** a simpleton, a fool. **2** (*sl.*) the head.

nook (nuk) *n.* **1** a corner. **2** a cosy place, as in an angle. **3** a secluded retreat.

nooky (nuk´i), **nookie** *n.* (*sl.*) sexual intercourse.

noon (noon) *n.* **1** the middle of the day, twelve o'clock. **2** (*fig.*) the culmination or height. **noonday** *n.*, *a.* **noontide, noontime** *n.*

noose (noos) *n.* **1** a loop with a running knot binding the closer the more it is pulled, as in a snare or a hangman's halter. **2** a tie, a bond, a snare. **3** (*facet.*) the marriage tie. ~*v.t.* **1** to catch in a noose; to entrap. **2** to tie a noose on. **3** to tie in a noose. **to put one's head in a noose** to put oneself into a dangerous or exposed situation.

nope (nōp) *adv.* (*coll.*) no.

nor (naw) *conj.* and not (a word marking the second or subsequent part of a negative proposition; occasionally used without the correlative).

Usage note See note under NEITHER.

nor' (naw) *n., a., adv.* north. **nor'-wester** (-wes´tə) *n.* **1** a north-wester. **2** a glass of strong liquor. **3** a sou'-wester hat.

noradrenalin (norədren´əlin), **noradrenaline** *n.* an amine related to adrenalin, used as a heart resuscitant.

Nordic (naw´dik) *a.* **1** of or relating to a tall, blond physical type inhabiting Scandinavia, parts of Scotland and other parts of N Europe. **2** of or relating to Scandinavia. **3** (of skiing) involving cross-country racing and jumping. ~*n.* a Nordic person.

Norfolk jacket (naw´fək), **Norfolk** *n.* a man's loose jacket with vertical pleats in the back and front, and a waistband.

nork (nawk) *n.* (*Austral., sl.*) a woman's breast.

norm (nawm) *n.* **1** a standard, model, pattern or type. **2** a standard structure, behaviour etc.

normal (naw´məl) *a.* **1** according to rule, standard, or established law; regular, typical, usual. **2** mentally and physically healthy. **3** (*Geom.*) perpendicular. **4** (*Chem.*) (of a solution) containing the equivalent of one gram of solute per litre. **5** mentally healthy, not suffering from any mental disorders. ~*n.* **1** the mean temperature, volume etc. **2** the usual state, quality, quantity etc. **3** (*Geom.*) a perpendicular line. **4** the average or mean value of observed quantities. **normalcy** *n.* **normal distribution** *n.* in statistics, the distribution of many random variables represented in a bell-shaped graph. **normality** (-mal´-) *n.* **normalize, normalise** *v.t.* **1** to make normal. **2** to cause to conform to normal standards etc. ~*v.i.* to become normal. **normalization** (-zā´shən) *n.* **normally** *adv.* **1** usually. **2** in the conventional way.

Norman (naw´mən) *n.* **1** a native or inhabitant of Normandy. **2** a member of a mixed people of Northmen and Franks established there in the 10th cent. **3** Norman French. **4** (*Archit.*) Norman architecture. **5** any of the kings of England from William I to Stephen. ~*a.* of or relating to Normandy or the Normans. **Norman architecture** *n.* a massive Romanesque style of architecture prevalent in Normandy (10th–11th cents.) and England (11th–12th cents.). **Norman Conquest** *n.* the conquest of England by Duke William of Normandy in 1066. **Norman French** *n.* **1** French as spoken by the Normans. **2** the form of this that continued in use in the English law courts. **Normanize, Normanise** *v.t.*

normative (naw´mətiv) *a.* of, relating to or establishing a norm. **normatively** *adv.* **normativeness** *n.*

Norse (naws) *n.* (*pl.* **Norse**) **1** the Norwegian language. **2** the Scandinavian languages, including early Swedish and Danish. **3** (*as pl.*) the Norwegians. **4** (*as pl.*) the Vikings. ~*a.* of or relating to Norway or ancient Scandinavia. **Norseman** *n.* (*pl.* **Norsemen**).

north (nawth) *n.* **1** one of the four cardinal points, the one to the right of a person facing the setting sun at the equinox. **2** a region or part north of any given point. **3** the northern part of any country. **4** the portion of the US to the north of the former slave-holding States. **5** the Arctic. **6** the industrialized nations. **7** in bridge, the player occupying the position at the table corresponding to north on the compass. **8** (*poet.*) the north wind. ~*a.* **1** situated in or towards the north. **2** (of the wind) blowing from the north. ~*adv.* towards or in the north. **north and south** along a line running to and from north and south. **north by east** one point east of north. **north by west** one point west of north. **north of** farther north than. **to the north** in a northerly direction. **North American** *a.* of or relating to North America. ~*n.* a native or inhabitant of North America. **northbound** *a.* heading towards the north. **North Country** *n.* the part of a country to the north, esp. northern England or the northern part of Great Britain. ~*a.* relating to or characteristic of this. **north-countryman** *n.* (*pl.* **north-countrymen**). **north-east** *n.* **1** the point midway between north and east. **2** a region lying in this quarter. ~*a.* of, relating to or coming from the north-east. ~*adv.* towards, at or in the north-east. **northeaster** *n.* a north-east wind. **northeasterly** *a., adv.* north-east. **north-eastern** *a.* **north-eastward** *a., adv.* towards the north-east. **north-eastwards** *a., adv.* north-eastward. **northerly** (-dhə-) *a., adv.* **1** towards or in the north. **2** (of the wind) blowing from the north. ~*n.* (*pl.* **northerlies**) a north wind. **northerliness** *n.* **northern** (-dhən) *a.* **1** of, relating to, situated, living in or proceeding from the north. **2** towards the north. **3** of the northern States of the US. **northerner** *n.* a native or inhabitant of the north. **northern hemisphere** *n.* the half of the earth which lies north of the equator. **northern lights** *n.pl.* the aurora borealis. **northernmost** *a.* **North Germanic** *n., a.* (of) the Scandinavian group of languages. **Northman** *n.* (*pl.* **Northmen**) an inhabitant of the north of Europe, esp. of Scandinavia. **north-north-east** *n.* the point midway between north and north-east. **north-north-west** *n.* the point midway between north and north-west. **North Pole** *n.* **1** the northernmost extremity of the axis on which the earth revolves. **2** the point in the northern sky round which the stars appear to revolve. **North Star** *n.* the pole star. **northward** (-wəd) *a., adv.* towards the north. ~*n.* a northward direction. **northwardly** *a., adv.* **northwards** *a., adv.* **north-west** *n.* **1** the point midway between north and west. **2** a region lying in this quarter. ~*a.* of, relating to or coming from the north-west. ~*adv.* towards, at or in the north-west. **northwester** *n.* a north-west wind. **north-westerly** *a., adv.* north-west. **north-western** *a.* **north-westward** *a., adv.* towards the north-west. **north-westwards** *a., adv.* north-westward.

Northants *abbr.* Northamptonshire.

Norway lobster (naw´wā) *n.* a small European

lobster, *Nephrops norvegicus*. **Norway rat** *n*. the brown rat, *Rattus norvegicus*.

Norwegian (nawwē´jən) *n*. **1** a native or inhabitant of Norway. **2** the language of Norway. ~*a*. of or relating to Norway.

Nos. *abbr.* numbers.

nose (nōz) *n*. **1** the projecting part or the face between the forehead and mouth, containing the nostrils and the organ of smell. **2** the power of smelling. **3** odour, scent; aroma, esp. the bouquet of wine. **4** a part of a thing resembling a nose, such as the nozzle of a pipe, tube or bellows, a beak, point, prow etc. **5** a nosing. **6** (*sl*.) a police informer. **7** (*fig*.) an instinctive ability to find something (*a nose for trouble*). ~*v.t*. **1** to perceive, trace or detect by smelling. **2** (*fig*.) to find out. **3** to rub or push with the nose. **4** to push (one's way). ~*v.i.* **1** to smell, to sniff. **2** (*fig*.) to search, to pry. **3** to push one's way, to push ahead. **as plain as the nose on your face** clearly to be seen. **by a nose** by the smallest possible margin. **to cut off one's nose to spite one's face** to harm oneself in the course of trying to harm someone else. **to follow one's nose** to act according to one's instincts. **to get up someone's nose** (*sl*.) to annoy someone. **to keep one's nose clean** (*sl*.) to behave well, to stay out of trouble. **to speak through one's nose** to have a nasal quality to one's voice. **to stick one's nose into** to meddle officiously in. **to turn up one's nose at** to show contempt for. **under someone's nose** in someone's actual presence or sight. **with one's nose in the air** in a haughty manner. **nosebag** *n*. **1** a bag containing fodder for hanging over a horse's head. **2** (*sl*.) a bag of provisions. **noseband** *n*. the part of a bridle passing over the nose and attached to the cheek-straps. **nosebleed** *n*. a bleeding from the nose. **nose-cone** *n*. the cone-shaped forward section of a rocket etc. **nosed** *a*. **nosedive** *n*. **1** a sudden plunge towards the earth made by an aircraft. **2** any sudden plunge. ~*v.i*. to make a nosedive. **nose flute** *n*. a type of flute blown through the nose. **noseless** *a*. **nose-rag** *n*. (*sl*.) a handkerchief. **nosering** *n*. **1** a ring worn in the nose as ornament. **2** a leading ring for a bull etc. **nose tackle** *n*. in American football, the defensive player in the centre of the linemen in formation. **nose-to-tail** *a., adv*. with the front of one vehicle close behind the back of another. **nose wheel** *n*. a landing wheel under the nose of an aircraft. **nosing** *n*. the prominent edge of a moulding, step etc. **nosy, nosey** *a*. (*comp*. **nosier,** *superl*. **nosiest**) **1** (*coll*.) very inquisitive. **2** having a large or prominent nose. **3** strong- or evil-smelling. ~*n*. (*pl*. **nosies**) a person with a large nose. **Nosy Parker** *n*. (*coll*.) a nosy person.

nosegay (nōz´gā) *n*. a bunch of flowers, esp. fragrant flowers.

nosh (nosh) *n*. (*sl*.) **1** food. **2** a meal. **3** (*N Am*.) a snack. ~*v.t., v.i*. **1** to eat. **2** (*N Am*.) to eat between meals. **noshery** *n*. (*pl*. **nosheries**) (*sl*.) a restaurant or café. **nosh-up** *n*. (*sl*.) a large meal, a feast.

nostalgia (nostal´jə) *n*. **1** a yearning for the past. **2** the evocation of a time in the past. **3** an acute longing for home, homesickness. **nostalgic** *a*. **nostalgically** *adv*.

nostril (nos´tril) *n*. either of the two apertures of the nose. **nostrilled** *a*.

nostrum (nos´trəm) *n*. (*pl*. **nostrums**) **1** a medicine based on a secret formula; a quack remedy. **2** a scheme for political or social reform. **nosy** NOSE.

not (not) *adv*. a particle expressing negation, denial, prohibition or refusal. **not at all** a polite way of acknowledging thanks. **not a thing** nothing at all. **not in the slightest** not at all. **not least** particularly, especially. **not on** **1** (*sl*.) not possible. **2** (*sl*.) not morally, socially etc. acceptable. **not out** having reached the end of a cricket innings or of play for the day without being dismissed. **not quite** **1** almost. **2** definitely not. **not that** it is not meant however that. **not (too) well** feeling rather unwell. **not very** **1** to a minor extent. **2** far from being.

nota bene (nōtə ben´ā) *v.t*. (*imper*.) note well, take note.

notable (nō´təbəl) *a*. **1** worthy of note; remarkable, memorable, distinguished. **2** excellent, capable. ~*n*. a notable person. **notableness** *n*. **notably** *adv*.

notary (nō´təri) *n*. (*pl*. **notaries**) a public official appointed to attest deeds, contracts etc., and administer oaths etc. **notarial** (-teə´ri-) *a*. **notarially** *adv*. **notarize, notarise** *v.t*. (*N Am*.) to certify as a notary. **notary public** *n*. (*pl*. **notaries public**) a notary.

notation (nōtā´shən) *n*. **1** the act or process of representing by signs, figures etc. **2** a system of signs, figures etc., employed in any science or art. **3** (*N Am*.) a note, an annotation; a record. **notate** (nōtāt´) *v.t*. to write in notation. **notational** *a*.

notch (noch) *n*. **1** a nick, a cut, a V-shaped indentation. **2** a tally point. **3** (*coll*.) a step on a scale, a degree. **4** (*N Am*.) an opening, narrow pass or short defile. ~*v.t*. **1** to cut a notch or notches in. **2** to score by notches. **3** to fix (stairs etc.) by means of notches. **to notch up** to score, to achieve. **notched** *a*. **notcher** *n*. **notchy** *a*. (*comp*. **notchier,** *superl*. **notchiest**).

note (nōt) *n*. **1** a brief record, a memorandum. **2** a short or informal letter. **3** a diplomatic communication. **4** a bank note or piece of paper money. **5** a written promise to pay a certain sum of money. **6** an annotation, a comment, explanation, or gloss, appended to a passage in a book etc. **7** notice, attention, observation. **8** distinction, repute, importance. **9** a sign representing the pitch and duration of a sound. **10** a musical sound. **11** a significant sound, tone or mode of expression. **12** a key in a musical instrument. **13** a bird's call. **14** a sign, mark or token. ~*v.t*. **1** to observe, to take notice of; to show respect to; to pay attention to. **2** to make a memorandum of; to set down or record as worth remembering. **3** to annotate. **4** (*chiefly pass.*) to make famous. **of note 1** important, distinguished. **2** worthy of attention. **to hit the right note** to behave in an appropriate or suitable manner. **to strike the right note** to hit the right note. **to take note** to pay attention. **notebook** *n.* **1** a book for writing notes in. **2** a small, portable, battery-operated computer, about the size of an exercise book. **notecase** *n.* a wallet for holding paper money. **noted** *a.* eminent, remarkable. **noteless** *a.* **notelet** *n.* a folded piece of paper with a decorative design on the front, for a short, informal letter. **notepad** *n.* a pad of paper for writing letters or notes on. **notepaper** *n.* paper for letters, esp. private correspondence. **noter** *n.* **noteworthy** *a.* **1** worth attention. **2** outstanding, famous. **noteworthiness** *n.*

nothing (nŭth´ing) *n.* **1** no thing. **2** not anything, nought. **3** no amount, zero, a nought. **4** nothingness, non-existence. **5** an insignificant or unimportant thing, a trifle. ~*a.* (*coll.*) insignificant, unimportant. ~*adv.* in no degree, in no way, not at all. **for nothing 1** free, without paying. **2** to no purpose. **no nothing** (*coll.*) (at the end of a list of negatives) not at all. **nothing else for it** no alternative. **nothing for it but** no alternative but. **nothing in it 1** untrue. **2** extremely easy. **3** very little difference between two alternatives. **nothing less than 1** positively, downright, absolutely. **2** (*dated*) anything rather than. **nothing to it** nothing in it. **think nothing of it** there is no need for apology or thanks. **to be nothing to 1** not to concern. **2** not to compare with. **to be nothing to do with** not to be connected or involved with. **to come to nothing 1** to turn out a failure. **2** to result in no amount. **to have nothing to do with** to be nothing to do with. **to make nothing of** to fail to understand or deal with. **nothingness** *n.*

notice (nō´tis) *n.* **1** observation, regard, attention. **2** intelligence, information, warning. **3** a written or printed paper giving information or directions. **4** an intimation or instruction. **5** intimation of the termination of an agreement, contract of employment etc., at a specified date. **6** an account of something in a newspaper etc., esp. a review of a book, play etc. **7** the act of noting. ~*v.t.* **1** to take notice of, to perceive. **2** to remark upon. **3** to pay respect to. **4** to serve a notice upon. **5** to give notice to. **at a moment's notice** with hardly any advance warning. **at short notice** with little advance warning. **to take no notice of** to pay no attention to; to ignore. **to take notice 1** to observe. **2** to show alertness. **to take notice of** to pay attention to, to heed. **under notice** served with a formal notice. **noticeable** *a.* easy to see, hear or recognize. **noticeably** *adv.* **noticeboard** *n.* a board exposed to public view on which notices are posted.

notify (nō´tifī) *v.t.* (*3rd pers. sing. pres.* **notifies,** *pres.p.* **notifying,** *past, p.p.* **notified**) **1** to give notice to, to inform (of or that). **2** to make known,

to announce, to declare, to publish. **notifiable** *a.* (esp. of cases of disease that must be reported to the sanitary authorities) to be notified. **notification** (-fikā´shən) *n.*

notion (nō´shən) *n.* **1** an idea, a conception. **2** an opinion, a view. **3** (*coll.*) an inclination, desire, intention or whim. **4** (*N Am.*) a small ingenious device or useful article, knick-knack. **5** (*pl., N Am.*) fancy goods, haberdashery, novelties etc. **notional** *a.* **1** of or relating to notions or concepts. **2** abstract, imaginary, hypothetical. **3** speculative, ideal. **4** (*Gram.*) (of a verb) having a full meaning of its own. **notionally** *adv.* **notionist** *n.*

notochord (nō´təkawd) *n.* the elastic cartilaginous band constituting a rudimentary form of the spinal column in the embryo and some primitive fishes.

notorious (nōtaw´riəs) *a.* widely or publicly or commonly known for something bad. **notoriety** (nōtərī´ə-) *n.* **notoriously** *adv.* **notoriousness** *n.*

notornis (nətaw´nis) *n.* (*pl.* **notornises**) a gigantic flightless New Zealand bird, *Porphyrio mantelli*, now very rare.

Notts. *abbr.* Nottinghamshire.

notwithstanding (notwidhstan´ding) *prep.* in spite of, despite. ~*adv.* nevertheless; in spite of this. ~*conj.* although, in spite of the fact that.

nougat (noo´gah, nŭg´ət) *n.* a confection made of nuts and sugar.

nought (nawt) *n.* **1** zero. **2** (*also poet.*) †nothing. **noughts and crosses** *n.* a game, the object of which is to complete a row of three noughts or three crosses in a grid of nine squares.

noun (nown) *n.* (*Gram.*) a word used as the name of anything. **nounal** *a.*

nourish (nŭr´ish) *v.t.* **1** to feed, to sustain, to support. **2** to maintain, to educate. **3** to foster, to cherish, to nurse. **nourisher** *n.* **nourishing** *a.* **nourishingly** *adv.* **nourishment** *n.* **1** food, sustenance. **2** the act of nourishing. **3** the state of being nourished.

nous (nows) *n.* **1** (*coll.*) sense, wit, intelligence. **2** (*Philos.*) mind, intellect.

nouveau (noo´vō), (*fem.*) **nouvelle** (-vel) *a.* new. **nouveau riche** (rēsh´) *n.* (*pl.* **nouveaux riches** (rēsh´)) a person who has recently acquired wealth but who has not acquired good taste or manners. **nouvelle cuisine** (kwizēn´) *n.* a style of simple French cooking which does not involve rich food, creamy sauces etc. and relies largely on artistic presentation. **nouvelle vague** (vahg´) *n.* a movement in the French cinema, dating from just before 1960, which aimed at imaginative quality in films.

Nov. *abbr.* November.

nova (nō´və) *n.* (*pl.* **novae** (-ē), **novas**) a star which flares up to great brightness and subsides after a time.

novel (nov´əl) *n.* **1** a fictitious narrative in prose, usu. of sufficient length to fill a volume. **2** this type of literature. ~*a.* **1** new, recent, fresh. **2** unusual, strange. **novelese** (-lēz´) *n.* (*derog.*) the language or style considered appropriate for inferior novels. **novelette** (-let´) *n*. 1 (*esp. derog.*) a short novel, usu. of a sentimental nature. 2 (*Mus.*) a kind of romance dealing freely with several themes. **novelettish** *a.* (*derog.*) cheaply sentimental. **novelish** *a.* **novelist** *n.* a writer of novels. **novelistic** (novəlis´-) *a.* **novelize, novelise** *v.t.* to make (a play, facts etc.) into a novel. **novelization** (-zā´shən) *n.* **novella** (nōvel´ə) *n.* (*pl.* **novellas**) 1 a tale, a short story. 2 a short novel. **novelly** *adv.* **novelty** *n.* (*pl.* **novelties**) 1 newness, freshness, originality. 2 something new. 3 a cheap, unusual object, sold as a gift or souvenir. ~*a.* having novelty value.

November (nōvem´bə) *n.* the 11th month of the year, the ninth of the Roman year.

novena (nōvē´nə) *n.* (*pl.* **novenas**) in the Roman Catholic Church, a devotion consisting of a prayer or service repeated on nine successive days.

novice (nov´is) *n.* 1 a person entering a religious house on probation before taking the vows. 2 a new convert. 3 a person who is new to any business, an inexperienced person, a beginner. 4 a person or an animal that has not won a specified prize in a race or competition. **noviciate** (nōvish´iət), **novitiate** *n.* 1 the term of probation passed by a novice. 2 a religious novice. 3 the part of a religious house allotted to novices. 4 any period of probation or apprenticeship.

Novocaine® (nō´vəkān), **novocaine** *n.* a synthetic produce derived from coal tar, used as a local anaesthetic.

now (now) *adv.* 1 at the present time. 2 at once, immediately. 3 very recently. 4 (in narrative) at this point or time, then. 5 in these circumstances. 6 on this further occasion. 7 used as an expletive in explaining, remonstrating, conciliating, threatening etc. ~*conj.* since, seeing that, this being the case. ~*n.* the present time. ~*a.* (*coll.*) present, existing. **as of now** from this time. **for now** until later. **now and again** from time to time, now and then. **now and then** from time to time; occasionally. **now or never** at this moment or the chance is gone for ever. **nowadays** *adv.* at the present time; in these days. ~*n.* the present time.

noway, noways NO¹.

nowhere (nō´weə) *adv.* not in, at, or to any place or state. ~*pron.* no place. **in the middle of nowhere** (*coll.*) in a remote location. **nowhere near** not nearly. **to come from nowhere** 1 to appear suddenly or unexpectedly. 2 to achieve sudden or unexpected success. **to come in nowhere** (*coll.*) to be badly defeated in a race or other contest. **to get nowhere** to make or cause to make little or no progress.

nowise NO¹.

noxious (nok´shəs) *a.* 1 hurtful, harmful, unwholesome. 2 pernicious, destructive. **noxiously** *adv.* **noxiousness** *n.*

nozzle (noz´əl) *n.* a spout, a projecting mouthpiece, or end of pipe or hose.

NP *abbr.* Notary Public.

Np *chem. symbol* neptunium.

n.p. *abbr.* 1 new paragraph. 2 no place of publication.

NPV *abbr.* net present value.

nr. *abbr.* near.

NS *abbr.* 1 new series. 2 new style.

ns *abbr.* nanosecond.

NSW *abbr.* New South Wales.

NT *abbr.* 1 New Testament. 2 Northern Territory (of Australia).

-n't (ənt) *contr.* not (*in comb.*, as in *isn't, doesn't*).

nth N¹.

NTP *abbr.* normal temperature and pressure.

nu (nu) *n.* the thirteenth letter of the Greek alphabet (v, N).

nuance (nū´ahns) *n.* 1 a delicate gradation in colour or tone. 2 a fine distinction between things, feelings, opinions etc. ~*v.t.* to give a nuance to.

nub (nŭb) *n.* 1 the pith or gist (of). 2 a small lump, as of coal. 3 a stub, something left over. 4 a tangle, a knot, a snarl. **nubble** (nŭb´əl) *n.* a small lump. **nubbly, nubby** *a.* (*comp.* **nubblier, nubbier,** *superl.* **nubbliest, nubbiest**).

nubile (nū´bīl) *a.* 1 (of a woman) marriageable. 2 sexually attractive. **nubility** (-bil´-) *n.*

nuci- (nū´si) *comb. form* of or relating to nuts.

nuclear (nū´kliə) *a.* 1 of or relating to atomic nuclei. 2 of or relating to the nucleus of a biological cell. 3 of or using nuclear power or weapons. **nuclear bomb** *n.* a bomb which explodes by using the energy released by nuclear fission or nuclear fusion. **nuclear charge** *n.* the positive electric charge in the nucleus of an atom. **nuclear disarmament** *n.* the reduction or giving up of a country's nuclear weapons. **nuclear energy** *n.* energy released during a nuclear reaction, whether by nuclear fission or nuclear fusion. **nuclear family** *n.* the basic family unit consisting of a mother and father and their children. **nuclear fission** *n.* the breaking up of a heavy atom, as of uranium, into atoms of smaller mass, causing a great release of energy. **nuclear force** *n.* the attractive force between nucleons in the atomic nucleus which holds the nucleus together. **nuclear-free** *a.* containing no nuclear weapons, nuclear installations or nuclear-waste dumps. **nuclear fuel** *n.* uranium, plutonium and other metals consumed to produce nuclear energy. **nuclear fusion** *n.* the creation of a new nucleus by merging two lighter ones, with release of energy. **nuclear magnetic resonance** *n.* resonance which can be produced in nuclei or in isotopes of the elements, used as an analytic technique and in diagnosis. **nuclear physics** *n.* the study of atomic nuclei. **nuclear power** *n.* power obtained from a controlled nuclear reaction. **nuclear-powered** *a.* nuclear **reactor** *n.* a structure of fissile material such as uranium, with a moderator such as carbon or heavy water, so arranged that nuclear energy is continuously released under control. **nuclear**

umbrella n. the protection provided by being allied with a nuclear power. **nuclear warfare** n. the use of nuclear weapons in warfare. **nuclear waste** n. radioactive waste material. **nuclear weapon** n. a missile or bomb which explodes by using the energy released by nuclear fission or nuclear fusion. **nuclear winter** n. a period of coldness and darkness predicted as likely to follow a nuclear war.

Usage note Pronunciation of *nuclear* as (nū′kūlə), as though the word were *nucular*, is best avoided.

nuclease (nū′kliāz) n. any of a group of enzymes which catalyse the breakdown of nucleic acids.
nucleate¹ (nū′kliət) a. having a nucleus, nucleated.
nucleate² (nū′kliāt) v.t. to form into a nucleus. ~v.i. to form a nucleus. **nucleation** (-ā′shən) n.
nuclei NUCLEUS.
nucleic acid (nūklē′ik) n. either of two complex organic acids forming part of nucleoproteins.
nucleo- (nū′kliō) comb. form of or relating to a nucleus.
nucleolus (nūkliō′ləs) n. (pl. **nucleoli** (-lī)) (Biol.) a nucleus of or within another nucleus. **nucleolar, nucleolated** (-əlātid) a.
nucleon (nū′klion) n. (Physics) a proton or neutron. **nucleonic** a.
nucleonics (nūklion′iks) n. the science of the nucleus of the atom.
nucleoprotein (nūkliōprō′tēn) n. a complex of nucleic acid and protein.
nucleoside (nū′kliəsīd) n. an organic compound containing a purine or pyrimidine base linked to a sugar.
nucleosynthesis (nūkliōsin′thisis) n. (Astron.) the cosmic formation of heavier elements from lighter by nuclear fusion.
nucleotide (nū′kliətīd) n. an organic compound containing a nucleoside linked to a phosphate group.
nucleus (nū′kliəs) n. (pl. **nuclei** (-ī)) **1** a central part about which aggregation, accretion or growth goes on. **2** a kernel. **3** (Physics) the charged centre of an atom consisting of protons and neutrons. **4** (Biol.) the central body in an ovule, seed, cell etc., constituting the organ of vitality, growth, or other functions. **5** a mass of grey matter in the central nervous system. **6** (fig.) a centre of growth, development, activity etc. **7** (Astron.) the brightest part of the head of a comet. **nucleal** a.
nuclide (nū′klīd) n. (Physics) a kind of atom characterized by a specific number of protons and neutrons. **nuclidic** (-klid′-) a.
nude (nūd) a. bare, naked, uncovered, unclothed. ~n. **1** an undraped figure in painting or sculpture. **2** a naked person. **the nude** the undraped human figure or the state of being undraped. **nudely** adv. **nudeness** n. **nudism** n. the

practice of going naked on beaches and other specially designated areas. **nudist** n. **nudity** n.
nudge (nŭj) v.t. **1** to push gently, esp. with the elbow. **2** to draw attention or give a hint with, or as if with, such a push. ~n. such a push. **nudger** n.
nudi- (nū′di) comb. form bare, naked.
nudism, nudist etc. NUDE.
nuevo sol (nwāvō sol′) n. the standard unit of currency of Peru.
nugatory (nū′gətəri) a. **1** trifling, insignificant, futile. **2** ineffective, inoperative.
nugget (nŭg′it) n. **1** a lump of metal, esp. of gold. **2** a lump of anything. **3** something small but valuable.
nuisance (nū′səns) n. **1** anything that annoys, irritates or troubles. **2** an offensive or disagreeable person, action, experience etc. **3** (Law) anything causing annoyance, inconvenience or injury to another. **nuisance value** n. the capacity to cause irritation, obstruction etc.
nuke (nūk) n. (coll.) a nuclear weapon. ~v.t. to attack with nuclear weapons.
null (nŭl) a. **1** (Law) having no legal force or validity. **2** non-existent. **3** (fig.) without character, expression, or individuality. **4** (Math., Logic) amounting to nothing, equal to zero, nil. **5** (Comput.) having no elements or only elements which are zeros. ~n. a dummy letter in a cipher. **null and void** having no legal force or validity. **null character** n. (Comput.) a character, usu. a zero, which represents nothing. **null hypothesis** n. in statistics, a hypothesis which suggests that the difference between samples does not mean that there is a difference between populations. **null link** n. (Comput.) a reference indicating that an item is the last item in a list.
nullify (nŭl′ifī) v.t. (3rd pers. sing. pres. **nullifies**, pres.p. **nullifying**, past, p.p. **nullified**) **1** to make void. **2** to cancel, to annul, to invalidate. **nullification** (-fikā′shən) n. **nullifier** n.
nullity (nŭl′iti) n. (pl. **nullities**) **1** (Law) invalidity. **2** an invalid act, instrument, etc. **3** nothingness, non-existence. **4** a nonentity, a mere cipher.
numb (nŭm) a. **1** deprived of sensation and motion. **2** torpid, stupefied, dulled. ~v.t. to benumb, to paralyse. **numb-fish** n. (pl. in general **numb-fish**, in particular **numb-fishes**) the electric ray. **numbly** adv. **numbness** n.
numbat (nŭm′bat) n. a small marsupial, *Myrmecobius fasciatus*, of Australia, with a bushy tail.
number (nŭm′bə) n. **1** a measure of discrete quantity. **2** a word or symbol representing a quantity, a numeral. **3** a sum or aggregate of people, things or abstract units. **4** one of a numbered series, for example a single issue of a periodical, one of the parts of a literary or other work so issued etc. **5** numerical reckoning. **6** arithmetic. **7** (often pl.) poetical measure, verse, rhythm. **8** (usu. pl.) plurality, multitude, numerical preponderance. **9** (Gram.) the distinctive

form of a word used to denote unity or plurality. **10** a song or piece of music forming part of a popular musician's act or repertoire. **11** a group of friends or associates (*one of our number*). **12** (*coll.*) a person or thing as specified (*a nifty little number*). **13** (*sl.*) a position or job, esp. an advantageous or lucrative one. *~v.t.* **1** to count, to reckon; to ascertain the number of. **2** to amount to. **3** to assign a number to, to distinguish with a number. **4** to include, to comprise (among etc.). **5** to have lived (a specified number of years). **a number of** several. **any number of 1** any particular number of. **2** (*coll.*) a large quantity of. **by numbers** performed in simple stages, esp. with each one numbered. **one's days are numbered** one will not live much longer. **one's number is up** (*coll.*) one is going to die. **to have someone's number** (*coll.*) to understand someone's intentions, motives or character. **to have someone's number on it** (of a bullet or bomb) to be destined to hit someone. **without number** too many to be counted. **number cruncher** *n.* (*Comput., Math., sl.*) a computer capable of large-scale processing of numbered information. **number crunching** *n.* **numbered** *a.* **numberer** *n.* **numberless** *a.* too many to be counted. **number one** *n.* **1** the first in a series. **2** (*coll.*) oneself. **3** (*coll.*) the most senior person in an organization. **4** (*coll.*) the product which is at the top of a sales chart, esp. a pop record. *~a.* most important. **number plate** *n.* the plate on a motor vehicle showing its registration number. **numbers game** *n.* **1** (*derog.*) the act or practice of considering only the numerical aspects of a situation. **2** (*NAm.*) a type of lottery based on a certain combination of numbers occurring in race results. **number two** *n.* a deputy.

Usage note Although singular in form, *number* is usually treated as a plural in uses such as *A number (of them) are staying.*

numbskull NUMSKULL.

numdah (nŭm´də) *n.* an embroidered felt rug from India etc.

numeral (nū´mərəl) *n.* a word, symbol or group of symbols denoting number. *~a.* of, relating to, consisting of or denoting number. **numerable** *a.* **numerably** *adv.* **numerally** *adv.* **numerical** (-mer´i-), **numeric** *a.* of or relating to numbers. **numerical analysis** *n.* the branch of mathematics dealing with developing numerical methods for problem-solving. **numerically** *adv.*

numerate[1] (nū´mərət) *a.* able to count; competent in mathematics. **numeracy** (-əsi) *n.*

numerate[2] (nū´mərāt) *v.t.* to reckon, to number. **numeration** (-ā´shən) *n.* **numerator** *n.* **1** the part of a vulgar fraction written above the line indicating how many fractional parts are taken. **2** a person who numbers.

numeric NUMERAL.

numerology (nūmərol´əji) *n.* the study of the

alleged significance of numbers. **numerological** (-loj´-) *a.* **numerologist** *n.*

numerous (nū´mərəs) *a.* **1** many in number. **2** consisting of a great number of individuals. **numerously** *adv.* **numerousness** *n.*

numinous (nū´minəs) *a.* **1** of or relating to divinity. **2** feeling awe of the divine.

numismatic (nūmizmat´ik) *a.* of or relating to coins or medals. **numismatically** *adv.* **numismatics, numismatology** (-mətol´-) *n.* the science or study of coins and medals. **numismatist** (-miz´-), **numismatologist** (-mətol´-) *n.*

numskull (nŭm´skŭl), **numbskull** *n.* a stupid person. **numskulled** *a.*

nun (nŭn) *n.* a woman devoted to a religious life and living in a convent under certain vows, usu. of poverty, chastity and obedience. **nunhood, nunship** *n.* **nunlike** *a.* **nunnery** *n.* (*pl.* **nunneries**) a religious home for nuns. **nunnish** *a.*

nuncio (nŭn´siō, -shiō) *n.* (*pl.* **nuncios**) a papal envoy or ambassador to a foreign power. **nunciature** (-shətūə) *n.*

nunnery, nunnish NUN.

nuptial (nŭp´shəl) *a.* of or relating to a wedding. **nuptials** *n.pl.* a wedding.

nurd NERD.

nurl KNURL.

nurse (nœs) *n.* **1** a person who tends to the sick, wounded or infirm. **2** (*Hist.*) a person employed to look after young children. **3** a wet-nurse. **4** a tree planted to protect another or others during growth. **5** (*Zool.*) a sexually imperfect bee, ant etc., which tends the young brood. **6** a person who or something which fosters or promotes. **7** the condition of being nursed (*at nurse*). **8** any of various sharks or dogfishes. *~v.t.* **1** to look after (a sick person). **2** to treat (an illness or injury). **3** to suckle; to give suck to or feed (an infant). **4** to rear, to nurture. **5** to hold or clasp, esp. on one's knees or lap. **6** to foster, to tend, to promote growth in. **7** to cherish, to brood over. **8** to manage with care. **9** to be economical with. *~v.i.* **1** to be a nurse. **2** to suckle a baby. **3** (of a baby) to suck milk from the breast. **nurse hound** *n.* a large NE Atlantic dogfish, *Scyliorhinus stellaris.* **nursemaid** *n.* **1** a woman in charge of young children. **2** a person who is very nurturing or protective of another. **nurser** *n.* **nurse shark** *n.* a slow-moving, brownish, Atlantic shark, *Ginglymostoma cirratum.* **nursing** *n.* the act of nursing or the profession of being a nurse. *~a.* of or relating to nursing (*nursing staff*). **nursing officer** *n.* any of several grades of nurse having administrative duties. **nursling** (-ling), **nurseling** *n.* an infant that is being breast-fed.

nursery (nœ´səri) *n.* (*pl.* **nurseries**) **1** a room set apart for young children. **2** a day nursery or nursery school. **3** a place or garden for rearing plants. **4** the place, sphere or condition in which persons, qualities etc. are bred or fostered. **5** a place where animal life is developed. **nurserymaid** *n.* a servant who looks after a children's nursery. **nurseryman** n. (pl. **nurserymen**) a man who raises plants in a nursery. **nursery rhyme** n. a traditional rhyme for children. **nursery school** n. a school for young children aged three to five. **nursery slopes** n.pl. gentle ski slopes set apart for novices. **nursery stakes** n.pl. a race for two-year-old horses.

nurture (nœ´chə) n. **1** the act of bringing up, training, fostering. **2** nourishment. **3** education, breeding. **4** active encouragement to help the development of something. ~v.t. **1** to nourish. **2** to rear, to train, to educate. **3** to help the development of. **nurturer** n.

☒ **nusance** common misspelling of NUISANCE.

nut (nŭt) n. **1** the fruit of certain trees, containing a kernel in a hard shell which does not open to set free the seeds. **2** the kernel itself. **3** a pod containing hard seeds. **4** a metal block with a hole for screwing on and securing a bolt, screw etc. **5** a screw fitted to a violin bow, for adjusting tension. **6** the ridge on the neck of stringed instruments over which the strings pass to the tuning pegs. **7** any of various parts of machinery, usu. one in which a screw works. **8** (sl.) the head. **9** (sl.) **a** a crazy or eccentric person. **b** a fanatic (a martial-arts nut). **10** a small lump of coal. **11** (pl., taboo sl.) testicles. ~v.i. (pres.p. **nutting**, past, p.p. **nutted**) to gather nuts. ~v.t. (sl.) to head-butt. **can't do something for nuts** (coll.) am/are/is very bad at doing something (he can't dance for nuts). **nuts and bolts** (coll.) the basic essential facts. **off one's nut 1** (sl.) mad. **2** (sl.) drunk. **to do one's nut** (sl.) to become very angry. **nut brown** n., a. (of) a dark reddish-brown colour. **nut-brown** a. **nutcase** n. (sl.) a crazy or eccentric person. **nutcracker** n. **1** (usu. pl.) an instrument for cracking nuts. **2** a crow of the genus Nucifraga. **nut cutlet** n. a preparation of crushed nuts etc., eaten by vegetarians as a substitute for meat. **nutgall** n. an oak gall, used in dyeing. **nuthatch** n. any small bird of the genus Sitta, allied to the woodpecker, esp. S. europaea. **nuthouse** n. (sl.) a psychiatric hospital. **nutlet** (-lit) n. **nutlike** a. **nut oil** n. oil obtained from hazelnuts, walnuts or other nuts. **nuts** a. (sl.) crazy, eccentric. ~int. (sl.) used to express contempt or defiance. **to be nuts about** (coll.) to delight in; to be very fond of. **nutshell** n. the hard shell enclosing the kernel of a nut. **in a nutshell** expressed in a very concise statement. **nutter** n. (sl.) a crazy or eccentric person. **nut tree** n. a tree bearing nuts, esp. a hazel. **nutty** a. (comp. **nuttier**, superl. **nuttiest**) **1** full of nuts. **2** tasting like nuts. **3** (sl.) crazy, eccentric. **nutty about** very fond of or enthusiastic about. **nuttiness** n.

nutate (nūtāt´) v.i. to nod, to bend forward, to droop. **nutant** (nū´-) a. (Bot.) drooping, hanging with the apex downwards. **nutation** (-ā´shən) n. **1** a nodding or oscillation. **2** a movement of the tips of growing plants, usu. towards the sun.

3 (Astron.) a periodical oscillation of the earth's axis due to the attractive influence of the sun and moon on the greater mass round the equator.

nutmeg (nŭt´meg) n. **1** an evergreen tree, Myristica fragrans, whose hard aromatic seed is used for flavouring and in medicine. **2** the seed of the nutmeg, often used grated in cookery. **nutmeg-apple** n. the pear-shaped fruit of the nutmeg tree. **nutmeggy** a.

nutria (nū´triə) n. **1** the coypu. **2** its skin or fur, formerly frequently used in hat-making.

nutrient (nū´triənt) n. a nutritious substance. ~a. nourishing; serving as or conveying nourishment. **nutriment** n. **1** any substance which nourishes or promotes growth, esp. food. **2** an intellectual stimulus. **nutrimental** (-men´-) a. **nutrition** (-trish´-) n. **1** the function or process of promoting the growth of organic bodies. **2** nourishment, food. **3** the study of nutrition. **nutritional** a. **nutritionally** adv. **nutritionist** n. **nutritious** a. affording nourishment, efficient as food. **nutritiously** adv. **nutritiousness** n. **nutritive** a., n. **nutritively** adv.

nux vomica (nŭks vom´ikə) n. **1** a S Asian tree, Strychnos nux-vomica. **2** the seed of the nux vomica, which yields strychnine.

nuzzle (nŭz´əl) v.t. **1** to rub or press the nose against. **2** to fondle. **3** to root up with the nose. ~v.i. **1** to root about with the nose. **2** to nestle, to hide the head, as a child in its mother's bosom.

NVQ abbr. National Vocational Qualification.

NW abbr. **1** north-west. **2** north-western.

nyala (nyah´lə), **inyala** (inyah´-) n. (pl. **nyala**, **inyala**) a large S African antelope, Tragelaphus angasi, with spiral horns.

nyctalopia (niktəlō´piə), **nyctalopy** (nik´təlōpi) n. (Med.) a disease of the eyes in which vision is worse in shade or twilight than in daylight, night-blindness.

nylon (nī´lən) n. **1** any of various thermoplastics, used largely for tights, shirts, dress fabrics, imitation furs, ropes, brushes etc. **2** a nylon fabric. **3** (pl.) nylon stockings. ~a. made of nylon.

nymph (nimf) n. **1** any one of a class of mythological youthful female divinities inhabiting groves, springs, mountains, the sea etc. **2** (poet.) a beautiful or attractive young woman. **3** a pupa or chrysalis. **nymphean** (-fē´ən), **nymphal** a. **nymphet** (nim´fet) n. a young girl who is very sexually attractive and precocious. **nymphish**, **nymphlike** a.

nymphalid (nimfal´id) a. of or relating to the family Nymphalidae of butterflies. ~n. a butterfly of the family Nymphalidae.

nympho (nim´fō) n. (pl. **nymphos**) (coll.) a nymphomaniac.

nymphomania (nimfəmā´niə) n. excessive sexual desire in a woman. **nymphomaniac** (-ak) n., a. **nymphomaniacal** (-mənī´ə-) a.

NZ abbr. New Zealand.

O

O¹ (ō), **o** (*pl.* **Os, O's**) the 15th letter of the English and other versions of the Roman alphabet, corresponding to the Greek omicron (o, O). It has four principal sounds: (1) low, back and short, as in *pot*, unmarked in this dictionary, o; (2) this raised and lengthened historically by a following *r*, as in *or*, marked aw; (3) as a rising diphthong, as in *go*, marked ō; (4) mid, central and short, as in *glove*, marked ŭ. In unstressed syllables *o* is often obscured, as in *bacon*, *tailor*, marked ə. In conjunction with other vowels *o* also represents a variety of sounds, as in *boat*, *foetus*, *join*, *pour* etc. ~*symbol* a blood type in the ABO system. ~*n.* **1** an O-shaped thing or mark. **2** a circle, oval, or any round or nearly round shape. **3** a nought, nothing, zero. **O-ring** *n.* a rubber ring used as a seal.

O² *chem. symbol* oxygen.

O³, **o** *abbr.* ordinary. **O grade** *n.* ORDINARY GRADE (under ORDINARY). **O level** *n.* ORDINARY LEVEL (under ORDINARY).

O⁴ (ō), **oh** *int.* an exclamation of earnest or solemn address, entreaty, invocation, pain, surprise, wonder etc. **oh well** used to express resignation.

O' (ō) *pref.* descendant of, in Irish surnames.

o' (ō, ə) *prep.* (*coll. or dial.*) of, on.

-o (ō) *suf.* (*coll.*) **1** serving as a diminutive, as in *cheapo*, *wino*. **2** forming an interjection, as in *cheerio*, *righto*.

-o- (ō) *suf.* used as the terminal vowel in combining forms, as in *Russo-*, *petro-*.

oaf (ōf) *n.* (*pl.* **oafs**) a silly, stupid person, a lout. **oafish** *a.* **oafishly** *adv.* **oafishness** *n.*

oak (ōk) *n.* **1** (*also* **oak tree**) any tree or shrub of the genus *Quercus*, esp. *Q. robur*, a forest tree much valued for its timber. **2** the wood of this. **3** any tree of the Australian genus *Casuarina*. **4** any of various trees and plants bearing a real or fancied resemblance to the oak. ~*a.* made of oak. **oak-apple** *n.* a gall or excrescence of various kinds produced on oaks by various gall-flies. **oaken** *a.* of the wood of the oak. **oaky** *a.* **1** full of oaks. **2** like oak.

oakum (ō'kəm) *n.* old rope, untwisted and pulled into loose fibres, used for caulking seams, stopping leaks etc. in ships.

O. & M. *abbr.* organization and method(s).

OAP *abbr.* old age pensioner, old age pension.

oar (aw) *n.* **1** a long pole with a flattened blade, for rowing, sculling or steering a boat. **2** a rower. **to put one's oar in 1** to intrude into a conversation. **2** to interfere, esp. with unasked-for advice.

to rest on one's oars 1 to cease rowing without shipping the oars. **2** to stop for rest, to cease working. **oared** *a.* **oarfish** *n.* (*pl. in general* **oarfish,** *in particular* **oarfishes**) a ribbonfish, *Regalecus glesne*. **oarless** *a.* **oarlike** *a.* **oarlock** *n.* (*N Am.*) a rowlock. **oarsman, oarswoman** *n.* (*pl.* **oarsmen, oarswomen**) a (skilled) rower. **oarsmanship** *n.* **oarweed, oreweed** *n.* any large marine alga, esp. of the genus *Laminaria*.

oasis (ōā'sis) *n.* (*pl.* **oases** (-sēz)) **1** a fertile spot in a waste or desert. **2** a thing or place offering peace, pleasure, refuge etc.

oast (ōst) *n.* a kiln for drying hops. **oast house** *n.*

oat (ōt) *n.* **1** (*usu. in pl.*) a cereal plant of the genus *Avena*, esp. *A. sativa*. **2** (*pl.*) the grain of this, used for food. **3** any related grass, esp. the wild oat, *A. fatua*. **4** (*poet.*) a musical pipe made from an oat-stem. **5** pastoral, bucolic poetry or song. **6** (*pl., sl.*) sexual gratification. **off one's oats** (*coll.*) off one's food; without appetite. **to feel one's oats** (*coll.*) to feel vitality or be full of self-esteem. **to get one's oats** (*sl.*) to have regular sexual intercourse. **to sow one's (wild) oats** to indulge in youthful (esp. sexual) excess. **oat-cake** *n.* a flat cake or biscuit made from oatmeal. **oaten** *a.* **oat-grass** *n.* any of various grasses, esp. of the genus *Arrhenatherum* or *Helictotrichon*. **oatmeal** *n.* **1** oats ground into meal, used chiefly for making porridge or oatcakes. **2** a fawny-grey colour (as of porridge). ~*a.* of this colour. **oaty** *a.*

oath (ōth) *n.* (*pl.* **oaths** (ōdhz)) **1** a solemn appeal to God or some holy or revered person or thing, in witness of the truth of a statement or of the binding nature of a promise, esp. in a court of law. **2** the form of an oath. **3** a profane imprecation or expletive, a curse. **4** a swear word. **on/ under/ upon oath** sworn to attesting the truth. **to swear an oath** to take an oath. **to take an oath** to swear formally to the truth of one's attestations.

OB *abbr.* outside broadcast.

ob. *abbr. obiit*, he/she died.

ob- (ob) *pref.* **1** toward, to, meeting, in, facing, as in *obvious*. **2** against, opposing, hindering, resisting, hostile, as in *obstinate*. **3** reversely, obversely, contrary to the normal, as in *obovate*.

obbligato (obligah'tō), **obligato** *a.* (*Mus.*) **1** not to be omitted. **2** indispensable to the whole. ~*n.* (*pl.* **obbligatos, obligatos, obbligati** (-tē), **obligati**) an instrumental part or accompaniment that forms an integral part of the composition or is independently important (usu. by a single instrument).

obdurate (ob´dūrət) *a.* **1** stubborn. **2** hardened in heart, esp. against moral influence. **obduracy, obdurateness** *n.* **obdurately** *adv.*

OBE *abbr.* Officer of (the Order of) the British Empire.

obeah (ō´biə), **obi** (ō´bi) *n.* a form of sorcery practised by blacks, esp. in the W Indies.

obedience (əbē´dyəns) *n.* **1** the act or practice of obeying. **2** dutiful submission to authority. **3** compliance with law, command or direction. **4** the authority of a Church or other body. **in obedience to** in accordance with. **obedient** *a.* **obediently** *adv.*

obeisance (əbā´səns) *n.* **1** a bow, a curtsy, or any gesture signifying deference, submission, respect or salutation. **2** homage. **obeisant** *a.* **obeisantly** *adv.*

obeli OBELUS.

obelisk (ob´əlisk) *n.* **1** a quadrangular stone shaft, usually monolithic and tapering, with a pyramidal apex. **2** an obelus.

obelus (ob´ələs) *n.* (*pl.* **obeli** (-lī)) **1** a mark (-, ÷, or †), used to mark spurious or doubtful passages in ancient manuscripts. **2** in printing, a dagger symbol (†) indicating a cross-reference, footnote or death date. **obelize, obelise** *v.t.*

obese (əbēs´) *a.* excessively fat, fleshy, corpulent. **obeseness, obesity** *n.*

obey (ōbā´) *v.t.* **1** to perform or carry out (a command, instruction or direction). **2** to be obedient to. **3** to yield to the direction or control of. **4** to act according to. **~v.i.** to do as one is directed or commanded. **obeyer** *n.*

obfuscate (ob´fəskāt) *v.t.* **1** to darken, to obscure. **2** to bewilder, to confuse. **obfuscation** (-kā´shən) *n.* **obfuscatory** *a.*

obi[1] (ō´bi) *n.* (*pl.* **obi, obis**) a coloured sash worn around a Japanese kimono.

obi[2] OBEAH.

obit (ob´it) *n.* **1** a memorial service or commemoration of a death. **2** (*coll.*) an obituary.

obituary (əbit´ūəri) *a.* relating to or recording a death or deaths. **~n.** (*pl.* **obituaries**) a notice of a death, usu. in the form of a short biography of the deceased. **obituarial** (-eə´riəl) *a.* **obituarist** *n.*

object[1] (əbjekt´) *v.t.* **1** to oppose. **2** to offer or adduce in opposition. **3** to allege (a fact, usu. with *that*) in criticism, disapproval, or condemnation. **~v.i.** **1** to make objections. **2** to be averse, to disapprove.

object[2] (ob´jikt) *n.* **1** anything presented to the senses or the mind, esp. anything visible or tangible. **2** a material thing. **3** that to which an action or feeling is directed; an aim, end, ultimate purpose. **4** (*derog.*) a person or thing of pitiable or ridiculous appearance. **5** (*Gram.*) a noun, or word, phrase or sentence equivalent to a noun, governed by a transitive verb or preposition. **6** a thing or idea regarded as external to, distinct from, or independent of the subjective consciousness. **7** (*Comput.*) a package of information. **object-ball** *n.* in billiards etc., the ball

at which a player aims with their cue ball. **object-glass** *n.* the lens or combination of lenses at the end of an optical instrument nearest the object. **objectify** (-jek´tifī) *v.t.* (*3rd pers. sing. pres.* **objectifies**, *pres.p.* **objectifying**, *past, p.p.* **objectified**) **1** to render objective. **2** to present to the mind as a concrete or sensible reality. **objectification** (-fikā´shən) *n.* **objection** (-jek´-) *n.* **1** the act of objecting. **2** an adverse argument, reason or statement. **3** disapproval, dislike, or the expression of this. **objectionable** *a.* **1** liable to objection, reprehensible. **2** offensive, unpleasant. **objectionability** (-bil´-) *n.* **objectionableness** *n.* **objectionably** *adv.* **objectless** *a.* **object lesson** *n.* a practical illustration. **objector** *n.* a person who objects.

objective (objek´tiv) *a.* **1** proceeding from the object of knowledge or thought as opposed to the perceiving or thinking subject. **2** external, actual, real, self-existent, substantive. **3** of, relating to or concerned with outward things as distinct from the subjective. **4** uninfluenced by emotion, impulse, prejudice etc. **5** (*Gram.*) denoting the case of the object of a transitive verb or preposition; accusative. **~n.** **1** an objective point, e.g. of military operations. **2** an aim, goal or target. **3** (*Gram.*) the objective case. **4** (*also* **objective lens**) an object-glass. **objectival** (objiktī´vəl) *a.* **objectively** *adv.* **objectiveness** *n.* **objectivism** *n.* **1** the tendency to give priority to what is objective. **2** the theory that stresses objective reality. **objectivist** *n.* **objectivistic** (-vis´-) *a.* **objectivity** (objiktiv´-) *n.* **objectivize, objectivise** *v.t., v.i.* **objectivization** (-zā´shən) *n.*

objet (ob´zhā) *n.* (*pl.* **objets** (-zhā)) an object. **objet d'art** (dah´) *n.* (*pl.* **objets d'art**) an art object.

objurgate (ob´jəgāt) *v.t., v.i.* to chide, to reprove. **objurgation** (-ā´shən) *n.* **objurgator** *n.* **objurgatory** *a.*

oblate[1] (ob´lāt) *a.* (*Geom.*) flattened at the poles, as opposed to *prolate*. **oblately** *adv.* **oblateness** *n.*

oblate[2] (ob´lāt) *n.* a person not under vows but dedicated to monastic or religious life or work. **oblation** (-lā´shən) *n.* the act of offering or anything offered in worship. **oblational, oblatory** *a.*

obligation (obligā´shən) *n.* **1** the binding power of a promise, contract, vow, duty, law etc. **2** a duty, responsibility, commitment. **3** (*Law*) a binding agreement, esp. one with a penal condition annexed. **of obligation** obligatory. **obligate** (ob´ligāt) *v.t.* **1** to place under an obligation, legal or moral. **2** to compel. **3** (*N Am.*) to commit (assets) as security. **obligator** *n.* **obligatory** (əblig´ə-) *a.* mandatory. **obligatorily** *adv.*

Usage note The meanings of the verbs *obligate* and *oblige* overlap, but *obligate* is usual for legal and moral binding, and *oblige* for other more general kinds of constraint or compulsion.

oblige (əblīj´) *v.t.* **1** to bind or constrain by legal, moral or physical force. **2** to place under a debt of gratitude by a favour or kindness. **3** to do a favour to, to gratify. **4** (*pass.*) to be under an obligation (to). **much obliged** used to express thanks. **obligee** (-jē´) *n.* (*Law*) a person to whom another is obligated. **obliger** *n.* **obliging** *a.* **1** kind, complaisant. **2** helpful, accommodating. **obligingly** *adv.* **obligingness** *n.* **obligor** (ob´ligaw) *n.* (*Law*) a person who is legally bound to another.

Usage note See note on *obligate* under OBLIGA-TION.

oblique (əblēk´) *a.* **1** slanting, deviating from the vertical or horizontal. **2** deviating from the straight or direct line, indirect, roundabout. **3** evasive, not to the point. **4** (*Geom.*) **a** inclined at an angle other than a right angle. **b** (of an angle) acute or obtuse. **5** (*Bot.*) (of leaves) unequal-sided. **6** (*Gram.*) of or relating to any grammatical cases other than the nominative or vocative. ~*n.* something that is at an angle or slanting, esp. a geometric figure, military advance, solidus etc. **obliquely** *adv.* **obliqueness** *n.* **obliquity** (əblik´wi-) *n.* (*pl.* **obliquities**).

obliterate (əblit´ərāt) *v.t.* **1** to efface, to erase. **2** to wear out, to destroy. **3** to reduce to an illegible or imperceptible state. **obliteration** (-ā´shən) *n.* **obliterative** *a.* **obliterator** *n.*

oblivion (əbliv´iən) *n.* **1** forgetfulness, unawareness. **2** the state of having forgotten. **3** the state of being forgotten. **4** an amnesty or pardon. **to fall into oblivion** to be forgotten. **oblivious** *a.* **1** forgetful (of). **2** unaware (of), paying no heed (to). **3** lost in thought or abstraction. **obliviously** *adv.* **obliviousness** *n.*

Usage note The use of *oblivious* to mean un-aware is still sometimes disapproved of, though it is very common.

oblong (ob´long) *a.* **1** longer than broad, of greater breadth than height esp. of rectangles with adjoining sides unequal. **2** (of leaves) elliptical. ~*n.* an oblong figure or object.

obloquy (ob´ləkwi) *n.* (*pl.* **obloquies**) **1** censorious language. **2** discredit, disgrace, infamy.

obnoxious (obnok´shəs) *a.* offensive, objectionable, hateful, odious. **obnoxiously** *adv.* **obnoxiousness** *n.*

obo *abbr.* (*N Am.*) or best offer.

oboe (ō´bō) *n.* **1** a woodwind instrument with a double reed, usu. of soprano pitch. **2** a person who plays this instrument in an orchestra. **3** a reed organ stop of similar tone. **oboe d'amore** (damaw´rā) *n.* an oboe pitched a minor third below a normal oboe, used in baroque music. **oboist** *n.*

obscene (əbsēn´) *a.* **1** repulsive, disgusting, indecent, lewd. **2** (*Law*) (of publications etc.) liable to corrupt or deprave. **obscenely** *adv.* **obsceneness** *n.* **obscenity** (-sen´-) *n.* (*pl.* **obscenities**) **1** the state or fact of being obscene. **2** an obscene word, gesture etc.

obscurant (əbskū´rənt) *n.* an opponent of intellectual progress. **obscurantism** (-rant´-) *n.* **obscurantist** *n.*, *a.*

obscure (əbskūə´) *a.* **1** dark, dim. **2** not clear, indefinite, indistinct. **3** abstruse. **4** difficult to understand. **5** unexplained, doubtful. **6** hidden, secluded, remote from public observation. **7** unknown, lowly, humble. **8** dull, dingy. ~*v.t.* **1** to make dark, to cloud. **2** to make less intelligible, visible or legible. **3** to dim, to throw into the shade, to outshine. **4** to conceal. ~*v.i.* to darken, to conceal. **obscuration** (obskūərā´shən) *n.* **obscurely** *adv.* **obscurer** *n.* **obscurity** *n.* (*pl.* **obscurities**) **1** the quality or state of being obscure. **2** an obscure person or thing.

❌ obsene common misspelling of OBSCENE.

obsequies (ob´sikwiz) *n.pl.* **1** funeral rites. **2** a funeral. **obsequial** (-sē´-) *a.*

obsequious (əbsē´kwiəs) *a.* servile, cringing, fawning, over-ready to comply with the desires of others. **obsequiously** *adv.* **obsequiousness** *n.*

observe (əbzœv´) *v.t.* **1** to regard attentively, to note, to take notice of, to perceive. **2** to examine and note scientifically. **3** to follow attentively, to heed. **4** to perform duly. **5** to comply with. **6** to celebrate. **7** to remark, to express as an opinion. ~*v.i.* to make a remark or remarks (upon). **observable** *a.*, *n.* **observably** *adv.* **observance** *n.* **1** the act of observing, complying with, keeping, following, performing etc. **2** a customary rite, form or ceremony. **3** a rule or practice, esp. in a religious order. **observancy** *n.* **observant** *a.* **1** watchful, attentive. **2** quick or strict in observing, esp. rules etc. **observantly** *adv.* **observation** (obzəvā´shən) *n.* **1** the act, habit or faculty of observing. **2** scientific watching and noting of phenomena as they occur, as distinct from experiment. **3** the result of such a scrutiny, a fact scientifically noted or taken from an instrument. **4** experience and knowledge gained by systematic observing. **5** a remark, an incidental comment or expression of opinion or reflection. **under observation** in a state of being watched carefully, undergoing scrutiny. **observational** *a.* **1** deriving from observation (rather than experiment). **2** containing or consisting of comment or observation. **observationally** *adv.* **observation car** *n.* (*esp. N Am.*) a railway carriage designed so that one can view passing scenery. **observation post** *n.* **1** (*Mil.*) a post from which an observer can watch the effect of artillery fire. **2** a position from which one observes. **observatory** *n.* (*pl.* **observatories**) an institution, building, room etc. for observation of astronomical or meteorological phenomena. **observer** *n.* **1** a person who observes. **2** an official looker-on at a proceeding.

obsess (əbses´) *v.t.* to preoccupy the mind of (as a fixed idea). ~*v.i.* (*N Am.*) to be continually preoccupied with (with *on*, *over*). **obsession** (-sesh´ən) *n.* (the condition of having) an unhealthily deep-rooted or persistent fixation. **obsessional** *a.*

obsessionalism *n.* **obsessionally** *adv.* **obsessive** *a.*, *n.* **obsessively** *adv.* **obsessiveness** *n.*

obsidian (obsid´iən) *n.* a black or dark-coloured vitreous lava.

obsolescent (obsəles´ənt) *a.* becoming obsolete. **obsolescence** *n.* **obsolete** (ob´səlēt) *a.* **1** passed out of use, no longer practised, current or accepted. **2** discarded, bygone, out of date. **3** (*Biol.*) imperfectly developed, atrophied. **obsoletely** *adv.* **obsoleteness, obsoletism** *n.*

obstacle (ob´stəkəl) *n.* an impediment, an obstruction. **obstacle race** *n.* a race in which the competitors have to surmount or avoid a series of natural or artificial obstacles.

obstetric (əbstet´rik), **obstetrical** (-əl) *a.* of or relating to childbirth or obstetrics. **obstetrically** *adv.* **obstetrician** (obstətrish´-) *n.* **obstetrics** *n.* the branch of medical science dealing with childbirth and ante- and post-natal care of women.

obstinate (ob´stinət) *a.* **1** pertinaciously adhering to one's opinion or purpose, stubborn, refractory. **2** not easily remedied, persistent. **obstinacy** *n.* (*pl.* **obstinacies**). **obstinately** *adv.*

obstreperous (əbstrep´ərəs) *a.* **1** noisy, clamorous. **2** boisterous, unruly. **obstreperously** *adv.* **obstreperousness** *n.*

obstruct (əbstrŭkt´) *v.t.* **1** to block up, to close by means of obstacles. **2** to hinder, to impede. **3** to hamper, to check, to retard, to stop. **obstructer** *n.* **obstruction** *n.* **obstructional** *a.* **obstructionism** *n.* deliberate obstruction of (legislative) business, procedure etc. **obstructionist** *n.* **obstructionistic** *a.* **obstructive** *a.* **1** causing or tending to cause obstruction. **2** intended to retard progress, esp. of parliamentary business. **~n.** **1** a person who causes obstruction, esp. in Parliament. **2** a hindrance. **obstructively** *adv.* **obstructiveness** *n.* **obstructor** *n.*

obtain (əbtān´) *v.t.* **1** to gain, to acquire, to secure. **2** to procure, to get. **3** to attain, to reach. **~v.i.** to be prevalent or accepted. **obtainable** *a.* **obtainer** *n.*

obtrude (əbtrood´) *v.t.* **1** (*usu. with on, upon*) to thrust out, forward or upon. **2** to introduce or thrust in without warrant or invitation. **~v.i.** to enter without right, to thrust oneself forward. **obtruder** *n.* **obtrusion** (-zhən) *n.* **obtrusive** *a.* **obtrusively** *adv.* **obtrusiveness** *n.* **1** a thrusting forward, a desire to be noticed. **2** undue prominence.

obtuse (əbtūs´) *a.* **1** blunt or rounded, not pointed or acute. **2** denoting an angle greater than a right angle. **3** dull, stupid, slow of apprehension. **obtusely** *adv.* **obtuseness** *n.* **obtusity** *n.*

obverse (ob´vœs) *a.* **1** (*Biol.*) (of leaves) having a base narrower than the apex. **2** forming a counterstatement, complementary. **~n.** **1** the face or front. **2** the side of a coin or medal bearing the main device. **3** the counterpart or complementary side or aspect of a statement, fact etc. **obversely** *adv.*

obviate (ob´viāt) *v.t.* to clear away, to remove, to overcome, counteract or neutralize (dangers, difficulties etc.). **obviation** (-ā´shən) *n.*

obvious (ob´viəs) *a.* **1** plain to the eye, perfectly manifest, immediately evident. **2** unsubtle. **~n.** what is obvious and needing no explanation. **obviously** *adv.* **obviousness** *n.*

OC *abbr.* Officer Commanding.

ocarina (okərē´nə) *n.* a musical instrument of terracotta with finger-notes and a mouthpiece, giving a mellow whistling sound.

⊠ ocasion common misspelling of OCCASION.

occasion (əkā´zhən) *n.* **1** an event, circumstance or position of affairs, giving an opportunity, reason, or motive for doing something. **2** motive, ground, reason, need. **3** an opportunity. **4** an incidental or immediate cause or condition. **5** a time or occurrence, esp. of special interest or importance. **~v.t.** **1** to cause directly or indirectly. **2** to induce, to influence. **as the occasion arises** when needful, when circumstances demand. **on occasion** now and then. **to rise to the occasion** to be equal to a demanding event or situation. **to take the occasion to** to take the opportunity of. **occasional** *a.* **1** happening, made, employed or done as opportunity arises. **2** irregular, infrequent, incidental, casual. **3** of or made for a special occasion. **occasional cause** *n.* a secondary cause. **occasionality** (-nal´-) *n.* **occasionally** *adv.* **occasional table** *n.* a small movable table (used as occasion demands).

Occident (ok´sidənt), **occident** *n.* (*poet.*) **1** the West. **2** western Europe, Europe and America. **3** the western hemisphere. **4** sunset. **Occidental** (-den´-) *a.* **1** western. **2** characteristic of Western culture, thoughts etc. **~n.** a westerner. **occidentalism** *n.* **occidentalist** *n.* **occidentalize, occidentalise** *v.t.* **occidentally** *adv.*

occiput (ok´siput) *n.* the back part of the head. **occipital** (-sip´i-) *a.* of or relating to the back part of the head. **~n.** the occipital bone. **occipital bone** *n.* the bone forming the back and part of the base of the skull. **occipitally** *adv.*

occlude (əklood´) *v.t.* **1** to shut or stop up. **2** to close, to bring together (the eyelids, the teeth). **3** to form or cause to form an occlusion. **4** (*Chem.*) (of metals etc.) to absorb (a gas). **occluded front** *n.* an occlusion. **occlusion** (-zhən) *n.* **1** a shutting or stopping up. **2** in meteorology, the closing of a cold front upon a warm one, which is narrowed and raised up, an occluded front. **3** the manner in which teeth come together, the bite. **occlusive** (-siv) *a.*, *n.*

occult (əkŭlt´, ok-) *a.* **1** supernatural, magical, mystical. **2** concealed, kept secret, esoteric. **3** mysterious, recondite, beyond the range of ordinary knowledge or perception. **~v.t.** (*Astron.*) to hide, to conceal, to cover or cut off from view (esp. during a planetary eclipse). **~n.** **1** that which is hidden, mysterious or magical. **2** the supernatural. **occultation** (-tā´shən) *n.* **occulted, occulting** *a.* (of a lighthouse beacon) temporarily

shut off, becoming invisible at regular intervals.
occultism *n.* **occultist** *n.* **occultly** *adv.* **occult-ness** *n.*

occupant (ok´ūpənt) *n.* **1** a person who occupies. **2** a person who resides or is in a place. **3** a person who establishes a claim by taking possession. **occupancy** *n.* (*pl.* **occupancies**). **occupation** (okūpā´shən) *n.* **1** the act of occupying or taking possession (e.g. of a country by a foreign army). **2** the state of being occupied. **3** occupancy, tenure. **4** the state of being employed or engaged in some way. **5** pursuit, employment, business, trade, calling, job. **occupational** *a.* caused by or related to employment. **occupationally** *adv.* **occupational therapy** *n.* treatment of various illnesses by providing a creative occupation or hobby. **occupational therapist** *n.*

occupy (ok´ūpī) *v.t.* (*3rd pers. sing. pres.* **occupies**, *pres.p.* **occupying**, *past, p.p.* **occupied**) **1** to take possession of. **2** to hold in possession, to be the tenant of. **3** to reside in, to be in. **4** to take up, to fill. **5** to employ, to engage (oneself, or in p.p.). **occupier** *n.* an occupant of a house etc.

occur (əkœ´) *v.i.* (*pres.p.* **occurring**, *past, p.p.* **occurred**) **1** to happen, to take place. **2** to be met with, to be found, to exist. **3** to present itself to the mind. **occurrence** (əkŭr´əns) *n.* **1** an event, an incident. **2** the happening or taking place of anything.

ocean (ō´shən) *n.* **1** the vast body of water covering about two-thirds of the surface of the globe. **2** any one of its principal divisions, the Antarctic, Atlantic, Arctic, Indian and Pacific Oceans. **3** the sea. **4** an immense expanse or quantity. **oceanarium** (-eə´riəm) *n.* (*pl.* **oceanariums**, **oceanaria** (-riə)) an aquarium for specimens of deep-sea animal life. **ocean-going** *a.* (suitable for) travelling on the ocean. **oceanic** (ōshian´-, ōsi-) *a.* **1** of, relating to, occurring in or (expansive) like the ocean. **2** (of a climate) governed by the ocean. **oceanography** (-og´-) *n.* the branch of science concerned with oceans and their biological, geographical and chemical features etc. **oceanographer** *n.* **oceanographic** (-graf´-), **oceanographical** *a.* **oceanward**, **oceanwards** *adv.*

ocelot (os´əlot, ō´-) *n.* **1** a small American feline, *Felis pardalis*, which has a yellow or orange coat marked with black stripes and spots. **2** its fur.

och (okh) *int.* (*Ir., Sc.*) used to express impatience, contempt, regret, surprise etc.

oche (ok´i), **hockey** (ok´i, hok´i) *n.* in darts, the line or mark behind which a player must stand when throwing at the dartboard.

ochre (ō´kə), (*N Am.*) **ocher** *n.* **1** a native earth consisting of hydrated peroxide of iron with clay in various proportions, used as a red or yellow pigment. **2** a yellow colour. ~*a.* of or relating to this pigment or colour. **ochraceous** (ōkrā´shəs), **ochreish** (ō´kərish), **ochreous** (ō´kriəs), **ochroid** (ō´kroid), **ochrous, ochry** *a.*

-ock (ək) *suf.* indicating smallness or youngness, as in *bullock*, *hillock*.

ocker (ok´ə) *n.* (*Austral., sl.*) a boorish, chauvinistic Australian.

o'clock (əklok´) *adv.* of the clock.

ocotillo (ōkōtē´yō) *n.* (*pl.* **ocotillos**) a cactus-like shrub, *Fouquiera splendens*, of Mexico and the south-western US.

OCR *abbr.* optical character reader, recognition.

Oct. *abbr.* October.

oct. *abbr.* octavo.

octa- (ok´tə), **oct-**, **octo-** (-tō) *comb. form* **1** having eight. **2** consisting of eight.

octad (ok´tad) *n.* a group or series of eight. **octadic** (-tad´-) *a.*

octagon (ok´təgən) *n.* **1** a plane figure of eight sides and angles. **2** any object or building of this shape. **octagonal** (-tag´-) *a.* **octagonally** *adv.*

octahedron (oktəhē´drən), **octohedron** *n.* (*pl.* **octahedra** (-drə), **octahedrons**, **octohedra**, **octohedrons**) a solid figure contained by eight plane faces. **octahedral** *a.*

octal (ok´təl) *a.* referring to or based on the number eight.

octamerous (oktam´ərəs) *a.* (*Biol.*) having parts in eights or in series of eight.

octane (ok´tān) *n.* (*Chem.*) a colourless liquid hydrocarbon of the alkane series that occurs in petroleum. **octane number**, **octane rating** *n.* a percentage measure of the antiknock quality of a liquid motor fuel.

octant (ok´tənt) *n.* **1** an arc comprising the eighth part of a circle's circumference. **2** an eighth of the area of a circle contained within two radii and an arc. **3** each of the eight parts into which a space is divided by three planes (usu. at right angles) intersecting at one point. **4** an instrument similar to a sextant for measuring angles, having a graduated arc of 45°.

octavalent (oktəvā´lənt) *a.* (*Chem.*) having a valency of eight.

octave (ok´tiv, -tāv) *n.* **1** (*Mus.*) **a** the interval between any musical note and that produced by twice or half as many vibrations per second (lying eight notes away inclusively). **b** a note at this interval above or below another. **c** two notes separated by this interval. **d** the scale of notes filling this interval. **2** any group of eight, such as the first eight lines of a sonnet or a stanza of eight lines. **octave coupler** *n.* a mechanism on an organ or harpsichord that allows keys or pedals that are an octave apart to be played simultaneously.

octavo (oktā´vō) *n.* (*pl.* **octavos**) **1** a book in which a sheet is folded into 8 leaves or 16 pages. **2** the size of such a book or paper (written 8vo).

octennial (okten´iəl) *a.* **1** recurring every eighth year. **2** lasting eight years.

octet (oktet´), **octette** *n.* **1** (*Mus.*) **a** a musical composition of eight parts or for eight instruments or singers. **b** a group of eight, esp. musicians or singers. **2** an octave (of verse). **3** (*Chem.*) a stable group of eight electrons.

octo- OCTA-.

October (oktō´bə) *n*. the tenth month of the year (the eighth of the Roman year).

octocentenary (oktōsentē´nəri, -ten´-) *n*. (*pl.* **octocentenaries**) an 800th anniversary. ~*a*. of or relating to an ocotocentenary.

octodecimo (oktōdes´imō) *n*. (*pl.* **octodecimos**) **1** a book having 18 leaves to the sheet. **2** the size of such a book (written 18mo). ~*a*. having 18 leaves to the sheet.

octogenarian (oktōjənee´riən) *n*. a person who is 80, or between 80 and 90 years old. ~*a*. of, relating to or being an octogenarian.

octopod (ok´təpod) *a*. having eight feet. ~*n*. any cephalopod of the order Octopoda, with eight arms and usually suckers.

octopus (ok´təpəs) *n*. (*pl.* **octopuses**) **1** any cephalopod mollusc of the genus *Octopus*, having eight arms furnished with suckers. **2** an organization or influence having far-extending powers (for harm).

octosyllabic (oktōsilab´ik) *a*. having eight syllables. ~*n*. a line of eight syllables. **octosyllable** (ok´-) *n*. a word of eight syllables.

octuple (ok´tūpəl) *a*. eightfold. ~*n*. the product of multiplication by eight. ~*v.t.*, *v.i.* to multiply by eight.

ocular (ok´ūlə) *a*. **1** of, relating to, by or with the eye or eyes, visual. **2** known from actual sight. ~*n*. an eyepiece. **ocularist** *n*. a maker of artificial eyes. **ocularly** *adv*. **ocular spectrum** *n*. an image persisting on the retina after the eyes are removed, an after-image. **oculate** (-lət), **oculated** (-lātid) *a*. **1** having eyelike spots. **2** having eyes or sight. **oculist** *n*. an ophthalmologist or optician. **oculistic** (-lis´-) *a*.

🅇 **ocult** common misspelling of OCCULT.

🅇 **ocupy** common misspelling of OCCUPY.

🅇 **ocur** common misspelling of OCCUR.

OD (ōdē´) *n*. (*sl.*) an overdose of a drug. ~*v.i.* (*3rd pers. sing. pres.* **OD's**, *pres.p.* **OD'ing**, *past, p.p.* **OD'd**) to take an overdose of a drug.

odalisque (ō´dəlisk), **odalisk** *n*. (*Hist.*) an Oriental female slave or concubine, esp. in a harem.

odd (od) *a*. **1** remaining after a number or quantity has been divided into pairs. **2** not even, not divisible by two. **3** bearing such a number. **4** lacking a match or pair. **5** singular, strange, eccentric, queer. **6** occasional, casual. **7** indefinite, incalculable. **8** (*ellipt.*) and more, with others thrown in (added to a round number in enumeration, as *two hundred odd*). ~*n*. **1** a handicap stroke in golf. **2** a stroke more than one's opponent's score. **oddball** *n*. a person who is eccentric or peculiar. ~*a*. eccentric, peculiar. **odd bod** *n*. (*sl.*) a person who is strange or eccentric. **oddish** *a*. **oddity** *n*. (*pl.* **oddities**) **1** oddness. **2** a peculiar feature or trait. **3** an odd person or thing. **odd job** *n*. a casual, irregular or occasional piece of work, esp. a domestic repair. **odd jobber**, **odd-job man**, **odd-job woman** *n*. **oddly** *adv*. **odd man out** *n*. **1** a person who is left when a number pair off. **2** a person who is at variance with, excluded from,

or stands out as dissimilar to a group etc. **oddment** *n*. **1** a remnant. **2** (*pl.*) odds and ends. **3** (*pl.*, *Print.*) matter other than the main part of a book, such as the preface. **oddness** *n*. **odds** *n.pl.* (*usu. as sing.*) **1** the ratio by which the amount staked by one party to a bet exceeds that by the other. **2** the chances in favour of a given event. **3** the balance of superiority, advantage. **4** an allowance to the weaker of two competitors. **5** inequality, difference. **6** variance, strife, dispute. **at odds** at variance. **by all odds** certainly. **over the odds** higher, more than is acceptable, necessary, usual etc. **to give odds** to lay odds. **to lay odds** to offer a bet with favourable odds. **to make no odds** to make no difference, not to matter. **to take odds** to accept a bet with favourable odds. **what's the odds?** (*coll.*) what difference does it make? **odds and ends** *n.pl.* miscellaneous remnants, trifles, scraps etc. **odds and sods** *n.pl.* (*coll.*) odds and ends. **odds-on** *a*. having a better than even chance of happening, winning, succeeding etc. ~*n*. a state when success is more likely than failure.

ode (ōd) *n*. a lyric poem in an elevated style, rhymed or unrhymed, of varied and often irregular metre, usu. in the form of an address or invocation.

-ode[1] (ōd) *suf*. denoting a thing resembling or of the nature of, as *geode*, *sarcode*.

-ode[2] (ōd) *suf*. denoting a path or way, as *anode*, *cathode*.

odious (ō´diəs) *a*. **1** hateful, repulsive. **2** offensive. **odiously** *adv*. **odiousness** *n*. **odium** (-əm) *n*. **1** general dislike, reprobation. **2** repulsion.

Usage note The adjectives *odious* and *odorous* should not be confused: *odious* means hateful, and *odorous* fragrant.

odometer (ōdom´itə), **hodometer** (hod-) *n*. an instrument attached to a vehicle for measuring and recording the distance travelled. **odometry** *n*.

odonto- (odont´ō), **odont-** *comb. form* having teeth or processes resembling teeth.

odour (ō´də), (*N Am.*) **odor** *n*. **1** a smell, whether pleasant or unpleasant. **2** (*coll.*) a bad smell. **3** repute, esteem. **odoriferous** (-rif´-) *a*. diffusing fragrance. **odoriferously** *adv*. **odorous** *a*. having a sweet scent, fragrant. **odorously** *adv*. **odorousness** *n*. **odourless** *a*.

Usage note See note on *odorous* under ODIOUS.

odyssey (od´isi) *n*. (*pl.* **odysseys**) (a story of) a long journey containing a series of adventures and vicissitudes. **Odyssean** (-sē´ən) *a*.

oedema (idē´ma), (*esp. N Am.*) **edema** *n*. swelling due to accumulation of serous fluid in the cellular tissue; dropsy. **oedematose** (-tōs), **oedematous** *a*.

Oedipus complex (ē´dipəs) *n*. (*Psych.*) a psychical impulse in offspring characterized by excessive love or sexual desire for the parent of the opposite sex and hatred for the parent of the same sex. **Oedipal, Oedipean** (-pē´ən) *a*.

oeno- (ē´nō), **oino-,** (*esp. N Am.*) **eno-, oen-** (ēn), **oin-,** (*esp. N Am.*) **en-** *comb. form* wine. **oenology** (ēnol´əji) *n.* the science or study of wines. **oenological** (-loj´-) *a.* **oenologist** *n.* **oenophile** (ē´nəfīl), **oenophil** (-fil), **oenophilist** (-nof´i-) *n.* a wine connoisseur. **oenophily** (-nof´ili) *n*.

o'er (aw) *prep., adv.* (*poet.*) over.

oersted (œ´sted) *n.* a unit of magnetic field or magnetizing force.

oesophagus (ēsof´əgəs), (*esp. N Am.*) **esophagus** *n.* (*pl.* **oesophagi** (-jī), **oesophaguses,** (*esp. N Am.*) **esophagi, esophaguses**) the gullet, the canal by which food passes to the stomach.

oestrogen (ē´strəjən, es´-), (*esp. N Am.*) **estrogen** *n.* 1 any of the female sex hormones which induce oestrus and encourage the growth of female secondary sexual characteristics. 2 a substance produced artificially that has these effects. **oestradiol** (-dī´ol) *n.* the major oestrogenic hormone in human females (used to treat breast cancer and oestrogen deficiency). **oestrogenic** (-jen´ik) *a.* **oestrogenically** *adv*.

oestrus (ē´strəs, es´-), **oestrum** (-trəm), (*esp. N Am.*) **estrus, estrum** *n.* the cyclical period of sexual receptivity in some female mammals, heat. **oestrous** *a*.

oeuvre (œ´vrə) *n.* the works of an author, painter etc.

of (ov, əv) *prep.* 1 denoting connection with or relation to in situation, origin or point of departure. 2 denoting connection with or relation to in motive, cause or agency. 3 denoting connection with or relation to in removal, separation or privation. 4 denoting connection with or relation to in substance. 5 denoting possession or inclusion. 6 denoting identity or equivalence. 7 denoting connection with or relation to in direction or distance. 8 denoting reference or respect to. 9 denoting connection with or relation to in quality or condition. 10 denoting the object of an action, feeling etc. 11 (*N Am.*) denoting time in relation to the next hour on the clock. **of an evening/ morning etc.** 1 (*coll.*) usually in the evening etc. 2 (*coll.*) at some point during most evenings etc.

ofay (ō´fā, ōfā´) *n.* (*N Am., sl., offensive*) (esp. used by blacks) a white person. ~*a.* white.

off (of) *adv.* 1 away, at a distance or to a distance in space or time (expressing removal, separation, suspension, discontinuance, decay or termination). 2 to the end, utterly, completely. 3 (*Naut.*) away from the wind. ~*prep.* from (denoting deviation, separation, distance, disjunction, removal etc.). ~*a.* 1 more distant, further, opp. to near. 2 right, as opposed to left. 3 removed or aside from the main street etc., divergent, subsidiary. 4 (*coll.*) unacceptable, unfair. 5 contingent, possible. 6 not occupied, disengaged, on bad form (*an off day*). 7 denoting that part of a cricket field to the left side of the bowler when the batsman

is right-handed. ~*n.* 1 the off side of a cricket field. 2 the beginning, start. ~*v.i.* 1 (*coll.*) to go off, to put off, to withdraw. 2 (*Naut.*) to go away from the land. ~*int.* away, begone. **off and on** intermittently, now and again. **to be off** to leave. **to take off** (of a plane) to leave the ground. **off-air** *a., adv.* 1 of or relating to the transmission of programmes by broadcasting. 2 connected with a radio or television programme but not broadcast. **offbeat** (of´bēt, ofbēt´) *a.* 1 (*Mus.*) in music, not coinciding with the beat. 2 (*coll.*) unconventional, unusual. ~*n.* (*Mus.*) any of the normally unaccented beats in a bar. **off-break** *n.* 1 in cricket, a ball which deviates inwards from the off side. 2 such deviation. **off-centre,** (*N Am.*) **off-center** *a.* not quite central. **off chance** *n.* a remote possibility. **on the off chance** in the slim hope (that), just in case. **off-colour,** (*N Am.*) **off-color** *a.* 1 out of sorts. 2 slightly obscene. **offcut** *n.* a section cut off the main piece of a material (of fabric, meat, paper, wood etc.). **off day** *n.* a day when one is on bad form. **off-drive** *v.t.* in cricket, to drive (the ball) off. ~*n.* a drive to the off side. **offhand** *adv.* 1 without consideration, preparation or warning. 2 casually, summarily, curtly or brusquely. ~*a.* 1 impromptu. 2 casual. 3 summary, curt or brusque. **offhanded** *a.* **offhandedly** *adv.* **offhandedness** *n.* **offing** *n.* that portion of the sea beyond the halfway line between the coast and the horizon. **in the offing** likely to occur soon. **offish** *a.* (*coll.*) inclined to be distant, reserved or stiff in manner. **offishly** *adv.* **offishness** *n.* **off-key** *a., adv.* 1 out of tune. 2 out of keeping. **off-licence** *n.* 1 a licence to sell intoxicating liquors to be consumed off the premises. 2 the premises operating under such a licence. **off-limits** *a.* out of bounds. **off-line** *a.* (*Comput.*) (of a computer peripheral) switched off, not under the control of a central processor. ~*adv.* with a delay between the production and processing of data. **offload** *v.i., v.t.* 1 to unload. 2 to get rid of (something or to someone else). **off of** *prep.* (*sl.*) off (*Get off of the floor*). **off-peak** *a.* (of a service) during a period of low demand. ~*adv.* at times of low demand. **off-piste** *a., adv.* away from regular ski runs. **off-price** *a.* (*N Am.*) (of goods) sold at lower than the manufacturer's recommended price. **offprint** *n.* a reprint of an article or separate part of a periodical etc. **off-putting** *a.* 1 disconcerting. 2 causing aversion, repellent. **off-puttingly** *adv.* **off-road** *a.* 1 on rough ground away from the road. 2 (of a vehicle etc.) designed for driving or riding on rough ground. **off-roader** *n.* **off-roading** *n.* **off-screen** *adv., a.* (appearing or happening) out of sight of the viewer of a film, television programme etc. **off-season** *a., adv.* out of season. ~*n.* a period of low (business) activity. **offset** *n.* 1 a lateral shoot or branch that takes root or is caused to take root and is used for propagation; an offshoot, a scion. 2 a spur or branch of a mountain range. 3 anything allowed as a counterbalance, equivalent, or compensation.

4 an amount set off (against). **5** in surveying, a short course measured perpendicularly to the main line. **6** (*Archit.*) a part where the thickness of a wall is diminished, usu. towards the top. **7** a bend or fitting bringing a pipe past an obstacle. ~*v.t.* (*pres.p.* **offsetting**, *past, p.p.* **offset**) **1** to balance by an equivalent. **2** to counterbalance, to compensate. **3** to print using the offset process. **offset printing** *n.* a (lithographic) printing process in which the image is first transferred from a plate on to a cylinder before it is printed on to paper. **offshoot** *n.* **1** a branch or shoot from a main stem. **2** a subsidiary matter. **offshore** *a.*, *adv.* **1** blowing off the land. **2** situated a short way from the land. **3** (made or registered) abroad. **offside** *n.* **1** in football etc., the field between the ball and the opponents' goal. **2** the right side of a horse etc. **3** the side of a vehicle away from the kerb. ~*a.* (of a player in football etc.) illegally ahead of the ball etc. when it is played. **offsider** *n.* (*Austral., coll.*) a friend, partner. **offspring** *n.* (*pl.* **offspring**) **1** issue, progeny. **2** (*collect.*) children, descendants. **3** a child. **4** a production or result of any kind. **off-stage** *a.*, *adv.* out of sight of the theatre audience. **off-street** *a.* (of parking) in a car park; away from the street. **off-the-shelf** *a.* (of goods) available from stock; ready-made. **off-the-shoulder** *a.* (of a dress etc.) cut so as to reveal the shoulders. **off-time** *n.* a time when little is happening. **off-white** *n.* a white colour with a tinge of grey, yellow etc. ~*a.* not quite white.

offal (of´əl) *n.* **1** parts of the carcass of an animal, including the head, tail, kidneys, heart, liver etc. (used as food). **2** refuse, rubbish, waste. **3** carrion.

offend (əfend´) *v.t.* **1** to wound the feelings of, to hurt. **2** to make angry, to cause displeasure or disgust in, to outrage, to annoy, to transgress. ~*v.i.* **1** to transgress or violate a law. **2** to cause anger, disgust etc., to scandalize. **offence** (əfens´), (*N Am.*) **offense** *n.* **1** the act of offending, an aggressive act. **2** an affront, an insult. **3** the state or a sense of being hurt, annoyed, or affronted; umbrage. **4** a breach of custom, a transgression, a sin. **5** an illegal act. **to give offence** to cause umbrage, to affront or insult. **to take offence** to be offended, to feel a grievance. **offenceless** *a.* **offendedly** *adv.* **offender** *n.* **offending** *a.* **offensive** *a.* **1** of, relating to or used for attack, aggressive. **2** causing or meant to cause offence. **3** irritating, vexing, annoying. **4** disgusting. **5** (*esp. N Am.*) of or relating to the team in possession of the ball etc. at a particular point during a game. ~*n.* **1** the attitude, method or act of attacking. **2** (*Mil.*) a strategic attack. **offensively** *adv.* **offensiveness** *n.*

offer (of´ə) *v.t.* **1** to present, to put forward, to tender for acceptance or refusal. **2** to present as an act of worship. **3** to sacrifice, to immolate. **4** to propose. **5** to bid (as a price). **6** to evince readiness (to do something). **7** to essay, to attempt. **8** to proffer, to make available for sale. **9** to show an intention (to). ~*v.i.* **1** to present or show itself, to appear, to occur. **2** to make an attempt (at). ~*n.* **1** an act of offering. **2** an expression of willingness or readiness (to). **3** a tender, proffer or proposal, to be accepted or refused. **4** a price or sum bid. **5** an attempt, an essay. **on offer** presented for sale, consumption etc., esp. at a bargain price. **under offer** provisionally sold prior to and subject to the signing of a contract. **offerer** *n.* **offering** *n.* **offeror** *n.* **offertory** (-təri) *n.* (*pl.* **offertories**) **1** that part of the Mass or liturgical service during which offerings or oblations are made. **2** in the Church of England, an anthem sung or the text spoken while these are being made. **3** the offering of these oblations. **4** the gifts offered. **5** any collection made at a religious service.

office (of´is) *n.* **1** a room, building or other place where business is carried on. **2** (*collect.*) the persons charged with business at a particular place, the official staff or organization as a whole. **3** a duty, charge, function; the task or service attached to a particular post or station. **4** a post of service, trust or authority, esp. under a public body. **5** a government department or agency. **6** (*N Am.*) a consulting room. **7** an act of worship of prescribed form, an act of help, kindness or duty. **8** (*often in pl.*) a service. **9** (*pl.*) the rooms or places in which the domestic duties of a house are discharged. **10** (*sl.*) a hint or signal. **office-bearer** *n.* a person who holds office. **office block** *n.* a large building containing offices. **office boy**, **office girl** *n.* a person employed to perform minor tasks in an office. **office hours** *n.pl.* the time during which an office is open for business. **officer** *n.* **1** a person holding a post or position of authority, esp. a government functionary. **2** a person elected to perform certain duties by a society, committee etc., or appointed to a command in the armed services or merchant navy. **3** a police officer. ~*v.t.* **1** to provide with officers. **2** to act as commander of. **office worker** *n.* an employee in an office. **official** (əfish´əl) *a.* **1** of or relating to an office or public duty. **2** holding an office, employed in public duties. **3** derived from or executed under proper authority. **4** duly authorized. **5** (*often derog.*) characteristic of persons in office. **6** (*Med.*) authorized by the pharmacopoeia, officinal. ~*n.* a person who holds a public office. **official birthday** *n.* the day in June when the British sovereign's birthday is observed. **officialdom**, **officialism** *n.* **officialese** (-ēz´) *n.* (*derog.*) official jargon. **officially** *adv.* **official receiver** *n.* an officer appointed by a receiving order to administer a bankrupt's estate. **official secrets** *n.pl.* confidential information relating to national security. **officiate** (əfish´-) *v.i.* **1** to perform official duties, to act in an official capacity. **2** to conduct public worship. **officiant** *n.* **officiation** (-ā´shən) *n.* **officiator** *n.*

Usage note See note on *official* under OFFICIOUS.

officinal (əfis´inəl, ofisī´-) *a.* **1** (of a pharmaceutical product) ready-prepared. **2** authorized by the pharmacopoeia. **3** used in medicine. **4** medicinal. *~n.* an officinal preparation or plant. **officinally** *adv.*

officious (əfish´əs) *a.* **1** aggressively interfering. **2** forward in doing or offering unwanted kindness, meddling, intrusive. **3** in diplomacy, informally related to official concerns or objects, not official. **officiously** *adv.* **officiousness** *n.*

Usage note The adjectives *officious* and *official* should not be confused: *officious* means meddlesome, and *official* relating to office or duty.

often (of´ən, -tən) *adv.* **1** frequently, many times. **2** in many instances. **as often as not** in roughly half of the instances. **more often than not** (quite) frequently. **oft** (oft) *adv.* (*poet.*) often (*esp. in comb.*).

ogee (ō´jē) *n.* **1** a wavelike moulding having an inner and outer curve like the letter S, a talon. **2** (*Archit.*) an ogee arch. *~a.* having such a double curve. **ogee arch** *n.* (*Archit.*) a pointed arch each side of which is formed of a concave and a convex curve. **ogee'd** *a.*

Ogen melon (ō´gən) *n.* a variety of small sweet melon resembling a cantaloupe.

ogive (ō´jīv, ōjīv´) *n.* **1** a diagonal rib of a vault. **2** a pointed or Gothic arch. **3** an S-shaped line. **4** a cumulative frequency graph. **ogival** (ōjī´-) *a.*

ogle (ō´gəl) *v.t.* to look or stare at with admiration, wonder etc., esp. amorously. *~v.i.* to cast amorous or lewd glances. *~n.* **1** an amorous glance or look. **2** a lewd stare. **ogler** *n.*

ogre (ō´gə) *n.* **1** a fairy-tale giant living on human flesh. **2** a monster, a barbarously cruel person. **ogreish, ogrish** *a.* **ogress** (ōg´ris) *n.* a female ogre.

oh O⁴.

o.h.c. *abbr.* overhead camshaft.

ohm (ōm) *n.* the unit of electrical resistance, that between two points on a conductor when a potential difference of one volt produces a current of one amp. **ohmic** *a.* **ohmmeter** *n.*

OHMS *abbr.* On Her/ His Majesty's Service.

oho (əhō´) *int.* used to express surprise, irony or exultation.

-oholic -AHOLIC.

OHP *abbr.* overhead projector.

o.h.v. *abbr.* overhead valve.

oi (oi) *int.* used to give warning, attract attention etc.

-oid (oid) *comb. form* forming adjectives and nouns denoting resemblance, as in *colloid, cycloid, rhomboid*. **-oidal** *comb. form* forming adjectives. **-oidally** *comb. form* forming adverbs.

oik (oik) *n.* (*coll.*) a stupid or uncouth person.

oil (oil) *n.* **1** an unctuous liquid, insoluble in water, soluble in ether and usually in alcohol, obtained from various animal and vegetable substances. **2** (*pl.*) oil colours, paints. **3** (*pl.*) oilskins. *~v.t.* **1** to smear, anoint, rub, soak, treat or impregnate with oil. **2** to lubricate with or as with

oil. *~v.i.* **1** to turn into oil. **2** to take oil aboard as fuel. **3** to become oily. **to burn the midnight oil** to study or work far into the night. **to oil someone's palm** to bribe someone. **to oil the wheels** to facilitate matters, to help things go smoothly. **oilbird** *n.* a nocturnal S American bird, *Steatornis caripensis*, the fat of whose young yields edible oil. **oilcake** *n.* the refuse after oil is pressed or extracted from linseed etc., used as fodder. **oil can** *n.* a can for holding oil, esp. one used for oiling machinery. **oilcloth** *n.* **1** a fabric coated with white lead ground in oil. **2** an oilskin. **oil colour,** (*NAm.*) **oil color** *n.* (an) oil paint. **oil drum** *n.* a metal drum in which oil is transported. **oil engine** *n.* an internal-combustion engine which burns vaporized oil. **oiler** *n.* **1** an oil can for lubricating machinery etc. **2** (*NAm.*) an oil well. **3** (*pl.*) oilskins. **4** an oil tanker. **oilfield** *n.* a region where mineral oil is obtained. **oil-fired** *a.* burning oil as fuel. **oil lamp** *n.* a lamp that uses oil as fuel. **oilless** *a.* **oilman** *n.* (*pl.* oilmen) a person who works in the oil industry. **oil-meal** *n.* oilcake ground into meal. **oil of turpentine** *n.* a volatile oil distilled from turpentine, used for mixing paint, varnishes etc. and in medicine. **oil of vitriol** *n.* sulphuric acid. **oil of wintergreen** *n.* an aromatic oil orig. made from the leaves of the checkerberry, *Gaultheria procumbens*. **oil paint** *n.* (a) paint made by grinding a pigment in oil. **oil painting** *n.* **1** the art of painting with oil paints. **2** a painting in oil paints. **no oil painting** physically unattractive. **oil-palm** *n.* a palm tree bearing fruits yielding palm oil, esp. *Elaeis guineensis* of W Africa. **oil pan** *n.* an engine sump. **oil platform** *n.* a floating or fixed offshore structure which supports an oil rig. **oil-press** *n.* a machine for pressing the oil from seeds, nuts etc. **oil rig** *n.* an installation for drilling and extracting oil and natural gas. **oil-sand** *n.* a stratum of porous rock impregnated with petroleum. **oilseed** *n.* any of various oil-yielding seeds including sesame and sunflower seeds. **oil-shale** *n.* a shale from which mineral oils can be distilled. **oilskin** *n.* **1** cloth rendered waterproof by treatment with oil. **2** a garment of this cloth. **3** (*pl.*) a suit of such garments. **oil slick** *n.* a patch of floating oil, usu. pollutant. **oilstone** *n.* a fine-grained whetstone lubricated with oil before use. **oil tanker** *n.* a large vessel for transporting oil. **oil well** *n.* a boring made for petroleum. **oily** *a.* (*comp.* oilier, *superl.* oiliest) **1** consisting of, containing, covered with or like oil. **2** unctuous, smooth, insinuating. **oilily** *adv.* **oiliness** *n.*

oink (oingk) *n.* the grunt of a pig.

ointment (oint´mənt) *n.* a soft unctuous preparation applied to diseased or injured parts or used as a cosmetic; an unguent.

OK (ōkā´), **okay** *a., int., adv.* (*coll.*) quite correct, all right. *~v.t.* (*3rd pers. sing. pres.* **OK's, okays,** *pres.p.* **OK'ing, okaying,** *past, p.p.* **OK'd, OKed, okayed**) to authorize, to endorse, to approve. *~n.* (*pl.* **OKs, okays**) approval, sanction, agreement.

okey-doke (ōkidōk´), **okey-dokey** (-dō´ki) *int.* (*coll.*) used as a casual or amiable form of assent or agreement.

okapi (ōkah´pi) *n.* (*pl. in general* **okapi**, *in particular* **okapis**) a ruminant mammal, *Okapia johnstoni*, with a dark chestnut coat and stripes on the hindquarters.

okra (ō´krə, ok´-) *n.* an African plant, *Abelmoschus esculentus*, cultivated for its green pods used in curries, soups, stews etc.; also called *gumbo* and *ladies' fingers*.

-ol (ol) *suf.* denoting a chemical compound containing an alcohol, or (loosely) an oil, as *benzol, menthol, phenol*.

old (ōld) *a.* (*comp.* **older, elder,** *superl.* **oldest, eldest**) **1** advanced in years or long in existence. **2** not young, fresh, new or recent. **3** like an old person, experienced, thoughtful. **4** crafty, cunning, practised (at), confirmed (in). **5** decayed by process of time, worn, dilapidated. **6** stale, trite. **7** customary, wonted. **8** obsolete, effete, out of date, antiquated, matured. **9** of any specified duration. **10** belonging to a former period, made or established long ago, ancient, bygone, long cultivated or worked. **11** early, previous, former, quondam. **12** (of a language) denoting the earliest known form. **13** (*coll.*) used to express familiarity or endearment. **14** (*coll.*) used to emphasize (*high old time*). **old age** *n.* the latter part of life. **old-age pension** *n.* RETIREMENT PENSION (under RETIRE). **old-age pensioner** *n.* **old bean** *n.* (*dated sl.*) old fellow, old chap. **Old Bill** *n.* (*sl.*) the police. **old bird** *n.* (*sl.*) a wary person. **old boy** *n.* **1** (*also* **Old Boy**) a former pupil of a school. **2** (*coll.*) used as a friendly form of address to a man or boy. **3** (*coll.*) an elderly man. **old boy network** *n.* (*coll.*) a network of former pupils of public schools and universities, who can use their contacts for employment opportunities etc. **old country** *n.* the country of origin of an immigrant or their ancestors. **old dear** *n.* (*coll.*) **1** an elderly person, esp. a woman. **2** one's mother. **olden** *a.* old, ancient, bygone. **Old English** *n.* the English language in use before about 1150, also called *Anglo-Saxon*. **Old English Sheepdog** *n.* a large English breed of sheepdog with a shaggy coat. **olde worlde** (ōldi wœ´ldi) *a.* (*often derog.*) (emphatically) old-fashioned and quaint. **old-fashioned** *a.* **1** out of date, outmoded. **2** quaint. **Old French** *n.* the French language of the period before *c.*1400. **old fruit** *n.* (*coll.*) a form of address to a man. **old fustic** *n.* **1** a tropical American tree, *Chlorophora tinctoria*. **2** the wood of this. **old girl** *n.* **1** (*also* **Old Girl**) a former pupil of a school. **2** (*coll.*) used as a friendly form of address to a woman or girl. **3** (*coll.*) an elderly woman. **old gold** *n.* a dull brownish-gold colour. **old-gold** *a.* **old guard** *n.* the old or conservative members of a party etc. **old hand** *n.* a person who is skilled or practised at a trade or craft of any kind. **old hat** *a.* (*coll.*) **1** outdated, old-fashioned. **2** familiar and dull. **Old High German** *n.* High

German before *c.*1200. **Old Icelandic** *n.* the Icelandic language up to the 16th cent. **oldie** *n.* (*coll.*) an old thing or person (e.g. an old song or film). **oldish** *a.* **old lady** *n.* (*coll.*) **1** a female sexual partner, a wife. **2** a mother. **old lag** *n.* a habitual convict. **old maid** *n.* **1** (*derog.*) an unmarried woman of advanced years or unlikely ever to marry. **2** a card game in which an unpaired queen at the end of a hand scores against one. **old-maidish** *a.* **old man** *n.* (*coll.*) **1** a male sexual partner, a husband. **2** a father. **3** used as a friendly form of address to a man. **old man's beard** *n.* traveller's joy. **old master** *n.* a masterly painter or painting of former times, esp. of the 16th–18th cents. **old moon** *n.* the moon at the end of its course, before the new moon. **oldness** *n.* **Old Nick** *n.* (*coll.*) the Devil. **Old Norse** *n.* the language of Norway and its territories until the 14th cent. **old retainer** *n.* an old and faithful servant. **Old Saxon** *n.* the dialect of the period *c.*1200 from which Low German developed. **old school** *n.* those who adhere to past traditions or principles. *~a.* of or relating to past traditions or principles. **old school tie** *n.* **1** a tie sporting a public school's colours worn by its former pupils. **2** a symbol of the mutual allegiance of a group of (esp. privileged or upper class) people. **old soldier** *n.* a former soldier or veteran. **old stager** *n.* an old hand. **oldster** *n.* an old or elderly person. **Old Style** *n.* (*Hist.*) the Julian method of reckoning dates, used till 1582. **Old Testament** *n.* the part of the Christian Bible that covers the old or Mosaic dispensation. **old-time** *a.* **1** old, ancient. **2** old-fashioned. **old-timer** *n.* (*coll.*) **1** an old man. **2** a veteran. **3** a person who has remained in a situation for a long time. **old wives' tale** *n.* a legend, a foolish story. **old woman** *n.* (*coll.*) **1** a wife or mother. **2** a timid, fidgety or fussy man. **old-womanish** *a.* **old-womanishness** *n.* **Old World** *n.* the eastern hemisphere. **old-world** *a.* **1** old-fashioned, quaint. **2** belonging to old times. **old year** *n.* the year just ended or on the point of ending.

oleaceous (ōliā´shəs) *a.* of the plant family Oleaceae, which includes ash, privet, olive, jasmine and lilac.

oleaginous (ōliaj´inəs) *a.* oily, greasy, unctuous. **oleaginously** *adv.* **oleaginousness** *n.*

oleander (ōlian´də) *n.* a poisonous evergreen shrub, *Nerium oleander*, with lanceolate leaves and pink or white flowers.

oleaster (ōlias´tə) *n.* **1** any shrub or tree of the genus *Elaeagnus*, esp. *E. angustifolia*, also called *Russian olive*. **2** the true wild olive, *Olea oleaster*.

olefin (ō´lifin), **olefine** (-fēn) *n.* (*Chem.*) any one of a group of hydrocarbons containing two atoms of hydrogen to one of carbon. **olefinic** (-fin´-) *a.*

oleic (ōlē´ik) *a.* of, relating to or derived from oil. **oleic acid** *n.* an unsaturated liquid fatty acid that occurs as a glyceride in many fats and oils. **oleiferous** (-if´-) *a.*

oleo- (ō´liō), **ole-** *comb. form* oil.
oleograph (ō´liəgrahf) *n.* a picture printed in oil colours to resemble a painting.
oleomargarine (ōliōmah´jərēn) *n.* 1 a yellow fatty substance from beef tallow, used in margarine. 2 (*esp. N Am.*) margarine.
oleoresin (ōliōrez´in) *n.* a mixture of an essential oil and a resin.
olfactory (olfak´təri) *a.* of, relating to or used in smelling. **olfaction** *n.* the sense or process of smelling. **olfactive** *a.*
oligarch (ol´igahk) *n.* a member of an oligarchy. **oligarchal** (-gah´-) *a.* **oligarchic** (-gah´-), **oligarchical** *a.* **oligarchically** *adv.* **oligarchy** *n.* (*pl.* **oligarchies**) 1 a form of government in which power is vested in the hands of a small exclusive class. 2 the members of such a class. 3 a state so governed.
oligo- (ol´igō), **olig-** *comb. form* denoting few, small.
Oligocene (ol´igəsēn) *a.* (*Geol.*) of or relating to the age or strata between the Eocene and Miocene. ~*n.* this epoch or system.
olio (ō´liō) *n.* (*pl.* **olios**) 1 a mixed dish. 2 a mixture, a medley, a variety, a pot-pourri.
olive (ol´iv) *n.* 1 an evergreen tree of the genus *Olea*, with narrow leathery leaves and clusters of oval drupes yielding oil when ripe and eaten unripe as a relish, esp. *O. europaea* and *O. africana*. 2 the fruit of this tree. 3 its wood. 4 the colour of the unripe olive, a dull yellowish green or brown. 5 (*Anat.*) either of a pair of olive-shaped swellings in the medulla oblongata. 6 any olive-shaped gastropod of the genus *Oliva*, or its shell. 7 (*usu. in pl.*) a slice of beef or veal rolled with onions etc., stewed. ~*a.* of an olive colour. **olivaceous** (-vā´shəs) *a.* live-coloured. **olivary** *a.* olive-shaped, oval. **olive branch** *n.* 1 a branch of the olive tree as an emblem of peace. 2 something which indicates a desire for peace (e.g. a goodwill gesture, an offer of reconciliation). **olive crown** *n.* a garland of olive leaves as a symbol of victory. **olive drab** *n.* (*N Am.*) 1 a dull olive-green colour. 2 a fabric or garment of this colour, esp. a US army uniform. **olive-drab** *a.* **olive green** *a., n.* (of) a dull yellowish green or brown colour. **olive oil** *n.* an oil extracted from olives. **olivine** (ol´ivēn, -vēn´) *n.* a mineral silicate of magnesium and iron.
olla (ol´ə) *n.* 1 an olio. 2 an olla podrida. **olla podrida** (pədrē´də) *n.* 1 a Spanish dish consisting of meat chopped fine, stewed with vegetables. 2 a multifarious or incongruous mixture.
ology (ol´əji) *n.* (*pl.* **ologies**) 1 a science. 2 any of the sciences whose names end in *-ology*.
-ology -LOGY.
oloroso (olərō´sō) *n.* (*pl.* **olorosos**) a medium-sweet golden sherry.
Olympiad (əlim´piad) *n.* 1 a period of four years, being the interval between the celebrations of the Olympic Games, a method of chronology used from 776 BC to AD 394. 2 (a staging of) an international contest, esp. the modern Olympic Games. **Olympian** *a.* 1 of or relating to Mount Olympus, the home of the Greek gods; celestial. 2 magnificent, lofty, superb. 3 Olympic. ~*n.* 1 any one of the twelve Greek gods regarded as living on Olympus. 2 a godlike person. 3 (*esp. N Am.*) a contestant in the Olympic Games. **Olympic** *a.* of or relating to Olympia or the Olympic Games. **Olympic Games** *n.pl.* 1 the greatest of the Greek national games, held every four years at Olympia, in honour of Zeus. 2 a revival (since 1896) of this festival, an international four-yearly sports meeting. **Olympics** *n.pl.* the modern Olympic Games.
OM *abbr.* Order of Merit.
-oma (ō´mə) *comb. form* (*pl.* **-omas, -omata** (-tə)) denoting a tumour or growth.
omasum (ōmā´səm) *n.* (*pl.* **omasa** (-sə)) (*Zool.*) the third stomach of a ruminant.
ombre (om´bə) *n.* a game of cards, for two, three or five players, popular in the 17th and 18th cents.
ombré (om´brā) *a.* (of a fabric etc.) with colours shading into each other from light to dark.
ombudsman (om´budzmən) *n.* (*pl.* **ombudsmen**) an official investigator of complaints against government bodies or employees; in the UK, the Parliamentary Commissioner for Administration. **ombudswoman** *n.* (*pl.* **ombudswomen**) a female ombudsman.
-ome (ōm) *comb. form* denoting a mass or part.
omega (ō´migə, om´-) *n.* 1 the last letter of the Greek alphabet (ω, Ω). 2 the last of a series. 3 the conclusion, the end, the last stage or phase.
omelette (om´lit), **omelet** *n.* a flat dish made with beaten eggs cooked in fat, eaten plain or seasoned and filled with herbs, cheese etc.
omen (ō´mən) *n.* 1 an incident, object or appearance taken as indicating a good or evil event or outcome; a portent etc. 2 prognostication or prophetic signification. ~*v.t.* to prognosticate, to portend. **omened** *a.*
omentum (əmen´təm) *n.* (*pl.* **omenta** (-tə)) a fold of the peritoneum connecting the viscera with each other. **omental** *a.*
omicron (ōmī´kron, om´i-) *n.* the 15th letter of the Greek alphabet (o, O), the short o.
ominous (om´inəs) *a.* 1 threatening, portending evil. 2 of evil omen, inauspicious. 3 relating to or containing an omen. **ominously** *adv.* **ominousness** *n.*
omit (əmit´) *v.t.* (*pres.p.* **omitting**, *past, p.p.* **omitted**) 1 to leave out, not to include, insert or mention. 2 to neglect, to leave undone. **omissible** *a.* **omission** (-shən) *n.* 1 the act of omitting or fact of being omitted. 2 something omitted. **omissive** *a.* **omitter** *n.*
omni- (om´ni) *comb. form* universally, in all ways, of all things.
omnibus (om´nibəs) *n.* 1 (*formal*) a bus. 2 a volume containing reprints of a number of

works, usually by the same author. ~*a.* inclusive, embracing several or various items, objects etc.

omnicompetence (omnikom´pitəns) *n.* competence in all areas or matters. **omnicompetent** *a.*

omnidirectional (omnidirek´shənəl) *a.* (capable of) moving, sending or receiving in every direction (of radio waves, a radio transmitter or receiver).

omnipotent (omnip´ətənt) *a.* **1** almighty. **2** having unlimited power. **omnipotence, omnipotency** *n.* **omnipotently** *adv.*

omnipresent (omniprez´ənt) *a.* present in every place at the same time. **omnipresence** *n.*

omniscience (omnis´iəns) *n.* infinite knowledge. **omniscient** *a.* **omnisciently** *adv.*

omnium (om´niəm) *n.* in the Stock Exchange, the aggregate value of the different stocks in which a loan is funded. **omnium gatherum** (gah´dhərəm) *n.* (*coll.*) a miscellaneous collection or assemblage, a medley.

omnivore (om´nivaw) *n.* a creature that eats any type of available food (i.e. vegetable matter and meat). **omnivorous** (-niv´ərəs) *a.* **1** all-devouring. **2** feeding on anything available. **3** reading or making use of anything and everything. **omnivorously** *adv.* **omnivorousness** *n.*

omphalo- (om´fəlō) *comb. form* relating to the navel. **omphalos** (-os) *n.* **1** the boss of an ancient Greek shield. **2** a stone in the temple of Apollo at Delphi, believed to be the middle point or navel of the earth. **3** a central point, a hub.

on (on) *prep.* **1** in or as in contact with, esp. as supported by, covering, encircling or suspended from the upper surface or level of. **2** into contact with the upper surface of, or in contact with from above. **3** in the direction of, tending toward, arrived at, against. **4** exactly at, next in order to, beside, immediately after, close to. **5** about, concerning, in the act of, in the making, performance, support, interest, process etc., of. **6** attached to. **7** present on. **8** carried with. **9** taking regularly (e.g. a drug). **10** at the expense of. **11** at the date, time or occasion of. **12** in a condition or state of. **13** sustained by. **14** by means of. **15** on the basis of. **16** in the manner of. ~*adv.* **1** so as to be in contact and supported by, covering, environing, suspended from or adhering to something. **2** in advance, forward, in operation, action, movement, progress, persistence, or continuance of action or movement. **3** (*coll.*) drunk, nearly drunk. **4** taking place. **5** arranged. ~*a.* **1** denoting the side of a cricket field to the left of the batsman. **2** operating. **3** (*coll.*) wagered. **4** performing, broadcasting, playing (e.g. of a batsman). **5** definitely happening as arranged. **6** acceptable, possible, tolerable. ~*n.* in cricket, the on side. **off and on** intermittently. **on and off** intermittently. **on and on** ceaselessly, continuously. **to be on about** to talk about, esp. tediously. **to be on at** (*coll.*) to nag or grumble at. **to**

be on to 1 to be aware of, to have twigged on to or tumbled to. **2** to get in touch with. **to go on at someone** to nag someone. **to go on to** to advance, progress, move or travel to (a further level, position or place). **on-board** *a.* on, installed in or carried on a vehicle, ship etc. **oncoming** *n.* the coming on, advance or approach (of). ~*a.* approaching. **oncost** *n.* a supplementary or additional expense, an overhead. **onflow** *n.* an onward flow. **onglaze** *a.* (of painting etc.) done on a glazed surface. **ongoing** *a.* **1** unceasing, continuous. **2** in progress. **ongoingness** *n.* **on-line** *a.*, *adv.* (*Comput.*) (of a computer peripheral) under the control of the central processor. **onlooker** *n.* a spectator, a person who looks on. **onlooking** *a.* **on-off** *a.* **1** (of a switch) having two positions, 'on' or 'off'. **2** intermittent. **onrush** *n.* a rushing on, an attack, an onset. **on-screen** *a.* appearing on a cinema, television or VDU screen. ~*adv.* **1** on or by means of a screen. **2** within the view shown on a film scene. **onset** *n.* **1** an attack, an assault, an onslaught. **2** the outset, beginning. **on-set** *a.* taking place on the set of a play or film. **onshore** *a.*, *adv.* towards the land. **onside** *a.*, *adv.* (of a player) in football etc., in a legal position, not offside. **on-site** *a.* taking place or available on a site. **onslaught** *n.* a furious attack or onset. **on-stage** *a.* on a part of the stage that the audience can see. **on-stream** *a.*, *adv.* (of a manufacturing plant, industrial installation etc.) in operation. **on-street** *a.* (of parking) at the side of the street. **on time** *adv.* punctually. **on to, onto** *prep.* to and upon, to a position on or upon. **onward** *adv.* towards the front or a point in advance, forward, on. ~*a.* **1** moving, tending or directed forward. **2** advancing, progressive. **onwards** *adv.*

Usage note The written form *onto* is still often disapproved of, though it parallels *into* and is very common.

-on (on) *suf.* **1** (*Chem.*) **a** denoting a chemical compound, as in *interferon.* **b** denoting an inert gas, as in *neon.* **2** (*Physics*) **a** denoting an elementary particle, as in *electron*, *neutron.* **b** denoting a quantum, as in *photon.*

onager (on´əjə) *n.* a wild ass, esp. *Equus hemionus* of Asian deserts.

onanism (ō´nənizm) *n.* **1** masturbation. **2** the withdrawal of the penis from the vagina prior to ejaculation. **onanist** *n.* **onanistic** (-nis´-) *a.*

once (wŭns) *adv.* **1** one time. **2** one time only. **3** at one time, formerly, at some past time. **4** at any time, ever, at all. **5** at some future time, some time or other. ~*n.* one time. ~*a.* former. ~*conj.* as soon as. **all at once** all together, simultaneously, suddenly. **at once 1** immediately, without delay. **2** simultaneously. **for once** for one time or occasion only. **once again** another time. **once (and) for all 1** finally. **2** definitively. **once in a while** occasionally. **once more** another time. **once or twice** a few times. **once upon a time** at some past date or period (usu. beginning a fairytale).

once-over n. (coll.) a look of appraisal. **oncer** n.
1 (Hist., sl.) a £1 note. **2** (coll.) something that
only happens once. **3** (Austral., coll.) (an election
of) an MP likely to serve only one term.

onco- (ong´kō) comb. form (Med.) denoting a
tumour.

oncogene (ong´kəjēn) n. (Med.) any of several
genes capable of causing cancer. **oncogenic**
(-jen´-), **oncogenous** (-koj´-) a. causing tumours.
oncogenicity (-nis´-), **oncogenesis** n.

oncology (ongkol´əji) n. (Med.) the study of
tumours and cancers. **oncologist** n.

ondes martenot (ōd mah´tənō) n. (pl. **ondes
martenot**) (Mus.) an electronic keyboard instrument producing one note of variable pitch.

one (wŭn) a. **1** single, undivided. **2** being a unit
and integral. **3** a or an. **4** single in kind, the only,
the same. **5** this, some, any, a certain. ~pron. **1** a
person or thing of the kind implied, someone or
something, anyone or anything. **2** a person unspecified. **3** (coll.) any person, esp. the speaker.
4 I. ~n. **1** a single unit, unity. **2** the number 1, a
thing or person so numbered. **3** one o'clock. **4** a
single thing or person. **5** (coll.) a drink. **6** (coll.) a
joke or story. **7** a blow, a setback. **all in one**
combined. **at one** in accord or agreement. **for one**
being one; even if the only one. **for one thing** as
a single consideration. **one and all** jointly and
severally. **one and only 1** unique. **2** unequalled.
one way and another altogether, on balance. **to
be one for** to be an enthusiast for. **one another**
pron. each other. **one-armed** a. having or executed by one arm. **one-armed bandit** n. (coll.) a
fruit machine operated by a single lever. **one by
one** adv. singly, individually, successively. **one-
day event** n. an equestrian competition taking
place over one day and including dressage,
show-jumping and cross-country riding. **one-
dimensional** a. superficial, shallow, flat. **onefold**
a. **1** having only one member or constituent.
2 single. **3** single-minded, simple in character.
one for the road n. (coll.) a last drink before
leaving. **one-horse** a. **1** drawn by a single horse.
2 (coll.) of meagre capacity, resources or efficiency. **3** (coll.) insignificant, petty. **one-horse
race** n. a race or competition which one particular person is certain to win. **one in the eye** n. a
disappointment or rebuff (for). **one-liner** n. (coll.)
a short punchy joke or witticism. **one-man** a. employing, worked by or consisting of one person.
oneness n. **1** singleness. **2** singularity, uniqueness. **3** unity, union, agreement, harmony. **4**
sameness. **one-night stand** n. **1** a single performance at one venue. **2** (coll.) a sexual encounter or
relationship lasting one evening or night. **3** a
person engaging in such an encounter. **one-off** a.
(coll.) unique, unrepeated. ~n. a unique object,
product, event etc. **one-piece** n. a garment consisting of one piece of material (e.g. a swimsuit).
~a. made in one piece. **oner** (wŭn´ə) n. (sl.) **1** £1.
2 a striking, extraordinary or pre-eminent person
or thing. **one-sided** a. **1** having or happening

on one side only. **2** partial, unfair, favouring one
side of an argument, topic etc. **3** more developed
on one side than another. **one-sidedly** adv. **one-
sidedness** n. **one-step** n. a quick-stepping type of
ballroom dancing. **one-time** a. former. **one-to-one**
a. **1** corresponding, esp. in mathematics, pairing
each element of a set with only one of another.
2 of one person to or with another (a one-to-
one relationship). **one-track** a. single-track. **one-
track mind** n. a mind preoccupied with one
thing. **one-two** n. (coll.) **1** in boxing, two successive blows rapidly delivered. **2** a type of football pass from and then immediately back to a
player. **one-up** a. (coll.) having, or in, a position
of advantage. **one-upmanship** n. (coll.) the art of
gaining or keeping an advantage over someone.
one-way a. **1** denoting a traffic system which
allows vehicles to go in one direction only
through certain streets. **2** unilateral. **3** valid for
travel in one direction only.

Usage note The pronoun one is formal: in gen-
eralizations, you is considered less stilted and
can often be used instead (as in You should
always be careful, meaning everyone should
take care); in speaking of oneself, simple I is
preferable.

-one (ōn) suf. (Chem.) denoting certain chemical
compounds, esp. hydrocarbons, as in acetone,
ketone, ozone.

oneiric (ōnī´rik), **oniric** a. of or relating to
dreams.

oneiro- (ōnī´rō) comb. form of or relating to
dreams.

oneiromancy (ōnī´rəmansi) n. divination by
dreams.

onerous (ō´nərəs) a. **1** burdensome, heavy,
weighty, troublesome. **2** (Law) involving heavy
obligations. **onerously** adv. **onerousness** n.

oneself (wŭnself´) pron. **1** the reflexive and
emphatic form one. **2** one's normal or usual self.
by oneself alone, unaided. **to be oneself** to act in
one's normal manner.

onion (-n´yən) n. **1** a plant, Allium cepa, with an
underground bulb of several coats and a pungent
smell and flavour, much used in cookery. **2** other
species of the genus Allium. **to know one's
onions** (coll.) to be knowledgeable in one's subject or competent in one's job. **onion dome** n.
a bulb-shaped dome characteristic of Russian
church architecture. **onion-skin** n. a thin glazed
paper. **oniony** a.

only (ōn´li) a. **1** solitary, single or alone in its or
their kind. **2** the single, the sole. ~adv. **1** solely,
merely, exclusively, alone. **2** with no other,
singly. **3** wholly. **4** not otherwise. **5** not earlier.
~conj. **1** except that. **2** but. **3** were it not (that).
only too true regrettably true. **only too willing**
more than willing. **onliness** n. **only-begotten** a.
begotten as the sole issue. **only child** n. a child
without brothers or sisters.

o.n.o. abbr. or near(est) offer.

onomastic (onəmas'tik) *a.* of or relating to a name. **onomastics** *n.* the study of proper names.
onomatopoeia (onəmatəpē'ə) *n.* **1** the formation of words in imitation of the sounds associated with or suggested by the things signified. **2** the rhetorical use of a word so formed. **onomatopoeic, onomatopoetic** (-pōet'-) *a.* **onomatopoeically, onomatopoetically** *adv.*
-ont (ont) *comb. form* (*Biol.*) denoting an individual of a specified type, as in *symbiont*.
onto ON.
ontogenesis (ontōjen'əsis) *n.* the origin and development of the individual organism. **ontogenetic** (-net'-), **ontogenic** *a.* **ontogenetically, ontogenically** *adv.* **ontogeny** (ontoj'əni) *n.*
ontology (ontol'əji) *n.* the branch of metaphysics dealing with the theory of pure being or reality. **ontologic** (-loj'-), **ontological** *a.* **ontologically** *adv.* **ontologist** *n.*
onus (ō'nəs) *n.* (*pl.* **onuses**) **1** a duty, obligation or responsibility. **2** a burden.
onward, onwards ON.
onyx (on'iks) *n.* a variety of quartz resembling agate, with variously-coloured layers. **onyx marble** *n.* a calcium carbonate mineral resembling marble.
oo- (ō'ə, ō'ō) *comb. form* of or relating to ova or an egg.
oocyte (ō'əsīt) *n.* the unfertilized ovum or egg cell.
oodles (oo'dəlz) *n.pl.* (*coll.*) a great quantity, superabundance.
oof (oof) *n.* (*sl.*) money. **oofy** *a.* rich. **oofiness** *n.*
ooh (oo) *int.* used to express delight, surprise, pain, admiration etc. *~v.i.* to say 'ooh'.
oolite (ō'əlīt) *n.* **1** a limestone composed of grains or particles of sand like the roe of a fish. **2** an oolith. **oolith** *n.* any of the rounded grains of which oolite is composed. **oolitic** (-lit'-) *a.*
oompah (oom'pah) *n.* (*coll.*) an imitation or representation of the sound of a large brass musical instrument. *~v.i.* to make such a sound.
oomph (umf), **oomf** *n.* (*sl.*) **1** vigour, energy. **2** sexual attractiveness, magnetism.
-oon (oon) *suf.* forming nouns, as in *balloon, poltroon*.
oophorectomy (ōəfərek'təmi) *n.* (*pl.* **oophorectomies**) (*Med.*) a surgical operation to remove an ovary.
oops (oops, ups) *int.* (*coll.*) used to express surprise, dismay, apology, esp. on having dropped something. **oops-a-daisy** UPSYDAISY.
Oort cloud (awt) *n.* (*Astron.*) a cloud of small frozen bodies orbiting the solar system.
ooze (ooz) *n.* **1** wet mud, slime. **2** a slimy deposit consisting of foraminiferal remains, found on ocean beds. **3** the liquor of a tanning vat, consisting of an infusion of bark etc. **4** a gentle, sluggish flow, an exudation. *~v.i.* **1** to flow or pass gently. **2** to percolate (through the pores of a body etc.). *~v.t.* to emit or exude. **oozy** *a.* (*comp.* **oozier**, *superl.* **ooziest**). **oozily** *adv.* **ooziness** *n.*

op (op) *n.* (*coll.*) (an) operation.
o.p. *abbr.* **1** out of print. **2** overproof.
op. *abbr.* **1** operator. **2** (*Mus.*) opus.
opacify, opacity OPAQUE.
opal (ō'pəl) *n.* an amorphous, transparent, vitreous form of hydrous silica, several kinds of which are characterized by a play of iridescent colours and used as gems. **opalescent** (-les'ənt) *a.* characterized by a play of iridescent colours. **opalesce** *v.i.* **opalescence** *n.* **opal glass** *n.* a semi-translucent white glass. **opaline** (-līn) *a.* of, relating to or like opal. *~n.* **1** a translucent variety of glass. **2** a yellow chalcedony.
opaque (əpāk') *a.* (*comp.* **opaquer**, *superl.* **opaquest**) **1** impervious to rays of light, not transparent or translucent. **2** impenetrable to sight. **3** obscure, unintelligible. **4** obtuse, unintelligent. *~n.* **1** opacity. **2** darkness. **3** an opaque thing or substance, esp. a pigment used in photography. **opacify** (ōpas'ifī) *v.t., v.i.* (*3rd pers. sing. pres.* **opacifies**, *pres.p.* **opacifying**, *past, p.p.* **opacified**) to make or become opaque. **opacifier** *n.* **opacity** (ōpas'-) *n.* **opaquely** *adv.* **opaqueness** *n.*
op art (op) *n.* a type of abstract art employing shapes arranged to produce an optical illusion, esp. that of movement.
op. cit. (op sit') *abbr. opere citato*, in the work cited.
open (ō'pən) *a.* **1** not closed, obstructed or enclosed. **2** affording entrance, passage, or access. **3** unclosed, unshut, having any barrier, gate, cover etc. removed, withdrawn or unfastened. **4** uncovered, bare, unsheltered, exposed. **5** unconcealed, undisguised, manifest. **6** unrestricted, not exclusive or limited. **7** ready to admit, receive or be affected. **8** liable, subject (to). **9** unoccupied, vacant. **10** disengaged, free. **11** affording wide views. **12** widely spaced. **13** loosely woven, latticed or having frequent gaps or spaces. **14** generous, liberal. **15** frank, candid. **16** spread out, unfolded. **17** not closed or decided, debatable, moot. **18** (of weather) not frosty. **19** (*Mus.*) not stopped, or produced from an unstopped pipe, string etc. **20** enunciated with the vocal organs comparatively unclosed. **21** (of a syllable) not ended by a consonant. *~n.* **1** unenclosed space or ground. **2** public view. **3** (**Open**) in sport, a tournament open to any class of player. *~v.t.* **1** to make open. **2** to unclose. **3** to unfasten, unlock. **4** to remove the covering from. **5** to unfold, spread out, expand. **6** to free from obstruction or restriction, to make free of access. **7** to reveal, to make manifest or public. **8** to announce open. **9** to widen, to enlarge, to develop. **10** to make a start in, to begin. **11** to set going. **12** (*Law*) to state (a case) before calling evidence. *~v.i.* **1** to become unclosed or unfastened. **2** to crack, to fissure, to gape. **3** to unfold, to expand. **4** to develop. **5** to make a start, to begin. **to be open with** to speak frankly to. **to bring into the open** to disclose (what was hitherto hidden or secret). **to open fire** to begin firing

ammunition. **to open out 1** to unfold, to expand. **2** to develop. **3** to become communicative. **4** (*Naut.*) to bring into full view. **5** to accelerate. **6** to begin firing. **to open someone's eyes** to astonish or enlighten someone. **to open up 1** to make accessible. **2** to reveal. **3** to discover, to explore, to colonize, to make ready for trade. **4** to accelerate. **5** to begin firing. **6** to talk openly. **with open arms** enthusiastically. **openable** *a.* **open air** *n.* an unenclosed space outdoors. **open-air** *a.* outdoor. **open-and-shut** *a.* needing little deliberation, easily solved, simple. **open-armed** *a.* ready to receive with cordiality. **open book** *n.* someone or something easily understood. **opencast** *a.* (*Mining*) of or relating to a surface excavation. **open college** *n.* an adult-education college. **open day** *n.* a day when an institution (e.g. a school or university) is open to the public. **open door** *n.* **1** free admission or unrestricted access. **2** a policy of equal trading with all nations. **open-door** *a.* **open-ended** *a.* having no set limit or restriction on duration, time, amount etc. **opener** *n.* **1** a person who opens something. **2** an implement for opening bottles, tins etc. **3** (*coll.*) the first of a series of performances, events etc. **for openers** (*coll.*) to start with. **open-eyed** *a.* **1** watchful, vigilant, aware. **2** astonished, surprised. **open-faced** *a.* innocent-looking, having a candid expression. **open-handed** *a.* generous, liberal. **open-handedly** *adv.* **open-handedness** *n.* **open-hearted** *a.* frank, ingenuous, sincere, candid, unsuspicious. **open-heartedly** *adv.* **open-heartedness** *n.* **open-heart surgery** *n.* surgery performed on a heart while its functions are temporarily performed by a heart-lung machine. **open house** *n.* **1** hospitality proffered to all comers. **2** (*NAm.*) an open day. **open ice** *n.* ice through which ships can navigate. **opening** *a.* **1** that opens. **2** beginning, first in order, initial. *~n.* **1** the act of making or becoming open. **2** a gap, a breach, an aperture. **3** a beginning, a commencement, the first part or stage, a prelude. **4** (*Law*) a counsel's statement of a case before evidence is called. **5** in chess etc., a series of moves beginning a game. **6** a vacancy, an opportunity. **7** the two facing pages of an open book. **opening time** *n.* the time at which bars and public houses can legally begin selling alcohol. **open letter** *n.* a letter addressed to an individual but published in a newspaper. **openly** *adv.* **open market** *n.* a market situation of unrestricted commerce and free competition. **open-minded** *a.* accessible to ideas, unprejudiced, candid, unreserved. **open mind** *n.* **open-mindedly** *adv.* **open-mindedness** *n.* **open-mouthed** *a.* **1** gaping with stupidity, surprise etc. **2** greedy, ravenous. **3** clamorous. *~adv.* with the mouth open in surprise etc. **openness** *n.* **open-plan** *a.* having no, or few, dividing partitions or walls. **open prison** *n.* a prison allowing greater than usual freedom of movement. **open question** *n.* a question that is undecided. **open sandwich** *n.* a sandwich without an upper slice of bread, exposing its filling. **open sea** *n.* sea not enclosed or obstructed by land. **open season** *n.* **1** a period during which it is legal to hunt or angle for various species of game or fish. **2** an unrestricted period for an attack or attempt (on). **open secret** *n.* an apparently undivulged secret which is however generally known. **open sesame** *int.* a magic formula for opening a door, mentioned in the *Arabian Nights*. *~n.* **1** a key to a mystery etc. **2** an easy means of entry to a profession etc. **open shop** *n.* an establishment where union membership is not a condition of employment. **open-top, open-topped** *a.* (of a vehicle) not having a fixed roof. **open verdict** *n.* a verdict which names no criminal or records no cause of death. **openwork** *n.* ornamental work showing openings.

opera[1] (op´ərə) *n.* **1** a dramatic entertainment in which music forms an essential part. **2** a composition comprising words and music for this. **3** the branch of the musical and dramatic arts concerned with this. **4** a company which performs opera. **5** an opera house. **opera glasses** *n.pl.* small binoculars for use in theatres. **opera hat** *n.* a collapsible tall hat for men. **opera house** *n.* a theatre in which opera is performed. **operatic** (-rat´-) *a.* **operatically** *adv.* **operatics** *n.pl.* **1** (*usu. sing. in constr.*) the producing or study of operas. **2** a display of exaggerated behaviour. **operetta** (-ret´ə) *n.* a short opera of a light character. **operettist** *n.*

opera[2] OPUS.

operate (op´ərāt) *v.t.* **1** to work or control the working of. **2** to control, manage, run (a business, an organization etc.). *~v.i.* **1** to work, to act. **2** to produce an effect. **3** to exert power, force, strength, influence etc. **4** (*Med.*) to produce a certain effect on the human system. **5** to perform a surgical operation (on). **6** (*Mil.*) to carry out strategic movements. **7** to trade, to carry on a business. **operable** *a.* **1** suitable for or capable of being operated (on). **2** practicable. **operability** (-bil´-) *n.* **operand** (-rand) *n.* (*Math.*) that which is operated on, esp. a quantity in mathematics. **operant** *a.*, *n.* **operating** *n.* **operating system** *n.* a program that controls the running of a computer system. **operating table** *n.* a table on which a patient lies during a surgical operation. **operating theatre,** (*NAm.*) **operating room** *n.* a specially-fitted room where surgery is performed. **operation** (-ā´shən) *n.* **1** the act or process of operating. **2** working, action, mode of working. **3** activity, performance of a function. **4** effect. **5** a planned campaign or series of military or naval movements. **6** a surgical act performed with or without instruments upon the body, to remove diseased parts, extract foreign matter, remedy infirmities etc. **7** (*Math.*) the act of altering the value or form of a number or quantity by such a process as multiplication or division. **8** a commercial or financial transaction. **9** a procedure, a process. **operational** *a.* **1** ready for or capable of action or use. **2** working, in operation. **3** of or relating to military operations. **operationalize, operationalise** *v.t.* to express in operational terms. **operationally** *adv.* **operative** *a.* **1** acting, exerting force. **2** producing the proper result. **3** efficacious, effective. **4** relevant, significant. **5** of or relating to a surgical operation. **6** practical, as distinguished from theoretical or contemplative. **~n. 1** a (skilled) worker, an operator. **2** (*N Am.*) a private detective or secret agent. **operatively** *adv.* **operativeness** *n.* **operator** *n.* **1** a person who runs or operates a machine, a telephone switchboard, a business etc. **2** (*Math., Logic*) a symbol etc. representing a function to be performed. **3** a financial speculator. **4** (*coll.*) a skilled manipulator. **operon** (op´əron) *n.* (*Biol.*) a group of genes controlled by another gene.

operculum (əpœ´kūləm) *n.* (*pl.* **opercula** (-lə)) **1** (*Bot.*) a lid or cover as of the leaf of the pitcher plant, *Nepenthes*, or of the spore vessel in mosses. **2** (*Zool.*) **a** the gill cover in fishes. **b** the plate closing the mouth of many univalve shells. **c** any of various similar parts. **opercular, operculate** (-lət), **operculated** (-lātid) *a.*

operetta, operettist OPERA¹.

operon OPERATE.

ophidian (ofid´iən) *n.* a reptile of the suborder Serpentes (formerly Ophidia). **~a. 1** of or relating to this suborder. **2** snakelike.

ophthalmia (ofthal´miə) *n.* inflammation of the eye.

ophthalmic (ofthal´mik) *a.* of or relating to the eye. **ophthalmic optician** *n.* an optician qualified to test eyesight and prescribe and dispense glasses or lenses.

ophthalmo- (ofthal´mō), **ophthalm-** *comb. form* of or relating to the eye.

ophthalmology (ofthalmol´əji) *n.* the science of the eye, its structure, functions and diseases. **ophthalmologic** (-loj´-), **ophthalmological** *a.* **ophthalmologist** *n.*

ophthalmoscope (ofthal´məskōp) *n.* an instrument for examining the inner structure of the eye. **ophthalmoscopic** (-skop´ik), **ophthalmoscopical** *a.*

-opia (ō´piə) *comb. form* denoting a condition or defect of the eye, as in *myopia, diplopia.*

opiate¹ (ō´piət) *n.* **1** a medicine compounded with opium. **2** a narcotic. **3** anything serving to dull sensation, relieve uneasiness or induce sleep. **~a. 1** soporific, narcotic, soothing. **2** consisting of or containing opium.

opiate² (ō´piāt) *v.t.* **1** to treat with opium. **2** to dull the sensibility of.

opine (əpīn´) *v.i., v.t.* **1** to think, to suppose (that). **2** to express an opinion (that).

opinion (əpin´yən) *n.* **1** a judgement, conviction or belief falling short of positive knowledge. **2** a view regarded as probable. **3** views, sentiments, esp. those generally prevailing. **4** one's judge-

ment, belief or conviction with regard to a particular subject. **5** (*Law etc.*) the formal statement of a judge, counsel, physician or other expert on a question submitted to them. **6** estimation, reputation. **opinionated** (-ātid), **opinionative** *a.* **1** obstinate in one's opinions. **2** dogmatic, stubborn. **opinionless** *a.* **opinion poll** *n.* a Gallup poll.

opioid OPIUM.

opium (ō´piəm) *n.* **1** an addictive narcotic drug prepared from the dried exudation of the unripe capsules of the poppy, esp. the opium poppy. **2** anything considered to be stupefying or tranquillizing. **opioid** (-oid) *n.* a compound resembling an opiate in effects. **~a.** of or relating to such compounds. **opium den** *n.* a place where opium is sold or used as a narcotic. **opium poppy** *n.* a poppy, *Papaver somniferum*, with red, white, pink or purple flowers.

❌ **oponent** common misspelling of OPPONENT.

opoponax (əpop´ənaks) *n.* **1** the resinous juice from the root of *Opoponax chironium*, formerly used as a stimulant and in medicine. **2** a gum resin from the tree *Commiphora kataf*, used in perfumery. **3** SPONGE TREE (under SPONGE).

❌ **oposite** common misspelling of OPPOSITE.

opossum (əpos´əm) *n.* (*pl. in general* **opossum**, *in particular* **opossums**) **1** an American marsupial quadruped of the family Didelphidae, with a prehensile tail and a thumb on the hind foot, most species of which are arboreal and one aquatic. **2** a similar marsupial of Australia and New Zealand, esp. the phalanger.

opp. *abbr.* **1** opera (pl. of opus). **2** opposite.

❌ **opperation** common misspelling of OPERATION (under OPERATE).

oppo (op´ō) *n.* (*pl.* **oppos**) (*coll.*) a colleague or friend.

opponent (əpō´nənt) *n.* **1** a person who opposes, esp. in a debate, argument or contest. **2** an adversary, an antagonist. **~a.** opposing, opposed, antagonistic, adverse. **opponency** *n.* **opponent muscle** *n.* a muscle that brings two parts, such as a finger and thumb, into opposition.

opportune (op´ətūn, -tūn´) *a.* **1** situated, occurring, done etc. at a favourable moment. **2** seasonable, timely, well-timed. **3** fit, suitable. **opportunely** *adv.* **opportuneness** *n.* **opportunism** *n.* **1** utilizing circumstances or opportunities to gain one's ends, esp. the act or practice of shaping policy according to the needs or circumstances of the moment. **2** acceptance of what may be realized as a partial advance towards an ideal. **3** sacrifice of principle to expediency. **opportunist** *n.* **opportunistic** (-nis´tik) *a.* **opportunistically** *adv.* **opportunity** (-tū´-) *n.* (*pl.* **opportunities**) **1** a chance, an opening. **2** a favourable circumstance. **3** an opportune or convenient time or occasion. **opportunity knocks** an opportunity occurs.

oppose (əpōz´) *v.t.* **1** to set against, to place or bring forward as an obstacle, adverse force, counterpoise, contrast or refutation (to). **2** to set oneself against or act against, to resist, withstand, obstruct. **3** to object to, to dispute. **4** (*in p.p.*) opposite, contrasted. ~*v.i.* to offer resistance or objection. **as opposed to** in contrast with. **opposable** *a.* **1** able to be opposed. **2** (*Zool.*) (of the thumb) capable of facing the fingers on the same hand. **opposer** *n.*

opposite (op´əzit) *a.* **1** situated in front of or contrary in position (to). **2** fronting, facing. **3** antagonistic, adverse, contrary, diametrically different (to or from). **4** (*Bot.*) (of leaves on a stem) placed in pairs on contrary sides on the same horizontal plane. ~*n.* **1** a person who or something which is opposite. **2** a contrary thing or term. ~*adv.* in an opposite place or direction. ~*prep.* **1** opposite to. **2** as a co-star with (in a play, film etc.). **opposite angles** *n.pl.* the angles between the opposite sides of the intersection of two lines. **oppositely** *adv.* **oppositeness** *n.* **opposite number** *n.* **1** a person in the corresponding position on another side. **2** a counterpart. **opposite prompt** *n.* the side of a theatre stage to an actor's right; stage right. **opposite sex** *n.* women in relation to men, or vice versa.

opposition (opəzish´ən) *n.* **1** the act or state of opposing. **2** antagonism, resistance, hostility. **3** the state of being opposite. **4** antithesis, contrast, contrariety. **5** (**Opposition**) the chief parliamentary party opposed to the party in office. **6** (*Astron., Astrol.*) the situation of two heavenly bodies when their longitudes differ by 180°. **oppositional** *a.*

oppress (əpres´) *v.t.* **1** to tyrannize over, to keep subservient. **2** to inflict hardships, cruelties, or exactions upon, to govern cruelly or unjustly. **3** to lie heavy on the mind of, to weigh down. **4** to overburden. **oppression** (-shən) *n.* **oppressive** *a.* **1** overbearing, exacting, tyrannous. **2** hard to tolerate. **3** (of the weather) close, muggy, sultry. **oppressively** *adv.* **oppressiveness** *n.* **oppressor** *n.*

opprobrium (əprō´briəm) *n.* **1** disgrace, infamy, ignominy, obloquy. **2** a cause of this. **opprobrious** *a.* abusive, vituperative, scornful. **opprobriously** *adv.*

oppugn (əpūn´) *v.t.* (*formal*) to oppose, to dispute, to call in question. **oppugner** *n.*

❌ **opress** common misspelling of OPPRESS.

opt (opt) *v.i.* to choose, to make a choice (for, between). **to opt out 1** to choose not to be involved in something. **2** (of a school, hospital etc.) to choose no longer to be under the control or management of a local authority. **opt-out** *n.* **1** the action of opting out. **2** an instance of this.

optative (op´tətiv, optā´-) *a.* (*Gram.*) expressing a wish or desire. ~*n.* **1** the optative mood. **2** a verbal form in this mood. **optatively** *adv.* **optative mood** *n.* a set of verb forms expressing a wish.

optic (op´tik) *a.* of or relating to vision or the eye. ~*n.* **1** a lens. **2** a glass device fixed to the neck of a bottle to measure out spirits. **3** (*facet.*) an eye.

optical *a.* **1** of or relating to sight, vision or the eye. **2** of or relating to optics. **optical brightener** *n.* any fluorescent substance used to make laundry whiter. **optical character recognition** *n.* the scanning and identification of printed characters using photoelectric means. **optical disk** *n.* (*Comput.*) an inflexible non-magnetic disk on which information is stored digitally by laser. **optical fibre**, (*N Am.*) **optical fiber** *n.* a thin glass fibre which can transmit light, used in communications and in fibre optics. **optical illusion** *n.* **1** an object which has an appearance so like something else that the eye is deceived. **2** an instance of such deception. **optically** *adv.* **optical microscope** *n.* a microscope used to view objects by the light it emits, as opposed to an electron microscope. **optical telescope** *n.* a telescope used to view objects by the light it emits, as opposed to a radio telescope. **optician** (-tish´ən) *n.* a person who prescribes or dispenses spectacles and contact lenses to correct eye defects. **optic lobe** *n.* the dorsal lobe in the brain, concerned with sight. **optic nerve** *n.* a nerve of sight connecting the retina with the brain. **optics** *n.* the science of the nature, propagation, behaviour and function of light.

optimism (op´timizm) *n.* **1** a sanguine temperament, disposition to take a hopeful view of things. **2** the view that the existing state of things is the best possible, orig. expounded by Leibnitz from the postulate of the omnipotence of God. **3** the view that the universe is tending towards a better state and that good must ultimately prevail. **optimist** *n.* **optimistic** (-mis´-) *a.* **optimistically** *adv.*

optimum (op´timəm) *n.* (*pl.* **optima** (-mə), **optimums**) **1** the most favourable condition. **2** the best compromise. ~*a.* (of conditions, circumstances etc.) best or most favourable. **optimal** *a.* optimum. **optimally** *adv.* **optimize, optimise** *v.t.* **1** to make the most of. **2** to organize or execute with maximum efficiency. ~*v.i.* to be an optimist. **optimization** (-zā´shən) *n.*

option (op´shən) *n.* **1** the right, power or liberty of choosing. **2** a choice, a preference. **3** the thing chosen or preferred. **4** the right to deliver or call for the delivery of securities, land, commodities etc. at a specified rate within a specified time. **to have no option but to** to have to. **to keep/ leave one's options open** to refrain from committing oneself. **optional** *a.* open to choice; not compulsory. **optional extra** *n.* an additional item which can be bought as part of another purchase. **optionality** (-nal´-) *n.* **optionally** *adv.*

opto- (op´tō), **opt-** *comb. form* of or relating to sight or optics.

optometer (optom´itə) *n.* an instrument for ascertaining the range of vision and other powers of the eye. **optometric** (-met´-) *a.* **optometrist** *n.* a person who practises optometry. **optometry** *n.* the occupation of an optician.

opulent (op´ūlənt) *a.* **1** rich, wealthy, affluent. **2**

abounding (in). **3** abundant, profuse, copious. **opulence** *n.* **opulently** *adv.*

opuntia (əpŭn´shiə, op-, ō-) *n.* a cactus of the genus *Opuntia*, the prickly pear.

opus (ō´pəs, op´-) *n.* (*pl.* **opera** (op´ərə), **opuses**) (*esp. Mus.*) **1** a work, esp. a musical composition. **2** a work numbered in order of publication.

OR *abbr.* other ranks.

or (aw) *conj.* **1** a disjunctive introducing an alternative. **2** used to connect synonyms, words explaining, correcting etc.

-or (ə) *suf.* denoting agency or condition, as *actor*, *author*, *creator*, *equator*.

orache (or´ich), **orach** *n.* a plant, *Atriplex hortensis*, sometimes used as a vegetable; also called *saltbush*.

oracle (or´əkəl) *n.* **1** the answer of a god or inspired priest to a request for advice or prophecy. **2** the agency or medium giving such responses. **3** the seat of the worship of a deity where these were sought. **4** a person of profound wisdom, knowledge or infallible judgement. **5** an utterance regarded as profoundly wise, authoritative or infallible. **6** a mysterious, ambiguous or obscure utterance. ~*v.i.* to speak as an oracle. ~*v.t.* to utter as an oracle. **oracular** (orak´ū-) *a.* **oracularity** (-lar´-) *n.* **oracularly** *adv.*

oracy (aw´rəsi) *n.* skill in spoken communication and self-expression.

oral (aw´rəl) *a.* **1** spoken, not written, by word of mouth. **2** of, at or near the mouth. **3** taken by mouth. **4** (*Psych.*) of or relating to the early stage of infantile sexual development when gratification is obtained from eating and sucking. ~*n.* (*coll.*) an oral examination. **orally** *adv.* **oral sex** *n.* sex involving contact between one person's mouth and another's genitals.

Usage note In standard English *oral* is pronounced the same as *aural*, and the two are easily confused or liable to misinterpretation. Some people try to distinguish them by giving *aural* the pronunciation (ow´-), but this is not a generally accepted practice. In some dialects they are in fact differentiated, with *oral* pronounced (or´-).

Orange (or´ənj) *a.* of or relating to the Orangemen. **Orangeism** *n.* the practices or principles of Orangemen. **Orangeman** *n.* (*pl.* **Orangemen**) a member of a society formed in 1795 to uphold the Protestant ascendancy in Ireland.

orange (or´ənj) *n.* **1** the large roundish cellular pulpy fruit of *Citrus aurantium* or *C. sinensis*. **2** (*also* **orange tree**) any of various trees or shrubs of the genus *Citrus* yielding this fruit. **3** a fruit or plant resembling this. **4** the colour of the fruit, reddish-yellow. ~*a.* of the colour of an orange. **orangeade** (-jād´) *n.* a fizzy drink flavoured with orange. **orange peel** *n.* **1** the rind of an orange. **2** a pitted effect on porcelain. **orangery** (-jəri) *n.*

(*pl.* **orangeries**) a building designed for the cultivation of orange trees in a cool climate. **orange squash** *n.* a concentrated orange drink. **orange stick** *n.* a thin piece of orange-tree wood used for manicure purposes.

orang-utan (orangutan´), **orang-outang** (-tang´), **orangutan**, **ourang-outang** *n.* a large, red-haired, arboreal anthropoid ape, *Pongo pygmaeus*, of Borneo and Sumatra.

oration (ərā´shən) *n.* a formal speech, dealing with some important subject in elevated language. **orate** *v.i.* (*esp. facet. or derog.*) **1** to make an oration. **2** to talk at length. **orator** (or´ə-) *n.* **1** a person who delivers an oration. **2** an eloquent speaker. **oratorial** (orətaw´ri-), **oratorical** (-tor´i-) *a.* **oratorically** *adv.* **oratory**[1] (or´ə-) *n.* **1** the art of public speaking, rhetoric. **2** eloquence. **3** rhetorical language.

oratorio (orətaw´riō) *n.* (*pl.* **oratorios**) a musical composition for voices and instruments, usually semi-dramatic in character, having a scriptural theme.

oratory[1] ORATION.

oratory[2] (or´ətəri) *n.* (*pl.* **oratories**) **1** a small chapel, esp. one for private devotions. **2** (*usu.* **Oratory**) any of several congregations of Roman Catholic priests living in a community without vows, the first of which was established at Rome by St Philip Neri in 1564 to preach and hold services among the people. **oratorian** (-taw´ri-) *a.*, *n.*

orb (awb) *n.* **1** a sphere, a globe. **2** (*poet.*) a heavenly body. **3** (*poet.*) an eye or eyeball. **4** the globe forming part of the regalia. **orbed** *a.* in the form of an orb. **orbicular** (-bik´ū-) *a.* **orbicularity** (-lar´-) *n.* **orbicularly** *adv.* **orbiculate** (-lət) *a.* (*Bot.*) (of a leaf etc.) circular.

orbit (aw´bit) *n.* **1** the path of a celestial body around another. **2** the path of an electron around the nucleus of an atom. **3** a course or sphere of action, a career. **4** the bony cavity of the eye. **5** the ring or border round the eye in insects, birds etc. ~*v.t.* (*pres.p.* **orbiting**, *past*, *p.p.* **orbited**) **1** to move in a curved path around. **2** to circle (a planet etc.) in space. **3** to send into an orbit. ~*v.i.* to revolve in an orbit. **orbital** *a.* **1** (*Astron.*) of an orbit or orbits. **2** (of a road) going around a town. **orbital sander** *n.* a sander with a circular motion. **orbiter** *n.* a spacecraft designed to orbit a planet etc.

orc (awk) *n.* a whale of the genus *Orca*, esp. *O. gladiator*, a grampus. **orca** (aw´kə) *n.* the killer whale.

Orcadian (awkā´diən) *a.* of or relating to the Orkney Islands. ~*n.* a native or inhabitant of the Orkney Islands.

orchard (aw´chəd) *n.* an enclosure containing fruit trees, or a plantation of these. **orchardist** *n.*

orchestra (aw´kistrə) *n.* **1** a body of musicians playing a variety of instruments, performing in a theatre, concert room etc. **2** (*also* **orchestra pit**) the place for the band, or band and chorus, in a theatre, concert room etc. **3** (*NAm.*) the stalls in a theatre. **orchestral** (-kes´-) *a.* **orchestrally** *adv.* **orchestra stalls** *n.pl.* seats just behind the orchestra in a theatre. **orchestrate** *v.t.* **1** to compose or arrange (music) for an orchestra. **2** to arrange, organize etc. to achieve the best effect. **orchestration** (-trā´shən) *n.* **orchestrator** *n.*

orchid (aw´kid) *n.* **1** any of a large order of monocotyledonous plants, the Orchidaceae, of which the genus *Orchis* is the type, characterized by tuberous roots and flowers usually of a fantastic shape and brilliant colours in which the pistils and stamens are united with the floral axis. **2** a flower of such a plant. **orchidaceous** (-dā´shəs), **orchidean** (-kid´i-), **orchideous** *a.* **orchidist** *n.* **orchidology** (-dol´-) *n.* the knowledge of orchids. **orchis** (-kis) *n.* (*pl.* **orchises**) **1** any orchid of the genus *Orchis*, usu. having pink, red or purple flowers and fleshy tubers. **2** any of various wild orchids.

orchido- (aw´kidō), **orchid-** *comb. form* (*Med.*) denoting a testicle or testicles.

orchil (aw´chil, -kil), **archil** (ah´chil, -kil), **orchilla** (-chil´ə, -kil´ə) *n.* **1** a violet, purple or red dye obtained from various lichens, esp. *Roccella tinctoria.* **2** this and other species of lichen yielding such dye.

orchis ORCHID.

orchitis (awkī´tis) *n.* (*Med.*) inflammation of the testicles.

ordain (awdān´) *v.t.* **1** to set apart for an office or duty, to appoint and consecrate, to confer holy orders on. **2** to decree, to establish, to destine. **ordainable** *a.* **ordainer** *n.* **ordainment** *n.*

ordeal (awdēl´) *n.* an experience testing endurance, patience, courage etc.

order (aw´də) *n.* **1** regular or methodical disposition or arrangement. **2** sequence, succession, esp. as regulated by a system or principle. **3** normal, proper or right condition. **4** a state of efficiency, a condition suitable for working. **5** tidiness, absence of confusion or disturbance. **6** established state of things, general constitution of the world. **7** customary mode of procedure, esp. the rules and regulations governing an assembly or meeting. **8** a rule, regulation. **9** a mandate, an injunction, an authoritative direction. **10** kind, sort, quality. **11** a class or body of persons united by some common purpose. **12** (*also* **Order**) a fraternity of monks or friars, or formerly of knights, bound by the same rule of life. **13** a grade of the Christian ministry. **14** (*pl.*) the clerical office or status. **15** (*also* **Order**) a body usu. instituted by a sovereign, graded like the medieval orders of knights, to which distinguished persons may be admitted as an honour. **16** the insignia worn by members of this. **17** any of the nine grades of angels and archangels. **18** a system of parts, ornaments and proportions of columns etc. distinguishing styles of architec-

ture, esp. classical, as the Doric, Ionic, Corinthian, Tuscan and Composite. **19** (*Math.*) degree of complexity. **20** (*Biol.*) a division below that of class and above that of family and genus. **21** (*esp. NAm.*) a portion or helping in a restaurant etc. ~*v.t.* **1** to direct, to command. **2** to instruct (a person, firm etc.) to supply goods or perform work. **3** to ordain. **4** to ordain. **5** to manage. **6** to arrange beforehand. **7** to direct the supplying, doing or making of. **8** to put in order. **by order** according to direction by proper authority. **in bad order** not working properly. **in good order** working properly. **in/on the order of** approximately the size or quantity specified. **in order 1** properly or systematically arranged. **2** in due sequence. **3** ready and fit for use. **in order that** so that. **in order to 1** to the end that. **2** so as to. **on order** having been ordered but not yet arrived. **out of order 1** disarranged. **2** untidy. **3** not consecutive. **4** not systematically arranged. **5** not fit for working or using. **6** (*coll.*) (of behaviour) not acceptable. **to order** according to, or in compliance with, an order. **to order about 1** to send from one place to another. **2** to domineer over. **to take orders 1** to accept commissions, commands etc. **2** to be ordained. **order book** *n.* a book, usu. with counterfoils and detachable leaves, on which orders for goods, work etc. are written. **orderer** *n.* **order form** *n.* a printed paper with blanks for a customer to enter goods to be supplied. **Order in Council** *n.* a sovereign's order on the advice of the Privy Council. **orderless** *a.* **orderly**[1] *a.* **1** in order. **2** methodical, regular. **3** keeping or disposed to keep order, free from disorder or confusion. **4** of or relating to orders and their execution. **orderliness** *n.* **order of magnitude** *n.* the approximate size of something, esp. measured in powers of ten. **order of the day** *n.* **1** business arranged beforehand, esp. the programme of business in a legislative assembly. **2** the prevailing state of things. **order paper** *n.* a paper on which the order of business, esp. in Parliament, is written or printed.

orderly[1] ORDER.

orderly[2] (aw´dəli) *n.* (*pl.* **orderlies**) **1** (*Mil.*) a soldier who attends on an officer to carry orders, messages etc. **2** a male hospital attendant. **orderly book** *n.* (*Mil.*) a book for regimental orders. **orderly officer** *n.* (*Mil.*) the officer of the day. **orderly room** *n.* (*Mil.*) a room in barracks used as the office for company or regimental business.

ordinal (aw´dinəl) *a.* **1** denoting order or position in a series. **2** (*Biol.*) of or relating to an order. ~*n.* **1** an ordinal number. **2** a book containing orders, rules, rubrics etc., esp. forms for ordination in the Church of England. **ordinal number** *n.* a number denoting order or position in a series, e.g. first, second.

ordinance (aw´dinəns) *n.* **1** an order, decree or regulation laid down by a constituted authority. **2** an established rule, rite or ceremony etc.

ordinand (-nənd) *n.* a person preparing for holy orders.

Usage note The nouns *ordinance, ordnance* and *ordonnance* should not be confused: an *ordinance* is an order or decree, *ordnance* heavy artillery or military stores, and *ordonnance* systematic arrangement.

ordinary (aw´dinəri) *a.* **1** usual, habitual, customary, regular, normal, not exceptional or unusual. **2** commonplace. **3** mediocre. **4** having immediate or ex officio jurisdiction. **5** not good-looking, plain. ~*n.* (*pl.* **ordinaries**) **1** a rule or order, as of the Mass. **2** a bishop or a bishop's deputy, esp. sitting as an ecclesiastical judge. **3** (*Her.*) any of the simplest and commonest charges, esp. the chief, pale, fesse, bend, bar, chevron, cross and saltire. **in ordinary** in actual and constant service. **in the ordinary way** in normal circumstances. **out of the ordinary** exceptional. **ordinarily** *adv.* **ordinariness** *n.* **ordinary grade** *n.* (a pass in) an examination at the lower of the two main levels of the Scottish Certificate of Education. **ordinary level** *n.* (*Hist.*) (a pass in) an examination at the lower of the two main levels of the General Certificate of Education in England and Wales. **ordinary seaman** *n.* a sailor not fully qualified as able seaman. **ordinary share** *n.* a share (in a company) which pays dividends according to profit only after the claims of preference shares have been met.

ordinate (aw´dinət) *n.* (*Math.*) a line drawn from a point parallel to one of a pair of reference lines, called the coordinate axes, and meeting the other. **ordination** (-ā´shən) *n.* **1** the act of ordaining. **2** arrangement in order, classification. **3** appointment, ordainment. **ordinee** (-nē´) *n.* a person who is newly ordained.

ordnance (awd´nəns) *n.* **1** heavy guns, cannon, artillery. **2** the department of public service dealing with military stores and equipment, except those of or relating to the quartermaster's department. **Ordnance Survey** *n.* the (Government map-making body responsible for the) survey of Great Britain and Northern Ireland.

Usage note See note under ordinance.

ordonnance (aw´dənəns) *n.* the arrangement of the elements of a picture, building, literary composition etc.

Usage note See note under ordinance.

Ordovician (awdōvish´iən) *n.* (*Geol.*) the middle period of the lower Palaeozoic era, which followed the Cambrian period. ~*a.* of or relating to this era.

ordure (aw´dyə) *n.* excrement, dung, filth.

ore (aw) *n.* a natural mineral substance from which metal may be profitably extracted.

öre (œ´rə) *n.* (*pl.* **öre**) a monetary unit in Sweden.

øre (œ´rə) *n.* (*pl.* **øre**) a monetary unit in Norway and Denmark.

oregano (origah´nō, oreg´ənō) *n.* (*pl.* **oreganos**) the (usu. dried) leaves of wild marjoram, *Origanum vulgare*, used as a culinary herb.

oreography orography.

oreweed oarweed (under oar).

orfe (awf) *n.* a small yellow or golden-coloured fish, *Leuciscus idus*, of the carp family.

organ (aw´gən) *n.* **1** a musical wind instrument composed of an assemblage of pipes sounded by means of a bellows and played by keys. **2** a wind instrument having some resemblance to this, played by keys or other mechanism. **3** an instrument. **4** a barrel organ. **5** a part of an animal or vegetable body performing some definite vital function. **6** a medium or agent of communication etc., such as a newspaper or other periodical. **organ-blower** *n.* a person or mechanism working an organ's bellows. **organ-grinder** *n.* a player on a barrel organ. **organist** *n.* a person who plays a church or other organ. **organ loft** *n.* **organ pipe** *n.* any one of the sounding-pipes of a pipe organ. **organ-screen** *n.* a screen or partition, usu. between the nave and the choir, on which the organ is placed in a large church. **organ stop** *n.* **1** the handle by which a set of pipes in an organ is put in or out of action. **2** the set of pipes or reeds of a certain quality controlled by this.

organdie (aw´gəndi), (*N Am.*) **organdy** *n.* (*pl.* **organdies**) a stiff, light transparent muslin.

organelle (awgənel´) *n.* (*Biol.*) a unit in a cell having a particular structure and function.

organic (awgan´ik) *a.* **1** of or relating to a bodily organ or organs. **2** of, relating to or of the nature of organisms or plants or animals. **3** having organs. **4** (*Med.*) (of diseases etc.) of, relating to or affecting an organ or organs. **5** (*Chem.*) (of a compound etc.) of, relating to or belonging to the class formed from carbons. **6** (of vegetables etc.) grown without artificial fertilizers, pesticides etc. **7** structural, fundamental, inherent, not accidental. **8** organized, systematic, coordinated. **9** of or relating to an organized system. **10** vital, not mechanical. **11** formed or developed using natural factors, rather than to a plan. **organically** *adv.* **organic chemistry** *n.* the study of the compounds of carbon. **organicism** (-sizm) *n.* (*Biol.*) the theory that all things in nature have an organic basis. **organic law** *n.* a law stating a country's constitution.

organism (aw´gənizm) *n.* **1** an organized body consisting of mutually dependent parts fulfilling functions necessary to the life of the whole. **2** an animal or a plant. **3** organic structure. **4** a whole having mutually related parts analogous to those of a living body.

organize (aw´gənīz), **organise** *v.t.* **1** to put into proper working order. **2** to arrange or dispose (things or a body of people) in order to carry out some purpose effectively. **3** to enlist (workers etc.) in a trade union. **4** to correlate the parts of and make into an organic whole. **5** to make organic, to make into an organism, to make into

a living part, structure or being. **organizable** *a.*
organization (-zā´shən) *n.* **1** the act of organizing.
2 the state of being organized. **3** an organized
system, body or society. **4** tidiness, method.
organizational *a.* **organizationally** *adv.* **organi-**
zer *n.* **1** a person who organizes. **2** a thing used
for organizing, esp. a personal organizer.
organo- (aw´gənō, -gan´-) *comb. form* **1** (*Biol.*)
organ. **2** (*Chem.*) organic.
organophosphate (awganōfos´fāt) *n.* an
organic compound that contains phosphate.
organotherapy (awgənōther´əpi) *n.* the treatment of disease by the administration of one or
more hormones in which the body is deficient.
organza (awgan´zə) *n.* a thin transparent fabric
of silk, rayon or nylon.
organzine (aw´gənzēn) *n.* silk thread made of
several threads twisted together in a direction
contrary to that of the strands; thrown silk.
orgasm (aw´gazm) *n.* **1** the culminating excitement in the sexual act. **2** a paroxysm of excitement or passion. ~*v.i.* to experience an orgasm.
orgasmic (-gaz´-) *a.* **orgasmically** *adv.* **orgastic**
(-gas´-) *a.* **orgastically** *adv.*
orgy (aw´ji) *n.* (*pl.* **orgies**) **1** a wild revel, a
drunken carouse, esp. involving indiscriminate
sexual activity. **2** a bout of indulgence. **3** (*pl.*)
revelry, debauchery. **orgiastic** (-as´-) *a.*
-orial -ORY¹.
oriel (aw´riəl) *n.* **1** a projecting polygonal recess
with a window or windows, usu. built out from
an upper storey and supported on corbels or a
pier. **2** (*also* **oriel window**) the window of such a
structure.
orient (aw´riənt) *n.* **1** (**Orient**) the East, the
countries east of S Europe and the
Mediterranean. **2** (*poet.*) (**Orient**) the eastern sky.
3 the peculiar lustre of a pearl of the finest
quality. **4** an orient pearl. ~*a.* **1** (*poet.*) eastern,
Oriental. **2** lustrous, perfect, without a flaw (of
pearls). ~*v.t.* **1** to adjust, align or bring into
position. **2** to determine the position of, with
reference to the east and accordingly to all points
of the compass. **3** to place (a church) so that the
chancel points due east. **4** to bury (a body) with
feet towards the east. **5** to find the bearings of. **6**
to find or correct one's mental relations and
principles. ~*v.i.* to turn or face towards the east.
to orient oneself to check one's position
according to one's surroundings. **oriental** (-en´-)
a. **1** (*also* **Oriental**) situated in, of or relating to
the East or the (esp. Asian) countries east of S
Europe and the Mediterranean. **2** (*also* **Oriental**)
derived from or characteristic of the civilization
etc. of the East. ~*n.* (*also* **Oriental**) a native or
inhabitant of the East. **orientalism** *n.* **orientalist**
n. **orientality** (-tal´-) *n.* **orientalize**, **orientalise**
v.t., *v.i.* **orientalization** (-zā´shən) *n.* **orientally**
adv.

Usage note Using *Oriental* of people can give
offence, and is best avoided.

orientate (aw´riəntāt) *v.t.*, *v.i.* ORIENT. **orientation**
(-tā´shən) *n.* **1** the act of orienting oneself. **2** the
state of being oriented. **3** (*Psych.*) awareness of
one's temporal, social and physical situation. **4**
an introduction or briefing. **orientational** *a.*
orientational course *n.* (*esp. N Am.*) a course
giving an introduction.
orienteering (awrientiə´ring) *n.* a sport in
which the contestants race cross-country
following checkpoints located by a map and
compass. **orienteer** *v.i.* to take part in orienteering. ~*v.i.* a person who orienteers.
orifice (or´ifis) *n.* an opening or aperture, as of a
tube etc.
origami (origah´mi) *n.* the (traditionally Japanese) art of paper folding.
origanum (ərig´ənəm) *n.* any plant of the genus
Origanum, esp. wild marjoram.
origin (or´ijin) *n.* **1** the beginning, commencement or rise (of anything). **2** derivation, a source.
3 extraction, a person's ancestry. **4** ground,
foundation, occasion. **5** (*Math.*) the point where
coordinate axes intersect. **6** (*Anat.*) the point of
attachment of a muscle, opposite to its insertion.
original (ərij´-) *a.* **1** of or relating to the origin,
beginning or first stage. **2** first, primary, primitive; initial, innate. **3** not copied or imitated, not
produced by translation; fresh, novel. **4** able to
devise, produce, think or act for oneself; inventive, creative. ~*n.* **1** the pattern, the archetype,
the first copy. **2** that from which a work is copied
or translated. **3** an eccentric person. **4** origin,
derivation, cause, primitive stock, ancestry.
original instrument *n.* a musical instrument, or a
copy of this, that dates from the time of the
music played on it. **originality** (-nal´-) *n.* **origin-**
ally *adv.* **original print** *n.* a print made directly
from a woodcut, etching etc. **original sin** *n.*
(*Theol.*) **1** the innate depravity of humankind. **2**
the sin of Adam in eating the forbidden fruit.
originate (ərij´-) *v.t.* **1** to cause to begin, to bring
into existence. **2** to be the origin of. ~*v.i.* to have
origin (in, from or with). **origination** (-ā´shən) *n.*
originative *a.* **originator** *n.*
orinasal (awrinā´zəl) *a.* of, relating to or sounded
by the mouth and nose. ~*n.* a vowel sounded by
the mouth and nose, such as the nasal vowels in
French.
oriole (aw´riōl, -riəl) *n.* **1** any bird of the genus
Oriolus, esp. *O. oriolus*, the golden oriole. **2** any
bird of the genus *Icterus*, such as the Baltimore
oriole, *I. galbula.*
orison (or´izon) *n.* (*usu. pl.*, *formal*) a prayer, a
supplication.
-orium (aw´riəm) *suf.* denoting a place where
something specific is done, as *sanatorium.*
orlop (aw´lop), **orlop deck** *n.* the lowest deck of a
vessel having three or more decks.
ormer (aw´mə) *n.* an edible mollusc, esp.
Haliotis tuberculata; also called *sea-ear.*
ormolu (aw´məloo) *n.* **1** a gold-coloured alloy of
copper, zinc and tin, used for cheap jewellery. **2**

gold leaf ground and used as a pigment for decorating furniture etc. **3** metallic ware, furniture etc. decorated with this.
ornament[1] (aw'nəmənt) *n.* **1** a thing or part that adorns. **2** an embellishment, a decoration. **3** ornamentation. **4** a person, possession or quality that reflects honour or credit. **5** a mark of distinction, a badge. **6** (*pl.*, *Mus.*) decorations such as trills, mordents etc. to be improvised. **ornamental** (-men'-) *a.* decorative, serving as an ornament. *~n.* an ornamental thing, esp. a plant cultivated for show. **ornamentalism** *n.* **ornamentalist** *n.* **ornamentally** *adv.*
ornament[2] (aw'nəmənt) *v.t.* to adorn, to decorate, to embellish. **ornamentation** (-tā'shən) *n.* **ornamenter** *n.*
ornate (awnāt') *a.* **1** adorned, ornamented, richly embellished. **2** (of literary style etc.) florid, elaborately finished. **ornately** *adv.* **ornateness** *n.*
ornery (aw'nəri) *a.* (*N Am.*, *coll.*) mean, low. **orneriness** *n.*
ornithischian (awnithis'kiən, -thish'-) *a.* of or relating to the order Ornithischia, an order of dinosaurs. *~n.* any dinosaur of this order, such as the stegosaurus or triceratops.
ornitho- (aw'nithō), **ornith-** *comb. form* of or relating to birds.
ornithology (awnithol'əji) *n.* the branch of zoology dealing with birds. **ornithological** (-loj'-) *a.* **ornithologically** *adv.* **ornithologist** *n.*
ornithopod (aw'nithəpod) *n.* any bipedal herbivorous dinosaur of the suborder Ornithopoda, including the iguanodon. *~a.* of or relating to this suborder.
ornithorhyncus (awnithōring'kəs) *n.* the duck-billed platypus, *Ornithorhyncus anatinus*, an Australian aquatic oviparous mammal.
oro- (or'ō) *comb. form* of or relating to mountains.
orogenesis (orōjen'əsis), **orogeny** (oroj'əni) *n.* the process of forming mountains. **orogenetic** (-net'-), **orogenic** (-jen'-) *a.*
orography (orog'rəfi), **oreography** (oriog'-) *n.* the branch of physical geography concerned with mountains and mountain systems. **orographic** (-graf'-) *a.* **orographical** *a.*
orotund (or'ətŭnd) *a.* **1** characterized by fullness and resonance. **2** (of the voice and utterance) rich and musical. **orotundity** (-tŭn'-) *n.* orotund quality of voice.

Usage note The uses of the adjectives *orotund* and *rotund* overlap, but *orotund* is usual of the voice, and of spoken and written words, and *rotund* of objects and people.

orphan (aw'fən) *n.* **1** a child bereft of one parent, or of both. **2** a person bereft of previous advantages. **3** (*Print.*) the first line of a paragraph at the foot of a page or column. *~a.* bereft of one parent, or of both. *~v.t.* to make an orphan of. **orphanage** (-ij) *n.* **1** an institution for bringing up orphans. **2** orphan condition. **orphanhood**, **orphanism** *n.* **orphanize**, **orphanise** *v.t.*

orphrey (aw'fri) *n.* (*pl.* **orphreys**) a band of gold and silver embroidery decorating an ecclesiastical vestment.
orpiment (aw'pimənt) *n.* **1** native yellow trisulphide of arsenic, used as a pigment and a dyestuff. **2** realgar.
orpine (aw'pīn), **orpin** (-pin) *n.* a fleshy-leaved plant, *Sedum telephium*, of the stonecrop family, with purple flowers.
orrery (or'əri) *n.* (*pl.* **orreries**) a mechanical model for illustrating the motions, magnitudes and positions of the planetary system.
orris (or'is) *n.* **1** any plant of the genus *Iris*, esp. *I. florentina*. **2** orris root. **orris root** *n.* the root of the orris, used as a perfume and in medicine.
ortanique (awtənēk') *n.* a citrus fruit, a cross between an orange and a tangerine.
ortho- (aw'thō) *comb. form* **1** straight. **2** upright; perpendicular. **3** correct. **4** (*Chem.*) denoting an organic compound having substituted atoms attached to two adjacent carbon atoms in a benzene ring. **5** (*Chem.*) denoting an oxyacid derived from an acid anhydride by combination with the largest number of water molecules.
orthodontics (awthədon'tiks), **orthodontia** (-tiə) *n.* dentistry dealing with the correction of irregularities of the teeth. **orthodontic** *a.* **orthodontist** *n.*
orthodox (aw'thədoks) *a.* **1** holding right or accepted views, esp. in matters of faith and religious doctrine. **2** in accordance with sound or accepted doctrine. **3** approved, accepted, conventional, not heretical, heterodox or original. **4** (**Orthodox**) of or relating to the Orthodox Church. **5** (**Orthodox**) adhering to the traditional doctrines and rituals of Judaism. **Orthodox Church** *n.* the Eastern Church, which has the patriarch of Constantinople as its head. **orthodoxy** *n.* (*pl.* **orthodoxies**) **1** the state of being orthodox. **2** orthodox belief or practice. **3** an instance of this. **4** the members of the Orthodox Church collectively. **5** Orthodox Jews collectively.
orthogon (aw'thəgon) *n.* **1** a rectangular figure. **2** a right-angled triangle. **orthogonal** (-thog'-) *a.* **orthogonally** *adv.* **orthogonal projection** *n.* projection by lines perpendicular to the plane of projection.
orthography (awthog'rəfi) *n.* (*pl.* **orthographies**) **1** correct spelling. **2** that part of grammar which deals with letters and spelling. **3** mode of spelling as regards correctness and incorrectness. **4** the art of drawing plans, levations etc. in accurate projection, as if the object were seen from an infinite distance. **orthographer**, **orthographist** *n.* **ortho- graphic** (-graf'-), **orthographical** *a.* **orthographically** *adv.*
orthopaedics (awthəpē'diks), (*esp. N Am.*) **orthopedics** *n.* the branch of medicine concerned with bones and joints; the act or art of curing muscular or skeletal deformities by surgery, esp.

in children. **orthopaedic, orthopaedical** *a.* **orthopaedist** *n.*

orthopteran (awthop´tərən) *n.* any insect of the order *Orthoptera*, with two pairs of wings, the hind wings membranous and those in front coriaceous and usually straight; any orthopterous insect. **orthopteral, orthopterous** *a.*

orthoptic (awthop´tik) *a.* relating to correct vision with both eyes. **orthoptics** *n.* (*Med.*) the correction of defective eyesight, e.g. by exercising weak eye muscles. **orthoptist** *n.*

orthorhombic (awthōrom´bik) *a.* (of a crystal) having three planes of dissimilar symmetry at right angles to each other.

ortolan (aw´tələn) *n.* (*Zool.*) 1 (*also* **ortolan bunting**) a small bunting, *Emberiza hortulana*, formerly esteemed as a delicacy. 2 any of several W Indian and American birds, esp. the bobolink.

-ory[1] (əri) *suf.* denoting place where or instrument, as *dormitory, lavatory, refectory.* **-orial** (aw´riəl) *suf.* forming adjectives, as *lavatorial.*

-ory[2] (əri) *suf.* forming adjectives, as *amatory, admonitory, illusory.*

oryx (or´iks) *n.* (*pl. in general* **oryx**, *in particular* **oryxes**) any straight-horned antelope of the genus *Oryx*, of Africa and Arabia.

OS *abbr.* 1 (*also* **o.s.**) Old Style. 2 operating system. 3 Ordinary Seaman. 4 Ordnance Survey. 5 out of stock. 6 outsize.

Os *chem. symbol* osmium.

Osage orange (ō´sāj, osāj´) *n.* 1 a thorny N American tree, *Maclura pomifera.* 2 the orange-like fruit of this. 3 the timber from this.

Oscar (os´kə) *n.* a gold-plated statuette awarded by the American Academy of Motion Picture Arts and Sciences to the actor, director, filmwriter etc. whose work is adjudged the best of the year.

oscillate (os´ilāt) *v.i.* 1 to swing, to move like a pendulum. 2 to vibrate. 3 to fluctuate, to vacillate, to vary. ~*v.t.* to cause to swing or vibrate. **oscillation** (-ā´shən) *n.* 1 the movement of oscillating. 2 the regular variation in an alternating current. 3 a single cycle (of something oscillating) from one extreme to the other. **oscillative, oscillatory** *a.* **oscillator** *n.* 1 someone or something that oscillates. 2 a device for producing alternating current. **oscillo-** (os´ilō) *comb. form* **oscillogram** (osil´əgram) *n.* **oscillograph** (os´iləgrahf) *n.* a device for giving a visible representation of the oscillations of an electric current. **oscillographic** (-graf´-) *a.* **oscillography** (-log´-) *n.* **oscilloscope** (osil´əskōp) *n.* an instrument which registers the oscillations of an alternating current or the fluorescent screen of a cathode ray tube. **oscilloscopic** (-skop´-) *a.*

osculate (os´kūlāt) *v.t.* 1 (*formal or facet.*) to kiss. 2 (*Geom.*) (of a curve) to have two branches with a common tangent with (another curve), where each branch extends in both directions of the tangent. ~*v.i.* to kiss. **osculant** *a.* **oscular** *a.* 1 of or relating to the mouth. 2 of or relating to kissing.

osculation (-lā´shən) *n.* **osculatory** (os´-) *a.*, *n.* (*pl. osculatories*). **osculum** (os´kūləm) *n.* (*pl. oscula* (-lə)) (*Zool.*) a pore or orifice, esp. an opening in a sponge, out of which water passes.

-ose[1] (ōs, ōz) *suf.* forming adjectives denoting fullness, abundance, as *grandiose, jocose, verbose.* **-osely** *suf.* forming adverbs. **-oseness** *suf.* forming nouns.

-ose[2] (ōs) *suf.* forming nouns denoting carbohydrates and isomeric compounds.

osier (ō´ziə) *n.* any of various willows, esp. *Salix viminalis,* the pliable shoots of which are used for basket-making. **osier bed** *n.* **osiered** *a.*

-osis (ō´sis) *comb. form* (*pl. -oses* (ō´sēz)) denoting conditions, esp. morbid states, as *chlorosis, necrosis.*

-osity (os´iti) *suf.* forming nouns from adjectives in -OSE[1] or -OUS, as *grandiosity, luminosity.*

osmic (oz´mik) *a.* of or relating to odours or the sense of smell. **osmically** *adv.*

osmium (oz´miəm) *n.* (*Chem.*) the heaviest known metallic element, at. no. 76, chem. symbol Os, usu. found in association with platinum. **osmic** *a.* containing osmium.

osmoregulation (ozmōregūlā´shən) *n.* (*Biol.*) the adjustment of osmotic pressure in a cell in relation to the surrounding fluid.

osmosis (osmō´sis, oz-) *n.* 1 (*Biol., Chem.*) the diffusion of a solvent through a semipermeable membrane into a more concentrated solution. 2 diffusion through any porous or porous barrier. 3 gradual absorption or adoption of ideas etc. **osmotic** (-mot´-) *a.* **osmotically** *adv.*

osprey (os´prā) *n.* (*pl. ospreys*) 1 a large bird, *Pandion haliaetus,* preying on fish; also known as the *sea eagle* or *fish-hawk.* 2 an egret plume used for trimming hats and bonnets.

ossein (os´iin) *n.* the gelatinous tissue left when mineral matter is eliminated from a bone.

osseous (os´iəs) *a.* 1 of the nature of or like bone, bony. 2 consisting of bone, ossified.

ossicle (os´ikəl) *n.* 1 (*Anat.*) a small bone. 2 a bony calcareous or chitinous part or process in various animals.

Ossie Aussie.

ossify (os´ifī) *v.t.* (*3rd pers. sing. pres.* **ossifies,** *pres.p.* **ossifying,** *past, p.p.* **ossified**) to turn into bone. ~*v.i.* 1 to become bone. 2 to become inflexible in attitudes, habits etc. **ossific** (-sif´-) *a.* **ossification** (-kā´shən) *n.*

osso bucco (osō boo´kō) *n.* a stew made from knuckle of veal and marrowbone.

ossuary (os´ūəri) *n.* (*pl. ossuaries*) 1 a charnel house. 2 an urn for bones. 3 a deposit of bones (as in a cave).

osteitis (ostiī´tis) *n.* inflammation of bone.

ostensible (osten´sibəl) *a.* 1 put forward for show or to hide the reality. 2 professed, pretended, seeming. **ostensibly** *adv.* **ostensive** *a.* 1 exhibiting, showing. 2 ostensible. 3 (*Logic*) setting forth a general principle obviously including the proposition to be proved. **ostensively**

adv. **ostensiveness** *n.* **ostensory** *n.* (*pl.* **ostensories**) in the Roman Catholic Church, a monstrance. **ostentation** (ostəntā´shən) *n.* **1** pretentious or ambitious display. **2** parade, pomp. **ostentatious** *a.* **ostentatiously** *adv.* **ostentatiousness** *n.*

osteo- (os´tiō), **oste-** (os´ti) *comb. form* bone.

osteoarthritis (ostiōahthrī´tis) *n.* degenerative arthritis, esp. of the weight-bearing joints of the spine, hips and knees. **osteoarthritic** (-thrit´-) *a.*

osteogenesis (ostiōjen´əsis) *n.* the formation of bone. **osteogenetic** (-net´-) *a.*

osteology (ostiol´əji) *n.* the branch of anatomy treating of bones, osseous tissue etc. **osteologic** (-loj´-), **osteological** *a.* **osteologically** *adv.* **osteologist** (-ol´-) *n.*

osteomalacia (ostiōmələ´shiə) *n.* softening of the bones. **osteomalacic** (-ā´sik) *a.*

osteomyelitis (ostiōmīəlī´tis) *n.* inflammation of the marrow of the bones.

osteopathy (ostiop´əthi) *n.* a method of treating diseases by eliminating structural derangement by manipulation, mainly of the spinal column. **osteopath** (os´tiəpath), **osteopathist** (-op´-) *n.*

osteoporosis (ostiōpawrō´sis) *n.* development of porous or brittle bones due to lack of calcium in the bone matrix.

ostinato (ostinah´tō) *n.* (*pl.* **ostinatos, ostinati** (-ti)) (*esp. Mus.*) a musical figure continuously reiterated throughout a composition.

ostium (os´tiəm) *n.* (*pl.* **ostia** (*Anat., Zool.*) the mouth or opening of a passage.

ostler (os´lə), **hostler** (hos´lə) *n.* (*Hist.*) a man who looks after horses at an inn, a stableman.

Ostmark (ost´mahk) *n.* (*Hist.*) the standard unit of currency in the Democratic Republic of Germany.

ostracize (os´trəsīz), **ostracise** *v.t.* to exclude from society, to ban, to send to Coventry. **ostracism** *n.*

ostrich (os´trich) *n.* (*pl. in general* **ostrich**, *in particular* **ostriches**) **1** a large African bird, *Struthio camelus*, having rudimentary wings, but capable of running with great speed, and valued for its feathers, which are used as plumes, and for its meat. **2** a person who refuses to recognize unpleasant facts.

OT *abbr.* Old Testament.

-ot[1] (ət) *suf.* forming nouns, originally diminutives, as *parrot*.

-ot[2] (ət) *suf.* forming nouns denoting persons, as *patriot*.

OTC *abbr.* Officers' Training Corps.

other (-dh´ə) *a.* **1** not the same as one specified or implied. **2** different, distinct in kind. **3** alternative, additional. **4** extra. **5** second, only remaining (of two alternatives). **6** opposite, contrary. ~*n., pron.* **1** an or the other person, thing, example, instance etc. **2** (*pl.*) the ones remaining. **3** (*sl.*) sexual intercourse. **4** (*Philos.*) (*usu.* **Other**) that which is distinct or different. ~*adv.* otherwise. **every other** every alternate (day, week

etc.). **of all others** out of the many possible or likely. **other things being equal** conditions being unchanged. **the other day** on a day recently. **the other night** on a night recently. **the other way round** in the opposite direction; in a reversed, inverted etc. position. **the other week** during a week recently. **other-directed** *a.* influenced in thought and action by values derived from external sources. **other fish to fry** *n.pl.* other more important matters to attend to. **other half** *n.* one's spouse or partner. **other man** *n.* the lover of a married or attached woman. **otherness** *n.* **other place** *n.* (*facet.*) **1** hell (as opposed to heaven). **2** the House of Lords as regarded by the House of Commons, and vice versa. **other ranks** *n.pl.* soldiers not holding a commissioned rank. **otherwhere** *adv.* (*poet.*) elsewhere. **otherwise** *adv.* **1** in a different way or manner. **2** in other respects. **3** by or from other causes. **4** in quite a different state. ~*conj.* **1** else, or. **2** but for this. **and/ or otherwise** the negation or opposite (of a specified thing). **other woman** *n.* the lover of a married or attached man. **other world** *n.* **1** the future life. **2** a world existing outside of or in a different mode from this. **other-worldly** *a.* **other-worldliness** *n.*

Usage note The use of *other* as an adverb (rather than *otherwise*) is sometimes disapproved of, though it is quite common, especially in North America.

otic (ō´tik) *a.* of or relating to the ear.

-otic (ot´ik) *suf.* forming adjectives corresponding to nouns ending in -OSIS, as *neurotic, osmotic*. **-otically** *suf.* forming adverbs.

otiose (ō´tiōs) *a.* **1** not wanted, useless, superfluous. **2** futile, sterile. **otiosely** *adv.* **otioseness** *n.*

otitis (ōtī´tis) *n.* inflammation of the ear.

otolaryngology (ōtōlaring-gol´əji) *n.* the study of diseases of the ear and throat. **otolaryngological** (-gəloj´-) *a.* **otolaryngologist** *n.*

otolith (ō´tōlith) *n.* a calcareous concretion found in the inner ear of vertebrates and some invertebrates. **otolithic** (-lith´ik) *a.*

otology (ōtol´əji) *n.* the science of the ear or of diseases of the ear. **otological** (-loj´-) *a.* **otologist** *n.*

otorhinolaryngology (ōtōrīnōlaring-gol´əji) *n.* ear, nose and throat medicine.

otoscope (ō´təskōp) *n.* an instrument for inspecting the ear and eardrum. **otoscopic** (-skop´-) *a.*

OTT *abbr.* (*coll.*) over the top.

otter (ot´ə) *n.* (*pl. in general* **otter**, *in particular* **otters**) **1** any of several semiaquatic mammals of the genus *Lutra* with dense fur and webbed feet. **2** the fur of this. **3** the sea otter. **4** a device for catching fish consisting usu. of a float armed with hooks. **5** a type of paravane. **otter-board** *n.* a device for keeping the mouth of a trawl net open. **otter-dog, otter-hound** *n.* a variety of dog used for hunting otters.

otto attar.

Ottoman (ot´əmən) *a.* (*Hist.*) **1** of or relating to the dynasty of Othman or Osman I. **2** of or relating to the Turks. ~*n.* (*pl.* **Ottomans**) a Turk.

ottoman (ot´əmən) *n.* (*pl.* **ottomans**) **1** a cushioned seat or sofa without back or arms, introduced from Turkey. **2** a heavy silk fabric.

oubliette (oobliet´) *n.* an underground dungeon in which persons condemned to perpetual imprisonment or secret death were confined.

ouch (owch) *int.* used to express sudden pain.

ought[1] (awt) *v.aux.* **1** to comply with duty or rightness (*You ought to be kind to animals*). **2** to comply with common sense or prudence (*I ought to save more money*). **3** to comply with expectation or probability (*The weather ought to be fine tomorrow*). **4** to comply with unfulfilled expectation or desire (*It ought to be finished by now*). **ought not** the negative form of ought.

ought[2] (awt), **aught** *n.* (*coll.*) a figure denoting nothing; nought.

oughtn't (aw´tənt) *contr.* ought not.

Ouija® (wē´jə), **Ouija board** *n.* a board inscribed with the letters of the alphabet, used for receiving messages etc. in spiritualistic manifestations.

ounce[1] (owns) *n.* **1** a unit of weight, of one-sixteenth of a pound avoirdupois (about 28 g). **2** a unit of one-twelfth of a pound troy, equal to 480 grains (about 31 g). **3** a small quantity.

ounce[2] (owns) *n.* a wild cat, *Panthera uncia*, of Asia; also called *mountain panther* and *snow leopard*.

our (owə) *a.* possessive of we. **Our Father** *n.* **1** the Lord's Prayer. **2** God. **Our Lady** *n.* the Virgin Mary. **Our Lady's bedstraw** *n.* lady's bedstraw (under lady). **Our Lord** *n.* **1** Jesus Christ. **2** God.

-our (ə) *suf.* forming nouns, as *ardour, clamour, favour.*

ours (owəz) *pron.* something which belongs to or is associated with us. **of ours** belonging or related to us.

Usage note (1) The pronoun *ours* does not have an apostrophe (it is not spelt *our's*). (2) *Ourselves* is preferred to *ourself* even where *we* refers to a singular collective noun (so *We regard ourselves as a team*).

ourselves (owəselvz´) *pron.* **1** we or us (objective), used to give emphasis. **2** the reflexive form of us. **3** our normal or usual selves. **by ourselves** alone, unaided. **to be ourselves** to act in our normal manner. **ourself** (-self´) *pron.* **1** †myself (used by a sovereign, newspaper editor etc.) (usu. in apposition). **2** ourselves.

-ous (əs) *suf.* **1** full of, abounding in, as *dubious, glorious.* **2** (*Chem.*) denoting a compound having more of the element indicated in the stem than those whose names end in -IC, as *nitrous, sulphurous.* **-ously** *suf.* forming adverbs. **-ousness** *suf.* forming nouns.

ousel ouzel.

oust (owst) *v.t.* **1** to eject, to expel, to turn out

(from). **2** to dispossess, to deprive (of). **ouster** *n.* **1** (*Law*) ejection, dispossession. **2** a person who ousts. **3** (*esp. N Am.*) dismissal, expulsion.

out (owt) *adv.* **1** from the inside or within. **2** not in, not within. **3** from among. **4** forth or away. **5** not at home, not in office. **6** no longer in prison. **7** not engaged or employed. **8** on strike. **9** not batting. **10** dismissed from the wicket. **11** in boxing, denoting defeat through inability to rise within the ten seconds allowed after being knocked down. **12** not in fashion. **13** not in practice. **14** in error, wrong. **15** at a loss. **16** at odds, not in agreement. **17** not to be thought of. **18** so as to be visible, audible, revealed, published etc. **19** introduced to society. **20** exhausted or extinguished. **21** clearly. **22** forcibly. **23** at full extent. **24** (*coll.*) no longer conscious. **25** (*esp. N Am.*) (of a homosexual man or woman) having declared publicly their sexual orientation. **26** to an end or conclusion, completely, thoroughly. **27** (of a tooth) extracted. **28** (of a bone etc.) dislocated. **29** (of a jury) considering its verdict. **30** (of a flower) open. **31** (of time) not spent working. **32** (of the tide) at the lowest point. ~*prep.* (*coll.*) from inside of. ~*n.* **1** (*usu. pl.*) those out of office, the opposition. **2** (*coll.*) a way of escape. **3** in baseball, the action or an act of putting a player out. ~*a.* **1** external. **2** outlying, remote, distant. **3** played away from the home ground. ~*int.* (*ellipt.*) begone! away! an expression of impatience, anger or abhorrence. ~*v.t.* **1** to put out or eject. **2** to knock out, to disable. **3** (*coll.*) to publicize, without permission, the supposed homosexuality of (esp. a person in public life). ~*v.i.* to come out or emerge. **all out** striving to the uttermost. **at outs** at variance, at odds. **from out** out of. **not out** (of a side or batsman in cricket) not having been caught, bowled etc. **out and about** able to get up and go outside. **out and away** beyond comparison. **out for** striving for. **out of it 1** not included, neglected. **2** at a loss. **3** in error, mistaken. **4** (*coll.*) unaware of one's surroundings due to drink, drugs etc. **out of one's way** away from one's intended or desired route. **out of the way 1** unusual. **2** remote. **out to** aiming to, working to. **out with 1** away with. **2** not friendly with. **out with it** say what you are thinking. **out and out** *a.* complete, thorough. ~*adv.* completely, unreservedly. **out-and-outer** *n.* **1** (*sl.*) a thorough-going person. **2** an extremist. **outer** *a.* **1** being on the exterior side, external. **2** farther from the centre or the inside. **3** objective, material, not subjective or psychical. ~*n.* **1 a** the part of a target outside the rings round the bull's-eye. **b** a shot striking this. **2** (*coll.*) a person who makes public a claim that another person is homosexual. **3** an outer garment. **4** (*Austral., sl.*) the part of the spectator area at a sports ground that is unsheltered. **5** an outer container. **outer garments** *n.pl.* clothes worn over other clothes. **outer man** *n.* external appearance, attire (of a man). **outermost, out-**

most *a.* **1** most or farthest out. **2** most distant. **outer space** *n.* the vast, immeasurable region beyond the earth. **outerwear** *n.* outer garments. **outer woman** *n.* external appearance, attire (of a woman). **outing** *n.* **1** an excursion, a pleasure-trip, an airing. **2** an appearance in a match, race etc. **3** (*coll.*) the practice or policy of publicizing the supposed homosexuality of a man or woman in public life. **out of** *prep.* **1** from the inside of. **2** from among. **3** beyond the reach of. **4** from (material, source, condition etc.). **5** born of. **6** without. **7** deprived of, having used up. **out-of-body experience** *n.* a sensation of being outside one's body. **out-of-court** *a.* (of a settlement) made or done without using a court. **out of date** *a.* no longer in fashion or use. **out of doors** *a.* in the open air. ~*adv.* into the open air. **out-of-pocket expenses** *n.pl.* the actual outlay of cash incurred. **out-of-town** *a.* situated or taking place outside a town. **out to lunch** *a.* (*coll.*) crazy.

out- (owt) *pref.* **1** out, towards the outside, external. **2** from within, forth. **3** separate, detached, at a distance. **4** denoting issue or result. **5** expressing excess, exaggeration, superiority, surpassing, defeating, enduring, getting through or beyond.

out- (+ a–e words) **outact** *v.t.* to exceed in action, to excel, to outdo. **outage** (owt´) *n.* a period of time during which a power supply, machine etc. is not operating. **outback** (owt´-) *n.*, *a.*, *adv.* (*esp. Austral.*) the hinterland, the bush, the interior. **outbacker** *n.* **outbalance** *v.t.* to outweigh, to exceed. **outbid** *v.t.* (*pres.p.* **outbidding**, *past* **outbad**, **outbade**, *p.p.* **outbidden**) **1** to bid more than. **2** to outdo by offering more. **outblaze** *v.i.* to blaze out or outwards. ~*v.t.* to blaze more brightly than. **outboard** (owt´-) *a.* **1** situated on or directed towards the outside of a ship. **2** having an engine and propeller outside the boat. ~*adv.* out from a ship's side or away from the centre. **outbound** (owt´-) *a.* outward bound. **outbrave** *v.t.* **1** to surpass in bravery, beauty, splendour etc. **2** to stand up against defiantly. **outbreak** (owt´-), **outbreaking** *n.* **1** a sudden bursting forth, an eruption. **2** a riot or insurrection. **3** an outcrop. **outbreeding** *n.* interbreeding of unrelated plants or animals. **outbreed** *v.i.*, *v.t.* (*past, p.p.* **outbred**). **outbuilding** (owt´-) *n.* a detached building, an outhouse. **outburst** (owt´-) *n.* **1** an outbreak, an explosion. **2** an outcry. **3** an outcrop. **outcast** (owt´-) *n.* **1** a castaway, a vagabond. **2** an exile. ~*a.* **1** rejected, cast out. **2** exiled. **outcaste**[1] (owt´-) *n.* **1** a person who has been expelled from a caste. **2** a person with no caste. **outcaste**[2] (-kahst´) *v.t.* to cause (someone) to lose their caste. **outclass** *v.t.* **1** to be of a superior class, kind or qualifications than. **2** to surpass as a competitor. **outcome** (owt´-) *n.* issue, result, consequence, effect. **outcrop** (owt´-) *n.* **1** (*Geol.*) the exposure of a stratum at the surface. **2** a noticeable manifestation or occurrence. ~*v.i.* (*pres.p.* **outcropping**, *past, p.p.* **outcropped**) to crop out at the surface. **outcry** (owt´-) *n.* (*pl.* **outcries**) **1** a

vehement or loud cry. **2** noise, clamour. **outdance** *v.t.* to surpass in dancing. **outdare** *v.t.* **1** to exceed in daring. **2** to defy. **outdated** *a.* obsolete, out of date. **outdistance** *v.t.* to outstrip. **outdo** *v.t.* (*3rd pers. sing. pres.* **outdoes**, *pres.p.* **outdoing**, *past* **outdid**, *p.p.* **outdone**) to excel, to surpass. **outdoor** (owt´-) *a.* **1** living, existing, being, happening etc. out of doors or in the open air. **2** fond of the open air. **outdoor pursuits** *n.pl.* sports or leisure activities undertaken out of doors. **outdoors** *adv.* in the open air, out of the house. ~*n.* the open air.

outer out.

out- (+ f– words) **outface** *v.t.* **1** to brave. **2** to confront boldly. **3** to stare down. **outfall** (owt´-) *n.* **1** the point of discharge of a river, drain etc. **2** an outlet. **outfield** (owt´-) *n.* **1** in cricket, baseball etc., the part of the field at a distance from the batsman. **2** the players occupying this. **outfielder** *n.* **outfight** *v.t.* (*past, p.p.* **outfought**) **1** to fight better than. **2** to beat in a fight. **outfit** (owt´-) *n.* **1** the act of equipping for a journey, expedition etc. **2** the tools and equipment required for a trade, profession etc. **3** a set of (esp. selected) clothes. **4** (*coll.*) a set or group of people who work as a team. ~*v.t.* (*pres.p.* **outfitting**, *past, p.p.* **outfitted**) to fit out, to provide with an outfit. **outfitter** *n.* a person who deals in outfits for journeys, athletic sports, ceremonies, schools etc. **outflank** *v.t.* **1** to extend beyond or turn the flank of. **2** to get the better of. **outflow** (owt´-) *n.* **1** the process of flowing out. **2** that which flows out. **outflung** *a.* flung out to one side. **outfly** *v.t.* (*3rd pers. sing. pres.* **outflies**, *pres.p.* **outflying**, *past* **outflew**, *p.p.* **outflown**) **1** to fly faster than. **2** to outstrip. **outfox** *v.t.* (*coll.*) to outwit.

out- (+ g–l words) **outgas** *v.i.* (*3rd pers. sing. pres.* **outgases**, *pres.p.* **outgassing**, *past, p.p.* **outgassed**) to release or give off an adsorbed or occluded gas or vapour. ~*v.t.* **1** to release or give off as a gas or vapour. **2** to drive off a gas or vapour from. **outgeneral** *v.t.* (*pres.p.* **outgeneralling**, (*N Am.*) **outgeneraling**, *past, p.p.* **outgeneralled**, (*N Am.*) **outgeneraled**) **1** to surpass in generalship. **2** to manoeuvre so as to get the better of. **outgo** (owt´-) *n.* (*pl.* **outgoes**) expenditure, outlay, cost, outflow, issue. **outgoing** (owt´-) *a.* **1** leaving. **2** friendly and sociable; extrovert. ~*n.* **1** a going out, departure, termination. **2** (*usu. in pl.*) outlay, expenditure. **outgrow** *v.t.* (*pres.p.* **outgrowing**, *past* **outgrew**, *p.p.* **outgrown**) **1** to surpass in growth. **2** to grow too much or too great for. **3** to grow out of. **to outgrow one's strength** to become thin and weak through too rapid growth. **outgrowth** (owt´-) *n.* **1** something, or the process of, growing out from a main body. **2** a result or by-product. **outguess** *v.t.* to guess what someone else intends. **outgun** *v.t.* (*pres.p.* **outgunning**, *past, p.p.* **outgunned**) **1** to defeat with superior weaponry. **2** to surpass. **outhouse** (owt´-) *n.* **1** a smaller building away from the main building. **2** (*N Am.*) an outdoor

lavatory. **outjockey** v.t. (3rd pers. sing. pres. **outjockeys,** pres.p. **outjockeying,** past, p.p. **outjockeyed**) to outwit. **outjump** v.t. to surpass in jumping. **outlander** n. **1** a foreigner, a stranger. **2** an alien settler. **outlast** v.t. **1** to last longer than. **2** to surpass in duration, endurance etc. **outlay** (owt´-) n. expenditure. **outlet** (owt´lit) n. **1** a passage outwards. **2** a vent. **3** a means of egress. **4** an agency or market for goods. **5** (N Am.) a power point. **outlier** (owt´-) n. **1** a person who lodges or resides away from their office or business. **2** (Geol.) a portion of a bed detached from the main mass by denudation of the intervening parts. **outline** (owt´-) n. **1** the line or lines enclosing and defining a figure. **2** a drawing of such lines without shading. **3** the first general sketch, rough draft or summary. **4** (pl.) general features, facts, principles etc. **5** the representation of a word in shorthand. ~v.t. **1** to draw the outline of. **2** to sketch. **in outline** sketched or represented as an outline. **outlive** v.t. **1** to survive. **2** to outlast. **3** to live through. **outlook** (owt´-) n. **1** the prospect, general appearance of things, esp. as regards the future. **2** a view, a prospect. **outlying** (owt´-) a. situated at a distance, or on the exterior frontier. **outlandish** (owtlan´dish) a. **1** foreign-looking, strange, extraordinary. **2** bizarre, unconventional. **outlandishly** adv. **outlandishness** n. **outlaw** (owt´law) n. **1** a lawless person. **2** (Hist.) a person deprived of the protection of the law. **3** †an exile, a fugitive. ~v.t. **1** to deprive of the protection of the law. **2** to make illegal. **outlawry** n.
out- (+ m–p words) outmanoeuvre, (N Am.) **outmaneuver** v.t. **1** to get the better of by manoeuvring. **2** to outdo in manoeuvring. **outmatch** v.t. to be more than a match for. **outmeasure** v.t. to exceed in quantity or extent. **outmoded** a. **1** out of fashion. **2** obsolete. **outmodedly** adv. **outmodedness** n. **outnumber** v.t. to exceed in number. **outpace** v.t. **1** to walk faster than. **2** to outdo. **outpatient** (owt´-) n. a patient receiving treatment at a hospital without being a resident. **outperform** v.t. to do much better than. **outperformance** n. **outplacement** (owt´-) n. professional relocation of redundant employees arranged by their former employer. **outplay** v.t. to play better than or defeat an opponent in a game. **outpoint** v.t. to score more points than. **outpost** (owt´-) n. a post or station at a distance from the main body. **outpour** v.t. to pour out, to discharge. **outpouring** n. **outpsych** v.t. (esp. N Am. coll.) to defeat using psychology.
outmost outermost (under out).
output (owt´put) n. **1** the produce of a factory, mine etc. **2** the aggregate amount produced. **3** the data produced by a computer. **4** the signal delivered by an electronic system or device. **5** the terminal for the output of a computer etc. ~v.t. (pres.p. **outputting,** past, p.p. **output, outputted**) **1** to produce output. **2** (of a computer) to supply (results etc.).

out- (+ r– words) outrange v.t. (of artillery) to have a longer range than. **outrank** v.t. to exceed in rank. **outreach**[1] v.t. **1** to exceed in reach, to surpass. **2** to overreach, to reach out. **outreach**[2] (owt´-) n. **1** a reaching out. **2** the extent or distance of this. **3** the involvement of an organization with the community, esp. a church or a charity's involvement for welfare purposes. **outride** v.t. (pres.p. **outriding,** past **outrode,** p.p. **outridden**) **1** to ride faster than. **2** (of a ship) to come safely through (a storm). **outrider** (owt´-) n. **1** an escort who rides ahead of or beside a carriage or other vehicle. **2** (N Am.) a cowboy keeping cattle within bounds. **outriding** n. **outrigger** (owt´-) n. **1** a projecting spar, boom, beam or framework extended from the sides of a ship for various purposes. **2** a bracket carrying a rowlock projecting from the sides of a boat to give increased leverage in rowing. **3** a boat with these. **4** a projecting beam or framework used in building etc. **5** a chassis extension supporting the body of a motor vehicle. **outrigged** (owt´-) a. (of a boat etc.) having outriggers. **outright**[1] (-rīt´) adv. **1** completely, entirely. **2** at once, once for all. **3** openly. **outright**[2] (owt´-) a. **1** downright, positive. **2** unrestrained, thorough. **outrival** v.t. (pres.p. **outrivalling,** (N Am.) **outrivaling,** past, p.p. **outrivalled,** (N Am.) **outrivaled**) to surpass as a rival. **outro** (owt´rō) n. (pl. **outros**) (coll.) a concluding section of a piece of music etc. **outrun** v.t. (pres.p. **outrunning,** past **outran,** p.p. **outrun**) **1** to run faster or farther than, to outstrip. **2** to escape by running. **3** to go beyond (a specified point). **outrush** (owt´-) n. **1** a rushing out. **2** a violent overflow.
outrage (owt´rāj) n. **1** wanton injury to or violation of the rights of others. **2** a gross offence against order or decency. **3** a flagrant insult. **4** fierce anger or indignation. ~v.t. **1** to commit an outrage on. **2** to injure or insult in a flagrant manner. **3** to shock and anger. **outrageous** (-rā´-) a. **1** flagrant, heinous, atrocious, extravagant. **2** excessive, shocking. **3** violent, furious. **4** grossly offensive or abusive. **outrageously** adv. **outrageousness** n.
outré (oo´trā) a. **1** extravagant, exaggerated, eccentric. **2** outraging convention or decorum.
out- (+ s– words) outsail v.t. to sail better or faster than. **outsell** v.t. (pres.p. **outselling,** past, p.p. **outsold**) to sell more or faster than. **outset** (owt´-) n. commencement, beginning, start. **at/ from the outset** at or from the beginning. **outshine** v.t. **1** to excel in lustre. **2** to surpass in splendour. **3** to surpass in ability, excellence etc. **outshoot** v.t. (pres.p. **outshooting,** past, p.p. **outshot**) **1** to shoot better or farther than. **2** (esp. N Am.) to attempt or score more goals etc. than. **outsit** v.t. (pres.p. **outsitting,** past, p.p. **outsat**) **1** to sit beyond the time of. **2** to sit longer than. **outsize** (owt´-) a. **1** abnormally large. **2** larger than the standard size. ~n. an exceptionally large person or thing, such as a garment. **outsized** a.

outskirt (owt´-) *n.* (*usu. in pl.*) the outer border. **outsmart** *v.t.* **1** (*coll.*) to outwit. **2** to get the better of. **outsource** (owt´-) *v.t.* (*esp. N Am.*) to subcontract work to another company, esp. as a means of reducing costs. **outspend** *v.t.* (*pres.p.* **outspending**, *past, p.p.* **outspent**) to spend more than. **outspoken** *a.* open, candid, frank in speech. **outspokenly** *adv.* **outspokenness** *n.* **outspread**[1] *v.t.* (*past, p.p.* **outspread**) to spread out. **outspread**[2] (owt´-) *a.* spread out. **outstanding** *a.* **1** remaining unpaid. **2** projecting outwards. **3** salient, conspicuous, prominent. **4** superior, excellent. **outstandingly** *adv.* **outstare** *v.t.* to outface, to abash by staring. **outstation** (owt´-) *n.* **1** (*Austral.*) a distant station. **2** a branch of an organization, business etc. which is remote from headquarters. **outstay** *v.t.* to stay longer than (a specified time or another person). **outstep** *v.t.* (*pres.p.* **outstepping**, *past, p.p.* **outstepped**) to overstep. **outstretch** *v.t.* **1** to stretch out. **2** to reach further than. **outstrip** *v.t.* (*pres.p.* **outstripping**, *past, p.p.* **outstripped**) **1** to outrun, to leave behind. **2** to surpass in progress. **outswinger** (owt´-) *n.* in cricket, a ball that swings away from the batsman.

outside (owtsīd´, owt´-) *n.* **1** the external part or surface, the exterior. **2** the external appearance, superficial aspect. **3** that which is without. **4** external space, region, position etc. **5** the utmost limit, the extreme. **6** the side of a path away from a wall or next to a road. **7** an outside player in football etc. ~*a.* **1** of or relating to, situated on, near, or nearer to the outside, outer. **2** external, superficial. **3** highest or greatest possible, extreme. **4** remote, most unlikely. **5** not of or belonging to an institution etc. ~*adv.* **1** to or on the outside. **2** without, not within. **3** (*sl.*) not in prison. ~*prep.* **1** at, on, to, or of the exterior of. **2** without, out from, forth from. **3** beyond the limits of. **at the outside** at the most. **outside and in** outside and inside. **outside in** having the outer side turned in, and vice versa. **to get outside of** (*sl.*) to eat or drink. **outside broadcast** *n.* a radio or television broadcast from outside the studio. **outside edge** *n.* in skating, a stroke on the outer edge of the skate. **outside interest** *n.* a hobby. **outside-left, outside-right** *n.* in football, hockey etc., an attacking player on the extreme left or right. **outside of** *prep.* **1** outside. **2** (*N Am., coll.*) apart from. **outsider** (-sī´-) *n.* **1** a person who is not a member of a profession, party, circle, coterie etc. **2** a person not admissible to decent society. **3** in racing etc., a horse or competitor not included among the favourites. **outside track** *n.* the outside lane of a sports track.

Usage note The use of *outside of* as a preposition (rather than simple *outside*) is sometimes disapproved of.

out- (**+ t—w words**) **out-take** (owt´-) *n.* an unreleased piece of recorded music, film or television. **out-talk** *v.t.* **1** to outdo in talking. **2** to

talk down. **out-think** *v.t.* (*past, p.p.* **out-thought**) **1** to outwit. **2** to outdo in thinking. **out-thrust**[1] (owt´-) *n.* **1** outward thrust or pressure. **2** the act or an instance of becoming noticeable. **out-thrust**[2] (-thrŭst´) *v.t.* (*past, p.p.* **out-thrust**) to thrust forth or forward. **out-top** *v.t.* to surmount or surpass in height etc. **out-tray** (owt´-) *n.* a tray in an office for outgoing documents, correspondence etc. **out-turn** (owt´-) *n.* **1** the quantity produced. **2** the result of a process, an outcome. **outvalue** *v.t.* (*3rd pers. sing. pres.* **outvalues**, *pres.p.* **outvaluing**, *past, p.p.* **outvalued**) to exceed in value. **outvote** *v.t.* **1** to outnumber in voting. **2** to cast more votes than. **outwalk** *v.t.* **1** to outdo or outstrip in walking. **2** to walk beyond. **outwash** (owt´-) *n.* a mass of gravel, sand etc. carried by melted water from a glacier and deposited. **outwatch** *v.t.* **1** to watch longer than. **2** to watch throughout (a specified time). **outwear**[1] (-weə´) *v.t.* (*pres.p.* **outwearing**, *past* **outwore**, *p.p.* **outworn**) **1** to wear out. **2** to last longer than. **outwear**[2] (owt´-) *n.* outer garments. **outweigh** *v.t.* **1** to weigh more than. **2** to be of more value, importance etc. than. **outwit** *v.t.* (*pres.p.* **outwitting**, *past, p.p.* **outwitted**) to defeat by superior ingenuity and cunning. **outwith** *prep.* (*Sc.*) outside, beyond. **outwork** (owt´-) *n.* **1** a work included in the defence of a place, but outside the parapet. **2** work done outside the shop, factory etc. **outworker** (owt´-) *n.* a person who works outside (a factory, shop etc.). **outworking** (owt´-) *n.* the action or process of working out. **outworn** *a.* **1** worn out. **2** obsolete. **outward** (owt´wəd) *a.* **1** exterior, outer. **2** tending or directed toward the outside. **3** (of a ship, voyage etc.) leaving for a particular destination. **4** external, visible, apparent, superficial. **5** material, worldly, corporeal, not spiritual. ~*adv.* (*also* **outwards**) in an outward direction. ~*n.* outward or external appearance. **outward bound** *a.* going away from home. **Outward Bound®** *n.* a movement that provides adventure training for young people. **outwardly** *adv.* **outwardness** *n.*

ouzel (oo´zəl), **ousel** *n.* **1** a thrush, *Turdus torquatus*, the ring ouzel. **2** the dipper, *Cinclus cinclus*, the water ouzel.

ouzo (oo´zō) *n.* (*pl.* **ouzos**) an aniseed-flavoured spirit from Greece.

ova ovum.

oval (ō´vəl) *a.* egg-shaped, roughly elliptical. ~*n.* **1** a closed convex curve with one axis longer than the other. **2** an egg-shaped figure or thing, e.g. a sports field. **ovality** (-val´-) *n.* **ovally** *adv.* **ovalness** *n.*

ovary (ō´vəri) *n.* (*pl.* **ovaries**) **1** each of the organs (two in number in the higher vertebrates) in a female in which the ova are produced. **2** (*Bot.*) the portion of the pistil in which the ovules are contained. **ovarian** (-veə´ri-) *a.* **ovariectomy** (-ekt´əmi) *n.* (*pl.* **ovariectomies**) the removal of the ovary by excision, or of a tumour from the ovary. **ovariotomy** (-ot´əmi) *n.* (*pl.* **ovariotomies**).

ovaritis (-rī'tis) *n.* inflammation of the ovary.
ovate (ō'vāt) *a.* (*Biol.*) egg-shaped.
ovation (ōvā'shən) *n.* a display of popular favour, an enthusiastic reception. **ovational** *a.*
oven (-v'ən) *n.* **1** a close chamber in which substances are baked etc. **2** a furnace or kiln for assaying, annealing etc. **ovenbird, ovenbuilder** *n.* any Central or S American bird of the family Furnariidae, which make domed nests. **ovenproof** *a.* suitable for use in an oven. **oven-ready** *a.* (of food) already prepared for immediate cooking in an oven. **ovenware** *n.* heat-resistant dishes used for cooking and serving food.
over (ō'və) *prep.* **1** above, in a higher position than. **2** above or superior to in excellence, dignity or value. **3** more than, in excess of. **4** in charge of, concerned or engaged with. **5** across from side to side of. **6** through the extent or duration of. **7** having recovered from the effect of. **8** (*Math.*) divided by. **9** transmitted by. **10** in comparison with. **11** so as to cover. ~*adv.* **1** so as to pass from side to side or across some space, barrier etc. **2** in width, in distance across. **3** on the opposite side. **4** from one side to another. **5** so as to be turned down or upside down from an erect position. **6** so as to be across or down from a brink, brim etc. **7** so as to traverse a space etc. **8** from end to end, throughout. **9** at an end. **10** in excess, in addition. **11** excessively, with repetition, again. **12** for or until a later time. ~*a.* **1** upper, outer. **2** superior. **3** extra. ~*int.* (*also* **over to you**) in radio signalling etc., indicating that a reply is expected. ~*n.* **1** in cricket, the interval between the times when the umpire calls 'over'. **2** the number of balls (6 or 8) delivered by one bowler during this. **not over** not very. **over all** taken as a whole. **over and above 1** in addition to. **2** besides. **over and over 1** so as to turn completely round several times. **2** repeatedly. **over the way** across the street. **to begin over** (*N Am.*) to start over. **to get it over with** to do something unpleasant that has to be done. **to start over** (*N Am.*) to start again. **over again** *adv.* afresh, anew. **over against** *prep.* **1** opposite. **2** in front of. **3** in contrast with. **over-the-counter** *a.* obtainable without a prescription. **over-the-top** *a.* extreme, outrageous.
over- (ō'və) *pref.* **1** above. **2** across. **3** outer, upper. **4** as a covering. **5** past, beyond. **6** extra. **7** excessively, too much, too great. **8** completely, utterly.
over- (+ a–t words) over-abundant *a.* in excessive quantity. **over-abundance** *n.* **over-abundantly** *adv.* **overachieve** *v.i.* to do more than might be expected. ~*v.t.* to achieve more than (a goal). **overachievement** *n.* **overachiever** *n.* **overact** *v.t.* to act (a part) in an exaggerated way. ~*v.i.* to act more than is necessary. **overactivity** *n.* **overactive** *a.* excessively active. **overage** (ō'vərij) *n.* a surplus or excess. **over-age** *n.* over a certain age limit. **overall**[1] (ō'-) *a.* from end to end, total. ~*n.* **1** an outer garment worn as a protection against dirt etc. **2** (*pl.*) trousers or other garments

worn over others as a protection against dirt etc. **3** (*pl.*) close-fitting trousers worn as part of army uniform. **overall**[2] (-awl') *adv.* everywhere, in all parts or directions. **overalled** *a.* **overambitious** *a.* too ambitious. **overambition** *n.* **overambitiously** *adv.* **over-anxious** *a.* excessively anxious. **over-anxiety** *n.* **over-anxiously** *adv.* **overarch** *v.t.* to form an arch over. ~*v.i.* to form an arch overhead. **overarching** *a.* **overarm** (ō'-) *a.* **1** in sports, esp. cricket, bowled or thrown with the arm raised above the shoulder. **2** in swimming, with the arm or arms lifted out of the water. ~*adv.* the arm raised above the shoulder. **overawe** *v.t.* **1** to hold in awe. **2** to control or restrain by awe. **overbalance** *v.t.* **1** to outweigh. **2** to destroy the equilibrium of. **3** to upset. ~*v.i.* **1** to lose one's equilibrium. **2** to topple over. **overbear** *v.t.* (*pres.p.* **overbearing,** *past* **overbore,** *p.p.* **overborne) 1** to bear down, to overpower. **2** to surpass in importance etc. **overbearing** *a.* arrogant, haughty, imperious. **overbearingly** *adv.* **overbearingness** *n.* **overbid** *v.t., v.i.* (*pres.p.* **overbidding,** *past, p.p.* **overbid) 1** to outbid. **2** to bid more than the value of (one's hand of cards). ~*n.* a higher bid. **overbidder** *n.* **overbite** (ō'-) *n.* in dentistry, the overlapping of the lower teeth by the upper. **overblouse** (ō'-) *n.* a garment worn like a blouse, worn outside other clothing. **overblown**[1] (-blōn') *a.* inflated, pretentious. **overblown**[2] (ō'-) *a.* more than full blown. **overboard** (ō'-) *adv.* over the side of a ship. **to go overboard 1** (*coll.*) to go to extremes of enthusiasm. **2** to go too far. **to throw overboard** to abandon, discard. **overbook** *v.t., v.i.* to make bookings for more places than are available (e.g. in a hotel, plane, ship etc.). **overboot** (ō'-) *n.* a boot worn over another boot or shoe. **overbuild** *v.t.* (*past, p.p.* **overbuilt) 1** to build too much upon (land etc.). **2** to build over or upon. **overburden** (-bœ'-) *v.t.* to overload, to overweigh. **overburdensome** *a.* **overbusy** *a.* excessively busy. **overcall**[1] (-kawl') *v.t.* to bid higher than a previous bid or player at bridge. **overcall**[2] (ō'-) *n.* a higher bid than the preceding one. **overcapacity** *n.* a state of saturation or an excess of productive capacity. **overcapitalize, overcapitalise** *v.t.* to rate or fix the nominal value of the capital of (a company etc.) at too high a figure. **overcareful** *a.* careful to excess. **overcarefully** *adv.* **overcast** *v.t.* (*pres.p.* **overcasting,** *past, p.p.* **overcast) 1** to darken, to cloud. **2** to render gloomy or depressed. **3** to sew (an edge etc.) with long stitches to prevent unravelling etc., or as embroidering. ~*a.* **1** clouded all over (of the sky). **2** sewn or embroidered by overcasting. **overcharge** *v.t.* **1** to charge with more than is properly due. **2** to overburden, to overload. **3** to load (a firearm) with an excessive charge. **4** to exaggerate. **overcoat** (ō'-) *n.* **1** a heavy coat. **2** a protective coat of paint etc. **overcome** *v.t.* (*pres.p.* **overcoming,** *past* **overcame,** *p.p.* **overcome**) to overpower, to vanquish, to conquer. ~*v.i.* to be victorious. ~*a.* exhausted, helpless, affected by emotion etc. **overcommit** *v.t.* (*pres.p.* **overcommitting**, *past*, *p.p.* **overcommitted**) (*usu. reflex.*) to commit to an excessive degree. **overcommitment** *n.* **overcompensate** *v.t.* to provide with too much in compensation. ~*v.i.* (*Psych.*) to react excessively to feelings of inferiority or inadequacy etc. **overcompensation** *n.* **overconfidence** *n.* excessive confidence. **overconfident** *a.* **overconfidently** *adv.* **overcook** *v.t.* to cook too much or for too long. **overcritical** *a.* excessively critical. **overcrowd** *v.t.*, *v.i.* to crowd to excess. **overcrowding** *n.* **overcurious** *a.* too curious. **overcuriosity** *n.* **overdelicate** *a.* excessively delicate. **overdelicacy** *n.* **overdetermine** *v.t.* to determine in more than one way, or with more conditions than are necessary. **overdetermination** *n.* **overdetermined** *a.* **overdevelop** *v.t.* (*pres.p.* **overdeveloping**, *past*, *p.p.* **overdeveloped**) 1 to develop (a photographic negative) too much so that the image is too dense. 2 to develop too much. **overdo** *v.t.* (*3rd pers. sing. pres.* **overdoes**, *pres.p.* **overdoing**, *past* **overdid**, *p.p.* **overdone**) 1 to do to excess. 2 to exaggerate. 3 to overact. 4 to cook to excess. 5 to fatigue, to wear out. **to overdo it** to exhaust oneself, do too much. **overdose**[1] (ō´-) *n.* an excessive dose. **overdose**[2] (-dōs´) *v.t.* to give too large a dose to. ~*v.i.* to take an overdose. **overdosage** *n.* **overdraft** (ō´-) *n.* 1 a withdrawal of money from a bank in excess of the amount to one's credit. 2 the amount of this. **overdramatic** *a.* excessively dramatic. **overdramatize**, **overdramatise** *v.t.* to be excessively dramatic in one's reaction, behaviour etc. **overdraw** *v.t.* (*past* **overdrew**, *p.p.* **overdrawn**) 1 to draw upon for a larger sum than stands to one's credit. 2 to exaggerate. ~*v.i.* to overdraw one's account. **overdrawer** *n.* **overdrawn** *a.* having overdrawn one's account. **overdress**[1] (-dres´) *v.t.*, *v.i.* to dress too formally or ostentatiously. **overdress**[2] (ō´-) *n.* a dress worn over other clothes. **overdrink** *v.i.* (*past* **overdrank**, *p.p.* **overdrunk**) to drink too much. **overdrive** (ō´-) *n.* 1 an extra high gear in a motor car which drives the propeller shaft at a higher speed than the engine crankshaft. 2 a state of great activity. **overdub** *v.t.* (*pres.p.* **overdubbing**, *past*, *p.p.* **overdubbed**) to add additional sounds to a recording. ~*n.* an act or instance of overdubbing. **overdue** *a.* 1 remaining unpaid after the date on which it is due. 2 not arrived at the time it was due. 3 (of a library book etc.) kept longer than the period allowed. **overeager** *a.* excessively eager. **overeagerly** *adv.* **overeagerness** *n.* **overeat** *v.i.* (*past* **overate**, *p.p.* **overeaten**) 1 to eat to excess. 2 (*reflex.*) to injure (oneself) by eating to excess. **over-elaborate** *a.* excessively elaborate. ~*v.t.* to explain in too much detail. **over-elaborately** *adv.* **over-elaboration** *n.* **over-emotional** *a.* excessively emotional. **over-emotionally** *adv.* **over-emphasis** *n.* excessive emphasis. **overemphasize**, **overemphasise** *v.t.*, *v.i.* **overenthusiasm** *n.* excessive enthusiasm. **overenthusiastic** *a.* over-

enthusiastically *adv.* **overestimate** *v.t.* to give too high a value to. ~*n.* too high an estimate. **overestimation** *n.* **overexcite** *v.t.* to excite excessively. **overexcitement** *n.* **over-exercise** *v.t.* to use too much. ~*v.i.* to take too much exercise. ~*n.* excessive exercise. **overexert** *v.t.* to exert too much. **overexertion** *n.* **overexpose** *v.t.* 1 to expose too much. 2 to expose (a film) to light too long so as to make the negative defective. **overexposure** *n.* **overextend** *v.t.* 1 to extend too far. 2 (*reflex.*) to take on too much work etc. 3 to impose too much work on. **overfall** *n.* 1 a turbulent race or current with choppy waves caused by shoals, the meeting of cross-currents etc. 2 a structure for the overflow of water from a canal etc. **overfamiliar** *a.* too familiar. **overfamiliarity** *n.* **overfatigue** *n.* excessive fatigue. **overfeed** *v.t.* (*past*, *p.p.* **overfed**) to surfeit with food. **overfill** *v.t.*, *v.i.* to fill to excess. **overfine** *a.* excessively fine or precise. **overfish** *v.t.* to deplete (a stream etc.) by too much fishing. **overflow**[1] (-flō´) *v.t.* 1 to flow over, to flood, to inundate. 2 to cover as with a liquid. ~*v.i.* 1 to run over. 2 to abound. 3 to overflow the banks (of a stream). 4 (*followed by with*) to be full of. **overflow**[2] (ō´-) *n.* 1 a flood, an inundation. 2 a superabundance, a profusion. 3 any outlet for surplus liquid. 4 (*Comput.*) the generation of a number having more digits than the assigned location. **overflow meeting** *n.* an extra meeting for people unable to attend the main meeting. **overfly** *v.t.* (*3rd pers. sing. pres.* **overflies**, *pres.p.* **overflying**, *past* **overflew**, *p.p.* **overflown**) to fly over or beyond. **overflight** *n.* **overfond** *a.* 1 too fond. 2 doting. **overfondly** *adv.* **overfull** *a.* 1 too full. 2 surfeited. **overgarment** *n.* a garment worn over other clothing. **overgeneralize**, **overgeneralise** *v.i.* 1 to draw general conclusions from inadequate data. 2 to argue more widely than is justified by the evidence etc. ~*v.t.* to draw an excessively general conclusion from (data etc.). **overgeneralization** *n.* **overgenerous** *a.* excessively generous. **overgenerously** *adv.* **overglaze** *n.* 1 a second glaze on ceramic ware. 2 decoration on a glazed surface. ~*a.* (of painting etc.) done on a glazed surface. **overgraze** *v.t.* 1 to allow (land) to be excessively grazed. 2 (of livestock) to feed on (land) too heavily so that the vegetation is damaged. **overground** (ō´-) *a.* situated or running above ground, as opposed to *underground*. ~*adv.* 1 above ground. 2 in or into the open. **overgrow** *v.t.* (*past* **overgrew**, *p.p.* **overgrown**) to cover with vegetation. ~*v.i.* to grow too large. **overgrown** *a.* **overgrowth** (ō´-) *n.* **overhand** (ō´-) *a.* thrown or done with the hand raised above the level of the shoulder or elbow (of a ball, bowling etc.). ~*adv.* in this manner. **overhand knot** *n.* a simple knot made by forming a loop and passing the free end through it. **overhang**[1] *v.i.* (*past*, *p.p.* **overhung**) to hang over, to jut out. ~*v.t.* 1 to hang or impend over. 2 to threaten. **overhang**[2] (ō´-) *n.* 1 the act or an instance of overhanging. 2 the part or thing that overhangs. **3** the amount by which a thing overhangs. **overhaste** *n.* excessive haste. **overhasty** *a.* **overhastily** *adv.* **overhaul**[1] *v.t.* **1** to turn over thoroughly for examination. **2** to examine thoroughly. **3** to overtake, to gain upon. **overhaul**[2] (ō´-) *n.* inspection, thorough examination. **overhead**[1] *adv.* **1** above the head, aloft. **2** in the zenith, ceiling, roof etc. ~*a.* **1** situated overhead. **2** working from above downwards. **3** all round, average, general. **overhead**[2] (ō´-) *n.* **1** a stroke in racket games made above head height. **2** (*pl., N Am. sing.*) expenses of administration etc. **overhead projector** *n.* a device that projects an enlarged image of a transparency on to a screen behind the operator. **overhear** *v.t.* (*past, p.p.* **overheard**) to hear (words not meant for one) by accident or stratagem. **overheat** *v.t.* **1** to heat to excess. **2** to stimulate or agitate. ~*v.i.* to become overheated. **over-indulge** *v.t., v.i.* (*often reflex.*) to indulge to excess. **over-indulgence** *n.* **over-indulgent** *a.* **over-insure** *v.t.* to insure (property etc.) for more than its real value. **over-insurance** *n.* **overjoy** *v.t.* to transport with joy. **overjoyed** *a.* **overkill** (ō´-) *n.* **1** destructive capability, esp. in nuclear weapons, in excess of military requirements. **2** something applied in excess of what is suitable or required. ~*v.t., v.i.* to kill or destroy to a greater extent than necessary. **overladen** *a.* overburdened. **overland** (ō´-) *a.* lying, going, made or performed by land. ~*adv.* across the land. ~*v.t.* (*Austral.*) to take livestock across country. ~*v.i.* (*Austral.*) to go a long distance overland. **overlander** *n.* (*Austral., New Zeal.*) **1** a person who takes livestock a great distance for sale to a new station. **2** (*sl.*) a tramp. **overlap**[1] *v.t.* (*pres.p.* **overlapping**, *past, p.p.* **overlapped**) **1** to lap or fold over. **2** to extend so as to lie or rest upon. ~*v.i.* to coincide. **overlap**[2] (ō´-) *n.* **1** an act, case or the extent of overlapping. **2** the part that overlaps something else. **overlarge** *a.* too large. **overlay**[1] (-lā´) *v.t.* (*past, p.p.* **overlaid**) **1** to cover or spread over the surface of. **2** to cover with a layer. **3** to overcast, to cloud. **4** to weigh down. **overlay**[2] (ō´-) *n.* **1** something laid over (as a covering, layer etc.). **2** (*Comput.*) **a** the process of transferring data etc. to replace what is already stored. **b** a section so transferred.

Usage note See note under overlie (under over- (+ A–T WORDS)).

overleaf *adv.* on the other side of the leaf (of a book etc.). **overleap** *v.t.* (*past, p.p.* **overleaped, overleapt**) **1** to leap over. **2** to leap beyond. **3** to leap too far over. **4** to omit. **overlie** *v.t.* (*pres.p.* **overlying**, *past.* **overlay**, *p.p.* **overlain**) **1** to lie above or upon. **2** to smother by lying on.

Usage note The meanings of *overlie* and *overlay* overlap, but in general *overlie* is preferred for lying on top of or smothering something, and *overlay* is the appropriate term for covering or coating a surface.

overload[1] (-lōd´) *v.t.* **1** to load too heavily. **2** to overcharge. **overload**[2] (ō´-) *n.* an excessive load. **overlong** *a., adv.* too long, excessively long. **overlook**[1] (-luk´-) *v.t.* **1** to look over, to pass over with indulgence, to disregard, to slight. **2** to view from a high place. **3** to be situated so as to command a view of from above. **4** to superintend, to oversee. **5** to inspect or peruse, esp. in a cursory way. **overlook**[2] (ō´-) *n.* (*N Am.*) a commanding position or view. **overlooker** (ō´-) *n.* **overlord** (ō´-) *n.* **1** a superior lord, one who is lord over other lords. **2** a person who is supreme over another or others. **overly** (ō´-) *adv.* excessively, too. **overman** (-man´) *v.t.* (*pres.p.* **overmanning**, *past, p.p.* **overmanned**) to furnish with too many people. **overmantel** (ō´-) *n.* ornamental woodwork placed over a mantelpiece. **over-many** *a.* too many. **overmaster** *v.t.* **1** to master completely. **2** to overcome, to subdue. **overmastery** *n.* **overmatch** *v.t.* to be more than a match for. **overmeasure** *n.* a measure above what is sufficient or due. **over-mighty** *a.* excessively powerful. **overmuch** *a.* too much, more than is sufficient or necessary. ~*adv.* in or to too great a degree. **overnice** *a.* too nice, scrupulous, or fastidious. **overniceness** *n.* **overnicety** *n.* **overnight** *a.* **1** done or happening the night before. **2** for use overnight. ~*adv.* **1** in the course of the night or evening. **2** during or through the night. **3** suddenly, immediately. **overnighter** *n.* **1** a person who stays somewhere overnight. **2** an overnight bag. **overoptimistic** *a.* excessively or unjustifiably optimistic. **overoptimism** *n.* **overpaint** *v.t.* to paint over. **overparticular** *a.* excessively particular. **overpass**[1] (-pahs´) *v.t.* (*past, p.p.* **overpassed, overpast**) **1** to pass or go over. **2** to overlook. **3** to pass or go beyond. **overpass**[2] (ō´-) *n.* a flyover. **overpay** *v.t., v.i.* (*past, p.p.* **overpaid**) **1** to pay more than is sufficient. **2** to pay in excess. **overpayment** *n.* **overpessimistic** *a.* **overpitch** *v.t.* **1** to bowl (a ball) so that it pitches too near the stumps. **2** to exaggerate. **overplay** *v.t.* **1** to exaggerate the importance of. **2** to over-emphasize. **to overplay one's hand 1** to overestimate one's capabilities. **2** to spoil one's case by exaggerating. **overplus** (ō´-) *n.* **1** surplus, excess. **2** an amount left over. **overpopulated** *a.* having too large a population. **overpopulation** *n.* **overpower** *v.t.* **1** to be too strong or powerful for. **2** to overcome, conquer, vanquish. **3** to overcome the feelings or judgement of, to overwhelm. **overpowering** *a.* **overpoweringly** *adv.* **overprescribe** *v.t.* to prescribe excessively. **overprescription** *n.* **overprice** *v.t.* to price too highly. **overprint**[1] (ō´-) *n.* printed matter added to a previously printed surface, esp. a postage stamp. **overprint**[2] (-print´) *v.t.* **1** to print on a previously printed surface. **2** in photography, to print (a positive) darker than was intended. **3** to print too many copies of (a work). **overproduction** *n.* production in excess of demand. **overproduce** *v.t., v.i.* **overproof** *a.* above proof, containing a larger proportion of alcohol than is contained in proof-spirit. **overprotective** *a.* excessively protective. **overqualified** *a.* too highly qualified. **overrate** *v.t.* to rate too highly. **overrated** *a.* **overreach** *v.t.* **1** to reach or extend beyond. **2** to get the better of, to outwit, to cheat. **to overreach oneself 1** to strain oneself by reaching too far. **2** to defeat one's object by going too far. **overreact** *v.i.* to respond excessively. **overreaction** *n.* **over-refine** *v.t.* to refine too much, to be oversubtle. **over-refinement** *n.* **override**[1] (-rīd´) *v.t.* (*pres.p.* **overriding,** *past* **overrode,** *p.p.* **overridden**) **1** to ride over. **2** to trample as if underfoot, to disregard, to set aside, to supersede. **3** to fatigue or exhaust by excessive riding. **4** to outride, to overtake. **5** to take manual control of an automatic system. **override**[2] (ō´-) *n.* **1** a device used to override automatic control. **2** the action or process of overriding. **overriding** (-rī´-) *a.* dominant, taking precedence. **overripe** *a.* ripe to excess. **overrule** *v.t.* **1** to control by superior power or authority. **2** to set aside. **3** to reject, to disallow. **overrun**[1] (-rŭn´) *v.t.* (*pres.p.* **overrunning,** *past* **overran,** *p.p.* **overrun**) **1** to run or spread over. **2** to grow over. **3** to invade or harass by hostile incursions. **4** to extend over. **5** to run beyond, to outrun. **6** in mechanics, to run faster than. **7** (*Print.*) to carry over and change the arrangement of (type set up). *~v.i.* **1** to overflow. **2** to extend beyond the proper limits. **overrun**[2] (ō´-) *n.* **1** an instance of overrunning. **2** the amount of this. **3** the movement of a vehicle at a speed greater than is imparted by the engine. **overscrupulous** *a.* excessively scrupulous. **oversea** *a.* **1** beyond the sea, foreign. **2** of or connected with movement over the sea. *~adv.* from beyond the sea. **overseas** *adv.* **from overseas** from abroad. **oversee** *v.t.* (*pres.p.* **overseeing,** *past* **oversaw,** *p.p.* **overseen**) **1** to superintend. **2** to overlook, to disregard, to neglect. **overseer** (ō´-) *n.* a superintendent, an inspector. **oversell** *v.t.* (*past, p.p.* **oversold**) **1** to sell more than. **2** to sell more of (stocks etc.) than one can deliver. **3** to exaggerate the merits (of a commodity). *~v.i.* to use aggressive sales methods. **oversensitive** *a.* excessively sensitive. **oversensitiveness** *n.* **oversensitivity** *n.* **overset** *v.t.* (*pres.p.* **oversetting,** *past, p.p.* **overset**) **1** to upset. **2** to overthrow. **3** (*Print.*) to set up too much type for (a page etc.). **oversew** *v.t.* (*past* **oversewed,** *p.p.* **oversewn, oversewed**) to sew (two pieces or edges) together by passing the needle through from one side only so that the thread between the stitches lies over the edges. **oversexed** *a.* **1** obsessed with sexual activity. **2** having an abnormally active sex life. **overshadow** *v.t.* **1** to throw shadow over, to shade over, to obscure with or as with cloud. **2** to shelter, to protect. **3** to tower high above, to exceed in importance. **overshoe** (ō´-) *n.* a shoe worn over another. **overshoot**[1] (-shoot´) *v.t.* (*past, p.p.* **overshot**) **1** to shoot over or beyond. **2** to go beyond, to overstep, to exceed. *~v.i.* to go beyond

the mark. **to overshoot the mark** to go beyond what is intended. **overshoot**[2] (ō´-) *n.* **1** the act of overshooting. **2** the amount of this. **overshot** *a.* **1** driven by water sent over the top. **2** projecting, overlapping. **overside** *adv.* over the side (as of a ship). **oversight** (ō´-) *n.* **1** superintendence, supervision, care. **2** a mistake, an inadvertence, an unintentional error or omission. **oversimplify** *v.t., v.i.* (*3rd pers. sing. pres.* **oversimplifies,** *pres.p.* **oversimplifying,** *past, p.p.* **oversimplified**) to distort the perception of (a problem etc.) by making it seem too simple. **oversimplification** *n.* **oversize** *n.* a size above the ordinary. **oversized** *a.* **overskirt** (ō´-) *n.* an outer skirt. **oversleep** *v.i., v.t.* (*past, p.p.* **overslept**) (*often reflex.*) to sleep too long. **oversleeve** (ō´-) *n.* a protective sleeve covering another sleeve. **oversolicitous** *a.* excessively worried, concerned etc. **oversolicitude** *n.* **overspecialize, overspecialise** *v.i.* to concentrate too much on one aspect or area. **overspecialization** *n.* **overspend** *v.t.* (*past, p.p.* **overspent**) **1** to spend too much of (income etc.). **2** to wear, to exhaust. *~v.i.* (*often reflex.*) to spend beyond one's means. **overspill** (ō´-) *n.* **1** something spilt over. **2** people who have moved from crowded cities into surrounding areas. **overspread** *v.t.* (*past, p.p.* **overspread**) **1** to spread over. **2** to cover (with). **3** to be spread over. **overstaff** *v.t.* to provide with too large a staff. **overstate** *v.t.* to state too strongly, to exaggerate. **overstatement** *n.* **overstay** *v.t.* to stay longer than or beyond the limits of. **oversteer**[1] (-stia´) *v.i.* (of a motor vehicle) to have a tendency to turn too sharply. **oversteer**[2] (ō´-) *n.* (of a motor vehicle) the tendency to turn too sharply. **overstep** *v.t.* (*pres.p.* **overstepping,** *past, p.p.* **overstepped**) to exceed, to transgress. **to overstep the mark** to violate conventions of behaviour. **overstitch** *n.* a stitch made over an edge or over another stitch. *~v.t.* to sew with an overstitch. **overstock**[1] (ō´-) *n.* superabundance, excess. **overstock**[2] (-stok´) *v.t.* to stock to excess. **overstrain** *v.i.* to strain or exert too much. **overstress**[1] (-stres´) *v.t.* to stress too much. **overstress**[2] (ō´-) *n.* an excessive degree of stress. **overstretch** *v.t.* to stretch too much, to make too many demands on. **overstrung**[1] (-strŭng´) *a.* too highly strung. **overstrung**[2] (ō´-) *a.* (of a piano) with strings in sets crossing each other obliquely. **overstudied** *a.* affected; excessively deliberate. **overstudy** *v.t., v.i.* (*3rd pers. sing. pres.* **overstudies,** *pres.p.* **overstudying,** *past, p.p.* **overstudied**) to study excessively. **overstuff** *v.t.* **1** to stuff more than is necessary. **2** to cover (furniture) with thick upholstery. **oversubscribe** *v.t.* to subscribe or apply for more than is available. **oversubscribed** *a.* **oversubscription** *n.* **oversubtle** *a.* too subtle. **oversupply** *v.t.* (*3rd pers. sing. pres.* **oversupplies,** *pres.p.* **oversupplying,** *past, p.p.* **oversupplied**) to supply with too much. *~n.* (*pl.* **oversupplies**) an excessive supply. **oversusceptible** *a.* too susceptible or vulnerable.

overtake *v.t.* (*pres.p.* **overtaking**, *past* **overtook**, *p.p.* **overtaken**) **1** to come up with, to catch. **2** to reach, to attain to. **3** to take by surprise, to come upon suddenly. **overtask** *v.t.* **1** to burden with too heavy a task. **2** to be too heavy a task for. **overtax** *v.t.* **1** to tax too heavily. **2** to overburden. **overthrow**[1] (-thrō') *v.t.* (*past* **overthrew**, *p.p.* **overthrown**) **1** to overturn, throw down, demolish. **2** to overcome, conquer, subvert. **overthrow**[2] (ō'-) *n.* **1** defeat, discomfiture. **2** ruin, destruction. **3** in cricket, a ball returned to but missed by the wicketkeeper, allowing further runs to be made. **4** such a run. **5** (*Archit.*) a panel of decorated wrought-iron work in an arch or gateway. **overthrust** (ō'-) *n.* **1** (*Geol.*) the thrust of strata over those on the other side of a fault. **2** the amount of this. **overtime** (ō'-) *n.* **1** time during which one works beyond the regular hours. **2** work done during this period. **3** the rate of pay for such work. **4** (*N Am.*) in sport, extra time. ~*adv.* in addition to regular hours. **overtire** *v.t.* (*also reflex.*) to exhaust or wear out. **overtone** (ō'-) *n.* **1** (*esp. Mus.*) a harmonic. **2** a secondary meaning, a nuance. **overtop** *v.t.* (*pres.p.* **overtopping**, *past, p.p.* **overtopped**) to tower over, to surmount, to surpass. **overtrain** *v.t.* to subject to excessive training. **overturn**[1] (-tœn') *v.t.* to turn over, to upset. ~*v.i.* to be upset or turned over. **overturn**[2] (ō'-) *n.* **1** the act of overturning. **2** the state of being overturned.

overt (ōvœt') *a.* open, plain, public, apparent. **overtly** *adv.* **overtness** *n.*

overture (ō'vətūə) *n.* **1** (*Mus.*) an introductory piece for instruments, a prelude to an opera or oratorio. **2** a single-movement orchestral piece. **3** (*usu. in pl.*) a preliminary proposal, an offer to negotiate, or of suggested terms.

over- (+ **u–z words**) **overuse**[1] (-ūz') *v.t.* to use too much. **overuse**[2] (-ūs') *n.* excessive use. **overvalue** *v.t.* (*3rd pers. sing. pres.* **overvalues**, *pres.p.* **overvaluing**, *past, p.p.* **overvalued**) to value too highly. **overvaluation** *n.* **overview** (ō'-) *n.* an inspection, a survey. **overwater**[1] (-waw'-) *v.t.* to water too much. **overwater**[2] (ō'-) *a.* situated above the water. **overweening** *a.* arrogant, conceited, presumptuous. ~*n.* excessive conceit. **overweeningly** *adv.* **overweeningness** *n.* **overweight** *v.t.* **1** to weigh down. **2** to give too much emphasis to. ~*n.* **1** excess of weight. **2** preponderance. ~*a.* exceeding the normal or accepted weight. **overwhelm** *v.t.* **1** to cover completely, to submerge. **2** to crush, to engulf. **3** to destroy utterly. **4** to overcome, to bear down, to overpower. **overwhelming** *a.* **overwhelmingly** *adv.* **overwhelmingness** *n.* **overwind**[1] (-wīnd') *v.t.* (*past, p.p.* **overwound**) to wind too much or too tight. **overwind**[2] (ō'-) *n.* an instance of overwinding. **overwinter** *v.i.* **1** to spend the winter. **2** (of insects, fungi etc.) to live through the winter. ~*v.t.* to keep (animals, plants etc.) alive through the winter. **overwork** *v.t.* **1** to impose too much work upon. **2** to exhaust with work. ~*v.i.* to work

to excess. ~*n.* work beyond what is required or regular. **overworked** *a.* **1** used or working excessively. **2** overdone, overwrought. **overwrite** *v.t.* (*pres.p.* **overwriting**, *past* **overwrote**, *p.p.* **overwritten**) **1** (*Comput.*) to write data into computer memory, or on to magnetic tape or disk, thereby erasing the existing contents. **2** to write in an artificial or ornate style. **3** to write on top of (other writing). ~*v.i.* **1** to write in an artificial or ornate style. **2** to write too much. **3** in shipping insurance, to accept more risk than the premium income limits allow. **overwriting** *n.* **overwrought** *a.* **1** excited, agitated, nervous. **2** elaborately decorated. **overzealous** *a.* too zealous.

oviduct (ō'vidŭkt) *n.* a passage through which ova pass from the ovary, esp. in oviparous animals. **oviducal** (-dū'kəl), **oviductal** (-dŭk'təl) *a.*

oviform (ō'vifawm) *a.* egg-shaped.

ovine (ō'vīn) *a.* of, relating to, or like sheep.

oviparous (ōvip'ərəs) *a.* (*Zool.*) producing young by means of eggs that are expelled and hatched outside the body. **oviparity** (-ar'-) *n.* **oviparously** *adv.* **oviparousness** *n.*

oviposit (ōvipoz'it) *v.i.* (*pres.p.* **ovipositing**, *past, p.p.* **oviposited**) (*Zool.*) to deposit eggs, esp. with an ovipositor. **oviposition** (-ish'-) *n.* **ovipositor** *n.* a tubular organ in many insects serving to deposit the eggs.

ovoid (ō'void) *a.* egg-shaped, oval with one end larger than the other, ovate. ~*n.* an ovoid body or figure.

ovoviviparous (ōvōvīvip'ərəs) *a.* (*Zool.*) producing young by ova hatched within the body of the parent. **ovoviviparity** (-par'-) *n.*

ovule (ov'ūl) *n.* the body in the ovary which develops into the seed after fertilization. **ovular** *a.* **ovulate** *v.i.* to produce or discharge ovaries or ovules. **ovulation** (-lā'shən) *n.* the periodical discharge of the ovum or egg cell from the ovary.

ovum (ō'vəm) *n.* (*pl.* **ova** (ō'və)) **1** the female egg cell, or gamete, produced within the ovary and capable, usu. after fertilization by the male, of developing into a new individual. **2** (*Bot.*) an ovule.

ow (ow) *int.* used to express pain.

owe (ō) *v.t.* **1** to be indebted to for a specified amount. **2** to be under obligation to pay or repay (a specified amount). **3** to be obliged or indebted for. **4** to have to thank for (a service, a grudge etc.). **to owe a person a grudge** to hold a grudge against a person. **to owe it to oneself** to feel the need to do something that is in one's own interests. **owing** *a.* **1** due as a debt. **2** attributable, ascribable, resulting from, on account of.

owl (owl) *n.* **1** any nocturnal raptorial bird of the order Strigiformes, with large head, short neck and short hooked beak, including barn owls, tawny owls etc. **2** a solemn-looking person. **owlery** *n.* (*pl.* **owleries**). **owlet** (-lit) *n.* **1** a young owl. **2** a small owl. **owlish** *a.* **owlishly** *adv.* **owlishness**

n. **owl-light** *n.* imperfect light, dusk, twilight. **owl-like** *a.*, *adv.*

own[1] (ōn) *a.* **1** belonging or proper to, particular, individual, not anyone else's (usu. appended as an intensive to the poss. pronoun, adjective etc.). **2** (*ellipt.*) in the closest degree, by both parents (of a brother or sister). **of one's own** belonging to oneself. **on one's own** without aid from other people, independently. **to come into one's own 1** to gain what one is due. **2** to have one's talents or potential acknowledged. **to get one's own back** to be even with. **own brand** *a.* (of goods on sale) displaying the name or label of the retailer rather than the producer. ~*n.* **1** such a make of goods. **2** a kind particular to a person or group. **own goal** *n.* **1** in football etc., a goal scored by a player against their own side by accident. **2** (*coll.*) any action which results in disadvantage to the person taking it.

own[2] (ōn) *v.t.* **1** to possess. **2** to have as property by right. **3** to acknowledge as one's own. **4** to recognize the authorship, paternity etc. of. **5** to admit, to concede as true or existent. ~*v.i.* to confess (to). **to own up** to confess, to make a clean breast (of). **owned** *a.* **owner** *n.* **1** a lawful proprietor. **2** (*sl.*) a ship's captain. **ownerless** *a.* **owner-occupier** *n.* someone who owns the house they live in. **owner-occupied** *a.* **ownership** *n.*

ox (oks) *n.* (*pl.* **oxen** (ok´sən)) **1** any bovine animal, esp. of domesticated species, large cloven-hoofed ruminants, usu. horned. **2** the castrated male of the domesticated *Bos taurus.* **oxbow** (-bō) *n.* **1** the bow-shaped piece of wood in an ox-yoke. **2** a bend in a river. **3** a lake formed by this. **oxer** *n.* **1** an ox-fence. **2** a similar fence used in showjumping. **ox-eye** *n.* any of various plants of the daisy family with dark centres, esp. *Leucanthemum vulgare*, also called *ox-eye daisy.* **ox-fence** *n.* a strong fence for keeping in cattle. **oxherd** *n.* a cowherd. **oxhide** *n.* **1** the skin of an ox. **2** leather made from this. **oxlip** *n.* **1** a primula, *Primula elatior*, which has pale yellow flowers. **2** a similar plant that is a hybrid between a primrose and a cowslip. **ox-pecker** *n.* any African bird of the genus *Buphagus*, which feeds from the hides of cattle. **oxtail** *n.* the tail of an ox, esp. when used for making soup. **ox-tongue** *n.* **1** the tongue of an ox, esp. used as food. **2** any plant of the genus *Picris*, with oblong bristly leaves.

oxalis (ok´səlis, -sal´-) *n.* any plant of the genus *Oxalis*, e.g. wood sorrel. **oxalate** (ok´sələt) *n.* a salt or ester of oxalic acid. **oxalic** (-sal´-) *a.* belonging to or derived from oxalis. **oxalic acid** *n.* (*Chem.*) a sour, highly-poisonous acid found in numerous plants.

Oxbridge (oks´brij) *n.* the Universities of Oxford and Cambridge, esp. seen as elitist educational establishments conferring social, economic and political advantages. ~*a.* of or relating to Oxbridge.

Oxford (oks´fəd) *a.* of, relating to, or derived from

Oxford. **Oxford bags** *n.pl.* trousers very wide at the ankles. **Oxford blue** *n.* a dark shade of blue. ~*a.* of the colour Oxford blue.

oxide (ok´sīd) *n.* (*Chem.*) a binary compound of oxygen with another element or an organic radical. **oxidant** (-si-) *n.* a substance used as an oxidizing agent. **oxidation** (-sidā´shən) *n.* the process of oxidizing. **oxidation number, oxidation state** *n.* **1** a number indicating the number of electrons lost or gained by an atom of an element when chemically combined. **2** the state represented by a value of this. **oxidative** (ok´si-) *a.* **oxidize** (-si-), **oxidise** *v.t.* **1** to combine with oxygen. **2** to cover with a coating of oxide, to make rusty. **3** to cause to undergo a loss of electrons. ~*v.i.* **1** to enter into chemical combination with oxygen. **2** to rust. **3** to undergo loss of electrons. **oxidizable** *a.* **oxidization** (-zā´shən) *n.* **oxidized** *a.* **oxidizer** *n.* **oxidizing agent** *n.* a substance that oxidizes another substance and is itself reduced.

Oxon (ok´son) *abbr.* **1** Oxfordshire. **2** of Oxford (used for degrees etc.).

Oxonian (oksō´niən) *n.* **1** a student or graduate of Oxford University. **2** a native or inhabitant of Oxford. ~*a.* belonging to Oxford or Oxford University.

oxy- (ok´si), **ox-** (oks) *comb. form* **1** sharp, keen. **2** (*Chem.*) denoting the presence of oxygen or its acids or an atom of hydroxyl substituted for one of hydrogen.

oxyacetylene (oksiəset´ilēn) *a.* yielding a very hot blowpipe flame from the combustion of oxygen and acetylene, used for welding metals etc.

oxyacid (oksias´id) *n.* (*Chem.*) an acid containing oxygen as distinguished from one formed with hydrogen.

oxygen (ok´sijən) *n.* (*Chem.*) a colourless, tasteless, odourless divalent element, at. no. 8, chem. symbol O, existing in a free state in the atmosphere, combined with hydrogen in water, and with other elements in most mineral and organic substances. **oxygenate** (-āt) *v.t.* to treat or impregnate with oxygen. **oxygenation** (-ā´shən) *n.* **oxygenator** *n.* **oxygenize, oxygenise** *v.t.* **oxygen mask** *n.* an apparatus for supplying oxygen in rarefied atmospheres to aviators etc. **oxygenous** *a.* **oxygen tent** *n.* an oxygen-filled tent placed over a patient to assist breathing.

oxyhaemoglobin (oksihēməglō´bin), (*N Am.*) **oxyhemoglobin** *n.* the bright red product formed when oxygen from the lungs combines with haemoglobin.

oxymoron (oksimaw´ron) *n.* a rhetorical figure in which an epithet of a quite contrary signification is added to a word for the sake of point or emphasis, e.g. a clever fool, a cheerful pessimist.

oxytetracycline (oksitetrəsī´klēn) *n.* a broad-spectrum antibiotic.

oxytocin (oksitō´sin) *n.* **1** a hormone secreted by

the pituitary gland that stimulates uterine muscle contraction during childbirth. **2** a synthetic form of this.

oyez (ō´yes, ōyez´, ōyā´), **oyes** *int.* repeated three times as introduction to any proclamation made by an officer of a court of law or public crier.

oyster (oi´stə) *n.* **1** any of various bivalve molluscs of the families Ostreidae and Aviculidae, esp. *Ostrea edulis*, found in salt or brackish water, eaten as food. **2** an oyster-shaped morsel of meat in the hollow on either side of a fowl's back. **3** something regarded as a source of advantage, delight etc. **oyster bank, oyster bed** *n.* a part of a shallow sea-bottom forming a breeding-place for oysters. **oystercatcher** *n.* any wading bird of the genus *Haematopus*, feeding on shellfish. **oyster mushroom** *n.* an edible fungus, *Pleurotus ostreatus.* **oyster-plant** *n.* **1** salsify. **2** a blue-flowered plant, *Mertensia maritima.* **oyster white** *n.* a greyish-white colour. **oyster-white** *a.*

Oz (oz) *n.* (*Austral., sl.*) **1** Australia. **2** an Australian. ~*a.* Australian.

oz, oz. *abbr.* ounce(s).

ozocerite (ōzō´kərīt, -siə´rīt, -zos´ə-), **ozokerite** (ōzō´kərīt, -kiə´rīt) *n.* a fossil resin like spermaceti in appearance, used for making candles, insulators etc.

ozone (ō´zōn) *n.* **1** (*Chem.*) an allotropic form of oxygen, having three atoms to the molecule, with a slightly pungent odour, found in the atmosphere, probably as the result of electrical action. **2** (*coll.*) fresh, invigorating air as found at the seaside. **ozone-friendly** *a.* (of sprays etc.) not damaging the ozone layer, not containing chlorofluorocarbon (cfc). **ozone hole** *n.* a hole in the ozone layer, allowing ultraviolet radiation on to the earth's surface beneath it. **ozonic** (-zon´-), **ozoniferous** (-nif´-) *a.* **ozonize, ozonise** *v.t.* to charge with ozone. **ozonization** (-zā´shən) *n.* **ozonizer** *n.* **ozonosphere** (ōzō´nəsfiə, -zon´-), **ozone layer** *n.* a layer of ozone in the stratosphere which protects the earth from the sun's ultraviolet rays.

Ozzie Aussie.

P

P¹ (pē), **p** (*pl.* **Ps, P's**) the 16th letter of the English and other versions of the Roman alphabet, corresponding to the Greek pi (π, Π). It is pronounced as a voiceless bilabial plosive. **to mind one's Ps & Qs** to be careful over details, esp. in behaviour.

P² *abbr.* **1** parking. **2** in chess, pawn. **3** (*also* **P**) proprietary.

P³ *chem. symbol* phosphorus.

p *abbr.* **1** page. **2** penny, pence. **3** (*Mus.*) piano, used as an instruction to play softly. **4** pico-.

PA *abbr.* **1** personal assistant. **2** public address (system).

Pa *chem. symbol* protactinium.

pa (pah) *n.* (*pl.* **pas**) (*coll.*) father (used by or to children).

p.a. *abbr.* per annum.

pa'anga (pahng´gə) *n.* (*pl.* **pa'angas**) the standard unit of currency of Tonga, in the SW Pacific.

pabulum (pab´ūləm) *n.* **1** food; nourishment. **2** nutriment of a physical, mental or spiritual kind.

PABX *abbr.* private automatic branch (telephone) exchange.

pace¹ (pās) *n.* **1** a step, the space between the feet in stepping (about 30 in., 76 cm). **2** gait, manner of going, either in walking or running. **3** the carriage and action of a horse etc. **4** rate of speed or progress. **5** (*Mus.*) speed, tempo. ~*v.i.* **1** to walk with slow or regular steps. **2** to amble. ~*v.t.* **1** to traverse in slow and measured steps. **2** to set the pace for. **3** to measure by carefully regulated steps. **to be put through one's paces** to be examined closely, to be tested. **to force the pace** to try to increase the speed or tempo of any activity. **to keep pace with** to go or progress at equal rate with. **to set the pace** to fix the rate of going in a race or any other activity. **to stand the pace** to keep up with other people. **pace bowler** *n.* in cricket, a fast bowler. **-paced** *a.* **pacemaker** *n.* **1** a rider or runner who sets the pace in a race. **2** a person who sets the pace in any form of activity. **3** a small device, usu. implanted in the chest, that corrects irregularities in the heartbeat. **pacemaking** *n., a.* **paceman** *n.* (*pl.* **pacemen**) a pace bowler. **pacer** *n.* **pace-setter** *n.* **1** a leader. **2** a rider or runner who sets the pace in a race. **pacesetting** *a., n.* **pacy, pacey** *a.* (*comp.* **pacier,** *superl.* **paciest**) (*coll.*) (of a story, film etc.) moving at a fast, exciting pace.

pace² (pā´si, pah´chā) *prep.* with the permission of; with due respect to (someone who disagrees).

pacha PASHA.

pachinko (pəching´kō) *n.* a Japanese form of pinball.

pachyderm (pak´idœm) *n.* any large, thick-skinned mammal, esp. an elephant, rhinoceros or hippopotamus.

Pacific (pəsif´ik) *a.* of or relating to the Pacific Ocean. ~*n.* the Pacific Ocean. **Pacific Ocean** *n.* the ocean between America and Asia. **Pacific Rim** *n.* the regions or countries bordering the Pacific Ocean. **Pacific (Standard) Time** *n.* the standard time in a zone on the Pacific coast of Canada and the US.

pacific (pəsif´ik) *a.* **1** inclined or tending to peace, conciliatory. **2** tranquil, quiet, peaceful. **pacifically** *adv.* **pacification** (pasifikā´shən) *n.* the act of pacifying. **pacificator** (-sif´-) *n.* **pacificatory** (-kā´-) *a.* **pacifism** *n.* the doctrine of non-resistance to hostilities and of total non-cooperation with any form of warfare. **pacifist** *n., a.* **pacify** (-fī) *v.t.* (*3rd pers. sing. pres.* **pacifies,** *pres.p.* **pacifying,** *past, p.p.* **pacified**) **1** to appease, to calm, to quiet. **2** to restore peace to. **pacifier** (pas´i-) *n.* **1** a person who or something which pacifies. **2** (*N Am.*) a baby's dummy.

pack (pak) *n.* **1** a bundle of things tied or wrapped together for carrying. **2** a backpack. **3** a parcel, a burden, a load. **4** a quantity going in such a bundle or parcel taken as a measure, varying with different commodities. **5** a small packet, e.g. of cigarettes. **6** (*usu. derog.*) a set, a crew, a gang. **7** a set of playing cards. **8** a number of dogs kept together. **9** a number of wolves or other beasts or birds, esp. grouse, going together. **10** a group of Cub Scouts or Brownies. **11** a quantity of broken ice floating in the sea. **12** in rugby, the forwards of a team. **13** the main group of competitors following the leader or leading group in a race. **14** a face pack. **15** a hot or cold pad for treating a wound. ~*v.t.* **1** to put together into a pack or packs. **2** to stow into a bag, suitcase etc. for transporting or storing. **3** to crowd closely together, to compress. **4** to fill completely. **5** to cram (with). **6** (*coll.*) to carry (a gun). **7** to load with a pack. **8** to select or bring together (a jury etc.) so as to obtain some unfair advantage. ~*v.i.* **1** to put things in a bag, suitcase etc. for transporting or storing. **2** to crowd together. **3** (of animals or rugby forwards) to form a pack. **4** to be suitable for packing. **5** to depart hurriedly. **to pack a punch 1** (*coll.*) to be able to punch hard. **2** (*coll.*) to be forceful or effective. **to pack in 1** (*coll.*) to stop doing (something). **2** (*coll.*) to stop going out with (someone). **to pack**

off (*coll.*) to send or go away. **to pack up 1** (*coll.*) to stop functioning; to break down. **2** (*coll.*) to pack in. **to send packing** (*coll.*) to dismiss summarily. **packable** *a.* **package** (-ij) *n.* **1** a parcel, a bundle. **2** the packing of goods, the manner in which they are packed. **3** the container, wrapper etc. in which a thing is packed. **4** a number of items offered together. **5** (*Comput.*) a piece of software which can be used for various applications. **6** a package holiday. ~*v.t.* **1** to place in a pack. **2** to bring (a number of items) together as a single unit. **package deal** *n.* a deal in which a number of items are offered together. **package holiday** *n.* a holiday where travel, accommodation, meals etc. are all included in the price. **packager** *n.* **packaging** *n.* **1** the wrapping, container etc. in which something is packaged. **2** the act of packing goods. **3** the presentation of a person or thing to the public in a particular, esp. favourable, way. **pack animal** *n.* an animal used for carrying packs. **pack drill** *n.* a form of military punishment consisting of high-speed drill in full kit. **packed** *a.* **packed lunch** *n.* lunch packed in a container or wrapping, to be transported to work, school etc. and eaten there. **packed out** *a.* (*coll.*) full of people. **packer** *n.* **1** a person who packs, esp. one employed to pack meat, fish, fruit etc. for the market. **2** a machine for doing this. **packhorse** *n.* a horse used for carrying goods. **pack ice** *n.* large pieces of ice floating in the polar seas. **packing** *n.* **1** the act of packing. **2** something which is used for packing. **packing case** *n.* a large box made of unplaned wood. **packman** *n.* (*pl.* **packmen**) a pedlar. **pack rat** *n.* **1** a rat of western N America, esp. *Neotoma cinerea*, with a long furry tail. **2** a hoarder. **packsaddle** *n.* a saddle for supporting packs. **packthread** *n.* strong thread for sewing or tying up parcels.

packet (pak´it) *n.* **1** a small package. **2** (*coll.*) a large sum of money. **3** (*Hist.*) a packet-boat. ~*v.t.* to make up in a packet. **packet-boat** *n.* (*Hist.*) a vessel conveying mail, goods and passengers at regular intervals. **packet switching** *n.* (*Comput.*) a system of communication in which a message is broken down into units and sent separately to a pre-allocated address.

pact (pakt) *n.* an agreement, a compact.

pad[1] (pad) *n.* **1** a soft cushion. **2** a bundle or mass of soft stuff of the nature of a cushion. **3** a cushion-like package, cap, guard etc., for stuffing, filling out, protecting parts of the body etc. **4** a number of sheets of paper fastened together at the edge for writing upon and then detaching. **5** a rocket-launching platform. **6** an area for take-off and landing, esp. for helicopters. **7** the cushion-like sole of the foot, or the soft cushion-like paw of certain animals. **8** (*coll.*) one's home or room, esp. a flat. **9** the floating leaf of a water lily. ~*v.t.* (*pres.p.* **padding**, *past, p.p.* **padded**) **1** to stuff or line with padding. **2** to furnish with a pad or padding. **3** to fill out (a sentence, article etc.) with unnecessary words. **padded** *a.* **padded cell** *n.* a room with padded walls for confining violent patients in a psychiatric hospital. **padding** *n.* **1** material used for stuffing a saddle, cushion etc. **2** unnecessary matter inserted to fill out an article, magazine or book. **padsaw** *n.* a small narrow saw for cutting curves.

pad[2] (pad) *v.i.* (*pres.p.* **padding**, *past, p.p.* **padded**) **1** to trudge. **2** to travel on foot. ~*v.t.* to tramp or travel over; to tread. ~*n.* the sound of trudging.

paddle[1] (pad´əl) *n.* **1** a broad short oar used without a rowlock. **2** a paddle-shaped instrument. **3** a blade of a paddle wheel or water wheel. **4** a paddle wheel. **5** a spell of paddling. **6** (*Zool.*) a broad, flat limb for swimming, a flipper. ~*v.t.* **1** to propel by means of paddles. **2** to row gently. **3** (*N Am.*) to spank. ~*v.i.* **1** to ply a paddle; to move along by means of a paddle. **2** to row gently. **3** to swim with short, downward strokes. **paddle boat** *n.* a boat propelled by a paddle wheel. **paddle steamer** *n.* a steamer propelled by a paddle wheel. **paddle wheel** *n.* a wheel with floats or boards projecting from the periphery for pressing against the water and propelling a vessel.

paddle[2] (pad´əl) *v.i.* **1** to wade in shallow water. **2** to dabble in the water with the hands or, more usually, the feet. ~*n.* the act of paddling. **paddler** *n.*

paddock (pad´ək) *n.* **1** a small field or enclosure, usu. under pasture and near a stable. **2** a turfed enclosure adjoining a racecourse where horses are kept before racing. **3** an area beside a motor-racing circuit where cars are parked, repaired etc. **4** (*Austral., New Zeal.*) any pasture land enclosed by a fence. ~*v.t.* to keep in a paddock.

Paddy (pad´i) *n.* (*pl.* **Paddies**) (*often offensive*) an Irishman. **paddy wagon** *n.* (*N Am., sl.*) a police van.

paddy[1] (pad´i) *n.* (*pl.* **paddies**) **1** a paddy field. **2** rice in the straw or in the husk. **paddy field** *n.* a field planted with rice.

paddy[2] (pad´i) *n.* (*pl.* **paddies**) (*coll.*) a rage, a temper.

padlock (pad´lok) *n.* a detachable lock with a bow or loop for fastening to a staple etc. ~*v.t.* to fasten with a padlock.

padouk (padowk´) *n.* **1** a leguminous tree of the genus *Pterocarpus*, of Africa and Asia. **2** the wood of the padouk.

padre (pah´drā) *n.* **1** father (used in addressing a priest in Italy, Spain and Spanish America). **2** a chaplain in the armed forces.

paean (pē´ən) *n.* a song of triumph or rejoicing.

paederast PEDERAST.

paediatrics (pēdiat´riks), (*N Am.*) **pediatrics** *n.* the branch of medicine dealing with children's diseases. **paediatric** *a.* **paediatrician** (-iətrish´ən) *n.*

paedo- (pē´dō), (*N Am.*) **pedo-, paed-,** (*N Am.*) **ped-** *comb. form* of or relating to children.

paedophilia (pēdōfil´iə), (*N Am.*) **pedophilia**

n. the condition of being sexually attracted to children. **paedophile** (pē´dəfīl) *n.* a person, usually a man, who is sexually attracted to children.

paella (pīel´ə) *n.* a Spanish dish of rice, seafood, meat and vegetables, flavoured with saffron.

paeony PEONY.

pagan (pā´gən) *n.* **1** a heathen; a barbarous or unenlightened person. **2** a person who has no religion or disregards Christian beliefs. **3** a person who finds spirituality in nature; a pantheist. ~*a.* **1** heathen, heathenish; unenlightened; irreligious. **2** finding spirituality in nature. **paganish** *a.* **paganism** *n.* **paganize, paganise** *v.t., v.i.*

page[1] (pāj) *n.* **1** either side of a leaf of a book etc. **2** a leaf of a book etc. **3** an episode. **4** a subdivision of a computer memory. ~*v.t.* to put numbers on the pages of (a book etc.). ~*v.i.* **1** to leaf through a book etc. **2** (*Comput.*) to display text one page at a time. **paginal** (paj´in-), **paginary** *a.* **paginate** (paj´-) *v.t.* **pagination** (-ā´shən) *n.*

page[2] (pāj) *n.* **1** a young male attendant on people of rank. **2** any of various functionaries attached to the royal household. **3** a boy acting as an attendant at a wedding. **4** a boy in livery employed to go on errands, attend to the door etc. **5** (*Hist.*) a youth in training for knighthood attached to a knight's retinue. ~*v.t.* **1** to summon (a person in a hotel etc.) by calling their name aloud. **2** to summon by using a pager. **page-boy** *n.* **1** a page. **2** a woman's medium-length hairstyle, with the ends curled under. **pager** *n.* a small, portable, electronic device which alerts the carrier that someone is trying to telephone them.

pageant (paj´ənt) *n.* **1** a brilliant display or spectacle, esp. a parade or procession of an elaborate kind. **2** a theatrical exhibition, usu. representing well-known historical events, and illustrating costumes, buildings, manners etc. **3** a tableau or allegorical design, usu. mounted on a car in a procession. **4** empty and specious show. **pageantry** *n.*

paginate, paginal etc. PAGE[1].

pagoda (pəgō´də) *n.* **1** a sacred temple, usu. in the form of a pyramidal tower in many receding storeys, all elaborately decorated, in China, Japan and other Eastern countries. **2** a building imitating this. **pagoda tree** *n.* a Chinese leguminous tree, *Sophora japonica*, shaped like a pagoda.

pah (pah) *int.* used to express disgust or contempt.

paid PAY[1].

pail (pāl) *n.* **1** an open vessel, usu. round, of metal or plastic, for carrying liquids. **2** a pailful. **pailful** *n.* (*pl.* **pailfuls**)

paillasse PALLIASSE.

pain (pān) *n.* **1** bodily or mental suffering (*excruciating pain*). **2** an instance of bodily or mental suffering (*a sharp pain*). **3** (*pl.*) effort, trouble. **4** (*coll.*) a nuisance. ~*v.t.* to inflict pain upon, to afflict or distress bodily or mentally. **in pain** feeling pain. **on pain of** subject to the penalty of. **to be at pains to** to take trouble to, to be careful to. **to take pains to** to take trouble, to labour hard or be exceedingly careful. **under pain of** on pain of. **pained** *a.* looking upset or annoyed. **painful** *a.* **1** (of a part of the body) hurting, sore. **2** causing mental or physical pain. **3** laborious, toilsome, difficult. **painfully** *adv.* **painfulness** *n.* **painkiller** *n.* a drug that alleviates pain. **painkilling** *a.* **painless** *a.* **painlessly** *adv.* **painlessness** *n.* **painstaking** *a.* extremely thorough. **painstakingly** *adv.* **painstakingness** *n.*

paint (pānt) *n.* a solid colouring substance or pigment, usu. dissolved in a liquid vehicle, used to give a coloured coating to surfaces. ~*v.t.* **1** to cover or coat with paint. **2** to give a specified colour to with paint. **3** to portray or represent in colours. **4** to depict vividly in words. ~*v.i.* to practise painting. **to paint out** to efface by painting over. **paintable** *a.* **paintball** *n.* **1** a game in which teams shoot pellets of coloured paint at each other in simulated battle. **2** a pellet of coloured paint used in paintball. **paintballer** *n.* **paintbox** *n.* a box in which oil paint or watercolours are kept in compartments. **paintbrush** *n.* **painted lady** *n.* an orange-red butterfly spotted with black and white. **painter** *n.* **1** a person whose occupation is to colour walls, woodwork etc. with paint. **2** an artist who paints pictures. **painterly** *a.* **1** of, relating to or having the qualities of painting. **2** (of a painting) without sharp outlines. **painterliness** *n.* **painting** *n.* **1** the act, art or occupation of laying on colours or producing representations in colours. **2** a painted picture. **paint shop** *n.* the part of a factory where goods are painted. **paintstick** *n.* a crayon-like stick of water-soluble paint. **paintwork** *n.* **1** the parts of a room or vehicle which are painted. **2** the work of painting. **painty** *a.* (*comp.* **paintier,** *superl.* **paintiest**) (*coll.*) **1** like paint in smell etc. **2** covered in paint.

painter (pān´tə) *n.* a bow-rope for fastening a boat to a ring, stake etc.

pair (peə) *n.* **1** two things or people of a kind, similar in form, or applied to the same purpose or use. **2** a set of two, a couple, usu. corresponding to each other. **3** an implement or article having two corresponding and mutually dependent parts, such as scissors, spectacles, trousers (*pair of knickers; pair of scales; pair of tongs*). **4** two playing cards of the same value. **5** an engaged or married couple. **6** a couple of mated animals. **7** two horses harnessed together. **8** either member of a matching pair. **9** two Members of Parliament of opposite views abstaining from voting by mutual agreement. ~*v.t.* **1** to make or arrange in pairs or couples. **2** to cause to mate. **3** to join in marriage. **4** in Parliament, to make a pair with. ~*v.i.* **1** to be arranged in pairs. **2** to mate. **3** to unite in love. **4** (*coll.*) to marry. **5** in Parliament, to make a pair. **in pairs** in twos. **to pair off 1** to separate into couples. **2** to go off in pairs. **pair bond** *n.* a lasting, exclusive relationship between a male and a female. **paired** *a.* occurring in pairs. **pairing** *n.* two people who work together as a pair. **pair of compasses** *n.* an instrument with two legs connected by a joint for describing circles, measuring distances etc. **pair of virginals** *n.* a keyed musical instrument, shaped like a box, used in the 16th 17th cents.

paisa (pī´sah) *n.* (*pl.* **paise** (-sā)) a monetary unit of countries of the Indian subcontinent, equal to one hundredth of a rupee or taka.

Paisley (pāz´li) *n.* **1** (a fabric with) a colourful pattern of small intricate curves. **2** a shawl made of this fabric. ~*a.* denoting this fabric or pattern.

pajamas PYJAMAS.

pakeha (pah´kihah) *n.* (*pl.* **pakehas**) (*New Zeal.*) a white person, as distinct from a Maori. ~*a.* of or relating to pakehas.

Paki (pak´i) *n.* (*pl.* **Pakis**) (*sl.*, *offensive*) a Pakistani.

Pakistani (pahkistah´ni) *n.* (*pl.* **Pakistanis**) a native or inhabitant of Pakistan, or a descendant of one. ~*a.* of or relating to Pakistan.

pakora (pəkaw´rə) *n.* an Indian dish of pieces of vegetable, chicken etc. dipped in spiced batter and deep-fried.

PAL (pal) *abbr.* phase alternation line, a system of colour television broadcasting used in Europe.

pal (pal) *n.* (*coll.*) a friend. ~*v.i.* (*pres.p.* **palling**, *past*, *p.p.* **palled**) (*coll.*) to be friends (with). **to pal up with** (*coll.*) to become friendly with. **pally** *a.* (*comp.* **pallier**, *superl.* **palliest**) (*coll.*) friendly.

palace (pal´is) *n.* **1** the official residence of a monarch, emperor, bishop or other distinguished personage. **2** a splendid mansion.

paladin (pal´ədin) *n.* (*Hist.*) **1** any one of Charlemagne's 12 peers. **2** a knight errant.

Palaearctic (paliahk´tik), **palaearctic**, (*N Am.*) **Palearctic, palearctic** *a.* of or relating to the Arctic and northern parts of the Old World. ~*n.* the Palaearctic region.

palaeo- (pal´iō), (*N Am.*) **paleo-, palae-,** (*N Am.*) **pale-** *comb. form* ancient, old, prehistoric.

palaeoanthropology (paliōanthrəpol´əji), (*N Am.*) **paleoanthropology** *n.* the branch of anthropology concerned with fossil hominids. **palaeoanthropological** (-loj´-) *a.* **palaeoanthropologist** *n.*

Palaeocene (pal´iəsēn), (*N Am.*) **Paleocene** *a.*, *n.* (*Geol.*) (of or relating to) the oldest epoch of the Tertiary period.

palaeoclimatology (paliōklīmatol´əji), (*N Am.*) **paleoclimatology** *n.* the science of the climates of the geological past. **palaeoclimatological** (-loj´-) *a.* **palaeoclimatologist** *n.*

palaeography (paliog´rəfi), (*N Am.*) **paleography** *n.* the art or science of deciphering ancient

inscriptions or manuscripts. **palaeographer** *n.* **palaeographic** (-graf´-) *a.*

palaeolithic (paliōlith´ik), (*N Am.*) **paleolithic** *a.* of or relating to the earlier Stone Age. ~*n.* the palaeolithic period.

palaeontology (paliəntol´əji), (*N Am.*) **paleontology** *n.* the science or the branch of biology or geology dealing with fossil animals and plants. **palaeontological** (-loj´-) *a.* **palaeontologist** *n.*

Palaeozoic (paliōzō´ik), (*N Am.*) **Paleozoic** *a.* (*Geol.*) of or relating to the lowest fossiliferous strata and the earliest forms of life. ~*n.* the Palaeozoic era.

palais (pal´ā), **palais de danse** (də dās´) *n.* (*pl.* **palais** (-āz), **palais de danse** (-ā)) (*coll.*) a dance hall.

palanquin (palənkēn´), **palankeen** *n.* a couch or litter in India and the East carried by four or six people on their shoulders.

palatable (pal´ətəbəl) *a.* **1** pleasing to taste. **2** agreeable, acceptable. **palatability** (-bil´-), **palatableness** *n.* **palatably** *adv.*

palate (pal´ət) *n.* **1** the roof of the mouth. **2** the sense of taste. **3** liking, fancy. **palatal** *a.* of, relating to or uttered with the aid of the palate. ~*n.* a sound produced with the palate, esp. the hard palate, such as *k*, *g*, *ch*, *y*, *s*, *n.* **palatalize, palatalise** *v.t.* **palatalization** (-ā´shən) *n.* **palatally** *adv.*

palatial (pələ´shəl) *a.* of, relating to or befitting a palace, magnificent, splendid. **palatially** *adv.*

palatine (pal´ətīn) *a.* possessing or exercising royal privileges. **palatinate** (-lat´inət) *n.* the territory of a palatine.

palaver (pələh´və) *n.* **1** (*coll.*) unnecessary fuss and bother, tedious activity. **2** talk, chatter. **3** cajolery, flattery.

pale[1] (pāl) *a.* **1** whitish, ashen, lacking in colour, not ruddy. **2** (of a colour or light) dim, faint. **3** poor, feeble, inadequate. ~*v.t.* to make pale. ~*v.i.* **1** to turn pale. **2** to be pale, dim or poor in comparison. **paleface** *n.* (supposedly among N American Indians) a white person. **palely** *adv.* **paleness** *n.* **palish** *a.*

pale[2] (pāl) *n.* **1** a pointed stake. **2** a narrow board used in fencing. **3** a limit or boundary. **4** a region, a district, a territory, a sphere. **5** (*Her.*) a vertical band down the middle of a shield. **beyond the pale** unacceptable. **paled** *a.* fenced in. **paling** *n.* **1** a fence made with pales. **2** material for making fences.

Palearctic PALAEARCTIC.

paleo- PALAEO-.

Palestinian (paləstin´iən) *a.* of or relating to Palestine, a region on the E Mediterranean coast. ~*n.* a native or inhabitant of Palestine, or a descendant of one.

palette (pal´it) *n.* **1** a flat board used by artists for mixing colours on. **2** the colours or arrangement of colours used for a particular picture or by a particular artist. **palette knife** *n.* **1** a thin, flexible knife for mixing and sometimes for applying colours. **2** a kitchen knife with a flat, blunt, rounded, flexible blade.

palfrey (pawl´fri) *n.* (*pl.* **palfreys**) a small horse, esp. to be ridden by a woman.

palimony (pal´iməni) *n.* (*esp. N Am., coll.*) alimony paid to an unmarried partner after the end of a long-term relationship.

palimpsest (pal´impsest) *n.* a manuscript on parchment or other material from which the original writing has been erased to make room for another record.

palindrome (pal´indrōm) *n.* a word, verse or sentence that reads the same backwards and forwards, e.g. 'Madam I'm Adam' (Adam's alleged self-introduction to Eve). **palindromic** (-drom´-) *a.* **palindromist** *n.*

paling PALE².

palisade (palisād´) *n.* **1** a fence or fortification of stakes, timbers or iron railings. **2** (*pl., N Am.*) a row of high cliffs. ~*v.t.* to enclose or to fortify with stakes.

pall¹ (pawl) *n.* **1** a large cloth, thrown over a coffin, hearse or tomb. **2** anything that covers or shrouds. **3** an oppressive atmosphere. **pall-bearer** *n.* a person who attends the coffin at a funeral, or who holds up the funeral pall.

pall² (pawl) *v.i.* to become vapid or insipid; to become boring. ~*v.t.* to cloy, to dull.

Palladian (pəlā´diən) *a.* (*Archit.*) of or relating to the Italian architect Andrea Palladio, 1518–80, or his school of architecture. **Palladianism** *n.*

palladium (pəlā´diəm) *n.* (*Chem.*) a greyish-white metallic element of the platinum group, at. no. 46, chem. symbol Pd, used as an alloy with gold and other metals.

pallet¹ (pal´it) *n.* **1** a straw mattress. **2** a small crude bed.

pallet² (pal´it) *n.* **1** a flat wooden structure on which boxes, crates etc. are stacked or transported. **2** a tool, usu. consisting of a flat blade and handle, used for mixing and shaping clay in pottery making, or for taking up gold leaf and for gilding or lettering in bookbinding. **3** a palette. **4** a pawl or projection on a part of a machine, for converting reciprocating into rotary motion or vice versa. **palletize, palletise** *v.t.* **palletization** (-zā´shən) *n.*

palliasse (pal´ias), **paillasse** *n.* a mattress of straw.

palliate (pal´iāt) *v.t.* **1** to excuse; to extenuate. **2** to mitigate or alleviate (a disease etc.) without curing. **palliation** (-ā´shən) *n.* **palliative** *n., a.* a substance serving to alleviate a disease etc. without curing it. **palliatively** *adv.* **palliator** *n.*

pallid (pal´id) *a.* pale, wan. **pallidity** (-lid´-) *n.* **pallidly** *adv.* **pallidness** *n.*

pallium (pal´iəm) *n.* (*pl.* **palliums, pallia** (-iə)) **1** a scarflike vestment of white wool with red crosses, worn by the Pope and certain metropolitans and archbishops. **2** (*Zool.*) the mantle of a bivalve. **pallial** *a.*

pallor (pal´ə) *n.* paleness, lack of healthy colour.

pally PAL.

palm¹ (pahm) *n.* **1** (*also* **palm tree**) a tree of the Palmae, a family of tropical or subtropical endogens, usu. with a tall branched stem and head of large fan-shaped leaves. **2** a palm branch or leaf as a symbol of victory or triumph. **3** victory, triumph, the prize, pre-eminence. **palmaceous** (palmā´shəs) *a.* **palm oil** *n.* an oil obtained from the fruit of certain kinds of palm. **Palm Sunday** *n.* the Sunday immediately preceding Easter, commemorating the triumphal entry of Christ into Jerusalem. **palmtop** *n.* a computer with a full keyboard, small enough to be held in one hand while being used. **palm wine** *n.* an alcoholic drink made from fermented palm sap. **palmy** *a.* (*comp.* **palmier,** *superl.* **palmiest**) **1** abounding in palms. **2** victorious, flourishing.

palm² (pahm) *n.* **1** the inner part of the hand. **2** the part of a glove covering this. **3** the broad flat part of an oar, tie, strut, antler etc. ~*v.t.* **1** to conceal in the palm. **2** to steal by concealing in the palm. **3** to pass off fraudulently. **in the palm of one's hand** under one's control; in one's power. **to palm off** to foist (on). **palmar** (pal´mə) *a., n.* **palmate** (pal´māt), **palmated** *a.* **1** resembling a hand with the fingers spread out. **2** (*Zool.*) (of the foot of a bird) webbed. **palmately** *adv.* **palmful** *n.* (*pl.* **palmfuls**). **palmistry** *n.* fortune-telling by examining the lines and marks on the palm of the hand. **palmist** *n.*

palmette (palmet´) *n.* (*Archit.*) a carved or painted ornament in the form of a palm leaf.

palmetto (palmet´ō) *n.* (*pl.* **palmettos**) **1** a small palm, esp. *Sabal palmetto*, a fan palm of the southern US. **2** the dwarf fan palm or any of various other species of *Chamaerops*.

palmier (pal´miā) *n.* (*pl.* **palmiers** (-miā)) a sweet pastry shaped like a palm leaf.

palmitic (palmit´ik) *a.* of or derived from palm oil. **palmitic acid** *n.* (*Chem.*) a white, crystalline solid, which is a saturated acid, found in palm oil and other fats.

palmyra (palmī´rə) *n.* an Asian palm, *Borassus flabellifer*, with fan-shaped leaves used for matmaking.

palomino (paləmē´nō) *n.* (*pl.* **palominos**) a cream, yellow or gold horse with a white mane and tail.

paloverde (palōvœ´di) *n.* any yellow-flowered American tree of the genus *Cercidium*.

palp (palp), **palpus** (-pəs) *n.* (*pl.* **palps, palpi** (-pī)) a jointed sense organ developed from the lower jaw of an insect etc., a feeler. **palpal** *a.*

palpable (pal´pəbəl) *a.* **1** easily perceived, plain, obvious. **2** perceptible to the touch. **palpability** (-bil´-) *n.* **palpably** *adv.*

palpate (pal´pāt) *v.t.* to feel, to handle, to examine by touch. **palpation** (-pā´shən) *n.*

palpitate (pal´pitāt) *v.i.* **1** (of the heart) to beat rapidly. **2** to throb, to pulsate, to flutter. **palpitant** *a.* **palpitation** (-ā´shən) *n.*

palpus PALP.

palsy (pawl´zi) *n.* (*pl.* **palsies**) **1** paralysis. **2** infirmity, inefficiency, helplessness. **3** a cause of helplessness. ~*v.t.* (*3rd pers. sing. pres.* **palsies**, *pres.p.* **palsying**, *past, p.p.* **palsied**) **1** to paralyse. **2** to make helpless.

palter (pawl´tə) *v.i.* **1** to equivocate, to shuffle, to haggle. **2** to trifle. **palterer** *n.*

paltry (pawl´tri) *a.* (*comp.* **paltrier,** *superl.* **paltriest**) mean, petty, despicable; trivial. **paltrily** *adv.* **paltriness** *n.*

paludal (pəlū´dəl), **paludinal** (-dinəl), **paludinous** (-dinəs) *a.* **1** of or relating to marshes or fens, marshy. **2** malarial. **paludism** (pal´-) *n.* malaria.

palynology (palinol´əji) *n.* the study of pollen grains and other spores. **palynological** (-loj´-) *a.* **palynologist** *n.*

pampas (pam´pəs) *n.pl.* the open, far-extending, treeless plains in S America, south of the Amazon. **pampas grass** *n.* a tall grass, *Cortaderia selloana*, originally from the pampas.

pamper (pam´pə) *v.t.* **1** to indulge (a person, oneself), often excessively. **2** to gratify (tastes etc.) to excess. **pamperer** *n.*

pamphlet (pam´flit) *n.* a small book of a few sheets, unbound, usu. on some subject of temporary interest. ~*v.t.* (*pres.p.* **pamphleting,** *past, p.p.* **pamphleted**) to give out pamphlets to. **pamphleteer** (-tiə´) *n.* a writer of pamphlets.

pan[1] (pan) *n.* **1** a broad shallow vessel of metal or earthenware, usu. for cooking. **2** a panful. **3** a vessel for boiling, evaporating etc., used in manufacturing etc. **4** a hollow in the ground for evaporating brine in salt making. **5** a sheet-iron dish used for separating gold from gravel etc., by shaking in water. **6** the part of a flintlock that holds the priming. **7** hardpan. **8** a lavatory bowl. **9** either of the two shallow receptacles of a pair of scales. **10** the act or process of panning a camera. **11** (*N Am., sl.*) the face. ~*v.t.* (*pres.p.* **panning,** *past, p.p.* **panned**) **1** (*coll.*) to criticize severely. **2** (*coll.*) to hit or punch. **3** (usu. with *out*) to wash (gold-bearing earth or gravel) in a pan. **4** to move (a camera) in panning. ~*v.i.* **1** to search for gold by panning earth or gravel. **2** to move the camera while taking the picture of a moving object. **to pan out** to have a specified result (*My plan panned out well*). **pancake** *n.* a thin flat cake of batter cooked in a frying-pan. ~*v.i., v.t.* to make or cause to make a pancake landing. **Pancake Day** *n.* Shrove Tuesday, when it is traditional to eat pancakes. **pancake landing** *n.* an emergency landing in an aircraft, involving alighting from a low altitude at a large angle of incidence, remaining on an even keel. **pan-fry** *v.t.* (*3rd pers. sing. pres.* **pan-fries,** *pres.p.* **pan-frying,** *past, p.p.* **pan-fried**) to fry in a frying pan. **panful** *n.* (*pl.* **panfuls**). **panlike** *a.*

pan[2] (pan) *n.* **1** a betel leaf. **2** a betel leaf wrapped around sliced betel nut mixed with spices, used for chewing.

pan- (pan) *comb. form* all.

panacea (panəsē´ə) *n.* (*pl.* **panaceas**) a universal remedy.

Usage note The phrase *universal panacea* is best avoided: a panacea is universal by definition.

panache (pənash´) *n.* show, swagger, bounce; style; airs.

panama (pan´əmah) *n.* a hat made from the undeveloped leaves of a pine tree.

Panamanian (panəmā´niən) *n.* a native or inhabitant of the Republic of Panama, Central America, or a descendant of one. ~*a.* of or relating to Panama.

panatella (panətel´ə) *n.* a type of long, slender cigar.

panchromatic (pankrōmat´ik) *a.* uniformly sensitive to all colours.

pancreas (pang´kriəs) *n.* (*pl.* **pancreases**) a gland near the stomach secreting a fluid that aids digestive action. **pancreatic** (-at´-) *a.* **pancreatin** (-tin) *n.* a protein compound found in the pancreas and the pancreatic juice. **pancreatitis** (-tī´tis) *n.*

panda (pan´də) *n.* **1** a large, black-and-white, bearlike mammal, *Ailuropoda melanoleuca*, from China and Tibet, a giant panda. **2** a small raccoon-like animal, *Aelurus fulgens*, from the SE Himalayas and Tibet, a red panda. **panda car** *n.* a police patrol car, usu. painted with a dark stripe on a light background.

pandanus (pandā´nəs) *n.* (*pl.* **pandanuses**) **1** a tropical tree or bush of the genus *Pandanus*, containing the screw pines. **2** pandanus fibre, used for making mats.

pandemic (pandem´ik) *a.* affecting a whole country or the whole world. ~*n.* a pandemic disease.

pandemonium (pandimō´niəm) *n.* **1** confusion, uproar. **2** a place or state of lawlessness, confusion or uproar.

pander (pan´də) *v.i.* to do something that someone wants (*She panders to his every whim*). ~*n.* **1** a procurer, a pimp, a go-between in an amorous intrigue. **2** a person who ministers to base or vulgar passions, prejudices etc.

pandit PUNDIT.

Pandora's box (pandaw´rəz) *n.* an action which triggers a series of problems.

p.& p. *abbr.* postage and packing.

pane (pān) *n.* **1** a sheet of glass in a window. **2** any square of the pattern in a plaid etc.

panegyric (panəjir´ik) *n.* a eulogy written or spoken in praise of some person, act or thing. **panegyrical** *a.* **panegyrist** *n.* **panegyrize** (pan´-), **panegyrise** *v.t.*

panel (pan´əl) *n.* **1** a rectangular piece (orig. of cloth). **2** a rectangular piece of wood, metal or other material inserted in or as if in a frame, forming a compartment of a door, wall, car body etc. **3** a thin board on which a picture is painted. **4** a flat section of metal, plastic etc. into which switches and instruments are set; a control panel. **5** a piece of material of a different colour let in lengthwise in a garment. **6** (*Law*) a list of persons summoned by the sheriff as jurors; a jury. **7** the team in a quiz game, discussion etc. **8** (*Sc. Law*) a prisoner or the prisoners at the bar. ~*v.t.* (*pres.p.* **panelling**, (*N Am.*) **paneling**, *past*, *p.p.* **panelled**, (*N Am.*) **paneled**) **1** to fit or furnish (a door, wall etc.) with panels. **2** to decorate (a garment) with panels. **panel beater** *n.* a person who repairs the damaged body panels of motor vehicles. **panel game** *n.* a quiz game on television or radio in which a panel of experts etc. answers questions from an audience or a chairman. **panel heating** *n.* a system of heating rooms by wall panels containing heating pipes. **panelling**, (*N Am.*) **paneling** *n.* **1** wood panels covering the walls of a room. **2** wood for making panels. **panellist**, (*N Am.*) **panelist** *n.* a member of a team in a quiz game, discussion etc. **panel pin** *n.* a short, thin nail with a small head. **panel saw** *n.* a saw used in panel-making. **panel truck** *n.* (*N Am.*) a delivery van.

pang (pang) *n.* a sudden paroxysm of extreme pain, either physical or mental; a throe, agony.

panga (pang´gə) *n.* (*pl.* **pangas**) a broad, heavy, African knife.

pangolin (pang-gō´lin) *n.* a scaly anteater, of various species belonging to the genus *Manis* or *Phataginus*.

panhandle (pan´handəl) *n.* (*N Am.*) a strip of territory belonging to one political division extending between two others. ~*v.t., v.i.* (*N Am.*, *coll.*) to beg. **panhandler** *n.*

panic¹ (pan´ik) *n.* **1** sudden, overpowering, unreasoning fear, esp. when many people are affected. **2** a general alarm about financial concerns, causing ill-considered action. ~*v.t., v.i.* (*pres.p.* **panicking**, *past, p.p.* **panicked**) to affect or be affected with panic. **panic button** *n.* a button, switch etc. operated to signal an emergency. **panicky** *a.* **panicmonger** *n.* a person who spreads panic. **panic stations** *n.pl.* a state of alarm or panic. **panic-stricken, panic-struck** *a.* struck with sudden fear.

panic² (pan´ik) *n.* **1** any of several species of the genus *Panicum*. **2** a cereal grass, *Setaria italica*.

panicle (pan´ikəl) *n.* (*Bot.*) a loose and irregular compound flower cluster. **panicled, paniculate** (-nik´ūlət) *a.*

panjandrum (panjan´drəm) *n.* (*pl.* **panjandrums**) **1** a mock title for a self-important or arrogant person. **2** a high-and-mighty functionary or pompous pretender.

panne (pan), **panne velvet** *n.* a soft, long-napped fabric.

pannier (pan´iə) *n.* **1** a large basket, esp. one of a pair slung over the back of a beast of burden. **2** each one of a pair of bags fixed on either side of the wheel of a bicycle or motorcycle. **3** a covered basket for drugs and surgical instruments for a military ambulance.

pannikin (pan´ikin) *n.* **1** a small drinking cup of metal. **2** the contents of a pannikin.

panoply (pan´əpli) *n.* (*pl.* **panoplies**) **1** a full, impressive array. **2** a complete suit of armour. **panoplied** *a.*

panoptic (panop´tik) *a.* **1** viewing all aspects. **2** all-embracing, comprehensive.

panorama (panərah´mə) *n.* **1** a continuous picture of a complete scene on a sheet unrolled before the spectator or on the inside of a large cylindrical surface viewed from the centre. **2** a complete view in all directions. **3** a general survey. **panoramic** (-ram´-) *a.* **panoramically** *adv.*

pan pipes (pan´pīps) *n.pl.* a musical instrument made of a number of pipes or reeds, a mouth organ, originally associated with Pan, the chief rural divinity of the Greeks.

pansy (pan´zi) *n.* (*pl.* **pansies**) **1** any of various garden plants of the genus *Viola*, with flowers of various rich colours. **2** (*coll., offensive*) **a** an effeminate man. **b** a homosexual man.

pant¹ (pant) *v.i.* **1** to breathe quickly, to gasp for breath. **2** to throb, to palpitate. **3** to long, to yearn for. ~*v.t.* to utter gaspingly or convulsively. ~*n.* **1** a gasp. **2** a throb, a palpitation. **pantingly** *adv.*

pant² (pant) *n.* (*N Am.*) pants. **pant suit** *n.* PANTS SUIT (under PANTS).

pantalets (pantəlets´), **pantalettes** *n.pl.* (*Hist.*) **1** loose drawers extending below the skirts, with frills at the bottom, worn by children and women in the early 19th cent. **2** drawers, cycling knickerbockers etc. for women.

pantaloons (pantəloonz´) *n.pl.* **1** tight trousers fastened below the shoe, as worn in the Regency period. **2** trousers, esp. loose-fitting ones gathered at the ankles.

pantechnicon (pantek´nikən) *n.* (*pl.* **pantechnicons**) a pantechnicon van. **pantechnicon van** *n.* a large van for removing furniture.

pantheism (pan´thēizm) *n.* **1** the doctrine that God and the universe are identical. **2** the heathen worship of all the gods. **pantheist** *n.* **pantheistic** (-is´-), **pantheistical** *a.* **pantheistically** *adv.*

pantheon (pan´thion) *n.* (*pl.* **pantheons**) **1** a building dedicated to the illustrious dead. **2** the divinities of a nation collectively. **3** any temple dedicated to all the gods. **4** a group of illustrious people.

panther (pan´thə) *n.* **1** a black leopard. **2** (*N Am.*) a puma.

panties (pan´tiz) *n.pl.* (*coll.*) women's or girls' short knickers.

pantihose PANTYHOSE.

pantile (pan´tīl) *n.* a tile having an S-shaped cross-section. **pantiled** *a.*

panto (pan´tō) *n.* (*pl.* **pantos**) (*coll.*) a (Christmas) pantomime.

panto- (pan´tō), **pant-** *comb. form* all.

pantograph (pan´təgrahf), **pantagraph, pentagraph** (pen´-) *n.* **1** a drawing instrument used to enlarge, copy or reduce plans etc. **2** a framework similar in appearance to this, attached to the roof of an electrically driven vehicle, for collecting electrical power from an overhead cable. **pantographic** (-graf´-), **pantographical** a.

pantomime (pan´təmīm) n. **1** a theatrical entertainment for children, usu. based on a fairy tale and produced at Christmas time. **2** representation in dumbshow. **3** (coll.) a muddled or farcical situation. ~v.t. to express or represent by dumbshow. **pantomimic** (-mim´-), **pantomimical** a.

pantothenic acid (pantəthen´ik) n. an oily acid, a member of the vitamin B complex.

pantry (pan´tri) n. (pl. **pantries**) **1** a room or cupboard in which dishes, cutlery etc. are kept. **2** a room or cupboard in which bread and other provisions are kept. **pantryman** n. (pl. **pantrymen**) a butler or a butler's assistant.

pants (pants) n.pl. **1** underpants for men and boys. **2** women's knickers. **3** (N Am.) trousers. **to be caught with one's pants down** (coll.) to be caught in an embarrassing or ill-prepared position. **to bore the pants off someone** (coll.) to bore someone greatly. **to scare the pants off someone** (coll.) to scare someone greatly. **pants suit** n. (N Am.) a trouser suit.

Usage note Also called *pair of pants*.

panty girdle (pan´ti) n. a girdle shaped like pants.

pantyhose (pan´tihōz), **pantihose** n.pl. women's tights.

panzer (pan´zə) n. **1** (pl.) armoured troops, esp. an armoured division, in the German army. **2** a vehicle in such a division, esp. a tank. ~a. heavily armoured.

pap¹ (pap) n. **1** soft or semi-liquid food for infants etc. **2** pulp. **3** trivial or insubstantial reading matter. **pappy** a.

pap² (pap) n. (also dial.) †a teat, a nipple.

†papa (pəpah´) n. (pl. **papas**) father (used by or to children).

papacy (pā´pəsi) n. (pl. **papacies**) **1** the office, dignity or tenure of office of a pope. **2** the papal system of government. **papal** a. of or relating to the Pope or his office, or the Roman Catholic Church.

paparazzo (papərat´sō) n. (pl. **paparazzi** (-sē)) a freelance professional photographer who specializes in photographing celebrities at private moments, usu. without their consent.

papaveraceous (pəpāvərā´shəs) a. of or relating to the poppy family Papaveraceae.

papaw, **papaya** PAWPAW.

paper (pā´pə) n. **1** a thin flexible substance made of wood pulp or similar material, used for writing and printing on, wrapping etc. **2** a piece, sheet or leaf of this. **3** a newspaper. **4** a written or printed document. **5** an essay, a dissertation. **6** a lecture. **7 a** a set of questions for an examination. **b** a student's answers to these questions. **8** negotiable documents such as bills of exchange. **9** paper money. **10** wallpaper. **11** (sl.) free passes,

or persons admitted to a theatre etc. by such passes. **12** (pl.) documents establishing identity etc. **13** (pl.) a ship's documents. ~a. **1** made of paper. **2** like paper. **3** stated only on paper, having no real existence. ~v.t. **1** to cover with or decorate with paper. **2** to wrap or fold up in paper. **3** to rub with sandpaper. **4** to furnish with paper. **5** (sl.) to admit a large number to (a theatre etc.) by free tickets. **on paper 1** written down. **2** theoretically, rather than in reality. **to paper over** to disguise, cover up (a dispute, mistake etc.). **paperback** n. a book with a soft cover of flexible card. ~a. being or relating to a paperback or paperbacks. **paper boy** n. a boy who delivers newspapers. **paperchase** n. a game in which one or more people (called the hares) drop pieces of paper as scent for pursuers (called the hounds) to track them by. **paper clip** n. a small clip of looped wire used to fasten pieces of paper together. **paper girl** n. a girl who delivers newspapers. **paperhanger** n. a person whose occupation is hanging wallpaper. **paperknife** n. (pl. **paperknives**) a tool shaped like a blunt knife, used to slit open envelopes. **paperless** a. **papermaker** n. **papermaking** n., a. **paper mill** n. a mill in which paper is manufactured. **paper money** n. banknotes or bills used as currency, as distinct from *coin*. **paper mulberry** n. a small tree from Asia, *Broussonetia papyrifera*, belonging to the mulberry family, which is used for making papers. **paper nautilus** n. (pl. **paper nautiluses**, **paper nautili** (-lī)) a cephalopod of the genus *Argonauta*, the female of which has a thin, papery shell. **paper round**, (N Am.) **paper route** n. a job of delivering newspapers on a particular route, usually done by schoolchildren. **paper tape** n. (Comput.) a strip of paper with holes punched in it, for conveying instructions to a computer. **paper-thin** a. exceedingly thin. ~adv. very thinly. **paper tiger** n. a person or thing that is apparently threatening or powerful, but is not so in reality. **paperweight** n. a small heavy object for keeping loose papers from being disturbed. **paperwork** n. clerical work, e.g. writing letters. **papery** a.

papier mâché (papiā mash´ā) n. a material made from pulped paper, moulded into trays, boxes etc. ~a. made of papier mâché.

papilionaceous (pəpiliənā´shəs) a. (Bot.) resembling a butterfly (used of plants with butterfly-shaped flowers, such as the pea).

papilla (pəpil´ə) n. (pl. **papillae** (-ē)) (Anat., Bot.) a small pap, nipple or similar process; a small protuberance on an organ or part of the body or on plants. **papillary**, **papillate** (pap´ilāt) a. **papilloma** (papilō´mə) n. (pl. **papillomas**, **papillomata** (-tə)) a tumour formed by the growth of a papilla or group of papillae, such as a wart, corn etc. **papillose** (pap´ilōs), **papillous** (-pil´-) a.

papillon (pap´ilon, pap´iyō) n. a breed of toy spaniel with large butterfly-shaped ears.

papist (pā´pist) n. (often derog.) a Roman

Catholic. ~*a*. of or relating to Roman Catholicism. **papism** *n*. **papistic** (-pis´-), **papistical** *a*. **papistry** *n*.

papoose (pəpoos´) *n*. a young N American Indian child.

pappus (pap´əs) *n*. (*pl*. **pappi** (-ī)) (*Bot*.) the calyx of composite plants, consisting of a tuft of down or fine hairs or similar agent for dispersing the seed. **pappose** (-ōs), **pappous** *a*.

paprika (pap´rikə, pəprē´kə) *n*. **1** (*Bot*.) a sweet variety of red pepper. **2** a powdered condiment made from paprika.

Pap test (pap), **pap test** *n*. a test for the early diagnosis of cervical cancer in which cells are scraped from the cervix, and examined under a microscope. **Pap smear** *n*. a cervical smear examined in a Pap test.

papule (pap´ūl), **papula** (-ūlə) *n*. (*pl*. **papules**, **papulae** (-lē)) **1** a pimple. **2** a small fleshy projection on a plant. **papular** *a*. **papulose** (-lōs), **papulous** *a*.

papyrology (papirol´əji) *n*. the study of ancient papyri. **papyrological** (-loj´-) *a*. **papyrologist** *n*.

papyrus (pəpīə´rəs) *n*. (*pl*. **papyri** (-rī)) **1** a rushlike plant of the genus *Cyperus papyrus*, formerly common on the Nile and still found in Ethiopia, Syria etc. **2** a writing material made from this by the Egyptians and other ancient peoples. **3** a manuscript written on this material.

par[1] (pah) *n*. **1** average or normal condition, rate etc. **2** a state of equality, parity. **3** in golf, the number of shots which a good player is expected to play in order to complete a hole. **4** equal value, esp. equality between the selling value and the nominal value expressed on share certificates and other scrip. **5** par of exchange. **above par** at a price above the face value, at a premium. **at par** at face value. **below par 1** at a discount. **2** tired, slightly unwell. **on a par with** of equal value, degree etc. to. **par for the course** *n*. what is to be expected, usual. **par of exchange** *n*. the value of a given amount of the currency of one country in terms of another currency.

par[2] (pah) *n*. (*coll*.) in journalism, a paragraph.

para[1] (par´ə) *n*. (*coll*.) short for PARATROOPER.

para[2] (par´ə) *n*. (*sl*.) short for PARAGRAPH.

para-[1] (par´ə), **par-** *comb. form* **1** denoting closeness of position, correspondence of parts, situation on the other side, wrongness, irregularity, alteration etc. **2** (*Chem*.) denoting substitution or attachment of carbon atoms directly opposite in a benzene ring.

para-[2] (par´ə) *comb. form* of or relating to protection.

parabiosis (parəbīō´sis) *n*. (*Biol*.) the anatomical union of two organisms with shared physiological processes. **parabiotic** (-ot´-) *a*.

parable (par´əbəl) *n*. **1** an allegorical narrative of real or fictitious events from which a moral is drawn. **2** an allegory, esp. of a religious kind. **parabolic**[1] (-bol´-), **parabolical** *a*. of, relating to

or of the nature of a parable; allegorical, figurative.

parabola (pərab´ələ) *n*. (*pl*. **parabolas, parabolae** (-lē)) (*Geom*.) a plane curve formed by the intersection of the surface of a cone with a plane parallel to one of its sides. **parabolic**[2] (parəbol´-) *a*. of, relating to or of the form of a parabola. **parabolically** *adv*. **paraboloid** (-loid) *n*. a solid of which all the plane sections parallel to a certain line are parabolas, esp. one generated by the revolution of a parabola about its axis. **paraboloidal** (-loi´-) *a*.

parabolic[1] PARABLE.

parabolic[2] PARABOLA.

paracetamol (parəsē´təmol, -set´-) *n*. **1** a painkilling drug. **2** a tablet of this.

parachronism (pərak´rənizm) *n*. an error in chronology, esp. post-dating of an event.

parachute (par´əshoot) *n*. an umbrella-shaped contrivance by which a safe descent is made from a height, esp. from an aircraft. ~*v.t., v.i.* (to cause) to land by means of a parachute. **parachutist** *n*.

parade (pərād´) *n*. **1** a muster of troops for inspection etc. **2** a parade ground. **3** show, ostentatious display. **4** a procession, esp. in celebration of an important event. **5** a public promenade. **6** a row of shops. ~*v.i.* **1** to be marshalled in military order for display or review. **2** to march in a parade. ~*v.t.* **1** to march through (streets) in a parade. **2** to display, esp. ostentatiously. **on parade 1** taking part in a parade. **2** being paraded, on display. **parade ground** *n*. an area where soldiers parade.

paradiddle (par´ədidəl) *n*. a simple drumming pattern consisting of four beats played either *left, right, left, right* or *right, left, right, left*.

paradigm (par´ədīm) *n*. **1** an example, a pattern. **2** an example of a word in its grammatical inflections. **paradigmatic** (-digmat´-) *a*. **paradigmatically** *adv*. **paradigm shift** *n*. a basic change in approach.

paradise (par´ədīs) *n*. **1** heaven. **2** a place or condition of perfect bliss. **paradisaical** (-disā´ikəl) *a*. **paradisal** (-dī´səl) *a*. **paradisiacal** (-disī´əkəl) *a*. **paradisical** (-dis´ikəl) *a*.

parador (par´ədaw) *n*. (*pl*. **paradors, paradores** (-daw´rez)) a Spanish state-owned hotel.

parados (par´ədos) *n*. (*pl*. **paradoses**) (*Mil*.) a rampart or earthwork to protect against fire from the rear.

paradox (par´ədoks) *n*. **1** a statement, view or doctrine contrary to received opinion. **2** an assertion seemingly absurd but really correct. **3** a self-contradictory or essentially false and absurd statement. **4** a person, thing or phenomenon at variance with normal ideas of what is probable, natural or possible. **paradoxer** *n*. **paradoxical** (-dok´si-) *a*. **paradoxically** *adv*.

paraesthesia (paristhēz´yə), (*N Am*.) **paresthesia** *n*. (*Med*.) disordered perception or hallucination.

paraffin (par´əfin) *n*. **1** (*also* **paraffin oil**) a mixture of liquid paraffins used as a lubricant or fuel. **2** (*Chem*.) an alkane. **paraffin wax** *n*. a colourless, tasteless, odourless, fatty substance consisting primarily of a mixture of paraffins, and obtained from distillation of coal, bituminous shale, petroleum, peat etc., used for making candles, waterproofing etc.

paragliding (par´əglīding) *n*. the sport of gliding while attached to a device like a parachute, in which one is pulled by an aircraft etc., then allowed to drift to the ground. **paraglide** *v.i.* **paraglider** *n*.

paragon (par´əgən) *n*. **1** a pattern of perfection. **2** a model, an exemplar (*a paragon of virtue*). **3** a person or thing of supreme excellence. **4** a diamond of 100 carats or more.

paragraph (par´əgrahf) *n*. **1** a distinct portion of a discourse or writing marked by a break in the lines. **2** (*Print*.) a reference mark (¶). ~*v.t.* to form into paragraphs. **paragraphic** (-graf´-), **paragraphical** *a*.

Paraguayan (parəgwī´ən) *n*. a native or inhabitant of Paraguay, in S America. ~*a*. of or relating to Paraguay.

parakeet (par´əkēt), **parrakeet** *n*. any one of the smaller long-tailed parrots.

paraldehyde (pəral´dihīd) *n*. (*Chem*.) a hypnotic used in asthma, respiratory and cardiac diseases and epilepsy.

paralegal (parəlē´gəl) *a*. (*N Am*.) of or relating to auxiliary aspects of the legal profession. ~*n*. a person who assists lawyers but who is not yet fully qualified.

⊠ **paralel** common misspelling of PARALLEL.

parallax (par´əlaks) *n*. **1** apparent change in the position of an object due to change in the position of the observer. **2** the angular amount of this. **parallactic** (-lak´-) *a*.

parallel (par´əlel) *a*. **1** (of lines etc.) having the same direction and equidistant everywhere. **2** having the same tendency, similar, corresponding. **3** (*esp. Comput*.) occurring or performed simultaneously. ~*n*. **1** a line which throughout its whole length is everywhere equidistant from another. **2** (*also* **parallel of latitude**) any one of the parallel circles on a map or globe marking degrees of latitude on the earth's surface. **3** a direction parallel to that of another line. **4** a comparison. **5** a person or thing corresponding to or analogous with another, a counterpart. **6** (*Print*.) a reference mark (‖) calling attention to a note etc. ~*v.t.* (*pres.p.* **paralleling**, *past, p.p.* **paralleled**) **1** to be parallel to, to match, to rival, to equal. **2** to put in comparison with. **3** to find a match for. **in parallel** (of electrical circuits) arranged across a common voltage supply. **parallel bars** *n.pl.* a pair of horizontal bars used for various exercises in gymnastics. **parallelism** *n*. **parallel parking** *n*. the act of parking a vehicle parallel to the kerb.

parallelepiped (parəleləpī´ped), **parallelepipedon** (-pidən) *n*. (*Geom*.) a regular solid bounded by six parallelograms, the opposite pairs of which are parallel.

parallelogram (parəlel´əgram) *n*. (*Geom*.) a four-sided rectilinear figure whose opposite sides are parallel and equal.

Paralympics (parəlim´piks) *n.pl.* an international sporting event for disabled people, modelled on the Olympic Games. **Paralympic** *a*.

paralyse (par´əliz), (*N Am*.) **paralyze** *v.t.* **1** to affect with paralysis. **2** to render powerless or ineffective. **3** to render immobile or unable to function. **paralysation** (-zā´shən) *n*. **paralysingly** *adv*.

paralysis (pəral´isis) *n*. (*pl.* **paralyses** (-sēz)) **1** total or partial loss of the power of muscular contraction or of sensation in the whole or part of the body; palsy. **2** complete helplessness or inability to act. **3** inability to move or function properly. **paralytic** (-lit´-) *a*. **1** of, relating to or characterized by paralysis. **2** afflicted with paralysis. **3** (*sl*.) very drunk. ~*n*. a paralysed or paralytic person. **paralytically** *adv*.

paramagnetic (parəmagnet´ik) *a*. having the property of being attracted by the poles of a magnet; magnetic, as distinct from *diamagnetic*. **paramagnetism** (-mag´-) *n*.

paramatta PARRAMATTA.

paramedic (parəmed´ik) *n*. a person who is trained to help doctors, e.g. an ambulance operative. **paramedical** *a*. auxiliary to the work of medical doctors.

parameter (pəram´itə) *n*. **1** (*Math*.) a quantity remaining constant for a particular case, esp. a constant quantity entering into the equation of a curve etc. **2** (*coll*.) a limiting factor, a constraint. **parametric** (parəmet´-) *a*. **parametrize, parametrise** *v.t.*

Usage note The use of *parameter* to mean a limiting factor is sometimes disapproved of.

paramilitary (parəmil´itəri) *a*. having a similar nature or structure to military forces. ~*n*. (*pl.* **paramilitaries**) a member of a paramilitary organization.

paramnesia (paramnēz´yə) *n*. (*Psych*.) déjà vu.

paramount (par´əmownt) *a*. **1** supreme, preeminent, most important. **2** having supreme authority. **paramountcy** (-si) *n*. **paramountly** *adv*.

paramour (par´əmooə) *n*. (*dated or derog*.) a lover, usu. an illicit one.

parang (pah´rang) *n*. a heavy sheath knife.

paranoia (parənoi´ə), **paranoea** (-nē´ə) *n*. **1** mental derangement, esp. in a chronic form characterized by delusions etc. **2** (*coll*.) a sense of being persecuted. **paranoiac** (-ak) *a*., *n*. **paranoiacally** *adv*. **paranoic** (-nō´-) *a*. **paranoid** (par´ənoid) *a*., *n*.

paranormal (parənaw´məl) *a*. not rationally explicable. ~*n*. paranormal events. **paranormally** *adv*.

parapet (par'əpit) *n.* **1** a low or breast-high wall at the edge of a roof, bridge etc. **2** a breast-high wall or rampart for covering troops from observation and attack. **parapeted** *a.*

paraph (par'af) *n.* a flourish after a signature, orig. intended as a protection against forgery.

paraphernalia (parəfənā'liə) *n.pl.* miscellaneous belongings, ornaments, trappings, equipment.

paraphrase (par'əfrāz) *n.* **1** a free translation or rendering of a passage. **2** a restatement of a passage in different terms. ~*v.t.* to express or interpret in other words. ~*v.i.* to make a paraphrase. **paraphrastic** (-fras'-) *a.*

paraplegia (parəplē'jə) *n.*(*Med.*) paralysis of the lower limbs and the lower part of the body. **paraplegic** *n., a.*

parapsychology (parəsikol'əji) *n.* the study of mental phenomena which are beyond the sphere of ordinary psychology. **parapsychological** (-loj'-) *a.* **parapsychologist** *n.*

paraquat (par'əkwot) *n.* a very poisonous weedkiller.

parasailing (par'əsāling) *n.* the sport of gliding through the air attached to the back of a motor boat while wearing an open parachute. **parasail** *v.i., n.*

parascending (par'əsending) *n.* **1** paragliding. **2** parasailing. **parascend** *v.i.* **parascender** *n.*

paraselene (parəsilē'ni) *n.* (*pl.* **paraselenae** (-nē)) a mock moon appearing in a lunar halo.

parasite (par'əsīt) *n.* **1** an animal or plant subsisting at the expense of another organism. **2** a person who lives off other people, a hanger-on, a sponger. **parasitic** (-sit'-), **parasitical** *a.* **parasitically** *adv.* **parasiticide** (-sit'isīd) *n.* **parasitism** *n.* **parasitize, parasitise** *v.t.* **parasitization** (-zā'shən) *n.* **parasitoid** (-sitoid) *n.* (*Zool.*) an insect whose larvae live as parasites, eventually killing their hosts. ~*a.* of or relating to parasitoids. **parasitology** (-tol'-) *n.* **parasitologist** *n.*

parasol (pa'rəsol) *n.* **1** a small umbrella used to give shelter from the sun, a sunshade. **2** any of several fungi of the genus *Lepiota*, having an umbrella-shaped cap.

parastatal (parəstā'təl) *a.* esp. in some African countries, having some political authority, but indirectly controlled by the State. ~*n.* a parastatal organization.

paratha (pərah'tə) *n.* in Indian cookery, a piece of flat, round, unleavened bread fried on a griddle.

parathion (parəthī'ən) *n.* a highly toxic insecticide.

parathyroid (parəthī'roid) *n.* (*Anat.*) a small endocrine gland, one of which is situated on each side of the thyroid. ~*a.* of or relating to the parathyroids.

paratrooper (par'ətroopə) *n.* a soldier belonging to a unit transported in aircraft and dropped by parachute, with full equipment, usu. behind enemy lines. **paratroop** *a.* **paratroops** *n.pl.*

paratyphoid (parətī'foid) *n.* an infectious fever of the enteric group, similar in symptoms to typhoid but of milder character. ~*a.* of or relating to paratyphoid.

paravane (par'əvān) *n.* a mine-sweeping appliance for severing the moorings of submerged mines.

par avion (pahr avyō') *adv.* by airmail.

parboil (pah'boil) *v.t.* to boil partially.

parcel (pah'səl) *n.* **1** a quantity of things wrapped up together. **2** a bundle, a package. **3** a distinct portion, for example of land. **4** a number or quantity of things dealt with as a separate lot. ~*v.t.* (*pres.p.* **parcelling**, (*N Am.*) **parceling**, *past, p.p.* **parcelled**, (*N Am.*) **parceled**) **1** to make into a parcel. **2** to divide (out) into parts or lots. **3** to wrap (a rope) with strips of canvas, or cover (a seam) with strips of canvas and pitch. **parcel post** *n.* a branch of the postal service for the delivery of parcels.

parch (pahch) *v.t.* to scorch or roast partially dry, to dry up. ~*v.i.* to become hot or dry. **parched** *a.* **1** dried up. **2** (*coll.*) very thirsty.

parchment (pahch'mənt) *n.* **1** the skin of calves, sheep, goats etc., prepared for writing upon, painting etc. **2** a manuscript written on this, esp. a deed. **3** VEGETABLE PARCHMENT (under VEGETABLE). ~*a.* made of or resembling parchment.

parclose (pah'klōz) *n.* a screen or railing enclosing an altar, tomb etc. in a church.

pard (pahd), **pardner** (-nə) *n.* (*N Am., dial. or facet.*) a partner.

pardalote (pah'dəlōt) *n.* any small, spotted Australian bird of the genus *Pardalotus*.

pardon (pah'dən) *n.* **1** the act of excusing or forgiving. **2** a complete or partial remission of the legal consequences of crime. **3** an official warrant of a penalty remitted. **4** a papal indulgence. ~*v.t.* **1** to forgive, to absolve from. **2** to remit the penalty of. **3** to refrain from exacting. **4** to excuse, to make allowance for. **I beg your pardon** excuse me, a polite apology for an action, contradiction or failure to hear or understand what is said. **pardon me** I beg your pardon. **pardonable** *a.* **pardonableness** *n.* **pardonably** *adv.* **pardoner** *n.* **1** (*Hist.*) a person licensed to sell papal pardons or indulgences. **2** a person who pardons.

pare (peə) *v.t.* **1** to cut or shave (away or off). **2** to cut away or remove the rind etc. of (fruit etc.). **3** to trim by cutting the edges or irregularities of. **4** to diminish by degrees. **parer** *n.* **paring** *n.* **1** the act of cutting off, pruning or trimming. **2** the part which is pared off; a shaving, rind etc.

paregoric (parigor'ik) *a.* assuaging or soothing pain. ~*n.* a camphorated tincture of opium for assuaging pain.

parenchyma (pəreng'kimə) *n.* **1** (*Anat.*) the soft cellular tissue of glands and other organs, as distinct from connective tissue etc. **2** (*Bot.*) thin cellular tissue in the softer part of plants, pith, fruit pulp etc. **parenchymal, parenchymatous** (-kim´-) *a*.

parent (peə´rənt) *n*. **1** a father or mother. **2** a person who acts as a parent, e.g. an adoptive parent. **3** an organism from which others are produced. **4** a source, origin, cause or occasion. **5** a company having control of one or more subsidiaries. ~*v.t.* to be a parent or the parent of. **parentage** (-ij) *n*. birth, extraction, lineage, origin. **parental** (pərən´-) *a*. **parentally** *adv*. **parent company** *n*. a company having control of one or more subsidiaries. **parenthood** (-hud) *n*. **parenting** *n*. the skills or activity of being a parent. **parentless** *a*.

parenthesis (pərən´thəsis) *n*. (*pl*. **parentheses** (-sēz)) **1** (*Gram.*) a word, phrase or sentence inserted in a sentence that is grammatically complete without it, usu. marked off by brackets, dashes or commas. **2** (*pl.*) round brackets () to include such words. **3** an interval, interlude, incident etc. **in parenthesis** as an aside, by the way. **parenthesize, parenthesise** *v.t.* **1** to insert as a parenthesis. **2** to place (a clause etc.) between parentheses. **parenthetic** (-thet´-), **parenthetical** *a*. **parenthetically** *adv*.

paresthesia PARAESTHESIA.

par excellence (pahr ek´sələns) *adv*. above all others, pre-eminently.

parfait (pahfā´) *n*. **1** a rich, cold dessert made with whipped cream, eggs, fruit etc. **2** a dessert made of layers of ice cream, meringue, fruit and sauce, served in a tall glass.

pargasite (pah´gəsīt) *n*. (*Geol.*) a greenish variety of hornblende.

parget (pah´jit) *v.t.* (*pres.p.* **pargeting**, *past, p.p.* **pargeted**) **1** to plaster over. **2** to roughcast. ~*n*. **1** plaster. **2** pargeting. **pargeter** *n*. **pargeting** *n*. plasterwork, esp. decorative plasterwork.

parhelion (pah·hē´liən) *n*. (*pl.* **parhelia** (-liə)) a mock sun or bright spot in a solar halo, due to ice crystals in the atmosphere. **parheliacal** (-hilī´-), **parhelic** *a*.

pariah (pərī´ə) *n*. **1** a social outcast. **2** (*Hist.*) **a** a member of a people of very low caste in S India and Burma. **b** a person of low caste or without caste. **pariah dog** *n*. a pye-dog.

Usage note As a social classification, *pariah* has been abolished in India, and its use can give offence to Indians.

parietal (pərī´itəl) *a*. **1** of or relating to a wall or walls, esp. those of the body and its cavities. **2** (*Bot.*) of, relating to or attached to the wall of a structure, esp. of a placenta or ovary. **3** (*N Am.*) of or relating to residence within a college. **parietal bone** *n*. (*Anat.*) either of the two bones forming part of the top and sides of the skull. **parietal lobe** *n*. either of the two lobes of the brain at the top of the head, concerned with the perception and interpretation of sensory information.

pari-mutuel (parimū´tūəl) *n*. **1** a system of

betting in which the winners divide the losers' stakes less a percentage for management. **2** a totalizator.

paring PARE.

pari passu (pari pas´oo) *adv*. (esp. in legal contexts) with equal pace, in a similar degree, equally.

parish (par´ish) *n*. **1** an ecclesiastical district with its own church and clergyman. **2** a civil district for the purposes of local government etc. **3** the people living in a parish. **parish clerk** *n*. a subordinate lay official in the church, formerly leading the congregation in the responses. **parish council** *n*. a local administrative body elected by the parishioners in rural districts. **parishioner** (-rish´ənə) *n*. a person who belongs to a parish. **parish pump** *a*. (*coll.*) of local interest only, parochial. ~*n*. a symbol of parochialism. **parish register** *n*. a register of christenings, marriages and burials, kept at a parish church.

Parisian (pəriz´iən) *a*. of or relating to Paris, France. ~*n*. **1** a native or inhabitant of Paris. **2** the dialect of French spoken in Paris.

parity[1] (par´iti) *n*. (*pl.* **parities**) **1** equality of rank, condition, value etc. **2** parallelism, analogy. **3** the amount of a foreign currency equal to a specific sum of domestic currency. **4** equivalence of a commodity price as expressed in one currency to its price expressed in another. **5** (*Math.*) the property of being odd or even. **6** (*Physics*) (of quantity) the condition of changing or not changing under a transformation of coordinates etc.

parity[2] (par´iti) *n*. (*Med.*) **1** the condition of having given birth. **2** the number of children a woman has given birth to.

park (pahk) *n*. **1** a piece of ground, ornamentally laid out, enclosed for public recreation. **2** a piece of land, usu. for ornament, pleasure or recreation, with trees, pasture etc., surrounding or adjoining a mansion. **3** a large tract or region, usu. with interesting physical features, preserved in its natural state for public enjoyment. **4** an enclosed area of land where wild animals are kept in captivity. **5** an area where vehicles can be parked. **6** the position in automatic gear transmission in which the vehicle's gears are locked. **7** an area set aside for a specific purpose (*a science park*). **8** (*N Am.*) a sports stadium or arena. **9** (*coll.*) a soccer pitch. ~*v.t.* **1** to leave (a vehicle) in a place allotted for the purpose. **2** (*coll.*) to leave temporarily. ~*v.i.* to leave a vehicle in a place allotted for the purpose. **to park oneself** (*coll.*) to sit down. **parking** *n*. **parking lot** *n*. (*N Am.*) a car park. **parking meter** *n*. a coin-operated appliance on a kerb, that charges for the time cars are parked there. **parking ticket** *n*. a document issued for a parking offence, requiring payment of a fine or appearance in court. **parkland** *n*. open land with grass and trees on it. **parkway** *n*. **1** (*N Am.*) a highway lined with trees and grass. **2** a railway station with a sizeable car park.

parka (pah´kə) *n.* a hooded jacket edged or lined with fur.

parkin (pah´kin) *n.* a biscuit made of gingerbread, oatmeal and treacle.

Parkinson's disease (pah´kinsənz), **Parkinsonism** (-sənizm) *n.* a chronic disorder of the central nervous system causing loss of muscle coordination and tremor.

Parkinson's law (pah´kinsənz) *n.* the supposed principle in office management etc. that work expands to fill the time available for its completion.

parky (pah´ki) *a.* (*comp.* **parkier**, *superl.* **parkiest**) (*coll.*) chilly.

parlance (pah´ləns) *n.* way of speaking, idiom.

parley (pah´li) *n.* (*pl.* **parleys**) a conference for discussing terms, esp. between enemies. *~v.i.* (*pres.p.* **parleying**, *past, p.p.* **parleyed**) **1** to confer with an enemy with peacemaking intentions. **2** to talk, to dispute.

parliament (pah´ləmənt) *n.* **1** a deliberative assembly. **2** a legislative body, esp. the British legislature, consisting of the Houses of Lords and Commons, together with the sovereign. **parliamentarian** (-teə´ri-) *n.* **1** a person well-versed in parliamentary rules and usages or in parliamentary debate. **2** a Member of Parliament. **3** (*Hist.*) a person who supported the Parliament against King Charles I in the time of the English Civil War. *~a.* parliamentary. **parliamentary** (-men´-) *a.* **1** of, relating to or enacted by (a) parliament according to the rules of (a) parliament. **2** (esp. of language) admissible in (a) parliament, civil.

Usage note Pronunciation as (pah´liəmənt) is best avoided.

parlour (pah´lə), (*N Am.*) **parlor** *n.* **1** the family sitting-room in a private house. **2** a room in a convent, hotel etc. for conversation. **3** any of various commercial establishments (*a beauty parlour*). **4** a building used for milking cows. *~a.* (*derog.*) of or relating to a person who professes certain political views but makes no attempt to practise them. **parlour game** *n.* an indoor game, such as charades, sometimes played at a party. **parlourmaid** *n.* (*Hist.*) a maid waiting at table.

†parlous (pah´ləs) *a.* (*also facet.*) **1** perilous, awkward, trying. **2** difficult, cunning, shrewd. **parlously** *adv.* **parlousness** *n.*

Parma ham (pah´mə) *n.* a type of ham eaten uncooked.

Parma violet (pah´mə) *n.* a variety of violet with a strong scent and lavender-coloured flowers.

Parmesan (pahmizan´) *n.* a kind of hard, dry cheese made at Parma and elsewhere in N Italy, used grated as a topping for pasta dishes.

Parnassian (pahnas´iən) *a.* **1** of or relating to Mount Parnassus. **2** poetic.

parochial (pərō´kiəl) *a.* **1** of or relating to a

parish. **2** petty, narrow in outlook. **parochialism**, **parochiality** (-al´-) *n.* **parochialize, parochialise** *v.t.* **parochially** *adv.*

parody (par´ədi) *n.* (*pl.* **parodies**) **1** a literary composition imitating an author's work for the purpose of humour. **2** a poor imitation, a mere travesty. *~v.t.* (*3rd pers. sing. pres.* **parodies**, *pres.p.* **parodying**, *past, p.p.* **parodied**) to turn into a parody, to burlesque. **parodic** (-rod´-) *a.* **parodist** *n.*

parole (pərōl´) *n.* **1** the release of a prisoner under certain conditions, esp. good behaviour. **2** a word of honour. *~v.t.* to put or release on parole. **on parole** (of a prisoner) released under certain conditions esp. good behaviour. **parolee** (-lē) *n.*

paronomasia (parənəmā´ziə) *n.* a play on words, a pun.

parotid (pərot´id) *a.* (*Anat.*) situated near the ear. *~n.* (*Anat.*) a parotid gland. **parotid duct** *n.* a duct from the parotid gland by which saliva is conveyed to the mouth. **parotid gland** *n.* either of a pair of salivary glands situated on either side of the cheek in front of the ear, with a duct to the mouth. **parotiditis** (-dī´tis), **parotitis** (parətī´tis) *n.* (*Med.*) **1** inflammation of the parotid gland. **2** mumps.

-parous (pərəs) *comb. form* producing, bringing forth, as *oviparous*.

paroxysm (par´əksizm) *n.* **1** a sudden and violent fit. **2** a fit of laughter or other emotion. **paroxysmal** (-siz´-), **paroxysmic** *a.*

parquet (pah´kā) *n.* **1** a flooring of parquetry. **2** (*N Am.*) the part of the floor of a theatre between the orchestra and the row immediately under the front of the gallery. *~v.t.* (*pres.p.* **parqueting**, *past, p.p.* **parqueted**) to floor (a room) with parquetry. **parquetry** (-itri) *n.* inlaid woodwork for floors.

parr (pah), **par** *n.* a young salmon.

parramatta (parəmat´ə), **paramatta** *n.* a light twilled dress fabric of merino wool and cotton (orig. from Parramatta in New South Wales).

parricide (par´isīd) *n.* **1** the murder of a parent or other close relative, or of a revered person. **2** a person who murders a parent or other close relative, or a revered person. **parricidal** (-sī´-) *a.*

Usage note The nouns *parricide* and *patricide* should not be confused: *parricide* refers to a parent, close relative or revered person, and *patricide* just to a father.

parrot (par´ət) *n.* **1** any of various tropical birds with brilliant plumage of the order Psittaciformes, remarkable for their faculty of imitating the human voice. **2** a person who repeats words or imitates actions mechanically or unintelligently. *~v.t.* (*pres.p.* **parroting**, *past, p.p.* **parroted**) to repeat mechanically or by rote. **parrot-fashion** *adv.* accurately but without understanding the meaning. **parrotfish** *n.* (*pl. in general* **parrotfish**, *in particular* **parrotfishes**) any fish of the genus *Scarus*, so called because of their brilliant colouring and the beaklike projection of their jaws. **parrotry** *n.*

parry (par´i) *v.t.* (*3rd pers. sing. pres.* **parries**, *pres.p.* **parrying**, *past, p.p.* **parried**) **1** to ward off (a blow or thrust). **2** to evade cleverly, to shirk. ~*n.* (*pl.* **parries**) the act of parrying.

parse (pahz) *v.t.* **1** to describe or classify (a word) grammatically, its inflectional forms, relations in the sentence etc. **2** to analyse (a sentence) and describe its component words and their relations grammatically. **3** (*Comput.*) to analyse (a string) syntactically. **parser** *n.*

parsec (pah´sek) *n.* a unit of length in calculating the distance of the stars, being 1.9×10^{13} miles (3×10^{13} km) or 3.26 light years.

Parsee (pah´sē) *n.* **1** a Zoroastrian, a descendant of the Persians who fled to India from the Muslim persecution in the 7th and 8th cents. **2** the Pahlavi language. **Parseeism, Parsiism** *n.*

parsimonious (pahsimō´niəs) *a.* **1** careful in the expenditure of money. **2** frugal, niggardly, stingy. **parsimoniously** *adv.* **parsimoniousness** *n.* **parsimony** (pah´-) *n.*

parsley (pahs´li) *n.* an umbelliferous herb, *Petroselinum crispum*, cultivated for its aromatic leaves used for seasoning and garnishing dishes. **parsley fern** *n.* a type of fern, *Cryptogramma crispa*, which has parsley-like leaves. **parsley-piert** (-piət´) *n.* a small plant, *Aphanes arvensis*, of the rose family.

parsnip (pah´snip) *n.* an umbelliferous plant, *Pastinaca sativa*, with an edible root used as a vegetable.

parson (pah´sən) *n.* **1** a rector, vicar or other clergyman holding a benefice. **2** (*coll.*) a member of the clergy, esp. a Protestant one. **parsonage** (-ij) *n.* the home of a parson. **parsonic** (-son´-) *a.* **parson's nose** *n.* the rump of a fowl.

part (paht) *n.* **1** a portion, piece or amount of a thing or number of things. **2** a portion separate from the rest or considered as separate. **3** a small component of a machine, vehicle etc. **4** a member, an organ. **5** a proportional quantity. **6** any of several equal portions, quantities or numbers into which a thing is divided, or of which it is composed. **7** (*pl.*) PRIVATE PARTS (under PRIVATE). **8** a section of a book, periodical etc., as issued at one time. **9** a share, a lot. **10** interest, concern. **11** a share of work etc., act, duty. **12** side, party. **13** the role, character, words etc. allotted to an actor. **14** a copy of the words so allotted. **15** a person's allotted duty or responsibility. **16** (*pl.*) qualities, accomplishments, talents. **17** (*pl.*) region, district, quarters. **18** (*Mus.*) one of the constituent melodies of a harmony. **19** (*Mus.*) a melody allotted to a particular voice or instrument. **20** (*N Am.*) a parting in the hair. ~*v.t.* **1** to divide into portions, shares, pieces etc. **2** to separate. **3** to brush or comb (the hair) with a division along the head. ~*v.i.* **1** to divide. **2** to separate from another person or other people. ~*adv.* partly. ~*a.* partial. **for my part** so far as I am

concerned. **in part/ parts** partly. **on the part of** done by or proceeding from. **part and parcel** an essential part or element. **to look the part** to appear to be exactly right for a role. **to part company** to separate. **to part with** to relinquish, to give up. **to play a part 1** to assist or be involved. **2** to act deceitfully. **3** to act in a play or film. **to take part** to assist or participate. **to take the part of** to back up or support. **part exchange** *n.* a form of purchase in which one item is offered as partial payment for another, the balance being paid as money. **part-exchange** *v.t.* to offer in part exchange. **part of speech** *n.* a grammatical class of words of a particular character, usu. being one of noun, pronoun, adjective, verb, adverb, preposition, conjunction, interjection. **part-song** *n.* a composition for at least three voices in harmony, usu. without accompaniment. **part-time** *a.*, *adv.* working or done for less than the usual number of hours. **part-timer** *n.* **part-way** *adv.* **1** to some extent. **2** partially. **part-work** *n.* a publication issued in instalments, intended to be bound to form a complete book or course of study.

partake (pahtāk´) *v.i.* (*pres.p.* **partaking**, *past* **partook** (-tuk´), *p.p.* **partaken** (-tā´kən)) **1** to take or have a part or share (of or in, with another or others). **2** to have something of the nature (of). **3** to eat and drink (of). **partakable** *a.* **partaker** *n.*

parterre (pahtee´) *n.* **1** an ornamental arrangement of flower beds, with intervening walks. **2** (*N Am.*) the ground floor of a theatre or the part of this behind the orchestra.

parthenogenesis (pahthinəjen´əsis) *n.* (*Biol.*) generation without sexual union. **parthenogenetic** (-net´-) *a.* **parthenogenetically** *adv.*

Parthian (pah´thiən) *a.* of or relating to Parthia, an ancient kingdom in W Asia. **Parthian shot** *n.* a look, word etc. delivered as a parting blow (like the arrows shot by the Parthians in the act of fleeing).

partial (pah´shəl) *a.* **1** affecting a part only, incomplete. **2** biased in favour of one side or party, unfair. **3** having a preference for something. ~*n.* (*Mus.*) any constituent of musical sound. **partial derivative** *n.* (*Math.*) a derivative obtained by varying only one of several variables. **partiality** (-al´-) *n.* **partially** *adv.* **partialness** *n.*

Usage note See note on *partially* under PARTLY.

participate (pahtis´ipāt) *v.i.* to have or enjoy a share, to partake (in). **participant** *n.*, *a.* **participation** (-ā´shən) *n.* **participative** *a.* **participator** *n.* **participatory** *a.*

participle (pah´tisipəl) *n.* (*Gram.*) a word partaking of the nature of a verb and of an adjective, a verbal adjective qualifying a noun. **participial** (-sip´-) *a.* **participially** *adv.*

particle (pah´tikəl) *n.* **1** an atom. **2** a minute part or portion. **3** (*Gram.*) a word not inflected, or not used except in combination. **particle board** *n.* chipboard. **particle physics** *n.* the branch of physics concerned with fundamental particles and their properties. **particulate** (-tik´ūlət) *a.*

particoloured (pah´tikŭləd), (*N Am.*) **parti-colored, party-coloured,** (*N Am.*) **party-colored** *a.* partly of one colour, partly of another; variegated.

particular (pətik´ūlə) *a.* **1** of or relating to a single person or thing as distinct from others. **2** special, peculiar, characteristic. **3** single, separate, individual. **4** minute, circumstantial. **5** fastidious, exact, precise. **6** remarkable, noteworthy. **7** (*Logic*) stating something about only some members of a class. ~*n.* **1** an item, a detail, an instance. **2** (*pl.*) a detailed account. **in particular** particularly. **particularism** *n.* **1** devotion to private interests or those of a party, sect etc. **2** the policy of allowing political independence to the separate states of an empire, confederation etc. **3** (*Theol.*) the doctrine of the election or redemption of particular individuals of the human race. **particularist** *n.* **particularity** (-lar´-) *n.* (*pl.* **particularities**) **1** the quality of being particular. **2** (*usu. pl.*) a minute point or instance, a detail. **particularize, particularise** *v.t.* **1** to mention individually. **2** to specify, to give the particulars of. **particularization** (-zā´shən) *n.* **particularly** *adv.* **particularness** *n.*

parting (pah´ting) *n.* **1** a departure, leave-taking. **2** a dividing line, esp. between sections of hair combed or falling in opposite directions. **3** separation, division. **4** a point of separation or departure. ~*a.* **1** given or bestowed on departure or separation. **2** serving to part. **parting shot** *n.* a Parthian shot.

parti pris (pahti prē´) *n.* (*pl.* **partis pris** (pahti prē´)) a preconceived view, bias, prejudice. ~*a.* biased, prejudiced.

partisan (pah´tizan, -zan´), **partizan** *n.* **1** an adherent of a party, faction, cause etc., esp. one showing unreasoning devotion. **2** (*Mil.*) a member of a body of irregular troops carrying out special enterprises, such as raids. ~*a.* of, relating or attached to a party. **partisanship** *n.*

partita (pahtē´tə) *n.* (*pl.* **partitas, partite** (-tā)) (*Mus.*) **1** a suite of music. **2** an air with variations.

partite (pah´tīt) *a.* **1** divided (*usu. in comb.* as *bipartite*). **2** (*Bot., Zool.*) divided nearly to the base.

partition (pahtish´ən) *n.* **1** division into parts, distribution. **2** something which separates into parts, esp. a wall or screen. **3** a separate part. ~*v.t.* **1** to divide into parts or shares. **2** to separate (off). **partitioned** *a.* **partitioner** *n.* **partitionist** *n.*

partitive (pah´-) *a.* (*Gram.*) denoting a part. ~*n.* a word denoting partition, such as *some* or *any.* **partitive genitive** *n.* a genitive which indicates a whole divided into parts, e.g. *of* in *some of them.* **partitively** *adv.*

partly (paht´li) *adv.* **1** in part. **2** to some extent, not wholly.

Usage note The uses of the adverbs *partially* and *partly* overlap, but *partly* is more usual to introduce an explanation, and when the adverb is repeated as a correlative (*partly for this reason, and partly for that*).

---

partner (paht´nə) *n.* **1** a person who shares with another, esp. one associated with others in business; an associate. **2** either of two people who dance together. **3** either of two playing on the same side in a game. **4** either party in a marriage or a romantic relationship. ~*v.t.* to join in partnership with, to be a partner of. **partnerless** *a.* **partnership** *n.* **1** the state of being a partner or partners. **2** a contractual relationship between a number of people involved in a business enterprise. **3** a pair or group of partners.

partook PARTAKE.

partridge (pah´trij) *n.* (*pl.* **partridge, partridges**) any game bird of the genus *Perdix*, esp. *P. perdix.*

parturient (pahtū´riənt) *a.* about to give birth. **parturition** (-rish´ən) *n.* (*formal*) the act of giving birth.

party (pah´ti) *n.* (*pl.* **parties**) **1** a social gathering, usually in someone's home, often to celebrate a special occasion such as a birthday. **2** a number of persons united together for a particular purpose, esp. a national political group. **3** each of the actual or fictitious personages on either side in a legal action, contract etc. **4** (*Law*) an accessory, a person concerned in any affair. **5** (*coll.*) a person. ~*v.i.* (*3rd pers. sing. pres.* **parties,** *pres.p.* **partying,** *past, p.p.* **partied**) to attend parties, go out drinking etc. ~*v.t.* to entertain at a party. **party-goer** *n.* a person who likes going to parties or who is at a particular party. **party line** *n.* **1** the policy laid down by a political party. **2** a telephone exchange line used by a number of subscribers. **party politics** *n.* politics relating to political parties rather than the public good. **party political** *a.* of or relating to party politics. ~*n.* (*also* **party political broadcast**) a short, promotional television or radio programme made by a political party, usually broadcast just before an election. **party-poop, party-pooper** *n.* (*esp. N Am., sl.*) a person who spoils other people's fun, a spoilsport. **party-pooping** *n.* **party-popper** *n.* a small device from which paper streamers shoot out, sometimes used at parties. **party wall** *n.* a wall separating two buildings etc., the joint property of the respective owners.

parvenu (pah´vənoo, -nū) *n.* (*pl.* **parvenus**) **1** a person who has risen socially or financially. **2** an upstart. ~*a.* of or relating to a parvenu or parvenue. **parvenue** *n.* a female parvenu.

parvovirus (pah´vōvīrəs) *n.* (*pl.* **parvoviruses**) any one of a group of viruses each of which affects a particular species, such as *canine parvovirus.*

pas (pah) *n.* (*pl.* **pas** (pah)) a dance step, esp. in ballet. **pas de deux** (dœ´) *n.* (*pl.* **pas de deux**) a dance for two people.

pascal (pas´kəl) *n.* the SI unit of pressure, 1 newton per square metre.

paschal (pas´kəl) *a.* of or relating to the Passover or to Easter.

pash (pash) *n.* (*sl.*) a violent infatuation, a crush.

pasha (pah´shə), **bashaw** (bəshaw´), **pacha** *n.* (*Hist.*) a Turkish title of honour, usu. conferred on officers of high rank, governors etc. **pashalic** (-shəlik) *n.* the jurisdiction of a pasha.

Pashto (pŭsh´tō), **Pushto, Pushtu** (-too) *n.* a language spoken in Afghanistan and parts of Pakistan.

paso doble (pasō dō´blā) *n.* **1** a Latin American ballroom dance in fast 2/4 time, based on a march step. **2** this march step.

pasque flower (pask) *n.* a plant of the buttercup family, *Pulsatilla vulgaris*, with bell-shaped purple flowers.

pass (pahs) *v.i.* **1** to move from one place to another, to proceed, to go (along, on, quickly etc.). **2** to get through. **3** to circulate, to be current. **4** to be changed from one state to another. **5** to change hands, to be transferred. **6** to disappear, to vanish. **7** (*euphem.*) to die. **8** to go by, to elapse. **9** to go through, to be accepted without censure or challenge. **10** (of a bill before parliament) to be enacted. **11** to receive current recognition. **12** to be successful in a test or examination. **13** to adjudicate. **14** to take place, to happen, to occur. **15** in team games, to kick or hit the ball to a team-mate. **16** in cards, to give up one's option of playing, making trumps etc. **17** to choose not to do something, esp. to answer a question. **18** (*Law*) to be transferred or handed on. ~*v.t.* **1** to go by, beyond, over or through. **2** to overtake (a vehicle). **3** to transfer, to hand round. **4** to circulate, to give currency to. **5** to spend (time etc.). **6** in team games, to kick or hit (the ball) to a team-mate. **7** to endure. **8** to admit, to approve, to enact. **9** to satisfy the requirements of (an examination etc.). **10** to outstrip, to surpass. **11** to move, to cause to move. **12** to cause to go by. **13** to allow (a bill, a candidate etc.) to go through after examination. **14** to pronounce, to utter. **15** to void, to discharge. **16** not to declare. **17** to overlook, to disregard, to reject. **18** to omit. ~*n.* **1** the act of passing. **2** a passage, avenue or opening, esp. a narrow or difficult way. **3** a narrow passage through mountains, a defile. **4** a navigable passage, esp. at the mouth of a river. **5** a written or printed permission to pass. **6** a ticket authorizing one to travel (on a railway etc.) or to be admitted (to a theatre etc.) free. **7** a critical state or condition of things. **8** the act of passing an examination, esp. without special merit or honours. **9** in fencing, a thrust. **10** (*coll.*) a sexual advance. **11** a passing of hands over anything (as in conjuring). **12** a juggling trick. **13** in team games, the act of passing the ball. **to make a pass at** (*coll.*) to attempt to seduce. **to pass as** to be

accepted as. **to pass away** (*euphem.*) to die, to come to an end. **to pass by 1** to go past. **2** to omit, to disregard. **to pass for** to be taken for. **to pass off 1** to disappear gradually. **2** to proceed in a specified manner (*to pass off without a hitch*). **3** to circulate as genuine, to palm off. **to pass out 1** to faint. **2** (*Mil.*) (of an officer cadet) to complete training at a military academy. **3** to hand out, to distribute. **to pass over 1** to go across. **2** to allow to go by without notice, to overlook. **3** to omit. **4** to die. **to pass the time of day** to exchange greetings. **to pass through** to undergo, to experience. **to pass up** (*coll.*) to renounce. **to pass water** to urinate. **to sell the pass** to betray a cause. **passable** *a.* **1** acceptable, tolerable, fairly good. **2** able to be passed. **passableness** *n.* **passably** *adv.* **passband** *n.* a frequency band in which there is very little attenuation. **passbook** *n.* a book in which a record is kept of transactions relating to a building society or bank account. **passed pawn** *n.* in chess, a pawn with no opposing pawn restricting its ability to queen. **passer** *n.* **passerby** *n.* (*pl.* **passers-by**) a person who passes by or near, esp. casually. **pass-key** *n.* **1** a key for passing in when a gate etc. is locked. **2** a master key. **pass-mark** *n.* the lowest mark required to pass an examination. **password** *n.* **1** (*Comput.*) a string of characters by which a particular user can gain access to a system. **2** a word by which to distinguish friends from strangers, a watchword.

Usage note The past tense and participle *passed* should not be spelt *past* like the noun, adjective, preposition etc. See also note on *passable* under PASSIBLE.

passacaglia (pasəkah´liə) *n.* (*Mus.*) an instrumental piece with a ground bass.

passage¹ (pas´ij) *n.* **1** the act of passing. **2** movement from one place to another, transit, migration. **3** transition from one state to another. **4** a journey, a voyage, a crossing. **5** a way by which one passes, a way of entrance or exit. **6** a corridor or gallery giving admission to different rooms in a building. **7** right or liberty of passing. **8** a separate portion of a book, piece of music etc. **9** the passing of a bill etc. into law. **10** (*pl.*) events etc. that pass between people, incidents, episodes. **11** (*Anat.*) a duct in the body. **passageway** *n.* a corridor.

passage² (pas´ij) *v.i.* in dressage, to move sideways with diagonal pairs of legs lifted alternately. ~*v.t.* to make (a horse) passage.

passé (pas´ā) *a.* old-fashioned, behind the times.

passementerie (pas´məntri) *n.* a trimming for dresses, esp. of gold and silver lace.

passenger (pas´injə) *n.* **1** a person who travels on a public conveyance. **2** (*coll.*) a person, esp. a member of a team who benefits from something without contributing to it. **passenger pigeon** *n.* an extinct N American migratory pigeon.

passepartout (paspah´too) *n.* **1** a master key. **2** a simple frame for a picture, photograph etc. **3** the sticky tape or paper used for such a frame.

passerine (pas´erīn) *a.* **1** of or relating to the order Passeriformes, which contains the great mass of the smaller perching birds, such as sparrows. **2** like a sparrow, esp. in size. *~n.* a passerine bird.

passible (pas´ibəl) *a.* (*Theol.*) capable of feeling or suffering, susceptible to impressions from external agents. **passibility** (-bil´-) *n.*

Usage note The adjectives *possible* and *passable* should not be confused: *possible* means capable of feeling or suffering, and *passable* able to be passed or acceptable.

passim (pas´im) *adv.* here and there, throughout (indicating the occurrence of a word, allusion etc. in a cited work).

passing (pah´sing) *a.* **1** going by, occurring. **2** incidental, casual, cursory. **3** transient, fleeting. *~n.* **1** the act of passing. **2** passage, transit, lapse. **3** (*euphem.*) death. **passingly** *adv.* **passing note** *n.* (*Mus.*) a note forming a transition between two others, but not an essential part of the harmony. **passing shot** *n.* in tennis, a stroke that wins the point by passing an opponent beyond their reach.

passion (pash´ən) *n.* **1** intense emotion, a deep and overpowering affection of the mind, such as grief, anger, hatred etc. **2** an outburst of violent anger. **3** strong sexual love. **4 a** zeal, ardent enthusiasm (for). **b** the object of this. **5** (*also* **Passion**) **a** the last agonies of Christ. **b** an artistic representation of this. **c** a musical setting of the Gospel narrative of the Passion. **passionate** (-nət) *a.* easily moved to strong feeling, esp. love or anger; excited, vehement, warm, intense. **passionately** *adv.* **passionateness** *n.* **passion flower** *n.* any plant of the genus *Passiflora*, chiefly consisting of climbers, with flowers bearing a fancied resemblance to the instruments of the Passion. **passion fruit** *n.* the edible fruit of a passion flower, a grenadilla. **passionless** *a.* **passion play** *n.* a mystery play representing the Passion. **Passion Sunday** *n.* the fifth Sunday in Lent.

passive (pas´iv) *a.* **1** suffering, acted upon, not acting. **2** (*Gram.*) (of a verb form) expressing an action done to the subject of a sentence. **3** (esp. of a metal) not chemically reactive. **4** inactive, inert, submissive, not opposing. **5** (of a debt) yielding no interest. *~n.* (*Gram.*) the passive voice of a verb. **passivate** *v.t.* to make passive. **passivation** (-ā´shən) *n.* **passively** *adv.* **passiveness** *n.* **passive resistance** *n.* inert resistance, without active opposition. **passive smoking** *n.* the inhalation of others' cigarette smoke by non-smokers. **passive vocabulary** *n.* all the words that a person understands. **passive voice** *n.* the form of a transitive verb representing the subject as the object of the action. **passivity** (-siv´-) *n.*

Passover (pah´sōvə) *n.* a Jewish feast, on the

14th day of the month Nisan, commemorating the destruction of the first-born of the Egyptians and the 'passing over' of the Israelites by the destroying angel (Exodus xii).

passport (pahs´pawt) *n.* **1** an official document authorizing a person to travel in a foreign country and entitling them to legal protection. **2** anything ensuring admission (a *passport to high society*).

past (pahst) *a.* **1** gone by, neither present nor future. **2** just elapsed. **3** (*Gram.*) denoting an action or state belonging to the past. **4** former. *~n.* **1** past times. **2** one's past career or the history of this, esp. a disreputable one. **3** the past tense of a verb. *~prep.* **1** beyond in time or place. **2** beyond the influence or range of. **3** more than. *~adv.* so as to go by. **not to put it past someone to do something** not to be surprised if someone does something (*I wouldn't put it past him to lie about his age*). **past it** (*coll.*) no longer young and vigorous. **past master** *n.* **1** a thorough master (of a subject etc.). **2** a person who has been master of a Freemasons' lodge, a guild etc. **past participle** *n.* (*Gram.*) a participle derived from the past tense of a verb, with a past or passive meaning. **past participial** *a.* **past perfect** *n.* PLUPERFECT.

pasta (pas´tə) *n.* **1** a flour and water dough, often shaped and eaten fresh or in processed form, e.g. spaghetti. **2** a dish made with this dough. **3** a particular type or shape of this dough.

paste (pāst) *n.* **1** a mixture of flour and water, usu. with butter, lard etc., kneaded and used for making pastry etc. **2** a sweet of similar consistency. **3** a spread made of ground meat or fish. **4** an adhesive compound of flour, water, starch etc. boiled. **5** any doughy or plastic mixture, esp. of solid substances with liquid. **6** a vitreous composition used for making imitations of gems. **7** a mixture of clay, water etc. used to make ceramics. *~v.t.* **1** to fasten or stick with paste. **2** (*sl.*) to thrash, to beat. **3** to bomb heavily. **pasteboard** *n.* a board made of sheets of paper pasted together or of compressed paper pulp. *~a.* **1** made of pasteboard. **2** thin, flimsy. **3** sham. **paste-up** *n.* a sheet of paper with proofs, drawings etc. pasted on to it prior to being photographed for a printing process.

pastel (pas´təl) *n.* **1** a dry paste composed of a pigment mixed with gum water. **2** a coloured crayon made from this. **3** a picture drawn with such crayons. **4** the art of drawing with these. **5** a pale, subdued colour. *~a.* of a pastel colour. **pastelist, pastellist** *n.*

pastern (pas´tən) *n.* the part of a horse's leg between the fetlock and the hoof.

pasteurism (pas´tərizm) *n.* a method of preventing or curing certain diseases, esp. hydrophobia, by progressive inoculation. **pasteurize** (-chərīz), **pasteurise** *v.t.* to subject to treatment by heat in order to destroy the organisms which may be present. **pasteurization** (-zā´shən) *n.* **pasteurizer** *n.*

pastiche (pastēsh´), **pasticcio** (-tich´ō) *n.* (*pl.* **pastiches, pasticcios**) a medley, musical work, painting etc. composed of elements drawn from other works or which imitates the style of a previous work.

pastille (pas´təl) *n.* **1** an aromatic lozenge. **2** a roll, cone or pellet of aromatic paste for burning as a fumigator or disinfectant.

pastime (pahs´tīm) *n.* something that makes time pass agreeably, a game, a recreation, sport, diversion.

pastis (pas´tis, pastēs´) *n.* (*pl.* **pastis**) an aniseed-flavoured alcoholic drink.

pastor (pahs´tə) *n.* **1** a minister in charge of a church and congregation. **2** a person acting as a spiritual guide. **3** a pink starling, *Sturnus roseus*, of Europe and Asia. **pastorate** (-rət) *n.* **pastorship** *n.*

pastoral (pahs´tərəl) *a.* **1** of or relating to shepherds. **2** (of land) used for pasture. **3** (of poetry etc.) portraying country life, rural, rustic. **4** of or relating to the cure of souls or the duties of a pastor. **5** befitting a pastor. **6** of or relating to the personal needs, as distinct from the educational needs, of school pupils. *~n.* **1** a pastoral poem, play, picture etc. **2** a letter or address from a pastor, esp. from a bishop to his diocese. **pastoralist** *n.* (*Austral.*) a sheep or cattle farmer, as distinct from an agriculturalist. **pastorality** (-ral´-) *n.* **pastorally** *adv.* **pastoral staff** *n.* a bishop's crosier.

pastorale (pastərahl´, -rah´li) *n.* (*pl.* **pastorales** (-ahlz´), **pastorali** (-ah´li)) **1** a simple rustic melody. **2** a cantata on a pastoral theme.

pastrami (pastrah´mi) *n.* a highly seasoned smoked beef.

pastry (pās´tri) *n.* (*pl.* **pastries**) **1** a dough of flour, fat and water, used baked to make pies. **2** articles of food made with a crust of such dough, baked. **3** an item of pastry, a cake. **pastry-cook** *n.*

pasture (pahs´chə) *n.* **1** ground suitable for the grazing of cattle etc., grass for grazing. **2** the act of putting cattle etc. out to pasture. *~v.t.* **1** to put (cattle etc.) on land to graze. **2** (of sheep etc.) to eat down (grassland), to feed by grazing. *~v.i.* to graze. **pasturage** (-ij) *n.* **pastureland** *n.*

pasty[1] (pās´ti) *a.* (*comp.* **pastier,** *superl.* **pastiest**) **1** of or like paste. **2** pale, unhealthy-looking. **pastily** *adv.* **pastiness** *n.*

pasty[2] (pas´ti) *n.* (*pl.* **pasties**) a small pie, usu. of meat, baked without a dish.

pat (pat) *v.t.* (*pres.p.* **patting,** *past, p.p.* **patted**) **1** to strike gently and quickly with something flat, esp. the fingers or hand. **2** to pat into a shape, esp. a flattened shape. **3** to tap, to stroke gently. *~v.i.* to strike gently. *~n.* **1** a light, quick blow with the hand; a tap, a stroke. **2** the sound of a light blow with something flat. **3** a small mass or lump (of butter etc.) moulded by patting. *~a.* **1** facile. **2** exactly suitable or fitting, opportune, apposite, apt. *~adv.* **1** facilely. **2** aptly, opportunely. **to have off pat** to have learned or pre-pared thoroughly. **to pat someone on the back** to praise or congratulate someone. **to stand pat 1** (*esp. N Am.*) to stand by one's decision or beliefs. **2** in poker, to play with the hand one has been dealt, without drawing other cards. **pat-a-cake** *n.* a child's game in which two people clap hands with each other whilst reciting a rhyme. **patball** *n.* **1** a game in which two players hit a ball back and forth between them. **2** (*derog.*) slow-paced tennis. **patly** *adv.* **patness** *n.* **pat on the back** *n.* a demonstration of approval.

pat. *abbr.* patent(ed).

pataca (pətah´kə) *n.* (*pl.* **patacas**) the standard unit of currency of Macao.

patch (pach) *n.* **1** a piece of cloth, metal or other material put on to mend anything. **2** a piece put on to strengthen a fabric etc. **3** a piece of cloth worn over an injured eye. **4** a dressing covering a wound etc. **5** a differently coloured part of a surface. **6** a small piece of ground, a plot. **7** (*coll.*) the district for which a police officer, social worker etc. has responsibility. **8** a number of plants growing together. **9** a scrap, a shred. **10** a temporary electrical connection. **11** (*Comput.*) a small piece of code used to correct or improve instructions. *~v.t.* **1** to put a patch or patches on. **2** to mend with a patch or patches (usu. with *up*). **3** to mend clumsily. **4** to put together or arrange hastily. **5** to connect by a temporary connection. **6** (*Comput.*) to correct or improve by means of a patch. **7** to serve as a patch for. *~v.i.* to be connected by a temporary connection. **not a patch on** (*coll.*) not nearly as good as. **to patch up** to mend. **to patch up a quarrel** to be reconciled, esp. temporarily. **patchboard** *n.* a board with a number of electrical sockets used for making temporary circuits. **patcher** *n.* **patch pocket** *n.* a pocket consisting of a flat piece of cloth sewn on to the outside of a garment. **patch test** *n.* an allergy test in which patches containing different allergenic substances are applied to the skin. **patchwork** *n.* **1** work composed of pieces of different colours, sizes etc., sewn together. **2** something composed of a variety of parts. *~a.* **1** made of patchwork. **2** resembling patchwork. **3** cobbled together. **patchy** *a.* (*comp.* **patchier,** *superl.* **patchiest**) **1** of inconsistent quality, frequency etc. **2** appearing in patches. **3** covered with patches. **patchily** *adv.* **patchiness** *n.*

patchouli (pach´uli, pəchoo´-) *n.* **1** an Indian shrub of the genus *Pogostemon*, yielding a fragrant oil. **2** a perfume prepared from this.

pate (pāt) *n.* (*facet.*) the head, esp. the top of the head.

pâte (paht) *n.* the paste from which porcelain is made.

pâté (pat´ā) *n.* a spread made of cooked, diced meat, fish or vegetables blended with herbs etc. **pâté de foie gras** (də fwah grah´) *n.* pâté made of fatted goose liver.

patella (pətel´ə) *n.* (*pl.* **patellae** (-lē)) the kneecap. **patellar, patellate** (-lət), **patelliform** (-ifawm) *a.*

paten (pat´ən) *n.* **1** a plate or shallow dish for receiving the Eucharistic bread. **2** a circular metal plate.

patent (pā´tənt, pat´-) *n.* **1** a grant from the Crown by letters patent of a title of nobility, or from the Crown or a government of the exclusive right to make or sell a new invention. **2** an invention so protected. **3** anything serving as a sign or certificate (of quality etc.). ~*a.* **1** plain, obvious, manifest. **2** protected or conferred by letters patent. **3** made under a patent, proprietary. **4** ingenious. **5** permitting free passage. **6** open to the perusal of all. ~*v.t.* to secure by patent. **patency** (-si) *n.* **patentable** *a.* **patentee** (-tē´) *n.* a person granted a right or privilege by patent. **patent leather** *n.* a leather with a shiny or varnished surface. **patently** *adv.* **patent medicine** *n.* a medicine sold under a licence with a registered name and trade mark. **patent office** *n.* a government department responsible for granting patents.

pater (pā´tə) *n.* (*sl., usu. facet.*) a father.

paterfamilias (patəfəmil´ias, pā-) *n.* (*pl.* **patresfamilias** (pahtrāz-)) the father of a family, the male head of a household.

paternal (pətœ´nəl) *a.* **1** of or relating to a father. **2** fatherly. **3** connected or related through the father. **4** (of a government) restricting freedom and responsibility through overprotectiveness. **paternalism** *n.* the exercise of benign, overprotective authority, esp. in a form of government, often seen as interference with individual rights. **paternalist** *n.* **paternalistic** (-lis´-) *a.* **paternalistically** *adv.* **paternally** *adv.* **paternity** *n.* **1** fatherhood. **2** ancestry or origin on the male side, descent from a father. **3** authorship, source. **paternity leave** *n.* paid leave granted to a man when his wife has a baby. **paternity suit** *n.* a lawsuit held to establish whether a particular man is the father of a particular child. **paternity test** *n.* a blood test used to establish whether a particular man may be or cannot be the father of a particular child.

paternoster (patənos´tə) *n.* **1** the Lord's Prayer, esp. in Latin. **2** every 11th bead of a rosary, indicating that the Lord's Prayer is to be said. **3** a rosary. **4** a type of lift with compartments attached to a continuous, circular belt.

path (pahth) *n.* (*pl.* **paths** (pahdhz)) **1** a footway, esp. one beaten only by feet. **2** a course or track. **3** a course of life, action etc. **4** a sequence of operations taken by a system. **pathfinder** *n.* **1** an explorer or pioneer. **2** a radar device used for navigational purposes or for targeting missiles. **pathless** *a.* **pathway** *n.* **1** a path. **2** sequence of reactions in a living organism.

-path (path) *comb. form* **1** a medical practitioner, as in *homoeopath*. **2** a person suffering from a pathological disorder, as in *psychopath*. **-pathy** (pathi) *comb. form* **1** disease, treatment of this, as in *homoeopathy*. **2** suffering, feeling, as in *sympathy*.

pathetic (pəthet´ik) *a.* **1** affecting or moving the feelings, esp. those of pity and sorrow. **2** (*coll.*) poor, weak or contemptible. **pathetically** *adv.* **pathetic fallacy** *n.* in literature, the attribution of human feelings to objects associated with nature such as trees.

patho- (path´ō), **path-** *comb. form* disease.

pathogen (path´əjən) *n.* any disease-producing substance or micro-organism. **pathogenic** (-jen´-) *a.* **pathogenicity** (-is´-) *n.* **pathogenous** (-thoj´-) *a.*

pathogenesis (pathəjen´əsis) *n.* the origin and development of disease. **pathogenetic** (-net´-) *a.* **pathogeny** (-thoj´-) *n.*

pathology (pathol´əjl) *n.* **1** the science of diseases, esp. of the human body. **2** the changes which characterize disease. **pathologic** (pathəloj´-), **pathological** *a.* **1** of or relating to pathology. **2** caused by or involving disease. **3** (*coll.*) driven or motivated by compulsion rather than reason. **pathologically** *adv.* **pathologist** *n.*

pathos (pā´thos) *n.* a quality or element in events or expression that excites emotion, esp. pity or sorrow.

-pathy -PATH.

patience (pā´shəns) *n.* **1** calm endurance of pain, provocation or other evils; fortitude. **2** a card game played by one person. **to have no patience with 1** to be unable to stand or put up with. **2** to be irritated by.

patient (pā´shənt) *a.* **1** capable of bearing pain, suffering etc. without fretfulness. **2** not easily provoked, indulgent. **3** persevering, diligent. ~*n.* a person under medical treatment. **patiently** *adv.*

patina (pat´inə) *n.* (*pl.* **patinas**) **1** the green incrustation that covers ancient bronzes. **2** a similar film on any surface. **3** a soft shine produced by age on woodwork. **patinated** (-nātid) *a.* **patination** (-ā´shən) *n.*

patio (pat´iō) *n.* (*pl.* **patios**) **1** a paved area beside a house, used for outdoor meals, sunbathing etc. **2** the open inner court of a Spanish or Spanish-American house. **patio rose** *n.* a miniature floribunda rose.

patisserie (pətē´səri) *n.* **1** a pastry-cook's shop. **2** pastries collectively.

Patna rice (pat´nə) *n.* a variety of long-grain rice used for savoury dishes.

patois (pat´wah) *n.* (*pl.* **patois** (-wahz)) a non-standard dialect of a district.

patri- (pat´ri) *comb. form* father.

patriarch (pā´triahk) *n.* **1** the head of a family or tribe, ruling by paternal right. **2** (*Bible*) any of the founding fathers Abraham, Isaac and Jacob, their forefathers, and the sons of Jacob. **3** in the Eastern and early Churches, a bishop, esp. of Alexandria, Antioch, Constantinople, Jerusalem and some other sees. **4** the highest grade in the hierarchy of the Roman Catholic Church. **5** the founder of a religion, science etc. **6** a venerable old man. **7** the oldest living person in a group. **patriarchal** (-ah´kəl) *a.* **patriarchally** *adv.* **patriarchate** (-kət) *n.* **patriarchy** *n.* (*pl.* **patriarchies**) a patriarchal system of government or social organization, esp. as distinct from *matriarchy*.

patrician (pətrish´ən) *n.* **1** a noble, an aristocrat, a member of the highest class of society. **2** (*N Am.*) a refined or sophisticated person. ~*a.* **1** noble, aristocratic. **2** (*N Am.*) refined, sophisticated. **patriciate** (-ət) *n.*

patricide (pat´risīd) *n.* **1** (the act of) killing one's father. **2** a person who commits patricide. **patricidal** (-sī´-) *a.*

Usage note See note under PARRICIDE.

patrimony (pat´riməni) *n.* (*pl.* **patrimonies**) **1** an estate or right inherited from one's father or ancestors. **2** a heritage. **3** a church estate or endowment. **patrimonial** (-mō´-) *a.* **patrimonially** *adv.*

patriot (pat´riət, pā´triət) *n.* a person who loves their country and is devoted to its interests, esp. its freedom and independence. **patriotic** (-ot´ik) *a.* **patriotically** *adv.* **patriotism** *n.*

patristic (pətris´tik), **patristical** (-kəl) *a.* of or relating to the ancient Fathers of the Christian Church or their writings. **patristics** *n.* the study of patristic writings.

patrol (pətrōl´) *n.* **1** the action of moving around an area, esp. at night, for the maintenance of order and for security. **2** the detachment of soldiers, police, firemen etc., or the soldier, officer etc., doing this. **3** a detachment of troops, sent out to reconnoitre. **4** such reconnaissance. **5** a routine operational voyage or flight. **6** a person who controls traffic so that children may cross the road safely. **7** a group of six to eight Scouts or Guides. ~*v.i.* (*pres.p.* **patrolling**, *past*, *p.p.* **patrolled**) to go on a patrol. ~*v.t.* to go round. **patrol car** *n.* a car in which police officers patrol an area. **patrolman** *n.* (*pl.* **patrolmen**) (*N Am.*) a low-ranking police officer.

patrology (pətrol´əji) *n.* (*pl.* **patrologies**) patristics.

patron (pā´trən) *n.* **1** a person who supports, fosters or protects a person, cause, art etc. **2** (*coll.*) a regular customer (at a shop etc.). **3** a person who holds the gift of a benefice. **patronage** (pat´rənij) *n.* **1** support, fostering, encouragement or protection. **2** the right of presentation to a benefice or office. **3** the act of patronizing. **patronal** (pətrō´-) *a.* **patroness** *n.* a female patron. **patronize** (pat´rənīz), **patronise** *v.t.* **1** to treat in a condescending way. **2** to act as a patron towards. **3** to frequent as a customer. **patronization** (-zā´shən) *n.* **patronizer** *n.* **patronizing** *a.* **patronizingly** *adv.* **patron saint** *n.* a saint regarded as the patron of a particular group, country etc.

patronymic (patrənim´ik) *n.* a name derived from a father or ancestor; a family name. ~*a.* (of a name) derived from a father or ancestor.

patsy (pat´si) *n.* (*pl.* **patsies**) (*N Am.*, *sl.*) a person who is easily deceived, cheated etc., a sucker, a scapegoat.

patten (pat´ən) *n.* (*Hist.*) a clog or overshoe

mounted on an iron ring etc., for keeping the shoes out of the mud or wet.

patter¹ (pat´ə) *v.i.* **1** (of rain) to fall with a quick succession of light, sharp sounds. **2** to move with short, quick steps. ~*v.t.* to cause (water etc.) to patter. ~*n.* a quick succession of sharp, light sounds or taps.

patter² (pat´ə) *n.* **1** rapid speech introduced impromptu into a song, comedy etc. **2** glib talk, chattering, gossip. **3** the patois or slangy lingo of a particular class or group. ~*v.t.* to say (one's prayers) in a mechanical, singsong way. ~*v.i.* **1** to talk glibly. **2** to pray in this manner.

pattern (pat´ən) *n.* **1** a decorative design for a carpet, wallpaper, fabric etc. **2** a type, style. **3** a model or original to be copied or serving as a guide in making something. **4** a shape used to make a mould into which molten metal is poured to make a casting. **5** a sample or specimen (of cloth etc.). **6** the marks made by shot on a target. ~*v.t.* **1** to copy, to model (after, from or upon). **2** to decorate with a pattern. **pattern bombing** *n.* bombing over a wide area.

patty (pat´i) *n.* (*pl.* **patties**) **1** a little pie. **2** a small, flat cake of minced food. **3** (*N Am.*) a small, round sweet. **pattypan** *n.* a pan for baking patties.

paucity (paw´siti) *n.* an insufficient amount; scarcity.

Pauline (paw´līn) *a.* of or relating to St Paul or his writings.

Paul Jones (pawl jōnz´) *n.* a ballroom dance in which partners are exchanged several times.

paulownia (pawlō´niə) *n.* any Chinese tree of the genus *Paulownia*, having purple flowers.

paunch (pawnch) *n.* **1** the belly, the abdomen. **2** a fat or protruding belly. **3** (*Naut.*) a thick mat or wooden shield fastened on a mast etc., to prevent chafing. ~*v.t.* to rip open the belly of, to disembowel, to stab in the belly. **paunchy** *a.* (*comp.* **paunchier**, *superl.* **paunchiest**). **paunchiness** *n.*

pauper (paw´pə) *n.* **1** a person without means of support, a destitute person, a beggar. **2** (*Hist.*) a person entitled to public assistance. **pauperdom**, **pauperism** *n.* **pauperize**, **pauperise** *v.t.* **pauperization** (-zā´shən) *n.*

pause (pawz) *n.* **1** a cessation or intermission of action, speaking etc. **2** a break in reading, speaking, music etc., esp. for the sake of emphasis. **3** (*Mus.*) a mark (∪ or ⌣) over a note etc., indicating that it is to be prolonged. **4** a control to interrupt the operation of a video recorder etc. ~*v.i.* **1** to make a pause or short stop; to wait. **2** to linger (upon or over). **to give someone pause** to cause someone to hesitate and reconsider.

pavane (pəvan´), **pavan** (pav´ən) *n.* **1** a slow and stately dance, usu. in elaborate dress, in vogue in the 16th and 17th cents. **2** music for this.

pave (pāv) *v.t.* **1** to make a hard, level surface upon, with stone, bricks etc. **2** to cover with or as if with a pavement. **to pave the way for** to prepare for, to make possible. **pavement** *n.* **1** a paved footway at the side of a street or road. **2** a hard level covering, bricks, tiles, wooden blocks. **3** (*N Am.*) the paved surface of a road. **4** (*Zool.*) a close, level structure or formation (e.g. of teeth) resembling a pavement. **pavement artist** *n.* a person drawing figures etc. on a pavement in the hope of being given money from passers-by. **paver** *n.* **paving** *n.* **paving stone** *n.* **paviour** (-yə), (*N Am.*) **pavior** *n.* **1** a person who lays pavements. **2** a machine for ramming paving stones. **3** a paving stone, block etc.

pavilion (pəvil´yən) *n.* **1** an ornamental building, usu. of light construction, for amusements etc., esp. one for spectators and players at a cricket ground etc. **2** a tent, esp. a large one, of conical shape. **3** a temporary or movable structure for entertainment, shelter etc. ~*v.t.* to furnish with or shelter in a pavilion.

pavlova (pavlō´və, pav´ləvə) *n.* a dessert consisting of a meringue base topped with fruit and whipped cream.

paw (paw) *n.* **1** the foot of an animal having claws, as distinct from a hoof. **2** (*sl.*) one's hand. ~*v.t.* **1** to scrape or strike with the forefoot. **2** (*coll.*) to handle roughly, familiarly, sexually or clumsily. ~*v.i.* (of a horse) to strike the ground with a hoof.

pawky (paw´ki) *a.* (*comp.* **pawkier,** *superl.* **pawkiest**) (*esp. Sc., North.*) **1** humorous, arch. **2** sly, shrewd. **pawkily** *adv.* **pawkiness** *n.*

pawl (pawl) *n.* **1** a hinged piece of metal or lever engaging with the teeth of a wheel etc., to prevent it from running back etc. **2** (*Naut.*) a bar for preventing the recoil of a windlass etc. ~*v.t.* to stop from recoiling with a pawl.

pawn[1] (pawn) *n.* **1** a piece of the lowest value in chess. **2** an insignificant person used by a cleverer one for their advantage.

pawn[2] (pawn) *v.t.* **1** to deliver or deposit as a pledge for the repayment of a debt or loan, or the performance of a promise. **2** to stake, to wager, to risk. ~*n.* something deposited as security for a debt or loan, a pledge. **at pawn** deposited as a pledge or security. **in pawn** at pawn. **pawnbroker** *n.* a person who lends money on the security of goods pawned. **pawnbroking** *n.* **pawner** *n.* **pawnshop** *n.* a place where goods can be pawned.

pawpaw (paw´paw), **papaw** (pəpaw´) *n.* **1** (*also* **papaya** (pəpī´ə)) a large, oblong, edible yellow fruit. **2** (*also* **papaya**) a tropical American tree, *Carica papaya,* which yields papain and bears the papaya fruit. **3** a N American tree, *Asimina triloba,* having purple flowers and edible fruit.

pax (paks) *n.* the kiss of peace. ~*int.* (*sl.*) used to express a call for a truce (in children's games).

pay[1] (pā) *v.t.* (*past, p.p.* **paid** (pād)) **1** to hand over to (someone) what is due in discharge of a debt or for services or goods. **2** to discharge (a bill, claim, obligation etc.). **3** to deliver as due. **4** to deliver the amount, defray the cost or expense of. **5** to reward or punish. **6** to compensate, to recompense, to requite. **7** to be remunerative or worthwhile to. **8** to bestow, to tender (a compliment, visit etc.). ~*v.i.* **1** to make payment. **2** to discharge a debt. **3** to make an adequate return (to). **4** to be remunerative or worthwhile. ~*n.* **1** wages, salary. **2** payment, compensation, recompense. **in the pay of** employed by. **to pay back 1** to repay. **2** to take revenge on. **3** to return (a favour etc.). **to pay dearly for 1** to pay with a lot of money or effort for. **2** to suffer as a result of. **to pay for 1** to make a payment for. **2** to suffer as a result of. **to pay heed** to take notice. **to pay in** to deposit in a bank account. **to pay its way** to cover costs. **to pay off 1** to make (an employee) redundant, with a final payment. **2** (*coll.*) to be profitable or rewarding. **3** to pay the full amount of, to pay in full and discharge. **to pay one's dues 1** (*esp. N Am.*) to fulfil one's obligations. **2** (*esp. N Am.*) to achieve success after enduring a period of hardship. **to pay one's way** to keep out of debt. **to pay out 1** to disburse. **2** to punish. **to pay through the nose** to pay an exorbitant price. **to pay up** to pay someone what is owed or due to them. **paid** *a.* **to put paid to** (*coll.*) to end, to destroy. **paid holidays** *n.pl.* holidays from work for which one is paid as normal. **paid-up member** *n.* **1** a member of a trade union etc. who has paid the full subscription. **2** (*coll.*) an enthusiastic or committed supporter of a cause or organization. **payable** *a.* **1** that can or must be paid. **2** profitable. ~*n.* (*pl.*) debts owed by a business. **pay-as-you-earn** *n.* a method of collecting income tax by deducting it before payment of the earnings. **pay-as-you-go** *n.* a system of paying debts and expenses as they arise. **payback** *n.* profit or benefit from an investment etc. **payback period** *n.* the time allowed for the repayment of a loan. **pay bed** *n.* a bed for a private patient in a National Health Service hospital. **pay claim** *n.* a demand for a pay increase, esp. by a trade union. **pay day** *n.* **1** the day on which one's wages or salary are paid. **2** on the Stock Exchange, the day on which transfers of stock are to be paid for. **pay dirt** *n.* (*N Am.*) **1** a deposit containing enough gold to make mining worthwhile. **2** anything profitable or useful. **payee** (-ē´) *n.* **payer** *n.* **paying guest** *n.* a lodger who lives with a family. **payload** *n.* **1** the part of a transport vehicle's load that brings profit. **2** the passengers, cargo or weaponry carried by an aircraft. **3** the explosive capacity of a bomb, missile warhead etc. **4** the equipment which a spacecraft carries as the purpose of its mission, contrasted with those things necessary for its operation. **paymaster** *n.* **1** a person who pays, esp. one who regularly pays wages etc. **2** an officer in the armed services whose duty it is to pay the wages. **Paymaster-General** *n.* the officer at the head of the Treasury department concerned with the payment of civil salaries and other expenses. **payment** *n.* **pay-off**

n. (*coll.*) **1** the final payment of a bill etc. **2** a return on an investment etc. **3** the final result or outcome. **pay-out** *n.* a sum paid to someone, by an insurance company or as a prize. **pay packet** *n.* an envelope containing a person's wages. **payphone** *n.* a public telephone operated by coins. **payroll** *n.* a list of employees. **payslip** *n.* a slip of paper giving details of one's pay, income tax deductions etc.

pay[2] (pā) *v.t.* (*past*, *p.p.* **payed**) (*Naut.*) to coat, cover or fill with hot pitch for waterproofing.

PAYE *abbr.* pay-as-you-earn.

payola (pāō´lə) *n.* (*esp. N Am.*) clandestine reward paid for illicit promotion of a commercial product, e.g. of a record by a disc jockey.

Pb *chem. symbol* lead.

PBX *abbr.* private branch exchange.

PC *abbr.* **1** Parish Council. **2** personal computer. **3** police constable. **4** political correctness. **5** politically correct. **6** Privy Counsellor.

p.c. *abbr.* **1** per cent. **2** postcard.

PCB *abbr.* **1** (*Chem.*) polychlorinated biphenyl. **2** (*Comput.*) printed circuit board.

PCM *abbr.* pulse code modulation.

pct *abbr.* (*N Am.*) per cent.

PD *abbr.* (*N Am.*) Police Department.

Pd *chem. symbol* palladium.

pd. *abbr.* paid.

p.d.q. *abbr.* (*coll.*) pretty damn quick.

PDT *abbr.* Pacific Daylight Time.

PE *abbr.* physical education.

pea (pē) *n.* **1** a leguminous plant, *Pisum sativum*, the seeds of which are used as food. **2** the seed of this. **3** any of various similar leguminous plants, e.g. the chickpea. **pea-brain** *n.* (*coll.*) a stupid person. **pea-brained** *a.* **pea green** *n.* a colour like that of fresh green peas. **pea-green** *a.* **peapod** *n.* the seed case of the pea. **pea-shooter** *n.* a tube through which dried peas are blown. **pea-souper** *n.* (*coll.*) a dense yellowish fog.

peace (pēs) *n.* **1** a state of quiet or tranquillity. **2** calmness of mind. **3** freedom from or cessation of war or hostilities. **4** a treaty reconciling two hostile nations. **5** absence of civil disturbance or agitation. **6** a liturgical greeting. **7** a state of friendliness. **at peace 1** in a state of harmony or tranquillity. **2** (*euphem.*) dead. **to hold one's peace** to stay silent. **to keep the peace 1** to abstain from strife. **2** to prevent a conflict. **to make one's peace with** to end one's quarrel with. **to make peace 1** to reconcile or be reconciled (with). **2** to bring about a treaty of peace. **peaceable** *a.* **1** disposed to peace. **2** peaceful, quiet. **peaceableness** *n.* **peaceably** *adv.* **peace dividend** *n.* public money which, in the absence of hostilities, no longer needs to be spent on defence and therefore is available for civilian projects. **peaceful** *a.* **1** quiet, peace-loving, mild. **2** free from noise or disturbance. **3** in a state of peace. **peacefully** *adv.* **peacefulness** *n.* **peacekeeper** *n.* a person or organization that preserves peace between hostile parties. **peacekeeping** *n.*,

a. **peacemaker** *n.* a person who reconciles. **peace-making** *n.*, *a.* **peace-offering** *n.* **1** a gift to procure peace or reconciliation. **2** (*Bible*) an offering to God as a token of thanksgiving. **peace pipe** *n.* a pipe smoked by N American Indians as a sign of peace. **peacetime** *n.* a time when there is no war.

Usage note The meanings of the adjectives *peaceable* and *peaceful* overlap, but in general *peaceable* is used of people, and *peaceful* of quiet or tranquil conditions.

peach[1] (pēch) *n.* **1** a fleshy, downy stone fruit with sweet yellow flesh and a pinkish-orange skin. **2** the tree, *Prunus persica*, on which peaches grow. **3** a pinkish-yellow colour. **4 a** (*coll.*) a pretty girl. **b** anything extremely good or pretty. *~a.* pinkish-yellow. **peaches and cream** *a.* (of a complexion) clear, smooth and creamy. **peach Melba** (mel´bə), **pêche Melba** (pesh) *n.* a dish of ice cream, peaches and sauce. **peachy** *a.* (*comp.* **peachier**, *superl.* **peachiest**). **peachiness** *n.*

peach[2] (pēch) *v.i.* to turn informer against an accomplice, to inform (against or upon).

peacock (pē´kok) *n.* **1** a male peafowl, having gorgeous plumage and a long tail capable of expanding like a fan. **2** a vain, arrogant person. **peacock blue** *n.* a rich greenish blue. **peacock-blue** *a.* **peacock butterfly** *n.* a butterfly, *Inachis io*, having eyelike markings on the wings. **peafowl** *n.* a pheasant of the genus *Pavo*, of which the peacock is the male. **pea-chick** *n.* a young peafowl. **peahen** *n.* a female peafowl.

pea-jacket (pē´jakit) *n.* a coarse, thick, loose overcoat worn by seamen.

peak[1] (pēk) *n.* **1** a sharp point or top, esp. of a mountain. **2** a mountain with a peak. **3** the projecting brim in front of a cap. **4** a pointed beard. **5** (*Naut.*) the upper outer corner of a sail extended by a gaff. **6** the culminating point of an electricity load curve during a specified period, and the maximum load of electricity required. **7** the point of greatest activity, use, demand etc. *~v.i.* to reach a peak. *~a.* of or relating to the point of greatest activity, use, demand etc. **peaked**[1] *a.* **peak hour** *n.* the time when there is most traffic, activity etc. **peak load** *n.* the maximum load of electricity required. **peaky**[1] *a.* (*comp.* **peakier**, *superl.* **peakiest**). **peakiness** *n.*

peak[2] (pēk) *v.i.* **1** to pine away. **2** to look sickly. **peaked**[2] *a.* sharp-featured or emaciated. **peaky**[2] *a.* (*comp.* **peakier**, *superl.* **peakiest**).

peaked[1] PEAK[1].

peaked[2] PEAK[2].

peaky[1] PEAK[1].

peaky[2] PEAK[2].

peal (pēl) *n.* **1** a loud, esp. a prolonged or repercussive, sound, as of thunder, bells etc. **2** a set of bells tuned to each other. **3** a series of changes rung on these. *~v.i.* to sound a peal, to resound. ~v.t. 1 to utter or give forth sonorously. 2 to cause to give out loud and solemn sounds.

peanut (pē´nŭt) n. 1 a plant, *Arachis hypogaea*, of the bean family with pods ripening underground, the seeds of which are edible and used for their oil. 2 the seed of the peanut plant. 3 (pl., coll.) an insignificant sum of money. **peanut butter** n. a paste made from ground roasted peanuts.

pear (peə) n. 1 the fleshy yellow or greenish fruit of the pear tree. 2 (also **pear tree**) any of various trees of the genus *Pyrus*, on which pears grow. **pear-shaped** a.

pearl[1] (pœl) n. 1 a smooth, white or bluish-grey, lustrous and iridescent, calcareous concretion, found in several bivalves, the best in the pearl-oyster, prized as a gem. 2 an imitation pearl. 3 (pl.) a pearl necklace. 4 mother-of-pearl. 5 anything exceedingly valuable, or the finest specimen of its kind. 6 something round and clear and resembling a pearl, such as a dewdrop, tooth etc. 7 a bluish grey. ~a. 1 of, relating to, containing or made of pearls. 2 bluish-grey. ~v.t. 1 (poet.) to sprinkle with pearly drops. 2 (poet.) to make pearly. 3 to rub and strip (barley) into pearly grains. ~v.i. 1 to fish for pearls. 2 (poet.) to form pearly drops or fragments. **to cast pearls before swine** to offer something valuable or beautiful to someone who does not appreciate it. **pearl ash** n. crude potassium carbonate. **pearl barley** n. barley stripped of the husk and ground to a small white grain. **pearl bulb** n. a translucent light bulb. **pearl button** n. a button made of mother-of-pearl. **pearl-diver** n. a person who dives for pearl-oysters. **pearled** a. 1 decorated with pearls. 2 in pearl-like drops. 3 of the colour of pearls. **pearler** n. **pearlescent** a. resembling mother-of-pearl. **pearl-fisher** n. a person who fishes for pearls. **pearl-fishing** n. **pearlized, pearlised** a. having a finish resembling mother-of-pearl. **pearl millet** n. a tall grass, *Pennisetum typhoides*, grown esp. as fodder in Africa, India and the southern US. **pearl onion** n. a very small onion used for pickling. **pearl-oyster** n. **pearl-ware** n. a kind of fine, white, glazed earthenware. **pearlwort** n. any herbaceous plant of the genus *Sagina*, found in rocky and sandy areas. **pearly** a. (comp. **pearlier**, superl. **pearliest**). **pearlies** (-liz) n.pl. 1 pearly kings and queens. 2 a pearly king's or queen's ceremonial costume, covered with pearl buttons. 3 (sl.) teeth. **pearliness** n. **Pearly Gates** n.pl. (coll., facet.) the entrance to Heaven. **pearly king** n. a male London costermonger wearing pearlies. **pearly nautilus** n. (pl. **pearly nautiluses, pearly nautili** (-lī)) a cephalopod of the genus *Nautilus*, with a many-chambered shell with nacreous divisions. **pearly queen** n. a female London costermonger wearing pearlies.

pearl[2] (pœl) n. a picot.

pearlite PERLITE.

pearmain (peə´mān) n. a kind of apple with firm, white flesh.

peasant (pez´ənt) n. 1 a rustic labourer. 2 (coll.) a countryman. 3 (derog.) a rough, uncouth person. **peasantry** n. (pl. **peasantries**). **peasanty** a.

pease (pēz) n.pl. peas. **pease pudding** n. a pudding made of peas.

peat (pēt) n. 1 decayed and partly carbonized vegetable matter found in boggy places and used as fuel. 2 a piece of peat. **peatbog** n. a bog containing peat. **peatland** n. land which consists of peat. **peatmoss** n. 1 a peatbog. 2 sphagnum. **peaty** a. (comp. **peatier**, superl. **peatiest**).

peau-de-soie (pōdəswah´) n. a rich, finely ribbed fabric of silk or rayon.

pebble (peb´əl) n. 1 a small stone rounded by the action of water. 2 a transparent rock crystal, used for spectacles etc. 3 a lens made of this. 4 an agate. **not the only pebble on the beach** able to be replaced easily. **pebbled** a. **pebble-dash** n. a coating for external walls consisting of small stones imbedded in mortar. **pebble-dashed** a. **pebbly** a. (comp. **pebblier**, superl. **pebbliest**).

p.e.c. abbr. photoelectric cell.

pecan (pē´kən, pikan´) n. a N American hickory, *Carya illinoensis*, or its fruit or nut.

peccadillo (pekədil´ō) n. (pl. **peccadilloes, peccadillos**) a minor sin or offence.

peccary (pek´əri) n. (pl. **peccaries**) any American piglike mammal of the family Tayassuidae.

peck[1] (pek) v.t. 1 to strike with a beak or pointed instrument. 2 to kiss lightly. 3 to pick up with or as if with a beak. 4 to break, open, eat etc. thus. 5 (coll.) to eat, esp. in small amounts. 6 to mark with short strokes. 7 to break (up or down) with a pointed implement. 8 to type. ~v.i. to strike or aim with a beak or pointed implement. ~n. 1 a sharp stroke with or as with a beak. 2 a mark made by this. 3 a light kiss. **to peck at 1** to nibble at. 2 to nag. 3 to bite at (something) with a beak. **pecker** n. 1 a bird which pecks. 2 (coll.) a woodpecker. 3 (N Am., taboo sl.) the penis. **to keep one's pecker up** (coll.) to stay cheerful. **pecking order** n. the hierarchical order of importance in any social group. **peckish** a. (coll.) 1 hungry. 2 (N Am.) irritable, bad-tempered. **peck order** n. pecking order.

peck[2] (pek) n. 1 a measure of capacity for dry goods, 2 gallons (about 9 l); the fourth part of a bushel. 2 a vessel used for measuring this.

pecorino (pekərē´nō) n. (pl. **pecorinos**) an Italian ewe's-milk cheese.

pecten (pek´ten) n. (pl. **pectens, pectines** (-tinēz)) (Zool.) 1 a comblike process forming a membrane in the eyes of birds and some reptiles. 2 an appendage behind the posterior legs in scorpions, and various other parts or organs. 3 any mollusc of the genus *Pecten*, containing the scallops.

pectin (pek´tin) n. a white, amorphous compound found in fruits and certain fleshy roots, formed from pectose by the process of ripening.

pectic *a.* **pectose** (-tōs) *n.* an insoluble compound allied to cellulose, found in unripe fruits and other vegetable tissue.

pectoral (pek´tərəl) *a.* (*Anat.*) of, relating to or for the breast or chest. ~*n.* 1 a pectoral muscle. 2 a pectoral fin. 3 an ornament worn on the breast, esp. the breastplate of a Jewish high priest. **pectoral muscle** *n.* (*Anat.*) either of the two muscles at the top of the chest on each side, controlling certain arm and shoulder movements.

peculate (pek´ūlāt) *v.t.*, *v.i.* to appropriate (money or goods entrusted to one's care) to one's own use. **peculation** (-lā´shən) *n.* **peculator** *n.*

peculiar (pikū´lyə) *a.* 1 singular, strange, odd. 2 belonging particularly and exclusively (to). 3 of or relating to the individual. 4 particular, special. 5 one's own, private, not general. **peculiarity** (-iar´iti) *n.* (*pl.* **peculiarities**) 1 the quality of being peculiar. 2 an idiosyncrasy. 3 a characteristic. **peculiarly** *adv.*

pecuniary (pikū´niəri) *a.* 1 of, relating to or consisting of money. 2 (of an offence) entailing a financial penalty. **pecuniarily** *adv.*

-ped -PEDE.

pedagogue (ped´əgog) *n.* a teacher of young children, a schoolmaster (usu. in contempt, implying conceit or pedantry). **pedagogic** (-gog´-, -goj´-), **pedagogical** *a.* **pedagogically** *adv.* **pedagogics** (-goj´-, -gō´jiks) *n.* the science of teaching. **pedagogy** (-gogi, -goji) *n.* pedagogics.

pedal[1] (ped´əl) *n.* 1 a lever acted on by the foot, e.g. on a bicycle or motor vehicle. 2 in an organ, a wooden key moved by the feet, or a foot-lever for working several stops at once, for opening and shutting the swell-box etc. 3 a foot-lever for lifting the damper of a piano, for muffling the notes, and other purposes. 4 (*Mus.*) a sustained note, usu. in the bass. ~*v.t.* (*pres.p.* **pedalling**, (*N Am.*) **pedaling**, *past, p.p.* **pedalled**, (*N Am.*) **pedaled**) to work (a bicycle, sewing machine etc.) by pedals. ~*v.i.* to play an organ or work a bicycle etc. by pedals. **pedal bin** *n.* a bin with a lid which can be opened by means of a pedal. **pedal cycle** *n.* a bicycle. **pedaller,** (*N Am.*) **pedaler** *n.* **pedalo** (-ō) *n.* (*pl.* **pedalos, pedaloes**) a small boat propelled by paddles operated with pedals. **pedal-pusher** *n.* (*coll.*) 1 a cyclist. 2 (*pl.*) women's calf-length trousers.

pedal[2] (ped´əl, pē´dəl) *a.* (*Zool.*) of or relating to a foot or footlike part (esp. of a mollusc).

pedant (ped´ənt) *n.* 1 a person who makes a pretentious show of book-learning, or lays undue stress on rules and formulas. 2 a person with more book-learning than practical experience or common sense. 3 a person obsessed by a theory. **pedantic** (pidan´-), **pedantical** *a.* **pedantically** *adv.* **pedantry** *n.* (*pl.* **pedantries**).

pedate (ped´āt) *a.* 1 (*Zool.*) having feet. 2 (*Bot.*) palmately divided with the two lateral lobes divided into smaller segments like digits or toes.

peddle (ped´əl) *v.t.* 1 to sell in small quantities, to retail as a pedlar. 2 to promote (an idea etc.).

3 to sell (illegal drugs). ~*v.i.* to travel about the country selling small wares. **peddler** *n.* 1 a person who sells illegal drugs. 2 (*N Am.*) PEDLAR.

Usage note British English generally distinguishes *peddler*, a seller of drugs, from *pedlar*, a hawker of small wares; in the US *peddler* is general.

-pede (pēd), **-ped** (ped) *comb. form* a foot, as in *centipede, quadruped.*

pederast (ped´ərast), **paederast** *n.* a man who practises sodomy with a boy. **pederasty** *n.*

pedestal (ped´istəl) *n.* 1 an insulated base for a column, statue etc. 2 either of the supports of a kneehole desk. 3 a base, foundation or support. 4 the china pan of a lavatory, or its base. **pedestal table** *n.* a table which sits on a single central support.

pedestrian (pədes´triən) *n.* 1 a person who is walking. 2 a person who takes part in walking races. ~*a.* 1 of or relating to walking. 2 going or performed on foot. 3 prosaic, dull, commonplace. **pedestrian crossing** *n.* a marked strip across a road where vehicles must stop to allow pedestrians to cross. **pedestrianism** *n.* **pedestrianize, pedestrianise** *v.t.*, *v.i.* to convert (a road etc.) so that it may be used only by pedestrians. **pedestrianization** (-zā´shən) *n.* **pedestrian precinct** *n.* an area of a city or town which can be used only by pedestrians.

pediatrics PAEDIATRICS.

pedicel (ped´isel) *n.* 1 (*Bot.*) the stalk supporting a single flower etc., as distinct from *peduncle.* 2 (*Zool., Anat.*) any small, stalklike structure.

pedicle (-ikəl) *n.* 1 (*Med.*) part of a graft still temporarily attached to its original place. 2 (*Anat., Zool.*) a small, stalklike structure, a pedicel or peduncle.

pedicure (ped´ikūə) *n.* 1 the surgical treatment of the feet. 2 cosmetic care of the feet. 3 a chiropodist. ~*v.t.* to treat (the feet).

pedigree (ped´igrē) *n.* 1 genealogy, lineage, esp. of a domestic or pet animal. 2 a genealogical table or tree. 3 derivation of a word, etymology. ~*a.* (of a horse, dog etc.) pure-bred, having a known ancestry. **pedigreed** *a.*

pediment (ped´imənt) *n.* 1 (*Archit.*) **a** the triangular part surmounting a portico, in buildings in the Grecian style. **b** a similar member crowning doorways, windows etc. in buildings in classical Renaissance styles. 2 (*Geol.*) a gently sloping rock surface at the foot of a mountain. **pedimental** (-men´-) *a.* **pedimented** *a.*

pedlar (ped´lə) *n.* 1 (*Hist.*) a travelling hawker of small wares, usu. carried in a pack. 2 a person who retails gossip etc. **pedlary** *n.*

Usage note See note under PEDDLE.

pedo- PAEDO-.

pedology (pədol´əji) *n.* the science of soils. **pedological** (pedəloj´-) *a.* **pedologist** *n.*

pedometer (pidom′itə) *n.* an instrument for measuring the distance covered on foot by registering the number of steps taken.

pedophilia PAEDOPHILIA.

peduncle (pidŭng′kəl) *n.* **1** (*Bot.*) a flower stalk, esp. of a solitary flower or one bearing the subsidiary stalks of a cluster, as distinct from *pedicel.* **2** (*Zool.*) a stalklike process for the attachment of an organ or an organism. **peduncular** (-kū-), **pedunculate** (-kūlət), **pedunculated** (-lātid) *a.* **pedunculate oak** *n.* an oak, *Quercus robur,* having clusters of acorns growing on long stalks.

pedway (ped′wā) *n.* (*esp. N Am.*) a pedestrian footpath in a city.

pee (pē) *v.i.* (*3rd pers. sing. pres.* **pees,** *pres.p.* **peeing,** *past, p.p.* **peed**) (*coll.*) to urinate. *~v.t.* to pass as or with urine. *~n.* **1** an act of urinating. **2** urine.

peek (pēk) *v.i.* to peer, to peep, to pry. *~n.* a peep. **peekaboo** (pē′kəboo) *a.* **1** (of a garment) revealing or almost revealing parts of the body. **2** (of a hairstyle) covering one eye. *~n.* a game used for amusing young children, in which the face is hidden and then suddenly revealed.

peel (pēl) *v.t.* **1** to strip the skin, bark or rind off. **2** to strip (rind etc.) off a fruit etc. **3** in croquet, to send (another player's ball) through a hoop. *~v.i.* **1** to lose the skin or rind, to become bare. **2** (of paint etc.) to flake off. **3** (*coll.*) to undress. *~n.* skin, rind. **to peel off 1** to leave and move away from (e.g. a column of marchers). **2** (*coll.*) to undress. **peeler** *n.* **peeling** *n.* the skin of a fruit etc. that has been peeled off.

peen (pēn) *n.* the point of a mason's hammer, opposite to the face. *~v.t.* to hammer.

peep¹ (pēp) *v.i.* **1** to look through a crevice or narrow opening. **2** to look slyly or furtively. **3** to show oneself or appear partially or cautiously, to come (out) gradually into view. **4** (of a quality or characteristic) to show itself unconsciously. *~n.* **1** a furtive look, a hasty glance, a glimpse. **2** the first appearance. **peep-bo** *n.* peekaboo. **peeper** *n.* **1** a person who peeps. **2** (*coll.*) an eye. **3** (*N Am., sl.*) a private detective. **peephole** *n.* a small hole for looking through. **peeping Tom** *n.* a person who is guilty of prurient curiosity, a voyeur. **peep-show** *n.* **1** an exhibition of pictures etc., shown through a small aperture containing a lens. **2** a sex show seen by customers in separate compartments fitted with a small window. **peepsight** *n.* a movable disc on the breech of a firearm pierced with a small hole through which aim can be taken with accuracy. **peep-toe** *a.* (of a shoe) cut away at the toe.

peep² (pēp) *v.i.* (of a young bird, a mouse etc.) to cry, chirp or squeak. *~n.* **1** a chirp, squeak etc. **2** (*coll.*) any spoken sound (*not a peep*).

peepul (pee′pəl), **pipal** *n.* the bo tree.

peer¹ (piə) *v.i.* **1** to look very closely (at, into etc.). **2** to peep out.

peer² (piə) *n.* **1** in the UK, a member of one of the degrees of nobility, comprising dukes, marquesses, earls, viscounts and barons. **2** a noble, esp. a member of a hereditary legislative body. **3** a person of the same rank. **4** an equal in any respect. *~v.t.* **1** to equal, to rank with. **2** (*coll.*) to make a peer. *~v.i.* to be equal. **peerage** (-rij) *n.* **1** the body of peers, the nobility, the aristocracy. **2** the rank of a peer or peeress. **3** a book containing particulars of the nobility. **peeress** (-ris) *n.* a woman holding the rank of a peer. **peer group** *n.* a group of people equal in status, age etc. **peerless** *a.* without an equal. **peer of the realm, peer of the United Kingdom** *n.* any of the British peers all of whom are entitled to sit in the House of Lords. **peer pressure** *n.* pressure to conform with the attitudes and behaviour of one's peers.

peevish (pē′vish) *a.* fretful, irritable, petulant, expressing discontent. **peeve** *v.t.* (*coll.*) to annoy, to irritate. *~n.* (*coll.*) **1** a person who or something which annoys. **2** vexation. **peeved** *a.* (*sl.*) irritated, annoyed. **peevishly** *adv.* **peevishness** *n.*

peewit (pē′wit), **pewit** *n.* **1** a lapwing. **2** its cry.

peg (peg) *n.* **1** a pin or bolt, usu. of wood, for holding parts of a structure or fastening articles together, hanging things on, supporting, holding, marking etc. **2** a clothes-peg. **3** a step, a degree. **4** an occasion, pretext, excuse or topic for discourse etc. **5** (*coll.*) a small drink of spirits or wine. *~v.t.* (*pres.p.* **pegging,** *past, p.p.* **pegged**) **1** to fix or fasten (down, in, out etc.) with a peg or pegs. **2** to fix (esp. prices) at an agreed level. **3** to mark (a score) with pegs on a cribbage board. **off the peg** ready-made. **square peg in a round hole** a person in an unsuitable job or function. **to peg away at** to work at or struggle with persistently. **to peg down** to restrict (to rules etc.). **2** to fasten down with pegs. **to peg out 1** (*sl.*) to die. **2** in cribbage, to win by attaining the final hole in the cribbage board. **3** in croquet, to go out by hitting the final peg. **4** to mark out the boundaries of. **to take (someone) down a peg (or two)** to humiliate, to deflate the ego of. **pegboard** *n.* a board with holes into which pegs can be fixed, used for scoring in games, or placed on a wall and used for hanging things. **pegged** *a.* **peg-leg** *n.* (*coll.*) **1** an artificial leg. **2** a person who has an artificial leg. **pegtop** *n.* a spinning top with a metal peg, usu. spun by means of a string which unwinds rapidly when the top is thrown from the hand. *~a.* (of a garment) wide at the top and narrowing towards the bottom.

pegmatite (peg′mətīt) *n.* a coarse-grained variety of granite, with a little mica.

✗ **peice** common misspelling of PIECE.

peignoir (pān′wah) *n.* a loose robe or dressing gown worn by a woman.

✗ **peirce** common misspelling of PIERCE.

pejorative (pijor′ətiv) *a.* depreciatory, disparaging. *~n.* a word or form expressing depreciation. **pejoratively** *adv.*

pekan (pek′ən) *n.* a N American marten, *Martes pennanti,* of the weasel family, prized for its fur.

Pekinese (pēkinēz´), **Pekingese** a. of or relating to Beijing (formerly Peking). ~n. (pl. **Pekinese, Pekingese**) **1** a rough-coated variety of Chinese pug. **2** a citizen of Beijing, China. **3** the dialect of Chinese spoken in Beijing. **peke** n. (coll.) a Pekinese dog.

pelage (pel´ij) n. the coat or hair of an animal, esp. of fur.

pelagian (pilā´jiən) a. inhabiting the deep sea. ~n. a pelagian animal.

pelagic (pilaj´ik) a. of or inhabiting the deep sea.

pelargonium (pelāgō´niəm) n. (pl. **pelargoniums**) an ornamental plant of the genus Pelargonium, popularly called the geranium.

pelf (pelf) n. (derog. or facet.) money, wealth.

pelham (pel´əm) n. a horse's bit having a curb and a snaffle.

pelican (pel´ikən) n. a large waterbird of the family Pelecanidae, with an enormous pouch beneath the mandibles for storing fish when caught. **pelican crossing** n. a type of pedestrian crossing controlled by pedestrian-operated traffic lights.

pelisse (pilēs´) n. (Hist.) **1** a woman's long cloak or mantle. **2** a fur-lined cloak worn by a hussar.

pelite (pē´līt) n. (Geol.) a rock made up of a claylike sediment.

pellagra (pelag´rə, -lā´-) n. a virulent disease attacking the skin and causing nervous disorders and mania, caused by deficiency of B vitamins. **pellagrous** a.

pellet (pel´it) n. **1** a little ball, esp. of bread, paper or something easily moulded. **2** a small pill. **3** a small shot. ~v.t. (pres.p. **pelleting**, past, p.p. **pelleted**) **1** to form into pellets. **2** to hit with pellets. **pelletize, pelletise** v.t.

pellicle (pel´ikəl) n. a thin skin, a membrane or film. **pellicular** (-lik´ū-) a.

pellitory (pel´itəri) n. **1** (also **pellitory of Spain**) a herb of the aster family, Anacyclus pyrethrum. **2** (also **pellitory of the wall**) a low, bushy plant, Parietaria judaica.

pell-mell (pelmel´) adv. **1** in disorderly haste. **2** in a confused or disorderly manner. ~a. confused, disorderly. ~n. **1** disorder, confusion. **2** a medley.

pellucid (piloo´sid) a. **1** clear, limpid, transparent. **2** clear in thought, expression or style. **pellucidity** (-sid´-) n. **pellucidly** adv.

pelmet (pel´mit) n. a canopy, built-in or detachable, which conceals the fittings from which curtains hang; a valance.

pelorus (pilaw´rəs) n. a sighting device on a ship's compass.

pelota (pilot´ə, -lō´-) n. (pl. **pelotas**) **1** a game similar to squash played with a ball and a curved racket fitting upon the hand, popular in Spain and the Basque country. **2** the ball used in pelota.

pelt[1] (pelt) v.t. **1** to strike or assail by throwing missiles. **2** to strike repeatedly. **3** to assail with insults or abuse. ~v.i. **1** (of rain etc.) to beat down heavily. **2** to hurry (along). **3** to keep on throwing, firing etc. (at). ~n. a blow from something thrown. **at full pelt** at full speed.

pelt[2] (pelt) n. **1** a hide or skin with the hair on, esp. of a sheep or goat. **2** an undressed fur skin. **3** a raw skin stripped of hair or wool. **4** (facet.) the human skin.

pelvis (pel´vis) n. (pl. **pelvises, pelves** (-vēz)) (Anat.) **1** the lower portion of the great abdominal cavity. **2** the bony walls of this cavity. **3** the interior cavity of the kidney. **pelvic** a. **pelvic girdle, pelvic arch** n. (Anat.) the arrangement of bones which supports the hind limbs of vertebrates and the lower limbs in humans.

pemmican (pem´ikən) n. **1** dried meat, pounded, mixed with a large proportion of melted fat and pressed into cakes. **2** a similar preparation of beef with currants.

pen[1] (pen) n. **1** an instrument for writing with ink. **2** writing. **3** a style of writing. **4** a writer, a penman. **5** (Zool.) the long internal shell of a squid. **6** a female swan. ~v.t. (pres.p. **penning**, past, p.p. **penned**) to write, to compose and write. **to put pen to paper** to write something in a purposeful way. **pen and ink** n.pl. **1** instruments for writing. **2** writing. **pen-and-ink** a. written or drawn with pen and ink. **pen-feather** n. a quill-feather. **penfriend** n. a person, usu. one living abroad and whom one has not met, with whom one corresponds. **pen holder** n. a rod of wood or other material forming a handle for a pen. **penknife** n. (pl. **penknives**) a small knife, usu. carried in the pocket. **penlight** n. a small torch in the shape of a fountain pen. **penman** n. (pl. **penmen**). **penmanship** n. **1** the art of writing. **2** style of writing. **pen-name** n. a literary pseudonym. **pen pal** n. (coll.) a penfriend. **pen-pusher** n. (coll., derog.) a person doing dull, routine, clerical work. **pen-pushing** n.

pen[2] (pen) n. **1** a small enclosure for cattle, sheep, poultry etc. **2** a place of confinement. **3** (N Am., sl.) a penitentiary, a prison. **4** an enclosure for submarines. ~v.t. (pres.p. **penning**, past, p.p. **penned**) to enclose, to confine, to shut or coop (up or in).

penal (pē´nəl) a. **1** enacting, inflicting, of or relating to punishment. **2** punishable, esp. by law. **3** of the nature of punishment, very harsh. **penalize, penalise** v.t. **1** to subject to a penalty or handicap. **2** to put under an unfair disadvantage. **3** to make or declare penal. **penalization** (-zā´shən) n. **penally** adv. **penal servitude** n. (Hist.) imprisonment with hard labour.

penalty (pen´əlti) n. (pl. **penalties**) **1** legal punishment for a crime, offence or misdemeanour. **2** a sum of money to be forfeited for non-performance or breach of conditions. **3** a fine, a forfeit. **4** a handicap imposed for a breach of rules or on the winner in a previous contest. **5** a penalty kick, hit etc. in a game. ~a. given against a side as a penalty. **on penalty of** under penalty of. **the penalty of** something unpleasant resulting from (an action or circumstance).

under penalty of under the threat of. **penalty area** *n.* in football, a rectangular area in front of the goal, where a foul against the attacking team results in a penalty and in which the goalkeeper is allowed to handle the ball. **penalty box** *n.* **1** the penalty area. **2** an area to which penalized players are confined in ice hockey. **penalty goal** *n.* in football, hockey etc., a goal scored from a penalty. **penalty kick** *n.* in football, a kick allowed to the attacking side when a foul has been committed in the penalty area. **penalty shoot-out** *n.* in football, a shoot-out, involving penalty shots. **penalty shot** *n.* in football, a shot on goal from the penalty spot, to break a tie etc. **penalty spot** *n.* in football, the point from which a penalty kick is taken.

penance (pen´əns) *n.* **1** sorrow for sin evinced by acts of self-mortification etc. **2** in the Roman Catholic and Greek Orthodox Churches, a sacrament consisting of contrition, confession and satisfaction, with absolution by the priest. **3** an act of self-mortification undertaken as a satisfaction for sin, esp. one imposed by a priest before giving absolution. ~*v.t.* to inflict penance on. **to do penance** to do something unpleasant as a penance.

pence PENNY.

penchant (pā´shā) *n.* a strong inclination or liking, a bias.

pencil (pen´səl) *n.* **1** a cylinder or slip of graphite, crayon etc., usu. enclosed in a casing of wood, used for writing, drawing etc. **2** any of various appliances in the form of a pencil, such as an eyebrow pencil. **3** anything long and slim. **4** in optics, a system of rays diverging from or converging to a point. **5** (*Geom.*) the figure formed by a series of straight lines meeting at a point. ~*a.* **1** of or relating to pencils. **2** long and slim (*a pencil skirt*). ~*v.t.* (*pres.p.* **pencilling**, (*N Am.*) **penciling**, *past, p.p.* **pencilled**, (*N Am.*) **penciled**) **1** to paint, draw, write or mark with a pencil. **2** to mark or shade in delicate lines. **to pencil in** to agree or arrange something provisionally. **pencil case** *n.* a case for holding pencils etc. **pencilled**, (*N Am.*) **penciled** *a.* **penciller**, (*N Am.*) **penciler** *n.* **pencilling**, (*N Am.*) **penciling** *n.* **pencil sharpener** *n.* a device for sharpening pencils by rotating them against a blade.

pendant (pen´dənt) *n.* **1** anything hanging down or suspended by way of ornament etc., such as an earring, a locket. **2** a pendant chandelier. **3** (*Naut.*) **a** a short rope hanging from a masthead etc. **b** a tapering flag or pennant. **4** a companion, a counterpart, a match. ~*a.* PENDENT.

pendent (pen´dənt) *a.* **1** hanging. **2** overhanging. **3** pending, undetermined. **pendency** *n.* **pendentive** (-den´-) *n.* (*Archit.*) any of the triangular pieces of vaulting resting on piers or arches and forming segments of a dome. **pendently** *adv.*

pending *a.* **1** depending, awaiting settlement, undecided. **2** about to happen. ~*prep.* **1** during. **2**

until. **pending tray** *n.* a tray for correspondence etc. waiting to be dealt with.

pendulous (pen´dūləs) *a.* **1** hanging, suspended. **2** swinging, oscillating. **penduline** (-līn) *a.* **1** (of a nest) hanging. **2** (of a bird) building a hanging nest. **pendulously** *adv.* **pendulousness** *n.*

pendulum (pen´dūləm) *n.* (*pl.* **pendulums**) a body suspended from a fixed point and oscillating freely by the force of gravity, esp. the weighted rod regulating the movement of the works in a clock.

peneplain (pē´niplān) *n.* (*Geol.*) an area of flat land produced by erosion.

penetrate (pen´itrāt) *v.t.* **1** to enter, to pass into or through. **2** to permeate, to saturate or imbue (with). **3** to reach or discern by the senses or intellect. **4** to move or affect the feelings of. **5** to pierce. **6** to put one's penis into the vagina of. ~*v.i.* **1** to be understood. **2** to make way, to pass (into, through, to etc.). **penetrable** (-trəbəl) *a.* **penetrability** (-bil´-) *n.* **penetrance** *n.* **penetrant** *a., n.* **penetrating** *a.* **1** subtle, discerning. **2** sharp, piercing. **penetratingly** *adv.* **penetration** (-ā´-shən) *n.* **penetrative** (-trətiv) *a.* **penetrator** *n.*

penguin (peng´gwin) *n.* a black-and-white bird of the family Spheniscidae, belonging to the southern hemisphere, consisting of seabirds with rudimentary wings or paddles and scalelike feathers.

penicillin (penisil´in) *n.* an ether-soluble substance produced from the mould *Penicillium* and having an intense growth-inhibiting action against various bacteria.

penile PENIS.

peninsula (pənin´sūlə) *n.* a piece of land almost surrounded by water, poss. connected to the mainland by an isthmus. **peninsular** *a., n.*

Usage note The spellings of the noun *peninsula* and the adjective *peninsular* should not be confused.

penis (pē´nis) *n.* (*pl.* **penises, penes** (-nēz)) **1** the copulatory and urethral organ of a male mammal. **2** the copulatory organ of the males of lower vertebrates. **penial, penile** (-nīl) *a.*

penitent (pen´itənt) *a.* contrite, repentant, sorry. ~*n.* **1** a person who is penitent, a contrite sinner. **2** a person submitting to penance under the direction of a confessor. **3** a member of any of various Roman Catholic orders devoted to the practice of penance and mutual discipline. **penitence** *n.* **penitential** (-ten´-) *a.* **1** of, relating to or expressing penitence. **2** relating to or of the nature of penance. **penitentially** *adv.* **penitentiary** (-ten´-) *n.* (*pl.* **penitentiaries**) **1** (*N Am.*) a prison. **2** in the Roman Catholic Church, a papal court granting dispensations and dealing with matters relating to confessions. ~*a.* **1** penitential. **2** of or relating to the reformatory treatment of criminals etc. **3** (*N Am.*) (of an offence) entailing a prison sentence. **penitently** *adv.*

pennant (pen´ənt) *n.* **1** (*Naut.*) **a** a long narrow

streamer borne at the masthead of a ship of war.
b a pendant. **2** a pennon. **3** (*N Am.*) a flag
indicating championship, e.g. in baseball.

penne (pen´i) *n.* pasta quills, pasta in short,
thick, ridged tube shapes.

penniless (pen´ilis) *a.* without money, destitute.
pennilessly *adv.* **pennilessness** *n.*

pennon (pen´ən) *n.* **1** a small pointed or
swallow-tailed flag, formerly carried on the
spears of knights and later as the ensign of a
regiment of lancers. **2** (*Naut.*) a long streamer
carried by a ship. **pennoned** *a.*

penn´orth PENNYWORTH (under PENNY).

penny (pen´i) *n.* (*pl.* **pennies** (-niz), **pence** (pens))
1 a bronze coin, a 100th part of a pound sterling.
2 (*Hist.*) a bronze coin, formerly a 12th part of a
shilling. **3** (*N Am.*) a one-cent piece. **4** (*Bible*) a
denarius. **a penny for your thoughts** what are
you thinking about? **a pretty penny** considerable
cost or expense. **in for a penny, in for a pound**
total commitment is advisable. **like a bad penny**
repeatedly returning, esp. when not wanted. **the
penny drops** (*coll.*) the truth is realized, something is made clear. **two a penny** having little
value because very common. **pennies from
heaven** *n.pl.* an unexpected bonus or advantage.
penny black *n.* (*Hist.*) the first ever adhesive
postage stamp, which cost one (old) penny.
penny cress *n.* a plant, *Thlaspi arvense*, which
has round, flat pods. **penny dreadful** *n.* a cheap
crime story. **penny-farthing** *n.* (*Hist.*) an early
type of bicycle with a large front wheel and
small back wheel. **penny-in-the-slot** *a.* denoting
an automatic machine for giving out small
articles, tickets etc. in return for a coin inserted
in a slot. **penny-pinch** *v.i.* to save money by being
miserly. **penny-pincher** *n.* **penny-pinching** *n.*
miserliness, niggardliness. ~*a.* miserly, niggardly. **pennyweight** *n.* 24 grains, or one-
twentieth of an ounce troy (1.5 g). **penny whistle**
n. a tin pipe with six holes, played as a whistle.
penny wise *a.* saving small sums. **pennywort** *n.*
any one of several plants with round peltate
leaves. **pennyworth** (pen´iwœth), **penn´orth**
(pen´əth) *n.* **1** as much as can be bought for a
penny. **2** a good (or bad) bargain. **3** a small
amount (*not a pennyworth*).

Usage note Use of *pence* as a singular (after *one*
etc.) is best avoided.

---

pennyroyal (peniroi´əl) *n.* **1** a kind of mint,
Mentha pulegium, formerly and still popularly
used for medicinal purposes. **2** (*N Am.*) a similar
plant, *Hedeoma pulegioides*.

penology (pēnol´əji), **poenology** *n.* the science of
punishment and prison management. **peno-
logical** (-loj´-) *a.* **penologist** *n.*

pensile (pen´sīl) *a.* **1** hanging, suspended,
pendulous. **2** (of a bird) constructing a pendent
nest.

pension¹ (pen´shən) *n.* **1** a periodical allowance
for past services paid by the government or an

employer. **2** a similar allowance to a person for
goodwill, to secure services when required etc.,
or to literary people, scientists etc., to enable
them to carry on their work. ~*v.t.* to grant a
pension to. **to pension off 1** to cease to employ
and to give a pension to. **2** to discard as useless,
worn etc. **pensionable** *a.* **pensionability** (-bil´-) *n.*
pensionary *a.* of or relating to a pension. ~*n.* (*pl.*
pensionaries) **1** a pensioner. **2** a hireling.
pensioner *n.* a person in receipt of a pension.
pensionless *a.*

pension² (pāsyō´) *n.* a boarding house.

pensive (pen´siv) *a.* **1** thoughtful. **2** serious,
anxious, melancholy. **pensively** *adv.* **pensive-
ness** *n.*

penstemon (penstē´mən), **pentstemon** *n.* any
herbaceous plant of the genus *Penstemon* with
showy tubular flowers.

pent (pent) *a.* penned in or confined, shut (up or
in). **pent-up** *a.* **1** not openly expressed. **2** suppressed.

penta- (pen´tə) *comb. form* five.

pentachord (pen´təkawd) *n.* (*Mus.*) **1** a musical
instrument with five strings. **2** a scale of five
notes.

pentacle (pen´təkəl) *n.* a figure like a star with
five points formed by producing the sides of a
pentagon in both directions to their points of
intersection.

pentad (pen´tad) *n.* **1** the number five. **2** a group
of five.

pentagon (pen´təgən) *n.* a plane (usu. rectilineal) figure having five sides and five angles.
pentagonal (-tag´-) *a.*

pentagram (pen´təgram) *n.* a pentacle.

pentahedron (pentəhē´drən) *n.* (*pl.* **pentahedra**
(-drə), **pentahedrons**) a figure having five sides,
esp. equal sides. **pentahedral** *a.*

pentameter (pentam´itə) *n.* a verse of five feet,
such as the iambic verse of ten syllables.

pentane (pen´tān) *n.* (*Chem.*) a volatile, fluid,
paraffin hydrocarbon contained in petroleum
etc.

pentangle (pen´tang-gəl) *n.* a pentagram.

pentaprism (pen´təprizm) *n.* a five-sided prism
used in reflex cameras to invert the image by
deflecting light from any direction through 90°.

Pentateuch (pen´tətūk) *n.* the first five books of
the Old Testament, usu. ascribed to Moses.
Pentateuchal (-tū´-) *a.*

pentathlon (pentath´lon) *n.* (*pl.* **pentathlons**) a
modern athletics contest comprising five events
for each competitor. **pentathlete** (-lēt) *n.*

pentatonic (pentəton´ik) *a.* (*Mus.*) **1** consisting
of five tones. **2** of or relating to a pentatonic
scale.

pentavalent (pentəvā´lənt) *a.* (*Chem.*) having a
valency of five.

Pentecost (pen´tikost) *n.* **1** Whit Sunday. **2** a
festival to celebrate the descent of the Holy
Spirit. **3** a solemn Jewish festival at the close of
harvest, held on the 50th day from the second

day of the Passover. **Pentecostal** (-kos´-) a. **1** of or relating to Pentecost. **2** of or relating to any of various fundamentalist Christian groups who stress the powers of the Holy Spirit, e.g. in healing. ~n. a follower of Pentecostalism. **Pentecostalism** n. **Pentecostalist** a., n.

penthouse (pent´hows) n. **1** a flat built on the rooftop of a tall building. **2** a roof or shed standing aslope against a main wall or building. **3** a shedlike structure against a wall, a canopy, a protection over a window or door etc.

Pentothal® (pen´təthal) n. thiopentone.

pent roof (pent) n. a lean-to roof.

pentstemon PENSTEMON.

penult (pinŭlt´) n. the last but one, esp. the last syllable but one of a word. ~a. last but one. **penultimate** (-mət) a. last but one. ~n. the last but one, esp. the last syllable but one of a word.

penumbra (pinŭm´brə) n. (pl. **penumbrae** (-brē), **penumbras**) **1** the partly shaded zone around the total shadow caused by an opaque body intercepting the light from a luminous body, esp. round that of the earth or moon in an eclipse. **2** (Astron.) the lighter fringe of a sunspot. **3** a partial shadow. **4** something obscure or uncertain. **penumbral** a.

penury (pen´ūri) n. (pl. **penuries**) **1** extreme poverty, destitution. **2** a lack or scarcity (of). **penurious** (pinū´-) a. **1** poor, penniless. **2** niggardly, stingy. **penuriousness** n.

peon (pē´on) n. **1** a Spanish-American day labourer etc. **2** (NAm.) a menial worker. **peonage** (-nij) n.

peony (pē´əni), **paeony** n. (pl. **peonies**, **paeonies**) any plant of the genus Paeonia, with large globular terminal flowers, usu. double in cultivated varieties.

people (pē´pəl) n. **1** (usu. as pl.) the persons composing a nation, community or race. **2** (usu. as pl.) any body of persons, such as those belonging to a place, a class, a congregation or company of any sort etc. **3** (as pl.) persons generally or indefinitely. **4** (as pl.) one's family, kindred or tribe. **5** (as pl., NAm.) one's ancestors. **6** (as pl.) followers, retinue, servants, workpeople etc. ~v.t. **1** to stock with inhabitants, to populate. **2** to occupy, to inhabit. **the people 1** the commonalty, the populace, as distinct from the self-styled higher orders. **2** the electorate. **people carrier** n. a people mover. **peopled** a. inhabited. **people mover** n. a large vanlike estate car with an extra row of seats.

PEP (pep) abbr. personal equity plan.

pep (pep) n. (coll.) vigour, spirit, energy. ~v.t. (pres.p. **pepping**, past, p.p. **pepped**) (coll.) to pep up. **to pep up** (coll.) to give energy, vigour etc. to. **pep pill** n. a pill containing a stimulant. **peppy** a. (comp. **peppier**, superl. **peppiest**) (coll.) full of vitality, energetic. **pep talk** n. (coll.) a talk intended to encourage or stimulate.

peperoni PEPPERONI.

peplum (pep´ləm), **peplus** (-ləs) n. (pl. **peplums**,

pepluses) a flared extension attached to the waist of a tight-fitting jacket or bodice.

pepper (pep´ə) n. **1** a pungent aromatic condiment made from the dried berries of Piper nigrum or other species of the genus Piper, used whole or ground into powder. **2** the pepper plant, P. nigrum, or other species of the genus Piper. **3** rough treatment, pungent criticism or sarcasm etc. **4** a capsicum. **5** cayenne. ~v.t. **1** to sprinkle or season with pepper. **2** to sprinkle. **3** to attack with pungent remarks. **4** to pelt with missiles. **5** to beat severely. **pepper-and-salt** a. (of hair) dark mingled with grey. **pepperbox** n. **1** a pepper pot. **2** a gun with revolving barrels. **peppercorn** n. **1** the dried fruit of the Piper nigrum, used as a condiment. **2** anything of little value. **peppercorn rent** n. a nominal rent. **pepper mill** n. a small hand-operated device for grinding peppercorns. **pepper pot** n. **1** a small container with a perforated top for sprinkling pepper on food. **2** a W Indian dish of meat or fish with okra, chillies etc., flavoured with cayenne. **pepper shaker** n. (NAm.) a pepper pot. **pepperwort** n. any plant of the genus Lepidium, esp. garden cress. **peppery** a. **1** tasting of or like pepper. **2** hot-tempered, irascible, hasty. **3** pungent, sharp. **pepperiness** n.

peppermint (pep´əmint) n. **1** a pungent aromatic herb, Mentha piperita. **2** an essential oil distilled from this plant. **3** a sweet flavoured with peppermint oil. **4** (Austral.) any of various eucalyptuses which yield an oil similar to peppermint oil. **pepperminty** a.

pepperoni (pepərō´ni), **peperoni** n. a dry sausage of pork and beef that is heavily seasoned, esp. with pepper.

peppy PEP.

pepsin (pep´sin) n. a protein-digesting enzyme contained in gastric juice. **peptic** (-tik) a. **1** of or relating to digestion. **2** promoting digestion. **peptic gland** n. a gland which secretes gastric juice. **peptic ulcer** n. an ulcer in the stomach, duodenum etc. caused by the action of pepsin and stomach acid. **peptide** (-tīd) n. a group of two or more amino acids, in which the carbon of one amino acid is linked to the nitrogen of another.

peptone (pep´tōn) n. any of the soluble compounds into which the proteins in food are converted by the action of pepsin. **peptonize** (-tə-), **peptonise** v.t.

per (pœ) prep. **1** for each. **2** by, through, by means of. **3** according to.

per- (pœ) pref. **1** through, completely. **2** very, exceedingly, to the extreme. **3** (Chem.) denoting the highest degree of combination or of valency in similar chemical compounds.

peradventure (pœrədven´chə, pər-) adv. (formal or facet.) perhaps. ~n. uncertainty, doubt, conjecture.

perambulate (pəram´būlāt) v.t. to walk over or through, esp. for the purpose of surveying or inspecting. ~v.i. to walk about. **perambulation**

(-lā´shən) n. **perambulator** n. (formal) a pram. **perambulatory** a.

per annum (pər an´əm) adv. yearly, each year.

percale (pəkāl´) n. a closely woven cotton cambric.

per capita (pə kap´itə), **per caput** (kap´ut) adv. for each person.

perceive (pəsēv´) v.t. 1 to observe, to see. 2 to apprehend with the mind, to discern, to understand. **perceivable** a. **perceiver** n.

per cent (pə sent´), (N Am.) **percent** adv. in terms of 100 parts of a whole. ~n. 1 a percentage. 2 one part per hundred. 3 (pl.) securities yielding interest as specified. **percentage** (-tij) n. 1 a rate or proportion expressed per cent. 2 (coll.) advantage, profit. 3 in commerce, allowance, commission, duty. **percentile** n. in statistics, one of 99 values of a variable dividing its distribution into 100 groups with equal frequencies.

perception (pəsep´shən) n. 1 the act or an instance of perceiving. 2 intuitive apprehension, insight or discernment. 3 an impression based on one's perception of something. 4 (Philos.) the mental action of knowing external things through the medium of sense presentations. **percept** (pœ´sept) n. 1 something that is perceived. 2 the mental product of perception. **perceptible** a. able to be perceived by the senses or intellect. **perceptibility** (-bil´-) n. **perceptibly** adv. **perceptional** a. **perceptive** a. 1 having the faculty of perceiving. 2 discerning, astute. **perceptively** adv. **perceptiveness** n. **perceptivity** (pœseptiv´-) n. **perceptual** (-tūəl) a. **perceptually** adv.

perch[1] (pœch) n. 1 a pole or bar used as a rest or roost for birds or anything serving this purpose. 2 a high seat or position. 3 (Hist.) a land measure of 5½ yd. (5.03 m). ~v.i. 1 (of a bird) to alight or rest. 2 to alight or settle on or as if on a perch. ~v.t. to set or place on or as if on a perch. **to knock someone off their perch 1** to beat or destroy someone. **2** to lower the esteem in which someone is held. **percher** n. any of the perching birds.

perch[2] (pœch) n. (pl. in general **perch**, in particular **perches**) a striped spiny-finned freshwater fish, Perca fluviatilis, or P. flavescens, the yellow perch of the US. **percoid** (pœ´koid) n., a.

†perchance (pəchahns´) adv. (also poet.) 1 by chance. 2 perhaps.

percipient (pəsip´iənt) a. 1 perceiving, apprehending, conscious. 2 discerning, perceptive. ~n. a person who perceives, esp. one receiving a supposed telepathic message. **percipience** n. **percipiently** adv.

percoid PERCH[2].

percolate (pœ´kəlāt) v.i. 1 to pass through small interstices, to filter (through). 2 (of an idea) to spread through a group of people. ~v.t. 1 to make (coffee) in a percolator. 2 to ooze through, to permeate. 3 to strain, to filter. **percolation** (-ā´shən) n. **percolator** n. a coffee pot in which the boiling water filters through the coffee.

percussion (pəkŭsh´ən) n. 1 (Mus.) a the production of sound by striking on an instrument. b musical instruments played by striking. 2 (Med.) medical examination by gently striking some part of the body with the fingers or an instrument. 3 forcible striking or collision. **percussion cap** n. a small metal or paper cap containing fulminating powder, used in toy guns and in percussion locks. **percussionist** n. a person who plays a percussion instrument. **percussive** a. **percussively** adv.

per diem (pœ dē´em) a., adv. by the day, for each day.

perdition (pədish´ən) n. the loss of the soul or of happiness in a future state, damnation.

perdurable (pədū´rəbəl) a. (formal) very lasting or durable, permanent, everlasting. **perdurability** (-bil´-) n. **perdurably** adv.

Père David's deer (peə dā´vidz) n. a large deer, Elaphurus davidianus, with antlers.

peregrination (perigrinā´shən) n. 1 a sojourning in foreign countries. 2 (formal or facet.) a travelling about.

peregrine (per´igrin) n. a peregrine falcon. **peregrine falcon** n. a falcon, Falco peregrinus, used for hawking.

peremptory (pəremp´təri) a. 1 precluding question or hesitation. 2 imperious, dogmatic, dictatorial. 3 (Law) final, determinate. 4 absolute, positive, decisive, determined. **peremptorily** adv. **peremptoriness** n. **peremptory challenge** n. (Law) a defendant's objection to a proposed juror without giving a reason.

perennial (pəren´iəl) a. 1 lasting throughout the year. 2 (of a plant) living for more than two years. 3 unfailing, unceasing, lasting long, never ceasing. 4 (of a stream) flowing through every season. ~n. a perennial plant. **perenniality** (-al´-) n. **perennially** adv.

perestroika (perəstroi´kə) n. in the former USSR, the policy of restructuring and reforming Soviet institutions initiated in the 1980s by Mikhail Gorbachev.

perfect[1] (pœ´fikt) a. 1 complete in all its parts, qualities etc. 2 finished, thoroughly versed, trained, skilled etc. 3 precise, exact. 4 of the best, highest and most complete kind. 5 entire, complete, unqualified. 6 (Gram.) expressing action completed. 7 without defect or fault. ~n. (Gram.) the perfect tense or a perfect form of a verb. **perfect binding** n. a type of bookbinding in which the leaves are glued to the spine. **perfect interval** n. (Mus.) a fourth or fifth as in a major or minor scale starting on the lower note of the interval. **perfection** (pəfek´-) n. 1 the act of making or the state of being perfect. 2 supreme excellence. 3 a perfect person or thing. 4 the highest degree, the extreme (of). 5 an excellent quality or acquirement. **to perfection** completely, perfectly. **perfectionist** n. 1 a person who strives after perfection and tolerates no faults. **2** a person who believes in the possibility of attaining moral or religious perfection. **perfectionism** *n.* **perfective** (-fek´-) *a.* (*Gram.*) expressing completed action as distinct from *imperfective*. **perfectly** *adv.* **perfectness** *n.* **perfect pitch** *n.* (*Mus.*) absolute pitch. **perfect square** *n.* a square number.

Usage note In general the adjective *perfect* is not gradable but absolute, so the comparative *more perfect* and superlative *most perfect* are best avoided.

perfect² (pǝfekt´) *v.t.* **1** to make perfect. **2** to finish or complete, to bring to perfection. **3** to print on the other side of (a sheet). **perfecter** *n.* **perfectible** *a.* **perfectibility** (-bil´-) *n.*

perfidy (pœ´fidi) *n.* (*pl.* **perfidies**) (a) violation of faith, allegiance or confidence. **perfidious** (-fid´-) *a.* **perfidiously** *adv.* **perfidiousness** *n.*

perforate¹ (pœ´fǝrāt) *v.t.* **1** to bore through, to pierce. **2** to make a row of holes in. **3** to pass or reach through. ~*v.i.* to penetrate (into or through). **perforation** (-ā´shǝn) *n.* **perforative** (-rǝtiv) *a.* **perforator** *n.*

perforate² (pœ´fǝrǝt) *a.* perforated.

†**perforce** (pǝfaws´) *adv.* of necessity, compulsorily.

perform (pǝfawm´) *v.t.* **1** to carry through, to execute, to accomplish. **2** to discharge, fulfil. **3** to represent on the stage. **4** to play, to render (music). ~*v.i.* **1** to act a part. **2** to play a musical instrument, sing etc. **3** to do tricks. **4** to do what is to be done. **5** to function (well). **6** (of an investment) to yield a return. **7** (*sl.*) to have sexual intercourse. **performable** *a.* **performability** (-bil´-) *n.* **performance** *n.* **1** execution, carrying out, completion. **2** a thing done, an action. **3** a feat, a notable deed. **4** a piece of work. **5** the performing of a play, display of feats etc. **6** an entertainment. **7** (of a vehicle etc.) the capacity to function (well). **8** (*coll.*) an elaborate or laborious action, a fuss. **9** a return on an investment. ~*a.* (of a car) capable of travelling very fast and accelerating quickly. **performance art** *n.* a theatrical presentation including various art forms. **performance artist** *n.* **performer** *n.* **performing** *a.* **performing art** *n.* an art form requiring performance before an audience.

perfume¹ (pœ´fūm) *n.* **1** a sweet smell. **2** a substance emitting a sweet odour, fragrance, scent. **perfumed** *a.* having a sweet, pleasant smell. **perfumy** *a.*

perfume² (pœ´fūm, pǝfūm´) *v.t.* to fill or impregnate with a scent or sweet odour; to scent. **perfumer** (-fū´-) *n.* a person who makes or sells perfumes. **perfumery** (-fū´-) *n.* (*pl.* **perfumeries**) **1** a place where perfumes are sold. **2** (the preparation of) perfumes.

perfunctory (pǝfŭngk´tǝri) *a.* **1** done merely as a duty, or routinely; done in a half-hearted or careless manner. **2** careless, negligent, super-

ficial, mechanical. **perfunctorily** *adv.* **perfunctoriness** *n.*

perfuse (pǝfūz´) *v.t.* **1** to besprinkle. **2** to spread over, to suffuse (with). **3** to pour (water etc.) over or through. **4** (*Med.*) to pass a fluid through. **perfusion** (-zhǝn) *n.* **perfusive** (-siv) *a.*

pergola (pœ´gǝlǝ) *n.* (*pl.* **pergolas**) a covered walk or arbour with climbing plants trained over posts, trellis-work etc.

perhaps (pǝhaps´) *adv.* **1** it may be, possibly. **2** please (*Perhaps you could take over from me?*).

peri- (per´i) *pref.* **1** around. **2** (*Astron.*) near.

perianth (per´ianth) *n.* the outer part of a flower.

pericardium (perikah´diǝm) *n.* (*pl.* **pericardia** (-diǝ)) (*Anat.*) the membrane enveloping the heart. **pericardiac** (-ak), **pericardial** *a.* **pericarditis** (-dī´tis) *n.*

pericarp (per´ikahp) *n.* the seed vessel or wall of the developed ovary of a plant.

perichondrium (perikon´driǝm) *n.* (*pl.* **perichondria** (-driǝ)) (*Anat.*) the membrane investing the cartilages except at joints.

perigee (per´ijē) *n.* the nearest point to the earth in the orbit of the moon, one of the planets or an artificial satellite, as distinct from *apogee*. **perigeal** (-jē´-), **perigean** *a.*

perihelion (perihē´liǝn) *n.* (*pl.* **perihelia** (-liǝ)) the part of the orbit of a planet, comet etc. nearest the sun, as distinct from *aphelion*.

peril (per´ǝl) *n.* danger, risk, hazard, jeopardy, exposure to injury, loss or destruction. ~*v.t.* (*pres.p.* **perilling**, (*N Am.*) **periling**, *past, p.p.* **perilled**, (*N Am.*) **periled**) to risk, to endanger. **at one's peril** at risk of harm to oneself. **in peril of** with great danger to. **perilous** *a.* **perilously** *adv.* **perilousness** *n.*

perilune (per´iloon) *n.* the point in the orbit of a body round the moon where the body is closest to the centre of the moon, as distinct from *apolune*.

perimeter (pǝrim´itǝ) *n.* **1** (*Geom.*) **a** the bounding line of a plane figure. **b** the length of this. **2** the boundary of a camp etc. **3** an instrument for measuring the field of vision. **perimetric** (-met´-) *a.*

perinatal (perinā´tǝl) *a.* of or relating to the period shortly before and after birth.

perineum (perinē´ǝm) *n.* (*pl.* **perinea** (-nē´ǝ)) (*Anat.*) the part of the body between the genital organs and the anus. **perineal** *a.*

period (piǝ´riǝd) *n.* **1** any specified portion of time. **2** a definite or indefinite portion of time, an age, an era, a cycle. **3** a portion of time marked off by some recurring event, esp. an astronomical phenomenon. **4** the time taken up by the revolution of a planet round the sun. **5** a length of time allotted to a school lesson. **6** a complete sentence, esp. a complex one in which the predicate is not fully stated till the end. **7** (*pl.*) rhetorical language. **8** (*N Am.*) **a** a pause. **b** a full stop (.) marking this. **9** (*Chem.*) any one of the horizontal rows of elements in the periodic table. **10** an end, a limit. **11** an occurrence of menstruation. **12** the interval between the recurrences of equal values in a periodic function. ~*a.* (of a picture, object etc.) characteristic of a certain period, belonging to a historical period. **periodic** (-od´-) *a.* **1** happening or appearing at fixed intervals. **2** of or relating to a period or periods. **3** performed in a regular revolution. **4** constituting a complete sentence. **periodical** *a.* **1** (of a magazine etc.) appearing at regular intervals. **2** periodic. ~*a.* a magazine or other publication published at regular intervals, e.g. monthly or quarterly. **periodically** *adv.* **periodic decimal** *n.* (*Math.*) a set of figures repeated in a recurring decimal. **periodicity** (-dis´-) *n.* **periodic table** *n.* a table showing the chemical elements in order of their atomic number, and grouped in rows to show similar properties. **period piece** *n.* an objet d'art, piece of furniture etc. belonging to a historical period, esp. one of value.

periodontal (periǝdon´tǝl) *a.* (of tissue) around a tooth. **periodontics** *n.* the treatment of periodontal disorders. **periodontist** *n.* **periodontology** (-tol´-) *n.* periodontics.

peripatetic (peripǝtet´ik) *a.* **1** (of a teacher) working in several schools. **2** walking about, itinerant. ~*n.* a peripatetic person, esp. a teacher. **peripatetically** *adv.* **peripateticism** (-sizm) *n.*

periphery (pǝrif´ǝri) *n.* (*pl.* **peripheries**) **1** the perimeter or circumference of a figure or surface. **2** the outer region. **peripheral** *a.* **1** of relatively little importance. **2** of or relating to a periphery. **3** (*Anat.*) near the surface of the body. **4** being an additional or auxiliary device, esp. in computing. ~*n.* (*Comput.*) a device, e.g. a printer, a VDU, connected to a computer for input/output, storage etc. **peripherality** (-al´-) *n.* **peripherally** *adv.* **peripheral nervous system** *n.* (*Anat.*) the nervous system outside the brain and the spinal cord.

periphrasis (pǝrif´rǝsis) *n.* (*pl.* **periphrases** (-sēz)) **1** roundabout speaking or expression, circumlocution. **2** a roundabout phrase. **periphrastic** (-fras´-) *a.* **1** of or using periphrasis. **2** (*Gram.*) using two words instead of an inflected form of one word. **periphrastically** *adv.*

periscope (per´iskōp) *n.* an apparatus enabling people inside a submarine, trench etc. to look about above the surface of the water etc. **periscopic** (-skop´-) *a.* **periscopical** *a.* **periscopically** *adv.* **periscopic lens** *n.* a lens which allows clear vision over a wide angle.

perish (per´ish) *v.i.* **1** to be destroyed, to come to nothing. **2** to die, to lose life or vitality in any way. **3** to decay, to wither. **perish the thought** used to express horror or disapproval. **perishable** *a.* liable to perish, subject to rapid decay. ~*n.* (*pl.*) foodstuffs and other things liable to rapid decay or deterioration. **perishability** (-bil´-), **perishableness** *n.* **perishably** *adv.* **perished** *a.* (*coll.*) **1** (of a person) very cold. **2** (of

rubber etc.) in poor condition due to age, damp etc. **perisher** *n.* (*sl.*) an irritating person, esp. a child. **perishing** *a.* (*coll.*) **1** infernal, damned. **2** freezing cold. **perishingly** *adv.* **perishless** *a.*

peristalsis (peristal´sis) *n.* the automatic, wavelike, contractile motion of the alimentary canal and similar organs by which the contents are propelled along. **peristaltic** *a.* **peristaltically** *adv.*

peristyle (per´istīl) *n.* **1** a row of columns surrounding a building, court etc. **2** a court etc. with a colonnade around it.

peritoneum (peritǝnē´ǝm) *n.* (*pl.* **peritoneums**, **peritonea** (-ǝ)) (*Anat.*) the serous membrane lining the abdominal cavity and enveloping all the abdominal viscera. **peritoneal** *a.* **peritonitis** (-nī´tis) *n.* (*Med.*) inflammation of the peritoneum.

periwig (per´iwig) *n.* (*Hist.*) a wig. **periwigged** *a.*

periwinkle[1] (per´iwingkǝl) *n.* any plant of the genus *Vinca*, comprising trailing evergreen shrubs with blue or white flowers.

periwinkle[2] (per´iwingkǝl) *n.* a winkle.

☒ **perjorative** common misspelling of PEJORATIVE.

perjure (pœ´jǝ) *v.t.* (*Law*) (*reflex.*) to forswear (oneself), to lie under oath. **perjured** *a.* forsworn, guilty of perjury. **perjurer** *n.* **perjurious** (-joo´-) *a.* **perjury** (-jǝri) *n.* (*pl.* **perjuries**) (*Law*) **1** the act of swearing falsely, the violating of an oath. **2** the act of wilfully giving false evidence.

perk[1] (pœk) *v.t.* **1** to hold or stick up. **2** to thrust (oneself) forward. ~*a.* pert, brisk, smart, trim. **to perk up** (*coll.*) (to cause) to be more cheerful, lively or smart. **perky** *a.* (*comp.* **perkier**, *superl.* **perkiest**) **1** lively. **2** cheerful, jaunty. **perkily** *adv.* **perkiness** *n.*

perk[2] (pœk) *n.* (*coll.*) a benefit enjoyed by an employee over and above their salary.

perk[3] (pœk) *v.i., v.t.* (*coll.*) to percolate.

perlite (pœ´līt), **pearlite** *n.* (*Geol.*) a glassy igneous rock characterized by spheroidal cracks formed by contractile tension in cooling.

perm[1] (pœm) *n.* a hairstyle in which hair is shaped and then set by chemicals, heat etc. ~*v.t.* to put a perm in (hair).

perm[2] (pœm) *n.* (*coll.*) a forecast of a number of football match results selected from a larger number of matches. ~*v.t.* to make a perm of.

permaculture (pœ´mǝkŭlchǝ) *n.* the development of self-sustaining agricultural ecosystems.

permafrost (pœ´mǝfrost) *n.* a layer of permanently frozen earth in very cold regions.

permalloy (pœ´mǝloi) *n.* an alloy with high magnetic permeability.

permanent (pœ´mǝnǝnt) *a.* lasting, remaining or intended to remain in the same state, place or condition, as distinct from *temporary*. **permanence**, **permanency** *n.* **permanentize**, **permanentise** *v.t.* **permanently** *adv.* **permanent magnet** *n.* a magnet which retains properties after the removal of the magnetic field producing the magnetization. **Permanent Secretary** *n.* a senior civil servant who acts as a permanent adviser to ministers in a particular government department. **permanent set** *n.* **1** the permanent deformation of a substance after subjection to stress. **2** the extent of permanent set. **permanent tooth** *n.* (*pl.* **permanent teeth**) an adult tooth, which grows in after a milk tooth has fallen out. **Permanent Under Secretary** *n.* **1** a senior permanent adviser to a Secretary of State. **2** a senior civil servant who is usually the head of a division within the State Department. **permanent wave** *n.* PERM¹. **permanent way** *n.* the finished roadbed of a railway.

permanganate (pəmang'gənət) *n.* (*Chem.*) a salt of permanganic acid. **permanganic** (pœmangan'-) *a.* (*Chem.*) of or containing manganese in its highest valency. **permanganic acid** *n.* an acid containing heptavalent manganese.

permeate (pœ'miāt) *v.t.* **1** to penetrate and pass through. **2** to pervade, to saturate. **3** to pass through the pores or interstices of. ~*v.i.* to be diffused (in, through etc.). **permeable** *a.* yielding passage to fluids, penetrable. **permeability** (-bil'-) *n.* **permeance** *n.* **permeant** *a.* **permeation** (-ā'shən) *n.* **permeator** *n.*

permethrin (pəmē'thrin) *n.* a garden pesticide, esp. used against whitefly.

Permian (pœ'miən) *a.* (*Geol.*) of or relating to the uppermost strata of the Palaeozoic series, consisting chiefly of red sandstone and magnesian limestone, which rest on the Carboniferous strata. ~*n.* the Permian period.

per mille (pœ mil'i), **per mil** (mil') *adv.* in every thousand.

permit¹ (pəmit') *v.t.* (*pres.p.* **permitting**, *past, p.p.* **permitted**) **1** to give permission to or for, to authorize. **2** to allow by consent. ~*v.i.* **1** to provide an opportunity. **2** to allow, to admit (of). **permissible** (-mis'-) *a.* **permissibility** (-bil'-) *n.* **permissibly** *adv.* **permission** (-mish'ən) *n.* **1** the act of permitting. **2** consent or authorization given. **permissive** *a.* **1** allowing great licence in social and sexual conduct. **2** granting liberty, leave or permission. **3** not hindering or forbidding. **permissively** *adv.* **permissiveness** *n.* **permittee** (pœmitē') *n.* **permitter** *n.* **permittivity** (-tiv'-) *n.* (*pl.* **permittivities**) a measure of a substance's ability to store potential energy in an electric field.

permit² (pœ'mit) *n.* an order to permit, a permission or warrant, esp. a written authority to land or remove dutiable goods.

permutation (pœmūtā'shən) *n.* **1** (*Math.*) **a** change of the order of a series of quantities. **b** each of the different arrangements, as regards order, that can be made in a permutation. **2** PERM². **3** alteration, transmutation. **permutate** (pœ'-) *v.t.* to change the order of. **permutational** *a.*

permute (pəmūt') *v.t.* **1** to change thoroughly. **2** (*Math.*) to subject to permutation. **permutable** *a.*

interchangeable. **permutableness** *n.* **permutably** *adv.*

pernicious (pənish'əs) *a.* **1** destructive, ruinous, deadly, noxious, hurtful. **2** malicious, wicked. **pernicious anaemia** *n.* a very severe, sometimes fatal, form of anaemia. **perniciously** *adv.* **perniciousness** *n.*

pernickety (pənik'əti), (*N Am.*) **persnickety** (-snik'-) *a.* (*coll.*) **1** fastidious, fussy. **2** overparticular. **3** awkward to handle, ticklish.

perorate (per'ərāt) *v.i.* **1** to deliver an oration. **2** (*coll.*) to speechify. **peroration** (-ā'shən) *n.* the concluding part of an oration.

peroxide (pərok'sīd) *n.* (*Chem.*) **1** hydrogen peroxide. **2** the oxide of a given base that contains the greatest quantity of oxygen. **3** any salt or ester of hydrogen peroxide. ~*a.* of or relating to hydrogen peroxide as used to lighten the hair (*a peroxide blonde*). ~*v.t.* (*coll.*) to bleach (hair) with hydrogen peroxide. **peroxidase** (-idāz) *n.* any of a class of enzymes which catalyse the oxidation of a compound by the decomposition of hydrogen peroxide. **peroxidation** (-idā'shən) *n.*

perpendicular (pœpəndik'ūlə) *a.* **1** at right angles to the plane of the horizon. **2** (*Geom.*) at right angles to a given line or surface. **3** (of a hill, road etc.) nearly vertical, extremely steep. **4** (*facet.*) perfectly upright or vertical. ~*n.* **1** a perpendicular line. **2** a plumb rule, plumb level or other instrument for determining the vertical. **3** perpendicular attitude or condition. **perpendicularity** (-lar'-) *n.* **perpendicularly** *adv.* **Perpendicular style** *n.* (*Archit.*) the style of pointed architecture in England succeeding the Decorated, characterized by the predominance of vertical, horizontal and rectangular lines, esp. in window tracery, flattish arches and profuse ornamentation.

perpetrate (pœ'pətrāt) *v.t.* to perform, to commit, to be guilty of. **perpetration** (-ā'shən) *n.* **perpetrator** *n.*

perpetual (pəpech'ūəl) *a.* **1** unending, eternal. **2** persistent, continual, constant. **3** permanent, for a lifetime. **4** (of a plant) blooming continually throughout the season. **perpetually** *adv.* **perpetual motion** *n.* the motion of a hypothetical machine which continues to move indefinitely without any external source of energy. **perpetuity** (pœpətū'-) *n.* (*pl.* **perpetuities**) **1** the state of being perpetual. **2** a perpetual annuity. **3** a perpetual possession. **in perpetuity** for ever.

perpetuate (pəpech'ūāt) *v.t.* **1** to make perpetual. **2** to preserve from extinction or oblivion. **perpetuance, perpetuation** (-ā'shən) *n.* **perpetuator** *n.*

perplex (pəpleks') *v.t.* **1** to puzzle, to bewilder, to embarrass, to make anxious. **2** to complicate, confuse or involve; to make difficult to understand or to unravel. **perplexed** *a.* confused, puzzled. **perplexedly** (-plek'sid-) *adv.* **perplexedness**

(-plek´sid-) *n.* **perplexing** *a.* **perplexingly** *adv.*
perplexity *n.* (*pl.* **perplexities**)
per pro. (pœ prō´) *abbr.* through the agency of.

Usage note Most commonly used where one
person signs a letter or other document on behalf
of another. In *AB per pro.* (or *pp*) *CD*, the person
who signs should be CD (so *per pro.* does not
mean 'on behalf of', as popularly interpreted,
because the signing is on behalf of the first person specified, AB).

perquisite (pœ´kwizit) *n.* **1** gain, profit or
emolument, over and above regular wages or
salary, a perk. **2** anything to which a servant etc.
has a prescriptive right after it has served its
purpose. **3** (*coll.*) a gratuity, a tip.

Usage note The nouns *perquisite* and *prerequisite* should not be confused: a *perquisite* is
an extra payment, and a *prerequisite* an advance
requirement.

perry (per´i) *n.* (*pl.* **perries**) a fermented liquor
made from the juice of pears.
per se (pœ sā´) *adv.* by itself, in itself.
persecute (pœ´sikūt) *v.t.* **1** to pursue in a hostile,
envious or malicious way; to afflict with
suffering or loss of life or property, esp. for
adherence to a particular opinion or creed. **2** to
harass, to worry, to importune. **3** to bombard
with questions. **persecution** (-ū´shən) *n.* **persecution complex, persecution mania** *n.* an irrational
conviction that others are conspiring against
one. **persecutor** *n.* **persecutory** *a.*
perseverate (pəsev´ərāt) *v.i.* **1** to persist in an
action for a long time. **2** (*Psych.*) to have a
tendency to continue with a response after the
original stimulus has stopped. **perseveration**
(-ā´shən) *n.*
persevere (pœsiviə´) *v.i.* to persist in or with any
undertaking, plan or course. **perseverance** *n.* **1**
persistent endeavour. **2** persistence in any plan
or undertaking.
Persian (pœ´zhən, -shən) *a.* of or relating to
Persia (now Iran). ~*n.* **1** a native or inhabitant of
Persia, a person of Persian descent. **2** the Persian
(or Iranian) language. **3** a Persian cat. **Persian cat**
n. a breed of cat with long silky hair. **Persian
lamb** *n.* the curly fur of a young karakul, used for
clothing.
persienne (pœsien´) *n.* **1** an Oriental cambric or
muslin. **2** (*pl.*) window blinds or shutters like
Venetian blinds.
persiflage (pœ´siflahzh) *n.* banter, raillery,
frivolous treatment of any subject.
persimmon (pəsim´ən) *n.* **1** any evergreen tree
of the genus *Diospyrus.* **2** the plumlike fruit of
the persimmon.
persist (pəsist´) *v.i.* **1** to continue steadfastly, in
the pursuit of any plan. **2** to remain, to continue,
to endure. **persistence** *n.* **persistency** *n.* **persistent** *a.* **1** persisting, persevering. **2** lasting,
enduring. **3** constantly repeated. **4** (*Biol.*) (of

leaves etc.) not falling off. **persistently** *adv.*
persistent vegetative state *n.* (*Med.*) an irreversible condition in which a person's body is
kept functioning by medical intervention but
there are no signs of higher brain function.
persnickety PERNICKETY.
person (pœ´sən) *n.* **1** a human being, an
individual. **2** a being possessed of personality. **3**
the living body of a human being. **4** a human
being or body corporate having legal rights and
duties. **5** (*Theol.*) each of the three individualities in the Godhead, Father, Son or Holy
Spirit. **6** (*Gram.*) each of the three relations of the
subject or object of a verb, as speaking, spoken to
or spoken of. **7** (*euphem.*) the genitals. **8** a part or
character (on the stage). **in one's own person** as
oneself. **in person** by oneself, not by deputy.
-person *comb. form* a person, esp. one in a
particular job or position, as in *salesperson,
chairperson.* **personable** *a.* attractive and likeable. **personableness** *n.* **personably** *adv.* **personage** (-nij) *n.* **1** a person. **2** a person of rank,
distinction or importance. **3** a character in a play,
story etc. **personal** *a.* **1** of or relating to a person
as distinct from a thing. **2** of, relating to or
affecting an individual. **3** individual, private. **4 a**
(of criticism etc.) reflecting on an individual,
esp. disparaging, hostile. **b** making or prone to
make such remarks. **5** of or relating to the
physical person, bodily, corporeal. **6** transacted
or done in person. **7** (*Gram.*) denoting or
indicating any of the three persons. **8** (*Law*) of or
relating to the person (applied to all property
except land or heritable interests in land). ~*n.*
(*esp. N Am.*) a personal ad. **personal ad** *n.* (*esp. N
Am.*) a notice in the personal column of a newspaper. **personal column** *n.* a newspaper column
in the classified advertisement section containing personal messages, requests for donations to
charity etc. **personal computer** *n.* a small computer designed for business or home use, e.g. for
keeping records, word processing etc. **personal
equity plan** *n.* a scheme under which individuals
may invest a fixed sum each year in UK shares
without paying tax on capital gains or dividend
income. **personal estate** *n.* personal property.
personal identification number *n.* a secret
number allotted to a person for use as a password for an automated cash dispenser etc.
personality (-nal´-) *n.* (*pl.* **personalities**) **1** the
quality or state of being a person. **2** individual
existence or identity. **3** the sum of qualities and
characteristics that constitute individuality. **4** a
distinctive personal character. **5** an important or
famous person, a celebrity. **6** a person who has a
strong or unusual character. **7** personal application of remarks etc. **8** (*pl.*) disparaging personal
remarks. **personality cult** *n.* the excessive
adulation and boosting of a person, esp. a
political leader. **personalize, personalise** *v.t.* **1** to
make personal. **2** to mark (something) so that it is
identifiable as belonging to a particular person.

3 to personify. **personalization** (-zā´shən) n. **personally** adv. **1** in person. **2** as regards oneself. **3** particularly, individually. **4** as a person. **personal organizer** n. **1** a portable personal filing system, usu. in the form of a small loose-leafed book, containing details of appointments, telephone numbers, memoranda etc. **2** a handheld microcomputer used for the same purpose. **personal pronoun** n. a pronoun, e.g. I, you, we, used to refer to a person or thing. **personal property** n. (Law) movable property, as distinct from real property. **personal stereo** n. (pl. **personal stereos**) a very small, portable stereo set with headphones, designed to be attached to a belt or held in the hand. **personal touch** n. an individual approach. **personalty** (-əlti) n. (pl. **personalties**) (Law) movable property as distinct from realty. **personhood** n. the state of being a person. **person-to-person** a. **1** between individuals. **2** (of a telephone call) arranged through the operator to a particular person, with no substitutes.

persona (pəsō´nə) n. (pl. **personas, personae** (-nē)) **1** a person's social façade, as distinct from anima. **2** (often pl.) a character in a play, novel etc. **persona grata** (grah´tə) n. (pl. **personae gratae** (-tē)) an acceptable person, esp. in diplomatic circles. **persona non grata** (non grah´tə) n. an unacceptable person.

personate (pœ´sənāt) v.t. **1** to assume the character or to act the part of. **2** to impersonate, esp. for the purpose of voting without being entitled to do so, or for any other fraudulent purpose. **personation** (-ā´shən) n. **personator** n.

personify (pəson´ifi) v.t. (3rd pers. sing. pres. **personifies,** pres.p. **personifying,** past, p.p. **personified**) **1** to regard or represent (an abstraction) as possessing the attributes of a living being. **2** to symbolize by a human figure. **3** to embody, to exemplify, to typify, in one's own person. **personification** (-fikā´shən) n. **personified** a. **personifier** n.

personnel (pœsənel´) n. **1** the body of persons engaged in some service, esp. a public institution, military or naval enterprise etc. **2** the staff of a business firm etc. **3** a personnel department. **personnel carrier** n. an armoured vehicle for transporting personnel. **personnel department** n. the department of a business firm etc. that deals with the appointment, records and welfare of personnel.

perspective (pəspek´tiv) n. **1** the art of representing solid objects on a plane surface exactly as regards position, shape and dimensions, as the objects themselves appear to the eye at a particular point. **2** the apparent relation of visible objects as regards position and distance. **3** a representation of objects in perspective. **4** the relation of facts or other matters as viewed by the mind. **5** a view, a vista, a prospect. **6** a point of view from which something is considered. ~a. **1** of or relating to perspective. **2** in perspective. **in perspective 1** according to the laws of perspective. **2** in due proportion. **out of perspective 1** not according to the laws of perspective. **2** not in due proportion. **perspectival** (-tī´vəl) a. **perspectively** adv.

Perspex® (pœ´speks) n. a transparent plastic, very tough and of great clarity.

perspicacious (pœspikā´shəs) a. quick-sighted, mentally penetrating or discerning. **perspicaciously** adv. **perspicacity** (-kas´-), **perspicaciousness** n.

Usage note The adjectives perspicacious and perspicuous should not be confused: perspicacious means discerning, and perspicuous clearly expressed.

perspicuous (pəspik´ūəs) a. **1** free from obscurity or ambiguity, clearly expressed, lucid. **2** expressing things clearly. **perspicuity** (-ū´-) n. **perspicuously** adv. **perspicuousness** n.

Usage note See note under PERSPICACIOUS.

perspire (pəspīə´) v.i. to sweat. ~v.t. to give out (the excretions of the body) through the pores of the skin, to sweat. **perspiration** (pœspirā´shən) n. **perspiratory** (-spir´-) a.

persuade (pəswād´) v.t. **1** to influence or convince by argument, advice, entreaty, or expostulation. **2** to induce. **3** to try to influence, to advise. **persuadable** a. **persuadability** (-bil´-) n. **persuader** n. **1** a person who persuades. **2** (sl.) a pistol, a firearm, a weapon. **persuasible** (-si-) a. **persuasibility** (-bil´-) n. **persuasion** (-zhən) n. **1** the act of persuading. **2** power to persuade, persuasiveness. **3** the state of being persuaded, a settled conviction. **4** creed, belief, esp. in religious matters. **5** a religious sect or denomination. **6** (coll. or facet.) a sort, a kind. **persuasive** (-siv) a. able or tending to persuade, winning. **persuasively** adv. **persuasiveness** n.

PERT abbr. programme evaluation and review technique.

pert (pœt) a. **1** saucy, forward. **2** sprightly, lively. **pertly** adv. **pertness** n.

pertain (pətān´) v.i. **1** to relate, to apply, to have reference (to). **2** to belong (to) as an attribute, an appendage, a part etc. **3** to be appropriate (to).

pertinacious (pœtinā´shəs) a. stubborn, persistent. **pertinaciously** adv. **pertinaciousness**, **pertinacity** (-nas´-) n.

pertinent (pœ´tinənt) a. relevant, apposite. **pertinence, pertinency** n. **pertinently** adv.

perturb (pətœb´) v.t. **1** to throw into confusion or physical disorder. **2** to disturb, to disquiet, to agitate. **3** to cause (a planet, electron etc.) to deviate from a regular path. **perturbable** a. **perturbation** (pœtəbā´shən) n. **perturbingly** adv.

pertussis (pətǔs´is) n. whooping cough.

peruke (pərook´), **perruque** n. (Hist.) a wig.

peruse (pərooz´) v.t. **1** to read. **2** to observe or examine carefully. **perusal** n. **peruser** n.

Peruvian (pəroo´viən) a. of or relating to Peru.

~*n.* a native or inhabitant of Peru, or a descendant of one. **Peruvian bark** *n.* the bark of several species of cinchona, used as a tonic in debility and intermittent fevers.

pervade (pəvād´) *v.t.* **1** to pass through. **2** to permeate, to saturate. **3** to be diffused throughout. **pervasion** (-zhən) *n.* **pervasive** (-siv) *a.* **pervasively** *adv.* **pervasiveness** *n.*

perve (pœv), **perv** *n.* (*sl.*) **1** a sexual pervert. **2** (*Austral.*) a lecherous gaze. ~*v.i.* **1** to behave like a sexual pervert. **2** (*Austral.*) to gaze lecherously (at).

perverse (pəvœs´) *a.* **1** wilfully or obstinately wrong. **2** turned against what is reasonable or fitting. **3** unreasonable, intractable, petulant, peevish. **4** perverted. **5** against the weight of evidence. **perversely** *adv.* **perverseness** *n.* **perversity** *n.* (*pl.* **perversities**).

perversion (pəvœ´shən) *n.* **1** the act of perverting. **2** a misinterpretation, misapplication or corruption. **3** abnormal sexual proclivity. **4** an act of perversion.

pervert[1] (pəvœt´) *v.t.* **1** to turn aside from the proper use, to put to improper use. **2** to misapply, to misinterpret. **3** to lead astray, to mislead, to corrupt. **perversive** *a.* **perverted** *a.* marked by (esp. sexual) perversion. **perverter** *n.*

pervert[2] (pœ´vœt) *n.* **1** a person who has been perverted. **2** a person with abnormal sexual proclivities.

pervious (pœ´viəs) *a.* **1** permeable. **2** allowing passage (to). **3** accessible (to facts, ideas etc.). **perviousness** *n.*

peseta (pəsā´tə) *n.* (*pl.* **pesetas**) the standard unit of currency of Spain and Andorra.

pesewa (pəsā´wah) *n.* a unit of currency of Ghana, worth 100th of a cedi.

pesky (pes´ki) *a.* (*comp.* **peskier**, *superl.* **peskiest**) (*esp. N Am., coll.*) annoying, troublesome. **peskiness** *n.*

peso (pā´sō) *n.* (*pl.* **pesos**) the standard unit of currency of several Central and S American countries and the Philippines.

pessary (pes´əri) *n.* (*pl.* **pessaries**) (*Med.*) **1** a device inserted in the vagina to prevent or remedy prolapse of the womb or as a contraceptive. **2** a medicated plug or suppository introduced into the vagina.

pessimism (pes´imizm) *n.* **1** the habit of taking a gloomy and despondent view of things. **2** (*Philos.*) the doctrine that pain and evil predominate enormously over good, or that there is a predominant tendency towards evil throughout the universe, as distinct from *optimism*. **pessimist** *n.* **pessimistic** (-mis´-) *a.* **pessimistically** *adv.*

pest (pest) *n.* **1** a person or something which is extremely destructive, hurtful or annoying. **2** any plant or animal that harms crops, livestock or humans. **pesticide** (pes´tisīd) *n.* a chemical used to kill pests that damage crops etc. **pesticidal** (-sī´-) *a.*

pester (pes´tə) *v.t.* to bother, to worry, to annoy. **pesterer** *n.*

pestiferous (pestif´ərəs) *a.* **1** pestilent. **2** hurtful or noxious in any way.

pestilence (pes´tiləns) *n.* any contagious disease that is epidemic and deadly, esp. bubonic plague. **pestilent** *a.* **1** noxious to health or life, deadly. **2** fatal to morality or society. **3** (*coll.*) vexatious, troublesome, mischievous. **pestilential** (-len´shəl) *a.* **1** of or relating to pestilence. **2** destructive, pestilent. **pestilentially** *adv.* **pestilently** *adv.*

pestle (pes´əl) *n.* **1** an implement used in pounding substances in a mortar. **2** any appliance used for pounding or crushing things. ~*v.t.* to pound with or as if with a pestle. ~*v.i.* to use a pestle.

pesto (pes´tō) *n.* an Italian sauce made of basil, garlic, pine nuts etc.

pet[1] (pet) *n.* **1** an animal kept in the house as a companion. **2** a darling, a favourite. ~*a.* **1** kept as a pet. **2** of or relating to pets. **3** (*often facet.*) petted, indulged, favourite. ~*v.t.* (*pres.p.* **petting**, *past, p.p.* **petted**) **1** to make a pet of, to pamper. **2** to fondle. ~*v.i.* to engage in amorous fondling. **pet aversion, pet hate** *n.* a thing especially disliked. **pet name** *n.* a name used to express affection or intimacy. **petter** *n.*

pet[2] (pet) *n.* a fit of peevishness or bad temper. **pettish** *a.* **pettishly** *adv.* **pettishness** *n.*

petal (pet´əl) *n.* any one of the divisions of a corolla of a flower. **petaline** (-līn) *a.* **petalled, petaled** *a.* **petal-like** *a.* **petaloid** *a.*

petard (pitahd´) *n.* (*Hist.*) a conical case or box of iron etc., formerly used for blowing open gates or barriers. **hoist with/ by one's own petard** caught in one's own trap.

peter[1] (pē´tə) *v.i.* in bridge, to play an echo. ~*n.* in bridge, an echo. **to peter out 1** to come to an end, to die out. **2** (of a lode or vein in mining) to thin or give out.

peter[2] (pē´tə) *n.* (*sl.*) **1** a prison cell. **2** a safe. **peterman** *n.* (*pl.* **petermen**) (*sl.*) a safe-breaker.

Peter Pan (pētə pan´) *n.* a man who looks youthful or who behaves in a youthful manner.

petersham (pē´təshəm) *n.* a thick corded-silk ribbon used for belts, hatbands etc.

pethidine (peth´idēn) *n.* a synthetic analgesic drug with sedative effects similar to but less powerful than morphine, used esp. in childbirth.

petiole (pet´iōl) *n.* the leaf-stalk of a plant. **petiolar, petiolate, petiolated** *a.*

petit (pet´i) *a.* (*esp. Law*) small, petty, inconsiderable, inferior. **petit bourgeois** (peti buə´zhwah) *n.* (*pl.* **petits bourgeois** (peti buə´zhwah)) a member of the petite bourgeoisie. **petit four** (peti faw´) *n.* (*pl.* **petits fours** (fawz´)) a small fancy cake or biscuit. **petit mal** (pətē mal´) *n.* **1** a mild form of epilepsy, as distinct from *grand mal.* **2** a mild epileptic fit. **petit point** (pətē pwā) *n.* **1** a kind of fine embroidery, as distinct from *gros point.* **2** tent stitch. **petits pois** (peti pwah´) *n.pl.* small, sweet green peas.

petite (pətēt´) *a.* **1** (of a woman) slight, dainty, graceful. **2** designed for a small woman. **petite bourgeoisie** *n.* the lower middle classes.

petition (pitish´ən) *n.* **1** an entreaty, a request, a supplication. **2** a formal written supplication to persons in authority, esp. to the people, Parliament etc. **3** the paper containing such supplication. **4** (*Law*) a formal written application to a court, as for a writ of habeas corpus, in bankruptcy etc. ~*v.t.* to address a petition to. ~*v.i.* to appeal humbly (to). **petitionable** *a.* **petitionary** *a.* **petitioner** *n.*

petrel (pet´rəl) *n.* any member of the family Procellariidae or Hydrobatidae, small dusky seabirds, with long wings and great power of flight.

Usage note The spellings of the nouns *petrel* (a bird) and *petrol* (refined petroleum) should not be confused.

Petri dish (pet´ri, pē´-) *n.* a shallow, circular, flat-bottomed dish used for cultures of micro-organisms.

petrify (pet´rifī) *v.t.* (*3rd pers. sing. pres.* **petrifies**, *pres.p.* **petrifying**, *past, p.p.* **petrified**) **1** to convert into stone or a stony substance. **2** to stupefy with fear, astonishment etc. **3** to make hard, callous, benumbed or stiffened. ~*v.i.* **1** to be converted into stone or a stony substance. **2** to become stiffened, benumbed, callous etc. **petrifaction** (-fak´-) *n.*

petro- (pet´rō) *comb. form* **1** stone. **2** petrol.

petrochemical (petrōkem´ikəl) *n.* any chemical obtained from petroleum. ~*a.* of or relating to petrochemicals or petrochemistry.

petrochemistry (petrōkem´istri) *n.* **1** the chemistry of rocks. **2** the chemistry of petroleum.

petrodollar (pet´rōdolə) *n.* a dollar earned from the exporting of petroleum.

petroglyph (pet´rōglif) *n.* a rock-carving.

petrography (petrog´rəfi) *n.* descriptive petrology. **petrographer** *n.* **petrographic** (-graf´-), **petrographical** *a.*

petrol (pet´rəl) *n.* a refined form of petroleum used in motor cars etc. ~*a.* of or relating to the supply of petrol. **petrolatum** (-lā´təm) *n.* (*N Am.*) a fatty compound of paraffin hydrocarbons obtained by refining the residue from petroleum after distillation, pure petroleum jelly. **petrol bomb** *n.* a bottle or other container full of petrol, used as an incendiary.

Usage note See note under PETREL.

petroleum (pitrō´liəm) *n.* an inflammable, oily liquid exuding from rocks or pumped from wells, used for lighting, heating and the generation of mechanical power. **petroleum ether** *n.* a volatile mixture of hydrocarbons, distilled from petroleum. **petroleum jelly** *n.* a product of petroleum used in pharmacy as a lubricant.

petrology (pitrol´əji) *n.* the study of the origin, structure and mineralogical and chemical composition of rocks. **petrologic** (-loj´-), **petrological** *a.* **petrologically** *adv.* **petrologist** *n.*

petrous (pet´rəs) *a.* **1** (*Anat.*) denoting the hard part of the temporal bone. **2** (*Geol.*) like stone, stony.

petticoat (pet´ikōt) *n.* **1** a loose underskirt. **2** (*sl.*) a woman, a girl. ~*a.* (*coll., often derog.*) of or relating to women, feminine. **petticoated** *a.* **petticoatless** *a.*

pettifog (pet´ifog) *v.i.* (*pres.p.* **pettifogging**, *past, p.p.* **pettifogged**) **1** to do legal business in a mean or tricky way, to practise chicanery. **2** to act in a mean, quibbling or shifty way. **pettifogger** *n.* **1** a petty, second-rate lawyer, esp. one given to sharp practices. **2** a petty or second-rate practitioner in any profession. **pettifoggery** *n.* **pettifogging** *a.* petty, trivial, quibbling.

petty (pet´i) *a.* (*comp.* **pettier**, *superl.* **pettiest**) **1** little, trifling, insignificant. **2** small-minded, mean. **3** minor, inferior, subordinate, on a small scale. **4** (*Law*) (of a crime) of minor importance. **pettily** *adv.* **pettiness** *n.* **petty bourgeois** *n.* a petit bourgeois. **petty bourgeoisie** *n.* the petite bourgeoisie. **petty cash** *n.* minor items of receipt and expenditure. **petty jury** *n.* a jury in criminal cases who try the bills found by the grand jury. **petty officer** *n.* a naval officer corresponding in rank to a non-commissioned officer. **petty treason** *n.* (*Hist.*) murder of one's master or husband.

petulant (pet´ūlənt) *a.* given to fits of bad temper, peevish, irritable. **petulance, petulancy** *n.* **petulantly** *adv.*

petunia (pitū´niə) *n.* any member of the genus *Petunia* of S American plants, allied to the tobacco plant, cultivated in gardens for their showy funnel-shaped flowers.

petuntse (pātŭnt´sə) *n.* (*Geol.*) a fusible substance similar to feldspar used for the manufacture of porcelain.

pew (pū) *n.* **1** a long bench with a back, for worshippers in church. **2** a boxlike enclosed seat in a church for a family etc. **3** (*coll.*) a seat, a chair. ~*v.t.* to furnish with pews. **to take a pew** (*coll.*) to sit down. **pewage** (-ij) *n.* **pewless** *a.*

pewee (pē´wē) *n.* a N American flycatcher of the genus *Contopus.*

pewit PEEWIT.

pewter (pū´tə) *n.* **1** an alloy usu. of tin and lead, sometimes of tin with other metals. **2** dishes or utensils made of this. **3** a pewter tankard or pot. ~*a.* made of pewter. **pewterer** *n.*

peyote (pāō´ti) *n.* **1** a Mexican cactus, *Lophophora williamsii.* **2** a hallucinogenic drug made from peyote.

pfennig (pfen´ig) *n.* (*pl.* **pfennigs, pfennige** (-igə)) a German unit of currency, worth one-hundredth of a mark.

PG *abbr.* **1** parental guidance (used to classify the content of cinema films). **2** paying guest.

pH 922 phase

pH (pēach´) *n.* (*Chem.*) a measure of the acidity or alkalinity of a solution on a scale from 0 to 14, with 7 representing neutrality, figures below it denoting acidity and those above it alkalinity.

phaeton (fā´tən) *n.* a light four-wheeled open carriage, usu. drawn by two horses.

phage (fāj) *n.* a bacteriophage.

-phage (fāj) *comb. form* eater, as *bacteriophage*. **-phagia** (fā´jiə), **-phagy** (fəji) *comb. form* eating, as *anthropophagia*.

phagocyte (fag´ōsīt) *n.* a leucocyte that absorbs microbes etc., protecting the system against infection. **phagocytic** (-sit´-) *a.* **phagocytosis** (-tō´sis) *n.* the destruction of microbes etc. by phagocytes.

-phagous (fəgəs) *comb. form* eating, devouring, as *anthropophagous*.

phalanger (fəlan´jə) *n.* any small, Australian, woolly-coated, arboreal marsupial of the family Phalangeridae, comprising the flying squirrel and flying opossum.

phalanx (fal´angks) *n.* (*pl.* **phalanxes**, (*Anat.*, *Bot.*) **phalanges** (fəlan´jēz)) **1** any compact body of troops or close organization of people. **2** (*Anat.*) any one of the small bones of the fingers. **3** (*Bot.*) any one of the bundles of stamens in polyadelphous flowers.

phalarope (fal´ərōp) *n.* any small wading bird of the subfamily Phalaropodidae, related to the snipes.

phallus (fal´əs) *n.* (*pl.* **phalli** (-lī), **phalluses**) **1** a penis. **2** a figure of a penis, venerated as a symbol of the fertilizing power in nature. **phallic** *a.* **phallically** *adv.* **phallicism** (-sizm), **phallism** *n.* **phallocentric** (falōsen´trik) *a.* centred on the phallus or on male attitudes. **phallocentricity** (-tris´-) *n.* **phallocentrism** *n.*

phanerogam (fan´ərōgam) *n.* (*Bot.*) a plant having pistils and stamens, a flowering plant. **phanerogamic** (-gam´-), **phanerogamous** (-rog´ə-) *a.*

phantasize FANTASIZE (under FANTASY).

phantasm (fan´tazm) *n.* **1** a phantom, an optical illusion. **2** a deception, a figment, an unreal likeness or presentation (of). **3** a vision or image of an absent or deceased person. **phantasmal** (-taz´-) *a.* **phantasmic** (-taz´-) *a.*

phantasmagoria (fantazməgor´riə), **phantasmagory** (-taz´məgəri) *n.* (*pl.* **phantasmagorias**, **phantasmagories**) a series of phantasms, fantastic appearances or illusions appearing to the mind as in nightmare, frenzy etc. **phantasmagorial, phantasmagoric** (-gor´-), **phantasmagorical** *a.*

phantasy FANTASY.

phantom (fan´təm) *n.* **1** an apparition, a ghost, a spectre. **2** a vision, an illusion, an imaginary appearance. **3** (*Med.*) a model of the human body used for demonstration or practice. ~*a.* seeming, apparent, illusory, imaginary, fictitious. **phantom circuit** *n.* an arrangement of

electrical wires equivalent to an extra circuit. **phantom limb** *n.* the sensation that a limb is still present after it has been amputated. **phantom pregnancy** *n.* (*Med.*) the manifestation of symptoms of pregnancy in a woman who is not pregnant.

Pharaoh (feə´rō) *n.* any one of the ancient Egyptian kings. **Pharaoh's ant** *n.* a small reddish-yellow ant, *Monomorium pharaonis*, of tropical regions, which has spread to other countries and infests heated buildings etc. **Pharaoh's serpent** *n.* a firework consisting of sulphocyanide of mercury, which fuses into a serpentine shape when lit. **Pharaonic** (-rāon´-) *a.*

Pharisee (far´isē) *n.* **1** a member of an ancient Jewish sect who rigidly observed the rites and ceremonies prescribed by the written law, and were marked by their exclusiveness towards the rest of the people. **2** a self-righteous person, an unctuous hypocrite. **Pharisaic** (-sā´ik) *a.* **Pharisaical** *a.* **Pharisaically** *adv.* **Pharisaism** (far´isā-) *n.*

pharmaceutical (fahməsū´tikəl) *a.* of, relating to or engaged in pharmacy. **pharmaceutically** *adv.* **pharmaceutics** *n.*

pharmacology (fahməkol´əji) *n.* the science of drugs and medicines. **pharmacological** (-kəloj´-) *a.* **pharmacologically** *adv.* **pharmacologist** *n.*

pharmacopoeia (fahməkəpē´ə) *n.* (*pl.* **pharmacopoeias**) **1** a book, esp. an official publication, containing a list of drugs, formulas, doses etc. **2** a collection of drugs. **pharmacopoeial** *a.*

pharmacy (fah´məsi) *n.* (*pl.* **pharmacies**) **1** the art or practice of preparing, compounding and dispensing drugs, esp. for medicinal purposes. **2** a chemist's shop, a dispensary. **pharmacist** *n.* a person who is trained in pharmacy and is legally entitled to sell drugs and poisons.

pharyngo- (fəring´gō), **pharyng-** *comb. form* of or relating to the pharynx.

pharyngotomy (faring-got´əmi) *n.* (*pl.* **pharyngotomies**) the surgical operation of cutting the pharynx.

pharynx (far´ingks) *n.* (*pl.* **pharynges** (fərin´jēz)) (*Anat.*, *Zool.*) the canal or cavity opening from the mouth into the oesophagus and communicating with the air passages of the nose. **pharyngal** (fəring´gəl), **pharyngeal** (fərin´jiəl) *a.* **pharyngitis** (-jī´-) *n.*

phase (fāz) *n.* **1** a stage of change or development. **2** a particular aspect of the illuminated surface of the moon or a planet, applied esp. to the successive quarters etc. of the moon. **3** (*Physics*) the relationship in time between the peaks of two alternating voltages etc. **4** a difficult period, esp. in adolescence. **5** a variation in an animal's coloration owing to seasonal changes etc. **6** (*Chem.*) a distinct, mechanically separable, homogeneous portion of matter that is part of a physical-chemical system. **7** a particular aspect or appearance. ~*v.t.* to carry out in phases. **in**

phase happening together or in harmony. **out of phase** not happening together or in harmony. **to phase in** to introduce gradually. **to phase out** to discontinue gradually. **phasic** *a*.

-phasia (fā´ziə) *comb. form* speech disorder, as *dysphasia*.

phatic (fat´ik) *a*. (of speech) used to express feelings, sociability etc., rather than to express meaning.

Ph.D. *abbr.* Doctor of Philosophy.

pheasant (fez´ənt) *n*. any game bird of the family Phasianidae, naturalized in Britain and Europe, noted for their brilliant plumage and delicate flesh. **pheasantry** *n*. (*pl.* **pheasantries**) a place where pheasants are kept.

phenacetin (finas´itin) *n*. a white crystalline compound used as an antipyretic.

phencyclidine (fensīk´lidēn) *n*. a hallucinogenic drug derived from piperidine.

phenix PHOENIX.

pheno- (fē´nō, fen´ō) *comb. form* **1** (*Chem.*) derived from coal tar, orig. in the production of coal gas for illuminating. **2** showing.

phenobarbitone (fēnōbah´bitōn), (*N Am.*) **phenobarbital** (-təl) *n*. a white, crystalline powder used as a sedative or hypnotic drug, esp. in cases of epilepsy.

phenocryst (fē´nōkrist) *n*. a large crystal in porphyritic rock.

phenol (fē´nol) *n*. (*Chem.*) **1** carbolic acid. **2** any of various weakly acidic compounds derived from benzene, and containing a hydroxyl group. **phenolic** (finol´-) *a*. **phenolphthalein** (fēnolfthal´ēn) *n*. (*Chem.*) a white, crystalline compound used as a laxative and as an acid-base indicator.

phenom (finom´) *n*. (*N Am., coll.*) an exceptionally gifted person.

phenomenon (finom´inən), **phaenomenon** *n*. (*pl.* **phenomena** (-nə), **phaenomena**) **1** something which appears or is perceived by observation or experiment, esp. a thing or occurrence whose cause is in question. **2** (*coll.*) a remarkable or unusual person or thing. **3** (*Philos.*) something which is apprehended by the mind, as distinguished from real existence. **phenomenal** *a*. **1** of or relating to phenomena, esp. as distinct from underlying realities or causes. **2** extraordinary, prodigious. **3** of the nature of a phenomenon, perceptible by the senses. **phenomenalism, phenomenism** *n*. (*Philos.*) the doctrine that phenomena are the sole material of knowledge, and that underlying realities and causes are unknowable. **phenomenalist, phenomenist** *n*. **phenomenalistic** (-lis´-) *a*. **phenomenalize, phenomenalise** *v.t.* **phenomenally** *adv.* **phenomenology** (-nol´-) *n*. (*Philos.*) **1** the science of phenomena, as distinct from *ontology*. **2** the division of any inductive science concerned with the phenomena forming its basis. **phenomenological** (-loj´-) *a*. **phenomenologically** *adv.* **phenomenologist** *n*.

Usage note *Phenomena* is sometimes used as a singular noun (*a phenomena*), and a plural *phenomenas* may also be encountered, but both these uses are best avoided.

phenotype (fē´nōtīp) *n*. (*Biol.*) the observable characteristics of an organism produced by the interaction of the genotype and the environment. **phenotypic** (-tip´ik) *a*. **phenotypical** *a*. **phenotypically** *adv.*

pheromone (fer´əmōn) *n*. any chemical substance secreted by an animal that stimulates responses from others of its species. **pheromonal** (-mō´-) *a*.

phew (fū) *int.* used to express relief, surprise, disgust etc.

phi (fī) *n*. the 21st letter of the Greek alphabet (ф, Ф).

phial (fī´əl) *n*. a small glass vessel or bottle, esp. for medicine or perfume.

phil- PHILO-.

-phil -PHILE.

philabeg FILIBEG.

philadelphus (filədel´fəs) *n*. a strongly-scented flowering shrub of the genus *Philadelphus*.

philander (filan´də) *v.i.* (of a man) to have casual affairs with women, to flirt. **philanderer** *n*.

philanthropy (filan´thrəpi) *n*. **1** love of humankind. **2** active benevolence towards one's fellow humans. **philanthrope** (fil´anthrōp) *n*. **philanthropic** (-throp´-), **philanthropical** *a*. **philanthropically** *adv.* **philanthropism** *n*. **philanthropist** *n*. **philanthropize, philanthropise** *v.t., v.i.*

philately (filat´əli) *n*. the collecting of postage stamps. **philatelic** (filətel´-) *a*. **philatelically** *adv.* **philatelist** *n*.

-phile (fīl), **-phil** (fil) *comb. form* a lover of, or loving, as *bibliophile*, *Anglophile*.

philharmonic (filəmon´ik) *a*. **1** loving music. **2** used as part of the name of an orchestra or choir.

philhellene (fil´helēn, filhel´ēn) *n*. a friend or lover of Greece and Greeks. *~a*. friendly to Greece. **philhellenic** (-lē´-) *a*. **philhellenism** (-hel´-) *n*. **philhellenist** (-hel´-) *n*.

-philia (fil´iə), **-phily** (fili) *comb. form* **1** love of, as *necrophilia*. **2** a strong tendency towards, as *haemophilia*. **-philiac** (fil´iak) *comb. form* **-philic** (fil´ik), **-philous** (fil´əs) *comb. form*

-philic -PHILIA.

philippic (filip´ik) *n*. a speech or declamation full of acrimonious invective.

Philippine (fil´ipēn) *a*. of or relating to the Philippines, in SE Asia.

Philistine (fil´istīn) *n*. **1** a member of an ancient warlike people in S Palestine who were hostile to the Jews. **2** (*usu.* **philistine**) a person of narrow or materialistic views or ideas; a person deficient in liberal culture. *~a*. **1** (*usu.* **philistine**) commonplace, uncultured, prosaic. **2** of or relating to the Philistines. **philistinism** (-tin-) *n*.

Phillips® (fil´ips) *a*. denoting a screw having a

cross-shaped slot in the head, or a screwdriver for use with such a screw.

phillumeny (filoo´məni) *n.* the collecting of matchboxes or matchbox labels. **phillumenist** *n.*

philo- (fil´ō), **phil-** *comb. form* fond of, affecting, inhabiting.

philodendron (filəden´drən) *n.* (*pl.* **philodendra** (-drə), **philodendrons**) any of various plants of the genus *Philodendron* (arum family), cultivated for their showy foliage.

philology (filol´əji) *n.* **1** the historical or comparative study of language. **2** love of learning or literature. **philologer, philologian** (filəlō´-), **philologist** *n.* **philological** (-loj´-) *a.* **philologically** *adv.* **philologize, philologise** *v.i.*

philosopher (filos´əfə) *n.* **1** a person who studies philosophy. **2** a person of philosophical disposition. **philosophers' stone, philosopher's stone** *n.* an imaginary stone, sought by the alchemists in the belief that it would change the baser metals into gold or silver.

philosophy (filos´əfi) *n.* (*pl.* **philosophies**) **1** the knowledge or investigation of ultimate reality or of general principles of knowledge or existence. **2** a particular system of philosophic principles. **3** the fundamental principles of a science etc. **4** practical wisdom, calmness and coolness of temper, serenity, resignation. **philosophical** (-əsof´-), **philosophic** *a.* **1** of, relating to or according to philosophy. **2** devoted to or skilled in philosophy. **3** wise, calm, temperate, unimpassioned. **philosophically** *adv.* **philosophize, philosophise** *v.t., v.i.* **philosophizer, philosophiser** *n.*

Usage note The uses of the adjectives *philosophic* and *philosophical* overlap, but *philosophical* is more usual for the sense calm or temperate.

-philous -PHILIA.

philtre (fil´tə), (*N Am.*) **philter** *n.* a love potion.

-phily -PHILIA.

phlebitis (flibī´tis) *n.* (*Med.*) inflammation of the inner membrane of a vein. **phlebitic** (-bit´-) *a.*

phlebotomy (flibot´əmi) *n.* the opening of a vein, bloodletting. **phlebotomist** *n.* **phlebotomize, phlebotomise** *v.t.*

phlegm (flem) *n.* **1** viscid mucus secreted in the air passages or stomach, esp. as a morbid product and discharged by coughing etc. **2** self-possession, coolness, sluggishness, apathy. **3** (*Hist.*) watery matter forming one of the four humours of the body. **phlegmatic** (flegmat´-), **phlegmatical** *a.* cool, sluggish, apathetic, unemotional. **phlegmatically** *adv.* **phlegmy** (flem´i) *a.* (*comp.* **phlegmier,** *superl.* **phlegmiest**)

phloem (flō´em) *n.* (*Bot.*) the softer cellular portion of fibrovascular tissue in plants, the bark and the tissues closely connected with it, as opposed to *xylem.*

phlogiston (fləjis´tən) *n.* (*Hist.*) the principle of inflammability formerly supposed to be a necessary constituent of combustible bodies.

phlox (floks) *n.* a plant of the genus *Phlox,* with clusters of showy flowers.

-phobe (fōb) *comb. form* a person who fears or hates, as *homophobe, Francophobe.* **-phobia** (fō´biə) *comb. form* fear, morbid dislike, as *claustrophobia, hydrophobia.* **-phobic** *comb. form*

phobia (fō´biə) *n.* (*pl.* **phobias**) an irrational fear or hatred. **phobic** *a., n.*

Phoenician (fənish´ən) *a.* of or relating to Phoenicia, an ancient Semitic country on the coast of Syria, or to its colonies. ~*n.* a native or inhabitant of Phoenicia or its colonies.

phoenix (fē´niks), (*N Am.*) **phenix** *n.* (*pl.* **phoenixes,** (*N Am.*) **phenixes**) **1** a mythical Arabian bird, the only one of its kind, said to live for 500 or 600 years in the desert, burn itself on a funeral pyre, and rise again in renewed youth. **2** a person or thing of extreme rarity or excellence, a paragon.

phone (fōn) *v.t., v.i.* to telephone. ~*n.* a telephone. **phone book** *n.* a telephone directory. **phonecard** *n.* a plastic card inserted into a slot in a cardphone, which cancels out the prepaid units on the card as the call is made. **phone-in** *n.* a radio or TV programme in which members of the audience at home telephone to make comments, ask questions etc., as part of a live broadcast.

-phone (fōn) *comb. form* **1** sound, voice, a device producing sound, as *telephone.* **2** (a person) speaking a specified language, as *Francophone.*

phoneme (fō´nēm) *n.* any one of the smallest distinctive group of phones in a language. **phonemic** (-nē´-) *a.* **phonemically** *adv.* **phonemics** *n.* the study of phonemes.

phonetic (fənet´ik) *a.* **1** of or relating to the voice or vocal sounds. **2** representing sounds, esp. by means of a distinct letter or character for each. **3** of or relating to phonetics. **phonetically** *adv.* **phonetician** (fōnətish´ən) *n.* **phoneticism** (-sizm) *n.* **phoneticist** (-sist) *n.* **phonetics** *n.* **1** vocal sounds and their classification. **2** the science of articulate sounds, phonology. **phonetist** (fō´-) *n.* **1** a person who is versed in phonetics, a phonologist. **2** an advocate of phonetic writing, a phoneticist.

phoney (fō´ni), (*esp. N Am.*) **phony** *a.* (*comp.* **phonier,** *superl.* **phoniest**) (*coll.*) **1** bogus, false. **2** fraudulent, counterfeit. **3** (of a person) pretentious. ~*n.* (*pl.* **phoneys, phonies**) a phoney person or thing. **phonily** *adv.* **phoniness** *n.*

phonic (fon´ik) *a.* **1** of or relating to sounds, acoustic. **2** of or relating to vocal sounds. **phonically** *adv.* **phonics** *n.* a method of teaching people to read by associating letters with their phonetic values.

phono (fō´nō) *a.* denoting a type of plug, and the socket with which it is used, in which one conductor is cylindrical and the other a longer, central part.

phono- (fō´nō), **phon-** *comb. form* sound.

phonogram (fō´nəgram) *n.* a written character indicating a particular spoken sound. **phonograph** (-grahf) *n.* **1** an instrument for automatically recording and reproducing sounds. **2** (*N Am.*) a gramophone. **phonographer** (-nog´-) *n.* a person who is skilled in phonography. **phonographic** (-graf´-) *a.* **phonographically** *adv.* **phonographist** (-nog´-) *n.* a phonographer. **phonography** (-nog´-) *n.* **1** a system of shorthand in which each sound is represented by a distinct character. **2** automatic recording and reproduction of sounds by phonograph.

phonology (fənol´əji) *n.* **1** the science of the vocal sounds. **2** the sounds and combinations of sounds in a particular language. **phonological** (fonəloj´-) *a.* **phonologically** *adv.* **phonologist** *n.*

phony PHONEY.

phooey (foo´i) *int.* (*coll.*) used to express disbelief or dismissal.

-phore (faw) *comb. form* bearer, as *gonophore*, *semaphore*. **-phorous** (fərəs) *comb. form* bearing, as *electrophorous, galactophorous.*

phosgene (foz´jēn) *n.* (*Chem.*) gaseous carbon oxychloride, used as a poison gas.

phosphate (fos´fāt) *n.* **1** (*Chem.*) any salt of phosphoric acid. **2** a phosphate of calcium, iron, alumina etc., used as fertilizing agents. **phosphatase** (fos´fətāz) *n.* any enzyme which catalyses the hydrolysis of an organic phosphate. **phosphatic** (-fat´-) *a.*

phosphide (fos´fīd) *n.* (*Chem.*) a combination of phosphorus with another element or radical.

phosphine (fos´fēn) *n.* (*Chem.*) a colourless, fishy-smelling gas, which is slightly soluble. **phosphinic** (-fin´-) *a.*

phosphite (fos´fīt) *n.* (*Chem.*) any salt of phosphorous acid.

phospho- (fos´fō), **phosph-** *comb. form* (*Chem.*) containing phosphorus.

phospholipid (fosfōlip´id) *n.* (*Chem.*) any lipid which consists of a phosphate group and one or more fatty acids.

phosphor (fos´fə) *n.* **1** phosphorus. **2** a substance that exhibits phosphorescence. **phosphor bronze** *n.* a combination of phosphorus with bronze. **phosphoresce** (-res´) *v.i.* to give out a light unaccompanied by perceptible heat or without combustion. **phosphorescence** *n.* **1** the emission of or the property of emitting light unaccompanied by perceptible heat or without combustion. **2** the emission of light caused by radiation bombardment, and continuing after the radiation has ceased. **phosphorescent** *a.*

phosphorus (fos´fərəs) *n.* (*Chem.*) a non-metallic element, at. no. 15, chem. symbol P, occurring in two allotropic forms, white phosphorus, which is waxy, poisonous, spontaneously combustible at room temperature and appears luminous, and red phosphorus which is non-poisonous and ignites only when heated. **phosphorate** (-rāt) *v.t.* to combine or impregnate

with phosphorus. **phosphoric** (-for´-) *a.* **1** (*Chem.*) of or relating to phosphorus in its higher valency. **2** phosphorescent. **phosphoric acid** *n.* a crystalline solid used to make fertilizer and soap, and in food processing. **phosphorite** (-rīt) *n.* a massive variety of phosphate of lime. **phosphorous** *a.* **1** (*Chem.*) of, relating to, of the nature of or obtained from phosphorus, esp. in its lower valency. **2** phosphorescent.

photic (fō´tik) *a.* **1** of or relating to light. **2** accessible to the sun's light; denoting the upper layers of the sea, which receive the sun's light.

photo (fō´tō) *n.* (*pl.* **photos**) a photograph. *~v.t.* (*3rd pers. sing. pres.* **photoes**, *pres.p.* **photoing**, *past, p.p.* **photoed**) to photograph. **photo finish** *n.* a close finish of a race or contest, in which only a photograph enables a judge to decide the winner. **photo opportunity**, (*N Am., coll.*) **photo op** (op) *n.* a photocall. **photo session** *n.* a session arranged for a photographer to take photographs of a person for an advertisement etc.

photo- (fō´tō), **phot-** *comb. form* of or relating to light or to photography.

photobiology (fōtōbīol´əji) *n.* the study of the effect of light on living organisms.

photocall (fō´tōkawl) *n.* an occasion when someone is photographed by arrangement for publicity purposes.

photocell (fō´tōsel) *n.* a photoelectric cell.

photochemical (fōtōkem´ikəl) *a.* of, relating to or produced by the chemical action of light. **photochemically** *adv.* **photochemistry** *n.*

photocomposition (fōtōkompəzish´ən) *n.* (*Print.*) filmsetting.

photocopy (fō´tōkopi) *n.* (*pl.* **photocopies**) a photographic reproduction of matter that is written, printed etc. *~v.t.* (*3rd pers. sing. pres.* **photocopies**, *pres.p.* **photocopying**, *past, p.p.* **photocopied**) to make a photocopy of. **photocopiable** *a.* **photocopier** *n.* a machine for making photocopies.

photodegradable (fōtōdigrā´dəbəl) *a.* capable of being decomposed by the action of sunlight.

photoelectric (fōtōilek´trik) *a.* of or relating to photoelectricity, or to the combined action of light and electricity. **photoelectric cell** *n.* a device for measuring light by a change of electrical resistance when light falls upon a cell, or by the generation of a voltage. **photoelectricity** (-tris´-) *n.* electricity produced or affected by light.

photofit (fō´tōfit) *n.* (a method of composing) a likeness of someone's face consisting of photographs of parts of faces, used for the identification of criminal suspects.

photogenic (fōtōjen´ik) *a.* **1** looking attractive in photographs or in cinema films. **2** (*Biol.*) producing light, phosphorescent. **photogenically** *adv.*

photograph (fō´təgrahf) *n.* a picture etc. taken by means of photography. *~v.t.* to take a photograph. *~v.i.* **1** to practise photography. **2** to appear (well or badly) in a photograph. **photographable** *a*. **photographer** (fətog´-) *n*. **photographic** (-graf´-) *a*. **photographically** *adv*. **photographic memory** *n*. the ability to memorize facts etc. in great detail, even after a very short exposure to them. **photography** (fətog´-) *n*. the process or art of producing images or pictures of objects by the chemical action of light on certain sensitive substances.

photogravure (fōtōgravūə´) *n*. **1** the process of producing an intaglio plate for printing by the transfer of a photographic negative to the plate and subsequent etching. **2** a picture produced by photogravure.

photojournalism (fōtōjœ´nəlizm) *n*. journalism featuring photographs more than or instead of text. **photojournalist** *n*.

photolithography (fōtōlithog´rəfi), **photolitho** (-lī´thō) *n*. a mode of producing by photography designs upon stones etc., from which impressions may be taken at a lithographic press. **photolithographer** *n*. **photolithographic** (-graf´-) *a*. **photolithographically** *adv*.

photometer (fōtom´itə) *n*. an instrument for measuring the relative intensity of light. **photometric** (fōtōmet´-) *a*. **photometry** *n*.

photomicrography (fōtōmīkrog´rəfi) *n*. the process of making magnified photographs of microscopic objects. **photomicrograph** (-mī´krəgrahf) *n*. **photomicrographer** *n*.

photomontage (fōtōmontahzh´) *n*. **1** a means of producing pictures by the montage of many photographic images. **2** the picture thus produced.

photon (fō´ton) *n*. (*pl*. **photons**) a quantum of radiant energy.

photonovel (fō´tōnovəl) *n*. a novel presented as a series of photographs with speech bubbles.

photo-offset (fōtōof´set) *n*. offset printing from photolithographic plates.

photophobia (fōtōfō´biə) *n*. abnormal shrinking from or intolerance of light. **photophobic** *a*.

photorealism (fōtōriə´lizm) *n*. meticulous realism in art, esp. depicting mundane or sordid subjects. **photorealist** *n*. **photorealistic** (-lis´-) *a*.

photoreceptor (fōt´ōriseptə) *n*. a nerve ending receptive to light.

photosensitive (fōtōsen´sitiv) *a*. sensitive to the action of light. **photosensitivity** (-tiv´-) *n*.

photosetting (fō´tōseting) *n*. filmsetting. **photoset** *v.t*. (*pres.p.* **photosetting**, *past, p.p.* **photoset**). **photosetter** *n*.

Photostat® (fō´təstat), **photostat** *n*. **1** a type of photocopier. **2** a type of photocopy. ~*v.t.* (*pres.p.* **photostatting**, *past, p.p.* **photostatted**) to make a photostat of. **photostatic** (-stat´-) *a*.

photosynthesis (fōtōsin´thəsis) *n*. the process by which carbohydrates are produced from carbon dioxide and water through the agency of light, esp. when it occurs in green plants. **photosynthesize, photosynthesise** *v.t., v.i.* **photosynthetic** (-thet´-) *a*. **photosynthetically** *adv*.

phototropism (fōtōtrō´pizm) *n*. tropism due to the influence of light. **phototropic** (-trop´-) *a*.

phototype (fō´tōtīp) *n*. **1** a printing plate produced by photoengraving. **2** a print from this. **phototypesetting** (fōtōtīp´seting) *n*. filmsetting. **phototypeset** *a*. **phototypesetter** *n*. a filmsetting machine.

photovoltaic (fōtōvoltā´ik) *a*. of or relating to the production of electric current caused by electromagnetic radiation.

phrase (frāz) *n*. **1** an expression denoting a single idea or forming a distinct part of a sentence. **2** a brief or concise expression. **3** a mode, manner or style of expression, diction. **4** an idiomatic expression. **5** (*Mus*.) a short, distinct passage forming part of a melody. ~*v.t.* **1** to express in words or phrases. **2** to divide up (a sentence) when reading aloud etc., by pausing slightly at appropriate points. **3** (*Mus*.) to divide up (a piece of music) into phrases when playing or singing. **phrasal** *a*. **phrasal verb** *n*. (*Gram*.) a combination of a verb and an adverb, or a verb and a preposition. **phrase book** *n*. a tourists' handbook of phrases or idioms in a foreign language. **phrasing** *n*.

phraseology (frāziol´əji) *n*. (*pl.* **phraseologies**) **1** a choice or arrangement of words. **2** a manner of expression, diction. **phraseological** (frāziəloj´-) *a*.

phrenology (frənol´əji) *n*. (*Hist*.) the theory that the mental faculties and affections are located in distinct parts of the brain denoted by prominences on the skull. **phrenological** (frenəloj´-) *a*. **phrenologist** *n*.

Phrygian (frij´iən) *a*. of or relating to Phrygia, an ancient country in Asia Minor. ~*n*. **1** a native or inhabitant of Phrygia. **2** the language of the Phrygians. **Phrygian bonnet, Phrygian cap** *n*. a conical cap worn by the ancient Phrygians, since adopted as an emblem of liberty.

phthisic (thī´sik, fthī´-) *a*. of or relating to phthisis. **phthisical** (thiz´-, fthiz´-), **phthisicky** *a*.

phthisis (thī´sis, fthī´-) *n*. (*Med*.) a wasting disease, esp. pulmonary tuberculosis.

phut (fŭt) *n*. a dull bang. **to go phut** (*coll*.) (of a plan) to falter, to be unsuccessful.

phycology (fīkol´əji) *n*. the botany of seaweeds or algae. **phycological** (-loj´-) *a*. **phycologist** *n*.

phyla PHYLUM.

phylactery (filak´təri) *n*. (*pl.* **phylacteries**) **1** a small leather box in which are enclosed slips of vellum inscribed with passages from the Pentateuch, worn on the head and left arm by Jews during morning prayer, except on the Sabbath. **2** a charm, spell or amulet worn as a preservative against disease or danger.

phyllo- (fil´ō), **phyll-** *comb. form* a leaf.

phyllophagous (filof´əgəs) *a*. (*Zool*.) feeding on leaves.

phylloquinone (filōkwin´ōn) *n*. a vitamin found in leafy green vegetables, and essential for blood-clotting; vitamin K_1.

phylloxera (filoksiəˊrə, -lokˊsərə) n. (pl. **phylloxeras**) an aphid or plant-louse, *Daktulosphaira vitifoliae*, orig. from America, very destructive to grapevines.

phylogeny (phīlojˊəni), **phylogenesis** (phīlōjenˊisis) n. (pl. **phylogenies, phylogeneses** (-sēz)) (*Biol.*) the evolution of a group, species or type of plant or animal life. **phylogenetic** (-jənetˊ-), **phylogenic** (-jenˊ-) a.

phylum (fīˊləm) n. (pl. **phyla** (-lə)) **1** (*Biol.*) a primary group consisting of related organisms descended from a common form. **2** a group of related languages.

physalis (fīˊsəlis, fis-ˊ, fīsāˊ-) n. any plant of the genus *Physalis*, having fruit in lantern-like calyxes.

physic (fizˊik) n. **1** a medicine, esp. a purge or cathartic. **2** the science or art of healing. **3** the medical profession. **physic garden** n. a garden where medicinal herbs are grown.

physical (fizˊikəl) a. **1** bodily, corporeal, as opposed to *spiritual*. **2** of or relating to matter, material. **3** obvious to or cognizable by the senses. **4** of or relating to physics, esp. as opposed to *chemical*. ~n. (*also* **physical examination**) an examination to ascertain physical fitness. **physical chemistry** n. the branch of chemistry concerned with the ways in which the physical properties and the chemical structure of a substance affect each other. **physical education** n. a school subject involving physical exercises and sports. **physical geography** n. the branch of geography concerned with the features of the earth's surface, the distribution of land and water, climate and the distribution of plants and animals. **physicalism** n. (*Philos.*) the theory that all phenomena can be described in the language of physics. **physicalist** n., a. **physicalistic** (-isˊ-) a. **physicality** (-kalˊ-) n. **physical jerks** n.pl. (*coll.*) physical exercises to promote fitness. **physically** adv. **physicalness** n. **physical science** n. any branch of science, such as physics, chemistry and geology, concerned with natural forces. **physical training** n. programmed physical exercise to promote fitness.

physician (fizishˊən) n. **1** a person versed in or practising the art of healing, including medicine and surgery. **2** a legally qualified practitioner who prescribes remedies for diseases. **3** any medical practitioner. **4** (*fig.*) a healer.

physicist (fizˊisist) n. a person versed in physics.

physico- (fizˊikō) comb. form physical.

physico-chemical (fizikōkemˊikəl) a. of or relating to physics and chemistry.

physics (fizˊiks) n. the science dealing with the phenomena of matter, esp. as affected by energy, and the laws governing these, excluding biology and chemistry.

physio (fizˊiō) n. (pl. **physios**) (*coll.*) short for PHYSIOTHERAPIST (under PHYSIOTHERAPY).

physio- (fizˊiō), **phys-** comb. form **1** of or relating to nature. **2** physical.

physiognomy (fizionˊəmi) n. (pl. **physiognomies**) **1** the art of reading character from features of the face or the form of the body. **2** the face or countenance as an index of character; cast of features. **3** (*coll.*) the face. **4** the lineaments or external features of a landscape etc. **5** an aspect, appearance, look of a situation, event etc. **physiognomic** (fiziənomˊ-), **physiognomical** a. **physiognomically** adv. **physiognomist** n.

physiography (fiziogˊrəfi) n. the scientific description of the physical features of the earth, and the causes by which they have been modified; physical geography. **physiographer** n. **physiographic** (fiziəgrafˊ-), **physiographical** a. **physiographically** adv.

physiology (fiziolˊəji) n. the science of the vital phenomena and the organic functions of animals and plants. **physiologic** (fiziəlojˊ-) a. **physiological** a. **physiologically** adv. **physiological saline** n. a solution of salts which is isotonic with the body fluids. **physiologist** n.

physiotherapy (fiziōtherˊəpi) n. a form of medical treatment in which physical agents such as movement of limbs, massage, electricity etc. are used in place of drugs or surgery. **physiotherapist** n.

physique (fizēkˊ) n. the physical structure or constitution of a person.

-phyte (fīt) comb. form denoting a vegetable organism, as *zoophyte*. **-phytic** (fitˊik) comb. form

phyto- (fīˊtō) comb. form plant.

phytochemistry (fītōkemˊistri) n. the chemistry of plants. **phytochemical** a. **phytochemist** n.

phytogeography (fītōjiogˊrəfi) n. the geographical distribution of plants.

phytopathology (fītōpətholˊəji) n. the science of the diseases of plants.

phytophagous (fītofˊəgəs) a. plant-eating.

phytoplankton (fīˊtōplangktən) n. plant life as a constituent of plankton.

pi[1] (pī) n. **1** the 16th letter of the Greek alphabet (π, Π). **2** the symbol representing the ratio of the circumference of a circle to the diameter, i.e. 3.14159265.

pi[2] (pī) a. (*sl.*) pious.

pi[3] PIE[3].

piaffe (piafˊ) v.i. (of a horse) to move at a piaffer. **piaffer** n. a movement like a trot but slower.

pia mater (pīəˊ māˊtə) n. (*Anat.*) a delicate membrane, the innermost of the three meninges enveloping the brain and spinal cord.

pianissimo (piənisˊimō) adv. (*Mus.*) very softly. ~a. to be played very softly. ~n. (pl. **pianissimos, pianissimi** (-mi)) a passage to be played pianissimo.

piano[1] (pianˊō) n. (pl. **pianos**) a musical instrument, the sounds of which are produced by blows on the wire strings from hammers acted upon by levers set in motion by keys. **pianism** (pēˊənizm) n. **1** piano playing. **2** the technique of this. **pianist** (pēˊ-) n. a piano player. **pianistic**

(-nis´-) *a.* **pianistically** *adv.* **piano accordion** *n.* an accordion with a keyboard resembling that of a piano. **pianoforte** (-faw´ti) *n.* (*esp. Mus., formal*) a piano. **Pianola**® (piənō´lə) *n.* 1 a type of player-piano. 2 in bridge, a hand which requires no skill. 3 an easy task. **piano organ** *n.* a mechanical organ worked on similar principles to those of the barrel organ. **piano-player** *n.* 1 a pianist. 2 a device for playing a piano mechanically. **piano trio** *n.* a trio for piano, violin and cello. **piano-tuner** *n.* a person whose occupation is tuning pianos.

piano² (pyah´nō) *adv.* 1 (*Mus.*) softly. 2 in a subdued manner. ~*a.* 1 (*Mus.*) to be played softly. 2 subdued. ~*n.* (*pl.* **pianos, piani** (-ni)) a passage to be played piano.

piano nobile (piahnō nō´bilā) *n.* (*Archit.*) the main floor of a large house.

piassava (pēəsah´və) *n.* 1 a coarse stiff fibre obtained from Brazilian palms, used esp. to make ropes and brushes. 2 a Brazilian palm yielding piassava.

piastre (pias´tə), (*N Am.*) **piaster** *n.* a small coin of Turkey and several former dependencies.

piazza (piat´sə) *n.* (*pl.* **piazzas**) 1 a square open space, public square or market place, esp. in an Italian town. 2 (*N Am.*) the veranda of a house.

pibroch (pē´brokh) *n.* a series of variations, chiefly martial, played on the bagpipes.

pic (pik) *n.* (*pl.* **pix** (piks), **pics**) (*coll.*) a picture.

pica (pī´kə) *n.* (*pl.* **picas**) (*Print.*) 1 a unit of type size (one sixth of an inch). 2 a size of type, the standard of measurement in printing.

picador (pik´ədaw) *n.* in Spanish bullfights, a horseman with a lance who goads the bull.

picaresque (pikəresk´) *a.* describing the exploits and adventures of rogues or vagabonds, of or relating to a style of fiction describing the episodic adventures of an errant rogue.

picayune (pikəyoon´) *n.* (*N Am.*) 1 a 5-cent piece or other small coin. 2 (*coll.*) something of small value. ~*a.* of little value, petty, trifling.

piccalilli (pik´əlili, pikəlil´i) *n.* (*pl.* **piccalillis**) a pickle of various chopped vegetables with pungent spices.

piccaninny (pik´ənini), (*N Am.*) **pickaninny** *n.* (*pl.* **piccaninnies,** (*N Am.*) **pickaninnies**) (*offensive*) a little black or Aboriginal child.

piccolo (pik´əlō) *n.* (*pl.* **piccolos**) 1 a small flute, with the notes one octave higher than the ordinary flute. 2 a piccolo player.

pick¹ (pik) *v.t.* 1 to choose, to select carefully. 2 to pluck, to gather. 3 to strike at with something pointed. 4 to remove extraneous matter from (the teeth etc.) by picking. 5 to clean by removing matter which adheres with the teeth, fingers etc. 6 to take up with a beak etc. 7 to eat in little bits. 8 to make (one's way) carefully on foot. 9 to find an occasion for (a quarrel etc.). 10 to steal the contents of. 11 to open (a lock) with an implement other than the key. 12 to pluck, to pull apart. 13 to twitch the strings of, to play (a guitar,

banjo etc.). 14 to break, pierce or indent with a pointed instrument. 15 to make (a hole) or to open by picking. ~*v.i.* 1 to make a careful choice. 2 to eat in little bits. 3 to pick a banjo, guitar etc. 4 to strike at with a pointed implement. 5 to pilfer. ~*n.* 1 choice, selection. 2 the best (of). **to pick and choose** to make a fastidious selection. **to pick at** 1 to eat sparingly. 2 to criticize in a cavilling way. **to pick off** 1 to gather or detach (fruit etc.) from a tree etc. 2 to shoot with careful aim one by one. 3 to eliminate (opposition) one by one. 4 in baseball, to put out by throwing the ball to a base. **to pick on** 1 to single out for unpleasant treatment, to bully. 2 to single out, to select. **to pick out** 1 to select. 2 to distinguish (with the eye) from surroundings. 3 to play (a tune) by ear on the piano etc. 4 to relieve or variegate with or as if with distinctive colours. 5 to gather (the meaning of a passage etc.). **to pick over** to examine carefully in order to reject unwanted items. **to pick someone's brains** to consult someone with special expertise or experience. **to pick to pieces** to analyse or criticize spitefully. **to pick up** 1 to take up with the fingers, beak etc. 2 to raise (oneself) after a fall. 3 to raise (one's feet) off the ground. 4 to gather or acquire here and there or little by little. 5 to collect and take away. 6 to accept and pay (a bill). 7 to arrest and detain (a suspect etc.). 8 to receive (an electronic signal etc.). 9 to make the acquaintance of. 10 to resume. 11 to regain or recover (health etc.). 12 to recover one's health. **to take one's pick** to make a choice. **picker** *n.* **pickings** *n.pl.* 1 profit or reward, esp. when obtained dishonestly. 2 gleanings, odds and ends. **picklock** *n.* 1 a person who picks locks, a thief. 2 an instrument for opening a lock without the key. **pick-me-up** *n.* 1 a drink or medicine taken to restore the nerves etc. 2 something which makes one feel better when tired or depressed. **pickpocket** *n.* a person who steals from other people's pockets. **pickpocketing** *n.* **pick-up** *n.* 1 (*also* **pick-up truck**) a vehicle with a driver's cab at the front, and an open back with sides and a tailboard. 2 a device holding a needle which follows the track of a gramophone record and converts the mechanical vibrations into acoustic or electrical vibrations. 3 a device on a musical instrument for converting sound vibrations into electrical signals for amplification. 4 a casual acquaintance, esp. one made for the purpose of having sexual intercourse. 5 the act of making such an acquaintance. 6 the act of picking up, esp. giving a lift. 7 a person or thing picked up. 8 an increase in trade, economy, speed etc. 9 (*Mus.*) the introductory notes to a tune. **picky** *a.* (*comp.* **pickier,** *superl.* **pickiest**) (*coll.*) excessively fastidious, choosy. **pickiness** *n.* **pick-your-own** *a.* (of commercially grown fruit etc.) available to be picked by customers.

pick² (pik) *n.* 1 a tool with a long iron head, usu. pointed at one end and pointed or chisel-edged at the other, fitted in the middle on a wooden shaft, used for breaking ground etc. **2** (*coll.*) a plectrum. **3** any of various implements used for picking. ~*v.t.* **1** to break with or as if with a pick. **2** to make (holes).

pickaback PIGGYBACK.

pickaninny PICCANINNY.

pickaxe (pik´aks), (*N Am.*) **pickax** *n.* an instrument for breaking ground etc., a pick. ~*v.t.* to break up with a pickaxe. ~*v.i.* to use a pickaxe.

picket (pik´it) *n.* **1** a person or group of people set by a trade union to watch a shop, factory etc., during labour disputes. **2** a person or group posted in a certain place as part of a protest or demonstration. **3** a pointed stake, post or peg, forming part of a palisade or paling, for tethering a horse to etc. **4** (*Mil., also* **picquet, piquet**) a small body of troops posted on the outskirts of a camp etc., as a guard, sent out to look for the enemy, or kept in camp for immediate service. ~*v.t.* (*pres.p.* **picketing,** *past, p.p.* **picketed**) **1** to set a picket or pickets at (the gates of a factory etc.). **2** to post as a picket. **3** to fortify or protect with stakes etc., to fence in. **4** to tether to a picket. ~*v.i.* to act as a picket. **picketer** *n.* **picket line** *n.* a group of people picketing a factory etc.

pickle (pik´əl) *n.* **1** a liquid, such as brine, vinegar etc., for preserving fish, meat, vegetables etc. **2** (*often pl.*) vegetables or other food preserved in pickle. **3** (*N Am.*) a pickled cucumber. **4** diluted acid used for cleaning etc. **5** (*coll.*) a disagreeable or embarrassing position. **6** (*coll.*) a troublesome child. ~*v.t.* **1** to preserve in pickle. **2** to treat with pickle. **pickled** *a.* (*coll.*) drunk. **pickler** *n.* **1** a person who pickles vegetables etc. **2** a vegetable suitable for pickling.

picnic (pik´nik) *n.* **1** an excursion into the country etc. with a packed lunch to be eaten outside. **2** an informal meal, eaten outside. ~*v.i.* (*pres.p.* **picnicking,** *past, p.p.* **picnicked**) to go on a picnic. **no picnic** (*coll.*) a difficult or unpleasant experience. **picnicker** *n.* **picnicky** *a.*

pico- (pē´kō, pī´kō) *comb. form* one millionth of a millionth part (10⁻¹²).

picot (pē´kō) *n.* a small loop of thread forming part of an ornamental edging.

picquet PICKET.

picric (pik´rik) *a.* having an intensely bitter taste. **picrate** (-rāt) *n.* **picric acid** *n.* (*Chem.*) an acid obtained by the action of nitric acid on phenol etc., used in dyeing and in certain explosives.

Pict (pikt) *n.* a member of an ancient people who once inhabited parts of Northern Britain. **Pictish** *a., n.*

pictograph (pik´təgrahf), **pictogram** (-gram) *n.* **1** a picture standing for an idea, a pictorial character or symbol. **2** a record or primitive writing consisting of these. **3** a diagram showing statistical data in pictorial form. **pictographic** (-graf´-) *a.* **pictography** (-tog´-) *n.*

pictorial (piktaw´riəl) *a.* **1** of, relating to, containing, expressed in or illustrated by pictures. **2**

picturesque. ~*n.* an illustrated journal etc. **pictorially** *adv.*

picture (pik´chə) *n.* **1** a painting or drawing representing a person, natural scenery or other objects. **2** a photograph, engraving or other representation on a plane surface. **3** (*coll.*) an image, a copy. **4** a perfect example. **5** (*coll., iron.*) a striking or funny sight. **6** (*coll., esp. iron.*) a beautiful object. **7** a scene, a subject suitable for pictorial representation. **8** a motion picture, a film. **9** the image on a television screen. ~*v.t.* **1** to represent by painting. **2** to form a mental likeness of, to imagine vividly. **3** to describe vividly. **in the picture** having all the relevant information. **out of the picture** not involved in a situation. **the pictures** (*coll.*) a public showing of motion pictures, the cinema. **to get the picture** to understand the situation. **picture book** *n.* an illustrated book, esp. for children. **picture frame** *n.* a frame for displaying a picture. **picture gallery** *n.* a gallery or large room in which pictures are exhibited. **picturegoer** *n.* a person who regularly goes to the cinema. **picture hat** *n.* a lady's hat with a wide, drooping brim (as seen in Reynolds's and Gainsborough's pictures). **picture-moulding** *n.* **1** material used to make picture frames. **2** a wooden rail near the top of a wall for hanging pictures from. **picture postcard** *n.* a postcard with a picture on one side. **picture-postcard** *a.* picturesque. **picture rail** *n.* a wooden rail near the top of a wall for hanging pictures from. **picture window** *n.* a large window, usu. with a single pane, framing an attractive view.

picturesque (pikchəresk´) *a.* **1** having those qualities that characterize a good picture. **2** (of language) graphic, vivid. **picturesquely** *adv.* **picturesqueness** *n.*

piddle (pid´əl) *v.i.* (*coll.*) **1** to urinate (used by or to children). **2** to work, act, behave etc., in a trifling way; to trifle. ~*n.* **1** an act of urinating (used by or to children). **2** urine (used by or to children). **piddler** *n.* **piddling** *a.* trifling.

pidgin (pij´in) *n.* a language that is a combination of two or more languages, used esp. for trading between people of different native languages. **pidgin English** *n.* a pidgin in which one of the languages is English.

pi-dog PYE-DOG.

pie¹ (pī) *n.* a pastry case filled with meat, fruit etc. **pie chart** *n.* a pictorial representation of relative quantities, in which the quantities are represented by sectors of a circle. **piecrust** *n.* the baked pastry crust of a pie. **piecrust table** *n.* a table which has a carved edge resembling a piecrust. **pie-eater** *n.* (*Austral., sl.*) an insignificant person. **pie-eyed** *a.* (*sl.*) drunk. **pie in the sky** *n.* an unrealistic aspiration. **pieman** (-mən) *n.* (*pl.* **piemen**) a man who sells pies.

†pie² (pī) *n.* **1** a magpie. **2** a pied animal.

pie³ (pī), (*N Am.*) **pi** *n.* **1** a confused mass of printers' type. **2** a jumble, disorder, confusion.

piebald (pī´bawld) *a.* **1** (of a horse or other

animal) having patches of two different colours, usu. black and white; particoloured, mottled. **2** motley, mongrel. ~*n*. a piebald horse or other animal.

piece (pēs) *n*. **1** a distinct part of anything. **2** a detached portion, a fragment (of). **3** a division, a section. **4** a plot or enclosed portion (of land). **5** a definite quantity or portion in which commercial products are made up or sold. **6** an example, an instance. **7** an artistic or literary composition or performance, usu. short. **8** a coin. **9** (*esp. N Am., sl.*) a gun, a firearm. **10** a man at chess, draughts etc. **11** (*offensive, sl.*) a woman. **12** (*coll.*) a share of something. ~*v.t.* **1** to add pieces to, to mend, to patch. **2** to eke out. **3** to form (a theory) by putting facts together. **4** to put together so as to form a whole, to join together. **5** to join (threads) together in spinning. ~*v.i.* to come together, to fit (well or ill). **by the piece** (of wages) according to the amount of work done. **in one piece 1** not broken. **2** not damaged or hurt. **in pieces** broken. **of a piece** of the same sort, uniform. **to give someone a piece of one's mind** to criticize or reprimand someone sharply. **to go to pieces** to collapse emotionally. **to say one's piece** to express one's opinion. **to take to pieces 1** to separate (something) into its various components. **2** to criticize harshly. **piece-goods** *n.pl.* fabrics woven in standard lengths. **piecemeal** *adv*. piece by piece, part at a time. ~*a*. fragmentary. **piece of cake** *n*. something very easy. **piece of eight** *n*. (*Hist.*) a Spanish dollar of eight reals, worth about 22 p. **piece of the action** *n*. (*coll.*) active involvement. **piece of water** *n*. a small lake. **piece of work** *n*. an object produced by working. **piecer** *n*. **piece-rate** *n*. a rate of pay for piecework. **piecework** *n*. work paid for by the piece or job.

pièce de résistance (pyes də rezis'tãs) *n*. (*pl.* **pièces de résistance** (pyes)) **1** an outstanding item. **2** the main dish of a meal.

pied (pīd) *a*. particoloured, variegated, spotted. **piedness** *n*. **Pied Piper** *n*. a person who entices people to follow them, esp. to their doom. **pied wagtail** *n*. a small, British, black-and-white wagtail *Motacilla alba*.

pied-à-terre (pyädəteə') *n*. (*pl.* **pieds-à-terre** (pyädəteə')) a flat or house for occasional use, e.g. a city apartment for a country dweller.

pie-dog PYE-DOG.

pier (piə) *n*. **1** a structure projecting into the sea, used as a landing stage, promenade etc. **2** a breakwater, mole, jetty. **3** a mass of masonry supporting an arch, the superstructure of a bridge or other building, a pillar, a column. **4** a solid portion of masonry between windows etc. **5** a covered passageway leading from an airport building to aircraft. **pier glass** *n*. a large ornamental mirror, orig. placed between windows.

pierce (piəs) *v.t.* **1** to penetrate or transfix with a pointed instrument. **2** (of a pointed instrument) to penetrate, to transfix, to prick. **3** to make a

hole in. **4** to make (a hole). **5** to affect or penetrate keenly. **6** to force a way into, to explore. **7** (of light) to shine through. **8** (of sound) to break (a silence etc.). ~*v.i.* to penetrate (into, through etc.). **pierceable** *a*. **piercer** *n*. **piercing** *a*. **1** penetrating. **2** affecting deeply. **piercingly** *adv*. **piercingness** *n*.

pierrot (pyer'ō, piə'-) *n*. a buffoon or itinerant minstrel, orig. French and usu. dressed in loose white costume with the face whitened. **pierrette** (-ret') *n*. a female pierrot.

pietà (piātah') *n*. a pictorial or sculptured representation of the Virgin Mary and the dead Christ.

pietist (pī'ətist) *n*. a person who makes a display of strong religious feelings. **pietism** *n*. **pietistic** (-tis'-), **pietistical** *a*.

piety (pī'əti) *n*. (*pl.* **pieties**) **1** the quality of being pious. **2** an act of piety.

piezoelectricity (pīēzōilektris'iti), **piezoelectric effect** (-lek'-) *n*. a property possessed by some crystals, e.g. those used in gramophone crystal pick-ups, of generating surface electric charges when mechanically strained. **piezoelectric** *a*. **piezoelectrically** *adv*.

piezometer (pīizom'itə) *n*. an instrument for determining the compressibility of liquids or other forms of pressure.

piffle (pif'əl) *n*. (*coll.*) trash, rubbish, twaddle. ~*v.i.* to talk or act in a feeble, ineffective or trifling way. **piffler** *n*. **piffling** *a*. small or unimportant.

pig (pig) *n*. **1** any ungulate, omnivorous mammal of the family Suidae, esp. the domesticated variety, *Sus scrofa*. **2** (*N Am.*) a piglet. **3** any similar animal, such as a guinea pig. **4** the flesh of the pig, pork. **5** (*coll.*) a greedy, gluttonous, filthy, obstinate, or annoying person. **6** (*coll.*) a very difficult or unpleasant thing. **7** (*sl., offensive*) a police officer. **8** (*sl.*) an oblong mass of metal (esp. iron or lead) as run from the furnace. ~*v.i.* (*pres.p.* **pigging**, *past, p.p.* **pigged**) **1** to give birth to piglets. **2** to be huddled together like pigs. ~*v.t.* (*past, p.p.* **pigged**) **1** to give birth to (piglets). **2** to overindulge oneself in (food). **in pig** (of a sow) pregnant. **to make a pig of oneself** to eat too much. **to make a pig's ear of** (*sl.*) to make a mess of, to botch. **to pig it** to live in squalor. **to pig out** (*esp. N Am., sl.*) to make a pig of oneself. **piggery** *n*. (*pl.* **piggeries**) **1** a pig farm. **2** a pigsty. **3** piggishness. **piggie** *n*. a piggy. **piggish** *a*. **1** of or relating to pigs. **2** like a pig, esp. in greed. **piggishly** *adv*. **piggishness** *n*. **piggy** *n*. (*pl.* **piggies**) (*coll.*) **1** a little pig. **2** a pig (used by or to a child). **3** a toe (used by or to children). **4** the game of tipcat. ~*a*. (*comp.* **piggier**, *superl.* **piggiest**) like a pig. **piggy bank** *n*. a bank in the shape of a pig. **piggy in the middle** *n*. pig in the middle. **pig-headed** *a*. stupidly obstinate or perverse. **pig-headedly** *adv*. **pig-headedness** *n*. **pig-ignorant** *a*. (*coll.*) very ignorant. **pig in a poke** *n*. goods purchased without being seen beforehand.

pig in the middle *n.* a person who is unwillingly involved in a dispute between two other parties. **pig-iron** *n.* crude iron from a furnace. **pig-jump** *v.i.* (*Austral., sl.*) (of a horse) to jump with all four legs without bringing them together. ~*n.* a jump made in this way. **piglet** (-lit) *n.* **piglike** *a.* **pigling** *n.* a piglet. **pig meat** *n.* pork, ham or bacon. **pig-nut** *n.* an earth-nut. **pigpen** *n.* (*N Am.*) a pigsty. **pigskin** *n.* 1 the skin of a pig. 2 leather made from this. 3 (*N Am.*) a football. 4 (*sl.*) a saddle. ~*a.* made of pigskin. **pig's swill, pigswill** (-swil) *n.* refuse from kitchens, etc., for feeding pigs. **pigsticking** *n.* 1 the sport of hunting wild boars with a spear. 2 pig-killing. **pig-sticker** *n.* **pigsty** *n.* (*pl.* **pigsties**) 1 an enclosure where pigs are kept. 2 a dirty place, a hovel. **pigtail** *n.* 1 a plait of hair. 2 tobacco prepared in a long twist. 3 the tail of a pig. **pigtailed** *a.* **pigweed** *n.* the goosefoot or other herb eaten by pigs.

pigeon[1] (pij´ən) *n.* 1 any grey-and-white bird of the family Columbidae, esp. *Columbia livia*; a dove. 2 (*sl.*) a gullible person, a simpleton. **pigeon-breast, pigeon-chest** *n.* a deformity in which the human breast is constricted and the sternum thrust forward. **pigeon-breasted, pigeon-chested** *a.* **pigeon fancier** *n.* a person who keeps pigeons as a hobby. **pigeon-fancying** *n.* **pigeon-hawk** *n.* a merlin. **pigeon-hearted** *a.* timid, easily frightened. **pigeon-hole** *n.* 1 a compartment in a cabinet etc., for papers, etc. 2 a nesting compartment for pigeons. 3 a category, esp. an oversimplified one. ~*v.t.* 1 to give a definite place to in the mind, to label, to classify. 2 to defer for future consideration, to shelve. 3 to put away in a pigeon-hole. **pigeon pair** *n.* 1 twins consisting of one boy and one girl. 2 the children of a family consisting of one boy and one girl. **pigeonry** *n.* (*pl.* **pigeonries**). **pigeon-toed** *a.* (of a person) having the toes turned in.

pigeon[2] (pij´in) *n.* 1 a pidgin. 2 (*coll.*) someone's business or concern. **not my pigeon** (*coll.*) not my business, not my concern.

piggery PIG.

piggyback (pig´ibak), **pickaback** (pik´əbak) *adv.* 1 on the back or shoulders, like a pack. 2 on the back or top of something larger. ~*v.i.* to ride piggyback. ~*v.t.* 1 to carry (a person) piggyback. 2 to carry or mount on top of something. ~*n.* an act of carrying a person piggyback.

pigment (pig´mənt) *n.* 1 colouring matter used as paint or dye. 2 a substance giving colour to animal or vegetable tissues. **pigmental** (-men´-), **pigmentary** (pig´-) *a.* **pigmentation** (-tā´shən) *n.*

pigmy PYGMY.

pi jaw (pī jaw´) *n.* a long, moralizing lecture.

pika (pī´kə) *n.* (*pl.* **pikas**) a small burrowing mammal of the genus *Ochotona*, related to the rabbit, a native of Asia and N America.

pike[1] (pīk) *n.* 1 a large slender voracious freshwater fish of the family Esocidae, with a long pointed snout. 2 a similar fish, such as the garpike. 3 (*Hist.*) a military weapon, consisting of

a narrow, elongated lance-head fixed to a pole. 4 a pickaxe, a spike. 5 a peak, a peaked or pointed hill, esp. in the English Lake District. 6 a diving position in which the legs are straight and the hips bent, and the hands clasp the feet or knees. **to pike on** (*esp. Austral., coll.*) to back out of, to withdraw timidly from. **pikeperch** *n.* (*pl.* **pikeperch**) any of various perches of the genus *Lucioperca* or *Stizostedion*, which resemble pike. **pikestaff** *n.* 1 (*Hist.*) the wooden shaft of a pike. 2 a pointed stick carried by pilgrims etc. **plain as a pikestaff** perfectly clear or obvious.

pike[2] (pīk) *n.* 1 a toll gate. 2 a turnpike road. **to come down the pike** (*N Am.*) to come to attention, to arrive.

pikelet (pīk´lit) *n.* (*North.*) a round, thin crumpet.

pilaf (pilaf´), **pilaff, pilau** (-low´), **pilaw** (-law´), **pillau** (-low´) *n.* a Middle Eastern or Indian mixed dish consisting of rice boiled with meat, poultry, or fish, together with raisins, spices etc.

pilaster (pilas´tə) *n.* (*Archit.*) a rectangular column projecting from a wall or pier. **pilastered** *a.*

pilchard (pil´chəd) *n.* a small sea fish, *Sardinia pilchardus*, allied to the herring, and an important food fish.

pile[1] (pīl) *n.* 1 a heap, a mass of things heaped together. 2 a funeral pyre, a heap of combustibles for burning a dead body. 3 a very large, massive or lofty building or a group of such buildings. 4 an accumulation. 5 (*coll.*) a great quantity or sum. 6 a series of plates of different metals arranged alternately so as to produce an electrical current. 7 an atomic pile. ~*v.t.* 1 to collect or heap up or together, to accumulate. 2 to load. 3 to stack (rifles) with butts on the ground and muzzles together. ~*v.i.* to move in a crowd. **to pile it on** (*coll.*) to exaggerate. **to pile up** 1 to accumulate. 2 to cause to be involved in a pile-up. **pile-up** *n.* (*coll.*) a crash involving several vehicles.

pile[2] (pīl) *n.* 1 a heavy timber driven into the ground, esp. under water, to form a foundation. 2 a sharp stake or post. ~*v.t.* 1 to furnish or strengthen with piles. 2 to drive piles into. **piledriver** *n.* a machine for driving piles into the ground. **piledriving** *n., a.* **pile dwelling** *n.* a dwelling built on piles.

pile[3] (pīl) *n.* 1 the nap of velvet, plush or other cloth, or of a carpet. 2 soft hair, fur, down, wool. **pileless** *a.*

piles (pīlz) *n.pl.* (*coll.*) haemorrhoids. **pilewort** *n.* the lesser celandine or figwort, supposed to be a remedy for piles.

pileus (pī´liəs) *n.* (*pl.* **pilei** (-liī)) the cap of a mushroom. **pileate** (-liət), **pileated** (-liātid) *a.* **pileated woodpecker** *n.* a large N American woodpecker, *Dryocopus pileatus*, having a red head.

pilfer (pil´fə) *v.t., v.i.* to steal in small quantities. **pilferage** (-rij) *n.* **pilferer** *n.* **pilfering** *n.* **pilferingly** *adv.*

pilgrim (pil´grim) *n.* **1** a person who travels a distance to visit some holy place for religious reasons. **2** a person journeying through life. **3** a traveller, a wanderer. **pilgrimage** (-mij) *n.* **1** a pilgrim's journey to some holy place. **2** the journey of human life. **3** any journey to a place of special significance. ~*v.i.* to go on a pilgrimage. **Pilgrim Fathers** *n.pl.* the English Puritan colonists who sailed to N America, and founded Plymouth, Massachusetts in 1620. **pilgrimize, pilgrimise** *v.i.*

pill (pil) *n.* **1** a little ball of some medicinal substance to be swallowed whole. **2** something unpleasant which has to be accepted or put up with. **3** (*coll.*) a ball. **the pill** (*coll.*) the contraceptive pill. **to gild/ sugar/ sweeten the pill** to make something unpleasant more acceptable. **pillbox** *n.* **1** a small box for holding pills. **2** a small round brimless hat worn by women. **3** (*Mil.*) a concrete blockhouse, used as a machine-gun emplacement or for other defensive purposes. **pill-popper** *n.* (*coll.*) **1** a person who takes a lot of pills. **2** a drug addict. **pill-popping** *n., a.* **pillwort** *n.* an aquatic plant of the genus *Pilularia globulifera*, with spore-producing globular bracts.

pillage (pil´ij) *n.* **1** the act of plundering. **2** plunder, esp. the property of enemies taken in war. ~*v.t.* **1** to strip of money or goods by open force. **2** to lay waste. ~*v.i.* to rob, to ravage, to plunder. **pillager** *n.*

pillar (pil´ə) *n.* **1** an upright structure of masonry, iron, timber etc., of considerable height in proportion to thickness, used for support, ornament or as a memorial; a column, a post, a pedestal. **2** an upright mass of anything analogous in form or function. **3** a mass of coal, stone etc., left to support the roof in a mine or quarry. **4** a person or group of people acting as chief support of an institution, movement etc. **from pillar to post 1** from one place to another. **2** from one difficult situation to another. **pillar box** *n.* a short hollow pillar in which letters may be placed for collection by the post office. **pillar-box red** *n., a.* vivid red (the colour of a pillar box). **pillared** *a.*

pillion (pil´yən) *n.* a passenger seat on a motorcycle. ~*a., adv.* (riding) on a pillion.

pillock (pil´ək) *n.* (*sl.*) a stupid person.

pillory (pil´əri) *n.* (*pl.* **pillories**) (*Hist.*) a wooden frame supported on a pillar and with holes through which the head and hands of a person were put, so as to expose them to public derision. ~*v.t.* (*3rd pers. sing. pres.* **pillories**, *pres.p.* **pillorying**, *past, p.p.* **pilloried**) **1** to hold up to ridicule. **2** (*Hist.*) to put in the pillory.

pillow (pil´ō) *n.* **1** a cushion filled with feathers or other soft material, used as a rest for the head of a person lying down, esp. in bed. **2** a block used as a cushion or support on a machine. **3** anything resembling a pillow in form or function. **4** a lace-pillow. ~*v.t.* **1** to lay or rest on

or as if on a pillow. **2** to prop up with a pillow. **pillowcase** *n.* a washable cover of linen etc., for a pillow. **pillow-fight** *n.* a game in which the participants strike each other with pillows. **pillow lace** *n.* lace made on a lace-pillow. **pillow lava** *n.* lava in pillow-shaped masses. **pillowslip** *n.* a pillowcase. **pillow talk** *n.* intimate conversation in bed. **pillowy** *a.*

pilose (pī´lōs), **pilous** (-ləs) *a.* covered with or consisting of hairs. **pilosity** (-los´-) *n.*

pilot (pī´lət) *n.* **1** a person directing the course of an aeroplane, spacecraft etc. **2** a person qualified to conduct ships into or out of harbour or along particular coasts, channels etc. **3** a radio or TV programme made to test its suitability to be extended into a series. **4** a guide or director, esp. in difficult or dangerous circumstances. ~*a.* serving as a preliminary test or trial. ~*v.t.* **1** to act as pilot on or direct the course of (esp. a ship, aircraft etc.). **2** to introduce or test (a new scheme etc.). **pilotage** (-tij) *n.* **pilot balloon** *n.* a small, hydrogen-filled balloon sent up to obtain the direction and velocity of the upper winds. **pilot-bird** *n.* a sweet-toned Australian scrub bird, *Pycnoptilus floccosus.* **pilot chute** *n.* a small parachute which brings the main parachute into operation. **pilot fish** *n.* a small sea fish, *Naucrates ductor*, said to act as a guide to sharks. **pilot house** *n.* a wheelhouse. **pilot-jacket** *n.* a pea-jacket. **pilotless** *a.* **pilot light** *n.* **1** a small jet of gas kept burning in order to light a boiler etc. **2** a small light on the dial of a radio etc. that goes on when the current is switched on. **pilot officer** *n.* a junior commissioned rank in the RAF corresponding to second lieutenant in the Army. **pilot whale** *n.* a small whale of the genus *Globicephalus.*

Pilsner (pilz´nə), **Pilsener** *n.* a pale beer with a strong flavour of hops.

pilule (pil´ūl) *n.* a pill, esp. a small pill. **pilular, pilulous** *a.*

pimento (pimen´tō) *n.* (*pl.* **pimentos**) **1** a pimiento. **2** (*esp. W Ind.*) allspice.

pimiento (pimien´tō) *n.* (*pl.* **pimientos**) a red pepper.

pimp (pimp) *n.* a man who finds customers for a prostitute or lives from her earnings. ~*v.i.* to act as a pimp.

pimpernel (pim´pənel) *n.* any plant of the genus *Anagallis*, esp. the scarlet pimpernel.

pimple (pim´pəl) *n.* **1** a small pustule, or inflamed swelling on the skin. **2** anything resembling a pimple. **pimpled** *a.* **pimply** *a.* (*comp.* **pimplier**, *superl.* **pimpliest**).

PIN (pin), **PIN number** *n.* a personal identification number.

pin (pin) *n.* **1** a short, slender, pointed piece of metal, wood etc., used for fastening parts of clothing, papers etc., together. **2** a peg or bolt of metal or wood used for various purposes, such as the bolt of a lock, a thole, a peg to which the strings of a musical instrument are fastened, a hairpin, a ninepin etc. **3** an ornamental device with a pin used as a fastening etc., or as a decoration. **4** a badge pinned to clothing. **5** anything of slight value. **6** (*pl.*, *coll.*) legs. **7** (*Med.*) a metal rod for joining together the ends of fractured bones while healing. **8** in golf, a small flagpole marking the position of the hole. **9** a keg or small cask. ~*v.t.* (*pres.p.* **pinning**, *past*, *p.p.* **pinned**) **1** to fasten (to, on, up etc.) with or as if with a pin. **2** to pierce, to transfix. **3** to place (the blame) (on). **4** to seize, to make fast, to secure. **on pins and needles** in a state of nervousness. **to pin down 1** to bind to a promise or obligation. **2** to force (someone) to make a decision. **3** to restrict the movements of. **4** to try to discover the identity or location of. **5** to hold down by force. **to pin one's faith on** to place full reliance on. **to pin one's hopes on** to pin one's faith on. **pinball** *n.* a game played on a machine with a sloping board on which a ball moves, propelled by flippers, striking targets and thus accumulating points. **pincushion** *n.* a small cushion for sticking pins into. **pin-down** *n.* the act of keeping children in care in solitary confinement for a long period of time. **pinhead** *n.* **1** the head of a pin. **2** a very small object. **3** (*coll.*) a very stupid person. **pinheaded** *a.* (*coll.*) very stupid. **pinheadedness** *n.* **pinhole** *n.* **1** a very small aperture. **2** a hole into which a pin or peg fits. **pinhole camera** *n.* a camera with a pinhole instead of a lens. **pin money** *n.* **1** (*Hist.*) an allowance of money for dress or other private expenses. **2** money earned or saved, esp. by a woman, for personal expenditure. **pinpoint** *n.* **1** the point of a pin. **2** anything sharp or painful. ~*v.t.* to locate accurately and precisely. ~*a.* **1** very small. **2** accurate and precise. **pinprick** *n.* **1** a prick or minute puncture with or as if with a pin. **2** a petty annoyance. **pins and needles** *n.pl.* a tingling sensation when a limb has been immobile for a long time. **pinstripe** *n.* **1** (a cloth with) a very narrow stripe. **2** (*sing. or pl.*) a pinstripe suit. ~*a.* made of pinstripe. **pinstriped** *a.* **pin-table** *n.* a table for playing pinball. **pintail** *n.* **1** a duck, esp. *Anas acuta*, with a pointed tail. **2** a grouse with a pointed tail. **pin-tuck** *n.* a narrow ornamental tuck on a shirt or dress. **pin-up** *n.* **1** a poster of an attractive person, often scantily clothed. **2** an attractive person who appears on posters. **pinwheel** *n.* **1** a small Catherine wheel. **2** a wheel with pins set in the face instead of cogs in the rim. ~*v.i.* to rotate like a pinwheel. **pinworm** *n.* a small threadworm, *Enterobius vermicularis*.

☒ **pinacle** common misspelling of PINNACLE.

pina colada (pēnə kəlah'də) *n.* a cocktail made from rum, pineapple juice and coconut juice.

pinafore (pin'əfaw) *n.* **1** an apron or sleeveless overall worn to protect the front of clothes. **2** a pinafore dress. **pinafored** *a.* **pinafore dress** *n.* a sleeveless dress worn over a blouse or sweater.

pince-nez (pansnā') *n.* (*pl.* **pince-nez**) a pair of armless eyeglasses held in place by a spring clipping the nose.

pincers (pin'səz) *n.pl.* **1** (*also* **pair of pincers**) a tool with two limbs working on a pivot as levers to a pair of jaws, for gripping, crushing, extracting nails etc. **2** a nipping or grasping organ, as in crustaceans. **pincer movement** *n.* (*Mil.*) a military manoeuvre in which one army encloses another on two sides at once.

pinch (pinch) *v.t.* **1** to nip or squeeze, to press so as to cause pain or inconvenience. **2** to take off or remove by nipping or squeezing. **3** to afflict, to distress, esp. with cold, hunger etc. **4** to straiten, to stint. **5** (*coll.*) to steal. **6** (*sl.*) to arrest, to take into custody. ~*v.i.* **1** to nip or squeeze anything. **2** to be niggardly. **3** to be straitened. **4** to cavil. ~*n.* **1** a sharp nip or squeeze, as with the ends of the fingers. **2** as much as can be taken up between the finger and thumb. **3** a pain, a pang. **4** distress, straits, a dilemma, stress, pressure. **5** (*sl.*) **a** an arrest. **b** a theft. **at a pinch** in an urgent case, if hard pressed. **to feel the pinch** to be affected by a lack of money. **pinched** *a.* thin and pale, esp. because of illness. **pinch-hitter** *n.* **1** a baseball player who bats as a substitute for another. **2** (*N Am.*) a substitute. **pinch-hit** *v.i.* (*pres.p.* **pinchhitting**, *past*, *p.p.* **pinch-hit**). **pinchingly** *adv.* **pinchpenny** *n.* (*pl.* **pinchpennies**) a miser. ~*a.* miserly. **pinch-run** *v.i.* (*pres.p.* **pinch-running**, *past*, *p.p.* **pinch-run**) in baseball, to run as a substitute for another, esp. at an important point in the game. **pinch-runner** *n.*

pinchbeck (pinch'bek) *n.* an alloy of copper, zinc, etc., formerly used for cheap jewellery. ~*a.* **1** specious, spurious. **2** cheap in quality.

pine[1] (pīn) *n.* **1** (*also* **pine tree**) any tree of the coniferous genus *Pinus*, consisting of evergreen trees with needle-shaped leaves. **2** the timber from a pine tree. **3** a pineapple. ~*a.* of pines or pine timber. **pineapple** *n.* **1** a tropical plant, *Ananas comosus*. **2** the large multiple fruit of the pineapple, having sweet, yellow flesh and a tough, brownish skin. **pine cone** *n.* the cone-shaped fruit of the pine tree. **pine marten** *n.* a European marten, *Martes martes*, having a dark brown coat and a yellowish throat. **pine needle** *n.* the needle-shaped leaf of the pine tree. **pine nut** *n.* the edible seed of some pine trees. **pinery** *n.* (*pl.* **pineries**). **pinewood** *n.* the timber of pine trees. **piny** (pī'ni), **piney** *a.* (*comp.* **pinier**, *superl.* **piniest**).

pine[2] (pīn) *v.i.* **1** to languish, waste away. **2** to long or yearn (for, after or to).

pineal (pin'iəl, pī'niəl) *a.* shaped like a pine cone. **pineal body** *n.* (*Anat.*) a dark grey conical structure situated behind the third ventricle of the brain which secretes melatonin into the bloodstream. **pineal gland** *n.* the pineal body.

ping (ping) *n.* a sharp ringing sound, like the sound of a bullet flying through the air. ~*v.i.* **1** to make such a sound. **2** (*N Am.*) (of an internal-combustion engine) to pink. ~v.t. to cause to make a pinging sound. **pinger** n.

ping-pong (ping'pong) n. table tennis.

pinguid (ping'gwid) a. (formal or facet.) fat, oily, greasy, unctuous.

pinion[1] (pin'yən) n. **1** the joint of a bird's wing remotest from the body. **2** (poet.) a wing. **3** a wing feather. ~v.t. **1** to cut off the pinion of to prevent flight. **2** to shackle, to fetter the arms of. **3** to bind fast (to).

pinion[2] (pin'yən) n. **1** the smaller of two cogwheels in gear with each other. **2** a cogged spindle engaging with a wheel.

pink[1] (pingk) n. **1** a pale rose colour or pale red slightly inclining towards purple. **2** any plant or flower of the genus Dianthus, largely cultivated in gardens. **3** any of several allied or similar plants, such as moss pink. **4** the supreme excellence, the very height (of). **5** a fox-hunter's scarlet coat or the cloth used to make one. **6** a fox-hunter. **7** (coll., often derog.) a moderately left-wing person. ~a. **1** pale red or rose. **2** (coll., often derog.) moderately left-wing. **3** (of wine) rosé. **in the pink** in fine condition. **pink-collar** a. (of an occupation) traditionally associated with women. **pink disease** n. a disease affecting young children in which the extremities turn pink. **pink elephants** n.pl. (coll.) hallucinations induced by intoxication with alcohol. **pink-eye** n. **1** a contagious influenza among horses, cattle and sheep, characterized by inflammation of the conjunctiva. **2** a form of conjunctivitis in humans. **pink gin** n. gin mixed with Angostura Bitters. **pinkish** a. **pinkly** adv. **pinkness** n. **pink noise** n. recordings of mid-to-low-frequency background noise, designed to be soothing to young babies. **pinko** n. (pl. **pinkos, pinkoes**) (esp. N Am., sl., usu. derog.) a person with (moderately) left-wing views. **pink slip** n. (esp. N Am.) a note given to an employee, terminating employment. **pinky** a. **pinkiness** n.

pink[2] (pingk) v.t. **1** to pierce, to stab. **2** to make a punched pattern in leather etc. for ornament. **3** to decorate in this manner. **pinking** n. **pinking shears, pinking scissors** n.pl. a pair of shears with zigzag cutting edges, used to cut cloth to prevent fraying.

pink[3] (pingk) v.i. (of an internal-combustion engine) to detonate prematurely, making a series of popping sounds.

pinkie (ping'ki), **pinky** n. (pl. **pinkies**) (esp. N Am., Sc., coll.) the little finger.

pinna (pin'ə) n. (pl. **pinnae** (-nē), **pinnas**) **1** the projecting upper part of the external ear. **2** (pl.) a leaflet of a pinnate leaf. **3** a wing, a fin, or an analogous structure.

pinnace (pin'is) n. (Naut.) a man-of-war's boat with six or eight oars.

pinnacle (pin'əkəl) n. **1** the apex, the culmination (of). **2** a pointed summit. **3** a turret, usu. pointed or tapering, placed as an ornament on the top of a buttress etc., or as a termination on

an angle or gable. ~v.t. **1** to set on or as if on a pinnacle. **2** to surmount as a pinnacle. **3** to furnish with pinnacles.

pinnate (pin'āt), **pennate** (pen'-), **pinnated** (-ātid), **pennated** a. **1** (Bot.) having leaflets arranged featherwise along the stem. **2** (Zool.) having lateral processes along an axis. **pinnately** adv. **pinnatifid** (-nat'ifid) a. (Bot.) divided into lobes nearly to the midrib. **pinnation** (-ā'shən) n.

pinni- (pin'i) comb. form a wing, a fin.

pinniped (pin'iped) a. having feet like fins. ~n. any member of a group of pinniped marine carnivores containing the seals, sea lions and walruses.

pinnule (pin'ūl) n. **1** (Bot.) any one of the smaller or ultimate divisions of a pinnate leaf. **2** (Zool.) a small fin, wing, barb of a feather etc. **pinnular** a.

pinny (pin'i) n. (pl. **pinnies**) (coll.) a pinafore, an apron.

pinochle (pē'nokəl), **penuchle** (-nŭkəl), **pinocle** n. **1** a card game similar to bezique, played with a 48-card pack by two or four players. **2** in pinochle, the combination of queen of spades and jack of diamonds.

piñon (pinyon'), **pinyon** n. **1** any of various low-growing pines of the west of N America, esp. Pinus edulis. **2** the edible seed of the piñon.

pint (pīnt) n. **1** a measure of capacity, the eighth part of a gallon (0.568 l). **2** (coll.) a pint of beer, milk etc. **3** the amount of shellfish contained in a pint mug. **pinta** (pīn'tə) n. (dated, coll.) a pint of milk. **pint pot** n. a vessel, esp. made of pewter, for holding a pint of beer. **pint-sized** a. (coll.) small.

pintle (pin'təl) n. a pin or bolt, esp. one used as a pivot.

pinto (pin'tō) a. (N Am.) piebald. ~n. (pl. **pintos**) a horse or pony with patches of white and another colour.

piny PINE[1].

Pinyin (pinyin') n. a system of romanized spelling used to transliterate Chinese characters.

pinyon PIÑON.

piolet (pyōlā') n. a climber's ice axe.

pion (pī'on) n. (pl. **pions**) (Physics) a meson with positive or negative or no charge, chiefly responsible for nuclear force. **pionic** (pīon'ik) a.

pioneer (pīəniə') n. **1** an early leader or developer of an enterprise. **2** an explorer. **3** (Mil.) a member of a body of soldiers whose duty it is to clear and repair roads, bridges etc., for troops on the march. ~v.t. **1** to initiate or develop (a new enterprise). **2** to act as pioneer to. **3** to lead, to conduct. ~v.i. to act as a pioneer.

pious (pī'əs) a. **1** reverencing God, religious, devout. **2** sanctimonious. **3** dutiful. **pious fraud** n. a deception in the interests of religion or of the person deceived. **piously** adv.

pip[1] (pip) n. the seed of an apple, orange etc. ~v.t. (pres.p. **pipping**, past, p.p. **pipped**) to remove the pips from (fruit). **pipless** a.

pip[2] (pip) n. a short, high-pitched sound.

pip³ (pip) *n.* **1** a spot on a playing card, domino, dice etc. **2** a star on an army officer's uniform indicating rank. **3** an image of an object on a radar screen.

pip⁴ (pip) *n.* **1** a disease in poultry etc., causing a secretion of thick mucus in the throat. **2** (*coll.*) a fit of bad temper. **3** (*facet.*) any of various human disorders.

pip⁵ (pip) *v.t.* (*pres.p.* **pipping**, *past*, *p.p.* **pipped**) (*coll.*) **1** to hit with a shot. **2** to beat, to get the better of. **3** to blackball. **to pip at the post** to beat, outdo etc. at the last moment, e.g. in a race or contest. **to pip out** to die. **to pip to the post** to pip at the post.

pipal PEEPUL.

pipe (pīp) *n.* **1** a long hollow tube or line of tubes, esp. for conveying liquids, gas etc. **2** a wind instrument consisting of a tube. **3** (*Mus.*) a tube producing a note of a particular tone in an organ. **4** (*pl.*) bagpipes. **5** (*pl.*) pan pipes. **6** a boatswain's whistle. **7** a signal on a boatswain's whistle. **8** a tubular organ, vessel, passage etc., in an animal body. **9** (*usu. pl.*) the windpipe. **10** a shrill note or cry of a bird etc. **11** a tube with a bowl for smoking tobacco. **12** a pipeful (of tobacco). **13 a** a large cask for wine. **b** this used as a measure of capacity, usu. 150 gall. (682 l). *~v.t.* **1** to play or execute on a pipe. **2** to whistle. **3** to utter in a shrill tone. **4** to lead or bring (along or to) by playing or whistling on a pipe. **5** to call or direct by a boatswain's pipe or whistle. **6** to furnish with pipes. **7** to trim or decorate with piping. **8** to convey or transmit along a pipe or wire. *~v.i.* **1** to play on a pipe. **2** to whistle, to make a shrill, high-pitched sound. **put that in your pipe and smoke it** (*coll.*) accept that unwelcome fact. **to pipe down 1** (*coll.*) to stop talking. **2** (*Naut.*) to dismiss from duty. **to pipe up 1** to begin to sing, to sing the first notes of. **2** (*coll.*) to begin to speak. **pipe band** *n.* a band consisting of pipers, drummers and a drum major. **pipeclay** *n.* a fine, white, plastic clay used for making tobacco pipes, and for cleaning military accoutrements etc. *~v.t.* **1** to whiten with pipeclay. **2** to put in order. **pipe-cleaner** *n.* a piece of twisted wire covered in fine yarn, used for cleaning tobacco pipes. **piped music** *n.* music recorded for playing in shops, restaurants etc. as background music. **pipe dream** *n.* a fantastic notion, an unrealistic hope. **pipefish** *n.* (*pl. in general* **pipefish**, *in particular* **pipefishes**) any fish of the family Syngnathidae, having an elongated snout. **pipeful** *n.* (*pl.* **pipefuls**). **pipeless** *a.* **pipeline** *n.* **1** a long pipe or conduit laid down from an oil well, or oil region, to convey the petroleum to a port etc. **2** a channel of communication. **in the pipeline** under preparation, soon to be supplied, produced etc. **pipe major** *n.* a non-commissioned officer in charge of pipers. **pipe of peace** *n.* a peace pipe. **pipe organ** *n.* (*Mus.*) an organ which uses pipes as well as reeds. **piper** *n.* a person who plays upon a pipe, esp. a strolling player or

a performer on the bagpipes. **pipe-rack** *n.* a stand for tobacco pipes. **pipe-stem** *n.* the tube of a tobacco pipe. **pipework** *n.* pipes collectively. **pipy** (pī'pi) *a.* (*comp.* **pipier**, *superl.* **pipiest**).

piperidine (piper'idēn) *n.* (*Chem.*) a liquid which smells like pepper, formed by the reduction of pyridine.

pipette (pipet') *n.* a fine tube for removing quantities of a fluid, esp. in chemical investigations. *~v.t.* to transfer or measure with a pipette.

piping (pī'ping) *n.* **1** the act of playing the pipes. **2** a shrill whistling or wailing sound, a fluting. **3** a covered cord for trimming dresses. **4** a cordlike decoration of icing, cream etc., on a cake or other dish. **5** a quantity, series or system of pipes. *~a.* **1** shrill, whistling. **2** playing upon a pipe. **piping hot** *a.* very hot.

pipistrelle (pipistrel') *n.* any small, reddish-brown bat of the genus *Pipistrellus*, the commonest British bat.

pipit (pip'it) *n.* any larklike bird of the genus *Anthus*.

pipkin (pip'kin) *n.* a small earthenware pot, pan or jar.

pippin (pip'in) *n.* **1** any of several varieties of apple. **2** (*coll.*) an outstanding person or thing.

pipsqueak (pip'skwēk) *n.* (*coll.*) a small, contemptible or insignificant person.

piquant (pē'kənt) *a.* **1** having an agreeably sharp, pungent taste. **2** interesting, stimulating, lively, sparkling. **piquancy** *n.* **piquantly** *adv.*

pique (pēk) *v.t.* (*pres.p.* **piquing**, *past, p.p.* **piqued**) **1** to irritate. **2** to touch the envy, jealousy or pride of. **3** to stimulate or excite (curiosity etc.). **4** to plume or congratulate (oneself on). *~n.* ill feeling, irritation, resentment.

piqué (pē'kā) *n.* a heavy cotton fabric with a corded surface, quilting.

piquet¹ (piket') *n.* a game of cards for two persons, with a pack of cards from which all below the seven have been withdrawn.

piquet² PICKET.

piracy PIRATE.

piranha (pirah'nə), **piraya** (-yə) *n.* a small, voracious, flesh-eating S American tropical fish, of the genus *Serrasalmus* which can attack and wound people and large animals.

pirate (pī'rət) *n.* **1** a robber on the high seas, a marauder. **2** a pirates' ship. **3** a person who infringes the copyright of another. **4** an unauthorized radio station. *~a.* denoting an unauthorized radio station, video copy etc. *~v.t.* **1** to publish (literary or other matter belonging to others) without permission or compensation. **2** to plunder. **piracy** (pī'rəsi) *n.* (*pl.* **piracies**) **1** the crime of a pirate, robbery on the high seas. **2** any similar illegal practice, such as hijacking. **3** unauthorized publication, infringement of copyright. **piratic** (-rat'-), **piratical** *a.* **piratically** *adv.*

piripiri (pir'ipiri) *n.* (*pl.* **piripiris**) (*New Zeal.*) a plant of the rose family, *Acaena anserinifolia*, having prickly burs.

pirouette (piruet´) *n.* a rapid whirling round on the point of one foot, in dancing. ~*v.i.* to dance or perform a pirouette.

piscatory (pis´kətəri) *a.* of or relating to fishers or fishing. **piscatorial** (-taw´ri-) *a.* **piscatorially** *adv.*

Pisces (pī´sēz) *n.* (*pl.* **Pisces**) **1** (*Astron.*) a large constellation representing two fishes joined by their tails. **2** (*Astrol.*) **a** the Fishes, the 12th sign of the zodiac. **b** a person born under the sign of Pisces. **Piscean** (-siən) *a.*

pisciculture (pis´ikŭlchə) *n.* the artificial breeding, rearing and preserving of fish. **piscicultural** (-kŭl´-) *a.* **pisciculturist** (-kŭl´-) *n.*

piscina (pisē´nə) *n.* (*pl.* **piscinae** (-nē), **piscinas**) **1** a stone basin with outlet beside the altar in some churches to receive the water used in purifying the chalice etc. **2** a fish pond. **piscinal** (pis´inəl) *a.*

piscine (pis´īn) *a.* of or relating to fish.

piscivorous (pisiv´ərəs) *a.* living on fish.

piss (pis) *v.i.* (*taboo sl.*) to urinate. ~*v.t.* **1** to discharge in the urine. **2** to wet with urine. ~*n.* **1** urine. **2** the act of urinating. **to piss about** to waste time in foolish behaviour. **to piss down** (*sl.*) to rain heavily. **to piss in the wind** to do something futile or detrimental to oneself. **to piss off 1** to go away. **2** to annoy, to bore, to make discontented. **to piss on** to treat with deep contempt, to humiliate. **to piss oneself 1** to urinate in one's clothes. **2** to laugh uncontrollably. **3** to be frightened, nervous. **to take the piss out of** to tease, to make fun of. **piss artist** *n.* **1** a habitual heavy drinker, a drunk. **2** a foolish or incompetent person. **3** a person who exaggerates or is insincere. **pissed** *a.* **1** drunk. **2** (*N Am.*) annoyed. **pissed off** *a.* annoyed. **pisspot** *n.* a chamber pot. **piss-take** *n.* the act of making fun of someone. **piss-taker** *n.* **piss-taking** *n.* **piss-up** *n.* a bout of drinking.

pissoir (pēs´wah) *n.* a public urinal.

pistachio (pistah´shiō) *n.* **1** an Asian tree, *Pistacia vera*, having a reddish fruit with an edible pale greenish kernel. **2** (*also* **pistachio nut**) the edible pale greenish kernel of the fruit of the pistachio. **3** a pale green colour.

piste (pēst) *n.* a slope prepared for skiing. **pisteur** (-tœ´) *n.* a person who prepares the snow on a skiing piste.

pistil (pis´til) *n.* (*Bot.*) the female organ in flowering plants, comprising the ovary and stigma, usu. with a style supporting the latter.

pistol (pis´təl) *n.* **1** a small firearm for use with one hand. **2** something shaped like a pistol. **pistol grip** *n.* a handle shaped like the butt of a pistol. **pistol shot** *n.* **1** the range of a pistol. **2** a shot from a pistol. **pistol-whip** *v.t.* (*pres.p.* **pistol-whipping**, *past, p.p.* **pistol-whipped**) to strike with a pistol.

piston (pis´tən) *n.* **1** a device fitted to occupy the sectional area of a tube and be driven to and fro by alternating pressure on its faces, so as to

impart or receive motion, as in a steam engine or a pump. **2** a valve in a musical wind instrument. **3** in an internal-combustion engine, a plunger which passes on the working pressure of the burning gases via the connecting rod to the crankshaft. **piston engine** *n.* an engine in which motion is derived from a piston or pistons. **piston-engined** *a.* **piston ring** *n.* a split ring encircling the piston in a groove. **piston rod** *n.* a rod attaching the piston to machinery.

pit[1] (pit) *n.* **1** a natural or artificial hole in the ground, esp. one of considerable depth in proportion to its width. **2** a pit made in order to obtain minerals or for industrial or agricultural operations. **3** a coal mine. **4** a hole dug and covered over as a trap for wild animals or enemies. **5** a hollow or depression in the surface of the ground, of the body etc. **6** a hollow scar, esp. one left by smallpox. **7** an orchestra pit. **8** the ground floor of the auditorium in a theatre, esp. behind the stalls, or the part of an audience occupying this. **9** an area on a motor-racing course where cars are repaired, their tyres are changed etc. **10** a sunken area in a car workshop giving access to the underside of cars. **11** an area for cock-fighting, a cockpit. **12** (*sl.*) a bed. **13** an abyss. ~*v.t.* (*pres.p.* **pitting**, *past, p.p.* **pitted**) **1** to match, to set in competition against. **2** to mark with pits or hollow scars, as with smallpox. **3** to put into a pit, esp. for storage. ~*v.i.* (of the flesh) to retain the impression of a finger when touched. **the pit 1** the grave. **2** hell. **the pits** (*sl.*) a very unpleasant person, thing, place or situation. **to dig a pit for** to try to trap. **pit bull terrier, pit bull** *n.* a sturdy, very fierce variety of bull terrier, sometimes used for dogfights. **pitfall** *n.* **1** a hidden danger. **2** a pit slightly covered so that animals may fall in, a trap. **pithead** *n.* (the area or buildings near) the top of a mine shaft. **pitman** *n.* **1** (*pl.* **pitmen**) a man who works in a pit, a coal miner. **2** (*pl.* **pitmans**) a connecting rod in machinery. **pit of the stomach** *n.* **1** the bottom of the stomach. **2** the hollow below the breastbone. **pit pony** *n.* (*pl.* **pit ponies**) (*Hist.*) a pony used for haulage in coal mines. **pit prop** *n.* a length of wood, metal etc. used to support the roof of a coal seam during and after mining. **pit stop** *n.* in motor racing, a stop at a pit for servicing and refuelling. **pitted** *a.* having pits or hollow scars, esp. left by smallpox. **pit viper** *n.* a N American viper of the subfamily Crotaline with a heat-sensitive pit on each side of the head.

pit[2] (pit) *n.* (*esp. N Am.*) the stone of a fruit. ~*v.t.* (*pres.p.* **pitting**, *past, p.p.* **pitted**) to remove the pit from (fruit).

pita PITTA.

pit-a-pat (pit´əpat), **pitter-patter** (pit´əpatə) *n.* a tapping, a flutter, a palpitation. ~*adv.* **1** with this sound. **2** palpitatingly, falteringly.

pitch[1] (pich) *v.t.* **1** to fix or plant in the ground. **2** to set in orderly arrangement, to fix in position.

3 to throw, to fling, esp. with an upward heave or underhand swing. **4** to pave with cobbles. **5** to expose for sale. **6** to set to a particular pitch or keynote. **7** to put or relate in a particular way. **8** (*coll.*) to tell (a story). **9** in baseball, to throw (the ball) to the batter. **10** in golf, to strike (the ball) with a lofted club. **11** to toss (hay) with a fork. ~*v.i.* **1** to encamp. **2** to light, to settle. **3** to plunge, to fall. **4** in cricket, (of a ball) to bounce. **5** to fall headlong. **6** (of a ship) to plunge at the bow or stern. **7** to move with a jolting motion. ~*n.* **1** the act of pitching. **2** mode of pitching. **3** the delivery of the ball in various games. **4** height, degree, intensity. **5** degree of slope in a roof. **6** the place or position taken up by a person for buying and selling, a stall. **7** (*coll.*) an attempt at persuasion, usu. to induce someone to buy something. **8** the place in which the wickets are placed or the distance between them. **9** any area marked out for playing sports, e.g. football. **10** the lineal distance between points etc., arranged in series, as between the teeth of a cog-wheel, between floats on a paddle-wheel, between successive convolutions of the thread of a screw etc. **11** (*Mus.*) the degree of acuteness or gravity of a tone. **12** in cricket, the point at which a bowled ball bounces. **13** in golf, a pitch shot. **to pitch in 1** (*coll.*) to begin or set to vigorously. **2** (*coll.*) to participate or contribute. **to pitch into 1** (*coll.*) to assail with blows, abuse, etc. **2** (*coll.*) to attack vigorously. **to pitch on** to select, to decide upon. **pitch-and-toss** *n.* a game in which coins are pitched at a mark, the player getting nearest having the right to toss all the others' coins into the air and take those that come down with heads up. **pitched** *a.* **pitched battle** *n.* **1** a fierce fight or argument. **2** (*Mil.*) a battle for which both sides have made deliberate preparations. **pitched roof** *n.* a sloping roof. **pitchfork** *n.* a large, two-pronged fork with a long handle, used for lifting hay, sheaves of corn etc. ~*v.t.* **1** to lift or throw with a pitchfork. **2** to place unexpectedly or unwillingly in a certain situation. **pitch-pipe** *n.* (*Mus.*) a small pipe which is blown to set the pitch for singing or tuning. **pitch shot** *n.* in golf, a shot in which the ball is struck with a lofted club.
pitch² (pich) *n.* **1** a dark brown or black resinous substance obtained from tar, turpentine and some oils, used for caulking, paving roads etc. **2** any of various bituminous substances. ~*v.t.* to cover, coat, line or smear with pitch. **pitch-black** *a.* deep black, as dark as pitch. **pitchblende** (-blend) *n.* native uranium oxide, the chief source of radium. **pitch pine** *n.* any of various highly resinous pines, esp. *Pinus rigida* or *P. palustris*, much used for woodwork. **pitchstone** *n.* (*Geol.*) a brittle, vitreous, volcanic rock almost identical to obsidian. **pitchy** *a.* (*comp.* **pitchier**, *superl.* **pitchiest**) like pitch; dark, dismal. **pitchiness** *n.*
pitcher¹ (pich´ə) *n.* **1** a large vessel, usu. of

earthenware, with a handle and a spout, for holding liquids. **2** (*N Am.*) a jug. **3** a pitcher-shaped leaf. **4** (*pl.*) pottery which has been crushed and reused. **pitcherful** *n.* (*pl.* **pitcherfuls**). **pitcher plant** *n.* any one of various plants with pitcher-shaped leaves of the families Nepenthaceae and Sarraceniceae.
pitcher² (pich´ə) *n.* **1** a person who or something which pitches. **2** a player delivering the ball in baseball and other games. **3** a block of stone used for paving.
piteous (pit´iəs) *a.* exciting or deserving pity, lamentable, sad, mournful. **piteously** *adv.* **piteousness** *n.*
pith (pith) *n.* **1** the soft, white tissue under the skin of an orange, grapefruit etc. **2** the essence, the essential part, the main substance. **3** (*Bot.*) a cellular spongy substance occupying the middle of a stem or shoot in dicotyledonous plants. **4** strength, vigour, energy. **pith hat, pith helmet** *n.* a lightweight sun-helmet made of pith. **pithless** *a.* **pithy** *a.* (*comp.* **pithier**, *superl.* **pithiest**) **1** condensed, sententious. **2** forcible, energetic. **3** consisting of, like, or containing a lot of pith. **pithily** *adv.* **pithiness** *n.*
pitiable, pitiful etc. PITY.
piton (pē´ton) *n.* a bar, staff or stanchion used for fixing ropes on precipitous mountainsides etc.
pitta (pit´ə), **pita** *n.* a flat, round, slightly leavened bread, hollow inside so that it can be filled with food.
pittance (pit´əns) *n.* **1** a dole, an allowance, esp. of a meagre amount. **2** a small number or quantity.
pitted PIT¹.
pitter-patter PIT-A-PAT.
pittosporum (pitos´pərəm) *n.* any evergreen shrub of the Australasian genus *Pittosporum*, having small, sweet-scented flowers.
pituitary (pitū´itəri) *a.* (*Anat.*) of or relating to the pituitary gland. ~*n.* (*pl.* **pituitaries**) the pituitary gland. **pituitary gland, pituitary body** *n.* a small structure attached by a pedicle to the base of the brain, secreting hormones which regulate growth, the production of other hormones etc.
pity (pit´i) *n.* (*pl.* **pities**) **1** a feeling of grief or tenderness aroused by the sufferings or distress of others, compassion. **2** a subject for pity, a cause of regret, an unfortunate fact. ~*v.t.* (*3rd pers. sing. pres.* **pities**, *pres.p.* **pitying**, *past, p.p.* **pitied**) to feel pity for. **more's the pity** unfortunately. **to take pity on** to feel compassionate or act compassionately towards. **pitiable** (pit´iəbəl) *a.* **1** deserving or calling for pity. **2** contemptible. **pitiableness** *n.* **pitiably** *adv.* **pitiful** *a.* **1** calling for pity. **2** pitiable, contemptible. **pitifully** *adv.* **pitifulness** *n.* **pitiless** *a.* **pitilessly** *adv.* **pitilessness** *n.* **pitying** *a.* **pityingly** *adv.*
pivot (piv´ət) *n.* **1** a pin, shaft or bearing on which anything turns or oscillates. **2** a thing or event on which an important issue depends. **3** (*Mil.*) a

soldier at the flank about whom a company wheels. ~*v.i.* (*pres.p.* **pivoting**, *past, p.p.* **pivoted**) **1** to turn on or as if on a pivot. **2** to hinge (on). ~*v.t.* to place on or provide with a pivot. **pivotable** *a.* **pivotability** (-bil´-) *n.* **pivotal** *a.* **1** acting as a pivot. **2** critical, crucial.

Usage note The use of the adjective *pivotal* in the sense critical or crucial is sometimes disapproved of.

pix¹ PIC.
pix² PYX.
pixel (pik´səl) *n.* any one of the minute units which together form an image, e.g. on a cathode-ray tube. **pixelate** (-lāt) *v.t.* to split into pixels. **pixelation** (-ā´shən) *n.*
pixie (pik´si), **pixy** *n.* (*pl.* **pixies**) a supernatural being akin to a fairy or an elf. **pixie hat** *n.* a child's hat with a pointed top.
pixilated (pik´silātid), **pixillated** *a.* mentally unbalanced, eccentric.
pizazz (pizaz´), **pizzazz, pzazz** *n.* (*sl.*) the quality of being exciting, lively and stylish.
pizza (pēt´sə) *n.* (*pl.* **pizzas**) a flat, round piece of baked dough covered with cheese and tomatoes, and also often with anchovies, mushrooms, slices of sausage etc. **pizzeria** (-rē´ə) *n.* (*pl.* **pizzerias**) a place where pizzas are made or sold.
pizzicato (pitsikah´tō) *a.* (*Mus.*) played by plucking the strings of a violin etc. with the fingers. ~*adv.* in this manner. ~*n.* (*pl.* **pizzicatos**, **pizzicati** (-ti)) a passage or work so played.
pl. *abbr.* **1** place. **2** plate. **3** (*esp. Mil.*) platoon. **4** plural.
placable (plak´əbəl) *a.* able to be appeased, ready to forgive, mild, complacent. **placability** (-bil´-), **placableness** *n.* **placably** *adv.*
placard (plak´ahd) *n.* a written or printed paper or bill posted up in a public place, a poster. ~*v.t.* **1** to post placards on. **2** to announce or advertise by placards. **3** to display as a placard.
placate (pləkāt´) *v.t.* to appease, to pacify, to conciliate. **placatingly** *adv.* **placation** (-ā´shən) *n.* **placatory** *a.*
place (plās) *n.* **1** a particular portion of space. **2** a spot, a locality. **3** a city, a town, a village. **4** a residence, an abode. **5** a building, esp. one devoted to some particular purpose. **6** a residence with its surroundings, esp. in the country. **7** an open space in a town. **8** a point or passage in a book etc. **9** a particular place on a surface, esp. on the skin. **10** position in a definite order, as of a figure in relation to others in a series or group. **11** stead, lieu. **12** space, room for a person. **13** rank, station in life, official position. **14** situation, employment, appointment, esp. under government. **15** a vacancy, e.g. for a student at a university. **16** duty, sphere, province. **17** a position among the competitors that have been placed. **18** (*N Am.*) the second position in a race or competition (*win, place or show*). ~*v.t.* **1** to put or set in a particular place. **2** to put, to set, to fix.

3 to arrange in proper places. **4** to identify. **5** to assign a class to. **6** to put in office, to appoint to a post. **7** to find an appointment, situation or living for. **8** to put in someone's care. **9** to put out at interest, to invest, to lend. **10** to dispose of (goods) to a customer. **11** to make (an order for goods). **12** to arrange (a bet). **13** to set or fix (confidence etc., in or on). **14** to assign a definite date, position etc. to, to locate. **15** in racing, to indicate the position of (a horse etc.), usu. among the first three passing the winning-post. **16** to get a goal by a place-kick. **all over the place** in a mess, in chaos. **in place 1** suitable, appropriate. **2** (*N Am.*) on the spot (*to run in place*). **in place of** instead of. **in places** at several points. **out of place 1** in the wrong position. **2** unsuitable, inappropriate. **to go places** (*coll.*) to be successful. **to keep someone in their place** to remind someone of their lowly status. **to put oneself in another's place** to imagine what one would do if one was in someone else's situation. **to put someone in their place** to humiliate someone who is arrogant, presumptuous etc. **to take one's place** to go to one's rightful position. **to take place** to happen, to occur. **to take the place of** to be substituted for. **place card** *n.* a small card with a person's name on it indicating their place at a table. **placed** *a.* **1** among the first three, or sometimes four, places in a race. **2** (*N Am.*) second in a race. **place in the sun** *n.* a favourable situation, scope for action etc. **place-kick** *n.* in football, rugby etc., a kick after the ball has been placed for the purpose. **place-kicker** *n.* **placeless** *a.* **placeman** *n.* (*pl.* **placemen**) a man holding an appointment, esp. under government. **place mat** *n.* a table mat. **placement** *n.* **place name** *n.* the name of a place, esp. as distinct from a personal name. **place setting** *n.* the plate, knife, fork etc. set for one person at a table. **placing** *n.*
placebo (pləsē´bō) *n.* (*pl.* **placebos**) **1** a medicine having no physiological action, given to humour the patient, to provide psychological comfort or as a control during experiments to test the efficacy of a genuine medicine. **2** something said or done to placate someone without addressing the cause of their anxiety. **placebo effect** *n.* an effect produced by the administration of a placebo, not produced by any property of the placebo.
placenta (pləsen´tə) *n.* (*pl.* **placentae** (-tē), **placentas**) **1** the organ by which the foetus is nourished in the higher mammals. **2** (*Bot.*) the part of the ovary to which the ovules are attached. **placental** *a.*
placer (plā´sə) *n.* an alluvial or other deposit containing valuable minerals.
placid (plas´id) *a.* **1** gentle, quiet. **2** calm, peaceful, serene, unruffled. **placidity** (pləsid´-) *n.* **placidly** *adv.* **placidness** *n.*
placket (plak´it) *n.* **1** the opening or slit in a garment. **2** the flap of fabric under a placket. **3** a woman's pocket.

plagiarize (plā´jərīz), **plagiarise** *v.t.*, *v.i.* to appropriate and give out as one's own (the writings, inventions, or ideas of another). **plagiarism** *n.* **1** the act of plagiarizing. **2** something plagiarized. **plagiarist** *n.* **plagiaristic** (-ris´-) *a.* **plagiarizer** *n.*

plague (plāg) *n.* **1** a pestilence, an intensely malignant epidemic, esp. the bubonic or pneumonic plague. **2** an infestation (*a plague of locusts*). **3** a blow, a calamity, an affliction. **4** (*coll.*) a nuisance, a trouble. ~*v.t.* (*pres.p.* **plaguing**, *past, p.p.* **plagued**) **1** to afflict with any calamity or evil. **2** to vex, to tease, to annoy. **3** to affect with a plague. **plaguesome** *a.*

plaice (plās) *n.* (*pl.* **plaice**) **1** a European flatfish, *Pleuronectes platessa*, much used for food. **2** AMERICAN PLAICE (under AMERICAN).

plaid (plad) *n.* **1** a long rectangular outer garment of tartan woollen cloth, worn by Scottish Highlanders. **2** tartan cloth. ~*a.* made of tartan. **plaided** *a.*

plain (plān) *a.* **1** clear, evident. **2** simple, without difficulties, easy to understand. **3** easily seen. **4** not intricate. **5** (of knitting) consisting of plain stitches, as distinct from *purl.* **6** without ornament. **7** unvariegated, uncoloured. **8** not seasoned highly. **9** (of flour) having no raising agent. **10** homely, unaffected, unsophisticated. **11** straightforward, sincere, frank. **12** direct, outspoken. **13** not luxurious. **14** ugly. ~*adv.* **1** plainly, clearly. **2** totally, utterly. ~*n.* a tract of level country. **plainchant** *n.* plainsong. **plain chocolate** *n.* dark chocolate with a slightly bitter flavour. **plain clothes** *n.pl.* private clothes, as distinct from *uniform.* **plain-clothes** *a.* wearing such clothes (*plain-clothes policeman*). **plain dealer** *n.* a person who speaks their mind plainly. **plain dealing** *n.* **plainly** *adv.* **plainness** *n.* **plain sailing** *n.* **1** sailing a straightforward course. **2** a simple course of action. **plainsman** *n.* (*pl.* **plainsmen**) a man who lives on plains. **plainsong** *n.* a variety of vocal music according to the ecclesiastical modes of the Middle Ages, governed as to time not by metre but by word accent, and sung in unison. **plain-spoken** *a.* speaking or said plainly and without reserve. **plain stitch** *n.* a simple stitch in knitting, in which a loop is made by passing wool round the right-hand needle and pulling it through a loop on the left-hand needle. **plain suit** *n.* a suit of cards which is not trumps. **plainswoman** *n.* (*pl.* **plainswomen**) a woman who lives on plains. **plain text** *n.* a text which is not in code. **plain time** *n.* working time which is not paid at overtime rates. **plain weaving** *n.* weaving in which the weft passes alternately over and under the warp.

plaint (plānt) *n.* **1** (*Law*) an accusation, a charge. **2** †a lamentation, a mournful song.

plaintiff (plān´tif) *n.* (*Law*) a person who brings a suit against another, a complainant, a prosecutor.

plaintive (plān´tiv) *a.* **1** expressive of sorrow or grief. **2** having a mournful sound. **plaintively** *adv.* **plaintiveness** *n.*

plait (plat), **plat** *n.* **1** a braid of several strands of hair, straw, twine etc. **2** a pleat. ~*v.t.* (*pres.p.* **plaiting**, **platting**, *past, p.p.* **plaited**, **platted**) **1** to braid, to form into a plait or plaits. **2** to make by plaiting. **plaiter** *n.*

plan (plan) *n.* **1** a drawing of a building, machine etc., by projection on a plane surface, usu. showing the relative positions of the parts on one floor or level. **2** a map of a town or estate, on a large scale. **3** a scheme, a project, a design. **4** an outline of a discourse, sermon etc. **5** method of procedure. **6** one of the ideal planes, perpendicular to the line of vision, passing through the objects in a picture, in which these appear of diminishing size according to the distance. ~*v.t.* (*pres.p.* **planning**, *past, p.p.* **planned**) **1** to design, to contrive, to scheme, to devise. **2** to draw a plan of. ~*v.i.* to make plans. **to plan on** (*coll.*) to intend. **planless** *a.* **planned** *a.* done according to a plan. **planned economy** *n.* COMMAND ECONOMY (under COMMAND). **planner** *n.* **planning** *n.* **planning permission** *n.* official permission from a local authority etc. to erect or convert a building or change its use.

planchette (plahnshet´) *n.* a small, usu. heart-shaped, board resting on two castors, and a pencil which makes marks as the board moves under the hands of the person resting upon it (believed by spiritualists to be a mode of communicating with the unseen world).

plane[1] (plān) *n.* **1** a surface such that a straight line joining any two points in it lies wholly within it. **2** such a surface imagined to extend to an indefinite distance, forming the locus for certain points or lines. **3** a level surface. **4** an even surface extending uniformly in some direction. **5** a level (of thought, existence etc.). ~*a.* **1** level, flat, without depressions or elevations. **2** lying or extending in a plane. ~*v.i.* **1** to glide, to soar. **2** to skim across water. **planar** (-nə) *a.* **plane chart** *n.* a chart used in plane sailing on which lines of latitude and longitude are represented by straight, parallel lines. **plane polarization** *n.* a type of polarization in which the vibrations of electromagnetic radiation are restricted to one direction. **plane sailing** *n.* **1** the art of determining a ship's position on the supposition that it is moving on a plane. **2** plain sailing. **plane-table** *n.* a surveying instrument marked off into degrees from the centre for measuring angles in mapping.

plane[2] (plān) *n.* a tool for smoothing boards and other surfaces. ~*v.t.* **1** to smooth or dress with a plane. **2** to remove (away) or pare (down) irregularities. **planer** *n.*

plane[3] (plān) *n.* any tree of the genus *Platanus*, having large, spreading branches with broad angular leaves palmately lobed. **plane tree** *n.*

plane[4] (plān) *n.* **1** an aeroplane. **2** each of the thin horizontal structures used as wings to sustain an aeroplane in flight.

planet (plan´it) *n.* a heavenly body revolving round the sun, either as a primary planet in a nearly circular orbit or as a secondary planet or satellite revolving round a primary. **the planet** the earth. **planetarium** (-eə´riəm) *n.* (*pl.* **planetariums, planetaria** (-riə)) **1** an apparatus for exhibiting the motions of the planets. **2** a building in which this is exhibited on a large scale. **3** an orrery. **planetary** *a.* **1** of or relating to the planets or the planetary system. **2** terrestrial, worldly. **3** wandering. **planetary nebula** *n.* a ring-shaped nebula round a star, consisting of a shell of gas. **planetoid** *n.* an asteroid.

plangent (plan´jənt) *a.* **1** sounding noisily. **2** resounding sorrowfully. **plangency** (-si) *n.* **plangently** *adv.*

planimeter (plənim´itə) *n.* an instrument for measuring the area of an irregular plane surface. **planimetric** (planimet´-), **planimetrical** *a.* **planimetry** *n.*

planish (plan´ish) *v.t.* **1** to flatten, smooth, or toughen (metal) by hammering or similar means. **2** to reduce in thickness by rolling. **planisher** *n.*

planisphere (plan´isfiə) *n.* a plane projection of a sphere, esp. of part of the celestial sphere. **planispheric** (-sfer´-) *a.*

plank (plangk) *n.* **1** a long piece of sawn timber thicker than a board. **2** an article or principle of a political programme. ~*v.t.* **1** to cover or lay with planks. **2** (*coll., esp. N Am.*) to lay down (money, etc.) as if on a board or table. **3** (*coll., esp. N Am.*) to put down roughly. **to walk the plank** to be compelled to walk blindfold along a plank thrust over a ship's side (a pirates' mode of putting to death). **plank bed** *n.* a bed of boards without a mattress (a form of prison discipline). **planking** *n.* planks collectively, for flooring.

plankton (plangk´tən) *n.* minute animals and plants or those of low organization, floating in water at any level. **planktonic** (-ton´-) *a.*

plano- (plā´nō) *comb. form* flat, level.

planoconcave (plānōkon´kāv) *a.* plane on one side and concave on the other.

planoconvex (plānōkon´veks) *a.* plane on one side and convex on the other.

plant (plahnt) *n.* **1** any vegetable organism of the kingdom Plantae, usu. one of the smaller plants as distinct from shrubs and trees. **2** a sapling. **3** a shoot, a slip, a cutting. **4** an offshoot, a descendant. **5** the tools, machinery, apparatus and fixtures used in an industrial concern. **6** a factory. **7** (*coll.*) a person or thing used to entrap another, esp. an article secretly left so as to be found in a person's possession and provide incriminating evidence. **8** mobile mechanical equipment used for earth-moving, road-building etc. ~*v.t.* **1** to set in the ground for growth. **2** to put (young fish, spawn etc.) into a river etc. **3** to furnish or lay out with plants. **4** to fix firmly, to station. **5** to settle, to found, to introduce, to establish. **6** to implant

(an idea etc.). **7** to aim and deliver (a blow etc.). **8** (*coll.*) to put into position secretly in order to observe, deceive or entrap. **9** to bury. ~*v.i.* **1** to sow seed. **2** to perform the act of planting. **to plant out** to plant (young plants) outdoors. **plantable** *a.* **plantation** (-tā´shən) *n.* **1** a large estate for the cultivation of sugar, cotton, coffee etc. **2** a large quantity of trees or growing plants that have been planted; a growing wood, a grove. **3** (*Hist.*) a colony or settlement, settling of colonists, colonization. **plantation song** *n.* a type of song formerly sung by black plantation workers in America. **planter** *n.* **1** a person who plants. **2** a person who owns or works a plantation. **3** an ornamental pot for plants. **4** an implement or machine for planting. **plantless** *a.* **plantlet** *n.* **plantlike** *a.* **plant-louse** *n.* (*pl.* **plant-lice**) an insect infesting plants, esp. the aphis. **plantsman** (-mən) *n.* (*pl.* **plantsmen**) a gardening expert. **plantswoman** *n.* (*pl.* **plantswomen**) a female gardening expert.

Plantagenet (plantaj´inət) *a.* of or relating to the kings of England from Henry II to Richard III. ~*n.* any one of these Plantagenet kings.

plantain[1] (plan´tin) *n.* any plant of the genus *Plantago*, with broad flat leaves and a spike of dull green flowers. **plantain lily** *n.* a hosta.

plantain[2] (plan´tin) *n.* **1** a tropical American herbaceous tree, *Musa paradisiaca*, closely related to the banana, and bearing similar fruit. **2** the fruit of the plantain.

plantar (plant´ə) *a.* of or relating to the sole of the foot.

plantigrade (plan´tigrād) *a.* walking on the sole of the foot as bears, badgers etc. ~*n.* a plantigrade animal.

plaque (plahk) *n.* **1** a plate, slab or tablet of metal, porcelain, ivory etc., usu. of an artistic or ornamental character. **2** a filmy deposit on the surface of the teeth consisting of mucus and bacteria. **3** (*Med.*) a patch or spot on the surface of the body. **4** a small plate worn as a badge or personal ornament. **plaquette** (plaket´) *n.*

plash[1] (plash) *n.* a large puddle, a marshy pool. **plashy** *a.* (*comp.* **plashier**, *superl.* **plashiest**)

plash[2] (plash) *v.t.* **1** to cause (water) to splash. **2** to dabble in. ~*v.i.* **1** to make a splash. **2** to dabble in water. ~*n.* **1** a splash, a plunge. **2** the sound made by a splash.

plash[3] (plash) *v.t.* **1** to bend down or cut partly and intertwine (branches), to form a hedge. **2** to make or repair (a hedge) in this way.

plasma (plaz´mə), **plasm** (plaz´əm) *n.* **1** the fluid part of the blood, lymph or milk. **2** sterilized blood plasma used for transfusions. **3** the viscous living matter of a cell, protoplasm. **4** a hot, ionized gas containing approximately equal numbers of positive ions and electrons. **5** a green variety of quartz allied to chalcedony. **plasmatic** (-mat´-), **plasmic** *a.* **plasmid** (-mid) *n.* (*Biol.*) a small circle of DNA found esp. in bacteria, which exists and replicates itself independently of the main bacterial chromosome.

plaster (plahs´tə) *n*. **1** a mixture of lime, sand etc., for coating walls etc. **2** a sticking plaster. **3** plaster of Paris. **4** (*Hist*.) an adhesive application of some curative substance, usu. spread on linen, muslin or a similar fabric, placed on parts of the body. ~*a*. made of plaster. ~*v.t*. **1** to cover with plaster or other adhesive substance. **2** to apply a sticking plaster or plaster cast to (a wound etc.). **3** to daub, to smear over, to smooth over. **4** to cause to lie flat or adhere. **5** to cover with excessive quantities of, to use excessively or tastelessly. **6** to stick (on) as if with plaster. **7** (*sl*.) to inflict heavy damage, injury, or casualties on. **plasterboard** *n*. (a thin, rigid board consisting of) a layer of plaster compressed between sheets of fibreboard, used in making partition walls, ceilings etc. **plaster cast** *n*. **1** a covering of plaster of Paris used to immobilize and protect a broken limb etc. **2** a plaster copy, made from a mould, of any object, esp. a statue. **plastered** *a*. (*sl*.) drunk. **plasterer** *n*. **plaster of Paris** *n*. gypsum, esp. calcined gypsum, used for making plaster casts. **plaster saint** *n*. (*iron*.) a person regarded as being extremely virtuous. **plasterwork** *n*. **plastery** *a*.

plastic (plas´tik) *n*. **1** any of a group of synthetic, polymeric substances which, though stable in use at ordinary temperatures, are plastic at some stage in their manufacture and can be shaped by the application of heat and pressure. **2** (*coll*.) plastic money. ~*a*. **1** made of plastic. **2** synthetic, insincere. **3** having the power of giving form or shape. **4** capable of being modelled or moulded. **5** (*Biol*.) capable of adapting to varying conditions. **6** (*Philos*.) formative, causing growth. **plastically** *adv*. **plastic art** *n*. art which is concerned with moulding, shaping or representation in three dimensions. **plastic bomb** *n*. a bomb containing plastic explosive. **plastic bullet** *n*. a cylinder of plastic approximately 4 in. (10 cm) long, less lethal than an ordinary bullet, used mainly for riot control. **plastic explosive** *n*. an adhesive, jelly-like explosive substance. **plasticity** (-tis´-) *n*. **plasticky** *a*. **plastic money** *n*. (*coll*.) credit cards, bank cards etc. **plastic surgery** *n*. the branch of surgery concerned with the restoration of missing, deformed or disfigured parts of the body or with the cosmetic improvement of any feature. **plastic wood** *n*. a malleable material which resembles wood when hardened, used for filling in cracks.

Plasticine® (plas´tisēn) *n*. a soft, modelling substance used esp. by children.

plastid (plas´tid) *n*. (*Biol*.) a small particle in the cells of plants and some animals containing pigment, starch, protein etc.

-plasty (plas´ti) *comb. form* formation or replacement by plastic surgery, as *rhinoplasty*.

platan (plat´ən) *n*. a plane tree.

plate (plāt) *n*. **1** a small shallow vessel, now usu. of crockery, for eating from. **2** a plateful, the contents of a plate, a portion served on a plate. **3** any shallow receptacle, esp. for taking a collection in church. **4** (*N Am*.) a main course of a meal. **5** (*collect*.) domestic utensils, such as spoons, forks, knives, cups, dishes etc., of gold, silver or other metal. **6** plated ware. **7** a flat, thin piece of metal etc., usu. rigid and uniform in thickness. **8** a very thin coating of one metal upon another. **9** (*Biol*.) a flat, rigid layer of bone, horn etc. forming part of an animal's body or shell. **10** (*Geol*.) a huge platelike section of the earth's crust. **11** a piece of metal with an inscription for attaching to an object. **12** a number plate. **13** a piece of metal used for engraving. **14** a print taken from a plate. **15** a sheet of glass or other material coated with a sensitized film for photography. **16** an electrotype or stereotype cast of a page of type, to be used for printing. **17** an illustration in a book, often on different paper from the text. **18** a device for straightening teeth. **19** the plastic base of a denture, fitting the gums and holding the false teeth. **20** in baseball, a flat piece of whitened marker which marks the position of a batter and pitcher. **21** (*N Am*.) the anode of a thermionic valve. **22** a horizontal timber laid on a wall as base for framing. **23** a cup or other article of gold or silver offered as a prize in a race etc. **24** a race for such a prize. ~*v.t*. **1** to coat with a layer of metal, esp. gold, silver or tin. **2** to cover with plates of metal for defence, ornament etc. **3** to make a plate of type for printing. **4** to roll or beat into thin plates. **handed to one on a plate** (*coll*.) obtained without effort. **to have on one's plate** to have waiting to be done, to be burdened with. **plate armour,** (*N Am*.) **plate armor** *n*. **1** armour composed of heavy plates of metal with which ships, forts etc., are covered to protect them against artillery fire. **2** defensive armour formerly worn by knights and men-at-arms, as distinct from chain or mail armour. **plateful** *n*. (*pl*. **platefuls**). **plate glass** *n*. a superior kind of glass made in thick sheets, used for mirrors, large windows etc. **platelayer** *n*. a person who fixes or repairs railway track. **plateless** *a*. **platelet** *n*. a small blood particle involved in clotting. **plater** *n*. **plate rack** *n*. a frame for holding plates and dishes. **plate tectonics** *n*. (*Geol*.) (the study of the earth's crust based on) the theory that the lithosphere is made up of a number of continually moving and interacting plates. **plating** *n*. **1** a coating of gold, silver or other metal. **2** in racing, competing for plates.

plateau (plat´ō) *n*. (*pl*. **plateaux** (-ōz), **plateaus**) **1** a tableland, an elevated plain. **2** a period of stability after or during an upward progression, a levelling-off. ~*v.i*. (*3rd pers. sing. pres*. **plateaus,** *pres.p*. **plateauing,** *past, p.p*. **plateaued**) to level off after an upward progression.

platen (plat´ən) *n*. **1** the part of a printing press which presses the paper against the type to give the impression. **2** the roller in a typewriter serving the same purpose.

platform (plat´fawm) *n.* **1** any flat or horizontal surface raised above some adjoining level. **2** a stage or raised flooring in a hall etc., for speaking from. **3** a raised pavement etc., beside the line at a railway station etc. **4** the small floor by which one enters or alights from a bus. **5** (a shoe with) a thick sole. **6** a political programme, the principles forming the basis of a party. ~*v.t.* to place on or as if on a platform. ~*v.i.* to speak from a platform.

platinum (plat´inəm) *n.* (*Chem.*) a heavy, ductile and malleable metallic element of a silver colour, at. no. 78, chem. symbol Pt, fusing only at extremely high temperatures, immune to attack by most chemical reagents. **platinic** (plətin´-) *a.* of or containing (tetravalent) platinum. **platinize, platinise** *v.t.* to coat with platinum. **platinization** (-zā´shən) *n.* **platinous** *a.* of or containing (divalent) platinum. **platinum-black** *n.* finely divided platinum in the form of a black powder, obtained by the reduction of platinum salts. **platinum blond** *a.* (of a man or boy) having hair so fair as to be almost white. ~*n.* a man or boy with platinum blond hair. **platinum blonde** *a.* (of a woman or girl) having hair so fair as to be almost white. ~*n.* a woman or girl with platinum blonde hair. **platinum disc** *n.* the highest award given to a recording artist, group etc. for sales of a particular record, CD etc. above a specified very high number of copies, often presented in the form of a platinum replica disc.

platitude (plat´itūd) *n.* **1** a trite remark, esp. of a didactic kind. **2** flatness, commonplaceness, insipidity, triteness. **platitudinize** (-tū´dinīz), **platitudinise** *v.i.* **platitudinous** (-tū´-) *a.*

Platonic (pləton´ik) *a.* **1** of or relating to Plato, the Greek philosopher, *c.*427–347 BC, or to his philosophy or school. **2** (**platonic**) not involving sexual desire or activity (*a platonic relationship*). **Platonically** *adv.* **Platonism** (plā´tə-) *n.* **Platonist** *n.*

platoon (plətoon´) *n.* **1** (*Mil.*) a subdivision, usu. half, of a company, formerly a tactical unit under a lieutenant. **2** a group of people.

platteland (plat´əland) *n.* (*S Afr.*) rural areas. **plattelander** *n.*

platter (plat´ə) *n.* **1** a large shallow dish or plate. **2** (*sl.*) a gramophone record. **3** the metal disc in the turntable of a record player. **4** (*Comput.*) a hard disk for storing data magnetically. **handed to one on a platter** (*coll.*) obtained without effort.

platy- (plat´i) *comb. form* broad, flat.

platyhelminth (platihel´minth) *n.* the flatworm.

platypus (plat´ipəs) *n.* (*pl.* **platypuses**) a small, aquatic, egg-laying mammal of E Australia having a broad bill and tail, thick fur and webbed feet; also *duck-billed platypus.*

platyrrhine (plat´irīn) *a.* (of monkeys) broadnosed, as distinct from *catarrhine.* ~*n.* a platyrrhine monkey.

plaudit (plaw´dit) *n.* (*usu. pl.*) an expression of applause.

plausible (plaw´zibəl) *a.* **1** apparently right, reasonable or probable, but specious. **2** apparently trustworthy, ingratiating, but insincere. **plausibility** (-bil´-) *n.* **plausibly** *adv.*

play (plā) *n.* **1** a series of actions engaged in for pleasure or amusement. **2** sport, exercise, amusement, fun. **3** playing in a game. **4** the manner or style of this. **5** the period during which a game is in progress. **6** a manoeuvre, esp. in a game. **7** free, light, aimless movement or activity. **8** freedom of movement or action. **9** space or scope for freedom of movement or action. **10** a state of activity. **11** gambling. **12** a dramatic composition or performance, a drama. **13** conduct or dealing towards others (esp. as fair or unfair). ~*v.i.* **1** to sport, to frolic. **2** to do something as an amusement. **3** to toy, to trifle (with). **4** to take part in a game. **5** (*coll.*) to participate, to cooperate. **6** (of a sports ground) to be likely to produce play as specified. **7** to take one's turn at performing an action specific to a game. **8** to perform in a specified position or manner in a game (*He plays in defence*). **9** to perform on a musical instrument. **10** to move about in a lively, light or aimless manner, to dance, frisk, shimmer etc. **11** to act or move freely. **12** (of a part of a machine etc.) to move loosely or irregularly. **13** (of water, light etc.) to be discharged or directed on to something. **14** to emit or reproduce sound. **15** to take part in a game of chance, to gamble. **16** to behave, to act, to conduct oneself in regard to others (*to play false*). **17** to play a part, esp. on stage. **18** (of a drama, show etc.) to be in performance. ~*v.t.* **1** to give a performance or performances of (a musical or dramatic work, the works of a specified composer or author). **2** to perform music on. **3** to cause to emit or reproduce sounds, esp. music. **4** to emit or reproduce (sounds, esp. music). **5** to act the role of. **6** to act, or stage a play, in (a specified theatre or town). **7** to pretend to be. **8** to handle, to deal with, to regard (as). **9** to perform (a trick etc.) esp. in jest or mockery. **10** to engage in (a game or sport). **11** to execute (a stroke, a shot etc.). **12** to proceed through (a game, a rubber etc.). **13** to oppose, to compete against. **14** to play in (a specified position) in a game. **15** to make use of (a player or an implement) in a game. **16** to bring (a card etc.) into operation in a game. **17** to cause (a ball etc.) to move in a certain direction by striking, kicking etc. **18** to gamble on. **19** to give (a fish) freedom to exhaust itself. **20** to accompany (someone entering or leaving a room) with music. **21** to discharge (guns, a hose etc.) continuously (on or upon). **22** to cause to move lightly or aimlessly (on). **at play** engaged in playing. **in play** in fun, not seriously. **to bring into play** to make operative. **to call into play** to put into operation, to introduce as an influence or factor. **to make a play for** (*coll.*) to try to get. **to make (great) play**

with to parade, to flourish ostentatiously. **to make play** to act effectively. **to play about** to act in a frivolous or irresponsible manner. **to play along (with)** to seem to agree or cooperate (with). **to play around 1** to play about. **2** to have casual sexual relationships. **to play at 1** to engage in (a game). **2** to perform or execute in a frivolous or half-hearted way. **3** to pretend to be. **to play back** to replay (something just recorded). **to play ball** (*coll.*) to cooperate, to comply. **to play by ear 1** to play without reading the printed music. **2** to react to (a situation) by responding instinctively to events as they occur, rather than by following a plan. **to play down** to treat as unimportant, not to stress. **to play false** to betray. **to play fast and loose 1** to be fickle. **2** to act recklessly. **to play for time** to protract something deliberately to allow other events to catch up. **to play hard to get** (*coll.*) to act coyly, esp. as a come-on. **to play into someone's hands** to unknowingly give the advantage to one's opponent. **to play it cool** (*coll.*) not to show emotion, to keep calm. **to play off 1** to oppose (one person) against another, esp. for one's own advantage. **2** to take part in a play-off. **3** in golf, to tee off. **to play on 1** to move about lightly or unsteadily on. **2** to continue to play. **3** to exploit. **4** to perform upon. **to play oneself in** to accustom oneself to the conditions in a game etc. **to play safe** to take no risks. **to play the man** to be brave or courageous, to be a man. **to play up 1** to cause trouble or suffering (to). **2** to misbehave. **3** to malfunction or function erratically. **4** to give prominence to. **5** to play more vigorously. **to play upon** to exploit (something or somebody). **to play up to** to humour, to flatter. **to play with 1** to treat with levity. **2** to amuse oneself with. **playable** *a.* **playability** (-bil´-) *n.* **play-act** *v.i.* **1** to act in a play. **2** to behave insincerely or overdramatically. *~v.t.* to act (a part). **play-acting** *n.* **play-actor** *n.* **playback** *n.* a reproduction, esp. immediately after the recording has been made, of recorded sound or vision. **playbill** *n.* a bill or programme announcing or giving the cast of a play. **playboy** *n.* a wealthy man who appears to live only for pleasure. **played out** *a.* tired out, worn out, used up. **player** *n.* **1** a person who plays. **2** a person engaged in a game. **3** a person skilled in a particular game. **4** an actor. **5** a performer on a musical instrument. **6** a device which plays records, tapes or compact discs. **7** an automatic device for playing a musical instrument. **player-manager** *n.* a member of a team who is also the manager of the team. **player-piano** *n.* a piano with a device by which it can be played automatically. **playfellow** *n.* a playmate. **playful** *a.* **1** frolicsome, sportive. **2** humorous, jocular, amusing. **playfully** *adv.* **playfulness** *n.* **playgirl** *n.* a wealthy woman who appears to live only for pleasure. **playgoer** *n.* a person who regularly goes to the theatre. **playground** *n.* **1** a piece of ground used for games, esp. one attached to a

school. **2** a favourite district for tourists, mountain climbers etc. **playgroup** *n.* a group of preschool children who meet regularly for supervised and usu. creative play. **playhouse** *n.* **1** a theatre. **2** a toy house for playing in. **playing** *n.* **playing card** *n.* any of a pack of 52 cards used for card games. **playing field** *n.* a field or open space used for sports. **playlet** *n.* **playlist** *n.* a list of records to be played in a radio show. *~v.t.* to put on a playlist. **playmaker** *n.* a member of a sports team who often sets up an attack. **playmate** *n.* **1** a companion one plays with. **2** a lover. **play-off** *n.* a game to decide the final winner of a competition, esp. an extra game when two competitors are tied. **play on words** *n.* a pun. **playpen** *n.* a portable framework inside which young children can play in safety. **play-reading** *n.* **1** the act of reading a play. **2** an instance of playreading. **playroom** *n.* a room for children to play in. **play school** *n.* a nursery school or playgroup. **plaything** *n.* **1** a toy. **2** a person used for one's amusement. **playtime** *n.* time in the school day which is allotted for play. **playwright** *n.* a person who writes plays. **playwriting** *n.*

plaza (plah´za) *n.* (*pl.* **plazas**) **1** a public square or open paved area. **2** (*esp. N Am.*) a shopping mall.

plc, PLC *abbr.* public limited company.

plea (plē) *n.* **1** an urgent entreaty. **2** (*Law*) the accused's answer to an indictment. **3** (*Law*) something alleged by a party to legal proceedings in support of a claim or defence. **4** an excuse. **plea bargaining** *n.* (*esp. N Am.*) the practice of arranging more lenient treatment by the court in return for an admission of guilt by the accused. **plea bargain** *n.*, *v.i.*

pleach (plēch) *v.t.* to interlace, to intertwine, to plash.

plead (plēd) *v.i.* (*past, p.p.* **pleaded,** (*esp. N Am.,* Sc., *dial.*) **pled** (pled)) **1** to speak or argue in support of a claim or in defence against a claim. **2** to supplicate earnestly. **3** (*Law*) to put forward a plea or allegation, to address a court on behalf of someone. **4** to urge arguments for or against something. *~v.t.* **1** to discuss, maintain or defend by arguments. **2** (*Law*) to allege in pleading or argument. **3** to offer in excuse, to allege in defence. **to plead guilty** (*Law*) to admit guilt or liability. **to plead not guilty** (*Law*) to deny guilt or liability. **pleadable** *a.* **pleader** *n.* **pleading** *n.* **1** (*Law*) a (usu. *pl.*) a written statement of a party in a suit at law. **b** the art or practice of drawing up such statements. **c** the act of making a plea. **2** entreating, imploring. **pleadingly** *adv.*

pleasant (plez´ənt) *a.* (*comp.* **pleasanter,** *superl.* **pleasantest**) **1** pleasing, agreeable, affording gratification to the mind or senses. **2** affable, friendly, good-humoured. **pleasantly** *adv.* **pleasantness** *n.* **pleasantry** (-tri) *n.* (*pl.* **pleasantries**) **1** (usu. *pl.*) an agreeable remark, made esp. for the sake of politeness. **2** (*esp. pl.*) a jest, a joke, an amusing trick. **3** jocularity, facetiousness.

please (plēz) *v.t.* **1** to give pleasure to, to be agreeable to. **2** to satisfy, to win approval from. **3** to be the desire or wish of. ~*v.i.* **1** to like, to think fit, to prefer. **2** to afford gratification to someone. ~*int.* a polite formula used in making requests. **if you please 1** if it is agreeable to you, with your permission. **2** (*iron.*) expressing sarcasm or protest. **please yourself** do as you wish. **pleased** *a.* **1** gratified, satisfied. **2** delighted, happy. **pleaser** *n.* **pleasing** *a.* **pleasingly** *adv.*

pleasure (plezh´ə) *n.* **1** the gratification of the mind or senses. **2** enjoyment, gratification, delight. **3** sensual gratification. **4** a source of gratification. **5** (*formal*) choice, wish, desire. ~*a.* for pleasure. ~*v.t.* to give pleasure to. ~*v.i.* to take pleasure (in). **to take pleasure in** to get enjoyment from. **with pleasure** gladly, willingly. **pleasurable** *a.* giving pleasure, pleasant, gratifying. **pleasurableness** *n.* **pleasurably** *adv.*

pleat (plēt) *n.* a flattened fold, a crease. ~*v.t.* to fold or double over, to crease.

pleb (pleb) *n.* (*derog.*) a common, vulgar person. **plebby** *a.* (*comp.* **plebbier,** *superl.* **plebbiest**).

plebeian (pləbē´ən) *n.* one of the common people. ~*a.* **1** of or relating to the common people. **2** ignorant, uncultured. **3** common, vulgar. **plebeianism** *n.*

plebiscite (pleb´isīt, -sit) *n.* **1** a direct vote of the whole body of citizens in a state on a definite question, a referendum. **2** an expression of opinion by the whole community. **plebiscitary** (-bis´itəri) *a.*

plectrum (plek´trəm) *n.* (*pl.* **plectrums, plectra** (-trə)) a small implement of ivory etc., with which players pluck the strings of the guitar, harp, lyre etc.

pled PLEAD.

pledge (plej) *n.* **1** anything given or handed over by way or guarantee of security for the repayment of money borrowed or for the performance of some obligation. **2** a thing put in pawn. **3** a promise of a donation to a charity, or the donation itself. **4** an earnest, a token. **5** an agreement, promise or binding engagement. **6** the state of being pledged. **7** a health, a toast. ~*v.t.* **1** to give as a pledge or security. **2** to deposit in pawn. **3** to promise solemnly. **4** to drink a toast to. **to take the pledge** to vow to abstain from alcoholic drink. **pledgeable** *a.* **pledgee** (-ē´) *n.* **pledger** *n.* **pledgor** *n.*

pledget (plej´it) *n.* a compress of lint for laying over an ulcer, wound etc.

pleiotropy (plīot´rəpi) *n.* (*Biol.*) the production of two or more apparently unrelated effects by a single gene. **pleiotropic** (-trō´pik) *a.* **pleiotropism** *n.*

Pleistocene (plīs´təsēn) *a.* (*Geol.*) of or relating to the strata or epoch overlying or succeeding the Pliocene formation. ~*n.* the Pleistocene epoch.

plenary (plē´nəri) *a.* **1** full, complete, entire, absolute. **2** attended by all members. **plenarily** *adv.*

plenipotentiary (plenipəten´shəri) *n.* (*pl.* **plenipotentiaries**) an ambassador or envoy to a foreign court, with full powers. ~*a.* **1** invested with full powers. **2** (of power) full, absolute.

plenitude (plen´itūd) *n.* completeness, abundance, fullness.

Usage note The form *plentitude* (after *plenty*) is best avoided.

plenty (plen´ti) *n.* **1** a large quantity or number, an ample supply, lots. **2** abundance, copiousness. ~*a.* (*coll.*) plentiful, abundant. ~*adv.* (*coll.*) very, abundantly. **plenteous** (-tiəs) *a.* (*poet.*) **plenteously** *adv.* **plenteousness** *n.* **plentiful** *a.* existing in abundance, copious. **plentifully** *adv.* **plentifulness** *n.*

plenum (plē´nəm) *n.* (*pl.* **plenums**) **1** a full meeting. **2** (*Physics*) space, as considered to be full of matter, opposed to *vacuum*.

pleonasm (plē´ənazm) *n.* redundancy of expression in speaking or writing. **pleonastic** (-nas´-) *a.* **pleonastically** *adv.*

❌ **plesant** common misspelling of PLEASANT.

plesiosaurus (plēsiəsaw´rəs), **plesiosaur** (plē´-) *n.* (*pl.* **plesiosauruses, plesiosaurs**) any member of the genus *Plesiosaurus* of extinct marine saurian creatures with long necks, small heads and four paddles.

plethora (pleth´ərə) *n.* **1** superabundance, excess. **2** (*Med.*) **a** excessive fullness of blood. **b** an excess of any body fluid. **plethoric** (-thor´-) *a.* **plethorically** *adv.*

pleura (pluər´ə) *n.* (*pl.* **pleurae** (ploo´rē)) (*Anat., Zool.*) **1** a thin membrane covering the interior of the thorax and enveloping the lungs. **2** a part of the body wall in arthropods. **pleural** *a.* **pleurisy** (-isi) *n.* (*Med.*) inflammation of the pleurae, usu. accompanied by fever, pain in the chest or side etc. **pleuritic** (-rit´-) *a.*

pleuro- (pluə´rō), **pleur-** *comb. form* **1** of or relating to the side or ribs. **2** of or relating to the pleura.

pleuron (pluə´ron) *n.* (*pl.* **pleura** (-rə)) (*Anat.*) a pleura.

pleuropneumonia (pluərōnūmō´niə) *n.* (*Med., Zool.*) inflammation of the lungs and pleurae, esp. as contagious disease among cattle.

Plexiglas® (plek´siglahs) *n.* a transparent plastic, the same as Perspex.

plexus (plek´səs) *n.* (*pl.* **plexus, plexuses**) **1** (*Anat.*) a network of veins, fibres or nerves. **2** a network, a complication. **plexiform** *a.*

pliable (plī´əbəl) *a.* **1** easily bent, flexible, pliant. **2** supple, limber. **3** yielding readily to influence or arguments. **pliability** (-bil´-), **pliableness** *n.* **pliably** *adv.* **pliant** *a.* pliable. **pliancy** (-ənsi) *n.* **pliantly** *adv.*

plicate (plī´kət, -kāt), **plicated** (-kā´tid) *a.* (*Biol., Geol.*) plaited, folded like a fan. **plication** (plikā´shən), **plicature** (plik´əchə) *n.*

plié (plē´ā) n. (pl. **pliés**) a ballet movement in which the knees are bent outwards while the back remains straight.

pliers (plī´əz) n.pl. small pincers with long jaws for bending wire etc.

plight¹ (plīt) n. condition, state, case, esp. one of distress or disgrace.

†**plight**² (plīt) v.t. to pledge, to promise, to engage (oneself, one's faith etc.).

plimsoll (plim´səl), **plimsole** n. a rubber-soled canvas shoe worn for physical education etc.

Plimsoll line (plim´səl), **Plimsoll mark** n. a line, required to be placed on every British ship, marking the level to which the authorized amount of cargo submerges it.

plinth (plinth) n. 1 (Archit.) a square member forming the lower division of a column etc. 2 a block serving as a pedestal.

Pliocene (plī´əsēn), **Pleiocene** n. (Geol.) the most modern epoch of the Tertiary. ~a. of or relating to the Pliocene period.

plissé (plē´sā) a. (of a fabric) having a wrinkled finish. ~n. (a fabric having) a wrinkled finish.

plod (plod) v.i. (pres.p. **plodding**, past, p.p. **plodded**) 1 to walk painfully, slowly and laboriously, to trudge. 2 to toil, to drudge. 3 to study with steady diligence. ~v.t. to make (one's way) thus. ~n. 1 a laborious walk, a trudge. 2 a wearisome piece of work. **plodder** n. **plodding** a. **ploddingly** adv.

-ploid (ploid) comb. form (Biol.) denoting the number of sets of chromosomes in a cell, as polypoid.

ploidy (ploi´di) n. (Biol.) the number of sets of chromosomes in a cell.

plonk¹ (plongk) v.t., v.i. to (be) put down or drop heavily, forcefully or with a plonk. ~n. 1 the act of plonking. 2 a heavy, hollow sound. **plonker** n. (sl.) 1 (derog.) a stupid person. 2 (taboo) the penis.

plonk² (plongk) n. (coll.) cheap (and inferior) wine.

plop (plop) n. 1 the sound of something falling heavily into water. 2 the act of falling with a plop. ~adv. suddenly and heavily, with a plop. ~v.i., v.t. (pres.p. **plopping**, past, p.p. **plopped**) to fall into water or drop with a plop.

plosion (plō´zhən) n. in phonetics, the abrupt release of air in the pronunciation of a plosive.

plosive (plō´siv) a. in phonetics, produced by stopping and then suddenly releasing the air-flow; explosive. ~n. a plosive consonant.

plot (plot) n. 1 a small piece of ground. 2 a plan of a field, farm, estate etc. 3 a complicated plan, scheme or stratagem; a conspiracy. 4 the plan or skeleton of the story in a play, novel etc. 5 a graphic representation. ~v.t. (pres.p. **plotting**, past, p.p. **plotted**) 1 to make a plan, map or diagram of. 2 to mark (e.g. the course of a ship or aircraft on a map etc.). 3 to locate and mark on a graph by means of coordinates. 4 to draw (a curve) through points so marked. 5 to lay out in

plots. 6 to plan, to devise, to contrive secretly. 7 to plan the plot of (a novel etc.). ~v.i. to form schemes or plots against another, to conspire. **plotless** a. **plotlessness** n. **plotter** n.

plough (plow), (esp. N Am.) **plow** n. 1 an implement for cutting, furrowing and turning over land for tillage. 2 arable land. 3 an implement or machine resembling a plough in form or function, such as a snowplough. 4 (**the Plough**) the seven brightest stars in Ursa Major, also called Charles's Wain and the Big Dipper. ~v.t. to turn up (ground) with a plough. 2 to make (a furrow) with a plough. 3 to furrow, groove or scratch, with or as if with a plough. ~v.i. 1 to turn up ground with a plough. 2 to advance laboriously through. **to plough back** 1 to plough (grass etc.) into the soil for enrichment. 2 to reinvest (profits). **to plough into** to collide with violently. **to plough out** to root out or remove by ploughing. **to plough through** 1 to smash a way through. 2 to work or read through laboriously. **to put one's hand to the plough** to begin a task or undertaking. **ploughable** a. **plougher** n. **ploughland** n. land fit for tillage, arable land. **ploughman** n. (pl. **ploughmen**) a person who ploughs. **ploughman's lunch**, **ploughperson's lunch** n. a cold snack of bread and cheese with pickle, served esp. in a pub. **ploughman's spikenard** n. a European composite plant, Inula conyzae, having fragrant purple-and-yellow flowers. **ploughshare** n. the blade of a plough.

plover (plŭv´ə) n. any one of several short-billed birds of the family Charadriidae, esp. the golden, yellow or green plover.

ploy (ploi) n. a manoeuvre, a tactic, a stratagem.

PLR abbr. Public Lending Right.

pluck (plŭk) v.t. 1 to pull off or out, to pick. 2 to pull, to twitch. 3 to strip by pulling out feathers. 4 to pull the strings of (a guitar etc.) with the fingers or a plectrum. 5 to plunder. 6 to fleece, to swindle. ~v.i. to pull, drag, or snatch (at). ~n. 1 courage, spirit. 2 the act of plucking. 3 the heart, lungs and liver of an animal as food. **plucker** n. **pluckless** a. **plucky** a. (comp. **pluckier**, superl. **pluckiest**) having pluck, spirit or courage. **pluckily** adv. **pluckiness** n.

plug (plŭg) n. 1 a piece of wood or other substance used to stop a hole; a stopper, a peg, a wedge. 2 anything wedged in or stopping up a pipe, or used to block the outlet to a wastepipe. 3 a mass of volcanic rock stopping a vent. 4 a cake, stick or small piece of compressed tobacco. 5 a spark plug. 6 a fireplug. 7 a device with a non-conducting case, having three or two pins, which is attached to an electrical cable to make an electrical connection with a suitable socket. 8 (coll.) an electrical socket. 9 (coll.) a piece of favourable publicity, esp. one inserted into other material. ~v.t. (pres.p. **plugging**, past, p.p. **plugged**) 1 to stop with a plug. 2 to insert as a plug. 3 (sl.) to shoot. 4 (sl.) to strike with the fist. 5 (coll.) to give favourable publicity to (something), esp. by alluding to it repeatedly. **to plug away at** to work doggedly and persistently at. **to plug in** to establish an electrical connection (with). **plugger** *n*. **plugging** *n*. **plughole** *n*. the outlet for waste water in a sink, bath etc., which can be closed with a plug. **plug-in** *a*. able to be connected by means of a plug. **plug-ugly** *n*. (*pl*. **plug-uglies**) (*NAm.*, *sl.*) a hooligan, a rowdy. ~*a*. looking like a hooligan.

plum (plŭm) *n*. **1** a small, sweet, fleshy fruit with reddish or purple skin. **2** (*also* **plum tree**) a tree of the genus *Prunus* bearing plums. **3** the wood of the plum tree. **4** a dried grape or raisin used in cakes, puddings etc. **5** plum colour. **6** the best part of anything, the choicest thing of a set. ~*a*. **1** dark reddish-purple. **2** choice, cushy (*a plum job*). **a plum in one's mouth** a voice which is rich to the point of affectation. **plum colour**, (*NAm.*) **plum color** *n*. dark reddish purple. **plum duff** *n*. a plain boiled flour pudding with raisins etc. **plummy** *a*. (*comp*. **plummier**, *superl*. **plummiest**) **1** full of or rich in plums. **2** luscious, inviting, desirable. **3** (of the voice) rich to the point of affectation. **plum pudding** *n*. a pudding containing raisins, currants, etc., esp. a rich one with spices etc., eaten at Christmas.

plumage, plumassier PLUME.

plumb¹ (plŭm) *n*. **1** a weight, usu. of lead, attached to a line, used to test perpendicularity. **2** a position parallel to this, the vertical. **3** a sounding lead, a plummet. ~*adv*. **1** exactly, correctly, right. **2** vertically. **3** (*NAm.*, *sl.*) completely, very (*plumb ugly*). ~*a*. **1** perpendicular, vertical. **2** downright, sheer, perfect, complete. **3** in cricket, (of a wicket) level. ~*v.t*. **1** to sound with a plummet, to measure the depth of. **2** to make vertical or perpendicular. **3** to experience in the extreme (*to plumb the depths of despair*). **4** to fathom, to understand. **out of plumb** not exactly vertical. **plumbeous** (-biəs) *a*. **1** consisting of or resembling lead. **2** glazed with lead. **plumbic** (-bik) *a*. **1** of, relating to, derived from or combined with lead. **2** due to the presence of lead. **plumbless** *a*. fathomless, too deep to measure. **plumb line** *n*. **1** the cord by which a plumb is suspended for testing perpendicularity. **2** a vertical line. **plumbous** (-bəs) *a*. (*Chem.*) containing lead in its divalent form.

plumb² (plŭm) *v.t*. **1** to provide with plumbing. **2** to plumb in. ~*v.i*. to work as a plumber. **to plumb in** to connect to a water main and/or drainage system.

plumbago (plŭmbā´gō) *n*. (*pl.* **plumbagos**) **1** graphite. **2** a perennial herb of the genus *Plumbago*, with blue, rose or violet flowers.

plumber (plŭm´ə) *n*. a person who fits and repairs cisterns, pipes, drains, gas fittings etc., in buildings. **plumber's snake** *n*. a long flexible wire for unblocking drains or cleaning obstacles in piping. **plumbing** *n*. **1** the arrangement of water pipes, gas installations etc. in a building. **2**

the work of a plumber. **3** (*coll.*) the lavatory or lavatories.

plume (ploom) *n*. **1** a feather, esp. a large or conspicuous one. **2** a feather-bunch or tuft of feathers, or anything resembling this worn as an ornament. **3** something resembling a plume (*a plume of smoke*). **4** (*Zool.*) a feather-like part or form. ~*v.t*. **1** to adorn with or as with feathers. **2** to pride oneself (on something). **3** to trim, dress, or arrange (feathers), to preen. **plumage** (-mij) *n*. a bird's entire covering of feathers. **plumaged** *a*. **plumeless** *a*. **plumelike** *a*. **plume moth** *n*. a small moth of the family Pterophoridae, having long legs and feathery wings. **plumery** *n*. **plumose** (-ōs), **plumous** *a*. resembling a feather or feathers, feathery. **plumy** *a*. (*comp*. **plumier**, *superl*. **plumiest**) **1** feathery. **2** adorned with plumes.

plummet (plŭm´it) *n*. **1** a weight attached to a line used for sounding. **2** a ball of lead for a plumb line. **3** a weight attached to a fishing line, used to keep the float upright. ~*v.i*. (*pres.p*. **plummeting**, *past*, *p.p*. **plummeted**) to fall sharply or rapidly.

plummy PLUM.

plump¹ (plŭmp) *a*. well-rounded, fat, fleshy, chubby. ~*v.t*. to make plump; to fatten, to distend. ~*v.i*. to grow plump; to swell (out or up). **plumpish** *a*. **plumply** *adv*. **plumpness** *n*. **plumpy** *a*. (*comp*. **plumpier**, *superl*. **plumpiest**).

plump² (plŭmp) *v.i*. to plunge or fall suddenly and heavily. ~*v.t*. **1** to fling or drop suddenly and heavily. **2** to say suddenly, to blurt out. ~*n*. a sudden plunge, a heavy fall. ~*adv*. (*coll.*) **1** suddenly and heavily. **2** directly, straight down. **3** flatly, bluntly. ~*a*. (*coll.*) downright, plain, blunt. **to plump for** to decide in favour of, to choose.

plumule (ploo´mūl) *n*. **1** the rudimentary stem in an embryo. **2** a little feather, one of the down feathers. **plumulaceous** (-lā´shəs), **plumular** *a*.

plumy PLUME.

plunder (plŭn´də) *v.t*. **1** to pillage, to rob, to strip. **2** to steal from. ~*n*. **1** forcible or systematic robbery. **2** spoil, booty. **3** (*coll.*) profit, gain. **plunderer** *n*.

plunge (plŭnj) *v.t*. **1** to force or thrust into water or other fluid. **2** to immerse. **3** to force, to drive (into a condition, action etc.). ~*v.i*. **1** to throw oneself, to dive (into). **2** to rush or enter impetuously (into a place, condition, etc.). **3** to fall or descend very steeply or suddenly. **4** to decrease quickly and suddenly. **5** (of a horse) to throw the body forward and the hind legs up. **6** (of a ship) to pitch. **7** (*coll.*) to gamble or bet recklessly, to spend money or get into debt heavily. ~*n*. **1** the act of plunging, a dive. **2** a sudden and violent movement. **to take the plunge** (*coll.*) to commit oneself after hesitating. **plunge neckline** *n*. a plunging neckline. **plunger** *n*. **1** a part of a machine working with a plunging motion, such as the long solid cylinder used as a piston in a force pump. **2** a rubber suction cup on a handle, used to unblock drains etc. **3** (*coll.*) a reckless gambler, speculator or spendthrift. **plunging** *a.*, *n.* **plunging neckline** *n.* a low-cut neckline on a woman's dress or top.

plunk (plŭngk) *n.* a dull, metallic sound. ~*v.t.* **1** to cause to emit a plunk. **2** to pluck the strings of (a banjo etc.). ~*v.i.* to emit a plunk.

pluperfect (ploopœˈfĭkt) *a.* (*Gram.*) expressing action or time prior to some other past time. ~*n.* **1** the pluperfect tense. **2** a pluperfect form.

plural (plooˈrəl) *a.* **1** consisting of more than one. **2** (*Gram.*) denoting more than one. ~*n.* (*Gram.*) **1** the form of a word which expresses more than one, or (in languages having a dual number) more than two. **2** the plural number. **pluralism** *n.* **1** the state of being plural. **2** the holding of more than one office, esp. an ecclesiastical benefice, at the same time. **3** (*Philos.*) the doctrine that there is more than one ultimate principle in the universe, as distinct from *monism*. **4** a social system in which members of diverse ethnic, cultural etc. groups coexist, preserving their own customs and lifestyle but having equal access to power. **pluralist** *n.* **pluralistic** (-lisˈ-) *a.* **pluralistically** *adv.* **plurality** (-ralˈ-) *n.* (*pl.* **pluralities**) **1** pluralism. **2** a majority, or the excess of (votes etc.) over the next highest number. **3** (*Math.*) a number consisting of two or more. **pluralize, pluralise** *v.t.* **pluralization** (-zāˈshən) *n.* **plurally** *adv.*

pluri- (plooˈri) *comb. form* several, more, more than one.

plus (plŭs) *prep.* **1** (*Math.*) with the addition of. **2** (of temperature) above zero. **3** (*coll.*) having gained. ~*a.* **1** at least (after a number). **2** better than (after an exam grade). **3** (*Math.*) above zero, positive. **4** electrified positively. **5** additional, extra, esp. additional and advantageous. ~*n.* **1** a plus sign. **2** an addition, a positive quantity. **3** an advantage, a positive feature. **4** a surplus. ~*conj.* (*coll.*) and in addition, and what is more. **plus fours** *n.pl.* long, baggy knickerbockers for men. **plus sign** *n.* a character (+) used as the sign of addition.

Usage note The use of *plus* as a conjunction is sometimes disapproved of.

plush (plŭsh) *n.* a cloth of various materials with a pile or nap longer than that of velvet. ~*a.* **1** made of plush. **2** plushy. **plushly** *adv.* **plushness** *n.* **plushy** *a.* (*comp.* **plushier**, *superl.* **plushiest**) (*coll.*) rich, luxurious, lavish. **plushiness** *n.*

plutarchy (plooˈtahki) *n.* (*pl.* **plutarchies**) (a) plutocracy.

Pluto (plooˈtō) *n.* the ninth planet in the solar system in order of distance from the sun. **Plutonian** (-tōˈ-) *a.* **1** of or relating to Pluto or the lower regions. **2** infernal, subterranean, dark. **plutonic** (-tonˈ-) *a.* **1** (*Geol.*) igneous. **2** (**Plutonic**) Plutonian.

plutocracy (plootokˈrəsi) *n.* (*pl.* **plutocracies**) **1** the rule of wealth or the rich. **2** a state ruled by a plutocracy. **3** a ruling class of rich people. **plutocrat** (plooˈtəkrat) *n.* (*esp. derog., facet.*) **1** a member of a plutocracy. **2** a wealthy, powerful person. **plutocratic** (-kratˈ-) *a.* **plutocratically** *adv.*

plutonium (plootōˈniəm) *n.* (*Chem.*) a radioactive element, at. no. 94, chem. symbol Pu, formed by the radioactive decay of neptunium.

pluvial (plooˈviəl) *a.* **1** of or relating to rain, rainy. **2** (*Geol.*) due to the action of rain. **pluviometer** (-omˈitə) *n.* a rain gauge. **pluviometric** (-metˈ-) *a.* **pluviometrical** *a.* **pluviometrically** *adv.* **pluvious** *a.*

ply[1] (plī) *n.* (*pl.* **plies**) **1** a thickness, a layer. **2** a fold, a plait, a twist, a strand (of a rope, twine etc.). **plywood** *n.* board consisting of three or more thin layers of wood glued together in such a manner that the grain of each is at right-angles to that of its neighbour.

ply[2] (plī) *v.t.* (*3rd pers. sing. pres.* **plies**, *pres.p.* **plying**, *past*, *p.p.* **plied**) **1** to use (a tool) vigorously or busily. **2** to work at, to employ oneself in. **3** to pursue, to press, to persist in questioning. **4** to supply (with) or subject (to) repeatedly. **5** to travel regularly along. ~*v.i.* **1** to go to and fro, to travel or sail regularly. **2** to stand or wait for custom. **3** (*Naut.*) to sail to windward.

Plymouth Brethren (plimˈəth) *n.pl.* a strict evangelical group formed at Plymouth about 1830, having no regular ministry and formulating no creed.

PM *abbr.* **1** Prime Minister. **2** post-mortem.

Pm *chem. symbol* promethium.

p.m. *abbr.* post meridiem (after noon).

PMG *abbr.* **1** Paymaster General. **2** Postmaster General.

PMS *abbr.* (*Med.*) premenstrual syndrome.

PMT *abbr.* premenstrual tension.

PNdB *abbr.* perceived noise decibel(s).

pneumatic (nūmatˈik) *a.* **1** of, relating to or consisting of air, gaseous. **2** actuated by means of compressed air or a vacuum. **3** containing or filled with air. **4** having air-filled cavities. **pneumatically** *adv.* **pneumatic drill** *n.* a rock drill in which compressed air reciprocates a loose piston which hammers a steel bit. **pneumaticity** (-tisˈ-) *n.* **pneumatics** *n.* the branch of science concerned with the mechanical properties of air and other gases. **pneumatic trough** *n.* a trough containing mercury or water used for the collection of gases in inverted vessels slightly immersed.

pneumo- (nūˈmō) *comb. form* of or relating to the lungs.

pneumococcus (nūmōkokˈəs) *n.* (*pl.* **pneumococci** (-kokˈsī)) (*Med.*) a bacterium which causes pneumonia.

pneumoconiosis (nūmōkōniōˈsis) *n.* any disease of the lungs or bronchi caused by habitually inhaling metallic or mineral dust.

pneumonia (nūmōˈniə) *n.* acute inflammation of a lung or the lungs. **pneumonic** (-monˈ-) *a.*

pneumonic plague *n.* a contagious bacterial disease causing fever, delirium and infection of the lungs.

PNG *abbr.* Papua New Guinea.

PO *abbr.* **1** Petty Officer. **2** Pilot Officer. **3** postal order. **4** Post Office.

Po *chem. symbol* polonium.

po (pō) *n.* (*pl.* **pos**) (*coll.*) a chamber pot.

poa (pō´ə) *n.* any plant of the genus *Poa* of grasses, meadow grass.

p.o.a. *abbr.* price on application.

poach[1] (pōch) *v.t.* to cook (an egg, fish etc.) in simmering liquid. **poacher**[1] *n.*

poach[2] (pōch) *v.t.* **1** to take (game, fish etc.) from another's lands or by illegitimate methods. **2** to take or use dishonestly or illegally. **3** in tennis, to take (a shot) when in one's partner's part of the court. ~*v.i.* **1** to encroach or trespass on another's lands, esp. to take game, fish etc. **2** to take game, fish etc. by illegal or unsportsmanlike methods. **3** to intrude or encroach upon another's rights, area of responsibility etc. **4** to take an advantage unfairly, e.g. in a race or game. **poacher**[2] *n.*

poacher[1] POACH[1].

poacher[2] POACH[2].

pochard (pō´chəd) *n.* (*pl.* **pochard, pochards**) any European diving sea duck of the genus *Aethya*, esp. *A. ferina.*

pochette (poshet´) *n.* a small handbag shaped like an envelope.

pock (pok) *n.* a pockmark. **pocked** *a.* **pockmark** *n.* **1** the pit or scar left by a pustule. **2** any similar mark or indentation. **pockmarked, pock-pitted** *a.* **pocky** *a.* (*comp.* **pockier**, *superl.* **pockiest**).

pocket (pok´it) *n.* **1** a small bag, sack or pouch, esp. a small bag inserted in the clothing, to contain articles carried about the person. **2** a pouchlike compartment in a car door etc. **3** pecuniary means. **4** an isolated area or patch. **5** (*Geol.*) a cavity in rock, containing foreign matter. **6** a small netted bag in snooker or pool to receive the balls. **7** an air pocket. ~*a.* **1** for the pocket. **2** small. ~*v.t.* (*pres.p.* **pocketing**, *past, p.p.* **pocketed**) **1** to put into a pocket. **2** to keep in or as if in the pocket. **3** to appropriate, esp. illegitimately. **4** to repress or conceal (one's feelings). **5** in snooker or pool, to drive (a ball) into a pocket. **6** to submit to (an insult etc.) without showing resentment. **in pocket 1** having made a profit. **2** (of money) available. **in someone's pocket 1** under someone's influence or control. **2** intimate with someone. **out of pocket** having made a loss, having less money than before. **to put one's hand in one's pocket** to spend or give money. **pocketable** *a.* **pocket battleship** *n.* (*Hist.*) a small battleship. **pocketbook** *n.* **1** a notebook or a book or case for carrying papers etc. in the pocket. **2** (*N Am.*) a purse or handbag. **3** (*N Am.*) a paperback book or any small book. **pocketful** *n.* (*pl.* **pocketfuls**). **pocket knife** *n.* a knife with blades shutting into the handle, for carrying in the pocket. **pocketless** *a.* **pocket money** *n.* **1** money for occasional expenses or amusements. **2** a small, regular allowance given to a child. **pockety** *a.*

pod[1] (pod) *n.* **1** a long capsule or seed vessel, esp. of leguminous plants. **2** any of various similar receptacles, such as the case enclosing the eggs of a locust, a silkworm cocoon, a narrow-necked eel-net etc. **3** a streamlined container, housing an engine, fuel, armaments etc., attached to the outside of an aircraft. **4** a detachable compartment on a spacecraft. ~*v.i.* (*pres.p.* **podding**, *past, p.p.* **podded**) to produce pods. ~*v.t.* to shell (peas etc.). **in pod** (*coll.*) pregnant.

pod[2] (pod) *n.* a flock, bunch or small herd of whales, seals etc.

podagra (pədag´rə) *n.* (*Med.*) gout, esp. in the foot. **podagral, podagric, podagrous** *a.*

podge (poj) *n.* a short and stout person. **podgy** *a.* (*comp.* **podgier**, *superl.* **podgiest**) **1** short and stout. **2** (of a face) plump. **podginess** *n.*

podiatry (pōdī´ətri) *n.* chiropody. **podiatrist** *n.*

podium (pō´diəm) *n.* (*pl.* **podiums, podia** (-diə)) **1** a low projecting wall or basement supporting a building etc. **2** a platform encircling the arena in an amphitheatre. **3** a continuous structural bench round a hall etc. **4** a small raised platform (for a conductor, lecturer etc.). **podial** *a.*

podzol (pod´zol), **podsol** (-sol) *n.* an infertile soil, with a greyish-white upper layer, like ash, and a brown subsoil.

poem (pō´im, -əm) *n.* **1** a metrical composition, esp. of an impassioned and imaginative kind. **2** an artistic and imaginative composition in verse or prose. **3** anything supremely beautiful, well-executed or satisfying.

poesy (pō´izi, -si) *n.* (*pl.* **poesies**) **1** the art of poetry. **2** metrical compositions collectively.

poet (pō´it) *n.* **1** a writer of poems or metrical compositions, esp. one possessing high powers of imagination and rhythmical expression. **2** a person possessed of high imaginative or creative power. **poetaster** (-tas´tə) *n.* an inferior or petty poet; a pitiful versifier. **poetess** (-tis) *n.* (*dated*) a woman poet. **poetic** (-et´-), **poetical** *a.* **1** of or relating to, or suitable for poetry or poets. **2** expressed in poetry, written in poetry. **3** having the finer qualities of poetry. **4** fit to be expressed in poetry. **poetically** *adv.* **poeticize** (-sīz), **poeticise** *v.t.* to make poetic. **poetic justice** *n.* punishment or reward ideally (often ironically) well-deserved. **poetic licence** *n.* the latitude in grammar etc. allowed to poets. **poetics** *n.* **1** the theory or principles of writing poetry. **2** the branch of literary criticism dealing with poetry. **Poet Laureate** *n.* (*pl.* **Poets Laureate**) an officer of the British royal household whose nominal duty is to compose an ode every year for the sovereign's birthday, for any great national victory etc. **poetry** (-ri) *n.* **1** the art or work of a poet. **2** a quality in anything that powerfully stirs the imagination or the aesthetic sense. **3** something resembling poetry in beauty, grace etc.

po-faced (pōfāst´) *a.* (*coll.*) **1** deadpan. **2** humourless, stolid. **3** stupidly solemn. **4** smug.

pogo (pō´gō), **pogo stick** *n.* (*pl.* **pogos, pogo sticks**) a toy consisting of a strong pole attached to a spring and having a handle at the top and a crossbar on which one stands to bounce along.

pogrom (pog´rəm, pəgrom´) *n.* an organized attack, usu. with pillage and massacre, upon a class of the population, esp. Jews.

poignant (poin´yənt) *a.* **1** sharp, painful to the emotions, moving. **2** stimulating to the palate, pungent. **3** keen, piercing. **4** bitter, painful. **poignance, poignancy** *n.* **poignantly** *adv.*

poikilothermal (poikiləthœ´məl), **poikilothermic** (-mik) *a.* having a body temperature which varies with the surrounding temperature. **poikilotherm** (poi´-) *n.* an animal of this type. **poikilothermia, poikilothermism, poikilothermy** *n.*

poinsettia (poinset´iə) *n.* a shrub of the S American and Mexican genus *Poinsettia*, with red leaflike bracts and small greenish-yellow flowerheads.

point (point) *n.* **1** a mark made by the end of anything sharp, a dot. **2** a dot used as a mark of punctuation, to indicate vowels (as in Hebrew) etc. **3** (*Print.*) a full stop, or decimal mark to separate integral from fractional digits in decimal numbers etc. **4** a particular item, a detail. **5** a particular place or position. **6** a specific position or stage in a development or on a scale. **7** a state or condition. **8 a** a particular moment. **b** the precise moment for an event, action etc., the instant. **9** the verge. **10** a step or stage in an argument, discourse etc. **11** a unit used in measuring or counting, in assessing superiority etc., in appraising qualities of an exhibit in a show, a racehorse etc., in reckoning odds given to an opponent in a game, in betting, or in scoring in games. **12** a success in argument. **13** a unit of weight etc. for diamonds (2 mg). **14** a salient quality, a trait, a characteristic. **15** the essential element, the exact object (of a discussion, joke etc.), the main purport, the gist. **16** the aim, the purpose; the value of an activity. **17** a conclusion. **18** a suggestion, a tip. **19** the sharp end of a tool, weapon etc., the tip. **20** a cape, a promontory (esp. in place names). **21** a tapering rail moving on a pivot for switching a train from one line to another. **22** (*pl.*) the contact-breakers in the distributor of an internal-combustion engine. **23** a power point. **24** pungency, effectiveness, force. **25** (*Geom.*) that which has position but not magnitude. **26** (*Print.*) the unit of measurement for type bodies, approx. 1/72 in. (0.351 mm). **27** a fielder or position on the offside square of, and close in to, the batsman in cricket. **28** (*Mil.*) the leading party of an advanced guard. **29** (*pl.*) the extremities of a horse, a dog etc. **30** in ballet, pointe. **31 a** the act

of pointing by a setter etc. **b** the position adopted by the dog. **32** in fencing, a twist. **33 a** a point of the compass. **b** a particular place on the horizon corresponding to one of these. **34** in boxing, the tip of the chin. **35** a patch of a different colour in the fur of some cats. ~*v.t.* **1** to sharpen. **2** to mark with points, to punctuate; to indicate the vowels of (as Hebrew). **3** to give force or point to. **4** to fill (the joints of masonry) with mortar or cement pressed in with a trowel. **5** to indicate, to show. **6** to direct (a finger etc. at). **7** to turn in a particular direction, to aim. **8** to give effect or pungency to (a remark, jest etc.). **9** to indicate the meaning or point of by a gesture. ~*v.i.* **1** to direct attention (to). **2** (of a pointer or setter) to draw attention to game by standing rigidly and looking at it. **3** to aim (at or towards). **4** to face or be directed (towards). **5** to tend towards. **6** to hint at, or to be evidence of. **at all points 1** in every part or direction. **2** completely, perfectly. **at/ on the point** on the verge (of). **off the point** beside the point. **on the point of** about to do. **to have a point** to have an effective or relevant argument. **to make a point 1** to score a point. **2** to establish a point in argument. **to make a point of 1** to attach special importance to. **2** to take special care to. **to make one's point** to establish a point in argument, to make one's opinion clear. **to point out** to indicate, to draw attention to. **to point up** to emphasize, to highlight. **to take someone's point** to understand someone's argument. **to the point** appropriate, apposite, pertinent. **to win on points** in boxing, to win by scoring more points, not by a knockout. **up to a point** partially, not completely. **point-blank** *a.* **1** aimed or fired horizontally directly at the mark making no allowance for the downward curve of the trajectory; hence very close (permitting such aim to be taken). **2** direct, blunt. ~*adv.* **1** at very close range; horizontally, with direct aim. **2** directly, bluntly. ~*n.* a point-blank shot. **point duty** *n.* the work of a police officer or traffic warden stationed at a junction of streets or other point to regulate traffic. **pointed** *a.* **1** having a sharp point. **2** having point, penetrating, cutting. **3** referring to some particular person or thing. **4** emphasized, made obvious. **pointedly** *adv.* **pointedness** *n.* **pointer** *n.* **1** a person or thing which points. **2** the index hand of a clock etc. **3** a rod used for pointing on a blackboard etc. **4** an indication, a hint, a tip. **5 a** a dog of a breed trained to point at game. **b** this breed of dog. **pointing** *n.* **1** the act of indicating, directing, sharpening etc. **2 a** the process of finishing or renewing a mortar-joint in a wall. **b** the mortar used in this process. **c** the finish produced. **3 a** punctuation. **b** division into groups of words or syllables for singing. **point lace** *n.* lace made with the point of a needle. **pointless** *a.* **1** having no point. **2** purposeless, futile. **3** in sport, without any points scored.

pointlessly *adv.* pointlessness *n.* point of honour *n.* a matter involving personal honour or reputation. point of no return *n.* 1 a critical point (at which one must commit oneself irrevocably to a course of action). 2 the point in a flight where shortage of fuel makes it necessary to go on as return is impossible. point of order *n.* a question of procedure in a debate etc. point of sale *n.* the place, esp. a retail shop, where the sale of an article physically takes place. point of the compass *n.* 1 each one of the 32 angular divisions of the compass. 2 the angle of 11° 15´ between two such points. point of view *n.* 1 the position from which a thing is looked at. 2 a way of regarding a matter. pointsman *n.* (*pl.* pointsmen) 1 a police officer or traffic warden on point duty. 2 a person in charge of the switches on a railway. point-to-point *a.* of or relating to a steeplechase or other race in a direct line from one point of a course to another. ~*n.* such a race. point-to-pointer *n.* point-to-pointing *n.* pointy *a.* (*comp.* pointier, *superl.* pointiest) having a sharp point or points.

pointe (pwăt) *n.* (*pl.* pointes (pwăt)) 1 (in ballet) the extreme tip of the toe. 2 a position in which the dancer balances on this.

pointillism (pwă´tilizm) *n.* (in painting) delineation by means of dots of various pure colours which merge into a whole in the viewer's eye. pointillist *n.*, *a.* pointillistic *a.*

poise (poiz) *v.t.* 1 to balance to hold or carry in equilibrium. 2 to place in a carefully balanced position. 3 to counterpoise. ~*v.i.* 1 to be balanced or in equilibrium. 2 to hang (in the air) over, to hover. ~*n.* 1 composure, assurance, self-possession. 2 equipoise, equilibrium. 3 a counterpoise. 4 a state of suspense, indecision etc. 5 physical balance. poised *a.* 1 balanced. 2 having or showing composure, self-possession etc. 3 in a state of readiness, all set (to).

poison (poi´zən) *n.* 1 a substance that injures or kills an organism into which it is absorbed. 2 anything destructive or corrupting. 3 (*Chem.*, *Physics*) a substance which retards catalytic activity or a chemical reaction, or, by absorbing neutrons, the course of a nuclear reaction. ~*v.t.* 1 to put poison in or upon; to infect with or administer poison. 2 to kill or injure by this means. 3 to embitter or turn (someone) against. 4 to taint, to corrupt, to vitiate, to pervert. poisoned chalice *n.* something apparently desirable which has a hidden inconvenience or disadvantage. poisoner *n.* poison gas *n.* (*Mil.*) poisonous or stupefying gas or vapour used in warfare to disable an enemy. poison ivy *n.* (*pl.* poison ivies) any of various N American shrubs or climbing plants of the genus *Rhus*, which cause an intensely itching skin rash. poison oak *n.* either of two N American shrubs, *Rhus toxicodendron* and *R. diversilobia*, related to poison ivy and causing a similar rash. poisonous *a.* poisonously *adv.* poisonousness *n.* poison

pen letter *n.* a letter written maliciously and usu. anonymously, to abuse or frighten the recipient. poison pill *n.* 1 a pill containing poison. 2 a tactic used by a company to make itself unattractive to a possible takeover bidder.

poke¹ (pōk) *v.t.* 1 to thrust, to push (in, out, through etc.) with the end of something. 2 to jab, to prod (with a finger, a stick etc.). 3 to stir (a fire) with a poker. 4 to cause to protrude. 5 to put, move etc. by poking. 6 to make (a hole etc.) by poking. 7 (*coll.*) to punch. 8 (*taboo sl.*) to have sexual intercourse with. 9 to shut (up) in a confined space. ~*v.i.* 1 to thrust, to jab. 2 to protrude. 3 (*coll.*) to pry, to search. 4 to dawdle, to busy oneself without any definite object. ~*n.* 1 a poking, a push, a thrust, a prod, a nudge. 2 a collar with a drag attached to prevent animals from breaking through fences etc. 3 (*coll.*) a punch. 4 (*taboo sl.*) an act of sexual intercourse. poky¹ *a.* (*comp.* pokier, *superl.* pokiest) 1 (of a room etc.) cramped, confined, stuffy. 2 slow, petty, dull. pokily *adv.* pokiness *n.*

poke² (pōk) *n.* (*esp. Sc.*) a bag, a sack.

poker¹ (pō´kə) *n.* 1 an iron rod used to stir a fire. 2 a metal rod used in pokerwork. pokerwork *n.* the production of decorative designs on wood by burning or scorching with a heated metal rod.

poker² (pō´kə) *n.* a card game in which the players bet on the value in their hands. poker dice *n.* a dice marked with designs of the playing cards from nine to ace, instead of spots. poker-face *n.* 1 an expressionless face. 2 a person with such a face. poker-faced *a.*

pokeweed (pōk´wēd) *n.* a N American herb, *Phytolacca americana*, with purple berries used medicinally.

poky¹ POKE¹.

poky² (pō´ki), **pokey** *n.* (*pl.* pokies, pokeys) (*sl.*) (a) prison.

Polack (pō´lak) *n.* (*sl.*, *offensive*) a Pole or a person of Polish origin.

polar (pō´lə) *a.* 1 of, relating to or situated near the poles of the earth or of the celestial sphere. 2 coming from the regions near the poles. 3 of or relating to a magnetic pole, having polarity, magnetic. 4 having two opposite elements or tendencies, esp. positive and negative electricity. 5 directly opposite in character or tendencies. 6 of or relating to the poles of a cell. polar bear *n.* a white arctic bear, *Thalarctos maritimus*. polar body *n.* (*Biol.*) a small cell produced from the ovum during its formation. polar coordinate *n.* (*Math.*) either one of a pair of coordinates which define the position of a point by means of a line from the point to the origin and the angle this makes with a fixed line through the origin. polar curve *n.* (*Math.*) a curve related to a given curve and to a fixed point, the pole. polar distance *n.* the angular distance of a point from the nearest pole. polarly *adv.* polar star *n.* the pole star.

polari- (pōˊləri), **polaro-** (-ō) *comb. form* of or relating to poles or polarized light.

polarimeter (pōlərimˊitə) *n.* an instrument for measuring the polarization of light, or the rotation of the plane of polarized light. **polarimetric** (-metˊ-) *a.* **polarimetry** *n.*

polariscope (pōlarˊiskōp) *n.* a polarimeter. **polariscopic** (-skopˊ-) *a.*

polarity (pōlarˊiti) *n.* (*pl.* **polarities**) 1 the state of having two opposite poles, or of having different or opposing properties in opposite parts or directions. 2 the tendency of a magnetized bar to point to the magnetic poles. 3 the quality (in electricity) of being attracted to one pole and repelled from the other. 4 the disposition in a body to place its mathematical axis in a particular direction. 5 diametric opposition in opinions etc.

polarize (pōˊlərīz), **polarise** *v.t.* 1 to cause to acquire polarity or polarization. 2 to restrict the vibrations of (a light wave) to one direction. 3 to reduce the voltage of (a battery) by the collection of hydrogen on the positive electrode. 4 to cause to divide into two opposing groups or camps. ~*v.i.* 1 to acquire polarity or polarization. 2 to split up into two opposing camps or groups. **polarizable** *a.* **polarization** (-zāˊshən) *n.* **polarizer** *n.*

polarography (pōlərogˊrəfi) *n.* (*Chem.*) the analysis of a substance by measuring the current produced by electrolysing it at different voltages. **polarographic** (-grafˊik) *a.*

Polaroid® (pōˊləroid) *n.* 1 a light-polarizing material used esp. in sunglasses. 2 a type of camera which produces a finished print from inside itself within seconds of the picture's being taken. 3 such a finished print.

polder (pōlˊdə) *n.* a tract of land below sea or river level, that has been drained and cultivated, esp. in the Netherlands.

Pole (pōl) *n.* 1 a native or inhabitant of Poland. 2 a person of Polish descent.

pole[1] (pōl) *n.* 1 a long slender piece of wood or metal, usu. rounded and tapering, esp. fixed upright in the ground as a flagstaff, support for a tent, telegraph wires etc. 2 the shaft of a large horse-drawn vehicle. 3 (*Hist.*) an instrument for measuring; a measure of length, a rod or perch, 5½ yd. (5 m). 4 the flexible rod of wood or fibreglass used in pole-vaulting. 5 (*esp. N Am.*) a simple fishing rod. ~*v.t.* to furnish or support with, to convey or push by a pole or poles. **up the pole 1** (*sl.*) crazy, mad. 2 mistaken, wrong. **pole position** *n.* the most advantageous position at the start of a race, esp. a motor or horse race. **pole vault** *n.* a field event in which the competitor attempts to clear a very high bar with the aid of a long flexible pole. **pole-vault** *v.i.* **pole-vaulter** *n.*

pole[2] (pōl) *n.* 1 either of the extremities, north and south, of the axis on which a sphere or spheroid, esp. the earth, revolves. 2 each of the points where the projection of the axis of the earth pierces the celestial sphere and round which the stars appear to revolve. 3 a point from which a pencil of rays radiates, a fixed point of reference. 4 either of the two points in a body where the attractive or repelling force is greatest, as in a magnet. 5 either of the two terminals, positive and negative, of an electric cell, battery etc. 6 (*Biol.*) the extremity of the axis of a cell nucleus etc. 7 either of the two polar regions. 8 either of two opposite extremes. 9 either of the two points where the axis of a circle cuts the surface of a sphere. 10 (*Geom.*) a fixed point. 11 (*poet.*) the sky, the firmament. **poles apart 1** as far apart as possible. 2 having widely divergent views, attitudes etc. **pole star** *n.* 1 (*Astron.*) a bright star, Polaris in Ursa Minor, within a degree and a quarter of the northern celestial pole. 2 a guiding principle. 3 a lodestar, a centre of attraction. **poleward** *a.* **polewards** *a., adv.*

Usage note It is conventional to use capital letters (*North Pole, South Pole*) when referring to the polar regions.

pole-axe (pōlˊaks), (*N Am.*) **poleax** *n.* 1 (*Hist.*) a form of battleaxe consisting of an axe set on a long handle. 2 a long-handled butcher's axe with a hammer at the back, used for slaughtering cattle. ~*v.t.* to strike, kill or destroy (as if) with a poleaxe.

polecat (pōlˊkat) *n.* (*pl. in general* **polecat**, *in particular* **polecats**) 1 a small carnivorous European weasel-like mammal, *Mustela putorius*, with two glands emitting an offensive smell. 2 (*N Am.*) a skunk.

polemic (pəlemˊik) *n.* 1 a controversy or controversial discussion. 2 (*pl.*) the art or practice of controversial discussion, esp. in theology. 3 an aggressive attack on, or rebuttal of, another's conduct or views. ~*a.* polemical. **polemical** *a.* 1 of or relating to controversy. 2 controversial, disputatious. **polemically** *adv.* **polemicist** (-sist) *n.* **polemicize** (-sīz), **polemicise**, **polemize** (polˊəmīz), **polemise** *v.i.*

polenta (pəlenˊtə) *n.* a kind of porridge made of maize meal, or less commonly from barley or chestnut meal, a common food in Italy.

police (pəlēsˊ) *n.* 1 a (*usu. as pl.*) a civil force organized by a state for the maintenance of order, the detection of crime, and the apprehension of offenders. b a similar force enforcing regulations on behalf of an official body (*military police*). 2 (*as pl.*) constables etc. belonging to this force. ~*v.t.* 1 to control by the use of police. 2 to provide with police. 3 to supervise, to regulate, to discipline. **police constable** *n.* a police officer of the lowest rank. **police dog** *n.* a dog, usu. an Alsatian, trained to assist police. **police force** *n.* a separately organized body of police. **police informer** *n.* a person who gives information to the police about criminals and their activities. **policeman** *n.* (*pl.* **policemen**) any male member of a police force, esp. a constable. **police state** *n.* a totalitarian state maintained by the use of political police. **police station** *n.* the headquarters of a local section of the police. **policewoman** *n.* (*pl.* **policewomen**) a female member of the police force.

policy[1] (pol´isi) *n.* (*pl.* **policies**) **1** a course of action or administration recommended or adopted by a party, government, firm, organization or individual. **2** prudent conduct. **3** prudence, foresight or sagacity in managing or conducting, esp. state affairs.

Usage note See note under POLITY.

policy[2] (pol´isi) *n.* (*pl.* **policies**) **1** a contract of insurance. **2** the document containing such a contract. **policyholder** *n.* a person or organization holding a contract of insurance.

poliomyelitis (pōliōmīəli´tis), **polio** *n.* (*Med.*) an acute infectious viral disease affecting the central nervous system, which can cause paralysis and muscle wasting.

Polish (pō´lish) *a.* of or relating to Poland or to its inhabitants or their language. ~*n.* **1** the language of the Poles. **2** (*pl.*) the Polish people. **Polish notation** *n.* (*Math.*) a notation which does not use brackets or punctuation and places operators before their arguments, also called *prefix notation*.

polish (pol´ish) *v.t.* **1** to make smooth or glossy, usu. by friction. **2** to refine, to free from roughness or coarseness. **3** to bring to a fully finished state. ~*v.i.* to take a polish. ~*n.* **1** a smooth glossy surface, esp. produced by friction. **2** friction applied for this purpose. **3** a substance applied to impart a polish. **4** the act, or an instance, of polishing. **5** refinement, elegance of manners. **to polish off 1** (*coll.*) to finish speedily. **2** to get rid of. **to polish up 1** to give a polish to. **2** to improve, or refresh (one's knowledge of something) by study. **polishable** *a.* **polished** *a.* **1** accomplished. **2** impeccably executed. **3** (of rice) having had the outer husk removed. **polisher** *n.*

politburo (pol´itbūrō) *n.* (*pl.* **politburos**) the political bureau of the Central Committee of the Communist Party of the former USSR.

polite (pəlīt´) *a.* (*comp.* **politer**, *superl.* **politest**) **1** refined in manners. **2** courteous. **3** cultivated. **4** (of literature) elegant, refined. **politely** *adv.* **politeness** *n.*

politic[1] (pol´itik) *a.* **1** prudent and sagacious. **2** prudently devised, judicious, expedient. **politicly** *adv.* artfully, cunningly.

politic[2] POLITICKING.

political (pəlit´ikəl) *a.* **1** of or relating to civil government and its administration. **2** of or relating to politics, esp. party politics. **3** taking or belonging to a side in politics. **4** interested or involved in politics. **5** of or relating to aspects of power and status in any organization, rather than to those of principle. **6** having an established system of government. **political asylum**

n. protection from extradition given by one country to a political refugee from another country. **political correctness** *n.* the avoidance of discrimination, in language or action, against minorities such as women, people of colour, lesbians and gays or people with disabilities. **political economy** *n.* the science of the production and distribution of wealth, the study of economics in relation to government. **political economist** *n.* **politically** *adv.* **politically correct**, **politically incorrect** *a.* of or relating to language, behaviour etc. associated with political correctness. **political prisoner** *n.* a person imprisoned for their political beliefs or activities. **political science** *n.* the study of government, politics and the state. **political scientist** *n.*

politician (politish´ən) *n.* **1** a person experienced or skilled in politics. **2** a person engaged in or devoted to party politics, usu. as a career.

politicize (pəlit´isīz), **politicise** *v.t.* **1** to give a political tone or scope to. **2** to make politically aware. **politicization** (-zā´shən) *n.*

politicking (pol´itiking) *n.* political activity, esp. vote-getting. **politic**[2], **politick** *v.i.* (*pres.p.* **politicking**, *past*, *p.p.* **politicked**) to engage in political activity. **politicker** *n.*

politico (pəlit´ikō) *n.* (*pl.* **politicos**, **politicoes**) (*coll.*) a politician.

politico- (pəlit´ikō) *comb. form* **1** political and. **2** politically.

politics (pol´itiks) *n.* **1** the art or science of civil government. **2** the relationships, involving power and authority, between people, or between people and organizations. **3** the profession of politics. **4** (*sing. or pl. in constr.*) political affairs. **5** (*as pl.*) the political dimension to any action or activity. **6** (*as pl.*) any activities concerned with the acquisition, apportionment or exercise of power within an organization, manoeuvring, intrigue. **7** (*as pl.*) a person's political views or sympathies.

polity (pol´iti) *n.* (*pl.* **polities**) **1** the form, system or constitution of the civil government of a State. **2** an organized community, a body politic. **3** the form of organization of an institution etc.

Usage note The nouns *polity* and *policy* should not be confused: a *polity* is a form of civil government, and a *policy* a course of action.

polka (pōl´kə, pol´-) *n.* (*pl.* **polkas**) **1** a lively round dance of Bohemian origin. **2** a piece of music in duple time for this. ~*v.i.* (*3rd pers. sing. pres.* **polkas**, *pres.p.* **polkaing**, *past*, *p.p.* **polkaed**, **polka'd**) to dance a polka. **polka dot** *n.* a small dot in a regular pattern of dots, esp. as a textile design.

poll[1] (pōl) *n.* **1** the voting at an election, the number of votes polled, or the counting of these. **2** the time or place of election. **3** an attempt to ascertain public opinion by questioning a few individuals. **4** a register or enumeration of heads or persons, esp. of persons entitled to vote at elections. **5** (*Sc., dial.*) **a** a human head. **b** the part of the head on which the hair grows. ~*v.t.* **1** to remove the top of (trees etc.). **2** to cut off the horns of. **3** to take the votes of. **4** to receive (a specified number of votes). **5** to give (one's vote). **6** to ascertain and record the opinion of, in a poll. ~*v.i.* to give one's vote. **pollable** *a.* **pollee** (-lē) *n.* **poller** *n.* **polling** *n.* **polling booth** *n.* a semi-enclosed structure in which a voter marks their ballot paper. **polling day** *n.* the day on which an election is held. **polling station** *n.* a building designated as a place where voters should go to cast their votes. **pollster** (-stə) *n.* a person who conducts or analyses an opinion poll. **poll tax** *n.* a capitation tax or one levied on every person.

poll² (pōl), **polled** (pōld) *a.* **1** (of cattle) having had the horns cut off. **2** hornless.

pollack (pol'ək), **pollock** *n.* (*pl. in general* **pollack, pollock,** *in particular* **pollacks, pollocks**) a sea fish, *Pollachius pollachius*, with a protruding lower jaw, used for food.

pollard (pol'əd) *n.* **1** a tree with its branches cut off so as to have a dense head of new young branches. **2** a stag or other animal that has cast its horns. **3** a polled or hornless ox, sheep or other animal. ~*v.t.* to lop the top of (a tree).

pollen (pol'ən) *n.* a powder of fine dustlike grains discharged from the anthers of flowers and able to fertilize in the ovules. **pollen count** *n.* a measure of the pollen present in the air, published to assist hay fever sufferers etc. **pollenless** *a.* **pollinate** *v.t.* to sprinkle (a stigma) with pollen so as to cause fertilization. **pollination** (-ā'shən) *n.* **pollinator** *n.*

pollute (pəloot') *v.t.* **1** to make foul or unclean. **2** to contaminate (an environment), esp. with man-made waste. **3** to defile; to corrupt the moral purity of. **4** to profane. **pollutant** *a., n.* **polluter** *n.* **pollution** (-shən) *n.*

polly (pol'i), **pollie** *n.* (*pl.* **pollies**) (*Austral., coll.*) a politician.

Pollyanna (polian'ə) *n.* (*pl.* **Pollyannas**) an excessively or irritatingly cheerful and optimistic person. **Pollyannaish** *a.* **Pollyannaism** *n.*

polo (pō'lō) *n.* (*pl.* **polos**) a game of Asian origin resembling hockey but played on horseback. **polo neck** *n.* (a jumper with) a close-fitting, doubled-over collar. **polo shirt** *n.* a short-sleeved knitted cotton shirt with a collar, opening only partly down the front. **polo stick** *n.* a long-handled mallet for playing polo.

polonaise (polənāz') *n.* **1** a slow dance of Polish origin. **2** a piece of music in 3/4 time for this.

polonium (pəlō'niəm) *n.* (*Chem.*) a radioactive element, at. no. 84, chem. symbol Po.

polony (pəlō'ni) *n.* (*pl.* **polonies**) a sausage of partly-cooked pork.

poltergeist (pōl'təgīst, pol'-) *n.* an alleged spirit which makes its presence known by noises and moving objects.

poltroon (poltroon') *n.* a contemptible coward.

poly (pol'i) *n.* (*pl.* **polys**) (*coll.*) short for POLYTECHNIC.

poly- (pol'i) *comb. form* **1** several, many. **2** excessive, abnormal. **3** (*Chem.*) denoting a polymer.

polyadelphous (poliədel'fəs) *a.* (*Bot.*) having many stamens arranged in three or more groups.

polyamide (poliam'īd, -ā'-) *n.* (*Chem.*) a synthetic, polymeric material such as nylon.

polyandry (pol'iandri) *n.* **1** the practice of a woman having more than one husband at a time. **2** (*Bot.*) the state of a flower having many stamens. **polyandrist** *n.* **polyandrous** *a.*

polyanthus (polian'thəs) *n.* (*pl.* **polyanthuses**) a garden variety of primula, prob. a development from the cowslip or oxlip.

polycarbonate (polikah'bənāt) *n.* any of a class of strong thermoplastics, mostly used as moulding materials.

polychaete (pol'ikēt) *a.* belonging to the Polychaeta, a class of marine worms with setae. ~*n.* a polychaete worm. **polychaetan** (-kē'-), **polychaetous** *a.*

polychlorinated biphenyl (poliklōrinātid bīfē'nil) *n.* any of various compounds with two benzene molecules in which chlorinated atoms have replaced hydrogens.

polychromatic (polikrəmat'ik) *a.* **1** exhibiting many colours or a play of colours. **2** (of radiation) containing more than one wavelength. **polychromatism** (-krō'mətizm) *n.* **polychrome** (pol'ikrōm) *n.* **1** a work of art executed in several colours, esp. a statue. **2** varied colouring. ~*a.* having or executed in many colours. **polychromic** (-krō'-), **polychromous** *a.* **polychromy** (pol'ikrōmi) *n.*

polycotton (polikot'ən) *n.* a fabric made of a mixture of polyester and cotton fabrics.

polycrystalline (polikris'təlīn) *a.* (of a solid substance) having constituent substances with differently-oriented crystals.

polycyclic (polisī'klik, -sik'lik) *a.* (*Chem.*) having more than one ring of atoms in the molecule.

polydactyl (polidak'til) *a.* having more than the normal number of fingers or toes.

polyester (polies'tə) *n.* **1** any of a group of synthetic polymers made up of esters, used esp. in making fibres for cloth, plastics and resins. **2** a fabric made of such fibres.

polyethene, polyethylene POLYTHENE.

polygamy (pəlig'əmi) *n.* **1** the practice or condition of having more than one wife or husband at the same time. **2** the state of having more than one mate. **3** (*Bot.*) the state of having male, female and hermaphrodite flowers on the same plant. **polygamic** (-gam'ik) *a.* **polygamist** *n.* **polygamous** *a.* **polygamously** *adv.*

polygene (pol'ijēn) *n.* (*Biol.*) any of a group of genes that together control a single characteristic.

polyglot (pol'iglot) *a.* expressed in or speaking many languages. ~*n.* **1** a polyglot person. **2** a book, esp. the Bible, written in or translated into many languages. **polyglottal** (-glot´-), **polyglottic** a. **polyglottism** n.

polygon (pol´igon) n. a closed plane figure, usu. rectilinear and of more than four angles or sides. **polygonal** (pəlig´ənəl), †**polygonous** (-lig´-) a. **polygon of forces** n. a polygon which represents the various forces acting on a body by the arrangement of its sides.

polygonum (pəlig´ənəm) n. any plant of the genus *Polygonum*, comprising the knotgrass etc., with jointed stems.

polygraph (pol´igrahf) n. an instrument which registers several small physiological changes simultaneously, e.g. in pulse rate, body temperature, often used as a lie detector.

polygyny (polij´ini) n. the practice or condition of having more than one wife at a time. **polygynous** (-lij´-) a.

polyhedron (polihē´drən) n. (pl. **polyhedrons**, **polyhedra** (-drə)) a solid bounded by many (usu. more than four) plane sides. **polyhedral**, **polyhedric**, **polyhedrous** a.

polymath (pol´imath) n. a person of great and varied learning. **polymathic** (-math´-) a. **polymathy** (-lim´-) n.

polymer (pol´imə) n. (Chem.) a compound, formed by polymerization, which has large molecules made up of many comparatively simple repeated units. **polymerase** (pol´imərāz, pəlim´ərāz) n. an enzyme which catalyses the polymerization of DNA or RNA. **polymeric** (-mer´ik) a. **polymerize, polymerise** v.t. to cause to undergo polymerization. ~v.i. to undergo polymerization. **polymerization** (-zā´shən) n. a chemical reaction in which two or more small molecules combine as repeating units in a much larger molecule. **polymerous** (-lim´-) a. (Biol.) consisting of many parts.

polymorphic (polimaw´fik) a. having, assuming, or occurring in many forms. **polymorphism** n. **polymorphous** a.

Polynesian (polinē´zhən) a. of or relating to Polynesia, a group of islands of the central and southern Pacific. ~n. **1** a native or inhabitant of Polynesia. **2** the group of related languages spoken in Polynesia, including Maori and Hawaiian.

polyneuritis (polinūrī´tis) n. (Med.) simultaneous inflammation of many nerves. **polyneuritic** (-nūrit´ik) a.

polynomial (polinō´miəl) a. (Math.) multinomial. ~n. a multinomial.

polyp (pol´ip) n. **1** (Zool.) any one of various coelenterates, such as the hydra, the sea anemone etc., an individual in a compound organism of various kinds. **2** (Med.) a polypus. **polypary** n. (pl. **polyparies**) the calcareous or chitonous structure supporting a colony of polyps.

polypeptide (polipep´tīd) n. (Chem.) any of a group of polymers made up of long amino-acid chains.

polyphagous (pəlif´əgəs) a. (Zool.) feeding on various kinds of food.

polyphase (pol´ifāz) a. (of a circuit or system) having, producing or using two or more alternating voltages of equal frequency, the phases of which are cyclically displaced by fractions of a period.

polyphone (pol´ifōn) n. a symbol or letter standing for more than one sound. **polyphonic** (-fon´-), **polyphonous** (-lif´-) a. **1** (of a symbol or letter) representing different sounds. **2** (Mus.) contrapuntal. **polyphonically** adv. **polyphony** n. (pl. **polyphonies**) **1** the state of being polyphonic. **2** (a) composition in parts, each part having an independent melody of its own, counterpoint.

polyphosphate (polifos´fāt) n. (Chem.) any of several complex phosphates, used as food additives.

polyphyletic (polifīlet´ik) a. (Biol.) (of a group of organisms) descended from more than one ancestral group.

polyploid (pol´iploid) a. (Biol.) having more than twice the basic (haploid) number of chromosomes. ~n. a polyploid organism or nucleus. **polyploidy** n.

polypod (pol´ipod) a. (Zool.) having numerous feet. ~n. a millipede, e.g. a woodlouse.

polypody (pol´ipōdi) n. (pl. **polypodies**) a fern of the genus *Polypodium*, growing on rocks, walls, trees etc.

polypoid (pol´ipoid) a. like a polyp or polypus. **polypose, polypous** a.

polypropylene (poliprō´pilēn), **polypropene** (-prō´pēn) n. (Chem.) any of various plastics or fibres that are polymers of propylene, used for laminates, pipes and various fibres.

polypus (pol´ipəs) n. (pl. **polypuses, polypi** (-pī)) (Med.) a usu. benign growth with ramifications growing in a mucous cavity; a polyp.

polysaccharide (polisak´ərīd) n. any of a class of carbohydrates, e.g. starch, insulin etc., whose molecules contain chains of monosaccharides.

polysemous (polisē´məs) a. having several meanings in one word. **polysemic** a. **polysemy** (pol´isēmi, pəlis´imi) n.

polystyrene (polistī´rēn) n. a thermoplastic polymer of styrene used esp. as a transparent plastic for moulded products or in expanded form, as a rigid white foam, for packaging and insulation.

polysyllabic (polisilab´ik) a. **1** (of a word) consisting of many syllables. **2** characterized by polysyllables. **polysyllabically** adv. **polysyllable** (pol´-) n. a polysyllabic word.

polytechnic (politek´nik) a. connected with, of or relating to, or giving instruction in many subjects, esp. technical ones. ~n. (Hist.) a college where degree and other advanced courses were given in technical, vocational and academic subjects.

polytetrafluoroethylene (politetrəfluərōeth´ilēn) n. (Chem.) a tough, translucent plastic used esp. for moulded articles and as a non-stick coating.

polytheism (pol´ithēizm, -thē´-) n. the belief in or worship of a plurality of gods. **polytheist** n. **polytheistic, polytheistical** a. **polytheistically** adv.

polythene (pol´ithēn), **polyethene** (-eth´ēn), **polyethylene** (polieth´ilēn) n. (Chem.) any of various thermoplastics that are polymers of ethylene, used for packaging, domestic utensils, insulation etc.

polytonality (politənal´iti) n. (Mus.) the use of two or more keys at the same time in a piece. **polytonal** (-tō´nəl) a.

polyunsaturated (poliŭnsat´ūrātid) a. (Chem.) (of certain animal and vegetable fats) having long carbon chains with many double bonds. **polyunsaturate** n. a polyunsaturated animal or vegetable fat.

polyurethane (poliŭ´rəthān) n. any of a class of polymeric resins used esp. as foam for insulation and packing or in paints.

polyvalent (polivā´lənt) a. MULTIVALENT.

polyvinyl (polivī´nil, -əl) n., a. (Chem.) (of, related to or being) a polymerized vinyl compound. **polyvinyl acetate** n. a soft colourless polymer used in paint, adhesives etc. **polyvinyl chloride** n. a tough transparent polymer used esp. for coating wires and cables, insulation etc.

polyzoan (polizō´ən) n. any member of a class of invertebrate animals, mostly marine, existing in coral-like or plantlike colonies.

Pom[1] POMMY.

Pom[2] (pom) n. (coll.) a Pomeranian dog.

pomace (pŭm´is) n. 1 the mashed pulp of apples crushed in a cider-mill, esp. the refuse after the juice has been pressed out. 2 any pulpy substance left after crushing, esp. of fish after oil has been extracted.

pomade (pəmād´, -mahd´) n. a perfumed ointment for dressing the hair and the scalp. ~v.t. to apply this to (the hair etc.).

pomander (pōman´də, pom-) n. 1 a perfumed ball or powder kept in a box, bag etc., used as a scent and formerly carried about the person to prevent infection. 2 the perforated box or hollow ball in which this is kept or carried. 3 a spiced orange similarly used.

pome (pōm) n. 1 a compound fleshy fruit, composed of an enlarged receptacle enclosing carpels containing the seeds, such as the apple, pear, quince etc. 2 (poet.) an apple. **pomiculture** (pō´mikŭlchə) n. fruit-growing. **pomiferous** (-mif´-) a. **pomology** (pəmol´-) n. the art or science of the cultivation of fruit. **pomological** (pōmələj´-) a. **pomologist** (pəmol´-) n.

pomegranate (pom´igranit) n. 1 the fruit of a N African and W Asian tree, Punica granatum, resembling an orange, with a thick, tough rind and acid red pulp enveloping numerous seeds. 2 the tree bearing this fruit.

pomelo (pom´ilō, pŭm´-) n. (pl. **pomelos**) 1 a shaddock. 2 a grapefruit.

Pomeranian (pomərā´niən) n. 1 a breed of dog, small with a foxlike pointed muzzle and long, silky hair. 2 a dog of this breed.

pomfret (pom´frit) n. (pl. in general **pomfret**, in particular **pomfrets**) 1 any of various food-fishes of the Indian and Pacific oceans, of the family Stromateidae. 2 a food-fish of northern oceans, Brama brama.

pommel (pom´əl, pŭm´əl) n. 1 a round ball or knob, esp. on the hilt of a sword. 2 the upward projection at the front of a saddle. 3 either of the two handles on top of a pommel horse. ~v.t. (pres.p. **pommelling**, (N Am.) **pommeling**, past, p.p. **pommelled**, (N Am.) **pommeled**) to pummel. **pommel horse** n. a vaulting horse with a pair of curved handles.

Pommy (pom´i), **Pommie, Pom** (pom) n. (pl. **Pommies, Poms**) (Austral., New Zeal., offensive) a British person, esp. an immigrant to Australia or New Zealand. ~a. British.

pomp (pomp) n. 1 a pageant. 2 ceremonial display, splendour. 3 ostentatious display or parade.

pompano (pom´pənō) n. (pl. in general **pompano**, in particular **pompanos**) a W Indian food-fish of various species belonging to the family Garangidae or Stromateidae.

pom-pom (pom´pom) n. an automatic quick-firing gun, usu. mounted for anti-aircraft defence.

pompon (pom´pon), **pompom** (-pom) n. 1 an ornament in the form of a tuft or ball of feathers, ribbon etc. worn on women's and children's hats, shoes etc., on the front of a soldier's shako, on a French sailor's cap etc. 2 a small compact chrysanthemum or dahlia.

pompous (pom´pəs) a. 1 exaggeratedly solemn or portentous, self-important. 2 ostentatious, pretentious. **pomposity** (-pos´-) n. (pl. **pomposities**). **pomposo** (-pō´sō) adv. (Mus.) in a stately or dignified manner. **pompously** adv. **pompousness** n.

ponce (pons) n. (sl.) 1 a prostitute's pimp. 2 (offensive) an effeminate man. ~v.i. to pimp. **to ponce about/ around** 1 to act in an ostentatious or effeminate manner. 2 to fool about, to waste time. **poncey, poncy** a. (comp. **poncier**, superl. **ponciest**).

poncho (pon´chō) n. (pl. **ponchos**) 1 a woollen cloak, worn in S America, with a slit in the middle through which the head passes. 2 a cycling-cape of this pattern.

pond (pond) n. 1 a body of still water, often artificial, smaller than a lake. 2 (facet.) the sea, esp. the Atlantic Ocean. **pond life** n. all the animals living in ponds. **pond-skater** n. any of various heteropterous insects of the family Gerridae, able to run on the surface of a pond supported by surface tension. **pond snail** n. a freshwater snail that lives in ponds, esp. one of the genus *Limnaea*. **pondweed** *n.* an aquatic plant growing on stagnant water, esp. species of *Potamogeton*.

ponder (pon´də) *v.t.* to weigh carefully in the mind; to think over, to consider deeply, to reflect upon. ~*v.i.* to think, to deliberate, to muse (on, over etc.). **ponderable** *a.* (*formal*) capable of being weighed, having appreciable weight, as distinct from *imponderable*. **ponderous** *a.* **1** very heavy or weighty. **2** bulky, unwieldy. **3** dull, tedious. **4** pompous, self-important. **ponderously** *adv.* **ponderousness** *n.*

ponderosa (pondərō´zə, -sə) *n.* **1** a N American pine tree, *Pinus ponderosa*. **2** the wood from this tree.

pone[1] (pōn) *n.* (*NAm.*) **1** a kind of bread made by N American Indians of maize meal. **2** a similar bread made with eggs, milk etc. **3** a loaf of this.

pone[2] (pōn, pō´ni) *n.* **1** the player to the dealer's right who cuts the cards. **2** in a two-handed card game, the non-dealer.

pong (pong) *n.* (*coll.*) a bad smell, a stink. ~*v.i.* to stink. **pongy** *a.* (*comp.* **pongier**, *superl.* **pongiest**).

pongee (pŭnjē´, pon-) *n.* **1** a soft unbleached kind of Chinese silk. **2** a fine cotton fabric resembling this.

pongid (pon´jid) *n.* any ape of the family Pongidae, incl. orang-utans, gorillas and chimpanzees. ~*a.* of or relating to this family of apes.

pongo (pong´gō) *n.* (*pl.* **pongos**) **1** the orang-utan. **2** (*Naut.*, *sl.*) a soldier. **3** (*Austral.*, *New Zeal.*, *sl.*, *offensive*) an Englishman.

poniard (pon´yəd) *n.* (*formal*) a small fine-bladed dagger.

pont (pont) *n.* (*S Afr.*) a small ferry boat, esp. one guided across a river by a cable.

pontiff (pon´tif) *n.* (*also* **sovereign pontiff**, **supreme pontiff**) the Pope. **pontifical** (-tif´-), †**pontific** *a.* **1** papal, popish. **2** with an assumption of authority, pompous, dogmatic. ~*n.* **1** a book containing the forms for rites and ceremonies to be performed by bishops. **2** (*pl.*) the vestments and insignia of a pontiff or bishop. **pontifically** *adv.* **pontifical Mass** *n.* a High Mass celebrated by a bishop, cardinal etc. **pontificate**[1] (-kət) *n.* the office, or period of office, of a bishop or pope.

pontificate[1] PONTIFF.

pontificate[2] (pontif´ikāt) *v.t.* to celebrate (Mass etc.) as a bishop. ~*v.i.* **1** to officiate as a pontiff or bishop, esp. at Mass. **2** to speak or behave in a pompous and dogmatic manner.

pontoon[1] (pontoon´) *n.* **1** a card game in which the object is to make the aggregate number of the pips on the cards as nearly as possible 21, without exceeding this number. **2** a hand making 21 at the first deal in this game.

pontoon[2] (pontoon´) *n.* **1** a flat-bottomed boat, cylinder or other buoyant structure supporting a floating bridge. **2** a caisson. **3** a pontoon bridge. ~*v.t.* to bridge with pontoons. **pontoon bridge** *n.* a platform or roadway laid across pontoons.

pony (pō´ni) *n.* (*pl.* **ponies**) **1** a horse of any small breed. **2** a small glass. **3** (*sl.*) 25 pounds sterling. **4** (*pl.*, *sl.*) racehorses. **ponytail** *n.* a hairstyle in which the hair is gathered at the back and hangs down over the nape of the neck like a tail. **pony-trekking** *n.* cross-country pony-riding in groups as a pastime. **pony-trekker** *n.*

poo POOH.

pooch (pooch) *n.* (*esp. N Am.*, *coll.*) a dog.

poodle (poo´dəl) *n.* **1** a breed of pet dog with long woolly hair, often clipped in a fanciful style. **2** a dog of this breed. **3** a servile follower. ~*v.i.* (*sl.*) to travel in a lazy or leisurely way.

poof[1] (puf, poof), **pooftah** (-tə), **poofter**, **poove** (poov), **pouf** *n.* (*sl.*, *offensive*) **1** a male homosexual. **2** an effeminate man. **poofy** *a.*

poof[2] (puf) *int.* **1** used to express rejection or contempt. **2** used to announce a disappearance as if by magic.

pooh (poo), **poo** *int.* **1** used to express contempt or impatience. **2** used to express disgust, esp. at a bad smell. ~*n.* excrement (used by or to children). **pooh-pooh** (-poo´) *v.t.* **1** to laugh or sneer at. **2** to make light of.

pooja PUJA.

pool[1] (pool) *n.* **1** a small body of water, still or nearly still. **2** a deep, still part of a stream. **3** a puddle. **4** a pond, natural or ornamental. **5** a swimming pool. **6** an underground accumulation of oil or gas. ~*v.i.* to gather or settle in a pool or pools; to form a pool. **poolside** *n.* the area round the side of a swimming pool. ~*a.*, *adv.* beside a pool.

pool[2] (pool) *n.* **1** a group of people, vehicles, tools etc. available for use when required. **2** a group of people who share duties or routine work. **3** a game played on a billiard table in which the players aim to drive different balls into the pockets in a certain order. **4** the collective stakes in a betting arrangement. **5** the receptacle for the stakes in certain games of cards. **6** (*pl.*) football pools. **7** a group of competitors who play against each other for the right to progress in a tournament. **8** a combination of persons, companies etc., for manipulating prices and suppressing competition. **9** a common stock or fund to be used for such manipulation. ~*v.t.* **1** to put (funds, risks etc.) into a common fund or pool. **2** to share (goods, resources) in common. **3** (*Austral.*, *sl.*) to inform on, involve (a person in a crime). **pool hall** *n.* a room, or an establishment, where pool is played. **pool room** *n.* (*N Am.*) a pool hall.

poop[1] (poop) *n.* **1** the stern of a ship. **2** a high deck over the after part of a spar-deck. **poop deck** *n.*

poop[2] (poop) *v.t.* (*esp. N Am.*, *coll.*) to render breathless, to exhaust. **pooped** *a.*

poop[3] (poop) *v.i.* (*coll.*) **1** to defecate. **2** to break wind. ~*n.* **1** faeces. **2** the act of defecating or breaking wind. **3** a toot. **poop scoop**, **pooper scooper** *n.* a device for cleaning dogs' excrement from a pavement etc.

poop⁴ (poop) n. (coll.) a stupid or ineffectual person.

poor (puə) a. **1** lacking enough money to live on, needy, indigent. **2** badly supplied, lacking (in). **3** (of land) barren, unproductive. **4** scanty, meagre, inadequate in quantity or quality, unsatisfactory. **5** uncomfortable. **6** inferior, sorry, paltry, miserable, contemptible. **7** (often iron.) insignificant, humble, meek. **8** unfortunate, pitiable, used as a term of slight contempt, pity or endearment. **the poor** those who are needy or indigent, esp. those who depend on charity or state benefit. **to take a poor view of** to regard unfavourably or pessimistically. **poor box** n. a money box, esp. in a church for charitable contributions. **poorly** adv. **1** with poor results, with little success. **2** defectively, imperfectly. **3** meanly, despicably. ~a. in delicate health; unwell, indisposed. **poorliness** n. **poor man's** a. cheap, inferior (substitute for something). **poorness** n. **poor relation** n. a person or thing looked down on, considered inferior, or shabbily treated in comparison to others. **poor show** n. something badly done. **poor-spirited** a. **1** timid, cowardly. **2** mean, base. **poor white** n. (usu. offensive) a member of a class of poverty-stricken and socially inferior white people in the southern US or S Africa.

pootle (poo'təl) v.i. (coll) to move along in a leisurely or lazy way.

poove POOF¹.

pop¹ (pop) v.i. (pres.p. **popping**, past, p.p. **popped**) **1** to make a short, sharp, explosive noise as of the drawing of a cork. **2** to burst open with such a sound. **3** (esp. of the eyes) to protrude as with amazement. **4** to enter or issue forth with a quick, sudden motion. **5** to move quickly. **6** to shoot (at) with a gun, pistol etc. ~v.t. **1** to push or thrust (in, out, up) suddenly. **2** to put (down etc.) quickly or hastily. **3** to fire off (a gun etc.). **4** to cause (a thing) to pop by breaking etc. **5** (sl.) to pawn. **6** (sl.) to take (drugs) orally or by injection. **7** to cause (maize kernels) to burst by heating. ~adv. **1** with a pop. **2** suddenly. ~n. **1** a short, sharp, explosive noise. **2** (coll.) an effervescing drink, esp. ginger beer or champagne. **in pop** (sl.) in pawn. **to go pop** to make, or burst with, a popping sound. **to pop off 1** (coll.) to leave hastily. **2** to die. **to pop the question** (coll.) to propose marriage. **to pop up** to appear suddenly. **popcorn** n. **1** maize kernels burst and puffed up by heating. **2** the kind of maize suitable for this. **pop-eyed** a. (coll.) **1** having bulging eyes. **2** wide-eyed with surprise or shock. **popgun** n. **1** a small toy gun used by children, shooting a pellet or cork with air compressed by a piston. **2** (derog.) a poor or defective firearm. **popper** n. **1** something that pops. **2** (coll.) a press stud. **popping-crease** n. in cricket, a line four feet in front of the stumps parallel with the bowling crease. **pop-shop** n. (sl.) a pawnshop. **pop socks** n.pl. knee-length women's stockings. **pop-up** a. **1** (of books) having illustrations etc. which stand up off the page when the book is opened to give a quasi-three-dimensional effect. **2** having a device which causes the contents to spring up, such as a toaster. **3** (Comput.) of, relating to or being a computer facility (e.g. a menu) which can be accessed during the running of a program.

pop² (pop) n. **1** pop music. **2** a pop record, a pop song. **3** (coll.) a popular piece of (usu. light) classical music. ~a. **1** popular or modern. **2** of or relating to pop music. **pop art** n. art incorporating everyday objects from popular culture and the mass media. **pop artist** n. **pop culture** n. behaviour, attitudes, consumption and consumables etc., based on popular music, art etc. **pop music** n. modern popular music, post 1950, esp. as characterized by a simple, heavy rhythmic beat and electronic amplification. **poppy¹** a.

pop³ (pop), **pops** (pops) n. (N Am., coll.) **1** father. **2** used as a familiar form of address to an old or elderly man.

pop. abbr. population.

popadum, popadam, popadom POPPADOM.

pope (pōp) n. **1** (Pope) the bishop of Rome as the head of the Roman Catholic Church. **2** a small freshwater fish, Gymnocephalus cernua, akin to the perch, the ruff. **popedom** n. **popeless** a. **Popemobile** n. (coll.) an open vehicle with a raised platform in it, used by the Pope when on tour. **popery** (-pəri) n. (derog.) the religion, ecclesiastical system or ceremonial of the Roman Catholic Church. **popish** a. **1** (often derog.) of or relating to the Pope. **2** (derog.) of or relating to popery, papistical. **popishly** adv.

popinjay (pop'injā) n. a conceited chattering fop.

poplar (pop'lə) n. **1** a large tree of the genus Populus, of rapid growth, and having a soft, light wood. **2** (N Am.) the tulip tree.

poplin (pop'lin) n. a fine cotton fabric with a ribbed surface.

poppa (pop'ə) n. (N Am., coll.) father (used esp. by children).

poppadom (pop'ədəm), **poppadum, popadum, popadam, popadom** n. a crisp, thin Indian bread, spiced and fried or roasted, often served with chutneys.

popper POP¹.

poppet (pop'it) n. **1** (coll.) a darling, a term of endearment. **2** a puppet, a marionette. **3** (Naut.) a piece of wood fitted inside the gunwale of a boat. **poppet-valve** n. a mushroom-shaped valve that can be lifted bodily.

poppy¹ POP².

poppy² (pop'i) n. (pl. **poppies**) **1** any of various plants or flowers of the genus Papaver, containing plants with large showy flowers chiefly of scarlet colour, with a milky juice having narcotic properties. **2** a poppy-head. **poppied** a. **Poppy Day** n. Remembrance Sunday. **poppy head** n. **1** the seed capsule of a poppy. **2** a finial of foliage or other ornamental top to ecclesiastical woodwork, esp. a pew-end.

poppycock (pop´ikok) *n.* (*sl.*) nonsense, balderdash.

Popsicle® (pop´sikəl) *n.* (*NAm.*) an ice lolly.

popsy (pop´si), **popsie** *n.* (*pl.* **popsies**) (*dated sl.*, *often derog.*) an attractive young woman.

populace (pop´üləs) *n.* the common people; the masses.

popular (pop´ülə) *a.* **1** pleasing to or esteemed by the general public or a specific group or an individual. **2** of, relating to, carried on by or prevailing among the general public or the common people. **3** suitable to or easy to be understood by ordinary people, not expensive, not abstruse, not esoteric. **4** democratic. **popular front** *n.* a coalition of left-wing parties in a common front, often against dictatorship. **popularism** *n.* **popularity** (-lar´-) *n.* **popularize, popularise** *v.t.* **1** to make popular. **2** to treat (a subject etc.) in a popular style. **3** to spread (knowledge etc.) among the people. **popularization** (-zā´shən) *n.* **popularizer** *n.* **popularly** *adv.* **popular music** *n.* music of an undemanding kind, appealing to a wide audience.

populate (pop´ülāt) *v.t.* **1** to furnish with inhabitants, to people. **2** to form the population of, to inhabit. **population** (-lā´shən) *n.* **1** the inhabitants of a country etc., collectively. **2** the number of such inhabitants. **3** the (number of) people of a certain class and/or in a specified area. **4** in statistics, the aggregate of individuals or items from which a sample is taken. **5** the group of organisms, or of members of a particular species, in a particular area. **6** the act of populating. **population explosion** *n.* a sudden and rapid increase in the size of a population.

populist (pop´ülist) *n.* **1** a person claiming to represent the interests of the common people. **2** a person who believes in the rights, virtues or wisdom of the common people. ~*a.* of or relating to a populist or to populism. **populism** *n.* **populistic** (-lis´-) *a.*

populous (pop´üləs) *a.* full of people; thickly populated. **populously** *adv.* **populousness** *n.*

porbeagle (paw´bēgəl) *n.* a large shark of the genus *Lamna*, a mackerel shark.

porcelain (paw´səlin, -slin) *n.* **1** a fine kind of earthenware, white, thin, and semi-transparent. **2** objects made of this. **porcelain clay** *n.* kaolin. **porcelainous** (-lā´-), **porcellanic** (-lan´-), **porcellanous** (-sel´ə-), **porcellaneous** (-lā´niəs) *a.*

porch (pawch) *n.* **1** a covered structure in front of, or extending from the entrance to, a building. **2** a covered approach to a doorway. **3** (*NAm.*) a veranda. **porched** *a.* **porchless** *a.*

porcine (paw´sīn) *a.* of, relating to or resembling a pig.

porcupine (paw´kūpīn) *n.* any individual of the families Hystricidae or Erethizontidae, rodent quadrupeds covered with erectile, quill-like spines. **porcupine fish** *n.* a tropical fish, *Diodon hystrix*, covered with spines.

pore¹ (paw) *n.* (*Biol.*) a minute opening, esp. a hole in the skin for absorption, perspiration etc. **porous** *a.* **1** having (many) pores. **2** permeable to liquids etc. **3** not fully secure. **porosity** (-ros´-) *n.* (*pl.* **porosities**). **porously** *adv.* **porousness** *n.*

pore² (paw) *v.i.* **1** to gaze at or study with steady, continued attention and application. **2** to meditate or study patiently and persistently (over, upon etc.). **porer** *n.*

poriferan (pərif´ərən) *n.* any aquatic invertebrate animal of the phylum Porifera, the sponges. ~*a.* of or relating to the Porifera or a poriferan. **poriferal** *a.*

pork (pawk) *n.* the flesh of pigs, esp. fresh, as food. **pork barrel** *n.* **1** (*NAm.*) a project involving spending large amounts of government money in a way that will please voters. **2** the government money spent. **pork-barrelling,** (*N Am.*) **pork-barreling** *n.* **pork butcher** *n.* **1** a person who kills pigs for sale. **2** a butcher who specializes in pork. **porker** *n.* a pig raised for killing, esp. a young fattened pig. **porklet** (-lit) *n.* **porkling** (-ling) *n.* a small or a young pig. **pork pie** *n.* a pie made of minced pork, usu. round with vertical sides. **pork-pie hat** *n.* a round hat with flat crown and rolled-up brim. **pork scratchings** *n.pl.* crisp pieces of pork fat strained out of melted lard. **porky** *a.* (*comp.* **porkier,** *superl.* **porkiest**) **1** like pork. **2** (*coll.*) fat, fleshy. ~*n.* (*rhyming sl.*) (*also* **porky-pie,** *pl.* **porkies, porky-pies**) a lie. **porkiness** *n.*

porn (pawn), **porno** (paw´nō) *n.* (*coll.*) pornography. ~*a.* pornographic.

pornography (pawnog´rəfi) *n.* **1** the obscene and exploitative depiction of erotic acts. **2** written, graphic etc. material consisting of or containing this. **pornographer** *n.* **pornographic** (-graf´-) *a.* **pornographically** *adv.*

porosity, porous PORE¹.

porphyria (pawfir´iə) *n.* any one of a group of inborn metabolic disorders characterized by an abnormal pigment in the urine, severe pain, photosensitivity, and periods of mental confusion. **porphyrin** *n.* any of a class of red or purple pigments found in animal and plant tissues.

porphyry (paw´firi) *n.* (*pl.* **porphyries**) **1** (*Geol.*) an igneous rock consisting of a felsitic or cryptocrystalline groundmass full of feldspar or quartz crystals. **2** a rock quarried in Egypt having a purple groundmass with enclosed crystals of feldspar. **porphyritic** (-rit´-) *a.*

porpoise (paw´pəs) *n.* (*pl. in general* **porpoise,** *in particular* **porpoises**) any small whale of the genus *Phocaena*, as an adult about 5 ft. (1.5 m) long, with a blunt snout.

porridge (por´ij) *n.* **1** a dish made by boiling oatmeal etc. in water or milk till it thickens. **2** (*sl.*) a term of imprisonment. **porridgy** *a.*

porringer (por´injə) *n.* a small basin or bowl out of which soup etc. is eaten.

port¹ (pawt) *n.* **1** (*Naut.*) a harbour, a sheltered piece of water into which vessels can enter and remain in safety. **2** a town or other place having a harbour, esp. where goods are imported or exported under the customs authorities. **port of call** n. **1** a port at which a ship stops during a voyage. **2** any stopping place on an itinerary.

port² (pawt) n. **1** (*Naut.*) **a** an opening in the side of a ship, allowing access to the holds etc. **b** a porthole. **2** (*Mil.*) an aperture in a wall or the side of an armoured vehicle for firing a gun through. **3** an opening in machinery for the passage of steam, gas, water etc. **4** a connector on a computer into which a peripheral can be plugged. **porthole** n. **1** a small window in the side of a ship or aircraft. **2** (*Naut., Hist.*) an aperture in a ship's side for light, air etc., and for firing guns through.

port³ (pawt) n. a fortified dessert wine (usu. dark-red or tawny) made in Portugal. **port wine** n.

port⁴ (pawt) n. (*Naut. etc.*) the left-hand side of a ship, aircraft etc., as one looks forward, as distinct from *starboard*. ~a. towards or on the left. ~v.t. to turn or put (the helm) to the left side of a ship. ~v.i. to turn to port (of a ship). **port watch** n. the watch comprising the officers and crew whose living quarters are on the port side of a ship.

port⁵ (pawt) v.t. (*Mil.*) to carry or hold (a rifle etc.) in a slanting position across the body in front. ~n. **1** (*Mil.*) the position of a weapon carried thus. **2** (*formal*) carriage, deportment.

port⁶ (pawt) n. (*Austral., coll.*) **1** a suitcase, a travelling bag. **2** a bag for carrying something specific, such as a shopping bag.

port⁷ (pawt) v.t. (*Comput.*) to transfer (software) from one system to another. **portable¹** a. **portability¹** (-bil´-) n.

porta (paw´tə) n. (*pl.* **portas, portae** (-ē)) the aperture where veins, ducts etc. enter an organ, esp. the transverse fissure of the liver.

portable¹ PORT⁷.

portable² (paw´təbəl) a. **1** capable of being easily carried, esp. about the person. **2** not bulky or heavy. **3** (of a pension etc.) transferable as the holder changes jobs or other circumstances. ~n. a portable version of anything. **portability²** (-bil´-) n. **portably** adv.

portage (paw´tij) n. **1** the act or an instance of carrying, carriage. **2** the cost of carriage. **3** a break in a line of water-communication over which boats, goods etc. have to be carried. **4** transportation of boats etc. over this. ~v.t. to carry (goods or a boat) over a portage. ~v.i. to make a portage.

Portakabin® (paw´təkabin) n. a portable building delivered intact to, or speedily erected on, a site as temporary offices etc.

portal¹ (paw´təl) n. a door, a gate, a gateway, an entrance, esp. one of an ornamental or imposing kind.

portal² (paw´təl) a. of, relating to or connected with the porta. **portal vein** n. the large vein conveying blood to the liver from the stomach, pancreas etc.

portamento (pawtəmen´tō) n. (*pl.* **portamentos, portamenti** (-tē)) (*esp. Mus.*) a smooth, continuous glide from one note to another across intervening tones.

portcullis (pawtkŭl´is) n. a strong timber or iron grating, sliding in vertical grooves over a gateway, and let down to close the passage in case of assault. **portcullised** a.

portend (pawtend´) v.t. **1** to indicate by previous signs, to presage, to foreshadow. **2** to be an omen or a warning of. **portent** (paw´tent) n. **1** something which portends. **2** an omen, esp. of evil. **3** a prodigy, a marvel. **portentous** (-ten´təs) a. **1** ominous. **2** impressive. **3** solemn. **4** self-consciously solemn or meaningful. **portentously** adv. **portentousness** n.

Usage note Pronunciation of *portentous* as (pawten´tiəs), as though the word were *portentious*, is best avoided.

porter¹ (paw´tə) n. **1** a person employed to carry loads, esp. parcels, luggage etc. at a railway station, airport or hotel, or goods in a market. **2** a person who transports patients and does other manual labour in a hospital. **3** a dark-brown beer made from charred or chemically-coloured malt etc. (perh. so called from having been made specially for London porters). **4** (*N Am.*) a sleeping-car attendant. **porterage** (-rij) n. **1** the work of carrying luggage etc. **2** a charge for such work. **porterhouse** n. **1** a tavern at which porter etc. is sold. **2** an eating house, a chophouse. **porterhouse steak** n. a choice cut of beefsteak next to the sirloin, and including part of the tenderloin. **porterly** a. **porter's knot** n. a pad worn on the shoulders by porters when carrying heavy loads.

porter² (paw´tə) n. a gatekeeper, a doorkeeper esp. of a large building, who usu. regulates entry and answers enquiries.

portfolio (pawtfō´liō) n. (*pl.* **portfolios**) **1** a portable case for holding papers, drawings etc. **2** a collection of such papers, esp. samples of recent work etc. **3** the office and duties of a minister of state. **4** the investments made, or securities held, by an investor.

portico (paw´tikō) n. (*pl.* **porticoes, porticos**) **1** a colonnade, a roof supported by columns. **2** a porch with columns. **porticoed** a.

portière (pawtyeə´) n. a door-curtain.

portion (paw´shən) n. **1** a part; a share, a part assigned, an allotment. **2** a helping. **3** a wife's fortune, a dowry. **4** one's destiny in life. ~v.t. **1** to divide into portions, to distribute. **2** to allot, to assign. **3** to give a dowry to. **portionless** a. without a dowry.

Portland (pawt´lənd) a. of or derived from Portland. **Portland cement** n. a cement having the colour of Portland stone. **Portland stone** n. a yellowish-white limestone, quarried in Portland, much used for building.

portly (pawt'li) *a.* (*comp.* **portlier,** *superl.* **portliest**) stout, corpulent. **portliness** *n.*

portmanteau (pawtman'tō) *n.* (*pl.* **portmanteaus, portmanteaux** (-tōz)) a travelling bag which opens out flat, for carrying clothes. ~*a.* combining several uses or qualities. **portmanteau word** *n.* an invented word combining the sense and the sound of two distinct words, as *chortle,* from *chuckle* and *snort,* coined by Lewis Carroll.

portrait (paw'trit) *n.* **1** a likeness or representation of a person or animal, esp. from life. **2** a vivid description. **3** a type, a similitude. ~*a.* (of an illustration in a book etc.) having its height greater than its width, as distinct from *landscape.* **portraitist** *n.* a painter or photographer who specializes in portraits. **portraiture** (-chə) *n.* **1** the art of painting portraits. **2** a portrait. **3** portraits collectively. **4** vivid description. **portray** (petrā') *v.t.* **1** to make a portrait of. **2** to describe. **3** to play the role of. **4** to present (as). **portrayable** *a.* **portrayal** *n.* **portrayer** *n.*

Portuguese (pawtūgēz') *a.* of or relating to Portugal, its people or its language. ~*n.* (*pl.* **Portuguese**) **1** a native or inhabitant of Portugal. **2** (*as pl.*) the people of Portugal. **3** the Portuguese language. **Portuguese man-of-war** *n.* a jellyfish of the genus *Physalia* with a poisonous sting.

POS *abbr.* point of sale.

pose[1] (pōz) *v.t.* **1** to place, to cause (an artist's model etc.) to take a certain attitude. **2** to affirm, to lay down. **3** to put forward, to ask (a question etc.). ~*v.i.* **1** to assume an attitude or character. **2** to attempt to impress by affecting an attitude or style, to behave affectedly. **3** to appear or set up (as). ~*n.* a bodily or mental attitude or position, esp. one put on for effect. **poser**[1] *n.* a person who poses. **2** a poseur. **poseur** (-zœ') *n.* an affected person. **poseuse** (-zœz') *n.* a female poseur. **posey** *a.* affected, pretentious.

pose[2] (pōz) *v.t.* to puzzle (a person), to cause to be at a loss. **poser**[2] *n.* **1** a person who or a thing which puzzles. **2** a puzzling question or proposition.

poser[1] POSE[1].

poser[2] POSE[2].

✗ **posess** common misspelling of POSSESS.

posh (posh) *a.* **1** (*coll.*) smart, elegant, fashionable. **2** (*sometimes derog.*) genteel, upper-class. ~*adv.* in a smart, or an upper-class, manner. **to posh up** to smarten up, to polish.

posit (poz'it) *v.t.* (*pres.p.* **positing,** *past, p.p.* **posited**) **1** to place, to set in position. **2** to lay down as a fact or principle, to assume, to postulate.

position (pəzish'ən) *n.* **1** a location, the place occupied by a person or thing. **2** the place belonging or assigned to a person or thing. **3** (*Mil.*) an occupied and defended or a defensible point or area. **4** a player's place in a team forma-

tion or usual area of operation on the field of play. **5** a posture. **6** arrangement, disposition. **7** a point of view, a stance. **8** a situation, a state of affairs. **9** a situation relative to other persons or things. **10** status, rank, condition. **11** an office, a post, an appointment. **12** (*Logic*) a principle laid down, a proposition. **13** any one of the basic poses in ballet. **14** the relative placing of chessmen during a game. ~*v.t.* to place in position; to locate. **in a position to** take up. **positional** *a.* **positionally** *adv.* **positioner** *n.* **position paper** *n.* a report setting out a person's point of view or plans in a particular matter.

positive (poz'itiv) *a.* **1** definitely, explicitly or formally laid down or affirmed. **2** explicit, express, definite. **3** intrinsic, inherent, absolute, not relative. **4** existing, real, actual. **5** incontestable, certain, undoubted. **6** fully convinced. **7** confident, cocksure, dogmatic. **8** (*coll.*) downright, thorough. **9** constructive, helpful. **10** (*Gram.*) not comparative or superlative. **11** (*Physics*) denoting the presence of some quality, not negative. **12** having the same polarity as the charge of a proton. **13** having relatively higher electrical potential. **14** (*Math.*) denoting increase or progress, additive, greater than zero. **15** (of a photograph) exhibiting lights and shades in the same relations as in nature. ~*n.* **1** that which may be affirmed. **2** (*Gram.*) the positive degree, a positive adjective. **3** (*Math.*) a positive quantity. **4** a photograph in which the lights and shades are shown as in nature. **positive discrimination** *n.* discrimination in favour of an individual or a group of people previously discriminated against or likely to be discriminated against in areas such as employment. **positive feedback** *n.* **1** a helpful response to a questionnaire etc. **2** the return of part of the output of an electronic system to the input, thus reinforcing the signal etc. **3** (*Biol.*) the adjusting of an effect in a cyclic process by its own influence on the process giving rise to it. **positive geotropism** *n.* (*Bot.*) the tendency of a root to grow downwards, towards the centre of the earth. **positively** *adv.* **positiveness** *n.* **positive pole** *n.* the north-seeking pole of a magnet. **positive prescription** *n.* (*Law*) long-continued or immemorial use or possession without interruption, as giving right or title. **positive sign** *n.* the sign +, denoting addition. **positive vetting** *n.* active investigation of a person's background etc. to check whether they are suitable for work involving national security. **positivism** *n.* **1** the philosophical system of Auguste Comte, 1798–1857, which recognizes only observed phenomena and rejects speculation or metaphysics. **2** the religious system based on this, professing to be a synthesis of all human conceptions of the external order of the universe, and to secure the victory of social feeling over self-love. **3** logical positivism. **positivist** *n.*, *a.* **positivistic** (-vis'-) *a.* **positivistically** *adv.* **positivity** (-tiv'-) *n.*

positron (poz´itron) *n.* (*Physics*) a subatomic particle having the same mass as an electron, but a positive charge.

posse (pos´i) *n.* **1** a body or force (of persons). **2** (*US*) a group of men called on by a sheriff to help with law enforcement. **3** a posse comitatus. **posse comitatus** (komitā´təs) *n.* a force which the sheriff of a county is empowered to raise in case of riot etc.

possess (pəzes´) *v.t.* **1** to have the ownership of, to own as property, to have full power over, to control (oneself, one's mind etc.). **2** to occupy, to dominate the mind of. **3** to have sexual intercourse with (a woman). **4** to imbue, to impress (with). **to be possessed of** to own. **to possess oneself of** to acquire, to obtain as one's own. **what possessed you?** a rhetorical question expressing shock or disapproval of another's actions. **possessor** *n.* **possessory** *a.*

possession (pəzesh´ən) *n.* **1** the act or state of possessing. **2** the state of being possessed or under physical or supernatural influence. **3** a person or thing which is possessed. **4** holding or occupancy as owner. **5** (*Law*) the exercise of such control as attaches to ownership, actual detention, or occupancy. **6** territory, esp. a subject dependency in a foreign country. **7** (*pl.*) property, goods, wealth. **8** in ball games, esp. football, control of the ball by a particular team or player. **9** self-possession. **in possession 1** in actual occupancy. **2** holding, possessing. **in possession of** owning, possessing. **in the possession of** owned or possessed by. **to take possession of 1** to become the possessor of. **2** to seize. **possessionless** *a.* **possession order** *n.* a court order entitling a landlord to evict a tenant or squatter and regain possession of the property.

possessive (pəzes´iv) *a.* **1** of or relating to possession. **2** showing a strong urge to possess or dominate, unwilling to share, unwilling to allow another to be independent of oneself. **3** (*Gram.*) denoting possession, genitive. ~*n.* **1** the possessive case. **2** a word in this case. **possessive case** *n.* **possessively** *adv.* **possessiveness** *n.* **possessive pronoun** *n.* any one of the pronouns indicating possession (as Eng. *mine*, *yours*, *his* etc.).

possible (pos´ibəl) *a.* **1** that may happen, be done, or exist. **2** not contrary to the nature of things. **3** feasible, practicable. **4** that may be dealt with or put up with, tolerable, reasonable. ~*n.* **1** something which is possible. **2** a person who is a possible competitor, member etc. **3** the highest score that can be made in shooting etc. **possibility** (-bil´-) *n.* (*pl.* **possibilities**) **1** the state, or the fact, of being possible. **2** a possible thing. **3** a person or thing which has an outside or moderate chance of success, selection etc. **4** (*usu. pl.*) potential. **possibly** *adv.* **1** by any possible means. **2** perhaps. **3** by remote chance.

possum (pos´əm) *n.* (*coll.*) an opossum. **to play possum** to feign ignorance or unawareness, to

dissemble (in allusion to the opossum's feigning death on the approach of danger).

post¹ (pōst) *n.* **1** a piece of timber, metal etc., set upright, and intended as a support to something, or to mark a boundary. **2** a pole for fastening notices to. **3** a starting or winning post. **4** an upright forming part of various structures, machines etc. ~*v.t.* **1** to fix (*usu.* up) on a post or in a public place. **2** to fasten bills etc., upon (a wall etc.). **3** to advertise, to make known. **4** to publish (the name of a ship) as overdue or missing. **5** (*N Am.*) to achieve (a score etc.) in a game. **post-mill** *n.* a windmill, the whole of which can turn round a central post to catch the wind.

post² (pōst) *n.* **1** a fixed place, position or station. **2** a military station. **3** the troops at such a station. **4** a fort. **5** a place established for trading purposes, esp. in a remote place. **6** a situation, an appointment. ~*v.t.* **1** to station, to place (an employee, soldiers etc.) in a particular position. **2** to transfer to another unit or location.

post³ (pōst) *n.* **1** an established system of conveyance and delivery of letters and parcels; orig. one of a series of men stationed at points along a road whose duty was to ride forward to the next man with letters. **2** a post office. **3** a postbox. **4** a single collection or dispatch of letters or parcels. **5** the letters delivered at a house at one time. ~*v.t.* **1** to transmit by post. **2** to put into a postbox for transmission. **3** to send with speed. **4** to transfer (accounts) to a ledger, to enter in this from a day-book etc. **5** to fill (a ledger) in this way. ~*v.i.* to travel rapidly, to hurry. **to keep someone posted** to keep someone supplied with up-to-date information. **to post up 1** to complete (a ledger) with entries of accounts from a day-book etc. **2** to supply with full information. **postbag** *n.* **1** a mailbag. **2** mail received (esp. by a public figure, magazine, radio show etc.). **postbox** *n.* a box where letters may be put for collection and subsequent delivery. **postcard** *n.* a card for sending by post without an envelope. **postcode** *n.* a code of letters and numbers denoting a particular subsection of a postal area, used to help in sorting mail. **post-haste** *adv.* with all speed. **post-horn** *n.* (*Hist.*) a long straight horn blown to announce the arrival of a mail coach. **postman** *n.* (*pl.* **postmen**) a person who collects and delivers mail. **postman's knock** *n.* a children's game in which a kiss is the reward for delivering an imaginary letter. **postmark** *n.* a mark stamped by post-office officials on letters etc., usu. stating place, date, and hour of dispatch, and serving to cancel the postage stamp. ~*v.t.* to stamp (an envelope etc.) with this. **postmaster** *n.* a man in charge of a post office. **postmistress** *n.* a woman in charge of a post office. **post office** *n.* **1** a place for the receipt and delivery of letters etc. **2** (**Post Office**) a government department or a national corporation in charge of the dispatch and delivery of letters and packets etc. **3** (*N Am.*) postman's knock. **post office box** *n.* a private numbered box at a post office in which the holder's mail is deposited awaiting collection. **post-paid** *a.*, *adv.* having the postage prepaid. **postperson** *n.* a postman or postwoman. **post room** *n.* a department in a company where incoming and outgoing mail is dealt with. **post town** *n.* a town in which there is a head post office. **postwoman** *n.* (*pl.* **postwomen**) a woman who collects and delivers mail.

post- (pōst) *pref.* **1** after, in time or order. **2** behind.

postage (pōs′tij) *n.* the fee for sending a letter etc. by post. **postage meter** *n.* (*N Am.*) a franking machine. **postage stamp** *n.* an embossed or printed stamp or an adhesive label to indicate how much postage has been paid.

postal (pōs′təl) *a.* **1** of or relating to the mail service. **2** carried on by post. ~*n.* (*US*) a postcard. **postal card** *n.* (*US*) a postcard. **postal code** *n.* POSTCODE (under POST³). **postally** *adv.* **postal note** *n.* (*Austral., New Zeal.*) a postal order. **postal order** *n.* an order for a sum of money (specified on the document) issued at one post office for payment at another. **postal vote** *n.* a vote submitted by post.

post- (+ **b–e words**) **post-classical** *a.* later than the classical writers, artists etc., esp. those of Greece and Rome. **post-coital** *a.* **post-coitally** *adv.* **post-date**¹ *v.t.* to assign or mark with a date later than the actual one. **post-date**² (pōst′-) *n.* a date later than the actual one. **post-doctoral** *a.* of or relating to studies, research etc. carried out after obtaining a doctorate. **post-entry** *n.* (*pl.* **post-entries**) **1** an additional or subsequent entry. **2** a late entry (for a race etc.).

poster (pōs′tə) *n.* **1** a large placard or advertising bill. **2** a person who posts this. **3** a large printed picture. **poster paint, poster colour** *n.* an opaque, gum-based watercolour paint.

poste restante (pōst res′tāt) *n.* **1** a department in a post office where letters are kept until called for. **2** an address on a letter to a poste restante department.

posterior (postiə′riə) *a.* **1** coming or happening after. **2** later. **3** situated behind or at the back. ~*n.* the buttocks. **posteriority** (-or′-) *n.* **posteriorly** *adv.*

posterity (pəster′iti) *n.* **1** those proceeding in the future from any person, descendants. **2** succeeding generations.

postern (pos′tən) *n.* **1** a small doorway or gateway at the side or back. **2** a private entrance, esp. to a castle, town etc.

post- (+ **f–h words**) **post-feminist** *a.* later than, or developed from, the ideas or attitudes characteristic of the original feminist movement. ~*n.* a person having such ideas or attitudes. **post-feminism** *n.* **postfix** *v.t.* to append (a letter etc.) at the end of a word. ~*n.* a suffix. **postglacial** *a.* later than the glacial period. ~*n.* a postglacial period.

postgrad *n.*, *a.* (*coll.*) (a) postgraduate. **postgraduate** *a.* **1** carried on or awarded after graduation. **2** working for a postgraduate qualification. ~*n.* a graduate who pursues a further course of study.

post-haste POST³.

posthumous (pos′tūməs) *a.* **1** (of a child) born after the death of the father. **2** happening after decease. **3** published after the death of the author or composer. **posthumously** *adv.*

post- (+ **i–k words**) **post-Impressionism** *n.* the doctrines and methods of a school of (esp. French) painters of the late 19th cent. who rejected the naturalism and momentary effects of Impressionism in favour of a use of pure colour for more formal or subjective ends. **post-Impressionist** *a.*, *n.* **post-industrial** *a.* of or relating to an economy or a society no longer dependent on heavy industry.

postilion (pəstil′yən), **postillion** *n.* the rider on the near horse of the leaders or of a pair drawing a carriage.

Post-it Note® (pōs′tit nōt) *n.* a small sheet of paper for writing messages, with a strip of adhesive along one edge which allows the note to be stuck to a surface and removed again without damaging the surface.

postlude (pōst′lood) *n.* (*Mus.*) a closing piece or voluntary.

post- (+ **m– words**) **post-millennial** *a.* of or relating to a period after the millennium. **post-millennialism** *n.* the doctrine that the second advent of Christ will follow the millennium. **post-millennialist** *n.* **postmodernism** *n.* in art, architecture, literature etc., a movement which rejects the basic tenets of 20th-cent. modernism. **postmodern** *a.* **postmodernist** *a.*, *n.* **postmodernity** *n.*

post meridiem (pōst mərid′iem) *adv.* after noon. **postmeridian** *a.* **1** of or belonging to the afternoon. **2** late.

post-mortem (pōstmaw′təm) *adv.* after death. ~*a.* made or occurring after death. ~*n.* **1** an examination of a dead body to determine the cause of death. **2** an analysis or review after a game etc., esp. after defeat or failure.

post- (+ **n–o words**) **post-natal** *a.* of, relating to or typical of the period after childbirth. **post-natal depression** *n.* depression suffered by a mother after childbirth. **post-natally** *adv.* **post-nuptial** *a.* made or happening after marriage. **post-operative** *a.* of or relating to the period just after a surgical operation.

post-obit (pōstō′bit, -ob′it) *a.* taking effect after death; post-mortem. ~*n.* a bond securing payment of a sum of money to a lender on the death of a specified person from whose estate the borrower has expectations.

post- (+ **p– words**) **postprandial** *a.* (*formal or facet.*) after lunch or dinner. **post-production** *a.* of or relating to editing etc. of a film or TV programme, done after shooting.

post-partum (pōstpah'təm) _a._ of or relating to the period immediately after childbirth.

postpone (pəspōn') _v.t._ to put off, to defer, to delay. **postponable** _a._ **postponement** _n._ **postponer** _n._

postposition (pōstpəzish'ən) _n._ **1** the act of placing after. **2** the state of being placed after or behind. **3** a word or particle placed after a word, esp. an enclitic. **postpose** (-pōz') _v.t._ to place (a word or particle) after another. **postpositional** _a._ **postpositive** (-poz'itiv) _a._ (_Gram._) placed after something else. ~_n._ a postpositive word or particle. **postpositively** _adv._

post- (+ s–t words) post-structuralism _n._ a development of structuralism, esp. as used in textual analysis. **post-structuralist** _n._, _a._ **post-tax** _a._ (of income) after taxes have been deducted. **post-traumatic stress disorder, post-traumatic stress syndrome** _n._ (_Psych._) a psychologically disturbed condition suffered by a person who has been through a very traumatic experience (e.g. a shipwreck or aeroplane crash), the symptoms including anxiety, guilt and depression.

postscript (pōst'skript) _n._ **1** a paragraph added to a letter after the writer's signature. **2** any supplement added on to the end of a book, document, talk etc.

postulant (pos'tūlənt) _n._ a candidate for entry into a religious order or for an ecclesiastical office.

postulate¹ (pos'tūlət) _n._ **1** a position assumed without proof as being self-evident. **2** a fundamental assumption. **3** a statement of the possibility of a simple operation such as a geometrical construction.

postulate² (pos'tūlāt) _v.t._ to demand, to claim, to assume without proof, to take as self-evident. **postulation** (-lā'shən) _n._ **postulator** _n._

❌ **postumous** common misspelling of POST-HUMOUS.

posture (pos'chə) _n._ **1** a pose, attitude or arrangement of the parts of the body. **2** the manner of holding the body. **3** a mental attitude. **4** a situation, condition, state (of affairs etc.). ~_v.t._ to arrange the body and limbs of (a person) in a particular posture. ~_v.i._ **1** to assume a posture, to pose. **2** to endeavour to look or sound impressive. **postural** _a._ **posturer** _n._

post- (+ v–w words) post-vocalic _a._ following a vowel. **post-war** _a._ existing or happening after a war, esp. the latest war.

posy (pō'zi) _n._ (_pl._ **posies**) **1** a bunch of flowers, a nosegay. **2** a motto or short inscription, esp. in a ring; _orig._ one in verse. **posy ring** _n._ a ring inscribed with a posy.

pot¹ (pot) _n._ **1** a round vessel of earthenware, metal or glass, usu. deep relative to the breadth, for holding liquids etc. **2** a vessel of this kind used for cooking. **3** a large drinking-cup of earthenware, pewter etc. **4** the quantity this holds. **5** a vessel used for various domestic or industrial purposes; a chamber pot, a coffee pot,

a flower pot, a teapot etc. **6** a chimney pot. **7** a wicker trap for catching lobsters etc. **8** (_coll._) a cup offered as a prize in a race etc. **9** (_often pl._, _coll._) a large sum of money. **10** the money or stakes in the pool in gambling games. **11** a pot belly. ~_v.t._ (_pres.p._ **potting**, _past_, _p.p._ **potted**) **1** to put into a pot or pots. **2** to season and preserve in a sealed pot. **3** to pocket a ball (in billiards etc.). **4** (_coll._) to shoot at or bring down, esp. with a pot-shot. **5** to bag, to secure. **6** to sit (a young child) on a potty. **7** to abridge (_a potted history_). ~_v.i._ (_coll._) to shoot (at). **to go to pot** (_sl._) to be ruined or done for, to degenerate. **to pot on** to transfer (a plant) to a larger pot. **to pot up** to plant (a seedling) into a pot. **pot belly** _n._ (_pl._ **pot bellies**) **1** a protuberant belly. **2** a pot-bellied person. **3** (_NAm._) a small bulbous stove burning wood or coal. **pot-bellied** _a._ **potboiler** _n._ **1** a work of art or literature produced merely for money. **2** a painter or writer who produces this. **pot-bound** _a._ (of a plant) filling the pot with its roots, not having room to grow. **pot cheese** _n._ (_NAm._) cottage cheese. **potful** _n._ (_pl._ **potfuls**). **pot-herb** _n._ any culinary herb. **pothole** _n._ **1** a cauldron-shaped cavity in the rocky bed of a stream. **2** a pitlike cavity or a system of caves in mountain limestone etc., usu. produced by a combination of faulting and water action. **3** a cavity in a roadway caused by wear or weathering. ~_v.i._ to explore cave systems. **potholer** _n._ a person who explores underground cave systems as a sport. **potholing** _n._ **pot-hook** _n._ **1** an S-shaped hook for suspending a pot or kettle over a fire. **2** a letter like a pot-hook, esp. in clumsy handwriting. **pot-luck, pot luck** _n._ **1** whatever food may be available without special preparation. **2** whatever luck or chance may offer. **pot of gold** _n._ an imaginary treasure, or one searched for in vain (traditionally found at the end of the rainbow). **pot pie** _n._ a pie with a crust, cooked in a stewpot. **pot plant** _n._ a plant grown in a flowerpot. **pot roast** _n._ a piece of meat stewed in a closed receptacle. **pot-roast** _v.t._ **potsherd** _n._ a broken piece of pottery, esp. as an archaeological find. **pot-shot** _n._ **1** a shot at game etc. that happens to be within easy range. **2** a random shot. **3** a shot for filling the pot, esp. one of an unsportsmanlike kind. **potting** _n._ **potting shed** _n._ a garden shed in which tools are kept, plants are potted etc.

pot² (pot) _n._ (_sl._) marijuana. **pothead** _n._ a person who takes marijuana regularly.

pot³ (pot) _n._ (_Austral._, _New Zeal._) a drop goal in rugby. ~_v.t._ (_pres.p._ **potting**, _past_, _p.p._ **potted**) to score (a drop goal).

potable (pō'təbəl) _a._ drinkable. ~_n._ (_usu. pl._) anything drinkable. **potability** (-bil'-) _n._ **potableness** _n._

potage (potahzh') _n._ thick soup.

potamic (pətam'ik) _a._ of or relating to rivers. **potamology** (potəmol'-) _n._ **potamological** (-loj'-) _a._ **potamologist** (-mol'-) _n._

potash (pot´ash) n. **1** a powerful alkali, consisting of potassium carbonate in a crude form, orig. obtained from the ashes of plants. **2** caustic potash. **3** potassium or a potassium compound.

potassium (pətas´iəm) n. (*Chem.*) a bluish or pinkish white metallic element, at. no. 19, chem. symbol K. **potassic** a. **potassium-argon dating** n. (*Geol.*) a method of dating rocks by measuring the ratio of potassium-40 to its decay product argon-40. **potassium carbonate** n. a white alkaline substance used in the manufacture of glass, soap etc. **potassium chloride** n. a white crystalline substance used as a fertilizer and in photographic processing. **potassium cyanide** n. a very poisonous soluble substance used in extracting gold and silver from their ores. **potassium iodide** n. a white crystalline substance used as an additive to table salt. **potassium permanganate** n. a purple, soluble crystalline substance, used in solution as a disinfectant, bleach etc.

potation (pōtā´shən) n. (*formal or facet.*) **1** the act, or an instance, of drinking. **2** a beverage. **3** (*usu. pl.*) tippling. **potatory** (pō´-, -tā´-) a.

potato (pətā´tō) n. (*pl.* **potatoes**) **1** a plant, *Solanum tuberosum*, with edible farinaceous tubers. **2** a tuber of this. **3** (*coll.*) a hole in a sock or stocking. **potato chip** n. **1** a long slice of potato fried in deep fat. **2** (*N Am., S Afr.*) a potato crisp. **potato crisp** n. a flake of potato fried in deep fat.

pot-au-feu (potōfœ´) n. (*pl.* **pot-au-feu**) **1** a traditional French stew of beef and vegetables. **2** the type of pot used for this stew. **3** the broth from this stew.

poteen (pətēn´), **potheen** (-chēn´) n. Irish whiskey illicitly distilled.

potent (pō´tənt) a. **1** (*formal*) powerful, mighty. **2** having great force or influence. **3** cogent. **4** strong, intoxicating. **5** (of a male) capable of having sexual intercourse. **potence, potency** n. (*pl.* **potences, potencies**). **potentate** (-tāt) n. **1** a person who possesses great power. **2** a monarch, a ruler. **potential** (-ten´shəl) a. **1** (of energy) existing but not in action, latent. **2** existing in possibility, not in actuality. ~n. **1** anything that may be possible. **2** a possibility. **3** as yet undeveloped value, resources or ability. **4** the work done in transferring a unit (of mass, electricity etc.) from infinity to a given point. **potential barrier** n. (*Physics*) an area of high potential in a field of force, where the passage of particles is impeded. **potential difference** n. the work required to move an electrical charge between two points, measured in volts. **potential energy** n. the energy possessed by virtue of the relative condition of parts of a body or of bodies to each other. **potentiality** (-shial´-) n. (*pl.* **potentialities**). **potentialize, potentialise** v.t. **potentially** adv. **potentiate** (-ten´shi-) v.t. **1** to make potent. **2** to make more effective. **3** to make possible. **potentiation** (-ā´shən) n. **potentiator** n. **potentiometer** (-om´itə) n. an instrument for measuring

electromotive force or potential difference. **potentiometric** (-əmet´rik) a. **potentiometry** (-om´itri) n. **potently** adv. **potentness** n.

potentilla (pōtəntil´ə) n. any plant or shrub of the genus *Potentilla*, comprising the cinquefoil, tormentil etc.

potheen POTEEN.

pother (podh´ə) n. bustle, confusion. ~v.i. to make a bustle or stir.

potion (pō´shən) n. a liquid mixture intended as a medicine, poison or a magic charm.

potlatch (pot´lach) n. a ceremonial feast among Indians of the northwestern US involving emulation in the giving of extravagant gifts.

potoroo (potōroo´) n. (*pl.* **potoroos**) the marsupial rat kangaroo.

pot-pourri (pōpərē´, pōpoo´ri) n. (*pl.* **pot-pourris**) **1** a mixture of dried flower-petals and spices, usu. kept in a bowl for perfuming a room. **2** a literary miscellany, a musical medley etc.

pottage (pot´ij) n. a kind of soup or stew.

potter[1] (pot´ə) n. a maker of pottery. **potter's wheel** n. a horizontal wheel on which pots are shaped. **pottery** n. (*pl.* **potteries**) **1** earthenware. **2** a place where this is manufactured, a potter's workshop. **3** the making of earthenware.

potter[2] (pot´ə), (*N Am.*) **putter** (pŭt´ə) v.i. **1** to busy oneself in a desultory but generally agreeable way. **2** to proceed in a leisurely and often random fashion. **3** to study or work (at) in a superficial way. ~v.t. to waste or pass (time away) in a desultory way. **potterer** n.

potting POT[1].

potty[1] (pot´i) a. (*comp.* **pottier**, *superl.* **pottiest**) **1** crazy, foolish. **2** insignificant. **pottiness** n.

potty[2] (pot´i) n. (*pl.* **potties**) (*coll.*) a chamber pot, esp. one for use by small children. **potty-train** v.t. to teach (a young child) to use a potty.

pouch (powch) n. **1** a small bag. **2** a purse, a detachable pocket. **3** the baglike pocket of skin in which marsupials carry their young. **4** a similar receptacle in other animals, e.g. in a rodent's cheeks. **5** a puffy fold of skin under the eye. **6** a bag for holding mail. **7** (*Bot.*) a pouchlike sac in plants. ~v.t. **1** to put into a pouch. **2** to put into a pocket. **3** to cause (a bodice etc.) to hang like a pouch. **pouched** a. **pouchy** a.

pouf[1] (poof), **pouffe** n. a large, solid cushion used as a seat or a footstool.

pouf[2] POOF[1].

poultice (pōl´tis) n. a heated and medicated composition, for applying to sore or inflamed parts of the body to reduce inflammation, a cataplasm. ~v.t. to apply a poultice to.

poultry (pōl´tri) n. domestic fowls, including chickens, geese, ducks, turkeys etc. **poult** (pōlt) n. a young pullet, partridge, turkey etc. **poulterer** n. a dealer in poultry for the table. †**poulter** n. a dealer in poultry for the table.

pounce (powns) n. **1** a pouncing, an abrupt swoop, spring etc. **2** the claw of a bird of prey. ~v.i. **1** to sweep down or spring upon and seize prey with the claws. **2** to seize (upon), to dart or dash (upon) suddenly. **3** to speak abruptly in reply to a remark etc. **pouncer** n.

pound[1] (pownd) n. **1** an avoirdupois unit of weight divided into 16 ounces and equal to approx. 0.454 kg. **2** a troy unit of weight divided into 12 ounces and equal to approx. 0.373 kg. **3** (also **pound sterling**, pl. **pound, pounds**) the basic monetary unit of the UK, divided into 100 (new) pence (formerly 20 shillings). **4** the standard monetary unit of various other countries. **poundage** (-dij) n. **1** an allowance, fee, commission etc., of so much in the pound. **2** a percentage of the aggregate earnings of an industrial concern paid as or added to wages. **3** a person's weight, esp. if considered excessive. **poundal** n. (Physics) a unit of force, that required to give an acceleration of one foot per second to a mass of one pound. **pound cake** n. a rich sweet cake, so called from the ingredients being pound for pound of each. **pound coin** n. a UK coin with the value of one pound sterling. **pounder**[1] n. **1** (usu. in comb.) a gun firing a shot of a specified number of pounds weight. **2** a person worth or possessing a specified sum in pounds sterling. **3** something weighing a pound, or a specified number of pounds, such as a fish. **pound-foolish** a. neglecting the care of large sums, esp. through trying to make small economies. **pound of flesh** n. the exact amount owing to one, esp. when recovering it involves one's debtor in considerable suffering or trouble. **pound sign** n. the sign £, representing a pound sterling.

pound[2] (pownd) n. **1 a** an enclosure for confining stray cattle etc. **b** a yard for keeping cars removed from the street by police, or distrained goods etc. **2** an enclosure, a pen. **3** a trap, a prison. ~v.t. to confine in or as in a pound. **pound lock** n. a lock with two gates and usu. a reservoir at the side to regulate the water level.

pound[3] (pownd) v.t. **1** to crush, to pulverize. **2** to beat, to strike heavily. **3** to thump, to pommel. ~v.i. **1** to strike heavy blows, to hammer (at, upon etc.). **2** to fire heavy shot (at). **3** to walk or go heavily (along). **4** (of the heart, a drum etc.) to beat heavily or very fast. **to pound out** to produce, as if with heavy blows (esp. on a typewriter). **pounder**[2] n.

pour (paw) v.t. **1** to cause (liquids etc.) to flow downwards. **2** to serve (a drink) by pouring. **3** to discharge, to emit copiously. **4** to send (forth or out) in a stream, or in great numbers. **5** to shed freely. **6** to utter, to give vent to. ~v.i. **1** to flow in a stream of rain, to fall copiously. **2** to rush in great numbers. **3** to come in a constant stream. **to pour oil on troubled waters** to exercise a soothing, calming or conciliatory influence. **pourable** a. **pourer** n.

pourboire (puǝbwah´) n. a gratuity, a tip.

poussin (poo´si) n. a young chicken reared for eating.

pout (powt) v.i. **1** to thrust out the lips in sullenness, displeasure, or contempt. **2** (of lips) to be

protruded or prominent. ~v.t. to thrust out (the lips). ~n. a protrusion of the lips. **the pouts** a fit of sullenness. **pouter** n. **1** a person who pouts. **2** a variety of pigeon which can inflate its crop. **poutingly** adv. **pouty** a.

poverty (pov´ǝti) n. **1** the state of being poor; want, destitution, indigence. **2** scarcity, meagreness, dearth (of). **3** deficiency (in). **4** inferiority. **5** renunciation (by monks etc.) of the right to hold property. **poverty line** n. a level of income below which one is in poverty. **poverty-stricken** a. very poor. **poverty trap** n. a situation in which any increase in one's earned income is immediately offset by a decrease in one's entitlement to state benefit, thus making it impossible to raise one's standard of living.

POW abbr. prisoner of war.

pow (pow) int. used to express the sound of an impact, blow etc.

powder (pow´dǝ) n. **1** any dry dustlike substance or fine particles. **2** dust. **3** a cosmetic in the form of fine dust. **4** a medicine in the form of powder. **5** gunpowder. ~v.t. **1** to reduce to powder. **2** to put powder on. **3** to sprinkle or cover with powder. **4** to sprinkle with fine spots or figures for decoration. **to keep one's powder dry** to take precautions and wait for an opportunity to act. **to take a powder** (N Am., coll.) to run away, leave quickly. **powder blue** n. a pale blue colour. ~a. having a pale blue colour. **powder flask, powder horn** n. (Hist.) a case or horn fitted to hold gunpowder. **powder keg** n. **1** a small barrel to hold gunpowder. **2** a potentially explosive place or situation. **powder metallurgy** n. the technology of making metal objects by compacting and sintering powdered metal. **powder monkey** n. (Naut.) a boy formerly employed to carry powder from the magazine to the guns. **powder puff** n. a soft pad for applying powder to the skin. **powder room** n. (coll.) a women's cloakroom. **powder snow** n. very fine dry snow. **powdery** a.

power (pow´ǝ) n. **1** the ability to do or act so as to effect something. **2** a mental or bodily faculty, or potential capacity. **3** strength, force, energy, esp. as actually exerted. **4** influence, dominion, authority (over). **5** legal authority or authorization. **6** political ascendancy. **7** a person, group or body invested with authority or having influence. **8** military strength. **9** a state having influence on other states. **10** (coll.) a great deal. **11** (Math.) **a** the product obtained by multiplication of a quantity or number into itself. **b** the index showing the number of times a factor is multiplied by itself. **12** mechanical energy as distinguished from hand labour. **13 a** electricity. **b** electrical energy or power. **14** the capacity (of a machine etc.) for performing mechanical work. **15** (Physics) the rate at which energy is emitted or transferred, esp. the rate of doing work, measured in watts (joules per second), footpounds per second, or ergs per second. **16** the magnifying capacity of a lens etc. **17** (*pl.*) the sixth order of angels. **18** a supernatural being having sway over some part of creation, a deity. *~v.t.* **1** to supply with esp. motive power. **2** (*coll.*) to cause to move with great speed or force. *~v.i.* (*coll.*) to move with great force or speed. **in someone's power 1** within the limits of someone's capabilities or authority. **2** under someone's control, at someone's mercy. **more power to your elbow!** (*coll.*) used to express one's approval of someone's efforts, urging someone to continue and even intensify them. **the powers that be** (*often facet.*) established authority. **to power down** to switch off, to decrease the power supply to. **to power up** to switch on, to increase the power supply to. **power-assisted** *a.* (of the steering or brakes in a motor car) made easier to use by added mechanical power. **power base** *n.* supporters etc. from whom one draws authority or power. **power behind the throne** *n.* a person with no official position in government who exercises a strong personal influence on a ruler. **power block** *n.* a group of nations etc. who together wield political, military etc. power. **powerboat** *n.* a boat propelled by a powerful motor, esp. a speedboat. **power-broker** *n.* a person who acts as an intermediary in setting up political alliances etc. **power-broking** *n.*, *a.* **power cut** *n.* an interruption or reduction in the supply of electricity. **power-dive** *n.* a steep dive of an aircraft under engine power. *~v.i.* to make such a dive. **power dressing** *n.* the wearing by businesswomen of plain suits tailored in a masculine style in order to give an impression of authority and power. **powered** *a.* **powerful** *a.* **1** having great strength or energy. **2** mighty, potent. **3** impressing the mind, forcible, efficacious. **4** producing great effects. **powerfully** *adv.* **powerfulness** *n.* **powerhouse** *n.* **1** a power station. **2** (*coll.*) a very forceful and dynamic person or thing. **powerless** *a.* **1** without strength or power. **2** unable (to). **powerlessly** *adv.* **powerlessness** *n.* **power line** *n.* a cable carrying electric power, esp. one supported on pylons or poles. **power of attorney** *n.* a written authority by which one person authorizes another to act in their stead. **power pack** *n.* **1** a unit for converting a power supply to the voltage required by an electronic circuit. **2** a unit for supplying power. **power plant** *n.* **1** a power station. **2** the machinery etc. used to generate power. **power play** *n.* **1** in team sports, aggressive tactics, esp. concentrating players on one part of the defence. **2** similar tactics in business or politics. **3** in ice hockey, a formation used when the opposing team are one or more players down. **power point** *n.* an electrical socket by which an appliance can be connected to the mains. **power politics** *n.* (*sometimes as pl.*) diplomacy backed by armed force or the threat of it. **power-sharing** *n.* the involvement of all the parties or groups in an organization in making and implementing policy. **power shovel** *n.* a mechanical excavator. **power station** *n.* an installation for the generation of power, esp. electrical power. **power steering** *n.* a system in which the torque applied to a vehicle's steering wheel is augmented by engine power. **power stroke** *n.* in an internal-combustion engine, the downward stroke of the piston. **power tool** *n.* an electrically-powered tool. **power train** *n.* the sequence of parts in a motor vehicle from the engine through the transmission to the axle and wheels.

powwow (pow´wow) *n.* a meeting, talk or conference, orig. among N American Indians. *~v.i.* to hold a powwow.

pox (poks) *n.* **1** any disease characterized by the formation of pustules that leave pockmarks. **2** syphilis. **3** a plant disease which causes spots like pox pustules. **poxy** *a.* (*comp.* **poxier,** *superl.* **poxiest**) **1** syphilitic. **2** (*sl.*) unpleasant, rotten.

pp *abbr.* **1** per pro. **2** pianissimo.

Usage note See note under PER PRO.

pp. *abbr.* pages.

p.p.m., ppm *abbr.* parts per million.

PPS *abbr.* **1** Parliamentary Private Secretary. **2** post-postscriptum, further postscript.

PR *abbr.* **1** proportional representation. **2** public relations.

Pr *chem. symbol* praseodymium.

pr. *abbr.* pair.

practicable (prak´tikəbəl) *a.* **1** capable of being done, feasible. **2** (of roads etc.) usable, passable. **practicability** (-bil´-), **practicableness** *n.* **practicably** *adv.*

Usage note The meanings of the adjectives *practicable* and *practical* overlap, but *practicable* usually means possible in practice, feasible, while *practical* contrasts practice or performance with theory or speculation, with reference either to a person or an action.

practical (prak´tikəl) *a.* **1** of or relating to action not theory or speculation. **2** realistic, down-to-earth. **3** (of a person) preferring action to speculation. **4** capable of being used, available, serving or suitable for use. **5** such in effect, virtual. **6** of, relating to or governed by practice. **7** derived from practice, experienced. *~n.* a practical examination, lesson etc. **practicality** (-kal´-) *n.* (*pl.* **practicalities**). **practical joke** *n.* a joke or trick entailing some action and intended to make the victim look foolish. **practical joker** *n.* **practically** *adv.* **1** in a practical manner. **2** virtually, in effect, as regards results. **practicalness** *n.*

Usage note See note under PRACTICABLE.

practice (prak´tis) *n.* **1** habitual or customary action or procedure. **2** a habit, a custom. **3** the continued or systematic exercise of any profession, art, craft etc. **4 a** professional work. **b**

the business of a professional person. **5** actual performance, doing or execution, as opposed to theory or intention. **6** (*often pl.*) conduct, dealings. **7 a** regular, repeated exercise in order to gain proficiency in something. **b** a session of such exercise. **8** legal procedure, the rules governing this. **in practice 1** in the sphere of action. **2** in training, in condition for working, acting, playing etc., effectively. **out of practice** out of training. **to put into practice** to convert (an idea or theory) into actuality, to do something previously only thought of. **practician** (-tish´ən) *n.* a person who works or practises, a practitioner.

practise (prak´tis), (*N Am.*) **practice** *v.t.* **1** to do or perform habitually; to carry out. **2** to exercise as a profession etc. **3** to exercise oneself in or on (to improve or maintain a skill etc.). **4** to instruct, to exercise, to drill (in a subject, art etc.). **5** to accustom. ~*v.i.* **1** to exercise oneself. **2** to exercise a profession or art. **3** to do a thing or perform an act habitually. **4** to use influence, to impose (upon). **practised** *a.* experienced, expert. **practiser** *n.* **practising** *a.* doing or actively engaged in now (*practising Christian*).

practitioner (praktish´ənə) *n.* a person who regularly practises any profession, esp. medicine.

praesidium PRESIDIUM.

praetor (prē´tə), (*N Am.*) **pretor** *n.* (*Hist.*) a Roman magistrate; orig. a consul as leader of the army, later a curule magistrate elected yearly to perform various judicial and consular duties. **praetorial** (pritaw´ri-) *a.* **praetorian** *a.*, *n.* **praetorship** *n.*

pragmatic (pragmat´ik) *a.* **1** concerned with practicalities or expediency rather than principles. **2** concerned with the causes and effects and the practical lessons of history. **3** pragmatical. **pragmatical** *a.* **1** officious, given to interfering in the affairs of others. **2** dogmatic. **3** relating to pragmatism. **pragmaticality** (-kal´-), **pragmaticalness** *n.* **pragmatically** *adv.* **pragmatics** *n.* in linguistics, the study of the social etc. aspects of language. **pragmatism** (prag´-) *n.* **1** pragmaticalness, officiousness. **2** treatment of things, esp. in history, with regard to causes and effects. **3** (*Philos.*) the doctrine that our only test of the truth of human cognitions or philosophical principles is their practical results. **pragmatist** *n.* **pragmatize, pragmatise** *v.t.* **1** to represent (an imaginary thing) as real. **2** to rationalize (a myth).

prairie (preə´ri) *n.* an extensive tract of level or rolling grassland, usu. destitute of trees, esp. in N America. **prairie chicken, prairie hen** *n.* a N American grouse, *Tympanuchus cupido.* **prairie dog** *n.* any small rodent of the genus *Cynomys,* living in large communities on the N American prairies. **prairie oyster** *n.* a pick-me-up made of raw egg, Worcester sauce etc. **prairie wolf** *n.* the coyote, *Canis latrans.*

praise (prāz) *v.t.* **1** to express approval and commendation of. **2** to extol, to glorify. ~*n.* the act, or an instance, of praising, approbation, encomium. **praise be!** an exclamation expressing gratitude and pleasure. **praiseful** *a.* **praiser** *n.* **praiseworthy** *a.* deserving of praise. **praiseworthily** *adv.* **praiseworthiness** *n.*

praline (prah´lēn) *n.* a confection of almond or other nut with a brown coating of sugar.

pram (pram) *n.* a four-wheeled conveyance for a baby, with a cradle-like body and pushed by a person walking.

prance (prahns) *v.i.* **1** to spring or caper on the hind legs, as a horse in high mettle. **2** to walk or strut in a pompous or swaggering style. ~*n.* **1** the act of prancing. **2** a prancing movement. **prancer** *n.*

prandial (pran´diəl) *a.* (*formal or facet.*) relating to lunch or dinner.

prang (prang) *v.t.* (*sl.*) **1** to crash. **2** to bomb heavily. **3** to strike. ~*n.* **1** a bombing raid. **2** a crash.

prank (prangk) *n.* **1** a wild frolic. **2** a trick, a playful act, a practical joke. **3** a gambol, a capricious action. **prankful** *a.* **prankish** *a.* **prankishness** *n.* **pranksome** *a.* **prankster** *n.* a person given to playing pranks or practical jokes. **pranky** *a.*

prase (prāz) *n.* a dull leek-green translucent quartz.

praseodymium (prāziōdim´iəm) *n.* (*Chem.*) a rare metallic element, at. no. 59, chem. symbol Pr, occurring in certain rare-earth minerals.

prat (prat) *n.* (*sl.*) **1** a stupid or contemptible person. **2** the buttocks. **pratfall** *n.* **1** (*esp. N Am.*) a fall on one's buttocks. **2** a humiliating blunder or mishap.

prate (prāt) *v.i.* **1** to chatter; to talk a lot and without purpose or reason. **2** to babble, to cackle. ~*v.t.* **1** to utter foolishly. **2** to boast idly about. ~*n.* idle or silly talk, unmeaning loquacity. **prater** *n.* **prating** *n.*, *a.* **pratingly** *adv.*

prattle (prat´əl) *v.i.* to talk in a childish or foolish manner. ~*v.t.* to utter or divulge thus. ~*n.* childish or idle talk. **prattler** *n.* **prattling** *n.*, *a.* **prattlingly** *adv.*

prawn (prawn) *n.* any of several small decapod crustaceans, like large shrimps. ~*v.t.* to fish for prawns. **prawn cracker** *n.* in Chinese cookery, a savoury puff made from rice flour flavoured with prawn.

praxis (prak´sis) *n.* (*pl.* **praxises, praxes** (-ēz)) **1** use, practice, accepted practice. **2** the practice of an art; the practical as distinct from the theoretical side.

pray (prā) *v.t.* **1** to ask for with earnestness or submission. **2** to beseech, to entreat, to supplicate. **3** to address devoutly and earnestly. ~*v.i.* **1** to address God with adoration or earnest entreaty. **2** to make supplication, to beg or petition (for). **prayer**[1] (prā´ə) *n.* a person who prays.

prayer[1] PRAY.

prayer[2] (preə) *n.* **1** the act of praying. **2** a solemn petition or a thanksgiving addressed to God or any object of worship. **3** the practice of praying, a formula for praying. **4** a prescribed formula of divine worship; a liturgy. **5** (*often pl.*) a religious service. **6** an entreaty. **7** something entreated or prayed for. **8** a memorial or petition. **not to have a prayer** (*N Am., coll.*) to have not the slightest chance or hope. **prayer book** *n.* a book containing prayers and forms of devotion, esp. the Anglican Book of Common Prayer. **prayerful** *a.* **1** given to prayer, devout. **2** devotional, characterized by prayer. **prayerfully** *adv.* **prayerfulness** *n.* **prayerless** *a.* **prayerlessly** *adv.* **prayer mat** *n.* a small carpet on which a Muslim kneels and prays. **prayer shawl** *n.* a tallith. **prayer wheel** *n.* a revolving wheel or cylinder on which written prayers are inscribed or fastened by Tibetan Buddhists.

pre- (prē) *pref.* **1** before, earlier than; in advance. **2** in front of, anterior to. **3** surpassingly.

pre- (+ a– words) pre-adolescent *a.* **1** (of a child) having nearly reached adolescence. **2** of or relating to the stage between childhood and adolescence. **~n.** a pre-adolescent child. **pre-adolescence** *n.* **preamp** (prē´amp) *n.* a preamplifier. **preamplifier** *n.* an amplifier used to boost a low-level signal and often to equalize it before feeding it to the main amplifier. **preamplified** *a.* **pre-arrange** *v.t.* to arrange in advance. **pre-arranged** *a.* **pre-arrangement** *n.* **preatomic** *a.* of or relating to the period before the use of atomic energy.

preach (prēch) *v.i.* **1** to deliver a sermon or public discourse on some religious subject. **2** to give earnest religious or moral advice, esp. in an obtrusive or persistent way. **~v.t. 1** to proclaim, to expound in a common or public discourse. **2** to deliver (a sermon). **3** to teach or advocate in this manner. **to preach to the converted** to advocate an opinion etc. to people already in favour. **preachable** *a.* **preacher** *n.* **preachify** (-ifī) *v.i.* (*3rd pers. sing. pres.* **preachifies,** *pres.p.* **preachifying,** *past, p.p.* **preachified**) to hold forth in a sermon, esp. tediously; to sermonize. **preachification** (-fikā´shən) *n.* **preachment** *n.* (*usu. derog.*) a discourse or sermon. **preachy** *a.* (*comp.* **preachier,** *superl.* **preachiest**) fond of preaching or sermonizing, disposed to preach. **preachiness** *n.*

preamble (prēam´bəl) *n.* **1** an introductory statement, esp. the introductory portion of a statute setting forth succinctly its reasons and intentions. **2** a preliminary event, fact etc. **preambular** (-bū-), **preambulary** *a.*

pre- (+ b– words) pre-book *v.t.* to reserve, to arrange in advance. **pre-bookable** *a.*

prebend (preb´ənd) *n.* **1** (*Hist.*) the stipend or maintenance granted to a canon of a cathedral or collegiate church out of its revenue. **2** (*Hist.*) the land or tithe yielding this. **3** a prebendary. **prebendal** *a.* of or relating to a prebend or a prebendary. **prebendary** *n.* (*pl.* **prebendaries**) **1** an honorary canon. **2** (*Hist.*) the holder of a prebend. **prebendaryship** *n.*

pre- (+ c– words) Precambrian *n., a.* (*Geol.*) (of or relating to) the earliest geological era, before the appearance of early life forms. **precancerous** *a.* (*Med.*) (of cells or tissues) showing changes which may lead to the development of cancer. **precast** *a.* (of concrete blocks, panels etc.) cast before being put in position. **pre-Christian** *a.* of or relating to the times before Christ or before Christianity. **preclassical** *a.* before the classical period, esp. in music and literature. **preclinical** *a.* (*Med.*) **1** of or relating to the early stages of a disease, before the symptoms are recognizable. **2** of or relating to the early stage of medical studies, before the student has practical experience with patients. **pre-Columbian** *a.* of or relating to the period in US history before the arrival of Columbus. **preconcert** (-sœt´) *v.t.* to contrive or agree on by previous arrangement. **precondition** *n.* a necessary preliminary condition. **~v.t.** to prepare beforehand, to put into a desired condition or frame of mind beforehand. **preconscious** *a.* (*Psych.*) **1** of or relating to a state antecedent to consciousness. **2** of or relating to ideas or memories which are not conscious but which can readily be recalled. **~n.** the part of the mind where preconscious ideas etc. exist. **preconsciousness** *n.* **pre-cook** *v.t.* to cook beforehand. **pre-cool** *v.t.* to cool beforehand. **precostal** *a.* in front of the ribs. **pre-cut** *v.t.* (*pres.p.* **pre-cutting,** *past, p.p.* **pre-cut**) to cut beforehand.

precarious (prikeə´riəs) *a.* **1** not well-established, insecure, unstable. **2** doubtful, dependent on chance, uncertain, hazardous. **precariously** *adv.* **precariousness** *n.*

precaution (prikaw´shən) *n.* **1** a measure taken beforehand to guard against or bring about something. **2** (*pl.*) contraceptive measures. **precautionary,** †**precautional** *a.*

precede (prisēd´) *v.t.* **1** to go before in time, order, rank or importance. **2** to walk in front of. **3** to cause to come before, to preface or prelude. **precedence** (pres´i-), **precedency** *n.* **1** priority. **2** the right to a higher position or a place in advance of others at public ceremonies, social functions etc. **to take precedence** to have a higher priority (over). **precedent**[1] (pres´idənt) *n.* something done or said which may serve as an example to be followed in a similar case, esp. a legal decision, usage etc. **precedented** *a.* having or warranted by a precedent. **precedent**[2] (prisē´dənt, pres´idənt) *a.* going before in time, order, rank etc. **precedently** *adv.*

precentor (prisen´tə) *n.* **1** a cleric who directs choral services in a cathedral. **2** a person who leads the singing of choir or congregation. **3** a person who leads the prayers in a synagogue. **precent** *v.i.* to act as precentor. **~v.t.** to lead the singing of (psalms etc.). **precentorship** *n.*

precept (prē´sept) *n.* **1** a command, a mandate. **2** a rule of conduct. **3** a maxim. **4** a writ, a warrant.

5 an order for the levying or collection of a rate.
preceptor (-sep´-) *n.* a teacher, an instructor.
preceptorial (-taw´ri-) *a.* **preceptorship** *n.* **preceptress** (-sep´tris) *n.* a woman teacher; a governess.
precession (prisesh´ən) *n.* the wobbling motion of the axis of a spinning body, so that it forms a cone-shape. **precessional** *a.* **precession of the equinoxes** *n.* (*Astron.*) a slow but continual shifting of the equinoctial points from east to west, occasioned by the earth's axis slowly revolving in a small circle about the pole of the ecliptic, causing an earlier occurrence of the equinoxes in successive sidereal years.
precinct (prē´singkt) *n.* **1** the space enclosed by the walls or boundaries of a place, esp. a church. **2** a boundary, a limit. **3** a pedestrianized area of a town set aside for a particular activity, usu. shopping. **4** (*US*) a municipal police district. **5** (*US*) a polling district. **6** (*pl.*) the environs or immediate surroundings (of).
precious (presh´əs) *a.* **1** of great price or value. **2** highly esteemed, dear, beloved. **3** affected, over-refined in manner, style, workmanship etc. **4** (*coll., iron.*) worthless, rascally; considerable. ~*adv.* (*coll.*) very, extremely. **preciosity** (-ios´-) *n.* (*pl.* **preciosities**) overfastidiousness or affected delicacy in the use of language, in workmanship etc. **preciously** *adv.* **precious metals** *n.pl.* gold, silver and platinum. **preciousness** *n.* **precious stone** *n.* a gem.
precipice (pres´ipis) *n.* **1** a vertical or very steep cliff. **2** the edge of a cliff, hence a situation of extreme danger. **precipiced** *a.*
precipitate¹ (prəsip´itāt) *v.t.* **1** to throw headlong. **2** to hasten; to bring on, esp. prematurely. **3** (*Chem.*) to cause (a substance) to be deposited at the bottom of a vessel, as from a solution. **4** (*Physics etc.*) **a** to cause (moisture) to condense and be deposited, as from vapour. **b** to cause to fall as rain, snow etc. **c** to cause (dust) to be deposited on a surface from the air. ~*v.i.* **1** (of a substance in solution) to fall to the bottom of a vessel. **2** (of vapour) to condense and be deposited in drops. **3** to fall as rain, snow etc. **precipitable** *a.* **precipitability** (-bil´-) *n.* **precipitation** (-ā´shən) *n.* **1** the act of precipitating, the state of being precipitated. **2** violent speed. **3** rash haste. **4** (the amount of) rain, snow, sleet etc. falling to the ground. **precipitator** *n.*
precipitate² (prisip´itāt) *a.* **1** headlong. **2** flowing or rushing with haste and violence. **3** hasty, rash, inconsiderate. **4** adopted without due deliberation. ~*n.* **1** (*Chem.*) a solid substance deposited from a state of solution. **2** (*Physics etc.*) moisture condensed from vapour and deposited, as rain, dew etc. **precipitance, precipitancy, precipitateness** *n.* **precipitant** *a.* headlong, precipitate. ~*n.* (*Chem.*) any substance that, being added to a solution, causes precipitation. **precipitately** *adv.*

Usage note See note under PRECIPITOUS.

precipitous (prisip´itəs) *a.* **1** like or of the nature of a precipice, very steep. **2** headlong, precipitate, hasty, rash. **precipitously** *adv.* **precipitousness** *n.*

Usage note The adjectives *precipitous* and *precipitate* should not be confused: *precipitous* means steep, and *precipitate* hasty or rash.

précis (prā´sē) *n.* (*pl.* **précis** (-sēz)) an abstract or summary. ~*v.t.* (*3rd pers. sing. pres.* **précises** (prā´sēz), *pres.p.* **précising** (prā´sēing), *past, p.p.* **précised** (prā´sēd)) to make a précis of.
precise (prisīs´) *a.* **1** definite, sharply defined or stated. **2** accurate, exact. **3** strictly observant of rule, punctilious, overnice, overscrupulous. **4** particular, identical. **precisely** *adv.* **1** in a precise manner. **2** exactly, quite so. **preciseness** *n.* **precision** (-sizh´ən) *n.* accuracy, exactness. ~*a.* **1** characterized by great accuracy in execution. **2** intended for very accurate measurement or operation. **precisionism** *n.* **precisionist** *n.*
preclude (priklood´) *v.t.* **1** to shut out, to exclude. **2** to hinder, to prevent. **preclusion** (-zhən) *n.* **preclusive** (-siv´) *a.*
precocious (prikō´shəs) *a.* **1** (*often derog.*) prematurely developed intellectually. **2** (*often derog.*) forward, pert. **3** characteristic of such development. **4** developing or ripe before the normal time. **precociously** *adv.* **precociousness** *n.* **precosity** (-kos´-) *n.*
precognition (prēkəgnish´ən) *n.* foreknowledge; clairvoyance. **precognitive** (-kog´nitiv) *a.*
preconceive (prēkənsēv´) *v.t.* to conceive or form (an opinion of) beforehand. **preconception** *n.*
precordia (prikaw´diə), **praecordia** *n.pl.* (*Med.*) the chest and the parts it contains, the region about the heart. **precordial** *a.*
precursor (prikœ´sə) *n.* **1** a forerunner, a harbinger. **2** a predecessor in office etc. **3** (*Chem.*) a substance from which another is formed by chemical reaction etc. **precursive** *a.* precursory. **precursory** *a.* **1** preceding and indicating as a forerunner or harbinger. **2** preliminary, introductory.
pre- (+ d– words) pre-date *v.t.* to exist or happen at an earlier date than. **predecease** *n.* the death of a person before some other person. ~*v.t.* to die before (a particular person). **pre-decimal** *a.* before the introduction of a decimal system, esp. of coinage. **predigest** *v.t.* **1** to digest partially before introducing into the stomach. **2** to render (literature or any difficult reading material) easier to understand by simplifying. **predigestion** *n.* **pre-doom** *v.t.* to doom in advance. **predorsal** *a.* in front of the dorsal region. **predynastic** *a.* of or relating to a time, esp. in ancient Egypt, before the emergence of dynasties.
predacious (pridā´shəs), **predaceous** *a.* **1** living by prey, predatory. **2** of or relating to animals living by prey. **predaciousness** *n.* **predacity** (-das´-) *n.*

predator (pred´ətə) *n.* **1** a predatory animal. **2** a predatory person. **predation** (-ā´shən) *n.* **1** (*Zool.*) the way of life of a predator, the relationship between a predator and its prey. **2** (*usu. pl.*) depredation. **predatory** *a.* **1** habitually hunting and killing other animals for food. **2** living by plunder. **3** of, relating to or characterized by plunder or pillage. **predatorily** *adv.* **predatoriness** *n.*

predecessor (prē´disesə) *n.* **1** a person who precedes another in any position, office etc. **2** a thing preceding another thing. **3** a forefather, an ancestor.

predestine (prēdes´tin) *v.t.* **1** to appoint beforehand by irreversible decree. **2** to preordain (to salvation, to do a certain deed etc.). **3** to predetermine. **predestinarian** (-neə´ri-) *a.* of or relating to predestination. ~*n.* a believer in predestination. **predestinate**[1] (-āt) *v.t.* to predestine. **predestinate**[2] (-ət) *a.* ordained or appointed beforehand. **predestination** (-ā´shən) *n.* (*Theol.*) the act of predestining, esp. the act of God in foreordaining some to salvation and some to perdition.

predetermine (prēditœ´min) *v.t.* **1** to determine or settle beforehand. **2** to foreordain, to predestine. **predeterminable** *a.* **predeterminate** (-nət) *a.* **predetermination** (-ā´shən) *n.* **predeterminer** *n.*

predicable (pred´ikəbəl) *a.* capable of being predicated or affirmed. **predicability** (-bil´-) *n.*

predicament (pridik´əmənt) *n.* **1** a particular state, condition or position, esp. a difficult or unpleasant one. **2** (*Philos.*) that which is predicted, a category.

predicate[1] (pred´ikāt) *v.t.* **1** to affirm, to assert as a property etc. **2** (*Logic*) to assert about the subject of a proposition. **3** to found, to base (an argument etc. on). **predication** (-ā´shən) *n.* **predicative** (-dik´-) *a.* **1** (*Gram.*) (of an adjective) occurring within the predicate, as distinct from *attributive*. **2** predicating, affirming. **predicatively** *adv.*

predicate[2] (pred´ikət) *n.* **1** (*Logic*) that which is predicated, that which is affirmed or denied of the subject. **2** (*Gram.*) the entire statement made about the subject, including the copula as well as the logical predicate.

predict (pridikt´) *v.t.* to forecast, to foretell, to prophesy. **predictable** *a.* **1** able to be forecast or foretold. **2** (occurring or apt to behave in a manner which is) easily foreseen. **predictability** (-bil´-), **predictableness** *n.* **predictably** *adv.* **prediction** (-dik´shən) *n.* **1** something predicted. **2** the act, or the art, of predicting. **predictive** *a.* **predictively** *adv.* **predictor** *n.*

predilection (prēdilek´shən, pred-) *n.* a prepossession in favour of something, a preference, a partiality.

predispose (prēdispōz´) *v.t.* **1** to dispose or incline beforehand (to some course of action etc.). **2** to make susceptible or liable to. **predisposition** (-zish´ən) *n.*

predominate (pridom´ināt) *v.i.* **1** to be superior in strength, influence or authority. **2** to prevail, to have the ascendancy (over). **3** to have control (over). **4** to preponderate. **predominance, predominancy** *n.* **predominant** *a.* **1** predominating (over). **2** superior, overruling, controlling. **predominantly** *adv.* **predominately** *adv.* **predominatingly** *adv.*

Usage note The adverb *predominantly* is preferred to *predominately*.

pre- (+ e– words) pre-echo *n.* (*pl.* **pre-echoes**) **1** a faint echo-like sound heard in a recording before the actual sound, caused by a transfer of signals between surfaces of the tape. **2** a foreshadowing; a foretaste. **pre-eclampsia** *n.* (*Med.*) a serious toxic condition occurring in late pregnancy, characterized by high blood pressure and oedema. **pre-eclamptic** *a.* **pre-elect** *v.t.* to elect beforehand. **pre-election** *n.* an election held previously. ~*a.* occurring or done before an election. **pre-embryo** *n.* (*pl.* **pre-embryos**) (*Med.*) the structure formed after fertilization of the human ovum, which will have developed into an embryo after 14 days. **pre-engage** *v.t.* **1** to engage by previous contract or pledge. **2** to preoccupy. **3** to engage in conflict beforehand. **pre-engagement** *n.* **pre-establish** *v.t.* to establish beforehand. **pre-exist** *v.i.* to exist previously. ~*v.t.* to exist earlier than. **pre-existence** *n.* **pre-existent** *a.*

pre-eminent (prēem´inənt) *a.* **1** eminent beyond others. **2** superior to or surpassing all others, paramount, outstanding. **pre-eminence** *n.* **pre-eminently** *adv.*

pre-empt (priempt´) *v.t.* **1 a** to secure by preemption. **b** to acquire in advance. **2** to seize on to the exclusion of others. **3** to act before another (in order to thwart), to anticipate. **pre-emption** *n.* **1** the act or right of buying before others. **2** anticipating, forestalling. **3** (*Mil.*) the making of a pre-emptive strike. **pre-emptive** *a.* **pre-emptive bid** *n.* in bridge, an unusually high bid intended to shut out opposition. **pre-emptive strike** *n.* an attack on enemy installations intended to forestall a suspected attack on oneself. **pre-emptor** *n.*

Usage note *Pre-empt* should not be used as though it simply meant to prevent.

preen (prēn) *v.t., v.i.* **1** to clean and arrange (feathers) using the beak. **2** to take great trouble with, or an excessive interest in (one's appearance). **3** to pride or congratulate oneself (on). **preener** *n.* **preen gland** *n.* in birds, a gland at the base of the tail which produces oil used in preening.

pre- (+ f– words) prefab (prē´fab) *n.* (*coll.*) a prefabricated building, esp. a small house. **prefabricate** (prēfab´rikāt) *v.t.* **1** to manufacture (the component parts of a structure) in advance for rapid on-site assembly. **2** to produce (objects) in a very standardized way. **prefabrication** n. **prefabricator** n. **pre-flight** a. happening or provided before an aircraft flight. **preform** v.t. to form beforehand. **preformation** n. **prefrontal** a. **1** situated in front of the frontal bone or the frontal region of the skull. **2** in the forepart of the frontal lobe of the brain.

preface (pref'əs) n. **1** something spoken or written as introductory to a discourse or book. **2** an introduction; an exordium, a preamble, a prelude. **3** the thanksgiving etc. forming the prelude to the consecration of the Eucharist. ~v.t. **1** to introduce (with preliminary remarks etc.). **2** to provide with a preface. **3** to serve as a preface or introduction to. **prefacer** n. **prefatorial** (-taw'ri-), **prefatory** (pref'-) a.

prefect (prē'fekt) n. **1** (Hist.) a Roman commander, a governor, a chief magistrate. **2** the civil governor of a department in France, or of a province in Italy. **3** in some schools, a senior pupil with limited disciplinary powers over others. **prefectoral** (-fek'-), **prefectorial** (-taw'ri-) a. **prefecture** (-chə) n. the office, jurisdiction, official residence, or the term of office of a prefect. **prefectural** (-fek'chə-) a.

prefer (prifœ') v.t. (pres.p. **preferring**, past, p.p. **preferred**) **1** to set before, to hold in higher estimation, to like better. **2** to bring forward, to submit. **3** to promote; to recommend, to favour. **preferable** (pref'ə-) a. **1** more desirable. **2** to be preferred. **preferability** (-bil'-) n. **preferably** adv. **preference** (pref'ə-) n. **1** the act of preferring one thing to another, or of being preferred. **2** liking for one thing more than another, predilection. **3** right or liberty of choice. **4** something which is preferred. **in preference to** rather than. **preference bond, preference share, preference stock** n. a bond, a share or stock entitled to a dividend before ordinary shares. **preferential** (prefərən'shəl) a. giving, receiving or constituting preference. **preferentially** adv. **preferential voting** n. a system of proportional representation in which the voter puts the candidates in order of preference. **preferment** n. advancement, promotion. **preferred** a. **preferred debt** n. a debt having priority of payment. **preferred share, preferred stock** n. (N Am.) preference share or preference stock. **preferrer** n.

Usage note (1) After prefer to the contrastive clause should be introduced by rather than, not simply than (I prefer to die rather than (to) submit). (2) The implicit double comparative more preferable is best avoided. (3) Pronunciation of preferable as (prifœ'rəbəl), with stress on the second syllable, is best avoided.

---

prefigure (prēfig'ə) v.t. **1** to represent beforehand by figures, types or similitudes; to foreshadow. **2** to picture to oneself beforehand. **prefiguration** (-rā'shən) n. **prefigurement** n.

prefix[1] (prēfiks') v.t. **1** to put, place or set in front of. **2** to attach at the beginning (as an intro-

duction, prefix etc.). **prefixation** (-ā'shən) n. **prefixion** (-shən), **prefixture** (-chə) n.

prefix[2] (prē'fiks) n. **1** a letter, syllable or word put at the beginning of a word to modify the meaning. **2** a title prefixed to a name. **prefixal** a.

pre- (+ g– words) preglacial a. belonging to the period before a glacial epoch.

pregnable (preg'nəbəl) a. capable of being taken by force.

pregnant (preg'nənt) a. **1** having a child or young developing in the womb. **2** full of meaning or suggestion, significant. **3** inventive, imaginative. **4** fruitful, big (with consequences etc.). **5** portentous, fraught. **pregnancy** n. (pl. **pregnancies**). **pregnantly** adv.

pre- (+ h– words) preheat v.t. to heat beforehand. **prehistoric** a. **1** of or relating to the time prior to that known to history. **2** (coll.) completely out of date. **prehistorian** n. **prehistorically** adv. **prehistory** n. (pl. **prehistories**). **prehuman** a. existing before the appearance of human beings.

prehensile (prihen'sīl) a. (Zool.) adapted to seizing or grasping, as the tails of monkeys. **prehensility** (prēhensil'-) n.

pre- (+ i– words) pre-ignition n. premature ignition of the explosive mixture in the cylinder of an internal-combustion engine. **pre-industrial** a. of, relating to or belonging to the time before the Industrial Revolution.

prejudge (prējŭj') v.t. **1** to form a premature opinion about. **2** to judge before a case has been fully heard, to condemn in advance. **prejudgement, prejudgment** n. **prejudger** n.

prejudice (prej'ədis) n. **1** opinion, bias or judgement formed without due consideration of facts or arguments. **2** intolerance or hostility toward a particular group, race etc. **3** mischief, damage or detriment arising from unfair judgement or action. ~v.t. **1** to prepossess with prejudice, to bias. **2** to affect injuriously, esp. to impair the validity of a right etc. **without prejudice** (Law) without impairing any pre-existing right, detracting from any subsequent claim, or admitting any liability. **prejudiced** a. prepossessed, biased, bigoted. **prejudicial** (-dish'əl) a. **1** causing prejudice or injury. **2** mischievous, detrimental. **prejudicially** adv.

pre- (+ l– words) prelapsarian a. **1** before the Fall of man. **2** without original sin, innocent. **prelingual, pre-linguistic** a. preceding the acquisition or development of language, as prelingual deafness. **preliterate** a. of or relating to a society in which writing has not been developed. **preliteracy** n.

prelate (prel'ət) n. an ecclesiastical dignitary of the highest order, such as an archbishop, bishop etc., formerly including abbot and prior. **prelacy** n. (pl. **prelacies**) **1** the office, dignity or see of a prelate. **2** prelates collectively. **3** episcopacy (in a hostile sense). **prelatic** (-lat'-), **prelatical** a.

preliminary (prilim'inəri) a. **1** introductory. **2**

previous to the main business or discourse. ~*n.*
(*pl.* **preliminaries**) **1** something introductory. **2**
(*pl.*) introductory or preparatory arrangements
etc. **3** a preliminary trial, examination etc. **preliminary to 1** in advance of. **2** as a preparation
for. **preliminarily** *adv.* **prelims** (prē´limz) *n.pl.* **1**
preliminary matter of a book. **2** preliminary
examinations at university or school.
prelude (prel´ūd) *n.* **1** something done,
happening etc., introductory or preparatory to
that which follows. **2** a harbinger, a precursor. **3**
(*Mus.*) **a** a short introductory strain preceding
the principal movement, a piece played as
introduction to a suite. **b** an independent piece
of a similar type. ~*v.t.* **1** to perform or serve as a
prelude to. **2** to introduce with a prelude. **3** to
usher in, to foreshadow. **preludial** *a.*
pre- (+ m– words) premarital *a.* occurring
before marriage. **premaritally** *adv.* **premaxillary**
a. situated in front of the maxilla or upper jaw.
pre-med *n.* **1** pre-medication. **2** (**premed**) a
premedical student, or premedical studies.
premedical *a.* of or relating to a course of study
undertaken before medical studies. **pre-
medication** *n.* drugs administered to sedate and
to prepare a patient for general anaesthesia. **premenstrual** *a.* preceding menstruation. **premen-
strually** *adv.* **premenstrual syndrome, premenstrual tension** *n.* any or all of a range of
symptoms, including nervous tension, fluid
retention etc., caused by the hormonal changes
which precede menstruation. **premillennial** *a.*
existing or happening before the millennium.
premolar *n.* any one of the eight teeth situated in
pairs in front of the molars. ~*a.* in front of a
molar tooth.
premature (prematūe´, prem´-) *a.* **1** ripe or
mature too soon. **2** happening, arriving, existing
or performed before the proper time. **3** overhasty. **4** (of a baby) born after a gestation period
of less than 37 weeks. **prematurely** *adv.* **prema-
tureness** *n.* **prematurity** (-tūe´-) *n.*
premeditate (primed´itāt) *v.t.* **1** to meditate on
beforehand. **2** to plan and contrive beforehand.
premeditation (-ā´shen) *n.*
premier (prem´ie) *a.* **1** first, chief, principal. **2**
the earliest created (*premier earl*). ~*n.* (*usu.*
Premier) a prime or chief minister, or any other
head of government. **premiership** *n.*
premiere (prem´iee, -ie), **première** *n.* a first
performance of a play or film. ~*v.t.* to give a first
performance of (a play or film). ~*v.i.* (of a play or
film) to have its first performance.
premise[1] (prem´is) *n.* **1** (*Logic*) a premiss. **2** (*pl.*) a
piece of land and the buildings upon it, esp.
considered as a place of business. **on the
premises** actually in the building referred to.
premise[2] (primīz´, prem´is) *v.t.* **1** to put forward
as preparatory to what is to follow. **2** to state as
an antecedent proposition or condition. **3** to
assume from a premiss.
premiss (prem´is) *n.* (*Logic*) **1** a statement from

which another is inferred. **2** either of the two
propositions of a syllogism from which the
conclusion is drawn.
premium (prē´miem) *n.* (*pl.* **premiums**) **1** a
payment (usu. periodical) made for insurance. **2**
a sum paid in addition to interest, wages etc., a
bonus. **3** a reward, a recompense, a prize. ~*a.* (of
goods etc.) the best quality, and hence more
expensive. **at a premium 1** above their nominal
value, above par. **2** in great esteem or demand
because scarce. **to put a premium on 1** to render
more than usually valuable or advantageous. **2** to
provide, or to be, an incentive to. **Premium
Bond, Premium Savings Bond** *n.* a British
government bond bearing no interest but subject
to a monthly draw for money prizes.
premonition (premenish´en) *n.* a foreboding, a
presentiment. **premonitor** (-mon´-) *n.*
premonitory *a.*
pre- (+ n– words) prenatal *a.* of or relating to
the period before birth. **prenatally** *adv.* **pre-
nominal** *a.* (of esp. an adjective) placed before a
noun. **prenuptial** *a.* existing or happening before
marriage.
pre- (+ o– words) preocular *a.* situated in front
of the eye. **preordain** *v.t.* to ordain or decide
beforehand. **pre-owned** *a.* (*esp. N Am.*) second-
hand.
preoccupy (priok´ūpī) *v.t.* (*3rd pers. sing. pres.*
preoccupies, *pres.p.* **preoccupying**, *past, p.p.*
preoccupied) **1** to pre-engage, to engross (the
mind etc.). **2** to occupy beforehand or before another. **preoccupation** (-ā´shen) *n.* **1** something
which preoccupies, such as a business affair etc.
2 the state of being preoccupied or engrossed
(with). **preoccupied** *a.* thinking about one thing
to the exclusion of all others; lost in thought.
prep (prep) *n.* **1** (*sl.*) preparation or private study
done at home or outside lesson time. **2** (*sl.*) the
time set aside for this. **3** (*N Am.*) a student at a
preparatory school. ~*a.* **1** of or relating to the
preparation of school work. **2** (*N Am.*) of or
relating to preparatory schools. ~*v.t.* (*pres.p.*
prepping, *past, p.p.* **prepped**) (*N Am.*) to prepare.
preppy, preppie *a.* (*comp.* **preppier**, *superl.*
preppiest) (*N Am.*) **1** denoting a young but
classic look in clothes, clean-cut, conventionally
smart. **2** holding (middle-class) values associated
with students at preparatory schools. ~*n.* (*pl.*
preppies) **1** (*N Am.*) a student at a preparatory
school. **2** a person who dresses in a preppy
fashion. **prep school** *n.* a preparatory school.
prep. *abbr.* preposition.
pre- (+ p– words) pre-pack, pre-package *v.t.* to
package (esp. food products) before they are
offered for sale. **prepaid** *a.* paid in advance (as
postage etc.). **prepay** *v.t.* (*pres.p.* **prepaying**, *past,
p.p.* **prepaid**) **1** to pay beforehand. **2** to pay
(postage) in advance, esp. by affixing a stamp to.
prepayable *a.* **prepayment** *n.* **pre-plan** *v.t.*
(*pres.p.* **pre-planning**, *past, p.p.* **pre-planned**) to
plan in advance. **prepose** *v.t.* to place (a word) in

front of another. **pre-prandial** *a.* (*formal or facet.*) done, happening etc. before lunch or dinner. **pre-preference** *a.* ranking before preference shares etc. **pre-print** *n.* a part of a publication printed in advance of the whole. **pre-process** *v.t.* to subject to preliminary processing. **pre-processor** *n.* (*Comput.*) a program that modifies data to suit the requirements of another program. **pre-production** *a.* of or relating to work done on a film or TV programme before shooting. **pre-program** *v.t.* (*pres.p.* **pre-programming**, *past, p.p.* **pre-programmed**) to program (a computer etc.) in advance. **pre-pubertal**, **pre-pubescent** *a.* **1** existing or happening (just) before puberty. **2** of or relating to a child who has not yet reached puberty. *~n.* such a child. **pre-publication** *a.* happening, or produced, before publication (of a book etc.). *~n.* publication in advance of some other event.

prepare (pripeə´) *v.t.* **1** to bring into a suitable condition, to fit for a certain purpose, esp. food for eating. **2** to make ready or fit (to do, to receive etc.). **3** to produce. **4** to construct, to put together, to draw up. **5** to get (work, a speech, a part etc.) ready by practice, study etc. **6** (*Mus.*) to lead up to (a discord) by sounding the dominant note in a consonance. *~v.i.* **1** to get everything ready. **2** to take the measures necessary (for). **3** to make oneself ready. **preparation** (prepərā´shən) *n.* **1** the act, or an instance, of preparing. **2** the state of being prepared. **3** (*often pl.*) a preparatory act or measure. **4** anything prepared by a special process, such as food, a medicine, a part of a body for anatomical study etc. **5** the preparing of lessons or school work. **6** (*Mus.*) the introduction of a note to be continued in a subsequent discord. **preparative** (-par´ə-) *a., n.* **preparatory** *a.* **1** tending or serving to prepare. **2** introductory (to). *~adv.* in a preparatory way. **preparatorily** *adv.* **preparatory school** *n.* **1** a private school for pupils usu. aged 6–13, which prepares them for entry to a public school. **2** (*N Am.*) a private secondary school which prepares students for college. **prepared** *a.* **to be prepared 1** to be ready (for). **2** to be willing (to). **preparedness** (-rid-) *n.* a state of readiness, esp. for war. **preparer** *n.*

prepense (pripens´) *a.* (*esp. Law*) (*usu. placed after the noun*) premeditated, deliberate. **prepensely** *adv.*

☒ **preperation** common misspelling of PREPARATION (under PREPARE).

preponderate (pripon´dərāt) *v.i.* to be superior or to outweigh in number, power, influence etc. **preponderance**, **†preponderancy** *n.* **preponderant** *a.* **preponderantly**, **preponderatingly** *adv.*

preposition (prepəzish´ən) *n.* (*Gram.*) a word or group of words, e.g. *at, by, in front of*, used to relate the noun or pronoun it is placed in front of to other constituent parts of the sentence. **prepositional** *a.* **prepositionally** *adv.* **prepositive** (pripoz´-) *a.* prefixed, intended to be placed before (a word).

prepossess (prēpəzes´) *v.t.* **1** to imbue (with an idea, feeling etc.). **2** to bias (esp. favourably). **3** (of an idea etc.) to preoccupy. **prepossessing** *a.* **1** tending to win favour, attractive. **2** biasing. **prepossession** (-shən) *n.*

preposterous (pripos´tərəs) *a.* **1** contrary to nature, reason or common sense. **2** obviously wrong, foolish, absurd. **preposterously** *adv.* **preposterousness** *n.*

preppy PREP.

prepuce (prē´pūs) *n.* **1** the foreskin, the loose covering of the glans penis. **2** a similar fold of skin over the clitoris. **preputial** (-pū´-) *a.*

pre- (+ q– words) pre-qualify *v.i.* (*3rd pers. sing. pres.* **pre-qualifies**, *pres.p.* **pre-qualifying**, *past, p.p.* **pre-qualified**) to qualify (for entry) in advance (of a sporting competition etc.).

prequel (prē´kwəl) *n.* a novel, film etc. which narrates the events leading up to those in an existing novel or film.

pre- (+ r– words) Pre-Raphaelite (prēraf´əlīt) *n.* a member of the Pre-Raphaelite Brotherhood. *~a.* **1** having the characteristics of Pre-Raphaelitism. **2** resembling those (esp. women) painted by the Pre-Raphaelites. **Pre-Raphaelite Brotherhood** *n.* a small group of painters formed in London in 1848, including Holman Hunt, Millais and D. G. Rossetti, to cultivate the spirit and methods of the early Italian painters, esp. in respect to truth to nature and vividness of colour. **Pre-Raphaelitism** *n.* **pre-record** *v.t.* to record beforehand. **prerequisite** *a.* required beforehand. *~n.* a requirement that must be satisfied in advance, a precondition.

Usage note See note under PERQUISITE.

prerogative (prirog´ətiv) *n.* **1** an exclusive right or privilege vested in a particular person or body of persons, esp. a sovereign, in virtue of their position or relationship. **2** any peculiar right, option, privilege, natural advantage etc.

Pres. *abbr.* President.

pre- (+ s– words) pre-school *a.* (for children who are) under school age. **pre-schooler** *n.* **pre-select** *v.t.* to select in advance. **pre-selection** *n.* **pre-selective** *a.* that can be selected in advance. **preselector** *n.* a device which preselects an electrical or mechanical operation, e.g. a gear change. **pre-senile** *a.* of or relating to the period before the onset of old age. **pre-set** *v.t.* (*pres.p.* **pre-setting**, *past, p.p.* **pre-set**) to set the controls of (an electric or electronic device) in advance, so that it starts to operate at the required time in the required way. **pre-shrink** *v.t.* (*past* **pre-shrank**, *p.p.* **pre-shrunk**) to shrink (fabric) before it is made up into garments. **prestressed** *a.* (of concrete) reinforced with stretched steel wires or rods. **presuppose** *v.t.* **1** to assume beforehand. **2** to imply as a necessary antecedent. **presupposition** *n.* **1** the act, or an instance, of presupposing. **2** a supposition adopted beforehand.

presage[1] (pres´ij) *n.* **1** something that foretells a future event, an omen, a prognostic. **2** foreboding, presentiment. **presageful** *a.*

presage² (prisāj´, pres´ij) *v.t.* **1** to foreshadow, to betoken. **2** to indicate by natural signs etc. **3** (of a person) to foretell, to have a presentiment of. **presager** *n.*

presbyopia (prezbiō´piə) *n.* a form of long-sightedness with indistinct vision of near objects, caused by alteration in the refractive power of the eyes with age. **presbyopic** (-op´-) *a.*

presbyter (prez´bitə) *n.* **1** an elder who had authority in the early Church. **2** in the Episcopal Church, a minister of the second order, a priest. **3** in the Presbyterian Church, a minister of a presbytery, an elder. **presbyterate** (-bit´ərət) *n.* **presbyterial** (-tiə´riəl) *a.* **Presbyterian** (-tiə´ri-) *n.* **1** any adherent of Presbyterianism. **2** a member of a Presbyterian Church. ~*a.* **1** of or relating to Church government by presbyters. **2** governed by presbyters. **Presbyterian Church** *n.* a Church governed by elders, including ministers, all equal in rank. **Presbyterianism** *n.* **presbytership** *n.* **presbytery** (-ri) *n.* (*pl.* **presbyteries**) **1** a court consisting of the pastors and ruling elders of the Presbyterian churches of a given district, ranking above the Kirk-session and below the synod. **2** in the Roman Catholic Church, a priest's residence. **3** the eastern portion of a chancel beyond the choir in a cathedral or other large church, the sanctuary.

prescient (pres´iənt) *a.* foreknowing, far-seeing. **prescience** *n.* **presciently** *adv.*

prescribe (priskrīb´) *v.t.* **1** to direct (a medicine etc.) to be used as a remedy. **2** to recommend (some course of action). **3** to lay down with authority; to appoint (a rule of conduct etc.). ~*v.i.* **1** to write directions for medical treatment. **2** (*Law*) to assert a prescriptive title (to or for). **prescriber** *n.* **prescript** (prē´skript) *n.* a direction, a command, a law. **prescription** (-skrip´-) *n.* **1** the act, or an instance, of prescribing. **2** something which is prescribed, esp. a written direction for the preparation of medical remedies, and the manner of using them. **3** (*Law*) POSITIVE PRESCRIPTION (under POSITIVE). **prescriptive** (-skrip´-) *a.* **1** prescribing. **2** laying down rules; concerned with rules. **3** acquired or authorized by long use. **4** based on long use or prescription. **prescriptively** *adv.* **prescriptiveness** *n.* **prescriptivism** *n.* **prescriptivist** *n.*

Usage note The verbs *prescribe* and *proscribe* should not be confused: something prescribed is to be taken, given, used or studied, and is assumed to be useful or beneficial; something proscribed is forbidden, and so assumed to be harmful.

❌ **presede** common misspelling of PRECEDE.

presence (prez´əns) *n.* **1** the quality or state of being present. **2 a** the immediate vicinity of a person. **b** the immediate vicinity of a person of high rank. **3** (a person with) an imposing or dig-

nified bearing. **4** personal magnetism, the ability to grasp and hold an audience's attention. **5** a group or force representing one's interests or exercising an influence on one's behalf. **6** an influence as of a being invisibly present. **in the presence of** in front of, within sight of (a person). **presence of mind** *n.* a calm, collected state of mind, esp. in danger or emergency.

present¹ (prez´ənt) *a.* **1** being here or in a place referred to, as distinct from *absent*. **2** being in view or at hand. **3** found or existing in the thing referred to. **4** being now under discussion, consideration etc. **5** now existing, occurring, going on etc. **6** (*Law*) instant, immediate. **7** (*Gram.*) expressing what is actually going on. **8** ready at hand, assisting in emergency, attentive, propitious. ~*n.* **1** the present time. **2** the present tense. **at present** at the present time, now. **by these presents** (*Law*) by this document. **for the present 1** for the time being. **2** so far as the time being is concerned. **present-day** *a.* contemporary, of the current time.

present² (prizent´) *v.t.* **1** to introduce to the acquaintance or presence of, esp. to introduce formally. **2** to introduce to a sovereign at Court. **3** to exhibit, to show, to offer to the sight. **4** to hold in position or point (a gun etc.). **5** to offer for consideration, to submit. **6** to offer or deliver (a cheque or an invoice). **7** to exhibit (an actor, a play etc.) on the stage. **8** to act as the presenter of (as a television programme). **9** to offer, to give, to bestow, esp. in a ceremonious way. **10** to invest or endow (with a gift). **11** to tender, to deliver. ~*v.i.* **1** (*Med.*) **a** to come forward as a patient (with). **b** (of an illness) to manifest itself. **2** (of a foetus) to be in a specified position during labour with respect to the mouth of the uterus. ~*n.* (*Mil.*) position for, or act of, aiming a firearm. **to present arms** to hold a rifle etc., in a perpendicular position in front of the body to salute a superior officer. **to present oneself** to appear, to come forward. **presentable** *a.* **1** fit to be presented. **2** of suitable appearance for company etc. **3** fit to be shown or exhibited. **4** suitable for offering as a gift. **presentability** (-bil´-) *n.* **presentableness** *n.* **presentably** *adv.*

present³ (prez´ənt) *n.* something which is presented, a gift. **to make a present of** to give as a gift.

presentation (prezəntā´shən) *n.* **1** the act, or an instance, of presenting, or the process of being presented. **2** a present, a gift. **3** an exhibition, a theatrical representation. **4** a verbal report on, or exposé of, a subject, often with illustrative material. **5** the manner of presenting, esp. the appearance, arrangement, neatness etc. of material submitted. **6** (*Med.*) the particular position of the foetus at birth. **presentational** *a.* **presentationally** *adv.*

presentee (prezəntē´) *n.* **1** a person receiving a present. **2** a person recommended for office. **3** a person presented at Court.

presenter (prizen´tə) n. **1** a person who presents. **2** a broadcaster who introduces and comperes, or provides a linking commentary for, a radio or television programme.

presentient (prizen´shənt, -sen´-) a. feeling or perceiving beforehand.

presentiment (prizen´timənt) n. apprehension or anticipation, more or less vague, of an impending event, esp. of evil, a foreboding.

presently (prez´əntli) adv. **1** soon, shortly. **2** (esp. N Am., Sc.) at the present time.

presentment (prizent´mənt) n. **1** the act of presenting (information). **2** (esp. US) a report by a grand jury respecting an offence, from their own knowledge.

preserve (prizœv´) v.t. **1** to keep safe, to guard, to protect. **2** to maintain in a good or the same condition. **3** to retain, to keep intact. **4** to keep from decay or decomposition by chemical treatment, boiling, pickling, freezing etc. **5** to keep (a stream, covert, game etc.) for private use by preventing poaching etc. ~n. **1** fruit boiled with sugar or preservative substances, jam. **2 a** a place where game is preserved. **b** water where fish are preserved. **3** a special domain, something reserved for certain people only. **preservable** a. **preservation** (prezəvā´shən) n. **1** the act, or an instance, of preserving, or the process of being preserved. **2** the state of being preserved. **preservationist** n. a person who is interested in preserving traditional and historic things. **preservative** a. tending to preserve. ~n. something which preserves, esp. a chemical substance used to prevent decomposition in foodstuffs. **preserver** n.

preside (prizīd´) v.i. **1** to be set in authority over others; to sit at the head of a table; to act as director, controller, chairman or president. **2** to lead, to superintend. **3** to officiate (at the organ, piano etc.). **presidency** (prez´idənsi) n. (pl. **presidencies**) the office, jurisdiction or term of office of a president. **president** (prez´idənt) n. **1** a person (usu. elected) presiding over a temporary or permanent body of persons. **2** the chief executive or elective head of government in a modern republic. **3** a person presiding over the meetings of a society. **4** the chief officer of certain colleges and universities, esp. in the US. **5** (N Am.) the permanent chairman and chief executive officer of a corporation, board of trustees, government department etc. **president-elect** n. (pl. **presidents-elect**) a president who has been elected but has not yet taken office. **presidential** (-den´-) a. **presidentially** adv. **presidentship** n. **presider** n.

presidium (prisid´iəm), **praesidium** n. (pl. **presidiums**, **presidia** (-diə), **praesidiums**, **praesidia** (-diə)) a permanent executive committee in a Communist country.

press[1] (pres) v.t. **1** to act steadily upon with a force or weight. **2** to push (something up, down, against etc.) with steady force. **3** to put or hold (upon etc.) with force. **4** to squeeze, to crush, to compress. **5** to make smooth by pressure (as cloth or paper). **6 a** to extract juice from (esp. fruit). **b** to extract (juice) from fruit. **7** to make by pressing in a mould, esp. to make (a gramophone record) from a matrix. **8** to clasp, to embrace, to hug. **9** to crowd upon. **10** to urge, to ply hard, to bear heavily on. **11** to invite with persistent warmth. **12** to put forward vigorously and persistently, to urge. **13** to weigh down, to distress. **14** to straiten, to constrain. **15** to enforce strictly, to impress. **16** to insist on the acceptance of (something). ~v.i. **1** to exert pressure; to bear heavily, or weigh heavily (on). **2** to be urgent. **3** to make demands (for). **4** to throng, to crowd, to encroach, to intrude. **5** to strive eagerly, to hasten, to strain, to push one's way. ~n. **1** the act, or an instance, of pressing, urging or crowding. **2** a crowd, a throng. **3** urgency, pressure, hurry. **4** (esp. Ir., Sc.) an upright case, cupboard or closet, for storing things, esp. linen; a bookcase. **5 a** an instrument or machine for compressing any body or substance, forcing it into a more compact form, shaping, extracting juice etc. **b** a device for keeping the shape of a tennis racket. **6** a machine for printing. **7** (**Press**) a printing establishment, or a publishing house. **8** the process or practice of printing. **9** the reaction of newspapers etc. to a person, event etc. (a good press). **at press** in press. **in (the) press** being printed. **the press 1** the news media collectively, esp. newspapers and periodicals. **2** journalists. **to be pressed for** to have very little of (esp. time). **to go to press** to start printing, to begin to be printed. **to press on/ ahead/ forward 1** to continue (determinedly) on one's way. **2** to proceed, esp. in spite of difficulties or opposition. **to press the button 1** to start a machine etc. by pressing a button. **2** (fig.) to set a train of events in motion. **to press the flesh** (sl.) (esp. of politicians) to shake hands. **to send to press** to send for printing. **press agent** n. a person employed to handle relations with the press, esp. to ensure good publicity for an actor, organization etc. **press box** n. an enclosure for reporters at a sports ground. **press-button** n., a. push-button. **press conference** n. a meeting with journalists to announce a policy etc., or answer their questions. **press cutting** n. a clipping from a newspaper. **presser** n. **press gallery** n. a gallery set aside for reporters, esp. in a legislative assembly. **pressing** a. urgent, importunate, insistent. ~n. **1** something made by pressing. **2** the gramophone records etc. made from a single matrix at one time. **pressingly** adv. **pressman** n. (pl. **pressmen**) **1** a journalist. **2** a person who operates a printing press. **press office** n. the department (of an organization, a ministry etc.) which releases information to the press etc. **press officer** n. **press-on** a. (of a fabric) able to be pressed on or ironed on to something. **press release** n. an official statement or report given to the press. **press stud** n. a fastener consisting of two small round buttons, one of which has a small raised knob which snaps into a hole in the other. **press-up** *n.* a gymnastic exercise in which the body is held rigid in a prone position and raised and lowered by bending and straightening the arms.

press² (pres) *v.t.* **1** (*Hist.*) to force into naval or military service. **2** (*fig.*) to bring into service. **press-gang** *n.* (*Hist.*) **1** a detachment of men employed to impress men, usu. into the navy. **2** a group of people using coercive methods. ~*v.t.* to force (a person) to do something.

pressie PREZZIE.

pressure (presh´ə) *n.* **1** the act of pressing. **2** the state of being pressed. **3** a force steadily exerted upon or against a body by another in contact with it. **4** the amount of this, usu. measured in units of weight upon a unit of area. **5** constraining force, compulsion. **6** moral force. **7** persistent attack. **8** stress, urgency. **9** trouble, affliction, oppression. ~*v.t.* **1** to apply pressure to. **2** to constrain, to subject to compelling moral force against one's will. **pressure cooker** *n.* an apparatus for cooking at a high temperature under high pressure of steam. **pressure-cook** *v.t.* **pressure gauge** *n.* an instrument which measures pressure (of steam etc.). **pressure group** *n.* a group or small party exerting pressure on government etc. to promote a particular interest. **pressure point** *n.* **1** any of various points on the body where a blood vessel may be pressed against a bone to check bleeding. **2** a point on the skin which is sensitive to pressure. **3** a policy area etc. where political pressure may be exerted. **pressure suit** *n.* an airman's suit that inflates automatically if there is a failure in the pressure cabin. **pressurize, pressurise** *v.t.* **1** to fit an aircraft cabin with a device that maintains normal atmospheric pressure at high altitudes. **2** to increase the pressure on. **3** to (seek to) coerce. **pressurization** (-zā´shən) *n.* **pressurized-water reactor** *n.* a type of nuclear reactor that uses water under pressure as coolant and moderator.

prestidigitation (prestidijitā´shən) *n.* (*formal*) sleight of hand, conjuring. **prestidigitator** (-dij´-) *n.*

prestige (prestēzh´) *n.* influence or weight derived from former fame, excellence, achievements etc. ~*a.* **1** having or conferring prestige. **2** superior, very high-quality, very stylish etc. **prestigeful** *a.* **prestigious** (-tij´əs) *a.* having, showing or conferring prestige. **prestigiously** *adv.* **prestigiousness** *n.*

presto (pres´tō) *adv.* (*Mus.*) quickly. ~*a.* quick. ~*n.* (*pl.* **prestos**) a quick movement or passage. ~*int.* (*also* **hey presto**) immediately (used to indicate the speed with which e.g. a conjuring trick is done).

presume (prizūm´) *v.t.* **1** to take for granted or assume without previous enquiry or examination. **2** to venture. **3** to be impudent enough (to). ~*v.i.* **1** to venture without previous leave, to take

liberties. **2** to form overconfident or arrogant opinions. **3** to behave with assurance or arrogance. **presumable** *a.* **presumably** *adv.* as can be presumed. **presumedly** (-mid-) *adv.* **presumer** *n.* **presuming** *a.* presumptuous. **presumingly** *adv.* **presumingness** *n.* **presumption** (-zŭmp´-) *n.* **1** the act of presuming. **2** assumption of the truth or existence of something without direct proof. **3** something which is taken for granted. **4** a ground for presuming. **5** overconfidence, arrogance, impudence, effrontery. **presumptive** *a.* giving grounds for, or based on, presumption. **presumptively** *adv.* **presumptiveness** *n.* **presumptuous** (-chuəs) *a.* full of presumption, arrogant, forward. **presumptuously** *adv.* **presumptuousness** *n.*

Usage note (1) *Presume* usually implies less tentativeness (and more arrogance) than *assume*. (2) The form *presumptious* for *presumptuous* is best avoided.

---

pre- (+ t– words) pre-tax *a.* (of income or profits) before taxes have been deducted. **preteen** *a.* of or relating to a child approaching the age of 13. ~*n.* such a child. **pre-term** *a.* born, or happening, prematurely. ~*adv.* prematurely. **pretreat** *v.t.* to treat beforehand. **pretreatment** *n.*

pretend (pritend´) *v.t.* **1** to assume the appearance of; to feign to be. **2** to simulate, to counterfeit in order to deceive. **3** to make believe in play, to imagine. **4** to allege or put forward falsely. **5** to put forward, to assert, to claim. ~*v.i.* **1** to feign, to make believe. **2** to put forward a claim (to). ~*a.* make-believe. **pretence** (-tens´), (*N Am.*) **pretense** *n.* **1** (an act of) pretending or feigning. **2** an excuse, a pretext. **3** a claim (true or false) (to). **4** a false profession. **5 a** display, show, ostentation. **b** affectation. **6** (a) semblance. **pretenceless** *a.* **pretender** *n.* **1** a person who makes a claim, esp. a claim that cannot be substantiated. **2** a claimant, esp. a claimant to a throne held by another. **pretension** (-shən) *n.* **1** (*often pl.*) a claim. **2** (*often pl.*) an aspiration. **3** a pretext. **4** pretentiousness, self-importance. **pretentious** (-shəs) *a.* **1** full of pretension; making specious claims to excellence etc. **2** ostentatious, arrogant, conceited. **pretentiously** *adv.* **pretentiousness** *n.*

preter- (prē´tə) *comb. form* **1** beyond. **2** more than.

preterite (pret´ərit), (*esp. N Am.*) **preterit** *a.* (*Gram.*) denoting completed action or existence in past time. ~*n.* **1** the preterite tense. **2** a verb in the preterite tense.

pretermit (prētəmit´) *v.t.* (*pres.p.* **pretermitting**, *past, p.p.* **pretermitted**) (*formal*) **1** to pass by or over, to neglect, to omit (to mention, to do etc.). **2** to discontinue. **pretermission** (-shən) *n.*

preternatural (prētənach´ərəl) *a.* beyond what is natural; out of the regular course of nature. **preternaturalism** *n.* **preternaturally** *adv.*

pretext (prē´tekst) *n.* **1** an excuse. **2** an ostensible reason or motive. **on/ under the pretext of** putting forward as an excuse.

pretor PRAETOR.

pretty (prit´i) a. (comp. **prettier,** superl. **prettiest**) **1** good-looking, attractive, appealing (though without the striking qualities or perfect proportions of beauty). **2** aesthetically pleasing (with the same qualification). **3** superficially or conventionally attractive. **4** (coll., derog.) (of a man) effeminate-looking. **5** (esp. iron.) nice, fine. **6** considerable, large. ~adv. **1** moderately, fairly. **2** very. ~n. (pl. **pretties**) a pretty thing or person. ~v.t. (3rd pers. sing. pres. **pretties,** pres.p. **prettying,** past, p.p. **prettied**) (often with up) to make pretty, to adorn. **prettify** (-fī) v.t. (3rd pers. sing. pres. **prettifies,** pres.p. **prettifying,** past, p.p. **prettified**) **1** to make pretty. **2** to express or depict in a pretty way. **prettification** (-fikā´shən) n. **prettifier** n. **prettily** adv. **prettiness** n. **prettyish** a. **pretty much, pretty nearly, pretty well** adv. (coll.) nearly, almost. **pretty-pretty** a. affectedly pretty, over-pretty.

pretzel (pret´səl) n. a crisp biscuit of wheaten flour flavoured with salt, usu. in the shape of a stick or a knot.

prevail (privāl´) v.i. **1** to have the mastery or victory (over, against etc.). **2** to predominate. **3** to be in force, to be in general use or in vogue; to be customary. **to prevail on/ upon** to succeed in persuading, to induce. **prevailing** a. **prevailingly** adv. **prevailing wind** n. the wind that blows most frequently in a particular place. **prevalence** (prev´ə-) n. **1** a superiority, predominance. **2** frequency, vogue, currency. **prevalent** a. **prevalently** adv.

prevaricate (privar´ikāt) v.i. **1** to quibble. **2** to act or speak evasively. **3** to equivocate. **prevarication** (-ā´shən) n. **prevaricator** (-var´-) n.

Usage note The verbs prevaricate and procrastinate should not be confused: prevaricate means to quibble, and procrastinate to delay action.

prevent (privent´) v.t. **1** to keep from happening. **2** to hinder, to thwart, to stop. **preventable, preventible** a. capable of prevention. **preventability** (-bil´-) n. **preventative** a. PREVENTIVE (under PREVENT). **preventatively** adv. **preventer** n. **prevention** n. **preventive** a. **1** tending to hinder or prevent. **2** prophylactic. ~n. **1** something which prevents. **2** a medicine or precaution to ward off disease. **3** a contraceptive. **preventively** adv.

preview (prē´vū) n. **1** an advance view, a foretaste. **2** an advance showing of a play, film, art exhibition etc. before its general presentation to the public. **3** a television or cinema trailer. ~v.t. to view or show in advance.

previous (prē´viəs) a. **1** going before in time or order; antecedent, prior (to). **2** (coll.) premature, hasty. ~adv. before, previously (to). **previously** adv. **previousness** n.

prevue (prē´vū) n. (esp. N Am.) a television or cinema trailer.

pre- (+ w– words) pre-war a. existing or happening before a war, esp. the latest war. **pre-wash** n. a preliminary wash, before the main one, in a washing machine. ~a. of or relating to such a wash. ~v.t. to give such a wash to.

prey (prā) n. **1** an animal which is or may be seized to be devoured by carnivorous animals. **2** booty, spoil, plunder. **3** a person who becomes a victim of an unscrupulous person, or is vulnerable to unpleasant influences etc. ~v.i. **1** to take booty or plunder. **2** to take food by violence. **to prey on 1** to rob, to plunder. **2** to chase and seize as food. **3** to make a victim of, to subject to robbery, extortion etc. **4** to have a depressing or obsessive effect on. **preyer** n.

prezzie (prez´i), **pressie** n. (coll.) a present, a gift.

priapism (prī´əpizm) n. **1** lasciviousness. **2** (Med.) continuous erection of the penis without sexual excitement. **priapean** (-pē´ən), **priapic** (-ap´-) a. phallic.

price (prīs) n. **1** the amount asked for a thing or for which it is sold. **2** the cost of a thing. **3** (coll.) the amount needed to bribe somebody. **4** that which must be expended, sacrificed, done etc., to secure a thing. **5** the odds in betting. **6** estimation, value, preciousness. ~v.t. **1** to fix the price of, to value, to appraise. **2** to ask the price of. **above price** beyond price. **a price on one's head** a reward offered for one's killing or capture. **at any price** no matter what the cost. **at a price** for a lot of money etc. **beyond price** priceless, invaluable. **not at any price** under no circumstances. **to price oneself out of the market** to lose trade by charging too high prices. **what price...? 1** what are the chances of (something) happening? **2** (iron.) so much for (something). **without price** priceless, invaluable. **priced** a. **price-fixing** n. the setting of prices by agreement between producers and distributors. **priceless** a. **1** invaluable, inestimable. **2** (sl.) very funny. **pricelessly** adv. **pricelessness** n. **price list** n. a list of the current prices of merchandise, stocks etc. **pricer** n. **price ring** n. a group of manufacturers or traders who cooperate to maintain prices at an agreed, high level. **price-sensitive** a. **1** (of a product) a variation in whose price might affect sales. **2** (of information) that could affect the price of something. **price tag** n. **1** the label attached to an object showing its price. **2** price, cost. **price war** n. competition among traders or manufacturers to lower prices and so increase sales. **pricey, pricy** a. (comp. **pricier,** superl. **priciest**) expensive. **priciness** n.

prick (prik) n. **1** the act, or an instance, of pricking. **2** the state or the sensation of being pricked. **3** a puncture; a dot, point or small mark made by or as by pricking. **4 a** a sharp, stinging pain. **b** a mental pain. **5** (taboo sl.) the penis. **6** (taboo sl., derog.) an obnoxious or inept man. ~v.t. **1** to pierce slightly, to puncture. **2** to make by puncturing. **3** to mark off or delineate with small holes or pricks. **4** to cause (the ears) to point upwards. **5** to goad, to rouse, to incite, to spur on. ~*v.i.* **1** to make a thrusting motion, as if to prick. **2** to point upward. **3** to feel as if pricked. **to kick against the pricks** to hurt oneself in unavailing struggle against something. **to prick off** to prick out. **to prick out 1** to mark a pattern out with dots. **2** to plant seedlings more widely apart with a view to transplanting later to their permanent quarters. **pricker** *n.*

prickle (prik´əl) *n.* **1** a small, sharp point. **2** (*Bot.*) a thornlike growth capable of being peeled off with the skin or bark, as opposed to a thorn or spine. **3** (*loosely*) a small thorn, spine etc. **4** a prickling sensation. **5** a spine of a hedgehog etc. ~*v.t.* **1** to prick slightly. **2** to give a pricking or tingling sensation to. ~*v.i.* **1** to have such a sensation. **2** to take offence or react defensively. **prickly** *a.* (*comp.* **pricklier,** *superl.* **prickliest**) **1** full of or armed with prickles. **2** tingling. **3** (of a person) oversensitive, ready to take offence. **prickliness** *n.* **prickly heat** *n.* an inflammatory skin condition characterized by itching and stinging sensations, prevalent in hot countries. **prickly pear** *n.* (the pear-shaped fruit of) any cactus of the genus *Opuntia,* usu. covered with prickles. **prickly poppy** *n.* an annual poppy, *Argemone mexicana,* of tropical America, with yellow or white flowers and prickly leaves.

pride (prīd) *n.* **1** generous elation or satisfaction arising out of some accomplishment, possession or relationship. **2** a source of such elation. **3** inordinate self-esteem, unreasonable conceit of one's own superiority; insolence, arrogance. **4** sense of dignity, self-respect, proper self-esteem. **5** the acme, the highest point, the best condition. **6** a collection of lions. **to pride oneself on** to be proud of oneself for. **to take (a) pride in 1** to be proud of. **2** to be conscientious about the maintenance of. **pride and joy** *n.* someone or something that one is very proud of. **prideful** *a.* **pridefully** *adv.* **pridefulness** *n.* **prideless** *a.* **pride of place** *n.* the highest, most prominent or most important position. **pride of the morning** *n.* a shower of rain or a mist as the sun comes up.

prie-dieu (prēdyœ´) *n.* (*pl.* **prie-dieux** (-dyœ´)) a kneeling-desk for prayers.

priest (prēst) *n.* **1** a person who officiates in sacred rites, esp. by offering sacrifice. **2** a minister in the Roman Catholic, Orthodox or Anglican Church, below a bishop and above a deacon, esp. as having authority to administer the sacraments and pronounce absolution. ~*v.t.* to ordain, to make (someone) a priest. **priestcraft** *n.* (*usu. derog.*) priestly policy based on material interests. **priestess** *n.* a woman priest, esp. pagan. **priesthood** *n.* **1** the office or position of a priest. **2** priests collectively. **priest-in-charge** *n.* (*pl.* **priests-in-charge**) a priest temporarily in charge of a parish which is without its own priest. **priestless** *a.* **priestlike** *a.* **priestling** *n.* **priestly** *a.*

(*comp.* **priestlier,** *superl.* **priestliest**) of, relating to or befitting a priest or the priesthood; sacerdotal. **priestliness** *n.* **priest's hole** *n.* (*Hist.*) a hiding place for fugitive Catholic priests, esp. in England under the penal laws.

prig (prig) *n.* a self-righteous, formal or moralistic person. **priggery** *n.* **priggish** *a.* **priggishly** *adv.* **priggishness** *n.*

prim (prim) *a.* (*comp.* **primmer,** *superl.* **primmest**) formal, affectedly proper, demure, prudish. ~*v.t.* (*pres.p.* **primming,** *past, p.p.* **primmed**) **1** to put (the lips, mouth etc.) into a prim expression. **2** to deck with great nicety or preciseness. **primly** *adv.* **primness** *n.*

prima (prē´mə) *a.* first, chief, principal. **prima ballerina** *n.* (*pl.* **prima ballerinas**) the leading female ballet dancer in a company. **prima donna** (don´ə) *n.* (*pl.* **prima donnas, prime donne** (-mā don´ā)) **1** a chief female singer in an opera or an opera company. **2** a person who is temperamental, hard to please, and given to histrionics. **prima-donnaish** *a.*

primacy (prī´məsi) *n.* (*pl.* **primacies**) **1** the dignity or office of a primate. **2** pre-eminence.

primaeval PRIMEVAL.

prima facie (prīmə fā´shi) *adv.* at first sight, on the first impression. ~*a.* based on first impressions.

primal (prī´məl) *a.* **1** primary, original, primitive. **2** fundamental, chief. **primally** *adv.*

primary (prī´məri) *a.* **1** first in time, order or origin. **2** original, radical, firsthand. **3** primitive, fundamental. **4** first in rank or importance, chief. **5** (*Biol.*) first or lowest in development, elementary. **6** (of education) for children between the ages of 5 and 11 (12 in Scotland). **7** of or relating to an industry that produces raw materials. **8** of or relating to the inducing current or its circuit in an induction coil or transformer. **9** (*Geol.*) (**Primary**) of or relating to the Palaeozoic strata. ~*n.* (*pl.* **primaries**) **1** something which stands first in order, rank or importance. **2** (*Astron.*) a celestial body round which other members of a system orbit. **3** a primary election. **4** a primary feather. **5** a primary colour. **6** a primary school. **7** (**Primary**) the Palaeozoic period. **primarily** (prī´-, -mar´i-) *adv.* **primariness** *n.* **primary cell** *n.* a battery in which an irreversible chemical action is converted into electrical energy (cp. SECONDARY cell (under SECONDARY)). **primary coil** *n.* a coil in a transformer to which current is supplied. **primary colour, (***N Am.***) primary color** *n.* any of the fundamental colours from which others can be obtained by mixing (for paints red, blue and yellow; for transmitted light red, blue and green). **primary education** *n.* the first formal and compulsory stage of education in primary, junior and infant schools. **primary election** *n.* a meeting or election for the selection of party candidates by voters of a state or region, esp. in the US. **primary feather** *n.* a large quill feather of a bird's wing. **primary school** *n.* a school providing primary education, usu. for children aged under 11 (England and Wales) or under 12 (Scotland).

primate (prī´māt, -mət) *n.* **1** a member of the Primates, the highest order of mammals, comprising humans, apes, monkeys and lemurs. **2** the chief prelate in a national episcopal church, an archbishop. **Primate of all England** *n.* the Archbishop of Canterbury. **Primate of England** *n.* the Archbishop of York. **primatology** (-tol´-) *n.* the branch of zoology concerned with the study of primates. **primatological** (-loj´-) *a.* **primatologist** (-tol´-) *n.*

primavera (prēməveə´rə) *n.* (*pl.* **primaveras**) **1** a tree bearing yellow flowers, *Cybistax donell-smithii*, growing in central America. **2** the wood of this tree, hard and light in colour.

prime[1] (prīm) *a.* **1** first in time, rank, excellence or importance. **2** (esp. of meat and provisions) chief, first-rate, excellent. **3** original, primary, fundamental. **4** in the vigour of maturity, blooming. **5** (*Math.*) (of a number) divisible by no integral factors except itself and unity (e.g. 2, 3, 5, 7, 11, 13). ~*n.* **1** the period or state of highest perfection. **2** the best part (of anything). **3** the first stage, the beginning (of anything). **4** the first canonical hour of the day, beginning at 6 a.m. or at sunrise. **5** in the Roman Catholic Church, the office for this hour. **6** dawn, spring, youth. **7** (*Math.*) a prime number. **8** the first of the eight parries in fencing, or a thrust in this position. **9** (*Print.*) a symbol (´) added to a letter etc. as a distinguishing mark, or to a number signifying minutes or feet. **prime cost** *n.* the cost of material and labour in the production of an article. **prime meridian** *n.* **1** a meridian from which longitude is reckoned, usu. that of Greenwich. **2** a corresponding line on a map. **prime minister** *n.* **1** the chief minister of a state. **2** the head of an elected government. **prime mover** *n.* **1** a person who or thing which originates a movement or an action, esp. the force putting a machine in motion. **2** the author, or the first promoter, of a project. **primeness** *n.* **prime number** *n.* a number that is divisible by no integral factors except itself and unity. **prime rate** *n.* the lowest commercial rate of interest charged by a bank at a particular time. **prime time** *n.* peak viewing or listening time for television or radio audiences, for which advertising rates are highest. **prime vertical** *n.* a great circle of the heavens passing through the east and west points of the horizon and the zenith.

prime[2] (prīm) *v.t.* **1** to prepare something, esp. a gun, for use. **2** to supply (with information). **3** to fill (a person) with food or drink in order to prepare them for some activity. **4** to fill (a pump) with fluid to expel the air before starting. **5** to inject fuel into (the float chamber of a carburettor). **6** to prepare (wood, metal etc.) for painting by applying primer. **primer**[1] *n.* **1** a person or thing that primes. **2** (a type of) paint

used as a sealant and a base for subsequent coats. **3** a detonator. **priming** *n.* **1** the act, or an instance, of preparing a firearm for discharge. **2** the powder placed in the pan of a flint gun. **3** a train of powder connecting a blasting-charge with the fuse. **4** a mixture used as a preparatory coat. **5** hasty instruction, cramming.

primer[1] PRIME[2].

primer[2] (prī´mə) *n.* **1** an elementary reading book for children. **2** a short introductory book.

primer[3] (prim´ə) *n.* (*Print.*) either one of two sizes of type, great primer and long primer.

primeval (prīmē´vəl), **primaeval** *a.* belonging to the earliest ages, ancient, original, primitive. **primevally** *adv.*

primigravida (prīmigrav´idə) *n.* (*pl.* **primigravidas, primigravidae** (-dē)) (*Med.*) a woman who is pregnant for the first time.

primipara (prīmip´ərə) *n.* (*pl.* **primiparas, primiparae** (-rē)) (*Med.*) a woman who is giving birth for the first time. **primiparous** *a.*

primitive (prim´itiv) *a.* **1** of or relating to the beginning or the earliest periods, early, ancient, original, primary, primordial. **2** rude, simple, plain, old-fashioned. **3** crude, uncivilized. **4** (of a culture or society) not advanced, lacking a written language and all but basic technical skills. **5** (*Gram.*) radical, not derivative. **6** (*Math.*) (of a line etc.) from which another is derived. **7** (*Geol.*) belonging to the lowest strata or the earliest period. **8** (*Biol.*) of or relating to an early stage of development. **9** (of art) belonging to the period before the Renaissance. **10** not conforming to the traditional standards of Western painting. ~*n.* **1** a primitive painter. **2** a picture by such a painter. **3** a primitive word. **Primitive Church** *n.* the Christian Church in its earliest form. **primitive colour**, (*N Am.*) **primitive color** *n.* a primary colour. **primitively** *adv.* **primitiveness** *n.* **primitivism** *n.* **1** the state of being primitive; primitive behaviour. **2** the belief that primitive things, ways etc. are superior to modern ones. **3** primitive art, culture, religion etc. **primitivist** *n.*, *a.*

primogeniture (prīmōjen´ichə) *n.* **1** seniority by birth amongst children of the same parents. **2** the right, system or rule under which, in cases of intestacy, the eldest son succeeds to the real estate of his father. **primogenital, primogenitary** *a.* **primogenitor** *n.* **1** the first father or ancestor. **2** an ancestor.

primordial (prīmaw´diəl) *a.* **1** first in order, primary, original, primitive. **2** existing at or from the beginning; first-formed. **primordiality** (-al´-), **primordialism** *n.* **primordially** *adv.*

primp (primp) *v.t.* to prink; to tidy up or smarten (oneself).

primrose (prim´rōz) *n.* **1** any plant of the genus *Primula*, esp. *Primula vulgaris*, a common British wild plant, flowering in early spring. **2** a pale yellow colour. ~*a.* **1** like a primrose. **2** of a pale yellow colour. **primrose path** *n.* the pursuit of ease and pleasure, esp. as leading to perdition. **primrose yellow** n., a.

primula (prim´ūlə) n. any plant of the genus of herbaceous plants *Primula*, belonging to the family Primulaceae, comprising the primrose, cowslip etc.

Primus® (prī´məs) n. a portable paraffin cooking stove used esp. by campers.

prince (prins) n. **1** a male member of a royal family, other than a reigning king. **2** (*also* **prince of the blood**) the son or grandson of a reigning monarch. **3** a member of a foreign order of nobility usu. ranking next below a duke. **4** the ruler of a principality or small state, usu. feudatory to a king or emperor. **5** a chief, leader or foremost representative. **Prince Charming** n. an ideal young suitor. **prince consort** n. a prince who is also the husband of a queen. **princedom**, †**princehood** n. **princekin, princelet, princeling** n. a young or petty prince. **princelike** a. **princely** a. (*comp.* **princelier**, *superl.* **princeliest**) **1** of, relating to or befitting a prince. **2** belonging to a prince. **3** having the rank of a prince. **4** stately, dignified. **5** generous, lavish. **princeliness** n. **Prince of Wales** n. the title customarily conferred on the heir-apparent to the British throne. **Prince Regent** n. a prince acting as regent. **prince royal** n. the eldest son of a sovereign. **prince's feather** n. a Mexican plant, *Amaranthus hypochondriacus*, tall, with small red flowers. **princeship** n. **prince's metal** n. an alloy of copper and zinc. **princess** (-ses, -ses´) n. **1** the wife of a prince. **2** a female member of a royal family, other than a reigning queen. **3** (*also* **princess of the blood**) the daughter or granddaughter of a sovereign. **4** a woman who is pre-eminent in her field. **5** (*also* **princesse**) a style of woman's dress, flared and with a close-fitting bodice, made up of panels from bodice to hem with no waist seam. **Princess Regent** n. **1** a princess acting as regent. **2** the wife of a Prince Regent. **Princess Royal** n. a title conferrable for life on the eldest daughter of a reigning sovereign.

principal (prin´sipəl) a. **1 a** chief, leading, main. **b** first in rank, authority, importance, influence or degree. **2** (of money) constituting the capital sum invested. ~n. **1** a chief or head. **2** a president, a governor, the head of a college etc. **3** a leader or chief actor in any transaction, the chief party, the person ultimately liable. **4** a person employing another as agent. **5** the actual perpetrator of a crime, the principal in the first degree, or one aiding and abetting, principal in the second degree. **6** a performer who takes a leading role. **7** a capital sum invested or lent, as distinguished from income. **8 a** a main rafter, esp. one extending to the ridge pole. **b** a main girder. **9** an organ stop of the open diapason family, usu. sounding an octave above standard pitch. **10** a civil servant of the grade below secretary. **11** a person for whom another becomes surety. **12** (*Mus.*) the leading player in each

section of an orchestra. **13** (*Hist.*) each of the two combatants in a duel. **principal boy** n. the leading male role in a pantomime, usu. taken by a woman. **principal clause** n. (*Gram.*) the main clause in a sentence, to which other clauses are subordinate. **principally** adv. chiefly, mainly, for the most part. **principal parts** n.pl. (*Gram.*) those inflected forms of a verb from which all other inflections can be derived. **principalship** n.

<hr>

Usage note The spellings of the adjective and noun *principal* (first, a head etc.) and the noun *principle* (a general rule, a moral standard etc.) should not be confused.

<hr>

principality (prinsipal´iti) n. (*pl.* **principalities**) **1** the territory or jurisdiction of a prince. **2** sovereignty, royal state or condition, superiority. **3** (*pl.*) one of the nine orders of angels.

principle (prin´sipəl) n. **1** a source, an origin; a fundamental cause or element. **2** a general truth forming a basis for reasoning or action. **3** a fundamental doctrine or tenet. **4** a rule of action or conduct deliberately adopted, as distinct from *impulse*. **5** the habitual regulation of conduct by moral law. **6** a law of nature by virtue of which a given mechanism etc. brings about certain results. **7** the mechanical contrivance, combination of parts, or mode of operation, forming the basis of a machine, instrument, process etc. **8** (*Chem.*) the constituent that gives specific character to a substance. **in principle** as far as the basic idea or theory is concerned. **on principle** because of the fundamental (moral) issue involved; in order to assert a principle. **principled** a. **1** guided by principle. **2** based on a principle.

<hr>

Usage note See note under PRINCIPAL: *principle* is never an adjective.

<hr>

prink (pringk) v.i. to make oneself smart, esp. excessively so. ~v.t. **1** to dress or smarten (oneself) up. **2** (of a bird) to preen.

print (print) n. **1** an indentation or other mark made by pressure, an imprint, an impression. **2** an impression from type, an engraved plate etc. **3** printed lettering. **4** printed matter. **5** a printed publication, esp. a newspaper. **6** the print run of a book etc. **7** a reproduction of a work of art made by a photographic process. **8** printed cotton cloth. **9** a positive photographic image produced from a negative. **10** a fingerprint. ~v.t. **1** to impress, to mark by pressure. **2** to take an impression of, to stamp. **3** to impress or make copies of (a book, picture etc.) by pressure, as from inked types, plates or blocks, on paper, cloth etc. **4** to cause (a book etc.) to be so impressed or copied. **5** to reproduce a design, writing etc. by any transfer process. **6** to mark with a design etc. by stamping. **7** to mark (a textile, ceramic etc.) with a decorative design. **8** to imprint, to form (letters etc.) in imitation of printing. **9** to impress (on the memory etc.) as if by printing. **10** to produce (a positive photographic image) from a negative. *~v.i.* **1** to practise the art of printing. **2** to publish books etc. **3** to form letters etc. in imitation of printing. **in print 1** in a printed form. **2** (of a printed book etc.) on sale. **out of print** no longer obtainable from the publisher. **to appear in print** to have one's work published. **to print out 1** to print. **2** to produce a printout (of). **printable** *a*. **1** able to be printed, or to be printed on or from. **2** fit to appear in print. **printability** (-bil´-) *n*. **printed circuit** *n*. an electronic circuit consisting of conductive material printed or etched on to an insulating base. **printer** *n*. **1** a person engaged in printing books, pamphlets, newspapers etc.; a typesetter, a compositor. **2** a person who carries on a printing business. **3** a person who prints textiles. **4** a machine or instrument for printing copies, designs etc. **5** a device for producing a printout. **printer's mark** *n*. an engraved design used as a device or trademark by a printer or publisher, an imprint. **printery** *n*. (*pl.* **printeries**) (*N Am.*) a printing office. **printhead** *n*. (*Comput.*) the component in a printer that forms and prints the characters. **printing** *n*. **1** the act, process or practice of impressing letters, characters or figures on paper, cloth or other material. **2** the business of a printer, the production of printed material. **3** a single impression of a book. **4 a** printed matter. **b** handwriting with separated letters looking like printed ones. **printing machine** *n*. a machine for taking impressions from type etc., esp. a power-operated one. **printing press** *n*. **1** a printing machine. **2** a handpress for printing. **printless** *a*. taking, or leaving, no impression. **printmaker** *n*. a person who makes prints. **printmaking** *n*. **printout** *n*. (a) printed copy produced by a computer. **print run** *n*. (the number of copies produced in) a single printing of a book etc. **printworks** *n.pl.* a factory for printing fabrics.

prion[1] (prī´on) *n*. (*pl.* **prions**) (*Biol.*) an infectious protein particle associated with diseases of the brain and nervous system in human beings and animals, such as BSE, Creutzfeldt Jakob disease, scrapie etc.

prion[2] (prī´ən) *n*. (*pl.* **prions**) any of various petrels of the genus *Pachyptila* with a serrated bill, living in the southern oceans.

prior[1] (prī´ə) *a*. **1** former, preceding; earlier, antecedent. **2** taking precedence. *~adv.* previously, antecedently (to).

prior[2] (prī´ə) *n*. **1** a superior of a monastic house or order next in rank below an abbot. **2** the deputy of an abbot. **priorate, priorship** *n*. **prioress** *n*. **1** the deputy of an abbess. **2** the superior of a priory of nuns. **priory** *n*. (*pl.* **priories**) a religious house governed by a prior or prioress.

priority (prīor´iti) *n*. (*pl.* **priorities**) **1** the fact or the state of going before, antecedence. **2** precedence, a superior claim or entitlement. **3** something given or meriting special attention. **4** the right to proceed while other vehicles wait.

~a. having or entitling to priority. **prioritize, prioritise** *v.t.* **1** to arrange (things to be done) in order of priority. **2** to give priority to. **prioritization** (-prī´-) *n*.

prise (prīz), (*N Am.*) **prize** *v.t.* **1** to wrench. **2** to force open with or as with a lever. **3** to extract with difficulty. *~n*. leverage.

prism (priz´m) *n*. **1** a solid having similar, equal and parallel plane bases or ends, its sides forming similar parallelograms. **2** a transparent solid of this form, usu. triangular, with two refracting surfaces set at an acute angle to each other, used as an optical instrument. **prismal** *a*. **prismatic** (-mat´-), †**prismatical** *a*. **1** of, relating to or resembling a prism. **2** formed, refracted or distributed by a prism. **prismatically** *adv*. **prismoid** (-moid) *n*. a solid like a prism, having similar but unequal ends. **prismoidal** *a*.

prison (priz´ən) *n*. **1** a place of confinement, esp. a public building for the confinement of criminals, persons awaiting trial etc. **2** confinement, captivity. **prison-breaker** *n*. a person who escapes from legal imprisonment. **prison-breaking** *n*. **prison camp** *n*. a camp for prisoners of war etc. **prisoner** *n*. **1** a person confined in a prison. **2** a person under arrest on a criminal charge. **3** a captive. **4** a prisoner of war. **to take prisoner 1** to capture. **2** to arrest and hold in custody. **prisoner at the bar** *n*. a person in custody or on trial upon a criminal charge. **prisoner of conscience** *n*. a person whose political, religious etc. beliefs have led to imprisonment. **prisoner of state** *n*. a person imprisoned for political reasons. **prisoner of war** *n*. a person captured in war. **prisoner's base**, †**prison bars** *n*. a children's game played by two sides occupying opposite goals or bases, the object being to touch and capture a player away from their base.

prissy (pris´i) *a*. (*comp.* **prissier**, *superl.* **prissiest**) prim, fussy, prudish. **prissily** *adv*. **prissiness** *n*.

pristine (pris´tēn, -tīn) *a*. **1** of or relating to an early or original state or time. **2** ancient, primitive. **3** pure, unadulterated, uncorrupted; as new.

Usage note The use of *pristine* in the sense 'as new' is sometimes disapproved of.

private (prī´vət) *a*. **1** not public; kept or withdrawn from publicity or observation; retired, secluded. **2** secret, confidential. **3** (of a person) not holding a public position. **4** not administered or provided by the state. **5** not official. **6** personal, not of or relating to the community. **7** one's own. **8** secretive, reticent. *~n*. **1** a soldier of the lowest rank. **2** (*pl.*) the private parts. **in private 1** privately, confidentially. **2** in private life. **privacy** (prī´vəsi, priv´-) *n*. **1** the state of being private. **2** (a person's right to) freedom from intrusion or publicity. **3** the avoidance of publicity or display. **private act, private bill** *n*. one affecting a private person or persons and not the general public. **private company** *n*. a company with a restricted number of shareholders, whose shares are not offered for sale to the general public. **private detective** n. a private person or an agent of a detective agency employed privately to investigate cases. **private enterprise** n. **1** economic activity undertaken by private individuals or organizations. **2** individual initiative. **private eye** n. (coll.) a private detective. **private hotel** n. a hotel or boarding house which is not obliged to take in chance travellers. **private house** n. a dwelling house belonging to a private individual, as distinct from a public building. **private investigator** n. a private detective. **private law** n. the branch of law which deals with individuals and their rights and duties, and private property. **private life** n. an individual's personal and family life, as distinct from work or public life. **privately** adv. **private means** n.pl. income from investments etc., as distinct from earned income. **private member** n. a member of Parliament who does not hold a government office. **private member's bill** n. a bill introduced and sponsored by a member of Parliament, not by the government. **privateness** n. **private parts** n.pl. the genitals. **private patient** n. a patient who is treated privately by a doctor, not under the National Health Service. **private press** n. a usu. small printing establishment run as a hobby rather than for profit. **private school** n. **1** a school run independently by an individual or group, esp. for profit. **2** (US) a school which is not supported by the state. **private secretary** n. (pl. **private secretaries**) **1** a secretary entrusted with personal and confidential matters. **2** a civil servant acting as an aide to a minister or senior government official. **private sector** n. the economy which is not state-owned or state-controlled. **private soldier** n. **1** a soldier of the lowest rank. **2** (US) a soldier who is not a recruit. **private view** n. an occasion when only those invited to an exhibition are admitted. **private war** n. **1** a war against citizens of another state conducted by private individuals, not by government. **2** a feud between persons or groups in which even murder may be committed. **private wrong** n. an offence committed against an individual, not against society. **privatize, privatise** v.t. to denationalize, to take back into the private sector, to return to private ownership. **privatization** (-zā´shən) n. **privatizer** n.

privateer (prīvətiə´) n. **1** an armed ship owned and officered by private persons commissioned by Government by letters of marque to engage in war against a hostile nation, esp. to capture merchant shipping. **2** a person who engages in privateering. ~v.i. to cruise or engage in hostilities in a privateer. **privateering** n. **privateersman** n. (pl. **privateersmen**).

privation (prīvā´shən) n. **1** deprivation or lack of what is necessary to a comfortable life; want, destitution. **2** absence, loss, negation (of). **privative** (priv´ə-) a. **1** causing privation. **2** con-

sisting in the absence or loss or removal of something. **3** (Gram.) expressing privation or absence of a quality etc., negative.

privet (priv´it) n. any evergreen, white-flowered shrub of the genus Ligustrum, esp. L. vulgare, largely used for hedges.

privilege (priv´ilij) n. **1** a benefit, right, advantage or immunity belonging to a person, class, office etc. **2** favoured status, the possession of privileges, a special advantage. **3** the rights and freedoms enjoyed by members of a legislative assembly. **4** a right of priority or precedence in any respect. **5** a franchise, monopoly or patent granted to an individual or a company. ~v.t. **1** to invest with a privilege. **2** to license, to authorize (to do). **3** to exempt (from). **privileged** a.

privy (priv´i) a. **1** secluded, hidden, secret, clandestine, private. **2** cognizant of something secret with another, privately knowing (with to). ~n. (pl. **privies**) **1** a lavatory, esp. an outside one. **2** (Law) a person having an interest in any action or thing. **privily** adv. **Privy Council** n. a committee of advisers to the British sovereign (the functions of which are now largely exercised by the Cabinet and committees), consisting of the princes of the blood, past and present government ministers, and members appointed by the Crown. **privy councillor, privy counsellor** n. **privy purse** n. **1** an allowance of money for the personal use of the sovereign. **2** the officer in charge of this.

prize[1] (prīz) n. **1** something which is offered or won as the reward of merit or superiority in any competition, contest, exhibition etc. **2** a sum of money or other object offered for competition in a lottery etc. **3** a well-paid appointment, a fortune, or other desirable object of perseverance, enterprise etc. ~a. **1** offered or gained as a prize. **2** gaining or worthy of a prize, first-class, of superlative merit. ~v.t. to value highly, to esteem. **prizefight** n. a boxing match fought for stakes. **prizefighter** n. **prizefighting** n. **prize-giving** n. a formal awarding of prizes, esp. at the end of a school year. **prizeless** a. **prize money** n. money offered as a prize. **prize ring** n. **1** the roped space (now usu. square) for a prizefight. **2** prizefighting. **prizewinner** n. the winner of a prize. **prizewinning** a.

prize[2] (prīz) n. **1** something which is taken from an enemy in war, esp. a ship or other property captured at sea. **2** a find, a windfall.

prize[3] PRISE.

PRO abbr. public relations officer.

pro[1] (prō) prep. **1** for. **2** in favour of. ~adv. in favour of. ~n. (pl. **pros**) an argument or a reason in favour of. ~a. in favour of. **pro and con** for and against; on both sides. **pros and cons** n.pl. reasons or arguments for and against.

pro[2] (prō) n. (pl. **pros**) **1** (coll.) a professional (actor, footballer etc.), or a person who behaves professionally. **2** (sl.) a prostitute. ~a. professional.

pro-¹ (prō) *pref.* **1** in favour of. **2** replacing, substituting for. **3** onward, forward, in front of.

pro-² (prō) *pref.* **1** before in time or position; earlier than. **2** projecting forward.

proactive (prōak´tiv) *a.* **1** energetic, enterprising, taking the initiative. **2** (*Psych.*) of or relating to a learned habit or mental conditioning which affects a later process. **proaction** (-ak´shən) *n.* **proactively** *adv.* **proactivity** (-tiv´iti) *n.*

pro-am (prō´am) *a.* involving both professionals and amateurs. *~n.* a pro-am tournament etc.

prob *abbr.* problem.

probabilistic (probəbilis´tik) *a.* **1** of or relating to probability. **2** based on probability. **3** of the nature of probabilism. **probabilistically** *adv.*

probability (probəbil´iti) *n.* (*pl.* **probabilities**) **1** the quality of being probable. **2** the likelihood of something happening. **3** something which is or appears probable or most probable. **4** (*Math.*) the likelihood of an event measured by the ratio of the favourable chances to the whole number of chances. **in all probability** most likely.

probable (prob´əbəl) *a.* likely to happen or prove true, having more evidence for than against, likely. *~n.* a person likely to be chosen for a team, post etc. **probably** *adv.*

probate (prō´bāt) *n.* **1** the official proving of a will. **2** a certified copy of a proved will. *~v.t.* (*N Am.*) to establish the validity of (a will).

probation (prəbā´shən) *n.* **1** (*Law*) a method of dealing with criminals by allowing them to go at large under supervision during their good behaviour. **2** a proving or testing of character, ability etc., esp. of a candidate for a religious ministry etc. by employment for a fixed period. **3** a moral trial, esp. the discipline undergone in this life as a means to salvation. **on probation 1** being tested for suitability etc. **2** (*Law*) under the supervision of a probation officer. **probational** *a.* **probationary** *a.*, *n.* (*pl.* **probationaries**). **probationer** *n.* **1** a person on probation or trial, esp. a divinity student licensed to preach and eligible for a charge, or a newly-appointed teacher or nurse. **2** an offender under probation. **probationership** *n.* **probation officer** *n.* a court official who supervises and assists offenders who are on probation.

probative (prō´bətiv) *a.* **1** proving or tending to prove. **2** serving as proof, evidential.

probe (prōb) *n.* **1** a surgical instrument, usu. a silver rod with a blunt end, for exploring cavities of the body, wounds etc. **2** a thorough investigation, as by a newspaper of e.g. alleged corruption. **3** an electric lead containing or connected to a monitoring circuit. **4** an unmanned spacecraft carrying equipment for collecting scientific measurements of conditions. **5** an exploratory survey. *~v.t.* **1** to search or examine (a wound, ulcer etc.) with, or as with, a probe. **2** to scrutinize or enquire into thoroughly. **3** to pierce with or as if with a probe. **probeable** *a.* **prober** *n.* **probingly** *adv.*

probity (prō´biti, prob´-) *n.* **1** honesty, sincerity or integrity. **2** uprightness, rectitude.

problem (prob´ləm) *n.* **1** a question proposed for solution. **2** a matter, situation or person that is difficult to deal with or understand. **3** a source of perplexity or distress. **4** (*Geom.*) a proposition requiring something to be done. **5** an investigation starting from certain conditions for the determination or illustration of a physical law etc. **6** an arrangement of pieces on a chessboard or of cards on a bridge board, from which a certain result has to be attained, usu. in a specified number of moves. *~a.* causing or posing a problem; hard to deal with. **problematic** (-mat´-), **problematical** *a.* **1** doubtful, questionable, uncertain. **2** (*Logic*) propounding or supporting that which is possible or probable but not necessarily true, contingent. **problematically** *adv.* **problematize**, **problematise** *v.t.* to make into a problem; to regard as a problem. **problematization** (-zā´shən) *n.*

pro bono (prō bō´nō) *a.* (*Law, US*) of or relating to legal work done without charge for poor clients, or to a lawyer who does such work.

proboscis (prəbos´is) *n.* (*pl.* **probosces** (-ēz), **proboscides** (-idēz), **proboscises**) **1** the trunk of an elephant or the elongated snout of a tapir etc. **2** the elongated mouth of some insects. **3** the suctorial organ of some worms etc. **4** (*facet.*) the human nose. **proboscidean** (probəsid´-) *a.* **1** having a proboscis. **2** of, relating to or like a proboscis. **3** of or relating to the Proboscidea, an order of mammals containing the elephants, the extinct mastodon etc. *~n.* any individual of the Proboscidea. **proboscis monkey** *n.* a monkey, *Nasalis larvatus*, of Borneo, the male having a long, flexible nose.

procaine (prō´kān), **procain** *n.* a synthetic crystalline substance used as a local anaesthetic, esp. in dentistry.

procaryote PROKARYOTE.

proceed (prəsēd´) *v.i.* **1** to go (in a specified direction or to a specified place). **2** to go on; to go forward, to advance, to continue to progress. **3** to carry on a series of actions, to go on (with or in). **4** to act in accordance with a method or procedure. **5** (of an action) to be carried on. **6** to issue or come forth, to originate (from). **7** to advance (to) a degree. **8** to take or carry on legal proceedings (against). **procedure** (-dyə) *n.* **1** an act, or a manner, of proceeding. **2** the (customary or established) mode of conducting business etc. esp. in a court or at a meeting. **3** a course of action. **4** an action, a step in a sequence of actions. **5** a proceeding. **6** (*Comput.*) a subroutine. **procedural** *a.* **procedurally** *adv.* **proceeding** *n.* **1** progress, advancement. **2** an action or line of conduct. **3** a transaction. **4** (*pl.*) events, what was going on. **5** (*pl.*) legal proceedings. **6** (*pl.*) the records of a learned society. **proceeds** (prō´-) *n.pl.* produce, material results, profits, e.g. the amount realized by the sale of goods.

process[1] (prō´ses) n. **1** a course or method of proceeding or doing, esp. a method of operation in manufacture, scientific research etc. **2** a natural series of continuous actions, changes etc. **3** a progressive movement or state of activity, progress, course. **4** the course of proceedings in an action at law. **5** a writ or order commencing this. **6** (*Anat., Zool., Bot.*) an outgrowth, an enlargement, a protuberance of a bone etc. ~*v.t.* **1** to subject to routine procedure, to deal with. **2** to institute legal proceedings against. **3** to serve a writ on. **4** to treat (food etc.) by a preservative or other process. **5** (*Comput.*) to perform operations on (data). **in process of time** as time goes on. **processable** *a.* **processor** *n.* **1** a person or thing that processes. **2** (*Comput.*) a device or program that processes data; a central processing unit. **3** a food processor.

process[2] (prəses´) *v.i.* to go in procession.

procession (prəsesh´ən) *n.* **1** a group of persons, vehicles etc. proceeding in regular order for a ceremony, display, demonstration etc. **2** the movement of such a train. **processional** *a.* of, relating to or used in processions. ~*n.* **1** a service book giving the ritual of, or the hymns sung in, religious processions. **2** a processional hymn. **processionally** *adv.* **processionary** *a.* **processionist** *n.*

pro-choice (prōchois´) *a.* in favour of a woman's right to choose whether or not to have an abortion.

proclaim (prəklām´) *v.t.* **1** to announce publicly, to promulgate. **2** to announce the accession of (a monarch). **3** to reveal or indicate. **4** to outlaw (a person) by public proclamation. **proclaimer** *n.* **proclamation** (prokləmā´shən) *n.* **proclamatory** (-klam´-) *a.*

proclitic (prōklit´ik) *a.* (*Gram*) (of a monosyllable) attached to and depending in accent upon a following word. ~*n.* a proclitic monosyllable. **proclitically** *adv.*

proclivity (prəkliv´iti) *n.* (*pl.* **proclivities**) a tendency, bent, propensity.

procrastinate (prōkras´tināt) *v.i.* **1** to put off action. **2** to be dilatory. **procrastination** (-ā´shən) *n.* **procrastinative, procrastinatory** *a.* **procrastinator** *n.*

Usage note See note under PREVARICATE.

procreate (prō´kriāt) *v.t.* to generate, to beget. ~*v.i.* to produce offspring. **procreant** *a.* **procreation** (-ā´shən) *n.* **procreative** *a.* **procreativeness** *n.* **procreator** *n.*

Procrustean (prəkrŭs´tiən) *a.* reducing to strict conformity by violent measures.

proctor (prok´tə) *n.* **1** an English University official (usu. one of two elected annually) with the duty of maintaining order and discipline. **2** (*US*) a supervisor or invigilator at examinations. **3** (*Law*) a person employed to manage another's cause, esp. in an ecclesiastical court. **4** in the Church of England, a representative of the clergy

at a convocation. **proctorial** (-taw´ri-) *a.* **proctorially** *adv.* **proctorship** *n.*

procumbent (prōkŭm´bənt) *a.* **1** lying down on the face; leaning forward. **2** (*Bot.*) lying or trailing along the surface of the ground.

procuration (prokūrā´shən) *n.* **1** (*formal*) the act of procuring or obtaining. **2** action on behalf of another, the management of another person's affairs.

procurator (prok´ūrātə) *n.* a person who manages another's affairs, esp. those of a legal nature, an agent, a proxy, an attorney. **procurator fiscal** *n.* (*Sc.*) the public prosecutor and coroner in a county or district. **procuratorial** (-taw´ri-) *a.* **procuratorship** *n.*

procure (prəkūə´) *v.t.* **1** to obtain, to get by some means or effort. **2** to bring about. **3** to acquire, to gain. **4** to obtain for purposes of prostitution. ~*v.i.* to act as procurer or procuress, to pimp. **procurable** *a.* **procural, procurance, procurement** *n.* **procurer** *n.* a person who procures or obtains, esp. one who procures women as prostitutes. **procuress** *n.* a woman procurer.

Prod (prod), **Proddie** (prod´i), **Proddy** *n.* (*pl.* **Prods, Proddies**) (*sl., offensive*) a Protestant (esp. in Ireland).

prod (prod) *n.* **1** a pointed instrument, a goad. **2** a poke with or as with this. **3** a stimulus to action. ~*v.t.* (*pres.p.* **prodding**, *past, p.p.* **prodded**) **1** to poke with or as with the finger or a pointed instrument. **2** to goad, to irritate, to incite. ~*v.i.* to make a prodding movement (at). **prodder** *n.*

prodigal (prod´igəl) *a.* **1** given to extravagant expenditure. **2** wasteful, lavish (of). ~*n.* a prodigal person, a spendthrift. **prodigality** (-gal´-) *n.* **prodigally** *adv.* **prodigal son** *n.* **1** a spendthrift son who repents. **2** a wanderer returned.

prodigy (prod´iji) *n.* (*pl.* **prodigies**) **1** something wonderful or extraordinary. **2** a wonderful example (of). **3** a person, esp. a child, or thing with extraordinary gifts or qualities. **4** something out of the ordinary course of nature, a monstrosity. **prodigious** (-dij´-) *a.* **1** wonderful, astounding. **2** enormous in size, quality, extent etc. **3** abnormal. **prodigiously** *adv.* **prodigiousness** *n.*

produce[1] (prədūs´) *v.t.* **1** to bring into view, to bring forward. **2** to publish, to exhibit. **3** to bring into existence, to bring forth. **4** to bear, to yield. **5** to manufacture, to make. **6** to bring about, to cause. **7** (*Geom.*) to extend, to continue (a line) in the same direction. **8** to act as producer of (a play of film). **producer** *n.* **1** a person who or thing which produces. **2** a person, or an organization, that produces goods or services for sale. **3** a person who exercises general administrative and financial control over a play, film or broadcast. **producible** *a.* **producibility** (-bil´-), †**producibleness** *n.*

produce[2] (prod´ūs) *n.* **1** goods produced or yielded. **2** the result (of labour, skill etc.). **3 a** the natural or agricultural products of a country etc.

collectively. **b** the amount of this. **4** in assaying, the percentage of copper or other metal yielded by a given amount of ore.

product (prod´ŭkt) *n.* **1** that which is produced by natural processes, labour, art or mental application. **2** an effect, a result. **3** (*Math.*) the quantity obtained by multiplying two or more quantities together. **production** (-dŭk´shən) *n.* **1** the act, or an instance, of producing, esp. as opposed to consumption. **2** the process of being manufactured. **3** a thing produced, a product. **4** the amount produced, the output. **5** in economics, the creation of goods and services with exchange value. **6** a play, film, broadcast etc., esp. in relation to its producers. **7** the work of a film etc. producer. **8** (preparation for) the public presentation of a stage work. **productional** *a.* **production line** *n.* a system of stage-by-stage manufacture in which a product undergoes various processes or operations as it passes along a conveyor belt. **productive** (-dŭk´-) *a.* **1 a** producing or tending to produce. **b** giving rise to. **2** yielding in abundance, fertile. **3** in economics, producing commodities having exchangeable value. **4** (*Gram.*) of or relating to an affix which is currently much used to produce new words. **productively** *adv.* **productiveness** *n.* **productivity** (prodŭktiv´-) *n.* **1** efficiency of production. **2** the capacity to produce. **3** yield in abundance.

proem (prō´em) *n.* a preface, a preamble, an introduction, a prelude. **proemial** (-ē´miəl) *a.*

Prof. *abbr.* Professor.

prof (prof) *n.* (*coll.*) a professor at a university etc.

profane (prəfān´) *a.* **1** not sacred, not inspired, not initiated into sacred or esoteric rites or knowledge; secular. **2** (of a person) irreverent towards holy things. **3** (of language) irreverent, impious, blasphemous. **4** heathenish. *~v.t.* **1** to treat with irreverence. **2** to desecrate, to violate, to pollute. **profanation** (profənā´shən) *n.* **profanely** *adv.* **profaneness** *n.* **profaner** *n.* **profanity** (-fan´-) *n.* (*pl.* **profanities**) **1** profane language, blasphemy; swearing. **2** a profane act.

profess (prəfes´) *v.t.* **1** to make open or public declaration of, to avow publicly. **2** to affirm one's belief in or allegiance to. **3** to undertake the teaching or practice of (an art, science etc.). **4** to teach (a subject) as a professor. **5** to lay claim to, to make a show of, to pretend (to be or do). **6** to receive into a religious order under vows. *~v.i.* to act as a professor. **professed** *a.* **1** avowed, declared, acknowledged. **2** pretending to be qualified (as a teacher, practitioner etc.). **3** in the Roman Catholic Church, of or relating to a religious person who has taken vows. **professedly** (-sid-) *adv.* **professor** *n.* **1** a public teacher of the highest rank, esp. in a university. **2** (*US*) any university or college teacher. **3** a person who makes profession, esp. of a religious faith. **professorate** (-ət) *n.* **professorial** (-saw´ri-) *a.* **professorially** *adv.* **professoriate** (-saw´riət) *n.* **professorship** *n.*

profession (prəfesh´ən) *n.* **1** the act of professing; a declaration, an avowal. **2** a protestation, a pretence. **3** an open acknowledgement of sentiments, religious belief etc. **4** a vow binding oneself to, or the state of being a member of, a religious order. **5** a calling, a vocation, esp. an occupation involving high educational or technical qualifications. **6** the body of persons engaged in such a vocation. **the oldest profession** (*coll. or facet.*) prostitution. **professional** *a.* **1** of or relating to a profession. **2** engaging in an activity as a means of livelihood, esp. as distinct from *amateur.* **3** characterized by, or conforming to, the technical or ethical standards of a profession. **4** competent, conscientious. **5** (*derog.*) permanently or habitually undertaking some activity perceived as undesirable. *~n.* **1** a member of a profession. **2** a person who makes a living by some art, sport etc., as distinguished from one who engages in it for pleasure. **professional foul** *n.* a deliberate foul in football etc., in order to prevent the opposition from scoring. **professionalism** *n.* **1** the qualities, stamp or spirit of a professional. **2** participation by professionals, esp. in sports. **professionalize, professionalise** *v.t.* **professionalization** (-zā´-shən) *n.* **professionally** *adv.* **professionless** *a.*

proffer (prof´ə) *v.t.* to offer or tender for acceptance. *~n.* (*formal*) an offer, a tender. **profferer** *n.*

proficient (prəfish´ənt) *a.* (of a person) well versed or skilled in any art, science etc.; expert, competent. *~n.* a person who is proficient, an adept, an expert. **proficiency** *n.* **proficiently** *adv.*

profile (prō´fīl) *n.* **1** an outline, a contour. **2** a side view, esp. of the human face. **3** a drawing, silhouette or other representation of this. **4** the outline of a vertical section of a building, the contour of architectural detail etc. **5** a vertical section of soil or rock showing the various layers. **6** a set of statistical data showing the salient features of some organization, e.g. a company. **7** a person's characteristic attitudes or behaviour. **8** a short biographical or character sketch. *~v.t.* **1** to draw in profile or in vertical section. **2** to shape (stone, wood, metal etc.) to a given profile. **3** to write a profile of. **in profile** as seen from the side. **profiler** *n.* **profilist** *n.*

profit (prof´it) *n.* **1** any advantage or benefit, esp. one resulting from labour or exertion. **2** (*often pl.*) excess of receipts or returns over outlay, financial gain. *~v.t.* (*pres.p.* **profiting**, *past, p.p.* **profited**) to benefit, to be of advantage to. *~v.i.* **1** to be of advantage (to). **2** to receive benefit or advantage (by or from). **at a profit** making a financial gain. **profit and loss** income and gains credited and expenditure and losses debited in an account so as to show the net loss or profit. **profitable** *a.* **1** yielding or bringing profit or gain, lucrative. **2** advantageous, beneficial, useful. **profitability** (-bil´-) *n.* **profitableness** *n.* **profitably** *adv.* **profiteer** (-tiə´) *v.i.* to make undue profits at the expense of the public, esp. in a time of shortage or other emergency. ~*n.* a person who profiteers. **profitless** *a.* **profitlessly** *adv.* **profitlessness** *n.* **profit margin** *n.* the amount of profit in a business after all outgoings etc. have been deducted. **profit-sharing** *n.* a system of remuneration by which the workers in an industrial concern are apportioned a percentage of the profits in order to give them an interest in the business. **profit-taking** *n.* the selling of shares etc. at a time when the selling price is expected to be at its highest.

profiterole (prəfit´ərōl) *n.* a small, hollow ball of choux pastry with a sweet filling, usu. served with chocolate sauce.

profligate (prof´ligət) *a.* **1** licentious, dissolute. **2** wildly extravagant. ~*n.* a profligate person. **profligacy, profligateness** *n.* **profligately** *adv.*

pro forma (prō faw´mə) *a., adv.* (done) as a matter of form, as a formality. ~*n.* a pro forma invoice. **pro forma invoice** *n.* an invoice made out in advance to show the market price of goods.

profound (prəfownd´) *a.* **1** having great intellectual penetration or insight. **2** having great knowledge. **3** requiring great study or research, abstruse, recondite. **4** (of a quality etc.) deep, intense. **5** deep-seated, far below the surface. **6** coming from a great depth, deep-drawn. **7** thoroughgoing, extensive. ~*n.* (*poet.*) **1** the depths of the earth, the abyss. **2** the deep, the ocean. **profoundly** *adv.* **profoundness** *n.* **profundity** (-fŭn´di-) *n.* (*pl.* **profundities**).

profuse (prəfūs´) *a.* **1** poured out lavishly, exuberant, copious, superabundant. **2** liberal to excess, prodigal, extravagant. **profusely** *adv.* **profuseness** *n.* **profusion** (-zhən) *n.*

prog (prog) *n.* (*coll.*) a radio or TV programme.

progenitor (prōjen´itə) *n.* **1** an ancestor in the direct line, a forefather, a parent. **2** a predecessor, an original. **progenitive** *a.* **1** of or relating to the bearing of offspring. **2** capable of bearing offspring. **progenitorial** (-taw´ri-) *a.* **progenitorship** *n.* **progeniture** (-chə) *n.* **1** the art, or an instance, of begetting, generation. **2** offspring.

progeny (proj´əni) *n.* (*pl.* **progenies**) **1** the offspring of human beings, animals or plants. **2** a child or children, descendants. **3** issue, results, consequences.

progesterone (prōjes´tərōn) *n.* a female steroid hormone that prepares and maintains the uterus for pregnancy. **progestogen** (-jən) *n.* any of a range of hormones of the progesterone type, synthetic progestogens being used in oral contraceptives.

prognathic (prognath´ik), **prognathous** (prog´nəthəs, -nā´thəs) *a.* **1** having the jaws projecting. **2** (of the jaws) projecting. **prognathism** (prog´-) *n.*

prognosis (prognō´sis) *n.* (*pl.* **prognoses** (-sēz)) **1** a forecast of the probable course or result of an illness. **2** a forecast, a prediction.

prognostic (prognos´tik) *n.* **1** a symptom on which a prognosis can be based. **2** a sign or indication of a future event; an omen, a token. **3** a prediction, a forecast. ~*a.* foreshowing, indicative of something future by signs or symptoms. **prognostically** *adv.* **prognosticate** *v.t.* **1** to foretell from present signs. **2** to foreshadow, to presage, to betoken. **prognostication** (-ā´shən) *n.* **prognosticative** *a.* **prognosticator** *n.* **prognosticatory** *a.*

programme (prō´gram), (*Comput., N Am.*) **program** *n.* **1** (a paper, booklet etc. giving) a list of the successive items of any entertainment, public ceremony, conference, course of study etc. plus other relevant information. **2** the items on such a list. **3** a broadcast presented at a scheduled time. **4** (*Comput.*) (**program**) a sequence of instructions which, when fed into a computer, enable it to process data in specified ways. **5** a curriculum or syllabus. **6** a plan or outline of proceedings or actions to be carried out. ~*v.t.* (*pres.p.* **programming**, (*N Am. also*) **programing**, *past, p.p.* **programmed**, (*N Am. also*) **programed**) **1** to arrange a programme for. **2** to enter in a programme. **3** to cause to conform to a certain pattern, esp. of thought, behaviour. **4** (*usu.* **program**) to prepare as a program for, to feed a program into (a computer). **programmable** (-gram´-) *a.* **programmability** (-bil´-) *n.* **programmatic** (-mat´-) *a.* **1** of or having a programme. **2** of, or of the nature of, programme music. **programmatically** *adv.* **programme music** *n.* music intended to suggest a definite series of scenes, incidents etc. **programmer** *n.*

progress[1] (prō´gres) *n.* **1** a moving or going forward; movement onward, advance. **2** advance towards completion, a specified destination, fruition or a higher state. **3** (*Hist.*) a journey of state, esp. by royalty. **in progress** going on, developing, proceeding. **progress-chaser** *n.* a person employed to check at each stage in a manufacturing etc. process that the work is on schedule. **progress report** *n.* a report setting out the progress that has been made in a project.

progress[2] (prəgres´) *v.i.* **1** to move forward, to advance; to be carried on, to proceed. **2 a** to advance, to develop. **b** to make improvement. **3** (*Hist.*) to travel in state. ~*v.t.* to cause (a project, a career etc.) to advance steadily. **progression** (-gresh´ən) *n.* **1** the act, or an instance, of progressing. **2** progress, motion onward; movement in successive stages. **3** (*Mus.*) a regular succession of notes or chords in melody or harmony. **4** (*Math.*) regular or proportional advance by increase or decrease of numbers. **progressional** *a.* **progressionism** *n.* **progressionist** *n.* **1** a believer in, or advocate of, social and political progress. **2** a person who believes that organisms have advanced from lower to higher forms, an evolutionist. **progressive** (-gres´-) *a.* **1** moving forward or onward; advancing. **2** (of a disease) increasing in extent or severity. **3** (of taxation) at a rate which increases as the taxable sum increases. **4** in a state of progression, proceeding step by step, successive. **5** continuously increasing. **6 a** believing in or advocating social and political reform. **b** modern or efficient. **7** (of a dance or a card game) involving a change of partner every so often. **8** denoting an educational system which allows flexibility and takes the needs and abilities of the individual child as its determinant. **9** (*Gram.*) denoting a verb form which expresses action in progress. ~*n.* **1** a progressive person. **2** the progressive form of a verb. **progressively** *adv.* **progressiveness** *n.* **progressivism** *n.* **progressivist** *n.*

prohibit (prəhib´it) *v.t.* (*pres.p.* **prohibiting**, *past*, *p.p.* **prohibited**) **1** to forbid authoritatively, to interdict. **2** to hinder, to prevent. **prohibiter**, **prohibitor** *n.* **prohibition** (prōibish´-) *n.* **1** the act, or an instance, of prohibiting. **2** an order or edict prohibiting. **3** (*Law*) a writ from a superior court forbidding an inferior court from proceeding in a matter beyond its jurisdiction. **4** the forbidding by law of the manufacture and the sale of intoxicating liquors for consumption as beverages. **prohibitionary** *a.* **prohibitionist** *n.* a person in favour of prohibiting the sale of intoxicating liquors. **prohibitionism** *n.* **prohibitive** *a.* **1** tending to prohibit or preclude. **2** (of costs, prices etc.) such as to debar purchase, use etc. **prohibitively** *adv.* **prohibitiveness** *n.*

project[1] (proj´ekt, prō´-) *n.* **1** a plan, a scheme, a design. **2** an (esp. large-scale) planned undertaking. **3** a piece of work undertaken by a pupil or group of pupils to supplement and apply classroom studies.

project[2] (prəjekt´) *v.t.* **1** to throw or shoot forward. **2** to cast (light, shadow, an image) on to a surface or into space. **3** to enable (one's voice) to be heard at a distance. **4** to express or present (oneself) in a way that creates a favourable image. **5** to transport (oneself) in the imagination. **6** to predict or expect (something) based on known data. **7** (*Psych.*) to impute (something in one's own mind) to another person, group or entity. **8** to contrive, to plan (a course of action etc.). **9 a** (*Geom.*) to draw straight lines from a given centre through every point of (a figure) so as to form a corresponding figure on a surface. **b** to draw (such lines). **c** to produce (such a projection). **10** to make a projection of (the earth, sky etc.). ~*v.i.* **1** to jut out, to protrude. **2** to make oneself audible at a distance. **3** to communicate effectively. **4** to express one's personality so as to create a favourable impression. **projectile** (-tĭl) *n.* **1** a body (e.g. a bullet, a spear) projected or thrown forward with force. **2** a self-propelling missile, esp. one adapted for discharge from a heavy gun. ~*a.* **1** impelling forward. **2** adapted to be forcibly projected, esp. from a gun. **projection** *n.* **1** the act or state of projecting, protruding, throwing or impelling. **2** a part or thing that projects, a prominence. **3** a mental image viewed as an external object. **4** the process whereby one ascribes to others one's own mental factors and

attributes. **5** the showing of films or slides by projecting images from them on to a screen. **6 a** prediction based on known data. **7** the representation of the terrestrial or celestial sphere, or a part of it, on a plane surface. **projectionist** *n.* a person who operates a film projector. **projective** *a.* **1** of, relating to or derived from projection. **2** (*Geom.*) such that they may be derived from one another by projection (of two plane figures). **3** (*Psych.*) externalizing or making objective. **projective geometry** *n.* the branch of geometry dealing with those properties of figures that are unchanged under projection. **projectively** *adv.* **projector** *n.* **1** an apparatus for projecting rays of light, images, slides or cinema films on to a screen. **2** a person who forms schemes.

prokaryote (prōkar´iot), **procaryote** *n.* an organism whose cells have no distinct nucleus, their genetic material being carried in a single filament of DNA. **prokaryotic** (-ot´ik) *a.*

prolactin (prōlak´tin) *n.* a hormone produced by the pituitary gland, which stimulates lactation.

prolapse (prō´laps, -laps´) *n.* **1** a falling down or slipping out of place of an organ or part, such as the uterus or rectum. **2** the displaced organ or part. ~*v.i.* to undergo prolapse. **prolapsus** (-lap´səs) *n.* a prolapse.

prolate (prō´lāt) *a.* **1** (*Geom.*) extended in the direction of the longer axis, elongated in the polar diameter, as distinct from *oblate*. **2** widespread; growing in width. **prolately** *adv.* **prolateness** *n.*

prole (prōl) *n., a.* (*coll.*, *derog.*) PROLETARIAN.

prolegomenon (prōligom´inən) *n.* (*pl.* **prolegomena** (-inə)) (*usu. pl.*) an introductory or preliminary discourse prefixed to a book etc. **prolegomenary**, **prolegomenous** *a.*

proletarian (prōləteə´riən) *a.* of or relating to the common people. ~*n.* a member of the proletariat. **proletarianism** *n.* **proletarianize**, **proletarianise** *v.t.* proletarianization (-zā´shən) *n.* **proletariat** (-riət, -at), **proletariate** *n.* **1** wage earners collectively, people without property who sell their labour. **2** (*derog.*) the lowest and most uncultured class.

pro-life (prōlīf´) *a.* favouring greater restrictions on the availability of legal abortions and/or a ban on the use of human embryos for experimental purposes. **pro-lifer** *n.*

proliferate (prəlif´ərāt) *v.i.* to grow or increase rapidly and abundantly. ~*v.t.* to produce (cells etc.) by proliferation. **proliferation** (-ā´shən) *n.* **proliferative** *a.* **proliferator** *n.* **proliferous** *a.* **1** producing new individuals from buds, parts etc. **2** spreading by proliferation. **proliferously** *adv.*

prolific (prəlif´ik) *a.* **1** producing offspring, esp. abundantly. **2** fruitful, productive, fertile. **3** abounding (in). **4** very productive (of). **prolificacy** *n.* **prolifically** *adv.* **prolificity** (prolifis´-), **prolificness** *n.*

proline (prō'lēn) *n.* an amino acid occurring in proteins, esp. collagen.

prolix (prō'liks) *a.* **1** long and wordy. **2** tedious, tiresome, diffuse. **prolixity** (-lik'si-), **prolixness** *n.* **prolixly** *adv.*

prologue (prō'log), (*N Am.*) **prolog** *n.* **1** an introductory discourse, esp. lines introducing a play. **2** an act or event forming an introduction to some proceeding or occurrence. **3** the speaker of a prologue. ~*v.t.* (*3rd pers. sing. pres.* **prologues**, (*NAm.*) **prologs**, *pres.p.* **prologuing**, (*NAm.*) **prologing**, *past, p.p.* **prologued**, (*N Am.*) **prologed** (-logd)) to introduce with a prologue. **prologize** (-gīz), **prologise**, **prologuize**, **prologuise** *v.i.* to write or speak a prologue.

prolong (prəlong') *v.t.* **1** to extend in duration (an action or a state). **2** to lengthen, to extend in space or distance. **prolongation** (prōlong-gā'-shən) *n.* **prolonged** *a.* lengthy. **prolongedly** (-idli) *adv.* **prolonger** *n.*

prolusion (prəloo'zhən) *n.* (*formal*) **1** a prelude. **2** a preliminary essay, exercise or attempt. **prolusory** (-səri) *a.*

prom (prom) *n.* (*coll.*) **1** a paved promenade. **2** a promenade concert. **3** (*N Am.*) a dance at a school etc.

promenade (promənahd', prom'-) *n.* **1** a walk, drive, or ride for pleasure, exercise or display. **2** a place for promenading, esp. a paved terrace on a seafront. **3** any paved public walk. **4** a processional sequence in a square or country dance. **5** (*N Am.*) a dance at a college, school, unit or association. ~*v.i.* **1** to take a walk etc. for pleasure, exercise or show. **2** to perform a promenade in dancing. ~*v.t.* **1** to take a promenade along, about or through (a place). **2** to lead (a person) about, esp. for display. **promenade concert, promenade performance** *n.* a concert or performance at which part of the floor of the hall is left bare for the audience to stand and to walk about. **promenade deck** *n.* an upper deck on a ship where passengers may stroll. **promenader** *n.* a standing member of the audience at a promenade concert or performance.

promethazine (prōmeth'əzēn) *n.* an antihistamine drug used to treat allergies, travel sickness etc.

Promethean (prəmē'thiən) *a.* of, relating to or like Prometheus; original, creative, daring. **promethium** (-thiəm) *n.* (*Chem.*) a radioactive metallic element, at. no. 61, chem. symbol Pm, obtained as a fission product of uranium.

prominent (prom'inənt) *a.* **1** standing out, jutting, projecting, protuberant. **2** conspicuous. **3** distinguished. **prominence, prominency** *n.* **1** the state of being prominent. **2** something which is prominent, such as an outcrop. **3** (*Astron.*) a cloud of incandescent gas erupting from the surface of the sun which can be seen during an eclipse. **prominently** *adv.* **prominent moth** *n.* a moth of the family Notodontidae, having tufts of scales on the forewing.

promiscuous (prəmis'kūəs) *a.* **1** indulging in casual indiscriminate sexual intercourse. **2** mixed together in a disorderly manner. **3** of different kinds mingled confusedly together. **4** (*coll.*) fortuitous, accidental, casual, heedless. **promiscuity** (promiskū'-) *n.* **promiscuously** *adv.* **promiscuousness** *n.*

promise (prom'is) *n.* **1** a verbal or written engagement to do or forbear from doing some specific act. **2** something which is promised. **3** a ground or basis of expectation, esp. of success, improvement or excellence. ~*v.t.* **1** to engage to do or not to do (something). **2** to engage to give or procure (something). **3** to make a promise of something to. **4** to give good grounds for expecting. ~*v.i.* **1** to bind oneself by a promise. **2** to give grounds for favourable expectations. **to promise ill** to hold out unfavourable prospects. **to promise oneself** to look forward to (something pleasant). **to promise well** to hold out favourable prospects. **promised land** *n.* **1** any place of expected happiness or prosperity. **2** heaven. **3** the land of Canaan promised to Abraham and his seed. **promiser** *n.* **promising** *a.* giving grounds for expectation or hope, likely to turn out well. **promisingly** *adv.* **promisor** *n.* (*Law*) a person who enters into a covenant. **promissory** *a.* containing, or of the nature of, a promise, esp. a promise to pay money. **promissory note** *n.* a signed engagement to pay a sum of money to a specified person or the bearer at a stated date or on demand.

prommer (prom'ə) *n.* (*coll.*) a person who attends a promenade concert, esp. regularly.

promo (prō'mō) *n.* (*pl.* **promos**) (*coll.*) something used to promote a product, esp. a pop video. ~*a.* promotional.

promontory (prom'əntəri) *n.* (*pl.* **promontories**) **1** a headland, a point of high land projecting into the sea. **2** (*Anat.*) a rounded protuberance. **promontoried** *a.*

promote (prəmōt') *v.t.* **1** to raise to a higher rank or position, to exalt, to prefer. **2** to transfer (a sports team) to a higher division of a league etc. **3** to forward, to advance, to contribute to the growth, increase or advancement of. **4** to support, to foster, to encourage. **5** to bring to the notice of the public, to encourage the sale of (a product) by advertising. **6** to help to ensure the passing of (an act of parliament). **promotable** *a.* **promotability** (-bil'-) *n.* **promoter** *n.* **1** a person who or thing which promotes or furthers. **2** a person who organizes a sporting event, esp. a boxing match. **3** (*Chem.*) a substance which increases the efficiency of a catalyst. **promotion** *n.* **promotional** *a.* **promotive** *a.*

prompt (prompt) *a.* **1** acting quickly or ready to act as occasion demands. **2** done, made or said with alacrity, or at once. **3** (of a payment) made without delay. ~*adv.* punctually. ~*n.* **1 a** the act of prompting, or the thing said to prompt an actor etc. **b** a person who prompts in a theatre etc. **2** (*Comput.*) a reminder to an operator, in the form of a question or statement appearing on the VDU, that the system is ready for input. ~*v.t.* **1** to urge or incite (to action or to do); to instigate. **2** to suggest to the mind, to inspire, to excite (thoughts, feelings etc.). **3** to assist (a speaker, actor etc.) when at a loss, by suggesting the words forgotten. ~*v.i.* to supply an actor etc. with forgotten words. **prompt book** *n.* a copy of a play for the use of the prompter at a theatre. **prompter** *n.* a person who prompts, esp. one employed at a theatre to prompt actors. **prompting** *n.* **promptitude** (-titūd), **promptness** *n.* **promptly** *adv.* **prompt side** *n.* the side of a stage on which the prompter stands, usu. to the left of the actor in Britain and to the right in the US.

promulgate (prom´əlgāt) *v.t.* **1** to make known to the public; to disseminate; to announce publicly. **2** to put (a law etc.) into effect by proclaiming it. **promulgation** (-gā´shən) *n.* **promulgator** (prom´-) *n.*

pronate (prō´nāt) *v.t.* to lay (a hand or forelimb) prone so as to have the palm downwards, as distinct from *supinate.* **pronation** (-nā´shən) *n.* **pronator** *n.* (*Anat.*) any muscle used to turn the palm downwards.

prone (prōn) *a.* **1** leaning or bent forward or downward. **2** lying with the face downward, as distinct from *supine.* **3** lying flat, prostrate. **4** disposed, inclined, apt (esp. in comb., as *accident-prone*). **pronely** *adv.* **proneness** *n.*

prong (prong) *n.* **1** any one of the spikes of a fork. **2** a sharp-pointed instrument or spikelike projection. ~*v.t.* **1** to pierce, stab or prick with a prong. **2** to dig (soil) with a fork. **prongbuck, pronghorn, prong-horned antelope** *n.* a N American ruminant, *Antilocapra americana.* **pronged** *a.*

pronominal (prōnom´inəl) *a.* **1** (*Gram.*) of, relating to or of the nature of a pronoun. **2** serving as a pronoun. **pronominalize, pronominalise** *v.t.* **pronominalization** (-zā´shən) *n.* **pronominally** *adv.*

pronoun (prō´nown) *n.* (*Gram.*) a word used in place of a noun to denote a person or thing already mentioned or implied.

pronounce (prənowns´) *v.t.* **1** to utter articulately, to say correctly. **2** to utter formally, officially or rhetorically (a judgement, a curse etc.). **3** to declare, to affirm. ~*v.i.* **1** to articulate sounds or words. **2** to declare one's opinion (on, for, against etc.). **pronounceable** *a.* **pronounceability** (-bil´-) *n.* **pronounced** *a.* **1** strongly marked, emphatic, decided. **2** conspicuous, obvious. **pronouncedly** (-sid-) *adv.* **pronouncement** *n.* a statement. **pronouncer** *n.* **pronunciation** (-nǔnsiā´shən) *n.* **1** the act, or an instance, of pronouncing words etc. **2** the correct pronouncing of words etc. **3** a person's way of pronouncing.

Usage note Pronunciation of *pronunciation* as (prənownsiā´shən) (after *pronounce*) and the corresponding spelling *pronounciation* are best avoided.

pronto (pron´tō) *adv.* (*coll.*) without delay; quickly.

pro-nuncio (prōnǔn´siō, -shō) *n.* (*pl.* **pro-nuncios**) a papal ambassador of lower status than a nuncio.

proof (proof) *n.* **1** the act of proving, a test, a trial. **2** testing, assaying, experiment. **3** demonstration. **4** a sequence of steps establishing the correctness of a mathematical or logical proposition. **5** convincing evidence of the truth or falsity of a statement, charge etc., esp. oral or written evidence submitted in the trial of a cause. **6** a standard degree of strength in distilled spirits. **7** (*Print.*) a trial impression from type for correction. **8** an impression of an engraving taken with special care before the ordinary issue is printed. **9** a first or early impression of a photograph, coin, medal etc. ~*a.* **1** proved or tested as to strength, firmness etc. **2** impenetrable. **3** able to resist physically or morally. **4** used in testing, verifying etc. **5** of a certain degree of alcoholic strength. ~*v.t.* **1** to make proof, esp. waterproof. **2** to make a proof of (printed matter, an engraving etc.). **above proof** (of alcoholic liquor) of a stronger than standard strength. **proofer** *n.* **proofing** *n.* **proofless** *a.* **proof-plane** *n.* a disc-shaped conductor with an insulating handle used in measuring the electrification of a body. **proof positive** *n.* convincing proof. **proof-read** *v.t.* (*past, p.p.* **proof-read** (-red)) to read and correct (printer's proofs). **proof-reader** *n.* **proof-reading** *n.* **proof-sheet** *n.* a sheet of printer's proof. **proof spirit** *n.* a mixture of alcohol and water containing a standard amount of alcohol, in Britain 57.1% by volume.

-proof (proof) *comb. form* (to make) resistant, impervious, immune to, as *rainproof, soundproof.*

prop[1] (prop) *n.* **1** a rigid support, esp. a loose or temporary one; a buttress, a pillar, a stay. **2** a person supporting a cause etc. **3** a prop forward. ~*v.t.* (*pres.p.* **propping**, *past, p.p.* **propped**) **1** to support or hold (up) with or as with a prop. **2** to support, to hold up (of a prop). **to prop up 1** to support in an upright position. **2** to keep going with financial etc. help. **prop forward** *n.* in rugby, either of the two forwards supporting the hooker in the front row of the scrum.

prop[2] (prop) *n.* a stage property. **props** *n.* (*also* **props man, props mistress**) PROPERTY MAN (under PROPERTY).

prop[3] (prop) *n.* (*coll.*) an aeroplane propeller. **prop-jet** *n.* TURBOPROP (under TURBO-).

propaganda (propəgan´də) *n.* **1** (*often derog.*) information, ideas, opinions etc. propagated as a means of winning support for, or fomenting opposition to, a government, cause, institution etc. **2** an organization, scheme or other means of propagating such information etc. **propagandist** *n.* a person devoted to, or engaged in, propaganda. *~a.* propagandistic. **propagandism** *n.* **propagandistic** (-dis´-) *a.* **propagandistically** *adv.* **propagandize, propagandise** *v.t.* **1** to spread by propaganda. **2** to subject to propaganda. *~v.i.* to spread propaganda.

propagate (prop´əgāt) *v.t.* **1** to cause to multiply by natural generation or other means; to reproduce. **2** to hand down (a characteristic) to the next generation. **3** to cause to spread or extend. **4** to diffuse, to disseminate. *~v.i.* **1** to be reproduced or multiplied by natural generation or other means. **2** to have offspring. **propagation** (-ā´shən) *n.* **propagative** *a.* **propagator** *n.* **1** a person or thing that propagates. **2** a heated, covered box for growing plants from seed or cuttings.

propane (prō´pān) *n.* (*Chem.*) a flammable, gaseous hydrocarbon used as fuel. **propanoic acid** PROPIONIC ACID. **propanol** *n.* propyl alcohol. **propanone** (-pə-) *n.* acetone.

propel (prəpel´) *v.t.* (*pres.p.* **propelling**, *past, p.p.* **propelled**) **1** to drive forward; to cause to move forward or onward. **2** to urge on, to encourage. **propellant** *a.* propellent. *~n.* something which propels, esp. the fuel mixture used by a rocket engine, the gas in an aerosol, or the explosive charge in a gun. **propellent** *a.* propelling; capable of propelling. **propeller** *n.* **1** a person who or thing which propels. **2** a rotating device, usu. consisting of two to four blades set at an angle and twisted like the thread of a screw, at the end of a shaft driven by steam, electricity etc., for propelling a vessel through the water or an aeroplane or airship through air. **propeller shaft** *n.* the shaft which transmits from an engine to a propeller in an aircraft or ship, or from a gearbox to the driving axle in a motor vehicle. **propeller turbine** *n.* a turboprop. **propelling pencil** *n.* a pencil having a metal or plastic casing which, when turned, extends or retracts a replaceable lead. **propelment** *n.*

propene (prō´pēn) *n.* (*Chem.*) propylene.

propensity (prəpen´siti) *n.* (*pl.* **propensities**) bent, natural tendency, inclination.

proper (prop´ə) *a.* **1** belonging or pertaining exclusively or peculiarly (to). **2** correct, just, accurate. **3** suitable, appropriate; fit, becoming. **4** decent, respectable; strictly decorous. **5** (*usu. following its noun*) real, genuine, according to strict definition. **6** own. **7** (*coll.*) thorough, complete. *~adv.* (*dial. or coll.*) **1** completely, exceedingly. **2** correctly, genteelly. **proper fraction** *n.* a fraction less than unity. **properly** *adv.* **1** in a proper manner, fitly, suitably. **2** rightly, justly, correctly, accurately. **3** (*coll.*) thoroughly, quite. **proper motion** *n.* (*Astron.*) part of the apparent motion of a star, responsible for the star's change of position relative to the sun over a long period of time. **proper name, proper noun** *n.* (*Gram.*) a

name or noun designating an individual person, animal, place etc., as distinct from a *common noun*. **properness** *n.* **proper pride** *n.* a person's sense of dignity or self-respect.

property (prop´əti) *n.* (*pl.* **properties**) **1** something which is owned; a possession, possessions, a piece of real estate. **2** a peculiar or inherent quality. **3** character, nature. **4** (*Law*) exclusive right of possession, ownership. **5** (*pl.*) articles required for the production of a play on the stage. **6** (*Logic*) an attribute which is common to a whole class, but not essential to it. **propertied** *a.* possessing property, esp. land. **property man, property master, property mistress, property woman** *n.* the man or woman in charge of theatrical properties. **property tax** *n.* a direct tax on property.

prophase (prō´fāz) *n.* (*Biol.*) the first stage of mitosis, or of meiosis.

prophecy (prof´əsi) *n.* (*pl.* **prophecies**) **1** a prediction, esp. one divinely inspired. **2** the prediction of future events. **3** the gift or faculty of prophesying.

prophesy (prof´əsī) *v.t.* (*3rd pers. sing. pres.* **prophesies**, *pres.p.* **prophesying**, *past, p.p.* **prophesied**) **1** to predict, to foretell. **2** to herald. *~v.i.* to utter prophecies. **prophesier** (-sīə) *n.*

prophet (prof´it) *n.* **1** a person who foretells future events, esp. under divine inspiration. **2** a revealer or interpreter of the divine will. **3** a religious leader, a founder of a religion. **4** a preacher or teacher of a cause etc. **5** (*sl.*) a tipster. **prophetess** *n.* a woman prophet. **prophethood, prophetship** *n.* **prophetic** (-fet´-), **prophetical** *a.* **1** of, relating to or containing prophecy. **2** predictive, anticipative. **prophetically** *adv.*

prophylactic (profilak´tik) *a.* **1** protecting against disease. **2** preventive. *~n.* **1** a preventive medicine. **2** (*esp. N Am.*) a condom. **prophylaxis** (-lak´sis) *n.* preventive treatment against disease.

propinquity (prəping´kwiti) *n.* **1** nearness in time, space or relationship. **2** similarity.

propionic acid (prōpion´ik), **propanoic acid** (prōpanō´ik) *n.* (*Chem.*) a colourless carboxylic acid used esp. to inhibit the growth of mould in bread.

propitiate (prəpish´iāt) *v.t.* to appease, to conciliate; to render well-disposed. **propitiation** (-ā´shən) *n.* **1** the act of propitiating, appeasement. **2** (*Bible*) atonement, esp. that of Christ. **propitiator** *n.* **propitiatory** *a.* intended or serving to propitiate. **propitiatorily** *adv.* **propitious** (-shəs) *a.* **1** (of an omen) favourable. **2** disposed to be kind or gracious. **3** auspicious, suitable (for etc.). **propitiously** *adv.* **propitiousness** *n.*

propolis (prop´əlis) *n.* a resinous substance obtained by bees from buds etc. and used to cement their combs, stop up crevices etc.

proponent (prəpō´nənt) *a.* proposing or advocating. *~n.* **1** a person who makes a proposal or proposition. **2** a person who argues for, an advocate.

proportion (prəpaw´shən) n. 1 the comparative relation of one part or thing to another with respect to magnitude, number or degree; ratio. 2 due relation, suitable or pleasing adaptation of one part or thing to others. 3 a proportional part, a share. 4 (pl.) dimensions. 5 (Math.) a equality of ratios between pairs of quantities. b a series of such quantities. ~v.t. 1 to adjust in suitable proportion. 2 to make proportionate (to). 3 to apportion. in proportion 1 in due relation as to magnitude, number etc. 2 consistent with the real importance of the matter in hand. out of proportion not in proportion. proportionable a. 1 capable of being made proportional. 2 being in proportion, corresponding, proportional. proportionably adv. proportional a. 1 having due proportion. 2 of or relating to proportion. 3 (Math.) having a constant ratio. ~n. a quantity in proportion with others, each of the terms of a ratio. proportionalist n. an advocate of proportional representation. proportionality (-nal´-) n. proportionally adv. proportional representation n. an electoral system in which the representation of parties in an elected body is as nearly as possible proportional to their voting strength. proportionate (-nət) a. in due or a certain proportion (to). proportionately adv. proportionateness n. proportioned a. proportionless a. proportionment n.

Usage note *Proportion* should not be used as though it meant simply a part (without implicit comparison).

propose (prəpōz´) v.t. 1 to put forward, to offer, to present for consideration. 2 to nominate for election. 3 to put forward as a plan, to purpose, to intend. 4 to present (a person etc.) as the subject for a toast. ~v.i. 1 to put forward a plan or intention. 2 to make an offer, esp. of marriage. proposable a. proposal n. 1 the act, or an instance, of proposing. 2 something proposed. 3 an offer of marriage. proposer n.

proposition (propəzish´ən) n. 1 something which is propounded. 2 a statement, an assertion. 3 (Logic) a sentence in which something is affirmed or denied. 4 (Math.) a formal statement of a theorem or problem, sometimes with the demonstration. 5 a proposal, a scheme proposed for consideration or adoption. 6 an invitation to have sexual intercourse. 7 (coll.) a person or thing that has to be dealt with, esp. when considered in terms of success or failure. ~v.t. (coll.) to make a proposition to, esp. to invite to have sexual intercourse. not a proposition not likely to succeed. propositional a.

propound (prəpownd´) v.t. 1 to state or set out for consideration, to propose. 2 (Law) to bring forward (a will etc.) for probate. propounder n.

proprietor (prəprī´ətə) n. an owner, esp. of a business; a person who has the exclusive legal

right or title to anything, whether in possession or not, a possessor in one's own right. proprietary a. 1 of or relating to a proprietor or proprietorship. 2 owned as property. 3 (of a product) made and marketed under a patent, trademark etc. proprietary name, proprietary term n. a name of a product registered as a trademark. proprietorial (-taw´ri-) a. proprietorially adv. proprietorship n. proprietress proprietrix n.

propriety (prəprī´əti) n. (pl. proprieties) 1 the quality of being conformable to an acknowledged or correct standard or rule. 2 fitness, correctness, rightness; correctness of behaviour, becomingness. 3 (pl.) the rules of correct or polite behaviour.

proprioception (prōpriəsep´shən) n. reception of, or activation by, stimuli from within the organism. proprioceptive a.

propulsion (prəpŭl´shən) n. the act, or an instance, of propelling, a driving forward. propulsive, †propulsory a.

propyl (prō´pīl, -pil) n. (Chem.) a hydrocarbon radical derived from propane. propyl alcohol n. an aliphatic alcohol, propanol. propylene (prop´ilēn) n. a colourless, gaseous alkene obtained from petroleum.

pro rata (prō rah´tə) a. proportional. ~adv. proportionally, in proportion.

prorate (prōrāt´, prō´-) v.t. (esp. N Am.) to distribute proportionally. proration (-ā´shən) n.

prorogue (prərōg´) v.t. (pres.p. proroguing, past, p.p. prorogued) to put an end to the meetings of (Parliament) without dissolving it. ~v.i. to be prorogued. prorogation (-ā´shən) n.

pros- (pros) pref. 1 to, towards. 2 before. 3 in addition.

prosaic (prəzā´ik) a. 1 of, relating to or resembling prose. 2 unpoetic, unimaginative. 3 dull, commonplace. prosaically adv. prosaicness n. prosaism n. prosaist (prō´-) n. 1 a writer of prose. 2 a prosaic person.

proscenium (prəse´niəm) n. (pl. prosceniums, proscenia (-niə)) 1 the part of a stage between the curtain and the orchestra. 2 (also proscenium arch) the frame through which the audience views the traditional type of stage.

prosciutto (proshoo´tō) n. (pl. prosciutti (-tē), prosciuttos) cured Italian ham, usu. eaten as an hors d'œuvre.

proscribe (prəskrīb´) v.t. 1 to interdict, to forbid. 2 to denounce as dangerous. proscriber n. proscription (-skrip´-) n. proscriptive (-skrip´-) a.

Usage note See note under PRESCRIBE.

prose (prōz) n. 1 ordinary written or spoken language not in metre, as distinct from verse. 2 a passage of prose for translation into a foreign language. 3 commonplaceness. 4 a tedious or unimaginative discourse. ~a. 1 written in or consisting of prose. 2 dull, commonplace, prosaic. ~v.i. to write or talk in a dull, tedious manner. ~v.t. **1** to write or utter in prose. **2** to turn into prose. **proselike** a. **prose poem, prose poetry** n. a piece of prose that has some of the characteristics of poetry. **proser** n. **prosify** (-fī) v.t. (3rd pers. sing. pres. **prosifies**, pres.p. **prosifying**, past, p.p. **prosified**) **1** to turn into prose. **2** to make prosaic. ~v.i. to write prose. **prosy** a. (comp. **prosier**, superl. **prosiest**) dull, tedious, long-winded. **prosily** adv. **prosiness** n.

prosecute (pros'ikūt) v.t. **1** to take legal proceedings against. **2** to seek to obtain by legal process. **3** to pursue or follow up with a view to attaining or accomplishing. **4** to carry on (work, trade etc.). ~v.i. **1** to act as a prosecutor. **2** to take legal proceedings against someone. **prosecutable** a. **prosecution** (-kū'shən) n. **1** the act, or an instance, of prosecuting. **2** the setting out of a charge against an accused person before a court. **3** the instituting and carrying on of a civil or criminal suit. **4** the prosecutor or prosecutors collectively. **prosecutor** n. a person who prosecutes, esp. in a criminal court. **prosecutorial** (-taw'riəl) a. **prosecutrix** (-triks) n. a woman prosecutor.

proselyte (pros'ilīt) n. a new convert to some religion, party or system, esp. a gentile convert to Judaism. ~v.t. (NAm.) to proselytize. **proselytism** (-li-) n. **proselytize** (-li-), **proselytise** v.t., v.i. **proselytization** (-zā'shən) n. **proselytizer** n.

prosify PROSE.

prosimian (prōsim'iən) a. (Zool.) of or relating to a primitive suborder of primates, Prosimii, which includes lemurs, lorises and tarsiers. ~n. any primate of the Prosimii.

prosody (pros'ədi) n. **1** the study of the art of versification, formerly regarded as a branch of grammar. **2** the study of the rhythms and intonation of a language. **prosodist** n.

prospect[1] (pros'pekt) n. **1** an extensive view of a landscape etc. **2** the way a house etc. fronts or looks. **3** a scene. **4** a pictorial representation of a view. **5** a mental picture of what is to come. **6** expectation, ground of expectation. **7** (pl.) expectation of money to come or of an advancement in career. **8** a prospective customer. **9** a place likely to yield ore. **10** a sample of ore for testing. **11** the mineral obtained by testing. **prospectless** a.

prospect[2] (prəspekt') v.i. **1** to search, to explore a place, esp. for minerals. **2** to work a mine experimentally. **3** to promise well or ill (of a mine). ~v.t. **1** to search or explore (a region) for minerals. **2** to promise (a good or poor yield). **prospection** n. **prospective** a. **1** of or relating to the future. **2** anticipated, expected, probable. **3** looking to the future. **prospectively** adv. **prospectiveness** n. **prospector** n. a person who searches for minerals or mining sites.

prospectus (prəspek'təs) n. (pl. **prospectuses**) a descriptive circular announcing the main objects and plans of a commercial scheme, institution, literary work etc.

prosper (pros'pə) v.i. to succeed; to thrive. ~v.t. to make successful or fortunate. **prosperity** (-sper'-) n. the condition of being prosperous; success, wealth. **prosperous** a. **1** successful, thriving, making progress, or advancement. **2** favourable, fortunate, auspicious. **prosperously** adv. **prosperousness** n.

prostaglandin (prostəglan'din) n. any of a group of hormone-like substances which have wide-ranging effects on body processes, e.g. muscle contraction.

prostate (pros'tāt) n. the prostate gland. ~a. situated in front. **prostatectomy** (-stətek'təmi) n. (pl. **prostatectomies**) surgical removal of the prostate gland. **prostate gland** n. a gland situated round the neck of the bladder in male mammals, secreting a fluid which forms part of semen. **prostatic** (-tat'-) a., n.

Usage note The noun and adjective *prostate* and the adjective *prostrate* should not be confused: there is only one *r* in the word for the male gland; *prostrate* means lying flat, overcome.

---

prosthesis (pros'thəsis, -thē'-) n. (pl. **prostheses** (-sēz)) **1** the addition of an artificial part for the body to supply a deficiency. **2** an artificial part thus supplied. **3** (Gram.) the addition of one or more letters to the beginning of a word. **prosthetic** (-thet'-) a. **prosthetically** adv. **prosthetics** n. the branch of surgery or dentistry concerned with prosthesis.

prostitute (pros'titūt) n. **1** a person (esp. a woman or girl) who engages in sexual activity for money. **2** a person who hires out their work, talent etc. for unworthy purposes. ~v.t. **1** to hire (oneself, another) out for sexual purposes. **2** to offer or sell for base or unworthy purposes. **3** to devote to unworthy uses. ~a. prostituted. **prostitution** (-tū'shən) n. **prostitutor** (pros'-) n.

prostrate[1] (pros'trāt) a. **1** lying flat or prone. **2** lying in a horizontal position, procumbent, lying in a posture of humility or at mercy. **3** overcome (by grief etc.), exhausted. **4** (Bot.) growing along the ground.

Usage note See note under PROSTRATE.

---

prostrate[2] (prostrāt') v.t. **1** to lay (a person etc.) flat. **2** to throw (oneself) down, esp. in reverence or adoration (before). **3** to throw down, to overthrow, to overcome, to demolish. **4** to reduce to physical exhaustion. **prostration** (-ā'shən) n.

prosy PROSE.

Prot. abbr. **1** Protectorate. **2** Protestant.

protactinium (prōtaktin'ium) n. (Chem.) a radioactive metallic element, at. no. 91, chem. symbol Pa, yielding actinium on disintegration.

protagonist (prətag'ənist) n. **1** an advocate, champion etc. (of a cause). **2** the leading character in any play or story. **3** a leading contestant.

protamine (prō´təmēn) *n.* any of a group of simple proteins occurring in the sperm of some fish.

protea (prō´tiə) *n.* any member of a S African genus of shrubs and small trees, *Protea*, with large cone-shaped flowers.

protean (prō´tiən, prōtē´ən) *a.* **1** readily assuming different shapes or aspects; variable, changeable. **2** (of an artist etc.) versatile.

protease (prō´tiāz) *n.* any enzyme which can hydrolyse proteins; a proteolytic enzyme.

protect (prətekt´) *v.t.* **1** to shield, defend or keep safe (from or against injury, danger etc.). **2** to support (industries) against foreign competition by imposing duties on imports. **3** to provide funds so as to guarantee payment of (bills etc.). **4** to screen (e.g. machinery) so as to minimize the risk of injury etc. **protectingly** *adv.* **protection** *n.* **1** the act, or an instance, of protecting. **2** the state of being protected. **3** something which protects, a covering, shield or defence. **4** a passport, a safe conduct. **5** protection money. **6** (*coll.*) freedom from injury, molestation etc. purchased by protection money. **7** (*N Am.*) a certificate of citizenship of the US issued to seamen by the customs authorities. **8** protectionism. **protectionism** *n.* the doctrine or system of protecting home industries against foreign competition by import duties etc. **protectionist** *n., a.* **protection money** *n.* a bribe extorted by gangsters from shopkeepers etc. by threats of damage to property, personal assault etc. **protection racket** *n.* an organized system whereby gangsters extort protection money. **protective** *a.* **1** affording protection; intended to protect. **2** (of a person) desirous of shielding another from harm or distress. **3** (of food) protecting against disease, esp. deficiency diseases. ~*n.* **1** something that protects. **2** a condom. **protective clothing** *n.* clothing, esp. covering the whole body, made of materials which protect the body from heat, toxic substances etc. **protective coloration, protective colouring** *n.* colouring that enables animals to escape detection by blending with their surroundings, camouflage. **protective custody** *n.* detention before trial in order to ensure an accused's personal safety. **protectively** *adv.* **protectiveness** *n.*

protector (prətek´tə) *n.* **1** a person who protects against injury or evil etc.; a guardian or patron. **2** a protective device, a guard. **3** (*Hist.*) (**Protector**) a person in charge of a kingdom during the minority, incapacity etc. of the sovereign. **4** (**Protector**) a title of Oliver Cromwell, Lord Protector of the Commonwealth, 1653–58, and his son Richard Cromwell, 1658–59. **protectoral** *a.* **protectorate** (-rət) *n.* **1** protection, usu. com-

bined with partial control, of a weak state by a more powerful one. **2** territory under such protection. **3** (**Protectorate**) the office of protector of a kingdom. **4** (**Protectorate**) the period of this, esp. that of Oliver and Richard Cromwell. **protectorless** *a.* **protectress, protectrix** *n.*

protégé (prot´āzhā, prō´-) *n.* a person under the protection, care, or patronage of another. **protégée** *n.* a female protégé.

protein (prō´tēn) *n.* **1** any of a class of complex organic compounds, containing carbon, oxygen, hydrogen and nitrogen, usu. with some sulphur, found in all living organisms and forming an essential constituent of animal foods. **2** such compounds collectively, esp. considered as a component in foodstuffs. **proteinaceous** (-nā´shəs), **proteinic** (-tē´-), **proteinous** (-tē´-) *a.*

pro tem (prō tem´), **pro tempore** (tem´pəri) *a.* temporary. ~*adv.* for the time being.

proteolysis (prōtiol´isis) *n.* (*Chem.*) the resolution or splitting up of proteins or peptides by the process of digestion or the application of enzymes. **proteolytic** (-lit´-) *a.*

Proterozoic (protərōzō´ik) *a.* (*Geol.*) of or relating to the later part of the Precambrian era, when the earliest forms of life appeared. ~*n.* this era.

protest[1] (prətest´) *v.i.* **1** to make a solemn affirmation. **2** to express dissent or objection. ~*v.t.* **1** to affirm or declare formally or earnestly. **2** to object (that). **3** (*N Am.*) to express one's disapproval of or objection to. **4** (*Law*) to make a formal declaration, usu. by a notary public, that payment (of a bill) has been demanded and refused. **protester** *n.* **protestingly** *adv.* **protestor** *n.*

protest[2] (prō´test) *n.* **1** the act, or an instance, of protesting. **2** a solemn or formal declaration of opinion, usu. of dissent or remonstrance. **3** an expression or demonstration of dissent, disapproval etc. **4** (*Law*) a formal declaration, by the holder, of the non-payment of a bill. **under protest** unwillingly; having expressed objections.

Protestant (prot´istənt) *n.* **1** a member of a Church upholding the principles of the Reformation, or (loosely) of any western Church not within the Roman communion. **2** (**protestant**) a person who makes a protest. ~*a.* **1** of or relating to the Protestants, or to Protestantism. **2** (**protestant**) making a protest. **Protestantism** *n.* **Protestantize, Protestantise** *v.t., v.i.*

protestation (protistā´shən) *n.* **1** a solemn affirmation or declaration. **2** a solemn declaration of dissent, a protest.

Proteus (prō´tiəs) *n.* (*pl.* **Proteuses**) **1** a changeable, shifty or fickle person or thing. **2** (**proteus**) an olm. **3** (**proteus**) a member of the genus *Proteus* of bacteria, found in animal intestines.

prothallium (prōthal´iəm) *n.* (*pl.* **prothallia**

prothallus

994 **prove**

(-iə)) (*Bot.*) a cellular structure bearing the sexual organs in vascular cryptogams.

prothallus (prōthal´əs) *n.* (*pl.* **prothalli** (-lī)) a prothallium.

protist (prō´tist) *n.* any organism of the kingdom Protista, microscopic organisms whose position (as animals or plants) is doubtful, incl. protozoans, algae and fungi. **protistology** (-tol´-) *n.*

protium (prō´tiəm) *n.* (*Chem.*) the ordinary isotope of hydrogen, of atomic weight 1, as distinct from *deuterium, tritium.*

proto- (prō´tō), **prot-** *comb. form* **1** chief. **2** earliest, original, primitive, ancestral. **3** denoting that chemical compound in a series in which the distinctive element or radical combines in the lowest proportion with another element. **4** denoting the earliest, reconstructed, form of a language, as *proto-Celtic, proto-Germanic.*

protocol (prō´təkol) *n.* **1** the original draft of an official document or transaction, esp. minutes or a rough draft of a diplomatic instrument or treaty, signed by the parties to a negotiation. **2** the formal etiquette and procedure governing diplomatic and ceremonial functions. **3** the customs and rules of etiquette governing any social or official occasion. **4** the official formulas used to start and finish diplomatic instruments, charters, wills etc. **5** an official memorandum or account. **6** an annexe to a treaty which adds to its provisions or clarifies them. **7** (*N Am.*) a record of observations in scientific experiments. **8** (*Comput.*) a set of rules governing the transmission of data between two devices which are not directly connected. ~*v.i.* (*pres.p.* **protocolling**, *past, p.p.* **protocolled**) to draft protocols. ~*v.t.* to reduce to or record in a protocol.

protolanguage (prō´tōlang·gwij) ´*n.* a hypothetical language, the earliest ancestor of any group of modern languages and reconstructed from them.

protomartyr (prōtōmah´tə) *n.* **1** a first martyr (applied esp. to St Stephen). **2** the first who suffers in any cause.

proton (prō´ton) *n.* (*pl.* **protons**) (*Physics*) a particle occurring in atomic nuclei and identical with the nucleus of the hydrogen atom, having an electric charge equal and opposite to that of the electron, and a mass 1840 times as great. **protonic** (-ton´-) *a.*

protopectin (prōtōpek´tin) *n.* pectose.

protophyte (prō´təfīt) *n.* a unicellular plant bearing gametes.

protoplasm (prō´tōplazm) *n.* (*Biol.*) the viscid semifluid substance composed of oxygen, hydrogen, carbon and nitrogen, constituting the living matter of a cell and its nucleus. **protoplasmal** (-plaz´-), **protoplasmatic** (-mat´-), **protoplasmic** (-plaz´-) *a.*

protoplast (prō´təplahst) *n.* (*Biol.*) a unit of protoplasm, the nucleus and cytoplasm of a cell, but not the cell wall. **protoplastic** (-plas´-) *a.*

prototherian (prōtəthiə´riən) *n.* any mammal of the subclass Prototheria, comprising the Monotremata and their ancestors. ~*a.* of or relating to the subclass Prototheria.

prototype (prō´tətīp) *n.* **1** an original or primary person or thing, an exemplar, an archetype. **2** a pre-production model on which tests can be carried out to trace design faults, indicate possible improvements etc. ~*v.t.* to make a prototype of. **prototypal** (-tī´-) *a.* **prototypical** (-tip´-), **prototypic** *a.* **prototypically** *adv.*

protozoan (prōtəzō´ən), **protozoon** (-zō´on) *n.* (*pl.* **protozoans, protozoa** (-zō´ə)) any member of the phylum Protozoa, consisting of microscopic unicellular organisms, amoebas, ciliates etc. ~*a.* of or relating to this phylum. **protozoal** *a.* **protozoic** *a.*

protract (prətrakt´) *v.t.* **1** to extend in duration, to prolong. **2** to draw (a map, plan etc.) to scale, esp. with a scale and protractor. **protracted** *a.* **protractedly** *adv.* **protractedness** *n.* **protracter** *n.* **protractile** (-tīl) *a.* (of the organ etc. of an animal) capable of extension. **protraction** *n.* **protractor** *n.* **1** an instrument, usu. in the form of a graduated arc, for laying down angles on paper etc. **2** a muscle that protracts or extends a limb.

protrude (prətrood´) *v.t.* **1** to thrust forward or out. **2** to cause to project or thrust out. ~*v.i.* to project, to be thrust forward, or above a surface. **protrudent** *a.* **protrusible** (-si-) *a.* **protrusile** (-sīl) *a.* (*Zool.*) capable of being thrust forward, as a limb, jaw etc. **protrusion** (-zhən) *n.* **protrusive** *a.* **protrusively** *adv.*

protuberant (prətū´bərənt) *a.* swelling, bulging out, prominent. **protuberance** *n.* **protuberantly** *adv.*

Usage note The forms *protruberant, protruberance* etc. (after *protrude*) are best avoided.

proud (prowd) *a.* **1** having high or inordinate self-esteem; haughty, arrogant. **2** having a due sense of dignity. **3** elated, exultant, feeling honoured, pleased, gratified. **4** grand, imposing. **5** (of words, looks etc.) stately, inspired by pride. **6** (of deeds etc.) inspiring pride, noble, grand. **7** projecting, standing out above a plane surface. **8** (of a stream) swollen, in flood. **to do someone proud 1** to entertain someone lavishly. **2** to give someone cause to be proud. **proud-hearted** *a.* proud in spirit, arrogant. **proudly** *adv.* **proudness** *n.*

prove (proov) *v.t.* (*past* **proved**, *p.p.* **proved**, **proven** (proo´vən, prō´-)) **1** to establish or demonstrate the truth of by argument, reasoning or testimony. **2** to test, to try by experiment, to make trial of. **3** to show to be true. **4** (*Math. etc.*) to test the accuracy of, esp. by an established procedure. **5** to have experience of, to undergo. **6** to establish the authenticity or validity of. **7** to obtain probate of (a will). **7** (*Print.*) to take a proof impression from. ~*v.i.* **1** to be found by experience or trial. **2** to turn out to be. **3** to turn out (to be). **4** to make a trial or attempt. **5** (of dough) to rise and become aerated before baking. **not proven** (*Sc. Law*) not proved (a verdict given when there is not sufficient evidence to convict). **to go to prove** to go to show. **to prove oneself** to do something which shows one's qualities, esp. courage. **provable** *a.* **provability** (-bil´-), **provableness** *n.* **provably** *adv.*

Usage note The past participle *proven* is largely encountered in Scottish and American English, although it occurs in a few fixed expressions (as *of proven ability*) and, increasingly, in television and radio advertising with overtones of the technical sense 'tested'.

provenance (prov´inəns) *n.* **1** an origin or source. **2** the place of origin of a work of art.

Provençal (provāsahl´) *n.* **1** a native or inhabitant of Provence (France). **2** the Romance language of Provence. ~*a.* of or relating to Provence, its language, or inhabitants.

provender (prov´əndə) *n.* **1** dry food for beasts, fodder. **2** (*facet.*) provisions, food.

provenience (prəvēn´yəns) *n.* (*esp. N Am.*) PROVENANCE.

proverb (prov´œb) *n.* **1** a short, pithy sentence, containing some truth or wise reflection proved by experience or observation; a maxim, a saw, an adage. **2** a typical example, a byword. **proverbial** (prəvœ´-) *a.* **1** like, or of the nature of, a proverb. **2** notorious. **proverbiality** (-al´-) *n.* **proverbially** *adv.*

provide (prəvīd´) *v.t.* **1** to procure or prepare beforehand. **2** to furnish, to supply. **3** to equip (with). **4** to lay down as a preliminary condition, to stipulate. ~*v.i.* **1** to make preparation or provision (for or against). **2** to furnish means of subsistence (for a person). **provided** *a.* **1** supplied, furnished. **2** laid down, stipulated. ~*conj.* on the understanding or condition (that). **provider** *n.* **1** a person or thing that provides. **2** the breadwinner of a family. **providing** *n.* the action of supplying, furnishing or preparing beforehand. ~*conj.* provided (that).

providence (prov´idəns) *n.* **1** the beneficent care or control of God or nature. **2** (**Providence**) God or nature regarded as exercising such care. **3** foresight, timely care or preparation. **4** frugality, economy, prudence. **provident** *a.* **1** making provision for the future, thrifty. **2** showing foresight, prudent. **providential** (-den´-) *a.* **1** due to or effected by divine providence. **2** lucky, fortunate, opportune. **providentially** *adv.* **providently** *adv.* **Provident Society** *n.* a Friendly Society.

province (prov´ins) *n.* **1** a large administrative division of a kingdom, country or state. **2** (*pl.*) all parts of a country except the metropolis. **3** a proper sphere of action, business, knowledge etc. **4** the territory under the authority of an archbishop or metropolitan. **provincial** (-vin´shəl) *a.* **1** of or relating to a province. **2**

constituting a province. **3** of, relating to or characteristic of the provinces. **4** narrow, rustic, unpolished, uncultured. ~*n.* **1** a person who belongs to a province or the provinces. **2** a narrow-minded or unsophisticated person. **3** the superior of a religious order etc., in a province. **provincialism** *n.* **1** the quality of being provincial. **2** a mode of speech, thought, behaviour etc., or a word or expression, peculiar to a province or the provinces. **3** the restricting of one's interest to local affairs, narrow-mindedness. **provincialist** *n.* **provinciality** (-shial´-) *n.* **provincialize, provincialise** *v.t.* **provincially** *adv.*

provision (prəvizh´ən) *n.* **1** the act, or an instance, of providing. **2** something provided, or prepared beforehand. **3** a stipulation or condition providing for something. **4** a clause in a law or a deed. **5** (*pl.*) a supply of food etc. for a household. **6** (*pl.*) food and drink prepared for an expedition. ~*v.t.* to provide with provisions. **provisional** *a.* **1** provided for present need; temporary, not permanent. **2** requiring future confirmation. **3** (**Provisional**) denoting the militant breakaway faction of the IRA or Sinn Fein. ~*n.* (**Provisional**) a member of the Provisional IRA. **provisionality** (-nal´-) *n.* **provisionally** *adv.* **provisionalness** *n.* **provisioner** *n.* **provisionless** *a.* **provisionment** *n.*

proviso (prəvī´zō) *n.* (*pl.* **provisos, provisoes**) **1** a provisional condition, a stipulation. **2** a clause in a covenant or other document rendering its operation conditional.

provisory (prəvī´zəri) *a.* **1** conditional. **2** provisional. **provisorily** *adv.*

Provo (prō´vō) *n.* (*pl.* **Provos**) (*coll.*) a member of the Provisional IRA.

provoke (prəvōk´) *v.t.* **1** to rouse; to incite or stimulate to action, anger etc. **2** to irritate, to incense, to exasperate. **3** to instigate, to call forth, to cause. **4** to tempt. **provocation** (provəkā´shən) *n.* **1** the act, or an instance, of provoking. **2** something that provokes or irritates. **3** (*Law*) an action that provokes a physical attack. **provocative** (-vok´-) *a.* **1** tending to provoke, esp. sexual desire. **2** irritating, annoying, esp. with the intention to excite anger or rouse to action. ~*n.* a provocative action, thing, word etc. **provocatively** *adv.* **provocativeness** *n.* **provokable** *a.* **provoker** *n.* **provoking** *a.* tending to provoke, annoying, exasperating. **provokingly** *adv.*

provost (prov´əst) *n.* **1** the head of some colleges or schools. **2** the head of a chapter, a prior, a dignitary in a cathedral corresponding to a dean. **3** (*Sc.*) the head of a municipal corporation or burgh. **4** in Germany, a Protestant minister in charge of the principal church in a town. **5** (*Hist.*) an officer in charge of a body of men, establishment etc. a steward, a provost marshal. **6** (*US*) a senior administrative officer in a university. **provost guard** (prəvō´) *n.* (*US*) a detachment of soldiers commanded by a provost marshal. **provost marshal** (prəvō´) *n.* **1** a commissioned officer, the head of the military police in a camp or in the field. **2** a naval officer in charge of prisoners awaiting court-martial. **provostship, provostry** *n.*

prow (prow) *n.* **1** the fore part of a vessel, the bow. **2** the projecting front part of anything, such as the nose of an aeroplane.

prowess (prow´is) *n.* **1** outstanding ability or skill. **2** valour, bravery, gallantry.

prowl (prowl) *v.i.* to rove (about) stealthily as if in search of prey. ~*v.t.* to go through or about (a place) in this way. ~*n.* the act or an instance of prowling. **on the prowl** prowling in search of prey. **prowl car** *n.* (*US*) a police patrol car. **prowler** *n.*

prox. *abbr.* proximo.

proxemics (proksē´miks) *n.* the study of the spatial relationships of people in ordinary conditions and activities.

proximal (prok´siməl) *a.* nearest the centre of the body or the point of attachment, as distinct from *distal*. **proximally** *adv.* **proximate** (-ət) *a.* **1** nearest, next. **2** immediately preceding or following. **3** approximate. **proximately** *adv.* **proximity** (-sim´-) *n.* immediate nearness in place, time, relation etc., esp. of kinship. **proximity fuse** *n.* an electronic device which detonates a missile when it gets near its target.

proximo (prok´simō) *a.* in or of the month succeeding the present, next month (in old commercial use).

proxy (prok´si) *n.* (*pl.* **proxies**) **1** the agency of a substitute for a principal. **2** a person deputed to act for another, esp. in voting. **3** a document authorizing one person to act or vote for another. **4** a vote given under this authority. ~*a.* done, made etc. by proxy. **proxyship** *n.*

prude (prood) *n.* a person who affects great modesty or propriety, esp. in regard to sexual matters. **prudery** (-əri) *n.* (*pl.* **pruderies**). **prudish** *a.* **prudishly** *adv.* **prudishness** *n.*

prudent (proo´dənt) *a.* **1** cautious, discreet, circumspect. **2** worldly-wise, careful of consequences. **3** showing good judgement or foresight. **prudence** *n.* **prudential** (-den´shəl) *a.* actuated òr characterized by prudence. **prudentialism** *n.* **prudentialist** *n.* **prudentiality** (-shial´-) *n.* **prudentially** *adv.* **prudentials** *n.pl.* **1** prudential considerations, matters of practical wisdom. **2** (*N Am.*) administrative or financial matters, esp. minor ones. **prudently** *adv.*

Usage note The meanings of the adjectives *prudent* and *prudential* overlap, but *prudent* is a term of approval, applied to people as well as actions, and *prudential* is more neutral and usually describes the conduct of business.

pruinose (proo´inōs) *a.* (*Bot.*) covered with a white powdery substance or bloom, frosted.

prune¹ (proon) *n.* **1** the dried fruit of various kinds of *Prunus domestica*, the common plum. **2** (*coll.*) a stupid or uninteresting person.

prune² (proon) *v.t.* **1** to cut or lop off the superfluous branches etc. from (a shrub or tree). **2** to cut or lop (branches etc.) from a shrub or tree. **3** to reduce (costs, administration etc.). **4** to free from anything superfluous or undesirable. ~*n.* an instance of pruning. **pruner** *n.* **pruning hook, pruning knife, pruning shears** *n.* an instrument of various forms for pruning trees etc.

prunella¹ (prunel´ə) *n.* any plant of the labiate genus *Prunella*, with purplish, bluish or white flowers, the common self-heal.

prunella² (prunel´ə) *n.* a smooth dark silk or woollen cloth, used for making the uppers of shoes and gaiters, and formerly for clergymen's and barristers' gowns.

prurient (prua´riənt) *a.* **1** disposed to, characterized by or arousing an unhealthy interest in sexual matters. **2** characterized by a morbid curiosity. **prurience, pruriency** *n.* **pruriently** *adv.*

prurigo (proori´gō) *n.* a papular disease of the skin producing severe itching. **pruriginous** (-rij´-) *a.* **pruritus** (-təs) *n.* (*Med.*) itching. **pruritic** (-rit´ik) *a.*

Prussian (prŭsh´ən) *a.* of or relating to Prussia, a former German state. ~*n.* (*Hist.*) a native or inhabitant of Prussia. **Prussian blue** *n.* a deep-blue pigment obtained from ferrocyanide or iron. **Prussian-blue** *a.* **prussic acid** (prŭs´-) *n.* hydrocyanic acid, first obtained from Prussian blue.

pry¹ (prī) *v.i.* (*3rd pers. sing. pres.* **pries**, *pres.p.* **prying**, *past, p.p.* **pried**) **1** to look closely or inquisitively; to peep, to peer. **2** to search or enquire curiously or impertinently (into). **prying** *a.* **pryingly** *adv.*

pry² (prī) *v.t.* (*3rd pers. sing. pres.* **pries**, *pres.p.* **prying**, *past, p.p.* **pried**) (*N Am.*) to prise.

PS *abbr.* **1** Police Sergeant. **2** postscript. **3** private secretary. **4** (in a theatre) prompt side.

psalm (sahm) *n.* **1** a sacred song or hymn. **2** (**Psalm**) any one of the sacred songs contained in the Book of Psalms. **psalm-book** *n.* a book, for use in church, containing psalms, esp. in metrical form. **psalmic** *a.* **psalmist** *n.* a composer of psalms. **psalmody** (sah´mədi, sal´-) *n.* (*pl.* **psalmodies**) **1** the act, art or practice of singing psalms, esp. in divine worship. **2** psalms collectively. **3** the setting to music of psalms. **psalmodic** (-mod´-) *a.* **psalmodist** (sah´-) *n.* **psalmodize, psalmodise** *v.i.*

psalter (sawl´tə) *n.* **1** (**Psalter**) The Book of Psalms. **2** a version of this. **3** a book containing the Psalms for use in divine service, esp. the version of the Psalms in the Prayer Book or the Latin collection used in the Roman Catholic Church.

psalterium (sawltiə´riəm) *n.* (*pl.* **psalteria** (-riə)) the third stomach of a ruminant, the omasum.

psaltery (sawl´təri) n. (pl. **psalteries**) a medieval stringed instrument somewhat resembling the dulcimer, but played by plucking the strings.

PSBR abbr. public sector borrowing requirement.

psephology (sefol´əji) n. the statistical and sociological study of elections, voting patterns etc. **psephological** (-loj´-) a. **psephologically** adv. **psephologist** n.

pseud (sūd) n. (coll.) an affected or pretentious person, a pretender, a sham. ~a. pseudo. **pseudery** n. **pseudo** (sū´dō) a. 1 false, sham, spurious. 2 affected, pretentious. ~n. (pl. **pseudos**) an insincere or pretentious person.

pseudo- (sū´dō), **pseud-** comb. form 1 false, counterfeit, spurious. 2 closely resembling, as pseudoclassical, pseudo-Gothic, pseudohistorical.

pseudocarp (sū´dōkahp) n. a fruit composed of other parts besides the ovary.

pseudomorph (sū´dəmawf) n. 1 a mineral having the crystalline form of another. 2 a false form. **pseudomorphic** (-maw´-) a. **pseudomorphism** (-maw´-) n. **pseudomorphous** (-maw´-) a.

pseudonym (sū´dənim) n. a fictitious name, esp. a pen name. **pseudonymity** (-nim´-) n. **pseudonymous** (-don´-) a. **pseudonymously** adv.

pseudopod (sū´dəpod) n. 1 a pseudopodium. 2 a protrusion from the bodywall of e.g. a caterpillar, used as a leg.

pseudopodium (sūdōpō´diəm) n. (pl. **pseudopodia** (-diə)) a temporary protrusion from the cell surface of a protozoan etc., used for movement or feeding. **pseudopodial** a.

pseudo-science (sūdōsī´əns) n. a spurious science, an untested set of beliefs that passes as a science. **pseudo-scientific** (-tif´-) a.

psi (sī) n. 1 the twenty-third letter of the Greek alphabet (Ψ, ψ), equivalent to ps. 2 paranormal or psychic phenomena collectively.

p.s.i. abbr. pounds per square inch.

psilocybin (sīlōsī´bin) n. a hallucinogenic drug obtained from Mexican mushrooms of the genus Psilocybe.

psilosis (sīlō´sis) n. (Med.) sprue.

psittaceous (sitā´shəs), **psittacine** (sit´əsīn) a. 1 belonging or allied to the parrots. 2 parrot-like. **psittacism** n. (formal) the mechanical repetition of words or ideas, without understanding. **psittacosis** (sitəkō´sis) n. a contagious disease of parrots communicable to humans, with symptoms like those of pneumonia.

psoas (sō´əs) n. (pl. **psoases**) either of the two large muscles involved in flexing and rotating the hip joint.

psoriasis (sərī´əsis) n. a dry, scaly skin disease. **psoriatic** (-at´-) a.

psst (pəst), **pst** int. used as a whispered call to attract someone's attention surreptitiously.

PST abbr. Pacific Standard Time.

PSV abbr. public service vehicle.

psych (sīk), **psyche** v.t. (coll.) 1 to psychoanalyse. 2 to psych out. ~v.i. to make a psychic bid. **to**

psych out 1 (N Am.) to work out, to divine, to anticipate correctly (a person's motivation etc.). 2 to intimidate or defeat by psychological means. 3 (coll.) to have a psychological breakdown. **to psych up** to prepare or stimulate psychologically as a preliminary to action.

psyche (sī´ki) n. the soul, the spirit, the mind.

psychedelic (sīkədel´ik) a. 1 of or relating to new, altered or heightened states of consciousness and sensory awareness as induced by the use of certain hallucinatory drugs. 2 (of drugs) capable of producing such states. 3 having an effect on the mind similar to that of psychedelic drugs. 4 resembling the phenomena of psychedelic experience. 5 (of colours) unnaturally vivid, fluorescent. ~n. a hallucinogenic drug. **psychedelia** (-dē´liə) n.pl. 1 psychedelic objects, clothing, art etc. 2 psychedelic drugs. **psychedelically** adv.

psychiatry (sīkī´ətri) n. the study and treatment of mental disorders. **psychiatric** (-kiat´-) a. **psychiatrical** a. **psychiatrically** adv. **psychiatric nurse** n. a nurse who works with mentally ill people. **psychiatric patient** n. a person who is being treated for mental illness. **psychiatrist** n.

psychic (sī´kik) a. 1 of or relating to the human soul, spirit or mind. 2 of or relating to phenomena that appear to be outside the domain of physical law, paranormal, extrasensory. 3 (of a person) believed to be sensitive to nonphysical or paranormal forces and influences. ~n. 1 a person believed to have psychic powers, a medium. 2 a psychic bid. 3 (pl.) psychology. **psychical** a. 1 of or relating to the soul or mind. 2 of or relating to paranormal phenomena. **psychically** adv. **psychic bid** n. in bridge, a bid that deliberately gives the impression of a stronger hand than is the case. **psychicism** (-isizm) n. psychical research. **psychicist** (-isist) n. **psychism** n.

psycho (sī´kō) n. (pl. **psychos**) a psychopath. ~a. psychotic, psychopathic.

psycho- (sī´kō), **psych-** comb. form 1 mental. 2 psychical.

psychoactive (sīkōak´tiv) a. (of drugs) capable of affecting the mind or behaviour.

psychoanalysis (sīkōənal´isis) n. a method devised by Sigmund Freud for exploring and bringing to light concepts, experience etc. hidden in the unconscious mind as a form of treatment for functional nervous diseases or mental illness. **psychoanalyse** (-an´əlīz), (N Am.) **psychoanalyze** v.t. to subject to, or treat by, psychoanalysis. **psychoanalyst** (-an´ə-) n. **psychoanalytic** (-anəlit´-), **psychoanalytical** a. **psychoanalytically** adv.

psychobabble (sī´kōbabəl) n. (coll., derog.) the excessive or inappropriate use of psychological jargon, esp. in popular psychotherapy.

psychobiology (sīkōbīol´əji) n. the study of the relationship between biology and mental and behavioural phenomena. **psychobiological** (-loj´-) a. **psychobiologist** (-ol´-) n.

psychodrama (sī´kōdrahmə) n. (pl. **psychodramas**) **1** an improvised dramatization of events from a patient's past life, used as a form of mental therapy. **2** a film or a play which concentrates on the psychological development of the characters.

psychodynamics (sīkōdīnam´iks) n. the study of mental and emotional forces and their effect on behaviour. **psychodynamic** a. **psychodynamically** adv.

psychogenesis (sīkōjen´əsis) n. (the study of) the origin or development of the mind.

psychographics (sīkōgraf´iks) n. the study of personalities, aspirations, attitudes etc., esp. in market research. **psychographic** a.

psychokinesis (sīkōkinē´sis) n. apparent movement or alteration in physical objects produced by mental effort alone.

psycholinguistics (sīkōling-gwis´tiks) n. the study of the psychology of language, its acquisition, development, use etc. **psycholinguist** (-ling´-) n. **psycholinguistic** (-gwis´-) a.

psychology (sīkol´əji) n. (pl. **psychologies**) **1** science of the human mind or soul. **2** a system or theory of mental laws and phenomena. **3** (characteristic) mentality or motivation. **4** (coll.) skill in understanding or motivating people. **psychological** (-loj´-) a. **1** of or relating to psychology. **2** relating to or affecting the mind. **3** existing only in the mind. **psychological block** n. a mental block. **psychologically** adv. **psychological moment** n. the critical moment, the exact time for action etc. **psychological warfare** n. the use of propaganda to reduce enemy morale. **psychologist** n. **psychologize, psychologise** v.t., v.i.

psychometrics (sīkōmet´riks) n. the branch of psychology dealing with the measurement of mental capacities and attributes, esp. by the use of psychological tests and statistical methods. **psychometric, psychometrical** a. **psychometrically** adv. **psychometrist** (-kom´-) n. **psychometry** n. **1** psychometrics. **2** the occult faculty of divining by touching a physical object, the character, surroundings, experiences etc. of persons who have touched it.

psychomotor (sīkōmō´tə) a. of or relating to muscular action proceeding from mental activity.

psychoneurosis (sīkōnūrō´sis) n. (pl. **psychoneuroses** (-sēz)) a neurosis, esp. one due to emotional conflict.

psychopath (sī´kəpath) n. **1** a person suffering from a severe personality disorder characterized by antisocial behaviour and a tendency to commit acts of violence. **2** (coll.) a mentally or emotionally unstable person. **psychopathic** (-path´-) a. **psychopathically** adv. **psychopathy** (-kop´əthi) n. psychologically abnormal behaviour.

psychopathology (sīkōpathol´əji) n. (the branch of psychology dealing with) mental and behavioural aberrance. **psychopathological** a.

psychophysics (sīkōfiz´iks) n. the science of the relations between mind and body, esp. between physical stimuli and psychological sensation. **psychophysical** a.

psychophysiology (sīkōfiziol´əji) n. the branch of physiology which deals with mental phenomena. **psychophysiological** (-loj´-) a.

psychosexual (sīkōsek´shəl, -sūəl) a. of or relating to the psychological aspects of sex. **psychosexually** adv.

psychosis (sīkō´sis) n. (pl. **psychoses** (-sēz)) a severe mental disorder, not due to organic lesion, characterized by distortion of the sufferer's concept of reality. **psychotic** (-kot´-) n., a. (a person) suffering from psychosis. **psychotically** adv.

psychosocial (sīkōsō´shəl) a. of or relating to the interaction of social and psychological factors, esp. in illness. **psychosocially** adv.

psychosomatic (sīkōsəmat´ik) a. **1** denoting a physical disorder caused by or influenced by the patient's emotional condition. **2** of or relating to the mind and the body considered together. **psychosomatically** adv.

psychosurgery (sīkōsœ´jəri) n. the use of brain surgery in the treatment of mental disorder. **psychosurgical** a.

psychotherapy (sīkōther´əpi) n. the treatment of mental disorder by psychological or hypnotic means. **psychotherapeutic** (-therəpū´tik) a. **psychotherapeutics** n. **psychotherapist** n.

psychotic PSYCHOSIS.

psychotropic (sīkōtrō´pik, -trop´-) a. psychoactive.

psychrometer (sīkrom´itə) n. the wet-and-dry bulb hygrometer for measuring the humidity of the atmosphere.

☒ psycology common misspelling of PSYCHOLOGY.

PT abbr. physical training.

Pt chem. symbol platinum.

pt. abbr. **1** part. **2** pint(s). **3** (Math.) point. **4** port.

PTA abbr. parent-teacher association.

ptarmigan (tah´migən) n. (pl. in general **ptarmigan**, in particular **ptarmigans**) any of various birds of the genus Lagopus, allied to the grouse, having grey or brown plumage in the summer and white in the winter, esp. Lagopus mutus, of subarctic regions.

Pte. abbr. (Mil.) Private.

pteridophyte (ter´idōfīt) n. any member of the division Pteridophyta including ferns, clubmosses and horsetails.

ptero- (ter´ō), **pteri-** (-i), **pter-** comb. form **1** winged. **2** having processes resembling wings.

pterodactyl (terədak´til) n. an extinct winged reptile from the Mesozoic strata with membranous wings and a long birdlike head.

pterosaur (ter´əsaw) n. any individual of the

Pterosauria, an order of flying reptiles of the Mesozoic age.

pterygoid (ter´igoid) a. (Anat.) wing-shaped. **pterygoid process** n. either of the winglike processes descending from the great wings of the sphenoid bone of the skull.

PTFE abbr. polytetrafluoroethylene.

PTO abbr. please turn over.

Ptolemaic (toləmā´ik) a. 1 of or relating to Ptolemy, Alexandrian astronomer (2nd cent. AD) who maintained that the earth was a fixed body in the centre of the universe, the sun and moon revolving round it. 2 (Hist.) of or relating to the Ptolemies, kings of Egypt, 323–30 BC. **Ptolemaic system** n. Ptolemy's conception of the universe.

ptomaine (tō´mān) n. (Chem.) any one of a class of sometimes poisonous amines derived from decaying animal and vegetable matter.

ptosis (tō´sis) n. (pl. **ptoses** (-sēz)) a drooping of the upper eyelid from paralysis of the muscle raising it. **ptotic** (tō´tik) a.

PTSD abbr. post-traumatic stress disorder.

ptyalin (tī´əlin) n. an enzyme contained in saliva, which converts starch into dextrin.

Pu chem. symbol plutonium.

pub (pŭb) n. 1 a public house. 2 (Austral., coll.) a hotel. ~v.i. (pres.p. **pubbing**, past, p.p. **pubbed**) to visit public houses. **pub crawl** n. (coll.) a drinking tour of a number of pubs.

puberty (pū´bəti) n. the period of life at which persons become capable of begetting or bearing children. **puberal** (-bərəl), **pubertal** a. **pubes** (-bēz, pūbz) n. (pl. **pubes**) 1 the hypogastric region which in the adult becomes covered with hair. 2 (coll.) the hair of the pubic region. **pubescence** (-bes´əns) n. 1 the state or age of puberty. 2 (Bot., Zool.) soft, hairy down on plants or parts of animals, esp. insects, downiness, hairiness. **pubescent** a. **pubic** a. of or relating to the pubes or pubis. **pubis** (-bis) n. (pl. **pubises**, **pubes** (-bēz)) either of two bones forming the anterior part of the pelvis.

public (pŭb´lik) a. 1 of, relating to or affecting the people as a whole, as distinct from personal or private. 2 open to the use or enjoyment of all, not restricted to any class. 3 done, existing or such as may be observed by all, not concealed or clandestine. 4 open, notorious. 5 a well-known, prominent. b of or relating to a person in their capacity as a public figure. 6 of or relating to the affairs or service of the people. 7 employed by, or provided by, local or central government. 8 of or for a university. ~n. 1 the people in general. 2 any particular section of the people. 3 (coll.) a public house, or a public bar. **in public** openly, publicly. **in the public eye** famous. **to go public 1** to become a public company. 2 to make publicly known. **public act** n. an act of parliament that affects the public as a whole. **public address system** n. a system of microphones, amplifiers, loudspeakers etc. used for addressing a large

audience. **public analyst** n. a chemist who carries out independent analyses of consumer products to check for toxins etc. **public bar** n. a bar in a public house, usu. less well appointed, and serving drinks at cheaper prices than a saloon bar. **public bill** n. a bill before parliament that affects the public as a whole. **public company** n. a company whose shares can be purchased on the Stock Exchange by members of the public. **public convenience** n. a public lavatory. **public enemy** n. a person, esp. a notorious criminal, considered to be a menace to the community. **public figure** n. a famous person. **public health** n. the field of responsibility for the general health of the community covering e.g. sanitation, food-handling in shops and restaurants, hygiene in public places. **public house** n. a house licensed for the retail of intoxicating liquors, an inn, a tavern. **public law** n. 1 the body of law governing the relations between individuals and the state. 2 a public act. **public lending right** n. the right of authors to royalties when their books are borrowed from public libraries. **public libel** n. (Law) a published libel. **publicly** adv. **publicness** n. **public nuisance** n. 1 (Law) an illegal act affecting the whole community rather than an individual. 2 (coll.) a generally objectionable person. **public opinion** n. the views of the general public or the electorate on political and social issues. **public orator** n. an officer at a university who acts as public speaker on ceremonial occasions. **public ownership** n. ownership by the state of e.g. large industries, utilities etc. **public prosecutor** n. (Law) an official who conducts criminal prosecutions on behalf of the state. **public purse** n. a national treasury. **public records** n.pl. official state papers to which the public has access. **public relations** n. 1 (sing. or pl. in constr.) the relationship between an organization and the public. 2 (a department entrusted with) the maintenance of goodwill towards, and a favourable image of, an organization in the mind of the public. **public school** n. 1 a non-fee-paying school under the control of a publicly elected body. 2 an independent fee-paying school (in England and Wales) esp. for boarders. **public sector** n. the state-owned part of the economy. **public servant** n. a government employee. **public spirit** n. interest in or devotion to the community. **public-spirited** a. **public-spiritedly** adv. **public-spiritedness** n. **public transport** n. a system of buses, trains etc. run by the State for use by the public. **public utility** n. an enterprise concerned with the provision of an essential service, e.g. gas, water, electricity, to the public. **public works** n.pl. roads, buildings etc. constructed for public use by or on behalf of the government. **public wrong** n. an offence committed against the public as a whole.

publican (pŭb´likən) n. 1 a keeper of a public house. 2 (Austral.) a keeper of a hotel. 3 (Hist.) a collector or farmer of the revenues, taxes etc. in the Roman empire.

publication (pŭblikā'shən) *n.* **1** the act, or an instance, of making publicly known. **2** the act of publishing a book, periodical, musical composition etc. **3** a work printed and published.

publicist (pŭb'lisist) *n.* **1** a writer on current social or political topics, esp. a journalist, a person who publicizes, esp. a press or publicity agent. **2** a public relations officer. **publicistic** (-sis'-) *a.*

publicity (pŭblis'iti) *n.* **1** the process of attracting public attention to a product, person etc. **2** anything calculated to arouse public interest, such as a newsworthy event or information, advertising etc. **3** public attention or interest. **publicity agent** *n.* a person employed to keep before the public the name of a product, film etc.

publicize (pŭb'lisīz), **publicise** *v.t.* to make known to the public; to advertise.

publish (pŭb'lish) *v.t.* **1** to make public, to promulgate, to announce publicly. **2** to issue or print and offer for sale (a book, newspaper etc.) to the public. **3** to issue the works of (an author). **4** to read (the banns of marriage). **5** (*Law*) to communicate (a libel) to someone apart from the person libelled. ~*v.i.* to print and offer for sale. **publishable** *a.* **published** *a.* (of a writer) having had one's works issued. **publisher** *n.* **1** a person or a company that publishes, esp. books and other literary productions. **2** (*N Am.*) a newspaper proprietor. **3** a person who makes anything public. **publishing** *n.*

puce (pūs) *n.* a dark reddish purple colour. ~*a.* of this colour.

puck[1] (pŭk) *n.* **1** a mischievous sprite, elf or fairy. **2** a mischievous child. **puckish** *a.* **puckishly** *adv.* **puckishness** *n.* **pucklike** *a.*

puck[2] (pŭk) *n.* a vulcanized rubber disc used instead of a ball in ice hockey.

pucka PUKKA.

pucker (pŭk'ə) *v.t.* to gather into small folds or wrinkles. ~*v.i.* to become wrinkled or gathered into small folds etc. ~*n.* a fold, a wrinkle, a bulge. **puckery** *a.*

pud (pud) *n.* (*coll.*) short for PUDDING.

pudding (pud'ing) *n.* **1** a sweet dish, usu. cooked, and usu. made with flour, eggs, milk etc. **2** a savoury dish, usu. meat with pastry or batter etc. **3** the dessert course of a meal. **4** a skin or intestine stuffed with minced meat etc., a large sausage. **5** (*N Am.*) a cold dessert, usu. creamy. **6** (*coll.*) a fat or stupid person. **in the pudding club** (*sl.*) pregnant. **pudding basin** *n.* a basin for steaming a pudding in. **pudding face** *n.* (*coll.*) a fat, round, smooth face. **pudding-faced** *a.* **pudding-head** *n.* (*coll.*) a stupid person. **pudding-stone** *n.* a conglomerate of pebbles in a siliceous matrix. **puddingy** *a.*

puddle (pŭd'əl) *n.* **1** a small pool, esp. of rainwater. **2** clay and sand worked together to form a watertight lining for a pond, canal etc. **3**

the patch of rough water left by the blade of an oar. ~*v.i.* **1** to dabble (in mud, water etc.). **2** to mess, to muddle (about). **3** to make puddle from clay and sand. ~*v.t.* **1** to work (clay etc.) into puddle. **2** to line or render watertight with puddle. **3** to stir up (molten iron) in a furnace so as to convert it into wrought iron. **4** to make dirty or muddy. **5** to work (clay and water) so as to separate gold or opals. **puddler** *n.* **puddly** *a.*

pudency (pū'dənsi) *n.* (*formal*) modesty, shamefacedness. **pudendum** (-den'dəm) *n.* (*pl.* **pudenda** (-də)) (*often pl.*) the genitals, esp. those of a woman. **pudendal** *a.*

pudge (pŭj) *n.* a short, thick or fat person or figure. **pudgy** *a.* (*comp.* **pudgier**, *superl.* **pudgiest**). **pudgily** *adv.* **pudginess** *n.*

pueblo (pweb'lō) *n.* (*pl.* **pueblos**) a village, town or settlement, esp. of the Indians of New Mexico etc.

puerile (pūə'rīl) *a.* childish, silly, inane. **puerilely** *adv.* **puerility** (-ril'-) *n.* (*pl.* **puerilities**) **1** the state of being childish or silly. **2** a puerile action, expression etc.

puerperal (pūœ'pərəl) *a.* of, relating to or resulting from childbirth. **puerperal fever** *n.* a fever, caused by infection of the genital tract, attacking women after childbirth.

Puerto Rican (pwœtō rē'kən) *n.* a native or inhabitant of Puerto Rico, in the Greater Antilles. ~*a.* of or relating to Puerto Rico or its inhabitants.

puff (pŭf) *v.i.* **1** to breathe, to blow, to emit or expel air, steam etc. in short, sudden blasts. **2** to move or go while puffing. **3** to breathe hard. **4** to come (out) in a short, sudden blast. **5** to become inflated or distended. ~*v.t.* **1** to emit, to blow out, with a short sudden blast or blasts. **2** to blow or drive (away) thus. **3** to draw at (a cigarette, pipe). **4** to utter pantingly. **5** to inflate, to blow (up or out). **6** to blow (away etc.). **7** to bid at an auction in order to inflate the price. **8** to cause to be out of breath. **9** to praise or advertise in an exaggerated or misleading way. ~*n.* **1** a short, sudden blast of breath, smoke, steam etc., a whiff, a gust. **2** the sound made by this. **3** a small amount of breath, smoke etc., emitted at one puff. **4** a light, puffy thing or small mass of any material. **5** a cake, tart etc. of light or spongy consistency. **6** a light wad, pad or tuft for applying powder to the skin. **7** an exaggerated or misleading advertisement, review etc. **8** a rolled mass of hair pinned over a pad. **9** (*N Am.*) an eiderdown. **10** (*sl.*, *derog.*) a male homosexual. **to puff and blow** to breathe hard or noisily. **puff-adder** *n.* a highly venomous African snake, *Bitis arietans*, which inflates part of its body when aroused. **puffball** *n.* **1** any of several fungi, the roundish spore case of which emits dry, dustlike spores. **2** a full skirt gathered in at the hem to make a rounded shape. **3** a powder puff. **puffed** *a.* **1** inflated. **2** (of a sleeve) short and full, gathered into a close fitting band. **3** (*coll.*) (*also* **puffed out**) out of breath. **puffed up 1** inflated. **2** swollen up with conceit or self-importance. **puffer** *n.* **1** a person or thing that puffs, esp. a steamboat, steam engine etc. **2** (**puffer fish**) a globe-fish. **puffery** *n.* (*pl.* **pufferies**) **1** exaggerated praise. **2** an instance of this. **puff pastry,** (*N Am.*) **puff paste** *n.* (a rich dough used to make) a light, flaky pastry etc. **puff-puff** *n.* a steam locomotive (used by or to children). **puffy** *a.* (*comp.* **puffier,** *superl.* **puffiest**) **1** puffing, blowing or breathing in puffs. **2** short-winded. **3** swollen, distended. **4** tumid, turgid, bombastic. **puffily** *adv.* **puffiness** *n.*

puffin (pŭf´in) *n.* any of various seabirds of the genus *Fratercula,* esp. the N Atlantic *F. arctica,* with black and white plumage and a brightly-coloured bill. **puffin crossing** *n.* a type of pelican crossing incorporating sensors which monitor the movements of pedestrians and keep the traffic lights red until the crossing is clear.

pug¹ (pŭg) *n.* **1** a pug-dog. **2** a pug-moth. **3** a fox. **pug-dog** *n.* a small, short-haired breed of dog with wrinkled face, up-turned nose and tightly curled tail. **pug-moth** *n.* a small geometrid moth, esp. of the genus *Eupithecia.* **pug-nose** *n.* a short squat nose. **pug-nosed** *a.*

pug² (pŭg) *n.* clay and other material mixed and prepared for making into bricks. ~*v.t.* (*pres.p.* **pugging,** *past, p.p.* **pugged**) **1** to grind and render plastic (clay etc.) for brick-making. **2** to puddle with clay. **3** to pack (a wall, floor etc.) with sawdust etc. to deaden sound. **pug-mill** *n.* a mill in which clay is made into pug.

pug³ (pŭg) *n.* (*sl.*) a boxer.

pugilist (pū´jilist) *n.* a boxer, a prizefighter. **pugilism** *n.* **pugilistic** (-lis´-) *a.*

pugnacious (pŭgnā´shəs) *a.* inclined to fight; quarrelsome. **pugnacity** (-nas´-), **pugnaciousness** *n.*

puisne (pū´ni) *a.* (*Law*) (of a judge) junior or inferior in rank.

puissant (pū´isənt, pwē´-) *a.* (*formal*) powerful, strong, mighty. **puissance** (pū´isəns, pwē´säs) *n.* **1** a showjumping event that tests a horse's power to jump high obstacles. **2** (*formal*) power, strength. **puissantly** *adv.*

puja (poo´jə), **pooja** *n.* a Hindu act of worship.

puke (pūk) *v.t., v.i.* (*sl.*) to vomit. ~*n.* **1** vomit. **2** the act of vomiting. **puker** *n.* **pukey, puky** *a.*

pukeko (poo´kikō, pŭk´-) *n.* (*pl.* **pukekos**) (*New Zeal.*) a wading bird, *Porphyrio porphyrio,* with bright plumage.

pukka (pŭk´ə), **pucka, pukkah** *a.* (*Ang.-Ind.*) **1** genuine. **2** superior. **3** durable, substantial. **4** of full weight.

pulchritude (pŭl´kritūd) *n.* (*formal or facet.*) beauty. **pulchritudinous** (-tū´din-) *a.*

pule (pūl) *v.i.* to cry plaintively or querulously, to whine, to whimper.

pull (pul) *v.t.* **1** to draw towards one by force. **2** to drag, to haul, to tug. **3** to draw (up, along, nearer etc.). **4** to move (a vehicle) in a particular direction. **5** to pluck. **6 a** to remove by plucking (a tooth, a cork etc.). **b** to remove (a weed) by the

root. **7** to draw (beer etc.) from a barrel etc. **8** to bring out (a weapon). **9** to strain (a muscle or tendon). **10 a** to row (a boat). **b** to take (a person in a boat) by rowing. **11** (*coll.*) to attract (a crowd, support etc.). **12** (*sl.*) to carry out, esp. with daring and imagination or with deceptive intent. **13** (*sl.*) to succeed in attracting sexually. **14** (*Print.*) to take (an impression), to take (a proof). **15** to strike (a cricket ball) from the off to the on side. **16** to strike a golf ball to the left. **17** to rein in (a horse), esp. so as to lose a race. ~*v.i.* **1** to give a pull. **2** to tug, to haul. **3** to move with difficulty, or effortfully. **4** (of a horse) to strain against the bit. **5** to draw, to suck (at a pipe). **6** to pluck, to tear (at). ~*n.* **1 a** the act of pulling, a tug. **b** the force exerted by this. **2** something which is pulled. **3** a handle by which beer is drawn, a door opened, a bell rung etc. **4** a quantity of beer etc. drawn. **5** a draught, a swig. **6** influence or advantage. **7** (*coll.*) a hold, unfair or illegitimate influence. **8** (*coll.*) a spell of hard exertion. **9** something which draws one's attention. **10** (*Print.*) a proof. **11** in cricket, a stroke by which a ball is sent from the off to the on side. **12** in golf, a stroke sending a ball to the left. **13** the checking of a horse by its rider, esp. to secure defeat in a race. **14** a spell of rowing. **15** a draw at a cigarette. **pull the other one** (*coll.*) used as an expression of disbelief (i.e. pull the other leg). **to pull about** to pull to and fro, to handle roughly. **to pull ahead** to move ahead, or into the lead. **to pull apart 1** to pull asunder or into pieces. **2** to become separated or severed. **3** to criticize severely. **to pull away** to move (further) into the lead. **to pull back** to retreat or cause to retreat; to withdraw. **to pull down 1** to demolish. **2** to degrade, to humble. **3** to weaken, to cause (prices etc.) to be reduced. **4** (*sl.*) to earn a (specified) amount of money. **to pull in 1** to retract, to make tighter. **2** (of a train) to enter a station. **3** (of a vehicle, driver) to stop (at), to pull over. **4** (*coll.*) to attract (audiences etc.). **5** (*sl.*) to arrest. **6** to earn. **to pull off 1** to remove by pulling. **2** to accomplish (something difficult or risky). **to pull oneself together** to regain one's composure or self-control. **to pull out 1** to remove by pulling. **2** to leave, to depart. **3** to withdraw. **4** to cease to participate in. **5** to move out from the side of the road or from behind another vehicle. **6** (of an aircraft) to level off after a dive. **to pull over** (of a vehicle) to draw in to the side of the road (and stop). **to pull round** to (cause to) recover. **to pull through** to (cause to) survive, recover or not fail against the odds. **to pull together** to cooperate. **to pull to pieces 1** to tear (a thing) up. **2** to criticize, to abuse. **to pull up 1** to drag up forcibly. **2** to pluck out of the ground. **3** to cause to stop. **4** to come to a stop. **5** to rebuke. **6** to gain on, to draw level (with). **pull-back** *n.* **1** a drawback, a restraint, hindrance. **2** a retreat, a withdrawal. **pull-down** *a.* **1** that can be pulled down. **2** (*Comput.*) of or relating to a menu which can be accessed during the running of the program and which brings a list of options down over the screen. ~*n.* a thing which can pull down or be pulled down. **puller** *n.* **pull-in** *n.* **1** a stopping place. **2** a transport café. **pull-off** *a.* that can be pulled off. ~*n.* **1** an act of pulling off. **2** a lay-by. **pull-on** *n., a.* (a garment) without fastenings, requiring simply to be pulled on. **pull-out** *n.* **1** a removable section of a magazine. **2** a large fold-out leaf in a book. **3** a withdrawal. **pullover** *n.* a knitted garment which is pulled on over the head. **pull-up** *n.* **1** the act, or an instance of pulling up. **2** a stop. **3** a lay-by. **4** an exercise in which one hangs by the hands from a bar and pulls oneself up until the chin is level with the bar.

pullet (pul´it) *n.* a young fowl, esp. a hen less than a year old.

pulley (pul´i) *n.* (*pl.* **pulleys**) **1** a wheel with a grooved rim, or a combination of such wheels, mounted in a block for changing the direction or for increasing the effect of a force. **2** a wheel used to transmit power or motion by means of a belt, chain etc. passing over its rim. ~*v.t.* (*3rd pers. sing. pres.* **pulleys**, *pres.p.* **pulleying**, *past, p.p.* **pulleyed**) **1** to lift or hoist with a pulley. **2** to furnish or fit with pulleys.

Pullman (pul´mən) *n.* (*pl.* **Pullmans**) **1** a Pullman car. **2** a train made up of these. **3** a similarly luxurious motor coach. **Pullman car** *n.* a luxurious railway saloon or sleeping car.

pullulate (pul´ūlāt) *v.i.* **1** (of a shoot etc.) to shoot, bud. **2** (of a seed) to germinate. **3** (of animals) to breed rapidly and prolifically. **4** to swarm, to abound. **5** to develop, to spring up. **pullulant** *a.* **pullulation** (-lā´shən) *n.*

pulmonary (pul´mənəri) *a.* **1** of or relating to the lungs. **2** having lungs or similar organs. **3** susceptible to lung diseases. **pulmonary artery** *n.* the artery carrying blood from the heart to the lungs. **pulmonary tuberculosis** *n.* a form of tuberculosis caused by inhaling the tubercle bacillus into the lungs. **pulmonary vein** *n.* the vein carrying oxygenated blood from the lungs back to the heart. **pulmonic** (-mon´-) *a., n.*

pulp (pulp) *n.* **1** any soft, moist, coherent mass. **2** the fleshy or succulent portion of a fruit. **3** the soft tissue of an animal body or in an organ or part, as in the internal cavity of a tooth. **4** the soft mixture of rags, wood etc. from which paper is made. **5** a magazine or book printed on cheap paper and sentimental or sensational in content. **6** fiction of the type published in such books and magazines. **7** (*Mining*) pulverized ore mixed with water. ~*v.t.* **1** to convert into pulp. **2** to extract the pulp from. ~*v.i.* to become pulpy. **pulper** *n.* **pulp-wood** *n.* softwood suitable for making into pulp. **pulpy** *a.* (*comp.* **pulpier**, *superl.* **pulpiest**). **pulpiness** *n.*

pulpit (pul´pit) *n.* **1** an elevated enclosed stand in a church from which a preacher delivers a sermon. **2** a railed area at the bow or stern of a boat. **the pulpit 1** preachers generally. **2** preaching.

pulque (pul´ki, -kā) *n.* a Mexican vinous beverage made by fermenting the sap of a species of agave. **pulque brandy** *n.* a liquor distilled from this.

pulsar (pul´sah) *n.* (*Astron.*) an interstellar source of regularly pulsating radio waves, prob. a swiftly rotating neutron star.

pulsate (pulsāt´, pul´-) *v.i.* **1** to move, esp. to expand and contract, with rhythmical alternation, to beat, to throb. **2** to vibrate, to thrill. **pulsatile** (pul´sətīl) *a.* **1** having the property of pulsation. **2** (*Mus.*) played by beating, percussive. **pulsation** (-ā´shən) *n.* **pulsator** (-sā´-) *n.* **pulsatory** (pul´-) *a.*

pulsatilla (pulsətil´ə) *n.* (*pl.* **pulsatillas**) the pasque flower, *Pulsatilla vulgaris.*

pulse¹ (puls) *n.* **1** the rhythmic beating of the arteries caused by the propulsion of blood along them from the heart. **2** a single beat of the arteries or the heart. **3** a pulsation, a vibration. **4** a short-lived variation in some normally constant value in a system, as in voltage etc. **5** an electromagnetic or sound wave of brief duration. **6** a quick, regular stroke or recurrence of strokes (as of oars). **7** a throb, a thrill. **8** the public mood or opinion. ~*v.i.* **1** to pulsate. **2** to be produced in pulses. ~*v.t.* to produce or transmit by or as by rhythmic beats. **pulse code** *n.* the coding of information using pulses. **pulse code modulation** *n.* a form of pulse modulation in which the information is carried by a sequence of binary codes. **pulsejet** *n.* a type of jet engine using a pulsating thrust. **pulseless** *a.* **pulselessness** *n.* **pulse modulation** *n.* a type of modulation in which a series of varied pulses is used to carry a signal. **pulsimeter** (-sim´itə) *n.* an instrument for measuring the rate, force, regularity etc. of a pulse.

pulse² (puls) *n.* **1** the edible seeds of leguminous plants. **2** a plant or plants producing such seeds.

pulverize (pul´vərīz), **pulverise** *v.t.* **1** to reduce to fine powder or dust. **2** (*coll.*) to demolish, to smash, to defeat utterly. ~*v.i.* to be reduced to powder. **pulverizable** *a.* **pulverization** (-zā´shən) *n.* **pulverizator** *n.* **pulverizer** *n.*

puma (pū´mə) *n.* (*pl.* **pumas**) the cougar, *Felis concolor*, a large feline carnivore of the Americas.

pumice (pum´is) *n.* **1** a light, porous or cellular kind of lava, used as a cleansing and polishing material. **2** a piece of this stone. ~*v.t.* to rub, polish or clean with pumice. **pumiceous** (pūmish´əs) *a.* **pumice stone** *n.* pumice.

pummel (pum´əl) *v.t.* (*pres.p.* **pummelling**, (*N Am.*) **pummeling**, *past, p.p.* **pummelled**, (*N Am.*) **pummeled**) to strike or pound repeatedly, esp. with the fists.

pump¹ (pump) *n.* **1** a device or machine usu. in the form of a cylinder and piston, for raising water or other liquid. **2** a similar machine for exhausting or compressing air, an air-pump. **3**

the act of pumping, a stroke of a pump. ~*v.t.* **1** to raise or remove (liquid or gas) with a pump. **2** to free from water, make dry or fill with air with a pump. **3** to propel, to pour, with or as with a pump. **4** to move up and down as if working a pump-handle. **5** to elicit information from by persistent interrogation. **6** to shake (someone's hand) vigorously. ~*v.i.* **1** to work a pump. **2** to raise water etc. with a pump. **3** to move up and down in the manner of a pump-handle. **to pump iron** to do weight-lifting exercises. **to pump up 1** to inflate (a pneumatic tyre). **2** to inflate the tyres of (a cycle etc.). **pump action** *a.* (of a repeating rifle or shotgun) requiring a pumplike movement to bring a shell into the chamber. **pump-brake** *n.* the handle of a pump, esp. with a transverse handle. **pumper** *n.* **pump-priming** *n.* **1** the introduction of fluid into a pump to expel the air before operation. **2** the investing of money to stimulate commercial activity esp. in stagnant or depressed areas. **pump room** *n.* **1** a room where a pump is worked. **2** a room at a spa where the waters from the medicinal spring are dispensed.

pump² (pŭmp) *n.* **1** a light low-heeled, slipperlike shoe worn with evening dress and for dancing. **2** a plimsoll. **3** (*NAm.*) a court shoe.

pumpernickel (pŭm´pənikəl) *n.* German wholemeal rye bread.

pumpkin (pŭmp´kin) *n.* **1** any plant of the genus *Cucurbita*, creeping plants with large lobed leaves. **2** the large globular edible fruit of *Cucurbita maxima*.

pun¹ (pŭn) *n.* the playful use of a word in two different senses or of words similar in sound but different in meaning. ~*v.i.* (*pres.p.* **punning**, *past*, *p.p.* **punned**) to make a pun. **punningly** *adv.* **punster** *n.* a person who makes puns.

pun² (pŭn) *v.t.* (*pres.p.* **punning**, *past*, *p.p.* **punned**) to pound, to crush, to consolidate by ramming. **punner** *n.*

Punch (pŭnch) *n.* the chief character in the popular puppet show of Punch and Judy, represented as a grotesque hump-backed man. **pleased as Punch** highly delighted.

punch¹ (pŭnch) *n.* **1** a tool, usu. consisting of a short cylindrical piece of steel tapering to a sharp or blunt end, for making holes, indenting, forcing bolts out of holes etc. **2** a machine in which a similar tool is used, esp. one for making holes in paper or cardboard. **3** a tool or machine for stamping a die or impressing a design. **4** a blow with the fist. **5** vigour, forcefulness. **6** striking power. ~*v.t.* **1** to stamp or perforate with a punch. **2** to make (a hole or indentation) thus. **3** to drive (out etc.) with a punch. **4** to strike, esp. with the fist. **5** to press in vigorously, as a key or button. **6** to record by pressing a key. **7** (*NAm.*) to drive (cattle) by pushing with or as with a stick. **to pull one's punches** (*usu. in neg.*) to strike or criticize with less than full force. **punchbag** *n.* a heavy, stuffed bag struck with the fists as exercise or by boxers in training. **punchball** *n.* **1**

a ball usu. suspended or on an elastic stand used for punching practice. **2** (*NAm.*) a game in which a ball is punched with the fist. **punch-drunk** *a.* suffering a form of cerebral concussion from having taken repeated blows to the head; dazed. **puncher** *n.* **punching bag** *n.* (*NAm.*) a punchbag. **punchline** *n.* the conclusion of a joke or story that shows the point of it, produces the laugh or reveals an unexpected twist. **punch-up** *n.* (*coll.*) a brawl, a fist fight. **punchy** *a.* (*comp.* **punchier**, *superl.* **punchiest**) (*coll.*) forceful, incisive. **punchily** *adv.* **punchiness** *n.*

punch² (pŭnch) *n.* a beverage made of wine or spirits, water or milk, lemons, sugar, spice etc., usu. served hot. **punchbowl** *n.* **1** a round bowl in which punch is made. **2** a round hollow in a hill.

puncheon (pŭn´chən) *n.* **1** a short upright timber, used for supporting the roof in a mine or as an upright in the framework of a roof. **2** a perforating or stamping tool, a punch.

puncta PUNCTUM.

punctate (pŭngk´tāt) *a.* (*Biol.*) covered with points, dots, spots etc. **punctation** (-tā´shən) *n.*

punctilio (pŭngktil´iō) *n.* (*pl.* **punctilios**) **1** a nice point in conduct, ceremony or honour. **2** precision in form or etiquette. **3** petty formality. **punctilious** *a.* **1** precise or exacting in punctilio. **2** strictly observant of ceremony or etiquette. **punctiliously** *adv.* **punctiliousness** *n.*

punctual (pŭngk´chuəl) *a.* **1** observant and exact in matters of time. **2** done, made or occurring exactly at the proper time. **punctuality** (-al´-) *n.* **punctually** *adv.*

punctuate (pŭngk´chuāt) *v.t.* **1** to mark (written matter) with stops, to divide into sentences, clauses etc. with stops. **2** to interrupt or intersperse. **punctuation** (-ā´shən) *n.* **punctuation mark** *n.* any of the marks used to punctuate written matter, such as the comma, colon etc.

punctum (pŭngk´təm) *n.* (*pl.* **puncta** (-tə)) (*Biol.*) a point, a speck, a dot, a minute spot of colour etc.

puncture (pŭngk´chə) *n.* **1** a small hole made with something pointed, a prick. **2** the act of pricking or perforating. **3** the perforation of a pneumatic tyre by e.g. a sharp stone on the road, and the consequent loss of pressure. ~*v.t.* **1** to make a puncture in. **2** to pierce or prick with something pointed. **3** (*coll.*) to deflate (a person's self-esteem or pomposity). ~*v.i.* (of a tyre, balloon etc.) to sustain a puncture. **puncturable** *a.* **puncturer** *n.*

pundit (pŭn´dit) *n.* **1** (*also* **pandit**) a Hindu learned in the Sanskrit language and the science, laws and religion of India. **2** a learned person. **3** (*iron.*) a pretender to learning. **punditry** *n.*

pungent (pŭn´jənt) *a.* **1** sharply affecting the senses, esp. those of smell or taste. **2** acrid, keen, caustic, biting. **3** piquant, stimulating. **4** (*Biol.*) sharp-pointed, adapted for pricking or piercing. **pungency** *n.* **pungently** *adv.*

Punic (pū´nik) *a.* of or relating to ancient

Carthage, the Carthaginians, or the Carthaginian language.

punily, puniness PUNY.

punish (pŭn´ish) v.t. **1** to inflict a penalty on (a person) for an offence. **2** to inflict a penalty for (an offence). **3** to inflict pain or injury on, to handle severely, to maul. **4** to give great trouble to (opponents in a game, race etc.). **punishable** a. **punisher** n. **punishing** a. severe, wearing. **punishingly** adv. **punishment** n. **1** the act, or an instance, of punishing. **2** the state of being punished. **3** the penalty or suffering inflicted. **4** (coll.) severe or rough treatment. **punitive** (pū´-), **punitory** (pū´-) a. **1** awarding or inflicting punishment. **2** retributive. **3** (of taxes) at a very high rate. **punitive damages** n.pl. (Law) vindictive damages. **punitively** adv.

Punjabi (pŭnjah´bi) n. (pl. **Punjabis**) **1** a native or inhabitant of the state of Punjab in India or the province of Punjab in Pakistan, or the larger area comprising both of these, formerly a province of British India. **2** the Indic language of these areas. ~a. of or relating to these areas, their inhabitants or their language.

punk¹ (pŭngk) n. **1 a** a worthless person or thing. **b** worthless articles. **2** nonsense. **3** (a follower of) a youth movement of the late 1970s and 1980s, characterized by a violent rejection of established society, outlandish (often multicoloured) hairstyles, and the use of worthless articles such as safety pins and razor blades as decoration. **4** punk rock. **5** (NAm.) a novice. **6** (NAm.) a petty criminal. **7** (NAm.) a passive male homosexual. ~a. **1** associated with the punk movement or punk rock. **2** (NAm.) inferior, rotten. **punkish** a. **punk rock** n. a style of popular music associated with the punk movement and characterized by a driving beat, crude or obscene lyrics and an aggressive performing style. **punk rocker** n. **punky** a. **punkiness** n.

punk² (pŭngk) n. (NAm.) wood decayed through the growth of a fungus, touchwood.

punkah (pŭng´kə) n. (Ind.) **1** a large portable fan made from a palm leaf. **2** a large screenlike fan suspended from the ceiling and worked by a cord.

punner PUN².

punnet (pŭn´it) n. a small, shallow basket for fruit, flowers etc.

punster PUN¹.

punt¹ (pŭnt) n. a shallow, flat-bottomed, square-ended boat, usu. propelled by pushing against the bottom of the stream with a pole. ~v.t. **1** to propel (a punt etc.) with a pole. **2** to convey in a punt. ~v.i. to go (about) in a punt. **punter¹** n.

punt² (pŭnt) v.i. **1** to stake against the bank in some card games. **2** (coll.) to bet on a horse etc. **3** (coll.) to speculate on the Stock Exchange. ~n. **1** a bet. **2** a point in the game of faro. **punter²** n. **1** a person who bets. **2** a small gambler on the Stock Exchange. **3** a prostitute's client. **4** (coll.) any member of the public, esp. when considered as a customer or client. **5** a point in faro.

punt³ (pŭnt) v.t. in ball games, to kick the ball after dropping it from the hand and before it touches the ground. ~n. such a kick. **punter³** n.

punt⁴ (punt) n. the standard monetary unit of the Republic of Ireland.

punter¹ PUNT¹.

punter² PUNT².

punter³ PUNT³.

puny (pū´ni) a. (comp. **punier**, superl. **puniest**) **1** small and feeble, tiny, undersized, weak, poorly developed. **2** petty, trivial. **punily** adv. **puniness** n.

pup (pŭp) n. **1** a puppy. **2** the young of other animals, such as the seal. **3** (sl., derog.) a conceited young man. ~v.t. (pres.p. **pupping**, past, p.p. **pupped**) to give birth to (pups). ~v.i. to give birth to pups, to whelp, to litter. **in pup** pregnant. **to sell a pup to** (sl.) to trick into buying something worthless; to swindle.

pupa (pū´pə) n. (pl. **pupae** (-pē), **pupas**) an insect at the immobile, metamorphic stage between larva and imago. **pupal** a. **pupate** (-pāt´) v.i. to become a pupa. **pupation** (-pā´shən) n. **pupiparous** a. (of insects) giving birth to young which are already at the pupal stage.

pupil¹ (pū´pil, -pəl) n. **1** a young person of either sex under the care of a teacher. **2** a person who is being, or has been, taught by a particular person. **3** (Law) a trainee barrister. **pupillage** (-ij), **pupilage** n. **1** the state or period of being a pupil. **2** (Law) the apprenticeship period of a barrister. **pupillary¹, pupilary** a. **pupilship** n.

pupil² (pū´pil, -pəl) n. the circular opening of the iris of the eye through which rays of light pass to the retina. **pupillar, pupilar** a. **pupillary²**, **pupilary** a. **pupillate** (-lət), **pupilled** a. having a central spot like a pupil (of ocelli).

pupillar PUPIL².

pupillary¹ PUPIL¹.

pupillary² PUPIL².

pupiparous PUPA.

puppet (pŭp´it) n. **1** an articulated toy figure moved by strings, wires or rods, a marionette. **2** a small figure with a hollow head and cloth body into which the operator's hand is inserted, a glove puppet. **3** a person whose actions are under another's control, a mere tool. **puppeteer** (-tiə´) n. **1** a person who manipulates puppets. **2** a person who manipulates other people. **puppeteering** n. **puppetry** n. **puppet state, puppet government** n. a country, or government, which appears to be independent but is in fact controlled from another country.

puppy (pŭp´i) n. (pl. **puppies**) **1** a young dog. **2** a silly young man, a coxcomb, a fop. **puppy fat** n. temporary plumpness in children or adolescents. **puppyhood** n. **puppyish** a. **puppy love** n. temporary infatuation in adolescence.

purblind (pœ´blīnd) a. **1** partially blind, near-sighted, dim-sighted. **2** obtuse, lacking insight or understanding. **purblindly** *adv.* **purblindness** *n.*

purchase (pœ´chis) *v.t.* **1** to obtain by payment of an equivalent value, to buy. **2** to acquire at the expense of some sacrifice, exertion, danger etc. **3** (*Naut.*) to haul up, hoist or draw in by means of a pulley, lever, capstan etc. ~*n.* **1** the act, or an instance, of purchasing or buying. **2** a thing which is purchased. **3** annual value, annual return, esp. from land. **4** (*Law*) the acquisition of property by payment of a price or value, any mode of acquiring property other than by inheritance. **5** advantage gained by the application of any mechanical power, leverage. **6** an appliance furnishing this, such as a rope, pulley etc. **7** an effective hold or position for leverage, a grasp, a foothold. **purchasable** *a.* **purchaser** *n.* **purchasing power** *n.* the ability of a person, or of their money, to buy (an amount of goods or services).

purdah (pœ´də) *n.* **1** the custom in some Muslim and Hindu societies of secluding women from the view of strangers. **2** a curtain or screen, esp. one keeping women secluded.

pure (pūə) *a.* **1** unmixed, unadulterated. **2** free from anything foul or polluting, clear, clean. **3** free from moral defilement, innocent, guiltless. **4** unsullied, chaste. **5** of unmixed descent, free from admixture with any other breed. **6** mere, sheer, absolute. **7** (of a sound) free from discordance, harshness etc., perfectly correct in tone intervals. **8** (of a vowel) having a single sound or tone, not combined with another. **9** (of sciences) entirely theoretical, not applied. **purebred** *a.* of a pure strain through many generations of controlled breeding. ~*n.* such an animal. **purely** *adv.* **1** in a pure way. **2** merely; entirely. **pure mathematics** *n.* the abstract science of magnitudes etc. **pureness** *n.* **pure science** *n.* a science based on self-evident truths, such as logic, mathematics etc., or one studied apart from any practical applications.

purée (pū´rā) *n.* (*pl.* **purées**) a smooth thick pulp of fruit, vegetables etc. obtained by liquidizing, sieving etc. ~*v.t.* (*3rd pers. sing. pres.* **purées**, *pres.p.* **puréeing**, *past, p.p.* **puréed**) to reduce to a purée.

purgation (pœgā´shən) *n.* **1** the act of purging, purification. **2** cleansing of the bowels by the use of purgatives. **purgative** (pœ´gə-) *a.* having the quality of cleansing, esp. evacuating the intestines, aperient. ~*n.* **1** something that purges. **2** an aperient or cathartic. **purgatively** *adv.*

purgatory (pœ´gətri, -təri) *n.* (*pl.* **purgatories**) **1** a place or state of spiritual purging, esp. a place or state succeeding the present life in which, according to the Roman Catholic Church, the souls of the faithful are purified from venial sins by suffering. **2** any place of temporary suffering or tribulation. **3** (*coll.*) an acutely uncomfortable experience. ~*a.* cleansing, purifying. **purgatorial** (-taw´ri-) *a.* **purgatorially** *adv.*

purge (pœj) *v.t.* **1** to cleanse or purify. **2** to remove

(off or away) by cleansing. **3** to clear (of an accusation, suspicion etc.). **4** to rid (a state or a party) of persons actively in opposition. **5** (*Law*) to clear oneself of, to atone for (an offence). **6** to atone for, expiate or annul (guilt, spiritual defilement etc.). **7 a** to cleanse (the bowels) by administering a laxative. **b** to empty (the bowels). ~*v.i.* to grow pure by clarification. ~*n.* **1** the act, or an instance, of purging. **2** a purgative medicine. **purger** *n.* **purging** *a., n.*

purify (pū´rifī) *v.t.* (*3rd pers. sing. pres.* **purifies**, *pres.p.* **purifying**, *past, p.p.* **purified**) **1** to make pure, to cleanse. **2** to free from sin, guilt, pollution etc. **3** to make ceremonially clean. **4** to clear of or from foreign elements, corruptions etc. **purification** (-fikā´shən) *n.* **purificatory** *a.* **purifier** *n.*

purin (pū´rin), **purine** (-rēn) *n.* (*Chem.*) **1** a crystalline solid derivable from uric acid. **2** any of a group of compounds derived from this, such as guanine and adenine.

purist (pū´rist) *n.* a person advocating or affecting purity, esp. in art or language. **purism** *n.* **puristic** (-ris´-), **puristical** *a.*

puritan (pū´ritən) *n.* **1** (**Puritan**) any one of a party or school of English Protestants of the 16th and 17th cents., who aimed at purifying religious worship from all ceremonies etc. not authorized by Scripture, and at the strictest purity of conduct. **2** (*usu. derog.*) any person practising or advocating extreme strictness in conduct or religion. **3** a purist. ~*a.* **1** (**Puritan**) of or relating to the Puritans. **2** excessively strict in religion or morals. **puritanic** (-tan´-), **puritanical** *a.* **puritanically** *adv.* **puritanism**, **Puritanism** *n.*

purity (pū´riti) *n.* **1** the state of being pure, cleanness. **2** freedom from pollution, adulteration or admixture of foreign elements. **3** moral cleanness, innocence, chastity.

purl¹ (pœl) *n.* **1** an edging or fringe of twisted gold or silver wire. **2** the thread or cord of which this is made. **3** a small loop on the edges of pillow lace. **4** a series of such loops as an ornamental hem or edging. **5** an inversion of the stitches in knitting. ~*a.* of or relating to an inverted stitch in knitting, made by putting the needle into the front of the stitch, as distinct from *plain*. ~*v.t.* **1** to border or decorate with purl or purls. **2** to knit with a purl stitch. ~*v.i.* to knit with a purl stitch.

purl² (pœl) *v.i.* **1** to flow with a soft, bubbling, gurgling or murmuring sound and an eddying motion. ~*n.* a gentle bubbling, gurgling or murmuring sound; an eddying motion. **purling** *n., a.*

purl³ (pœl) *v.t., v.i.* to upset, to overturn. **purler** *n.* (*coll.*) a heavy or headlong fall or throw.

purlieu (pœ´lū) *n.* (*pl.* **purlieus**) **1** (*usu. pl.*) the bounds or limits within which one ranges, one's usual haunts. **2** (*pl.*) outlying parts, outskirts, environs.

purlin (pœ´lin) *n.* a horizontal timber resting on the principal rafters and supporting the common rafters or boards on which the roof is laid.

purloin (pœloin´) v.t. (formal or facet.) to steal, to take by theft. **purloiner** n.

purple (pœ´pəl) a. **1** of the colour of red and blue blended, the former predominating. **2** (Hist.) of the crimson colour obtained from molluscs esp. of the genus Murex. ~n. **1** a purple colour. **2** a purple pigment or dye. **3** a purple dress or robe, esp. of an emperor, king, Roman consul or a bishop. **4 a** (fig.) **(the purple)** imperial or regal power. **b** any position of authority or privilege. ~v.t. to make or dye purple. ~v.i. to become purple. **born in the purple** of high and wealthy, esp. royal or imperial, family. **purple emperor** n. a variety of butterfly, Apatura iris, having purple wings. **purple heart** n. **1** a mauve, heart-shaped, amphetamine tablet taken as a stimulant. **2 (Purple Heart)** a US decoration for wounds received on active service. **purpleness** n. **purple passage** n. **1** (also **purple patch**) a passage of over-ornate writing. **2** (coll.) a period of success or good fortune. **purple prose** n. obtrusively elevated or ornate writing. **purplish, purply** a.

purport[1] (pəpawt´) v.t. **1** to convey as the meaning, to imply, to signify. **2** to profess, to be meant to appear (to). **purportedly** adv.

purport[2] (pœ´pawt) n. **1** meaning, tenor, sense. **2** object, purpose.

purpose (pœ´pəs) n. **1** an end in view, an object, an aim. **2** determination, resolution. ~v.t. to intend, to design. **on purpose** intentionally, designedly, not by accident. **to no purpose** with no useful result. **to the purpose 1** with close relation to the matter in hand, relevantly. **2** usefully. **purpose-built** a. constructed to serve a specific purpose. **purposeful** a. **1** having a definite end in view. **2** determined, resolute. **purposefully** adv. **purposefulness** n. **purposeless** a. having no purpose, aimless. **purposelessly** adv. **purposelessness** n. **purposely** adv. on purpose, intentionally, not by accident. **purpose-made** a. made for a specific purpose. **purposive** a. **1** having or serving a purpose. **2** purposeful. **3** done with a purpose. **purposively** adv. **purposiveness** n.

purpura (pœ´pūrə) n. (Med.) a skin rash consisting of small purple spots caused by internal bleeding from the small blood vessels. **purpuric** (-pū´-) a. **purpurin** (-rin) n. a red colouring matter used in dyeing, orig. obtained from madder.

purr (pœ) n. a soft vibratory murmuring as of a cat when pleased. ~v.i. **1** (of a cat) to make this sound. **2** (of a person) to express satisfaction with or as if with this sound. **3** (of machinery, a car engine etc.) to make a similar soft sound. ~v.t. to signify, express or utter thus. **purring** a., n. **purringly** adv.

purse (pœs) n. **1** a small bag or pouch for money, usu. carried in the pocket. **2** (N Am.) a woman's handbag. **3** money, funds, resources, a treasury. **4** a sum of money subscribed or collected or offered as a gift, prize etc. **5** a baglike receptacle, a pouch. ~v.t. to wrinkle, to pucker. ~v.i. to

become wrinkled or puckered. **purse net** n. a net the mouth of which can be drawn together with cords like an old-fashioned purse. **purse seine** n. a large purse net for sea-fishing. **purse strings** n.pl. strings for drawing together the mouth of an old-fashioned purse. **to hold the purse strings** to control the expenditure (of a household etc.).

purser (pœ´sə) n. an officer on board ship or on an aircraft in charge of the provisions, pay and the general welfare of the passengers.

purslane (pœs´lin) n. any of various herbs of the genus Portulaca, esp. the succulent herb, Portulaca oleracea, used as a salad and pot-herb.

pursue (pəsū´, -soo´) v.t. (pres.p. **pursuing**, past, p.p. **pursued**) **1** to follow with intent to seize, kill etc. **2** to try persistently to gain or obtain, to seek. **3** to continue with, to be engaged in (a course of action, studies). **4** to proceed in accordance with. **5** (of misfortune, consequences etc.) to attend persistently, to haunt. **6** to try persistently to make the acquaintance of, or to gain the attention of (a person). **7** to continue to discuss, to follow up. ~v.i. to go in pursuit. **pursuable** a. **pursuance** n. the carrying out, performance, implementation (of a plan etc.). **pursuant** a. pursuing. ~adv. in accordance or conformably (to). **pursuantly** adv. **pursuer** n. **pursuit** (-sūt, -soot) n. **1** the act, or an instance, of pursuing, a following. **2** a prosecution, an endeavour to attain some end. **3** an employment, occupation, business or recreation that one follows persistently. **4** a kind of cycle race in which two competitors at a time set off at opposite sides of the track and try to overtake each other. **in pursuit of** pursuing.

pursuivant (pœ´sivənt, -swi-) n. (Her.) an attendant on a herald, an officer of the College of Arms of lower rank than a herald.

pursy (pœ´si) a. (comp. **pursier**, superl. **pursiest**) **1** short-winded, asthmatic. **2** fat, corpulent. **pursiness** n.

purulent (pū´rələnt) a. consisting of or discharging pus or matter. **purulence, purulency** n. **purulently** adv.

purvey (pəvā´) v.t. to provide, to supply, esp. provisions. ~v.i. **1** to make provision. **2** to act as a supplier. **purveyance** n. **purveyor** n.

purview (pœ´vū) n. **1** extent, range, scope, intention. **2** range of vision, knowledge etc.

pus (pŭs) n. the thick yellowish liquid secreted from inflamed tissues, the produce of suppuration.

push (push) v.t. **1** to press against with force, tending to urge forward or away. **2** to move (a body along, up, down etc.) thus. **3** to make (one's way) vigorously. **4** to impel, to drive. **5** to cause to put forth or project. **6** to put pressure on (a person). **7** to pursue (a claim etc.). **8** to develop or carry (a point, an argument etc.), esp. to extremes. **9** (with a number) to approach. **10** to seek to promote, esp. to promote the sale or use of. **11** (coll.) to peddle (drugs). ~v.i. **1** to exert pressure (against, upon etc.). **2** to press forward, to make one's way vigorously, to hasten forward energetically. **3** to protrude or project. **4** to thrust or butt (against). **5** to be urgent and persistent. ~*n*. **1** the act, or an instance, of pushing, a thrust, a shove. **2** a vigorous effort, an attempt, an onset. **3** pressure. **4** an exigency, a crisis, an extremity. **5** persevering energy, self-assertion. **6** the use of influence to help (a person or a cause). **7** (*Mil.*) an offensive. **8** (*Austral.*) a gang of larrikins, a clique or party. **at a push** if really necessary. **to be pushed for** (*coll.*) to be short of (time or money). **to get/ give the push** (*sl.*) to dismiss, be dismissed, esp. from a job. **to push about/ around 1** (*coll.*) to bully, to treat with contempt. **2** to move around roughly or aimlessly. **to push along** (*coll.*) to go away. **to push for** (*coll.*) to advocate vigorously, to make strenuous efforts to achieve. **to push in** (*coll.*) to force one's way into (esp. a queue) ahead of others. **to push off 1** to push against the bank with an oar so as to move a boat off. **2** (*coll.*) to go away. **to push on 1** to press forward, to hasten. **2** to urge or drive on. **to push one's luck** (*coll.*) to take risks, esp. by overplaying an existing advantage. **to push through** to secure the acceptance of (a plan, proposal etc.) speedily or by compulsion. **when push comes to shove** (*coll.*) when the time for action comes. **push-bike, push-bicycle** *n.* (*coll.*) a bicycle worked by foot pedals as distinguished from a motor-bicycle. **push-button** *n.* a device for opening or closing an electric circuit by the pressure of the finger on a button. ~*a.* (of machinery etc.) operated by means of a push-button. **pushcart** *n.* (*N Am.*) a barrow. **pushchair** *n.* a light, folding chair on wheels for a child. **pusher** *n.* **1** a person or thing that pushes, esp. a device used in conjunction with a spoon for feeding very young children. **2** (*coll.*) a pushful person. **3** (*coll.*) a drug peddler. **pushful** *a.* (*coll.*) self-assertive, energetic, vigorous or persistent in advancing oneself. **pushfully** *adv.* **pushing** *a.* **1** enterprising, energetic. **2** self-assertive; encroaching. **3** (*coll.*) having almost reached (a specified age). **pushover** *n.* (*coll.*) **1** something easy to do. **2** a person, team etc. easy to defeat. **push-pull** *a.* of or relating to any piece of apparatus in which electrical or electronic devices, e.g. two transistors in an amplifier, act in opposition to each other. **pushrod** *n.* in an internal-combustion engine, a metal rod that opens and closes the valves. **push-start** *v.t.* to set (a vehicle) in motion by pushing, then engaging a gear to start the engine. ~*n.* the act, or an instance, of starting an engine thus. **push-up** *n.* (*N Am.*) a press-up. **pushy** *a.* (*comp.* **pushier**, *superl.* **pushiest**) (*coll.*) pushful. **pushily** *adv.* **pushiness** *n.*

pusillanimous (pūsilan´imǝs) *a.* lacking courage, firmness or strength of mind, faint-hearted. **pusillanimity** (-nim´-) *n.* **pusillanimously** *adv.*

puss (pus) *n.* **1** a pet name for a cat, esp. in calling. **2** a hare. **3** (*coll.*) a child, a girl. **puss moth** *n.* a large bombycid moth, *Cerura vinula.* **pussy** *n.* (*pl.* **pussies**) **1** (*coll.*) a cat. **2** (*taboo sl.*) the female pudenda. **3** (*offensive*) women generally considered as sexual objects. **pussy cat** *n.* a cat. **pussyfoot** *v.i.* **1** to move stealthily or warily. **2** to avoid committing oneself. **pussyfooter** *n.* **pussy willow** *n.* **1** a small American willow, *Salix discolor*, with silvery catkins. **2** any of various similar willows.

pustule (pŭs´tūl) *n.* **1** a small vesicle containing pus, a pimple. **2** a small excrescence, a wart, a blister. **pustular** *a.* **pustulate**[1] (-lāt) *v.t., v.i.* to form into pustules. **pustulate**[2] (-lǝt) *a.* covered with pustules or excrescences. **pustulation** (-lā´shǝn) *n.* **pustulous** *a.*

put[1] (put) *v.t.* (*pres. p.* **putting**, *past, p.p.* **put**) **1** to move so as to place in some position. **2** to bring into some particular state or condition. **3** to assign. **4** to express, to state. **5** to render, to translate (into). **6** to substitute (one thing for another). **7** to apply, to set, to impose. **8** to stake (money on). **9** to invest (e.g. money in). **10** to inflict (something on somebody). **11** to subject (a person) to. **12** to advance, to propose (for consideration etc.), to submit (to a vote). **13** to imagine (oneself) in a position etc. **14** to constrain, to incite, to force, to make (a person do etc.). **15** to repose (trust, confidence etc.). **16** to estimate (at a specified amount). **17** to hurl, to cast, to throw (a weight etc.) as a sport. ~*v.i.* **1** (*Naut.*) to go, to proceed, to steer one's course (in a specified direction). **2** (*N Am.*) (of a river) to flow in a specified direction. ~*n.* **1** the act, or an instance, of putting. **2** a cast, a throw (of a weight etc.). **3** an agreement to sell or deliver (stock, goods etc.) at a stipulated price within a specified time. **not to know where to put oneself** (*coll.*) to be very embarrassed. **not to put it past somebody** to consider a person capable of (the activity under discussion). **to put about 1** to inconvenience. **2** (*Naut.*) to go about, to change the course of to the opposite tack. **3** (*coll.*) to make public, to spread abroad. **to put across 1** to communicate effectively. **2** to make acceptable. **to put away 1** to return to its proper place. **2** to lay by. **3** to shut up (in a prison, mental institution etc.). **4** (*coll.*) to consume (food or drink). **5** to put (an animal) to death because of old age etc. **6** to remove. **to put back 1** to retard, to check the forward motion of. **2** to postpone. **3** to move the hands of (a clock) back. **4** to replace. **to put by** to put, set or lay aside for future use. **to put down 1** to suppress, to crush. **2** to take down, to snub, to degrade. **3** to confute, to silence. **4** to reduce, to diminish. **5** to write down, to enter, to subscribe. **6** to reckon, to consider, to attribute. **7** to put (a baby) to bed. **8** to kill, esp. an old or ill animal. **9** to pay (as a deposit). **10** (of an aircraft) to land. **11** (of a bus etc.) to stop to let (passengers) off. **12** to preserve, to store, to pickle. **to put forth 1** (*formal*) **a** to present to notice. **b** to publish, to put into circulation. **2** to extend. **3** to shoot out. **4** to exert. **5** (of a plant) to produce (buds, shoots). **to put forward 1** to set forth, to advance, to propose. **2** to thrust (oneself) into prominence. **3** to move the hands of (a clock) onwards. **to put in 1** to introduce, to interject, to interpose. **2** to insert, to enter. **3** to install in office etc. **4 a** to present, to submit, as an application, request etc. **b** to submit a claim (for something). **5** to be a candidate (for). **6** to enter a harbour. **7** (*coll.*) to spend, to pass (time), to devote (effort). **to put it across someone** (*coll.*) to defeat someone by ingenuity. **to put it on 1** to pretend (to be ill etc.). **2** to exaggerate. **to put it to someone 1** to suggest to a person (that). **2** to challenge a person to deny (that). **to put off 1** to lay aside, to discard, to take off. **2 a** to postpone (an appointment). **b** to postpone an appointment with (a person). **3** to disappoint, to evade (a person). **4** to hinder, to distract the attention of. **5** to dissuade (from). **6** to cause aversion to. **7** to foist, to palm off (with). **to put on 1** to take on. **2** to clothe oneself with. **3 a** to assume (a disguise etc.). **b** to pretend to feel (an emotion). **4** to add, to affix, to apply. **5** to add on (weight etc.). **6** to bring into play, to exert. **7** to cause to operate (a light etc.). **8** to cause to be available. **9** to stage, to produce (a play etc.). **10** to appoint. **11** to move the hands of (a clock) forward. **12** to send (a bowler) on to the field in cricket. **to put one over on** (*coll.*) to deceive into believing or accepting. **to put on to** to make (a person) aware of; to put (a person) in touch with. **to put out 1** to eject. **2** to extinguish (a light). **3** to disconcert; to annoy, to irritate. **4** to inconvenience (oneself). **5** to exert (strength). **6** to dislocate (a joint). **7** to publish, to broadcast. **8** to give out (work) to be done at different premises. **9** to render unconscious. **10** to invest, to place (at interest). **11** in cricket, to dismiss (a batsman or a side). **12** to blind (someone's eyes). **to put over 1** to communicate effectively. **2** (*N Am.*) to postpone. **3** (*N Am.*) to pass off. **to put through 1** to connect (someone) by telephone (to someone else). **2** to see to a conclusion, to accomplish. **3** to cause to undergo (esp. suffering). **to put together** to assemble (things, parts) to form a finished whole. **to put to it 1** to distress. **2** to press hard. **to put under** to render unconscious by the use of an anaesthetic. **to put up 1** to raise (a hand etc.). **2** to erect, to build. **3** to offer, to present, as for sale, auction. **4** to increase (a price etc.). **5** to give, to show, as a fight, resistance etc. **6** to lodge and entertain. **7** to take lodgings. **8** to display (a notice etc.). **9** to publish (banns etc.). **10** to provide (money, a prize). **11** to offer (oneself) as a candidate. **12** to present as a candidate. **13** to pack up. **14** to place in a safe place. **15** to lay aside. **16** to sheathe (a sword). **17** to cause (game birds) to come out of cover. **to put upon 1** to impose upon; to take undue advantage of. **2** to victimize. **to put up to 1** to incite to. **2** to make conversant with. **to put**

up with to tolerate, to submit to. **put-down** *n.* a snub, an action or remark intended to humiliate. **put-in** *n.* in rugby football, the action of putting the ball into the scrum. **put-off** *n.* an evasion, an excuse. **put-on** *n.* an attempt to deceive or mislead. **putter**¹ *n.* **1** a person who puts. **2** a shot-putter. **putting (the shot)** *n.* the act or sport of throwing a heavy weight from the shoulder by an outward thrust of the arm. **put-up job** *n.* something secretly pre-arranged for purposes of deception. **put-you-up** *n.* a makeshift temporary bed for a visitor.

put² PUTT.

putative (pū′tətiv) *a.* **1** reputed, supposed. **2** commonly regarded as. **putatively** *adv.*

putlog (pŭt′log), **putlock** (-lok) *n.* a short horizontal piece of timber for the floor of a scaffold to rest on.

put-put (pŭt′pŭt) *v.i.* (*pres.p.* **put-putting**, *past*, *p.p.* **put-putted**) **1** (of a petrol engine) to make a rapid popping sound. **2** (of a vehicle) to travel along while making this sound. ~*n.* this sound.

putrefy (pū′trifī) *v.t.* (*3rd pers. sing. pres.* **putrefies**, *pres.p.* **putrefying**, *past*, *p.p.* **putrefied**) to make putrid, to cause to rot or decay. ~*v.i.* **1** to become putrid, to rot, to decay. **2** to fester, to suppurate. **3** to become corrupt. **putrefaction** (-fak′-) *n.* **putrefacient** (-fā′shənt) *a.* **putrefactive** *a.* **putrescence** (-tres′əns) *n.* the process of rotting. **putrescent** *a.*

putrid (pū′trid) *a.* **1** in a state of putrefaction, decomposition, or decay. **2** tainted, foul, noxious. **3** (*fig.*) corrupt. **4** (*sl.*) of very poor quality. **putridity** (-trid′-), **putridness** *n.* **putridly** *adv.*

putsch (puch) *n.* a sudden rising, revolt; a coup d'état.

putt (pŭt), **put** *v.i.* (*3rd pers. sing. pres.* **putts, puts**, *pres.p.* **putting**, *past*, *p.p.* **putted**) to strike a golf ball with a putter. ~*v.t.* to strike (the ball) gently with a putter so as to get it into a hole on a putting green. ~*n.* this stroke. **putter**² *n.* **1** a short, stiff golf club, used for striking the ball on a putting green. **2** a person who putts. **putting green** *n.* **1** the piece of ground around each hole on a golf course, usu. kept rolled, closely mown and clear of obstacles. **2** an area of smooth grass with several holes for putting games.

puttee (pŭt′i, -ē) *n.* **1** a long strip of cloth wound spirally round the leg, usu. from ankle to knee, as a form of gaiter. **2** (*N Am.*) a leather legging.

putter¹ PUT¹.

putter² PUTT.

putter³ (pŭt′ə) *v.i.* to put-put. ~*n.* a put-putting sound.

putter⁴ POTTER².

putto (put′ō) *n.* (*pl.* **putti** (-ē)) a figure of a small boy, cherub or cupid in Renaissance and baroque art.

putty (pŭt′i) *n.* (*pl.* **putties**) **1** whiting and linseed oil beaten up into a tenacious cement, used in glazing etc. **2** fine lime mortar used by plasterers for filling cracks etc. **3** calcined tin or lead used by jewellers as polishing powder for glass, metal etc. *~v.t.* (*3rd pers. sing. pres.* **putties,** *pres.p.* **puttying,** *past, p.p.* **puttied**) to fix, cement, fill up or cover with putty. **to be putty in someone's hands** to be easily manipulated by someone. **putty-root** *n.* an American orchid, *Aplectrum hyemale,* the root of which contains glutinous matter sometimes used as cement.

puzzle (pŭz'əl) *n.* **1** a perplexing problem, question or enigma. **2** a toy, riddle or other contrivance for exercising ingenuity or patience. *~v.t.* to perplex, to embarrass, to mystify. *~v.i.* to be bewildered or perplexed. **to puzzle out** to discover, or work out by mental labour. **puzzle-dom** (-dəm), **puzzlement** *n.* **puzzler** *n.* a person who or a thing which puzzles. **puzzling** *a.* **puzzlingly** *adv.*

PVA *abbr.* polyvinyl acetate.

PVC *abbr.* polyvinyl chloride.

Pvt. *abbr.* (*Mil.*) Private.

PW *abbr.* policewoman.

p.w. *abbr.* per week.

PWA (pēdŭbəlūā') *n.* (*pl.* **PWAs**) a person with Aids.

PWD *abbr.* Public Works Department.

PWR *abbr.* pressurized-water reactor.

pyaemia (pīe'miə), (*N Am.*) **pyemia** *n.* (*Med.*) blood poisoning, due to the spread of pus-forming bacteria in the system causing multiple abscesses. **pyaemic** *a.*

pycnic PYKNIC.

pye-dog (pī'dog), **pie-dog, pi-dog** *n.* a stray mongrel dog, esp. in India.

pyelitis (pīəlī'tis) *n.* (*Med.*) inflammation of the pelvis of the kidney.

pygmy (pig'mi), **pigmy** *n.* (*pl.* **pygmies, pigmies**) **1** a member of any of various dwarf peoples living in Malaysia or Central Africa. **2** a dwarf, a small person, anything very diminutive. **3** a person having a certain faculty or quality in relatively a very small degree; an insignificant person. *~a.* **1** of or relating to pygmies; diminutive, dwarf. **2** small and insignificant. **pygmaean** (-mē'ən), **pygmean** *a.* **pygmy chimpanzee** *n.* an anthropoid ape of central and W Africa, *Pan paniscus.* **pygmy hippopotamus** *n.* (*pl.* **pygmy hippopotamuses, pygmy hippopotami**) a quadruped, *Choeropsis liberiensis,* related to but smaller than *Hippopotamus amphibius.*

pyjamas (pəjah'məz), (*N Am.*) **pajamas** *n.pl.* **1** a sleeping suit consisting of a loose jacket and trousers. **2** loose trousers of silk, cotton etc. worn by both sexes among Muslims in India and Pakistan. **pyjama** *a.* of or relating to either the jacket or the trousers of pyjamas.

pyknic (pik'nik), **pycnic** *a.* (of a body type) characterized by short stature, relatively short arms and legs, a large abdomen and a short neck. *~n.* a person of this body type.

pylon (pī'lən) *n.* **1** a structure, usu. of steel, supporting an electric cable. **2** a rigid, streamlined support (for an engine etc.) on the outside of an aircraft. **3** a stake marking out the path for aircraft at an airfield. **4** a gateway of imposing form or dimensions, esp. the monumental gateway of an Egyptian temple.

pylorus (pīlaw'rəs) *n.* (*pl.* **pylori** (-rī)) (*Anat.*) the contracted end of the stomach leading into the small intestine. **pyloric** (-lor'ik) *a.*

pyorrhoea (pīərē'ə), (*N Am.*) **pyorrhea** *n.* **1** inflammation of the gums leading to the discharge of pus and loosening of the teeth; periodontal disease. **2** any discharge of pus.

pyracantha (pī'rəkanthə), **pyracanth** (-kanth) *n.* (*pl.* **pyracanthas, pyracanths**) any evergreen thorny shrub of the genus *Pyracantha,* with white flowers and coral-red berries, also called the firethorn, commonly trained against walls as an ornamental climber.

pyralid (pīral'id, -rā'lid) *n.* any of various moths of the family *Pyralidae,* small and slender with long legs. *~a.* of or relating to this family.

pyramid (pir'əmid) *n.* **1** a monumental structure of masonry, with a square base and triangular sloping sides meeting at the apex. **2** a similar solid body, with a triangular or polygonal, but usu. square, base. **3** a pile or heap of this shape. **4** a game of pool played with fifteen coloured balls and a cue ball. **pyramidal** (-ram'-), **pyramidic** (-mid'-), **pyramidical** *a.* **pyramidally, pyramidically** *adv.* **pyramid selling** *n.* a system of selling whereby batches of goods are sold to agents who sell smaller batches at increased prices to subagents and so on.

pyre (pīə) *n.* **1** a funeral pile for burning a dead body. **2** any pile of combustibles.

pyrethrum (pīrē'thrəm) *n.* (*pl.* **pyrethrums**) **1** any of several plants of the genus *Tanacetum* of the Compositae, esp. *T. coccineum.* **2** an insecticide made from the dried heads of these. **pyrethrin** (-thrin) *n.* either of two oily, insecticidal compounds found in pyrethrum flowers. **pyrethroid** *n.* (*Chem.*) any one of a group of synthetic compounds with similar insecticidal properties.

pyretic (pīret'ik) *a.* of, relating to or producing fever.

Pyrex® (pī'reks) *n.* a heat-resistant glass containing oxide of boron. *~a.* (of a cooking or laboratory container) made of Pyrex.

pyrexia (pīrek'siə) *n.* (*Med.*) fever, feverish condition. **pyrexial, pyrexic, pyrexical** *a.*

pyridine (pir'idēn, pī'-) *n.* (*Chem.*) a liquid alkaloid obtained from bone oil, coal tar etc., used as a solvent etc. **pyridoxine** (-dok'sēn) *n.* a derivative of pyridine found in yeast, vitamin B_6.

pyrimidine (pirim'idēn) *n.* **1** (*Chem.*) a cyclic organic nitrogenous base, with the formula $C_4H_4N_2$. **2** any of several compounds derived from this including constituents of nucleic acids.

pyrites (pīrī'tēz) *n.* a native sulphide of iron, one of two common sulphides, chalcopyrite, yellow or copper pyrites, or marcasite, usu. called iron pyrites. **pyrite** (pī´rīt) *n.* iron pyrites. **pyritic** (-rit´-), **pyritous** (pī´ri-) *a.* **pyritiferous** (-tif´-) *a.* **pyritize** (pī´ri-), **pyritise** *v.t.*

pyro- (pī´rō), **pyr-** *comb. form* **1** fire, heat. **2** (*Chem.*) obtained (as if) by heating or by the elimination of water. **3** (*Mineral.*) changing under the action of heat. **4** having a red or yellow colour like fire.

pyroclastic (pīrōklas´tik) *a.* formed from or consisting of the fragments broken up or ejected by volcanic action. **pyroclast** (pī´-) *n.* **pyroclastic flow** *n.* (*Geol.*) a mixture of hot ash, lava and gases flowing at high speed from a volcanic crater.

pyroelectric (pīrōilek´trik) *a.* (of some minerals) becoming electrically charged on heating. **pyroelectricity** (-eliktris´-) *n.*

pyrogen (pī´rəjen) *n.* a substance, such as ptomaine, that produces fever on being introduced into the body. **pyrogenetic** (-net´-), **pyrogenic** (-jen´-) *a.* **1** producing heat. **2** producing feverishness. **3** pyrogenous. **pyrogenous** (-roj´-) *a.* produced by fire or by volcanic processes, igneous.

pyrography (pīrog´rəfi) *n.* (*pl.* **pyrographies**) the art of making designs in wood by means of fire, pokerwork.

pyrolysis (pīrol´isis) *n.* the chemical decomposition of a substance by heat. **pyrolyse** (pī´rəlīz), (*N Am.*) **pyrolyze** *v.t.* to subject to this process. **pyrolytic** (-lit´-) *a.*

pyromania (pīrəmā´niə) *n.* an irresistible desire to set things on fire. **pyromaniac** (-ak) *n.*

pyrometer (pīrom´itə) *n.* an instrument for measuring high temperatures. **pyrometric** (-met´-), **pyrometrical** *a.* **pyrometrically** *adv.* **pyrometry** (-om´-) *n.*

pyrope (pī´rōp) *n.* a deep-red garnet.

pyrophoric (pīrəfor´ik) *a.* (of a chemical) igniting spontaneously on contact with air.

pyrophosphoric (pīrōfosfor´ik) *a.* derived by heat from phosphoric acid.

pyrosis (pīrō´sis) *n.* (*Med.*) heartburn.

pyrotechnic (pīrōtek´nik) *a.* **1** of or relating to fireworks or their manufacture. **2** of the nature of fireworks. **3** (*fig.*) resembling a firework show, brilliant, dazzling. **pyrotechnical** *a.* **pyrotechnically** *adv.* **pyrotechnics** *n.* **1** the art of making fireworks. **2** (*sing. or pl.*) a display of fireworks. **3** (*sing. or pl.*) a dazzling or virtuoso display. **pyrotechnist** *n.* **pyrotechny** (pī´rətekni) *n.*

pyroxene (pī´roksēn, -rok´-) *n.* any of a group of silicates of lime, magnesium, iron or manganese, of various forms and origin.

pyroxylin (pīrok´silin), **pyroxyle** (-sil) *n.* a nitrocellulose, gun cotton, used in the manufacture of plastics and lacquers.

Pyrrhic (pir´ik) *a.* of or relating to Pyrrhus. **pyrrhic victory, Pyrrhic victory** *n.* a victory that is as costly as a defeat.

pyruvate (pīroo´vāt) *n.* (*Chem.*) any salt or ester of pyruvic acid. **pyruvic acid** *n.* an organic acid occurring as an intermediate in the metabolism of proteins and carbohydrates.

Pythagorean (pīthagərē´ən) *n.* a follower of Pythagoras. *~a.* of or relating to Pythagoras or his philosophy. **Pythagoras's theorem** (pīthag´ə-rəsiz) *n.* the theorem, attributed to Pythagoras, that the square on the hypotenuse of a right-angled triangle is equal to the sum of the squares on the other two sides.

python (pī´thən) *n.* a large non-venomous serpent of the family Pythonidae, that crushes its prey. **pythonic** (-thon´-) *a.*

pyuria (pīū´riə) *n.* (*Med.*) the presence of pus in the urine.

pyx (piks), **pix** *n.* the covered vessel, usu. of precious metal, in which the Eucharistic host is kept. **pyxidium** (-sid´iəm) *n.* (*pl.* **pyxidia** (-diə)) (*Bot.*) a capsule or seed vessel dehiscing by a transverse suture, as in the pimpernel. **pyxis** (-sis) *n.* (*pl.* **pyxides** (-sidēz)) **1** a box, a casket. **2** (*Bot.*) a pyxidium.

pzazz PIZAZZ.

Q

Q[1] (kū), **q** (*pl.* **Qs, Q's**) the 17th letter of the English and other versions of the Roman alphabet. It is pronounced as a voiceless velar plosive like *k* and is normally followed by *u*, the combination of *qu* usually having the sound of *kw*. ~*symbol* **1** (*Theol.*) the alleged source of the material found in the gospels of both Matthew and Luke but not in Mark. **2** (*Physics*) heat.

Q[2] *abbr.* **1** Queen. **2** Queen's.

QC *abbr.* (*Law*) Queen's Counsel.

QED *abbr.* L *quod erat demonstrandum*, which was to be proved.

qindar (kindah´), **qintar** (-tah´) *n.* a unit of Albanian currency equal to one hundredth of a lek.

Qld. *abbr.* Queensland.

QM *abbr.* quartermaster.

QMG *abbr.* Quartermaster General.

QMS *abbr.* Quartermaster Sergeant.

qr. *abbr.* quarter(s).

qt. *abbr.* **1** quart, quarts. **2** (*also* **q.t.**) quiet. **on the qt.** (*coll.*) secretly, on the sly.

qu *abbr.* **1** query. **2** question.

qua (kwā, kwah) *conj.* in the character of, by virtue of being, as.

quack[1] (kwak) *v.i.* **1** to make the harsh cry of a duck or a similar sound. **2** (*coll.*) to chatter loudly or boastfully. ~*n.* the cry of a duck.

quack[2] (kwak) *n.* **1** an unqualified practitioner of medicine, esp. one offering ineffectual remedies. **2** (*sl.*) a doctor. **3** a mere pretender to knowledge or skill. ~*a.* of or relating to quacks or quackery (*quack remedies*). **quackery, quackism** *n.* **quackish** *a.*

quad[1] (kwod) *n.* a quadrangle or court, as of a college etc.

quad[2] (kwod) *n.* (*coll.*) each child of quadruplets.

quad[3] (kwod) *a.* quadraphonic. ~*n.* quadraphonics.

Quadragesima (kwodrəjes´imə) *n.* (*also* **Quadragesima Sunday**) the first Sunday in Lent. **quadragesimal** *a.* **1** (of a fast) lasting 40 days. **2** of, relating to or used in Lent; Lenten.

quadrangle (kwod´rang-gəl) *n.* **1** a plane figure having four angles and four sides, esp. a square or rectangle. **2** an open square or four-sided court surrounded by buildings. **3** such a court together with the surrounding buildings. **quadrangular** (-rang´gū-) *a.*

quadrant (kwod´rənt) *n.* **1** the fourth part of the circumference of a circle, an arc of 90°. **2** a plane figure contained by two radii of a circle at right angles to each other and the arc between them. **3** a quarter of a sphere. **4** any of the four sections into which something, esp. a plane, is divided by two lines that intersect at right angles. **5** an object or part shaped like a quadrant of a circle. **6** an instrument shaped like a quarter-circle graduated for taking angular measurements, esp. one formerly used by sailors and astronomers for taking the altitude of the sun or stars. **quadrantal** (-ran´-) *a.*

quadraphonic (kwodrəfon´ik), **quadrophonic** *a.* of, relating to or being a system of recording and reproducing sound using four independent sound signals or speakers. **quadraphonically** *adv.* **quadraphonics** *n.* **quadraphony** (-raf´əni) *n.*

quadrat (kwod´rət) *n.* a square of vegetation marked out for ecological study.

quadrate[1] (kwod´rət) *a.* square; rectangular. ~*n.* **1** (*Anat.*) the quadrate bone. **2** (*Anat.*) a quadrate muscle. **3** a square, cubical or rectangular object. **quadrate bone** *n.* (*Anat., Zool.*) in birds and reptiles, a bone by means of which the jaws are articulated with the skull. **quadrate muscle** *n.* a square-shaped muscle in the hip, forearm etc.

quadratic (-rat´-) *a.* (*Math.*) **1** involving the second and no higher power of the variable or unknown quantity. **2** square. ~*n.* **1** a quadratic equation. **2** (*pl.*) the part of algebra dealing with quadratic equations.

quadrate[2] (kwodrāt´, kwod´-) *v.t.* **1** to square. **2** to make conformable. ~*v.i.* to agree, to match, to correspond.

quadrennial (kwodren´iəl) *a.* **1** lasting four years. **2** recurring every four years. **quadrennially** *adv.* **quadrennium** (-iəm) *n.* (*pl.* **quadrenniums, quadrennia** (-iə)) a period of four years.

quadri- (kwod´ri), **quadr-** *comb. form* four.

quadriceps (kwod´riseps) *n.* (*Anat.*) a four-headed muscle at the front of the thigh, acting as extensor to the leg.

quadrilateral (kwodrilat´ərəl) *n.* a plane figure or area with four straight sides. ~*a.* having four sides and four angles. **quadrilaterality** (-ral´-), **quadrilateralness** *n.*

quadrille[1] (kwədril´) *n.* **1** a dance consisting of five figures executed by four sets of couples. **2** a piece of music for such a dance.

quadrille[2] (kwədril´) *n.* a game of cards played by four persons with 40 cards, fashionable in the 18th cent.

quadrillion (kwədril´yən) *n.* (*pl.* **quadrillion, quadrillions**) **1** the fifth power of a thousand, one followed by 15 zeros. **2** (in Britain, esp. formerly) the number produced by raising a million to its fourth power, represented by one followed by 24 zeros. **quadrillionth** *n.*, *a.*

quadrinomial (kwodrinō′miəl) *a.* consisting of four terms. *~n.* (*Math.*) a mathematical expression consisting of four algebraic terms.

quadripartite (kwodripah′tīt) *a.* **1** divided into or consisting of four parts. **2** affecting or shared by four parties.

quadriplegia (kwodriplē′jə, -jiə) *n.* (*Med.*) paralysis of all four limbs. **quadriplegic** *a.*, *n.*

quadrivalent (kwodrivā′lənt) *a.* (*Chem.*) having a valency or combining power of four, tetravalent.

quadroon (kwədroon′) *n.* the offspring of a mulatto and a white person; a person of one quarter black and three-quarters white blood.

quadrophonic QUADRAPHONIC.

quadrumanous (kwodroo′mənəs), †**quadrimanous** *a.* of, relating to or belonging to a group of mammals in which the hind as well as the fore feet have an opposable digit and are used as hands, containing the monkeys, apes, baboons and lemurs.

quadruped (kwod′ruped) *n.* a four-footed animal, esp. a mammal. *~a.* having four legs and feet. **quadrupedal** (-pē′dəl, -ped′əl, -roo′pidəl) *a.*

quadruple (kwod′rupəl, -roo′-) *a.* **1** consisting of four parts. **2** involving four members, units etc. **3** equal to four times the number or quantity of, fourfold. **4** (*Mus.*) (of musical time) having four beats in a bar. *~n.* a number or quantity four times as great as another. *~v.i.* to increase fourfold, to become four times as much. *~v.t.* to multiply fourfold, to make four times as much. **quadruplet** (-plit) *n.* **1** any one of four children born of the same mother at one birth. **2** a compound or combination of four things working together. **3** (*Mus.*) four notes to be played in a time value of three. **quadruplicate**[1] (-roo′plikāt) *v.t.* to make fourfold, to quadruple. **quadruplicate**[2] (-roo′plikət) *a.* **1** four times as many or as much, fourfold. **2** four times copied. **in quadruplicate** written out or copied four times. **quadruplication** (-ā′shən) *n.* **quadruplicity** (-plis′-) *n.* the state of being quadruple. **quadruply** *adv.*

quaff (kwof) *v.t.* **1** to drink in large draughts. **2** to drink from in large draughts. *~v.i.* to drink copiously. *~n.* a copious draught. **quaffable** *a.* **quaffer** *n.*

quag (kwag, kwog) *n.* a piece of marshy or boggy ground. **quaggy** *a.* (*comp.* **quaggier**, *superl.* **quaggiest**) **quagginess** *n.*

quagga (kwag′ə) *n.* (*pl. in general* **quagga**, *in particular* **quaggas**) a S African quadruped, *Equus quagga*, intermediate between the ass and the zebra, now extinct.

quagmire (kwag′mīə, kwog′-) *n.* **1** an area of soft marshy ground that moves or sinks under the feet. **2** an awkward or difficult predicament.

quail[1] (kwāl) *v.i.* **1** to shrink back with fear, to be

cowed, to lose heart. **2** to give way (before or to).

quail[2] (kwāl) *n.* (*pl. in general* **quail**, *in particular* **quails**) a small migratory bird of the genus *Coturnix*, allied to the partridge, esp. a European game bird *C. coturnix*.

quaint (kwānt) *a.* **1** old-fashioned and odd, pleasing by virtue of strangeness, oddity or fancifulness. **2** odd, whimsical, singular. **quaintly** *adv.* **quaintness** *n.*

quake (kwāk) *v.i.* **1** to shake, to tremble, to quiver. **2** to rock, to vibrate. *~n.* **1** a tremulous motion, a shudder. **2** (*coll.*) an earthquake. **quaking** *a.* **1** trembling. **2** unstable. **quaking-grass** *n.* a grass of the genus *Briza*, the spikelets of which have a tremulous motion. **quaky** *a.* (*comp.* **quakier**, *superl.* **quakiest**). **quakiness** *n.*

Quaker (kwā′kə) *n.* a member of the Society of Friends. *~a.* of or relating to Quakers or their religious belief. **Quakerish** *a.* **Quakerism** *n.*

qualify (kwol′ifī) *v.t.* (*3rd pers. sing. pres.* **qualifies**, *pres.p.* **qualifying**, *past*, *p.p.* **qualified**) **1** to invest or furnish with the requisite qualities. **2** to make competent, fit, or legally capable (to be or do, or for any action, place, office or occupation). **3** to modify, to limit, to narrow the scope, force etc. of (a statement, opinion or word). **4** to moderate, to mitigate, to temper. **5** to reduce the strength or flavour of (spirit etc.) with water, to dilute. **6** (*esp. Gram.*) to attribute a quality to, to describe or characterize as. *~v.i.* **1** to become qualified or fit. **2** to make oneself competent, suitable or eligible (for). **qualifiable** *a.* **qualification** (-fikā′shən) *n.* **1** the act of qualifying or the state of being qualified. **2** modification, restriction or limitation of meaning; exception or partial negation restricting completeness or absoluteness. **3** any natural or acquired quality fitting a person or thing (for an office, employment etc.). **4** a condition that must be fulfilled for the exercise of a privilege etc. **qualificative**, **qualificatory** *a.* **qualifier** *n.* **qualifying** *n.*, *a.* **qualifying round** *n.* a preliminary round in a competition.

quality (kwol′iti) *n.* (*pl.* **qualities**) **1** a distinctive property or attribute, that which gives individuality. **2** relative nature or kind, distinguishing character. **3** a mental or moral trait or characteristic. **4** particular capacity, value, or function. **5** degree of excellence, relative goodness. **6** a high standard of excellence. **7** (*Logic*) the affirmative or negative nature of a proposition. **8** that which distinguishes sounds of the same pitch and intensity, timbre. *~a.* **1** having or displaying excellence. **2** (of a newspaper) aimed at an educated readership. **qualitative** (-tativ) *a.* of, relating to or concerned with quality (as opposed to *quantitative*). **qualitative analysis** *n.* (*Chem.*) the detection of the constituents of a compound body. **qualitatively** *adv.* **quality control** *n.* the testing of manufactured products to ensure they are up to standard. **quality con-**

troller *n.* **quality time** *n.* time spent constructively in improving family relationships, lifestyle etc.

qualm (kwahm) *n.* **1** a sensation of fear or uneasiness. **2** a misgiving, a scruple, compunction. **3** a sensation of nausea, a feeling of sickness. **qualmish** *a.* **qualmishly** *adv.* **qualmishness** *n.* **qualmy** *a.* (*comp.* **qualmier,** *superl.* **qualmiest**).

quandary (kwon´dəri) *n.* (*pl.* **quandaries**) **1** a state of difficulty or perplexity. **2** an awkward predicament, a dilemma.

quango (kwang´gō) *n.* (*pl.* **quangos**) a board set up by central government to supervise activity in a specific field, e.g. the Race Relations Board.

quanta, quantal QUANTUM.

quantify (kwon´tifī) *v.t.* (*3rd pers. sing. pres.* **quantifies,** *pres.p.* **quantifying,** *past, p.p.* **quantified**) **1** to determine the quantity of, to measure as to quantity. **2** to express the quantity of. **3** (*Logic*) to define the application of as regards quantity. **quantifiable** *a.* **quantification** (-fikā´shən) *n.* **quantifier** *n.*

quantity (kwon´titi) *n.* (*pl.* **quantities**) **1** that property by virtue of which anything may be measured. **2** extent, measure, size, greatness, volume, amount or number. **3** a sum, a number. **4** a certain or a large number, amount or portion. **5** (*pl.*) large quantities, abundance. **6** (*Math.*) **a** a thing having such relations, of number or extension, as can be expressed by symbols. **b** a symbol representing this. **7** the duration of a syllable or vowel sound. **8** (*Logic*) the extent to which a predicate is asserted of the subject of a proposition. **quantitative** (-tātiv, -tətiv), **quantitive** *a.* **1** of, relating to or concerned with quantity (as opposed to *qualitative*). **2** relating to or based on the quantity of vowels (as accent, verse etc.). **quantitative analysis** *n.* (*Chem.*) the determination of the amounts and proportions of the constituents of a compound body. **quantitatively** *adv.* **quantity mark** *n.* a mark placed over a vowel to indicate quantity. **quantity surveyor** *n.* a person employed to estimate the quantities of materials needed to erect a building. **quantity theory** *n.* the economic theory that prices vary directly with the amount of money in circulation and the speed at which it circulates.

quantum (kwon´təm) *n.* (*pl.* **quanta** (-tə)) **1** (*Physics*) the smallest possible amount into which a physical property such as energy or momentum can be subdivided and by which the value of that property can change. **2** a quantity, an amount. **3** an amount required, allowed or sufficient. **quantal** *a.* of or relating to a quantum; composed of discrete values. **quantum jump, quantum leap** *n.* **1** (*coll.*) a sudden transition. **2** an unexpected and spectacular advance. **3** (*Physics*) the sudden transition of an atom, electron etc. from one energy level to another. **quantum mechanics** *n.* (*Physics*) a branch of physics based on quantum theory, applied to elementary particles and atoms which do not

behave according to Newtonian mechanics. **quantum mechanical** *a.* **quantum mechanically** *adv.* **quantum theory** *n.* (*Physics*) the theory that energy, esp. radiant energy, occurs in quanta and that energy transferences take place in discrete increments.

quarantine (kwor´əntēn) *n.* **1** the enforced isolation, esp. of people and animals coming from places infected with contagious disease. **2** the prescribed period of isolation imposed. ~*v.t.* to isolate or put in quarantine.

quark[1] (kwahk) *n.* (*Physics*) any of several hypothetical particles thought to be the fundamental units of other subatomic particles.

quark[2] (kwahk) *n.* a low-fat soft cheese made from skimmed milk.

quarrel[1] (kwor´əl) *n.* **1** a noisy or violent contention or dispute, an altercation, a brawl, a petty fight. **2** a falling-out or breach of friendship. **3** a ground or cause of complaint or dispute, a reason for strife or contention. ~*v.i.* (*pres.p.* **quarrelling,** (*N Am.*) **quarreling,** *past, p.p.* **quarrelled,** (*N Am.*) **quarreled**) **1** to dispute violently, to wrangle, to squabble. **2** to fall out, to break off friendly relations (with). **3** to cavil, to take exception, to find fault (with). **quarreller,** (*N Am.*) **quarreler** *n.* **quarrelsome** (-səm) *a.* inclined or apt to quarrel, contentious. **quarrelsomely** *adv.* **quarrelsomeness** *n.*

quarrel[2] (kwor´əl) *n.* a square or diamond-shaped pane of glass used in lattice windows.

quarry[1] (kwor´i) *n.* (*pl.* **quarries**) **1** a place from which building-stone, slates etc. are dug, cut, blasted etc. **2** a source from which information is extracted. ~*v.t.* (*3rd pers. sing. pres.* **quarries,** *pres.p.* **quarrying,** *past, p.p.* **quarried**) to dig or take from or as from a quarry. **quarryman** *n.* (*pl.* **quarrymen**) a person employed in a quarry.

quarry[2] (kwor´i) *n.* (*pl.* **quarries**) **1** any animal pursued by hounds, hunters, a bird of prey etc. **2** game, prey. **3** any object of pursuit.

quarry[3] (kwor´i) *n.* (*pl.* **quarries**) **1** a square or diamond-shaped pane of glass, a quarrel. **2** a square stone or tile. **quarry tile** *n.* an unglazed floor tile.

quart[1] (kwawt) *n.* **1** a measure of capacity, the fourth part of a gallon, two pints (1.136 l). **2** a measure, bottle or other vessel containing such a quantity. **to fit a quart into a pint pot 1** (*usu. neg.*) to cram a large amount into a small space, esp. too small a space. **2** (*usu. neg.*) to attempt something impossible or barely possible.

quart[2] (kaht) *n.* **1** a sequence of four cards of the same suit in piquet etc. **2** QUARTE.

quarte (kaht), **quart, carte** *n.* the fourth of eight parrying or attacking movements in fencing.

quarter (kwaw´tə) *n.* **1** a fourth part, any of four equal parts. **2** the fourth part of the year, three calendar months. **3** a point of time 15 minutes before or after the hour. **4** the fourth part of a dollar, 25 cents; a coin of this value. **5** any one of four equal periods into which a game or match is divided. **6** (*coll.*) **a** the fourth part of a pound weight (4 oz.). **b** the fourth part of a hundredweight (28 lb., 12.7 kg). **c** a grain measure of 8 bushels (2.91 hl). **d** the fourth part of a fathom. **7 a** the fourth part of a period of the moon. **b** any one of the four phases of increase or decrease of the moon's face during a lunation. **8** one of the four chief points of the compass. **9** a particular direction, region, or locality. **10** place of origin or supply, source. **11** a division of a town, esp. one assigned to or occupied by a particular class or group. **12** (*esp. Mil.*) **a** (*pl.*) a place of lodging or abode, that is occupied by troops etc. **b** (*usu. in pl.*) allotted position, proper place or station, esp. for troops. **13** a haunch. **14** mercy, clemency. **15** exception from death allowed in war to a surrendered enemy. ~*v.t.* **1** to divide into four equal parts. **2** (*Hist.*) to cut the body of (a traitor etc.) into quarters. **3 a** to put into quarters, to assign quarters to. **b** to provide (esp. soldiers) with lodgings and food. **4** (of a hound etc.) to range over (a field) in all directions. **5** (*Her.*) to bear or arrange (charges or coats of arms) quarterly on a shield etc. ~*v.i.* **1** to be stationed or lodged. **2** to range in search of game. **3** (of the wind) to blow on a ship's quarter. **quarterage** (-rij) *n.* a quarterly payment, wages, allowance etc. **quarterback** *n.* a player in American football who directs the attacking play of the team. **quarter-binding** *n.* a type of bookbinding in which the back is of leather, cloth etc. and the sides and corners of another usu. inferior material. **quarter day** *n.* the day beginning each quarter of the year (Lady Day, 25 Mar., Midsummer Day, 24 June, Michaelmas Day, 29 Sept. and Christmas Day, 25 Dec.) on which tenancies etc. begin and end, payments are due etc. **quarterdeck** *n.* the upper deck extending from the stern to the mainmast, usu. assigned for the use of officers and cabin passengers. **quarterfinal** *n.* the round before the semi-final, in a knockout competition. **quarter-finalist** *n.* **quarter-hour** *n.* **1** a quarter of an hour. **2** a point of time 15 minutes before or after the hour or sometimes 30 minutes after the hour. **quartering** *n.* **1** a dividing into quarters or fourth parts. **2** the assignment of quarters or lodgings. **3** (*pl.*) the grouping of several coats of arms on a shield. **quarter-light** *n.* the small window in the front door of a car, often for ventilation. **quarter-line** *n.* a line 22 m from the goal-line in rugby, or the space enclosed by it. **quarterly** *a.* **1** containing a quarter. **2** occurring or done every quarter of a year. **3** (of a shield) divided into quarters. ~*adv.* **1** once in each quarter of the year. **2** in quarters, arranged in the four quarters of the shield. ~*n.* (*pl.* **quarterlies**) a periodical published every quarter. **quartermaster** *n.* **1** a regimental officer appointed to provide and assign quarters, lay out camps, and issue rations, clothing, ammunition etc. **2** a petty officer, having charge of the steering, signals, stowage etc. **Quartermaster-General**

n. a staff officer in charge of the department dealing with quartering, encamping, moving, or embarking troops. **quartermaster sergeant** *n.* a sergeant assisting the quartermaster. **quarter note** *n.* (*Mus.*, *esp. N Am.*) a crotchet. **quarter of an hour** *n.* a period of 15 minutes. **quarter-plate** *n.* **1** a photographic plate measuring 4¼ × 3¼ in. (10.8 × 8.3 cm). **2** a picture produced from this. **quarter-pounder** *n.* a hamburger weighing a quarter of a pound. **quarter-tone** *n.* (*Mus.*) an interval of half a semitone.

quartet (kwawtet´), **quartette** *n.* **1** (*Mus.*) **a** a musical composition for four voices or instruments. **b** the performers of such a composition, a group of four musicians playing together. **2** a group or set of four people or four similar things. **quartile** (kwaw´tīl) *a.* (*Astrol.*) denoting the aspect of two heavenly bodies when distant from each other a quarter of a circle. ~*n.* **1** a quartile aspect. **2** any of three values of a variable that divide a statistical survey into four equal parts, each containing a quarter of the individuals surveyed.

quarto (kwaw´tō) *n.* (*pl.* **quartos**) **1** a size obtained by folding a sheet of paper twice, making four leaves or eight pages (usu. written *4to*). **2** a book, pamphlet etc. having pages of this size. ~*a.* having the sheet folded into four leaves (*quarto paper*).

quartz (kwawts) *n.* a mineral consisting of pure silica or silicon dioxide, either massive or crystallizing hexagonally. **quartz clock** *n.* an electric clock of high accuracy in which the alternating current frequency is determined by the mechanical vibrations of a quartz crystal. **quartz (iodine) lamp** *n.* a light source, based on iodine vapour, used for high-intensity lighting in car headlamps, cine projectors etc. **quartzite** (-īt) *n.* a massive or schistose metamorphic rock consisting of sandstone with a deposition of quartz about each grain. **quartz watch** *n.* a watch operated by the vibrations of a piezoelectric quartz crystal as in a quartz clock. **quartzy** *a.*

quasar (kwā´zah) *n.* (*Astron.*) any of a group of unusually bright, starlike objects outside our galaxy, that exhibit large red-shifts and are a powerful source of radio waves and other energy emissions.

quash (kwosh) *v.t.* **1** to annul or make void. **2** to put an end to, esp. by legal procedure. **3** to suppress, to extinguish, to crush.

Usage note The verbs *quash* and *squash* should not be confused: *quash* means to annul, and *squash* to crush.

quasi (kwā´zī, -sī, kwah´zī) *adv.* as if; as it were.
quasi- (kwā´zī, -sī, kwah´zī) *comb. form* **1** apparently, seeming, not real, as *quasi-scientific*. **2** partly, not quite, to some degree, as *quasi-judicial*.
quassia (kwosh´ə, -iə) *n.* **1** a tree of a S American genus *Quassia*, esp. *Q. amara*, the bitter wood,

bark and oil of which yield a tonic and insecticide. **2** the wood or bark of this or a related W Indian tree.

quatercentenary (kwatəsəntē´nəri, -ten´-) *n.* (*pl.* **quatercentenaries**) **1** a 400th anniversary. **2** its celebration.

Usage note Pronunciation and spelling as *quarter-* are best avoided.

quaternary (kwətœ´nəri) *a.* **1** (*Chem.*) consisting of four, having four parts, esp. being or composed of an atom bound to four other atoms or radicals. **2** fourth in order. **3** (*Geol.*) (**Quaternary**) of, relating to or being the most recent geological period or rock strata. ~*n.* (*pl.* **quaternaries**) **1** a set of four. **2** (*Geol.*) (**Quaternary**) the Quaternary period or system of rock.

quatrain (kwot´rān) *n.* a stanza of four lines, usu. rhyming alternately.

quatrefoil (kat´rəfoil, kat´ə-), **quaterfoil**, **quarterfoil** *n.* an opening, panel or other figure in ornamental tracery, divided by cusps into four foils.

Quattrocento (kwatrōchen´tō, kwah-) *n.* the 15th cent., regarded as a distinctive period in Italian art and literature. **quattrocentist** *n.*

quaver (kwā´və) *v.i.* **1** to quiver, to tremble, to vibrate. **2** to sing or play with tremulous modulations or trills. ~*v.t.* to sing or utter with a tremulous sound. ~*n.* **1** a shake or rapid vibration of the voice, a trill. **2** a quiver or shakiness in speaking. **3** (*Mus.*) a note equal in duration to half a crotchet or one-eighth of a semibreve. **quaverer** *n.* **quaveringly** *adv.* **quavery** *a.*

quay (kē) *n.* a landing place or wharf, usu. of masonry and stretching along the side of or projecting into a harbour, for loading or unloading ships. **quayage** (-ij) *n.* **quayside** *n.* the edge of a quay.

queasy (kwē´zi) *a.* (*comp.* **queasier**, *superl.* **queasiest**) **1** sick at the stomach, affected with nausea. **2** easily nauseated. **3** fastidious, squeamish, uneasy (*a queasy conscience*). **queasily** *adv.* **queasiness** *n.*

Quechua (kech´wə), **Quichua** (kich´-) *n.* (*pl.* **Quechuas, Quechua, Quichuas, Quichua**) **1** a member of any of various groups of S American Indian peoples, including the Incas. **2** their language. **Quechuan** *a.*

queen (kwēn) *n.* **1** a female sovereign, esp. a hereditary sovereign of an independent state. **2** the wife of a king. **3** a queen dowager. **4** a court card bearing a representation of a queen. **5** the most powerful piece in chess. **6** the fertile female in a colony of bees, ants, etc. **7** a woman who or thing which is pre-eminent in any sphere or is regarded as the supreme example of its class. **8** a woman of majestic presence. **9** a woman or girl masquerading as a sovereign or presiding at some festivity. **10** (*sl., offensive*) an effeminate male homosexual, often an ageing one. **11** a female cat. ~*v.t.* **1** to make (a woman) queen. **2** in

chess, to make (a pawn) into a queen. ~*v.i.* **1** to act as a queen. **2** to reign as queen. **3** to become a queen in chess. **queen high** in a card game, having the queen as the top-ranking card. **to queen it** to act in a superior or arrogant way (over). **Queen Anne** *a.* **1** of, relating to or denoting the architectural style prevalent in the reign of Queen Anne (*c*.1700–20), characterized by plain and unpretentious design with classic details. **2** of or relating to a style of decorative art typified by Chippendale furniture. **Queen Anne's lace** *n.* (*Bot.*) the wild carrot, *Daucus carota.* **queen bee** *n.* **1** a fully-developed female bee. **2** a woman in a dominating position, socially or in business. **queen cake** *n.* a small, soft, usu. heart-shaped currant cake. **queen consort** *n.* the wife of a king. **queendom** *n.* **queen dowager** *n.* the widow of a king. **queenhood** *n.* **queening** (kwē´ning) *n.* a variety of apple. **queenless** *a.* **queenlike** *a.* **queenly** *a.* (*comp.* **queenlier**, *superl.* **queenliest**) **1** appropriate to a queen. **2** like a queen, majestic. **queenliness** *n.* **queen mother** *n.* a queen dowager who is also the mother of the reigning sovereign. **queen of puddings** *n.* a pudding made with a breadcrumb and custard mixture topped with meringue. **Queen of the May** *n.* MAY QUEEN (under MAY). **queen of the meadows** *n.* (*Bot.*) meadowsweet. **queen post** *n.* either of two suspending or supporting posts between the tie-beam and rafters in a roof. **queen's bishop** *n.* the bishop on the queen's side of a chessboard at the beginning of a game. **Queen's Counsel** *n.* counsel to the Crown, an honorary title which gives precedence over ordinary barristers. **Queen's English** *n.* correct English as spoken by educated people. **Queen's evidence** *n.* (*Law*) evidence given against one's accomplice in return for a free pardon or reduction in sentence, during the reign of a queen. **Queen's Guide** *n.* a Guide who has reached the highest level of proficiency, during the reign of a queen. **Queen's highway** *n.* a public road, a right-of-way. **queenship** *n.* **queen-size, queen-sized** *a.* (of a bed etc.) larger than is usual or regular but smaller than king-size. **queen's knight** *n.* the knight on the queen's side of a chessboard at the beginning of a game. **queen's pawn** *n.* the pawn in front of the queen at the beginning of a game of chess. **queen's rook** *n.* the rook on the queen's side of a chessboard at the beginning of a game. **Queen's Scout** *n.* a Scout or Guide who has passed the highest tests of proficiency and ability. **Queen's Speech** *n.* during the reign of a queen, an address by the queen to Parliament at the beginning of every session, outlining the government's proposed legislation.

Queensberry Rules (kwēnz´bəri) *n.pl.* standard rules of boxing drawn up by the 8th Marquess of Queensberry in 1867.

queer (kwiə) *a.* **1** strange, odd; singular, droll. **2** questionable, suspicious. **3** out of sorts, slightly unwell, faint. **4** (*sl., offensive*) homosexual. **5**

(*coll.*) mentally unbalanced. ~*n.* (*sl.*, *derog.*) a homosexual, esp. a male homosexual. ~*v.t.* (*coll.*) to spoil, to put out of order. **to queer someone's pitch** to spoil one's chances. **queerish** *a.* **queerly** *adv.* **queerness** *n.* **Queer Street** *n.* (*coll.*) trouble, esp. financial difficulty.

Usage note Some homosexuals now use *queer* of themselves, but its use by non-homosexuals remains offensive.

---

quell (kwel) *v.t.* **1** to suppress, to put down, to subdue. **2** to crush. **3** to cause to subside; to calm, to allay, to quiet. **queller** *n.*

quench (kwench) *v.t.* **1** to extinguish, to put out, esp. with water. **2 a** to cool (heat or a heated thing), esp. with water. **b** to cool (hot metal) rapidly by immersing in oil, water etc. **3** to satisfy (thirst) by drinking. **4** to allay, to slake. **5** to suppress, to subdue. **6** (*Physics*) to reduce or inhibit (luminescence, oscillation etc.). **quenchable** *a.* **quencher** *n.* **quenchless** *a.*

quenelle (kənel´) *n.* a ball of savoury paste made of meat or fish, usu. served as an entrée.

quern (kwœn) *n.* **1** a simple hand-mill for grinding corn, usu. consisting of two stones resting one on the other. **2** a small hand-mill for grinding spices. **quernstone** *n.*

querulous (kwer´ələs, -ū-) *a.* **1** complaining. **2** discontented, peevish, fretful. **querulously** *adv.* **querulousness** *n.*

query (kwiə´ri) *n.* (*pl.* **queries**) **1** a question (often used absolutely as preface to a question). **2** a point or objection to be answered, a doubt. **3** a mark of interrogation (?). ~*v.i.* (*3rd pers. sing. pres.* **queries**, *pres.p.* **querying**, *past, p.p.* **queried**) to put a question. ~*v.t.* **1** to express as a question. **2** to question, to call in question. **3** to express doubt concerning. **4** to mark with a query.

quest (kwest) *n.* **1** the act of seeking, a search. **2** an expedition or venture in search or pursuit of some object, esp. embarked on by a medieval knight. **3** the object of such a venture. ~*v.i.* **1** to go on a quest (after), to search (for). **2** (of a dog) to search about for game. ~*v.t.* (*poet.*) to seek out or for. **in quest of** searching for. **quester** *n.* **questingly** *adv.*

question (kwes´chən) *n.* **1** a sentence requiring an answer, an interrogative sentence. **2** the act of asking or enquiring. **3** doubt, uncertainty, objection. **4** a point at issue, a matter to be resolved, a problem requiring solution. **5** a subject to be discussed. **6** a proposition or subject to be debated and voted on, esp. in a deliberative assembly. ~*v.t.* **1** to ask a question or questions of, to interrogate, to examine by asking questions. **2** to study (phenomena etc.) with a view to acquiring information. **3** to call in question, to treat as doubtful or unreliable, to raise objections to. ~*v.i.* **1** to ask a question or questions. **2** to doubt, to be uncertain. **beyond (all) question** undoubtedly, unquestionably. **in question** re-

ferred to, under discussion. **out of the question** not worth discussing, impossible. **past question** undoubtedly. **to call in/ into question** to dispute. **to put the question** to put to the vote, to divide the meeting or House upon. **questionable** *a.* **1** open to doubt or suspicion, esp. with regard to honesty, morality etc. **2** disputable. **questionability** (-bil´-), **questionableness** *n.* **questionably** *adv.* **questioner** *n.* **questioningly** *adv.* **questionless** *a.* **question mark** *n.* **1** a mark of interrogation (?). **2** a cause for doubt or suspicion. **question master** *n.* a person who puts questions, esp. the person who asks the questions in a quiz or game. **questionnaire** (-neə´) *n.* **1** a series of questions designed to collect information, esp. for statistical purposes. **2** a form containing these. **question time** *n.* time set aside each day in Parliament where ordinary members may question ministers.

quetzal (kwet´səl) *n.* (*pl.* **quetzals**, **quetzales** (-sah´lēz)) **1** a Central American bird, *Pheromacrus mocinno*, of the trogon family, with brilliantly coloured plumage. **2** the basic unit of currency of Guatemala.

queue (kū) *n.* **1** a line of people, vehicles etc. waiting their turn. **2** a sequence of items to be dealt with or processed in the order in which they were received. **3** WAITING LIST (under WAIT). **4** a plaited tail hanging at the back of the head, either of the natural hair or a wig, a pigtail. ~*v.t.* (*pres.p.* **queuing, queueing,** *past, p.p.* **queued**) to arrange or place in a queue. ~*v.i.* to form into a waiting queue, to take one's place in a queue. **queue-jumping** *n.* going to the beginning of a queue instead of to the end. **queue-jump** *v.i.* **queue-jumper** *n.*

quibble (kwib´əl) *n.* **1** a trivial or petty objection, argument or distinction, esp. one exploiting a verbal ambiguity. **2** an evasion of the point, an equivocation. **3** a play upon words; a pun. ~*v.i.* **1** to raise trivial objections, to argue over unimportant, esp. verbal, details. **2** to evade the point in question. **3** to pun. **quibbler** *n.* **quibbling** *a.* **quibblingly** *adv.*

quiche (kēsh) *n.* a pastry shell filled with a savoury egg custard to which cheese, onion or other vegetables, bacon etc. have been added.

Quichua QUECHUA.

quick (kwik) *a.* **1** rapid in movement, acting swiftly, swift, nimble. **2** done or happening in a short time, taking only a short time. **3** speedy, expeditious, prompt. **4** lively, vigorous, alert, acutely sensitive or responsive, intelligent. **5** (of a temper) irritable, easily aroused. **6** rash, precipitate, hasty. **7** eager, ready (to act or respond). ~*adv.* in a short space of time, at a rapid rate; quickly. ~*int.* come, move, act etc. quickly. ~*n.* **1** sensitive living flesh, esp. the sensitive flesh under the nails. **2** the feelings, the seat of the feelings. **the quick and the dead** the living and the dead. **quick-fire** *a.* **1** rapid, following in rapid succession. **2** (of a quiz etc.) consisting of quick-fire questions. **3** designed to fire shots in rapid succession. **quick fix** *n.* a rapidly accomplished, usu. temporary, solution. **quick-freeze** *v.t.* (*past* **quick-froze,** *p.p.* **quick-frozen**) to freeze (food) rapidly in order to retain the natural qualities. **quickie** *n.* (*coll.*) **1** something that is done rapidly. **2** a swift act of sexual intercourse. **3** a swiftly consumed (alcoholic) drink. **quicklime** *n.* burned lime not yet slaked; calcium oxide. **quickly** *adv.* **quick march** *n.* (*Mil.*) **1** a march in quick time. **2** the music for such a march. *~int.* the command to start a quick march. **quickness** *n.* **quick one** *n.* (*coll.*) a quickie. **quicksand** *n.* **1** loose wet sand easily yielding to pressure and engulfing people, animals etc. **2** a bed of such sand. **3** something treacherous and engulfing. **quickset** *a.* (of a hedge) composed of living plants, esp. hawthorn bushes. *~n.* **1** slips of plants, esp. hawthorn, put in the ground to form a quickset hedge. **2** a quickset hedge. **quicksilver** *n.* **1** mercury. **2** an unpredictable temperament. *~v.t.* to coat (the glass of a mirror) with an amalgam of quicksilver and tinfoil. **quickstep** *n.* **1** a fast foxtrot. **2** (*Mil.*) (**quick step**) the step used in marching at quick time. **3** a march tune or lively piece of music to accompany either of these. *~v.i.* (*pres.p.* **quickstepping,** *past, p.p.* **quickstepped**) to dance a quickstep. **quick-tempered** *a.* easily irritated, irascible. **quick-thorn** *n.* the hawthorn, esp. when planted as a hedge. **quick time** *n.* (*Mil.*) the ordinary rate of marching in the British Army, usu. reckoned at about 120 paces to the minute or 4 miles (6.44 km) an hour. **quick trick** *n.* **1** a trick won during the opening rounds of play in a game of bridge. **2** a card that should win this. **quick-witted** *a.* having a keen and alert mind. **quick-wittedness** *n.*

quicken (kwik´ən) *v.t.* **1** to make faster, to accelerate. **2** to give or restore life or animation to. **3** to stimulate, to rouse, to inspire, to kindle. **4** to cheer, to refresh. *~v.i.* **1** to move with increased rapidity. **2** to receive life, animation or vigour. **3** to come to life. **4** to be in that state of pregnancy in which the child gives signs of life. **5** (of a foetus) to give signs of life in the womb. **quickener** *n.*

quid[1] (kwid) *n.* (*pl.* **quid**) (*sl.*) a pound (sterling). **quids in** (*sl.*) in a profitable position.

quid[2] (kwid) *n.* a piece of tobacco for chewing.

quiddity (kwid´iti) *n.* (*pl.* **quiddities**) **1** the essence of a thing. **2** a quibble, a trifling or captious subtlety. **quiddative, quiddiative** (-itātiv) *a.*

quid pro quo (kwid prō kwō´) *n.* (*pl.* **quid pro quos**) something in return or exchange (for something), an equivalent.

quiescent (kwies´ənt) *a.* **1** at rest, still, not moving, inert, inactive, dormant. **2** (*formal*) tranquil, calm, free from anxiety, agitation or emotion. **quiescence, quiescency** *n.* **quiescently** *adv.*

quiet (kwī´ət) *a.* **1** making little or no noise, silent, hushed. **2** in a state of rest, motionless. **3** calm, unruffled, placid, tranquil, peaceful, undisturbed. **4** gentle, mild, peaceable. **5** unobtrusive, not glaring or showy. **6** not overt, private. **7** retired, secluded. *~n.* **1** silence, stillness, peace, calmness. **2** a state of rest or repose. **3** freedom from disturbance, tranquillity. **4** peace of mind, calm, patience, placidness. *~v.t., v.i.* to quieten. **on the quiet** (*coll.*) secretly. **to keep quiet (about)** to refrain from talking or disclosing information (about). **quieten** *v.t.* **1** to make quiet. **2** to soothe, to calm, to appease. *~v.i.* to become quiet or calm. **quietism** *n.* **1** a state of calmness and placidity. **2** (**Quietism**) a form of religious mysticism based on the doctrine that the essence of religion consists in the withdrawal of the soul from external objects and in fixing it upon the contemplation of God. **quietist** *a., n.* **quietistic** (-tis´-) *a.* **quietly** *adv.* **quietness, quietude** *n.*

quietus (kwīē´təs) *n.* (*pl.* **quietuses**) **1** a final discharge or settlement. **2** release from life, death. **3** something that represses or quietens.

quiff (kwif) *n.* **1** a tuft of hair brushed up and back from the forehead. **2** a curl lying flat on the forehead.

quill (kwil) *n.* **1** the hollow stem or barrel of a feather. **2** any of the large strong feathers of a bird's wing or tail. **3** a pen, esp. one made from such a feather. **4** a spine of a porcupine. **5** a musical pipe made from a hollow cane, reed etc. *~v.t.* to form into rounded folds, flutes etc., to goffer. **quill-feather** *n.* a large wing or tail feather. **quilling** *n.* **1** lace, tulle or ribbon gathered into small rolls resembling quills. **2** the process of making ornamental designs from this.

quilt (kwilt) *n.* **1** a bed-cover or bedspread made by stitching one cloth over another with some soft warm material as padding between them. **2** a duvet. *~v.t.* **1** to fill, cover or line with padded material. **2 a** to stitch together (two pieces of cloth) with soft material in between, esp. using crossing lines of stitching. **b** to make (a cover, jacket etc.) in this way. **3** to stitch in crossing lines or ornamental figures, like the stitching in a quilt. **4** to sew up between two layers of material. **quilter** *n.* **quilting** *n.* **1** the process of making quilted work. **2** material for making quilts. **3** quilted work.

quim (kwim) *n.* (*taboo sl.*) the female genitals.

quin (kwin) *n.* (*coll.*) each child of quintuplets.

quince (kwins) *n.* **1** a hard, acid, yellowish fruit used in cookery for flavouring and for preserves etc. **2** a small tree or shrub, *Cydonia oblonga*, that bears quinces. **3** Japanese quince, japonica.

quincentenary (kwinsəntē´nəri, -ten´-) *n.* (*pl.* **quincentenaries**) **1** a 500th anniversary. **2** a 500th anniversary celebration. **quincentennial** (-ten´-) *a.*

quincunx (kwin´kŭngks) *n.* (*pl.* **quincunxes**) an arrangement of five things in a square or rectangle, one at each corner and one in the middle, esp. such an arrangement of trees in a plantation. **quincuncial** (-kŭn´shəl) *a*. **quincuncially** *adv*.

quinine (kwin´ēn, -ēn´) *n*. a bitter alkaloid obtained from cinchona bark formerly widely used, esp. in the form of its salts, to relieve fever, in the treatment of malaria and as a tonic.

Quinquagesima (kwinkwəjes´imə) *n*. (*also* **Quinquagesima Sunday**) the Sunday before Lent (about 50 days before Easter).

quinque- (kwin´kwi), **quinqui-** *comb. form* five.

quinquennial (kwinkwen´iəl) *a*. **1** lasting five years. **2** recurring every five years. **quinquennially** *adv*. **quinquennium** (-iəm) *n*. (*pl*. **quinquenniums, quinquennia**) a period of five years.

quinquevalent (kwinkwivā´lənt), **quinquivalent** *a*. (*Chem*.) having a valency or combining power of five, pentavalent.

quinsy (kwin´zi) *n*. inflammatory sore throat, esp. with suppuration of one tonsil or of both. **quinsied** *a*.

quint (kwint) *n*. (*N Am*.) QUIN.

quinte (kāt) *n*. the fifth of eight parrying or attacking movements in fencing.

quintessence (kwintes´əns) *n*. **1** the essential principle or pure embodiment (of a quality, class of things etc.). **2** the pure and concentrated essence of any substance, a refined extract. **quintessential** (-tisen´shəl) *a*. **quintessentially** *adv*.

quintet (kwintet´), **quintette** *n*. **1** (*Mus*.) **a** a musical composition for five voices or instruments. **b** the performers of such a composition, a group of five musicians playing together. **2** a group or set of five people or five similar things.

quintillion (kwintil´yən) *n*. (*pl*. **quintillion, quintillions**) **1** the sixth power of a thousand, one followed by 18 zeros. **2** in Britain, esp. formerly, the number produced by raising a million to its fifth power, represented by one followed by 30 zeros. **quintillionth** *n*., *a*.

quintuple (kwin´tūpəl, -tū´-) *a*. **1** consisting of five parts. **2** involving five members etc. **3** equal to five times the number of a quantity of, fivefold. **4** (of musical time) having five beats in a bar. ~*n*. a number or amount five times as great as another. ~*v.i.* to increase fivefold, to become five times as much. ~*v.t.* to multiply fivefold, to make five times as much. **quintuplet** (-plit) *n*. **1** a set of five things. **2** any one of five children born of the same mother at one birth. **3** (*Mus*.) five notes played in the time of four. **quintuplicate¹** (-tū´plikāt) *v.t.* to make fivefold, to multiply by five. **quintuplicate²** (-tū´plikət) *a*. **1** five times as much or as many, fivefold. **2** five times copied. **in quintuplicate** written out or copied five times. **quintuplication** (-ā´shən) *n*.

quip (kwip) *n*. **1** a sarcastic jest or sally. **2** a witty retort, a smart saying. **3** a quibble. ~*v.i.* (*pres.p.* **quipping**, *past*, *p.p.* **quipped**) to make quips, to scoff. **quippish** *a*. **quipster** (-stə) *n*.

quire (kwīə) *n*. **1** 24, or now usu. 25, sheets of paper. **2** a set of four sheets of paper or parchment folded into eight leaves, as in medieval manuscripts. **3** a small book, pamphlet etc.

quirk (kwœk) *n*. **1** a mannerism. **2** an artful trick, evasion or subterfuge, a shift. **3** a twist or flourish in drawing or writing. **4** a fantastic turn or flourish in music. **5** (*Archit*.) an acute recess between a moulding proper and a fillet or soffit. **quirkish** *a*. **quirky** *a*. (*comp*. **quirkier**, *superl*. **quirkiest**). **quirkily** *adv*. **quirkiness** *n*.

quirt (kwœt) *n*. a riding whip with a short handle and a long, braided leather lash. ~*v.t.* to strike with a quirt.

quisling (kwiz´ling) *n*. **1** a person who openly allies themselves with their nation's enemies. **2** a traitor.

quit (kwit) *v.t.* (*pres.p.* **quitting**, *past*, *p.p.* **quitted**, **quit**) **1** to give up, to renounce, to abandon. **2** to leave, to depart from. **3** (*esp. N Am*.) to cease, to desist from. ~*v.i.* **1** to leave, to depart. **2** to stop doing something, esp. to give up one's job. ~*a*. free, clear, absolved, rid (of). **to be quits** to be even or left on even terms, so that neither has the advantage. **quittance** *n*. **1** (*formal or poet*.) a discharge or release from a debt or obligation. **2** (*formal*) a receipt, an acquittance. **quitter** *n*. **1** a person who quits. **2** a shirker, a coward.

quitch (kwich), **quitch-grass** *n*. couch grass.

quite (kwīt) *adv*. **1** completely, entirely, altogether, to the fullest extent, absolutely, perfectly. **2** to some extent, somewhat, fairly. **3** certainly, yes (used to indicate agreement). **quite something** a remarkable person or thing. **quite the thing** quite proper or fashionable.

quiver¹ (kwiv´ə) *v.i.* **1** to tremble or be agitated with a rapid tremulous motion. **2** to shake, to shiver. ~*v.t.* to cause (wings etc.) to quiver. ~*n*. a quivering motion. **quiverer** *n*. **quiveringly** *adv*. **quivery** *a*.

quiver² (kwiv´ə) *n*. a portable case for arrows. **quivered** *a*. **quiverful** *n*. (*pl*. **quiverfuls**).

qui vive (kē vēv´) *int*. who lives, who goes there? **on the qui vive** on the lookout, alert, expectant.

quixotic (kwiksot´ik) *a*. **1** extravagantly romantic and chivalrous. **2** aiming at lofty but impracticable ideals, visionary. **quixotically** *adv*. **quixotism** *n*. **quixotry** (kwik´sətri) *n*.

quiz (kwiz) *n*. (*pl*. **quizzes**) **1** a set of questions designed to test knowledge. **2** an entertainment, such as a radio or television game based on this. **3** an investigation by questioning, an interrogation. ~*v.t.* (*3rd pers. sing. pres.* **quizzes**, *pres.p.* **quizzing**, *past*, *p.p.* **quizzed**) to examine by questioning. **quizmaster** *n*. a person who puts the questions to contestants in a quiz. **quiz show** *n*. a radio or television quiz. **quizzable** *a*. **quizzer** *n*. a person given to quizzing. **quizzery** *n*. **quizzical** *a*. **1** questioning, mocking. **2** slightly eccentric, amusingly odd. **quizzicality** (-kal´-), **quizzicalness** *n*. **quizzically** *adv*.

quod (kwod), **quad** *n*. (*sl*.) prison, jail.

quoin (koin) *n*. **1** the external angle of a building.

2 a large stone, brick etc. at the external angle of a wall, a cornerstone. **3** a wedge-shaped block of wood used for various purposes, such as locking up type in a forme, raising the level of a gun etc. *~v.t.* to raise or secure with a quoin or wedge. **quoining** *n.*

quoit (koit, kwoit) *n.* **1** a flattish circular ring of iron, rope etc. for throwing at a peg or similar mark. **2** (*pl., usu. sing. in constr.*) a game of throwing such rings. **3** a dolmen or the horizontal stone cover of this. **quoiter** *n.*

quondam (kwon´dam) *a.* having formerly been, sometime, former (*his quondam friend*).

Quonset hut® (kwon´sit) *n.* (*N Am.*) a hut similar to a Nissen hut.

Quorn® (kwawn) *n.* a textured vegetable protein used as a meat substitute.

quorum (kwaw´rəm) *n.* (*pl.* **quorums**) the minimum number of officers or members of a society, committee etc. that must be present to transact business. **quorate** (-rət, -rāt) *a.* being or consisting of a quorum, having a quorum present.

quota (kwō´tə) *n.* (*pl.* **quotas**) **1** a proportional share, part or contribution. **2** a prescribed number or quantity, e.g. of students to be admitted to a given college at the beginning of each year.

quote (kwōt) *v.t.* **1** to adduce or cite from (an author, book etc.), esp. in illustration or support of a point, statement etc. **2** to repeat or copy out

the words of (another person, a passage in a book etc.). **3** to enclose in quotation marks. **4** to state (the current price) of a commodity, job of work etc. *~v.i.* **1** to cite or adduce a passage (from). **2** to state a price (for), to supply an estimate of costs (for). *~n.* (*usu. in pl., coll.*) a quotation mark. **quotable** *a.* worth quoting. **quotability** (-bil´-), **quotableness** *n.* **quotation** (-tā´shən) *n.* **1** the act of quoting. **2** a passage or phrase quoted. **3** a price listed or stated as current on the Stock Exchange. **4** an estimate supplied by a contractor for a job of work. **5** (*Mus.*) a short passage taken from one piece and used in another. **quotation mark** *n.* either of a pair of punctuation marks (in English usu. double (" ") or single (' ')) used to indicate the beginning and end of a passage quoted, and sometimes to enclose words considered slang, jargon etc. **quoted** *a.* quoted company *n.* a company whose shares are quoted on the Stock Exchange. **quoter** *n.* **quoteworthy** *a.*

quotidian (kwətid´iən) *a.* **1** daily. **2** (esp. of a fever) recurring every day. **3** commonplace, everyday. *~n.* a fever, esp. malaria, in which the paroxysms return every day.

quotient (kwō´shənt) *n.* the result obtained by dividing one quantity by another.

Quran, Qur'an KORAN.

q.v. *abbr.* L *quod vide*, which see (*imper.*), an instruction to look up a cross-reference.

qwerty (kwœ´ti), **QWERTY** *n.* the standard English typewriter or keyboard layout.

R

R¹ (ah), **r** (*pl.* **Rs, R's**) the 18th letter of the English and other versions of the Roman alphabet, corresponding to the Greek rho (ρ, P). It has two sounds: (1) when it precedes a vowel, as in *ran, morose*, it is usually an alveolar continuant; (2) at the end of syllables and when it is followed by a consonant, as in *her, martyr, heard*, it is no longer pronounced in standard English. **R months** *n.pl.* those months with an 'r' in the spelling (September to April), when oysters are in season.

R² *abbr.* **1** (*Chem.*) radical. **2** radius. **3** rand. **4** Réaumur. **5** Regina. **6** (*also* ®) registered (trademark). **7** (*Physics*) resistance. **8** reverse (gear). **9** Rex. **10** right. **11** River. **12** rook.

r *abbr.* **1** radius. **2** recto. **3** right. **4** run, runs.

RA *abbr.* **1** (*Astron.*) right ascension. **2** Royal Academy; Royal Academician. **3** Royal Artillery.

Ra *chem. symbol* radium.

rabbet (rab´it), **rebate** (rē´bāt, rab´it) *v.t.* (*pres.p.* **rabbeting, rebating,** *past, p.p.* **rabbeted, rebated**) **1** to cut a groove or slot along the edge of (a board) so that it may receive the edge of another piece cut to fit it. **2** to unite or fix in this way. ~*n.* a groove or slot made in the edge of a board so that it may join with another. **rabbet plane** *n.* a plane for cutting rabbets.

rabbi (rab´ī) *n.* (*pl.* **rabbis**) **1** a Jewish doctor or teacher of the law, esp. one ordained and having certain legal and ritual functions. **2** the leader of a Jewish congregation. **rabbinate** (-nət) *n.* **1** the office of rabbi. **2** rabbis collectively. **rabbinical, rabbinic** *a.* of or relating to rabbis, their opinions, learning or language. **rabbinically** *adv.*

rabbit (rab´it) *n.* **1** a burrowing mammal, *Oryctolagus cuniculus*, allied to the hare, killed for its flesh and fur and kept as a pet. **2** the fur of a rabbit. **3** (*coll.*) a bungling player at an outdoor game. **4** (*N Am.*) a hare. ~*v.i.* (*pres.p.* **rabbiting,** *past, p.p.* **rabbited**) **1** to hunt rabbits. **2** (*coll.*) (*often with on*) to talk at length, often aimlessly. **rabbit punch** *n.* a sharp blow to the back of the neck that can cause unconsciousness or death. **rabbit warren** *n.* a piece of ground where rabbits live and breed in burrows. **rabbity** *a.*

rabble (rab´əl) *n.* **1** a noisy crowd of people, a mob. **2** the common people, the mob, the lower orders. **rabble-rouser** *n.* a person who stirs up the common people to mass anger or violence; a demagogue. **rabble-rousing** *a., n.*

Rabelaisian (rabəlā´ziən) *a.* **1** of, relating to or characteristic of the French satirical humorist

François Rabelais, 1483–1553. **2** extravagant, grotesque, coarsely and boisterously satirical.

rabid (rab´id) *a.* **1** mad, raging, furious, violent. **2** fanatical, headstrong, excessively zealous or enthusiastic, unreasoning. **3** relating to or affected with rabies. **rabidity** (-bid´-), **rabidness** *n.* **rabidly** *adv.*

rabies (rā´biz) *n.* an often fatal viral disease of the nervous system transmitted through the saliva of a rabid animal and characterized by hydrophobia and convulsions.

raccoon (rəkoon´), **racoon** *n.* (*pl. in general* **raccoon, racoon,** *in particular* **raccoons, racoons**) **1** a greyish-black furry ring-tailed N American carnivore of the genus *Procyon*, esp. *P. lotor*. **2** the fur of a raccoon.

race¹ (rās) *n.* **1** a contest of speed between horses, runners, boats, motor-vehicles etc. **2** (*pl.*) a series of racing contests for horses, dogs etc. **3** (*fig.*) any competitive contest or rivalry, esp. one depending chiefly on speed. **4** a rapid current of water, esp. in the sea or a tidal river. **5** a channel of a stream, esp. an artificial one. ~*v.i.* **1** to take part in a race. **2** to contend in speed (with). **3** to run or move swiftly. **4** to go at full speed. **5** to go at a violent pace owing to diminished resistance (as a propeller when lifted out of the water). **6** to attend races. ~*v.t.* **1** to contend against in speed or in a race. **2** to cause (e.g. a horse) to participate in a race. **3** to cause to go or move at full speed. **racecard** *n.* a programme of a race meeting with particulars of the horses, prizes etc. **racecourse** *n.* a piece of ground on which horse races are run. **racegoer** *n.* a person who frequently goes to race meetings. **racegoing** *n.* **racehorse** *n.* a horse bred for racing. **race meeting** *n.* a meeting for horse racing. **racer** *n.* **1** a person, animal or machine that races or contends in a race. **2** a yacht, cycle, car etc. built for racing. **3** a rail or turntable for traversing a heavy gun. **racetrack** *n.* **1** a racecourse. **2** a circuit for motor racing. **racing** *n.* **racing car** *n.* a car specially built to go at high speeds in competition. **racing driver** *n.* a person who drives racing cars. **racy¹** *a.* (*comp.* **racier,** *superl.* **raciest**) designed or fitted for racing.

race² (rās) *n.* **1** a major division of human beings descended from a common stock and distinguished by physical characteristics. **2** a particular ethnic stock. **3** division of humankind into races. **4** a group or division of living creatures (*the human race*). **5** a genus, species, stock, strain or variety, of plants or animals, persisting

through several generations. **6** (*fig.*) lineage, pedigree, descent. **7** a clan, a family, a house.
race relations *n.pl.* **1** the relations between people of different races within a single community. **2** (*as sing.*) the study of such relations.
race riot *n.* a riot caused by a feeling of being discriminated against on grounds of race. **racial** (-shəl) *a.* **1** of or relating to race or lineage. **2** on grounds of or resulting from difference in race. **racially** *adv.* **racism, racialism** *n.* **1** a belief in the superiority of one race over another. **2** discrimination or prejudice based on this belief. **3** antagonism between different races or towards races other than one's own. **4** the theory that race determines human development. **racist, racialist** *n.*, *a.*
raceme (ras´ēm, rəsēm´) *n.* (*Bot.*) a centripetal inflorescence in which the flowers are attached separately by nearly equal stalks along a common axis. **racemate** (ras´əmāt) *n.* (*Chem.*) a racemic compound. **racemic** (-sē´-) *a.* (*Chem.*) consisting of equal parts of dextrorotatory and laevorotatory forms of the same compound. **racemose** (ras´əmōs), **racemous** (-əs) *a.* having the form of a raceme. **racemose gland** *n.* (*Anat.*) a gland consisting of branching ducts.
rachis (rāk´is), **rhachis** *n.* (*pl.* **rachides** (rak´idēz, rā´-), **rhachides, rachises** (rak´isēz, rā´-), **rhachises**) **1** (*Bot.*) **a** the axis of an inflorescence. **b** the axis of a pinnate leaf or frond. **2** (*Anat.*) the spinal column. **3** (*Zool.*) the shaft of a feather, esp. the part bearing the barbs.
rachitis (rəkī´tis) *n.* rickets. **rachitic** (-kit´-) *a.*
Rachmanism (rak´mənizm) *n.* the conduct of an unscrupulous landlord who exploits tenants and charges extortionate rents for slum property.
racial, racialism etc. RACE².
racing RACE¹.
rack¹ (rak) *n.* **1** an open framework or set of rails, bars, woven wire etc. for placing articles on. **2** a grating or framework of metal or wooden rails or bars for holding cattle fodder etc. **3** a bar or rail with teeth or cogs for engaging with a gearwheel, pinion or worm. **4** (*Hist.*) an apparatus for torture consisting of a framework on which the victim was laid, the wrists and ankles being tied to rollers which were turned so as to stretch the joints, sometimes to the extent of dislocation. ~*v.t.* **1** to cause intense pain or anguish to. **2** to strain, tear or shake violently. **3** (*fig.*) to strain, to stretch. **4** to place on or in a rack. **5** (*Hist.*) to torture on the rack. **on the rack 1** under torture. **2** under great stress. **to rack one's brains** to use great mental effort. **to rack up** (*esp. N Am.*) to accumulate (points or a score). **rack and pinion** *n.* a device for converting rotary motion into linear motion and vice versa, with a gearwheel which engages in a rack. **rack railway** *n.* a railway, usu. on a steep incline, with a cogged rail between the bearing rails. **rack-rent** *n.* an exorbitant rent, approaching the value of the property or land. ~*v.t.* to extort such a rent from

(a tenant) or for (land etc.). **rack-wheel** *n.* a cogwheel.
rack² (rak) *n.* destruction. **to go to rack and ruin** to fall into a state of complete ruin or neglect.
rack³ (rak) *v.t.* to draw off (wine etc.) from the lees.
rack⁴ (rak) *n.* **1** a joint of lamb comprising the front rib section. **2** the neck and spine of a forequarter of veal or mutton.
rack⁵ (rak) *n.* light vapoury clouds, cloud-drift. ~*v.i.* to fly, as cloud or vapour before the wind.
racket¹ (rak´it), **racquet** *n.* **1** a bat with a network of catgut etc. instead of a blade, with which players at tennis, squash, badminton or rackets strike the ball. **2** a snow-shoe resembling this. ~*v.t.* to strike with or as with a racket. **rackets** *n.* a ball game resembling tennis, played against a wall in a four-walled court.
racket² (rak´it) *n.* **1** a clamour, a confused noise, a din. **2** a commotion, a disturbance, a fuss. **3** a frolic, a spree, uproarious gaiety, excitement or dissipation. **4** (*sl.*) a scheme, a dodge, an underhand plan. **5** an organized illegal or unethical activity. **6** (*sl.*) a line of business. ~*v.i.* (*pres.p.* **racketing**, *past*, *p.p.* **racketed**) to make a noise or din. **racketeer** (-tiə´) *n.* a member of a gang engaged in systematic blackmail, extortion or other illegal activities for profit. ~*v.t.* to operate an illegal business or enterprise for profit. **racketeering** *n.* **rackety** *a.*
raconteur (rakontœ´) *n.* a (good, skilful etc.) storyteller. **raconteuse** (-tœz´) *n.* a female raconteur.
racoon RACCOON.
racquet RACKET¹.
racy¹ RACE¹.
racy² (rā´si) *a.* (*comp.* **racier**, *superl.* **raciest**) **1** lively, spirited, stimulating. **2** suggestive, bordering on the indecent, risqué. **3** strongly flavoured, piquant, pungent. **4** having the characteristic qualities in high degree. **racily** *adv.* **raciness** *n.*
rad¹ (rad) *n.* (*Physics*) a unit measuring the dosage of ionized radiation absorbed, equivalent to 0.01 joule of energy per kilogram of mass of irradiated material.
rad² (rad) *n.* (*coll.*) a radiator.
rad³ (rad) *a.* (*comp.* **radder**, *superl.* **raddest**) (*sl.*) excellent, very good.
radar (rā´dah) *n.* **1** a system which employs reflected or retransmitted radio waves to locate the presence of objects and to determine their angular position and range. **2** the equipment used for this. **radar trap** *n.* a device which uses radar to allow the police to identify vehicles exceeding the speed limit.
raddle (rad´əl) *n.* ruddle. ~*v.t.* **1** to paint or colour with ruddle. **2** to apply rouge to (the face) excessively or badly. **raddled** *a.* **1** unkempt. **2** haggard-looking because of age or debauchery.
radial (rā´diəl) *a.* **1** of, relating to or resembling a ray, rays or radii. **2** extending or directed from a

centre as rays or radii; divergent. **3** having radiating parts, lines etc. **4** positional as or acting along a radius. **5** (*Anat.*) of or relating to the radius of the forearm. ~*n.* **1** a radiating part, line, bone, nerve, artery etc. **2** a radial-ply tyre. **radial engine** *n.* an internal-combustion engine which has its cylinders arranged radially. **radial keratotomy** *n.* keratotomy to correct short-sightedness. **radially** *adv.* **radially symmetrical** *a.* showing radial symmetry. **radial-ply** *a.* (of a motor vehicle tyre) having the fabric in the casing placed radially at right angles to the circumference for increased flexibility. **radial symmetry** *n.* the state of having several planes arranged symmetrically around a common axis, as in a starfish. **radial velocity** *n.* (*pl.* **radial velocities**) (*Astron.*) the component of velocity of an object along the line of sight between the observer and the object, esp. a star.

radian (rā´diən) *n.* (*Geom.*) **1** an arc equal in length to the radius of its circle. **2** the angle subtending such an arc, 57.296°.

radiant (rā´diənt) *a.* **1** emitting rays of light or heat. **2** issuing in rays. **3** (*fig.*) shining, beaming (with joy, love etc.). **4** splendid, brilliant. **5** extending, arranged or acting radially, radiating. **6** emitting radiant heat. ~*n.* the point from which light or heat radiates. **radiance,** †**radiancy** *n.* (*pl.* **radiances,** †**radiancies**). **radiant heat** *n.* heat transmitted by radiation. **radiant heater** *n.* **radiantly** *adv.*

radiate (rā´diāt) *v.i.* **1** to emit rays of light, heat or other electromagnetic radiation. **2** to issue or be emitted in rays from or as from a centre. **3** to proceed or spread from a central point. ~*v.t.* **1** to emit or send out as rays or from a central point. **2** to exhibit, to demonstrate (vitality, happiness etc.). **3** to send forth in all directions, to disseminate. **radiation** (-ā´shən) *n.* **1** (*Physics*) **a** the act of radiating or emitting rays, esp. the emission of heat, light etc. in the form of electromagnetic waves or particles. **b** energy transmitted as waves or particles. **2** a travelling outwards, as radii, to the periphery. **radiational** *a.* **radiation sickness** *n.* illness caused by too great absorption of radiation in the body, whose symptoms include fatigue, nausea, vomiting, internal bleeding, loss of hair and teeth, and in extreme cases, leukaemia. **radiative** (-ətiv), **radiatory** (-ətəri) *a.* **radiator** *n.* **1** something that radiates. **2** a vessel, chamber or coil of pipes charged with hot air, water, steam etc. for radiating heat in a building. **3** a device for dissipating the heat absorbed by the cooling water of an engine jacket. **radiator grille** *n.* a grille on the front of a motor vehicle that protects the radiator and allows cooling air to circulate round it.

radical (rad´ikəl) *a.* **1** of or relating to the root, source or origin. **2** inherent, fundamental. **3** going to the root, thorough-going, extreme. **4 a** being, relating to or according to radical politics,

favouring extreme action or changes. **b** of or belonging to a political party advocating extreme measures. **5** original, basic, primary. **6** (*Med.*) relating to or being surgery intended to remove all traces of diseased tissue. **7** (*Math.*) of or relating to the root of a number or quantity. **8** of or relating to the root of a word, primary, underived. **9** (*sl.*) excellent, very good, outstanding. ~*n.* **1** a person promoting extreme measures or holding advanced views on either side of the political spectrum. **2** (*Math.*) a quantity that is, or is expressed as, the root of another. **3** (*Chem.*) **a** an element, atom or group of atoms forming part of a compound and not decomposed by the reactions that normally alter the compound. **b** a free radical. **4** the root of a word. **5** a fundamental principle. **6** any of the set of basic characters in the Chinese writing system. **radicalism** *n.* **radicality** (-kal´-), **radicalness** *n.* **radicalize, radicalise** *v.t., v.i.* **radicalization** (-zā´shən) *n.* **radically** *adv.* thoroughly, fundamentally, essentially. **radical sign** *n.* the symbol ($\sqrt{}$) placed before a number to show that the square root, or some higher root as shown by a superscript number (e.g. $\sqrt[3]{}$), is to be calculated.

radicchio (rədē´kiō) *n.* (*pl.* **radicchios**) a type of chicory from Italy with purple and white leaves eaten raw in salads.

radices RADIX.

radicle (rad´ikəl) *n.* **1** the part of a plant embryo that develops into the main root. **2** a small root, a rootlet. **3** a rootlike part of a nerve, vein etc. **radicular** (-dik´ū-) *a.*

radii RADIUS.

radio (rā´diō) *n.* (*pl.* **radios**) **1** electromagnetic waves used in two-way broadcasting. **2** the process or system of transmitting and receiving sound signals, messages, music etc. by means of electromagnetic waves of radio frequency. **3** any device which can send signals through space using electromagnetic waves. **4** an apparatus capable of demodulating and transmitting a signal sent using electromagnetic waves. **5** a radio receiving set. **6** sound broadcasting. **7** the programmes broadcast on the radio. **8** a sound broadcasting station, channel or organization. ~*v.t.* (*3rd pers. sing. pres.* **radioes,** *pres.p.* **radioing,** *past, p.p.* **radioed**) **1** to send or communicate by radio. **2** to send a radio message to. ~*v.i.* to use a radio or the system of radio to communicate. **radio astronomy** *n.* the study of radio waves received back from celestial objects. **radio cab, radio car** *n.* (*dated*) a taxi equipped with a two-way radio. **radio control** *n.* remote control using radio signals. **radio-controlled** *a.* **radio fix** *n.* the position of a ship, aeroplane etc. as determined by radio signals. **radio frequency** *n.* (*pl.* **radio frequencies**) **1** radio spectrum. **2** a frequency or band of frequencies used for radio transmission. **radio galaxy** *n.* (*pl.* **radio galaxies**) a galaxy which is a strong source of radio waves. **radio ham** *n.* a licensed amateur operator of a radio transmitting and receiving system. **radio spectrum** *n.* the range of electromagnetic frequencies, between 10 kHz and 300,000 MHz, used in radio transmissions. **radio telescope** *n.* an apparatus for collecting radio waves from outer space.

radio-¹ (rā´diō) *comb. form* **1** of or relating to radio, radio frequency or broadcasting. **2** of, relating to or connected with radiation or radioactivity. **3** radioactive, radioactive isotope of (an element).

radio-² (rā´diō) *comb. form* **1** radiate. **2** (*Anat.*) of or relating to the outer bone of the forearm.

radioactive (rādiōak´tiv) *a.* of or exhibiting radioactivity. **radioactively** *adv.* **radioactivity** (-tiv´-) *n.* **1** the spontaneous emission of usu. penetrating radiation, as alpha and beta particles, that accompanies the disintegration of atomic nuclei of unstable elements or isotopes. **2** radioactive substances. **3** radiation emitted by radioactive substances.

radiocarbon (rādiōkah´bən) *n.* carbon-14, a radioactive carbon isotope. **radiocarbon dating** *n.* CARBON DATING (under CARBON).

radio-element (rādiōel´imənt) *n.* a radioactive chemical element.

radiogenic (rādiōjēn´ik) *a.* **1** produced by radioactivity. **2** suitable for radio broadcasting. **radiogenically** *adv.*

radiogram (rā´diōgram) *n.* (*dated*) **1** a combined radio and record player. **2** a photograph produced by X-rays, gamma rays etc. **3** a radiotelegraphic message.

radiograph (rā´diōgrahf) *n.* **1** a negative produced by X-rays, gamma rays etc. **2** a print from this. *~v.t.* to obtain a photographic image of by means of such rays. **radiographer** (-og´-) *n.* a person who takes X-ray pictures of parts of the body. **radiographic** (-graf´-) *a.* **radiographically** *adv.* **radiography** (-og´-) *n.*

radioimmunology (rādiōimūnol´əji) *n.* immunology that employs the techniques of radiology. **radioimmunological** (-loj´-) *a.*

radioisotope (rādiōī´sətōp) *n.* a radioactive isotope of a chemical element. **radioisotopic** (-top´-) *a.* **radioisotopically** *adv.*

radiolarian (rādiōlee´riən) *n.* a marine rhizopod protozoan of the superclass Actinopoda, having radiating filamentous pseudopodia and abounding in warm seas.

radiology (rādiol´əji) *n.* the branch of medical science concerned with radioactivity, X-rays and other diagnostic or therapeutic radiations. **radiologic** (-loj´-), **radiological** *a.* **radiologist** *n.*

radiometer (rādiom´itə) *n.* an instrument for measuring the intensity of radiant energy. **radiometric** (-met´-) *a.* **radiometric dating** *n.* a method of dating geological material by measuring the relative amounts of the isotopes of a particular radioactive element.

radionics (rādion´iks) *n.* a form of complementary medicine that bases diagnoses on the analysis of energy supposedly emitted from items, e.g. hair, belonging to the patient.

radionuclide (rādiōnū´klīd) *n.* a radioactive nuclide.

radiopaque (rādiōpāk´), **radio-opaque** (rādiōōpāk´) *a.* not allowing X-rays or other radiation to pass through. **radiopacity** (-pas´-) *n.*

radiophonic (rādiōfon´ik) *a.* of, relating to or being music or other sounds produced electronically.

radioscopy (rādios´kəpi) *n.* examination of bodies by means of X-rays.

radiosonde (rā´diōsond) *n.* a miniature radio transmitter sent up in a balloon and dropped by parachute, for sending information of pressures, temperatures etc.

radio-telegram (rādiōtel´igram) *n.* a message sent by radio-telegraphy, esp. from a ship to land. **radio-telegraph** *n.* **radio-telegraphic** (-graf´-) *a.* **radio-telegraphy** (-tǝleg´-) *n.* telegraphy which transmits messages using radio waves.

radio-telephone (rādiōtel´ifōn) *n.* an apparatus for sending telephone messages using radio waves. *~v.t.* to telephone using a radio-telephone. **radio-telephonic** (-fon´-) *a.* **radiotelephony** (-tǝlef´-) *n.* telephony which transmits messages using radio waves.

radiotelex (rādiotel´eks) *n.* a telex sent using radio-teletype apparatus.

radiotherapy (rādiother´əpi) *n.* the treatment of disease by means of X-rays or other radiation, esp. from radioactive sources. **radiotherapeutic** (-pū´tik) *a.* **radiotherapist** *n.*

radish (rad´ish) *n.* **1** a cruciferous plant, *Raphanus sativus*, cultivated for its pungent root, which is eaten as a salad vegetable. **2** this root.

radium (rā´diəm) *n.* (*Chem.*) a highly radioactive metallic element, at. no. 88, chem. symbol Ra, occurring in pitchblende, used in making luminous materials and in radiotherapy. **radium therapy** *n.* the treatment of disease, esp. cancer, using radiation from radium.

radius (rā´diəs) *n.* (*pl.* **radii** (-dii)) **1** (*Math.*) a straight line from the centre of a circle or sphere to any point on the circumference. **2** (*Math.*) the length of this, half the diameter. **3 a** a circular area measured by its usu. specified radius. **b** any circumscribed area. **4** the shorter of the two long bones of the forearm. **5** the corresponding bone in animals and birds. **6** a radiating line, part, object etc., such as a spoke. **7** (*Geom.*) the distance from a focus to a point on a curve. **8** (*Bot.*) **a** the outer zone of a composite flower. **b** a floret in this. **c** a branch of an umbel. **9** an arm of a starfish.

radix (rā´diks) *n.* (*pl.* **radices** (-disēz)) **1** (*Math.*) a quantity or symbol taken as the base of a system of numbering, logarithms etc. **2** a source or origin. **3** a root.

radon (rā´don) *n.* (*Chem.*) a gaseous radioactive

element, at. no. 86, chem. symbol Rn, formed by the disintegration of radium.

raffia (raf´iə), **raphia** n. 1 a Madagascan palm, *Raphia ruffia*, with a short stem and gigantic pinnate leaves. 2 fibre prepared from the leaves, used for tying, ornamental work etc.

raffish (raf´ish) a. 1 disreputable, disorderly, dissipated-looking, rakish. 2 vulgar, tawdry. **raffishly** adv. **raffishness** n.

raffle (raf´əl) n. a lottery in which one or more articles are put up to be disposed of by drawing lots among a number of people buying tickets for the draw. ~v.t. to dispose of by means of a raffle.

raft[1] (rahft) n. 1 a flat floating framework of planks or other material used for supporting or carrying people, goods etc. on water. 2 a small, often inflatable boat for use in an emergency. 3 a floating accumulation of driftwood, ice etc. in a river. 4 a number of logs or pieces of timber fastened together for transport by floating down a river etc. ~v.t. 1 to transport on or as on a raft. 2 to cross (a river etc.) on a raft. 3 to make into a raft. 4 to transport in the form of a raft. ~v.i. to travel on a raft. **rafter**[1] n. a person who manages or works on a raft. **raftsman** n. (pl. **raftsmen**).

raft[2] (rahft) n. (coll.) a large number, a crowd, a lot.

rafter[1] RAFT[1].

rafter[2] (rahf´tə) n. any of the sloping pieces of timber supporting a roof or forming the framework on which the tiles etc. or the roof are laid. **raftered** a.

rag[1] (rag) n. 1 a torn or worn piece of cloth, esp. an irregular piece detached from a fabric by wear and tear. 2 (pl.) tattered or shabby clothes. 3 (collect.) torn fragments of cloth, linen etc., used as material for paper, stuffing etc. 4 (sl.) a handkerchief. 5 (derog.) a newspaper. 6 (derog.) a flag, sail, drop-curtain etc. 7 a remnant, a scrap, the smallest piece (of anything). **rag-and-bone man** n. (pl. **rag-and-bone men**) an itinerant dealer in old or unwanted clothes, household items etc. **ragbag** n. 1 a miscellaneous collection. 2 a bag for scraps of cloth. 3 (coll.) a carelessly dressed or dishevelled woman. **rag bolt** n. a bolt with jags on the shank to prevent its being easily withdrawn. **rag book** n. a book for a young child made out of cloth instead of paper. **rag doll** n. a doll made from cloth. **rag paper** n. paper made from rags. **rags-to-riches** a. denoting someone who starts off poor and becomes rich, or a story describing this progress. **ragtag, ragtag and bobtail** n. (derog.) the riff-raff, the rabble. **ragtail** a. (esp. N Am.) confused, badly organized, straggly. **rag trade** n. (coll.) the clothing industry. **ragweed** n. ragwort. **ragworm** n. any of several burrowing marine worms used as bait in fishing. **ragwort** n. a yellow-flowered plant with deeply cut leaves of the genus *Senecio*, esp. *S. jacobaea*, a common weed.

rag[2] (rag) v.t. (pres.p. **ragging**, past, p.p. **ragged**) 1 to tease, irritate or play rough practical jokes on.

2 to reprove, to talk to severely. ~v.i. to engage in rough or noisy horseplay. ~n. 1 a programme of entertainments, stunts, processions etc. organized by students to raise money for charity. 2 a prank. 3 the act of ragging. 4 a piece of boisterous and disorderly conduct.

rag[3] (rag) n. (Mus.) 1 a piece of ragtime music. 2 ragtime.

rag[4] (rag) n. 1 (also **ragstone**) a hard, coarse, rough stone, usu. breaking up into thick slabs. 2 a large roofing slate with a rough surface on one side.

raga (rah´gə), **rag** (rahg) n. 1 in traditional Indian music, a form or a mode which forms the basis for improvisation. 2 a composition following such a pattern.

ragamuffin (rag´əmŭfin) n. 1 a ragged unkempt person, esp. a child. 2 ragga. 3 (also **raggamuffin**) a follower of ragga music.

rage (rāj) n. 1 violent anger, fury. 2 a fit of passionate anger. 3 (fig.) extreme violence, vehemence or intensity (of). 4 a violent desire or enthusiasm (for). 5 (coll.) an object of temporary pursuit, enthusiasm or devotion. 6 intense emotion, passion or ardour. 7 (Austral., New Zeal., coll.) a party. ~v.i. (pres.p. **raging**) 1 to storm, to rave, to be furious with anger, to be violently incensed or agitated. 2 to express anger or passion violently. 3 to be violent, to be at the highest state of vehemence, intensity or activity. 4 (Austral., New Zeal., coll.) to have a good time. **all the rage** an object of general desire, quite the fashion. **rager** n.

ragga (rag´ə) n. a form of popular dance music incorporating elements of reggae and hip hop.

raggamuffin RAGAMUFFIN.

ragged (rag´id) a. 1 worn into rags, tattered. 2 rough, shaggy. 3 broken, jagged, or uneven in outline or surface. 4 disjointed, irregular, imperfect. 5 lacking in uniformity, finish etc. 6 harsh, dissonant. 7 wearing tattered clothes. 8 shabby, poor, miserable in appearance. **raggedly** adv. **raggedness** n. **ragged robin** n. a pink-flowered plant, *Lychnis floscuculi*, the petals of which have a tattered appearance. **raggedy** a. tattered.

raggle-taggle (rag´əltag´əl), **wraggle-taggle** a. unkempt, untidy.

raglan (rag´lən) n. a loose overcoat with no seams on the shoulders, the sleeves going up to the neck. ~a. cut in this way. **raglan sleeve** n. a sleeve which continues to the collar, with no seams on the shoulders.

ragout (ragoo´) n. a highly seasoned dish of small pieces of stewed meat and vegetables. ~v.t. to make into a ragout.

ragtime (rag´tīm) n. a style of jazz music popular esp. in the early 20th cent., characterized by a syncopated melody and played esp. on the piano. ~a. disreputable, unruly.

rah (rah) int. (esp. N Am., coll.) hurrah. **rah-rah** a. (N Am., coll.) marked by or demonstrating extreme, esp. noisy enthusiasm. **rah-rah skirt** n. a short flared skirt as worn by a cheerleader.

rai (rī) *n.* a form of popular music originating in Algeria that incorporates elements of traditional Bedouin music and Western rock.

raid (rād) *n.* **1** a sudden hostile or predatory incursion as of armed troops, criminals etc. **2** a sudden surprise invasion or descent of police or customs officers etc. **3** an air raid. **4** an attempt by speculators to lower stock market prices by concerted selling. **5** (*esp. facet.*) an excursion or foray to obtain something (*a raid on the larder*). *~v.t.* to make a raid upon. **raider** *n.*

rail[1] (rāl) *n.* **1** a bar of wood or metal or series of such bars resting on posts or other supports, forming part of a fence, banisters etc. **2** a continuous line of iron or steel bars, resting on sleepers etc. laid on the ground, usu. forming one of a pair of such lines constituting the track of a railway or tramway. **3** any of the iron or steel bars forming such a line. **4** either of a similar pair of lines serving as track for part of a machine. **5** the railway as a means of travel or transportation. **6** a bar fixed on a wall on which to hang things. **7** a horizontal structural support in a door. **8** (*pl.*) a barrier at the side of a racecourse. *~v.t.* **1** to enclose with rails. **2** to furnish or fill with rails. **3** to lay down rails upon. **4** to send by rail. **to go off the rails 1** to go mad. **2** to go awry. **railage** *n.* **railcar** *n.* a self-powered single railway carriage. **rail card** *n.* an identity card issued to certain people (e.g. pensioners and students) allowing the holder cheaper rail fares. **rail gun** *n.* an electromagnetic anti-missile projectile launcher. **railhead** *n.* **1** a terminus. **2** the farthest point to which rails have been laid. **railing** *n.* **1** (*often pl.*) a fence made of wooden or other rails. **2** materials for railings. **railless** *a.* **railman** *n.* (*pl.* **railmen**) a railway worker. **railroad** *n.* (*esp. N Am.*) a railway. *~v.t.* **1** to force hurriedly to a conclusion. **2** to send to prison on a false charge. **railway** (rāl′wā) *n.* **1** a permanent track formed of rails of iron or steel along which trains and vehicles are driven, usu. by locomotives. **2** a system of tracks, stations, rolling stock and other apparatus worked by one company or organization. **3** an organization that runs such a system. **4** a track laid with rails for the passage of cranes, trucks etc. **railwayman, railwaywoman** *n.* (*pl.* **railwaymen, railwaywomen**) a railway worker. **railway yard** *n.* a place where rolling stock is kept.

rail[2] (rāl) *v.i.* **1** to use abusive or derisive language. **2** to scoff (at or against). **railer** *n.* **raillery** *n.* (*pl.* **railleries**) **1** good-humoured ridicule or pleasantry, banter. **2** a bantering comment.

rail[3] (rāl) *n.* a wading bird of the family Rallidae, esp. the water rail and the corncrake or landrail.

raiment (rā′mənt) *n.* (*dated or poet.*) dress, apparel, clothes.

rain (rān) *n.* **1** the condensed moisture of the atmosphere falling in drops. **2** a fall of such drops. **3** a similar fall or shower of liquid, particles or objects. **4** (*fig.*) a large quantity of anything falling quickly. **5** rainy weather. **6** (*pl.*) the rainy season in a tropical country. *~v.i.* **1** (*usu. impers.*) to fall in drops of water from the clouds. **2** to fall in showers like rain. **3** to send down rain. *~v.t.* **1** to pour down (rain). **2** to send down in showers like rain. **to be rained off** to be cancelled or postponed because of rain or bad weather. **to be rained out** (*N Am.*) to be rained off. **rainbird** *n.* any of various birds supposed to foretell rain, esp. the green woodpecker. **rainbow** (-bō) *n.* **1** a luminous arc showing the prismatic colours, appearing opposite the sun during rain, caused by the reflection, double refraction and dispersion of the sun's rays passing through the drops. **2** any similar effect or display of colours. **3** a wide assortment (*a rainbow of opinions*). *~a.* **1** coloured like the rainbow. **2** many-coloured. **rainbow coalition** *n.* a political alliance of minority groups. **rainbow trout** *n.* a brightly-coloured trout, *Onchorhyncus mykiss*, of N American origin. **rain check** *n.* (*esp. N Am.*) **1** a ticket for a sports event which allows re-admission on another day if rain stops play. **2** an extension of an offer to a later, more convenient time. **to take a rain check** to postpone accepting an invitation till a later date. **rain cloud** *n.* a cloud producing rain, a nimbus. **raincoat** *n.* a waterproof coat or cloak for wearing in wet weather, a mackintosh. **raindrop** *n.* a particle of rain. **rainfall** *n.* **1** a shower of rain. **2** the amount of rain which falls in a particular district in a given period. **rainforest** *n.* a dense tropical forest of mostly evergreen trees with a very heavy rainfall. **rainless** *a.* **rainmaker** *n.* **1** a person who professes to cause rain by incantations or magic. **2** (*N Am., sl.*) a successful business person who generates a high level of income for an employer. **rainmaking** *n.* the artificial production of rain, e.g. by seeding clouds. **rainproof** *a.* impervious or resistant to rain. *~v.t.* to make impervious to rain. **rain shadow** *n.* the leeward side of hills, which has a relatively light rainfall compared to the windward side. **rainstorm** *n.* a storm with very heavy rain. **rainswept** *a.* exposed to the rain. **rainwater** *n.* water that has fallen in the form of rain. **rainwear** *n.* rainproof clothing. **rain-worm** *n.* an earthworm. **rainy** *a.* (*comp.* **rainier,** *superl.* **rainiest**) **1** characterized by much rain. **2** showery, wet. **3** bearing rain. **rainily** *adv.* **raininess** *n.* **rainy day** *n.* a time of misfortune or distress, esp. pecuniary need.

raise (rāz) *v.t.* **1** to move or put into a higher position. **2** to cause to rise, to elevate. **3** to cause to stand up, to set upright. **4** to increase the amount or value of. **5** to increase the strength or intensity of (*to raise one's voice*). **6** to erect, to build, to construct. **7** to restore to life or from sleep. **8** to rouse, to excite, to stir up. **9** to produce, to create, to cause. **10** to set up, to cause to be heard or known, to suggest (a point etc.). **11** to occasion. **12** to bring up, to rear. **13** to grow or breed. **14** to collect, to procure, to levy (money etc.). **15** to advance, to promote, to heighten, to make higher or nobler, to cause to ascend. **16** to remove, to bring to an end (a ban, blockade, siege etc.). **17** (*Math.*) to multiply (a number) by itself a specified number of times. **18** to cause to increase in volume by the addition of a raising agent. **19** to cause (a blister, lump etc.) to form or swell. **20** to bid more money than (a previous player) at cards. **21 a** in bridge, to make a higher bid in (the suit of one's partner). **b** to increase (a bid) in this way. **22** to establish radio links with. **23** to put a nap on (cloth). ~*n.* (*N Am.*) a rise in salary. **raised beach** *n.* (*Geol.*) an ancient beach or shore, of a lake or sea, left high and dry by elevation of the land or recession of the water. **raiser** *n.* **raising** *n.* **raising agent** *n.* a natural or chemical substance which causes dough or cakes to rise.

raisin (rā´zin) *n.* a dried grape, the partially dried fruit of various species of vine. **raisiny** *a.*

raison d'être (rāzōn det´rə) *n.* (*pl.* **raisons d'être** (rāzŏn det´rə)) the reason for a thing's existence.

raita (rah-ē´tə, rāē´tə, rīē´tə, rī´ta) *n.* an Indian side dish of chopped cucumber or other salad vegetables in yogurt.

raj (rahj) *n.* (in the Indian subcontinent) rule, government. **the Raj** the British rule of India before 1947.

raja (rah´jə), **rajah** *n.* **1** an Indian king, prince or tribal chief, a dignitary or noble. **2** a Malayan or Javanese chief. **rajaship** *n.*

rake¹ (rāk) *n.* **1** an implement having a long handle with a cross-bar set with teeth, used for drawing loose material together, smoothing soil etc. **2** a similar implement for collecting light articles. **3** (*Hist.*) a two-wheeled implement drawn by a horse for gathering hay together etc. ~*v.t.* **1** to collect or gather (up or together) with a rake. **2** to scrape, scratch, smooth, clean etc. (soil) with a rake. **3** to search with or as with a rake, to scour, to ransack. **4** to fire along the length of, to enfilade. **5** (of shot) to pass from end to end of. **6** (*fig.*) to command from end to end with the eye. ~*v.i.* **1** to use or work with a rake. **2** to search (about etc.) with or as with a rake. **to rake in** (*coll.*) to accumulate (usu. money). **to rake off** (*coll.*) to receive a share of the profits from an illegal job. **to rake over** (*coll.*) to dwell on the memory of (a quarrel, the past etc.). **to rake up** (*coll.*) to revive the memory of (a quarrel, the past etc.). **rake-off** *n.* (*coll.*) **1** commission on a job. **2** more or less illicit profits from a job. **raker** *n.*

rake² (rāk) *n.* a dissolute or immoral man, a debauchee, a libertine. **rakish**¹ *a.* of, resembling or characteristic of a rake. **rakishly** *adv.* **rakishness** *n.*

rake³ (rāk) *n.* **1** inclination, slope, esp. backward slope. **2** (*Naut.*) the slope of a mast or funnel towards the stern. **3** the angle between the face of a cutting tool and a plane perpendicular to the

working surface. **4** the angle of sweepback of an aircraft's wing. ~*v.i.* to slope, esp. backwards, from the perpendicular. ~*v.t.* to give such an inclination to.

raki (rahkē´, rak´i), **rakee** *n.* (*pl.* **rakis, rakees**) an aromatic liquor made from spirit or grape juice, usu. flavoured with mastic, used in the E Mediterranean region.

rakish¹ RAKE².

rakish² (rā´kish) *a.* **1** (*Naut.*) with masts sharply inclined. **2** apparently built for speed. **3** smart-looking with a suggestion of the pirate or smuggler. **4** dashing, jaunty.

rallentando (rələntan´dō) *adv., a.* (*Mus.*) gradually slower. ~*n.* (*pl.* **rallentandos, rallentandi** (-dē)) **1** a gradual slowing in the speed at which music is played. **2** a passage to be played in this way.

rally¹ (ral´i) *v.t.* (*3rd pers. sing. pres.* **rallies,** *pres.p.* **rallying,** *past, p.p.* **rallied**) **1** to reunite, to bring (disordered troops) etc. together again. **2** to gather or bring together for a common purpose. **3** to restore, to reanimate, to revive, to pull together. ~*v.i.* **1** to reassemble, to come together again after a reverse or rout. **2** to come together for a cause or purpose. **3** to regain strength, to recover tone or spirit, to return to a state of health, vigour or courage. **4** (of share prices) to increase after a period of decline. ~*n.* (*pl.* **rallies**) **1** the act of rallying or recovering order, strength, health, energy etc. **2** an assembly, a reunion. **3** a large gathering of supporters of a cause, or of people with a common interest. **4** in tennis etc., a rapid or lengthy exchange of strokes. **5** a sharp increase in trade on the Stock Exchange after a period of decline. **6** a motoring contest designed to test driving and navigational skills in which cars are raced over a usu. unknown route on public roads and rough terrain. **to rally round** to come to someone's aid morally or financially. **rallier** *n.* **rallycross** *n.* a form of motor racing in which specially adapted saloon cars race over a circuit containing both paved and rough, uneven surfaces (e.g. grass).

rally² (ral´i) *v.t.* (*3rd pers. sing. pres.* **rallies,** *pres.p.* **rallying,** *past, p.p.* **rallied**) to ridicule or tease in a good-humoured way.

RAM (ram) *n.* (*Comput.*) a temporary storage space in a computer from which data can be accessed directly in any order and altered.

ram (ram) *n.* **1** an uncastrated male sheep, a tup. **2** (*Hist.*) a battering-ram. **3** the drop-weight of a piledriver or steam hammer. **4** a hydraulic engine for raising water, lifting etc. ~*v.t.* (*pres.p.* **ramming,** *past, p.p.* **rammed**) **1** to beat, drive, press or force (down, in, into etc.) by heavy blows. **2** to stuff, to compress, to force (into) with pressure. **3** to make firm by ramming. **4** to crash against with force. **5** to drive or impel (a thing against, into etc.) forcefully or with violence. ~*v.i.* to crash or collide violently. **the Ram** the constellation or zodiacal sign Aries. **to ram**

home to force recognition or acceptance of.
ramjet *n.* (*also* **ramjet engine**) a form of aero-engine where the compressed air produced by the forward movement of the aircraft is used to burn the fuel. **rammer** *n.* **1** someone who or something which rams. **2** an instrument for pounding, driving etc. **ram-raid** *n.* a robbery from a shop etc., using a vehicle to break into the premises. **ram-raider** *n.* **ram-raiding** *n.* **ramrod** *n.* **1** a rod for forcing down the charge of a muzzle-loading gun. **2** a stiff or rigid person or thing.

Ramadan (ram´ədan, -dahn´), **Ramadhan** *n.* the ninth and holiest month of the Islamic year, the time of the great annual fast.

ramble (ram´bəl) *v.i.* **1** to walk or move about freely, as for recreation, or aimlessly. **2** to wander or be incoherent in speech, writing etc. **3** (of a plant) to grow in a straggling random manner. ~*n.* **1** a walk for pleasure or without a definite object, a stroll. **2** a roaming about. **rambler** *n.* **1** a person who rambles about, esp. a person who takes long walks in the countryside. **2** a vigorous climbing rose with lax stems. **rambling** *a.* **1** wandering about. **2** desultory, disconnected, incoherent. **3** irregular, straggling. **4** (of a plant) climbing with trailing stems. **ramblingly** *adv.*

rambunctious (rambŭngk´shəs) *a.* (*esp.* N Am., *coll.*) unruly, boisterous, exuberant. **rambunctiously** *adv.* **rambunctiousness** *n.*

rambutan (ramboo´tən) *n.* **1** the red, hairy, pulpy fruit of a Malaysian tree, *Nephelium lappaceum*. **2** this tree.

ramekin (ram´ikin), **ramequin** *n.* **1** a dish of cheese, eggs, breadcrumbs etc., baked in a small dish or mould. **2** (*also* **ramekin dish**) the mould itself.

ramie (ram´i), **ramee** *n.* **1** a bushy Chinese and E Asian plant, *Boehmeria nivea*, of the nettle family. **2** the fine fibre of this woven as a substitute for cotton.

ramification (ramifikā´shən) *n.* **1** the act of ramifying, the state of being ramified. **2** a subdivision in a complex system, structure etc. **3** a consequence, esp. one that causes complications. **ramify** (ram´ifī) *v.i.* (*3rd pers. sing. pres.* **ramifies**, *pres.p.* **ramifying**, *past, p.p.* **ramified**) **1** to divide into branches or subdivisions, to branch out, to send out offshoots. **2** to develop a usu. complicated consequence. ~*v.t.* to cause to divide into branches etc.

rammer RAM.

ramp[1] (ramp) *v.i.* **1** to dash about, to rage, to storm. **2** to act in a violent or aggressive manner. **3** (*Archit.*) (of a wall) to ascend or descend to another level. **4** (*Her.*) (of a heraldic lion) to rear or stand up on the hind legs, with the forelegs raised. ~*v.t.* to build or provide with ramps. ~*n.* **1** a slope or inclined plane or way, esp. leading from one level to another. **2** a movable stairway for boarding or leaving a plane. **3** a hump in the road, often designed to slow traffic down. **4** a

sloping part in the top of a handrail, wall, coping etc. **5** the act of ramping.

ramp[2] (ramp) *v.t.* (*sl.*) to force to pay large amounts of money, esp. by swindling. ~*v.i.* to engage in a ramp. ~*n.* a swindle, esp. one involving artificially inflated prices.

rampage[1] (rampāj´) *v.i.* to dash about, to storm, to rage, to behave violently or boisterously. **rampager** *n.*

rampage[2] (ram´pāj, -pāj´) *n.* boisterous, excited, violent behaviour. **on the rampage 1** violently excited. **2** on a drunken spree. **rampageous** (-pā´-) *a.*

rampant (ram´pənt) *a.* **1** unrestrained, aggressive, wild, violent. **2** (of weeds etc.) rank, luxuriant. **3** (*Her.*) (of a heraldic animal) standing upright on the hind legs, ramping. **rampancy** *n.* (*pl.* **rampancies**). **rampantly** *adv.*

rampart (ram´paht) *n.* **1** an embankment, usu. surmounted by a parapet, round a fortified place, or such an embankment together with the parapet. **2** (*fig.*) a defence. ~*v.t.* to fortify or defend with or as with a rampart.

rampion (ram´piən) *n.* **1** a bellflower, *Campanula rapunculus*, with red, purple or blue blossoms. **2** any of several related plants of the genus *Phyteuma* with clusters of bluish flowers.

ramrod RAM.

ramshackle (ram´shakəl) *a.* (of a building, vehicle etc.) tumbledown, rickety, shaky.

ramsons (ram´zəns, -səns) *n.* (*pl.* **ramsons**) the broad-leaved garlic, *Allium ursinum*, or its bulbous root, eaten as a relish.

ran RUN.

ranch (rahnch) *n.* **1** a farm for rearing cattle and horses, esp. in western N America. **2** any large farm devoted to rearing a particular animal or crop. **3** a ranch house. ~*v.t.* to manage or work on a ranch. **rancher** *n.* a person who owns, manages or works on a ranch. **ranch house** *n.* **1** a house belonging to a ranch. **2** (*N Am.*) an open-plan single-storey house.

rancid (ran´sid) *a.* having the taste or smell of stale oil or fat. **rancidity** (-sid´-), **rancidness** *n.*

rancour (rang´kə), (*N Am.*) **rancor** *n.* inveterate spite, resentment or enmity, malignancy, deep-seated malice. **rancorous** *a.* **rancorously** *adv.*

rand[1] (rand, rant) *n.* **1** the standard monetary unit of S Africa. **2** (*S Afr.*) the high land bordering a river valley.

rand[2] (rand) *n.* a strip of leather between the sole and heel-piece of a boot or shoe.

R & B, R. & B. *abbr.* (*Mus.*) rhythm and blues.

R & D, R. & D. *abbr.* research and development.

random (ran´dəm) *a.* **1** done, made etc. without calculation or method; left to or occurring by chance. **2** having a value or outcome which cannot be determined, only defined in terms of probability (*a random variable*). **3** relating to, being or consisting of items or individuals having equal probabilities of occurring or being chosen (*a random sample*; *random numbers*).

4 (of masonry) consisting of stones etc. of irregular size and shape. **at random** without direction or definite purpose, haphazardly. **random access** n. (*Comput.*) direct access to specific data in a larger store of computer data, without reading the entire store sequentially. **random-access memory** n. RAM. **randomize, randomise** v.t. **randomization** (-zā´shən) n. **randomizer** n. **randomly** adv. **randomness** n.

R and R, R. and R. abbr. **1** rescue and resuscitation. **2** rest and recreation. **3** rock and roll.

randy (ran´di) a. (*comp.* **randier,** *superl.* **randiest**) lustful, on heat, sexually eager or excited. **randily** adv. **randiness** n.

ranee (rah´ni), **rani** n. (*pl.* **ranees, ranis**) **1** a Hindu queen. **2** the consort of a raja.

rang RING².

range (rānj) n. **1** the extent of variation in something. **2** the limits between which such variation occurs. **3** the area, extent, scope, compass or sphere of power, activity, variation, voice-pitch etc. **4** the entire collection of products of a designer, manufacturer, stockist etc. **5 a** the extreme horizontal distance attainable by a gun or missile. **b** the distance between a gun or missile and its target. **6 a** a piece of ground with targets etc. for firing practice. **b** an area used for testing military equipment. **7** a row, rank, line, chain or series (e.g. of mountains). **8** a cooking-stove or fireplace, usu. containing a boiler, oven or ovens, hotplate etc. **9** a stretch, a tract, esp. of grazing or hunting ground. **10** the distance between a camera and the photographic subject. **11** the geographical area over which a plant or animal is naturally distributed. **12** the set of values of a dependent variable in statistics. ~v.t. (*pres.p.* **ranging**) **1** to set in a row or rows. **2** to arrange in definite order, place, company etc., to classify, to array. **3** to roam or pass over, along or through. **4** to make straight, level or flush, to align. ~v.i. **1** to lie, extend or reach. **2** to vary (between specified limits or from one specified point to another). **3** to roam, to wander, to rove, to sail (along etc.). **4** to be level, straight or flush. **5** to rank, to be in place (among, with etc.). **6 a** to carry (a specified distance) in a particular direction. **b** (of a gun etc.) to have a specified range. **rangefinder** n. an instrument for measuring the distance of an object from the observer, used in shooting a gun or focusing a camera. **ranger** n. **1** the superintendent of a forest, nature reserve etc. **2** (*N Am.*) a commando in the US army. **3** a member of a body of mounted troops. **4** (**Ranger**) a Guide of 16 and upwards. **5** a person who ranges, a rover, a wanderer. **rangership** n. **ranging-pole, ranging-rod** n. a usu. red and white striped rod used in surveying. **rangy** a. (*comp.* **rangier,** *superl.* **rangiest**) tall, wiry, strong.

rani RANEE.

rank¹ (rangk) n. **1** relative degree of excellence etc. **2** high station, dignity, eminence. **3** relative position, degree, standing, station, class. **4** a row, a line. **5** a row of soldiers ranged side by side, as opposed to file. **6** a row of taxis for hire. **7** order, array. **8** a line of squares stretching across a chessboard from side to side. ~v.t. **1** to classify, to estimate, to give a (specified) rank to. **2** to draw up or arrange in rank or ranks. **3** (*N Am.*) to take precedence over, to have a higher rank than. ~v.i. **1** to hold a (specified) rank. **2** to have a place or position (among, with etc.). **3** (*N Am.*) to take precedence (over). **the ranks** ordinary soldiers, as distinct from officers. **to break rank/ ranks 1** (of soldiers) to fall out of line. **2** to lose solidarity. **to close ranks** to maintain solidarity. **to keep rank** (of soldiers) to remain in line. **to pull rank** to take precedence by virtue of higher rank, sometimes unfairly. **to rise from the ranks 1** (of a soldier) to be promoted from the ranks, to receive a commission. **2** to achieve success by one's own efforts. **rank and file** n. (*often constr. as pl.*) **1** common soldiers. **2** (*fig.*) ordinary people. **rank and filer** n. **ranker** n. **1** a soldier in the ranks. **2** a commissioned officer promoted from the ranks. **ranking** a. (*N Am.*) highly placed, prominent. ~n. a position on a scale of excellence.

rank² (rangk) a. **1** excessively luxuriant in growth, over-fertile, over-abundant. **2** rancid, offensive, strong, evil-smelling. **3** indecent, obscene. **4** strongly marked, thorough, flagrant, arrant, utter. **5** coarse, gross. **6** complete, total (*a rank outsider*). ~adv. rankly. **rankly** adv. **rankness** n.

rankle (rang´kəl) v.i. to continue to cause irritation, anger or bitterness.

ransack (ran´sak) v.t. **1** to pillage, to plunder. **2** to search thoroughly. **ransacker** n.

ransom (ran´səm) n. **1** a sum of money demanded or paid for the release of a person from captivity or for goods captured by an enemy. **2** release from captivity in return for such a payment. ~v.t. **1** to redeem from captivity or obtain the restoration of (property) by paying a sum of money. **2** to demand or exact a ransom for, to hold to ransom. **3** to release in return for a ransom.

rant (rant) v.i. **1** to use loud, bombastic or violent language. **2** to declaim or preach in a theatrical or noisy fashion. ~v.t. to declaim or utter loudly or theatrically. ~n. **1** bombastic or violent declamation. **2** a tirade, a noisy declamation. **3** inflated talk. **to rant and rave** to express anger in a loud uncontrolled manner. **ranter** n. **rantingly** adv.

ranunculus (rənŭngk´ūləs) n. (*pl.* **ranunculuses, ranunculi** (-lī)) a plant of the genus *Ranunculus*, typified by the buttercup. **ranunculaceous** (-ā´shəs) a. relating or belonging to the Ranunculaceae, a family of plants including the buttercup.

rap¹ (rap) v.t. (*pres.p.* **rapping,** *past, p.p.* **rapped**) **1** to strike with a slight, sharp blow. **2** to rebuke. **3**

(*usu. with out*) to utter in a quick, abrupt way. ~*v.i.* **1** to strike a sharp, quick blow, esp. at a door. **2** to make a sharp, quick sound like a light blow. **3** (*sl.*) to talk. **4** to perform a rap or rap music. ~*n.* **1** a slight, sharp blow. **2** a sound like the blow from a knocker, the knuckles etc. on a door. **3** a similar sound made by some agency as a means of communicating messages at a spiritualistic séance. **4** a sharp rebuke. **5** (*coll.*) blame, punishment. **6** (*sl.*) an informal talk, chat. **7 a** a rhythmic, often impromptu monologue, over music. **b** (*also* **rap music**) a style of popular music characterized by a heavy, rhythmic beat over which a rap is recited. **8** (*esp. N Am., sl.*) a legal or criminal charge. **to beat the rap** (*N Am., sl.*) to be acquitted of a crime, to escape punishment. **to rap over the knuckles** to reprove, reprimand. **to take the rap** (*coll.*) to take the blame for another. **rapper** *n.*

rap² (rap) *n.* (*with a neg.*) the least amount.

rapacious (rəpā′shəs) *a.* **1** grasping, extortionate. **2** given to plundering or seizing by force, predatory. **3** (of animals) living on food seized by force. **rapaciously** *adv.* **rapaciousness** *n.* **rapacity** (-pas′-) *n.*

rape¹ (rāp) *v.t.* **1** to force to have sexual intercourse, to commit rape on. **2** (*fig.*) to despoil, to violate. ~*n.* **1** penetrative sexual intercourse with someone, usu. a woman, against the person's will. **2** (*fig.*) violation, despoiling (e.g. of the countryside). **raper** *n.* **rapist** *n.* a person who commits rape.

rape² (rāp) *n.* a plant, *Brassica napus*, allied to the turnip, grown as food for animals and for its seed which yields oil. **rape-cake** *n.* the compressed seeds and husks of rape after the oil has been expressed, used for feeding cattle and as manure. **rapeseed** *n.* the seed of the rape plant.

raphia RAFFIA.

rapid (rap′id) *a.* **1** very swift, quick, speedy. **2** done, acting, moving or completed in a very short time. **3** descending steeply. ~*n.* (*usu. pl.*) a sudden descent in a stream, with a swift current. **rapid eye movement** *n.* the rapid movement of the eyes under closed eyelids which usu. occurs during the dreaming phase of sleep. **rapid-fire** *a.* **1** (of guns) quick-firing. **2** done, occurring etc. in rapid succession. **rapidity** (-pid′-), **rapidness** *n.* **rapidly** *adv.* **rapid transit** *n.* (*N Am.*) fast passenger transport, usu. by underground, in urban areas.

rapier (rā′piə) *n.* a light, narrow sword, used only in thrusting. ~*a.* sharp, penetrating (*rapier wit*).

rapine (rap′īn) *n.* (*formal or poet.*) the act of plundering or carrying off by force.

rapist RAPE¹.

rappel (rəpel′) *n.* abseiling. ~*v.i.* (*pres.p.* **rappelling**, *past, p.p.* **rappelled**) to abseil.

rapport (rəpaw′) *n.* **1** correspondence, sympathetic relationship, agreement, harmony. **2** communication via a spiritualist.

rapprochement (raprosh′mā) *n.* reconciliation,

re-establishment of friendly relations, esp. between nations.

rapscallion (rapskal′iən) *n.* (*dated or facet.*) a rascal, a scamp, a good-for-nothing.

rapt (rapt) *a.* **1** transported, carried away by one's thoughts or emotions, enraptured. **2** absorbed, engrossed. **raptly** *adv.* **raptness** *n.*

raptor (rap′tə) *n.* a bird of prey. **raptorial** (-taw′ri-) *a.* **1** catching and feeding on prey, predatory. **2** of or relating to a bird of prey. **3** (of a bird's talons) adapted for seizing prey. ~*n.* a predatory animal or esp. bird.

rapture (rap′chə) *n.* **1** ecstasy, transport, ecstatic joy. **2** (*pl.*) a fit or transport of delight. **rapturous** *a.* **rapturously** *adv.* **rapturousness** *n.*

rare¹ (reə) *a.* **1** exceptional, seldom existing or occurring, not often met with, unusual, scarce, uncommon. **2** especially excellent, singularly good, choice, first-rate. **3** (esp. of the atmosphere) of sparse, tenuous, thin or porous substance, not dense. **rare earth** *n.* **1** an oxide of a lanthanide. **2** (*also* **rare-earth element, rare-earth metal**) a lanthanide. **rare gas** *n.* an inert gas. **rarely** *adv.* **1** seldom. **2** exceptionally. **3** remarkably well. **rareness** *n.* **rarity** (reə′riti) *n.* (*pl.* **rarities**) **1** the quality or state of being rare, rareness. **2** a rare thing or person, esp. a thing of exceptional value through being rare.

rare² (reə) *a.* (of meat) half-cooked, underdone.

rarebit (reə′bit) *n.* WELSH RABBIT.

rarefy (reə′rifi), **rarify** *v.t.* (*3rd pers. sing. pres.* **rarefies, rarifies**, *pres.p.* **rarefying, rarifying**, *past, p.p.* **rarefied, rarified**) **1** to make rare, thin, porous or less dense and solid. **2** (*fig.*) to purify, to refine, to make less gross. ~*v.i.* to become less dense. **rarefaction** (-fak′shən), **rarefication** (-fikā′shən) *n.* **rarefactive** (-fak′-) *a.*

raring (reə′ring) *a.* ready, eager. **raring to go** eager to get started.

❌ **rasberry** common misspelling of RASPBERRY.

rascal (ras′kəl, rahs′-) *n.* **1** a mischievous or slightly naughty person or animal, esp. a child (*used playfully or affectionately*). **2** a mean rogue, a tricky, dishonest or contemptible fellow, a knave, a scamp. **rascality** (-kal′-) *n.* (*pl.* **rascalities**). **rascally** *a., adv.*

rase RAZE.

rash¹ (rash) *a.* **1** hasty, precipitate, impetuous, venturesome. **2** reckless, thoughtless, acting or done without reflection. **rashly** *adv.* **rashness** *n.*

rash² (rash) *n.* **1** an eruption of spots or patches on the skin. **2** a series of unwelcome, unexpected events.

rasher (rash′ə) *n.* a thin slice of bacon or ham for frying.

rasp (rahsp) *v.t.* **1** to rub down, scrape or grate with a coarse, rough implement. **2** to file with a rasp. **3** to utter in harsh or grating tones. **4** to irritate, to grate upon (feelings etc.). ~*v.i.* **1** to rub, to grate. **2** to make a grating sound. ~*n.* **1** an instrument like a coarse file with projections or raised teeth for scraping away surface material.

2 a harsh, grating noise. **rasping, raspy** *a.* **raspingly** *adv.*

raspberry (rahz´bəri) *n.* (*pl.* **raspberries**) **1** the fruit of various species of *Rubus*, esp. *R. idaeus*, consisting of red or sometimes white or yellow drupes set on a conical receptacle. **2** a shrub that bears raspberries. **3** (*coll.*) a rude derisive sound made with the lips. **4** a pinkish to purplish-red colour. **raspberry cane** *n.* a long woody shoot of a raspberry plant.

Rastafarian (rastəfeeˊriən) *n.* a member of the religious and political, largely Jamaican, sect which believes Haile Selassie, the former Emperor of Ethiopia, to be God. ~*a.* of or relating to Rastafarians or Rastafarianism. **Rasta** (rasˊ-) *n., a.* Rastafarian. **Rastafarianism** *n.*

raster (rasˊtə) *n.* the pattern of scanning lines which appears as a patch of light on a television screen and which reproduces the image. **rasterize, rasterise** *v.t.* (*Comput.*) to convert (a digitized image) into a pattern of signals which can be displayed on a screen. **rasterization** (-zāˊshən) *n.* **rasterizer** *n.*

rat (rat) *n.* **1** any of several rodents of the genus *Rattus* that are similar to but larger than mice, esp. the black rat, *R. rattus*, and *R. norvegicus*, the grey, brown or Norway rat. **2** any of various similar or related rodents. **3** a person who is considered to have deserted their party or friends, a turncoat. **4** (*coll.*) a contemptible person. ~*v.i.* (*pres.p.* **ratting**, *past, p.p.* **ratted**) **1** to hunt or kill rats (esp. of dogs). **2** (*coll.*) to play the rat in politics, in a strike etc. **to rat on** (*coll.*) to betray, to divulge secret information, to inform against. **to smell a rat** to be suspicious. **rat-arsed** *a.* (*sl.*) drunk. **ratbag** *n.* (*sl.*) a disagreeable or despicable person. **rat-catcher** *n.* a person who earns a living by ridding buildings etc. of rats. **rat kangaroo** *n.* any kangaroo-like marsupial of the family Potoroidea, about the size of a rabbit. **rat race** *n.* the continual competitive scramble of everyday life. **rat-run** *n.* a minor road or route of minor roads used by drivers to avoid traffic congestion during a rush hour. **rats!** *int.* (*sl.*) an exclamation of incredulity or derision. **ratsbane** *n.* poison for rats. **rat's-tail** *n.* a thing, esp. a file, like the tail of a rat. **rat-tail** *n.* **1** the grenadier fish. **2** a horse's tail with little or no hair. **3** a horse with such a tail. **rat-tailed** *a.* **rat-tail spoon, rat-tailed spoon** *n.* a spoon with a tapering, ridged moulding along the underside of the bowl. **ratted** *a.* (*sl.*) drunk. **ratter** *n.* **1** a person or animal, esp. a dog or cat, that catches rats. **2** a person who is considered to have deserted their party or friends. **ratty** *a.* (*comp.* **rattier**, *superl.* **rattiest**) **1** infested with or characteristic of rats. **2** (*sl.*) annoyed, ill-tempered. **3** (*coll.*) unkempt, untidy, shabby. **rattily** *adv.* **rattiness** *n.*

ratable RATEABLE (under RATE¹).

ratafia (ratəfeeˊə) *n.* **1** a liqueur or cordial flavoured with the kernels of cherry, peach, almond or other kinds of fruit. **2** a sweet almond-flavoured biscuit eaten with this.

ratan RATTAN.

rataplan (ratˊəplan) *n.* a noise like the rapid beating of a drum. ~*v.t.* (*pres.p.* **rataplanning**, *past, p.p.* **rataplanned**) to beat out (a tune) on or as if on a drum. ~*v.i.* to make a rataplan on a drum.

ratatat, rat-a-tat RAT-TAT.

ratatouille (ratətweˊ) *n.* a vegetable casserole from Provence, France, made with aubergines, tomatoes, peppers etc., stewed slowly in olive oil.

ratch (rach) *n.* a ratchet or ratchet-wheel. **ratchet** (-it) *n.* **1** a wheel or bar with inclined angular teeth, between which a pawl drops, permitting motion in one direction only. **2** the pawl or detent that drops between the teeth of a ratchet-wheel. ~*v.t.* (*pres.p.* **ratcheting**, *past, p.p.* **ratcheted**) **1** to furnish with a ratchet. **2** to move as if by a ratchet. ~*v.i.* to operate by or as by a ratchet. **ratchet-wheel** *n.* a wheel with a toothed edge.

rate¹ (rāt) *n.* **1** the proportional measure of something in relation to some other thing, ratio, comparative amount, degree etc. **2** a standard by which any quantity or value is fixed. **3** a price, cost, charge, value etc. **4** relative speed of movement, change, progress etc. **5** (*usu. pl.*) a sum levied upon commercial property and (formerly) dwellings for local purposes. **6** rank or class. ~*v.t.* **1** to estimate the value or relative worth of. **2** to assign a value, rank, position on a scale etc. to. **3** to consider, to regard as. **4** to merit, to deserve. **5** (*coll.*) to think highly of. **6 a** to assess for local rates. **b** to subject to payment of local rates. **7** to fix the rank of (a seaman etc.). ~*v.i.* to be rated or ranked (as). **at any rate 1** in any case. **2** even so. **at that rate** if that is so, typical or true. **at this rate** if this is so, typical or true. **rateable, ratable** *a.* **1** liable to be rated, subject to assessment for local rates. **2** capable of being rated or valued. **rateability** (-bilˊ-) *n.* **rateable value** *n.* the estimated value of a commercial property and formerly a dwelling, used annually to assess the rates chargeable on the property. **rateably** *adv.* **ratepayer** *n.* a person who was formerly liable to pay rates; a householder.

rate² (rāt) *v.t.* to chide angrily, to scold. ~*v.i.* to chide, to storm (at).

ratel (rāˊtəl) *n.* a nocturnal carnivore of the genus *Mellivora*, allied to the badger, esp. *M. capensis*, the honey badger of W and S Africa which feeds on small animals and honey, and *M. indicus* from India.

rathe (rādh), **†rath** (rahth) *a.* coming, appearing, ripening etc. early or before the usual time.

rather (rahˊdhə) *adv.* **1** more readily or willingly, preferably, for choice, sooner. **2** with more reason, more properly, rightly, truly or accurately. **3** in a greater degree, to a greater extent. **4** to a certain extent. **5** slightly, somewhat. **6** on the contrary. **7** (*coll.*) very much, assuredly, yes, certainly. **had/ would rather** would prefer to.

Usage note See note under PREFER.

ratify (rat´ifī) *v.t.* (*3rd pers. sing. pres.* **ratifies**, *pres.p.* **ratifying**, *past, p.p.* **ratified**) to confirm, to establish or make valid (by formal consent or approval). **ratifiable** *a.* **ratification** (-fikā´shən) *n.* **ratifier** *n.*

rating[1] (rā´ting) *n.* **1** the act of assessing, judging, ranking etc. **2** a classification according to grade, a rank; relative standing or position. **3** an estimate of the financial standing or creditworthiness of a person or business. **4** (*pl.*) an evaluation of the popularity of radio or television programmes based on estimated audience size. **5** (*Naut.*) an ordinary seaman.

rating[2] (rā´ting) *n.* a scolding, a harsh reprimand.

ratio (rā´shiō) *n.* (*pl.* **ratios**) the relation of one quantity or magnitude to another of a similar kind, measured by the number of times one is contained by the other, either integrally or fractionally.

ratiocinate (rashios´ināt) *v.i.* (*formal*) **1** to reason or argue. **2** to deduce consequences from premises or by means of syllogisms. **ratiocination** (-nā´shən) *n.* **ratiocinative** (-ətiv), **ratiocinatory** (-ətawri, -ətri) *a.* **ratiocinator** *n.*

ration (rash´ən) *n.* **1** a fixed statutory allowance of food or other provisions in a time of shortage (e.g. war). **2** (*usu. pl.*) a fixed daily allowance of food, a portion allotted or allowed to an individual. **3** (*pl.*) provisions, esp. food. ~*v.t.* **1** to supply with rations, to put on fixed rations. **2** to limit to a fixed allowance or amount. **3** to distribute in fixed, esp. small, quantities. **ration book, ration card** *n.* a book or card containing coupons etc. authorizing the holder to draw a ration.

rational (rash´ənəl) *a.* **1** having the faculty of reasoning, endowed with mental faculties. **2** agreeable to reasoning, reasonable, sensible, not foolish, not extravagant. **3** based on or conforming to what can be tested by reason. **4** (*Math.*) (of a number, quantity etc.) expressible as the ratio of two integers. ~*n.* (*Math.*) a rational number. **rationale** (rashənahl´) *n.* **1** a statement or exposition of reasons or principles. **2** the logical basis or fundamental reason (of anything). **rational horizon** *n.* CELESTIAL HORIZON (under CELESTIAL). **rationalism** (rash´-) *n.* **1** reliance on reason rather than intuition, religious authority etc. **2** the determination of all questions of belief, esp. in religious matters, by the reason, rejecting supernatural revelation. **rationalist** *n.* **rationalistic** (-lis´-) *a.* **rationalistically** *adv.* **rationality** (-nal´-) *n.* (*pl.* **rationalities**). **rationalize, rationalise** *v.t.* **1** to offer a rational explanation for, esp. to justify, explain or excuse (behaviour, actions etc.) by offering plausible reasons. **2** to render rational or reasonable. **3** to reorganize (e.g. a business) so as to make more

efficient and economic. **4** (*Math.*) to clear (an equation etc.) of radical signs. ~*v.i.* **1** to provide plausible explanations for behaviour, actions etc. **2** to think or act as a rationalist. **rationalization** (-zā´shən) *n.* **rationalizer** *n.* **rationally** *adv.* **rationalness** *n.*

ratline (rat´lin), **ratlin, ratling** (-ling) *n.* any of the small ropes extended across the shrouds on each side of a mast, forming steps or rungs.

ratoon (rətoon´), **rattoon** *n.* a sprout from the root of a sugar cane that has been cut down. ~*v.i.* to send up ratoons.

ratsbane RAT.

rattan (rətan´, rat´-), **ratan** *n.* **1** any of various species of Malaysian climbing palms of the genus *Calamus* with long, thin pliable stems. **2** the stem or part of a stem of such a plant. **3** a switch or walking stick of this material.

rat-tat (rat-tat´), **ratatat** (ratətat´), **rat-a-tat, ratatat-tat** (ratətat-tat´), **rat-a-tat-tat** *n.* a rapid knocking sound as of a knocker on a door.

ratted RAT.

ratter RAT.

rattle (rat´əl) *v.i.* **1** to make a rapid succession of sharp noises, as of things clattered together or shaken in a hollow vessel. **2** to talk rapidly, noisily or foolishly. **3** to move, go or act with a rattling noise. **4** to run, ride or drive rapidly. ~*v.t.* **1** to cause to make a rattling noise, to make (a window, door etc.) rattle. **2** to utter, recite, play etc. (off, away etc.) rapidly. **3** to stir up, to disconcert, to alarm, to frighten. **4** to cause to move quickly with noise, esp. to drive fast. ~*n.* **1** a rapid succession of sharp noises. **2** an instrument, esp. a child's toy, with which such sounds are made. **3** a rattling noise in the throat. **4** rapid, noisy or empty talk, chatter. **5** noise, bustle, racket, boisterous gaiety. **6** the horny articulated rings in the tail of the rattlesnake, which make a rattling noise. **7** a plant having seeds that rattle in their cases. **rattler** *n.* **1** someone who or something which rattles. **2** (*coll.*) a rattlesnake. **3** (*sl.*) a first-rate specimen. **rattlesnake** *n.* any of various snakes of the American genera *Crotalus* or *Sistrurus*, having a tail furnished with a rattle. **rattletrap** *n.* (*coll.*) **1** a rickety object, esp. a vehicle. **2** (*pl.*) valueless articles, rubbishy curios. ~*a.* rickety, rubbishy. **rattling** *a.* **1** making a rapid succession of sharp noises. **2** (*coll.*) brisk, vigorous. ~*adv.* (*coll.*) extremely, very (*a rattling good time*). **rattly** *a.* **rattliness** *n.*

ratty RAT.

raucous (raw´kəs) *a.* hoarse, rough or harsh in sound. **raucity** (-si-) *n.* **raucously** *adv.* **raucousness** *n.*

raunchy (rawn´chi) *a.* (*comp.* **raunchier**, *superl.* **raunchiest**) (*coll.*) **1** earthy, sexual. **2** (*esp. N Am.*) slovenly. **raunchily** *adv.* **raunchiness** *n.*

ravage (rav´ij) *n.* **1** devastation, ruin, havoc, waste. **2** (*usu. pl.*) devastating effects. ~*v.t.* to devastate, to spoil, to pillage. ~*v.i.* to wreak havoc. **ravager** *n.*

Usage note The verbs *ravage* and *ravish* should not be confused: *ravage* means to devastate, and *ravish* to rape.

rave (rāv) *v.i.* **1** to wander in mind, to be delirious, to talk wildly, incoherently or irrationally. **2** to speak in a furious way (against, at etc.). **3** to be excited, to go into raptures (about etc.). **4** to act, move or dash furiously, to rage. **5** (*coll.*) to enjoy oneself wildly. ~*v.t.* to utter in a wild, incoherent or furious manner. ~*n.* **1** the act of raving. **2** extravagant enthusiasm (*a rave review*). **3** (*coll.*) (*also* **rave-up**) a very lively party. **4** an often large-scale party for dancing to fast, non-stop electronic music, typically held in the early hours of the morning in a marquee, disused building or outside. **5** a raving sound as of the wind or sea. **6** (*sl.*) an infatuation. **raver** *n.* **1** (*coll.*) a person who leads a wild social life. **2** (*coll.*) a person who attends raves. **3** a frenzied or delirious person. **raving** *a.* **1** frenzied. **2** (*coll.*) marked (*a raving beauty*). ~*n.* (*pl.*) extravagant, irrational utterances.

ravel (rav´əl) *v.t.* (*pres.p.* **ravelling**, (*N Am.*) **raveling**, *past, p.p.* **ravelled**, (*N Am.*) **raveled**) **1** to entangle, to confuse, to complicate. **2** to untwist, to disentangle, to separate the component threads of. **3** to fray. ~*v.i.* **1** to become tangled. **2** to become untwisted, unravelled or unwoven. **3** to fray (out). **ravelling**, (*N Am.*) **raveling** *n.* **1** the act of entangling, confusing etc. **2** the act of unravelling. **3** anything, such as a thread, separated in the process of unravelling.

raven¹ (rā´vən) *n.* a large, black, omnivorous bird, *Corvus corax*, of the crow family. ~*a.* resembling a raven in colour, glossy black.

raven² (rav´ən) *v.t.* (*esp. poet.*) **1** to devour with voracity. **2** to ravage, to plunder. ~*v.i.* **1** to plunder. **2** to go about ravaging. **3** to prowl after prey. **4** to be ravenous. **5** to feed with voracity. **ravening** *n., a.*

ravenous (rav´ənəs) *a.* **1** voracious, hungry, famished. **2** furiously rapacious, eager for gratification. **ravenously** *adv.* **ravenousness** *n.*

ravine (rəvēn´) *n.* a long, deep hollow caused esp. by a torrent, a gorge, a narrow gully or cleft. **ravined** *a.*

raving RAVE.

ravioli (raviō´li) *n.* small pasta cases with a savoury filling.

ravish (rav´ish) *v.t.* **1** to violate, to rape. **2** to carry away, to enrapture, to transport (with pleasure etc.). **ravisher** *n.* **ravishing** *a.* enchanting, charming, entrancing, transporting, filling one with rapture. **ravishingly** *adv.* **ravishment** *n.*

Usage note See note under RAVAGE.

raw (raw) *a.* **1** uncooked. **2** in the natural state. **3** not manufactured, processed or refined; requiring further industrial treatment. **4** not modified or adjusted (*raw data*). **5** (of spirits) not blended or diluted. **6** crude, untempered. **7** untrained,

unskilled, inexperienced, undisciplined, immature, fresh. **8** having the skin off, having the flesh exposed, galled, inflamed, chafed. **9** sore or sensitive as if from chafing (*a raw throat*; *touched a raw nerve*). **10** (of weather) cold and damp, bleak. **11** (of a fabric edge) unhemmed. ~*n.* a raw place on the body, a sore, a gall. **in the raw 1** in its natural state. **2** naked. **to come the raw prawn** (*Austral., sl.*) to try to deceive. **to touch on the raw** to wound in a sensitive spot. **raw-boned** *a.* having bones scarcely covered with flesh, gaunt. **raw deal** *n.* (*coll.*) unfair treatment. **rawhide** *n.* **1** untanned leather. **2** a whip made of this. **rawish** *a.* **rawly** *adv.* **raw material** *n.* the material of any manufacturing process. **rawness** *n.* **raw sienna** *n.* the yellowish-brown colour of untreated sienna. **raw umber** *n.* umber in the natural state; the colour of this.

Rawlplug® (rawl´plŭg) *n.* a thin ridged or toothed tube, usu. of plastic, inserted in masonry to provide a fixing for a screw.

ray¹ (rā) *n.* **1** a line or beam of light proceeding from a radiant point. **2** (*often pl.*) a narrow beam of radiant energy or a stream of particles (*alpha rays*; *cosmic rays*). **3** a straight line along which radiant energy, esp. light or heat, is propagated. **4** (*fig.*) a gleam, a vestige or slight manifestation (of hope, enlightenment etc.). **5** any of a series of radiating lines or parts. **6** (*Math.*) a straight line extending from a point. **7** (*Bot.*) the outer whorl of florets in a composite flower. ~*v.t.* to shoot out (rays), to radiate. ~*v.i.* to issue or shine forth in rays. **rayed** *a.* **ray gun** *n.* in science fiction, a gun which sends out rays to kill or stun. **rayless** *a.* **raylet** *n.*

ray² (rā) *n.* any of several large cartilaginous fish allied to the sharks, with a broad flat body, the eyes on the upper surface and a long, slender tail.

ray³ (rā), **re** (rā) *n.* (*Mus.*) **1** the second note of a major scale in the tonic sol-fa system of notation. **2** the note *D* in the fixed-doh system.

rayon (rā´on) *n.* an artificial textile fibre or fabric made from cellulose.

raze (rāz), **rase** *v.t.* **1** to demolish, to level to the ground, to destroy. **2** to erase, to obliterate. **3** to scratch (out). **razed** *a.* **razer** *n.*

razor (rā´zə) *n.* a sharp-edged cutting instrument for shaving off the hair of the beard, head etc. ~*v.t.* **1** to shave with a razor. **2** to shave, to cut (down) close. **razorback** *n.* **1** an animal with a sharp back like a razor. **2** a rorqual. ~*a.* having a sharp back or ridge like a razor. **razorbacked** *a.* **razorbill** *n.* a bird with a bill like a razor, esp. the razor-billed auk, *Alca torda*. **razor blade** *n.* a blade used in a razor, for cutting or shaving. **razor cut** *n.* a haircut trimmed or shaped with a razor, esp. one tapering at the neck. ~*v.t.* (*pres.p.* **razor cutting**, *past, p.p.* **razor cut**) to cut or trim (hair) with a razor. **razor edge, razor's edge** *n.* **1** the edge of a razor. **2** a keen edge. **3** a sharp crest or ridge, as of a mountain. **4** a critical situation, a crisis. **5** a sharp line of demarcation, esp. between parties or opinions. **razor-edged** *a.* **razor-fish** *n.* (*pl. in general* **razor-fish**, *in particular* **razor-fishes**) a razor-shell. **razor-shell** *n.* a bivalve mollusc with a narrow, curved shell like the handle of a cut-throat razor. **razor wire** *n.* strong wire set across with pieces of sharp metal, used for fences or on top of walls etc.

razz (raz) *n.* (*esp. N Am., sl.*) a sound of contempt, a raspberry. ~*v.t.* to jeer at, to heckle.

razzle-dazzle (raz´əldazəl) *n.* (*coll.*) **1** bewilderment, excitement, stir, bustle. **2** a spree. **3** noisy or showy fuss. **on the razzle** on a spree or binge, esp. involving excessive drinking.

razzmatazz (razmətaz´), **razzamatazz** (razə-) *n.* (*coll.*) **1** colourful, noisy, lively atmosphere or activities, razzle-dazzle. **2** insincere deceptive talk.

Rb *chem. symbol* rubidium.

RC *abbr.* **1** reinforced concrete. **2** Roman Catholic.

RD *abbr.* **1** refer to drawer. **2** (Royal Naval) Reserve Decoration.

Rd *abbr.* Road.

RDA *abbr.* recommended daily allowance.

RDF *abbr.* radio direction-finder.

RE *abbr.* religious education.

Re *chem. symbol* rhenium.

re[1] (rā) *prep.* **1** in the matter of. **2** (*coll.*) as regards, about.

Usage note The use of *re* in the middle of a sentence for 'about' is sometimes disapproved of.

---

re[2] RAY[3].

re- (rē) *pref.* **1** again, again and again, afresh, anew, repeatedly. **2** back, backward, back again. **3** in return, mutually. **4** against, in opposition. **5** after, behind. **6** off, away, down. **7** UN-[1].

Usage note In its main productive use, *re-* usually forms hyphenated words where the second element begins with *e* (as *re-echo*), or where a solid form could be confused with another word (as *re-form* and *reform*).

're *contr.* are (*we're*; *they're*; *you're*).

re- (+ ab–ac words) reabsorb *v.t.* to absorb anew or again. **reabsorption** *n.* **reaccept** *v.t.* to accept again. **reacceptance** *n.* **reaccustom** *v.t.* to accustom again. **reacquaint** *v.t.* to make acquainted again. **reacquaintance** *n.* **reacquire** *v.t.* to acquire anew. **reacquisition** *n.* **reactivate** *v.t.* to restore to a state of activity, to make functional or operational again. **reactivation** *n.*

reach (rēch) *v.t.* **1** to stretch out, to extend. **2** to extend towards so as to touch, to extend as far as, to attain, to arrive at. **3** to make contact with, to communicate with. **4** to affect, to influence. **5** to hand, to deliver, to pass. ~*v.i.* **1** to reach out, to extend. **2** to reach or stretch out the hand. **3** to make a reaching effort, to put forth one's powers, to be extended so as to touch. **4** to have extent in time, space etc. **5** to attain (to). **6** (*Naut.*) to sail

on a tack with the wind from the side. ~*n.* **1** the act or power of reaching. **2** extent, range, compass, power, attainment. **3** an unbroken stretch of water, as between two bends on a river. **4** (*Naut.*) the direction or distance travelled by a vessel on a tack. **5** the estimated number of people exposed to a marketing campaign or who select a particular radio or television programme or channel. **out of reach** unable to be reached or gained. **reachable** *a.* **reacher** *n.* **reach-me-down** *a.* (of clothes) cheap ready-made or second-hand. ~*n.pl.* ready-made or second-hand clothes.

react (riakt´) *v.i.* **1** to act in response (to a stimulus etc.). **2** to act or tend in an opposite manner, direction etc. **3** to have a reciprocal effect, to act upon the agent. **4** (*Chem.*) to exert chemical action upon another substance, to undergo a chemical reaction. **5** (*Physics*) to exert an equal and opposite force to that exerted by another body. ~*v.t.* (*Chem.*) to cause to react (with another substance). **reactance** *n.* the part of the opposition to the flow of an electric current that is due to capacitance or inductance in a circuit; the component of impedance that is not due to resistance. **reactant** *n.* (*Chem.*) a substance that takes part in a chemical reaction, esp. one that undergoes change. **reactive** *a.* **1** reacting or exhibiting reaction. **2** tending to react, liable to react readily. **3** occurring as a reaction, esp. produced in response to stress etc. (*reactive depression*). **4** of or relating to reactance. **reactively** *adv.* **reactivity** (-tiv´-), **reactiveness** *n.* **reactor** *n.* **1** a substance which undergoes a reaction. **2** NUCLEAR REACTOR (under NUCLEAR). **3** a vessel in which chemical reaction takes place. **4** (*Med.*) a person sensitive to a given drug or medication. **5** a component that introduces reactance into an electrical circuit.

reaction (riak´shən) *n.* **1** the response of an organ etc. to stimulation. **2** a mental or emotional response. **3** reciprocal action. **4** contrary action or condition following the first effects of an action. **5** action in an opposite direction, esp. in politics after a reform movement, revolution etc. **6** an effect, esp. an adverse effect, produced in response to a drug, medical treatment etc. **7** the chemical action of one substance upon another, resulting in the formation of one or more new substances. **8** a process involving change within atomic nuclei. **9** the equal and opposite force exerted upon the agent by a body acted upon. **reactionary** *a.* involving or tending towards reaction, esp. political reaction, retrograde, conservative. ~*n.* (*pl.* **reactionaries**) a reactionary person. **reactionism** *n.* **reactionist** *n.*

read (rēd) *v.t.* (*past, p.p.* **read** (red)) **1** to perceive and understand the meaning of (printed, written or other characters, signs, symbols, significant features etc.); to peruse. **2** to discover the meaning of by observation; to interpret, to explain. **3** to accurately deduce or comprehend. **4** to learn or ascertain by reading. **5** to study by reading.

6 to bring into a specified condition by reading. 7 to study for an examination. 8 a (of a meteorological instrument etc.) to indicate or register. b to take a reading from (such an instrument). 9 to hear and understand a message transmitted by radio from (a person). 10 (*Comput.*) to retrieve (copy) or transfer (data) from a storage device, such as magnetic tape. 11 to substitute as a (correct or preferred) reading (*read mouse for moose*). ~*v.i.* 1 to follow or interpret the meaning of a book etc. 2 to pronounce written or printed matter aloud. 3 to render written music vocally or instrumentally (well, easily etc.). 4 to acquire information (about). 5 to study by reading. 6 to mean or be capable of interpretation (in a certain way etc.). 7 to sound or affect (well, ill etc.) when perused or uttered. ~*n.* 1 an act of reading, a perusal. 2 something to be read (*an interesting read*). **to read in** to transfer (data) into a computer memory etc. **to read into** to extract or assume (a meaning not explicit). **to read off** to take (a reading or information) from a recording instrument, e.g. a thermometer. **to read out 1** to read aloud. **2** (*N Am.*) to expel from a political party or other organization. **to read someone like a book** to have full understanding of a person's motives etc. **to read someone's mind** to make an accurate guess as to what someone is thinking. **to read up** to get information about by reading. **to take as read** to assume, to accept without discussion. **readable** *a.* worth reading, interesting, legible. **readability** (-bil'-), **readableness** *n.* **readably** *adv.* **reader** *n.* **1** a person who reads or reads much. **2** a textbook, a book of selections for translation, a reading-book for schools. **3** a person employed by a publisher to read and report upon manuscripts etc. offered for publication. **4** a proof-reader. **5** (*also* **Reader**) a lecturer in some universities ranking below a professor. **6** a device for projecting a large-scale image of microfilm etc. **readership** *n.* **1** a body of readers, esp. of a particular newspaper, magazine etc. or author. **2** (*also* **Readership**) the post of university reader. **read-only memory** *n.* (*Comput.*) ROM. **read-out** *n.* **1** a record or display of the data retrieved from a computer or of a measurement made by a scientific recording instrument. **2** the act of retrieving data from computer storage facilities for display on screen or as a printout. **read-write head** *n.* (*Comput.*) the electromagnetic head in a computer diskdrive which reads or writes data on magnetic tape or disk.

re- (+ ad– words) readapt *v.t., v.i.* to adapt again or to suit a new purpose. **readaptation** *n.* **readdress** *v.t.* **1** to put a new, esp. a corrected address upon. **2** to deal with (a problem etc.) again or in a different way. **3** to write or speak to anew. **readjust** *v.t.* to arrange or adjust afresh. **readjustment** *n.* **readmit** *v.t.* (*pres.p.* **readmitting,** *past, p.p.* **readmitted**) to admit again. **re-**

admission, **readmittance** *n.* **readopt** *v.t.* to adopt again. **readoption** *n.* **re-advertise** *v.t., v.i.* to advertise again. **re-advertisement** *n.*

readily, readiness READY.

reading (rē'ding) *n.* **1** the act, practice or art of reading. **2** matter for reading. **3** the study or knowledge of books, literary research, scholarship. **4** a public recital or entertainment at which selections etc. are read to the audience. **5** an observation made by examining a recording instrument, a measurement. **6** the way in which a passage reads. **7** an interpretation of a piece of music. **8** the form of a passage given by a text, editor etc. **9** the recital of the whole or part of a Bill as a formal introduction or measure of approval in a legislative assembly. **reading age** *n.* a person's reading ability calculated with reference to the average ability of a whole population at a particular age (*a reading age of nine*).

ready (red'i) *a.* (*comp.* **readier,** *superl.* **readiest**) **1** in a state of preparedness, fit for use or action. **2** willing, apt, disposed. **3** on the point of, about (to). **4** quick, prompt. **5** able, expert, facile. **6** at hand, within reach, handy, quickly available. ~*adv.* (*usu. in comb. with p.p.*) in a state of preparedness, beforehand. ~*n.* (*coll.*) ready money. ~*v.t.* (*3rd pers. sing. pres.* **readies,** *pres.p.* **readying,** *past, p.p.* **readied**) to make ready, to prepare. **at/ to the ready 1** prepared for action. **2** (of a firearm) held in the position preparatory to aiming and firing. **ready, steady, go!** the usual words used to start a race. **ready to hand** nearby. **to make ready** to prepare. **readies** *n.pl.* (*coll.*) ready money, esp. banknotes. **readily** *adv.* **1** willingly, without reluctance. **2** without trouble or difficulty, easily. **readiness** *n.* **ready-made** *a.* (esp. of clothing in standard sizes) made beforehand, not made to order. **ready-mix** *n.* **1** a food or concrete mix which only needs liquid to be added to make it ready for use. **2** concrete which is delivered in liquid state ready for use. **readymixed** *a.* **ready money** *n.* actual cash, ready to be paid down. **ready-money** *a.* **ready reckoner** *n.* a book with tables of interest etc. for facilitating business calculations. **ready-to-wear** *a.* off-the-peg.

re- (+ af–al words) reaffirm *v.t.* to affirm again. **reaffirmation** *n.* **reafforest** *v.t.* to convert back into forest. **reafforestation** *n.* **realign** *v.t.* **1** to align again. **2** to group together on a new basis. **realignment** *n.* **reallocate** *v.t.* to allocate again or differently. **reallocation** *n.* **reallot** *v.t.* (*pres.p.* **reallotting,** *past, p.p.* **reallotted**) to allot again or differently. **reallotment** *n.*

reagent (riā'jənt) *n.* (*Chem.*) **1** a substance in a chemical reaction, esp. used to detect the presence of other substances or in chemical synthesis. **2** a force etc. that reacts. **reagency** *n.* reciprocal action.

real[1] (riəl) *a.* **1** actually existing; not fictitious, affected, imaginary, apparent, theoretical or nominal. **2** true, genuine, not counterfeit, not spurious. **3** having substantial existence, objective. **4** measured by purchasing power (*real income*). **5** (*Law*) consisting of fixed or permanent things, such as lands or houses, as distinct from *personal*. **6** (*coll.*) complete, utter (*a real beauty*). *~adv.* (*N Am., coll.*) very. **for real 1** (*coll.*) in reality, genuine. **2** in earnest. **the real McCoy 1** the genuine article. **2** the best. **the real thing** the genuine article and not a substitute. **real ale** *n.* beer which is allowed to ferment and mature in the cask and is not pumped up from the keg with carbon dioxide. **real life** *n.* actual human life, as distinct from fictional representation of human life. **real live** *a.* (*coll., often facet.*) actual, real. **really** *adv.* **1** in fact, in reality. **2** positively, truly. **3** I assure you. **4** is that so? **realness** *n.* **real number** *n.* any rational or irrational number. **real tennis** *n.* the earliest form of tennis, played in a walled indoor court. **real time** *n.* the actual time during which an event occurs. **real-time** *a.* **1** (*Comput.*) of or relating to the processing of data by a computer as it is generated. **2** responding instantly to events as they occur.

real² (rā´al) *n.* (*pl.* **reals, reales** (-lēz)) **1** the standard monetary unit of Brazil. **2** (*Hist.*) a Spanish silver coin or money of account.

realgar (rial´gah) *n.* an orange-red mineral consisting of a sulphide of arsenic, used as a pigment and in the manufacture of fireworks.

realism (riə´lizm) *n.* **1** the practice of regarding, accepting and dealing with people, circumstances etc. as they are; concern with what is factual and practicable. **2** the practice of representing objects, people, scenes etc. as they are or as they appear to the painter, novelist etc., rather than an idealized or romantic interpretation. **3** the scholastic doctrine that every universal or general idea has objective existence, as distinct from *nominalism* and *conceptualism*. **4** the doctrine that the objects of perception have real existence, as distinct from *idealism*. **realist** *n.* **1** a practical person. **2** a believer in or adherent of realism. **realistic** (-lis´-) *a.* **1** of or relating to realism. **2** matter-of-fact, common-sense. **realistically** *adv.*

reality (rial´iti) *n.* (*pl.* **realities**) **1** the quality of being real, actuality, actual existence, being, that which underlies appearances. **2** that which is real and not counterfeit, imaginary, supposed etc. **3** the real nature (of). **in reality** in fact.

realize (riə´līz), **realise** *v.t.* **1** to perceive as a reality. **2** to apprehend clearly and vividly, to become aware of. **3** to bring into actual existence, to give reality to, to achieve. **4** to present as real, to impress on the mind as real, to make realistic. **5** to convert into money. **6** to bring in, as a price. **realizable** *a.* **realization** (-ā´shən) *n.* **realizer** *n.*

realm (relm) *n.* **1** (*esp. Law, formal*) a kingdom. **2** domain, region, sphere, field of interest.

realpolitik (rāahl´politēk) *n.* politics based on practical reality rather than moral or intellectual ideals.

realty (riəl´ti) *n.* (*Law*) real property. **Realtor**® (-tə, -taw) *n.* (*N Am.*) a member of the National Association of Real Estate Boards. **realtor** *n.* (*N Am.*) an estate agent.

ream¹ (rēm) *n.* **1** 500 sheets of paper, formerly 480 sheets or 20 quires. **2** (*usu. pl., coll.*) a large amount, esp. of written material.

ream² (rēm) *v.t.* **1** to enlarge the bore of (a hole in metal etc.). **2** (*Naut.*) to open (a seam) for caulking. **3** (*N Am.*) to squeeze the juice from (citrus fruit). **reamer** *n.*

re- (+ **an–ap words**) **reanimate** *v.t.* **1** to restore to life. **2** to revive, to encourage, to give new spirit to. **reanimation** *n.* **reappear** *v.i.* to appear again. **reappearance** *n.* **reapply** *v.t.* (*3rd pers. sing. pres.* **reapplies**, *pres.p.* **reapplying**, *past, p.p.* **reapplied**) to apply again, esp. to submit a second application (e.g. for a job). **reapplication** *n.* **reappoint** *v.t.* to appoint again. **reappointment** *n.* **reapportion** *v.t.* to share out again. **reapportionment** *n.* **reappraise** *v.t.* to revalue, to reassess. **reappraisal** *n.*

reap (rēp) *v.t.* **1** to cut (a crop) with a scythe, sickle or reaping-machine. **2** to cut the harvest off (ground etc.). **3** to obtain as return for labour, deeds etc. **reaper** *n.* **1** a person who reaps. **2** a reaping-machine. **the (Grim) Reaper** death. **reaping-machine** *n.* a machine for cutting grain.

rear¹ (riə) *n.* **1** the back or hindmost part. **2** (*Mil.*) the hindmost division of a military or naval force. **3** a place or position at the back. **4** (*euphem.*) the buttocks. *~a.* of or at the rear. **to bring up the rear** to come last. **rear admiral** *n.* a naval officer next below the rank of vice admiral. **rear commodore** *n.* an officer of a yacht club below vice commodore. **rearguard** *n.* **1** (*Mil.*) a body of troops protecting the rear of an army. **2** an element in a political party, organization etc. holding entrenched or conservative views. *~a.* **1** of or characteristic of the rearguard. **2** (*Mil.*) defensive in the face of defeat (*rearguard action*). **rear lamp, rear light** *n.* a red light at the back of a bicycle or motor vehicle. **rearmost** *a.* coming or situated last of all. **rear sight** *n.* the sight of a firearm nearest the breach. **rear-view mirror** *n.* a small mirror in a motor vehicle which allows the driver to observe the traffic behind. **rearward** (-wəd) *a.* situated in or towards the rear. *~adv.* (*also* **rearwards**) towards the rear. *~n.* the rear. **rear-wheel drive** *n.* a system in which power is transmitted to and by the rear wheels of a motor vehicle.

rear² (riə) *v.t.* **1** to bring up, to breed, to educate. **2** to raise, to set up, to elevate to an upright position. **3** to raise, to cultivate, to grow. **4** to build, to erect, to uplift, to place or hold on high. *~v.i.* **1** (of a horse) to stand on the hind legs. **2** (*fig.*) to rise to a great height, to tower. **rearer** *n.*

re- (+ **ar–at words**) **rearm** *v.t.* to arm afresh, esp. with more modern weapons. **rearmament** *n.* **rearouse** *v.t.* **rearrange** *v.t.* **1** to arrange in a new way or order. **2** to alter the arrangements for (a meeting etc.). **rearrangement** n. **rearrest** v.t. to arrest again. ~n. a second arrest. **reascend** v.t., v.i. to ascend again. **reascension, reascent** n. **reassemble** v.t., v.i. to assemble or collect together again. **reassembly** n. (pl. **reassemblies**). **reassert** v.t. to assert anew. **reassertion** n. **reassess** v.t. to make a new assessment of. **reassessment** n. **reassign** v.t. **1** to assign again. **2** to transfer back or to another what has been already assigned. **reassignment** n. **reassume** v.t. **1** to take up again. **2** to take upon oneself again. **reassumption** n. **reassure** v.t. **1** to assure or confirm again. **2** to give fresh courage to, to restore to confidence. **reassurance** n. **reassuring** a. **reassuringly** adv. **reattach** v.t. to attach afresh. **reattachment** n. **reattain** v.t. to attain again. **reattainment** n. **reattempt** v.t. to attempt afresh.

reason (rē'zən) n. **1** that which is adduced to support or justify, or serves as a ground or motive for an act, opinion etc. **2** that which accounts for anything, a final cause. **3** the intellectual faculties, esp. the group of faculties distinguishing man from animals. **4** the exercise of the rational powers. **5** good sense, judgement, sanity. **6** sensible conduct, moderation. **7** the intuitive faculty which furnishes a priori principles, categories etc. **8** (Logic) the premise of an argument, esp. the minor premise when stated after the conclusion. **9** the power of consecutive thinking, the logical faculty. ~v.i. **1** to use the faculty of reason. **2** to argue, esp. to employ argument (with) as a means of persuasion. **3** to reach conclusions by way of inferences from premises. ~v.t. **1** to debate, discuss or examine by means of the reason or reasons and inferences. **2** to assume, conclude or prove by way of argument. **3** to persuade or dissuade by argument. **4** to set forth in orderly argumentative form. **by reason of** because, on account of, in consequence of. **in/ within reason** in moderation. **it stands to reason** it follows logically. **to listen to reason** to be persuaded to act in a sensible manner. **to see reason** to recognize and accept the logical force of an argument. **with reason** with justifiable cause, for a good reason. **reasonable** a. **1** rational, reasoning, governed by reason. **2** conformable to reason, sensible, proper. **3** not extravagant, moderate, esp. in price; fair, not extortionate. **4** willing to listen to reason. **5** average, quite good (reasonable weather). **reasonableness** n. **reasonably** adv. **reasoned** a. well-thought-out, well-argued. **reasoner** n. **reasoning** n. **reasonless** a.

Usage note The reason (why)...is that... is preferred to the reason (why)...is because.

re- (+ aw- words) reawake v.t., v.i. (past **reawoke**, p.p. **reawoken**) to awake again. **reawaken** v.t., v.i. **1** to reawake. **2** to arouse afresh. **reawakening** n.

re- (+ b- words) rebadge v.t. to give a new badge or logo to. **rebase** v.t. to give a new base or basis

to. **rebid**[1] (rēbid', rē'-) v.i. (pres.p. **rebidding**, past, p.p. **rebid**) to bid again, esp. to bid on the same suit as the previous bid in a game of bridge. ~v.t. to bid (the same suit as a previous bid) at a higher level. **rebid**[2] (rē'bid) n. **1** an act of rebidding. **2** a bid made in this way. **rebind** v.t. (past, p.p. **rebound**) **1** to bind again. **2** to give a new binding to. **rebirth** n. **1** a second birth, esp. an entrance into a new sphere of existence, as in reincarnation. **2** a revival. **3** a spiritual renewal. **rebirthing** n. a type of psychotherapy that involves reliving the experience of being born, used as a treatment for anxieties, neuroses etc. **rebirther** n. **reboot** v.t. (Comput.) to boot again. **rebore**[1] v.t. to bore again, esp. to widen the bore of (a cylinder in an internal-combustion engine). **rebore**[2] (rē'baw) n. the process of reboring the cylinders of a worn vehicle engine. **rebroadcast** v.t. (past **rebroadcast, rebroadcasted**, p.p. **rebroadcast**) to broadcast again. ~a. broadcast again. ~n. a second broadcast. **rebuild** v.t. to build again, to reconstruct. **rebuilder** n. **rebury** v.t. (3rd pers. sing. pres. **reburies**, pres.p. **reburying**, past, p.p. **reburied**) to bury again. **reburial** n.

rebarbative (ribah'bətiv) a. (formal or poet.) repellent, grim, forbidding.

rebate[1] (rē'bāt, -bāt') n. **1** a refund of part of an amount paid. **2** a deduction from an account payable. ~v.t. to give a rebate of. **rebatable, rebateable** a.

rebate[2] RABBET.

rebel[1] (reb'əl) n. **1** a person who forcibly resists the established government or renounces allegiance to it. **2** a person who resists authority or control. ~a. **1** rebellious. **2** of or relating to rebellion or to rebels.

rebel[2] (ribel') v.i. (pres.p. **rebelling**, past, p.p. **rebelled**) **1** to act in rebellion (against). **2** to refuse to conform, to revolt (against any authority, control etc.). **3** to feel or show repugnance. **rebellion** (-bel'yən) n. **1** organized, esp. armed, resistance to the established government. **2** opposition to any authority. **3** an instance of rebelling. **rebellious** (-bel'yəs) a. **1** disposed to rebel, insubordinate, difficult to manage or control. **2** engaged in rebellion. **3** resisting treatment, refractory, unyielding. **rebelliously** adv. **rebelliousness** n.

rebound[1] (ribownd') v.i. **1** to bound back, to recoil (from a blow etc.). **2** to react, esp. adversely (on or upon the perpetrator).

rebound[2] (rē'bownd) n. **1** the act of rebounding, a recoil. **2** a reaction (of feeling etc.). **on the rebound 1** in the act of bouncing back. **2** as a reaction to a disappointment, esp. in love.

rebuff (ribŭf') n. **1** a rejection, a check (to an offer or a person who makes advances etc.). **2** a curt denial, a snub. **3** a defeat, a sudden or unexpected repulse. ~v.t. to give a rebuff to, to repel.

rebuke (ribūk') v.t. to reprove, to reprimand, to

chide. ~*n.* **1** the act of rebuking. **2** a reproof. **rebuker** *n.* **rebukingly** *adv.*

rebus (rē´bəs) *n.* (*pl.* **rebuses**) a picture or figure enigmatically representing a word, name or phrase, usu. by objects suggesting words or syllables.

rebut (ribŭt´) *v.t.* (*pres.p.* **rebutting**, *past, p.p.* **rebutted**) **1** to contradict or refute by plea, argument or countervailing proof. **2** to thrust back, to check, to repel. **rebutment, rebuttal** *n.* **rebuttable** *a.* **rebutter** *n.* **1** a person who, or argument etc. that rebuts. **2** (*Law*) the answer of a defendant to a plaintiff's surrejoinder.

rec (rek) *n.* (*coll.*) a recreation ground.

re- (+ ca– words) **recalculate** *v.t.* to calculate again. **recalculation** *n.* **recapitalize, recapitalise** *v.t.* to convert into capital again. **recapitalization** *n.* **recapture** *v.t.* **1** to capture again, to recover (as a prize from the captor). **2** to re-experience or renew (a past feeling etc.). ~*n.* the act of recapturing. **recast** *v.t.* (*past, p.p.* **recast**) **1** to put into a new form, to fashion again, to remodel. **2** to cast, found or mould again. **3 a** to change the cast of (a play etc.). **b** to assign a different part to (an actor). ~*n.* **1** that which has been recast. **2** the process or result of recasting.

recalcitrant (rikal´sitrənt) *a.* refractory, obstinately resisting authority or control. ~*n.* a recalcitrant person. **recalcitrance** *n.* **recalcitrantly** *adv.*

recall[1] (rikawl´) *v.t.* **1** to call back, to summon to return. **2** to bring back to mind, to recollect. **3** to remind one of. **4** to revoke, to annul, to take back. **5** to take back. **recallable** *a.*

recall[2] (rē´kawl) *n.* **1** a calling back, a summons to return. **2** the act or power of remembering. **3** the possibility of revoking, annulling or cancelling.

recant (rikant´) *v.t.* to retract, to renounce, to abjure. ~*v.i.* to disavow or abjure opinions or beliefs formerly avowed, esp. with a formal acknowledgement of error. **recantation** (rēkantā´shən) *n.* **recanter** *n.*

recap (rē´kap, -kap´) *v.t., v.i.* (*pres.p.* **recapping**, *past, p.p.* **recapped**) to recapitulate. ~*n.* recapitulation.

recapitulate (rēkəpit´ūlāt) *v.t.* to repeat in brief (as the principal points or headings of a discourse), to sum up, to summarize. **recapitulation** (-lā´shən) *n.* **1** the act of recapitulating, e.g. at the end of a speech. **2** (*Mus.*) the repeating of earlier themes in a piece of music. **recapitulative** (-lətiv), **recapitulatory** (-lətri) *a.*

recce (rek´i) *n.* (*pl.* **recces**) (*coll.*) a reconnaissance. ~*v.t., v.i.* (*3rd pers. sing. pres.* **recces**, *pres.p.* **recceing**, *past, p.p.* **recced**) to reconnoitre.

☒ **reccommend** common misspelling of RECOMMEND.

recd. *abbr.* received.

re- (+ ce–cl words) **re-cede** *v.t.* to cede again, to restore to a former possessor. **recharge**[1] (-chahj´) *v.t.* **1** to charge again. **2** to put a new charge into. **recharge**[2] (rē´-) *n.* a new charge or a charge in

return. **rechargeable** *a.* **recharger** *n.* **recheck**[1] (-chek´) *v.t., v.i.* to check again. **recheck**[2] (rē´-) *n.* the act of checking something again. **rechristen** *v.t.* **1** to christen again. **2** to give a new name to. **recirculate** *v.t., v.i.* to pass or go round again. **recirculation** *n.* **reclassify** *v.t.* (*3rd pers. sing. pres.* **reclassifies**, *pres.p.* **reclassifying**, *past, p.p.* **reclassified**) to classify again or elsewhere. **reclassification** *n.* **reclothe** *v.t.* to clothe again.

recede (risēd´) *v.i.* **1** to go back or away (from). **2** to be gradually lost to view by distance. **3** to incline, slope or tend backwards or away. **4** to decline, to retrograde. **5** (of hair) to cease to grow at the temples. **6** to draw back, e.g. from a promise.

re-cede RE- (+ CE–CL WORDS).

receipt (risēt´) *n.* **1** a written acknowledgement of money or goods received. **2** the act or fact of receiving or being received. **3** (*usu. pl.*) that which is received, esp. money. ~*v.t.* **1** to give a receipt for. **2** (*esp. N Am.*) to write an acknowledgement of receipt on (a bill etc.). **in receipt of** having received.

receive (risēv´) *v.t.* **1** to obtain, get or take as a thing due, offered, sent, paid or given. **2** to be given, to be furnished or supplied with, to acquire. **3** to encounter, to experience. **4** to understand, to perceive, to regard (in a particular light). **5** to support the face or weight of, to bear. **6** to be a receptacle for. **7** to admit to one's presence, to welcome, to entertain as a guest. **8** to accept for consideration. **9** to accept with approval or consent, to admit, as proper or true. **10** to accept (stolen goods) from a thief. **11** to convert (incoming electrical signals) into sounds, pictures etc. by means of a receiver. **12** to return the service in tennis or squash. **to be at/ on the receiving end** to be the recipient of something unpleasant. **receivable** *a.* **received** *a.* generally accepted or believed. **received pronunciation, Received Pronunciation** *n.* the non-localized pronunciation of British English, taken as the standard. **receiver** (risē´və) *n.* **1** a person who receives. **2** a part of a telephonic or telegraphic apparatus for receiving messages or current, esp. the part of a telephone containing the earpiece and mouthpiece. **3** an officer appointed by a court to administer property under litigation, esp. that of bankrupts. **4** an apparatus that converts incoming radio, television or telephone signals into an audible or visual form. **5** a person who receives stolen goods. **6** (*Chem.*) a vessel for receiving the products of distillation or for collecting gas. **receivership** *n.* **1** the office of a receiver, esp. an official receiver. **2** the state of being administered by a receiver. **receiving order** *n.* an order from a bankruptcy court staying separate action against a debtor and placing affairs in the hands of an official receiver.

recent (rē´sənt) *a.* **1** of, relating to or being the present or time not long past. **2** that happened, existed or came into existence lately. **3** modern, fresh, newly begun or established. **4** (*Geol.*) (**Recent**) of, relating to or being the existing epoch of geological time; Holocene. ~*n.* (**Recent**) Holocene. **recency** (-si), **recentness** *n.* **recently** *adv.*

receptacle (risep´təkəl) *n.* **1** something which receives, holds or contains. **2** a vessel, space or place of deposit. **3** (*Bot.*) a part forming a support, such as the axis of a flower cluster, the spore-bearing structure of a fern or alga etc.

reception (risep´shən) *n.* **1** the act of receiving. **2** the state of being received or the manner in which something is received. **3** receipt, acceptance, admission. **4** an occasion of formal or ceremonious receiving of visitors. **5** a formal welcome. **6** an area of a hotel, office etc. where people report or are received on arrival. **7** the quality of received radio or television signals. **receptionist** *n.* a person at a hotel or elsewhere, whose duty it is to receive and look after visitors or clients. **reception order** *n.* the official order required for detention in a psychiatric hospital. **reception room** *n.* a room in a house to which visitors are admitted, as distinct from bedrooms, kitchen etc. **receptive** (risep´tiv) *a.* **1** quick to receive impressions, ideas etc. **2** having the ability or capacity to receive. **receptively** *adv.* **receptivity** (rēseptiv´-), **receptiveness** *n.* **receptor** *n.* **1** any of various devices which receive signals or information. **2** (*Biol.*) **a** an organ adapted for receiving stimuli. **b** a sensory nerve ending which changes stimuli into nerve impulses.

recess (rises´, rē´ses) *n.* **1** a part that recedes, a depression, indentation, hollow, niche or alcove. **2 a** a cessation or suspension of public or other business, a vacation. **b** (*NAm.*) a short break (e.g. between school classes). **3** (*often pl.*) a secluded or secret place, a nook. ~*v.t.* **1** to put into a recess. **2** to build a recess in (a wall etc.). **3** (*NAm.*) to interrupt temporarily, to adjourn. ~*v.i.* (*NAm.*) to adjourn.

recession (risesh´ən) *n.* **1** a slump, esp. in trade or economic activity. **2** the act of receding, withdrawal, retirement. **3** a receding part or object. **recessional** *a.* of or relating to the recession of the clergy and choir from the chancel. ~*n.* a hymn sung during this ceremony. **recessionary** *a.* **recessive** *a.* **1** tending to recede. **2** relating to or controlled by a recessive gene. **3** (of a stress accent) tending to move towards the beginning of a word. **recessive gene** *n.* a gene that must be inherited from both mother and father in order to show its effect in the individual. **recessively** *adv.* **recessiveness** *n.*

réchauffé (rāshōfā´) *n.* **1** a dish warmed up again. **2** a rehash.

recherché (rəshœ´shā) *a.* **1** out of the common, rare, choice, exotic. **2** affected, precious, far-fetched.

recidivist (risid´ivist) *n.* a relapsed or inveterate criminal, usu. one serving or who has served a

second term of imprisonment. **recidivism** *n.* **recidivistic** (-vis´-) *a.*

☒ **recieve** common misspelling of RECEIVE.

recipe (res´ipi) *n.* **1** a list of ingredients and directions for preparing a dish. **2** a remedy, expedient, device or means for effecting some result. **3** a formula or prescription for compounding medical or other mixtures.

recipient (risip´iənt) *n.* a person who receives something. ~*a.* **1** receiving. **2** receptive. **recipience, recipiency** *n.*

reciprocal (risip´rəkəl) *a.* **1** acting, done or given in return, mutual. **2** mutually interchangeable. **3** inversely correspondent, complementary. **4** (*Gram.*) expressing mutual action or relation. ~*n.* (*Math.*) the quotient resulting from dividing unity by a given quantity. **reciprocality** (-kal´-) *n.* **reciprocally** *adv.*

reciprocate (risip´rəkāt) *v.i.* **1** to return an equivalent, to make a return in kind. **2** to alternate, to move backwards and forwards. ~*v.t.* **1** to give in return. **2** to give and take mutually, to interchange. **3** to give alternating or backward-and-forward motion to. **reciprocating engine** *n.* an engine in which the reciprocating motion of a piston is transformed into rotary motion of a crankshaft. **reciprocation** (-kā´shən) *n.* **reciprocator** *n.* **reciprocity** (resipros´iti) *n.* (*pl.* **reciprocities**) **1** the state of being reciprocal, reciprocation of rights or obligations. **2** mutual action or the principle of give-and-take, esp. interchange of commercial privileges between two nations.

recitative (resitətēv´) *n.* **1** a style of rendering vocal passages intermediate between singing and ordinary speaking, as in oratorio and opera. **2** a piece or part to be sung in recitative.

recite (risīt´) *v.t.* **1** to repeat aloud or declaim from memory, esp. before an audience. **2** to give details of, to relate in full. **3** to enumerate. ~*v.i.* to give a recitation. **recital** *n.* **1** the act of reciting. **2** a musical performance, esp. by one person or of the works of one person. **3** an enumeration or narrative of facts or particulars, a story. **4** (*Law*) the part of a document formally stating facts, reasons, grounds etc. **recitalist** *n.* **recitation** (-ā´shən) *n.* **1** the recital of prose or poetry, esp. the delivery of a composition committed to memory. **2** a composition intended for recital. **reciter** *n.*

reck (rek) *v.t.* (*poet.*) to care about, to heed. ~*v.i.* to have a care or thought (of).

reckless (rek´lis) *a.* heedless of the consequences or danger, rash, foolhardy. **recklessly** *adv.* **recklessness** *n.*

reckon (rek´ən) *v.t.* **1** to count, to add (up), calculate or compute. **2** to count or include (in or among). **3** to regard (as), to account, to esteem, to consider (to be). **4** to be of the opinion, to calculate, to guess (that). **5** (*sl.*) to think highly of, to regard favourably. ~*v.i.* **1** to compute, to calculate. **2** to settle accounts (with). **3** to rely, to count, to place dependence (upon). **4** to suppose, to believe, to guess, to calculate. **to be reckoned with** meriting consideration because formidable, influential etc. **reckoner** *n.* any of several devices or tables for quick calculations, esp. a ready reckoner. **reckoning** *n.* **1** the act of calculating or counting. **2** an appraisal, an estimation, an opinion. **3** a statement of accounts or charges, a bill. **4** a settling of accounts.

reclaim (riklām´) *v.t.* **1** to claim or demand back, to claim the restoration of. **2** to bring (e.g. marshland) under cultivation. **3** to recover (usable substances) from waste products. **4** to bring back from error, vice, wildness etc., to reform, to tame, to civilize. ~*n.* the act of reclaiming or being reclaimed, reclamation. **reclaimable** *a.* **reclaimer, reclaimant** *n.* **reclamation** (rekləmā´shən) *n.*

recline (riklīn´) *v.i.* **1** to assume or be in a leaning or recumbent posture, to lie down or lean back upon cushions or other supports. **2** to incline backwards. ~*v.t.* **1** to lay or lean (one's body, head, limbs etc.) back, esp. in a horizontal or nearly horizontal position. **2** to cause (e.g. the back of a car seat) to lean backwards from the vertical. **reclinable** *a.* **reclinate** (rek´lināt) *a.* (*Bot.*) (of plant parts) inclined from an erect position, bending downwards. **reclination** (-ā´shən) *n.* **recliner** *n.* **1** a type of armchair having a back which can be adjusted to recline backwards. **2** a person who or thing which reclines.

recluse (rikloos´) *n.* a person who lives retired from the world, esp. a religious devotee who lives in a solitary cell and practises austerity and self-discipline, a hermit, an anchorite or anchoress. **reclusion** (-kloo´zhən) *n.* **reclusive** *a.*

re- (+ co- words) recode *v.t.* to code again or differently. **re-collect** *v.t.* **1** to collect or gather together again. **2** to collect or compose (one's ideas, thoughts or feelings) again. **recolonize, recolonise** *v.t.* to colonize afresh. **recolonization** *n.* **recolour,** (*N Am.*) **recolor** *v.t.* to colour again. **recombine** *v.t., v.i.* to combine or join together again or differently. **recommence** *v.i., v.t.* to begin again. **recommencement** *n.* **recommission** *v.t.* to commission anew. **recommit** *v.t.* (*pres.p.* **recommitting,** *past, p.p.* **recommitted**) **1** to commit again. **2** to refer back (to a committee etc.). **recommitment, recommittal** *n.* **recompose** *v.t.* **1** to compose or put together again. **2** to rearrange. **3** to restore the composure of, to make tranquil again. **recondition** *v.t.* to repair, to make as good as new. **reconfigure** *v.t.* to configure again or differently. **reconfiguration** *n.* **reconfirm** *v.t.* to confirm or ratify again. **reconfirmation** *n.* **reconnect** *v.t., v.i.* to connect again. **reconnection** *n.* **reconquer** *v.t.* to conquer again. **reconquest** *n.* **reconsecrate** *v.t.* to consecrate afresh. **reconsecration** *n.* **reconsider** *v.t.* to consider (a decision) again (esp. with a view to rescinding). **reconsideration** *n.* **reconsign** *v.t.* to consign again. **reconsignment** *n.* **reconsolidate** *v.t., v.i.* to

consolidate again. **reconsolidation** *n.* **reconstitute** *v.t.* **1** to constitute again. **2** to build up again, to reconstruct, to re-form. **3** to restore (esp. dried food) to a former condition by adding liquid. **4** to give a new constitution to, to reorganize. **reconstitution** *n.* **reconstruct** *v.t.* **1** to construct again. **2** to rebuild. **3 a** to build up a picture of (a past event) from the available evidence. **b** to act out (a crime) as part of a police investigation. **reconstructable, reconstructible** *a.* **reconstruction** *n.* **reconstructive, reconstructional, reconstructionary** *a.* **reconstructor** *n.* **reconvene** *v.t., v.i.* to convene or assemble again. **reconvert** *v.t.* to convert again, back to its previous state, religion etc. **reconversion** *n.* **reconvict** *v.t.* to convict again. **reconviction** *n.* **recount** (-kownt´) *v.t.* to count over again. **re-count** (rē´-) *n.* a new or second count, esp. of votes in an election. **re-cover** *v.t.* to cover again, to put a new covering on.

recognition (rekəgnish´ən) *n.* **1** the act of recognizing. **2** the state of being recognized. **recognitive** (rekog´-), **recognitory** (-kog´-) *a.*

recognizance (rekog´nizəns), **recognisance** *n.* (*Law*) **1** a bond or obligation entered into in a court or before a magistrate to perform a specified act, fulfil a condition etc. (such as to keep the peace or appear when called upon). **2** a sum deposited as pledge for the fulfilment of this.

recognize (rek´əgnīz), **recognise** *v.t.* **1** to know again, to recall the identity of. **2** to be aware, to realize or perceive the nature of. **3** to acknowledge, to admit the truth, validity, existence etc. of. **4** to reward, to thank. **5** to show appreciation of. **6** to give a sign of knowing (a person). **recognizable** *a.* **recognizability** (-bil´-) *n.* **recognizably** *adv.* **recognizant** (rikog´nizənt) *a.* (*formal*) **1** conscious (of). **2** showing recognition or acknowledgement (of). **recognizer** *n.*

Usage note Pronunciation with just (-n-), rather than (-gn-) is best avoided.

recoil[1] (rikoil´) *v.i.* **1** to shrink back, as in fear or disgust. **2** to start or spring back. **3** to rebound. **4** to go wrong and harm the perpetrator. **5** (of a firearm) to be driven back when fired. **6** to retreat.

recoil[2] (rikoil´, rē´-) *n.* **1** the act of recoiling. **2** the act or feeling of shrinking back, as in fear or disgust. **3** the backward kick of a gun when fired.

recollect (rekəlekt´) *v.t.* to recall to memory, to remember, to succeed in recalling the memory of. ~*v.i.* to succeed in remembering. **recollection** (-lek´shən) *n.* **1** the act or power of recollecting. **2** a memory, a reminiscence. **3** a person's memory. **4** the period of past time over which a person's memory extends. **recollective** *a.*

re-collect RE- (+ CO- WORDS).

recombinant (rikom´binənt) *a.* (*Biol.*) found by or exhibiting genetic recombination. ~*n.* a recombinant organism, cell or cell nucleus. **recombinant DNA** *n.* DNA prepared in the laboratory by combining DNA molecules from different individuals or species. **recombination** n. (*Biol.*) the process whereby genetic material from different sources is combined, esp. the interchange of sections of parental chromosomes resulting in new combinations of genes in the offspring.

recommend (rekəmend´) v.t. **1** to commend to another's notice, use or favour, esp. to represent as suitable for an office or employment. **2** to advise (a certain course of action etc.), to counsel. **3** (of qualities etc.) to make acceptable, desirable or serviceable. **recommendable** a. **recommendation** (-dā´shən) n. **recommendatory** a. **recommender** n.

recompense (rek´əmpens) v.t. **1** to make a return or give an equivalent for, to requite, to repay (a person, a service, an injury etc.). **2** to indemnify, to compensate (for), to make up (for). ~n. that which is given as a reward, compensation, requital or satisfaction (for a service, injury etc.).

❌ **reconaisance** common misspelling of RECONNAISSANCE.

reconcile (rek´ənsīl) v.t. **1** to restore to friendship after an estrangement. **2** to make content, acquiescent or submissive (to). **3** to harmonize, to make consistent or compatible (with). **4** to adjust, to settle (differences etc.). **reconcilable** a. **reconcilability** (-bil´-), †**reconcilableness** n. **reconcilement** n. **reconciler** n. **reconciliation** (-siliā´shən) n. **reconciliatory** (-sil´iətri) a.

recondite (rek´əndīt, rikon´-) a. **1** out of the way, abstruse, little known, obscure. **2** of or relating to abstruse or special knowledge, profound. **reconditely** adv. **reconditeness** n.

❌ **reconize** common misspelling of RECOGNIZE.

reconnaissance (rikon´əsəns) n. **1** a preliminary examination or survey. **2** an exploratory survey of a tract of country or a coastline in wartime to ascertain the position of the enemy, the strategic features etc.

reconnoitre (rekənoi´tə), (*N Am.*) **reconnoiter** v.t. to make a reconnaissance of. ~v.i. to make a reconnaissance. ~n. a reconnaissance.

record¹ (rikawd´) v.t. **1** to register, to write an account of, to set down permanent evidence of. **2 a** to transfer (sound, a programme etc.) by electronic means on to a storage medium for later reproduction or broadcast. **b** to make a recording of (the voice etc.). **3** to bear witness to, to be evidence of. ~v.i. to make a recording. **recordable** a. **recorded** a. **recorded delivery** n. a postal service in which an official record of posting and delivery is kept. **recording** n. **1** the process of making a record of sound or image on record, tape or film. **2** the record, tape or film so produced. **3** a radio or television programme which has been recorded. **recordist** n. a person who records a sound.

record² (rek´awd, -əd) n. **1** a written or other permanent account or statement of a fact, event etc. **2** a register, a report, a minute or minutes of proceedings. **3** a trace or series of marks made by

a recording instrument. **4** a thin plastic disc on to which sound is recorded. **5** the past history of a person's career, achievements etc. esp. as an index of character and abilities. **6** a list or history of criminal convictions. **7** the best performance, as in sport, or the most striking event of its kind recorded. **8** the state of being recorded. **9** a portrait, monument or other memento of a person, event etc. **10** (*Comput.*) a group of items handled as a unit. **off the record** in confidence, not said officially. **on record 1** recorded, esp. with legal or official authentication. **2** publicly known. **to beat/ break the record** to surpass all former achievements or events of the kind. **to go on record** to state one's beliefs publicly. **to have a record** to be a known, previously convicted criminal. **to put/ set the record straight** to correct an error or false impression. **record breaker** n. a person who breaks a world, national etc. record, esp. in sport. **record-breaking** n., a. **record holder** n. a person who holds a record, esp. in sport. **record player** n. a machine for playing and reproducing sounds on a gramophone record.

recorder (rikaw´də) n. **1** a person or thing which records. **2** a machine for recording sound on to tape, a tape recorder. **3** a form of flute blown through a mouthpiece at the end. **4** a barrister or solicitor with a minimum of ten years' standing, appointed as a part-time judge in the Crown court. **5** a person who keeps records. **recordership** n.

recount (rikownt´) v.t. to relate in detail, to narrate.

re-count RE- (+ CO- WORDS).

recoup (rikoop´) v.t. **1** to reimburse, to indemnify for a loss or expenditure. **2** to recover, to make up for (a loss, expenditure etc.). **3** (*Law*) to keep back (a part of something due). **recoupable** a. **recoupment** n.

Usage note The verbs *recoup* and *recuperate* should not be confused: *recoup* refers to recovering loss or expenditure, and *recuperate* to recovering health or strength.

---

recourse (rikaws´) n. **1** resorting or applying (to) as for help. **2** a source of help, that which is resorted to. **to have recourse to** to turn or apply to for help. **without recourse** an endorsement of a bill of exchange etc. protecting the endorser from liability for non-payment.

recover (rikŭv´ə) v.t. **1** to regain, to repossess oneself of, to win back. **2** to obtain by legal process. **3** to save (the reusable by-products of an industrial process). **4** to extract (valuable matter) from an ore. **5** to make up for, to retrieve. **6** to bring (a weapon) back after a thrust etc. ~v.i. **1** to regain a former state, esp. after sickness, misfortune etc. **2** to come back to consciousness, life, health etc. **3** in fencing, to come back to a posture of defence after making an attack. ~n. **1** the position of a weapon or the body after a thrust etc. **2** the act of coming back to this.

recoverable *a.* **recoverability** (-bil´-), **recoverableness** *n.* **recoverer** *n.* **recovery** *n.* (*pl.* **recoveries**) **1** the act of recovering or the state of having recovered. **2** a golf stroke played on to the fairway or green from a bunker or the rough.

re-cover RE- (+ CO- WORDS).

re- (+ cr- words) **recreate** *v.t.* to create anew. **recreation** *n.* **recross** *v.t.*, *v.i.* to cross or pass over again. **recrystallize**, **recrystallise** *v.t.*, *v.i.* to crystallize again. **recrystallization** *n.*

recreant (rek´riənt) *a.* (*formal or poet.*) **1** craven, cowardly. **2** disloyal. ~*n.* a coward, an apostate, a deserter. **recreance**, **recreancy** *n.* **recreantly** *adv.*

recreation (rekriā´shən) *n.* **1** the act or process of refreshing oneself or renewing one's strength after toil. **2** a pleasurable or entertaining exercise or activity. **recreational** *a.* **recreationally** *adv.* **recreation ground** *n.* a communal open space in an urban area. **recreative** *a.*

re-creation RE- (+ CR- WORDS).

recriminate (rikrim´ināt) *v.i.* to return an accusation, to bring countercharges. **recrimination** (-ā´shən) *n.* **recriminative**, **recriminatory** *a.*

recrudesce (rēkrudes´) *v.i.* (*formal*) to break out or become active again. **recrudescence** *n.* **recrudescent** *a.*

recruit (rikroot´) *v.t.* **1** to enlist (esp. soldiers, sailors or airmen). **2** to raise or increase the strength of (an army, regiment, crew etc.) by enlisting recruits. **3** to enrol (members). **4** to replenish with fresh supplies, to fill gaps in. **5** to restore to health, to refresh, to reinvigorate. ~*v.i.* **1** to enlist recruits for military service. **2** to gain new members, supplies etc. ~*n.* **1** a serviceman or servicewoman newly enlisted. **2** a person who has newly joined a society etc. **recruitable** *a.* **recruiter** *n.* **recruitment** *n.*

recta, **rectal** etc. RECTUM.

rectangle (rek´tang-gəl) *n.* a plane quadrilateral figure with four right angles. **rectangular** (-tang´gūlə) *a.* **1** shaped like a rectangle. **2** having an angle or angles of 90°. **3** placed or having parts placed at right angles. **4** having a base, surface or section shaped like a rectangle. **rectangularity** (-lar´-) *n.* **rectangularly** *adv.*

rectify (rek´tifī) *v.t.* (*3rd pers. sing. pres.* **rectifies**, *pres.p.* **rectifying**, *past, p.p.* **rectified**) **1** to set right, to correct, to amend, to adjust, to reform, to supersede by what is right or just. **2** to refine or purify (spirit etc.) by repeated distillations and other processes. **3** to transform (alternating current) into direct current. **4** to determine the length of (an arc etc.). **rectifiable** *a.* **rectification** (-fikā´shən) *n.* **rectifier** *n.* **1** someone who or something which rectifies. **2** any of various electrical devices used in power supply circuits to change alternating current into direct current.

rectilinear (rektilin´iə), **rectilineal** (-iəl) *a.* **1** consisting of, lying or proceeding in a straight line. **2** bounded by straight lines. **rectilinearity** (-niar´iti) *n.* **rectilinearly**, **rectilineally** *adv.*

rectitude (rek´titūd) *n.* **1** uprightness, rightness

of moral principle, conformity to truth and justice. **2** righteousness. **3** freedom from error, correctness in judgement etc.

recto (rek´tō) *n.* (*pl.* **rectos**) **1** the right-hand page of an open book (usu. bearing an odd number) as distinct from *verso*. **2** the front of a printed sheet of paper.

rector (rek´tə) *n.* **1** the incumbent of a Church of England parish in which tithes were formerly paid to the incumbent. **2** a Roman Catholic priest in charge of a religious institution or church. **3** a clergyman in charge of a parish in the Episcopalian Church. **4** the head of certain universities, colleges and schools. **rectorate** (-rət) *n.* **rectorial** (-taw´ri-) *a.*, *n.* **rectorship** *n.* **rectory** *n.* (*pl.* **rectories**) **1** the house of a rector. **2** the benefice or living of a Church of England rector with all its rights, property etc.

rectum (rek´təm) *n.* (*pl.* **rectums**, **recta** (-tə)) (*Anat.*) the lowest portion of the large intestine extending to the anus. **rectal** *a.* **rectally** *adv.*

re- (+ cu-cy words) **recut** *v.t.* (*pres.p.* **recutting**, *past, p.p.* **recut**) to cut again. **recycle** *v.t.* to pass again through a system of treatment or series of changes, esp. to process (a waste product, such as paper or glass) so as to be reusable. **recyclable** *a.* **recycler** *n.*

recumbent (rikŭm´bənt) *a.* lying down, reclining. **recumbence**, **recumbency** *n.* **recumbently** *adv.*

recuperate (rikoo´pərət, -kū´-) *v.i.* to recover from sickness, exhaustion, loss of power, a loss etc. ~*v.t.* to recover, to regain (health, strength etc.). **recuperable** *a.* **recuperation** (-ā´shən) *n.* **recuperative** *a.* **recuperator** *n.*

Usage note The use of *recuperate* as a transitive verb is sometimes disapproved of. See also note under RECOUP.

recur (rikœ´) *v.i.* (*pres.p.* **recurring**, *past, p.p.* **recurred**) **1** to happen again, to happen repeatedly. **2** to come back to one's mind. **3** (*Math.*) to be repeated indefinitely. **4** to return, to go back (to) in thought etc. **recurrence** (-kŭr´əns) *n.* **recurrent** (rikŭr´ənt) *a.* **1** returning, recurring, esp. at regular intervals. **2** (*Anat.*) (of veins, nerves etc.) turning in the opposite direction, running in an opposite course to those from which they branch. **recurrently** *adv.* **recurring** *a.* happening again or being repeated. **recurring decimal** *n.* (*Math.*) a decimal fraction in which one digit or a sequence of digits recurs over and over again indefinitely. **recursion** (-shən) *n.* **1** the act of returning. **2** (*Math.*) the repeated application of a mathematical procedure to a preceding result to generate a sequence of values. **recursive** *a.* **1** recurring, repeating. **2** (*Math.*) relating to or involving mathematical recursion. **3** (*Comput.*) relating to or being a computer program or subroutine which calls itself into operation. **recursively** *adv.*

recurve (rikœv´) *v.t.*, *v.i.* to bend backwards.

recurvate (-vət, -vāt) *a.*, †*v.t.* **recurvature** (-vəchə) *n.*

recusant (rek´ūzənt) *a.* **1** obstinately refusing to conform. **2** (*Hist.*) refusing to attend the services of the Church of England. ~*n.* **1** a person who refuses to submit or comply. **2** (*Hist.*) a person, esp. a Roman Catholic, who refused to attend the services of the Church of England. **recusance, recusancy** *n.*

red (red) *a.* (*comp.* **redder,** *superl.* **reddest**) **1** of a bright warm colour, such as blood, usu. including crimson, scarlet, vermilion etc.; of the colour at the least refracted end of the spectrum or that farthest from the violet. **2** tinged with red. **3** (of hair) reddish-brown, auburn, tawny, ginger, russet. **4** flushed, suffused with blood, esp. as a sign of anger or shame. **5** involving bloodshed or violence, bloody. **6** revolutionary, anarchistic. **7** (*coll. or derog.*) (*also* **Red**) left-wing, communist, socialist. **8** (*Hist.*) (*also* **Red**) Soviet. **9** denoting danger. ~*n.* **1** a red colour or a shade of this. **2** a red pigment. **3** red clothes. **4** the red ball in billiards, snooker etc. **5** the red colour in roulette etc. **6** a red light. **7** (*coll. or derog.*) a revolutionary, an extreme radical, an anarchist. **8** a member of a Communist or Socialist party, state or country, esp. the former Soviet Union. **in the red** overdrawn at the bank. **to paint the town red** to have a riotous time. **to see red** to become enraged. **red admiral** *n.* a butterfly, *Vanessa atalanta*, with reddish-banded wings. **red arsenic** *n.* realgar. **red-back, red-back spider** *n.* a venomous Australian spider, *Latrodectus hasselti*, with red spots on its back. **red bark** *n.* a variety of cinchona. **red biddy** *n.* red wine mixed with methylated spirits. **red blood cell, red blood corpuscle** *n.* a blood cell containing haemoglobin, an erythrocyte. **red-blooded** *a.* vigorous, virile. **red-bloodedness** *n.* **redbreast** *n.* (*coll.*) the robin, *Erythacus rubecula*. **redbrick** *a.* relating to, being or characteristic of any of the pre-1939 provincial universities in Britain. **redcap** *n.* **1** (*coll.*) a member of the military police. **2** (*N Am.*) a porter at a railway station. **red card** *n.* a piece of red cardboard shown by a soccer referee to a player to indicate that they are being sent off the field. **red carpet** *n.* **1** a strip of red carpet put out for a celebrity or important person to walk on. **2** deferential treatment shown to such a person. **red cedar** *n.* any of various species of cedar, esp. a N American juniper, *Juniperus virginiana*, with fragrant, red wood. **red cell** *n.* an erythrocyte. **red cent** *n.* (*N Am., coll.*) a trifling amount of money. **redcoat** *n.* **1** (*Hist.*) a British soldier (so called from the scarlet tunics worn by line regiments). **2** an entertainments officer at a Butlin's holiday camp. **red coral** *n.* any of several pinkish-red corals of the genus *Corallium* used to make ornaments and jewellery. **red corpuscle** *n.* an erythrocyte. **redcurrant** *n.* **1** the small, red, edible berry from a shrub of the gooseberry family. **2** a shrub, *Ribes rubrum*, that bears redcurrants. **red deer** *n.* a large species of deer, *Cervus elaphus*, with reddish coat and branching antlers, occurring wild in the Scottish Highlands, on Exmoor etc. **redden** *v.t.* to make red. ~*v.i.* to become red, esp. to blush. **reddish, reddy** *a.* **reddishness** *n.* **red dwarf** *n.* a star with a relatively small mass and low luminosity. **red ensign** *n.* a red flag with the Union Jack in one corner, used as the ensign of the British Merchant Navy. **red-eye** *n.* **1** (*N Am., coll.*) low quality whisky. **2** the effect on a photograph of a person's eyes appearing red, caused by light from a flashgun etc. being reflected from the retina. **3** the rudd. **4** (*N Am., coll.*) (*also* **red-eye flight**) a long-distance overnight aeroplane flight. **red-faced** *a.* **1** flushed with embarrassment. **2** with a red, florid complexion. **redfish** *n.* **1** a male salmon in the spawning season. **2** any of various fishes with a reddish colour, esp. of the genus *Sebastes*. **red flag** *n.* **1** the symbol of revolution or of communism. **2** a danger signal. **red fox** *n.* the common European fox, *Vulpes vulpes*. **red giant** *n.* a giant star with high luminosity that emits red light. **red grouse** *n.* a grouse, *Lagopus scoticus*. **red gum** *n.* **1** an eruption of red pimples in infants, caused by teething. **2** any of various species of Australian eucalyptus yielding reddish resin. **3** such a resin. **red-handed** *a., adv.* in the very act of committing a crime or doing something wrong. **red hat** *n.* **1** a cardinal's hat. **2** the rank or office of a cardinal. **redhead** *n.* a person with red hair. **red-headed** *a.* **1** (of a person) having red hair. **2** (of a bird etc.) having a red head. **red heat** *n.* **1** the temperature at which a thing is red-hot. **2** the state of being red-hot. **red herring** *n.* **1** herring, dried and smoked. **2** anything which diverts attention from the real issue or line of enquiry. **red-hot** *a.* **1** heated to redness. **2 a** excited, keen, wildly enthusiastic. **b** full of energy or activity. **3** intense, ardent, passionate. **4** furious, violent. **5** very recent, topical, new. **red-hot poker** *n.* a plant of the S African genus *Kniphofia*, esp. *K. uvaria* cultivated for its tall stout stems bearing terminal spikes of orange and yellow flowers. **Red Indian** *n.* (*offensive*) a N American Indian. **red lead** *n.* red oxide of lead used as a pigment. **red Leicester** *n.* orange-coloured Leicester cheese. **red-letter day** *n.* an auspicious or memorable day (because these were marked in red on the calendar). **red light** *n.* **1** a red light used as a signal to stop, esp. a red traffic light. **2** a danger signal. **3** any signal or indication to stop. **red-light area, red-light district** *n.* an area or district in a town where there is a collection of brothels etc. **redly** *adv.* **red man** REDSKIN (under RED). **red meat** *n.* dark-coloured meat, esp. beef or lamb. **red mullet** *n.* an edible mullet of the family Mullidae, found in European waters. **redneck** *n.* (*N Am., derog. or offensive*) a poor white farm labourer in the South. **redness** *n.* **red orpiment** *n.* REALGAR. **red**

panda *n.* a small raccoon-like animal, *Aelurus fulgens*, from the SE Himalayas and Tibet. **red pepper** *n.* the red fruit of the sweet pepper. **redpoll** (red´pol, -pōl) *n.* any of several small finches of the genus *Acanthis*, the males of which have a red or rosy crown, esp. *A. flammea* and *A. hornemanni*. **red rag** *n.* anything that excites rage (as a red object is supposed to enrage a bull). **red rattle** *n.* a pink-flowered European plant, *Pedicularis palustris*, of marshland. **red rose** *n.* the emblem of the House of Lancaster during the Wars of the Roses, 1455–85. **red sandalwood** *n.* **1** a SE Asian tree, *Pterocarpus santalinus*, with hard, fragrant dark red wood. **2** the wood of this tree used for cabinetwork and to make dyes. **redshank** *n.* either of two red-legged sandpipers, *Tringa totanus* or *T. erythropus*. **red shift** *n.* the shift of lines in the spectrum towards the red, caused by a receding light source. **redskin, red man** *n.* (*offensive*) a N American Indian. **red snapper** *n.* any of several edible fish of the snapper family. **red spider, red spider mite** *n.* a mite of the family Tetranychidae, infesting house and garden plants. **red squirrel** *n.* **1** a reddish squirrel, *Sciurus vulgaris*, found in Europe and some parts of Asia. **2** a small, widely distributed N American squirrel, *Tamiasciurus hudsonicus*. **red tape** *n.* extreme adherence to official routine and formality (from the red tape once used in tying up official documents). **red tide** *n.* sea water, when discoloured and made toxic by red protozoans. **red valerian** *n.* a Mediterranean plant, *Centranthus ruber*, with red spurred flowers. **redwater, redwater fever** *n.* (*Zool.*) **1** haematuria in cattle and sheep, the most marked symptom of which is red urine. **2** a disease of cattle caused by the tick-borne protozoan *Babesia boris*, resulting in haematuria. **redwing** *n.* **1** a European thrush, *Turdus iliacus*, with red patches under the wings. **2** a N American blackbird, *Agelaius phoeniceus*, with red wing patches. **redwood** *n.* any of various trees with reddish timber, esp. the gigantic Californian sequoia, *Sequoia sempervirens*.

-red (rid) *suf.* condition, as hatred, kindred.

redaction (ridak´shǝn) *n.* **1** reduction to order, esp. revising, rearranging and editing a literary work. **2** a revised or rearranged edition. **redact** *v.t.* to reduce to a certain form, esp. a literary form, to edit, to prepare for publication. **redactor** *n.*

redan (ridan´) *n.* a fortification having two faces forming a salient angle towards the enemy.

redden RED.

reddle RUDDLE.

re- (+ **de–dy words**) **redecorate** *v.t.* to decorate afresh. **redecoration** *n.* **rededicate** *v.t.* to dedicate anew. **rededication** *n.* **redefine** *v.t.* to define again or afresh. **redefinition** *n.* **redeploy** *v.t.* **1** to transfer (troops, labour force) from one area to another. **2** to assign a new task to. **redeployment** *n.* **redesign**[1] (rēdizīn´) *v.t.* to make a new design

of, incorporating improvements. **redesign**[2] (rē´-) *n.* a new or changed design. **redetermine** *v.t.* to determine again. **redetermination** *n.* **redevelop** *v.t.* **1** to develop again. **2** to renovate and build in (a depressed urban area). **redeveloper** *n.* **redevelopment** *n.* **redial** *v.t., v.i.* (*pres.p.* **redialling**, (*N Am.*) **redialing**, *past, p.p.* **redialled**, (*N Am.*) **redialed**) to dial again. **redirect** *v.t.* **1** to direct again. **2** to readdress (a letter, parcel etc.). **redirection** *n.* **rediscover** *v.t.* to discover afresh. **rediscovery** *n.* (*pl.* **rediscoveries**). **redissolve** *v.t., v.i.* to dissolve again. **redissolution** *n.* **redistribute** *v.t.* to distribute again. **redistribution** *n.* the act of distributing again. **redistributive** *a.* **redivide** *v.t.* to divide again. **redivision** *n.* **redo** *v.t.* (*3rd pers. sing. pres.* **redoes**, *pres.p.* **redoing**, *past* **redid**, *p.p.* **redone**) **1** to do again. **2** to redecorate. **redouble** *v.t.* to increase by repeated additions, to intensify, to multiply. ~*v.i.* **1** to become increased by repeated additions, to grow more intense, numerous etc. **2** to double an opponent's double in bridge. ~*n.* the act of redoubling. **redraft**[1] (-drahft´) *v.t.* to draft or draw up a second time. **redraft**[2] (rē´-) *n.* a second or revised draft. **redraw** *v.t.* (*past* **redrew**, *p.p.* **redrawn**) to draw again. **re-dress** *v.t., v.i.* **1** to dress again. **2** to dress in different clothes. **re-dye** *v.t.* (*3rd pers. sing. pres.* **re-dyes**, *pres.p.* **re-dyeing**, *past, p.p.* **re-dyed**) to dye again.

redeem (ridēm´) *v.t.* **1** to buy back, to recover by paying a price. **2** to recover (mortgaged property), to discharge (a mortgage), to buy off (an obligation etc.). **3** to exchange (coupons, tokens etc.) for goods or cash. **4** to deliver, to save, to rescue, to reclaim. **5** to atone for, to make amends for. **6** to make good. **7** to recover from captivity by purchase, to ransom. **8** (of Christ) to deliver from sin and its penalty. **9** to perform (a promise). **redeemable** *a.* **redeemer** *n.* **1** a person who redeems. **2** (**Redeemer**) Christ, as Saviour of the world.

redemption (ridemp´shǝn) *n.* **1** the act of redeeming or the state of being redeemed. **2** (*Theol.*) salvation from sin and damnation by the atonement of Christ. **3** that which redeems. **redemptive, redemptory** *a.*

rediffusion (rēdifū´zhǝn) *n.* a system of relaying radio or television programmes via cables.

redingote (red´ing-gōt) *n.* a woman's long double-breasted coat.

redintegrate (redin´tigrāt) *v.t.* **1** to restore to completeness, to make united or perfect again. **2** to renew, to re-establish. **redintegration** (-grā´shǝn) *n.* **redintegrative** (-grǝtiv) *a.*

redolent (red´ǝlǝnt) *a.* **1** suggestive, reminding one (of). **2** fragrant. **3** giving out a strong smell. **redolence, redolency** *n.* **redolently** *adv.*

redoubt (ridowt´) *n.* (*Mil.*) a detached outwork or fieldwork enclosed by a parapet without flanking defences.

redoubtable (ridow´tǝbǝl) *a.* **1** formidable. **2** valiant. **redoubtably** *adv.*

redound

redound (ridownd´) *v.i.* **1** to have effect, to contribute (to one's credit etc.). **2** to result, to act in return or recoil (on or upon).

redox (rē´doks) *a.* (*Chem.*) of, relating to or being a chemical reaction where one agent is reduced and another oxidized. ~*n.* oxidation and reduction.

redress (ridres´) *v.t.* **1** to remedy, to amend, to make reparation for. **2** to set straight or right again, to readjust, to rectify. ~*n.* **1** redressing of wrongs or oppression. **2** reparation. **3** rectification. **to redress the balance** to make equal again. **redressable** *a.* **redressal, redressment** *n.* **redresser, redressor** *n.*

re-dress RE- (+ DE–DY WORDS).

redstart (red´staht) *n.* **1** a red-tailed migratory songbird, *Phoenicurus phoenicurus*. **2** a N American warbler of the genus *Setophaga*.

reduce (ridūs´) *v.t.* **1** to make smaller or less in size, number, degree, extent etc. **2** to bring or force into a specified condition, state, action etc. **3** to convert from one form into another, esp. simpler, form. **4** to set out in systematic form, to modify or simplify so as to conform (to a rule, formula, fundamental classification etc.). **5** to bring down, to lower, to degrade, to diminish, to weaken. **6** to lower the price of. **7** to impoverish. **8** to subdue, to conquer. **9** (*Math.*) to change from one denomination to another. **10** (*Chem.*) **a** to cause to lose oxygen atoms from. **b** to cause to combine or react with hydrogen. **c** to cause to gain electrons. **11** to convert (e.g. iron ore) to a metal. **12** to lessen the density of (a photographic print or negative). **13** to correct (a bone fracture, dislocation etc.) by restoring to the proper position. **14** to concentrate (a stock, sauce etc.) by boiling. ~*v.i.* **1** to become smaller or less. **2** to lose weight. **3** (*Chem.*) to become reduced, to undergo reduction. **to reduce to the ranks** (*Mil.*) to demote to the rank of private soldier. **reduced** *a.* **in reduced circumstances** poor, hard-up. **reducer** *n.* **reducible** *a.* **reducibility** (-bil´-), **reducibleness** *n.* **reducing** *a.*

reductio ad absurdum (ridŭktiō ad absœ´dəm) *n.* proof of the falsity of a proposition by showing the absurdity of its logical consequence.

reduction (ridŭk´shən) *n.* **1** the act or process of reducing. **2** the state of being reduced. **3** the amount by which something is reduced, a decrease, a diminution. **4** a reduced copy of anything. **5** (*Mus.*) a piano score arranged from an orchestral score. **reductionism** *n.* **1** the explaining of complex data or phenomena in simpler terms. **2** (*derog.*) oversimplification. **reductionist** *n.*, *a.* **reductionistic** (-nis´-) *a.* **reductive** *a.*

redundant (ridŭn´dənt) *a.* **1** superfluous, excessive, superabundant, unnecessary. **2** deprived of one's job as no longer necessary. **3** using more words than are necessary, pleonastic, tautological. **4** (*Comput.*) included as a back-up in

case of failure (*redundant components*). **redundancy, redundance** *n.* (*pl.* **redundancies, redundances**). **redundantly** *adv.*

reduplicate (ridū´plikāt) *v.t.* **1** to double, to repeat. **2** to repeat (a letter or syllable) to form a tense. **reduplication** (-ā´shən) *n.* **reduplicative** *a.*

re- (+ e– words) re-echo *v.t.* (*3rd pers. sing. pres.* **re-echoes**, *pres.p.* **re-echoing**, *past, p.p.* **re-echoed**) **1** to echo or repeat again. **2** to return (an echo), to resound. ~*v.i.* **1** to echo again. **2** to reverberate. **re-edit** *v.t.* to edit afresh. **re-educate** *v.t.* to cause to develop new or different attitudes, habits, beliefs etc. **re-education** *n.* **re-elect** *v.t.* to elect again, esp. for another term in office. **re-election** *n.* **re-eligible** *a.* eligible to be re-elected to the same position. **re-embark** *v.t., v.i.* to embark again. **re-embarkation** *n.* **re-emerge** *v.i.* to emerge again. **re-emergence** *n.* **re-emergent** *a.* **re-emphasize, re-emphasise** *v.t.* to emphasize again or more strongly. **re-employ** *v.t.* to employ again. **re-employment** *n.* **re-enact** *v.t.* to enact again, to act out (a past event). **re-enactment** *n.* **re-enlist** *v.t., v.i.* to enlist again. **re-enter** *v.t., v.i.* to enter again. **re-entrant** *a.* **1** re-entering. **2** pointing inwards. ~*n.* a re-entrant angle, esp. in fortification, as distinct from *salient*. **re-entry** *n.* (*pl.* **re-entries**) **1** the act of re-entering. **2** (*Law*) an act of retaking possession, esp. of leased premises by the leasor. **3** the re-entry of a spacecraft into the earth's atmosphere. **re-equip** *v.t.* (*pres.p.* **re-equipping**, *past, p.p.* **re-equipped**) to equip again. **re-erect** *v.t.* to erect again. **re-erection** *n.* **re-establish** *v.t.* to establish anew, to restore. **re-establishment** *n.* **re-evaluate** *v.t.* to evaluate again or differently. **re-evaluation** *n.* **re-examine** *v.t.* to examine again or further. **re-examination** *n.* **re-explore** *v.t.* to explore again. **re-exploration** *n.* **re-export** *v.t.* **1** to export again. **2** to export after having been imported. **3** to export (imported goods) after processing. ~*n.* **1** the act of re-exporting. **2** a commodity re-exported. **re-exportation** *n.* **re-exporter** *n.*

reebok RHEBOK.

reed (rēd) *n.* **1** any of various water or marsh plants with long straight stems, esp. of the genera *Phragmites* or *Arundo*. **2 a** the stem of a reed. **b** (*collect.*) reeds as material for thatching etc. **3 a** a thin strip of metal or wood inserted in an opening in a musical instrument and set in vibration by a current of air to produce the sound. **b** (*usu. pl.*) a musical instrument or organ pipe constructed with this. **c** (*usu. pl.*) the section of an orchestra that plays reed instruments. **4** a musical pipe made from a reed, a shepherd's pipe. ~*v.t.* **1** to thatch with reed. **2** to fit (an organ pipe etc.) with a reed. **reedbuck** *n.* a buff-coloured antelope of the genus *Redunca*, found south of the Sahara in Africa. **reed bunting** *n.* a common European bunting with a black head, *Emberiza schoeniclus*. **reeded** *a.* (*Mus.*) (of a musical instrument) having a reed. **reeding** *n.* (*Archit.*) a semicylindrical architectural moulding or series of these set parallel to one another. **reed instrument** *n.* a woodwind instrument with a reed, such as an oboe. **reedless** *a.* **reedling** *n.* the bearded tit. **reed mace** *n.* a reedlike marsh or water plant of the genus *Typha*, esp. *T. latifolia* which bears tiny spikes of furry brown flowers. **reed-organ** *n.* a musical instrument with a keyboard, the sounds of which are produced by reeds of the organ type. **reed pipe** *n.* **1** a reed instrument. **2** a reeded organ pipe. **3** a musical pipe made of a reed. **reed-stop** *n.* an organ stop controlling a set of reed pipes. **reed warbler** *n.* any of various common Eurasian warblers of the genus *Acrocephalus*, esp. *A. scirpaceus*, that frequent marshy areas. **reedy** *a.* (*comp.* **reedier**, *superl.* **reediest**) **1** abounding in reeds. **2** like a reed. **3** sounding like a reed instrument, thin or sharp in tone. **4** thin, frail in form. **reedily** *adv.* **reediness** *n.*

reef[1] (rēf) *n.* a ridge of rock, coral, sand etc. in the sea at or near the surface of the water.

reef[2] (rēf) *n.* (*Naut.*) any of the horizontal portions across the top of a square sail or the bottom of a fore-and-aft sail, which can be rolled up or wrapped and secured in order to shorten sail. ~*v.t.* **1** to reduce the extent of (a sail) by taking in a reef or reefs. **2** to take in a part of (a bowsprit, topmast etc.) in order to shorten it. **reefer**[1] *n.* **1** a person who reefs. **2** a reefing-jacket. **reefing-jacket** *n.* a stout, close-fitting double-breasted jacket. **reef knot** *n.* a square or symmetrical double knot. **reef-point** *n.* a short length of rope stitched to a sail, for securing a reef.

reefer[1] REEF[2].

reefer[2] (rē′fə) *n.* (*sl.*) a marijuana cigarette.

reek (rēk) *v.i.* **1** to give off a strong disagreeable odour. **2** to give a strong impression (of something offensive or undesirable). **3** to emit smoke, fumes, vapour or steam. ~*n.* **1** a foul, stale or disagreeable odour, a foul atmosphere. **2** (*esp. Sc.*) **a** smoke. **b** vapour, steam, fume. **reeky** *a.* (*comp.* **reekier**, *superl.* **reekiest**).

reel[1] (rēl) *n.* **1** a rotatory frame, cylinder or other device on which thread, cord, wire, paper etc. can be wound, either in the process of manufacture or for winding and unwinding as required. **2** a quantity of material wound on a reel. ~*v.t.* **1** to wind on a reel. **2** to unwind or take (off) a reel. **to reel in 1** to draw (a fish etc.) towards one by using a reel. **2** to wind (thread, a line etc.) on a reel. **to reel off 1** to unwind or pay out from a reel. **2** to tell (a story) fluently and without a hitch. **to reel up 1** to wind up entirely on a reel. **2** to reel in. **reeler** *n.*

reel[2] (rēl) *v.i.* **1** to stagger, to sway. **2** to go (along) unsteadily. **3** to have a whirling sensation, to be dizzy. **4** to whirl, to rock. ~*n.* a staggering or swaying motion or sensation.

reel[3] (rēl) *n.* **1** a lively esp. Scottish dance in which the couples face each other and describe figures of eight. **2** a piece of music for this. ~*v.i.* to dance a reel.

reeve[1] (rēv) *n.* **1** (*Hist.*) a chief officer or magistrate of a town or district, holding office usu. under the monarch but sometimes by election. **2** †a bailiff, a steward. **3** (*Can.*) the presiding officer of a township or village council.

reeve[2] (rēv) *v.t.* (*past, p.p.* **reeved, rove** (rōv)) (*Naut.*) **1** to pass (the end of a rope, a rod etc.) through a ring, a hole in a block etc. **2** to fasten (a rope etc.) round some object by this means.

reeve[3] (rēv) *n.* the female of the ruff.

ref[1] (ref) *n.* a referee.

ref[2] *abbr.* **1** reference. **2** refer to.

re- (+ fa–fl words) **reface** *v.t.* to put a new face or surface on (a wall, building etc.). **refashion** *v.t.* to fashion anew. **refasten** *v.t.* to fasten again. **refill**[1] (rēfil′) *v.t.* to fill again. **refill**[2] (rē′-) *n.* **1** something which is used to refill. **2** a fresh or replacement fill (as of lead for a propelling pencil, tobacco for a pipe etc.). **refillable** *a.* **refilm** *v.t.* **1** to film again. **2** to make a new film version of. **refinance** *v.t.* to finance again, to provide further capital for. **refinish** *v.t.* to give a new finish or surface to. **refinisher** *n.* **refit**[1] *v.t.* (*pres.p.* **refitting**, *past, p.p.* **refitted**) to make fit for use again, to repair, to re-equip, to fit out anew (esp. a ship). ~*v.i.* (of ships) to undergo repair of damages. **refit**[2] (rē′-) *n.* the repairing or renewing of what is damaged or worn out, esp. the repairing of a ship. **refitment** *n.* **refitter** *n.* **reflag** *v.t.* (*pres.p.* **reflagging**, *past, p.p.* **reflagged**) to change the country of registration of (a ship). **refloat** *v.t., v.i.* to float again.

refectory (rifek′təri) *n.* (*pl.* **refectories**) a room or hall where meals are taken in colleges, religious houses etc. **refection** (rifek′shən) *n.* (*formal*) **1** refreshment by food. **2** a light meal, a repast. **refectory table** *n.* a long narrow dining table, esp. on two trestles.

refer (rifœ′) *v.t.* (*pres.p.* **referring**, *past, p.p.* **referred**) **1** to trace back, to assign (to a certain cause, source, class, place etc.). **2** to hand over (for consideration and decision). **3** to send or direct (a person) for information, aid, treatment etc. **4** to fail (an examinee). ~*v.i.* **1** to apply for information. **2** to appeal, to have recourse. **3** to cite, to allude, to direct attention (to). **4** to be concerned with, to have relation (to). **referable** (refœ′rəbəl, ref′ə-), **referrable, referrible** (-fœ′-) *a.* **referral** *n.* the act of referring or being referred, esp. to another person or organization for treatment, consideration etc. **referred** *a.* **referred pain** *n.* pain localized at a different point from the part actually causing it. **referrer** *n.*

referee (refərē′) *n.* **1** an umpire in football, boxing etc. **2** a person to whom a point or question is referred. **3** a person who is prepared to testify to the abilities and character of someone, and who furnishes a reference, testimonial etc. ~*v.i.* (*3rd pers. sing. pres.* **referees**, *pres.p.* **refereeing**, *past, p.p.* **refereed**) to act as a referee (in football etc.).

reference (ref′ərəns) *n.* **1** the act of referring. **2**

relation, respect, correspondence (to). **3** allusion, directing of attention (to). **4 a** a note or mark referring from a book to another work or from the text to a commentary, diagram etc. **b** that which is referred to. **5** a testimonial, esp. one not seen by the person described within it. **6** a person referred to for information, evidence of character etc., a referee. ~*v.t.* (*usu. p.p.*) to furnish (a work) with cross-references, references to authorities etc. **in/with reference to** with regard to, as regards, concerning. **without reference to** irrespective of, regardless of. **reference book** *n.* an encyclopedia, dictionary or the like, consulted when occasion requires, not for continuous reading. **reference library** *n.* a library where books may be consulted but not borrowed. **referent** (ref´ə-) *n.* the thing to which a word or phrase refers. **referential** (refəren´-) *a.* **referentially** *adv.*

referendum (refəren´dəm) *n.* (*pl.* **referendums, referenda** (-də)) **1** the submission of a political question to the whole electorate for a direct decision by general vote. **2** a vote taken in this manner.

Usage note The plural *referendums* is preferred to *referenda*.

refine (rifīn´) *v.t.* **1** to clear from impurities, defects etc., to purify. **2** to free from coarseness, to educate, to polish, to cultivate the taste, manners etc. of. **3** to make (a statement, idea etc.) more subtle, complex or abstract. ~*v.i.* **1** to become pure or clear. **2** to become polished or more highly cultivated in talk, manners etc. **3** to draw subtle distinctions (upon). **refinable** *a.* **refined** *a.* **1** freed from impurities. **2** highly cultivated, polished, elegant. **refinement** *n.* **1** the act or process of refining. **2** the state of being refined. **3** elegance of taste, manners, language etc. **4** an additional feature or development, an improvement, an elaboration. **5** a subtle distinction or piece of reasoning. **refiner** (rifī´nə) *n.* **1** someone who or something which refines. **2** a person or company whose business is to refine metals, oil etc. **refinery** *n.* (*pl.* **refineries**) a place for refining raw materials, such as sugar and oil.

reflate (rēflāt´) *v.t.* to inflate again. **reflation** (-ā´shən) *n.* an increase in economic activity, esp. through an increase in the supply of money and credit. **reflationary** *a.*

reflect (riflekt´) *v.t.* **1** to turn or throw back (light, heat, sound etc.) esp. in accordance with certain physical laws. **2** to mirror, to throw back an image of. **3** to reproduce exactly, to correspond in features or effects. **4** to show, to give an idea of. **5** to cause to accrue or to cast (honour, disgrace etc.) upon. **6** to remind oneself (that). ~*v.i.* **1** to throw back light, heat, sound etc. **2** to turn the thoughts back, to think, to ponder, to meditate. **3** to bring shame or discredit (on or upon). **reflectance** *n.* (*Physics*) a measure of the ability of a surface to reflect light or other

radiation; the ratio of the amount of light reflected by a surface to that falling on the surface. **reflection** (-flek´shən), **reflexion** *n.* **1** the act of reflecting. **2** the state of being reflected. **3** rays of light, heat etc. or an image thrown back from a reflecting surface. **4 a** continued consideration, thought, meditation. **b** the act or process by which the mind takes cognizance of its own operations. **5** a thought, idea, comment or opinion resulting from deliberation. **6** discredit, censure, reproach (brought or cast on or upon a person etc.). **7** that which entails censure or reproach (upon). **reflective** *a.* **1** throwing back an image, rays of light, heat etc. **2** of, relating to or concerned with thought or reflection. **3** meditative, thoughtful. **reflectively** *adv.* **reflectiveness** *n.* **reflectivity** (rēflektiv´-) *n.* (*Physics*) **1** the ability to reflect light or other radiation. **2** reflectance when measured independently of the thickness of the material of which a reflecting surface is composed. **reflector** *n.* **1** someone who or something which reflects. **2** a reflecting surface that throws back rays of light, heat etc., usu. a polished, concave surface, as in a lamp, lighthouse, telescope, surgical instrument etc. **3** a small piece of red, orange or clear plastic glass used (e.g. on a bicycle) to reflect the light from vehicle headlights. **4** a reflecting telescope.

reflex (rē´fleks) *a.* **1** involuntary, produced independently of the will under stimulus from impressions on the sensory nerves. **2** done or produced as a reaction or response to a situation without apparent intervention of conscious thought; automatic, mechanical. **3** turned or bent backward. **4** (of an angle) greater than 180°. **5** introspective. **6** reactive, turned back upon itself or the source, agent etc. **7** reflected, lighted by reflected light. ~*n.* **1** a reflex action. **2** a mechanical or automatic response. **3** (*pl.*) the power or capacity to respond rapidly. **4** a reflected image, reproduction or secondary manifestation. **5** reflected light, colour etc. **6** a word formed by development from a form in an earlier stage of a language. **reflex arc** *n.* (*Anat.*) the nervous pathway which nerve impulses travel along to produce a reflex action. **reflex camera** *n.* a camera in which the viewfinder is integrated with the main lens. **reflexed** *a.* bent backwards or downwards. **reflexible** *a.* **reflexibility** (-bil´-) *n.* **reflexive** *a.* **1** denoting action upon the agent. **2** (*Gram.*) implying action by the subject upon itself or themselves or referring back to the grammatical subject. **reflexively** *adv.* **reflexiveness, reflexivity** *n.* **reflexly** *adv.* **reflexology** (rēfleksol´-) *n.* **1** a form of complementary medical therapy where the soles of the feet are massaged to stimulate the circulation and nerves, and so release tension. **2** (*Psych.*) the interpretation of behaviour in terms of reflex actions and responses. **reflexologist** *n.*

reflexion REFLECTION (under REFLECT).

refluent (ref´luənt) *a.* (*formal*) **1** flowing back. **2** ebbing. **refluence** *n.*

reflux (rē´flŭks) *n.* **1** (*Chem.*) the boiling of liquid in a flask fitted with a condenser, so that the vapour condenses and flows back into the flask. **2** a flowing back. ~*v.t., v.i.* to boil under reflux conditions.

re- (+ **fo–fu** words) **refocus** *v.t.* (*3rd pers. sing. pres.* **refocuses, refocusses,** *pres.p.* **refocusing, refocussing,** *past, p.p.* **refocused, refocussed**) **1** to focus again. **2** to change or adjust the focus of. **reforest** *v.t.* to reafforest. **reforestation** *n.* **reforge** *v.t.* **1** to forge over again. **2** to refashion. **re-form** *v.t., v.i.* to form again or anew. **re-formation** *n.* **reformat** *v.t.* (*pres.p.* **reformatting,** *past, p.p.* **reformatted**) **1** to put into a new format. **2** (*Comput.*) to format again. **reformulate** *v.t.* to formulate again. **reformulation** *n.* **refreeze** *v.t.* (*past* **refroze,** *p.p.* **refrozen**) to freeze again. **refuel** *v.t.* (*pres.p.* **refuelling,** (*N Am.*) **refueling,** *past, p.p.* **refuelled,** (*N Am.*) **refueled**) to provide with fresh fuel. ~*v.i.* to take on fresh fuel. **re-fund** *v.t.* to pay off (an old debt) by borrowing more money. **refurnish** *v.t.* **1** to furnish anew. **2** to supply with new furniture. **re-fuse** *v.t.* to fuse or melt again.

reform (rifawm´) *v.t.* **1** to change from worse to better by removing faults, imperfections, abuses etc. **2** to improve, to amend, to redress, to cure, to remedy. ~*v.i.* to amend one's habits, morals, conduct etc. ~*n.* **1** the act of reforming, esp. the correction of political, social or legal abuses. **2** an alteration for the better, an amendment, an improvement. **reformable** *a.* **reformation** (refəmā´shən) *n.* **1** the act of reforming. **2** the state of being reformed. **3** redress of grievances or abuses, esp. a thorough change or reconstruction in politics, society or religion. **the Reformation** the great religious revolution in the 16th cent. which resulted in the establishment of the Protestant Churches. **reformationist** *n.* **reformative** *a.* tending to produce reform. **reformatory** *a.* reformative. ~*n.* (*pl.* **reformatories**) (*Hist., also N Am.*) a reform school. **reformed** *a.* corrected, amended, purged of errors and abuses. **Reformed Church** *n.* a Protestant Church that adopted Calvinistic doctrines and principles, as distinct from Lutheran Churches. **reformer** (rifaw´mə) *n.* **1** a person who effects a reformation. **2** a person who favours political reform. **reformism** *n.* any policy advocating religious or political reform. **reformist** *n., a.* **reform school** *n.* an institution for the detention and reformation of juvenile offenders.

re-form RE- (+ FO–FU WORDS).

refract (rifrakt´) *v.t.* **1** (*Physics*) (of water, glass etc.) to cause (a ray of light etc.) to undergo refraction. **2** to measure the refractive capacity of (the eye, a lens etc.). **refraction** *n.* (*Physics*) the deflection that takes place when a ray of light, heat etc. passes at any angle other than a right angle from the surface of one medium into an-

other medium of different density. **refractive** *a.* of or relating to refraction. **refractive index** *n.* **1** the amount by which a medium refracts light. **2** the ratio of the speed of light or other radiation in free space to its speed in any other medium. **refractively** *adv.* **refractiveness, refractivity** (rēfraktiv´-) *n.* **refractometer** (rēfraktom´itə) *n.* any instrument which measures the refractive index of a medium. **refractometric** (-təmet´-) *a.* **refractometry** *n.* **refractor** *n.*

refractory (rifrak´təri) *a.* **1** perverse, insubordinate, obstinate in opposition or disobedience, unmanageable. **2** (*Med.*) **a** not amenable to ordinary treatment. **b** immune or resistant to infection. **3** not easily fused or reduced, not easily worked. **refractorily** *adv.* **refractoriness** *n.*

refrain¹ (rifrān´) *v.i.* to abstain (from an act or doing), to forbear. **refrainer** *n.* **refrainment** *n.*

refrain² (rifrān´) *n.* **1** a recurring phrase or line, esp. repeated at the end of every stanza, a chorus. **2** the music to accompany this.

refrangible (rifran´jibəl) *a.* capable of being refracted. **refrangibility** (-bil´-), **refrangibleness** *n.*

refresh (rifresh´) *v.t.* **1** to make fresh again, to reanimate, to reinvigorate. **2** to revive or restore after depression, fatigue etc. **3** to freshen up, to stimulate (one's memory). **4** to restore, to repair, to renovate. **5** to replenish. **refresher** *n.* **1** someone who or something which refreshes. **2** (*coll.*) a drink. **3** (*Law*) an extra fee paid to counsel when a case is adjourned or continued from one term or sitting to another. **refresher course** *n.* a course to bring up to date knowledge of a particular subject. **refreshing** *a.* **1** reinvigorating, reanimating. **2** welcome or pleasing because different or new. **refreshingly** *adv.* **refreshment** *n.* **1** the act of refreshing. **2** the state of being refreshed. **3 a** that which refreshes. **b** (*usu. pl.*) food or drink.

refrigerate (rifrij´ərāt) *v.t.* **1** to make cool or cold. **2** to freeze or keep at a very low temperature in a refrigerator so as to preserve in a fresh condition. ~*v.i.* to become cold or chilled. **refrigerant** *n.* **1** the working fluid in a refrigerator or freezer that removes heat and transfers it to the surroundings. **2** (*Med.*) a medicine for allaying fever or inflammation. ~*a.* cooling, allaying heat. **refrigeration** (-ā´shən) *n.* **refrigerative** *a., n.* **refrigerator** (rifrij´ərātə) *n.* an apparatus for keeping meat and other provisions at a low temperature, in order to preserve their freshness.

refringent (rifrin´jənt) *a.* (*Physics*) refractive. **refringence, refringency** *n.*

refuge (ref´ūj) *n.* **1** shelter or protection from danger or distress. **2** a place, thing, person or course of action that shelters or protects from danger, distress or calamity. **3** an expedient, a subterfuge. **4** a traffic island. **refugee** (-jē´) *n.* a person who flees to a place of refuge, esp. one who takes refuge in a foreign country in time of war or persecution or political commotion.

refulgent (riful´jənt) a. (poet.) shining brightly, brilliant, radiant, splendid. **refulgence, †refulgency** n. **refulgently** adv.

refund[1] (rifŭnd´) v.t. **1** to pay back, to repay, to restore. **2** to reimburse. **refundable** a.

refund[2] (re¯´fŭnd) n. **1** an act of refunding money. **2** an amount refunded.

re-fund RE- (+ FO–FU WORDS).

refurbish (refœ´bish) v.t. to freshen up by renovating, redecorating etc. **refurbishment** n.

refuse[1] (rifūz´) v.t. **1** to decline (to do, yield, grant etc.). **2** to decline to accept or consent to. **3** to deny the request of. **4** (of a horse) to decline to jump over (a ditch etc.). ~v.i. **1** to decline to comply. **2** (of a horse) to fail to jump. **refusable** a. **refusal** (rifū´zəl) n. **1** the act of refusing. **2** first refusal. **refusenik** (-nik), **refusnik** n. **1** (Hist.) a Soviet Jew who was refused permission to emigrate. **2** (coll.) a person who refuses to cooperate in some way. **refuser** n.

refuse[2] (ref´ūs) a. rejected as valueless. ~n. something which is refused or rejected as worthless, waste or useless matter.

re-fuse RE- (+ FO–FU WORDS).

refute (rifūt´) v.t. **1** to prove (a statement, argument etc.) false or erroneous, to disprove. **2** to prove wrong, to rebut in argument, to confute. **3** to declare to be false, to deny. **refutable** a. **refutal, refutation** (refūtā´shən) n. **refuter** n.

Usage note The use of refute where there is no argument or proof is often disapproved of: deny or repudiate can be used instead.

reg (rej) n. (coll.) registration mark.

re- (+ ga–gi words) regather v.t., v.i. to gather or collect together again. **regelate** v.i. to freeze together again. **regelation** n. **regerminate** v.i. to germinate anew. **regermination** n. **regild** v.t. (p.p. **regilded, regilt**) to gild again.

regain (rigān´) v.t. **1** to recover possession of. **2** to reach again.

regal (re¯´gəl) a. of, relating to or fit for a king or queen, royal. **regalism** n. the doctrine of royal supremacy in ecclesiastical affairs. **regality** (rigal´-) n. (pl. **regalities**) **1** the state of being royal, royalty. **2** sovereign jurisdiction. **3** a country or territory under royal jurisdiction, a monarchical state, a kingdom. **regally** adv.

regale (rigāl´) v.t. **1** to entertain sumptuously with food and drink. **2** to amuse, to divert, to give entertainment to. **3** to delight, to gratify (with something rich or choice). **regalement** n.

regalia (rigā´liə) n.pl. **1** the insignia of royalty, esp. the emblems worn or displayed in coronation ceremonies etc. **2** the emblems or insignia of an office or order.

Usage note Regalia should not be used as a singular.

regard (rigahd´) v.t. **1** to look upon or view in a specified way or with fear, reverence etc., to consider (as). **2** to look at, to observe, to notice. **3** to value, to pay honour to, to esteem. **4** to affect, to relate to, to concern. **5** to give heed to, to pay attention to, to take into account. ~v.i. **1** to look. **2** to pay attention. ~n. **1** observant attention, heed, care, consideration. **2** esteem, kindly or respectful feeling. **3** a look, a gaze. **4** reference. **5** relation. **6** (pl.) compliments, good wishes. **as regards** regarding. **in/ with regard to 1** regarding. **2** in connection with. **regarder** n. **regardful** a. heedful, mindful (of). **regarding** prep. respecting, concerning. **regardless** a. heedless, careless, negligent (of). ~adv. despite everything, without concern for the consequences, drawbacks etc. **regardlessly** adv. **regardlessness** n.

regatta (rigat´ə) n. a sporting event comprising a series of yacht or boat races.

regd. abbr. registered.

regency REGENT.

regenerate[1] (rijen´ərāt) v.t. **1** to generate anew, to give new existence to. **2** to impart fresh vigour or higher life to. **3** to change fundamentally and reform the moral and spiritual nature of. **4** (Biol.) to replace (a lost or damaged body part or tissue) by new growth. ~v.i. to become regenerated. **regeneration** (-ā´shən) n. **regenerative** (-rət-), **regeneratory** a. **regeneratively** adv. **regenerator** n.

regenerate[2] (rijen´ərət) a. **1** regenerated, renewed. **2** reformed, converted.

regent (re¯´jənt) n. **1** a person appointed to govern a country during the minority, absence or disability of a monarch. **2** (N Am.) a member of the governing body of a State university. ~a. exercising the authority of regent (usu. following its noun). **regency** n. (pl. **regencies**) **1** the office, commission or government of a regent. **2** a body entrusted with the office or duties of a regent. **3** the period of office of a regent or a body so acting. **the Regency** the period (1810–20) when George, Prince of Wales, was regent for George III. **regentship** n.

reggae (reg´ā) n. a form of rhythmical W Indian rock music in 4/4 time.

regicide (rej´isīd) n. **1** the killing of a king. **2** a person who takes part in killing a king. **regicidal** (-sī´-) a.

regime (rāzhēm´), **régime** n. **1** a mode or prevailing system of government or management. **2** the prevailing social system or general state of things. **3** a prevailing set of conditions. **4** a regimen.

regimen (rej´imən) n. (Med.) a systematic plan or course of diet, exercise etc. for the preservation or restoration of health.

regiment[1] (rej´imənt) n. **1** a body of soldiers forming the largest permanent unit of the army, usu. divided into two battalions comprising several companies or troops, and commanded by a colonel. **2** a large number or a group. **regimental** (-men´-) a. of or relating to a regiment. ~n.pl. military uniform. **regimentally** adv. **regimental sergeant major** n. the chief sergeant of a regiment, a squadron of cavalry or a battery of artillery.

regiment² (rej´iment) *v.t.* **1** to force order or discipline on, harshly. **2** to organize into a system of bodies or groups. **3** to form into a regiment or regiments. **regimentation** (-tā´shən) *n.*

Regina (riji´nə) *n.* a reigning queen.

region (rē´jən) *n.* **1** a tract of land, sea, space etc. of large but indefinite extent, often having certain prevailing characteristics, as of fauna or flora. **2** a district, a sphere, a realm. **3** a part of the body surrounding an organ etc. **4** a civil division of a town, district or country. **5** one of the strata into which the atmosphere or the sea may be divided. **in the region of** approximately. **regional** *a.* **regionalism** *n.* **regionalist** *n., a.* **regionalize, regionalise** *v.t.* to organize into administrative regions. **regionalization** (-zā´shən) *n.* **regionally** *adv.*

register (rej´istə) *n.* **1** an official or authoritative list of names, facts etc., as of births, marriages, deaths, people entitled to vote at elections, shipping etc. **2** a book, roll or other document in which such a record is kept. **3** a mechanical device for recording data automatically. **4** a cash register. **5** a computer device which can store small amounts of data. **6** (*Mus.*) **a** the range or compass of a voice or instrument. **b** a particular portion of this. **7** a form of language used in a particular situation. **8** a contrivance for regulating the admission of air or heat to a room, ventilator, fireplace etc. **9** a sliding device in an organ for controlling a set of pipes. **10** (*Print.*) **a** precise correspondence of lines etc. on one side of the paper to those on the other. **b** exact overlaying of the different colours used in colour printing. **11** an act of registering, registration. *~v.t.* **1** to enter or cause to be entered in a register. **2** to record or note as if in a register. **3** to note mentally. **4** to express (an emotion) facially or by one's bearing. **5** (of an instrument) to record, to indicate. **6** to send (a letter etc.) by registered post. **7** to cause (printed material etc.) to correspond precisely. *~v.i.* **1** to enter one's name in or as in a register. **2** to make an impression. **3** (of an emotion) to be expressed in the face, bearing etc. **4** to be shown by a recording instrument. **5** to be in register. **in register** (of printed matter, photographic and colour plates etc.) exactly corresponding. **registered** *a.* **registered nurse** *n.* a nurse registered with the United Kingdom Central Council for Nursing, Midwifery and Health Visiting. **registered post** *n.* **1** a Post Office service where a registration fee is paid for mail and compensation paid in case of loss. **2** mail sent by this service. **registered trademark** *n.* a trademark which is legally registered and protected. **register office** *n.* a registrar's office where civil marriages are performed and births, marriages and deaths are recorded. **register ton** *n.* a unit used to measure the internal capacity of a ship, equal to 100 cu. ft. (about 3

m³). **registrable** *a.* **registrar** (-strah´, rej´-) *n.* **1** an official keeper of a register or record. **2** an administrative officer in a college or university responsible for enrolment, student records etc. **3** a hospital doctor between the grades of houseman and consultant. **4** a court official with administrative and judicial functions. **registrarship** *n.* **registration** *n.* **1** the act of registering. **2** the state of being registered. **3** an entry in a register. **4** a group of people all registered at a single time. **registration document** *n.* a document which shows the official details of a motor vehicle. **registration mark, registration number** *n.* a combination of letters and numbers corresponding to a place and (time of) year of registration, displayed by and identifying every motor vehicle. **registry** *n.* (*pl.* **registries**) **1** an office or other place where a register is kept. **2** registration. **registry office** *n.* a register office.

re- (+ gl–gr words) reglaze *v.t.* to glaze again. **regorge** *v.t.* **1** to disgorge, to vomit up. **2** to swallow back again. *~v.i.* to gush or flow back (from a river etc.). **regrade** *v.t.* to grade again or differently. **regroup** *v.t., v.i.* to group again. **regroupment** *n.* **regrow** *v.t., v.i.* (*past* **regrew,** *p.p.* **regrown**) to grow again. **regrowth** *n.*

regnal (reg´nəl) *a.* of or relating to a reign. **regnal year** *n.* the year of a reign dating from the sovereign's accession (used in dating some documents). **regnant** *a.* **1** reigning, ruling, exercising regal authority (*often following its noun* as queen regnant). **2** predominant, prevalent. **regnancy** *n.*

rego (rej´ō) *n.* (*Austral., sl.*) motor vehicle registration.

regression (rigresh´ən) *n.* **1** a backward movement, a return. **2** reversion to type. **3** (*Psych.*) return to an earlier stage of development or a form of behaviour characteristic of this. **4** the statistical analysis between dependent and independent variables. **regress**¹ (rigres´) *v.i.* (*esp. Psych.*) to move back, to return, esp. to a former state, condition or mode of behaviour. *~v.t.* to cause psychological regression in. **regress**² (rē´gres) *n.* **1** passage back, return, regression. **2** the act of reasoning backwards from effect to cause. **regressive** (ri-) *a.* **1** regressing or characterized by regression. **2** (of a tax) decreasing in rate as the amount to be taxed increases. **regressively** *adv.* **regressiveness, regressivity** (rēgresiv´iti) *n.*

regret (rigret´) *n.* **1** distress or sorrow for a disappointment, loss or want. **2** grief, repentance or remorse for a wrongdoing, fault or omission. **3** (*pl.*) an expression of sorrow or disappointment, esp. in declining an invitation. *~v.t.* (*pres.p.* **regretting,** *past, p.p.* **regretted**) **1** to be distressed or sorry for (a disappointment, loss etc.). **2** to regard (a fact, action etc.) with sorrow or remorse. **regretful** *a.* feeling regret, esp. sorry for past action. **regretfully** *adv.* **regretfulness** *n.*

regrettable *a.* to be regretted, unwelcome, undesirable. **regrettably** *adv.*

Usage note *Regretfully* should not be used to express general regret (as a sentence adverb) instead of *regrettably*.

Regt *abbr.* Regiment.
regular (reg´ūlə) *a.* **1** conforming to or governed by rule, law, type or principle. **2** systematic, methodical, consistent. **3** acting, done or happening in an orderly, uniform, constant or habitual manner; not casual, fortuitous or capricious. **4** symmetrical, unvarying, harmonious, normal. **5** conforming to custom, etiquette etc.; not infringing conventions. **6** duly authorized, properly qualified. **7** (*Geom.*) (of a geometrical figure) having the sides and angles equal. **8** (*Gram.*) conforming to the normal type of inflection. **9** belonging to the permanent standing army. **10** (*coll.*) belonging to a religious or monastic order. **11** complete, thorough, out-and-out, unmistakable. **12** (*N Am., Can.*) popular, likeable. **13** defecating or menstruating at uniform or normal intervals. ~*n.* **1** a soldier belonging to a permanent army. **2** (*coll.*) a person permanently employed or constantly attending (as a customer etc.). **3** a member of the regular clergy. **regularity** (-lar´-) *n.* **regularize, regularise** *v.t.* **regularization** (-zā´shən) *n.* **regularly** *adv.*

Usage note Pronunciation of *regularly* as (reg´ūli) is best avoided.

regulate (reg´ūlāt) *v.t.* **1** to adjust, control or order by rule. **2** to subject to restrictions. **3** to adjust to requirements, to put or keep in good order. **regulable** (-ləbəl) *a.* **regulation** (-lā´shən) *n.* **1** the act of regulating. **2** the state of being regulated. **3** a prescribed rule, order or direction. ~*a.* **1** prescribed by regulation. **2** formal, normal, accepted. **3** (*coll.*) ordinary, usual. **regulative** (-lət-), **regulatory** *a.* **regulator** (reg´ūlātə) *n.*
regulo (reg´ūlō) *n.* the temperature of a gas oven, expressed as a particular number.
regurgitate (rigœ´jitāt) *v.t.* **1** to bring back (partially digested food) into the mouth after swallowing. **2** to throw or pour back again. ~*v.i.* to gush or be poured back. **regurgitation** (-ā´shən) *n.*
re- (+ h– words) rehandle *v.t.* to handle or deal with again. **rehang** *v.t.* (*past, p.p.* **rehung**) to hang again (e.g. curtains). **rehash**[1] *v.t.* **1** to work over again. **2** to remodel, esp. in a perfunctory or ineffective manner. **rehash**[2] (rē´-) *n.* something presented under a new form. **rehear** *v.t.* (*past, p.p.* **reheard**) **1** to hear a second time. **2** to try over again in a law court. **reheat**[1] (-hēt´) *v.t.* **1** to heat again. **2** to inject fuel into (a jet aircraft's exhaust gases) to produce more thrust. **reheat**[2] (rē´-) *n.* the process by which thrust is produced in an aircraft by the ignition fuel added to exhaust gases. **reheater** *n.* **reheel** *v.t.* to heel (a shoe etc.) again. **rehire** *v.t.* to hire again (usu. after

dismissal). **rehome** *v.t.* to find a new home for.
rehouse *v.t.* to house anew. **rehydrate** *v.t.* **1** to add water to (esp. dehydrated food). **2** to restore fluid lost by dehydration to (a person). ~*v.i.* to take up water or other fluid after dehydration. **rehydratable** *a.* **rehydration** *n.*
rehab (rē´hab) *n.* (*coll.*) rehabilitation.
rehabilitate (rēhəbil´itāt) *v.t.* **1** to make fit after disablement, illness, imprisonment etc. for making a living or playing a part in the life of society. **2** to restore to a former rank, position, office or privilege, to reinstate. **3** to re-establish the character or reputation of. **rehabilitation** (-ā´shən) *n.* **rehabilitative** (-ətiv) *a.*
rehearse (rihœs´) *v.t.* **1** to recite or practise (a play, musical performance, part etc.) before public performance. **2** to train for a public performance by rehearsal. **3** to repeat, to recite. **4** to relate, to recount, to enumerate. ~*v.i.* to take part in a rehearsal. **rehearsal** *n.* **1** the act of rehearsing. **2** a preparatory performance of a play etc. **rehearser** *n.*
rehoboam (rēəbō´əm) *n.* a wine bottle, especially a champagne bottle, which holds six times the amount of a standard bottle, approximately 156 fl. oz. (about 4.6 l).
re- (+ i– words) reignite *v.t.* to ignite again.
reimport[1] (rēimpawt´) *v.t.* **1** to import again after exportation. **2** to import (goods made from exported raw materials). **reimport**[2] (rēim´pawt) *n.* **1** the act of reimporting. **2** something reimported. **reimportation** *n.* **reimpose** *v.t.* to impose again. **reimposition** *n.* **reincarnate** *v.t.* **1** to incarnate anew. **2** to cause to be born again. ~*a.* born again in a new body. **reincarnation** *n.* **1** the rebirth of the soul in a new body after death. **2** the embodiment of a concept, idea etc. in a new form. **reincorporate** *v.t.* to incorporate again. **reincorporation** *n.* **reindustrialize, reindustrialise** *v.t.* to redevelop the industry of. **reindustrialization** *n.* **reinfect** *v.t.* to infect again. **reinfection** *n.* **reinsert** *v.t.* to insert again. **reinsertion** *n.* **reinstate** *v.t.* **1** to restore, to replace (in a former position, state etc.). **2** to restore to a former rank, status etc. **reinstatement, reinstation** *n.* **reinsure** *v.t.* to insure against insurance risks. **reinsurance** *n.* **reinsurer** *n.* **reintegrate** *v.t.* **1** to integrate again (as into society). **2** to redintegrate. **reintegration** *n.* **reinter** *v.t.* to inter or bury again. **reinterment** *n.* **reinterpret** *v.t.* to interpret again or differently. **reinterpretation** *n.* **reintroduce** *v.t.* to introduce or bring back into. **reintroduction** *n.* **reinvent** *v.t.* **1** to invent again. **2** to produce or create again or in a new or different form. **reinvest** *v.t.* to invest again. **reinvestment** *n.* **reinvigorate** *v.t.* **1** to reanimate. **2** to give fresh vigour to. **reinvigoration** *n.* **reissue** *v.t., v.i.* (*pres.p.* **reissuing**, *past, p.p.* **reissued**) to issue again. ~*n.* a second issue.
Reich (rīkh) *n.* the German realm considered as an empire made up of subsidiary states.
reify (rē´ifī) *v.t.* (*3rd pers. sing. pres.* **reifies**, *pres.p.*

reifying, *past*, *p.p.* reified) to make (an abstract idea) concrete, to treat as real. **reification** (-fikā´shən) *n.* **reificatory** *a.*

reign (rān) *n.* **1** the period during which a sovereign reigns. **2** a period during which a person or thing is predominant or prevalent. **3** supreme power, sovereignty, dominion. **4** rule, sway, control, influence. ~*v.i.* **1** to exercise sovereign authority, to be a king or queen. **2** to predominate, to prevail. **reigning** *a.* currently holding the title as most recent winner of a contest etc.

reimburse (rēimbœs´) *v.t.* **1** to repay (a person who has spent money). **2** to refund (expenses etc.). **reimbursable** *a.* **reimbursement** *n.*

rein (rān) *n.* (*often pl.*) **1** a long narrow strip, usu. of leather, attached at each end to a bit for guiding and controlling a horse or other animal in riding or driving. **2** a similar device for controlling a young child. **3** a means of restraint or control. ~*v.t.* **1** to check, to control, to manage with reins. **2** to pull (in, up or back) with reins. **3** to govern, to curb, to restrain. **to draw rein 1** to stop one's horse, to pull up. **2** to abandon an effort, enterprise etc. **to give (free) rein to** to leave unrestrained, to allow to proceed without check. **to keep on a tight rein** to control carefully. **reinless** *a.*

reindeer (rān´diə) *n.* a deer, *Rangifer tarandus,* now inhabiting the subarctic parts of the northern hemisphere, domesticated for the sake of its milk and as a draught animal. **reindeer lichen, reindeer moss** *n.* a lichen, *Cladonia rangiferina,* which forms the winter food of the reindeer.

reinforce (rēinfaws´) *v.t.* to add new strength, support or emphasis to. **reinforceable** *a.* **reinforced concrete** *n.* concrete given great tensile strength by the incorporation of rods, wires etc. of iron or steel; ferroconcrete. **reinforcement** *n.* **1** the act of reinforcing. **2** the state of being reinforced. **3** anything that reinforces. **4** (*usu. in pl.*) additional troops, ships etc. **reinforcer** *n.*

reiterate (rēit´ərāt) *v.t.* to repeat again and again. **reiteratedly** *adv.* **reiteration** (-ā´shən) *n.* **reiterative** (-ətiv) *a., n.*

re- (+ j–k words) rejig (rējig´) *v.t.* (*pres.p.* **rejigging,** *past, p.p.* **rejigged**) **1** to re-equip (e.g. a factory). **2** to rearrange or adjust, sometimes in an unethical way. **rejoin**[1] *v.t.* **1** to join again. **2** to join together again, to reunite after separation. ~*v.i.* to come together again. **rekey** *v.t.* (*Comput.*) to retype, esp. to re-enter (data) using a computer keyboard. **rekindle** *v.t.* to kindle again. ~*v.i.* to ignite again.

reject[1] (rijekt´) *v.t.* **1** to put aside, to discard, to cast off. **2** to refuse to accept, receive, grant etc., to deny (a request etc.). **3** (*Med.*) to fail to accept (an implanted organ, tissue graft etc.) because of immunological incompatibilities. **4** to rebuff (a person). **5** to repel, to cast up again, to vomit. **rejectable** *a.* **rejecter, rejector** *n.* **rejection** (-jek´-

shən) *n.* **rejectionist** *n.* a person who refuses to accept a peace treaty, policy etc. **rejective** *a.*

reject[2] (rē´jekt) *n.* **1** someone or something which has been rejected. **2** something which is substandard and offered for sale at discount.

rejoice (rijois´) *v.i.* **1** to feel joy or gladness in a high degree. **2** to be glad (that or to). **3** to delight or exult (in). **4** to express joy or gladness, to celebrate, to make merry. ~*v.t.* to make joyful, to gladden. **to rejoice in 1** to be glad because of. **2** to be fortunate to have (*He rejoices in the name of Rufus T. Firefly*). **rejoicer** *n.* **rejoicing** *n.* **1** joyfulness. **2** (*often pl.*) the expression of joyfulness, making merry, celebrating a joyful event. **rejoicingly** *adv.*

rejoin[1] RE- (+ J–K WORDS).

rejoin[2] (rijoin´) *v.t.* to answer to a reply, to retort. ~*v.i.* (*Law*) to answer to a charge or pleading, esp. as the defendant to the plaintiff's replication. **rejoinder** (-də) *n.* **1** an answer to a reply, a retort. **2** (*Law*) the answer of a defendant to the plaintiff's replication.

rejuvenate (rijoo´vənāt) *v.t.* **1** to make young again. **2** to restore to vitality or a previous condition. **rejuvenation** (-ā´shən) *n.* **rejuvenator** *n.* **rejuvenesce** (-nes´) *v.i.* **1** to grow young again. **2** (*Biol.*) (of cells) to acquire fresh vitality. ~*v.t.* to give fresh vitality to. **rejuvenescence** *n.* **rejuvenescent** *a.*

re- (+ la–le words) relabel *v.t.* (*pres.p.* **relabelling,** (*N Am.*) **relabeling,** *past, p.p.* **relabelled,** (*N Am.*) **relabeled**) to label again. **relaunch**[1] (-lawnch´) *v.t.* **1** to launch again. **2** to reintroduce (a product) on to the market, usu. with some modifications. **relaunch**[2] (rē´-) *n.* **1** the act of relaunching. **2** something relaunched. **relay**[1] (rēlā´) *v.t.* (*past, p.p.* **relaid**) to lay again. **relearn** *v.t.* (*past, p.p.* **relearned, relearnt**) to learn again. **relet** *v.t.* (*pres.p.* **reletting,** *past, p.p.* **relet**) to let again.

relapse (rilaps´) *v.i.* to fall or slip back (into a former bad state, condition or practice). **2** to become ill again after partial recovery. ~*n.* a falling or sliding back into a former bad state, esp. in a patient's state of health after partial recovery. **relapser** *n.* **relapsing fever** *n.* an epidemic infectious disease characterized by frequent attacks of fever, caused by spirochaetes of the genus *Borrelia.*

relate (rilāt´) *v.t.* **1** to tell, to narrate, to recount. **2** to bring into relation or connection (with). **3** to ascribe to as source or cause, to show a relation (to). ~*v.i.* **1** to have relation or regard (to). **2** to refer (to). **3** to get on well with. **relatable** *a.* **related** *a.* **1** connected. **2** connected or allied by blood or marriage. **relatedness** *n.* **relater** *n.*

relation (rilā´shən) *n.* **1** the condition of being related or connected. **2** the way in which a thing or person stands or is conceived in regard to another, as dependence, independence, similarity, difference, correspondence, contrast etc. **3** connection by blood or marriage, kinship. **4** a person so connected, a relative, a kinsman or kinswoman. **5** respect, reference. **6** (*pl.*) dealings, affairs with. **7** (*pl.*, *euphem.*) sexual intercourse. **8** the act of relating. **9** a narrative, an account, a story. **relational** *a.* **1** of, characterized by or indicating relation. **2** having kinship. **relational database** *n.* (*Comput.*) a database structured so that related items of data are recognized as such and can be accessed together. **relationally** *adv.* **relationship** *n.* **1** the state of being related. **2** connection by blood etc., kinship. **3** mutual connection between people or things. **4** an emotional or sexual affair.

relative (rel'ətiv) *a.* **1** not absolute but depending on relation to something else. **2** considered or being in relation to something else, correlative. **3** resulting from relation, proportionate to something else, comparative. **4 a** having reference, relating (to). **b** relevant, pertinent, closely related (to). **5** having mutual relation, corresponding, related. **6** (*Gram.*) referring or relating to another word, sentence or clause (the antecedent). **7** (*Mus.*) having the same key signature. ~*n.* **1** a person connected by blood or marriage, a kinsman or kinswoman, a relation. **2** an animal or plant related to another by common origin. **3** a relative word, esp. a pronoun. **4** something relating to or considered in relation to another thing, a relative term. **relatival** (-tī'vəl) *a.* **relative atomic mass** *n.* the ratio of the average mass of one atom of an element to one-twelfth of the mass of an atom of carbon-12. **relative density** *n.* (*Chem.*) the ratio of density of a substance to the density of a standard substance under the same, or specified, conditions. **relative humidity** *n.* the amount of water vapour present in the air expressed as a percentage of the amount that would be present in the same volume of saturated air at the same temperature. **relatively** *adv.* **relative molecular mass** *n.* the ratio of the average mass of one molecule of an element or compound to one-twelfth of the mass of an atom of carbon-12. **relativeness** *n.* **relativism** *n.* **1** the doctrine that ethical truths, moral principles etc. are not absolute but may vary between individuals and cultures. **2** the doctrine that knowledge is not absolute but relative to the thinking mind; relativity of knowledge. **relativist** *n.* **relativistic** (-vis'-) *a.* **1** (*Physics*) of, concerned with or described by the theory of relativity. **2** of or relating to relativism. **relativity** (-tiv'-) *n.* **1** the fact or condition of being relative, relativeness. **2** (*Physics*) (*also* **relativity theory**) either of two theories enunciated by Albert Einstein founded on the postulates that motion is relative and that the velocity of light is constant, and developing the Newtonian concept of space, time, motion and gravitation.

relator (rilā'tə) *n.* **1** (*Law*) an informer, a complainant, esp. one who institutes proceedings by way of a relation or information to the Attorney-General. **2** a relater, a narrator.

relax (rilaks') *v.i.* **1** to become less tense, rigid, stern or severe. **2** to take relaxation. **3** to become less energetic, to diminish. **4** to become less formal or inhibited. ~*v.t.* **1** to allow to become less tense or rigid. **2** to slacken, to loosen. **3** to lessen the force or intensity of. **4** to make less strict or severe. **5** to relieve from strain, effort or nervous tension. **relaxable** *a.* **relaxant** *a.* relaxing. ~*n.* a medicine etc. that relaxes. **relaxation** (rēlaksā'shən) *n.* **1** the act of relaxing. **2** the state of being relaxed. **3** cessation from work, indulgence in recreation, amusement. **4** a diminution of tension, severity, application or attention. **5** remission of a penalty etc. **6** (*Physics*) a return to equilibrium. **relaxed** *a.* informal. **relaxedly** (-sid-) *adv.* **relaxedness** *n.* **relaxer** *n.* **relaxing** *a.* producing or conducive to relaxation.

relay¹ RE- (+ LA–LE WORDS).

relay² (rē'lā) *n.* **1** a supply of fresh horses, workers, hounds etc. to relieve others when tired. **2** a supply of materials, people etc. to be ready when required. **3** a relay race. **4** a contrivance for receiving, reinforcing and retransmitting radio, television etc. signals. **5** an electrical control device that responds to variations in the current, voltage etc. of a circuit by activating switches and other devices in the same or a different circuit. **6** a message etc. that is relayed. **relay race** *n.* a race between teams, each member of which covers a certain distance.

relay³ (rē'lā, rilā') *v.t.* **1** to spread (information etc.) by relays. **2 a** to receive and transmit by a relay. **b** to broadcast (a signal or programme) from a particular place. **3** to arrange in or provide with relays.

release (rilēs') *v.t.* **1** to set free from restraint or confinement, to liberate. **2** to free from obligation or penalty. **3** to deliver from pain, care, trouble, grief or other evil. **4** to move from a fixed position. **5** to allow to pass from a place of origin or storage, to emit. **6** to issue (a recording, film etc.) for general sale, exhibition etc. **7** to make (information, news etc.) public. **8** (*Law*) to surrender, to quit, to remit (a right, debt, claim etc.). ~*n.* **1** liberation from restraint, confinement, pain, care, obligation or penalty. **2** a discharge from liability, responsibility etc. **3** the act of releasing or issuing a recording, film etc. **4** anything newly issued for sale or to the public. **5** a news item available for publication or broadcasting. **6** a handle, catch or other device by which a piece of mechanism is released. **7** (*Law*) **a** surrender or conveyance of property or right to another. **b** the instrument by which this is carried out. **releasable** *a.* **releasee** (-sē') *n.* a person to whom property is released. **releaser** *n.* **releasor** *n.* (*Law*) a person releasing property or a claim to another.

relegate (rel'igāt) *v.t.* **1** to consign or dismiss (to some inferior position etc.). **2** to demote (e.g. a football team) to a lower division. **3** (*formal*) to refer, commit, or hand over (to). **4** (*formal*) to assign to a category or class. **5** to send away, to banish. **relegable** *a.* **relegation** (-gā´shən) *n.*

❎ **releive** common misspelling of RELIEVE.

relent (rilent´) *v.i.* **1** to give way to compassion, to yield. **2** to become less harsh, severe or obdurate. **relentless** (-lis) *a.* **1** merciless, pitiless. **2** sustained, incessant, unremitting. **relentlessly** *adv.* **relentlessness** *n.*

relevant (rel´əvənt) *a.* pertinent, applicable, bearing on the matter in hand, apposite. **relevance, relevancy** *n.* **relevantly** *adv.*

re- (**+ li–lo words**) **relight** *v.t.* (*past, p.p.* **relighted, relit**) to light, kindle or illumine afresh. ~*v.i.* to ignite again. **reline** *v.t.* to line again, to give a new lining to. **relive** *v.t.* to live over again, esp. in the imagination. **reload** *v.t.* to load again. ~*v.i.* to load a firearm again. **relocate** *v.t.* to move (e.g. a factory, workers, business) to a new location. ~*v.i.* to move to a new place or area, esp. for employment or business reasons. **relocation** *n.*

reliable, reliance etc. RELY.

relic (rel´ik), **†relique** (rəlēk´, rel´ik) *n.* **1** any ancient object of historical interest. **2** something remaining or kept in remembrance of a person, esp. a part of the body or other object religiously cherished from its having belonged to some saint. **3** a custom etc. that has survived from the past. **4** a keepsake, a souvenir, a memento. **5** (*usu. pl.*) some part or thing remaining after the loss or decay of the rest, a remnant, a fragment, a scrap, a survival, a trace. **6** (*pl.*) a dead body, a corpse, remains.

relict (rel´ikt) *n.* **1** a plant or animal existing as a remnant of a formerly widely distributed group in a previous geological era. **2** a geological or geographical feature, such as a mountain, which is a remnant of an earlier formation.

relief[1] (rilēf´) *n.* **1** alleviation of pain, grief, discomfort etc. **2** the feeling of comfort or cheerfulness that follows the removal of pain, distress etc. **3** anything that breaks monotony or relaxes tension. **4** assistance given to people in poverty, need or distress. **5** release from a post or duty by a person or persons acting as substitute. **6** such a substitute. **7** a supplementary vehicle for transporting passengers at peak times. **8** assistance in time of stress or danger, the raising of the siege of a besieged town. **9** an army or detachment carrying this out. **10** (*Law*) redress of a grievance etc., esp. by legal remedy or compensation. **on relief** (*esp. N Am.*) in receipt of government financial assistance. **relief road** *n.* a road taking traffic round a congested urban area.

relief[2] (rilēf´) *n.* **1** the projecting of carved or moulded figures or designs from a surface in approximate proportion to the objects represented. **2** a piece of sculpture, moulding etc. with the figures etc. projecting. **3** apparent projection of forms and figures due to drawing, colouring and shading. **4** distinctness of contour, clearness, vividness. **relief map** *n.* **1** a map in

which hills and valleys are indicated by shading, hachures, contour lines etc. **2** a three-dimensional map in which hills and valleys are shown by prominences and depressions, usu. in exaggerated proportion, instead of contour lines.

relieve (rilēv´) *v.t.* **1** to alleviate, to mitigate, to relax, to lighten. **2** to free wholly or partially from pain, grief, discomfort etc. **3** to provide aid or assistance to. **4** to release from a post, duty, responsibility etc., esp. to take turn on guard or at a post. **5** to remove a burden or responsibility from. **6** to break or mitigate the monotony, dullness etc. of. **7** to raise the siege of. **8** (*coll.*) to take or steal from, to deprive (one of). **9** to give relief or prominence to, to bring out or make conspicuous by contrast. **relievable** *a.* **relieved** *a.* experiencing relief, esp. from worry or emotion. **relievedly** (-vid-) *adv.* **reliever** *n.*

relievo (relē´vō), **rilievo** *n.* (*pl.* **relievi** (-vē), **rilievi**) raised or embossed work, relief.

religion (rilij´ən) *n.* **1** belief in a superhuman being or beings, esp. a personal god, controlling the universe and entitled to worship and obedience. **2** the feelings, effects on conduct and the practices resulting from such belief. **3** a system of faith, doctrine and worship. **4** the monastic state, the state of being bound by religious vows. **5** anything of great personal importance. **religionism** *n.* excessive or exaggerated religious zeal. **religionist** *n.*, *a.* **religionless** *a.* **religiose** (-iōs) *a.* **1** morbidly affected with religious emotion. **2** pious, sanctimonious. **religiosely** *adv.* **religiosity** (-ios´-) *n.* religious sentimentality or emotionalism. **religious** *a.* **1** of, relating to or concerned with religion. **2** imbued with religion, pious, devout. **3** bound by vows to a monastic life, belonging to a monastic order. **4** conscientious, rigid, strict. ~*n.* (*pl.* **religious**) a person bound by monastic vows. **religiously** *adv.* **religiousness** *n.*

relinquish (riling´kwish) *v.t.* **1** to give up a claim to, to surrender. **2** to forsake, to abandon, to resign. **3** to let go of. **relinquisher** *n.* **relinquishment** *n.*

reliquary (rel´ikwəri), **reliquaire** (relikweə´) *n.* (*pl.* **reliquaries, reliquaires**) a depository for relics, a casket for keeping a relic or relics in.

relish (rel´ish) *n.* **1** great enjoyment, gusto, appetite, zest, fondness, liking. **2** pleasing anticipation. **3** something taken with food to give a flavour, a condiment. **4** the effect of anything on the palate, taste, distinctive flavour, esp. a pleasing taste or flavour. **5** a pleasing quality. **6** a slight admixture or flavouring, a smack, a trace (of). ~*v.t.* **1** to be gratified by, to enjoy. **2** to look forward to with pleasure. **3** to give agreeable flavour to, to make piquant etc. **relishable** *a.*

reluctant (rilŭk´tənt) *a.* unwilling, averse, disinclined (to). **reluctance, †reluctancy** *n.* **reluctantly** *adv.*

rely (rilī´) *v.i.* (*3rd pers. sing. pres.* **relies**, *pres.p.* **relying**, *past, p.p.* **relied**) **1** to trust or depend (on or upon) with confidence. **2** to be dependent (on). **reliable** *a.* **1** that may be relied on. **2** trustworthy. **reliability** (-bil´-), **reliableness** *n.* **reliably** *adv.* **reliance** *n.* **1** confident dependence (on or upon), trust. **2** a ground of confidence, that on which one relies. **reliant** *a.* **reliantly** *adv.*

REM (rem) *abbr.* rapid eye-movement.

rem (rem) *n.* (*pl.* **rems**) a unit of radiation dosage which has the same biological effect as one roentgen of X-ray or gamma radiation.

re- (+ ma–mi words) remake[1] (rēmāk´) *v.t.* (*past, p.p.* **remade**) to make again or anew. **remake**[2] (rē´māk) *n.* **1** anything made again from the original materials. **2** a new version of an old film, record etc. **reman** *v.t.* (*pres.p.* **remanning**, *past, p.p.* **remanned**) **1** to man (a ship, gun etc.) again. **2** to equip with a new complement of men. **remarry** *v.t., v.i.* (*3rd pers. sing. pres.* **remarries**, *pres.p.* **remarrying**, *past, p.p.* **remarried**) to marry again. **remarriage** *n.* **remaster** *v.t.* to make a new master recording from (an older or original recording to improve the sound quality). **rematch** (rē´-) *n.* a second or return match or game. **remeasure** *v.t.* to measure again. **remeasurement** *n.* **remix**[1] *v.t.* **1** to mix again. **2** to change the balance of (a sound recording). **remix**[2] (rē´-) *n.* a remixed version of a sound recording. **remixer** *n.*

remain (rimān´) *v.i.* **1** to stay behind or be left after use, separation, destruction etc. **2** to continue in a place or state. **3** to last, to abide, to continue, to endure. **4** to continue to be. **5** to be still to be done or dealt with. **remainder** (-də) *n.* **1** anything left over after a part has been taken away, used etc.; the rest, the residue. **2** the quantity left over after subtraction, the excess remaining after division. **3** the copies of a book left unsold after the initial demand for it has ceased, offered at a reduced price. **4** (*Law*) an interest in an estate limited to take effect and be enjoyed after a prior estate is determined. ~*v.t.* to offer (unsold copies of a book) at a reduced price. **remains** *n.pl.* **1** that which remains behind. **2** ruins, relics. **3** a dead body, a corpse. **4** literary productions published after one's death.

remand (rimahnd´) *v.t.* to recommit to custody after a partial hearing. ~*n.* **1** the act of remanding. **2** the state of being remanded. **to be on remand** to be in custody awaiting trial. **remand centre** *n.* a place of detention for people awaiting trial.

remanent (rem´ənənt) *a.* remaining, left behind, surviving. **remanence** *n.*

remark (rimahk´) *v.t.* **1** to utter by way of comment, to comment (that). **2** to take notice of, to observe with particular attention, to perceive. ~*v.i.* to make a comment or observation (on). ~*n.* **1** an observation, a comment. **2** the act of noticing, observation. **3** (*usu. pl., coll.*) anything said, conversation.

remarkable (rimah´kəbəl) *a.* **1** worthy of special observation or notice, notable. **2** unusual, extra-

ordinary, striking. **remarkableness** *n.* **remarkably** *adv.*

remedy (rem´ədi) *n.* (*pl.* **remedies**) **1** something which cures a disease. **2** medicine, healing treatment. **3** something which serves to remove, counteract or repair any evil. **4** redress, reparation. **5** the tolerated variation in the standard weight of coins. ~*v.t.* (*3rd pers. sing. pres.* **remedies**, *pres.p.* **remedying**, *past, p.p.* **remedied**) **1** to cure, to heal. **2** to repair, to rectify, to redress. **remediable** (rimē´-) *a.* **remedial** (rimē´-) *a.* **1** affording or intended as a remedy. **2** of or relating to the teaching of slow learners and people with special needs. **remedially** *adv.*

remember (rimem´bə) *v.t.* **1** to bear or keep in mind, not to forget. **2** to recall to mind, to recollect. **3** to hold in the memory, to know by heart. **4** to keep in mind with gratitude, reverence, respect etc. **5** to commemorate (e.g. the dead). **6** (*coll.*) to convey a greeting from (*remember me to your father*). **7** to be good to, to make a present to, to tip. ~*v.i.* **1** to have the power of memory, to exercise the memory. **2** to have a remembrance or recollection. **rememberer** *n.* **remembrance** (-brəns) *n.* **1 a** the act of remembering. **b** memory. **2** the state of being remembered. **3** a recollection, a memory. **4** a keepsake, a memento, a memorial. **5** (*pl.*) regards, greetings.

remind (rimīnd´) *v.t.* **1** to put in mind (of). **2** to cause to remember (to do etc.). **reminder** *n.* **1** someone who or something which reminds. **2** a memento. **remindful** *a.* serving to remind.

reminiscence (reminis´əns) *n.* **1** the act or power of remembering or recalling past knowledge. **2** a past event, experience etc. which is remembered. **3** an account of or the narration of this. **4** (*pl.*) a collection of personal recollections of past events etc. **5** something reminding or suggestive (of something else). **reminisce** *v.i.* to talk, think or write about past experiences. **reminiscent** *a.* **1** reminding or suggestive (of). **2** of the nature of or relating to reminiscence. **3** recalling or given to recalling past events. **reminiscently** *adv.* **reminiscer** *n.*

remiss (rimis´) *a.* **1** careless or lax in the performance of duty or business, heedless, negligent. **2** slow, slack, languid. **remissly** *adv.* **remissness** *n.*

remission (rimish´ən) *n.* **1** the reduction of a prison sentence. **2** abatement (e.g. in the symptoms of a disease), diminution of force or intensity, reduction. **3** the remitting or discharge of a debt, penalty etc. **4** forgiveness, pardon. **remissible** (rimis´əbəl) *a.* that may be remitted. **remissive** (rimis´-), **remissory** *a.*

remit[1] (rimit´) *v.t.* (*pres.p.* **remitting**, *past, p.p.* **remitted**) **1** to transmit (cash, payment etc.), esp. by post. **2** to refrain from exacting etc., to forgo, to discharge from (a fine, penalty etc.). **3** to relax, to slacken, to mitigate, to desist from partially or entirely. **4** to refer or submit, to send back for consideration. **5** to refer (a case) to a lower court. **6** to defer, to put off. **7** to send or put back. **8** (*Theol.*) to pardon, to forgive. ~*v.i.* to become less intense, to abate. **remittable** *a.* **remittal** *n.* **remittance** *n.* **1** the act of remitting money or the like, in payment for goods etc. or as an allowance. **2** the sum so remitted. **remittee** (-ē´) *n.* **remittent** *a.* (of an illness or symptom) having alternate increase and decrease of intensity. **remittently** *adv.* **remitter** (rimit´ə) *n.*

remit[2] (rē´mit, rimit´) *n.* **1** the extent of responsibility, authority or concern of a person, committee etc. **2** something remitted, esp. a matter remitted for consideration.

remnant (rem´nənt) *n.* **1** that which is left after a larger part has been separated, used, lost or destroyed. **2** the last part of a piece of cloth etc., esp. a portion offered at a reduced price. **3** a scrap, a fragment, a surviving trace.

re- (+ mo– words) remodel *v.t.* (*pres.p.* **remodelling**, (*N Am.*) **remodeling**, *past, p.p.* **remodelled**, (*N Am.*) **remodeled**) **1** to model again. **2** to refashion. **remodify** *v.t.* (*3rd pers. sing. pres.* **remodifies**, *pres.p.* **remodifying**, *past, p.p.* **remodified**) to modify again. **remodification** *n.* **remonetize, remonetise** *v.t.* to reinstate (a metal etc.) as legal currency. **remonetization** *n.* **remortgage** *v.t.* to take out a second or further mortgage on (a property). ~*n.* a second or further mortgage. **remould**[1] (-mōld´), (*N Am.*) **remold** *v.t.* **1** to mould, fashion or shape anew. **2** to bond a new tread on to (a tyre). **remould**[2] (rē´-) *n.* a used tyre which has a new tread bonded into the casing and the walls coated with rubber. **remount**[1] (-mownt´) *v.t.* **1** to mount again. **2** to reascend. **3** to mount or set up (a gun, jewellery, a picture etc.) again. **4** to supply (a person, regiment etc.) with a fresh horse or horses. ~*v.i.* to mount a horse again. **remount**[2] (rē´-) *n.* a fresh horse for riding on.

remonstrance (rimon´strəns) *n.* **1** the act of remonstrating. **2** an expostulation, a protest. **remonstrant** *a., n.*

remonstrate (rem´ənstrāt) *v.i.* to make a protest, to argue or object forcibly. ~*v.t.* to say or state in protest or opposition. **remonstration** (-strā´shən) *n.* **remonstrative** (rimon´strətiv), **remonstratory** (rem´-) *a.* **remonstrator** *n.*

remontant (rimon´tənt) *a.* (esp. of a rose) blooming more than once in the season. ~*n.* a remontant rose.

remorse (rimaws´) *n.* **1** the pain caused by a sense of guilt, bitter regret or repentance. **2** compunction, reluctance to commit a wrong or to act cruelly. **remorseful** *a.* feeling remorse. **remorsefully** *adv.* **remorsefulness** *n.* **remorseless** *a.* **1** without compassion or compunction, cruel. **2** unrelenting. **remorselessly** *adv.* **remorselessness** *n.*

remote (rimōt´) *a.* **1** far off, distant in time or space. **2** out of the way, far away from a centre of population, isolated. **3** not closely connected or related. **4** removed in likeness or relation, separated, different. **5** (*usu. superl.*) slight, inconsiderable, least. **6** (of a person) aloof, cold. **remote control** *n.* **1** electronic or radio control of apparatus etc. from a distance. **2** a device allowing remote control (e.g. of a television set). **remote-controlled** *a.* **remotely** *adv.* **remoteness** *n.* **remote sensing** *n.* the scanning of the earth or another planet from space, esp. by satellites equipped with cameras, radar etc., in order to obtain data.

remove (rimoov´) *v.t.* **1** to move or take from a place or position. **2** to move to another place. **3** to take away, to get rid of. **4** to transfer to another post or office. **5** to dismiss. **6** (*euphem.*) to kill, to murder. **7** (*formal*) to act as the removers of or for. ~*v.i.* to go away (from), esp. to change one's place or abode. ~*n.* **1** a distance, a degree of separation. **2** a degree of difference or gradation. **3** a class or form (in some schools). **removable** *a.*, *n.* **removability** (-bil´-) *n.* **removal** *n.* **1** the act of removing or displacing. **2** change of place, site or abode. **3** the transfer of furniture etc. from one house etc. to another. **removed** *a.* **1** distant in space or time. **2** distant in condition, character, association or relationship. **3** separated by a specified number of intervals of descent. **remover** *n.* **1** someone who or something which removes. **2** (*often pl.*) a company whose business is to remove furniture from one house etc. to another.

remunerate (rimū´nərāt) *v.t.* **1** to reward, to recompense, to pay for a service etc. **2** to serve as recompense or equivalent for or to. **remuneration** (-ā´shən) *n.* **remunerative** (-ətiv) *a.*

re- (+ n– words) rename *v.t.* to name anew, to give a new name to. **renationalize, renationalise** *v.t.* to bring (a privatized industry) back under state control. **renationalization** *n.* **renegotiate** *v.t.* to negotiate again, esp. on different terms. **renegotiable** *a.* **renegotiation** *n.* **renominate** *v.t.* to nominate again. **renomination** *n.* **renumber** *v.t.* to number again.

Renaissance (rinā´səns) *n.* **1** the revival of art and letters in the 14th 16th cents. **2** the period of this. **3** the style of architecture, painting, literature and science that was developed under it. **4** (**renaissance**) any revival of a similar nature, a rebirth.

renal (rē´nəl) *a.* of or relating to the kidneys.

renascent (rinas´ənt, -nā´-) *a.* coming into being again, reborn, renewed. **renascence** *n.* **1** rebirth, renewal, a springing into fresh life. **2** the Renaissance.

rend (rend) *v.t.* (*past, p.p.* **rent** (rent) (*dated or poet.*) **1** to tear, pull or wrench (off, away, apart, asunder etc.). **2** to split or separate with violence. **3** to lacerate, to cause anguish to. **4** to pierce or disturb (the air, silence etc.), with sound. ~*v.i.* to be or become torn or pulled apart.

render (ren´də) *v.t.* **1** to make, to cause to be. **2** to bestow, to give, to pay, to furnish. **3** to pay or give back. **4** to present, to submit, to hand in. **5** to reproduce, to express, to represent, to interpret, to translate, to perform, to execute. **6** to boil down, to melt and clarify (fat). **7** to give the first coat of plaster to. **renderer** n. **rendering** n. **1** a performance, an execution, an interpretation (of a piece of music, a dramatic part etc.). **2** a translation, a version. **3** the first coat of plaster on brickwork etc. **rendition** n. **1** translation, interpretation. **2** execution, performance, rendering (of music etc.).

rendezvous (ron´dāvoo, rā´-) n. (pl. **rendezvous** (-vooz)) **1** a place agreed upon for meeting. **2** a meeting at an arranged place and time. **3** a place appointed for assembling, esp. of troops or warships. ~v.i. (3rd pers. sing. pres. **rendezvouses** (-vooz), pres.p. **rendezvousing** (-vooing), past, p.p. **rendezvoused** (-vood)) to meet or assemble at a rendezvous.

rendition RENDER.

renegade (ren´igād) n. **1** a deserter. **2** a turncoat. **3** a rebel, an outlaw. ~a. **1** having deserted or turned against a cause, faith etc., traitorous. **2** rebellious. ~v.i. to turn renegade.

renege (rināg´, -nēg´), **renegue** v.i. **1** to go back (on one's promise, commitments etc.). **2** to break one's word. **3** to fail to follow suit in cards, to revoke. ~v.t. to deny, to renounce. **reneger** n.

Usage note Pronunciation of renege with (-j-) instead of (-g-) is best avoided.

renew (rinū´) v.t. **1** to make new again or as good as new, to renovate. **2** to make fresh or vigorous again, to reanimate, to revivify, to regenerate. **3** to replace (something old or worn out) with new. **4** to replenish. **5** to get, make, do, say etc. over again, to recommence, to repeat. **6** to grant or be granted a further period of validity or effective-ness of (a lease, patent, mortgage, licence etc.). **renewable** a. **renewability** (-bil´-) n. **renewal** n. **renewer** n.

rennet (ren´it) n. **1** curdled milk containing rennin, obtained from the stomach of an unweaned calf etc. or an aqueous infusion of the stomach membrane of the calf, used to coagulate milk. **2** a similar preparation from seeds or other vegetable sources. **rennin** (-in) n. an enzyme occurring in the digestive juice of young calves or related mammals that causes coagulation of milk protein and is used in making cheese, junket etc.

renounce (rinowns´) v.t. **1** to surrender or give up (a claim, right etc.) esp. by formal declaration. **2** to declare against, to reject or cast off formally, to repudiate, to disclaim, to disown. **3** to forsake, to abandon, to give up, to withdraw from. ~v.i. **1** (Law) to decline or resign a right or trust. **2** in cards, to fail to follow suit through having none left of that suit. **renouncement** n. **renouncer** n.

renovate (ren´əvāt) v.t. **1** to restore to a state of soundness or good condition, to repair. **2** to

make new again. **renovation** (-ā´shən) n. **renovator** n.

renown (rinown´) n. exalted reputation, fame, celebrity. **renowned** a. famous, celebrated.

rent[1] (rent) n. **1** a sum of money payable periodically for the use of land, buildings etc. **2** payment for the use of any kind of property. **3** the return from cultivated land after production costs have been subtracted. ~v.t. **1** to occupy, hold in tenancy or use in return for rent. **2** to let for rent. **3** to impose rent upon. **4** (esp. N Am.) to hire. ~v.i. **1** to be let (at a certain rent). **2** to allow or obtain the use of property in return for rent. **for rent** available for use or tenancy on payment of a rent. **rent-a-** comb. form (often facet.) rented or hired, e.g. rent-a-crowd, rent-a-mob. **rentable** a. **rentability** (-bil´-) n. **rental** n. **1** an amount paid or received as rent. **2** the act of renting. **3** property available for rent. **rental library** n. (pl. **rental libraries**) (N Am.) a library that hires out books for a fee. **rent boy** n. a young male prostitute. **renter** n. **1** a tenant. **2** a person who lets property for rent. **3** a distributor of cinema films. **4** (sl.) a male prostitute. **rent-free** a. exempted from the payment of rent. ~adv. without payment of rent.

rent[2] (rent) n. **1** a tear, slit or breach, an opening made by or as if by rending or tearing asunder. **2** a cleft, a fissure, a chasm.

rent[3] REND.

rente (rāt) n. (pl. **rentes** (rāt)) annual income or revenue from capital investment. **rentier** (-tiā) n. a person drawing income from rentes or investments.

renunciation (rinŭnsiā´shən) n. **1** the act of renouncing. **2** a declaration or document ex-pressing this. **3** self-denial, self-sacrifice, self-resignation. **renunciant** n., a. **renunciative**, **re-nunciatory** (-nŭn´-) a.

re- (+ o— words) **reoccupy** v.t. (3rd pers. sing. pres. **reoccupies**, pres.p. **reoccupying**, past, p.p. **reoccupied**) to occupy again. **reoccupation** n. **reoccur** v.i. (pres.p. **reoccurring**, past, p.p. **re-occurred**) to occur again. **reoccurrence** n. **reoffend** v.i. to offend again, to commit a second offence. **reoffender** n. **reopen** v.t., v.i. to open again. **reorder** v.t. **1** to put in order again, to rearrange. **2** to order or command again. ~n. a repeat order for goods. **reorganize**, **reorganise** v.t. to order anew. **reorganization** n. **reorganizer** n. **reorient** v.t. **1** to orient again. **2** to change the outlook or attitude of or restore the normal outlook of. **reorientate** v.t. to reorient. **reorientation** n.

Rep abbr. **1** (N Am.) Representative. **2** (N Am.) Republican.

rep[1] (rep) n. (coll.) **1** repertory. **2** a repertory company or theatre.

rep[2] (rep) n. a representative, esp. a sales repre-sentative. ~v.i. (pres.p. **repping**, past, p.p. **repped**) to act or be employed as a sales representative.

rep[3] (rep), **repp** *n.* a textile fabric of wool, cotton or silk, with a finely-corded surface. **repped** *a.* having a surface like rep.

rep[4] (rep) *n.* (*NAm., sl.*) reputation.

re- (+ **pa–pl words**) **repack** *v.t.* to pack again. **repackage** *v.t.* to package again. **repackaging** *n.* **repaginate** *v.t.* to renumber the pages of. **repagination** *n.* **repaint**[1] (-pānt) *v.t., v.i.* to paint again. **repaint**[2] (rē´-) *n.* **1** an act of repainting. **2** something repainted, esp. a golf ball. **repaper** *v.t.* to paper (walls etc.) again. **repartition** *v.t.* to partition, to allot again. **repass** *v.t.* **1** to pass again. **2** to go past again. ~*v.i.* to pass again (into, through etc.). **repeople** *v.t.* to repopulate. **rephrase** *v.t.* to express in a different way, esp. so as to make clearer. **replan** *v.t.* (*pres.p.* **replanning**, *past, p.p.* **replanned**) to plan again or anew. **replant** *v.t.* **1** to plant (a tree etc.) again or in a new site. **2** to plant (ground) again. **replay**[1] (-plā´) *v.t.* to play again (a record, game etc.). **replay**[2] (rē´-) *n.* **1** a second game between two contestants. **2** the playing again of a recording or part of a broadcast match or game.

repair[1] (ripeə´) *v.t.* **1** to restore to a good or sound state after dilapidation or wear. **2** to make good the damaged or dilapidated parts of, to renovate, to mend. **3** to remedy, to set right, to make amends for. ~*n.* **1** restoration to a sound state. **2** a part that has been mended or repaired. **3** good or comparative condition. **repairable** *a.* **repairer** *n.* **repairman** *n.* (*pl.* **repairmen**) a person who repairs machinery, appliances etc.

Usage note See note under REPARATION.

repair[2] (ripeə´) *v.i.* to go, to betake oneself, to resort (to).

reparation (repərā´shən) *n.* **1** the act of making amends. **2** satisfaction for wrong or damage, amends, compensation. **3** (*usu. pl.*) compensation for war damage payable by a defeated nation. **4** the act of repairing or restoring. **5** the state of being repaired. **reparable** (rep´ərəbəl) *a.* capable of being made good, repaired or remedied. **reparative, reparatory** *a.*

Usage note The uses of the adjectives *reparable* and *repairable* overlap, but *reparable* is usual of abstract effects, and *repairable* of physical damage or wear.

repartee (repahtē´) *n.* **1** sharp, witty remarks or retorts or conversation consisting of these. **2** a smart or witty rejoinder. **3** skill in repartee, adroitness and wit in reply.

repast (ripahst´) *n.* (*formal*) **1** a meal. **2** food, victuals.

repat (rē´pat, -pat´) *n.* (*coll.*) **1** a repatriate. **2** repatriation.

repatriate (rēpat´riāt, -pā´-) *v.t.* to restore (someone) to their country. ~*v.i.* to return to one's country. ~*n.* a person who has been repatriated. **repatriation** (-ā´shən) *n.*

repay (ripā´) *v.t.* (*past, p.p.* **repaid** (-pād´)) **1** to pay back, to refund. **2** to return, to deal (a blow etc.) in retaliation or recompense. **3** to pay (a creditor etc.). **4** to make recompense for, to requite. ~*v.i.* to make a repayment or requital. **repayable** *a.* **repayment** *n.*

repeal (ripēl´) *v.t.* to revoke, to rescind, to annul (a law etc.). ~*n.* abrogation, revocation, annulment. **repealable** *a.* **repealist** *n.*

repeat (ripēt´) *v.t.* **1** to do, make or say over again. **2** to recite from memory, to rehearse. **3** to reproduce, to imitate. ~*v.i.* **1** to do something over again. **2** to recur, to happen again. **3** (of a watch etc.) to strike over again the last hour or quarter-hour struck. **4** (of food) to rise to the mouth, to be tasted again. **5** (of a firearm) to fire several shots without reloading. ~*n.* **1** the act of repeating, repetition. **2** something repeated. **3** a radio or television programme broadcast for the second time or more. **4 a** a supply of goods corresponding to the previous one. **b** the order for this. **5** (*Mus.*) **a** a passage to be repeated. **b** a sign indicating this. **to repeat itself** to recur in the same form or order. **to repeat oneself** to say or do the same thing over again. **repeatable** *a.* **repeatability** (-bil´-) *n.* **repeatedly** *adv.* **repeater** *n.* **1** someone who or something which repeats. **2** a repeating firearm. **3** a watch or clock striking the hours and parts of hours when required. **4** a repeating signal etc. **5** a device for transmitting or amplifying electrical signals. **repeating decimal** *n.* a recurring decimal.

repechage (rep´əshahzh) *n.* a heat, esp. in rowing or fencing, where contestants beaten in earlier rounds get another chance to qualify for the final.

repel (ripel´) *v.t.* (*pres.p.* **repelling**, *past, p.p.* **repelled**) **1** to drive or force back. **2** to repulse, to ward off, to keep at a distance. **3** to produce aversion or disgust in, to be repulsive or distasteful to. **4** to resist mixing with, absorbing or adherence of. **5** to tend to force away or apart. **repellent** *a.* **1** repelling or tending to repel. **2** repulsive. ~*n.* that which repels. **repellence, repellency** *n.* **repellently** *adv.* **repeller** *n.*

Usage note See note on *repellent* under REPULSE.

repent (ripent´) *v.i.* to feel sorrow, regret or pain for something done or left undone, esp. to feel such sorrow for sin as leads to amendment, to be penitent or contrite. ~*v.t.* **1** to feel contrition or remorse for, to regret. **2** to affect (oneself) with penitence. **repentance** *n.* **repentant** *a.* **repentantly, repentingly** *adv.* **repenter** *n.*

repercussion (rēpəkŭsh´ən) *n.* **1** an effect or consequence of an act, action or event, esp. one that is indirect and wide-ranging. **2** a recoil after impact. **3** an echo, a reverberation. **repercussive** *a.*

repertoire (rep´ətwah) *n.* **1** a stock of plays, musical pieces, songs etc., that a person, company etc. is ready to perform. **2** a stock or range of items, techniques, skills etc. available or regularly used.

repertory (rep'ətəri) *n.* (*pl.* **repertories**) **1** a repertoire. **2** the staging of several different plays in a season by one company. **3** a repertory company. **4** a repertory theatre. **5** a store, a collection, esp. of information, statistics etc. **repertory company** *n.* a theatrical company that presents a number of different plays, esp. at one theatre. **repertory theatre** *n.* a theatre with a permanent repertory company.

repetition (repitish'ən) *n.* **1** the act of repeating, reiteration. **2** recital from memory. **3** that which is repeated, a piece set to be learnt by heart. **4** a copy, a reproduction, a replica. **5** (*Mus.*) the ability of a musical instrument to repeat a note in rapid succession. **repetitional, repetitionary** *a.* **repetitious** (repitish'-) *a.* characterized by repetition, esp. when tedious or superfluous. **repetitiously** *adv.* **repetitiousness** *n.* **repetitive** (ripet'-) *a.* of, relating to or characterized by repetition. **repetitively** *adv.* **repetitiveness** *n.* **repetitive strain injury** *n.* (*Med.*) a condition in which the joints and tendons of usu. the hands become inflamed, typically as the result of repeated use of (usu. industrial) apparatus, machinery, computers etc.

Usage note The meanings of the adjectives *repetitious* and *repetitive* overlap, but *repetitious* suggests undesirable and tedious repetition, whereas *repetitive* can be neutral.

repine (ripīn') *v.i.* (*formal*) **1** to fret, to be discontented (at). **2** to complain, to grumble.

⊠ repitition common misspelling of REPETITION.

replace (riplās') *v.t.* **1** to put back again in place. **2** to take the place of, to succeed. **3** to be a substitute for. **4** to supersede, to displace. **5** to put a substitute in place of, to fill the place of (with or by). **6** to put in a fresh place. **replaceable** *a.* **replacement** *n.* **1** the act of replacing. **2** a person who or thing which replaces another. **replacer** *n.*

replenish (riplen'ish) *v.t.* **1** to fill up again. **2** to renew, to replace with new supplies. **3** to fill completely. **replenisher** *n.* **replenishment** *n.*

replete (riplēt') *a.* **1** abundantly supplied or stocked (with). **2** filled to excess, sated, gorged (with). **3** completely filled. **repletion** (-ē'shən), **repleteness** *n.*

replica (rep'likə) *n.* (*pl.* **replicas**) **1** a duplicate of a picture, sculpture etc. by the artist who executed the original. **2** an exact copy, a facsimile. **3** a copy on a smaller scale.

replicate¹ (rep'likāt) *v.t.* **1** to repeat (e.g. an experiment) exactly. **2** to reproduce, to make a replica of. **3** to fold back on itself. *~v.i.* to produce a replica of itself, to undergo biological replication. **replicable** (-kəbəl) *a.* **replicability** (-bil'-) *n.* **replication** (-kā'shən) *n.* **1** the act of replicating, repeating or reproducing. **2** a reproduction, a copy. **3** the production of an exact copy or a

duplicate of itself by a virus, cell structure or complex molecule, esp. DNA or RNA. **4** (*Law*) the reply of a plaintiff to the defendant's plea. **replicative** *a.*

replicate² (rep'likət) *a.* (*Bot.*) folded back on itself. *~n.* (*Mus.*) a tone one or more octaves above or below a given tone.

reply (riplī') *v.i.* (*3rd pers. sing. pres.* **replies**, *pres.p.* **replying**, *past, p.p.* **replied**) **1** to answer, to respond, to make answer orally, in writing, or by action. **2** (*Law*) to plead in answer to a defendant's plea. *~v.t.* **1** to return as in answer. **2** to answer (that etc.). *~n.* **1** the act of replying. **2** that which is said, written or done in answer, a response. **replier** *n.* **reply coupon** *n.* a coupon exchangeable in any country for stamps to be used on a letter or reply. **reply-paid** *a.* (of an envelope etc.) provided by and having the postage paid by the person requesting a reply.

re- (+ po–pu words) **repoint** *v.t.* to repair the joints of (brickwork etc.) with new cement or mortar. **repolish** *v.t.* to polish again. **repopulate** *v.t.* **1** to populate again. **2** to increase the population of. **repopulation** *n.* **reposition** *v.t.* to place in a new or different position. *~v.i.* to alter one's position. **repossess** *v.t.* **1** to possess again, to regain possession of. **2** to take back possession of (property and goods) for failure to make loan repayments. **repossession** *n.* **repot** *v.t.* (*pres.p.* **repotting**, *past, p.p.* **repotted**) to put (a plant) into a fresh pot. **re-present** *v.t.* to present again. **re-presentation** *n.* **reprice** *v.t.* to price again or anew. **reprint¹** (-print') *v.t.* to print (a book etc.) again. **reprint²** (rē'-) *n.* a new edition or impression of a printed work without much alteration of the contents. **reprocess** *v.t.* **1** to process again. **2** to treat (a substance or material) in order to make it reusable in a new form. **reprocessing** *n.*, *a.* **reprogram, reprogramme** *v.t.* (*pres.p.* **reprogramming**, *past, p.p.* **reprogrammed**) to program again or in a different way. **reprogrammable** *a.* **reproof¹** *v.t.* **1** to make waterproof again. **2** to make a fresh proof of. **republish** *v.t., v.i.* **1** to publish again. **2** to print a new edition (of). **republication** *n.* **repurchase** *v.t., v.i.* to purchase back or again. *~n.* **1** the act of buying again. **2** something which is bought again. **repurify** *v.t.* (*3rd pers. sing. pres.* **repurifies**, *pres.p.* **repurifying**, *past, p.p.* **repurified**) to purify again. **repurification** *n.*

report (ripawt') *v.t.* **1** to give an account of, to describe or to narrate, esp. as an eyewitness. **2** to bring back as an answer. **3** to state as a fact or as news. **4** to prepare a record of, esp. for official use or for publication. **5** to give information against. **6** (of a parliamentary committee etc.) to return (a bill) with conclusions and amendments. *~v.i.* **1** to make or tender a report. **2** to act as a reporter. **3** to present oneself (at a certain place etc.). **4** to be responsible (to an employer or supervisor). **5** to give an account of one's condition or opinion as specified (*to report sick*).

~n. **1** that which is reported, esp. the formal statement of the result of an investigation, trial etc. **2** a detailed account of a speech, meeting etc., esp. for publication in a newspaper. **3** common talk, popular rumour. **4** an account or statement of the merits of a person or thing. **5** an end-of-term statement of a pupil's work and behaviour at school. **6** a loud noise, esp. of an explosive kind. **7** fame, repute, accepted character. **to report back 1** to submit a report to the person, company etc. for whom one is acting. **2** to present oneself as having returned. **reportable** *a.* **reportage** (ripawt´ij, rɔpawtahj´) *n.* **1** the art of reporting news. **2** writing in a factual or journalistic style. **reported** *a.* **reportedly** *adv.* according to common talk or rumour. **reported speech** *n.* indirect speech. **reporter** *n.* **1** a person who gathers news etc. for a newspaper or broadcasting company. **2** a person who reports. **3** a person authorized to draw up official statements of law proceedings and decisions of legislative debates. **reportorial** (repawtaw´riəl) *a.* (*esp. N Am.*) of or relating to newspaper reporters. **reportorially** *adv.* **report stage** *n.* the stage of progress with a Bill in the House of Commons or House of Lords when a committee has reported.

reposal¹ REPOSE¹.

reposal² REPOSE².

repose¹ (ripōz´) *n.* **1** rest, cessation of activity, excitement, toil etc. **2** sleep. **3** quiet, tranquillity, calmness. **4** composure, ease of manner etc. **5** in art, moderation and harmony of colour and treatment. ~*v.i.* **1** to lie at rest. **2** to be laid or be in a recumbent position, esp. in sleep or death. **3** to rest or be supported (on). ~*v.t.* **1** to lay (oneself etc.) to rest, to rest. **2** to refresh with rest. **reposal**¹, **reposedness** *n.* **reposeful** *a.* **reposefully** *adv.* **reposefulness** *n.*

repose² (ripōz´) *v.t.* to place, to put (confidence etc. in). **reposal**² *n.*

repository (ripoz´itəri) *n.* (*pl.* **repositories**) **1** a place or receptacle in which things are deposited for safety or preservation. **2** a person, book etc. regarded as a store of information or knowledge. **3** a person to whom a secret etc. is confided.

repp, repped REP³.

reprehend (reprihend´) *v.t.* **1** to find fault with. **2** to censure, to blame. **reprehensible** (-hen´sibəl) *a.* open to censure or blame. **reprehensibility** (-bil´-), **reprehensibleness** *n.* **reprehensibly** *adv.* **reprehension** *n.*

represent (reprizent´) *v.t.* **1** to stand for, to correspond to. **2** to be an example or specimen of. **3** to serve as symbol for. **4** (of a picture etc.) to serve as a likeness of, to depict. **5** to present to or bring before the mind by describing, portraying, imitating etc. **6** to take the place of as deputy, substitute etc. **7** to act as agent or spokesman for (e.g. in a representative chamber). **8** to describe (as), to make out (to be). **9** to set forth. **10** to state (that). **11** to enact (a play etc.) on the stage, to

personate, to play the part of. **representable** *a.* **representability** (-bil´-) *n.* **representation** (-tā´shən) *n.* **1** the act of representing. **2** something that represents, a likeness, a picture, an image. **3** (*often pl.*) a statement of facts, arguments etc. **4** the system of representing bodies of people in a legislative assembly. **representational** *a.* **1** of or relating to representation. **2** (of art) depicting objects etc. in a realistic manner. **representationalism** *n.* **1** representational art. **2** representationism. **representationalist** *n.* **representationism** *n.* the doctrine that the immediate object in perception is only an idea, image or other representation of the external thing. **representationist** *n.* **representative** *a.* **1** serving to represent or symbolize, able or fitted to represent, typical. **2** similar or corresponding to others of its kind. **3** acting as agent, delegate, deputy etc. **4** consisting of delegates etc. **5** based on representation by delegates. **6** presenting images or ideas to the mind. **7** (of art) representational. ~*n.* **1** someone who or something which represents. **2** an example, a specimen, a typical instance or embodiment. **3** an agent, deputy or substitute, esp. a person chosen by a body of electors. **4** a travelling salesperson, a sales representative. **representatively** *adv.* **representativeness** *n.* **representer** *n.*

re-present RE- (+ PO–PU WORDS).

repress (ripres´) *v.t.* **1** to restrain, to keep under restraint. **2** to put down, to suppress, to quell. **3** to banish (unpleasant thoughts etc.) to the unconscious. **repressed** *a.* (of a person) repressing or tending to repress unacceptable thoughts, feelings etc. **represser** *n.* **repressible** *a.* **repression** (-shən) *n.* **repressive** *a.* **repressively** *adv.* **repressor** *n.* a substance, esp. a protein, produced by a regulator gene that indirectly represses the expression of a gene responsible for protein synthesis.

reprieve (riprēv´) *v.t.* **1** to suspend the execution of (someone) for a time. **2** to grant a respite to. **3** to rescue, to save (from). ~*n.* **1** the temporary suspension of a sentence on a prisoner. **2** the warrant authorizing this. **3** a respite. **reprieval** *n.*

reprimand¹ (rep´rimahnd) *n.* a severe reproof, a rebuke, esp. a public or official one.

reprimand² (reprimahnd´) *v.t.* to reprove severely, to rebuke, esp. publicly or officially.

reprisal (riprī´zəl) *n.* an act of retaliation.

reprise (riprēz´) *n.* (*Mus.*) a repeated phrase, theme etc., a refrain. ~*v.t.* **1** to repeat (an earlier phrase, theme etc.). **2** to repeat or restage the performance of.

repro (rē´prō) *n.* (*pl.* **repros**) a reproduction, a copy.

reproach (riprōch´) *v.t.* to censure, to upbraid. ~*n.* **1** censure mixed with disappointment. **2** a rebuke, a censure. **3** shame, infamy, disgrace. **4** an object or cause of scorn or derision. **above reproach** perfect, blameless. **beyond reproach** above reproach. **reproachable** *a.* **reproacher** *n.*

reproachful *a.* containing or expressing reproach, upbraiding, opprobrious, abusive. **reproachfully** *adv.* **reproachfulness** *n.* **reproachingly** *adv.* **reproachless** *a.* **reproachlessness** *n.*

reprobate (rep´rəbāt) *n.* **1** a wicked, depraved wretch. **2** a person who is condemned by God. ~*a.* **1** depraved. **2** abandoned to sin, condemned by God. ~*v.t.* **1** to express disapproval and detestation of, to condemn severely. **2** (of God) to abandon to wickedness and eternal punishment. **reprobation** (-ā´shən) *n.*

reproduce (rēprədūs´) *v.t.* **1** to copy. **2** to produce again. **3** (*Biol.*) to produce (new life) through sexual or asexual processes. ~*v.i.* **1** to produce offspring. **2** to come out (well, badly etc.) as a copy. **reproducer** *n.* **reproducible** *a.* **reproducibility** (-bil´-) *n.* **reproducibly** *adv.* **reproduction** (-dŭk´-) *n.* **1** the act of reproducing. **2** (*Biol.*) any of the sexual or asexual processes by which animals or plants produce offspring. **3** a copy, an imitation. **4** the quality of the sound of a recording. ~*a.* made in imitation of a particular style or period. **reproductive** *a.* **reproductively** *adv.* **reproductiveness, reproductivity** (-tiv´-) *n.*

reprography (riprog´rəfi) *n.* the art or process of reproducing printed matter e.g. by photocopying. **reprographic** (rēprəgraf´-) *a.* **reprographically** *adv.* **reprographics** *n.*

reproof[1] RE- (+ PO—PU WORDS).

reproof[2] (riproof´)*n.* **1** censure, blame, reprehension. **2** an expression of blame. **reprove** (-proov´) *v.t.* to rebuke, to censure, esp. to one's face, to chide. **reprovable** *a.* **reprover** *n.* **reprovingly** *adv.*

reptile (rep´tīl) *n.* **1** a crawling animal; a member of the Reptilia, a class of animals comprising the snakes, lizards, turtles, crocodiles etc. **2** a grovelling, mean, despicable person. **reptilian** (-til´-) *a., n.*

republic (ripŭb´lik) *n.* **1** a state or a form of political constitution in which the supreme power is vested in the people or their elected representatives; a commonwealth. **2** a society in which all the members are equal. **republican** *a.* **1** of, relating to or consisting of a republic. **2** characteristic of the principles of a republic. **3** believing in or advocating the principles of a republic. ~*n.* (*also* **Republican**) **1** a person who favours or advocates a republican form of government. **2** a member of the Republican Party in the US. **3** a supporter of republicanism in N Ireland. **republicanism** *n.*

repudiate (ripū´diāt) *v.t.* **1** to refuse to acknowledge, to disown, to disclaim (a debt etc.). **2** to disavow, to reject, to refuse to admit, accept, recognize etc. **repudiable** *a.* **repudiation** (-ā´shən) *n.* **repudiator** *n.*

repugnance (ripŭg´nəns), **repugnancy** *n.* **1** antipathy, dislike, distaste, aversion. **2** inconsistency, incompatibility or opposition, of mind, disposition, statements, ideas etc. **repugnant** *a.* **repugnantly** *adv.*

repulse (ripŭls´) *v.t.* **1** to beat or drive back, by force of arms. **2** to reject, esp. in a rude manner, to rebuff, to snub. **3** to disgust, to be repulsive to. **4** to defeat in argument. ~*n.* **1** the act of repulsing. **2** the state of being repulsed. **3** a rebuff, a refusal, a failure, a disappointment. **repulser** *n.* **repulsion** (-shən) *n.* **1** disgust, repugnance, aversion. **2** (*Physics*) the tendency of certain bodies to repel each other, as distinct from *attraction.* **repulsive** *a.* **1** repellent, loathsome, disgusting. **2** (*Physics*) acting by repulsion. **repulsively** *adv.* **repulsiveness** *n.*

Usage note The meanings of the adjectives *repulsive* and *repellent* overlap, but *repulsive* expresses much stronger aversion than *repellent.*

reputable (rep´ūtəbəl) *a.* being of good repute, respectable, creditable. **reputably** *adv.*

reputation (repūtā´shən) *n.* **1** the estimation in which one is generally held, repute. **2** the repute, honour or credit derived from favourable public opinion or esteem.

repute (ripūt´) *n.* character attributed by public report; reputation, fame. ~*v.t.* (*chiefly in p.p.*) to consider, to report, to regard (as). **reputed** *a.* generally regarded (usu. with implication of doubt) (*She is reputed to be the richest woman in the country*). **reputedly** *adv.*

re- (+ r– words) reread[1] (rērēd´) *v.t.* (*past, p.p.* **reread** (rēred´)) to read again. **reread**[2] (rē´rēd) *n.* the act of reading again. **re-readable** *a.* **re-record** *v.t.* to record again. **re-release** *v.t.* to release (a record etc.) again. ~*n.* a record etc. which has been re-released. **re-roof** *v.t.* to provide with a new roof. **re-route** *v.t.* (*pres.p.* **re-routeing, re-routing**, *past, p.p.* **re-routed**) to transport or redirect by a different route. **rerun**[1] *v.t.* (*pres.p.* **rerunning**, *past* **reran**, *p.p.* **rerun**) **1** to run (a race) again. **2** to show (a film or television programme) again. **rerun**[2] (rē´rŭn) *n.* **1** a repeated film, television programme etc. **2** a race run a second time.

request (rikwest´) *n.* **1** an expression of desire or the act of asking for something to be granted or done; a petition. **2** something which is asked for. **3** the state of being demanded or sought after. **4 a** a request for a particular song to be played by a disc jockey or performer. **b** the song requested. ~*v.t.* **1** to ask for. **2** to address a request to. **3** to ask (that). **on request** if or when asked for. **requester** *n.* **request programme** *n.* a radio programme consisting of requests from listeners. **request stop** *n.* a stop on a route where a bus will stop only if signalled to do so.

requiem (rek´wiəm) *n.* **1** (**Requiem**) in the Roman Catholic Church, a mass for the repose of the soul of a dead person. **2** (*Mus.*) the musical setting of this, a dirge. **3** a memorial (for).

require (rikwīə´) *v.t.* **1** to have need of, to depend upon for completion etc. **2** to ask or claim as a right or by authority, to order. **3** to command, to instruct. **4** to demand (something of a person), to insist (on having, that etc.). **5** to want to have. **requirable** *a.* **requirement** *n.* **requirer** *n.*

requisite (rek´wizit) *a.* required by the nature of things, necessary for completion etc., indispensable. *~n.* something which is required, a necessary part or quality. **requisitely** *adv.* **requisiteness** *n.*

requisition (rekwizish´ən) *n.* **1** an authoritative order for the supply of provisions etc. **2** a formal and usu. written demand or request for the performance of a duty. **3** the state of being called upon or put in use. *~v.t.* to demand by requisitions. **under requisition** in use, being applied. **requisitioner** *n.* **requisitionist** *n.*

requite (rikwīt´) *v.t.* **1** to make return for. **2** to reward or avenge. **3** to repay, to make return to, to recompense. **4** to give or deal in return. **requital** *n.*

reredos (riə´dos) *n.* (*pl.* **reredoses**) the ornamental screen at the back of an altar.

re- (+ sa–so words) **resale** *n.* **1** a second, i.e. retail, sale. **2** a sale at second hand. **resaleable**, **resalable** *a.* **resale price maintenance** *n.* the practice by which a manufacturer sets a minimum resaleable price for goods. **reschedule** *v.t.* to change the schedule of. **reseal** *v.t.* to seal again. **resealable** *a.* **reseat** *v.t.* **1** to seat again. **2** to furnish (a church etc.) with new seats. **3** to realign (a nail etc.) into its correct position. **reseed** *v.t.* to sow (land) with seed again. **reselect** *v.t.* to select again or in a different way. **reselection** *n.* **resell** *v.t.* (*past, p.p.* **resold**) to sell again. **reseller** *n.* **re-serve** *v.t., v.i.* to serve again. **reset** *v.t.* (*pres.p.* **resetting**, *past, p.p.* **reset**) to set (type, a jewel etc.) again. **resettable** *a.* **resettle** *v.t., v.i.* to settle again. **resettlement** *n.* **reshape** *v.t.* to shape again. **reshuffle**[1] (-shŭf´-) *v.t.* **1** to shuffle again. **2** to rearrange or reorganize (esp. the Cabinet or a government department). **reshuffle**[2] (rē´-) *n.* the act of reshuffling. **re-sign** *v.t., v.i.* to sign again. **resignal** *v.t.* (*pres.p.* **resignalling**, (*N Am.*) **resignaling**, *past, p.p.* **resignalled**, (*N Am.*) **resignaled**) to supply with signals again. **resit**[1] (-sit´) *v.t., v.i.* (*pres.p.* **resitting**, *past, p.p.* **resat**) to sit (an examination) again after failing. **resit**[2] (rē´-) *n.* an examination which one must sit again, having failed initially. **resite** *v.t.* to move to another site. **resize** *v.t.* to change the size of. **reskill** *v.t.* to provide with new skills. **re-soluble** *a.* able to be dissolved again. **re-sort** *v.t.* to sort again.

rescind (rinsind´) *v.t.* to annul, to cancel, to withdraw. **rescindable** *a.* **rescission** (-sizh´ən) *n.*

rescue (res´kū) *v.t.* (*3rd pers. sing. pres.* **rescues**, *pres.p.* **rescuing**, *past, p.p.* **rescued**) **1** to save from confinement, danger, evil or injury. **2** (*Law*) to liberate by unlawful means from custody. **3** (*Law*) to recover (property etc.). *~n.* **1** the act of saving from confinement, danger, evil or injury. **2** forcible seizure (of a person, property etc.) from the custody of the law. **rescuable** *a.* **rescue bid** *n.* in bridge, a bid made in order to

rescue one's partner from a difficult situation. **rescuer** *n.*

research (risœch´) *n.* **1** systematic study of phenomena etc., a course of critical investigation. **2** diligent and careful inquiry or investigation. *~v.t.* to make careful and systematic investigation into. *~v.i.* to make researches. **researchable** *a.* **research and development** *n.* in industry, work concerned with the application of scientific research in the development of new products etc. **researcher** *n.*

Usage note Pronunciation as (rē´-), with stress on the first syllable, is best avoided.

resect (risekt´) *v.t.* **1** (*Med.*) to excise a section of (an organ or part). **2** to cut or pare down (bone etc.). **resection** (-sek´shən) *n.* **resectional** *a.* **resectionist** *n.*

resemble (rizem´bəl) *v.t.* to be like, to be similar to; to have features, nature etc., like those of. **resemblance** *n.* similarity, likeness. **resemblant** *a.* **resembler** *n.*

resent (rizent´) *v.t.* to regard as an injury or insult, to feel or show displeasure or indignation at, to cherish bitter feelings about. **resenter** *n.* **resentful** *a.* **resentfully** *adv.* **resentfulness** *n.* **resentment** *n.*

reserpine (risœ´pin) *n.* an alkaloid extracted from plants of the *Rauwolfia* genus, used to treat high blood pressure and as a sedative.

reservation (rezəvā´shən) *n.* **1** the act of reserving. **2** something which is reserved. **3** the booking of accommodation in a hotel, train, ship etc. **4** an expressed or tacit limitation, exception, or qualification. **5** a strip of land separating a dual carriageway. **6** a tract of land reserved for indigenous peoples or for public use.

reserve (rizœv´) *v.t.* **1** to keep back for future use, enjoyment, treatment etc.; to postpone, to keep in store. **2** to retain for oneself or another, esp. as an exception from something granted. **3** to book, keep or set apart. *~n.* **1** something which is reserved. **2** a sum of money or a fund reserved, esp. by bankers, to meet any demand. **3** a reservation of land for a special use. **4** troops kept for any emergency, such as to act as reinforcements or cover a retreat. **5** a part of the military or naval forces not embodied in the regular army and navy, but liable to be called up in case of emergency. **6** a member of these forces, a reservist. **7** the state of being reserved or kept back for a special purpose. **8** in sport, a substitute. **9** (*pl.*) in sport, the second-choice team. **10** mental reservation, exception or qualification. **11** reticence, self-restraint, caution in speaking or action. **12** lack of exaggeration in artistic or literary expression. **13** a company's profit added to capital. **in reserve** reserved and ready for use in an emergency. **to reserve judgement** to delay making a judgement about someone or something until more information is available. **reservable** *a.* **reserved** *a.* **1** reticent, backward in communicating one's thoughts or feelings, undemonstrative, distant. **2** retained for a particular use, person etc. **reservedly** (-vid-) *adv.* **reservedness** (-vid-) *n.* **reserved occupation** *n.* vital employment which exempts a person from military service in the event of war. **reserve price** *n.* in an auction, a price below which no offer will be accepted. **reserver** *n.* **reservist** *n.* a member of the military or naval reserve.

re-serve RE- (+ SA–SO WORDS).

reservoir (rez´əvwah) *n.* **1** a receptacle of earthwork or masonry for the storage of water in large quantity. **2** a lake used as a water supply. **3** a receptacle in which a quantity of anything, esp. fluid, may be kept in store. **4** a part of an implement, machine, animal or vegetable organ etc., acting as a receptacle for fluid. **5** a reserve supply or store of anything.

reside (rizīd´) *v.i.* **1** to dwell permanently or for a considerable length of time, to have one's home (at). **2** to be in official residence. **3** (of qualities, rights etc.) to inhere, to be vested (in), to be precipitated, to sink. **residence** (rez´i-) *n.* **1** the act or state of residing in a place. **2** the act of living or remaining where one's duties lie. **3** the place where one dwells, one's abode. **4** a house of some size or pretensions. **in residence 1** actually resident. **2** (of an artist, writer etc.) acting in a regular capacity for a limited period at a gallery, university etc. **residency** *n.* (*pl.* **residencies**) **1** a residence. **2** (*N Am.*) a period of specialized training undertaken by a doctor following internship. **3** a musician's or band's regular engagement at a venue. **resident** (rez´i-) *n.* **1** a person who dwells permanently in a place, as distinct from a visitor. **2** a non-migratory bird or animal. **3** a hotel guest. **4** (*N Am.*) a boarder at a boarding school. **5** (*N Am.*) a junior doctor who lives and works in a hospital to gain specialized experience. ~*a.* **1** residing. **2** having a residence, esp. official quarters in connection with one's duties. **3** working regularly in a particular place. **4** non-migratory. **5** inherent. **residential** (reziden´shəl) *a.* **1** suitable for residence or for residences. **2** of or relating to residence. **residentially** *adv.* **residentship** *n.*

residue (rez´idū) *n.* **1** what is left or remains over, the rest, the remainder. **2** (*Law*) what remains of an estate after payment of all charges, debts and particular bequests. **3** (*Chem.*) a residuum. **residual** (-zid´-) *a.* **1** of the nature of a residue or residuum, remaining after a part has been taken away. **2** (*Math.*) left by a process of subtraction. **3** remaining unexplained or uneliminated. ~*n.* **1** a residual quantity, a remainder. **2** the difference between the computed and the observed value of a quantity at any given moment, a residual error. **residually** *adv.* **residuary** (-zid´-) *a.* **1** of or relating to the residue of an estate. **2** of, relating to or forming a residue, residual, remaining. **residuum** (-zid´ūəm) *n.* (*pl.* **residua** (-ə)) **1** (*Chem.*) a substance which is left after any

process of separation or purification, esp. after combustion, evaporation etc. **2** the remainder left by subtraction or division, a residual error.

resign (rizīn´) *v.i.* **1** to give up office, to retire (from). **2** in chess, to admit defeat. ~*v.t.* **1** to give up, to surrender, to relinquish. **2** to hand over (to). **3** to give up, to abandon. **4** to yield, to submit, to reconcile (oneself, one's mind etc. to). **resignation** (rezignā´shən) *n.* **1** the act of resigning, esp. an office. **2** a document announcing this. **3** the state of being resigned, patience, acquiescence, submission. **resigned** *a.* submissive, patiently acquiescent or enduring. **resignedly** (-nid-) *adv.* **resignedness** (-nid-) *n.*

re-sign RE- (+ SA–SO WORDS).

resilience (rizil´yəns), **resiliency** *n.* **1** elasticity. **2** (of a person) an ability to recover quickly from illness or misfortune. **resilient** *a.* **resiliently** *adv.*

resin (rez´in) *n.* **1** an amorphous inflammable vegetable substance secreted by plants and usu. obtained by exudation, esp. from the fir and pine. **2** a similar substance obtained by the chemical synthesis of various organic materials, used esp. in making plastics. ~*v.t.* (*pres.p.* **resining**, *past*, *p.p.* **resined**) to treat with resin. **resinate** *v.t.* **resinoid** (-noid) *a.*, *n.* **resinous** *a.*

resist (rizist´) *v.t.* **1** to stand or strive against, to act in opposition to, to try to frustrate. **2** to oppose successfully, to withstand, to stop, to repel, to frustrate, to be proof against. **3** not to yield to (temptation or pleasure). ~*v.i.* to offer resistance. ~*n.* a substance applied to a surface etc. to prevent the action of a chemical agent, such as the mordant used in dyeing calico. **unable to resist** strongly inclined to, strongly attracted to. **resistance** *n.* **1** the act or power of resisting. **2** opposition, refusal to comply. **3** (*esp. Med.*) something which hinders or retards, esp. the opposition exerted by a fluid to the passage of a body. **4** (*Physics*) the opposition exerted by a substance to the passage of electric current, heat etc. through it, or a measure of this. **5** (*Biol.*) the ability to withstand adverse conditions. **6** (*Med.*) the body's natural power to withstand disease. **7** a resistor. **8** a resistance movement. **resistance movement** *n.* an underground organization of civilians and others in an enemy-occupied country whose aim is to sabotage the invaders' plans and render their position as difficult as possible. **resistant** *a.* **resister** *n.* **resistible** *a.* **resistibility** *n.* **resistive** *a.* **resistivity** (rēzistiv´-) *n.* the power of a material to resist the passage of electrical current through it. **resistor** *n.* an electronic component with a specified resistance.

Usage note It is conventional to use *resistEr* for a person, *resistOr* for an electrical device.

resoluble (rizol´ūbəl) *a.* able to be dissolved, resolved or analysed.

re-soluble RE- (+ SA–SO WORDS).

resolute (rez´əloot) *a.* having a fixed purpose,

determined, constant in pursuing an object. **resolutely** *adv.* **resoluteness** *n.* **resolution** (-loo´shən) *n.* **1** resoluteness, determination, firmness and boldness in adhering to one's purpose. **2** a resolve, a settled purpose. **3** a formal proposition, statement of opinion, or decision by a legislative or corporate body or public meeting. **4** mental analysis, solution of a problem etc. **5** (*Chem.*) the act or process of resolving or separating anything into the component parts, decomposition, analysis. **6** analysis of a force into two or more jointly equivalent forces. **7** analysis or conversion into a different format. **8** (*Mus.*) the conversion of a discord into a concord. **9** (*Physics*) the smallest interval which can be measured by a scientific instrument. **10** the definition of a television or film image. **resolutive** *a.* (*Med.*) having the power or tending to resolve, dissolve or relax. **resolutive condition** *n.* (*Law*) a condition whose fulfilment terminates a contract.

resolve (rizolv´) *v.t.* **1** to cause (someone) to decide or determine. **2** to pass by vote or resolution (that). **3** to separate into the component parts; to dissolve, to analyse, to disintegrate, to dissipate; to reduce to the constituent parts or elements. **4** to analyse mentally. **5** to solve, to explain, to clear up, to answer. **6** to convert into by analysis. **7** (*Mus.*) to convert (a discord) into a concord. **8** to decide, to determine on. ~*v.i.* **1** to make one's mind up, to decide or determine (upon). **2** to separate into the component parts, to dissolve, to break up, to be analysed. **3** to be converted. **4** to reduce by mental analysis (into). **5** (*Mus.*) to be converted from discord into concord. **6** to pass a resolution. ~*n.* **1** a resolution, a firm decision or determination. **2** (*N Am.*) a resolution by a deliberative assembly. **3** resoluteness, firmness of purpose. **resolvable** *a.* **resolvability** (-bil´-) *n.* **resolved** *a.* determined, resolute. **resolvedly** (-vid-) *adv.* **resolver** *n.* **resolving power** *n.* the ability of a microscope or telescope to distinguish or produce separable images of small adjacent objects.

resonant (rez´ənənt) *a.* **1** (of a sound) prolonged or reinforced by vibration or reverberation. **2** having the property of prolonging or reinforcing sound, esp. by vibration. **3** capable of returning sound, re-echoing, resounding. **resonance** *n.* **1** the quality or state of being resonant. **2** sympathetic vibration. **3** (*Chem.*) the description of the electronic structure of a molecule in certain compounds in terms of different arrangements of two or more bonds. **resonantly** *adv.* **resonate** *v.i.* to resound, to reverberate. **resonator** *n.* (*Mus.*) **1** a body or system that detects and responds to certain frequencies. **2** a device for enriching or amplifying sound.

resorb (risawb´) *v.t.* to absorb again. **resorbence** *n.* **resorbent** *a.*

resorcin (rizaw´sin), **resorcinol** (-nol) *n.* (*Chem.*)

a crystalline phenol used as a dyestuff in resins, adhesives and in medicine.

resort (rizawt´) *n.* **1** a place frequented by holidaymakers. **2** something to which one has recourse, an expedient. **3** recourse (to). **4** the act of frequenting a place. **5** the state of being frequented. ~*v.i.* **1** to go, to repair, to betake oneself. **2** to have recourse, to apply, to turn to (for aid etc.). **resorter** *n.*

re-sort RE- (+ SA—SO WORDS).

resound (rizownd´) *v.i.* **1** to ring, to re-echo, to reverberate (with). **2** (of a place) to be filled with sound. **3** (of sounds, instruments etc.) to be re-echoed, to be repeated, reinforced, or prolonged. **4** (of news, events etc.) to be talked about, to make a sensation. ~*v.t.* **1** to spread the fame of. **2** to sound again, to return the sound of. **resounding** *a.* **1** ringing, resonant. **2** clear, decisive (*a resounding success*). **resoundingly** *adv.*

resource (risaws´, -zaws´) *n.* **1** an expedient, a device. **2** a means of aid, support or safety. **3** (*usu. pl.*) stocks or supply available. **4** (*pl.*) means of support and defence, esp. of a country. **5** a leisure pursuit. **6** capacity for finding or devising means. **7** skill in devising expedients, practical ingenuity. ~*v.t.* to provide with resources. **one's own resources** one's own abilities. **resourceful** *a.* **resourcefully** *adv.* **resourcefulness** *n.* **resourceless** (-lis) *a.* **resourcelessness** *n.*

re- (+ sp—su words) **respell** *v.t.* (*past, p.p.* **respelt, respelled**) to spell again. **respray**[1] (-sprā´) *v.t.* to spray again. **respray**[2] (rē´-) *n.* the act of respraying. **restage** *v.t.* to stage again or in a different way. **restart**[1] (-staht´) *v.t., v.i.* to start afresh. **restart**[2] (rē´-) *n.* **1** a new beginning. **2** a new start to a race, match etc. after a false start, stoppage etc. **restate** *v.t.* to state again or express differently. **restatement** *n.* **restock** *v.t., v.i.* to stock again. **restring** *v.t.* (*past, p.p.* **restrung**) **1** to provide (a musical instrument or tennis racket) with new strings. **2** to put (beads etc.) on to a new string. **restructure** *v.t.* to change the structure or organization (of). **restudy** *v.t.* (*3rd pers. sing. pres.* **restudies**, *pres.p.* **restudying**, *past, p.p.* **restudied**) to study again. **restyle**[1] (-stīl´) *v.t.* **1** to give a new style to. **2** to give a new name or title to. **restyle**[2] (rē´-) *n.* a new or different style. **resubmit** *v.t.* to submit (an application, a proposal etc.) again. **resupply** *v.t.* (*3rd pers. sing. pres.* **resupplies**, *pres.p.* **resupplying**, *past, p.p.* **resupplied**) to provide with fresh supplies. ~*v.i.* to obtain fresh supplies. ~*n.* **1** the act of resupplying. **2** something which is resupplied. **resurface** *v.t.* to put a new surface on (a road etc.). ~*v.i.* to appear again. **resurvey**[1] (rēsəvā´) *v.t.* to survey again, to read and examine again. **resurvey**[2] (rēsə´vā) *n.* a renewed survey.

respect (rispekt´) *n.* **1** esteem, deferential regard. **2** attention (to), heed (to), regard (to or of). **3** a particular, an aspect. **4** relation, regard, reference. **5** (*pl.*) expressions of esteem sent as a complimentary message. ~*v.t.* **1** to esteem, to regard with deference. **2** to treat with consideration, to spare from insult, injury, interference etc. **in respect of** with regard to, concerning. **with (all due) respect** a polite phrase used to precede an expression of disagreement. **with respect to** with regard to, concerning. **respectable** *a.* **1** worthy of respect, of good repute. **2** of fair social standing. **3** honest, decent, not disreputable. **4** not mean, not inconsiderable, above the average in number, quantity, merit etc. **5** fairly good, tolerable, passable. **6** appropriate for a respectable person. **respectability** (-bil´-) *n.* **1** the quality or character of being respectable. **2** people who are respectable. **respectableness** *n.* **respectably** *adv.* **respecter** *n.* **respectful** *a.* **respectfully** *adv.* **respectfulness** *n.* **respecting** *prep.* in regard to, concerning. **respective** *a.* relating severally to each of those in question; several, comparative, relative. **respectively** *adv.*

respire (rispīə´) *v.i.* **1** to breathe. **2** to inhale or take air into and exhale it from the lungs. **3** (of a plant) to carry out respiration. **4** to recover breath. **5** to recover hope, spirit etc. ~*v.t.* **1** to inhale and exhale. **2** to breathe out, to emit (perfume etc.). **respirable** (res´pir-) *a.* **respirability** (-bil´-) *n.* **respirate** (-rāt) *v.t.* to give artificial respiration to. **respiration** (respirā´shən) *n.* **1** the act or process of breathing. **2** a single act of inhaling and exhaling. **3** (*Biol.*) the absorption of oxygen and emission of carbon dioxide by living organisms. **respirator** (res´pir-) *n.* **1** an appliance worn over the mouth or mouth and nose to exclude poisonous gases, fumes etc., or to protect the lungs from the sudden inspiration of cold air; a gas mask. **2** (*Med.*) an apparatus for providing artificial respiration. **respiratory** (-spir´-) *a.*

respite (res´pīt) *n.* **1** an interval of rest or relief, a reprieve. **2** a temporary intermission of labour, effort, suffering etc., esp. a delay in the execution of a sentence. ~*v.t.* **1** to grant a respite to, to reprieve. **2** to suspend the execution of (a sentence). **3** to relieve by a temporary cessation of labour, suffering etc. **4** to postpone, to defer, to delay. **respiteless** *a.*

resplendent (risplen´dənt) *a.* shining with brilliant lustre, vividly or gloriously bright. **resplendence, resplendency** *n.* **resplendently** *adv.*

respond (rispond´) *v.i.* **1** to answer, to reply. **2** (of a congregation) to return set answers to a priest. **3** to perform an act or show an effect in answer or correspondence to something. **4** to react (to an external irritation or stimulus). **5** to be responsive, to show sympathy or sensitiveness (to). **6** in bridge, to bid in response to a partner's bid. ~*v.t.* to answer, to say in response. **respondence, †respondency** *n.* **respondent** *n.* **1** (*Law*) a person who answers in a suit at law, a defendant, esp. in a divorce case. **2** a person who answers. **3** a person who maintains a thesis in reply. ~*a.* **1**

giving response, answering. **2** responsive (to). **3** in the position of defendant. **responder** *n.*

response (rispons´) *n.* **1** the act of answering. **2** an answer, a reply, a reaction. **3** (*often pl.*) a versicle or other portion of a liturgy said or sung in answer to the priest, a responsory. **4** in bridge, a bid made in responding. **5** the reaction of an organism to stimulation. **responsive** *a.* **1** answering or inclined to answer. **2** of the nature of an answer. **3** reacting to stimulus. **4** responding readily, sympathetic, impressionable. **responsively** *adv.* **responsiveness** *n.* **responsorial** (-saw´-) *a.* of or relating to liturgical responses. **responsory** *n.* (*pl.* **responsories**) an anthem said or sung alternately by the soloist and a choir after one of the lessons.

responsible (rispon´sibəl) *a.* **1** answerable, liable, accountable (to or for). **2** morally accountable for one's actions, able to discriminate between right and wrong. **3** respectable, trustworthy. **4** being the cause. **5** involving responsibility. **responsibility** (-bil´-) *n.* **1** the state of being responsible. **2** something for which one is responsible. **on one's own responsibility** without authorization. **responsibly** *adv.*

rest[1] (rest) *v.i.* **1** to cease from exertion, motion or activity. **2** to be relieved from work or exertion, to repose. **3** to lie in sleep or death, to lie buried. **4** to be still, to be without motion. **5** to be free from care, disturbance or molestation, to be tranquil, to be at peace. **6** (of land) to be allowed to lie fallow. **7** to be spread out. **8** to be supported or fixed, to be based, to lean, to recline, to stand (on). **9** to depend, to rely (on). **10** to trust or put one's confidence (in). **11** (of eyes) to be fixed, to be directed steadily (upon). **12** to remain without further discussion. **13** (*US*) (of an attorney) to call no more evidence. ~*v.t.* **1** to cause to cease from exertion. **2** to give repose to, to lay at rest. **3** (*in p.p.*) to refresh by resting. **4** to give (oneself) rest. **5** to place for support, to base, to establish, to lean, to lay, to support. ~*n.* **1** cessation from bodily or mental exertion or activity, repose, sleep. **2** freedom from care, disturbance or molestation, peace, tranquillity. **3** a period of such cessation or freedom, esp. a brief pause or interval. **4** a stopping place, a place for lodging. **5** a shelter for taxi drivers, sailors etc. **6** something on which anything stands or is supported, a prop, a support, a device for steadying a rifle on in taking aim, for supporting the cutting tool in a lathe etc. **7** a long cue with a crosspiece at one end used as a support for a snooker cue in playing. **8** (*Mus.*) an interval of silence. **b** the sign indicating this. **9** a pause in a verse, a caesura. **10** death. **at rest 1** reposing, not in motion, still. **2** not disturbed, agitated or troubled. **3** (*euphem.*) dead, in the grave. **to rest one's case** to conclude one's arguments. **to rest up** (*N Am.*) to have a rest. **to set at rest** to ease (someone's mind). **rest-cure** *n.* seclusion and rest (usu. in bed) as a method of treatment for nervous disorders. **restful** *a.* **1** inducing rest, soothing, free from disturbance. **2** at rest, quiet. **restfully** *adv.* **restfulness** *n.* **rest home** *n.* an institution where old people live and are looked after. **restless** *a.* **1** not resting, never still, agitated, uneasy, fidgety, unsettled, turbulent. **2** not affording sleep, sleepless. **restlessly** *adv.* **restlessness** *n.* **restroom** *n.* (*N Am.*) a room with toilet facilities etc. in a public building.

rest² (rest) *n.* the remaining part or parts, the residue, the remainder; the others. *~v.i.* to remain, to stay, to continue (in a specified state). **and all the rest** and all the others. **for the rest** as regards the remaining persons, matters or things, as regards anything else. **to rest with** to be left in the hands of.

restaurant (res´tərənt, -trənt, -trā) *n.* a place for refreshment, a public eating house. **restaurant car** *n.* a dining car on a train. **restaurateur** (-tərətœ´) *n.* the keeper of a restaurant.

Usage note The form *restauranteur* (after *restaurant*) for *restaurateur* is best avoided.

restitution (restitū´shən) *n.* **1** the act of restoring something taken away or lost. **2** making good, reparation, indemnification. **3** (*esp. Theol.*) restoration to a former state or position. **4** the resumption of its former shape by an elastic body. **restitutive** (res´-), **restitutory** (-tū´-) *a.*

restive (res´tiv) *a.* **1** restless, fidgety. **2** (of a horse) unwilling to go forward, standing still, refractory. **3** impatient of control, unmanageable. **restively** *adv.* **restiveness** *n.*

Usage note The meanings of the adjectives *restive* and *restless* overlap, but *restive* should imply some impending (usually rebellious) action, whereas *restless* is more simply descriptive of a state.

restore (ristaw´) *v.t.* **1** to bring back to a former state, to repair, to reconstruct. **2** to put back, to replace, to return. **3** to bring back to health, to cure. **4** to bring back to a former position, to reinstate. **5** to bring into existence or use again, to re-establish, to renew. **6** to give back, to make restitution of. **restorable** *a.* **restoration** (restərā´shən) *n.* **1** the act of restoring. **2** a building etc., restored to its supposed original state. **3** a skeleton of an extinct animal built up of its remains. **4** a drawing, model, or other representation of a building, extinct animal etc., in its supposed original form. **5** the re-establishment of a monarchy, or the period of this. *~a.* (**Restoration**) of or relating to the literary period following the Restoration of Charles II (*Restoration comedy*). **restorative** (-stor´-) *a.* tending to restore health or strength. *~n.* food, drink, a medicine etc., for restoring strength, vigour etc.; a stimulant, a tonic. **restoratively** *adv.* **restorer** *n.*

restrain (ristrān´) *v.t.* **1** to hold back, to check, to curb. **2** to keep under control, to repress, to hold in check, to restrict. **3** to confine, to imprison.

restrainable *a.* **restrainedly** (-nid-) *adv.* **restrainer** *n.* **restraint** *n.* **1** the act of restraining. **2** the state of being restrained. **3** check, repression, control, self-repression, avoidance of excess. **4** constraint, reserve. **5** something used to retain a person or animal physically. **in restraint of** in order to restrain.

restrict (ristrikt´) *v.t.* **1** to limit, to confine, to keep within certain bounds. **2** to subject to limitation. **3** to withhold from disclosure. **restricted** *a.* **1** limited, confined. **2** out of bounds to the general public. **3** denoting a zone where a speed limit or waiting restrictions apply for vehicles. **restrictedly** *adv.* **restrictedness** *n.* **restriction** *n.* **1** something that restricts. **2** a restrictive law or regulation. **3** restricting or being restricted. **restrictionist** *a.*, *n.* **restrictive** *a.* **1** restricting or tending to restrict. **2** (*Gram.*) denoting a relative clause or phrase which restricts the application of the antecedent noun etc. **restrictively** *adv.* **restrictiveness** *n.* **restrictive practice** *n.* **1** a trading agreement contrary to the public interest. **2** a practice by a trade union, e.g. the closed shop, regarded as limiting managerial flexibility.

result (rizŭlt´) *v.i.* **1** to have an issue, to terminate or end (in). **2** to be the actual, or follow as, the logical consequence; to ensue (from). *~n.* **1** consequence, issue, outcome, effect. **2** a favourable outcome. **3** a quantity, value, or formula obtained from a calculation. **4** a final score in a game or contest. **resultant** *a.* **1** resulting, following as a result. **2** resulting from the combination of two factors, agents etc. **resultless** *a.*

resume (rizūm´) *v.t.* **1** to begin again, to recommence, to go on with after interruption. **2** to take back, to take again, to reoccupy, to recover. *~v.i.* to continue after interruption, to recommence. **resumable** *a.*

résumé (rez´ūmā) , **resumé** *n.* **1** a summary, a recapitulation, a condensed statement. **2** (*esp. N Am.*) a curriculum vitae.

resumption (rizŭmp´shən) *n.* the act of resuming. **resumptive** *a.*

resurgent (risœ´jənt) *a.* rising again, esp. in popularity. **resurgence** *n.*

resurrect (rezərekt´) *v.t.* **1** (*coll.*) to bring again into vogue or currency, to revive. **2** to exhume. **3** to bring back to life. *~v.i.* to come back to life. **resurrection** *n.* **1** (**Resurrection**) a rising again from the dead, esp. the rising of Christ from the dead, and the rising of all the dead at the Last Day. **2** the state of being risen again. **3** a springing again into life, vigour, vogue or prosperity. **4** exhumation, resurrecting, body snatching. **resurrectional** *a.* **resurrectionism** *n.* belief in the Christian doctrine of Resurrection. **resurrection plant** *n.* any of various desert plants which curl into a tight ball in drought and unfold when moistened.

resuscitate (risŭs´itāt) *v.t.* **1** to revive, to restore from apparent death. **2** to restore to vigour, animation, usage etc. ~*v.i.* to revive, to come to life or prominence again. **resuscitable** *a.* **resuscitation** (-ā´shən) *n.* **resuscitative** *a.* **resuscitator** *n.*

re- (+ ta–to words) retake[1] (-tāk´) *v.t.* (*pres.p.* **retaking,** *past* **retook,** *p.p.* **retaken**) **1** to take again. **2** to recapture. **retake**[2] (rē´-) *n.* **1** the act of retaking. **2** something retaken. **3** a second photographing (of a scene). **4** a rerecording. **reteach** *v.t.* (*past, p.p.* **retaught**) to teach again or in a different way. **retell** *v.t.* (*past, p.p.* **retold**) to tell again or in a different way. **retexture** *v.t.* to treat (clothing) so as to restore the original texture. **rethink**[1] (-thingk´) *v.t.* (*past, p.p.* **rethought**) to think again, to reconsider (a plan, decision etc.) and take an alternative view. **rethink**[2] (rē´-) *n.* the act of rethinking. **retie** *v.t.* (*pres.p.* **retying,** *past, p.p.* **retied**) to tie again. **re-time** *v.t.* to set a new time or timetable for. **retitle** *v.t.* to give a new title to. **retouch** *v.t.* **1** to improve (a photograph, picture etc.) by new touches. **2** to touch again. ~*n.* **1** the act of retouching. **2** a photograph, painting etc. that has been retouched. **retoucher** *n.*

retable (ritā´bəl) *n.* a shelf, ledge or panelled frame above the back of an altar for supporting ornaments.

retail[1] (rē´tāl) *n.* the sale of commodities in small quantities, as distinct from *wholesale.* ~*a.* of or relating to selling by retail. ~*adv.* at a retail price. **retail price index** *n.* an index of the cost of living, based on average retail prices of selected goods, usu. updated monthly.

retail[2] (rē´tāl, ritāl´) *v.t.* **1** to sell in small quantities. **2** to tell (a story etc.) in detail, to retell, to spread about. ~*v.i.* to be sold by retail (at or for a specified price). **retailer** *n.*

retain (ritān´) *v.t.* **1** to hold or keep possession of, to keep. **2** to continue to have, to maintain, to preserve. **3** to remember. **4** to hold back, to keep in place. **5** to hire, to engage the services of (someone) by paying a preliminary fee. **retainable** *a.* **retainability** (-bil´-) *n.* **retainer** *n.* **1** someone who or something which retains. **2** (*Law*) an agreement by which an attorney acts in a case. **3** a preliminary fee paid (esp. to a counsel) to secure someone's services. **4** an attendant, a follower, esp. of a feudal chieftain. **5** (*facet.*) a long-serving, faithful servant. **6** a reduced rent paid on accommodation during a period of non-occupancy. **retaining wall** *n.* a massive wall built to support and hold back the earth of an embankment, a mass of water etc. **retainment** *n.*

retaliate (rital´iāt) *v.i.* to repay an injury or result, to make reprisals. ~*v.t.* to repay (an injury or insult). **retaliation** (-ā´shən) *n.* **retaliative** (-tal´yətiv) *a.* **retaliator** *n.* **retaliatory** (-tal´yətəri) *a.*

retard (ritahd´) *v.t.* **1** to cause to move more slowly. **2** to hinder, to impede, to delay the growth, advance, arrival or occurrence of. ~*n.* delay, retardation. **retardant** *n.* a substance that slows a process down (*fire retardant*). ~*a.* serving to delay or slow down. **retardation**

(rētahdā´shən) *n.* **retardative, retardatory** *a.* **retarded** *a.* underdeveloped intellectually or emotionally. **retarder** *n.* **retardment** *n.*

retch (rech) *v.i.* **1** to make an effort to vomit. **2** to strain, as in vomiting. ~*n.* the act or sound of retching.

retd. *abbr.* **1** retired. **2** returned.

retention (riten´shən) *n.* **1** the act of retaining. **2** the state of being retained. **3** the power of retaining, esp. ideas in the mind. **4** (*Med.*) failure to evacuate urine etc. **retentive** *a.* **retentively** *adv.* **retentiveness** *n.*

reticent (ret´isənt) *a.* **1** reserved in speech. **2** not disposed to communicate one's thoughts or feelings. **3** keeping something back. **reticence** *n.* **reticently** *adv.*

reticle (ret´ikəl) *n.* a network of fine lines etc., drawn across the focal plane of an optical instrument.

reticular (ritik´ūlə) *a.* **1** having the form of a net or network. **2** formed with interstices.

reticulate[1] (ritik´ūlāt) *v.t.* to make, divide into or arrange in a network, to mark with fine, intersecting lines. ~*v.i.* to be divided into or arranged in a network. **reticulation** (-lā´shən) *n.*

reticulate[2] (ritik´ūlət) *a.* formed into or resembling a network.

reticule (ret´ikūl) *n.* **1** a reticle. **2** a kind of bag, orig. of network.

reticulum (ritik´ūləm) *n.* (*pl.* **reticula** (-lə)) **1** a netlike or reticulated structure, membrane etc. **2** (*Zool.*) the second stomach of a ruminant.

retiform (rē´tifawm, ret´-) *a.* netlike, reticulated.

retina (ret´inə) *n.* (*pl.* **retinas, retinae** (-nē)) (*Anat.*) a netlike layer of sensitive nerve-fibres and cells behind the eyeball in which the optic nerve terminates. **retinal** *a.*

retinue (ret´inū) *n.* the group of attendants accompanying a distinguished person.

retire (ritīə´) *v.i.* **1** to withdraw, to go away, to fall back, to retreat, to recede. **2** to withdraw from business to a private life. **3** to resign one's office or appointment, to cease from or withdraw from active service. **4** to go to or as to bed. **5** to go into privacy or seclusion. **6** in cricket, to end one's innings without being out. ~*v.t.* **1** to cause to retire or resign. **2** to order (troops) to retire. **3** (of a cricket captain) to cause (a batsman) to end his innings. **4** in baseball, to put out (a batter). **retiral** *n.* (*esp. Sc.*) retirement from work. **retired** *a.* **1** having retired from work. **2** of or relating to retired people. **3** private, withdrawn from society, given to privacy or seclusion. **4** secluded, sequestered. **retirement** *n.* **retirement age** *n.* the age at which people usually retire from work. **retirement home** *n.* **1** a house or flat to which an old person moves after retirement. **2** an institution where old people live and are looked after. **retirement pension** *n.* a state pension paid to people who have reached retirement age. **retirer** *n.* **retiring** *a.* shy, not forward, unsociable. **retiringly** *adv.*

retort[1] (ritawt´) *n.* **1** the turning of a charge, taunt, attack etc. against the originator or aggressor. **2** an angry reply. **3** a retaliation. *~v.t.* **1** to say, make or do as a retort. **2** to turn (an argument, accusation, etc.) on or against the originator or aggressor. **3** to pay back (an attack, injury etc.) in kind. **4** to turn or throw back. *~v.i.* to turn an argument or charge against the originator or aggressor. **retorted** *a.* recurved, bent or twisted back. **retorter** *n.*

retort[2] (ritawt´) *n.* **1** a container with a bulblike receptacle and a long neck bent downwards used for distillation of liquids etc. **2** a large receptacle of fireclay, iron etc., of similar shape, used for the production of coal gas. *~v.t.* to purify (mercury etc.) by treatment in a retort.

re- (**+ tr–ty words**) **retrace** *v.t.* **1** to go over (one's course or track) again. **2** to trace back to the beginning, source etc. **3** to go over again in memory, to try to recollect. **retrain** *v.t.* to teach new skills to. *~v.i.* to learn new skills. **retranslate** *v.t.* **1** to translate again. **2** to translate back into the original language. **retranslation** *n.* **retransmit** *v.t.* (*pres.p.* **retransmitting**, *past, p.p.* **retransmitted**) to transmit again or to a greater distance. **retransmission** *n.* **retread**[1] (-tred´) *v.t.* (*past* **retrod**, *p.p.* **retrodden**) **1** to tread again. **2** to remould (a tyre). **retread**[2] (rē´-) *n.* **1** a remoulded tyre. **2** something unoriginal, using ideas which have been used before. **retrial** (rē´trīəl) *n.* (*Law*) a second trial. **retry** *v.t.* (*3rd pers. sing. pres.* **retries**, *pres.p.* **retrying**, *past, p.p.* **retried**) to try again. **retune** *v.t.* to tune again or in a different way. **returf** *v.t.* to turf again. **retype** *v.t.* to type again, correcting errors.

retract (ritrakt´) *v.t.* **1** to take back, to revoke, to acknowledge to be false or wrong. **2** to draw back or in. *~v.i.* **1** to withdraw a statement, declaration, promise etc. **2** to withdraw, to shrink back. **retractable** *a.* **retractile** (-tīl) *a.* capable of being retracted. **retractility** (-til´-) *n.* **retraction** (-trak´-shən) *n.* **retractive** *a.* **retractor** *n.* **1** a muscle used for drawing back. **2** (*Med.*) an instrument or bandage used by a surgeon for holding back parts.

retreat (ritrēt´) *v.i.* **1** to move back, to retire, esp. before an enemy or from an advanced position. **2** to recede. **3** to withdraw to a place of privacy, seclusion or security. *~v.t.* to cause to retreat. *~n.* **1** the act of withdrawing or retiring, esp. the retiring of an army before an enemy. **2** (*Mil.*) **a** a signal to retreat. **b** a bugle call at sunset. **3** retirement for meditation, prayer etc. **4** a state of retirement or seclusion. **5** a place of retirement, security, privacy or seclusion.

retrench (ritrench´) *v.t.* **1** to cut down, to reduce, to curtail, to diminish. **2** to shorten, to abridge, to cut out or pare down. **3** (*esp. Austral.*) to make redundant. *~v.t.* to curtail expenses, to make economies. **retrenchment** *n.*

retribution (retribū´shən) *n.* recompense, a

suitable return, esp. for evil, requital, vengeance. **retributive** (ritrib´-) *a.* **retributory** (-trib´-) *a.*

retrieve (ritrēv´) *v.t.* **1** (of a dog) to find and bring in (game, a stick, a ball etc.). **2** to recover by searching or recollecting, recall to mind. **3** to regain (something which has been lost, impaired etc.). **4** to rescue (from). **5** to restore, to reestablish (one's fortunes etc.). **6** to remedy, to make good, to repair. **7** in tennis etc., to return (a difficult ball) successfully. **8** to recover (data stored in a computer system). **retrievable** *a.* **retrievability** (-bil´-) *n.* **retrievably** *adv.* **retrieval** *n.* **retriever** *n.* **1** a dog of a breed used to fetch in game. that has been shot. **2** a person who retrieves.

retro (ret´rō) *n.* (*pl.* **retros**) **1** an object made in the style of a past era. **2** a style or fashion mimicking one from a past era. *~a.* mimicking the style of a past era.

retro- (ret´rō) *comb. form* **1** back, in return. **2** (*Anat., Med.*) located behind.

retroact (retrōakt´) *v.i.* **1** to act backwards or in return. **2** to act retrospectively. **3** to react. **retroaction** (-ak´shən) *n.* **retroactive** *a.* **retroactively** *adv.* **retroactivity** (-tiv´-) *n.*

retrocede (retrōsēd´) *v.i.* **1** to move backwards. **2** to recede. *~v.t.* to cede back again, to restore (territory etc.).

retrofit (ret´rōfit) *v.t.* (*pres.p.* **retrofitting**, *past, p.p.* **retrofitted**) to equip or modify (an aircraft, car etc.) with new parts or safety equipment after manufacture.

retroflected (retrōflek´tid), **retroflex** (ret´rəfleks), **retroflexed** (ret´rəflekst) *a.* **1** (*Anat., Med., Bot.*) turned or curved backward. **2** (of a vowel or consonant) articulated with the tip of the tongue bent upwards and backwards. **retroflection** (-flek´shən), **retroflexion** *n.*

retrograde (ret´rəgrād) *a.* **1** going, moving, bending or directed backwards. **2** inverted, reversed. **3** declining, degenerating, deteriorating. *~n.* **1** a degenerate person. **2** a backward movement or tendency, deterioration, decline. *~v.i.* **1** to move backwards, to recede. **2** to decline, to deteriorate, to revert. **retrogradation** (-grədā´shən) *n.* **retrogradely** *adv.*

retrogress (retrōgres´) *v.i.* **1** to go backward, to retrograde. **2** to degenerate. **retrogression** (-gresh´ən) *n.* **retrogressive** *a.* **retrogressively** *adv.*

retroject (retrōjekt´) *v.t.* to throw backwards, as distinct from *project.*

retro-rocket (ret´rōrokit) *n.* a small rocket on a spacecraft, satellite etc. which produces thrust in the opposite direction to flight for deceleration or manoeuvring.

retrorse (ritraws´) *a.* (*Biol.*) turned or bent backwards, reverted. **retrorsely** *adv.*

retrospect (ret´rəspekt) *n.* **1** view of, regard to, or consideration of previous conditions etc. **2** a review of past events. **in retrospect** looking back on something that has happened. **retrospection**

(-spek´-) *n*. **retrospective** (-spek´-) *a*. **1** in retrospection, viewing the past. **2** of or relating to an exhibition of an artist's life work. **3** applicable to what has happened. **4** towards the rear. ~*n*. an exhibition of an artist's life work. **retrospectively** *adv*.

retroussé (ritroo´sā) *a*. (of the nose) turned up at the end.

retrovert (rētrəvœt´) *v.t*. (*esp. Med*.) to turn back (esp. of the womb). **retroversion** (-vœ´shən) *n*.

retrovirus (ret´rōvīərəs) *n*. (*pl*. **retroviruses**) (*Biol*.) any of a group of viruses which use RNA to synthesize DNA, reversing the normal process of cellular transcription of DNA into RNA; many cause cancer in animals and one is the cause of Aids in humans.

retsina (retsē´nə) *n*. a resin-flavoured white wine from Greece.

return (ritœn´) *v.i*. **1** to come or go back, esp. to the same place or state. **2** to revert, to happen again, to recur. ~*v.t*. **1** to bring, carry or convey back. **2** to give, render or send back. **3** to repay, to put or send back or in return, to requite. **4** to yield (a profit). **5** to say in reply, to retort. **6** in cricket etc., to hit (the ball) back. **7** to report officially. **8** to elect. ~*n*. **1** the act of coming or going back. **2** the act of giving, paying, putting or sending back. **3** something which is returned. **4** a return ticket. **5** an official account or report. **6** the act of electing or returning. **7** the state of being elected. **8** (*often pl*.) the proceeds or profits on labour, investments etc. **9** in sport, a stroke, thrust etc. in return. **10** a return match or game. **by return (of post)** by the next post back to the sender. **in return** in reply or response, in requital. **many happy returns (of the day)** a birthday greeting. **returnable** *a*. **returnee** (-nē´) *n*. **1** a person who returns home after being abroad for a long time. **2** a person who returns to work after a period looking after their children. **returner** *n*. **return game** *n*. a return match. **returning officer** *n*. the presiding officer at an election. **return key** *n*. a key on a computer keyboard pressed to return to the beginning of the next line. **returnless** *a*. **return match** *n*. a second meeting of the same clubs or teams. **return ticket** *n*. a ticket for a journey to a place and back again.

re- (+ u– words) reunify *v.t*. (*3rd pers. sing. pres*. **reunifies**, *pres.p*. **reunifying**, *past, p.p*. **reunified**) to join together (territories which have been divided). **reunification** *n*. **reunite** *v.t*. **1** to join again after separation. **2** to reconcile after variance. ~*v.i*. to become united again. **reupholster** *v.t*. to upholster again. **reupholstery** *n*. **reuse**[1] (rēūz´) *v.t*. to use again. **reusable** *a*. **reuse**[2] (rēūs´) *n*. the act of using again. **reutilize, reutilise** *v.t*. to utilize again or in a different way. **reutilization** *n*.

reunion (rēū´nyən) *n*. **1** the act of reuniting. **2** the state of being reunited. **3** a meeting or

social gathering, esp. of friends, associates or partisans.

Rev. *abbr*. Reverend.

rev (rev) *n*. a revolution in an engine. ~*v.t., v.i*. (*pres.p*. **revving**, *past, p.p*. **revved**) to run (an engine) quickly by increasing the speed of revolution. **rev counter** *n*. a revolution counter.

re- (+ v– words) revaccinate *v.t*. to vaccinate again. **revaccination** *n*. **revalue** *v.t*. (*pres.p*. **revaluing**, *past, p.p*. **revalued**) **1** to adjust the exchange rate of (a currency) usu. upwards, as distinct from *devalue*. **2** to reappraise. **revaluation** *n*. **revamp** *v.t*. to renovate, to restore the appearance of. **revarnish** *v.t*. to varnish again. **revegetate** *v.t*. to produce new vegetation on. **revegetation** *n*. **reverify** *v.t*. (*3rd pers. sing. pres*. **reverifies**, *pres.p*. **reverifying**, *past, p.p*. **reverified**) to verify again. **reverification** *n*. **revisit** *v.t*. (*pres.p*. **revisiting**, *past, p.p*. **revisited**) to visit again. **revitalize, revitalise** *v.t*. to vitalize again. **revitalization** *n*. **revivify** *v.t*. (*3rd pers. sing. pres*. **revivifies**, *pres.p*. **revivifying**, *past, p.p*. **revivified**) to restore to life, to reanimate, to reinvigorate, to put new life into, to revive. **revivification** *n*.

Revd *abbr*. Reverend.

reveal[1] (rivēl´) *v.t*. **1** to allow to appear. **2** to disclose, to divulge (something secret, private or unknown), to betray. **3** to make known by supernatural or divine means. **revealable** *a*. **revealer** *n*. **revealing** *a*. **1** significant. **2** (of a dress etc.) exposing more of the body than is usual. **revealingly** *adv*. **revealment** *n*.

reveal[2] (rivēl´) *n*. the depth of a wall as revealed in the side of an aperture, doorway or window.

reveille (rival´i) *n*. a morning signal by drum or bugle to awaken soldiers or sailors.

revel (rev´əl) *v.i*. (*pres.p*. **revelling**, (*N Am*.) **reveling**, *past, p.p*. **revelled**, (*N Am*.) **reveled**) **1** to make merry, to carouse, to be boisterously festive. **2** to take great enjoyment (in). ~*v.t*. to spend or waste in revelry. ~*n*. (*often pl*.) an act of revelling, a carousal, a merrymaking. **reveller**, (*N Am*.) **reveler** *n*. **revelry** (-ri) *n*. (*pl*. **revelries**).

revelation (revəlā´shən) *n*. **1** the act of revealing, a disclosing of knowledge or information. **2** knowledge or information which is revealed, esp. by God to humans. **3** an astonishing disclosure. **revelational** *a*. **revelationist** *n*. a person who believes in divine revelation. **revelative** (rev´əlā-), **revelatory** (rev´ələ-) *a*.

revenant (rev´ənənt) *n*. a person who returns from the grave or from exile, esp. a ghost.

revenge (rivenj´) *n*. **1** retaliation, retribution or spiteful return for an injury. **2** a means, mode or act of revenging. **3** the desire to inflict revenge, vindictiveness. **4** in a game, the chance to win following an earlier defeat. ~*v.t*. **1** to take satisfaction or retribution for, to retaliate. **2** to avenge or satisfy (oneself) with such retribution or retaliation. ~*v.i*. to take vengeance. **revengeful**

a. **revengefully** *adv.* **revengefulness** *n.* **revengeless** *a.* **revenger** *n.*

Usage note The usual constructions of *revenge* are *revenge oneself* (*on* or *upon*) and *be revenged* (*on* or *upon*). See also notes under AVENGE, VENGEANCE.

revenue (rev´ənū) *n.* **1** (*often pl.*) income, esp. of a considerable amount from many forms of property. **2** the annual income of a state, derived from taxation, customs, excise etc. **3** the department of the civil service collecting this. **revenue tax** *n.* a tax for raising revenue, as distinct from *protective tax*, designed to affect trade.

reverberate (rivœ´bərāt) *v.i.* **1** (of sound, light or heat) to be driven back or to be reflected, to resound, to re-echo. **2** (of an event or idea) to have a powerful, long-lasting effect. **3** to rebound, to recoil. ~*v.t.* to send back, to re-echo, to reflect (sound, light or heat). **reverberant** *a.* **reverberantly** *adv.* **reverberation** (-ā´shən) *n.* **reverberative** (-bərə-) *a.* **reverberator** *n.* **reverberatory** *a.* producing or acting by reverberation.

revere (riviə´) *v.t.* to regard with awe mingled with affection, to venerate. **reverence** (rev´ər-) *n.* **1** the act of revering, veneration. **2** a feeling of or the capacity for feeling reverence. **3** (**Reverence**) a title given to the clergy. ~*v.t.* to regard or treat with reverence, to venerate. **reverencer** *n.* **reverend** (rev´ə-) *a.* worthy or entitled to reverence or respect, esp. as a title of respect given to members of the clergy. ~*n.* (*coll.*) a member of the clergy. **reverent** (rev´ər-) *a.* **1** feeling or expressing reverence. **2** submissive, humble. **reverential** (revərən´-) *a.* **reverentially** *adv.* **reverently** *adv.*

Usage note (1) In referring to persons with the title 'Reverend', *the Reverend Dr Smith*, *the Reverend Bill Smith* and *the Reverend W. Smith* are the recommended styles: always include *the* and a name, initial or other title along with the surname. (2) The adjectives *reverend* and *reverent* should not be confused: *reverend* means worthy of reverence, and *reverent* feeling reverence. The uses of *reverent* also overlap with those of *reverential*, but *reverent* is stronger and requires sincere feeling.

reverie (rev´əri) *n.* **1** listless musing, a daydream, a loose or irregular train of thought. **2** (*Mus.*) a dreamy musical composition.

revers (riviə´) *n.* (*pl.* **revers** (-viəz´)) a part of a coat, esp. a lapel, turned back so as to show the lining.

reverse (rivœs´) *v.t.* **1** to turn in the contrary direction, to turn the other way round, upside down, or inside out. **2** to invert, to transpose. **3** to cause to go backwards. **4** to cause to have a contrary motion or effect. **5** to revoke, to annul, to nullify. ~*v.i.* **1** to change to a contrary condition, direction etc. **2** to put a car into reverse

gear. ~*a.* **1** having an opposite direction, contrary. **2** turned backwards, inverted, reversed, upside down. ~*n.* **1** the contrary, the opposite. **2** the opposite of the usual manner. **3** the back surface (of a coin etc.), as distinct from *obverse*. **4** a complete change of affairs for the worse, a check, a defeat. **5** reverse gear. **6** the verso of a page. **to reverse arms** to hold a rifle with the butt upwards. **to reverse the charges** to make a telephone call for which the recipient pays. **reversal** *n.* **reverse-charge** *a.* denoting a telephone call for which the recipient pays. **reverse fault** *n.* (*Geol.*) an oblique fault with the upper rock strata displaced upwards in relation to the lower strata. **reverse gear** *n.* the gear which makes a vehicle go backwards. **reversely** *adv.* **reverser** *n.* **reverse take-over** *n.* the take-over of a larger company by a smaller one. **reversible** *a.* **reversibility** (-bil´-) *n.* **reversibly** *adv.* **reversing** *n.*, *a.* **reversing light** *n.* a light on the rear of a motor vehicle which is lit when reverse gear is engaged. **reversion** (-shən) *n.* **1** return to a former condition, habit etc. **2** (*Biol.*) the tendency of an animal or a plant to revert to ancestral type or character. **3** the right of succeeding to an estate after the death of the grantee etc. **4** a sum payable upon a person's death, esp. an annuity or life assurance. **reversional** *a.* **reversionary** *a.* **reversioner** *n.* a person who holds the reversion to an estate etc.

revert (rivœt´) *v.i.* **1** to go back, to fall back, to return (to a previous condition, habits, type etc., esp. to a wild state). **2** (*Law*) to come back by reversion to the possession of the former proprietor. **3** to recur, to turn the attention again (to). ~*v.t.* to turn (esp. the eyes) back. **reverter** *n.* **revertible** *a.*

revet (rivet´) *v.t.* (*pres.p.* **revetting**, *past*, *p.p.* **revetted**) to face (a wall, scarp, parapet etc.) with masonry. **revetment** *n.* **1** a facing of stones, concrete etc. to protect a wall or embankment. **2** a retaining wall.

review (rivū´) *n.* **1** a final examination, esp. by people in authority. **2** a repeated examination, a reconsideration, a second view. **3** a retrospective survey. **4** a critical account of a book etc. **5** a periodical publication containing essays and criticisms. **6** a display or a formal or official inspection of military or naval forces. ~*v.t.* **1** to view again. **2** to look back on, to go over in memory, to revise. **3** to survey, to look over carefully and critically. **4** to write a critical review of. **5** to hold a review of, to inspect. ~*v.i.* to write reviews. **reviewable** *a.* **reviewer** *n.*

Usage note The spellings of the nouns *review* (a second view, a critical account, etc.) and *revue* (an entertainment) should not be confused.

revile (rivīl´) *v.t.* to abuse, to vilify. ~*v.i.* to be abusive. **revilement** *n.* **reviler** *n.* **reviling** *a.*

revise (rivīz´) *v.t.* **1** to look over, to re-examine for correction or emendation. **2** to correct, alter or amend. **3** to reread (course notes etc.) for an examination. ~*v.i.* to reread course notes etc. for an examination. ~*n.* (*Print.*) a proof-sheet in which corrections made in rough proof have been embodied. **revisable** *a.* **revisal** *n.* **reviser** *n.* **revision** (-vizh´ən) *n.* **1** the act or process of revising. **2** a revised version. **revisional, revisionary** *a.* **revisionist** *n.* **1** a person in favour of revision. **2** a person who believes in the broadening and evolution of the theories of Marxism. **3** (*derog.*) a person who departs from the principles of orthodox Communism. **revisionism** *n.* **revisory** *a.*

revive (riviv´) *v.i.* **1** to return to life, consciousness, vigour, popularity, activity, vogue, the stage etc. **2** to come back to the mind again, to reawaken. ~*v.t.* to bring back to life, consciousness, vigour, etc. **revivable** *a.* **revival** *n.* **1** the act of reviving. **2** the state of being revived. **3** a new production of a dramatic work previously neglected or forgotten. **4** a religious awakening, esp. a movement for the renewal of religious fervour by means of special services etc. **revivalism** *n.* **revivalist** *n.* **revivalistic** (-lis´-) *a.* **reviver** *n.*

reviviscent (revivis´ənt) *a.* recovering life and strength, reviving.

revoke (rivōk´) *v.t.* to annul, to cancel (a law etc.). ~*v.i.* in cards, to fail to follow suit when this would have been possible. ~*n.* the act of revoking at cards. **revocable** (rev´əkəbəl) *a.* **revocation** (revəkā´shən) *n.* **revocatory** (rev´əkətəri) *a.* **revokable** *a.* **revoker** *n.*

revolt (rivōlt´) *v.i.* **1** to renounce allegiance, to rise in rebellion or insurrection. **2** to feel disgust (at), to feel repugnance (at). ~*v.t.* to repel, to nauseate, to disgust. ´~*n.* **1** a renunciation of allegiance and subjection. **2** a rebellion, an uprising, an insurrection. **3** revulsion. **4** a mood of defiance. **revolted** *a.* having revolted. **revolter** *n.* **revolting** *a.* horrible, disgusting, repulsive. **revoltingly** *adv.*

revolute (rev´əloot) *a.* (*Bot.*) (of a leaf) rolled backwards from the edge.

revolution (revəloo´shən) *n.* **1** a fundamental change in government, esp. by the forcible overthrow of the existing system and substitution of a new ruler or political system. **2** a radical change or reversal of circumstances, conditions, relations or things. **3** the act or state of revolving. **4** the circular motion of a body on its axis, rotation. **5** the motion of a body round a centre. **6** a complete rotation or movement round a centre. **7** the period of this. **8** a round or cycle or regular recurrence or succession. **revolutionary** *a.* **1** bringing about great changes. **2** of, relating to or tending to produce a revolution in government. **3** of or relating to a particular revolution. ~*n.* **1** an advocate of revolution. **2** a person who takes an active part in a revolution. **revolutionism** *n.* **revolutionist** *n.* **revolutionize, revolutionise** *v.t.* to cause radical change in.

revolve (rivolv´) *v.i.* **1** to turn round. **2** to move round a centre, to rotate. **3** to move in a circle, orbit or cycle. ~*v.t.* **1** to cause to revolve or rotate. **2** to turn over and over in the mind, to meditate on, to ponder over. **to revolve around** to have (something) as an important central feature or focus (*His life revolves around his family*). **revolver** *n.* **1** a pistol having a revolving breech cylinder by which it can be fired several times without reloading. **2** something which revolves. **revolving door** *n.* a door, usu. with four leaves at right angles, which rotates about a vertical axis.

revue (rivū´) *n.* a light entertainment with songs, dances etc., representing topical characters, events, fashions etc.

Usage note See note under REVIEW.

revulsion (rivŭl´shən) *n.* **1** a strong feeling of disgust. **2** a sudden or violent change or reaction, esp. of feeling.

re- (+ w- words) rewind[1] *v.t.* (*past, p.p.* **rewound**) to wind (a film or tape) back to the beginning. **rewind**[2] (rē´-) *n.* **1** a mechanism for rewinding a film or tape. **2** the act of rewinding. **rewinder** *n.* **rewire** *v.t.* to install new electrical wiring in (a house etc.). **reword** *v.t.* to put into different words. **rework** *v.t.* **1** to treat or use again. **2** to revise. **3** to reprocess for renewed use. **reworking** *n.* **rewrap** *v.t.* (*pres.p.* **rewrapping**, *past, p.p.* **rewrapped**) to wrap again or in a different way. **rewrite**[1] (-rīt´) *v.t.* (*pres.p.* **rewriting**, *past* **rewrote**, *p.p.* **rewritten**) **1** to write over again. **2** to revise. **rewrite**[2] (rē´-) *n.* **1** the act of rewriting. **2** something rewritten.

reward (riwawd´) *n.* **1** something which is given in return usu. for good done or received. **2** a recompense, a requital, retribution. **3** a sum of money offered for the detection of a criminal or for the restoration of anything lost. ~*v.t.* to repay, to requite, to recompense (a service or offence, a doer or offender). **rewarder** *n.* **rewarding** *a.* **1** personally satisfying. **2** profitable. **rewardingly** *adv.* **rewardless** *a.*

Rex (reks) *n.* a reigning king (the official title used by a king, esp. on documents, coins etc.).

RF, r.f. *abbr.* radio frequency.

Rf *chem. symbol* rutherfordium.

RFC *abbr.* Rugby Football Club.

Rh[1] *chem. symbol* rhodium.

Rh[2] *abbr.* (*Med.*) rhesus factor.

r.h. *abbr.* right hand.

Rhaetian (rē´shən), **Rhetian** *n.* Rhaeto-Romance. ~*a.* of or relating to the Rhaeto-Romance dialects. **Rhaeto-Romance** (rētō-rōmans´), **Rhaeto-Romanic** (-rōman´ik) *a.* of or relating to the Romance peoples of SE Switzerland and the Tyrol or their dialects, esp. Romansh and Ladin. ~*n.* any of the Rhaeto-Romance dialects.

rhapsody (rap´sədi) *n.* (*pl.* **rhapsodies**) **1** a high-flown, enthusiastic composition or utterance. **2** (*Mus.*) an irregular and emotional composition, esp. of the nature of an improvisation. **rhapsodic**

(-sod´-), **rhapsodical** *a.* **rhapsodically** *adv.*
rhapsodist *n.* **rhapsodize, rhapsodise** *v.i.* to
recite or write rhapsodies.
rhatany (rat´əni), **ratany** *n.* (*pl.* **rhatanies,
ratanies**) a Peruvian shrub, *Krameria triandra,*
or its root, from which an extract is obtained
for use in medicine and for adulterating port
wine.
rhea (rē´ə) *n.* any flightless bird of the family
Rheidae of S America, smaller than ostriches
and with three toes.
rhebok (rē´bok), **reebok** *n.* a small antelope of
southern Africa, *Pelea capreolus,* having a long
neck and short, straight horns.
Rhenish (ren´ish) *a.* of or relating to the Rhine or
the Rhineland. ~*n.* Rhine wine, hock.
rhenium (rē´niəm) *n.* (*Chem.*) a metallic element, at. no. 75, chem. symbol Re, occurring in
certain platinum and molybdenum ores.
rheostat (rē´əstat) *n.* a variable resistance for
adjusting and regulating an electric current.
rheostatic (-stat´-) *a.*
rhesus (rē´səs), **rhesus monkey** *n.* a macaque,
Macaca mulatta, held sacred in some parts of
India. **rhesus baby** *n.* (*pl.* **rhesus babies**) a baby
born with a blood disorder because its own
rhesus-positive blood is incompatible with its
mother's rhesus-negative blood. **rhesus factor** *n.*
an antigen substance occurring in the red blood
corpuscles of most human beings and many
mammals (e.g. the rhesus monkey). **rhesus negative** *a.* not having the rhesus factor. **rhesus positive** *a.* having the rhesus factor.
rhetoric (ret´ərik) *n.* **1** the art of effective
speaking or writing, the rules of eloquence. **2** the
use of language for effect or display, esp. affected
or exaggerated oratory or declamation. **rhetorical**
(ritor´-) *a.* **1** designed for effect or display, florid,
showy, affected, declamatory. **2** of, relating to or
of the nature of rhetoric. **rhetorically** *adv.* **rhetorical question** *n.* a question asked merely for
the sake of emphasis and requiring no answer.
rhetorician (retərish´ən) *n.* **1** a skilled orator. **2** a
teacher of rhetoric. **3** a flamboyant or affected
speaker.
rheum (room) *n.* the thin serous fluid secreted by
the mucous glands as tears, saliva, or mucus.
rheumatic (roomat´ik) *a.* of, relating to, suffering from or subject to rheumatism. ~*n.* a person
who suffers from rheumatism. **rheumatically**
adv. **rheumatic fever** *n.* (*Med.*) a disease characterized by fever, acute pain in the joints and
potential inflammation of the heart and pericardium. **rheumaticky** *a.* **rheumatics** *n.* (*coll.*)
rheumatism. **rheumatism** (roo´mətizm) *n.* an
inflammatory disease which affects the muscles
and joints of the human body, causing swelling
and pain. **rheumatoid** (roo´mə-) *a.* resembling
rheumatism. **rheumatoid arthritis** *n.* (*Med.*) a
chronic disease which causes inflammation and
pain in the joints.
rheumatology (roomətol´əji) *n.* the study of

rheumatism. **rheumatological** (-loj´-) *a.* **rheuma-
tologist** *n.*
rhinestone (rīn´stōn) *n.* a colourless artificial
gem cut to look like a diamond.
rhinitis (rīnī´tis) *n.* (*Med.*) inflammation of the
mucous membrane of the nose.
rhino (rī´nō) *n.* (*pl.* **rhinos, rhino**) a rhinoceros.
rhino- (rī´nō), **rhin-** *comb. form* (*Anat.*) of or
relating to the nose or nostrils.
rhinoceros (rīnos´ərəs) *n.* (*pl.* **rhinoceros,
rhinoceroses**) a large grey-coloured quadruped
of the family Rhinocerotidae, now found only in
Africa and S Asia, with one or two horns on the
nose. **rhinoceros beetle** *n.* a large horned beetle
of the subfamily Dynastinae. **rhinoceros bird** *n.*
the ox-pecker. **rhinoceros horn** *n.* the keratinized
fibres forming rhinoceros's horns, supposed to
have aphrodisiac or reinvigorating qualities.
rhinocerotic (-rot´-) *a.*
rhinoplasty (rī´nōplasti) *n.* (*Med.*) plastic
surgery of the nose. **rhinoplastic** (-plas´-) *a.*
rhizo- (rī´zō), **rhiz-** *comb. form* (*Bot.*) having roots
or rootlike processes.
rhizobium (rīzō´biəm) *n.* a soil bacterium of the
genus *Rhizobium,* occurring in the root nodules
of leguminous plants.
rhizoid (rī´zoid) *a.* (*Bot.*) rootlike. ~*n.* a filament
or hairlike organ in mosses etc.
rhizome (rī´zōm) *n.* (*Bot.*) a prostrate, thickened,
rootlike stem, sending roots downwards and
producing aerial shoots etc. annually. **rhi-
zomatous** (-zom´-) *a.*
rho (rō) *n.* (*pl.* **rhos**) the 17th letter of the Greek
alphabet (ρ, P).
rhodium (rō´diəm) *n.* (*Chem.*) a greyish-white
metallic element, at. no. 45, chem. symbol Rh,
belonging to the platinum group.
rhodo- (rō´dō), **rhod-** *comb. form* **1** rose. **2**
roselike.
rhododendron (rōdəden´drən) *n.* (*pl.* **rhodo-
dendrons**) any evergreen shrub of the genus
Rhododendron akin to the azaleas, with brilliant
flowers.
rhodopsin (rōdop´sin) *n.* a purplish pigment
found in the retina, visual purple.
rhodora (rōdaw´rə) *n.* a N American flowering
shrub, *Rhodora canadensis,* belonging to the
family Ericaceae, growing in boggy ground.
rhomb (rom, romb) *n.* a rhombus. **rhombic**
(rom´bik) *a.*
rhombi RHOMBUS.
rhombohedron (rombōhē´drən) *n.* (*pl.*
rhombohedra (-drə), **rhombohedrons**) **1** a solid
figure bounded by six equal rhombuses. **2** in
crystallography, a crystal in the form of a
rhombohedron. **rhombohedral** *a.*
rhomboid (rom´boid) *a.* having the shape or
nearly the shape of a rhomboid. ~*n.* a parallelogram, the adjoining sides of which are not equal
and which contains no right angle. **rhomboidal**
(-boi´-) *a.*
rhombus (rom´bəs) *n.* (*pl.* **rhombuses, rhombi**

(-bī)) (*Geom.*) an oblique parallelogram with equal sides.

rhubarb (roo´bahb) *n.* **1** any herbaceous plant of the genus *Rheum*, esp. *R. rhaponticum*, the fleshy and juicy leaf-stalks of which are cooked and eaten. **2** the root of several central Asian species of *Rheum*, from which purgative medicines are prepared. **3** the sound supposedly made by actors to simulate background conversation. **4** nonsense. **5** (*N Am.*, *sl.*) a loud argument, an angry quarrel. **rhubarby** *a.*

rhumb (rŭm) *n.* **1** any one of the 32 principal points of the compass. **2** the angular distance between any successive pair of these. **3** (*Naut.*) a line cutting all the meridians at the same angle, such as a ship would follow sailing continuously on one course. **rhumb line** *n.*

rhumba RUMBA.

rhyme (rīm), †**rime** *n.* **1** a correspondence of sound in the final accented syllable or group of syllables of a line of verse with that of another line, consisting of identity of the vowel sounds and of all the consonantal sounds but the first. **2** (*sing. or pl.*) verse characterized by rhyme. **3** a word rhyming with another. ~*v.i.* **1** to make a rhyme with another word or verse. **2** to be in accord, to harmonize (with). **3** to make rhymes, to versify. ~*v.t.* **1** to put into rhyme. **2** to treat (a word) as rhyming with another. **without rhyme or reason** unreasonable, purposeless. **rhymeless** *a.* **rhymer** *n.* **rhymester** (-sta), **rhymist** *n.* a poet, esp. of inferior talent; a poetaster. **rhyming slang** *n.* a form of slang originating among Cockneys in London in which a word is replaced by a rhyming phrase of which often only the first element is used, so that the rhyme itself disappears (e.g. *Barnet fair* becomes *Barnet* meaning *hair*).

rhyolite (rī´əlīt) *n.* (*Geol.*) an igneous rock with a structure showing the effect of lava-flow, composed of quartz and feldspar with other minerals.

rhythm (ridh´m) *n.* **1** movement characterized by action and reaction or regular alternation of strong and weak impulse, stress, accent, motion, sound etc. **2** the regulated succession of musical notes according to duration. **3** a structural system based on this. **4** in art, correlation of parts in a harmonious whole. **5** any alternation of strong and weak states or movements. **6** a sense of rhythm. **rhythm and blues** *n.* a style of popular music integrating elements of folk, rock and roll, and blues. **rhythmic, rhythmical** *a.* **rhythmically** *adv.* **rhythmic gymnastics** *n.pl.* (*sometimes sing.*) a kind of gymnastics incorporating elements of dance and often using ribbons or hoops. **rhythmicist** (-sist) *n.* **rhythmist** *n.* **rhythmless** *a.* **rhythm method** *n.* a method of contraception requiring sexual abstinence during the period when ovulation is most likely to occur. **rhythm section** *n.* the section of instruments (usu. piano, double bass and drums) in a band whose main task is to provide the rhythm.

RI *abbr.* **1** King and Emperor (L *rex et imperator*). **2** Queen and Emperor (L *regina et imperatrix*). **3** religious instruction.

rial (rē´ahl), **riyal** *n.* the standard unit of currency in Iran, Oman, Saudi Arabia, Qatar and Yemen.

rib[1] (rib) *n.* **1** (*Anat.*) any one of the bones extending outwards and forwards from the spine, and in human beings forming the walls of the thorax. **2** a ridge, strip, line etc., analogous in form or function to this. **3** a cut of meat including one or more ribs. **4** a curved timber extending from the keel for supporting the side of a ship etc. **5** a raised moulding or groin on a ceiling or vaulted roof. **6** a hinged rod forming part of an umbrella-frame. **7** a main vein in a leaf. **8** a raised row in a knitted or woven fabric. **9** a structural member in an aerofoil. ~*v.t.* (*pres.p.* **ribbing**, *past*, *p.p.* **ribbed**) **1** to provide with ribs. **2** to mark with ribs or ridges. **3** to enclose with ribs. **4** to plough leaving spaces between furrows. **ribbed** *a.* **ribbing**[1] *n.* a system or arrangement of ribs, as in a vaulted roof etc. **ribcage** *n.* the structure of ribs and tissue which forms the enclosing wall of the chest. **ribless** *a.* **ribwort** *n.* the narrow-leaved plantain, *Plantago lanceolata*.

rib[2] (rib) *v.t.* (*pres.p.* **ribbing**, *past*, *p.p.* **ribbed**) (*coll.*) to tease, make fun of. **ribbing**[2] *n.*

ribald (rib´əld) *a.* (of language) coarse, licentious, lewd. ~*n.* a low or indecent person, esp. one using coarse language. **ribaldry** (-ri) *n.*

ribbing[1] RIB[1].

ribbing[2] RIB[2].

ribbon (rib´ən), **riband** (rib´ənd) *n.* **1** a narrow woven strip or band of silk, satin etc., used for ornamenting dress etc. **2** such a strip or band worn as a distinctive mark of an order, college, club etc. **3** a narrow strip of anything. **4** an ink-impregnated cloth strip used in typewriters etc. **5** (*pl.*) torn shreds, ragged strips. **ribbon development** *n.* urban extension in the form of a single depth of houses along roads radiating from a town. **ribboned** *a.* **ribbonfish** *n.* (*pl.* **ribbonfish**) a long, narrow, flattish fish, esp. of the families Trachipteridae and Regalecidae. **ribbon worm** *n.* a nemertean.

riboflavin (rībōflā´vin), **riboflavine** (-vēn) *n.* a yellow vitamin of the B complex, found esp. in milk and liver, which promotes growth in children; vitamin B_2.

ribonucleic acid (rībōnuklē´ik) *n.* any of a group of nucleic acids present in all living cells and playing an essential role in the synthesis of proteins.

ribose (rī´bōz) *n.* a pentose sugar occurring in ribonucleic acid and riboflavin.

ribosome (rī´bəsōm) *n.* any of numerous minute granules containing ribonucleic acid and protein in a cell, which are the site for protein synthesis. **ribosomal** *a.*

rice (rīs) *n.* the white grain or seeds of *Oryza sativa*, an Asian aquatic grass extensively cultivated in warm climates for food. **rice bowl** *n.* an

area where rice is produced in large quantities.
rice-paper *n.* **1** a thin edible paper made from rice straw, used in baking. **2** a paper made from the pith of the Taiwanese *Tetrapanax papyriferum* and used by Chinese artists for painting on. **ricer** *n.* a device with small holes through which potatoes etc. are pressed to make a coarse mash.

rich (rich) *a.* **1** wealthy, having a lot of valuable possessions, abounding (in resources, productions etc.). **2** abundantly supplied (in or with). **3** producing ample supplies. **4** fertile, abundant, well-filled. **5** valuable, precious, costly. **6** elaborate, splendid. **7** abounding in qualities pleasing to the senses, sweet, luscious, high-flavoured, containing a lot of fat, oil, sugar, spices etc. **8** containing a large proportion of fuel. **9** vivid, bright. **10** (of a sound) mellow, deep, full, musical. **11** comical, funny, full of humorous suggestion. **richen** *v.i., v.t.* **riches** *n.pl.* valuable possessions and large amounts of money. **richly** *adv.* **1** in a rich manner. **2** abundantly, thoroughly. **richness** *n.*

Richter scale (rik´tə) *n.* a logarithmic scale for registering the magnitude of earthquakes.

ricin (rī´sin) *n.* a toxic substance obtained from castor oil beans.

rick[1] (rik), **wrick** *n.* a stack of corn, hay etc., built in a regular shape and thatched. ~*v.t.* to make or pile into a rick.

rick[2] (rik) *v.t.* to wrench or sprain. ~*n.* a wrench or sprain.

rickets (rik´its) *n.* (*Med.*) a disease of children resulting in the softening of the bones, esp. the spine, bow-legs, emaciation etc., owing to lack of mineral matter in the bones. **rickety** *a.* **1** shaky, tumbledown, fragile, unsafe. **2** feeble in the joints. **3** affected with or of the nature of rickets. **ricketiness** *n.*

rickettsia (riket´siə) *n.* (*pl.* **rickettsiae** (-siē)) any of a group of microorganisms of the genus *Rickettsia* found in lice, ticks etc. which when transmitted to human beings cause serious diseases, e.g. typhus. **rickettsial** *a.*

rickrack RICRAC.

rickshaw (rik´shaw), **ricksha** (-shah) *n.* a light two-wheeled hooded carriage drawn by one or two people, or attached to a bicycle etc.

ricochet (rik´əshā) *n.* **1** a rebounding or skipping of a stone, projectile or bullet off a hard or flat surface. **2** the act of aiming so as to produce this, or a hit so made. ~*v.i.* (*pres.p.* **ricocheting** (-shāing), **richochetting** (-sheting), *past, p.p.* **ricocheted** (-shād), **richochetted** (-shetid)) to skip or bound in this way.

ricotta (rikot´ə) *n.* a soft white Italian cheese made from sheep's milk.

ricrac (rik´rak), **rickrack** *n.* a zigzag braid for trimming garments.

rictus (rik´təs) *n.* (*pl.* **rictuses, rictus**) **1** (*Zool., Anat.*) the expanse of a person's or animal's open mouth, gape. **2** a grimace. **rictal** *a.*

rid (rid) *v.t.* (*pres.p.* **ridding**, *past* **rid**, *p.p.* **ridded**) to free, to clear, to disencumber (of). **to get rid of** to free oneself of or become free of. **riddance** *n.* clearance, deliverance, relief.

ridden etc. RIDE.

-ridden (rid´ən) *comb. form* oppressed, dominated by or excessively concerned with, as *debt-ridden.*

riddle[1] (rid´əl) *n.* **1** a question or proposition put in ambiguous language to exercise ingenuity; a puzzle, conundrum or enigma. **2** any person, thing or fact of an ambiguous, mysterious or puzzling nature. ~*v.i.* to speak in riddles. ~*v.t.* **1** to solve, to explain (a riddle, problem etc.). **2** to be a riddle to. **riddler** *n.* **riddling** *a.* puzzling. **riddlingly** *adv.*

riddle[2] (rid´əl) *v.t.* **1** to pass through a riddle, to sift. **2** to perforate with holes, esp. with gunshot. **3** to assail with arguments, questions, facts etc. ~*n.* a coarse sieve for sifting gravel, cinders etc. or washing ore. **riddled with** full of.

ride (rīd) *v.i.* (*pres.p.* **riding**, *past* **rode** (rōd), *p.p.* **ridden** (rid´ən), †**rid**) **1** to sit and be carried along, as on a horse, cycle, public conveyance etc., esp. to go on horseback. **2** to practise horsemanship. **3** to float, to seem to float. **4** to lie at anchor. **5** to be supported by, to be on something, esp. in motion. **6** (of an animal) to serve for riding. ~*v.t.* **1** to sit on and be carried along by (a horse etc.). **2** (*N Am.*) to travel in (a vehicle). **3** to traverse on a horse, cycle etc. **4** to compete in (a race). **5** to cause to ride, to give a ride to. **6** to be carried by, to float over. **7** to yield to (a blow). **8** to oppress, to tyrannize, to domineer (over). **9** (*taboo sl.*) to copulate with. **10** (*N Am.*) to annoy, to pester. ~*n.* **1** the act of riding. **2** a journey on horseback or in a public conveyance. **3** a path for riding on, esp. through a wood. **4** a journey or an experience of a specified nature (*a rough ride*). **5** a fairground device or structure, such as a roller-coaster, which people ride for fun. **6** (*taboo sl.*) an act of copulation. **7** (*taboo sl.*) a sexual partner. **to let something ride** to let something continue without interference. **to ride down 1** to overtake by riding. **2** to trample on in riding. **to ride for a fall** to act recklessly. **to ride high** to be popular or successful. **to ride out 1** to come safely through (a storm etc.). **2** to endure successfully. **to ride shotgun 1** (*esp. N Am.*) to travel as a guard, sitting beside the driver of a vehicle. **2** (*esp. N Am.*) to travel in the passenger seat of a vehicle. **3** (*esp. N Am.*) to act as a protector. **to ride up** (of a skirt etc.) to work up out of the normal position. **to take for a ride** (*coll.*) to play a trick on. **rideable, ridable** *a.* **ride-off** *n.* in a riding competition, a qualifying round. **ride-on** *a.* (of a lawnmower) designed to be ridden on while operated. **rider** *n.* **1** a person who rides, esp. on a horse. **2** an additional clause to a document, act etc., an opinion, recommendation etc. added to a verdict. **3** a subsidiary problem, a corollary, an obvious supplement. **4** a part in a machine which surmounts or bridges other parts. **5** (*pl.*) an additional timber or plate for strengthening the framework of a ship. **riderless** *a.* **riding**[1] *n.* **1** the act or state of a person who rides. **2** a path for riding on, esp. through a wood. **riding habit** *n.* a woman's costume for riding on horseback. **riding light** *n.* a light shown by a ship at anchor. **riding-master** *n.* a man who teaches riding. **riding school** *n.* a place where riding is taught.

ridge (rij) *n.* **1** the long horizontal angle formed by the junction of two slopes. **2** a long and narrow hilltop or mountain crest. **3** a continuous range of hills or mountains. **4** a strip of ground thrown up by a plough or other implement. **5** the spine of an animal. **6** an elongated area of high pressure on a weather map. **7** a raised hotbed for melons. ~*v.t.* **1** to mark or cover with ridges. **2** to break (a field etc.) into ridges. **3** to plant in ridges. **4** to gather into ridges. ~*v.i.* to gather into ridges. **ridge piece** *n.* a horizontal timber along the ridge of a roof. **ridge-pole** *n.* **1** the horizontal pole of a long tent. **2** a ridge piece. **ridge tile** *n.* a tile used to make a roof ridge. **ridge tree** *n.* a ridge piece. **ridgeway** *n.* a road or way along a ridge. **ridgy** *a.*

ridicule (rid´ikūl) *n.* **1** derision, mockery. **2** words or actions intended to express contempt and excite laughter. ~*v.t.* to treat with ridicule, to laugh at, to make fun of, to expose to derision. **ridiculer** *n.* **ridiculous** (-dik´-) *a.* **1** meriting or exciting ridicule. **2** absurd, foolish. **ridiculously** *adv.* **ridiculousness** *n.*

riding[1] RIDE.

riding[2] (rī´ding) *n.* **1** each of the three former administrative divisions of Yorkshire (*East Riding, North Riding, West Riding*). **2** an electoral division of Canada.

riel (rē´əl) *n.* the standard monetary unit of Cambodia.

rife (rīf) *a.* occurring in great quantity, number etc., current, prevalent. **rifely** *adv.* **rifeness** *n.*

riff (rif) *n.* (*Mus.*) a phrase or figure played repeatedly in jazz or rock music, usu. as background to an instrument solo. ~*v.i.* to play riffs.

riffle (rif´əl) *v.t.* **1** to ruffle, to flick through rapidly (the pages of a book etc.). **2** to shuffle (playing cards) by halving the deck and flicking the corners together using both thumbs. ~*v.i.* to flick cursorily (through). ~*n.* the act of riffling.

riff-raff (rif´raf) *n.* worthless people, rabble.

rifle (rī´fəl) *n.* **1** a firearm having the barrel spirally grooved so as to give a rotary motion to the projectile. **2** (*pl.*) troops armed with rifles. ~*v.t.* **1** to furnish (a firearm or the bore or barrel of a firearm) with spiral grooves in order to give a rotary motion to the projectile. **2** to plunder, to pillage, to strip. **3** to search and rob. **4** to snatch and carry off. ~*v.i.* **1** to search (through). **2** to shoot with a rifle. **rifle bird** *n.* any Australian bird of the genus *Ptilorrhis*, with velvety black

plumage. **rifleman** *n.* (*pl.* **riflemen**). **rifle range** *n.* an area for target practice using rifles. **rifleshot** *n.* **1** the distance a projectile from a rifle will carry. **2** a marksman with a rifle. **rifling** *n.* the spiral grooves in the bore of a firearm which cause the rotation of the projectile fired.

rift (rift) *n.* **1** a cleft, a fissure. **2** a wide crack, rent or opening, made by splitting. **3** a break in cloud. **4** a serious quarrel causing a split between people. ~*v.t.* to cleave, to split. ~*v.i.* to break open. **riftless** *a.* **rift valley** *n.* a narrow valley formed by the subsidence of the earth's crust between two faults.

rig[1] (rig) *v.t.* (*pres.p.* **rigging**, *past, p.p.* **rigged**) **1** to furnish or fit (a ship) with spars, gear or tackle. **2** to dress, clothe or fit up or out. **3** to put together or fit up in a hasty or makeshift way. **4** to assemble the parts of (an aircraft). ~*n.* **1** the way in which the masts and sails of a ship are arranged. **2** equipment for a particular purpose. **3** an oil rig. **4** (*coll.*) the style or look of a person's clothes etc., an outfit, a turn-out. **5** (*esp. N Am., Austral.*) an articulated lorry. **in full rig** (*coll.*) smartly or formally dressed. **rigged** *a.* **rigger**[1] *n.* **1** a person who rigs ships etc. **2** a person who erects scaffolding. **3** an outrigger. **4** a person who works on an oil rig. **-rigger** *comb. form* a ship rigged in the specified manner. **rigging** *n.* **1** the system of tackle, ropes etc. supporting the masts and controlling the sails etc. of a ship. **2** the adjustment or alignment of the components of an aeroplane. **rig-out** *n.* (*coll.*) dress, outfit.

rig[2] (rig) *v.t.* (*pres.p.* **rigging**, *past, p.p.* **rigged**) **1** to manipulate fraudulently. **2** to hoax, to trick. ~*n.* **1** a swindling scheme, a dodge, a trick. **2** a prank, a frolic, a practical joke. **to rig the market** to manipulate the market so as to raise or lower prices for underhand purposes. **rigger**[2] *n.*

rigger[1] RIG[1].

rigger[2] RIG[2].

right (rīt) *a.* **1** required by or acting, being or done in accordance with truth and justice. **2** correct, true. **3** fit, suitable, most suitable, the preferable, the more convenient. **4** sound, sane, well. **5** properly done, placed etc., not mistaken, satisfactory. **6** real, genuine, veritable. **7** on or towards the side of the body which is to the south when the face is to the sunrise. **8** (*also* **Right**) politically conservative, right-wing. ~*adv.* **1** in accordance with truth and justice, justly, equitably, rightly. **2** exactly, correctly, properly. **3** satisfactorily, well. **4** to or towards the right hand. **5** straight. **6** (*coll.*) immediately. **7** all the way (to). **8** completely. ~*n.* **1** what is right or just. **2** the cause or party having justice on its side. **3** just claim or title, esp. a claim enforceable at law, justification. **4** something which one is entitled to. **5** (*coll.*) the right hand. **6** the right-hand side, part or surface of anything. **7** (*often* **Right**) **a** the party sitting on the right of the president in a foreign legislature, usu. the more conservative party. **b** conservatives collectively. **8** in marching etc., the right foot. **9** the right wing of an army. ~*v.t.* **1** to set in or restore to an upright, straight, correct or proper position; to correct, make right, to rectify. **2** to relieve from wrong or injustice. ~*v.i.* to resume a vertical position. ~*int.* (*coll.*) used to express approval, compliance or enthusiasm. **by right** properly, with justice. **in the right** correct, in accordance with reason or justice. **of right** legally or morally entitled. **right and left 1** in all directions. **2** on every side. **right away** at once, immediately. **right ho!** righto! **right, left and centre** in or from all directions. **right off** right away. **right oh!** righto! **right on! right on!** (*sl*) used to express support or approval. **right you are!** (*coll.*) used to express agreement or compliance. **too right** (*coll.*) used to express agreement. **to put right** to correct, to rectify. **to put to rights** to put in order. **to set right** to put right. **to set to rights** to put to rights. **rightable** *a.* **right about** *n.* **1** (*esp. Mil.*) the opposite direction, a reverse to face in the opposite direction. **2** a reversal of policy. **3** a retreat. **right about-face** *n.* (*esp. Mil.*) a right about. **right about-turn** *n.* a right about. **right angle** *n.* an angle formed by two lines meeting perpendicularly. **at right angles** placing at or forming a right angle. **right-angled** *a.* **right arm** *n.* one's best or most efficient assistant, aid or support. **right ascension** *n.* (*Astron.*) the distance from the first point of Aries, measured along the celestial equator. **right-back** *n.* in football, hockey etc., a defensive player playing mainly on the right side of the pitch. **right bank** *n.* the bank of a river which is on the right facing downstream. **righten** *v.t.* **righter** *n.* **right field** *n.* in baseball, the part of the outfield to the right of the batter when facing the pitcher. **right-footed** *a.* **1** using the right foot more readily and effectively than the left, in football etc. **2** done by the right foot. **rightful** *a.* **1** entitled, holding or held by legitimate claim. **2** just, equitable, fair. **rightfully** *adv.* **rightfulness** *n.* **right hand** *n.* **1** one's best assistant etc. **2** the hand on the right side, esp. as the better hand. **3** a position on or direction to this side. **right-hand** *a.* **1** situated on or towards the right hand. **2** done with the right hand. **3** (of a screw) right-handed. **4** denoting a person whose help is most useful or necessary. **right-handed** *a.* **1** (of a screw) turning to the right. **2** (of a tool) used by or fitted for use by the right hand. **3** done with the right hand. **4** using the right hand more readily and effectively than the left. **right-handedly** *adv.* **right-handedness** *n.* **right-hander** *n.* **1** a right-handed person. **2** a blow with the right hand. **right-hand man** *n.* (*pl.* **right-hand men**) one's best or most efficient assistant, aid or support. **Right Honourable** *n.* a title given to peers, peeresses, Privy Councillors etc. **rightish** *a.* **rightist** *n.* a conservative, an adherent of the right in politics. ~*a.* conservative, rightwing. **rightism** *n.* **rightless** *a.* **rightlessness** *n.* **rightly** *adv.* **1** justly, fairly, equitably. **2** honestly, uprightly. **3** correctly, accurately, properly. **right-**

minded *a.* having fair, honourable or sensible views. **right-mindedness** *n.* **rightmost** *a.* furthest right. **rightness** *n.* **righto** (-ō´) *int.* used to express agreement or compliance. **right of abode** *n.* a person's right to be resident in a country. **right of primogeniture** *n.* the right, system or rule under which, in cases of intestacy, the eldest son succeeds to the real estate of his father. **right of way** *n.* **1** the right established by usage or dedication to the public to use a track, path, road etc. across a person's land. **2** a track, path or road subject to such a right. **3** the right of a vehicle or ship to take precedence in passing according to law or custom. **right-on** *a.* (*sl.*) **1** up to date, modern, fashionable. **2** having modern, liberal views. **Right Reverend** *n.* the title of a bishop. **right side** *n.* the outer side of a fabric or garment. **on the right side of 1** pleasing, in the favour of. **2** below (a specified age). **right side out** with the correct side facing outwards. **right sphere** *n.* the sphere of the heavens where there is a right angle between the equator and the horizon. **right-thinking** *a.* right-minded. **right-to-life** *a.* pro-life. **rightward** *a.,adv.* **right whale** *n.* any whale of the family Balaenidae, yielding the best whalebone etc. **right wing** *n.* **1** the conservative section of a political party or grouping. **2** the right side of an army, football team etc. **right-wing** *a.* **1** having or relating to conservative political views. **2** of or on the right wing. **right-winger** *n.* **righty-ho** (rītihō´) *int.* righto!

righteous (rī´chəs) *a.* **1** just, upright, morally good. **2** equitable, deserved, justifiable, fitting. **righteously** *adv.* **righteousness** *n.*

rigid (rij´id) *a.* **1** stiff, not easily bent, not pliant, unyielding. **2** rigorous, strict, inflexible, harsh, stern. **rigidify** (-jid´ifī) *v.i.* (*3rd pers. sing. pres.* **rigidifies,** *pres.p.* **rigidifying,** *past, p.p.* **rigidified**) to make or become rigid. **rigidity** (-jid´-), **rigidness** *n.* **rigidly** *adv.*

rigmarole (rig´mərōl) *n.* **1** a long, complicated procedure. **2** a long unintelligible story. **3** loose disjointed talk. ~*a.* incoherent.

rigor (rī´gaw, rig´ə) *n.* **1** (*Med.*) a feeling of chill, a shivering accompanied by stiffening, premonitory of fever etc. **2** a state of rigidity assumed by certain animals and commonly known as 'shamming dead'. **rigor mortis** (maw´tis) *n.* the stiffening of the body following death.

rigour (rig´ə), (*N Am.*) **rigor** *n.* **1** strictness, exactness in enforcing rules. **2** stiffness or inflexibility of opinion, doctrine, observance etc., austerity of life. **3** sternness, harshness. **4** inclemency of the weather etc., hardship, distress. **5** (*pl.*) harsh conditions. **rigorous** *a.* **1** strict, precise, severe, stern, inflexible. **2** logically accurate, precise, stringent. **3** inclement, harsh. **rigorously** *adv.* **rigorousness** *n.*

rile (rīl) *v.t.* **1** (*coll.*) to make angry, to vex, to irritate. **2** (*N Am.*) to make turbulent or muddy.

rilievo RELIEVO.

rill (ril) *n.* **1** a small stream, a rivulet. **2** a trench or furrow. **3** a rille.

rille (rill) *n.* (*Astron.*) a furrow, trench or narrow valley on Mars or the moon.

rim (rim) *n.* **1** an outer edge, border or margin, esp. of a vessel or other circular object. **2** a ring or frame. **3** the peripheral part of the framework of a wheel, between the spokes or hub and the tyre. ~*v.t.* (*pres.p.* **rimming**, *past, p.p.* **rimmed**) **1** to furnish with a rim. **2** to serve as rim to. **3** to edge, to border. **rim-brake** *n.* a brake acting on the rim, not the hub, of a wheel. **rimless** *a.* **rimmed** *a.*

rime (rīm) *n.* **1** a deposit of ice caused by freezing fog or low temperatures. **2** (*poet.*) hoar frost. ~*v.t.* to cover with rime. **rimy** *a.* (*comp.* **rimier**, *superl.* **rimiest**)

rind (rīnd) *n.* the outer coating of trees, fruits etc.; bark, peel, husk, skin. ~*v.t.* to strip the bark from. **rinded** *a.* (*usu. in comb.*, as *coarse-rinded*). **rindless** *a.* **rindy** *a.*

rinderpest (rin´dəpest) *n.* a malignant contagious disease attacking ruminants, esp. cattle.

ring[1] (ring) *n.* **1** a circlet. **2** a circlet of gold etc., worn usu. on a finger or in the ear as an ornament, token etc. **3** anything in the form of a circle. **4** a line, mark, moulding, space or band round, or the rim of, a circular or cylindrical object or sphere. **5** an annual ring. **6** a group or concourse of people, things etc. arranged in a circle. **7** a circular space, enclosure or arena for circus performances etc. **8** an enclosed space with seats round it, for boxing or wrestling. **9** a combination of people acting together, often illegally for commercial or political ends. **10** a circular course. **11** a gas ring. **12** (*Chem.*) a closed chain of atoms. ~*v.t.* (*past, p.p.* **ringed**) **1** to put a ring round. **2** to encircle, to enclose, to hem in. **3** to fit with a ring. **4** to put a ring on or in. ~*v.i.* to form a ring. **the ring 1** boxing. **2** bookmakers collectively. **to make/ run rings round** (*coll.*) to be much more successful or skilful than. **ringbark** *v.t.* to cut a ring of bark from (a tree) in order to check growth, kill it or induce it to fruit. **ring-binder** *n.* a binder consisting of metal rings which hold loose-leaf pages by means of perforations in the paper. **ringbolt** *n.* a bolt with a ring or eye at one end. **ring circuit** *n.* an electrical circuit in which power points are connected to the supply in a continuous closed circuit. **ring-dove** *n.* **1** the wood pigeon. **2** the collared dove. **ringed** *a.* **ringed plover** *n.* either of two small plovers, *Charadrius hiaticula* and *C. dubius.* **ringer**[1] *n.* **1** (*Austral.*) the fastest shearer in a shearing shed. **2** a person who rings. **ring-fence** *n.* **1** a fence encircling a whole estate or piece of land. **2** a complete barrier. ~*v.t.* **1** to encircle with a ring-fence. **2** to protect completely. **ring finger** *n.* the third finger, esp. of the left hand, on which the wedding ring is worn. **ringleader** *n.* the leader of a riot, mutiny, piece of mischief etc. **ringless** *a.* **ringlet** *n.* **1** a curl, a curly

lock of hair. **2** a butterfly, *Aphantopus hyperantus,* having spots on its wings. **3** a small ring or circle. **ringletted, ringleted** *a.* **ringlety** *a.* **ringlike** *a.* **ring main** *n.* **1** an electrical supply in which outlet sockets are connected to the mains supply through a ring circuit. **2** a ring circuit. **ringmaster** *n.* the manager and master of ceremonies of a circus performance. **ring-neck** *n.* any of various ring-necked birds. **ring-necked** *a.* (*Zool.*) having a band or bands of colour round the neck. **ring ouzel** *n.* a thrush, *Turdus torquatus,* having a white band on the breast. **ringpull** *n.* a metal ring attached to a can of soft drink, beer etc. which opens it when pulled. **ring road** *n.* a road circumnavigating an urban centre. **ringside** *n.* **1** the area or seats immediately beside a boxing or wrestling ring or any sporting arena. **2** any position affording a close and unobstructed view. ~*a.* of or relating to a ringside (*a ringside seat; a ringside view*). **ringsider** *n.* **ringtailed** *a.* **1** having a tail marked with rings or bands of colour. **2** having a tail curled at the end. **ringworm** *n.* a contagious skin disease caused by a white fungus.

ring[2] (ring) *v.i.* (*past* **rang** (rang), *p.p.* **rung** (rŭng)) **1** to give a clear vibrating sound, like a sonorous metallic body when struck. **2** to re-echo, to resound, to reverberate, to continue to sound. **3** (of the ears) to have a sensation as of vibrating metal, to tingle. **4** to give a summons or signal by ringing. **5** to telephone someone. ~*v.t.* **1** to cause to ring. **2** to telephone. **3** to sound (a knell, peal etc.) on a bell or bells. **4** to summon, signal, announce, proclaim, celebrate etc. by ringing. **5** to usher (in or out) with bell-ringing. ~*n.* **1** the sound of a bell or other resonant body. **2** the act of ringing a bell. **3** a set of bells tuned harmonically. **4** a ringing sound, a continued or reverberated sound. **5** (*coll.*) a telephone call. **6** the quality of resonance. **7** the characteristic sound of a voice, statement etc. **to ring back** to make a return telephone call to. **to ring down the curtain** to lower the curtain in a theatre. **to ring false** to appear insincere. **to ring in 1** to report in by telephone. **2** (*Austral., New Zeal., sl.*) to substitute fraudulently. **to ring off** to end a telephone call; to hang up the receiver. **to ring round** to telephone several people. **to ring true** to seem genuine. **to ring up** to call on the telephone. **to ring up the curtain** to raise the curtain in a theatre. **ringer**[2] *n.* **1** a person or thing almost identical to another. **2** a horse, athlete etc. racing under the name of another. **3** a person who rings, e.g. church bells. **4** a device for ringing, a bell pull. **to be a ringer for** to look exactly like. **ringing** *a., n.* **ringingly** *adv.* **ringing tone** *n.* the tone heard on a telephone after an unengaged number is dialled.

Usage note In standard English, the past tense of the verb *ring* is *rang,* not *rung.*

ringer[1] RING[1].

ringer[2] RING[2].

ringgit (ring´git) *n.* the standard unit of currency of Malaysia, the Malaysian dollar.

rink (ringk) *n.* **1** a prepared floor for roller skating or an area of artificially formed ice for ice-skating. **2** the building or structure housing a skating rink. **3** a strip of ice or of a green marked off for curling. **4** a division of a side playing bowls or curling.

🅇 **rinoceros** common misspelling of RHINOCEROS.

rinse (rins) *v.t.* **1** to wash, to cleanse with clean water. **2** to apply liquid to. **3** to remove (soap) by rinsing. **4** to clear by rinsing. ~*n.* **1** the act of rinsing. **2** an antiseptic mouthwash. **3** a hair tint. **rinser** *n.*

riot (rī´ət) *n.* **1** a disturbance, an outbreak of lawlessness, a tumult, an uproar. **2** wanton or unrestrained conduct, loose living, revelry. **3** unrestrained indulgence in something. **4** luxuriant growth, lavish display. **5** (*Law*) a tumultuous disturbance of the peace by three or more persons. **6** (*coll.*) a person or thing which is hilariously funny. ~*v.i.* **1** to take part in a riot. **2** to revel, to behave or live licentiously. **to run riot 1** to act without control or restraint. **2** to grow luxuriantly. **Riot Act** *n.* (*Hist.*) an Act of 1715 enjoining riotous people to disperse within an hour of the Act being read by a magistrate. **to read the riot act** to give a severe warning that something must stop; to reprimand severely. **rioter** *n.* **riot gear** *n.* protective clothing for police or prison officers in the event of a riot. **riotous** *a.* **riotously** *adv.* **riotousness** *n.*

RIP *abbr.* may he, she or they rest in peace.

rip[1] (rip) *v.t.* (*pres.p.* **ripping**, *past, p.p.* **ripped**) **1** to tear or cut forcibly (out, off, up etc.). **2** to rend, to split. **3** to saw (wood) with the grain. **4** to make a long tear or rent in. **5** to make (a passage, opening etc.) by ripping. **6** to utter (an oath etc.) with violence. ~*v.i.* **1** to come or be torn forcibly apart, to tear. **2** to go (along) at a great pace. ~*n.* **1** a rent made by ripping, a tear. **2** the act of ripping. **to let rip 1** (*coll.*) to speak, act or proceed without restraint. **2** (*coll.*) not to check the speed of. **to rip into** to attack or criticize verbally. **to rip off 1** (*coll.*) to cheat. **2** (*coll.*) to steal (from). **ripcord** *n.* a cord which, when pulled, releases a parachute from its pack or opens the gasbag of a balloon allowing it to descend. **rip-off** *n.* **1** (*coll.*) a cheat. **2** (*coll.*) an exploitative imitation. **3** (*coll.*) a theft. **ripper** *n.* **1** a person who rips or tears. **2** a murderer who mutilates victims' bodies. **ripping** *a.* (*dated, coll.*) excellent, fine, splendid. **rippingly** *adv.* **rip-roaring** *a.* (*coll.*) **1** noisy, unrestrained, exuberant. **2** excellent, fine, splendid. **ripsaw** *n.* a saw for sawing along the grain. **ripsnorter** *n.* (*coll.*) a forceful or excellent person or thing. **ripsnorting** *a.* **ripsnortingly** *adv.* **ripstop** *a.* woven in such a way as to prevent tears. ~*n.* a ripstop fabric.

rip[2] (rip) *n.* an eddy, a stretch of broken water, a rip tide. **rip current** *n.* a rip caused by tidal currents flowing away from the land. **rip tide** *n.* **1** a rip current. **2** an eddy, a stretch of broken water. **3** a conflict of psychological forces.

rip[3] (rip) *n.* (*coll.*) **1** a disreputable person. **2** a worthless horse.

riparian (rīpeə´riən) *a.* (*esp. Law*) of, relating to or dwelling on the banks of a river. **riparial** *a.*

ripe (rīp) *a.* **1** ready for reaping or gathering. **2** mature, come to perfection in growth, fully developed, mellow, fit for use, ready or in a fit state (for). **3** resembling ripe fruit, rosy, rounded, luscious. ~*v.t., v.i.* to ripen. **ripely** *adv.* **ripen** *v.t.* to make ripe. ~*v.i.* to become ripe. **ripeness** *n.*

riposte (ripost´) *n.* **1** a quick reply, a retort. **2** in fencing, a quick lunge or return thrust. ~*v.i.* to make a riposte.

ripper RIP[1].

ripple (rip´əl) *v.i.* **1** to run in small waves or undulations. **2** to sound like water running over a rough surface. ~*v.t.* to cause to run in small waves or undulations. ~*n.* **1** the ruffling of the surface of water, a wavelet. **2** a sound as of rippling water. **3** an undulation (of water, hair etc.). **4** a kind of ice cream with streaks of syrup etc. through it. **ripply** *a.*

riprap (rip´rap) *n.* (*N Am.*) a foundation of loose stones, e.g. in deep water or on a soft bottom.

RISC (risk) *n.* (*Comput.*) **1** a computer which performs a limited number of operations at high speed. **2** computing with a RISC computer.

rise (rīz) *v.i.* (*pres.p.* **rising**, *past* **rose** (rōz), *p.p.* **risen** (riz´ən)) **1** to move upwards, to ascend, to leave the ground, to mount, to soar. **2** to get up from a lying, kneeling or sitting position, or out of bed, to become erect, to stand up. **3** to adjourn, to end a session. **4** to come to life again. **5** to swell or project upwards. **6** to increase, to become high or tall. **7** (of the sun or moon) to appear above the horizon. **8** to be promoted, to thrive. **9** to increase in confidence, cheerfulness, energy, force, intensity, value, price etc. **10** to slope up. **11** to arise, to come into existence, to originate. **12** to come to the surface, to come into sight. **13** to become audible. **14** to become higher in pitch. **15** to respond, esp. with annoyance. **16** to be built. **17** to swell by the action of yeast. **18** to become equal (to). **19** to break into insurrection, to revolt, to rebel (against). **20** (of the wind) to start to blow. **21** (of a barometer) to indicate a higher atmospheric pressure. ~*n.* **1** the act of rising. **2** ascent, elevation. **3 a** an upward slope. **b** the degree of this. **4** a hill, a knoll. **5** source, origin, start. **6** an increase in volume, price, value, power, rank, age, prosperity, height, amount, salary etc. **7** the rising of a feeding fish to the surface. **8** the vertical part of an arch, step etc. **9** appearance above the horizon, rising (of the sun or moon). **on the rise** increasing. **rise and shine** (*coll.*) get up out of bed. **to get a rise out of** (*coll.*) to tease, to provoke. **to give rise to** to cause. **to rise above 1** to be superior to. **2** to remain unaffected by (problems or adverse conditions). **to take a rise out of** to get a rise out of. **riser** *n.* **1** someone who or something which rises (*an early riser*). **2** the vertical part of a step etc. **3** a vertical pipe for liquid or gas. **rising** *n.* **1** a revolt, an insurrection. **2** the agent causing dough to rise. **3** a mounting up or ascending. **4** a protuberance, a tumour, a knoll. ~*a.* **1** increasing. **2** growing. **3** advancing. **4** sloping upwards. ~*adv.* (*coll.*) approaching, nearing. **rising damp** *n.* the absorption of ground moisture into the fabric of a building.

rishi (rish´i) *n.* (*pl.* **rishis**) a seer, a saint, an inspired poet, esp. each of the seven sages said to have communicated the Hindu Vedas to humankind.

risible (riz´ibəl) *a.* **1** exciting laughter. **2** inclined to laugh. **risibility** (-bil´-) *n.* **risibly** *adv.*

risk (risk) *n.* **1** a hazard, a chance of harm, injury, loss etc. **2** a person or thing liable to cause a hazard or loss. ~*v.t.* **1** to expose to risk or hazard. **2** to venture on, to take the chance of. **at one's (own) risk** accepting responsibility. **at risk** in danger, vulnerable. **at the risk of** with the possibility of (unpleasant consequences). **to put at risk** to expose to danger. **to risk one's neck** to do something very dangerous. **to run a risk** to risk danger. **to run the risk** to take the chance (of danger). **to take a risk** to run a risk. **risk capital** *n.* money invested in a speculative enterprise. **risker** *n.* **riskful** *a.* **risky** *a.* (*comp.* **riskier,** *superl.* **riskiest**) **1** dangerous, hazardous, venturesome, daring. **2** risqué. **riskily** *adv.* **riskiness** *n.*

risotto (rizot´ō) *n.* (*pl.* **risottos**) an Italian dish of rice cooked in butter and stock or broth, with onions, cheese, chicken, ham etc.

risqué (rēs´kā) *a.* suggestive of indecency, indelicate.

rissole (ris´ōl) *n.* a ball or flat cake of minced meat, fish etc., coated with breadcrumbs and fried.

rit. *abbr.* (*Mus.*) ritardando.

ritardando (ritahdan´dō) *adv.*, *a.*, *n.* (*pl.* **ritardandos, ritardandi** (-dē)) (*Mus.*) (a) slowing down.

rite (rīt) *n.* **1** a religious or solemn prescribed act, ceremony or observance. **2** (*pl.*) the prescribed acts, ceremonies or forms of worship of any religion. **riteless** *a.* **rite of passage, rite de passage** (rēt də pasahzh´) *n.* a ceremony marking an individual's change of status, esp. into adulthood or matrimony.

ritual (rich´uəl) *n.* **1** a prescribed manner of performing divine service. **2** performance of rites and ceremonies, esp. in an elaborate or excessive way. **3** any formal or customary act or series of acts consistently followed. ~*a.* of, relating to, consisting of or involving rites. **ritualism** *n.* punctilious or exaggerated observance of ritual. **ritualist** *n.* **ritualistic** (-lis´-) *a.* **ritualistically** *adv.* **ritualize, ritualise** *v.t.*, *v.i.* **ritualization** (-zā´shən) *n.* **ritually** *adv.*

ritzy (rit´si) *a.* (*comp.* **ritzier,** *superl.* **ritziest**) (*coll.*) elegant, showy, luxurious, rich. **ritzily** *adv.* **ritziness** *n.*

rival (rī´vəl) *n.* **1** one's competitor for something. **2** a person or thing considered as equal to another. **3** a person who strives to surpass another in a quality, pursuit etc. ~*a.* being a rival, having the same claims or pretensions, in competition. ~*v.t.* (*pres.p.* **rivalling,** (*N Am.*) **rivaling,** *past, p.p.* **rivalled,** (*N Am.*) **rivaled**) **1** to vie with, to emulate, to strive to equal or surpass. **2** to be, or almost be, the equal of. **rivalry** (-ri) *n.* (*pl.* **rivalries**). **rivalship** *n.*

river (riv´ə) *n.* **1** a large stream of water flowing in a channel over a portion of the earth's surface and discharging itself into the sea, a lake, a marsh or another river. **2** a large and abundant stream, a copious flow. **to sell down the river** (*coll.*) to let down, to betray. **river blindness** *n.* a tropical skin disease caused by the parasitic threadworm *Onchocerca volvulus*, whose larvae can cause blindness if they enter the eyes. **riverboat** *n.* a boat for use on rivers. **river capture** *n.* the diversion of a mountain stream into a stronger one. **rivered** *a.* **riverine** (-rīn) *a.* of, relating to, resembling or produced by a river; riparian. **riverless** *a.* **riverside** *n.* the ground along the bank of a river. ~*a.* built on the bank of a river.

rivet (riv´it) *n.* a short bolt, pin or nail, usu. with a flat head at one end, the other end being flattened and clinched by hammering, used for fastening metal plates together. ~*v.t.* (*pres.p.* **riveting,** *past, p.p.* **riveted**) **1** to join or fasten together with a rivet or rivets. **2** to clinch. **3** to fasten firmly. **4** to fix (attention, eyes etc. upon). **5** to engross the attention of. **riveter** *n.* **riveting** *a.* extremely interesting, engrossing.

riviera (rivieə´rə) *n.* a coastal strip with a subtropical climate.

rivulet (riv´ulit) *n.* a small stream.

riyal RIAL.

RN *abbr.* **1** Registered Nurse. **2** Royal Navy.

Rn *chem. symbol* radon.

RNA *abbr.* ribonucleic acid.

roach[1] (rōch) *n.* (*pl.* **roach**) a freshwater fish, *Rutilus rutilus,* allied to the carp.

roach[2] (rōch) *n.* **1** (*N Am., coll.*) a cockroach. **2** (*sl.*) the butt or filter of a cannabis cigarette.

roach[3] (rōch) *n.* (*Naut.*) **1** a curved part of a fore-and-aft sail projecting beyond an imaginary straight line between its corners. **2** the extent of such projections. **3** the upward curve in the foot of a square sail.

road[1] (rōd) *n.* **1** a track or way for travelling on, esp. a broad strip of ground suitable for motor vehicles, forming a public line of communication between places, a highway. **2** a way of going anywhere, route, course. **3** (*N Am.*) a railway. **4** (*usu. pl.*) a place in the open water beyond a harbour where ships can ride at anchor, a roadstead. **by road** using transport on the roads. **in someone's road** (*coll.*) in the road. **in the road**

(*coll.*) obstructing someone. **on the road** passing through, travelling, touring (often as a way of life). **to hit the road** (*sl.*) to leave, to begin travelling. **to take to the road** to set out, to begin travelling. **roadbed** *n.* **1** the foundation upon which a railway track or highway is laid. **2** (*N Am.*) the part of a road on which vehicles travel. **roadblock** *n.* a road obstructed by the army or police checking for escaped criminals, terrorists etc. **road fund licence** *n.* a paper disc displayed on a vehicle to prove that the owner has paid road tax. **road hog** *n.* (*coll.*) a selfish motorist or cyclist paying no regard to the convenience of other people using the road. **road-holding** *n.* the capacity of a motor vehicle to remain stable at high speeds, on wet roads etc. **roadhouse** *n.* a public house, restaurant etc. on a highway, which caters for motorists. **road hump** *n.* a sleeping policeman. **roadie** *n.* a person employed to transport, set up and dismantle the instruments and equipment of a touring band. **road manager** *n.* a person who organizes and supervises a band's tour. **road metal** *n.* broken stones for road-making. **road movie** *n.* a film or genre of film which has a central plot involving a journey by road. **road-pricing** *n.* a method of reducing traffic on busy roads by making drivers pay to use them. **road rage** *n.* violent aggression towards other motorists. **roadroller** *n.* a vehicle with a large metal roller for compacting the surface of a newly-laid road. **roadrunner** *n.* a bird of Mexican and US deserts, *Geococcyx californianus*, which can run very fast. **road sense** *n.* the instinct of a road-user which enables them to cope with a traffic emergency, avoid an accident etc. **roadshow** *n.* **1** a touring group of performers. **2** a musical or theatrical performance by such a group. **3** a live or prerecorded outside broadcast by a touring radio or television unit. **4** a touring political or advertising campaign. **roadside** *n.* the border of a road. *~a.* situated or growing by the roadside. **road sign** *n.* a sign giving instructions to road users. **roadstead** *n.* an anchorage for ships some distance from the shore. **roadster** (-stə) *n.* **1** a horse, cycle or car suitable for the road. **2** a two-seater car. **road test** *n.* a test of the performance of a vehicle on a road. **road-test** *v.t.* to give a road test to. **road train** *n.* (*esp. Austral.*) a large lorry pulling one or more trailers. **roadway** *n.* **1** a road. **2** the central part of a highway, used by vehicles etc. **roadwork** *n.* **1** (*pl.*) repairs to or under a section of road. **2** physical training comprising running or jogging along roads. **roadworthy** *a.* fit for use or travel on a road. **roadworthiness** *n.*

road² (rōd) *v.t.* (of a dog) to follow (a game bird) by its scent.

roam (rōm) *v.i.* to wander about without any definite purpose, to rove, to ramble. *~v.t.* to range, to wander, to rove over. *~n.* the act of roaming. **roamer** *n.*

roan¹ (rōn) *a.* **1** (of an animal, esp. a horse) of a

bay, sorrel or dark colour, with spots of grey or white thickly interspersed. **2** of a mixed colour, having a decided shade of red. *~n.* **1** a roan animal, esp. a horse. **2** a roan colour.

roan² (rōn) *n.* a soft flexible leather made of sheepskin tanned with sumac. *~a.* made of roan.

roar (raw) *n.* **1** a loud, deep, hoarse, continued sound, as of a lion etc. **2** a burst of mirth or laughter. **3** a loud engine noise. *~v.i.* **1** (of a lion etc.) to make a loud, deep, hoarse, continued sound. **2** (of a person in rage or distress; loud laughter, the sea, thunder, guns, a fire) to make a confused din like this. **3** (of a diseased horse) to make a noise in breathing. **4** (of a place) to resound, to re-echo, to be full of din. **5** (of a vehicle) to travel at high speed, making a loud noise. *~v.t.* to shout, say, sing or utter with a roaring voice. **roarer** *n.* **roaring** *a.* **1** shouting, noisy, boisterous, stormy. **2** brisk, active. *~adv.* extremely, boisterously. **roaring drunk** *a.* extremely and noisily drunk. **roaringly** *adv.* **roaring trade** *n.* (*coll.*) thriving and profitable business.

roast (rōst) *v.t.* **1** to cook by exposure to the direct action of radiant heat, esp. at an open fire or in an oven. **2** to dry (coffee beans etc.) by exposure to heat. **3** to heat excessively or violently. **4** to heat (ore etc.) highly without fusing, to drive out impurities. **5** (*coll.*) to criticize strongly. *~v.i.* **1** to be roasted. **2** to heat oneself excessively. *~a.* roasted. *~n.* **1** something which is roasted, roast meat or a dish of this, a roast joint. **2** the act or operation of roasting. **3** (*N Am.*) a party where roasted food is served. **roaster** *n.* **1** someone who or something which roasts. **2** a kind of oven for roasting. **3** a contrivance for roasting coffee. **4** a fowl, animal, vegetable etc. suitable for roasting. **roasting** *a.* (*coll.*) very hot. *~n.* **1** the act of roasting. **2** a severe criticism.

rob (rob) *v.t.* (*pres.p.* **robbing**, *past, p.p.* **robbed**) **1** to take something by unlawful violence or secret theft from. **2** to plunder, to pillage, to deprive, to strip (of). *~v.i.* to commit robbery. **to rob Peter to pay Paul 1** to take away from one person in order to give to another. **2** to pay off one debt by incurring a new one. **robber** *n.* **robbery** *n.* (*pl.* **robberies**) **1** the act or practice of robbing. **2** an instance of robbing. **3** extortion, overpricing.

robe (rōb) *n.* **1** a long, loose outer garment. **2** (*often pl.*) a dress, gown or vestment of state, rank or office. **3** a dressing gown, a bathrobe. **4** a long, white dress worn by a baby at its christening. **5** (*N Am.*) a fur blanket or wrap. *~v.t.* **1** to clothe, to dress. **2** to invest with a robe or robes. *~v.i.* to put on a robe or dress.

robin (rob´in) *n.* **1** a small brown European bird, *Erithacus rubecula*, the male adult having a red throat and breast. **2** a N American red-breasted thrush, *Turdus migratorius*.

robinia (rəbin´iə) *n.* any member of the genus *Robinia* of leguminous shrubs and trees including the false acacia.

robot (rō´bot) *n.* **1** a machine capable of acting and speaking in a human manner; a humanoid, an automaton. **2** a brutal, mechanically efficient person who has no sensitivity. **3** (*S Afr.*) a traffic light. **robotic** (-bot´-) *a.* **robotically** *adv.* **robotics** *n.* the branch of technology concerned with the design, construction, application etc. of robots. **robotize, robotise** *v.t.* to cause (work etc.) to be done by a robot. **robotization** (-zā´shən) *n.*

robust (rōbŭst´) *a.* **1** strong, hardy, vigorous, capable of endurance, having excellent health and physique. **2** (of wine) full-bodied. **3** (of exercise, sport, discipline etc.) requiring muscular strength, invigorating. **4** mentally vigorous, firm, self-reliant. **robustly** *adv.* **robustness** *n.*

robusta (rōbus´tə) *n.* **1** coffee beans from an American plant, *Coffea canephora*. **2** the plant itself.

roc (rok) *n.* a legendary bird of immense size and strength.

rocaille (rōkī´) *n.* decorative work of rock, shell or a similar material.

rocambole (rok´əmbōl) *n.* a plant related to the leek, *Allium scorodoprasum*, Spanish garlic.

rochet (roch´it) *n.* an open-sided vestment with tight sleeves, resembling a surplice, worn by bishops and abbots.

rock[1] (rok) *n.* **1** the solid matter constituting the earth's crust, or any portion of this. **2** a similar material from any other planet. **3** (*Geol.*) any solid, hard or stony part of this, a mass of it, esp. forming a hill, promontory, islet, cliff etc. **4** a detached block of stone, a boulder. **5** (*N Am.*) a stone, a pebble. **6** (*pl., N Am., sl.*) money. **7** (*sl.*) a diamond or other precious or large gem. **8** a hard sweet, often in the form of a stick, esp. as a souvenir. **9** anything dangerous. **10** a person or thing providing refuge, stability, supportiveness etc. **11** (*sl.*) a solid form of cocaine. **12** (*pl., taboo sl.*) the testicles. **between a rock and a hard place** (*N Am.*) having to decide between two equally unpleasant courses of action. **on the rocks 1** (*coll.*) poor, hard up. **2** (*coll.*) (of a marriage) at an end, destroyed. **3** (of a drink) served with ice. **to get one's rocks off** (*sl.*) to achieve esp. sexual gratification. **rock-bed** *n.* a base of rocks. **rock-bottom** *n.* **1** the lowest stratum reached in excavating, mining etc. **2** the lowest point (e.g. of despair). ~*a.* (of prices) lowest possible. **rock-bound** *a.* hemmed in by rocks. **rockburst** *n.* a sudden collapse of rock in a mine. **rock cake** *n.* a bun with a hard, rough surface. **rock-candy** *n.* (*N Am.*) a hard sweet often found in the form of a stick. **rock-climber** *n.* a person who climbs rock faces for enjoyment. **rock-climbing** *n.* **rock cress** *n.* arabis. **rock-crystal** *n.* the finest and most transparent kind of quartz, usu. found in hexagonal prisms. **rock dove** *n.* the European wild dove, *Columba livia*, supposed to be the ancestor of the domesticated varieties. **rockery** *n.* (*pl.* **rockeries**) a mound or slope of rocks, stones and earth, for growing

alpine and other plants. **rock face** *n.* the surface of a vertical or nearly vertical cliff or mountainside. **rockfall** *n.* **1** a fall of loose rocks. **2** a mass of fallen rocks. **rockfish** *n.* (*pl.* **rockfish**) **1** a black goby. **2** any of several wrasses etc. which frequent rocks. **rock garden** *n.* **1** a rockery. **2** a garden containing a rockery or rockeries. **rockhopper** *n.* a crested penguin, *Eudyptes crestatus*, of the Antarctic and New Zealand. **rockless** *a.* **rocklet** *n.* **rocklike** *a.* **rockling** *n.* a small gadoid fish, esp. of the genus *Cilata* or *Rhinomenus*, found in pools among rocks. **rock plant** *n.* any of various plants growing among rocks, esp. alpines. **rock pool** *n.* a small pool between rocks. **rock rabbit** *n.* a hyrax, esp. *Procavia capensis*. **rock rose** *n.* the helianthemum. **rock salmon** *n.* dogfish or other coarse fish disguised for the market. **rock salt** *n.* salt found in stratified beds. **rock-wool** *n.* mineral wool. **rocky**[1] *a.* (*comp.* **rockier**, *superl.* **rockiest**) **1** full of or abounding with rocks. **2** consisting of or resembling rock. **rockiness**[1] *n.* **Rocky Mountain goat** *n.* an animal of NW America, *Oreamnos americanus*, resembling a goat. **Rocky Mountain spotted fever** *n.* a tick-borne rickettsial disease with high fever and a skin rash.

rock[2] (rok) *v.t.* **1** to move backwards and forwards. **2** to shock, to distress. ~*v.i.* **1** to move backwards and forwards. **2** to dance to or play rock music. ~*n.* **1** an act or spell of rocking. **2** a rocking motion. **3** rock music. **4** rock and roll. ~*a.* of or relating to rock music. **rockabilly** (-əbili) *n.* a quick-paced type of Southern US rock and country music originating in the 1950s. **rock and roll, rock 'n' roll** *n.* **1** a type of music, popular from the mid-1950s, which combines blues and country-and-western music. **2** the type of dancing done to this music. **rock and roller** *n.* **rocker** *n.* **1** someone who or something which rocks. **2** a rocking chair. **3** a curved piece of wood on which a cradle, rocking chair etc., rocks. **4** a rock musician. **5** a member of a teenage band of leather-clad motorcyclists of the 1960s, as opposed to the *Mods*. **6** a low skate with a curved blade. **7** (of machinery) any one of various devices and fittings having a rocking motion. **off one's rocker** (*coll.*) crazy. **rocking** *n., a.* **rocking chair** *n.* a chair mounted on rockers. **rocking horse** *n.* a large toy horse mounted on rockers. **rocking stone** *n.* a stone so balanced on a natural pedestal that it can be rocked. **rocky**[2] *a.* (*comp.* **rockier**, *superl.* **rockiest**) (*coll.*) unsteady, tottering, fragile. **rockily** *adv.* unsteadily. **rockiness**[2] *n.*

rockery ROCK[1].

rocket[1] (rok´it) *n.* **1** a firework consisting of a cylindrical case of paper or metal filled with a mixture of explosives and combustibles, used for display, signalling, conveying a line to stranded vessels and in warfare. **2** a device with a warhead containing high explosive and propelled by the mechanical thrust developed by gases generated through the use of chemical fuels. **3** (*coll.*) a severe scolding, a telling-off. ~*v.t.* (*pres.p.* **rocketing**, *past, p.p.* **rocketed**) **1** to bombard with rockets. **2** to propel by means of a rocket. ~*v.i.* **1** to fly straight up or to fly fast and high. **2** (of prices) to rise rapidly. **3** (of a promoted person) to advance to a high position speedily. **rocketeer** (-tiə´) *n.* **1** a person who flies rocket-propelled missiles. **2** a person who works with or is interested in space rockets. **rocketry** (-ri) *n.* the scientific study of rockets.

rocket² (rok´it) *n.* **1** any of various plants of the genus *Hesperis* or *Sisymbrium*. **2** (*also* **roquette**) a variety of the cruciferous plant *Eruca vesicaria*, used for salads.

rocky¹ ROCK¹.

rocky² ROCK².

rococo (rəkō´kō) *n.* **1** a florid style of ornamentation (in architecture, furniture etc.) flourishing in the 18th cent. **2** design or ornament of an eccentric and over-elaborate kind. ~*a.* in this style.

rod (rod) *n.* **1** a straight, slender piece of wood, a stick, a wand. **2** this or a bundle of twigs etc. as an instrument of punishment. **3** a baton, a sceptre. **4** a fishing rod. **5** an angler using a fishing rod. **6** a magician's wand. **7** a slender bar of metal, esp. forming part of machinery etc. **8** (*Hist.*) a unit of linear measure, equal to 5½ yards (about 5 m). **9** (*N Am., sl.*) a hot rod. **10** (*N Am., sl.*) a revolver. **11** (*Anat.*) a rodlike body or structure in the retina of the eye. **to make a rod for one's own back** to do something that will cause one trouble later. **rodless** *a.* **rodlet** *n.* **rodlike** *a.*

rode RIDE.

rodent (rō´dənt) *n.* any animal of the order Rodentia, having two (or sometimes four) strong incisors and no canine teeth, including the squirrel, beaver, rat etc. ~*a.* **1** (*Med.*) gnawing. **2** of or relating to the Rodentia.

rodeo (rō´diō, rədā´ō) *n.* (*pl.* **rodeos**) **1** a driving together or rounding-up of cattle. **2** a place they are rounded up in. **3** an outdoor entertainment or contest exhibiting the skills involved in this. **4** an exhibition of motorcycling skills etc.

roe¹ (rō) *n.* **1** the mass of eggs forming the spawn of fishes, amphibians etc. **2** the sperm or milt. **roed** *a.* **roe-stone** *n.* oolite.

roe² (rō) *n.* (*pl.* **roe, roes**) a small species of deer, *Capreolus capreolus*. **roebuck** *n.* the male roe. **roe-deer** *n.* the roe.

roentgen (rŭnt´yən, rœnt´-), **röntgen** *n.* the international unit of quantity of X- or gamma-rays. **roentgenography** (-nog´-) *n.* photography using X-rays. **roentgenology** (-nol´-) *n.* radiology.

rogation (rōgā´shən) *n.* (*usu. pl.*) a solemn supplication, esp. one chanted in procession on the Rogation Days. **rogational** *a.* **Rogation Days** *n.pl.* the Monday, Tuesday and Wednesday preceding Ascension Day, marked by prayers, processions and supplications. **rogatory** (rog´ə-) *a.* (*Law*) seeking information.

roger (roj´ə) *int.* **1** in radio communication, your message is received and understood. **2** (*sl.*) I agree. ~*v.t.* (*taboo sl.*) (of a man) to have sexual intercourse with. ~*v.i.* (*taboo sl.*) to have sexual intercourse.

rogue (rōg) *n.* **1** a dishonest person, a criminal. **2** (*facet.*) a mischievous person, esp. a child. **3** a vicious wild animal cast out or separate from the herd, esp. an elephant. **4** a shirking or vicious racehorse or hunter. **5** an inferior or intrusive plant among seedlings. **6** a variation from the standard type or variety. ~*a.* **1** irresponsible, destructive. **2** roguish. **roguery** *n.* (*pl.* **rogueries**). **rogues' gallery** *n.* a collection of photographic portraits kept in police records for identification of criminals. **roguish** *a.* mischievous, high-spirited. **roguishly** *adv.* **roguishness** *n.*

roil (roil) *v.t.* **1** to make turbid, as by stirring or shaking up. **2** (*N Am.*) to make angry, to irritate, to rile.

roister (rois´tə), **royster** *v.i.* **1** to behave uproariously, to revel boisterously. **2** to swagger. **roisterer** *n.* **roisterous** *a.*

role (rōl), **rôle** *n.* **1** a part or character taken by an actor. **2** any part or function one is called upon to perform. **role model** *n.* a person who is admired and emulated by many people. **role-play** *n.* role-playing. **role-playing** *n.* an enactment of a possible situation or playing of an imaginary role, as therapy, training etc. **role reversal** *n.* the reversing of roles which have been traditionally or formerly taken.

roll (rōl) *n.* **1** anything rolled up, a cylinder of any flexible material formed by or as by rolling or folding over on itself. **2** a small individual loaf of bread. **3** a pastry or cake rolled round a filling (*a sausage roll*). **4** a document, an official record, a register, a list, esp. of names of solicitors, soldiers, schoolchildren etc. **5** a cylindrical or semicylindrical mass of anything. **6** a rolling motion or gait. **7** the act of rolling. **8** a gymnastic exercise in which the body is curled up and rolled over either forwards or backwards. **9** a resounding peal of thunder etc. **10** a continuous beating of a drum with rapid strokes. **11** a complete lateral revolution of an aircraft. **12** (*N Am.*) a wad of money. ~*v.t.* **1** to send, push or cause to move along by turning over and over on its axis. **2** to cause to rotate. **3** to cause to revolve between two surfaces. **4** to knead, press, flatten or level with or as with a roller or rollers. **5** to form into a cylindrical shape by wrapping round and round or turning over and over. **6** to carry or impel forward with a sweeping motion. **7** to carry (along) with a swinging gait. **8** to convey in a wheeled vehicle. **9** to cause to operate. **10** to display (the credits for a film or television programme) by rolling them up the screen. **11** to utter with a prolonged, deep, vibrating sound. ~*v.i.* **1** to move along by turning over and over and round and round. **2** to revolve. **3** to operate or cause to operate. **4** to move along on wheels.

5 to be conveyed (along) in a wheeled vehicle. **6** (*coll.*) to progress. **7** (of eyes etc.) to move or slip about with a rotary motion. **8** to wallow about. **9** to sway, to reel, to go from side to side; to move along with such a motion. **10** (of film or television credits) to be displayed by rolling up the screen. **11** to make a prolonged, deep, vibrating sound. **12** (of a ship) to turn back and forth on the longitudinal axis. **13** (of an aircraft) to make a full corkscrew revolution about the longitudinal axis. **14** to undulate or sweep along. **15** to be formed into a cylindrical shape by turning over upon itself. **16** to grow into a cylindrical or spherical shape by turning over and over. **17** to spread (out) under a roller. **on a roll** (*sl.*) having a period of great success. **roll on!** (of a day, date or event) hurry along, come quickly (*Roll on the holidays!*). **to roll back** (*N Am.*) to cause to decrease. **to roll in 1** to come in quantities or numbers. **2** (*coll.*) to arrive in a casual manner. **to roll up 1** (*coll.*) to assemble, to come up. **2** to make (a cigarette) by hand. **3** to wind into a cylinder. **rollable** *a.* **roll-back** *n.* a reduction in prices, taxes or wages. **roll bar** *n.* a metal strengthening bar which reinforces the frame of a (racing) vehicle which may overturn. **roll-call** *n.* the act of calling a list of names to check attendance. **rolled** *a.* **rolled gold** *n.* metal covered by a thin coating of gold. **rolled oats** *n.pl.* oats which have been husked and crushed. **roller** *n.* **1** a cylindrical body turning on its axis, employed alone or forming part of a machine, used for inking, printing, smoothing, spreading out, crushing etc. **2** a small cylinder for curling the hair, a curler. **3** a long, heavy, swelling wave. **4** (*also* **roller bandage**) a long, broad bandage, rolled up for convenience. **5** someone who or something which rolls. **rollerball** *n.* a type of pen with a nib consisting of a rolling ball which controls the flow of ink. **roller bearing** *n.* a bearing comprised of strong steel rollers for giving a point of contact. **Rollerblade**® *n.* a type of roller skate with a single row of small wheels fitted to the side of the boot. **rollerblade** *v.i.* to skate wearing Rollerblades. **rollerblader** *n.* **roller blind** *n.* a window blind fitted on a roller. **roller coaster** *n.* a switchback railway at an amusement park, carnival, fair etc. **roller-coaster** *a.* having many sudden dramatic changes. *~v.i.* to have many sudden and dramatic changes. **roller-coast** *v.i.* to roller-coaster. **roller derby** *n.* a (boisterous) roller-skating race. **roller skate** *n.* a skate mounted on wheels or rollers for skating on a hard surface etc. *~v.i.* to skate wearing roller skates. **roller skater** *n.* **roller skating** *n.* **roller towel** *n.* a continuous towel hung on a roller. **rolling** *a., n., adv.* **to be rolling in** to have a lot of. **to be rolling (in it)** (*coll.*) to be extremely wealthy. **rolling drunk** *a.* staggering through drunkenness. **rolling mill** *n.* a factory in which metal is rolled out by machinery into plates, sheets, bars etc. **rolling pin** *n.* a hard wooden etc.

roller for rolling out dough, pastry etc. **rolling stock** *n.* **1** the carriages, vans, locomotives etc. of a railway. **2** (*N Am.*) the road vehicles of a business firm. **rolling stone** *n.* a person who cannot settle down in one place. **rollmop** *n.* a rolled-up fillet of herring pickled in vinegar. **roll-neck** *n.* **1** a jumper with a high neck folded over. **2** such a neck on a garment. *~a.* having a roll-neck. **roll of honour** *n.* a list of people who are being honoured. **roll-on** *a.* (of a deodorant) applied by a plastic rolling ball in the neck of its container. *~n.* **1** a step-in elastic corset which fits by stretching. **2** a roll-on deodorant. **roll-on roll-off** *a.* (of a ship) carrying motor vehicles which drive on and off when embarking and disembarking. **roll-out** *n.* **1** the official presentation of a new aircraft or spacecraft. **2** the official launch of a new product. **3** the part of a landing when an aircraft travels along the runway gradually losing speed. **roll-over** *n.* **1** the extension of a debt for a longer period. **2** (*coll.*) the act of overturning a vehicle. *~n., a.* (relating to) the extension of the period of validity of a prize, competition etc. **roll-top desk** *n.* a desk with a flexible cover sliding in grooves. **roll-up** *n.* **1** (*coll.*) a hand-made cigarette made with tobacco and a cigarette paper. **2** (*Austral.*) attendance, turnout.

rollick (rol´ik) *v.i.* to behave in a careless, merry fashion; to frolic, to revel, to be merry or enjoy life in a boisterous fashion. *~n.* **1** exuberance, high spirits. **2** a frolic, a spree, an escapade. **rollicking** *a.* boisterous, carefree. *~n.* (*coll.*) a severe reprimand (euphem. for *bollocking*).

roly-poly (rōlipō´li) *n.* (*pl.* **roly-polies**) **1** (*also* **roly-poly pudding**) a pudding made of a sheet of suet pastry, spread with jam, rolled up and baked or boiled. **2** a plump or dumpy person. *~a.* plump, dumpy.

ROM (rom) *n.* (*Comput.*) a data-storage device in computers which retains information in an unalterable state.

rom. *abbr.* roman (type).

romaine (rōmān´) *n.* (*N Am.*) a cos lettuce.

Roman (rō´mən) *a.* **1** of or relating to the modern or ancient city of Rome or its territory or people. **2** of or relating to the Roman Catholic Church, papal. **3** dating from a period of rule by the ancient Romans. **4** belonging to the Roman alphabet. **5** (**roman**) denoting ordinary upright characters used in print as distinct from italic or Gothic. *~n.* **1** an inhabitant or citizen of Rome. **2** a soldier of the ancient Roman Empire. **3** a Roman Catholic. **4** roman type. **Roman candle** *n.* a firework consisting of a tube from which coloured fireballs are discharged. **Roman Catholic** *a.* of or relating to the Church of Rome, a Christian denomination with the Pope as its head. *~n.* a member of this Church. **Roman Catholicism** *n.* **Roman holiday** *n.* an entertainment or enjoyment which depends on others suffering. **Romanic** (-man´-) *a.* **1** derived from Latin,

Romance

roof

Romance. **2** derived or descended from the Romans. ~*n.* Romance. **Romanism** *n.* Roman Catholicism. **Romanist** *n.* **1** a student of Roman history etc. or of the Romance languages. **2** a Roman Catholic. **romanize, romanise** *v.t.* **1** to make Roman in character. **2** to convert to the Roman Catholic religion. **3** to put into the Roman alphabet or roman type. **romanization** (-zā´shən) *n.* **romanizer** *n.* **Roman law** *n.* the system of law evolved by the ancient Romans which forms the basis of many modern legal codes. **Roman nose** *n.* a nose with a high bridge, an aquiline nose. **Roman numeral** *n.* a roman letter representing a (cardinal) number as in the ancient Roman system of numbering, occasionally still in use. **Romano-** *comb. form* Roman.

Romance (rōmans´) *n.* any one of a group of languages derived from Latin, e.g. French, Spanish or Romanian. ~*a.* of or relating to this group of languages.

romance (rōmans´) *n.* **1** the spirit or atmosphere of imaginary adventure, chivalrous or idealized love, strangeness and mystery. **2** an episode, love affair or series of facts having this character. **3** a modern literary genre of sentimental love stories, romantic fiction. **4** a work of this genre. **5** a medieval tale, usu. in verse, describing the adventures of a hero of chivalry. **6** a fabrication, a fiction, a falsehood. **7** (*Mus.*) a short musical composition of a simple character, usu. suggestive of a love-song. ~*v.i.* **1** to make false, exaggerated or imaginary statements. **2** to imagine or tell romantic or extravagant stories. ~*v.t.* to have a love affair with. **romancer** *n.*

Usage note The pronunciation (rō´-), with stress on the first syllable, should only be used facetiously or mockingly.

Romanesque (rōmənesk´) *a.* of the styles of architecture that succeeded the Roman and lasted till the introduction of Gothic. ~*n.* Romanesque art, architecture etc.

Romanian (rumā´niən), **Rumanian, Roumanian** *a.* of or relating to the country of Romania, its people or language. ~*n.* **1** a native or inhabitant of Romania, or a person of Romanian descent. **2** the language of Romania.

romantic (rōman´tik) *a.* **1** of, relating to, of the nature of or given to romance. **2** imaginative, visionary, poetic, extravagant, fanciful. **3** (of conduct etc.) fantastic, unpractical, sentimental. **4** (of scenery etc.) wild, picturesque, suggestive of romance. **5** (*also* **Romantic**) of or relating to the movement in literature and art tending away from the moderation and harmonious proportion of classicism towards the less restrained expression of ideal beauty and grandeur. ~*n.* **1** a romantic person, a person given to sentimental thoughts or acts of love. **2** a romantic poet, novelist etc., a romanticist. **romantically** *adv.* **romanticism** (-sizm) *n.* **1** the reaction from classical to medieval forms and to the less

restrained expressions of romantic ideals which originated in Germany about the middle of the 18th cent., and reached its culmination in England and France in the first half of the 19th cent. **2** the quality or state of being romantic. **romanticist** *n.* **romanticize** (-sīz), **romanticise** *v.t., v.i.* **romanticization** (-zā´shən) *n.*

Romany (rom´əni, rō´-) *n.* (*pl.* **Romanies**) **1** a gypsy. **2** the gypsy language. ~*a.* gypsy.

romer (rō´mə) *n.* a small piece of card or plastic marked with graduations for measuring map references.

romneya (rom´niə) *n.* any plant of the genus *Romneya*, having large, poppy-like flowers.

romp (romp) *v.i.* **1** to play or frolic roughly or boisterously. **2** (*coll.*) to go rapidly (along, past etc.) with ease. ~*n.* **1** rough or boisterous play. **2** an easy win. **3** a swift run. **to romp home/ in** (*coll.*) to win easily. **romper** *n.* **1** a person who romps. **2** (*also* **romper suit**) a one-piece playsuit for infants. **rompy** *a.* (*comp.* **rompier**, *superl.* **rompiest**).

rondavel (rondah´vəl) *n.* a round hut or building in S Africa.

rondeau (ron´dō) *n.* (*pl.* **rondeaux** (ron´dōz, ron´dō)) a poem in iambic verse of eight or ten syllables and ten or thirteen lines, with only two rhymes, the opening words coming twice as a refrain. **rondo** (-dō) *n.* (*pl.* **rondos**) (*Mus.*) a musical composition having a principal theme which is repeated after each subordinate theme, often forming part of a symphony etc.

röntgen ROENTGEN.

roo (roo), **'roo** *n.* (*pl.* **roos**, **'roos**) (*Austral., coll.*) kangaroo.

rood (rood) *n.* **1** the cross of Christ, a crucifix, esp. one set on a beam or screen in a church. **2** a quarter of an acre (about 0.1 ha). **rood-screen** *n.* a stone or wood screen between the nave and choir of a church, usu. elaborately designed and decorated with carving etc., orig. supporting the rood.

roof (roof) *n.* (*pl.* **roofs**, **rooves** (roovz)) **1** the upper covering of a house or other building. **2** the covering or top of a vehicle etc. **3** any analogous part, e.g. of a furnace, oven etc. **4** a house, shelter etc. **5** an upper limit, a ceiling. ~*v.t.* **1** to cover with or as if with a roof. **2** to be the roof of. **3** to shelter. **a roof over one's head** a place to live. **to go through the roof 1** (*coll.*) (of prices etc.) to increase suddenly and quickly. **2** to hit the roof. **to hit/ raise the roof** (*coll.*) to lose one's temper. **under one roof** in the same building. **under one's roof** in one's home. **roofage** *n.* the expanse of a roof. **roofed** *a.* **roofer** *n.* a person who builds and repairs roofs. **roof garden** *n.* a garden of plants and shrubs growing in soil-filled receptacles on a flat roof. **roofing** *n.* **1** material used for roofs. **2** the act of roofing buildings. **roofless** *a.* **rooflike** *a.* **roof of the mouth** *n.* the palate. **roof-rack** *n.* a detachable rack on the roof of a motor vehicle for holding luggage etc. **rooftop** *n.* the outside surface of a roof. **to shout from the rooftops** to announce publicly. **roof-tree** *n.* the ridge-pole of a roof. **roofy** *a.*

Usage note The plural *roofs* is preferred to *rooves*.

---

rook[1] (ruk) *n.* **1** a gregarious bird, *Corvus frugilegus*, of the crow family with glossy black plumage. **2** (*sl.*) a cheat, a swindler, a sharper, esp. at cards, dice etc. ~*v.t.* **1** to charge extortionately. **2** to cheat, to swindle. **rookery** *n.* (*pl.* **rookeries**) **1** a colony of rooks. **2** a wood or clump of trees where rooks nest. **3** a place frequented by seabirds or seals for breeding. **4** a colony of seals etc. **rookish** *a.*

rook[2] (ruk) *n.* the castle in chess.

rookie (ruk´i), **rooky** *n.* (*pl.* **rookies**) (*sl.*) a raw recruit or beginner.

room (room) *n.* **1** space regarded as occupied or available for occupation, accommodation, capacity, vacant space or standing ground. **2** opportunity, scope. **3** a portion of space in a building enclosed by walls, floor and ceiling. **4** the people present in a room. **5** (*pl.*) apartments, lodgings, accommodation for a person or family. ~*v.i.* to occupy rooms, to lodge. **to give/ leave/ make room** to withdraw so as to leave space for other people. **-roomed** *a.* **roomer** *n.* (*N Am.*) a lodger. **roomful** *n.* (*pl.* **roomfuls**). **roomie** *n.* (*N Am., coll.*) a room-mate. **rooming** *a., n.* **rooming house** *n.* a lodging-house. **room-mate**, (*N Am.*) **roommate** *n.* a person with whom someone shares a room or lodgings. **room service** *n.* in a hotel, the serving of food and drink to guests in their rooms. **roomy** *a.* (*comp.* **roomier**, *superl.* **roomiest**) having ample room, spacious, extensive. **roomily** *adv.* **roominess** *n.*

roost (roost) *n.* **1** a pole or perch for birds to rest on. **2** a place for fowls to sleep on at night. **3** a resting place, a room, esp. a bedroom. ~*v.i.* **1** to perch on or occupy a roost, to sleep on a roost. **2** to stay the night. **rooster** *n.* (*esp. N Am., Austral.*) the domestic cock.

root[1] (root) *n.* **1** the descending part of a plant which fixes itself in the earth and draws nourishment from it. **2** (*pl.*) the ramifying parts, rootlets or fibres into which this divides, or the analogous part of an epiphyte etc. **3** a young plant for transplanting. **4** a vegetable with an edible root, such as a carrot or turnip. **5** an edible root. **6** the part of an organ or structure that is embedded. **7** the cause or source. **8** the basis, the bottom, the fundamental part or that which supplies origin, sustenance, means of development etc. **9** (*pl.*) one's ancestry, origins, place of origin or belonging. **10** the elementary, unanalysable part of a word as distinct from its inflectional forms and derivatives. **11** (*Math.*) **a** the quantity or number that, multiplied by itself a specified number of times, yields a given quantity. **b** a square root. **c** a value of an unknown quantity which satisfies a given equation. **12** (*Austral., New Zeal., taboo sl.*) **a** an act of sexual intercourse. **b** a sexual partner. ~*v.i.* to take root. ~*v.t.* **1** to cause to take root. **2** to fix or implant firmly (to the spot). **3** to pull or dig (up) by the roots. **4** (*Austral., New Zeal., taboo sl.*) **a** to have sexual intercourse with. **b** to exhaust. **root and branch** utterly, radically. **to pull up by the roots 1** to uproot. **2** to destroy. **to put down roots 1** to draw nourishment from the soil. **2** to become established. **to root out 1** to uproot. **2** to extirpate. **to strike at the root/ roots of** to destroy deliberately. **to strike root** to take root. **to take root 1** to become planted and send out living roots or rootlets. **2** to become immovable or established. **root beer** *n.* (*N Am.*) a fizzy soft drink made from herbs and the roots of plants. **root canal** *n.* the pulp cavity in the root of a tooth. **rooted** *a.* firmly established. **rootedly** *adv.* **rootedness** *n.* **rootless** *a.* **rootlet** *n.* **rootlike** *a.* **root-mean-square** *n.* (*Math.*) the square root of the average of the squares of a set of values. **root sign** *n.* (*Math.*) a radical sign. **rootstock** *n.* **1** a rhizome. **2** a plant into which a graft is inserted. **3** the original source or primary form of anything. **rootsy** *a.* (*coll.*) (of music) authentic, uncommercialized, incorporating elements of traditional folk music. **root vegetable** *n.* a vegetable that is or has an edible root. **rooty** *a.* **rootiness** *n.*

root[2] (root) *v.t.* to dig, turn or grub (up) with the snout, beak etc. ~*v.i.* **1** to turn up the ground in this manner in search of food. **2** to hunt (up or out), to rummage (about, in etc.). **rootle** (-təl) *v.t., v.i.* to root.

root[3] (root) *v.i.* (*coll.*) to cheer, to shout encouragement to, to give support (*I'm rooting for you*). **rooter** *n.*

rooves ROOF.

rope (rōp) *n.* **1** a stout cord of twisted fibres of hemp, flax, sisal, cotton, nylon etc., or wire. **2** a lasso. **3** cordage over one inch (2.5 cm) in circumference. **4** a series of things strung together in a line, e.g. of garlic, onions, pearls. **5** (*pl.*) the ropes enclosing a boxing or wrestling ring. ~*v.t.* **1** to tie, fasten or secure with a rope. **2** to enclose or close (in) with rope. **3** to fasten (people) together or to tie (a person on) with a rope when climbing. ~*v.i.* **1** to put a rope on for climbing. **2** to climb (down or up) using a rope. **on the ropes 1** in boxing, forced against the ropes by one's opponent. **2** nearly defeated. **the rope 1** a hangman's noose. **2** death by hanging. **to rope in** to enlist or persuade (someone) to join a group or enter into an activity. **to rope into** to persuade (someone) to enter into (an activity). **ropeable**, **ropable** *a.* **1** capable of being roped. **2** (*Austral., New Zeal., sl.*) wild, intractable, bad-tempered. **rope ladder** *n.* a ladder made of two ropes connected by rungs usu. of wood. **ropemanship** *n.* skill in tightrope walking or climbing with ropes. **rope-moulding** *n.* a moulding cut in imitation of rope-strands. **roper** *n.* **rope-walker** *n.* a tightrope artist. **rope-walking** *n.* **ropeway** *n.* a cable railway. **rope-yard** *n.* an establishment where rope is made. **ropy, ropey** *a.* (*comp.* **ropier,** *superl.* **ropiest**) **1** (*coll.*) inferior, shoddy. **2** (*coll.*) unwell. **3** resembling a rope. **ropily** *adv.* **ropiness** *n.*

Roquefort (rok´faw) *n.* a French blue cheese made from ewes' milk.

roquette ROCKET².

ro-ro (rō´rō) *a.* roll-on roll-off.

rorqual (raw´kwəl) *n.* a baleen whale with dorsal fins, of the family Balaenopteridae, the finback.

Rorschach test (raw´shahk) *n.* (*Psych.*) a test for personality traits and disorders based on the interpretation of random ink blots.

rosace (rō´zās) *n.* **1** a rose window. **2** a rose-shaped centrepiece or other ornament, a rosette. **rosaceous** (-zā´shəs) *a.* **1** (*Bot.*) of or relating to the Rosaceae family of plants to which the rose belongs. **2** roselike, rose-coloured. **rosarian** (-zeə´ri-) *n.* a cultivator of roses. **rosarium** (-əm) *n.* (*pl.* **rosariums**) a rose garden.

rosaline (rō´zəlēn) *n.* fine needlepoint or pillow lace.

rosaniline (rōzan´ilēn, -līn, -lin) *n.* **1** a compound having powerful basic properties, derived from aniline. **2** a salt of this used as a dyestuff under the names aniline red, magenta etc.

rosarian, rosarium ROSACE.

rosary (rō´zəri) *n.* (*pl.* **rosaries**) **1** a form of prayer in the Roman Catholic Church in which three sets of five decades of aves, each decade preceded by a paternoster and followed by a gloria, are repeated. **2** this series of prayers. **3** a string of beads by means of which account is kept of the prayers uttered. **4** a similar string of beads used in other religions. **5** a rose garden, a rose plot.

roscoe (ros´kō) *n.* (*N Am., sl.*) a gun.

rose¹ (rōz) *n.* **1** any plant or flower of the genus *Rosa,* consisting of prickly bushes or climbing and trailing shrubs bearing single or double flowers, usu. scented, of all shades of colour from white and yellow to dark crimson. **2** any of various other flowers or plants having some resemblance to the rose (*a Christmas rose*). **3** a light crimson or pink colour. **4** (*pl.*) a complexion of this colour. **5** a device, rosette, knot, ornament or other object shaped like a rose. **6** a perforated nozzle for a hose or watering can. ~*a.* coloured like a rose, pink or pale red. **all roses** completely pleasant, unproblematic or easy. **under the rose** in secret, privately, confidentially, sub rosa. **rose-apple** *n.* **1** a tropical tree of the genus *Syzygium,* cultivated for its foliage, flowers and fruit. **2** the fruit of the rose-apple. **roseate** (-ziət) *a.* **1** rose-coloured, rosy. **2** having a partly pink plumage. **rosebay** *n.* **1** (*also* **rosebay willowherb**) the willowherb *Chamerion angustifolium.* **2** the azalea. **3** the oleander. **rosebowl** *n.*

a bowl-shaped ornamental vase for roses. **rosebud** *n.* **1** a flower bud of a rose. **2** an attractive young woman. **rose bush** *n.* a rose plant. **rosechafer** *n.* a European beetle, *Cetonia aurata,* infesting roses. **rose colour,** (*N Am.*) **rose color** *n.* a deep pink. **rose-coloured** *a.* **1** of rose colour. **2** sanguine, optimistic. **to see through rose-coloured spectacles** to take an overoptimistic or unrealistic view (of). **rose-cut** *a.* (of a diamond etc.) cut with a flat surface below and a hemispherical or pyramidal part above covered with facets. **rose diamond** *n.* a rose-cut diamond. **rose-fish** *n.* (*pl.* **rose-fish**) a red-coloured food fish, *Sebastes marinus,* of the N Atlantic. **rose geranium** *n.* a sweet-scented pelargonium, *Pelargonium graveolus.* **rose-hip** *n.* a red berry, the fruit of the rose plant. **rose leaf** *n.* a petal (or leaf) of a rose. **roseless** *a.* **roselike** *a.* **rose madder** *n.* a pale pink pigment. **rose-mallow** *n.* a hibiscus. **rose of Sharon** (sheə´rən, shar´ən) *n.* **1** a species of hypericum, *Hypericum calycinum,* having golden-yellow flowers. **2** (*Bible*) an Eastern plant not clearly identified. **3** a species of garden hibiscus, *Hibiscus Syriacus.* **rose pink** *n.* rose colour. **rose-pink** *a.* rose-coloured. **rose-point** *n.* a point lace with a rose design. **rose quartz** *n.* a rose-pink variety of quartz. **rose red** *n.* the colour of a red rose. **rose-red** *a.* **rose-root** *n.* a yellow-flowering plant, *Rhodiola rosea,* having a fragrant root. **rosery** (-zəri) *n.* (*pl.* **roseries**) a place where roses grow, a rose garden. **rose-tinted** *a.* rose-coloured. **rose tree** *n.* a rose plant. **rose water** *n.* scented water distilled from rose leaves. **rose window** *n.* a circular window filled with tracery branching from the centre, usu. with mullions arranged like the spokes of a wheel. **rosewood** *n.* **1** a hard close-grained fragrant wood of a dark-red colour obtained chiefly from various species of *Dalbergia.* **2** any tree yielding rosewood. **rosy** *a.* (*comp.* **rosier,** *superl.* **rosiest**) **1** of the colour of a pink or red rose. **2** healthy, blooming. **3** favourable, auspicious. **rosily** *adv.* **rosiness** *n.* **rosy-cheeked** *a.*

rose² RISE.

rosé (rō´zā) *n.* a pink-coloured wine, having had only brief contact with red grape skins.

rosella (rōzel´ə) *n.* (*pl.* **rosellas**) (*Austral.*) a variety of brightly-coloured parakeet, *Platycerus eximius.*

rosemary (rōz´məri) *n.* (*pl.* **rosemaries**) an evergreen fragrant shrub, *Rosmarinus officinalis,* of the mint family, with leaves which yield a perfume and oil and which are used in cooking etc.

rosery ROSE¹.

rosette (rōzet´) *n.* **1** a rose-shaped ornament, knot or badge. **2** a bunch of ribbons, worsted, strips of leather etc. arranged concentrically more or less as the petals of a rose (usu. worn as a badge or given as a prize). **3** (*Archit.*) **a** a carved or painted ornament in the conventional form of a rose. **b** a rose window. **4** (*Bot.*) **a** a circular group of leaves usu. round the base of a stem. **b** markings resembling a rose. **5** a rose diamond. **rosetted** *a.*

Rosh Hashana (rosh həshah´nə), **Rosh Hashanah** *n.* the Jewish New Year.

rosin (roz´in) *n.* resin, esp. the solid residue left after the oil has been distilled from crude turpentine. *~v.t.* (*pres.p.* **rosining**, *past, p.p.* **rosined**) to rub, smear etc. (esp. the bow of a stringed instrument) with rosin. **rosined** *a.* **rosiny** *a.*

roster (ros´tə) *n.* **1** a list showing the order of rotation in which employees, officers, members etc. are to perform their turns of duty. **2** a list of names, e.g. of sports players, available for selection to a team. *~v.t.* to put on a roster.

rostrum (ros´trəm) *n.* (*pl.* **rostra** (-trə), **rostrums**) **1** a platform, a pulpit. **2** (*Zool., Bot.*) a beak, bill or beaklike snout, part or process. **rostral** *a.* **1** (*Zool.*) of, relating to, situated on or resembling a rostrum or beak. **2** (*Anat.*) nearer the hypophysial area, or the nose-and-mouth area. **rostrally** *adv.* **rostrate** (-trət), **rostrated** (-trātid) *a.* (*Zool., Bot.*) having or ending in a part resembling a bird's beak.

rosy ROSE¹.

rot (rot) *v.i.* (*pres.p.* **rotting**, *past, p.p.* **rotted**) **1** to decay, to decompose through natural change, to putrefy. **2** to crumble (away) through decomposition. **3** to be affected with rot or some other decaying disease. **4** to pine away. **5** to die out gradually. *~v.t.* to cause to rot, to decompose, to make putrid. *~n.* **1** putrefaction, rottenness. **2** dry rot, wet rot. **3** (*coll.*) nonsense, rubbish. **4** a rapid deterioration. *~int.* used to express disbelief or disagreement. **rotgut** *n.* (*coll.*) any alcoholic drink of inferior quality.

rota (rō´tə) *n.* (*pl.* **rotas**) a list of names, duties etc., a roster.

rotary (rō´təri) *a.* **1** acting or characterized by rotation. **2** rotating on its axis. *~n.* (*pl.* **rotaries**) **1** a rotary machine. **2** (*N Am.*) a traffic roundabout. **Rotary, Rotary International** *n.* an international business club for mutual benefit and service. **Rotarian** (-teə´ri-) *n.* a member of Rotary. *~a.* of or relating to Rotary. **Rotarianism** *n.* **Rotary club** *n.* a local branch of Rotary. **rotary cultivator** *n.* a horticultural machine with revolving blades or claws for tilling. **rotary-wing** *a.* (of an aircraft) deriving lift from rotary aerofoils. **Rotavator**® (-vātə), (*N Am.*) **Rotovator** *n.* a rotary cultivator. **rotavate**, (*N Am.*) **rotovate** *v.t.* to till with a rotary cultivator.

rotate¹ (rōtāt´) *v.i.* **1** to revolve round an axis or centre. **2** to act in rotation. *~v.t.* **1** to cause (a wheel etc.) to revolve. **2** to arrange (crops etc.) in rotation. **rotatable** *a.* **rotation** (-shən) *n.* **1** the act of rotating, rotary motion. **2** alternation, recurrence, regular succession. **3** a system of growing different kinds of crop in a regular order. **rotational** *a.* **rotationally** *adv.* **rotative** (rō´-) *a.* **rotator** *n.* **1** something which moves in or gives a circular motion. **2** (*Anat.*) a muscle imparting rotatory motion. **rotatory** (rō´tə-) *a.*

rotate² (rō´tāt) *a.* (*Bot.*) (of a calyx, corolla etc.) wheel-shaped.

rote (rōt) *n.* mere repetition of words, phrases etc. without understanding; mechanical, routine memory or knowledge. **rote learning** *n.* learning by rote.

rotifer (rō´tifə) *n.* any member of the Rotifera, a phylum of minute aquatic animals with swimming organs appearing to have a rotary movement. **rotiferal** (-tif´-), **rotiferous** *a.*

rotisserie (rōtis´əri) *n.* **1** a device with a spit on which food, esp. meat, is roasted or barbecued. **2** a restaurant specializing in meat cooked in this way.

rotor (rō´tə) *n.* **1** the rotating part of an electric machine. **2** any system of revolving blades that produces lift in aircraft.

rotten (rot´ən) *a.* **1** decomposed, decayed, decaying, tainted, putrid, fetid. **2** morally corrupt, unhealthy, untrustworthy. **3** (*coll.*) poor or contemptible in quality. **4** (*coll.*) disagreeable, annoying, unpleasant. **5** (*coll.*) unwell. **rotten apple** *n.* (*coll.*) a member of a group who is immoral or corrupt. **rottenly** *adv.* **rottenness** *n.* **rotter** *n.* (*coll.*) a good-for-nothing or detestable person.

Rottweiler (rot´vīlə, -wī-) *n.* a large German breed of dog with a smooth black-and-tan coat.

rotund (rōtŭnd´) *a.* **1** rounded, circular or spherical. **2** (of speech or language) sonorous, magniloquent. **3** plump, well-rounded. **rotunda** (-də) *n.* (*pl.* **rotundas**) a circular building, hall etc., esp. with a dome. **rotundity** *n.* **rotundly** *adv.*

Usage note See note under OROTUND.

rouble (roo´bəl), **ruble** *n.* the standard monetary unit of Russia, Belarus and Tajikistan.

roué (roo´ā) *n.* a rake, a debauchee.

rouge (roozh) *n.* **1** a cosmetic used to colour the cheeks red. **2** red oxide of iron used for polishing metal, glass etc. *~v.t.* to colour with rouge. *~v.i.* **1** to colour one's cheeks etc. with rouge. **2** to blush. **rouge-et-noir** (ānwah´) *n.* a gambling card game played by a 'banker' and a number of people on a table marked with four diamonds, two red and two black.

rough (rŭf) *a.* **1** having an uneven, broken or irregular surface, having prominences or inequalities, not smooth, level or polished. **2** shaggy, hairy. **3** of coarse texture. **4** rugged, hilly. **5** harsh to the senses, astringent, discordant, severe. **6** violent, boisterous, tempestuous. **7** (of language) coarse, crude. **8** turbulent. **9** disorderly. **10** (of wine) sharp-tasting. **11** harsh or rugged in temper or manners. **12** cruel, unfeeling. **13** rude, unpolished. **14** lacking finish or completeness, not completely wrought, crude. **15** approximate, not precise or exact, general. **16** difficult, hard (to bear). **17** unwell or low in spirits (*feeling rough*). *~adv.* roughly, in a rough manner. *~n.* **1** a rough or unfinished state. **2**

rough ground. **3** the rough ground to right and left of a golf fairway. **4** a rough person, a rowdy. **5** a draft, a rough drawing. **6** rough or harsh experiences, hardships. ~*v.t.* **1** to make rough, to roughen. **2** to plan or shape (out) roughly or broadly. **the rough edge/ side of one's tongue** (*coll.*) a scolding, a rebuke. **to rough in** to outline, to draw roughly. **to rough it** to put up with hardships, to live without the ordinary conveniences. **to rough up 1** to ruffle (fur, hair or feathers) by rubbing in the wrong direction. **2** (*sl.*) to beat up, to injure during a beating. **roughage** (-ij) *n.* **1** food materials containing a considerable quantity of cellulose, which resist digestion and promote peristalsis. **2** coarse fodder. **rough-and-ready** *a.* hastily prepared, without finish or elaboration; provisional, makeshift. **rough-and-tumble** *a.* disorderly, irregular, haphazard. ~*n.* an irregular fight, contest, scuffle etc. **rough breathing** *n.* (*Gram.*) in Greek, a sign (-) over an initial vowel indicating that it is aspirated, as distinct from a *smooth breathing*. **roughcast** *n.* **1** a rough model or outline. **2** a coarse plastering, usu. containing gravel, for outside walls etc. ~*a.* **1** formed roughly, without revision or polish. **2** coated with roughcast. ~*v.t.* (*past, p.p.* **roughcast**) **1** to form or compose roughly. **2** to coat (a wall) with roughcast. **rough cut** *n.* the first assembly of a film by an editor from the selected takes which are joined in scripted order. **rough deal** *n.* harsh or unfair treatment. **rough diamond** *n.* a person with rough exterior or manners but a genuine or warm character. **rough-dry** *v.t.* (*3rd pers. sing. pres.* **rough-dries,** *pres.p.* **rough-drying,** *past, p.p.* **rough-dried**) to dry without smoothing or ironing. **roughen** *v.t., v.i.* **rough-handle** *v.t.* to handle roughly. **rough-hew** *v.t.* (*past* **rough-hewed,** *p.p.* **rough-hewn**) to hew out roughly, to give the first crude form to. **rough-hewn** *a.* **1** cut out roughly. **2** rugged, rough, unpolished. **rough hound** *n.* a dogfish, *Scyliorhinus canicula.* **rough house** *n.* (*sl.*) horseplay, brawling. **rough-house** *v.t.* to handle roughly. ~*v.i.* to create a disturbance. **roughish** *a.* **rough justice** *n.* **1** justice appropriate to a crime but not strictly legal. **2** a sentence or verdict hastily reached and executed. **roughly** *adv.* **1** in a rough manner. **2** approximately. **roughneck** *n.* **1** a rowdy, a hooligan. **2** an oilworker employed to handle drilling equipment on a rig. **roughness** *n.* **rough passage** *n.* **1** a voyage over rough sea. **2** a difficult period. **rough ride** *n.* a difficult experience. **rough-rider** *n.* a horsebreaker, a bold, skilful horseman able to ride unbroken horses. **roughshod** *a.* (of a horse) shod with roughened shoes. **to ride roughshod over** to treat in a domineering and inconsiderate way. **rough stuff** *n.* (*sl.*) violence, violent behaviour. **rough tongue** *n.* a rough manner of speech. **rough trade** *n.* (*sl.*) a usu. casual homosexual partner who is uncultivated or aggressive. **rough work** *n.* **1** preliminary work.

2 (*coll.*) violence. **3** a piece of work which requires the use of force.

roulade (rulahd´) *n.* **1** a rolled piece of veal or pork. **2** a thin slice of meat spread with a stuffing and rolled into a sausage shape. **3** (*Mus.*) a run of notes on one syllable, a flourish.

rouleau (roo´lō) *n.* (*pl.* **rouleaux** (-lōz), **rouleaus**) **1** a small roll, esp. a pile of coins done up in paper. **2** a trimming of decorative piping.

roulette (rulet´) *n.* **1** a gambling game played with a ball on a table with a revolving disc. **2** a wheel with points for making dotted lines, used in engraving, for perforating etc. **3** (*Math.*) a curve that is the locus of a point rolling on a curve. **rouletted** *a.*

Roumanian ROMANIAN.

round (rownd) *a.* **1** spherical, circular, cylindrical or approximately so. **2** convexly curved in contour or surface; full, plump, not hollow, corpulent. **3** going from and returning to the same point, with circular or roughly circular course or motion. **4** continuous, unbroken. **5** plain, open, frank, candid, fair. **6** (of pace etc.) quick, smart, brisk. **7** full-toned, resonant. **8** (of a sound) articulated with lips formed into a circle. **9** composed of tens, hundreds etc., esp. evenly divisible by ten, approximate, without fractions. ~*n.* **1** a round object, piece, slice etc. **2** a ladder rung, a circle, coil, sphere or globe. **3** a sandwich made with two slices of bread. **4** something which surrounds, circumference, extent. **5** a circular course, a circuit, a recurrent series. **6** a heat, a cycle. **7** a bout, a session, a spell. **8** an allowance. **9** a series of actions. **10** an order of drinks for several people, each of whom is buying drinks for the group in turn. **11** a burst of applause. **12** a single shot or volley fired from a firearm or gun. **13** ammunition for this. **14** the state of being completely carved out in the solid, as distinct from RELIEF². **15** (*Mil.*) a circuit of inspection, the route taken. **16** (*Mus.*) a piece of music sung by several voices each taking it up in succession. ~*adv.* **1** on all sides so as to encircle. **2** so as to come back to the same point. **3** to or at all points on the circumference or all members of a party etc. **4** by a circuitous route. **5** with rotating motion. **6** to an opposite opinion or view. **7** to one's house. **8** into a more convenient position. **9** in girth. ~*prep.* **1** on all sides of. **2** so as to encircle. **3** to or at all parts of the circumference of. **4** in relation to as a body is to its axis or centre, in all directions from. **5** revolving round. **6** visiting each of. **7** to the other side of. ~*v.t.* **1** to make round or curved. **2** to pass, go or travel round. **3** to change (an amount or figure) to the nearest large number or round number. **4** to collect together, to gather (up). **5** to fill out, to complete. **6** to pronounce fully and smoothly. ~*v.i.* **1** to grow or become round. **2** (of a guard etc.) to go the rounds. **3** (*chiefly Naut.*) to turn round. **in the round 1** all things considered. **2** able to be viewed from every side. **round about**

1 in or as if in a circle (round), all round. **2** approximately. **3** in an opposite direction. **4** circuitously, indirectly. **round and round** several times round. **to get round 1** to coax by flattery or deception. **2** to evade (a law or rule). **to go the round(s)** (of news, a joke etc.) to be passed from person to person. **to make one's rounds** to make a series of visits to different people or places. **to make the round of** to go round. **to round down** to lower (a number) to avoid fractions or reach a convenient figure. **to round off 1** to finish off, to complete, to perfect. **2** to shape (angles etc.) to a round or less sharp form. **to round on** to turn upon, to attack. **to round out 1** to finish off, to complete, to perfect. **2** to provide more information about. **3** to fill out, to become more plump. **to round up 1** to gather (horse, cattle etc.) together. **2** to raise (a number) to avoid fractions or reach a convenient figure. **roundabout** *n.* **1** a device at a crossroads whereby traffic circulates in one direction only. **2** a merry-go-round. **3** a circular revolving device for riding on in a children's playground. *~a.* circuitous, indirect, loose. **round-arm** *a.* in cricket, (of bowling) performed with a swing in which the arm turns at shoulder level. **round brackets** *n.pl.* parentheses. **round dance** *n.* a dance in which the performers are ranged or move in a circle, esp. a waltz. **rounded** *a.* **roundedness** *n.* **rounder** *n.* **1** (*pl.*) a game with a short bat and a ball, between two sides, with four bases around which a player hitting the ball has to run without the ball being returned to the base ahead. **2** a complete run through all the bases in rounders. **Roundhead** *n.* a Parliamentarian in the English Civil War. **roundhouse** *n.* **1** a circular building containing a turntable for servicing railway locomotives. **2** (*sl.*) a blow with a wide sweep of the arm. **roundhouse kick** *n.* in karate, a kick with a wide sweep of the leg. **roundish** *a.* **roundly** *adv.* **1** bluntly, straightforwardly, plainly, emphatically. **2** energetically, thoroughly. **3** in a round or roundish form. **roundness** *n.* **round robin** *n.* **1** a petition with the signatures placed in a circle so that no name heads the list. **2** a tournament in which each contestant plays every other contestant. **round-shouldered** *a.* having the shoulders bent forward so that the back is rounded. **roundsman** (-mən) *n.* (*pl.* **roundsmen**) **1** a man who makes calls to collect orders, deliver goods etc. **2** (*N Am.*) a police officer making a round of inspection. **3** (*Austral.*) a journalist covering a particular topic. **round table** *n.* a conference or meeting at which all parties are on an equal footing. **round-the-clock** *a.* continuous, lasting 24 hours a day. **round trip** *n.* a journey to a place and back. *~a.* (*N Am.*) return. **round-up** *n.* **1** a gathering together of cattle etc. **2** a similar gathering of people, objects, news, facts etc.; a news round-up. **roundworm** *n.* a parasitic elongated worm, a nematode.

roundel (rown′dəl) *n.* (*Her. etc.*) a round disc, panel, heraldic circular charge etc.
roundelay (rown′dəlā) *n.* a simple song, usu. with a refrain.
rouse (rowz) *v.t.* **1** to wake. **2** to excite to thought or action. **3** to provoke, to stir (up), to agitate. **4** to startle (game) from a covert. *~v.i.* **1** to wake or be wakened. **2** to start up, to be excited or stirred (up) to activity etc. **to rouse oneself** to abandon inactivity. **rousable** *a.* **rouseabout** *n.* (*Austral., New Zeal.*) an odd-job man in a shearing shed or on a station. **rouser** *n.* **rousing** *a.* **1** having power to awaken, excite or rouse. **2** blazing strongly. **rousingly** *adv.*
roust (rowst) *v.t.* **1** to rouse, to rout (out). **2** (*N Am., sl.*) to jostle or harass. **to roust around** to rummage. **roustabout** *n.* **1** an unskilled worker on an oil rig. **2** a casual labourer. **3** a labourer on wharves. **4** (*N Am.*) a labourer in a circus. **5** (*Austral.*) a rouseabout.
rout[1] (rowt) *n.* **1** an utter defeat and overthrow. **2** a disorderly and confused retreat of a defeated army etc. **3** a crowd, a miscellaneous or disorderly gathering. **4** a riot, a brawl, an uproar, a disturbance. *~v.t.* to defeat utterly and put to flight. **to put to rout** to defeat utterly.
rout[2] (rowt) *v.t.* **1** to root (up or out). **2** to gouge, to scoop, to tear (out etc.). *~v.i.* to root up or out. **to rout out** to hunt out. **router** *n.* **1** a plane, a saw or any of various other tools for hollowing out or cutting grooves. **2** someone who or something which routs.
route (root) *n.* **1** the course, way or road(s) travelled or to be travelled. **2** (*N Am.*) a course travelled in delivering or selling. *~v.t.* (*pres.p.* **routeing, routing**) **1** to send by a certain route. **2** to arrange or plan the route of. **routeman** *n.* (*pl.* **routemen**) (*N Am.*) a roundsman. **route march** *n.* (*Mil.*) an arduous military-training march.
routine (rootēn′) *n.* **1** a course of procedure, business or official duties etc., regularly pursued. **2** any regular or mechanical habit or practice. **3** a sequence of jokes, movements, steps etc. regularly performed by a comedian, dancer, skater, stripper etc. **4** (*Comput.*) a computer program or part of one which performs a particular task. *~a.* **1** tiresome, repetitive, commonplace. **2** of or relating to a set procedure. **routinely** *adv.* **routinism** *n.* adherence to routine. **routinist** *n., a.* **routinize, routinise** *v.t.* **routinization** (-zā′shən) *n.*
roux (roo) *n.* (*pl.* **roux**) a sauce base, the thickening element in a sauce made from fat and flour cooked together.
rove[1] (rōv) *v.i.* **1** to wander, to ramble, to roam. **2** (of eyes) to look round, to wander. *~v.t.* to wander over, through etc. *~n.* the act of roving, a ramble. **rove-beetle** *n.* a beetle of the family Staphylinidae, having an elongated body. **rover** *n.* **1** a wanderer. **2** in American football, a defensive linebacker moving around in anticipation of the opposition's play. **3** a pirate, a buccaneer.

rover ticket *n.* a ticket which can be used for unlimited travel on public transport within a defined area for a certain period. **roving** *n., a.* **roving commission** *n.* a commission without a rigidly defined area of authority. **roving eye** *n.* a promiscuous sexual interest. **rovingly** *adv.*

rove² REEVE².

row¹ (rō) *n.* **1** a series of persons or things in a straight or nearly straight line. **2** a line, a rank (of seats, vegetables etc.). **3** a street usu. of identical houses. **hard row to hoe** a difficult task. **in a row** **1** (placed) one after the other. **2** (ordered) in succession. **row house** *n.* (*N Am.*) a terrace house.

row² (rō) *v.t.* **1** to propel by oars. **2** to convey by rowing. **3** to make (a stroke) in rowing. **4** to take part in (a rowing race). *~v.i.* **1** to row a boat. **2** to be impelled by oars. *~n.* **1** a spell at rowing. **2** an excursion in a rowing boat. **rowable** *a.* **row-boat** *n.* (*N Am.*) a rowing boat. **rower** *n.* **rowing** *n., a.* **rowing boat** *n.* a boat propelled by rowing. **rowing machine** *n.* an exercise machine fitted with oars and a sliding seat. **rowlock** (rol´ǝk), **rollock** *n.* a crotch, notch or other device on the gunwale of a boat serving as a fulcrum for an oar.

row³ (row) *n.* (*coll.*) **1** a noisy disturbance, a noise, a din, a commotion, a tumult. **2** a quarrel. **3** a scolding. *~v.t.* to scold, to reprimand. *~v.i.* to make a row, to quarrel.

rowan (row´ǝn, rō´-) *n.* **1** the mountain ash, *Sorbus aucuparia.* **2** (*N Am.*) a similar tree, *Sorbus americana,* of America. **rowan berry** *n.* the small red fruit of the rowan. **rowan tree** *n.*

rowdy (row´di) *a.* (*comp.* **rowdier,** *superl.* **rowdiest**) rough, riotous. *~n.* (*pl.* **rowdies**) a noisy, rough or disorderly person. **rowdily** *adv.* **rowdiness** *n.* **rowdyish** *a.* **rowdyism** *n.*

rowel (row´ǝl) *n.* a spiked disc or wheel on a spur. *~v.t.* (*pres.p.* **rowelling,** (*N Am.*) **roweling,** *past, p.p.* **rowelled,** (*N Am.*) **roweled**) to prick or goad with a rowel.

rowlock ROW².

royal (roi´ǝl) *a.* **1** of, relating to, suitable to or befitting a king or queen. **2** under the patronage or in the service of a king or queen. **3** regal, kingly, princely. **4** noble, magnificent, majestic. **5** extremely fine, on a great scale, splendid, first-rate. *~n.* **1** (*coll.*) a member of a royal family. **2** a royal stag. **3** a royal mast or sail next above the topgallant. **Royal Air Force** *n.* the air force of Great Britain. **royal assent** *n.* the sovereign's assent to a bill passed by Parliament. **royal blue** *n.* a deep blue. **royal-blue** *a.* **royal burgh** *n.* a burgh holding its municipal authority by royal charter. **Royal Commission** *n.* a commission of inquiry ordered by Parliament. **royal duke** *n.* a duke who is also a prince. **royal family** *n.* the sovereign and the sovereign's family. **royal fern** *n.* a flowering fern, *Osmunda regalis.* **royal flush** *n.* a flush with cards in a sequence headed by the ace. **royal icing** *n.* a hard icing on wedding cakes, fruit cakes etc. **royalist** *n.* **1** an adherent or supporter of royalism or of monarchical govern-

ment, esp. a supporter of the royal cause in the English Civil War. **2** (*N Am.*) a reactionary or conservative person. *~a.* of or relating to royalists. **royalism** *n.* **royal jelly** *n.* the food secreted and fed by worker bees to developing queen bees. **royally** *adv.* **royal mast** *n.* the topmost part of a mast above the topgallant. **royal oak** *n.* a sprig of oak worn on 29 May to commemorate King Charles II. **royal plural** *n.* the royal 'we'. **royal prerogative** *n.* the constitutional authority and privilege invested in a sovereign. **royal sail** *n.* a sail above a topgallant sail. **royal stag** *n.* a stag with antlers having 12 or more points. **royal standard** *n.* a flag with the royal arms. **royal tennis** *n.* real tennis. **royalty** *n.* (*pl.* **royalties**) **1** the office or dignity of a king or queen, sovereignty. **2** a royal person or persons. **3** a member of a royal family. **4** a right or prerogative of a sovereign. **5** royal rank, birth or lineage. **6** (*usu. pl.*) a share of profits paid to a landowner for the right to work a mine, to a patentee for the use of an invention, to an author on copies of books sold etc. **Royal Victorian Order** *n.* an order founded by Queen Victoria and conferred for special services to the sovereign. **royal warrant** *n.* a warrant authorizing the supply of goods to a royal household. **royal 'we'** *n.* the customary use of the first person plural by a sovereign referring to themselves.

rozzer (roz´ǝ) *n.* (*sl.*) a police officer.

RP *abbr.* received pronunciation.

RPI *abbr.* retail price index.

r.p.m. *abbr.* **1** revolutions per minute. **2** resale price maintenance.

rpt *abbr.* repeat.

Rs. *abbr.* rupee(s).

RSA *abbr.* Republic of South Africa.

RSI *abbr.* repetitive strain injury.

RSM *abbr.* Regimental Sergeant Major.

RSV *abbr.* Revised Standard Version (of the Bible).

RSVP *abbr.* please reply.

RT *abbr.* **1** radio-telegraphy. **2** radio-telephony.

Rt. Hon. *abbr.* Right Honourable.

Rt. Revd., Rt. Rev. *abbr.* Right Reverend.

Ru *chem. symbol* ruthenium.

rub¹ (rŭb) *v.t.* (*pres.p.* **rubbing,** *past, p.p.* **rubbed**) **1** to apply friction to, to move one's hand or other object over the surface of. **2** to polish, to clean, to scrape, to graze. **3** to slide or pass (a hand or other object) along, over or against something. **4** to make sore by rubbing. **5** to take an impression of (a design) with chalk and graphite on paper laid over it. **6** to spread on or mix into something by rubbing. *~v.i.* **1** to move or slide along a surface, to grate, to graze, to chafe (against, on etc.). **2** to cause pain or fraying by rubbing. **3** in bowling, to meet with a hindrance. **4** to proceed (along, on, through etc.) with difficulty. *~n.* **1** the act or a spell of rubbing. **2** a hindrance, an obstruction, a difficulty. **3** in bowling, an unevenness of the ground which impedes the bowl. **to rub along 1** (*coll.*) to manage, to just succeed, to cope despite difficulties. **2** (*coll.*) to keep on friendly terms. **to rub down 1** to clean or dry by rubbing. **2** to make smooth. **to rub elbows with** (*N Am.*) to rub shoulders with. **to rub in** to force in by friction. **to rub it in** to keep reminding someone of something embarrassing. **to rub off** to remove by rubbing. **to rub off on someone** to pass on to someone by example or close association. **to rub one's hands** to express expectation, glee, satisfaction etc. by rubbing one's hands together. **to rub out 1** to remove or erase by friction. **2** (*N Am., sl.*) to kill. **to rub shoulders with** to associate or mix with. **to rub someone's nose in it** to refer to or remind someone of an error, indiscretion or misfortune. **to rub up 1** to polish, to burnish. **2** to freshen (one's recollection of something). **3** to mix into a paste etc. by rubbing. **to rub (up) the wrong way** to irritate. **rubbing** *n.* **1** the act of rubbing. **2** an impression made on paper laid over an image and rubbed with chalk, wax etc. **rub-down** *n.* the act of rubbing down. **rub of the green, rub on the green** *n.* **1** in golf, an accidental interference with the ball. **2** (*coll.*) good fortune. **rub-up** *n.* the act of rubbing up.

rub² (rŭb) *n.* a rubber of bridge.

rubato (rubah´tō) *n.* (*pl.* **rubatos, rubati** (-tē)) (*Mus.*) **1** flexibility of rhythm, fluctuation of tempo within a musical piece. **2** an instance of this. ~*a.* to be performed in this manner.

rubber¹ (rŭb´ə) *n.* **1** a soft, elastic substance obtained from the coagulated juice of several tropical plants. **2** a piece of rubber for erasing pencil marks etc. **3** (*coll.*) a condom. **4** (*pl., N Am.*) galoshes, rubber overshoes. **5** someone who or something which rubs. ~*a.* made of, yielding or relating to rubber. **rubber band** *n.* a continuous band of rubber for securing packages, the hair etc. **rubber bullet** *n.* a baton round made of rubber. **rubberize, rubberise** *v.t.* to treat with rubber. **rubberneck, rubbernecker** *n.* (*coll.*) **1** a sightseer. **2** a person who gapes out of curiosity. ~*v.i.* **1** to sightsee. **2** to gape foolishly. **rubber plant** *n.* **1** a plant, *Ficus elastica*, common to Asia and related to the fig, with large shiny leaves, grown as a popular house plant. **2** (*also* **rubber tree**) any one of various tropical, latex-yielding trees, esp. *Hevea brasiliensis*. **rubber solution** *n.* a liquid adhesive which dries to a rubber-like material. **rubber stamp** *n.* **1** a device with a rubber pad for marking or imprinting. **2** a person who makes routine authorizations, a cipher. **3** a routine seal of approval, an automatic endorsement. ~*v.t.* **1** to approve or endorse as a matter of routine. **2** to imprint with a rubber stamp. **rubbery** *a.* **rubberiness** *n.*

rubber² (rŭb´ə) *n.* **1** a series of three games at whist, bridge, backgammon etc. **2** two games out of three or the game that decides the contest.

rubbish (rŭb´ish) *n.* **1** waste, broken or rejected matter, refuse, junk, litter, trash. **2** nonsense. ~*a.*

(*coll.*) bad, useless, distasteful etc. ~*v.t.* **1** to criticize. **2** to reject as rubbish. **rubbish heap** *n.* **1** a pile of or place for waste. **2** a state of uselessness. **on the rubbish heap** (*coll.*) discarded as ineffective or worthless. **rubbishing** *a.* **rubbishy** *a.*

rubble (rŭb´əl) *n.* **1** rough, broken fragments of stone, brick etc. **2** (*Geol.*) disintegrated rock. **3** water-worn stones. **rubbly** *a.*

rube (roob) *n.* (*N Am., coll.*) an unsophisticated country dweller, a country bumpkin.

rubella (rubel´ə) *n.* (*Med.*) a mild, infectious disorder resembling measles which, if contracted by a pregnant woman, may cause birth deformities in her unborn child; German measles. **rubellite** (roo´bəlīt, rubel´-) *n.* a pinkish-red tourmaline. **rubeola** (-bē´ələ) *n.* (*Med.*) measles.

Rubicon (roo´bikən) *n.* an irrevocable step, a point of no return.

rubicund (roo´bikənd) *a.* ruddy, rosy, red-faced. **rubicundity** (-kŭn´-) *n.*

rubidium (rubid´iəm) *n.* (*Chem.*) a silvery-white metallic element, at. no. 37, chem. symbol Rb, belonging to the potassium group. **rubidic** *a.*

Rubik's cube® (roo´biks) *n.* a puzzle consisting of a cube, each face of which is divided into nine coloured segments which can be revolved to obtain the same colour on each face.

ruble ROUBLE.

rubric (roob´rik) *n.* **1** a title, chapter heading, entry, set of rules, commentary or direction, orig. printed in red or distinctive lettering, esp. a liturgical direction in the Prayer Book etc. **2** explanatory notes, instructions, rules. **3** an established custom. ~*a.* red, marked with red. **rubrical** *a.* **rubricate** *v.t.* **1** to mark, distinguish, print or illuminate with red. **2** to furnish with a rubric or rubrics. **rubrication** (-ā´shən) *n.* **rubricator** *n.*

ruby (roo´bi) *n.* (*pl.* **rubies**) **1** a precious stone of a red colour, a variety of corundum. **2** the colour of ruby, a purplish red. ~*a.* **1** of the colour of a ruby. **2** marking a 40th anniversary. **ruby glass** *n.* glass coloured with oxides of copper, iron, lead etc. **ruby-tail** *n.* a wasp, *Chrysis ignita*, with a bluish-green back and red abdomen. **ruby wedding** *n.* a 40th wedding anniversary.

ruche (roosh) *n.* a pleated strip of gauze, lace, silk or the like used as a frill or trimming. **ruched** *a.* **ruching** *n.*

ruck¹ (rŭk) *n.* **1** a multitude, a crowd, esp. the mass of horses left behind by the leaders in a race. **2** the common run of people or things. **3** in rugby, a gathering of players round the ball when it is on the ground. **4** in Australian Rules football, three players who follow the play without fixed positions. ~*v.i.* to form a ruck in rugby.

ruck² (rŭk) *v.i., v.t.* to wrinkle, to crease. ~*n.* a crease, a wrinkle, a fold, a pleat. **ruckle** (-əl) *v.t., v.i.* to ruck. ~*n.* a ruck.

rucksack (rŭk´sak) *n.* a bag carried on the back by means of straps by campers, hikers, climbers etc.

ruckus (rŭk´əs) *n.* (*esp. N Am.*) a row, a disturbance, an uproar.

ruction (rŭk´shən) *n.* (*coll.*) **1** a commotion, a disturbance, a row. **2** (*pl.*) trouble, arguments.

rudbeckia (rŭdbek´iə) *n.* a plant of the genus *Rudbeckia* of N American plants of the aster family.

rudd (rŭd) *n.* a fish, *Scardinius erythrophthalmus*, resembling a roach.

rudder (rŭd´ə) *n.* **1** a flat wooden or metal framework or solid piece hinged to the sternpost of a boat or ship and serving as a means of steering. **2** a vertical moving surface in the tail of an aircraft for providing directional control and stability. **3** any steering device. **4** a principle etc. which guides, governs or directs the course of anything. **rudderless** *a.*

ruddle (rŭd´əl), **reddle** (red´əl) *n.* a variety of red ochre used for marking sheep, raddle. ~*v.t.* to colour or mark with ruddle.

ruddy (rŭd´i) *a.* (*comp.* **ruddier,** *superl.* **ruddiest**) **1** of a red or reddish colour. **2** (of a healthy complexion) fresh-coloured. **3** bloody. ~*v.t.* (*3rd pers. sing. pres.* **ruddies,** *pres.p.* **ruddying,** *past, p.p.* **ruddied**) to make ruddy. ~*v.i.* to grow red. **ruddily** *adv.* **ruddiness** *n.* **ruddy duck** *n.* an American duck, *Oxyura jamaicensis*, which has reddish-brown plumage in the male.

rude (rood) *a.* **1** impolite, uncivil, insolent, offensive, insulting. **2** unformed, unfinished. **3** simple, primitive, crude, uncultivated, uncivilized, unsophisticated, unrefined, rough, rugged. **4** violent, boisterous, abrupt, tempestuous. **5** coarse, uncouth, indecent, vulgar. **6** hearty, robust, strong. **to be rude to** to speak impolitely to. **rudely** *adv.* **rudeness** *n.* **rudery** *n.* **rudish** *a.*

rudiment (roo´dimənt) *n.* **1** (*usu. pl.*) an elementary or first principle of knowledge etc. **2** (*pl.*) the undeveloped or imperfect form of something, a beginning, a germ. **3** (*Biol.*) a partially developed, aborted or stunted organ, structure etc., a vestige. **rudimentary** (-men´-) *a.* **rudimentarily** *adv.* **rudimentariness** *n.*

rue¹ (roo) *v.t.* (*pres. p.* **rueing, ruing,** *past, p.p.* **rued**) to grieve or be sorry for, to regret, to repent of. **rueful** *a.* regretful, sorrowful. **ruefully** *adv.* **ruefulness** *n.*

rue² (roo) *n.* a plant of the genus *Ruta*, esp. *R. graveolens*, a shrubby evergreen plant, having a strong smell and acrid taste, formerly used as a stimulant etc. in medicine.

ruff¹ (rŭf) *n.* **1** a broad pleated or fluted collar or frill of linen or muslin worn by both sexes, esp. in the 16th cent. **2** a growth like a ruff, such as the ring of feathers round the necks of some birds. **3** a bird, *Philomachus pugnax*, of the sandpiper family (perh. from the conspicuous ruff in the male in the breeding season). **ruffed** *a.* **rufflike** *a.*

ruff² (rŭf) *n.* **1** (*also* **ruffe**) a small freshwater fish, *Gymnocephalus cernua*, related to and resembling the perch. **2** (*esp. Austral.*) a marine food fish, *Arripis georgianus*, related to the Australian salmon.

ruff³ (rŭf) *n.* the act of trumping when one cannot follow suit. ~*v.t., v.i.* to trump.

ruffian (rŭf´iən) *n.* a low, lawless, brutal person, a bully, a violent hoodlum. **ruffianism** *n.* **ruffianlike, ruffianly** *a.*

ruffle (rŭf´əl) *v.t.* **1** to disorder, to disturb the smoothness or order of, to rumple, to disarrange. **2** to annoy, to disturb, to upset, to discompose. **3** to gather into a ruffle. **4** (of a bird) to make (the feathers) stand out, when cleaning or in anger etc. ~*v.i.* to grow rough or turbulent, to move or toss about loosely, to flutter. ~*n.* **1** a strip or frill of fine, pleated or goffered lace etc., attached to some part of a garment, esp. at the neck or wrist. **2** a bird's ruff. **3** a ripple on water. **ruffled** *a.*

rufiyaa (roofē´yah) *n.* the standard unit of currency of the Maldives.

rufous (roo´fəs) *a.* of a brownish red.

rug (rŭg) *n.* **1** a thick, heavy wrap, coverlet etc., usu. woollen with a thick nap, or of skin with the hair or wool left on. **2** a carpet or floor mat of similar material. **3** (*coll.*) a hairpiece, a wig. **to pull the rug from under** to put (someone) in a defenceless or discomposed state, to undermine (someone).

rugby (rŭg´bi), **Rugby, rugby football** *n.* a game of football in which players are allowed to use their hands in carrying and passing the ball and tackling their opponents. **Rugby League** *n.* a form of rugby played by teams consisting of 13 players of amateur or professional status. **Rugby Union** *n.* a form of rugby played by teams of 15 players of largely amateur status. **rugger** *n.* (*coll.*) rugby.

rugged (rŭg´id) *a.* **1** having an extremely uneven surface full of inequalities; broken and irregular. **2** rocky, craggy, of abrupt contour. **3** (of a man) having strong, virile features. **4** (of a sound) harsh, grating. **5** rough in temper, stern, unbending, severe. **6** strenuous, hard. **7** hardy, sturdy. **ruggedized** *a.* (*esp. N Am.*) designed to be hardwearing. **ruggedization** (-zā´shən) *n.* **ruggedly** *adv.* **ruggedness** *n.*

rugger RUGBY.

ruin (roo´in) *n.* **1** a disastrous change or state of wreck or disaster, an overthrow, a downfall. **2** bankruptcy. **3** a cause of destruction, downfall or disaster. **4** the state of being ruined or destroyed. **5** (*often in pl.*) the remains of a structure, building, city etc. that has been demolished or has decayed. **6** a person who has suffered a downfall, e.g. a bankrupt. ~*v.t.* (*pres.p.* **ruining,** *past, p.p.* **ruined**) **1** to bring to ruin. **2** to reduce to ruins, to dilapidate. **3** to destroy, to overthrow, to subvert. **4** to harm, to spoil, to disfigure. **5** to bankrupt. **in ruins 1** in a state of ruin or decay. **2** completely spoiled. **ruinable** *a.* **ruination** (-ā´shən) *n.* **ruiner** *n.* **ruinous** *a.* **1** causing ruin, destructive, pernicious. **2** fallen into ruin, dilapidated. **ruinously** *adv.* **ruinousness** *n.*

rule (rool) *n.* **1** something which is established as a principle, standard or guide of action or procedure. **2** a line of conduct, a regular practice, an established custom, canon or maxim. **3** the act of ruling or the state or period of being ruled, government, authority, sway, direction, control; method, regularity. **4** a strip of wood, plastic, metal etc. usu. graduated in centimetres or inches and millimetres or fractions of an inch, used for linear measurement or guidance. **5** (*Print.*) **a** a thin metal strip for separating columns, headings etc. **b** a thin printed line. **6** an authoritative form, direction or regulation, a body of laws or regulations, to be observed by an association, religious order etc. and its individual members. **7** (*Law*) an order, direction or decision by a judge or court, usu. with reference to a particular case only. **8** (**Rules**) Australian Rules football. ~*v.t.* **1** to govern, to manage, to control, to curb, to restrain. **2** to be the ruler, governor or sovereign of. **3** to lay down as a rule or as an authoritative decision. **4** to mark (paper etc.) with straight lines. **5** to draw (a straight line) using a rule. ~*v.i.* **1** to exercise supreme power (usu. over). **2** to decide, to make a decision. **3** to dominate, to be prevalent. **as a rule** usually, generally. **by rule** mechanically, automatically. **to be ruled by** to be guided by. **to rule out** to exclude, to eliminate (as a possibility). **to rule the roast** to rule the roost. **to rule the roost** to be the leader, to be dominant. **rulable** *a.* **ruleless** *a.* **rule of the road** *n.* a regulation governing the methods of passing each other for vehicles on the road, vessels on the water etc. **rule of thumb** *n.* practical experience, as distinct from theory, as a guide in doing anything. **ruler** *n.* **1** a person who rules or governs. **2** an instrument with straight edges or sides, used as a guide in drawing straight lines, a rule. **rulership** *n.* **ruling** *n.* **1** an authoritative decision, esp. with regard to a special legal case. **2** a ruled line or lines. ~*a.* **1** predominant, pre-eminent. **2** having or exercising authority or control. **ruling passion** *n.* a strong feeling which influences someone's actions.

rum[1] (rŭm) *n.* **1** a spirit distilled from fermented molasses or cane juice. **2** (*N Am.*) any alcoholic drink. **rum baba** *n.* a small cake soaked in rum. **rum butter** *n.* butter mixed with sugar and flavoured with rum.

rum[2] (rŭm) *a.* (*comp.* **rummer**, *superl.* **rummest**) (*sl.*) strange, singular, odd, queer. **rumly** *adv.* **rumness** *n.*

Rumanian ROMANIAN.

rumba (rŭm′bə), **rhumba** *n.* **1** a complex and rhythmic Cuban dance. **2** a ballroom dance developed from this dance. **3** a piece of music for this dance. ~*v.i.* (*3rd pers. sing. pres.* **rumbas**, **rhumbas**, *pres.p.* **rumbaing**, **rhumbaing**, *past,*

p.p. **rumbaed, rumba'd, rhumbaed, rhumba'd**) to dance the rumba.

rumble (rŭm′bəl) *v.i.* **1** to make a low, heavy, continuous sound, as of thunder, heavy vehicles etc. **2** to move (along) with such a sound. ~*v.t.* **1** to cause to move with a rumbling noise. **2** to utter with such a sound. **3** (*sl.*) to discover the truth about, to see through. ~*n.* **1** a rumbling sound. **2** (*N Am.; sl.*) a gang fight. **rumbler** *n.* **rumble seat** *n.* (*N Am.*) an outside folding seat on some early motor vehicles. **rumble strip** *n.* a series of raised strips set into a road to make vehicles vibrate as a warning to drivers. **rumbling** *a.* **rumblingly** *adv.* **rumblings** *n.pl.* signs that an unpleasant situation is about to develop. **rumbly** *a.*

rumbustious (rŭmbŭs′chəs) *a.* (*coll.*) boisterous, turbulent, cheerful and noisy. **rumbustiously** *adv.* **rumbustiousness** *n.*

rumen (roo′men) *n.* (*pl.* **rumens, rumina** (-minə)) (*Zool.*) the first cavity of the complex stomach of a ruminant.

ruminant (roo′minənt) *n.* **1** any member of the division of cud-chewing animals with a complex stomach, including cattle, sheep, deer etc. **2** any other cud-chewing animal (e.g. the camel). ~*a.* **1** of or relating to the ruminants. **2** meditative, contemplative. **ruminantly** *adv.* **ruminate** (-nāt) *v.i.* **1** to muse, to meditate (over). **2** to chew the cud. ~*v.t.* **1** to ponder over. **2** to chew again (what has been regurgitated). **rumination** (-ā′shən) *n.* **ruminative** (-nətiv) *a.* **ruminatively** *adv.* **ruminator** *n.*

rummage (rŭm′ij) *v.t.* **1** to make a search in or through, to ransack, esp. by throwing the contents about. **2** to find or uncover by such searching. **3** to disarrange or throw into disorder by searching. ~*v.i.* to make a search (through, among, in). ~*n.* **1** the act of rummaging, a search. **2** miscellaneous articles, odds and ends (found by rummaging). **rummager** *n.* **rummage sale** *n.* (*esp. N Am.*) a jumble sale.

rummy (rŭm′i) *n.* any of several card games in which the object is to collect combinations and sequences of cards.

rumour (roo′mə), (*N Am.*) **rumor** *n.* **1** popular report, hearsay, common talk. **2** a current story without any known authority. ~*v.t.* to report or circulate as a rumour. **rumorous** *a.* **rumourer** *n.* **rumour-monger** *n.* a person who spreads rumours. **rumour-mongering** *n.*

rump (rŭmp) *n.* **1** the end of the backbone of a mammal with the adjacent parts, the posterior, the buttocks. **2** in birds, the terminal part of the body. **3** the tail-end of anything. **rumpless** *a.* **rump steak** *n.* a beefsteak cut from the rump.

rumple (rŭm′pəl) *v.t.* to wrinkle, to make uneven, to crease, to disorder. ~*v.i.* to become wrinkled or creased. **rumply** *a.*

rumpus (rŭm′pəs) *n.* (*pl.* **rumpuses**) (*coll.*) a disturbance, an uproar, a row. **rumpus room** *n.* (*N Am., Austral., New Zeal.*) a playroom or games room, esp. for children.

run (rŭn) *v.i.* (*pres.p.* **running**, *past* **ran** (ran), *p.p.* **run**) **1** to move or pass over the ground by using the legs more quickly than in walking, esp. with a springing motion, so that both feet are never on the ground at once. **2** (of a horse etc.) to amble, trot, or canter. **3** to flee, to try to escape. **4** to make a run at cricket. **5** to compete in a race. **6** to complete a race in a specified position. **7** to seek election etc. **8** to move or travel rapidly. **9** to make a quick or casual trip or visit. **10** to be carried along violently. **11** to move along on or as if on wheels. **12** to be in continuous motion, to be in action or operation. **13** to go smoothly. **14** to glide, to elapse. **15** to flow. **16** to fuse, to melt, to dissolve and spread. **17** to flow (with), to be wet, to drip, to emit liquid, mucus etc. **18** to spread or circulate rapidly or in profusion. **19** (of a shoal of fish) to migrate, esp. upstream for spawning. **20** to extend, to take a certain course, to proceed, to go on, to continue (for a certain distance or duration). **21** to be played, featured or published etc. **22** to tend, to incline. **23** to be current, valid, in force or effect. **24** to occur inherently, persistently or repeatedly. **25** to pass freely or casually. **26** to occur in sequence. **27** to perform, quickly or in sequence. **28** to be allowed to wander unrestrainedly or grow (wild). **29** to elapse. **30** (of a loan, debt etc.) to accumulate. **31** (of stockings, tights etc.) to ladder, to unravel. ~*v.t.* **1** to cause to run or go. **2** to cause or allow to pass, penetrate etc., to thrust with. **3** to drive, to propel. **4** to track, to pursue, to chase, to hunt. **5** to press (hard) in a race, competition etc. **6** to accomplish (as if) by running. **7** to perform or execute (a race, an errand etc.). **8** to follow or pursue (a course etc.). **9** to cause to ply. **10** to bring to a specific state as if by running. **11** to keep going, to manage, to conduct, to carry on, to work, to operate. **12** to enter or enrol (as a contender). **13** to introduce or promote the election of (a candidate). **14** to get past or through (e.g. a blockade). **15** to cross, to traverse. **16** to cause to extend or continue. **17** to discharge, to flow with. **18** to cause to pour or flow. **19** to fill (a bath) from a flowing tap. **20** to convey in a motor vehicle, to give a lift to. **21** to be affected by or subjected to. **22** to graze (animals) in open pasture. **23** in billiards, cricket etc., to hit or score (a successful sequence of shots, runs etc.). **24** to sew quickly. **25** to have or keep current. **26** to publish. **27** to cast, to found, to mould. **28** to deal in, to smuggle. **29** to incur, to expose oneself to, to hazard. **30** to allow (a bill etc.) to accumulate before paying. ~*n.* **1** an act or spell of running. **2** the distance or duration of a run or journey. **3** a trip, a short excursion. **4** the running of two batsmen from one wicket to the other in cricket without either's being put out. **5** a complete circuit of the bases by a player in baseball etc. **6** a continuous course, a sustained period of operation or performance. **7** a sequence, series, stretch or succession (e.g. of

cards, luck etc.). **8** a succession of demands (on a bank etc.). **9** the quantity of a product produced by a factory at any one time. **10** the ordinary succession, trend or general direction, the way things tend to move. **11** a rapid motion. **12** a ladder or rip in a stocking, jumper, pair of tights etc. **13** a line of goods. **14** general nature, character, class or type. **15** a batch, flock, drove or shoal of animals, fish etc. born together or migrating together. **16** a periodical passage or migration. **17** an inclined course esp. for winter sports. **18** a habitual course or circuit. **19** a regular track (of certain animals), a burrow. **20** a grazing ground. **21** an enclosure for fowls. **22** free use or access, unrestricted enjoyment. **23** a mission involving travel (*a smuggling run*; *a bombing run*). **24** (*Mus.*) a rapid scale passage. **a (good) run for one's money 1** a strong challenge. **2** pleasure derived from an activity. **3** return for one's money or effort. **at a/ the run** running, in haste. **on the run 1** in flight, fugitive. **2** rushing about. **run off one's feet** extremely busy. **the runs** (*coll.*) diarrhoea. **to run about 1** to rush from place to place. **2** (of children) to play freely, without restraint. **to run across 1** to encounter by chance, to discover by accident. **2** to make a quick visit (to). **3** to cross at a run. **to run after 1** to try to form a sexual or romantic relationship with. **2** to cultivate, to devote oneself to. **3** to chase. **to run against** to compete against (someone) for election. **to run along** (*coll.*) to leave, to go away. **to run around 1** to transport from place to place by car. **2** to deceive repeatedly. **3** (*coll.*) to have casual sexual relations (with). **to run at** to rush at, to attack. **to run a temperature** to have an abnormally high body temperature. **to run away 1** to flee, to abscond. **2** to elope. **3** (of a horse) to bolt. **to run away with 1** to carry off. **2** to win (an easy victory). **3** to accept (an idea) rashly. **4** to cost (a lot of money). **5** (of a horse) to bolt with. **6** to elope with. **7** (of enthusiasm, emotions etc.) to deprive of self-control and common sense. **to run down 1** to stop through not being wound up, recharged etc. **2** to make enfeebled by overwork etc. **3** to pursue and overtake. **4** to search for and discover. **5** to disparage, to abuse. **6** to run against or over and sink or collide with. **7** to reduce in size or amount. **to run dry 1** to stop flowing. **2** (of a supply) to end. **to run for it** to make an escape attempt, to run away. **to run in 1** (*coll.*) to arrest, to take into custody. **2** to break in (a motor vehicle, machine etc.) by running or operating. **to run in the family/ blood** to be hereditary. **to run into 1** to incur, to fall into. **2** to collide with. **3** to reach (a specified number, amount etc.). **4** to meet by chance. **5** to be continuous with. **to run into the ground** (*coll.*) to exhaust or wear out with overwork. **to run its course** to develop naturally and come to a natural end. **to run low (on)** to have a depleted supply (of). **to run off 1** to print. **2** to decide (a race or contest) after a series of heats. **3** to cause to pour or flow out. **4** to write fluently. **5** to digress. **to run off with 1** to elope with. **2** to steal, remove. **to run on 1** to continue without a break. **2** to talk volubly or incessantly. **3** to elapse. **4** (of the mind) to be absorbed by. **to run out 1** to come to an end. **2** to leak. **3** in cricket, to dismiss a batsman by breaking the wicket when they are not in their ground. **4** (of a rope) to pass out. **5** to end a contest in a specified position. **to run out of** to have no more supplies of. **to run out on** (coll.) to abandon. **to run over 1** to review or examine cursorily. **2** to recapitulate. **3** to overflow. **4** to pass, ride or drive over. **5** to touch (piano keys) lightly in quick succession. **6** to go for a quick visit (to). **to run someone close/ hard** to be a serious challenge to. **to run someone ragged** to exhaust someone. **to run the show** (coll.) to manage, to have control of something in one's own hands. **to run through 1** to go through or examine rapidly. **2** to take, deal with, spend etc. one after another, to squander. **3** to pass through by running. **4** to pervade. **5** to transfix, to pierce with a weapon. **6** to strike out by drawing a line through. **to run to 1** to afford. **2** to extend to. **3** to have a tendency to. **4** to amount to. **5** to have the resources for. **6** to fall into (ruin). **to run to earth** to track down, to find after hard or prolonged searching. **to run to ground** to run to earth. **to run to meet** to anticipate (one's problems or troubles). **to run up 1** to grow rapidly. **2** (of prices) to increase quickly. **3** to accumulate (a debt etc.). **4** to force up (prices etc.). **5** to amount (to). **6** to make a quick visit (to). **7** to build, make or sew in a hasty manner. **8** to raise or hoist. **to run up against** to encounter (problems). **to run upon** to dwell on, to be absorbed by. **runabout** n. a light motor car or aeroplane. **run-around** n. evasive and deceitful treatment (He gave me the run-around). **runaway** n. **1** a person who flees from danger, restraint or service; a deserter, a fugitive. **2** an animal or vehicle which is out of control. ~a. **1** breaking from restraint. **2** out of control. **3** (of a success etc.) prodigious, decisive, easily won. **4** accomplished by flight. **5** fleeing as a runaway. **rundown** n. **1** a reduction in number, speed, power etc. **2** a brief or rapid résumé. **run-down** a. **1** dilapidated. **2** exhausted, worn out. **run-in** n. **1** (coll.) an argument, a row. **2** an approach. **runnable** a. **runner** n. **1** a person who runs, a racer. **2** a messenger, a scout, a spy. **3** a person who solicits custom etc., an agent, a collector, a tout. **4** (sl.) a smuggler. **5** a blockade-runner. **6** something on which anything runs, revolves, slides etc. **7** the blade of a skate. **8** a piece of wood or metal on which a sleigh runs. **9** a groove, rod, roller etc. on which a part slides or runs, esp. in machinery. **10** a sliding ring, loop etc. on a strap, rod etc. **11** (Naut.) a rope run through a single block with one end attached to a tackle block and the other having a hook. **12** a creeping stem thrown out by a plant, such as a

strawberry, tending to take root. **13** a twining or climbing plant, esp. a kidney bean. **14** a running bird, esp. the water rail. **15** in cricket, a player who runs for an injured batsman during their innings. **16** a long strip of carpet for a passage etc., or cloth for a table etc. **to do a runner** (sl.) to leave, esp. in order to avoid paying for something. **runner bean** n. a trailing bean plant, *Phaseolus coccineus*, having long, green seed pods. **runner-up** n. (pl. **runners-up, runner-ups**) the competitor in a race etc. who takes second place. **running** n. **1** the action of RUN. **2** the sport of running competitively. ~a. **1** moving at a run. **2** (of handwriting) cursive. **3** flowing. **4** continuous, uninterrupted. **5** discharging matter. **6** following in succession, repeated. **7** (of plants) trailing. **8** current, done at, or accomplished with, a run. **in the running** having a chance of winning. **to make the running** to set the pace. **running account** n. a current account. **running back** n. in American football, a back whose main task is to advance the ball from the scrimmage by running with it. **running battle** n. **1** a battle between pursuers and pursued. **2** a continuous or long-running argument. **running-board** n. the footboard of an (early) motor-car. **running commentary** n. (pl. **running commentaries**) an oral description, usu. by broadcasting, of an event in progress, e.g. a race. **running gear** n. **1** the wheels, axles or other working parts of a vehicle etc. **2** the rope and tackle used in handling a boat. **running head, running headline** n. the title of a book or similar heading used as a headline throughout a sequence of pages. **running knot** n. a knot which slips along the rope, line etc. **running light** n. a light visible on a moving vehicle, ship or aircraft at night. **runningly** adv. **running mate** n. **1** a subordinate candidate, one standing for the less important of two linked offices in a US election, esp. the vice-presidency. **2** (esp. US) a horse teamed or paired with another in a race. **running repairs** n.pl. repairs carried out while a machine etc. is in operation, minor repairs. **running sore** n. a suppurating sore. **running stitch** n. **1** a simple continuous stitch used for gathering or tacking. **2** a line of running stitches. **running title** n. a running head. **running water** n. water flowing from a tap. **runny** a. (comp. **runnier**, superl. **runniest**) **1** (of a nose or eyes) having liquid flowing from it or them. **2** excessively liquid. **run-off** n. **1** an additional tie-breaking contest, race etc. **2** overflow or liquid drained off. **3** (New Zeal.) an area of land where young animals are kept. **run-of-the-mill** a. undistinguished, ordinary, mediocre. **run-on** n. (Print.) continuous printed matter. **run-out** n. in cricket, the dismissal of a batsman by running them out. **run through** n. a quick examination, perusal or rehearsal. **run-up** n. **1** an approach. **2** a period preceding an event etc., e.g. a general election. **runway** n. **1** a landing strip for aircraft. **2** a trail to a watering place. **3** a ramp, passageway or chute. **4** a raised gangway in a theatre.

runcible (rŭn´sibəl), **runcible spoon** *n.* a three-pronged fork hollowed out like a spoon and with one of the prongs having a cutting edge.

rune (roon) *n.* **1** a letter or character of the earliest Germanic alphabet, formed from the Greek alphabet by modifying the shape to suit carving, used chiefly by the Scandinavians and Anglo-Saxons. **2** any mysterious mark or symbol. **runic** *a.*

rung[1] (rŭng) *n.* **1** a stick or bar forming a step in a ladder. **2** a rail or spoke in a chair etc. **runged** *a.* **rungless** *a.*

rung[2] RING[2].

runlet (rŭn´lit) *n.* a small stream, a runnel.

runnel (rŭn´əl) *n.* **1** a rivulet, a little brook. **2** a gutter.

runner, running etc. RUN.

runt (rŭnt) *n.* **1** the smallest or feeblest animal in a litter esp. a piglet. **2** any animal or person who is stunted in growth, deficient or inferior. **runty** *a.*

rupee (rupē´) *n.* the standard monetary unit of various Asian countries including India, Pakistan, Sri Lanka, Nepal, Bhutan, the Maldives, Mauritius and the Seychelles.

rupiah (roopē´ə) *n.* the standard monetary unit of Indonesia.

rupture (rŭp´chə) *n.* **1** the act of breaking or the state of being broken or violently parted, a break, a breach. **2** a breach or interruption of friendly relations. **3** (*Med.*) hernia. ~*v.t.* **1** to burst, to break, to separate by violence. **2** to sever (a friendship etc.). **3** to affect with a hernia. ~*v.i.* to suffer a breach or rupture. **rupturable** *a.*

rural (roo´rəl) *a.* **1** of or relating to the country, as distinct from *urban*. **2** pastoral, agricultural. **3** suiting or resembling the country, rustic. **rural dean** *n.* a member of the clergy, ranking below an archdeacon, charged with the inspection of a district. **ruralism** *n.* **ruralist** *n.* **rurality** (-ral´-), **ruralness** *n.* **ruralize, ruralise** *v.i., v.t.* **ruralization** (-zā´shən) *n.* **rurally** *adv.*

ruse (rooz) *n.* a stratagem, trick or wile.

rush[1] (rŭsh) *v.t.* **1** to drive, urge, force, move or push with violence and haste, to hurry. **2** to perform or complete quickly. **3** to force (someone) to act quickly. **4** to take by sudden assault. **5** to surmount, to pass, to seize and occupy, with dash or suddenness. **6** (*coll.*) to cheat, to swindle by overcharging. **7** in American football, to hinder by charging. ~*v.i.* **1** to move or run impetuously or precipitately. **2** to enter or go (into) with undue eagerness or lack of consideration. **3** to run, flow or roll with violence and impetuosity. ~*n.* **1** the act of rushing. **2** a violent or impetuous movement, advance, dash or onslaught. **3** a sudden onset of activity, movement or thronging of people (to a gold field etc.). **4** (*pl., coll.*) the first print from a film. **5** a violent demand (for) or run (on) a commodity etc. **6** (*sl.*)

a surge of euphoria induced by or as if by a drug. **7** in American football, a charge at the quarterback. ~*a.* characterized by or requiring much activity, speed or urgency. **to rush one's fences** to act too hastily or precipitously. **rusher** *n.* **rush hour** *n.* a period when traffic is very congested owing to people going to or leaving work. **rushingly** *adv.*

rush[2] (rŭsh) *n.* **1** a plant with long thin stems or leaves, of the family Juncaceae, growing mostly on wet ground, used for making baskets, mats, seats for chairs etc., and formerly for strewing floors. **2** a stem of this plant. **3** any of various other similar plants, e.g. the bulrush. **4** rushes collectively. **rushlike** *a.* **rushy** *a.*

rusk (rŭsk) *n.* a piece of bread or cake crisped and browned in the oven, given to babies.

russet (rŭs´it) *a.* of a reddish-brown colour. ~*n.* **1** a reddish-brown colour. **2** a rough-skinned reddish-brown variety of apple. **russety** *a.*

Russian (rŭsh´ən) *a.* of or relating to Russia. ~*n.* **1** a native or inhabitant of Russia, or a descendant of one. **2** the Russian language. **Russian boot** *n.* a wide-topped, calf-length boot. **Russianness** *n.* **Russian olive** *n.* an oleaster. **Russian roulette** *n.* **1** a test of courage or act of bravado involving firing a revolver loaded with a single bullet at one's own head after spinning the chamber. **2** any very dangerous undertaking. **Russian salad** *n.* a salad of pickles and diced vegetables in a mayonnaise dressing. **Russian tea** *n.* tea drunk with lemon instead of milk. **Russify** (rŭs´ifī) *v.t.* (*3rd pers. sing. pres.* **Russifies,** *pres.p.* **Russifying,** *past, p.p.* **Russified**) to make Russian in character. **Russification** (-fikā´shən) *n.* **Russki** (rŭs´ki), **Russky** *n.* (*pl.* **Russkis, Russkies**) (*sl., offensive*) **1** a Russian. **2** (*Hist., loosely*) a Soviet citizen.

Russophile (rŭs´ōfīl) *n.* a friend or admirer of Russia or the Russians.

Russophobe (rŭs´ōfōb) *n.* a person who fears or is an opponent of Russia or the Russians.

rust (rŭst) *n.* **1** the red incrustation on iron or steel caused by its oxidation when exposed to air and moisture. **2** a similar incrustation on other metals. **3** a plant disease caused by parasitic fungi of the order Urediniomycetes; blight. **4** any of these fungi. **5** the colour of rust, an orangey-red shade of brown. ~*a.* rust-coloured. ~*v.i.* **1** to contract rust, to be oxidated. **2** to become rust-coloured. **3** to be attacked by blight. **4** to degenerate through idleness or disuse. ~*v.t.* **1** to affect with rust, to corrode. **2** to impair by idleness, disuse etc. **rust belt** *n.* (*coll.*) a region of formerly profitable manufacturing industry, now in decline. **rust-coloured,** (*N Am.*) **rust-colored** *a.* **rustless** *a.* **rustproof** *a.* impervious to corrosion. ~*v.t.* to make rustproof. **rusty** *a.* (*comp.* **rustier,** *superl.* **rustiest**) **1** covered or affected with or as if with rust. **2** faded, discoloured by age. **3** impaired by disuse, inaction, neglect etc. **4** rust-coloured. **5** antiquated in appearance. **6** (of a voice) harsh, husky. **rustily** *adv.* **rustiness** *n.*

rustic (rŭs'tik) *a.* **1** like or characteristic of country life or people, unsophisticated, simple, artless. **2** awkward, uncouth. **3** of rough workmanship, coarse, plain. **4** made of rough timber. **5** loosely formed. **6** (*Archit.*) having a rough surface. ~*n.* a country person or dweller. **rustically** *adv.* **rusticate** *v.t.* **1** to suspend for a time from residence at a university; to exile to the country, as a punishment. **2** to make rustic in style, finish etc. **3** to give a rough surface and chamfered joints to (masonry). ~*v.i.* **1** to retire or to live in the country. **2** to become rustic. **rustication** (-ā'shən) *n.* **rusticity** (-tis'-) *n.*

rustle (rŭs'əl) *v.i.* **1** to make a quick succession of small sounds like the rubbing of silk or dry leaves. **2** to move or go along with a rustling sound. **3** to steal cattle, horses or sheep. **4** (*N Am., coll.*) to bustle, to move quickly and energetically. ~*v.t.* **1** to cause to make a rustling sound. **2** to steal (cattle, horses or sheep). ~*n.* a rustling. **to rustle up 1** (*coll.*) to prepare or make quickly, or without preparation or prior notice. **2** to gather up, to put together. **rustler** *n.*

rut¹ (rŭt) *n.* **1** a sunken track made by wheels or vehicles, a hollow, a groove. **2** a settled habit or course. ~*v.t.* (*pres.p.* **rutting**, *past, p.p.* **rutted**) to make ruts in. **in a rut** stuck in tedious routine. **rutty** *a.*

rut² (rŭt) *n.* the sexual excitement or heat of deer and some other animals. ~*v.i.* (*pres.p.* **rutting**, *past, p.p.* **rutted**) to be in a period of rut. **ruttish** *a.*

rutabaga (rootəbā'gə) *n.* (*N Am.*) a swede.

ruthenium (ruthē'niəm) *n.* (*Chem.*) a white, spongy metallic element of the platinum group, at. no. 44, chem. symbol Ru.

rutherfordium (rŭdhəfaw'diəm) *n.* (*Chem.*) a proposed name for the artificial radioactive elements of at. nos. 104 and 106.

ruthless (rooth'lis) *a.* pitiless, merciless, cruel. **ruthlessly** *adv.* **ruthlessness** *n.*

rutile (roo'til, -tīl) *n.* red titanium dioxide.

RV *abbr.* **1** (*N Am.*) recreational vehicle. **2** Revised Version (of the Bible).

Rwanda (ruan'də) *n.* the official language of Rwanda, central Africa. **Rwandan** *a.* of or relating to Rwanda. ~*n.* a native or inhabitant of Rwanda, or a descendant of one.

-ry (ri), **-ery** (əri) *suf.* a business, a place of business, cultivation etc., conduct, things connected with or of the nature etc., as *foundry, poultry, yeomanry.*

rye (rī) *n.* **1** the seeds or grain of *Secale cereale*, a cereal allied to wheat, used to make (black) bread, whisky etc. **2** the plant bearing this. **3** rye whisky. **4** (*N Am.*) rye bread. ~*a.* of rye. **ryegrass** *n.* any one of various grasses of the genus *Lolium*, cultivated for fodder grass. **rye whisky** *n.* whisky distilled from rye.

❌ **rythm** common misspelling of RHYTHM.

S

S¹ (es), **s** (*pl.* **Ss, S's**) the 19th letter of the English and other versions of the Roman alphabet, corresponding to the Greek sigma (σ, Σ). It has four sounds: (1) a voiceless labiodental fricative or sibilant, with a hard sound as in *sin, so*; (2) its voiced equivalent, the sound of z, as in *music, muse* etc.; (3) a voiceless palatal affricate, with the sound of *sh* in *sugar, mission*; (4) its voiced equivalent, marked in this dictionary zh, as in *measure, vision*. ~*n.* an S-shaped object or curve. **S-bend** *n.* an S-shaped bend.

S² *chem. symbol* sulphur.

S³, S. *abbr.* **1** Saint. **2** South, Southern. **3** Special (in *S level*). **S level** *n.* in England, Wales and N Ireland, an examination taken in conjunction with an A level in the same subject, but with a more advanced syllabus.

s *abbr.* **1** second(s). **2** shilling(s). **3** singular. **4** son. **5** succeeded.

-s¹ (s, z) *suf.* forming plurals of most nouns.

-s² (s, z) *suf.* **1** forming adverbs. **2** forming possessive pronouns.

-s³ (s, z) *suf.* forming nicknames or pet names.

-s⁴ (s, z) *suf.* forming the 3rd pers. sing. pres. tense of most verbs.

-s' (s, z) *suf.* forming the genitive (possessive) case of plural nouns and sometimes sing. nouns ending in *s*.

-'s¹ (s, z, iz) *suf.* forming the genitive (possessive) case of sing. nouns and pl. nouns not ending in *s*.

-'s² (s, z, iz) *suf.* var. of -s¹, forming plurals of letters or symbols.

-'s³ (s, z) *suf.* **1** short for IS, HAS. **2** short for US. **3** short for *does*, 3rd pers. sing. pres. of DO¹.

SA *abbr.* **1** sex appeal. **2** South Africa. **3** South America. **4** South Australia.

sab (sab) *n.* (*sl.*) a hunt saboteur. ~*v.t.* (*pres.p.* **sabbing**, *past, p.p.* **sabbed**) to disrupt (a hunt).

sabadilla (sabədil´ə) *n.* **1** a Mexican and Central American liliaceous plant, *Schoenocaulon officinale*, yielding acrid seeds from which veratrine is obtained. **2** a preparation of the barley-like seeds of this.

Sabbatarian (sabətəə´riən) *n.* **1** a Jew who strictly observes Saturday as a day of rest and divine worship. **2** a Christian who observes Sunday as a sabbath, or who is specially strict in its observance. **3** a Christian who observes Saturday as the sabbath. ~*a.* observing or inculcating the observance of the sabbath or Sunday. **Sabbatarianism** *n.*

sabbath (sab´əth) *n.* **1** (*also* **sabbath day**) the seventh day of the week, Saturday, set apart, esp. by the Jews, for rest and divine worship. **2** the Christian Sunday observed as a day of rest and worship. **3** a time of rest. **4** a witches' sabbath. **sabbatic** (-hat´-) *a.* **sabbatical** *a.* **1** of, relating to or befitting the sabbath. **2** of or relating to an extended period of leave from one's work. ~*n.* an extended period of leave from one's work. **sabbatically** *adv.*

saber SABRE.

sabicu (sabikoo´) *n.* **1** a W Indian tree, *Lysiloma latisiliqua*. **2** its mahogany-like wood.

Sabin vaccine (sā´bin) *n.* a vaccine taken orally to immunize against poliomyelitis.

sable (sā´bəl) *n.* **1** a small arctic and subarctic carnivorous quadruped, *Martes zibellina*, allied to the marten, the brown fur of which is very highly valued. **2** its skin or fur. **3** a painter's brush made of its hair. **4** (*Her.*) black. **5** (*poet.*) black, esp. as the colour of mourning. **6** (*pl.*) mourning garments. ~*a.* **1** (*Her., poet.*) black. **2** (*poet.*) dark, gloomy. **sable antelope** *n.* a large black E African antelope, *Hippotragus niger*, with long, backward-curving horns. **sabled** *a.* **sably** *a.*

sabot (sab´ō) *n.* **1** a simple wooden shoe, usu. made in one piece. **2** a wooden-soled shoe. **3** (*Austral.*) a small sailing boat. **saboted** *a.*

sabotage (sab´ətahzh) *n.* **1** malicious damage to a railway, industrial plant, machinery etc., as a protest by discontented workers, or as a non-military act of warfare. **2** any action designed to hinder or undermine. ~*v.t.* **1** to commit sabotage on. **2** to hinder or undermine. **saboteur** (-tœ´) *n.* a person who commits sabotage.

sabra (sab´rə) *n.* an Israeli born in Israel.

sabre (sā´bə), (*N Am.*) **saber** *n.* **1** a cavalry sword having a curved blade. **2** (*pl.*) cavalry. **3** a light fencing-sword with a tapering blade. ~*v.t.* to cut or strike down or kill with the sabre. **sabre-cut** *n.* **1** a blow with a sabre. **2** a wound or scar from such a blow. **sabre-rattling** *n.* a display of military power or aggression. **sabre saw** *n.* a portable electric jigsaw. **sabre-toothed tiger, sabre-toothed cat** *n.* a large extinct feline mammal with long upper canines, esp. of the genus *Smilodon*. **sabreur** (sabrœ´) *n.* a person who fights with the sabre. **sabrewing** *n.* a S American hummingbird of the genus *Campylopterus*.

SAC *abbr.* Senior Aircraftman.

sac (sak) *n.* **1** a pouch, a cavity or receptacle in an animal or vegetable. **2** a pouch forming the envelope of a tumour, cyst etc. **saccate** (-āt) *a.*

(*Bot.*) **1** having the form of a pouch. **2** contained in a sac. **sacciform** (sak´sifawm) *a.* sac-shaped.

saccate SAC.

sacchar- (sak´ə), **saccharo-** (-rō) *comb. form* sugar. **saccharide** (-īd) *n.* (*Chem.*) a carbohydrate, esp. a sugar. **saccharimeter** (-im´itə) *n.* an instrument for determining the quantity of sugar in solutions, esp. by means of a polarized light. **saccharin** (-ərin) *n.* an intensely sweet compound obtained from toluene, a product of coal-tar, used as a sugar substitute in food. **saccharine** (-īn, -ēn, -in) *a.* **1** of or relating to sugar. **2** having the qualities of sugar. **3** sickly sweet, sugary. **4** ingratiatingly pleasant or polite. **saccharometer** (-om´itə) *n.* a saccharimeter, esp. a hydrometer for measuring sugar concentration. **saccharose** (-ōs) *n.* (*Chem.*) sucrose. **saccharous** *a.*

sacciform SAC.

sacerdotal (sasədō´təl, sak-) *a.* **1** of or relating to priests or the priesthood. **2** (of a doctrine etc.) attributing sacrificial power and supernatural or sacred character to priests. **3** claiming or suggesting excessive emphasis on the authority of the priesthood. **sacerdotalism** *n.* **sacerdotalist** *n.* **sacerdotally** *adv.*

sachem (sā´chəm) *n.* **1** a chief of certain tribes of N American Indians. **2** (*N Am., coll.*) a magnate, a prominent person.

sachet (sash´ā) *n.* **1** a small ornamental bag or other receptacle containing perfumed powder for scenting clothes etc. **2** a small packet of shampoo etc.

sack¹ (sak) *n.* **1** a large, usu. oblong bag of strong coarse material, for holding coal, vegetables etc. **2** the quantity a sack contains, as a unit of capacity and weight. **3** a sack together with its contents. **4** a loose coat. **5** a loose-fitting waistless dress. **6** (*coll.*) dismissal from employment. **7** (*esp. N Am., sl.*) bed. *~v.t.* **1** to put into a sack. **2** (*coll.*) to give the sack to. **to get the sack** to be dismissed from employment. **to give the sack** to dismiss from employment. **to hit the sack** (*coll.*) to go to bed. **sackable** *a.* **sackcloth** *n.* **1** sacking. **2** this worn formerly in token of mourning or penitence. **sackful** *n.* (*pl.* **sackfuls**). **sacking** *n.* coarse stuff of which sacks, bags etc. are made. **sacklike** *a.* **sack race** *n.* a race in which the competitors are tied up to the waist or neck in sacks.

sack² (sak) *v.t.* **1** to plunder or pillage (a place taken by storm). **2** to ransack, to loot. *~n.* the pillaging of a captured place. **sacker** *n.*

sack³ (sak) *n.* (*Hist.*) a white wine, esp. one from Spain and the Canaries.

sackbut (sak´bŭt) *n.* a medieval bass trumpet with a slide like the modern trombone.

sacra, sacral SACRUM.

sacrament (sak´rəmənt) *n.* **1** a religious rite instituted as an outward and visible sign of an inward and spiritual grace. **2** the Lord's Supper, the Eucharist. **3** the consecrated elements of the Eucharist. **4** a sacred token, symbol, influence etc. **5** a solemn oath or engagement. **sacramental**

(-men´-) *a.* **1** of, relating to or constituting a sacrament. **2** bound by oath, consecrated. *~n.* a rite or observance ancillary or analogous to the sacraments. **sacramentalism** *n.* the doctrine of the spiritual efficacy of the sacraments. **sacramentalist** *n.* **sacramentality** (-tal´-) *n.* **sacramentally** *adv.*

sacred (sā´krid) *a.* **1** dedicated to religious use. **2** set apart, reserved or specially appropriated (to). **3** of, relating to or hallowed by religion or religious service, consecrated. **4** sanctified by religion, reverence etc., not to be profaned. **sacred cow** *n.* (*coll.*) an institution, custom etc. regarded with reverence and as beyond criticism. **Sacred Heart** *n.* **1** the physical heart of Christ. **2** a representation of this. **sacred ibis** *n.* (*pl.* **sacred ibises**) an ibis, *Threskiornis aethiopicus*, venerated by the ancient Egyptians. **sacredly** *adv.* **sacredness** *n.* **sacred number** *n.* a number associated with religious symbolism, such as the number seven.

sacrifice (sak´rifis) *n.* **1** the giving up of anything for the sake of another person, object or interest. **2** that which is offered or given up, a victim, an offering. **3** the act of offering an animal, person etc., esp. by ritual slaughter, or the surrender of a valued possession to a deity, as an act of propitiation, atonement or thanksgiving. **4** (*Theol.*) **a** the Crucifixion as Christ's offering of himself. **b** the Eucharist as a renewal of this or as a thanksgiving. **5** the sale of goods at a loss. **6** a great loss or destruction (of life etc.). *~v.t.* **1** to surrender for the sake of another person, object etc. **2** to offer to a deity as a sacrifice. **3** (*coll.*) to sell at a much reduced price. **sacrifice hit** *n.* in baseball, a hit to enable another player to score or reach a base. **sacrificer** *n.* **sacrificial** (-fish´əl) *a.* **sacrificially** *adv.*

sacrilege (sak´rilij) *n.* **1** the violation or profanation of sacred things. **2** irreverence towards something or someone (considered) sacred. **sacrilegious** (-lij´əs) *a.* **sacrilegiously** *adv.* **sacrilegiousness** *n.*

sacrist (sā´krist) *n.* an officer in charge of the sacristy of a church or religious house with its contents. **sacristan** (sak´ristən) *n.* a sacrist. **sacristy** (sak´risti) *n.* (*pl.* **sacristies**) an apartment in a church in which the vestments, sacred vessels, books etc. are kept.

sacro- (sak´rō, sā´-) *comb. form* sacrum, sacral. **sacroiliac** (-il´iak) *a.* (*Anat.*) of or relating to the sacrum and the ilium.

sacrosanct (sak´rəsangkt) *a.* **1** inviolable by reason of sanctity. **2** regarded with extreme respect, revered. **sacrosanctity** (-sangk´titi) *n.*

sacrum (sāk´rəm, sak´-) *n.* (*pl.* **sacra** (-rə), **sacrums**) (*Anat.*) a composite bone formed by the union of vertebrae at the base of the spinal column, constituting the dorsal part of the pelvis. **sacral** *a.*

SACW *abbr.* Senior Aircraftwoman.

SAD *abbr.* seasonal affective disorder.

sad (sad) *a.* (*comp.* **sadder**, *superl.* **saddest**) **1** sorrowful, mournful. **2** expressing sorrow. **3** causing sorrow, unfortunate. **4** bad, shocking. **5** (of bread, cake etc.) heavy, not well raised. **6** dull, dark-coloured. **7** (*sl.*) pathetic, contemptible. **sadden** *v.t.* to make sad. ~*v.i.* to become sad. **saddish** *a.* **sad-iron** *n.* a solid smoothing iron. **sadly** *adv.* **sadness** *n.* **sad sack** *n.* (*N Am.*, *coll.*) an inept person.

saddle (sad´əl) *n.* **1** a seat placed on an animal's back, to support a rider. **2** a similar part of the harness of a draught animal. **3** a seat on a bicycle, agricultural machine etc. **4** an object resembling a saddle. **5** a saddle-shaped marking on an animal's back. **6** the rear part of a male fowl's back. **7** a joint of mutton, venison etc., including the loins. **8** a supporting piece in various machines, suspension bridges, gun-mountings, tackle etc. **9** a depressed part of a ridge between two summits, a col. **10** a raised and symmetrical anticlinal fold. **11** a bar for supporting ceramic ware in a kiln. ~*v.t.* **1** to put a saddle on. **2** to load or burden with a duty etc. **3** (of a trainer) to enter (a horse) for a race. **in the saddle 1** mounted. **2** in control. **saddleback** *n.* **1** (*Archit.*) a roof or coping sloping up at both ends or with a gable at each end. **2** a saddlebacked hill. **3** an animal with a marking suggestive of a saddle. **4** a black pig with a white band across the back. **5** any of various birds with a saddle-like marking, esp. a New Zealand bird *Creadion carunculatus.* ~*a.* saddlebacked. **saddlebacked** *a.* **1** (of a horse) having a low back with an elevated neck and head. **2** curving up at each end. **saddlebag** *n.* **1** each of a pair of bags connected by straps slung across a horse etc. from the saddle. **2** a bag attached to the back of the saddle of a bicycle etc. **saddle bow** *n.* the pommel. **saddle-cloth** *n.* a cloth laid on a horse under the saddle. **saddle-horse** *n.* a horse for riding. **saddleless** *a.* **saddler** *n.* a maker or dealer in saddles and harness. **saddlery** *n.* (*pl.* **saddleries**) **1** the trade or shop of a saddler. **2** saddles and harnesses collectively. **saddle-sore** *a.* chafed with riding. **saddle stitch** *n.* a stitch or staple passed through the centre of a booklet etc. **saddle-stitch** *v.t.* **saddle tree** *n.* **1** the frame of a saddle. **2** the tulip tree.

Sadducee (sad´ūsē) *n.* a member of a sect among the Jews, arising in the 2nd cent. BC, who adhered to the written law to the exclusion of tradition, and denied the resurrection from the dead, existence of spirits etc. **Sadducean** (-sē´ən) *a.*

sadhu (sah´doo), **saddhu** *n.* a Hindu usu. mendicant holy man.

sadism (sā´dizm) *n.* **1** sexual perversion characterized by a passion for cruelty. **2** (*coll.*) pleasure derived from inflicting pain. **sadist** *n.* **sadistic** (sədis´-) *a.* **sadistically** *adv.* **sadomasochism** (-dōmas´əkizm) *n.* sadism and masochism combined in one person. **sadomasochist** *n.* **sadomasochistic** (-kis´-) *a.*

sae *abbr.* **1** self-addressed envelope. **2** stamped addressed envelope.

safari (səfah´ri) *n.* (*pl.* **safaris**) **1** a hunting or scientific expedition, esp. in E Africa. **2** a sightseeing trip to see African animals in their natural habitat. **safari jacket** *n.* a light, usu. cotton jacket with breast pockets and a belt. **safari park** *n.* a park containing uncaged wild animals, such as lions and monkeys. **safari suit** *n.* a suit having a safari jacket.

safe (sāf) *a.* **1** free or secure from danger or damage. **2** uninjured, unharmed. **3** affording security. **4** not dangerous or risky. **5** cautious, prudent. **6** certain, sure. **7** no longer dangerous, secure from escape or from doing harm. ~*n.* **1** a receptacle for keeping things safe, a steel fireproof and burglarproof receptacle for valuables, a strong-box. **2** a cupboard or other receptacle for keeping meat and other provisions. **on the safe side** as a precaution. **safe and sound** secure and unharmed. **safe bet** *n.* a bet that is certain to succeed. **safe-blower, safe-breaker,** (*N Am.*) **safe-cracker** *n.* a person who opens safes to steal. **safe conduct** *n.* **1** an official document or passport ensuring a safe passage, esp. in a foreign country or in time of hostilities. **2** the protection given by such a document. **safe deposit** *n.* a specially-constructed building or basement with safes for renting. **safeguard** *n.* **1** a person who or thing which protects. **2** a precaution, circumstance etc. that tends to save loss, trouble etc. **3** a safe conduct, a passport. ~*v.t.* to make safe or secure by precaution, stipulation etc. **safe house** *n.* a place that can be used as a refuge. **safe keeping** *n.* secure guardianship. **safe light** *n.* a filtered light used in a darkroom. **safely** *adv.* **safeness** *n.* **safe sex** *n.* sexual activity avoiding penetration or using physical protection such as condoms, to prevent the transmission of disease, esp. Aids.

safety (sāf´ti) *n.* (*pl.* **safeties**) **1** freedom from injury, danger or risk. **2** safe keeping or custody. **3** a safety catch. **4** (*coll.*) a safety bicycle. **5** in American football, the defensive back furthest back in the field. **safety first** used to advise caution. **safety belt** *n.* **1** a seat belt. **2** a belt fastening a person to a fixed object to prevent falling. **safety catch, safety lock** *n.* a device in a firearm to prevent accidental discharge. **safety curtain** *n.* a fireproof curtain in a theatre that cuts off the stage from the audience. **safety film** *n.* a photographic film with a non-flammable or slow-burning base. **safety glass** *n.* glass treated to prevent splintering when broken. **safety harness** *n.* a system of belts used to prevent a person falling or being injured. **safety lamp** *n.* a miner's lamp protected by wire or gauze so as not to ignite combustible gas. **safety match** *n.* a match that ignites only on a surface treated with a special ingredient. **safety net** *n.* **1** a net to catch tightrope and trapeze performers if they should fall. **2** a safeguard, precaution. **safety pin** *n.* a pin with a part for keeping it secure and guarding the point. **safety razor** n. a razor mounted on a handle with a guard to prevent cutting the skin. **safety valve** n. **1** a valve on a boiler automatically opening to let steam escape to relieve pressure and prevent explosion. **2** any harmless means of relieving anger, excitement etc.

safflower (saf'lowə) n. **1** a thistle-like plant, *Carthamus tinctorius*, with orange flowers yielding a red dye, and seeds rich in oil. **2** the petals of this, or the dye made from them.

saffron (saf'rən) n. **1** the dried deep orange stigmas of a crocus, *Crocus sativus*, used for colouring and flavouring food. **2** this plant. **3** the colour deep orange. **4** the meadow saffron, *Colchicum autumnale*. ~a. saffron-coloured, deep yellow. **saffrony** a. **safranin** (-nin, -nēn), **safranine** n. any of a series of basic compounds used in dyeing.

sag (sag) v.i. (*pres.p.* **sagging**, *past*, *p.p.* **sagged**) **1** to droop or give way esp. in the middle, under weight or pressure. **2** to bend, to hang sideways. **3** to lose vigour. **4** (of prices, esp. of stocks) to decline. **5** (*Naut.*) to drift to leeward. ~v.t. to cause to give way, bend, or curve sideways. ~n. **1** the act or state of sagging or giving way. **2** the amount of this. **3** (*Naut.*) a sideways drift or tendency to leeward. **sag bag** n. a large bean bag used for sitting on. **saggy** a. (*comp.* **saggier**, *superl.* **saggiest**).

saga (sah'gə) n. **1** a medieval prose narrative recounting family or public events in Iceland or Scandinavia, usu. by contemporary or nearly contemporary native writers. **2** a story of heroic adventure. **3** a series of books relating the history of a family. **4** a long involved story or account.

sagacious (səgā'shəs) a. **1** intellectually keen or quick to understand or discern. **2** (of policy etc.) characterized by wisdom and discernment. **sagaciously** adv. **sagaciousness** n. **sagacity** (-gas'-) n.

sage[1] (sāj) n. a grey-leaved aromatic plant of the genus *Salvia*, esp. *S. officinalis*, formerly much used in medicine, now employed in cookery. **sage and onion** n. a kind of stuffing used with meat or poultry. **sagebrush** n. **1** a shrubby plant of the various species of *Artemisia*, esp. *A. tridentata*, abounding in the plains of the W US. **2** an area covered in this. **sage Derby (cheese)** n. a cheese flavoured with sage. **sage green** n. a greyish green. **sage-green** a. **sage grouse** n. the largest of the American grouse, *Centrocercus urophasianus*, frequenting the sagebrush regions. **sage tea** n. a medicinal infusion of sage leaves. **sagy** a.

sage[2] (sāj) a. **1** wise, prudent. **2** judicious, well-considered. **3** (*often iron.*) grave, serious- or solemn-looking. ~n. (*sometimes iron.*) a person of great wisdom, esp. one of past times with a traditional reputation for wisdom. **sagely** adv. **sageness** n. **sageship** n.

sagittal (sojit'əl) a. **1** (*Anat.*) of or relating to the join between the two parietal bones forming the sides and top of the skull. **2** in or parallel to the mid-plane of the body. **Sagittarius** (sajitee'riəs) n. (*Astrol.*) **1** (*Astron.*) the Archer, a zodiacal constellation and the ninth sign of the zodiac, which the sun enters on 22 Nov. **2** a person born under this sign. **Sagittarian** n., a. **sagittate** (saj'itāt) a. (*esp. Bot.*) (esp. of a leaf) shaped like an arrowhead.

sago (sā'gō) n. (*pl.* **sagos**) **1** a starchy substance obtained from the soft inner portion of the trunk of several palms or cycads and used as food. **2** a sago palm. **sago palm** n. any of several tropical palms and cycads, esp. *Cycas circinalis* and *Metroxylon sagu*.

saguaro (səgwah'rō), **sahuaro** (səwah'rō) n. (*pl.* **saguaros**, **sahuaros**) a large Central American cactus, *Carnegiea gigantea*, with edible fruit.

sahib (sah'ib) n. (in India) a polite form of address for a man; a gentleman.

said SAY.

sail (sāl) n. **1** (*Naut.*) **a** a piece of canvas or other fabric spread on rigging to catch the wind, and cause a ship or boat to move in the water. **b** some or all of a ship's sails. **c** a ship or vessel with sails. **d** a specified number of ships in a squadron etc. **2** an excursion by sail or (*loosely*) by water. **3** anything like a sail in form or function. **4** the arm of a windmill. **5 a** the dorsal fin of some fish. **b** the tentacle of a nautilus. **c** the float of a Portuguese man-of-war. ~v.i. **1** to move or be driven forward by the action of the wind upon sails. **2** to be conveyed in a vessel by water. **3** to set sail. **4** to handle or make journeys in a vessel equipped with sails as a sport or hobby. **5** to pass gently (along), to float (as a bird). **6** to go along in a stately manner. **7** (*usu. with through, coll.*) to succeed easily. ~v.t. **1** to pass over in a ship, to navigate. **2** to perform by sailing. **3** to manage the navigation of (a ship). **4** to cause to sail, to set afloat. **to sail into** (*coll.*) to attack vigorously. **to set sail** to begin a voyage. **to take in sail 1** to furl the sails of a vessel. **2** to moderate one's ambitions. **under sail** with sails spread. **sailable** a. **sail-arm** n. an arm of a windmill. **sailboard** n. a moulded board with a single mast and sail, used in windsurfing. **sailboarder** n. **sailboarding** n. **sailcloth** n. **1** canvas etc. for making sails. **2** a kind of dress material. **sailed** a. (*also in comb.*) **sailer** n. a ship (with reference to her power or manner of sailing). **sailfish** n. (*pl. in general* **sailfish**, *in particular* **sailfishes**) **1** any large fish of the genus *Istiophorus*, with a tall dorsal fin. **2** a basking shark. **sail-fluke** n. a deep-water flatfish, the megrim. **sailing** n. **sailing boat**, (*N Am.*) **sailboat** n. a boat with sails. **sailing master** n. an officer whose duty it is to navigate a yacht etc. **sailing orders** n.pl. instructions to the captain of a ship. **sailing ship** n. a ship with sails. **sailless** a. **sailmaker** n. a person who makes, repairs or alters sails. **sailmaking** n. **sailplane** n. a glider that rises in an upward air current.

sailor (sā'lə) n. a member of the crew of a boat or ship, as distinguished from an officer. **sailor**

hat *n.* a flat-crowned narrow-brimmed straw hat worn by women, or one with a turned-up brim for children. **sailoring** *n.* **sailorless** *a.* **sailorlike, sailorly** *a.* **sailor suit** *n.* a child's navy and white suit like a sailor's.

sainfoin (sān´foin, san´-) *n.* a leguminous herb, *Onobrychis viciifolia,* resembling clover, grown for fodder.

saint (sānt, sənt) *n.* **1** a person eminent for piety and virtue, a holy person. **2** any of the blessed in heaven. **3** a person canonized or recognized by the Church as pre-eminently holy and deserving of veneration. **4** a member of the Mormons and some other sects (used in speaking of themselves). ~*v.t.* **1** to canonize. **2** to regard or address as a saint. **saintdom, sainthood** *n.* **sainted** *a.* **1** canonized. **2** gone to heaven. **3** holy, pious. **saintlike** *a.* **saintling** *n.* **saintly** *a.* (*comp.* **saintlier,** *superl.* **saintliest**). **saintliness** *n.* **saintpaulia** (səntpaw´liə) *n.* AFRICAN VIOLET (under AFRICAN). **saint's day** *n.* a day dedicated to the commemoration of a particular saint, esp. the patron saint of a church, school etc. **saintship** *n.* **St Andrew's cross** *n.* an X-shaped cross. **St Anthony cross, St Anthony's cross** *n.* a T-shaped cross. **St Anthony's fire** *n.* erysipelas (from the tradition that those stricken by the pestilence of erysipelas, or sacred fire, in 1809, were cured through the intercession of St Anthony). **St Bernard (dog)** *n.* a large and powerful breed of dog orig. kept by the monks of the Hospice in the Great St Bernard Pass to rescue travellers. **St Elmo's fire** (el´mōz) *n.* the corposant (from its being regarded as a sign of protection from St Elmo, patron saint of sailors). **St George's cross** *n.* a Greek cross used on the British flag. **St John's wort** *n.* any plant of the genus *Hypericum,* esp. *H. androsaemum.* **St Luke's summer** *n.* a spell of mild weather in the autumn (usually around 18 Oct., the feast day of Saint Luke). **St Martin's summer** *n.* a spell of mild weather in late autumn (usually around 11 Nov., the feast day of Saint Martin of Tours).

saithe (sāth) *n.* the coalfish, *Pollachius virens.*

sake¹ (sāk) *n.* **1** purpose. **2** desire of obtaining. **3** reason, cause. **for Christ's sake** used as a solemn adjuration or an expression of exasperation etc. **for God's sake** used as a solemn adjuration or an expression of exasperation etc. **for goodness' sake** a solemn adjuration. **for heaven's sake** a solemn adjuration. **for mercy's sake** a solemn adjuration or appeal. **for old times' sake** in memory of days gone by. **for Pete's sake** used as expression of annoyance. **for pity's sake** a solemn adjuration. **for someone's sake** because of someone, out of consideration for someone. **for the sake of** because of, out of consideration for.

sake² (sak´ā, sah´ki) **saké, saki** *n.* a fermented liquor made from rice.

sal¹ (sal) *n.* (*Chem.*) salt (used only with qualifying word). **sal ammoniac** (əmō´niak) *n.* ammonium chloride. **sal volatile** (vəlat´ili) *n.* an aromatic solution of ammonium carbonate.

sal² (sahl) *n.* a large Indian timber tree, *Shorea robusta.*

salaam (səlahm´) *n.* a ceremonious salutation or obeisance in Eastern countries. ~*v.i.* to make a salaam. ~*v.t.* to make a salaam to (a person).

salable SALE.

salacious (səlā´shəs) *a.* **1** lustful, lecherous. **2** arousing lust, erotic. **salaciously** *adv.* **salaciousness** *n.* **salacity** (-las´-) *n.*

salad (sal´əd) *n.* **1** a dish of (mixed) raw vegetables. **2** a cold dish of precooked vegetables, or of fruit, often mixed with a dressing. **3** any herb or other vegetable suitable for eating raw. **salad cream** *n.* a kind of mayonnaise. **salad days** *n.pl.* the time of youth and inexperience. **salad dressing** *n.* a mixture of oil, vinegar, mustard etc., for dressing salads.

salamander (sal´əmandə) *n.* **1** (*Zool.*) an amphibian of the family *Urodela,* esp. the genus *Salamandra.* **2** a lizard-like animal anciently believed to be able to live in fire. **3** a spirit or genie fabled to live in fire. **4** any of various implements and utensils used in a heated state. **salamandrian** (-man´dri-), **salamandrine** (-man´drin) *a.* **salamandroid** (-man´droid) *n., a.*

salami (səlah´mi), **salame** *n.* (*pl.* **salamis, salames**) a highly-seasoned Italian sausage.

salary (sal´əri) *n.* (*pl.* **salaries**) a fixed payment given periodically, usu. monthly, esp. for work not of a manual or mechanical nature. ~*v.t.* (*3rd pers. sing. pres.* **salaries,** *pres.p.* **salarying,** *past, p.p.* **salaried**) to pay a salary to. **salariat** (səleə´riət) *n.* the salaried class. **salaried** *a.* **salaryman** *n.* (*pl.* **salarymen**) in Japan, a white-collar worker.

salchow (sal´kō) *n.* an ice-skating jump with turns in the air.

sale (sāl) *n.* **1** the act of selling. **2** the exchange of a commodity for money or other equivalent. **3** an event at which goods are sold. **4** an auction. **5** a disposal of a shop's remaining goods at reduced prices. **6** (*pl.*) quantity of goods sold. **7** (*pl.*) the activities involved in selling goods collectively. **on/ for/ up for sale** offered for purchase. **saleable, salable** *a.* **saleability** (-bil´-) *n.* **saleableness** *n.* **sale of work** *n.* a sale of home-made goods for charitable purposes. **sale or return** *n.* an arrangement by which a retailer may return unsold goods to the wholesaler. **sale ring** *n.* a circle of buyers at an auction. **saleroom** *n.* (*N Am.*) **salesroom** *n.* a room in which goods are sold, an auction room. **sales clerk** *n.* (*N Am.*) a shop assistant. **sales department** *n.* the part of a firm that deals with selling. **sales engineer** *n.* a salesperson who has technical knowledge of their goods and market. **salesgirl** *n.* a saleswoman. **saleslady** *n.* (*pl.* **salesladies**) a saleswoman. **salesman, saleswoman** *n.* (*pl.* **salesmen, saleswomen**) **1** a person employed to sell goods, esp. in a shop. **2** a sales representative. **salesmanship** *n.* the art of selling, skill in persuading prospective purchasers. **salesperson** *n.* (*pl.* **salespersons,**

salespeople) a salesman or saleswoman. **sales representative** *n.* a person employed to secure orders for a company's products, usu. in an assigned geographical area. **sales resistance** *n.* opposition of a prospective customer to purchasing a product. **sales talk** *n.* persuasive or attractive arguments to influence a possible purchaser. **sales tax** *n.* a tax on the sale of goods and services.

saleratus (salərā´təs) *n.* (*N Am.*) an impure bicarbonate of potash or soda, much used as baking powder.

salicin (sal´isin), **salicine** (-sēn) *n.* a bitter crystalline compound obtained from the bark of willows and poplars, used medicinally. **salicylic** (-sil´-) *a.* **1** derived from the willow. **2** belonging to a series of benzene derivatives of salicin. **3** derived from salicylic acid. **salicylic acid** *n.* an acid whose derivatives, including aspirin, are used to relieve pain and to treat rheumatism.

salient (sā´liənt) *a.* **1** conspicuous, prominent. **2** pointing or projecting outwards. ~*n.* **1** a salient angle. **2** a portion of defensive works or of a line of defence projecting towards the enemy. **salience, saliency** *n.* **saliently** *adv.* **salient point** *n.* a significant point.

saliferous (səlif´ərəs) *a.* (*Geol.*) (of rock strata) bearing or producing salt.

saline (sā´līn) *a.* **1** consisting of or having the characteristics of salt. **2** containing or impregnated with salt or salts. **3** (*Med.*) containing a salt or salts of alkaline metals or magnesium. ~*n.* **1** a salina. **2** a saline substance, esp. a purgative. **3** a saline solution, esp. with the same concentration as body fluids. **salina** (səlī´nə) *n.* **1** a salt marsh, lake, spring etc. **2** salt works. **salineness** *n.* **salinity** (səlin´-) *n.* **salinization** (salinīzā´shən), **salinisation** *n.* **salinometer** (salinom´itə) *n.*

saliva (səlī´və) *n.* an odourless, colourless, somewhat viscid liquid secreted by glands into the mouth where it lubricates ingested food, spittle. **salivary** (sal´i-, səlī´-) *a.* of or producing saliva. **salivate** (sal´i-) *v.t.* to excite an unusual secretion and discharge of saliva in, as by the use of mercury. ~*v.i.* to secrete or discharge saliva in excess. **salivation** (-ā´shən) *n.* **saliva test** *n.* a scientific test based on a sample of saliva.

Salk vaccine (sawlk) *n.* a vaccine against poliomyelitis.

sallee (sal´i), **sally** *n.* (*pl.* **sallees, sallies**) (*Austral.*) any of several eucalypts and acacias resembling the willow.

sallow¹ (sal´ō) *n.* **1** a willow tree, esp. one of the low shrubby varieties. **2** a willow-shoot, an osier. **sallowy** *a.*

sallow² (sal´ō) *a.* of a sickly yellowish or pale brown colour. ~*v.t.* to make sallow. ~*v.i.* to become sallow. **sallowish** *a.* **sallowness** *n.*

sally¹ (sal´i) *n.* (*pl.* **sallies**) **1** a sudden rushing out or sortie of troops from a besieged place against besiegers. **2** an issuing forth, an excursion. **3** a sudden or brief outbreak of spirits etc.,

an outburst. **4** a flight of fancy or wit, a bantering remark etc. ~*v.i.* (*3rd pers. sing. pres.* **sallies,** *pres.p.* **sallying,** *past, p.p.* **sallied**) **1** (of troops) to rush out suddenly. **2** to go (out or forth) on a journey, excursion etc.

sally² (sal´i) *n.* (*pl.* **sallies**) **1** the part of a bellringer's rope covered with wool for holding. **2** the first movement of a bell when set for ringing. **sally-hole** *n.* the hole through which the bell rope is passed.

sally³ SALLEE.

salmagundi (salməgŭn´di) *n.* (*pl.* **salmagundis**) **1** a dish of chopped meat, anchovies, eggs, oil, vinegar etc. **2** a multifarious mixture, a medley, a miscellany.

salmanazar (salmənā´zə)*n.* a large wine bottle, holding about 12 times as much as a standard bottle.

salmi (sal´mē), **salmis** *n.* (*pl.* **salmis**) a ragout, esp. of game birds stewed with wine.

salmon (sam´ən) *n.* (*pl. in general* **salmon,** *in particular* **salmons**) **1** a larger silvery, pink-fleshed fish of the family Salmonidae, esp. of the genus *Salmo*, fished both for food and sport. **2** any of various fish resembling the salmon such as the Australian salmon and an American sea trout of the genus *Cynoscion*. **3** salmon pink. ~*a.* salmon-coloured. **salmonid** (sal´mənid, -mon´-) *a.* of or relating to the family Salmonidae. ~*n.* a fish of this family. **salmon-ladder, salmon-leap, salmon-pass, salmon-stair, salmon-weir** *n.* a series of steps, zigzags, or other contrivances to enable salmon to get past a dam or waterfall. **salmon pink** *n.* the colour of salmon flesh. **salmon-pink** *a.* **salmon trout** *n.* **1** an anadromous fish, *Salmo trutta*, resembling the salmon but smaller. **2** any of various similar fishes. **salmony** *a.*

salmonella (salmənel´ə) *n.* (*pl.* **salmonellae** (-lē)) **1** any bacterium of the genus *Salmonella*, many of which cause food poisoning. **2** food poisoning caused by infection with salmonellae. **salmonellosis** (-ō´sis) *n.*

salon (sal´on) *n.* **1** a reception room, esp. in a great house in France. **2** the business premises of a hairdresser, beautician etc. **3** (*Hist.*) a periodical reunion of eminent people in the house of someone socially fashionable, esp. a lady. **4** (*N Am.*) a meeting of esp. intellectuals in the house of a celebrity or socialite. **5** (**Salon**) an annual exhibition of paintings etc. held in Paris. **salon music** *n.* light music, usu. classical.

saloon (səloon´) *n.* **1** a large room or hall, esp. one suitable for social receptions, public entertainments etc., or used for a specified purpose. **2** a large room for passengers on board ship. **3** (*also* **saloon car**) a closed motor car with no internal partitions. **4** (*esp. N Am., coll.*) a drinking bar, a public house. **5** a saloon bar. **6** (*also* **saloon car, saloon carriage**) a large railway carriage without compartments, often arranged as a drawing room. **saloon bar** *n.* the more reserved bar in a public house. **saloon deck** n. a deck reserved for first-class or saloon passengers. **saloon-keeper** n. (N Am.) a publican or bartender.

salopettes (saləpets´) n.pl. thick usu. quilted trousers with shoulder straps, used for skiing.

Salopian (səlō´piən) n. a native or inhabitant of Shropshire. ~a. of or relating to Shropshire.

salpiglossis (salpiglos´is) n. any plant of the genus *Salpiglossis*, with trumpet-shaped flowers.

salpinx (sal´pingks) n. (pl. **salpinges** (-pin´jēz)) the Fallopian tube. **salpingectomy** (salpinjek´-təmi) n. (pl. **salpingectomies**) (Med.) the surgical removal of a Fallopian tube. **salpingitis** (-jī´tis) n. (Med.) inflammation of a Fallopian tube.

salsa (sal´sə) n. **1** a Puerto Rican dance or the music for this. **2** a spicy sauce, esp. served with Mexican food.

salsify (sal´sifi) n. (pl. **salsifies**) **1** a composite plant, *Tragopogon porrifolius*, the long whitish root of which is eaten. **2** this root.

salt (sawlt) n. **1** chloride of sodium, used for seasoning and preserving food, obtained from sea water or brine. **2** a compound formed by the union of basic and acid radicals, an acid the hydrogen of which is wholly or partially replaced by a metal. **3** wit, repartee in talk etc. **4** that which gives flavour. **5** a salt cellar. **6** (pl.) any of various mineral salts used as a medicine, esp. as a purgative. **7** (pl.) smelling salts. **8** a salt marsh. **9** a sailor. ~a. **1** impregnated or flavoured with or tasting of salt. **2** cured with salt (*salt beef*). **3** living or growing in salt water. **4** (of wit etc.) pungent. **5** (of grief) bitter. ~v.t. **1** to sprinkle or cover with salt. **2** to season with salt. **3** to cure or preserve with salt. **4** to make salt. **5** in photography, to treat (paper etc.) with a solution of a salt. **6** to add liveliness to (a story etc.). **above the salt** at the higher part of a table, above the salt cellar. **below the salt** among the less distinguished company. **in salt** sprinkled with salt or steeped in brine for curing. **not worth one's salt** not worth keeping, not useful. **to eat someone's salt** to accept someone's hospitality. **to salt away/ down** (sl.) to save or hoard (money etc.). **with a grain of salt** with doubt or reserve. **with a pinch of salt** with doubt or reserve. **worth one's salt** worth keeping, useful. **salt-and-pepper** a. (esp. of hair) with light and dark colours mixed together. **saltbush** n. ORACHE. **salt-cat** n. a mixture of salt, gravel, cumin seed and stale urine given to pigeons. **salt cellar** n. **1** a vessel for holding salt at table. **2** (coll.) either of the two deep hollows formed above the collarbones. **salt dome, salt plug** n. a domelike structure formed when rock salt is forced up through upper rock strata. **salted** a. **1** seasoned, preserved or treated with salt. **2** experienced or hardened. **salter** n. **1** a person who salts (fish etc.). **2** a person who makes or sells salt. **3** a worker at a salt works. **saltern** (-tən) n. **1** a salt manufactory. **2** a series of pools for evaporating sea water. **salt fish** n. (W Ind.) preserved cod. **salt-glaze** n. a glaze

produced on pottery by putting salt into the kiln after firing. ~v.t. to apply salt-glaze to. **salt grass** n. (N Am.) grass growing in salt meadows or alkaline regions. **salting** n. **1** the application of salt for preservation etc. **2** (pl., Geol.) salt lands, a salt marsh. **saltish** a. **saltishly** adv. **salt lake** n. an inland body of salt water. **saltless** a. **salt lick** n. **1** a place to which cattle go to lick ground impregnated with salt. **2** a block of this salt. **salt marsh** n. land liable to be overflowed by the sea, esp. used for pasturage or for collecting salt. **salt meadow** n. a meadow liable to be overflowed with salt water. **salt mine** n. a mine for rock salt. **saltness** n. **salt of the earth** n. a person of the utmost worth. **salt pan** n. **1** a shallow depression in the land in which salt water evaporates to leave salt. **2** a vessel in which brine is evaporated at a salt works. **salt shaker** n. (N Am.) a container of salt; a salt cellar. **salt spoon** n. a small spoon for use at the table. **salt water** n. **1** sea water. **2** (sl.) tears. **salt-water** a. living in, of or relating to salt water, esp. the sea. **salt well** n. a bored well yielding brine. **salt works** n. a factory for making salt. **saltwort** n. any of various plants of the genus *Salsola* or *Salicornia*, growing in salt marshes and on seashores. **salty** a. (comp. **saltier**, superl. **saltiest**) **1** of or containing salt. **2** tasting (strongly) of salt. **3** of the sea or life at sea. **4** witty. **5** earthy, coarse. **6** (sl.) tough, aggressive. **saltily** adv. **saltiness** n.

saltation (saltā´shən, sawl-, sol-) n. **1** a leaping or bounding. **2** (Biol.) an abrupt transition or variation in the form of an organism. **saltatorial** (-tətaw´ri-), **saltatorian**, **saltatorious**, **saltatory** (sal´tətəri) a.

saltire (sal´tīə, sawl´-) n. (Her.) an ordinary in the form of a St Andrew's cross or the letter X.

saltpetre (sawltpē´tə), (N Am.) **saltpeter** n. potassium nitrate.

salubrious (səloo´briəs)a. **1** (of climate etc.) promoting health, wholesome. **2** spiritually wholesome, respectable. **3** (of surroundings etc.) agreeable. **salubriously** adv. **salubriousness**, **salubrity** n.

saluki (səloo´ki) n. (pl. **salukis**) a Persian greyhound.

salutary (sal´ūtəri) a. promoting good effects, beneficial, corrective, profitable.

Usage note The adjectives *salutary* and *salutatory* should not be confused: *salutary* means beneficial, and *salutatory* relating to salutation.

salute (səloot´, -lūt´) v.t. **1** (Mil.) to show respect to (a military superior) by a salute. **2** to greet with a gesture or words of welcome, respect or recognition. **3** to praise, acknowledge. **4** to honour by the discharge of ordnance etc. **5** to meet (the eye etc.). ~v.i. to perform a salute. ~n. **1** gesture of welcome, recognition etc. **2** (Mil.) a a prescribed method of doing honour or paying a compliment or respect, as discharge of ordnance, dipping colours, presenting arms etc.

b the attitude taken by a soldier, sailor etc. in giving a salute. **3** in fencing, a conventional series of movements performed before engaging. **to take the salute 1** (*Mil.*) (of an officer) to acknowledge a salute. **2** to receive ceremonial salutes. **salutation** (salūtā´shən) *n.* **1** the act of saluting. **2** that which is said or done in the act of greeting. **3** (*pl.*) words of greeting or communicating good wishes or courteous inquiries. **salutational** *a.* **salutatory** (səlū´tətəri) *a.*, *n.* (*pl.* **salutatories**). **saluter** *n.*

Usage note See note on *salutatory* under SALUTARY.

Salvadorean (salvədaw´riən) *a.* of or relating to El Salvador. ~*n.* a native or inhabitant of El Salvador.

salvage (sal´vij) *n.* **1** the act of saving a ship, goods etc. from shipwreck, capture, fire etc. **2** compensation allowed for such saving. **3** property so saved. **4** the saving and recycling of waste or scrap material. **5** material saved for re-use. ~*v.t.* **1** to save or recover from wreck, fire etc. **2** to save from ruin or destruction. **salvageable** *a.* **salvager** *n.*

salvation (salvā´shən) *n.* **1** the act of saving from destruction. **2** deliverance, preservation from danger, evil etc. **3** (*Theol.*) deliverance of the soul, or of believers from sin and its consequences. **4** a person who or thing which delivers, preserves etc. **salvationism** *n.* **salvationist** *n.*

salve[1] (salv) *n.* **1** a healing ointment. **2** anything that soothes or palliates. ~*v.t.* to soothe, to ease.

salve[2] (salv) *v.t.* **1** to save from destruction. **2** to salvage. **3** to preserve unhurt.

salver (sal´və) *n.* a tray, usu. of silver, brass, electroplate etc., on which refreshments, visiting cards etc. are presented.

salvia (sal´viə) *n.* any plant of the genus *Salvia*, labiate plants comprising the common sage and many cultivated species with brilliant flowers.

salvo[1] (sal´vō) *n.* (*pl.* **salvoes, salvos**) **1** a discharge of guns etc. as a salute. **2** a concentrated fire of artillery, release of missiles etc. **3** a volley of cheers etc.

salvo[2] (sal´vō) *n.* (*pl.* **salvos**) **1** a saving clause, a proviso. **2** a mental reservation, an evasion, an excuse. **3** an expedient to save one's reputation etc.

sal volatile SAL[1].

salvor (sal´və, -vaw) *n.* a person or ship effecting salvage.

SAM *abbr.* surface-to-air missile.

samara (səmah´rə) *n.* (*Bot.*) a one-seeded indehiscent dry fruit with winglike extensions, produced by the sycamore, ash etc.

Samaritan (səma´ritən) *n.* **1** a kind, charitable person, in allusion to the 'good Samaritan' of the parable (Luke x.30–37); also *good Samaritan*. **2** a member of a voluntary organization formed to give help to people in despair. **3** a native

or inhabitant of Samaria. ~*a.* of or relating to Samaria or the Samaritans. **Samaritanism** *n.*

samarium (səmeə´riəm) *n.* (*Chem.*) a silvery-grey metallic chemical element, at. no. 62, chem. symbol Sm, one of the rare earth metals.

samba (sam´bə) *n.* **1** a Brazilian dance. **2** a ballroom dance in imitation of this. **3** music for this. ~*v.i.* (*pres.p.* **sambaing**, *past, p.p.* **sambaed, samba'd**) to dance the samba.

sambar SAMBUR.

Sam Browne (sam brown´), **Sam Browne belt** *n.* a military officer's belt with a light strap over the right shoulder.

sambur (sam´bə), **sambar** *n.* a large deer or elk, *Cervus unicolor*, from S Asia.

same (sām) *a.* **1** identical. **2** not other, not different. **3** identical or similar in kind, quality, degree etc. **4** exactly alike. **5** just mentioned, aforesaid. **6** unchanged, uniform. ~*pron.* **1** the same person or thing. **2** the aforesaid. ~*adv.* similarly; in the same way. **all the same 1** nevertheless. **2** notwithstanding what is said, done, altered etc. **just the same** nevertheless, yet. **same here** (*coll.*) me too. **the same to you!** likewise. **to be all the same to someone** used to express indifference. **sameness** *n.* **samey** *a.* (*comp.* **samier**, *superl.* **samiest**) (*coll.*) monotonous, repetitive. **sameyness** *n.*

Usage note The adverbial or conjunctive use of *(the) same as* (as in *I use dictionaries, (the) same as you (do)*) is informal and sometimes disapproved of: *in the same way as* can often be used instead. See also note under AS.

samizdat (sam´izdat, -miz´-) *n.* **1** the clandestine publishing of banned literature in the former Communist countries of eastern Europe. **2** this literature.

Samoan (səmō´ən) *n.* **1** a native or inhabitant of Samoa. **2** the language of Samoa. ~*a.* of or relating to Samoa or its language.

samosa (səmō´sə) *n.* (*pl.* **samosas, samosa**) an Indian savoury of spiced meat or vegetables in a triangular pastry case.

samovar (sam´əvah) *n.* a Russian tea urn heated by burning charcoal in an inner tube.

Samoyed (sam´əyed) *n.* (*pl.* **Samoyed, Samoyeds**) **1** a member of a Mongolian people inhabiting middle Siberia. **2** their language. **3** (*also* **samoyed**) a breed of white sledge-dog. **Samoyedic** (-yed´-) *a.* of or relating to this people. ~*n.* their language.

samp (samp) *n.* (*NAm.*) maize coarsely ground or made into porridge.

sampan (sam´pan) *n.* a Chinese flat-bottomed river boat, frequently used as a houseboat.

samphire (sam´fiə) *n.* **1** a herb, *Crithmum maritimum*, growing on sea-cliffs, the aromatic leaves of which are pickled as a condiment. **2** a glasswort of the genus *Salicornia*.

sample (sam´pəl, sahm´-) *n.* **1** a part taken, offered or used as illustrating the whole, an example. **2** in electronics, a sound created by sampling. ~*v.t.* **1** to take samples of, to test, to try. **2** to have an experience of. **3** to present samples of. **sample bag** *n.* (*Austral.*) a bag of advertisers' samples. **sampler** *n.* **1** a person who or thing which takes samples. **2** a piece of embroidered work done as a specimen of skill. **3** an electronic device used for sampling. **4** (*N Am.*) a collection of representative items etc. **sampling** *n.* **1** the act of sampling. **2** (*Mus.*) the taking of sounds, such as extracts from existing popular songs, and putting them together to form a new piece. **sampling error** *n.* error in a statistical analysis when the sample is unrepresentative. **sampling frame** *n.* an enumeration of a population for the purposes of sampling.

Samson (sam´sən) *n.* a man of extraordinary strength (Judges xiv.6 *passim*).

samurai (sam´urī) *n.* (*pl.* **samurai**) **1** a Japanese army officer. **2** (*Hist.*) a member of the military caste under the Japanese feudal regime, or a military retainer.

sanatorium (sanətaw´riəm), (*esp. N Am.*) **sanitarium** (-teə´-) *n.* (*pl.* **sanatoriums, sanatoria** (-riə), (*esp. N Am.*) **sanitariums, sanitaria**) **1** an institution for the treatment of chronic diseases. **2** an institution for invalids, esp. convalescents. **3** a sickroom, esp. in a boarding school.

sanctify (sangk´tifi) *v.t.* (*3rd pers. sing. pres.* **sanctifies,** *pres.p.* **sanctifying,** *past, p.p.* **sanctified**) **1** to make holy, to consecrate. **2** to set apart or observe as holy. **3** to purify from sin. **4** to give a sacred character to, to sanction. **5** to render productive of holiness. **sanctification** (-fikā´shən) *n.* **sanctifier** *n.*

sanctimonious (sangktimō´niəs) *a.* making a show of piety or saintliness. **sanctimoniously** *adv.* **sanctimoniousness** *n.* **sanctimony** (sangk´-timəni) *n.*

sanction (sangk´shən) *n.* **1** the act of ratifying, confirmation by superior authority. **2** a provision for enforcing obedience, a penalty or reward. **3** anything that gives binding force to a law, oath etc. **4** support, encouragement conferred by usage etc. **5** that which makes any rule of conduct binding. **6** (*usu. in pl.*) a coercive measure taken by one state against another to force compliance with international law or a change in policy etc. ~*v.t.* **1** to authorize, to ratify. **2** to approve. **3** to enforce by penalty etc. **sanctionable** *a.* **sanctionless** *a.*

sanctity (sangk´titi) *n.* (*pl.* **sanctities**) **1** the state of being holy, holiness. **2** spiritual purity, saintliness. **3** sacredness, inviolability. **4** (*pl.*) sacred things, feelings etc.

sanctuary (sangk´chuəri) *n.* (*pl.* **sanctuaries**) **1** a holy place. **2** a church, temple or other building or enclosure devoted to sacred uses, esp. an inner shrine or most sacred part of a church etc. **3** a place where deer, birds etc. are left undisturbed. **4** a place of immunity, a refuge. **5** immunity, protection. **6** (*Hist.*) a church or

other consecrated place in which debtors and malefactors were free from arrest. **to take sanctuary** to hide in a place of refuge.

sanctum (sangk´təm) *n.* (*pl.* **sanctums, sancta** (-tə)) **1** a sacred or private place. **2** (*coll.*) a private room, retreat.

sanctus (sangk´təs), **Sanctus** *n.* **1** the liturgical phrase 'Holy, holy, holy', in Latin or English. **2** the music for this. **sanctus bell** *n.* a bell, usu. in a turret or bell-cote over the junction of nave and chancel, rung at the sanctus before the Canon of the Mass.

sand (sand) *n.* **1** comminuted fragments of rock, esp. of chert, flint and other quartz rocks, reduced almost to powder. **2** (*pl.*) tracts of sand, stretches of beach or shoals or submarine banks of sand. **3** (*pl.*) particles of sand in an hourglass. **4** (*N Am. coll.*) grit, endurance, pluck. **5** a yellowish-brown colour. ~*v.t.* **1** to smooth or rub with sandpaper or a similar abrasive. **2** to sprinkle or treat with sand. **3** to cover or overlay with or bury under sand. **4** to mix sand with, to adulterate. **5** to drive (a ship) on a sandbank. **sandbag** *n.* a bag or sack filled with sand, used in fortification for making defensive walls, as ballast, for stopping crevices, draughts etc., as a cushion for supporting an engraver's plate, as a weapon for stunning a person etc. ~*v.t.* (*pres.p.* **sandbagging,** *past, p.p.* **sandbagged**) **1** to fortify or stop up with sandbags. **2** to strike or fell with a sandbag. **3** (*N Am.*) to coerce by harsh means. ~*v.i.* to deliberately underperform in e.g. a race, to gain an unfair advantage. **sandbagger** *n.* **sandbank** *n.* a bank or shoal of sand, esp. in the sea, a river etc. **sandbar** *n.* a ridge of sand built up by currents in a sea or river. **sand-bath** *n.* a vessel containing hot sand used for heating, tempering etc. **sand-bed** *n.* a layer of sand. **sandblast** *n.* a jet of sand used for engraving and cutting glass, cleaning stone surfaces etc. ~*v.t.* to cut, clean etc. with a sandblast. **sandblaster** *n.* **sandbox** *n.* **1** a box containing sand carried by a locomotive etc., for sprinkling the rails when slippery. **2** in golf, a box for sand used in teeing. **3** a large open box containing sand for children to play in, a sandpit. †**sandboy** *n.* a boy carting or hawking sand. **happy as a sandboy** happily engrossed. **sandcastle** *n.* a model of a castle in sand. **sand cloud** *n.* driving sand in a simoom. **sand-crack** *n.* **1** a fissure in the hoof of a horse, liable to cause lameness. **2** a crack in the human foot, caused by walking on hot sand. **3** a crack or flaw in a brick due to defective mixing. **sand dollar** *n.* any flat sea urchin of the order Clypeasteroida. **sand dune** *n.* a ridge of loose sand formed by the wind. **sand eel** *n.* any eel-like fish of the family Ammodytidae or Hypotychidae. **sander** *n.* a person who or thing which sands, esp. a power tool for smoothing etc. by means of an abrasive belt or disc. **sand flea** *n.* **1** a chigger. **2** a sand-hopper. **sandfly** *n.* (*pl.* **sandflies**) **1** any biting blackfly of the genus *Simulium*. **2** any tropical biting fly of the genus *Phlebotomus*. **sand-glass** *n.* an hourglass. **sandgrouse** *n.* a seed-eating bird of the family Pteroclididae, found in dry regions of the Old World. **sandhill** *n.* a sand dune. **sandhog** *n.* (*N Am.*) a person who works underwater or underground on construction projects etc. **sandhopper** *n.* any of various small jumping crustaceans of the order Amphipoda. **sandlike** *a.* **sandlot** *n.* (*N Am.*) a sandy area where children can play. **sandman** *n.* (*pl.* **sandmen**) a being in fairy lore who makes children sleepy by casting sand in their eyes. **sand martin** *n.* a small swallow, *Riparia riparia*, which makes its nest in sandbanks etc. **sandpaper** *n.* a paper or thin cloth coated with sand, used for smoothing wood etc. *~v.t.* to rub or smooth with this. **sandpiper** *n.* any of various wading birds of the family Scolopacidae. **sandpit** *n.* a container of sand for children to play in. **sand-shoe** *n.* a light shoe, usu. of canvas with a rubber sole, for walking on sand. **sand-skipper** *n.* a sand-hopper. **sandsoap** *n.* a gritty general-purpose soap. **sand spurrey** *n.* a pink-flowered plant, *Spergularia rubra*, which grows on sandy soil. **sandstock** *n.* a brick made with sand dusted on the surface. **sandstone** *n.* stone composed of an agglutination of grains of sand. **sandstorm** *n.* a storm of wind carrying along volumes of sand in a desert. **sandwort** *n.* any plant of the genus *Arenaria*, low herbs growing in sandy soil. **sandy** *a.* (*comp.* **sandier**, *superl.* **sandiest**) **1** consisting of or abounding in sand. **2** of the colour of sand. **3** (of hair) yellowish red. **4** having hair of this colour. **sandiness** *n.* **sandyish** *a.* **sand yacht** *n.* a yachtlike vehicle with wheels and sails for use on sand.

sandal¹ (san´dəl) *n.* **1** a kind of shoe consisting of a sole secured by straps passing over the foot and often round the ankle. **2** a strap for fastening a low shoe. *~v.t.* (*pres.p.* **sandalling**, (*N Am.*) **sandaling**, *past, p.p.* **sandalled**, (*N Am.*) **sandaled**) **1** to put sandals on. **2** to fasten with a sandal.

sandal² (san´dəl) *n.* sandalwood. **sandal tree** *n.* any tree yielding sandalwood. **sandalwood** *n.* **1** the fragrant wood of various trees of the genus *Santalum*, esp. *S. album*, much used for cabinetwork; also called *white sandalwood*. **2** a tree that yields sandalwood. **3** a similar wood or a tree that yields it. **4** a perfume derived from sandalwood. **sandalwood oil** *n.* an aromatic oil made from the white sandalwood.

sandarac (san´dərak), **sandarach** *n.* **1** a whitish-yellow gum-resin obtained from a NW African tree, *Tetraclinis articulata*. **2** this tree. **3** realgar.

sanderling (san´dəling) *n.* a small wading bird, *Calidris alba*.

sandwich (san´wich, -wij) *n.* **1** two slices of bread, usu. spread with butter or a similar substance, with meat etc. between them. **2** anything resembling a sandwich in layered arrangement. *~v.t.* to put, lay or insert between two things of a dissimilar kind. **sandwich-board** *n.* either of

two advertisement boards worn by a sandwich-man. **sandwich course** *n.* an educational course containing one or more periods of practical work. **sandwich-man** *n.* (*pl.* **sandwich-men**) a person carrying two advertisement boards hung from their shoulders, one in front and one behind.

Sandwich tern (san´wich) *n.* a crested tern, *Sterna sandvicensis*.

sane (sān) *a.* **1** sound in mind, not deranged. **2** (of views etc.) sensible, reasonable. **sanely** *adv.* **saneness** *n.*

Sanforized® (san´fərīzd), **Sanforised** *a.* (of fabric) pre-shrunk by a patented process.

sang SING.

sang-froid (sāfrwah´) *n.* calmness, composure in danger etc.

sangria (sang-grē´ə) *n.* a Spanish drink of diluted (red) wine and fruit juices.

sanguinary (sang´gwinəri) *a.* **1** accompanied by bloodshed or carnage. **2** delighting in bloodshed, murderous. **3** (of laws) inflicting death freely. **sanguinarily** *adv.* **sanguinariness** *n.*

sanguine (sang´gwin) *a.* **1** cheerful, confident. **2** (of the complexion) ruddy, florid. **3** having the colour of blood. *~n.* **1** blood colour, deep red. **2** a crayon of this colour prepared from iron oxide. **sanguinely** *adv.* **sanguineness** *n.* **sanguineous** (-gwin´-) *a.* **1** (*Med.*) of, relating to, forming or containing blood. **2** sanguinary. **3** of a blood colour. **4** full-blooded, plethoric.

Sanhedrin (san´idrin, -hē´-, -hed´-), **Sanhedrim** (-rim) *n.* (*Hist.*) the supreme court of justice and council of the Jewish nation, down to AD 425, consisting of 71 priests, elders and scribes.

sanicle (san´ikəl) *n.* any small woodland plant of the umbelliferous genus *Sanicula*, allied to the parsley.

sanify (san´ifī) *v.t.* (*3rd pers. sing. pres.* **sanifies**, *pres.p.* **sanifying**, *past, p.p.* **sanified**) to make healthy or more sanitary.

sanitary (san´itəri) *a.* **1** relating to or concerned with the preservation of health, of or relating to hygiene. **2** free from dirt, disease-causing organisms etc., hygienic. **sanitarian** (-teə´ri-) *n., a.* **sanitarily** *adv.* **sanitariness** *n.* **sanitarium** SANATORIUM. **sanitary engineer** *n.* a civil engineer dealing with disposal of waste, provision of clean water etc. **sanitary napkin** *n.* (*esp. N Am.*) a sanitary towel. **sanitary towel** *n.* an absorbent pad used for menstruation. **sanitary ware** *n.* porcelain for lavatories, baths etc. **sanitate** *v.t.* to improve the sanitary condition of. *~v.i.* to carry out sanitary measures. **sanitation** (-ā´shən) *n.* **1** sanitary conditions. **2** measures for the maintenance of health and the prevention of disease. **sanitationist** *n.* **sanitize, sanitise** *v.t.* **1** to make sanitary. **2** to remove offensive language etc. from, make respectable. **sanitization** (-za´shən) *n.* **sanitizer** *n.*

sanity (san´iti) *n.* **1** saneness, mental soundness. **2** reasonableness, moderation.

sank SINK.

sans (sanz, sã) *prep.* (*Shak.*, *also facet.*) without.

sans-culotte (sākulot´, sanzkū-) *n.* **1** (*Hist.*) a republican in the French Revolution. **2** a radical extremist, a revolutionary. **sans-culottism** *n.* **sans serif** (san ser´if), **sanserif** *n.* a printing type without serifs. ~*a.* without serifs.

Sanskrit (san´skrit) *n.* the ancient language of the Hindu sacred writings. **Sanskritic** (-krit´-) *a.* **Sanskritist** *n.*

Santa Claus (san´tǝ klawz, klawz´), **Santa** *n.* a mythical white-bearded old man bringing presents at Christmas and putting them in children's stockings, made popular in Britain in the late 19th cent.

santolina (santǝlē´nǝ) *n.* any fragrant shrubby composite plant of the genus *Santolina.*

santonica (santon´ikǝ) *n.* **1** a shrubby plant, *Artemisia cina.* **2** the unexpanded flower heads of this, containing santonin. **santonin** (san´tǝnin) *n.* the bitter principle of santonica, used as an anthelmintic.

✗ sanwich common misspelling of SANDWICH.

sap[1] (sap) *n.* **1** the watery juice or circulating fluid of living plants. **2** the sapwood of a tree. **3** vital fluid, strength. **4** (*sl.*) a gullible person, a saphead. **5** (*N Am.*, *sl.*) any object used as a bludgeon. ~*v.t.* (*pres.p.* **sapping**, *past*, *p.p.* **sapped**) **1** to draw off sap. **2** to exhaust the strength or vitality of. **3** (*N Am.*, *sl.*) to hit with a sap. **sapful** *a.* **sap green** *n.* **1** a green pigment obtained from the juice of blackthorn berries. **2** the colour of this. **sap-green** *a.* **saphead** *n.* (*sl.*) a softhead, a ninny. **sapless** *a.* **sapling** (-ling) *n.* **1** a young tree. **2** a youth. **3** a young greyhound. **sappy** *a.* (*comp.* **sappier**, *superl.* **sappiest**). **sappily** *adv.* **sappiness** *n.* **sapsucker** *n.* a small woodpecker of the genus *Sphyrapicus*, which feeds on sap from trees. **sapwood** *n.* the soft new wood next to the bark, alburnum.

sap[2] (sap) *v.t.* (*pres.p.* **sapping**, *past*, *p.p.* **sapped**) **1** to undermine. **2** to approach by mines, trenches etc. **3** to render unstable by wearing away the foundation. **4** to subvert or destroy insidiously. ~*v.i.* to make an attack or approach by digging trenches or undermining. ~*n.* **1** the act of sapping. **2** a deep trench or mine for approach to or attack on a fortification. **3** insidious undermining or subversion of faith etc. **sapper** *n.* **1** a person who digs trenches. **2**(*coll.*) an officer or private of the Royal Engineers. **3** (*N Am.*) a military engineer who lays or detects mines.

sapanwood (sap´ǝnwud), **sappanwood** *n.* a brownish-red dyewood obtained from trees of the genus *Caesalpinia*, esp. *C. sappan*, from S Asia and Malaysia.

sapele (sǝpē´li) *n.* **1** any of several W African trees of the genus *Entandrophragma.* **2** the reddish-brown wood, resembling mahogany, obtained from these trees.

✗ saphire common misspelling of SAPPHIRE.

sapid (sap´id) *a.* **1** possessing flavour that can be

relished, savoury. **2** not insipid, vapid or uninteresting. **sapidity** (-pid´-), **sapidness** *n.*

sapient (sā´piǝnt) *a.* wise, sagacious, discerning, sage (often ironical). **sapience** *n.* **sapiential** (-en´shǝl) *a.* of or conveying wisdom. **sapiential books** *n.pl.* (*Bible*) Proverbs, Ecclesiastes, Ecclesiasticus, The Book of Wisdom, The Canticles. **sapiently** *adv.*

sapling SAP[1].

sapodilla (sapǝdil´ǝ), **zapotilla** (zapǝtil´ǝ) *n.* **1** a large evergreen tree, *Manilkara zapota*, growing in the W Indies and Central America. **2** the edible fruit of this. **3** its durable wood.

saponaceous (sapǝnā´shǝs) *a.* resembling, containing or having the qualities of soap.

saponify (sǝpon´ifi) *v.t.* (*3rd pers. sing. pres.* **saponifies**, *pres.p.* **saponifying**, *past*, *p.p.* **saponified**) **1** to convert into soap by combination with an alkali. **2** to convert to an acid and an alcohol as a result of treatment with an alkali. ~*v.i.* (of an oil, fat etc.) to become converted into soap. **saponifiable** *a.* **saponification** (-fikā´shǝn) *n.*

saponin (sap´ǝnin) *n.* any of various glucosides obtained from the soapwort, horse chestnut etc. that produce a soapy foam and are used in detergents.

sappanwood SAPANWOOD.

sapper SAP[2].

Sapphic (saf´ik) *a.* **1** of or relating to Sappho, a poetess (*c.*600 BC) from the Greek island of Lesbos. **2** (*also* **sapphic**) lesbian.

sapphire (saf´īǝ) *n.* **1** any transparent blue variety of corundum. **2** an intense and lustrous blue, azure. **3** a S American hummingbird with a blue throat. ~*a.* sapphire-blue. **sapphire blue** *n.* a bright blue colour. **sapphire-blue** *a.* **sapphire wedding** *n.* a 45th wedding anniversary. **sapphirine** (-rīn) *a.*, *n.*

sappy SAP[1].

sapro- (sap´rō), **sapr-** *comb. form* (*Biol.*) indicating rotting or dead matter.

saprogenic (saprǝjen´ik) *a.* producing or produced by putrefaction.

saprophagous (sǝprof´ǝgǝs) *a.* feeding on decomposing matter.

saprophile (sap´rǝfīl) *n.* a bacterium feeding on decomposed matter. **saprophilic** (-fil´-), **saprophilous** (-prof´-) *a.*

saprophyte (sap´rǝfīt) *n.* a plant, bacterium or fungus that grows on decaying organic matter. **saprophytic** (-fit´-) *a.*

saraband (sar´ǝband), **sarabande** *n.* **1** a slow and stately Spanish dance. **2** a piece of music for this in strongly accented triple time.

Saracen (sar´ǝsǝn) *n.* (*Hist.*) a Muslim or Arab at the time of the Crusades. ~*a.* of or relating to the Saracens. **Saracenic** (-sen´-) *a.*

sarcasm (sah´kazm) *n.* **1** an ironical or wounding remark. **2** bitter or contemptuous irony. **sarcastic** (-kas´-) *a.* **1** containing or characterized by sarcasm. **2** given to using sarcasm. **sarcastically** *adv.*

sarcenet (sah´snit), **sarsenet** *n.* a thin, fine soft-textured silk used chiefly for linings, ribbons etc.

sarcoma (sahkō´mə) *n.* (*pl.* **sarcomas, sarcomata** (-tə)) a tumour of connective tissue. **sarcomatosis** (-tō´sis) *n.* **sarcomatous** *a.*

sarcophagus (sahkof´əgəs) *n.* (*pl.* **sarcophagi** (-jī, -gī), **sarcophaguses**) a stone coffin, esp. one of architectural or decorated design.

sarcous (sah´kəs) *a.* composed of flesh or muscle tissue.

sard (sahd) *n.* a precious stone, a variety of cornelian.

sardelle (sahdel´), **sardel** *n.* a small Mediterranean clupeoid fish like, and prepared as, the sardine.

sardine (sahdēn´) *n.* **1** a fish, *Clupea pilchardus*, caught off Brittany and Sardinia, and cured and preserved in oil. **2** any of various other small fish preserved in the same way. **like sardines** (packed) closely together.

Sardinian (sahdin´iən) *a.* of or relating to the island or the former kingdom of Sardinia, or its language. ~*n.* **1** a native or inhabitant of Sardinia. **2** the Romance language of Sardinia.

sardonic (sahdon´ik) *a.* **1** forced, insincere. **2** (of laughter etc.) sneering, bitterly ironical. **sardonically** *adv.* **sardonicism** (-sizm) *n.*

sardonyx (sah´dəniks) *n.* a variety of onyx composed of white chalcedony alternating with layers of sard.

saree SARI.

☒ sargant common misspelling of SERGEANT.

sargasso (sahgas´ō), **sargassum** (-gas´əm) *n.* (*pl.* **sargassos, sargassa**) any seaweed of the genus *Sargassum*, found floating esp. in the Sargasso Sea in the N Atlantic.

sarge (sahj) *n.* (*sl.*) short for SERGEANT.

sari (sah´ri), **saree** *n.* (*pl.* **saris, sarees**) a Hindu woman's traditional dress, formed from a length of material draped around the body.

sarin (sah´rin) *n.* a compound of phosphorus used as a nerve gas.

sarky (sah´ki) *a.* (*comp.* **sarkier**, *superl.* **sarkiest**) **1** (*coll.*) sarcastic. **2** (*sl.*) bad-tempered. **sarkily** *adv.* **sarkiness** *n.*

sarmentose (sahmen´tōs), **sarmentous** (-təs) *a.* (*Bot.*) having or producing runners.

sarnie (sah´ni) *n.* (*coll.*) a sandwich.

sarong (sərong´) *n.* a loose, skirtlike garment traditionally worn by men and women in the Malay Archipelago.

sarsaparilla (sahspəril´ə) *n.* **1** the dried roots of various species of smilax, used as a flavouring and formerly in medicine as an alterative and tonic. **2** a plant yielding this. **3** a carbonated drink flavoured with sassafras.

sarsen (sah´sən) *n.* (*Geol.*) a sandstone boulder such as those scattered over the chalk downs of Wiltshire.

sarsenet SARCENET.

sartorial (sahtaw´riəl) *a.* **1** of or relating to a tailor or tailored clothing. **2** of or relating to the elegance etc. of clothes.

SASE, s.a.s.e. *abbr.* (*N Am.*) self-addressed, stamped envelope.

sash[1] (sash) *n.* an ornamental band or scarf worn round the waist or over the shoulder, frequently as a badge or part of a uniform. **sashed**[1] *a.*

sash[2] (sash) *n.* **1** a frame of wood or metal holding the glass of a window. **2** a sliding light in a greenhouse etc. ~*v.t.* to furnish with sashes. **sash cord, sash line** *n.* a stout cord attached to a sash and the sash weights. **sashed**[2] *a.* **sash tool** *n.* a glazier's or painter's brush. **sash weight** *n.* a weight used to balance a sash and hold it in an open position. **sash window** *n.* a window having a movable sash or sashes.

sashay (sashā´) *v.i.* (*esp. N Am.*) to walk or move in a nonchalant or sauntering manner.

sashed[1] SASH[1].

sashed[2] SASH[2].

sashimi (sashim´i) *n.* a Japanese dish of thin slices of raw fish.

sasin (sas´in) *n.* the common Indian antelope, *Antilope cervicapra*, also called *blackbuck*.

Sasquatch (sas´kwach) *n.* a hairy humanoid creature reputedly living in W Canada.

sass (sas) *n.* (*N Am., coll.*) impudence, cheek, sauce. ~*v.t.* to talk impudently to. **sassy** *a.* (*comp.* **sassier**, *superl.* **sassiest**) cheeky, saucy. **sassily** *adv.* **sassiness** *n.*

sassaby TSESSEBI.

sassafras (sas´əfras) *n.* **1** a N American tree, *Sassafras albidum*, of the laurel family. **2** the dried bark of its root used as an aromatic stimulant and flavouring.

Sassenach (sas´ənakh) *n.* (*Sc. and Ir.*, *usu. derog.*) a Saxon, an English person. ~*a.* English.

sassy SASS.

sastrugi (sastroo´gi), **zastrugi** (zas-) *n.pl.* wavelike ridges on snow-covered plains caused by winds.

SAT *abbr.* standard assessment task.

Sat. *abbr.* Saturday.

sat SIT.

Satan (sā´tən), **Satanas** (sat´ənas) *n.* the archfiend, the Devil. **satanic** (sətan´-), **satanical** *a.* **1** of, relating to, emanating from or having the qualities of Satan. **2** devilish, infernal. **satanically** *adv.* **Satanism** *n.* **1** a diabolical disposition, doctrine or conduct. **2** the deliberate pursuit of wickedness. **3** Satan-worship. **Satanist** *n.* **Satanize, Satanise** *v.t.*

Satano- (sā´tənō) *comb. form* of or relating to Satan. **Satanology** (-o´ləji) *n.* (*pl.* **Satanologies**) the study of or a treatise on doctrines relating to Satan.

satay (sat´ā), **satai, saté** *n.* a Malaysian and Indonesian dish of cubed meat served with a spicy peanut sauce.

SATB *abbr.* (*Mus.*) soprano, alto, tenor, bass.

satchel (sach´əl) *n.* a small rectangular bag, often suspended by a strap passing over one shoulder, esp. for schoolchildren to carry books etc. in. **satchelled,** (*N Am.*) **satcheled** *a.*

sate (sāt) *v.t.* **1** to satisfy (an appetite or desire). **2** to satiate, to surfeit, to glut, to cloy. **sateless** *a.* (*poet.*)

sateen (sətēn´) *n.* a glossy woollen or cotton fabric made in imitation of satin.

satellite (sat´əlīt) *n.* **1** a secondary planet revolving round a primary one. **2** a man-made device projected into space to orbit the earth, moon etc., used for communications, weather forecasting, surveillance etc. **3** something dependent on another. **4** an obsequious follower, dependant. ~*a.* **1** transmitted by satellite. **2** on the periphery. **satellite dish** *n.* a dish-shaped aerial for receiving broadcasting signals from a satellite. **satellite town** *n.* a small town dependent upon a larger town in the vicinity. **satellitic** (-lit´ik) *a.* **satellitism** *n.*

sati SUTTEE.

satiate (sā´shiāt) *v.t.* **1** to satisfy (as a desire or appetite) fully. **2** to sate, to surfeit. **satiation** (-ā´shən) *n.* **satiety** (səti´əti) *n.* **1** the state of being sated or glutted. **2** excess of gratification producing disgust. **to satiety** to an extent beyond what is desired.

satin (sat´in) *n.* a silken fabric with an overshot weft and a highly-finished glossy surface on one side only. ~*a.* made of or resembling this, esp. in smoothness. ~*v.t.* (*pres.p.* **satining**, *past, p.p.* **satined**) to give (paper etc.) a glossy surface like satin. **satinet** (-net´), **satinette** *n.* **1** a thin satin. **2** a glossy fabric made to imitate satin. **satin finish** *n.* **1** a lustrous polish given to silverware with a metallic brush. **2** any effect resembling satin produced on materials. **satinflower** *n.* **1** the greater stitchwort, *Stellaria holostea.* **2** any other plant whose flowers have a satiny sheen. **satinize, satinise** *v.t.* to satin. **satinized** *a.* **satin paper** *n.* a fine, glossy writing paper. **satin spar** *n.* a finely fibrous variety of aragonite, calcite, or gypsum. **satin stitch** *n.* a stitch in parallel lines giving the appearance of satin. **satinwood** *n.* **1** a tree, *Chloroxylon swietenia*; also called *Ceylon satinwood* or *Sri Lanka satinwood.* **2** a tree, *Fagara flava*; also called *West Indian satinwood* or *Jamaican satinwood.* **3** the yellow ornamental wood of these. **satiny** *a.*

satire (sat´īə) *n.* **1** ridicule, sarcasm. **2** a composition in which wickedness or folly or individual persons are held up to ridicule. **3** satirical writing as a genre. **satirical** (-tir´-), **satiric** *a.* **satirically** *adv.* **satiricalness** *n.* **satirist** (sat´irist) *n.* a person who writes or employs satire. **satirize** (-i-), **satirise** *v.t.* to ridicule by means of satire. **satirization** (-ā´shən) *n.*

Usage note See note under SATYR.

satisfy (sat´isfī) *v.t.* (*3rd pers. sing. pres.* **satisfies**, *pres.p.* **satisfying**, *past, p.p.* **satisfied**) **1** to supply or gratify to the full. **2** to gratify, to please. **3** to pay (a debt etc.). **4** to fulfil. **5** to be sufficient for,

to meet the desires, expectations or requirements of. **6** (*Math., Logic*) to fulfil the conditions of. **7** to free from doubt. **8** to convince. **9** to meet (a doubt, objection etc.) adequately. ~*v.i.* **1** to give satisfaction. **2** to make payment or reparation. **to satisfy oneself** to be certain in one's own mind. **satisfaction** (-fak´-) *n.* **1** the act of satisfying. **2** the state of being satisfied. **3** gratification, contentment. **4** payment of a debt, fulfilment of an obligation. **5** a source of satisfaction. **6** compensation, amends. **7** (*Theol.*) atonement, esp. the atonement for sin achieved by Christ's death. **8** the performance of penance. **to one's satisfaction** so that one is satisfied. **satisfactory** (-fak´-) *a.* meeting all needs, desires or expectations. **satisfactorily** *adv.* **satisfactoriness** *n.* **satisfiable** *a.* **satisfiability** (-bil´-) *n.* **satisfiedly** *adv.* **satisfier** *n.* **satisfying** *a.* **satisfyingly** *adv.*

satnav (sat´nav) *abbr.* (*Naut.*) satellite navigation.

satori (sətaw´ri) *n.* in Zen Buddhism, an intuitive enlightenment.

satsuma (satsoo´mə, sat´sumə, -sū-) *n.* **1** a seedless type of mandarin orange. **2** a tree that bears such fruit. **Satsuma ware** *n.* a cream-coloured variety of Japanese pottery.

saturate (sach´ərāt) *v.t.* **1** to soak or imbue thoroughly. **2** to fill or charge (a body, substance, gas, fluid etc.) with another substance, fluid, electricity etc. to the point where no more can be held. **3** (*Chem.*) to cause (a chemical compound) to combine until no further addition is possible. **4** to overwhelm (a target) with bombs or projectiles. **5** to supply (a market) with more than is necessary. **saturable** *a.* **saturated** *a.* **1** (of a solution) containing as much dissolved material as possible at a given temperature. **2** full of water, soaked. **3** (of an organic compound) containing only single bonds between carbon atoms and not reacting to add further groups to the molecule. **4** (of a colour) deep, free from white. **saturated fat** *n.* a fat containing mostly saturated fatty acids. **saturater** *n.* **saturation** (-ā´shən) *n.* **saturation bombing** *n.* (*Mil.*) bombing that completely covers a target area. **saturation point** *n.* the point at which no more can be taken in, held etc.

Saturday (sat´ədi, -dā) *n.* the seventh day of the week, following Friday. ~*adv.* (*coll.*) on Saturday. **Saturdays** *adv.* (*coll.*) on Saturdays, each Saturday.

Saturn (sat´ən) *n.* the sixth of the major planets in distance from the sun. **saturnalia** (-nā´liə) *n.* (*pl.* **saturnalia, saturnalias**) **1** (*Hist.*) (*usu.* **Saturnalia**) an ancient Roman annual festival held in December in honour of Saturn, regarded as a time of unrestrained licence and merriment. **2** (*sing. or pl.*) a season or occasion of unrestrained revelry. **saturnalian** *a.* **Saturnian** (-tœ´ni-) *a.* **1** of or relating to the planet Saturn. **2** of a saturnine temperament. **saturniid** (sətœ´niid) *n.* any large moth of the family Saturniidae. **saturnine** (-nīn) *a.* dull, phlegmatic, gloomy, morose.

satyr (sat´ə) *n.* **1** any of a class of ancient sylvan Greek gods represented with the legs of a goat, budding horns, and goatlike ears, identified by the Romans with the fauns. **2** a lascivious man. **3** SATYRID (under SATYR). **satyriasis** (-rī´əsis) *n.* (*Med.*) unrestrained sexual appetite in men. **satyric** (sətir´-) *a.* **satyrid** (sat´irid) *n.* any butterfly of the family Satyridae.

Usage note The nouns *satyr* and *satire* should not be confused: a *satyr* is a mythological creature, and a *satire* a work ridiculing vice or folly. The corresponding adjectives *satyric* and *satiric* (pronounced the same) should also be distinguished.

sauce (saws) *n.* **1** a preparation, usu. liquid, taken with foods as an accompaniment or to enhance the taste. **2** anything that gives piquancy or makes palatable. **3** (*coll.*) impertinence, impudence. **4** (*N Am.*) stewed fruit, esp. apples. ~*v.t.* (*coll.*) to be saucy or impudent towards. **sauceboat** *n.* a low broad jug for holding sauce. **sauceless** *a.* **saucepan** *n.* a metal pan or pot, usu. cylindrical with a long handle, for boiling or stewing, orig. a pan for cooking sauces. **saucepanful** *n.* (*pl.* **saucepanfuls**). **sauce tartare** *n.* TARTARE SAUCE (under TARTARE). **saucy** *a.* (*comp.* **saucier**, *superl.* **sauciest**) **1** impudent, cheeky. **2** (*coll.*) smart, sprightly. **3** (*coll.*) smutty, suggestive. **saucily** *adv.* **sauciness** *n.*

saucer (saw´sə) *n.* **1** a shallow dish for placing a cup on and catching drips. **2** any small flattish vessel, dish or receptacle of similar use. **saucerful** *n.* (*pl.* **saucerfuls**). **saucerless** *a.*

Saudi (sow´di, saw´-), **Saudi Arabian** *n.* (*pl.* **Saudis, Saudi Arabians**) **1** a native or inhabitant of Saudi Arabia. **2** a member of the dynasty founded by King Saud. ~*a.* of or relating to Saudi Arabia or the dynasty founded by King Saud.

sauerkraut (sow´əkrowt) *n.* finely chopped cabbage compressed with salt until it ferments.

sauger (saw´gə) *n.* (*N Am.*) the smaller N American pikeperch, *Stizostedion canadense.*

sauna (saw´nə) *n.* **1** a Finnish-style steam bath. **2** a building or room used for saunas. **3** a period spent in a sauna.

saunter (sawn´tə) *v.i.* **1** to wander about idly and leisurely. **2** to walk leisurely (along). ~*n.* **1** a leisurely ramble or stroll. **2** a sauntering gait. **saunterer** *n.* **saunteringly** *adv.*

saurian (saw´riən) *a.* of, relating to or resembling the Sauria, an order of reptiles formerly including the crocodiles and lizards, but now the lizards alone.

saurischian (sawris´kiən, -rish´iən) *a.* of or relating to the Saurischia, an order of dinosaurs. ~*n.* a dinosaur of this order.

sauropod (saw´rəpod) *n.* any of the Sauropoda, an extinct order of gigantic herbivores.

saury (saw´ri) *n.* (*pl.* **sauries**) a sea fish, *Scomberesox saurus,* with elongated body ending in a beak.

sausage (sos´ij) *n.* **1** an article of food consisting of pork or other meat minced, seasoned and stuffed into a length of animal's gut or a similar receptacle. **2** anything of similar cylindrical shape. **not a sausage** (*coll.*) nothing at all. **sausage dog** *n.* (*coll.*) a dachshund. **sausage machine** *n.* **1** a machine used in manufacturing sausages. **2** a relentlessly uniform process. **sausage meat** *n.* meat used for stuffing sausages, esp. cooked separately as stuffing etc. **sausage roll** *n.* sausage meat enclosed in pastry and baked.

sauté (sō´tā) *a.* lightly fried. ~*v.t.* (*pres.p.* **sautéing,** *past, p.p.* **sautéd, sautéed**) to fry lightly. ~*n.* a dish of sautéd food.

Sauternes (sōtœn´) *n.* a sweet white Bordeaux wine.

savage (sav´ij) *a.* **1** fierce, cruel. **2** uncivilized, in a primitive condition. **3** untamed, wild. **4** (*coll.*) extremely angry, enraged. ~*n.* **1** a person of extreme brutality. **2** (*offensive*) †a human being in a primitive state, esp. a member of a nomadic tribe living by hunting and fishing. ~*v.t.* **1** (esp. of an animal) to attack violently. **2** to attack or criticize. **savagedom, savagism** *n.* **savagely** *adv.* **savageness** *n.* **savagery** *n.* (*pl.* **savageries**).

savannah (səvan´ə), **savanna** *n.* an extensive treeless plain covered with low vegetation, esp. in tropical America.

savant (sav´ənt) *n.* a person of learning, esp. an eminent scientist. **savante** (sav´ənt) *n.* a female savant.

savate (savaht´) *n.* a style of boxing in which the feet are used as well as the hands.

save (sāv) *v.t.* **1** to preserve, rescue or deliver as from danger or harm. **2** to deliver from sin. **3** to keep undamaged or untouched. **4** to keep from being spent, used or lost. **5** to refrain from spending or using. **6** to spare. **7** to prevent. **8** to prevent or obviate the need for. **9** to be in time for, to catch. **10** to preserve an opponent from scoring (a goal etc.). ~*v.i.* **1** to avoid waste or undue expenditure. **2** to set aside money for future use. ~*prep.* **1** except, saving. **2** leaving out, not including. ~*conj.* (*poet.*) unless. ~*n.* **1** the act of preventing an opponent from scoring a goal. **2** in bridge, a sacrifice-bid. **savable, saveable** *a.* **save-all** *n.* anything that prevents things from being wasted. **save-as-you-earn** *n.* a government savings scheme in which regular contributions are deducted from earnings. **saver** *n.* **1** a person who or thing which saves, (*usu. in comb.,* as *lifesaver*). **2** a cheap fare. **3** (*sl.*) in racing, a hedging bet. **saving** *a.* **1** preserving from danger, loss etc. **2** (*often in comb.*) economical, frugal. **3** reserving or expressing a reservation, stipulation etc. ~*n.* **1** the act of economizing. **2** (*usu. pl.*) that which is saved, an economy. **3** (*pl.*) money saved, esp. regularly or over a period of time. ~*prep.* **1** save, except. **2** with due respect to. **saving clause** *n.* (*Law*) a clause containing a stipulation of exemption etc. **saving grace** *n.* a virtue or quality in a person or thing that compensates for other less admirable characteristics. **savingly** adv. **savings account** n. a deposit account. **savings and loan** n. (N Am.) a cooperative association similar to a building society. **savings bank** n. a bank receiving small deposits and usu. devoting any profits to the payment of interest. **savings certificate** n. an interest-bearing document issued by the Government for savers.

saveloy (sav'əloi) n. a highly-seasoned dried sausage of salted pork (orig. of brains).

savin (sav'in), **savine** n. **1** an evergreen bush or low tree, *Juniperus sabina*, with bluish-green fruit, yielding an oil formerly used medicinally. **2** (N Am.) RED CEDAR (under RED).

saviour (sā'vyə), (N Am.) **savior** n. a person who preserves, rescues, or redeems. **our/ the Saviour** Christ, as the redeemer of humankind.

savoir faire (savwah feə') n. quickness to do the right thing, esp. in social situations.

savory (sā'vəri) n. (pl. **savories**) a plant of the aromatic genus *Satureja*, esp. *S. hortensis* and *S. montana*, used in cookery.

savour (sā'və), (N Am.) **savor** n. **1** (characteristic) flavour, taste, relish. **2** a particular taste or smell. **3** characteristic quality. **4** suggestive quality. ~v.t. **1** to relish, to enjoy the savour of. **2** to give a flavour to. **3** to perceive, to discern. ~v.i. to have a particular smell or flavour. **savourless** a. **savoury** a. **1** having a pleasant savour. **2** palatable, appetizing. **3** free from offensive smells. **4** salty, spicy etc. (as opposed to sweet). **5** respectable, wholesome. ~n. (pl. **savouries**) a savoury dish, esp. as served as an appetizer or digestive. **savourily** adv. **savouriness** n.

savoy (səvoi') n. a hardy variety of cabbage with wrinkled leaves.

savvy (sav'i) v.t., v.i. (3rd pers. sing. pres. **savvies**, pres.p. **savvying**, past, p.p. **savvied**) (sl.) to know, to understand. ~n. understanding, knowingness, cleverness. ~a. (comp. **savvier**, superl. **savviest**) (esp. N Am.) knowing, wise.

saw[1] (saw) n. **1** a cutting-instrument, usu. of steel, with a toothed edge, worked by hand, or power-driven, as in circular or ribbon form. **2** a tool or implement used as a saw. **3** (Zool. etc.) a serrated body part or organ. ~v.t. (past **sawed**, p.p. **sawn** (sawn), **sawed**) **1** to cut with a saw. **2** to form or make with a saw. **3** to make motions through as if sawing. ~v.i. **1** to use a saw. **2** to undergo cutting with a saw. **3** to make motions of one sawing. **sawbench** n. a circular saw with a bench. **sawbill** n. a duck with a serrated beak, esp. the merganser. **sawbones** n. (sl.) a surgeon or doctor. **sawbuck** n. (N Am.) **1** a sawhorse. **2** (sl.) a $10 note. **saw-doctor** n. a machine for cutting teeth in a saw. **sawdust** n. small fragments of wood produced in sawing, used for packing etc. **saw-edged** a. serrated. **sawfish** n. (pl. in general **sawfish**, in particular **sawfishes**) a fish of the family Pristidae, with an elongated, sawlike snout. **sawfly** n. (pl. **sawflies**) any of various hymenopterous insects of the superfamily Tenthredinoidea,

furnished with a sawlike ovipositor. **saw frame**, **saw-gate** n. a frame in which a saw blade is held taut. **saw-gin** n. a cotton gin with serrated edges. **sawgrass** n. (esp. N Am.) a sedge of the genus *Cladium*. **sawhorse** n. a rack on which wood is laid for sawing. **sawlike** a. **sawmill** n. a mill with machinery for sawing timber. **sawn-off**, (N Am.) **sawed-off** a. **1** (of a shotgun) having the end of the barrel cut off with or as with a saw. **2** (coll.) (of a person) short. **saw-pit** n. a pit over which timber is sawed, one person standing above and the other below the log. **saw-set, saw-wrest** n. a tool for slanting the teeth of a saw alternately outward. **sawtooth** a. **1** (also **sawtoothed**) shaped like the teeth of a saw. **2** (of a waveform) showing a slow linear rise and rapid linear fall. **saw-wort** n. a plant of the daisy family, *Serratula tinctoria*, having serrated leaves yielding a yellow dye. **sawyer** (-yə) n. **1** a person employed in sawing timber into planks, or wood for fuel. **2** (N Am.) a tree fallen into a river and swept along, sawing up and down in the water. **3** (New Zeal.) a kind of grasshopper.

saw[2] (saw) n. a saying, a proverb.

saw[3] SEE[1].

sax[1] (saks) n. (coll.) **1** a saxophone. **2** a saxophone-player. **saxist** n.

sax[2] (saks), **zax** (zaks) n. a slate-cutter's chopping and trimming tool with a point for making holes.

saxboard (saks'bawd) n. the uppermost strake of an open boat.

saxe (saks) n. saxe blue. **saxe blue** n. a light greyish blue. **saxe-blue** a.

saxhorn (saks'hawn) n. a brass musical wind instrument with a long winding tube, a wide opening and several valves.

saxifrage (sak'sifrāj) n. any plant of the genus *Saxifraga*, consisting largely of Alpine or rock plants with tufted, mossy or encrusted foliage and small flowers.

Saxon (sak'sən) n. **1** (Hist.) a member of a Germanic people from N Germany who conquered England in the 5th and 6th cents. **2** an Anglo-Saxon. **3** the Old Saxon or the Anglo-Saxon language. **4** a native or inhabitant of modern Saxony. **5** the Germanic elements of English. ~a. **1** (Hist.) of or relating to the Saxons, their country or language. **2** Anglo-Saxon. **3** of or relating to Saxony or its inhabitants. **Saxon architecture** n. a style of architecture used in England before the Norman Conquest. **Saxon blue** n. indigo dissolved in sulphuric acid, used by dyers. **Saxondom** n. **Saxonism** n. **Saxonist** n. **Saxonize**, **Saxonise** v.t., v.i.

saxony (sak'səni) n. a fine wool or woollen material produced in Saxony.

saxophone (sak'səfōn) n. **1** a brass musical wind instrument with a single reed used as a powerful substitute for the clarinet. **2** a saxophone-player. **saxophonic** (-fon'-) a. **saxophonist** (-sof'ə-, -əfōn-) n.

say (sā) v.t. (3rd pers. sing. pres. **says** (sez), †**saith** (seth), pres.p. **saying**, past, p.p. **said** (sed)) **1** to utter in or as words, to speak. **2** to repeat. **3** to tell, to state. **4** to allege, to report. **5** to give as an opinion or answer, to decide. **6** to convey (meaning or intention). ~v.i. to speak, to answer. ~n. **1** what one says or has to say, a statement. **2** (coll.) one's turn to speak. **3** authority, influence. ~adv. **1** approximately, about. **2** for example. ~int. (N Am.) used to express surprise, to attract attention etc. **I'll say** (coll.) used to express agreement. **I say!** an exclamation of mild surprise, protest etc. or calling for attention. **it is said** it is generally reported or rumoured. **not to say** indeed one might say, perhaps even. **says/ sez you!** (sl.) used to express incredulity. **say when** (coll.) tell me when to stop. **that is to say 1** in other words. **2** or at least. **they say** it is said. **to say for oneself** to say by way of conversation etc. **to say much for** to show the high quality of. **to say no** to refuse or disagree. **to say nothing of** not to mention. **to say out** to express fully. **to say something** to make a short speech. **to say something for** to say much for. **to say the word 1** to say that you agree. **2** to give the order etc. **to say yes** to agree. **what do/ would you say to?** how about? **when all is said and done** in the long run. **you can say that again!** (coll.) used to express agreement. **you don't say so** (coll.) used to express amazement, disbelief etc. **you said it!** (coll.) used to express agreement. **said** a. (Law or facet.) before-mentioned. **saying** n. a maxim, an adage. **as the saying goes** used to introduce a proverb, cliché etc. **there is no saying** it is impossible to know. **to go without saying** to be extremely obvious. **say-so** n. (pl. **say-sos**) **1** an unfounded assertion. **2** right of decision, authority.

SAYE abbr. save-as-you-earn.
Sb chem. symbol antimony.
SBN abbr. Standard Book Number.
S by E abbr. South by East.
S by W abbr. South by West.
SC abbr. special constable.
Sc chem. symbol scandium.
sc abbr. **1** scilicet (namely). **2** (also **s.c.**) small capitals.

scab (skab) n. **1** an incrustation formed over a sore etc., in healing. **2** (coll., derog.) a worker who refuses to join in a strike or who takes the place of a striker, a blackleg. **3** a highly contagious skin disease resembling mange, attacking horses, cattle and esp. sheep. **4** any one of various fungoid plant diseases. **5** a despicable scoundrel. ~v.i. (pres.p. **scabbing**, past, p.p. **scabbed**) **1** to form a scab. **2** (derog.) to work as a scab or blackleg. **scabbed** a. **scabby** a. (comp. **scabbier**, superl. **scabbiest**). **scabbily** adv. **scabbiness** n. **scablike** a.

scabbard (skab´əd) n. **1** the sheath of a sword or similar weapon. **2** (N Am.) the sheath of a revolver etc. **scabbard-fish** n. (pl. **scabbard-fish**)

1 a small silver sea fish, Lepidopus caudatus, with a bladelike body. **2** any of various related fishes.
scabies (skā´biz, -biēz) n. a contagious skin disease, caused by the itch mite.
scabious (skā´biəs) a. consisting of or covered with scabs. ~n. a plant of the herbaceous genus Scabiosa, Knautia etc., having involucrate heads of blue, pink and white flowers.
scabrous (skā´brəs, skab´-) a. **1** rough, rugged or uneven. **2** scaly, scurfy. **3** difficult, thorny, awkward to handle. **4** approaching the indecent, indelicate. **scabridity** (skəbrid´-), **scabrousness** n. **scabrously** adv.

Usage note Scabrous should not be used as though it meant scurrilous or scathing.
---

scad (skad) n. (pl. in general **scad**, in particular **scads**) any fish of the family Carangidae, usu. having large spiky scales, esp. the horse mackerel Trachurus trachurus.
scads (skadz) n.pl. (N Am., coll.) large amounts.
scaffold (skaf´əld, -ōld) n. **1** a temporary structure of poles and ties supporting a platform for the use of workers building or repairing a house or other building. **2** (Hist.) a temporary raised platform for the execution of criminals. **3** a platform, or stage for shows or spectators. **4** the bony framework of a structure, esp. one to be covered by developed parts. **5** (fig.) capital punishment. ~v.t. **1** to furnish with a scaffold. **2** to uphold, to support. **scaffolder** n. **scaffolding** n. **1** a scaffold or system of scaffolds for builders, shows, pageants etc. **2** a framework. **3** materials for scaffolds.
scalar (skā´lə) a. (Math., Physics) of the nature of a scalar. ~n. (Math.) a quantity having magnitude but no direction (e.g. time).
scalawag SCALLYWAG.
scald (skawld) v.t. **1** to burn with or as with a hot liquid or vapour. **2** to clean (out) with boiling water. **3** to cook briefly in hot water or steam. **4** to raise (milk) nearly to boiling point. **5** to treat (poultry) with boiling water to remove feathers etc. ~n. **1** an injury to the skin from hot liquid or vapour. **2** a fruit disease characterized by discoloration, caused by exposure to sunlight, gases etc. **like a scalded cat** moving very fast. **scalder** n.
scale[1] (skāl) n. **1** each of the thin horny plates forming a protective covering on the skin of fishes, reptiles etc. **2** (Bot.) a modified leaf, hair, feather or other structure resembling this. **3** a thin flake of dry skin. **4** a scab. **5** an incrustation. **6** a coating deposited on the insides of pipes, kettles etc. by hard water. **7** a small plate or flake of metal etc. **8** plaque formed on teeth. ~v.t. **1** to strip the scales off. **2** to remove in scales or layers. **3** to deposit scale on. ~v.i. **1** to form scales. **2** to come off in scales. **3** to become coated with scale. **to remove the scales from someone's eyes** to reveal the

truth to someone who has been deceived. **scale-board** *n.* a thin board for the back of a picture etc. **scale-bug** *n.* a scale insect. **scaled** *a.* **scale-fern** *n.* any of various spleenworts, esp. *Asplenium ceterach.* **scale insect** *n.* an insect, esp. of the family Coccidae, whose female secretes a protective waxy shell and lives attached to a host plant. **scale-leaf** *n.* a modified leaf that resembles a scale. **scaleless** *a.* **scale-moss** *n.* a type of liverwort with scalelike leaves. **scaler**[1] *n.* **scale-winged** *a.* having the wings covered with scales, lepidopterous. **scaly** *a.* (*comp.* **scalier,** *superl.* **scaliest**). **scaliness** *n.* **scaly anteater** *n.* the pangolin.

scale[2] (skāl) *n.* **1** the dish of a balance. **2** (*usu. pl.*) a simple balance. **3** (*usu. pl.*) a machine for weighing. **4** (**Scales**) Libra. ~*v.t.* to amount to in weight. **to throw into the scale** to add as a factor in a contest, debate etc. **to tip the scales 1** to cause one pan of a scales to become lower than the other because of greater weight, to weigh in (at). **2** to make the significant difference. **to turn the scales** to tip the scales.

scale[3] (skāl) *n.* **1** anything graduated or marked with lines or degrees at regular intervals, such as a scheme for classification. **2** (*Math.*) a basis for a numerical system in which the value of a figure depends on its place in the order. **3** a system of correspondence between different magnitudes, relative dimensions etc. **4** a set of marks or a rule or other instrument marked with these showing exact distances, proportions, values etc., used for measuring, calculating etc. **5** (*Mus.*) all the tones of a key arranged in ascending or descending order according to pitch. ~*v.t.* **1** to climb by or as by a ladder. **2** to clamber up. **3** to draw or otherwise represent to scale or proper proportions. **4** to alter the scale of. **5** to arrange, estimate or fix according to a scale. ~*v.i.* to have a common scale, to be commensurable. **in scale** in proportion to the surroundings etc. **to play scales** to play the notes of a scale as a musical exercise. **to scale** in proportion to actual dimensions. **to scale down** to make smaller proportionately. **to scale up** to make larger proportionately. **to sing scales** to sing a scale as an exercise for the voice. **scalable** *a.* **scalability** (-bil´-) *n.* **scale of notation** *n.* (*Math.*) the ratio between units in a numerical system. **scaler**[2] *n.* **scaling-ladder** *n.* (*Hist.*) a ladder used in storming fortified places.

scalene (skā´lēn) *a.* **1** (of a triangle) having no two sides equal. **2** (of a cone or cylinder) having the axis inclined to the base. ~*n.* a scalene triangle.

scaler[1] SCALE[1].

scaler[2] SCALE[3].

scallion (skal´yən) *n.* a variety of onion or shallot.

scallop (skol´əp, skal´-), **scollop** (skol´-) *n.* **1** any of various bivalve molluscs of the genus *Pecten* or a related genus, with ridges and flutings radiating from the middle of the hinge and an undulating margin. **2** the large adductor muscle of a scallop eaten as food. **3** (*Hist.*) a single shell of a scallop worn as a pilgrim's badge. **4** (*also* **scallop shell**) such a shell or a small shallow dish or pan used for cooking and serving oysters etc. in. **5** (*pl.*) an ornamental undulating edging cut like that of a scallop shell. **6** ESCALOPE. ~*v.t.* (*pres.p.* **scalloping,** *past, p.p.* **scalloped**) **1** to cut or indent the edge of, like a scallop shell. **2** to cook in a scallop. **scalloper** *n.*

scallywag (skal´iwag), **scalawag** (-əwag), **scallawag** *n.* a scamp, a rascal.

scalp (skalp) *n.* **1** the top of the head. **2** (*Hist.*) the skin of this with the hair belonging to it, torn off by N American Indians as a trophy of victory. **3** a trophy or token signifying conquest. ~*v.t.* **1** (*Hist.*) to tear or take the scalp from. **2** to criticize or abuse savagely. **3** (*N Am.*) to defeat or humiliate. **4** (*esp. N Am., coll.*) to buy (cheaply) and resell so as to make a large profit. **5** (*N Am.*) to buy and sell so as to take small quick profits on (stocks etc.). ~*v.i.* (*N Am.*) to take small profits to minimize risk. **scalper** *n.* **1** a person who or thing which scalps. **2** a wood engraver's tool. **scalpless** *a.*

scalpel (skal´pəl) *n.* a small knife used in surgical operations and anatomical dissections.

scaly SCALE[1].

scam (skam) *n.* (*N Am., sl.*) **1** a trick or swindle. **2** a story or rumour. ~*v.i.* (*pres.p.* **scamming,** *past, p.p.* **scammed**) to commit fraud. ~*v.t.* to swindle. **scammer** *n.*

scamp[1] (skamp) *n.* (*coll.*) **1** a worthless person, a knave, a rogue. **2** a mischievous child. **scampish** *a.*

scamp[2] (skamp) *v.t.* to do or execute (work etc.) in a careless manner or with bad material.

scamper (skam´pə) *v.i.* to run rapidly, playfully, hastily, or impulsively. ~*n.* a hasty or playful run.

scampi (skam´pi) *n.* **1** (*pl.*) large prawns such as the Norway lobster or Dublin (Bay) prawn, esp. when fried in breadcrumbs or batter. **2** (*sing.*) (*pl.* **scampi, scampis**) a dish of these.

scan (skan) *v.t.* (*pres.p.* **scanning,** *past, p.p.* **scanned**) **1** to examine closely or intently. **2** to examine and produce an image of (a body part) using X-rays etc. **3** to observe with a radar beam. **4** to continuously traverse (an area or object) with a beam of laser light, electrons etc. in order to examine or to produce or transmit an image. **5** to count, mark or test the metrical feet or the syllables of (a line of verse). **6** to examine sequentially or systematically. **7** to glance at or read through hastily. ~*v.i.* to be metrically correct, to agree with the rules of scansion. ~*n.* **1** an act of scanning. **2** an image or display produced by scanning. **scannable** *a.* **scanner** *n.* **1** a person who or thing which scans. **2** the aerial of a radar device. **3** an instrument used in scanning the human body, esp. one that takes radiographic photographs from various angles and combines them into a three-dimensional image. **scanning** *n.*, *a.* **scanning electron microscope** *n.* an electron microscope in which a beam of electrons scans an object to produce a three-dimensional image.

scandal (skan´dəl) *n.* **1** a disgraceful action, person etc. **2** offence or censure at some act or conduct, esp. as expressed in common talk. **3** damage to reputation, shame. **4** malicious gossip. **5** (*Law*) a defamatory statement, esp. of an irrelevant nature. **scandalize, scandalise** *v.t.* to offend by improper or outrageous conduct. **scandalmonger** *n.* a person who disseminates scandal. **scandalous** *a.* **scandalously** *adv.* **scandalousness** *n.* **scandal sheet** *n.* (*derog.*) a newspaper which publishes scandal or gossip.

Scandinavian (skandinā´viən) *a.* of or relating to Scandinavia (Norway, Sweden, Denmark and Iceland), its language or literature. ~*n.* **1** a native or inhabitant of Scandinavia. **2** the languages of Scandinavia collectively.

scandium (skan´diəm) *n.* (*Chem.*) a rare metallic element, at. no. 21, chem. symbol Sc, discovered in certain Swedish yttrium ores.

scannable, scanner etc. SCAN.

scansion (skan´shən) *n.* **1** the act of scanning verse. **2** a system of scanning.

scant (skant) *a.* **1** scarcely sufficient, not enough, deficient. **2** short (of). **scantly** *adv.* **scantness** *n.* **scanty** *a.* (*comp.* **scantier,** *superl.* **scantiest**) **1** deficient, insufficient. **2** scarcely adequate in extent, size or quantity. **scantily** *adv.* **scantiness** *n.*

scantling (skant´ling) *n.* **1** a beam less than 5 in. (12.7 cm) in breadth and thickness. **2** the sectional measurement of timber. **3** the measurement of stone in all three dimensions. **4** a set of fixed dimensions, esp. in shipbuilding.

scape (skāp) *n.* **1** a leafless radical stem bearing the flower. **2** the basal part of an insect's antenna.

-scape (skāp) *comb. form* scene, view, as in *seascape, townscape.*

scapegoat (skāp´gōt) *n.* a person made to bear blame due to another. ~*v.t.* to make a scapegoat of. **scapegoater** *n.* **scapegoating** *n.*

scapegrace (skāp´grās) *n.* a graceless, good-for-nothing person, esp. a child.

scaphoid (skaf´oid) *a.* boat-shaped, navicular. ~*n.* (*Anat.*) a scaphoid bone. **scaphoid bone** *n.* (*Anat.*) a bone of the carpus or tarsus.

scapula (skap´ūlə) *n.* (*pl.* **scapulae** (-lē), **scapulas**) the shoulder blade. **scapular** *a.* of or relating to the scapula or shoulder. ~*n.* **1** in the Roman Catholic Church, a vestment usu. consisting of two strips of cloth worn by certain monastic orders across the shoulders and hanging down the breast and back. **2** a bandage for the shoulder blade. **3** any of a series of feathers springing from the base of the humerus in birds, and lying along the side of the back. **scapular feather** *n.* a feather covering the shoulder. **scapulary** *n.* (*pl.*

scapularies) **1** in the Roman Catholic Church, a scapular. **2** a scapular feather.

scar[1] (skah) *n.* **1** a mark left by a wound, burn, ulcer etc. **2** the mark left by the fall of a leaf, stem, seed, deciduous part etc. **3** the after-effects of emotional distress. ~*v.t.* (*pres.p.* **scarring,** *past, p.p.* **scarred**) **1** to mark with a scar or scars. **2** to leave with lasting adverse effects. ~*v.i.* to form a scar, to cicatrize. **scarless** *a.*

scar[2] (skah), **scaur** (skaw) *n.* a crag, a cliff, a precipitous escarpment.

scar[3] (skah) *n.* a parrotfish.

scarab (skar´əb) *n.* **1** an ancient Egyptian sacred beetle, *Scarabaeus sacer.* **2** a seal or gem cut in the shape of a beetle, worn as an amulet by the Egyptians. **3** a scarabaeid. **scarabaeid** (-bē´id) *a.* of or relating to the Scarabaeidae, a family of beetles containing the dung-beetles. ~*n.* a beetle of this family.

scarce (skeəs) *a.* **1** infrequent, uncommon. **2** insufficient, not plentiful. ~*adv.* hardly, scarcely. **to make oneself scarce 1** (*coll.*) to keep out of the way. **2** (*coll.*) to be off, to decamp. **scarcely** *adv.* **1** hardly, barely. **2** only with difficulty. **3** not quite (used as a polite negative). **4** certainly not. **scarceness** *n.* **scarcity** *n.* (*pl.* **scarcities**) a deficiency or dearth (of).

Usage note When *scarcely* refers to time ('only just'), a following *when* is preferable to *than* (so *She had scarcely got in when the phone rang*).

scare (skeə) *v.t.* **1** to frighten, to alarm. **2** to drive (away) through fear. ~*v.i.* to become frightened. ~*n.* **1** a sudden fright, a panic. **2** a widespread terror of e.g. invasion, epidemic etc. **3** a financial panic. **to scare out** to scare up. **to scare up 1** (*esp. NAm.*) to beat up (game). **2** (*coll.*) to find or produce quickly. **scarecrow** *n.* **1** a figure set up to frighten birds away from crops etc. **2** (*coll.*) a shabby or absurd-looking person, a guy. **scared** *a.* **scaredy-cat** (skeə´di-) *n.* (*coll.*) a person who is easily frightened. **scaremonger** *n.* a person who causes scares, esp. by circulating unfounded reports etc. **scaremongering** *n.* **scarer** *n.* **scary** *a.* (*comp.* **scarier,** *superl.* **scariest**). **scarily** *adv.* **scariness** *n.*

scarf[1] (skahf) *n.* (*pl.* **scarfs, scarves** (-vz)) a long strip or square of some material worn round the neck and shoulders or over the head for warmth or decoration. **scarfed** *a.* **scarf pin, scarf ring** *n.* a pin or ring, usu. of gold, used to fasten a scarf. **scarf-skin** *n.* the outer layer of skin, the cuticle.

Usage note The plural *scarfs* is preferred to *scarves.*

scarf[2] (skahf) *v.t.* **1** to join the ends of (timber) by means of a scarf joint. **2** to cut a scarf in or on. **3** to strip the blubber or skin from (a whale). ~*n.* (*pl.* **scarfs**) **1** (*also* **scarf joint**) a joint made by bevelling or notching so that the thickness is not increased, and then bolting or strapping together. **2** a bevelled or notched end that forms such a joint. **3** an incision or groove cut along the body of a whale before stripping off the blubber.

scarf[5] (skahf) v.t. (N Am., coll.) to eat or drink greedily (usu. with down).

scarify[1] (skeə'rifī, skar´-) v.t. (3rd pers. sing. pres. **scarifies**, pres.p. **scarifying**, past, p.p. **scarified**) **1** to scratch or make slight incisions in. **2** to loosen the surface (of soil). **3** to pain, to torture, to criticize mercilessly. **scarification** (-fikā'shən) n. **scarifier** n. **1** a person who scarifies. **2** an implement or machine for breaking up soil etc.

scarify[2] (skeə'rifī) v.t. (3rd pers. sing. pres. **scarifies**, pres.p. **scarifying**, past, p.p. **scarified**) (coll.) to scare, frighten. ~v.i. to be scared or frightened. **scarifyingly** adv.

scarily, scariness SCARY (under SCARE).

scarious (skeə'riəs), **scariose** (-ōs) a. (of bracts etc.) membraneous and dry.

scarlatina (skahlətē'nə) n. (a mild form of) scarlet fever.

scarlet (skah'lit) n. **1** a bright red colour tending towards orange. **2** cloth or dress of this colour, esp. official robes or uniform. ~a. **1** of a scarlet colour. **2** dressed in scarlet. **scarlet fever** n. an infectious fever characterized by the eruption of red patches on the skin. **scarlet hat** n. **1** a cardinal's hat. **2** the rank of cardinal. **scarlet pimpernel** n. a small annual wild plant, *Anagallis arvensis*, which has flowers that close in bad weather; also called *poor man's weather-glass*. **scarlet rash** n. roseola. **scarlet runner** n. a trailing bean, *Phaseolus coccineus*, with scarlet flowers. **scarlet woman** n. (pl. **scarlet women**) (derog.) a prostitute.

scaroid SCARUS.

scarp (skahp) n. **1** a steep or nearly perpendicular slope. **2** the interior slope of the ditch at the foot of the parapet of a fortification. ~v.t. to cut down so as to be steep or nearly perpendicular. **scarped** a. precipitous, abrupt.

scarper (skah'pə) v.i. (sl.) **1** to leave in a hurry. **2** to go away without notice or warning.

Scart (skaht), **SCART** n. a 24-pin socket used to connect video equipment.

scarus (skeə'rəs) n. any fish of the genus *Scarus*, which have brightly coloured scales; also called *parrotfish*. **scaroid** (-roid) a., n.

scarves SCARF[1].

scary SCARE.

scat[1] (skat) int. go away!, be off! ~v.i. (pres.p. **scatting**, past, p.p. **scatted**) (coll.) **1** to depart hastily. **2** (esp. N Am.) to move quickly.

scat[2] (skat) n. jazz singing in meaningless syllables. ~v.i. (pres.p. **scatting**, past, p.p. **scatted**) to sing in this way.

scat[3] (skat) n. **1** excrement. **2** animal droppings.

scathe (skādh) v.t. **1** (poet.) to hurt, to harm, to injure, esp. by scorching. **2** to attack severely with sarcasm, criticism etc. **scatheless** a. **scathing** a. **1** hurtful, harmful. **2** (of sarcasm etc.) very bitter or severe. **scathingly** adv.

scatology (skətol'əji) n. **1** interest in or literature

characterized by obscenity. **2** the study of fossil excrement or coprolites. **3** the biological study of excrement, esp. to determine diet. **scatological** (skatəloj´-) a. **scatophagous** (-tof'əgəs) a. feeding on dung.

scatter (skat'ə) v.t. **1** to throw loosely about, to fling in all directions. **2** to strew. **3** to cause to separate in various directions, to disperse. **4** to dissipate. **5** (Physics) to diffuse (radiation etc.) or cause to spread out. **6** to fire (a charge) diffusely. ~v.i. **1** to disperse. **2** to be dissipated or diffused. **3** to fire a charge of shot diffusely. ~n. **1** the act of scattering. **2** a small number scattered about. **3** the extent of scattering. **scatterbrain** n. a person who is incapable of thinking seriously or unable to concentrate. **scatterbrained** a. **scatter cushion, scatter rug** n. a small cushion or rug which can be moved to any position in a room. **scatter diagram, scatter plot** n. a graph that plots the values of two variables along two axes at right angles to each other. **scattered** a. **1** irregularly situated, not together. **2** widely apart. **scatterer** n. **scatter-gun** n. (esp. N Am.) a shotgun. ~a. scattershot. **scattering** n. **1** the act of dispersing or strewing something. **2** a small amount or number irregularly strewn. **3** the deflecting or spreading out of a beam of radiation in passing through matter. **scatteringly** adv. **scattershot** a. (esp. N Am.) random, haphazard.

scatty (skat'i) a. (comp. **scattier**, superl. **scattiest**) (coll.) incapable of prolonged concentration, empty-headed, giddy. **scattily** adv. **scattiness** n.

scaup (skawp), **scaup duck** n. a diving duck of the genus *Aythya*, esp. *A. marila*, found in the northern regions.

scauper (skaw'pə) n. a wood engraver's gouge-like tool.

scaur SCAUR[2].

scavenger (skav'ənjə) n. **1** a person who collects waste or discarded objects. **2** an organism feeding on refuse, carrion etc. **scavenge** v.t. to search for or salvage (something usable) from among waste or discarded material. ~v.i. **1** to act as a scavenger. **2** to search for usable material. ~n. the action or process of scavenging. **scavengery** n.

Sc.D abbr. Doctor of Science.

SCE abbr. Scottish Certificate of Education.

scena (shā'nə) n. (pl. **scene** (-nā)) (Mus.) a long elaborate solo piece or scene in opera.

scenario (sinah'riō) n. (pl. **scenarios**) **1** a sketch or outline of the scenes and main points of a play etc. **2** the script of a film with dialogue and directions for the producer during the actual shooting. **3** an account or outline of projected or imagined future events. **scenarist** n.

Usage note *Scenario* should not be used as though it meant simply a scene or situation.

scend SEND.

scene (sēn) n. **1** the place where anything occurs or is exhibited as on a stage. **2** the place in which the action of a play or story is supposed to take place. **3** a single event, situation or incident in a play or film. **4** a description of an incident, situation etc. from life. **5** a striking incident, esp. an exhibition of feeling or passion. **6** a division of a play comprising so much as passes without change of locality or break of time, or, in French drama, without intermediate entrances or exits. **7** a film or television sequence. **8** a landscape, regarded as a piece of scenery. **9** (*coll.*) one's usual or preferred social environment, area of interest etc. **10** (*coll.*) an area of activity or business. **11** any of the painted frames, hangings or other devices used to give an appearance of reality to the action of a play. **behind the scenes 1** at the back of the stage. **2** in possession of facts etc., not generally known. **to come on the scene** to arrive, to appear. **to quit the scene** to die or to leave. **to set the scene 1** to describe the location of events. **2** to give background information. **scene-dock** *n.* a place near the stage in a theatre for storing scenery. **scenery** (-əri) *n.* (*pl.* **sceneries**) **1** the various parts or accessories used on the stage to represent the actual scene of the action. **2** the views presented by natural features, esp. when picturesque. **scene-shifter** *n.* a person employed in a theatre to move scenery. **scene shifting** *n.* **scenic** *a.* **1** characterized by beautiful natural scenery. **2** of or relating to natural scenery. **3** (of a painting etc.) depicting a scene or incident. **4** of or relating to the stage. **5** arranged for effect. **scenically** *adv.* **scenic railway** *n.* **1** a miniature railway that runs through artificial representations of picturesque scenery. **2** a switchback railway at a funfair.

scent (sent) *v.t.* **1** to perceive by smell. **2** to recognize the odour of. **3** to begin to suspect. **4** to trace or hunt (out) by or as by smelling. **5** to perfume. ~*v.i.* **1** to exercise the sense of smell. **2** to give forth a smell. ~*n.* **1** odour, esp. of a pleasant kind. **2** the odour left by an animal forming a trail by which it can be followed. **3** pieces of paper left as a trail in a paperchase. **4** a trail to be pursued. **5** a clue. **6** a liquid essence containing fragrant extracts from flowers etc. **7** the sense of smell, esp. the power of recognizing or tracing things by smelling. **on the scent** having a useful clue, lead etc. **to put someone off the scent** to throw someone off the scent. **to scent out** to discover by smelling or searching. **to throw someone off the scent** to mislead someone. **scent-bag** *n.* a bag containing aniseed etc., used to leave a track of scent for hounds to follow. **scented** *a.* **scent gland** *n.* a gland secreting an odorous substance, as in the musk deer, civet etc. **scentless** *a.* **scent organ** *n.* a scent gland.

sceptic (skep´tik), (*esp. N Am.*) **skeptic** *n.* **1** a person of a questioning habit of mind. **2** a person who casts doubt on any statement, theory etc., esp. in a cynical manner. **3** a person who doubts the truth of a revealed religion. ~*a.* sceptical. **sceptical** *a.* **1** given to doubting or questioning. **2** doubting or denying the truth of revelation, or

the possibility of knowledge. **3** of, relating to or characteristic of a sceptic. **sceptically** *adv.* **scepticism** (-sizm) *n.*

sceptre (sep´tə), (*esp. N Am.*) **scepter** *n.* **1** a staff or baton borne by a sovereign as a symbol of authority. **2** royal authority. **sceptred** *a.* invested with a sceptre or with royal authority.

sch. *abbr.* **1** scholar. **2** (*also* **Sch.**) school. **3** schooner.

schadenfreude (shah´dənfroidə) *n.* pleasure in others' misfortunes.

schappe (shap, shap´ə) *n.* a fabric or yarn made from waste silk.

schedule (shed´ūl, sked´-) *n.* **1** a timetable. **2** a planned programme of events, tasks etc. **3** a written or printed list or inventory (appended to a document). ~*v.t.* **1** to enter in a schedule. **2** to make a list of. **3** to arrange for a particular time. **4** to include (a building) in a list for preservation or protection. **according to schedule** as planned. **behind schedule** late; not keeping up to an arranged timetable. **on schedule** on time. **schedular** *a.* **scheduled flight, scheduled service** *n.* a flight or service that is part of a regular service. **scheduled territories** *n.pl.* STERLING AREA (under STERLING). **scheduler** *n.*

scheelite (shē´līt) *n.* a vitreous variously-coloured mineral, a tungstate of calcium.

schema (skē´mə) *n.* (*pl.* **schemata** (-tə), **schemas**) **1** a scheme, summary, outline or conspectus. **2** a chart or diagram. **3** (*Logic*) the abstract figure of a syllogism. **schematic** (-mat´-) *a.* having, or in the nature of, a plan or schema. ~*n.* a schematic diagram, esp. of an electrical circuit. **schematically** *adv.* **schematism** *n.* **schematize, schematise** *v.t.* **1** to formulate or express by means of a scheme. **2** to apply the Kantian categories to. **schematization** (-ā´shən) *n.*

scheme (skēm) *n.* **1** a proposed method of doing something. **2** a plot, a conspiracy. **3** a table or schedule of proposed acts, events etc. **4** a systematic arrangement of facts, principles etc. **5** a table of classification. ~*v.t.* to plan, to plot. ~*v.i.* **1** to form plans. **2** to plot. **schemer** *n.* **scheming** *a.* given to forming schemes. ~*n.* the forming of schemes. **schemingly** *adv.*

schemozzle SHEMOZZLE.

scherzo (skœt´sō) *n.* (*pl.* **scherzi** (-sē), **scherzos**) (*Mus.*) a light playful movement in music, usu. following a slow one, in a symphony or sonata. **scherzando** (-san´dō) *adv.* (*Mus.*) playfully. ~*n.* (*pl.* **scherzandi** (-dē), **scherzandos**) a passage or movement played in this way.

schilling (shil´ing) *n.* **1** the standard monetary unit of Austria. **2** a coin of this value.

schism (siz´m, skiz´m) *n.* **1** a split or division in a community. **2** division in a Church, esp. secession of a part or separation into two Churches. **3** the sin of causing such division. **schismatic** (-mat´-) *a., n.* **schismatical** *a.* **schismatically** *adv.*

schist (shist) *n.* a rock of a more or less foliated or laminar structure, tending to split easily.

schistoid (-toid), **schistose** (-tōs), **schistous** *a.* of the nature or structure of schist.

schistosome (shis'təsōm) *n.* a tropical flatworm of the genus *Schistosoma*. **schistosomiasis** (-səmī'əsis) *n.* a disease caused by infestation with worms of the genus *Schistosoma*; bilharzia.

schizanthus (skitsan'thəs) *n.* any plant of the genus *Schizanthus*, with much-divided leaves and showy flowers.

schizo (skit'sō) *n.* (*pl.* **schizos**) (*coll., offensive*) a schizophrenic. ~*a.* schizophrenic.

schizocarp (skit'səkahp) *n.* (*Bot.*) a fruit splitting into several one-seeded portions without dehiscing. **schizocarpic** (-kah´-), **schizocarpous** *a.*

schizoid (skit'soid, skid´zoid) *a.* 1 showing qualities of a schizophrenic personality. 2 (*coll.*) characterized by inconsistency, contradiction etc. ~*n.* a schizoid person. **schizoidal** (-soi´-) *a.*

schizophrenia (skitsəfrē'niə) *n.* 1 (*Psych.*) a severe psychological disorder characterized by loss of contact with reality, personality disintegration, hallucinations, delusions etc. 2 (*coll.*) behaviour characterized by inconsistency, contradictions etc. **schizophrenic** (-fren´-) *a., n.*

schlemiel (shləmēl´), **schlemihl, shlemiel** *n.* (*esp. N Am., coll.*) a bungling clumsy person who is easily victimized.

schlepp (shlep) *v.t.* (*pres.p.* **schlepping**, *past, p.p.* **schlepped**) (*esp. N Am., coll.*) to drag, pull. ~*n.* 1 a tedious journey. 2 an unlucky or incompetent person.

schlock (shlok) *n.* (*N Am., coll.*) shoddy, cheap goods; trash. ~*a.* shoddy, cheap, trashy.

schloss (shlos) *n.* a castle (in Germany).

schlump (shlump) *n.* (*esp. N Am., sl.*) a slovenly person, a slob.

schmaltz (shmawlts), **schmalz** *n.* (*esp. N Am., coll.*) over-sentimentality, esp. in music. **schmaltzy** *a.* (*comp.* **schmaltzier**, *superl.* **schmaltziest**).

schmuck (shmŭk) *n.* (*esp. N Am., sl.*) a fool.

schnapps (shnaps) *n.* any of various spirits resembling genever gin.

schnauzer (shnow'zə, -tsə) *n.* a breed of wirehaired German terrier.

schnitzel (shnit'səl) *n.* an escalope of meat, esp. veal.

schnorkel SNORKEL.

schnorrer (shnor'ə, shnaw´-) *n.* (*esp. N Am., sl.*) a beggar.

scholar (skol'ə) *n.* 1 a learned person. 2 an undergraduate on the foundation of a college and receiving assistance from its funds, usu. after a competitive examination. 3 a person acquiring knowledge, a (good or apt) learner. 4 a disciple. **scholarlike** *a.* **scholarly** *a.* 1 befitting a scholar. 2 learned. **scholarliness** *n.* **scholarship** *n.* 1 high attainments in literature or science. 2 education, instruction. 3 education, usu. with maintenance, free or at reduced fees, granted to a successful candidate after a competitive examination. 4 the

emoluments so granted to a scholar. 5 the qualities of a scholar. **scholar's mate** *n.* in chess, a series of four moves by a player resulting in checkmate.

scholastic (skəlas'tik) *a.* 1 of or relating to school, schools, universities etc. 2 educational, academic. 3 pedagogic, pedantic. 4 (*Hist.*) of, relating to or characteristic of the schoolmen of the Middle Ages. **scholastically** *adv.* **scholasticism** (-sizm) *n.*

school[1] (skool) *n.* 1 an institution for the education of children. 2 a faculty of a university. 3 an establishment offering specialized teaching. 4 the building or buildings of a school. 5 the body of pupils of a school. 6 a session or time during which teaching is carried on. 7 the body of disciples or followers of a philosopher, artist etc., or of adherents of a principle, system of thought etc. 8 (*Mus.*) a book of instruction, a manual. 9 any sphere or circumstances serving to discipline or instruct. 10 a group of people assembled for a common purpose, such as playing poker. ~*v.t.* 1 to instruct, to educate. 2 to train, to drill. 3 to discipline, to bring under control. 4 to send to school. ~*a.* of school, schools or the school. **at school** attending lessons etc. **in school** (*N Am.*) attending lessons, at school. **to go to school** 1 to begin one's schooling. 2 to attend lessons. **to leave school** to finish one's schooling. **schoolable** *a.* **school age** *n.* the age at which children attend school. **schoolbag** *n.* a bag for carrying schoolbooks etc. **schoolboy** *n.* a boy attending a school. ~*a.* of or relating to schoolboys. **schoolboyish** *a.* **schoolchild** *n.* (*pl.* **schoolchildren**) a child attending a school. **schoolday** *n.* 1 a day on which schools are open. 2 (*pl.*) the time of being a school pupil. **schoolfellow** *n.* a person who attends the same school. **schoolfriend** *n.* a friend from school. **schoolgirl** *n.* a girl attending a school. ~*a.* of or relating to schoolgirls. **schoolgirlish** *a.* **schoolhouse** *n.* 1 a building used as a school. 2 a dwelling house provided for a schoolmaster or schoolmistress. **schoolie** *n.* (*Austral., sl., dial.*) a schoolteacher. **schooling** *n.* 1 education at school. 2 training, tuition. 3 the training of a horse for riding, or in dressage, jumping etc. **school inspector** *n.* an official appointed to examine schools. **school leaver** *n.* a pupil who is about to leave or has recently left school. **school-leaving age** *n.* the minimum age at which a child may leave school. **schoolma'am, school-marm** *n.* (*N Am., coll.*) a schoolmistress. **school-marmish** *a.* (*esp. N Am., coll.*) prim and fussy. **schoolman** *n.* (*pl.* **schoolmen**) 1 (*Hist.*) a teacher or professor in a medieval university. 2 (*Hist.*) a person versed in the theology, logic or metaphysics of the medieval schools or the niceties of academic disputation. 3 (*N Am.*) a male teacher. **school-marm, schoolmarmish** SCHOOL-MA'AM (under SCHOOL[1]). **schoolmaster** *n.* a male head or assistant teacher in a school. **schoolmastering** *n.* **schoolmasterly** *a.*

schoolmate *n.* a person attending the same school. **schoolmistress** *n.* a female head or assistant teacher in a school. **schoolmistressy** *a.* **school of hard knocks** *n.* experience gained from a difficult life. **schoolroom** *n.* a room where teaching is given, in a school, house etc. **school-ship** *n.* a training ship. **schoolteacher** *n.* a person who teaches in a school. **schoolteaching** *n.* **school time** *n.* **1** lesson time. **2** schooldays. **schoolwork** *n.* work done at or for school. **school year** *n.* an academic year, usu. from September to the end of July.

school² (skool) *n.* a shoal of fish, porpoises etc. ~*v.i.* to form a school, swim in a school.

schooner (skoo´nə) *n.* **1** a vessel with two or more masts with fore-and-aft rigging. **2** (*N Am., Austral.*) a tall glass for beer or ale. **3** a tall glass for sherry.

schorl (shawl) *n.* black tourmaline.

schottische (shotēsh´, shot´ish) *n.* **1** a dance resembling a polka. **2** the music for it.

schuss (shus) *n.* **1** a straight fast ski slope. **2** a run made on this. ~*v.i.* to make such a run.

schwa (shwah, shvah) *n.* **1** a neutral unstressed vowel sound. **2** the symbol ə used to represent this.

sciatic (sīat´ik) *a.* **1** of or relating to the hip. **2** of or affecting the sciatic nerve. **3** of the nature of or affected by sciatica. **sciatica** (-kə) *n.* neuralgia of the hip and thigh. **2** pain in the great sciatic nerve. **sciatically** *adv.* **sciatic nerve** *n.* the nerve that extends from the pelvis down the back of the thigh.

science (sī´əns) *n.* **1** systematized knowledge about the physical world, developed by observation and experiment. **2** a department of systematized knowledge, a system of facts and principles concerning any subject. **3** a natural science. **4** the pursuit of such knowledge or the principles governing its acquirement. **to blind someone with science** to overawe someone with esp. spurious knowledge. **science fiction** *n.* fiction dealing with space travel, life on one of the planets etc. **science park** *n.* a place where academic scientific research is applied to commercial developments. **sciential** (-en´shəl) *a.* **1** of or producing science. **2** having knowledge. **scientially** *adv.* **scientific** (-tif´-) *a.* **1** of, relating to, used or engaged in science. **2** treating of or devoted to science. **3** made or done according to the principles of science. **scientifically** *adv.* **scientism** *n.* **1** scientific methods or attitudes. **2** (*often derog.*) (belief in) the application of scientific methods to investigate and explain social and psychological phenomena. **scientistic** *a.* **scientist** *n.* a person who studies or is expert in a (physical or natural) science. **Scientology®** (-tol´əji) *n.* a religious movement advocating self-improvement of one's physical and mental condition through psychological and scientific means. **Scientologist** *n.*

sci-fi (sī´fī) *n.* (*coll.*) science fiction.

scilicet (sī´liset, skē´liket) *adv.* to wit, videlicet, namely.

scilla (sil´ə) *n.* (*pl.* **scillas**) any plant of the genus *Scilla*, liliaceous plants with bell-shaped flowers.

Scillonian (silō´niən) *n.* a native or inhabitant of the Scilly Isles. ~*a.* of or relating to the Scilly Isles.

scimitar (sim´itə) *n.* a short Oriental sword, single-edged, curved and broadest towards the point.

scintilla (sintil´ə) *n.* (*pl.* **scintillas**) **1** a spark. **2** a trace, hint. **scintillant** *a.* **scintillate** (sin´-) *v.i.* **1** to be brilliantly witty or interesting. **2** to sparkle, to twinkle. **3** to emit sparks. **4** (*Physics*) to emit flashes of light when bombarded by electrons, photons etc. **scintillating** *a.* **scintillatingly** *adv.* **scintillation** (-ā´shən) *n.* **counter** *n.* an instrument for measuring radiation from a source by electronically counting the flashes of light produced by the absorption of radioactive particles by a phosphor. **scintiscan** (sin´tiskan) *n.* an image or other record showing radioactive traces in the body.

scion (sī´ən) *n.* **1** (*N Am. also* **cion**) a shoot, esp. for grafting or planting. **2** a descendant, a child.

scirocco SIROCCO.

scirrhus (sir´əs, skir´-) *n.* (*pl.* **scirrhi** (-ī)) a hard (cancerous) tumour. **scirrhoid** (-oid), **scirrhous** *a.* **scirrhosity** (-os´-) *n.*

scissile (sis´īl) *a.* that may be cut. **scission** (sish´ən) *n.* **1** the act of cutting or dividing. **2** a division, separation or split.

scissors (siz´əz) *n.pl.* **1** a cutting instrument consisting of two blades pivoted together that cut objects placed between them; also called *pair of scissors*. **2** a gymnastic movement in which the legs open and close with a scissor-like action. **3** a scissors hold. **scissor** *v.t.* **1** to cut with scissors. **2** to clip or cut (out) with scissors. **scissor-beak**, **scissor-bill** *n.* a skimmer, a bird of the genus *Rhynchops*. **scissor-bird**, **scissor-tail** *n.* a N American fork-tailed flycatcher, *Tyrannus forficatus*. **scissors-and-paste** *a.* of compilation, as distinguished from original literary work. **scissors and paste** *n.* **scissors hold** *n.* a wrestling hold in which the legs lock round the opponent's head or body. **scissorwise** *adv.*

sclera (sklíə´rə) *n.* the white of the eye; the sclerotic. **scleral** *a.* **scleritis** (sklərī´tis) *n.* (*Med.*) sclerotitis.

sclerenchyma (skləreng´kimə) *n.* the strong tissue forming the hard or fibrous parts of plants, such as the walls of nuts and fruit-stones, leaf midribs etc.

sclerite (sklíə´rīt) *n.* (*Zool.*) any one of the definite component parts of the hard integument of various invertebrates. **scleritic** (-rit´-) *a.*

scleroderm (sklĕr´ədœm) *n.* a hardened integument or exoskeleton, esp. of corals. **scleroderma** (-dœ´-), **sclerodermia** (-miə) *n.* (*Med.*) a chronic induration of the skin. **sclerodermatous** (-dœ´-), **sclerodermic** *a.*

scleroid (sklia´roid) *a.* (*Bot., Zool.*) hard in texture.

scleroma (sklerō´ma) *n.* (*pl.* **scleromata** (-ta)) hardening of cellular tissue, scleriasis.

sclerometer (skliarom´ita, sklar-) *n.* an instrument for determining the hardness of a mineral or a metal.

sclerophyll (sklia´rafil) *n.* any woody plant with leathery leaves. **sclerophyllous** (-rof´-) *a.*

scleroprotein (skliaroprō´tēn) *n.* an insoluble protein, such as keratin, forming the skeletal tissues of the body.

sclerosis (sklarō´sis) *n.* (*pl.* **scleroses** (-ō´sēz)) **1** hardening of a plant cell wall by the deposit of sclerogen. **2** thickening or hardening of a body tissue. **3** MULTIPLE SCLEROSIS (under MULTIPLE). **sclerosed** (sklia´rōzd) *a.*

sclerotic (sklarot´ik) *a.* (*Med.*) **1** (of the outer coat or tunic of the eye) hard, indurated. **2** of or affected with sclerosis.~*n.* the firm white membrane forming the outer coat of the eye, the white of the eye. **sclerotitis** (skliaratī´tis) *n.* (*Med.*) inflammation of the sclerotic.

sclerous (sklia´ras) *a.* hard, indurated, ossified.

SCM *abbr.* State Certified Midwife.

scoff¹ (skof) *v.i.* to mock or jeer (at). ~*n.* **1** an expression of contempt, derision or mockery. **2** an object of derision, a laughing stock. **scoffer** *n.* **scoffingly** *adv.*

scoff² (skof) *v.t.* (*coll.*) to eat ravenously. ~*n.* food.

scold (skōld) *v.i.* **1** to find fault noisily or angrily. **2** to rail (at). ~*v.t.* to chide or find fault with noisily or angrily. **scolder** *n.* **scolding** *a.,* *n.* **scoldingly** *adv.*

scollop SCALLOP.

scolopendrium (skolapen´driam) *n.* any of a genus of ferns containing the hart's tongue, *Phyllitis scolopendrium.*

scombroid (skom´broid) *n.* any marine fish of the family Scombridae or the superfamily Scombroidea including the mackerels, tunas and swordfishes. ~*a.* of or belonging to the Scombridae or Scombroidea. **scombrid** (-brid) *n.*

sconce¹ (skons) *n.* **1** a flat candlestick with a handle. **2** a candleholder fixed to a wall.

sconce² (skons) *n.* a blockhouse, a bulwark, a small detached fort. ~*v.t.* to fortify with a sconce.

scone (skon, skōn) *n.* a soft plain cake, usu. in small round or triangular pieces, cooked on a griddle or in an oven.

scoop (skoop) *n.* **1** a short-handled shovel-like implement for lifting and moving loose material such as coal or grain. **2** a large ladle or dipping-vessel. **3** a gougelike implement used by grocers, surgeons etc. or for spooning out shaped pieces of ice cream or other soft food. **4** the bucket of a dredging machine. **5** a coal scuttle. **6** the act or movement of scooping. **7** the amount scooped at once. **8** a large profit made in a speculation or competitive transaction. **9** the publication

or broadcasting of a piece of sensational news in advance of rival newspapers etc. **10** a news item so published. **11** (*Mus.*) a singer's exaggerated portamento. **12** a scooped-out hollow etc. ~*v.t.* **1** to ladle or to hollow (out) with a scoop. **2** to lift (up) with a scoop. **3** to scrape or hollow (out). **4** to gain (a large profit) by a deal etc. **5** to forestall (rival newspapers etc.) with a piece of sensational news. **scooper** *n.* **scoopful** *n.* (*pl.* **scoopfuls**). **scoop neck** *n.* a rounded low neckline on a garment. **scoop-net** *n.* a net so formed as to sweep the bottom of a river etc.

scoot (skoot) *v.i.* (*coll.*) to dart off, bolt, to scurry away. ~*n.* the act or an instance of scooting. **scooter** *n.* **1** a two-wheeled toy vehicle on which a child can ride with one foot, propelling with the other. **2** a larger, motorized two-wheeled vehicle with a seat. **3** (*N Am.*) a sailboat that can travel on water or ice. ~*v.i.* to travel or ride on a scooter. **scooterist** *n.*

scope¹ (skōp) *n.* **1** range of action or observation. **2** extent of or room for activity, development etc. **3** outlet, opportunity. **4** (*Naut.*) the length of cable at which a vessel rides. **scopeless** *a.*

scope² (skōp) *n.* (*coll.*) a periscope, telescope, oscilloscope etc.

-scope (skōp) *comb. form* denoting an instrument of observation etc., as in *microscope, spectroscope.* **-scopic** (skop´ik) *comb. form* of or relating to this or to observation etc., as in *microscopic, spectroscopic.* **-scopy** (skapi) *comb. form* observation by the instrument etc., specified, as in *microscopy, spectroscopy.*

scopolamine (skapol´amēn) *n.* hyoscine hydrobromide, a hypnotic drug used, among other purposes, with morphine for producing twilight sleep.

scorbutic (skawbū´tik) *a.* of, relating to, like or affected with scurvy. ~*n.* a person affected with scurvy. **scorbutically** *adv.*

scorch (skawch) *v.t.* **1** to burn the outside of so as to injure or discolour without consuming. **2** to affect harmfully with or as with heat. **3** to criticize or censure severely. ~*v.i.* **1** to be singed or dried up with or as with heat. **2** (*coll.*) to go at an excessive rate of speed. ~*n.* **1** a mark caused by scorching. **2** (*coll.*) an act or spell of scorching. **scorched** *a.* **scorched earth** *n.* the destruction of everything in a country that might be of service to an invading army. **scorched earth policy** *n.* **scorcher** *n.* **1** a person who or thing which scorches. **2** an extremely hot day. **3** (*coll.*) a striking or staggering example, a stunner. **scorching** *a.* **scorchingly** *adv.*

score (skaw) *n.* **1** the points made by a player or side at any moment in, or in total in certain games and contests. **2** the record of this. **3** the act of gaining a point in a game or contest. **4** (*pl.* **score, scores**) twenty, a set of twenty. **5** (*pl.*) large numbers. **6** account, reason. **7** (*Mus.*) **a** a copy of a musical work in which all the component parts are shown, either fully or in a compressed form.

b the music for a film, play etc. **8** the notation for a choreographed work. **9** (*sl.*) a remark etc. in which one scores off another person. **10** (*coll.*) the situation, the facts. **11** a scratch, incision. **12** an account, a debt. **13** (*Naut.*) a groove in a block etc., for receiving a strap. **14** a notch or mark on a tally. **15** anything laid up or recorded against one. **16** a mark from which a race starts, competitors fire in a shooting match etc. **17** a line drawn or scratched through writing etc. ~*v.t.* **1** to gain (a point, a win etc.) in a game or contest. **2** to count for a score of (points etc.). **3** to mark (up) or enter in a score. **4** to mark with notches, lines etc. **5** (*Mus.*) **a** to orchestrate. **b** to arrange for an instrument. **c** to prepare the sound script for (a film). **d** to arrange in score. **6** to groove, to furrow. **7** to make or mark (lines etc.). **8** to mark (out) with lines. **9** to mentally record (an offence etc.). **10** (*N Am.*) to criticize severely. ~*v.i.* **1** to win points, advantages etc. **2** to keep a score. **3** (*sl.*) to obtain illegal drugs. **4** (*sl.*) to successfully seduce someone into having sexual intercourse. **on that score** so far as that is concerned. **to score off 1** (*coll.*) to get the better of. **2** (*coll.*) to triumph over in argument, repartee etc. **to score out** to cross out, cancel. **to score points off** to get the better of in an argument. **to score under** to underline. **scoreboard** *n.* a board on which the score at any point in a game or contest is displayed. **scorecard** *n.* **score draw** *n.* a draw in football in which goals are scored. **scoreless** *a.* **scoreline** *n.* a score in a match etc. **scorer** *n.*

scoria (skaw´riə) *n.* (*pl.* **scoriae** (-riē)) **1** cellular lava or ashes. **2** the refuse of fused metals, dross. **scoriaceous** (-ā´shəs), **scoriform** (-fawm) *a.* **scorify** (-rifi) *v.t.* (*3rd pers. sing. pres.* **scorifies**, *pres.p.* **scorifying**, *past*, *p.p.* **scorified**) **1** to reduce to dross. **2** to assay (metal) by fusing its ore in a scorifier with lead and borax. **scorification** (-fikā´shən) *n.*

scorn (skawn) *n.* **1** contempt, disdain. **2** mockery, derision. **3** a subject or object of extreme contempt. ~*v.t.* **1** to hold in extreme contempt or disdain. **2** to regard as unworthy, paltry or mean. **to pour scorn on** to express contempt or disdain for. **scorner** *n.* **scornful** *a.* **scornfully** *adv.* **scornfulness** *n.*

Scorpio (skaw´piō) *n.* (*pl.* **Scorpios**) (*Astrol.*) **1** the eighth sign of the zodiac. **2** a person born under this sign. **Scorpian** *a.*, *n.* **scorpioid** (-oid) *a.* **1** (*Bot.*) curled up like the end of a scorpion's tail and uncurling as the flowers develop. **2** (*Zool.*) of, relating to as or resembling a scorpion. ~*n.* a scorpioid inflorescence.

scorpion (skaw´piən) *n.* **1** an arachnid of the order Scorpiones, with claws like a lobster and a sting in the jointed tail. **2** a smaller, similar arachnid of the order Pseudoscorpiones, a false scorpion. **scorpion fish** *n.* any of various marine fish of the family Scorpaenidae. **scorpion fly** *n.* any insect of the order Mecoptera, esp. of the genus *Panorpa*, named from the forceps-like

point of the abdomen. **scorpion grass, scorpion wort** *n.* the myosotis or forget-me-not.

scorzonera (skawzəniə´rə) *n.* **1** a plant of the family *Scorzonera hispanica* with long tapering roots. **2** this root eaten as a vegetable.

Scot (skot) *n.* **1** a native of Scotland. **2** a person of Scottish descent. **3** (*Hist.*) a member of a Gaelic people migrating to Scotland from Ireland in the 5th or 6th cent.

scot (skot) *n.* (*Hist.*) a payment, an assessment, a tax. **scot and lot** *n.* a town or parish tax levied according to ability to pay. **to pay scot and lot** to settle outstanding accounts, obligations etc. **scot-free** *a.* **1** unhurt, safe. **2** unpunished.

Scotch (skoch) *a.* Scottish. ~*n.* **1** (Scotch) whisky. **2** a drink of this. **3** the Scots. **Scotch broth** *n.* a clear broth containing barley and chopped vegetables. **Scotch cap** *n.* a brimless woollen cap, either a balmoral or a glengarry. **Scotch catch, Scotch snap** *n.* (*Mus.*) a short note followed by a long note in two played to the same beat. **Scotch egg** *n.* a hard-boiled egg encased in sausage meat and breadcrumbs. **Scotch fir** *n.* the Scots pine. **Scotchman** *n.* (*pl.* **Scotchmen**) a Scotsman. **Scotch mist** *n.* **1** a wet dense mist. **2** fine drizzle. **3** a retort made to someone who hasn't understood something. **Scotchness** *n.* **Scotch pancake** *n.* a drop scone. **Scotch pebble** *n.* agate, jasper, cairngorm etc. found in Scotland. **Scotch snap** SCOTCH CATCH (under SCOTCH). **Scotch tape**® *n.* adhesive transparent tape. **Scotch whisky** *n.* whisky distilled in Scotland. **Scotchwoman** *n.* (*pl.* **Scotchwomen**) a Scotswoman.

Usage note The use of *Scotch* other than of whisky or in the established compounds above can offend Scots: *Scottish* and *Scots* are acceptable alternatives.

scotch[1] (skoch) *v.t.* to put an end to, frustrate. ~*n.* a mark for hopping from, as in the game of hopscotch.

scotch[2] (skoch) *n.* a block for a wheel or other round object. ~*v.t.* **1** to block, wedge or prop (a wheel, barrel etc.) to prevent rolling. **2** to frustrate (a plan etc.).

scoter (skō´tə) *n.* (*pl.* **scoter, scoters**) a large sea duck of the genus *Melanitta*.

Scoticism SCOTTICISM (under SCOTTISH).

Scoticize SCOTTICIZE (under SCOTTISH).

Scotland Yard (skot´lənd) *n.* **1** the headquarters of the London Metropolitan Police. **2** the Criminal Investigation Department of the police. **3** police detectives.

scotoma (skotō´mə) *n.* (*pl.* **scotomas, scotomata** (-tə)) a blind spot in the field of vision.

Scots (skots) *a.* Scottish (applied to the people, language and law). ~*n.* **1** the form of the English language used in Scotland. **2** the people of Scotland. **Scotsman, Scotswoman** *n.* (*pl.* **Scotsmen, Scotswomen**). **Scots pine** *n.* a European pine, *Pinus sylvestris*, prob. indigenous in N Britain.

Scottish (skot´ish) *a.* of or relating to Scotland or its people. ~*n.* **1** the Scots language. **2** (*as pl.*) the people of Scotland. **Scotticism** (-sizm), **Scoticism** *n.* a Scottish idiom. **Scotticize, Scoticize, Scotticise, Scoticise** *v.t.* to make Scottish. ~*v.i.* to imitate the Scottish. **Scottie, Scotty** *n.* (*pl.* **Scotties**) (*coll.*) **1** a nickname for a Scotsman. **2** (*also* **Scottie dog**) a Scottish terrier. **Scottishness** *n.* **Scottish terrier** *n.* a breed of small terrier with short legs and a rough coat.

scoundrel (skown´drəl) *n.* an unprincipled person, a rogue. **scoundreldom, scoundrelism** *n.* **scoundrelly** *a.*

scour[1] (skow´ə) *v.t.* **1** to clean or polish by friction. **2** to remove or clean (away, off etc.) by rubbing. **3** to flush or clear out. **4** (of water etc.) to pass swiftly through or over. ~*v.i.* **1** to clean. **2** to be scoured or cleaned (well, easily etc.). **3** to be purged to excess. ~*n.* **1** scouring. **2** the clearing action of this. **3** dysentery in cattle etc. **4** a cleanser for various fabrics. **scourer** *n.* **scouring** *n.* **scouring pad** *n.* an abrasive pad used for cleaning pans etc. **scouring powder** *n.* an abrasive powder used esp. in the kitchen. **scouring-rush** *n.* any of various horsetails, esp. *Equisetum hyemale*, formerly used for scouring and polishing.

scour[2] (skow´ə) *v.i.* **1** to rove, to range. **2** to skim, to scurry. **3** to search about. ~*v.t.* **1** to move rapidly over, esp. in search. **2** to search thoroughly.

scourge (skœj) *n.* **1** a whip with thongs used as an instrument of punishment. **2** any means of inflicting punishment or suffering. **3** a pestilence or plague. ~*v.t.* **1** to whip with or as with a scourge. **2** to afflict, to chastise. **scourger** *n.*

Scouse (skows) *n.* **1** the dialect of Liverpool. **2** (*also* **Scouser**) a native or inhabitant of Liverpool. **3** (**scouse**) LOBSCOUSE. ~*a.* of or relating to Liverpool.

scout[1] (skowt) *n.* **1** a person sent out to bring in information, esp. one employed to watch the movements etc. of an enemy. **2** a person employed to search for people with talent in a particular field, new sales markets etc. **3** the act of watching or bringing in such information. **4** a scouting expedition. **5** (**Scout**) a member of a worldwide organization, intended to train and develop qualities of leadership, responsibility etc., orig. in boys. **6** a ship or aircraft used for reconnaissance. ~*v.t.* (*coll.*) to explore to get information about. ~*v.i.* **1** to act as a scout. **2** to make a search. **Scouter** *n.* an adult leader of Scouts. **scouter** *n.* **Scoutmaster** *n.* the leader of a group of Scouts.

scout[2] (skowt) *v.t.* to treat with contempt and disdain, to reject contemptuously.

scow (skow) *n.* a large flat-bottomed, square-ended boat.

scowl (skowl) *v.i.* to look sullen or ill-tempered. ~*n.* a look of sullenness, ill-temper or discontent. **scowler** *n.* **scowlingly** *adv.*

scr. *abbr.* scruple(s) (of weight).

scrabble (skrab´əl) *v.i.* **1** to scratch or grope (about) as if to obtain something. **2** to scramble. ~*n.* **1** a scramble, struggle. **2** a scratching or scraping. **Scrabble®** *n.* a word-building board game. **Scrabbler** *n.* (*coll.*) a person who plays Scrabble.

scrag (skrag) *n.* **1** a lean or bony piece of meat, esp. the lean end of neck of mutton. **2** a lean or bony person or animal. **3** (*coll.*) a person's neck. ~*v.t.* (*pres.p.* **scragging**, *past, p.p.* **scragged**) (*sl.*) **1** to wring the neck of, to throttle. **2** to kill by hanging. **3** to handle roughly; beat up. **scraggy** *a.* (*comp.* **scraggier**, *superl.* **scraggiest**). **scraggily** *adv.* **scragginess** *n.*

scraggly (skrag´li) *a.* (*comp.* **scragglier**, *superl.* **scraggliest**) sparse and irregular.

scram (skram) *int.* (*coll.*) get out of it! go away!

scramble (skram´bəl) *v.i.* **1** to climb or move along by clambering, esp. with the hands and knees. **2** to move with urgent or disorderly haste. **3** to seek or struggle (for, after etc.) in a rough-and-tumble or eager manner. **4** to climb or spread irregularly. **5** (of an aircraft or its crew) to take off immediately. ~*v.t.* **1** to put together hurriedly or haphazardly. **2** to mix or jumble up. **3** to prepare (eggs) by breaking into a pan and stirring up during cooking. **4** to order (an aircraft or crew) to scramble. **5** to make (a radiotelephonic conversation) unintelligible without a decoding receiver by altering the frequencies. **6** (*coll.*) to execute (an action etc.) inefficiently. ~*n.* **1** the act of scrambling. **2** a climb over rocks etc., or in a rough-and-tumble manner. **3** a rough or unceremonious struggle for something. **4** an emergency take-off of fighter aircraft. **5** a motorcycle race over rough ground. **scrambled egg** *n.* **1** a dish of eggs cooked by scrambling. **2** (*coll., facet.*) gold embroidery on a military officer's cap. **scrambler** *n.* **1** a person who scrambles. **2** an electronic device for scrambling speech transmitted by radio or telephone. **3** a motorcycle for racing over rough ground. **4** a plant with long weak shoots which it uses to climb over other plants.

scrap[1] (skrap) *n.* **1** a small detached piece, a bit. **2** a picture, paragraph etc., cut from a newspaper etc., for preservation. **3** waste, esp. old pieces of discarded metal collected for melting down etc. **4** (*pl.*) bits, odds and ends, leavings. **5** (*pl.*) leftover fragments of food. **6** (*usu. pl.*) refuse of fat from which the oil has been expressed. ~*v.t.* (*pres.p.* **scrapping**, *past, p.p.* **scrapped**) **1** to consign to the scrap heap. **2** to discard as worn out, obsolete etc. **scrapbook** *n.* a blank book into which pictures, cuttings from newspapers etc. are pasted for preservation. **scrap heap** *n.* **1** a heap of scrap metal. **2** a rubbish heap. **on the scrap heap** no longer useful. **scrap iron, scrap metal** *n.* discarded metal for reprocessing. **scrap merchant** *n.* a dealer in scrap. **scrappy** *a.* (*comp.* **scrappier**, *superl.* **scrappiest**) **1** consisting or made up of scraps. **2** disconnected. **scrappily**

adv. **scrappiness** *n.* **scrapyard** *n.* a place where scrap, esp. scrap metal, is collected or stored.

scrap² (skrap) *n.* (*coll.*) a fight, a scuffle. ~*v.i.* (*pres.p.* **scrapping**, *past, p.p.* **scrapped**) to engage in a fight. **scrapper** *n.*

scrape (skrāp) *v.t.* **1** to rub the surface of with something rough or sharp. **2** to abrade or smooth (a surface) with something rough or sharp. **3** to remove, to clean (off, out etc.) thus. **4** to rub or scratch (out). **5** to excavate or hollow (out) by scraping. **6** to rub against with a rasping or grating noise. **7** to draw or rub along something with a scraping noise. **8** to damage or graze by rubbing on a rough surface. **9** to collect or get together by scraping. **10** to save or amass with difficulty or by small amounts. **11** to clear (a ship's bottom) of barnacles etc. **12** to draw (the hair) tightly back off the forehead. ~*v.i.* **1** to rub the surface of something with a rough or sharp instrument. **2** to abrade, to smooth something with a rough or sharp instrument. **3** to rub (against something) with a scraping or rasping noise. **4** to make such a noise. **5** to get through with difficulty or by a close shave. **6** to be parsimonious. **7** to play awkwardly on a violin etc. **8** to make an awkward bow with a drawing back of the foot. **9** to barely manage. **10** to pass an examination etc. with difficulty. ~*n.* **1** the act, sound or effect of scraping. **2** a scraped place (on the skin etc.). **3** a thin layer of butter etc. **4** an awkward bow with a drawing back of the foot. **5** (*coll.*) an awkward predicament, esp. one due to one's own conduct. **to scrape acquaintance with** to contrive to make the acquaintance of. **to scrape along** (*coll.*) to keep going somehow. **to scrape away** to abrade, to reduce by scraping. **to scrape by** (*coll.*) to keep going somehow. **to scrape down 1** to scrape away. **2** to scrape from head to foot or top to bottom. **3** to silence or put down by scraping the feet. **scraper** *n.* **1** a person who scrapes. **2** an instrument for scraping, esp. for cleaning the dirt off one's boots before entering a house. **scraperboard** *n.* a board with a surface that can be scraped off to form a design. **scraping** *n.*

scrapie (skrā´pi) *n.* an encephalopathy affecting sheep, thought to be caused by a prion.

scrapper SCRAP².

scrappy SCRAP¹.

scratch (skrach) *v.t.* **1** to tear or mark the surface of lightly with something sharp. **2** to wound slightly. **3** to rub or scrape with the nails. **4** to hollow out with the nails or claws. **5** to chafe the surface of. **6** to write hurriedly; to scribble. **7** to erase, to score (out, through etc.). **8** to expunge (esp. the name of a horse in a list of entries for a race). **9** to withdraw from a contest. **10** to cancel (a match, game etc.). **11** to form by scratching. **12** to scrape (up or together). ~*v.i.* **1** to use the nails or claws in tearing, scraping etc. **2** to scrape one's skin with the nails. **3** to chafe, rub. **4** to scrape the ground as in searching. **5** to make a grating noise. **6** to withdraw one's entry from a

contest. **7** to manage with difficulty. ~*n.* **1** a mark made by scratching. **2** a slight wound. **3** a sound of scratching. **4** an act or spell of scratching. **5** a mark from which competitors start in a race, or a line across a prize ring at which boxers begin. **6** in golf, a handicap of zero. **7** (*sl.*) money. **8** in music, the technique of scratching. ~*a.* **1** improvised. **2** put together hastily or haphazardly. **3** in sport, without handicap. **to scratch along** to scrape along. **to scratch one's head** to be puzzled. **to scratch the surface 1** to gain a superficial understanding. **2** to investigate further. **to start from scratch** to start from the very beginning, with no advantage. **up to scratch** fulfilling the desired standard or requirements. **scratch card** *n.* a lottery card etc. whose surface has an opaque coating which is scratched off to reveal the figures, letters etc. underneath. **scratcher** *n.* **scratching** *n.* **1** a scratchy sound effect produced by manually rotating a (pop) record backwards and forwards, used in some styles of pop music. **2** (*pl.*) PORK SCRATCHINGS (under PORK). **scratch pad** *n.* **1** (*esp. N Am.*) a notebook, a scribbling block. **2** (*Comput.*) a small fast memory for storing computer data. **scratch video** *n.* a collage on video of previously existing pieces of television and cinema film. **scratchy** *a.* (*comp.* **scratchier**, *superl.* **scratchiest**) **1** consisting of or characterized by scratches. **2** tending to scratch or rub. **scratchily** *adv.* **scratchiness** *n.*

scrawl (skrawl) *v.t.* to draw or write clumsily, hurriedly or illegibly. ~*v.i.* to mark with illegible writing etc. ~*n.* a piece of hasty, clumsy or illegible writing. **scrawler** *n.* **scrawly** *a.* (*comp.* **scrawlier**, *superl.* **scrawliest**)

scrawny (skraw´ni) *a.* (*comp.* **scrawnier**, *superl.* **scrawniest**) excessively lean, bony. **scrawnily** *adv.* **scrawniness** *n.*

scream (skrēm) *v.i.* **1** to make a piercing, prolonged cry as if in extreme pain or terror. **2** to give out a shrill sound. **3** to be over-conspicuous or vivid. **4** (*coll.*) to turn informer. ~*v.t.* to utter or say in a screaming tone. ~*n.* **1** a loud, shrill, prolonged cry, as of one in extreme pain or terror. **2** a similar, loud sound. **3** (*coll.*) something or someone excruciatingly funny. **screamer** *n.* **1** a person who or something which screams, esp. the swift. **2** any bird of the S American semiaquatic family Anhimidae, from their harsh cry. **3** (*N Am., coll.*) a sensational headline. **4** (*coll.*) a person who or thing which makes one laugh. **screamingly** *adv.* extremely. **screamy** *a.* **screamily** *adv.* **screaminess** *n.*

scree (skrē) *n.* **1** loose fragments or debris of rock on a steep slope. **2** a slope covered with this.

screech (skrēch) *v.i.* to scream out with a sharp, harsh, shrill voice. ~*v.t.* to utter or say with such a voice. ~*n.* a shrill, harsh cry as of terror or pain. **screecher** *n.* **screech owl** *n.* an owl that screeches instead of hooting, esp. the barn owl or a small American owl, *Otus asio.* **screechy** *a.*

(*comp.* **screechier,** *superl.* **screechiest**). **screechily** *adv.* **screechiness** *n.*

screed (skrēd) *n.* **1** a long harangue or tirade. **2** a strip of mortar, wood etc. put on a wall etc. that is to be plastered, as a guide to evenness of surface etc. **3** a screeding. **4** a long and tedious piece of writing. **screeding** *n.* the final rendering of concrete to get a smooth surface.

screen (skrēn) *n.* **1** a partition separating a portion of a room from the remainder. **2** a movable piece of furniture, usu. consisting of a light framework covered with paper, cloth etc., used to shelter from excess of heat, draught etc. **3** anything serving to protect or conceal. **4** a surface on which images can be projected. **5** the film industry, moving pictures collectively. **6** the part of a television set, VDU etc. on which the image appears. **7** in cricket, a sight-screen. **8** a windscreen. **9** a frame containing a mesh placed over a window, door etc. to keep out flies. **10** (*Physics*) a body affording a shield against electric or magnetic induction. **11** in photography, a device for modifying the effect of light passing through a lens. **12** a coarse sieve or riddle. **13** a board or structure on which notices etc. can be posted. **14** a system for selecting, checking etc. **15** (*Print.*) a plate or film for half-tone reproduction. **16** (*Mil.*) a body of troops etc. used as a cover. ~*v.t.* **1** to shelter or protect from inconvenience, hurt or pain. **2** to hide, to conceal wholly or partly. **3** to prevent from causing, or protect from, electrical interference. **4** to separate with a screen. **5** to test for the presence of disease, weapons etc. **6** to examine or check thoroughly in order to assess suitability, sort into categories etc. **7** to project (a film) on a screen. **8** to sift. **screenable** *a.* **screener** *n.* **screening** *n.* **screenings** *n.pl.* small stuff or refuse separated by screening. **screenplay** *n.* a film script including stage directions and details of characters and sets. **screen printing, screen process** *n.* SILK-SCREEN PRINTING (under SILK). **screen print** *n.* **screen-print** *v.t.* **screen-printed** *a.* **screen saver** *n.* (*Comput.*) a computer program which uses moving images to prevent a monitor becoming damaged. **screen test** *n.* a filmed test of an actor to judge their suitability for a film. **screenwriter** *n.* a writer of screenplays. **screenwriting** *n.*

screw (skroo) *n.* **1** a cylinder with a spiral ridge or groove round its outer surface (called a male screw) or round its inner surface (called a female screw). **2** a male screw used for fastening boards etc. together. **3** a male or female screw forming part of a tool, mechanical appliance or machine and conveying motion to another part or bringing pressure to bear. **4** (*also* **screw-bolt**) a metal male screw with a blunt end, used to bolt things together. **5** a piece in spiral form. **6** (*sing. or pl.*) an instrument of torture. **7** a screw propeller. **8** a turn of a screw. **9** a sideways motion or tendency like that of a screw, a twist. **10** backspin given to a ball in snooker, billiards etc. **11** a twisted-up

paper (of tobacco etc.). **12** (*sl.*) a stingy person. **13** (*sl.*) salary. **14** (*sl., offensive*) a prison warder. **15** (*taboo sl.*) an act of sexual intercourse. **16** (*sl.*) a partner in sexual intercourse. ~*v.t.* **1** to fasten, join etc. with a screw or screws. **2** to turn (a screw). **3** to turn round or twist as a screw. **4** to give a spiral thread or groove to. **5** to oppress, esp. by exactions. **6** to extort (money etc.) out of. **7** to cheat. **8** to contort (as the face). **9** (*taboo sl.*) to have sexual intercourse with. **10** to cause (esp. a billiard ball) to swerve. **11** (*sl.*) to bungle. ~*v.i.* **1** to turn as a screw. **2** to move obliquely or spirally. **3** (*taboo sl.*) to have sexual intercourse. **to have a screw at** (*Austral., coll.*) to take a look at. **to have a screw loose** (*coll.*) to be slightly crazy. **to put the screws on** (*coll.*) to put pressure on. **to screw around** (*taboo sl.*) to have sexual intercourse with many partners. **to screw up 1** to tighten up with or as with a screw. **2** to fasten with a screw or screws. **3** (*sl.*) to bungle, mess up. **4** (*sl.*) to make confused or neurotic. **5** to summon (one's courage). **to screw up courage** to summon up resolution. **screwable** *a.* **screwball** *a.* (*esp. N Am., coll.*) eccentric, crazy, zany. ~*n.* **1** an eccentric person. **2** in baseball, a ball that spins against the natural curve. **screw cap** *n.* SCREW TOP (under SCREW). **screw-coupling** *n.* a collar with threads for joining pipes etc. together. **screwdriver** *n.* a tool like a blunt chisel for turning screws. **screwed** *a.* **1** twisted. **2** (*sl.*) ruined. **3** (*sl.*) drunk, tipsy. **screwer** *n.* **screw eye** *n.* a screw with a loop instead of a slotted head, for attaching cords to picture frames etc. **screw gear** *n.* an endless screw or worm for working a cogwheel etc. **screw hook** *n.* a hook which has a screw point for fastening it. **screw-jack** *n.* a lifting-jack with a screw rotating in a nut. **screw pine** *n.* any tree of the tropical genus *Pandanus*, with leaves clustered spirally. **screw-plate** *n.* a steel plate used for making male screws. **screw-press** *n.* a press worked by means of a screw. **screw propeller** *n.* a form of propeller with twisted blades which act like a screw. **screw-tap** *n.* a tool for making female screws. **screw top** *n.* a top for a bottle, jar etc., that opens and closes with a screwing motion. **screw-top, screw-topped** *a.* **screw-up** *n.* (*sl.*) a mess, bungle. **screw valve** *n.* a stopcock opened and shut by a screw. **screwy** *a.* (*comp.* **screwier,** *superl.* **screwiest**) **1** (*coll.*) mad, crazy. **2** (*coll.*) eccentric, absurd, zany. **screwiness** *n.*

scribal SCRIBE.

scribble (skrib´əl) *v.i.* **1** to write hastily or illegibly. **2** to make random or meaningless marks with a pen, crayon etc. **3** (*derog.*) to be a journalist or author. ~*v.t.* to write hastily, carelessly or without regard to correctness. ~*n.* **1** hasty or careless writing. **2** a scrawl. **3** something written hastily or carelessly. **scribblement** *n.* **scribbler** *n.* **scribbly** *a.*

scribe (skrīb) *n.* **1** a writer. **2** a secretary, a copyist. **3** (*Hist.*) an ancient Jewish writer or keeper of official records, one of a class of commentators, interpreters and teachers of the sacred law. **4** (*also* **scribe-awl**) a pointed instrument for marking lines on wood, bricks etc., a scriber. ~*v.t.* to mark with a scriber. **scribal** *a.* **scriber, scribing-awl, scribing-iron, scribing-tool** *n.* a tool used for scoring or marking lines etc.

scrim (skrim) *n.* strong cotton or linen cloth used for lining in upholstery and for cleaning.

scrimmage (skrim´ij) *n.* **1** a tussle, a confused or rough-and-tumble struggle, a skirmish. **2** in rugby football, a scrummage. **3** in American football, the period or activity between the ball coming into play and the time it is dead. ~*v.i.* to engage in a scrimmage. ~*v.t.* in American football, to put (the ball) into a scrimmage. **scrimmager** *n.*

scrimp (skrimp) *v.t.* **1** to make small, scant or short. **2** to limit, to skimp. ~*v.i.* to be niggardly. **scrimpy** *a.*

scrimshander (skrim´shandə) *v.t.* to scrimshaw. ~*n.* a person who scrimshaws.

scrimshank (skrim´shangk) *v.i.* (*esp. Mil., sl.*) to avoid work, to get out of doing one's duty. **scrimshanker** *n.*

scrimshaw (skrim´shaw) *v.t.* to decorate (ivory, shells etc.) with carvings and coloured designs. ~*n.* a piece of such work.

scrip (skrip) *n.* **1** a provisional certificate given to a subscriber for stock of a bank or company. **2** such certificates collectively. **3** an extra share or shares instead of a dividend.

script (skript) *n.* **1** a piece of writing. **2** handwriting as distinct from print. **3** printed cursive characters, type in imitation of writing. **4** an alphabet or system of writing. **5** handwriting in imitation of type. **6** the written text or draft of a film, play or radio or television broadcast as used by the actors or performers. **7** (*Law*) a writing, an original document. **8** an answer paper in an examination. ~*v.t.* to write the script for. **scriptorium** (-taw´ri-) *n.* (*pl.* **scriptoriums, scriptoria** (-riə)) a writing room, esp. in a monastery. **scriptorial** *a.* **scriptwriter** *n.* a person who writes scripts, esp. for broadcasting or for the cinema. **scriptwriting** *n.*

scripture (skrip´chə) *n.* **1** a sacred writing or book. **2** (**Scripture**) the Bible, esp. the books of the Old and New Testament without the Apocrypha. **3** a passage from the Scriptures. **the Scriptures** the Bible. **scriptural** *a.* of, relating to, derived from, based upon, or contained in a scripture, esp. the Bible. **scripturally** *adv.*

scrivener (skriv´ənə) *n.* (*Hist.*) a person whose business was to draw up contracts or other documents, a notary.

scrod (skrod) *n.* (*N Am.*) a young cod or haddock, esp. when prepared for cooking.

†scrofula (skrof´ūlə) *n.* a form of tuberculosis affecting esp. the lymph glands of the neck. **scrofulous** *a.*

scroll (skrōl) *n.* **1** a roll of paper or parchment.

2 an ancient book or volume in this form. **3** a convolved or spiral ornament more or less resembling a scroll of parchment, such as a volute, the curved head of a violin etc., a band or ribbon bearing an inscription, a flourish, or tracery consisting of spiral lines. ~*v.t.* **1** to roll up like a scroll. **2** to decorate with scrolls. **3** to enter in a scroll. **4** (*Comput.*) to move (text) up, down or across a screen. ~*v.i.* **1** to curl up like a scroll. **2** (*Comput.*) to move text up, down or across a screen so as to display the next line or section. **scroll bar** *n.* the part at the edge of a computer display which can be clicked on to scroll text etc. **scrolled** *a.* **scroller** *n.* **scroll saw** *n.* a fretsaw for cutting scrolls. **scrollwork** *n.* ornamental work in spiral lines, esp. cut out with a scroll saw.

Scrooge (skrooj) *n.* a miserly person.

scrotum (skrō´təm) *n.* (*pl.* **scrota** (-tə), **scrotums**) the pouch enclosing the testes in the higher mammals. **scrotal** *a.*

scrounge (skrownj) *v.t.* (*coll.*) **1** to pilfer. **2** to cadge. ~*v.i.* **1** to hunt around. **2** to cadge things. ~*n.* an act of scrounging. **on the scrounge** engaged in scrounging. **scrounger** *n.*

scrub¹ (skrŭb) *v.t.* (*pres.p.* **scrubbing,** *past, p.p.* **scrubbed**) **1** to rub hard with something coarse and rough, esp. with soap and water used with a scrubbing-brush for the purpose of cleaning or scouring. **2** to purify (a gas) with a scrubber. **3** (*coll.*) to get rid of, cancel. **4** to slow down by allowing (one's tyres) to scrape the road. ~*v.i.* **1** to clean or brighten things by rubbing hard. **2** to work hard. **3** to scrub the hands and arms before carrying out surgery. **4** (of tyres) to scrape, esp. when cornering. ~*n.* **1** the act of scrubbing. **2** a lotion containing abrasive granules for cleansing the skin. **to scrub round** (*coll.*) to avoid or ignore. **scrubber** *n.* **1** a person who or thing which scrubs. **2** a gas-purifier for removing tar and ammonia by spraying with water. **3** (*sl., offensive*) a prostitute or promiscuous woman. **scrubbing** *n.*, *a.* **scrubbing-brush,** (*N Am.*) **scrub-brush** *n.* a stiff brush for scrubbing floors etc.

scrub² (skrŭb) *n.* **1** (a tract of) undergrowth or stunted trees. **2** a stunted tree, bush etc. **3** (*esp. N Am.*) an inferior animal. **4** something mean or despicable. **5** (*N Am.*) a player not of the first team. **scrubby** *a.* (*comp.* **scrubbier,** *superl.* **scrubbiest**). **scrubland** *n.* **scrub turkey** *n.* a megapode. **scrub typhus** *n.* a febrile disease transmitted by mites.

scruff¹ (skrŭf) *n.* the nape or back of the neck, esp. as grasped by a person dragging another.

scruff² (skrŭf) *n.* (*coll.*) an unkempt or scruffy person. **scruffy** *a.* (*comp.* **scruffier,** *superl.* **scruffiest**) untidy, dirty. **scruffily** *adv.* **scruffiness** *n.*

scrum (skrŭm) *n.* **1** a set struggle in rugby between the forwards of both sides grappling in a compact mass with the ball on the ground in the middle. **2** (*coll.*) a disorderly crowd. ~*v.i.* (*pres.p.* **scrumming,** *past, p.p.* **scrummed**) **1** to form a scrum. **2** (*coll.*) to jostle or crowd. **to scrum down** to scrum. **scrum-half** *n.* the half-back who puts the ball into the scrum.

scrummage (skrŭm´ij) *n.* a rugby scrum. ~*v.i.* to scrum in rugby. **scrummager** *n.*

scrump (skrŭmp) *v.t., v.i.* (*coll.*) to steal (apples) from an orchard. **scrumpy** *n.* (*pl.* **scrumpies**) (*coll.*) (a) rough cider.

scrumple (skrŭm´pəl) *v.t.* to crumple, wrinkle.

scrumptious (skrŭmp´shəs) *a.* (*coll.*) **1** (of food) delicious. **2** first-class, stylish. **scrumptiously** *adv.* **scrumptiousness** *n.*

scrunch (skrŭnch) *v.t.* **1** to crunch. **2** to crush, to crumple. **3** to hunch up. **4** to style (hair) by crushing it. ~*v.i.* to make or move with a crunching sound. ~*n.* a crunch. **scrunch-dry** *v.t.* (*3rd pers. sing. pres.* **scrunch-dries**, *pres.p.* **scrunch-drying**, *past, p.p.* **scrunch-dried**) to dry (the hair) with a hairdryer whilst crushing in the hand, to give body. **scrunchy, scrunchie** *n.* (*pl.* **scrunchies**) an elastic loop covered in pleated fabric, for holding the hair in a ponytail.

scruple (skroo´pəl) *n.* **1** a doubt or hesitation from conscientious or moral motives. **2** (*Hist.*) a weight of 20 grains (1.296 g), the third part of a dram (apothecaries' weight). ~*v.i.* to hesitate, to be reluctant (to do etc.). **scrupler** *n.* **scrupulous** (-pū-) *a.* **1** influenced by scruples. **2** careful, cautious. **scrupulosity** (-los´-) *n.* **scrupulously** *adv.* **scrupulousness** *n.*

scrutiny (skroo´tini) *n.* (*pl.* **scrutinies**) **1** close observation or investigation. **2** an official examination of votes given at an election to verify the correctness of a declared result. **scrutineer** (-niə´) *n.* a person who examines something, esp. who acts as examiner in a scrutiny of votes. **scrutinize, scrutinise** *v.t.* to examine minutely. **scrutinization** (-zā´shən) *n.* **scrutinizer** *n.*

scry (skrī) *v.i.* (*3rd pers. sing. pres.* **scries**, *pres.p.* **scrying**, *past, p.p.* **scried**) to practise crystalgazing. **scryer** *n.*

scuba (skoo´bə, skū´-) *n.* (*pl.* **scubas**) an aqualung. **scuba-diving** *n.* underwater swimming with an aqualung. **scuba-dive** *v.i.* **scuba-diver** *n.*

scud (skŭd) *v.i.* (*pres.p.* **scudding**, *past, p.p.* **scudded**) **1** to run or fly swiftly. **2** (*Naut.*) to run fast before a gale with little or no sail spread. ~*n.* **1** the act or a spell of scudding. **2** a scudding motion. **3** loose, vapoury clouds driven swiftly by the wind. **4** a light passing shower. **5** windblown spray.

scuff (skŭf) *v.i.* **1** to drag or scrape with the feet in walking. **2** to become abraded or roughened, esp. by use. ~*v.t.* **1** to scrape or shuffle (the feet). **2** to touch lightly. **3** to roughen the surface of. ~*n.* a mark or roughened place caused by scuffing. **scuffed** *a.* worn, shabby.

scuffle (skŭf´əl) *v.i.* to fight or struggle in a roughand-tumble way. ~*n.* a confused and disorderly fight or struggle. **scuffler** *n.*

sculduggery SKULDUGGERY.

scull (skŭl) *n.* **1** either of a pair of short oars used

by one person for propelling a boat. **2** an oar used with twisting strokes over the stern. **3** a person who sculls a boat. **4** a boat propelled by sculling. **5** (*pl.*) a race between boats rowed by one person. ~*v.t.* to propel (a boat) by a scull or sculls. **sculler** *n.* **1** a person who sculls. **2** a boat rowed thus.

Usage note The spellings of the nouns *scull* (an oar) and *skull* (the cranium) should not be confused.

scullery (skŭl´əri) *n.* (*pl.* **sculleries**) a place where dishes and utensils are washed up, vegetables prepared etc.

†**scullion** (skŭl´yən) *n.* a servant who cleans pots, dishes etc., a kitchen drudge.

sculp (skŭlp) *v.t.* (*coll.*) to carve, to sculpture.

sculpin (skŭl´pin) *n.* any of various N American sea fishes with large spiny heads.

sculpture (skŭlp´chə) *n.* **1** the art of cutting, carving, modelling or casting wood, stone, clay, metal etc. into representations of natural objects or designs in round or in relief. **2** carved or sculptured work collectively. **3** a piece of work cut, carved, modelled or cast from wood, stone, clay, metal etc. **4** (*Zool.*) raised or sunk markings on a shell. ~*v.t.* **1** to represent in or by sculpture. **2** to ornament with sculpture. **3** to shape by or as by carving, moulding etc. ~*v.i.* to practise sculpture. **sculpt** *v.t., v.i.* to sculpture. **sculptor** *n.* a person who sculptures. **sculptress** *n.* a female sculptor. **sculptural** *a.* **sculpturally** *adv.* **sculpturesque** (-resk´) *a.*

scum (skŭm) *n.* **1** impurities that rise to the surface of liquid, esp. in fermentation or boiling. **2** the scoria of molten metal. **3** froth or any film of floating matter. **4** (*fig.*) the vile and worthless part. **5** (*coll.*) a worthless person or group. ~*v.t.* (*pres.p.* **scumming**, *past, p.p.* **scummed**) **1** to clear of scum, to skim. **2** to be or form a scum on. ~*v.i.* to become covered with scum. **scumbag** *n.* (*sl.*) a despicable or disgusting person. **scummy** *a.* (*comp.* **scummier**, *superl.* **scummiest**).

scumble (skŭm´bəl) *v.t.* **1** to cover (an oil painting) lightly with opaque or semi-opaque colours so as to soften the outlines or colours. **2** to produce a similar effect on (a drawing) by lightly rubbing. ~*n.* **1** a material for scumbling. **2** the effect produced.

scuncheon (skŭn´chən) *n.* a bevelling, splay or elbow in a window opening etc.

scupper[1] (skŭp´ə) *n.* a hole or tube through a ship's side to carry off water from the deck.

scupper[2] (skŭp´ə) *v.t.* **1** (*sl.*) to sink (a ship). **2** (*sl.*) to ruin, to do for. **3** (*sl.*) to kill.

scurf (skœf) *n.* **1** flakes or scales thrown off by the skin, esp. of the head. **2** any loose scaly matter adhering to a surface. **scurfy** *a.*

scurrilous (skŭr´iləs) *a.* using or expressed in grossly abusive or indecent language. **scurrility** (-ril´-) *n.* (*pl.* **scurrilities**). **scurrilously** *adv.* **scurrilousness** *n.*

scurry (skŭr´i) *v.i.* (*3rd pers. sing. pres.* **scurries,** *pres.p.* **scurrying,** *past, p.p.* **scurried**) to go with great haste, to hurry. *~n.* (*pl.* **scurries**) **1** an act or the noise of scurrying. **2** bustle, haste. **3** a flurry of rain or snow.

scurvy (skœ´vi) *n.* a disease caused by lack of vitamin C and characterized by swollen gums, extravasation of blood and general debility, arising orig. esp. among those on shipboard from a deficiency of vegetables. *~a.* (*comp.* **scurvier,** *superl.* **scurviest**) mean, contemptible. **scurvied** *a.* **scurvily** *adv.* **scurviness** *n.* **scurvy grass** *n.* any plant of the genus *Cochlearia*, formerly used as a remedy for scurvy.

scut (skŭt) *n.* a short tail, esp. of a hare, rabbit or deer.

scuta SCUTUM.

scutcheon (skŭch´ən) *n.* **1** an escutcheon. **2** a cover or frame for a keyhole. **3** a nameplate. **scutcheoned** *a.*

scute SCUTUM.

scutter (skŭt´ə) *v.i.* to scurry, scuttle. *~n.* the act or an instance of scuttering.

scuttle[1] (skŭt´əl) *n.* **1** a metal or other receptacle for carrying or holding coals, esp. for a fireplace, usu. called a coal scuttle. **2** the part of a motorcar body immediately behind the bonnet.

scuttle[2] (skŭt´əl) *n.* a hole with a movable lid or hatch in a wall or roof or the deck or side of a ship. *~v.t.* **1** to cut holes through the bottom or sides of (a ship). **2** to sink by cutting such holes. **scuttlebutt** *n.* **1** a cask of drinking water, usu. with a hole for dipping through, kept on the deck of a ship. **2** (*coll.*) rumour, gossip.

scuttle[3] (skŭt´əl) *v.i.* **1** to hurry along, to scurry. **2** to make off, to bolt. *~n.* **1** a hurried run or gait. **2** a hasty flight, a bolt. **scuttler** *n.*

scutum (skū´təm) *n.* (*pl.* **scuta** (-tə)) a scute. **scutal** *a.* **scutate** (-tət) *a.* **scute** *n.* (*Zool.*) a shield-like plate, scale or bony or horny segment as of the armour of a crocodile, turtle etc.

scuzzy (skŭz´i) *a.* (*comp.* **scuzzier,** *superl.* **scuzziest**) (*sl.*) squalid or disgusting. **scuzz** *n.*

scye (sī) *n.* the opening of a coat etc. where the sleeve is inserted.

scythe (sīdh) *n.* a long curved blade with a crooked handle used for mowing or reaping. *~v.t.* to cut with a scythe.

SDR *abbr.* special drawing right(s).

SE *abbr.* **1** south-east. **2** south-eastern.

Se *chem. symbol* selenium.

sea (sē) *n.* **1** the body of salt water covering the greater part of the earth's surface. **2** a definite part of this, or a very large enclosed body of (usu. salt) water. **3** the swell or motion of the sea. **4** a great wave, a billow. **5** the set or direction of the waves. **6** a vast quantity or expanse, a flood (of people, troubles etc.). *~a.* of, relating to, living, growing or used in, on or near the sea. **all at sea** perplexed, uncertain. **at sea 1** on the open sea. **2** out of sight of land. **3** perplexed, uncertain, wide of the mark. **by sea** in a ship. **on the sea 1** in a

ship at sea. **2** situated on the coast. **to go to sea** to become or to be a sailor. **to put (out) to sea** to leave port or land. **sea anchor** *n.* a sail stretched by spars and thrown overboard to lessen the leeway of a drifting ship. **sea anemone** *n.* any of various coelenterates of the order Actinaria, having a polypoid body with oral rings of tentacles. **sea-angel** *n.* the angelfish. **sea bass** *n.* a serranoid food-fish, esp. *Centropristis striatus*, common on the Atlantic shores of the US. **seabed** *n.* the floor of the sea. **seabird** *n.* **seaboard** *n.* **1** land bordering on the sea. **2** the seacoast. **3** the seashore. **seaborne** *a.* conveyed by sea. **sea bream** *n.* a marine fish of the family Sparidae, esp. of the genus *Pagellus* or *Spondyliosoma*. **sea breeze** *n.* a breeze blowing from the sea, usu. by day, in alternation with a land breeze at night. **sea buckthorn** *n.* a shrub, *Hippophae rhamnoides*, which grows on seacoasts. **sea change** *n.* a transformation or transmutation. **sea-chest** *n.* a sailor's storage chest. **seacock** *n.* a valve through which the sea can be admitted into the hull of a ship. **sea cow** *n.* a sirenian. **sea cucumber, sea gherkin** *n.* a holothurian such as the trepang. **sea dog** *n.* an old sailor, esp. of the Elizabethan era. **sea eagle** *n.* any of various fishing eagles, esp. of the genus *Haliaeetus*, and other large seabirds. **sea-ear** *n.* an ormer or mollusc of the genus *Haliotis*. **sea elephant** *n.* the elephant seal. **sea fan** *n.* a coral of the genus *Gorgonia* or a related genus, having fanlike branches. **seafarer** *n.* **1** a sailor. **2** a traveller by sea. **seafaring** *a.* **1** travelling by sea. **2** following the occupation of a sailor. *~n.* **1** travel by sea. **2** the occupation of a sailor. **seafood** *n.* edible salt-water fish and crustaceans, esp. shellfish. **seafront** *n.* the part of a town that faces the sea. **sea-girt** *a.* (*poet.*) surrounded by the sea. **seagoing** *a.* **1** making foreign voyages, as opposed to *coasting*. **2** seafaring. **sea gooseberry** *n.* any ctenophore with a rounded body and numerous cilia. **sea green** *n.* a faint bluish green. **sea-green** *a.* **seagull** *n.* a gull (family Laridae). **sea hare** *n.* any mollusc of the genus *Aplysia* with earlike tentacles. **sea hog** *n.* the common porpoise. **sea holly** *n.* an umbelliferous plant, *Eryngium maritimum*, with spiny leaves. **sea horse** *n.* **1** any of various upright fish of the family Syngnathidae, esp. *Hippocampus hippocampus*. **2** a fabulous animal, half horse and half fish. **sea-island cotton** *n.* a fine variety of cotton originally grown on the islands off the coasts of Georgia, S Carolina and Florida. **seajack** *v.t.* to hijack at sea. *~n.* an act of seajacking. **seajacker** *n.* **seakale** *n.* a cruciferous plant, *Crambe maritima*, grown as a culinary vegetable for its young shoots. **seakale beet** *n.* CHARD. **sea lane** *n.* a route for ships at sea. **sea lavender** *n.* any maritime plant of the genus *Limonium*, which have spikes of white, pink or mauve flowers. **sea legs** *n.pl.* ability to walk on the deck of a vessel at sea on a stormy day. **sea level** *n.* a level continuous with that of the surface of the sea at mean tide, taken as a basis for surveying etc. (in Britain at Newlyn, Cornwall). **sea lily** n. (pl. **sea lilies**) any echinoderm of the class Crinoidea, esp. of the genus *Ptilocrinus*. **sea lion** n. a large-eared seal, esp. of the genus *Zalophus* or *Otaria*. **sea loch** n. (*Sc.*) a lakelike arm of the sea. **Sea Lord** n. either of two senior naval officers (First Sea Lord and Second Sea Lord) on the admiralty board of the Ministry of Defence. **seaman** n. (pl. **seamen**) **1** a mariner, a sailor, esp. one below the rank of officer. **2** a person able to navigate a ship. **seamanlike**, **seamanly** a. **seamanship** n. **sea mile** n. a nautical mile. **sea mouse** n. an iridescent sea worm, *Aphrodite aculeata*. **sea onion** n. the squill. **sea otter** n. a marine otter, *Enhydra lutris*, of the shores of the N Pacific. **sea pen** n. any of various coelenterates of the genus *Pennatula*, which form feather-like colonies. **sea pink** n. thrift, *Armeria maritima*. **seaplane** n. an aeroplane fitted with floats to enable it to take off from and alight on the water. **seaport** n. a town with a harbour on the coast. **sea power** n. **1** a nation that has great naval strength. **2** naval strength. **sea purse** n. the leathery envelope in which sharks and rays deposit their eggs. **seaquake** n. an earthquake at sea. **sea room** n. room to handle a ship without danger of running ashore or of collision. **sea salt** n. salt obtained from sea water by evaporation. **seascape** n. a picture representing a scene at sea. **Sea Scout** n. a member of a branch of the Scouts specializing in sailing etc. **sea serpent** n. **1** a sea snake. **2** a creature of immense size and serpentine form, believed by mariners to inhabit the depths of the ocean. **sea shanty** n. SHANTY². **seashell** n. the shell of a marine mollusc. **seashore** n. **1** the shore, coast or margin of the sea. **2** (*Law*) the space between high and low water marks. **3** land adjacent to the sea. **seasick** a. suffering from seasickness. **seasickness** n. a peculiar functional disturbance characterized by nausea and vomiting, brought on by the motion of a ship. **seaside** n. a place or district close to the sea, esp. a holiday resort. **sea slug** n. any of various shell-less marine gastropod molluscs, esp. of the order Nudibranchia. **sea snail** n. **1** any snail-like marine gastropod such as a whelk. **2** a slimy fish of the family Liparididae, esp. *Liparis liparis*, the unctuous sucker. **sea snake** n. a venomous marine snake of the family Hydrophidae inhabiting the Indian Ocean and other tropical seas. **sea snipe** n. **1** the snipe fish. **2** the dunlin, *Calidris alpina*. **sea squirt** n. an ascidian. **sea trout** n. the salmon trout, bulltrout and some other fishes. **sea urchin** n. an echinus. **sea wall** n. a wall or embankment for protecting land against encroachment by the sea. **seaward** a. directed or situated towards the sea. ~adv. towards the sea. ~n. a seaward side or aspect. **seawards** adv. **seaware** n. any large coarse seaweed, esp. when used as a fertilizer. **sea wasp** n. a jellyfish of the order Cubomedusae, of

Australian tropical waters. **sea water** n. water of or from the sea. **seaway** n. **1** an inland waterway on which ocean-going ships can travel. **2** a ship's progress. **3** a clear way for a ship at sea. **seaweed** n. **1** any alga or other plant growing in the sea. **2** such algae collectively. **seaworthy** a. (of a ship) in a fit state to go to sea. **seaworthiness** n. **sea wrack** n. coarse seaweed, esp. thrown up by the waves.

seaborgium (sēbaw´giəm) n. (*Chem.*) (a name proposed for) the artificial radioactive element, at. no. 106, chem. symbol Sg.

seal¹ (sēl) n. **1** a carnivorous amphibious marine mammal of various species of the family Phocidae, having flipper-like limbs adapted for swimming and thick fur. **2** any allied mammal belonging to the family Otariidae, distinguished by having visible external ears, comprising the sea lions and fur seals. **3** sealskin. ~v.i. to hunt seals. **sealer**¹ n. a ship or person engaged in hunting seals. **sealskin** n. **1** the underfur of the fur seal, esp. prepared for use as material for jackets etc. **2** a sealskin garment.

seal² (sēl) n. **1** a die or stamp having a device, usu. in intaglio, for making an impression on wax or other plastic substance. **2** a piece of wax, lead or other material stamped with this and attached to a document as a mark of authenticity etc., or to an envelope, package, box etc. to prevent its being opened without detection etc. **3** a special official mark or design; the impression made with a stamp on wax or other plastic substance. **4** a stamped wafer- or other mark affixed to a document in lieu of this. **5** any device that must be broken to give access. **6** any act, gift or event regarded as authenticating, ratifying or guaranteeing. **7** a symbolic, significant or characteristic mark or impress. **8** a decorative adhesive stamp. **9** a vow of secrecy. **10** anything used to close a gap, prevent the escape of gas etc. **11** water in the trap of a drainpipe preventing the ascent of foul air. ~v.t. **1** to affix a seal to. **2** to stamp with a seal or stamp, esp. as a mark of correctness or authenticity. **3** to fasten with a seal. **4** to close hermetically, to shut up. **5** to close (the lips etc.) tightly. **6** to confine securely. **7** to secure against leaks, draughts etc. **8** to make (e.g. wood) impermeable to rain, etc. by applying a coating. **9** to confirm. **10** to ratify, to certify. **one's lips are sealed** one must keep a secret. **to set one's seal on** to authorize. **sealable** a. **sealant** n. a substance for sealing wood, stopping up gaps etc. **sealed** a. **sealed-beam** a. of or relating to electric lights, such as car headlights, in which the reflector and bulb are in one sealed unit. **sealed book** n. something beyond one's knowledge or understanding. **sealed orders** n.pl. orders that must not be read until a specified time. **sealer**² n. **1** a device or substance that seals. **2** (*Can.*) (*also* **sealer jar**) a jar used for preserving fruit etc. **sealing wax** n. a composition of shellac and turpentine with a pigment used for sealing letters etc. **seal-ring** n. a finger ring with a seal. **seals of office** *n.pl.* seals held by the Lord Chancellor, Secretary of State etc. as a symbol of office.

sealer[1] SEAL[1].

sealer[2] SEAL[2].

Sealyham (sē′lihəm, -liəm), **Sealyham terrier** *n.* a breed of Welsh terrier.

seam (sēm) *n.* **1** a ridge or other visible line of junction between two parts or things, esp. two pieces of cloth etc. sewn together. **2** (*Anat.*) a suture. **3** a crack, a fissure. **4** a line on the surface of anything, esp. the face. **5** a thin layer separating two strata of rock. **6** a thin stratum of coal. **7** (*N Am.*) a piece of sewing. ~*v.t.* **1** to join together with or as with a seam. **2** to mark with a seam, furrow, scar etc. **seam bowler** *n.* in cricket, a bowler who makes the ball bounce on its seam so that it changes direction. **seam bowling** *n.* **seamer, seaming machine** *n.* **seamless** *a.* **seamlessly** *adv.* **seamstress** (-stris), **sempstress** (semp′-) *n.* a woman whose occupation is sewing. **seamy** *a.* (*comp.* **seamier,** *superl.* **seamiest**) **1** showing the seams. **2** disreputable, unpleasant. **seaminess** *n.*

seance (sā′ons, -äs), **séance** *n.* a meeting for exhibiting, receiving or investigating spiritualistic manifestations.

sear (siə), **sere** *v.t.* **1** to burn or scorch the surface of to dryness and hardness. **2** to cauterize. **3** (*fig.*) to brand. **4** to cause pain or anguish to. **5** to brown (meat) at a high temperature so that the juices are retained. **6** to make callous or insensible. ~*a.* (*poet.*) (of leaves etc.) dried up, withered. **searing** *a.*

search (sœch) *v.t.* **1** to go over and examine for what may be found or to find something. **2** to examine (esp. a person) for concealed weapons etc. **3** to explore, to probe. **4** to look for, to seek (out). ~*v.i.* to make a search or investigation. ~*n.* **1** the act of seeking, looking or inquiring. **2** investigation, examination. **in search of** trying to find. **search me!** (*coll.*) how should I know?, I have no idea. **searchable** *a.* **search engine** *n.* (*Comput.*) a program that searches for data, files etc. **searcher** *n.* **searching** *a.* **1** making search or inquiry. **2** penetrating, thorough. **searchingly** *adv.* **searchlight** *n.* an electric arc light or other powerful illuminant concentrated into a beam that can be turned in any direction for lighting channels, discovering an enemy etc. **search party** *n.* a party going out to search for a lost, concealed or abducted person or thing. **search warrant** *n.* a warrant granted by a Justice of the Peace, authorizing entry into a house etc. to search for stolen property etc.

season (sē′zən) *n.* **1** any one of the four divisions of the year, spring, summer, autumn, winter. **2** a period of time of a specified or indefinite length. **3** the period of the greatest activity of something, or when it is in vogue, plentiful, at its best etc. **4** a favourable time. **5** a period when a mammal is on heat. **6** (*coll.*) a season ticket. ~*v.t.* **1** to render

palatable or give a higher relish to by the addition of condiments etc. **2** to make more piquant or pleasant. **3** to make sound or fit for use by preparation, esp. by maturing, acclimatizing etc. **4** to make mature or experienced. **5** to moderate (justice with mercy etc.). ~*v.i.* **1** to become inured, habituated, accustomed etc. **2** (of timber) to become hard and dry. **in season 1** in vogue. **2** in condition for shooting, hatching, use, mating, eating etc. **3** (of a mammal) on heat. **4** at a fit or opportune time. **seasonable** *a.* **1** occurring or done at the proper time. **2** suitable to the season. **seasonableness** *n.* **seasonably** *adv.* **seasonal** *a.* **1** of or occurring at a particular season. **2** required, done etc. according to the season. **seasonal affective disorder** *n.* a state of fatigue and depression occurring in the winter months, thought to be caused by lack of sunlight. **seasonality** (-nal′-) *n.* **seasonally** *adv.* **seasoner** *n.* **seasoning** *n.* **1** anything added to food to make it more palatable. **2** anything that increases enjoyment. **season ticket** *n.* a railway or other ticket, usu. issued at a reduced rate, valid for any number of journeys etc., for the period specified.

Usage note The adjectives *seasonable* and *seasonal* should not be confused: *seasonable* means suitable to the season, and *seasonal* relating to or done at a particular season.

seat (sēt) *n.* **1** something on which a person sits or may sit. **2** the part of a chair etc. on which a person's weight rests in sitting. **3** the part of a machine or other structure on which another part is supported. **4** the buttocks or the part of trousers etc. covering them. **5** a place for sitting or where one may sit. **6** the place where anything is, location. **7** a place in which authority is vested. **8** a country residence. **9** the right of sitting, esp. in a legislative body. **10** manner or posture of sitting. ~*v.t.* **1** to cause to sit down. **2** to assign seats to. **3** to provide (a church etc.) with seats. **4** to settle, to establish. **be seated** sit down. **by the seat of one's pants** (*coll.*) by intuition or instinct. **to take a seat** to sit down. **seat belt** *n.* a strap to hold a person in a seat in a car, aeroplane etc. **seater** *n.* (*usu in comb.,* as *two-seater*). **seating** *n.* **1** the provision of seats. **2** the seats provided or their arrangement. **seatless** *a.*

sebaceous (sibā′shəs) *a.* **1** fatty. **2** made of fatty or oily matter. **3** (of glands, ducts, follicles etc.) containing, conveying, or secreting fatty or oily matter to the skin or hair. **seborrhoea** (sebərē′ə), (*N Am.*) **seborrhea** *n.* (*Med.*) excessive secretion of sebum. **seborrhoeic** *a.* **sebum** (sē′bəm) *n.* the fatty matter secreted by the sebaceous glands, which lubricates the hair and skin.

Sec. *abbr.* secretary.

sec[1] (sek) *n.* (*coll.*) a second (of time).

sec[2] (sek) *a.* (of wine) dry.

sec[3] (sek) *abbr.* secant.

sec. *abbr.* second(s).

secant (sē′kənt) *a.* (*Math.*) **1** cutting. **2** dividing into two parts. ~*n*. **1** a straight line intersecting a curve, esp. a radius of a circle drawn through the second extremity of an arc of this and terminating in a tangent to the first extremity. **2** the ratio of this to the radius. **3** the ratio of the hypotenuse to the base of a right-angled triangle formed by drawing a perpendicular to either side of the angle.

secateurs (sekətœz´) *n.pl.* pruning scissors.

secco (sek´ō) *n.* (*pl.* **seccos**) tempera-painting on dry plaster.

secede (sisēd´) *v.i.* to withdraw from membership, association or communion, as with a Church. **seceder** *n.*

secession (sisesh´ən) *n.* **1** the act of seceding. **2** (*Hist.*) (**Secession**) the withdrawal of 11 southern states from the US Union in 1860. **secessional** *a.* **secessionism** *n.* **secessionist** *n.*

seclude (siklood´) *v.t.* to shut up or keep (a person, place etc.) apart or away from society. **secluded** *a.* **1** hidden from view, private. **2** away from others, solitary. **secludedly** *adv.* **secludedness** *n.* **seclusion** (-zhən) *n.* **seclusionist** *n.* **seclusive** *a.*

second¹ (sek´ənd) *a.* **1** immediately following the first in time, place or position. **2** next in value, authority, rank or position. **3** secondary, inferior. **4** other, alternate. **5** additional. **6** subordinate, derivative. **7** (*Mus.*) lower in pitch. **8** (*Mus.*) performing a subordinate part. ~*n.* **1** the next after the first in rank, importance etc. **2** a second class in an examination etc. **3** a person taking this. **4** another or an additional person or thing. **5** a person who supports another, esp. one who attends on the principal in a duel, boxing match etc. **6** the 60th part of a minute of time or angular measurement. **7** (*coll.*) a very short time. **8** (*pl.*) goods that have a slight flaw or are of second quality. **9** (*pl.*) coarse, inferior flour, or bread made from this. **10** (*Mus.*) the interval of one tone between two notes, either a whole tone or a semitone. **11** (*Mus.*) the next tone above or below. **12** (*Mus.*) two tones so separated combined together. **13** (*Mus.*) a lower part added to a melody when arranged for two voices or instruments. **14** (*coll.*) an alto. **15** second gear. **16** (*pl., coll.*) a second helping or course of a meal. ~*v.t.* **1** to support. **2** to support (a resolution) formally to show that the proposer is not isolated. **in the second place** as a second consideration etc. **second to none** unsurpassed. **second advent** *n.* the return of Christ to establish His personal reign on earth. **second ballot** *n.* a procedure in an election to choose a clear winner after some candidates have been eliminated in a first ballot. **second-best** *a.* next after best, of second quality. ~*n.* an alternative. **second cause** *n.* (*Logic*) a cause that is itself caused. **second chamber** *n.* the upper house in a legislative body having two chambers. **second childhood** *n.* a person's dotage. **second class** *n.* **1** the category next to the first or highest. **2** the second level of an honours

degree. **3** the class of mail not given priority. **4** (*N Am.*) a class of mail for newspapers etc. **second-class** *a.* **1** of second or inferior quality, rank etc., second-rate. **2** treated as inferior or second-rate. **3** of the second class. ~*adv.* by second class. **second coming** *n.* (*Theol.*) the second advent. **second cousin** *n.* the child of a parent's cousin. **second-degree** *a.* (*Med.*) (of burns) that cause blistering but not permanent scars. **seconder** *n.* **second floor** *n.* **1** the second from the ground floor. **2** (*US*) the first storey. **second gear** *n.* the forward gear next above first gear in a car etc. **second-generation** *a.* **1** of an improved stage of development. **2** denoting the children of a first generation. **second-guess** *v.t.* **1** (*coll.*) to forestall (a person) by guessing their actions, reactions etc. in advance. **2** to re-evaluate (a situation etc.) with hindsight. **second hand** *n.* the hand on a watch or clock that indicates seconds. **second-hand** *a.* **1** not primary or original. **2** not new, sold or for sale after having been used or worn. **3** dealing in second-hand goods. ~*adv.* at second hand. **at second hand** as one deriving or learning through another purchaser, owner, hearer etc. **second honeymoon** *n.* a holiday taken by a married couple after some years of marriage. **second in command** *n.* the next under the commanding officer, person in charge etc. **second intention** *n.* **1** (*Med.*) the healing of a wound by granulation after suppuration. **2** (*pl., Logic*) secondary conceptions formed by the action of the mind upon first intentions and their interrelations. **second lieutenant** *n.* the lowest commissioned rank in the British army. **secondly** *adv.* **1** in the second place. **2** as the second item. **second name** *n.* a surname. **second nature** *n.* something that has become effortless or instinctual through constant practice. **second officer** *n.* an assistant mate on a merchant ship. **second person** *n.* (*Gram.*) the form of a pronoun, verb etc. indicating the person or persons addressed. **second-rate** *a.* of inferior quality, size, value etc. **second rater** *n.* **second reading** *n.* a general approval of the principles of a bill. **second self** *n.* a close friend or associate. **second sight** *n.* the power of seeing things at a distance in space or time as if they were present, clairvoyance. **second-sighted** *a.* **second string** *n.* **1** an alternative course of action. **2** (*N Am.*) a reserve for a sports team etc. **second teeth** *n.pl.* a mammal's permanent teeth. **second thoughts** *n.pl.* reconsideration of a previous opinion or decision. **second wind** *n.* a renewed burst of energy, stamina etc. after a concentrated effort.

second² (sikond´) *v.t.* to transfer temporarily or release for temporary transfer to another position, branch of an organization etc. **secondee** (-dē´) *n.* **secondment** *n.*

secondary (sek´əndəri) *a.* **1** coming next in order of place or time to the first. **2** not primary, subordinate. **3** of the second or of inferior rank, importance etc. **4** revolving round a primary planet. **5** between the tertiary geological formation above and the primary below, Mesozoic. **6** of or being a feather on the second joint of a bird's wing. **7** of, relating to or carrying an induced current. ~n. (pl. **secondaries**) **1** a delegate or deputy. **2** a secondary planet, a satellite. **3** the secondary geological epoch or formation. **4** a secondary feather. **5** a hind wing in an insect. **6** a secondary coil, circuit etc. **secondarily** adv. **secondariness** n. **secondary cell** n. a rechargeable cell or battery using reversible chemical reactions to convert chemical into electrical energy. **secondary coil** n. a coil in which the current in the primary winding induces the electric current. **secondary colour**, (N Am.) **secondary color** n. any of the colours produced by combinations of two primary colours. **secondary education** n. education provided for children who have received primary education. **secondary picketing** n. picketing of an organization by workers with whom there is no direct dispute. **secondary rainbow** n. a reversed rainbow sometimes seen inside or outside a rainbow. **secondary school** n. a school for pupils in secondary education. **secondary sex characteristics, secondary sexual characteristics** n.pl. attributes related to the sex of an individual that develop from puberty.

seconde (sikond´, səgŏd´) n. in fencing, a position in parrying or lungeing.

☒ **secratary** common misspelling of SECRETARY.

secrecy (sē´krəsi) n. (pl. **secrecies**) **1** the state of being secret. **2** the quality of being secretive. **sworn to secrecy** having promised to keep something a secret.

secret (sē´krit) a. **1** concealed from notice, kept or meant to be kept private. **2** occult, mysterious. **3** given to secrecy, secretive. **4** secluded. ~n. **1** something to be kept back or concealed. **2** a thing kept back from general knowledge. **3** a mystery, something that cannot be explained. **4** the explanation or key to a mystery. **5** secrecy. **in (on) the secret** among the people who know a secret. **in secret** secretly, privately. **to keep a secret** not to reveal a secret. **secret agent** n. an agent of the secret service. **secret ballot** n. a ballot in which votes are cast in secret. **secretly** adv. **secretness** n. **secret police** n. a police force operating in secret, usu. dealing with political rather than criminal matters. **secret service** n. **1** a government service for obtaining information, or other work of which no account is given to the public. **2** (Secret Service) in the US, a branch of the Treasury Department responsible for protecting the President etc. **secret society** n. a society that is kept secret from non-members.

secretaire (sekrəteə´) n. an escritoire, a bureau.

secretary (sek´rətəri) n. (pl. **secretaries**) **1** a person employed to assist in clerical work, correspondence, arranging meetings etc., either by an individual or in an office. **2** an officer appointed by a company, firm, society etc. to conduct its correspondence, keep its records and represent it in business transactions etc. **3** a Secretary of State. **4** the principal assistant or deputy of an ambassador. **secretarial** (-teə´ri-) a. **secretariat** (-teə´riət) n. **1** the post of a secretary. **2** an administrative office headed by a secretary. **3** the administrative workers of an organization. **secretary bird** n. a S African bird, Sagittarius serpentarius, preying on snakes etc. (named from its penlike tufts in the ear). **Secretary-General** n. (pl. **Secretary-Generals**) the person in charge of the administration of an organization. **Secretary of State** n. **1** a minister in charge of a government department. **2** the Foreign Secretary of the US. **secretaryship** n.

Usage note Pronunciation as (sek´ət-), without the first r, is best avoided.

secrete (sikrēt´) v.t. **1** to conceal, to hide. **2** (Biol.) to separate from the blood, sap etc. by the process of secretion. **secretion** (-shən) n. **1** (Biol.) **a** the process of separating materials from the blood, sap etc. for the service of the body or for rejection as excreta. **b** any matter thus secreted, such as mucus, gastric juice, urine etc. **2** the act of secreting or concealing. **secretor** n. **secretory** a.

secretive (sē´krətiv) a. given to secrecy, uncommunicative. **secretively** adv. **secretiveness** n.

sect (sekt) n. **1** (usu. derog.) a body of persons who have separated from a larger body, esp. an established Church, on account of philosophical or religious differences. **2** a religious denomination, a nonconformist Church (as regarded by opponents). **3** the body of adherents of a particular philosopher, school of thought etc. **4** a party, a faction. **sectarian** a., n. **sectarianism** n. **sectarianize, sectarianise** v.t. **sectary** n. (pl. **sectaries**) a member of a sect.

sect. abbr. section.

section (sek´shən) n. **1** separation by cutting. **2** that which is cut off or separated. **3** each of a series of parts into which anything naturally separates or is constructed so as to separate for convenience in handling etc. **4** a division or subdivision of a book, chapter, statute etc. **5** a distinct part of a country, people, community, class etc. **6** a section-mark. **7** (N Am.) any one of the portions of a square of 640 acres (259 hectares) into which public lands are divided. **8** a thin slice of any substance prepared for microscopic examination. **9** a cutting of a solid figure by a plane, or the figure so produced. **10** a vertical plan of a building etc. as it would appear upon an upright plane cutting through it. **11** a part of an orchestra consisting of all the instruments of one class. **12** (N Am.) a particular district of a town. ~v.t. **1** to divide or arrange in sections. **2** to represent in sections. **3** to cause (a person) to be committed to a psychiatric hospital under the mental health legislation. **4** (Biol.) to cut into thin slices for microscopic examination. **sectional** a.

sectionalism *n.* **sectionalist** *n.* **sectionalize, sectionalise** *v.t.* **sectionally** *adv.* **section-mark** *n.* the sign § marking a reference or the beginning of a section of a book, chapter etc.

sector (sek´tə) *n.* **1** a distinct part, a section. **2** (*Mil.*) a section of a battle front. **3** (*Math.*) **a** a portion of a circle or other curved figure included between two radii and an arc. **b** a mathematical rule consisting of two hinged arms marked with sines, tangents etc. **sectoral** *a.* **sectorial** (-taw´ri-) *a.* **1** denoting a tooth on each side of either jaw, adapted for cutting like scissors with the corresponding one, as in many Carnivora. **2** sectoral. ~*n.* a sectorial tooth.

secular (sek´ūlə) *a.* **1** of or relating to the present world or to things not spiritual or sacred, not ecclesiastical or monastic. **2** (of education etc.) not concerned with religion. **3** lasting, extending over, occurring in or accomplished during a century, an age or a very long period of time. **4** of or relating to secularism. ~*n.* **1** a lay person. **2** a Roman Catholic priest bound only by the vow of chastity and belonging to no regular order. **secularism** *n.* **1** the state of being secular. **2** the belief that religion should not be part of education etc. **secularist** *n.*, *a.* **secularity** (-lar´-) *n.* **secularize, secularise** *v.t.* **secularization** (-zā´shən) *n.* **secularly** *adv.*

secure (sikūə´) *a.* **1** free from danger or risk. **2** safe from attack, impregnable. **3** certain, sure (of). **4** in safe keeping, safe not to escape. **5** firmly fixed or held. **6** trustworthy. ~*v.t.* **1** to make safe or secure. **2** to put into a state of safety from danger. **3** to close or confine securely. **4** to make safe against loss, to guarantee payment of. **5** to gain possession of. **6** (*Med.*) to compress (a vein etc.) to prevent bleeding. **to secure arms** (*Mil.*) to hold rifles muzzle downwards with the lock under the armpit as a protection from rain. **securable** *a.* **securely** *adv.* **securement** *n.* **secureness** *n.* security. **securer** *n.*

security (sikū´riti) *n.* (*pl.* **securities**) **1** the state of being or feeling secure. **2** freedom from danger or risk, safety. **3** certainty, assurance. **4** that which guards or secures. **5** (an organization which sees to) the protection of premises etc. against burglary, espionage etc. **6** a pledge, a guarantee. **7** something given or deposited as a pledge for payment of a loan, fulfilment of obligation etc., to be forfeited in case of non-performance. **8** a person who becomes surety for another. **9** a document constituting evidence of debt or of property, a certificate of stock etc. **on security of** using as a guarantee. **securitization** (-zā´shən), **securitisation** *n.* the putting together of a number of stocks, mortgages etc. into a single bond which is traded like a security. **securitize** *v.t.* **security blanket** *n.* **1** an official sanction or set of measures used in the interest of security. **2** a blanket or piece of material used to comfort a young child. **security guard** *n.* a person employed to guard buildings, money in transit etc.

security risk *n.* a person or thing considered to be a threat to (national) security.

sedan (sidan´) *n.* **1** (*also* **sedan chair**) a covered chair for one person, carried by two people by means of a pole on each side. **2** (*NAm.*) a closed car with a single compartment for driver and passengers, a saloon car.

sedate (sidāt´) *a.* calm, staid. ~*v.t.* to administer a sedative to. **sedately** *adv.* **sedateness** *n.* **sedation** (-ā´shən) *n.* **1** a state of calmness or relaxation, esp. produced by a sedative drug. **2** the administration of a sedative. **sedative** (sed´ə-) *a.* allaying nervous irritability, soothing. ~*n.* a sedative medicine, influence etc.

sedentary (sed´əntəri) *a.* **1** sitting. **2** accustomed or obliged by occupation, to sit a great deal. **3** involving or requiring much sitting. **4** (*Zool.*) not migratory, attached to one place, not free-moving. **sedentarily** *adv.* **sedentariness** *n.*

Seder (sā´də) *n.* a ceremonial meal eaten on the first night (or the first two nights) of Passover.

sedge (sej) *n.* **1** any coarse grasslike plant of the genus *Carex*, usu. growing in marshes or beside water. **2** any coarse grass growing in such spots. **sedge bird, sedge warbler, sedge wren** *n.* a reed warbler, *Acrocephalus schoenobaenus*, haunting sedgy places. **sedgy** *a.* (*comp.* **sedgier**, *superl.* **sedgiest**).

sediment (sed´imənt) *n.* **1** the matter which subsides to the bottom of a liquid. **2** lees, dregs. **3** (*Geol.*) deposited material. **sedimentary** (-men´-) *a.* **sedimentary rocks** *n.pl.* rocks or strata laid down as sediment from water. **sedimentation** (-ā´shən) *n.* **sedimented** *a.*

sedition (sidish´ən) *n.* **1** disorder or commotion in a state, not amounting to insurrection. **2** conduct tending to promote treason or rebellion. **seditious** *a.* **seditiously** *adv.* **seditiousness** *n.*

seduce (sidūs´) *v.t.* **1** to lead astray, esp. to induce (someone) to sexual intercourse. **2** to entice or lure, esp. by offering rewards. **seduced** *a.* beguiled. **seducement** *n.* **seducer** *n.* **seducible** *a.* **seduction** (-dŭk´shən) *n.* **1** the act of seducing, esp. of persuading someone to sexual intercourse. **2** the state of being seduced. **3** that which seduces, an enticement, an attraction, a tempting or attractive quality, a charm. **seductive** *a.* **seductively** *adv.* **seductiveness** *n.* **seductress** (-tris) *n.* a female seducer.

sedulous (sed´ūləs) *a.* assiduous, constant, steady and persevering in business or endeavour; industrious, diligent. **sedulity** (-dū´-), **sedulousness** *n.* **sedulously** *adv.*

sedum (sē´dəm) *n.* any fleshy-leaved plant of the genus *Sedum*, including the stonecrop, orpine etc.

see[1] (sē) *v.t.* (*past* **saw** (saw), *p.p.* **seen** (sēn)) **1** to perceive by the eye. **2** to discern, to look at. **3** to perceive mentally, to understand. **4** to experience, to go through. **5** to be a spectator of. **6** to imagine, to picture to oneself. **7** to ascertain or establish. **8** to call on, to pay a visit to.

9 to escort, to conduct (a person home etc.). **10** in poker etc., to accept (a challenge, bet etc., or person offering this). **11** to ensure. **12** to consider; to deduce. **13** to meet socially, esp. regularly as a boyfriend or girlfriend. **14** to consult. **15** to find attractive (*What does he see in her?*). **16** to supervise (an action etc.). **17** (*impers.*) to refer to. ~*v.i.* **1** to have or exercise the power of sight. **2** to discern. **3** to inquire. **4** to reflect, to consider carefully. **5** to ascertain by reading. **6** to take heed. **7** to give attention. **8** to make provision. **9** to look out. **10** to take care (that). **as far as I can see** to the best of my understanding, judgement etc. **as I see it** in my opinion. **do you see?** do you understand? **I'll be seeing you** (*coll.*) goodbye. **I see** I understand. **let me see** used to ask for time to consider or reflect. **see you (later)** (*coll.*) goodbye for the present. **to have seen better days** to be on the decline. **to see about 1** to give attention to. **2** to make preparations for etc. **to see after 1** to take care of. **2** to see about. **to see daylight** (*coll.*) to begin to comprehend. **to see fit** to think advisable. **to see into** to investigate. **to see life** to gain experience of the world, esp. by dissipation. **to see off 1** to escort on departure. **2** (*coll.*) to get rid of. **to see one's way clear to** to feel able to. **to see out 1** to escort out of a house etc. **2** to outlive, outlast. **3** to last to the end of. **4** to finish. **to see over** to inspect. **to see someone damned first** (*coll.*) to refuse categorically to do what someone wants. **to see someone right** (*coll.*) to make sure that someone is taken care of, rewarded etc. **to see the light 1** to be born. **2** to realize the truth. **3** to be converted to a religion or to any other belief. **to see the light of day** to come into existence. **to see things** to see things that are not there. **to see through 1** to penetrate, not to be deceived by. **2** to persist (in a task etc.) until it is finished. **3** to help through a difficulty, danger etc. **to see to** to look after. **to see to it that** to take care that. **you see 1** you understand. **2** you will understand when I have explained. **seeable** *a.* **seeing** *n.* **1** sight. **2** (*Astron.*) atmospheric conditions for observation. ~*conj.* inasmuch as, since, considering (that). **seer** *n.* **1** a person who sees. **2** a person who foresees, a prophet. **see-through** *a.* (esp. of clothing) (semi-)transparent.

see² (sē) *n.* the diocese or jurisdiction of a bishop or archbishop.

seed (sēd) *n.* **1** the mature fertilized ovule of a flowering plant, consisting of the embryo germ or reproductive body and its covering. **2** (*collect.*) seeds, esp. in quantity for sowing. **3** the male fertilizing fluid, semen. **4** the germ from which anything springs, beginning. **5** a seeded player. **6** a crystal added to induce crystallization. **7** a small container for the application of radium etc. ~*v.t.* **1** to sow or sprinkle with seed. **2** to put a small crystal into (a solution) to start crystallization. **3** to scatter solid particles in (a cloud) to bring on rain. **4** to remove the seeds from (fruit etc.). **5** in sport, to arrange the draw in

(a tournament) so that the best players do not meet in the early rounds. **6** to classify (a good player) in this way. ~*v.i.* **1** to sow seed. **2** to run to seed. **3** to produce or drop seed. **to go to seed** to run to seed. **to run to seed 1** to cease flowering as seeds are produced. **2** to become shabby. **3** to lose self-respect. **seedbed** *n.* **1** a piece of ground where seedlings are grown. **2** a place where anything develops. **seed cake** *n.* a sweet cake containing aromatic seeds, esp. caraway. **seed-coat** *n.* the integument of a seed. **seed coral** *n.* coral in small seedlike pieces. **seedcorn** *n.* **1** corn set aside for sowing. **2** assets reused for future profit. **seed crystal** *n.* a crystal used to cause crystallization. **seed-eater** *n.* a granivorous bird. **seeder** *n.* **1** a device for planting seeds. **2** a device for removing the seeds from raisins etc. **3** a seedfish. **4** a person who seeds. **seed-fish** *n.* (*pl. in general* **seed-fish**, *in particular* **seed-fishes**) a fish that is ready to spawn. **seed-head** *n.* a flower head in seed. **seed-leaf** *n.* a cotyledon. **seedless** *a.* **seedling** (-ling) *n.* **1** a plant reared from seed. **2** a very young plant. **seed-lip** *n.* a basket in which a sower carries seed. **seed money** *n.* the money with which a project is set up. **seedpearl** *n.* a small seedlike pearl. **seed-plot** *n.* **1** a piece of ground on which seeds are sown. **2** a nursery or hotbed (of seditions etc.). **seed potato** *n.* (*pl.* **seed potatoes**) a potato tuber used for planting. **seedsman** *n.* (*pl.* **seedsmen**) a person who deals in seeds. **seed-time** *n.* the season for sowing. **seed vessel** *n.* the pericarp. **seedy** *a.* (*comp.* **seedier**, *superl.* **seediest**) **1** abounding in seeds. **2** run to seed. **3** (*coll.*) shabby, down at heel. **4** (*coll.*) off colour, as after a debauch. **5** (*coll.*) out of sorts. **seedily** *adv.* **seediness** *n.*

seek (sēk) *v.t.* (*past, p.p.* **sought** (sawt)) **1** to go in search of. **2** to try to find, to look for. **3** to ask, to solicit (a thing of a person). **4** to resort to. ~*v.i.* **1** to make search or inquiry (after or for). **2** to try (to do). **far/ much to seek 1** seriously lacking or insufficient. **2** a long way off being found yet. **to seek 1** lacking, insufficient. **2** not found yet. **to seek out 1** to search for. **2** to cultivate the friendship of. **seeker** *n.* **sought-after** *a.* desired as a possession etc., much in demand.

seem (sēm) *v.i.* **1** to give the impression of being, to be apparently though not in reality. **2** to appear (to do, to have done, to be true or the fact that). **3** to be evident. **do not seem to** (*coll.*) somehow do not. **I can't seem to** (*coll.*) I am unable to. **it seems** it appears, it is reported (that). **it would seem** it appears, it seems to one. **seeming** *a.* **1** appearing, apparent, but not real. **2** apparent and perhaps real. **seemingly** *adv.* **seemingness** *n.*

seemly (sēm'li) *a.* (*comp.* **seemlier**, *superl.* **seemliest**) **1** becoming, decent. **2** suited to the occasion, purpose etc. **seemliness** *n.*

seen SEE¹.

seep (sēp) *v.i.* to percolate, to ooze. ~*n.* (*N Am.*) a spring or place where oil, water etc. oozes out of the ground. **seepage** (-ij) *n.*

seer SEE[1].

seersucker (siə´sŭkə) *n.* a thin striped linen or cotton fabric with a puckered appearance.

see-saw (sē´saw) *n.* **1** a game in which two persons sit one on each end of a board balanced on a support in the middle and move alternately up and down. **2** the board so used. **3** alternate or reciprocating motion. **4** a contest in which the advantage changes sides repeatedly. ~*a.* **1** moving up and down or to and fro. **2** vacillating. ~*adv.* with a see-saw movement. ~*v.t.* to cause to move in a see-saw fashion. ~*v.i.* **1** to play on a see-saw. **2** to move up and down or backwards and forwards. **3** to act in a vacillating manner. **to go see-saw** to vacillate.

seethe (sēdh) *v.t.* (*past* **seethed,** †**sod** (sod), *p.p.* **seethed,** †**sodden** (sod´ən)) to boil. ~*v.i.* **1** to be in a state of ebullition. **2** to be agitated, to bubble over. **seether** *n.* **seethingly** *adv.*

segment (seg´mənt) *n.* **1** (*esp. Biol.*) a portion cut or marked off as separable, a section, a division, esp. one of a natural series (as of a limb between the joints, the body of an articulate animal, a fruit or plant organ divided by clefts). **2** (*Geom.*) a part cut off from any figure by a line or plane. **3** in linguistics, the smallest distinct part of a spoken utterance. ~*v.i.* **1** to divide or be divided into segments. **2** (of a cell) to undergo cleavage. ~*v.t.* to divide into segments. **segmental** (-men´-), **segmentary, segmentate** (-tət) *a.* **segmentalize** (-men´-), **segmentalise** *v.t.* **segmentalization** (-ā´shən) *n.* **segmentally** *adv.* **segmentation** (-ā´shən) *n.*

sego (sē´gō), **sego lily** *n.* (*pl.* **segos, sego lilies**) a N American liliaceous plant, *Calochortus nuttallii.*

segregate (seg´rigāt) *v.t.* **1** to separate from others. **2** to place in a separate class. **3** to split (a community) into separate parts on the basis of race. ~*v.i.* **1** (*Biol.*) (of a pair of alleles) to become separated during meiosis. **2** (*Mineral.*) (of crystals) to separate from a mass and collect about nuclei and lines of fracture. **segregable** *a.* **segregation** (-ā´shən) *n.* **1** the act of segregating. **2** separation of a community on racial grounds. **segregational** *a.* **segregationist** *n.* **segregative** *a.*

segue (seg´wā) *v.i.* (*3rd pers. sing. pres.* **segues,** *pres.p.* **seguing,** *past, p.p.* **segued**) (*Mus.*) to follow on immediately. ~*n.* an act or result of seguing.

seguidilla (segidēl´ya) *n.* **1** a lively Spanish dance in triple time. **2** the music for this.

sei (sā), **sei whale** *n.* a rorqual, *Balaenoptera borealis.*

seif (sēf, sāf), **seif dune** *n.* a long sand dune in the form of a ridge.

❌ **seige** common misspelling of SIEGE.

seigneur (senyœ´), †**seignior** (sān´yə) *n.* (*Hist.*) a feudal lord. **seigneurial** *a.* **seigneury** (sā´-) *n.* (*pl.* **seigneuries**) (*Hist.*) the territory or lordship of a seigneur.

seine (sān) *n.* a large fishing net with floats at the top and weights at the bottom for encircling. ~*v.t.*

to catch with this. ~*v.i.* to fish with it. **seine-net** *n.* **seiner** *n.*

seise (sēz) *v.t.* (*usu. in p.p., Law*) to put in possession of. **seised of** in legal possession of. **seisable** *a.* **seisin** (-zin) *n.* **1** possession of land under a freehold. **2** the act of taking such possession. **3** the thing so possessed.

seismic (sīz´mik), **seismal** (-məl) *a.* **1** of, relating to or produced by an earthquake. **2** of, relating to or involving artificially induced vibrations of the earth. **3** of enormous proportions or effect. **seismical** *a.* **seismically** *adv.* **seismicity** (-mis´iti) *n.* seismic activity, esp. liability to or frequency of earthquakes. **seismic survey** *n.* a survey which uses seismic methods to find oil and gas.

seismo- (sīz´mō) *comb. form* of or relating to an earthquake.

seismogram (sīz´məgram) *n.* a record given by a seismograph. **seismograph** (sīz´məgrahf) *n.* an instrument for recording the period, extent and direction of the vibrations of an earthquake. **seismographic** (-graf´-), **seismographical** *a.* **seismography** (-mog´-) *n.*

seismology (sīzmol´əji) *n.* the study or science of earthquakes. **seismological** (-məloj´-) *a.* **seismologically** *adv.* **seismologist** *n.*

seize (sēz) *v.t.* **1** to grasp or lay hold of suddenly. **2** to grasp mentally, to comprehend. **3** to affect suddenly and forcibly. **4** (*Naut.*) to fasten, to lash with cord etc. **5** (*Law*) to seise. **6** to take possession of. **7** to confiscate. ~*v.i.* **1** to lay hold (upon). **2** to become stuck. **3** (of a body part) to become stiff. **seized of 1** in legal possession of. **2** aware or informed of. **seizable** *a.* **seizer** *n.* **seizin** (-zin) *n.* SEISIN (under SEISE). **seizing** *n.* (*Naut.*) a cord or cords used for seizing. **seizure** (-zhə) *n.* **1** the act of seizing. **2** a sudden attack, as of a disease.

selachian (silā´kiən) *n.* a fish of the subclass Selachii comprising the sharks, dogfish etc. ~*a.* of or relating to this subclass. **selachoid** (sel´-əkoid) *n., a.*

seldom (sel´dəm) *adv.* rarely, not often. ~*a.* rare.

select (silekt´) *a.* **1** chosen, picked out. **2** taken as superior to or more suitable than the rest. **3** strict in selecting new members etc., exclusive. ~*v.t.* to choose, to pick out (the best etc.). **select committee** *n.* members of parliament specially chosen to examine a particular question and to report on it. **selectee** (-tē´) *n.* (*N Am.*) a conscript. **selection** *n.* **1** the act of selecting. **2** the right or opportunity of selecting, choice. **3** that which is selected. **4** (*Biol.*) a natural or artificial process of sorting out organisms suitable for survival. **5** a range of goods (as in a shop) from which to choose. **selectional** *a.* **selectionally** *adv.* **selective** *a.* **1** of or relating to selection. **2** capable of selecting. **3** given to selecting only what suits. **selectively** *adv.* **selectiveness** *n.* **selectivity** (sēlektiv´-, sil-, sel-) *n.* **selectness** *n.* **selector** *n.*

selenium (silē´niəm) *n.* (*Chem.*) a non-metallic element, at. no. 34, chem. symbol Se, obtained as a by-product in the manufacture of sulphuric acid, similar in chemical properties to sulphur and tellurium, utilized for its varying electrical resistance in light and darkness. **selenic** (silen´ik, -lē´-) *a.* **selenious** *a.* **selenite** (sel´init) *n.* a transparent variety of gypsum or sulphate of lime. **selenitic** (selinit´-) *a.* **selenium cell** *n.* a type of photoelectric cell using a strip of selenium.

seleno- (silē´nō), **selen-, seleni-** (-ni) *comb. form* **1** of or relating to the moon. **2** of, relating to or containing selenium.

self (self) *n.* (*pl.* **selves** (selvz)) **1** the individuality of a person or thing, as the object of reflexive consciousness or action. **2** one's individual person. **3** one's private interests etc. **4** furtherance of these. **5** (*pl.* **selfs**) a flower of a uniform or of the original wild colour. *~a.* **1** self-coloured. **2** uniform, pure, unmixed. **3** of one piece or the same material throughout. *~pron.* (*coll., facet.*) myself, yourself etc. *~v.t.* (*Bot.*) to self-fertilize. **one's better self** one's nobler impulses. **one's former self** oneself as one was before. **one's old self** one's former self. **selfhood, selfness** *n.* **selfish** *a.* **1** attentive only to one's own interests. **2** not regarding the interests or feelings of others. **3** actuated by or proceeding from self-interest. **selfishly** *adv.* **selfishness** *n.* **selfless** *a.* having no regard for self, unselfish. **selflessly** *adv.* **selflessness** *n.*

self- (self) *comb. form* **1** expressing direct or indirect reflexive action, as in *self-command.* **2** expressing action performed independently, or without external agency, as in *self-acting, self-fertilization.* **3** expressing relation to the self, as in *self-conscious, self-suspicious.* **4** expressing uniformity, naturalness etc., as in *self-coloured, self-glazed.*

self- (+ a–i words) **self-abandon** *n.* the abandonment of oneself. **self-abandoned** *a.* **self-abandonment** *n.* **self-abasement** *n.* the abasement or humiliation of oneself. **self-abhorrence** *n.* self-hatred. **self-abnegation** *n.* self-denial. **self-absorbed** *a.* absorbed in oneself. **self-absorption** *n.* **1** absorption in oneself. **2** (*Physics*) the absorption of radiation in a material by the material itself. **self-abuse** *n.* **1** masturbation. **2** the revilement of oneself. **self-accusation** *n.* the accusation of oneself. **self-accusatory** *a.* **self-acknowledged** *a.* acknowledged by oneself. **self-acting** *a.* automatic. **self-action** *n.* **self-activity** *n.* **self-actualization, self-actualisation** *n.* (*Psych.*) the realization of one's personality and development of this. **self-addressed** *a.* (of an envelope) addressed to oneself (for the sending of a reply). **self-adhesive** *a.* (of a label etc.) adhesive; able to stick without extra glue etc. **self-adjusting** *a.* (of machinery etc.) adjusting itself. **self-adjustment** *n.* **self-admiration** *n.* the admiration of oneself. **self-advancement** *n.* the advancement of oneself or one's interests. **self-advertisement** *n.* the promotion of oneself. **self-advertiser** *n.* **self-affirmation** *n.* (*Psych.*) the recognition of the existence of the self. **self-aggrandizement, self-aggrandisement** *n.* the act or process of trying to

make oneself more important. **self-aggrandizing** *a.* **self-analysis** *n.* (*Psych.*) the analysis of oneself. **self-analysing,** (*N Am.*) **self-analyzing** *a.* **self-appointed** *a.* appointed by oneself. **self-appointment** *n.* **self-appreciation** *n.* appreciation of oneself. **self-approbation** *n.* approval of oneself. **self-approval** *n.* self-appreciation. **self-assembly** *n.* the construction of furniture etc. using parts that come in a kit. **self-assertion** *n.* the assertion of one's views etc. **self-asserting, self-assertive** *a.* **self-assertiveness** *n.* **self-assured** *a.* confident in one's own abilities etc. **self-assurance** *n.* **self-assuredly** *adv.* **self-aware** *a.* conscious of one's own feelings, motives etc. **self-awareness** *n.* **self-basting** *a.* (of poultry etc.) not requiring basting during cooking. **self-betrayal** *n.* **1** the betrayal of oneself. **2** the revelation of one's real thoughts etc. **self-binder** *n.* a reaping machine with an automatic binding device. **self-born** *a.* born of itself. **self-build** *n.* the building of a house by the person who is going to live in it. *~a.* of or relating to such building. **self-builder** *n.* **self-catering** *a.* (of holiday accommodation) not providing meals, cleaning etc. **self-censorship** *n.* censorship of oneself. **self-centred,** (*N Am.*) **self-centered** *a.* interested solely in oneself and one's own affairs, egotistic. **self-centredly** *adv.* **self-centredness** *n.* **self-certify** *v.t.* (*3rd pers. sing. pres.* **self-certifies,** *pres.p.* **self-certifying,** *past, p.p.* **self-certified**) to attest to in writing (one's financial standing etc.). **self-certification** *n.* **self-certified** *a.* **self-cleaning** *a.* (esp. of an oven) cleaning itself. **self-closing** *a.* (of a door etc.) closing automatically. **self-cocking** *a.* (of a gun or gun hammer) cocking automatically. **self-collected** *a.* self-possessed, composed. **self-colour,** (*N Am.*) **self-color** *n.* **1** a colour uniform throughout. **2** a pure or unmixed colour. **3** a colour not changed by cultivation. **self-coloured** *a.* **self-command** *n.* self-control. **self-communion** *n.* meditation, mental converse with oneself. **self-conceit** *n.* self-satisfaction. **self-conceited** *a.* **self-condemned** *a.* condemned by oneself (openly or inadvertently). **self-condemnation** *n.* **self-confessed** *a.* openly admitting oneself to be. **self-confident** *a.* self-assured. **self-confidence** *n.* **self-confidently** *adv.* **self-congratulation** *n.* congratulation of oneself. **self-congratulatory** *a.* **self-conquest** *n.* the overcoming of one's weak points etc. **self-conscious** *a.* **1** conscious of one's actions, situation etc., esp. as observed by others. **2** (*Philos.*) conscious of one's own activities, states etc. **3** able to reflect on these. **self-consciously** *adv.* **self-consciousness** *n.* **self-consistent** *a.* consistent with other parts (of a whole). **self-consistency** *n.* **self-constituted** *a.* self-appointed. **self-contained** *a.* **1** reserved, not communicative. **2** complete in itself. **self-containment** *n.* **self-contempt** *n.* contempt for oneself. **self-contemptuous** *a.* **self-content** *n.* satisfaction with oneself. **self-contented** *a.* **self-contradiction** *n.* internal inconsistency.

self-contradictory *a.* **self-control** *n.* power of controlling one's feelings, impulses etc. **self-controlled** *a.* **self-convicted** *a.* convicted by one's own acts etc. **self-correcting** *a.* correcting itself. **self-created** *a.* brought into existence by one's or its own power or vitality. **self-creation** *n.* **self-critical** *a.* critical of oneself. **self-criticism** *n.* **self-deceiver** *n.* a person who deceives themselves. **self-deceit, self-deception** *n.* **self-deceiving** *a.* **self-deceptive** *a.* **self-defeating** *a.* doomed to failure because of flaws within it. **self-defence,** (*N Am.*) **selfdefense** *n.* the act or art of defending one's own person, property or reputation. **self-defensive** *a.* **self-delight** *n.* delight in oneself. **self-delusion** *n.* the delusion of oneself. **self-denial** *n.* refusal to gratify one's own appetites or desires. **self-denying** *a.* **self-dependent** *a.* dependent on oneself. **self-dependence** *n.* **self-deprecation** *n.* the disparagement of oneself. **self-deprecating** *a.* **self-deprecatingly** *adv.* **self-deprecatory** *a.* **self-depreciation** *n.* self-deprecation. **self-depreciative** *a.* **self-depreciatory** *a.* **self-despair** *n.* despair with oneself. **self-destroying** *a.* destroying oneself or itself. **self-destruct** *v.i.* (of a bomb etc.) to explode automatically at a pre-set time. *~a.* able to self-destruct. **self-destruction** *n.* **1** the destruction of something by itself. **2** suicide. **self-destructive** *a.* **self-destructively** *adv.* **self-determination** *n.* **1** determination of one's own will, as opposed to *fatalism.* **2** the right of a group (local or racial) to decide to what state it will adhere. **3** the liberty of a state to determine its own form of government. **self-determined, self-determining** *a.* **self-development** *n.* the development of oneself. **self-devotion** *n.* the devotion of oneself to a cause; self-sacrifice. **self-discipline** *n.* discipline of oneself; self-control. **self-disciplined** *a.* **self-discovery** *n.* the process of gaining insight into one's character etc. **self-disgust** *n.* disgust with oneself. **self-distrust** *n.* distrust of oneself. **self-doubt** *n.* lack of confidence in one's abilities. **self-drive** *a.* (of a hired vehicle) driven by the hirer. **self-educated** *a.* educated by oneself. **self-education** *n.* **self-effacement** *n.* modesty; timidity. **self-effacing** *a.* **self-effacingly** *adv.* **self-elect, self-elected** *a.* elected by oneself or (as a committee) by its own members, co-opted. **self-election** *n.* **self-elective** *a.* **self-employed** *a.* running one's own business, or working freelance. **self-employment** *n.* **self-esteem** *n.* a good opinion of oneself. **self-estimation** *n.* self-evident *a.* obvious in itself, not requiring proof or demonstration. **self-evidence** *n.* **self-evidently** *adv.* **self-examination** *n.* **1** the examination of one's own behaviour etc. **2** the examination of one's body. **self-executing** *a.* (*Law*) (of a law) providing for its own enforcement independently of other legislation. **self-existent** *a.* existing independently, underived, unconditioned. **self-existence** *n.* **self-explanatory, self-explaining** *a.* not needing explanation. **self-expression** *n.* the

expression of one's own personality (through art etc.). **self-expressive** *a.* **self-faced** *a.* (of stone) having its natural face, unhewn. **self-feeder** *n.* **1** a machine, furnace etc. that feeds itself. **2** a machine for feeding animals automatically. **self-feeding** *a.* **self-fertile** *a.* (of plants) fertilized by their own pollen. **self-fertility** *n.* **self-fertilization, self-fertilisation** *n.* **self-fertilized, self-fertilizing** *a.* **self-financing** *a.* (of a project etc.) that finances itself. **self-financed** *a.* **self-flattery** *n.* self-appreciation. **self-flattering** *a.* **self-forgetful** *a.* oblivious of self, unselfish. **self-forgetfulness** *n.* **self-fulfilling** *a.* (of a prophecy etc.) bound to come true as a result of its being made. **self-fulfilment,** (*N Am.*) **self-fulfillment** *n.* the fulfilment of one's desires etc. **self-generating** *a.* generated by itself or oneself. **self-glorification** *n.* the glorification of oneself. **self-governing** *a.* **1** controlling oneself. **2** autonomous. **self-governed** *a.* **self-government** *n.* **self-hate** *n.* self-hatred. **self-hatred** *n.* hatred of oneself. **self-heal** *n.* a plant having healing virtues, esp. *Prunella vulgaris.* **self-help** *n.* the act or practice of attaining one's ends without help from others. *~a.* of or relating to self-help. **self-hypnotism** *n.* hypnotism of oneself. **self-hypnosis** *n.* one's own idea of what one is. **self-immolation** *n.* the offering of oneself as a sacrifice. **self-important** *a.* conceited, pompous. **self-importance** *n.* **self-importantly** *adv.* **self-imposed** *a.* imposed on and by oneself. **self-improvement** *n.* improvement of one's social or economic position by one's own efforts. **self-induced** *a.* **1** induced by oneself or itself. **2** produced by self-induction. **self-inductance** *n.* the property of an electric circuit that causes an electromotive force to be generated in it by a change in the current flowing through it. **self-induction** *n.* production of an induced electric current in the circuit by the variation of the current in the circuit. **self-inductive** *a.* **self-indulgent** *a.* gratifying one's inclinations etc. **self-indulgence** *n.* **self-indulgently** *adv.* **self-inflicted** *a.* inflicted by and on oneself. **self-interest** *n.* **1** one's personal advantage. **2** absorption in selfish aims. **self-interested** *a.* **self-involved** *a.* wrapped up in oneself. **self-involvement** *n.*

selfish SELF.

self- (+ j–l words) **self-justification** *n.* justifying or providing excuses for oneself. **self-justifying** *a.* **self-knowledge** *n.* the understanding of oneself. **self-loading** *a.* (of a firearm) reloading automatically. **self-loader** *n.* **self-locking** *a.* locking itself. **self-love** *n.* **1** undue regard for oneself or one's own interests. **2** selfishness. **3** conceit.

selfless SELF.

self- (+ m–w words) **self-made** *a.* **1** successful, wealthy etc. through one's own exertions. **2** made by oneself. **self-mastery** *n.* self-control. **selfmate** *n.* in chess, checkmate in which a player is forced to achieve checkmate. **self-mocking** *a.* mocking oneself or itself. **self-mockery** *n.*

self-motivated a. motivated by one's own interest, enthusiasm etc. **self-motivation** n. **self-murder** n. suicide. **self-murderer** n. **self-mutilation** n. mutilation of oneself. **self-neglect** n. neglect of oneself. **self-opinion** n. high opinion of oneself or one's opinion. **self-opinioned, self-opinionated** a. conceitedly or obstinately adhering to one's own views. **self-parody** n. (pl. **self-parodies**) (a) parody of oneself or one's work. **self-parodying** a. **self-perpetuating** a. perpetuating itself or oneself. **self-perpetuation** n. **self-pity** n. pity for oneself. **self-pitying** a. **self-pityingly** adv. **self-pollination** n. pollination by pollen from the same plant. **self-pollinated** a. **self-pollinating** a. **self-pollinator** n. **self-portrait** n. a portrait of oneself. **self-possessed** a. calm, having presence of mind. **self-possession** n. **self-praise** n. praise of oneself; boasting. **self-preservation** n. 1 preservation of oneself from injury. 2 the instinct impelling one to this. **self-proclaimed** a. proclaimed by oneself or itself. **self-propagating** a. able to propagate itself. **self-propelled** a. moving using its own means of propulsion. **self-propelling** a. **self-protection** n. self-defence; protecting oneself. **self-protective** a. **self-publicist** n. a person who tries to get publicity for themselves. **self-publicity** n. **self-raising**, (N Am.) **self-rising** a. (of flour) having the raising agent already added. **self-realization** n. 1 full development of one's faculties. 2 this as an ethical principle. **self-recording** a. self-registering. **self-referential** a. making reference to itself or oneself. **self-referentiality** n. **self-regard** n. 1 consideration or respect for oneself. 2 selfishness. 3 conceit. **self-regarding** a. **self-registering** a. (of a scientific instrument etc.) recording its movements etc. automatically. **self-regulating** a. regulating oneself or itself. **self-regulation** n. **self-regulatory** a. **self-reliant** a. independent; confident in one's abilities. **self-reliance** n. **self-reliantly** adv. **self-renewal** n. renewing oneself or itself. **self-renunciation** n. 1 self-sacrifice. 2 unselfishness. **self-reproach** n. blame directed at oneself. **self-reproachful** a. **self-respect** n. 1 due regard for one's character and position. 2 observing a worthy standard of conduct. **self-respectful, self-respecting** a. **self-restrained** a. restrained by oneself. **self-restraint** n. **self-revealing** a. revealing one's character, motives etc. **self-revelation** n. **self-righteous** a. pharisaical. **self-righteously** adv. **self-righteousness** n. **self-righting** a. righting itself (as when capsized). **self-rising** SELF-RAISING (under SELF- (+ M—W WORDS)). **self-rule** n. self-government. **self-sacrifice** n. surrender or subordination of one's own interests and desires to those of others. **self-sacrificing** a. **selfsame** a. exactly the same, absolutely identical. **self-satisfaction** n. conceit; complacence. **self-satisfied** a. **self-sealing** a. able to seal itself. **self-seed** v.i. (of a plant) to propagate itself by seed. **self-seeder** n. **self-seeding** a. **self-seeker** n. a

person selfishly pursuing their own interests. **self-seeking** n., a. **self-selection** n. the act of selecting oneself or itself. **self-selecting** a. **self-service** n., a. (a restaurant, shop etc.) where customers help themselves and pay a cashier on leaving. **self-serving** a. giving priority to one's own interests. **self-slaughter** n. suicide. **self-sown** a. growing from seed sown naturally by the parent plant. **self-starter** n. 1 an automatic device for starting a motor car. 2 a person who is ambitious and strongly motivated. **self-sterile** a. (Biol.) incapable of self-fertilization. **self-sterility** n. **self-styled** a. assuming a name or title oneself without authorization, would-be, pretended. **self-sufficient, self-sufficing** a. 1 capable of fulfilling one's own requirements, needs etc. without aid. 2 conceited, overbearing. **self-sufficiency** n. **self-sufficiently** adv. **self-suggestion** n. suggestion arising reflexively within the self, esp. in hypnotic states. **self-supporting** a. 1 financially independent. 2 able to support itself without help. **self-support** n. **self-surrender** n. surrender of oneself or one's will. **self-sustained, self-sustaining** a. sustaining oneself or itself. **self-tapping** a. (of a screw) able to cut its own thread. **self-taught** a. taught by oneself. **self-torture** n. the inflicting of pain on oneself. **self-understanding** n. 1 comprehension of one's actions etc. 2 awareness of oneself. **self-will** n. obstinacy. **self-willed** a. **self-winding** a. (of a clock etc.) winding itself automatically. **self-worth** n. self-esteem.

sell (sel) v.t. (past, p.p. **sold** (sōld)) 1 to transfer or dispose of (property) to another for an equivalent in money. 2 to yield or give up (one's life etc.) exacting some return. 3 to be a regular dealer in. 4 to surrender for a reward or bribe. 5 (sl.) to cheat. 6 to inspire others with a desire to possess. 7 (of a publication or recording) to attain sales of (a specified number of copies). 8 to cause to be sold. ~v.i. 1 to be a shopkeeper or dealer. 2 to be purchased, to find purchasers. 3 to have a specified price (to sell for £10). ~n. 1 (sl.) a disappointment, a fraud. 2 a manner of selling. **sold on** enthusiastic about. **to sell off** 1 to sell the remainder of (goods). 2 to clear out (stock), esp. at reduced prices. **to sell oneself** 1 to try to persuade someone of one's abilities. 2 to offer one's services for money etc. **to sell out** 1 to sell off (one's stock etc.). 2 to sell completely. 3 to dispose of (one's shares in a company etc.). 4 to betray. **to sell up** 1 to sell the goods of (a debtor) to pay their debt. 2 to sell one's business, one's house and possessions etc. **sellable** a. **sell-by date** n. 1 a date marked on the packaging of a perishable product, by which day the product should be withdrawn from sale. 2 (coll.) a date after which decay or decline begins. **seller** n. 1 a person who sells. 2 something that sells well or badly. **seller's market, sellers' market** n. a market in which demand exceeds supply and sellers make the price. **selling** n. **selling point** n. a good feature. **selling race** n. a horse race, the

winner of which is sold by auction. **sell-off** n.
1 the privatization of a company by selling
shares. **2** (esp. N Am.) a sale of bonds, shares etc.
leading to a fall in price. **3** a sale. **sell-out** n. **1** a
betrayal. **2** a performance etc. for which all the
tickets have been sold. **sell-through** n. the retail
of articles also commonly rented out, such as
videos.

Sellotape® (sel´ətāp) n. a cellulose or plastic adhesive tape for mending, binding etc. **sellotape**
v.t. to fix or fasten with Sellotape.

seltzer (selt´sə), **seltzer water** n. **1** an effervescing
mineral water. **2** an artificial substitute for this.

selvage (sel´vij) n. **1** a rope or ring made of spun
yarns etc., laid parallel and secured by lashings.
2 SELVEDGE.

selvedge (sel´vij) n. **1** the edge of cloth woven so
as not to unravel. **2** a narrow strip of different
material woven along the edge of cloth etc. and
removed or hidden in seaming. **3** the edge-plate
of a lock with an opening for the bolt. **4** (Geol.)
an alteration zone at the edge of a rock mass.

selves SELF.

SEM abbr. scanning electron microscope.

semantic (siman´tik) a. of or relating to semantics; concerned with the meaning of words
and symbols. **semantically** adv. **semantician**
(-tish´ən) n. **semanticist** (-sist) n. **semantics** n. the
area of linguistics concerned with meaning.

semaphore (sem´əfaw) n. **1** (Mil.) a system of
signalling using the arms or two flags to represent letters of the alphabet. **2** an apparatus
for signalling by means of oscillating arms or
flags or the arrangement of lanterns etc. **sema-
phoric** (-for´-), **semaphorical** a. **semaphoric-
ally** adv.

semasiology (simāziol´əji) n. semantics. **semasi-
ological** (-əloj´-) a. **semasiologist** n.

semblance (sem´bləns) n. **1** external appearance, seeming. **2** a likeness, an image. **semblable**
(sem´bləbəl) n. (one's) like or fellow.

semeiology SEMIOLOGY.

semeiotics SEMIOTICS.

semen (sē´mən) n. the fertilizing fluid containing
spermatozoa, produced by the generative organs
of a male animal.

semester (simes´tə) n. a college half-year in German, some American and other universities.

semi (sem´i) n. (pl. **semis**) (coll.) **1** a semi-
detached house. **2** a semi-final.

semi- (semi) pref. **1** half. **2** partially, imperfectly.
3 once every half.

semi- (+ a–m words) semi-annual a. occurring
every six months, half-yearly. **semi-annually**
adv. **semiaquatic** a. living or growing close to
or partly in water. **semi-automatic** a. **1** partly
automatic. **2** (of a firearm) self-loading. **semi-
autonomous** a. **1** partly self-governing. **2** having
some freedom to act independently. **semi-
basement** n. a storey in a building which is
partly below ground level. **semi-bold** a. printed
in a darker type than normal but not bold.

semibreve (sem´-) n. (Mus.) a note equal to half a
breve, or two minims. **semicircle** (sem´-) n. **1** a
half circle. **2** half the circumference of a circle.
3 a series of objects etc. arranged like this.
semicircular a. **semicircular canal** n. each of
three fluid-filled tubes in the inner ear, concerned with the maintenance of balance. **semi-
civilized, semi-civilised** a. partially civilized.
semicolon n. a mark (;) used in punctuation, now
usu. intermediate in value between the period
and the comma. **semiconductor** n. **1** a substance
(such as silicon) whose electrical conductivity
lies between those of metals and insulators and
increases as its temperature rises. **2** a device
using such a substance. **semiconducting** a. **semi-
conscious** a. partially conscious. **semicylinder**
n. half of a cylinder divided along the plane of
its axis. **semicylindric, semicylindrical** a. **semi-
darkness** n. partial darkness. **semi-derelict** a.
partially derelict. **semi-detached** a. partially detached, esp. being one of two houses built as a
pair. ~n. a semi-detached house. **semidiameter** n.
half a diameter. **semi-documentary** n. (pl. **semi-
documentaries**) a film using a mixture of fact
and fiction. **semi-dome** n. **1** a half-dome, usu. a
structure like a dome divided vertically. **2** a
structure resembling a dome. **semi-double** a. (of
a flower) intermediate between single and
double. **semi-final** n. the match or round before
the final. **semi-finalist** n. **semi-finished** a. (of
metal etc.) prepared for the final stage in the
manufacturing process. **semi-fitted** a. (of a garment) shaped but not closely fitted. **semi-fluid** a.
imperfectly fluid. ~n. a semi-fluid substance.
semi-independent a. partially independent.
semi-infinite a. (Math.) limited in one direction
and extending to infinity in the other. **semi-
invalid** n. a person who is partially disabled.
semi-liquid n., a. semi-fluid. **semi-literate** a.
1 hardly able to read and write. **2** (derog.) (of a
text) showing a lack of literacy. **semi-literacy** n.
semi-lunar a. resembling or shaped like a half-
moon or crescent. **semi-lunar bone** n. a bone of
this shape in the carpus. **semi-lunar cartilage** n.
a cartilage of this shape in the knee. **semi-lunar
valve** n. either one of two half-moon-shaped
valves in the heart. **semi-metal** n. an element
having metallic properties but non-malleable.
semi-metallic a. **semi-monthly** a. **1** occurring
twice a month. **2** issued at half-monthly intervals. ~adv. twice a month.

semi- (+ n–o words) semi-nude a. half-naked.
semi-nudity n. **semi-official** a. partly or virtually
official. **semi-officially** adv. **semi-opaque** a.
partly opaque.

seminal (sem´inəl) a. **1** of or relating to semen or
reproduction. **2** formative. **3** important to the
future development of anything. **seminal fluid** n.
semen. **seminally** adv.

seminar (sem´inah) n. **1** a group of students
undertaking an advanced course of study or
research together, usu. under the guidance of a

professor. **2** such a course. **3** a discussion group, or a meeting of it.

seminary (sem´inəri) n. (pl. **seminaries**) a place of education, a college, esp. a (foreign) Roman Catholic school for training priests. **seminarian** (-neə´ri-) n., a. **seminarist** n.

semination (seminā´shən) n. the natural dispersal of seeds by plants. **seminiferous** (-nif´-) a. **1** bearing or producing seed. **2** conveying semen.

semiology (semiol´əji), **semeiology** n. **1** the study of signs and symbols. **2** the study of the symptoms of disease. **semiological** (-loj´-) a. **semiologist** n.

semiotics (semiot´iks), **semeiotics** n. **1** the study of signs and symbols and their relationships in language. **2** (Med.) symptomatology. **semiotic** a. **semiotical** a. **semiotically** adv. **semiotician** (-tish´-) n.

semi- (+ p–t words) **semipalmate, semipalmated** a. (Zool.) half-webbed, as the toes of many shorebirds. **semi-permanent** a. long-lasting, but not permanent. **semi-permeable** a. permeable by small molecules but not by large ones. **semipiscine** a. partly resembling a fish. **semiplume** (sem´-) n. a feather with a stiff stem but a downy web. **semi-precious** a. valuable, but not regarded as a precious stone. **semi-pro** n. (pl. **semi-pros**) (N Am., coll.) a semi-professional. ~a. semi-professional. **semi-professional** n. a person who is paid for an activity but does not do it for a living. ~a. of or relating to semi-professionals. **semi-professionally** adv. **semiquaver** (sem´-) n. (Mus.) a note of half the duration of a quaver. **semi-retired** a. partially retired. **semi-retirement** n. **semi-rigid** a. (of an airship) having a flexible gas container and a rigid keel. **semi-skilled** a. (of a worker) having some basic skills but not highly trained. **semi-skimmed** a. (of milk) containing less fat than full-cream milk. **semi-smile** n. a half or forced smile. **semi-soft** a. (of cheese) fairly soft. **semi-solid** a. so viscous as to be almost solid. **semi-sweet** a. slightly sweetened. **semi-synthetic** a. (Chem.) (of a substance) prepared synthetically but deriving from a material that occurs naturally. **semitone** (sem´-) n. (Mus.) an interval equal to half a major tone on the scale. **semi-trailer** n. a trailer which has back wheels but is supported in front by the towing vehicle. **semi-transparent** a. almost transparent. **semi-transparency** n. **semi-tropical** a. partly within or bordering on the tropics. **semi-tropics** n.pl.

Semite (sem´īt, sē´-) n. a descendant of Shem, or a member of one of the peoples (including Jews, Phoenicians, Assyrians, Arabs and Ethiopians) reputed to be descended from Shem. ~a. Semitic. **Semitic** (simit´-) a. of or relating to the Semites or their languages. ~n. any one of the Semitic group of languages, including Arabic and Hebrew. **Semitism** (semi´-) n. **Semitist** n. **Semitize** (semi´-), **Semitise** v.t. **Semitization** (-ā´shən) n.

semi- (+ v–w words) **semivocal, semivocalic** a. of or relating to a semivowel. **semivowel** (sem´-)

n. **1** a sound having the character of both vowel and consonant, as w and y. **2** a character representing such a sound. **semi-weekly** a. occurring, issued etc. twice a week. ~adv. twice a week.

semolina (seməlē´nə) n. the hard grains of wheat left after bolting, used for puddings etc.

sempervivum (sempəvē´vəm) n. a fleshy plant of the genus Sempervivum, containing the houseleeks.

sempstress SEAMSTRESS (under SEAM).

Semtex® (sem´teks) n. a malleable plastic explosive.

SEN abbr. State Enrolled Nurse.

Sen. abbr. **1** (N Am.) Senate. **2** (N Am.) Senator. **3** Senior.

senate (sen´ət) n. **1** (also Senate) an assembly or council performing legislative or administrative functions. **2** (Hist.) (also Senate) the state council of the ancient Roman republic and empire of ancient Athens, Sparta etc., of the free cities of the Middle Ages etc. **3** (also Senate) the upper legislative house in various bicameral parliaments, as of the US and France. **4** the governing body of various universities. **senator** n. **1** a member of a senate. **2** in Scotland, a Lord of Session. **senatorial** (-taw´ri-) a. **senatorship** n.

send (send) v.t. (past, p.p. **sent** (sent), (Naut.) **sended**) **1** to arrange for (a letter, message etc.) to go or be taken to some destination. **2** to cause (a signal) to be broadcast or transmitted. **3** to cause to go (in, up, off, away etc.). **4** to propel, to hurl. **5** to cause to come or befall. **6** to bestow, to inflict. **7** to cause to be, to bring about. **8** (sl.) to affect emotionally; to move to rapture. ~v.i. **1** to dispatch a messenger or letter. **2** (Naut., also **scend**) to pitch or plunge deeply into the trough of the sea. ~n. (Naut., also **scend**) **1** the impetus or drive of the sea. **2** the act of sending or pitching into the trough of the sea. **to send away for** to order (goods) by post. **to send down 1** to suspend from university. **2** to send to prison. **3** in cricket, to bowl (a ball or an over). **to send for 1** to require the attendance of a person or the bringing of a thing. **2** to order. **to send in 1** to cause to go in. **2** to submit (something, such as a competition entry). **to send off 1** to dispatch. **2** to give a send-off to (a person who is departing). **3** in sport, to order (a player) off the field because of an infringement of the rules. **to send off for** to send away for. **to send on 1** to forward (mail). **2** to send (luggage) in advance. **to send up 1** to parody. **2** to ridicule. **3** to cause to go up. **4** (N Am.) to send to prison. **5** to pass to a higher authority. **to send word** to send information. **sendable** a. **sender** n. **send-off** n. **1** a start, as in a race. **2** a leave-taking, a friendly demonstration to a person departing on a journey. **send-up** n. (coll.) a parody or imitation.

senecio (sinē´shiō) n. (pl. **senecios**) any plant of the genus Senecio, including the groundsel and the ragwort. **senecioid** (-oid) a.

senescent (sines´ənt) *a.* growing old. **senesce** *v.i.* **senescence** *n.*

seneschal (sen´ishəl) *n.* **1** (*Hist.*) an officer in the houses of princes and high dignitaries in the Middle Ages having the superintendence of feasts and domestic ceremonies, sometimes dispensing justice; a steward or major-domo. **2** a judge in Sark. **seneschalship** *n.*

senhor (senyaw´) *n.* **1** a man, in a Portuguese-speaking country. **2** the Portuguese or Brazilian title corresponding to the English Mr or sir. **senhora** (-rə) *n.* **1** a lady (in Portugal, Brazil etc.). **2** Mrs, madam. **senhorita** (-rē´tə) *n.* **1** a young unmarried girl (in Portugal, Brazil etc.). **2** Miss.

senile (sē´nīl) *a.* **1** of, relating to or proceeding from the infirmities etc. of old age. **2** suffering from the (mental) infirmities associated with old age. ~*n.* a senile person. **senile dementia** *n.* dementia starting in old age, characterized by the loss of memory and inability to control one's bodily functions. **senility** (sinil´-) *n.*

senior (sēn´yə) *a.* **1** elder (appended to names to denote the elder of two persons with identical names, esp. father and son). **2** older or higher in rank or service. **3** (of a school) having pupils in an older age range. **4** (*N Am.*) of the final year at university or high school. ~*n.* **1** a person older than another. **2** a person older or higher in rank, service etc. **3** (*N Am.*) a student in their third or fourth year. **4** an aged person. **senior aircraftman** *n.* (*pl.* **senior aircraftmen**) the rank above aircraftman in the RAF. **senior aircraftwoman** *n.* (*pl.* **senior aircraftwomen**). **senior citizen** *n.* an elderly person, usu. an old-age pensioner. **senior college** *n.* (*N Am.*) a college in which students complete the last two years of a bachelor's degree. **senior high school** *n.* (*N Am.*) a secondary school comprising usu. the three highest grades. **seniority** (-nior´-) *n.* (*pl.* **seniorities**). **senior management** *n.* the highest level of management below the board of directors. **senior nursing officer** *n.* a person in a hospital who is in charge of the nursing services. **senior officer** *n.* an officer to whom a junior officer is responsible. **senior partner** *n.* the head of a firm. **senior registrar** *n.* a hospital doctor one grade below a consultant. **senior service** *n.* the Royal Navy. **senior tutor** *n.* a college tutor in charge of teaching arrangements.

Usage note An implicit double comparative *more senior* is occasionally encountered, but is best avoided: *senior* already includes the notion of 'more'. However *senior* does not function as a true comparative in English, and should not be followed by *than* (the correct form is *senior to*).

senna (sen´ə) *n.* **1** the dried, purgative leaflets or pods of several species of cassia. **2** a cassia tree.

señor (senyaw´) *n.* (*pl.* **señores** (-riz)) **1** a man, in a Spanish-speaking country. **2** the Spanish form

of address equivalent to Mr or sir. **señora** (-rə) *n.* **1** a lady (in Spain etc.). **2** Mrs, madam. **señorita** (-yərē´tə) *n.* **1** a young unmarried girl (in Spain etc.). **2** Miss.

Senr. *abbr.* Senior.

sensation (sensā´shən) *n.* **1** the mental state or affection resulting from the excitation of an organ of sense, the primary element in perception or cognition of an external object. **2** a state of excited feeling or interest, esp. affecting a number of people. **3** the thing or event exciting this. **to create a sensation** to cause surprise and excitement. **sensate** (sen´sət) *a.* perceived by the senses. **sensational** *a.* **1** causing, of or relating to sensation. **2** intending to shock or excite people. **3** (*coll.*) very good. **sensationalism** *n.* **1** the employment of sensational methods in literary composition, political agitation etc. **2** (*Philos.*) the theory that all knowledge is derived from sensation. **sensationalist** *n.* **sensationalistic** (-lis´-) *a.* **sensationalize, sensationalise** *v.t.* **sensationally** *adv.*

sense (sens) *n.* **1** any one of the five faculties by which sensation is received through special bodily organs (sight, hearing, touch, taste, smell). **2** the faculty of sensation, perception. **3** bodily feeling, sensuousness. **4** intuitive perception. **5** consciousness, conviction (of). **6** sound judgement, good mental capacity. **7** meaning, signification. **8** general feeling or judgement, consensus of opinion. **9** (*pl.*) normal command or possession of the senses, sanity. **10** (*Math.*) a direction of movement. ~*v.t.* **1** to perceive by the senses. **2** (of a computer) to detect (a signal, a hole in a punched tape etc.). **3** (*N Am.*) to understand. **in a sense** in a way. **in one sense** in a sense. **in one's senses** sane. **out of one's senses** insane. **to bring someone to their senses 1** to make someone understand that they are doing something wrong, silly etc. **2** to make someone conscious after they have been unconscious. **to make sense** to be intelligible. **to make sense of** to understand. **sense datum** *n.* an item of experience received directly through a sense organ. **sense impression** *n.* an impression on the mind through the medium of sensation. **senseless** *a.* **1** incapable of sensation. **2** contrary to reason, foolish. **senselessly** *adv.* **senselessness** *n.* **sense of direction** *n.* the ability to know in which direction one should be travelling. **sense of humour** *n.* the capacity of perceiving the ludicrous elements in life or art. **sense organ** *n.* a bodily organ concerned in the production of sensation. **sense-perception** *n.* perception by the senses.

sensible (sen´sibəl) *a.* **1** acting with or characterized by good sense or judgement. **2** perceptible by the senses. **3** appreciable. **4** (of clothing etc.) practical. **5** having perception (of). **sensibility** (-bil´-) *n.* (*pl.* **sensibilities**) **1** capacity to see or feel. **2** susceptibility of impression. **3** sensitivity to sensory stimuli. **sensible horizon**

n. the circular line where the sky and the earth seem to meet. **sensibleness** *n.* **sensibly** *adv.*

Usage note The nouns *sensibility* and *sensibleness* should not be confused: *sensibility* is the capacity to feel, and *sensibleness* reasonableness or common sense.

sensitive (sen´sitiv) *a.* **1** readily or acutely affected by external influences. **2** impressible, delicately susceptible. **3** of or depending on the senses, sensory. **4** (of photographic materials) susceptible to the action of light. **5** (of information) secret. **6** (of a market) liable to quick price changes. ~*n.* a person who is sensitive or abnormally sensitive. **sensitively** *adv.* **sensitiveness, sensitivism** *n.* **sensitive plant** *n.* **1** a plant, *Mimosa pudica* or *M. sensitiva*, the leaves of which shrink from the touch. **2** a sensitive person. **sensitivity** (-tiv´-) *n.* (*pl.* **sensitivities**). **sensitize, sensitise** *v.t.* **sensitization** (-zā´shən) *n.* **sensitizer** *n.* **sensitometer** (-tom´itə) *n.* an apparatus for determining the sensitiveness of photographic plates, films etc.

sensor (sen´sə) *n.* an instrument which responds to, and signals, a change in a physical stimulus, for information or control purposes.

sensorium (sensaw´riəm) *n.* (*pl.* **sensoria** (-riə), **sensoriums**) **1** the seat or organ of sensation, the brain. **2** (*Biol.*) the nervous system, comprising the brain, spinal cord etc. **sensorial** *a.* **sensorially** *adv.* **sensory** (sen´səri) *a.* **1** sensorial. **2** of the senses or of sensation.

sensual (sen´shuəl, -sū-) *a.* **1** of, relating to or affecting the senses, carnal. **2** of, relating to or devoted to the indulgence of the appetites or passions, esp. those of sex. **3** (*Philos.*) of, relating to or according to sensationalism. **4** of or relating to sense or sensation, sensory. **sensualism** *n.* **sensualist** *n.* **sensuality** (-al´-) *n.* indulgence of the appetites or passions, voluptuousness. **sensualize, sensualise** *v.t.* **sensualization** (-zā´shən) *n.* **sensually** *adv.*

Usage note The adjectives *sensual* and *sensuous* should not be confused: *sensual* is more associated with bodily appetites, and *sensuous* with aesthetic pleasures.

sensuous (sen´shuəs, -sū-) *a.* **1** of, relating to or derived from the senses. **2** abounding in or suggesting sensible images. **3** readily affected through the senses. **sensuously** *adv.* **sensuousness** *n.*

Usage note See note under SENSUAL.

sent SEND.
sentence (sen´təns) *n.* **1** (*Gram.*) a series of words, containing a subject, predicate etc., expressing a complete thought. **2** (*Law*) **a** a penalty or declaration of penalty upon a condemned person. **b** a judicial decision, verdict. **3** (*Logic*) an expression that is well-formed, without variables. ~*v.t.* **1** to pronounce judgement on. **2** to

condemn to punishment. **under sentence of** condemned to. **sentential** (-ten´shəl) *a.* of a sentence.

sententious (senten´shəs) *a.* **1** characterized by many pithy sentences, axioms or maxims. **2** terse, brief and energetic. **3** pompous in tone. **sententiously** *adv.* **sententiousness** *n.*

sentient (sen´shiənt, -tiənt) *a.* having the power of sense-perception. **sentience** *n.* **sentiency** *n.* **sentiently** *adv.*

sentiment (sen´timənt) *n.* **1** (*often pl.*) an opinion or attitude. **2** a thought or mental tendency derived from or characterized by emotion. **3** mental feeling excited by aesthetic, moral or spiritual ideas. **4** susceptibility to emotion.

sentimental (sentimen´təl) *a.* **1** characterized by sentiment. **2** swayed by emotion. **3** showing too much emotion, mawkish. **4** susceptible to emotion. **sentimentalism** *n.* **1** unreasonable or uncontrolled emotion. **2** mawkishness. **sentimentalist** *n.* **sentimentality** (-tal´-) *n.* **sentimentalize, sentimentalise** *v.i.* to affect sentimentality. ~*v.t.* to make sentimental. **sentimentalization** (-zā´shən) *n.* **sentimentally** *adv.* **sentimental value** *n.* the value of an object in terms not of money but of associations, memories etc.

sentinel (sen´tinəl) *n.* a person who keeps watch to prevent surprise, esp. a soldier on guard. ~*v.t.* (*pres.p.* **sentinelling**, (*N Am.*) **sentineling**, *past*, *p.p.* **sentinelled**, (*N Am.*) **sentineled**) **1** (*poet.*) to watch over, to guard. **2** to set sentinels at or over.

sentry (sen´tri) *n.* (*pl.* **sentries**) a sentinel, a soldier on guard. **sentry box** *n.* a shelter for a sentry. **sentry-go** *n.* a sentry's duty of pacing to and fro.

sepal (sep´əl) *n.* (*Bot.*) any one of the segments, divisions or leaves of a calyx.

separate[1] (sep´ərāt) *v.t.* **1** to set or keep apart. **2** to break up into distinct parts, to disperse. **3** to come or be between. **4** to sort or divide. **5** (*N Am.*) to discharge, dismiss. ~*v.i.* **1** to withdraw (from). **2** to disperse. **3** (of a married couple) to agree to live apart. **separable** *a.* **separability** (-bil´-) *n.* **separableness** *n.* **separably** *adv.* **separation** (-ā´shən) *n.* **1** the act of separating or the state of being separated, esp. partial divorce, consisting of cessation of cohabitation between married persons. **2** any of three or more monochrome reproductions which can combine to make a full colour picture. **separation order** *n.* a court order for judicial separation. **separatist** *n.* a person who advocates secession, from a Church, political party, federation etc. **separatism** *n.* **separative** *a.* **separator** *n.* **1** a person who separates. **2** a machine that separates the cream from milk. **separatory** (-rətəri) *a.*

separate[2] (sep´ərət) *a.* **1** disconnected, considered apart. **2** distinct, individual. ~*n.* **1** (*pl.*) women's clothes that cover part of the body and are worn together, e.g. skirts and jackets. **2** an offprint. **separately** *adv.* **separateness** *n.*

❌ **seperate** common misspelling of SEPARATE[1].

Sephardi (sifah´di) *n.* (*pl.* **Sephardim** (-dim)) a Jew of Spanish, Portuguese or N African descent. **Sephardic** *a.*

sepia (sē´piə) *n.* **1** a dark reddish-brown colour. **2** a dark brown pigment. **3** this pigment prepared from the black secretion of the cuttlefish. **4** the fluid secreted by cuttlefish. **5** a watercolour drawing in sepia. ~*a.* **1** made in sepia. **2** of the colour sepia.

sepoy (sē´poi) *n.* (*Hist.*) an Indian soldier under European discipline, esp. one in the former British Indian army.

sepsis (sep´sis) *n.* (*pl.* **sepses** (-sēz)) **1** septic condition, putrefaction. **2** infection by disease-causing bacteria, e.g. from a wound, blood poisoning.

Sept. *abbr.* **1** September. **2** Septuagint.

sept (sept) *n.* a clan or branch of a clan, esp. in Scotland or Ireland.

septa SEPTUM.

September (septem´bə) *n.* the ninth month of the year (the seventh after March, first month of the ancient Roman year).

septet (septet´), **septette** *n.* (*Mus.*) **1** a group of seven, esp. singers, voices, instruments etc. **2** a musical composition for seven performers.

septi- (sep´ti), **sept-** *comb. form* seven.

septic (sep´tik) *a.* (*Med.*) causing or tending to promote putrefaction, not aseptic. **septicaemia** (-sē´miə), (*N Am.*) **septicemia** *n.* an abnormal state of the blood caused by the absorption of poisonous or putrid matter, blood poisoning. **septicaemic** *a.* **septically** *adv.* **septicity** (-tis´-) *n.* **septic tank** *n.* a tank in which sewage is partially purified by the action of bacteria.

septimal (sep´timəl) *a.* of, relating to or based on the number seven. **septime** (sep´tēm) *n.* the seventh parry in fencing.

septuagenarian (septūəjineə´riən) *n.* a person of 70 years of age, or between 70 and 80. ~*a.* of such an age.

septum (sep´təm) *n.* (*pl.* **septa** (-tə)) (*Biol.*) a partition, as in a chambered cell, the cell of an ovary, between the nostrils etc. **septal** *a.*

septuple (sep´tūpəl) *a.* sevenfold. ~*n.* **1** a set of seven things. **2** a sevenfold number or amount. ~*v.t.*, *v.i.* to multiply by seven. **septuplet** (-tū´plit) *n.* each of seven children born at a birth.

sepulchre (sep´əlkə), (*N Am.*) **sepulcher** *n.* **1** a tomb, esp. one hewn in the rock or built in a solid and permanent manner. **2** a burial vault. ~*v.t.* **1** to place in a sepulchre, to entomb. **2** to serve as a sepulchre for. **sepulchral** (-pŭl´krəl) *a.* **1** of or relating to burial, the grave or to monuments raised over the dead. **2** suggestive of a sepulchre, grave, dismal, funereal. **sepulchrally** *adv.*

seq. *abbr.* **1** the following (L *sequens*). **2** and in what follows (L *sequente*).

seqq. *abbr.* **1** (*pl.*) the following (L *sequentes*, *sequentia*). **2** in the following places (L *sequentibus*).

sequacious (sikwā´shəs) *a.* logically consistent and coherent. **sequaciously** *adv.* **sequacity** (-kwas´-) *n.*

sequel (sē´kwəl) *n.* **1** that which follows. **2** a succeeding part, a continuation (of a story etc.). **3** the consequence or result (of an event etc.). **in the sequel** as things developed afterwards.

sequence (sē´kwəns) *n.* **1** succession, the process of coming after in space, time etc. **2** a series of things following one another consecutively or according to a definite principle. **3** a set of consecutive cards. **4** (*Mus.*) a succession of similar harmonious formations or melodic phrases at different pitches. **5** a scene in a film. ~*v.t.* **1** to arrange in definite order. **2** to discover the sequence of. **sequence of tenses** *n.* (*Gram.*) the relation of tense in a subordinate clause to the tense of the principal verb. **sequencer** *n.* **1** (*Mus.*) an electronic device which can be programmed with musical notes, chords etc., connected to a synthesizer. **2** a device for performing operations in a sequence, esp. in data processing. **3** an apparatus for determining the sequence of monomers in a biological polymer. **sequent** *a.* **sequential** (sikwen´shəl) *a.* **sequentiality** (-shial´-) *n.* **sequentially** *adv.* **sequently** *adv.*

sequester (sikwes´tə) *v.t.* **1** (*esp. in p.p.*) to set apart, to isolate, to seclude. **2** (*Law*) to separate (property etc.) from the owner temporarily; to take possession of (property in dispute) until some case is decided or claim is paid. **3** to confiscate, to appropriate. **4** (*Chem.*) to remove (a metal ion) by adding a reagent that forms a complex with it. **sequestrable** *a.* **sequestrate** (sē´kwistrāt) *v.t.* (*Law*) to sequester. **sequestration** (-ā´shən) *n.* **sequestrator** *n.*

sequin (sē´kwin) *n.* a small disc of shiny metal, jet etc., used as trimming for dresses etc. **sequinned, sequined** *a.*

sequoia (sikwoi´ə) *n.* either of two gigantic conifers of California, *Sequoia sempervirens* and *Sequoiadendron giganteum*.

sera SERUM.

serac (serak´, ser´-) *n.* any of the large angular or tower-shaped masses into which a glacier breaks up at an icefall.

seraglio (siral´yō) *n.* (*pl.* **seraglios**) **1** a harem. **2** (*Hist.*) a walled palace, esp. the old palace of the Turkish Sultan, with its mosques, government offices etc. at Istanbul.

serai (sərī´) *n.* a caravanserai.

seraph (ser´əf) *n.* (*pl.* **seraphs, seraphim** (-fim)) an angel of the highest order. **seraphic** (-raf´-) *a.* **1** of or like a seraph. **2** ecstatic, rapturous. **seraphically** *adv.*

Serb (sœb) *n.* **1** a native or inhabitant of Serbia in SE Europe. **2** a person of Serbian descent; a person belonging to a Slav ethnic group of Serbia. **3** Serbian. ~*a.* of or relating to the Serbs, Serbian. **Serbian** *a.* of or relating to Serbia, its people or their language. ~*n.* **1** a native or inhabitant of Serbia, a Serb. **2** the language of Serbia, one of the two main dialects of Serbo-Croat. **Serbo-** (sœ´bō) *comb. form* Serbian (and). **Serbo-Croat** (-krō´at), **Serbo-Croatian** (-krōä´shən) *n.* the Slavonic language which has Serbian and Croat as its main dialects. *~a.* of or relating to this language.

sere[1] (siə) *n.* a series of ecological communities following one another in one area.

sere[2] SEAR.

serein (sərān´) *n.* a fine rain falling from a clear sky after sunset, esp. in tropical regions.

serenade (serənād´) *n.* **1** a song or piece of music played or sung in the open air at night, esp. by a lover beneath his lady's window. **2** a nocturne, a serenata. *~v.t.* to sing or play a serenade to or in honour of. *~v.i.* to perform a serenade. **serenader** *n.* **serenata** (-nah´tə) *n.* (*Mus.*) a cantata or simple form of symphony, usu. with a pastoral subject, for the open air.

serendipity (serəndip´iti) *n.* the happy knack of making unexpected and delightful discoveries by accident. **serendipitous** *a.* **serendipitously** *adv.*

serene (sərēn´) *a.* **1** placid, tranquil. **2** (of the sky, atmosphere etc.) calm and clear. **3** honoured; applied as a title to certain continental princes. **all serene** (*sl.*) all right. **Serene Highness** *n.* title accorded to certain European princelings. **serenely** *adv.* **serenity** (-ren´-), **sereneness** *n.*

serf (sœf) *n.* **1** (*Hist.*) a feudal labourer attached to an estate, a villein. **2** a slave, a drudge. **serfage** (-ij), **serfdom, serfhood** (-hud), **serfism** *n.*

serge (sœj) *n.* a strong and durable twilled cloth, of worsted, cotton, rayon etc.

sergeant (sah´jənt) *n.* **1** (*Mil.*) a non-commissioned Army or Air Force officer ranking next above corporal, teaching drill, commanding small detachments etc. **2** a police officer ranking next below an inspector. **3** (*N Am.*) a police officer ranking next below a lieutenant. **sergeancy** (-si) *n.* (*pl.* **sergeancies**). **Sergeant Baker** *n.* (*Austral.*) a large brightly coloured fish, *Aulopus purpurissatus*, found in temperate waters. **sergeant-fish** *n.* (*pl.* in general **sergeant-fish**, in particular **sergeant-fishes**) a fish with lateral stripes resembling a chevron, *Rachycentron canadum*. **sergeant major** *n.* (*Mil.*) the chief sergeant of a regiment, a squadron of cavalry or a battery of artillery. **sergeantship** *n.* **serjeant-at-arms, sergeant-at-arms** *n.* (*pl.* **serjeants-at-arms, sergeants-at-arms**) any one of several court and city officers with ceremonial duties. **serjeant-at-law** *n.* (*pl.* **serjeants-at-law**) (*Hist.*) a member of the highest order of barristers, abolished in 1877. **serjeantship** *n.*

Sergt. *abbr.* Sergeant.

serial (siə´riəl) *a.* **1** of, relating to, consisting of or having the nature of a series. **2** (of a novel, story etc.) published, broadcast or shown at a cinema in instalments. **3** occurring as part of a series of a set of repeated occurrences (*serial murder*). **4** (*Comput.*) of or relating to the computer

processing of tasks one after another. **5** (*Mus.*) (of music) based on a fixed, arbitrary series of notes, not on a traditional scale. *~n.* **1** a serial story, play, film etc. **2** a serial publication, a periodical. **serialism** *n.* **serialist** *n.* **seriality** (-al´-) *n.* **serialize, serialise** *v.t.* **1** to publish (a novel) in instalments. **2** to arrange in a series. **3** (*Mus.*) to compose (music) using a serial technique. **serialization** (-zā´shən) *n.* **serial killer** *n.* a killer who commits a series of apparently unconnected murders. **serially** *adv.* **serial number** *n.* a number stamped on an item which identifies it in a large series of identical items. **serial rights** *n.pl.* the right to publish as a serial. **seriate**[1] (-āt) *v.t.* to arrange in a series or regular sequence. **seriate**[2] (-ət), **seriated** (-ātid) *a.* arranged in a series or regular sequence. **seriately** *adv.* **seriatim** (-ā´tim) *adv.* **1** in regular order. **2** one point etc. after the other. **seriation** (-ā´shən) *n.*

sericeous (sirish´iəs), **sericate** (ser´ikət), **sericated** (-kātid) *a.* (*Bot., Zool.*) silky, downy, soft and lustrous.

sericulture (ser´ikŭlchə) *n.* the breeding of silk-worms and the production of raw silk. **sericultural** (-kŭl´-) *a.* **sericulturist** (-kŭl´-) *n.*

series (siə´riz) *n.* (*pl.* **series**) **1** a number, set or continued succession of things similar to each other or each bearing a definite relation to that preceding it. **2** a set of radio or television programmes or of lectures complete in themselves but featuring the same characters, subject matter etc. **3** a set of volumes, parts, articles, periodicals etc., consecutively numbered or dated or issued in the same format under one general title. **4** a sequence of games between the same teams. **5** (*Math.*) a number of terms, the successive pairs of which are related to each other according to a common law or mode of derivation, a progression. **6** the connection of two or more electric circuits so that the same current traverses all the circuits. **7** (*Geol.*) a group of allied strata forming a subdivision of a geological system. **8** (*Mus.*) an arrangement of 12 notes used as a basis for composition. **9** (*Chem.*) a set of related elements or compounds. **in series 1** in ordered succession. **2** (of circuits etc.) arranged in a series.

serif (ser´if), **ceriph** *n.* any of the fine cross-lines at the top and bottom of printed letters of the alphabet. **seriffed** *a.*

serigraph (ser´igrahf) *n.* a silk-screen print. **serigrapher** (-ig´rəphə) *n.* **serigraphy** (-ig´-) *n.*

serin (ser´in) *n.* a small yellow or green finch, *Serinus serinus*, the wild canary.

serine (siə´rēn, ser´-) *n.* a hydrophilic amino acid involved in the synthesis of cysteine.

seringa (səring´gə) *n.* **1** a Brazilian rubber tree, *Hevea brasiliensis*. **2** syringa.

serious (siə´riəs) *a.* **1** grave, thoughtful. **2** in earnest, not pretended. **3** not merely entertaining, not frivolous. **4** of great importance, momentous. **5** having serious consequences, dangerous. **6** (*coll.*) significantly costly. **serio-comic,**

serio-comical *a.* mingling the serious and the comic; serious in meaning with the appearance of comedy, or comic with a grave appearance. **serio-comically** *adv.* **seriously** *adv.* **1** in a serious manner. **2** to a serious extent. **3** (*coll.*) very. **seriousness** *n.*

serjeant SERGEANT.

sermon (sœ´mən) *n.* **1** a discourse founded on a text of Scripture delivered in church. **2** a similar discourse delivered elsewhere. **3** a moral reflection. **4** a serious exhortation or reproof. *~v.t.* **1** to deliver a sermon to. **2** to lecture. **sermonet** (-nit), **sermonette** (-net´) *n.* a short sermon. **sermonize, sermonise** *v.i.,v.t.* **sermonizer** *n.*

serology (siərol´əji) *n.* the study of blood serum, its composition and properties. **serological** (-əloj´-) *a.* **serologist** *n.*

seronegative (siərōneg´ətiv) *a.* (*Med.*) (of a person whose blood has been tested) not showing the presence of a virus etc.

seropositive (siərōpoz´itiv) *a.* (*Med.*) (of a person whose blood has been tested) showing the presence of a virus etc.

serotine (ser´ətīn), **serotine bat** *n.* a small reddish bat, *Eptesicus serotinus*, flying in the evening.

serotonin (serətō´nin, sirot´ənin) *n.* (*Biol.*) a compound found in many body tissues which acts as a vasoconstrictor.

serous (siə´rəs) *a.* of, relating to or resembling serum. **serosity** (-os´-) *n.* **serous gland, serous membrane** *n.* a thin, transparent membrane lining certain large body cavities, and secreting a thin fluid which allows movement of the organs in the cavities.

serpent (sœ´pənt) *n.* **1** a reptile with an elongated scaly body and no limbs, a snake. **2** a treacherous, insinuating person. **3** (*Mus.*) an old-fashioned wind instrument of serpentine form. **serpentine** (-tīn) *a.* **1** of, relating to, resembling or having the qualities of a serpent. **2** coiling, winding, twisting, sinuous. **3** subtle, wily, treacherous. *~n.* **1** a massive or fibrous rock consisting of hydrated silicate of magnesia richly coloured and variegated and susceptible of a high polish, used for making various ornamental articles. **2** a skating figure consisting of three circles in a line. *~v.i.* **1** to wind in and out like a serpent. **2** to meander. **serpentinely** *adv.* **serpentine verse** *n.* a verse beginning and ending with the same word.

SERPS (sœps), **Serps** *abbr.* State earnings-related pension scheme.

serra (ser´ə) *n.* (*pl.* **serrae** (-ē)) a sawlike organ, part or structure.

serradilla (serədil´ə) *n.* (*pl.* **serradillas**) a species of clover, *Ornithopus sativus*, grown for fodder.

serranid (sərən´id, ser´ə-) *n.* any marine fish of the family Serranidae, comprising the sea basses, sea perches and groupers. *~a.* of or relating to this family.

serrate[1] (ser´āt) *a.* (*Biol.*) notched on the edge, like a saw, serrated.

serrate[2] (sərāt´) *v.t.* (*usu. p.p.*) to cut into notches and teeth, to give a sawlike edge to. **serrated** *a.* **serration** (-ā´shən), **serrature** (ser´əchə) *n.*

serried (ser´id) *a.* (esp. of soldiers) close-packed, in compact order.

serrulate (ser´ūlāt), **serrulated** (-lātid) *a.* (*Biol.*) finely serrated, having minute notches. **serrulation** (-ā´shən) *n.*

serum (siə´rəm) *n.* (*pl.* **serums, sera** (-rə)) **1** the thin transparent part that separates from the blood in coagulation. **2** (*Med.*) animal serum used as an antitoxin etc. **3** a constituent of milk and other animal fluids, lymph. **4** whey. **serum sickness** *n.* (*Med.*) an allergic reaction to a serum injection, such as fever, rashes etc.

serval (sœ´vəl) *n.* an African wild cat with long legs and a black-spotted tawny coat, *Felis serval.*

servant (sœ´vənt) *n.* **1** a person employed by another person to work under direction for wages, esp. in the house of the employer and undertaking domestic tasks or acting as a personal attendant. **2** a devoted follower, a person willing to perform the will of another.

serve (sœv) *v.t.* **1** to act as servant to, to be in the employment of. **2** to be useful to, to render service to. **3** to attend to as a shop assistant. **4** to be subservient or subsidiary to. **5** to satisfy, to suffice. **6** to supply, to perform (a purpose, function etc.). **7** to carry out the duties of, to do the work of (an office etc.). **8** to undergo the punishment prescribed by (a sentence) or for (a specified time). **9** to treat (well, badly etc.). **10** to dish (up) for eating, to bring to and set on the table. **11** to distribute to those at table. **12** to supply (a person with). **13** to deliver (a summons, writ etc.) in the manner prescribed by law. **14** to throw or send (a ball etc.) to begin or resume play in tennis, badminton etc. **15** (of a male animal) to mate with, to cover, esp. for hire. **16** (*Mil.*) to keep (a gun etc.) firing. **17** (*Naut.*) to lash or whip (a rope) with thin cord to prevent fraying. *~v.i.* **1** to be employed, to perform the duties of or to hold an office etc. **2** to perform a function. **3** to be used (as), to be a satisfactory substitute (for). **4** to be satisfactory, favourable or suitable. **5** to be in subjection. **6** to deliver the ball to begin or resume play in tennis, badminton etc. **7** to attend a celebrant at the altar. **8** to be a member of an armed force. **9** to act as a waiter. *~n.* **1** the act of or turn for serving at tennis, badminton etc. **2** (*Austral., sl.*) a reprimand. **to serve at table** to act as waiter or waitress. **to serve one's need/needs** to be adequate. **to serve one's time 1** to serve one's sentence. **2** to go through an apprenticeship. **3** to hold an office etc. for the full period. **to serve out** to distribute (portions of food) to those at table. **to serve out one's time** (*esp. N Am.*) to serve one's time. **to serve someone right** to be what someone deserved (as a punishment or misfortune). **to serve the purpose of** to be used as. **to serve the turn** to be adequate. **to serve up** to serve out (food).

server *n.* **1** a person who serves at table. **2** a utensil (such as a tray or spoon) used to serve food. **3** in tennis, badminton etc., the person who serves. **4** a person who assists the celebrant at mass. **5** (*Comput.*) **a** a computer program to manage shared access to a network service. **b** a device on which this is run. **servery** (-vəri) *n.* (*pl.* **serveries**) a counter or room from which food is served. **serving** *n.* a portion of food, a helping.

service¹ (sœ´vis) *n.* **1** the act of serving. **2** work done for an employer or for the benefit of another. **3** a benefit or advantage conferred on someone. **4** the state of being a servant, esp. the place or position of a domestic servant. **5** a department of state or public work or duty, the organization performing this. **6** use, assistance. **7** a liturgical form for worship. **8** a performance of this. **9** (*Law*) formal legal delivery, posting up or publication (of a writ, summons etc.). **10** a set of dishes, plates etc. required for serving a meal. **11** that which is served at table. **12** the act of serving the ball at tennis, badminton etc. **13** maintenance work undertaken by the vendor after a sale. **14** (*pl.*) the armed forces. **15** (*pl.*) the service area of a motorway. **16** (*pl.*) provision of water, electricity etc. to a property. ~*v.t.* **1** to repair or maintain (a car etc.) after sale. **2** to meet interest on (a debt). **3** (of a male animal) to serve. **4** to provide service or services for. **at someone's service** ready to help someone. **in/ on active service** on service. **in service 1** working as a servant. **2** available for use. **on service** engaged in actual duty in the army, navy etc. **out of service** not available for use. **to be of service** to be available to help. **to see service 1** to have experience, esp. as a soldier or sailor. **2** to be put to long or hard use. **to take service with** to become a servant to. **serviceable** *a.* **1** able or willing to render service. **2** useful, beneficial, advantageous. **3** durable, fit for service. **serviceability** (-bil´-), **serviceableness** *n.* **serviceably** *adv.* **service area** *n.* **1** an area served by a broadcasting station within which efficient transmission can be guaranteed. **2** a place beside a motorway where petrol, food etc. are available. **service book** *n.* a book containing the church offices, esp. the Book of Common Prayer. **service bus, service car** *n.* (*New Zeal.*) a long-distance bus. **service charge** *n.* a percentage of a bill, charged in addition to the total, to pay for service. **service dress** *n.* in the armed forces, uniform other than full dress. **service flat** *n.* a flat for which an inclusive sum is charged for rent and full hotel service. **service game** *n.* in tennis etc., a game in which a particular player serves. **service industry** *n.* (*pl.* **service industries**) an industry concerned with providing a service to its customers, rather than with manufacturing. **service line** *n.* in tennis etc., either of two lines marking the limit within which the serve must fall. **serviceman** *n.* (*pl.* **servicemen**) **1** a member of the armed forces. **2** a man whose job is to provide service or maintenance. **service road** *n.* a minor road running alongside a main road and carrying local traffic only. **service station** *n.* a roadside establishment providing petrol etc. to motorists. **servicewoman** *n.* (*pl.* **servicewomen**) a woman member of the armed forces.

service² (sœ´vis) *n.* the service tree. **service-berry** *n.* (*pl.* **service-berries**) **1** the fruit of the service tree. **2** any shrub of the genus *Amelanchier*. **3** the fruit of this. **service tree** *n.* **1** a European tree, *Sorbus domestica*, with small pearlike fruit. **2** the wild service tree, *Sorbus torminalis*.

serviette (sœviet´) *n.* a table napkin.

servile (sœ´vīl) *a.* **1** cringing, fawning. **2** of, relating to or befitting a slave or slaves. **servilely** *adv.* **servility** (-vil´-) *n.*

serving SERVE.

servitude (sœ´vitūd) *n.* **1** the condition of a slave, slavery, bondage. **2** subjection to or as to a master. **3** (*Law*) the subjection of property to an easement for the benefit of a person other than the owner or of another estate.

servo (sœ´vō) *n.* (*pl.* **servos**) a servo-mechanism or servo-motor. **servo-mechanism** *n.* an automatic device using a small amount of power which controls the performance of a much more powerful system. **servo-motor** *n.* a motor which powers a servo-mechanism.

sesame (ses´əmi) *n.* **1** an African plant, *Sesamum orientale*, with oily seeds used as food. **2** these seeds. **sesamoid** (-moid) *a.* shaped like a sesame seed, nodular. ~*n.* a sesamoid bone, any of several small bones developed in tendons as in the kneecap, the sole of the foot etc.

sesqui- (ses´kwi) *comb. form* denoting a proportion of 1½ to 1 or 3 to 2.

sesquicentenary (seskwisəntē´nəri, -ten´-, -sen´tin-) *n.* (*pl.* **sesquicentenaries**) a 150th anniversary. **sesquicentennial** (-ten´-) *n.*, *a.*

sess (ses) *n.* CESS¹.

sessile (ses´īl) *a.* **1** (*Zool.*, *Bot.*) attached by the base, destitute of a stalk or peduncle. **2** sedentary; immobile. **sessile oak** *n.* the durmast. **sessility** (-sil´-) *n.*

session (sesh´ən) *n.* **1** a sitting or meeting of a court, council etc. for the transaction of business. **2** the time of such meeting. **3** the period during which such meetings are held at short intervals. **4** a period devoted to an activity. **5** (*coll.*) a period of heavy drinking. **6** the lowest court of the Presbyterian Church. **7** the act of sitting or being assembled. **in session** assembled for business. **sessional** *a.*

sestet (sestet´) *n.* **1** the last six lines of a sonnet. **2** a composition for six instruments or voices, a sextet.

set¹ (set) *v.t.* (*pres.p.* **setting**, *past*, *p.p.* **set**) **1** to place, to put. **2** to fix. **3** to plant (usu. *out*). **4** to bring or put in a specified or right position, direction or state. **5** to arrange for use, display etc. **6** to apply (a thing to something else). **7** to attach, to fasten. **8** to determine, to appoint. **9** to cause to sit. **10** to apply (oneself, one's energies etc., to). **11** to cause (to work etc.). **12** to present, to offer (an example, task etc.). **13** to stud, to make insertions in (a surface etc.). **14** to arrange, to compose (type). **15** to fix (the hair) in waves etc. **16** to adapt or fit (words etc.) to music usu. composed for the purpose. **17** (*Naut.*) to spread (sail). *~v.i.* **1** to become solid or firm from a fluid condition, to congeal. **2** to take shape. **3** to move or incline in a definite or specified direction. **4** (of flowers or fruit) to mature, to develop. **5** (of a dog) to point. **6** to face one's partner (in dancing). **7** to pass below the horizon. **8** to decline, to pass away. *~a.* **1** fixed, immovable. **2** determined, intent (on or upon). **3** motionless, stationary. **4** established, prescribed. **5** regular, in due form. **dead set against** utterly opposed to. **dead set on** determined on. **of set purpose** intentionally, deliberately. **to set about 1** to begin. **2** (*coll.*) to attack. **to set against 1** to oppose. **2** to balance (one thing) against another. **3** to make (a person) unfriendly to or prejudiced against. **to set apart** to separate, to reserve (for some special purpose). **to set aside 1** to reserve. **2** to reject. **3** to annul, to quash. **to set at ease 1** to relieve of anxiety, fear, bashfulness etc. **2** to make comfortable. **to set back 1** to turn backwards. **2** to hinder the progress of, to impede. **3** (*coll.*) to cost. **to set by 1** (*esp. N Am.*) to reserve. **2** (*esp. N Am.*) to lay by, to save. **to set down 1** to put on the ground. **2** to let (a passenger) alight from a vehicle. **3** to put in writing, to note. **4** to attribute. **5** to explain (as). **to set forth 1** to start (on a journey etc.). **2** to show, to demonstrate, to make known. **to set forward 1** to promote, to help. **2** to begin going forward. **to set free** to release. **to set in 1** to begin in a steady manner. **2** to come into fashion. **3** (of the tide) to move steadily shoreward. **4** (of the weather) to become settled. **5** to insert (esp. a sleeve). **to set in order 1** to arrange, to adjust. **2** to reform. **to set little by** to value little. **to set much by** to value highly. **to set off 1** to make more attractive or brilliant by contrast. **2** to beautify, to adorn. **3** to place over, against, as an equivalent. **4** to start (laughing etc.). **5** to set out. **6** to detonate. **to set on 1** to incite, to urge (to attack). **2** to employ (on a task). **3** to make an attack on. **to set oneself up as** to pretend to be. **to set one's hand to 1** to begin (a task). **2** to sign (a document). **to set one's seal to** to seal (a document). **to set one's teeth 1** to clench the teeth. **2** to be obstinate or determined. **to set out 1** to start (upon a journey etc.). **2** to intend. **3** to display, to state at length. **4** to mark off. **5** to assign, to allot. **6** to equip. **7** to adorn, to embellish. **8** to plant out. **to set over** to put in authority over or in control of. **to set right** to correct. **to set the stage** to prepare for (an event etc.). **to set to 1** to apply oneself vigorously. **2** to begin to fight. **to set to work 1** to begin on a task. **2** to cause to begin working. **to set up 1** to erect, to display.

2 to raise, to exalt. **3** to establish. **4** to start a business (as). **5** to cause to develop, to occasion. **6** to begin to utter. **7** (*coll.*) to arrange for (someone else) to be blamed, to frame. **8** to compose (type). **9** to put (copy etc.) in type. **10** to supply the needs of. **11** to prepare. **12** to restore the health of. **13** to put forward (a theory). **to set upon** to set on. **set-aside** *n.* **1** the act of setting aside. **2** the policy of taking farmland out of production to reduce surpluses or maintain prices of a crop. **setback** *n.* **1** a check, an arrest. **2** an overflow, a counter-current. **3** a relapse. **set fair** *a.* (of the weather) fine and settled. **set menu** *n.* a limited menu which has a set number of courses. **set-off** *n.* **1** a thing set off against another. **2** an offset, a counterpoise, a counter-claim. **3** a decorative contrast, an embellishment. **4** (*Print.*) an accidental transference of ink from one printed sheet to another. **set phrase** *n.* an invariable combination of words. **set piece** *n.* **1** a carefully prepared and usually elaborate performance. **2** an elaborate, formalized piece of writing, painting etc. **3** a carefully arranged display of fireworks or a large firework built up with scaffolding. **4** in sport, a formal movement to put the ball back into play. **set screw** *n.* a screw which secures parts of machinery together and prevents relative movement. **set scrum** *n.* a scrum in rugby ordered by the referee. **set square** *n.* a right-angled triangular piece of wood etc. used in mechanical drawing. **setter** *n.* **1** a person who or thing which sets (type, gems, music to words etc.). **2** a large dog trained to point at game by standing rigid. **setting** *n.* **1** the action of a person who or thing which sets. **2** the result of this. **3** hardening. **4** the framing etc. in which something (such as a jewel) is set. **5** the framing, surroundings or environment of a thing, event etc. **6** the scenery and other stage accessories of a play. **7** a set of eggs. **8** the music to which words, a song etc. are fitted. **9** one person's cutlery etc. at a table. **10** a level at which a machine or device is set to operate. **setting lotion** *n.* lotion used for setting hair. **set-to** *n.* (*pl.* **set-tos**) (*coll.*) **1** a fight, esp. with the fists. **2** a heated argument. **set-up** *n.* **1** an arrangement. **2** a situation. **3** (*coll.*) a situation in which someone is tricked or framed.

set[2] (set) *n.* **1** a number of similar, related or complementary things or persons, a group. **2** a number of things intended to be used together or required to form a whole. **3** (*Math.*) a collection of mathematical objects, numbers etc. **4** a clutch of eggs. **5** a group of games played together, counting as a unit, esp. in tennis. **6** the direction of a current, opinion etc., drift. **7** a predisposition to respond in a certain way to a psychological stimulus. **8** posture. **9** the way a dress etc. sits. **10** permanent inclination, bias. **11** the act of pointing at game etc. (by a setter). **12** a young plant for setting out, a shoot, a slip for planting. **13** a distance set off for excavation. **14** a timber framing for supporting the roof. **15** a set theatre scene. **16** a built-up cinema scene. **17** an apparatus for radio or television receiving. **18** a class of pupils of the same or similar ability. **19** the adjustment or setting of a machine. **20** (*Austral., coll.*) a grudge. **21** a sequence of songs or pieces of music to be performed. **22** a set hairstyle. **23** a badger's sett. **24** a sett used for paving. **25** a number of people performing a square dance. **to make a dead set at 1** to attack with determination. **2** to try to win the affections of. **set point** *n.* in tennis etc., a point which, if won by one of the players, will win the set. **set theory** *n.* a branch of mathematics which studies the properties and relationships of sets.

seta (sē′tə) *n.* (*pl.* **setae** (-tē)) (*Biol.*) a bristle or bristle-like plant or animal part. **setaceous** (sitā′shəs) *a.* **setiferous** (-tif′-), **setiform** (sē′tifawm), **setigerous** (-tij′-), **setose** (sē′tōs) *a.*

seton (sē′tən) *n.* a twist of silk, cotton or similar material inserted in a wound to maintain drainage and as a counterirritant, esp. in veterinary surgery.

sett (set) *n.* **1** a small rectangular block of stone used for road paving. **2** a badger's burrow.

settee (sitē′) *n.* a long seat with a back for several persons; a sofa.

setter SET[1].

setting SET[1].

settle[1] (set′əl) *v.t.* **1** to place firmly, to put in a permanent or fixed position. **2** to cause to sit down or to become fixed. **3** to determine, to decide. **4** to plant with inhabitants, to colonize. **5** to settle in as colonists. **6** to cause to sink or subside. **7** to clear of dregs. **8** to deal with, to finish with. **9** to adjust and liquidate (a disputed account). **10** to pay (an account). **11** to secure (property, an income etc., on). **12** to adjust, to accommodate (a quarrel, dispute etc.). ~*v.i.* **1** to sit down, to alight. **2** to cease from movement, agitation etc. **3** to become motionless, fixed or permanent. **4** to take up a permanent abode, mode of life etc. **5** to become established, to become a colonist (in). **6** to subside, to sink to the bottom. **7** to become clarified. **8** to determine, to resolve (upon). **9** to adjust differences, claims or accounts. **to settle down 1** to become regular in one's mode of life. **2** to begin to apply oneself (to a task etc.). **3** to stop being excited, to calm down. **to settle for** to accept, to be content with. **to settle in** to make or become comfortably established. **to settle one's affairs** to make sure one's finances etc. are in order before one dies. **to settle up 1** to pay what is owing. **2** to finally arrange (a matter). **to settle with 1** to pay money due to (a creditor). **2** to deal with. **settleable** *a.* **settlement** *n.* **1** the act of settling an agreement; an official agreement. **2** the state of being settled. **3** the act of paying back money. **4** a subsidence. **5** a place or region newly settled, a colony. **6** (*Law*) the conveyance of property or creation of an estate to make provision for the support of a

person or persons or for some other object. **7** the property so settled. **settler** *n.* **1** a person who settles, esp. a colonist. **2** (*sl.*) a knock-down blow, a decisive argument etc. **settling** *n.*, *a.* **settling day** *n.* a day for the settling-up of accounts, esp. on the Stock Exchange. **settlor** *n.* (*Law*) a person who makes a settlement.

settle[2] (set′əl) *n.* a long, high-backed seat or bench for several persons.

seven (sev′ən) *n.* **1** the number or figure 7 or vii. **2** the age of seven. **3** the seventh hour after midnight or midday. **4** (*pl.*) a rugby game or tournament played with teams of seven players. **5** a set of seven persons or things, esp. a card with seven pips. **6** a size etc. denoted by the number seven. **7** a team or set of seven people. ~*a.* **1** seven in number. **2** aged seven. **seven deadly sins** *n.pl.* pride, covetousness, lust, gluttony, anger, envy, sloth. **sevenfold** *a., adv.* **seven seas** *n.pl.* the N and S Atlantic, N and S Pacific, Arctic, Antarctic and Indian oceans. **seven year itch** *n.* the supposed onset of boredom, leading to infidelity, after seven years of marriage.

seventeen (seventēn′, sev′-) *n.* **1** the number or figure 17 or xvii. **2** the age of 17. **3** a size etc. denoted by the number seventeen. ~*a.* **1** 17 in number. **2** aged 17. **seventeenth** *n.* **1** any one of 17 equal parts. **2** the last of 17 (people, things etc.). **3** the next after the 16th. ~*a.* that is the seventeenth.

seventh (sev′ənth) *n.* **1** any one of seven equal parts. **2** (*Mus.*) the interval between a given tone and the seventh above it (inclusively) on the diatonic scale. **3** a combination of these two tones. **4** the last of seven (people, things etc.). **5** the next after the sixth. ~*a.* **1** the last of seven (people, things etc.). **2** the next after the sixth. **Seventh-Day Adventist** *n.* a member of a sect that believes in the imminent second advent of Christ and observes Saturday as the sabbath. **seventhly** *adv.*

seventy (sev′ənti) *n.* (*pl.* **seventies**) **1** the number or figure 70 or lxx. **2** the age of 70. ~*a.* **1** 70 in number. **2** aged 70. **seventies** *n.pl.* **1** the period of time between one's 70th and 80th birthdays. **2** the range of temperature between 70° and 80°. **3** the period of time between the 70th and 80th years of a century. **seventieth** (-əth) *n.* **1** any one of 70 equal parts. **2** the last of 70 (people, things etc.). **3** the next after the 69th. ~*a.* that is the seventieth. **seventy-first, seventy-second** etc. *a., n.* the ordinal numbers corresponding to seventy-one, seventy-two etc. **seventy-one, seventy-two** etc. *n., a.* the cardinal numbers between seventy and eighty.

sever (sev′ə) *v.t.* **1** to part, to separate. **2** to divide, to cleave. **3** to cut or break off (apart from the whole). **4** to keep distinct or apart. **5** to end the contract of. ~*v.i.* to separate, to part. **severable** *a.* **severance** *n.* **severance pay** *n.* a sum of money paid to a worker as compensation for loss of employment.

several (sev´ərəl) *a.* **1** consisting of a number, more than two but not many. **2** separate, distinct. **3** not common, not shared with others, of or relating to individuals. ~*n.* a few, an indefinite number, more than two but not many. **severally** *adv.* **severalty** (-ti) *n.* (*pl.* **severalties**) (*Law*) exclusive tenure or ownership.

severe (siviə´) *a.* **1** rigorous, strict. **2** trying, hard to endure or sustain. **3** distressing, bitter. **4** grave, serious. **5** rigidly conforming to rule, unadorned. **severely** *adv.* **severity** (-ver´i-) *n.* (*pl.* **severities**).

Seville orange (səvil´, sev´-) *n.* a bitter orange used to make marmalade.

sew (sō) *v.t.* (*p.p.* **sewn** (sōn), **sewed**) **1** to fasten together by thread worked through and through with a needle. **2** to make, mend etc. by sewing. ~*v.i.* to work with a needle and thread. **to sew up 1** to mend, join etc. by sewing. **2** (*sl.*) to complete satisfactorily. **sewer**[1] *n.* **sewing** *n.* **sewing machine** *n.* a machine for stitching etc. driven electrically or by a treadle or a crank turned by hand.

Usage note The spellings of the verbs *sew* (of needlework) and *sow* (of seed) should not be confused.

---

sewer[1] SEW.

sewer[2] (soo´ə, sū´ə) *n.* a channel, underground conduit or tunnel for carrying off the drainage and liquid refuse of a town etc. **sewage** (-ij) *n.* the waste matter, esp. excrement, carried off through the sewers. ~*v.t.* to manure with sewage. **sewage farm** *n.* a place where sewage is treated for use as manure. **sewage works** *n.* a place where sewage is treated before being discharged (into the sea etc.). **sewerage** (-rij) *n.* **1** the system of draining by means of sewers. **2** sewers, drains etc. collectively. **3** (*N Am.*) sewage. **sewer rat** *n.* the common brown rat.

sewn SEW.

sex (seks) *n.* **1** the sum total of the physiological, anatomical and functional characteristics which distinguish male and female. **2** either of the divisions according to this. **3** the quality of being male or female. **4** (*collect.*) males or females, men or women. **5** (*coll.*) sexual intercourse. **6** sexual instincts, desires etc. ~*v.t.* to determine the sex of. ~*a.* **1** of or relating to sex. **2** arising from or based on sexual differences. **sex act** *n.* an act of sexual intercourse. **sex appeal** *n.* what makes a person attractive to the opposite sex. **sex change** *n.* the use of surgery, hormone treatment etc. to enable a person to change sex. **sex chromosome** *n.* the chromosome responsible for the initial determination of sex. **sexed** *a.* **sexer** *n.* **sex hormone** *n.* a hormone involved in sexual development. **sexism** *n.* discrimination (esp. against women) on the grounds of sex. **sexist** *n.* **sex kitten** *n.* (*coll.*) a young woman who plays up her sex appeal. **sexless** *a.* **sexlessly** *adv.* **sexlessness** *n.* **sex life** *n.* a person's sexual activity. **sex-linked**

a. **1** (of a gene) located on a sex chromosome. **2** (of a character) determined by a sex-linked gene. **sex maniac** *n.* (*coll.*) a person who needs or wants sexual gratification to an excessive degree. **sex object** *n.* a person perceived solely as an object of sexual desires and fantasies. **sex offender** *n.* a person who commits a crime of a sexual nature. **sexology** (-ol´-) *n.* the science dealing with the sexes and their relationships. **sexological** (-əloj´-) *a.* **sexologist** (-ol´-) *n.* **sexpot** *n.* (*coll.*) a sexy person. **sex-starved** *a.* suffering from a lack of sexual activity. **sex symbol** *n.* a person who is acknowledged to have sex appeal. **sexy** *a.* (*comp.* **sexier**, *superl.* **sexiest**) **1** sexually stimulating. **2** sexually aroused. **3** of or relating to sex. **4** (*coll.*) interesting, in fashion, appealing. **sexily** *adv.* **sexiness** *n.*

sexagenarian (seksəjineə´riən) *a.* 60 years of age or between 60 and 70. ~*n.* a sexagenarian person.

sexcentenary (seksəntē´nəri, -ten´-, -sen´tin-) *a.* of, relating to or consisting of 600 years. ~*n.* (*pl.* **sexcentenaries**) **1** a 600th anniversary. **2** a celebration of this.

sexennial (seksen´iəl) *a.* **1** occurring once every six years. **2** lasting six years. **sexennially** *adv.*

sexfoil (seks´foil) *n.* an architectural or other ornament of six-lobed foliation.

sexology SEX.

sexpartite (sekspah´tīt) *a.* divided into six.

sexploitation (seksploitā´shən) *n.* the portrayal or manipulation of sex for financial profit in films, magazines etc.

sext (sekst) *n.* in the Roman Catholic Church, the office for the sixth hour or noon.

sextant (sek´stənt) *n.* an instrument used in navigation and surveying for measuring angular distances or altitudes. **sextantal** (-tan´-) *a.*

sextet (sekstet´), **sextette** *n.* **1** (*Mus.*) **a** a composition for six instruments or voices. **b** a group of six musicians or singers performing such a composition. **2** any group of six.

sexton (sek´stən) *n.* an officer having the care of a church, its vessels, vestments etc., and frequently acting as parish clerk and a gravedigger. **sexton beetle** *n.* a beetle of the genus *Nicrophorus* that buries carrion to serve as a nidus for its eggs. **sextonship** *n.*

sextuple (seks´tūpəl) *a.* **1** six times as many. **2** having six parts. ~*n.* a sextuple amount. ~*v.i.* to multiply by six. **sextuplet** (-tū´plit) *n.* **1** each of six born at one birth. **2** (*Mus.*) a group of six notes played in the time of four.

sexual (sek´sūəl, -shəl) *a.* **1** of, relating to or based on sex or the sexes or on the distinction of sexes. **2** of or relating to generation or copulation, venereal. **sexual harassment** *n.* unwanted attention of a sexual nature, esp. in the workplace. **sexual intercourse** *n.* a sexual act in which the male's erect penis is inserted into the female's vagina. **sexuality** (-al´-) *n.* **sexual-ize**, **sexualise** *v.t.* **sexualization** (-ā´shən) *n.* **sexually** *adv.*

sexy SEX.

SF *abbr.* science fiction.

sf. *abbr.* (*Mus.*) sforzando.

sforzando (sfawtsan´dō), **sforzato** (-tsah´tō) *adv.* (*Mus.*) emphatically, with sudden vigour. ~*a.* emphatic, vigorous. ~*n.* (*pl.* **sforzandos, sforzandi** (-dē), **sforzatos, sforzati** (-tē)) **1** a note or group of notes emphasized in this way. **2** an increase in emphasis.

sfumato (sfumah´tō) *a.* (of art) with misty outlines. ~*n.* (*pl.* **sfumatos**) **1** the technique of blending areas of different colours. **2** this effect.

sfz *abbr.* (*Mus.*) sforzando.

SG *abbr.* **1** (*N Am.*) senior grade. **2** (*Law*) Solicitor-General. **3** specific gravity.

SGML *abbr.* (*Comput.*) Standard Generalized Mark-up Language.

sgraffito (sgrafē´tō) *n.* (*pl.* **sgraffiti** (-tē)) **1** decoration by means of scratches through plaster or slip, revealing a differently coloured ground. **2** an example of this.

Sgt, sgt *abbr.* sergeant.

sh (sh) *int.* used to call for silence.

s.h. *abbr.* second-hand.

shabby (shab´i) *a.* (*comp.* **shabbier,** *superl.* **shabbiest**) **1** ragged, threadbare. **2** in ragged or threadbare clothes. **3** mean, despicable. **4** of poor quality. **shabbily** *adv.* **shabbiness** *n.* **shabby-genteel** *a.* aspiring to gentility, although shabby. **shabbyish** *a.*

shack (shak) *n.* a rude cabin, esp. one built of logs. **to shack up (with)** (*sl.*) to live (with), usu. having a sexual relationship.

shackle (shak´əl) *n.* **1** a fetter or handcuff. **2** a coupling link. **3** (*pl.*) restraints, impediments. ~*v.t.* **1** to chain, to fetter. **2** to impede, to hamper. **shackle-bolt** *n.* **1** a bolt passing through holes in a shackle to fasten it. **2** a bolt with a shackle at the end.

shad (shad) *n.* (*pl. in general* **shad,** *in particular* **shads**) any of several anadromous deep-bodied food-fish of the genus *Alosa,* esp. the American or white shad.

shaddock (shad´ək) *n.* **1** the large orange-like fruit of a Malaysian and Polynesian tree, *Citrus grandis.* **2** the tree bearing this.

shade (shād) *n.* **1** obscurity or partial darkness caused by the interception of the rays of light. **2** gloom, darkness. **3** a place sheltered from the sun. **4** the dark or darker part of a picture. **5** a screen for protecting from or moderating light, esp. a covering for a lamp, or a shield worn over the eyes. **6** (*N Am.*) a window blind. **7** a glass cover for protecting an object. **8** a colour. **9** gradation of colour, esp. with regard to its depth or its luminosity. **10** a scarcely perceptible degree, a small amount. **11** something unsubstantial, unreal or delusive. **12** the soul after its separation from the body, a spectre. **13** (*pl.*) the abode of spirits, Hades. **14** (*pl., coll.*) sunglasses. **15** (*pl.*) undertones (of). ~*v.t.* **1** to shelter or screen from light or heat. **2** to obscure, to darken (an object in

a picture) so as to show gradations of colour or effects of light and shade. **3** to graduate as to light and shade or colour. **4** to cause to pass or blend with another colour. ~*v.i.* to pass off by degrees or blend (with another colour). **to put in the shade** to be superior to; to outdo. **shadeless** *a.* **shading** *n.* **shady** (shā´di) *a.* (*comp.* **shadier,** *superl.* **shadiest**) **1** sheltered from the light and heat of the sun. **2** casting shade. **3** shunning the light. **4** disreputable, of equivocal honesty. **shadily** *adv.* **shadiness** *n.*

shadow (shad´ō) *n.* **1** shade. **2** a patch of shade. **3** the dark figure of a body projected on the ground etc. by the interception of light. **4** an inseparable companion. **5** a person who follows another closely and unobtrusively. **6** darkness, obscurity. **7** protection, shelter. **8** the dark part of a picture, room etc. **9** an imperfect or faint representation. **10** a dim foreshadowing, a premonition. **11** a faint trace, the slightest degree. **12** something unsubstantial or unreal. **13** a phantom, a ghost. **14** eyeshadow. **15** gloom or sadness. ~*v.t.* **1** to darken, to cloud. **2** to set (forth) dimly or in outline, to typify. **3** to watch secretly, to spy upon. **4** to accompany so as to learn what a job involves. **shadow-boxing** *n.* boxing against an imaginary opponent when training. **shadow cabinet** *n.* a group of leading members of a party out of office, who would probably constitute the cabinet if in power. **shadower** *n.* **shadowgraph** *n.* **1** an image or photograph produced by X-rays. **2** an image produced by a shadow on a screen. **3** an image formed by light refracted by a fluid. **shadowless** *a.* **shadow theatre,** (*N Am.*) **shadow theater** *n.* a puppet show using shadows on a screen. **shadowy** *a.* **shadowiness** *n.*

shaft (shahft) *n.* **1** the slender stem of a spear, arrow etc. **2** an arrow. **3** anything more or less resembling this, such as a ray (of light) or a bolt of lightning. **4** (*Archit.*) **a** a column between the base and the capital. **b** a small column in a cluster or in a window joint. **5** any long, straight and more or less slender part. **6** (*sl.*) a penis. **7** the handle of a tool. **8** either one of the bars between a pair of which a horse is harnessed. **9** a large axle or long cylindrical bar, esp. rotating and transferring motion. **10** (*Mining*) a well-like excavation, usu. vertical, giving access to a mine. **11** an upward vent to a mine, tunnel etc. **12** (*N Am., coll.*) unfair treatment. ~*v.t.* **1** (*N Am., coll.*) to cheat, to treat unfairly. **2** (*sl.*) to have sexual intercourse with. **3** to fit with a shaft. **shafting** *n.* **1** a system of shafts for the transmission of power. **2** material from which shafts are cut.

shag (shag) *n.* **1** a rough coat of hair, a bushy mass. **2** cloth having a long coarse nap. **3** strong tobacco cut into fine shreds. **4** the crested cormorant, *Phalacrocorax aristotelis.* **5** (*taboo sl.*) an act of sexual intercourse. ~*v.t., v.i.* (*pres.p.* **shagging,** *past, p.p.* **shagged**)(*taboo sl.*) to have sexual intercourse (with). **shagged out** *a.* tired out. **shagger**

n. **shaggy** *a.* (*comp.* **shaggier**, *superl.* **shaggiest**)
1 rough-haired, hairy, hirsute. **2** coarse, tangled,
unkempt. **shaggily** *adv.* **shagginess** *n.* **shaggy-dog
story** *n.* a long, inconsequential story, funny but
lacking a punchline.

shagreen (shəgrēn´) *n.* **1** a kind of leather with
a granular surface which is prepared without
tanning from the skins of horses, asses, camels,
sharks and seals, usu. dyed green. **2** the skins
of various sharks, rays etc., covered with hard
papillae, used for polishing etc.

shah (shah) *n.* (*Hist.*) a sovereign of Iran. **shah-
dom** *n.*

shaikh SHEIK.

shake (shāk) *v.t.* (*past* **shook** (shuk), *p.p.* **shaken**
(shā´kən)) **1** to move forcibly or rapidly to and
fro or up and down. **2** to cause to tremble or
quiver. **3** to shock, to disturb. **4** to brandish. **5** to
weaken the stability of. **6** to trill. **7** (*coll.*) to upset the composure of. **8** (*Austral.*, *sl.*) to steal.
9 (*esp. N Am.*, *coll.*) to shake off. ~*v.i.* **1** to move
quickly to and fro or up and down, to tremble,
to totter, to shiver. **2** to quiver. **3** to change the
pitch or power of the voice, to make trills.
4 (*coll.*) to shake hands. ~*n.* **1** the act or an act of
shaking. **2** a jerk, a shock. **3** the state of being
shaken, agitation. **4** (*Mus.*) a trill. **5** a milk shake.
6 (*N Am.*, *Austral.*) an earthquake. **in two shakes
(of a lamb's/ dog's tail)** very quickly. **no great
shakes** (*coll.*) of no great account. **the shakes**
(*coll.*) a fit of trembling, caused by fever, withdrawal from alcohol etc. **to shake down 1** to
bring down (fruit etc.) by shaking. **2** to cause
(grain etc.) to settle into a compact mass. **3** to
become compact. **4** to settle down into a comfortable or harmonious state. **5** (*N Am.*, *sl.*) to extort
money from. **to shake in one's shoes** to be very
frightened. **to shake off 1** to get rid of by shaking,
to cast off. **2** to get rid of (someone who is following one). **to shake one's head** to move the
head from side to side in token of refusal, dissent, disapproval etc. **to shake out 1** to open out
or empty by shaking. **2** (*coll.*) to reduce (staff) as
part of a drastic reorganization. **to shake up 1** to
mix, disturb etc. by shaking. **2** (*coll.*) to reorganize drastically. **3** to reshape by shaking. **4** to
rouse or shock. **shakeable**, **shakable** *a.* **shake-
down** *n.* **1** a makeshift bed. **2** a period or process
of adjustment. **3** (*esp. N Am.*, *sl.*) a swindle. ~*a.* of
or relating to a familiarization or test voyage.
shake-out *n.* **Shaker** *n.* a member of an American
millenarian sect believing in a life of simplicity
and celibacy (from their religious dances).
Shakeress (-ris) *n.* a female Shaker. **Shakerism** *n.*
shaker *n.* **1** a container for mixing or sprinkling
by shaking. **2** a person who or thing which
shakes. **shake-up** *n.* **shaky** *a.* (*comp.* **shakier**,
superl. **shakiest**) **1** liable to shake, unsteady. **2** of
doubtful integrity, solvency, ability etc. **shakily**
adv. **shakiness** *n.*

Shakespearean (shākspiə´riən), **Shakespear-
ian** *a.* of, relating to or resembling Shakespeare

or his style. ~*n.* a student of Shakespeare's
works.

shako (shak´ō) *n.* (*pl.* **shakos**) a military cylindrical hat, usu. flat-topped, with a peak in
front, and decorated with a pompom, plume or
tuft.

shale (shāl) *n.* a laminated argillaceous rock
resembling soft slate, often containing much
bitumen. **shale oil** *n.* oil from bitumen shale.
shaly *a.*

shall (shal) *v.aux.* (*2nd pers. sing. pres.* †**shalt**
(shalt), *3rd pers. sing. pres.* **shall**, *past, subj.*
should (shud, shəd), *2nd pers.* †**shouldst**,
†**shouldest**) **1** (in the 1st pers.) used to express
simple futurity or a conditional statement or
(stressed) strong intention. **2** (in the 2nd and 3rd
pers.) used to express a command, intention,
promise, permission etc. **3** used to express future
or conditional obligation, duty etc. **4** used to
form a conditional protasis etc. **shall I?** do you
want me to?

Usage note In British English, *shall* is now
used less frequently than *will* (or, in spoken and
informal written English, *'ll*, which blurs the distinction between the two). The traditional rules
for using *shall* (or *should*) and *will* (or *would*) are
basically as follows: in expressing the future and
in conditional sentences (with *if*, *lest*) *shall* is
used in the first person and *will* in the second
and third persons (*I shall go*; *If you go we will be
sad*; *They will go*; *If she goes you will be sad* etc.);
in other contexts the distribution is reversed,
with *will* for the first person and *shall* for others
(*I will go, you can't stop me*; *He shall go, I'll force
him* etc.). Nowadays, however, uses such as *I will
go* (future) and *We shall go, definitely* are also
generally acceptable.

shallot (shəlot´) *n.* a plant, *Allium ascalonicum*,
allied to garlic with similar but milder bulbs.

shallow (shal´ō) *a.* **1** not having much depth.
2 trivial, silly. ~*n.* a shallow place, a shoal. ~*v.i.*
to become shallow or shallower. ~*v.t.* to make
shallow. **shallowly** *adv.* **shallowness** *n.*

shalom (shəlom´) *n.*, *int.* peace (a greeting used
esp. by Jewish people).

sham (sham) *v.t.* (*pres.p.* **shamming**, *past, p.p.*
shammed) to feign, to make a pretence of. ~*v.i.* to
feign, to pretend. ~*n.* **1** an imposture, a pretence.
2 a fraud, a person who or thing which pretends
to be someone or something else. ~*a.* feigned,
pretended. **shammer** *n.*

shamanism (shah´mənizm, shā´-) *n.* a form of
religion based on the belief in good and evil
spirits which can be influenced by shamans, prevailing among some Siberian and N American
peoples. **shaman** *n.* a priest, exorcist or medicine man among shamanists. **shamanist** *n.*, *a.*
shamanistic (-nis´-) *a.*

shamateur (sham´ətə) *n.* (*derog.*) a person
classed as an amateur in sport, but who accepts
payment. **shamateurism** *n.*

shamble (sham´bəl) *v.i.* to walk in an awkward, shuffling or unsteady manner. ~*n.* a shambling walk or gait. **shambling** *a.*

shambles (sham´bəlz) *n.* **1** (*coll.*) utter confusion, a disorganized mess. **2** a butcher's slaughterhouse. **3** a place of carnage or execution.

shambolic (shambol´ik) *a.* (*coll.*) chaotic, utterly confused.

shame (shām) *n.* **1** a painful feeling due to consciousness of guilt, humiliation etc. **2** the instinct to avoid this, modesty. **3** a state of disgrace. **4** anything that brings dissappointment. ~*v.t.* **1** to make ashamed. **2** to bring shame on, to cause to feel disgraced. **3** to force (into or out of) by shame. **for shame!** used to reprove someone who should be ashamed. **shame on you!** you should be ashamed. **to put to shame** to humiliate by exhibiting better qualities. **shamefaced** *a.* bashful, easily abashed. **shamefacedly** (-fāst´li, -fā´sid-) *adv.* **shamefacedness** *n.* **shameful** *a.* **shamefully** *adv.* **shamefulness** *n.* **shameless** *a.* **shamelessly** *adv.* **shamelessness** *n.* **shamer** *n.*

shammer SHAM.

shammy (sham´i), **†shamoy** (-oi) *n.* (*pl.* **shammies**, **†shamoys**) (*coll.*) CHAMOIS LEATHER (under CHAMOIS).

shampoo (shampoo´) *v.t.* (*3rd pers. sing. pres.* **shampoos**, *pres.p.* **shampooing**, *past, p.p.* **shampooed**) **1** to wash with shampoo. **2** to wash the hair of with shampoo. ~*n.* (*pl.* **shampoos**) **1** a liquid soap or detergent used for washing the hair. **2** a similar cleaner for a car, carpet, upholstery etc. **3** an act of shampooing.

shamrock (sham´rok) *n.* a species of trefoil, esp. *Trifolium minus, T. repens* or *Medicago lupulina*, forming the national emblem of Ireland.

shamus (shā´məs) *n.* (*pl.* **shamuses**) (*N Am., sl.*) a detective.

shandy (shan´di) *n.* (*pl.* **shandies**) a mixture of beer and ginger beer or lemonade.

shanghai (shanghī´) *v.t.* (*3rd pers. sing. pres.* **shanghais**, *pres.p.* **shanghaiing**, *past, p.p.* **shanghaied**) **1** to drug and ship as a sailor while stupefied. **2** to kidnap. **3** (*coll.*) to trick into performing an unpleasant task.

shank (shangk) *n.* **1** the leg, esp. the part from the knee to the ankle. **2** the shin bone. **3** a bird's tarsus. **4** the shaft of a column. **5** the straight part of an instrument, tool etc. connecting the acting part with the handle. **6** the narrow part of the sole of a shoe. **7** the lower foreleg of an animal, esp. as a cut of meat. **shanked** *a.* **shanks's pony**, **shanks's mare** *n.* one's legs for walking as opposed to riding etc.

shanny (shan´i) *n.* (*pl.* **shannies**) a blenny, *Blennius pholis*.

shan't (shahnt) *contr.* shall not.

shantung (shantŭng´) *n.* a plain fabric woven in coarse silk yarns.

shanty¹ (shan´ti) *n.* (*pl.* **shanties**) **1** a rude hut or cabin. **2** a hastily built or rickety building. **shanty town** *n.* a poor part of a town consisting mainly of shanties.

shanty² (shan´ti), **chanty** *n.* (*pl.* **shanties**, **chanties**) a song sung by sailors, esp. one with a strong rhythm sung while working.

shape (shāp) *v.t.* (*p.p.* **shaped**, **†shapen** (-pən)) **1** to form, to create. **2** to make into a particular form, to fashion. **3** to adapt, to make conform (to). **4** to regulate, to direct. **5** to conceive, to conjure up. ~*v.i.* **1** to take shape, to come into shape, to develop (well, ill etc.). **2** to become fit or adapted (to). ~*n.* **1** the outward form or figure. **2** outward aspect, appearance. **3** concrete form, embodiment, realization. **4** fit or orderly form or condition. **5** kind, sort. **6** an image, an apparition. **7** a pattern, a mould. **to shape up 1** to develop a shape. **2** to develop satisfactorily. **to take shape** to become recognizable as or develop into something definite. **shapeable**, **shapable** *a.* **shaped** *a.* **shapeless** *a.* **1** having no regular form. **2** lacking in symmetry. **shapelessly** *adv.* **shapelessness** *n.* **shapely** *a.* (*comp.* **shapelier**, *superl.* **shapeliest**) **1** well-formed, well-proportioned. **2** having beauty or regularity. **shapeliness** *n.* **shaper** *n.*

shard (shahd), **sherd** (shœd) *n.* **1** a potsherd. **2** a fragment of volcanic rock. **3** the wing-case of a beetle.

share¹ (sheə) *n.* **1** a part or portion detached from a common amount or stock. **2** a part to which one has a right or which one is obliged to contribute, a fair or just portion. **3** an allotted part, esp. any one of the equal parts into which the capital of a company is divided. ~*v.t.* **1** to divide into portions, to distribute among a number, to apportion. **2** to give away a portion of. **3** to have or endure with others, to participate in. ~*v.i.* **1** to have a share or shares (in). **2** to be a sharer or sharers (with). **3** to participate. **share and share alike** in equal shares. **to share out** to divide into equal shares and distribute. **shareable**, **sharable** *a.* **sharecropper** *n.* (*esp. N Am.*) a tenant farmer who pays over part of the crop as rent. **sharecrop** *v.i., v.t.* (*pres.p.* **sharecropping**, *past, p.p.* **sharecropped**). **share-farmer** *n.* (*Austral.*) a tenant farmer who shares in the profits. **shareholder** *n.* a person who holds a share or shares in a joint-stock company etc. **shareholding** *n.* **shareout** *n.* **sharer** *n.* **shareware** *n.* (*Comput.*) computer software which is free to users for a certain time.

share² (sheə) *n.* **1** a ploughshare. **2** a blade of a cultivator, seeder etc.

sharia (shərē´ə), **shariah** *n.* the body of Islamic religious law.

shark (shahk) *n.* **1** a selachoid sea fish of various species with lateral gill openings and an inferior mouth, mostly large and voracious and armed with formidable teeth. **2** (*coll.*) a rogue, a swindler. **sharkskin** *n.* **1** the skin of a shark. **2** a smooth woven fabric of rayon etc.

sharon fruit (shar´ən) *n.* a kind of persimmon.

sharp (shahp) *a.* **1** having a keen edge or fine point. **2** terminating in a point or edge. **3** angular, abrupt. **4** clearly outlined or defined. **5** pungent, sour. **6** (of sand) gritty. **7** shrill, piercing. **8** harsh, sarcastic. **9** acute, keen-witted. **10** attentive, alert. **11** (*derog.*) alive to one's interests, dishonest. **12** quick, energetic. **13** (*Mus.*) above the true pitch, esp. a semitone higher. **14** (*coll.*) stylish. *~adv.* **1** punctually, exactly. **2** at a sharp angle. **3** above the true pitch. **4** suddenly, abruptly. *~n.* **1** a note a semitone above the true pitch. **2** the sign # indicating this. **3** a long and slender sewing-needle. **4** (*coll.*) a cheat. **sharpen** *v.t., v.i.* to make sharp. **sharpener** *n.* **sharp end** *n.* **1** (*facet.*) the bow of a ship. **2** (*coll.*) the place where things are happening. **sharper** *n.* **1** (*coll.*) a swindler, a rogue. **2** a person who lives by their wits. **sharp-featured** *a.* having well-defined facial features. **sharpish** *a.* (*coll.*) rather sharp. *~adv.* **1** rather quickly. **2** rather sharply. **sharply** *adv.* **sharpness** *n.* **sharp practice** *n.* (*coll.*) underhand or questionable dealings. **sharp-set** *a.* **1** set with a sharp edge. **2** ravenous. **sharpshooter** *n.* a skilled marksman. **sharpshooting** *n.* **sharp-tongued** *a.* having critical or sarcastic speech. **sharp-witted** *a.* having a keen wit, judgement or discernment. **sharp-wittedly** *adv.* **sharp-wittedness** *n.*

shat SHIT.

shatter (shat´ə) *v.t.* **1** to break up at once into many pieces. **2** to destroy, dissipate, to overthrow, to ruin. **3** to upset, distress. **4** (*sl.*) to tire out. *~v.i.* to break into fragments. **shattered** *a.* **shatterer** *n.* **shattering** *a.* **shatteringly** *adv.*

shave (shāv) *v.t.* (*p.p.* **shaved**, †**shaven** (-vən)) **1** to remove hair from (the face, a person etc.) with a razor. **2** to remove (usu. off) from a surface with a razor. **3** to pare or cut thin slices off the surface of (leather, wood etc.). **4** to pass by closely with or without touching, to brush past, to graze. *~v.i.* to shave oneself. *~n.* **1** the act of shaving or the process of being shaved. **2** a knife for shaving, paring or scraping, esp. a blade with a handle at each end for shaving hoops etc. **3** a thin slice. **4** a narrow escape or miss. **shaven** *a.* **shaver** *n.* **1** a barber. **2** an electric razor. **3** (*coll.*) a young boy. **shaving** *n.* **1** the act of a person who shaves. **2** a thin slice pared off.

Shavian (shā´viən) *a.* of, relating to or characteristic of the writings of George Bernard Shaw, 1856–1950. *~n.* a follower of Shaw.

shaw (shaw) *n.* the stalk and leaves of a root-crop plant, e.g. a potato.

shawl (shawl) *n.* a square or oblong garment worn chiefly by women as a loose wrap for the upper part of the person. **shawl collar** *n.* (on a coat etc.) a collar of a rolled shape that tapers down the front of the garment. **shawled** *a.*

she (shē) *pron.* **1** the female person, animal or personified thing mentioned or referred to. **2** (*Austral., coll.*) it. *~n.* a female. *~a.* female (*esp. in*

comb., as *she-cat*, *she-devil*, *she-goat* etc.). **she-devil** *n.* a spiteful woman.

Usage note *She* is sometimes used as an objective pronoun (after a verb or preposition), especially when joined by *and* to a personal name or pronoun, *she and X*, but this is best avoided. See also note under THEY.

s/he *pron.* a written representation of 'he or she'.

shea (shē, shē´ə) *n.* a tropical African tree, *Vitellaria paradoxa*, yielding a kind of butter. **shea-butter** *n.*

sheading (shē´ding) *n.* any one of the six divisions of the Isle of Man.

sheaf (shēf) *n.* (*pl.* **sheaves** (-vz)) a quantity of things bound or held together lengthwise, esp. a bundle of wheat, oats, barley etc. *~v.t.* to collect and bind into sheaves, to sheave.

shear (shiə) *v.t.* (*past* **sheared**, †**shore** (shaw), *p.p.* **shorn** (shawn), **sheared**) **1** to cut or clip with shears. **2** to reduce or remove nap from (cloth etc.) by clipping. **3** to remove (wool etc.) thus. **4** to fleece, to plunder, to strip. **5** to subject to a shear. *~v.i.* **1** to use shears. **2** to cut, to penetrate. **3** to undergo a shear. *~n.* **1** (*pl.*) a cutting instrument with two large blades crossing each other like scissors and joined together by a spring; also called *pair of shears*. **2** a strain caused by pressure upon a solid body in which the layers of its substance move in parallel planes. **3** (*Geol.*) alteration of structure by transverse pressure. **to shear off** to break off vertically. **shearer** *n.* a person who shears sheep. **shearling** (-ling) *n.* **1** a sheep that has been shorn once. **2** wool from a shearling. **shearwater** *n.* **1** any seabird of the family Procellariidae, allied to the petrels. **2** any seabird of the genus *Rhynchops*; the skimmer.

sheath (shēth) *n.* (*pl.* **sheaths** (shēths, shēdhz)) **1** a case for a blade, weapon or tool, a scabbard. **2** (*Biol., Zool.*) an envelope, a case, a cell-covering, investing tissue, membrane etc. **3** a condom. **4** the protective covering of an electric cable. **sheathe** (shēdh) *v.t.* **1** to put into a sheath. **2** to protect by a casing or covering. **sheathing** (-dh-) *n.* anything which sheathes, esp. a metal covering for a ship's bottom. **sheath knife** *n.* (*pl.* **sheath knives**) a large case knife. **sheathless** *a.*

sheave[1] (shēv) *n.* the grooved wheel in a block or pulley over which the rope runs.

sheave[2] (shēv) *v.t.* to gather into sheaves, to sheaf.

sheaves SHEAF.

shebang (shibang´) *n.* (*N Am., sl.*) **1** a business, concern, affair. **2** a shed or hut.

shebeen (shibēn´) *n.* an unlicensed house where excisable liquors are sold.

shed[1] (shed) *v.t.* (*pres.p.* **shedding**, *past, p.p.* **shed**) **1** to let fall, to drop. **2** to throw off. **3** to take off (clothes). **4** to reduce (an electrical power load). **5** to reduce one's number of (employees). **shedder** *n.* **1** a person who or thing which sheds. **2** a female salmon after spawning.

shed[2] (shed) *n.* **1** a slight simple building, usu. a roofed structure with the ends or ends and sides open. **2** a hut. *~v.t.* (*pres.p.* **shedding**, *past, p.p.* **shedded**) to park in a shed. **shedhand** *n.* (*Austral.*) a worker in a sheep-shearing shed.

she'd (shid, shēd) *contr.* **1** she had. **2** she would.

sheen (shēn) *n.* **1** brightness, splendour. **2** lustre, glitter. **sheeny** *a.*

sheep (shēp) *n.* (*pl.* **sheep**) **1** a gregarious ruminant animal of the genus *Ovis*, esp. the domesticated *O. aries*, or any of its numerous breeds, reared for the sake of their flesh and wool. **2** a timid, subservient, unoriginal person who follows the crowd. **3** a bashful or embarrassed person. **4** (*pl.*) the members of a minister's flock. **to separate the sheep from the goats** to sort a group into inferior and superior members. **sheep-dip** *n.* **1** a preparation for killing ·vermin or preserving the wool on sheep. **2** a place for dipping sheep in this. **sheepdog** *n.* **1** a collie. **2** a breed of heavy, rough-coated, short-tailed dogs employed by shepherds. **sheepfold** *n.* a pen or enclosure for sheep. **sheepish** *a.* **1** like a sheep. **2** bashful, timid. **3** ashamed. **sheepishly** *adv.* **sheepishness** *n.* **sheeplike** *a.* **sheep-run** *n.* a large tract of land for pasturing sheep. **sheep's-bit** *n.* a plant with blue flowers like the scabious, *Jasione montana.* **sheepshank** *n.* a knot used to shorten a rope temporarily. **sheepskin** *n.* **1** the skin of a sheep, esp. used as a coat or rug. **2** leather prepared therefrom, used for bookbinding etc. **sheepwalk** *n.* land for pasturing sheep, usu. of less extent than a sheep-run.

sheer[1] (shiə) *a.* **1** pure, absolute. **2** perpendicular. **3** (of a fabric) very thin, diaphanous. *~adv.* **1** vertically. **2** entirely, outright. **sheerly** *adv.* **sheerness** *n.*

sheer[2] (shiə) *v.i.* **1** (*esp. Naut.*) to deviate from a course. **2** to go (away or off), esp. from someone or something one does not like. *~n.* a swerving or curving course. **to sheer off** to move off, to go away.

sheerlegs (shiə'legz), **shearlegs** *n.* an apparatus consisting of two masts, or legs, secured at the top, for hoisting heavy weights, esp. in dockyards.

sheet[1] (shēt) *n.* **1** a thin, flat, broad piece of anything, esp. a rectangular piece of linen, cotton or nylon used in a bed to keep the blankets etc. from a sleeper's body. **2** a piece of metal etc., rolled out, hammered, fused etc. into a thin sheet. **3** a piece of paper of a regular size, esp. complete as it was made, reckoned as the 24th part of a quire. **4** (*derog.*) a newspaper. **5** a broad expanse or surface. **6** a set of unseparated postage stamps. *~v.t.* **1** to cover, wrap or shroud in a sheet or sheets. **2** to form into sheets. *~v.i.* (of rain) to come down in sheets, very heavily. **in sheets 1** (of a book) not bound. **2** (of rain) very heavy. **sheeting** *n.* fabric used for making sheets. **sheet lightning** *n.* lightning in wide extended flashes. **sheet metal, sheet copper, sheet iron, sheet lead** *n.* metal rolled out, hammered or

fused into thin sheets. **sheet music** *n.* music printed on unbound sheets of paper.

sheet[2] (shēt) *n.* **1** a rope attached to the clew of a sail for moving, extending it etc. **2** (*pl.*) the space at the bow or stern of a boat. **sheet anchor** *n.* **1** a large anchor, usu. one of two carried outside the waist of a ship for use in emergencies. **2** a chief support, a last refuge. **sheet bend** *n.* a kind of knot used for joining ropes of different thicknesses.

sheik (shāk, shēk), **sheikh, shaikh** *n.* **1** the head of a Bedouin family, clan or tribe. **2** a Muslim leader. **sheikdom** *n.*

sheila (shē'lə) *n.* (*Austral., sl.*) a girl, a young woman.

shekel (shek'əl) *n.* **1** the main unit of currency of Israel. **2** (*pl., coll.*) money, riches. **3** a Hebrew weight of ¹/₆₀ of a mina. **4** (*Hist.*) a silver coin of this weight.

sheldrake (shel'drāk) *n.* (*pl.* **sheldrake, sheldrakes**) a large wild duck with vivid plumage, of the genus *Tadorna* or *Cascarca*, esp. *T. tadorna*, breeding on sandy coasts. **shelduck** *n.* (*pl.* **shelduck, shelducks**) a female sheldrake.

shelf (shelf) *n.* (*pl.* **shelves** (-vz)) **1** a horizontal board or slab set in a wall or forming one of a series in a bookcase, cupboard etc., for standing vessels, books etc. on. **2** a projecting layer of rock, a ledge. **3** a reef, a shoal, a sandbank. **on the shelf 1** put aside, discarded. **2** (of a woman) considered too old to marry. **shelfful** *n.* (*pl.* **shelffuls**). **shelf-life** *n.* (*pl.* **shelf-lives**) the length of time a foodstuff or manufactured item can be stored before deteriorating. **shelflike** *a.* **shelf mark** *n.* a mark on a library book indicating its place on the shelves. **shelf room** *n.* room available on a shelf.

shell (shel) *n.* **1** a hard outside covering etc. **2** the hard but fragile outside covering of an egg. **3** the hard outside case of a mollusc. **4** the wing-case or pupa-case of an insect. **5** the carapace of a tortoise, turtle etc. **6** the exoskeleton of an arthropod. **7** the hard outside covering of a seed etc., a pod. **8** the framework or walls of a house, ship etc., with the interior removed or not yet built. **9** the outline of a plan etc. **10** a light, long and narrow racing boat. **11** a hollow pastry case. **12** a hollow projectile containing a bursting-charge, missiles etc., exploded by a time or percussion fuse. **13** a case of paper or other material containing the explosive in fireworks, cartridges etc. **14** (*N Am.*) a cartridge. **15** mere outer form or semblance. **16** a spherical area outside the nucleus of an atom occupied by electrons of almost equal energy. *~v.t.* **1** to strip or break off the shell from. **2** to take out of the shell. **3** to cover with a shell or with shells. **4** to throw shells at, to bombard. *~v.i.* to cast the husk or shell. **to come out of one's shell** to stop being shy or reserved. **to shell out** (*coll.*) to pay up, to pay the required sum. **shellback** *n.* an old sailor. **shell-bit** *n.* a gouge-shaped boring bit. **shell company** *n.* a company with a Stock Exchange listing used to form a new company. **shelled** *a.* (*usu. in comb.*, as *hard-shelled*). **shell egg** *n.* an egg in its shell. **shellfire** *n.* the firing of artillery shells. **shellfish** *n.* (*pl. in general* **shellfish,** *in particular* **shellfishes**) any aquatic mollusc or crustacean having a shell. **shell game** *n.* (*N Am.*) thimblerig. **to play a shell game** (*coll.*) to trick or deceive someone. **shell-jacket** *n.* (*Mil.*) an undress or fatigue jacket. **shell-less** *a.* **shell-like** *a.* **shell-lime** *n.* lime obtained by burning seashells. **shell-money** *n.* wampum. **shell-out** *n.* **1** the act of shelling out. **2** a variety of pool etc. played on the billiard table. **shell pink** *n.* a pale yellow-tinged pink colour. **shell-pink** *a.* **shell program** *n.* (*Comput.*) a basic computer program used as a framework to develop one's own requirements. **shell-shock** *n.* COMBAT FATIGUE (under COMBAT). **shell-shocked** *a.* **shell suit** *n.* a nylon tracksuit worn as leisure wear. **shell-work** *n.* work composed of or ornamented with shells. **shelly** *a.*

she'll (shēl) *contr.* she will, she shall.

shellac (shəlak´) *n.* a thermoplastic resin obtained by purifying the resinous excreta of certain jungle insects, used in the manufacture of varnishes. ~*v.t.* (*pres.p.* **shellacking,** *past, p.p.* **shellacked**) **1** to varnish with this. **2** (*N Am.*) to defeat or thrash.

Shelta (shel´tə) *n.* a secret jargon made up largely of Gaelic or Irish words, used by tinkers, beggars etc.

shelter (shel´tə) *n.* **1** anything that covers or shields from injury, danger etc. **2** being sheltered, security. **3** a place of safety. **4** a light building affording protection from the weather to persons, instruments etc. **5** an air-raid shelter. ~*v.t.* **1** to shield from injury, danger etc. **2** to protect, to cover. **3** to conceal, to screen. ~*v.i.* to take shelter (under). **shelter belt** *n.* a row of trees planted to provide shelter for crops. **sheltered accommodation, sheltered housing** *n.* accommodation consisting of individual homes which have some shared facilities and are looked after by a warden, used esp. by elderly people. **shelterer** *n.* **shelterless** *a.*

shelty (shel´ti), **sheltie** *n.* (*pl.* **shelties**) a Shetland pony or sheepdog.

shelve[1] (shelv) *v.t.* **1** to place on a shelf or shelves. **2** to defer indefinitely. **3** to fit with shelves. **shelver** *n.* **shelving** *n.* **1** shelves collectively. **2** material for making shelves.

shelve[2] (shelv) *v.i.* to slope gradually.

shemozzle (shimoz´əl), **schemozzle** *n.* (*sl.*) **1** an uproar, a violent row. **2** a confused situation.

shenanigan (shinan´igən) *n.* (*often pl., coll.*) **1** trickery, deception. **2** noisy, boisterous behaviour.

shepherd (shep´əd) *n.* **1** a person employed to tend sheep at pasture. **2** a pastor, a Christian minister. ~*v.t.* **1** to tend, as a shepherd. **2** to drive or gather together. **shepherd dog** *n.* a sheepdog. **shepherdess** *n.* a female shepherd. **shepherd's**

crook *n.* a long staff armed with an iron crook, used to catch or hold sheep. **shepherd's needle** *n.* a plant, *Scandix pecten-veneris*; also called *Venus's comb.* **shepherd's pie** *n.* cooked minced meat, covered with mashed potatoes and baked in an oven. **shepherd's plaid** *n.* **1** black and white checked cloth. **2** this pattern. **shepherd's purse** *n.* a common cruciferous weed, *Capsella bursa-pastoris.*

sherardize (sher´ədīz), **sherardise** *v.t.* to coat (iron or steel) with zinc by heating it in a container with zinc dust.

sherbet (shœ´hit) *n.* **1** an effervescent powder used in sweets or to make fizzy drinks. **2** (*esp. N Am.*) a water ice. **3** an oriental cooling drink, made of diluted fruit juices. **4** (*Austral., facet.*) beer.

sherd SHARD.

sheriff (sher´if) *n.* **1** HIGH SHERIFF (under HIGH). **2** (*N Am.*) an elected county official responsible for keeping the peace etc. **3** an honorary elected official in some towns. **sheriff court** *n.* (*Sc.*) a sheriff's court, hearing civil and criminal cases. **sheriffdom, sheriffhood, sheriffship** *n.*

Sherpa (shœ´pə) *n.* (*pl.* **Sherpa, Sherpas**) a member of a mountaineering people living on the southern slopes of the Himalayas.

sherry (sher´i) *n.* (*pl.* **sherries**) **1** a fortified Spanish white wine orig. from Xeres. **2** a glass of this.

she's (shiz, shēz) *contr.* **1** she is. **2** she has.

Shetland (shet´lənd) *n.* a Shetland pony. **Shetlander** *n.* a native of the Shetland Islands. **Shetland pony** *n.* a very small variety of horse with flowing mane and tail, orig. from Shetland. **Shetland wool** *n.* the fine wool from Shetland sheep.

Shia (shē´ə), **Shiah, Shi'a** *n.* (*pl.* **Shia, Shias, Shiah, Shiahs, Shi'a, Shi'as**) **1** one of the two main branches of Islam (see also SUNNA), which regards Ali (Muhammad's cousin and son-in-law) as the first rightful imam or caliph and rejects the three Sunni caliphs. **2** a Shi'ite. ~*a.* belonging to, or characteristic of, the Shia branch of Islam. **Shi'ism, Shiism** *n.* adherence to Shia. **Shi'ite** (-īt), **Shiite** *n.* a member of the Shia branch of Islam. ~*a.* of or relating to Shia.

shiatsu (shiat´soo) *n.* a massage in which pressure is applied to the acupuncture points of the body.

shibboleth (shib´ələth) *n.* a criterion, test or watchword of a party etc.

shicer (shī´sə) *n.* (*Austral.*) **1** (*sl.*) a crook, a welsher. **2** (*Mining*) a useless mine. **3** (*sl.*) a useless thing.

shicker (shik´ə) *a.* (*Austral., New Zeal., sl.*) drunk. **shickered** *a.*

shield (shēld) *n.* **1** a broad piece of defensive armour made of wood, leather or metal, usu. carried on the left arm to protect the body, usu. straight across the top and tapering to a point at the bottom. **2** a shield-shaped trophy in, e.g., a sporting competition. **3** a wooden screen or framework or a metal plate used in tunnelling, machinery etc., as a protection when working a gun etc. **4** a shieldlike part in an animal or a plant. **5** (*Her.*) an escutcheon or field bearing a coat of arms. **6** defence, a protection. **7** (*N Am.*) a sheriff's or detective's badge. **8** a structure of lead, concrete etc., round something highly radioactive to protect against radiation. **9** (*Geol.*) a mass of very ancient rock at the centre of a continent. ~*v.t.* to screen or protect with or as with a shield. **shield bug** *n.* a shield-shaped insect of the family Pentatomidae. **shield fern** *n.* **1** a fern of the genus *Polystichum* having shield-shaped covers protecting the sori. **2** a fern of the genus *Dryopteris*; also called *buckler*. **shieldless** *a.* **shield volcano** *n.* (*Geol.*) a broad domed volcano.

shift (shift) *v.t.* **1** to move from one position to another. **2** to remove, esp. with an effort. **3** (*N Am.*) to change (gear). **4** (*sl.*) to dispose of, sell. **5** (*sl.*) to consume hastily or in large quantities. ~*v.i.* **1** to move or be moved about. **2** to change place or position. **3** to change into a different form, state etc. **4** to resort to expedients, to do the best one can. **5** to prevaricate, to practise evasion. **6** (*sl.*) to move quickly. **7** (*N Am.*) to change gear. ~*n.* **1** a change of place, form or character. **2** a substitution of one thing for another. **3** a change of clothing. **4** a relay of workers. **5** the period of time for which a shift works. **6** a chemise. **7** a woman's loose, unshaped dress. **8** a device, an expedient. **9** a trick, an artifice. **10** a displacement of spectral lines. **11** a key on a keyboard which switches between upper and lower case. **12** in bridge, a change of suit in bidding or playing. **13** the overlapping of bricks so that the ends of rows do not coincide. **14** (*N Am.*) a gear lever or its mechanism. **to make shift** to manage, to contrive (to do, to get on etc.). **to shift for oneself** to depend on one's own efforts. **to shift off** to get rid of, to defer. **shiftable** *a.* **shifter** *n.* **shiftingly** *adv.* **shiftless** *a.* **1** lazy. **2** incompetent, incapable, without forethought. **shiftlessly** *adv.* **shiftlessness** *n.* **shift work** *n.* work in shifts. **shifty** *a.* (*comp.* **shiftier**, *superl.* **shiftiest**) (*coll.*) furtive, sly. **shiftily** *adv.* **shiftiness** *n.*

Shi'ism, Shi'ite etc. SHIA.

shiitake (shitah´kā), **shiitake mushroom** *n.* a mushroom, *Lentinus edodes*, used in Oriental cookery.

shiksa (shik´sə), **schicksa, shikse** *n.* (*offensive*) a non-Jewish woman.

shill (shil) *n.* (*N Am.*) a decoy or person employed to entice others into buying etc.

shillelagh (shilā´li, -lə) *n.* (*Ir.*) an oak or blackthorn sapling used as a cudgel.

shilling (shil´ing) *n.* **1** (*Hist.*) a former British silver (or, later, cupronickel), coin and money of account, equal in value to 12 old pence (5 new pence). **2** the standard monetary unit of several E African countries. **to take the King's shilling** (*Hist.*) to enlist during the reign of a king (with

alln. to the former practice of giving recruits a shilling as token of a contract). **to take the Queen's shilling** to enlist during the reign of a queen.

shilly-shally (shil´ishali) *v.i.* (*3rd pers. sing. pres.* **shilly-shallies**, *pres.p.* **shilly-shallying**, *past, p.p.* **shilly-shallied**) **1** to act in an irresolute manner, to hesitate. **2** to be undecided. ~*n.* **1** irresolution, hesitation. **2** foolish trifling. ~*a.* vacillating. **shilly-shallyer, shilly-shallier** *n.*

shim (shim) *n.* a wedge, piece of metal etc., used to tighten up joints, fill in spaces etc. ~*v.t.* (*pres.p.* **shimming**, *past, p.p.* **shimmed**) to fill in, wedge or fit with this.

shimmer (shim´ə) *v.i.* **1** to emit a faint or tremulous light. **2** to beam or glisten faintly. ~*n.* a faint or tremulous light. **shimmeringly** *adv.* **shimmery** *a.*

shimmy (shim´i) *n.* (*pl.* **shimmies**) **1** (*Hist.*) an orig. N American dance in which the body is shaken rapidly. **2** abnormal vibration in an aircraft or motor car. ~*v.i.* (*3rd pers. sing. pres.* **shimmies**, *pres.p.* **shimmying**, *past, p.p.* **shimmied**) **1** (*Hist.*) to dance a shimmy. **2** (of a car or aircraft) to vibrate.

shin (shin) *n.* **1** the forepart of the human leg between the ankle and the knee. **2** a cut of beef, the lower foreleg. ~*v.i.* (*pres.p.* **shinning**, *past, p.p.* **shinned**) to climb up a tree etc. by means of the hands and legs alone. ~*v.t.* to climb. **shin bone** *n.* the tibia. **shin-guard** *n.* a padded guard for the shin worn at football etc. **shin-pad** *n.* a shin-guard.

shindig (shin´dig) *n.* (*coll.*) a noisy or rowdy ball or dance.

shindy (shin´di) *n.* (*pl.* **shindies**) **1** a row, a disturbance, a rumpus, a brawl. **2** a rowdy party or dance.

shine (shīn) *v.i.* (*past, p.p.* **shone** (shon), **shined**) **1** to emit or reflect rays of light. **2** to be bright, to beam, to glow. **3** to be brilliant or conspicuous. **4** to be lively or animated. ~*v.t.* **1** to cause to shine, to polish. **2** (*N Am.*) to clean (shoes etc.). ~*n.* **1** (*coll.*) fair weather, brightness. **2** an act of shining esp. shoes. **to take a shine to** to like at first sight. **to take the shine off 1** to surpass, eclipse. **2** to spoil the brilliance etc. of. **shiner** *n.* **1** a person who or thing which shines. **2** (*coll.*) a black eye. **shiningly** *adv.* **shiny** *a.* (*comp.* **shinier**, *superl.* **shiniest**). **shinily** *adv.* **shininess** *n.*

shingle[1] (shing´gəl) *n.* **1** a thin piece of wood laid in overlapping rows as a roof-covering. **2** †a woman's haircut in which the hair is layered like shingles, showing the shape of the head. **3** (*N Am.*) a small signboard or plate, such as that of a doctor. ~*v.t.* **1** to roof with shingles. **2** †to cut (hair) in a shingle.

shingle[2] (shing´gəl) *n.* coarse rounded gravel on the seashore. **shingly** *a.*

shingles (shing´gəlz) *n.pl.* (*usu. treated as sing.*) a viral infection, *Herpes zoster*, marked by pain and inflammation of the skin along the path of an affected nerve (usu. on the chest or abdomen).

Shinto (shin´tō) n. the indigenous religion of the people of Japan existing along with Buddhism, a species of nature- and ancestor-worship. **Shintoism** n. **Shintoist** n.

shinty (shin´ti) n. (pl. **shinties**) **1** a game somewhat resembling hockey, played by teams of 12 people. **2** a stick or ball used in shinty.

shiny SHINE.

ship (ship) n. **1** a large seagoing vessel. **2** a large sailing vessel with three or more square-rigged masts. **3** (coll.) an aircraft, a spacecraft. **4** a boat, esp. a racing boat. ~v.t. (pres.p. **shipping**, past, p.p. **shipped**) **1** to put on board a ship. **2** to send or carry in a ship. **3** to engage for service on board a ship. **4** to fix (a mast, rudder etc.) in the proper place on a ship. **5** to send (goods) by any recognized means of conveyance. **6** (Naut.) to take in (water) over the side. **7** to bring (oars) inside a vessel. ~v.i. **1** to embark on a ship. **2** to engage for service as a sailor. **to ship a sea** to have a wave come over the side of a vessel. **to ship off 1** to send by ship. **2** (coll.) to send (a person) away. **to take ship** to embark. **when one's ship comes in** when one becomes rich. **ship biscuit, ship's biscuit** n. (Hist.) a hard coarse kind of bread or biscuit used on board ship, hard tack. **shipboard** n. the deck or side of a ship. **on shipboard** on board ship. **shipbroker** n. **1** a person who transacts all necessary business for a ship when in port. **2** a marine insurance agent. **shipbuilder** n. **1** a shipwright. **2** a naval architect. **shipbuilding** n. **ship canal** n. a canal along which ocean-going vessels can pass. **ship chandler, ship's chandler** n. a person who deals in cordage, canvas and other commodities for fitting out ships. **ship-fever** n. typhus. **shipless** a. **shipload** n. the quantity of cargo, passengers etc. that a ship carries. **shipmate** n. a person who serves or sails in the same ship, esp. a fellow-sailor. **shipment** n. **1** the act of shipping. **2** goods or commodities shipped, a consignment. **ship of the desert** n. a camel. **ship of the line** n. (Hist.) a warship suitable for taking its place in a line of battle. **shipowner** n. a person who owns a ship or ships or shares therein. **shippable** a. **shipper** n. a person who ships or sends goods by a common carrier. **shipping** a. of or relating to ships. ~n. **1** the act of putting on board ship, sending goods etc. **2** ships collectively, esp. the ships of a country or port. **shipping agent** n. a person or company managing the administrative business of a ship. **ship-rigged** a. having three or more square-rigged masts. **ship's biscuit** SHIP BISCUIT (under SHIP). **ship's boat** n. a small boat carried on a ship. **ship's chandler** SHIP CHANDLER (under SHIP). **ship's company** n. the crew of a ship. **ship's corporal** n. a sailor who attends to police matters under the master-at-arms. **shipshape** a. well arranged, neat. **ship-to-shore** a. from a ship to land. ~n. a radio-telephone used from a ship to the land.

shipworm n. a bivalve that bores into ships' timbers, piles etc.; a teredo. **shipwreck** n. **1** the destruction or loss of a ship, by foundering, striking a rock or other cause. **2** destruction, ruin. ~v.t. to cause to suffer shipwreck. ~v.i. to suffer shipwreck. **shipwright** n. **1** a shipbuilder. **2** a ship's carpenter. **shipyard** n. a yard etc. where ships are built and repaired.

-ship (ship) suf. **1** denoting state, condition, the quality of being so-and-so, as in fellowship, friendship. **2** status, office, as in judgeship, ladyship. **3** tenure of office, as in chairmanship. **4** skill in the capacity specified, as in marksmanship, scholarship. **5** the whole group of people of a specified type, as in membership.

shiralee (shir´əlē) n. (Austral.) a swag, a tramp's bundle.

shire (shīə) n. **1** an administrative division of England, a county, esp. one whose name ends in '-shire'. **2** (Austral.) a rural district with an elected council. **-shire** (shə, shiə) suf. forming the names of counties. **shire county** n. a non-metropolitan county. **shire-horse** n. a large breed of draught horse, orig. raised in the midland shires.

shirk (shœk) v.t. to avoid or get out of unfairly. ~v.i. to avoid the performance of work or duty. ~n. a person who shirks. **shirker** n.

shirr (shœ) n. **1** an elastic cord or thread inserted in cloth etc. to make it elastic. **2** a gathering or fulling. ~v.t. **1** to draw (a sleeve, dress etc.) into gathers by means of elastic threads. **2** (N Am.) to bake (eggs) in a buttered dish. **shirring** n.

shirt (shœt) n. **1** a loose garment of linen, cotton, wool, silk or other material, extending from the neck to the thighs, and usu. showing at the collar and wristbands, worn by men and boys under the outer clothes. **2** (also **shirt blouse**) a woman's blouse with collar and cuffs. **3** a nightshirt. **the shirt off one's back** (coll.) one's last remaining possessions. **to keep one's shirt on** (coll.) to keep calm. **to lose one's shirt** (coll.) to lose all one has. **to put one's shirt on** (coll.) to bet all one has on. **shirt-dress** n. a shirtwaister. **shirted** a. **shirt-front** n. the part of a shirt covering the breast, esp. if stiffened and starched. **shirting** n. **shirtless** a. **shirtsleeve** n. (usu. in pl.) the sleeve of a shirt. **in one's shirtsleeves** with one's coat off. **shirt-tail** n. the curved part at the back of a shirt below the waist. **shirtwaist** n. (esp. N Am.) a woman's blouse similar to a shirt. **shirtwaister** n. a woman's dress with a bodice similar to a shirt. **shirty** a. (comp. **shirtier**, superl. **shirtiest**) (sl.) cross, ill-tempered. **shirtily** adv. **shirtiness** n.

shish kebab (shish) n. a skewer of marinated and cooked meat and vegetables.

shit (shit) v.i. (pres.p. **shitting**, past, p.p. **shit, shitted, shat** (shat)) (taboo sl.) to empty the bowels. ~n. **1** ordure, excrement. **2** an act of defecating. **3** a worthless or despicable person or thing. **4** nonsense. **5** a drug such as cannabis. ~int. used to express anger, disappointment etc.

in the shit in trouble. **not to give a shit** not to care at all. **the shits** diarrhoea. **shitbag, shithead** *n.* a worthless person. **shite** (shīt) *n., int.* **shithouse** *n.* **1** a lavatory. **2** a dirty or inferior place. **shit-scared** *a.* terrified. **shitty** *a. (comp.* **shittier,** *superl.* **shittiest) 1** soiled with excrement. **2** very bad or inferior. **3** despicable. **shittily** *adv.* **shittiness** *n.*

shivaree CHARIVARI.

shiver[1] (shiv′ə) *v.i.* to tremble or shake, as with fear, cold or excitement. ~*n.* a shivering movement. **the shivers 1** a feeling or movement of horror. **2** a chill, ague. **shiverer** *n.* **shiveringly** *adv.* **shivery** *a.*

shiver[2] (shiv′ə) *n.* a tiny fragment, a sliver. ~*v.t., v.i.* to break into shivers. **shiver my timbers** an oath supposedly used by pirates.

shoal[1] (shōl) *n.* a large number, a multitude, a crowd, esp. of fish moving together. ~*v.i.* (of fish) to form a shoal or shoals.

shoal[2] (shōl) *n.* **1** a shallow, a submerged sandbank. **2** (*esp. pl.*) hidden danger or difficulty. ~*v.i.* to become shallower. **shoaly** *a.*

shoat (shōt) *n.* (*N Am.*) a young hog.

shock[1] (shok) *n.* **1** an impact, a blow. **2** a sudden and violent sensation, such as that produced on the nerves by a discharge of electricity. **3** prostration brought about by a violent and sudden disturbance of the system. **4** (*coll.*) a stroke caused by thrombosis etc. **5** a sudden mental agitation, a violent disturbance (of belief, trust etc.). **6** (*esp. N Am.*) a shock absorber. ~*v.t.* **1** to give a violent sensation of disgust, horror or indignation to. **2** to shake or jar by a sudden collision. **3** to affect with a shock. ~*v.i.* to behave or appear in an improper or scandalous fashion. **shockable** *a.* **shockability** (-bil′-) *n.* **shock absorber** *n.* an apparatus to neutralize the shock of axle-springs on recoil. **shock cord** *n.* **1** heavy elasticated cord designed to absorb shock. **2** a piece of this. **shocker** *n.* (*coll.*) **1** something that shocks, esp. a sensational story. **2** a staggering specimen or example of anything. **3** a shock absorber. **shocking** *a.* **1** causing a shock. **2** disgraceful. **3** dreadful. ~*adv.* (*coll.*) shockingly; extremely. **shockingly** *adv.* **shockingness** *n.* **shocking pink** *n.* a garish, intense shade of pink. **shocking-pink** *a.* **shock-proof** *a.* resistant to damage from shock. **shock stall** *n.* loss of lift and air resistance experienced by aircraft approaching the speed of sound. **shock tactics** *n.pl.* **1** any sudden and violent action. **2** (*Mil.*) a cavalry charge relying on weight of numbers for success. **shock therapy, shock treatment** *n.* (*Psych.*) the treatment of certain mental and other disorders by administering an electric shock. **shock troops** *n.pl.* selected soldiers employed on tasks requiring exceptional endurance and courage. **shock wave** *n.* a very strong sound wave, accompanied by a rise in pressure and temperature, caused by an explosion or by something travelling supersonically.

shock[2] (shok) *n.* a collection of sheaves of grain, usu. 12 but varying in number. ~*v.i.* to collect sheaves into shocks.

shock[3] (shok) *n.* a thick, bushy mass or head of hair.

shod SHOE.

shoddy (shod′i) *a.* (*comp.* **shoddier,** *superl.* **shoddiest) 1** inferior. **2** not genuine, sham. **3** made of shoddy. ~*n.* (*pl.* **shoddies) 1** fibre obtained from old cloth torn to pieces and shredded. **2** inferior cloth made from a mixture of this with new wool etc. **3** anything of an inferior, sham or adulterated kind. **shoddily** *adv.* **shoddiness** *n.*

shoe (shoo) *n.* (*pl.* **shoes,** †**shoon** (shoon)) **1** an outer covering for the foot, esp. one distinguished from a boot by not coming up to the ankles. **2** (*N Am.*) a boot. **3** a metallic rim or plate nailed to the hoof of a horse, ox or ass, to preserve it from wear and damage. **4** anything resembling a shoe in form or function, such as a socket, ferrule, wheel-drag or parts fitted to implements, machinery etc. to take friction, thrust etc. **5** the apparatus by which a tractor collects current from a live rail. ~*v.t.* (*pres.p.* **shoeing,** *past, p.p.* **shod** (shod)) **1** to furnish (esp. a horse) with shoes. **2** to cover at the bottom or tip. **to be in another's shoes** to be in another's place or plight. **where the shoe pinches** where one's problem is. **shod** *a.* having shoes (*esp. in comb.,* as *dry-shod*). **shoebill, shoe-billed stork** *n.* a whale-headed stork. **shoeblack** *n.* a person earning a living by cleaning the shoes of passers-by. **shoebox** *n.* **1** a box for shoes. **2** (*coll.*) a very small space, house etc. **shoehorn** *n.* a device to assist one in putting on a shoe. ~*v.t.* to force into a space that is too small. **shoelace** *n.* a string of cotton etc. for fastening on a shoe. **shoe leather** *n.* **1** leather for making shoes. **2** shoes. **shoeless** *a.* **shoemaker** *n.* **shoemaking** *n.* **shoeshine** *n.* (*esp. N Am.*) a polish on shoes. **shoestring** *n.* **1** a shoelace. **2** (*coll.*) an inadequate or barely adequate sum of money. ~*a.* **1** barely adequate. **2** produced, run etc. on a minimum of capital. **shoe-tree** *n.* a shaped block inserted in a shoe when it is not being worn.

shogun (shō′gun) *n.* (*Hist.*) the hereditary commander-in-chief of the army and virtual ruler of Japan under the feudal regime, abolished in 1868. **shogunate** (-ət) *n.*

shone SHINE.

shoo (shoo) *int.* begone, be off. ~*v.t.* (*pres.p.* **shooing,** *past, p.p.* **shooed**) to drive (birds etc. away) by crying 'shoo'. ~*v.i.* to cry 'shoo'. **shoo-in** *n.* (*N Am.*) a sure thing; a certain winner.

shook SHAKE.

shoot (shoot) *v.i.* (*past, p.p.* **shot** (shot)) **1** to go or come (out, along, up etc.) swiftly. **2** to put out buds etc. to extend in growth. **3** to protrude, to jut out. **4** to discharge a missile, esp. from a firearm. **5** to hunt game etc. thus. ~*v.t.* **1** to discharge or send with sudden force. **2** to cause (a bow, firearm etc.) to discharge a missile. **3** to hit, wound or kill with a missile from a firearm. **4** to pass swiftly through, over or down. **5** to protrude, to push out. **6** to put forth. **7** in various games, to hit or kick at a goal. **8** to take (photographs) or record (on film). **9** (*N Am.*, *coll.*) to play a game of (pool etc.). **10** (*N Am.*, *coll.*) to throw (a die or dice). **11** (*coll.*) in golf, to make (a specified score). **12** (*coll.*) to go through (a red traffic light). ~*n.* **1** a young branch or sprout. **2** an inclined plane or trough down which water, goods etc. can slide, a chute, a rapid. **3** a place where game can be shot. **4** a shooting party, match or expedition, a hunt. **5** an act or an instance of shooting. ~*int.* **1** (*esp. N Am.*) speak out! say it! **2** (*N Am.*, *sl.*, *euphem.*) used to express disappointment, disgust etc. **to shoot ahead** to get swiftly to the front in running, swimming etc. **to shoot a line** (*sl.*) to boast, to exaggerate. **to shoot down 1** to destroy, kill, by shooting. **2** to defeat the argument of. **to shoot down in flames 1** to criticize severely. **2** to defeat soundly. **to shoot from the hip** (*coll.*) to speak plainly or carelessly. **to shoot home** to hit the target or mark. **to shoot it out** (*sl.*) to fight using guns in order to settle a dispute. **to shoot one's bolt** to do all in one's power. **to shoot one's mouth off** (*sl.*) to speak boastfully or ill-advisedly. **to shoot through** (*Austral.*, *sl.*) to depart; to escape. **to shoot up 1** to grow rapidly. **2** (*sl.*) to inject a drug into a vein. **3** to terrorize (an area) by shooting. **shootable** *a.* **shooter** *n.* **1** a person who shoots, esp. at a goal. **2** a thing that shoots, esp. a pistol (*usu. in comb.*, as *six-shooter*). **shooting** *n.* **1** the act of discharging firearms or arrows. **2** a piece of land rented for shooting game. **3** the right to shoot over an estate etc. ~*a.* moving or growing quickly. **whole shooting match** (*coll.*) everything. **shooting box** *n.* a small house or lodge for use during the shooting season. **shooting brake**, **shooting break** *n.* an estate car. **shooting gallery** *n.* a piece of ground or an enclosed space with targets and measured ranges for practice with firearms. **shooting iron** *n.* (*esp. N Am.*, *coll.*) a firearm, esp. a revolver. **shooting range** *n.* a shooting gallery. **shooting star** *n.* an incandescent meteor shooting across the sky. **shooting stick** *n.* a walking stick that may be adapted to form a seat. **shooting war** *n.* a war in which there is shooting. **shoot-out** *n.* (*coll.*) **1** a fight, esp. to the death, using guns. **2** a direct confrontation. **3** in football, a tie-breaker decided by shots at goal.

shop (shop) *n.* **1** a building in which goods are sold by retail. **2** a building in which a manufacture, craft or repairing is carried on. **3** (*coll.*) one's business, profession etc. or talk about this. **4** (*sl.*) a berth, a job. **5** (*coll.*) an act of shopping. **6** (*coll.*) an institution, place of business etc. ~*v.i.* (*pres.p.* **shopping**, *past*, *p.p.* **shopped**) to visit shops for the purpose of purchasing goods. ~*v.t.* (*sl.*) to inform against to the police. **all over the shop 1** (*coll.*) scattered around. **2** (*coll.*) in every

place. **3** (*coll.*) wildly. **to set up shop** to start a business. **to shop around** to try several shops to find the best value. **to shut up shop** to give up doing something. **shopaholic** *n.* (*coll.*) a compulsive shopper. **shop assistant** *n.* a person who serves in a retail shop. **shopfitter** *n.* a person who fits shelves etc. in shops. **shopfitting** *n.* **shop floor** *n.* **1** the part of a workshop where the machinery is situated. **2** the workforce as opposed to the management. **shopfront** *n.* a shop's façade. **shop girl** *n.* a girl employed in a shop. **shopkeeper** *n.* the owner of a shop, a trader who sells goods by retail. **shopkeeping** *n.* **shopless** *a.* **shoplifter** *n.* a person who steals from a shop under pretence of purchasing. **shoplift** *v.t.*, *v.i.* **shoplifting** *n.* **shopman** *n.* (*pl.* **shopmen**) **1** a shopkeeper or a man employed to assist in a shop. **2** a workman in a repair shop. **shopper** *n.* **1** a person who shops. **2** a bag or trolley for carrying shopping. **3** a small-wheeled bicycle. **4** (*sl.*) an informer. **shopping** *n.* **1** the act or an instance of buying goods from shops. **2** goods purchased from shops. **shopping cart** *n.* a supermarket trolley. **shopping centre**, (*N Am.*) **shopping center** *n.* an area where there are many shops. **shop-soiled** *a.* **1** dirty or faded from being displayed in a shop. **2** tarnished. **3** hackneyed. **shop steward** *n.* a trade union member elected from the workforce to represent them. **shop talk** *n.* talk about one's job. **shopwalker** *n.* a person employed in a large shop to direct customers etc. **shop window** *n.* **1** a shop's display window. **2** a place or opportunity for one to display one's talents. **shop worker** *n.* a worker in a shop. **shopworn** *a.* shop-soiled.

shoran (shaw´ran, shor´-) *n.* a system of aircraft navigation using two radar signals.

shore[1] (shaw) *n.* **1** the land on the borders of a large body of water, the sea, a lake etc. **2** (*usu. pl.*) a country or sea coast. **3** (*Law*) the land between high- and low-water marks. **in shore** on the water near to the shore. **on shore** ashore. **shorebased** *a.* operating from a base on shore. **shorebird** *n.* a bird such as a wader which frequents the shore, esp. those of the families Charadriiformes or Scolopacidae. **shore leave** *n.* (*Naut.*) **1** permission to go on shore. **2** the period of this. **shoreless** *a.* **shoreline** *n.* the line along which water meets the shore. **shoreward** *a.*, *adv.* **shorewards** *adv.* **shoreweed** *n.* a perennial plant, *Littorella uniflora*, which grows in shallow water.

shore[2] (shaw) *n.* **1** a prop, a stay. **2** a support for a building or a vessel on the stocks. ~*v.t.* to support or hold (up) with shores. **shoring** *n.*

†**shore**[3], **shorn** SHEAR.

short (shawt) *a.* **1** measuring little in linear extension, not long. **2** not extended in time or duration. **3** below the average in stature, not tall. **4** not coming up to a certain standard. **5** deficient, in want (of). **6** breaking off abruptly. **7** brief, curt. **8** crumbling or breaking easily. **9** (*coll.*) neat, undiluted. **10** (of vowels and syllables) not prolonged, unaccented. **11** not having goods, stocks etc. in hand at the time of selling. **12** (of stocks etc.) not in hand, sold. ~*adv.* **1** abruptly, at once. **2** without having stocks etc. in hand. ~*n.* **1** a short syllable or vowel, or a mark (˘) indicating that a vowel is short. **2** a short circuit. **3** a single-reel film. **4** (*pl.*) knee- or thigh-length trousers; also called *pair of shorts.* **5** (*pl., esp. N Am.*) underpants; also called *pair of shorts.* **6** a drink of, or containing, spirits. **7** (*pl.*) short-dated bonds. **8** a person who sells short on the Stock Exchange. ~*v.t.* to short-circuit. ~*v.i.* to short-circuit. **for short** as an abbreviation. **in short** briefly, in few words. **in short order** (*N Am.*) straightaway. **in short supply** scarce. **in the short run** over a short period of time. **in the short term** in the short run. **short and sweet** (*esp. iron.*) brief and pleasant. **short for** a shortened form of. **short of 1** deficient in; lacking. **2** less than. **3** distant from. **4** except. **short of breath** short-winded. **short on** (*coll.*) deficient in; lacking. **to be caught short** to be taken short. **to be taken short 1** (*coll.*) to feel a sudden need to urinate or defecate. **2** to be put at a disadvantage. **to bring up short** to check or pause abruptly. **to come short** to be deficient, to fail. **to go short** not to have enough. **to have by the short and curlies** (*coll.*) to have (someone) in one's power. **to make short work of** to deal with quickly and expeditiously. **to pull up short** to bring up short. **to run short** to exhaust the stock in hand (of a commodity). **to sell short 1** to sell (stocks) for future delivery. **2** to cheat. **3** to disparage. **to stop short 1** to come to a sudden stop. **2** to fail to reach the point aimed at. **shortage** (-tij) *n.* **1** a deficiency. **2** the amount of this. **short back and sides** *n.* a short haircut. **shortbread** *n.* a brittle, dry cake like a biscuit made with much butter and sugar. **shortcake** *n.* **1** shortbread. **2** a cake made with short pastry and containing fruit and cream in layers. **short-change** *v.t.* **1** to give too little money as change to. **2** (*sl.*) to cheat. **short change** *n.* **short circuit** *n.* an accidental crossing of two conductors carrying a current by another conductor of negligible resistance, which shortens the route of the current. **short-circuit** *v.t.* **1** to introduce a short circuit into. **2** to dispense with (intermediaries). **3** to take a short cut in undertaking. ~*v.i.* to form a short circuit. **shortcoming** *n.* a failure of performance of duty etc. **shortcrust (pastry)** *n.* a crumbly type of pastry. **short cut** *n.* **1** a shorter route than the usual. **2** a quicker way of doing something. **short-dated** *a.* (of a security etc.) having only a little time to run. **short division** *n.* (*Math.*) the division of numbers that can be worked out in one's head rather than on paper. **short drink** *n.* a small measure of a strong alcoholic drink. **short-eared owl** *n.* a migratory owl, *Asio flammeus.* **shorten** *v.t.* **1** to make short in time, extent etc. **2** to curtail. **3** (*Naut.*) to reduce the amount of (sail spread). ~*v.i.* to become short. **shortener** *n.* **shortening** *n.* **1** making

or becoming shorter. **2** fat used for making pastry. **shortfall** *n.* the amount by which something falls short, deficit. **short fuse** *n.* (*coll.*) a quick temper. **short game** *n.* in golf, play on and around the green. **shorthand** *n.* a system of contracted writing used for reporting etc., stenography. **shorthand typist** *n.* a typist qualified to use shorthand. **short-handed** *a.* short of workers, helpers etc. **short haul** *n.* **1** transport etc. over a short distance. **2** a short-term effort. **short head** *n.* in racing, a distance less than the length of a horse's head. **shorthold** *a.* (of a tenancy or lease) lasting a short fixed term. **shorthorn** *n.* an animal of a breed of cattle with short horns. **shortie** (-ti), **shorty** *n.* (*pl.* **shorties**) (*coll.*) a shorter than average person, garment etc. **shortish** *a.* **shortlist**, (*esp. Sc.*) **short leet** *n.* a selected list of candidates from whom a final choice will be made. ~*v.t.* to put on such a list. **short-lived** (-livd´) *a.* not living or lasting long, brief. **shortly** *adv.* **short measure** *n.* less than the correct or promised amount. **shortness** *n.* **short notice** *n.* a small length of warning time. **short odds** *n.pl.* in betting, a nearly equal chance. **short order** *n.* (*N Am.*) an order in a restaurant for food that can be prepared quickly. **short-order** *a.* **short-range** *a.* having a small range, in time or distance. **short shrift** *n.* summary treatment. **short sight** *n.* **1** inability to see clearly at a distance, myopia. **2** lack of foresight. **short-sighted** *a.* **short-sightedly** *adv.* **short-sightedness** *n.* **short-sleeved** *a.* having sleeves reaching not below the elbow. **short-staffed** *a.* short-handed. **shortstop** *n.* in baseball, a fielder between second and third base. **short story** *n.* a story that is not as long as a novel. **short suit** *n.* in cards, a suit of which one has fewer than four cards. **short-tempered** *a.* having little self-control, irascible. **short temper** *n.* **short-term** *a.* of or covering a short period of time. **short-termism** *n.* concentrating on short-term gain. **short time** *n.* the condition of working fewer than the normal number of hours per week. **short ton** *n.* (*N Am.*) a measure of weight equal to 2000 lb. (907.18 kg). **short view** *n.* a view only of the present. **short waist** *n.* **1** a high waist of a dress. **2** a short upper body. **short-waisted** *a.* **short wave** *n.* a radio wave of between 10 and 100 metres wavelength. **short weight** *n.* weight less than it should be. **short wind** *n.* breath that is quickly exhausted. **short-winded** (-win´-) *a.* **1** easily put out of breath. **2** incapable of sustained effort. **short-windedness** *n.* **shorty** SHORTIE (under SHORT).

shot[1] (shot) *n.* **1** a missile for a firearm, esp. a solid or non-explosive projectile. **2** the act of shooting. **3** the discharge of a missile from a firearm or other weapon. **4** an attempt to hit an object with such a missile. **5** a photographic exposure. **6** the film taken between the starting and stopping of a cine-camera. **7** (*coll.*) an injection by hypodermic needle. **8** a stroke at various games. **9** an attempt to guess etc. **10** the distance reached by a missile, the range of a firearm, bow etc. **11** a marksman. **12** (*pl.* **shot, shots**) a small lead pellet, a quantity of which is used in a charge or cartridge for shooting game. **13** a remark aimed at someone. **14** (*coll.*) a drink of esp. spirits. ~*v.t.* (*pres.p.* **shotting**, *past*, *p.p.* **shotted**) to load or weight with shot. **like a shot** immediately, eagerly. **to get shot of** (*coll.*) to get rid of. **to give it one's best shot** (*coll.*) to try one's very best. **to have shot one's bolt** to be unable to take further action. **shot across the bows** *n.* a warning. **shotgun** *n.* a light gun for firing small shot. **shotgun marriage, shotgun wedding** *n.* (*coll.*) a hurried wedding esp. because the bride is pregnant. **shot in the arm** *n.* (*coll.*) **1** a hypodermic injection. **2** something which encourages or invigorates. **shot in the dark** *n.* a random guess. **shot-put** *n.* an athletic contest in which a shot is thrown. **shot-putter** *n.* **shot-putting** *n.*

shot[2] (shot) *a.* **1** that has been shot. **2** (of fabric) having a changeable colour.

shot[3] (shot) *n.* a reckoning, a bill.

shot[4] SHOOT.

shotten (shot'ən) *a.* (of a herring etc.) having ejected the spawn.

should SHALL.

shoulder (shōl'də) *n.* **1** the part of the body at which the arm, foreleg or wing is attached to the trunk. **2** one's power to sustain burdens, responsibility etc. **3** (*pl.*) the upper part of the back. **4** the forequarter of an animal cut up as meat. **5** anything resembling a shoulder. **6** a projecting part of a mountain, tool etc. **7** the verge of a road. ~*v.t.* **1** to push with the shoulder. **2** to jostle, to make (one's way) thus. **3** to take on one's shoulders. **4** to accept (a responsibility). ~*v.i.* to make one's way by jostling. **shoulder to shoulder 1** (standing in rank) with shoulders nearly touching. **2** with hearty cooperation, with mutual effort. **to give someone the cold shoulder** (*coll.*) to shun or snub someone. **to put one's shoulder to the wheel** to set to work enthusiastically or in earnest. **to shoulder arms** to hold a rifle with the barrel against one's shoulder. **shoulder bag** *n.* a bag worn over the shoulder. **shoulder-belt** *n.* a baldric, bandolier etc. passing across the shoulder. **shoulder blade, shoulder bone** *n.* (*Anat.*) the scapula. **shouldered** *a.* **shoulder-high** *a.*, *adv.* up to the shoulders. **shoulder joint** *n.* the place where the upper arm joins the collarbone and blade-bone. **shoulder pad** *n.* a pad sewn into the shoulder of a garment. **shoulder strap** *n.* **1** a strap worn over the shoulder, esp. by soldiers, bearing the initials or number of the regiment etc. **2** either one of two strips of cloth that suspend a garment from the shoulders. **3** a strap of a bag.

shouldn't (shud'ənt) *contr.* should not.

shout (showt) *n.* **1** a loud, vehement and sudden call or expression of a strong emotion such as anger or joy. **2** (*coll.*) a round of drinks; one's turn to buy this. ~*v.i.* **1** to utter a loud cry or call. **2** to

speak at the top of one's voice. **3** (*Austral.*, *coll.*) to buy a round of drinks. ~*v.t.* **1** to utter with a shout. **2** to say at the top of one's voice. **3** (*Austral.*, *coll.*) to buy or stand someone (a drink). **all over bar the shouting** (*coll.*) virtually decided. **to shout down** to silence or render inaudible by shouting. **to shout for** to call for by shouting. **shouter** *n.* **shout-up** *n.* (*coll.*) a noisy argument.

shove (shŭv) *v.t.* **1** to push, to move forcibly along. **2** to push against. **3** (*coll.*) to put. ~*v.i.* to make one's way (along etc.) by pushing. ~*n.* **1** a strong or hard push. **2** an act of prompting into action. **to shove off 1** to push off from the shore etc. **2** (*sl.*) to go away. **shove-halfpenny** *n.* a game in which coins are slid over a flat board which is marked off into sections.

shovel (shŭv'əl) *n.* **1** an implement consisting of a wide blade or scoop with a handle, used for shifting loose material. **2** a machine with a similar function. ~*v.t.* (*pres.p.* **shovelling**, (*N Am.*) **shoveling**, *past*, *p.p.* **shovelled**, (*N Am.*) **shoveled**) **1** to shift, gather together or take up and throw with a shovel. **2** (*coll.*) to move (esp. food) roughly. **shovelful** *n.* (*pl.* **shovelfuls**). **shovelhead** *n.* the shark *Sphyrna tibura*; also called *bonnethead*. **shoveller**, (*N Am.*) **shoveler** *n.* **1** a person who shovels. **2** (*also* **shoveler**) the spoonbill duck, *Anas clypeata*.

shovelboard (shŭv'əlbawd) *n.* a game played (now usu. on a ship's deck) by shoving wooden discs with the hand or a mace towards marked compartments.

show (shō), †**shew** *v.t.* (*past* **showed**, †**shewed**, *p.p.* **shown** (shōn), †**shewn**, †**showed**, †**shewed**) **1** to cause or allow to be seen, to reveal. **2** to make clear, to explain. **3** to cause (a person) to see or understand. **4** to conduct (round or over a house etc.). ~*v.i.* **1** to become visible or noticeable. **2** to have a specific appearance. **3** (*N Am.*) to finish third or in the first three in a race. ~*n.* **1** the act of showing. **2** outward appearance, semblance. **3** ostentation, pomp. **4** a spectacle, an entertainment. **5** (*coll.*) an opportunity, a concern. **6** (*Med.*) a discharge from the vagina marking the start of childbirth. **nothing to show for** no visible result of (one's efforts etc.). **on show** being displayed. **to give the (whole) show away 1** to let out the real nature of something pretentious. **2** to blab. **to go to show** to be evidence or proof (that). **to show cause** (*Law*) to allege with justification. **to show in** to lead in. **to show off 1** to set off, to show to advantage. **2** (*coll.*) to make a display of oneself, one's talents etc. **to show oneself 1** to appear in public. **2** to exhibit oneself (to be). **to show out** to lead out. **to show the way** to show what has to be done, which way to go etc. by leading. **to show through 1** to be visible through. **2** to be revealed inadvertently. **to show up 1** to expose. **2** to be clearly visible. **3** to be present. **4** (*coll.*) to embarrass or humiliate. **showband** *n.* **1** a jazz band. **2** a band playing cover versions of popular songs. **showbiz** n. (*coll.*) show business. **showboat** n. (*N Am.*) a steamboat fitted as a theatre. **show business** n. (*coll.*) the entertainment industry, theatre, television, cinema. **showcase** n. **1** a glass case for exhibiting specimens, articles on sale etc. **2** a place where something is presented. ~*v.t.* to display in or as in a showcase. **showdown** n. **1** an open or final confrontation. **2** in poker, putting one's cards face up on the table. **showgirl** n. an actress working in variety theatre. **showground** n. a piece of land where a show is staged. **show house**, **show home** n. one of a group of new houses, open to the public as an example of the type. **showing** n. **showjumping** n. competitive riding over a set course containing obstacles. **showjumper** n. **showman** n. (*pl.* **showmen**) **1** the manager or proprietor of a menagerie, circus etc. **2** a person skilled in publicizing esp. themselves. **showmanship** n. **show-off** n. (*coll.*) a person who shows off, an exhibitionist. **show of force** n. a demonstration of willingness to use force. **show of hands** n. the raising of hands in voting. **showpiece** n. a particularly fine specimen, used for display. **showplace** n. a place tourists etc. go to see. **showroom** n. a room where goods are set out for inspection. **show-stopper** n. (*coll.*) a performance where the audience applaud for such a long time that the show is interrupted. **show-stopping** a. **show trial** n. a judicial trial to demonstrate a state's power. **showy** a. (*comp.* **showier**, *superl.* **showiest**) ostentatious, gaudy. **showily** adv. **showiness** n.

shower (show´ə) n. **1** a fall of rain, hail or snow. **2** a brief fall of arrows, bullets etc. **3** a copious supply (of). **4** a shower-bath. **5** (*esp. N Am.*) a party (e.g. for a bride-to-be or expectant mother) at which gifts are given. **6** (*sl., derog.*) a collec-tion of (inferior etc.) people. ~*v.t.* **1** to sprinkle or wet with a shower. **2** to discharge or deliver in a shower. ~*v.i.* **1** to fall in a shower. **2** to have a shower. **shower-bath** n. a bath in which a stream of water is sprayed over the body. **showerless** a. **showerproof** a. **showery** a. **showeriness** n.

shrank SHRINK.

shrapnel (shrap´nəl) n. **1** bullets enclosed in a shell with a small charge for bursting in front of the enemy and spreading in a shower. **2** shell-splinters from a high-explosive shell.

shred (shred) n. **1** a piece torn off. **2** a strip, a fragment. ~*v.t.* (*pres.p.* **shredding**, *past, p.p.* **shredded, shred**) to tear or cut into shreds. **to tear to shreds** to completely refute or demolish (an argument). **shredder** n. **shreddy** a. **shredless** a.

shrew (shroo) n. **1** a small mouselike mammal of the family Soricidae. **2** a bad-tempered, scolding woman, a virago. **shrewish** a. **shrewishly** adv. **shrewishness** n.

shrewd (shrood) a. astute, discerning. **shrewdly** adv. **shrewdness** n.

shriek (shrēk) v.i. **1** to utter a sharp, shrill, inarticulate cry. **2** to laugh wildly. ~*v.t.* **1** to utter with a shriek. **2** to reveal blatantly. ~n. a sharp, shrill, inarticulate cry. **to shriek of** to give a clear indication of, to reveal blatantly. **to shriek out** to utter in a shriek. **to shriek with laughter** to laugh uncontrollably. **shrieker** n.

†shrift (shrift) n. **1** confession to a priest. **2** absolution, esp. of one about or appointed to die.

shrike (shrīk) n. a bird of the family Laniidae, especially the butcher-bird, feeding on insects and small birds and having the habit of impaling them on thorns for future use.

shrill (shril) a. **1** high-pitched and piercing in tone. **2** (*derog.*) noisy, importunate. ~*v.i.* **1** to utter a piercing sound. **2** to sound shrilly. ~*v.t.* to cause to utter in a shrill tone. **shrillness** n. **shrilly** adv.

shrimp (shrimp) n. (*pl. in general* **shrimp**, *in particular* **shrimps**) **1** a slender long-tailed edible crustacean, allied to the prawn. **2** (*coll.*) a very small person. ~*v.i.* to fish for shrimps. **shrimper** n.

shrine (shrīn) n. **1** a chest or casket in which sacred relics were deposited. **2** a tomb, altar, chapel etc. of special sanctity. **3** a place hallowed by its associations. **4** a Shinto place of worship. ~*v.t.* (*poet.*) to place in a shrine.

shrink (shringk) v.i. (*past* **shrank** (shrangk), *p.p.* **shrunk** (shrŭngk), **shrunken** (-kən)) **1** to grow smaller. **2** to draw back, to recoil. **3** to flinch. ~*v.t.* to cause to shrink, to make smaller. ~n. **1** shrinkage, shrinking. **2** (*sl.*) a psychiatrist. **to shrink into oneself** to become withdrawn. **shrinkable** a. **shrinkage** (-ij) n. **1** the process of shrinking, a shrunken condition. **2** the amount of this. **3** a deduction from one's takings to allow for loss. **shrinker** n. **shrinking** a. **shrinkingly** adv. **shrinking violet** n. (*coll.*) a shy, hesitant person. **shrink-resistant** a. resistant to shrinkage. **shrink-wrap** v.t. (*pres.p.* **shrink-wrapping**, *past, p.p.* **shrink-wrapped**) to wrap in plastic film, which is then shrunk, e.g. by heating, to make a tight-fitting, sealed package. **shrunken** a.

Usage note In standard English, the past tense of *shrink* is *shrank*, not *shrunk*.

†shrive (shrīv) v.t. (*past* **shrove** (shrōv), *p.p.* **shriven** (shriv´ən)) **1** to confess, impose penance on and absolve. **2** to confess (oneself) and receive absolution.

shrivel (shriv´əl) v.i. (*pres.p.* **shrivelling**, (*N Am.*) **shriveling**, *past, p.p.* **shrivelled**, (*N Am.*) **shriveled**) to contract, to wither. ~*v.t.* to cause to contract or become wrinkled.

shroud (shrowd) n. **1** a winding sheet. **2** anything that covers or conceals. **3** (*pl.*) ropes extending from the lower mast-heads to the sides of the ship, serving to steady the masts. ~*v.t.* **1** to dress for the grave. **2** to cover, disguise or conceal. **shroudless** a.

shrove SHRIVE.

shrub[1] (shrŭb) *n.* a woody plant smaller than a tree, with branches proceeding directly from the ground without any supporting trunk. **shrub-bery** *n.* (*pl.* **shrubberies**) a plantation of shrubs. **shrubby** *a.* (*comp.* **shrubbier**, *superl.* **shrubbiest**). **shrubbiness** *n.* **shrubless** *a.*

shrub[2] (shrŭb) *n.* a drink composed of the sweetened juice of lemons or other fruit with spirit.

shrug (shrŭg) *v.t.* (*pres.p.* **shrugging**, *past, p.p.* **shrugged**) to draw up (the shoulders) to express dislike, doubt etc. ~*v.i.* to draw up the shoulders. ~*n.* this gesture. **to shrug off 1** to disregard, to ignore. **2** to throw off, to get rid of.

shrunk, shrunken SHRINK.

shuck (shŭk) *n.* (*esp. N Am.*) **1** a shell, husk or pod. **2** (*pl.*) something utterly valueless. ~*v.t.* to remove the shell etc. from. **to shuck off** to strip off. **shucker** *n.* **shucks** *int.* (*coll.*) used to express contempt, annoyance, embarrassment etc.

shudder (shŭd´ə) *v.i.* **1** to shiver suddenly as with fear; to quake. **2** to vibrate. ~*n.* a sudden shiver or trembling. **the shudders** (*coll.*) a state of shuddering. **shudderingly** *adv.* **shuddery** *a.*

shuffle (shŭf´əl) *v.t.* **1** to shift to and fro or from one to another. **2** to move (cards) over each other so as to mix them up. **3** to mix (up), to throw into disorder. **4** to put aside, to throw (off). **5** to put or throw (on) hastily. ~*v.i.* **1** to change the relative positions of cards in a pack. **2** to shift ground. **3** to prevaricate. **4** to move (along) with a dragging gait. ~*n.* **1** the act of shuffling. **2** a shuffling movement of the feet etc. **3** the shuffling of cards. **4** a mix-up, a general change of position. **5** an evasive or prevaricating piece of conduct. **shuffle-board** *n.* (*N Am.*) SHOVELBOARD. **shuffler** *n.* **shufflingly** *adv.*

shufti (shŭf´ti, shuf´-), **shufty** *n.* (*pl.* **shuftis, shufties**) (*sl.*) a (quick) look (at something).

shun (shŭn) *v.t.* (*pres.p.* **shunning**, *past, p.p.* **shunned**) to avoid, to keep clear of.

'shun (shŭn) *int.* (*Mil.*) short for ATTENTION.

shunt (shŭnt) *v.t.* **1** to turn (a train etc.) on to a side track. **2** to get rid of, suppress or defer discussion or consideration of. **3** to get (a person) out of the way, or keep (a person) inactive. ~*v.i.* (of a train etc.) to turn off on to a side track. ~*n.* **1** the act of shunting. **2** a conductor joining two points of a circuit through which part of an electric current may be diverted. **3** (*sl.*) a car crash. **shunter** *n.*

shush (shush, shŭsh) *int.* used to call for silence. ~*v.i.* to be quiet. ~*v.t.* to make quiet. ~*n.* an utterance of 'shush' to call for silence.

shut (shŭt) *v.t.* (*pres.p.* **shutting**, *past, p.p.* **shut**) **1** to close by means of a door, lid, cover etc. **2** to cause (a door, lid, cover etc.) to close an aperture. **3** to keep (in or out) by closing a door. **4** to bar (out), to exclude, to keep from entering or participating in. **5** to bring (teeth etc.) together. ~*v.i.* **1** to become closed. **2** (of teeth, scissor-blades etc.) to come together. ~*a.* **1** closed. **2** made fast.

to be shut of (*sl.*) to be rid of. **to get shut of** (*sl.*) to get rid of. **to shut down 1** to pull or push down (a window-sash etc.). **2** (of a factory) to stop working. **3** to stop (a factory etc.) from operating. **to shut in 1** to confine. **2** to encircle. **3** to prevent egress or prospect from. **to shut off 1** to stop the inflow or escape of (gas etc.) by closing a tap etc. **2** to separate. **to shut out 1** to exclude, to bar. **2** to prevent the possibility of. **3** to block from the memory. **4** (*N Am.*) to prevent from scoring. **to shut the door on** to prevent the possibility of. **to shut to 1** to close (a door). **2** (of a door) to shut. **to shut up 1** to close all the doors, windows etc. of (a house). **2** to close and fasten up (a box etc.). **3** to put away in a box etc. **4** to confine. **5** (*coll.*) to stop, to make an end. **6** to confute, to silence. **shutdown** *n.* **shut-eye** *n.* (*coll.*) sleep. **shut-off** *n.* **1** something used for stopping an operation. **2** cessation. **shutout** *n.* (*N Am.*) the act of preventing an opponent from scoring.

shutter (shŭt´ə) *n.* **1** a person who or thing which shuts. **2** a cover of wooden battens or panels or metal slats for sliding, folding, rolling or otherwise fastening over a window to exclude light, burglars etc. **3** a device for admitting and cutting off light to a photographic lens. ~*v.t.* **1** to put up the shutters of. **2** to provide or fit with a shutter or shutters. **to put up the shutters** to cease business. **shutterless** *a.*

shuttle (shŭt´əl) *n.* **1** a boat-shaped contrivance enclosing a bobbin, used by weavers for passing the thread of the weft between the threads of the warp. **2** the sliding holder carrying the lower thread for making lock-stitches in a sewing machine. **3** a shuttle service. **4** a vehicle used on a shuttle service or one that goes between two points. **5** a space shuttle. ~*v.i.* to move or travel regularly between two points or places. ~*v.t.* to cause to move in this way. **shuttle diplomacy** *n.* negotiations by a mediator travelling between two heads of state etc. **shuttle service** *n.* transport service running to and fro between two points. **shuttlewise** *adv.*

shuttlecock (shŭt´əlkok) *n.* **1** a light cone-shaped object with feathered flights, used in the games of battledore and badminton. **2** anything repeatedly passed to and fro.

shy[1] (shī) *a.* (*comp.* **shyer, shier,** *superl.* **shyest, shiest**) **1** fearful, timid. **2** bashful, shrinking from approach or familiarity. **3** careful, watchful (of). ~*adv.* (*coll.*) short of, lacking. ~*v.i.* (*3rd pers. sing. pres.* **shies**, *pres.p.* **shying**, *past, p.p.* **shied**) **1** (of a horse) to start or turn aside suddenly. **2** to shrink (from). ~*n.* (*pl.* **shies**) the act of shying. **-shy** *comb. form* showing reluctance or aversion, as in *work-shy*. **shyly** *adv.* **shyness** *n.*

shy[2] (shī) *v.t., v.i.* (*3rd pers. sing. pres.* **shies**, *pres.p.* **shying**, *past, p.p.* **shied**) (*coll.*) to fling, to throw. ~*n.* (*pl.* **shies**) **1** the act of shying. **2** a try, an attempt. **shyer** *n.*

shyster (shī´stə) *n.* (*esp. N Am.*) **1** a tricky or disreputable lawyer. **2** (*coll.*) a tricky person.

SI *abbr.* **1** (Order of the) Star of India. **2** *Système International* (*d'Unités*), the now universally used system of scientific units, the basic units of which are the metre, second, kilogram, ampere, kelvin, candela and mole.

Si *chem. symbol* silicon.

si (sē) *n.* (*Mus.*) te.

sial (sī'əl) *n.* (*Geol.*) the outer layer of the earth's crust, rock rich in silicon and aluminium.

Siamese (sīəmēz') *a.* of or relating to Siam, now Thailand, a country of SE Asia, or to its inhabitants or their language. *~n.* **1** (*pl.* **Siamese**) a native or inhabitant of Siam, now a Thai. **2** the language of Siam, now Thai. **3** (*pl.* **Siameses**) a Siamese cat. **Siamese cat** *n.* a breed of cat with blue eyes and dark-coloured ears, face, tail and paws. **Siamese fighting fish** *n.* a colourful freshwater fish, *Betta splendens*, of SE Asia, the male of which has sail-like fins and is highly aggressive. **Siamese twins** *n.pl.* identical twins born joined together at some part of the body.

sib (sib) *n.* **1** a brother or sister. **2** any blood relative. **3** those regarded as blood relatives, kindred. **sibling** (-ling) *n.* each of two or more children that have one or both parents in common.

sibilant (sib'ilənt) *a.* **1** hissing. **2** (of a letter of the alphabet etc.) having a hissing sound. *~n.* a letter which is pronounced with a hissing sound, as *s* or *z*. **sibilance, sibilancy** *n.* **sibilantly** *adv.* **sibilate** *v.t., v.i.* **sibilation** (-ā'shən) *n.*

sibyl (sib'il) *n.* a prophetess, a sorceress. **sibylline** (-īn) *a.* **1** of or relating to, or composed or uttered by, a sibyl. **2** prophetic, oracular, cryptic, mysterious.

sic (sēk, sik) *adv.* thus, so (usu. printed after a doubtful word or phrase to indicate that it is quoted exactly as in the original).

sice (sīs) *n.* the number six on dice.

Sicilian (sisil'yən) *a.* of or relating to Sicily, an island off S Italy, or its inhabitants. *~n.* a native or inhabitant of Sicily. **siciliana** (-siliah'nə), **siciliano** (-ah'nō) *n.* (*pl.* **sicilianas, sicilianos**) **1** a graceful dance of the Sicilian peasantry. **2** the music (in 6/8 time) for this.

sick[1] (sik) *a.* **1** ill, in bad health. **2** affected with nausea, inclined to vomit. **3** feeling disturbed, upset. **4** pining or longing (for). **5** mentally ill, or having a warped personality. **6** tired (of). **7** (of a room, quarters etc.) set apart for sick people. **8** (of humour) macabre, cruel, referring to subjects not usu. considered suitable for jokes. *~n.* (*coll.*) vomit. *~v.t.* (*coll.*) to vomit (up) (food etc.). **sick and tired of** bored and exhausted by, fed up with. **sick to/ at one's stomach 1** (*esp. N Am.*) affected with nausea, vomiting. **2** (*esp. N Am.*) disgusted, revolted. **the sick** those who are ill. **to go sick** to be absent from one's work or duties through illness (real or claimed). **to look sick** (*coll.*) to be outranked or outshone, to be deficient in comparison. **sickbay** *n.* **1** a part of a ship used for the sick and injured. **2** any area set aside for the sick. **sickbed** *n.* a bed occupied

by someone who is ill. **sick benefit** *n.* SICKNESS BENEFIT (under SICK[1]). **sick building syndrome** *n.* (*Med.*) a combination or pattern of ailments, such as headaches and dizziness, thought to be caused by working in a fully air-conditioned building. **sicken** *v.i.* **1** to grow ill. **2** to develop the symptoms (for a particular illness). **3** to feel disgust (at). *~v.t.* **1** to make sick. **2** to affect with nausea. **3** to disgust. **sickener** *n.* **1** (*coll.*) a circumstance that causes disgust or acute disappointment. **2** a toadstool of the genus *Russula*, esp. a poisonous one. **sickening** *a.* **1** disgusting, offensive. **2** horrifying. **3** (*coll.*) very annoying, or acutely disappointing. **sickeningly** *adv.* **sick headache** *n.* a migraine. **sickie** *n.* (*coll.*) (*Austral., New Zeal.*) a day's sick leave, sometimes taken when one is not ill. **sickish** *a.* **sickishly** *adv.* **sickishness** *n.* **sick leave** *n.* leave of absence on account of illness. **sick list** *n.* a list of people, e.g. staff, students, or members of a military unit, laid up by illness. **sickly** *a.* (*comp.* **sicklier,** *superl.* **sickliest**) **1** weak in health, affected by illness. **2** ill-looking. **3** nauseating. **4** sentimental. **sickliness** *n.* **sick-making** *a.* (*coll.*) sickening. **sickness** *n.* **1** the condition of being ill. **2** nausea, vomiting. **3** an illness, a disease. **sickness benefit** *n.* a benefit paid to someone who is off work through illness. **sicko** (sik'ō) *n.* (*pl.* **sickos**) (*N Am., coll.*) someone mentally ill, or with a warped personality. **sick pay** *n.* the salary or wages paid to a worker on sick leave. **sickroom** *n.* **1** a room in which a sick person is laid up. **2** a room adapted to accommodate the sick.

sick[2] (sik) *v.t.* (*pres.p.* **sicking,** *past, p.p.* **sicked**) to chase or attack, to set upon.

sickle (sik'əl) *n.* an implement consisting of a long curved blade with a short handle, used for reaping, lopping etc. **sickle-cell anaemia,** (*N Am.*) **sickle-cell anemia** *n.* a severe form of anaemia, hereditary and typically affecting black peoples, in which the red blood cells become narrow and curved like a sickle, as a result of the production of abnormal haemoglobin.

side (sīd) *n.* **1** any of the bounding surfaces (or lines) of a material object, esp. a more or less vertical inner or outer surface (as of a building, a room, a natural object etc.). **2** such a surface as distinct from the top and bottom, back and front, or the two ends. **3** a part of an object, region etc. to left or right of its main axis or aspect facing oneself. **4 a** either surface of a plate, sheet, layer etc. (*Write on one side only*). **b** the writing etc. on one side of a sheet of paper etc. **5** the right or left half of a person or animal, esp. of the part between the hip and shoulder. **6** a direction or position, esp. to right or left, in relation to a person or thing. **7** (*esp. in combination*) a position close to something or someone (*on the lakeside; never left my side*). **8** an aspect or partial view of a thing (*see the funny side; his nice side*). **9** either of two opposing bodies, parties, teams or sects. **10** either of the opposing views or causes represented. **11** the line of descent through one's father or mother (*There's red hair on my mother's side*). **12** twist or spin given to a billiard or snooker ball. **13** a television channel (*Try the other side*). **14** (*sl.*) swagger, bumptiousness, pretentiousness. *~v.i.* to align oneself (with one of two opposing parties). *~a.* **1** situated at or on the side. **2** being from or towards the side, oblique. **by the side of 1** alongside, close to. **2** in comparison with. **from side to side 1** all the way across. **2** one way then the other from a central line or path. **on one side 1** away in one direction from a central or principal position. **2** aside. **on the side 1** in addition to the usual, principal or known. **2** in addition to, or apart from, the main aim, or one's main occupation or income, applied esp. to an underhand or illicit arrangement. **side by side** close together (for strength or support etc.). **this side of** not going as far as, short of (*Keep this side of plagiarism*). **to change sides** to alter one's allegiance, to change one's party. **to choose sides** (of team leaders) to select team members from the group available. **to let the side down** (*coll.*) to disgrace one's colleagues, relations etc. by failing to live up to their standards. **to take sides** to support one side in an argument etc. **side arms** *n.pl.* weapons, such as swords or pistols, carried at the side. **side-bet** *n.* a bet in addition to the ordinary stakes. **sideboard** *n.* **1** a flat-topped table or cabinet placed at the side of a room to support decanters, dining utensils etc. **2** (*pl.*) side-whiskers. **sideburns** *n.pl.* side-whiskers. **sidecar** *n.* a car with seats, attached to the side of a motorcycle. **side chapel** *n.* a chapel at the side of a church, in or with an entrance from an aisle. **sided** *a.* **side dish** *n.* a supplementary dish accompanying a course at dinner etc. **side door** *n.* **1** a door at the side of a building, or beside the main entrance. **2** an indirect or unexpected means of attaining something. **side drum** *n.* a small double-headed drum with snares, orig. carried at the drummer's side. **side effect** *n.* a secondary effect (e.g. of a drug), often adverse. **side issue** *n.* a subsidiary matter. **sidekick** *n.* (*coll.*) a close associate or assistant, often in a shady enterprise. **sidelamp** *n.* a lamp at the side of something, esp. at the side of a vehicle for warning of its presence. **sideless** *a.* **sidelight** *n.* **1** light admitted into a building etc. from the side. **2** an incidental illustration or piece of information. **3** either of two small lights at the side of a vehicle, for warning of its presence. **4** (*Naut.*) either of the two navigational lights carried by a ship at night. **sideline** *n.* **1** an incidental branch of business. **2** a line marking the side of a sports pitch, tennis court etc. *~v.t.* to remove from participation in a game or other activity. **on the sidelines 1** watching a game etc. from the side of the pitch etc. **2** not participating directly in an activity. **sidelong** *adv.* from the side, obliquely rather than directly. *~a.* (of a look or glance) oblique, rather than direct. **side note**

n. a marginal note as distinct from a footnote. **side-on** *adv., a.* **1** with a side facing in the forward or leading direction. **2** in profile, showing the profile. **side plate** *n.* the smallest size of plate in a dinner service, laid to the side of a place setting, and used for bread etc. **side road, side street** *n.* a minor road or street leading off the main road or street. **sidesaddle** *n.* a saddle designed for sitting on a horse with both legs on one side. *~adv.* in this position on horseback. **side salad** *n.* a portion of salad served as a side dish. **sideshow** *n.* a subordinate show, business affair etc. **sidesman** *n.* (*pl.* **sidesmen**) a church officer assisting the churchwarden. **sidespin** *n.* a horizontal spinning motion imparted to a ball in various ball games. **side-splitting** *a.* (of laughter, a joke etc.) causing one to double up. **sidestep** *n.* a step or movement to one side. *~v.t.* (*pres.p.* **sidestepping**, *past, p.p.* **sidestepped**) **1** to dodge (a tackle in football etc.) by stepping sideways. **2** to avoid confronting and dealing with (a question or issue), to evade. **sidestepper** *n.* **sidestroke** *n.* **1** a stroke delivered sideways or on the side of a thing. **2** a swimming stroke performed lying on one's side. **3** an incidental action. **sideswipe** *n.* **1** a glancing blow. **2** an incidental criticism. *~v.t.* to hit with a sideswipe. **side table** *n.* a table for use at the side of a room or alongside a main table. **sidetrack** *n.* **1** a diversion or digression. **2** a railway siding. *~v.t.* **1** to divert or distract from the main purpose or intended course. **2** to defer indefinitely. **3** (*N Am.*) to turn into a railway siding. **side view** *n.* a view from the side, a profile. **sidewalk** *n.* (*N Am.*) a pavement. **sideward** (-wəd) *adv., a.* sideways. **sidewards** (-wədz) *adv.* sideways. **sideways, sidewise** *adv.* **1** towards or from the side. **2** with one side facing forward (*sitting sideways on the chair*). *~a.* **1** directed or moving towards or from the side (*a sideways movement, glance*). **2** unconventional, from an unusual point of view. **side-whiskers** *n.pl.* hair grown by a man on either side of the face in front of the ears. **side wind** *n.* **1** a wind from the side. **2** an indirect influence, agency etc. **sidewinder** (-wīndə) *n.* a N American rattlesnake that moves by a kind of sideways looping movement. **siding** *n.* **1** a short track connected to and positioned alongside a railway line, for shunting trains or facilitating overtaking. **2** weatherproof cladding for the outside of a building.

sidereal (sīdiə´riəl) *a.* of or relating to the fixed stars or the constellations. **sidereal day** *n.* the time between two successive upper culminations of a fixed star or of the vernal equinox, about four minutes shorter than the solar day. **sidereal month** *n.* the mean period required by the moon to make a circuit among the stars, amounting to 27.32166 days. **sidereal time** *n.* time as measured by the movement of the earth in relation to the fixed stars. **sidereal year** *n.* the time occupied by a complete revolution of the earth round the sun, longer than the solar year.

siderite (sid´ərīt) *n*. **1** native ferrous carbonate. **2** an iron meteorite. **sideritic** (-rit´-) *a*.

siding SIDE.

sidle (sī´dəl) *v.i.* to move or edge sideways (e.g. up to someone), esp. in a stealthy or ingratiating manner.

SIDS *abbr.* sudden infant death syndrome.

siege (sēj) *n*. **1** (*Mil.*) the military operation of surrounding a town or fortified place with troops, cutting its supply lines, and subjecting it to constant bombardment, in order to force its surrender. **2** a police operation conducted on comparable lines, usu. to force an armed and dangerous person out of a building. **under siege 1** being besieged. **2** subjected to constant attack or criticism. **siege train** *n*. the artillery and other equipment carried by an army for conducting a siege.

siemens (sē´mənz) *n*. the SI unit of electrical conductance, equal to one reciprocal ohm.

sienna (sien´ə) *n*. **1** a pigment composed of a native clay coloured with iron and manganese. **2** the colour of this pigment, raw or burnt sienna.

sierra (sieə´rə) *n*. (*pl*. **sierras**) in Spanish-speaking countries and the US, a long mountain chain, jagged in outline.

siesta (sies´tə) *n*. (*pl*. **siestas**) a short midday sleep, esp. in hot countries.

sieve (siv) *n*. an instrument for separating the finer particles of substances from the coarser, or liquids from solids, having meshes or perforations through which liquid or fine particles pass, while solids or coarse particles are retained. *~v.t.* **1** to pour or pass through a sieve, to sift. **2** to examine minutely to identify or separate out elements of (*They sieved the evidence for clues*). **to have a head like a sieve** (*coll.*) to be very forgetful. **sievelike** *a*.

sievert (sē´vət) *n*. the SI unit of ionizing radiation, equal to 100 rems.

☒ sieze common misspelling of SEIZE.

sift (sift) *v.t.* **1** to separate into finer and coarser particles by means of a sieve. **2** to separate (from, out etc.). **3** to sprinkle (sugar, flour etc.) as with a sieve. **4** to examine minutely. **sifter** *n*.

sigh (sī) *v.i.* **1** to inhale and exhale deeply and audibly, as an involuntary expression of grief, fatigue, relief etc. **2** to yearn (for). **3** to make a sound like sighing. *~v.t.* to utter with sighs (*'It's too late,' she sighed*). *~n.* an act or sound of sighing. **sigher** *n*. **sighingly** *adv*.

sight (sīt) *n*. **1** the faculty of seeing. **2** the act of seeing. **3** view, range of vision (*The island was already within sight*). **4** one's point of view, judgement or estimation (*In his sight she was perfect*). **5** that which is seen, a scene, esp. a delightful or shocking one. **6** something interesting, or worth going to see (*the sights of London*). **7** a device on a firearm, optical instrument etc. for enabling one to direct it accurately to any point. *~v.t.* **1** to see, catch sight of (*The vehicle was sighted again at 10.45 heading for the coast*).

2 to adjust the sights of (a firearm or optical instrument). **3** to aim (a firearm) by means of sights. **a sight** (*coll.*) a great deal (*She's got a sight more common sense than you have*). **at first sight** immediately on seeing someone or something, as a first impression. **at sight** on sight. **by a long sight** by a long way (*not finished by a long sight*). **in sight 1** visible. **2** having a view (of). **3** not far off. **on sight 1** as soon as seen, immediately. **2** (of a bill, to be paid) on presentation. **out of sight 1** not in a position to be seen, or to have a view, or be in view (of). **2** having disappeared, e.g. into the distance. **3** forgotten, ignored. **4** (*coll.*) excellent. **to catch sight of** to begin to see, to glimpse or notice. **to get a sight of** to glimpse, to manage to see. **to have lost sight of** to have fallen out of touch with, no longer to know the whereabouts of. **to look a sight** to look untidy or disreputable. **to lose sight of 1** to cease to see. **2** to overlook, to forget, to cease to take cognizance of. **to lower one's sights** to settle for less, to become less ambitious. **to set one's sights on** to have as one's goal, or the object of one's desires or ambition. **within sight** in sight. **sighted** *a*. **1** having the faculty of sight. **2** (*in comb.*) having vision of a specified kind, as *short-sighted*. **3** (of a gun) fitted with a sight. **sighter** *n*. **sight for sore eyes, sight for the gods** *n*. (*coll.*) a person or thing one is pleased to see, a welcome visitor. **sighting** *n*. an instance of seeing or catching sight of someone or something. **sightless** *a*. **1** not having the faculty of sight, blind. **2** (*poet.*) invisible. **sightlessly** *adv*. **sightlessness** *n*. **sightline** *n*. the line from one's eye to the object one is seeing. **sightly** *a*. **1** pleasing to the eye, attractive. **2** (*N Am.*) affording a pleasant view. **sightliness** *n*. **sight-read** *v.t.* (*past, p.p.* **sight-read**) to play or sing (music) at sight, without having previously seen it. **sight-reader** *n*. **sight-reading** *n*. **sight screen** *n*. a white screen set on the boundary of a cricket field to help the batsman see the ball. **sightseeing** *n*. the activity of going to see the sights or notable features of a place. **sightseer** *n*. **sightsee** (-sēə) *n*. **sight-sing** *v.t.*, *v.i.* (*past* **sight-sang**, *p.p.* **sight-sung**) to sing (music) at sight. **sight unseen** *adv*. without previous inspection (of the object to be bought etc.).

sigma (sig´mə) *n*. the eighteenth letter of the Greek alphabet (σ, Σ, or when final, ς, or, in uncial form, c or C). **sigmoid** (-moid) *a*. **1** curved like the uncial sigma C, crescent-shaped. **2** curved like an S, having a double or reflexed curve. **sigmoid flexure** *n*. (*Anat.*) a C-shaped or S-shaped curve or bend, esp. the final section of the descending colon, leading to the rectum. **sigmoidoscope** (-moi´-) *n*. (*Med.*) an instrument that is inserted through the anus for examining the inside of the rectum and the sigmoid colon. **sigmoidoscopy** (-os´kəpi) *n*.

sign (sīn) *n*. **1** a mark expressing a particular meaning. **2** (*Math.*) a conventional mark used for a word or phrase to represent a mathematical process (as + or -). **3** a symptom or proof (of), esp. a miracle as evidence of a supernatural power. **4** (*Med.*) any external indication of illness, as distinct from symptoms felt by the patient. **5** a password, a secret formula or gesture by which confederates etc. recognize each other. **6** a motion, action or gesture used instead of words to convey information, commands etc., e.g. one used in a sign language. **7** a board or panel giving information or indicating directions etc. **8** a device, usu. painted on a board, displayed as a token or advertisement of a trade. ~*v.t.* **1** to mark with a sign, esp. with one's signature, initials or an accepted mark as an acknowledgement, guarantee, ratification etc. **2** to write (one's name) by way of official acknowledgement, ratification etc. **3** to order, request or make known by a gesture. ~*v.i.* **1** to write one's name by way of official acknowledgement, ratification etc. **2** to communicate by gesture or movement. **3** to communicate in a sign language. **to sign away** to transfer or convey by signing a deed. **to sign for** to acknowledge receipt of by signing. **to sign in** to record arrival by signing. **to sign off 1** to stop work for the time. **2** to end a letter by signing. **3** to stop broadcasting, with a verbal announcement etc. **4** to discharge from employment. **5** formally to cease collecting unemployment benefit. **6** in bridge, to make a conventional bid indicating that one wishes to end the bidding. **to sign on 1** to commit (oneself or another) to an undertaking or employment. **2** to register as unemployed. **3** to begin broadcasting, with a verbal announcement etc. **to sign out** to record departure by signing. **to sign up 1** to commit (oneself or another) to an undertaking or employment. **2** to enlist, enrol. **signable** *a.* **signage** *n.* **1** signs collectively, advertising boards, or their design. **2** the use of a sign language, signing. **signboard** *n.* a board on which a tradesman's sign or advertisement is painted. **signer** *n.* **signing** *n.* **1** the use of, or the art of using, a sign language. **2** a recently signed-up member of a professional sports team. **sign language** *n.* a system of communication that uses visual signals rather than the spoken word, esp. any system of hand and finger movements used by the deaf. **sign-off** *n.* in bridge, an act of signing off. **sign of the cross** *n.* in Christianity, a gesture made tracing the shape of a cross, either in front of one in the air, or from the forehead to chest and to each shoulder, as a way of invoking God's grace. **sign of the times** *n.* anything that serves as an indication of sociological change or development. **sign of the zodiac** *n.* each of the 12 equal parts into which the zodiac has anciently been divided, orig. corresponding to the constellations bearing the same names, but now, through the precession of the equinoxes, coinciding with the constellations bearing the names next in order. **sign-painter** *n.* a person whose job is painting signboards etc. **signpost** *n.* **1** a post supporting a

sign, e.g. at a crossroads, indicating the direction of, and often distance to, particular places. **2** (*fig.*) something that indicates the right direction or course, a pointer. ~*v.t.* **1** to provide with signposts. **2** to point to or indicate (a direction or course to be followed). **signwriter** *n.* a person who paints the lettering on signboards. **signwriting** *n.*

signal (sig′nəl) *n.* **1** a sign in the form of an action, light or sound, agreed upon or understood as conveying information. **2** an event that is the occasion or cue for some action. **3** the apparatus used for conveying information, e.g., on the railway, a pole with a movable arm or coloured light, indicating whether the line is clear. **4** a set of transmitted electrical impulses received as a sound or image on radio or television. ~*v.t.* (*pres.p.* **signalling**, (*N Am.*) **signaling**, *past, p.p.* **signalled**, (*N Am.*) **signaled**) **1** to make signals to (*to signal someone to move on*). **2** to convey, announce, order etc. by signals (*to signal one's assent*). **3** (of an event) to signify or indicate (a certain change or development). ~*v.i.* to make signals. ~*a.* conspicuous, notable (*a signal victory*). **signal box** *n.* an elevated cabin beside a railway track, from which signals and points are worked. **signalize, signalise** *v.t.* **1** to make signal or remarkable, to give distinction to. **2** to point out or indicate particularly. **signaller**, (*N Am.*) **signaler** *n.* **signally** *adv.* **signalman** *n.* (*pl.* **signalmen**) **1** a person who works railway signals. **2** (*Mil.*) a person who receives or transmits signals. **signal-to-noise ratio** *n.* the ratio of the strength of a desired electrical signal to that of the noise or interference from an unwanted signal, usu. expressed in decibels.

signature (sig′nəchə) *n.* **1** one's name, initials or mark written or impressed with one's own hand in signing a document etc. **2** the act of signing one's name on a document etc. **3** (*Mus.*) a symbol indicating key (*key signature*) or time (*time signature*) at the beginning of a stave to the right of the clef, or wherever there is a change. **4** a distinguishing mark, feature, characteristic or pattern. **signatory** (-təri) *n.* (*pl.* **signatories**) any one of those who have signed an agreement, treaty etc., e.g. on behalf of a state; the state thus represented. ~*a.* having signed a document or agreement, bound by one's signature. **signature dish** *n.* a particular dish invented by, and regarded as the speciality of, a certain chef. **signature tune** *n.* a distinctive piece of music used to introduce a particular programme, performer etc., and therefore associated with them.

signet (sig′nit) *n.* a small seal, esp. for use in lieu of or with a signature as a mark of authentication. **signet ring** *n.* a finger ring set with a seal.

signify (sig′nifī) *v.t.* (*3rd pers. sing. pres.* **signifies**, *pres.p.* **signifying**, *past, p.p.* **signified**) **1** to make known by signs, gestures or words (*to signify one's agreement with a nod*). **2** to communicate, to announce. **3** to be a sign of, to indicate (*Raised *eyebrows usually signify surprise).* **4** to mean or denote, to have as its meaning *(A thumbs-up sign signifies OK).* ~*v.i.* (*dated*) to be of consequence, to matter. **significance** (-nif´ikəns) *n.* **1** importance, moment, consequence *(an event of little significance).* **2** meaning, real import *(The significance of this passage has evidently escaped most of you).* **3** the quality of being significant. **4** in statistics, the measurable probability that data not conforming to a hypothesis are substantial enough to refute the hypothesis. **5** particular emphasis or expressiveness used to convey a hint. **significant** *a.* **1** meaning something. **2** meaning something important, and relevant. **3** expressing or suggesting something more than appears on the surface *(with a significant nod).* **4** in statistics, having significance. **significant figures, significant digits** *n.pl.* (*Math.*) digits that contribute to a number, as distinct from zeros filling vacant spaces at the beginning or end. **significantly** *adv.* **significant other** *n.* (*N Am., coll.*) one's spouse, partner or lover. **signification** (-fikā´shən) *n.* **1** the act of signifying. **2** that which is signified, the precise meaning, sense or implication (of a term etc.). **significative** (-nif´-ikətiv) *a.*

signor (sēn´yaw) *n.* (*pl.* **signori** (sēnyaw´rē)) **1** an Italian man. **2** the Italian form of address corresponding to *sir* or *Mr.* **signora** (-yaw´rə) *n.* (*pl.* **signore** (-yaw´rā)) **1** a married Italian woman. **2** the Italian form of address to a married woman, corresponding to *Madam* or *Mrs.* **signorina** (-yərē´nə) *n.* (*pl.* **signorine** (-nā)) **1** an Italian unmarried girl. **2** the Italian form of address to an unmarried girl or woman, corresponding to *Miss* or to French *mademoiselle.*

sika (sē´kə) *n.* a small deer, *Cervus nippon,* native to Japan but introduced into other countries, including Britain.

Sikh (sēk) *n.* a member of a monotheistic religion that takes the Granth as its scripture, founded in the 16th cent. in the Punjab. ~*a.* of or relating to Sikhs or Sikhism. **Sikhism** *n.*

silage (sī´lij) *n.* **1** any green crop, esp. grass or clover, stored by ensilage, that is, compressed into pits, for use as fodder. **2** the making of silage. ~*v.t.* to store in a silo.

sild (sild) *n.* a young herring, esp. one canned in Norway.

silence (sī´ləns) *n.* **1** the absence of noise, stillness. **2** avoidance of comment, or withholding of information, secrecy. **3** uncommunicativeness, taciturnity. **4** absence of mention, oblivion. **5** a period during which conversation or communication lapses. ~*v.t.* **1** to reduce to silence with an unanswerable argument. **2** to fit (e.g. a firearm) with a silencer. **in silence** without a word or sound. **silencer** *n.* **1** a person who or something that silences. **2** a device for reducing or muffling noise, fitted to firearms, or to the exhaust of a motor on a vehicle etc.

silent (sī´lənt) *a.* **1** not speaking, not making any

sound. **2** (of a letter) written but not pronounced, as the unpronounced *k* in *knee.* **3** uncommunicative, taciturn. **4** saying nothing (about or on a topic), making no mention. **5** (of a film) not having a synchronized soundtrack. **silently** *adv.* **silent majority** *n.* the large majority of a population who have moderate views but who do not bother to express them. **silentness** *n.* **silent partner** *n.* a partner in a business who has no voice in its management.

silhouette (siluet´) *n.* **1** a portrait in profile or outline, usu. black on a white ground or cut out in paper etc. **2** the outline of a figure as seen against the light or cast as a shadow. ~*v.t.* (*usu. in pass.*) to represent or cause to be visible in silhouette. **in silhouette** as a dark shape or outline.

silica (sil´ikə) *n.* (*Chem.*) a hard, crystalline silicon dioxide, occurring in various mineral forms, esp. as sand, flint, quartz etc. **silica gel** *n.* a granular form of hydrated silica, used to absorb water and other vapours. **silicate** (-kət) *n.* any of many salts of silicic acid, common in the rocks forming the earth's crust. **siliceous** (-lish´əs), **silicious** *a.* of or containing silica. **silicic** (-lis´-) *a.* of or containing silica or silicon. **silicify** (-lis´ifi) *v.t.* (*3rd pers. sing. pres.* **silicifies**, *pres.p.* **silicifying**, *past, p.p.* **silicified**) to convert into or impregnate with silica. **silicification** (-fikā´shən) *n.* **silicon** (-kən) *n.* (*Chem.*) a non-metallic semiconducting element, at. no. 14, chem. symbol Si, usu. occurring in combination with oxygen as quartz or silica, and next to oxygen the most abundant of the elements. **silicon carbide** *n.* CARBORUNDUM. **silicon chip** *n.* a microchip composed of silicon, on to which an integrated microcircuit can be printed. **silicone** (-kōn) *n.* any of numerous water-repellent oils of low melting-point, the viscosity of which changes little with temperature, used as lubricants, constituents of polish etc. ~*v.t.* to treat with silicone. **Silicon Valley** *n.* an area that has a high concentration of industries concerned with information technology and electronics. **silicosis** (-kō´sis) *n.* an occupational disease of the lungs occasioned by the inhalation of silica dust.

siliqua (sil´ikwə) *n.* (*pl.* **siliquae** (-kwē)) a dry, elongated pericarp or pod containing seeds, as in plants of the mustard family. **silique** (silēk´) *n.*

silk (silk) *n.* **1** a fine soft glossy fibre spun by the larvae of certain moths, esp. the common silkworm, *Bombyx mori.* **2** similar thread spun by the silk spider and other arachnids. **3** cloth made of silk. **4** (*pl.*) varieties of this or garments made of it, esp. as worn by jockeys. **5** (a skein of) fine thread for embroidery. **6** a King's or Queen's Counsel, or their rank (from their right to wear a silk gown). ~*a.* made of silk, silken, silky. **to take silk** to exchange a gown of ordinary fabric for one of silk, esp. to become a KC or QC. **silk cotton** *n.* the silky covering of the seed pods of the bombax and other trees. **silken** *a.* **1** made of silk. **2** soft and glossy like silk. **3** silk-clad.

4 (of someone's manner) suave, plausible, ingratiating. **silk-fowl** *n.* a breed of fowl that has silky plumage. **silklike** *a.* **silk moth** *n.* any of various moths whose caterpillars make a silken cocoon, esp. the moth which metamorphoses from the silkworm. **silk-screen** *a.* denoting a stencil method of printing in which paint or ink is forced through a screen of silk or other fine-meshed fabric. ~*v.t.* to print or decorate using the silk-screen method. **silk-screen printing** *n.* **silk spider** *n.* a spider spinning a silky substance, esp.*Nephela plumipes*. **silkworm** *n.* the larva of *Bombyx mori* or allied moths which enclose their chrysalis in a cocoon of silk. **silky** *a.* (*comp.* **silkier**, *superl.* **silkiest**) like silk, glossy, soft. **silkily** *adv.* **silkiness** *n.*

sill (sil), **cill** *n.* **1** a block or timber forming a basis or foundation in a structure, esp. a slab of timber or stone at the foot of a door or window. **2** a piece of timber forming the horizontal base of a lock or dock gate. **3** (*Geol.*) a sheet of intrusive igneous rock between other strata.

sillabub SYLLABUB.

sillimanite (sil´imənīt) *n.* the mineral aluminium silicate, found as orthorhombic crystals or fibrous masses.

silly (sil´i) *a.* (*comp.* **sillier**, *superl.* **silliest**) **1** foolish, weak-minded. **2** showing poor judgement, unwise. **3** mentally weak, imbecile. **4** senseless as a result of a blow (*The blow knocked him silly*). **5** in cricket, close to the batsman's wicket. ~*n.* (*pl.* **sillies**) a silly person. **sillily** *adv.* **silliness** *n.* **silly billy** *n.* (*pl.* **silly billies**) (*coll.*) a foolish person. **silly season** *n.* the late summer, when newspapers are traditionally full of trivial stories, for lack of anything serious to print.

silo (sī´lō) *n.* (*pl.* **silos**) **1** a store-pit or airtight chamber for pressing and preserving green fodder. **2** a tall construction in which grain etc. can be stored. **3** an underground store and launch pad for a guided missile. ~*v.t.* (*3rd pers. sing. pres.* **siloes**, *pres.p.* **siloing**, *past, p.p.* **siloed**) **1** to put in a silo. **2** to convert into silage.

❌ **silouette** common misspelling of SILHOUETTE.

silt (silt) *n.* fine sediment deposited by water. ~*v.t.* to choke or fill (up) with silt. ~*v.i.* to be choked (up) with silt. **siltation** (-tā´shən) *n.* **silty** *a.* (*comp.* **siltier**, *superl.* **siltiest**).

Silurian (silūe´riən, sī-) *a.* (*Geol.*) of or relating to the period called Silurian or its rock system. ~*n.* **1** the lowest subdivision of the Palaeozoic strata, next above the Cambrian (well developed in S Wales, where these strata were first examined). **2** the geological period during which these strata formed.

silva SYLVA.

silver (sil´və)*n.* **1** (*Chem.*) a precious ductile and malleable metallic element of a white colour, at. no. 47, chem. symbol Ag. **2** domestic utensils, esp. cutlery, implements, ornaments etc. made of silver, usu. combined with a harder metal. **3** silver or cupronickel coins. **4** the colour or lustre of

or as of silver. **5** a silver medal. ~*a.* **1** made of silver. **2** resembling silver, white or lustrous like silver. ~*v.t.* **1** to coat or plate with silver or a silver substitute. **2** to back (mirror glass) with an amalgam of tin and mercury. **3** to give a silvery colour or lustre to. **4** to tinge (hair) with white or grey. ~*v.i.* to acquire a silvery appearance, e.g. (of hair) to turn grey or white. **silver band** *n.* a band whose instruments are silver-plated. **silver birch** *n.* a common variety of birch, *Betula alba*, with a silvery-white trunk. **silverer** *n.* **silver fern** *n.* **1** a tree fern of New Zealand, *Cyaltea dealbata*, with leathery leaves. **2** a silver fern leaf on a black background, as the symbol of New Zealand. **silver fir** *n.* any of various fir trees of the genus *Abies* with needles that are silvery-white on the underside. **silverfish** *n.* any of various small wingless insects of the *Lepisma* genus, esp. *Lepisma saccharina*, which infest buildings and can be destructive to books, cloth etc. **silver fox** *n.* **1** a variety of common American red fox in a phase during which its coat becomes black mixed with silver. **2** the pelt of this animal. **silver gilt** *n.* **1** gilded silver or silverware. **2** an imitation gilding consisting of silver foil varnished with yellow lacquer. **silver grey** *n.*, *a.* pale luminous grey. **silver jubilee** *n.* (a celebration of) a 25th anniversary, esp. of a monarch's reign. **silver leaf** *n.* **1** silver beaten out into thin leaves or plates. **2** (**silver-leaf**) a disease of plum trees. **silverlike** *a.* **silver lining** *n.* the bright or compensating side of any misfortune, trouble etc. (from the proverb 'Every cloud has a silver lining'). **silver medal** *n.* in athletics competitions etc., the silver-coloured medal awarded as a second prize. **silver paper** *n.* **1** silver-coloured wrapping material, e.g. for confectionery, usu. consisting of aluminium foil or sometimes tin foil, often with a backing of greaseproof paper. **2** fine tissue paper, (orig. for wrapping silverware). **silver plate** *n.* **1** silverware. **2** (metal articles coated with) a thin layer of silver, electroplate. **silver-plate** *v.t.* to coat with a thin layer of silver, to electroplate. **silver sand** *n.* fine white sand used in gardening. **silver screen** *n.* **1** the cinema screen. **2** motion pictures generally, cinematography. **silverside** *n.* **1** the upper and choicer part of a round of beef. **2** (*also* **silversides**) any of several small sea fishes with a silver side-marking, e.g. *Atherina presbyter*. **silversmith** *n.* a maker of or worker in silver articles. **silversmithing** *n.* **silver tongue** *n.* eloquence. **silver-tongued** *a.* **silverware** *n.* articles of silver or silver plate, esp. cutlery and often tableware. **silver wedding** *n.* a 25th wedding anniversary. **silverweed** *n.* any of various silvery-leaved plants, esp. *Potentilla anserina*. **silvery** *a.* **1** having the appearance of silver. **2** (of hair) white, with a bright sheen. **3** having a soft clear sound. **silveriness** *n.*

silviculture (sil´vikŭlchə), **sylviculture** *n.* the cultivation of trees, forestry. **silvicultural** (-kŭl´-) *a.* **silviculturist** (-kŭl´-) *n.*

sima (sī´mə) n. (Geol.) **1** the inner part of the earth's crust, lying deep to the ocean bed as well as to the continental masses. **2** the silica- and magnesia-rich material of which this layer consists.

simian (sim´iən) a. **1** of or relating to the anthropoid apes. **2** apelike or monkey-like in appearance or movement. ~n. an ape or monkey.

similar (sim´ilə) a. **1** having a resemblance (to) (Her nose was similar to her mother's; They've got a van similar to ours). **2** resembling each other, alike (Our views are similar, though not exactly the same; We have similar interests). **3** (Geom.) made up of the same number of parts arranged in the same manner, corresponding. **similarity** (-lar´-) n. (pl. **similarities**). **similarly** adv.

Usage note Similar should be followed by to (and not as).

simile (sim´ili) n. a figure of speech that highlights a particular quality that something has by comparing it, esp. using like or as, to something else proverbial for that quality, as of eyes like stars; a heart as pure as the driven snow. **similitude** (-mil´itūd) n. **1** likeness, resemblance. **2** semblance, guise.

simmer (sim´ə) v.i. **1** to boil gently. **2** to be just below boiling point. **3** to be in a state of suppressed emotion, esp. rage. ~v.t. **1** to boil gently. **2** to keep just below boiling point. ~n. a state of simmering. **to simmer down** to become less agitated or excited, to calm down.

simnel (sim´nəl), **simnel cake** n. a rich fruit cake decorated with marzipan, traditionally eaten on Mothering Sunday, Easter Day and Christmas Day.

simony (sim´əni, sī´-) n. the buying or selling of ecclesiastical preferments or privileges. **simoniac** (-mō´niak), **simoniacal** (-nī´əkəl) a.

simoom (simoom´), **simoon** (-moon´) n. a hot dry wind blowing over the desert, esp. of Arabia, raising great quantities of sand and causing intense thirst.

simpatico (simpat´ikō) a. congenial, agreeable, likeable.

simper (sim´pə) v.i. to smile in an affected manner, to smirk. ~v.t. to utter with a simper. ~n. an affected smile or smirk. **simperer** n. **simpering** a. **simperingly** adv.

simple (sim´pəl) a. (comp. **simpler**, superl. **simplest**) **1** clear, easy to understand. **2** not difficult, easy to do. **3** not complicated, straightforward. **4** not elaborate, not adorned. **5** all of one kind or consisting of only one thing, not analysable. **6** absolute, nothing but (It's simple jealousy). **7** weak in intellect. **8** unsophisticated, artless. **9** humble, of low degree. **simple eye** n. in insects etc., an eye that has only one lens. **simple fracture** n. a fracture in which the surrounding skin is not injured. **simple interest** n. in money loans, interest payable upon the principal, i.e. the capital sum, only. **simple-minded** a. **1** foolish, stupid.

2 mentally deficient, feeble-minded. **simple-mindedly** adv. **simple-mindedness** n. **simpleness** n. **simple sentence** n. a sentence consisting of a single main clause. **simple time** n. (Mus.) a tempo that has two, three or four beats to the bar. **simpleton** (-tən) n. a silly, gullible or feeble-minded person. **simplex** (-pleks) a. **1** simple, not compound. **2** (Comput. etc.) in computing and telecommunications, allowing the transmission of a signal in only one direction at a time. **simplicity** (-plis´-) n. **simplify** (-plifī) v.t. (3rd pers. sing. pres. **simplifies**, pres.p. **simplifying**, past, p.p. **simplified**) **1** to make simple. **2** to make simpler or easier to understand, to reduce to essentials. **simplification** (-fikā´shən) n. **simplifier** n. **simplism** n. **1** the affectation of simplicity. **2** the fault of being simplistic, oversimplification. **simplistic** (-plis´-) a. **1** oversimplified, naive, superficial, unrealistically limited, shallow etc. **2** oversimplifying. **simplistically** adv. **simply** adv. **1** in a clear, straightforward manner. **2** in a simple or plain manner (simply delicious). **3** in an unsophisticated, artless manner. **4** absolutely, without qualification. **5** merely, only (I'm simply wanting to help).

simulacrum (simūlā´krəm) n. (pl. **simulacra** (-krə)) **1** an image or likeness. **2** a deceptive or superficial likeness, a spurious substitute. **3** a mere semblance or pretence.

simulate (sim´ūlāt) v.t. **1** to assume the likeness or mere appearance of. **2** to counterfeit, to feign, to imitate, to put on, to mimic. **3** to reproduce the structure, movement or conditions of (a situation or environment) e.g. in an experiment, by computer etc. **simulated** a. **simulation** (-lā´shən) n. **simulative** (-lətiv) a. **simulator** (-lātə) n. **1** a person or thing that simulates something. **2** a device that simulates a certain environment, set of conditions, or process, used for testing or training purposes.

simulcast (sim´əlkahst) n. (the transmission of) a simultaneous broadcast on radio and television. ~v.t. to broadcast (a programme) simultaneously on radio and television.

simultaneous (siməltā´niəs) a. **1** happening, done or acting at the same time. **2** coincident or concurrent (with). **simultaneity** (-tənā´-) n. **simultaneous equations** n.pl. a set of two or more equations in both or all of which the variables have the same values. **simultaneously** adv. **simultaneousness** n.

sin[1] (sin) n. **1** transgression of duty, morality, or the law of God. **2** wickedness, moral depravity. **3** a transgression, an offence. **4** a breach of etiquette, social standards etc. ~v.i. (pres.p. **sinning**, past, p.p. **sinned**) **1** to commit a sin. **2** to offend (against). **as sin** (coll.) to a degree, extremely, very (ugly as sin). **for one's sins** (facet.) literally, as a judgement upon one, meaning little more than 'as it happens'. **like sin** (coll.) intensely (She hates him like sin). **to live in sin** (of a couple) to cohabit without being married.

sin bin *n.* **1** (*sl.*) in ice hockey etc., an area to the side of the pitch where players who have committed fouls are temporarily sent. **2** (*coll.*) an independent unit where disruptive school pupils can be sent for temporary attendance. **sinful** *a.* **1** (of a person) frequently or habitually sinning. **2** (of an act) reprehensible, or entailing sin. **sinfully** *adv.* **sinfulness** *n.* **sinless** *a.* **sinlessly** *adv.* **sinlessness** *n.* **sinner** *n.* someone who habitually sins, a sinful person.

sin² (sin) *abbr.* SINE¹.

since (sins) *adv.* **1** after or from a time specified or implied till now (*I've been scared ever since*). **2** at some time after such a time and before now (*It's happened twice since*). **3** before this, before now, ago (*I gave up hoping long since*). ~*prep.* **1** from the time of. **2** throughout or during the time after. **3** after (a certain event, time or date) and before now. ~*conj.* **1** from the time when, during the time after. **2** inasmuch as. **3** because.

sincere (sinsiə´) *a.* (*comp.* **sincerer,** *superl.* **sincerest**) **1** being in reality as in appearance or profession. **2** not feigned or put on, genuine. **sincerely** *adv.* in a sincere manner. **yours sincerely** a conventional way of ending a formal or business letter. **sincereness** *n.* **sincerity** (-ser´i-) *n.*

Usage note In closing letters, *Yours sincerely* is a formal style, and goes with an opening in which an individual is addressed by name (*Dear John, Dear Miss X* etc.).

sinciput (sin´sipŭt) *n.* (*Anat.*) the upper part of the head, especially from the forehead to the crown. **sincipital** (-sip´-) *a.*

sine¹ (sīn) *n.* (*Math.*) a trigonometric function that is the ratio of the length of the line opposite the angle to the length of the hypotenuse in a right-angled triangle. **sine curve** *n.* a curve representing the relationship between the size of an angle and its sine, a sinusoid. **sine wave** *n.* any oscillation whose representation is a sine curve.

sine² (sin´i, sī´-) *prep.* without, lacking. **sine die** (dī´ē, dē´ā) *adv., a.* without any day (being fixed). **sine qua non** (sī´ni kwā non, sin´i kwah nōn) *n.* (*pl.* **sine qua nons**) an essential condition or indispensable requirement.

sinecure (sin´ikūə, sī´-) *n.* **1** an ecclesiastical benefice without cure of souls. **2** any paid office with few or no duties attached. **sinecurism** *n.* **sinecurist** *n.*

sinew (sin´ū) *n.* **1** a tendon, a fibrous cord connecting muscle and bone. **2** (*pl.*) muscles. **3** (*often in pl.*) that which gives strength or power, e.g. to a state, organization or policy, muscle, clout. **sinewed** *a.* **sinewless** *a.* **sinewy** *a.* **sinewiness** *n.*

sing (sing) *v.i.* (*past* **sang** (sang), *p.p.* **sung** (sŭng)) **1** to utter words in a tuneful manner, to render a song vocally, to make vocal melody. **2** (of birds, or certain insects) to emit sweet or melodious sounds. **3** (of a kettle, the wind etc.) to make a

murmuring or whistling sound. **4** (of the ears) to ring. **5** (*sl.*) to confess, to inform. **6** to tell (of) in song or poetry. ~*v.t.* **1** to utter (words, a song, tune etc.) in a tuneful or melodious manner. **2** to relate, proclaim or celebrate in verse or poetry. **3** to accompany with singing; to greet, acclaim, lull (to sleep), usher (in or out) etc., with singing. **to sing out** to call out loudly, to shout. **to sing the praises of** to commend warmly, to proclaim the virtues of. **to sing up** to sing more loudly and enthusiastically. **singable** *a.* **singalong** *n.* **1** (*often attrib.*) a tune or song that an audience can join in with, or sing in accompaniment to. **2** an occasion or event at which the audience can join in with the performer in singing popular or familiar songs. **to sing along** (of an audience) to accompany a performer in singing popular songs. **singer** (sing´ə) *n.* **singer-songwriter** *n.* someone who writes songs and performs them, esp. professionally. **singing** *a., n.* **singingly** *adv.* **singsong** *a.* **1** (of a voice, accent etc.) having a rising and falling inflection. **2** having a monotonous rhythm. ~*n.* **1** a monotonous rising and falling (of a voice etc.). **2** an informal session of singing usu. well-known songs. ~*v.i., v.t.* (*past, p.p.* **singsonged**) to utter, to recite, sing etc. in a sing-song manner.

Usage note In standard English, the past tense of *sing* is *sang*, not *sung*.

singe (sinj) *v.t.* (*pres.p.* **singeing,** *past, p.p.* **singed**) **1** to burn slightly, to burn the surface of. **2** to burn bristles or nap off (an animal carcass or fabric). ~*n.* a slight or superficial burn. **singed** *a.*

Singhalese SINHALESE.

single (sing´gəl) *a.* **1** consisting of one only, sole. **2** simple, not compound, double or complex, not combined with others. **3** individual, solitary. **4** (*with neg.*) even one (*not a single offer*). **5** (*used for emphasis*) individual (*every single person*). **6** unmarried, or without a current partner. **7** involving or performed by one or by one on each side. **8** designed for use by or with one person, thing etc. **9** (of a travel ticket) valid for the outward journey only. ~*n.* **1** a single thing, item, quantity or measure. **2** a rail, bus etc. ticket for a journey in one direction. **3** a gramophone record with only one track recorded on each side. **4** a single round or game, a hit for one run in cricket or a one-base hit in baseball. **5** (*pl.*) a game, esp. of tennis, consisting of a single player on either side. **6** (*usu. in pl.*) an unmarried person. **7** (*N Am., coll.*) a one-dollar bill. ~*v.t.* to pick (out) from among others. **single acrostic** *n.* an acrostic that uses only the first letter of each line. **single-breasted** *a.* (of a jacket, coat etc.) having only one thickness of cloth over the breast when closed, with one central set of buttons, holes etc.; not overlapping. **single combat** *n.* a duel. **single cream** *n.* pouring cream of a less fatty consistency than double cream. **single-decker** *n.* a bus with a single floor or deck of seats. **single entry**

n. in bookkeeping, the system of entering transactions in one account only. **single figures** *n.pl.* a number etc. under ten. **single file** *n.* a line of people, vehicles etc. standing or moving one behind the other. *~adv.* one behind the other. **single-handed** *a.* **1** done without assistance. **2** unassisted, alone. **3** (of e.g. a player in certain games etc.) using only one hand. *~adv.* without assistance, alone. **single-handedly** *adv.* **single-handedness** *n.* **single market** *n.* an association of countries trading freely with one another, esp. the single internal market of the European Union. **single-minded** *a.* intent on one purpose only. **single-mindedly** *adv.* **single-mindedness** *n.* **singleness** *n.* **single parent** *n.* one parent raising a child or children alone. **single pneumonia** *n.* pneumonia affecting one lung only. **singles bar, singles club** *n.* a bar or club where unmarried people meet. **single-seater** *n., a.* (a) vehicle, vessel etc., having seating for only one person. **singlet** (-glit) *n.* **1** an undershirt, a vest. **2** (*Physics*) a single line in a spectrum. **singleton** (-tən) *n.* **1** a card that is the only one of its suit in a player's hand at whist, bridge etc. **2** a single object, person etc. as opposed to a group or pair. **singletree** *n.* (*N Am., Austral.*) a swingletree. **singly** *adv.*

singular (sing´gūlə) *a.* **1** out of the usual, remarkable. **2** peculiar, odd. **3** (of a word or inflected form of a word) denoting or referring to one person or thing; not plural. **4** (of a logical proposition) referring to a specific thing or person, not general. **5** single, individual. *~n.* **1** (*Gram.*) the singular number. **2** a word denoting this. **singularity** (-lar´-) *n.* (*pl.* **singularities**) **1** the state of being singular. **2** an odd mannerism or trait. **singularize, singularise** *v.t.* **singularization** (-zā´shən) *n.* **singularly** *adv.*

sinh (shīn, sinch, sīnāch´) *abbr.* (*Math.*) a hyperbolic sine.

Sinhalese (sinhəlēz´), **Singhalese,** †**Cingalese** (sing-gə-) *a.* of or relating to Sri Lanka (formerly Ceylon), or to its majority people or their language; Sri Lankan. *~n.* (*pl.* **Sinhalese, Singhalese,** †**Cingalese**) **1** a native or inhabitant of Sri Lanka. **2** a member of the Sinhalese people constituting the majority of the inhabitants of Sri Lanka. **3** the official language of Sri Lanka and the Sinhalese people.

sinister (sin´istə) *a.* **1** ill-looking, malevolent. **2** nefarious or criminal. **3** ill-omened, inauspicious. **4** (*Her.*) on the left side (of a shield etc.), the side to the right of the observer. **sinisterly** *adv.* **sinisterness** *n.* **sinistral** *a.* **1** left-handed. **2** of, on, or towards the left. **3** (of a flatfish) having the left side uppermost. **4** (of a spiral shell) with a whorl turning (unusually) to the left. **sinistrality** (-tral´-) *n.* **sinistrally** *adv.* **sinistro-** *comb. form* on or towards the left; laevo-. **sinistrorse** (-traws) *a.* (*Bot.*) rising and twining to the left, from the observer's point of view.

sink (singk) *v.i.* (*past* **sank** (sangk), **sunk** (sŭngk),

p.p. **sunk,** *part. a.* **sunken** (-kən)) **1** to go downwards, to fall gradually. **2** to disappear below the horizon. **3** to drop below the surface of a liquid. **4** (of a ship) to go down to the sea bed etc. **5** to fall or descend by force of gravity. **6** to decline to a lower level of health, morals etc. **7** to deteriorate. **8** to droop, to despond. **9** to subside or decline. **10** to become lower in intensity, price etc. **11** to become shrunken or hollow, to slope downwards. **12** to go deep or deeper (into), to be impressed (into) to be absorbed. **13** (of darkness) to fall (on a place). *~v.t.* **1** to cause to sink. **2** to submerge (as) in a fluid, to send below the surface. **3** to excavate, to make by excavating. **4** to inset or inlay into a surface. **5** to pocket (the ball) in snooker etc. **6** in golf, to hole (the ball or a putt). **7** to allow to fall or droop. **8** to lower, to ruin. **9 a** to invest (money in an enterprise). **b** to invest unprofitably, to lose, to waste, to squander. **10** (*coll.*) to drink, to quaff. **11** (*usu. in pass.*) to absorb or preoccupy (*to be sunk in thought*). *~n.* **1** a plastic, porcelain or metal basin, usu. fitted to a water supply and drainage system in a kitchen. **2** a cesspool or sewer. **3** a place of iniquity. **4** (*Physics*) a device, body or process which absorbs or dissipates energy, as *heat sink*. **to sink in 1** to become absorbed, to penetrate. **2** to become understood. **to sink or swim** to either succeed or fail (in a venture etc.). **sinkable** *a.* **sinkage** (-kij) *n.* **sinker** *n.* **1** a person who or something that sinks. **2** a weight used to sink a fishing line, net etc. **3** (*N Am.*) a doughnut. **4** (*N Am.*) in baseball, a ball that drops after being pitched or hit. **sinking** *a., n.* **sinking feeling** *n.* the uncomfortable feeling in the abdomen brought on by e.g. nervousness or hunger. **sinking fund** *n.* a fund set aside for the reduction of a debt.

Usage note In standard English, the past tense of *sink* is *sank*, not *sunk*.

sinner SIN¹.

Sino- (sī´nō) *comb. form* Chinese, or Chinese and, as in *Sino-Tibetan.*

sinology (sīnol´əji) *n.* the study of Chinese languages, culture, literature etc. **sinological** (-nəloj´-) *a.* **sinologist** *n.* **sinologue** (sī´nəlog, sin´-) *n.* an expert or specialist in sinology, a sinologist.

sinter (sin´tə) *n.* a calcareous or siliceous rock precipitated from (hot) mineral waters. *~v.t.* to form (metal powder, ceramics, glass etc.) into a solid mass by pressure or heating at a temperature below melting point. *~v.i.* to be formed into such a mass.

sinuate (sin´ūət), **sinuated** (-ātid) *a.* (*esp. Bot.*) (esp. of the edges of leaves etc.) bending, curving or winding in and out.

sinuous (sin´ūəs) *a.* **1** bending in and out. **2** winding, serpentine, tortuous. **sinuosity** (-os´-) *n.* (*pl.* **sinuosities**) **1** the quality of being sinuous. **2** a bend or series of bends and curves. **sinuously** *adv.* **sinuousness** *n.*

sinus (sī´nəs) *n.* (*pl.* **sinuses**) **1** a cavity or pouch-like hollow, esp. in bone or tissue. **2** the cavity in the skull which connects with the nose. **3** (*Med.*) a fistula. **4** (*Bot.*) a rounded recess or curve, as in the margin of a leaf. **sinusitis** (-sī´tis) *n.* (painful) inflammation of a nasal sinus. **sinusoid** *n.* **1** (*Math.*) a sine curve. **2** any of the small blood vessels that replace the capillaries in a bodily organ, esp. the liver.

Sion ZION.

-sion (shən, zhən) *suf.* forming nouns from Latin past participles with a stem in -*s*-, as *revulsion, immersion, fusion.*

Sioux (soo) *n.* (*pl.* **Sioux**) **1** a member of a N American Indian people of the upper Mississippi and Missouri rivers, a Dakota. **2** any of the various Siouan languages spoken by this group. ~*a.* of or relating to the Sioux. **Siouan** *n.* **1** a family of central and eastern N American languages. **2** a Sioux. ~*a.* of or relating to the Sioux or their languages.

sip (sip) *v.t.*, *v.i.* (*pres.p.* **sipping**, *past*, *p.p.* **sipped**) to drink or imbibe in small quantities using the lips. ~*n.* **1** a very small draught of liquid. **2** an act of sipping. **sipper** *n.* **sippet** (-it) *n.* **1** a small piece of toast or fried bread garnishing a dish of mince etc. **2** a small piece of bread or other food soaked in broth etc. **3** any small piece or fragment.

siphon, siphonal etc. SYPHON.

sir (sœ) *n.* **1** a form of courteous address to a man. **2** (**Sir**) a title prefixed to the names of baronets and knights and formerly clergymen.

sire (sīə) *n.* **1** the male parent of an animal, esp. a stallion. **2** †a title used in addressing a king or a sovereign prince. **3** (*poet.*) †a father, a progenitor. ~*v.t.* (esp. of stallions or male domestic animals) to beget.

siren (sī´rən) *n.* **1** an apparatus for producing a loud warning sound by means of a rotating perforated disc through which steam or compressed air is emitted. **2** an electrical warning device emitting a similarly piercing sound. **3 a** a charming or seductive woman, esp. a dangerous temptress. **b** (*sometimes attrib.*) an alluring distraction. **4** a sweet singer. **sirenian** (-rē´-) *n.* any of the Sirenia, an order of marine herbivorous mammals, allied to the whales, but having the fore limbs developed into paddles, comprising the manatees and dugongs. ~*a.* of or relating to the Sirenia. **siren suit** *n.* a suit in one piece, closed with a zip fastening (designed for wearing in air-raid shelters).

sirloin (sœ´loin) *n.* the loin or upper part of the loin of beef.

sirocco (sirok´ō), **scirocco** (shi-) *n.* (*pl.* **siroccos, sciroccos**) **1** a hot oppressive wind blowing from N Africa across to Italy etc., often carrying dust or rain. **2** a sultry southerly wind in Italy.

sirree (sirē´) *n.* (*N Am.*, *coll.*) sir (used for emphasis often with *yes* or *no*).

sirup SYRUP.

☒ **sirynge** common misspelling of SYRINGE.

sis (sis), **siss** *n.* (*coll.*) short for SISTER. **sissy** (sis´i), **cissy** *n.* (*pl.* **sissies, cissies**) an effeminate, feeble or cowardly boy or man. ~*a.* (*comp.* **sissier**, *superl.* **sissiest**) effeminate, feeble, cowardly.

sisal (sī´səl), **sisal-grass, sisal-hemp** *n.* the fibre of the Mexican agave used for cordage etc.

siskin (sis´kin) *n.* a small migratory songbird, *Carduelis spinus*, related to the goldfinch.

☒ **sisors** common misspelling of SCISSORS.

sissy, siss SIS.

sister (sis´tə) *n.* **1 a** a female born of the same parents as oneself. **b** a half-sister, a foster sister or, formerly, a sister-in-law. **2** (*esp. N Am.*, *coll.*) used as a form of address to a female companion or friend. **3** a female fellow member of the same group, society, trade union etc., esp. now a fellow feminist. **4** a senior nurse, usu. one in charge of a hospital ward. **5** a member of a female religious order. **6** any thing, quality etc. closely resembling the one in question. ~*a.* closely related, similar, of the same design, type, origins, as *sister ships*. **sister city** *n.* (*pl.* **sister cities**) a city that is twinned with one's own. **sister german** *n.* (*pl.* **sisters german**) a sister having the same parents as oneself. **sisterhood** *n.* **1** the state of being a sister, the relationship of sisters. **2** a religious community of women bound together by monastic vows. **3** a community or body of women, such as the Women's Movement, bound together by common interests. **sister-in-law** *n.* (*pl.* **sisters-in-law**) **1** one's husband's or wife's sister. **2** one's brother's wife. **sisterless** *a.* **sister-like** *a.* **sisterly** *a.* **sisterliness** *n.* **sister uterine** *n.* (*pl.* **sisters uterine**) a sister having the same mother, but not the same father, as another.

sit (sit) *v.i.* (*pres.p.* **sitting**, *past*, *p.p.* **sat** (sat)) **1** to set oneself or be in a resting posture with the body nearly vertical supported on the buttocks. **2** (of birds and various animals) to be in a resting posture. **3** to perch. **4** (of a bird) to cover eggs in order to hatch, to brood. **5** to be in a specified position, quarter etc. **6** to be situated. **7** (of clothes etc.) to suit, to fit. **8** to rest, press or weigh (on). **9** to meet, to hold a session. **10** to hold or occupy a seat (on a deliberative body or in a specified capacity e.g. as a magistrate). **11** to babysit (for someone). ~*v.t.* **1** to cause to sit, to set. **2** to place (oneself) in a seat. **3** to hold or keep a sitting position on (a horse etc.). **4** to be a candidate for (an examination). **5** (*in comb.* as *babysit*) to stay in with so as to look after. ~*n.* **1** an act or time of sitting. **2** a sit-down, a rest. **sitting pretty** in an advantageous position. **to sit at the feet of** to be taught by (a certain teacher, esp. a famous one). **to sit back** to withdraw from active participation. **to sit by** to observe without taking an active part. **to sit down 1** to place oneself on a seat, or in a sitting position, after standing. **2** to place in a sitting position, to cause to sit. **to sit down under** to submit meekly to (an insult or insulting treatment). **to sit for 1** to take (an examination). **2** to represent (a constituency in parliament). **3** to pose for (a portrait). **to sit heavy on the stomach** to be difficult to digest. **to sit in** to take part in a sit-in. **to sit in judgement** to pass judgement on the actions of others, to be critical. **to sit in on** to observe, be present at, or participate in (a discussion, meeting, lecture etc.) as a visitor. **to sit on 1** to hold a meeting, discussion or investigation over. **2** (*coll.*) to repress severely, to snub. **3** (*coll.*) to suppress or prevent from circulating. **to sit on one's hands 1** not to act or intervene. **2** not to applaud. **to sit out 1** to sit out of doors. **2** to sit apart from (a dance, meeting etc.). **3** to stay till the end of (a concert etc., or an uncomfortable episode). **4** to stay longer than (other visitors). **to sit tight** to hold firm and do nothing. **to sit up 1** to rise from a recumbent position. **2** to sit with the body erect. **3** suddenly to pay attention, take notice, become alert, esp. in *to sit up and take notice.* **4** not to go to bed. **sit-down** *n.* **1** (*coll.*) a spell of sitting, a rest, a break. **2** a protest in which participants sit down in a public place, or occupy their workplace, as a form of passive resistance. **3** a sit-down strike. ~*a.* (of a meal) eaten while seated at a table. **sit-down strike** *n.* a strike in which employees occupy their place of work. **sit-in** *n.* the occupation of premises (e.g. at a university) as a form of protest. **sitter** *n.* **1** a person who sits, esp. for a portrait. **2** (*coll.*) something easy to achieve or accomplish, esp. an easy catch or shot. **3** a babysitter. **4** a hen that sits on a clutch of eggs to incubate them. **sitting** *n.* **1** a period of continuous sitting (e.g. for a portrait). **2** a session of one particular activity. **3** a meeting of a body, esp. the time when business is officially in progress. **4** a meal-serving session (*first sitting for lunch*). **5** (*Law*) a term. **6** a clutch of eggs for hatching or the process of brooding on them. ~*a.* **1** seated. **2** (of a bird or animal) remaining still, not flying or running. **3** (of a hen) sitting on eggs to hatch them, brooding. **4** holding office or (of a Member of Parliament) current. **5** in session. **sitting duck** *n.* an easy target, someone in a defenceless position. **sitting room** *n.* **1** a room for sitting in, a living room or lounge. **2** room or space for people to sit down. **sitting target** *n.* a sitting duck. **sitting tenant** *n.* the person currently occupying or in possession of a flat, house etc. **sit-up** *n.* a physical exercise in which the upper torso is raised from a reclining into a sitting position using the abdominal muscles without the help of the hands. **sit-upon** *n.* (*coll.*) the bottom, buttocks.

sitar (sitah´, sit´-) *n.* an Indian stringed musical instrument with a long neck. **sitarist** (-tah´-) *n.*

sitcom (sit´kom) *n.* (*coll.*) a situation comedy.

site (sīt) *n.* **1** the ground on which anything, esp. a building, stands, has stood, or will stand. **2** (*esp. in comb.*) a place or centre of a particular activity or procedure (*a camping site; building site*). ~*v.t.* to position, locate. **on site** (available) at the workplace or place of activity.

Sitka (sit´kə), **Sitka spruce** *n.* a quick-growing

spruce fir, *Picea sitchensis*, cultivated for its timber, native to N America.

situate[1] (sit´ūāt) *v.t.* (*usu. in pass.*) **1** to place. **2** to locate. **3** to place in certain circumstances. **situation** (-ā´shən) *n.* **1** the place in which something is situated, position. **2** a state of affairs or set of circumstances. **3** (*dated*) a paid office, post or place. **situational** *a.* **situation comedy** *n.* a serialized comedy on radio or esp. television involving the same set of characters in a different comic situation in each episode. **situationism** *n.* the argument that people's behaviour is influenced or dictated more by their circumstances or environment than by their qualities or personality. **situationist** *n.*

situate[2] (sit´ūət) *a.* (*usu. Law*) situated.

sitz-bath (sits´-bahth) *n.* a bath in which a person sits, a hip bath.

six (siks) *n.* **1** the number or figure 6 or vi. **2** the age of six. **3** the time of six o'clock, the sixth hour after midday or midnight. **4** the sixth in a series. **5** a size represented by 6. **6** a card etc. bearing six symbols. **7** that which represents, amounts to or is worth six, e.g. a hit to the boundary, worth six runs in cricket. **8** a set or team of six, e.g. any of the divisions in a Cub-Scout or Brownie pack. ~*a.* **1** six in number. **2** aged six. **at sixes and sevens** in disorder or confusion. **six of one and half a dozen of the other** a dilemma presenting alternatives of equal acceptability, merit etc. **to knock for six 1** to overcome completely, to defeat. **2** to astonish. **3** to stagger. **sixer** *n.* **1** the leader of a Cub-Scout or Brownie six. **2** anything representing, worth or equal to six, e.g. a boundary hit in cricket. **sixfold** *a., adv.* **1** six times as much or as many. **2** in six parts or divisions. **six-footer** *n.* (*coll.*) a person six ft. tall. **six-gun** *n.* a six-shooter. **six of the best** *n.* a severe beating, esp. with a cane. **six-pack** *n.* a pack of six cans or bottles, esp. of beer. **sixpence** *n.* (*Hist.*) a cupronickel coin equivalent to six old pennies, the equivalent of 2½p. **on a sixpence 1** within a small area. **2** easily, quickly. **sixpenny** *a.* worth or costing sixpence, esp. before decimalization. **six-shooter** *n.* a six-chambered revolver. **sixth** *n.* **1** any one of six equal parts. **2** a sixth form. **3** (*Mus.*) **a** a musical interval of six consecutive notes on the diatonic scale. **b** a note separated from another by this interval. **c** a tone and the sixth note above or below it sounded together. ~*n., a.* **1** (the) last of six (people, things etc.). **2** the next after the fifth. **sixth form** *n.* the highest form in a secondary school. **sixth-form college** *n.* a college for pupils over 16, where subjects are taught at sixth-form level. **sixth-former** *n.* **sixthly** *adv.* **sixth sense** *n.* the power of intuition, or extrasensory perception.

sixte (sikst) *n.* a parry in fencing (the sixth of eight parrying positions) in which the hand is opposite the right breast and the point of the sword raised and a little to the right.

sixteen (sikstēn´) *n.* **1** the number/figure 16 or xvi. **2** the age of 16. **3** a size etc. represented by 16. ~*a.* **1** 16 in number. **2** aged 16. **sixteenmo** (-mō) *n.* in bookbinding, sextodecimo. **sixteenth** *n.* any one of 16 equal parts. ~*n.*, *a.* **1** (the) last of 16 (people, things etc.). **2** the next after the 15th.

sixty (siks´ti) *n.* (*pl.* **sixties**) **1** the number/ figure 60 or lx. **2** the age of 60. ~*a.* **1** 60 in number. **2** aged 60. **sixties** *n.pl.* **1** the period of time between one's 60th and 70th birthdays. **2** the rango of temperature (Fahrenheit) between 60 and 70 degrees. **3** the period of time between the 60th and 70th years of a century. **sixtieth** *n.* any one of 60 equal parts. ~*n.*, *a.* **1** (the) last of 60 (people, things etc.). **2** the next after the 59th. **sixty-first, sixty-second** etc. *n.*, *a.* the ordinal numbers corresponding to sixty-one etc. **sixty-four thousand dollar question** *n.* the crucial question (from the top prize-winning question in a television quiz show). **sixty-one, sixty-two** etc. *n.*, *a.* the cardinal numbers between 60 and 70.

size¹ (sīz) *n.* **1** extent, dimensions. **2** any one of a series of standard grades or classes with which garments and other things are divided according to their relative dimensions. ~*v.t.* **1** to sort or arrange according to size. **2** to cut or shape to a required size. **of a size** all having the same size. **of some size** fairly big. **the size of** as large as. **the size of it** the situation as it really is. **to size up 1** to form a rough estimate of the size of. **2** to judge the capacity of (a person). **what size?** how big? **sizeable, sizable** *a.* of considerable size. **sizeably** *adv.* **sized** *a.* **1** having a particular size (*usu. in comb.*, as *small-sized*). **2** sorted or graded according to size. **sizeism, sizism** *n.* discrimination on the grounds of size. **sizeist** *n.*, *a.* **sizer** *n.*

size² (sīz) *n.* a gluey, gelatinous solution used to glaze surfaces (e.g. of paper), stiffen fabrics, prepare walls for papering etc. ~*v.t.* to coat, glaze or prepare with size. **sizing** *n.* materials for making size. **sizy** *a.* (*comp.* **sizier**, *superl.* **siziest**). **siziness** *n.*

sizzle (siz´əl) *v.i.* **1** to make a hissing noise as of frying. **2** (*coll.*) to be extremely hot. **3** (*coll.*) to be in a rage or in a state of extreme excitement. ~*n.* **1** a hissing noise. **2** a state of heat or excitement. **sizzler** *n.* (*coll.*) **1** a hot day. **2** anything which is striking or racy (e.g. a dress, a novel). **sizzling** *a.* **1** very hot. **2** scurrilous or risqué. ~*adv.* (*coll.*) very, as in *sizzling hot*.

sjambok (sham´bok), **jambok** (jam´-) *n.* (*S Afr.*) a short heavy whip, usu. of rhinoceros hide.

ska (skah) *n.* an early form of reggae music originating in Jamaica.

skag (skag) *n.* (*esp. N Am.*, *sl.*) **1** a cigarette or the stub of one. **2** heroin.

skat (skat) *n.* a three-handed card game resembling piquet.

skate¹ (skāt) *n.* **1** (each of a pair of boots fitted with) a steel blade or runner for gliding on ice, an ice-skate. **2** a four-wheeled device for fitting to the sole of a shoe, for gliding on a smooth surface, a roller skate. **3** a board or plate, often with wheels, for putting under a heavy or cumbersome object to enable it to be moved around. **4** a period of skating. ~*v.i.* to move over ice or a smooth surface on skates. ~*v.t.* to perform or describe (a particular figure) on skates. **to get one's skates on** (*coll.*) to hurry up. **to skate around** to avoid talking about or confronting (an issue, subject etc.) directly. **to skate on thin ice** to take up a risky stance when not altogether certain of one's ground. **to skate over** to gloss over or hurry over (a topic that calls for direct confrontation). **skateboard** *n.* a board mounted on roller-skate wheels on which both feet can be placed when momentum is achieved, propulsion being effected by pushing one foot against the ground. ~*v.i.* to ride on a skateboard. **skateboarder** *n.* **skatepark** *n.* a place designed for skateboarding, with ramps etc. **skater** *n.* **skating rink** *n.* a place with an artificial floor or sheet of ice for skating.

skate² (skāt) *n.* (*pl. in general* **skate**, *in particular* **skates**) a fish of the genus *Raja*, distinguished by having a long pointed snout.

skate³ (skāt) *n.* (*sl.*) a mean or dishonest person.

sked (sked) *n.* (*N Am.*, *coll.*) a schedule. ~*v.t.* (*pres.p.* **skedding**, *past*, *p.p.* **skedded**) to schedule.

skedaddle (skidad´əl) *v.i.* (*coll.*) to run away, as in haste or panic.

skeet (skēt) *n.* a type of clay-pigeon shooting in which targets are hurled in different directions, angles etc. from two traps, to simulate a bird in flight.

skeeter¹ (skē´tə) *n.* (*N Am.*, *Austral.*, *coll.*, *dial.*) a mosquito.

skeeter² SKITTER.

skein (skān) *n.* **1** a quantity of yarn, silk, wool, cotton etc., wound in a coil which is folded over and knotted. **2** something resembling this. **3** a flock of wild geese, swans etc. in flight. **4** a tangle, a web.

skeleton (skel´itən) *n.* **1** the hard supporting or protective framework of an animal or vegetable body, comprising bones, cartilage, shell and other rigid parts. **2** the bones of a person or animal dried, preserved and fastened together in the posture of the living creature. **3** a very lean person or emaciated animal. **4** the supporting framework of any structure. **5** the essential portions, the nucleus (of an organization). **6** an outline or rough draft. **7** all that is left of something when bereft of life or purpose, a hulk. ~*a.* reduced to the essential parts or a minimum. **skeletal** (skel´itəl, skəlē´təl) *a.* **1** of or relating to the skeleton. **2** thin, emaciated. **skeletal muscle** *n.* striated muscle, associated with voluntary movements. **skeleton in the cupboard, skeleton in the closet** *n.* an unpleasant or shameful secret from the past. **skeletonize, skeletonise** *v.t.* **skeleton key** *n.* a key with most of the inner bits removed or filed down, used as a master key or pass-key, or for picking locks.

skep (skep) *n*. **1** a basket or similar receptacle of wicker, wood etc., or the amount it can carry. **2** a beehive of straw or wicker.

skeptic SCEPTIC.

skerrick (sker´ik) *n*. (*esp. Austral., New Zeal.*) a tiny amount.

sketch (skech) *n*. **1** a rough, hasty, unfinished or tentative drawing or painting, often one done in preparation for a larger work. **2** a preliminary study, a rough draft, an outline, a short account without details. **3** a comedy act, or humorous one-scene play, esp. as part of a programme or revue. **4** a one-movement musical composition. **5** a descriptive essay of a brief, unelaborated or slight character. ~*v.t.* **1** to make a sketch of. **2** to present in rough draft or outline without details. ~*v.i.* to make a sketch or sketches. **to sketch in/ out** to indicate roughly or in outline only. **sketchable** *a*. **sketcher** *n*. **sketch map** *n*. a map drawn quickly and roughly, e.g. to show the position of something. **sketchy** *a*. (*comp.* **sketchier,** *superl.* **sketchiest**) **1** like a sketch in being rough or vague, with few details. **2** hasty and inadequate. **sketchily** *adv*. **sketchiness** *n*.

skew (skū) *a*. **1** oblique, slanting, crooked, twisted, turned askew. **2** (*esp. Math.*) distorted, unsymmetrical. ~*n*. **1** a slant or oblique position, an oblique course or movement. **2** (*Math.*) in statistics, skewness. **3** a sloping coping, or a stone supporting the coping of a gable. ~*v.i.* to move sideways, to turn aside, to swerve or twist. ~*v.t.* **1** to make skew. **2** to distort. **on the skew** skewed, slanting, crooked. **skew arch** *n*. an arch (e.g. that of a bridge) set obliquely to its span or abutments. **skewback** *n*. a stone, plate or course of masonry at the top of an abutment taking the spring of an arch. **skew bridge** *n*. a bridge having its arch or arches set obliquely to its span or abutments. **skew chisel** *n*. a chisel that has an oblique edge. **skewed** *a*. **skew gear** *n*. a gear consisting of two cogwheels whose axes are not parallel and do not intersect. **skewness** *n*. **1** the quality of being skew. **2** in statistics, a measure, or the degree, of asymmetry in a frequency distribution. **skew-whiff** *a., adv.* (*coll.*) askew, to one side.

skewbald (skū´bawld) *a*. (of an animal, esp. a horse) with spots of white and a colour other than black, as distinct from piebald. ~*n*. an animal of this colour.

skewer (skū´ə) *n*. **1** a long pin of wood or metal for holding meat together during cooking. **2** a similar implement used for various other purposes. ~*v.t.* **1** to fasten with a skewer. **2** to pierce with or as with a skewer, to transfix. **3** (*esp. NAm.*) to criticize harshly.

ski (skē) *n*. (*pl.* **skis, ski**) **1** either of a pair of long narrow runners of waxed wood, metal, plastic etc., usu. pointed and curved upwards at the front, fastened one to each foot and used for

sliding over snow. **2** a similar piece of apparatus fitted to the underside of a vehicle or aircraft. **3** WATER-SKI (under WATER). ~*a*. for use or wear while skiing. ~*v.i.* (*3rd pers. sing. pres.* **skis,** *pres.p.* **skiing, ski-ing,** *past, p.p.* **skied** (skēd), **ski'd**) to move on skis. ~*v.t.* to ski at (a certain venue) or on (a certain route, slope etc.). **skiable** *a*. **ski-bob** (-bob) *n*. a bicycle-like snow vehicle with a low seat and steering device, supported on two skis. **ski-bobber** *n*. **ski-bobbing** *n*. **skier** *n*. **ski jump** *n*. a ski slope or run surmounted by a ramp from which skiers jump. **ski-jump** *v.i.* to execute a jump from this. **ski jumper** *n*. **ski lift** *n*. any of various forms of lifting apparatus for transporting skiers up a slope (e.g. a chair lift). **ski pole** *n*. a ski stick. **ski run** *n*. a slope for skiing on. **ski slope** *n*. a ski run. **ski stick** *n*. each of a pair of pointed sticks used in skiing to balance or propel.

skid (skid) *v.i.* (*pres.p.* **skidding,** *past, p.p.* **skidded**) **1** (of wheels or vehicles) to slip sideways or diagonally on a slippery surface. **2** to slide or slip. **3** (*coll.*) to decline or fail, or to err or slip up. ~*v.t.* **1** to move, support, check or brake with a skid. **2** to cause to skid. ~*n*. **1** an instance of skidding, a slip on muddy ground, an icy road etc. **2** a support or prop, usu. of wood. **3** a shoe or other device acting as a brake. **4** the runner on the underside of an aircraft. **on the skids 1** (*coll.*) due to be abandoned or defeated. **2** (*coll.*) due to be launched. **to hit the skids** (*coll.*) to deteriorate fast. **to put the skids under 1** (*coll.*) to speed the collapse or departure of. **2** (*coll.*) to hurry (someone) up. **skid-pad** *n*. a slippery area of ground for training drivers to control a skidding vehicle. **skid-pan** *n*. **1** a skid-pad. **2** a shoe or drag usu. put under a wheel as a brake on a slope etc. **skid row** *n*. (*N Am., coll.*) a quarter inhabited by alcoholics and vagrants.

skiff (skif) *n*. a small light boat.

skiffle (skif´əl) *n*. a type of music popular in the 1950s played on unconventional percussion instruments and guitars.

skill (skil) *n*. **1** familiar knowledge of any art or science combined with dexterity. **2** practical mastery of a craft, trade, sport etc., often attained by training. **3** tact, diplomacy. **skilful,** (*N Am.*) **skillful** *a*. **1** having or showing skill (at or in something). **2** requiring or involving skill. **skilfully** *adv*. **skilfulness** *n*. **skilled** *a*. **1** having skill, skilful (in or at something). **2** (of a worker) experienced, highly trained. **3** (of a job) involving or requiring skill or specialized training. **skill-less, †skilless** *a*.

skillet (skil´it) *n*. **1** a long-handled cooking pot. **2** (*N Am.*) a frying pan.

skim (skim) *v.t.* (*pres.p.* **skimming,** *past, p.p.* **skimmed**) **1** to clear the scum etc. from the surface of. **2** to take (cream etc.) from the surface of a liquid. **3** to touch lightly or nearly touch the surface of, to graze. **4** to throw so as to cause to graze or pass lightly over a surface. **5** to glance over or read superficially. **6** to deal with cursorily. **7** (*N Am.*, *sl.*) to redirect or conceal (income) to avoid tax. ~*v.i.* **1** to pass lightly and rapidly (over or along a surface). **2** to glance (over or through) rapidly and superficially. ~*n.* **1** the act or process of skimming. **2** the thick matter which forms on or is removed from, the surface of a liquid, scum. **skimmer** *n.* **1** someone who or something that skims. **2** a perforated ladle for skimming. **3** a flat, usu. broad-brimmed, straw hat. **4** a bird of the N American genus *Rhynchops*, which takes small fishes from the water by flying along with its lower mandible under the surface. **skim milk, skimmed milk** *n.* milk from which the cream has been skimmed.

skimp (skimp) *v.t.* **1** to supply in a niggardly manner, to stint (a person, provisions etc.). **2** to perform with insufficient attention or inadequate effort. ~*v.i.* to be stingy or parsimonious. **skimpingly** *adv.* **skimpy** *a.* (*comp.* **skimpier**, *superl.* **skimpiest**) **1** meagre, inadequate. **2** (of clothing) covering the body minimally, scanty, short or tight. **skimpily** *adv.* **skimpiness** *n.*

skin (skin) *n.* **1** the natural membraneous outer covering of an animal body. **2** the hide or integument of an animal removed from the body, with or without the hair. **3** one's colouring or complexion (*people with fair skins*). **4** a vessel made of the skin of an animal for holding liquids (e.g. wine). **5** the outer layer or covering of a plant, fruit etc. **6** a film, e.g. the skinlike film that forms on certain liquids. **7** a membrane. **8** the outer layer or covering of an object, structure etc. **9** the outer cladding of a vessel, rocket etc. ~*v.t.* (*pres.p.* **skinning**, *past*, *p.p.* **skinned**) **1** to strip the skin from, to flay, to peel. **2** to graze (e.g. one's knee). **3** to cover (over) with or as with skin. **4** (*sl.*) to cheat, to swindle. ~*v.i.* to become covered (over) with skin, to cicatrize. **by/ with the skin of one's teeth** very narrowly, by a close shave. **no skin off someone's nose** making no difference to someone, possibly even encouraging rather than perturbing to someone. **to be skin and bone** to be extremely thin or emaciated. **to get under one's skin** to interest or annoy one intensely. **to have a thick skin** to be impervious to insults or criticism. **to have a thin skin** to be sensitive to slights or criticism. **to save one's skin** to escape injury, to get off unscathed. **to the skin** right through one's clothing, as in *soaked to the skin*. **skincare** *n.* the care and protection of the skin and complexion through the use of beauty products and cosmetics. **skin-deep** *a.* superficial, not deep. ~*adv.* superficially. **skin diver** *n.* someone who dives in deep water usu. with flippers and an aqualung, but no diving suit, as, orig., a pearl-diver. **skin-diving** *n.* **skin-flick** *n.* (*sl.*) an overtly pornographic film that features nudity and sex scenes. **skinflint** *n.* a niggardly person, a miser. **skinful** *n.* (*pl.* **skinfuls**) (*sl.*) enough alcohol to intoxicate one. **skin graft**

n. the transfer of skin from a sound to a disfigured or injured part. **skin-grafting** *n.* **skinhead** *n.* **1** a young person with close-cropped hair, esp. as a member of a gang of aggressive and often racist youths wearing heavy-duty boots and braces. **2** (*N Am.*) a recruit in the Marines. **skinless** *a.* **skinlike** *a.* **skinned** *a.* **skinner** *n.* **skinny** *a.* (*comp.* **skinnier**, *superl.* **skinniest**) **1** very lean or thin. **2** (of garments, esp. knitted ones) tight-fitting. **3** resembling skin. **skinniness** *n.* **skinny-dip** *v.i.* (*pres.p.* **skinny-dipping**, *past*, *p.p.* **skinny-dipped**) (*coll.*) to swim in the nude. **skin test** *n.* a test performed on the skin to determine its resistance to disease or to detect substances liable to cause an allergic reaction. **skintight** *a.* (of garments) tight, clinging.

skink (skingk) *n.* a small lizard of the family Scincidae, of Africa and SW Asia.

skint (skint) *a.* (*sl.*) hard up for money, penniless.

skip[1] (skip) *v.i.* (*pres.p.* **skipping**, *past*, *p.p.* **skipped**) **1** to progress by hopping on each foot in turn. **2** to move about with light bounds or capers. **3** to jump repeatedly over a skipping rope. **4** to pass rapidly (from one thing to another). **5** to make omissions. **6** (*sl.*) to make off hurriedly, to bolt (off), to abscond. ~*v.t.* **1** to cause (a stone) to skim over water, bouncing off its surface at intervals. **2** to miss deliberately, to absent oneself from (a meal, a class etc.). **3** (*esp. N Am.*) to leave (town) quickly and quietly, to abscond from. ~*n.* **1** a step and a hop on one foot, or a type of forward movement hopping on each foot in turn. **2** a light leap or spring. **3** an act of omitting, leaving out or passing over. **skip it!** (*coll.*) forget it! never mind! **skipjack** *n.* **1** any of various kinds of fish that jump out of the water. **2** (*also* **skipjack tuna**) a striped tropical tuna, *Katsuwonus pelamis*, important as a food fish. **skipper**[1] *n.* **skipping** *n.* the act, recreation or exercise of jumping over a rope repeatedly. **skipping rope**, (*N Am.*) **skip-rope** *n.* a rope or cord used for skipping over as a game or form of physical exercise.

skip[2] (skip) *n.* **1** a container for collecting and moving refuse, building materials etc. **2** a box cage or bucket lift in a mine for hoisting people or materials.

skip[3] (skip) *n.* in bowls or curling, the captain of a side. ~*v.t.* (*pres.p.* **skipping**, *past*, *p.p.* **skipped**) to be the skip of (a side).

skipper[1] SKIP[1].

skipper[2] (skip′ə) *n.* **1** a sea captain, the master of a vessel. **2** the captain of a team or side. **3** an aircraft captain. ~*v.t.* to act as skipper of.

skirl (skœl) *n.* (*Sc.*) the shrill sound of the bagpipes. ~*v.i.* (of bagpipes) to produce their characteristic shrill sound.

skirmish (skœ′mish) *n.* **1** a slight or irregular fight, esp. between small parties or scattered troops. **2** a struggle, esp. of a preliminary or minor nature. ~*v.i.* to engage in a skirmish. **skirmisher** *n.*

skirt (skœt) *n.* **1** a woman's garment hanging from the waist. **2** the part of a dress or coat hanging below the waist. **3** the outer flap surrounding the base of a hovercraft. **4** a part of an aircraft or vehicle that hides and protects the wheels or underside. **5** the flap of a saddle. **6** (*often pl.*) the edge, border, margin or outer extremities of something. **7** a cut of beef from the flank. **8** the diaphragm and other membranes as a meat dish. **9** (*sl., offensive*) a woman or girl as a sexual object. ~*v.t.* **1** to lie or go along or by the edge of. **2** to pass round (the edge of), to avoid. **3** to border. ~*v.i.* to lie or move (along, round the side or edge of something). **skirted** *a.* **skirting** *n.* **1** a skirting board. **2** material suitable for skirts. **3** (*pl., Austral., New Zeal.*) the inferior parts of wool trimmed from a fleece. **skirting board** *n.* a narrow board running round the bottom of the wall of a room. **skirtless** *a.*

skit (skit) *n.* a satirical piece, lampoon or humorous theatrical sketch (on a certain situation or topic).

skite (skīt) *v.i.* (*Austral., New Zeal., coll.*) to boast or brag. ~*n.* **1** a braggart or boaster. **2** boastful talk, swagger.

skitter (skit´ə), **skeeter** (skē´tə) *v.i.* **1** to glide, skim or skip rapidly (esp. along a surface). **2** to dart or scurry (about, off). **skittery** *a.* nervous, restless, fidgety.

skittish (skit´ish) *a.* **1** (of horses) excitable, nervous, easily frightened. **2** capricious, uncertain, coquettish, wanton, too lively. **skittishly** *adv.* **skittishness** *n.*

skittle (skit´əl) *n.* **1** any one of the pins set up to be bowled at in skittles or ninepins. **2** (*pl.*) ninepin bowling, a game in which nine wooden pins are set up at the far end of an alley, and the player has to knock as many as possible down by bowling a wooden ball or disc at them. **3** TABLE SKITTLES. ~*v.i.* to play at ninepins. **to skittle out** in cricket, to dismiss (batsmen) in quick succession.

skive[1] (skīv) *v.t.* **1** to split (leather) into thin layers. **2** to shave or pare (hides).

skive[2] (skīv) *v.i.* (*coll.*) **1** to avoid performing a duty, task etc. **2** to take time (off work or school) illicitly. ~*n.* **1** a period of shirking or an evasion of duty etc. **2** a task or piece of work etc. which is far from onerous. **skiver** *n.*

skivvy (skiv´i) *n.* (*pl.* **skivvies**) (*sl., derog.*) **1** a maid or general servant. **2** a person who does menial work. ~*v.i.* (*3rd pers. sing. pres.* **skivvies**, *pres.p.* **skivvying**, *past, p.p.* **skivvied**) to work as a skivvy, do menial work (for someone).

skua (skū´ə) *n.* (*pl.* **skuas**) a dark-coloured predatory seabird of the family Stercorariidae, allied to the gulls.

skulduggery (skŭldŭg´əri), **sculduggery, skull-duggery** *n.* (*coll.*) underhand behaviour, trickery, cheating or malpractice.

skulk (skŭlk) *v.i.* **1** to lurk, to withdraw and conceal oneself. **2** to sneak away, esp. from duty, work, danger etc. **skulker** *n.*

skull (skŭl) *n.* **1** the bony case enclosing the brain, the cranium. **2** the whole head, esp. as part of the skeleton, without skin or soft tissue. **3** an image or representation of this. **out of one's skull 1** (*sl.*) out of one's mind, crazy. **2** (*sl.*) helplessly drunk. **skull and crossbones** *n.* (*usu. sing.*) a representation of a human skull surmounting two crossed thigh bones, used as an emblem of death or danger. **skullcap** *n.* **1** a light, brimless cap fitting closely to the head. **2** the sinciput. **3** a plant of the genus *Scutellaria*, with blue, helmet-shaped flowers. **skulled** *a.*

Usage note See note under SCULL.

skunk (skŭngk) *n.* **1** a N American carnivorous quadruped, *Mephitis mephitica*, with a bushy tail and white stripes down the back, which when on the defence ejects a fetid secretion from the anal glands. **2** the pelt of this animal. **3** (*coll., offensive*) a base or obnoxious person. **skunk-cabbage** *n.* (*N Am.*) either of two plants of the arum family, *Symplocarpus foetidus* or *Lysichitum americanum*, which give off a fetid odour.

sky (skī) *n.* (*pl.* **skies**) (*used in sing. or pl.*) **1** the apparent vault of heaven, the firmament. **2** the upper region of the atmosphere, the region of clouds. **3** the climate, the weather. **4** the celestial regions, the heavens. ~*v.t.* (*3rd pers. sing. pres.* **skies**, *pres.p.* **skying**, *past, p.p.* **skied**) **1** to hit (a ball) high into the air. **2** to hang (a picture) in the top tier at an exhibition. **to the skies** lavishly, extravagantly (*praise someone to the skies*). **under the open sky** outside, out of doors. **sky-blue** *n., a.* (of) a pale blue. **skydive** *v.i.* to jump from an aircraft and delay opening the parachute, esp. in order to execute acrobatic manoeuvres. ~*n.* an instance of this. **skydiver** *n.* **skyey, skiey** *a.* **sky-high** *adv., a.* high as the sky, very high. **skyjack** (-jak) *v.t.* to hijack (an aircraft). ~*n.* an act of skyjacking. **skyjacker** *n.* **skylark** *n.* a lark, *Alauda arvensis*, that flies singing high into the air. ~*v.i.* (*coll.*) to lark, to frolic, to play practical jokes etc. **skyless** *a.* **skylight** *n.* a window set in a roof or ceiling. **skyline** *n.* the outline against the sky of the configuration of the land or buildings. **sky pilot** *n.* (*sl.*) a clergyman, a priest, a preacher. **skyrocket** *n.* a rocket. ~*v.i.* (*pres.p.* **skyrocketing**, *past, p.p.* **skyrocketed**) to rise rapidly to a high level. **skyscape** *n.* a picture or view chiefly of the sky or clouds. **skyscraper** *n.* **1** a very high multi-storeyed building. **2** a triangular skysail. **sky-sign** *n.* an advertisement on a roof. **skywalk** *n.* a high-level covered walkway bridging two buildings. **skyward** *a., adv.* **skywards** *adv.* **skyway** *n.* **1** a route or lane used by aircraft. **2** the sky as a means of transport. **3** SKYWALK (under SKY). **sky-writing** *n.* (the formation of) writing, esp. for advertising purposes, traced in the sky by smoke discharged from an aeroplane. **sky-writer** *n.*

slab (slab) *n.* **1** a thin, flat, regularly shaped piece of anything, esp. of stone, concrete etc. **2** a large slice of bread, cake etc. **3** the outside piece sawn from a log in squaring the side. **4** (*Austral., New Zeal.*) a plank. **5** the table on which a corpse is laid out in a mortuary.

slack[1] (slak) *a.* **1** not drawn tight, loose. **2** limp, relaxed. **3** careless, negligent. **4** (of trade or the market) sluggish, slow. **5** (of the tide) neither ebbing nor flowing. **6** in phonetics, pronounced with relaxed vocal muscles. ~*n.* **1** the part of a rope etc. that hangs loose. **2** a slack period in trade etc. **3** a lazy fit, a spell of inactivity. **4** a cessation of flow, slack water. **5** (*pl.*) loosely cut casual trousers. ~*v.i.* **1** to abate. **2** to become loose or looser. **3** to become slower, to fail. **4** to neglect, or take a break from, one's work, to become remiss or lazy. ~*v.t.* **1** to slow. **2** to lessen. **3** to cause to abate. **4** to loosen, to relax. **to slack off 1** to loosen, to reduce the tension on (a rope etc.). **2** to lose speed or momentum. **to slack up 1** to slow down (a train) before stopping. **2** to ease off. **to take up the slack 1** to gather up the loose portion of a rope. **2** to use surplus resources or time to good effect. **slacken** *v.i., v.t.* to become or make slack or slacker. **to slacken off** to slack off. **slacker** *n.* a shirker, a lazy or remiss person. **slackly** *adv.* **slackness** *n.*

slack[2] (slak) *n.* small pieces of coal, or coal dust.

slag (slag) *n.* **1** the fused refuse or dross separated in the reduction of ores, clinker. **2** volcanic scoria. **3** a mixture of mineral dross and dust produced in coal mining. **4** (*sl., offensive*) a slovenly or immoral woman. ~*v.i.* (*pres.p.* **slagging**, *past, p.p.* **slagged**) to form slag, to combine in a slaggy mass. ~*v.t.* **1** to convert into slag. **2** (*sl.*) to criticize, to disparage. **to slag off** (*sl.*) to make disparaging remarks about. **slaggy** *a.* (*comp.* **slaggier**, *superl.* **slaggiest**). **slagheap** *n.* a hill or heap of waste material produced in coal mining.

slain SLAY.

slake (slāk) *v.t.* **1** to quench, to assuage, to satisfy, to appease (one's thirst, desire etc.). **2** to mix (lime) with water so as to form a chemical combination. **slakeable, slakable** *a.* **slaked lime** *n.* calcium hydroxide, produced by adding water to quicklime.

slalom (slah´ləm) *n.* **1** a downhill ski race on a zigzagged course marked with artificial obstacles. **2** a similarly zigzagged obstacle race in canoes or vehicles, or on water-skis or skateboards.

slam[1] (slam) *v.t.* (*pres.p.* **slamming**, *past, p.p.* **slammed**) **1** to shut (a door, lid etc.) suddenly with a loud noise. **2** to put (a thing down on a surface) thus. **3** (*coll.*) to thrash, to defeat completely. **4** (*coll.*) to criticize severely. **5** to put into action suddenly or violently (*He slammed the brakes on*). ~*v.i.* **1** (of a door) to shut violently or noisily. **2** (*coll.*) to move, esp. to enter or leave, angrily or violently (*She slammed out of the room*). ~*n.* **1** a noise as of the violent shutting of a door. **2** an act of slamming. **3** (*N Am., sl.*)

prison. **slam dunk, slamdunk** *n.* in basketball, the action of jumping high and ramming the ball down through the basket. **slammer** *n.* (*sl.*) prison.

slam[2] (slam) *n.* in whist etc., the winning of every trick (a *grand slam*), or all but one trick (a *little slam* or *small slam*). ~*v.t.* (*pres.p.* **slamming**, *past, p.p.* **slammed**) to beat (one's opponents) by achieving a slam.

slander (slahn´də) *n.* **1** a false statement maliciously uttered to injure a person. **2** the making of malicious and untrue statements, defamation. **3** (*Law*) false defamatory language or statements. ~*v.t.* to injure by the malicious utterance of a false report. **slanderer** *n.* **slanderous** *a.* **slanderously** *adv.* **slanderousness** *n.*

slang (slang) *n.* very informal vocabulary or phraseology that would be out of place in a formal context, and is often confined to a specific context, culture or profession. ~*a.* of the nature of slang (*slang expressions*). ~*v.i.* to use slang. ~*v.t.* to abuse with slang. **slanging** *n.,* *a.* **slanging match** *n.* a quarrel in which strong insults are exchanged. **slangy** *a.* (*comp.* **slangier**, *superl.* **slangiest**). **slangily** *adv.* **slanginess** *n.*

slant (slahnt) *v.i.* **1** to slope. **2** to incline from or be oblique to a vertical or horizontal line. **3** to be biased (towards). ~*v.t.* **1** to cause to slant. **2** to present (a report etc.) in a biased or unfair way. ~*a.* sloping, oblique. ~*n.* **1** a slope. **2** inclination from the vertical or horizontal. **3** an oblique line, a solidus. **4** an angle of approach, a point of view. **5** a bias or unfair emphasis. **on a/the slant** sloping, aslant. **slantly, slantways, slantwise** *adv.*

slap (slap) *v.t.* (*pres.p.* **slapping**, *past, p.p.* **slapped**) **1** to strike with the open hand, to smack. **2** to lay or throw forcefully or quickly (*He slapped a note on the counter*). **3** to put (on) or apply hastily (*She slapped on some make-up*). ~*n.* a blow, esp. with the open hand. ~*adv.* with the suddenness and impact of a slap, headlong, slap bang. **to slap down** to rebuff or rebuke curtly and unequivocally. **to slap on the back** to congratulate. **slap and tickle** *n.* flirtatious romping, kissing and cuddling. **slap bang** *adv.* **1** suddenly, violently, headlong. **2** exactly, precisely. **3** conspicuously, in an obvious position. **slapdash** *a.* hasty, impetuous, careless, happy-go-lucky. ~*adv.* in a careless, rash, impetuous manner. **slap-happy** *a.* **1** careless, irresponsible. **2** happy-go-lucky, carefree. **3** punch-drunk. **slap in the face** *n.* a rebuff. **slap on the back** *n.* an offer of congratulations. **slap on the wrist** *n.* a reprimand. **slapstick** *n.* **1** broad comedy or knockabout farce. **2** a clown's implement that makes a noise like a resounding slap when used to strike someone. ~*a.* of, relating to or in the style of slapstick. **slap-up** *a.* (*coll.*) **1** first-rate. **2** lavish.

slash (slash) *v.t.* **1** to cut by striking violently at random. **2** to make long incisions or narrow gashes in. **3** to reduce (prices etc.) drastically. **4** to criticize severely. **5 a** to lash (with a whip etc.). **b** to crack (a whip). ~*v.i.* **1** to strike (at etc.) violently and at random with a knife, sword etc. **2** (of a tail etc.) to lash. ~*n.* **1** a long cut or incision. **2** a slashing cut or stroke. **3** a solidus. **4** (*sl.*) an act of urinating. **slasher** *n.* **1** a person or thing that slashes. **2** a slasher film or movie. **slasher film, slasher movie** *n.* a film showing violent knife attacks.

slat (slat) *n.* a thin narrow strip, usu. of wood or metal, used in Venetian blinds, crates etc. **slatted** *a.*

slate[1] (slāt) *n.* **1** a fine-grained laminated rock easily splitting into thin, smooth, even slabs. **2** a slab or trimmed piece of this, esp. for use as a roofing-tile. **3** a tablet of slate, usu. with a wooden frame, for writing on. **4** (*esp. N Am.*) a preliminary list of candidates liable to revision. **5** the colour of slate, a dull blue-grey. ~*v.t.* **1** to cover or roof with slates. **2** (*esp. N Am.*) to place (a candidate) on a list. ~*a.* **1** made or consisting of slate. **2** slate-coloured. **on the slate** on credit, on the tab, recorded as a debt. **to have a slate loose** (*coll.*) to be slightly mentally unbalanced. **to wipe the slate clean** to start afresh, to erase past crimes, errors etc. **slate-black, slate-grey** *a.* of the dark, blue or grey colour characteristic of slate. **slate-pencil** *n.* a stick of soft slate for writing on slates with. **slater** *n.* **1** a person who slates roofs. **2** a woodlouse. **slating** *n.* **slaty** *a.* (*comp.* **slatier**, *superl.* **slatiest**). **slatiness** *n.*

slate[2] (slāt) *v.t.* to criticize savagely, to abuse, to berate.

slattern (slat´ən) *n.* an untidy or sluttish woman. **slatternly** *a.* **slatternliness** *n.*

slaughter (slaw´tə) *n.* **1** the killing of animals for market. **2** wholesale or indiscriminate killing. ~*v.t.* **1** to kill wantonly or ruthlessly, to massacre. **2** to kill (animals) for market. **3** (*coll.*) to defeat decisively. **slaughterer** *n.* **slaughterhouse** *n.* a place where beasts are slaughtered, a shambles. **slaughterous** *a.* **slaughterously** *adv.*

Slav (slahv) *n.* a member of any of various peoples inhabiting eastern Europe who speak a Slavonic language, including the Russians, Poles, Serbs, Croats, Bulgarians and Slovenes. ~*a.* **1** of or relating to the Slavs. **2** Slavonic. **Slavic** *a.*, *n.* Slavonic. **Slavonic** (sləvon´-) *a.* **1** of or relating to a group of languages belonging to the Indo-European family including Russian, Bulgarian, Polish, Serbo-Croat and Czech etc. **2** of or relating to the peoples who speak these languages. ~*n.* the Slavonic group of languages.

slave (slāv) *n.* **1** a person who is the property of and bound in obedience to another. **2** a person who is entirely under the domination (of another person), the influence (of e.g. fashion) or a helpless victim (to a habit, drugs etc.). **3** a person who works like a slave esp. for low wages, a drudge. **4** a machine or device which is entirely controlled by another, or imitates the action of a similar device. ~*v.i.* to toil like a slave, to drudge. **slave-driver** *n.* **1** an overseer of slaves. **2** an

exacting or over-demanding taskmaster. **slave-drive** *v.t.* **slave-holder** *n.* a person who owns slaves. **slave-holding** *n.* **slave labour,** (*N Am.*) **slave labor** *n.* (the work of) people employed as or like slaves. **slavelike** *a.* **slaver**[1] *n.* **1** a person who deals in slaves. **2** a slave ship. **slavery** (-vəri) *n.* **1** the condition of being a slave. **2** the practice of owning slaves. **slave ship** *n.* a vessel engaged in the slave trade. **slave trade** *n.* the trade of procuring, buying and transporting slaves, esp. from Africa to America in the 16th–18th cents. **slave trader** *n.* **slavish** *a.* **1** of or relating to or characteristic of a slave. **2** subservient, servile, base, abject, ignoble. **3** entirely imitative, devoid of originality. **slavishly** *adv.* **slavishness** *n.*

slaver[1] SLAVE.

slaver[2] (slav´ə) *v.i.* **1** to let saliva flow from the mouth, to slabber, to dribble. **2** to fawn, to flatter, to drool. ~*n.* **1** saliva dribbling from the mouth. **2** (*coll.*) nonsense, drivel. **slaverer** *n.*

Slavic SLAV.

Slavonic SLAV.

slaw (slaw) *n.* (*N Am.*) sliced cabbage served as a salad, coleslaw.

slay (slā) *v.t.* (*past* **slew** (sloo), *p.p.* **slain** (slān)) **1** to put to death, to kill. **2** (*coll.*) **a** (*past, p.p. also* **slayed**) to impress powerfully. **b** to amuse to an overwhelming degree. **slayer** *n.*

sleaze (slēz) *n.* (*coll.*) **1** that which is squalid, distasteful, disreputable, esp. with reference to corrupt behaviour by politicians. **2** sleazy conditions, sleaziness. **3** a person of doubtful morality. **sleazeball, sleazebag** *n.* (*sl.*) a morally disreputable person. **sleazy** *a.* (*comp.* **sleazier**, *superl.* **sleaziest**) **1** squalid or seedy (*sleazy nightclubs*). **2** slatternly. **3** (of fabric) thin, wanting in substance, flimsy. **sleazily** *adv.* **sleaziness** *n.*

sled (sled) *n.* (*N Am.*) a sledge. ~*v.i.* (*pres.p.* **sledding**, *past, p.p.* **sledded**) to travel by sled. ~*v.t.* to convey by sled.

sledge[1] (slej) *n.* **1** a vehicle on runners instead of wheels, used for carrying passengers or hauling loads etc., esp. over snow or ice, drawn variously by dogs, horses, reindeer or people; a sleigh. **2** a toboggan. ~*v.i.* to travel by sledge. ~*v.t.* to carry or convey on a sledge. **sledger** *n.*

sledge[2] (slej) *n.* a sledgehammer. **sledgehammer** *n.* a heavy hammer wielded by both hands. ~*a.* (of a blow etc.) imitating the action of a sledgehammer, clumsy, hard-hitting.

sleek (slēk) *a.* **1** (of fur, skin etc.) smooth, glossy. **2** well-groomed and well-fed, prosperous-looking. **3** unctuous, smooth-spoken. ~*v.t.* to make (hair etc.) sleek. **sleeken** *v.t.* **sleekly** *adv.* **sleekness** *n.* **sleeky** *a.* (*comp.* **sleekier**, *superl.* **sleekiest**).

sleep (slēp) *n.* **1** a state of rest in which consciousness is almost entirely suspended, the body is relaxed, the eyes are closed, and the vital functions are inactive. **2** a period or spell of this (*have a short sleep*). **3** a state with the characteristics of sleep, such as rest, death or the hibernating state of certain animals. **4** (*coll.*) mucous matter which collects at the corner of the eye, esp. during sleep. ~*v.i.* (*past, p.p.* **slept** (slept)) **1** to take rest in sleep. **2** to be or lie dormant, inactive or in abeyance. **3** to be dead. **4** to fall asleep. ~*v.t.* **1** to spend (time) in sleep (*slept the night on the floor*; *sleep the whole morning away*). **2** to provide with accommodation for sleeping, to lodge (a certain number). **3** to rest in (sleep, as cognate object). **in one's sleep** while asleep (*talks in her sleep*). **to get to sleep** to manage to go to sleep. **to go to sleep** to fall asleep. **to put to sleep 1** to anaesthetize. **2** (*euphem.*) to kill (an animal) painlessly, usu. by injection. **to sleep around** (*coll.*) to be sexually promiscuous. **to sleep in 1** to sleep on the premises. **2** to oversleep. **to sleep off** to rid or recover from (e.g. the effects of alcohol) by sleeping. **to sleep on it** to postpone making a decision until the next day. **to sleep out 1** to sleep out of doors. **2** to have one's sleeping accommodation away from one's place of work. **to sleep over** to spend the night where one is visiting. **to sleep rough** to sleep out of doors, esp. on the street. **to sleep together/with** (*euphem.*) to have sexual intercourse (with), esp. in bed. **sleeper** *n.* **1** a person who sleeps, or is asleep. **2** a wooden beam or other support for the rails on a railway track. **3** a sleeping berth, compartment or carriage on a train. **4** a train with these. **5** a small stud or hoop earring worn to keep the hole in a pierced ear open. **6** a sleeping suit. **7** (*coll.*) a person (e.g. a secret agent) who lies dormant before coming into action. **8** (*coll.*) something (e.g. a film, a book) which becomes valuable or popular after a period of being neither. **sleeping** *a., n.* **sleeping bag** *n.* a padded bag of warm material for sleeping in, esp. when camping. **sleeping car, sleeping carriage** *n.* a railway carriage fitted with berths for sleeping in. **sleeping draught** *n.* a drink containing a drug to make one go to sleep. **sleeping partner** *n.* a partner having no share in the management of a business, a silent partner. **sleeping pill** *n.* a sedative in tablet form for inducing sleep. **sleeping policeman** *n.* (*pl.* **sleeping policemen**) (*coll.*) a hump on the surface of a road for slowing traffic. **sleeping sickness** *n.* a disease characterized by fever and mental and physical lethargy, almost always fatal, endemic in tropical Africa, and caused by a parasite *Trypanosoma gambiense*. **sleeping suit** *n.* a baby's one-piece suit for sleeping in. **sleepless** *a.* **1** unable to sleep. **2** (of a night) during which one cannot get to sleep. **3** constantly watchful and active. **sleeplessly** *adv.* **sleeplessness** *n.* **sleepwalk** *v.i.* to walk about or perform actions while asleep. **sleepwalker** *n.* **sleepwalking** *n.* **sleepy** *a.* (*comp.* **sleepier,** *superl.* **sleepiest**) **1** inclined to sleep, drowsy. **2** lazy, habitually inactive. **3** tending to induce sleep. **sleepily** *adv.* **sleepiness** *n.* **sleepyhead** *n.* a lazy or sleepy person.

sleet (slēt) *n.* hail or snow mingled with rain. ~*v.i.* to snow or hail with a mixture of rain. **sleety** *a.* (*comp.* **sleetier,** *superl.* **sleetiest**). **sleetiness** *n.*

sleeve (slēv) *n.* **1** the part of a garment that covers the arm. **2** the cardboard cover for a gramophone record. **3** a tube, pipe or cylindrical sheath enclosing a revolving shaft, connecting lengths of pipe etc. **4** a windsock. ~*v.t.* to provide or fit with a sleeve or sleeves. **to have up one's sleeve** to hold secretly in reserve or in readiness. **to roll up one's sleeves** to get ready for hard work, a fight etc. **sleeved** *a.* **sleeveless** *a.* **sleeving** *n.* the outer insulating cover on an electric cable.

sleigh (slā) *n.* a vehicle mounted on runners for driving over snow or ice, a sledge, esp. for carrying passengers rather than goods. ~*v.i.* to travel by sleigh. **sleigh bell** *n.* any of a set of small bells hung on a sleigh or its harness.

sleight (slīt) *n.* **1** dexterity, skill in manipulating things. **2** a trick or stratagem so dexterously performed as to escape detection. **3** trickery, cunning. **sleight of hand** *n.* deceptive movement of the hands, esp. in conjuring, legerdemain.

slender (slen´də) *a.* (*comp.* **slenderer,** *superl.* **slenderest**) **1** small in circumference or width as compared with length. **2** attractively or gracefully thin. **3** slight, inadequate. **4** (of hopes etc.) not strong or well-founded. **slenderize, slenderise** *v.t.* to make slender or slim. ~*v.i.* to slim. **slender loris** *n.* one of two types of loris, *Loris tardigradus.* **slenderly** *adv.* **slenderness** *n.*

slept SLEEP.

sleuth (slooth) *n.* (*coll.*) a detective. ~*v.i.* to act as a detective. ~*v.t.* to track or investigate. **sleuthhound** *n.* **1** a bloodhound. **2** (*coll.*) a detective.

slew[1] SLAY.

slew[2] (sloo), **slue** *v.t., v.i.* to turn, twist or swing (round, about etc.) as on a pivot. ~*n.* such a turn or twist.

slew[3] (sloo), **slue** *n.* (*N Am., coll.*) a great quantity or large number.

slice (slīs) *n.* **1** a broad thin piece cut off, esp. from bread etc., or a wedge cut from a circular pie, tart, cake etc. **2** a part, share etc., separated or allotted from a larger quantity. **3** a spatula or other similarly shaped blade for lifting fish etc. from a frying pan or for serving it. **4** a slicing stroke in tennis or golf. ~*v.t.* **1** to cut (*usu.* up) into broad, thin pieces. **2** to cut (off) slices from. **3** to cut, to divide. **4** to strike (a ball) with a drawing motion so that it curves to the right (or to the left for a left-handed player). ~*v.i.* to cut (through a medium) with a slicing action. **sliceable** *a.* **slicer** *n.* **slice of life** *n.* an experience that brings home the grim realities of life.

slick (slik) *a.* **1** (*coll.*) dexterous, adroit. **2** neatly or deftly performed. **3** clever, smart, specious. **4** oily, smooth of speech, glib etc. **5** smooth, sleek. **6** polished, glossy. ~*n.* **1** a smooth or slippery surface patch, esp. of oil spilt on water. **2** a smooth racing-car tyre. ~*v.t.* to make smooth or sleek, esp. to flatten or smooth (the hair back or down). **slicker** *n.* (*N Am.*) **1** a waterproof, an oilskin. **2** (*coll.*) a plausible, cunning person, a swindler. **3** CITY SLICKER (under CITY). **slickly** *adv.* **slickness** *n.*

slide (slīd) *v.i.* (*past* **slid** (slid), *p.p.* **slid**, †**slidden** (-dən)) **1** to move smoothly along a surface with continuous contact, esp. to glide over ice, snow or other slippery surface, without skates. **2** to pass (away, into etc.) smoothly, gradually or imperceptibly. **3** to move secretly or unobtrusively. **4** to glide or gloss (over a subject best avoided). ~*v.t.* **1** to cause to move smoothly along with a slippery motion (*slid the glass across the bar*). **2** to cause to move or slip unobtrusively (*She slid her hand into his*). ~*n.* **1 a** an act of sliding. **b** a downward turn (e.g. in value), a rapid deterioration. **2** a piece or part that slides (e.g. on a machine). **3** a thin glass plate carrying an object to be viewed in a microscope. **4** a photographic transparency mounted in card or plastic, for projection on to a screen. **5** a surface, series of grooves, guide-bars etc., on which a part slides, a slideway. **6** an inclined channel, chute etc., esp. which children slide down for fun. **7** a polished track on ice for people to slide on. **8** a prepared slope on snow for tobogganing. **9** a landslip. **10** a clasp for the hair. **11** a series of musical tones passing smoothly one into another. **to let things slide** to leave things undone, or take no positive action over them, to allow things to deteriorate. **slidable** *a.* **slide fastener** *n.* (*N Am.*) a zip fastener. **slider** *n.* **slide rule** *n.* a device, consisting of one rule sliding within another, whereby several mathematical processes can be performed mechanically. **slideway** *n.* in machinery etc., the projection, channel or grooves along which a sliding part moves. **sliding scale** *n.* a scale of duties, prices, wages etc., varying directly or inversely according to fluctuations of value or other conditions.

slight (slīt) *a.* (*comp.* **slighter**, *superl.* **slightest**) **1** inconsiderable, insignificant. **2** small in amount, intensity etc. **3** inadequate, negligible. **4** frail, weak. **5** (of a person's figure) small and slender. **6** (*in superl.*) (*usu. with neg. or interrog.*) the least (*hadn't the slightest inkling this would happen*). ~*n.* an act of disregard, disrespect or neglect, a snub. ~*v.t.* **1** to treat, or speak about, as of little importance, to disregard. **2** to treat disrespectfully, to snub. **slighter** *n.* **slightingly** *adv.* **slightish** *a.* **slightly** *adv.* **slightness** *n.*

slily SLYLY (under SLY).

slim (slim) *a.* (*comp.* **slimmer**, *superl.* **slimmest**) **1** tall and narrow in shape. **2** slender, gracefully thin, of slight shape or build. **3** poor, slight, inadequate. **4** slick, crafty, clever. ~*v.i.* (*pres.p.* **slimming**, *past, p.p.* **slimmed**) to diet and exercise in order to become slimmer. ~*v.t.* to make slim or slimmer. **slimline** *a.* **1** slim in shape. **2** (of a drink etc.) aiding slimness. **slimly** *adv.* **slimmer** *n.* **slimmish** *a.* **slimness** *n.*

slime (slīm) *n.* any soft, glutinous or viscous substance, esp. mucus or soft, moist and sticky earth. ~*v.t.* to smear or cover with slime. **slime mould,** (*N Am.*) **slime mold** *n.* a myxomycete or other micro-organism that secretes slime. **slimy** *a.* (*comp.* **slimier**, *superl.* **slimiest**) **1** consisting of, or of the nature of, slime. **2** covered with or abounding in slime. **3** slippery, difficult to grasp. **4** repulsively mean or cringing. **slimily** *adv.* **sliminess** *n.*

sling[1] (sling) *n.* **1** a band or other arrangement of rope, chains etc., for suspending, hoisting or transferring anything. **2** a band of cloth for supporting an injured arm, suspended from the neck. **3** a short leather strap having a string at each end for hurling a small missile by hand. **4** an act of slinging. ~*v.t.* (*past, p.p.* **slung** (slŭng)) **1** to hurl from a sling. **2** (*coll.*) to throw, to hurl. **3** (*coll.*) to cast (out). **4** to hang loosely so as to swing. **5** to hoist by means of a sling. **6** (*coll.*) to pass, hand, give (someone something). ~*v.i.* **1** to hurl missiles with or as with a sling. **2** to move swiftly or violently. **sling-back** *n.* a backless shoe with a narrow strap round the back of the ankle. **sling-bag** *n.* a bag with a long strap, for carrying over the shoulder. **slinger** *n.* **slingshot** *n.* **1** SLUNG SHOT (under SLING[1]). **2** (*esp. N Am.*) a catapult. **slung shot** *n.* a heavy metal ball attached by a thong or strap to the wrist for use as a weapon.

sling[2] (sling) *n.* a sweetened drink of water mixed with spirits, esp. gin.

slink (slingk) *v.i.* (*past, p.p.* **slunk** (slŭngk)) **1** to steal or sneak (away etc.) in a furtive or cowardly manner. **2** to move sinuously and provocatively. **slinky** *a.* (*comp.* **slinkier**, *superl.* **slinkiest**) **1** sinuous, slender. **2** (of clothes) clinging, figure-hugging. **slinkily** *adv.* **slinkiness** *n.*

slip[1] (slip) *v.i.* (*pres.p.* **slipping**, *past, p.p.* **slipped**) **1** to slide unintentionally and miss one's footing. **2** to slide, to glide. **3** to move, go or pass unnoticed or quickly. **4** to go (along) swiftly. **5 a** to get (out, through etc.), become free, or escape thus. **b** to drop (out of someone's grasp, fingers etc.). **6** to commit a small mistake or oversight. **7** to decline (*Standards are slipping*). **8** (*coll.*) to lose one's customary skill or grip, to lose control of a situation. **9** (of time) to elapse. **10** (of a clutch) to fail to engage. ~*v.t.* **1** to cause to move in a sliding manner. **2** to put (on or off) or to insert (into) with a sliding, hasty or careless motion. **3** to let loose. **4** to put (a garment on) or take (a garment off) speedily or easily. **5** to escape or free oneself from (*The dog slipped its collar*). **6** to escape (one's memory). **7** to dislocate (a bone). **8** to keep (a clutch) partially engaged. **9** to transfer (an unworked stitch) from one knitting needle to the other. **10** to detach (a carriage) from a train in motion. **11** to detach (an anchor) from a ship. ~*n.* **1** an instance of slipping. **2** an unintentional error, a small offence, a lapse, an indiscretion. **3** a garment that a woman wears under her dress or skirt. **4** a leash for slipping a dog or hounds. **5** (*pl.*) in cricket, any of three off-side positions or the fielders playing in these positions. **6 a** backward movement of a belt on a pulley, due to slipping. **b** the difference between the pitch of a propeller and the distance travelled through the surrounding medium in a single revolution. **to give the slip** to escape from, to evade. **to let slip through one's fingers 1** to lose hold of. **2** to miss the chance of getting. **to slip away/ off** to leave quickly or unobtrusively. **to slip up** to make a mistake. **slip case** *n.* an open-ended cover for one or more books which reveals the spines. **slip cover** *n.* **1** a loose cover for fitting over a chair or sofa. **2** a dust jacket or slip case for a book. **slip-knot** *n.* **1** a knot that can be undone with a pull. **2** a knot that slips up and down the string etc. on which it is made, a running knot. **slip of the pen** *n.* a mistake in writing. **slip of the tongue** *n.* a mistake in speaking. **slip-on** *a.*, *n.* (a garment or item of footwear) which can be put on or removed easily and quickly, usu. without fasteners. **slipover** *a.* (of a garment) easily put on over the head. ~*n.* a pullover. **slippage** (-ij) *n.* an act, instance, amount or degree of slipping or failure to meet a target. **slipped disc** *n.* a displacement of one of the discs between the vertebrae, causing painful pressure on spinal nerves. **slipper** *n.* **1** a loose comfortable shoe, for wearing indoors, esp. with nightclothes. **2** a light slip-on dancing shoe. **slippered** *a.* **slipperwort** *n.* a calceolaria. **slippery** *a.* **1** so smooth, wet or slimy as to be difficult to hold. **2** so smooth, wet, muddy etc. as to cause slipping. **3** elusive. **4** shifty, dishonest. **5** unstable. **slipperiness** *n.* **slippery elm** *n.* **1** a N American elm, *Ulmus fulvus.* **2** its medicinal inner bark. **slippery slope** *n.* a disastrous course. **slippy** *a.* (*comp.* **slippier,** *superl.* **slippiest**) (*coll.*) slippery. **to look slippy** (*coll.*) to hurry, to look sharp. **slippiness** *n.* **slip road** *n.* an access or exit road on to or off a motorway. **slipshod** *a.* **1** careless, slovenly. **2** down-at-heel. **slip stitch** *n.* **1** a hidden stitch used in hemming. **2** in knitting, a stitch passed unworked from one needle to the other. **slip-stitch** *v.t.* to sew with a slip stitch. **slipstream** *n.* **1** the stream of air behind an aircraft propeller. **2** a similar stream behind any moving body, object, vehicle etc. **slip-up** *n.* an error, a blunder. **slipway** *n.* a slip for the repair, laying up or launch of vessels.

slip² (slip) *n.* a creamy mixture of clay and water used to coat or decorate pottery. **slipware** *n.* pottery which has been decorated with slip.

slip³ (slip) *n.* **1** a small piece of paper for writing messages etc. on. **2** a small form for filling in. **3** a long narrow strip of paper, wood or other material. **4** (*Print.*) a galley proof. **5** a cutting for grafting or planting. **a slip of a** merely a slight young (girl etc.).

slipper, slippery etc. SLIP¹.

slit (slit) *n.* a long cut or narrow opening. ~*v.t.* (*pres.p.* **slitting,** *past, p.p.* **slit**) **1** to make a long

cut in. **2** to cut into long pieces or strips. **slitter** *n.* **slitty** *a.* (*comp.* **slittier,** *superl.* **slittiest**) (*usu. derog.*) (of eyes) narrow.

slither (slidh´ə) *v.i.* **1** to slip, to slide unsteadily (along etc.). **2** to move with a slipping or sliding motion like a snake. ~*n.* a sliding motion. **slithery** *a.*

sliver (sliv´ə) *n.* **1** a thin piece cut from something. **2** a piece of wood or similar material torn off. ~*v.t.* **1** to form or divide into long, thin pieces. **2** to cut or break into slivers. ~*v.i.* to split, to splinter, to break into slivers.

Sloane (slōn), **Sloane Ranger** *n.* (*dated*) an upper-class young person, typically female and cultivating the casually elegant look, living in any of the fashionable parts of London.

slob (slob) *n.* (*coll.*) a messy, slovenly or boorish person. **slobbish** *a.* **slobby** *a.* (*comp.* **slobbier,** *superl.* **slobbiest**) slovenly, messy.

slobber (slob´ə) *v.i.* **1** to let saliva run from the mouth, to dribble, to slaver. **2** to talk or behave sentimentally (over). ~*n.* **1** saliva or spittle running from the mouth. **2** over-sentimental talk or behaviour. **slobberer** *n.* **slobbery** *a.* **slobberiness** *n.*

sloe (slō) *n.* the fruit of the blackthorn, *Prunus spinosa,* or the shrub bearing it. **sloe-eyed** *a.* having dark, slanted or almond-shaped eyes. **sloe gin** *n.* gin flavoured with sloes.

slog (slog) *v.t.* (*pres.p.* **slogging,** *past, p.p.* **slogged**) to hit vigorously and at random, esp. in batting or with the fists. ~*v.i.* **1** to work (away) hard. **2** to move slowly or cumbersomely. ~*n.* **1** a spell of hard work. **2** a heavy blow. **3** an exhausting walk. **slogger** *n.*

slogan (slō´gən) *n.* **1** a catchy advertising phrase or word. **2** a political catchword.

sloop (sloop) *n.* a fore-and-aft rigged vessel with one mast.

slop (slop) *v.t.* (*pres.p.* **slopping,** *past, p.p.* **slopped**) **1** to spill or allow to overflow. **2** to soil by spilling liquid upon. ~*v.i.* **1** to spill (over), to overflow the side of a vessel. **2** to tramp through slush or mud. ~*n.* **1** water or other liquid carelessly thrown about. **2** sentimental or maudlin speech or writing. **3** (*pl.*) dirty water, liquid refuse. **4** (*pl.*) liquid food refuse fed to animals, esp. pigs. **5** (*Naut.*) a rough sea. **to slop about** to shamble or slouch. **to slop out** (of prisoners) to clean out slops from a chamber pot. **slop basin, slop bowl** *n.* a basin for emptying the dregs of cups etc. into at table. **slop bucket** *n.* a bucket for taking away slops from the bedroom or kitchen. **sloppy** *a.* (*comp.* **sloppier,** *superl.* **sloppiest**) **1** wet, splashed, covered with spilt water or puddles. **2** (of food) watery and insipid. **3** (of work) done carelessly. **4** (of clothes) untidy, badly fitting. **5** weakly sentimental, maudlin or effusive. **6** (*Naut.*) (of the sea) rough, choppy. **sloppily** *adv.* **sloppiness** *n.*

slope (slōp) *n.* **1** an inclined surface, line or direction. **2** a piece of ground whose surface makes an angle with the horizon. **3** the degree of such inclination, the difference in level between two ends or sides of something, or the rate at which this becomes greater with distance. **4** a downhill skiing course on a hillside. **5** the position of a rifle when carried on the shoulder. ~*v.i.* to be inclined at an angle to the horizon. ~*v.t.* to place or form with a slope, to hold or direct obliquely. **to slope arms** to position a rifle on the shoulder with the barrel pointing up and back. **to slope off** (*coll.*) to leave, esp. furtively, to sneak away. **sloping** *a.* **slopingly** *adv.* **slopy** *a.* (*comp.* **slopier,** *superl.* **slopiest**).

slosh (slosh) *v.t.* **1** (*coll.*) to strike hard. **2** (*coll.*) to splash, spread or pour (liquid) carelessly. **3** to move (something) about in liquid. **4** to wet by splashing. ~*v.i.* **1** to move or splash through slush, mud, water etc. **2** (*coll.*) to hit. ~*n.* **1** (*coll.*) a heavy blow. **2** a liquid or semi-liquid medium, such as slush, mud etc. **3** the slapping or splashing sound of liquid. **sloshed** *a.* (*coll.*) drunk.

slot (slot) *n.* **1** the aperture into which coins are put in a slot machine. **2** a groove or opening, esp. in a machine for some part to fit into. **3** a place or niche (e.g. in an organization). **4** a (usu. regular) position in a sequence or schedule (e.g. of a television programme). ~*v.t.* (*pres.p.* **slotting,** *past, p.p.* **slotted**) **1** to fit or place (as) into a slot. **2** to make a slot in. ~*v.i.* to fit (together or into) by means of a slot or slots. **slot machine** *n.* **1** a machine for dispensing sweets, drinks etc., operated by means of coins or tokens pushed or dropped through a narrow aperture, a vending machine. **2** a similarly operated machine allowing a spell of play at pinball. **3** (*N Am.*) a fruit machine. **slotter** *n.*

sloth (slōth) *n.* **1** laziness, indolence, sluggishness, reluctance to exert oneself. **2** a S American arboreal edentate mammal of the family Bradypodidae characterized by its slow and awkward movements on the ground. **slothful** *a.* **slothfully** *adv.* **slothfulness** *n.*

slouch (slowch) *n.* **1** an ungainly or negligent drooping or stooping gait, or movement. **2** a downward bend of the hat-brim. **3** (*sl.*) an awkward, slovenly or incapable person. **4** a slouch hat. ~*v.i.* **1** to stand or move in a drooping or ungainly attitude. **2** to droop or hang down. ~*v.t.* to bend the brim of (a hat) so that it hangs down on one side. **sloucher** *n.* **slouch hat** *n.* any soft hat with a brim that can be pulled down, esp. one worn with the brim down at one side. **slouching** *a.* **slouchy** *a.* (*comp.* **slouchier,** *superl.* **slouchiest**). **slouchiness** *n.*

slough[1] (slow) *n.* **1** a place full of mud, a bog, a quagmire. **2** a marsh, a swamp. **3** a state of abject depression or degradation. **Slough of Despond** *n.* extreme despondency (from the name of a place in John Bunyan's *Pilgrim's Progress*). **sloughy**[1] *a.* (*comp.* **sloughier,** *superl.* **sloughiest**).

slough[2] (slŭf) *n.* **1** the cast skin of a snake. **2** a covering or other part or thing cast off. ~*v.t.* to

cast off (a skin, dead tissue etc.). ~*v.i.* **1** to peel and come (off, away etc.). **2** to cast off slough. **sloughy**[2] *a.* (*comp.* **sloughier,** *superl.* **sloughiest**).

sloughy[1] SLOUGH[1].

sloughy[2] SLOUGH[2].

Slovak (slō′vak) *n.* **1** any member of a Slavonic people inhabiting Slovakia, formerly the eastern part of Czechoslovakia, but now an independent republic. **2** the Slavonic language of this people, closely related to Czech. ~*a.* of or relating to this people, their language or the region they inhabit. **Slovakian** (-vak′-) *n., a.*

sloven (slŭv′ən) *n.* a person who is careless about dress or negligent about cleanliness; an untidy, careless, lazy person. **slovenly** *a., adv.* **slovenliness** *n.*

Slovene (slōvēn′, slō′-) *n.* **1** a member of a S Slavonic people inhabiting Slovenia, a republic of S central Europe, formerly part of Yugoslavia. **2** the language of this people. ~*a.* of or relating to the Slovenes, their language or the region they inhabit. **Slovenian** (-vē′-) *n., a.*

slow (slō) *a.* **1** not quick, of low velocity, moving at a low speed. **2** taking a long time in acting or doing something. **3** deliberate (of speech etc.). **4** gradual, e.g. in growth or development. **5** not prompt or willing (to do something). **6** not hasty, not precipitate. **7** tardy, backward (*slow learners*). **8** stupid, dull. **9** (of a party or similar event) lifeless. **10** (of business, trade etc.) slack. **11** (of a clock or watch) behind the right time. **12** not allowing fast movement (*in the slow lane*). **13** (of a fire or oven) producing little heat. **14** (of a cricket pitch or tennis court) causing the ball to roll or bounce sluggishly. **15** (of a photographic film) needing a long exposure. **16** (of a lens) having a small aperture. ~*adv.* slowly. ~*v.i.* to slacken or moderate speed (up or down). ~*v.t.* to reduce the speed of. **slow but sure** finally achieving results. **slowcoach** *n.* a person who is slow in moving, acting, deciding etc. **slowdown** *n.* **1** the act or process of slowing down. **2** a go-slow protest. **slow handclap** *n.* a slow regular clapping by an audience, expressing discontent. **slowish** *a.* **slow loris** *n.* (*pl.* **slow loris**) one of two types of loris, *Nycticebus coucang*. **slowly** *adv.* **slow march** *n.* a marching tempo used by the military at funerals etc. **slow motion** *n.* **1** in film and video, a slow-projection or fast-exposure technique which allows action to appear slower than normal. **2** artificially slow movement or action imitating this. **slow-motion** *a.* **slowness** *n.* **slowpoke** *n.* (*N Am., coll.*) a slowcoach. **slow-witted** *a.* dull, slow to react.

slow-worm (slō′wœm) *n.* a small limbless viviparous snakelike lizard, *Anguis fragilis*, the blindworm.

slub (slŭb) *n.* **1** a knob or lump in yarn. **2** fabric woven with this kind of yarn. ~*a.* (of a fabric) having a lumpy appearance.

sludge (slŭj) *n.* **1** thick mud. **2** an oozy or slimy sediment, as of ore and water. **3** a hard precipitate produced in the treatment of sewage. **4** a residue of dirty oil in the sump of an internal-combustion engine. **5** (*Geol.*) sea ice beginning to form in small accumulations. **sludgy** *a.* (*comp.* **sludgier,** *superl.* **sludgiest**).

slue SLEW².

slug¹ (slŭg) *n.* **1** a shell-less air-breathing gastropod, very destructive to plants. **2** a sea slug. **3 a** a bullet, esp. an irregularly shaped one. **b** a pellet for an airgun. **4** a small, roughly rounded lump of metal. **5** (*coll.*) a quantity of liquor which can be gulped at one go. ~*v.t.* (*pres.p.* **slugging,** *past,* *p.p.* **slugged**) to gulp (liquor) down, to swig. **sluggard** (-əd) *n.* a habitually lazy person. **sluggardly** *a.* **sluggish** *a.* **1** habitually lazy, inactive. **2** slow in movement or response, inert. **sluggishly** *adv.* **sluggishness** *n.*

slug² (slŭg) *v.t.* (*pres.p.* **slugging,** *past,* *p.p.* **slugged**) to hit hard. ~*n.* a hard blow. **to slug it out 1** to fight it out. **2** to stick it out, to keep going to the end. **slugger** *n.*

sluice (sloos) *n.* **1** a waterway with a sliding gate or hatch by which the level of a body of water is controlled, a sluice-gate or floodgate. **2** the stream above, below, or passing through a floodgate. **3** an inclined trough or channel for washing ore, floating logs down etc., a sluice-way. **4** a place for, or an act of, rinsing. ~*v.t.* **1** to flood or drench by means of a sluice or sluices. **2** to provide with a sluice. **3** to drench, to wash thoroughly, to rinse. **4** to let out or drain by a sluice. ~*v.i.* to pour out (as) through a sluice. **sluice-gate** *n.* a floodgate. **sluice-valve** *n.* a valve controlling the level of a sluice. **sluice-way** *n.* a channel into which water passes from a sluice.

slum (slŭm) *n.* **1** a squalid, usu. overcrowded, neighbourhood in a town or city, inhabited by the very poor. **2** a house, flat etc. which is overcrowded, in a deteriorated condition etc. ~*v.i.* (*pres.p.* **slumming,** *past,* *p.p.* **slummed**) **1** to live in squalid or poverty-stricken conditions. **2** to visit a place or affect a lifestyle inferior to what one is accustomed to, out of curiosity or for amusement. **to slum it** (*coll.*) to make do with less comfortable or luxurious conditions than one is used to. **slummer** *n.* **slummy** *a.* (*comp.* **slummier,** *superl.* **slummiest**). **slumminess** *n.*

slumber (slŭm´bə) *v.i.* (*poet.*) **1** to sleep, esp. lightly. **2** to be inactive or dormant. ~*n.* **1** light sleep, or a spell of this. **2** a state of dormancy, inactivity. **slumberer** *n.* **slumberous** *a.* **slumberously** *adv.* **slumberousness** *n.* **slumberwear** *n.* nightclothes.

slump (slŭmp) *v.i.* **1** to fall or sink (down) heavily. **2** to decline quickly or drastically. ~*n.* **1** an act of slumping. **2** a heavy fall or decline, a collapse (of prices etc.).

slung SLING¹.

slunk SLINK.

slur (slœ) *v.t.* (*pres.p.* **slurring,** *past,* *p.p.* **slurred**) **1** to pronounce indistinctly. **2** to blur or smudge (writing). **3** (*Mus.*) **a** to sing or play legato. **b** to

mark (notes) to be slurred. **4** to speak slightingly of. **5** to pass lightly over. ~*v.i.* **1** to speak or articulate indistinctly. **2** to pass lightly or slightingly (over). ~*n.* **1** a reproach or disparagement. **2** a blurred impression in printing. **3** a slurring in pronunciation or singing. **4** a curved line placed over or under notes, denoting that they are to be played or sung legato. **5** the performance of such notes.

slurp (slœp) *n.* a sucking sound produced when eating or drinking noisily. ~*v.i., v.t.* to eat or drink noisily.

slurry (slŭr´i) *n.* (*pl.* **slurries**) **1** a thin, fluid paste made by mixing certain materials (esp. cement) with water. **2** liquid manure.

slush (slŭsh) *n.* **1** half-melted snow. **2** liquid mud, sludge. **3** (*sl.*) mawkishly sentimental talk or writing, gush. **slush fund** *n.* a fund of money used to finance corrupt business or political practices. **slushy** *a.* (*comp.* **slushier,** *superl.* **slushiest**). **slushiness** *n.*

slut (slŭt) *n.* (*offensive*) a dirty, slovenly or sexually promiscuous woman. **sluttish** *a.* **sluttishly** *adv.* **sluttishness** *n.*

sly (slī) *a.* (*comp.* **slyer, slier,** *superl.* **slyest, sliest**) **1** crafty, cunning. **2** furtive, not open or frank. **3** playfully roguish. **on the sly** slyly, in secret, on the quiet. **slyboots** *n.* (*coll.*) a sly person, esp. in keeping something dark. **slyly, slily** *adv.* **slyness** *n.*

SM *abbr.* **1** sadomasochism. **2** sergeant major.

Sm *chem. symbol* samarium.

smack¹ (smak) *n.* **1** a blow with the flat of the hand, a slap. **2** in cricket, a hard hit. **3** a loud kiss. **4** a quick, smart report as of a blow with something flat, a crack of a whip etc. ~*v.t.* **1** to strike with the flat of the hand, to slap. **2** to separate (the lips) with a sharp noise, as an indication that one is enjoying, or is about to enjoy, something, esp. food. **3** to hit, put down, crack (a whip), kiss etc. with a sharp noise. ~*v.i.* to produce a sharp noise. ~*adv.* headlong, plump, directly (*ran smack into her*). **to have a smack at** (*coll.*) to tackle, have a go at. **smacker** *n.* **1** a noisy kiss. **2** a resounding blow. **3** (*sl.*) a pound or dollar note. **smack in the eye, smack in the face** *n.* (*coll.*) a snub or rebuff.

smack² (smak) *n.* **1** a slight taste or flavour (of). **2** a suggestion, trace, tincture or dash (of). **3** a very tiny amount, a smattering (of). ~*v.i.* to have a taste, flavour or suggestion (of).

smack³ (smak) *n.* a one-masted vessel, like a sloop or cutter, used in fishing etc.

smack⁴ (smak) *n.* (*sl.*) heroin or some other illegally sold drug.

small (smawl) *a.* **1** deficient or relatively little in size, stature, amount etc. **2** of less dimensions than the standard kind. **3** composed of little pieces (*small shot*). **4** of minor importance, slight, trifling, petty. **5** concerned or dealing with business etc., of a restricted or minor kind (*small shopkeepers*). **6** of low degree, poor, humble.

7 ignoble, narrow-minded. ~*adv.* into small pieces (*cut the vegetables up small*). ~*n.* **1** the slender part of anything (*a pain in the small of the back*). **2** (*pl., coll.*) small items of washing, esp. undergarments. **in a small way** on a small or unambitious scale. **no small** considerable, substantial, significant, rather a lot of (*no small feat; with no small dismay*). **small wonder 1** it is hardly surprising (that etc.). **2** naturally, of course. **small arms** *n.pl.* portable firearms, such as rifles, pistols etc. **small calorie** *n.* a unit of heat, equalling 4.1868 joules; the quantity of heat required to raise the temperature of 1 gram of water by 1°C. **small capital** *n.* a capital letter lower in height than the regular capital of the same font. **small change** *n.* coins as distinct from notes, esp. of low denominations. **small circle** *n.* a circle dividing a sphere into two unequal parts. **small craft** *n.pl.* fishing vessels and other small boats. **small deer** *n.pl.* small insignificant animals. **small fortune** *n.* a large sum of money. **small fry** *n.pl.* **1** small or young fishes. **2** (*coll.*) children. **to be small fry** to be insignificant or unimportant. **smallholder** *n.* the farmer or tenant of a smallholding. **smallholding** *n.* (the working of) a portion of agricultural land of limited area smaller than a farm. **small hours** *n.pl.* the time from midnight till 3 or 4 a.m., the early hours of the morning. **small intestine** *n.* the long narrow part of the intestine comprising the duodenum, jejunum and the ileum. **smallish** *a.* **small letter** *n.* a lowercase letter. **small-minded** *a.* restricted in outlook, petty. **small-mindedly** *adv.* **small-mindedness** *n.* **smallness** *n.* **small potatoes** *n.* (*sl.*) an insignificant person or unimportant matter. **smallpox** *n.* variola, an acute contagious disease with fever and an outbreak of pustules on the skin that leave permanent pockmarks, now eradicated through vaccination and surviving only in a few laboratories. **small print** *n.* **1** matter printed in a small typeface. **2** the unobtrusively printed reservations or restrictions in a policy or contract document. **small-scale** *a.* of limited scope or extent. **small talk** *n.* light social conversation on superficial topics. **small-time** *a.* (*coll.*) **1** insignificant, unimportant. **2** amateurish. **small-timer** *n.* **small-town** *a.* (*derog.*) characteristic of a small town in all its lack of sophistication, provinciality and pettiness.

smarm (smahm) *v.t.* (*coll.*) to plaster, to flatten (hair down) with hair oil etc. ~*v.i.* to fawn, to ingratiate oneself, to make (up to someone). ~*n.* gush, fawning behaviour. **smarmy** *a.* (*comp.* **smarmier,** *superl.* **smarmiest**) **1** sleek and smooth. **2** having a wheedling manner. **smarmily** *adv.* **smarminess** *n.*

smart (smaht) *a.* **1** spruce, formal and stylish. **2** astute, intelligent. **3** shrewd, quick to spot a chance and take advantage of it. **4** (of dealings) verging on the unethical (*a bit of smart practice*). **5** (of equipment etc.) clean, bright and in good repair. **6** (of a resort, rendezvous etc.) stylish,

fashionable. **7** (of people in society) sophisticated. **8** vigorous, lively. **9** stinging, severe. ~*v.i.* **1** to feel or give or cause sharp pain or mental distress (*The chlorine made his eyes smart*). **2** (of a rebuff or injustice) to rankle. **3** to feel wounded (*was smarting from the rebuff*). **4** to suffer punishment (*You'll smart for this!*). ~*adv.* smartly. ~*n.* **1** a sharp pain, a stinging sensation. **2** a feeling of resentment. **3** distress, anguish. **smart alec** (alik), **smart aleck, smart alick** *n.* (*coll.*) a know-all. **smart-alecky** *a.* **smart-arse,** (*N Am.*) **smart-ass** *n.* (*sl.*) a smart alec. **smart card** *n.* a plastic card containing a microprocessor for effecting point-of-sale debits etc. **smarten** *v.t., v.i.* **smartish** *adv.* **smartly** *adv.* **smart money** *n.* **1** money paid to buy oneself off from an unpleasant engagement etc., or paid as a penalty or in compensation. **2** money bet or invested by experienced gamblers or business people. **smartness** *n.* **smart set** *n.* those in society who are admired for their sophistication, glamour and know-how. **smarty** *n.* (*pl.* **smarties**) (*coll.*) **1** a smart alec. **2** a smartly dressed person, a member of the smart set. **smarty pants, smarty boots** *n.* (*pl.* **smarty pants, smarty boots**) (*coll.*) a know-all, a smart alec.

smash (smash) *v.t.* **1** to break to pieces by violence, to shatter. **2** to hit with a crushing blow. **3** to overthrow completely, to rout. **4** to hit (a shuttlecock, tennis ball etc.) with a forceful overhead stroke. ~*v.i.* **1** to break to pieces. **2** to go bankrupt. **3** to crash (into). **4** to perform a smash (in badminton, tennis etc.). **5** to come to pieces under force. ~*n.* **1** an act or instance of smashing. **2** a smash-up, a crash between vehicles. **3** (*coll.*) a smash hit. **4** in badminton, tennis etc., a forceful overhead stroke. **5** a violent blow with the fist. **6** a collapse; the bankruptcy or ruin of a person or concern. ~*adv.* with a smash. **smashable** *a.* **smash-and-grab** *a.* (*coll.*) (of a theft) in which a shop window is broken and goods inside hurriedly removed. **smashed** *a.* **1** broken. **2** (*sl.*) very drunk. **smasher** *n.* **1** (*sl.*) an outstandingly attractive or amiable person. **2** (*sl.*) something of staggering size, quality, effectiveness etc. **3** someone who or something that smashes. **smash hit** *n.* (*coll.*) a song, show, performer etc. that is a great success. **smashing** *a.* (*coll.*) very fine, wonderful. **smashingly** *adv.* **smash-up** *n.* a violent collision between vehicles, a car crash.

smatter (smat'ə) *n.* a smattering. **smatterer** *n.* a dabbler. **smattering** *n.* **1** a slight superficial knowledge. **2** a small quantity.

smear (smiə) *v.t.* **1** to rub or daub with anything greasy or sticky. **2** to apply thickly. **3** to soil, stain or dirty. **4** to malign (someone) or blacken (their name) publicly. ~*v.i.* to become blurred, smudged etc. ~*n.* **1** a stain or mark made by smearing. **2** an attack on a person's reputation. **3** (*Med.*) a substance (e.g. vaginal secretion) smeared on a glass slide for examination under a microscope. **smear campaign** *n.* a series of orchestrated attacks on the reputation of a politician, institution etc. **smearer** *n.* **smear test** *n.* a microscopic examination of a smear, e.g. for cervical cancer. **smeary** *a.* (*comp.* **smearier**, *superl.* **smeariest**). **smearily** *adv.* **smeariness** *n.*

smell (smel) *n.* **1** the sense by which odours are perceived. **2** the sensation or the act of smelling. **3** that which affects the organs of smell. **4** a bad odour. **5** a characteristic quality, a trace. ~*v.t.* (*past, p.p.* **smelt** (smelt), **smelled** (smeld, smelt)) **1** to notice or perceive through the sense of smell (*I smell burning*). **2** to scent or detect (*She could smell a bargain a mile off*). ~*v.i.* **1** to give out an odour (of etc.) (*His breath smelt of garlic*). **2** to have a specified smell (*You smell lovely*). **3** to suggest, to indicate, to smack (of) (*It smells of corruption*). **4** to have or exercise the sense of smell (*Here, smell*). **5** to stink. **to smell out 1** to detect by instinct or prying. **2** to pollute (e.g. a room with smoke). **smeller** *n.* **smelling** *n.* **smelling salts** *n.pl.* an aromatic preparation of ammonium carbonate used in cases of faintness etc. **smell-less** *a.* **smelly** *a.* (*comp.* **smellier**, *superl.* **smelliest**) malodorous. **smelliness** *n.*

smelt¹ (smelt) *v.t.* **1** to fuse (an ore) so as to extract the metal. **2** to extract (metal) from ore thus. **smelter** *n.* **smeltery** *n.* (*pl.* **smelteries**).

smelt² (smelt) *n.* (*pl.* **smelt, smelts**) a small food fish, *Osmerus eperlanus*, allied to the salmon.

smelt³ SMELL.

smidgen (smij´in), **smidgeon, smidgin** *n.* (*coll.*) a tiny amount.

smile (smīl) *v.i.* **1** to express amusement, kindness or pleasure by an instinctive lateral movement of the lips with an upward turn at the corners. **2** (of the weather, fortune etc.) to look favourably (on or upon someone). ~*v.t.* **1** to express by or as by a smile. **2** to bring or drive (into, out of, away etc.) thus. ~*n.* **1** an act of smiling. **2** a cheerful or favourable expression. **smileless** *a.* **smiler** *n.* **smiley** *a.* **smilingly** *adv.*

smirch (smœch) *v.t.* to soil, to smear, to stain, to defile, to defame (someone's name or reputation). ~*n.* **1** a stain, a smear. **2** a stain or blot on one's reputation.

smirk (smœk) *v.i.* to smile affectedly or smugly. ~*n.* an affected or smug smile, a simper. **smirker** *n.* **smirkingly** *adv.* **smirky** *a.* (*comp.* **smirkier**, *superl.* **smirkiest**). **smirkily** *adv.*

smite (smīt) *v.t.* (*past* **smote** (smōt), †**smit** (smit), *p.p.* **smitten** (smit´ən)) (*poet. or facet.*) **1** to strike, to deal a severe blow to. **2** to inflict injury, death, defeat, damage or disaster upon. **3** (*usu. p.p.*) to strike or affect (by or with a feeling, disease etc.) (*smitten with paralysis*; *smitten by her charms*). **smiter** *n.* **smitten** *a.* (*coll.*) enamoured.

smith (smith) *n.* **1** a person who works in metals, esp. someone who forges iron with the hammer, a blacksmith. **2** (*usu. in comb.*) a person who makes or crafts something (*a locksmith*; *a wordsmith*; *a songsmith*). **smithy** (smidh´i) *n.* (*pl.* **smithies**) a blacksmith's workshop.

smithereens (smidhərēnz´), **smithers** (smidh´-əz) *n.pl.* little bits, tiny fragments (*blew the place to smithereens*).

smitten SMITE.

smock (smok) *n.* **1** a loose dress or shirt with a yoke, or smocking forming one, or an artist's overall of similar shape. **2** (*Hist.*) (*also* **smock-frock**) a farm labourer's yoked or smocked shirt-like overall. ~*v.t.* to decorate with smocking. **smocking** *n.* decorative gathering on a shirt or dress, across the yoke or round the wrists or waist.

smog (smog) *n.* fog thickened by smoke and by fumes from industrial plants or motor vehicles. **smoggy** *a.* (*comp.* **smoggier**, *superl.* **smoggiest**).

smoke (smōk) *n.* **1** volatile products of combustion, esp. carbonaceous and other matter in the form of visible vapour or fine particles escaping from a burning substance. **2** an act of smoking a cigarette, pipe, cigar etc. (*was outside having a quick smoke*). **3** (*sl.*) a cigarette. ~*v.i.* **1** to draw into the mouth or inhale and exhale the smoke of tobacco etc. **2** to emit smoke. **3** to emit vapour, fumes etc., to reek. **4** (of a chimney etc.) to send smoke into a room, to fail to draw. ~*v.t.* **1** to draw with the mouth or inhale and exhale the smoke of (a cigarette, pipe etc.). **2** to apply smoke to. **3** to blacken, flavour etc., with smoke. **the Smoke** (*coll.*) a big city, esp. London. **to end up in smoke** to go up in smoke. **to go up in smoke 1** (of a scheme, a desire) to come to nothing. **2** to be destroyed by fire. **to smoke out 1** to exterminate or drive out with smoke. **2** to discover, to force into the open. **smokable, smokeable** *a.* **smoke bomb** *n.* a bomb that produces dense smoke on exploding. **smoked** *a.* **smoked glass** *n.* glass darkened by being exposed to smoke. **smokehouse** *n.* a building where meat, fish etc. is cured by smoking. **smokeless** *a.* (of e.g. fuel) emitting little or no smoke. **smokeless zone** *n.* an area in which it is forbidden to emit smoke from chimneys, and where smokeless fuel only may be burnt. **smoker** *n.* **1** a person who smokes tobacco. **2** a person who dries, cures, fumigates etc., with smoke. **3** a smoking compartment. **4** (*N Am.*) an all-male get-together. **5** an apparatus for smoking bees. **smoke ring** *n.* cigarette smoke exhaled in the shape of a ring. **smokescreen** *n.* **1** a dense volume of smoke produced by chemicals used to conceal the movements of ships, troops etc., from the enemy. **2** a ploy used to obscure or deceive. **smoke signal** *n.* **1** a message conveyed by a series of puffs of smoke. **2** (*coll.*) a private signal from one person to another. **smokestack** *n.* a funnel, esp. on a steamer. **smoking** *n.*, *a.* **smoking carriage, smoking compartment, smoking room** *n.* a railway carriage or compartment, or a room in a club etc., reserved for smokers. **smoking gun, smoking pistol** *n.* a piece of incontestably incriminating evidence. **smoking jacket** *n.* a velvet jacket, orig. used by men when smoking. **smoky** *a.* (*comp.* **smokier**, *superl.* **smokiest**)

1 resembling smoke in colour, smell, flavour etc. **2** filled with smoke. **3** emitting smoke. **4** dirtied by smoke. **smokily** *adv.* **smokiness** *n.*

smolder SMOULDER.

smolt (smōlt) *n.* a salmon in its second year when it acquires its silvery scales.

smooth (smoodh) *a. (comp.* **smoother,** *superl.* **smoothest) 1** having a continuously even surface, free from roughness. **2** not hairy. **3** (of water) unruffled. **4** (of liquids or semi-liquids) without lumps. **5** free from obstructions or impediments. **6** (of sound, taste etc.) not harsh. **7** (of e.g. breathing or movement) flowing rhythmically or evenly. **8** calm, pleasant. **9** suave, flattering. *~v.t.* (*also* **smoothe) 1** to make smooth, to even (out). **2** to flatten (lumps or projections out) or ease (difficulties or problems away). **3** to free from obstructions, irregularities etc. **4** to extenuate, to alleviate. *~v.i.* **1** to become smooth, to even (out). **2** (of problems or upsets) to abate, to heal (over). *~n.* **1** an act of smoothing, stroking or patting down. **2** a smooth place or part. **3** (*coll.*) that which is pleasant or easy (*take the rough with the smooth*). **smoothable** *a.* **smooth-bore, smooth-bored** *a.* (of a gun) not rifled. *~n.* a smooth-bore gun. **smooth breathing** *n.* (*Gram.*) in Greek, a sign (') over an initial vowel indicating that it is unaspirated, as distinct from a *rough breathing.* **smoothen** *v.t., v.i.* to make or become smooth or smoother. **smoother** *n.* **smoothie** (-i), **smoothy** *n.* (*pl.* **smoothies**) (*coll.*) an excessively suave or plausible person, esp. a man. **smoothing** *n., a.* **smoothing iron** *n.* (*dated*) a flat iron, an iron for pressing clothes and linen. **smoothish** *a.* **smoothly** *adv.* **smooth muscle** *n.* muscle (e.g. in the intestine, the wall of a blood vessel) capable of involuntary contractions, as distinct from striated muscle. **smoothness** *n.* **smooth-spoken, smooth-tongued** *a.* polite, plausible, flattering. **smooth talk** *n.* suave, specious or hypocritical talk. **smooth-talk** *v.t.* to attempt to win over by such talk.

smorgasbord (smaw´gəsbawd) *n.* **1** a buffet or hors d'œuvre of open sandwiches. **2** a buffet comprising an assortment of hors d'oeuvres and other dishes.

smote SMITE.

smother (smŭdh´ə) *v.t.* **1** to suffocate, to stifle. **2** to kill by suffocation etc. **3** to keep (a fire) down by covering it with ashes etc. **4** to hide, to conceal (the truth etc.). **5** to overcome, to overwhelm (*smothered the baby with kisses*). **6** to cover thickly, to enclose (*likes his food smothered in gravy*). **7** (*N Am.*) to defeat fast and thoroughly. *~v.i.* to be suffocated, to be prevented from breathing freely. *~n.* a stifling cloud of dust, smoke, vapour etc. **smothery** *a.* **smotheriness** *n.*

smoulder (smōl´də), (*esp. N Am.*) **smolder** *v.i.* **1** to burn in a smothered way without flames. **2** to exist in a suppressed or latent condition. **3** to feel or show strong repressed emotions (such as

anger, jealousy). *~n.* **1** a smouldering state. **2** a smouldering fire. **smoulderingly** *adv.*

smudge (smŭj), **smutch** (smŭch) *n.* a dirty mark, a smear, a blur. *~v.t.* **1** to smear or blur (writing, drawing etc.). **2** to make a dirty smear, blot or stain on. **3** to soil, to smirch, to defile, to sully (purity, reputation etc.). *~v.i.* to become smeared or blurred. **smudgeless** *a.* **smudgy** *a.* (*comp.* **smudgier,** *superl.* **smudgiest**). **smudginess** *n.*

smug (smŭg) *a.* (*comp.* **smugger,** *superl.* **smuggest**) self-satisfied, complacent. **smugly** *adv.* **smugness** *n.*

smuggle (smŭg´əl) *v.t.* **1** to import or export illegally without paying customs duties. **2** to take (out) or bring (in) secretly, to convey clandestinely. **3** to hide (away). **smuggled** *a.* **smuggler** *n.* **smuggling** *n.*

smut (smŭt) *n.* **1** a particle of soot or other dirt, a mark or smudge made by this. **2** obscene or ribald talk, language, stories etc. **3** a disease of corn caused by parasitic fungi, that turns parts of the ear to black powder. **4** any fungus of the order *Ustilaginales* that causes smut. *~v.t.* (*pres.p.* **smutting,** *past, p.p.* **smutted) 1** to stain or mark with smut. **2** to infect with smut. *~v.i.* (of corn etc.) to be attacked by smut. **smutty** *a.* (*comp.* **smuttier,** *superl.* **smuttiest**). **smuttily** *adv.* **smuttiness** *n.*

Sn *chem. symbol* tin.

snack (snak) *n.* **1** a quick light meal. **2** a dish of something, or a small quantity of food, taken between main meals. *~v.i.* to have a snack. **snack bar** *n.* a café, self-service restaurant or other place offering light meals or refreshments.

snaffle (snaf´əl) *n.* a bridle-bit usu. with a joint in the middle. *~v.t.* **1** to provide or control with a snaffle. **2** (*coll.*) to steal, to appropriate for oneself. **snaffle-bit** *n.* a snaffle.

snafu (snafoo´) *n.* (*esp. N Am., sl.*) a state of total confusion or chaos. *~a.* in total chaos or confusion.

snag (snag) *n.* **1** an unexpected or concealed difficulty. **2** a jagged projection, as the stumpy base of a branch left in pruning. **3** a tree stump projecting from the bed of a river (constituting a navigational hazard). **4** a tear, a flaw in fabric. *~v.t.* (*pres.p.* **snagging,** *past, p.p.* **snagged) 1** to catch or damage on a snag. **2** to clear of snags. **3** (*esp. N Am.*) to hinder, to halt, to impede. **snagged** *a.* **snaggy** *a.* (*comp.* **snaggier,** *superl.* **snaggiest**).

snail (snāl) *n.* **1** a gastropod mollusc of various species with a spirally coiled shell. **2** the sea snail. **3** a sluggish person or thing. **snailery** *n.* (*pl.* **snaileries**) a place where edible snails are cultivated. **snail-like** *a.* **snail's pace** *n.* a slow rate of progress. **snaily** *a.* (*comp.* **snailier,** *superl.* **snailiest**).

snake (snāk) *n.* **1** a limbless reptile of the suborder Ophidia, of a venomous or non-venomous type and having a forked tongue and the ability to swallow prey whole. **2** a snakelike limbless lizard or amphibian. **3** a sneaking, treacherous person. **4** anything resembling a snake in appearance or movement, esp. a tool for unblocking drains, a plumber's snake. ~*v.i.* to wind, to move quietly or snakily. **snake-charmer** *n.* an entertainer who appears to mesmerize snakes by playing music. **snake-charming** *n.* **snake in the grass** *n.* a treacherous or underhand person. **snakelike** *a.* **snake oil** *n.* (*coll.*) a panacea or quack remedy. **snake-pit** *n.* **1** a pit full of snakes. **2** any arena where people are viciously fighting each other for power. **snakeroot** *n.* **1** the root of various N American plants supposed to be an antidote for snake bites. **2** any of these plants. **snakes and ladders** *n.pl.* a board game in which counters can advance more speedily up ladders or move backwards down snakes. **snake's-head** *n.* the fritillary. **snakeskin** *n.*, *a.* (made of) the skin of a snake. **snakish** *a.* **snaky** *a.* (*comp.* **snakier**, *superl.* **snakiest**). **snakily** *adv.* **snakiness** *n.*

snap (snap) *v.i.* (*pres.p.* **snapping**, *past*, *p.p.* **snapped**) **1** to break with a sharp report. **2** to make a sharp, quick sound, like a crack or slight explosion. **3** to part, close or fit into place suddenly with a sharp click. **4** (of a dog) to make a biting movement (at). **5** to snatch or grasp (at an opportunity, chance etc.). **6** to speak or shout sharply or irritably (at someone). **7** to collapse (under pressure, strain of work etc.). **8** to move smartly (e.g. into action). ~*v.t.* **1** to break (something) with a sharp report. **2** to cause to click (shut, open etc.). **3** to cause (a whip, one's fingers etc.) to make a sharp crack or report. **4** to say abruptly or irritably. **5** to photograph casually. **6** to seize suddenly, to take advantage of eagerly. ~*n.* **1** the act or an instance or the sound of snapping. **2** a crisp ginger-flavoured biscuit (*a ginger snap*; *a brandy snap*). **3** a snapshot. **4** a sudden spell of severe weather. **5** a children's card game in which players shout 'Snap!' when two identical cards are turned face up. **6** vigour, briskness. **7** (*N Am.*, *coll.*) something that is easy or profitable, a cinch. **8** an abrupt reply or retort. ~*a.* **1** done, taken etc., suddenly or on the spur of the moment (*snap judgements*). **2** closing or fastening with a snap. **3** (*N Am.*, *coll.*) easy, profitable, cheap. ~*adv.* with (the sound of) a snap. ~*int.* **1** uttered when playing the game of snap. **2** used to indicate similarity, identicalness or synchronicity. **to snap off 1** to break off. **2** to bite off. **to snap one's fingers (at)** to show contempt or defiance (of). **to snap out** to say crossly. **to snap out of it** to change one's mood abruptly (for the better). **to snap someone's head off** to retort abruptly, irritably or rudely. **to snap up 1** to take quick advantage of (a bargain etc.), to purchase eagerly. **2** to grab quickly. **snap bean** *n.* a bean whose pods are broken in pieces and eaten. **snapdragon** *n.* a plant of the genus *Antirrhinum*, with a flower opening like a dragon's mouth. **snap fastener** *n.* a press-stud. **snappable** *a.* **snapper** *n.* **1** any of a number of reddish sea fish

of the family Lutjanidae. **2** a spotted food fish of Australia and New Zealand. **3** a snapping turtle. **4** a person who or something that snaps. **snapping** *n.*, *a.* **snappingly** *adv.* **snapping turtle** *n.* a fierce and voracious N American freshwater turtle, *Chelydra serpentina*, a snapper. **snappish** *a.* given to snapping or biting, given to sharp replies, spiteful, irascible. **snappishly** *adv.* **snappishness** *n.* **snappy** *a.* (*comp.* **snappier**, *superl.* **snappiest**) **1** snappish. **2** irritable, cross. **3** sharp, lively. **4** smart, stylish. **to make it snappy** to hurry up. **snappily** *adv.* **snapshot** *n.* a photograph taken casually, as distinct from a posed photograph taken in a studio.

snare (snee) *n.* **1** a trap, usu. consisting of a noose, for catching birds or other animals. **2** a trick, trap, stratagem or allurement by which one is brought into difficulty, defeat, disgrace, sin etc. **3** (*Mus.*) a string of gut, wire or hide stretched inside the head of a drum making a rattling sound when the head is struck. ~*v.t.* **1** to catch in a snare. **2** to ensnare, entrap or inveigle. **snare drum** *n.* (*Mus.*) a small drum with two heads, the lower of which is fitted with a snare. **snarer** *n.*

snarl[1] (snahl) *v.i.* **1** (of a dog) to growl in a sharp tone with teeth bared. **2** to speak in a harsh, surly or savage manner. ~*v.t.* to express or say with a snarl. ~*n.* **1** a sharp-toned growl. **2** a savage remark or exclamation. **snarler** *n.* **snarlingly** *adv.* **snarly** *a.* (*comp.* **snarlier**, *superl.* **snarliest**).

snarl[2] (snahl) *v.t.* **1** to entangle. **2** to cause to become confused or complicated. ~*v.i.* to become entangled, muddled, complicated, jammed etc. ~*n.* **1** a tangle, a knot of hair, thread etc. **2** a knot in wood. **3** (*fig.*) an entanglement, embarrassing difficulty. **to snarl up** to (cause to) become tangled, disordered, inoperable, immobile etc. **snarled** *a.* **snarl-up** *n.* an instance or state of confusion, obstruction, disorder etc. (e.g. a traffic jam).

snatch (snach) *v.t.* **1** to seize suddenly, eagerly or without permission or ceremony. **2** to steal, grab. **3** to remove or rescue (from, away etc.) suddenly or hurriedly. **4** to win or gain narrowly. **5** to grab (a chance or opportunity). ~*v.i.* to try to seize, to make a sudden motion (at) as if to seize. ~*n.* **1** an act of snatching, a grab (at). **2** that which is snatched; a short spell e.g. of rest, work. **3** a fragment of talk, song etc. **4** in weightlifting, a kind of lift in which the weight is raised overhead in one motion. **5** (*coll.*) a robbery, a kidnapping. **by/ in snatches** desultorily, in fits and starts. **snatcher** *n.* **snatchy** *a.* (*comp.* **snatchier**, *superl.* **snatchiest**). **snatchily** *adv.*

snazzy (snaz´i) *a.* (*comp.* **snazzier**, *superl.* **snazziest**) (*sl.*) up to date, showy, smart, attractive (e.g. of clothes). **snazzily** *adv.* **snazziness** *n.*

sneak (snēk) *v.i.* (*past*, *p.p.* **sneaked**, (*coll.*) **snuck** (snŭk)) **1** to creep (about, away, off etc.), as if afraid or ashamed to be seen. **2** to behave in a mean, cringing, cowardly or underhand way. **3** to tell tales. ~*v.t.* **1** (*sl.*) to steal. **2** to place or remove stealthily. ~*n.* **1** a person who sneaks. **2** a tale-bearer. **sneaker** *n.* **1** a rubber-soled shoe. **2** a person who sneaks. **sneaking** *a.* **1** unacknowledged but persistent (*have a sneaking admiration for someone*). **2** niggling, half-formed (*a sneaking suspicion*). **sneakingly** *adv.* **sneak thief** *n.* a pilferer, someone who steals from open windows or doors. **sneaky** *a.* (*comp.* **sneakier**, *superl.* **sneakiest**). **sneakily** *adv.* **sneakiness** *n.*

sneer (snia) *n.* a smile, laugh or verbal expression of contempt. ~*v.i.* **1** to show contempt by a smile, grin or laugh. **2** to scoff, to express derision or contempt (at). ~*v.t.* to say or express with a sneer. **sneerer** *n.* **sneering** *n.*, *a.* **sneeringly** *adv.* **sneery** *a.* (*comp.* **sneerier**, *superl.* **sneeriest**).

sneeze (snēz) *v.i.* to eject air etc. through the nostrils audibly and convulsively, owing to irritation of the inner membrane of the nose. ~*n.* an act of sneezing or the noise produced by it. **not to be sneezed at** not to be despised, worth consideration. **sneezer** *n.* **sneezy** *a.* (*comp.* **sneezier**, *superl.* **sneeziest**).

snick (snik) *v.t.* **1** to cut, to nick, to notch, to snip. **2** in cricket, to hit (the ball) lightly with a glancing stroke. ~*n.* **1** a slight cut, nick or notch. **2** a light glancing hit, in cricket.

snicker (snik´ə) *v.i.* **1** to snigger. **2** to neigh, to nicker. ~*v.t.* to say with a snigger. ~*n.* a snigger. **snickerer** *n.* **snickeringly** *adv.* **snickery** *a.*

snide (snīd) *a.* (*comp.* **snider**, *superl.* **snidest**) **1** malicious, sneering, disparaging, sly, mean. **2** sham, bogus, counterfeit. ~*n.* **1** a snide person. **2** a snide remark. **snidely** *adv.* **snideness** *n.*

sniff (snif) *v.i.* to draw air audibly up the nose in order to smell, clear the nasal passages, inhale a drug, express contempt etc. ~*v.t.* **1** to draw (up) with the breath through the nose. **2** to smell, to perceive or investigate by sniffing. ~*n.* **1** an act or the sound of sniffing. **2** that which is sniffed in (e.g. a scent). **to sniff at 1** to investigate by sniffing. **2** to express contempt or disdain for. **to sniff out** to discover (as if) by sniffing, to find through investigation. **sniffer** *n.* **1** (*often in comb.*) someone who sniffs, esp. a person who sniffs a drug, glue etc. (*glue-sniffers*). **2** (*sl.*) the nose. **3** (*coll.*) any of various devices for detecting gas, drugs, explosives, radiation etc. **sniffer dog** *n.* a dog trained to smell out drugs or explosives. **sniffle** (-əl) *v.i.* to sniff (as with a cold, when weeping etc.), to snuffle. ~*n.* **1** an act or sound of sniffling. **2** a snuffle. **3** (*usu. pl.*) a slight cold, a runny nose. **sniffler** *n.* **sniffly** *a.* **sniffy** *a.* (*comp.* **sniffier**, *superl.* **sniffiest**) (*coll.*) given to sniffing, disdainful. **sniffily** *adv.* **sniffiness** *n.*

snifter (snif´tə) *n.* **1** (*coll.*) a small drink of spirits. **2** a short-stemmed glass with a wide bowl and narrow top (for brandy, liqueur etc.).

snigger (snig´ə) *v.i.* to laugh in a half-suppressed or discourteous manner. ~*n.* a suppressed laugh. **sniggerer** *n.* **sniggeringly** *adv.*

snip (snip) *v.t.* (*pres.p.* **snipping**, *past, p.p.* **snipped**) **1** to cut (cloth etc.) or cut (a hole) in something, quickly and sharply with scissors or shears. **2** to cut or clip (off) sharply or quickly with shears or scissors. ~*v.i.* to make a quick sharp cutting movement with scissors or shears (at). ~*n.* **1** an act, movement or sound of snipping. **2** a cut with scissors or shears. **3** a small piece snipped off. **4** (*coll.*) a bargain. **5** (*pl.*) shears used to cut sheet metal by hand. **snipper** *n.* **snippet** (-it) *n.* **1** a small bit snipped off. **2** a scrap of information or news. **3** a short extract from a book etc. **snippety** *a.* **snipping** *n.* a piece snipped off.

snipe (snīp) *n.* (*pl. in general* **snipe**, *in particular* **snipes**) **1** a long-billed marsh- and shore-bird of the genus *Gallinago*, esp. the British *G. coelestis.* **2** a gunshot, usu. fired from cover. **3** a verbal attack or criticism, usu. made from a secure position. ~*v.i.* **1** to criticize, to find fault, carp (at), esp. slyly or snidely. **2** to pick off members of the enemy, usu. from cover. **3** to shoot or hunt snipe. ~*v.t.* to shoot at or kill from cover. **sniper** *n.* **sniping** *n.*

snitch (snich) *v.i.* (*sl.*) to inform, to peach (on). ~*v.t.* to steal, to pilfer. ~*n.* **1** the nose. **2** a tell-tale, an informer. **3** a minor robbery.

snivel (sniv´əl) *v.i.* (*pres.p.* **snivelling**, (*N Am.*) **sniveling**, *past, p.p.* **snivelled**, (*N Am.*) **sniveled**) **1** to weep with nose running, to be tearful. **2** to run at the nose, sniffing continually. ~*n.* **1** mucus running from the nose. **2** audible or affected weeping. **3** hypocrisy. **sniveller**, (*N Am.*) **sniveler** *n.* **snivellingly** *adv.* **snivelly**, (*N Am.*) **snively** *a.*

snob (snob) *n.* **1** a person who cultivates or behaves obsequiously towards those of higher social position, or regards the claims of wealth and position with an exaggerated and contemptible respect. **2** a person who condescends to, patronizes, or avoids those felt to be of lower standing. **snobbery** *n.* (*pl.* **snobberies**). **snobbish** *a.* **snobbishly** *adv.* **snobbishness** *n.* **snobby** *a.* (*comp.* **snobbier**, *superl.* **snobbiest**).

snog (snog) *v.i.* (*pres.p.* **snogging**, *past, p.p.* **snogged**) (*coll.*) to kiss and cuddle. ~*n.* an act or an instance of this. **snogger** *n.*

snood (snood) *n.* **1** a crocheted net to contain a woman's back-hair. **2** a knitted tube worn as a hood. **snooded** *a.*

snook (snook) *n.* a gesture of derision made with the thumb to the nose and the fingers spread. **to cock a snook 1** to make this gesture (at). **2** to express defiance or laugh (at someone's authority etc.).

snooker (snoo´kə) *n.* **1** a game played on a billiard table, in which a white cue ball is used to pocket the other 21 balls (15 red and 6 coloured). **2** a shot or situation in this game in which the cue ball is blocked by another ball, making a direct stroke impossible. ~*v.t.* **1** to put (one's opponent or oneself) in this position. **2** to put (someone) in a difficult position, to obstruct, to thwart. **3** to defeat. **snookered** *a.* thwarted, foiled, outwitted.

snoop (snoop) *v.i.* to go about in an inquisitive or sneaking manner, to pry. ~*n.* **1** an act or instance of snooping. **2** a snooper, a detective. **snooper** *n.* a prying busybody. **snoopy** *a.* (*comp.* **snoopier,** *superl.* **snoopiest**).

snoot (snoot) *n.* (*coll.*) the nose. **snooty** *a.* (*comp.* **snootier,** *superl.* **snootiest**) supercilious, snobbish. **snootily** *adv.* **snootiness** *n.*

snooze (snooz) *v.i.* to take a short sleep, esp. in the day. ~*n.* a short sleep, a nap. **snoozer** *n.* **snoozy** *a.* (*comp.* **snoozier,** *superl.* **snooziest**).

snore (snaw) *v.i.* to breathe through the mouth and nostrils with a snorting noise in sleep. ~*n.* an act or sound of snoring. **snorer** *n.* **snoring** *n.*

snorkel (snaw´kəl), **schnorkel** (shnaw´-) *n.* **1** a breathing apparatus used in diving and swimming consisting of a tube which extends from the mouth to above the surface of the water. **2** a device on a submarine for taking in and expelling air when at periscope depth. ~*v.i.* (*pres.p.* **snorkelling,** (*N Am.*) **snorkeling,** *past, p.p.* **snorkelled,** (*N Am.*) **snorkeled**) to swim with a snorkel. **snorkeller,** (*N Am.*) **snorkeler** *n.*

snort (snawt) *v.i.* **1** to force air violently and loudly through the nostrils like a frightened or excited horse (e.g. as an expression of contempt). **2** (of e.g. an engine) to make a noise like this. **3** (*sl.*) to inhale drugs, esp. habitually. ~*v.t.* **1** to utter or throw (out) with a snort. **2** (*sl.*) to inhale (a drug). ~*n.* **1** an act or sound of snorting. **2** (*sl.*) an instance of inhaling a drug, or the amount inhaled in one snort. **3** (*coll.*) a small drink of spirits, a snifter. **snorter** *n.* **1** a person or animal that snorts. **2** (*coll.*) anything of extraordinary size, excellence, violence etc. (such as a strong wind).

snot (snot) *n.* (*sl.*) **1** mucus from the nose. **2** a low or contemptible person. **snot-rag** *n.* a handkerchief. **snotty** *a.* (*comp.* **snottier,** *superl.* **snottiest**) **1** (*coll.*) soiled with nasal mucus. **2** (*sl.*) contemptible, low. **3** (*sl.*) snobbish, snooty. **snottily** *adv.* **snottiness** *n.*

snout (snowt) *n.* **1** the projecting nose or muzzle of an animal. **2** (*sl., derog.*) the human nose. **3** a nozzle. **4** a projecting front, as of a glacier, a cliff etc. **5** (*sl.*) cigarette tobacco. **6** (*sl.*) an informer, esp. a police one. **snouted** *a.* **snoutless** *a.* **snoutlike** *a.* **snouty** *a.* (*comp.* **snoutier,** *superl.* **snoutiest**).

snow (snō) *n.* **1** watery vapour in the atmosphere frozen into crystals and falling to the ground in flakes. **2** a fall of this or the layer it forms on the ground. **3** anything resembling snow, esp. in whiteness. **4** a gas in the form of frozen vapour, esp. carbon dioxide. **5** (*sl.*) cocaine. **6** a mass of white dots on a television or radar screen caused by interference. **7** a dessert resembling snow in appearance, texture and whiteness. ~*v.i.* **1** (with subject *it*) to fall in or as snow. **2** to come or arrive in large quantities. ~*v.t.* **1** to cover (over) or

block (up) with snow. **2** to confine or hem (in) with snow. **3** to send, sprinkle or scatter down as snow. **to snow under** (*usu. pass.*) to overwhelm (with work etc.). **snowball** *n.* a round mass of snow pressed together in the hands and flung as a missile. ~*v.t.* to pelt with snowballs. ~*v.i.* **1** to throw snowballs. **2** to accumulate with increasing rapidity, to accelerate. **snowberry** *n.* (*pl.* **snowberries**) **1** the N American shrub, *Symphoricarpos racemosus.* **2** any of various other white-berried ornamental shrubs. **3** the berry of these shrubs. **snow-blind** *a.* partially or totally blinded, usu. temporarily, through the glare of reflected light from the surface of snow. **snowblindness** *n.* **snowboard** *n.* a wide ski for sliding downhill on. **snowbound** *a.* imprisoned or kept from travelling by snow. **snowdrift** *n.* a mass of snow accumulated by the wind. **snowdrop** *n.* a bulbous plant, *Galanthus nivalis,* with a white drooping flower appearing in early spring. **snowfall** *n.* **1** a fall of snow. **2** the amount of snow falling in a given place during a given time. **snowfield** *n.* an expanse of snow, esp. in polar or lofty mountain regions. **snowflake** *n.* a fleecy cluster of ice crystals, or a single six-branched ice crystal, falling as snow. **snow goose** *n.* a white Arctic goose with black wing-tips. **snowless** *a.* **snowlike** *a., adv.* **snowline** *n.* the lowest limit of perpetual snow on mountains etc. **snowman** *n.* (*pl.* **snowmen**) a human-like figure built with packed snow. **snowmobile** *n.* a motor vehicle with runners or Caterpillar tracks enabling it to travel over snow. **snow pea** *n.* (*esp. N Am.*) a mangetout. **snowplough,** (*N Am.*) **snowplow** *n.* **1** an implement used to clear a road or railway track of snow. **2** a skiing position in which the tips of the skis meet to form a V shape. ~*v.i.* to ski in this position in order to slow or stop. **snowscape** *n.* a snow-covered landscape. **snowshoe** *n.* a long, light, racket- or ski-shaped frame worn to prevent sinking when walking on snow. **snowshoe hare, snowshoe rabbit** *n.* a N American hare, white-coated in winter, that has long hind feet. **snowstorm** *n.* a heavy fall of snow, esp. accompanied by wind. **snow-white** *a.* as white or pure as snow. **snowy** *a.* (*comp.* **snowier,** *superl.* **snowiest**) **1** resembling snow, white like snow. **2** (of weather etc.) bringing a lot of snow. **3** covered with snow. **4** spotless, unblemished. **snowily** *adv.* **snowiness** *n.*

Snr., snr. *abbr.* senior.

snub (snŭb) *v.t.* (*pres.p.* **snubbing,** *past, p.p.* **snubbed**) to rebuke with sarcasm or contempt, to slight in a pointed or offensive manner. ~*n.* an act of snubbing, a rebuff, a slight. ~*a.* short, stubby. **snubber** *n.* **snubbingly** *adv.* **snub nose** *n.* a short upturned nose. **snub-nosed** *a.*

snuck SNEAK.

snuff (snŭf) *n.* the charred part of the wick in a candle or lamp. ~*v.t.* **1** to trim (a wick, candle etc.) by removing this. **2** to extinguish (a flame) by or as by snuffing. **to snuff it** (*sl.*) to die. **to**

snuff out 1 to put out, extinguish (a candle etc.). **2** (*sl.*) to kill. **snuffer** *n.* **1** a long-handled instrument with a cone-shaped cap at the end for extinguishing candles. **2** (*pl.*) a scissor-like instrument for trimming away snuff from the wick of a candle. **snuff movie, snuff film, snuff video** *n.* (*sl.*) a pornographic film whose climax is the actual murder of an unsuspecting member of the cast.

snuff² (snŭf) *n.* **1** powdered tobacco or other substance inhaled through the nose. **2** a pinch of this. **3** an act of snuffing. **4** a sniff. ~*v.t.* to draw in through the nostrils, to sniff, to scent. ~*v.i.* **1** to sniff. **2** to take snuff. **up to snuff 1** knowing, sharp, not easily imposed upon. **2** in good condition, up to scratch. **snuffbox** *n.* a small container for carrying snuff. **snuffy** *a.* (*comp.* **snuffier,** *superl.* **snuffiest**). **snuffiness** *n.*

snuffle (snŭf´əl) *v.i.* **1** to breathe noisily or make a sniffing noise as when the nose is obstructed. **2** to talk through the nose. **3** to snivel, to whine. ~*v.t.* **1** to say through the nose. **2** to sniff. ~*n.* **1** an act or sound of snuffling. **2** (*pl.*) a slight cold, the sniffles. **3** a nasal tone or voice. **snuffler** *n.* **snuffly** *a.*

snug (snŭg) *a.* (*comp.* **snugger,** *superl.* **snuggest**) **1** sheltered and comfortable. **2** cosy, comfortable. **3** compact, trim, well secured. ~*v.i.* (*pres.p.* **snugging,** *past, p.p.* **snugged**) to lie close, to nestle, to snuggle. ~*n.* a snuggery. **snuggery** *n.* (*pl.* **snuggeries**) a snug place or room, esp. in a pub or bar. **snuggle** (-əl) *v.i.* to move or lie close (up to) for warmth. ~*v.t.* to draw close to one. ~*n.* an act of snuggling. **snuggly** *a.* **snugly** *adv.* **snugness** *n.*

So. *abbr.* south, southern.

so¹ (sō) *adv.* **1** (*usu. with neg.*) in such a manner or to such an extent, degree etc. (with *as* expressed or understood) (*not so confident now; not so easy as it used to be; not so stupid as to believe that; never heard so blatant a lie!*). **2** in the manner or to the extent, degree, intent, result etc. (with *that*) (*was so tired that he fell asleep in the armchair*). **3** also, in addition (*He needs a holiday and so do I*). **4** therefore; with the result that (*I've got a dental appointment, so I'll be a bit late*). **5** on condition, provided (that) (*just so (that) you realize you're not the only one round here*). **6** well (*So, next we tried the window*). **7** extremely, very (*You've been so patient; Things are not so good*). **8** thus, this, that, as follows, as demonstrated (*I think so too; People thought her bad-tempered, but I never found her so; Place your feet so*). **9** in such a case, or state (*He's in a coma and likely to remain so for weeks*). ~*conj.* in order that (*Listen carefully so you miss nothing*). ~*int.* used to express surprise, dawning awareness or dissent etc. (*So! This is where you've been hiding!*). ~*a.* **1** true (*That is so*). **2** put in a set order, right (*likes things just so*). ~*pron.* the same, as much (*If you haven't yet registered, please do so now; You're too shy – you told me so yourself*). **and so**

forth and the rest, and so on, and the like. **and so on** and so forth. **or so** or thereabouts, or about that. **so as to** in order to (*I kept pinching myself so as to keep awake*). **so be it** let it be thus (in affirmation, resignation etc.). **so long!** (*coll.*) au revoir, goodbye. **so long as** as long as, on condition that (*So long as you play quietly, you can stay up till 9.30*). **so much 1** a great deal, to a great extent (*She's so much better!*). **2** a certain (limited) amount (*I only have so much patience*). **3** (*with neg.*) to a lesser degree (*not so much a fashion as a fad*). **so much as** (*with neg.*) (not) even (*without so much as a wave*). **so much for 1** I don't think much of (*So much for her fabled speed, if she can't be accurate*). **2** there is nothing more to be said about (*So much for that*). **so much so** to such a degree, extent (that). **so that** in order that (*We moved into town so that we could be nearer my mother*). **so what?** what about it? **so-and-so** *n.* (*pl.* **so-and-sos**) **1** an indefinite person or thing. **2** an unpleasant person or disliked thing. **so-called** *a.* usually called thus (with implication of doubt). **so so** *a.* indifferent, middling, mediocre. ~*adv.* indifferently.

so² SOH.

-so (sō) *comb. form* of any kind, -soever.

soak (sōk) *v.t.* **1** to put (something) in liquid to become permeated, to steep. **2** to wet thoroughly. **3** to suck (in or up), to absorb (liquid). **4** to extract, remove or wash (out) by steeping in a liquid. **5** (*coll.*) to tax heavily. ~*v.i.* **1** to lie in liquid so as to become permeated. **2** to permeate (into, through etc.). **3** (*coll.*) to drink excessively. ~*n.* **1** an act of soaking or an instance of being soaked. **2** the liquid that something is immersed in or the period for which something is immersed. **3** (*sl.*) a heavy drinker. **4** (*coll.*) a drinking bout. **5** (*Austral.*) low-lying land where water is retained. **to soak in** to become fully understood, appreciated, felt etc., to penetrate. **to soak oneself in** to become thoroughly acquainted or steeped in (a subject etc.). **soakage** (-ij) *n.* **soakaway** *n.* a hole or depression dug in the ground to allow drainage to percolate into the soil. **soaker** *n.* **soaking** *a.* wet through. ~*n.* an act of wetting, steeping etc.; the state of being soaked. **soaking wet** *a.* wet through.

soap (sōp) *n.* **1** a compound of a fatty acid and a base of sodium or potassium, producing a lather in water, and used for washing and cleansing. **2** a solid piece or bar of this, esp. for cleansing the body with. **3** INSOLUBLE SOAP (under INSOLUBLE). **4** (*coll.*) a soap opera. ~*v.t.* to rub or wash with soap. **soapbox** *n.* **1** a box for packing soap. **2** a box or improvised stand used as a platform by a street orator. **soapless** *a.* **soap opera** *n.* a serialized, long-running television or radio drama usu. following a regular set of characters through various domestic or sentimental situations (orig. sponsored by soap manufacturers). **soapstone** *n.* steatite. **soapsuds** *n.pl.* water impregnated with soap to form a foam. **soapwort**

n. a trailing herbaceous plant, *Saponaria officinalis*, the juice of which forms a lather with water. **soapy** *a.* (*comp.* **soapier**, *superl.* **soapiest**) **1** of the nature of or resembling soap. **2** smeared or combined with soap. **3** unctuous, flattering, smooth. **soapily** *adv.* **soapiness** *n.*

soar (saw) *v.i.* **1** to fly into the air, to rise. **2** (of a bird, aircraft etc.) to sail, float at a great height. **3** to rise intellectually or in spirit, status, position etc. **4** to increase or rise rapidly in amount, degree etc. **5** to tower. **soarer** *n.* **soaringly** *adv.*

sob (sob) *v.i.* (*pres.p.* **sobbing**, *past, p.p.* **sobbed**) **1** to weep violently, catching one's breath in a convulsive manner. **2** to gasp convulsively from physical exhaustion or distress. ~*v.t.* **1** to say with a sob or sobs. **2** to bring (oneself into a certain state) by sobbing (*She sobbed herself to sleep*). ~*n.* a convulsive catching of the breath, as in weeping. **sobbingly** *adv.* **sob sister** *n.* (*coll.*) **1** a female journalist who writes about personal relationships and problems. **2** a female actor who plays sentimental roles. **sob story** *n.* (*pl.* **sob stories**) a hard-luck story intended to elicit pity.

sober (sō´bə) *a.* (*comp.* **soberer**, *superl.* **soberest**) **1** not drunk; temperate in the use of alcoholic liquors etc. **2** well-balanced, sane. **3** self-possessed, calm. **4** (of a view, facts, the truth etc.) objective, not exaggerated. **5** (of colours etc.) subdued, quiet. ~*v.t., v.i.* to make or become sober. **sobering** *a.* **soberingly** *adv.* **soberly** *adv.* **soberness** *n.* **sobersided** *a.* of a sober, serious or sedate disposition. **sobersides** *n.* (*pl.* **sobersides**) a person of this disposition. **sobriety** (-brī´ə-) *n.*

sobriquet (sō´brikā), **soubriquet** (soo´-) *n.* **1** a nickname. **2** an assumed name.

Soc., soc. *abbr.* **1** socialist. **2** society.

soca (sō´kə) *n.* a type of music popular in the E Caribbean which blends elements of soul and calypso.

soccer (sok´ə) *n.* Association Football.

sociable (sō´shəbəl) *a.* **1** fit or inclined to associate or be friendly, companionable. **2** (of a party etc.) of a friendly, not formal, character. **sociability** (-bil´-), **sociableness** *n.* **sociably** *adv.*

social (sō´shəl) *a.* **1** of or relating to society, its organization or its divisions, or to the intercourse, behaviour or mutual relations of humans. **2** living in communities, tending to associate with others. **3** existing only as a part or member of a multiple organism. **4** (of insects) organized or existing in such a community. **5** of, relating to, or conducive to shared activities or companionship (*social gatherings*). **6** relating to the classes in society, esp. the upper class or fashionable society (*social background; social poise*). **7** sociable, companionable. ~*n.* a social gathering. **social anthropology** *n.* a discipline within the social sciences concerned with systems of belief and cultural organization in a society. **social climber** *n.* (*derog.*) a person who constantly looks for ways of improving their social status, esp. by ingratiating themselves

with people of a higher class. **social climbing** *n.* **social contract, social compact** *n.* a collective agreement between members of a society and a government that secures the rights and liberties of each individual to the extent of not interfering with another's rights and liberties. **social democracy** *n.* the theories and practices of socialists who believe in transforming a capitalist society into a socialist one by democratic means. **social democrat** *n.* **social engineering** *n.* the management and adjustment of society carried out on sociological principles. **social engineer** *n.* **socialism** *n.* the doctrine that the political and economic organization of society should be based on the subordination of the individual to the interests of the community, involving the collective ownership of the sources and instruments of production, democratic control of industries, cooperation instead of individual private gain, state distribution of the products instead of payment by wages, free education etc. **socialist** *n., a.* **socialistic** (-is´-) *a.* **socialistically** *adv.* **socialite** (-līt) *n.* a person who is constantly to be found in fashionable society. **sociality** (-shial´-) *n.* **socialize, socialise** *v.i.* to behave in a convivial or sociable manner, to mix socially. ~*v.t.* **1** to prepare, make fit for social life. **2** (*esp. N Am.*) to constitute or transform according to socialist principles. **socialization** (-zā´shən) *n.* **socialized medicine** *n.* (*N Am., derog.*) the providing of medical services to all through public funds. **socially** *adv.* **social order** *n.* the complex interdependent hierarchy that constitutes society, esp. with reference to one's place in it. **social realism** *n.* the realistic presentation of social conditions in art etc. **social science** *n.* **1** the study of society and the interaction and behaviour of its members. **2** any one of the subjects included in this, e.g. sociology, economics, political science, anthropology and psychology. **social scientist** *n.* **social secretary** *n.* a person whose job is to arrange the social engagements and activities of an organization or individual. **social security** *n.* state provision for the unemployed, aged or sick through a system of pensions or benefits. **social service** *n.* work for the benefit of one's fellow human beings, philanthropic work. **social services** *n.pl.* welfare services provided by the state or a local authority. **social work** *n.* any of various types of welfare service (for the aged, disabled etc.) provided by the social services and carried out by trained employees. **social worker** *n.*

society (səsī´əti) *n.* (*pl.* **societies**) **1** a social community. **2** the general body of persons, communities or nations constituting the human race regarded as a community. **3** social organization. **4** the privileged and fashionable classes of a community or some subdivision or quasi-subdivision of them, as *high society, polite society*. **5** a body of persons associated for some common object or collective interest, a club or an association. **6** the company of other people, companionship (*She enjoyed his society*; *She began to shun society*). **7** a group of plants or animals of the same species or sharing the same needs, characteristics etc. ~*a.* of or relating to fashionable society. **societal** *a.* of or relating to (human) society. **societally** *adv.*

socio- (sō´siō) *comb. form* **1** social. **2** society.

sociobiology (sōsiōbīol´əji) *n.* the study of human or animal behaviour from a genetic or evolutionary basis. **sociobiological** (-əloj´-) *a.* **sociobiologically** *adv.* **sociobiologist** *n.*

socio-economic (sōsiōēkənom´ik, -ek-) *a.* of, relating to or involving social and economic factors. **socio-economically** *adv.*

sociolinguistic (sōsiōling-gwis´tik) *a.* of or relating to the social aspects of language. **sociolinguist** (-ling´gwist) *n.* **sociolinguistically** *adv.* **sociolinguistics** *n.*

sociology (sōsiol´əji) *n.* **1** the science of the organization and dynamics of human society. **2** the study or investigation of social problems. **sociological** (-əloj´-) *a.* **sociologically** *adv.* **sociologist** *n.*

sociopolitical (sōsiōpəlit´ikəl) *a.* of, relating to or involving social and political factors.

sock¹ (sok) *n.* (*pl.* **socks,** (*commercial*) **sox**) **1** a short stocking. **2** a removable inner sole. **put a sock in it** (*sl.*) be quiet, shut up. **to blow the socks off** to astonish. **to knock the socks off 1** (*coll.*) to defeat resoundingly. **2** to astonish. **to pull one's socks up** to make a vigorous effort to do better.

sock² (sok) *v.t.* (*sl.*) to hit or punch (esp. a person) hard with a blow. ~*n.* a hard hit, punch or blow. **to sock it to** to address or attack with great vigour or force.

socket (sok´it) *n.* a natural or artificial hollow place or fitting adapted for receiving and holding another part or thing, e.g. an implement or electric plug, or for holding a revolving part such as a limb, eye, head of an instrument etc. ~*v.t.* (*pres.p.* **socketing,** *past, p.p.* **socketed**) to fit into or furnish with a socket.

sockeye (sok´ī) *n.* a Pacific blueback salmon, *Oncorhynchus nerka*, with red flesh highly esteemed as a food.

Socratic (səkrat´ik), †**Socratical** *a.* of, relating to or according to Socrates, Greek philosopher, 469–399 BC.

sod¹ (sod) *n.* **1** a piece of surface soil cut away, a turf. **2** surface soil filled with the roots of grass etc., turf, sward. **under the sod** in one's grave.

sod² (sod) *n.* (*taboo sl.*) **1** a despicable person, esp. male. **2** a person, chap (*the lucky sod*). ~*int.* curse (someone or something). **sod all** nothing at all. **sod off** go away, get lost. **sodding** *a.* accursed. ~*adv.* used as an intensive before adjectives and adverbs. **Sod's law** (sodz) *n.* a wry maxim saying that anything which can possibly go wrong will do so.

soda (sō´də) *n.* **1** (*Chem.*) any of various compounds of sodium, e.g. sodium carbonate, sodium hydroxide, sodium bicarbonate. **2** soda water. **3** (*N Am.*) a fizzy soft drink. **soda bread, soda scone** *n.* a type of bread or scone made with baking soda, esp. in Ireland. **soda fountain** *n.* **1** a device for dispensing soda water. **2** (*N Am.*) a counter serving soft drinks, ice creams etc. **soda syphon** *n.* a pressurized bottle for dispensing soda water. **soda water** *n.* an effervescent drink composed of water charged with carbon dioxide.

sodden (sod´ən) *a.* **1** soaked, saturated. **2** (of bread etc.) not properly baked, heavy, doughy. **3** bloated and stupid, esp. with drink. **soddenly** *adv.* **soddenness** *n.*

sodding SOD².

sodium (sō´diəm) *n.* (*Chem.*) a silver-white metallic element, at. no. 11, chem. symbol Na, the base of soda. **sodium bicarbonate** *n.* a white powder used in baking powder, effervescent drinks, antacid preparations and fire extinguishers, baking soda. **sodium carbonate** *n.* a crystalline salt used in the manufacture of cleaning agents, glass etc., washing soda. **sodium chloride** *n.* a colourless crystalline compound occurring in sea water, common salt. **sodium hydroxide** *n.* a deliquescent alkali used in manufacturing paper and soap, caustic soda. **sodium lamp, sodium-vapour lamp** *n.* an electric lamp used esp. in street lighting, consisting of a glass tube containing sodium vapour and neon which emits an orange light when current is passed through it. **sodium nitrate** *n.* a white crystalline salt occurring naturally as Chile saltpetre, used in fertilizers, explosives etc.

Sodom (sod´əm) *n.* a place of utter wickedness or depravity. **sodomite** (-mīt) *n.* a person who practises sodomy. **sodomitic** (-mit´-), **sodomitical** *a.* **sodomy** (-i) *n.* anal intercourse with a man or woman, or sexual relations with an animal (supposedly the characteristic sexual behaviour of the people of Sodom, Gen. xix.24).

soever (sōev´ə), **-soever** *adv.* appended, sometimes as a suffix, and sometimes after an interval, to pronouns, adverbs or adjectives to give an indefinite or universal meaning (*wheresoever I find her*; *in what place soever she dwells*).

sofa (sō´fə) *n.* a long stuffed couch or seat with raised back and ends. **sofa bed** *n.* a sofa that can be extended so as to serve as a bed.

soffit (sof´it) *n.* the undersurface of a cornice, lintel, balcony, arch etc.

soft (soft) *a.* **1** yielding easily to pressure, easily moulded, cut or worked. **2** smooth to the touch. **3** not loud or harsh. **4** affecting the senses in a mild or delicate manner. **5** (of a day, a breeze etc.) balmy, gentle. **6** (of light colours) not brilliant, not glaring. **7** (of radiation rays) low in energy. **8** (of water) free from mineral salts that prevent lathering, suitable for washing. **9** (of a drug) relatively harmless or non-addictive. **10** gentle or mild in disposition, yielding. **11** (of the wing of a political party) willing to compromise, moderate. **12** impressionable, sympathetic. **13** easily imposed on, lenient. **14** silly, simple. **15** amorous, sentimental. **16** (of a job) easy. **17 a** in phonetics, not guttural or explosive, sibilant (as *c* in *cede* or *g* in *gem*). **b** voiced or unaspirated (as *b*, *d* and *g*). *~adv.* softly, gently, quietly. **to be soft on 1** to be lenient or sympathetic towards. **2** to be amorously inclined towards. **to have a soft spot for** to be fond of (a person). **softball** *n.* **1** a game resembling baseball played with a larger and softer ball. **2** the ball used in this game. **soft-boiled** *a.* (of an egg) lightly boiled, so as to leave the yolk runny. **soft-centred**, (*N Am.*) **soft-centered** *a.* **1** (of a chocolate) with a soft filling. **2** (of a person) kind or sentimental at heart. **soft-core** *a.* (of pornography) relatively inexplicit. **soft drink** *n.* a non-intoxicant beverage. **soften** (sof´ən) *v.t.* to make soft or softer. *~v.i.* to become soft or softer. **to soften up 1** to make more sympathetic to. **2** to break down the resistance of. **3** to reduce the effectiveness of the defences of (a targeted position etc.) e.g. by preliminary bombing. **softener** *n.* **softening** *n.* **soft-focus** *n., a.* (having, designed to produce) a slightly out-of-focus image with blurred edges. **soft fruit** *n.* small stoneless berries such as strawberries, raspberries, blackcurrants, redcurrants and blackberries. **soft furnishings** *n.pl.* textile furnishings such as carpets, curtains, chair covers etc. **soft-headed** *a.* silly, stupid. **soft-headedness** *n.* **soft-hearted** *a.* tender-hearted, compassionate. **soft-heartedly** *adv.* **soft-heartedness** *n.* **softie**, **softy** *n.* (*pl.* **softies**) **1** a silly, weak-minded person. **2** a person who is physically unfit or flaccid. **3** a tender-hearted person. **softish** *a.* **soft-land** *v.i., v.t.* to land or cause (a spacecraft) to land gently on the moon or a planet, without incurring damage. **soft landing** *n.* **softly** *adv.* **softly-softly** *a.* (of tactics) deceptively gentle, but insidious nonetheless. **softness** *n.* **soft option** *n.* an option offering least difficulty. **soft palate** *n.* the posterior part of the palate terminating in the uvula. **soft-paste** *n.* porcelain, made from bone ash, clay etc. **soft pedal** *n.* (*Mus.*) a foot pedal for subduing the tone of notes played on the piano. **soft-pedal** *v.i., v.t.* (*pres.p.* **soft-pedalling**, (*N Am.*) **soft-pedaling**, *past, p.p.* **soft-pedalled**, (*N Am.*) **soft-pedaled**) to play down, avoid the issue of. **soft porn** *n.* soft-core pornography. **soft roe** *n.* the roe of a male fish. **soft sell** *n.* selling by means of gentle persuasiveness or suggestion. **soft-sell** *v.t.* (*past, p.p.* **soft-sold**). **soft soap** *n.* **1** semi-liquid soap made with potash. **2** (*coll.*) flattery, blarney. **soft-soap** *v.t.* (*coll.*) to flatter for some ulterior object. **soft-spoken** *a.* **1** speaking softly. **2** mild, affable, conciliatory. **soft target** *n.* an easily attacked, undefended target. **soft tissues** *n.pl.* the soft bodily parts as distinct from bone or cartilage. **soft-top** *n.* **1** a car with a flexible roof that can be folded back. **2** the roof of a car like this. **soft touch**

n. (*sl.*) someone easily influenced or imposed upon. **software** *n.* computer programs designed to perform various applications, e.g. word processing. **softwood** *n.* **1** the wood of a coniferous tree such as the pine. **2** a conifer yielding this wood. **softy** SOFTIE (under SOFT).

soggy (sog´i) *a.* (*comp.* **soggier**, *superl.* **soggiest**) **1** soaked, sodden, thoroughly wet. **2** (*coll.*) dull, heavy, spiritless. **soggily** *adv.* **sogginess** *n.*

soh (sō), **so**, **sol** (sol) *n.* (*Mus.*) **1** the fifth note of a major scale in the tonic sol-fa system. **2** the note G in the fixed-doh system.

soigné (swahn´yā), (*fem.*) **soignée** *a.* **1** well-turned-out, well-groomed. **2** elegant, tasteful.

soil¹ (soil) *n.* **1** the ground, esp. the top stratum of the earth's crust, composed of a mixture of crumbled rock and organic matter, whence plants derive their mineral food. **2** territory, region (*on German soil*; *back on my native soil*). **3** the earth with reference to agriculture and cultivation (*a man of the soil*). **soil-less** *a.* **soil science** *n.* the scientific study of soils, pedology. **soily** *a.* (*comp.* **soilier**, *superl.* **soiliest**).

soil² (soil) *v.t.* **1** to make dirty. **2** to tarnish, to pollute. *~v.i.* to become sullied or dirty, to tarnish. *~n.* **1** a dirty spot or defilement. **2** any foul matter, filth. **soiled** *a.* **soil pipe** *n.* a pipe carrying waste material and water from a toilet.

soirée (swah´rā) *n.* an evening party or gathering for conversation and social intercourse etc., usu. with music.

sojourn (soj´œn, sō´-) *v.i.* to stay or reside (in, among etc.) temporarily. *~n.* a temporary stay or residence. **sojourner** *n.*

sol¹ (sol) *n.* (*Chem.*) a colloidal solution.

sol² SOH.

sola (sō´lə) *n.* **1** an E Indian plant with a pithy stem, *Aeschynomene indica.* **2** the pith of this plant, used for making sun helmets. **sola topi**, **sola topee** *n.* a helmet affording protection from the sun, made from sola.

solace (sol´əs) *n.* comfort in grief, trouble etc. *~v.t.* to comfort or console in trouble etc. **to solace oneself with** to find comfort in.

solan (sō´lən), **solan goose** *n.* the gannet, *Sula bassana.*

solanum (səlā´nəm) *n.* any plant of the genus *Solanum*, containing the potato, eggplant, nightshades and tobacco. **solanaceous** (solənā´shəs) *a.*

solar (sō´lə) *a.* of or relating to, proceeding from, measured by or powered by the sun. **solar battery** *n.* a battery consisting of one or more solar cells. **solar cell** *n.* a cell that converts solar energy into electricity. **solar day** *n.* the interval between successive traverses of the meridian (at any particular place) by the sun. **solar eclipse** *n.* an eclipse of the sun in which it is obscured by the moon. **solar energy** *n.* **1** radiant energy produced by the sun. **2** energy derived from the sun, solar power. **solarium** (-leə´riəm) *n.* (*pl.* **solaria** (-riə), **solariums**) a room or building constructed for the enjoyment of, or therapeutical exposure

of the body to, the rays of the sun. **solar panel** *n.*
a panel of solar cells functioning as a power
source. **solar plexus** *n.* the epigastric plexus, a
network of nerves behind the stomach. **solar
power** *n.* solar energy. **solar system** *n.* the sun
and the various heavenly bodies revolving about
it. **solar time** *n.* time as reckoned by the apparent
motion of the sun. **solar year** *n.* the time taken by
the earth to make a single circuit of the sun, 365
days, 5 hours, 48 minutes and 46 seconds.

sold SELL.

solder (sōl´də) *n.* **1** a fusible alloy for uniting the
edges etc. of less fusible metals. **2** anything that
cements or unites. ~*v.t.* to unite or mend with or
as with solder. ~*v.i.* to become united or mended
(as) with solder. **solderable** *a.* **solderer** *n.*

soldier (sōl´jə) *n.* **1** a person engaged in military
service, esp. a private or non-commissioned officer. **2** a person of military skill or experience,
esp. a tried and successful commander. **3** a person who works diligently for a cause. **4** a soldier
ant, soldier beetle, or soldier crab. **5** an oblong
piece of toast for dipping into a soft-boiled egg.
~*v.i.* to serve as a soldier. **to soldier on** to persevere doggedly in the face of difficulty. **soldier
ant** *n.* any of the asexual fighting ants or termites
of a community, with a large head and jaws.
soldier beetle *n.* a reddish beetle that preys
on the larvae of other insects. **soldier crab** *n.*
a species of hermit crab. **soldier-like** *a.* **soldierly**
a. **soldier of fortune** *n.* a military adventurer
ready to fight in any army for pay, a mercenary.
soldiership *n.* **soldiery** *n.* (*pl.* **soldieries**) **1** soldiers collectively. **2** a body of soldiers. **3** the profession of soldiers, soldiership.

sole[1] (sōl) *n.* **1** the flat underside or bottom of the
foot. **2** the part of a boot or shoe under the foot,
esp. the part in front of the heel. **3** the bottom or
lower part (of a plane, a plough, the head of a
golf club, various engines etc.). **4** the floor of a
ship's cabin. ~*v.t.* to provide or fit (a boot etc.)
with a sole. **-soled** *a.*

sole[2] (sōl) *n.* a flatfish of various species of the
family Soleidae, highly esteemed as food.

sole[3] (sōl) *a.* single, only (*Her sole aim in life is
shopping; is the sole prerogative of the Speaker*).
solely *adv.* **soleness** *n.*

solecism (sol´isizm) *n.* **1** a deviation from correct
idiom or grammar. **2** a breach of good manners,
an impropriety. **solecist** *n.* **solecistic** (-sis´-),
solecistical *a.*

Usage note The nouns *solecism* and *solipsism*
should not be confused: a *solecism* is a lapse in
language or manners, and *solipsism* a philosophical theory.

---

solemn (sol´əm) *a.* **1** performed with or accompanied by ceremonies or due formality. **2** awe-
inspiring, impressive. **3** serious, momentous.
4 formal, pompous. **5** dull, sombre. **solemness**,
solemnness *n.* **solemnity** (-lem´ni-) *n.* (*pl.* **solem-
nities**) **1** solemness, impressiveness. **2** affected

gravity or formality. **3** (*often pl.*) a rite or ceremony, esp. one performed with religious rever-
ence. **solemnize** (-nīz), **solemnise** *v.t.* **1** to dignify
or to celebrate with solemn formalities or ceremonies. **2** to make solemn. **solemnization** (-zā´-
shən) *n.* **solemnizer** *n.* **solemnly** *adv.* **Solemn
Mass** *n.* HIGH MASS (under HIGH).

solenoid (sol´ənoid, sō´-) *n.* a magnet consisting
of a cylindrical coil traversed by an electric current. **solenoidal** (-noi´-) *a.*

sol-fa (solfah´) *n.* solmization, tonic sol-fa.

soli SOLO.

solicit (səlis´it) *v.t.* (*pres.p.* **soliciting**, *past, p.p.*
solicited) **1** to make earnest or importunate
requests for. **2** to make earnest or persistent requests or appeals to. **3** to entice or incite (someone) to do something illegal or immoral. **4** (of a
prostitute) openly to offer sexual relations to in
exchange for money. ~*v.i.* **1** to make earnest or
importunate appeals. **2** (of a prostitute) to proposition someone as a potential client. **solicita-
tion** (-ā´shən) *n.* **solicitor** *n.* **1** a legal practitioner
authorized to advise clients and prepare causes
for barristers but not to appear as advocate in the
higher courts. **2** a person who solicits. **Solicitor
General** *n.* (*pl.* **Solicitors General**) (*Law*) a law
officer of the British Crown ranking next to the
Attorney General, appointed by the government
in power to advise and represent it in legal
matters. **solicitorship** *n.* **solicitous** *a.* **1** anxious,
concerned, apprehensive, disturbed (about, for
etc.). **2** eager (to). **solicitously** *adv.* **solicitous-
ness** *n.* **solicitude** (-tūd) *n.* **1** a solicitous state
of mind, or solicitous behaviour. **2** anxiety,
concern.

solid (sol´id) *a.* (*comp.* **solider**, *superl.* **solidest**)
1 firm, unyielding. **2** composed of particles
closely cohering; not hollow (*a solid block of concrete*). **3** uniform, the same throughout (*solid
gold*). **4** substantial, not flimsy (*good solid walls*).
5 (*Geom.*) of or in three dimensions. **6** reliable,
well-grounded (*a solid argument*). **7** thinking,
feeling or acting unanimously. ~*adv.* **1** in a solid
manner. **2** so as to be solid (*set solid*). **3** unanimously. ~*n.* **1** a rigid, compact body. **2** (*Geom.*) a
body or magnitude possessing length, breadth
and depth, having thickness or volume. **solidify**
(-lid´ifi) *v.t., v.i.* (*3rd pers. sing. pres.* **solidifies**,
pres.p. **solidifying**, *past, p.p.* **solidified**) to make
or become solid. **solidifiable** *a.* **solidification**
(-fikā´shən) *n.* **solidifier** *n.* **solidity** (-lid´-), **solid-
ness** *n.* **solidly** *adv.* **solid-state** *a.* **1** of or relating
to solid matter or substances. **2** of, composed of,
or relating to semiconductor materials.

solidarity (solidar´iti) *n.* **1** cohesion, mutual
dependence. **2** community of interests, feelings,
responsibilities etc.

solidus (sol´idəs) *n.* (*pl.* **solidi** (-dī)) **1** the stroke
(/) formerly denoting a shilling (as in 2/6), also
used in writing fractions (e.g. 1/4), separating
numbers (e.g. in dates) or alternative words (as
in *him/ her*) etc. **2** (*in full* **solidus curve**) in a

graph representing the composition and temperature of a mixture, a curve below which the mixture is completely solid.

soliloquy (səlil´əkwi) *n.* (*pl.* **soliloquies**) **1** the activity of talking to oneself. **2** a speech or discourse, esp. in a play, uttered to oneself, a monologue. **soliloquist** *n.* **soliloquize, soliloquise** *v.i.* **soliloquizer** *n.*

solipsism (sol´ipsizm) *n.* the philosophical theory that the only knowledge possible is that of oneself, absolute egoism. **solipsist** *n., a.* **solipsistic** (-sis´-) *a.*

Usage note See note under SOLECISM.

solitaire (sol´iteə) *n.* **1** a gem, esp. a diamond, set singly in a ring or other jewel. **2** a jewel, esp. a ring, set with a single gem. **3** a game for one player, played on a board with hollows and marbles or holes and pegs, in which marbles or pegs are removed from the board as others are jumped over them, till only one remains. **4** (*esp. N Am.*) a card game for one player, patience.

solitary (sol´itəri) *a.* **1** living or being alone. **2** (*Bot.*) (of plants) growing singly. **3** passed or spent alone (*a solitary life*). **4** (of a place) unfrequented, secluded. **5** single, individual (*can't think of a solitary reason*). *~n.* (*pl.* **solitaries**) **1** a person who lives in solitude, a recluse. **2** (*coll.*) solitary confinement. **solitarily** *adv.* **solitariness** *n.* **solitary confinement** *n.* in a prison, incarceration without the company of others, isolation.

solitude (sol´itūd) *n.* **1** seclusion, loneliness. **2** somewhere isolated and empty of people.

solmization (solmizā´shən), **solmisation** *n.* (*Mus.*) the association of the syllables *doh, ray, me, fah, soh, lah, te* with the notes of the musical scale, *doh* being C in the fixed-doh system, or the keynote in tonic sol-fa.

solo (sō´lō) *n.* (*pl.* **solos, soli** (-lē)) **1** a composition or passage played by a single instrument or sung by a single voice, usu. with an accompaniment. **2** solo whist. **3** a solo flight. **4** any unaided or unaccompanied effort by one person. *~a., adv.* unaccompanied, alone. *~v.i.* (*3rd pers. sing. pres.* **soloes**, *pres.p.* **soloing**, *past, p.p.* **soloed**) **1** to perform a musical solo. **2** to fly an aircraft unaccompanied. **solo climbing** *n.* rock-climbing without ropes or the assistance of a partner. **solo flight** *n.* a flight in an aircraft by a single person. **soloist** *n.* **solo whist** *n.* a card game for four people somewhat resembling whist.

Solomon (sol´əmən) *n.* a very wise man (after King Solomon of Israel, d. *c.*930 BC). **Solomonic** (-mon´-) *a.*

solstice (sol´stis) *n.* either of the times (about 21 June and 22 Dec.) and points at which the sun is farthest from the celestial equator (north in summer and south in winter). **solstitial** (-stish´əl) *a.*

soluble (sol´ūbəl) *a.* **1** capable of being dissolved in a fluid. **2** capable of being solved. **solubility** (-bil´-) *n.* **solubilize, solubilise** *v.t.* **solubilization**

(-zā´shən) *n.* **solute** (-ūt) *n.* a dissolved substance.

solution (səloo´shən) *n.* **1** the resolution or act or process of solving a problem, difficulty etc. **2** the correct answer to a problem, puzzle etc. or the means of solving it. **3** the liquefaction of a solid or gaseous body by mixture with a liquid. **4** the liquid combination so produced. **5** the condition of being dissolved. **6** separation, dissolution, disintegration.

solve (solv) *v.t.* to resolve or find an answer to (a problem etc.). **solvable** *a.* **solvability** (-bil´-) *n.* **solvation** (-vā´shən) *n.* **solvent** (-vənt) *a.* **1** having the power to dissolve. **2** able to pay all just debts or claims. *~n.* **1** a liquid that can dissolve a substance. **2** something which solves. **solvency** *n.* **solvent abuse** *n.* the using of solvents (such as glue or petrol) as drugs by inhaling their fumes. **solver** *n.*

Som. *abbr.* Somerset.

soma (sō´mə) *n.* (*pl.* **somata** (sō´mətə)) **1** the body as distinguished from soul and spirit. **2** the body of an organism excluding its reproductive cells. **somatic** (səmat´ik) *a.* of or relating to the body as distinct from the mind, corporeal, physical.

Somali (səmah´li) *n.* (*pl.* **Somalis, Somali**) **1** a member of a people inhabiting Somalia in NE Africa. **2** the language of this people. *~a.* of or relating to this people, their language or their country.

sombre (som´bə), (*N Am.*) **somber** *a.* **1** dark, gloomy. **2** solemn, melancholy. **3** grave, worrying (*a sombre outlook*). **sombrely** *adv.* **sombreness** *n.*

sombrero (sombreə´rō) *n.* (*pl.* **sombreros**) a wide-brimmed hat worn esp. in Mexico.

some (sŭm) *a.* **1** an indeterminate quantity, number etc. of. **2** an appreciable if limited amount etc. of. **3** several. **4** (at least) a few, a little (*I do have some common sense*). **5** a considerable quantity, amount etc. of (*It'll take some time to sort out*). **6** a certain, a particular but not definitely known or specified (person or thing) (*Some psychologist said so*). **7** certain (members of a group) or a certain (proportion of a total amount) in contrast to the others or the rest (*Some people are allergic to gluten*). **8** used to present an approximate number (*some 200 people*). **9** (*esp. N Am.*) striking, outstanding (*That's some kitchen*). *~adv.* (*coll.*) to some extent (*You've certainly improved some*). *~pron.* **1** a particular but unspecified amount or quantity. **2** certain unspecified ones. **and then some** (*sl.*) and a lot more. **somebody** *pron.* some person. *~n.* (*pl.* **somebodies**) a person of consequence. **someday, some day** *adv.* at some unspecified time in the future. **somehow** *adv.* **1** in some indeterminate way, for some unknown reason (*Somehow I miss him still*). **2** in some way or other, no matter how (*I must see you somehow*). **3** by some indeterminate means. **someone** *pron., n.* somebody. **someone or other, something or other** *pron.* an unspecified person or thing. **someplace** *adv.*

(*esp. N Am.*) somewhere. **something** *pron., n.*
1 some indeterminate, unknown or unspecified
thing (*Have something to eat; Something's happened; He's an expert on something, I forget
what*). **2** some quantity or portion (*She has something of her mother in her*). **3** a thing of consequence or importance (*You made it – that's
quite something*). **or something** used to indicate
a further unspecified possibility (*The train must
be late or something*). **something of** by way of
being (*She's something of an expert on early
music*). **to see something of** to meet (someone)
occasionally. **something else** *n.* (*esp. N Am., sl.*) a
person or thing inspiring wonder, awe, disbelief
etc. **sometime** *adv.* at some unspecified time. *~a.*
former, late. **sometimes** *adv.* occasionally, now
and then. **someway** *adv.* in some unspecified
way. **somewhat** *adv.* to some extent, rather. **more
than somewhat** considerably (*I was more than
somewhat annoyed*). **somewhen** *adv.* (*coll.*) at
some time. **somewhere** *n., adv.* **1** (in, at or to)
some unknown or unspecified place. **2** (in) some
place or other. **somewhere about** approximately
(*aged somewhere about 45*). **to get somewhere** to
make headway, to progress.
-some¹ (səm) *suf.* **1** forming adjectives from
verbs, nouns or adjectives, denoting qualities, as
wearisome, loathsome, toothsome, wholesome.
2 forming nouns from numbers, denoting groups
of a certain number of people, as *threesome,
foursome, eightsome* etc.
-some² (sōm) *comb. form* a body, as in *chromosome.*
somersault (sŭm´əsawlt), **summersault** *n.* a
leap, or a forward roll on the ground, in which
one turns head over heels and lands on one's
feet. *~v.i.* to execute a somersault.
somnambulance (somnam´būləns) *n.* sleepwalking. **somnambulant** *n., a.* **somnambulate**
v.i. to sleepwalk. **somnambulation** (-lā´shən) *n.*
somnambulator *n.* **somnambulism** *n.* **somnam-
bulist** *n.* **somnambulistic** (-lis´-) *a.*
somnolent (som´nələnt) *a.* **1** sleepy, drowsy.
2 inducing sleep or drowsiness. **somnolence,
somnolency** *n.* **somnolently** *adv.*
son (sŭn) *n.* **1** a male child in relation to a parent
or parents. **2** a male descendant. **3** a form of
address used by an old person to a youth, or by
a priest or teacher to a disciple etc. **4** a native (of
a country). **5** an inheritor, exponent or product
(of a quality, art, occupation etc.) (*the sons
of toil*). **the Son** Christ as the second person
of the Trinity. **son-in-law** *n.* (*pl.* **sons-in-law**) a
daughter's husband. **sonless** *a.* **sonny** *n.* a familiar, often patronizing or belittling term of address to a boy or man. **son of a bitch, sonofabitch**
n. (*pl.* **sons of bitches**) (*derog.*) a man. **son of a
gun** *n.* a rascal. **sonship** *n.*
sonant (sō´nənt) *a.* voiced and syllabic. *~n.* **1** a
vowel or other voiced sound or letter. **2** a syllabic
consonant, e.g. syllabic *l, m* or *n.*
sonar (sō´nah) *n.* a device which detects the

presence and position of underwater objects by
means of echo-soundings or emitted sound.
sonata (sənah´tə) *n.* a musical composition for
one instrument, or for one instrument accompanied on the piano, usu. of three or four movements in different rhythms.
son et lumière (son ā loomieə´) *n.* an outdoor
entertainment at a historic location which re-
creates past events associated with it using
sound effects, a spoken narration, music, and
special lighting.
song (song) *n.* **1** a short poem intended or suitable
for singing, esp. one set to music. **2** a musical
composition accompanied by words for singing.
3 an instrumental piece of a similar character.
4 musical or modulated utterance with the voice,
singing (*She would break into song occasionally*).
5 a melodious utterance, as the musical cry of a
bird. **for a song** for a trifle, very cheaply (*bought
it for a song; going for a song*). **to be on song** to be
in top form, to be performing at one's best. **to
make a song and dance** to make a fuss (about).
songbird *n.* **1** any bird with a musical cry or call.
2 (*Zool.*) any perching bird of the suborder
Oscines, having a syrinx. **songbook** *n.* a book of
songs with music. **song cycle** *n.* a sequence of
songs concerned with the same subject or theme.
songless *a.* **songster** (-stə) *n.* **1** a person skilled
in singing. **2** a songbird. **songstress** (-stris) *n.* a
female singer. **song thrush** *n.* a European thrush,
Turdus philomelos, whose song is partly imitated from that of other birds. **songwriter** *n.* a
writer or composer of esp. popular songs. **song-
writing** *n.*
sonic (son´ik) *a.* **1** of, relating to or producing
sound waves. **2** travelling at about the speed of
sound. **sonically** *adv.* **sonic barrier** *n.* the sound
barrier. **sonic boom, sonic bang** *n.* the loud noise
caused by a shock wave produced by an aircraft
or projectile travelling at supersonic speed.
sonnet (son´it) *n.* a poem of 14 iambic pentameter (ten-syllable) lines, usu. consisting of an
octave rhyming *a b b a a b b a*, and a sestet with
three rhymes variously arranged.
sonny SON.
sonogram (sō´nəgram) *n.* **1** a visual representation of a sound produced by means of a sonograph. **2** (*Med.*) a sonogram produced from an
ultrasound examination. **sonograph** (-grahf) *n.*
an instrument for scanning and recording sound,
showing the distribution of energy at various
frequencies.
sonorous (son´ərəs) *a.* **1** giving out sound,
resonant. **2** loud-sounding, sounding rich or
full. **3** high-sounding, impressive. **sonorant** *n.* **1** a
frictionless continuant or nasal (*l, r, m, n, ng*)
which has a consonantal or vocalic function
depending on its position within a syllable.
2 either of the consonants represented by *w* or *y*
which have consonantal or vocalic articulations,
a semivowel. **sonority** (sənor´-), **sonorousness** *n.*
sonorously *adv.*

sool (sool) *v.t.* (*Austral., New Zeal., coll.*) **1** to incite (esp. a dog) to attack. **2** (of a dog) to attack or worry (an animal). **sooler** *n.*

soon (soon) *adv.* (*comp.* **sooner**, *superl.* **soonest**) **1** in a short time from now (*You'll be eighteen soon*). **2** in a short time after a specified or established time (*I soon regretted it*). **3** early (*How soon can you come?*). **4** readily, willingly (*We'd as soon pay now*). **as soon as 1** at the moment that (*I'll ring as soon as I hear; Ring as soon as possible*). **2** immediately after (*As soon as she'd said it, she realized her gaffe*). **3** not later than (*He went to bed as soon as the clock struck eleven*). **so soon as** as soon as. **sooner** *adv.* **1** in a shorter time. **2** earlier. **3** rather, more willingly. **no sooner...than** immediately (*No sooner did she make the promise than she withdrew it*). **sooner or later 1** sometime or other. **2** inevitably, eventually. **soonest** *adv.* (*coll.*) **1** in the shortest time. **2** earliest. **3** as soon as possible. **soonish** *adv.*

Usage note *No sooner...than* is preferred to *no sooner...when*.

soot (sut) *n.* a black substance composed of carbonaceous particles rising from fuel in a state of combustion and deposited in a chimney etc. ~*v.t.* to cover, manure or soil with soot. **sootless** (-lis) *a.* **sooty** *a.* (*comp.* **sootier**, *superl.* **sootiest**) **sootily** *adv.* **sootiness** *n.*

sooth (sooth) †*n.* truth, reality. **soothsayer** *n.* a prognosticator, a diviner.

soothe (soodh) *v.t.* **1** to calm, to tranquillize. **2** to mitigate, to assuage. **soother** *n.* **soothing** *a.* **soothingly** *adv.*

sop (sop) *n.* **1** a piece of bread etc. steeped or dipped and softened in milk, broth, gravy etc. **2** something done or given to bribe or pacify. ~*v.t.* (*pres.p.* **sopping**, *past.*, *p.p.* **sopped**) **1** to dip or steep in broth etc. **2** to take (up) by absorption. ~*v.i.* (*usu. pres.p.*) to be thoroughly wet or soaked. **sopping** *a.* wet through, soaking. **sopping wet** *a.* wet through. **soppy** *a.* (*comp.* **soppier**, *superl.* **soppiest**) (*coll.*) **1** maudlin, sentimental, weak-minded. **2** foolishly doting (on). **3** wet through. **soppily** *adv.* **soppiness** *n.*

sophism (sof'izm) *n.* a plausible but specious or fallacious argument. **sophist** *n.* a plausible but fallacious reasoner, a quibbler or casuist. **sophistic** (səfis'-), **sophistical** *a.* **sophisticate**¹ (-fis'-tikāt) *v.t.* **1** to make (a person) more cultivated or refined. **2** to make (machinery or methods) more complex or refined. **3** to deprive (a person or thing) of simplicity, to make perverted, adulterated or artificial. **sophisticate**² (-kət) *n.* a sophisticated person. **sophisticated** *a.* **1** worldly-wise; refined. **2** complex, highly developed. **sophisticatedly** *adv.* **sophistication** (-kā'shən) *n.* **sophisticator** *n.* **sophistry** *n.* (*pl.* **sophistries**) **1** the use, or art of using, plausible but specious arguments to persuade hearers, casuistry, sophism. **2** a plausible but fallacious argument.

sophomore (sof'əmaw) *n.* (*esp.* N Am.) a second-year student. **sophomoric** (-mor'-), **sophomorical** *a.*

soporific (sopərif'ik) *a.* causing or tending to cause sleep. ~*n.* a soporific medicine or agent. **soporifically** *adv.*

sopping, soppy SOP.

soprano (səprah'nō) *n.* (*pl.* **sopranos**, **soprani** (-nē)) **1** the highest singing voice, treble. **2** a boy or female singer with this voice. **3** a musical part for this voice. **4** an instrument that has the highest range within a family of instruments. **5** the player of such an instrument. ~*a.* (*Mus.*) of, or having, a treble part, voice or pitch. **sopranist** *n.* **soprano recorder** *n.* (N Am.) a descant recorder.

sorb (sawb) *n.* **1** (*also* **sorb-apple**) the service tree. **2** its fruit. **sorbitol** (-itol) *n.* a white crystalline substance obtained from sugar and often used as a sugar substitute or in the manufacture of synthetic resins.

sorbet (saw'bā) *n.* **1** an ice flavoured with fruit juice, spirit etc., a water ice. **2** sherbet.

sorcerer (saw'sərə) *n.* a person who uses magic, witchcraft, spells or enchantments, a wizard or magician. **sorceress** (-ris) *n.* a female magician or enchanter, a witch. **sorcerous** *a.* **sorcery** *n.* (*pl.* **sorceries**).

sordid (saw'did) *a.* **1** foul, dirty. **2** mean, ignoble. **3** avaricious, niggardly. **sordidly** *adv.* **sordidness** *n.*

sore (saw) *a.* **1 a** (of a part of the body) tender and painful to the touch, esp. through disease, injury or irritation. **b** (of a person) suffering pain. **2** mentally distressed, vexed (at). **3** (*coll.*) annoyed. **4** causing annoyance or distress, exasperating. ~*n.* **1** a sore place on the body where the surface is bruised, broken or inflamed by a boil, ulcer etc. **2** that which excites resentment, remorse, grief etc. **to stick out like a sore thumb** to be highly conspicuous. **sorehead** *n.* (N Am., *coll.*) an irritable person. **sorely** *adv.* **1** extremely, strongly (*was sorely tempted to be rude back*). **2** severely, gravely (*sorely insulted*). **soreness** *n.* **sore point** *n.* a subject etc. which arouses irritation, annoyance, retrospective hurt feelings etc. **sore throat** *n.* an inflamed condition of the membranous lining of the gullet etc., usu. due to a cold.

sorghum (saw'gəm) *n.* any member of the genus *Sorghum*, which includes the Indian millet, durra etc., much cultivated in the US for fodder etc.

soroptimist (sərop'timist) *n.* a member of an international organization of women's clubs, Soroptimist International.

sororal (səraw'rəl), **sororial** (-riəl) *a.* of, relating to or characteristic of a sister or sisters. **sorority** (-ror'i-) *n.* (*pl.* **sororities**) **1** (N Am.) a society of women students. **2** a body or association of women, a sisterhood.

sorrel¹ (sor'əl) *n.* **1** a herb with acid leaves,

Rumex acetosa, allied to the dock. **2** any of various plants with similar leaves, as wood sorrel.

sorrel² (sor´əl) *a.* of a reddish- or yellowish-brown. ~*n.* **1** this colour. **2** a horse or other animal of this colour.

sorrow (sor´ō) *n.* **1** mental pain or distress from loss, disappointment etc. **2** an event, thing or person causing this, a misfortune. **3** mourning, lamentation. ~*v.i.* **1** to grieve. **2** to lament. **sorrower** *n.* **sorrowful** *a.* **sorrowfully** *adv.* **sorrowfulness** *n.* **sorrowing** *a.*, *n.*

sorry (sor´i) *a.* **1** penitent, apologetic (*I'm sorry for causing all this trouble*; *Sorry about the mess*). **2** feeling or showing grief, regretful (that) (*I'm sorry (that) you've been ill*). **3** feeling pity (for) (*was very sorry for the victims*). **4** paltry, pitiful (*a sorry sight*; *a sorry effort*). ~*int.* used to express apology. **sorrily** *adv.* **sorriness** *n.*

sort (sawt) *n.* **1** a group of instances of a certain thing identifiable, by having the same set of characteristics, a kind (*What sort of dog?*; *several sorts of humour*). **2** a more or less adequate example or instance of a kind (*A cassowary is a sort of bird*; *thinks she's some sort of expert*). **3** (*coll.*) a person, a type (of person) (*She's a good sort*; *He's not the complaining sort*). **4** a letter or other piece of printing type considered as part of a font. ~*v.t.* **1** to separate into sorts, classes etc. **2** (*esp. Sc.*) to fix or punish. **after a sort** in a (usu. inadequate) way or fashion. **in some sort** after a sort, to a certain extent. **of a sort** of sorts. **of sorts** of an inferior or inadequate kind (*a dancer of sorts*). **out of sorts 1** irritable, moody. **2** slightly unwell. **sort of** rather, to a degree, as it were (*sort of unsettled*). **to sort out 1** to solve or resolve. **2** to clear out; to tidy up. **3** to separate. **4** to arrange. **5** (*coll.*) to beat, to punish. **sortable** *a.* **sorted** *a.* **1** arranged in sorts etc., classified. **2** (*coll.*) dealt with, put in order. **3** (*sl.*) reduced to submission, under control. **4** (*coll.*) (of a person) well-balanced. **sorter** *n.* a person who or something that sorts (e.g. mail). **sorting** *n.* **sorting office** *n.* an office where mail is sorted. **sort-out** *n.* an act of sorting out.

Usage note *Sort of* should not be used as a plural (as in *those sort of men*) or followed by the indefinite article *a*, *an* (as in *this sort of a woman*).

---

sortie (saw´ti) *n.* **1** a sally, esp. of troops from a besieged place in order to attack or raid. **2** a mission or attack by a single aircraft. ~*v.i.* (*3rd pers. sing. pres.* **sorties**, *pres.p.* **sortieing**, *past*, *p.p.* **sortied**) **1** to sally. **2** to make a sortie.

SOS (esōes´) *n.* (*pl.* **SOSs**) **1** an internationally recognized distress call in Morse code. **2** any distress call or plea for help (e.g. an emergency broadcast on television or radio).

sostenuto (sostinoo´tō) *a.*, *adv.* (*Mus.*) (played) in a steadily sustained manner. ~*n.* (*pl.* **sostenutos**) a passage to be played thus.

sot (sot) *n.* a habitual drunkard, a person habitually muddled (as if) with excessive drinking. **sottish** *a.*

sotto voce (sotō vō´chi) *adv.* under one's voice, in an undertone.

sou (soo) *n.* (*pl.* **sous**) **1** (*Hist.*) a French copper coin worth one-twelfth of a livre. **2** (*with neg.*) a very small amount of money (*haven't a sou*).

soubrette (soobret´) *n.* a mischievous coquettish scheming female character in a comedy, esp. the role of a lady's maid, or an actress or singer practised in such roles.

soubriquet SOBRIQUET.

souffle (soo´fəl) *n.* (*Med.*) a low whispering or murmur heard in the auscultation of an organ etc.

soufflé (soo´flā) *n.* any of various savoury or sweet, cooked or uncooked dishes made of beaten whites of eggs etc. ~*a.* made light and frothy by beating etc. **souffléed** *a.*

sough (sow, sŭf, sookh) *v.i.* to make a murmuring, sighing sound, like the wind. ~*n.* such a sound.

sought SEEK.

souk (sook) *n.* an outside, often covered market in a Muslim country (esp. in N Africa and the Middle East).

soul (sōl) *n.* **1** the spiritual part of a person. **2** a spiritual being. **3** the moral and emotional part of a person. **4** the essential or animating or inspiring force or principle, the energy in anything. **5** a person regarded as providing this, a leader. **6** a disembodied spirit (*lost souls*). **7** a human being, a person (*haven't seen a soul all day*). **8** an embodiment or exemplification (*I'll be the soul of tact*). **9** soul music. **to be the life and soul of** to be the liveliest or most entertaining person at (a party etc.). **upon my soul!** good gracious! goodness me! **soul brother**, **soul sister** *n.* a fellow black person. **soul-destroying** *a.* unrewarding, frustrating, boring. **souled** *a.* **soul food** *n.* (*coll.*) the traditional foods of American blacks in the south (e.g. yams, chitterlings). **soulful** *a.* **1** rich in, satisfying or expressing the spiritual, emotional or higher intellectual qualities. **2** sad, longing, yearning, mournful. **soulfully** *adv.* **soulfulness** *n.* **soulless** *a.* **1** impersonal, dull, uninteresting. **2** lacking sensitivity or finer feeling. **soullessly** *adv.* **soullessness** *n.* **soul mate** *n.* a person with whom one feels a close affinity. **soul music** *n.* a type of music made popular by American blacks, combining elements of blues, gospel, jazz and pop. **soul-searching** *n.* a critical and close examination of one's motives, actions etc. ~*a.* manifesting a tendency towards such self-examination.

sound¹ (sownd) *n.* **1** the sensation produced through the organs of hearing. **2** that which causes this sensation, the vibrations affecting the ear. **3** MUSICAL SOUND (under MUSIC). **4** vibration. **5** that which can be heard. **6** a specific tone or note. **7** an articulate utterance corresponding to a particular vowel or consonant. **8** an impression given by words (*don't like the sound of his illness*). **9** dialogue, music etc. accompanying visual images. ~*v.i.* **1** to make or give out sound. **2** to convey a particular impression by sound or word (*She sounded upset; Their kitchen sounds great*). **3** to give out a sound by way of summons, call or signal (*when the alarm sounded*). **4** to resonate. ~*v.t.* **1** to cause to sound. **2** to utter (a letter etc.) audibly. **3** to give a signal for by sound (*sound the alarm*). **4** to make known, to proclaim (*sounding her praises*). **5** to test (e.g. the lungs) by the sound produced. **to sound off 1** to boast. **2** to speak loudly, volubly, angrily etc. **sound barrier** *n.* the build-up of air resistance to an aircraft etc. as it attains the speed of sound. **sound bite** *n.* a brief pithy, telling or representative extract from a recorded interview. **soundcheck** *n.* a check made on sound equipment prior to recording. **sound effect** *n.* (*often pl.*) an imitation or reproduction of a sound used in the performance of a play or on the soundtrack of a film or broadcast. **sounding**[1] *a.* **1** making or giving out sound. **2** sonorous, resonant, noisy. **sounding board** *n.* **1** a canopy-like structure of wood or metal placed over a pulpit etc. to reflect sound towards the audience. **2** a person, institution, group etc., used to test reaction to a new idea or plan. **soundless** *a.* **soundlessly** *adv.* **soundlessness** *n.* **soundproof** *a.* impenetrable to sound. ~*v.t.* to make impenetrable to sound, to insulate against sound. **sound spectrograph** *n.* an instrument for making a graphic representation of the frequency, intensity etc. of sound. **sound system** *n.* a set of apparatus for sound reproduction. **soundtrack** *n.* **1** the synchronized sound recording accompanying a film etc. **2** the portion along the side of a film which bears the continuous recording of the accompanying sound. **soundwave** *n.* a sound-propagating wave of disturbance in a medium such as air.

sound[2] (sownd) *a.* **1** free from injury, defect or decay. **2** not diseased or impaired. **3** well-grounded, wise. **4** orthodox. **5** stable, firm. **6** trustworthy, honest. **7** solvent. **8 a** (of sleep) deep, unbroken. **b** (of a sleeper) tending to sleep deeply. ~*adv.* soundly, fast (asleep). **soundly** *adv.* **soundness** *n.*

sound[3] (sownd) *v.t.* **1** to measure the depth of (a sea, channel etc.) or test the quality of (its bed) with a sounding line. **2** to gather information about pressure, temperature and humidity from (the upper atmosphere). **3** to test or examine by means of a probe etc. ~*v.i.* **1** to take soundings, to ascertain the depth of water. **2** (of a whale etc.) to dive deeply. ~*n.* an instrument for exploring cavities of the body, a probe. **to sound out 1** to test, to examine, to endeavour to discover (intentions, feelings etc.). **2** to test the reaction of (someone) to a proposed move etc. **sounder** *n.* a device for taking soundings. **sounding**[2] *n.* **1** (*Naut.*) **a** the act of measuring the depth of

water, esp. by means of an echo. **b** (*usu. pl.*) a measurement of depth taken thus. **2** the act of collecting a sample of opinions etc., esp. unofficially. **3** a test, an examination, a probe. **sounding line** *n.* a weighted wire or line for measuring the depth of water. **sounding rod** *n.* a graduated iron rod, used to ascertain the depth of water in a ship's hold.

sound[4] (sownd) *n.* **1** a narrow passage of water, such as a strait connecting two seas. **2** the swimbladder of a fish.

sounding[1] SOUND[1].

sounding[2] SOUND[3].

soup (soop) *n.* **1** a liquid food made from meat, fish or vegetables and stock. **2** anything resembling soup in consistency etc. **3** (*coll.*) a thick fog. **in the soup** (*sl.*) in difficulties, in trouble. **to soup up** to modify (the engine of a car or motorcycle) in order to increase its power. **souped-up** *a.* (of a vehicle engine) modified to increase its power. **soup kitchen** *n.* **1** a public establishment for supplying soup to the poor. **2** a mobile army kitchen. **soupy** *a.* (*comp.* **soupier**, *superl.* **soupiest**). **soupily** *adv.* **soupiness** *n.*

soupçon (soop´sŏ) *n.* a mere trace, taste or flavour (of).

sour (sowǝ) *a.* **1** sharp or acid to the taste, like a lemon, tart. **2** tasting sharp through fermentation, rancid. **3** bad-tempered, morose. **4** disagreeable, inharmonious. **5** (of soil) excessively acidic or infertile. ~*v.t.* **1** to cause to have a sour taste. **2** to cause (a relationship) to become unfriendly. ~*v.i.* to become sour. ~*n.* (*esp. N Am.*) a cocktail usu. made with a spirit and lemon juice, sugar and ice. **to go/ turn sour 1** to become sour. **2** to lose attraction or become distasteful. **sour cream** *n.* fresh cream soured by the introduction of bacteria, used in salads, cooking etc. **sourdough** *n.* fermenting dough, orig. from a previous baking, used as leaven. **sour grapes** *n.pl.* peevish disdain for a desired object that is out of one's reach. **sourish** *a.* **sourly** *adv.* **sourness** *n.* **sourpuss** *n.* (*coll.*) a habitually morose person.

source (saws) *n.* **1** the spring or fountainhead from which a stream of water proceeds; cause. **2** an origin, a beginning. **3** a person who or something that initiates or creates something. **4** a person or thing that provides inspiration or information. **5** a body that emits radiation. **6** (*Physics*) a point from which a current or fluid flows. ~*v.t.* **1** to obtain (components, materials etc.) from a particular source. **2** to establish the source of. **at source** at the point of issue.

sousaphone (soo´zǝfōn) *n.* a brass wind instrument like a long curved tuba, carried so as to encircle the player's waist. **sousaphonist** *n.*

souse (sows) *v.t.* **1** to pickle. **2** to plunge into or drench thoroughly with water etc. **3** (*usu. p.p., sl.*) to inebriate. ~*v.i.* to plunge into water or another liquid. ~*n.* **1** pickle made with salt. **2** anything steeped or preserved in pickle, esp. mackerel and herring. **3** a dip or plunging into liquid. **4** (*sl.*) a drunkard. **5** (*sl.*) a drinking bout. **soused** *a.*

soutane (sootan´) *n.* a cassock.

south (sowth) *n.* **1** that one of the four cardinal points of the compass directly opposite to the north, or the direction in which this lies. **2** (*usu.* **the South**) **a** the southern part of a region, e.g. the part of England south of the Wash, or the American states south of the Mason Dixon line. **b** the less developed countries of the world. **3** a wind from the south. **4** at cards, the player or position facing north. ~*a.* **1** situated in the south. **2** facing in the southern direction. **3** (of the wind) coming from the south. ~*adv.* **1** towards the south. **2** (of the wind) from the south. **south by east** between south and south-south-east. **south by west** between south and south-south-west. **south of** further south than. **to the south** in a southerly direction. **South African** *a.* of or relating to the Republic of South Africa, its inhabitants or any of their languages. ~*n.* a native, citizen or inhabitant of South Africa. **South American** *a.* of or relating to South America, its inhabitants or any of their languages. ~*n.* a native, citizen or inhabitant of any of the South American countries. **southbound** *a.* going or leading south. **south-east** *n.* **1** the point of the compass equally distant from the south and the east, or the direction in which this lies. **2** (*usu.* **the South-East**) the part of a town or a region lying towards the south-east, esp. the south-eastern area of Britain, including London. ~*a.* of or relating to, approaching or coming from the south-east. ~*adv.* at, towards or near the south-east. **southeaster** *n.* a south-east wind. **south-easterly** *a., adv.* south-east. ~*n.* (*pl.* **south-easterlies**) a south-east wind. **south-eastern** *a.* **south-eastward** *a., adv.* (moving) towards the south-east. ~*n.* a south-easterly direction or south-eastern area. **south-eastwards** *adv.* **southerly** (sŭdh´əli) *a., adv.* **1** (positioned) in, or (tending) towards the south. **2** (of a wind) blowing from the south. ~*n.* (*pl.* **southerlies**) a south wind. **southerliness** *n.* **southern** (sŭdh´ən) *a.* **1** of or relating to or situated in or towards the south. **2** coming from or inhabiting the south. **Southern Cross** *n.* a cross-shaped constellation visible in the southern hemisphere. **Southerner, southerner** *n.* an inhabitant or native of the south, esp. of southern England or the southern states of the US. **southern hemisphere** *n.* the half of the earth south of the equator. **southern lights** *n.pl.* the aurora australis. **southernmost** *a.* **southernwood** *n.* a shrubby species of wormwood, *Artemisia abrotanum*. **southmost** *a.* **south-paw** *n., a.* (of or relating to) a left-handed person, esp. a left-handed boxer. **South Pole** *n.* the most southerly point on the earth's axis or the celestial sphere. **south seas** *n.pl.* the seas south of the equator. **south-south-east** *n.* the compass point, or the direction, midway between south and south-east. **south-south-west** *n.* the compass point, or the direction, midway between south

and south-west. **southward** (sowth´wəd, sŭdh´-əd) *a., adv.* (moving) towards the south. **southwardly** *a., adv.* **southwards** *a., adv.* **south-west** *n.* **1** the point of the compass equally distant from the south and the west, or the direction in which this lies. **2** (*usu.* **the South-West**) the part of a town or region lying towards the south-west, esp. the south-western part of Britain. ~*a.* of or relating to, approaching or coming from the south-west. ~*adv.* at, towards or near the south-west. **southwester** *n.* a wind from the south-west. **southwesterly** *a., adv.* south-west. **south-western** *a.* **south-westward** *a., adv.* (moving) towards the south-west. **south-westwards** *adv.* **sou'wester** (sow-wes´tə) *n.* **1** a southwester. **2** a waterproof hat with a wide brim hanging down behind, worn by sailors etc.

souvenir (soovəniə´) *n.* a keepsake, a memento.

sou'wester SOUTH-WEST (under SOUTH).

sovereign (sov´rən) *a.* **1** supreme. **2** possessing supreme power, dominion or jurisdiction. **3** royal. **4** (of a remedy) effectual. **5** utter, absolute (*sovereign disdain*). ~*n.* **1** a supreme ruler, a monarch. **2** a former English gold coin, worth one pound. **sovereignly** *adv.* **sovereign pontiff** *n.* the Pope. **sovereignty** (-ti) *n.* (*pl.* **sovereignties**) **1** lordship, supremacy. **2** an independent, self-governing state. **3** self-government, independence.

Usage note The form *sovereignity* for *sovereignty* is best avoided.

---

soviet (sō´viət, sov´-) *n.* **1** a local council elected by workers and inhabitants of a district in the former Soviet Union. **2** a regional council selected by a number of these. **3** the national congress consisting of delegates from regional councils. **4** (*pl.*) (*usu.* **Soviet**) the government or people of the former Soviet Union. ~*a.* (*usu.* **Soviet**) of or relating to the former Soviet Union, its government or its people. **sovietize, sovietise** *v.t.* **sovietization** (-zā´shən) *n.*

sow¹ (sō) *v.t.* (*past* **sowed**, *p.p.* **sown** (sōn), **sowed**) **1** to scatter (seed) for growth. **2** to scatter seed over (ground etc.). **3** to scatter over, to cover thickly with. **4** to disseminate, to spread. **5** to implant, to initiate. ~*v.i.* to scatter seed for growth. **to sow the seeds/ seed of** to introduce, initiate or implant (a doubt, a suspicion etc.). **sower** *n.* **sowing** *n.*

Usage note See note under SEW.

---

sow² (sow) *n.* **1** a female pig. **2** the female of other animals, e.g. the guinea pig. **3** (*esp. N Am.*) (*also* **sow bug**) a woodlouse. **sowthistle** *n.* a plant of the genus *Sonchus*, with toothed leaves and milky juice.

sox SOCK¹.

soy (soi) *n.* **1** (*also* **soy sauce**) a thin brown salty sauce made from fermented soya beans, used extensively in Japanese and Chinese cookery. **2** the soya plant.

soya (soi′ə) *n.* **1** a leguminous herb, *Glycine soja,* native to SE Asia, grown for its seeds. **2** (*also* **soya bean**) the seed of this plant, used as a source of oil and flour, as a substitute for animal protein and to make soy sauce and tofu. **3** (*also* **soya sauce**) soy.

sozzled (soz′əld) *a.* (*coll.*) drunk.

spa (spah) *n.* (*pl.* **spas**) **1** a mineral spring. **2** a resort or place where there is such a spring.

space (spās) *n.* **1** continuous extension in three dimensions or any quantity or portion of this. **2** the universe beyond the earth's atmosphere, outer space. **3** an interval between points etc. **4** emptiness. **5** room. **6 a** an unoccupied seat. **b** welcome isolation. **7** an interval of time. **8** advertising slots in newspapers etc., or on radio or television. **9** an interval between written or printed words or lines. *~v.t.* **1** to set so that there will be spaces between. **2** to put the proper spaces between (words, lines etc.). **to space out** to place at wider intervals. **space age** *n.* the era in which space travel and exploration have become possible. **space-age** *a.* **1** of or relating to the space age. **2** modern. **space bar** *n.* a bar on a typewriter or computer keyboard for making spaces (between words etc.). **space blanket** *n.* a heat-retaining aluminium-coated wrapping for the body, carried e.g. by mountaineers for emergencies. **space capsule** *n.* a small information-gathering spacecraft. **spacecraft** *n.* a manned or unmanned craft for travelling through outer space. **spaced-out** *a.* (*pred.* **spaced out**) (*dated sl.*) unnaturally euphoric, high on drugs. **space flight** *n.* **1** a voyage in space. **2** space travel. **spaceman, spacewoman** *n.* (*pl.* **spacemen, spacewomen**) a space traveller. **space platform, space station** *n.* a large artificial satellite serving as a landing stage in space travel and as a base for scientific investigations. **space probe** *n.* an unmanned spacecraft carrying equipment for collecting scientific measurements of conditions in space. **spacer** *n.* **space rocket** *n.* a rocket for launching spacecraft or for travelling in space. **space-saving** *a.* economic on space, occupying very little space. **spaceship** *n.* a manned spacecraft. **space shuttle** *n.* **1** a spacecraft designed to carry people and materials to and from a space station. **2** a reusable rocket-launched manned spacecraft that returns to earth. **space station** SPACE PLATFORM (under SPACE). **spacesuit** *n.* an all-in-one garment specially adapted for space travel. **space-time, space-time continuum** *n.* (*Physics*) the four-dimensional manifold for continuum which in accordance with Einstein's theory of relativity, is the result of fusing time with three-dimensional space. **space travel** *n.* travel in outer space. **space traveller,** (*N Am.*) **space traveler** *n.* **space vehicle** *n.* a spacecraft. **space walk** *n.* a trip by an astronaut outside a spacecraft when it is in space. **spacewalk** *v.i.* **spacial** SPATIAL. **spacious** (-shəs) *a.* **1** having

ample room. **2** roomy, extensive. **spaciously** *adv.* **spaciousness** *n.*

spade¹ (spād) *n.* **1** an implement for digging, having a broad blade fitted on to a long handle, and worked with both hands and one foot. **2** a tool of similar form employed for various purposes. **3** anything resembling a spade in shape etc. *~v.t.* **1** to dig with a spade. **2** to cut out with a spade. **to call a spade a spade** to be outspoken, not to mince matters. **spadeful** *n.* (*pl.* **spadefuls**) **spadework** *n.* tedious but necessary preliminary work.

spade² (spād) *n.* **1** a playing card with a black figure or figures shaped like a heart with a small triangular handle. **2** (*pl.*) this suit of cards. **3** (*offensive, sl.*) a black person. **in spades** (*coll.*) to an extreme degree.

spadix (spā′diks) *n.* (*pl.* **spadices** (-sēz)) (*Bot.*) a spike of flowers on a fleshy stem, usu. enclosed in a spathe.

spaghetti (spəget′i) *n.* a variety of pasta made in long thin cylindrical strings. **spaghetti Bolognese** (bolənāz′) *n.* spaghetti with a minced-beef sauce. **spaghetti junction** *n.* a multi-intersection road junction, esp. at a motorway, with criss-crossing flyovers. **spaghetti western** *n.* a film about the American West made cheaply in Italy or Spain, often with a violent or melodramatic content.

Spam® (spam) *n.* a tinned luncheon meat of chopped and spiced ham.

span¹ (span) *n.* **1** the space from end to end of a bridge etc. **2** the horizontal distance between the supports of an arch. **3** an entire stretch of distance or time (e.g. a lifespan, attention span). **4** a brief space of distance or time. **5** the wingspan of a bird or aeroplane. **6** the space from the tip of the thumb to the tip of the little finger when extended, esp. as a former measure, 9 in. (23 cm). *~v.t.* (*pres.p.* **spanning**, *past, p.p.* **spanned**) **1** (of a bridge etc.) to extend from side to side of (a river etc.). **2** (of an engineer etc.) to build a bridge across (a river etc.). **3** to measure or cover the extent of (e.g. an octave) with one's hand expanded. **4** to cover (a range, a period of time).

span² (span) *a.* absolutely new, brand new.

span³ SPIN.

spandrel (span′drəl), **spandril** *n.* (*Archit.*) the space between the shoulder of an arch and the rectangular moulding etc. enclosing it, or between the shoulders of adjoining arches and the moulding etc.

spangle (spang′gəl) *n.* **1** a small disc of glittering metal or metallic material, used for ornamenting dresses etc., a sequin. **2** any small sparkling object. *~v.t.* to set or adorn with spangles. **spangled** *a.* **spangler** *n.* **spangly** *a.*

Spaniard (span′yəd) *n.* **1** a native or inhabitant of Spain. **2** (*usu.* **spaniard**) any of various sharp-leaved plants of the New Zealand genus *Aciphylla;* also called *wild spaniard.*

spaniel (span′yəl) *n.* **1** any of various breeds of dog, distinguished by large drooping ears, long silky or curly coat and a gentle disposition. **2** a servile, cringing person, esp. someone's minion.

Spanish (span´ish) *a.* of or relating to Spain, its people or their language. ~*n.* **1** the language of Spain and South America. **2** (*as pl.*) the Spaniards. **Spanish chestnut** *n.* the true chestnut tree, *Castanea sativa.* **Spanish fly** *n.* (*pl.* **Spanish flies**) **1** a bright green beetle that raises blisters, *Lytta vesicatoria.* **2** a (supposedly aphrodisiac) preparation made from this, cantharides. **Spanish guitar** *n.* **1** a traditional six-stringed acoustic guitar. **2** classical guitar music. **Spanishness** *n.* **Spanish omelette** *n.* an omelette with a filling of tomato, peppers (traditionally pimento) or other chopped vegetables. **Spanish onion** *n.* a large variety of onion with a mild flavour.

spank (spangk) *v.t.* to strike with the open hand, to slap, esp. on the buttocks. ~*v.i.* (of a horse) to trot fast, almost approaching a gallop. ~*n.* a resounding blow with the open hand, a slap, esp. on the buttocks. **spanker** *n.* **1** a person who spanks another. **2** (*Naut.*) a fore-and-aft sail set by two spars on the after side of the mizzenmast. **3** a fast horse. **4** (*coll.*) an exceptionally fine specimen, a stunner. **spanking** *n.* a series of slaps on the buttocks, as a punishment. ~*a.* (*coll.*) **1** dashing, brisk, stunning. **2** (of a breeze) strong. ~*adv.* exceptionally.

spanner (span´ə) *n.* an instrument for tightening up or loosening the nuts on screws, a wrench. **spanner in the works** *n.* an impediment, a cause of confusion or difficulty.

spar[1] (spah) *n.* **1** a round timber, a pole, esp. used as a mast, yard, boom, shears etc. **2** the longitudinal supporting beam of an aircraft wing. **spar-deck** *n.* the upper deck of a vessel stretching from stem to stern.

spar[2] (spah) *v.i.* (*pres.p.* **sparring**, *past, p.p.* **sparred**) **1** to move the arms about in defence or offence as in boxing. **2** to engage in a contest of words etc. ~*n.* **1** a sparring movement. **2** a boxing match. **3** a verbal contest, an argument. **sparrer** *n.* **sparring** *n.* **sparring partner** *n.* **1** a boxer with whom one in training practises. **2** a person with whom another engages in lively repartee.

spar[3] (spah) *n.* any of various lustrous minerals occurring in crystalline or vitreous form, e.g. *feldspar, fluorspar.* **sparry** *a.* (*comp.* **sparrier**, *superl.* **sparriest**).

spare (spee) *a.* **1** not needed for routine purposes, able to be spared. **2** available for use in emergency etc. **3** unoccupied, not in use (*a spare seat; a spare keyboard*). **4** (of someone's figure) thin, lean. **5** (of style) concise, not wasting words (*her spare prose*). **6** (of diet etc.) meagre, frugal. ~*v.t.* **1** to be able to afford (*can't spare the money; Can you spare a moment?*). **2** to dispense with or do without (*can't spare her just now*). **3** to relieve, to release (*was trying to spare her feelings*). **4** to refrain from punishing, destroying etc. (*spared the prisoners*). **5** to refrain from inflicting (*Spare us the sob story*). **6** to use frugally (*no expense spared; Don't spare the horses*). **7** to refrain from using (*Spare the rod and spoil the child*). ~*n.* that which is surplus to immediate requirements and available for use, such as a copy or duplicate of something (*I'd lend you a key but I haven't got a spare*). **not to spare oneself** to do one's utmost, to give utterly dedicated service. **to go spare** (*coll.*) to become excessively angry, agitated or distraught. **to spare** extra, surplus, more than required (*plenty to spare*). **sparely** *adv.* **spareness** *n.* **spare part** *n.* a replacement for a machine part which may break, wear out etc. **sparer** *n.* **spare rib** *n.* a piece of pork consisting of a rib with only a little meat. **spare time** *n.* time when one is at leisure, or not engaged in one's regular work or activities. **spare-time** *a.* **spare tyre** *n.* **1** a tyre carried in a vehicle as a replacement in case of a puncture. **2** (*coll.*) a bulge of fat around the midriff. **sparing** *a.* **sparingly** *adv.* **sparingness** *n.*

spark (spahk) *n.* **1** an incandescent particle thrown off from a burning substance, or produced from a match, flint etc. **2** the luminous effect of a disruptive electrical discharge. **3** such an electrical discharge as the igniting device in an internal-combustion engine. **4** a flash of wit, a particle of life or energy. **5** a trace, a hint (of kindled interest etc.). **6** a vivacious and witty person. **7** a brilliant point, facet etc. ~*v.t.* to cause or start. ~*v.i.* **1** to give out sparks. **2** to produce sparks at the point of broken continuity in an electrical circuit. **to make sparks fly** to start a violent quarrel, to cause a row. **to spark off 1** to kindle (a process, someone's interest etc.). **2** to galvanize into activity. **sparkless** *a.* **spark plug, sparking plug** *n.* a device for igniting the explosive mixture in the cylinder of an internal-combustion engine. **sparky** *a.* (*comp.* **sparkier**, *superl.* **sparkiest**).

sparkle (spah´kal) *n.* **1** a gleam, glitter. **2** vivacity, wit. **3** effervescence. ~*v.i.* **1** to emit sparks. **2** to glisten, to twinkle. **3** (of some wines, mineral waters etc.) to emit carbon dioxide in little bubbles. **4** to be vivacious or witty. **sparkler** *n.* **1** something that sparkles. **2** (*sl.*) a diamond. **3** a hand-held firework that emits fizzling sparks. **sparkling** *a.* **1** effervescent. **2** twinkling, scintillating. **sparklingly** *adv.*

sparrow (spar´ō) *n.* **1** a small brownish-grey bird of the genus *Passer*, esp. *P. domesticus*, the house sparrow. **2** any of various other small birds resembling this, e.g. the hedge sparrow, *Prunella modularis.* **sparrowhawk** *n.* a small hawk, *Accipiter nisus*, preying on small birds etc.

sparse (spahs) *a.* thinly scattered, not dense. **sparsely** *adv.* **sparseness, sparsity** *n.*

Spartan (spah´tən) *n.* **1** a native or inhabitant of Sparta. **2** a person bearing pain, enforcing discipline etc., like a Spartan. ~*a.* **1** of or relating to Sparta or the Spartans. **2** like a Spartan, hardy, strict etc. **3** austere, rigorous.

spasm (spaz´m) *n.* **1** a convulsive and involuntary muscular contraction. **2** a sudden or convulsive act, movement etc. **3** a burst of emotion or effort. **spasmodic** (-mod´-) *a*. **1** caused or affected by a spasm or spasms. **2** happening at irregular intervals. **spasmodical** *a*. **spasmodically** *adv*. **spastic** (spas´tik) *a*. **1** of, affected by, resembling or characterized by spasms. **2** (*sl., offensive*) ineffectual, incapable. ~*n*. **1** a sufferer from cerebral palsy. **2** (*sl., offensive*) an ineffectual, clumsy person. **spastically** *adv*. **spasticity** (-tis´-) *n*.

Usage note The term *spastic* gives offence: it is better to express in terms of *cerebral palsy* instead.

spat¹ (spat) *n*. **1** (*usu. pl., Hist.*) a short gaiter fastening over and under the shoe. **2** a cover for the top part of an aircraft wheel.

spat² (spat) *n*. **1** (*esp. N Am., coll.*) a petty quarrel. **2** a slap, a smack. ~*v.t*. (*pres.p.* **spatting**, *past, p.p.* **spatted**) to slap. ~*v.i*. (*N Am., New Zeal.*) to engage in a petty argument.

spat³ (spat) *n*. the spawn of shellfish, esp. oysters. ~*v.i*. (*pres.p.* **spatting**, *past, p.p.* **spatted**) (of an oyster) to spawn. ~*v.t*. to deposit (spawn).

spat⁴ SPIT¹.

spatchcock (spach´kok) *n*. a fowl opened out along the backbone and fried or grilled flat. ~*v.t*. to cook (poultry) in this way.

spate (spāt) *n*. **1** a heavy flood, esp. in a mountain stream or river. **2** a sudden onrush, influx or outburst. **3** a sudden downpour.

spathe (spādh) *n*. (*Bot.*) a large bract or pair of bracts enveloping the spadix of a plant. **spathaceous** (spədhā´shəs) *a*.

spatial (spā´shəl), **spacial** *a*. of, relating to, existing or occurring in space. **spatiality** (-al´-) *n*. **spatialize**, **spatialise** *v.t*. **spatially** *adv*. **spatiotemporal** (spāshiōtem´pərəl) *a*. (*Physics, Philos.*) **1** of space-time. **2** of, concerned with or existing in both space and time. **spatio-temporally** *adv*.

spatter (spat´ə) *v.t*. **1** to scatter or splash (water etc.) about. **2** to sprinkle or splash (someone etc.) with water, mud etc. ~*v.i*. **1** to sprinkle drops about. **2** to be scattered about in drops. ~*n*. **1** a shower, a sprinkling, a pattering. **2** something spattered or soiled.

spatula (spat´ūlə) *n*. a broad knife or trowel-shaped tool used for spreading plasters, working pigments, mixing foods etc. **spatular** *a*. **spatulate** (-lət) *a*.

spavin (spav´in) *n*. a disease in horses affecting the hock joint with swelling or a hard excrescence. **spavined** *a*.

spawn (spawn) *v.t*. **1** (of fish, amphibians etc.) to deposit or produce (eggs, young etc.). **2** (*derog.*) (of human beings) to give birth to, to beget (children). **3** (*coll.*) to produce, to generate, to give rise to. ~*v.i*. **1** (of fish etc.) to deposit eggs. **2** (*derog.*) to issue, to be brought forth, esp. in abundance. ~*n*. **1** the eggs of fish, frogs and molluscs. **2** white fibrous matter from which fungi

are produced, mycelium. **3** (*derog.*) offspring. **spawner** *n*.

spay (spā) *v.t*. to destroy or remove the ovaries of (female animals) so as to make them infertile, to sterilize.

speak (spēk) *v.i*. (*past* **spoke** (spōk), †**spake** (spāk), *p.p.* **spoken** (spō´kən)) **1** to utter articulate sounds or words in the ordinary tone as distinct from singing. **2** to talk, to converse. **3** to deliver a speech or address. **4** to communicate by other means. **5** (of a picture etc.) to be highly expressive or lifelike. **6** to be on speaking terms. **7** (of a musical instrument etc.) to produce a (characteristic) sound. **8** (of a dog) to bark. ~*v.t*. **1** to utter articulately. **2** to declare (one's thoughts, opinions etc.). **3** to talk or converse in (a language). **nothing to speak of** nothing important or significant, none worth mentioning. **spoken for** allocated, reserved, claimed. **to speak for 1** to be spokesperson for. **2** to act as an advocate for, to represent, to witness to. **to speak for itself** (of a circumstance) to be of self-evident significance. **to speak for oneself** to be one's own advocate. **to speak of** to mention. **to speak one's mind** to speak freely and frankly. **to speak out 1** to speak loudly and articulately. **2** to express one's opinion frankly. **to speak to 1** to address. **2** to speak in support or confirmation of (*spoke to the general view*). **3** (*coll.*) to reprimand, to reprove (*shall have to speak to him*). **to speak up 1** to speak loudly. **2** to speak without constraint, to express one's opinion freely. **to speak volumes 1** (of a circumstance) to be of great or peculiar significance. **2** to constitute abundant evidence (for). **speakable** *a*. **speakeasy** *n*. (*pl.* **speakeasies**) (*Hist., N Am.*) a premises where illicit liquor was sold during the time of Prohibition. **speaker** *n*. **1** a person who speaks, esp. someone who delivers a speech. **2** (*in comb.*) a person who speaks a specified language (*English-speakers*). **3** (**Speaker**) an officer presiding over a deliberative assembly, esp. the House of Commons. **4** a loudspeaker. **speakership** *n*. **speaking** *n*. the activity or an instance of uttering words etc. ~*a*. **1** (of a likeness etc.) animated, vivid, expressive. **2** able to speak. **3** (*in comb.*) able to speak a specific language, or having a specific language as one's native tongue (*the German-speaking Czechs*). **4** transmitting speech. **5** giving an estimate or opinion from a specified angle (*technically speaking; roughly speaking*). **on speaking terms 1** amicable towards one another. **2** slightly acquainted. **speaking acquaintance** *n*. **1** a person whom one knows slightly. **2** slight familiarity with someone. **speaking clock** *n*. a recorded-speech telephone service giving the correct time.

spear (spiə) *n*. **1** a weapon with a pointed head on a long shaft. **2** a sharp-pointed instrument with barbs, for stabbing fish etc. **3** a pointed shoot, esp. a stem of broccoli or asparagus. **4** a blade or stalk of grass. ~*v.t*. to pierce, kill or capture with a spear. **spear-grass** *n*. grass of various species having long, sharp leaves. **speargun** *n.* a gun for firing spears under water. **spearhead** *n.* **1** the pointed end of a spear. **2** the person or group leading a campaign, thrust or attack. ~*v.t.* to lead (a campaign, an assault etc.). **spearmint** *n.* the garden mint, *Mentha spicata*, used as a flavouring.

spec[1] (spek) *n.* (*coll.*) short for SPECIFICATION (under SPECIFY) (*a job spec*).

spec[2] (spek) *n.* (*coll.*) short for SPECULATION (under SPECULATE). ~*a.* (*Austral., New Zeal.*) short for SPECULATIVE (under SPECULATE). **on spec** (*coll.*) on the off chance, in the hope of success, as a gamble.

special (spesh´əl) *a.* **1** exceptionally good or important (*a special day*). **2** particular, not ordinary or general (*has a special meaning in this context*). **3** for a particular purpose, environment or occasion (*requires no special qualifications*). **4** close, intimate (*a special friend*). **5** additional, extra (*special buses*). **6** individual (*They have their own special chairs*). **7** denoting the educational needs of children who are handicapped etc. ~*n.* **1** a person or thing dedicated to a special purpose etc. **2** a special train, constable, edition of a newspaper, item on a menu etc. **Special Branch** *n.* a branch of the British police force dealing with political security. **special constable** *n.* a citizen sworn in to aid the police force in times of war, civil commotion etc. **special correspondent** *n.* a journalist or reporter who writes on special topics for a newspaper. **special delivery** *n.* express delivery. **special edition** *n.* an extra edition of a newspaper with updated news. **special effect** *n.* an extraordinary visual or sound effect, esp. one created on a film, video tape, or television or radio broadcast. **specialism** *n.* a special area of expertise etc., a speciality. **specialist** *n.* **1** a person who is trained in a particular branch of a profession etc. (*a specialist in obstetrics*). **2** a person whose studies particularly or exclusively concern a certain subject or branch of one. **speciality** (-shial´-) *n.* (*pl.* **specialities**) **1** a particular area of expertise, a pursuit, occupation, service, commodity, product etc., which is the special concern of a certain person or business. **2** a person's special characteristic or feature, peculiarity or skill. **specialize, specialise** *v.t.* (*Biol.*) to differentiate, limit, adapt or apply to a specific use, function, environment, purpose or meaning. ~*v.i.* **1** to become differentiated, adapted or applied thus. **2** to employ oneself as or train oneself to be a specialist. **specialization** (-zā´shən) *n.* **special licence** *n.* a licence authorizing marriage without banns. **specially** *adv.* **specialness** *n.* **special pleading** *n.* **1** (*Law*) the allegation of special or new matter in a legal case. **2** specious or unfair argument. **special school** *n.* a school established to meet the educational needs of handicapped children. **specialty** *n.* (*pl.* **specialties**) **1** (*Law*) a legal agreement expressed in a sealed deed. **2** (*esp. N Am.*) a speciality.

species (spē´shiz) *n.* (*pl.* **species**) **1** a class of things with certain characteristics in common. **2** (*Biol.*) a group of organisms (taxonomically subordinate to a genus) generally resembling each other and capable of reproduction. **3** (*Logic*) a group of individuals having certain common attributes and designated by a common name (subordinate to a genus). **4** a kind, a sort. **speciation** (-ā´shən) *n.* (*Biol.*) the development of new biological species in the course of evolution. **specie** (-shē) *n.* coin as distinct from paper money.

specify (spes´ifi) *v.t.* (*3rd pers. sing. pres.* **specifies**, *pres.p.* **specifying**, *past, p.p.* **specified**) **1** to mention expressly. **2** to stipulate, to state as a condition (that). **3** to include in a specification. **specifiable** *a.* **specific** (spəsif´-) *a.* **1** clearly specified or particularized, precise (*Can you be more specific?*; *specific instructions*). **2** constituting, of or relating to, characterizing or particularizing a species (*specific difference*; *the creature's specific name*). **3** special, peculiar (to) (*no specific treatment for Aids-related illnesses*; *symptoms specific to mercurial poisoning*; *gender-specific diseases*). ~*n.* **1** †a medicine, remedy, agent etc. for a particular part of the body. **2** that which is particular or specific. **specifically** *adv.* **specification** (spesifikā´shən) *n.* **1** the act of specifying. **2** an article or particular specified. **3** a detailed statement of particulars, esp. of materials, work, workmanship to be undertaken or supplied by an architect, builder, manufacturer etc. **4** a detailed description of an invention by an applicant for a patent. **specific difference** *n.* a characteristic that differentiates a species. **specific gravity** *n.* the relative weight or density of a solid or fluid expressed by the ratio of its weight to that of an equal volume of a substance taken as a standard, water in the case of liquids and solids, air for gases. **specificity** (spesifis´-) *n.* **specificness** *n.* **specified** *a.* **specifier** *n.*

specimen (spes´imən) *n.* **1** a part or an individual intended to illustrate or typify the nature of a whole or a class. **2** (*Med.*) a sample of blood, urine etc. taken for medical analysis. **3** (*coll.*) a person or animal (*a splendid specimen*).

specious (spē´shəs) *a.* **1** apparently, but not actually, right or fair, plausible (*specious arguments*). **2** deceptively pleasing to the eye, showy. **speciosity** (-shios´-), **speciousness** *n.* **speciously** *adv.*

speck (spek) *n.* **1** a small spot or blemish. **2** a minute particle (*not a speck of dust anywhere*). **3** a rotten patch in a piece of fruit. ~*v.t.* to mark with a speck or specks. **speckle** *n.* a small spot, stain or patch of colour, light etc. ~*v.t.* to mark (as) with speckles. **speckled** *a.* **speckless** *a.* **specky** *a.* (*comp.* **speckier**, *superl.* **speckiest**).

specs (speks) *n.pl.* (*coll.*) spectacles, glasses.

spectacle (spek´təkəl) *n.* **1** something exhibited to the view, a show. **2** (*coll.*) a sight attracting ridicule, laughter etc. **to make a spectacle of oneself** to do something that makes people stare or laugh at one. **spectacled** *a.* **1** wearing spectacles. **2** (of an animal etc.) having eye markings like spectacles. **spectacles** *n.pl.* an optical instrument, consisting of a lens for each eye mounted in a light frame for resting on the nose and ears, used to assist the sight; also called *pair of spectacles.* **spectacular** (-tak´ū-) *a.* **1** of the nature of a public spectacle. **2** marked by great display, lavish. **3** dramatic; thrilling; stunning, striking. ~*n.* an elaborate show, esp. a musical, in a theatre, on television etc. **spectacularly** *adv.*

spectator (spektā´tə) *n.* a person who looks on, esp. at a show or spectacle. **spectate** *v.i.* to look on, to be an observer or onlooker. **spectatorial** (-tətaw´ri-) *a.* **spectatorship** *n.* **spectator sport** *n.* a sport that attracts a large number of spectators or viewers.

spectra SPECTRUM.

spectral[1] SPECTRE.

spectral[2] SPECTRUM.

spectre (spek´tə), (*N Am.*) **specter** *n.* **1** an apparition, a ghost. **2** an unpleasant thought or image that haunts one (*the spectre of poverty*). **spectral**[1] *a.* **1** of or relating to ghosts. **2** ghostlike, phantom-like. **spectrality** (-tral´-) *n.* **spectrally** *adv.*

spectro- (spek´trō) *comb. form* spectrum.

spectrograph (spek´trəgrahf) *n.* an apparatus for photographing or otherwise reproducing spectra. **spectrogram** (-gram) *n.* a record produced by a spectrograph. **spectrographic** (-graf´-) *a.* **spectrographically** *adv.* **spectrography** (-trog´-rəfi) *n.*

spectrometer (spektrom´itə) *n.* an instrument for measuring the refractive index of substances. **spectrometric** (-met´-) *a.* **spectrometry** *n.*

spectroscope (spek´trəskōp) *n.* an instrument for forming and analysing the spectra of rays emitted by bodies. **spectroscopic** (-skop´-), **spectroscopical** *a.* **spectroscopically** *adv.* **spectroscopist** (-tros´-) *n.* **spectroscopy** (-tros´-) *n.*

spectrum (spek´trəm) *n.* (*pl.* **spectra** (-trə)) **1** the rainbow-like range of colours into which white light is dispersed, according to the degrees of refrangibility of its components, when passing through a prism, from violet (with the shortest wavelength) to red (with the longest wavelength). **2** the complete range of wavelengths of electromagnetic radiation. **3** any particular distribution of electromagnetic radiation, esp. as characteristic of a particular substance when emitting or absorbing radiation. **4** any similar range, e.g. of sound frequencies, or of particles distributed according to energy. **5** a complete range, of e.g. opinion, interests, activities, abilities etc. **spectral**[2] *a.* **spectrum analyser,** (*N Am.*) **spectrum analyzer** *n.* a device for breaking down oscillation into its individual components. **spectrum analysis, spectral analysis** *n.* chemical analysis with a spectroscope.

speculate (spek´ūlāt) *v.i.* **1** to pursue an inquiry or form conjectures or views (on or upon). **2** to

guess or conjecture. **3** to make purchases, investments etc. on the chance of profit. **4** to gamble wildly or recklessly. **speculation** (-lā´shən) *n.* **speculative** (-lətiv) *a.* **speculatively** *adv.* **speculativeness** *n.* **speculator** *n.*

speculum (spek´ūləm) *n.* (*pl.* **specula** (-lə)) **1** a surgical instrument for dilating the passages or cavities of the body, to facilitate inspection. **2** a mirror, esp. one of polished metal, used as a reflector in a telescope. **3** a lustrous spot or coloured area on the wing of certain birds. **specular** *a.*

sped SPEED.

speech (spēch) *n.* **1** the faculty or act of uttering articulate sounds or words. **2** a public address, an oration. **3** an individual's characteristic manner of speech. **4** that which is spoken, an utterance. **5** the language or dialect of a nation, region etc. **speech day** *n.* the annual prize-giving day in some schools, with ceremonial speeches etc. **speechful** *a.* **speechify** *v.i.* (*3rd pers. sing. pres.* **speechifies,** *pres.p.* **speechifying,** *past, p.p.* **speechified**) (*often derog.*) to make a speech or speeches, esp. pompous or lengthy, to harangue. **speechification** (-fikā´shən) *n.* **speechifier** *n.* **speechless** *a.* **1** unable to speak, silent, esp. through emotion. **2** dumbfounded. **speechlessly** *adv.* **speechlessness** *n.* **speech therapy** *n.* treatment for improving speech, enunciation etc. **speech therapist** *n.*

speed (spēd) *n.* **1** rapidity, swiftness. **2** rate of motion, the ratio of the distance covered to the time taken by a moving body. **3** the numerical expression of the sensitivity of a photographic plate, film or paper to light. **4** a measure of the power of a lens to take in light. **5 a** any of the gear ratios on a bicycle. **b** (*esp. N Am.*) a gear in a motor vehicle. **6** (*sl.*) amphetamine. ~*v.i.* (*past, p.p.* **sped** (sped)) **1** to move rapidly, to hasten. **2** (*past, p.p.* **speeded**) to drive, to travel at an excessively high, dangerous or illegal speed. ~*v.t.* **1** (*past, p.p.* **speeded**) to regulate the speed of, to set (an engine etc.) at a fixed rate of speed. **2** to cause to go fast, to urge, to send at great speed. **at speed** while moving quickly. **to speed up 1** to progress faster. **2** to cause to progress faster, to expedite. **speedboat** *n.* a light motor boat designed for high speed. **speed bump, speed hump** *n.* a widthways ridge on a road for slowing traffic down. **speeder** *n.* **speeding** *n.* (the offence of) driving at an excessive, dangerous or illegal speed. ~*a.* travelling at such a speed. **speed limit** *n.* the legal limit of speed for a road vehicle, vessel etc. in a particular area or in particular conditions. **speed merchant** *n.* (*coll.*) a motorist who habitually drives fast. **speedo** (-ō) *n.* (*pl.* **speedos**) (*coll.*) a speedometer. **speedometer** (-dom´itə) *n.* a device fitted in a vehicle to measure and indicate its speed. **speed trap** *n.* a stretch of road monitored by police using radar devices to catch speeding drivers. **speed-up** *n.* an increase in speed, an acceleration. **speedway** *n.*

1 the sport of motorcycle racing on a track. **2** a racecourse, stadium or track for motorcycle racing. **3** (*N Am.*) a road or track for motor-car racing. **4** (*N Am.*) a highway for fast traffic. **speedwell** *n.* a flowering herb, any of various species of *Veronica*. **speedy** *a.* (*comp.* **speedier,** *superl.* **speediest**). **speedily** *adv.* **speediness** *n.*

spelean (spilē´ən), **spelaean** *a.* **1** of or relating to a cave or caves. **2** cave-dwelling. **speleology** (spēliol´əji) *n.* the scientific study or exploration of caves. **speleological** (-liəloj´-) *a.* **speleologist** *n.*

spell[1] (spel) *v.t.* (*past, p.p.* **spelt** (spelt), **spelled** (speld, spelt)) **1** to say or write the letters forming (a word). **2** (of letters) to form (a word). **3** to mean, to import, to portend, entail or involve (*a formula that spells disaster*). ~*v.i.* to put letters together in such a way as to (correctly) form a word (*He never could spell*). **to spell out 1** to utter or write letter by letter. **2** to make clear, easy to understand. **3** to puzzle out. **spellable** *a.* **spellcheck** *n.* a check made by a spelling checker of the spelling in a computer file. ~*v.t.* to check the spelling in (a file) with a spelling checker. **spellchecker** *n.* a spelling checker. **speller** *n.* a person who spells well, badly etc. (*a good speller*). **spelling** *n.* **1** the activity or process of writing or saying the letters of a word. **2** the particular formation of letters making up a word, orthography. **3** one's ability to spell (*My spelling's awful*). **spelling-bee** *n.* a competition in spelling. **spelling checker** *n.* a computer program that checks the spelling of words keyed, usu. against a stored list of vocabulary.

spell[2] (spel) *n.* **1** a series of words used as a charm, an incantation. **2** the power of an occult force. **3** a powerful attraction or fascination. **under a spell** dominated by, or as if by, a spell. **spellbind** *v.t.* (*past, p.p.* **spellbound**) **1** to put a spell on. **2** to entrance. **spellbinder** *n.* **spellbinding** *a.* **spellbindingly** *adv.* **spellbound** *a.*

spell[3] (spel) *n.* **1** a shift or turn of work. **2** a (usu. short) period of time. **3** a period of weather of a certain kind (*a cold spell*). **4** a period characterized by some experience (*a spell of ill health*; *having a bad spell*). **5** (*Austral.*) a rest from work. ~*v.i.* (*Austral.*) to rest briefly.

spellican SPILLIKIN.

spelt[1] SPELL[1].

spelt[2] (spelt) *n.* a variety of wheat, *Triticum spelta*, formerly much cultivated in S Europe etc.

spelunker (spilŭng´kə) *n.* (*N Am.*) a person who explores or studies caves as a sport or hobby. **spelunking** *n.*

spencer (spen´sə) *n.* **1** a short overcoat or jacket, for men or women. **2** a woman's undergarment, a vest.

spend (spend) *v.t.* (*past, p.p.* **spent** (spent)) **1** to pay out (money etc.) on something or someone (*spent £40 on a new pair of shoes*; *seemed reluctant to spend money on his children*). **2** to use up, to expend (time, energy etc.). **3** to pass (time) (*spending a week in Venice*). **4** to wear out (*The*

storm had spent itself). ~*v.i.* to expend money. ~*n.* **1** the activity of spending money. **2** a sum spent, expenditure. **to spend a penny** (*coll.*) to urinate. **spendable** *a.* **spender** *n.* **spending** *n.* **spending money** *n.* pocket money, money for spending. **spendthrift** *n.* a prodigal or wasteful person. ~*a.* prodigal, wasteful. **spent** *a.* exhausted, tired out (*feeling spent*; *spent inspiration*).

sperm (spœm) *n.* (*pl.* **sperm, sperms**) **1** a spermatozoon, a male gamete. **2** the seminal or reproductive fluid of male animals. **3** a sperm whale or cachalot. **sperm bank** *n.* a supply of semen stored ready for using in artificial insemination. **sperm count** *n.* the number of spermatozoa found in a single ejaculation, or in any measured quantity of semen. **spermicide** (-misīd) *n.* a substance that kills spermatozoa. **spermicidal** (-sī´-) *a.* **sperm oil** *n.* oil from the head of a sperm whale, used as a lubricant. **sperm whale** *n.* a large whale, *Physeter macrocephalus*, yielding sperm oil, spermaceti and ambergris.

spermaceti (spœməsē´ti, -set´i) *n.* a white waxy, buoyancy-promoting substance, existing in solution in the oily matter in the head of the sperm whale, used for candles, ointments etc. **spermacetic** *a.*

spermatic (spœmat´ik) *a.* consisting of, of or relating to or conveying sperm or semen.

spermato- (spœ´mətō), **spermat-, sperm-, spermo-** *comb. form* (*Biol.*) a seed or sperm.

spermatozoon (spœmətōzō´on, -mat´ə-) *n.* (*pl.* **spermatozoa** (-zō´ə)) any of the millions of mature male sex cells contained in the semen. **spermatozoal** (-zō´əl), **spermatozoan** (-zō´ən), **spermatozoic** (-zō´ik) *a.*

spermicide SPERM.

spew (spū), **spue** *v.t.* **1** to vomit (up). **2** to spit out. **3** to emit or eject violently or in great quantity. ~*v.i.* **1** to vomit. **2** to stream, gush or flood out. ~*n.* vomit, matter ejected with great force or in great quantity. **spewer** *n.* **spewy** *a.* (*comp.* **spewier,** *superl.* **spewiest**).

SPF *abbr.* sun protection factor (an indication of the protective strength of sun creams or lotions).

sp. gr. *abbr.* specific gravity.

sphagnum (sfag´nəm) *n.* (*pl.* **sphagna** (-nə)) any moss of the genus *Sphagnum*, found in peat or bogs, and used as a fertilizer and as packing material. **sphagnous** *a.* **sphagnum moss** *n.*

sphere (sfiə) *n.* **1** a solid bounded by a surface every part of which is equally distant from a point within called the centre. **2** a ball, a globe, esp. one of the heavenly bodies. **3 a** a globe representing the earth or the apparent heavens. **b** any of the spherical shells revolving round the earth as centre in which, according to ancient astronomy, the heavenly bodies were set. **c** (*poet.*) the sky, the heavens. **4** an area of knowledge or a discipline. **5** field of action, influence etc. position; social class. **spheral** *a.* **spheric** (sfer´ik) *a.* spherical. **spherical** (sfer´ikəl) *a.*

1 sphere-shaped, globular. **2** relating to spheres or their properties. **spherical aberration** n. the deterioration of an image from a lens or mirror with a spherical surface as a result of the different focal points of rays striking its edge and centre. **spherically** adv. **sphericity** (-ris´-) n. **spheroid** (sfiə´roid) n. **1** a body nearly spherical. **2** a solid generated by the revolution of an ellipse about its minor axis (called an *oblate spheroid*) or its major axis (called a *prolate spheroid*). **spheroidal** (-roi´-) a. **spheroidally** adv. **spheroidic, spheroidical** a. **spheroidicity** (-dis´-) n.

sphincter (sfingk´tə) n. (*Anat.*) a ring muscle that contracts or shuts any orifice or tube. **sphincteral, sphincterial** (-tiə´riəl), **sphincteric** (-ter´ik) a.

sphinx (sfingks) n. **1** any of several ancient Egyptian figures with the body of a lion and a human or animal head. **2** a taciturn or enigmatic person.

sphygmomanometer (sfigmōmənom´itə) n. an instrument for measuring the tension of blood in an artery. **sphygmomanometric** (-manəmet´-) a.

spic (spik), **spick, spik** n. (*N Am.*, *offensive*) **1** a Spanish-speaking American, esp. a Mexican. **2** the Spanish spoken by such a person.

spic and span SPICK AND SPAN.

spice (spīs) n. **1** any aromatic and pungent vegetable substance used for seasoning food. **2** such substances collectively (*sugar and spice*). **3** a touch, a trace. **4** zest or interest (*adds a bit of spice*). ~v.t. **1** to season with spice. **2** to add interest to. **spicebush**, (*N Am.*) **spicewood** n. the wild allspice, *Lindera benzoin*, an American shrub. **spicy, spicey** a. (*comp.* **spicier,** *superl.* **spiciest**) **1** flavoured with spice. **2** abounding in spices. **3** pungent, piquant. **4** suggestive of scandal. **5** showy, smart. **spicily** adv. **spiciness** n.

spick and span (spik ən span´), **spic and span** a. new and fresh, clean and smart.

spicy SPICE.

spider (spī´də) n. **1** an eight-legged arachnid of the order Araneae, usu. equipped with a spinning apparatus utilized by most species for making webs to catch their prey. **2** an arachnid resembling this. **3** a spider-like thing, esp. a three-legged frying-pan, gridiron, frame etc. **4** a long-legged rest for a cue in snooker. ~v.i., v.t. to (cause to) move in a spider-like way. **spider crab** n. a crab with long thin legs. **spiderish** a. **spiderlike** a., adv. **spiderman** n. (*pl.* **spidermen**) (*coll.*) a construction worker who works at great heights. **spider mite** n. RED SPIDER (under RED). **spider monkey** n. any monkey belonging to the American genus *Ateles* or *Brachyteles* with long limbs, a slender body, and a prehensile tail. **spider plant** n. a southern African house plant of the lily family, *Chlorophytum comosum*, having streamers of long narrow leaves with central white or yellow stripes. **spiderwort** n. any plant of the genus *Tradescantia*, esp. *Tradescantia virginiana*, whose flowers have long hairy stamens.

spidery a. (esp. of handwriting) attenuated, spindly.

spiel (shpēl, spēl) n. the sales patter of a practised dealer, or anyone's well-rehearsed or familiar tale. ~v.i. to talk with glib or practised ease. ~v.t. to reel off (patter). **spieler** n. (*sl.*) **1** (*esp. N Am.*) a person who spiels or holds forth. **2** (*Austral., New Zeal.*) a gambler, card-sharper or trickster.

spiffing (spif´ing) a. (*dated coll.*) **1** excellent. **2** smart, spruce, well-dressed. **spiffy** a. (*comp.* **spiffier,** *superl.* **spiffiest**) (*esp. N Am.*) spiffing.

spignel (spig´nəl), **spicknel** (spik´nəl) n. an umbelliferous plant, *Meum athamanticum*, with an aromatic root used in medicine, and finely cut, ornamental leaves, also called *baldmoney*.

spigot (spig´ət) n. **1** a peg or plug for stopping the vent-hole in a cask. **2** (*N Am.*) a faucet, a tap. **3** (*N Am.*) the turning-plug in a tap.

spike¹ (spīk) n. **1** any pointed object, a sharp point. **2** a pointed piece of metal, e.g. one of a number fixed on the top of a railing or fence. **3 a** any of a number of metal points fitted to the sole of a boot or running shoe, to prevent slipping. **b** (*pl.*) a pair of running shoes with spikes. **4** a pointed metal rod set vertically into a base, on which to impale bills or, in journalism, rejected news stories. **5** a large nail or pin, used in structures built of large timbers, on railways etc. **6** (*sl.*) a hypodermic needle. **7** (*sl.*) a doss-house. **8** an electrical pulse characterized by a rapid increase and equally rapid decrease in voltage. ~v.t. **1** to fasten with spikes. **2** to provide or fit with spikes. **3** to pierce with or impale on a spike. **4** (of a news editor) to file (a story) as rejected (by impaling it on a spike). **5** to lace (a drink) with spirits. **6** to render useless. **to spike someone's guns** to foil someone's plans. **spike heel** n. a high heel tapering to a point. **spiky** a. (*comp.* **spikier,** *superl.* **spikiest**). **spikily** adv. **spikiness** n.

spike² (spīk) n. (*Bot.*) an inflorescence closely attached to a common stem. **spikelet** (-lit) n. a small spike, esp. as part of the inflorescence of most grasses, with two bracts at the base.

spikenard (spīk´nahd) n. **1 a** a Himalayan herb, *Nardostachys jatamansi*, related to the valerian. **b** an ancient and costly aromatic ointment prepared chiefly from the root of this. **2** a European and African plant, *Inula conyza*, with yellow flowers and aromatic roots.

spill¹ (spil) v.t. (*past, p.p.* **spilt** (spilt), **spilled** (spild, spilt)) **1** to cause (liquid, powder etc.) to fall or run out of a vessel, esp. accidentally. **2** to shed. **3** (*coll.*) to throw out of a vehicle or from a saddle. **4** (*sl.*) to give away, disclose (information). ~v.i. **1** (of liquid) to run or fall out of a vessel. **2** (of a crowd) to pour (out of a place). ~n. **1** an instance of spilling, or the amount spilt. **2** a fall, esp. from a vehicle or saddle. **to spill over 1** to overflow. **2** (of excess population) to be forced to move or spread. **to spill someone's blood** to be responsible for someone's death. **to**

spill the beans to divulge a secret. **spillage** (-lij) *n*. **spillover** *n*. **1** an instance, or the process, of spilling over. **2** that which spills over. **3** a repercussion or knock-on effect. **spillway** *n*. a passage for the overflow of water from a reservoir etc. **spilth** (-th) *n*. **1** that which is spilt. **2** an instance of spilling. **3** excess of supply.

spill² (spil) *n*. a slip of paper or wood used to light a candle, pipe etc.

spillikin (spil´ikin), **spellican** (spel´ikən) *n*. a small strip or pin of bone, wood etc., used in spillikins. **spillikins** *n*. a game in which players attempt to remove spillikins from a pile one at a time without disturbing the others.

spin (spin) *v.t.* (*pres.p.* **spinning**, *past* **spun** (spŭn), **span** (span), *p.p.* **spun**) **1** to make (something or someone) rotate or whirl round rapidly. **2 a** to draw out and twist (wool, cotton etc.) into threads. **b** to make (yarn etc.) thus. **3** (of spiders etc.) to produce (a web, cocoon etc.) by drawing out a thread of viscous substance. **4** to tell, compose etc. (a tale), at great length. **5** to hit (a ball) so that it twists in flight. **6** to shape in a lathe etc. **7** to fish with a revolving bait. **8** to toss (a coin). **9** to spin-dry. **~v.i. 1** to turn round quickly. **2** (of a ball) to twist in flight. **3** (of one's head) to be dizzy with amazement or excitement. **4** to draw out and twist cotton etc., into threads. **5** to make yarn etc., thus. **6** to fish with a spinning bait. **7** (of a vehicle etc.) to go (along) with great swiftness. **~n. 1** the act or motion of spinning, a whirl. **2** a rapid diving descent by an aircraft accompanied by a continued gyration. **3** a twisting motion imparted to a ball, or to a rifle bullet. **4** (*coll.*) a brief run in a car, aircraft etc. **5** (*Physics*) the angular momentum of a subatomic particle in default of orbital motion. **6** (*N Am.*) a cosmetic twist given to information in presentation. **in a flat spin** in a state of agitation. **to spin a yarn** to tell a story. **to spin off** to throw off, or be thrown off, by centrifugal force while spinning. **to spin out 1** to compose or tell (a yarn etc.) at great length. **2** to prolong, to protract. **3** to spend (time) in tedious discussion etc. **4** (*N Am.*) (of e.g. a vehicle) to go out of control in a skid etc. **spin bowling** *n*. in cricket, a style of bowling in which the ball is delivered slowly with an imparted spin to make it bounce unpredictably. **spin bowler** *n*. **spin doctor** *n*. (*coll.*) in politics, a spokesperson employed to give a favourable twist to events for the benefit of the media. **spindryer, spin-drier** *n*. a machine with a rotating perforated drum in which the water is extracted from washing by centrifugal force. **spin-dry** *v.t.* (*3rd pers. sing. pres.* **spin-dries,** *pres.p.* **spindrying,** *past, p.p.* **spin-dried**). **spinner** *n*. **1** a person or thing that spins. **2** a machine for spinning thread. **3 a** in cricket, a ball bowled with a spin. **b** a spin bowler. **4** a spider's spinneret. **5** in fishing, a lure designed to revolve in the water. **6** a mayfly or other fly used in fishing. **7** a spindryer. **spinneret** (spin´əret) *n*. **1** the spinning

organ of a spider through which the silk issues. **2** the orifice through which liquid cellulose is projected to form the threads of rayon or artificial silk. **spinning** *n*. **spinning jenny** *n*. (*pl.* **spinning jennies**) a spinning frame with several spindles invented by Hargreaves in 1764 for spinning more than one thread at once. **spinning machine** *n*. a machine for spinning fibres continuously. **spinning wheel** *n*. a machine for home spinning, with a spindle driven by a wheel operated by the foot or hand, formerly used for spinning wool, cotton, or flax. **spin-off** *n*. a byproduct or incidental benefit, something derived from an existing idea or product.

spina bifida SPINE.

spinach (spin´ich, -ij) *n*. **1** an annual herb of the genus *Spinacia*, esp. *S. oleracea*, with succulent leaves cooked as food. **2** the leaves of this plant. **spinach beet** *n*. a variety of beet of which the leaves are eaten as spinach. **spinachy** *a*.

spinal SPINE.

spindle (spin´dəl) *n*. **1** a pin or rod in a spinning wheel for twisting and winding the thread. **2** a rod used for the same purpose in hand-spinning. **3** a pin bearing the bobbin in a spinning machine. **4** a rod, axis, or arbor which revolves, or on which anything revolves. **5** (*Biol.*) a spindle-shaped structure formed in a cell during cell division. **spindle-legs, spindle-shanks** *n*. **1** (*as pl.*) long thin legs. **2** (*as sing.*) a person with long thin legs. **spindle-shaped** *a*. tapering from the middle towards both ends, fusiform. **spindly** *a*. (*comp.* **spindlier,** *superl.* **spindliest**) **1** tall and thin. **2** elongated.

spindrift (spin´drift) *n*. fine spray blown up from the surface of water.

spine (spīn) *n*. **1** the spinal column, the backbone. **2** (*Bot.*) a thorn. **3** (*esp. Zool.*) a sharp projection, outgrowth etc. **4** the narrow back part of a book or its cover, that usu. faces outwards on a shelf and bears the title and the author's name. **spina bifida** (spīna bif´ida) *n*. a congenital condition in which one or more vertebrae fail to unite during the embryo stage, so that the spinal cord and meninges protrude, resulting in paralysis of the lower body in some cases. **spinal** *a*. **spinal column** *n*. the backbone, an interconnected series of vertebrae in the skeleton which runs the length of the trunk and encloses the spinal cord, giving support to the thorax and abdomen. **spinal cord** *n*. a cylindrical structure of nerve fibres and cells within the vertebral canal, forming part of the central nervous system. **spinally** *adv*. **spine-chiller** *n*. a book, film, event etc. that causes terror. **spine-chilling** *a*. **spined** *a*. **spineless** *a*. **1** without a spine; invertebrate. **2** (of a plant or animal) without spines. **3** of weak character, lacking decision. **spinose** (-nōs), **spinous** *a*. (*Bot., Zool.*) having spines, spiny. **spiny** *a*. (*comp.* **spinier,** *superl.* **spiniest**). **spininess** *n*. **spiny anteater** *n*. ECHIDNA. **spiny lobster** *n*. any of several large spiny crustaceans, lacking large anterior claws, esp. *Palinuris vulgaris.*

spinel (spinel´) *n.* **1** a vitreous aluminate of magnesium, of various colours, crystallizing isometrically. **2** any of various other minerals of similar structure. **spinel ruby** *n.* a dark red variety of spinel, used in jewellery etc.

spinet (spinet´) *n.* **1** an obsolete musical instrument, similar in construction to but smaller than the harpsichord. **2** (*N Am.*) a kind of small upright piano.

spinifex (spī´nifeks) *n.* any coarse, spiny Australian grass of the genus *Spinifex*, growing in sandhills etc. in the arid regions of Australia, and often covering enormous areas of ground.

spinnaker (spin´əkə) *n.* a large jib-shaped sail carried opposite the mainsail on the mainmast of a racing yacht.

spinner, spinneret etc. SPIN.

spinney (spin´i) *n.* (*pl.* **spinneys**) a small wood with undergrowth, a copse.

spinose, spinous SPINE.

spinster (spin´stə) *n.* **1** an unmarried woman. **2** a woman unlikely to get married, esp. an elderly one. **spinsterhood** *n.* **spinsterish** *a.* **spinsterishness** *n.*

spiny SPINE.

spiracle (spī´rəkəl), **spiraculum** (-rak´ūləm) *n.* (*pl.* **spiracles, spiracula** (-lə)) an external breathing hole in insects, certain fish, and whales. **spiracular** (-rak´ū-), **spiraculate** (-lət), **spiraculiform** (-kū´lifawm) *a.*

spiraea (spīrē´ə), (*N Am.*) **spirea** *n.* any flowering plant belonging to the *Spiraea* genus of Rosaceae, including the meadowsweet.

spiral (spī´rəl) *a.* **1** forming a spire, spiral, or coil. **2** continually winding about, and receding from, or advancing on, a centre, in a flat plane, or rising or descending in a cone. **3** continually winding, as the thread of a screw. ~*n.* **1** a plane or three-dimensional spiral curve, formed by a point revolving round a central point while continuously advancing on or receding from it. **2** a formation or object with this shape, such as a spring, a shell formation, or a spiral galaxy. **3** a continuous upward or downward movement, e.g. of prices and wages, a decrease or increase in the one causing a corresponding movement in the other. **4** flight in a spiral motion. ~*v.i.* (*pres.p.* **spiralling,** (*N Am.*) **spiraling,** *past, p.p.* **spiralled,** (*N Am.*) **spiraled**) **1** to move upwards, downwards, or in a plane, in a spiral. **2** (esp. of prices and wages) to rise or fall rapidly. ~*v.t.* to make spiral. **spiral galaxy** *n.* (*pl.* **spiral galaxies**) a galaxy comprising an ellipsoidal nucleus around which two arms revolve and spiral outwards. **spirality** (-ral´-) *n.* **spirally** *adv.* **spiral staircase** *n.* a staircase rising in a spiral round a central column.

spirant (spī´rənt) *n.* a consonant produced with a continuous expulsion of breath, esp. a fricative. ~*a.* denoting this kind of consonant.

spire (spīə) *n.* **1** a tapering, conical, or pyramidal structure, esp. the tapering portion of a steeple. **2** a stalk of grass, the tapering part of a tree above the point where branching begins. **3** the spike of a flower, or any similarly tapering object. ~*v.t.* to furnish with a spire or spires. **spiry** *a.* (*comp.* **spirier,** *superl.* **spiriest**).

spirea SPIRAEA.

spirit (spir´it) *n.* **1 a** the vital principle animating a person or animal. **b** the non-physical, immaterial part of a person, the soul. **2** a rational being unconnected with a physical body. **3** a disembodied soul; an incorporeal or supernatural being, such as a ghost. **4** a person considered with regard to their individual qualities of mind or temperament. **5** a person of strong mental or moral force. **6** vivacity, enthusiasm (*lacks spirit*). **7** (*often pl.*) mood, humour (*in high spirits*). **8** mental attitude (*take it in the right spirit*). **9** real meaning or intent (*the spirit of the law*). **10** characteristic quality or tendency (*the spirit of the age*). **11** (*usu. pl.*) distilled alcoholic liquors, such as brandy, whisky, gin etc. **12** (*often pl., N Am.*) a liquid distilled essence. **13** distilled alcohol. **14** a solution of a volatile principle in alcohol. ~*v.t.* (*pres.p.* **spiriting,** *past, p.p.* **spirited**) **1** to convey (away, off etc.) secretly and rapidly. **2** to animate, to inspirit. **if the spirit moves one** if one feels inclined. **in spirit 1** inwardly, in one's heart. **2** as a supportive presence, though not in person (*They are with us today in spirit*). **spirit duplicator** *n.* a duplicator that reproduces copies from a master sheet with the use of an alcoholic solution. **spirited** *a.* **1** full of spirit or life, animated, lively. **2** (*in comb.*) having a particular mental attitude, as in *high-spirited*. **spiritedly** *adv.* **spiritedness** *n.* **spirit gum** *n.* a fast-drying gum solution used for sticking on false hair etc. **spirit lamp** *n.* a lamp burning methylated or other spirit. **spiritless** *a.* lacking strength of character or purpose. **spiritlessly** *adv.* **spiritlessness** *n.* **spirit level** *n.* an instrument used for determining the horizontal through the position of an air bubble in a glass tube containing alcohol. **spiritous** *a.* spirituous. **spiritual** (-chuəl, -tūəl) *a.* **1** of or relating to the spirit as distinct from matter. **2** immaterial, incorporeal. **3** of or relating to the soul or the inner nature. **4** derived from or of or relating to God, holy. **5** of or relating to sacred things, not lay or temporal. ~*n.* a type of hymn sung by black people of the southern US, a negro spiritual. **spiritualism** *n.* **1** a system of professed communication with the spirits of the dead, chiefly through people called mediums; belief in this. **2** (*Philos.*) the doctrine that the spirit exists as distinct from matter or as the only reality. **spiritualist** *n.* **spiritualistic** (-lis´-) *a.* **spirituality** (-al´-) *n.* **spiritualize, spiritualise** *v.t.* **1** to elevate (thoughts etc.), to render spiritual. **2** to give a spiritual rather than literal meaning to. **spiritualization** (-zā´shən) *n.* **spiritually** *adv.* **spiritualness** *n.* **spirituous** (-tūəs) *a.*

containing spirit, alcoholic; distilled as distinct from fermented. **spirituousness** *n.*

spirochaete (spī´rōkēt), (*N Am.*) **spirochete** *n.* any spiral-shaped bacterium of the genus *Spirochaeta*, which includes the causative agents of syphilis, relapsing fever, and epidemic jaundice.

spirogyra (spīrəjī´rə) *n.* (*pl.* **spirogyras**) any alga of the genus *Spirogyra*, whose cells contain spiral bands of chlorophyll.

spirt SPURT.

spit[1] (spit) *v.t.* (*pres.p.* **spitting**, *past, p.p.* **spat** (spat), †**spit**) **1** to eject (saliva etc.), throw (out) from the mouth. **2** to utter or throw (out) in a violent or spiteful way (*'Bitch!' he spat*; *He spat out a curse*). ~*v.i.* **1** to eject saliva from the mouth. **2** (of an angry cat) to make a spitting noise. **3** (of a frying pan, fire etc.) to throw out hot fat, sparks etc. **4** (*impers.*) to drizzle with rain. ~*n.* **1** spittle, saliva. **2** an act of spitting. **3** the foamy liquid that certain insects secrete to protect their young. **4** the exact likeness or double (of). **to spit it out** (*coll.*) to say what is concerning one, to come clean. **to spit up** (*N Am.*) (usu. of a baby) to vomit. **spit and polish** *n.* **1** the activities of cleaning and polishing, esp. as a soldier's duties. **2** (*coll.*) (obsessive) cleanliness, attention to details, as in the army. **spitball** *n.* (*N Am.*) a ball of chewed paper thrown as a missile. ~*v.i.* to toss out ideas for discussion. **spitfire** *n.* an irascible person. **spitter** *n.* **spitting** *n.* **spitting cobra** *n.* a black-necked cobra native to Africa that spits out its venom, as distinct from striking. **spitting distance** *n.* a very small distance. **spitting image** *n.* (*coll.*) an exact likeness; a person or thing that exactly resembles another. **spittle** (spit´əl) *n.* saliva, esp. ejected from the mouth. **spittly** *a.* **spittoon** (-toon´) *n.* a receptacle for spittle.

spit[2] (spit) *n.* **1** a long pointed rod on which meat for roasting is skewered and rotated over a fire. **2** a point of land or a narrow shoal extending into the sea. **3** a long narrow underwater ridge. ~*v.t.* (*pres.p.* **spitting**, *past, p.p.* **spitted**) **1** to fix (meat) upon a spit. **2** to pierce, to transfix. **spitty** *a.* (*comp.* **spittier**, *superl.* **spittiest**).

spit[3] (spit) *n.* (*pl.* **spit**, **spits**) a spade's depth of earth.

spite (spīt) *n.* **1** ill will, malice. **2** a grudge. ~*v.t.* **1** to thwart maliciously. **2** to vex or annoy. **in spite of** notwithstanding, despite. **in spite of oneself** though behaving contrary to one's inclinations. **spiteful** *a.* **spitefully** *adv.* **spitefulness** *n.*

spitter, spittle etc. SPIT[1].

spitz (spits) *n.* a sharp-muzzled breed of dog, also called *Pomeranian.*

spiv (spiv) *n.* a man who dresses flashily and lives by dubious dealing and trading, e.g. in black-market goods. **spivvish** *a.* **spivvy** *a.* (*comp.* **spivvier**, *superl.* **spivviest**).

splash (splash) *v.t.* **1** to bespatter with water, mud etc. **2** to dash (liquid etc., about, over, etc.). **3** to make (one's way) e.g. through water, scattering it about. **4** to spend recklessly. **5** to display

prominently in a newspaper (*Her name was splashed across the front page*). **6** to decorate with bright scattered patches of colour. ~*v.i.* **1** to dash water or other liquid about. **2** to dabble, to plunge. **3** to move or to make one's way (along etc.) thus. ~*n.* **1** the act of splashing. **2** water or mud splashed about. **3** a noise as of splashing. **4** a spot or patch of liquid, colour etc. **5** a vivid display. **6** a conspicuously presented news item. **7** a dash; a small amount of soda water etc. mixed with an alcoholic drink. **to make a splash** (*sl.*) to make a sensation, display, etc. **to splash down** (of a spacecraft) to land on water when returning to earth. **splashback** *n.* a washable surface or panel behind a sink to protect the wall from splashes. **splashdown** *n.* the landing of a spacecraft on the ocean. **splashy** *a.* (*comp.* **splashier**, *superl.* **splashiest**).

splat[1] (splat) *n.* a flat strip of wood forming the central part of a chair back.

splat[2] (splat) *n.* **1** the slapping sound made by a soft or wet object striking a surface. **2** a cracking, splitting or squashing sound. ~*adv.* with such a sound (*was spreadeagled splat against the wall*). ~*v.t., v.i.* (*pres.p.* **splatting**, *past, p.p.* **splatted**) to hit or fall with a splat.

splatter (splat´ə) *v.t.* **1** to bespatter, to splash with dirt, mud, water etc. **2** to display or present (news, pictures etc.) conspicuously. **3** to splutter. ~*v.i.* **1** to spatter. **2** to make a continuous splash or splashing noise. ~*n.* **1** a noisy splash. **2** an untidy spread of colour.

splay (splā) *v.t.* **1** to form (a window opening, doorway etc.) with diverging sides. **2** to spread out (one's arms, legs etc.). ~*v.i.* (of e.g. an embrasure or other opening, or its sides) to widen, to diverge. ~*n.* an oblique surface, side, or widening of a window etc. ~*a.* **1** wide and flat. **2** turned outwards. **splay-foot** *n.* (*pl.* **splay-feet**) a broad flat foot turned outwards. **splay-footed** *a.*

spleen (splēn) *n.* **1** a soft vascular organ situated to the left of the stomach in most vertebrates which produces lymphocytes and antibodies, and filters the blood. **2** spitefulness, ill temper. **3** low spirits, melancholy. **spleeny** *a.* (*comp.* **spleenier**, *superl.* **spleeniest**).

splendid (splen´did) *a.* **1** magnificent, sumptuous. **2** glorious, illustrious. **3** brilliant, dazzling. **4** fine, excellent. **splendidly** *adv.* **splendidness** *n.* **splendiferous** (-dif´-) *a.* (*facet.*) splendid. **splendour**, (*N Am.*) **splendor** *n.* **splendorous** *a.*

splenetic (splinet´ik) *a.* **1** affected with spleen; peevish, ill-tempered. **2** of or relating to the spleen. **splenetically** *adv.*

splenic (splen´ik, splē´nik) *a.* of or relating to or affecting the spleen. **splenitis** (-nī´tis) *n.* **splenoid** (splē´noid) *a.*

splice (splīs) *v.t.* **1** to unite (two ropes etc.) by interweaving the strands of the ends. **2** to unite (timbers etc.) by bevelling, overlapping, and fitting the ends together. **3** (*coll.*) to unite in marriage (*get spliced*). ~*n.* **1** a union of ropes, timbers etc., by splicing. **2** the point of juncture between two pieces of film. **3** the joint on the handle of a cricket bat which fits into the blade. **splicer** *n.*

spliff (splif) *n.* (*sl.*) a cannabis cigarette.

splint (splint) *n.* **1** a thin piece of wood or other material used to keep the parts of a broken bone together. **2** a thin strip of wood used in basket-making etc., or one used to light a fire, pipe etc. **3** a splint-bone. **4** a callous tumour on the splint-bone of a horse. ~*v.t.* to secure or support with splints. **splint-bone** *n.* **1** either of two small bones in a horse's leg extending from the knee to the fetlock. **2** a human fibula.

splinter (splin'tə) *n.* **1** a thin piece of wood, glass, stone, metal etc. broken, split, or shivered off. **2** a needle-like piece of wood, esp. when embedded in the flesh. ~*v.t.* to split, shiver or rend into splinters or fragments. ~*v.i.* to split or shiver into splinters. **splinter group, splinter party** *n.* a small group that has broken away from its parent political etc. organization. **splintery** *a.*

split (split) *v.t.* (*pres.p.* **splitting**, *past, p.p.* **split**) **1** to break, cleave, tear or divide, esp. longitud-inally or with the grain. **2** to divide into two or more thicknesses, sections etc. **3** to break or separate (off or away). **4** to divide (up) into parts or groups. **5** to divide into opposed parties (*The issue has split the government*; *are split over finance*; *split on education*). **6** (*coll.*) (esp. of accomplices) to divide (a haul of money etc.) between members of the group; to divide (pro-ceeds) in this way. **7** to cause (one's head) to ache or throb. **8** to bring about the fission of (an atom). ~*v.i.* **1** to be broken or divided, esp. longitud-inally or with the grain. **2** to break (up), to come to pieces. **3** to divide into opposed parties. **4** (of a couple etc.) to break (up), to separate or stop associating (with one another). **5** (*sl.*) to betray the secrets of, to inform (on). **6** (*coll.*) (of one's head) to ache acutely. **7** (*coll.*) to burst with laughter. **8** (*sl.*) to depart. ~*n.* **1** an instance, or the resultant state, of splitting. **2** a crack, rent, tear or fissure. **3** a separation, a rupture, a schism, a division into opposing parties. **4** (*pl.*) an acrobat's feat of leaping, or sitting down, with the legs fully stretched out forwards and back-wards, or right and left. **5** a dessert of sliced fruit, esp. banana, and ice cream etc. **6** something split, a split osier for basketwork, a single thick-ness of split hide etc. **7** (*sl.*) a half bottle of soda water. **8** a half glass of liquor. **9** (*coll.*) a division of proceeds, a haul of money etc. ~*a.* **1** having been split. **2** fractured. **3** having splits. **to split one's sides** to laugh uproariously. **to split the difference** to compromise by taking the average of two amounts. **split end** *n.* **1** (*usu. pl.*) the tip of a hair that has split from dryness etc. **2** in American football, an offensive player who lines up some distance from the formation. **split in-finitive** *n.* an infinitive phrase where an adverb has been inserted between *to* and the verb, as in *to completely destroy*, considered by some a

stylistic solecism, but in many cases allowable. **split-level** *a.* (esp. of a one-storey house) built on more than one level. **split pea** *n.* a dried pea split in half and used in soups etc. **split personality** *n.* (*pl.* **split personalities**) a personality comprising two or more dissociated groups of attitudes and behaviour, as a manifestation of mental illness. **split pin** *n.* a pin with a divided end which is splayed apart to keep the pin in place. **split ring** *n.* a metal ring constructed in two spiral turns, so that keys etc. can be put on it or taken off. **split-screen** *n.* a cinematic or computing technique in which different images are displayed simul-taneously on separate sections of the screen. **split second** *n.* an instant, a fraction of a second. **split-second** *a.* **1** very rapid. **2** precise to a frac-tion of a second (*split-second timing*). **split shift** *n.* a work period divided into two parts separ-ated by a long interval. **splitter** *n.* **splitting** *a.* (of a headache) acute, severe.

splodge (sploj) *n.* a daub, a blotch, an irregular stain. ~*v.t.* to make a daub or blotch on. **splodgy** *a.* (*comp.* **splodgier**, *superl.* **splodgiest**).

splosh (splosh) *v.i., v.t.* (*coll.*) to splash; to move with a splashing sound. ~*n.* **1** a splash or a splashing sound. **2** (*sl.*) money.

splotch (sploch) *n.* a splodge. ~*v.t.* to make a splodge on, to cover with splodges. **splotchy** *a.* (*comp.* **splotchier**, *superl.* **splotchiest**).

splurge (splœj) *n.* **1** an exuberant or extravagant display. **2** a bout of extravagance. ~*v.i.* **1** to make an exuberant or extravagant display. **2** to spend a lot of money (on).

splutter (splŭt'ə) *v.i.* **1** to speak in an agitated, incoherent manner. **2** to emit drops of saliva etc. from the mouth. **3** (of a fire, frying food etc.) to emit sparks, hot fat etc. with a spitting noise. ~*v.t.* to utter in a spluttering way. ~*n.* a splutter-ing sound or utterance. **splutterer** *n.* **spluttering** *a.* **splutteringly** *adv.* **spluttery** *a.*

spoil (spoil) *v.t.* (*past, p.p.* **spoilt** (spoilt), **spoiled** (spoild, spoilt)) **1** to mar, to damage, to vitiate; to impair the goodness, usefulness, value etc., of. **2** to detract from one's enjoyment of, to mar (*The rain completely spoilt our holiday*). **3** to impair the character of by over-indulgence (*mustn't spoil the children*). **4** to invalidate (a ballot paper) by marking it incorrectly. ~*v.i.* **1** (of per-ishable food) to decay, to deteriorate through keeping. **2** (*with neg.*) (of long-sustained jokes or secrets) to get stale. **3** to be eager or only too ready (for a fight). ~*n.* **1** (*usu. pl.*) plunder, booty. **2** offices, honours, or emoluments acquired as the result of a party victory, esp. in the US. **3** waste material obtaining in mining, quarrying, excavating etc. **spoilt for choice** faced with so many attractive possibilities that one cannot choose between them. **spoilage** (-ij) *n.* **1** an amount wasted or spoiled, e.g. of paper in the printing process. **2** the act of spoiling or process of being spoiled. **spoiler** *n.* **1** a person or thing that spoils something. **2** an aerodynamic device fitted to an aircraft wing to increase drag and reduce lift. **3** a similar device fitted to the front or rear of a motor vehicle to maintain stability at high speeds. **spoilsport** *n.* a person who interferes with other people's enjoyment.

spoke[1] (spōk) *n.* **1** any one of the rods connecting the hub with the rim of a wheel. **2** a rung of a ladder. **3** any of the projecting radial handles of a ship's steering wheel. *~v.t.* **1** to fit or provide with spokes. **2** to check (a wheel) with a spoke. **to put a spoke in someone's wheel** to thwart someone. **spokeshave** *n.* a plane with a handle at each end for dressing spokes, curved work etc.

spoke[2], **spoken** SPEAK.

spokesman (spōks'mən), **spokesperson, spokeswoman** *n.* (*pl.* **spokesmen, spokespersons, spokespeople, spokeswomen**) **1** a person who speaks on behalf of another or others. **2** a person delegated to give the views etc. of a group or body.

spoliation (spōliā'shən) *n.* **1** robbery, pillage, the act or practice of plundering, esp. of neutral commerce, in time of war. **2** extortion. **3** (*Law*) destruction, mutilation, or alteration of a document to prevent its use as evidence. **4** taking the emoluments of an ecclesiastical benefice under an illegal title. **spoliator** (spō'-) *n.* **spoliatory** (spō'liətəri) *a.*

spondee (spon'dē) *n.* a metrical foot consisting of two long syllables.

spondulicks (spondū'liks) *n.pl.* (*sl.*) money, cash.

spondylitis (spondilī'tis) *n.* inflammation of the vertebrae.

sponge (spŭnj) *n.* **1** any marine animal of the phylum Porifera, with pores in the body wall. **2** the skeleton or part of the skeleton of a sponge or colony of sponges, esp. of a soft, elastic kind used as an absorbent pad in bathing, cleansing etc. **3** a synthetic imitation of this. **4** any sponge-like substance or implement, e.g. a piece of absorbent material impregnated with spermicide, used in the vagina as a contraceptive. **5** an act of cleansing or wiping with a sponge. **6** sponge cake. **7** a parasite, a scrounger. **8** (*coll.*) a heavy drinker. *~v.t.* (*pres.p.* **sponging, spongeing**) **1** to wipe, wet or cleanse with a sponge; to sluice (down or over). **2** to obliterate, to wipe (out or away) with or as with a sponge. **3** to absorb, to take (up) with a sponge. **4** to extort or obtain by scrounging. *~v.i.* **1** to suck in like a sponge. **2** to live parasitically (on) or scrounge (off). **3** to gather sponges. **spongeable** *a.* **sponge bag** *n.* a small waterproof bag for carrying toiletries. **sponge bath** *n.* a cleansing of the body e.g. of a bedridden patient, with a wet sponge or cloth. **sponge cake** *n.* **1** a light porous cake, made with eggs, sugar and flour but without fat. **2** a basic cake made with eggs, fat, sugar and flour. **sponge cloth** *n.* **1** loosely-woven fabric with a wrinkled surface. **2** (a piece of) thin spongy material used for cleaning. **spongelike** *a.* **sponge pudding** *n.* a

baked or steamed pudding usu. made of a Victoria sponge mixture. **sponger** *n.* **1** a scrounger or parasite. **2** a person or thing that sponges. **sponge tree** *n.* a thorny tropical acacia, *Acacia farnesiana*, with rounded heads of yellow flowers that yield a perfume; the opopanax. **spongiform** (-jifawm) *a.* **1** like a sponge in porosity or texture. **2** denoting diseases in which diseased tissues have a spongelike appearance or texture. **spongy** *a.* (*comp.* **spongier,** *superl.* **spongiest**). **spongily** *adv.* **sponginess** *n.*

sponsor (spon'sə) *n.* **1** a person or organization that provides esp. financial support for another person or group or for some activity. **2** a person who promises to pay a sum of money usu. to charity, the amount of which is determined by the performance of an entrant in a fund-raising event. **3** a person or firm that pays the costs of mounting a radio or TV programme in exchange for advertising time. **4** a member who introduces a bill into a legislative assembly. **5** a godfather or godmother. **6** a surety, a person who undertakes to be responsible for another. *~v.t.* to act as a sponsor for. **sponsorial** (-saw'ri-) *a.* **sponsorship** *n.*

spontaneous (spontā'niəs) *a.* **1** arising, occurring, done, or acting without external cause. **2** not due to external constraint or suggestion, voluntary. **3** not due to conscious volition or motive. **4** (*esp. Biol.*) instinctive, automatic, involuntary. **spontaneity** (-tənē'-, -nā'-) *n.* **spontaneous combustion** *n.* the ignition of a body by the development of heat within itself. **spontaneously** *adv.* **spontaneousness** *n.*

spoof (spoof) *n.* **1** a deception, a hoax. **2** a parody, humorous take-off (of a play, poem etc.). *~v.t.* **1** to hoax, to fool. **2** to parody. **spoofer** *n.* **spoofery** *n.* (*pl.* **spooferies**).

spook (spook) *n.* (*coll.*) **1** a ghost. **2** (*esp. N Am.*) a spy. *~v.t.* (*esp. N Am.*) to startle or frighten. *~v.i.* (*esp. N Am.*) to become frightened. **spookish** *a.* **spooky** *a.* (*comp.* **spookier,** *superl.* **spookiest**) **1** ghostly. **2** (*coll.*) eerie, weird. **3** frightening. **4** (*N Am., sl.*) of or relating to spies. **spookily** *adv.* **spookiness** *n.*

spool (spool) *n.* **1** a small cylinder for winding thread, photographic film etc., on. **2** the central bar of an angler's reel. **3** a reel (of cotton etc.). *~v.t.* to wind on a spool.

spoon (spoon) *n.* **1** a domestic utensil consisting of a shallow bowl on a stem or handle, used for conveying liquids or liquid food to the mouth etc. **2** an implement or other thing shaped like a spoon, such as an oar with the blade curved lengthwise, a golf club with a lofted face, a spoon-bait etc. **3** a spoonful. **4** (*pl., Mus.*) a pair of spoons played as a musical instrument. *~v.t.* **1** to take (up etc.) with a spoon. **2** in cricket, to hit a ball (usu. up) with little force. *~v.i.* **1** to fish with a spoon-bait. **2** (*dated*) to indulge in demonstrative lovemaking. **born with a silver spoon in one's mouth** fortunate in being born

into a family with wealth and social class.
spoon-bait *n.* a spoon-shaped piece of bright
metal with hooks attached used as a revolving
lure in fishing. **spoon-beak, spoonbill** *n.* a bird
with a broad, flat bill, esp. of the genus *Platalea.*
spoon-bread *n.* (*N Am.*) soft bread made from
maize. **spooner** *n.* (*coll.*) a person who behaves in
a foolishly or mawkishly amorous way. **spoon-
feed** *v.t.* (*past, p.p.* **spoon-fed**) **1** to feed (a baby)
with a spoon. **2** to teach by presenting
(information) to (students etc.) in such a manner
that no individual effort or research is required
on the part of those being taught. **spoon-fed** *a.*
spoonful *n.* (*pl.* **spoonfuls**).
spoonerism (spoo´nərizm) *n.* an accidental or
facetious transposition of the initial letters or
syllables of words, e.g. 'I have in my breast a
half-warmed fish'.
spoor (spuə) *n.* the track of a wild animal. ~*v.i.* to
follow a spoor. **spoorer** *n.*
sporadic (spərad´ik), †**sporadical** *a.* separate,
scattered, occurring here and there or irregularly.
sporadically *adv.*
sporangium (spəran´jiəm) *n.* (*pl.* **sporangia**
(-jiə)) (*Bot.*) a sac in which spores are formed.
sporangial *a.*
spore (spaw) *n.* **1** the reproductive body in a
cryptogam, usu. composed of a single cell not
containing an embryo. **2** a minute organic body
that develops into a new individual, as in
protozoa etc.
sporran (spor´ən) *n.* a pouch, usu. covered with
fur, hair etc., worn by Scottish Highlanders in
front of the kilt.
sport (spawt) *n.* **1** a game, a competitive pastime,
esp. an athletic or outdoor pastime, such as
hunting, fishing, football, racing, running etc. **2**
such games or pastimes collectively. **3** (*pl.*) a
meeting for outdoor games etc. **4** diversion,
amusement, fun, jest, pleasantry. **5** (*coll.*) a
sportsman, a fair or obliging person. **6** a person
who behaves in a specified way on losing (*a good
sport*). **7** (*Austral.*) used as a form of address, esp.
between males. **8** (*N Am., coll.*) a playboy. **9**
(*Biol.*) an animal or plant deviating remarkably
from the normal type. **10** a plaything. ~*v.i.* **1** to
play, to divert oneself. **2** to trifle, to jest, to make
merry (with a person's feelings etc.). **3** (*Biol.*) to
vary remarkably from the normal type. ~*v.t.* to
wear or display in an ostentatious manner. **in
sport** in fun, as a joke. **to make sport of** to jeer at,
to ridicule. **sporter** *n.* **sportful** *a.* **sportfully** *adv.*
sportfulness *n.* **sporting** *a.* **1** relating to, used in,
or fond of sports. **2** calling for sportsmanship.
3 involving a risk, as in sports competition.
sporting chance *n.* some chance of succeeding.
sportingly *adv.* **sportive** *a.* frolicsome, playful.
sportively *adv.* **sportiveness** *n.* **sportless** *a.* **sports**
a. (of clothing etc.) suitable for sports. **sports car**
n. a low usu. two-seater car built for high-speed
performance. **sportscast** *n.* (*N Am.*) a broadcast of
sports news. **sportscaster** *n.* **sports coat, sports**

jacket *n.* a casual jacket for men, usu. made of
tweed. **sports ground** *n.* an area of ground
equipped for competitive outdoor sports.
sportsman *n.* (*pl.* **sportsmen**) **1** a person who
participates in sport, esp. professionally. **2**
a person who goes hunting or shooting. **3** a
person who acts fairly towards opponents or
who faces good or bad luck with equanimity.
sportsmanlike *a.* **sportsmanly** *a.* **sportsmanship**
n. **sportsperson** *n.* (*pl.* **sportspeople, sports-
persons**). **sportswear** *n.* clothes worn for sport,
or for casual wear. **sportswoman** *n.* (*pl.* **sports-
women**). **sports writer** *n.* a newspaper columnist
who writes on sport. **sporty** *a.* (*comp.* **sportier,**
superl. **sportiest**) **1** taking pleasure in sports. **2**
(of clothes etc.) suitable as sportswear. **3** (of a car
etc.) resembling a sports car. **4** vulgar, showy.
sportily *adv.* **sportiness** *n.*
spot (spot) *n.* **1** a small part of a surface of distinctive colour or texture, esp. round or roundish
in shape. **2** a small mark or stain, a speck, a blot.
3 a pimple or blemish on the skin. **4** a mark, e.g.
a circle, or one of a set of such marks, distinguishing the face of a playing card, dice,
domino etc. **5** a stain on one's character or
reputation. **6** a small extent of space (*find a
sheltered spot*). **7 a** a particular place, a definite
locality (*landed on this spot*). **b** the place where
one is, or is standing or sitting (*remain on the
spot; move off the spot*). **8** (*often in comb.*) a place
used for a certain activity; a place of entertainment. **9** PENALTY SPOT (under PENALTY). **10** a place
on one's body (*a tender spot*). **11** an aspect of
one's character (*a weak spot*). **12** an aspect of a
situation (*a bright spot*). **13** (*coll.*) a small amount
(of anything) (*a spot of dinner; a spot of luck; a
spot of bother; a spot of rain*). **14** a place on a
television or radio programme for an entertainer.
15 an opportunity in the interval between
programmes for advertisers. **16** a spotlight. **17** a
mark near the top of a billiard or snooker table
on which the red ball or cue ball is placed at
certain times. ~*v.t.* (*pres.p.* **spotting,** *past, p.p.*
spotted) **1** to pick out beforehand (e.g. the
winner of a race). **2** to recognize, to detect. **3** to
watch out for and note (*train-spotting*). **4** to catch
sight of (*spotted her in the crowd*). **5** (*Mil.*) to
pinpoint (the enemy's position), esp. from the
air. **6** to mark, stain, or discolour with a spot or
spots. **7** to sully, to blemish (someone's reputation). **8** to place (a ball) on the spot at billiards or
snooker. **9** (*impers.*) to rain slightly. ~*v.i.* to
become or be liable to be marked with spots. **in
a spot** in an awkward situation. **in a tight spot** in
a dangerous or complicated situation. **on the
spot 1** at the scene of action. **2** in the position of
having to act or respond quickly. **3** at once,
without change of place, there and then. **4** alert,
wide awake. **to change one's spots** to reform
one's ways. **to hit the spot** (*coll.*) to be just what
is needed. **to knock spots off** to outdo easily. **to
run on the spot** to make running movements

with the legs without moving forwards, for exercise. **spot cash** *n.* (*coll.*) money down. **spot check** *n.* a random examination or check without prior warning. **spot-check** *v.t.* **spotlamp** *n.* a spotlight. **spotless** *a.* **spotlessly** *adv.* **spotlessness** *n.* **spotlight** *n.* **1** a lamp for throwing a concentrated beam of light, esp. on a performer on the stage. **2** the patch of light thus thrown. **3** the glare of publicity. *~v.t.* (*past, p.p.* **spotlighted, spotlit**) **1** to direct a spotlight on to. **2** to direct attention towards. **spot-on,** (*pred.*) **spot on** *a.* (*coll.*) absolutely accurate. **spotted** *a.* **spotted dick** *n.* a steamed suet pudding with currants. **spotted dog** *n.* **1** a Dalmatian. **2** spotted dick. **spotted fever** *n.* **1** cerebrospinal meningitis, characterized by spots on the skin. **2** typhus. **3** ROCKY MOUNTAIN SPOTTED FEVER (under ROCK[1]). **spottedness** *n.* **spotter** *n.* **1** (*Mil.*) an observer trained to detect the approach of enemy aircraft. **2** (*in comb.*) a person whose hobby or job is spotting or noting things (*a talent-spotter; a plane-spotter*). **spotting** *n.* (*often in comb.*, as *talent-spotting, train-spotting*). **spotty** *a.* (*comp.* **spottier,** *superl.* **spottiest**) **1** covered or marked with spots. **2** having pimples or blemishes on the skin. **3** patchy, uneven, irregular. **spottily** *adv.* **spottiness** *n.* **spot-weld** *v.t.* to join (two pieces of metal) with a circular weld. **spot weld** *n.* **spot-welder** *n.*

spouse (spows) *n.* a husband or wife. **spousal** (-zəl) *a.*, †*n.* **spouseless** *a.*

spout (spowt) *n.* **1** a short pipe, tube, or channelled projection for carrying off water from a gutter, conducting liquid from a vessel etc. **2** a chute or trough down which things may be shot into a receptacle. **3** a continuous stream, jet, or column of water etc. **4** a waterspout. **5** (*also* **spout-hole**) a whale's spiracle or blowhole. *~v.t.* **1** to pour out or discharge with force or in large volume. **2** to utter or recite in a declamatory manner. *~v.i.* **1** to pour out or issue forcibly or copiously. **2** to declaim, to hold forth. **up the spout 1** (*sl.*) ruined, failed. **2** (*sl.*) at the pawnbroker's, in pawn. **3** (*sl.*) pregnant. **spouter** *n.* **spoutless** *a.*

sprain (sprān) *v.t.* to twist or wrench the muscles or ligaments of (a joint) so as to injure without dislocation. *~n.* such a twist or wrench or the bruising and swelling caused by it.

sprang SPRING.

sprat (sprat) *n.* **1** a small food fish, *Clupea sprattus*, related to the herring. **2** the young of the herring and other small fish.

sprawl (sprawl) *v.i.* **1** to lie or stretch out the body and limbs in a careless or awkward posture. **2** (of a town, plant etc.) to straggle, to be spread out in an irregular or ungraceful form. *~v.t.* to spread out (one's body or limbs) in an ungainly fashion. *~n.* **1** a sprawling posture. **2** irregular or ungraceful form. **sprawler** *n.* **sprawling** *a.* **sprawlingly** *adv.* **sprawly** *a.*

spray[1] (sprā) *n.* **1** water or other liquid flying in small, fine drops. **2** a perfume or other liquid applied in fine particles with an atomizer. **3** (*often in comb.*) an appliance for spraying (*a hairspray*). *~v.t.* **1** to throw or apply (liquid) in the form of spray. **2** to treat with a spray, e.g. to sprinkle (a plant) with an insecticide. *~v.i.* (of a male cat or other male animal) to sprinkle its territory with urine. **sprayable** *a.* **spray-dry** *v.t.* (*3rd pers. sing. pres.* **spray-dries,** *pres.p.* **spray-drying,** *past, p.p.* **spray-dried**) to dry (a liquid, e.g. milk) by spraying it into hot air etc. **sprayer** *n.* **spray gun** *n.* a gunlike appliance which sprays paint etc. **spray-paint** *v.t.* to paint (a surface) using a spray.

spray[2] (sprā) *n.* **1** a small branch or sprig, esp. with branchlets, leaves, flowers etc. **2** a decorative bouquet of this shape. **3** a brooch or other ornament resembling a sprig of leaves, flowers etc. **sprayey** (-i) *a.*

spread (spred) *v.t.* (*past, p.p.* **spread**) **1** to extend in length and breadth by opening (out), unrolling, unfolding, flattening out etc. **2** to scatter, to diffuse, to smooth into a thin wide layer (*spread jam on bread*). **3** to disseminate, to publish (*spread the word*). **4** to cover the surface of (*spread bread with jam*). **5** to display, lay (out) before the eye or mind (*the landscape that was spread out before us*). **6** to lay (a table). *~v.i.* **1** to be extended in length and breadth. **2** to be scattered, diffused, smoothed out thinly or disseminated. **3** to extend, stretch (out) widely. *~n.* **1** an act of spreading. **2** breadth, extent, compass, expansion. **3** an aircraft's wingspan. **4** diffusion, dissemination. **5** expanding girth (*middle-age spread*). **6** the gap between two prices, e.g. the bid and offer price of shares. **7** (*coll.*) a meal set out, a feast. **8** a sweet or savoury paste for spreading over bread etc. **9** a coverlet, a bedspread. **10** two facing pages in a book, magazine etc. **11** (*N Am.*) an extensive ranch. **spreadable** *a.* **spread eagle** *n.* (*Her.*) an eagle with wings and legs extended. **spreadeagle** *v.t.* to cause to stand or lie with arms and legs stretched out. **spreader** *n.* **spreadsheet** *n.* a computer program which can perform rapid calculations on figures displayed on a VDU in rows and columns, used for business accounting and financial planning.

spree (sprē) *n.* **1** a lively frolic, esp. with drinking. **2** a bout of extravagance or excess, esp. involving an outing (*a spending spree; a shopping spree*). *~v.i.* (*3rd pers. sing. pres.* **sprees,** *pres.p.* **spreeing,** *past, p.p.* **spreed**) to have a spree. **on the spree** having a spree.

sprig[1] (sprig) *n.* **1** a small branch, twig, or shoot. **2** an ornament resembling this, esp. as a pattern on fabric. **3** (*derog.*) a scion, a young fellow. *~v.t.* (*pres.p.* **sprigging,** *past, p.p.* **sprigged**) **1** to print or embroider (fabric) with sprigs. **2** to ornament (pottery) with applied decoration.

sprig[2] (sprig) *n.* a small headless nail or brad.

sprightly (sprīt′li) **spritely** *a.* (*comp.* **sprightlier,**

superl. **sprightliest**) lively, spirited, gay, vivacious, brisk or agile. **sprightliness** *n.*

spring (spring) *v.i.* (*past* **sprang** (sprang), *p.p.* **sprung** (sprŭng)) **1** to leap, to bound, to jump (*sprang to her feet*; *sprang across the room*; *sprang to my help*). **2** to move suddenly by or as by the action of a spring (*The lid sprang open*; *The branches sprang back*). **3** to rise, to come (up) from or as from a source, to arise, to originate, to appear, esp. unexpectedly (*A storm sprang up*; *Where could that idea have sprung from?*). **4** (of wood etc.) to warp, to split. ~*v.t.* **1** to cause to move, fly, act etc., suddenly by or as by releasing a spring (*sprang the trap*). **2** to produce unexpectedly (*always springing surprises*). **3** (*sl.*) to bring about the escape from prison of. **4** to rouse or start (game) from earth or covert. **5** to provide (a vehicle etc.) with springs (*fully sprung seats*). **6** to cause (timber, a wooden implement etc.) to warp, crack, or become loose. **7** (of a vessel) to develop (a leak) thus. ~*n.* **1** a leap, jump. **2** a backward movement as from release from tension, a recoil, a rebound. **3** elasticity, resilience (*a dance floor with plenty of spring*; *My feet are losing their spring*). **4** an elastic body or structure, usu. of bent or coiled metal used to prevent jar, to convey motive power in a watch etc. **5** the first of the four seasons of the year, preceding summer, roughly March, April and May in the N hemisphere. **6** (*Astron.*) the period lasting from the vernal equinox to the summer solstice. **7** the early part (of life, a relationship etc.), youth. **8** the spring tide. **9** a natural issue of water, oil etc. from the earth, or the site of this. **10** a source, an origin. **11** a source of energy, a cause of action, a motive. **spring balance** *n.* a balance weighing objects by the tension of a spring. **springboard** *n.* **1** a springy board giving impetus in leaping, diving etc. **2** anything that provides a starting point or initial impetus. **spring chicken** *n.* **1** (*N Am.*) a tender young chicken, usu. from 2 to 10 months old. **2** (*usu. with neg., coll.*) a young, active, inexperienced person (*and he's no spring chicken*). **spring-clean** *v.t.* to clean (a house) thoroughly in preparation for summer. ~*n.* a thorough cleaning of this kind. **spring equinox** *n.* **1** the equinox that occurs about 20 March in the N hemisphere and 22 September in the S hemisphere. **2** (*Astron.*) the March equinox. **springer** *n.* **1** a person or thing that springs. **2** a breed of spaniels used to rouse game; a spaniel of this breed. **spring fever** *n.* **1** a restless feeling associated with spring. **2** (*facet.*) lethargy, lassitude. **spring greens** *n.pl.* the young leaves of a type of cabbage that does not develop a heart. **springless** *a.* **springlet** *n.* **springlike** *a.* **spring-loaded** *a.* having a spring, secured by means of a stretched or compressed spring. **spring mattress** *n.* **spring onion** *n.* an onion with a tiny thin-skinned bulb and long leaves, eaten in salads. **spring roll** *n.* a Chinese dish comprising a thin deep-fried pancake filled with a

savoury mixture. **springtail** *n.* any insect of the wingless order Collembola, having bristles on its under side enabling it to leap. **spring tide** *n.* **1** a high tide occurring a day or two after the new or the full moon. **2** (*poet.*) (*usu.* **springtide**) springtime. **springtime** *n.* the season of spring. **spring water** *n.* water from a spring, as distinct from rainwater or river water. **springy** *a.* (*comp.* **springier**, *superl.* **springiest**) **1** elastic or resilient, like a spring. **2** (of movement) lively, bouncy. **springily** *adv.* **springiness** *n.*

Usage note In standard English, the past tense of *spring* is *sprang*, not *sprung*.

---

springbok (spring'bok) *n.* **1** a southern African gazelle, *Antidorcas marsupialis*, that runs with a high leaping movement. **2** (**Springbok**) a sportsman or sportswoman representing South Africa in international competitions.

sprinkle (spring'kəl) *v.t., v.i.* to scatter in small drops or particles. ~*v.t.* to shower (a surface with) small drops or particles. ~*n.* a sprinkling, a light shower. **sprinkler** *n.* that which sprinkles, e.g. a rotating device that waters a lawn. **sprinkling** *n.* a small quantity or number (of).

sprint (sprint) *v.i., v.t.* to run (a short distance) at top speed. ~*n.* **1** a short burst of running, cycling etc. at top speed. **2** a running race of 400 metres or less. **sprinter** *n.*

sprit (sprit) *n.* a small spar set diagonally from the mast to the top outer corner of a sail. **spritsail** (-səl, -sāl) *n.* a sail extended by a sprit.

sprite (sprīt) *n.* a fairy, an elf.

spritely SPRIGHTLY.

spritzer (sprit'sə) *n.* a drink made from white wine and soda water.

sprocket (sprok'it) *n.* **1** each of a set of teeth on a wheel etc., engaging with the links of a chain. **2** a sprocket-wheel. **sprocket-wheel** *n.* a wheel set with sprockets.

sprog (sprog) *n.* (*coll.*) a baby, an infant, a child.

sprout (sprowt) *v.i.* **1** to shoot forth, to develop shoots, to germinate. **2** to grow, like the shoots of plants. ~*v.t.* **1** to put forth or produce (shoots etc.). **2** to grow (e.g. a beard or moustache) or put forth (e.g. a television aerial). **3** to cause to put forth sprouts or to grow. ~*n.* **1** a new shoot on a plant. **2** a Brussels sprout.

spruce[1] (sproos) *a.* neat, trim, smart. ~*v.t.* to smarten (up). **sprucely** *adv.* **spruceness** *n.*

spruce[2] (sproos) *n.* any conifer of the genus *Picea*, of a distinctive cone shape, with dense foliage and four-angled needles.

sprung SPRING.

spry (sprī) *a.* (*comp.* **spryer**, **sprier**, *superl.* **spryest**, **spriest**) active, lively, nimble, agile. **spryly** *adv.* **spryness** *n.*

spud (spŭd) *n.* **1** (*coll.*) a potato. **2** a short spadelike tool for cutting up weeds by the roots etc. ~*v.t.* (*pres.p.* **spudding**, *past, p.p.* **spudded**) to dig (up) or clear (out) with a spud. **to spud in** **1**

to begin drilling an oil well. **2** (*coll.*) to start work. **spud-bashing** *n.* (*coll.*) peeling potatoes.

spue SPEW.

spumante (spooman´ti) *n.* (*pl.* **spumantes** (-tiz)) a sparkling Italian wine.

spume (spūm) *n.* froth, foam. *~v.i.* to froth, to foam. **spumy** *a.* (*comp.* **spumier**, *superl.* **spumiest**). **spuminess** *n.*

spun SPIN.

spunk (spŭngk) *n.* **1** mettle, spirit, pluck. **2** touchwood, tinder. **3** (*taboo sl.*) semen. **4** (*Austral.*, *sl.*) a sexually attractive person. **spunky** *a.* (*comp.* **spunkier**, *superl.* **spunkiest**) **1** plucky, spirited. **2** (*Austral.*, *sl.*) sexually attractive.

spur (spœ) *n.* **1** an instrument worn on a horseman's heel having a sharp or blunt point or a rowel. **2** instigation, incentive, stimulus, impulse. **3** (*Bot.*) a spur-shaped projection, attachment, or part, such as the pointed projection on a cock's leg, or a steel point or sheath fastened on this in cockfighting. **4** a ridge or buttress projecting from a mountain range. **5** a tubular projection on the columbine and other flowers. **6** a branch road, or a railway siding or branch line. *~v.t.* (*pres.p.* **spurring**, *past*, *p.p.* **spurred**) **1** to prick with spurs. **2** to urge (on), to incite. **3** to stimulate (interest, enthusiasm etc.). **4** to provide or fit with spurs. *~v.i.* to ride hard, to press (on or forward). **on the spur of the moment** on impulse, impromptu. **spurless** *a.* **spur-wheel** *n.* a gearwheel with radial teeth projecting from the rim.

spurge (spœj) *n.* a plant of the genus *Euphorbia* with milky, usu. acrid juice. **spurge laurel** *n.* a bushy evergreen shrub, *Daphne laureola*, with glossy leaves, greenish flowers, and poisonous berries.

spurious (spū´riəs) *a.* **1** not genuine, not proceeding from the true or pretended source, false, counterfeit (*a spurious interest*). **2** like a specified part or organ in form or function but physiologically or morphologically different. **3** (of children) illegitimate. **spuriously** *adv.* **spuriousness** *n.*

spurn (spœn) *v.t.* **1** to reject with disdain; to treat with scorn. **2** to thrust or kick away with the foot. *~v.i.* to kick (at or against). *~n.* the act of spurning, scornful rejection. **spurner** *n.*

spurrey (spŭr´i), **spurry** *n.* (*pl.* **spurreys**, **spurries**) a low annual weed of the genus *Spergula* of the family Silenaceae.

spurt (spœt) *v.i.* **1** (*also* **spirt**) to gush out in a jet or sudden stream. **2** to make a sudden intense effort. *~v.t.* to send or force out in a jet or stream. *~n.* **1** (*also* **spirt**) a forcible gush or jet of liquid. **2** a short burst of intense effort or speed.

sputnik (spŭt´nik, spoot´-) *n.* any of a series of Russian artificial earth satellites, the first of which was launched in 1957.

sputter (spŭt´ə) *v.i.* **1** (of frying food etc.) to emit spitting sounds. **2** to emit saliva in scattered drops, to splutter. **3** to speak in a jerky, in-

coherent, or excited way. *~v.t.* **1** to emit with a spluttering noise. **2** to utter rapidly and indistinctly. *~n.* **1** an act, or a sound, of sputtering. **2** (an instance of) confused, incoherent speech. **sputterer** *n.* **sputteringly** *adv.*

sputum (spū´təm) *n.* (*pl.* **sputa** (-tə)) **1** spittle, saliva. **2** (*Med.*) a morbid mixture of saliva and mucus expectorated from the respiratory tract.

spy (spī) *n.* (*pl.* **spies**) **1** a person employed by a government or business to obtain information about, and report on, the movements and operations of an enemy, business rival etc. **2** a person who keeps a constant secret or surreptitious watch on the actions, movements etc., of others. *~v.t.* (*3rd pers. sing. pres.* **spies**, *pres.p.* **spying**, *past*, *p.p.* **spied**) **1** to see, to detect, to discover, esp. by close observation. **2** to explore or search (out) secretly. **3** to discover thus. *~v.i.* **1** to act as a spy, to keep a surreptitious watch (on). **2** to search narrowly, to pry (into). **spyglass** *n.* a small telescope. **spyhole** *n.* a peephole. **spymaster** *n.* the person at the head of a spy organization.

Sq *abbr.* Square (in addresses).

Sqn *abbr.* squadron. **Sqn Ldr** *abbr.* Squadron Leader.

squab (skwob) *n.* **1** a short fat person. **2** a young bird, esp. an unfledged pigeon. **3** a stuffed cushion; a sofa padded throughout; an ottoman; the padded side or back of a car seat. *~a.* fat, short, squat. **squabby** *a.* (*comp.* **squabbier**, *superl.* **squabbiest**) short and fat, squat.

squabble (skwob´əl) *n.* a petty or noisy quarrel, a wrangle. *~v.i.* to engage in a petty or noisy quarrel, to wrangle. **squabbler** *n.*

squad (skwod) *n.* **1** a small party of people, e.g. engaged in a task together. **2** (*Mil.*) a small number of soldiers assembled for drill or inspection. **3** a sports team. **4** a specialized body within the police force (*usu. in comb.*, as *the drug squad*). **squad car** *n.* a police car linked to headquarters by radio. **squaddie**, **squaddy** *n.* (*pl.* **squaddies**) (*Mil.*, *coll.*) a private soldier.

squadron (skwod´rən) *n.* **1** an organized group of people. **2** a main division of a cavalry regiment, usu. consisting of two troops containing 120 to 200 men. **3** a detachment of several warships employed on some particular service. **4** a division of a naval fleet under a flag-officer. **5** a Royal Air Force unit with 10 to 18 aircraft. **squadron leader** *n.* a commissioned officer in the Royal Air Force immediately junior to a wing commander, the equivalent in rank to a major in the army.

squalid (skwol´id) *a.* **1** repulsively dirty, filthy. **2** mean, poverty-ridden. **3** sordid. **squalidity** (-lid´-) *n.* **squalidly** *adv.* **squalidness** *n.* **squalor** (skwol´ə) *n.*

squall (skwawl) *n.* **1** a sudden, violent gust or succession of gusts of wind, esp. accompanied by rain, hail, snow etc. **2** a harsh, discordant scream, esp. of a child. **3** (*often pl.*) an upset, quarrel or commotion (*domestic squalls*). ~*v.i.,* *v.t.* **1** to cry out. **2** to scream discordantly. **squaller** *n.* **squally** *a.* (*comp.* **squallier,** *superl.* **squalliest**).

squander (skwon´də) *v.t.* **1** to spend (money, time etc.) wastefully. **2** to dissipate by foolish prodigality. **3** to waste (one's talents etc.) by misapplication. **squanderer** *n.* **squanderingly** *adv.*

square (skweə) *n.* **1** a rectangle with equal sides. **2** any surface, area, object, part etc., of this shape. **3** a rectangular division of a chessboard or draughtboard, window pane etc. **4** a square scarf. **5** an open quadrilateral area surrounded by buildings, usu. laid out with trees, flower beds, lawns etc. **6** an open area at a street junction. **7** (*N Am.*) a block of buildings bounded by four streets. **8** in cricket, a close-trimmed area at the centre of the ground, from which the playing strip can be selected. **9** (*Mil.*) **a** a body of infantry formed into a rectangular figure. **b** a drilling area inside barracks. **10** the product of a quantity multiplied by itself (*The square of 9 is 81*). **11** an L- or T-shaped instrument for laying out and testing right angles. **12** (*sl.*) a conventional, old-fashioned person, someone out of touch with modern ways of thought. **13** an arrangement of words, figures etc., with as many rows as columns (usu. reading alike perpendicularly or across). ~*a.* **1** having four equal sides and four right angles. **2** (of corners or angles) of right-angled shape, measuring 90°, rectangular. **3** at right angles (to). **4** angular as distinct from rounded (*a square jaw*). **5** denoting a unit of measure representing the area of a square whose side is the unit specified (*a square metre*). **6** level or parallel (with). **7** even (with), quits (with). **8** in football, in a straight line across the pitch. **9** in cricket, at right angles to the wicket, on a line through the stumps. **10** just, fair, honest. **11** in proper order. **12** not in debt, owing no money. **13** evenly balanced, even, settled, complete, thorough, absolute. **14** in golf etc., having the same score as one's opponent. **15** (of scores) equal. **16** direct, uncompromising (*a square denial*). **17** (*coll.*) (of a person or their tastes) dull, conventional, old-fashioned. ~*adv.* **1** evenly (*not lying square*). **2** honestly; fairly (*not playing square with me*). **3** at right angles (*a workbench placed square to the window*). ~*v.t.* **1** to make square or rectangular. **2** to give a rectangular cross-section to (timber). **3** to multiply (a number or quantity) by itself. **4** to adjust, to bring into conformity (with or to), to reconcile (*square the account with the facts*). **5** to mark (paper etc.) out in squares. **6** to settle, to pay (a bill). **7** to hold (one's shoulders) back, and at an even height, presenting a square front. **8** (*coll.*) to bribe, to win over with gifts, money etc. **9** to even the scores in (a match etc.). ~*v.i.* **1** to conform precisely, to agree, to harmonize (with) (*Your story doesn't square with the facts*). **2** to put

oneself in an attitude for boxing. **3** to be at right angles (with). **all square** with no party in debt to any other, even, quits. **back to square one** back to where one started without having made any progress. **on the square 1** at right angles. **2** fair, honest; fairly, honestly. **3** belonging to the Freemasons. **out of square** not square, not at right angles. **to square the circle 1** to construct geometrically a square equal in area to a given circle. **2** to attempt impossibilities. **to square up** to settle an account. **to square up to 1** to face (someone) in a fighting attitude. **2** to face up to, to tackle positively (one's problems etc.). **square-bashing** *n.* (*Mil., sl.*) military drill. **square brackets** *n.pl.* a pair of angular brackets [] as distinct from parentheses. **square-built** *a.* broadly built. **square dance** *n.* a dance for four couples forming a square set. **square-dancer** *n.* **square-dancing** *n.* **square deal** *n.* **1** a fair bargain. **2** a fair deal, fair treatment. **square-eyed** *a.* (*facet.*) watching, or affected by watching, too much television. **square leg** *n.* in cricket, a fielder standing about 20 metres directly behind the batsman on strike. **squarely** *adv.* **square meal** *n.* a meal which is full and satisfying. **square measure** *n.* a system of measures expressed in square feet, square metres etc. **squareness** *n.* **square number** *n.* the product of a number multiplied by itself. **squarer** *n.* **square-rigged** *a.* (*Naut.*) having the principal sails extended by horizontal yards suspended by the middle from the mast. **square root** *n.* the quantity that, multiplied by itself, will produce the given quantity (*The square root of 49 is 7*). **square sail** (səl, sāl) *n.* a four-cornered sail set on a yard, esp. on a fore-and-aft rigged vessel. **square-shouldered** *a.* having the shoulders held well up and back, as opposed to round sloping shoulders. **square wave** *n.* (*Physics*) an oscillation that gives a rectangular waveform. **squarish** *a.*

squash¹ (skwosh) *v.t.* **1** to crush, to press flat or into a pulp. **2** to pack (people or things) tight, to crowd. **3** to put down, to snub (someone) with a crushing remark. **4** to dismiss (a suggestion, proposal etc.). **5** to put down, to quash (a rebellion). ~*v.i.* **1** to be crushed or beaten to pulp by a fall. **2** to squeeze (into). ~*n.* **1** a throng, a crowd packed tight. **2** the fall of a soft body. **3** the sound of this. **4** a drink made from usu. concentrated fruit juice from crushed fruit, diluted with water. **5** (*also* **squash rackets**) a game with rackets and a small soft ball, played against the walls of a closed court. **6** a thing or mass crushed or squeezed to pulp. **squasher** *n.* **squashy** *a.* (*comp.* **squashier,** *superl.* **squashiest**). **squashily** *adv.* **squashiness** *n.*

Usage note See note under QUASH.

squash² (skwosh) *n.* **1** the fleshy edible gourdlike fruit of any of several trailing plants of the genus *Cucurbita,* cooked and eaten as a vegetable. **2** the plant producing this fruit.

squat (skwot) *v.i.* (*pres.p.* **squatting,** *past,* *p.p.* **squatted**) **1** to sit down or crouch on the haunches. **2** (chiefly of animals) to crouch close to the ground, to cower. **3** (*coll.*) to sit. **4** to settle on land or occupy a building without any title. ~*v.t.* to put (oneself) in a crouching posture. ~*a.* (*comp.* **squatter,** *superl.* **squattest**) **1** short, thick, dumpy. **2** in a squatting position. ~*n.* **1** a squatting posture. **2** a building occupied by squatters, or the illegal occupation of a building by squatters. **squatly** *adv.* **squatness** *n.* **squatter** *n.* **1** a person who occupies property or land without legal title to it. **2** (*Austral.*) a sheep farmer. **3** a person who sits on the haunches. **squat thrust** *n.* an exercise in which, from a squatting position with hands on the floor in front, the legs are thrust out backwards to full length, and then drawn in again.

squaw (skwaw) *n.* (*now offensive*) a N American Indian woman or wife.

squawk (skwawk) *n.* **1** a raucous squeal, esp. as the cry of a fowl. **2** (*coll.*) a complaint or protest. ~*v.i.* **1** to utter a squawk. **2** (*coll.*) to protest loudly. ~*v.t.* to utter with a squawk. **squawk-box** *n.* an intercom or loud speaker. **squawker** *n.*

squeak (skwēk) *n.* **1** a sharp, shrill cry, like that of a mouse. **2** a high-pitched whine produced e.g. by an unoiled door hinge. **3** (*coll.*) a narrow escape or margin, a close shave. ~*v.i.* **1** to utter or make a squeak. **2** (*coll.*) to get (by, through, past etc.) narrowly. **3** (*sl.*) to break silence or secrecy, esp. to turn informer. ~*v.t.* to utter with a squeak. **squeaker** *n.* **squeaky** *a.* (*comp.* **squeakier,** *superl.* **squeakiest**) **squeakily** *adv.* **squeakiness** *n.* **squeaky-clean** *a.* **1** utterly clean (orig. from the squeaking noise made by newly washed hair when rubbed). **2** (*coll.*) above reproach.

squeal (skwēl) *n.* a more or less prolonged shrill cry, like that made by a pig or a baby. ~*v.i.* **1** to utter a more or less prolonged shrill cry as in pain, etc. **2** (*sl.*) to turn informer. **3** (*coll.*) to complain loudly. ~*v.t.* to utter with a squeal. **squealer** *n.*

squeamish (skwē´mish) *a.* **1** easily nauseated, disgusted or offended. **2** fastidious, finicky, hypercritical, excessively nice, prudish, unduly scrupulous. **squeamishly** *adv.* **squeamishness** *n.*

squeegee (skwē´jē) *n.* a rubber-bladed implement fixed to a handle, for cleaning surfaces such as windows or wiping them dry. ~*v.t.* (*3rd pers. sing. pres.* **squeegees,** *pres.p.* **squeegeeing,** *past, p.p.* **squeegeed**) to wipe, smooth etc., with a squeegee.

squeeze (skwēz) *v.t.* **1** to press closely, esp. between two bodies or with the hand, so as to force moisture etc., out. **2** to crush (out), to extract (moisture etc.) thus. **3** to reduce the size of, or alter the shape of, by pressing closely. **4** to force (oneself etc., or one's way, into, out of etc. a narrow space etc.). **5** to extort money etc., from, to harass by exactions. **6** to exact (money etc.) by extortion etc. **7** to put pressure on, to oppress, to constrain by arbitrary or illegitimate means. **8** to press (someone's hand) to express affection, sympathy etc. ~*v.i.* to press, to push, to force one's way (into, through etc.). ~*n.* **1** an act of squeezing or the condition of being squeezed. **2** pressure. **3** a close embrace. **4** a throng, a crush. **5** a small amount of juice etc. produced by squeezing (*a squeeze of lemon*). **6** an illicitly exacted commission, or other such extortion. **7** an economic situation, e.g. during a financial crisis, in which there are restrictions on investment and borrowing. **to put the squeeze on** (*coll.*) to put pressure on (someone), to coerce. **squeezable** *a.* **squeezability** (-bil´-) *n.* **squeeze bottle,** **squeezy bottle** *n.* a flexible plastic bottle that is squeezed to extract the contents. **squeeze-box** *n.* (*coll.*) an accordion or concertina. **squeezer** *n.* **squeezy** *a.* (*comp.* **squeezier,** *superl.* **squeeziest**) (of a container) flexible, able to be squeezed to extract the contents.

squelch (skwelch) *v.i.* **1** to make a noise as of treading in wet snow. **2** to move with this sound (*squelched across the field*). ~*v.t.* **1** to crush. **2** to silence, to extinguish, to discomfit. ~*n.* an act of squelching; a squelching noise. **squelcher** *n.* **squelchy** *a.* (*comp.* **squelchier,** *superl.* **squelchiest**)

squib (skwib) *n.* **1** a firework emitting sparks and hisses, and exploding with a bang. **2** a short satire or lampoon.

squid (skwid) *n.* (*pl.* **squid, squids**) any cephalopod mollusc of the order Teuthoidea, similar to a cuttlefish but with eight arms and two long tentacles, esp. an edible variety of the genus *Loligo.*

squidgy (skwij´i) *a.* (*comp.* **squidgier,** *superl.* **squidgiest**) (*coll.*) soft and squashy.

squiffy (skwif´i) *a.* (*comp.* **squiffier,** *superl.* **squiffiest**) (*coll.*) slightly drunk. **squiffed** *a.* squiffy.

squiggle (skwig´əl) *n.* a wriggly line. ~*v.i.* **1** to squirm, to wriggle, to twist. **2** to make wriggly lines. ~*v.t.* to scrawl or scribble (a word, signature etc.). **squiggler** *n.* **squiggly** *a.* (*comp.* **squigglier,** *superl.* **squiggliest**)

squill (skwil) *n.* **1** any of several liliaceous plants of the genus *Scilla,* e.g. the striped squill, *Puschkinia scilloides,* typically with small blue flowers. **2** a white-flowered Mediterranean plant *Drimia* or *Urginea maritima;* also called *sea onion.* **3** the sliced bulb of this used as an expectorant, diuretic etc.

squinch (skwinch) *v.t.* **1** to screw (one's face or one's eyes up). **2** to squeeze or compress, to squash (up, down). ~*v.i.* (of eyes) to squint or narrow.

squint (skwint) *v.i.* **1** to be affected with strabismus, to have a squint. **2** to look obliquely or with half-closed eyes (at). ~*v.t.* **1** to shut or contract (the eyes) quickly. **2** to keep (the eyes) half shut. ~*a.* **1** squinting. **2** looking obliquely; looking askance. **3** (*coll.*) askew, crooked. ~*n.* **1**

an affection of the eyes causing the axes to be differently directed, strabismus. **2** a stealthy look, a sidelong glance. **3** (*coll.*) a look (*had a squint at the document*). **4** an obliquely set opening through the wall of a church, giving a view of the altar. **squinter** *n.* **squint-eyed** *a.* **1** squinting. **2** ill-willed, malevolent. **squinting** *a.* **squintingly** *adv.* **squinty** *a.* (*comp.* **squintier**, *superl.* **squintiest**).

squire (skwīə) *n.* **1** a country gentleman, esp. the chief landowner in a place. **2** (*Hist.*) an attendant on a knight. **3** a man who attends a lady, a beau, a gallant. **4** (*facet.*) used as a form of address to a man. ~*v.t.* to attend as a squire, to escort (a woman). **squirearchy** (-ahki), **squirarchy** *n.* (*pl.* **squirearchies**, **squirarchies**) **1** landed proprietors collectively. **2** the political influence of, or government by these. **squirearch** *n.* **squirearchical** (-ah´-), **squirarchal** *a.* **squiredom** *n.* **squireship** *n.*

squirm (skwœm) *v.i.* **1** to wriggle, to writhe about; to move (up, through etc.) by wriggling. **2** to display discomfort, embarrassment etc. ~*n.* a wriggling movement. **squirmer** *n.* **squirmy** *a.* (*comp.* **squirmier**, *superl.* **squirmiest**).

squirrel (skwir´əl) *n.* **1** any bushy-tailed rodent of the family Sciuridae, with reddish fur (*red squirrel*) or grey fur (*grey squirrel*) living chiefly in trees. **2** the fur of a squirrel. **3** (*coll.*) a person who hoards things. ~*v.t.* (*pres.p.* **squirreling**, (*N Am.*) **squirreling**, *past, p.p.* **squirrelled**, (*N Am.*) **squirreled**) to hoard or hide (things away). ~*v.i.* to bustle or scurry (about). **squirrelly** *a.* **squirrelmonkey** *n.* a small S American monkey, *Saimiri sciureus*, with soft golden fur.

squirt (skwœt) *v.t.* **1** to eject (liquid etc.) in a jet or stream from a narrow orifice. **2** to splash with such a jet or stream (*squirted her with water from the hosepipe*). ~*v.i.* (of liquid) to be so ejected. ~*n.* **1** a jet (of liquid etc.), or a small quantity produced by squirting (*a squirt of soda water*). **2** a syringe. **3** (*coll.*) a pert, conceited or insignificant person. **squirter** *n.*

squish (skwish) *n.* a moist squashing or squelching sound. ~*v.t.* to crush so as to make a squelching or sucking noise. ~*v.i.* to make a squelching or sucking sound. **squishy** *a.* (*comp.* **squishier**, *superl.* **squishiest**).

squit (skwit) *n.* **1** (*sl.*) an insignificant person. **2** (*pl., coll., dial.*) (*usu.* **the squits**) diarrhoea. **squitters** *n.pl.* (*coll., dial.*) diarrhoea.

Sr *chem. symbol* strontium.

Sri Lankan (shrēlang´kən, srē-) *n.* **1** a native or inhabitant of Sri Lanka (formerly Ceylon). **2** a person of Sri Lankan parentage or descent. ~*a.* of or relating to Sri Lanka or its people. **Sri Lanka satinwood** *n.* CEYLON SATINWOOD (under CEYLON MOSS).

SRN *abbr.* State Registered Nurse.

SS *abbr.* **1** Saints. **2** (*Hist.*) Hitler's bodyguard, used as security police, concentration-camp guards etc. (G *Schutzstaffel*, elite guard). **3** steamship.

SSE *abbr.* south-south-east.

SSSI *abbr.* Site of Special Scientific Interest.

SSW *abbr.* south-south-west.

St, St. *abbr.* **1** Saint. **2** Strait. **3** Street.

Usage note Names spelt St are conventionally alphabetized as if *Saint*: see SAINT for entries.

st. *abbr.* **1** stone. **2** in cricket, stumped by.

stab (stab) *v.t.* (*pres.p.* **stabbing**, *past, p.p.* **stabbed**) **1** to pierce or wound with a pointed, usu. short, weapon. **2** to plunge (a weapon, into). **3** to inflict pain upon or to injure by slander etc. ~*v.i.* **1** to aim a blow with or as with a pointed weapon (at). **2** (of a pain etc.) to produce a feeling like being stabbed. ~*n.* **1** a blow or thrust with a pointed weapon. **2** a wound inflicted thus. **3** a secret malicious injury. **to have/ make a stab at** (*coll.*) to attempt, to have a go at (doing something). **to stab in the back 1** (*fig.*) to betray. **2** (*fig.*) to injure the reputation of (esp. a colleague, friend etc.). **stabber** *n.* **stabbing** *a., n.* **stabbingly** *adv.* **stab in the back** *n.* a treacherous act.

stable[1] (stā´bəl) *a.* (*comp.* **stabler**, *superl.* **stablest**) **1** firmly fixed, established. **2** not to be moved, shaken or destroyed easily. **3** firm, resolute, constant; not changeable, unwavering. **4** mentally and emotionally steady. **5** (*Chem.*) durable, not readily decomposed. **6** (*Physics*) not radioactive, not subject to radioactive decay. **stabilator** (-bilātə) *n.* a device combining the functions of stabilizer and elevator at the tail of an aircraft. **stability** (stəbil´-) *n.* **stabilize, stabilise** *v.t.* to make stable. ~*v.i.* to become stable. **stabilization** (-zā´shən) *n.* **stabilizer** *n.* **1** anything that stabilizes. **2** a device working on gyroscopic principles that prevents a ship rolling. **3** (*N Am.*) the horizontal member of the tailplane of an aircraft. **4** (*pl.*) a pair of small wheels fitted on either side of the rear wheel of a child's bicycle. **5** a food additive which retards chemical action. **stable equilibrium** *n.* the tendency of any body to recover equilibrium when moved. **stableness** *n.* **stably** *adv.*

stable[2] (stā´bəl) *n.* **1** a building or part of a building for horses or (sometimes) cattle. **2** an establishment for housing and training racehorses. **3** the racehorses belonging to a particular stable. **4** a group of people with particular skills, e.g. athletes under one manager. **5** any collection or group, e.g. of products, from a common source. **6** a source from which such a group or collection proceeds. ~*v.t.* to put or keep (a horse) in a stable. ~*v.i.* (of horses etc.) to lodge in a stable. **stable boy** *n.* a boy employed in a stable. **stable companion** *n.* a person with whom one shares rooms etc. **stable door** *n.* **1** a horizontally divided door for a stable, of which the upper half can be left open while the lower half remains closed. **2** a similarly designed door as the door, esp. the front door, of a house. **stableful** *n.* (*pl.* **stablefuls**). **stable girl** *n.* a girl or woman employed at a stable. **stable lad** *n.* a groom in a racing stable. **stableman** *n.* (*pl.* **stablemen**) a person employed at a stable. **stable mate** *n.* a stable companion. **stabling** *n.* accommodation for horses.

staccato (stəkah´tō) *a., adv.* (*Mus.*) (played) with each note sharply distinct and detached, as opposed to *legato*. ~*n.* (*pl.* **staccatos**) **1** a passage of music played in this way. **2** a staccato style of playing.

stack (stak) *n.* **1** a pile, a heap, esp. of an orderly kind. **2** a round or rectangular pile of corn in the sheaf, or of hay, straw etc., usu. with a thatched top, a rick. **3** (*often pl.*, *coll.*) a great quantity (*stacks of homework*). **4** a funnel, a smokestack. **5** a tall factory chimney. **6** the part of a chimney projecting above the roof of a building, supporting one or more chimney pots. **7** an accumulation of aircraft circling an airport at different altitudes waiting for instructions to land. **8** (*usu. pl.*) compact bookshelves in a library, usu. with restricted public access. **9** a vertically arranged set of hi-fi or public-address-system components. **10** a towering isolated mass of rock, esp. off the coast of N Britain. ~*v.t.* **1** to pile in a stack or stacks. **2** to assign (waiting aircraft) to a particular altitude in preparation for landing at an airport. **to stack up** (*N Am.*, *coll.*) to measure up, to compare satisfactorily. **stackable** *a.* **stacker** *n.* **stack-room** *n.* in a library, the area containing the stacks. **stack-yard** *n.* a yard or enclosure for stacks of hay, straw etc.

stadium (stā´diəm) *n.* (*pl.* **stadiums**, **stadia** (-diə)) **1** a sports arena with tiers of benches for spectators. **2** (*Hist.*) a race course for foot races or chariot races. **3** a stage of development, e.g. in geology, or in the course of a disease.

Usage note The plural *stadiums* is preferred to *stadia* when referring to modern structures.

staff[1] (stahf) *n.* **1** a stick carried for help in walking, climbing etc., or as a weapon. **2** a rod carried as a symbol of authority. **3** a shaft or pole serving as a support, e.g. a flagstaff. **4** a thing or person that affords support or sustenance (*Bread is the staff of life; the staff of my old age*). **5** a rod used in surveying etc. **6** a body of employees, e.g. in a firm under a manager, or on a newspaper under an editor. **7** the body of those in authority in an organization, esp. the teachers of a school collectively. **8** (*Mil.*) a body of officers assisting an officer in high command, whose duties are concerned with a regiment, or with an army, fleet or air force as a whole. **9** (**Staff**) a staff sergeant. **10** (*Mus.*) (*pl.* **staffs**, **staves**) the set of five parallel lines on which and between which notes are written, their position indicating their pitch. ~*v.t.* to supply (a firm, hospital, school etc.) with staff (*inadequately staffed wards*). **staff college** *n.* **1** (*Mil.*) a college at which military officers receive training for staff duties. **2** a college for the staff of a particular organization. **staffed** *a.* **staffer** *n.* (*N Am.*) a member of a staff,

esp. that of a newspaper. **staff nurse** *n.* a qualified nurse immediately below a sister in rank. **staff officer** *n.* (*Mil.*) an officer serving on a staff. **staffroom** *n.* **1** a common room for staff, esp. in a school or college. **2** the staff using such a room (*staffroom politics*). **staff sergeant** *n.* **1** the senior sergeant of a non-infantry company. **2** (*N Am.*) a non-commissioned officer immediately above a sergeant in rank.

staff[2] (stahf) *n.* a composition of plaster of Paris, cement etc., used as building material etc., esp. in temporary structures.

Staffordshire bull terrier (staf´ədshə) *n.* a smooth-coated breed of terrier of stocky build.

stag (stag) *n.* **1** the male of the red deer, esp. from its fifth year. **2** the male of other large deer. **3** a male unaccompanied by a woman at a social function. **4** in Stock Exchange dealings, a person who stags. ~*v.t.* (*pres.p.* **stagging**, *past*, *p.p.* **stagged**) (*sl.*) to watch closely, to spy on. ~*v.i.* in Stock Exchange dealings, to apply for or to purchase stock or shares in a new issue solely with the object of selling at a profit immediately on allotment. **stag beetle** *n.* any beetle of the family Lucanidae, with large mandibles, in the male branching like a stag's horns. **staghound** *n.* a large hound used for hunting stags. **stag-night**, **stag-party** *n.* (*coll.*) a party for men only, esp. one given for a man about to be married.

stage (stāj) *n.* **1** a point in a progressive movement, a definite period or phase in development (*is at a difficult stage; in the early stages; at the planning stage; at the embryonic stage*). **2 a** a raised platform on which theatrical or other performances take place before an audience. **b** any elevated platform, such as a scaffold for workers erecting or repairing a building, or a shelf on which objects may be exhibited or examined etc. **3** the theatre, drama, the profession of an actor, actors collectively. **4** the scene of action. **5** a dock, often floating, for the embarkation or disembarkation of passengers or goods. **6** any one of a series of regular stopping places on a route. **7** the distance between two such places. **8** a definite portion of a journey (*a fare stage*). **9** (*Hist.*) a stagecoach. **10** a detachable propulsion unit of a rocket. **11** (*Geol.*) a band of strata constituting a subdivision of a series or formation. **12** the small platform on a microscope where the slide is mounted for examination. ~*v.t.* **1** to put (a play etc.) on the stage. **2** to plan and execute (an event). **to go on the stage** to become a professional actor or actress. **to hold the stage** to dominate proceedings, to take the leading role, e.g. in a discussion. **to set the stage** to arrange things in preparation (for an event etc.). **stageable** *a.* **stageability** (-bil´-) *n.* **stagecoach** *n.* (*Hist.*) a horse-drawn coach that ran regularly by stages for conveyance of parcels, passengers etc. **stagecraft** *n.* the art of writing or staging plays. **stage direction** *n.* an instruction respecting the movements etc. of actors in a play.

stage door *n.* a door to a theatre for the use of actors, workers etc. **stage effect** *n.* **1** in the theatre, an effect contrived by lighting etc. **2** generally, something done to add theatricality to an occasion. **stage fright** *n.* a fit of nervousness in facing an audience. **stagehand** *n.* a worker who moves scenery etc. in a theatrical production. **stage left** *n.*, *adv.* (the area of the stage) to the left of an actor facing the audience. **stage-manage** *v.t.* to direct or supervise (a play, performance, show etc.) from behind the scenes. **stage management** *n.* **stage manager** *n.* a professional name used by an actor etc. **stage play** *n.* a play performed on stage, as distinct from radio or television. **stager** *n.* a person of long experience in anything (esp. in *old-stager*). **stage right** *n.*, *adv.* (the area of the stage) to the right of an actor facing the audience. **stage-struck** *a.* smitten with the theatre, esp. with an overwhelming desire to act. **stage whisper** *n.* **1** an audible aside. **2** something meant for the ears of people other than the person ostensibly addressed. **stagey** STAGY (under STAGE). **staging** *n.* **1** the business or process of putting a play on the stage. **2** a platform or scaffolding, usu. temporary. **3** shelving for greenhouse plants. **staging post** *n.* a regular stopover point on an air route. **stagy, stagey** *a.* (*comp.* **stagier**, *superl.* **stagiest**) theatrical, melodramatic, histrionic, artificial. **stagily** *adv.* **staginess** *n.*

stagflation (stagflā´shən) *n.* a state of the economy in which there is a combination of high inflation and falling industrial output and employment.

stagger (stag´ə) *v.i.* **1** to move unsteadily in walking, to totter, to reel. **2** to begin to give way, to waver, to hesitate. *~v.t.* **1** to cause to reel. **2** to cause to hesitate. **3** to amaze or shock. **4** to overlap, to place zigzag. **5** to arrange (working hours, holidays etc.) so as not to coincide. **6** to design (a crossroads) so that the side roads do not meet opposite one another. **7** to set (the spokes of a wheel) alternately leaning in and out. *~n.* **1** a staggering movement. **2** an overlapping, overhanging, zigzag or slantwise arrrangement of things in a series or structure. **staggerer** *n.* **staggering** *a.* **staggeringly** *adv.* **staggers** *n.* **1** a disease affecting the brain and spinal cord of horses and cattle, causing staggering and a loss of balance. **2** giddiness, vertigo.

stagnant (stag´nənt) *a.* **1** (of water) still, without current, motionless. **2** (of people or their lives, of business etc.) dull, sluggish. **stagnancy** *n.* **stagnantly** *adv.* **stagnate** (-nāt´, stag´-) *v.i.* to become stagnant. **stagnation** (-nā´shən) *n.*

stagy STAGE.

staid (stād) *a.* sober, steady, sedate. **staidly** *adv.* **staidness** *n.*

stain (stān) *v.t.* **1** to discolour, to soil, to sully. **2** to tarnish, to blemish (a reputation etc.). **3** to colour by means of dye or another agent acting chemically or by absorption. **4** to impregnate (an object for microscopic examination) with a colouring matter affecting certain parts more powerfully than others. *~v.i.* **1** to cause discoloration. **2** to take stains. *~n.* **1** a discoloration. **2** a spot of a distinct colour. **3** a blot, a blemish. **stainable** *a.* **stained glass** *n.* glass coloured for use in windows. **stainer** *n.* **stainless** *a.* **1** without a stain, immaculate. **2** resistant to rust or tarnish. **stainlessly** *adv.* **stainlessness** *n.* **stainless steel** *n.* a rustless alloy steel used for cutlery etc.

stair (steə) *n.* **1** each one of a series of steps, esp. for ascending from one storey of a house to another. **2** (*usu. pl.*) a flight of stairs. **staircase** *n.* a flight of stairs with banisters, supporting structure etc. **stairhead** *n.* the landing at the top of a flight of stairs. **stairlift** *n.* a mechanism fitted to a staircase, with a chair in which an elderly or disabled person can be carried up and down stairs. **stair-rod** *n.* a rod for fastening a stair carpet into the angle between two stairs. **stairway** *n.* a staircase. **stairwell** *n.* the vertical shaft which contains a staircase.

stake¹ (stāk) *n.* **1** a stick or post pointed at one end and set in the ground, as a support, part of a railing etc. **2** (*Hist.*) a post to which persons condemned to death by burning were bound. **3** death by this method; martyrdom. **4** a prop or upright part or fitting for supporting a machine etc. **5** in basket-weaving, any of the uprights acting as supports for the woven strands. *~v.t.* **1** to fasten, support, or protect with a stake or stakes. **2** to mark (out or off) with stakes. **to stake one's claim** to assert one's right to possess something, to register or establish one's claim (to something). **to stake out** to place under surveillance. **stake-boat** *n.* an anchored boat marking a point on a boat-race course. **stake-net** *n.* a fishing net stretched on stakes. **stake-out** *n.* a (police) surveillance operation covering a particular building or area.

stake² (stāk) *n.* **1** anything, esp. a sum of money, wagered on a competition or contingent event, esp. deposited with a stakeholder. **2** (*pl.*) money competed for in a race etc. **3** (*pl.*) the race itself. **4** an interest or involvement (in some concern). *~v.t.* **1** to wager, to venture (something, esp. a sum of money, on an event etc.). **2** to risk. **3** (*N Am., coll.*) to support financially or otherwise. **at stake 1** likely to be lost or damaged, at risk, endangered (*Many lives are at stake*). **2** at issue. **stakeholder** *n.* **1** an independent person with whom each party making a wager deposits their stake. **2** a person with an interest or involvement in something, such as a business concern or the society in which they live. **staker** *n.*

stalactite (stal´əktīt) *n.* a deposit of carbonate of lime, hanging from the roof of a cave etc., in the form of a thin tube or a large icicle, produced by the evaporation of percolating water. **stalactitic** (-tit´-) *a.*

Usage note See note under STALAGMITE.

stalagmite (stal´əgmīt) *n.* a deposit of the same material as in a stalactite, in the form of a pointed column or a mound, rising from the floor of a cave. **stalagmitic** (-mit´-) *a.*

Usage note A *stalagmite* (with *g* for *ground*) rises from the floor, and a *stalactite* (with *c* for *ceiling*) hangs from the roof.

stale¹ (stāl) *a.* (*comp.* **staler,** *superl.* **stalest**) **1** not fresh; dry, musty. **2** insipid or tasteless from being kept too long. **3** (of jokes etc.) trite; (of news) old. **4** (of e.g. an athlete or person studying) in a debilitated condition from overtraining or overexertion. ~*v.t.* to make stale. ~*v.i.* to become stale. **stalely** *adv.* **staleness** *n.*

stale² (stāl) *n.* the urine of horses or cattle. ~*v.i.* (of horses or cattle) to urinate.

stalemate (stāl´māt) *n.* **1** in chess, the position when the king, not actually in check, is unable to move without placing itself in check, and there is no other piece that can be moved. **2** a situation of deadlock. ~*v.t.* **1** in chess, to reduce (one's opponent) to a stalemate. **2** to bring to a standstill.

Stalinism (stah´linizm) *n.* the rigid authoritarianism, totalitarianism and centralization associated with the regime of the dictator of the former Soviet Union Joseph Stalin, 1879–1953, developed from the communist ideology of Marxism-Leninism. **Stalinist** *n.*

stalk¹ (stawk) *n.* **1** the stem or axis of a plant. **2** in a plant, a slender attachment such as the peduncle of a flower or petiole of a leaf. **3** the supporting peduncle of a crinoid, barnacle etc.; any slender attachment for an organ in an animal. **4** any long slender linking or supporting shaft, such as the stem of a wineglass. **stalked** *a.* **stalk-eyed** *a.* (of certain crustaceans) having the eyes set on peduncles. **stalkless** *a.* **stalklet** *n.* **stalklike** *a.* **stalky** *a.* (*comp.* **stalkier,** *superl.* **stalkiest**)

stalk² (stawk) *v.t.* **1** to pursue (game or other prey, or an enemy) stealthily by the use of cover. **2** to follow (a person, esp. a public figure) persistently and with a sinister or unwelcome purpose. ~*v.i.* **1** to go stealthily, to steal (up to game or prey) under cover. **2** to walk with a stately stride. ~*n.* **1** the act of stalking game or prey. **2** stately gait. **stalker** *n.* **stalking-horse** *n.* **1** a horse or figure like a horse behind which a hunter hides when stalking game. **2** a mask or pretence concealing one's true purpose.

stall¹ (stawl) *n.* **1** a booth or shed in a market, street etc., or a bench, table etc. in a building for the sale of goods. **2** a cowshed or stable. **3** a division or compartment for a horse, ox etc., in a stable or byre. **4** a seat in the choir of a large church, enclosed at the back and sides and usu. canopied, for a clergyman, chorister etc. **5** (*usu. pl.*) each one of a set of seats in a theatre, usu. in the front part of the pit. **6** in public washing or toilet facilities, a compartment for one person,

containing a shower or lavatory. **7** STARTING STALL (under START). **8** an instance of an aircraft or motor stalling, or the resulting condition. **9** a sheath or holder for something (*a finger-stall*). ~*v.i.* **1** (of a vehicle or its engine) to cease working suddenly, e.g. when the fuel supply is inadequate. **2** (of an aircraft or pilot) to lose forward impetus and thus sustaining power if there is not enough airspace underneath for recovering lift. ~*v.t.* **1** to cause (a vehicle, aircraft or engine) to stall. **2** to put or keep (esp. cattle) in a stall for fattening.

stall² (stawl) *v.i.* to play for time; to be evasive. ~*v.t.* to obstruct or delay. ~*n.* an act of stalling.

stallion (stal´yən) *n.* an uncastrated male horse, esp. one kept for breeding purposes.

stalwart (stawl´wət, stal´-) *a.* **1** strong in build, sturdy. **2** stout-hearted, determined, resolute. ~*n.* a strong, resolute, dependable person, esp. a valiant supporter or partisan. **stalwartly** *adv.* **stalwartness** *n.*

stamen (stā´mən) *n.* (*pl.* **stamens, stamina** (stam´inə)) (*Bot.*) the pollen-bearing male organ of a flower. **stamened** *a.* **staminate** (-nāt) *a.* (*Bot.*) having stamens (but no pistils). **staminiferous** (-nif´-) *a.*

stamina (stam´inə) *n.* power of endurance, ability to tolerate long periods of mental or physical stress.

stammer (stam´ə) *v.i.* to speak with halting articulation, nervous hesitation, or repetitions of the same sound; to stutter. ~*n.* **1** this kind of speech disorder; a tendency to stammer or stutter. **2** a stammering utterance. **stammerer** *n.* **stammeringly** *adv.*

stamp (stamp) *v.t.* **1** to bring (one's foot) down heavily. **2** to crush or flatten with one's foot thus. **3** to impress (a mark, pattern, initials etc.) on a surface with a die or similar rubber, metal or wooden implement. **4** to make a mark or impression upon (a surface) thus. **5** to impress (a scene, an experience, a fact, on or in the mind or memory). **6** to affix a postage stamp or other stamp to (an envelope etc.). **7** to characterize distinctively (*the pusillanimous attitude that stamps a coward; They were put in the top class and stamped as bright*). ~*v.i.* **1** to bring one's foot down heavily or forcibly on the ground. **2** to walk heavily. ~*n.* **1** an instrument for stamping marks, designs etc. **2** the mark made, or the blow imparted, by this. **3** an official mark set on things chargeable with some duty or tax, to show that it is paid. **4** a small piece of adhesive paper for affixing to letters, receipts etc., to show that the required charge has been paid. **5** a label, imprint, or other mark certifying ownership, quality, genuineness etc., affixed to or impressed on goods etc. **6** a distinguishing mark or impress. **7** a kind, sort or type (*people of this stamp*). **8** a downward blow with the foot, or an act of bringing it down heavily. **9** the sound of this. **to stamp on** to suppress, to crush out of existence.

to stamp out 1 to extinguish (a fire) by stamping. **2** to suppress, extirpate. **stamp-collector** *n.* a person who collects specimens of postage stamps. **stamp collecting** *n.* **stamp duty** *n.* a duty imposed on certain legal documents. **stamper** *n.* **stamp hinge** *n.* a transparent paper holder with adhesive backing for sticking postage stamps into a stamp album. **stamping ground** *n.* a habitual meeting place, a favourite resort.

stampede (stampēd´) *n.* **1** a sudden headlong rush of startled animals, esp. cattle. **2** a sudden rush of people, esp. in panic. **3** any impulsive or unreasoning movement on the part of a large number of people. *~v.i.* to take part in a stampede. *~v.t.* **1** to cause to do this. **2** to rush (people into acting without due thought).

stance (stans, stahns) *n.* **1** the position taken for a stroke in golf, cricket etc. **2** a personal attitude, political position etc. **3** the position adopted by a person when standing.

stanch[1] STAUNCH[1].

stanch[2] STAUNCH[2].

stanchion (stan´shən) *n.* **1** a prop, post, pillar etc., forming a support or part of a structure. **2** a vertical bar or pair of bars for confining cattle in a stall.

stand (stand) *v.i.* (*past, p.p.* **stood** (stud)) **1** to be in, take or keep an upright position, esp. on the feet, or on a base. **2** to be located or situated (*On this spot stood the gallows*). **3** to have a specified height or stature (*stood barely five foot*). **4** to be in a specified state, attitude, position, situation, rank etc. (*The score stands at three-nil; He stood in awe of the prefects; stand accused of murder*). **5** to move into a specified position and remain in it (*stood to one side*). **6** to take a certain attitude (*stand aloof*). **7** to remain firm or constant, to abide, to endure, to persist. **8** to be or remain in a stationary position, to cease from motion, to stop, to be or remain immovable, not to give way. **9** (of rules, laws, conditions etc.) to hold good, to remain valid or unimpaired. **10** (of water) to be motionless, to lie stagnant. **11** (*Naut.*) to hold a specified course, to steer. **12** to become a candidate (for). **13** to act or serve in a specified role or capacity (*stand surety; stand proxy*). *~v.t.* **1** to set in an erect or a specified position (*stood the vase on the piano*). **2** to endure, to sustain, without giving way or complaining (*can't stand the pain*). **3** to treat (someone) to (a drink etc.) (*I'll stand you dinner*). **4** to undergo (a trial etc.). *~n.* **1** a cessation of motion or progress, a stop, a halt, a state of inactivity, a standstill, a stoppage. **2** the act of standing, esp. with firmness, in a fixed or stationary position, place or station (*took her stand at the entrance*). **3** a show of resistance, opposition, defensive effort etc. (*make a stand against racism*). **4** in cricket, a lengthy partnership between two batsmen at the wicket. **5** someone's attitude, position or standpoint in regard to an issue. **6** a small frame or piece of furniture for supporting anything, a

base, rack or holder (*an inkstand; a hatstand*). **7** a trading stall in a street or market, or a commercial company's information booth at a conference etc. **8** a place in a town where cabs etc. stand for hire. **9** an erection with banks of seats or steps for spectators to stand or sit on. **10** (*N Am.*) the witness box in a court of law. **11** a halt somewhere for a performance by a performer on tour. **12** a clump of plants or trees (*a stand of willows*). **as it stands 1** in its present state, without alteration. **2** in the present circumstances, as things are. **as things stand** in the present circumstances, as things are. **stand and deliver!** (*Hist.*) the traditional utterance of a highwayman at a hold-up, ordering the victims to hand over their money and valuables. **to stand alone** to be unique or unrivalled. **to stand back 1** to retire to a position further from the front. **2** to withdraw mentally from close involvement, usu. in order to get an objective view. **to stand by 1** to be present as a bystander; to look on passively. **2** to uphold, to support firmly. **3** to abide by (one's decision etc.). **4** to stand near in readiness to act promptly as directed. **5** (*Naut.*) to post oneself ready to operate (the anchor etc.). **to stand down 1** to withdraw or resign from a body, competition etc. **2** to leave the witness box in a law court. **3** (*Mil.*) to come off duty. **4** (of a committee) to be dissolved. **to stand fast** to stay firm, to be unmoved. **to stand for 1** to represent, to imply. **2** (*usu. with neg.*) to allow, to tolerate, to endure. **3** to support the cause of. **to stand good** to remain valid. **to stand in for 1** to deputize for, to act in place of. **2** to take the place of (an actor etc. whose special skills are temporarily not required). **to stand off** to move away; to keep at a distance. **to stand on** to insist on (ceremony etc.). **to stand one's ground** to remain resolute, to stay fixed in position. **to stand on one's own (two) feet** to manage without the help of others. **to stand out 1** to be conspicuous, prominent or outstanding. **2** to persist in opposition or support, to hold out (for or against). **3** to endure without giving way. **to stand over 1** to supervise closely in an irksome or threatening way. **2** to be deferred, to be postponed. **to stand to 1** (*Mil.*) to stand ready for an attack, e.g. after dark or before dawn. **2** to be liable to (lose, gain etc. something). **to stand up 1** to rise to one's feet. **2** to be or remain erect; to set erect. **3** (of an argument etc.) to be valid, to hold water. **4** (*coll.*) to fail to keep an appointment with. **to stand up for** to maintain, to support, to take the side of. **to stand upon** to stand on (ceremony etc.). **to stand up to** to oppose with determination. **to stand well with** to be on good terms with, to be in the favour of. **to take one's stand on** to have as the basis of one's argument. **stand-alone** *a.* (of a computer) working independently, not part of an interdependent network etc. **standby** *n.* (*pl.* **standbys**) a substitute or replacement kept esp. for use in an emergency. *~a.* (of a ticket) not booked in advance, subject to availability. **on standby 1** held in readiness for use or service in an emergency etc. **2** (of an airline passenger) awaiting an empty seat, not having booked in advance. **standee** *n.* (*coll.*) a person who is having to stand because all the seats are occupied. **stander** *n.* **stand-in** *n.* a substitute or deputy. **standing** *a.* **1** erect. **2** not cut down. **3** remaining on the spot, not moving or progressing. **4** fixed, established, permanent, not temporary or for a special occasion. **5** stagnant. ~*n.* **1** repute, estimation, esp. good estimation. **2** relative place or position. **3** the position or activity of a person that stands. **4** duration, existence (*a partnership of long standing*). **to be left standing** to prove much the weaker competitor, to be left at the starting post. **standing army** *n.* (*pl.* **standing armies**) a peacetime army of professional soldiers. **standing joke** *n.* a subject of constant ridicule. **standing order** *n.* **1** an instruction to a bank by a customer to pay fixed sums at regular intervals in payment of bills etc. **2** (*pl.*) orders made by a deliberative assembly as to the manner in which its business should be conducted. **standing ovation** *n.* a prolonged spell of applause during which the audience rise to their feet in their enthusiasm. **standing room** *n.* room for standing, esp. after all seats are filled. **standing wave** *n.* (*Physics*) the pattern of maximum and minimum amplitude that occurs when two waves vibrating at the same frequency are travelling in opposed directions. **stand-off, stand-off half** *n.* a rugby halfback acting as a link between the scrum-half and the three-quarters. **stand-offish** *a.* cold, distant, reserved in manner. **stand-offishly** *adv.* **stand-offishness** *n.* **standpipe** *n.* an upright pipe serving as a hydrant, to provide a head of water for pressure etc. **standpoint** *n.* a point of view or viewpoint, whether topographical or mental. **standstill** *n.* a stoppage, a cessation of progress. **stand-to** *n.* (*Mil.*) a state of readiness for action, the activity of standing ready. **stand-up** *a.* **1** (of a meal) taken standing. **2 a** (of a fight) fully physical and violent. **b** in boxing, unflinching. **3** (of a collar) upright. **4** (of a comedian) telling jokes etc. directly to the audience in a solo performance.

standard (stanʹdəd) *n.* **1** a measure of extent, quantity, value etc. established by law or custom as an example or criterion for others. **2** any type, fact, thing etc., serving as a criterion. **3** the degree of excellence required for a particular purpose (*not up to standard*; *below standard*). **4** any particular level of quality or competence (*a low standard of workmanship*). **5** the ordinary quality of product etc., as distinct from one including extra features. **6** a flag as the distinctive emblem of an army, government etc. **7** an upright pillar, post or other support. **8** an upright water pipe or standpipe. **9** a tree or shrub growing on a single upright stem, or supported on its own

stem. **10** a shrub grafted on to an upright stem. **11** a document dictating the required specifications, nationally or internationally, of manufactured goods. **12** something taken as a model to imitate. **13** a well-established and popular tune or song. ~*a.* **1** serving as a standard; used as a standard. **2** being of the normal or regulation quality, size etc. **3** recognized as having lasting value; accepted as authoritative. **4** (of language) conforming to the usage of educated native speakers. **to raise the standard** to rally supporters to the cause in preparation for war or some other campaign. **standard assessment task** *n.* a standard test taken by schoolchildren in any of the core subjects in the national curriculum, which indicates their progress in it. **standard-bearer** *n.* **1** a soldier carrying a standard. **2** a leader of a movement or cause. **standard deviation** *n.* a measure of the scatter of the value of a variable about a mean in a frequency distribution. **standardize, standardise** *v.t.* to bring into line with a standard. ~*v.i.* to model oneself (on). **standardizable** *a.* **standardization** (-zāʹshən) *n.* **standardizer** *n.* **standard lamp** *n.* a movable lamp on a tall pedestal. **standard of living** *n.* the level of subsistence or material welfare of an individual, group or community. **standard time** *n.* the method of reckoning time from a conventionally adopted meridian (for most purposes this is the meridian of Greenwich).

stank STINK.

Stanley knife® (stanʹli) *n.* (*pl.* **Stanley knives**) a sharp trimming knife with a replaceable blade.

stannary (stanʹəri) *n.* (*pl.* **stannaries**) a tin-mining district.

stanza (stanʹzə) *n.* a recurring group of lines of poetry adjusted to each other in a definite scheme, often with rhyme. **stanza'd, stanzaed** (-zəd), **stanzaic** (-zāʹ-) *a.*

stapes (stāʹpēz) *n.* (*pl.* **stapes**) (*Anat.*) the innermost of the three small bones of the middle ear, shaped like a stirrup and transmitting vibrations to the middle ear from the incus.

staphylococcus (stafiləkokʹəs) *n.* (*pl.* **staphylococci** (-kokʹsī)) any micro-organism of the genus *Staphylococcus*, forming the bacteria most frequently found in suppurative infections of the skin or mucous membrane. **staphylococcal** *a.*

staple[1] (stāʹpəl) *n.* **1** a U-shaped piece of metal driven into a post, wall etc., to receive part of a fastening or to hold wire etc. **2** a similarly shaped piece of thin wire for driving through sheets of paper and clamping them together. ~*v.t.* to fasten, attach or support with staples. **staple gun** *n.* a hand tool for propelling staples into a surface. **stapler** *n.* a device for inserting or driving in staples.

staple[2] (stāʹpəl) *n.* **1** the principal commodity sold or produced in any place, country etc. **2** the main element of diet etc. **3** the chief material or substance of anything. **4** raw material. **5** the length, strength etc. of the fibre of wool, cotton etc., as a criterion of quality. ~*a.* **1** (of a commodity or product) predominating in the home consumption or exports of a nation or region. **2** chief, principal, main. ~*v.t.* to sort or classify (wool etc.) according to staple.

star (stah) *n.* **1** (*Astron.*) **a** any celestial body appearing as a luminous point, esp. one of the fixed stars or those so distant that their relative position in the heavens appears constant, as distinct from planets or comets. **b** any heavenly body that is really a gaseous mass giving out heat and light. **2** a heavenly body regarded as having influence over a person's life. **3** an object, figure or device resembling a star. **4** such a figure with radiating points used as an emblem, e.g. as a military decoration, part of the insignia of an order or as indicating a grade of excellence (*a three-star hotel*). **5** a brilliant or prominent person, esp. an actor or singer. ~*a.* **1** outstanding, brilliant (*a star student*). **2** of or relating to stars of the stage or screen (*star quality*). ~*v.t.* (*pres.p.* **starring**, *past, p.p.* **starred**) **1** to set, spangle, or decorate with stars. **2** to put an asterisk against (a name etc.). ~*v.i.* (of an actor, singer etc.) to appear as a star. **starburst** *n.* **1** a pattern of diverging lines around a source of light. **2** (*Astron.*) the explosion of a star. **3** a photographic lens attachment that makes a light source appear with divergent rays. **4** (*Astron.*) a period of star-formation in a galaxy. **stardom** *n.* the state or status of being a star in films etc. **stardust** *n.* **1** (*Astron.*) a large concentration of distant stars appearing as dust. **2** dust that supposedly fills the eyes with romantic illusions. **starfish** *n.* (*pl. in general* **starfish,** *in particular* **starfishes**) an echinoderm, *Asterias rubens,* with five or more rays or arms. **star fruit** *n.* the yellow edible fruit, star-shaped in section, of a SE Asian tree, *Averrhoa carambola.* **stargazer** *n.* (*usu. derog. or facet.*) an astronomer or astrologer. **stargaze** *v.i.* **stargazing** *n.* **starless** *a.* **starlet** *n.* **1** a young actress who is being trained and promoted as a future star performer. **2** a little star. **starlight** *n.* the light of the stars. ~*a.* **starlit. starlike** *a.* **starlit** *a.* **1** lit by the stars. **2** with the stars visible in the heavens. **Star of David** *n.* the emblem of Judaism and the State of Israel, consisting of a six-pointed star made from two superimposed equilateral triangles. **starry** *a.* (*comp.* **starrier,** *superl.* **starriest**) **1** filled or adorned with stars. **2** shining like, or illuminated by, stars. **3** resembling a star. **starrily** *adv.* **starriness** *n.* **starry-eyed** *a.* acting or thinking in a dreamy, over-optimistic manner. **Stars and Stripes** *n.pl.* the national flag of the US. **star shell** *n.* a shell bursting in the air and emitting luminous stars, used to light up an enemy's position. **starship** *n.* in science fiction, a manned spacecraft for interstellar travel. **star-spangled** *a.* covered with stars. **star-struck** *a.* obsessed with the glamour of stardom or of film stars etc. **star-studded** *a.* **1** covered with stars. **2**

(of a film, play etc.) having a large proportion of famous performers. **star turn** *n.* the principal performance in an entertainment.

starboard (stah´bawd, -bəd) *n.* (*Naut.*) the right-hand side of a vessel looking forward. ~*v.t.* **1** to put (the helm) to starboard. **2** to make (a vessel) turn to starboard. **starboard watch** *n.* the watch taken by crew members with bunks on the starboard side.

starch (stahch) *n.* **1** a white, tasteless, odourless, amorphous compound, found in all plants except fungi, but esp. in cereals, potatoes, beans etc., an important constituent of vegetable foods, and used as a soluble powder to stiffen linen etc. **2** stiffness, preciseness, formality. ~*a.* stiff, precise, prim. ~*v.t.* to stiffen with starch. **starched** *a.* **starchedly** (stah´chidli) *adv.* **starchedness** (stah´chid-) *n.* **starcher** *n.* **starchly** *adv.* **starchness** *n.* **starchy** *a.* (*comp.* **starchier,** *superl.* **starchiest**) **1** of or relating to starch. **2** stiff, unyielding. **starchily** *adv.* **starchiness** *n.*

stare (stee) *v.i.* **1** to look with eyes fixed and wide open, as in admiration, surprise, horror etc. **2** (of the eyes) to be wide open and gazing fixedly. **3** to stand out, to be prominent. ~*v.t.* to reduce to a specified state by staring (*stared her into submission*). ~*n.* a staring gaze. **to be staring one in the face 1** to be only too obvious. **2** to be imminent, to be inexorably awaiting one. **to stare down** to outstare. **to stare out** to outstare. **starer** *n.* **staring** *a.*

stark (stahk) *a.* **1** (of a landscape etc.) bare, desolate. **2** plain, simple, esp. harshly so (*a stark contrast*; *the stark realities*). **3** stubborn, inflexible. **4** complete, downright, sheer (*stark madness*). ~*adv.* wholly, absolutely (*stark mad*). **stark staring mad** completely crazy. **starkers** (-kəz) *a.* (*coll.*) stark naked. **starkly** *adv.* **stark naked** *a.* completely naked. **starkness** *n.*

starling (stah´ling) *n.* a small black and brown speckled bird of the genus *Sturnus,* esp. *S. vulgaris.*

starry STAR.

start (staht) *v.i.* **1** to commence, to come into existence (*The programme starts at 8.30*). **2 a** to make a beginning (on a task, journey etc.). **b** to begin a meal etc. (with a certain item) (*usually start with soup*). **3** to begin moving, to make as if to move (*She started after him, then changed her mind*). **4** to set out, to leave, to begin a journey (*If we start at six, we'll be there by eleven*). **5** (of a machine, engine etc.) to begin operating (*The car won't start*). **6** (*coll.*) to begin complaining (*Now don't you start*). **7** to make a sudden involuntary movement, as from fear, surprise etc. **8** to shrink, to wince. **9** to move abruptly, to spring (*aside* etc.). **10** to appear or well up suddenly (*The pain made tears start in his eyes*). ~*v.t.* **1** to begin (*started work*; *start singing*; *started to laugh*). **2** to set going, to set in motion (*start the proceedings*; *started a fire*). **3** to set (someone) up (in business etc.). **4** to originate, to set going (*start a business*).

5 to cause (someone) to begin (reacting in some way) (*started us all laughing*; *started me coughing*). **6** to cause (a machine, engine etc.) to begin operating. **7** to give the signal to (competitors) to start in a race. **8** to cause to start, to rouse (game etc.). **9** to conceive (a baby). ~*n.* **1** the beginning of a journey, enterprise etc., a setting-out. **2** a starting-place. **3** the amount of lead given to a competitor at the beginning of a race etc. (*a ten-second start*). **4** an advantageous initial position in life, in business etc. **5** a sudden involuntary movement, as of fear, surprise etc. **6** (*usu. pl.*) a spasmodic effort, as in *fits and starts*. **7** (*coll.*) an odd or queer occurrence (*a rum start*). **for a start** in the first place, as the first consideration of several. **to start in 1** to begin. **2** (*NAm.*) to make a beginning (on). **to start off 1** to begin (*start off with introductions*). **2** to set out on a journey. **to start on** (*coll.*) to pick a fight with, to nag, to bully. **to start out 1** to begin a journey. **2** to begin in a certain way (*He started out as an airman but eventually became an archaeologist*). **to start up 1** to come into notice or occur to the mind suddenly; to arise, to occur. **2** (of an engine, machine etc.) to start. **3** to rise suddenly. **4** to establish (a business etc.). **to start with 1** in the first place, as the first consideration (*should never have bought it to start with*). **2** in the beginning (*There were eight of us to start with*). **starter** *n.* **1** a person who or thing that starts. **2** a device for starting an internal-combustion engine. **3** a person who gives the signal for starting a race etc. **4** a horse or other competitor starting in a race (*There are ten starters*). **5** (*sometimes pl.*) the first course of a meal. **6** anything that initiates a process. **for starters** (*coll.*) in the first place, to begin with, as the first consideration. **under starter's orders** (of racehorses etc.) ready to race, awaiting the signal to go. **starting** *n., a.* **starting block** *n.* (*usu. pl.*) a device consisting of angled wooden blocks or metal pads used by sprinters to brace their feet in crouch starts. **starting gate** *n.* in horse racing, a set of starting stalls. **starting grid** *n.* in motor racing, a system of markings on the track to indicate starting positions. **starting pistol** *n.* a pistol used to give the starting signal for a race. **starting point** *n.* a point of departure for a journey, argument, procedure etc. **starting post** *n.* a post from which competitors start in a race. **starting price** *n.* the odds on a horse at the beginning of a race. **starting stall** *n.* a compartment for one horse in the line-up for a race, with a movable barrier that is lifted at the starting signal. **start-up** *n.* an act, or the process, of starting, esp. in reference to setting a machine in motion or establishing a business.

startle (stah'təl) *v.t.* to alarm, to shock; to cause to start in surprise etc. **startler** *n.* **startling** *a.* surprising, alarming. **startlingly** *adv.*

starve (stahv) *v.i.* **1** to die of hunger. **2** to suffer

severely from hunger or malnourishment. **3** to be in need or penury. **4** (*used in continuous tenses, coll.*) to be very hungry (*I'm starving*). **5** to suffer from a lack of mental or spiritual nourishment. **6** to long (for e.g. affection, stimulation). ~*v.t.* **1** to cause to die, or suffer extremely, from lack of food. **2** to deprive (of affection etc.). **3** to deprive of mental or spiritual nourishment. **4** to force (into surrender, out of a stronghold etc.) by starving. **starvation** (-vā'shən) *n.*

stash (stash) *v.t.* (*coll.*) to store, (money etc.) in a secret place (usu. with *away*). ~*n.* **1** a secret store. **2** a hiding place, hideaway or hideout.

stasis (stā'sis, stas'-) *n.* (*pl.* **stases** (-sēz)) **1** a state of equilibrium or inaction. **2** stagnation of the blood, esp. in the small vessels or capillaries, or any stoppage in the flow of a bodily fluid.

stat[1] (stat) *n.* (*coll.*) a thermostat.

stat[2] (stat) *n.* **1** (*esp. pl.*) a statistic. **2** statistics.

state (stāt) *n.* **1** the condition, mode of existence, situation, or relation to circumstances, of a person or thing (*in a poor state of health*; *in a reasonable state*). **2** (*coll.*) a nervous or excited condition (*Don't get in such a state*). **3** (*coll.*) an untidy or confused condition. **4** (*often* **State**) a political community organized under a government, a commonwealth, a nation, the body politic. **5** such a community forming part of a federal republic, esp. *the United States*. **6** civil government (*Ministers of State*; *Church and State*). **7** dignity, rank, pomp, splendour. ~*a.* **1** (*often* **State**) **a** of or relating to the state or body politic (*state secrets*; *state papers*). **b** used or reserved for ceremonial occasions (*the State apartments*). **c** involving ceremony (*a state visit*; *the state opening of Parliament*). ~*v.t.* **1** to set forth in speech or writing, esp. with explicitness and formality (*stated her intentions*). **2** to fix, to determine, to specify (*only at stated times*). **3** (*Law*) to present the facts of (a case) for review. **4** (*Mus.*) to play (a theme) so as to acquaint the listener with it. **in state** with proper ceremony (*was received in state*). **of state** relating to government (*affairs of state*). **to lie in state** (of an important dead person) to lie in a coffin in some place where the public may come to visit as a token of respect. **statable** *a.* **statecraft** *n.* statesmanship. **statedly** *adv.* **statehood** *n.* **state house** *n.* **1** the building which houses a US state legislature. **2** in New Zealand, a private residence built with government funds. **stateless** *a.* (of a person) without nationality or citizenship. **statelessness** *n.* **stately** *a.* (*comp.* **statelier**, *superl.* **stateliest**) grand, lofty, dignified, elevated, imposing. **stateliness** *n.* **stately home** *n.* a large country mansion, usu. of historic interest and open to public view. **statement** *n.* **1** the act of stating; the expression of something in words. **2** that which is stated; a declaration. **3** a formal account, recital, or narration (*make a statement to the police*). **4** an itemized record of additions to and withdrawals from a bank account. **5** a formal presentation of money owed for goods, services etc. **state of emergency** n. the situation of a country at a time of peril or disaster, esp. justifying the suspension of the normal running of the constitution. **state of grace** n. the spiritual condition of forgiveness or release from one's sins. **state-of-the-art** a. using the most advanced technology available at the time. **state of war** n. the situation following a declaration of war, or when war is in progress. **state pension** n. a pension paid by the state to a person of pensionable age. **state prisoner** n. a person imprisoned for an offence against the state. **stateroom** n. **1** a room reserved for ceremonial occasions, a state apartment. **2** a private sleeping apartment on a liner etc. or, in N America, a train. **state school** n. a government-financed school for the provision of free education. **state's evidence** n. King's or Queen's evidence. **stateside** a., adv. (coll.) of, in or towards the US. **statesman, stateswoman** n. (pl. **statesmen, stateswomen**) **1** a person skilled in the art of government. **2** a person taking a leading part in the administration of the state. **statesmanlike, statesmanly** a. **statesmanship** n. **statesperson** n. (pl. **statespersons, statespeople**) a statesman or stateswoman. **statewide** a., adv. (N Am.) (happening, applying etc.) throughout the whole state. **statism** n. (belief in) the centralized control of economic and social affairs by the state. **statist** n.

static (stat'ik) a. **1** stationary; not moving, acting or altering; stable, passive. **2** (Physics) **a** of or relating to bodies at rest or in equilibrium. **b** acting as weight without producing motion. **c** of or relating to or causing stationary electric charges. **3** of or relating to interference of radio or television signals. **4** of or relating to statics. ~n. **1** static electricity. **2** atmospherics; electrical interference of radio or television signals causing crackling, hissing and a speckled picture. **statically** adv. **static electricity** n. electrical effects caused by stationary charges, as opposed to charged particles flowing in a current. **statics** n. the branch of dynamics concerned with the relations between forces in equilibrium.

station (stā'shən) n. **1** a place where railway trains stop to set down or take up passengers or goods, usu. with a platform and administrative buildings and public facilities. **2** such buildings and facilities. **3** a similarly equipped terminus or assembly point for coaches or buses. **4** the place where a person or thing stands, esp. an appointed or established place. **5** a place where a particular service or operation is based (a police station; a coastguard station; a polling station; a petrol station). **6** a particular broadcasting establishment, or the radio or television channel it serves. **7** position, occupation, standing, rank, esp. high rank (one's station in life; ideas above one's station). **8** (Austral.) the ranch house or homestead of a sheep farmer. ~v.t. to assign to or place in a particular station, to post. **stationary**

a. **1** remaining in one place, not moving. **2** intended to remain in one place; fixed, not portable. **3** not changing in character, condition, magnitude etc. **4** (of planets) having no apparent movement in longitude. **stationariness** n. **station house** n. a police station. **stationmaster** n. the official in charge of a railway station. **station of the cross** n. in the Roman Catholic Church, any of a series of 14 images or pictures in a church etc. depicting successive scenes in Christ's passion. **station wagon** n. (esp. N Am.) an estate car.

Usage note The spellings of the adjective stationary (not moving) and the noun stationery (writing materials) should not be confused.

stationer (stā'shənə) n. a person who sells papers, pens, ink and writing materials. **stationery** n. writing materials and related goods sold by a stationer.

Usage note See note on stationery under STATION.

statism, statist STATE.

statistics (stətis'tiks) n. **1** (as sing.) the science of collecting, organizing, and analysing numerical data, esp. on a large scale, with the purpose of extrapolating trends in a whole from the representative sample studied. **2** (as pl.) numerical facts, arranged and classified, esp. respecting social conditions. **statistic** n. a statistical fact, a figure or total. ~a. statistical. **statistical** a. of or relating to statistics. **statistically** adv. **statistical significance** n. a measure of the amount of significance assignable to a deviant result. **statistician** (statistish'ən) n.

statue (stat'ū) n. a representation of a person or animal sculptured or cast, e.g. in marble or bronze, esp. about life-size. **statuary** a. of or for statues. ~n. (pl. **statuaries**) **1** statues collectively. **2** the art of making statues. **3** a sculptor. **statued** a. **statuesque** (-esk´) a. like a statue; having the dignity or beauty of a statue. **statuesquely** adv. **statuesqueness** n. **statuette** (-et´) n. a small statue, less than life-size.

stature (stach'ə) n. **1** the natural height of a body, esp. of a person. **2** eminence or social standing. **3** mental or moral standing. **statured** a.

status (stā'təs) n. **1** relative standing, rank, or position in society. **2** (Law) a person's legal identity, e.g. whether alien or citizen. **3** the current situation or state of affairs. **status symbol** n. a possession regarded as indicative of a person's elevated social rank or wealth.

status quo (stātəs kwō´) n. the existing state of affairs.

statute (stat'ūt) n. **1** a written law enacted by a legislative body. **2** an ordinance of a corporation or its founder intended as a permanent law. **statute book** n. a book in which statutes are published. **statute law** n. law enacted by a legislative body. **statute mile** n. a unit of distance equivalent to 1,760 yards (1.609 kilometres). **statutory** *a.* enacted, regulated, enforced or recognized by statute. **statutorily** *adv.* **statutory rape** *n.* (*Law, N Am.*) the act of having sexual intercourse with a minor.

staunch[1] (stawnch), **stanch** (stawnch) *a.* **1** loyal, constant, trustworthy. **2** (of a ship) seaworthy, watertight. **3** (of a joint etc.) firm, stout. **staunchly** *adv.* **staunchness** *n.*

staunch[2] (stawnch), **stanch** (stahnch, stawnch) *v.t.* to stop (blood) flowing, or stop blood flowing from (a wound).

stave (stāv) *n.* **1** each of the curved strips forming the side of a cask etc. **2** a strip of wood or other material used for a similar purpose. **3** a stanza, a verse. **4** (*Mus.*) a staff. ~*v.t.* (*past, p.p.* **staved, stove** (stōv)) **1** to crush the staves of (a cask, boat etc.). **2** to make (a hole) thus. **3** to furnish or fit with staves. **4** (*past, p.p.* **staved**) to stop, avert or ward (off). **to stave in** to crush.

staves STAFF[1].

stay[1] (stā) *v.i.* **1** to continue in a specified place or state, not to move or change. **2** to remain (e.g. calm, cheerful). **3** to reside temporarily (at, with etc.). **4** (*Sc., S Afr.*) to live, to dwell permanently (somewhere). **5** to remain somewhere long enough to be included in something (*stay to dinner; stay for evensong*). **6** to keep going or last out in a race etc., or till some other conclusion. ~*v.t.* **1** to spend (a period of time) somewhere (*stayed a week with her parents*). **2** to hinder, to stop the progress etc. of (e.g. a disease). **3** temporarily to satisfy (someone's hunger). **4** to postpone, to suspend (judgement, a decision etc.). ~*n.* **1** the circumstance, or a period, of staying or dwelling. **2** continuance in a place etc. **3** a suspension of judicial proceedings (*a stay of execution*). **to be here to stay** to be a fixture, to have come for good. **to stay in** to remain at home, to remain indoors. **to stay over** (*coll.*) to remain overnight. **to stay put** to remain where put or placed; to remain on the spot. **to stay the night** to remain somewhere, esp. to sleep, until the next day. **to stay up** not to go to bed till after one's normal bedtime. **stay-at-home** *a., n.* (a person who is) unenterprising or unadventurous. **stayer** *n.* a person with stamina and the will-power to go on; a horse or person that can stay the course. **staying power** *n.* stamina.

stay[2] (stā) *n.* **1** a support, a prop. **2** (*pl.*) a corset. ~*v.t.* to prop (usu. up), to support.

stay[3] (stā) *n.* **1** (*Naut.*) a rope supporting a mast. **2** a guy rope or other rope supporting a flagstaff. **3** a supporting brace in an aircraft. ~*v.t.* **1** to support by stays. **2** (*Naut.*) to put (a sailing ship) on the other tack. **staysail** (-səl) *n.* a sail extended by a stay.

STD *abbr.* **1** sexually transmitted disease. **2** subscriber trunk dialling.

stead (sted) *n.* place or room which another had or might have had. **in someone's stead** instead of someone. **in something's stead** instead of some-

thing. **to stand someone in good stead** to be of service to someone.

steadfast (sted´fəst, -fahst) *a.* firm, resolute, unwavering. **steadfastly** *adv.* **steadfastness** *n.*

steading (sted´ing) *n.* (*Sc., North.*) a farmstead.

steady (sted´i) *a.* (*comp.* **steadier,** *superl.* **steadiest**) **1** firmly fixed, not wavering. **2** moving or acting in a regular way, uniform, constant. **3** free from intemperance or irregularity, constant in mind or conduct. **4** persistent, tenacious. **5** serious, reliable and conscientious. **6** well controlled (*a steady hand; steady nerves*). **7** (of a ship) upright and on course. ~*v.t.* (*3rd pers. sing. pres.* **steadies,** *pres.p.* **steadying,** *past, p.p.* **steadied**) to make steady. ~*v.i.* to become steady. ~*n.* (*pl.* **steadies**) **1** (*coll.*) a regular boyfriend or girlfriend. **2** a rest or support for keeping the hand etc. steady. ~*adv.* steadily (*held them steady*). ~*int.* careful! take care! **steady on!** calm down! take it easy! **steadier** *n.* **steadily** *adv.* **steadiness** *n.* **steady-going** *a.* sober, dependable. **steady state** *n.* (*Physics*) a state of dynamic equilibrium.

steak (stāk) *n.* **1** a thick slice of beef, other meat, or fish cut for grilling, frying etc. **2** any of several cuts of beef such as *stewing steak, braising steak.* **steakhouse** *n.* a restaurant that specializes in serving steaks. **steak knife** *n.* (*pl.* **steak knives**) a knife with a serrated blade, for eating steak with.

steal (stēl) *v.t.* (*past* **stole** (stōl), *p.p.* **stolen** (stō´lən)) **1** to take (someone else's property) away without right or permission or intention of returning it, to take feloniously. **2** to secure covertly or by surprise (*steal a kiss*). **3** to secure (e.g. someone's affections) insidiously. **4** in various sports, to get (a run, the ball etc.) stealthily or fortuitously. **5** in baseball, to run to (a base) while the pitcher is delivering. ~*v.i.* **1** to take anything feloniously. **2** to go or come furtively, silently or unnoticed (*She stole out of the house; The minutes stole past; A thought stole into his head*). ~*n.* (*coll.*) **1** an act of stealing. **2** something stolen. **3** a bargain. **to steal someone's thunder 1** to spoil the effect someone had hoped to achieve with a particular idea by using the idea oneself first. **2** to attract publicity away from someone towards oneself. **stealer** *n.* **stealingly** *adv.*

stealth (stelth) *n.* furtiveness, secrecy. **by stealth** furtively, surreptitiously. **stealthy** (-thi) *a.* (*comp.* **stealthier,** *superl.* **stealthiest**). **stealthily** *adv.* **stealthiness** *n.*

steam (stēm) *n.* **1** water in the form of vapour or the gaseous form to which it is changed by boiling. **2** the visible mass of particles of water into which this condenses. **3** any vaporous exhalation. **4** power or energy generated by steam under pressure. ~*a.* powered by steam, as in *steam engine,* or relating to energy from steam under pressure. ~*v.i.* **1** to give off steam. **2** to rise in steam or vapour. **3** to move by the agency of steam (*steamed across the bay*). **4** (*sl.*) (of a gang) to push through a crowd robbing people in the process. ~*v.t.* **1** to cook (food) in steam. **2** to treat (e.g. timber) with steam for the purpose of softening. **3** to ease (an envelope) open or (a stamp) off by applying steam to the gum. **to get up steam 1** to build up steam pressure, esp. sufficient to run a steam engine. **2** to collect one's forces or energy. **3** to work oneself up into an excited state. **to let off steam** to give vent to one's feelings. **to run out of steam** to lose momentum or energy. **to steam in** (*sl.*) to initiate or join a fight, to weigh in. **to steam up** to (cause to) become covered with condensed steam. **under one's own steam** by one's own efforts, without help. **steam bath** *n.* a steam-filled room in which to cleanse oneself. **steamboat** *n.* a vessel propelled by a steam engine. **steamed up** *a.* **1** (of windows etc.) clouded by steam. **2** (*coll.*) angry, indignant. **steam engine** *n.* an engine worked by the pressure of steam on a piston moving in a cylinder etc. **steamer** *n.* **1** a person or thing that steams. **2** a vessel propelled by steam. **3** a receptacle for steaming articles, esp. for cooking food. **steam hammer** *n.* a steam-powered forging hammer. **steam iron** *n.* an electric iron with a compartment in which water is heated and then emitted as steam through holes in its base to aid pressing and ironing. **steam power** *n.* force applied by the agency of steam to machinery etc. **steamroll** *v.t.* (*N Am.*) to steamroller. **steamroller** *n.* **1** a heavy roller propelled by steam, used in road-making and road-repairing. **2** any crushing force. ~*v.t.* **1** to crush (opposition etc.) by overwhelming pressure. **2** to force (legislation through) in a legislative assembly by such means. **steamship** *n.* a ship propelled by a steam engine. **steam train** *n.* a train powered or drawn by a steam engine. **steam turbine** *n.* a machine in which steam acts on moving blades attached to a drum. **steamy** *a.* (*comp.* **steamier**, *superl.* **steamiest**) **1** of, like, full of, emitting or covered with steam. **2** (*sl.*) erotic. **steamily** *adv.* **steaminess** *n.*

stearin (stiə'rin), **stearine** *n.* **1** a usu. white crystalline glyceryl ester of stearic acid. **2** stearic acid as used for candles. **3** a fatty compound contained in the more solid animal and vegetable fats. **stearic** (stiar'-) *a.* of or relating to stearin or stearic acid. **stearic acid** *n.* a fatty acid obtained from solid animal or vegetable fats and used in making candles and soap.

steatite (stē'ətīt) *n.* soapstone or some other impure form of talc. **steatitic** (-tit'-) *a.*

steed (stēd) *n.* (*poet.*) a horse, esp. a warhorse.

steel (stēl) *n.* **1** iron combined with carbon in various proportions, remaining malleable at high temperatures and capable of being hardened by cooling. **2** a quality of hardness, toughness etc. in a person. **3** a steel rod with a roughened surface for sharpening knives. **4** (*poet.*) weaponry consisting of a sword or swords. ~*a.* **1** made of steel. **2** like steel in being e.g. hard and cold. ~*v.t.* **1** to harden (one's heart etc. against), to brace (oneself for). **2** to cover, point or face with steel. **steel**

band *n.* a type of band (orig. from the Caribbean islands) which plays percussion instruments made from oil drums. **steel grey, steel blue** *a., n.* bluish-grey like steel. **steel wool** *n.* fine steel shavings bunched together for cleaning and polishing. **steelwork** *n.* articles or parts of a structure made of steel. **steelworker** *n.* **steelworks** *n.sing. or pl.* a plant where steel is made. **steely** *a.* (*comp.* **steelier**, *superl.* **steeliest**) **1** of steel; like steel in being cold, bright, hard or grey. **2** strong, cold and ruthless or inflexible (*steely determination*). **steeliness** *n.*

steelyard (stēl'yahd) *n.* a balance with unequal arms, the article weighed being hung from the shorter arm and a weight moved along the other till they balance.

steep[1] (stēp) *a.* **1** sharply inclined, sloping at a high angle. **2** (of a rise or fall) swift, sudden. **3** (*coll.*) (of a price, demand etc.) excessive, exorbitant, unreasonable. **4** (of a story) difficult to credit, incredible. ~*n.* **1** a steep slope. **2** a precipice. **steepen** *v.t., v.i.* **steepish** *a.* **steeply** *adv.* **steepness** *n.*

steep[2] (stēp) *v.t.* **1** to soak (in liquid); to wet thoroughly. **2** to imbue, to immerse (in a subject, tradition etc.). ~*n.* **1** an act of steeping; the process of being steeped. **2** a liquid for steeping. **steeper** *n.*

steeple (stē'pəl) *n.* a lofty structure rising above the roof of a building, esp. a church tower with a spire. **steeplechase** *n.* **1** a horse race across country (orig. with a visible steeple as the finishing point) in which hedges etc. have to be jumped. **2** a track race over obstacles including hurdles and water jumps. **steeplechaser** *n.* **steeplechasing** *a., n.* **steepled** *a.* **steeplejack** *n.* a person who climbs steeples etc., to do repairs etc.

steer[1] (stiə) *v.t.* **1** to guide (a ship, aeroplane, vehicle etc.) by a rudder, wheel, handle etc. **2** to direct (one's course) in this way. **3** to guide the movement or direction of by suggestion, instruction etc. ~*v.i.* **1** to guide a ship, vehicle etc., or direct one's course by or as by this means. **2** (of a vehicle etc.) to allow itself to be steered (easily etc.). **to steer clear of** to avoid. **steerable** *a.* **steerage** (-rij) *n.* **1** the activity or process of steering. **2** (*esp. Hist.*) the part of a ship, usu. forward and on or below the main deck, allotted to passengers travelling at the lowest rate. **steerer** *n.* **steering** *n.* **steering column** *n.* a shaft in a motor vehicle carrying the steering wheel at the top. **steering committee** *n.* a committee which determines the order of business for a legislative assembly or other body. **steering wheel** *n.* the wheel which controls the rudder of a ship, or the stub axles of the front wheels of a vehicle. **steersman** *n.* (*pl.* **steersmen**) a person who steers a vessel, a helmsman.

steer[2] (stiə) *n.* a young male of the ox kind, esp. a castrated bullock.

stegosaur (steg'əsaw), **stegosaurus** (-saw'rəs) *n.* a quadrupedal herbivorous dinosaur of the

Jurassic period, with a double ridge of bony plates along its back.

stein (stīn) *n.* a large, usu. earthenware beer mug, often with a hinged lid.

stellar (stel´ə) *a.* of or relating to stars. **stellate** (-āt, -ət), **stellated** (-ātid) *a.* star-shaped, radiating.

stem¹ (stem) *n.* **1** the stock, stalk, or ascending axis of a tree, shrub, or other plant. **2** the slender stalk or peduncle of a flower, leaf etc. **3** the slender part between the body and foot of a wineglass etc. **4** the tube of a tobacco-pipe. **5** a vertical stroke e.g. in a letter or musical note. **6** the winding-shaft of a watch. **7** (*Gram.*) the main part of a noun, verb etc., to which inflectional endings etc. are affixed, or that remains unchanged when suffixes etc. are added to form derivatives. **8** (*Naut.*) the upright piece of timber or iron at the fore end of a ship to which the sides are joined. ~*v.t.* (*pres.p.* **stemming**, *past, p.p.* **stemmed**) **1** to remove the stem or stems of. **2** (of a ship) to make headway or hold its position against (the tide etc.). **to stem from** to originate in, to spring from. **stemless** *a.* **stemlike** *a.* **stemmed** *a.* **stem stitch** *n.* an embroidery stitch used for the stems of flowers etc. **stemware** *n.* (*N Am.*) glasses with stems, wineglasses.

stem² (stem) *v.t.* (*pres.p.* **stemming**, *past, p.p.* **stemmed**) **1** to draw up, to check, to hold back. **2** to dam up (a stream etc.). ~*v.i.* in skiing, to slow down by pushing the heel of one or both skis outward from the direction of travel. ~*n.* in skiing, the process of stemming, used to turn or slow down. **stem turn** *n.* in skiing, a turn executed by stemming with one ski.

stench (stench) *n.* a foul or offensive smell.

stencil (sten´sil) *n.* **1** (*also* **stencil-plate**) a thin plate of metal or other material out of which patterns have been cut for painting through the spaces on to a surface. **2** the decoration, lettering etc. produced thus. **3** a waxed sheet used for preparing a stencil with a typewriter. ~*v.t.* (*pres.p.* **stencilling**, (*N Am.*) **stenciling**, *past, p.p.* **stencilled**, (*N Am.*) **stenciled**) **1** to paint (letters, designs etc.) by means of a stencil. **2** to decorate (a wall etc.) thus. **stenciller**, (*N Am.*) **stenciler** *n.*

Sten gun (sten) *n.* a light sub-machine gun.

stenograph (sten´əgrahf) *n.* **1** a character used in shorthand. **2** a form of typewriter using stenographic characters. **stenographer** (-nog´-), **stenographist** (-nog´-) *n.* a shorthand writer. **stenography** (-nog´-) *n.* the art of writing in shorthand by hand or by machine.

Stentor (sten´taw), **stentor** *n.* a person with a loud, strong voice. **stentorian** (-taw´ri-) *a.* (of someone's voice) carrying, powerful, loud.

step (step) *v.i.* (*pres.p.* **stepping**, *past, p.p.* **stepped**) **1** to lift and set down a foot or the feet alternately, to walk a short distance in a specified direction. **2** to walk or dance slowly or with dignity. ~*v.t.* to go through, perform, or measure by stepping. ~*n.* **1** a single complete

movement of one leg in the act of walking, dancing etc. (*Take one step back*). **2** the distance traversed in this. **3** a sequence constituting a unit of movement in dancing. **4** an action or measure taken in a series directed to some end (*take steps to halt the spread of the disease*; *What's the next step?*). **5** the level-topped, block-shaped structure on which the foot is placed in ascending or descending, a single stair or a tread in a flight of stairs. **6** a rung of a ladder, a support for the foot in stepping in or out of a vehicle, a doorstep etc. **7** in climbing, a foothold cut in ice or snow. **8** a footprint. **9** the noise made by a foot in walking etc. **10** the distinctive sound or look of someone's manner of walking. **11** a short distance. **12** (*pl.*) a self-supporting stepladder with fixed or hinged prop; also called *pair of steps*. **13** a degree or grade in progress, rank or precedence. **14** one of a sequence of fixed levels on a payscale etc. **in someone's steps** following the example of someone. **in step 1** in marching, dancing etc., in conformity or time with others. **2** (*coll.*) in agreement (with). **out of step 1** not in step. **2** (*coll.*) not in agreement or harmony (with others). **step by step** gradually, with deliberation, taking one step at a time. **to mind one's step** to watch one's step. **to step down 1** to resign, retire, relinquish one's position etc. **2** to decrease the voltage etc. of. **to step in 1** to enter a house or room, esp. briefly. **2** to intervene. **3** to stand in as a substitute for someone. **to step it** (*poet.*) to dance. **to step on it** (*coll.*) to hurry, to increase speed. **to step out 1** to leave a room, house etc. briefly. **2** to be socially active. **3** (*N Am., dial., coll.*) to date, to go out (with). **4** to take longer, faster strides. **to step out of line** to depart from normal or acceptable behaviour. **to step up 1** to advance by one or more stages. **2** to increase the voltage etc. of. **3** to come forward. **to turn one's steps towards** to head for, to walk in the direction of. **to watch one's step** to take care, to guard one's behaviour. **step aerobics** *n.* a form of aerobics in which participants step on to and down from a portable plastic block. **stepladder** *n.* a ladder with flat treads or rungs. **steplike** *a.* **stepped** *a.* **stepper** *n.* **stepping stone** *n.* **1** a raised stone in a stream or swampy place on which one steps in crossing. **2** a means to an end. **stepwise** *adv.* proceeding, or arranged, in steps.

step- (step) *comb. form* denoting a family relationship resulting from a remarriage.

stepbrother (step´brŭdhə) *n.* a son of a stepparent by a marriage other than with one's mother or father.

stepchild (step´chīld) *n.* (*pl.* **stepchildren** (-children)) a child of one's husband or wife by a previous marriage.

stepdaughter (step´dawtə) *n.* a female stepchild.

stepfamily (step´famili) *n.* (*pl.* **stepfamilies**) a family that contains a stepchild or stepchildren.

stepfather (step´fahdhə) *n.* a male step-parent.

stephanotis (stefənō´tis) *n.* any tropical climbing plant of the genus *Stephanotis*, with fragrant waxy flowers.

stepmother (step´mŭdhə) *n.* a female stepparent.

step-parent (step´peərənt) *n.* the later husband or wife of a mother or father.

steppe (step) *n.* a vast plain devoid of forest, esp. in Russia and Siberia.

stepsister (step´sistə) *n.* a daughter of a stepparent by a marriage other than with one's mother or father.

stepson (step´sŭn) *n.* a male stepchild.

-ster (stə) *suf.* denoting a person belonging to a certain category, or involved in a certain activity, as in *youngster, songster, gamester, gangster.*

stereo (ster´iō, stiə´riō) *n.* (*pl.* **stereos**) **1** stereophonic reproduction, stereophony. **2** a piece of stereophonic equipment such as a record player, tape deck etc. **3** stereoscopic photography. **4** a stereoscope. **5** a stereoscopic photograph. **6** (*Print.*) (a) stereotype. ~*a.* **1** stereophonic. **2** stereoscopic.

stereo- (ster´iō, stiə´riō) *comb. form* solid, threedimensional.

stereophonic (steriōfon´ik, stiəriō-) *a.* denoting a sound-recording or reproduction system involving the use of two or more separate microphones and loudspeakers to split the sound into separate channels to create a spatial effect. **stereophonically** *adv.* **stereophony** (-of´əni) *n.*

stereoscope (ster´iōskōp, stiə´riō-) *n.* a binocular instrument for blending into one two pictures taken from slightly different positions, thus giving an effect of three dimensions. **stereoscopic** (-skop´-), **stereoscopical** *a.* **stereoscopically** *adv.* **stereoscopy** (-os´-) *n.*

stereotype (ster´iōtīp, stiə´riō-) *n.* **1** a person or thing that conforms to a standardized image. **2** a hackneyed convention, idea etc. **3** a printing-plate cast from a mould taken from movable type. ~*v.t.* **1** to fix or establish in a standard form. **2** to print from a stereotype. **3** to make a stereotype of. **stereotyped** *a.* hackneyed, unoriginal; formulaic, conventional. **stereotyper** *n.* **stereotypic** (-tip´-), **stereotypical** *a.* **stereotypically** *adv.* **stereotypy** (-tīpi) *n.*

steric (ster´ik), **sterical** (-kəl) *a.* (*Chem.*) of or relating to the spatial arrangement of atoms in a molecule.

sterile (ster´īl) *a.* **1** barren, unfruitful; not producing crops, fruit, young etc. **2** (of arguments etc.) barren of results; unproductive, pointless. **3** containing no living bacteria, microbes etc., sterilized. **4** destitute of ideas or sentiment; mentally unproductive. **sterilely** *adv.* **sterility** (stəril´-) *n.* **sterilize** (-ri-), **sterilise** *v.t.* **1** to rid of living bacteria; to make sterile. **2** to render incapable of procreation. **sterilizable** *a.* **sterilization** (-zā´shən) *n.* **sterilizer** *n.*

sterling (stœ´ling) *a.* **1** of, relating to, or in, British money (*in pounds sterling*). **2** (of coins and precious metals) of standard value, genuine, pure. **3** (of work, efforts etc.) sound, of intrinsic worth, not showy. ~*n.* **1** British (as distinct from foreign) money. **2** genuine British money. **sterling area** *n.* a group of countries that keep their reserves in sterling rather than in gold or dollars. **sterlingness** *n.* **sterling silver** *n.* silver that is 92¼ per cent pure.

stern[1] (stœn) *a.* **1** severe, grim, forbidding, austere. **2** harsh, rigid, strict. **3** ruthless, unyielding, resolute. **sternly** *adv.* **sternness** *n.*

stern[2] (stœn) *n.* **1** the hind part of a ship or boat. **2** any rear part, e.g. the rump or tail of an animal. **sterned** *a.* **sternmost** *a.* **sternpost** *n.* (*Naut.*) a timber or iron post forming the central upright of the stern and usu. carrying the rudder. **sternward** *a., adv.* **sternwards** *adv.* **sternway** *n.* (*Naut.*) the movement of a ship backwards.

sternum (stœ´nəm) *n.* (*pl.* **sternums, sterna** (-nə)) the breastbone. **sternal** *a.* **sternal rib** *n.* a true rib, attached to the breastbone, not floating.

steroid (stiə´roid, ster´-) *n.* any of a group of compounds of similar chemical structure, including sterols, bile acids and various hormones. **steroidal** *a.*

sterol (ster´ol, stiə´rol) *n.* (*Chem.*) any of various solid alcohols, such as cholesterol, ergosterol.

stertorous (stœ´tərəs) *a.* (of breathing) characterized by deep snoring or snorelike sounds. **stertorously** *adv.* **stertorousness** *n.*

stet (stet) *v.i.* (*pres.p.* **stetting**, *past, p.p.* **stetted**) in proof-reading etc., to let the original stand (cancelling a previous correction), usu. as an instruction 'let it stand'. ~*v.t.* to write 'stet' against.

stethoscope (steth´əskōp) *n.* an instrument used in listening to the movement of the heart and lungs, consisting of a disc for placing against the chest, attached to a tube dividing into two branches with earpieces. **stethoscopic** (-skop´-) *a.* **stethoscopically** *adv.* **stethoscopist** (-thos´-kəpist) *n.* **stethoscopy** (-thos´-) *n.*

stetson (stet´sən) *n.* a broad-brimmed slouch hat.

stevedore (stē´vədaw) *n.* a person whose occupation is to load and unload ships.

stew (stū) *v.t., v.i.* to cook by boiling slowly or simmering in a closed dish or pan. ~*v.i.* **1** to be stifled or oppressed by a close atmosphere. **2** (*coll.*) to be anxious or agitated; to fret or agonize (over). **3** (of tea) to become bitter from overlong brewing. **4** (*coll.*) to study hard, to sweat or pore (over). ~*n.* **1** a meat dish etc. cooked by stewing. **2** (*coll.*) a state of mental agitation or worry (*get in a stew*). **to stew in one's own juice** to suffer alone the consequences of one's folly. **stewed** *a.* **1** (of meat etc.) cooked by stewing. **2** (*coll.*) drunk.

steward (stū´əd) *n.* **1** a passengers' attendant on a ship, aircraft or train, in charge of provisions, accommodation etc. **2** any one of the officials superintending a ball, show, public meeting etc. **3** a shop steward. **4** a person employed to manage the property or affairs of another person, esp. the paid manager of a large estate or household. **5** a person in charge of provisions etc., in a college, club etc. **6** the title of certain officers of state, or of the royal household. **stewardess** (-dis) *n.* a female steward, esp. on an aircraft. **stewardship** *n.*

stick[1] (stik) *n.* **1** a shoot or branch of a tree or shrub broken or cut off. **2** a slender piece of wood or other material used, esp. specially trimmed and shaped, as a rod, staff, walking cane etc. **3** (*often in comb.*) any of various long slender implements with a specialized use, e.g. a *candlestick*, *drumstick*, *cocktail stick*, *fiddlestick*, *broomstick*, *matchstick*, or for hitting the ball with in games, e.g. a *hockey stick*, *polo stick*, *lacrosse stick*. **4** (*pl.*) in hockey, the offence of raising the stick above the shoulder. **5** a slender piece of something, e.g. *a stick of celery, rhubarb, rock*. **6** a conductor's baton. **7** the gear lever of a motor vehicle or the control rod of an aircraft. **8** a number of bombs or paratroops dropped in succession. **9** (*Naut.*) a mast, a spar. **10** (*coll.*) blame, hostile criticism (*got a lot of stick for his opinions*). **11** (*coll.*) a piece of wood representing an item of furniture etc. (*one or two sticks of furniture*). **12** a person, esp. someone elderly and old-fashioned. **13** (*coll.*) (**the sticks**) areas remote from the city, esp. as rustic and unsophisticated, or inaccessible. **14** (*pl., Austral., coll.*) goalposts. ~*v.t.* (*past, p.p.* **sticked**) to provide (a plant) with sticks for support. **stick insect** *n.* an insect belonging to the Phasmidae, which resembles dry twigs. **stickless** *a.* **sticklike** *a.*

stick[2] (stik) *v.t.* (*past, p.p.* **stuck** (stŭk)) **1** to thrust the point of (in, into, through etc.). **2** to pierce, to stab. **3** to fix or insert (in, into) (*stuck posts into the ground*). **4** to fix or impale on or as on, by or as by, a point. **5** to thrust (out, up, through etc.). **6** to set with pointed objects (*an orange stuck with cloves*). **7** to cause to adhere (*sticking stamps on envelopes; stuck a poster on the wall*). **8** (*coll.*) to put (something somewhere) (*Stick those boxes in the spare room*). **9** (*coll.*) to tolerate, endure. **10** (*sl.*) to try to put the blame for (something on someone) (*You can't stick that one on me*). ~*v.i.* **1** to be inserted or thrust, to poke (into). **2** to protrude, project, or stand (up, out etc.). **3** to become fixed, to adhere (*These stamps don't stick very well*). **4** to remain attached (to) (*The burrs stuck to her clothing*). **5** to be inseparable, to be constant (to), to stay (with) (*Stick with me; She stuck to him loyally*). **6** to endure or persist (*The image stuck in her mind*). **7** to stay, remain (*I'll stick here for a while*). **8** to persist, to persevere (at) (*I stuck at that job for four years*). **9** to be stopped, hindered, or checked (*We got so far, then stuck*). **10** to have scruples or misgivings, to hesitate (at). **stick 'em up!** (*coll.*) hands up! **to be stuck 1** to be unable to progress further. **2** to be confined (somewhere) (*I don't want to be stuck in the house all day*). **to be stuck**

for to lack, to need (*I'm a bit stuck for cash*). **to be stuck on** (*coll.*) to be very keen on, or infatuated with. **to be stuck with** (*coll.*) to have no choice but to have, to be landed with (*I'm stuck with a husband who won't dance*). **to stick around** (*coll.*) to remain in the vicinity. **to stick at it** to persevere. **to stick at nothing** not to be deterred or feel scruples. **to stick by 1** to stay close to. **2** to remain faithful to, to support. **to stick fast 1** to adhere strongly. **2** to be fixed or trapped immovably. **to stick in one's throat** to be repugnant to one, to be against one's principles. **to stick it on 1** (*coll.*) to overcharge. **2** (*coll.*) to exaggerate. **to stick it out** to put up with something as long as is demanded of one. **to stick one's chin out** to be resolute, to show determination. **to stick one's neck out 1** (*coll.*) to invite trouble. **2** (*coll.*) to take a risk. **to stick out 1** to (cause to) protrude. **2** to be conspicuous or obvious. **to stick out a mile** to be only too obvious. **to stick out for** to demand, to insist upon. **to stick together** to remain loyal to one another. **to stick to it** to persevere. **to stick to someone's fingers** (*coll.*) (of money) to be embezzled by someone. **to stick up 1** to put up, to erect. **2** to stand up, to be prominent. **3** to paste or post up. **4** (*coll.*) to hold up; to rob at gunpoint. **to stick up for** to take the part of, to defend. **stickability** (-bil´-) *n.* (*coll.*) perseverance, staying power. **sticker** *n.* **1** an adhesive label or poster. **2** a person or thing that sticks. **3** a conscientious, persevering person. **4** an importunate person. **sticking** *n., a.* **sticking place**, **sticking point** *n.* **1** the place where a screw etc., becomes fixed or jammed. **2** the point at which difficulties arise, and prevent progress. **sticking plaster** *n.* an adhesive plaster for wounds etc. **stick-in-the-mud** *a.* dull, slow, unprogressive. ~*n.* an unenterprising person. **stickpin** *n.* (*NAm.*) a tiepin. **stick-up** *n.* (*sl.*) an armed robbery. **sticky** *a.* (*comp.* **stickier**, *superl.* **stickiest**) **1** tending to stick, adhesive. **2** viscous, glutinous. **3** (*coll.*) difficult, painful. **stickily** *adv.* **stickiness** *n.* **stickybeak** *n.* (*Austral., New Zeal., sl.*) an inquisitive person, a nosy parker. ~*v.i.* to be inquisitive, to pry. **sticky end** *n.* (*coll.*) a disagreeable end or death. **sticky-fingered** *a.* (*coll.*) given to stealing. **sticky wicket** *n.* **1** a damp cricket pitch which is difficult to bat on. **2** (*coll.*) a difficult situation. **stuck-up** *a.* puffed up, conceited, giving oneself airs.

stickle (stik´əl) *v.i.* to contend pertinaciously (for some trifle). **stickler** *n.* a person who argues contentiously (for something, esp. a nice point of style, punctuation or etiquette).

stickleback (stik´əlbak) *n.* a small spiny-backed, freshwater fish, esp. *Gasterosteus aculeatus*.

stiff (stif) *a.* **1** rigid, not easily bent or moved. **2** not pliant, not flexible, not yielding, not working freely. **3** hard to deal with or accomplish; difficult. **4** (of a person or their manner) constrained, not easy, not graceful, awkward, formal, precise, affected. **5** obstinate, stubborn, firm, persistent (*stiff resistance*). **6** severe, harsh, strong (*a stiff fine*; *encountered a stiff breeze*). **7** (of muscles or limbs) painful to use because of immediately previous, esp. unwonted, exercise. **8** (*used predic.*, *coll.*) to an intense degree (*worried stiff*; *bored stiff*; *frozen stiff*). **9** (of liquor) strong. **10** (of a mixture etc.) not fluid, thick and tenacious, viscous. ~*n*. (*sl.*) a corpse. **stiff with** (*coll.*) packed with, full of (*stiff with holidaymakers*). **stiffen** *v.t.*, *v.i.* **stiffening** *n.* **stiffish** *a.* **stiffly** *adv.* **stiff neck** *n.* rheumatism affecting the muscles of the neck. **stiff-necked** *a.* stubborn, self-willed. **stiffness** *n.* **stiff upper lip** *n.* fortitude in adversity (*keep a stiff upper lip*).

stifle (stī´fəl) *v.t.*, *v.i.* to smother, to suffocate; to kill or die by suffocation (*nearly stifled by the heat*; *We'll stifle if we stay indoors*). ~*v.t.* **1** to suppress (*I had to stifle a yawn*). **2** to stamp out, quash, extinguish. **stifler** *n.* **stifling** *a.* (of heat, the atmosphere etc.) choking, suffocating. **stiflingly** *adv.*

stigma (stig´mə) *n.* (*pl.* **stigmas, stigmata** (-mətə, -mah´tə)) **1** a mark of discredit or infamy. **2** a distinguishing mark (of), a typical characteristic (of). **3** (*Bot.*) the part of a pistil of a flower that receives the pollen. **4** (*pl.*) in Christian dogma, the marks left on Christ's body from the process of crucifixion, believed also to have been divinely imprinted on the body of St Francis of Assisi and other saintly people. **5** a mark or spot on a butterfly's wing. **6** (*Med.*) a visible sign of a disease. **7** an insect's spiracle. **stigmatic** (-mat´-) *a.*, *n.* **stigmatically** *adv.* **stigmatize** (stig´mətīz), **stigmatise** *v.t.* **1** to represent (as something disgraceful or unworthy). **2** to produce stigmata on. **stigmatization** (-zā´shən) *n.*

stile[1] (stīl) *n.* a series of steps or other contrivance by which one may get over a wall etc.

Usage note See note under STYLE.

stile[2] (stīl) *n.* a vertical piece in the frame of a panelled door or wainscot, or in a window frame.

Usage note See note under STYLE.

stiletto (stilet´ō) *n.* (*pl.* **stilettos**) **1** a small dagger. **2** a pointed instrument for making eyelet-holes etc. **3** a stiletto heel. **4** a shoe with a stiletto heel. ~*v.t.* (*3rd pers. sing. pres.* **stilettoes**, *pres.p.* **stilettoing**, *past*, *p.p.* **stilettoed**) to stab with a stiletto. **stiletto heel** *n.* a high, very tapered heel for a woman's shoe.

still[1] (stil) *a.*, *adv.* **1** at rest, motionless. **2** (of sea, weather, air etc.) quiet, calm. **3** (of e.g. an audience) silent, noiseless, hushed. **4** (of drinks) not effervescent or sparkling. ~*n.* **1** stillness, calm, quiet (*in the still of the evening*). **2** an ordinary photograph, or one from a single frame of a cinema film for record or publicity purposes. ~*adv.* **1** without moving. **2** as previously, without

stopping or altering (*still jogs several miles a day*; *They're still in love*). **3** even to this or that time, yet (*It's still dark*; *happened when I was still a child*). **4** nevertheless, all the same, in spite of that (*I'm still unconvinced*; *Still, there are advantages*). ~*v.t.* **1** to quiet, to calm. **2** to silence. **3** to appease. **still and all** (*coll.*) nevertheless, in spite of that. **stillbirth** *n.* **1** the birth of a dead child. **2** a child born dead. **stillborn** *a.* **still life** *n.* (*pl.* **still lifes**) the representation of fruit, flowers and other inanimate objects in painting; a painting of this kind. **stillness** *n.* **stilly** (stil´li) *adv.*

still[2] (stil) *n.* a vessel or apparatus employed in distillation, esp. of spirits, consisting of a boiler, a tubular condenser or worm enclosed in a refrigerator, and a receiver. ~*v.t.* to distil. **still room** *n.* **1** a room for distilling. **2** a storeroom for liquors, preserves etc.

stillage (stil´ij) *n.* a frame, stool, bench etc., for placing things on for draining, waiting to be packed up etc.

Stillson (stil´sən), **Stillson wrench** *n.* a powerful wrench whose jaws tighten with increased pressure.

stilt (stilt) *n.* **1** a pole having a rest for the foot, used in pairs, to raise a person above the ground in walking. **2** any of a number of tall supports or columns for raising a building above the ground. **3** a long-legged three-toed wading bird related to the plover. **stilted** *a.* **1** raised on or as if on stilts. **2** (of literary style etc.) bombastic, inflated. **stiltedly** *adv.* **stiltedness** *n.*

Stilton® (stil´tən) *n.* a rich white or blue veined cheese orig. sold at Stilton, in Cambridgeshire.

stimulus (stim´ūləs) *n.* (*pl.* **stimuli** (-lī)) **1** something that stimulates one to activity, or energizes one; an incitement, a spur. **2** something that excites reaction in a living organism. **stimulant** *a.* **1** serving to stimulate. **2** producing a quickly diffused and transient increase in physiological activity. ~*n.* something that stimulates, such as a drug or alcoholic drink. **stimulate** *v.t.* **1** to rouse to action or greater exertion. **2** to spur on, to incite. **3** to excite (organic action). ~*v.i.* to act as a stimulus. **stimulating** *a.* **stimulatingly** *adv.* **stimulation** (-lā´shən) *n.* **stimulative** (-lətiv) *a.* **stimulator** *n.* **stimulatory** (-lətəri) *a.*

Usage note The meanings of the nouns *stimulus* and *stimulant* overlap, but *stimulant* is usual for something that stimulates physiological activity (as alcohol or drugs), and *stimulus* for an incitement or incentive.

stimy STYMIE.

sting (sting) *n.* **1** a sharp-pointed defensive or offensive organ, often conveying poison, with which certain insects, scorpions and plants are armed. **2** the act of stinging. **3** the wound or pain so caused. **4** any acute pain, ache, smart, stimulus etc. **5** pungent or forceful quality. **6** (*sl.*) a swindle. ~*v.t.* (*past*, *p.p.* **stung** (stŭng)) **1** to pierce or wound with a sting. **2** to cause acute physical or mental pain to (*was stung by his criticism*). **3** to goad (into). **4** (*coll.*) to cheat, to overcharge. ~*v.i.* **1** to have or use a sting (*Do those insects sting?*). **2** to have an acute and smarting pain. **stinger** *n.* **1** something that stings, such as a nettle, insect, snake etc. **2** a smarting blow. **stinging nettle** *n.* a nettle, *Urtica dioica*, covered with stinging hairs. **sting in the tail** *n.* an unexpected or ironic twist to finish with. **stingless** *a.* **stingray** *n.* a tropical ray with a venomous spine on its tail.

stingy (stin´ji) *a.* (*comp.* **stingier**, *superl.* **stingiest**) tight-fisted, mean, parsimonious, niggardly. **stingily** *adv.* **stinginess** *n.*

stink (stingk) *v.i.* (*past* **stank** (stangk), **stunk** (stŭngk), *p.p.* **stunk**) **1** to emit a strong, offensive smell. **2** (*coll.*) to have an evil reputation. **3** (*coll.*) to smack of disreputable dealings; to be scandalous. ~*v.t.* to drive (someone out of a place) by a stink. ~*n.* **1** a strong, offensive smell, a stench. **2** (*sl.*) a disagreeable exposure, a scandal, a row. **like stink** (*sl.*) intensely, very hard. **to raise a stink 1** (*sl.*) to complain. **2** (*sl.*) to stir up trouble, esp. adverse publicity. **to stink out 1** to drive out by creating an offensive smell. **2** to cause (a room etc.) to stink. **stink bomb** *n.* a small glass sphere which releases a foul-smelling liquid when broken. **stinker** *n.* **1** a stinking person, animal etc. **2** (*sl.*) an unpleasant person or thing. **3** (*sl.*) a difficult task or problem. **stinkhorn** *n.* an evil-smelling fungus, esp. *Phallus impudicus*. **stinking** *a.* **1** emitting an offensive smell. **2** (*coll.*) offensive, repulsive, objectionable. **3** (*coll.*) extremely drunk. ~*adv.* (*coll.*) extremely, very (*They're stinking rich*). **stinkingly** *adv.* **stinky** *a.* (*comp.* **stinkier**, *superl.* **stinkiest**).

Usage note In standard English, the preferred past tense of *stink* is *stank*, not *stunk*.

stint (stint) *v.t.* **1** to give or allow (someone) money, food etc. scantily or grudgingly. **2** to supply (food etc.) scantily or grudgingly. ~*v.i.* to be too sparing or parsimonious (of a certain commodity). ~*n.* **1** limit, bound, restriction (*gave her services without stint*). **2** an allotted amount, quantity, turn of work etc. (*when you've done your stint*). **3** a small sandpiper, esp. the dunlin. **stintingly** *adv.* **stintless** *a.* **1** unstinted. **2** abundant.

stipe (stīp) *n.* (*Bot.*, *Zool.*) a stalk, stem or stemlike support.

stipend (stī´pend) *n.* a periodical payment for services rendered, a salary, esp. of a member of the clergy. **stipendiary** (-pen´-) *a.* performing services for or receiving a stipend. ~*n.* (*pl.* **stipendiaries**) a person receiving a stipend, esp. a paid magistrate. **stipendiary magistrate** *n.* a magistrate who receives a salary.

stipple (stip´əl) *v.t.* **1** to engrave, paint or draw by means of dots or light dabs instead of lines etc. **2** to roughen the surface of (wall paint, cement

etc.). ~*v.i.* to use dots or light dabs in engraving, painting or drawing. ~*n.* **1** the technique or work of stippling. **2** the effect produced by stippling. **stippler** *n.* **stippling** *n.*

stipulate (stip´ūlāt) *v.t.* to lay down or specify as an essential condition to an agreement, contract or bargain. ~*v.i.* **1** to make a specific demand (for). **2** to settle terms. **stipulation** (-lā´shən) *n.* **stipulator** *n.*

stir[1] (stœ) *v.t.* (*pres.p.* **stirring**, *past*, *p.p.* **stirred**) **1** to move a spoon etc. round and round in (a liquid or liquid mixture) to blend the ingredients. **2** to cause to move, to agitate, to disturb. **3** to move vigorously, to bestir (oneself etc.). **4** to rouse (up), to excite, to animate, to inflame (*stirred their imaginations*; *were stirred to fury*). ~*v.i.* **1** to move, to be in motion, not to be still. **2** to wake up, or get up after sleep. **3** (*esp. with neg.*) to go (out of the house etc.). **4** (*coll.*) to cause trouble by gossip or subversive innuendo. ~*n.* **1** an act of stirring (*give it another stir*). **2** agitation, commotion, bustle, excitement (*caused a stir in the community*). **3** (*with neg.*) a movement (*not a stir*). **to stir in** to mix (an ingredient) into a mixture by stirring. **to stir one's stumps** (*coll.*) to become active, to get going. **to stir the blood** to rouse one emotionally, to evoke strong feelings, e.g. of patriotism. **to stir up 1** to mix by stirring vigorously. **2** to incite (trouble, rebellion etc.). **3** to agitate, to excite, to arouse. **stir-fry** *v.t.* (*3rd pers. sing. pres.* **stir-fries**, *pres.p.* **stir-frying**, *past*, *p.p.* **stir-fried**) to cook by the Chinese method of frying in hot oil while stirring and tossing. ~*n.* (*pl.* **stir-fries**) a stir-fried meal or dish. **stirless** *a.* **stirrer** *n.* **1** a person or thing that stirs. **2** (*coll.*) a person who likes fomenting ill feeling, a troublemaker. **stirring** *a.* **1** moving. **2** animating, rousing, exciting, stimulating. ~*n.pl.* initial signs or indications of something (*the first stirrings of a renaissance*; *felt the stirrings of an unfamiliar emotion*). **stirringly** *adv.*

stir[2] (stœ) *n.* (*sl.*) prison. **stir-crazy** *a.* (*sl.*) mentally unhinged as a result of prolonged imprisonment or confinement.

stirrup (stir´əp) *n.* a horse rider's foot support, usu. consisting of an iron loop suspended from the saddle by a strap. **stirrup cup** *n.* a parting cup, orig. given to someone about to leave on horseback. **stirrup pump** *n.* a portable hand pump with a length of hose, to be worked by one or two people, for extinguishing small fires.

stitch (stich) *n.* **1** a single pass of the needle in sewing. **2** a single turn of the wool or thread round a needle in knitting, crocheting etc. **3** the link of thread, wool etc., thus inserted. **4** a sequence of moves in knitting or sewing that produces a distinctive pattern (*Can you teach me cable stitch?*). **5** (*with neg.*) the least item of clothing (*emerged without a stitch on*). **6** a sharp intense pain in the side, brought on by running or other exercise. ~*v.t.*, *v.i.* to sew. **in stitches** helpless with laughter. **to stitch up 1** to sew together or mend. **2** (*sl.*) to incriminate by informing on or concocting evidence against. **stitcher** *n.* **stitchery** *n.* **stitch in time** *n.* a timely repair or remedy. **stitchless** *a.* **stitch-up** *n.* (*sl.*) **1** an act of incriminating someone for a crime. **2** (*derog.*) an act of securing a desirable outcome for oneself, esp. unfairly. **stitchwort** *n.* any plant of the genus *Stellaria*, esp. *Stellaria holostea*, with starry white flowers, common in hedges.

stoat (stōt) *n.* the ermine, *Mustela erminea*, esp. in its brownish summer coat.

stock (stok) *n.* **1** the aggregate of goods ready for sale or distribution. **2** a supply of anything, available for use (*the stock of data*). **3** equipment or raw material for use in the course of business etc. (*new rolling stock*; *run down stationery stocks*). **4** the beasts, or livestock, on a farm, or implements of husbandry and produce. **5** livestock when fattened for slaughter, fatstock. **6** the capital of a corporate company divided into shares entitling the holders to a proportion of the profits. **7** (*pl.*) the shares of such capital. **8** money lent to a government represented by certificates entitling the holders to fixed interest; the right to receive this interest. **9** (*N Am.*) a stock company, a repertory company, or its repertoire. **10** one's reputation or standing (*My stock is low enough as it is*). **11** any cruciferous plant of the genus *Matthiola* or *Malcolmia*, esp. the stock-gilly-flower. **12** a plant that receives a graft. **13** the trunk or main stem of a tree or other plant. **14 a** a family, a breed, a line of descent (*came of Manx stock*). **b** any analogous system of branches emerging from a main stem, such as a distinct group of languages. **15** liquor from boiled meat, bones etc., used as a basis for soup, sauce, gravy etc. **16** (*pl.*) a frame of timber with holes in which the ankles, and sometimes also the wrists, of petty offenders were formerly confined as a punishment. **17** (*pl.*) a timber framework on which a vessel rests during building. **18** the principal supporting or holding part of anything, the handle, block, base, body etc. **19** a band of silk, leather etc., worn as a cravat e.g. by horse-riders. **20** solid brick pressed in a mould. ~*a.* **1** kept in stock (*stock sizes*). **2** habitually used, standing, permanent (*the stock reply*). ~*v.t.* **1** to provide (e.g. shops) with goods, (farms) with livestock etc. **2** to keep (goods) in stock. **3** to fit with a handle, butt etc. **in stock** available to be sold immediately. **on the stocks** in preparation for construction. **out of stock** not available for sale, not in stock. **to stock up** to take in supplies, lay in stock. **to take stock 1** to make an inventory of goods etc. on hand. **2** to survey one's position, prospects etc. **3** to examine, to form an estimate (of a person, etc.). **stockbreeder** *n.* a farmer who raises livestock. **stockbreeding** *n.* **stockbroker** *n.* a person engaged in the purchase and sale of stocks on commission. **stockbrokerage** *n.* **stockbroker belt** *n.* (*coll., usu. derog.*) the prosperous commuter area around London. **stock-broking** *n.* **stock car** *n.* **1** a production (saloon) car modified for racing. **2** (*N Am.*) a railway truck for transporting livestock. **stock company** *n.* (*pl.* **stock companies**) (*N Am.*) a repertory company. **stock dove** *n.* a European wild pigeon, *Columba oenas*, smaller and darker than the ring-dove. **stocker** *n.* **Stock Exchange** *n.* **1** (*also* **stock exchange**) the place where stocks or shares are publicly bought and sold. **2** the dealers who work there. **stock-gillyflower** *n.* a fragrant, bright-flowered herbaceous plant, *Matthiola incana*. **stockholder** *n.* a proprietor of stock in the public funds or shares in a stock company. **stockholding** *n.* **stock-in-trade** *n.* **1** goods, tools and other requisites of a trade etc. **2** resources, capabilities. **stockist** *n.* a shopkeeper etc. who keeps certain goods in stock. **stockjobber** *n.* **1** (*Hist.*) a dealer who speculated in stocks so as to profit by fluctuations of price and acted as an intermediary between the buying and selling stockbrokers. **2** (*N Am.*) a broker. **stockless** *a.* **stocklist** *n.* a publication giving current prices etc. of stocks. **stockman** *n.* (*pl.* **stockmen**) a man in charge of livestock. **stock market** *n.* a Stock Exchange or the business transacted there. **stockpile** *n.* an accumulated reserve of goods, weapons etc. ~*v.t.* to accumulate (commodities, esp. reserves of raw materials). **stockpiler** *n.* **stockpot** *n.* a pot for making or storing stock for soup, sauces etc. **stockroom** *n.* a room for storing the stock of goods available for sale. **stock-still** *a., adv.* motionless. **stocktaking** *n.* **1** the job of preparing an inventory of the stock in a shop, warehouse etc. **2** the activity of reviewing one's position and assets. **stocktake** *v.i.* **stocktaker** *n.* **stocky** *a.* (*comp.* **stockier**, *superl.* **stockiest**) thickset, short and stout, stumpy. **stockily** *adv.* **stockiness** *n.* **stockyard** *n.* an enclosure with pens etc., for cattle at market etc.

stockade (stokād´) *n.* **1** a line or enclosure of posts or stakes. **2** (*N Am.*) a prison, esp. a military one. ~*v.t.* to surround or fortify with a stockade.

stockfish (stok´fish) *n.* (*pl.* **stockfish**) cod, ling etc. split open and dried in the sun without salting.

stocking (stok´ing) *n.* **1** (*usu. in pl.*) a close-fitting covering for the foot and leg. **2** (*esp. N Am.*) a sock. **3** a close-fitting garment (*a bodystocking*). **4** a horse's lower leg when of a contrasting colour, esp. white. **5** CHRISTMAS STOCKING (under CHRISTMAS). **in one's stocking feet/ soles** without one's shoes, e.g. when having one's height measured. **stockinet** (-net´), **stockinette** *n.* an elastic knitted material for undergarments etc. **stockinged** *a.* **in one's stockinged feet/ soles** in one's stocking feet. **stocking filler**, (*N Am.*) **stocking stuffer** *n.* a gift suitable for inclusion in a Christmas stocking. **stockingless** *a.* **stocking stitch** *n.* in knitting, alternate rows of plain and purl stitches, giving a smooth surface on one side..

stodge (stoj) *n.* (*coll.*) **1** heavy, starchy, filling food, esp. steamed or baked pudding. **2** turgid literary matter. **3** anything boring, a dull person etc. **stodgy** *a.* (*comp.* **stodgier**, *superl.* **stodgiest**) **1** (of food) heavy, stiff, indigestible, lumpy. **2** dull, turgid, matter-of-fact. **stodgily** *adv.* **stodginess** *n.*

stoep (stoop) *n.* (*S Afr.*) an open, roofed platform in front of a house, a veranda.

stogy (stō´gi), **stogie** *n.* (*pl.* **stogies**) (*N Am.*) **1** a long cheaply made cigar. **2** a heavy boot.

Stoic (stō´ik) *n.* **1** a philosopher or member of the school founded by Zeno, *c.* 308 BC, teaching that virtue is the highest good, and that the passions and appetites should be rigidly subdued. **2** (**stoic**) a stoical, long-suffering person. ~*a.* **1** of or relating to the Stoics. **2** stoical. **stoical** *a.* resigned, impassive. **stoically** *adv.* **stoicism** (-sizm) *n.* **1** (**Stoicism**) the philosophy of the Stoics. **2** indifference to pleasure or pain. **3** fortitude in pain or adversity.

stoke (stōk) *v.t.* to tend (a furnace, esp. of a steam engine). ~*v.i.* to act as stoker. **to stoke up 1** to feed a fire or furnace with fuel. **2** to fill oneself with food. **stokehole** *n.* **1** the mouth of a furnace. **2** an aperture in a blast furnace etc. for a stirring tool and adding fuel. **stoker** *n.* a person who stokes a furnace.

STOL (stol) *n.* a system by which aircraft take off and land over a short distance.

stole¹ (stōl) *n.* **1** a broad band of fabric, fur etc. worn round the neck and shoulders by women. **2** a narrow band of silk etc. worn over both shoulders as an ecclesiastical vestment by priests.

stole², **stolen** STEAL.

stolid (stol´id) *a.* dull, impassive, phlegmatic; lacking emotion, or showing none. **stolidity** (-lid´-), **stolidness** *n.* **stolidly** *adv.*

stoma (stō´mə) *n.* (*pl.* **stomas, stomata** (-mətə)) **1** (*Bot.*) an aperture for respiration in a leaf. **2** a surgically made opening in the abdominal wall. **stomal** *a.*

stomach (stŭm´ək) *n.* **1** the digestive cavity, formed by a dilatation of the alimentary canal, or (in certain animals) one of several such cavities. **2** the belly, the abdomen; a prominent belly. **3** appetite (for food) or an inclination or liking (for some enterprise). ~*v.t.* **1** to accept as palatable. **2** to put up with, to brook. **stomach-ache** *n.* an abdominal pain. **stomachal** *a.* **stomachful** *n.* (*pl.* **stomachfuls**). **stomachic** (-mak´-) *a.*, *n.* **stomach pump** *n.* a syringe for withdrawing the contents of the stomach, or for forcing liquid etc. into it. **stomach upset** *n.* a spell of nausea, diarrhoea or abdominal pain caused by a disorder of the digestive system.

stomal, stomata STOMA.

stomp (stomp) *v.i.* to stamp with the feet. ~*n.* **1** a lively jazz dance involving heavy stamping of the feet. **2** an early jazz composition with a heavily stressed rhythm. **stomper** *n.*

stone (stōn) *n.* **1** the non-metallic mineral material of which rock is composed. **2** an esp.

small piece of this, a pebble, cobble, or chip etc. used e.g. in road-making. **3** rock as material for building, paving etc., often specifically limestone or sandstone. **4** (*in comb.*) a piece of stone shaped and prepared for a specific purpose, e.g. *a millstone, grindstone, tombstone, curling stone* etc. **5** a gem, a precious stone. **6** a thing like stone in its hardness or form (*a hailstone*). **7** the hard case of the kernel in a drupe or stone fruit (*peach stones*). **8** (*Med.*) **a** a concretion in a bodily organ, a calculus (*gallstones; a kidney stone*). **b** the condition of a person with such a concretion. **9** a stony meteorite, an aerolite. **10** (*usu pl.*) a testicle. **11** (*pl.* **stone**) a unit of weight equivalent to 14 lb. (6.35 kg). **12** a greyish-brown colour. ~*a.* **1** made of stone or a hard material like stone. **2** of a greyish-brown colour. ~*v.t.* **1** to pelt with stones. **2** to put to death by this means. **3** to remove stones from (fruit). **4** to face, wall or pave with stone. **to cast/ throw stones** to go in for criticizing people. **to cast/ throw the first stone** to be the first to accuse or criticize, though not oneself blameless. **to leave no stone unturned** to use all available means to effect an object. **Stone Age** *n.* the period in which primitive humans used implements of stone, not metal. **stonechat** *n.* the wheatear, *Saxicola torquata.* **stone circle** *n.* a ring of prehistoric monoliths. **stone-cold** *a.* completely cold. **stone-cold sober** *a.* utterly sober. **stonecrop** *n.* any species of *Sedum*, esp. *S. acre.* **stone curlew** *n.* a curlew-like bird, *Burhinus oedicnemus*, frequenting stony open ground, or any bird of the family Burhinidae. **stonecutter** *n.* a person whose occupation is to cut stones for building etc. **stonecutting** *n.* **stoned** *a.* (*sl.*) under the influence of drugs or alcohol. **stone-dead** *a.* completely dead. **stone-deaf** *a.* completely deaf. **stone fruit** *n.* a fruit with seeds covered by a hard shell, such as peaches, plums etc., a drupe. **stoneground** *a.* (of flour) ground between millstones. **stonehatch** *n.* the ringed plover. **stoneless** *a.* **stonemason** *n.* a person who dresses stones or builds with stone. **stonemasonry** *n.* **stoner** *n.* **stone's throw, stone's cast** *n.* a short distance. **stonewall** *v.t.* to obstruct (e.g. parliamentary business, a discussion etc.) by giving lengthy or evasive answers etc. ~*v.i.* **1** to behave obstructively in this way. **2** in cricket, to stay in batting without trying to make runs. **stoneware** *n.* pottery made from clay and flint or a hard siliceous clay. **stone-washed** *a.* (of clothes, denim etc.) given a faded surface by the abrasive action of small pieces of pumice. **stonework** *n.* masonry. **stony** *a.* (*comp.* **stonier**, *superl.* **stoniest**) **1** of or relating to, made or consisting of, abounding in or resembling stone. **2** (of a meteorite) composed of silicates and other non-metals. **3** hard, cruel, pitiless; incapable of feeling or emotion. **4** obdurate, perverse. **stonily** *adv.* **stoniness** *n.* **stony-broke** *a.* (*sl.*) destitute or nearly destitute of money. **stony-hearted** *a.* unfeeling.

stonkered (stong'kəd) *a.* (*Austral., New Zeal., sl.*) totally exhausted. **stonking** *a.* (*sl.*) great, impressive. *~adv.* extremely.

stood STAND.

stooge (stooj) *n.* **1** a butt, a confederate, a decoy. **2** a subordinate. **3** a meek or complaisant person. *~v.i.* **1** to act as a stooge (for). **2** to move or potter (about, around) aimlessly.

stook (stuk) *n.* a bundle of sheaves set up on end. *~v.t.* to set up in stooks.

stool (stool) *n.* **1** a seat without a back, for one person, usu. with three or four legs. **2** a low bench for kneeling or resting the feet on; a footstool. **3** (*esp. pl.*) the faeces. **4** the stump of a timber tree from which shoots are thrown up. **5** a plant or stock from which young plants are produced by layering etc. **6** (*NAm.*) a decoy bird used in hunting. *~v.i.* (of a plant) to shoot out stems from the root. **stoolball** *n.* a game like cricket, played in S England. **stoolie** *n.* (*NAm., sl.*) a stool-pigeon, an informer. **stool-pigeon** *n.* **1** a person used as a decoy. **2** an informer for the police.

stoop[1] (stoop) *v.i.* **1** to bend the body downward and forward. **2** to have a habitual forward inclination of the head and shoulders. **3** to condescend, to lower or bring oneself down (to some demeaning act). **4** (of a hawk etc.) to pounce, to swoop towards a prey. *~v.t.* to incline (one's head, shoulders etc.) downwards and forwards. *~n.* **1** the act of stooping. **2** a habitual inclination of the shoulders etc. **3** the swoop of a bird on its prey. **stoopingly** *adv.*

stoop[2] (stoop) *n.* (*NAm.*) a flight of steps, a porch, or a small veranda in front of a house.

stop (stop) *v.t.* (*pres.p.* **stopping**, *past, p.p.* **stopped**) **1** to cause to cease moving, going, working, or acting. **2** to impede; to hinder; to prevent (from doing something). **3** to prevent the doing or performance of. **4** to discontinue (*stopped talking*; *stopped work*). **5** to cause to cease action; to foil or defeat. **6 a** in boxing, to knock out, or defeat with a knockout. **b** to parry (a blow). **7** to close by filling or obstructing, to staunch, to plug (up). **8** to fill (a crack or a cavity); to put a filling in (a tooth etc.). **9** to keep back, to cut off, to suspend (wages etc.). **10** to instruct a bank to withhold payment on (a cheque). **11** (*Mus.*) to press (a string), close (an aperture etc.) so as to alter the pitch. **12** to remove leaves or buds from (a plant) to encourage thick growth, to pinch back. **13** to make (something, e.g. a clock) cease working. *~v.i.* **1** to come to an end; to discontinue, to cease or desist. **2** to halt; to pause; to come to rest. **3** (*coll.*) to stay, to remain temporarily, to sojourn (*Why not stop here for the night?*). *~n.* **1** an act of stopping or state of being stopped, a cessation, a pause, an interruption. **2** a regular halt for a bus or train, a place where passengers get on or off. **3** a punctuation mark indicating a pause, esp. a full point; in telegrams etc., a full point. **4** a block, peg, pin etc. used to

stop the movement of something at a particular point. **5** (*Mus.*) the pressing down of a string, closing of an aperture etc., effecting a change of pitch. **6** a key, lever or other device employed in this. **7** a set of pipes in an organ having tones of a distinct quality. **8** a knob bringing these into play. **9** a perforated diaphragm for regulating the passage of light in a camera. **10** the diameter of a camera lens. **11** a device for reducing the diameter of a lens. **12** a unit of alteration of exposure or aperture such that a reduction of one stop is the equivalent of halving it. **13** a sound produced by closure of the mouth or throat, a plosive or mute consonant. **to pull out all the stops 1** to make the utmost effort. **2** to play at maximum volume. **to put a stop to** to cause to cease, esp. abruptly. **to stop at nothing** to be ruthless, to be ready to do anything to achieve one's ends. **to stop by** to break one's journey (at a particular place) for a visit. **to stop dead** to stop short. **to stop down** in photography, to reduce the aperture of (a lens) by means of a diaphragm. **to stop off/ over** to break one's journey (at a particular place). **to stop one's ears 1** to put one's fingers in one's ears so as not to hear. **2** to refuse to listen. **to stop out 1** to stay out. **2** in printing etc., to cover (part of a surface) to prevent printing, etching etc. **stopcock** *n.* a valve operated externally to stop the flow of fluid in a pipe. **stopgap** *n.* a temporary substitute or expedient. **stop-go** *a.* (of a policy etc.) alternately active and inactive or stimulating and restrictive. **stop lamp** *n.* a rear light on a vehicle showing when the brake is being used. **stop light** *n.* **1** a traffic light at red. **2** a stop lamp. **stopoff, stopover** *n.* a break in a journey. **stoppable** *a.* **stoppage** (-ij) *n.* **1** the state of being hindered or stopped. **2** a deduction from pay. **3** a cessation of work, as in a strike. **stopper** *n.* **1** a plug for closing a bottle etc. **2** a person or thing that stops, or stops something. *~v.t.* to close or secure with a stopper. **to put a stopper on 1** to prevent the continuance of. **2** to keep (someone) quiet. **stopping** *n.* **1** a filling in a tooth or material for this; the dental operation itself. **2** plastic material for filling holes and cracks in wood etc. before painting. **stopple** (stop'əl) *n.* something that stops or closes the mouth of a vessel, a stopper, plug, bung etc. **stop press** *n.* late news inserted in a paper after the printing has commenced. **stop-press** *a.* **stop valve** *n.* a valve that stops the flow of liquid through a pipe. **stop-volley** *n.* in tennis, a volley close to the net and not followed through, dropping the ball just over the net. **stopwatch** *n.* a watch with an additional hand which can be stopped by a special device at any second or fraction of a second, used for timing races etc.

storax (staw'raks) *n.* **1** a vanilla-scented resin obtained from *Styrax officinalis*, formerly used in medicine etc. **2** the tree itself. **3** a balsam obtained from *Liquidambar orientalis*.

store (staw) n. 1 a stock laid up for drawing upon. 2 (often pl.) an abundant supply, plenty, abundance. 3 a place where things are laid up or kept for sale, a storehouse, a warehouse. 4 a large establishment where articles of various kinds are sold, a department store. 5 (N Am.) a shop. 6 (sometimes in pl.) a shop selling basic commodities. 7 (pl.) articles kept on hand for special use, esp. ammunition, arms, military and naval provisions etc.; a supply of such articles. 8 (Comput.) the memory in a computer. ~v.t. 1 to deposit (furniture etc.) in a warehouse etc. for safe keeping. 2 to accumulate or lay (usu. up or away) for future use. 3 to stock or supply (with). 4 to have a capacity for holding a reserve, e.g. of water (The leaves store moisture). 5 (Comput.) to enter (data) into a computer memory or in a storage device. **in store 1** in reserve. **2** ready for use. **3** on hand. **4** awaiting one in the future. **to set store by/ on** to value highly. **storable** a. **storage** (-rij) n. 1 the storing or warehousing of goods etc. 2 the price paid for or the space reserved for this. 3 the storing of data in a computer memory or on disk etc. **storage battery, storage cell** n. an accumulator. **storage heater** n. a type of radiator which stores heat during periods of off-peak electricity. **store card** n. a credit card issued to customers by a department store etc. **storefront** n. 1 (esp. N Am.) the side of a shop that faces the street. 2 a room in the front of a shop. **storehouse** n. 1 a place where things are stored up, a warehouse, granary, repository etc. 2 a great quantity. **storekeeper** n. 1 a person who has the charge of stores. 2 (N Am.) a shopkeeper. **storeman** n. (pl. **storemen**) a person in charge of stored goods or equipment. **storer** n. **storeroom** n.

storey (staw´ri), (N Am. also) **story** n. (pl. **storeys, stories**) a horizontal division of a building, esp. a set of rooms on the same floor. **storeyed, storied** a.

storied STORY¹.

stork (stawk) n. 1 a long-necked, long-legged wading bird of the genus Ciconia, allied to the heron, esp. the white or house-stork C. alba, nesting on buildings. 2 this bird as the traditional bringer of babies.

storm (stawm) n. 1 a violent disturbance of the atmosphere accompanied by wind, rain, snow, hail, or thunder and lightning, a tempest. 2 a wind of force 10 or 11, between a gale and a hurricane. 3 a violent disturbance or agitation of society, life, the mind etc., a tumult, commotion etc. 4 a hail or shower (of blows or missiles). 5 a violent outburst (of cheers etc.). 6 a direct assault on, or the capture of, a fortified place. ~v.i. 1 to bluster, to fume, to rage (at etc.), to behave violently. 2 to move somewhere in violent and angry haste (stormed out of the house). 3 (of wind, rain etc.) to rage. ~v.t. to take (a stronghold etc.) by storm. **to take by storm 1** to capture by means of a violent assault. **2** to captivate,

overwhelm (an audience, (the people of) a city etc.). **stormbound** a. stopped or delayed by storms. **storm centre,** (N Am.) **storm center** n. 1 the place of lowest pressure in a cyclonic storm. 2 any focus of violent debate, controversy or conflict. **storm cloud** n. 1 a heavy dark rain cloud. 2 a threat of imminent trouble. **storm-door** n. an extra outer door for protection in severe weather. **storm in a teacup** n. a fuss about nothing. **storming** a. 1 that storms or rages. 2 characterized by vigour, speed, dynamism etc. **storm lantern** n. HURRICANE LAMP (under HURRICANE). **stormless** a. **storm petrel** n. 1 a small black and white petrel of the N Atlantic, Hydrobates pelagicus. 2 a seditious person, a troublemaker. **stormproof** a. **storm troops** n.pl. 1 shock troops. 2 (Hist.) the Nazi political militia. **storm trooper** n. **storm window** n. an outer sash window to provide extra insulation. **stormy** a. (comp. **stormier,** superl. **stormiest**) 1 characterized or affected by storms. 2 (of winds) tempestuous. 3 violent, vehement, passionate. **stormily** adv. **storminess** n. **stormy petrel** n. STORM PETREL (under STORM).

story¹ (staw´ri) n. (pl. **stories**) 1 a narrative or recital in prose or verse, of actual or fictitious events, a tale, short novel, romance, anecdote, legend or myth. 2 the plot or incidents of a novel, epic or play; a storyline. 3 a series of facts of special interest connected with a person, place etc. 4 an account of an incident, experience etc. 5 a descriptive article in a newspaper. 6 (coll.) a falsehood, a fib. **the story goes** it is commonly said. **to cut/ make a long story short** used to announce that one is omitting many details and coming directly to the point. **storied** a. (poet.) 1 adorned with scenes from stories or history. 2 celebrated in stories or history. **storyboard** n. (a board displaying) a series of shots or sketches indicating the sequence of images to be used in a cinema film, television programme or television advertisement. **story book** n. a book containing a story or stories. **story-book** a. fairy-tale, romantic. **storyline** n. the main plot of a book, film etc. **storyteller** n. 1 a person who tells stories. 2 (coll.) a person who tells lies. **storytelling** n.

story² STOREY.

stoup (stoop) n. a basin for holy water.

stout (stowt) a. 1 corpulent, bulky, fleshy. 2 strong, sound, sturdy, well-built. 3 staunch, lusty, vigorous, brave, resolute, intrepid. ~n. a type of strong beer made from roasted malt or barley. **stout heart** n. courage, fortitude. **stout-hearted** a. **stout-heartedly** adv. **stout-heartedness** n. **stoutish** a. **stoutly** adv. **stoutness** n.

stove¹ (stōv) n. 1 an apparatus, wholly or partially closed, in which fuel is burned for heating, cooking etc. 2 a hothouse in which a high temperature is maintained. **stove-enamel** n. enamel made heatproof by treating in a stove. **stove-enamelled,** (N Am.) **stove-enameled** a. **stove-**

pipe *n.* a pipe for conducting smoke etc. from a stove to a chimney.

stove² STAVE.

stow (stō) *v.t.* **1** (*esp. Naut.*) to put or pack (often away) in a suitable or convenient place or position. **2** to pack or fill compactly with things. **to stow away 1** to put (something) where it will be tidily out of the way; to pack or fold away. **2** to be a stowaway on board a ship or aircraft. **stowage** (-ij) *n.* **1** an area or place for stowing goods or the charge for this. **2** the act of stowing or state of being stowed. **stowaway** *n.* a person who conceals themselves on a ship, aircraft etc. in order to get a free passage. **stower** *n.*

strabismus (strəbiz′məs) *n.* (*Med.*) squinting, a squint, produced by a muscular defect of the eye. **strabismal, strabismic** *a.*

straddle (strad′əl) *v.t.* **1** to stand or sit astride of (something) with legs well apart. **2** (of a town etc.) to be situated on both sides of, or across (e.g. a border, road etc.). **3** to part (one's legs) widely. **4** to shoot or drop bombs beyond and short of (a target) to determine the range. ~*v.i.* **1** to stand, walk or sit with the legs wide apart. **2** (of the legs) to be well apart. **3** to trim, to sit on the fence. ~*n.* **1** an act of straddling. **2** a high-jumping technique in which the legs straddle the bar while the body is parallel to it. **straddle-legged** *a.* **straddler** *n.*

strafe (sträf, strahf) *v.t.* **1** to bombard heavily. **2** to rake with machine-gun fire from the air. **3** to reprimand or punish severely. **4** to abuse or do a serious and deliberate injury to. ~*n.* **1** an act of strafing. **2** an attack from the air.

straggle (strag′əl) *v.i.* **1** to spread irregularly, to lose tightness or compactness. **2** to become dispersed, sporadic or irregular. **3** to wander away from or trail behind the main body. **4** (of e.g. a beard or a plant) to grow in an uncontrolled, untidy way. ~*n.* a straggling group or growth. **straggler** *n.* **stragglingly** *adv.* **straggly** *a.* (*comp.* **stragglier,** *superl.* **straggliest**).

straight (strāt) *a.* **1** extending uniformly in one direction, not bent, curved or crooked. **2** (*Geom.*) (of a line) lying along the shortest path between any two of its points. **3** (*esp. N Am.*) successive, in an unbroken run (*got straight As in her grade exams*). **4** unobstructed, uninterrupted; coming direct from its source. **5** level, even (*That picture's not straight*). **6** in proper order or condition; arranged to one's satisfaction. **7** clear (*Let's get this straight*). **8 a** upright, honest, not deviating from truth or fairness, correct, accurate, right. **b** reliable, trustworthy, authoritative; not evasive or ambiguous. **9** (of drama or some other art) serious, not comic or popular; using conventional techniques and ideas. **10 a** unmodified, unmitigated. **b**(of a drink) undiluted. **11** (of a person) conventional, not outrageous. **12** (*sl.*) heterosexual. **13** (of hair) not curly or wavy. **14** (of legs or back) not bent, bowed or bandy. **15** (of a garment) not full or flared. **16** (of an aim or

shot) going direct to its mark. **17** (of a look) direct, uncompromising. ~*n.* **1** a straight part, piece or stretch of anything. **2** a straight condition or state. **3** in poker, five cards in sequence irrespective of suit. **4** (*coll.*) a conventional person. **5** (*sl.*) a heterosexual person. **6** the straight part of a racetrack. ~*adv.* **1** in a straight line, direct. **2** directly. **3** without deviation, ambiguity or circumlocution. **4** with an accurate aim (*can't shoot straight*). **5** clearly (*can't see straight*). **straight away** at once, without delay. **straight from the shoulder 1** (of a physical blow) squarely delivered. **2** (of criticism etc.) frank, direct. **straight off/ out** (*coll.*) without needing time for checking or deliberation (*couldn't tell you the date straight off*). **straight up 1** (*coll.*) honestly, truly. **2** (*N Am., coll.*) without dilution or admixture. **the straight and narrow** the honest and virtuous way of life. **to go straight** to abandon criminal activities and become honest. **straightaway** *adv.* straight away, immediately. **straight-edge** *n.* a strip of metal or wood having one edge straight, used as a ruler etc. **straighten** *v.t.* to make straight or symmetrical. **to straighten out** to resolve, unscramble. **to straighten up** to stand erect after bending. **straightener** *n.* **straight face** *n.* a controlled expression, usu. concealing an inclination to laugh. **straight-faced** *a.* **straight fight** *n.* a contest between two candidates or sides only. **straightforward** *a.* **1** upright, honest, frank, open. **2** (of a task) simple, presenting no difficulties. **3** straight. **straightforwardly** *adv.* **straightforwardness** *n.* **straightish** *a.* **straight-jacket** STRAITJACKET (under STRAIT). **straight-laced** STRAIT-LACED (under STRAIT). **straightly** *adv.* **straight man** *n.* (*pl.* **straight men**) a person who acts as a stooge to a comedian. **straightness** *n.* **straight-out** *a.* (*N Am., coll.*) outright, complete, blunt, honest. **straight-up** *a.* (*coll.*) **1** trusty, honest, reliable. **2** (*N Am.*) pure, unmixed, unadulterated.

Usage note The spellings of the current adjective *straight* (not curved) and the noun *strait* (a narrow passage of water) should not be confused. The archaic adjective *strait* (narrow) is represented in the verb *straiten*, which should be distinguished from *straighten*, and in *straitjacket* and *strait-laced*, which now vary with *straightjacket* and *straight-laced*, but remain the preferred spellings.

strain¹ (strān) *v.t.* **1** to stretch tight; to make taut. **2** to exert (e.g. oneself, one's senses, one's eyes, ears etc.) to the utmost. **3** to force beyond due limits. **4** to weaken, injure or distort by excessive effort or over-exertion. **5** to purify from extraneous matter by passing through a colander or other strainer. **6** to remove (solid matter) by filtering (out). **7** to constrain, to make unnatural, artificial, or uneasy. **8** to press closely, to embrace. ~*v.i.* **1** to become taut, tense or fully stretched. **2** to exert oneself, to make violent efforts (after etc.). **3** to pull or tug (at). **4** to toil or labour (under a burden etc.). **5** to be filtered, to percolate. ~*n.* **1** an act of straining, a violent effort, a pull. **2** the force thus exerted; tension. **3** an injury, distortion, or change of structure, caused by excessive effort, exertion, or tension. **4** mental tension, fatigue from overwork etc. **5** a song, a tune, a melody, a piece of poetry. **6** tone, spirit, manner, style, pitch. **to strain oneself 1** to do oneself an injury through effort or straining. **2** (*often with neg., facet*) to try unduly hard. **strainable** *a.* **strained** *a.* **1** unnatural. **2** forced. **3** tense. **4** stressful. **strainer** *n.* **1** a filter. **2** a sieve, colander. **strain gauge** *n.* an engineer's device for testing the strain being put on a material or structure, at any point where it is attached.

strain² (strān) *n.* **1** race, stock, family, breed. **2** natural tendency or disposition.

strait (strāt) *n.* **1** (*often pl.*) a narrow passage of water between two seas. **2** (*usu. pl.*) a trying position, distress, difficulty. **straiten** *v.t.* **1** to distress. **2** to place in difficulty. **straitened circumstances** *n.pl.* poverty, financial hardship. **straitjacket, straightjacket** *n.* a garment with very long sleeves that are crossed in front and tied behind, for confining the arms of a violent prisoner or mental patient. ~*v.t.* (*pres.p.* **straitjacketing, straightjacketing,** *past, p.p.* **straitjacketed, straightjacketed**) **1** to confine in a straitjacket. **2** to restrict irksomely. **strait-laced, straight-laced** *a.* **1** puritanically strict in morals or manners. **2** laced or braced tightly. †**straitly** *adv.* †**straitness** *n.*

Usage note See note under STRAIGHT.

strake (strāk) *n.* **1** a continuous line of planking or plates from stem to stern of a vessel. **2** part of the metal rim on a cartwheel.

strand¹ (strand) *v.t.* **1** to run or force aground. **2** (*esp. in p.p.*) to bring to a standstill or into straits, esp. from lack of funds. ~*v.i.* to run aground. ~*n.* (*esp. poet.*) a shore or beach of the sea, lake or large river. **stranded** *a.* **1** left in difficulties. **2** without resources.

strand² (strand) *n.* **1** each of the fibres, threads, wires etc. of which a rope etc. is composed. **2** a thin lock of hair. **3** a string (of pearls, beads etc.). **4** any of the threads or elements composing a complex structure. ~*v.t.* **1** to break a strand in (a rope). **2** to make (a rope etc.) by twisting strands together.

strange (strānj) *a.* **1** unusual, singular, extraordinary, queer, surprising, unaccountable. **2** not well known, unfamiliar, new (to) (*an experience quite strange to us*). **3** alien, foreign (*strange lands*). **4** fresh or unused (to), unacquainted (*was strange to the work*). **5** awkward, shy. ~*adv.* (*coll.*) oddly (*began acting strange*). **strangely** *adv.* **strangeness** *n.* **1** the quality of being strange. **2** (*Physics*) the quantum number, conserved in strong but not in weak interactions, introduced

to explain the paradoxically long lifetimes of certain elementary particles.

stranger (strān´jə) *n.* **1** a person from another place; someone who does not know, or is not known in, a certain place. **2** a foreigner. **3** a person unknown (to one). **4** a person unaccustomed (to) (*a stranger to violence*).

strangle (strang´gəl) *v.t.* **1** to kill by compressing the windpipe, to choke, to throttle. **2** to suppress, to stifle. **stranglehold** *n.* **1** a choking grip used in wrestling. **2** a restrictive force or influence that squeezes the life out of something. **3** a monopoly; exclusive control. **strangler** *n.* **strangles** *n.* an infectious disease of the respiratory tract, affecting horses etc.

strangulate (strang´gūlāt) *v.t.* **1** to strangle. **2** (*Med.*) to compress (a blood vessel, intestine etc.). **strangulated** *a.* **strangulated hernia** *n.* (*Med.*) a hernia so constricted by surrounding tissue that its blood supply is cut off. **strangulation** (-lā´shən) *n.*

strap (strap) *n.* **1** a long narrow strip of leather or similar material, usu. with a buckle, for fastening round things. **2** a strip of fabric holding a garment in position on the body (*a shoulder strap*). **3** in a vehicle, train etc., a loop for grasping to steady oneself. **4** a strip, band or plate for holding parts together or for mounting things on. ~*v.t.* (*pres.p.* **strapping,** *past, p.p.* **strapped**) **1** to fasten (down, up etc.) with a strap. **2** to beat with a strap. **straphanger** *n.* (*coll.*) a standing passenger in a bus or train. **strap-hang** *v.i.* **strapless** *a.* **strapped** *a.* (*coll.*) short, in difficulties (for something) (*a bit strapped for cash*). **strapper** *n.* **strapping** *a.* tall, lusty, strong, muscular. **strappy** *a.* (*comp.* **strappier,** *superl.* **strappiest**).

strata STRATUM.

stratagem (strat´əjəm) *n.* **1** an artifice, trick or manoeuvre, esp. for deceiving an enemy. **2** trickery, deception.

stratal STRATUM.

strategy (strat´əji) *n.* (*pl.* **strategies**) **1** the art of war, generalship, esp. the art of directing military movements so as to secure the most advantageous positions and combinations of forces. **2** a long-term plan aimed at achieving a specific goal. **3** a stratagem. **strategic** (-tē´-), **strategical** *a.* **1** of, relating to, used in or of the nature of strategy. **2** (of materials) essential for the conduct of war. **3** (of missiles etc.) for use against an enemy's homeland rather than on the battlefield. **strategically** *adv.* **strategics** *n.* **strategist** (strat´ijist) *n.*

strath (strath) *n.* in the Scottish Highlands, a wide valley through which a river runs. **strathspey** (-spā´) *n.* **1** a Scottish dance slower than a reel. **2** music in 4/4 time for this.

strati STRATUS.

stratify (strat´ifī) *v.t.* (*3rd pers. sing. pres.* **stratifies,** *pres.p.* **stratifying,** *past, p.p.* **stratified**) **1** to form, deposit or arrange in strata. **2** to construct or design in layers, or according to a hierarchy. **stratification** (-fikā'shən) n. **stratified** a.

stratigraphy (strətig'rəfi) n. (Geol.) **1** the branch of geology dealing with the succession, classification, nomenclature etc. of stratified rocks. **2** the analysis of layers in archaeology. **stratigrapher** n. **stratigraphic** (-graf'-), **stratigraphical** a.

stratosphere (strat'əsfiə) n. the layer of atmosphere above the troposphere, extending to about 50 km above the earth's surface, in the lower part of which temperature does not vary very much and in the upper part of which temperature increases with height. **stratospheric** (-fer'-) a.

stratum (strah'təm, strā'-) n. (pl. **strata** (-tə)) **1** a horizontal layer of any material. **2** (Geol.) a bed of sedimentary rock. **3** a layer of tissue or cells. **4** a layer of sea or atmosphere. **5** a social level, a class. **6** (Math.) in statistics, each of the bands into which a population is divided for the purpose of stratified sampling. **stratal** a.

Usage note Strata is sometimes used as a singular noun (a strata), and a plural stratas may also be encountered, but both uses are best avoided.

stratus (strah'təs) n. (pl. **strati** (-tī)) a continuous horizontal sheet of cloud.

straw (straw) n. **1** the dry, ripened stalks of certain species of grain, esp. wheat, rye, oats etc., used as cattle fodder or material for packing, thatching, hat-making etc. **2** a single stalk of this kind, or a piece of one. **3** a long narrow plastic or paper tube for sucking up a drink. **4** (usu. with neg.) anything proverbially worthless (not worth a straw). **5** the colour of straw, a pale yellow. **6** a straw hat. ~a. **1** made of straw. **2** pale yellow. **to catch at straws/ a straw** to resort to desperate or manifestly inadequate remedies or measures. **to draw the short straw** to be the one selected, orig. by lot, for a difficult or unpleasant task. **straw hat** n. a hat made of plaited straw. **straw in the wind** n. a hint or indication of future events. **straw poll, straw vote** n. an unofficial ballot taken as a test of opinion. **strawy** a.

strawberry (straw'bəri) n. (pl. **strawberries**) **1** a low, stemless perennial plant of the genus Fragaria, with trifoliate leaves and white flowers, bearing a fleshy red fruit. **2** the fruit itself, its surface studded with small achenes. ~a. of the colour (pinkish-red) or flavour of strawberries. **strawberry blonde** a., n. (a woman) with reddish-blonde hair. **strawberry mark** n. a soft reddish birthmark. **strawberry roan** a. (of an animal's coat) chestnut mixed with grey or white. ~n. an animal with a coat of this colour.

stray (strā) v.i. **1** to wander from the direct or proper course, to go wrong, to lose one's way. **2** to wander from the path of rectitude, to err or sin, to go astray. ~n. **1** any domestic animal that has gone astray. **2** a straggler, a waif. ~a. **1** gone astray. **2** straggling, occasional, sporadic (a stray visitor; heard a few stray shots). **3** (Physics) waste, unwanted (stray light; stray magnetic fields). **strayed** a. having strayed or gone astray. **strayer** n.

streak (strēk) n. **1** an esp. irregular line or long narrow mark of a distinct colour from the background; a strip or band. **2** a vein or element (had a streak of selfishness). **3** a run or stretch, esp. of good or bad luck (on a winning streak). **4** a line of bacteria etc. on a culture medium. ~v.t. to mark with streaks. ~v.i. **1** to move in a straight line at speed. **2** (coll.) to run naked through a public place as a prank. **streaker** n. **streaking** n. **streak of lightning** n. a jagged flash of lightning. **streaky** a. (comp. **streakier**, superl. **streakiest**) **1** marked with streaks; striped. **2** (of bacon) having alternate layers of meat and fat. **streakily** adv. **streakiness** n.

stream (strēm) n. **1** a body of flowing water; a small river, a brook. **2** a moving body of fluid, e.g. lava, or anything in a state of continuous progressive movement, a moving throng of people etc. **3** a steady flow, a current, a drift (against the stream). **4** a band of schoolchildren of the same general academic ability, taught as a group. ~v.i. **1** to flow, move or issue in or as a stream. **2** to pour out or emit liquid abundantly (eyes streaming with tears). **3** to float, hang or wave in the wind etc. (hair streaming in the wind). ~v.t. **1** to pour out or flow with (liquid) abundantly (The wound was streaming blood). **2** to group (schoolchildren) into streams. **on stream** (of a factory etc.) in operation, in production. **to go with the stream** to do the same as other people, to behave conventionally. **streamer** n. **1** a long narrow flag, a pennon. **2** a narrow roll of paper or ribbon that unrolls when thrown. **3** a column of light shooting across the sky, as in the aurora borealis or australis. **streamless** a. **streamlet** n. **streamline** n. **1** the direction of an air current or of the particles of air impinging on a moving body. **2** the shape given to aircraft, vehicles etc., in order to cause the minimum of resistance. ~v.t. **1** to shape an aircraft, vehicle etc. in this manner. **2** to make an organization, process etc. simpler or more efficient. **streamlined** a. **stream of consciousness** n. **1** (Psych.) the flow of thoughts and feelings forming an individual's conscious experience. **2** a literary technique used to express the unspoken thoughts and emotions of a fictional character, without using conventional narrative or dialogue. **streamy** a. (comp. **streamier**, superl. **streamiest**).

street (strēt) n. **1** a road in a city or town with houses on one side or on both. **2** the part of the road used by vehicles. **3** the people living in a street. **on the streets 1** living by prostitution. **2** homeless, destitute. **streets ahead of** far better than. **up one's street** ideally suited to one's talents, inclinations etc. **streetcar** n. (N Am.) a tram. **street credibility**, (coll.) **street cred** n.

knowledge of the customs, language etc. associated with the urban subculture. **street door** *n.* a main house door opening on to the street. **streeted** *a.* **street entertainer** *n.* a juggler, acrobat, musician, mime or other performer who entertains people in the street, usu. for donations of money. **street entertainment** *n.* **street furniture** *n.* objects for public use or convenience in the street such as litter bins, postboxes, lamp-posts etc. **street lamp** *n.* a street light. **street light** *n.* a light, esp. on a post, illuminating a street. **street lighting** *n.* **street trader** *n.* a person who sells goods from a street stall. **street value** *n.* the monetary value of a commodity, esp. drugs, in terms of the price paid by the ultimate user. **streetwalker** *n.* a prostitute. **streetwalking** *n.*, *a.* **streetward** *a.*, *adv.* **streetwise** *a.* familiar with life among the poor, criminals etc. in an urban environment.

strelitzia (strəlit´siə) *n.* any southern African plant of the genus *Strelitzia*, with showy flowers that have a projecting tongue.

strength (strength) *n.* **1** the quality of being strong. **2** the relative degree to which, or aspect in which, a person or thing is strong. **3** someone or something that supplies support, power or force. **4** an attribute or quality seen as a character asset (*Detachment is her great strength*). **5** the number of people present or available. **6** the full number or complement (*The staff is below strength*). **from strength** from a strong position, for the purpose of negotiation etc. **from strength to strength** with continually increasing success. **in strength** in considerable numbers. **on the strength of 1** in reliance on. **2** on the faith of. **the strength of** the essence, gist or main thrust of (*That's about the strength of it*). **strengthen** *v.t.* to make strong or stronger. ~*v.i.* to increase in strength. **to strengthen someone's hand/hands** to empower someone to take action. **strengthener** *n.* **strengthless** *a.*

Usage note Pronunciation as (strenth) is best avoided.

strenuous (stren´ūəs) *a.* **1** energetic, vigorous, zealous, ardent. **2** requiring effort. **strenuously** *adv.* **strenuousness** *n.*

streptococcus (streptōkok´əs) *n.* (*pl.* **streptococci** (-kok´sī)) any bacterium of the chain-forming genus *Streptococcus*, some of which cause infectious diseases. **streptococcal** (-kok´əl), **streptococcic** (-kok´sik) *a.*

streptomycin (streptōmī´sin) *n.* an antibiotic obtained from a soil bacterium and used in the treatment of tuberculosis and other bacterial infections.

stress (stres) *n.* **1** tension, pressure or strain exerted on an object; a measure of this, or its amount. **2** constraining or impelling force. **3** demands made on one physically, mentally or emotionally. **4** physical, mental or emotional strain resulting from this. **5** weight, importance,

emphasis. **6** accentuation of, or emphasis on, a word or syllable; the chief accent in a word (*The stress comes on the third syllable*). ~*v.t.* **1** to emphasize. **2** to put the stress or accent on. **3** to subject to physical or mental stress or mechanical force. ~*v.i.* (*usu. with out, coll.*) (of a person) to feel stress. **to lay stress on** to emphasize, to accord importance to. **stressed out** *a.* frantic or exhausted as a result of stress. **stressful** *a.* **stressfully** *adv.* **stressfulness** *n.* **stressless** *a.*

stretch (strech) *v.t.* **1** to draw out, to extend in any direction or to full length. **2** to tighten, to draw tight, to make taut; to make longer or wider by tension. **3** to extend lengthwise, to straighten (a limb etc.). **4** to hit so as to prostrate (*The blow stretched him full length*). **5** to distend, to strain. **6** to do violence to; to exaggerate (e.g. the truth). **7** to utilize fully or challenge sufficiently (*I don't feel this job is stretching me*). ~*v.i.* **1** to be extended in length or breadth. **2** to have a specified extension in space or time, to reach or last. **3** to be drawn out or admit of being drawn out (*fabrics that stretch*). **4** to extend or straighten one's body or limbs (*yawned and stretched*). ~*n.* **1** a reach, sweep, or tract (of land, water etc.). **2** an act of stretching or state of being stretched. **3** extent or reach. **4** (*coll.*) a period of a prison sentence. **5** (*coll.*) a period of service. ~*a.* **1** (of fabric etc.) able to stretch (*stretch jeans*). **2** (of a vehicle, aircraft etc.) modified to accommodate extra seating etc. (*a stretch limousine*). **at a stretch 1** at one go. **2** continuously. **at full stretch** working etc. to full capacity, using all resources. **to stretch a point** to go beyond what might be expected. **to stretch out 1** to extend (e.g. a hand or foot). **2** to lie or recline at full length. **3** to eke (money etc.) out. **4** to prolong. **stretchable** *a.* **stretchability** (-bil´-) *n.* **stretched** *a.* **stretcher** *n.* **1** a framework consisting of canvas extended on two poles, for carrying a sick, wounded, dead or disabled person in a recumbent position. **2** a brick or stone laid lengthwise in a course in a wall (cp. HEADER). **3** a wooden frame with canvas stretched across it. ~*v.t.* to carry on a stretcher (*stretchered off the field*). **stretch marks** *n.pl.* translucent linear markings on the skin resulting from weight gain or pregnancy. **stretchy** *a.* (*comp.* **stretchier**, *superl.* **stretchiest**). **stretchiness** *n.*

strew (stroo) *v.t.* (*p.p.* **strewn** (stroon), **strewed**) **1** to scatter, to spread. **2** to cover (with) by scattering over. **3** to be scattered over, to cover sporadically. **strewer** *n.*

strewth (strooth), **struth**, **'struth** *int.* used to express surprise or alarm etc.

stria (strī´ə) *n.* (*pl.* **striae** (strī´ē)) a superficial furrow, a thin line or groove, mark or ridge. **striate**[1] (-ət) *a.* marked with striae. **striately** *adv.* **striate**[2] (strīāt´) *v.t.* to mark with striae. **striated** (-ā´tid) *a.* **striated muscle** *n.* (*Anat.*) skeletal or voluntary muscle, with contractile fibrils lying side by side, having a striped appearance, as distinct from smooth muscle. **striation** (-ā´shən), **striature** (strī´chə) n.

stricken (strik´ən) a. (often in comb.) affected, esp. severely, by e.g. disease, disaster or sorrow (the stricken city; disaster-stricken areas; grief-stricken parents; stricken by polio).

strict (strikt) a. **1** defined or applied exactly, accurate, precise; admitting of no exception (must be kept in strict isolation). **2** enforcing or observing rules precisely, not lax. **3** rigorous, severe, stringent. **strictly** adv. **1** in a strict manner. **2** (also **strictly speaking**) confining words to their exact sense (strictly (speaking), the spider is not an insect). **3** (N Am., coll.) definitely. **strictness** n.

stricture (strik´chə) n. **1** a censure, a sharp criticism. **2** (Med.) a morbid contraction of a duct or channel, as of the urethra. **strictured** a.

stride (strīd) v.i. (past **strode** (strōd), p.p. **stridden** (strid´ən)) **1** to walk with long steps. **2** to sit or stand with legs apart, to straddle. ~v.t. **1** to pass over in one step. **2** to bestride. ~n. **1** a long or measured step or the distance covered by this. **2** (pl., esp. Austral., coll.) men's trousers. **to make great strides** to progress or develop rapidly. **to take in one's stride 1** to jump (an obstacle) without adjusting one's gait. **2** to achieve (something) or override (something) without difficulty or effort. **strider** n.

stridence (strī´dəns), **stridency** (-si) n. loudness or harshness of tone. **strident** a. **stridently** adv.

stridulate (strid´ūlāt) v.i. (of insects, esp. cicadas and grasshoppers) to make a shrill creaking noise by rubbing the legs or wing-cases or other hard parts together. **stridulation** (-lā´shən) n.

strife (strīf) n. **1** contention, conflict, hostile struggle. **2** (Austral., coll.) any kind of trouble. **strifeful** a.

strike (strīk) v.t. (past **struck** (strŭk), p.p. **struck**, †**stricken** (strik´ən)) **1** to hit, to deliver a blow or blows upon; to deliver, to deal, to inflict (a blow etc.) (struck him a blow on the shoulder). **2** to come into violent contact with; to bring or cause to come into violent contact (struck his fist on the table; The ship struck a sandbank). **3** to drive, to send (a ball etc.) with force. **4** to attack (an enemy craft, location etc.). **5 a** to produce, make, form, effect, or bring into a particular state by a stroke, e.g. to ignite (a match), to stamp or mint (a coin), to render (deaf, dumb or blind). **b** to afflict (was struck by a virus). **6** to effect forcibly, to impress strongly, to occur suddenly to the mind of (A thought struck me; That strikes me as a waste of time). **7** to cause (a bell, musical note etc.) to sound. **8** to notify (the time) by sound (The clock struck twelve). **9** to cause to penetrate, to thrust (into) (The noise struck fear into us). **10** to make (a bargain). **11** to lower (sails, a flag, tent etc.). **12** to determine or find (a balance, average etc.). **13** to assume (an attitude). **14** to discover, to come across. **15** to find by drilling, excavating

etc. (strike oil; strike gold). ~v.i. **1** to try to hit, to deliver a blow or blows (at, upon); to collide, to dash (against, upon etc.); to be driven on shore, a rock etc. **2** to sound the time; (of time) to be sounded (Has the clock struck yet?; Twelve had already struck). **3** to leave off work to enforce a demand for higher wages etc. **4** to arrive suddenly, to happen (upon). **5** to enter or turn (in a certain direction) (We struck south-west). **6** to lower sails, a flag etc. in token of surrender etc. ~n. **1** an act of striking. **2** an act of striking for an increase of wages etc. **3** a refusal to take part in some other activity or perform a task expected of one. **4** an attack upon an enemy location, craft etc.; an attack on a target from the air. **5** a discovery (as of oil). **6** a lucky find, unexpected success. **7** in tenpin bowling, the knocking down of all ten pins with the first bowl, or the score in doing this. **8** in baseball, a good pitched ball missed by the batter and counting against them. **9** in cricket, a position to receive the bowling. **on strike** participating in an industrial strike. **strike a light!** used to express astonishment. **struck on** (coll.) enamoured of, infatuated with. **to strike a light** to strike a match. **to strike back** to return a blow, to retaliate. **to strike down 1** to knock down. **2** to make ill or cause to die, esp. suddenly. **3** to bring low. **to strike home 1** to hit the intended target. **2** to achieve the desired effect. **to strike (it) lucky** to have a success. **to strike it rich 1** to find a deposit of oil, minerals etc. **2** to make an unexpected large financial gain. **to strike off 1** to remove, separate, dislodge etc. by a blow. **2** to erase, to delete, to strike out (e.g. someone, or their name, from a register). **3** to print (copies of a document). **to strike out 1** to hit from the shoulder (e.g. in boxing). **2** to take vigorous action. **3** to delete, to expunge. **4** to set off (We struck out northwards). **5** to make vigorous strokes (in skating, swimming etc.). **6** to devise, to contrive (a plan etc.). **7** in baseball, to dismiss (a batter) or be dismissed after three strikes. **to strike through** to delete (a word etc.) by drawing a line through it. **to strike up 1** to enter into, to start (a conversation etc.). **2** to begin to play or sing. **to strike upon 1** to think of or hit upon (an idea, solution etc.). **2** (of light) to shine upon, to illuminate. **to strike while the iron is hot** to take an opportunity while it presents itself. **strikebound** a. (of a factory etc.) closed or disrupted because of a strike. **strikebreaker** n. **1** a blackleg. **2** a worker brought in to replace one out on strike. **strike-break** v.i. (past **strike-broke**, p.p. **strike-broken**). **strike call** n. a directive to union members to go on strike. **strike force** n. a police force or military force equipped for immediate action. **strike-out** n. in baseball, an out called after three strikes by the batter. **strike pay** n. an allowance for subsistence from a trade union to workers on strike. **striker** n. **1** a person or thing that strikes, esp. a worker on strike. **2** in soccer, an attacking player, a forward. **strike rate** *n.* a success rate e.g. in goal-scoring or run-scoring. **striking** *a.* surprising, forcible, impressive, noticeable. **within striking distance** near enough to strike, reach or achieve. **striking-circle** *n.* in hockey, the semi-circular area in front of the goal from within which the ball must be struck to score. **strikingly** *adv.* **strikingness** *n.*

Strimmer® (strim´ə)*n.* an electrically operated grass-trimmer with a rapidly rotating nylon cutting cord.

Strine (strīn) *n.* Australian English, comically transliterated, e.g. *afferbeck lauder*, for *alphabetical order.*

string (string) *n.* **1** twine, a fine line, usu. thicker than thread and thinner than cord. **2** a length of this or strip of leather, tape, or other material, used for tying, fastening, binding together, connecting etc. **3** a stringlike fibre, tendon, nerve etc., e.g. the tough piece connecting the two halves of a bean pod. **4** a piece of wire, catgut etc., yielding musical sounds or notes when caused to vibrate in a piano, violin etc.; each of the interwoven pieces of catgut stretched across the head of a tennis racket. **5** (*pl.*) the stringed instruments in an orchestra. **6** a cord or thread upon which anything is strung; a series of things or persons connected together or following in close succession (*a string of pearls*; *a string of visitors*; *came out with a string of expletives*). **7** the horses under training at a particular racing stable. **8** (*pl.*) conditions, complications. **9** (*Comput.*) a sequence of alphabetic or numeric characters in a computer program. ~*v.t.* (*past, p.p.* **strung** (strŭng)) **1** to supply with a string or strings. **2** to fit the strings on (a bow). **3** to tie with string. **4** to thread (beads etc.) on a string. **5** to strip (beans etc.) of strings or fibres. **no strings attached** (*coll.*) with no conditions or restrictions. **on a string 1** totally dependent, e.g. emotionally. **2** held in suspense. **to pull strings** to exert influence unobtrusively. **to string along 1** (*coll.*) to accompany. **2** to agree with, go along with. **3** (*coll.*) to fool, deceive. **to string out** to prolong, esp. unnecessarily. **to string up** (*coll.*) to hang (by the neck). **string bass** *n.* (*Mus.*) a double bass. **string bean** *n.* **1** (*esp. N Am.*) a runner bean, a French bean. **2** (*coll.*) a tall thin person. **stringcourse** *n.* a projecting horizontal band, moulding or raised course of bricks running along a building. **stringed** *a.* **stringed instrument** *n.* a musical instrument in which sounds are generated by the vibration of strings. **stringer** *n.* **1** a long horizontal member in a structural framework. **2** (*coll.*) a journalist who works part-time for a newspaper or news agency in a particular area. **3** a person who strings. **stringless** *a.* **stringlike** *a.* **string vest** *n.* a wide-meshed vest. **stringy** *a.* (*comp.* **stringier**, *superl.* **stringiest**) consisting of strings or small threads, fibrous, ropy, viscous. **stringiness** *n.* **strung up** *a.* (*coll.*) **1** in a highly nervous state. **2** hanged.

stringent (strin´jənt) *a.* strict, precise, binding, rigid. **stringency** *n.* **stringently** *adv.* **stringentness** *n.*

strip¹ (strip) *v.t.* (*pres.p.* **stripping**, *past, p.p.* **stripped**) **1** to pull the clothes or covering from, to denude, to skin, to peel, to husk, to clean. **2** to deprive (of e.g. titles or property), to despoil, to plunder. **3** to remove (clothes, bark, rigging, branches etc.) (*stripped off his clothes*; *stripped the leaves off the stem*). **4** to remove fittings from. **5** to sell off (the assets of a company) for profit. **6** to tear the thread from (a screw), or the teeth from (a gear). **7** to remove (paint) from (a surface). ~*v.i.* **1** to take (off) one's clothes, to undress. **2** to come away in strips. **3** (of a screw) to have the thread torn off. **4** (of a projectile) to be discharged without spin. ~*n.* **1** an act of stripping. **2** a striptease. **3** the clothes worn by a football team etc. **to strip down** to dismantle. **stripagram**, **strippergram** *n.* a telegram delivered by a person who does a striptease for the entertainment of the recipient. **strip club** *n.* a club in which striptease artistes perform. **stripper** *n.* **strip-search** *n.* a body search requiring the removal of all clothing. ~*v.t.* to search in this way. **striptease** *n.* a cabaret turn in which a performer partially or wholly undresses.

strip² (strip) *n.* **1** a long narrow piece. **2** a narrow stretch of land (*an airstrip*). **3** a strip cartoon. **to tear someone off a strip** (*coll.*) to scold someone angrily. **strip cartoon** *n.* a comic strip. **strip light** *n.* a tubular fluorescent light. **strip lighting** *n.*

stripe (strīp) *n.* **1** a long, narrow band of a distinctive colour or texture. **2** (*Mil.*) a chevron on the sleeve of a uniform indicating rank. **3** (*N Am.*) a cast of character or opinion (*people of that stripe*). ~*v.t.* to mark with stripes. **striped** *a.* **stripy** *a.* (*comp.* **stripier**, *superl.* **stripiest**). **stripiness** *n.*

stripling (strip´ling) *n.* a youth, a lad.

strive (strīv) *v.i.* (*past* **strove** (strōv), **strived**, *p.p.* **striven** (striv´ən), **strived**) **1** to try hard, to make a great effort (for something, to do something etc.). **2** to struggle or contend (against). **striver** *n.* **strivingly** *adv.*

strobe (strōb) *n.* **1** a stroboscope. **2** a stroboscopic lamp. **3** (*N Am.*) an electronic flash for a camera. ~*v.t.* to illuminate intermittently as though by stroboscope. ~*v.i.* **1** to flash intermittently. **2** (of a television screen etc.) to show strobing. **strobing** *n.* **1** the appearance of jerkily moving lines or stripes in a television picture. **2** in cinematography, undesirable jerkiness in the movement portrayed. **stroboscope** (-bəskōp) *n.* (*Physics*) an instrument for observing or timing periodic motion such as rotation by making the moving body visible at intervals through the use of an intermittently flashing light. **stroboscopic** (-skop´-), **stroboscopical** *a.*

strobile (strō´bīl), **strobilus** (-biləs) *n.* (*Bot.*) **1** a pine cone or a multiple fruit such as this. **2** a conelike structure, such as the flower of the hop plant.

strode STRIDE.

stroke[1] (strōk) *n.* **1** an act of striking, a blow; the impact, shock, noise etc., of this. **2** a sudden attack of illness etc., esp. a thrombosis in the brain, sometimes causing unconsciousness or paralysis. **3** a player's action in hitting the ball etc. in various games, such as golf, tennis, cricket; such a hit as the scoring unit in golf. **4** a single movement of something, esp. any one of a series of recurring movements, as of the heart, an oar, wing, piston etc. **5** the length, manner, rate etc. of such a movement. **6** (*with neg.*) the slightest such movement or action (*haven't done a stroke of work*). **7** a mark made by a single movement of a pen, pencil etc.; a touch or detail, e.g. in a description. **8** a move, action or happening (*a stroke of policy*; *a stroke of fate*). **9** each strike of a clock. **10** the stroke oar of a boat. ~*v.t.* to act as stroke for (a boat or crew). **at a stroke** by a single action. **off one's stroke** not at one's best. **on the stroke** punctually. **on the stroke of** exactly at the time when the clock starts striking (a particular time). **stroke oar** *n.* **1** the rower nearest the stern, who sets the rowing speed. **2** the oar of this rower. **stroke of genius** *n.* a brilliantly inspired idea. **stroke of (good) luck** *n.* a piece of good fortune. **stroke play** *n.* in golf, scoring by counting the number of strokes played as opposed to the number of holes won.

stroke[2] (strōk) *v.t.* to pass the hand over the surface of (fur, hair, an animal etc.) caressingly. ~*n.* an act of stroking or a spell of this. **stroker** *n.*

stroll (strōl) *v.i.* **1** to walk in a leisurely way, to saunter. **2** to achieve the desired result easily. ~*n.* **1** a leisurely ramble. **2** an easy success. **stroller** *n.* **1** a person who strolls. **2** (*N Am.*) a pushchair. **strolling players** *n.pl.* (a troupe of) actors who move from place to place giving performances.

strong (strong) *a.* (*comp.* **stronger** (strong´gə), *superl.* **strongest** (strong´gist)) **1** able to withstand or resist force; not easily damaged (*strong walls*). **2** able to withstand opposition or bear adverse fortune etc. (*a strong will*; *a strong personality*). **3** (of a person or their constitution) able to fight off illness, or not prone to suffer from it. **4** fully healthy, esp. after illness (*strong and well*). **5** (of people's nerves) not easily shattered; proof against shocks. **6** (of a market) maintaining high or rising prices. **7** powerful; muscular; full of stamina; capable of sustained effort. **8** effective, forceful (*strong opposition*; *a strong lobby*). **9** firm, not wavering (*strong beliefs*). **10** (of a position or argument) difficult to attack, invulnerable, convincing. **11** (of the wind or weather) violent. **12** having a powerful impact on the senses or emotions (*strong sunlight*; *a strong performance*). **13** (of e.g. a military force, team etc.) powerful, numerous, well-trained, of high quality. **14** likely to be successful or to win (*a strong contestant*; *a strong combination*). **15** (of

a beverage or a solution) concentrated; containing a high proportion of the active ingredient (*strong black coffee*). **16** (*Chem.*) (of an acid or base) having a high concentration of hydrogen or hydroxide ions in aqueous solution. **17** used (following the number) to specify numbers present, the size of a gathering etc. (*a band of protesters about 300 strong*). **18** (of someone's voice) loud, carrying, powerful. **19** (of food, its flavour or smell) pungent. **20** (of someone's breath) foul-smelling. **21** (of moves or measures) forceful, drastic. **22** (*Gram.*) (of Germanic verbs) forming inflections through a vowel change (as *run, ran, sing, sang, sung*), not by the addition of a suffix (as *walk, walked*). **going strong 1** continuing to flourish. **2** still in action. **strong-arm** *a.* using or involving physical force. **strongbox** *n.* a safe or robust trunk for storing valuables. **stronghold** *n.* **1** a fortress, a fastness. **2** a refuge. **strongish** *a.* **strong language** *n.* **1** swearing. **2** forceful or emphatic phraseology. **strongly** *adv.* **strongman** *n.* (*pl.* **strongmen**) **1** a person who performs muscular feats of strength. **2** (*coll.*) an autocratic leader. **strong meat** *n.* theories or doctrines demanding courageous thought. **strong-minded** *a.* resolute,determined. **strong-mindedly** *adv.* **strong-mindedness** *n.* **strong point** *n.* **1** something at which one excels; one's forte. **2** a particularly strongly fortified or defended position. **strongroom** *n.* a specially reinforced room for storing valuables. **strong stomach** *n.* a constitution or digestive system not prone to nausea. **strong suit** *n.* **1** in card-playing, a suit in which one can take tricks. **2** one's forte or strong point.

strontium (stron´tiəm, -shəm) *n.* (*Chem.*) a soft silvery-white metallic element, at. no. 38, chem. symbol Sr, resembling calcium. **strontia** (-tiə, -shə) *n.* strontium oxide. **strontium-90** *n.* strontium with atomic weight of 90, a radioactive product of nuclear fission which tends to accumulate in bones. **strontium oxide** *n.* a white compound used in manufacturing fireworks.

strop (strop) *n.* a strip of leather etc., for sharpening razors etc. on. ~*v.t.* (*pres.p.* **stropping**, *past, p.p.* **stropped**) to sharpen with or on a strop.

strophe (strō´fi) *n.* a number of lines constituting a section of a lyric poem. **strophic** *a.*

stroppy (strop´i) *a.* (*comp.* **stroppier**, *superl.* **stroppiest**) (*coll.*) **1** rowdy, angry. **2** awkward, quarrelsome. **stroppily** *adv.* **stroppiness** *n.*

strove STRIVE.

struck STRIKE.

structure (strŭk´chə) *n.* **1** a combination of parts, as a building, machine, organism etc., esp. the supporting or essential framework. **2** the manner in which a complex whole is constructed, put together, or organically formed. **3** the arrangement of parts, organs, atoms etc., in a complex whole (*sentence structure*). ~*v.t.* to give a structure to. **structural** *a.* **1** of or relating to structure. **2** having a structure. **3** forming part of a structure, integral to the structure. **structuralism** *n.* an approach to the human sciences, literature, linguistics etc. as coded systems comprising self-sufficient and self-determining structures of interrelationships and rules of combination through which meaning or function is generated and communicated. **structuralist** *n.*, *a.* **structural linguistics** *n.* the study of language as a complex structure of interconnected elements. **structurally** *adv.* **structural psychology** *n.* the study of the nature and arrangement of mental states and processes. **structured** *a.* **structureless** *a.*

strudel (strooˊdəl) *n.* a thin pastry rolled up with a filling (e.g. apple) and baked.

struggle (strŭgˊəl) *v.i.* **1** to make violent movements in trying to break free from restraint etc. **2** to make great efforts, esp. against difficulties or opposition. **3** to strive (for something, or to do something). **4** to contend (with or against). **5** to make one's way (along etc.) against difficulties, opposition etc. **6** (of a writer, artist etc.) to have difficulty making a name for oneself. *~n.* **1** an act or spell of struggling. **2** a strenuous effort. **3** a fight or contest, esp. of a confused character. **struggler** *n.* **struggling** *a.*

strum (strŭm) *v.t., v.i.* (*pres.p.* **strumming**, *past*, *p.p.* **strummed**) to play noisily or carelessly, to thrum on a stringed instrument. *~n.* **1** the sound of strumming. **2** an act of strumming. **strummer** *n.*

†strumpet (strŭmˊpit) *n.* a prostitute, a harlot.

strung STRING.

strut[1] (strŭt) *v.i.* (*pres.p.* **strutting**, *past*, *p.p.* **strutted**) to walk with a pompous, conceited gait. *~n.* such a gait. **strutter** *n.* **struttingly** *adv.*

strut[2] (strŭt) *n.* a timber or iron beam inserted in a framework so as to keep other members apart, a brace. *~v.t.* (*pres.p.* **strutting**, *past*, *p.p.* **strutted**) to brace with a strut or struts.

struth, **'struth** STREWTH.

strychnine (strikˊnēn) *n.* a highly poisonous alkaloid obtained from certain plant species of the genus *Strychnos*, esp. *S. nux-vomica*, used in medicine as a stimulant etc. **strychnic** *a.*

stub (stŭb) *n.* **1** a stump, end or remnant of anything, e.g. of a cigarette or a pencil. **2** the stump of a tree, tooth etc. **3** a counterfoil, esp. of a cheque or receipt. *~v.t.* (*pres.p.* **stubbing**, *past*, *p.p.* **stubbed**) **1** to strike (one's toe) against something. **2** to extinguish (a cigarette etc.), to put (out) with a squashing action. **stubby** *a.* (*comp.* **stubbier**, *superl.* **stubbiest**) short and thickset. *~n.* (*pl.* **stubbies**) (*Austral., coll.*) a small squat beer bottle. **stubbily** *adv.* **stubbiness** *n.*

stubble (stŭbˊəl) *n.* **1** the stumps of wheat, barley etc. covering the ground after harvest. **2** short, bristly hair, whiskers etc. **3** an unshaven growth of facial hair. **stubbled** *a.* **stubbly** *a.* (*comp.* **stubblier**, *superl.* **stubbliest**).

stubborn (stŭbˊən) *a.* **1** unreasonably obstinate, not to be persuaded. **2** obdurate, inflexible, in-

tractable, refractory. **3** unyielding, immovable. **stubbornly** *adv.* **stubbornness** *n.*

stucco (stŭkˊō) *n.* (*pl.* **stuccoes**, **stuccos**) **1** fine plaster for coating walls or moulding into decorations in relief. **2** any plaster used for coating the outside of buildings. *~v.t.* (*3rd pers. sing. pres.* **stuccoes**, *pres.p.* **stuccoing**, *past*, *p.p.* **stuccoed**) to coat with stucco. **stuccoer** *n.*

stuck STICK[2].

stud[1] (stŭd) *n.* **1** a large-headed nail, knob, head of a bolt etc., esp. fixed as an ornament. **2** a small jewel for wearing in pierced ears or a pierced nose. **3** an ornamental button for wearing in a shirt-front etc. **4** a crosspiece in each link of chain cable. **5** a marker let into a road surface so as to project slightly. *~v.t.* (*pres.p.* **studding**, *past*, *p.p.* **studded**) **1** to set with studs or ornamental knobs. **2** to set thickly, to bestrew. **studded** *a.*

stud[2] (stŭd) *n.* **1** a number of horses kept for riding, racing, breeding etc. **2** an animal-breeding establishment. **3** a stallion or other male animal used for breeding. **4** (*sl.*) a sexually potent esp. young man. **5** stud poker. *~a.* (of a stallion or other male animal) kept for breeding. **at stud** (of a stallion) available for breeding, for a fee. **stud book** *n.* a register of pedigrees of horses or cattle. **stud farm** *n.* a farm where horses are bred. **stud-horse** *n.* a stallion. **stud poker** *n.* a variety of poker in which cards are dealt face up.

studding-sail (stŭdˊingsāl, stŭnˊsəl), **stunsail** (stŭnˊsəl), **stuns'l** *n.* (*Naut.*) an additional sail set beyond the sides of a square sail in light winds.

student (stūˊdənt) *n.* **1** a person engaged in study, esp. someone receiving instruction at a university, college or other institution for higher education or technical training. **2** (*esp. N Am.*) a schoolboy or schoolgirl. **3** a studious person. **4** a person at the trainee or apprentice stage (*student nurses*). **studentship** *n.*

studio (stūˊdiō) *n.* (*pl.* **studios**) **1** the working room of a sculptor, painter, photographer etc. **2** the room in which records, radio and television programmes are recorded, or films made. **3** the place from which television and radio programmes are broadcast. **4** (*pl.*) the buildings used for making films by a television or film company. **studio couch** *n.* a couch that converts into a bed. **studio flat** *n.* a flat with one main room, or with a room suitable as an artist's studio.

studious (stūˊdiəs) *a.* **1** devoted to study. **2** studied, deliberate, intended. **3** eager, diligent, anxious (to do something, in something). **studiously** *adv.* **studiousness** *n.*

study (stŭdˊi) *n.* (*pl.* **studies**) **1** mental application to books, art, science etc., the pursuit of knowledge. **2** (*usu. pl.*) a subject that is studied or worth studying; the pursuit of such subjects (*She returned to England to complete her studies*). **3** a room devoted to study, literary work etc. **4** a sketch or other piece of work done for practice or as a preliminary design for a picture etc. **5** (*Mus.*) a composition designed to test or develop technical skill. ~*v.t.* (*3rd pers. sing. pres.* **studies,** *pres.p.* **studying,** *past, p.p.* **studied**) **1** to apply the mind to for the purpose of learning. **2** to inquire into, to investigate. **3** to contemplate, to consider attentively. **4** to commit (the words of one's role etc.) to memory. **5** to read (a book etc.) carefully and analytically. **6** to apply thought and pains to, to be zealous for. ~*v.i.* to apply oneself to study, esp. to reading. **to make a study of** to examine or investigate thoroughly. **studied** *a.* deliberate; contrived (*with studied indifference*). **studiedly** *adv.* **studiedness** *n.* **study-bedroom** *n.* a room, esp. for a student, in which to sleep and to study. **study group** *n.* a number of people involved in investigating a particular topic, meeting regularly for discussion etc.

stuff (stŭf) *n.* **1** the material of which anything is made or may be made. **2** the fundamental substance, essence, or elements of anything. **3** household goods, furniture, utensils etc. **4** things said, done, written etc. (*all that stuff about Aids prevention*). **5** a textile fabric, esp. woollen, as opposed to silk or linen. **6** worthless matter, nonsense, trash. ~*v.t.* **1** to cram, to pack, to fill or stop (up). **2** to cram, press, ram, or crowd into a receptacle, confined space etc.; to push roughly (*stuffed my books into my rucksack*). **3** to fill the skin of (a dead animal) so as to restore its natural form. **4** to fill (a fowl etc.) with stuffing or seasoning for cooking. **5** to fill with food (*stuffing themselves as usual*). **6** to fill with ideas, notions, nonsense etc. **7** (*sl., offensive*) used to express contemptuous dismissal or rejection (*Tell them to stuff their offer*). **8** (*taboo sl.*) to have sexual intercourse with (a woman). ~*v.i.* to cram oneself with food. **stuff and nonsense!** an expression of contemptuous disbelief. **that's the stuff!** that is just what is needed. **to do one's stuff** (*coll.*) to act as one is expected. **stuffed** *a.* **1** (of poultry etc.) filled with stuffing. **2** having blocked nasal passages, bunged (up). **get stuffed!** (*offensive*) used to express anger, contempt etc. against another person. **stuffed shirt** *n.* (*coll.*) a pompous person. **stuffer** *n.* **stuffing** *n.* **1** material used to stuff something. **2** a mixture of ingredients used to stuff poultry etc. before it is cooked. **to knock the stuffing out of** to beat (an opponent) thoroughly. **stuffy** *a.* (*comp.* **stuffier,** *superl.* **stuffiest**) **1** ill-ventilated, close, fusty. **2** boring, uninspiring. **3** strait-laced, conventional, dull. **4** (of one's nose etc.) stuffed up. **stuffily** *adv.* **stuffiness** *n.*

stultify (stŭl´tifī) *v.t.* (*3rd pers. sing. pres.* **stultifies,** *pres.p.* **stultifying,** *past, p.p.* **stultified**) to dull the mind of. **stultification** (-fikā´shən) *n.* **stultifier** *n.*

stumble (stŭm´bəl) *v.i.* **1** to trip in walking or to strike the foot against something without falling, to have a partial fall. **2** to move (along) unsteadily. **3** to read or speak blunderingly. **4** to come (upon) by chance. ~*n.* an act of stumbling. **stumblebum** *n.* (*N Am., coll.*) a clumsy person.

stumbler *n.* **stumbling** *n., a.* **stumbling-block** *n.* an obstacle, an impediment, a cause of difficulty or hesitation etc. **stumblingly** *adv.*

stump (stŭmp) *n.* **1** the part left in the earth after a tree has fallen or been cut down. **2** any part left when the rest of a branch, limb, tooth etc., has been cut away, amputated, destroyed, or worn out; a stub, a butt. **3** in cricket, each of the three posts of a wicket. **4** (*pl., facet.*) the legs. ~*v.i.* **1** to walk stiffly, awkwardly, or noisily, as on wooden legs. **2** to make stump speeches, to go about doing this. ~*v.t.* **1** (of a question or problem) to baffle; to be too difficult for. **2** to put out (the batsman) at cricket by touching the wicket while they are out of the crease. **3** to go about (a district) making stump speeches. **on the stump** going about making political speeches. **to stump up 1** to pay up. **2** to produce the money required. **up a stump** (*N Am.*) in difficulties. **stumped** *a.* **stumper** *n.* **1** a baffling question. **2** a wicket-keeper. **stump speech** *n.* **1** a speech from some improvised platform, orig. a tree stump. **2** an electioneering speech. **stumpy** *a.* (*comp.* **stumpier,** *superl.* **stumpiest**) **1** short, thickset, stocky. **2** full of stumps, stubby. **stumpily** *adv.* **stumpiness** *n.*

stun (stŭn) *v.t.* (*pres.p.* **stunning,** *past, p.p.* **stunned**) **1** to render senseless with a blow. **2** to stupefy, to shock or overwhelm. **3** to daze or deafen with noise. **stun gun** *n.* a gun that stuns, using ultrasound or electric shock, without causing serious injury. **stunner** *n.* **1** (*sl.*) something astonishing or first-rate. **2** a person or thing that stuns. **stunning** *a.* **1** stupefying. **2** (*sl.*) wonderfully good, fine etc. **stunningly** *adv.*

stung STING.

stunk STINK.

stunsail, stuns'l STUDDING-SAIL.

stunt¹ (stŭnt) *v.t.* to check in growth or development, to dwarf, to cramp. **stunted** *a.* **stuntedness** *n.*

stunt² (stŭnt) *n.* **1** a thing done to attract attention. **2** a performance serving as a display of strength, skill, or the like, a feat. **stuntman** *n.* (*pl.* **stuntmen**) a person who performs dangerous feats (esp. as a stand-in for an actor). **stuntwoman** *n.* (*pl.* **stuntwomen**).

stupefy (stū´pəfī) *v.t.* (*3rd pers. sing. pres.* **stupefies,** *pres.p.* **stupefying,** *past, p.p.* **stupefied**) **1** to make stupid or senseless. **2** to stun, to astonish. **stupefacient** (-fā´shənt) *a., n.* **stupefaction** (-fak´shən) *n.* **stupefier** *n.* **stupefying** *a.* **stupefyingly** *adv.*

stupendous (stūpen´dəs) *a.* astounding in magnitude, force, degree etc., marvellous, amazing, astonishing. **stupendously** *adv.* **stupendousness** *n.*

stupid (stū´pid) *a.* (*comp.* **stupider,** *superl.* **stupidest**) **1** slow or dull in apprehension, wit or understanding, unintelligent, obtuse. **2** senseless, nonsensical. **3** in a state of stupor, stupefied. **4** used in irritation for general disparage-

ment (*Move your stupid guitar, can't you?*).
stupidity (-pid´-) *n.* (*pl.* **stupidities**). **stupidly** *adv.*
stupidness *n.*

stupor (stū´pə) *n.* a dazed condition, torpor, deadened sensibility. **stuporous** *a.*

sturdy[1] (stœ´di) *a.* (*comp.* **sturdier**, *superl.* **sturdiest**) **1** robust, lusty, vigorous, hardy. **2** of strong or stocky build. **3** determined (*sturdy opposition*). **sturdily** *adv.* **sturdiness** *n.*

sturdy[2] (stœ´di) *n.* a disease in sheep characterized by giddiness caused by a tapeworm in the brain. **sturdied** (-did) *a.*

sturgeon (stœ´jən) *n.* a large anadromous fish of the genus *Acipenser*, characterized by bony scales, esp. *A. sturio*, which yields caviare and isinglass.

stutter (stŭt´ə) *v.i.* to keep hesitating or repeating sounds spasmodically in the articulation of words. ~*v.t.* to utter in this way, to stammer (out). ~*n.* the act or habit of stuttering or stammering. **stutterer** *n.* **stutteringly** *adv.*

sty[1] (stī) *n.* (*pl.* **sties**) **1** a pen or enclosure for pigs. **2** a mean or filthy habitation. **3** a place of debauchery.

sty[2] (stī), **stye** *n.* (*pl.* **sties**, **styes**) a small inflamed swelling on the edge of the eyelid.

style (stīl) *n.* **1** a sort, kind, make, pattern, esp. with reference to appearance. **2** manner of writing, expressing ideas, speaking, behaving, doing etc., as distinct from the matter expressed or done. **3** the general characteristics of literary diction, artistic expression, or mode of decoration, distinguishing a particular people, person, school, period etc. **4** a manner or form of a superior or fashionable kind, fashion, distinction (*arrived in style*). **5** a mode of designation or address, title, description. **6** (*Bot.*) the extension of an ovary supporting the stigma. ~*v.t.* **1** to design or shape. **2** to designate, to describe formally by name and title. **styleless** *a.* **stylelessness** *n.* **styler** *n.* **stylish** *a.* fashionable in style, smart, showy. **stylishly** *adv.* **stylishness** *n.* **stylist** *n.* **1** a clothes designer. **2** a hairdresser who styles hair. **3** a writer having or cultivating a good style. **4** a person, esp. an athlete or musician, who performs stylishly. **stylistic** (-lis´-) *a.* **stylistically** *adv.* **stylistics** *n.* the study of style in literary language. **stylize, stylise** *v.t.* to give (something) a conventional, non-naturalistic form in drawing, painting or other artistic representation. **stylization** (-zā´shən) *n.* **stylized** *a.*

Usage note The spellings of the nouns *style* (a manner etc.) and *stile* (steps, part of a door frame etc.) should not be confused.

styloid (stī´loid) *a.* penlike, stylus-like. ~*n.* (*also* **styloid process**) a spine projecting from the base of the temporal bone.

stylus (stī´ləs) *n.* (*pl.* **styli** (-lī, -li), **styluses**) **1** a pointed instrument for writing by means of carbon paper. **2** a device, esp. a diamond or sapphire point, attached to the cartridge in the arm

of a record player that follows the groove in a record.

stymie (stī´mi), **stimy** *n.* (*pl.* **stymies**, **stimies**) **1** in golf, the position when an opponent's ball lies between the player's ball and the hole. **2** a difficult position or situation. ~*v.t.* (*3rd pers. sing. pres.* **stymies**, **stimies**, *pres.p.* **stymieing**, **stymying**, **stimying**, *past, p.p.* **stymied**, **stimied**) **1** to cause difficulties for, to check. **2** in golf, to hinder by a stymie.

styptic (stip´tik) *a.* (of a drug or application) that stops bleeding.

styrax (stī´raks) *n.* any tree or shrub of the genus *Styrax*, certain species of which yield benzoin and storax. **styrene** *n.* (*Chem.*) a colourless volatile liquid derived from benzene used in the manufacture of plastics and synthetic rubber.

styrofoam (stī´rəfōm) *n.* (*esp. N Am.*) a type of expanded polystyrene.

suable (soo´əbəl) *a.* capable of being sued. **suability** (-bil´-) *n.*

suasion (swā´zhən) *n.* (*formal*) persuasion as opposed to compulsion.

suave (swahv) *a.* agreeable, bland, gracious, polite. **suavely** *adv.* **suaveness** *n.* **suavity** *n.* (*pl.* **suavities**).

sub (sŭb) *n.* (*coll.*) **1** short for SUBMARINE. **2** short for SUBSCRIPTION (under SUBSCRIBE). **3** short for SUBSTITUTE. **4** short for SUB-EDITOR (under SUB-EDIT). **5** a small loan or advance payment of wages etc. ~*v.i.* (*pres.p.* **subbing**, *past, p.p.* **subbed**) **1** to act as a substitute (for) or as a sub-editor. **2** to receive pay in advance on account of wages due later. ~*v.t.* **1** to grant (a small loan or advance) to. **2** to sub-edit.

sub- (sŭb) *pref.* **1** to, at or from a lower position, as in *submerge*, *substratum*, *subvert*. **2** inferior in importance, secondary, as in *subcommittee*, *subplot*. **3** almost, bordering on, as in *subarctic*, *subtropical*. **4** forming verbs expressing secondary action, as in *subcontract*, *subdivide*. **5** signifying support, as in *subsistence*. **6** (*Chem.*) (of a salt) basic.

subacid (sŭbas´id) *a.* slightly acid or sour. **subacidity** (-sid´-) *n.*

subacute (sŭbəkūt´) *a.* (*Med.*) (of illness) intermediate between acute and chronic.

subadult (sŭbad´ŭlt, -ədŭlt´) *a.* (*Zool.*) (of an animal) not quite adult. ~*n.* a subadult animal.

subagent (sŭbā´jənt) *n.* a person employed by an agent. **subagency** *n.* (*pl.* **subagencies**) a subordinate agency.

subalpine (sŭbal´pīn) *a.* of or relating to elevated regions not above the timberline.

subaltern (sŭb´əltən) *n.* (*Mil.*) a junior army officer, one below the rank of captain. ~*a.* subordinate; of inferior rank.

subantarctic (sŭbantahk´tik) *a.* of or relating to the region bordering on the Antarctic.

sub-aqua (sŭbak´wə) *a.* of or relating to underwater sports. **subaquatic** (-kwat´-) *a.* **1** partially aquatic. **2** subaqueous. **subaqueous** (-kwiəs) *a.* **1**

being or formed under water. **2** feeble, wishy-washy.

subarctic (sŭbahk´tik) *a.* of or relating to the region bordering on the Arctic.

subatomic (sŭbətom´ik) *a.* **1** of or occurring inside an atom. **2** making up an atom. **3** smaller than an atom.

subaxillary (sŭbak´siləri) *a.* (*Biol.*) situated beneath the armpit or the wing cavity, or under the axil formed by a petiole and stem etc.

sub-basement (sŭb´bāsmənt) *n.* a storey underneath a basement.

sub-branch (sŭb´brahnch) *n.* a subordinate branch.

subcategory (sŭb´katəgəri) *n.* (*pl.* **subcategories**) a secondary or subordinate category. **subcategorize**, **subcategorise** *v.t.* **subcategorization** (-zā´shən) *n.*

subclass (sŭb´klahs) *n.* **1** a secondary or subordinate class. **2** (*Bot., Biol.*) a taxonomic subdivision of a class.

sub-clause (sŭb´klawz) *n.* **1** (*Law*) a subsidiary part of a clause. **2** (*Gram.*) a subordinate clause.

subclinical (sŭbklin´ikəl) *a.* (*Med.*) having symptoms sufficiently slight as to be undetectable clinically.

subcommittee (sŭb´kəmiti) *n.* a small committee appointed from among its members by a larger committee to consider and report on a particular matter.

subconscious (sŭbkon´shəs) *a.* **1** existing in the mind but without one's full awareness. **2** of or relating to the subconscious. **3** slightly or partially conscious. ~*n.* **1** (*usu.* **the subconscious**) that part of the field of consciousness which at any given moment is outside the range of one's attention. **2** (*usu.* **the subconscious**) the accumulation of past conscious experiences which are forgotten or for the moment are out of one's thoughts. **subconsciously** *adv.* **subconsciousness** *n.*

subcontinent (sŭbkon´tinənt) *n.* **1** a large land mass, not of sufficient size to be a continent. **2** a large geographically independent land mass forming part of a continent. **subcontinental** (-nen´-) *a.*

subcontract[1] (sŭbkəntrakt´) *v.t.* to employ a company etc. to carry out (work) as part of a larger project. ~*v.i.* to make a subcontract or carry out a subcontract. **subcontractor** *n.*

subcontract[2] (sŭbkon´trakt) *n.* a secondary or subsidiary contract, e.g. to supply labour, materials or equipment.

subculture (sŭb´kŭlchə) *n.* a social or ethnic group with a characteristic culture differing from that of the national or predominant culture. **subcultural** (-kŭl´-) *a.*

subcutaneous (sŭbkūtā´niəs) *a.* beneath the skin. **subcutaneously** *adv.*

subdivide (sŭbdivīd´) *v.t., v.i.* to divide again or into smaller parts. **subdivisible** (-viz´-) *a.* **subdivision** (-vizh´ən, sŭb´-) *n.* **1** the act of

subdividing, or an instance of this. **2** a secondary or subsidiary division. **3** (*N Am., Austral.*) a piece of land divided into plots for sale.

subdominant (sŭbdom´inənt) *a., n.* (*Mus.*) (of or relating to) the tone next below the dominant, the fourth of the scale.

subduction (sŭbdŭk´shən) *n.* (*Geol.*) the sideways and downward thrust of the edge of a tectonic plate into the mantle beneath another plate.

subdue (səbdū´) *v.t.* (*3rd pers. sing. pres.* **subdues**, *pres.p.* **subduing**, *past, p.p.* **subdued**) **1** to conquer, to bring to subjection, to vanquish, to overcome. **2** to tame, to render gentle or mild. **3** to tone down, to soften, to make less glaring. **subduable** *a.* **subdued** *a.* **subduer** *n.*

sub-edit (sŭb´edit) *v.t.* (*pres.p.* **sub-editing**, *past, p.p.* **sub-edited**) to prepare (a manuscript) for printing. **sub-editor** *n.* **1** a person who sub-edits manuscripts. **2** an assistant editor. **sub-editorial** (-taw´-) *a.*

subentry (sŭb´entri) *n.* (*pl.* **subentries**) a subsidiary entry.

subfamily (sŭb´famili) *n.* (*pl.* **subfamilies**) **1** (*Biol.*) a taxonomic subdivision of a family. **2** any subdivision or subclass of a group.

subform (sŭb´fawm) *n.* a secondary form.

sub-frame (sŭb´frām) *n.* a supporting frame, e.g. for a door frame or window frame.

subfusc (sŭb´fŭsk) *a.* (*formal*) **1** dusky, sombre. **2** drab, dingy.

subgenus (sŭb´jenəs, -jē´-) *n.* (*pl.* **subgenera** (-ərə), **subgenuses**) (*Biol.*) a taxonomic subdivision of a genus. **subgeneric** (-jiner´ik) *a.*

sub-group (sŭb´groop), (*Math.*) **subgroup** *n.* a subdivision of a group.

sub-head (sŭb´hed), **sub-heading** (-heding) *n.* a heading, often explanatory, underneath the main heading of a book, article etc.

subhuman (sŭbhū´mən) *a.* **1** less than human or that which is normal to humans. **2** of or relating to animals lower than, or closely related to, humans.

subjacent (sŭbjā´sənt) *a.* underlying; lower in position.

subject[1] (sŭb´jikt) *n.* **1** the theme of discussion or description, or artistic expression or representation. **2 a** that which is treated or to be treated in any specified way. **b** the cause or occasion (for) (*a subject for rejoicing*). **3** a branch of learning or study. **4** (*Gram.*) the noun or its equivalent about which something is affirmed, the nominative of a sentence. **5** someone under the dominion or political rule of a person or state; a person owing allegiance to a sovereign; a member of a state as related to the sovereign or government; any person bound in obedience to another. **6** the ego, as distinguished from the object or non-ego, the mind, the conscious self. **7** (*Mus.*) the leading phrase or motif in music. **8** a person regarded as subject to any specific disease, mental tendency, psychic influence etc. (*a neurotic subject*). **9**

(Logic) that member of a proposition about which something is predicated. ~a. **1** being under the power, control or authority of another, owing obedience (to). **2** exposed, liable, prone, disposed (to) (*subject to pneumonia*). **3** dependent, conditional (*subject to their approval*). **on the subject of** concerning. **subjective** (-jek´-) a. **1** due to or proceeding from the individual mind, personal. **2** concerned with or proceeding from the consciousness or the mind, as opposed to objective or external things. **3** lacking reality, fanciful, imaginary. **4** (*Gram.*) denoting the case of the subject of a verb, nominative. ~n. the subjective case. **subjectively** adv. **subjectiveness** n. **subjectivism** n. the doctrine that human knowledge is purely subjective, and therefore relative. **subjectivist** n. **subjectivity** (-tiv´-) n. **subjectless** a. **subject matter** n. the object of consideration, discussion etc.

subject² (səbjekt´) v.t. **1** to expose, to make liable (to). **2** to cause to undergo. **3** to subdue, to reduce to subjection (to). **subjection** n.

subjoin (subjoin´) v.t. to add at the end, to append, to affix. **subjoinder** (-də) n. a remark made in response to a previous one, a rejoinder. **subjoint** (sub´joint) n. a secondary joint e.g. in an insect's leg.

sub judice (sub joo´disi) a. (*Law*) under consideration, esp. by a court or judge.

subjugate (sub´jugāt) v.t. to subdue, to conquer, to bring into subjection, to enslave. **subjugable** a. **subjugation** (-gā´shən) n. **subjugator** n.

subjunctive (səbjŭngk´tiv) a. (*Gram.*) denoting the mood of a verb expressing condition, wishes, hypothesis or contingency. ~n. **1** the subjunctive mood. **2** a word or form in the subjunctive mood. **subjunctively** adv.

subkingdom (sub´kingdəm) n. (*Biol.*) a primary division of the animal or plant kingdom.

sub-lease¹ (sub´lēs) n. a lease of property by a tenant or lessee.

sub-lease² (sublēs´) v.t. to grant or obtain a sublease of (property). **sub-lessee** (-ē´) n. **sublessor** (-les´ə) n.

sub-let¹ (sub´let) n. **1** a sub-letting, a sub-lease. **2** (*coll.*) sub-let property.

sub-let² (sublet´) v.t. (*pres.p.* **sub-letting**, *past, p.p.* **sub-let**) to sub-lease, to let (property already rented or held on lease).

sublibrarian (sublībreə´riən) n. a subordinate librarian.

sub lieutenant (sub leften´ənt) n. a British naval officer next in rank below a lieutenant.

sublimate¹ (sub´limāt) v.t. **1** (*Psych.*) to divert by sublimation. **2** (*Chem.*) to convert (a solid substance) by heat directly to vapour without passing through the liquid state (followed by an equivalent return to solidity by cooling). **3** to refine, to purify, to etherealize. **sublimation** (-ā´shən) n. **1** (*Psych.*) the diversion by the subject of certain instinctive impulses, esp. sexual, into altruistic or socially acceptable channels. **2**

the act of sublimating a solid etc. **3** the result of sublimating.

sublimate² (sub´limət) n. (*Chem.*) the product of sublimation.

sublime (səblīm´) a. (*comp.* **sublimer**, *superl.* **sublimest**) **1** of the most lofty or exalted nature. **2** characterized by grandeur, nobility or majesty. **3** (of e.g. indifference, ignorance, impudence) unparalleled, outstanding. ~v.t. **1** (*Chem.*) to sublimate. **2** to elevate, to purify. **3** to make sublime. ~v.i. **1** to pass directly from solid to vapour, to be sublimated. **2** to be elevated or purified. **sublimely** adv. **sublimeness** n. **sublimity** (-lim´-) n.

subliminal (səblim´inəl) a. (*Psych.*) **1** not reaching the threshold of consciousness, hardly perceived. **2** of or relating to subconsciousness. **subliminal advertising** n. (*Psych.*) advertising directed to and acting on the unconscious. **subliminally** adv.

Sub-Lt. abbr. Sub Lieutenant.

sublunary (subloo´nəri), **sublunar** a. **1** situated beneath the moon. **2** (*Astron.*) **a** within the orbit of the moon. **b** subject to the moon's influence. **3** of or relating to this world, mundane.

sub-machine gun (submashēn´) n. a light automatic or semiautomatic rapid-firing gun fired from the hip or shoulder.

submarine (submərēn´, sub´-) n. a vessel, esp. a warship, that may be submerged, equipped with a periscope. ~a. situated, acting or growing beneath the surface of the sea. **submariner** (-mar´inə) n. a sailor in a submarine.

submediant (submē´diənt) a., n. (*Mus.*) (of) the sixth note of the diatonic scale.

submerge (səbmœj´) v.t. **1** to put under water etc., to flood. **2** to inundate, to overwhelm. ~v.i. to sink or dive under water etc. **submergence** n. **submergible** a. **submersion** (-shən) n.

submicroscopic (submīkrəskop´ik) a. too small to be viewed under a normal microscope.

subminiature (submin´ichə) a. **1** of very reduced size. **2** (of a camera) very small, using a 16mm film.

submission (səbmish´ən) n. **1** the act of submitting, or the process of being submitted. **2** something that is submitted. **3** the state of being submissive; compliance, obedience, resignation, meekness. **4** (*Law*) a theory or argument presented by counsel to a judge or jury. **5** the surrender of a wrestler overcome by the pain of a hold. **submissive** (-mis´-) a. **submissively** adv. **submissiveness** n.

submit (səbmit´) v.t. (*pres.p.* **submitting**, *past, p.p.* **submitted**) **1** to yield or surrender (oneself) to the domination of someone else. **2** to present or refer for consideration, decision etc. (*submit my application*). **3** (*esp. Law*) to put forward (a theory etc.) deferentially. **4** to subject (to a process, treatment etc.). ~v.i. **1** to yield, to surrender, to give in (*refuse to submit*; *submit to defeat and humiliation*). **2** to be submissive. **submitter** n.

subnormal (sŭbnaw´məl) *a.* **1** less than normal, below the normal standard. **2** having lower intelligence than is normal. **subnormality** (-mal´-) *n.*

suboptimal (sŭbop´timəl) *a.* less than optimal; not of the best kind or quality.

suborder (sŭb´awdə) *n.* (*Biol.*) a subdivision of a taxonomic order. **subordinal** (-aw´-) *a.*

subordinate[1] (səbaw´dinət) *a.* **1** inferior (to) in order, rank, importance, power etc. **2** subject, subservient, subsidiary (to). ~*n.* a person working under another or inferior in official standing. **subordinate clause** *n.* (*Gram.*) a clause that functions as a noun, adjective or adverb and qualifies the main clause. **subordinately** *adv.* **subordinateness** *n.*

subordinate[2] (səbaw´dināt) *v.t.* **1** to make subordinate. **2** to treat or consider as of secondary importance (to). **3** to make subject or subservient (to). **subordination** (-ā´shən) *n.*

suborn (səbawn´) *v.t.* to induce (e.g. a witness) by underhand means, esp. bribery, to commit perjury or some other criminal act. **subornation** (-nā´shən) *n.* **suborner** *n.*

subphylum (sŭbfī´ləm) *n.* (*pl.* **subphyla** (-lə)) (*Biol.*) a taxonomic subdivision of a phylum.

sub-plot (sŭb´plot) *n.* a secondary or subordinate plot in a novel, play etc.

subpoena (səpē´nə) *n.* (*Law*) a writ commanding a person's attendance in a court of justice under a penalty. ~*v.t.* (*pres.p.* **subpoenaing**, *past, p.p.* **subpoenaed** (-nəd), **subpoena'd**) to serve with such a writ.

sub-postmaster (sŭbpōst´mahstə), **subpostmistress** (sŭbpōst´mistris) *n.* a person in charge of a sub-post office.

sub-post office (sŭbpōst´ofis) *n.* a small local post office offering a restricted range of services.

sub rosa (sŭb rō´zə) *adv.* **1** secretly. **2** in confidence.

subroutine (sŭb´rootēn) *n.* a sequence of computer instructions for a particular, usu. recurring, task that can be used at any point in a program.

sub-Saharan (sŭbsəhah´rən) *a.* of, relating to, or forming part of the regions of Africa south of the Sahara desert.

subscribe (səbskrīb´) *v.t.* **1** to contribute or pledge to contribute (an annual or other specified sum) to or for a fund, object etc. **2** to write (one's name etc.) at the end of a document etc. **3** to sign (a document, promise etc.). ~*v.i.* **1** to engage to pay a contribution, to allow one's name to be entered in a list of contributors. **2** to assent or give support (to an opinion etc.). **3** to write one's name at the end of a document. **4** to undertake to receive and pay for shares or a periodical, service etc. **to subscribe to** to arrange to take (a periodical) regularly. **subscribable** *a.* **subscriber** *n.* **subscriber trunk dialling** *n.* a telephone dialling system allowing subscribers to dial direct to any number in the system. **subscript** (sŭb´skript) *n., a.* (a character) written or printed below and usu. to the right of another or below the base line. **subscription** (-skrip´-) *n.* **1** the act of subscribing. **2** a contribution to a fund etc. **3** a membership fee. **4** an advance payment for several issues of a periodical. **5** a raising of money from subscribers. **6** a signature. **subscription concert** *n.* each concert of a series for which seats are sold in advance.

subsection (sŭb´sekshən) *n.* a subdivision of a section.

subsequent (sŭb´sikwənt) *a.* coming immediately after in time or order; following, succeeding, posterior (to). **subsequently** *adv.*

subserve (səbsœv´) *v.t.* to serve as a means or instrument in promoting (an end etc.). **subservient** *a.* **1** obsequious, servile. **2** useful as an instrument or means. **3** subordinate (to). **subservience**, **subserviency** *n.* **subserviently** *adv.*

subset (sŭb´set) *n.* (*esp. Math.*) a set contained within a larger set.

subshrub (sŭb´shrŭb) *n.* a low-growing woody plant with nonwoody tips.

subside (səbsīd´) *v.i.* **1** to settle down, to abate, to become tranquil. **2** to sink, to fall in level. **3** to sink in, to collapse. **4** to settle lower into the ground. **5** (*facet.*) (of a person) to drop plumply (into a chair etc.). **subsidence** (-sī´-, sŭb´si-) *n.*

subsidiary (səbsid´iəri) *a.* **1** aiding, auxiliary, supplemental. **2** subordinate or secondary in importance. ~*n.* (*pl.* **subsidiaries**) **1** a subsidiary person or thing, an auxiliary, an accessory. **2** a company whose shares are mostly owned by another. **subsidiarily** *adv.* **subsidiarity** (-ar´-) *n.* **1** the state of being subsidiary. **2** the principle of keeping central authorities subsidiary and devolving or delegating power to the lowest practicable level.

subsidy (sŭb´sidi) *n.* (*pl.* **subsidies**) **1** money granted by the state or a public body to keep down the price of essential commodities. **2** a contribution by the state, a public corporation etc., to a commercial or charitable undertaking of benefit to the public. **3** financial aid. **subsidize**, **subsidise** *v.t.* **subsidization** (-zā´shən) *n.* **subsidizer** *n.*

subsist (səbsist´) *v.i.* **1** to exist, to remain in existence. **2** to live, to have means of living, to find sustenance, to be sustained (on). **3** to inhere (in), to be attributable to. **subsistence** *n.* **1** the state or means of subsisting. **2** the minimum required to support life. **subsistence allowance**, **subsistence money** *n.* an advance of wages, or a special payment, made to enable an employee to meet immediate needs. **subsistence farming** *n.* farming in which most of the yield is consumed by the farmer with little over for sale. **subsistence level** *n.* a living standard that provides only the basic necessities for life. **subsistence wage** *n.* a wage sufficient only to provide the basic necessities of life. **subsistent** *a.*

subsoil (sŭb´soil) *n.* the stratum of earth immediately below the surface soil.

subsonic (sŭbson´ik) *a.* of, relating to, using or travelling at speeds less than that of sound.

subspecies (sŭb´spēshiz, -siz) *n.* (*Biol.*) a taxonomic subdivision of a species. **subspecific** (-spəsif´-) *a.*

substance (sŭb´stəns) *n.* **1** that of which a thing consists. **2** matter, material, as opposed to form. **3** matter of a definite or identifiable chemical composition. **4** the essence, the essential part, pith, gist or main purport. **5** that which is real, solidity, firmness, solid foundation. **6** material possessions, property, wealth, resources. **7** (*Philos.*) the permanent substratum in which qualities and accidents are conceived to inhere, the self-existent ground of attributes and phenomena. **8** a narcotic or intoxicating drug or chemical, esp. an illegal one.

sub-standard (sŭbstan´dəd) *a.* below an accepted or acceptable standard.

substantial (səbstan´shəl) *a.* **1** of considerable importance, value, extent, amount etc. **2** material, practical, virtual. **3** solid, stout, strongly constructed, durable. **4** possessed of substance, having sufficient means, well-to-do, financially sound. **5** having physical substance; real, actually existing, not illusory. ~*n.* (*usu. pl.*) the essential parts, reality. **substantiality** (-shial´-) *n.* **substantialize, substantialise** *v.t., v.i.* **substantially** *adv.*

substantiate (səbstan´shiāt) *v.t.* **1** to establish, to prove, to make good (a statement etc.). **2** to make real or actual. **substantiation** (-ā´shən) *n.*

substantive (sŭb´stəntiv) *a.* **1** independently existent, not merely implied, inferential or subsidiary. **2** of or relating to the essence or substance of anything. **3** solidly based; important, substantial. **4** (*Gram.*) **a** expressing existence. **b** denoting or functioning as a noun. **5** (of a dye or dyeing process) not requiring a mordant. **6** (*Mil.*) (of rank) permanent. ~*n.* (*Gram.*) a noun or part of a sentence used as a noun. **substantival** (-tī´-) *a.* **substantivally** *adv.* **substantively** *adv.* **substantive verb** *n.* the verb 'to be'.

sub-station (sŭb´stāshən) *n.* a subsidiary station, esp. one in which electric current from a generating station is modified before distribution.

substitute (sŭb´stitūt) *n.* **1** a person or thing put in the place of or serving for another. **2** an artificial replacement for a natural substance (*milk substitute*). ~*v.t.* **1** to put or use in exchange (for) another person or thing. **2** (*coll.*) to replace (a person or thing by or with another). ~*v.i.* to act as a substitute (for). **substitutable** *a.* **substitutability** (-bil´-) *n.* **substitution** (-ū´shən) *n.* **1** the act of substituting. **2** a replacement. **substitutive** *a.*

substratum (sŭb´strahtəm) *n.* (*pl.* **substrata** (-tə)) **1** that which underlies anything. **2** a layer or stratum lying underneath. **3** the ground or basis of phenomena etc., foundation. **substrate**

(-strāt) *n.* **1** a substratum. **2** a surface for painting or printing on. **3** (*Biol.*) the substance on which an enzyme acts. **4** a base on which something lives or is formed.

substructure (sŭb´strŭkchə) *n.* an understructure or foundation.

subsume (səbsūm´) *v.t.* to include under a more general class or category. **subsumable** *a.* **subsumption** (-sŭmp´-) *n.*

subsurface (sŭb´sœfis) *n.* the stratum or strata below the surface of the earth. ~*a.* **1** of or relating to the subsurface. **2** below the ground.

subsystem (sŭb´sistəm) *n.* a system within a larger system.

subtenant (sŭbten´ənt) *n.* a tenant holding property from someone who is also a tenant. **subtenancy** *n.* (*pl.* **subtenancies**).

subtend (sŭbtend´) *v.t.* **1** (of a chord relatively to an arc, or the side of a triangle to an angle) to extend under or be opposite to. **2** (*Bot.*) to be lower than and enclose.

subterfuge (sŭb´təfūj) *n.* **1** a deception, prevarication etc. used to avoid an inference, censure etc., or to evade or conceal something. **2** the practice of using subterfuges.

subterranean (sŭbtərā´niən) *a.* **1** underground. **2** hidden, concealed. **subterraneous** *a.* **subterraneously** *adv.*

subtext (sŭb´tekst) *n.* an unstated message or theme in a speech or piece of writing, conveyed in the tone of voice, choice of words etc.

subtitle (sŭb´tītəl) *n.* **1** an additional or subsidiary title of a book etc. **2** a printed explanatory caption to a silent film or a printed translation of the dialogue in a foreign film. ~*v.t.* to provide a subtitle for.

subtle (sŭt´əl) *a.* **1** rarefied, attenuated, delicate, hard to seize, elusive. **2** difficult to comprehend, not obvious, abstruse. **3** making fine distinctions, acute, discerning. **4** ingenious, skilful, clever. **subtleness** *n.* **subtlety** (-ti) *n.* (*pl.* **subtleties**). **subtly** (sut´li) *adv.*

subtonic (sŭbton´ik) *n.* (*Mus.*) the note next below the tonic.

subtopia (sŭbtō´piə) *n.* (*derog.*) unsightly suburbs, badly planned rural or urban areas. **subtopian** *a.*

subtotal (sŭb´tōtəl) *n.* the total resulting from adding a group of figures which form part of the overall total.

subtract (səbtrakt´) *v.t.* to take away (a part, quantity etc.) from the rest, to deduct. **subtracter** *n.* **subtraction** *n.* **subtractive** *a.* **subtractor** *n.*

subtropical (sŭbtrop´ikəl) *a.* of or relating to the regions near the tropics. **subtropics** *n.pl.*

suburb (sŭb´œb) *n.* an outlying part of a city or town. **suburban** (-œ´-) *a.* **1** of or relating to a suburb or the suburbs. **2** (*derog.*) denoting an outlook on life limited by certain narrow conventions. **suburbanite** (-nīt) *n.* **suburbanize, suburbanise** *v.t.* **suburbanization** (-zā´shən) *n.* **suburbia** (-œ´biə) *n.* (*often derog.*) **1** (the inhabitants of) residential suburbs collectively. **2** the lifestyle, culture etc. held to be characteristic of suburbia.

subvene (səbvēn´) *v.i.* to happen so as to aid or effect a result. **subvention** (-ven´-) *n.* a grant in aid, a subsidy.

subvert (səbvœt´) *v.t.* to overthrow, to destroy, to overturn. **subversion** (-shən) *n.* **subversive** *a.* intending to weaken or destroy a government etc. ~*n.* a subversive person. **subversively** *adv.* **subversiveness** *n.* **subverter** *n.*

subway (sŭb´wā) *n.* **1** an underground passage, tunnel, conduit etc. **2** (*Sc., N Am.*) an underground railway.

subwoofer (sŭb´wufə) *n.* a component in a loudspeaker which reproduces very low bass frequencies.

sub-zero (sŭbziə´rō) *a.* below zero (degrees).

succeed (səksēd´) *v.i.* **1** to be successful, to attain a desired object, to end well or prosperously. **2** to follow in time or order, to be subsequent. **3** to be the heir or successor (to an office, estate etc.). ~*v.t.* **1** to follow, to come after (in time or order), to be subsequent to. **2** to take the place previously occupied by, to be heir or successor to. **succeeder** *n.*

success (səkses´) *n.* **1** the act of succeeding, favourable result, attainment of what is desired or intended. **2** attainment of prosperity or high position. **successful** *a.* **successfully** *adv.* **successfulness** *n.*

succession (səksesh´ən) *n.* **1** a following in order. **2** a series of things following in order. **3** the act or right of succeeding to an office or inheritance. **4** the order in which persons so succeed. **5** the line of persons so succeeding. **in succession** one after another. **in succession to** as the successor to or of. **successional** *a.* **successionally** *adv.* **successor** *n.* a person who or something which succeeds another.

successive (səkses´iv) *a.* following in order or uninterrupted succession, consecutive. **successively** *adv.* **successiveness** *n.*

succinct (səksingkt´) *a.* compressed into few words, brief, concise. **succinctly** *adv.* **succinctness** *n.*

Succoth (sukōt´, sŭk´əth) *n.* the Jewish harvest festival commemorating the Israelites' sheltering in the wilderness.

succour (sŭk´ə), (*N Am.*) **succor** *n.* aid in time of difficulty or distress. ~*v.t.* to come to the aid of; to help or relieve in difficulty or distress. **succourer** *n.* **succourless** *a.*

succuba (sŭk´ūbə), **succubus** (-bəs) *n.* (*pl.* **succubae** (-bē), **succubi** (-bī)) a demon believed to assume the shape of a woman and have sexual intercourse with men in their sleep.

succulent (sŭk´ūlənt) *a.* **1** juicy and delicious. **2** (*coll.*) desirable. **3** (*Bot.*) (of a plant, stem etc.) thick and fleshy. ~*n.* (*Bot.*) a succulent plant, such as a cactus. **succulence** *n.* **succulently** *adv.*

succumb (səkŭm´) *v.i.* **1** to cease to resist etc.,

to give way (to); to yield, to submit (to). **2** (*euphem.*) to die.

succuss (səkŭs´) *v.t.* to shake suddenly, esp. in medical diagnosis. **succussion** (-kŭsh´ən) *n.*

X sucess common misspelling of SUCCESS.

such (sŭch) *a.* **1** of that, or the same, or the like kind or degree (as). **2** of the kind or degree mentioned or implied. **3** being the same in quality, degree etc. **4** so great, intense etc. (as, that). **5** (*Law, also formal*) of the aforesaid kind. ~*adv.* so (*such a nice day*). ~*pron.* **1** such a person, persons or things (as). **2** the aforesaid thing or things. **3** suchlike. **as such** loosely as described (*He has no qualifications as such*). **such a one 1** such a person or thing. **2** †some unspecified person or thing. **such as 1** for example. **2** of a kind that. **3** those who. **such as it is** despite its inadequacies. **such-and-such** *a.* not known or specified, some. ~*n.* an unknown or unspecified person or thing. **such-and-such a person** *n.* an unknown or unspecified person. **suchlike** *pron.* things of that sort. ~*a.* of such a kind.

suck (sŭk) *v.t.* **1** to draw (milk etc.) into the mouth by the action of the lips. **2** to draw liquid from with or as with the mouth. **3** to take and hold in the mouth with a sucking action. **4** to imbibe, to drink in, to absorb, to gain. **5** to engulf, to draw (in). ~*v.i.* **1** to draw liquid etc. in by suction. **2** to draw milk, nourishment etc. in thus. **3** to make the sound of sucking or a sound like sucking. **4** (*N Am., sl.*) to be very bad or contemptible. ~*n.* **1** an act or spell of sucking, suction. **2** force of suction. **3** a small draught or drink. **to suck dry 1** to empty by sucking. **2** to use up the sympathy, tolerance etc. of. **to suck in 1** to absorb. **2** to engulf, to draw (in). **3** to involve unwillingly in a bad situation. **to suck up 1** (*coll.*) to act in an obsequious manner, toady. **2** to absorb. **sucker** *n.* **1** a person who or something which sucks. **2** a suckling. **3** (*coll.*) a gullible person. **4** (*coll.*) a person who is very fond of or unable to resist a specified thing (*I'm a sucker for romance*). **5** (*esp. N Am., coll.*) something not named or specified. **6** a sucking-disc. **7** (*Biol.*) an organ acting on the same principle as a sucking-disc. **8** (*Bot.*) a shoot from a root or a subterranean part of a stem. **9** a fish which sucks in food or has a suctorial mouth. **10** (*N Am., coll.*) a lollipop. ~*v.t.* **1** (*Bot.*) to strip suckers from. **2** (*esp. N Am., coll.*) to dupe, to trick. ~*v.i.* (*Bot.*) to send out suckers. **suck-in** *n.* (*sl.*) a deception, a fiasco. **sucking** *a.* **1** deriving nourishment from the breast; not yet weaned. **2** (*Zool.*) unfledged. **sucking-disc** *n.* a disc of leather, rubber etc. adhering firmly to a smooth surface when wetted. **sucking-pig** *n.* a pig not yet weaned. **sucks** *int.* (*coll.*) used to express disappointment or derision.

suckle (sŭk´əl) *v.t.* **1** to give milk from the breast or udder to. **2** to nourish. ~*v.i.* to feed by sucking milk from the mother's breast or udder. **suckler** *n.* **suckling** *n.* a child or animal not yet weaned.

sucre (soo'krā) *n.* the standard unit of currency of Ecuador.

sucrose (soo'krōz) *n.* (*Chem.*) sugar as obtained from sugar cane or sugar beet.

suction (sŭk'shən) *n.* **1** the act or process of sucking. **2** the production of a vacuum in a confined space causing fluid to enter, or a body to adhere to something, under atmospheric pressure. **3** the force produced by this process. **suction pump** *n.* a pump in which liquid is forced up by atmospheric pressure. **suctorial** (-taw'ri-) *a.* (*Zool.*) adapted for sucking or for adhering by suction. **suctorian** (-riən) *n.*

☒ **suculent** common misspelling of SUCCULENT.

☒ **sucumb** common misspelling of SUCCUMB.

Sudanese (soodənēz') *a.* of or relating to Sudan, NE Africa. ~*n.* (*pl.* **Sudanese**) a native or inhabitant of Sudan, or a descendant of one.

sudden (sŭd'ən) *a.* **1** happening unexpectedly, without warning. **2** instantaneous, abrupt, swift, rapid. **all of a sudden** suddenly; unexpectedly. **sudden death** *n.* (*coll.*) an extended period of play to decide a tie in a game or contest, ending when one side scores. **sudden infant death syndrome** *n.* (*Med.*) cot death. **suddenly** *adv.* **suddenness** *n.*

sudoriferous (soodərif'ərəs) *a.* producing or secreting perspiration. **sudorific** *a.* causing perspiration. ~*n.* a sudorific drug.

suds (sŭdz) *n.pl.* **1** soapy water forming a frothy mass. **2** (*N Am.*, *coll.*) beer. ~*v.i.* to form suds. ~*v.t.* to wash in soapy water. **sudsy** *a.*

sue (soo) *v.t.* (*3rd pers. sing. pres.* **sues**, *pres.p.* **suing**, *past*, *p.p.* **sued**) **1** (*Law*) to prosecute or to pursue a claim (for) by legal process. **2** to entreat, to petition. ~*v.i.* **1** (*Law*) to take legal proceedings (for). **2** to make entreaty or petition (to or for). **suer** *n.*

suede (swād) *n.* **1** undressed kid or similar leather given a nap surface by rubbing. **2** (*also* **suede-cloth**) a fabric resembling suede. ~*a.* made of suede.

suet (soo'it) *n.* the hard fat about the kidneys and loins of oxen, sheep etc. **suet pudding** *n.* a boiled or steamed pudding made of suet etc. **suety** *a.*

suffer (sŭf'ə) *v.i.* **1** to undergo or endure pain, grief, injury, loss etc. **2** to be at a disadvantage. ~*v.t.* **1** to experience or undergo (something painful, disagreeable or unjust). **2** to tolerate, to put up with. **sufferable** *a.* **sufferableness** *n.* **sufferably** *adv.* **sufferance** *n.* tacit or passive permission, toleration, allowance. **on sufferance** merely tolerated. **sufferer** *n.* **suffering** *n.*, *a.*

suffice (səfīs') *v.i.* to be enough, to be adequate or sufficient (for or to do etc.). ~*v.t.* to be enough for, to content, to satisfy. **suffice it to say** I will say only this. **sufficiency** (-fish'ənsi) *n.* (*pl.* **sufficiencies**) an adequate supply (of). **sufficient** (-fish'ənt) *a.* enough, adequate, sufficing (for). ~*n.* (*coll.*) enough, a sufficiency. **sufficiently** *adv.*

suffix[1] (sŭf'iks) *n.* **1** a letter or syllable appended to the end of a word to form an inflection or derivative. **2** (*Math.*) a subscript. **suffixal** *a.*

suffix[2] (sŭf'iks, səfiks') *v.t.* to add as a suffix, to append. **suffixion** (sŭfik'shən), **suffixation** (-sā'shən) *n.*

suffocate (sŭf'əkāt) *v.t.* **1** to choke, to kill by stopping respiration. **2** to smother, to stifle. **3** to cause difficulty of respiration to. ~*v.i.* to be or feel suffocated. **suffocating** *a.* **suffocatingly** *adv.* **suffocation** (-ā'shən) *n.* **suffocative** *a.*

Suffolk (sŭf'ək) *n.* a breed of black-faced sheep.

suffragan (sŭf'rəgən) *a.* assisting: denoting a bishop consecrated to assist another bishop or any bishop in relation to the metropolitan (*suffragan bishop*; *bishop suffragan*). ~*n.* a suffragan or auxiliary bishop. **suffraganship** *n.*

suffrage (sŭf'rij) *n.* **1** the right to vote, esp. in parliamentary elections. **2** a vote in support of an opinion etc., or of a candidate for office. **suffragette** (-rəjet') *n.* (*Hist.*) a female agitator for women's right to vote. **suffragist** *n.* (*esp. Hist.*) an advocate of extension of the right to vote, esp. to women. **suffragism** *n.*

suffuse (səfūz') *v.t.* **1** (of a blush, fluid etc.) to overspread from within. **2** to cover with colour. **suffusion** (-zhən) *n.*

Sufi (soo'fi) *n.* (*pl.* **Sufis**) a Muslim pantheistic philosopher and mystic. **Sufic** *a.* **Sufism** *n.*

sug (sŭg) *v.t.* (*pres.p.* **sugging**, *past*, *p.p.* **sugged**) (*sl.*) to pretend to be conducting market research while actually trying to sell a product to.

sugar (shug'ə) *n.* **1** a sweet, crystalline substance obtained from the expressed juice of various plants, esp. the sugar cane and the sugar beet. **2** (*Chem.*) any one of various sweet or sweetish soluble carbohydrates, such as glucose, sucrose, lactose etc. **3** (*esp. N Am.*, *coll.*) a term of affection, dear. **4** flattering or seductive words, esp. used to mitigate or disguise something distasteful. **5** something used to make an unpleasant thing more acceptable. ~*v.t.* **1** to sweeten, cover or sprinkle with sugar. **2** to mitigate, disguise or render palatable. **sugar beet** *n.* a beet, *Beta vulgaris*, from which sugar is extracted. **sugar-candy** *n.* candy. **sugar cane** *n.* a very tall grass, *Saccharum officinarum*, with tall jointed stems, from the juice of which sugar is made. **sugar-coated** *a.* **1** covered with sugar. **2** made superficially attractive, esp. to hide something less pleasant. **3** excessively sentimental. **sugar daddy** *n.* (*pl.* **sugar daddies**) (*sl.*) a well-to-do, elderly man who spends money on a young woman. **sugarless** *a.* **sugar loaf** *n.* (*pl.* **sugar loaves**) a conical mass of refined sugar. **sugar maple** *n.* a N American tree, *Acer saccharum*, the sap of which yields sugar. **sugar pea** *n.* a mangetout. **sugar snap**, **sugar snap pea** *n.* a mangetout. **sugar soap** *n.* an alkaline preparation for cleaning or stripping paint. **sugary** *a.* **1** containing or resembling sugar. **2** excessively sweet or sentimental. **3** exaggeratedly charming or flattering. **sugariness** *n.*

suggest (səjest´) v.t. **1** to propose (a plan, idea etc.) for consideration. **2** to cause (an idea etc.) to arise in the mind. **3** to hint at, indicate. **to suggest itself** to arise in the mind. **suggester** n. **suggestible** a. **1** able to be suggested. **2** readily yielding to suggestion. **suggestibility** (-bil´-) n. **suggestion** (-jes´chən) n. **1** the act of suggesting. **2** something which is suggested. **3** a hint, an insinuation. **4** (Psych.) insinuation of an idea or impulse into the mind. **suggestive** a. **1** containing or conveying (a) suggestion. **2** tending to suggest thoughts of a prurient nature. **suggestively** adv. **suggestiveness** n.

suicide (soo´isid) n. **1** the act of intentionally taking one's own life. **2** a person who takes their own life intentionally. **3** any self-inflicted action of a disastrous nature. ~a. (Mil.) denoting an extremely dangerous operation. ~v.i. to commit suicide. **suicidal** (-sī´-) a. **suicidally** adv. **suicide pact** n. an agreement between people to commit suicide at the same time.

sui generis (sooī jen´əris, sooē) a. unique, of its own kind.

suit (soot, sūt) n. **1** a set of outer clothes (now usu. a jacket and trousers or a skirt), esp. when made of the same cloth. **2** a set of clothes or an article of clothing for a particular purpose (a diving suit). **3** any one of the four sets in a pack of playing cards. **4** (also **suit at law**) a legal prosecution or action for the recovery of a right etc. **5** the act of suing, a petition, a request. **6** a set (of sails or other articles used together). **7** (sl.) a person who wears a business suit, esp. a bureaucrat without character or individuality. ~v.t. **1** to agree with, to be appropriate to, to make (one) look attractive. **2** to satisfy, to please, to meet the desires etc. of. **3** to adapt, to accommodate, to make fitting (to). ~v.i. to agree, to accord, to correspond; to be convenient. **to follow suit 1** to play a card of the suit led by someone else. **2** (fig.) to follow someone's example. **to suit oneself 1** to do what one wants, regardless of other people's feelings. **2** to find something which pleases one. **suitable** a. suited, fitting, convenient, proper, becoming. **suitability** (-bil´-) n. **suitableness** n. **suitably** adv. **suitcase** n. a case with a handle for carrying clothes etc. while travelling. **suitcaseful** n. (pl. **suitcasefuls**). **suiting** n. cloth for suits.

suite (swēt) n. **1** a set (of connecting rooms, matching furniture etc.). **2** (Mus.) a series of instrumental compositions, orig. of dance tunes. **3** (Mus.) a set of selected musical pieces played as one instrumental work. **4** a company, a retinue.

suitor (soo´tə, sū´-) n. **1** a man who wants to marry a particular woman. **2** a party to a lawsuit. **3** a company seeking to buy another company.

sukiyaki (sukiyak´i) n. a Japanese dish of thin slices of meat and vegetables cooked together with soy sauce, saki etc.

sulcate (sŭl´kāt) a. having longitudinal furrows, grooves or channels.

sulfur SULPHUR.

sulk (sŭlk) v.i. to be silent and bad-tempered. ~n. (often pl.) a fit of sulking. **sulker** n. **sulky** a. (comp. **sulkier**, superl. **sulkiest**) sullen, morose, bad-tempered, resentful. ~n. (pl. **sulkies**) a light, two-wheeled vehicle for a single person. **sulkily** adv. **sulkiness** n.

sullen (sŭl´ən) a. **1** persistently morose, bad-tempered, cross. **2** slow, sluggish. **3** dismal, forbidding. **sullenly** adv. **sullenness** n.

sully (sŭl´i) v.t. (3rd pers. sing. pres. **sullies**, pres.p. **sullying**, past, p.p. **sullied**) **1** to defile, to disgrace. **2** (poet.) to soil, to tarnish. ~v.i. to be soiled or tarnished.

sulpha (sŭl´fə), (esp. N Am.) **sulfa** n. any drug derived from sulphonamide. **sulpha drug** n.

sulphamic acid (sŭlfam´ik), (esp. N Am.) **sulfamic acid** n. an amide of sulphuric acid, used in weedkiller. **sulphamate** (sŭl´fəmāt) n.

sulphate (sŭl´fāt), (esp. N Am.) **sulfate** n. a salt of sulphuric acid.

sulphide (sŭl´fīd), (esp. N Am.) **sulfide** n. a compound of sulphur, with an element or radical.

sulphite (sŭl´fīt), (esp. N Am.) **sulfite** n. a salt of sulphurous acid.

sulphonamide (sŭlfon´əmīd), (esp. N Am.) **sulfonamide** n. **1** an amide of a sulphonic acid. **2** a sulpha drug.

sulphone (sŭl´fōn), (esp. N Am.) **sulfone** n. an organic compound containing the divalent group SO_2 linked to two carbon atoms. **sulphonic** (-fon´-) a. **sulphonic acid** n. any of a class of strong organic acids used in making dyes, drugs and detergents.

sulphur (sŭl´fə), (esp. N Am.) **sulfur** n. **1** (Chem.) a pale yellow non-metallic element, at. no. 16, chem. symbol S, insoluble in water, occurring in crystalline or amorphous forms, used in the manufacture of chemicals, gunpowder, matches etc. **2** the material of which hellfire was supposed to consist; brimstone. **3** any one of various pale yellow butterflies. ~a. of the colour of sulphur, pale yellow. **sulphur dioxide** n. a pungent gas used industrially and as a bleach and food preservative, which is a major source of air pollution. **sulphureous** (-fū´ri-) a. **1** consisting of or having the qualities of sulphur. **2** sulphur-coloured. **sulphuric** (-fū´-) a. (Chem.) derived from or containing sulphur, esp. in its highest valency. **sulphuric acid** n. a corrosive, oily, liquid acid, oil of vitriol. **sulphurous**[1] (sŭl´fərəs) a. sulphureous. **sulphurous**[2] (sŭlfū´rəs) a. containing sulphur in its lower valency. **sulphurous acid** n. an unstable acid used as a preservative and a bleaching agent. **sulphur spring** n. a spring of water impregnated with sulphur or sulphide etc. **sulphury** (-fəri) a.

sultan (sŭl´tən) n. a Muslim sovereign, esp. a former ruler of Turkey. **sultana** (-tah´nə) n. **1** a seedless raisin. **2** a small yellow grape from which a sultana is produced. **3** the wife, mother or daughter of a sultan. **4** the mistress of a king, prince etc. **sultanate** (-nāt) *n.* **sultanship** *n.*

sultry (sŭl´tri) *a.* (*comp.* **sultrier,** *superl.* **sultriest**) **1** very hot, close and heavy, oppressive. **2** passionate, sensual. **sultrily** *adv.* **sultriness** *n.*

sum (sŭm) *n.* **1** the aggregate of two or more numbers, magnitudes, quantities or particulars, the total. **2** substance, essence, summary. **3** a particular amount of money. **4** an arithmetical problem or the process of working it out. **5** (*pl.*) elementary arithmetic. ~*v.t.* (*pres.p.* **summing,** *past, p.p.* **summed**) to add, collect or combine into one total or whole. **in sum** briefly, in summary. **to sum up 1** to recapitulate. **2** to form a rapid opinion or estimate of. **3** to put in a few words, to condense. **summing-up** *n.* **1** a summary of the evidence and arguments of a case by the judge to the jury at the end of a trial. **2** a recapitulation. **sum total** *n.* the sum of two or more numbers etc., the total.

sumac (soo´mak, shoo´-), **sumach** *n.* **1** a tree or shrub of the genus *Rhus* or *Cotinus,* the dried and powdered leaves of which are used in tanning, dyeing etc. **2** a preparation of the dried leaves.

summary (sŭm´əri) *n.* (*pl.* **summaries**) an abridged or condensed statement. ~*a.* **1** condensed into few words, abridged, concise. **2** done briefly or unceremoniously. **summarily** *adv.* **summariness** *n.* **summarist** *n.* **summarize, summarise** *v.t.* to make or be a summary of. **summarizable** *a.* **summarization** (-zā´shən) *n.* **summarizer** *n.* **summary conviction** *n.* (*Law*) a conviction made by a judge or magistrate with no jury. **summary jurisdiction** *n.* (*Law*) the authority of a court to adjudicate summarily on a matter arising during proceedings. **summary offence** *n.* (*Law*) an offence tried in a magistrate's court.

summation (səmā´shən) *n.* **1** the act or process of making a sum, addition. **2** a summing-up; a summary. **summational** *a.* **summative** (sŭm´-ətiv) *a.*

summer (sŭm´ə) *n.* **1** the season of the year when the sun shines most directly upon a region, the warmest season of the year. **2** (*Astron.*) the period from the summer solstice to the autumnal equinox. **3** the hot weather associated with the summer. **4** the time of greatest happiness or achievement. **5** (*pl., poet.*) years of age. ~*a.* of, relating to or used in summer. ~*v.i.* to pass the summer. ~*v.t.* to feed or keep (cattle etc.) during the summer. **summer house** *n.* a light building in a garden, for shade etc. in summer. **summerless** *a.* **summer pudding** *n.* a pudding of soft fruit in a bread casing. **summer school** *n.* a course of study held during the summer vacation. **summer solstice** *n.* (*Astron.*) one of the times (about 21 June in the northern hemisphere) and points at which the sun is farthest from the celestial equator. **summer time** *n.* the official time of one hour in advance of Greenwich Mean Time which comes into force between stated dates in the summer in Britain. **summertime** *n.* the period of summer. **summery** *a.*

summersault SOMERSAULT.

summing-up SUM.

summit (sŭm´it) *n.* **1** the highest point, the top. **2** the utmost elevation, degree etc. **3** a summit conference. **summit conference** *n.* a conference between heads of states. **summiteer** (-tiə´) *n.* **1** a person taking part in a summit conference. **2** a person who has climbed to the summit of a mountain. **summitless** *a.* **summit meeting** *n.* a summit conference. **summit talks** *n.pl.* a summit conference.

summon (sŭm´ən) *v.t.* **1** to call, cite or command to meet or attend. **2** to order by a summons to appear in court. **3** to call upon to do something. **4** to rouse, to call (up) (courage etc.). **summonable** *a.* **summoner** *n.*

summons (sŭm´ənz) *n.* (*pl.* **summonses**) **1** the act of summoning. **2** (*Law*) an authoritative call or citation, esp. to appear before a court or judge. ~*v.t.* to serve with a summons, to summon.

summum bonum (suməm bon´əm) *n.* the highest or supreme good.

sumo (soo´mō) *n.* traditional Japanese wrestling in which a contestant attempts to force his opponent out of the designated area or to touch the ground with a part of the body other than the feet. ~*a.* of or relating to sumo (*a sumo wrestler*).

sump (sŭmp) *n.* **1** a well in the floor of a mine, to collect water for pumping. **2** a receptacle for lubricating oil in the crankcase of an internal-combustion engine. **3** a pit to collect metal at its first fusion.

sumptuary (sŭmp´tūəri) *a.* of, relating to or regulating expenditure. **sumptuary edict** *n.* an edict restraining private excess in dress, luxury etc.

sumptuous (sŭmp´tūəs) *a.* **1** costly, expensive. **2** showing lavish expenditure. **3** splendid, magnificent. **sumptuosity** (-os´-) *n.* **sumptuously** *adv.* **sumptuousness** *n.*

Sun. *abbr.* Sunday.

sun (sŭn) *n.* **1** the heavenly body round which the earth revolves and which gives light and heat to the earth and other planets of the solar system. **2** the light or warmth of the sun, sunshine, a sunny place. **3** a fixed star that has satellites and is the centre of a system. **4** (*poet.*) a day, a sunrise. **5** (*poet.*) anything splendid or luminous, or a chief source of light, honour etc. ~*v.t.* (*pres.p.* **sunning,** *past, p.p.* **sunned**) to expose to the rays of the sun. ~*v.i.* to sun oneself. **against the sun** anticlockwise. **beneath the sun** under the sun. **in the sun** exposed to the rays of the sun. **to catch the sun 1** to be in a sunny place. **2** to become sunburnt. **under the sun** in the world, on earth. **with the sun** clockwise. **sun and planet** *n.* a system of gearing cogwheels. **sun-baked** *a.* dried or hardened by the sun's heat. **sunbathe** *v.i.* to expose the body to the sun in order to get a suntan. **sunbather** *n.* **sunbeam** *n.* a ray of sunlight. **sunbed** *n.* **1** an array of ultraviolet-emitting light tubes under which one lies to tan the skin. **2** a portable folding bed used for sunbathing. **sunbelt** *n.* a strip of land which has a warm, sunny climate. **sunblind** *n.* a window shade or awning. **sunblock** *n.* a cream, lotion etc. for the skin which blocks out the sun's ultraviolet rays; a sunscreen. **sun-bonnet** *n.* a large bonnet of light material with projections at the front and sides and a pendant at the back. **sunburn** *n.* reddening and inflammation of the skin due to over-exposure to the sun. *~v.i.* (*past, p.p.* **sunburnt, sunburned**) to suffer from sunburn. **sunburnt, sunburned** *a.* **sunburst** *n.* **1** an object made in the shape of the sun with its rays. **2** a strong or sudden burst of sunlight. **sun cream** *n.* cream used to protect the skin from the sun's rays. **sun deck** *n.* **1** the upper deck of a passenger ship. **2** (*N Am.*) a terrace, attached to a house, used for sunbathing. **sundew** *n.* any low, hairy, insectivorous bog plant of the genus *Drosera.* **sundial** *n.* an instrument for telling the time of day by means of the shadow of a gnomon cast on a dial etc. **sundown** *n.* sunset. **sundowner** *n.* (*coll.*) **1** (*Austral., New Zeal.*) a tramp who times his arrival at sundown in order to get a night's lodging. **2** an alcoholic drink taken at sunset. **sundress** *n.* a lightweight, lowcut, sleeveless dress for wearing in the sun. **sun-dried** *a.* dried in the sun. **sunfish** *n.* (*pl.* **sunfish**) a large fish of various species with a body like a sphere truncated behind. **sunflower** *n.* any plant of the genus *Helianthus,* esp. *H. annus,* with yellow-rayed flowers. **sunglasses** *n.pl.* darkened glasses for protecting the eyes from glare. **sun-god** *n.* the sun worshipped as a deity. **sunhat** *n.* a light hat with a broad brim etc., to protect the head from the sun. **sun-helmet** *n.* (*Hist.*) a cork or pith helmet worn by white people in the tropics. **sunkissed** *a.* lightened or warmed by the sun. **sunlamp** *n.* **1** a lamp which gives out ultraviolet rays for curative purposes or tanning the skin. **2** in film-making, a large lamp with a parabolic reflector. **sunless** *a.* **sunlessness** *n.* **sunlight** *n.* **sunlit** *a.* **sunlike** *a.* **sun lounge** *n.* a room with large windows to admit sunlight. **sunlounger** *n.* a portable folding bed used for sunbathing. **sunny** *a.* (*comp.* **sunnier,** *superl.* **sunniest**) **1** bright with or warmed by sunlight. **2** bright, cheerful, cheery, genial. **3** proceeding from the sun. **sunnily** *adv.* **sunniness** *n.* **sunray** *n.* **1** (*usu. pl.*) a sunbeam. **2** (*pl.*) ultraviolet rays used in heat treatment. **sunrise** *n.* **1** the first appearance of the sun above the horizon. **2** the colours and light in the sky at sunrise. **3** the time of sunrise. **sunrise industry** *n.* a high-technology industry with good prospects for the future. **sunroof** *n.* (*pl.* **sunroofs, sunrooves**) **1** a car roof with a panel that slides or lifts open. **2** such a panel. **sunroom** *n.* **1** a sun lounge. **2** (*esp. N Am.*) a solarium. **sunscreen** *n.* a substance included in suntan

preparations to protect the skin by screening out some of the ultraviolet radiation from the sun. **sunset** *n.* **1** the disappearance of the sun below the horizon. **2** the colours and light in the sky at sunset. **3** the time of sunset. **4** the decline (of life etc.). **sunshade** *n.* a parasol, awning, blind etc. used as a protection against the sun. **sunshine** *n.* **1** the light of the sun. **2** the space lit by this. **3** warmth, brightness. **4** cheerfulness, favourable influence. **5** (*coll.*) a form of address. **sunshine roof** *n.* (*pl.* **sunshine roofs, sunshine rooves**) a sunroof. **sunshiny** *a.* **sunspot** *n.* a dark patch sometimes seen on the surface of the sun. **sunstroke** *n.* heatstroke due to exposure to the sun in hot weather. **suntan** *n.* a browning of the skin caused by the formation of pigment induced by exposure to the sun or a sunlamp. *~v.i.* (*pres.p.* **suntanning,** *past, p.p.* **suntanned**) to get a suntan. **suntanned** *a.* **suntrap** *n.* a sheltered sunny place, for example in a garden. **sunup** *n.* (*esp. N Am.*) sunrise. **sun visor** *n.* a movable shield attached to the top of a car's windscreen to shield the eyes from the sun. **sunward** *a., adv.* **sunwards** *adv.*

sundae (sŭn´dā, -di) *n.* an ice cream served with fragments of nuts and various fruits.

Sunday (sŭn´dā, -di) *n.* **1** the 1st day of the week, the Christian Sabbath. **2** a newspaper published on a Sunday. *~adv.* (*coll.*) on Sunday. **Sunday best** *n.* (*coll., often facet.*) one's best clothes. **Sunday driver** *n.* a person who drives mainly at weekends, esp. one who is slow or lacks confidence. **Sundays** *adv.* (*coll.*) every Sunday. **Sunday school** *n.* a school held on Sundays for the religious instruction of children.

sundry (sŭn´dri) *a.* several, various, miscellaneous. *~n.* (*pl.* **sundries**) **1** (*pl.*) matters, items or miscellaneous articles, too trifling or numerous to specify. **2** (*Austral.*) in cricket, a run scored otherwise than off the bat, an extra.

sung SING.

sunk, sunken SINK.

Sunna (sun´ə, sŭn´ə) *n.* the traditional part of the Muslim law, based on the sayings or acts of Muhammad, accepted as of equal authority to the Koran by one branch of Islam, the Sunni, but rejected by the Shiites. **Sunni** (-i) *n.* (*pl.* **Sunni, Sunnis**) **1** the branch of Islam which rejects Ali as Muhammad's first successor, as distinct from *Shia.* **2** an adherent of the Sunni. *~a.* of or relating to Sunni.

sunny SUN.

sup (sŭp) *v.t.* (*pres.p.* **supping,** *past, p.p.* **supped**) **1** to take (soup etc.) in successive sips or spoonfuls. **2** (*esp. North., coll.*) to drink (alcohol). *~v.i.* to take in liquid or liquid food by sips or spoonfuls. *~n.* a mouthful (of a drink, soup etc.).

super[1] (soo´pə) *a.* (*coll.*) excellent, very good, enjoyable. **super-duper** (-doo´pə) *a.* (*coll.*) excellent, very good, enjoyable.

super[2] (soo´pə) *n.* (*coll.*) **1** a supernumerary actor. **2** a superintendent. **3** superphosphate. **4** an extra or superfluous person, a supernumerary. **5** superfine cloth or manufacture.

super- (soo´pə) *comb. form* **1** above, beyond or over. **2** to a great degree or extent. **3** particularly good or large of its kind. **4** of a higher kind.

superable (soo´pərəbəl) *a.* able to be overcome, conquerable. **superableness** *n.* **superably** *adv.*

superabound (soopərəbownd´) *v.i.* to be more than enough. **superabundance** (-bŭn´-) *n.* **super-abundant** *a.* **superabundantly** *adv.*

superadd (sooпərad´) *v.t.* to add over and above (something else). **superaddition** (-ish´ən) *n.*

superannuate (soopərən´ūāt) *v.t.* **1** to pension off on account of age. **2** to dismiss, discard, disqualify or incapacitate on account of age. **3** to make pensionable. **superannuable** *a.* **super-annuated** *a.* too old, no longer for use. **super-annuation** (-ā´shən) *n.* **1** a regular payment made by an employee to a pension scheme. **2** the pension paid after retirement. **3** the act of super-annuating. **4** the state of being superannuated.

superb (soopœb´) *a.* **1** grand, majestic, imposing, magnificent, splendid, stately. **2** (*coll.*) excellent, first-rate. **superbly** *adv.* **superbness** *n.*

supercargo (soopəkah´gō) *n.* (*pl.* **supercargoes**, **supercargos**) an officer in a merchant ship who superintends sales etc. and has charge of the cargo.

supercede SUPERSEDE.

supercharge (soo´pəchahj) *v.t.* **1** to charge or fill greatly or to excess with emotion, vigour etc. **2** to fit a supercharger to. **supercharger** *n.* a mechanism in an internal-combustion engine which provides for the complete filling of the cylinder with explosive material when going at high speed.

supercilious (soopəsil´iəs) *a.* contemptuous, overbearing, haughtily indifferent, arrogant, disdainful. **superciliously** *adv.* **superciliousness** *n.*

superclass (soo´pəklahs) *n.* a taxonomic category between a phylum or division and a class.

supercomputer (soo´pəkəmpūtə) *n.* a very powerful computer capable of over 100 million arithmetic operations per second. **super-computing** *n.*

superconductivity (soopəkondŭktiv´iti) *n.* (*Physics*) the total loss of electrical resistance exhibited by some metals and alloys at very low temperatures. **superconducting** (-kəndŭk´-), **superconductive** *a.* **superconductor** (-kəndŭk´-) *n.*

supercontinent (soo´pəkontinənt) *n.* (*Geol.*) any of several large land masses believed to have split to form the present continents.

supercool (soo´pəkool) *v.t.* (*Chem.*) to cool (a liquid) below its freezing point without solidification. ~*v.i.* to be cooled in this way. ~*a.* (*sl.*) extremely cool, wonderful.

supercritical (soopəkrit´ikəl) *a.* (*Physics*) of more than critical mass.

superego (soopərē´gō) *n.* (*pl.* **superegos**) (*Psych.*) the unconscious inhibitory morality in the mind

which criticizes the ego and condemns the unworthy impulses of the id.

superelevation (soopərelivā´shən) *n.* the difference in height between the opposite sides of a curved section of road, railway track etc.

supererogation (soopərerəgā´shən) *n.* performance of more than duty requires. **supererogate** (-er´ə-) *v.i.* **supererogatory** (-irog´ətəri) *a.*

superfamily (soo´pəfamili) *n.* (*pl.* **superfamilies**) a taxonomic category between a suborder and a family.

superfetation (soopəfētā´shən), **superfoetation** *n.* **1** (*Med., Zool.*) the conception of a second embryo or litter during the gestation of the first. **2** (*Bot.*) the fertilization of an ovule by different kinds of pollen.

superficial (soopəfish´əl) *a.* **1** of or relating to or lying on the surface. **2** not penetrating deep, cursory. **3** apparent, but not in reality. **4** not deep or profound in character, shallow. **superficiality** (-shial´-) *n.* (*pl.* **superficialities**). **superficially** *adv.* **superficialness** *n.*

superficies (soopəfish´iēz) *n.* (*pl.* **superficies**) **1** (*Geom.*) a surface. **2** the area of a surface. **3** external appearance or form.

superfine (soo´pəfin) *a.* **1** exceedingly fine, of extra quality. **2** extremely fine in size. **super-fineness** *n.*

superfluidity (soopəflooid´iti) *n.* the property of flowing without friction or viscosity. **super-fluid** (-floo´-) *n., a.*

superfluous (supœ´fluəs) *a.* more than is necessary or sufficient, excessive, redundant. **superfluity** (soopəfloo´-) *n.* (*pl.* **superfluities**) **1** the state of being superfluous. **2** something unnecessary. **3** an excess, a superabundance. **superfluously** *adv.* **superfluousness** *n.*

supergiant (soo´pəjīənt) *n.* a very large, very bright star of low density.

superglue (soo´pəgloo) *n.* an adhesive that gives an extremely strong bond on contact. ~*v.t.* (*3rd pers. sing. pres.* **superglues**, *pres.p.* **supergluing**, **superglueing**, *past, p.p.* **superglued**) to stick with superglue.

supergrass (soo´pəgrahs) *n.* (*coll.*) a police informer whose information implicates many people or concerns major criminals or criminal activities.

superheat (soopəhēt´) *v.t.* (*Physics*) **1** to heat (a liquid) above boiling point without vaporization. **2** to heat to excess. **3** to heat (steam) above the boiling point of water so no condensation occurs. **superheater** (soo´-) *n.*

superhero (soo´pəhiərō) *n.* (*pl.* **superheroes**) a comic-strip character with superhuman powers who fights against evil.

superhighway (soo´pəhīwā) *n.* **1** (*N Am.*) a motorway. **2** INFORMATION SUPERHIGHWAY (under INFORM).

superhuman (soopəhū´mən) *a.* **1** beyond normal human ability. **2** higher than human. **superhumanly** *adv.*

superimpose (sooperimpōz´) v.t. to lay on top of something else. **superimposition** (-pezish´-) n.

superincumbent (sooperinkŭm´bent) a. lying or resting on something.

superinduce (sooperindūs´) v.t. to bring in as an addition. **superinduction** (-dŭk´-) n.

superintend (sooperintend´) v.t. to have or exercise the management or oversight of, to direct, to control. ~v.i. to supervise, to inspect. **superintendence** n. **superintendency** n. (pl. **superintendencies**). **superintendent** n. 1 a person who superintends. 2 a director of an institution. 3 a police officer ranking above an inspector. 4 (N Am.) any high-ranking official, esp. the chief of a police department. 5 (N Am.) the caretaker of a building. ~a. superintending.

superior (supiə´riə) a. 1 upper, of higher position, class, grade, rank, excellence, degree etc. 2 better or greater relatively (to). 3 of a quality above the average. 4 situated near the top, in the higher part or above. 5 (Bot.) (of the calyx or the ovary) growing above another. 6 above being influenced by or amenable (to). 7 supercilious. 8 of wider application. 9 (Print.) set above the line. ~n. 1 a person superior to another or others, one's better. 2 the head of a monastery or other religious house. **superioress** n. the head of a convent or other religious house. **superiority** (-or´i-) n. **superiority complex** n. (Psych.) an inflated opinion of one's worth. **superiorly** adv. **superior planet** n. any planet further from the sun than the earth is.

Usage note Superior does not function as a true comparative in English, and should not be followed by than (the correct form is superior to).

superjacent (sooperjā´sent) a. lying on or above something.

superlative (supœ´lətiv) a. 1 of the highest degree, consummate, supreme. 2 (Gram.) expressing the highest or utmost degree. ~n. 1 (Gram.) a the superlative degree. b a word or phrase in the superlative degree. 2 something which is supreme or excellent. 3 an exaggeration. **superlatively** adv. **superlativeness** n.

superluminal (sooperloo´minel) a. (Physics) of or relating to a speed greater than the speed of light.

superlunar (sooperloo´ne), **superlunary** (-neri) a. above the moon, celestial, not mundane.

superman (soo´peman) n. (pl. **supermen**) 1 (Philos.) a hypothetical superior being, esp. one who is advanced in intellect and morals. 2 (coll.) a man of outstanding ability or strength.

supermarket (soo´pemahkit) n. a large, self-service shop where food and domestic goods are sold.

supermodel (soo´pemodel) n. a well-known, highly-paid fashion model.

supermundane (soopermŭn´dān) a. above or superior to worldly things.

supernatural (soopernach´erel) a. existing by,

due to, or exercising powers above the usual forces of nature, outside the sphere of natural law. **the supernatural** supernatural forces. **supernaturalism** n. **supernaturalist** n. **supernaturalize**, **supernaturalise** v.t. supernaturally adv. **supernaturalness** n.

supernormal (soopernaw´mel) a. beyond what is normal. **supernormality** (-mal´-) n. **supernormally** adv.

supernova (soopernō´ve) n. (pl. **supernovae** (-vē), **supernovas**) (Astron.) a nova up to 100 million times brighter than the sun, produced by the eruption of a star following its implosion.

supernumerary (soopernū´mereri) a. 1 being in excess of a prescribed or customary number. 2 employed for extra work. 3 (of an actor) having a non-speaking role. ~n. (pl. **supernumeraries**) a supernumerary person or thing, esp. a person appearing on the stage without a speaking role.

superorder (soo´perawde) n. (Biol.) a taxonomic category between an order and a subclass or a class. **superordinal** a.

superordinate (sooperaw´dinet) a. 1 superior in rank or status. 2 having the relation of superordination. ~n. 1 a superordinate person or thing. 2 a word whose meaning includes the meaning of another word. **superordination** (-ā´shen) n. (Logic) the relation of a universal proposition to a particular proposition that it includes.

superphosphate (sooperfos´fāt) n. 1 a mixture of phosphates used as a fertilizer. 2 a phosphate containing the greatest amount of phosphoric acid that can combine with the base.

superphysical (sooperfiz´ikel) a. 1 unable to be explained by physical causes. 2 beyond the physical.

superpose (sooperpōz´) v.t. (esp. Geom.) to lay over or on something. **superposable** a. **superposition** (-ish´en) n.

superpower (soo´pepowe) n. a very powerful nation, esp. the US or the former USSR.

supersaturated (sooperisach´urātid) a. containing more material than a saturated solution or vapour. **supersaturate** v.t. **supersaturation** (-ā´shen) n.

superscribe (soo´peskrīb, -skrīb´) v.t. 1 to write on the top or outside of something or above. 2 to write a name, inscription, address etc. on the outside or top of. **superscript** (soo´-) a. 1 written at the top or outside. 2 set above the line, superior. ~n. a superior character. **superscription** (-skrip´shen) n.

supersede (soopesēd´), **supercede** v.t. 1 to put a person or thing in the place of. 2 to set aside, to annul. 3 to take the place of, to displace, to supplant. **supersedence** n. **supersedure** (-je) n. **supersession** (-sesh´en) n.

X **supersilious** common misspelling of SUPER-CILIOUS.

supersonic (soopeson´ik) a. 1 of or relating to sound waves with such a high frequency that they are inaudible. **2** above the speed of sound. **3** travelling at or using such speeds. **supersonically** *adv.* **supersonics** *n.* ultrasonics.

superstar (soo´pəstah) *n.* a very popular film, music, sports etc. star. **superstardom** *n.*

superstate (soo´pəstāt) *n.* a powerful political state formed from a union of several nations.

superstition (soopəstish´ən) *n.* **1** credulity regarding the supernatural, the occult or the mysterious. **2** an ignorant or unreasoning dread of the unknown. **3** a religion, particular belief or practice originating in this, esp. a belief in omens, charms etc. **superstitious** *a.* **superstitiously** *adv.* **superstitiousness** *n.*

superstore (soo´pəstaw) *n.* a very large supermarket; a very large store selling goods other than food.

superstratum (soopəstrah´təm, -strā´-) *n.* (*pl.* **superstrata** (-tə)) a stratum resting on another.

superstructure (soo´pəstrŭkchə) *n.* **1** the part of a building above the ground. **2** an upper part of a structure. **3** a concept or idea based on another. **superstructural** *a.*

supertanker (soo´pətangkə) *n.* a very large tanker ship.

supertax (soo´pətaks) *n.* a tax in addition to the basic income tax, levied on incomes above a certain level.

supertonic (soopəton´ik) *n.* (*Mus.*) the note next above the tonic in the diatonic scale.

supervene (soopəvēn´) *v.i.* to come or happen as something extraneous or additional. **supervenient** *a.* **supervention** (-ven´-) *n.*

supervise (soo´pəvīz) *v.t.* to have oversight of, to oversee, to superintend. **supervision** (-vizh´ən) *n.* **supervisor** *n.* **supervisory** *a.*

superwoman (soo´pəwumən) *n.* (*pl.* **superwomen** (-wimin)) (*coll.*) an exceptionally strong or capable woman.

supinate (soo´pināt) *v.t.* to turn the palm of (the hand) upwards or forwards, as distinct from *pronate.* **supination** (-ā´shən) *n.* **supinator** *n.* (*Anat.*) either of two muscles which supinate the hand.

supine (soo´pīn) *a.* **1** lying on the back with the face upwards, as distinct from *prone.* **2** having the front or the palm upwards. **3** negligent, indolent, listless, careless. **supinely** *adv.* **supineness** *n.*

☒ **supose** common misspelling of SUPPOSE.

supper (sŭp´ə) *n.* **1** the last meal of the day, esp. a light one. **2** an evening social affair including supper. **to sing for one's supper** to perform a task in order to receive a benefit. **supperless** *a.*

supplant (səplahnt´) *v.t.* to take the place of or oust, esp. by craft or treachery. **supplantation** (sŭplahntā´shən) *n.* **supplanter** *n.*

supple (sŭp´əl) *a.* **1** pliant, flexible, easily bent. **2** lithe, able to move and bend easily. **3** yielding, compliant, soft, submissive, obsequious, servile. **supplely** (sŭp´əlli) *adv.* **suppleness** *n.* **supply**[1] (sŭp´li) *adv.*

supplement[1] (sŭp´limənt) *n.* **1** an addition, esp. one that supplies a deficiency. **2** an addition or update to a book, newspaper or periodical. **3** an additional charge for additional facilities or services. **4** (*Geom.*) the angle that added to another will make the sum two right angles. **supplemental** (-men´-) *a.* **supplementally** *adv.* **supplementary** *a.* serving as a supplement, additional. ~*n.* (*pl.* **supplementaries**) a supplementary thing, esp. a question. **supplementarily** *adv.* **supplementary benefit** *n.* (*Hist.*) money paid regularly by the state to people whose income fell below a certain minimum level.

supplement[2] (sŭp´limənt, sŭpliment´) *v.t.* to make additions to; to complete by additions. **supplementation** (-tā´shən) *n.*

suppliant (sŭp´liənt) *a.* **1** entreating, supplicating. **2** expressing entreaty or supplication. ~*n.* a person making a humble request. **suppliance** *n.* **suppliantly** *adv.*

supplicate (sŭp´likāt) *v.t.* (*formal*) **1** to beg or ask for earnestly and humbly. **2** to beg humbly (to grant etc.). **3** to address in earnest prayer. ~*v.i.* to petition earnestly, to beseech. **supplicant** *a.*, *n.* **supplicatingly** *adv.* **supplication** (-ā´shən) *n.* **supplicatory** (-kətəri) *a.*

supply[1] SUPPLE.

supply[2] (səplī´) *v.t.* (*3rd pers. sing. pres.* **supplies**, *pres.p.* **supplying**, *past, p.p.* **supplied**) **1** to furnish with what is wanted, to provide (with). **2** to furnish, to provide. **3** to serve instead of. **4** to fill (the place of), to make up for (a deficiency etc.). ~*n.* (*pl.* **supplies**) **1** the act of supplying things needed. **2** what is supplied; a sufficiency of things available for use. **3** (*often pl.*) necessary stores or provisions. **4** the quantity of goods or services offered for sale at a particular time. **5** a person who fills a position temporarily,a substitute. ~*a.* **1** filling a position temporarily (a *supply teacher*). **2** providing supplies. **on supply** (of a teacher etc.) acting as a supply. **supplier** *n.* **supply and demand** *n.* the amount of a product that is available and the amount that is required, as factors in regulating price. **supply-side** *a.* denoting an economic policy of low taxation and other incentives to stimulate production.

support (səpawt´) *v.t.* **1** to bear the weight of, to hold up, to sustain. **2** to keep from yielding or giving way. **3** to give strength or endurance to. **4** to furnish with necessaries, to provide for. **5** to give assistance to, to defend, to back up, to second. **7** to promote, to encourage. **8** to bear out, to substantiate, to corroborate. **9** to take a keen interest in (a sports team etc.); to want (a team etc.) to win. **10** to bear; to endure, to put up with. **11** to subscribe to (a charity or other institution). **12** to play a secondary role to (the main character) in a film or play. **13** to accompany (a band, feature film etc.) in a subordinate role. ~*n.* **1** the act of supporting or the state of being supported. **2** a person who or something which supports. **3** a band etc. supporting another in a concert. **4** subsistence, livelihood. **5** aid, assistance. **in support of** in order to support. **supportable** *a.* **supportability** (-bil´-) *n.* **supportably** *adv.* **supporter** *n.* **supporting** *a.* **1** playing or having a secondary or subordinate role. **2** giving support. **supporting film** *n.* a less important film in a programme. **supportingly** *adv.* **supportive** *a.* providing support, esp. moral or emotional encouragement. **supportively** *adv.* **supportiveness** *n.* **supportless** *a.*

suppose (səpōz´) *v.t.* **1** to take to be the case, to accept as probable, to surmise. **2** to lay down without proof, to assume by way of argument or illustration. **3** to imagine, to believe. **4** to involve or require as a condition, to imply. **5** (*usu. pass.*) to require or expect, to oblige (to). **6** to believe (to). **I suppose so** used to express agreement with a degree of uncertainty. **supposable** *a.* **supposed** *a.* believed to be so. **supposedly** (-zid-) *adv.* allegedly. **supposer** *n.* **supposition** (sŭpəzish´ən) *n.* **suppositional** *a.* **suppositionally** *adv.*

supposititious (sŭpəzish´əs), **suppositious** (səpozitish´əs) *a.* substituted for something else, not genuine, spurious. **suppositiously** *adv.* **suppositiousness** *n.* **supposititiously** *adv.* **supposititiousness** *n.*

suppository (səpoz´itəri) *n.* (*pl.* **suppositories**) a solid block of medicine introduced into the vagina or rectum, and left to dissolve.

suppress (səpres´) *v.t.* **1** to put down, to overpower, to subdue, to quell. **2** to keep in or back, to withhold, to stifle, to repress. **3** to keep back from disclosure or circulation, to conceal. **4** to eliminate (electrical interference). **suppressant** *n.* something which suppresses, esp. a drug which suppresses the appetite. **suppressible** *a.* **suppression** (-presh´ən) *n.* **suppressive** *a.* **suppressor** *n.*

suppurate (sŭp´ūrāt) *v.i.* to generate pus, to fester. **suppuration** (-ā´shən) *n.* **suppurative** (-rətiv) *a.*

supra (soo´prə) *adv.* above; earlier on.

supra- (soo´prə) *pref.* **1** above. **2** beyond.

supramaxillary (sooprəmaksil´əri) *a.* of or relating to the upper jaw.

supramundane (sooprəmŭn´dān) *a.* above the world.

supranational (sooprənash´ənəl) *a.* overriding national sovereignty. **supranationalism** *n.* **supranationality** (-nal´-) *n.*

supreme (suprēm´) *a.* **1** highest in authority or power. **2** highest in degree or importance, utmost, extreme, greatest possible. **3** last, final. **supremacy** (-prem´-) *n.* the quality or state of being supreme. **supremacist** (-prem´əsist) *n.* a person who believes or promotes the supremacy of a particular group, esp. a racial group. ~*a.* of or relating to supremacism. **supremacism** *n.* **Supreme Being** *n.* the deity, God. **Supreme Court** *n.* the highest judicial court in a state. **supremely** *adv.* **supremeness** *n.* **supreme pontiff** *n.* the Pope.

supremo (suprē´mō) *n.* (*pl.* **supremos**) a supreme leader or head.

Supt. *abbr.* Superintendent.

sura (suə´rə), **surah** *n.* a chapter of the Koran.

surah (sūə´rə) *n.* a soft, twilled, usu. self-coloured silk material.

surcharge[1] (sœ´chahj) *n.* **1** an extra charge or cost. **2** another valuation or other matter printed on a postage or revenue stamp. **3** an excessive load, burden or charge. **4** an amount surcharged on official accounts.

surcharge[2] (sœ´chahj, sœchahj´) *v.t.* **1** to put an extra charge on. **2** to overprint (a stamp) with a surcharge. **3** to overload, to overburden, to overfill. **4** to impose payment of (a sum) or on (a person) for amounts in official accounts disallowed by an auditor.

surcingle (sœ´sing-gəl) *n.* a belt or girth put round the body of a horse etc., for holding a saddle or blanket on its back.

surculus (sœ´kūləs) *n.* (*pl.* **surculi** (-lī)) (*Bot.*) a shoot rising from a rootstock, a sucker. **surculose** (-lōs) *a.*

surd (sœd) *a.* **1** (*Math.*) not capable of being expressed in rational numbers. **2** (of a sound) uttered with the breath and not with the voice. ~*n.* **1** (*Math.*) an irrational quantity. **2** a surd consonant, such as *p*, *f* or *s*.

sure (shuə, shaw) *a.* **1** certain, confident, undoubting. **2** free from doubts (of). **3** positive, believing, confidently trusting (that). **4** infallible, certain (to). **5** safe, reliable, trustworthy, unfailing. **6** unquestionably true. **7** certain (of finding, gaining etc.). ~*adv., int.* (*coll.*) surely, certainly; yes. **for sure** (*coll.*) surely, certainly. **sure as fate** without doubt, undoubtedly. **sure enough 1** (*coll.*) in reality, not merely in expectation. **2** (*coll.*) with near certainty. **to be sure 1** not to fail (to). **2** without doubt, certainly, of course. **3** it must be admitted. **to make sure** to make certain, to ascertain. **to make sure of** to establish the truth of. **sure-fire** *a.* (*coll.*) bound to succeed, assured. **sure-footed** *a.* not liable to stumble or fall. **sure-footedly** *adv.* **sure-footedness** *n.* **surely** *adv.* **1** undoubtedly. **2** certainly (frequently used by way of asseveration or to deprecate doubt). **3** securely, safely. **sureness** *n.*

surety (shuə´rəti, shaw´ti) *n.* (*pl.* **sureties**) **1** a person undertaking responsibility for payment of a sum, discharge of an engagement or attendance in court by another, a guarantor. **2** a pledge deposited as security against loss or damage or for payment or discharge of an engagement etc. **3** a guarantee. **4** certainty. **to stand surety** to act as a surety. **suretyship** *n.*

surf (sœf) *n.* **1** the swell of the sea breaking on the shore, rocks etc. **2** the foam produced by this. ~*v.i.* **1** to ride on the surf, to engage in surfing. **2** (*sl.*) to travel illicitly on the roof or outside of a train. ~*v.t.* to browse electronically through (esp. the Internet). **surfboard** *n.* a long narrow board used in surfing. **surfer** *n.* **surfie** *n.* (*esp. Austral.*)

a person whose life centres round surfing. **surfing** *n.* **1** surf-riding. **2** browsing through the Internet. **3** (*sl.*) travelling illicitly on the roof or outside of a train. **surf-riding** *n.* the sport of riding on the surf on a surfboard. **surfy** *a.*

surface (sœ'fis) *n.* **1** the exterior part of anything, the outside, the superficies. **2** any one of the limits bounding a solid. **3** (*Geom.*) something which has length and breadth but no thickness. **4** something which is apparent at first view or on slight consideration. ~*a.* **1** of or relating to the surface. **2** superficial. ~*v.t.* **1** to put a surface on. **2** to bring to the surface. ~*v.i.* **1** to rise to the surface. **2** to become known. **3** (*coll.*) to wake up or get out of bed. **to come to the surface** to appear after being hidden. **surface-active** *a.* capable of lessening the surface tension of a liquid. **surfaced** *a.* **surface mail** *n.* mail sent by land or sea. **surfacer** *n.* **surface tension** *n.* the tension of a liquid causing it to act as an elastic enveloping membrane tending to contract to the minimum area, as seen in the bubble, the drop etc. **surface-to-air** *a.* of or relating to missiles launched from land to an airborne target. **surface-to-surface** *a.* of or relating to missiles launched from one point on land to another.

surfactant (səfak'tənt) *n.* a surface-active substance, such as a detergent.

surfeit (sœ'fit) *n.* **1** excess, esp. in eating or drinking. **2** oppression resulting from this, satiety, nausea. **3** an excessive supply or amount. ~*v.t.* **1** to fill or feed to excess. **2** to overload, to cloy. ~*v.i.* **1** to overeat. **2** to feel uncomfortable through excess. **surfeiter** *n.*

surge (sœj) *n.* **1** a sudden onset. **2** a large wave, a billow, a swell. **3** a heaving and rolling motion. **4** a sudden increase or rise. ~*v.i.* **1** (of waves) to swell, to heave, to move up and down. **2** to well up, to move with a sudden rushing or swelling motion. **3** to increase or rise suddenly.

surgeon (sœ'jən) *n.* **1** a medical practitioner treating injuries, deformities and diseases by manual procedure, often involving operations. **2** a medical officer in the army or navy or in a military hospital. **surgeonfish** *n.* any sea fish of the genus *Acanthurus*, with lancelike spines at the tail. **surgeon general** *n.* (*pl.* **surgeons general**) **1** the head of the public health service in the US. **2** the chief medical officer in the US Army or Navy. **surgeonship** *n.*

surgery (sœ'jəri) *n.* (*pl.* **surgeries**) **1** (the branch of medicine dealing with) the treatment of injuries, deformities or diseases by manual procedure, often operations. **2** the office or consulting room of a doctor, dentist etc., or its hours of opening. **3** a place where an MP is available for consultation, or the time when they are available. **surgical** *a.* **surgically** *adv.* **surgical spirit** *n.* methylated spirit with oil of wintergreen and castor oil used for sterilizing, cleaning the skin etc.

suricate (sū'rikāt) *n.* a small S African meerkat, *Suricata suricata*, allied to the weasel.

Surinamese (suərinamēz') *a.* of or relating to Suriname, S America. ~*n.* (*pl.* **Surinamese**) a native or inhabitant of Suriname.

surly (sœ'li) *a.* (*comp.* **surlier**, *superl.* **surliest**) rude and bad-tempered. **surlily** *adv.* **surliness** *n.*

surmise (səmīz') *n.* a supposition on slight evidence, a guess, a conjecture. ~*v.t.* **1** to guess, to imagine, with little evidence; to conjecture, to suspect. **2** to suspect the existence of. ~*v.i.* to conjecture, to guess, to suppose. **surmisable** *a.* **surmiser** *n.*

surmount (səmownt') *v.t.* **1** to overcome, to vanquish, to rise above. **2** to overtop, to cap. **3** to get or climb to the top of and beyond. **surmountable** *a.* **surmountableness** *n.* **surmounter** *n.*

surname (sœ'nām) *n.* a name added to the first or Christian name; a family name (orig. an appellation signifying occupation etc., or a nickname ultimately becoming hereditary). **surnamed** *a.* having as a surname.

surpass (səpahs') *v.t.* to excel, to go beyond in amount, degree etc. **surpassable** *a.* **surpassing** *a.* excellent, exceptional. **surpassingly** *adv.* **surpassingness** *n.*

surplice (sœ'plis) *n.* a loose, flowing vestment of white linen, with full sleeves, worn by clergy and choristers at divine service. **surpliced** *a.*

surplus (sœ'pləs) *n.* **1** an amount which remains over, excess beyond what is used or required. **2** the balance in hand after all liabilities are paid. **3** the residuum of an estate after all debts and legacies are paid. ~*a.* being more than is needed.

surprise (səprīz') *n.* **1** an unexpected event. **2** emotion excited by something sudden or unexpected, astonishment. **3** the act of taking someone unawares or unprepared. ~*a.* unexpected. ~*v.t.* **1** to strike with astonishment, to be contrary to or different from expectation. **2** (*usu. p.p.*) to shock, to scandalize. **3** to come or fall upon suddenly and unexpectedly, esp. to attack unawares. **4** to disconcert. **5** to lead or drive unawares (into an act etc.). **to take by surprise** to strike with astonishment, to take unawares. **surprisal** *n.* **surprisedly** (-zid-) *adv.* **surpriser** *n.* **surprising** *a.* **surprisingly** *adv.* **surprisingness** *n.*

surreal (səriəl') *a.* **1** having the qualities of surrealism. **2** strange, weird, bizarre. **surreality** (-al'-) *n.* **surreally** *adv.*

surrealism (səriə'lizm) *n.* an artistic and literary movement of the 20th cent. which aimed at expressing the subconscious activities of the mind by presenting images with the chaotic incoherency of a dream. **surrealist** *n.*, *a.* **surrealistic** (-lis'-) *a.* **surrealistically** *adv.*

surrebut (sūribŭt') *v.i.* (*pres.p.* **surrebutting**, *past*, *p.p.* **surrebutted**) (*Law*) to reply to a defendant's rebutter. **surrebutter** *n.* (*Law*) the plaintiff's reply to the defendant's rebutter.

surrejoin (sūrijoin') *v.i.* (*Law*) to reply to a

defendant's rejoinder. **surrejoinder** (-də) n. the plaintiff's reply to the defendant's rejoinder.

surrender (sərən´də) v.t. 1 to give up possession of, esp. upon compulsion or demand. 2 to yield up to the power or control of another. 3 to yield (oneself) to any influence, habit, emotion etc. 4 to relinquish (a life-insurance policy) in return for a smaller, immediate payment. ~v.i. 1 to yield something or to give oneself up into the power of another, esp. to an enemy in war. 2 to give in, to yield, to submit. 3 to yield to any influence, habit, emotion etc. ~n. the act of surrendering or the state of being surrendered. **surrenderer** n. **surrender value** n. a payment made in return for the voluntary relinquishing of a life insurance policy by its holder.

surreptitious (sŭrəptish´əs) a. 1 done by stealth or fraud. 2 secret, clandestine. **surreptitiously** adv. **surreptitiousness** n.

surrey (sŭr´i) n. (pl. **surreys**) (NAm.) a light, four-wheeled horse-drawn carriage.

surrogate (sŭr´əgət) n. 1 a deputy; a substitute. 2 a deputy of a bishop or his chancellor appointed to grant marriage licences and probates. **surrogacy** (-si), **surrogateship** n. **surrogate mother** n. 1 a person taking the role of a mother. 2 a woman who bears a child for a childless couple, often after artificial insemination or embryo implantation.

surround (sərownd´) v.t. 1 to lie or be situated all round, to encompass, to encircle, to enclose. 2 to cause to be surrounded in this way. ~n. 1 an edging, a border. 2 the floor covering, or staining of floorboards, between the skirting and the carpet. 3 the structure built round a fire etc. **surrounding** a. **surroundings** n.pl. things around a person or thing, environment, circumstances.

surtax (sœ´taks) n. an additional tax. ~v.t. to impose a surtax on.

surtitle (sœ´tītəl) n. a printed translation of part of the text of an opera etc. projected on a screen above the stage. ~v.t. to provide with surtitles.

surveillance (səvā´ləns, -vā´əns) n. observation, close watch, supervision.

Usage note The pronunciation with (l) is preferred to that without.

---

survey¹ (səvā´) v.t. 1 to look over, to take a general view of. 2 to examine and ascertain the condition, value etc. of (a building etc.). 3 to determine by accurate observation and measurement the boundaries, extent, position, contours etc. of (a tract of country, coast, estate etc.). ~v.i. to carry out a survey. **surveyable** a. **surveying** n. **surveyor** n. 1 a person who surveys, esp. one who measures land. 2 an inspector (of customs, weights and measures etc.). **surveyorship** n.

survey² (sœ´vā) n. 1 the act or process of surveying. 2 a general view. 3 a careful examination, investigation, inspection or scrutiny. 4 an account based on this. 5 the operation of

surveying land etc. 6 a map, plan etc. recording the results of this.

survive (səvīv´) v.i. to be still alive or in existence. ~v.t. 1 to live longer than, to outlive, to outlast. 2 to be alive after, to live through, to outlive or outlast (an event, period etc.). **survivable** a. **survival** n. 1 the act or condition of surviving. 2 a person, thing, custom, opinion etc. surviving into a new state of things. 3 the activity of coping with harsh conditions, either as a sport or as a training exercise. **survivalism** n. 1 a policy of taking measures to ensure one's own survival. 2 the activity of practising outdoor survival skills as a sport. **survivalist** n., a. **survival kit** n. emergency rations etc., carried by members of the armed forces etc. **survival of the fittest** n. 1 the preservation of forms of life that have proved themselves best adapted to their environment, the process or result of natural selection. 2 the success of the most adaptable or efficient businesses, people etc. **survivor** n. **survivorship** n.

sus¹ (sŭs) n. (sl.) suspicion of loitering with criminal intent.

sus² SUSS.

susceptible (səsep´tibəl) a. 1 impressionable, sensitive. 2 capable of being influenced or affected, accessible, liable (to). 3 admitting (of). **susceptibility** (-bil´-) n. (pl. **susceptibilities**) 1 the condition or quality of being susceptible. 2 (pl.) sensitive feelings, sensibilities. **susceptibly** adv. **susceptive** a. 1 readily receiving impressions etc., susceptible. 2 receiving emotional impressions. **susceptiveness, susceptivity** (sŭseptiv´-) n.

sushi (soo´shi) n. a Japanese dish of cold rice cakes with a vinegar dressing and garnishes of raw fish etc.

suspect¹ (səspekt´) v.t. 1 to imagine to exist, to have an impression of the existence of without proof, to surmise. 2 to be inclined to think. 3 to be inclined to believe to be guilty but upon slight evidence, to doubt the innocence of. 4 to believe to be uncertain, to doubt, to mistrust.

suspect² (sŭs´pekt) n. a person suspected of crime etc. ~a. 1 suspected, under suspicion, suspicious. 2 doubtful, uncertain.

suspend (səspend´) v.t. 1 to hang up, to hang from something above. 2 to sustain from falling or sinking. 3 to render temporarily inoperative or cause to cease for a time, to intermit; to defer. 4 to debar temporarily from a privilege, office etc. **suspended** a. (of particles) held in a suspension. **suspended animation** n. temporary ceasing of the body's vital functions. **suspended sentence** n. a prison sentence that is not served unless a further crime is committed. **suspender** n. 1 an attachment to hold up a stocking or sock. 2 (pl., N Am.) braces. 3 a person who or something which suspends. **suspender belt** n. a belt with stocking suspenders attached.

suspense (səspens´) n. 1 a state of uncertainty,

doubt or apprehensive expectation or waiting. **2**
(*Law*) a temporary cessation of a right etc. **to
keep in suspense** to delay giving (someone) vital
information. **suspenseful** *a.* **suspension** (-shən)
n. **1** the act of suspending. **2** the state of being
suspended. **3** a system of springs etc. that
supports the body of a vehicle on the axles. **4** a
dispersion of solid particles in a fluid. **suspension bridge** *n.* a bridge sustained by flexible
supports passing over a tower or elevated pier
and secured at each extremity. **suspensive** *a.*
suspensory *a.*
suspicion (səspish′ən) *n.* **1** the act or feeling of a
person who suspects. **2** belief in the existence of
wrong or guilt on inadequate proof, doubt,
mistrust. **3** a very slight amount; a trace. **above
suspicion** too honest or good to be suspected.
under suspicion suspected. **suspicionless** *a.* **suspicious** *a.* **1** inclined to suspect. **2** entertaining
suspicion. **3** expressing or showing suspicion. **4**
exciting or likely to excite suspicion. **suspiciously** *adv.* **suspiciousness** *n.*
suss (sŭs), **sus** *v.t.* (*pres.p.* **sussing**, *past*, *p.p.*
sussed) (*sl.*) **1** to suspect of a crime. **2** to work out
or discover the true facts of. ~*n.* **1** a suspect. **2** a
suspicion. **on suss** on suspicion (of having
committed a crime). **to suss out** to investigate, to
find out about.
sustain (səstān′) *v.t.* **1** to bear the weight of, to
hold up, to keep from falling. **2** to stand, to
undergo without yielding. **3** to experience, to
suffer. **4** to nourish, to provide sustenance for. **5**
to enable to bear something, to keep from failing,
to strengthen, to encourage, to keep up. **6** to
prolong. **7** to maintain, to uphold. **8** to establish
by evidence. **9** to support, to confirm, to bear out,
to substantiate. **sustainable** *a.* **1** (of sources of
raw materials) capable of being replaced at the
same rate as they are used, minimizing damage
to the environment. **2** able to be sustained. **sus-
tainedly** (-idli) *adv.* **sustainer** *n.* **sustainment** *n.*
sustenance (sŭs′tinəns) *n.* **1** something which
sustains, the means of support or maintenance. **2**
the nourishing element in food. **3** food, subsistence.
☒ **sutle** common misspelling of SUBTLE.
sutler (sŭt′lə) *n.* (*Hist.*) a person following an
army and selling provisions, liquor etc.
Sutra (soo′trə) *n.* **1** in Hindu literature, a rule, a
precept, an aphorism. **2** (*pl.*) Brahminical books
of rules, doctrine etc.
suttee (sŭtē′, sŭt′i), **sati** (sŭt′i) *n.* (*pl.* **suttees**,
satis) (*Hist.*) **1** a Hindu custom by which the
widow was burnt on the funeral pyre with her
dead husband. **2** a widow so burnt.
suture (soo′chə) *n.* **1** (*Biol.*) the junction of two
parts by their margins as if by sewing, esp. of the
bones of the skull. **2** (*Med.*) the uniting of two
body surfaces, esp. the edges of a wound, by
stitching. **3** catgut, silk etc. used in uniting body
surfaces. **4** a stitch or seam made in this way.
~*v.t.* to unite by a suture. **sutural** *a.* **sutured** *a.*

suzerain (soo′zərān) *n.* **1** (*Hist.*) a feudal lord. **2** a
state having sovereignty or control over another.
suzerainty *n.*
s.v. *abbr.* (L) *sub verbo*, *sub voce*, under the word
or heading.
svelte (svelt) *a.* (esp. of a woman's figure) slender,
lissom.
Svengali (sven-gah′li) *n.* (*pl.* **Svengalis**) a person
who control's another's mind, esp. for a sinister
purpose.
SW *abbr.* **1** south-west. **2** south-western.
swab (swob), **swob** *n.* **1** a mop for cleaning floors,
decks, the bore of a gun etc. **2** a small piece of
cotton wool or gauze used for removing blood,
dressing wounds, taking specimens etc. **3** a
specimen taken with a swab for examination.
~*v.t.* (*pres.p.* **swabbing**, **swobbing**, *past*, *p.p.*
swabbed, **swobbed**) to rub, wipe or clean with a
swab or mop. **swabber** *n.*
swaddle (swod′əl)*v.t.* **1** to wind or swathe in or
as in a bandage, wrap or wraps. **2** to wrap in
swaddling-clothes to restrict movement.
swaddling-clothes *n.pl.* (*Hist.*) cloth bands used
for swaddling an infant.
swag (swag) *n.* **1** (*sl.*) booty obtained by robbery,
esp. burglary. **2** an ornamental festoon. **3** a heavy,
loosely hanging fold of fabric. **4** (*Austral.*, *New
Zeal.*) a pack or bundle of personal effects, baggage. ~*v.t.* (*pres.p.* **swagging**, *past*, *p.p.* **swagged**)
1 to hang or arrange in swags. **2** to cause to sway
or sag. ~*v.i.* to hang loose and heavy; to sag.
swagman *n.* (*pl.* **swagmen**) (*Austral.*, *New Zeal.*) a
man who carries his swag about with him in
search of work.
swagger (swag′ə) *v.i.* **1** to walk, strut or go (about
etc.) with an air of defiance, self-confidence or
superiority. **2** to talk or behave in a blustering,
boastful or hectoring manner. ~*v.t.* to bluster or
bluff (a person into, out of etc.). ~*n.* **1** a
swaggering walk, gait or manner. **2** bluster, dash,
conceit. **3** smartness. ~*a.* (*coll.*) smart, fashionable. **swaggerer** *n.* **swaggeringly** *adv.* **swagger
stick** *n.* a short cane with a metal head, carried
by soldiers.
Swahili (swəhē′li, swah-) *n.* (*pl.* **Swahili**) **1** a
member of a Bantu-speaking people of Tanzania.
2 their language, Kiswahili.
swain (swān) *n.* **1** †a young rustic; a country
gallant. **2** (*poet.*) a male lover.
swallow[1] (swol′ō) *v.t.* **1** to take through the
mouth and throat into the stomach. **2** to absorb,
to engulf, to overwhelm, to consume (up). **3** to
accept with credulity. **4** to accept without
resentment, to put up with. **5** to refrain from
showing or expressing. **6** to retract, to recant. **7** to
say indistinctly. ~*v.i.* to perform the action of
swallowing. ~*n.* **1** the act of swallowing. **2** the
amount swallowed at once. **swallowable** *a.*
swallower *n.*
swallow[2] (swol′ō) *n.* **1** any small, swift,
migratory bird of the family Hirundinidae, with
long, pointed wings and a forked tail. **2** a swift or

other bird resembling the swallow. **swallow-dive** *n.* a dive with the arms outstretched. **swallowtail** *n.* **1** a deeply forked tail. **2** a butterfly or hummingbird with such a tail. **3** (*often pl.*) a swallow-tailed coat, a dress coat. **swallow-tailed** *a.*

swam SWIM.

swami (swah´mi) *n.* (*pl.* **swamis**) a Hindu religious teacher.

swamp (swomp) *n.* a tract of wet, spongy land, a bog, a marsh. ~*v.t.* **1** to cause (a boat etc.) to be filled with or to sink in water. **2** to plunge or sink into a bog. **3** to overwhelm, to render helpless with difficulties, numbers etc. ~*v.i.* to fill with water, to sink, to founder. **swampland** *n.* land consisting of swamps. **swampy** *a.* (*comp.* **swampier**, *superl.* **swampiest**).

swan (swon) *n.* a large, web-footed aquatic bird of the genus *Cygnus*, with a long neck and usu. white plumage, noted for its grace in the water. ~*v.i.* (*pres.p.* **swanning**, *past, p.p.* **swanned**) to wander aimlessly (about, around etc.). **swan-dive** *n.* (*N Am.*) a swallow-dive. **swanlike** *a.* **swan-neck** *n.* a pipe, tube, rail etc. curved like a swan's neck, esp. the end of a discharge pipe. **swannery** *n.* (*pl.* **swanneries**) a place where swans are kept or bred. **swansdown** *n.* **1** down obtained from a swan. **2** a thick cotton cloth with a downy nap on one side. **swansong** *n.* **1** the last or dying work, esp. of a poet. **2** any final work, performance etc.

swank (swangk) *n.* (*coll.*) swagger, bluster. ~*v.i.* to swagger, to show off, to bluster. ~*a.* (*esp. N Am.*) swanky. **swankpot** *n.* (*coll.*) a person who swanks. **swanky** *a.* (*comp.* **swankier**, *superl.* **swankiest**) (*coll.*) **1** stylish, showy. **2** showing off. **swankily** *adv.* **swankiness** *n.*

swap (swop), **swop** *v.t., v.i.* (*pres.p.* **swapping**, **swopping**, *past, p.p.* **swapped, swopped**) to exchange, to barter. ~*n.* **1** an act of exchanging, a barter. **2** something suitable for swapping. **3** something exchanged in a swap. **swapper** *n.*

sward (swawd) *n.* (*poet.*) **1** a surface of land covered with thick short grass. **2** turf. **swarded** *a.* **swardy** *a.*

swarf (swawf) *n.* grit, metal filings, chips, grindings.

swarm[1] (swawm) *n.* **1** a cluster of bees issuing from a hive with a queen bee and seeking a new home. **2** a large number of small animals, insects, people etc., esp. when moving in a confused mass. **3** (*pl.*) great numbers. ~*v.i.* **1** (of bees) to collect together in readiness for emigrating, to leave (or go out of) a hive in a swarm. **2** to move (about etc.) in a swarm. **3** to congregate, to throng, to be very numerous. **4** (of places) to be thronged or overcrowded (with).

swarm[2] (swawm) *v.i.* (*with up*) to climb up (a tree, rope, pole etc.) by embracing it with the arms and legs. ~*v.t.* to swarm up.

swarthy (swaw´dhi) *a.* (*comp.* **swarthier**, *superl.* **swarthiest**) dark or dusky in complexion. **swarthily** *adv.* **swarthiness** *n.*

swash (swosh) *v.i.* **1** to make a noise as of splashing water. **2** (of liquid) to wash or splash about. ~*n.* a washing, dashing or splashing of water. **swashbuckler** *n.* **1** an adventurer, a daredevil. **2** a film or book about the adventures of a swashbuckler. **swashbuckling** *a.*

swastika (swos´tikə) *n.* a cross with arms bent at a right angle, used as a symbol of anti-Semitism or Nazism.

swat (swot) *v.t.* (*pres.p.* **swatting**, *past, p.p.* **swatted**) **1** to hit sharply. **2** to crush (a fly) with a sharp blow. ~*n.* a sharp blow. **swatter** *n.*

Usage note The spellings of the verbs *swat* (to crush) and *swot* (to study hard) should not be confused.

swatch (swoch) *n.* **1** a sample of cloth. **2** a collection of samples.

swath (swawth, swoth), **swathe** (swādh) *n.* (*pl.* **swaths** (swawths, swawdhz, swoths), **swathes**) **1** a row or ridge of grass, corn etc. cut and left lying on the ground. **2** the space cut by a scythe, machine etc. in one course. **3** a broad strip or band.

swathe (swādh) *v.t.* to bind or wrap in or as in a bandage, cloth etc. ~*n.* a bandage, a wrapping.

sway (swā) *v.i.* **1** to move backwards and forwards, to swing, to oscillate irregularly. **2** to be unsteady, to waver, to vacillate. **3** to lean or incline to one side or in different directions. ~*v.t.* **1** to cause to oscillate, waver, or vacillate. **2** to bias; to influence, to control, to rule. **3** to cause to incline to one side. ~*n.* **1** rule, dominion, control. **2** the act of swaying, a swing.

swear (sweə) *v.i.* (*past* **swore** (swaw), †**sware** (sweə), *p.p.* **sworn** (swawn)) **1** to affirm solemnly invoking God or some other sacred person or object as witness or pledge, to take an oath. **2** to appeal (to) as witness of an oath. **3** to use profane or obscene language. **4** to give evidence on oath. **5** to make a promise on oath. ~*v.t.* **1** to utter or affirm with an oath. **2** to take an oath (that). **3** to cause to take an oath, to administer an oath to, to bind by an oath. **4** (*coll.*) to declare, to vow. **5** to promise or testify upon oath. **6** to utter profanely or obscenely. ~*n.* **1** an act or spell of swearing. **2** a profane oath. **to swear blind** (*coll.*) to state solemnly or emphatically. **to swear by** (*coll.*) to have or profess great confidence in. **to swear in** to induct into office with the administration of an oath. **to swear off** (*coll.*) to renounce solemnly. **to swear to** to testify firmly to the truth of. **swearer** *n.* **swear word** *n.* an obscene or taboo word.

sweat (swet) *n.* **1** the moisture exuded from the skin of a person or animal. **2** the act or state of sweating. **3** (*coll.*) a state of anxiety, a flurry. **4** (*coll.*) drudgery, toil, hard labour, exertion. **5** moisture exuded from or deposited in drops on any surface. ~*v.i.* (*past, p.p.* **sweated**, (*N Am.*) **sweat**) **1** to exude sweat, to perspire. **2** to emit moisture. **3** (of moisture) to exude. **4** to collect surface moisture. **5** to be in a flurry or state of anxiety, panic etc. **6** to toil, to labour, to drudge. ~*v.t.* **1** to cause to emit moisture in drops on a surface. **2** to emit as or like sweat. **3** to make (an animal or athlete) sweat by exertion. **4** to employ at starvation wages, to exact the largest possible amount of labour from at the lowest pay, by utilizing competition. **5** (*coll.*) to subject to extortion, to bleed. **6** to heat (meat or vegetables) in fat until the juices exude. **by the sweat of one's brow** by working hard. **no sweat** (*sl.*) no difficulty or problem, without trouble. **to sweat blood** (*sl.*) to work or worry to an extreme degree. **to sweat out 1** to remove or get rid of by sweating. **2** (*coll.*) to endure, to live through. **sweatband** *n.* a band of absorbent material round the forehead or wrist, worn in some sports to keep sweat out of the eyes or from the hands. **sweater** *n.* a pullover. **sweat gland** *n.* a gland below the skin which exudes sweat. **sweatpants** *n.pl.* loose, warm trousers with an elasticated or drawstring waist, worn for leisure or exercise. **sweatshirt** *n.* a loose, long-sleeved sweater made from cotton jersey. **sweatshop** *n.* a factory or other workplace that employs the sweating system. **sweat sock** *n.* (*NAm.*) either one of a pair of thick, absorbent, cotton socks, worn with trainers. **sweatsuit** *n.* a suit consisting of a sweatshirt and sweatpants, worn for leisure or exercise. **sweaty** *a.* (*comp.* **sweatier,** *superl.* **sweatiest**) covered with or causing sweat. **sweatily** *adv.* **sweatiness** *n.*

Swede (swēd) *n.* a native or inhabitant of Sweden, or a descendant of one. **swede, swede turnip** *n.* a large turnip, *Brassica rutabaga*, having yellow flesh.

Swedish (swē´dish) *a.* of or relating to Sweden. ~*n.* the language of the Swedes.

sweep (swēp) *v.t.* (*past, p.p.* **swept** (swept)) **1** to clear dirt etc. from or clean with or as with a broom. **2** to collect or gather (up) with or as with a broom. **3** to propel with sweeps. **4** to cause to move with a sweeping motion. **5** to carry (along, away etc.) with powerful or unchecked force. **6** to wipe out, remove, destroy. **7** to move swiftly and powerfully over, across or along, to range, to scour. **8** (esp. of the eyes) to pass over in swift survey. **9** to pass over destructively. **10** (*NAm.*) to gain an overwhelming victory in. ~*v.i.* **1** to clear or clean a place with a broom. **2** to glide, move or pass along with a strong, swift continuous motion. **3** to go with a stately motion. **4** (of land, a curve etc.) to extend continuously. **5** (of the eye) to range unchecked. ~*n.* **1** the act of sweeping. **2** a clearance, a riddance. **3** a sweeping motion. **4** a sweeping curve, direction, piece of road etc. **5** a broad expanse. **6** the range, reach or compass of a sweeping motion or of an instrument, weapon, implement etc. having this motion. **7** a survey of an area made in an arc. **8** a chimney sweep. **9** a sortie by aircraft. **10** (*coll.*) a sweepstake. **to make a clean sweep of 1** to get rid

of entirely. **2** to win all the prizes in (a competition etc.). **to sweep aside** to remove quickly and completely. **to sweep away** to sweep aside. **sweepback** *n.* the angular relation of an aircraft wing to the axis. **sweeper** *n.* **1** a person who sweeps. **2** a carpet sweeper. **3** a defensive player in soccer positioned behind the main defensive line. **sweeping** *a.* **1** covering a wide area. **2** wideranging, comprehensive. **3** without discrimination or qualification. **4** that sweeps. **sweepingly** *adv.* **sweepingness** *n.* **sweepings** *n.pl.* things collected by sweeping. **swept-back** *a.* (of an aircraft wing) slanting backwards, set back at an angle. **swept-wing** *a.* (of an aircraft) having swept-back wings.

sweepstake (swēp´stāk), (*esp. N Am.*) **sweepstakes** *n.* **1** a lottery in which a number of people stake sums on an event, esp. on a horse race, the total amount staked being divided among the winning betters. **2** a race with betting of this kind. **3** a prize won in a sweepstake.

sweet (swēt) *a.* **1** having a taste like the taste of honey or sugar. **2** pleasing to the senses. **3** fragrant. **4** pleasant or melodious in sound. **5** fresh, not salt or salted, not sour, bitter, stale or rancid. **6** pleasant to the mind, agreeable, delightful. **7** charming, amiable, gracious. **8** (*coll.*) lovable, dear, beloved. ~*n.* **1** a sweet thing. **2** a piece of confectionery, such as a toffee or a chocolate. **3** a sweet dish, such as a tart, pudding or ice cream; this served as a course of a meal, after the main course. **4** the sweetness or the sweet part of anything. **5** dear one, darling. ~*adv.* (*coll.*) sweetly. **to be sweet on** to be in love with; to be very fond of. **sweet alyssum** *n.* a cruciferous plant, *Lolularia maritima*, with clusters of small flowers. **sweet and sour** *a.* cooked in a sauce made with sugar and vinegar or lemon juice. **sweet basil** *n.* the culinary herb *Ocimum basilicum*. **sweet bay** *n.* the bay tree or bay laurel, *Laurus nobilis*. **sweetbread** *n.* the pancreas or thymus gland of a calf or sheep, used as food. **sweet-brier** *n.* a Eurasian wild rose, *Rosa eglanteria*, having small, fragrant flowers. **sweet chestnut** *n.* the tree *Castanea sativa*. **sweet cicely** *n.* MYRRH². **sweetcorn** *n.* **1** a variety of maize with kernels rich in sugar. **2** the kernels eaten as a vegetable when young. **sweeten** *v.t.* **1** to make sweet or sweeter. **2** to make more agreeable or less unpleasant. **3** to mollify, to pacify. ~*v.i.* to become sweet or sweeter. **sweetener** *n.* **1** a sugar-free sweetening agent. **2** (*sl.*) a bribe. **sweetening** *n.* **sweet fennel** FENNEL. **sweet gale** *n.* the bog myrtle, the gale. **sweetheart** *n.* a lover, a boyfriend or girlfriend (used as a term of endearment). **sweetheart agreement, sweetheart contract, sweetheart deal** *n.* (*coll.*) an agreement reached between an employer and a trade union with advantages to both parties. **sweetie, sweety** *n.* (*pl.* **sweeties**) **1** a piece of confectionery, a sweet. **2** (*also* **sweetie-pie**) a term of endearment. **sweetish** *a.* **sweetishness** *n.* **sweetly** *adv.* **sweet**

marjoram *n.* the herb *Marjorana hortensis*, used in cooking. **sweetmeal** *n.* **1** sweetened wholemeal. **2** a biscuit made of sweetmeal. **†sweetmeat** *n.* **1** a piece of confectionery, a sweet. **2** a small, fancy cake. **sweetness** *n.* **sweet nothings** *n.pl.* words of endearment. **sweet pea** *n.* an annual leguminous climbing plant, *Lathyrus odoratus*, with showy flowers. **sweet pepper** *n.* a mild-flavoured capsicum. **sweet potato** *n.* (*pl.* **sweet potatoes**) a tropical climbing plant, *Ipomoea batatas*, with an edible root. **sweet rocket** *n.* any of various plants of the genus *Hesperis* or *Sisymbrium*. **sweetshop** *n.* a shop where sweets are sold. **sweet talk** *n.* (*coll.*) flattery, blandishment. **sweet-talk** *v.t.* (*coll.*) to flatter, esp. in order to coax or persuade. **sweet tooth** *n.* a fondness for sweet-tasting things. **sweet violet** *n.* the violet *Viola odorata*. **sweet william** (wil´yəm) *n.* a biennial species of pink, *Dianthus barbatus*, with dense clusters of showy, fragrant flowers. **sweety** SWEETIE (under SWEET).

swell (swel) *v.i.* (*p.p.* **swollen** (swō´lən), **swelled**) **1** to dilate or increase in bulk or extent, to expand. **2** to rise (up) from the surrounding surface. **3** to bulge, to belly (out). **4** to become greater in volume, strength or intensity. **5** to be puffed up, to be elated, to strut. **6** to be inflated with emotion. ~*v.t.* **1** to increase the size, bulk, volume or dimensions of. **2** to raise (up) from the surrounding surface. **3** to inflate, to puff up. ~*n.* **1** the act or effect of swelling. **2** a rise, an increase, an augmentation. **3** a succession of long, unbroken waves in one direction, for example after a storm. **4** a bulge, a bulging part. **5** (*Mus.*) an increase followed by a decrease in the volume of sound; a combined crescendo and diminuendo. **6** (*Mus.*) a contrivance for gradually increasing and diminishing sound in an organ etc. **7** (*dated coll.*) a person of high standing or importance, a showy, dashing or fashionable person. ~*a.* (*esp.* N *Am.*, *coll.*) excellent, fine. **swelled head** *n.* (*coll.*) a high opinion of oneself. **swelling** *n.* **1** an unnatural enlargement or protuberance of a body part. **2** the act of expanding, or the state of being swollen or augmented. **swellish** *a.* **swollen head** *n.* (*coll.*) a swelled head.

swelter (swel´tə) *v.i.* **1** (of the weather etc.) to be hot, moist and oppressive, to cause faintness, languor or oppression. **2** to sweat profusely. ~*n.* a sweltering condition. **sweltering** *a.* oppressively hot. **swelteringly** *adv.* **sweltry** (-tri) *a.*

swept SWEEP.

swerve (swœv) *v.i.* to turn to one side, to deviate, to diverge from the direct or regular course. ~*v.t.* to cause to diverge, to deflect. ~*n.* **1** the act of swerving. **2** a sudden divergence or deflection. **swerveless** *a.* **swerver** *n.*

swift (swift) *a.* **1** moving or able to move with great rapidity, rapid, quick, speedy. **2** ready, prompt, expeditious. **3** passing rapidly, soon over, brief, unexpected, sudden. ~*n.* a small,

long-winged insectivorous bird of the family Apodidae, closely resembling the swallow. **swiftly** *adv.* **swiftness** *n.*

swig (swig) *v.t.*, *v.i.* (*pres.p.* **swigging**, *past*, *p.p.* **swigged**) (*coll.*) to drink in large draughts. ~*n.* a large drink of liquor. **swigger** *n.*

swill (swil) *v.t.*, *v.i.* **1** to wash, to rinse. **2** to drink greedily. ~*n.* **1** the act of rinsing. **2** liquid food for animals, esp. pigs. **3** (liquid) rubbish, slops. **4** poor-quality alcoholic liquor. **5** a swig. **swiller** *n.*

swim (swim) *v.i.* (*pres.p.* **swimming**, *past* **swam** (swam), *p.p.* **swum** (swŭm)) **1** to move progressively in the water by the motion of the hands and feet, or fins, tail etc. **2** to float or be supported on water or other liquid. **3** to glide along. **4** to be drenched or flooded (with water etc.). **5** to seem to reel or whirl round one. **6** to have a feeling of dizziness. ~*v.t.* **1** to pass, traverse or accomplish by swimming. **2** to compete in (a race) by swimming. **3** to perform (a particular swimming stroke). **4** to cause (a horse, boat etc.) to swim or float. **5** to bear up, to float (a ship etc.). ~*n.* **1** the act or a spell of swimming. **2** a pool or run frequented by fish in a river. **3** the main current of life, business etc. **in the swim** involved in the main current activity. **swim-bladder** *n.* the air-bladder or sound of a fish. **swimmable** *a.* **swimmer** *n.* **swimming** *n.*, *a.* **swimming bath** *n.* an artificial pool for swimming in. **swimming costume** *n.* a swimsuit. **swimmingly** *adv.* smoothly, easily, without impediment. **swimming pool** *n.* an artificial pool for swimming in. **swimming trunks** *n.pl.* a man's or boy's shorts worn for swimming. **swimsuit** *n.* a woman's or girl's one-piece garment for swimming. **swimsuited** *a.* **swimwear** *n.* clothes worn for swimming.

Usage note In standard English, the past tense of *swim* is *swam*, not *swum*.

swindle (swin´dəl) *v.t.*, *v.i.* **1** to cheat. **2** to obtain by cheating. ~*n.* **1** the act or process of swindling. **2** a thing that is not what it pretends to be, a deception, a fraud. **3** a gross fraud or imposition, a fraudulent scheme. **swindler** *n.*

swine (swīn) *n.* (*pl.* **swine**, **swines**) **1** (*formal or* N *Am.*) a pig, a hog. **2** (*coll.*) a greedy, vicious or debased person. **3** (*coll.*) something difficult or unpleasant. **swine fever** *n.* an infectious lung disease affecting pigs. **swine vesicular disease** *n.* an infectious viral disease of pigs causing fever and blisters. **swinish** *a.* **swinishly** *adv.* **swinishness** *n.*

swing (swing) *v.i.* (*past*, *p.p.* **swung** (swŭng)) **1** to move to and fro, like an object suspended by a point or one side, to sway, hang freely like a pendulum, to oscillate, to rock. **2** to turn on or as on a pivot, to move or wheel (round etc.) through an arc. **3** to go with a swaying, undulating or rhythmical gait or motion. **4** to go to and fro by swinging. **5** (*coll.*) to hit out (at) with a swinging arm movement. **6** (*coll.*) to be hanged. **7** to play swing-music. **8** to have the rhythmical quality of swing-music. **9** to fluctuate between emotions, decisions etc. **10** (*coll.*) to be lively or up to date. **11** (*coll.*) to be promiscuous. **12** (*coll.*) (of a party) to be lively and exciting. **13** (of a cricket ball) to be bowled with a swing. ~*v.t.* **1** to cause to move to and fro, to sway, to oscillate. **2** to wave to and fro, to brandish. **3** to cause to turn or move around, as on a pivot or through an arc. **4** to throw (a punch). **5** to play or perform in the style of swing-music. **6** (*coll.*) to manipulate, to influence. **7** (*coll.*) to cause to happen, to bring about. **8** in cricket, to cause (the ball) to swing. ~*n.* **1** the act or state of swinging. **2** a swinging or oscillating motion. **3** a swinging gait or rhythm. **4** the compass or sweep of a moving body. **5** a curving or sweeping movement. **6** a blow delivered with a sweeping arm movement. **7** free course, unrestrained liberty. **8** regular course of activity. **9** a seat suspended by ropes etc., on which a person, esp. a child, may swing to and fro. **10** a spell of swinging on this. **11** swing-music. **12** the rhythmic feeling of swing-music. **13** a shift in opinion, condition etc. **in full swing** in full activity or operation. **swings and roundabouts** a situation in which there are as many gains as losses. **swingbin** *n.* a plastic bin with a lid which can be swung open and shut. **swingboat** *n.* a boat-shaped carriage for swinging in at fairs etc. **swing bowler** *n.* in cricket, a bowler who swings the ball. **swing bowling** *n.* **swingbridge** *n.* a drawbridge opening by turning horizontally. **swing-door** *n.* a door which can swing open in either direction. **swinger** *n.* **swinging** *a.* **1** that swings. **2** (*coll.*) lively or up to date. **3** (*coll.*) promiscuous. **swingingly** *adv.* **swing-music** *n.* a style of playing jazz in which the basic melody and rhythm persist through individual interpretations of the theme, impromptu variations etc. **swing-wing** *n.* an aircraft having movable wings allowing varying degrees of sweepback at different speeds. **swingy** *a.* (*comp.* **swingier**, *superl.* **swingiest**).

swingeing (swin´jing) *a.* severe, great, huge. **swingeingly** *adv.*

swingle (swing´gəl) *n.* **1** a wooden instrument for beating flax to separate the woody parts from the fibre. **2** the swinging part of a flail. ~*v.t.* to clean (flax) by beating with a swingle. **swingletree** *n.* a crossbar pivoted in the middle on a cart etc. to which traces are attached.

swinish SWINE.

swipe (swīp) *v.t.* (*coll.*) **1** to hit with great force. **2** to pilfer. **3** to pass (a swipe card) through a machine which can electronically read its encoded information. ~*v.i.* to hit out with a swipe. ~*n.* a hard, swiping blow. **swipe card** *n.* a credit card, debit card etc. having magnetically encoded information which can be read by an electronic device. **swiper** *n.*

swirl (swœl) *v.i.* to form eddies, to whirl about. ~*v.t.* to carry (along, down etc.) with an eddying

motion. ~*n.* **1** a whirling motion, an eddy. **2** the act of swirling. **3** a winding or curling pattern or figure. **swirly** *a.* (*comp.* **swirlier**, *superl.* **swirliest**).

swish (swish) *v.i.* **1** to make a whistling sound in cutting through the air. **2** to move with such a sound. ~*v.t.* **1** to make such a whistling movement with. **2** to strike or cut (off) with such a sound. ~*n.* a whistling sound, movement or blow. ~*a.* (*coll.*) smart, elegant. **swishy** *a.* (*comp.* **swishier**, *superl.* **swishiest**) **1** making a swishing sound. **2** (*sl.*) effeminate.

Swiss (swis) *a.* of or relating to Switzerland. ~*n.* (*pl.* **Swiss**) a native or inhabitant of Switzerland, or a descendant of one. **Swiss chard** *n.* a variety of beet, *Beta vulgaris*, with stalks and leaves eaten as a vegetable. **Swiss cheese plant** *n.* a climbing house plant, *Monstera deliciosa*, with holes in the leaves. **Swiss roll** *n.* a thin sponge cake, rolled up around a filling, esp. of jam.

switch (swich) *n.* **1** a mechanism for diverting railway trains or vehicles from one line to another, or for completing or interrupting an electric circuit, transferring current from one wire to another etc. **2** a shift, change. **3** an exchange. **4** a small flexible twig or rod. **5** a (false) tress of hair. **6** a computer system which transfers funds between point-of-sale terminals and institutions. ~*v.t.* **1** to turn (on or off) with a switch. **2** to move, to whisk or snatch (away etc.) with a jerk. **3** (*esp. N Am.*) to shift (a train etc.) from one line to another. **4** to lash or beat with a switch. **5** to change, to divert. ~*v.i.* **1** to turn an electrical device (on or off) with a switch. **2** to make a change, to shift. **3** to move or swing with a careless or jerking movement, to whisk. **4** to cut (off) connection on a telephone etc. **to switch off** (*coll.*) to stop listening or paying attention, to lose interest. **to switch on** (*coll.*) to become alive or responsive (to). **to switch over** to change, to change over. **switchable** *a.* **switchback** *n.* **1** a railway on which the vehicles are carried over a series of ascending inclines by the momentum of previous descents, used for amusement at fairs etc. **2** a zigzag railway for ascending or descending steep inclines. **3** a steeply ascending and descending road, track etc. **switchblade** *n.* a flick knife. **switchboard** *n.* a board on which switches are fixed controlling electric or telephonic circuits. **switched-on** *a.* (*sl.*) **1** up to date, clued up. **2** high, under the influence of drugs. **switcher** *n.* **switchgear** *n.* **1** the switching equipment used to open and close electric circuits. **2** the switches in a motor vehicle. **switch-over** *n.* the act of switching over.

swivel (swiv´əl) *n.* a link or connection comprising a ring and pivot or other mechanism allowing the two parts to revolve independently. ~*v.i., v.t.* (*pres.p.* **swivelling**, (*N Am.*) **swiveling**, *past, p.p.* **swivelled**, (*N Am.*) **swiveled**) to turn on a swivel or pivot. **swivel chair** *n.* a chair that revolves on its base.

swizz (swiz), **swiz** n. (coll.) **1** something unfair; a disappointment. **2** a swindle.

swizzle (swiz´əl) n. (coll.) **1** a mixed alcoholic drink of various kinds. **2** a cheat, a fraud. ~v.t. to stir with a swizzle-stick. **swizzle-stick** n. a stick used for frothing or mixing drinks.

swob SWAB.

swollen SWELL.

swoon (swoon) v.i. (poet.) to fall into a fainting fit, esp. from excitement. ~n. a faint. **swooningly** adv.

swoop (swoop) v.i. **1** (of a bird of prey) to descend upon prey etc. suddenly. **2** to come (down upon), to attack suddenly. ~v.t. (coll.) to snatch (up). ~n. **1** a sudden plunge of or as of a bird of prey on its quarry. **2** a sudden descent, attack, seizing or snatching.

swoosh (swoosh) v.i. to move with or make a rushing sound. ~n. such a sound.

swop SWAP.

sword (sawd) n. **1** a weapon, usu. consisting of a long blade fixed in a hilt with a guard for the hand, used for cutting or thrusting. **2** the power of the sword, military power or sovereignty. **3** war, destruction or death in war. **to put to the sword** to kill (esp. those captured or defeated in war). **swordbill** n. a S American hummingbird, _Ensifera ensifera_, with a long, sword-shaped bill. **sword dance** n. **1** a dance in which swords are brandished or clashed together or in which women pass under crossed swords. **2** a Highland dance performed over two swords laid crosswise on the floor. **swordfish** n. (pl. **swordfish**) a sea fish, _Xiphias gladius_, allied to the mackerel, having the upper jaw prolonged into a swordlike weapon. **swordless** a. **swordlike** a. **sword of Damocles** n. a situation of impending disaster. **swordplay** n. **1** a combat between gladiators, fencing. **2** repartee. **swordplayer** n. **swordproof** a. **swordsman** (-mən) n. (pl. **swordsmen**) **1** a man who carries a sword. **2** a man skilled in the use of the sword. **swordsmanship** n. **swordstick** n. a hollow walking stick enclosing a long, pointed blade.

swore, sworn SWEAR.

swot (swot) v.i., v.t. (pres.p. **swotting**, past, p.p. **swotted**) (coll.) to study hard. ~n. **1** a person who studies hard. **2** hard study.

Usage note See note under SWAT.

swum SWIM.

swung SWING.

-sy (si) suf. forming diminutive adjectives and nouns, as in _folksy, mumsy_ etc.

sybarite (sib´ərīt) n. a sensual and luxurious person. ~a. sensual and luxurious. **sybaritic** (-rit´-), **sybaritical** a. **sybaritically** adv. **sybaritism** n.

sybil SIBYL.

sycamore (sik´əmaw) n. **1** a large Eurasian maple, _Acer pseudoplatanus_, having winged seeds. **2** the wood of the sycamore.

sycophant (sik´əfant)n. a servile flatterer, a parasite. **sycophancy** n. **sycophantic** (-fan´-) a. **sycophantically** adv. **sycophantish** (-fan´-) a. **sycophantize, sycophantise** v.i.

syllabi SYLLABUS.

syllable (sil´əbəl) n. **1** a sound forming a word or part of a word, containing one vowel sound, with or without a consonant or consonants, and uttered at a single effort or vocal impulse. **2** the characters representing a syllable. **3** the least expression or particle of speech. ~v.i. to pronounce by syllables, to articulate. **syllabary** n. (pl. **syllabaries**) **1** a catalogue of characters representing syllables. **2** such characters collectively, serving the purpose of an alphabet in certain languages. **syllabic** (-ab´-) a. of, relating to, consisting of or based on a syllable or syllables. **syllabically** adv. **syllabicity** (-bis´-) n. **syllabled** a.

syllabub (sil´əbŭb), **sillabub** n. a dessert made by mixing cream with wine etc., adding flavouring and frothing it up.

syllabus (sil´əbəs) n. (pl. **syllabuses, syllabi** (-bī)) **1** a list, outline, summary, abstract etc., giving the principal points or subjects of a course of lectures, teaching or study, examination requirements, hours of attendance etc. **2** a statement of requirements for an examination.

syllepsis (silep´sis) n. (pl. **syllepses** (-sēz)) **1** the application of a word in both the literal and metaphorical senses at the same time. **2** the connection of a verb or adjective with two nouns, with only one of which it is in syntactical agreement. **sylleptic** a. **sylleptically** adv.

syllogism (sil´əjizm) n. a form of argument consisting of three propositions, a major premiss or general statement, a minor premiss or instance, and a third deduced from these, called the conclusion. **syllogistic** (-jis´-) a. **syllogistically** adv.

sylph (silf) n. **1** a supposed elemental being inhabiting the air, intermediate between material and immaterial beings. **2** a graceful and slender woman or girl. **3** any S American hummingbird of the genus _Aglaiocercus_, with a long, brilliantly-coloured tail. **sylphlike** a.

sylva (sil´və), **silva** n. (pl. **sylvae** (-vē), **sylvas, silvae, silvas**) **1** the trees of a particular time or place. **2** a catalogue or study of such trees. **sylvan** a. (poet.) **1** wooded. **2** of or relating to a wood or forest. **3** rural, rustic.

sylviculture SILVICULTURE.

symbiont (sim´biont) n. an organism living in a state of symbiosis. **symbiontic** (-on´-) a. **symbiosis** (-ō´sis) n. (pl. **symbioses** (-sēz)) **1** the vital union or partnership of certain organisms, such as the fungus and alga in lichens, as distinct from _antibiosis_. **2** a mutually beneficial relationship between people, things or groups. **3** an instance of symbiosis. **symbiotic** (-ot´-) a. **symbiotically** adv.

symbol (sim´bəl) n. **1** an object typifying or representing something by resemblance, association etc., a type, an emblem. **2** a mark, character or letter accepted as representing or signifying some thing, idea, relation, process etc., such as the letters of the alphabet, those representing chemical elements or the signs of mathematical relations. **symbolic** (-bol´-), **symbolical** *a.* of, relating to, serving as or using symbols. **symbolically** *adv.* **symbolicalness** *n.* **symbolic logic** *n.* logic that uses symbols to represent and clarify principles etc. **symbolism** *n.* **1** representation by symbols or signs. **2** a system of symbols. **3** symbolic significance. **4** the use of symbols, esp. in art and literature. **5** a late-19th-cent. movement among artists and writers using symbolic images to express or suggest the essential nature of things, mystical ideas, emotions etc. **symbolist** *n.* **symbolistic** (-lis´-) *a.* **symbolize**, **symbolise** *v.t.* **1** to be the symbol of, to typify. **2** to represent by symbols. **3** to treat as symbolic, not literal, to make symbolic or representative of something. **symbolization** (-zā´shən) *n.* **symbolizer** *n.*

symmetry (sim´itri) *n.* (*pl.* **symmetries**) **1** due proportion of the several parts of a body or any whole to each other, congruity, parity, regularity, harmony. **2** beauty of form arising from this. **3** arrangement of parts on either side of a dividing line or point so that the opposite parts are exactly similar in shape and size. **4** regularity of structure so that opposite halves exactly correspond. **5** (*Bot.*) regularity of number in sepals, petals, stamens etc., each whorl composed of the same number or multiples of this. **symmetric** (-met´-), **symmetrical** *a.* **symmetrically** *adv.* **symmetricalness** *n.*

sympathy (sim´pəthi) *n.* (*pl.* **sympathies**) **1** the quality of being affected with the same feelings as another person, or of sharing emotions, affections, inclinations etc. with another person. **2** fellow feeling, agreement, harmony. **3** (*often pl.*) a feeling of accord (with). **4** loyalty or support. **5** compassion (for). **6** unity or correlation of action. ~*a.* showing loyalty or support (a *sympathy strike*). **in sympathy with 1** showing sympathy for. **2** showing loyalty or support for. **sympathetic** (-thet´-) *a.* **1** of, relating to, expressive of or due to sympathy. **2** having sympathy or common feeling with another, sympathizing. **3** being or acting in sympathy or agreement, concordant. **4** in accord with one's mood or disposition, congenial. **5** of, relating to or mediated by the sympathetic nervous system. **6** (of acoustic, electrical, and other vibrations) produced by impulses from other vibrations. **sympathetically** *adv.* **sympathetic nervous system** *n.* the part of the autonomic nervous system in which nerve impulses are transmitted chiefly by adrenalin and related substances. **sympathize**, **sympathise** *v.i.* **1** to have or express sympathy with another, in pain, pleasure etc. **2** to be of the same disposition, opinion etc. **sympathizer** *n.*

sympatric (simpat´rik) *a.* (*Biol.*) occurring in the same geographical area, as distinct from *allopatric*.

symphony (sim´fəni) *n.* (*pl.* **symphonies**) **1** a complex and elaborate composition for an orchestra, usu. consisting of four varied movements. **2** a symphony orchestra. **symphonic** (-fon´-) *a.* **symphonically** *adv.* **symphonic poem** *n.* a tone poem. **symphonious** (-fō´-) *a.* **symphonist** *n.* a composer or performer of symphonies. **symphony orchestra** *n.* a large orchestra containing wind, string and percussion sections.

symposium (simpō´ziəm) *n.* (*pl.* **symposia** (-ziə), **symposiums**) **1** a conference or formal meeting at which several speakers give addresses on a particular topic. **2** a series of brief articles expressing the views of different writers, in a magazine etc. **3** a drinking party.

symptom (simp´təm) *n.* **1** (*Med.*) a perceptible change in the appearance or functions of the body indicating disease. **2** a sign, a token, an indication. **symptomatic** (-mat´-), **symptomatical** *a.* **symptomatically** *adv.* **symptomatology** (-mətol´-) *n.* **1** a branch of medicine concerned with disease symptoms. **2** the symptoms associated with a disease. **symptomless** *a.*

syn- (sin) *pref.* **1** with. **2** together. **3** alike.

synaesthesia (sinisthē´ziə), (*N Am.*) **synesthesia** *n.* **1** (*Psych.*) the subjective sensation of a sense other than the sense being stimulated. **2** sensation experienced at a point distinct from the point of stimulation. **synaesthetic** (-thet´-) *a.*

synagogue (sin´əgog) *n.* **1** a Jewish congregation for religious instruction and observances. **2** a building or place of meeting for this. **synagogal** (-gog´-), **synagogical** (-goj´-) *a.*

synapse (sī´naps) *n.* (*Anat.*) the point at which a nerve impulse is transmitted from one neuron to another. **synapsis** (sinap´sis) *n.* (*pl.* **synapses** (-sēz)) **1** (*Anat.*) a synapse. **2** (*Biol.*) the pairing of homologous chromosomes occurring at the start of cell division by meiosis. **synaptic** (sin-) *a.* **synaptically** *adv.*

synarthrosis (sinahthrō´sis) *n.* (*pl.* **synarthroses** (-sēz)) (*Anat.*) a fixed bone joint.

sync (singk), **synch** *n.* (*coll.*) synchronization. ~*v.t.*, *v.i.* (*pres.p.* **syncing**, **synching**, *past, p.p.* **synced**, **synched**) to synchronize. **in sync** well matched, working well together. **out of sync** badly matched, not working well together.

syncarp (sin´kahp) *n.* an aggregate fruit, such as the blackberry. **syncarpous** (-kah´-) *a.*

synchondrosis (singkondrō´sis) *n.* (*pl.* **synchondroses** (-sēz)) (*Anat.*) the almost immovable articulation of bones by means of cartilage, as in the vertebrae.

synchro- (sing´krō) *comb. form* **1** synchronized. **2** synchronous.

synchromesh (sing´krəmesh) *a.* of or relating to a system of gearing in which the drive and driving members are automatically synchronized before engagement, thus avoiding shock and noise in changing gear. *~n.* such a system.

synchronous (sing´krənəs) *a.* **1** occurring simultaneously. **2** operating or recurring together at the same rate. **synchronal** *a.* **synchronic** (-kron´-) *a.* applied to the study of a subject, e.g. language, at a particular time, as distinct from *diachronic.* **synchronically** *adv.* **synchronicity** (-nis´-) *n.* **1** an apparently significant simultaneous occurrence of events with no obvious connection. **2** synchrony. **synchronism** *n.* **1** synchrony. **2** the process of matching the soundtrack of a film exactly with the picture. **synchronistic** (-nis´-) *a.* **synchronistically** *adv.* **synchronize, synchronise** *v.t.* **1** to cause to occur in unison or at the same time. **2** (*loosely*) to combine, coordinate. **3** to cause to agree in time or indicate the same time. **4** to match the soundtrack of (a film) exactly with the picture. *~v.i.* **1** to concur in time, to happen at the same time. **2** (of clocks or watches) to be synchronized. **synchronization** (-zā´shən) *n.* **synchronized swimming** *n.* a sport in which a team of swimmers performs a series of coordinated dancelike movements to music. **synchronizer** *n.* **synchronously** *adv.* **synchronous motor** *n.* an electric motor whose speed is proportional to the frequency of the supply current. **synchrony** *n.* **1** the state of being synchronous or synchronic. **2** the treatment of occurrences as being synchronous.

Usage note The use of *synchronize* to mean combine or coordinate is sometimes disapproved of.

---

synchrotron (sing´krətron) *n.* (*Physics*) a very high-energy particle accelerator.

synclinal (singklī´nəl) *a.* sloping downwards towards a common point or line, as distinct from *anticlinal.* **syncline** (sing´-) *n.* a synclinal flexure or axis.

syncopate (sing´kəpāt) *v.t.* **1** (*Mus.*) to modify (a musical note, rhythm etc.) by beginning on an unaccented and continuing with an accented beat. **2** to contract (a word) by omitting one or more letters or syllables from the middle. **syncopation** (-ā´shən) *n.* **syncopator** *n.*

syncope (sing´kəpi) *n.* **1** (*Gram.*) the elision of a letter or syllable from the middle of a word. **2** (*Med.*) a faint. **syncopal, syncopic** (-kop´-) *a.*

syncretism (sing´kritizm) *n.* **1** (*Philos., Theol.*) the attempted reconciliation of various philosophic or religious schools or systems of thought, for example against a common opponent. **2** the fusion of inflectional varieties in the development of a language. **syncretic** (-kret´-) *a.* **syncretist** *n.* **syncretistic** (-tis´-) *a.* **syncretize, syncretise** *v.t.*

syndic (sin´dik) *n.* **1** an officer or magistrate invested with varying powers in different places and times. **2** a business agent of a university, corporation etc. **syndical** *a.*

syndicalism (sin´dikəlizm) *n.* (*Hist.*) the economic doctrine that all the workers in any trade or industry should participate in the management and control and in the division of the profits. **syndicalist** *n.*

syndicate[1] (sin´dikət) *n.* **1** an association of people or firms formed to promote some special interest or undertake a joint project. **2** an agency which supplies material for simultaneous publication in several newspapers or periodicals.

syndicate[2] (sin´dikāt) *v.t.* **1** to combine in a syndicate. **2** to sell for simultaneous publication in several newspapers or periodicals. **3** to sell (a television programme) for broadcasting by several different stations. **syndication** (-ā´shən) *n.*

syndrome (sin´drōm) *n.* **1** the aggregate of symptoms characteristic of any disease or disorder. **2** a pattern or set of feelings, actions etc. characteristic of a condition or problem. **syndromic** (-drom´-) *a.*

synecdoche (sinek´dəki) *n.* a figure of speech by which a part is put for the whole or the whole for a part. **synecdochic** (-dok´-), **synecdochical** *a.*

synecology (sinikol´əji) *n.* the ecology of plant and animal communities. **synecologic** (-ēkəloj´-), **synecological** *a.* **synecologist** *n.*

synergy (sin´əji) *n.* (*pl.* **synergies**) **1** the working together of two drugs, muscles etc. so that their combined action exceeds the sum of their individual actions. **2** an instance of synergy. **synergism** (-jizm) *n.* **synergetic** (-jet´-) *a.* **synergetically** *adv.* **synergic** *a.* **synergist** *n.* something that acts with, or increases the effect of, another thing. **synergistic** (-jis´-) *a.*

synesthesia SYNAESTHESIA.

synod (sin´əd) *n.* **1** an ecclesiastical council. **2** a Presbyterian council intermediate between the presbyteries and the General Assembly. **3** a deliberative assembly, a meeting for discussion. **synodal** *a.* **synodic** (-nod´-) *a.* (*Astron.*) of or relating to the conjunction of heavenly bodies. **synodical** *a.* **synodically** *adv.* **synodic period** *n.* the time between the conjunctions of a planet with the sun.

synonym (sin´ənim) *n.* **1** a word having much the same meaning as another of the same language. **2** a word denoting the same thing but differing in some senses, or in range of application. **synonymatic** (-nonimat´-), **synonymatical, synonymic** (-nim´-) *a.* **synonymity** (-nim´-) *n.* **synonymous** (-non´-) *a.* **1** having the same meaning, conveying the same idea. **2** expressing the same thing by a different word or words. **synonymously** *adv.* **synonymousness** *n.* **synonymy** (-non´imi) *n.* (*pl.* **synonymies**) **1** the condition or fact of being synonymous, synonymity. **2** the use of synonyms for emphasis. **3** a treatise on synonyms; a dictionary or list of synonyms.

synopsis (sinop´sis) *n.* (*pl.* **synopses** (-sēz)) a

general view, a conspectus, a summary. **synopsize, synopsise** v.t. **synoptic** a. **1** of or relating to a synopsis. **2** affording a general view. **3** of or relating to the Synoptic Gospels. **4** giving a general view of the weather. **synoptical** a. **synoptically** adv. **Synoptic Gospels** n.pl. the Gospels of Matthew, Mark and Luke. **synoptist** n. the writer of any of the Synoptic Gospels.

synovia (sīnō´viə) n. an albuminous lubricating fluid secreted by the synovial membranes lining joints and tendon sheaths. **synovial** a. of, relating to or secreting synovia. **synovial membrane** n. a membrane of connective tissue secreting synovial fluid. **synovitis** (-əvī´tis) n. inflammation of the synovial membrane.

syntax (sin´taks) n. **1** (the part of grammar that deals with) the due arrangement of words forming units or the construction of sentences etc. **2** a set of rules for constructing sentences etc. **3** a treatise on syntax. **syntactic** (-tak´-) a. of, relating to or according to the rules of syntax. **syntactical** a. **syntactically** adv.

synth (sinth) n. (coll.) a synthesizer.

synthesis (sin´thəsis) n. (pl. **syntheses** (-sēz)) **1** the building up of a complex whole by the union of elements, esp. the process of forming concepts, general ideas, theories etc. **2** the putting of two or more things together, combination, composition. **3** (Chem.) the production of a substance by chemical reaction. **4** the uniting of divided parts in surgery. **synthesist** n. **synthesize, synthesise** v.t. **1** to make a synthesis of. **2** to combine into a synthesis. **synthesizer** n. **1** a keyboard-operated electronic instrument which can produce and manipulate a wide variety of sounds, imitate conventional musical instruments etc. **2** a person who or something which synthesizes. **synthetic** (-thet´-), **synthetical** a. **1** artificially produced, man-made. **2** false, sham. **3** of, relating to or consisting in synthesis. **synthetically** adv. **synthetic resin** n. a substance similar to vegetable resin obtained by the chemical synthesis of various organic materials. **synthetist** n.

syphilis (sif´ilis) n. an infectious venereal disease caused by the spirochaete Treponema, introduced into the system by direct contact or due to heredity, affecting first the genitals, then the skin and mucous membranes and finally the muscles, bones and brain. **syphilitic** (-lit´-) a. **syphilize, syphilise** v.t. **syphiloid** a.

syphon (sī´fən), **siphon** n. **1** a tube shaped like an inverted U or V, having one branch longer than the other, used for conveying liquid over the edge of a cask, tank etc., to a lower level, through the force of atmospheric pressure. **2** a bottle for holding aerated water, discharging through a syphon-like tube through the pressure of the gas, a soda syphon. **3** (Zool.) (siphon) a suctorial or other tubular organ, esp. in cephalopods, gastropods etc. **~v.t.** to convey or draw (off) by a syphon. **~v.i.** to flow or be conveyed by a syphon.

syphonage (-nij) n. **syphonal** a. **syphonic** (-fon´-) a.

Syrian (sir´iən) a. of or relating to Syria in the Middle East. **~n.** a native or inhabitant of Syria, or a descendant of one.

syringa (siring´gə) n. (pl. **syringas**) **1** the mock orange. **2** any plant of the genus Syringa, containing the lilacs.

syringe (sirinj´) n. (esp. Med.) a cylindrical instrument with a piston used to draw in a quantity of liquid by suction and eject or inject it in a stream, spray or jet. **~v.t.** (pres.p. **syringing**) to water, spray or cleanse with a syringe.

syrinx (sir´ingks) n. (pl. **syrinxes, syringes** (-in´jēz)) **1** a set of pan pipes. **2** a narrow gallery cut in the rock in ancient Egyptian tombs. **3** the organ of song in birds, the inferior larynx, a modification of the trachea where it joins the bronchi.

syrup (sir´əp), (N Am.) **sirup** n. **1** a saturated solution of sugar in water, usu. combined with fruit juice etc. for use in cookery, as a beverage etc., or with a medicinal substance. **2** the uncrystallizable fluid separated from sugar-cane juice in the process of refining molasses, treacle. **3** excessive sweetness or sentimentality. **syrupy** a.

SYSOP (sis´op) n. (Comput.) a system operator.

systaltic (sistal´tik) a. (of the heart) alternately contracting and dilating, pulsatory.

system (sis´təm) n. **1** coordinated arrangement, organized combination, organization, method. **2** an established method or procedure. **3** a coordinated body of principles, facts, theories, doctrines etc. **4** a logical grouping, a method or plan of classification. **5** a coordinated arrangement or organized combination or assembly of things or parts, for working together, performing a particular function etc. **6** a group of related or linked natural objects, such as mountains, the rocks of a geological period etc. **7** any complex and coordinated whole. **8** any organic structure taken as a whole, such as the animal body, the universe etc. **9** a method of selecting one's procedure in gambling etc. **10** (Comput.) a group of related hardware units or programs. **11** (Mineral.) any of seven types of crystal structure. **12** (Mus.) the braced staves of a score. **the system** the establishment, bureaucracy or society generally, esp. when regarded as a destroyer of individualism. **to get something out of one's system** (coll.) to rid oneself of a worry or a preoccupation. **systematic** (-mat´-), **systematical** a. **1** methodical. **2** done, formed or arranged on a regular plan, not haphazard. **systematically** adv. **systematics** n. the study of classification, taxonomy. **systematism** n. **systematist** n. **systematize, systematise** v.t. **1** to make systematic. **2** to create a system for. **systematization** (-zā´shən) n. **systematizer** n. **systemic** (-stem´-, -stē´-) a. **1** of, relating to or affecting the bodily system as a whole. **2** (of blood circulation) not pulmonary. **3**

(of an insecticide etc.) absorbed by the tissues of a plant etc., thus making it toxic. **systemically** *adv.* **systemize, systemise** *v.t.* to systematize. **systemization** (-zā´shən) *n.* **systemizer** *n.* **systemless** *a.* **system operator** *n.* (*Comput.*) a person who is in charge of the running of an electronic bulletin board. **systems analysis** *n.* the analysis of an industrial, medical, business etc.

procedure or task in order to identify its requirements and devise a computer system to fulfil these. **systems analyst** *n.* **systems operator** *n.* (*Comput.*) a person who is in chargeof the running of complexelectronic systems.

systole (sis´təli) *n.* the contraction of the heart forcing the blood outwards, as distinct from *diastole*. **systolic** (-tol´-) *a.*

T

T¹ (tē), **t** (*pl.* **Ts, T's**) the 20th letter of the English and other versions of the Roman alphabet, corresponding to the Greek tau (τ, T). It is pronounced as a voiceless dental or alveolar plosive or, if followed by *h*, as a voiced or voiceless dental or alveolar fricative, as in *then, think* etc. ~*n.* a T-shaped thing or part. **to a T** perfectly, to a nicety (*The working hours suit her to a T*). **T-bar** *n.* **1** a metal etc. bar in the shape of a 'T'. **2** a T-bar lift. **3** a shoe or sandal fastening with one strap coming up the foot and another crossing over it. **T-bar lift** *n.* a ski lift made up of a series of inverted T-bars. **T-bone** *n.* a bone in the shape of a T, as in a sirloin steak. **T-junction** *n.* a place where a road joins another road at right angles without crossing over it. **T-shirt** *n.* an informal light-weight, short-sleeved garment for the upper body (so called because when it is laid out flat it resembles the shape of the letter T). **T-square** *n.* a T-shaped ruler used for measuring and drawing right angles.

T² *chem. symbol* tritium.

T³ *abbr.* **1** temperature. **2** tera-. **3** tesla. **4** thymus. **T-lymphocyte, T-cell** *n.* a type of lymphocyte produced or processed by the thymus gland.

t, t. *abbr.* **1** ton(s). **2** tonne(s).

't (t) *pron.* (*poet. or coll.*) it (*'Tis true*).

Ta *chem. symbol* tantalum.

ta (tah) *int.* (*coll.*) thank you.

TAB *abbr.* typhoid-paratyphoid A and B (vaccine).

tab¹ (tab) *n.* **1** a small flap, tag, tongue etc., as the flap of a shoe, the tag or tip of lace etc. **2** a small paper flap attached to a file for identification purposes. **3** a strap, a loop. **4** (*Mil.*) military insignia. **5** (*N Am., coll.*) the bill, the cost (*The company picked up the tab for the meal*). **6 a** any of several loops that hold up a stage curtain. **b** the stage curtain itself. ~*v.t.* (*pres.p.* **tabbing,** *past, p.p.* **tabbed**) to put a tab or tabs on something. **to keep tabs on 1** (*coll.*) to keep a watch on. **2** (*coll.*) to keep a record or account of.

tab² (tab) *n.* (*coll.*) a tabulator on a computer or typewriter keyboard (*Input the data and then press tab*). ~*v.t.* (*pres.p.* **tabbing,** *past, p.p.* **tabbed**) to tabulate.

tab³ (tab) *n.* (*sl.*) a tablet or small piece of paper impregnated with a drug, esp. an illegal one.

tabard (tab'əd) *n.* **1** a sleeveless jacket, tunic or overall. **2** an outer garment worn over armour. **3** a herald's sleeveless coat blazoned with the arms of the sovereign.

Tabasco® (təbas'kō) *n.* a hot, capsicum sauce, used for flavouring Mexican dishes, tomato juice etc.

tabbouleh (təboo'lā) *n.* a type of Mediterranean salad made from cracked wheat, tomatoes and cucumber and flavoured with mint, lemon juice and olive oil.

tabby (tab'i) *n.* (*pl.* **tabbies**) **1** a tabby cat. **2** a cat, esp. a female cat. **3 a** silk or other fabric with a watered appearance. **b** a garment of this. ~*a.* **1** wavy, watered. **2** striped. **tabby cat** *n.* a grey or brownish cat with dark stripes.

tabernacle (tab'ənakəl) *n.* **1** (*Bible*) a tent, booth or other building of light construction, and usu. movable, used as a habitation, temple etc. **2** (*Hist.*) a tentlike structure used by the Jews as a sanctuary before settlement in Palestine. **3** a place of nonconformist worship. **4** an ornamental receptacle for the consecrated elements or the pyx. **tabernacled** *a.*

tabla (tab'lə) *n.* a pair of small Indian drums with variable pitch, played with the hands.

table (tā'bəl) *n.* **1** an article of furniture consisting of a flat surface resting on one or more supports, used for serving meals, working, writing, playing games etc. **2** this used for meals. **3** the food served on a table. **4** the company sitting at a table. **5 a** a table or board adapted for a particular game (*usu. in comb.,* as *billiard-table*). **b** a table or board designed for a particular purpose (*bird table*). **6** a part of a machine or machine-tool where the work to be operated on is put. **7** a slab of wood or other material. **8** such a slab with writing or an inscription. **9** the contents of such writing etc. **10** a list of numbers, references, or other items arranged systematically, esp. in columns. **11** a multiplication table. **12** a plateau, a tableland. **13** (*Archit.*) a flat surface, usu. rectangular, a horizontal band of moulding. ~*v.t.* **1** to put forward (a motion) for debate at a meeting. **2** (*Naut.*) to strengthen (a sail) with wide hems. **at table** taking a meal. **to lay on the table 1** to put forward for debate or discussion. **2** (*esp. N Am.*) to set aside indefinitely. **to turn the tables** to reverse the conditions or relations. **under the table 1** illicit, secret. **2** (*coll.*) drunk. **tablecloth** *n.* a cloth for covering a table, esp. at mealtimes. **tabled** *a.* **table d'hôte** (tahbəl dōt') *n.* (*pl.* **tables d'hôte** (tahbəl)) a hotel or restaurant meal at a fixed price, limited to certain dishes arranged by the proprietor. **tableful** *n.* **table knife** *n.* a knife for use at meals. **table lamp** *n.* a small lamp for standing on a table etc. **tableland** *n.* a plateau. **table licence** *n.* a licence which permits the

tableau 1275 **tack**

holder, usually a restaurateur, to serve alcohol with food. **table linen** *n.* (*collect.*) tablecloths, napkins etc. **table manners** *n.pl.* accepted behaviour during meals. **table mat** *n.* a mat placed on a table to protect the surface from hot dishes or moisture. **table napkin** *n.* a napkin used to wipe the hands at table etc., a serviette. **table of contents** *n.* a list or summary of the chapters etc. in a book or periodical. **table salt** *n.* fine, free-flowing salt used at table. **table skittles** *n.pl.* a game of skittles set up on a board, and knocked down by a ball suspended above the board. **tablespoon** *n.* 1 a large spoon, usu. four times the size of a teaspoon and holding a fluid ounce (approx. 0.028 l). 2 a tablespoonful. **tablespoonful** *n.* the amount contained in a tablespoon. **table talk** *n.* 1 talk at table or meals. 2 familiar conversation, miscellaneous chat. **table tennis** *n.* a game based on tennis and played with small bats and hollow balls on a table with a net. **table top** *n.* 1 the flat top of a table. 2 any flat top. **table-top** *a.* that can be put on a table top. **tableware** *n.* dishes, plates, knives, forks etc., for use at meals. **table wine** *n.* an unfortified wine drunk with meals.

tableau (tab´lō) *n.* (*pl.* **tableaux** (-lōz, -lō)) 1 a presentation resembling a picture. 2 a striking or vivid representation or effect. **tableau vivant** (vē´vä) *n.* (*pl.* **tableaux vivants** (-lō vē´vä)) a motionless group of performers dressed and arranged to represent some scene or event.

tablet (tab´lit) *n.* 1 a small solid measure of medicine or other substance. 2 a thin flat piece of wood, ivory or other material for writing on. 3 a small table or slab, esp. used as a memorial. 4 a shaped slab (of soap). 5 (*NAm.*) a writing pad.

tabloid (tab´loid) *n.* 1 a newspaper measuring about 12 in. (30 cm) by 16 in. (40 cm), informal in style, often with lots of photographs. 2 a compressed dose of a drug etc. **tabloid journalism** *n.* newspaper writing that tends to highlight the sensational and salacious issues of the day.

taboo (təboo´), **tabu** *n.* (*pl.* **taboos, tabus**) 1 something which is very strongly disapproved of in a particular society etc. (*Most societies label incest as a taboo; Smoking is a taboo in this office.*) 2 a custom among the Polynesians etc., of prohibiting the use of certain persons, places or things. ~*a.* banned, prohibited, by social, religious or moral convention. ~*v.t.* (*3rd pers. sing. pres.* **taboos, tabus,** *pres.p.* **tabooing, tabuing,** *past, p.p.* **tabooed, tabued**) 1 to put under taboo. 2 to forbid the use of (something).

tabor (tā´bə), **tabour** *n.* (*Hist.*) a small drum used to accompany the pipe. **taborer** *n.*

tabouret (tab´ərit), (*NAm.*) **taboret** *n.* 1 a small seat, usu. without arms or back. 2 an embroidery frame.

tabular (tab´ūlə) *a.* 1 set out, arranged in, or computed from tables. 2 in the form of a table, having a broad flat surface. 3 (of a crystal) having two flat faces. **tabula rasa** (rah´zə) *n.* (*pl.* **tabulae**

rasae (-zē)) 1 the mind in its supposedly original state, before any impressions have been made on it. 2 a tablet with no writing on it. **tabularize, tabularise** *v.t.* **tabularly** *adv.* **tabulate** (-lāt) *v.t.* to reduce to or arrange (figures etc.) in tabular form. **tabulation** (-lā´shən) *n.* **tabulator** *n.* 1 (*Comput.*) a key on a computer or typewriter keyboard (orig. a separate attachment to a typewriter) which moves to a preset position to facilitate tabulation work etc. 2 someone or something that tabulates. **tabulatory** *a.*

tacamahac (tak´əməhak) *n.* 1 a resin obtained from various S American trees, esp. of the genus *Calophyllum.* 2 the balsam poplar. 3 the resin of this tree.

tach (tak) *n.* (*NAm., coll.*) short for TACHOMETER.

tache TASH.

tachism (tash´izm), **tachisme** *n.* a form of action painting with haphazard blobs of colour.

tacho (tak´ō) *n.* (*pl.* **tachos**) (*coll.*) 1 short for TACHOMETER. 2 short for TACHOGRAPH.

tacho- (tak´ō) *comb. form* speed.

tachograph (tak´əgrahf) *n.* a tachometer in a motor vehicle, esp. a lorry or bus, which records its speed and the distance travelled between stops.

tachometer (takom´itə) *n.* an instrument for measuring the rate of rotation of a revolving shaft in a vehicle's engine and which can therefore also indicate the vehicle's speed.

tachy- (tak´i) *comb. form* swift.

tachycardia (takikah´diə) *n.* (*Med.*) abnormally rapid beating of the heart.

tachymeter (təkim´itə), **tacheometer** (takiom´-) *n.* 1 a surveying instrument for measuring distances rapidly. 2 an instrument for indicating speed.

tacit (tas´it) *a.* implied but not actually expressed. **tacitly** *adv.* **tacitness** *n.*

taciturn (tas´itœn) *a.* habitually silent, reserved or uncommunicative. **taciturnity** (-tœ´-) *n.* **taciturnly** *adv.*

tack¹ (tak) *n.* 1 a small, sharp, flat-headed nail. 2 (*esp. NAm.*) a drawing pin. 3 a stitch, esp. one of a series of long stitches for fastening fabric in dressmaking temporarily. 4 (*Naut.*) **a** a course of a ship as determined by the position of the sails. **b** the act of tacking or changing direction to take advantage of a side wind etc. 5 a course of action, a policy (*and, if that doesn't work, try a different tack*). 6 a rope by which the forward lower corner of certain sails is fastened. 7 the part of a sail to which such rope is fastened. 8 stickiness, tackiness. ~*v.t.* 1 to fasten with tacks. 2 to stitch (fabric) temporarily or together in a hasty manner. 3 to change the course of a ship to the opposite tack. 4 to annex, to append (to or on to). ~*v.i.* 1 to change the course of a ship by shifting the tacks and position of the sails. 2 to zigzag. 3 to alter one's conduct or policy. **on the right tack** on the right lines. **on the wrong tack** on the wrong lines. **to come down to brass tacks**

to face realities, to state facts. **tacker** *n.* **tacky** *a.*
(*comp.* **tackier**, *superl.* **tackiest**) **1** sticky. **2** (*coll.*)
cheap or shoddy, vulgar and ostentatious, seedy.
tackily *adv.* **tackiness** *n.*

tack² (tak) *n.* a horse's saddle, bridle, harness etc.
tack room *n.* a room or area in a riding stable
where the horses' tack is kept and cleaned.

tack³ (tak) *n.* (*coll.*) **1** something shoddy, cheap or
vulgarly ostentatious. **2** shoddiness, cheapness,
vulgar ostentation.

tack⁴ (tak) *n.* food, fare.

tackle (tak´əl) *n.* **1** apparatus, esp. of ropes,
pulleys etc., for lifting, hoisting etc., or for working spars, sails etc. **2** a windlass or winch with
its ropes etc. **3** the implements, gear or outfit for
carrying on any particular work or sport (*fishing
tackle*). **4** in football, hockey etc., an attempt to
get the ball etc. away from the player who
currently has possession of it (*got booked for a
reckless tackle on the keeper*). **5** in American
football, the position outside the guard, next to
the end in the forward line, or the player in this
position. ~*v.t.* **1** to grapple with. **2** in football,
hockey etc., to make a tackle on (an opponent). **3**
to confront, to collar. **4** (*coll.*) to set to work
vigorously upon. **5** to secure or make fast with
tackle. **tackle-block** *n.* the pulley that a rope runs
over. **tackler** *n.* **tackling** *n.* (*collect.*) tackle.

tacky TACK¹.

taco (tah´kō) *n.* (*pl.* **tacos**) a type of thin pancake
or tortilla from Mexico, usually with a spicy
meat or vegetable filling.

tact (takt) *n.* **1** an intuitive sense of what is fitting
or right. **2** adroitness in doing or saying the
proper thing. **tactful** *a.* **tactfully** *adv.* **tactfulness**
n. **tactless** *a.* **tactlessly** *adv.* **tactlessness** *n.*

tactics (tak´tiks) *n.* **1** (*sing. or pl.*) the art of
manoeuvring military or naval forces, esp. in
actual contact with the enemy. **2** (*pl.*) procedure
or devices to attain some end (*stooped to using
devious tactics*). **tactic** (tak´tik) *n.* a way of doing
or achieving something (*His usual tactic is just
to wait and see what happens*). **tactical** *a.*
1 skilful, diplomatic. **2** (of a military strike or
the weapons used in one) immediately supportive, as opposed to *strategic*. **3** carefully planned
or executed. **tactically** *adv.* **tactical voting** *n.* the
practice of voting for the candidate most likely to
defeat the favourite candidate, rather than for
one's preferred candidate. **tactician** (-tish´ən) *n.*

tactile (tak´tīl) *a.* **1** of, relating to or perceived by
the sense of touch. **2** capable of being touched. **3**
pleasant or distinctive to the touch (*Velvet is a
very tactile material*). **tactility** (-til´-) *n.* **tactual** *a.*
1 caused by touch. **2** tactile.

tad (tad) *n.* (*N Am., coll.*) a small amount. **a tad**
slightly, a little (*This wine is a tad too sweet for
me*).

tadpole (tad´pōl) *n.* the larva of an amphibian,
esp. of a frog or toad, before the gills and tail disappear.

tae kwon do (tī kwon dō´) *n.* a type of Korean

martial art, similar to karate, involving kicks and
punches.

taffeta (taf´itə) *n.* **1** a light, thin, glossy silk fabric.
2 (*loosely*) a silk and linen or silk and wool
fabric.

taffrail (taf´rāl) *n.* (*Naut.*) the rail round a ship's
stern.

Taffy (taf´i) *n.* (*pl.* **Taffies**) (*coll., often offensive*) a
Welshman.

taffy (taf´i) *n.* (*pl.* **taffies**) **1** TOFFEE. **2** (*esp. US*,
coll.) insincere flattery.

tag (tag) *n.* **1** any small appendage, such as a metal
point at the end of a lace. **2** a label, esp. one tied
onto an item for sale to show its price or onto a
suitcase etc. to show its intended destination. **3**
an electronic device attached to goods for sale
which will set off an alarm if taken out of the
shop door. **4** an electronic tracking device, used
to monitor prisoners on remand or wildlife. **5** a
loop for pulling a boot on. **6** (*N Am.*) a vehicle
licence plate. **7** a loose or ragged end or edge. **8** a
loose tuft of wool on a sheep. **9** the tail or tip of
the tail of an animal. **10** anything tacked on at
the end. **11** the refrain of a song, the closing
speech in a play addressed to the audience. **12** a
well-worn phrase or quotation. **13** a children's
game in which the players try to escape being
touched by the one chosen to be 'it'. **14** the act of
tagging in wrestling. **15** the act of tagging a
runner out in baseball. ~*v.t.* (*pres.p.* **tagging**, *past*,
p.p. **tagged**) **1** to fit or mark with a tag, to attach
a tag to. **2** (*Comput.*) to attach a special code to (a
piece of data) so that it can be easily identified or
retrieved. **3** to attach (to, on to or together). **4** to
touch in the game of tag. **5** in wrestling, to touch
a team-mate's hand as a signal that it is their turn
in the ring. **6** in baseball, to touch (a runner) with
the ball or with a hand with the ball in it, putting
the runner out. **7** (*coll.*) to follow closely or persistently (after). **8** to remove tags from (a sheep).
to tag along with to go along with (someone), to
follow. **tag end** *n.* (*esp. N Am.*) the final part of
something. **tag team** *n.* a pair of wrestlers who
either fight together as a team or who take
alternate turns in the ring. **tag-team** *a.*

tagetes (təjē´tēz) *n.* any plant of the genus
Tagetes of the aster family.

tagliatelle (talyətel´i) *n.* pasta in the form of thin
strips.

Tahitian (tah-hē´shən) *n.* **1** a native or inhabitant
of Tahiti, an island in the S Pacific. **2** the language spoken there. ~*a.* belonging or relating to
Tahiti, its people or its language.

t'ai chi ch'uan (tī chē chwahn´), **t'ai chi** (chē´)
n. a Chinese form of exercise and self-defence
based on slow controlled movements.

taiga (tī´gə) *n.* the spruce-dominated coniferous
forests found in subarctic N America and
Eurasia.

tail¹ (tāl) *n.* **1** the part of an animal, bird, fish or
insect that extends from the end or the back of
the body, esp. when it forms a movable or flex-

ible appendage. **2** anything that resembles this kind of appendage in form, position or function (*a shirt tail*; *a long tail of traffic*). **3** the rear or last part or parts of something (*joined the tail of the queue*; *the tail of the storm*). **4** the rear of an aeroplane, including the rudder and the tailplane. **5** the rear part of a motor vehicle. **6** (*Astron.*) the luminous trail of particles that can be seen to follow a comet. **7** (*in pl.*) **a** a tailcoat. **b** (*coll.*) men's evening wear. **8** (*in pl.*) the obverse side of a tossed coin. **9** (*sl.*) the buttocks. **10** (*taboo sl.*) the female genitals. **11** (*sl.*) a woman, esp. one thought of in sexual terms. **12** (*taboo sl.*) sexual intercourse. **13** the route that someone or something travelling or running away takes (*That police car's been on my tail since we left*). **14** (*coll.*) a person who follows and watches another person or people (*put a tail on the suspected drug dealer*). **15** in music notation, the lower part of a note. **16** the part of a written letter such as a *g*, *j*, *p*, *q* or *y* that lies below the line. **17** in cricket, the less talented batsmen who play last in a batting order. ~*v.t.* **1** to follow and keep under surveillance. **2** to dock the tail of (a lamb). **3** (*coll.*) to remove the tails or ends from (fruit) (*top and tail the blackcurrants*). **4** to provide with a tail. **5** to join (on to another thing). ~*v.i.* to follow closely (after). **on someone's tail** very close behind someone. **to tail away** to dwindle. **to tail back** to form a tailback. **to tail off** to come to and end, or almost to an end (*Public interest in the issue has tailed off*). **to turn tail 1** to run away. **2** to turn one's back. **with one's tail between one's legs** beaten, in a state of defeat. **with one's tail up** in good spirits. **tailback** *n*. a queue of traffic stretching back from an obstruction or traffic problem. **tailboard** *n*. the hinged or sliding board at the back of a cart, wagon etc. **tailcoat** *n*. a man's morning or evening coat that is elongated and divided in two at the back. **tailcoated** *a*. **tail covert** *n*. any of the covert feathers around a bird's tail. **tailed** *a*. **tail-end** *n*. **1** the last or concluding part (*only heard the tail-end of the story*). **2** the lowest or rearmost part. **3** in cricket, the last of the batting order. **tail-ender** *n*. **tailfeather** *n*. a flight feather in a bird's tail. **tailgate** *n*. **1** the lower gate of a canal lock. **2** (*esp. N Am.*) a tailboard. **3** (*esp. N Am.*) the upward-lifting door at the back of a hatchback or estate car. ~*v.t.* (*esp. N Am., coll.*) to follow (the vehicle in front) very closely, often too closely to allow for a safe braking distance. ~*v.i.* to drive very closely behind another vehicle. **tailgater** *n*. **tailless** *a*. **tail light, tail lamp** *n*. a red warning light at the rear of a motor vehicle etc. **tail-off** *n*. a dwindling, a gradual ending. **tailpiece** *n*. **1** an ornamental design at the end of a chapter or section of a book. **2** a triangular block on a violin etc., to which the strings are attached. **3** the end or last part of something. **4** any rear appendage. **tailpipe** *n*. the rearmost part of a vehicle's exhaust pipe. **tailplane** *n*. the fixed horizontal portion of

the tail of an aeroplane. **tail-race** *n*. the part of a mill-race below a waterwheel. **tailskid** *n*. a device to take the weight at the rear end of an aeroplane's fuselage while taxiing. **tailspin** *n*. **1** a vertical, nose-foremost dive by an aeroplane, during which it describes a spiral. **2** a state of upheaval or loss of control. ~*v.i.* (*pres.p.* **tailspinning**, *past* **tailspun, tailspan**, *p.p.* **tailspun**) to put an aeroplane into a tailspin. **tailstock** *n*. an adjustable casting on a lathe which supports the free end of a workpiece. **tailwheel** *n*. a supporting wheel below the tail of an aeroplane. **tailwind** *n*. a wind blowing in the same direction as one is travelling in.

tail² (tāl) *n*. (*Law*) limitation of ownership, limited ownership. ~*a*. limited in this way. **in tail** controlled by or under limited ownership (*estate in tail*).

tailor (tāˊlə) *n*. a person whose occupation is to cut out and make clothes, esp. outer clothes for men. ~*v.i.* to work as a tailor. ~*v.t.* **1** to make (clothes) (*tailored the jacket to a perfect fit*). **2** (*coll.*) to adapt for a particular purpose or need (*tailored her working hours to give her time with the children*). **tailor-bird** *n*. any of several Asian warblers of the genus *Orthotomus*, that sew together leaves to form their nests. **tailored** *a*. well-cut, close-fitting. **tailoring** *n*. **tailor-made** *a*. **1** made by a tailor, well cut and close-fitting. **2** perfectly suited or adapted (*The flats are tailor-made for elderly people*). ~*n*. a tailored article of clothing. **tailor's twist** *n*. a strong silk thread.

taint (tānt) *n*. **1** a stain, a blemish, a disgrace. **2** a corrupting influence, infection. **3** a trace of decay, unsoundness, disease etc. ~*v.t.* **1** to imbue or infect with a noxious, poisonous or corrupting element. **2** to dirty, sully or tarnish. ~*v.i.* **1** to be infected or affected with incipient putrefaction. **2** to weaken. **tainted** *a*. **taintless** *a*.

taipan¹ (tīˊpan) *n*. a large and extremely venomous Australian snake, *Oxyuranus microlepidotus*.

taipan² (tīˊpan) *n*. the head of a foreign business in China.

take¹ (tāk) *v.t.* (*past* **took** (tuk), *p.p.* **taken** (tāˊkən)) **1** to lay hold of, grasp, seize, capture etc. (*took the CD from its case*; *took his rook easily*; *broke into the off-licence and took hundreds of cigarettes*; *took her to the dance*). **2** to carry off, remove, carry away, transport etc. (*took the cat to the vet*; *took the wrong jacket by mistake*). **3** to remove without permission (*OK, who's taken my pen?*). **4** to go by means of (*took the bus*; *let's take the shortcut*). **5** to lead in a certain direction (*the road that takes you into town*). **6** to have, receive, obtain, procure, acquire, appropriate, opt for etc. (*took a look out of the window*; *take the opportunity to thank everyone*; *took early retirement*). **7** to eat, consume, drink or swallow (*We usually take lunch at one o'clock*; *Do you take sugar in your coffee?*). **8** to indulge in (*used to take cocaine*). **9** to use or make use of (*Take 100g of* butter and 175g of sugar; a car that takes unleaded petrol). **10** to choose to go along (a specified road, direction etc.) (Take the first right; took a wrong turning). **11** to go for or perform (an action) (took a walk; took a run in the car). **12** to put up with, endure, accept etc. (told the class she wouldn't take any nonsense; I really can't take her rudeness). **13** to ascertain and record by weighing, measuring etc. (had her temperature taken). **14** to understand, detect, apprehend, grasp, suppose, consider, conclude etc. (took him to be telling the truth; took what he said to be true). **15** to be infected or ill with (a disease, virus etc.). **16** to feel or show (a specified response, esp. an emotional one) (took offence at her criticisms; takes great pride in her work). **17** to treat or regard in a specified way (takes his duties as a father very seriously; took the whole thing as a joke). **18** (coll.) to need (a specified person or thing, esp. to ensure the desired outcome or action) (took four of us to move the piano; It will take a miracle for us to win now). **19** to have or spend (time etc.) (took a day's sick leave; took his annual holiday in France). **20** to use up or last (a specified length of time) (The flight takes six hours). **21** to accommodate or have room for (This box will take up to 30 CDs). **22** to act upon or learn from (Take my advice and stay in bed). **23** to note down or write up (The police took her name and address; Take the minutes of the meeting). **24** to put (a specified course of action) in place or into effect (took preventative measures; took the decision to expand the company). **25** to choose to pursue (a specified course of action etc.) (took the initiative; always takes the easy way out). **26** to accept or choose to accept (took £200 for the car; took a job in London; took his word for it). **27** to hold, believe in or support (took the party line; took a different view). **28** to follow or teach (a specified subject, course of study etc.) (is taking a degree in physics; He takes the senior classes). **29** to sit an examination in (a specified subject or at a particular level) (took her English finals last month). **30** to photograph (took over 50 holiday snaps; I'll take you with the Eiffel Tower in the background). **31** to buy or subscribe to (a specified newspaper or other publication), esp. on a regular basis (We take 'The Guardian'). **32** to occupy, esp. temporarily (You can take the seat next to me). **33** to act as the leader, speaker, chairperson etc. of (He takes a local scout group; took the floor; Will you take this meeting?). **34** to look at, use or cite as a prime or illustrative example (Underfunding is widespread take education or health for a start). **35** to wear (a specified size of clothes or shoes) (What shoe size do you take?). **36** (Gram.) (of a part of speech) to have as the usual syntactic construction (The noun 'deer' can take singular and plural verb forms). **37** to use (text written by someone else) as a quote etc. (took a passage from Ulysses to

illustrate the point). **38** (dated) to have sexual intercourse with (a woman). ~v.i. **1** to be successful or have the desired effect (The skin graft has taken well). **2** (of plants) to begin to grow by sending out roots (The seedlings have taken and we can put them outside now). **3** (coll.) to become suddenly ill (took sick at school and was sent home). **take that!** used when delivering a blow etc. **to be taken with** to be charmed by or very pleased with. **to have what it takes** (coll.) to show the necessary talent, qualities or stamina. **to take after** to resemble physically, mentally etc. **to take against** to form a dislike for. **to take apart 1** to separate. **2** (coll.) to criticize severely. **3** (coll.) esp. in sport, to outplay, outclass or defeat (Aberdeen took Rangers apart). **to take aside** to disengage and talk privately to. **to take away 1** to subtract. **2** to remove. **3** to buy ready to eat, for consumption elsewhere. **to take away from** to detract from. **to take back 1** to withdraw, to retract. **2** to stimulate memories, esp. nostalgically (These photos take me back to when I was a lad). **3** (Print.) to reset on the previous line. **4** to return or accept the return of (something bought) for a replacement or refund. **5** to accept back into a relationship that had earlier been ended. **to take down 1** to write down. **2** to lower (a garment) to one's knees or ankles, esp. temporarily (took down her jeans). **3** to take apart, to pull to pieces. **4** to humiliate, to humble. **to take for** to mistake for. **to take from 1** to deduct from. **2** to diminish, to lessen. **3** to quote from (This passage is taken from Joyce's 'Ulysses'). **to take in 1** to admit, to receive (takes in lodgers). **2** to undertake (washing, typewriting etc.) at home for pay. **3** to include, to comprise. **4** to understand, to receive into the mind, to accept as true. **5** to deceive, to cheat. **6** to contract, to furl (sails). **to take it 1** to accept misfortune or punishment. **2** to understand by deduction (So am I to take it that you want to hand in your notice?). **to take it on/upon oneself** to decide (to do) without prompting or authority. **to take it or leave it 1** to accept something, including its problems, or not at all. **2** to have a lukewarm reaction to something. **to take it out of 1** (coll.) to get revenge, compensation or satisfaction from. **2** (coll.) to exhaust the strength or freshness of. **to take it out on** to vent one's anger or frustration on. **to take off 1** to remove, to withdraw. **2** to begin flight. **3** to become popular (Cyber cafés are taking off in a big way now). **4** to carry away. **5** to deduct (from). **6** to spend (an amount of time) away from work etc., esp. by choice. **7** to jump (from). **8** to leave suddenly or hastily. **9** (coll.) to mimic, to ridicule (an impersonator who takes off MPs so well). **to take on 1** to engage for work etc. **2** to undertake to do (work etc.). **3** to accept a challenge from, to engage in a contest with. **4** to acquire, to adopt. **5** (coll.) to be violently affected, to be upset. **to take oneself off** to go away, to leave. **to take out 1** to remove, to extract. **2** to invite and accompany on an outing etc. **3** to obtain for one-self, to procure. **4** (*Law*) to have (a summons, injunction etc.) put in place. **5** (*N Am.*) to buy ready to eat, for consumption elsewhere. **6** (*sl.*) to murder, to put out of action. **to take over 1** to assume the management, ownership etc. of. **2** to assume control of. **3** (*Print.*) to reset on the next line. **to take someone out of themselves** to distract someone from their problems or shyness. **to take someone up on 1** to argue or disagree with someone about. **2** to accept someone's challenge or offer of (*I'll take you up on that offer of a lift*). **to take to 1** to resort to. **2** to form a habit of. **3** to adapt to. **4** to form a liking for. **to take up 1** to lift (up). **2** to begin to engage or take an interest in. **3** to adopt as a protégé. **4** to agree to act on. **5** to resume, to pursue. **6** (of an object) to occupy or fill physically. **7** (of an activity) to occupy, to engage, to engross. **8** to accept as an office. **9** to interrupt, esp. to criticize. **10** to shorten, esp. by sewing in place. **11** to receive into a vehicle. **12** to absorb. **to take up with to** begin to associate with. **takable** *a.* **takeaway** *a.* denoting food bought from a restaurant for consumption elsewhere. *~n.* **1** a restaurant or shop where takeaway food is bought. **2** a take-away meal. **take-home pay** *n.* the amount of salary left after deductions (income tax, National Insurance etc.). **take-off** *n.* **1** the rising of an aircraft into the air. **2** (*coll.*) an act of mimicking, a caricature. **3** the spot from which one's feet leave the ground in leaping. **take-out** *a., n.* (*esp. N Am.*) TAKEAWAY (under TAKE¹). **takeover** *n.* **1** an act of seizing control. **2** the buying out by one company of another. **taker** *n.* a person who takes something, esp. a person who accepts a bet (*I reckon he'll get the sack any takers?*). **take-up** *n.* the act of claiming something, esp. of services or state benefit. **taking** *a.* **1** pleasing, alluring, attractive. **2** infectious. *~n.* **1** the act of someone who takes. **2** capture, arrest. **3** (*pl.*) money taken (*The takings are well down on last week's*). **takingly** *adv.*

take² (tāk) *n.* **1** something which is taken. **2** the amount (of fish etc.) taken at one catch or in one season. **3** takings. **4** the amount of copy taken at one time. **5** a scene that has been filmed. **on the take** making money dishonestly.

talc (talk) *n.* **1** talcum powder. **2** a fibrous, greasy magnesium silicate occurring in prisms and plates, used as a lubricator etc. *~v.t.* (*pres.p.* **talcing, talcking,** *past, p.p.* **talced, talcked**) to treat (something) with talc in order to dry it or lubricate it. **talcum** (-kəm) *n.* **1** cosmetic talcum powder. **2** talc (magnesium silicate). *~v.t.* (*pres.p.* **talcuming,** *past, p.p.* **talcumed**) to use talcum powder to dry or freshen (the body) (*talcumed the baby's bottom*). **talcum powder** *n.* **1** a usu. perfumed powder made from purified talc, used, esp. after a bath or shower, to absorb excess body moisture. **2** powdered magnesium silicate. **talcy** *a.*

tale (tāl) *n.* **1** a narrative, an account, a story, true or fictitious, esp. an imaginative or legendary story. **2** an idle or malicious report. **to tell tales 1** to report malicious stories to someone in authority. **2** to tell lies. **talebearer** *n.* a person who spreads malicious reports or breaks confidences. **talebearing** *n., a.* **taleteller** *n.* **1** a storyteller. **2** a talebearer.

talent (tal´ənt) *n.* **1** a particular aptitude, gift or faculty. **2** mental capacity of a superior order. **3** a talented person; talented people (*an exhibition of work from the talent of this year's art department*). **4** (*coll.*) attractive members of the opposite sex, collectively. **talented** *a.* endowed with talents or ability. **talentless** *a.* **talent scout** *n.* a person who is employed to discover talented people, e.g. for sports clubs or the entertainment industry. **talent show** *n.* a show which gives amateur entertainers the chance to display their ability. **talent spotter** *n.* a talent scout. **talent-spot** *v.t., v.i.* (*pres.p.* **talent-spotting,** *past, p.p.* **talent-spotted**).

tali TALUS.

talisman (tal´izmən) *n.* (*pl.* **talismans**) **1** a charm or an amulet that is believed to have magical powers, esp. one thought to protect the wearer from evil and to bring them good luck. **2** (*fig.*) something producing wonderful effects. **talismanic** (-man´-) *a.* **talismanically** *adv.*

talk (tawk) *v.i.* **1** to communicate ideas or thoughts in spoken words. **2** to exchange thoughts in spoken words. **3** to have the power of speech. **4** to reveal secret or confidential information. **5** to be influential (*money talks*). **6** to communicate by radio or electronic signals. **7** to make sounds in speech. **8** to gossip. *~v.t.* **1** to express in speech. **2** to converse about, to discuss. **3** to speak as a language, to use (a specified language) (*They talk Gaelic at home*). **4** to persuade or otherwise affect by talking. *~n.* **1** conversation, chat. **2** a subject of conversation. **3** gossip, rumour. **4** a short speech or address. **5** a specified form of speaking (*small talk*). **6** boastful claims (*says her dad's a millionaire, but I think it's all talk*). **7** (*in pl.*) discussion to negotiate something (*held talks about the gun control proposals*). **now you're talking** (*coll.*) at last you're saying something I can agree with or relate to. **talking of** while on the subject of, concerning (*Talking of Helen, where is she working now?*). **to know what one is talking about** to be an expert on a particular subject. **to talk about 1** to discuss. **2** to gossip about. **3** used to express ironic or disparaging emphasis (*Talk about ignorant! He thought Cyprus was in Asia!*). **to talk back 1** to reply. **2** to answer impudently. **to talk big** to boast. **to talk down 1** to silence by loud or persistent talking. **2** to guide (a pilot or aeroplane) in to land by giving verbal instructions. **to talk down to** to speak to in a patronizing or condescending way. **to talk into** to persuade to do by argument. **to talk of 1** to discuss. **2** to mention. **3** (*coll.*) to suggest, esp. tentatively. **to**

talk out to kill (a motion) by discussing it until the time of adjournment. **to talk out of** to dissuade from doing by argument. **to talk over 1** to discuss at length. **2** to persuade or convince by talking. **to talk round 1** to discuss without coming to a decision. **2** to persuade. **to talk shop** to talk about work, esp. tediously or at an inappropriate time. **to talk through 1** to explain the stages of (a procedure). **2** to discuss thoroughly and come to a resolution about. **to talk to 1** to speak to. **2** (*coll.*) to remonstrate with, to reprove. **to talk up 1** to speak loudly, boldly. **2** to praise. **you can/ can't talk** used to remind the listener that what is being said also applies to them. **talkative** *a.* given to talking a lot. **talkatively** *adv.* **talkativeness** *n.* **talkback** *n.* a two-way radio system. **talker** *n.* **talkie** *n.* (*coll.*) an early film with sound. **talking** *a.* **1** that talks. **2** able to talk. **talking book** *n.* an audiotape of someone reading a book, usu. a novel in abridged form. **talking film, talking picture** *n.* a film with a soundtrack. **talking head** *n.* (*coll.*) on television, a person shown from the shoulders up only, unaccompanied by action or illustrative material. **talking point** *n.* a matter to be or being talked about. **talking shop** *n.* (*often derog.*) a meeting or institution where issues will be discussed but no action will follow. **talking-to** *n.* (*coll.*) a telling-off, a reproof. **talk-show** *n.* a chat show.

tall (tawl) *a.* **1** high in stature, above the average height. **2** having a specified height. **3** (*sl.*) extravagant, boastful (*a bit of a tall story; a tall order*). **4** exorbitant, excessive. *~adv.* **1** in a way that suggests great height. **2** proudly (*walk tall*). **tallboy** *n.* a high chest of drawers, often on legs. **tall hat** *n.* TOP HAT (under TOP¹). **tallish** *a.* **tallness** *n.* **tall order** *n.* a difficult or demanding task, an exacting or unreasonable demand. **tall ship** *n.* a square-rigged sailing ship.

tallith (tal´ith) *n.* a fringed scarf worn over the head and shoulders by Jewish men during prayer.

tallow (tal´ō) *n.* a substance composed of the harder or less fusible fats, chiefly of animals, esp. beef or mutton fat, used for making candles, soap etc. **tallowish, tallowy** *a.*

tally (tal´i) *n.* (*pl.* **tallies**) **1** a reckoning, an account. **2** a number reckoned or registered, a score. **3** (*Hist.*) a stick in which notches are cut as a means of keeping accounts. **4** a mark registering number (of things received, delivered etc.). **5** anything made to correspond with something else, a counterpart, a duplicate (of). **6** a label or tag for identification. *~v.t.* (*3rd pers. sing. pres.* **tallies,** *pres.p.* **tallying,** *past, p.p.* **tallied**) to score as on a tally, to record, to register. *~v.i.* to agree, to correspond (with). **tallier** *n.* **tallyman, tallywoman** *n.* (*pl.* **tallymen, tallywomen**) **1** a person who keeps a tally. **2** a person who collects hire purchase payments.

tally-ho (talihō´) *int.* used to encourage hounds when the quarry is sighted. *~n.* (*pl.* **tally-hos**) a shout of this. *~v.i.* (*3rd pers. sing. pres.* **tally-hoes,** *pres.p.* **tally-hoing,** *past, p.p.* **tally-hoed**) to utter this cry. *~v.t.* to urge on (hounds) with this cry.

Talmud (tal´mud) *n.* the body of Jewish civil and religious law not included in the Pentateuch, including the Mishna and the Gemara. **Talmudic** (-mud´-), **Talmudical** *a.* **Talmudist** *n.* a student of or expert in the Talmud.

talon (tal´ən) *n.* **1** a claw, esp. of a bird of prey. **2** anything hooked or clawlike. **3** (*Archit.*) an ogee moulding. **taloned** *a.*

talus (tā´ləs) *n.* (*pl.* **tali** (-lī)) (*Anat.*) the anklebone.

tam (tam) *n.* (*coll.*) a tam-o'-shanter.

tamarillo (taməril´ō) *n.* (*pl.* **tamarillos**) the fruit of the tree tomato.

tamarin (tam´ərin) *n.* any small monkey of the genera *Saguinus* or *Leontopithecus* of the forests of Central and S America.

tamarind (tam´ərind) *n.* **1** a tropical tree, *Tamarindus indica.* **2** its pulpy leguminous fruit, used in making drinks, as a food flavouring and as a laxative. **3** its wood.

tamarisk (tam´ərisk) *n.* an evergreen shrub of the genus *Tamarix*, with slender feathery branches and white and pink flowers.

tambour (tam´buə) *n.* **1** a drum, esp. a bass drum. **2** a circular frame on which silk etc., is embroidered. **3** silk or other fabric embroidered thus. *~v.t., v.i.* to embroider with or on a tambour.

tambourine (tambərēn´) *n.* a small percussion instrument composed of a hoop with parchment stretched across one head and loose jingling discs in the sides, played by striking with the hand etc. **tambourinist** *n.*

tame (tām) *a.* **1** (of an animal) having lost its native wildness, domesticated, not wild. **2** tractable, docile. **3** subdued, spiritless. **4** dull, insipid (*an incredibly tame production of 'Hamlet'*). **5** (*US, coll.*) (of land) cultivated. **6** (of a plant) produced by cultivation. *~v.t.* to make tame. **tameable, tamable** *a.* capable of being tamed. **tameability** (-bil´-) *n.* **tameableness** *n.* **tamely** *adv.* **tameness** *n.* **tamer** *n.*

Tamil (tam´il) *n.* **1** a member of the Dravidian people who inhabit S India and Sri Lanka. **2** the language of this people. *~a.* of or relating to the Tamils or their language.

tammy (tam´i) *n.* (*pl.* **tammies**) (*coll.*) a tam-o'-shanter.

tam-o'-shanter (taməshan´tə) *n.* a cap fitted closely round the brows but wide and full above.

tamp (tamp) *v.t.* **1** to fill up (a blast-hole) with rammed clay above the charge. **2** to ram down (railway ballast, road-metal, soil, tobacco etc.). **tamper**¹ *n.* **tamping** *n.* material used to tamp a hole. **tampon** (-pon) *n.* a plug of lint etc. used for stopping haemorrhage and to absorb bodily secretions such as menstrual blood. *~v.t.* (*pres.p.* **tamponing,** *past, p.p.* **tamponed**) to plug with a tampon. **tamponade** (-nād´) *n.* **1** cardiac tamponade. **2** the surgical use of a tampon.

tamper[1] TAMP.

tamper[2] (tam´pə) v.i. **1** to meddle (with). **2** to interfere illegitimately (with), esp. to alter documents etc., to adulterate. **3** to employ blackmail. **tamperer** n. **tampering** n. **tamper-proof** a. made to be very difficult to tamper with.

tampon etc. TAMP.

tam-tam (tam´tam) n. a large metal gong.

tan[1] (tan) n. **1** a deepening of the skin's colour, esp. from pinkish-white to bronze, caused by exposure to the sun's rays or to artificial ultraviolet rays. **2** a yellowish-brown colour. **3** the bark of the oak or other trees, bruised and broken in a mill and used for tanning hides. ~a. yellowish-brown. ~v.t. (pres.p. **tanning**, past, p.p. **tanned**) **1** to make brown by exposure to the sun or to artificial ultraviolet rays. **2** to convert (raw hide) into leather by steeping in an infusion of tannin or by the action of some mineral or chemical salt. **3** (coll.) to flog, to thrash. ~v.i. to become brown by exposure to the sun or to artificial ultraviolet rays. **tanbark** n. the bark of some trees, such as the oak, a source of tannin. **tannable** a. **tanner** n. a person who tans hides. **tannery** n. (pl. **tanneries**) a place where tanning is done. **tannic** a. of, relating to or derived from tanbark. **tannic acid** n. tannin. **tannin** (-in) n. an astringent substance obtained from oak-bark etc., used in tanning leather, making writing ink etc., and in medicine. **tanning** n. **tannish** a.

tan[2] (tan) abbr. tangent.

tanager (tan´əjə) n. an American bird of the subfamily Thraupinae, related to the finches, usu. with brilliantly coloured plumage.

tandem (tan´dəm) n. **1** a bicycle or tricycle for two riders one behind the other. **2** a vehicle with two or more horses harnessed one behind the other. **3** an arrangement of two things one behind the other. ~adv. **1** with horses harnessed one behind the other. **2** (harnessed) one behind the other. **in tandem 1** with one thing behind another. **2** in partnership, together.

tandoor (tanduə´) n. a clay oven as used in N India and Pakistan. **tandoori** (-doo´ri) a. cooked in such a clay oven (tandoori chicken). ~n. food so cooked.

tang[1] (tang) n. **1** a strong taste or flavour. **2** a distinctive quality. **3** a projecting piece, tongue etc., such as the shank of a knife, chisel etc., inserted into the haft. **4** a smell. **5** piquancy; an exciting quality. **tangy** a. (comp. **tangier**, superl. **tangiest**). **tanginess** n.

tang[2] (tang) n. a ringing or clanging sound. ~v.t. to ring or clang. ~v.i. to cause to ring or clang.

tanga (tang´gə) n. pants, briefs or bikini bottoms that consist of two small joined triangular pieces, held in place by a string or thong waistband.

tangelo (tan´jəlō) n. (pl. **tangelos**) a tangerine and pomelo hybrid.

tangent (tan´jənt) n. **1** a straight line meeting a circle or curve without intersecting it. **2** in

trigonometry, the ratio of the sine to the cosine. **to go/ fly off at a tangent** to diverge suddenly from a course of thought or action. **tangency** n. **tangential** (-jen´shəl) a. **1** relating to or characteristic of a tangent. **2** along the line of a tangent. **3** digressive, irrelevant. **tangentially** adv.

tangerine (tanjərēn´) n. **1** a small, loose-skinned orange. **2** a bright orange colour. ~a. bright orange.

tangible (tan´jibəl) a. **1** perceptible by touch. **2** definite, capable of realization, not visionary. **3** corporeal. ~n. (usu. pl.) a tangible thing or property as opposed to goodwill. **tangibility** (-bil´-), **tangibleness** n. **tangibly** adv.

tangle (tang´gəl) v.t. **1** to knot together or intertwine in a confused mass. **2** to entangle, to ensnare, to entrap. **3** to complicate. ~v.i. **1** to become thus knotted together or intertwined. **2** to come into conflict with. ~n. **1** a confused mass of threads, hairs etc., intertwined. **2** a state of confusion. **3** a complicated situation or problem. **tangled** a. **tangler** n. **tangly** a. (comp. **tanglier**, superl. **tangliest**).

tango (tang´gō) n. (pl. **tangos**) **1** a Latin American dance that is characterized by highly stylized, often erotic, body movements punctuated by glides and pauses. **2** a piece of music for this dance. ~v.i. (3rd pers. sing. pres. **tangoes**, pres.p. **tangoing**, past, p.p. **tangoed**) to dance the tango.

tangram (tang´gram) n. a Chinese puzzle consisting of a square cut into seven differently shaped pieces which have to be fitted together.

tanh (than, tansh, tanäch´) n. hyperbolic tangent.

tank (tangk) n. **1** a cistern or vessel of large size for holding liquid, gas etc. **2** a heavily-armoured motor vehicle running on caterpillar tractors and carrying guns of various calibres. **3** a reservoir in a motor vehicle where the fuel goes. ~v.t. **1** to store or treat in a tank. **2** (sl.) to defeat. ~v.i. to move quickly and deliberately (tanked up the road). **to tank up 1** to fill a vehicle with fuel. **2** to drink, or cause to drink, a large quantity of alcohol. **tanked-up** a. (sl.) drunk, inebriated with drugs. **tank engine** n. a locomotive with a water tank over the boiler, and without a tender. **tanker** n. a specially-built ship, aircraft or vehicle fitted with tanks for carrying a cargo of oil or other liquids. ~v.t. to transport using a tanker. **tankful** n. (pl. **tankfuls**). **tankless** a. **tanklike** a. **tank top** n. a sleeveless top with low neck, usually worn over a shirt or blouse.

tankard (tang´kəd) n. **1** a large drinking-vessel, usu. of metal and often with a cover. **2** the amount a tankard holds.

Tannoy® (tan´oi) n. a public announcement and loudspeaker system.

tansy (tan´zi) n. (pl. **tansies**) a yellow-flowered perennial herb, Tanacetum vulgare, with muchdivided, bitter, aromatic leaves, formerly used in cookery and medicine.

tantalize (tan´təlīz), **tantalise** v.t. **1** to torment or tease by seeming to offer something badly wanted but continually withholding it. **2** to raise and then disappoint the hopes of. **tantalization** (-zā´shən) *n.* **tantalizer** *n.* **tantalizing** *a.* **tantalizingly** *adv.*

tantalum (tan´tələm) *n.* (*Chem.*) a rare hard greyish-white metallic element, at. no. 73, chem. symbol Ta, which is highly resistant to heat and acid corrosion. **tantalic** *a.*

tantalus (tan´tələs) *n.* a spirit-stand in which the decanters remain in sight but are secured by a lock.

tantamount (tan´təmownt) *a.* equivalent (to) in value or effect.

tantra (tan´trə) *n.* any of a class of later Sanskrit Hindu and Buddhist textbooks dealing chiefly with magical powers. **tantric** *a.* **tantrism** *n.* **tantrist** *n.*

tantrum (tan´trəm) *n.* a burst of ill temper, a fit of passion.

Taoiseach (tē´shəkh, -shək) *n.* the Prime Minister of the Republic of Ireland.

Taoism (tow´izm, tah´ōizm) *n.* the Chinese religious system based on the teachings of Laoze (b. 604 BC), primarily concerned with achieving harmony with the universe. **Taoist** (-ist) *n.*

tap[1] (tap) *v.t.* (*pres.p.* **tapping**, *past, p.p.* **tapped**) **1** to strike lightly or gently. **2** to strike lightly with. **3** to make with a tapping noise (*tapped the beat with her fingers*). *~v.i.* **1** to strike a gentle blow. **2** to tap-dance. *~n.* **1** a light or gentle blow, a rap. **2** the sound of this. **3** (*pl.*) a military signal for putting lights out in quarters or given at a military funeral. **4** a small piece of metal on the heel or toe of a tap-dancer's shoe designed to make the tapping noise. **5** tap-dancing (*learning ballet and tap*). **tap-dance** *n.* a step dance where the performers wear shoes with metal studs in the heels and toes to make a rhythmic sound as they dance. *~v.i.* to perform such a dance. **tap-dancer** *n.* **tap-dancing** *n.* **tapper**[1] *n.* **tapping** *n., a.*

tap[2] (tap) *n.* **1** a device that allows water or other fluid to be drawn out at a controlled rate; a faucet, a spigot. **2** a device connected secretly to a telephone and allowing someone other than the user to listen in to calls. **3** an act of listening in to a telephone call between other people. **4** (*coll.*) a taproom. **5** a tool for cutting female or internal screw-threads. *~v.t.* (*pres.p.* **tapping**, *past, p.p.* **tapped**) **1** to pierce (a cask etc.) so as to let out a liquid. **2** to let out or draw off (a liquid) in this way. **3** to provide with a tap or cock. **4** to draw (fluid) from a person's body. **5** to draw fluid from (a person) in this way. **6** (*fig.*) to draw upon (a source of supply) usually for the first time. **7** (*coll.*) to obtain money etc. from (*tapped his mum for £10*). **8** to divert current from (a wire). **9** to attach a device to (a telephone) in order to listen in to other people's conversations. **10** to make an internal screw in. **on tap 1** (of a cask etc.) tapped so that liquor can be drawn off. **2** (of liquor) ready to be drawn off by tap. **3** (*coll.*) freely available for use. **tappable** *a.* **tapper**[2] *n.*

taproom *n.* a room where alcoholic drinks, esp. beer on tap, are served. **tap root** *n.* the main root of a plant penetrating straight downwards for some depth. **tapster** (-stə) *n.* a person who serves liquor in a bar. **tap water** *n.* water from a tap, rather than from a bottle.

tapas (tap´as) *n.pl.* various light savoury snacks or appetizers, as served in Spain. **tapas bar** *n.* a bar serving this kind of food.

tape (tāp) *n.* **1** a continuous strip of paper or magnetized flexible material on which sound, pictures or other data can be recorded using various types of recording machines. **2** a unit containing a roll of tape for recording (*put the tape into the video*). **3** a narrow strip of woven linen, cotton etc., used for tying things together, in dressmaking, bookbinding etc. **4** a narrow strip of adhesive material, used for sticking things down or together, as insulation etc. **5** a strip of material stretched across a racecourse at the winning post. **6** a tape-measure. **7** a strong flexible band rotating on pulleys in printing and other machines. *~v.t.* **1** to record (sound, pictures or other data) on magnetic tape. **2** to provide, fasten or tie up with tapes. **3** to bind (sections of a book) with narrow bands. **4** to get a measure of. **on tape** recorded on magnetic tape. **to have taped** (*coll.*) to have a complete understanding of (a person or thing). **tapeable** *a.* **tape deck** *n.* a machine for recording sound on to magnetic tape and which replays this sound through an independent amplifier. **tape machine** *n.* a telegraphic instrument that receives and records news, stock prices etc. **tape-measure, tape-line** *n.* a tape or strip of metal, marked with centimetres, inches etc. for measuring, usu. coiled in a round flat case. **tape-record** *v.t.* to record using a tape recorder. **tape recorder** *n.* an electronic apparatus for recording music etc. on magnetic tape and which can also reproduce recorded sounds from such tapes. **tape recording** *n.* **tapeworm** *n.* a cestoid worm that parasitically infests the alimentary canal of humans and other vertebrates.

taper (tā´pə) *n.* **1** a small wax candle. **2** anything giving a very feeble light. *~v.i.* **1** to become gradually smaller or narrower towards one end. **2** to become gradually smaller or less important. *~v.t.* to make gradually smaller, narrower or less important. **tapered** *a.* tapering in form.

tapestry (tap´istri) *n.* (*pl.* **tapestries**) **1** a textile fabric in which the wool is supplied by a spindle instead of a shuttle, with designs or pictures applied by stitches across the warp. **2** any ornamental fabric with designs or pictures applied in this manner. **3** anything that is perceived as being intricate or interwoven (*the tapestry of life*). *~a.* of tapestry. **tapestried** *a.*

tapioca (tapiō´kə) *n.* a starchy, granular substance produced by beating cassava, forming a light farinaceous food.

tapir (tā´pə) *n.* an ungulate mammal of the genus

Tapirus of Central and S America and parts of Asia, related to the rhinoceros and the horse, with a short, flexible snout which it uses for feeding on vegetation.

tapper[1] TAP[1].

tapper[2] TAP[2].

tappet (tap´it) *n.* a projecting arm or lever that gives intermittent motion to some part in machinery.

tapster TAP[2].

tar[1] (tah) *n.* **1** a thick, dark, viscid oily liquid produced by the dry distillation of organic bodies and bituminous minerals, used in surfacing roads, preserving wood and the manufacture of antiseptics. **2** a similar by-product of burning tobacco. *~v.t.* (*pres.p.* **tarring**, *past, p.p.* **tarred**) to cover with tar. **tarred with the same brush** having the same bad characteristics. **to tar and feather** to smear with tar and then cover with feathers as a form of punishment. **tarbrush** *n.* a brush used to apply tar. **Tarmac** (-mak), **tarmac** *n.* **1** TARMACADAM (under TAR[1]). **2** a road or other surface made of this (*The plane taxied down the tarmac*). **tarmac** *v.t.* (*pres.p.* **tarmacking**, *past, p.p.* **tarmacked**) to put a layer of tarmacadam on (a surface such as a road). **tarmacadam** (-məka´dəm) *n.* a mixture of stones or slag held together by tar and used in surfacing roads, runways etc. **tarry**[1] *a.* (*comp.* **tarrier**, *superl.* **tarriest**) **tarriness** *n.*

tar[2] (tah) *n.* (*coll.*) a sailor.

taradiddle (tar´ədidəl), **tarradiddle** *n.* (*coll.*) **1** a lie, a fib. **2** nonsense.

taramasalata (tarəməsəlah´tə), **tarama** (tar´ə-mə) *n.* a pale pink creamy Greek pâté, made from smoked cod roe or, less commonly, the roe of other fish, blended with olive oil and garlic.

tarantella (tarəntel´ə), **tarantelle** (-tel´) *n.* **1** a rapid S Italian dance in triplets for one couple. **2** the music for such a dance.

tarantula (təran´tūlə) *n.* (*pl.* **tarantulas**) **1** any large hairy spider of the family Theraphosidae, found in tropical regions. **2** a large, hairy, black wolf spider, *Lycosa tarentula*, found in S Europe.

tarboosh (tahboosh´), **tarboush, tarbush** *n.* a brimless cap or fez, usu. red.

tardigrade (tah´digrād) *n.* any of various slow-moving invertebrates of the phylum Tardigrada, which have eight legs and live in wet soil, ditches etc.

tardy (tah´di) *a.* (*comp.* **tardier**, *superl.* **tardiest**) **1** moving slowly, slow, sluggish. **2** late, delayed, after the expected or proper time. **tardily** *adv.* **tardiness** *n.*

tare[1] (teə) *n.* **1** a vetch, esp. *Vicia sativa*, the common vetch. **2** (*Bible*) a weed that grows in fields of grain and which, when it is young, resembles corn.

tare[2] (teə) *n.* **1** an allowance for the weight of boxes, wrapping etc. in which goods are packed. **2** the weight of a motor vehicle without fuel, load, passengers or equipment.

targa (tah´gə) *n.* a sports car that has a removable hard roof which fits over a roll bar or goes into the boot when not in use. *~a.* relating to this kind of sports car (*a targa top*).

target (tah´git) *n.* **1** an object set up as a mark to be fired at in archery etc., painted with concentric bands surrounding a bull's eye. **2** any person or thing made the object of attack, criticism etc., a butt. **3** the specific objective or aim of any (concerted) effort. **4** the objective of an air-raid. *~v.t.* (*pres.p.* **targeting**, *past, p.p.* **targeted**) **1** to make a target of. **2** to aim at. **3** to direct the resources of the social services to. **on target 1** on the right course. **2** on schedule. **targetable** *a.*

tariff (tar´if) *n.* **1** a table of charges. **2** a list or table of duties or customs payable on the importation or export of goods. **3** a duty on any particular kind of goods. **4** a law imposing such duties. *~v.t.* to draw up a list of duties or charges on (goods etc.).

tarlatan (tah´lətən) *n.* a fine, transparent muslin.

Tarmac, tarmacadam TAR[1].

tarn (tahn) *n.* a small mountain lake.

tarnish (tah´nish) *v.t.* **1** to diminish or destroy the lustre of. **2** to sully, to stain. *~v.i.* to lose lustre. *~n.* **1** loss of lustre, a stain, a blemish. **2** the film of discoloration forming on the exposed face of a mineral or metal. **tarnishable** *a.* **tarnisher** *n.*

taro (tah´rō) *n.* (*pl.* **taros**) a tropical plant of the arum family, esp. *Colocasia esculenta* and *C. macrorhiza*, the roots of which are used as food by Pacific islanders.

tarot (tar´ō) *n.* **1** a figured playing card, one of a pack of 78, used in an old (orig. Italian) card game. **2** a pack of such cards, consisting of four suits of 14 plus a fifth suit of 22 permanent trump cards, used for fortune-telling. **3** (any of) these 22 cards. **4** any game played with tarot cards.

tarp (tahp) *n.* (*coll.*) (a) tarpaulin.

tarpaulin (tahpaw´lin) *n.* **1** a canvas cloth coated with tar or other waterproof compound. **2** a sheet of this.

tarpon (tah´pon) *n.* **1** a large and powerful game fish, *Tarpon atlanticus*, of the herring family, found in tropical Atlantic waters. **2** a similar fish, *Megalops cyprinoides*, found in the Pacific.

tarradiddle TARADIDDLE.

tarragon (tar´əgən) *n.* a perennial herb, *Artemisia dracunculus*, related to wormwood, used as a flavouring in cookery etc.

☒ **tarrif** common misspelling of TARIFF.

tarry[1] TAR[1].

†**tarry**[2] (tar´i) *v.i.* (*3rd pers. sing. pres.* **tarries**, *pres.p.* **tarrying**, *past, p.p.* **tarried**) **1** to stay, to remain behind, to wait. **2** to linger, to delay, to be late.

tarsier (tah´siə) *n.* a small nocturnal arboreal primate of the genus *Tarsius* found in the

Philippines and Malaysia, with very large eyes and ears, and long tarsal bones.

tarsus (tah´səs) *n.* (*pl.* **tarsi** (-sī)) **1** (*Anat.*) the set of bones (seven in humans) between the lower leg and the metatarsus, the ankle. **2** (*Zool.*) the shank of a bird's leg. **3** (*Zool.*) the terminal segment in the leg of an insect or crustacean. **tarsal** *a., n.*

tart[1] (taht) *n.* **1** a pie containing fruit or some other sweet filling. **2** a pastry case with a covering or filling of jam etc. **tartlet** *n.*

tart[2] (taht) *n.* (*sl.*) **1** a prostitute, a promiscuous woman. **2** (*offensive*) a girl or woman, esp. when thought of in sexual terms. **to tart up 1** to make more showy. **2** to dress cheaply, in a vulgar way. **tarty** *a.* (*comp.* **tartier**, *superl.* **tartiest**). **tartiness** *n.*

tart[3] (taht) *a.* **1** sharp to the taste, acid. **2** biting, cutting, piercing. **tartish** *a.* **tartly** *adv.* **tartness** *n.*

tartan (tah´tən) *n.* **1** a chequered pattern of crossing stripes of various colours, esp. one of those distinguishing the various Scottish Highland clans. **2** a woollen etc. fabric with this pattern. ~*a.* consisting of, made of or like tartan.

Tartar (tah´tə), **Tatar** *n.* **1** a member of a group of peoples, such as the Mongols and Turks, who live in central Asia. **2** their language. **3** (**tartar**) a person of an intractable, irritable temper or more than one's match. ~*a.* of or relating to the Tartars or their language. **Tartarian** (-teə´ri-) *a., n.*

tartar (tah´tə) *n.* **1** a yellowish incrustation of calcium phosphate deposited on the teeth. **2** partially purified argol, the impure tartrate of potassium deposited from wines. **3** CREAM OF TARTAR (under CREAM). **tartaric** (-tar´-) *a.* (*Chem.*) of, relating to or containing tartar or tartaric acid. **tartaric acid** *n.* (*Chem.*) a crystalline acid from plants, used as a food additive (E334) and in medicines. **tartarize, tartarise** *v.t.* **tartar sauce** *n.* TARTARE SAUCE (under TARTARE). **tartrate** (-trāt) *n.* (*Chem.*) a salt or ester of tartaric acid. **tartrazine** (-trəzēn) *n.* (*Chem.*) a yellow dye used in textiles, medicines and food (E102).

tartare (tahtah´) *a.* (*usu. following the n.*) in cookery, in a Tartar style. **tartare sauce** (tah´tə) *n.* a relish made from mayonnaise, chopped capers, herbs etc. and usually served with fish.

Tarzan (tah´zən) *n.* a man of great physical strength and agility.

Tas. (tas) *abbr.* Tasmania.

tash (tash), **tache** *n.* (*coll.*) short for MOUSTACHE.

task (tahsk) *n.* **1** a piece of work. **2** (*Comput.*) an action or process to be carried out. **3** a piece of work undertaken voluntarily. ~*v.t.* **1** to impose a task upon. **2** to strain, to overtax. **to take to task** to reprove, to reprimand. **tasker** *n.* **task force**, **task group** *n.* **1** a group formed to carry out a specific task. **2** (*Mil.*) a military or police group formed to undertake a specific mission. **taskmaster, taskmistress** *n.* a person who gives someone work to do, esp. on a regular basis or with a strict deadline.

Tasmanian (tazmā´niən) *a.* of or relating to Tasmania. ~*n.* a native or inhabitant of Tasmania. **Tasmanian devil** *n.* a small fierce carnivorous nocturnal marsupial, *Sarcophilus harrisii*, now found only in Tasmania. **Tasmanian tiger, Tasmanian wolf** *n.* THYLACINE.

tassel[1] (tas´əl) *n.* **1** a pendent ornament, usu. composed of a tuft of threads, cords, silk etc. attached to the corners of cushions, curtains etc. **2** the pendent head of a flower, esp. one, such as the maize plant, with visible tassel-like stamens. ~*v.t.* (*pres.p.* **tasselling**, (*N Am.*) **tasseling**, *past, p.p.* **tasselled**, (*N Am.*) **tasseled**) **1** to provide or adorn with tassels. **2** to remove the tassels from (maize) to strengthen the plant. ~*v.i.* to form tassels.

tassel[2] (tas´əl), **torsel** (taw´səl) *n.* a small piece of wood or stone fixed into a wall for a beam or joist to rest on.

taste (tāst) *n.* **1** the sensation excited by the contact of various soluble substances with certain organs in the mouth, flavour. **2** the sense by which this is perceived. **3** the act of tasting. **4** a small quantity tasted, drunk, eaten or experienced, a bit taken as a sample. **5** the mental faculty or power of apprehending and enjoying the beautiful and the sublime in nature and art, or of appreciating and discerning between degrees of artistic excellence. **6** manner, style, execution, as directed or controlled by this. **7** an inclination, a predilection (for). ~*v.t.* **1** to try the flavour of by taking into the mouth. **2** to perceive the flavour of. **3** to experience. **4** (*coll.*) to eat a little of. ~*v.i.* **1** to have a specified taste, to have a smack or flavour (of) (*This tastes awful; This tastes of vinegar*). **2** to experience the sensation of taste. **3** to take or eat a small portion of food etc., to partake (of). **4** to have experience (of). **to leave a bad/ bitter taste (in one's mouth)** (of an unpleasant experience etc.) to make one upset, regretful etc. **to one's taste** to one's liking. **to taste** in the amount preferred or needed to give a pleasant taste (*Add seasoning to taste*). **taste-able, tastable** *a.* **taste bud** *n.* any of the tiny organs on the tongue sensitive to taste. **tasteful** *a.* **1** having or showing aesthetic taste. **2** having, characterized by, or done with good taste. **tastefully** *adv.* **tastefulness** *n.* **tasteless** *a.* **1** having no flavour, insipid. **2** vapid, dull. **3** having, characterized by or done with bad taste. **4** inappropriate, indecorous, tactless. **tastelessly** *adv.* **tastelessness** *n.* **taster** *n.* **1** a person who tastes, esp. a person employed to test the quality of teas, liquors etc. by tasting, orig. one employed to taste food and drink before it was served. **2** an implement for cutting a small cylindrical sample from cheese. **3** a small cup used by a wine taster etc. **4** a small sample. **tasting** *n.* a social event where samples, esp. of wine, are tasted and assessed for quality, sometimes as a prelude to buying. **tasty** *a.* (*comp.* **tastier**, *superl.* **tastiest**) **1** noticeably pleasant to the taste. **2** (*coll.*) in good taste. **3** (*coll.*) attractive. **4** (*coll.*) sexually alluring. **tastily** *adv.* **tastiness** *n.*

tat¹ (tat), **tatt** *n.* **1** rubbish, rags. **2** something which is pretentious but of little real value. **3** an unkempt or shabby person.

tat² (tat) *v.t.* (*pres.p.* **tatting**, *past, p.p.* **tatted**) to make by knotting. ~*v.i.* to make tatting. ~*n.* tatting. **tatting** *n.* **1** knotted work or lace used for edging etc. **2** the process of making this.

ta-ta (tatah´) *int.* (*coll.*) goodbye.

tatami (tətah´mi) *n.* (*pl.* **tatamis**) a traditional woven straw or rush mat of standard size, used as a floor covering in Japanese houses. **tatami mat** *n.*

Tatar TARTAR.

tater (tā´tə), **tatie** (-ti) *n.* (*coll.*) a potato.

tatter (tat´ə) *n.* (*usu. in pl.*) **1** a rag. **2** a torn and hanging piece or shred. **in tatters 1** torn to pieces. **2** in a state of ruin or irretrievable breakdown. **tattered** *a.* in tatters. **tattery** *a.*

tattie (tat´i) *n.* (*coll.*) a potato.

tatting TAT².

tattle (tat´əl) *v.i.* **1** to chatter, to gossip. **2** to tell tales or secrets. ~*n.* **1** prattle, gossip, idle talk. **2** a gossip. **tattler** *n.* **tattle-tale** *n.* (*N Am.*) a tell-tale.

tattoo¹ (tatoo´) *n.* (*pl.* **tattoos**) **1** the beat of drum recalling soldiers to their quarters. **2** a military pageant, esp. by night. **3** (the sound of) a regular or rhythmic tapping or drumming.

tattoo² (tatoo´) *v.t.* (*3rd pers. sing. pres.* **tattoos**, *pres.p.* **tattooing**, *past, p.p.* **tattooed**) to mark (the skin) by pricking and inserting pigments. ~*n.* (*pl.* **tattoos**) a mark or pattern so produced. **tattooer** *n.* **tattooist** *n.*

tatty (tat´i) *a.* (*comp.* **tattier**, *superl.* **tattiest**) (*coll.*) **1** untidy, unkempt. **2** shabby, of poor quality. **3** gaudy, tawdry. **tattily** *adv.* **tattiness** *n.*

tau (taw, tow) *n.* **1** the 19th letter of the Greek alphabet (τ, Τ). **2** a tau cross. **tau cross** *n.* a cross shaped like a T, a St Anthony's cross. **tau particle** *n.* (*Physics*) an elementary particle of the lepton family that has a negative electric charge.

taught TEACH.

taunt (tawnt) *v.t.* **1** to reproach or upbraid sarcastically or contemptuously. **2** to tease or tantalize. ~*n.* a bitter or sarcastic reproach. **taunter** *n.* **tauntingly** *adv.*

taupe (tōp) *n.* a brownish-grey colour. ~*a.* of this colour.

Taurus (taw´rəs) *n.* **1** (*Astron.*) a constellation close to Orion, said to represent a bull; the Bull. **2** (*Astrol.*) **a** the second sign of the zodiac, which the sun enters around 21 April. **b** a person born under this sign. **Taurean** *n.* a person born under the sign of Taurus. ~*a.* born under Taurus. **taurine** (-rīn) *n.* (*Chem.*) a colourless amino acid derivative that was first discovered in ox bile and which plays an important part in metabolizing fats. ~*a.* bull-like.

taut (tawt) *a.* **1** tight, not slack. **2** (of nerves) tense. **3** (of a ship) in good order, trim. **tauten** *v.t., v.i.* **tautly** *adv.* **tautness** *n.*

tautology (tawtol´əji) *n.* (*pl.* **tautologies**) **1** repetition of the same thing in different words. **2** (*Logic*) a statement that is always true. **tautological** (-loj´-), **tautologic** *a.* repetitive. **tautologically** *adv.* **tautologist** *n.* **tautologize, tautologise** *v.i.* **tautologous** (-gəs) *a.*

tavern (tav´ən) *n.* (*dated or poet.*) a public house, an inn. **taverna** (-vœ´nə) *n.* **1** a Greek hotel with its own bar. **2** a Greek restaurant.

taw¹ (taw) *v.t.* to dress or make (skins) into leather with mineral agents, as alum, instead of tannin. **tawer** *n.*

taw² (taw) *n.* **1** a game of marbles. **2** the line from which players throw their marbles. **3** a large marble.

tawdry (taw´dri) *a.* (*comp.* **tawdrier**, *superl.* **tawdriest**) **1** showy without taste or elegance. **2** gaudy and of little or no value. ~*n.* tasteless or worthless finery. **tawdrily** *adv.* **tawdriness** *n.*

tawny (taw´ni) *a.* (*comp.* **tawnier**, *superl.* **tawniest**) brownish-yellow, tan-coloured. ~*n.* this colour. **tawniness** *n.* **tawny eagle** *n.* a tawny-coloured eagle, *Aquila rapax*, found in Africa and Asia. **tawny owl** *n.* **1** a European owl, *Strix aluco*, with reddish-brown plumage. **2** (*coll.*) (**Tawny Owl**) an assistant leader of a Brownie Guide pack (officially an *Assistant Brownie Guider*).

tax (taks) *n.* (*pl.* **taxes**) **1** a compulsory contribution levied on a person, property or business to meet the expenses of government or other public services. **2** a heavy demand, requirement, strain etc. ~*v.t.* (*3rd pers. sing. pres.* **taxes**) **1** to impose a tax on. **2** to deduct tax from (someone's income, etc.). **3** to lay a heavy burden or strain upon, to make demands upon. **4** to pay a tax on (*taxed the car for a year*). **5** (*formal*) to accuse (of) (*taxed him with taking the money*). **6** (*Law*) to assess (costs of an action etc.). **taxable** *a.* **taxability** (-bil´-) *n.* **taxation** (-sā´shən) *n.* **tax avoidance** *n.* legal minimization of tax. **tax break** *n.* (*coll.*) an opportunity to reduce or minimize tax, allowed by the government. **tax-deductible** *a.* (of expenses) able or liable to be legally deducted before assessment for tax. **tax disc, tax disk** *n.* a paper disc on a motor vehicle's windscreen showing payment of road tax. **taxer** *n.* **tax evasion** *n.* illegal non-payment or underpayment of tax. **tax-free** *a.* exempt from taxation. **tax haven** *n.* a country where taxes are low, and which attracts tax exiles. **taxing** *a.* demanding, difficult (*a very taxing job*). **taxman** *n.* (*pl.* **taxmen**) (*coll.*) **1** a person employed by the Inland Revenue (Inland Revenue Service in US) to collect taxes and often adjudicate on matters relating to taxes. **2** the department responsible for tax collection, typically represented as uncaring and money-grasping. **taxpayer** *n.* **tax return** *n.* a (usu. yearly) statement of one's income and tax paid. **tax year** *n.* FINANCIAL YEAR (under FINANCE).

taxa TAXON (under TAXONOMY).

taxi (tak´si) *n.* (*pl.* **taxis**) a motor car usu. fitted with a taximeter and licensed to carry fare-paying passengers. *~v.i.* (*3rd pers. sing. pres.* **taxies**, *pres.p.* **taxiing, taxying**, *past, p.p.* **taxied**) (of an aircraft or pilot) to travel along the ground before take-off or after landing. **taxicab** *n.* a taxi. **taxi rank, taxi stand** *n.* a place where taxis can queue to pick up fares. **taxiway** *n.* a marked path from an airport terminal to a runway.

taxidermy (tak´sidœmi) *n.* the art of preparing and mounting the skins of animals so that they resemble the living forms. **taxidermal** (-dœ´-), **taxidermic** *a.* **taxidermist** *n.*

taximeter (tak´simētə) *n.* an automatic instrument fitted in a cab for registering the distance travelled on a particular journey and the fare to be paid.

taxonomy (takson´əmi) *n.* (*pl.* **taxonomies**) 1 the branch of natural history that deals with the principles, theories and techniques of classification. 2 a scheme of classification. **taxon** (tak´-) *n.* (*pl.* **taxa** (-sə)) any taxonomical category or group. **taxonomic** (-nom´-), **taxonomical** *a.* **taxonomically** *adv.* **taxonomist** *n.*

tayberry (tā´bəri) *n.* (*pl.* **tayberries**) 1 a type of hybrid plant produced by crossing blackberry and raspberry plants. 2 the fruit of this plant.

TB *abbr.* 1 torpedo boat. 2 tubercle bacillus. 3 tuberculosis.

Tb *chem. symbol* terbium.

t.b.a. *abbr.* to be announced, to be arranged.

tbs, tbsp *abbr.* tablespoon(s), tablespoonful(s).

tbsps *abbr.* tablespoonfuls.

Tc *chem. symbol* technetium.

TD *abbr.* Teachta Dála, member of the Dáil.

Te *chem. symbol* tellurium.

te (tē), (*N Am.*) **ti** *n.* (*pl.* **tes**, (*N Am.*) **tis**) (*Mus.*) 1 the seventh note of a major scale in the sol-fa system of notation. 2 the note B in the fixed-doh system.

tea (tē) *n.* (*pl.* **teas**) 1 a small evergreen shrub or tree, *Camellia sinensis*, grown in India, China, Japan and other parts of SE Asia for its leaves. 2 the leaves of this plant dried and shredded. 3 a drink made from these leaves by infusing them in boiling water. 4 a similar drink made by infusing the leaves of another plant, or by infusing another substance, in boiling water (*blackcurrant tea*; *beef tea*). 5 a light meal, usu. served in the late afternoon, typically consisting of small sandwiches, scones, cakes and biscuits etc. accompanied by cups of tea. 6 the main meal of the day, usu. served in the early evening and often consisting of a cooked dish followed by a pudding or cakes, biscuits etc. 7 (*esp. N Am.*) an afternoon social gathering at which tea is drunk. **tea bag** *n.* a small perforated bag containing tea. **tea-bread** *n.* light, spongy fruit bread. **tea caddy** *n.* a small box in which tea is kept. **teacake** *n.* a bun of light sweet bread, often toasted for eating at tea. **tea ceremony** *n.* (*pl.* **tea ceremonies**) in Japan, a ritualized procedure for preparing,

serving and drinking green tea. **tea chest** *n.* a light box lined with thin sheet metal, in which tea is imported. **tea cloth** *n.* a tea towel. **tea cosy** *n.* (*pl.* **tea cosies**) a cover for a teapot to keep the contents hot. **teacup** *n.* a small cup for drinking tea from. **teacupful** *n.* **tea dance** *n.* an afternoon tea combined with a dance. **tea garden** *n.* a garden where tea and other refreshments are served to the public. **tea lady** *n.* (*pl.* **tea ladies**) a woman employed to make tea for workers in an office etc. **tea leaf** *n.* (*pl.* **tea leaves**) 1 a leaf of tea or the tea plant. 2 (*pl.*) such leaves after infusion. **tea party** *n.* (*pl.* **tea parties**) a party at which tea is served. **tea plant** *n.* the plant *Camellia sinensis*. **tea planter** *n.* a person who cultivates tea plants. **teapot** *n.* a vessel in which tea is infused, with a handle and spout for pouring. **tearoom** *n.* a restaurant etc. where afternoon teas are provided. **tea rose** *n.* a rose, *Rosa odorata*, with scent supposed to resemble tea. **tea service, teaset** *n.* a collection of crockery used in serving tea, including teacups, tea saucers and teapot. **teaspoon** *n.* 1 a small spoon for stirring tea in a teacup. 2 a teaspoonful. **teaspoonful** *n.* (*pl.* **teaspoonfuls**). **teatime** *n.* the time of the day when the meal called tea is eaten. **tea towel** *n.* a small towel used for drying dishes etc. that have been washed. **tea tray** *n.* a tray on or from which tea is served. **tea-tree** *n.* 1 any Australasian myrtaceous plant of the genera *Melaleuca, Leptospermum* etc., used as a tea substitute by early settlers. 2 a red-berried shrub, *Lycium barbarum*, of the nightshade family.

teach (tēch) *v.t.* (*past, p.p.* **taught** (tawt)) 1 to cause (a person etc.) to learn (to do) or acquire knowledge or skill in, to instruct or train in (*taught her brother to drive*; *taught me how to knit*). 2 to impart knowledge or information concerning (a subject etc.), to give lessons in (*teaches English*). 3 to impart instruction to, to educate (*teaches the sixth form*). 4 to explain, to show, to disclose, to make known. 5 to make (someone) understand by example, experience, etc. (*Her lies taught him not to trust her*). *~v.i.* to teach people as an occupation. **to teach school** (*esp. N Am.*) to be a schoolteacher. **teachable** *a.* 1 (of a subject etc.) able to be taught. 2 disposed to learn, docile. **teachability** (-bil´-) *n.* **teachableness** *n.* **teacher** *n.* a person who teaches others, esp. a schoolteacher. **teacherly** *a.* **teach-in** *n.* 1 an informal conference on a specific subject involving specialists and students. 2 a group of these, usu. on a connected theme. **teaching** *n.* 1 the work or profession of a teacher. 2 (*often in pl.*) something which is taught, a doctrine (*according to the teachings of Freud*). **teaching hospital** *n.* a hospital where medical students are trained.

teak (tēk) *n.* 1 a large tree, *Tectona grandis*, grown in India and SE Asia for its heavy timber which does not crack, warp, shrink or corrode iron, used largely for shipbuilding, furniture etc. 2 this timber.

teal (tēl) *n.* (*pl.* **teal, teals**) **1** a small Eurasian freshwater duck of the genus *Anas*, esp. *A. crecca*, the common teal, related to the mallard. **2** teal blue. ~*a.* of the colour teal blue. **teal blue** *n.*, *a.* (of) a deep greenish-blue colour.

team (tēm) *n.* **1** a group of people who form a side in a game or sport. **2** a group of people who work together etc. **3** two or more horses, oxen etc., harnessed together. ~*v.t.* **1** to join (with others) in a common bond or for the same purpose (*Workers teamed up with the management against the takeover*). **2** to harness or join together in a team. **3** to match (*teamed a plain black sweater with her orange and black skirt*). **team-mate** *n.* a fellow member of a team, group, playing side etc. **team player** *n.* a person who works or plays well in a team and who puts this before personal achievement. **team spirit** *n.* the willingness to act as a team, or for the good of the team. **teamster** (-stə) *n.* **1** (*N Am.*) a person who drives a lorry or truck. **2** a person who drives a team of oxen, horses etc. **team-teaching** *n.* teaching done by two or more teachers each of whom has specialist knowledge, skills etc. **teamwork** *n.* effective cooperation with other members of a team or group.

tear[1] (tea) *v.t.* (*past* **tore** (taw), *p.p.* **torn** (tawn)) **1** to pull forcibly apart. **2** to make a hole in, to rip, to lacerate. **3** to make (a hole, rent, tear, wound etc.) by tearing (*tore a hole in my tights*). **4** to pull violently (away, out etc.). **5** to drag, remove or sever. ~*v.i.* **1** to pull violently (at). **2** to part or separate on being pulled. **3** (*coll.*) to rush, move or act with speed or violence (*tore up the road to catch the bus*). ~*n.* **1** a hole or rip. **2** a torn part of cloth etc. **that's torn it** (*sl.*) that's spoiled things. **to be torn between** to be unable to choose, or have difficulty choosing, between. **to tear apart 1** to devastate, disrupt or divide. **2** to make a mess of (a place), esp. when trying to find something. **3** to criticize severely. **to tear a strip off** (*coll.*) to reprimand. **to tear into 1** to reprimand or criticize forcefully. **2** to embark on energetically. **to tear oneself away** to leave reluctantly. **to tear one's hair 1** to be overcome with grief. **2** to be very puzzled. **to tear to shreds 1** to ruin or destroy completely. **2** to ridicule or criticize mercilessly. **tearable** *a.* **tearaway** *n.* (*coll.*) a reckless, sometimes violent, young person. ~*a.* reckless, impetuous. **tearer** *n.* **tearing** *a.* (*coll.*) violent, furious, tremendous (*Can't stop, I'm in a tearing hurry*). **tear-off** *a.* (of a strip of paper etc.) able to be easily detached, usu. along a perforation.

tear[2] (tiə) *n.* **1** a drop of the saline liquid secreted by the lachrymal glands, moistening the eyes or flowing down in strong emotion etc. **2** a drop of liquid. **3** a solid, transparent drop or droplike object. **in tears** crying, weeping. **teardrop** *n.* **tear duct** *n.* a short tube that runs from the inner corner of the lower eyelid down into the nasal passage, allowing tears to drain away. **tearful** *a.*

1 shedding or about to shed tears. **2** causing or characterized by sadness. **tearfully** *adv.* **tearfulness** *n.* **tear gas** *n.* (*pl.* **tear gases**, (*N Am.*) **tear gasses**) a poison gas that affects the lachrymal glands and causes violent watering of the eyes. **tear-gas** *v.t.* (*3rd pers. sing. pres.* **tear-gases**, (*N Am.*) **tear-gasses**, *pres.p.* **tear-gassing**, *past*, *p.p.* **tear-gassed**) to attack using tear gas. **tear-jerker** *n.* a book, film or song which is excessively sentimental. **tear-jerking** *n.*, *a.* **tearless** *a.* not tearful or crying. **tearlessly** *adv.* **tearlessness** *n.* **tear-stained** *a.* **1** wet with tears. **2** (*poet.*) sorrowful, sad.

tease (tēz) *v.t.* **1** to annoy, torment, irritate or vex with petty requests, importunity, jesting or raillery. **2** to arouse sexual desire in without any intention of satisfying it. **3** to pull apart or separate the fibres of. **4** to dress (cloth), esp. using teasels. ~*n.* **1** a person who teases or irritates. **2** an act or instance of teasing. **to tease out** to disentangle. **teaser** *n.* **1** (*coll.*) an awkward question, problem, or situation, a poser. **2** (*esp. N Am.*) a short trailer for a film etc. **3** a person who teases. **teasing** *a.* **teasingly** *adv.*

teasel (tē´zəl), **teazel, teazle** *n.* **1** a plant of the genus *Dipsacus*, with large burs or heads covered with stiff, hooked awns, used for raising a nap on cloth. **2** a bur or head of this kind. **3** a machine used as a substitute for this. ~*v.t.* (*pres.p.* **teaselling**, (*N Am.*) **teaseling**, *past*, *p.p.* **teaselled**, (*N Am.*) **teaseled**) to dress (cloth) with teasels. **teaseller**, (*N Am.*) **teaseler** *n.*

teat (tēt) *n.* **1** the nipple of the mammary gland, esp. of an animal, through which milk is drawn. **2** a projection or appliance resembling this, such as the attachment on a baby's feeding bottle through which milk etc. is sucked.

tec (tek) *n.* (*coll.*) a detective, esp. a private detective.

tech (tek) *n.* **1** (*also* **tec**) a technical college. **2** technology (esp. in *high-tech*).

techie (tek´i), **techy** *n.* (*pl.* **techies**) (*esp. Comput.*, *coll.*) a person with a great enthusiasm for or a good understanding of the latest technology (esp. computing).

technetium (teknē´shiəm) *n.* (*Chem.*) a chemical element, at. no. 43, chem. symbol Tc, whose radioisotope is used in radiotherapy.

technic (tek´nik) *n.* **1** (*usu. in pl.*) **a** technology. **b** technical jargon, procedures etc. **2** technique. ~*a.* technical. **technicist** (-sist) *n.*

technical (tek´nikəl) *a.* **1** of or relating to the mechanical arts and applied sciences. **2** of or relating to any particular art, science, business etc. **3** using or requiring specialist knowledge, language etc. (*This manual is far too technical*). **4** caused by a problem or breakdown in machinery etc. (*We've got some technical difficulties*). **5** due to or existing because of the strict interpretation of a law, rule etc. (*got off due to a technical loophole in the law*). **technical hitch** *n.* **1** a failure or breakdown, usually temporary, caused by a fault

in a mechanism etc. **2** a snag or hold-up.
technicality (-kal´-) *n.* (*pl.* **technicalities**) **1**
technicalness. **2** a technical term, expression etc.
3 a petty or formal detail. **technical knockout** *n.*
in boxing, the referee's decision to end the fight
because one boxer is too badly injured to
continue and to award the fight to the other
boxer. **technically** *adv.* **technicalness** *n.*

technician (teknish´ən) *n.* **1** a person skilled in
the technical side of a subject, a technical expert.
2 a person employed in a laboratory etc. to use
and look after technical equipment.

Technicolor® (tek´nikŭlə) *n.* **1** a colour cinematography process. **2** (*coll.*) (*also* **technicolor,**
technicolour) vivid colour or detail.

technique (teknēk´) *n.* **1** a mode of artistic
performance or execution. **2** mechanical skill in
art, craft etc. **3** proficiency in some skill. **4** a
particular way of carrying out or performing
something.

techno (tek´nō) *n.* a type of dance music with
insistent repetitive beats performed on electronic instruments (*techno-beat, techno-music*).

technobabble (tek´nōbabəl) *n.* (*coll.*) meaningless technical jargon.

technocracy (teknok´rəsi) *n.* (*pl.* **technocracies**)
1 government or industrial control by technical
experts. **2** an example of this. **technocrat** (tek´nō-
krat) *n.* **technocratic** (-krat´-) *a.* **technocratically**
adv.

technology (teknol´əji) *n.* (*pl.* **technologies**) **1**
the study of the mechanical arts and applied
sciences; the practical application of science to
industry and other fields. **2** the total technical
means and skills available to a particular human
society. **technological** (-loj´-) *a.* **technologist** *n.*

technophile (tek´nōfīl) *n.* a person with an
enthusiasm for new technology. ~*a.* **1** of or
relating to technophiles. **2** conforming to or
compatible with new technology. **technophilia**
(-fil´-) *n.* **technophilic** *a.*

technophobe (tek´nōfōb) *n.* a person who
distrusts, avoids or cannot master new
technology. **technophobia** (-fō´-) *n.* **techno-
phobic** *a.*

techy TECHIE.

tectonic (tekton´ik) *a.* **1** of or relating to building
or construction. **2** (*Geol.*) relating to, resulting
from or causing structural deformation of the
earth's crust. **tectonically** *adv.* **tectonics** *n.* **1**
(*Geol.*) the study of the structure of the earth's
crust and the forces that cause it to change. **2**
(*Archit.*) the art of designing and constructing
buildings etc. that combine practicality and
beauty.

Ted (ted), **ted** *n.* (*coll.*) a Teddy boy.

teddy (ted´i) *n.* (*pl.* **teddies**) **1** (*also* **teddy bear**) a
stuffed toy bear. **2** a woman's one-piece under-
garment.

Teddy boy (ted´i) *n.* (*coll.*) a young man, esp. of
the 1950s, characteristically wearing a long
jacket, drainpipe trousers and other styles

of dress associated with the Edwardian
period.

tedious (tē´diəs) *a.* boring, tiring and continuing
for a long time. **tediously** *adv.* **tediousness** *n.*
tedium (-əm) *n.* monotony, boredom.

tee[1] (tē) *n.* **1** in golf, the area at the start of each
hole where players strike the first ball of the
hole. **2** a means of raising and steadying a golf
ball for the first stroke at each hole, now usu. a
small wooden or plastic cup with a pointed stem
to dig into the ground. ~*v.t.* (*3rd pers. sing. pres.*
tees, *pres.p.* **teeing,** *past, p.p.* **teed**) to put (the
ball) on a tee. **to tee off 1** to play from a tee. **2**
(*coll.*) to begin.

tee[2] (tē) *n.* (*pl.* **tees**) the 20th letter of the alphabet,
T, t. **to a tee** perfectly, to a nicety. **tee shirt** *n.* T-
SHIRT (under T[1]).

tee-hee (tēhē´), **te-hee** *int.* used to express
restrained amusement. ~*n.* a restrained laugh, a
chuckle, a titter. ~*v.i.* (*3rd pers. sing. pres.* **tee-
hees,** **te-hees,** *pres.p.* **tee-heeing, te-heeing,** *past,
p.p.* **tee-heed, te-heed**) to give a restrained laugh,
to titter.

teem[1] (tēm) *v.i.* **1** to be prolific or abundant (*flies
teeming in the heat*). **2** to be abundantly stocked
(with) (*The place was teeming with flies*).

teem[2] (tēm) *v.i.* to pour (down), as rain etc. (*Rain
was teeming down the window*).

teen (tēn) *a.* teenage (*teen culture*). ~*n.* a teenager.
-teen (tēn) *suf.* denoting the addition of 10 (in
numbers 13–19). **-teenth** (-th) *suf.*

teens (tēnz) *n.pl.* the time in a person's life from
age 13 to 19 years. **teenage, teenaged** *a.* **1** aged
between 13 and 19 years. **2** of or relating to
teenagers. **teenager** *n.* a person aged between 13
and 19 years. **teeny-bopper** *n.* (*coll.*) a young
teenager, usu. a girl, who follows the latest
trends in clothes and pop music with great
enthusiasm.

teensy (tēn´zi, -si) *a.* (*comp.* **teensier,** *superl.*
teensiest) (*coll.*) tiny. **teensy-weensy** (-wēn´zi,
-si) *a.* (*comp.* **teensy-weensier,** *superl.* **teensy-
weensiest**) (*coll.*) very tiny.

teeny (tē´ni) *a.* (*comp.* **teenier,** *superl.* **teeniest**)
(*coll.*) tiny. **teeny-weeny** (-wē´ni) *a.* (*comp.* **teeny-
weenier,** *superl.* **teeny-weeniest**) very tiny.

teeny-bopper TEENS.

teepee TEPEE.

teeter (tē´tə) *v.i.* **1** to move to and fro unsteadily,
to sway or wobble. **2** to hesitate or waver.

teeth TOOTH.

teethe (tēdh) *v.i.* to cut or develop teeth, esp. first
or milk teeth. **teething** *n., a.* **teething ring** *n.* a ring
for a teething baby to chew on. **teething troubles**
n.pl. **1** the problems or difficulties that arise at
the beginning of a new venture etc. and which
can usu. be put right quite easily. **2** the soreness
and irritation caused when cutting the first teeth.

teetotal (tētō´təl) *a.* characterized by, relating to,
pledged to or advocating total abstinence from
intoxicants, esp. alcoholic drink. **teetotalism** *n.*
teetotaller, (*N Am.*) **teetotaler** *n.* **teetotally** *adv.*

teff (tef) *n.* an African cereal, *Eragrostis tef*, used as a fodder-plant and sometimes as a source of flour.

TEFL (tef´əl) *abbr.* teaching English as a foreign language.

Teflon® (tef´lon) *n.* polytetrafluoroethylene, used as a non-stick coating for saucepans etc.

te-hee TEE-HEE.

tektite (tek´tīt) *n.* (*Geol.*) a small, dark, glassy stone, thought to be of meteoric origin.

telco (tel´kō) *n.* (*pl.* **telcos**) (*N Am.*) a company in the telecommunications industry.

tele- (tel´i) *comb. form* **1** far, distant, as in *teleport*. **2** television, as in *teletext*. **3** relating to instruments that function over long distances, as in *telephone*. **4** relating to or conducted over the telephone, as in *telemarketing*.

tele-ad (tel´iad) *n.* a classified advertisement sent to a newspaper etc. by telephone.

telebanking (tel´ibangking) *n.* a computerized system of banking that allows transactions to be carried out by telephone.

telecamera (tel´ikamərə) *n.* **1** a camera designed for filming in television studios. **2** a camera fitted with a telephoto lens.

telecast (tel´ikahst) *n.* a programme or item broadcast by television. *~v.t.* (*past, p.p.* **telecast**) to broadcast by television. **telecaster** *n.*

telecommunication (telikəmūnikā´shən) *n.* **1** communication at a distance, by cable, telephone, radio etc. **2** (*pl.*) the science or technology of telecommunication.

telecommute (telikəmūt´) *v.i.* to work at home, keeping in contact with the office etc. by telephone, e-mail, fax, the Internet etc. **telecommuter** *n.*

telecoms (tel´ikomz), **telecomms** *n.* (*coll.*) telecommunications.

teleconference (tel´ikonfərəns) *n.* a meeting, discussion or conference where the participants are linked by video, audio or computer connections. **teleconferencing** *n.*

telecottage (tel´ikotij) *n.* a place with personal computers, fax, e-mail, Internet etc. facilities where people can work away from a central office while still being in close contact with it. **telecottaging** *n.*

tele-evangelist TELEVANGELIST.

telefacsimile (telifaksim´ili) *n.* an act or the process of sending a fax.

Telefax® (tel´ifaks), **telefax** *n.* **1** TELEFACSIMILE. **2** a document etc. sent by telefacsimile.

telegenic (telijen´ik) *a.* (of a person) having the looks or personal qualities desirable for working in or appearing on television.

telegram (tel´igram) *n.* a communication sent by telegraph, now only used for international messages and superseded in 1981 by the telemessage for internal messages.

telegraph (tel´igrahf) *n.* **1** an apparatus or device for transmitting messages or signals to a distance, esp. by making and breaking electrical connections. **2** (*in full* **telegraph-board**) a board at sports grounds, racecourses etc. displaying scores and other information in a format large enough to be read at a distance. *~v.t.* **1** to transmit (a message etc.) by telegraph. **2** to give advance warning (of something). *~v.i.* **1** to send a message by telegraph. **2** to signal (to etc.). **telegrapher** (tel´-, tileg´-) *n.* **telegraphese** (-ēz´) *n.* (*facet.*) jargon used in telegrams. **telegraphic** (-graf´-) *a.* **1** of or relating to the telegraph, sent by telegraph. **2** suitable for the telegraph, esp. in being brief, concisely worded. **telegraphically** *adv.* **telegraphist** (tileg´-) *n.* **telegraph plant** *n.* an Asian plant, *Codariocalyx motorius*, which has leaves that make jerking movements in response to being stimulated by sunshine. **telegraph pole**, **telegraph post** *n.* a pole that supports telegraph and telephone wires. **telegraphy** (tileg´rəfi) *n.* the art or practice of communicating by telegraph or of constructing or managing telegraphs.

telekinesis (telikinē´sis) *n.* (*Psych.*) the movement of objects at a distance supposedly without their being physically touched or interfered with. **telekinetic** (-net´-) *a.*

telemark (tel´imahk) *n.* a swinging turn in skiing, performed to change direction or to stop. *~v.i.* to make this kind of turn.

telemarketing (tel´imahkiting) *n.* a way of trying to boost the sales of a product by making unsolicited telephone calls to potential customers. **telemarketer** *n.*

telemessage (tel´imesij) *n.* a message sent by telex or telephone (superseding the telegraph).

telemeter (tilem´itə) *n.* a device that records readings, esp. meteorological data, and transmits it by way of electric or radio signals to a distant point. *~v.t.* to obtain and transmit (data) from a distance. *~v.i.* to record and send data readings. **telemetric** (telimet´-) *a.* **telemetry** (-tri) *n.*

teleology (teliol´əji, tē-) *n.* (*pl.* **teleologies**) **1** (*Philos.*) the doctrine that asserts that everything in the universe has been designed for a purpose. **2** (*Theol.*) the belief that, as things can be shown to have a design and purpose, there must be some form of designer (God) in control. **teleologic** (-loj´-), **teleological** *a.* **teleologically** *adv.* **teleologism** *n.* **teleologist** *n.*

telepathy (tilep´əthi) *n.* the supposed communication between minds at a distance without using any of the five recognized senses, thought-transference, mind-reading. **telepathic** (telipath´-) *a.* **telepathically** *adv.* **telepathist** *n.* **telepathize, telepathise** *v.t., v.i.*

telephone (tel´ifōn) *n.* **1** a means of transmitting sounds to distances by a wire or cord, esp. by converting sound vibrations into electrical signals. **2** an instrument for sending and receiving messages of this kind. **3** a communications network of telephones. *~v.t.* **1** to speak to (a person) by means of a telephone. **2** to transmit by means of a telephone. *~v.i.* to make a telephone call. **on the telephone 1** connected to a telephone system. **2** using the telephone. **over the telephone** by means of or using the telephone. **telephone book** *n.* a telephone directory. **telephone box, telephone booth, telephone kiosk** *n.* a public place where telephone calls can be made. **telephone call** *n.* **1** a conversation by way of a telephone. **2** an act of telephoning. **telephone directory** *n.* (*pl.* **telephone directories**) a book listing names, addresses and telephone numbers in a given area. **telephone exchange** *n.* a centralized place where telephone connections are made, formerly by operators but now usu. by a system of computers. **telephone number** *n.* **1** a particular number that is assigned to a specified telephone and which callers must dial to be connected to that telephone. **2** (*usu. in pl., coll.*) any very high number with lots of digits, esp. one that refers to money (*I don't know how much her new car cost, but we're talking telephone numbers*). **telephone operator** *n.* a person who works in a telephone exchange, making connections and sometimes also helping callers and answering queries. **telephonic** (-fon´-) *a.* **telephonically** *adv.* **telephonist** (tilef´-) *n.* a person who operates a telephone switchboard. **telephony** (-lef´əni) *n.* **1** a system of telephones. **2** communication by way of this.

telephotograph (telifō´təgrahf) *n.* a picture obtained by telephotography. **telephoto** (tel´ifōtō) *a.* telephotographic. ~*n.* (*pl.* **telephotos**) a telephoto lens. **telephoto lens** *n.* a lens of long focal length, for obtaining photographs of very distant objects. **telephotographic** (-graf´-) *a.* **telephotography** (-fətog´rəfi) *n.* the act or process of photographing objects beyond the limits of ordinary vision.

telepoint (tel´ipoint) *n.* **1** a type of socket where a cordless telephone can be connected to a telephone system. **2** a system of such sockets.

telepresence (tel´iprezəns) *n.* **1** the use of virtual reality technology esp. for remotely controlling machinery or for allowing someone to seem to take part in events that are happening at some distance. **2** the sensation of taking part in distant events that using this technology creates.

teleprinter (tel´iprintə) *n.* a telegraphic apparatus with a keyboard transmitter and a receiver which prints incoming messages.

teleprompter (tel´ipromptə) *n.* an apparatus which enables a speaker on television to see the text without this being visible to the viewers.

telerecording (tel´irikawding) *n.* a recording for broadcasting on television. **telerecord** *v.t.*

telesales (tel´isālz) *n.pl.* the selling of items by telephone.

telescope (tel´iskōp) *n.* **1** an optical instrument that uses lenses, mirrors or both for increasing the apparent size of distant objects. **2** RADIO TELESCOPE (under RADIO). ~*v.t.* **1** to drive or force (sections etc.) into each other, like the sliding sections of a telescope. **2** to condense (something) so that it takes up less space or time

(*telescoped two lectures into one hour*). ~*v.i.* to move or be forced into each other in this way. **telescopic** (-skop´-) *a.* **1** performed by, characteristic of or relating to, a telescope. **2** capable of retraction and protraction. **3** only able to be seen by using a telescope. **telescopically** *adv.* **telescopic sight** *n.* a small telescope mounted on a rifle, used as a sight to increase the accuracy of aim.

teleshopping (tel´ishoping) *n.* the buying of goods (usu. displayed or listed on a television or computer screen) through a telephone or computer link.

teletext (tel´itekst) *n.* data, such as news, local information etc., transmitted by television companies and viewable as text and graphics on a television that has a special adaptor or decoder.

telethon (tel´ithon) *n.* a very long television programme, usu. to raise funds for charities.

Teletype® (tel´itīp) *n.* a brand of teleprinter. **teletype** *v.t.* to send (a message etc.) using this kind of teleprinter. ~*v.i.* to use this kind of teleprinter. **teletypewriter** (-tīp´-) *n.* a teleprinter.

televangelist (telivan´jəlist), **tele-evangelist** (teliiv-) *n.* a person who regularly appears on television to hold religious services, preach (often a fundamentalist doctrine) and appeal for funds. **televangelism** *n.*

televiewer (tel´ivūə) *n.* a person who watches television. **televiewing** *n.*

television (tel´ivizhən) *n.* **1** the transmission by radio or other means of visual images, usu. with accompanying sound, so that they are displayed on a cathode-ray tube screen. **2** (*in full television set*) a device designed to receive and decode incoming electrical television signals. **3** the business of broadcasting television programmes (*works in television*). **televise** (-vīz) *v.t.* to transmit by television. **televisable** *a.* **televisual** (-vizh´ūəl) *a.* of or relating to television. **televisually** *adv.*

telework (tel´iwœk) *v.i.* TELECOMMUTE. **teleworker** *n.*

telex (tel´eks), **Telex** *n.* **1** an international telegraphy service that uses public telecommunications systems to send and receive printed messages by way of teleprinters. **2** the message sent. ~*v.t.* to send a message by telex.

tell (tel) *v.t.* (*past, p.p.* **told** (tōld)) **1** to relate, to recount. **2** to make known, to express in words, to communicate, to divulge. **3** to inform, to assure. **4** to give an order to, to direct. **5** to distinguish (*I can tell you are lying*). **6** to ascertain by observing. **7** to predict, to warn. **8** to judge, to decide, to find out. **9** to assure emphatically. ~*v.i.* **1** to give information or an account (of). **2** (*coll.*) to inform (*If you do that, I'll tell*). **3** to produce a marked effect. **4** to reveal the truth (*Only time will tell*). **5** to be an implicating factor, to have an effect. **all told** all included. **tell me another** (*coll.*) used to express disbelief. **that would be telling** (*coll.*) used to express a disinclination to give out any more information, esp. because doing so would disclose a secret. **there's no telling** it would be impossible to know or guess. **to tell off** to distinguish between. **to tell off 1** (*coll.*) to scold. **2** to count off. **3** to select or detach on some special duty. **to tell on** to report (someone). **to tell the time** to read the time from a clock or watch. **you're telling me** (*coll.*) I completely agree with what you are saying. **tellable** *a.* **teller** *n.* **1** an officer in a bank etc. appointed to receive or pay out money. **2** a person who numbers or counts, esp. one of four appointed to count votes in the House of Commons. **3** a person who tells. **tellership** *n.* **telling** *a.* **1** producing a striking effect. **2** revelatory, significant (*a telling remark*). **tellingly** *adv.* **telling-off** *n.* (*pl.* **tellings-off**) a rebuke, a mild scolding. **tell-tale** *n.* **1** a person who tells tales, esp. about the private affairs of others. **2** any automatic device for giving information as to condition, position etc. **~a. 1** revealing, implicating (*left tell-tale footprints*). **2** given to telling tales about people.

tellurian (teluˊriən) *a.* of, relating to or living on the earth. **~n.** an inhabitant of the earth.

telluric (teluˊrik) *a.* **1** of or relating to the earth's status as a planet. **2** of or relating to soil. **3** (*Chem.*) of or relating to tellurium, esp. in its higher valency.

tellurium (teluˊriəm) *n.* (*Chem.*) a rare silvery-white non-metallic element, at. no. 52, chem. symbol Te, found in association with gold, silver and bismuth. **telluride** (telˊurīd) *n.* **tellurite** (telˊurīt) *n.* **1** native oxide of tellurium. **2** a salt of tellurous acid. **tellurous** *a.* of or relating to tellurium, esp. in its lower valency.

telly (telˊi) *n.* (*pl.* **tellies**) (*coll.*) **1** television. **2** a television set.

telophase (teˊləfāz) *n.* (*Biol.*) the final stage in cell division which results in the formation of the nuclei of the daughter cells.

telpher (telˊfə) *n.* a form of suspended monorail on which a truck runs, carrying its load hanging below the level of the truck and rail. **telpherage** *n.*

temerity (timerˊiti) *n.* **1** excessive rashness, recklessness. **2** impertinence, audacity.

temp (temp) *n.* a temporary, usu. secretarial or clerical, worker. **~v.i.** to work as a temp.

temp. *abbr.* **1** temperature. **2** temporary.

temper (temˊpə) *n.* **1** a disposition of mind, esp. with regard to emotional stability (*a volatile temper, an even temper*). **2** composure, self-command (*always losing his temper*). **3** anger, irritation, passion (*stamped her feet in temper*). **4** a tendency to have angry emotional outbursts (*He's got a real temper*). **5** the state of a metal as regards hardness and elasticity. **~v.t. 1** (*fig.*) to qualify, to moderate, to tone down, to mitigate (*Temper your disgust with some sympathy*). **2** to bring (steel etc.) to a proper degree of hardness by heating and cooling. **3** to bring (clay etc.) to a proper consistency by mixing, kneading

etc. **4** to adjust the tones of (an instrument) according to a particular temperament. **out of temper** irritable, in a bad temper. **temperative** *a.* **tempered** *a.* **temperer** *n.*

tempera (temˊpərə) *n.* **1** a method of artistic painting that uses an emulsion of powdered pigment mixed with egg yolk and water. **2** the emulsion itself.

temperament (temˊpərəmənt) *n.* **1** a person's individual character, natural disposition. **2** manifest sensitivity or emotionality. **3** the adjustment of the tones of an instrument to fit the scale in any key, esp. by a compromise in the case of instruments of fixed intonation, such as an organ or piano. **temperamental** (-menˊ-) *a.* **1** having an erratic or neurotic temperament. **2** (*coll.*) unreliable, liable to break down (*a temperamental old car*). **3** resulting from or connected with temperament. **temperamentally** *adv.*

temperance (temˊpərəns) *n.* moderation, self-restraint, esp. where indulgence in food, alcohol etc. is concerned. **~a.** advocating or promoting moderation, esp. in alcoholic drinks.

temperate (temˊpərət) *a.* **1** self-restrained. **2** moderate. **3** (of climate) not liable to excess of heat or cold, mild. **4** abstemious. **5** abstemious or abstinent in the use of intoxicants. **temperately** *adv.* **temperateness** *n.* **temperate zone** *n.* the part of the earth which lies between the tropics and the polar circles and has a moderate climate.

temperature (temˊprəchə) *n.* **1** degree of heat or cold in a body or the atmosphere, esp. as registered by a thermometer. **2** (*Med.*) the degree of the body's internal heat. **3** (*coll.*) body temperature above normal. **4** the extent of excitement, enthusiasm etc. that a subject, discussion etc. generates. **to take someone's temperature** to use a device such as a thermometer to measure a person's (or an animal's) body heat, esp. as a way of checking on their health. **temperature inversion** *n.* the reversal of the usual variation of air temperature with height.

tempest (temˊpəst) *n.* **1** a violent storm of wind, esp. with heavy rain, hail or snow. **2** (*fig.*) violent tumult or agitation. **tempestuous** (-pesˊtū-) *a.* **1** (of the weather) very stormy. **2** (of a person, relationship etc.) turbulent, emotional, passionate. **tempestuously** *adv.* **tempestuousness** *n.*

tempi TEMPO.

template (temˊplət), **templet** *n.* **1** a pattern, gauge or mould, usu. of thin wood or metal, used as a guide in shaping, turning or drilling. **2** a short timber or stout stone placed in a wall to distribute the pressure of beams etc. **3** (*Chem.*) the coded information that is contained in the structure of a molecule which serves as the pattern for the production of another specific compound.

temple[1] (temˊpəl) *n.* **1** an edifice dedicated to the service of some deity or deities, esp. of the ancient Egyptians, Greeks or Romans. **2** either of the two successive buildings that were the seat of Jewish worship at Jerusalem.

temple² (tem´pəl) *n*. the flat part at either side of the head between the forehead and ear. **temple block** *n*. a hollow wooden percussion instrument played by striking it with a stick.

temple³ (tem´pəl) *n*. an attachment in a loom for keeping the fabric stretched.

templet TEMPLATE.

tempo (tem´pō) *n*. (*pl*. **tempi** (-pē), **tempos**) **1** (*Mus*.) the specified speed at which a piece of music is or should be played. **2** pace or rate (*the tempo of modern life*).

temporal¹ (tem´pərəl) *a*. **1** of or relating to this life. **2** secular, as opposed to spiritual. **3** of, relating to or expressing time. **4** (*Gram*.) denoting or relating to tense or to the linguistic expression of time ('*Slowly' is a temporal adverb*). **temporality** (-ral´-) *n*. (*pl*. **temporalities**) **1** temporariness. **2** (*pl*.) a secular possession, esp. the revenues of a religious corporation or an ecclesiastic. **temporally** *adv*. **temporalness** *n*.

temporal² (tem´pərəl) *a*. (*Anat*.) positioned at the temples. **temporal lobe** *n*. a large lobe on either side of the brain, associated with hearing and speech.

temporary (tem´pərəri) *a*. lasting, designed or intended only for a limited length of time (*temporary staff*). ~*n*. (*pl*. **temporaries**) a person working on a short-term contract. **temporarily** (tem´-, rar´i-, -reə´ri-) *adv*. **temporariness** *n*.

Usage note The pronunciation of *temporarily* with stress on the third syllable is sometimes disapproved of.

temporize (tem´pəriz), **temporise** *v.i.* **1** to pursue an indecisive, procrastinating or time-serving policy. **2** to comply with or humour or yield to the requirements of time and occasion. **temporization** (-zā´shən) *n*. **temporizer** *n*. **temporizingly** *adv*.

☒ temprature common misspelling of TEMPERATURE.

tempt (tempt) *v.t.* **1** to incite or entice (to or to do something wrong or forbidden). **2** to attract, to allure, to invite. **3** to risk provoking (*You're tempting fate*). **to be tempted to** to be inclined to (*I'm tempted to tell her*). **temptable** *a*. **temptability** (-bil´-) *n*. **temptation** (-tā´shən) *n*. **1** the act or an instance of tempting, enticement to do something, esp. something wrong. **2** the condition of being tempted. **3** an inviting prospect or thing. **tempter** *n*. **tempting** *a*. **1** enticing, inviting. **2** enticing to evil. **temptingly** *adv*. **temptress** (-tris) *n*.

tempura (tem´pʊrə) *n*. a Japanese dish of vegetables, seafood and fish coated in batter and deep-fried.

ten (ten) *n*. **1** the number or figure 10 or X. **2** the age of 10. **3** the 10th hour after midnight or midday. **4** a group of 10 people or things. **5** a playing card with 10 pips. **6** a size of shoe or

article of clothing designated by the number 10. ~*a*. **1** 10 in number. **2** aged 10. **3** an arbitrary use of the number used to express a large amount (*earns ten times as much as me*). **ten to one** very likely or probably. **tenfold** *a., adv.* **1** 10 times as much. **2** made up of 10 parts. **ten-gallon hat** *n*. a wide-brimmed hat worn by some Texans and American cowboys. **tenner** *n*. (*coll*.) a ten-pound or ten-dollar note. **tenpence** *n*. **tenpenny** *a*. priced or sold at tenpence. **tenpin** *n*. a type of skittle used in tenpin bowling. **tenpin bowling**, **tenpins** *n*. a game similar to ninepins but played with ten pins in a skittle-alley. **tenth** (-th) *n*. any one of 10 equal parts. ~*n., a*. **1** (the) last of 10 (people, things etc.). **2** the next after the 9th. **tenthly** *adv*. **tenth-rate** *a*. of very poor quality.

tenable (ten´əbəl) *a*. **1** capable of being held, retained or maintained against attack. **2** (of a position, office etc.) intended to be held (for a specified period or by a particular person). **tenability** (-bil´-) *n*. **tenableness** *n*.

tenacious (tənā´shəs) *a*. **1** holding fast. **2** inclined to hold fast, obstinate, unyielding. **3** persistent, determined. **4** retentive, adhesive, sticky. **5** highly cohesive, tough. **tenaciously** *adv*. **tenaciousness** *n*. **tenacity** (-nas´-) *n*.

tenant (ten´ənt) *n*. **1** a person who rents land or property from a landlord. **2** (*Law*) a person who holds land or property by any kind of title. **3** (*loosely*) an occupant, a dweller, an inhabitant. ~*v.t.* to hold as tenant, to occupy. **tenancy** (-si) *n*. (*pl*. **tenancies**) **1** the holding of land, property etc. under a lease. **2** the period of this. **3** the status of being a tenant. **tenantable** *a*. fit for occupation by a tenant. **tenant farmer** *n*. a person who cultivates land leased from the owner. **tenantless** *a*. **tenantry** (-ri) *n*. (*collect*.) tenants. **tenantship** *n*.

tench (tench) *n*. (*pl*. **tench**) a freshwater fish, *Tinca tinca*, of the carp family.

tend¹ (tend) *v.i.* **1** to have a bent, inclination or attitude, to be inclined (to). **2** to move, hold a course or be directed (in a certain direction etc.). **tendency** (-dənsi) *n*. (*pl*. **tendencies**) **1** bent, drift, inclination, disposition. **2** a faction or sub-group within a political party or movement. **3** a direction in which something moves. **tendentious** (-den´shəs) *a*. (*derog*.) with an underlying purpose, intended to further a cause. **tendentiously** *adv*. **tendentiousness** *n*.

tend² (tend) *v.t.* to attend, to watch, to look after, to take charge of. ~*v.i.* **1** to attend, to wait (upon). **2** to pay attention (to). **tended** *a*. **tender**¹ (ten´də) *n*. **1** a person who tends. **2** a truck attached to a steam locomotive carrying the supply of fuel, water etc. **3** a vessel attending a larger one, to supply provisions, carry dispatches etc.

tender¹ TEND².

tender² (ten´də) *a*. **1** (of food) easily chewed. **2** sensitive, caring and gentle. **3** easily broken, bruised etc., soft, delicate, fragile, weakly, frail. **4** painful when touched. **5** loving, affectionate, fond. **6** careful, solicitous, considerate (of). **7** requiring to be treated delicately or cautiously, ticklish. **8** young, early. **tenderfoot** *n.* (*pl.* **tenderfoots, tenderfeet**) **1** (*N Am., Austral., sl.*) a newcomer in the bush etc., a novice. **2** a newly enrolled Scout or Guide. **tender-hearted** *a.* **1** kind and thoughtful. **2** easily made to feel pity or love. **tender-heartedly** *adv.* **tender-heartedness** *n.* **tenderize, tenderise** *v.t.* to make tender (e.g. meat), e.g. by pounding and so breaking down the fibres. **tenderization** (-zā´shən) *n.* **tenderizer** *n.* **tenderloin** *n.* **1** the tenderest part of the loin in beef or pork. **2** (*N Am.*) the undercut, fillet. **tenderly** *adv.* **tender mercies** *n.pl.* (*iron.*) care or treatment which may ultimately be beneficial but which also involves a degree of discomfort, unpleasantness etc. **tenderness** *n.* **tender spot** *n.* (*fig.*) a subject or issue that someone is inclined to be touchy about.

tender[3] (ten´də) *v.t.* **1** to offer, to present for acceptance (*tendered her resignation*). **2** to offer in payment. ~*v.i.* to make a tender (to do certain work or supply goods etc.). ~*n.* **1** an offer in writing to do certain work or supply certain articles, at a certain sum or rate. **2** an offer for acceptance. **3** (*Law*) a formal offer of money or other things in satisfaction of a debt or liability. **to put out to tender** to invite or seek tenders (for work, services etc.). **tenderer** *n.*

tendon (ten´dən) *n.* (*Anat.*) **1** any of the strong bands or cords of connective tissue forming the termination or connection of the fleshy part of a muscle. **2** the hamstring of a quadruped. **tendinitis** (-ī´tis), **tendonitis** *n.* **tendinous** *a.*

tendril (ten´dril) *n.* a leafless organ by which a plant clings to another body for support.

tenement (ten´əmənt) *n.* **1** an apartment or set of apartments used by one family or set of residents. **2** a dwelling house. **3** (*Sc., US*) (*also* **tenement house**) a house that is divided into separate flats or apartments. **4** (*Law*) any kind of permanent property that may be held, such as lands, houses etc. **tenemental** (-men´-) *a.* **tenementary** *a.*

tenet (ten´it, tē´-) *n.* an opinion, principle, doctrine or dogma held by a person, school or organization.

tenner TEN.

tennis (ten´is) *n.* a racket game for two (singles) or four (doubles) players where the object is to hit the ball over a net so that it lands within the confines of a grass or hard court. **tennis ball** *n.* a ball used in playing tennis. **tennis court** *n.* a court laid out for playing tennis. **tennis elbow** *n.* an elbow strained or sprained in playing tennis, or through other exercise. **tennis racket** *n.* a racket used in playing tennis. **tennis shoe** *n.* a light shoe worn for playing tennis or with casual clothing.

tenon (ten´ən) *n.* the projecting end of a piece of timber fitted for insertion into a mortise etc. ~*v.t.* **1** to cut a tenon on. **2** to join by a tenon. **tenoner**

n. **tenon saw** *n.* a thin saw with a strong brass or steel back used for cutting tenons etc.

tenor (ten´ə) *n.* **1** the highest of male voices between baritone and alto. **2** a musical part for this voice. **3** a person with such a voice. **4** an instrument, esp. a recorder, saxophone or viola, playing a part between bass and alto. **5** the exact purport or meaning, also an exact transcript or copy. **6** a settled course, tendency or direction. **7** general purport or drift (of thought etc.). ~*a.* **1** of a voice, singer, instrument etc.) that is a tenor. **2** of, relating to or adapted for singing or playing the tenor part. **tenor clef** *n.* (*Mus.*) the C clef placed upon the fourth line of the stave. **tenorist** *n.* a person who sings or plays a tenor part.

tenosynovitis (tēnōsīnōvī´tis, ten-) *n.* swelling and inflammation in the tendons, usu. in joints, caused by repetitive use of the joint concerned.

tenotomy (tinot´əmi) *n.* (*pl.* **tenotomies**) the cutting of a tendon.

tense[1] (tens) *a.* **1** stretched tight, strained to stiffness (*a tense rope; tense nerves*). **2** suffering from emotional stress (*felt tense before the interview*). **3** producing emotional stress. **4** (of a phonetic sound) produced with relatively great muscular effort. ~*v.t.* to make tense. ~*v.i.* to become tense. **to tense up** to make or become tense. **tensely** *adv.* **tenseness** *n.* **tensile** (-sīl) *a.* **1** of or relating to tension. **2** capable of extension. **tensile strength** *n.* the greatest stress a given substance can withstand before breaking. **tensility** (-sil´-) *n.* **tensity** *n.* **tensorial** (-saw´riəl) *a.*

tense[2] (tens) *n.* (*Gram.*) **1** a form taken by a verb to indicate the time, and also the continuance or completedness, of an action. **2** a set of forms of this kind indicating also person and number. **tenseless** *a.*

tension (ten´shən) *n.* **1** the act of stretching. **2** the state of being stretched. **3** strain, stress, effort. **4** mental strain, stress or excitement. **5** a state of hostility, strain or anxiety. **6** in mechanics, a state of strain that results from forces acting in opposition to each other. **7** the expansive force of a gas or vapour. **8** electromagnetic force. **9** in knitting, the relative tightness or looseness of a piece of work. **tensional** *a.* **tensionally** *adv.* **tensioner** *n.* **tensionless** *a.*

tent (tent) *n.* **1** a portable shelter consisting of canvas or other flexible material stretched over and supported on poles. **2** (*Med.*) OXYGEN TENT (under OXYGEN). ~*v.t.* to cover with or lodge in a tent. ~*v.i.* to camp in a tent. **tentage** *n.* tents and camping equipment generally. **tent coat, tent dress** *n.* a very roomy style of coat or dress. **tented** *a.* consisting of tents (*a tented village*). **tent stitch** *n.* **1** embroidery consisting of a series of close parallel stitches made diagonally on a canvas etc. **2** a single stitch of this kind.

tentacle (ten´təkəl) *n.* **1** (*Zool.*) a long slender organ, esp. in invertebrates, such as an arm of an octopus, used for touching, grasping, moving etc. and, if suckers are present, for attaching the animal to a surface. **2** anything, such as a feeler, that resembles this. **3** (*Bot.*) a sensitive hair. **tentacled** *a.* **tentacular** (-tak´ū-), **tentaculate** (-tak´ūlət), **tentaculated** (-lātid), **tentaculoid** (-loid) *a.*

tentative (ten´tətiv) *a.* **1** consisting or done as a trial, experimental. **2** hesitant, uncertain. **tentatively** *adv.* **tentativeness** *n.*

tenter (ten´tə) *n.* **1** a frame or machine for stretching cloth to dry to make it set even and square. **2** a tenterhook. **tenterhook** *n.* any one of a set of hooks used in stretching cloth on the tenter. **on tenterhooks** in a state of suspense and anxiety, usu. because of uncertainty or awaiting an outcome or result.

tenth TEN.

tenuity (tinū´iti) *n.* **1** thinness, slenderness. **2** rarity. **3** meagreness.

tenuous (ten´ūəs) *a.* **1** insignificant, not able to stand up to much scrutiny (*formed a tenuous connection*). **2** thin, slender, small, minute. **3** rare, rarefied, subtle, over-refined. **tenuously** *adv.* **tenuousness** *n.*

tenure (ten´yə) *n.* **1** the act, manner or right of holding property, esp. real estate or office. **2** the manner or conditions of holding. **3** the period or term of holding. **4** the holding of a university or college post for an assured period of time, esp. following a probationary period. **tenured** *a.* **1** (of a teaching or lecturing post) guaranteed to be permanent or to last for a specified time. **2** (of a teacher or lecturer) holding this kind of post. **tenurial** (tenūə´riəl) *a.* **tenurially** *adv.*

tepal (tep´əl) *n.* (*Bot.*) any of the subdivisions of a perianth which is not clearly differentiated into the calyx and corolla.

tepee (tē´pē), **teepee**, **tipi** *n.* (*pl.* **tepees**, **teepees**, **tipis**) a N American Indian tent, usu. coneshaped and made by stretching animal skins over a framework of poles.

tepid (tep´id) *a.* **1** moderately warm, lukewarm. **2** unenthusiastic. **tepidity** (-pid´-), **tepidness** *n.* **tepidly** *adv.*

tequila (tikē´lə) *n.* a Mexican spirit distilled from agave which forms the basis of many drinks.

ter- (teə) *comb. form* three, thrice, three times, as in *tertiary*.

tera- (te´ə) *comb. form* 10 to the power of 12.

teraflop (te´rəflop) *n.* (*Comput.*) a unit of computing speed equal to one million million floating-point operations per second.

teratogen (te´rətəjən, tərat´-) *n.* (*Med.*) something which results in the malformation of an embryo. **teratogenic** (-jen´-) *a.* **teratogeny** (-toj´-) *n.*

teratology (terətol´əji) *n.* (*Med., Biol.*) the study of congenital malformations. **teratological** (-loj´-) *a.* **teratologist** *n.*

teratoma (terətō´mə) *n.* (*pl.* **teratomata** (-tə), **teratomas**) (*Med.*) a tumour or group of tumours composed of tissue that is foreign to the site of growth, most usually occurring in the testes or ovaries.

terawatt (te´rəwot) *n.* a unit of power equivalent to 10^{12} watts or a million megawatts.

terbium (tœ´biəm) *n.* (*Chem.*) a rare metallic element, at. no. 65, chem. symbol Tb, found in association with erbium and yttrium.

terce (tœs) *n.* in the Roman Catholic Church, the third canonical hour of divine office when prayers are said around 9 a.m.

tercel TIERCEL.

tercentenary (tœsəntē´nəri) *n.* (*pl.* **tercentenaries**) **1** a 300th anniversary. **2** a celebration to mark this. ~*a.* of or relating to a tercentenary. **tercentennial** (-ten´-) *a.* **1** happening every 300 years. **2** lasting for 300 years. ~*n.* a 300th anniversary.

tercet (tœ´sit), **tiercet** (tiə´-) *n.* in prosody, a set of three consecutive lines of verse that either all rhyme or which rhyme with another set of three lines coming before it or after it.

terebene (ter´ibēn) *n.* a liquid hydrocarbon obtained by treating oil of turpentine with sulphuric acid, used as an antiseptic, disinfectant, expectorant etc.

terebinth (ter´əbinth) *n.* **1** a small tree, *Pistacia terebinthus*, found around the Mediterranean and once used as a source of a form of turpentine. **2** its resin. **terebinthine** (-bin´thīn) *a.* **1** of or relating to the terebinth. **2** relating to or characteristic of turpentine.

teredo (tərē´dō) *n.* (*pl.* **teredos**) any of several molluscs, esp. *Teredo navalis*, that bore into submerged timber, the shipworm.

terete (tərēt´) *a.* (*Biol.*) rounded, cylindrical and smooth.

tergiversate (tœ´jivəsāt) *v.i.* **1** to change sides. **2** to practise evasions or subterfuges, to equivocate. **3** to turn one's back. **tergiversation** (-ā´shən) *n.* **tergiversator** *n.*

-teria (tiə´riə) *suf.* indicating that an establishment is self-service, as in *washeteria*.

term (tœm) *n.* **1** a word or expression that has a precise meaning and is used in a particular, often specialized, field (*a computing term*). **2** (*pl.*) any language or expressions used (*gave an answer in ambiguous terms*). **3** (*pl.*) conditions, stipulations (*under the terms of the contract*). **4** (*pl.*) prices, charges, rates of payments. **5** (*pl.*) relative position, relation, footing (*on friendly terms*). **6 a** a limited period of time, bounded by holidays or vacations, during which students etc. are taught. **b** a similar period during which a law court is in session. **c** a period of imprisonment (*did a two-year term for robbery*). **7 a** a limited period of time during which a specified state pertains or a particular activity is carried out (*her term of office*). **b** a less specific period of time (*in the long term*). **8** an appointed day or date, such as a Scottish quarter day. **9** the end of the normal length of a pregnancy (*carried the baby to term this time*). **10** (*Logic*) a word or group of words that may be the subject or predicate of a proposition. **11** (*Math.*) the antecedent or consequent of a ratio. **12** (*Math.*) any one of the parts of an expression connected by the plus or minus signs. **13** (*Math.*) each value in a sequence or series. ~*v.t.* to designate, to call, to denominate. **in set terms** expressed in a specific way. **in terms** explicitly. **in terms of 1** as measured or indicated by. **2** in relation to, with reference to. **on terms 1** friendly. **2** of equal status or standing. **to bring to terms** to force or induce to accept conditions. **to come to terms** to yield, to give way. **to come to terms with 1** to find a way of coping and living with (some difficulty). **2** to make an agreement with. **to make terms** to conclude an agreement. **termless** *a.* **termly** *a.* occurring every term. ~*adv.* **1** term by term. **2** every term. **3** periodically. **terms of reference** *n.pl.* **1** the specific points which a committee or other body is charged to decide. **2** the outlined scope for an inquiry, report etc. **terms of trade** *n.pl.* the ratio of export prices to import prices. **term-time** *n.* the period of time when teaching is done. ~*a.* of, relating to or characteristic of this period.

termagant (tœ´məgənt) *n.* a shrewish, abusive, violent woman. **termagancy** *n.* **termagantly** *adv.*

terminal (tœ´minəl) *a.* **1** (of a disease) ending in death. **2** (of someone suffering from a disease) about to die. **3** (of a morbid condition) forming the final stage of a fatal disease. **4** (*coll.*) extreme, acute, incurable (*suffers from terminal pessimism*). **5** (*Zool.*) occurring at the end of a series. **6** (*Bot.*) growing or appearing at the end of a stem (*terminal buds*). **7** relating to, done, submitted etc. during or at the end of a term or each term. **8** later, last. ~*n.* **1** a building or area at an airport that arriving and departing passengers pass through. **2** a main terminus or station at the end of a railway line or for long-distance buses or coaches. **3** (*Comput.*) a device, usu. consisting of a screen and keyboard, that allows data or information to enter or leave a computer or communications system. **4** something that forms an end, an extremity. **5** a point in an electric circuit or device where a connection can be made or broken. **6** a storage point at a port or at the end of a pipeline where oil is stored until distribution. **terminally** *adv.*

terminate (tœ´mināt) *v.t.* **1** to put an end to. **2** (*Med.*) to bring (a pregnancy) to an end artificially and prematurely. **3** to bound, to limit. **4** to form the extreme point or end of. ~*v.i.* to stop, to end (in etc.). **terminable** *a.* **1** capable of being terminated. **2** having a given term or period. **terminableness** *n.* **termination** (-ā´shən) *n.* **1** the act, process or state of terminating. **2** the state of being terminated. **3** (*Med.*) the act or an instance of artificially and prematurely bringing a pregnancy to an end. **4** a specific kind of ending or outcome. **to bring to a termination** to put a termination to. **to put a termination to** to end with no possibility of resumption. **termina-**

tional *a.* **terminative** *a.* **terminator** *n.* **1** a person who or thing which terminates. **2** the dividing line between the illuminated and the dark part of a heavenly body. **terminatory** *a.*

terminology (tœminol´əji) *n.* (*pl.* **terminologies**) **1** the set of terms used in any art, science, discipline etc. **2** the science or study of the (correct) use of terms. **terminological** (-loj´-) *a.* **terminological inexactitude** *n.* (*facet.*) a lie. **terminologically** *adv.* **terminologist** *n.*

terminus (tœ´minəs) *n.* (*pl.* **termini** (-nī), **terminuses**) **1** the point where a railway or bus route ends. **2** the town, building or buildings at this point. **3** a storage place at the end of an oil pipeline etc. **4** a final point, a goal.

termite (tœ´mīt) *n.* any of several kinds of small social insects of the order Isoptera, found chiefly in tropical regions and often causing damage to trees and wood in buildings, also called *white ant*. **termitarium** (-mitəə´riəm), **termitary** (-təri) *n.* (*pl.* **termitaria** (-riə), **termitaries**) a nest of a termite colony.

tern[1] (tœn) *n.* any small gull-like seabird of the family Sternidae, having slenderly-built bodies, forked tails and narrow, sharp-pointed wings.

tern[2] (tœn) *a.* ternate. ~*n.* **1** a set of three, esp. three lottery numbers winning a large prize if won together. **2** the prize won in this way. **ternary** *a.* **1** consisting of three parts. **2** (*Math.*) based on the number three (*ternary scale*). ~*n.* (*pl.* **ternaries**) a group of three, a triad. **ternate** (-nət, -nāt) *a.* **1** arranged in threes. **2** (*Bot.*) a composed of three leaflets. **b** in whorls of three. **ternately** *adv.*

terne (tœn) *n.* **1** (*in full* **terne metal**) an alloy of lead and 10–20% tin, often also with a small percentage of antimony. **2** (*in full* **terne-plate**) thin sheet iron or steel coated with this alloy.

terotechnology (terōteknol´əji) *n.* the application of managerial, financial and engineering skills to the installation and efficient operation of equipment and machinery.

terpene (tœ´pēn) *n.* (*Chem.*) any one of various isomeric oily hydrocarbons derived chiefly from coniferous plants.

terra (ter´ə) *n.* (*pl.* **terrae** (-rē)) in legal contexts, earth or land. **terra firma** (fœ´mə) *n.* dry land, firm ground. **terra incognita** (inkognē´tə) *n.* unknown country, unexplored territory.

terrace (ter´əs) *n.* **1** a raised level space or platform, artificially constructed or natural and used for growing grapes etc. **2** a paved patio or balcony next to a house. **3** a row of houses, esp. running along the side of a slope. **4** a row of houses all of the same kind. **5** (*pl.*) **a** open tiers around a sports stadium, formerly esp. a football stadium, where spectators stand. **b** (*usu.* the **terraces**) the standing spectators themselves. **6** (*Geol.*) an old shoreline or raised beach. ~*v.t.* to form into or provide with terraces. **terraced** *a.* in terraces. **terraced house, terrace house** *n.* a house which is usu. joined to its neighbour on either side and which forms part of a terrace. **terraced roof** *n.* a flat roof, esp. on an Indian or other Asian house.

terracotta (terəkot´ə) *n.* **1** a hard, unglazed earthenware used as a decorative building material and for making pottery, models etc. **2** a statue or figure in this. **3** the brownish-orange colour of terracotta. ~*a.* **1** made of this earthenware. **2** having a brownish-orange colour.

terrain (tərān´) *n.* **1** a region, a tract, an extent of land of a definite geological character or as thought of in terms of military operations. **2** a field or sphere of interest, influence or knowledge.

terrapin (ter´əpin) *n.* **1** any of several small turtles of the family Emydidae, esp. *Emys orbicularis*, which lives on land and in freshwater ponds and rivers in Europe. **2** a small edible turtle, *Malaclemys terrapin*, which lives in the marshy areas along the S Atlantic and Gulf coasts in the US. **Terrapin**® *n.* a type of prefabricated house with only one storey.

terrarium (tereə´riəm) *n.* (*pl.* **terrariums, terraria** (-riə)) **1** an enclosed container where small land animals are kept. **2** a large heavy sealed glass bulb where a variety of plants can be grown.

terrazzo (terat´sō) *n.* (*pl.* **terrazzos**) a mosaic floor-covering made by setting marble or other chips into cement, which is then polished.

terrene (terēn´) *a.* **1** of or relating to the earth, earthly. **2** characteristic of or relating to earth or soil, earthy. **3** terrestrial.

terrestrial (təres´triəl) *a.* **1** of or relating to or existing on the earth, not celestial. **2** consisting of land, not water. **3** (*Zool., Bot.*) living on the ground, not aquatic, arboreal etc. **4** (*Astron.*) (of a planet) similar in size, density etc. to the earth. **5** of or relating to this world, worldly. **6** (of broadcasting) not done by way of satellites. **7** (of a telephone) connected to a telephone system as opposed to using a cellular radio system. ~*n.* an inhabitant of the earth. **terrestrial globe** *n.* a sphere representing the earth and its geography. **terrestrially** *adv.* **terrestrial telescope** *n.* a type of telescope designed for looking at the earth's surface rather than for astronomical observations.

terrible (ter´ibəl) *a.* **1** (*coll.*) dreadful, appalling. **2** (*coll.*) very great or bad, extreme (*a terrible gossip*). **3** (*coll.*) completely useless or incompetent. **4** (*coll.*) ill or unwell. **5** (*coll.*) remorseful, regretful, guilty. **6** causing real terror, fear or dread (*a terrible curse*). **terribleness** *n.* **terribly** *adv.* **1** (*coll.*) very, extremely (*That's terribly good of you*). **2** to a great extent, in a terrible way.

terrier (ter´iə) *n.* **1** a small active dog of various breeds orig. bred to pursue its quarry underground. **2** any of these breeds. **3** a tenacious and hard-working person or animal.

terrific (tərif´ik) *a.* **1** (*coll.*) excellent, wonderful. **2** (*coll.*) huge (*made a terrific effort*). **3** (*coll.*)

dreadful, very unpleasant (*a terrific mess*). **4** (*coll.*) very powerful, forceful etc. **5** causing real fear, terror, awe etc. (*a terrific scream*). **terrifically** *adv.* **1** (*coll.*) exceedingly, surprisingly. **2** frighteningly. **terrify** (ter´ifī) *v.t.* (*3rd pers. sing. pres.* **terrifies**, *pres.p.* **terrifying**, *past, p.p.* **terrified**) to strike with terror, to frighten. **terrified** *a.* **terrifier** *n.* **terrifying** *a.* **terrifyingly** *adv.*

terrine (tərēn´) *n.* **1** a type of coarse pâté, usu. made by incorporating vegetables into a meat or fish base. **2** an earthenware container, esp. one that this type of pâté is cooked in and which is sometimes sold along with the pâté.

territory (ter´itəri) *n.* (*pl.* **territories**) **1** the extent of land within the jurisdiction of a particular sovereign, state or other power. **2** (**Territory**) a division of a country not yet granted full state rights. **3** a field of action, interest, thinking etc. **4** an assigned area of a commercial traveller, goods distributor etc. **5** (*Zool.*) the area defended by an animal or bird. **6** in sport, an area that a player or team tries to defend. **7** a large tract of land. **8** land of a specified nature. **territorial** (-taw´ri-) *a.* **1** of or relating to territory. **2** limited to a given district. **3** (of an animal, bird etc.) characterized by marking out and defending its own territory. **4** (of a person) inclined to be possessive about a particular field of action, interest etc. **5** (**Territorial**) of or relating to a Territory, esp. one of the US or Canada. ~*n.* (*coll.*) (**Territorial**) a member of the Territorial Army. **Territorial Army** *n.* a reserve military force of trained volunteers intended to provide a back-up service to the regular armed forces in an emergency. **territoriality** (-al´-) *n.* **territorialize, territorialise** *v.t.* **territorialization** (-zā´shən) *n.* **territorially** *adv.* **territorial waters** *n.pl.* the area of sea, usu. three miles out, adjoining the coast and adjudged to be under the jurisdiction of the country occupying that coast.

terror (ter´ə) *n.* **1** extreme fear. **2** a person or thing that causes fear. **3** (*coll.*) an exasperating nuisance, bore, troublesome child etc. **4** government or revolution by terrorism. **terrorism** *n.* organized violence and intimidation, usu. for political ends. **terrorist** *n.* a person who uses or advocates intimidation, violence etc., esp. for political reasons. **terroristic** (-ris´-) *a.* **terroristically** *adv.* **terrorize, terrorise** *v.t.* **1** to terrify. **2** to coerce with threats of violence etc. **terrorization** (-zā´shən) *n.* **terrorizer** *n.* **terror-stricken, terror-struck** *a.* terrified, paralysed with fear.

terry (ter´i) *n.* (*pl.* **terries**) a pile fabric in which the loops are not cut, used esp. for towels, bathrobes etc. ~*a.* made from this material.

terse (tœs) *a.* (*comp.* **terser**, *superl.* **tersest**) **1** (of style, language etc.) neat and compact. **2** concise, abrupt, often to the point of being rude. **tersely** *adv.* **terseness** *n.*

tertiary (tœ´shəri) *a.* **1** of the third order, rank or formation. **2** (*Geol.*) (**Tertiary**) of or relating to the first period of the Cenozoic period. ~*n.* (*pl.* **tertiaries**) **1** (*Geol.*) (**Tertiary**) the first period of the Cenozoic era, characterized by the appearance of modern flora and mammals. **2** in the Roman Catholic Church, a member of the third order of a monastic body. **tertiary education** *n.* education that follows primary and secondary education, usu. at a college or university.

Terylene® (ter´ilēn) *n.* a synthetic polyester used as a textile fibre.

TESL (tes´əl) *abbr.* teaching of English as a second language.

tesla (tes´lə) *n.* the SI unit of magnetic flux density equal to a flux of one weber per square metre.

TESSA (tes´ə), **Tessa** *n.* a tax exempt special savings account.

tessellate (tes´əlāt) *v.t.* **1** to make (a mosaic, pattern etc.) using tesserae or checks. **2** (*Math.*) to cover (a plane surface) by repeatedly using the same shape. **tessellated** *a.* **1** composed of tesserae, inlaid, like a mosaic. **2** (*Bot., Zool.*) coloured or marked in chequered squares. **tessellation** (-ā´shən) *n.*

tessera (tes´ərə) *n.* (*pl.* **tesserae** (-rē)) a small cubical piece of marble, earthenware etc., used in mosaics.

tessitura (tesituə´rə) *n.* (*Mus.*) **1** the range that encompasses most of the tones of a voice part. **2** the natural pitch of a voice or piece of vocal music.

test[1] (test) *n.* **1** a critical trial or examination. **2** a means of trial, a standard, a criterion. **3** a minor examination in a school etc. **4** TEST MATCH (under TEST[1]). **5** (*Chem.*) a substance employed to detect one or more of the constituents of a compound. ~*v.t.* **1** to put to the test, to try, to prove by experiment. **2** to try severely, to tax (someone's endurance etc.). **3** (*Chem.*) to examine by the application of some reagent. **to test out** to put to a practical test. **testable** *a.* **testability** (-bil´-) *n.* **test bed** *n.* an area for testing machinery etc., esp. aircraft engines under simulated working conditions. **test card** *n.* a still television image that is broadcast outside the usual hours of programme transmission and designed to be used as a guide for optimum reception. **test case** *n.* (*Law*) a case taken to trial in order that the court may decide some question that affects other cases. **test drive** *n.* a trial drive of a car or other motor vehicle to assess its performance, before purchase. **test-drive** *v.t.* (*past* **test-drove**, *p.p.* **test-driven**). **tester**[1] *n.* **1** a person or thing that tests. **2** a sample, esp. of a cosmetic, paint etc., that allows a customer to try a product out before buying it. **test flight** *n.* a trial flight of a new aircraft to assess its performance. **test-fly** *v.t.* (*3rd pers. sing. pres.* **test-flies**, *pres.p.* **test-flying**, *past* **test-flew**, *p.p.* **test-flown**). **testing** *n.* an act or the process of putting someone or something through a test. ~*a.* **1** characterized by trouble, difficulties etc. (*living in testing times*). **2** causing

or requiring a lot of effort. **testing ground** *n.* **1** a means of trying something out to gauge its merits, value etc. **2** a site set aside for trying out new weapons etc. **test match** *n.* a cricket or rugby match forming one of a series of international matches. **test paper** *n.* **1** an examination, usu. one that is taken prior to sitting a more important examination. **2** (*Chem.*) bibulous paper saturated with a chemical solution that changes colour when exposed to the action of certain chemicals. **test pilot** *n.* a pilot who test-flies new aircraft. **test tube** *n.* a narrow glass tube closed at one end, used in chemical tests. **test-tube** *a.* **test-tube baby** *n.* **1** a baby born from an ovum fertilized in vitro in a laboratory, then implanted into the mother's womb. **2** (*loosely*) a baby conceived by artificial insemination.

test[2] (test) *n.* (*Biol.*) a shell, a hard covering or exoskeleton.

testa (tes´tə) *n.* (*pl.* **testae** (-tē)) (*Bot.*) a hard seed covering.

testaceous (testā´shəs) *a.* (*Biol.*) **1** characterized by a hard outer covering. **2** (*Bot.*) reddish-brown in colour.

testacy TESTATE.

testament (tes´təmənt) *n.* **1** a solemn instrument in writing by which a person disposes of their personal estate after death, a will. **2** something which testifies proof, attestation. **3** (*Bible*) a covenant made between God and humankind. **4** either of the two main divisions of the Christian Scriptures. **5** (*coll.*) a copy of the New Testament. **testamentary** (-men´-), †**testamental** (-men´-) *a.* of or relating to a will, by a will.

testate (tes´tāt) *a.* having made and left a valid will. ~*n.* a person who has left a will in force. **testacy** (-təsi) *n.* (*pl.* **testacies**). **testator** (-tā´-) *n.* a person who dies testate. **testatrix** (-tā´triks) *n.* a female testator.

tester[1] TEST[1].

tester[2] (tes´tə) *n.* a canopy, esp. over a four-poster bedstead.

testes TESTIS.

testicle (tes´tikəl) *n.* (*Anat.*) either of the two reproductive glands which secrete the seminal fluid in males. **testicular** (-tik´ū-) *a.* **testiculate** (-tik´ūlət) *a.* **1** having testicles. **2** shaped like testicles; having a part so shaped.

testify (tes´tifī) *v.i.* (*3rd pers. sing. pres.* **testifies**, *pres.p.* **testifying**, *past, p.p.* **testified**) **1** to bear witness (to, against, concerning etc.). **2** (*Law*) to give evidence. **3** to make a solemn declaration. ~*v.t.* **1** to bear witness to. **2** to affirm or declare. **3** to be evidence of, to serve as proof of. **testification** (-fikā´shən) *n.* **testifier** *n.*

testimony (tes´timəni) *n.* (*pl.* **testimonies**) **1** (*Law*) a statement under oath or affirmation. **2** a solemn declaration or statement. **3** evidence, proof, confirmation. **testimonial** (-mō´-) *n.* **1** a certificate of character, services, qualifications etc., of a person. **2** a formal statement of fact. **3** a gift formally (and usu. publicly) presented to a person as a token of esteem and acknowledgement of services etc.

testis (tes´tis) *n.* (*pl.* **testes** (-tēz)) (*Anat.*) a testicle.

testosterone (testos´tərōn) *n.* (*Biol.*) a steroid hormone secreted by the testes, controlling the growth and functioning of male sex organs and stimulating the development of male secondary sexual characteristics.

testy (tes´ti) *a.* (*comp.* **testier**, *superl.* **testiest**) irritable, peevish, pettish, petulant. **testily** *adv.* **testiness** *n.*

tetanus (tet´ənəs) *n.* **1** a disease caused by the bacterium *Clostridium tetani* and marked by long-continued spasms of voluntary muscles, esp. those of the jaws. **2** the long-continued spasm of a muscle. **tetanic** (titan´-) *a.*, *n.* **tetany** (-ni) *n.* a disease brought on by a deficiency of calcium in the blood which causes intermittent painful muscular spasms.

tetchy (tech´i) *a.* (*comp.* **tetchier**, *superl.* **tetchiest**) fretful, irritable, touchy. **tetchily** *adv.* **tetchiness** *n.*

tête-à-tête (tātahtāt´, tetahtet´) *n.* (*pl.* **têtes-à-têtes** (tātahtāts´, tetahtets´), **tête-à-têtes**) **1** a private interview, a close or confidential conversation. **2** a sofa for two persons, esp. with seats facing in opposite directions so that the occupants face one another. ~*a.* private, confidential. ~*adv.* in private or close intimacy.

tether (tedh´ə) *n.* **1** a rope or halter by which an animal is prevented from moving too far. **2** prescribed range, scope. ~*v.t.* to confine with or as with a tether.

tetra (tet´rə) *n.* (*pl.* **tetras**) any of various small tropical fish of the characin family that are often kept in home aquaria for their attractive brightly-coloured appearance.

tetra- (tet´rə), **tetr-** *comb. form* **1** four, as in *tetragon.* **2** (*Chem.*) containing four atoms, radicals or groups, as in *tetraethyl.*

tetrachord (tet´rəkawd) *n.* (*Mus.*) **1** a scale series of four notes where the interval between the first and last notes encompasses a perfect fourth, esp. as used in ancient music. **2** a musical instrument that has four strings.

tetracyclic (tetrəsī´klik) *a.* **1** (*Bot.*) having four circles or whorls. **2** (*Chem.*) having four fused hydrocarbon rings. **tetracycline** (tetrəsī´klēn, -klin) *n.* any of several antibiotics with molecules of four rings.

tetrad (tet´rad) *n.* **1** a collection, group or set of four things. **2** the number four.

tetradactyl (tetrədak´til) *n.* (*Zool.*) an animal having four digits on each limb. **tetradactylous** *a.*

tetraethyl (tetrəē´thīl, -eth´il) *a.* having four ethyl groups. **tetraethyl lead** *n.* an antiknock, insoluble liquid used in petrol.

tetragon (tet´rəgon) *n.* a plane figure having four angles and four sides. **tetragonal** (titrag´ə-) *a.* **1** having the form of a tetragon. **2** of or relating to the crystal system characterized by three axes at

right angles, of which only two are equal. **tetragonally** *adv.*

tetragynous (titraj´inəs) *a.* (*Bot.*) (of a flower) having four pistils.

tetrahedron (tetrəhē´drən) *n.* (*pl.* **tetrahedra** (-drə), **tetrahedrons**) a solid figure bounded by four planes, esp. equilateral, triangular faces. **tetrahedral** *a.*

tetralogy (titral´əji) *n.* (*pl.* **tetralogies**) a collection of four dramatic works, esp. in ancient Greek a trilogy or three tragedies, followed by a satyric piece.

tetramerous (titram´ərəs), **tetrameral** (-ərəl) *a.* consisting of four parts.

tetrameter (titram´itə) *n.* in prosody, a verse consisting of four measures.

tetrandrous (titran´drəs) *a.* (*Bot.*) (of a flower) having four stamens.

tetraplegia (tetrəplē´jə) *n.* (*Med.*) quadriplegia, paralysis of both arms and both legs. **tetraplegic** *n.*, *a.*

tetraploid (tet´rəploid) *a.* (*Biol.*) having four times the haploid number of chromosomes. ~*n.* a tetraploid nucleus or cell.

tetrapod (tet´rəpod) *n.* **1** (*Zool.*) a four-footed animal. **2** an object or structure with four supporting legs. **tetrapodous** (titrap´-) *a.*

tetrapterous (titrap´tərəs) *a.* (*Zool.*) having four wings.

tetrasyllable (tet´rəsiləbəl) *n.* a word of four syllables. **tetrasyllabic** (-lab´-) *a.*

tetrathlon (tetrath´lon) *n.* a competition that comprises four distinct events, esp. a sporting one featuring running, swimming, shooting and riding events.

tetratomic (tetrətom´ik) *a.* (*Chem.*) having four atoms to a molecule.

tetravalent (tetrəvā´lənt) *a.* (*Chem.*) having a valency of four, quadrivalent.

tetrode (tet´rōd) *n.* a thermionic valve containing four electrodes.

Teuton (tū´tən) *n.* a member of any Teutonic people, esp. a German. **Teutonic** (-ton´-) *a.* **1** of or relating to the Germanic peoples, including Scandinavians, Anglo-Saxons etc., as well as the Germans, or to their languages. **2** German. ~*n.* **1** early Germanic. **2** the language or languages of the Teutons collectively. **Teutonicism** (-ton´-), **Teutonism** *n.*

Texan (tek´sən) *n.* a native or inhabitant of Texas, a southern US state. ~*a.* of or relating to Texas.

Tex-Mex (teks´meks) *a.*, *n.* (of, relating to or denoting) the Texan version of something Mexican, such as food, music, language etc.

text (tekst) *n.* **1** the words of something as printed, written or displayed on a video display unit. **2** the original words of an author, esp. as opposed to a translation, commentary or revision etc. **3** the actual words of a book or poem, as opposed to notes, appendices etc. **4** a verse or passage of Scripture, esp. one selected as the theme of a discourse. **5** a subject, a topic.

6 any book or novel which is studied as part of an educational course. **textbook** *n.* a standard book for a particular branch of study. ~*a.* **1** ideal. **2** typical. **textbookish** *a.* **text editor** *n.* (*Comput.*) a program that will allow the user to enter and edit text while simultaneously displaying the text entered or changes made on a VDU screen. **textless** *a.* **text processing** *n.* (*Comput.*) the management of textual data, esp. when it involves converting the data into different formats. **textual** (-tū-) *a.* belonging or relating to or contained in the text. **textual criticism** *n.* **1** the study of texts, esp. the Bible, to establish the original text. **2** a close reading and analysis of any literary text. **textualist** *n.* a person who adheres strictly to the text. **textualism** *n.* **textuality** (-al'-) *n.* **textually** *adv.*

Usage note The adjectives *textual* and *textural* should not be confused: *textual* relates to text, and *textural* to texture.

---

textile (teks'tīl) *n.* **1** a woven, bonded or felted fabric. **2** a fibre or yarn for making into cloth. ~*a.* **1** woven. **2** suitable for weaving. **3** of or relating to weaving.

texture (teks'chə) *n.* **1** the quality of something as perceived by touch. **2** the particular arrangement or disposition of threads, filaments etc., in a textile fabric. **3** the disposition of the constituent parts of any body, structure or material. ~*v.t.* to give texture to. **textural** *a.* **texturally** *adv.* **textured** *a.* **textureless** *a.* **texturize, texturise** *v.t.* to give a particular texture to. **texturized vegetable protein** *n.* a meat substitute made from soya beans to resemble meat in texture and taste.

Usage note See note on *textual* under TEXT.

Th *chem. symbol* thorium.

Th. *abbr.* Thursday.

-th[1] (th), **-eth** (əth) *suf.* forming ordinal and fractional numbers from the cardinal number four and upwards, as in *sixth, sixteenth, sixtieth.*

-th[2] (th) *suf.* **1** forming nouns from verbs of action of process, as in *growth.* **2** forming nouns from adjectives, as in *width, strength.*

Thai (tī) *n.* (*pl.* **Thai, Thais**) **1** a native or inhabitant of Thailand (formerly Siam). **2** a member of the predominant ethnic group in Thailand. **3** the language of Thailand. ~*a.* of or relating to Thailand, its people or its language.

thalamus (thal'əməs) *n.* (*pl.* **thalami** (-mī)) **1** (*Anat.*) either of two oval masses of grey matter at the base of the brain whose function is to relay sensory information to the cerebral cortex. **2** (*Bot.*) the receptacle of a flower. **thalamic** (thəlam'-) *a.*

thalassaemia (thaləsē'miə), (*N Am.*) **thalassemia** *n.* (*Med.*) a hereditary disorder of the blood due to defects in the synthesis of haemoglobin, sometimes fatal in children.

thalassic (thəlas'ik) *a.* of or relating to the sea or

seas, marine. **thalassotherapy** (-ōther'-) *n.* a type of alternative medicine using mud, seaweed, seawater etc. as relaxing agents and for detoxifying the body.

thalidomide (thəlid'əmīd) *n.* a drug formerly used as a sedative, withdrawn from use in 1961, as it was shown to be associated with malformation of the foetus when taken by pregnant women. **thalidomide baby, thalidomide child** *n.* a baby or child born showing the effects, such as shortened malformed limbs, of thalidomide.

thalli THALLUS.

thallium (thal'iəm) *n.* (*Chem.*) a rare soft, white, crystalline metallic element, at. no. 81, chem. symbol Tl, the spectrum of which contains a bright-green line from which it was named, used in alloys and glass-making. **thallic, thallous** *a.*

thallophyte (thal'ōfīt) *n.* (*Bot.*) any plant, such as algae, fungi and lichens, that has a thallus. **thallophytic** (-fit'-) *a.*

thallus (thal'əs) *n.* (*pl.* **thalluses, thalli** (-ī)) a plant-body without vascular tissue and lacking differentiation into root, stem or leaves. **thalloid** (-oid) *a.*

than (dhan, dhən) *conj., prep.* **1** used to introduce the second element in a comparison (*taller than his brother; colder than yesterday*). **2** used after adverbs, such as *rather, other, otherwise, sooner,* to introduce a less preferable or rejected option or to introduce an alternative (*try to keep calm rather than panic; had no choice other than to agree*).

Usage note After *than,* the objective pronoun (*me, him, us* etc.) is the everyday choice. The subjective (*I, he, we* etc.), though formerly demanded by strict grammatical rule, is now considered rather pedantic except with a following verb. So *I am better than him, He hit harder than her* are generally acceptable; *I am better than he is, He hit harder than she did* are more formal equivalents, with *better than he, harder than she* very careful and formal alternatives indeed.

---

thanatology (thanətol'əji) *n.* the scientific study of death.

thane (thān) *n.* (*Hist.*) **1** in feudal times in England, a freeman holding land by military service and ranking between ordinary freemen and the nobles. **2** in medieval Scotland, a man who held land from a king (not necessarily in return for military service or support), ranking with the son of an earl; a clan chief.

thank (thangk) *v.t.* **1** to express gratitude (to or for). **2** to blame or hold responsible (*I have only myself to thank for the mess I'm in*). ~*n.* (*pl.*) **1** an expression of gratitude (*Pass on my thanks for the flowers*). **2** a formula of acknowledgement of a favour, kindness, benefit etc. (*gave thanks to God*). **3** used as a formula expressing gratitude, thank you (*Thanks a lot*). **no (small) thanks to** despite having the handicap of. **thank goodness/**

God/ heavens/ the Lord etc. **1** (*coll.*) used to express relief, pleasure etc. **2** used to express pious gratitude. **thanks to** because of, owing to. **thank you** used as a formula expressing thanks, polite refusal etc. **to give thanks** to say grace before a meal. **thankful** *a.* **1** grateful, glad, appreciative. **2** expressive of thanks. **3** indebted (to). **thankfully** *adv.* **1** in a grateful, appreciative etc. way. **2** (*coll.*) fortunately, we should all be glad that (*Thankfully, the police arrived*). **thankfulness** *n.* **thankless** *a.* **1** insensible to kindness, ungrateful. **2** not deserving thanks. **3** not appreciated or profitable. **thanklessly** *adv.* **thanklessness** *n.* **thank-offering** *n.* an offering made as an expression of gratitude, esp. a Jewish sacrifice of thanksgiving. **thanksgiving** *n.* **1** the act of returning thanks or expressing gratitude, esp. to God. **2** a form of words expressive of this. **thank-you** *n.* (*coll.*) **1** an instance of saying 'thank you'. **2** a gift etc. given in appreciation. ~*a.* expressing gratitude, appreciation etc. (*a thank-you present*).

Usage note The use of *thankfully* to express thankfulness (as a sentence adverb) is sometimes disapproved of, though it is quite common.

that (dhat, dhət) *pron.* (*pl.* **those** (dhōz)) **1** used to refer to someone or something already known, indicated, mentioned etc. **2** used to refer to the more distant, less obvious etc. example of two similar things, often contrasting with *this* (*This book is more interesting than that*). **3** (*coll.*) used as an emphatically positive response to what has just been said ('*You must have been relieved.*' '*I was that!*'). **4** the one, usu. used with relative or complementary information (*Those who were late must stay behind*; *has a fiery temper just like that of her brother*). **5** (*pl.* **that**) used like *which* or *who* to introduce defining information (*the recipe that Martin gave me*; *the people that enjoyed her first film*). ~*a.* (*pl.* **those**) **1** denoting someone or something already known, indicated, mentioned etc. **2** used with *this* in contrasting or differentiating statements. **3** used for emphasis (*With all its mishaps, that holiday is one I'll never forget*). ~*adv.* **1** to the degree or extent specified or understood (*I can't walk that fast*). **2** (*coll.*) very, much, so, too (*The play wasn't that enjoyable*; *I was that annoyed I nearly hit him*). **3** at which, on which, when etc. (*was away on holiday the day that it happened*). ~*conj.* **1** indicating reason, purpose, consequence etc. (*so drunk that he couldn't stand*; *What happened next was that he fell over*). **2** expressing a wish or desire (*Oh, that this night would never end!*). **all that** (*coll.*) very, particularly (*wasn't all that bad*). **and (all) that** (*coll.*) and all the other things associated with what has just been mentioned. **like that 1** of the kind referred to. **2** in that way. **3** (*coll.*) effortlessly, without hesitation. **that is (to say)** used to introduce a rewording, a simpler version or an

explanation of what has just been said. **that's** (*coll.*) you are (*You got an A+! That's my clever girl!*). **that's right** used to express approval, agreement etc. **that's that** used to indicate that there is nothing more to be said or done about something. **that there** (*coll.*) used to indicate something emphatically (*That there dress is the one I want*). **that will do** used to indicate that no more is wanted or needed.

Usage note The introductory *that* of a defining or object clause is often omitted: *the dictionary* (*that*) *I bought, I said* (*that*) *I bought a dictionary.*

thatch (thach) *n.* (*pl.* **thatches**) **1** a roof covering of straw, rushes, reeds etc. **2** (*coll.*) anything that resembles this, esp. a thick head of hair. ~*v.t.* to cover with this. ~*v.i.* to do thatching. **thatched** *a.* **thatcher** *n.* **thatching** *n.* **1** the act of thatching. **2** the materials used in thatching.

Thatcherism (thach´erizm) *n.* the political, economic etc. philosophy and policies of Margaret Thatcher, British Prime Minister, 1979–90. **Thatcherite** (-īt) *n.* a supporter of Margaret Thatcher or her policies. ~*a.* of or relating to Margaret Thatcher or her policies.

thaw (thaw) *v.i.* **1** (of ice, snow etc.) to melt, dissolve or become liquid. **2** (of the weather) to become warm enough to melt frost, ice or snow. **3** to become warm enough to lose numbness etc. **4** to relax one's stiffness, to unbend, to become genial. ~*v.t.* **1** to cause to melt, dissolve etc. **2** to infuse warmth, animation, conviviality etc. into. ~*n.* **1** the act of thawing or the state of being thawed. **2** warm weather that thaws. **3** a relaxation of tension, an increase in friendliness. **to thaw out 1** to return to normal from a frozen condition. **2** to become more relaxed or more friendly. **thawless** *a.*

the (dhə, dhi, dhē) *a.* **1** used to refer to a particular person or thing, or to particular people or things, already mentioned, known to be familiar etc. (*took the dog to the vet*; *laid the table*). **2** used to refer to a unique person or thing (*the Pope*; *Aberdeen straddles the Dee and the Don*). **3** used before an adjective to denote which is, who are etc. (*Pitt the Younger*). **4** used before an adjective functioning as a collective or generic noun (*the poor*). **5** used before a gerund or verbal noun (*The singing was beautiful*). **6** used to denote a familiar cultural concept or activity (*goes to the football every week*; *reads the news*; *off to the cinema*). **7** (pronounced with stress) used to denote something or someone considered to be the best, most desirable etc. of its kind (*Planet Hollywood is the place to be seen*). **8** used before a noun that is followed by some defining, qualifying, relative, complementary etc. information (*the least you could do*; *the first of many*; *the love between them*; *the film we watched last night*). **9** used before a singular noun when it functions generically (*The pig is a clean animal*; *teaches a course on the Western*; *is *learning the piano).* **10** used before a figurative noun (*end up in the gutter; wants to take her band on the road*). **11** used after a preposition to introduce a quantity, time etc. (*does 45 miles to the gallon; gets paid by the hour*). **12** (*coll.* or *dated*) used before a noun denoting an affliction, condition etc. (*in bed with the cold; enough to give you the willies*). **13** used in formulaic constructions of time etc. to denote a notion of currency, the present etc. (*man of the match*). **14** (*coll.*) my, our (*Come back to the house for a drink; I'd better ask the wife first*). ~*adv.* **1** used in comparative constructions to indicate correlation or interdependency (*the sooner the better*). **2** used for emphasis or to indicate supremacy etc., usu. before comparatives or superlatives (*felt the better for telling him; This one is the most useful*). **all the** to, into, in etc. an even greater extent.

theatre (thē´ətə), (*N Am.*) **theater** *n.* **1** a building or outdoor area designed for the performance of plays, ballets, operas etc. **2** (*esp. N Am., Austral., New Zeal.*) (*in full* **picture theatre**) a cinema. **3** the business of writing, directing, producing etc. plays. **4** the acting profession (*been in the theatre since she was five*). **5** suitable material for putting on the stage. **6** (*in full* **lecture theatre**) a large room with rising tiered seating suitable for delivering lectures etc. **7** OPERATING THEATRE (under OPERATE). **8** a place where action or events take place (*Bombing turned the city into a theatre of destruction*). **9** the audience of a play, ballet, opera etc. (*The whole theatre was in convulsions*). ~*a.* (*attrib.*) (of weapons etc.) between strategic and tactical. **theatregoing** *n.* attendance at the theatre, esp. regularly or frequently. ~*a.* that attends the theatre, of or relating to attendance at the theatre. **theatregoer** *n.* **theatre-in-the-round** *n.* (*pl.* **theatres-in-the-round**) **1** a theatre which has the stage at the middle with sections of rising tiered seats all around it. **2** drama written or adapted to be staged in this kind of setting. **theatre sister** *n.* the nurse in charge of the nursing staff, equipment etc. in an operating theatre.

theatrical (thiat´rikəl) *a.* **1** of or relating to the theatre. **2** befitting the stage, dramatic. **3** suitable or calculated for display, pompous, showy. **4** befitting or characteristic of actors, stagy, affected. ~*n.* a professional theatre actor or actress. **theatric** *a.* theatrical. **theatrics** *n.pl.* theatrical actions, gestures etc. **theatricality** (-kal´-) *n.* **theatricalize, theatricalise** *v.t.* **theatricalization** (-zā´shən) *n.* **theatrically** *adv.* **theatricals** *n.pl.* **1** dramatic performances, esp. private ones. **2** theatrical actions, gestures etc. **3** professional theatre actors.

theca (thē´kə) *n.* (*pl.* **thecae** (-sē)) **1** (*Bot.*) a part in a non-flowering plant such as moss that functions in a similar way to a receptacle. **2** (*Zool.*) a sheath or casing covering an organ or organism. **thecate** (-kət, -kāt) *a.*

†**thee** (dhē) *pron.* objective (accusative and dative) of THOU¹.

theft (theft) *n.* **1** the act or an instance of stealing. **2** (*Law*) the dishonest taking of another person's property with no intention of ever returning it. **3** something which is stolen.

theine (thē´īn, -in) *n.* caffeine (found in tea leaves).

their (dheə) *a.* **1** possessive of THEY. **2** (**Their**) used in titles (*Their Royal Highnesses*). **3** (*coll.*) his or her (*Everyone must make up their own mind*).

Usage note The spellings of the adjective *their*, adverb *there* and contraction *they're* (they are) should not be confused. See also note under THEY.

theirs (dheəz) *pron.* something belonging to or associated with them (*It's good, but theirs is better*). **of theirs** belonging or relating to, known by etc. them (*a cousin of theirs*).

Usage note The pronoun *theirs* does not have an apostrophe (not *their's*), and should be distinguished from the contraction *there's* (there is).

theism (thē´izm) *n.* **1** belief in the existence of gods or a God, as opposed to atheism. **2** belief in a righteous God supernaturally revealed, as opposed to deism. **theist** *n.* **theistic** (-is´-), **theistical** *a.* **theistically** *adv.*

them (dhem, dhəm) *pron.* **1** objective (accusative and dative) of THEY. **2** (*coll.*) they (esp. after *to be*). ~*a.* (*esp. dial.*) those.

Usage note See note under THEY.

theme (thēm) *n.* **1** a subject on which a person thinks, writes or speaks. **2** (*esp. N Am.*) a short dissertation or essay by a student, school pupil etc. on a certain subject. **3** (*Mus.*) a melodic subject usu. developed with variations. **4** (*Logic*) the subject of thought. **5** an underlying unifying principle. ~*v.t.* to use a particular theme in the design of (a restaurant, leisure complex etc.). **thematic** (thimat´-) *a.* **1** of or relating to topics, by topics (*a thematic thesaurus*). **2** (*Mus.*) of or relating to melodic subjects. **thematically** *adv.* **theme park** *n.* a park designed for leisure, where all the activities are based on a single subject. **theme song, theme tune, theme music** *n.* **1** a recurring melody in a film, musical etc. which is associated with the production or a specific character. **2** a signature tune. **3** (*coll.*) a person's characteristic complaint, repeated phrase etc.

themselves (dhəmselvz´) *pron.* **1** the emphatic and reflexive form of THEM. **2** himself or herself. **3** their usual or normal selves. **to be themselves** to act in their normal unconstrained manner. **themself** *pron.* (*coll.*) **1** himself, herself. **2** himself or herself (*anyone could teach themself*).

Usage note When referring to a singular indefinite form, *themselves* should still be used, not *themself*. See note under THEY.

then (dhen) *adv.* **1** at that time. **2** afterwards, soon after, after that, next. **3** at another time. *~conj.* in that case, therefore, consequently, this being so, accordingly. *~a.* (*coll.*) of or existing at that time. *~n.* that time, the time mentioned or understood. **then and there** on the spot, immediately.

thenar (thē´nah) *n.* (*Anat.*) the part of the palm at the base of the thumb.

thence (dhens) *adv.* (*formal*) **1** from that place. **2** for that reason, from that source. **3** from that time. **from thence** thence. **thenceforth, thenceforward** *adv.* from that time onward. **from thenceforth** thenceforth.

theo- (thē´ō), **the-** *comb. form* of or relating to God or a god.

theobromine (thēōbrō´mēn, -min) *n.* a bitter alkaloid resembling caffeine contained in cacao seeds.

theocentric (thēōsen´trik) *a.* having God as its centre.

theocracy (thiok´rəsi) *n.* (*pl.* **theocracies**) **1** government by the immediate direction of God or through a class of priests. **2** a state so governed. **theocrat** (thē´əkrat) *n.* **theocratic** (-krat´-), **theocratical** *a.* **theocratically** *adv.*

theodolite (thiod´əlīt) *n.* a portable surveying instrument for measuring horizontal and vertical angles. **theodolitic** (-lit´-) *a.*

theology (thiol´əji) *n.* (*pl.* **theologies**) **1** the study of theistic religion, esp. Christianity. **2** a system of theistic religion, esp. Christianity. **theologian** (thēəlō´-), **theologist** *n.* **theological** (thēəloj´-) *a.* **theologically** *adv.* **theologize, theologise** *v.i.* to speculate on theology. *~v.t.* to make theological. **theologizer** *n.*

theophylline (thēəfil´ēn, -in) *n.* a white alkaloid similar to theobromine found in plants such as tea, used to treat heart disease and headaches.

theorem (thē´ərəm) *n.* **1** (*Math.*) a rule or law, esp. one expressed by symbols etc. **2** a proposition to be proved. **3** a principle to be demonstrated by reasoning. **theorematic** (-mat´-), **theorematical** *a.*

theoretical (thēəret´ikəl) *a.* of, relating to or founded on theory not facts or knowledge, not practical, speculative. **theoretic** *n.* theoretics. *~a.* theoretically *adv.* **theoretician** (-ritish´ən) *n.* a person interested in the theory rather than the practical application of a given subject. **theoretics** *n.* the speculative parts of a science.

theory (thē´əri) *n.* (*pl.* **theories**) **1** a supposition explaining something, esp. a generalization explaining phenomena as the results of assumed natural causes. **2** a speculative idea of something. **3** mere hypothesis, speculation, abstract knowledge. **4** an exposition of the general principles of a science etc. **5** a body of

theorems illustrating a particular subject. **theorist** *n.* a person who theorizes. **theorize, theorise** *v.i.* **theorization** (-zā´shən) *n.* **theorizer** *n.*

theosophy (thios´əfi) *n.* (*pl.* **theosophies**) **1** a form of speculation, mysticism or philosophy aiming at the knowledge of God by means of intuition and contemplative illumination or by direct communion. **2** a system founded in the US, in 1875, which claims to show the unity of all religions in their esoteric teaching, manifested by occult phenomena. **theosopher** *n.* **theosophic** (thēəsof´-), **theosophical** *a.* **theosophically** *adv.* **theosophist** *n.*

therapeutic (therəpū´tik) *a.* **1** of or relating to healing or curing disease. **2** curative. **3** contributing to well-being. **therapeutical** *a.* **therapeutically** *adv.* **therapeutics** *n.* (*Med.*) the branch of medical science dealing with the treatment of disease and the action of remedial agents in both health and disease. **therapeutist** *n.* **therapy** (ther´əpi) *n.* (*pl.* **therapies**) **1** the treatment of disease or physical and mental disorders from a curative and preventive point of view, therapeutics. **2** psychiatric or psychological therapy. **3** physiotherapy. **therapist** *n.*

there (dhea, dhə) *adv.* **1** in or at that place, point or stage. **2** to that place, thither. **3** used before or (in questions) after the verb *to be* to express fact or existence (*Is there a doctor in the house?*; *There was an old woman who lived in a shoe*). **4** in that regard. *~n.* that place. *~int.* **1** used to express direction, confirmation, triumph, alarm etc. **2** used (esp. redupl.) to soothe a child. **all there 1** (*coll.*) of normal intelligence. **2** (*coll.*) fully competent, knowing all about it. **so there!** used to express derision or triumph. **there and then** at that place and immediately. **there it is** that is the situation. **there you are 1** here is what you wanted. **2** used to express confirmation of a situation in a triumphant or resigned way. **there you go** there you are. **to have been there before** to have experienced the same thing previously and to know all about it. **thereabouts, thereabout** *adv.* near that place, number, degree etc. **thereafter** (-ah´-) *adv.* (*formal*) **1** after that. **2** according to that. **thereby** (-bī´) *adv.* (*formal*) **1** by that means. **2** in consequence of that. **therefore** *adv.* for that reason, consequently, accordingly. †**therefrom** (-from´) *adv.* from this or that time, place etc. **therein** (-in´) *adv.* (*formal*) in that or this time, place, respect etc. **thereinafter** (-ah´-) *adv.* (*formal*) later in the same (document etc.). **thereof** (-ov´) *adv.* (*formal*) of that or it. †**thereon** (-on´) *adv.* on that or it. **there's** *contr.* **1** there is. **2** (*coll.*) and by that you are or will be (*Fill my glass, there's a love*). **thereto** (-too´) *adv.* (*formal*) **1** to that or this. **2** besides, over and above. **theretofore** (-faw´) *adv.* (*formal*) before that time. **thereupon** (-pon´) *adv.* **1** immediately after or following that. **2** in consequence of that. **3** †upon that. †**therewith** (-widh´) *adv.* **1** with that. **2** immediately after or following that, thereupon.

therm (thœm) *n.* a British unit of heat, equal to 100,000 British thermal units.

thermal (thœ´məl) *a.* **1** of or relating to heat. **2** (of clothing) insulating the body against very low temperatures. ~*n.* **1** a rising current of warm air. **2** (*pl.*) thermal (under)clothes. **thermal capacity** *n.* (*Physics*) the number of heat units required to raise the temperature of a body, system etc. by one degree. **thermal imaging** *n.* the use of the heat given off by a person, object etc. to produce a visual image, for the purposes of medical diagnosis, location of bodies underground etc. **thermalize, thermalise** *v.i., v.t.* **thermalization** (-zā´shən) *n.* **thermally** *adv.* **thermal springs** *n.pl.* hot springs. **thermal unit** *n.* a unit for measuring heat. **thermic** *a.*

thermion (thœ´mion) *n.* (*Physics*) an ion or electron emitted by an incandescent body. **thermionic** (-on´-) *a.* **thermionics** *n.* **1** the branch of electronics dealing with the emission of electrons from hot bodies. **2** the study of the behaviour of these electrons in a vacuum. **thermionic valve,** (*N Am.*) **thermionic tube** *n.* a vacuum tube in which a stream of electrons flows from one electrode to another and is controlled by one or more other electrodes.

thermistor (thœmis´tə) *n.* (*Physics*) a semiconducting device whose resistance decreases with rising temperature.

thermo- (thœ´mō) *comb. form* heat.

thermochemistry (thœmōkem´istri) *n.* the branch of chemistry dealing with the relations between chemical reactions and the heat liberated or absorbed. **thermochemical** *a.*

thermocline (thœ´mōklīn) *n.* a layer of water in a lake etc., in which the water temperature decreases rapidly between the epilimnion and hypolimnion.

thermocouple (thœ´mōkŭpəl) *n.* a device for measuring temperature consisting of two wires of differing metals joined at both ends, one wire of a fixed temperature, the other at the temperature to be measured, the voltage developed being proportional to the difference in temperature.

thermodynamics (thœmōdīnam´iks) *n.* the branch of physics dealing with the relations between heat and other forms of energy. **thermodynamic, thermodynamical** *a.* **thermodynamically** *adv.* **thermodynamicist** (-sist) *n.*

thermoelectricity (thœmōilektris´iti) *n.* electricity generated by differences of temperature. **thermoelectric** (-lek´-) *a.* **thermoelectrically** *adv.*

thermography (thœmog´rəfi) *n.* (*Med.*) the use of thermographic imaging to detect abnormalities in the body. **thermogram** (thœ´məgram) *n.* **thermograph** (-grahf) *n.* **1** an instrument for automatically recording variations of temperature. **2** (*Med.*) an instrument for obtaining an image produced by infrared radiation in the body. **thermographic** (-graf´-) *a.*

thermoluminescence (thœmōloomines´əns) *n.* phosphorescence produced by heating an irradiated substance. **thermoluminescent** *a.*

thermometer (thəmom´itə) *n.* an instrument for measuring temperature, usu. by the expansion or contraction of a column of mercury or alcohol in a graduated tube of small bore with a bulb at one end. **thermometric** (thœmōmet´-), **thermometrical** *a.* **thermometrically** *adv.* **thermometry** (-tri) *n.*

thermonuclear (thœmōnū´kliə) *a.* **1** (*Physics*) relating to the fusion of nuclei at very high temperatures. **2** of or relating to weapons in which an explosion is produced by thermonuclear reaction.

thermophile (thœ´məfil), **thermophil** (-fil) *n.* (*Biol.*) a bacterium thriving in a high temperature. **thermophilic** (-fil´-) *a.*

thermopile (thœ´məpīl) *n.* a series of thermocouples, esp. one employed to measure small quantities of radiant heat.

thermoplastic (thœmōplas´tik) *n., a.* (a substance) which softens under heat without undergoing any chemical change, and can therefore be heated repeatedly.

Thermos® (thœ´mos), **thermos, thermos flask,** (*N Am.*) **thermos bottle** *n.* a vacuum flask.

thermosetting (thœ´mōseting) *a.* (of plastics) softening initially under heat but subsequently hardening and becoming infusible and insoluble. **thermoset** *a.*

thermosphere (thœ´məsfiə) *n.* the part of the earth's atmosphere above the mesosphere, from about 50 miles (80 km), in which the temperature rises steadily with height.

thermostat (thœ´məstat) *n.* an automatic device for regulating temperatures. **thermostatic** (-stat´-) *a.* **thermostatically** *adv.*

thesaurus (thisaw´rəs) *n.* (*pl.* **thesauruses, thesauri** (-rī)) **1** a collection of words, phrases etc. arranged as groups of synonyms or by concept. **2** a dictionary or encyclopedia.

these THIS.

thesis (thē´sis) *n.* (*pl.* **theses** (-sēz)) **1** a proposition advanced or maintained. **2** an essay or dissertation, esp. one submitted by a candidate for a degree etc.

thespian (thes´piən) *a.* of or relating to tragedy or drama. ~*n.* an actor.

theta (thē´tə) *n.* the eighth letter of the Greek alphabet (Θ, θ), corresponding to *th*.

thew (thū) *n.* **1** (*usu. in pl., poet.*) muscles, sinews. **2** (*poet.*) strength, vigour.

they (dhā) *pron.* **1** the plural of HE, SHE or IT (subjective). **2** people in general. **3** those in authority. **4** (*coll.*) he or she (referring to an indefinite pron.). **they'd** (dhād) *contr.* **1** they had. **2** they would. **they'll** (dhāl) *contr.* they will. **they're** (dheə) *contr.* they are. **they've** (dhāv) *contr.* they have.

Usage note This dictionary accepts and uses the (plural) pronouns *they, them, their* to refer back to singular indefinites (*someone, a person* etc.). The traditionally prescribed masculine singular (*he, him, his*) has increasingly come to be regarded as sexist. *They* and its forms are already the natural choices in spoken English, and the explicit alternatives *he or she, him or her, his or her* can be cumbersome. In other formal written contexts, however, *he or she* etc. may be preferred, and outside dictionary definitions indefinite sentences can often conveniently be recast in the plural.

THI *abbr.* temperature-humidity index.

thiamine (thī´əmēn), **thiamin** (-min) *n.* a vitamin found in unrefined cereals, beans and liver, important for metabolism and nerve function, the lack of which can cause beriberi; vitamin B_1.

thick (thik) *a.* **1** having great or specified extent or depth from one surface to the opposite. **2** arranged, set or planted closely, crowded together, close packed. **3** abounding (with), following in quick succession. **4** dense, muddy, impure, cloudy, foggy. **5** (*coll.*) not very intelligent, stupid. **6** (of articulation etc.) indistinct, muffled. **7** (*coll.*) very friendly, familiar (*as thick as thieves*). **8** stiff, not flowing easily. **9** (of an accent) clearly belonging to a particular place; marked, pronounced. *~adv.* **1** thickly. **2** in close succession (*thick and fast*). **3** indistinctly. *~n.* the thickest part. **a bit thick** (*coll.*) unreasonable. **in the thick** at the busiest part (of). **through thick and thin** under any conditions, undauntedly, resolutely. **thick ear** *n.* (*coll.*) a swollen ear as a result of a blow. **thicken** *v.t., v.i.* **thickener** *n.* **thickening** *n.* **thicket** *n.* a thick growth of small trees, bushes etc. **thickhead** *n.* (*coll.*) a blockhead. **thick-headed** *a.* **thick-headedness** *n.* **thickish** *a.* **thickly** *adv.* **thickness** *n.* **1** the extent from the upper surface to the lower. **2** the state of being thick. **3** a sheet or layer of cardboard etc. **4** a thick part. **5** the state of being arranged, set or planted closely, crowded together. **6** stiffness, the state of not flowing easily. **7** indistinct or muffled articulation. **8** an accent or pronunciation that clearly belongs to a particular place. **9** the state of being very friendly or familiar. **thickset** *a.* **1** solidly built, stout, stumpy. **2** planted, set or growing close together. *~n.* a thicket. **thick-skinned** *a.* insensitive to taunts, criticism etc.

thief (thēf) *n.* (*pl.* **thieves** (thēvz)) a person who steals, esp. furtively and without violence. **thieve** (thēv) *v.i.* to practise theft, to be a thief. *~v.t.* to take by theft. **thievery** (-vəri) *n.* (*pl.* **thieveries**) the act or practice of stealing. **thieves' Latin** *n.* cant or jargon employed as a secret language by thieves. **thievish** *a.* **thievishly** *adv.* **thievishness** *n.*

thigh (thī) *n.* **1** the thick, fleshy portion of the leg between the hip and knee in humans. **2** the corresponding part in other animals. **thigh bone** *n.* (*Anat.*) the principal bone between the hip and the knee, the femur. **thighed** *a.*

thill (thil) *n.* the shaft of a cart, carriage or other vehicle.

thimble (thim´bəl) *n.* **1** a cap of metal, plastic etc., worn to protect the end of the finger in sewing. **2** a sleeve or short metal tube. **3** a ferrule. **4** (*Naut.*) an iron ring having an exterior groove worked into a rope or sail to receive another rope or lanyard. **thimbleful** *n.* (*pl.* **thimblefuls**) **1** as much as a thimble holds. **2** a very small quantity. **thimblerig** (-rig) *n.* a sleight-of-hand trick with three thimbles or cups and a pea, persons being challenged to guess which cover the pea is under. **thimblerigger** *n.*

thin (thin) *a.* (*comp.* **thinner**, *superl.* **thinnest**) **1** having the opposite surfaces close together, of little thickness, slender. **2** not close-packed, not dense. **3** sparse, scanty, meagre. **4** lean, not plump. **5** not full, scant, bare. **6** flimsy, easily seen through. **7** of a watery consistency. **8** weak in sound, not full-toned. **9** (of an excuse, reason etc.) unconvincing, weak. *~adv.* thinly. *~v.t.* (*pres.p.* **thinning**, *past, p.p.* **thinned**) **1** to make thin or thinner. **2** to dilute. *~v.i.* **1** to become thin or thinner. **2** to waste away. **3** to become less dense. **on thin ice** in a vulnerable or dangerous situation. **thin on the ground** not numerous, sparse. **thin on top** balding. **to thin out** to remove fruit, flowers etc. from (a tree or plant) or some of a crop of (seedlings etc.) to improve the rest. **thin air** *n.* invisibility, a state of apparent non-existence. **thinly** *adv.* **thinner, thinners** *n.* a solvent used to thin, e.g. paint. **thinness** *n.* **thinnings** *n.pl.* branches, trees etc. removed in the course of thinning out an overgrown area. **thinnish** *a.* **thin-skinned** *a.* sensitive, easily offended. **thin time** *n.* a period of hardship, misery etc.

†thine (dhīn) *a.* THY (before a vowel). *~pron.* something or someone of or belonging to thee (you).

thing (thing) *n.* **1** any thought. **2** whatever exists or is conceived to exist as a separate entity, esp. an inanimate object as distinct from a living being. **3** an act, a fact, affair, circumstance etc. **4** a quality, a feature. **5** (*coll.*) a person or other animate object regarded with commiseration, disparagement etc. **6** a specimen, a style. **7** a remarkable fact. **8** (*pl.*) belongings, luggage etc. **9** clothes. **10** (*pl.*) the current or usual state of affairs. **11** (*pl., Law*) property. **12** a fact, point. **13** a statement. **(just) one of those things** a happening that one cannot do anything about. **one's thing** (*coll.*) one's usual sphere of interest or competence. **the thing 1** the proper thing (to do etc.). **2** the thing to be decided. **3** the important thing. **to do one's own thing** (*coll.*) to do what one likes or what one pleases. **to do things to** to affect (someone) in a strange and remarkable way. **to have a thing about 1** to have an unaccountable prejudice or fear about. **2** to have a strong liking for or preoccupation with. **to make a thing 1** to make an issue (of), to cause a fuss. **2** to exaggerate the importance (of). **thingamabob** (-əməbob), **thingamajig** (-jig), **thingumabob, thingumajig, thingummyjig** *n.* (*coll.*) THINGUMMY (under THING). **thingummy** (-əmi), **thingamy, thingy** (-i) *n.* (*pl.* **thingummies, thingamies, thingies**) (*coll.*) **1** a thing whose name one is unable to specify (through ignorance, forgetfulness or reluctance), a what-d'you-call-it. **2** used instead of a person's name (one does not know, has forgotten or wishes not to specify).

think (thingk) *v.t.* (*past, p.p.* **thought** (thawt), (*facet.*) **thunk** (thŭngk)) **1** to regard or examine in the mind, to reflect, to ponder (over etc.). **2** to consider, to be of the opinion, to believe (that), to judge (to be). **3** to design, to intend (to do). **4** to effect by thinking. **5** (*coll.*) to remember, to recollect (to do). **6** to imagine, to recognize. **7** to expect. ~*v.i.* **1** to exercise the mind actively, to reason. **2** to meditate, to cogitate, to consider (on, about etc.). ~*n.* (*coll.*) **1** an act of thinking. **2** a thought. **to think again 1** to reconsider a previous decision. **2** to change a previous plan or decision. **to think aloud** to speak about one's thoughts as they occur. **to think back** to reflect on the past, a past event etc. **to think better of** to change one's mind, to decide not to pursue (a course of action). **to think for oneself** to be independent-minded. **to think highly of** to hold in high regard. **to think on/ upon** to consider, to think about. **to think out 1** to devise. **2** to solve by long thought. **to think over** to consider (a proposition etc.). **to think through** to think fully about a situation, decision etc. and its consequences. **to think twice 1** to give extra thought to, to hesitate. **2** to change a decision. **to think up** to devise, to invent. **thinkable** *a.* **thinker** *n.* a person who thinks deeply, an intellectual person. **thinking** *n.* **1** the process of thought. **2** the opinion, received viewpoint etc. at a given time. ~*a.* **1** of or related to thought. **2** given to thinking deeply. **thinkingly** *adv.* **think-tank** *n.* a group of experts in any field who meet to solve problems and produce new ideas in that field.

thinner, thinnings etc. THIN.

thio- (thīˊō) *comb. form* sulphur.

thiopentone (thīōpenˊtōn) *n.* (*Chem.*) a barbiturate drug used, as a sodium salt, in medicine as a general anaesthetic and hypnotic.

thiosulphuric (thīōsŭlfūˊrik), (*esp. N Am.*) **thiosulfuric** *a.* (*Chem.*) applied to an acid corresponding to sulphuric acid in which one atom of oxygen is replaced by one of sulphur. **thiosulphate** (-sŭlˊfāt) *n.*

third (thœd) *n.* **1** any one of three equal parts. **2** the 60th part of a second of time or angular measurement. **3** (*Mus.*) **a** an interval between a tone and the next but one on the diatonic scale. **b** a tone separated by this interval. **c** the

consonance of two such tones. **4** (*pl.*) the third part of a deceased husband's estate, sometimes assigned as her share to the widow. **5** a third-class honours degree. **6** the third gear in a motor vehicle. ~*n., a.* **1** (the) last of three (people, things etc.). **2** the next after the second. **third age** *n.* old age, the period of retirement. **third-class** *a.* **1** inferior, worthless. **2** of the class coming next to the second. ~*adv.* by the third class. ~*n.* the third-best category of hotel, train travel etc. **third cousin** *n.* the child of a parent's second cousin. **third degree** *n.* (*sl.*) intimidation or torture, esp. to extract information. **third-degree** *a.* **1** (of burns) most severe, affecting lower layers of tissue. **2** (of an interrogation etc.) very demanding, perh. using torture. **third force** *n.* a moderate political party acting as a check on two parties with more extreme views. **third gear** *n.* in a motor vehicle, cycle etc., the third lowest gear. **thirdly** *adv.* **third man** *n.* (*pl.* **third men**) **1** in cricket, a fielder placed towards the boundary behind the slips. **2** this position. **third party** *n.* (a person) other than the principals (in a contract etc.). **third-party** *a.* (of insurance) covering damage, injury etc. to those other than the insured person(s). **third person** *n.* (*Gram.*) the form of a pronoun, verb etc. indicating persons or things referred to, as distinct from the speaker or addressee(s). **third-rate** *a.* inferior, worthless. **third reading** *n.* the final acceptance of a bill together with the amendments passed in committee.

thirst (thœst) *n.* **1** the uneasiness or suffering caused by the need to drink liquid. **2** a desire to drink liquid. **3** eager longing or desire. ~*v.i.* **1** to feel thirst (for or after). **2** to feel eager longing or desire (for or after). **thirstless** *a.* **thirsty** *a.* (*comp.* **thirstier,** *superl.* **thirstiest**) **1** feeling thirst, dry, parched. **2** (*coll.*) causing thirst (*thirsty work*). **3** eager (for). **thirstily** *adv.* **thirstiness** *n.*

thirteen (thœtēnˊ) *n.* **1** the number or figure 13 or xiii. **2** the age of 13. ~*a.* **1** 13 in number. **2** aged 13. **thirteenth** (-th) *n.* any one of 13 equal parts. ~*n., a.* **1** (the) last of 13 (people, things etc.). **2** the next after the 12th.

thirty (thœˊti) *n.* (*pl.* **thirties**) **1** three times ten. **2** the number or figure 30 or xxx. **3** the age of 30. ~*a.* **1** 30 in number. **2** aged 30. **thirties** *n.pl.* **1** the period of time between one's 30th and 40th birthdays. **2** the range of temperature between 30 and 40 degrees. **3** the period of time between the 30th and 40th years of a century. **thirtieth** (-əth) *n.* any one of 30 equal parts. ~*n., a.* **1** (the) last of 30 (people, things etc.). **2** the next after the 20th. **thirty-first, thirty-second** etc. *n., a.* the ordinal numbers corresponding to thirty-one etc. **thirty-fold** *a., adv.* **1** made up of 30 parts. **2** 30 times as much or as many. **thirty-one, thirty-two** etc. *n., a.* the cardinal numbers between thirty and forty. **thirty-something** *n., a.* (of) an unspecified age between 30 and 40. **thirty-two-mo** *n.* (*pl.* **thirty-two-mos**) **1** (of a book) a size in which each leaf is one-thirty-second the size of a printing sheet. **2** a book of this size.

this (dhis) *a., pron. (pl.* **these** (dhēz)) used to denote the person or thing that is present or near in place or time, or already mentioned, implied or familiar. *~adv.* to this extent. **this and that** *(coll.)* random and usu. unimportant subjects of conversation. **this here** *(sl.)* this particular (person, object etc.). **this world** existence, this mortal life.

thistle (this´əl) *n.* any plant of the genera *Circium, Carlina, Carduus* etc. having prickly stems, leaves and involucres. **thistledown** *n.* the light fluffy down surrounding thistle seeds. **thistly** *a.*

thither (dhidh´ə) *adv. (formal, poet.)* **1** to that place. **2** to that end, point or result. **thitherward** *adv.*

tho' THOUGH.

thole (thōl), **thole-pin** *n.* a pin in the gunwale of a boat serving as fulcrum for the oar.

-thon (thon) *comb. form* a large-scale event or related series of events lasting a long time or demanding endurance of the participants, as *telethon.*

thong (thong) *n.* **1** a strip of leather used as a whiplash, for reins, or for fastening anything. **2** *(Austral., N Am.)* a flip-flop (sandal). **3** a skimpy bathing garment that covers the genitals while leaving the buttocks bare. *~v.t.* **1** to fit or provide with a thong. **2** to fasten or thrash with a thong.

thorax (thaw´raks) *n. (pl.* **thoraces** (-rəsēz), **thoraxes**) **1** *(Anat.)* the part of the trunk between the neck and the abdomen. **2** *(Zool.)* the middle division of the body of insects. **thoracal** (-rəkəl) *a.* **thoracic** (thəras´-) *a.*

thorium (thaw´riəm) *n. (Chem.)* a radioactive metallic element, at. no. 90, chem. symbol Th, found chiefly in thorite and monazite.

thorn (thawn) *n.* **1** a spine, a sharp-pointed projection on a plant, a prickle. **2** a thorny shrub, tree or herb *(usu. in comb.* as *blackthorn, whitethorn).* **on thorns** restless, uneasy. **thorn apple** *n.* **1** a plant with prickly seed capsules, *Datura stramonium.* **2** the fruit of this. **thornback** *n.* a ray, *Raja clavata,* the back and tail of which are covered with spines. **thorn bush, thorn tree** *n.* a thorn-bearing tree. **thorn in one's side, thorn in one's flesh** *n.* a constant source of trouble. **thornless** *a.* **thornproof** *a.* **thorny** *a. (comp.* **thornier,** *superl.* **thorniest) 1** having many thorns. **2** difficult to resolve, problematical. **thornily** *adv.* **thorniness** *n.*

thorough (thŭr´ə) *a.* **1** complete, total, unqualified, not superficial. **2** very carefully, meticulously. **3** absolutely, utterly. **thorough bass** (bās) *n. (Mus.)* a bass part accompanied by shorthand marks, usu. figures, written below the stave, to indicate the harmony. **thoroughbred** *a.* **1** of pure breed. **2** of the best quality. *~n.* **1** a thoroughbred animal, esp. a horse. **2** **(Thoroughbred)** a British breed of racehorses originating from Arab sires

and English mares. **thoroughfare** *n.* **1** a road or street for public traffic. **2** a passage through from one street etc., to another, an unobstructed road or street. **thoroughgoing** *a.* **1** thorough, uncompromising. **2** going or ready to go to any lengths. **thoroughly** *adv.* **thoroughness** *n.*

those THAT.

†thou[1] (dhow) *pron.* the second personal pronoun singular (subjective), denoting the person spoken to.

thou[2] (thow) *n. (pl.* **thou, thous) 1** *(coll.)* short for THOUSAND. **2** a thousandth of an inch (0.0254 mm).

though (dhō), **tho'** *conj.* **1** notwithstanding that, despite the fact that. **2** even if, granting or supposing that. **3** nevertheless. **4** in spite of being. *~adv. (coll.)* however, all the same.

thought[1] (thawt) *n.* **1** the act or process of thinking. **2** reflection, serious consideration, meditation. **3** a conception, an idea, a reflection, a judgement, conclusion etc. **4** deep concern or solicitude. **5** the faculty of thinking or reasoning. **6** that which is thought. **7** *(pl.)* one's views, ideas, opinions etc. **8** expectation, hope. **9** an aim, intention. **a thought** *(coll.)* a very small degree, etc. a shade, somewhat. **to give thought to** to consider. **to take thought** to consider something carefully. **thoughted** *a.* **thoughtful** *a.* **1** engaged in thinking. **2** reflecting serious consideration. **3** considerate, careful. **thoughtfully** *adv.* **thoughtfulness** *n.* **thoughtless** *a.* **1** inconsiderate, careless. **2** reflecting absence of serious consideration. **thoughtlessly** *adv.* **thoughtlessness** *n.* **thought-provoking** *a.* mentally stimulating, engendering serious thought. **thought-reader** *n.* a person who appears to perceive by telepathy what is passing through another person's mind. **thought-reading** *n.* **thought-transference** *n.* telepathy.

thought[2] THINK.

thousand (thow´zənd) *n. (pl.* **thousand, thousands) 1** ten hundred, 1000. **2** a great many. *~a.* amounting to a thousand. **thousandfold** *a., adv.* **thousandth** (-th) *a., n.*

thrall (thrawl) *n. (poet.)* **1** a state of slavery or enthralment. **2** a slave, a serf. *~v.t.* to enthral, to enslave. **thraldom, thralldom** *n.*

thrash (thrash) *v.t.* **1** to beat severely, esp. with a stick etc. **2** to defeat, conquer, beat convincingly. *~v.i.* **1** to strike out wildly and repeatedly. **2** *(Naut.)* to strike the waves repeatedly. *~n.* **1** a thrashing. **2** *(sl.)* a party. **to thrash out** to discuss thoroughly in order to find a solution. **thrasher** *n.* **1** a person who thrashes. **2** a thresher. **thrashing** *n.* a severe beating.

thread (thred) *n.* **1** a slender cord consisting of two or more yarns doubled or twisted, for sewing or weaving. **2** a single filament of cotton, silk, wool etc. **3** anything resembling this. **4** the continuing theme or linking element in an argument or story. **5** the spiral on a screw. **6** a fine line of colour etc. **7** a thin seam or vein. **8** a continuous course (of life etc.). ~*v.t.* **1** to pass a thread through the eye or aperture of (a needle etc.). **2** to string (beads etc.) on a thread. **3** to pick (one's way) or to go through an intricate or crowded place etc. **4** to cut a thread on (a screw). **to hang by a thread** to be in a very precarious state. **threadbare** *a.* **1** so worn that the thread is visible, having the nap worn off. **2** (of an excuse, phrase etc.) worn, trite, hackneyed. **threadbareness** *n.* **threader** *n.* **threadlike** *a.*, *adv.* **thread vein** *n.* (*Med.*) a very fine vein on the surface of the skin. **threadworm** *n.* a threadlike nematode worm, esp. a pinworm. **thready** *a.* (*comp.* **threadier,** *superl.* **threadiest**) **1** threadlike. **2** (of the pulse) very weak, only faintly perceptible.

threat (thret) *n.* **1** a declaration of an intention to inflict punishment, loss, injury etc. **2** a menace. **3** an indication of an imminent danger. **threaten** *v.t.* **1** to use threats to. **2** to announce a damaging intention (to do). **3** to announce one's intention to inflict (injury etc.). **4** to indicate an imminent danger of. **5** to be a threat to, to endanger. ~*v.i.* **1** to use threats. **2** to have a threatening appearance. **3** to be imminent, to loom. **threatened** *a.* (of a species of animal, plant etc.) at risk, endangered. **threatener** *n.* **threatening** *a.* **1** serving as a threat, menacing. **2** ominous. **threateningly** *adv.*

three (thrē) *n.* **1** the number or figure 3 or iii. **2** the age of three. **3** the third hour after midnight or midday. **4** a group of three. ~*a.* **1** three in number. **2** aged three. **three-cornered** *a.* having three corners or angles. **three-day event** *n.* an equestrian competition taking place over three days and including dressage, show-jumping and cross-country riding. **three dimensions** *n.pl.* length, breadth and thickness. **three-dimensional** *a.* having or seeming to have three dimensions. **threefold** *a.*, *adv.* **1** made up of three parts. **2** three times as much or as many. **three-handed** *a.* **1** (of a card game) for three players. **2** having three hands. **three-legged race** *n.* a novelty race in which people run in pairs with one leg tied to a leg of their partner. **three-line whip** *n.* a written notice to MPs urging them to attend a parliamentary vote, underlined three times to denote its importance. **three parts** *n.pl.* three-quarters. **three-parts** *a.* **threepence** (threp´əns, thrip´-, thrŭp´-) *n.* the sum of three pence, esp. before decimal currency. **threepenny** (threp´ni, thrip´-, thrŭp´-) *a.* **threepenny bit** *n.* (*Hist.*) a small coin of the value of three old pence. **three-piece** *a.* consisting of three matching pieces, as a suit of clothes, a suite of furniture etc. **three-ply** *a.* having three strands, thicknesses etc. ~*n.* plywood of three layers. **three-point turn** *n.* an about-turn in a narrow space made by a vehicle moving obliquely forwards, backwards and forwards again. **three-pronged** *a.* (of an attack, strategy etc.) having three elements, goals etc. **three-pronged attack** *n.* an attack on three separate points at the same

time. **three-quarters** *n.pl.* three parts out of four equal parts of a whole. ~*adv.* **1** to the extent of three-quarters. **2** almost (*three-quarters drowned*). **three-quarter** *a.* **1** of three-fourths the usual size or number. **2** (of portraits) showing three-quarters of the face, or going down to the hips. ~*n.* a three-quarter back. **three-quarter back** *n.* in rugby football, each of three or four players between the full-back and the half-backs. **three R's** *n.pl.* reading, writing, arithmetic, the basic subjects of education. †**threescore** *a.* sixty. ~*n.* the age of 60. **threesome** (-səm) *n.* **1** a group of three. **2** a game for three.

threnody (thren´ədi), **threnode** (thre´nōd, thren´-) *n.* (*pl.* **threnodies, threnodes**) **1** a song of lamentation. **2** a poem on the death of a person. **threnodial** (thrinō´-), **threnodic** (-nod´-) *a.* **threnodist** (thren´-) *n.*

threonine (thre´ənēn) *n.* an amino acid essential for growth and health found in certain proteins.

thresh (thresh) *v.t.* **1** to beat out or separate the grain (from corn etc.). **2** to thrash. ~*v.i.* **1** to thresh corn. **2** to thrash. **to thresh out** to thrash out. **thresher** *n.* **1** a person who threshes. **2** a threshing machine. **3** a shark, *Alopias vulpinus*, having a long whiplike tail with which it directs its prey. **threshing** *n.* **threshing floor** *n.* a floor or area on which grain is threshed. **threshing machine** *n.* a powered machine for threshing corn etc.

threshold (thresh´ōld) *n.* **1** the stone or plank at the bottom of a doorway. **2** an entrance, a doorway. **3** a beginning. **4** (*Med., Psych.*) the minimum strength of a stimulus etc., that will produce a response (*threshold of pain*). **5** the minimum level at which changes in taxation etc. become operative.

threw THROW.

thrice (thrīs) *adv.* **1** three times. **2** (*usu. in comb., poet.*) very much.

thrift (thrift) *n.* **1** frugality. **2** good husbandry, economical management. **3** any plant of the genus *Armeria*, esp. the sea pink, *A. maritima*. **thriftless** *a.* extravagant. **thriftlessly** *adv.* **thriftlessness** *n.* **thrift shop, thrift store** *n.* (*N Am.*) a shop selling things for charity, a charity shop. **thrifty** *a.* (*comp.* **thriftier,** *superl.* **thriftiest**) frugal, careful, economical. **thriftily** *adv.* **thriftiness** *n.*

thrill (thril) *v.t.* **1** to affect with emotion so as to give a sense as of vibrating or tingling. **2** (of emotion) to excite greatly. ~*v.i.* **1** (of emotion) to penetrate, vibrate, or quiver (through, along etc.). **2** to have a vibrating, shivering or tingling sense of emotion. ~*n.* **1** an intense vibration, shiver. **2** a wave of strong emotion, such as joy or excitement. **3** (*coll.*) anything exciting. **thrilled** *a.* **thriller** *n.* a sensational or exciting novel, film etc., esp. one involving crime and detection. **thrilling** *a.* **thrillingly** *adv.* **thrillingness** *n.*

thrips (thrips) *n.* (*pl.* **thrips**) a minute insect of the order Thysanoptera, often injurious to plants, esp. grain, the thunderfly.

thrive (thrīv) *v.i.* (*past* **throve** (thrōv), **thrived**, *p.p.* **thriven** (thriv´en), **thrived**) **1** to prosper, to be fortunate, to be successful. **2** to grow vigorously. **thriver** *n.* **thriving** *a.* **thrivingly** *adv.* **thrivingness** *n.*

thro' THROUGH.

throat (thrōt) *n.* **1** the front part of the neck, containing the gullet and windpipe. **2** the gullet, the pharynx; the windpipe, the larynx. **3** a throat-shaped inlet, opening, or entrance, a narrow passage, strait etc. **4** (*poet.*) a voice; a bird's song. **throated** *a.* **throaty** *a.* (*comp.* **throatier**, *superl.* **throatiest**) **1** guttural. **2** hoarse. **throatily** *adv.* **throatiness** *n.*

throb (throb) *v.i.* (*pres.p.* **throbbing**, *past*, *p.p.* **throbbed**) **1** to vibrate, to quiver. **2** (of the heart or pulse) to beat rapidly or forcibly. **3** to beat with pain. ~*n.* a strong pulsation, a palpitation. **throbbingly** *adv.*

throe (thrō) *n.* **1** (*pl.*) the pains of childbirth or death. **2** a violent pain, a pang of anguish. **in the throes of** struggling with (a task etc.).

Usage note The spellings of the noun *throe* (a pang), and especially its plural *throes*, and the verb and noun *throw(s)* (cast) should not be confused.

thrombosis (thrombō´sis) *n.* (*pl.* **thromboses** (-sēz)) **1** (*Med.*) local coagulation of the blood in the heart or a blood vessel. **2** (*coll.*) a coronary thrombosis. **thrombotic** (-bot´-) *a.*

throne (thrōn) *n.* **1** a royal seat, a chair or seat of state for a sovereign, bishop etc. **2** sovereign power. ~*v.t.* to enthrone.

throng (throng) *n.* a multitude of people or living things pressed close together, a crowd. ~*v.i.* **1** to crowd or press together. **2** to come in multitudes. ~*v.t.* **1** to crowd, to fill to excess. **2** to fill with a crowd. **3** to press or impede by crowding upon.

throstle (thros´el) *n.* the song thrush.

throttle (throt´el) *n.* **1** a throttle-lever. **2** a throttle-valve. **3** the windpipe, the gullet, the throat. ~*v.t.* **1** to choke, to strangle. **2** to use a throttle-lever to control (an engine). **to throttle back** to reduce the speed of an engine by controlling the throttle. **to throttle down** to throttle back. **throttle-lever** *n.* a pedal, lever etc. operating a throttle-valve. **throttler** *n.* **throttle-valve** *n.* a valve to shut off, reduce or control the flow of steam in a steam engine or of explosive mixture to an internal-combustion engine.

through (throo), **thro'**, (*N Am.*) **thru** *prep.* **1** from end to end of, from side to side of, between the sides or walls of. **2** over the whole extent of, in the midst of, throughout. **3** by means, agency or fault of, on account of. **4** (*N Am.*) up to and including (*Monday through Friday*). ~*adv.* **1** from end to end or side to side, from beginning to end. **2** to a final (successful) issue. **3** completely. ~*a.* **1** going through or to the end, proceeding right to

the end or destination, esp. (of travel tickets etc.) involving several legs of a journey. **2** direct. **through and through 1** completely, in every way. **2** searchingly. **3** through again and again. **to be through** (*coll.*) to have finished. **throughout** *adv.* right through, in every part, from beginning to end. ~*prep.* right through, from beginning to end of. **throughput** *n.* (*esp. Comput.*) the amount of raw material put through or processed in e.g. a factory, computer.

Usage note The spellings of *through* and *threw*, the past tense of *throw*, should not be confused.

throve THRIVE.

throw (thrō) *v.t.* (*past* **threw** (throo), *p.p.* **thrown** (thrōn)) **1** to fling, to hurl, to cast, esp. to a distance with some force. **2** to cast down, to cause to fall, to prostrate. **3** to drive, to impel, to dash. **4** to make (a cast) with dice; to score with a cast of a dice. **5** to put on (clothes etc.) hastily or carelessly. **6** to twist, to wind into threads. **7** to shape on a potter's wheel. **8** to move so as to operate (a lever etc.). **9** (*coll.*) to hold (a party). **10** (*coll.*) to puzzle or astonish. **11** (*sl.*) to lose (a contest) deliberately. **12** in cricket, to bowl illegally with a straightening of the arm. **13** to unseat (a rider). ~*v.i.* **1** to hurl or fling a missile (at etc.). **2** to cast dice. ~*n.* **1** the act of throwing. **2** a cast of the dice. **3** the distance to which a missile is thrown. **4** (*N Am.*) a throw rug. **to be thrown back on** to be forced to resort to or rely on. **to throw about 1** to throw carelessly in various directions. **2** to spend (money) recklessly or ostentatiously. **to throw around** to throw about. **to throw away 1** to cast from one, to discard. **2** to reject carelessly. **3** to spend recklessly, to squander. **4** to lose through carelessness or neglect. **5** to fail to take advantage of. **6** to say in a deliberately unemphatic way. **to throw back 1** to reflect, as light etc. **2** to revert (to ancestral traits). **to throw good money after bad** to waste further money in a futile attempt to rectify a bad situation that has already cost money. **to throw in 1** to interject, to interpolate. **2** to put in without extra charge, to add as a contribution or extra. **3** in soccer, to restart play by throwing the ball two-handed from the place at which it went out. **4** in cricket etc., to throw (the ball) from the outfield. **to throw off 1** to cast off, to get rid of, to abandon, to discard. **2** to produce without effort. **3** to evade (pursuit). **to throw oneself at** to make a determined and blatant attempt to make (someone) become a sexual partner or spouse. **to throw oneself into** to take up (an activity) with enthusiasm and energy. **to throw oneself on/ upon** to commit oneself to the protection, favour etc. of. **to throw one's hand in 1** to stop participating in a particular hand of a gambling card game. **2** to give up a job etc. as hopeless. **to throw open 1** to open suddenly and completely. **2** to make freely accessible. **3** to open (a discussion etc.) to the audience. **to throw out 1** to cast out, to reject. **2** to expel. **3** to emit. **4** to give utterance to, to suggest. **5** to discomfit so as to lose the thread of argument etc. **to throw over** to abandon, to desert. **to throw stones** to criticize, to cast aspersions. **to throw together 1** to put together hurriedly or carelessly. **2** to bring into casual contact. **to throw up 1** to raise, erect or lift quickly. **2** to abandon, to resign from. **3** (*coll.*) to vomit. **4** to draw attention to. **throwable** *a.* **throwaway** *a.* **1** disposable. **2** (of something written or said) deliberately casual (*a throwaway line*). ~*n.* a disposable item. **throwback** *n.* a reversion to an earlier type. **thrower** *n.* **throw-in** *n.* in soccer, an act of throwing in the ball back in play from touch to restart play. **throw-over** *a.* able to be thrown over a bed, sofa etc. as a decorative cover. **throw rug** *n.* (*N Am.*) a rug or decorative cloth put over a piece of furniture. **throwster** (-stə) *n.* a person who throws silk.

Usage note See notes under THROE, THROUGH.

thru THROUGH.

thrum[1] (thrŭm) *v.i.* (*pres.p.* **thrumming**, *past, p.p.* **thrummed**) **1** to play carelessly or unskilfully (on a stringed instrument). **2** to tap, to drum monotonously (on a table etc.). ~*v.t.* **1** to play (an instrument) in this way. **2** to tap or drum on. ~*n.* the act or sound of such drumming or playing.

thrum[2] (thrŭm) *n.* **1** the fringe of warp threads left when the web has been cut off, or one of such threads. **2** a loose thread, fringe etc., a tassel. ~*v.t.* (*pres.p.* **thrumming**, *past, p.p.* **thrummed**) to cover or trim with thrums.

thrush[1] (thrŭsh) *n.* a bird of the family Turdidae, esp. the song thrush, *Turdus philomelos* or mistle thrush, *T. viscivorus.*

thrush[2] (thrŭsh) *n.* **1** a disease of the mouth and throat, usu. affecting children, caused by the fungus *Candida albicans* and resulting in white patches. **2** a similar infection of the vagina, caused by the same fungus.

thrust (thrŭst) *v.t.* (*past, p.p.* **thrust**) **1** to push suddenly or forcibly. **2** to stab. **3** to impose forcibly (on). **4** to force (one's way). ~*v.i.* **1** to make a sudden push or lunge (at), to stab (at). **2** to force or squeeze (in etc.). ~*n.* **1** a sudden or violent push or lunge. **2** an attack as with a pointed weapon, a stab. **3** a pointed remark. **4** force exerted by one body against another, esp. horizontal outward pressure, as of an arch against its abutments. **5** the forceful part, or gist, of an argument etc. **6** a strong attack or onslaught. **7** drive, determination. **to thrust oneself in 1** to intrude. **2** to interfere. **to thrust one's nose in** to interfere. **thruster** *n.* **1** a person who or thing which thrusts. **2** a small rocket engine used to correct altitude, course etc. on a spacecraft. **thrusting** *a.* aggressively ambitious.

thud (thŭd) *n.* a dull sound as of a blow on something soft. ~*v.i.* (*pres.p.* **thudding**, *past, p.p.* **thudded**) **1** to make a thud. **2** to fall with a thud. **thuddingly** *adv.*

thug (thŭg) *n.* **1** a violent or brutal ruffian. **2** (**Thug**) a member of a fraternity of religious assassins in India (suppressed 1828–35). **thuggery** *n.* **thuggish** *a.* **thuggishly** *adv.* **thuggishness** *n.*

thuja (thū´jə), **thuya** (-yə) *n.* any coniferous tree or shrub of the genus *Thuja*, also called *arbor vitae.*

thulium (thū´liəm) *n.* (*Chem.*) a rare silver-grey malleable metallic element, at. no. 69, chem. symbol Tm.

thumb (thŭm) *n.* **1** the short thick digit of the human hand. **2** the corresponding digit in animals. **3** the part of a glove which covers the thumb. ~*v.t.* **1** to turn (the pages of a book) with the thumb. **2** to soil or mark with the thumb. **to be all thumbs** to be clumsy and fumbling with one's hands. **to thumb a lift** to get a lift from a passing car by signalling with a raised thumb. **to thumb one's nose** to cock a snook. **under someone's thumb** completely under someone's power or influence. **thumbed** *a.* **thumb index** *n.* an index in a book in which the letters are printed on the fore-edge, spaces being cut away from preceding pages to expose them to sight. **thumb-indexed** *a.* **thumbless** *a.* **thumbmark** *n.* a mark made with a (dirty) thumb. **thumbnail** *n.* the nail of one's thumb. **thumbnail sketch** *n.* a brief, vivid description. **thumbprint** *n.* the impression left by the markings of a person's thumb. **thumbscrew** *n.* an instrument of torture for compressing the thumb. **thumbs down** *n.* an indication of failure or disapproval. **thumbs up** *n.* an indication of success or approval. **thumbtack** *n.* (*N Am.*) a drawing pin.

thump (thŭmp) *v.t.* **1** to strike with something giving a dull sound, esp. with the fist. **2** to hammer out (a tune) on a piano etc. ~*v.i.* **1** to beat, to knock, to hammer (on, at etc.). **2** to throb or pulsate violently. ~*n.* **1** a blow giving a dull sound. **2** the sound of this. **thumper** *n.* **1** a person who or thing which thumps. **2** (*coll.*) anything very large, excellent or remarkable. **thumping** *a.* (*coll.*) very large.

thunder (thŭn´də) *n.* **1** the sound following a flash of lightning, due to the disturbance of the air by the electric discharge. **2** a loud noise resembling atmospheric thunder. **3** a vehement denunciation or threat. ~*v.i.* **1** (*impers.*) to produce thunder. **2** to make the noise of thunder. **3** to make a loud noise. **4** to make loud denunciations etc. ~*v.t.* to emit or utter as with the sound of thunder. **thunderbolt** *n.* **1** an electric discharge with lightning and thunder. **2** an irresistible force, hero, a daring denunciation etc. **3** a supposed missile or mass of heated matter formerly believed to be discharged in a thunderbolt. **thunderclap, thundercrack, thunderpeal** *n.* **1** the noise of a single instance of thunder. **2** something alarming and unexpected. **thundercloud** *n.* a cloud from which lightning and thunder are produced. **thunderer** *n.*

thunderflash *n.* a blank shell, cartridge etc. which when fired makes a flash and a loud noise, used in military exercises. **thunderfly** *n.* (*pl.* **thunderflies**) a thrips. **thunderhead** *n.* an anvil-shaped cumulonimbus cloud indicative of thunder. **thundering** *a.* **1** producing thunder or a loud sound like thunder. **2** (*sl.*) extreme, remarkable, tremendous, out-and-out. **thunderingly** *adv.* **thunderless** *a.* **thunderous** *a.* **1** very loud. **2** angry, threatening. **thunderously** *adv.* **thunderousness** *n.* **thundershower, thunderstorm** *n.* a storm with thunder. **thunderstruck** *a.* **1** amazed, astounded. **2** struck by lightning. **thundery** *a.*

thunk (thŭngk) *n.* (*coll.*) a thud. ~*v.i.* to thud.

Thur. *abbr.* Thursday.

thurible (thū´ribəl) *n.* a censer. **thurifer** (-fə) *n.* an acolyte who carries a censer.

Thurs. *abbr.* Thursday.

Thursday (thoez´dā, -di) *n.* the fifth day of the week, following Wednesday. ~*adv.* (*coll.*) on Thursday. **Thursdays** *adv.* (*coll.*) on Thursday, every Thursday.

thus (dhŭs) *adv.* (*formal*) **1** in this manner. **2** in the way indicated or about to be indicated. **3** accordingly. **4** to this extent.

thuya THUJA.

thwack (thwak) *v.t.* to hit with a loud heavy blow, esp. with something flat. ~*n.* this blow or its sound.

thwart (thwawt) *v.t.* to cross, to frustrate. ~*n.* a transverse plank in a boat serving as seat for a rower.

†**thy** (dhī) *a.* of or relating to you (*thy goodness and mercy*). †**thyself** *pron.* **1** emphatic form of THOU[1]. **2** reflexive form of THEE.

thylacine (thī´ləsēn, -sīn, -sin) *n.* a carnivorous marsupial of Tasmania, *Thylacinus cynocephalus*, perhaps extinct.

thyme (tīm) *n.* any plant of the genus *Thymus*, esp. the garden thyme, *T. vulgaris*, a pungent aromatic herb used in cookery. **thymy** (-i) *a.*

Usage note The name of the plant should not be spelt *time*.

thymol (thī´mol) *n.* (*Chem.*) a phenol obtained from oil of thyme, used as an antiseptic.

thymus (thī´məs) *n.* (*pl.* **thymi** (-mī)) (*Anat.*) a gland situated in the lower region of the neck, usu. degenerating after puberty. **thymus gland** *n.*

thyroid (thī´roid) *n.* (*Anat.*) the thyroid gland. ~*a.* **1** shield-shaped. **2** of or connected with the thyroid gland or cartilages. **thyroid cartilage** *n.* (*Anat.*) a large cartilage in the larynx, the Adam's apple. **thyroid gland, thyroid body** *n.* a large ductless gland consisting of two lobes situated on each side of the larynx and the upper part of the windpipe, which regulates metabolism and hence growth and development. **thyroxine** (thīrok´sēn), **thyroxin** *n.* the main hormone produced by the thyroid gland, an amino acid containing iodine.

Ti *chem. symbol* titanium.

ti TE.

tiara (tiah´rə) *n.* **1** a jewelled coronet or headband worn as an ornament by women. **2** the triple crown worn by the Pope as a symbol of his temporal, spiritual, and purgatorial power.

Tibetan (tibet´ən) *a.* of or relating to the country of Tibet or its language. ~*n.* **1** a native or inhabitant of Tibet. **2** the language of Tibet.

tibia (tib´iə) *n.* (*pl.* **tibiae** (-biē), **tibias**) **1** (*Anat.*) the shin bone, the anterior and inner of the two bones of the leg. **2** (*Zool.*) the fourth joint of the leg in an insect. **tibial** *a.* **tibiotarsus** (-tah´səs) *n.* (*pl.* **tibiotarsi** (-sī)) (*Zool.*) in a bird, the bone that corresponds to the tibia.

tic (tik) *n.* a habitual convulsive twitching of muscles, esp. of the face.

tich TITCH.

tick[1] (tik) *v.i.* **1** to make a small regularly recurring sound like that of a watch or clock. **2** to function, to operate. ~*v.t.* to mark (off) with a tick. ~*n.* **1** the sound made by a going watch or clock. **2** (*coll.*) a moment. **3** a small mark used in checking items and indicating correctness. **in two ticks** (*coll.*) a very short time. **to tick off 1** to mark off (a series) by ticks. **2** (*coll.*) to reprimand, to tell off. **to tick over 1** (of an engine) to run slowly with gear disconnected. **2** to operate smoothly, at a low level of activity. **what makes a person tick** (*coll.*) a person's main motivation or interest. **ticker** *n.* (*coll.*) **1** the heart. **2** a watch. **3** (*N Am.*) a tape machine printing up-to-date information on Stock Exchange prices. **ticker tape** *n.* **1** the long strip of material from a ticker machine. **2** similar material thrown from city windows during a procession etc. **tickless** *a.* **tick-tack, tic-tac** *n.* a code of signalling employed by bookmakers at race meetings whereby their agents can keep them informed of the betting odds. **tick-tack-toe** *n.* (*N Am.*) noughts and crosses. **tick-tock** (-tok) *n.* the noise of a clock ticking.

tick[2] (tik) *n.* **1** any of various parasitic arachnids of the order Acarina, infesting some animals and occasionally humans. **2** any of various insects of the family Hippoboscidae, infesting sheep and birds.

tick[3] (tik) *n.* (*coll.*) credit, trust. **on tick** bought on credit, hire purchase etc.

tick[4] (tik) *n.* **1** a cover or case for the filling of mattresses and beds. **2** ticking. **ticking** *n.* the material for this, usu. strong striped cotton or linen cloth.

ticket (tik´it) *n.* **1** a card or paper with written or printed contents entitling the holder to admission to a concert etc., conveyance by train etc., or other privilege. **2** a tag or label giving the price etc. of a thing it is attached to. **3** a receipt for something to be collected later. **4** (*coll.*) a parking ticket. **5** (*coll.*) the correct thing. **6** (*coll.*) a certificate of discharge from the Army. **7** (*Naut.*) a master's certificate. **8** (*coll.*) a pilot's certificate. **9** (*NAm.*) **a** the list of candidates put up by a party. **b** the principles or programme of a party. *~v.t.* (*3rd pers. sing. pres.* **tickets**, *pres.p.* **ticketing**, *past, p.p.* **ticketed**) to put a ticket on. **(just) the ticket** (*coll.*) the right, desirable or appropriate thing. **ticket collector** *n.* a person employed to collect tickets from rail passengers etc. **ticketed** *a.* **ticket-holder** *n.* a person with a valid ticket for a match, concert, journey etc. **ticketless** *a.* **ticket office** *n.* an office where tickets for travel, entertainment etc. are sold. **ticket tout** *n.* a person who offers scarce tickets for unauthorized resale at inflated prices, esp. outside the venue concerned.

tickle (tik´əl) *v.t.* **1** to touch lightly so as to cause a thrilling sensation usually producing laughter. **2** to please, to gratify, to amuse. **3** to rub (a trout etc.) so that it backs into the hand and can be caught. *~v.i.* **1** to feel the sensation of tickling. **2** to produce the sensation of tickling. *~n.* the act or sensation of tickling. *~a.* (*coll.*) ticklish, uncertain. **tickled pink, tickled to death** *a.* (*coll.*) very amused, very pleased. **tickler** *n.* **ticklish** *a.* **1** sensitive to the feeling of tickling. **2** difficult, critical, precarious, needing tact or caution. **ticklishly** *adv.* **ticklishness** *n.*

tidal TIDE.

tidbit TITBIT.

tiddledywink TIDDLYWINK.

tiddler (tid´lə) *n.* (*coll.*) **1** a stickleback or other very small fish. **2** anything very small. **tiddly**[1] *a.* (*comp.* **tiddlier**, *superl.* **tiddliest**) very small or insignificant.

tiddly[1] TIDDLER.

tiddly[2] (tid´li) *a.* (*comp.* **tiddlier**, *superl.* **tiddliest**) (*coll.*) slightly drunk, drunk.

tiddlywink (tid´liwingk), (*NAm.*) **tiddledywink** (tid´əldi-) *n.* **1** a small counter or disc flicked into a cup or tray with another. **2** (*pl.*) the game involving flicking such counters.

tide (tīd) *n.* **1** the alternative rise and fall of the sea, due to the attraction of the sun and moon. **2** a rush of water, a flood, a torrent, a stream. **3** the course or tendency of events. **4** time, season, hour. *~v.i.* (*Naut.*) (of a ship) to work in or out of a river or harbour by the help of the tide. **to tide over** (to help) to surmount difficulties in a small way or temporarily. **tidal** *a.* **1** of or relating to the tides. **2** periodically rising and falling or ebbing and flowing, as the tides. **tidal bore** *n.* a large wave caused by water from a spring tide entering a constricted and shallower stretch of a river. **tidal flow** *n.* the regulated movement of traffic along the central lanes of a road in differing directions according to the time of the day. **tidally** *adv.* **tidal river** *n.* a river in which the tides act a long way inland. **tidal wave** *n.* **1** a large wave due to an earthquake etc. **2** a great movement of popular feeling. **tideless** *a.* **tideline** *n.* the farthest extent of the tide's ingress, often defined by a line of driftwood, seaweed etc. on the shore. **tidemark** *n.* **1** a line along a shore

showing the highest level of the tide. **2** (*coll.*) a dirty line round a bath indicating the level of the bath water. **3** (*coll.*) a line on the body showing the limit of washing. **tidewater** *n.* **1** water affected by the movement of the tide. **2** (*NAm.*) low-lying coastal land. **tideway** *n.* **1** the channel in which the tide runs. **2** the ebb or flow of the tide in this.

tidings (tī´dingz) *n.pl.* (*poet.*) news, intelligence, a report.

tidy (tī´di) *a.* (*comp.* **tidier**, *superl.* **tidiest**) **1** in good order, neat, trim. **2** (*coll.*) considerable, fairly large (*a tidy sum*). *~n.* (*pl.* **tidies**) **1** a receptacle for odds and ends. **2** an act of tidying a room etc. **3** (*NAm.*) an ornamental covering for a chair-back etc. *~v.t.* (*3rd pers. sing. pres.* **tidies**, *pres.p.* **tidying**, *past, p.p.* **tidied**) to make tidy, to put in order, to clear (up). **tidily** *adv.* **tidiness** *n.*

tie (tī) *v.t.* (*3rd pers. sing. pres.* **ties**, *pres.p.* **tying**, *past, p.p.* **tied**) **1** to fasten with a cord etc., to secure, to attach, to bind. **2** to arrange together and draw into a knot, bow etc. **3** to form (a knot, bow etc.) by securing cords etc. together. **4** to bind together, to unite. **5** to confine, to restrict, to bind (down etc.). **6** (*Mus.*) **a** to unite (notes) by a tie. **b** to perform as a single note. *~v.i.* to be exactly equal (with) in a score. *~n.* **1** something used to tie things together. **2** a necktie. **3** a bond, an obligation. **4** a beam or rod holding parts of a structure together. **5** (*Mus.*) a curved line placed over two or more notes to be played as one. **6** an equality of votes, score etc., among candidates, competitors etc. **7** a match between any pair of a number of players or teams. **to tie in 1** to agree or coordinate (with). **2** to be associated or linked (with). **to tie up 1** to fasten securely to a post etc. **2** to restrict, to bind by restrictive conditions. **3** to be compatible or coordinated (with). **4** to keep occupied to the exclusion of other activities. **5** to truss up. **6** to invest. **7** to bring to a close. **tie-back** *n.* a strip of fabric, cord etc. holding a curtain at the side of a window. **tie-beam** *n.* a horizontal beam connecting rafters. **tie-break, tie breaker** *n.* a contest to decide the winner after a tied game etc. **tie-clip** *n.* a clasp which holds a necktie against a shirt. **tied** *a.* **1** (of a public house) bound to obtain its supplies from one brewer etc. **2** (of a dwelling house) owned by an employer and rented to a current employee. **tie-dye, tie and dye** *n.* a method of dyeing in which parts of the fabric are knotted or tied tightly to avoid being coloured. *~v.t.* to dye by this process. **tie-in** *n.* **1** a connection. **2** something linked to something else, esp. a book to a film. **tiepin** *n.* a pin for holding a necktie in place. **tie-up** *n.* a link or connection.

tier (tiə) *n.* **1** a row, a rank, esp. one of several rows placed one above another. **2** (*Naut.*) a length of coiled cable; a place for this. **tiered** *a.*

tierce (tiəs) *n.* **1** in fencing, the third position for guard, parry or thrust. **2** the canonical office for the third hour.

tiercel (tiə´səl), **tercel** n. a male falcon.
tiercet TERCET.
tiff (tif) n. a slight quarrel.
tiffin (tif´in) n. (*Hist.*) a lunch or light repast between breakfast and dinner, formerly taken by the British in India.
tig (tig) v.t. (*pres.p.* **tigging**, *past*, *p.p.* **tigged**) to touch in the game of tag. ~n. the children's game of tag.
tiger (tī´gə) n. **1** a large Asian carnivorous feline mammal, *Panthera tigris*, tawny with black stripes. **2** a fierce, relentless, very energetic and forceful or cruel person. **tiger-cat** n. a wild cat of various species. **tigerish** a. **tiger lily** n. a lily, *Lilium tigrinum*, with orange-spotted flowers. **tiger moth** n. any moth of the family Arctiidae, with streaked hairy wings. **tiger shark** n. a striped or spotted shark, esp. *Galeocerdo cuvieri* or *Stegosoma tigrinum*. **tigress** (-gris) n. **1** a female tiger. **2** a fierce or forceful woman.
tight (tīt) a. (*comp.* **tighter**, *superl.* **tightest**) **1** drawn, fastened, held, or fitting closely. **2** compactly built or put together. **3** impervious, not leaky, impermeable (*often in comb.* as *watertight*). **4** tense, stretched to the full, taut. **5** involving great pressure. **6** (*coll.*) mean, parsimonious, tight-fisted. **7** under strict control. **8** demanding effort, stringent. **9** (of money etc.) not easily obtainable. **10** (*coll.*) awkward, difficult. **11** (*sl.*) drunk. **12** limited, restricted. **13** close, even. **14** concise, succinct. ~adv. tightly. **tight corner, tight spot, tight place** n. a difficult situation with little scope for manoeuvre. **tighten** v.t., v.i. **tight end** n. in American football, a player positioned at the outside of the offensive line, close to the tackle. **tight-fisted** a. mean, stingy. **tight-fitting** a. (of a garment) fitting close or too close to the body. **tight-knit**, **tightly-knit** a. tightly integrated or organized. **tight-lipped** a. **1** having the lips pressed tightly together, in anger etc. **2** taciturn. **tightly** adv. **tightness** n. **tightrope** n. a rope stretched between two points upon which an acrobat walks, dances etc. **tights** n.pl. a close-fitting garment of nylon or wool etc. covering the legs and the body below the waist and worn by women, male acrobats, ballet dancers etc., also called *pair of tights*.
tike TYKE.
tikka (tik´ə, tē´-) n. an Indian dish of kebabs (esp. chicken or lamb) marinated in spices and dry-roasted in a clay oven.
tilapia (tilā´piə, -lap´-) n. any freshwater mouthbrooding fish of the African genus *Tilapia* or related genera.
tilde (til´də, tild) n. a diacritical sign (~) in Spanish put over *n* to indicate the sound *ny* as in *señor*, in Portuguese and phonetics put over vowels to indicate nasalization.
tile (tīl) n. **1** a thin slab of baked clay, used for covering roofs, paving floors, constructing drains etc. **2** a similar slab of porcelain or other material used for ornamental paving. **3** a rectangular

block used in playing games, esp. mah-jong, and Scrabble. ~v.t. to cover with tiles. **on the tiles** (*coll.*) enjoying oneself wildly, usu. drunkenly. **tiler** n. **tiling** n. an area of tiles.
till[1] (til) *prep.* up to, up to the time of, until. ~*conj.* up to the time when.

Usage note See note under UNTIL.

---

till[2] (til) n. **1** a money drawer in or on a counter. **2** a cash register.
till[3] (til) v.t. to cultivate for crops. **tillable** a. **tillage** (-ij) n. **1** the cultivation of land for crops. **2** tilled land. **tiller**[1] n.
tiller[1] TILL[3].
tiller[2] (til´ə) n. the lever on the head of a rudder by which this is turned.
tilt (tilt) v.i. **1** to heel over, to tip, to be in a slanting position. **2** to charge with a lance, to joust, as in a tournament. **3** to compete (with). ~v.t. **1** to raise at one end, to cause to heel over, to tip, to incline. **2** to thrust or aim (a lance). ~n. **1** an inclination from the vertical, a slanting position. **2** a tilting, a tournament, a charge with the lance. **3** an attack on an opponent, a jibe. **at full tilt** at full speed or force. **tilter** n.
tilth (tilth) n. **1** tillage, cultivation. **2** the depth or condition of soil tilled.
timbale (tambahl´) n. a dish of meat or fish pounded and mixed with white of egg, cream etc., and cooked in a drum-shaped mould.
timber (tim´bə) n. **1** wood suitable for building, carpentry etc. **2** trees yielding wood suitable for constructive purposes, trees generally. **3** a piece of wood prepared for building, esp. one of the curved pieces forming the ribs of a ship. ~v.t. to provide or construct with timber. ~*int.* used as a warning shout that a tree is about to fall. **timbered** a. **1** (of a building) made of or containing timber. **2** (of countryside) wooded (*usu. in comb.*, as *well-timbered*). **timberland** n. (*N Am.*) a forested area yielding timber. **timberline** n. the line or level on a mountain above which no trees grow, the tree line. **timber wolf** n. (*pl.* **timber wolves**) a grey-coloured type of wolf once common in N America. **timberyard** n. a yard where timber is stored etc.
timbre (tam´bə) n. the quality of tone distinguishing particular voices, instruments etc., due to the individual character of the sound waves.
time (tīm) n. **1** the general relation of sequence or continuous or successive existence. **2** duration or continuous existence regarded as divisible into portions or periods, a particular portion of this. **3** (*sometimes in pl.*) a period characterized by certain events, persons, manners etc., an epoch, an era. **4** a portion of time allotted to a specified purpose. **5** the time available at one's disposal. **6** a portion of time allotted to one. **7** the end of an allotted portion of time, as of legal drinking hours. **8** the period of an apprenticeship, of gestation, of a round at boxing etc. **9** a portion of time as characterized by circum-

stances, conditions of existence etc. **10** a point in time, a particular moment, instant or hour. **11** a date, a season, an occasion, an opportunity. **12** time as reckoned by conventional standards, as sidereal time, solar time etc. **13** the relative duration of a note or rest. **14** rate of movement, tempo. **15** style of movement, rhythm. **16** (*sl.*) a term of imprisonment. *~v.t.* **1** to ascertain or mark the time, duration or rate of. **2** to adapt to the time or occasion. **3** to do, begin or perform at the proper season. **4** to regulate as to time. **5** to measure, as in music. **6** to arrange the time of, to schedule. *~v.i.* to keep time (with). **against time** in a great hurry, at utmost speed in order to achieve a goal by a specified time, to a deadline. **ahead of one's time** having progressive or revolutionary ideas that it is thought would be more generally acceptable at a future time. **ahead of time** earlier than anticipated. **all the time 1** continuously. **2** throughout a given period of time. **3** at all times. **at a time** separately at any one time (referring to a specified group or number) (*two at a time*). **at one time 1** once, in the past (referring to an unspecified time). **2** simultaneously. **at times** at intervals, now and then. **before one's time** prematurely. **for the time being** for the present. **in less than no time** very quickly. **in no time** very quickly. **in one's own good time** at a pace and time decided by oneself. **in one's own time** outside working hours. **in one's time 1** in one's prime, in one's heyday. **2** in a previous period of one's life. **in time 1** not too late, early enough. **2** in the course of time, some time or other, eventually. **3** in accordance with the time, rhythm etc. **not before time 1** at the appropriate moment. **2** later than the appropriate moment (*You're here, and not before time!*). **no time** a very short space of time. **on time** punctually. **out of time 1** unseasonable. **2** too late. **3** not keeping rhythm correctly. **time after time** repeatedly. **time and again** repeatedly. **time and a half** payment at one and a half times the normal rate, usu. for working overtime, weekends etc. **time and time again** repeatedly. **time enough** soon enough. **time was** (*coll.*) there was once a time (*Time was when you could buy a loaf for a halfpenny*). **to have no time for 1** to dislike. **2** to be unwilling or unable to spend time on (something). **to have the time 1** to be able to spend the required time. **2** to know what the time is. **to keep bad time 1** to be habitually unpunctual. **2** (of a clock etc.) to be unreliable. **to keep good time 1** to be habitually punctual. **2** (of a clock etc.) to be reliable. **to keep time** to move, sing etc. in time with something else, esp. music. **to know the time of day** to know what is going on, to be well informed. **to lose no time** to act immediately. **to lose time 1** to delay or be delayed. **2** (of a watch) to go more slowly than required. **to pass the time of day** to greet each other, to exchange casual remarks. **to take one's time** to proceed steadily and without hurry.

time-and-motion *a.* relating to the investigation of working methods with a view to increasing efficiency. **time bomb** *n.* a bomb set to explode at some prearranged time. **time capsule** *n.* a box containing objects typical of the period in which it was prepared, hidden, e.g. within a memorial, for later generations to examine. **time clock** *n.* **1** a clock that records the hours of workers' arrival and departure. **2** a switch activated at pre-set times by a built-in clock. **time-consuming** *a.* (of an activity) occupying a considerable amount of one's time. **time exposure** *n.* (a photograph taken by) exposure of a film for a relatively long time. **time factor** *n.* time as an element in scheduling a task etc. **time-frame** *n.* a limited period of time, e.g. as allotted for a planned activity. **time-fuse** *n.* a fuse in a bomb etc., graduated to ignite the charge at a certain time. **time-honoured**, (*N Am.*) **time-honored** *a.* of venerable age. **time immemorial** *n.* time beyond legal memory, a very long time ago. **timekeeper** *n.* **1** a person who records time, e.g. of workers, races. **2** a clock, watch or chronometer. **3** a person considered in terms of punctuality (*a good timekeeper*). **timekeeping** *n.* **time lag** *n.* the interval that elapses between cause and result. **time-lapse photography** *n.* a method of filming a slow process by taking still photographs at regular intervals and showing them as a normal-speed film. **timeless** *a.* **1** without end, eternal, ageless. **2** not restricted to a particular period. **timelessly** *adv.* **timelessness** *n.* **time limit** *n.* the period within which a task must be completed. **time lock** *n.* a security device by which safes, computer programs etc. can only be operated at certain times. **time-locked** *a.* **timely** *a.* (*comp.* **timelier**, *superl.* **timeliest**) opportune, occurring at the right time. **timeliness** *n.* **time of day 1** the hour by the clock. **2** a greeting appropriate to this. **time off** *n.* time away from work, for rest, recreation etc. **time-out** *n.* **1** (*N Am.*) a short break in a game such as basketball. **2** time off. **time out of mind** *n.* a longer time than anyone can remember. *~adv.* many times. **timepiece** *n.* a clock or watch. **timer** *n.* **1** an instrument which measures or records time. **2** an instrument which operates a machine etc., at a pre-set time. **times** *prep.* multiplied by. **timescale** *n.* the time period in which something is expected or scheduled to happen expressed in broad terms. **time-served** *a.* having completed a substantial period of occupational training, such as an apprenticeship. **time-server** *n.* a person who suits their conduct, opinions and manners to those in power. **time-serving** *a., n.* **time-sharing** *n.* **1** the purchase of the use of holiday accommodation for the same period every year. **2** simultaneous access to a computer by several users on different terminals. **timeshare** *n.* **1** a share in property under a time-sharing scheme. **2** this property. **time sheet** *n.* a sheet of paper on which hours of work are recorded. **time-shift** *n.* a rapid movement from one time to another. ~*v.t.* to move (something) in this way. **time signal** *n.* a signal issued by an observatory or broadcasting station to indicate the exact time. **time signature** *n.* (*Mus.*) an indication of time at the beginning of a piece of music. **time span** *n.* the amount of time taken up by an activity, historical period etc. **time switch** *n.* a switch with a built-in clock that operates at pre-set times. **timetable** *n.* **1** a printed list of the times of departure and arrival of trains etc. **2** a record of times of events, school lessons etc. ~*v.t.* **1** to put (an event etc.) on a timetable. **2** to arrange in a timetable. **time travel** *n.* (in stories, films etc.) travel through time. **time trial** *n.* a race (esp. cycling, motor sports) in which competitors are timed individually rather than racing together. **time warp** *n.* **1** (in science fiction) a hypothetical distortion of space and time in which people or objects from one age can be directly transferred to another. **2** a situation where people living in one period retain the dress, mannerisms, lifestyle etc. of a past period. **time-waster** *n.* a person who wastes their own or other people's time. **time-wasting** *n.* **1** the act of wasting time. **2** in sport, the deliberate slowing down of play in order to preserve the current score. **timeworn** *a.* antiquated, dilapidated. **time zone** *n.* a geographical region in which the same standard time is used. **timing** *n.* **1** reckoning the time taken. **2** the choosing of the best time (to do something). **3** the precise instant at which ignition occurs in an internal-combustion engine, and at which the valves open and close.

timid (tim´id) *a.* (*comp.* **timider**, *superl.* **timidest**) easily frightened, shy. **timidity** (-id´-), **timidness** *n.* **timidly** *adv.*

timorous (tim´ərəs) *a.* fearful, timid. **timorously** *adv.* **timorousness** *n.*

timpani (tim´pəni), **tympani** *n.pl.* (*Mus.*) orchestral kettledrums. **timpanist** *n.*

tin (tin) *n.* **1** (*Chem.*) a lustrous white metallic element, at. no. 50, chem. symbol Sn, easily beaten into thin plates, much used for cooking utensils etc., esp. in the form of thin plates of iron coated with tin. **2** a tin can. **3** a pot or other utensil made of tin. ~*v.t.* (*pres.p.* **tinning**, *past*, *p.p.* **tinned**) **1** to preserve (meat, fruit etc.) in tins. **2** to coat or overlay with tin. **tin can** *n.* a tin plate container that can be hermetically sealed to preserve food or drink. **tinfoil** *n.* tin, tin alloy or aluminium beaten into foil for wrapping foodstuffs etc. **tin-glaze** *n.* a glaze for pottery etc. made white and opaque by the addition of tin oxide. **tin god** *n.* **1** a person of local, undeserved importance. **2** a self-important person. **tin hat** *n.* a steel shrapnel helmet. **tinny** *a.* (*comp.* **tinnier**, *superl.* **tinniest**) **1** of or like tin. **2** making a thin, metallic sound. **3** cheap, made of flimsy materials. **tinnily** *adv.* **tinniness** *n.* **tinny, tinnie** *n.* (*pl.* **tinnies**) (*Austral., sl.*) a can of beer. **tin-opener** *n.* an implement for opening airtight tins of preserved meat, fruit etc. **tin plate** *n.* sheet

iron or sheet steel coated with tin. **tin-plate** *v.t.* to coat with tin. **tinpot** *a.* worthless, rubbishy. **tinsmith** *n.* a person who makes articles of tin or tin plate. **tinsnips** *n.pl.* hand-held cutters for cutting sheet tin. **tin soldier** *n.* **1** a toy soldier made of tin or other metal. **2** (*often derog.*) a person who enjoys playing at being a soldier. **tintack** *n.* a tack coated with tin. **tin whistle** *n.* a penny whistle.

tincture (tingk´chə) *n.* **1** a slight taste or flavour, a spice (of). **2** a tinge or shade (of colour), a tint. **3** an alcoholic or other solution of some principle, usu. vegetable, used in medicine. **4** (*Her.*) any one of the colours, metals or furs used in emblazoning. ~*v.t.* **1** to imbue with a colour or tint, to tinge. **2** to flavour. **3** to give a flavour or tinge (of some quality etc.).

tinder (tin´də) *n.* any dry, very combustible substance used to kindle fire from a spark. **tinderbox** *n.* (*Hist.*) a box furnished with tinder, flint and steel, for this purpose. **tindery** *a.*

tine (tīn) *n.* the prong, point or spike of an antler, fork, harrow etc. **tined** *a.*

ting (ting) *n.* a tinkling sound, as of a small bell. ~*v.i.* to make this sound. ~*v.t.* to cause to make this sound. **ting-a-ling** (-əling´) *n.*

tinge (tinj) *v.t.* (*pres.p.* **tingeing, tinging**) **1** to colour slightly, to stain (with). **2** to modify the character or qualities of. ~*n.* **1** a slight admixture of colour, a tint. **2** a smack, flavour.

tingle (ting´gəl) *v.i.* **1** to feel a stinging, prickly sensation. **2** to give this sensation. ~*v.t.* to cause to tingle. ~*n.* a tingling sensation. **tingly** *a.* (*comp.* **tinglier**, *superl.* **tingliest**).

tinker (ting´kə) *n.* **1** an itinerant mender of pots, kettles, pans etc. **2** (*Sc., Ir.*) a gypsy. **3** the act of tinkering, patching, botching. ~*v.t.* **1** to mend, alter or patch up in a rough-and-ready way, or in a clumsy, makeshift or ineffective manner. **2** to mend pots, kettles etc. ~*v.i.* **1** to work in this way (at or with). **2** to interfere, to meddle. **3** to experiment (with). **tinkerer** *n.*

tinkle (ting´kəl) *v.i.* **1** to make a succession of sharp, metallic sounds as of a bell. **2** (*coll.*) to urinate. ~*v.t.* to cause to tinkle, to ring. ~*n.* **1** a tinkling sound. **2** (*coll.*) a telephone call. **3** (*coll.*) the act of urination. **tinkler** *n.* **tinkly** *a.*

tinnitus (tinī´təs, tin´ītəs) *n.* (*Med.*) ringing in the ears.

tinny TIN.

tinsel (tin´səl) *n.* **1** brass, tin or other lustrous metallic substances in extremely into thin sheets and used in strips, discs or spangles to give a sparkling effect in decoration. **2** superficial brilliance, gaudy display. ~*a.* gaudy, showy, superficially fine. ~*v.t.* (*pres.p.* **tinselling**, (*N Am.*) **tinseling**, *past, p.p.* **tinselled**, (*N Am.*) **tinseled**) to adorn with tinsel. **tinselled, tinselly** *a.*

tint (tint) *n.* **1** a variety of colour, esp. one produced by admixture with another colour, esp. white. **2** a slight tinge (of another colour). **3** a faint or pale colour spread over a surface. **4** a dye or wash. ~*v.t.* **1** to give a tint or tints to. **2** to tinge. **tinter** *n.*

tintinnabulation (tintinabūlā´shən) *n.* a ringing, tinkling or jingling of bells, plates etc.

tiny (tī´ni) *a.* (*comp.* **tinier,** *superl.* **tiniest**) very small. **tinily** *adv.* **tininess** *n.*

-tion (shən) *suf.* denoting action or condition, as in *mention, expectation, vacation.*

tip[1] (tip) *n.* **1** the point, end or extremity, esp. of a small or tapering thing. **2** a small piece or part attached to anything to form a point or end, such as a ferrule or the tip of a cue. **3** a leaf bud of tea. ~*v.t.* (*pres.p.* **tipping,** *past, p.p.* **tipped**) **1** to put a tip on. **2** to form the tip of. **on the tip of one's tongue** about to be uttered, esp. if difficult to recall. **tipless** *a.* **tip of the iceberg** *n.* the small and most obvious part of a difficulty, problem etc., that is much larger. **tipstaff** *n.* **1** a metal-tipped staff carried by a sheriff's officer. **2** a sheriff's officer. **tiptoe** *v.i.* (*3rd pers. sing. pres.* **tiptoes,** *pres.p.* **tiptoeing,** *past, p.p.* **tiptoed**) to walk or stand on tiptoe. ~*n.* the tips of the toes. **on tiptoe** on the tip of the toes. **tiptop** *a.* of extremely high quality. ~*n.* the highest point, the very best.

tip[2] (tip) *v.t.* (*pres.p.* **tipping,** *past, p.p.* **tipped**) **1** to cause to lean, to tilt (up, over etc.). **2** to overturn, to upset. **3** to discharge (the contents of a cart, vessel etc.) thus. **4** to strike lightly, to tap, to touch. **5** to give a small gratuity to. **6** to toss or throw lightly. **7** (*coll.*) to give private information to about a horse, an investment etc. ~*v.i.* **1** to lean over, to tilt. **2** to upset. ~*n.* **1** a small present in money, a gratuity. **2** a piece of private information, esp. for betting or investment purposes. **3** a place where rubbish is dumped. **4** a slight touch, push or hit. **5** a small piece of practical advice. **to tip off 1** to give a warning hint. **2** in basketball, to start play by throwing the ball high between players of the two sides. **to tip (someone) the wink** (*coll.*) to give a hint, to inform furtively. **tipcat** *n.* **1** a game with a piece of wood pointed at both ends which is hit with a stick. **2** the tapering piece of wood. **tip-off** *n.* a piece of confidential information, warning etc., esp. given discreetly and in advance of the events concerned. **tipper** *n.* **1** someone who or something which tips. **2** a lorry or truck whose platform can be tilted towards the rear to empty out the load. **tipster** (-stə) *n.* a person who supplies tips about races etc. **tip-up** *a.* (of a (theatre) seat) able to be tilted up on a hinge or pivot.

tipi TEPEE.

tippet (tip´it) *n.* **1** (*Hist.*) a fur covering for the neck and shoulders, worn by women. **2** an ecclesiastical vestment. **3** part of the official costume of judges etc.

Tipp-Ex® (tip´eks), **Tippex** *n.* a usu. white correction fluid. ~*v.t.* to blank out (typing, writing etc.) using correction fluid.

tipple (tip´əl) *v.i.* to drink alcoholic liquors habitually. ~*v.t.* **1** to drink (alcoholic liquors) habitually. **2** to sip repeatedly. ~*n.* **1** one's favourite (alcoholic) drink. **2** strong drink. **tippler** *n.*

tipsy (tip´si) *a.* (*comp.* **tipsier,** *superl.* **tipsiest**) **1** fuddled, partially intoxicated. **2** proceeding from or inducing intoxication. **tipsily** *adv.* **tipsiness** *n.*

tiptoe, tip-top TIP[1].

TIR *abbr.* international road transport.

tirade (tīrād´) *n.* a long, vehement speech, declamation, or harangue, esp. of censure or reproof.

tire[1] (tīə) *v.t.* **1** to exhaust the strength of by toil or labour, to fatigue, to weary. **2** to exhaust the patience or attention of. ~*v.i.* **1** to become weary or exhausted. **2** to become bored. **tired** *a.* **1** fatigued. **2** bored, impatient, irritated. **3** stale, hackneyed. **tiredly** *adv.* **tiredness** *n.* **tireless** *a.* unwearied, endlessly energetic. **tirelessly** *adv.* **tirelessness** *n.* **tiresome** *a.* **1** wearisome, tedious. **2** annoying. **tiresomely** *adv.* **tiresomeness** *n.* **tiring** *a.*

Usage note See note under TYRE.

---

tire[2] (tīə) *n.* **1** a band of iron, steel etc., placed round the rim of a wheel. **2** see TYRE.

tiro TYRO.

†'tis (tiz) *contr.* it is.

tisane (tizan´), **ptisan** *n.* **1** a herbal tea. **2** a medicinal infusion of dried leaves or flowers, orig. made with barley.

tissue (tish´oo) *n.* **1** a fabric of cells and their products, forming the elementary substance of plant and animal organs. **2** a paper handkerchief. **3** tissue paper. **4** a fabrication, a connected series (of lies, accidents etc.). **5** any fine, gauzy or transparent woven fabric. **tissue paper** *n.* a thin, gauzy, unsized paper, used for wrapping articles, protecting engravings etc.

tit[1] (tit) *n.* any small songbird, esp. of the family Paridae and esp. of the genus *Parus*, e.g. the blue tit, great tit, a titmouse.

tit[2] (tit) *n.* **1** (*taboo sl.*) a woman's breast. **2** a teat or nipple. **titty** *n.* (*pl.* **titties**) **1** (*sl. or facet.*) a woman's breast. **2** a teat or nipple (used by or to children).

tit[3] (tit) *n.* (*taboo sl.*) an unpleasant or contemptible person.

tit[4] (tit) *n.* a tap, a slight blow. **tit for tat** blow for blow, retaliation in kind.

titan (tī´tən) *n.* a person of superhuman strength or genius. ~*a.* titanic. **titanic** (-tan´-) *a.* huge, colossal. **titanically** *adv.*

titanium (titā´niəm, tī-) *n.* (*Chem.*) a dark-grey metallic element, at. no. 22, chem. symbol Ti, found in small quantities in various minerals.

titbit (tit´bit), (*N Am.*) **tidbit** (tid´-) *n.* **1** a delicate or dainty morsel of food. **2** an interesting piece of gossip.

titch (tich), **tich** *n.* (*coll.*) **1** a very small person. **2** a very small amount. **titchy** *a.* (*comp.* **titchier,** *superl.* **titchiest**).

tithe (tīdh) *n.* **1** (*Hist.*) a tax of one-tenth, esp. of the yearly proceeds from land and personal industry, payable for the support of the clergy and Church. **2** the tenth part of anything. ~*v.t.* to impose tithes upon. **tithable** *a.* **tithe barn** *n.* a barn in which the corn and other tithes of a parish were formerly stored.

Titian (tish′ən) *a.* (of hair) reddish-brown in colour.

titillate (tit′ilāt) *v.t.* **1** to excite or stimulate pleasurably. **2** to tickle. **titillating** *a.* **titillatingly** *adv.* **titillation** (-ā′shən) *n.*

Usage note The verbs *titillate* and *titivate* should not be confused: *titillate* means to excite pleasantly, and *titivate* to dress up or smarten.

titivate (tit′ivāt), **tittivate** *v.t.*, *v.i.* to dress up, to adorn, to make smart. **titivation** (-ā′shən) *n.*

Usage note See note under TITILLATE.

title (tī′təl) *n.* **1** an inscription serving as a name or designation, esp. of a book, chapter, poem etc. **2** a personal appellation denoting office, nobility, distinction, or other qualification. **3** (*Law*) the right to ownership of property. **4** the legal evidence of this, a title deed. **5** an acknowledged claim, the grounds of this. **6** a book or publication. **7** (*often pl.*) a credit or caption in a film, broadcast etc. **8** in a sport, a championship. **9** the distinguishing formula at the head of a legal document, statute etc. ~*v.t.* to give a title to. **titled** *a.* bearing a title of nobility. **title deed** *n.* a legal instrument giving the evidence of a person's right to property. **titleless** *a.* **title-page** *n.* the page at the beginning of a book giving the subject, author's name etc. **title role** *n.* the character or part from whose name the title of a play is taken.

titmouse (tit′mows) *n.* (*pl.* **titmice** (-mīs)) the small insectivorous songbird, the tit.

titrate (tī′trāt) *v.t.* (*Chem.*) to determine the amount of a particular constituent in (a solution) by adding a known quantity of another chemical capable of reacting with it. **titratable** *a.* **titration** (-rā′shən) *n.*

titter (tit′ə) *v.i.* to laugh in a restrained manner, to snigger, to giggle. ~*n.* a restrained laugh. **titterer** *n.* **titteringly** *adv.*

tittivate TITIVATE.

tittle (tit′əl) *n.* a particle, an iota.

tittle-tattle (tit′əltatəl) *n.* gossip. ~*v.i.* to gossip.

tittup (tit′əp) *v.i.* (*pres.p.* **tittuping, tittupping,** *past, p.p.* **tittuped, tittupped**) (*coll.*) to go, act or behave in a lively manner, to prance, to frisk. ~*n.* a tittuping action or movement.

titty TIT².

titular (tit′ūlə) *a.* **1** existing in name or in title only, or holding a title without the office or duties attached, nominal. **2** of, relating to or held in virtue of a title. **titularly** *adv.*

tizzy (tiz′i) **tizz, tiz** *n.* (*pl.* **tizzies, tizzes**) (*coll.*) a state of extreme agitation.

TKO *abbr.* technical knockout.

Tl *chem. symbol* thallium.

TLC *abbr.* (*coll.*) tender loving care.

TM *abbr.* **1** trademark. **2** Transcendental Meditation.

Tm *chem. symbol* thulium.

tn *abbr.* (*N Am.*) ton(s).

TNT *abbr.* trinitrotoluene (an explosive).

to (tu, tə, too) *prep.* **1** in a direction towards (a place, person, thing, state or quality). **2** as far as. **3** no less than, in comparison with, in respect of, in correspondence with. **4** concerning. **5** with the result of becoming. **6** against, adjoining. **7** before. **8** accompanied by (music). **9** preceding the indirect object or the person or thing affected by the action etc. **10** the sign of the infinitive, expressing futurity, purpose, consequence etc., limiting the meaning of adjectives, or forming verbal nouns. **11** (*ellipt.*) denoting the infinitive of a verb mentioned or understood. **12** as the cost of (in accounting). ~*adv.* **1** towards the condition or end required. **2** into the normal condition, esp. to a standstill or a state of adjustment. **-to-be** *a.* about to be (always after the noun, as *mother-to-be*). **to-do** (tədoo′) *n.* (*pl.* **to-dos**) (*coll.*) a fuss, a commotion. **toing and froing** *n.* (*pl.* **toings and froings**) bustle, constant movement back and forth, coming and going.

Usage note See note under TOO.

toad (tōd) *n.* **1** a tailless amphibian of the family Bufonidae, esp. of the genus *Bufo*, being like a frog, usu. with a warty body, terrestrial except during breeding. **2** a repulsive or detestable person. **toadflax** *n.* a perennial herb of the genus *Linaria*, usu. with yellow or bluish personate flowers. **toad-in-the-hole** *n.* sausages etc. baked in batter.

toadstool (tōd′stool) *n.* an umbrella-shaped fungus, esp. a poisonous mushroom.

toady (tō′di) *n.* (*pl.* **toadies**) an obsequious person, a sycophant. ~*v.t.* (*3rd pers. sing. pres.* **toadies,** *pres.p.* **toadying,** *past, p.p.* **toadied**) to fawn upon, to be obsequious to. **toadyish** *a.* **toadyism** *n.*

toast (tōst) *n.* **1** a slice of bread browned by radiant heat. **2** a drinking or a call for drinking to the health of some person, cause, sentiment etc. **3** the person or other object of this. **4** a celebrity (of a place), a person thought to be toasted often (*the toast of the town*). ~*v.t.* **1** to brown (bread), cook (bacon etc.) by radiant heat. **2** to warm (the feet etc.) at a fire. **3** to drink to the health or in honour of. ~*v.i.* to brown or warm at a fire etc. **toaster** *n.* an electrical apparatus for making toast. **toasting** *n.* **toasting-fork** *n.* a fork to hold bread etc., for toasting by a fire. **toastmaster, toastmistress** *n.* an official who announces the toasts at public dinners etc. **toastrack** *n.* a rack for holding slices of toast. **toasty** *a.* (*comp.* **toastier,** *superl.* **toastiest**) **1** warm and comfortable. **2** of or resembling toast. ~*n.* (*pl.* **toasties**) (*coll.*) a toasted sandwich.

tobacco (təbak´ō) *n.* (*pl.* **tobaccos**) **1** a plant of American origin of the genus *Nicotiana*, with narcotic leaves which are used, after drying and preparing, for smoking, chewing, snuff etc. **2** the leaves of this, esp. prepared for smoking. **tobacconist** *n.* a retailer of tobacco products. **tobacco pipe** *n.* a pipe used in smoking tobacco. **tobacco plant** *n.*

toboggan (təbog´ən) *n.* a long low sled used for sliding down snow or ice-covered slopes. ~*v.i.* to slide on a toboggan. **tobogganer, tobogganist** *n.* **tobogganing** *n.*

toby jug (tō´bi) *n.* a mug or jug shaped like an old man wearing a three-cornered hat.

toccata (təkah´tə) *n.* (*Mus.*) a keyboard composition orig. designed to exercise or display the player's touch.

tocopherol (tokof´ərol) *n.* any of a group of antioxidants thought to be required for healthy animal and human reproduction and found in wheatgerm, egg yolk etc.; vitamin E.

tocsin (tok´sin) *n.* an alarm bell, signal etc.

tod (tod) *n.* own: only as below. **on one's tod** (*sl.*) on one's own.

today (tədā´) *adv.* **1** on or during this or the present day. **2** at the present day, nowadays. ~*n.* **1** this day. **2** this present era. **today fortnight** on this day a fortnight hence, two weeks today. **today week** on this day next week, a week today.

toddle (tod´əl) *v.i.* **1** to walk with short unsteady steps, as a child does. **2** to walk in a careless or leisurely way, to saunter. ~*v.t.* to walk (a certain distance etc.) in this way. ~*n.* **1** a toddling walk. **2** a stroll. **toddler** *n.* (*coll.*) a toddling child. **toddlerhood** *n.*

toddy (tod´i) *n.* (*pl.* **toddies**) **1** a beverage of spirit and hot water sweetened. **2** the fermented juice of various palm trees.

to-do TO.

toe (tō) *n.* **1** any one of the five digits of the foot. **2** the part of a shoe, sock etc., covering the toes. **3** the fore-part of the hoof of a horse etc. **4** (*Archit.*) a projection from the foot of a buttress etc., to give it greater stability. **5** the lower end or a projecting part in a shaft, spindle, rod, lever, organ pipe etc. ~*v.t.* (*3rd pers. sing. pres.* **toes**, *pres.p.* **toeing**, *past, p.p.* **toed**) **1** to touch (a line, mark etc.) with the toes. **2** to furnish (socks, shoes etc.) with toes. **on one's toes** alert, ready to act. **to toe the line** to conform, to bow to discipline. **to turn up one's toes** (*sl.*) to die. **toecap** *n.* a stiffened part of a boot or shoe covering the toes. **toe clip** *n.* a clip on the pedal of a bicycle to prevent the foot from slipping. **toed** *a.* **toehold** *n.* **1** in climbing, a small foothold. **2** any slight or precarious means of access or progress. **toeless** *a.* **toenail** *n.* the nail at the end of each toe. **toe-rag** *n.* (*sl.*) a mean or despicable person.

toff (tof) *n.* (*sl.*) a swell, a dandy, a person of consequence.

toffee (tof´i), **toffy** *n.* (*pl.* **toffees, toffies**) **1** boiled sugar or molasses and butter made for sucking or chewing. **2** a sweet made of this. **for toffee** (*coll.*) at all (*He couldn't play for toffee*). **toffee apple** *n.* a toffee-coated apple on a stick. **toffee-nosed** *a.* (*sl.*) conceited, arrogant, snobbish.

tofu (tō´foo) *n.* unfermented soya bean curd.

tog¹ (tog) *v.t.* (*pres.p.* **togging**, *past, p.p.* **togged**) (*coll.*) to dress (up or out), esp. in one's best (*all togged up*). **togs** *n.pl.* clothes.

tog² (tog) *n.* a unit of measurement of the heat insulation of clothing, fabrics etc.

toga (tō´gə) *n.* a loose flowing robe, the principal outer garment of an ancient Roman citizen. **togaed** (-gəd), **toga'd** *a.*

together (təgedh´ə) *adv.* **1** in company or union, conjointly, unitedly. **2** at the same time. **3** into union, so as to unite or be joined. **4** without cessation or intermission. **5** in a well-organised way. ~*a.* (*coll.*) competent, assured, composed, well-organized. **together with** as well as, in addition to. **togetherness** *n.* a friendly feeling of being together as a group.

toggle (tog´əl) *n.* **1** a crosspiece for fastening a garment, securing a watch-chain etc. **2** a pin put through a loop or eye at the end of a rope for securing this. **3** (*Comput.*) a switch which is pressed in the same way to turn a feature both on and off. **toggle switch** *n.* **1** an electric switch with a projecting lever which is pushed, usu. up or down. **2** (*Comput.*) a toggle.

toil (toil) *v.i.* **1** to labour with pain and fatigue of body or mind. **2** to move or progress painfully or laboriously. ~*n.* hard and unremitting work, labour, drudgery. **toiler** *n.* **toilsome** *a.* **toilsomely** *adv.* **toilsomeness** *n.*

toile (twahl) *n.* **1** cloth, esp. for clothes. **2** a model of a garment made up in cheap cloth.

toilet (toi´lit) *n.* **1** a lavatory. **2** the act or process of washing oneself, dressing etc. ~*v.t.* (*pres.p.* **toileting**, *past, p.p.* **toileted**) to assist (a child, invalid etc.) to use the lavatory. **toilet paper** *n.* paper for wiping oneself after urination or defecation. **toilet roll** *n.* a roll of toilet paper. **toiletry** (-ri) *n.* (*pl.* **toiletries**) (*often pl.*) an article or preparation used in washing or beautifying oneself. **toilet set** *n.* a set of utensils for a dressing table. **toilet soap** *n.* a soap for personal washing. **toilette** (twahlet´) *n.* the process of washing, dressing etc. **toilet tissue** *n.* soft toilet paper. **toilet-training** *n.* training a child to use a lavatory correctly and at the appropriate time. **toilet-train** *v.t.* **toilet water** *n.* a form of perfume lighter than an essence.

toils (toilz) *n.pl.* a net or snare.

token (tō´kən) *n.* **1** something representing or recalling another thing, event etc. **2** a sign, a symbol. **3** an evidence, an indication, a symptom. **4** a memorial of love or friendship, a keepsake. **5** a metal or plastic disc used instead of a coin, e.g. in a slot machine. **6** a voucher that can be used as payment for goods to a certain value. **7** a sign proving authenticity. ~*a.* **1** serving as a token. **2** nominal, perfunctory, done, given, invited etc. for form's sake only (*a token gesture*). **by the same token** similarly, in corroboration. **tokenism** *n.* the practice of making only a token effort, esp. as a political gesture. **tokenistic** (-is´-) *a.* **tokenless** *a.* **token vote** *n.* a parliamentary vote of money in which the sum stipulated is not binding.

told TELL.

tolerate (tol´ərāt) *v.t.* **1** to suffer, to endure, to permit by not preventing or forbidding. **2** to abstain from judging harshly or condemning (persons, religions, votes, opinions etc.). **3** to sustain, to endure (pain, toil etc.). **4** to sustain (a drug etc.) with impunity. **tolerable** *a.* **1** endurable, supportable. **2** passable, fairly good. **tolerability** (-bil´-) *n.* **tolerableness** *n.* **tolerably** *adv.* **tolerance** *n.* **1** the act or state of toleration. **2** permissible variation in weight, dimension, fitting etc. **3** the ability to endure pain, toil etc. **4** permitting other people to say and do as they like. **tolerant** *a.* showing toleration. **tolerantly** *adv.* **toleration** (-ā´shən) *n.* **1** the act of tolerating. **2** the spirit of tolerance. **3** recognition of the right of private judgement in religious matters and of freedom to exercise any forms of worship. **tolerator** *n.*

toll[1] (tōl) *n.* **1** a tax or duty charged for some privilege, service etc., esp. for the use of a road, bridge, market etc. **2** damage, deaths etc., suffered in an accident, natural disaster etc. **3** (*N Am.*) the charge for a long-distance telephone call. **to take its toll** to have a damaging effect in terms of loss, injury, deterioration etc. **toll bridge** *n.* a bridge where a toll is charged for passing over it. **toll call** *n.* (*N Am.*) a long-distance telephone call. **toll gate, toll bar** *n.* a gate or bar placed across a road to stop passengers or vehicles till a toll is paid. **toll-house** *n.* (*Hist.*) the house at a toll gate occupied by a toll collector. **tollroad** *n.* a road on which a toll is charged.

toll[2] (tōl) *v.t.* **1** to cause (a bell) to sound with strokes slowly and uniformly repeated. **2** (of a bell, clock etc.) to give out (a knell etc.) with a slow, measured sound. **3** to ring on account of. ~*v.i.* (of a bell) to sound or ring with slow, regular strokes. ~*n.* a tolling or a stroke of a bell. **toller** *n.*

tolu (təloo´) *n.* a balsam derived from the S American trees *Myroxylon balsamum* and *M. toluifera.* **toluene** (tol´ūēn), **toluol** *n.* (*Chem.*) a liquid compound belonging to the aromatic series, methyl benzene, orig. obtained from tolu. **toluic** (tol´-) *a.*

tom (tom) *n.* a male animal, esp. a tom-cat. **tomboy** *n.* a girl who likes boys' activities. **tomboyish** *a.* **tomboyishness** *n.* **tom-cat** *n.* a male cat. **Tom, Dick and Harry** *n.* (*derog.*) average commonplace people, any taken at random. **tomfool** *n.* a ridiculous fool, a trifler. ~*a.* very foolish. **tomfoolery** *n.* (*pl.* **tomfooleries**). **Tom Thumb** *n.* **1** a very short man. **2** (*also* **tom thumb**) **a** a dwarf variety of a plant or vegetable. **b** a small wild flower. **tomtit** *n.* a small bird, a tit, esp. a blue tit.

tomahawk (tom´əhawk) *n.* **1** a N American Indian battleaxe or hatchet with a stone, horn or steel head. **2** (*Austral.*) a hatchet. ~*v.t.* to strike or kill with a tomahawk.

tomatillo (tomətil´yō, -til´ō) *n.* (*pl.* **tomatillos**) **1** a Mexican ground cherry, *Physalis philadelphica.* **2** the edible berry of this.

tomato (təmah´tō) *n.* (*pl.* **tomatoes**) **1** the red or yellow pulpy edible fruit (used as a vegetable) of a trailing plant, *Lycopersicon esculentum*, of the nightshade family or Solanaceae, orig. S American. **2** the plant itself. **tomatoey** *a.*

tomb (toom) *n.* **1** a grave. **2** a vault for the dead. **3** a sepulchral monument. ~*v.t.* to bury, to entomb. **the tomb** the state of death. **tombless** *a.* **tombstone** *n.* a stone placed as a memorial over a grave.

tombola (tombō´lə) *n.* an instant lottery at a fête etc.

tome (tōm) *n.* a volume, esp. a ponderous one.

-tome (tōm) *comb. form* **1** forming nouns denoting instruments for cutting. **2** forming nouns denoting a section or segment.

tommy (tom´i) *n.* (*pl.* **tommies**) (**Tommy**) a British private soldier (from *Tommy Atkins*, a name used on sample forms). **tommy bar** *n.* a short rod inserted to turn a box spanner. **tommy-gun** *n.* a short-barrelled sub-machine gun (from General J. T. Thompson, US soldier and inventor). **tommyrot** *n.* (*coll.*) nonsense.

tomography (təmog´rəfi) *n.* diagnostic radiography of plane sections of the human body. **tomogram** (tō´-, tom´-) *n.*

tomorrow (təmor´ō) *n.* **1** the next day after today. **2** the near future. ~*adv.* on, during or in this. **like there's no tomorrow** (*coll.*) recklessly, extravagantly. **tomorrow afternoon** (on) the afternoon of tomorrow. **tomorrow morning** (on) the morning of tomorrow. **tomorrow week** on the day a week later than tomorrow, a week tomorrow.

tom-tom (tom´tom) *n.* a long, narrow, handbeaten drum used in India, Africa etc.

-tomy (təmi) *comb. form* (*pl.* **-tomies**) forming nouns denoting cutting, esp. of the surgical type, as in *lobotomy, phlebotomy.*

ton (tŭn) *n.* **1** any of various measures of weight or volume, usu. large, as the long ton, short ton etc. **2** a measure of refrigeration, the power able to freeze 2,000 lb. (907.2 kg) of water at 0°C in 24 hours. **3** a measure of timber, 40 cu. ft. (1.132 cu. m). **4** an unspecified great weight. **5** (*usu. pl., coll.*) a large quantity. **6** (*sl.*) £100. **7** (*sl.*) 100 m.p.h. **to weigh a ton** to be heavy to lift, carry etc. **-tonner** *comb. form* a ship of a specified tonnage (*3,000-tonner*). **ton-up** *n.* 100 m.p.h. ~*a.* achieving this speed, esp. recklessly and on a regular basis (*ton-up kid*).

tonal (tō´nəl) *a.* **1** of or relating to tone or tonality. **2** having tonality. **3** (*Mus.*) (of a fugue etc.) repeating the subject in the same key but at different pitches. **tonality** (-nal´-) *n.* (*pl.* **tonalities**) **1**

(*Mus.*) the character or quality of a tone or tonal system. **2** a system of tones, a key. **3** adherence to a single tonic key. **4** in fine art, the general colour scheme of a picture. **tonally** *adv.*

tone (tōn) *n.* **1** sound, with reference to pitch, quality and volume. **2** modulation or inflection of the voice to express emotion etc. **3** general disposition, temper, mood, prevailing sentiment, spirit. **4** (*Mus.*) **a** a musical sound. **b** an interval of a major second. **5** an intonation distinguishing sounds otherwise similar. **6** degree of luminosity of a colour. **7** the general effect of a picture, esp. as regards colour and luminosity, the tint or shade of colour. **8** the shade or colour of a photographic print. **9** healthy general condition of the bodily organs, tissues etc. ~*v.t.* **1** to give tone or quality to. **2** to modify the tone of, to tune. **3** to modify the colour of (a photographic picture). ~*v.i.* **1** to attune (to). **2** to harmonize (with) in colour, tint etc. **to tone down 1** to subdue, to soften (the tint, tone, pitch, intensity etc. of). **2** to modify, to reduce, to soften (a statement, demands etc.). **3** to become softer, less emphatic etc. **to tone up 1** (of muscles etc.) to become firmer or more vigorous. **2** to heighten, to intensify. **tone arm** *n.* the pick-up arm of a record player. **tone control** *n.* a switch to vary the frequencies of sound from a radio, hi-fi unit etc. **tone-deaf** *a.* unable to distinguish accurately between musical sounds of different pitch. **tone-deafness** *n.* **tone language** *n.* a language such as Chinese in which variation of tone serves to distinguish between words otherwise pronounced in the same way. **toneless** *a.* **tonelessly** *adv.* **tone poem** *n.* an orchestral composition in one movement which illustrates a train of thought external to the music. **toner** *n.* **1** a black powder used in photocopiers, computer printers etc. **2** a lotion applied to the face to tighten the pores. **3** a person who or thing which tones. **4** a chemical used in photographic processing. **tone-row** *n.* the basic series of notes in serial music.

tongs (tongz) *n.pl.* an implement consisting of two limbs, usu. connected near one end by a pivot, used for grasping coals etc.; also called *pair of tongs*.

tongue (tŭng) *n.* **1** a fleshy muscular organ in the mouth, used in tasting, swallowing and (in humans) speech. **2** the tongue of an ox, sheep etc., as food. **3** a tongue-shaped thing or part. **4** the clapper of a bell. **5** the pin in a buckle. **6** a piece of leather closing the gap in the front of a laced shoe. **7** a projecting edge for fitting into a groove in wood. **8** a long low promontory, a long narrow inlet. **9** speech, utterance, the voice. **10** manner of speech. **11** a language. **to find one's tongue** to express oneself after a period of remaining silent. **to give tongue 1** to speak one's mind. **2** to bark esp. (of a hound) when in contact with the quarry. **to hold one's tongue** to keep quiet. **to keep a civil tongue in one's head** to remain polite. **to lose one's tongue** to become

silent. **with one's tongue hanging out** eagerly, with avid expectation. **with one's tongue in one's cheek** ironically. **tongue-and-groove** *n.* planking that fits together for floors, walling etc. with a projecting strip on one side and a corresponding groove on the other. **tongued** *a.* **tongue-in-cheek** *a.* said with irony, mischievously and drily humorous. ~*adv.* **1** ironically. **2** insincerely. **tongue-lashing** *n.* a severe scolding. **tongueless** *a.* **tongue-tie** *n.* shortness of fraenum impeding movement of the tongue. **tongue-tied** *a.* **1** afraid of or prevented from speaking freely. **2** impeded in speech by tongue-tie. **tongue-twister** *n.* a series of words difficult to articulate without stumbling. **tonguing** *n.* (*Mus.*) the technique of playing wind instruments, using the tongue to control the notes produced.

tonic (ton´ik) *n.* **1** a tonic medicine. **2** tonic water. **3** (*Mus.*) the keynote. **4** something that makes someone feel better, a boost. ~*a.* **1** invigorating, bracing. **2** of or relating to tones. **3** (*Mus.*) of, relating to or founded on the keynote. **tonically** *adv.* **tonicity** (-nis´-) *n.* **1** the state of being tonic. **2** tone. **3** elasticity or contractility of the muscles. **tonic sol-fa** *n.* (*Mus.*) a system of notation in which diatonic scales are written always in one way (the keynote being indicated), the tones being represented by syllables or initials, and time and accents by dashes and colons. **tonic spasm** *n.* (*Med.*) a continuous muscular spasm, as opposed to *clonus*. **tonic water** *n.* a carbonated drink flavoured with quinine, often used as a mixer with alcoholic drinks.

tonight (tənīt´) *n.* **1** the present night. **2** the night of today. ~*adv.* on or during this.

tonnage (tŭn´ij) *n.* **1** the carrying capacity or internal cubic capacity of a vessel expressed in tons. **2** the aggregate freightage of a number of vessels, esp. of a country's merchant navy. **3** a duty on ships, formerly assessed on tonnage, now on dimensions.

tonne (tŭn) *n.* the metric ton.

-tonner TON.

tonsil (ton´sil) *n.* (*Anat.*) either of two organs situated to the rear of the mouth on each side of the fauces. **tonsillar** *a.* **tonsillectomy** (-lek´təmi) *n.* (*pl.* **tonsillectomies**) surgical removal of the tonsils. **tonsillitis** (-lī´tis) *n.* inflammation of the tonsils. **tonsillitic** (-lit´-) *a.*

tonsorial (tonsaw´riəl) *a.* (*usu. facet.*) of or relating to a hairdresser or hairdressing.

tonsure (ton´shə) *n.* **1** the shaving of the crown (as in the Roman Catholic Church before 1972) or of the whole head (as in the Greek Church) on admission to the priesthood or a monastic order. **2** the part of the head shaved in this way. ~*v.t.* to shave the head of, to confer the tonsure on.

too (too) *adv.* **1** in excessive quantity, degree etc. **2** as well, also, in addition, at the same time. **3** moreover. **4** more than enough (*You are too kind!*). **5** (*coll.*) extremely, superlatively. **none too** hardly, not very, rather less than (*The* *weather was none too promising*). **too bad** (of circumstances etc.) beyond rectification, esp. in a dismissive sense (*It's too bad we didn't win the lottery*).

Usage note The spellings of the adverb *too*, the numeral *two*, and the preposition and adverb *to* should not be confused.

toodle-oo (toodəloo´) *int.* (*coll.*) goodbye.
took TAKE¹.
tool (tool) *n.* **1** a simple implement, esp. one used in manual work. **2** a machine used in the making of machines. **3** anything used as a means to an end (*a mathematical tool*). **4** (*taboo sl.*) the penis. **5** a person employed as an instrument or agent. **6** in bookbinding, a hand-stamp or design used in tooling. ~*v.t.* to impress designs on (a bookcover). ~*v.i.* **1** to work with a tool. **2** (*sl.*) to drive, to ride, esp. at a moderate speed (*tooling along*). **tooled-up** *a.* (*sl.*) carrying firearms. **tooler** *n.* **tooling** *n.* **1** the process of dressing stone with a chisel. **2** the process of decorating leather, book covers etc. with tools. **tool kit** *n.* **1** a set of tools. **2** (*Comput.*) a set of software utilities. **toolmaker** *n.* a worker who makes and repairs machine tools in a workshop etc. **toolmaking** *n.* **toolpusher** *n.* the supervisor of drilling at an oil rig or oil well. **tool shed** *n.* a shed in which tools are kept.
toot (toot) *v.i.* **1** to make a short sharp noise like that of a horn, whistle etc. **2** (of a horn, whistle etc.) to give out its characteristic sound. ~*v.t.* **1** to sound (a horn etc.). **2** to give out (a blast etc.) on a horn. ~*n.* **1** a tooting sound or blast. **2** (*N Am., sl.*) cocaine; a snort of this. **tooter** *n.*
tooth (tooth) *n.* (*pl.* **teeth** (tēth)) **1** any one of the hard dense structures, originating in the epidermis, growing in the mouth or pharynx of vertebrates, and used for mastication. **2** a false or artificial tooth made by a dentist. **3** a toothlike projection on the margin of a leaf etc. **4** a projecting pin, point, cog etc. **5** a discriminating taste, a palate. **6** (*pl.*) powers, esp. to compel compliance. ~*v.t.* **1** to furnish with teeth. **2** to indent. ~*v.i.* to interlock. **armed to the teeth** armed with every possible weapon. **in the teeth of 1** in spite of. **2** in direct opposition to. **3** in the face of (the wind). **long in the tooth** elderly, old (as in horses). **to fight tooth and nail** to fight with all one's power. **to get one's teeth into** to tackle (a task etc.) in a determined and satisfying manner. **to show one's teeth** to adopt a threatening attitude. **toothache** *n.* pain in the teeth. **tooth-billed** *a.* (*Zool.*) having toothlike processes on the bill. **toothbrush** *n.* a small brush for the teeth. **toothcomb** *n.* a fine-tooth comb. **toothed** *a.* **toothed whale** *n.* any whale of the suborder Odonticeti, having simple teeth, such as porpoises etc. **tooth-glass** *n.* a glass for holding dentures or for rinsing the mouth out after cleaning the teeth. **toothing** *n.* **1** fitting with teeth. **2** projecting stones or bricks left in the end of a wall for

bonding it to a continuation. **toothless** *a.* **toothlike** *a.* **toothpaste, tooth powder** *n.* paste or powder for cleaning the teeth. **toothpick** *n.* a pointed instrument of plastic, wood etc., for removing particles of food etc., from between the teeth. **toothsome** *a.* palatable, pleasing to the taste. **toothsomely** *adv.* **toothsomeness** *n.* **toothwort** *n.* a herb, *Lathraea squamaria*, allied to the broomrape, with toothlike scales on the rootstock. **toothy** *a.* (*comp.* **toothier**, *superl.* **toothiest**) having prominent teeth.
tootle (too´təl) *v.i.* **1** to toot gently or continuously, as on a flute. **2** (*coll.*) to amble, to trot.
tootsy (tut´si), **tootsie** *n.* (*pl.* **tootsies**) **1** a foot or toe (used by or to children). **2** (*N Am.*) a woman. **3** (*N Am.*) a female lover.
top¹ (top) *n.* **1** the highest part or point of anything, the summit. **2** the upper side or surface. **3** the upper part of a shoe etc. **4** the cover of a carriage etc. **5** (*N Am.*) the hood of a car. **6** the head of a page in a book. **7** the part of a plant above ground. **8** the crown of the head. **9** a garment for the upper body or the upper part of a two-piece garment. **10** something which covers or closes something, a lid. **11** the upper end or head of a table. **12** the highest position, place, rank etc. **13** the highest degree, the apex, the culmination, the height. **14** (*Naut.*) a platform round the head of a lower mast, forming an extended base for securing the topmast shrouds. ~*v.t.* (*pres.p.* **topping**, *past, p.p.* **topped**) **1** to rise to the top of, to surmount. **2** to excel, to surpass, to be higher than. **3** to remove the top or extremity of (a plant etc.). **4** to put a top or cap on. **5** to be (of a specified height). **6** to cover the top of. **7** (*Naut.*) to tip (a yard) so as to bring one end above the other. **8** (*sl.*) to execute by hanging. **9** in golf, to hit (a ball) above its centre, thus reducing the distance it travels. **10** to be at the head of. ~*a.* **1** being on or at the top or summit. **2** highest in position, degree etc. **3** maximum. **at the top (of the tree)** being the most successful, esp. in a particular field of achievement. **from top to toe** completely, from head to foot. **off the top of one's head** without preparation, impromptu. **on top 1** in the lead. **2** in control. **on top of 1** added to. **2** in control of. **on top of the world 1** very happy indeed, exuberant. **2** at the height of fame, achievement etc. **over the top 1** on the attack. **2** to excess. **the tops** someone or something that is absolutely the best in quality. **to come to the top** to achieve distinction. **to top off 1** to complete by putting the top or uppermost part to. **2** to finish, to complete. **to top oneself** (*sl.*) to commit suicide. **to top out** to put the last or highest girder etc. on (a building). **to top up** to fill up (with petrol, oil etc.). **top-boot** *n.* a boot having high tops, usu. of distinctive material and colour. **top brass** *n.* (*sl.*) the highest-ranking officials or officers. **topcoat** *n.* **1** an overcoat. **2** a final coat of paint. **top dog** *n.* (*coll.*) the uppermost person, the boss. **top-down** *a.* **1** hier-

archical, controlled from the top echelons of management. **2** going from the general to the particular. **top drawer** *n.* **1** the uppermost drawer in a chest of drawers. **2** the highest social background or status. **top-drawer** *a.* **top dress** *v.t.* to manure on the surface, as distinct from digging or ploughing in. **top dressing** *n.* **top-flight** *a.* of the highest rank or quality. **topgallant** (təgal'ənt, top-) *n., a.* (*Naut.*) (denoting) the mast, rigging and sail, next above the topmast. **top gear** *n.* the highest gear in a motor vehicle or on a bicycle. **top hat** *n.* a tall silk cylindrical hat. **top-heavy** *a.* having the top or upper part too heavy for the lower. **top-heaviness** *n.* **topknot** *n.* **1** an ornamental knot or bow worn on the top of the head. **2** a tuft or crest growing on the head. **topless** *a.* **1** without a top. **2** (of women's clothing) leaving the breasts bare. **3** (of an entertainment etc.) featuring women who are topless. **toplessness** *n.* **top-level** *a.* at the highest level, of the greatest importance, prestige etc. **top-line** *a.* of the highest quality or popular status (*top-line entertainers*). **topmast** *n.* (*Naut.*) the mast next above the lower mast. **topmost** *a.* **1** highest, uppermost. **2** leading, foremost. **top-notch** *a.* (*coll.*) first-rate, excellent. **top-notcher** *n.* **topper** *n.* **1** (*coll.*) a top hat. **2** a person who or thing which tops. **topping** *n.* something which forms a top layer, esp. a sauce for food. **topsail** (top'səl) *n.* (*Naut.*) **1** a square sail next above the lowest sail on a mast. **2** a fore-and-aft sail above the gaff. **top secret** *a.* requiring the highest level of secrecy. **topside** *n.* **1** a cut of beef from the thigh. **2** (*pl.*) the sides of a vessel above the waterline. **topsoil** *n.* the upper layer of soil. **topspin** *n.* in tennis etc., a forward spin imparted to the ball by hitting the top of the ball with the racket etc. angled forward and upward. **top-up** *n.* an additional amount of something that raises or returns it to the desired level. ~*a.* used as a top-up.

top² (top) *n.* a wooden or metal toy, usu. conical or pear-shaped, made to rotate with great velocity on a metal point underneath, by the rapid unwinding of a string or spring or with the hand. **to sleep like a top** to sleep very soundly.

topaz (tō'paz) *n.* a transparent or translucent aluminium silicate, usu. white or yellow, but sometimes green, blue, red or colourless, valued as a gem.

tope¹ (tōp) *v.i.* to drink alcoholic liquors excessively or habitually, to tipple. **toper** *n.*

tope² (tōp) *n.* a small European shark, *Galeorhinus galeus*.

topi (tō'pi), **topee** *n.* (*pl.* **topis, topees**) a sunhat, a pith helmet.

topiary (tō'piəri) *n.* (*pl.* **topiaries**) **1** the art of cutting and clipping trees or shrubs etc. into fanciful shapes. **2** an example of this. ~*a.* shaped by cutting or clipping. **topiarian** (-eə'ri-) *a.* **topiarist** *n.*

topic (top'ik) *n.* the subject of a discourse, argument, literary composition or conversation.

topical *a.* **1** of or relating to news and current affairs. **2** of or relating to a particular place, local. **3** (*Med.*) of or relating to a particular external part of the body. **4** of or relating to topics. **topicality** (-kal'-) *n.* **topically** *adv.*

topography (təpog'rəfi) *n.* **1** the detailed description of particular places. **2** representation of local features on maps etc. **3** the artificial or natural features of a place or district. **4** (*Anat.*) the mapping of the surface or the anatomy of particular regions of the body. **topographer** *n.* **topographic** (topəgraf'ik), **topographical** *a.* **topographically** *adv.*

topology (təpol'əji) *n.* (*Math.*) the study of geometrical properties and relationships which are not affected by distortion of a figure. **topological** (topəloj'-) *a.* **topologically** *adv.* **topologist** *n.*

toponym (top'ənim)*n.* **1** a place name. **2** a descriptive place name, usu. derived from a geographical feature. **toponymic** (-nim'-), **toponymical** *a.* **toponymy** (təpon'-) *n.* the science of place names.

topper, topping TOP¹.

topple (top'əl) *v.i.* **1** to totter and fall. **2** to project as if about to fall. ~*v.t.* **1** to cause to topple, to overturn. **2** to overthrow (a government or leader).

topsy-turvy (topsitœ'vi) *a.* **1** upside down. **2** in an upset or disordered condition. ~*adv.* in a confused manner. ~*n.* a topsy-turvy state. **topsy-turvily** *adv.* **topsy-turviness** *n.*

toque (tōk) *n.* a small, brimless, close-fitting hat.

tor (taw) *n.* a prominent hill or rocky peak, esp. on Dartmoor and in the Peak District.

Torah (taw'rə) *n.* **1** the Pentateuch. **2** the scroll containing this, used in synagogue services. **3** the will of God, the Mosaic law.

torch (tawch) *n.* **1** an electric torch. **2** a light made of resinous wood, twisted flax, hemp etc., soaked in oil or tallow, for carrying in the hand. **3** an oil, electric or other lamp used for this purpose, esp. when raised aloft on a pole etc. ~*v.t.* (*sl.*) to set fire to (something) deliberately. **to carry a torch** to suffer from unrequited love (for). **to put to the torch** to burn down (as an act of war etc.). **torch-bearer** *n.* **1** a person who leads the way or inspires others. **2** a person who carries a torch in ceremonies etc. **torch-fishing** *n.* fishing at night by torchlight. **torchlight** *n.* **torchlit** *a.* **torch song** *n.* a sad song about unrequited love. **torch singer** *n.* **torch-thistle** *n.* any cactus of the genus *Cereus*, having flowers which open at night.

tore TEAR¹.

toreador (toriədaw', tor'-) *n.* a bullfighter, esp. one who fights on horseback. **toreador pants** *n.pl.* close-fitting calf-length trousers worn by women.

torero (toreə'rō) *n.* (*pl.* **toreros**) a bullfighter, esp. one who fights on foot.

tori, toric TORUS.

torment[1] (taw´ment) *n.* **1** extreme pain or anguish of body or mind. **2** a source or cause of this.
torment[2] (tawment´) *v.t.* **1** to subject to torment. **2** to annoy, to vex, to irritate. **tormentedly** *adv.* **tormentingly** *adv.* **tormentor** *n.*
tormentil (taw´mentil) *n.* a low-growing herb, *Potentilla erecta*, with four-petalled yellow flowers, the astringent rootstock of which is used for medicine.
torn TEAR[1].
tornado (tawnā´dō) *n.* (*pl.* **tornadoes, tornados**) **1** a storm of extreme violence covering a very small area at once, but progressing rapidly, usu. having a rotary motion with electric discharges. **2** (*loosely*) a very strong wind, a hurricane. **3** a sudden strong outburst, discharge etc. (of). **tornadic** (-nad´-) *a.*
toroid (tor´oid) *n.* a figure shaped like a torus. **toroidal** (-roi´-) *a.* **toroidally** *adv.*
torpedo (tawpē´dō) *n.* (*pl.* **torpedoes**) **1** a long, cigar-shaped, self-propelled apparatus charged with explosive, used for attacking a hostile ship below the waterline. **2** (*Zool.*) an electric ray, a sea fish having an electrical apparatus for disabling or killing its prey. ~*v.t.* (*3rd pers. sing. pres.* **torpedoes**, *pres.p.* **torpedoing**, *past, p.p.* **torpedoed**) **1** to attack, blow up or sink with a torpedo. **2** to destroy or wreck suddenly. **torpedo boat** *n.* a small swift vessel fitted for firing torpedoes. **torpedo-like** *a.*
torpid (taw´pid) *a.* **1** dull, sluggish, inactive. **2** numb. **3** (of a hibernating animal) dormant. **torpefy** (-pifi) *v.t.* (*3rd pers. sing. pres.* **torpefies**, *pres.p.* **torpefying**, *past, p.p.* **torpefied**) to make numb or torpid. **torpidity** (-pid´-) *n.* **torpidly** *adv.* **torpidness** *n.* **torpor** *n.* **torporific** (-rif´-) *a.*
torque (tawk) *n.* the movement of a system of forces causing rotation. ~*v.t.* to apply a twisting force to, to apply torque to. **torque converter** *n.* a device applying the correct amount of torque from an engine to the driving axle of a motor vehicle. **torquey** *a.*
torr (taw) *n.* (*pl.* **torr**) a unit of pressure, equal to 133.32 pascals, $^1/_{760}$ of a standard atmosphere.
torrefy (tor´ifi) *v.t.* (*3rd pers. sing. pres.* **torrefies**, *pres.p.* **torrefying**, *past, p.p.* **torrefied**) **1** to dry or parch. **2** to roast (ores etc.). **torrefaction** (-fak´shen) *n.*
torrent (tor´ent) *n.* **1** a violent rushing stream (of water, lava etc.). **2** a flood (of abuse, passion etc.). **torrential** (teren´shel) *a.* **torrentially** *adv.*
torrid (tor´id) *a.* **1** dried up with heat, parched, scorching, very hot. **2** intense, passionate. **torridity** (-rid´-) *n.* **torridness** *n.* **torridly** *adv.* **torrid zone** *n.* the broad belt of the earth's surface between the tropics.
torsion (taw´shen) *n.* **1** (*esp. Biol.*) the act of twisting or the state of being twisted. **2** (*Physics*) the force with which a body tends to return to its original state after being twisted. **3** (*Med.*) the twisting of the cut end of an artery for checking

haemorrhage after an operation. **torsional** *a.* **torsionally** *adv.* **torsion balance** *n.* an instrument for estimating very minute forces by the action of a twisted wire. **torsion bar** *n.* a metal bar, part of a vehicle's suspension, that twists to absorb the vertical movement of the wheels. **torsionless** *a.* **torsion pendulum** *n.* a pendulum that works by rotation rather than by swinging back and forth.
torso (taw´sō) *n.* (*pl.* **torsos**, (*N Am.*) **torsi** (-sē)) **1** the trunk of a statue or body without the head and limbs. **2** an unfinished or partially destroyed work of art or literature.
tort (tawt) *n.* (*Law*) a private or civil wrong leading to liability for damages. **tortious** (-shes) *a.* **tortiously** *adv.*
torte (taw´te, tawt) *n.* (*pl.* **torten, tortes**) a rich gateau or tart, with fruit, cream etc.
tortelli (tawtel´i) *n.* a dish of small pasta parcels filled with a meat, cheese or vegetables mixture.
tortellini (-lē´ni) *n.* tortelli rolled and formed into small rings.
tortilla (tawtē´ye) *n.* in Mexican cooking, a thin flat maize cake baked on an iron plate.
tortoise (taw´tes) *n.* **1** a slow-moving herbivorous land reptile of the family Testudinidae, having a dome-shaped leathery shell. **2** a very slow person. **tortoise-like** *a.*, *adv.* **tortoiseshell** *n.* the mottled horny plates of the carapace of some marine turtles, used for combs, ornaments, inlaying etc. ~*a.* **1** made of this. **2** resembling this in marking and colour. **tortoiseshell butterfly** *n.* (*pl.* **tortoiseshell butterflies**) any butterfly of the genera *Nymphalis* and *Aglais*, with mottled yellow, orange and black wings. **tortoiseshell cat** *n.* a domestic cat with a mottled yellow, brown and black coat.
tortuous (taw´tūes) *a.* **1** twisting, winding, crooked. **2** roundabout, not direct. **3** devious, not open and straightforward. **tortuously** *adv.* **tortuousness** *n.*

Usage note The adjectives *tortuous* and *torturous* should not be confused: *tortuous* means twisting, and *torturous* relating to torture.

torture (taw´che) *n.* **1** the infliction of extreme physical pain as a punishment or to extort confession etc. **2** excruciating pain or anguish of mind or body. ~*v.t.* **1** to subject to torture. **2** to cause great mental or physical suffering to. **3** to wrest from the normal position, to distort. **4** to pervert the meaning of (a statement etc.). **torturable** *a.* **torturer** *n.* **torturingly** *adv.* **torturous** *a.* **torturously** *adv.*

Usage note See note on *torturous* under TORTUOUS.

torus (taw´res) *n.* (*pl.* **tori** (-rī), **toruses**) **1** (*Geom.*) a ring-shaped surface generated by a circle rotated about a line which does not intersect the circle. **2** (*Bot.*) the receptacle or thalamus of a flower, the modified end of a stem supporting the floral organs. **3** (*Archit.*) a semicircular projecting moulding, esp. in the base of a column. **4** (*Anat.*) a rounded ridge of bone or muscle. **toric** *a.*

Tory (taw´ri) *n.* (*pl.* **Tories**) **1** (*coll.*) a member of the Conservative Party. **2** (*Hist.*) a member of the party opposed to the exclusion of the Duke of York (James II) from the throne and to the Revolution of 1688, opposed to *Whig.* ~*a.* of or relating to the Tories. **Toryism** *n.*

tosa (tō´sə) *n.* a smooth-haired large heavy dog bred from the mastiff, orig. kept for dogfighting.

tosh (tosh) *n.* (*sl.*) rubbish, nonsense.

toss (tos) *v.t.* **1** to throw up with the hand, esp. palm upward. **2** to throw, to pitch, to fling, with an easy or careless motion. **3** to throw back (the head) with a jerk. **4** to throw about or from side to side, to cause to rise and fall, to agitate. **5** to exchange views on, to debate. **6 a** to throw up (a coin) into the air to decide a bet etc., by seeing which way it falls. **b** to settle a wager or dispute with (a person) in this way. **7** to turn or shake (a salad etc.) with a dressing or coating. ~*v.i.* **1** to roll and tumble about, to be agitated. **2** to throw oneself from side to side. **3** to toss a coin (for). ~*n.* **1** the act of tossing. **2** the state of being tossed. **3** a fall from a horse etc. **to take a toss** to be thrown by a horse. **to toss a pancake** to turn a pancake over in the pan by flipping it in the air. **to toss oars** to salute by raising oars to an upright position. **to toss off 1** to swallow at a draught. **2** to produce or do quickly or perfunctorily. **3** (*taboo sl.*) to masturbate. **to toss one's head** to throw one's head back in anger, disgust, impatience etc. **to toss up** to toss a coin. **tosser** *n.* **1** (*taboo sl.*) an unpleasant or contemptible person. **2** a person who or thing which tosses. **tossing the caber** *n.* a Scottish sport which involves heaving a large pole as far as possible having balanced it upright by the end. **toss-up** *n.* **1** the tossing up of a coin. **2** a doubtful point, an even chance.

tot¹ (tot) *n.* **1** a small child. **2** (*coll.*) a dram of liquor.

tot² (tot) *v.t.* (*pres.p.* **totting**, *past, p.p.* **totted**) to add (up). ~*v.i.* to mount (up). **to tot up to** to total, to amount to. **totting-up** *n.* adding together to make a total, esp. driving offences until there are sufficient to cause disqualification.

total (tō´təl) *a.* **1** complete, comprising everything or constituting the whole. **2** absolute, entire, thorough. ~*n.* **1** the total sum or amount. **2** the aggregate. ~*v.t.* (*pres.p.* **totalling**, (*N Am.*) **totaling**, *past, p.p.* **totalled**, (*N Am.*) **totaled**) **1** to ascertain the total of. **2** to amount to as a total. **3** (*N Am., sl.*) to wreck (a vehicle) completely in a crash. ~*v.i.* to amount (to) as a total. **total abstinence** *n.* complete abstinence from alcoholic drink. **total eclipse** *n.* an eclipse in which the entire visible surface of the sun, moon etc. is temporarily obscured. **totalitarian** (-taliteə´ri-) *a.* **1** permitting no rival parties or policies. **2** controlling the entire national resources of trade, natural wealth and manpower. ~*n.* a person in

favour in such a system. **totalitarianism** *n.* **totality** (-tal´-) *n.* **1** the total sum or amount. **2** (*Astron.*) the period of total eclipse during an eclipse. **3** the whole of something, the entirety. **totalize, totalise** *v.t.* to total. ~*v.i.* to use a totalizator. **totalization** (-zā´shən) *n.* **totalizator** *n.* a machine for showing the total amount of bets staked on a race in order to divide the whole among those betting on the winner. **totally** *adv.* **Total Quality Management** *n.* in industry, a systematic commitment to quality of product and customer service while increasing efficiency and reducing costs. **total recall** *n.* the ability to remember the past in great detail. **total war** *n.* warfare in which all available resources, military and civil, are employed.

tote¹ (tōt) *v.t.* **1** to carry, to bear. **2** to lead, to haul. **tote bag** *n.* a large bag for shopping etc. **tote box** *n.* (*N Am.*) a small rigid container for goods.

tote² (tōt) *n.* short for TOTALIZATOR (under TOTAL).

totem (tō´təm) *n.* **1** a natural object, usu. an animal, taken as a badge or emblem of an individual or clan on account of a supposed relationship. **2** an image of this. **totemic** (-tem´-), **totemistic** (-mis´-) *a.* **totemism** *n.* **totemist** *n.* **totem pole** *n.* a post on which totems are carved or hung.

totter (tot´ə) *v.i.* **1** to walk or stand unsteadily, to stagger. **2** to be on the point of falling. **totterer** *n.* **totteringly** *adv.* **tottery** *a.*

toucan (too´kən) *n.* a brilliantly-coloured tropical American bird of the family Ramphastidae, with an enormous beak.

touch (tŭch) *v.t.* **1** to meet the surface of, to have no intervening space between at one or more points, to be in contact with, to come into contact with. **2** to bring or put the hand or other part of the body or a stick etc., into contact with. **3** to cause (two objects) to come into contact. **4** to put the hand to (the hat etc.). **5** to reach, to attain. **6** to meddle, to interfere with. **7** to affect with tender feeling, to soften. **8** to approach, to compare with. **9** (*sl.*) to beg or borrow money from. **10** to concern, to relate to. **11** to mention hastily or lightly. **12** to strike lightly, to tap, to play upon lightly, to mark or delineate lightly, to put (in) fine strokes with a brush etc. **13** to produce a mental impression on. **14** to injure slightly. **15** to excite the anger of, to rouse, to irritate. **16** to impair. **17** to be associated with. **18** to eat or drink, to consume. ~*v.i.* **1** (of two or more objects) to come into contact. **2** to deal with or mention in a slight or hasty manner, to touch on. ~*n.* **1** the act of touching. **2** the state of touching or being touched, contact. **3** the sense by which contact, pressure etc. are perceived. **4** a slight effort, a light stroke with brush or pencil. **5** a stroke, a twinge (*a touch of gout*). **6** a trace, a minute quantity, a tinge. **7 a** a characteristic manner or method of handling, working, executing, playing on the keys or strings of a musical instrument etc. **b** the manner in which the keys of a piano etc. respond to this. **8** characteristic impress (*the master's touch*). **9** in football, rugby etc., the part of the field outside the touchlines and between the goal lines. **at a touch** with very little manual effort (*The door opened at a touch*). **in touch 1** in communication (with). **2** up to date, au fait with events etc. **3** aware, understanding of, conscious of, empathetic. **out of touch 1** not up to date or well-informed. **2** not in regular communication (with). **to lose one's touch** to cease to be skilful. **to lose touch 1** to cease regular communication (with). **2** to cease to be well-informed. **to touch at** (of a ship) to come to land or call at (a port etc.). **to touch down 1** in rugby, American football etc., to touch the ground with the ball behind the opponents' goal. **2** (of an aircraft or spacecraft) to make contact with the ground after a flight. **to touch off 1** to cause to begin, to trigger. **2** to set alight. **to touch on/ upon 1** to allude to. **2** to deal with or mention in a slight or hasty manner. **to touch up 1** to correct or improve by slight touches, as paint or make-up, to retouch. **2** to fondle (someone) in a sexual way. **to touch wood** to touch something wooden as a supposed protection against bad luck. **touchable** *a.* **touch-and-go** *a.* highly uncertain, very risky or hazardous. **touchback** *n.* in American football, a touchdown behind one's own goal. **touchdown** *n.* the moment or an act of touching down. **touched** *a.* **1** moved by some emotion, e.g. pity or gratitude. **2** (*coll.*) slightly insane. **touch-hole** *n.* the priming hole or vent of a gun. **touching** *a.* affecting, moving, arousing pathos. ~*prep.* concerning, with regard to. **touchingly** *adv.* **touchingness** *n.* **touch-in-goal** *n.* in rugby, the areas at the end of the pitch between the goal line and the dead-ball line. **touch judge** *n.* a linesman in rugby. **touchlines** *n.pl.* in certain sports, the two longer or side boundaries of the field. **touch-me-not** *n.* any of several plants of the genus *Impatiens* whose ripe seed pods burst open when touched, noli-me-tangere. **touch of nature** *n.* **1** a natural characteristic. **2** overt human feelings with which others sympathize. **touch of the sun** *n.* **1** slight sunstroke. **2** a brief period of sunlight. **touchpaper** *n.* paper saturated with nitre for igniting gunpowder, fireworks etc. **touch rugby, touch football** *n.* a form of rugby or American football, used esp. in training, where touching replaces tackling. **touch screen** *n.* a VDU screen that can be touched to activate menu choices. **touchstone** *n.* **1** a dark stone, usu. jasper, schist or basanite used in conjunction with touch-needles for testing the purity of gold and other alloys. **2** a standard, a criterion. **touch-type** *v.i.* to type without looking at the typewriter keyboard. **touch-typing** *n.* **touch-typist** *n.* **touch-up** *n.* a small action or series of actions to improve something in a minor way. **touchwood** *n.* a soft white substance into which wood is converted by the action of fungi, easily ignited

and burning like tinder. **touch wood** *int.* used esp. within a sentence as a substitute for the superstitious practice of touching wood to avert bad luck (*The weather, touch wood, will be fine*).

touché (tooshā´) *int.* used to acknowledge a hit in fencing, or a point scored in argument.

touchy (tŭch´i) *a.* (*comp.* **touchier,** *superl.* **touchiest**) apt to take offence, irascible, irritable. **touchily** *adv.* **touchiness** *n.*

tough (tŭf) *a.* **1** firm, strong, not easily broken, resilient, not brittle. **2** able to endure hardship. **3** stiff, tenacious. **4** stubborn, unyielding. **5** aggressive, violent. **6** laborious (*tough work*). **7** difficult (*a tough question*). **8** (*coll.*) (of luck etc.) unjust, hard, severe. **9** (of meat etc.) hard to cut or chew. ~*n.* a burly lout, a bully. **to tough it (out)** to withstand difficult circumstances, to persevere with something difficult. **toughen** *v.t., v.i.* **toughener** *n.* **tough guy** *n.* (*coll.*) **1** a hard, resilient person. **2** an aggressive person. **toughie** *n.* (*coll.*) a tough person or problem. **toughish** *a.* **tough luck** *int.* (*sl.*) hard luck (used esp. where no sympathy is being offered). ~*n.* misfortune, undeserved lack of success. **toughly** *adv.* **tough-minded** *a.* **1** practical and realistic, not sentimental. **2** resilient in the face of opposition or hardship. **tough-mindedness** *n.* **toughness** *n.* **tough nut to crack** *n.* a difficult problem to solve.

toupee (too´pā), **toupet** (too´pā, -pit) *n.* a small wig to cover a bald spot, a hairpiece.

tour (tuə) *n.* **1** a journeying round from place to place in a district, country etc. **2** an extended excursion or ramble. **3** a circuit. **4** a shift or turn of work or duty, esp. a period of service abroad. **5** a trip made by a theatre company, band, sports team etc., stopping at various places to play. **6** a brief visit to a place to look round it. ~*v.i.* to make a tour. ~*v.t.* to make a tour through. **on tour** (of a sports team, theatre company, band etc.) engaged in touring. **touring car, tourer** *n.* (*dated*) a large, long car with room for a lot of luggage. **tourism** *n.* the business of attracting and providing for holidaymakers. **tourist** *n.* a person making a tour, esp. a holidaymaker or member of a sports team. **tourist class** *n.* the lowest category of passenger accommodation in a ship or aircraft. **touristic** *a.* **touristically** *adv.* **touristy** *a.* **1** full of tourists. **2** (*usu. derog.*) designed to attract tourists. **tour operator** *n.* a travel agency which organizes package tours.

tour de force (tuə də faws´) *n.* (*pl.* **tours de force** (tuə)) an outstanding feat of performance, skill, strength etc.

tourism, tourist etc. TOUR.

tourmaline (tuə´məlēn) *n.* a black or coloured transparent or translucent silicate with electrical properties, some varieties of which are used as gems.

tournament (tuə´nəmənt) *n.* **1** any contest of skill in which a number of people take part. **2** (*Hist.*) a contest, exercise or pageant in which mounted knights contested, usu. with blunted lances etc.

tournedos (tuə´nədō) *n.* (*pl.* **tournedos** (-dōz)) a thick round fillet steak.

tourney (tuə´ni) *n.* (*pl.* **tourneys**) a tournament. *~v.i.* (*3rd pers. sing. pres.* **tourneys,** *pres.p.* **tourneying,** *past, p.p.* **tourneyed**) to engage in a tournament.

tourniquet (tuə´nikā) *n.* a bandage for compressing an artery and checking haemorrhage.

tousle (tow´zəl) *v.t.* **1** to disarrange, to rumple, to dishevel, to put into disorder. **2** to pull about. **tously** *a.*

tout (towt) *n.* **1** a person employed to tout. **2** a person who watches horses in training and supplies information. **3** TICKET TOUT (under TICKET). *~v.i.* **1** to solicit custom in an obtrusive way. **2** to observe secretly, to spy (esp. on horses in training for a race). *~v.t.* to solicit the custom of or try to obtain in an obtrusive way. **touter** *n.*

tow¹ (tō) *v.t.* **1** to pull (a vehicle) behind another. **2** to pull (a boat, ship etc.) through the water by a rope etc. **3** to drag (a net) over the surface of water to obtain specimens. **4** to pull, to drag behind one. *~n.* **1** the act of towing. **2** the state of being towed. **to have in tow 1** to have on tow (a boat etc.). **2** to be accompanied by, esp. as the person in charge. **to have on tow** to be towing (a vehicle etc.). **towable** *a.* **towage** (-ij) *n.* **tow bar** *n.* a strong bar on the back of a vehicle for attaching a trailer. **towboat** *n.* a tug. **towpath, towing-path** *n.* a track beside a canal or river, formerly for horses towing barges etc. **towplane** *n.* an aircraft that tows gliders prior to release. **towrope, towing-rope, towline** *n.* a hawser or rope used in towing.

tow² (tō) *n.* the coarse broken part of hemp or flax after combing out. **tow-coloured,** (*N Am.*) **tow-colored** *a.* (of hair) very light in colour. **tow-headed** *a.* having very pale hair.

toward (təwawd´, twawd, tawd) *prep.* TOWARDS.

towards (təwawdz´, twawdz, tawdz) *prep.* **1** in the direction of. **2** as regards, with respect to. **3** for, for the purpose of. **4** near, about.

towel (tow´əl) *n.* **1** an absorbent cloth for wiping and drying after washing, washing up etc. **2** a piece of absorbent paper similarly used. **3** SANITARY TOWEL (under SANITARY). *~v.t.* (*pres.p.* **towelling,** (*N Am.*) **toweling,** *past, p.p.* **towelled,** (*N Am.*) **toweled**) to wipe with a towel. *~v.i.* to wipe oneself with a towel. **to throw in the towel 1** (of a boxer or their second) to throw a towel into the ring as a sign of submission. **2** (*coll.*) to admit defeat. **towel-horse** *n.* a wooden stand on which to hang towels. **towelling,** (*N Am.*) **toweling** *n.* cloth for making towels. **towel rail** *n.* a rail, esp. in a bathroom, on which towels are hung.

tower (tow´ə) *n.* **1** a structure lofty in proportion to the area of its base, and circular, square or polygonal in plan, frequently of several storeys, often forming part of a church, castle or other large building. **2** a similarly-proportioned structure for industrial or other purposes (*cooling tower; control tower; scaffold tower*). *~v.i.* **1** to rise to a great height, to soar. **2** to be relatively high, to reach high (above). **tower block** *n.* a very tall residential or office building. **towered** *a.* **towering** *a.* **1** very high, lofty. **2** (of passion etc.) violent, outrageous. **3** very great. **Tower of Babel** *n.* a visionary or impractical plan (Gen. xi.1–9). **tower of strength** *n.* a person who gives strong, stable, reliable support, esp. in another's time of difficulty. **towery** *a.*

town (town) *n.* **1** an urban area larger than a village, esp. one not constituting a city. **2** such an area as contrasted with the country. **3** the centre of a town. **4** the chief town of a district or neighbourhood, esp. London. **5** the people of a town. **6** the people of a university town who are not members of the university. **7** (*N Am.*) a township. **on the town** (*coll.*) out to enjoy oneself amongst the amusements and entertainments of a city at night. **to go to town** to let oneself go, to drop all reserve. **town clerk** *n.* (*Hist.*) **1** the clerk to a municipal corporation. **2** the keeper of the records of a town. **town council** *n.* the governing body in a town. **town councillor** *n.* **town crier** *n.* an officer who makes public proclamations e.g. of sales, lost articles etc. **town hall** *n.* a large public building for the transaction of municipal business, public meetings, entertainments etc. **town house** *n.* **1** a private residence in town, as opposed to a country house. **2** a modern urban terraced house, often with a garage at the front on the ground floor. **townie, townee** (-i) *n.* (*derog.*) a person who habitually or for preference lives in town. **townish** *a.* **townlet** *n.* **town planning** *n.* the regulating of the laying out or growth of a town. **town planner** *n.* **townscape** *n.* **1** the visual design of an urban development. **2** a picture of an urban scene. **townsfolk** *n.pl.* the people of a town or city. **township** *n.* **1** (*Hist.*) in S Africa, an urban area formerly designated for black people. **2** (*N Am.*) a territorial district subordinate to a county invested with certain administrative powers. **3** (*Austral.*) any town or settlement, however small. **4** a new area being developed by settlers, speculators etc. **townsman, townswoman** *n.* (*pl.* **townsmen, townswomen**) **1** an inhabitant of a town. **2** a fellow citizen. **townspeople** *n.pl.* townsfolk. **townward** *a., adv.* **townwards** *adv.*

toxaemia (toksē´miə), (*esp. N Am.*) **toxemia** *n.* (*Med.*) **1** blood poisoning. **2** a condition during pregnancy in which there is a sudden rise in blood pressure. **toxaemic** *a.*

toxic (tok´sik) *a.* **1** poisonous. **2** of or relating to poison. **toxically** *adv.* **toxicant** *n.* a poison. **toxicity** (-sis´-) *n.* **toxic shock syndrome** *n.* (*Med.*) a group of symptoms in women including vomiting, fever and diarrhoea, usu. attributable to bacterial infection from an unremoved tampon or an IUD etc.

toxicology (toksikol´əji) *n*. the branch of medicine treating of poisons and their antibodies. **toxicological** (-loj´-) *a*. **toxicologically** *adv*. **toxicologist** *n*.

toxin (tok´sin) *n*. a poisonous compound causing a particular disease.

toxocara (toksəkah´rə) *n*. any parasitic worm of the genus *Toxocara*, esp. the common roundworm causing toxocariasis. **toxocariasis** (-kərī´əsis) *n*. a disease in humans caused by the larvae of the toxocara worm found in cats and dogs, causing damage to the liver and eyes.

toxoplasmosis (toksōplazmō´sis) *n*. (*Med*.) an infectious disease caused by the sporozoan *Toxoplasma gondii*, characterized by jaundice, enlarged liver and spleen and convulsions, transmitted esp. through badly-prepared food and cat faeces.

toy (toi) *n*. **1** a plaything, esp. for a child. **2** something of an amusing or trifling kind, not serious or for actual use. **3** a very small breed of dog etc. **4** a replica in miniature. *~v.i.* to trifle, to amuse oneself, to sport, to dally. *~a.* **1** replica. **2** a small variety. **to toy with 1** to trifle with. **2** to touch or move idly. **3** to touch and nibble rather than eating normally. **4** to consider casually. **toy-box** *n*. a large box for keeping toys in. **toyboy** *n*. (*coll*.) a (woman's) much younger lover. **toyer** *n*. **toyingly** *adv*. **toylike** *a*. **toyshop** *n*. a shop where toys are sold. **toy soldier** *n*. **1** a miniature model of a soldier. **2** (*coll., derog*.) a peacetime soldier, i.e. one who has not experienced battle conditions.

TQM *abbr.* Total Quality Management.

trace¹ (trās) *n*. **1** a token, vestige, or sign of something that has existed or taken place. **2** a minute quantity. **3** (*usu. in pl*.) a mark left by a person or animal walking or thing moving, a track, a trail, a footprint, a rut etc. **4** a line made by a recording instrument. *~v.t.* **1** to follow the traces or track of. **2** to note the marks and vestiges of. **3** to ascertain the position or course of. **4** to pursue one's way along. **5** to copy (a drawing etc.) by marking the lines on transparent paper etc. laid on it or on carbon paper. **6** to delineate, to mark out. **7** to sketch out (a plan, scheme etc.). *~v.i.* to be followed back to the origins, to date back. **traceable** *a*. **traceability** (-bil´-), **traceableness** *n*. **traceably** *adv*. **trace element** *n*. a chemical element present in small quantities, esp. one that is valuable for an organism's physiological processes. **traceless** *a*. **tracer** *n*. **1** a person who or thing which traces. **2** (*Mil*.) a tracer bullet, shell etc. **3** an artificially produced radioactive isotope introduced into the human body where its course can be followed by the radiation it emits. **tracer bullet, tracer shell** *n*. (*Mil*.) a bullet or shell whose course is marked by a smoke trail or a phosphorescent glow. **tracery** (-əri) *n*. (*pl*. **traceries**) **1** ornamental stone openwork in Gothic windows etc. **2** any decorative work or natural markings

resembling this. **traceried** *a*. **tracing** *n*. **1** a traced copy of a drawing etc. **2** a trace made by a recording instrument. **tracing paper** *n*. a thin transparent paper used for copying drawings etc. by tracing.

trace² (trās) *n*. either of the two straps, chains or ropes by which a vehicle is drawn by horses etc. **in the traces** in harness. **trace-horse** *n*. a horse that draws a vehicle, using traces.

trachea (trəkē´ə, trā´kiə) *n*. (*pl*. **tracheae** (trəkē´ē, trā´kiē), **tracheas**) (*Anat*.) the windpipe, the air passage from the larynx to the bronchi and lungs. **tracheal** *a*. **tracheate** (trā´kiət) *a*.

tracheotomy (trakiot´əmi) *n*. (*pl*. **tracheotomies**) (*Med*.) the operation of making an opening into the windpipe. **tracheotomy tube** *n*. a tube inserted in the windpipe to enable breathing after a tracheotomy.

tracing TRACE¹.

track (trak) *n*. **1** a series of marks left by the passage of a person, animal or thing, a trail. **2** (*usu. in pl*.) a series of footprints. **3** a path, esp. one not constructed but beaten by use. **4** a racecourse, a route for racing. **5** a course of action. **6** a process of thought. **7** a set of rails, a monorail or a continuous line of railway. **8** a soundtrack. **9** the groove in a gramophone record in which the needle travels. **10** any one of several paths on a magnetic recording device on which esp. sound from a single input channel is recorded. **11** a course, the route followed by spaceships, ships etc. **12** (*N Am*.) an educational stream of schoolchildren taught together. **13** the endless band on which a Caterpillar tractor, tank etc. propels itself. **14** the conveyor which carries the items being assembled in a factory. **15** a single item, e.g. a song, recorded on a CD, tape etc. *~v.t.* **1** to follow the track or traces of. **2** to trace, to follow out (the course of anything). **3** to follow the flight of (a spacecraft etc.) by receiving signals emitted by or reflected from it. **4** to film (a subject) by moving the camera along a fixed path. **5** (*N Am*.) to stream (a pupil) according to educational attainment. **6** (*N Am*.) to leave a track of (dirt etc.); to leave a track of dirt etc. on. *~v.i.* **1** (of the stylus of a pick-up arm) to follow the groove on a record. **2** (of a camera) to move along a fixed path while shooting. **3** (of wheels) to take exactly the same track. **off the track** away from the subject in hand. **on someone's track 1** in pursuit of a person. **2** having knowledge of someone's plans, conduct etc. **on the right track** following the correct line of thought, inquiry etc. **on the wrong side of the tracks** in a poor, less socially prestigious area of town. **on the wrong track** following the incorrect line of thought, inquiry etc. **to keep track of** to remain aware of (events, developments etc.). **to lose track of** to cease to be aware of (events, developments etc.). **to make tracks** to run away, to bolt, to leave. **to make tracks for 1** to head for. **2** to go in pursuit of. **to track down** to discover by tracking. **to track with**

(*Austral.*) to associate with, to go out with. **trackage** (-ij) *n.* **trackball** *n.* on a portable computer, a built-in rolling ball that guides the cursor on screen. **tracker** *n.* **tracker dog** *n.* a dog that uses its sense of smell to find e.g. drugs, persons or smuggled goods, used by the police etc. **track events** *n.pl.* in athletics, running events on the track, as distinct from field events such as throwing and jumping. **tracking** *n.* **1** the act or process of following someone or something. **2** a leakage of electric current from an insulated unit along a conducting path created by dirt, moisture etc. **tracking station** *n.* an establishment using radio signals, radar etc. to track objects in the sky. **trackless** *a.* **track record** *n.* the past achievements, performance, experience etc. of a person or thing. **track shoe** *n.* a light running shoe with spikes on the sole to improve grip. **tracksuit** *n.* a light, loose-fitting suit for wearing before and after vigorous exercise, or as a leisure garment. **trackway** *n.* a long-established path or track.

tract[1] (trakt) *n.* **1** a region or area of land or water of a considerable but undefined extent. **2** (*Anat.*) the region of an organ or system.

tract[2] (trakt) *n.* a short treatise or pamphlet, esp. on religion or morals.

tractable (trak´təbəl) *a.* easily led, managed, or controlled, docile, manageable. **tractability** (-bil´-) *n.* **tractableness** *n.* **tractably** *adv.*

tractate (trak´tāt) *n.* a treatise.

traction (trak´shən) *n.* **1** the act of drawing something along a surface, esp. by motive power. **2** the state of being drawn in this way. **3** (*Med.*) **a** the sustained pulling on muscles, tone structure etc. by a system of weights and pulleys. **b** contraction. **4** grip on a surface, as of a tyre on the road. **tractional** *a.* **traction engine** *n.* a steam locomotive formerly used for drawing heavy loads on ordinary roads. **traction wheel** *n.* the wheel to which the force is applied in a locomotive etc.

tractor (trak´tə) *n.* **1** a motor vehicle capable of drawing other vehicles, farm implements etc. **2** a traction engine.

trad (trad) *n.* traditional jazz. ~*a.* (*coll.*) traditional.

trade (trād) *n.* **1** the exchange of commodities, buying and selling, commerce. **2** a business, handicraft etc. carried out for profit as distinct from agriculture, unskilled labour etc. **3** a business, handicraft etc., requiring training or an apprenticeship. **4** the amount of business done in a particular year, place etc. **5** the people engaged in a particular trade (*the motor trade*). **6** an exchange of one thing for another. **7** (*coll.*) in business or politics, a deal, a bargain. **8** (*pl.*) the trade winds. ~*v.i.* **1** to buy and sell, to barter, to exchange, to traffic, to deal (in). **2** to carry on commerce or business (with). **3** to carry merchandise (between etc.). **4** to be bought and sold. ~*v.t.* **1** to sell or exchange in commerce, to

barter. **2** to swap. **3** to exchange verbally. **to trade in** to give in part payment. **to trade off** to exchange (one thing for another), esp. as a compromise. **to trade on** to take advantage of. **tradable, tradeable** *a.* **trade cycle** *n.* the recurrent alternation of prosperity and depression in trade. **trade gap, trade deficit** *n.* the amount by which a country's visible imports exceeds its visible exports. **trade-in** *n.* **1** a transaction in which an item is given in part payment for another. **2** the item given in part payment. **trade journal, trade paper** *n.* a periodical containing information and comment concerning a particular industry, trade, profession etc. **tradeless** *a.* **trade mark, trademark** *n.* **1** a registered symbol or name used by a manufacturer or merchant to guarantee the genuineness of goods. **2** a distinguishing feature of a person or thing. **trademark** *v.t.* **trade name** *n.* **1** the name by which an article is called in the trade. **2** the name of a proprietary article. **trade-off** *n.* the exchange of one thing for another, esp. as a compromise. **trade paper** TRADE JOURNAL (under TRADE). **trade plates** *n.pl.* number plates used by people in the motor trade in moving otherwise unlicensed cars. **trade price** *n.* the price charged to dealers for articles to be sold again. **trader** *n.* **1** a person engaged in trade, a merchant, a tradesman. **2** a vessel employed in trade, a merchant ship. **trade secret** *n.* a process, formula etc. used to make a commercial product, known to only one manufacturer. **tradesman, tradeswoman** *n.* (*pl.* **tradesmen, tradeswomen**) a retail dealer, a shopkeeper. **tradespeople** *n.pl.* people engaged in trades, tradesmen or tradeswomen and their families. **trade union, trades union** *n.* an organized body of workers in any trade, formed for the promotion and protection of their common interests. **Trades Union Congress** *n.* the body representing trade unions collectively. **trade unionism, trades unionism** *n.* **trade unionist, trades unionist** *n.* **trade-weighted** *a.* (of exchange rates) weighted according to the significance of the trade with the various countries listed. **trade wind** *n.* **1** a wind blowing from the north or south towards the equator and deflected in a westerly direction by the easterly rotation of the earth. **2** (*pl.*) these and the anti-trades. **trading** *n.* the act or process of engaging in trade. **trading estate** *n.* an area of buildings intended for commercial or light industrial use, an industrial estate. **trading post** *n.* a store established in a remote, esp. little-populated, region. **trading stamp** *n.* a stamp given free with a purchase, which can be saved and later exchanged for goods. **trading station** *n.* (*Hist.*) an overseas settlement established or place visited for trading purposes.

tradescantia (tradiskan´tiə) *n.* any usu. trailing plant of the genus *Tradescantia*, with large colourful flowers and striped variegated leaves.

tradition (trədish´ən) *n.* **1** the handing down of

opinions, practices, customs etc., from ancestors to posterity, esp. by oral communication. **2** a belief, custom etc. so handed down. **3** (*coll.*) a regular practice, a custom. **4** the principles, maxims etc., derived from the usage and experience of artists, dramatists, actors etc. **5** (*Law*) formal delivery (of property). **traditional** *a.* **1** of or relating to tradition, based on tradition. **2** of or relating to a type of jazz which began in New Orleans in the 1900s. **3** of or relating to a regular practice or custom. **traditionalism** *n.* adherence to tradition, esp. superstitious regard to tradition in religious matters. **traditionalist** *n.* **traditionalistic** (-lis´-) *a.* **traditionally** *adv.* **traditionary** *a.*

traduce (tradūs´) *v.t.* to defame, to misrepresent, to speak ill of. **traducement** *n.* **traducer** *n.* **traducingly** *adv.*

traffic (traf´ik) *n.* **1** the vehicles etc. passing on a road etc. **2** the passing to and fro of people, vehicles etc. on a road etc. **3** the movement of ships, aircraft etc. **4** the transportation of people, animals or goods by road, rail, sea or air. **5** the amount of goods or number of people conveyed. **6** the trade in a particular commodity etc., esp. the illegal trade. **7** the exchange of goods by barter or by the medium of money, trade, commerce. **8** the messages, signals etc. handled by a communications system. **9** communication or dealing (with). ~*v.i.* (*pres.p.* **trafficking**, *p.p.* **trafficked**) **1** to deal (in) certain goods. **2** to deal (in) illegally. **3** to trade, to buy and sell goods, to have business (with). ~*v.t.* to barter. **traffic calming** *n.* measures taken to slow traffic down in locations where speed would be dangerous. **traffic island** *n.* an area in the middle of a road that acts as a refuge for pedestrians. **traffic jam** *n.* a line or build-up of vehicles that are stationary or slow-moving because of the large volume of traffic, an obstruction in the road etc. **trafficker** *n.* **trafficless** *a.* **traffic light**, **traffic lights**, **traffic signal** *n.* coloured lights at street intersections to control the flow and direction of traffic. **traffic warden** *n.* a person employed to enforce observance of parking restrictions, esp. by issuing parking tickets.

tragacanth (trag´əkanth) *n.* **1** a whitish or reddish demulcent gum obtained from the Asian plant of *Astragalus gummifer*, used in pharmacy, calico-printing etc. **2** this plant.

tragedy (traj´idi) *n.* (*pl.* **tragedies**) **1** a fatal or calamitous event, esp. a murder or fatal accident. **2** a serious event, a misfortune. **3** a drama in verse or elevated prose dealing with a lofty theme of a sad, pathetic or terrible kind, usu. with an unhappy ending. **4** the genre of such drama. **tragedian** (trəjē´diən) *n.* **1** a writer of tragedies. **2** an actor in tragedy. **tragedienne** (trəjēdien´) *n.* an actress in tragedy.

tragic (traj´ik) *a.* **1** lamentable, sad, calamitous. **2** characterized by loss of life. **3** of the nature or in the style of tragedy. **tragical** *a.* lamentable, sad,

calamitous. **tragicality** (-kal´-), **tragicalness** *n.* **tragically** *adv.* **tragic irony** *n.* a situation in a play etc. where the irony is clear to the audience but not to the characters. **tragicomedy** (-kom´-) *n.* (*pl.* **tragicomedies**) a drama in which tragic and comic scenes or features are mingled. **tragicomic**, **tragicomical** *a.* **tragicomically** *adv.*

trail (trāl) *v.t.* **1** to drag along behind, esp. along the ground. **2** to follow by the track or trail. **3** to lag behind in a contest, race etc. **4** to show an excerpt of as advance publicity. ~*v.i.* **1** to be dragged along behind, to hang down loosely or grow to some length along the ground, over a wall etc. **2** to lag behind. **3** to be losing in a contest etc. **4** to tail (off), to fall (away). ~*n.* **1** a track left by an animal etc. **2** the scent followed in hunting. **3** a beaten track through forest or wild country. **4** anything trailing behind a moving thing, a train, a floating appendage etc. **to trail arms** (*Mil.*) to carry (a rifle etc.) in a horizontal or oblique position in the right hand with the arm extended. **to trail oneself** to move wearily or reluctantly. **trail bike** *n.* a light motorcycle for riding on rough tracks etc. **trailblazer** *n.* **1** a pioneer in a field of endeavour. **2** a person who blazes a trail. **trailblazing** *n.*, *a.* **trailer** *n.* **1** any vehicle, sled etc. drawn behind another. **2** a person who or thing which trails. **3** a trailing plant. **4** (*N Am.*) a caravan. **5** a short piece of film, video etc. giving advance publicity to a forthcoming item. **trailer park** *n.* a caravan park or caravan site. **trailing** *a.* **trailing edge** *n.* in aircraft, the rear edge of a wing or of a control surface.

train (trān) *n.* **1** a series of railway carriages or trucks, either self-powered or drawn by an engine. **2** a line or long series or succession of people or things. **3** process, orderly succession, progressive condition. **4** something drawn or dragged along behind. **5** an extended part of a gown, robe etc. trailing behind the wearer. **6** a retinue, a suite. **7** a set of wheels, pinions etc., transmitting motion. **8** a line of combustible material leading fire to a charge or mine. ~*v.t.* **1** to bring to a state of proficiency by prolonged instruction, practice etc. **2** to instruct, to drill, to accustom (to perform certain acts or feats). **3** to prepare by diet and exercise (for a race etc.). **4** to bring (a plant etc.) by pruning, manipulation etc. into a desired shape, position etc. **5** to bring to bear, to point or aim (a cannon, camera etc. on). ~*v.i.* **1** to prepare oneself or come into a state of efficiency (for a race, match etc.). **2** (*coll.*) to go by train. **3** to prepare oneself for a career, to study. **in someone's train** following behind a person. **in the train of** as a consequence or sequel of. **in train** in progress, happening according to an organized schedule. **trainable** *a.* **trainability** (-bil´-) *n.* **trainee** (-nē´) *n.* a person undergoing training. **traineeship** *n.* **trainer** *n.* **1** a person who trains, esp. one who prepares athletes, sportspeople, horses etc. **2** a training shoe; a similar shoe worn for leisure purposes. **3** an aircraft or simulator for training pilots. **training** n. **1** the preparation of a person or animal for a particular activity, occupation etc. **2** the state of making oneself physically fit. **in training 1** at present undergoing physical training. **2** physically fit because of this. **out of training** not physically fit. **training college** n. (Hist.) a college for training teachers. **training ship** n. a ship for instructing young people in navigation, seamanship etc. **training shoe** n. a shoe made of light leather, canvas, plastic etc. for physical training. **train-load** n. the quantity of people or goods on a train. **trainman** n. (pl. **trainmen**) a railway employee who works on a train. **train-shed** n. the usu. glass and metal roof over the platforms of a railway station, as distinct from other buildings at the station. **trainsick** a. affected by nausea during train travel. **train-spotter** n. a person whose hobby is to collect train numbers. **train-spotting** n.

train-oil (trā′noil) n. oil obtained from the blubber or fat of whales.

traipse (trāps), **trapes** v.i. (coll.) **1** to trudge, to drag along wearily. **2** to go (about) on errands on foot. ~n. a trudge, a weary journey on foot.

trait (trāt, trā) n. **1** a distinguishing or peculiar feature, esp. of a person's character or behaviour. **2** a stroke, a touch (of).

traitor (trā′tə) n. a person guilty of disloyalty, treason or treachery, esp. to their country. **traitorous** a. of or like a traitor. **traitorously** adv. **traitorousness** n. **traitress** (-tris) n. a female traitor.

trajectory (trəjek′təri) n. (pl. **trajectories**) the path taken by a body, comet, projectile etc., under the action of given forces. **trajection** (-jek′shən) n.

tram (tram) n. **1** (also **tramcar**) a public passenger vehicle, usu. powered electrically from an overhead cable, running on lines set in or near ordinary roads. **2** a four-wheeled truck or car used in coal mines. **tramline** n. **1** a rail of a tramway. **2** each of the lines at the side of a tennis court which mark the boundaries of the singles and doubles court. **3** a course which cannot be deviated from. **tramway** n. **1** a public transport system using trams. **2** the route of this.

trammel (tram′əl) n. **1** (usu. in pl.) anything restraining freedom or activity. **2** a trammel net. ~v.t. (pres.p. **trammelling**, (N Am.) **trammeling**, past, p.p. **trammelled**, (N Am.) **trammeled**) to confine, to hamper, to restrict. **trammel net** n. a dragnet formed by a combination of three seines, in which fish become entangled.

tramp (tramp) v.i. **1** to walk, to go on foot, esp. for a considerable distance. **2** to walk or tread heavily. ~v.t. **1** to go over or traverse, or to perform (a journey etc.) on foot. **2** to tread heavily on, to trample. ~n. **1** an itinerant beggar, a vagrant. **2** the sound of the tread of people etc. walking or marching, or of horses' hooves. **3** a

walk, a journey on foot. **4** (sl., offensive) a promiscuous girl or woman. **tramper** n. **trampish** a.

trample (tram′pəl) v.t. **1** to tread underfoot, esp. carelessly or in scorn, triumph etc. **2** to tread down, to crush in this way. **3** to treat with arrogance or contemptuous indifference. ~n. the act or sound of trampling. **to trample on 1** to tread heavily on. **2** to tread on with contempt. **trampler** n.

trampoline (tram′pəlēn) n. a sheet of canvas suspended by springs from a frame, used for bouncing on or for assisting jumps in gymnastics. ~v.i. to use a trampoline. **trampolinist** n.

trance (trahns) n. **1** a state of mental abstraction, with no response to external surroundings or stimuli. **2** a hypnotic state, esp. of a spiritualistic medium. **3** a cataleptic state. **4** a state of ecstasy, rapture. ~v.t. (poet.) to entrance, to enchant. **trancelike** a.

tranche (trahnsh) n. a portion, esp. of a larger sum of money, block of shares etc.

tranny (tran′i) n. (pl. **trannies**) (coll.) a transistor radio.

tranquil (trang′kwil) a. **1** (of a person) calm and not showing any worry, excitement or strong feeling. **2** (of a place) peaceful, serene, quiet, undisturbed. **tranquillity** (-kwil′-), **tranquility** n. **tranquillize, tranquillise**, (N Am.) **tranquilize** v.t. to make calm, to reduce anxiety in, esp. with a sedative drug. **tranquillization** (-zā′shən) n. **tranquillizer** n. **1** a sedative drug, a drug to reduce anxiety. **2** anything that promotes tranquillity. **tranquillizingly** adv. **tranquilly** adv. **tranquilness** n.

trans- (tranz) pref. **1** across, over. **2** beyond, on the other side. **3** through. **4** into another state or place. **5** surpassing. **6** (Chem.) higher in atomic number than. **7** (Chem.) being an isomer with two atoms or groups on the opposite side of a given plane.

transact (tranzakt′) v.t. to do, to perform, to manage, to carry out. ~v.i. to do business, to conduct matters (with). **transaction** n. **1** the management or carrying out of a piece of business etc. **2** something transacted, a piece of business, an affair, a proceeding. **3** (pl.) the reports of the proceedings of a learned society. **transactional** a. **transactionally** adv. **transactor** n.

transalpine (tranzal′pīn) a. lying or situated beyond the Alps (usu. as seen from Italy). ~n. a person living beyond the Alps.

transatlantic (tranzətlan′tik) a. **1** lying or being beyond the Atlantic; American as seen from Europe, European as seen from N America. **2** crossing the Atlantic.

transceiver (transē′və) n. a device for transmitting and receiving radio signals.

transcend (transend′) v.t., v.i. **1** to rise above, to surpass, to excel, to exceed. **2** to pass or be beyond the range, sphere or power (of human understanding etc.). **transcendent** a. **1** excelling, surpassing, supremely excellent. **2** above and independent of the material universe. **transcendence, transcendency** n. **transcendental** (-den´-) a. **1** belonging to the a priori elements of experience, implied in and necessary to experience. **2** explaining matter and the universe as products of mental conception. **3** transcending ordinary ideas. **4** abstruse, speculative, vague, obscure. **transcendentalism** n. **transcendentalist** n. **transcendentalize, transcendentalise** v.t. **transcendentally** adv. **Transcendental Meditation** n. a form of meditation intended to induce spiritual balance and harmony through silent repetition of a mantra. **transcendently** adv.

transcontinental (tranzkontinen´təl) a. extending or travelling across a continent. **transcontinentally** adv.

transcribe (transkrīb´) v.t. **1** to copy in writing, to write out in full (shorthand notes etc.). **2** to translate, to transliterate. **3** to transfer (data) from one recording medium to another. **4** (Mus.) to arrange (a vocal composition) for an instrument, to readjust (a composition) for another instrument. **5** to record (spoken sounds) in the form of phonetic symbols. **6** to record for broadcasting. **transcriber** n. **transcript** (tran´skript) n. **1** a written or recorded copy. **2** any form of copy. **transcription** (-krip´shən) n. **1** the act of transcribing, the state of being transcribed. **2** a transcript. **3** (Biol.) the copying of nucleotides from DNA during the synthesis of an RNA molecule. **transcriptional, transcriptive** a.

transducer (tranzdū´sə) n. a power-transforming device for which the input and output are of different kinds, electrical, acoustic, optical etc., e.g. loudspeaker, microphone, photoelectric cell etc. **transduce** v.t. **transduction** (-dŭk´shən) n.

transept (tran´sept) n. **1** either of the transverse arms extending north and south in a cruciform church. **2** the area including both these arms. **transeptal** a.

transexual TRANSSEXUAL.

transfer[1] (transfœ´) v.t. (pres.p. **transferring**, past, p.p. **transferred**) **1** to convey, remove or shift from one place or person to another. **2** (esp. Law) to make over the possession of. **3** to remove to another club, department etc. **4** to convey (a design etc.) from one surface to another, esp. in lithography. **5** to use in a figurative or extended sense; to change (meaning) in this way. ~v.i. **1** to move from one place to another. **2** to change from one bus, train etc. to another. **3** to move to another club, department etc. **transferable** a. **transferability** (-bil´-) n. **transferable vote** n. in a system of proportional representation, a vote that can be transferred to a second candidate if the first loses a preliminary ballot. **transferee** (-rē´) n. **transference** (trans´fər-) n. **transferral** n. **transferrer, transferror** n.

transfer[2] (trans´fœ) n. **1** the removal or conveyance of a thing from one person or place to another. **2** the act of conveying a right, property etc. from one person to another. **3** the deed by which this is effected. **4** something which is transferred. **5** a design conveyed from paper etc. to some other surface. **6** a soldier transferred from one regiment, troop etc. to another. **7** a footballer etc. transferred from one club to another. **8** the removal of someone to another club, department etc. **transfer fee** n. the fee paid to one sports club by another for the transfer of a player. **transfer list** n. a list of footballers available for transfer to other clubs. **transfer RNA** n. an RNA that carries a particular amino acid to a ribosome in protein synthesis.

transfiguration (transfigūrā´shən) n. a change of form or appearance, esp. that of Christ on the Mount (Matt. xvii.1–9). **transfigure** (-fig´ə) v.t. to change the outward appearance of, esp. so as to elevate and glorify.

transfix (transfiks´) v.t. **1** to pierce through, to impale. **2** to render motionless with shock, fear etc. **transfixion** (-fik´shən) n.

transform (transfawm´) v.t. **1** to change the form, shape or appearance of, to metamorphose. **2** to change in disposition, character etc. **3** to change the voltage etc. of (an electrical current). ~v.i. to undergo a transformation. **transformable** a. **transformation** (-fəmā´shən) n. **1** the act of transforming. **2** the state of being transformed. **transformational** a. **transformationally** adv. **transformation scene** n. a scene in a pantomime etc. which changes suddenly and dramatically as the audience looks on. **transformative** a. **transformer** n. **1** a device which changes the circuit of an alternating electrical supply, thereby altering the voltage. **2** a person or thing which transforms.

transfuse (transfūz´) v.t. **1** to permeate, to cause to pass from one vessel etc. into another. **2** to transfer (blood) from the veins of one person or animal to those of another. **3** to inject (a liquid) into a blood vessel or cavity to replace loss or wastage. **transfusible** a. **transfusion** (-zhən) n. **transfusive** a.

transgenic (tranzjen´ik) a. (Biol.) (of an animal or plant) containing genetic material artificially transferred from another species.

transgress (tranzgres´) v.t. **1** to break (a rule or rules), to violate, to infringe. **2** (Geol.) (of the sea) to overspread (the land). ~v.i. to offend by violating a law or rule, to sin. **transgression** (-shən) n. **transgressive** a. **transgressively** adv. **transgressor** n.

tranship TRANS-SHIP.

transhumance (tranz·hū´məns) n. the seasonal migration of livestock from one grazing ground to another.

transient (tran´siənt, -ziənt) a. **1** not lasting or durable, temporary. **2** transitory, momentary, hasty, brief. **3** (Mus.) passing, serving merely to connect or introduce. **transience, transiency** n. **transiently** adv.

transistor (tranzis'tə) *n.* **1** a device made primarily of a semiconductor (germanium or silicon) capable of giving current and power amplification. **2** (*coll.*) a transistor radio. **transistorize, transistorise** *v.t.* **1** to equip with transistors. **2** to design with or convert to transistors. **transistorization** (-zā'shən) *n.* **transistor radio** *n.* a small portable radio with transistors.

transit (tran'zit, -sit) *n.* **1** the act of passing, conveying or being conveyed, across, over or through. **2** a line of passage, a route. **3** (*Astron.*) **a** the apparent passage of a heavenly body over the meridian of a place. **b** the passage of a heavenly body across the disc of another, esp. of Venus or Mercury across the sun's disc. **4** (*N Am.*) local public transport. ~*v.t.* (*pres.p.* **transiting**, *past*, *p.p.* **transited**) to pass across (the disc of the sun etc.). ~*v.i.* to make a transit. **in transit** being conveyed. **transit camp** *n.* a camp where people stay temporarily before moving on to another place. **transit lounge** *n.* a lounge at an airport for passengers from one flight waiting to join another. **transit visa** *n.* a visa allowing a person only to pass through a country, not to stay there.

transition (tranzish'ən) *n.* **1** passage or change from one place, state or action to another. **2** a change in architecture, painting, literature etc. **3** (*Mus.*) a change from one musical key to another or from the major to the relative minor. **4** in rhetoric, a passing from one subject to another. **5** (*Physics*) a change from one quantum stage to another. **transitional, transitionary** *a.* **transitionally** *adv.*

transitive (tran'sitiv) *a.* **1** (*Gram.*) (of verbs) expressing an action passing over from a subject to an object, having a direct object. **2** (*Logic*) denoting a relation between members of a sequence that necessarily holds between any two members if it holds between every pair of successive members. **transitively** *adv.* **transitiveness** *n.* **transitivity** (-tiv'-) *n.*

transitory (tran'sitəri) *a.* lasting only a short time, transient, not durable, short-lived. **transitorily** *adv.* **transitoriness** *n.* **transitory action** *n.* (*Law*) an action that can be brought in any country regardless of where the issue concerned originated.

translate (translāt') *v.t.* **1** to render or express the sense of (a word, passage or work) into or in another language. **2** to express in clearer terms. **3** to express, paraphrase or convey (an idea etc.) from one art or style into another. **4** to interpret (as). **5** to transform, to change. **6** to remove from one office to another (esp. a bishop to another see). **7** (*Theol.*) to convey to heaven without death. ~*v.i.* **1** to be engaged in translation. **2** to allow of translation, to be translatable. **3** to be changed (into). **translatable** *a.* **translatability** (-bil'-) *n.* **translation** *n.* **1** the act or process of translating. **2** the product of translating; a rendition of the sense of a passage etc. in another language. **3** the act of expressing in clearer terms.

4 the act of transforming or changing. **translational** *a.* **translationally** *adv.* **translator** *n.* **1** a person engaged in translation. **2** a computer program that translates from one (natural or programming) language to another. **3** a television transmitter. **translatory** *a.*

transliterate (tranzlit'ərāt) *v.t.* to represent (words, sounds etc.) in the corresponding or approximately corresponding characters of another language or alphabet. **transliteration** (-ā'shən) *n.* **transliterator** *n.*

translocation (tranzləkā'shən) *n.* movement from one place to another. **translocate** *v.t.*

translucent (transloo'sənt) *a.* **1** allowing light to pass through but not transparent. **2** (*loosely*) transparent. **translucence, translucency** *n.* **translucently** *adv.*

transmigrate (tranzmīgrāt') *v.i.* **1** to pass through one place, country or jurisdiction en route to another, to migrate. **2** (*Theol.*) (of the soul) to pass from one body into another, to undergo metempsychosis. **transmigrant** (-mī'-) *n.* an alien passing through one country on the way to another. ~*a.* in the process of transmigrating. **transmigration** *n.* **transmigrator** *n.* **transmigratory** (-mī'grə-) *a.*

transmit (tranzmit') *v.t.* (*pres.p.* **transmitting**, *past*, *p.p.* **transmitted**) **1** to send, transfer or convey from one person or place to another. **2** to communicate from one person or place to another. **3** to suffer to pass through, to act as a medium for, to conduct. **4** to broadcast (a TV or radio programme). **transmissible** (-mis'-) *a.* **transmissibility** (-bil'-) *n.* **transmission** (-shən) *n.* **1** the act of sending something from one person or place to another. **2** the act of communicating something from one person or place to another. **3** the act of broadcasting a TV or radio programme. **4** signals sent out by a transmitter. **5** a radio or TV broadcast. **6** the gear by which power is conveyed from an engine to the live axle in a motor vehicle. **transmittable** *a.* **transmittal** *n.* **transmittance** *n.* (*Physics*) the ratio of the light energy falling on a body to that transmitted onward by it. **transmitter** *n.* **1** a person or thing that transmits. **2** any form of machine that transmits electromagnetic waves, esp. for radio and television. **3** the apparatus required for this. **4** a neurotransmitter.

transmogrify (tranzmog'rifī) *v.t.* (*3rd pers. sing. pres.* **transmogrifies**, *pres.p.* **transmogrifying**, *past*, *p.p.* **transmogrified**) (*esp. facet.*) to transform, esp. as if by magical means. **transmogrification** (-fikā'shən) *n.*

transmute (tranzmūt') *v.t.* to change from one form, nature or substance into another; to transform (into). **transmutable** *a.* **transmutability** (-bil'-) *n.* **transmutably** *adv.* **transmutation** (-tā'shən) *n.* **transmutational** *a.* **transmutative** *a.* **transmuter** *n.*

transoceanic (tranzōshian'ik) *a.* **1** situated or

coming from beyond the ocean. **2** crossing the ocean.

transom (tran´səm) *n.* **1** a horizontal bar of wood or stone across a window or other opening. **2** (*N Am.*) a fanlight. **3** each of the beams bolted across the sternpost of a ship, supporting the after-end of the deck. **4** a beam across a saw-pit. **transomed** *a.* **transom window** *n.* **1** a window divided by a transom. **2** a window over the transom of a door.

transonic (transon´ik), **trans-sonic** *a.* relating to or being a speed near the speed of sound.

transpacific (tranzpəsif´ik) *a.* **1** lying or being beyond the Pacific. **2** crossing the Pacific.

transparent (transpar´ənt, -peə´-) *a.* **1** having the property of transmitting rays of light without diffusion, so that objects are distinctly visible. **2** easily seen through. **3** plain, evident, clear. **4** frank, sincere. **5** (*Physics*) permitting heat or electromagnetic radiation to pass through. **transparency** *n.* (*pl.* **transparencies**) **1** the state of being easily seen through, clearness. **2** the state of being obvious or evident. **3** frankness, sincerity. **4** a thing that is transparent, esp. a picture, inscription, photograph etc. painted on glass, muslin or other transparent or semi-transparent material, to be exhibited by means of light shining through it. **5** a positive photograph on a transparent base mounted on a frame for viewing by means of a projector. **transparence** *n.* **transparently** *adv.* **transparentness** *n.*

transpersonal (tranzpɜ´sənəl) *a.* **1** going beyond the personal. **2** (*Psych.*) of or relating to psychology or psychotherapy based on mystical, psychical or spiritual experience.

transpire (transpīə´) *v.t.* to emit through the excretory organs (of the skin or lungs), to emit as vapour, to exhale. ~*v.i.* **1** (of perspiration etc.) to be emitted through the the excretory organs, to pass off as vapour. **2** to leak out, become known. **3** to happen. **transpirable** *a.* **transpiration** (-pirā´shən) *n.* **transpiratory** *a.*

Usage note The use of *transpire* to mean to happen is sometimes disapproved of.

transplant[1] (transplahnt´) *v.t.* **1** to remove and plant in another place. **2** to remove from one place and establish in another. **3** to transfer (living tissue) from one part or person to another. **transplantable** *a.* **transplantation** (-tā´shən) *n.* **transplanter** *n.*

transplant[2] (trans´plahnt) *n.* **1** the surgical procedure for transplanting an organ. **2** an organ surgically transplanted. **3** a thing which is transplanted, such as a plant.

transponder (transpon´də) *n.* a radio or radar device which automatically transmits a signal in response to a signal received.

transpontine (transpon´tīn) *a.* **1** on the other side of a bridge. **2** on or from the other side of the ocean.

transport[1] (transpawt´) *v.t.* **1** to carry or convey

from one place to another. **2** (*Hist.*) to remove (a criminal) to a penal colony. **3** (*chiefly in p.p.*) to carry away by powerful emotion, to entrance, to ravish. **transportable** *a.* **1** that may be transported. **2** (*Hist.*) (of an offence) involving transportation. **transportability** (-bil´-) *n.* **transportation** (-tā´shən) *n.* **1** the act of transporting or conveying. **2** the state of being transported. **3** (means of) conveyance. **4** carriage of persons or things from one place to another. **5** (*Hist.*) banishment to a penal colony. **transportedly** *adv.* **transporter** *n.* **1** a person who or device that transports. **2** a large vehicle for transporting goods. **transporter bridge** *n.* a device for carrying road traffic across a river on a moving platform.

transport[2] (trans´pawt) *n.* **1** transportation, conveyance from one place to another. **2** a vehicle, aircraft etc. used for transporting people or goods. **3** (*Hist.*) a transported convict or a convict sentenced to transportation. **4** ecstasy. **transport café** *n.* a roadside café used predominantly by lorry drivers.

transpose (transpōz´) *v.t.* **1** to cause to change places. **2** to change the order or position of (words or a word) in a sentence. **3** (*Math.*) to transfer (a term) from one side of an equation to the other, changing the sign. **4** (*Mus.*) to write or play in a different key. **transposable** *a.* **transposal** *n.* **transposer** *n.* **transposition** (-pəzish´ən) *n.*

transputer (transpū´tə) *n.* a powerful microchip which has its own RAM facility and is designed to process in parallel rather than sequentially.

transsexual (trans-sek´shuəl), **transexual** (transek´shuəl) *n.* **1** a person who dresses and lives for all or most of the time as a member of the opposite sex. **2** a person who has undergone surgery and medical treatment to adopt the physical characteristics of the opposite sex. ~*a.* that is a transsexual; of or relating to transsexuals. **transsexualism** *n.*

trans-ship (trans-ship´), **tranship** (tranship´) *v.t.* (*pres.p.* **trans-shipping, transhipping**, *past, p.p.* **trans-shipped, transhipped**) to transfer from one ship, vehicle etc., to another. **trans-shipment** *n.*

trans-sonic TRANSONIC.

transubstantiate (transəbstan´shiāt) *v.t.* to change the substance of. **transubstantiation** (-ā´shən) *n.* **1** change from one substance into another, a change of essence. **2** (*Theol.*) conversion of the whole substance of the bread and wine in the Eucharist into the body and blood of Christ.

transuranic (tranzūran´ik) *a.* (*Chem.*) (of an atomic element) having an atomic number higher than uranium.

transverse (tranzvœs´, tranz´-) *a.* lying, being or acting across or in a cross direction. **transverse flute** *n.* a modern type of flute with the mouthpiece on the side. **transversely** *adv.*

transvestism (tranzves´tizm) *n.* the wearing of clothing belonging to the opposite sex, esp. for sexual stimulation. **transvestite** (-tīt) *n.* a person who practises transvestism. **transvestitism** (-tit-) *n.*

trap[1] (trap) *n.* **1** a contrivance for catching an animal, consisting of an enclosure or mechanical arrangement, esp. with a spring, often baited. **2** a trick or artifice for misleading or betraying a person, an ambush, a stratagem. **3** a device to catch someone, such as a motorist who is speeding. **4** a device for suddenly releasing a bird or propelling an object into the air to be shot at. **5** a compartment from which a racing greyhound is released. **6** a U-shaped bend or other contrivance in a soil pipe etc., for sealing this with a body of liquid and preventing the return flow of foul gas. **7** a trapdoor. **8** a two-wheeled vehicle on springs. **9** (*sl.*) the mouth. **10** (*esp. pl., sl.*) a percussion instrument in a jazz band. *~v.t.* (*pres.p.* **trapping**, *past, p.p.* **trapped**) **1** to catch in or as in a trap. **2** to retain, to hold back. **3** to stop or hold (gas etc.) in a trap. **4** to provide (a place) with traps. **5** to deceive, to ensnare. *~v.i.* to catch animals in traps. **trap-ball** *n.* a children's game played with a wooden device having a pivoted bar for sending a ball into the air on being hit with a bat. **trapdoor** *n.* a door in a floor or roof opening and shutting like a valve. **traplike** *a.* **trapper** *n.* a person who traps animals, esp. for furs. **trap-shooting** *n.* clay pigeon shooting. **trap-shooter** *n.*

trap[2] (trap), **trap-rock** *n.* a dark igneous rock, esp. a variety of dolerite or basalt, presenting a columnar or stairlike aspect.

trap[3] (trap) *v.t.* (*pres.p.* **trapping**, *past, p.p.* **trapped**) to adorn, to caparison. **trappings** *n.pl.* **1** decorations, adornments, esp. those of or relating to an office etc., finery. **2** ornamental harness or housing. **traps** *n.pl.* (*coll.*) one's personal belongings, luggage, baggage.

trapes TRAIPSE.

trapeze (trəpēz´) *n.* an apparatus consisting of a suspended bar or set of bars on which acrobats perform swinging, balancing and other feats. **trapezium** (-iəm) *n.* (*pl.* **trapezia** (-ziə), **trapeziums**) **1** a quadrilateral figure only two sides of which are parallel. **2** (*N Am.*) a trapezoid. **trapezius** *n.* (*pl.* **trapezii** (-ziī), **trapeziuses**) (*Anat.*) either of two flat triangular muscles on the back and shoulders that rotate the shoulder blades. **trapezoid** (trap´izoid, trəpē´-) *n.* **1** a quadrilateral no two of whose sides are parallel. **2** (*N Am.*) a quadrilateral figure only two sides of which are parallel. *~a.* shaped like a trapezoid, trapezoidal. **trapezoidal** (-zoi´-) *a.*

trapper TRAP[1].

trappings TRAP[3].

Trappist (trap´ist) *n.* a member of a Cistercian order, following the strict rule of La Trappe, a monastery founded at Soligny-la-Trappe, France, in 1664. *~a.* of or relating to this order.

traps TRAP[3].

trash (trash) *n.* **1** any waste or worthless matter, refuse, rubbish. **2** nonsense. **3** (*esp. N Am.*)

domestic refuse. **4** (*esp. N Am.*) nonsense. **5** a poor or worthless person or group of people. **6** a rubbishy article or production of any kind. *~v.t.* **1** (*esp. N Am., coll.*) to wreck. **2** (*coll.*) to subject to criticism, to denigrate. **trash can** *n.* (*N Am.*) a dustbin. **trashery** *n.* **trashy** *a.* (*comp.* **trashier**, *superl.* **trashiest**). **trashily** *adv.* **trashiness** *n.*

trattoria (tratərē´ə) *n.* (*pl.* **trattorias, trattorie** (-rē´ā)) an Italian restaurant.

trauma (traw´mə, trow´-) *n.* **1** (*Psych.*) a psychological shock having a lasting effect on the subconscious. **2** a distressing experience. **3** a wound or external injury. **4** physical shock produced by a wound or injury. **5** distress, anguish. **traumatic** (-mat´-) *a.* **1** of or causing trauma. **2** (*coll.*) distressing. **3** of, relating to or adapted to the cure of wounds. **traumatism** *n.* **traumatize, traumatise** *v.t.* to inflict a trauma on. **traumatization** (-zā´shən) *n.*

travail (trav´āl) *n.* (*poet.*) **1** painful toil, painful exertion or effort. **2** the pangs of childbirth. *~v.i.* **1** to toil painfully. **2** to suffer the pangs of childbirth.

travel (trav´əl) *v.i.* (*pres.p.* **travelling**, (*N Am.*) **traveling**, *past, p.p.* **travelled**, (*N Am.*) **traveled**) **1** to make a journey, esp. to distant or foreign lands. **2** (of a machine or part) to move (along, in, up and down etc.). **3** to move, to go, to pass through space. **4** to make journeys as a commercial traveller for securing orders etc. **5** (*coll.*) (of food or drink) to survive transportation in a specified way. **6** (*coll.*) to move quickly. *~v.t.* **1** to journey over. **2** to cause to travel. *~n.* **1** the act of travelling. **2** (*pl.*) an account of travelling, usu. in distant countries. **3** the length of stroke, the range or scope of a piston etc. **travel agent** *n.* a person who sells holidays, air, train or bus tickets etc. **travel agency** *n.* (*pl.* **travel agencies**). **travel bureau** *n.* a travel agency. **travelled,** (*N Am.*) **traveled** *a.* **1** having travelled. **2** experienced in travelling (*often in comb., as muchtravelled*). **traveller,** (*N Am.*) **traveler** *n.* **1** a person who travels. **2** a commercial traveller. **3** (*Austral.*) a swagman. **4** a gypsy. **5** an itinerant person who lives an alternative or New Age lifestyle. **traveller's cheque,** (*N Am.*) **traveler's check** *n.* a cheque available in various denominations, sold by a financial institution for use abroad by a traveller, who signs it on receipt and countersigns it in order to cash it. **traveller's joy** *n.* the wild clematis, *Clematis vitalba*. **travelling** *a., n.* **travelling crane** *n.* a crane that can move on rails. **travelling rug** *n.* a rug used while travelling. **travelling salesman** *n.* (*pl.* **travelling salesmen**) a person who travels from place to place promoting and selling the products or services of their company. **travelling salesperson** *n.* **travelogue** (-log), (*N Am.*) **travelog** *n.* a lecture or talk on travel illustrated by pictures or films. **travel-sick** *a.* suffering from nausea caused by being in a moving car, ship etc. **travel-sickness** *n.*

traverse¹ (trəvœs´, trav´-) *v.t.* **1** to travel across. **2** to make a traverse along (a cliff etc.). **3** to lie across or through. **4** to examine, consider or discuss thoroughly. **traversable** *a.* **traversal** *n.* **traverser** *n.*

traverse² (trav´œs) *a.* lying or being across, transverse. *~n.* **1** the act of traversing or travelling across. **2** the sideways travel of part of a machine. **3** anything, esp. a part of a building or mechanical structure, crossing something else. **4** a sideways movement of climbers or skiers on a mountainside or precipice to avoid obstacles.

travesty (trav´əsti) *n.* (*pl.* **travesties**) a parody, burlesque imitation or ridiculous misrepresentation. *~v.t.* (*3rd pers. sing. pres.* **travesties**, *pres.p.* **travestying**, *past*, *p.p.* **travestied**) to make a travesty of, to burlesque.

trawl (trawl) *n.* **1** (*also* **trawl net**) a net, shaped like a flattened bag, for dragging along the sea bottom. **2** a trawl line. **3** the act of trawling. *~v.i.* **1** to fish with a trawl net. **2** to gather data etc. from a great number of different sources. **trawl boat** *n.* **trawler** *n.* **1** a person who trawls. **2** a fishing vessel using a trawl net. **trawlerman** *n.* (*pl.* **trawlermen**) a man who works on a trawler. **trawling** *n.* **trawl line** *n.* a line of great length, with short lines carrying baited hooks, buoyed up at intervals, for deep-sea fishing.

tray (trā) *n.* **1** a flat shallow vessel, used for holding or carrying small articles on. **2** a shallow coverless box, esp. one forming a compartment in a trunk etc. **trayful** *n.* (*pl.* **trayfuls**).

treacherous (trech´ərəs) *a.* **1** violating allegiance, disloyal, perfidious. **2** deceptive, illusory. **3** unreliable, unsafe. **treacherously** *adv.* **treacherousness** *n.* **treachery** *n.* (*pl.* **treacheries**) the state of being treacherous.

treacle (trē´kəl) *n.* **1** a syrup drained from sugar in refining. **2** molasses. **3** excessive sentimentality. **treacly** *a.* (*comp.* **treaclier**, *superl.* **treacliest**). **treacliness** *n.*

tread (tred) *v.i.* (*past* **trod** (trod), *p.p.* **trod**, **trodden** (trod´ən)) **1** to set the foot on the ground. **2** to walk, to step, to go. **3** to deal (cautiously etc.). **4** (of a male bird) to copulate with a hen. *~v.t.* **1** to step or walk on. **2** to crush with the feet. **3** to trample on. **4** to walk (a distance, journey etc.). **5** to dance (a measure etc.). **6** (of a male bird) to copulate with, to cover. *~n.* **1** the act or manner of walking. **2** the sound of walking, a footstep. **3** (*also* **tread-board**) the flat part of a stair or step. **4** the part of a wheel that bears upon the ground. **5** the outer face of a tyre that is in contact with the road. **6** the part of a rail on which the wheels bear. **7** the part of a sole that rests on the ground. **8** the act of copulating in birds. **to tread on 1** to trample on. **2** to set the foot on. **3** to follow closely. **to tread on someone's toes** to offend someone's susceptibilities. **to tread out 1** to press out (wine etc.) with the feet. **2** to extinguish by stamping on. **to tread the boards** to go on stage, to be an actor. **to tread**

under foot 1 to destroy. **2** to treat with scorn. **to tread water 1** to remain upright and afloat by making walking motions with the legs. **2** to undergo a period of relative inactivity. **treader** *n.*

treadmill *n.* **1** a mechanism, usu. in the form of a revolving cylinder driven by the weight of a person or people, horses etc., treading on movable steps on the periphery, formerly used as a punishment in prisons. **2** a similar mechanism used for physical exercise. **3** wearisome monotony or routine. **treadwheel** *n.* a treadmill.

treadle (tred´əl) *n.* a lever worked by the foot giving motion to a lathe, sewing machine, bicycle etc. *~v.i.* to work a treadle.

treason (trē´zən) *n.* **1** a violation of allegiance by a subject against the sovereign or government, esp. an overt attempt to subvert the government, high treason. **2** (*Hist.*) murder of one's master or husband, petty treason. **3** an act of treachery, a breach of faith. **treasonable** *a.* consisting of or involving treason. **treasonableness** *n.* **treasonably** *adv.* **treasonous** *a.*

treasure (trezh´ə) *n.* **1** precious metals in any form, or gems. **2** a quantity of these hidden away or kept for future use, a hoard. **3** accumulated wealth. **4** anything highly valued, a precious or highly-prized thing, esp. if portable. **5** (*coll.*) a person greatly valued, a beloved person. *~v.t.* **1** to lay (up) as valuable, to hoard, to store (up). **2** to prize, to lay (up) in the memory as valuable. **treasure hunt** *n.* a game in which people compete to be the first to find something hidden. **treasure trove** *n.* **1** (*Law*) money, gold, silver, plate or bullion found hidden in the earth or a private place, the owner being unknown, but now becoming the property of the Crown. **2** a collection of valuable etc. items.

treasurer (trezh´ərə) *n.* **1** an officer who receives and disburses the public revenue from taxes, duties etc. **2** a person who has the charge of the funds of a company, society, club etc. **treasurership** *n.*

treasury (trezh´əri) *n.* (*pl.* **treasuries**) **1** a place or building in which treasure is stored. **2** (**Treasury**) a government department in charge of the public revenue. **3** a repository, a book etc. full of information on any subject. **4** the funds or revenue of a society etc. **treasury bill** *n.* an instrument of credit issued by the government as an acknowledgement of money lent by a private person for three, six or twelve months. **treasury note** *n.* (*Hist.*, *also* N Am.) a note issued by the Treasury for use as currency.

treat (trēt) *v.t.* **1** to act or behave to or towards. **2** to deal with or manipulate for a particular result, to apply a particular process to, to subject to the action of a chemical agent etc. **3** to apply medical care to. **4** to handle or present or express (a subject etc.) in a particular way. **5** to supply with food, drink or entertainment at one's expense. *~v.i.* **1** to arrange terms (with), to negotiate. **2** to discuss, to discourse (of). *~n.* **1** an entertainment, esp. out of doors, given to schoolchildren etc. **2** an unusual pleasure or gratification. **a treat** (*coll.*) excellently, very well. **to stand treat** (*coll.*) to pay for drinks etc. **treatable** *a.* **treater** *n.*

treatise (trē´tiz, -is) *n.* a literary composition expounding, discussing and illustrating some particular subject in a thorough way.

treatment (trēt´mənt) *n.* **1** any medical procedure intended to bring about a cure. **2** the act or manner of treating. **the treatment** (*coll.*) the usual way of dealing with something in a particular situation.

treaty (trē´ti) *n.* (*pl.* **treaties**) **1** an agreement formally concluded and ratified between different states. **2** an agreement between persons etc.

treble (treb´əl) *a.* **1** triple, threefold. **2** (*Mus.*) soprano. **3** (of a voice) high-pitched. ~*n.* **1** (*Mus.*) **a** a soprano voice, singer or part. **b** a high-pitched musical instrument. **2** the higher part of the frequency range, esp. in electronic sound reproduction. **3** a type of bet in which the stake and winnings of a bet on one race are carried forward to the next of three races. **4** a treble quantity or thing. **5** in darts, a hit scoring treble. **6** three sporting victories in the same season, event etc. ~*v.t.* to multiply by three. ~*v.i.* to become threefold. **treble chance** *n.* a type of bet in football pools in which one wins by accurately predicting the number of draws, and home and away wins. **treble clef** *n.* the clef that places G above middle C on the second line of the staff. **trebly** *adv.*

☒ **trecherous** common misspelling of TREACHEROUS.

tree (trē) *n.* **1** a perennial woody plant rising from the ground with a single supporting trunk or stem. **2** a similar plant having a tall straight stem, as a palm. **3** a thing resembling a tree, esp. in having a stem and branches. **4** a family or genealogical tree. **5** (*esp. Math.*) a tree diagram. **6** a timber beam or framework, such as an axle-tree, swingletree etc. **7** a last for a boot or shoe. ~*v.t.* (*3rd pers. sing. pres.* **trees**, *pres.p.* **treeing**, *past, p.p.* **treed**) **1** to drive or force to take refuge in a tree. **2** (*esp. N Am.*) to put into a difficult situation. **3** to stretch on a shoe-tree. **to grow on trees** (*usu. with neg.*) to be plentiful. **up a tree** (*esp. N Am.*) in a fix, cornered. **treecreeper** *n.* any small bird of the family Certhiidae which creeps up trees to feed on insects. **tree diagram** *n.* (*esp. Math.*) a diagram with branching lines. **tree fern** *n.* a fern with a vertical rhizome like a tree trunk. **tree frog** *n.* any frog with arboreal habits, esp. of the family Hylidae. **tree house** *n.* a small house in a tree for children to play in. **tree kangaroo** *n.* any arboreal kangaroo of the genus *Dendrolagus*. **treeless** *a.* **treelessness** *n.* **treelike** *a.* **tree line** *n.* the timberline. **tree of knowledge** *n.* **1** (*Bible*) a tree in the Garden of Eden, the fruit of which gave knowledge of good and evil (Gen. iii). **2** the branches of knowledge. **tree ring** *n.* ANNUAL RING

(under ANNUAL). **tree surgeon** *n.* an expert in the treatment of diseased trees. **tree surgery** *n.* **tree tomato** *n.* **1** a S American shrub, *Cyphomandra betacea*, which has edible red fruit. **2** the fruit of this; also called *tamarillo*. **treetop** *n.* the topmost part of a tree. **tree trunk** *n.* the trunk of a tree.

trefoil (tref´oil, trē´-) *n.* **1** a plant with three leaflets or three-lobed leaves, esp. of the genus *Trifolium*, such as the clover, the black medick etc. **2** a three-lobed or three-cusped ornament in window tracery etc. **3** any object in this shape. **trefoiled** *a.* (*also in comb.*).

trek (trek) *v.i.* (*pres.p.* **trekking**, *past, p.p.* **trekked**) **1** to journey, esp. with difficulty on foot. **2** (*Hist., esp. S Afr.*) to travel by ox-wagon. **3** (*S Afr.*) (of oxen) to draw a vehicle or load. ~*n.* **1** any long, arduous journey, esp. on foot. **2** a stage or day's march. **3** a journey with a wagon. **trekker** *n.*

trellis (trel´is) *n.* **1** (*also* **trellis-work**) openwork of strips of wood crossing each other and nailed together, used for verandas, summer houses etc. **2** a summer house, screen or other structure made of this. ~*v.t.* (*pres.p.* **trellising**, *past, p.p.* **trellised**) **1** to interlace into a trellis. **2** to provide with a trellis.

trematode (trem´ətōd) *n.* any parasitic flatworm of the class Trematoda, esp. a fluke.

tremble (trem´bəl) *v.i.* **1** to shake involuntarily, as with fear, cold, weakness etc. **2** to be in a state of fear or agitation. **3** to be alarmed (for). **4** to totter, to oscillate, to quaver. ~*n.* **1** the act or state of trembling. **2** the act or state of quavering or oscillating. **3** fear. **all of a tremble 1** (*coll.*) trembling. **2** (*coll.*) very agitated. **trembler** *n.* **1** a person who trembles. **2** an automatic vibrator for making or breaking an electrical circuit. **trembling** *a.* **tremblingly** *adv.* **trembling poplar** *n.* an aspen. **trembly** *a.* (*comp.* **tremblier**, *superl.* **trembliest**).

tremendous (trimen´dəs) *a.* **1** terrible, dreadful. **2** of overpowering magnitude, violence etc. **3** (*coll.*) extraordinary, considerable. **tremendously** *adv.* **tremendousness** *n.*

tremolo (trem´əlō) *n.* (*pl.* **tremolos**) (*Mus.*) **1** a tremulous or quavering effect in singing, playing etc. **2** an organ or harmonium stop producing a vibrating tone. **3** (*also* **tremolo arm**) a lever on an electric guitar used to vary the pitch of a played note.

tremor (trem´ə) *n.* **1** a trembling, shaking or quivering. **2** a thrill. **3** a small earthquake. ~*v.i.* to tremble.

tremulous (trem´ūləs) *a.* **1** trembling, shaking, quivering. **2** timid, irresolute, wavering. **tremulously** *adv.* **tremulousness** *n.*

trench (trench) *n.* **1** (*esp. Mil.*) a long narrow cut or deep furrow in the earth, a ditch, esp. a long narrow ditch, usu. with a parapet formed by the excavated earth, to cover besieging troops etc. **2** a long narrow groove in the ocean bed. ~*v.t.* **1** to cut a trench or trenches in (ground etc.). **2** to turn over (ground) by cutting a successive series of trenches and filling in with the excavated soil. **trench coat** n. **1** a soldier's heavy, lined mackintosh crossing over in front and having a belt. **2** a similar raincoat, worn by men or women. **trench foot** n. a gangrenous condition of the foot caused by prolonged standing in cold water. **trench mortar** n. a mortar used for throwing bombs. **trench warfare** n. type of warfare in which soldiers take up positions in trenches facing the enemy.

trenchant (tren´chənt) a. cutting, biting, incisive. **trenchancy** n. **trenchantly** adv.

trencher (tren´chə) n. a wooden plate of a type formerly used for serving food, now for cutting bread on. **trencherman** n. (pl. **trenchermen**) a (good or poor) feeder or eater.

trend (trend) n. **1** a general tendency, bent or inclination. **2** a mode, fashion. ~v.i. **1** to bend (away etc.). **2** to have a general tendency or direction. **trendsetter** n. a person who originates or dictates fashions. **trendsetting** a. **trendy** a. (comp. **trendier**, superl. **trendiest**) (coll., sometimes derog.) following the latest trends, fashionable. ~n. (pl. **trendies**) a trendy person. **trendily** adv. **trendiness** n.

trepan (tripan´) n. a surgeon's cylindrical saw for removing portions of the skull. ~v.t. (pres.p. **trepanning**, past, p.p. **trepanned**) to perforate with a trepan. **trepanation** (trepənā´shən), **trepanning** n.

trepidation (trepidā´shən) n. **1** a state of alarm or agitation. **2** a trembling of the limbs, as in paralysis.

trespass (tres´pəs) n. **1** (Law) a wrongful act involving injury to the person or property of another, esp. unauthorized entry into another's land. **2** †a transgression against law, duty etc., an offence, a sin. ~v.i. **1** (Law) to commit an illegal intrusion (upon the property or personal rights of another). **2** to intrude, encroach or make undue claims (upon). **3** †to transgress (against). **trespasser** n.

tress (tres) n. **1** a lock or plait of hair, esp. from the head of a girl or woman. **2** (pl.) hair. **tressed**, **tressy** a.

trestle (tres´əl) n. **1** a movable frame for supporting a table, platform etc., usu. consisting of a pair of divergent legs, fixed or hinged. **2** (also **trestle-work**) an open braced framework of timber or iron for supporting the horizontal portion of a bridge etc. **3** a trestle-tree. **4** a trestle-table. **trestle-table** n. a table formed of boards supported on movable trestles. **trestle-tree** n. (Naut.) either of a pair of horizontal fore-and-aft timbers fixed to a lower mast to support the crosstrees.

trevally (trival´i) n. (pl. **trevallies**) any Australian fish of the genus Caranx.

trews (trooz) n.pl. trousers, esp. made of tartan.

trey (trā) n. (pl. **treys**) the three at cards or dice.

tri- (trī) comb. form three, three times, triple.

triable (trī´əbəl) a. **1** subject to judicial trial. **2** that may be tried or tested.

triacetate (trīas´itāt) n. a cellulose derivative containing three acetate groups.

triad (trī´ad) n. **1** a collection of three. **2** the number three. **3** a Chinese secret society, often engaging in illegal activities. **4** a member of such a society. **5** (Mus.) a chord of three notes. **triadic** (-ad´-) a.

triage (trī´əj, trē´ahzh) n. **1** the sorting of hospital patients, casualties in war etc. according to urgency of treatment and likelihood of survival. **2** the act of sorting according to quality, prioritization.

trial (trī´əl) n. **1** (Law) the judicial examination and determination of the issues in a cause between parties before a judge, judge and jury or a referee. **2** the act or process of trying or testing. **3** experimental treatment. **4** a test, an examination, an experiment. **5** a person who or thing which tries or tests strength, endurance, and other qualities. **6** hardship, trouble, suffering etc. **7** a sports match to test ability. **8** a motorcycle journey to test skill. **9** a contest for dogs, horses etc. ~v.t. (pres.p. **trialling**, (N Am.) **trialing**, past, p.p. **trialled**, (N Am.) **trialed**) to subject to a performance test. ~v.i. to undergo a performance test. **on trial 1** undergoing a test. **2** being tried in a law court. **trial and error** n. a method of solving problems by trying several solutions and choosing the most successful. **trialist, triallist** n. **1** a person taking part in a trial. **2** a person involved in a judicial trial. **trial run** n. a preliminary test of a new procedure etc.

triangle (trī´ang-gəl) n. **1** a figure, esp. a plane figure, bounded by three lines, esp. straight lines. **2** any three things in the shape of a triangle, joined by imaginary lines. **3** a drawing implement or other thing or ornament of this shape. **4** a musical instrument consisting of a steel rod bent into a triangle and sounded by striking with a steel rod. **5** any situation involving three people or elements. **triangular** (-ang´gū-) a. **1** having the shape of a triangle. **2** involving three people or elements. **3** (of a pyramid) having a base with three sides. **triangularity** (-lar´-) n. **triangularly** adv. **triangulate** (-lāt) v.t. **1** to make triangular. **2** to divide into triangles, esp. (an area) in surveying. **3** to ascertain by this means. **triangulation** (-lā´shən) n.

Trias (trī´əs) n. (Geol.) the division of rock strata between the Carboniferous and the Jurassic (divided in Germany into three groups, whence the name). **Triassic** (-as´-) a., n.

triathlon (trīath´lon) n. an athletic contest consisting of three events. **triathlete** n.

triatomic (trīətom´ik) a. (Chem.) having three atoms in the molecule.

tribal (trī´bəl) a. belonging to, of or relating to a tribe. **tribalism** n. **1** tribal organization. **2** loyalty to a tribe or group. **tribalist** n. **tribalistic** (-lis´-) a. **tribally** adv.

tribasic (trībā´sik) *a.* (*Chem.*) having three atoms of hydrogen replaceable by a base or basic radical.

tribe (trīb) *n.* **1** a group of people ethnologically related and forming a community or a political division. **2** a group claiming common descent or affinity, a clan or group of clans, esp. a group of clans under a chief. **3** (*usu. derog.*) a number of persons of the same character, profession etc. **4** a family, esp. a large one. **5** (*Biol.*) a more or less indefinite group of plants or animals, usu. above a genus and below an order. **tribesman, tribeswoman** *n.* (*pl.* **tribesmen, tribeswomen**). **tribespeople** *n.pl.*

tribology (trībol´əji) *n.* the study of friction, lubrication and wear between interacting surfaces. **tribologist** *n.*

tribulation (tribūlā´shən) *n.* **1** severe affliction, suffering, distress. **2** a cause of this.

tribunal (trībū´nəl, trib-) *n.* **1** a court of justice. **2** a board of arbitrators etc. **3** a seat or bench for judges, magistrates etc., a judgement-seat.

tribune¹ (trib´ūn) *n.* **1** a champion of popular rights and liberties. **2** (*Hist.*) (*also* **tribune of the people**) each of two (later ten) representatives elected by the people of ancient Rome to protect their rights and liberties against the patricians. **3** (*Hist.*) any one of various ancient Roman civil, fiscal and military officers. **tribunate** (-nət, -nāt), **tribuneship** *n.*

tribune² (trib´ūn) *n.* **1** a bishop's throne in an apse; an apse containing this. **2** a platform with seats. **3** a rostrum, a pulpit. **4** a raised floor for the curule chairs of the magistrates in the apse of a Roman basilica.

tributary (trib´ūtəri) *n.* (*pl.* **tributaries**) **1** a stream or river flowing into a larger one or a lake. **2** (*Hist.*) a person or state subject to tribute. ~*a.* **1** serving to increase a larger stream or river etc. **2** (*Hist.*) paying or subject to tribute. **tributarily** *adv.* **tributariness** *n.*

tribute (trib´ūt) *n.* **1** a contribution, gift or offering (of praise etc.). **2** (*Hist.*) a sum of money or other valuable thing paid by one ruler or state to another in token of submission, for peace or protection, or by virtue of a treaty. **3** a praiseworthy thing attributable (to).

trice (trīs) *n.* an instant. **in a trice** in a moment.

tricentenary (trīsentē´nəri, -ten´-, trīsen´tin-) *n.* (*pl.* **tricentenaries**) TERCENTENARY.

triceps (trī´seps) *a.* (of muscles) three-headed, having three points of attachment. ~*n.* a triceps muscle, esp. the large muscle at the back of the upper arm.

triceratops (trīser´ətops) *n.* a large herbivorous dinosaur of the Cretaceous period, of the genus *Triceratops*, with three horns and a bony crest on the hood.

trichina (trikī´nə) *n.* (*pl.* **trichinae** (-nē)) any hairlike nematode parasitic worm of the genus *Trichinella*, esp. *T. spiralis*, infesting the intestine or muscles of pigs, humans etc. **trichiniasis** (trikinī´əsis), **trichinosis** (-nō´-) *n.* a disease due to the presence of trichinae in the system. **trichinosed** (trik´inōzd), **trichinotic** (trikinot´-), **trichinous** *a.*

tricho- (trī´kō, trik´ō) *comb. form* hair.

trichology (trikol´əji) *n.* the study of the human hair. **trichologist** *n.*

trichomonad (trikəmon´ad, -kō-) *n.* any parasitic protozoan of the order Trichomonadida, occurring in the digestive system of humans and animals such as cattle.

trichomoniasis (trikəmənī´əsis, -kō-) *n.* an infection caused by trichomonads, esp. a vaginal infection, *Trichomonas vaginalis*.

trichopathy (trikop´əthi) *n.* (*pl.* **trichopathies**) the treatment of hair-diseases. **trichopathic** (-əpath´-) *a.*

trichroism (trī´krōizm) *n.* the property of exhibiting different colours in three different directions when viewed by transmitted light. **trichroic** (-krō´-) *a.*

trichromatic (trīkrōmat´ik) *a.* three-coloured, having the normal three fundamental colour-sensations (of red, green and purple). **trichromatism** (-krō´-) *n.*

trick (trik) *n.* **1** an artifice, an artful device or stratagem. **2** an optical illusion. **3** an ingenious or peculiar way of doing something, a knack. **4** a feat of dexterity, esp. of legerdemain or sleight of hand. **5** a foolish or malicious act, a prank, a practical joke. **6** a particular habit or practice, a mannerism, a personal peculiarity. **7** the whole number of cards played in one round. **8** a round. **9** a point gained as the result of a round. **10** (*sl.*) a session with a prostitute. **11** (*sl.*) a client of a prostitute. ~*a.* using trickery, illusion etc. ~*v.t.* **1** to cheat, to deceive, to delude, to inveigle (into, out of etc.). **2** to dress, to deck (out or up). ~*v.i.* to practise trickery. **how's tricks?** (*coll.*) how are you? **to do the trick** (*coll.*) to achieve the required effect. **to turn a trick** (*sl.*) (of a prostitute) to have sexual relations with a client. **up to one's tricks** (*coll.*) behaving badly. **trick cyclist** *n.* **1** a cyclist performing tricks. **2** (*sl.*) a psychiatrist. **tricker** *n.* **trickery** *n.* (*pl.* **trickeries**). **trickish** *a.* **trick of the trade** *n.* a trade secret. **trick or treat** *n.* (*esp. N Am.*) the Hallowe'en custom of children in fancy dress knocking on people's doors and asking for sweets etc., threatening to play a trick if not given anything. **trickster** (-stə) *n.* **tricksy** (-si) *a.* (*comp.* **tricksier**, *superl.* **tricksiest**) playful, sportive. **tricksily** *adv.* **tricksiness** *n.* **tricky** *a.* (*comp.* **trickier**, *superl.* **trickiest**) **1** difficult, awkward. **2** requiring tactful or skilful handling. **3** deceitful. **trickily** *adv.* **trickiness** *n.*

trickle (trik´əl) *v.i.* to flow in drops or in a small stream. ~*v.t.* **1** to cause to flow in this way. **2** to come out slowly or gradually. ~*n.* **1** a trickling. **2** a small stream, a rill. **trickle charger** *n.* a battery charger which is mains-operated. **tricklet** *n.* **trickly** *a.*

triclinic (trīklin´ik) a. 1 (of a mineral) having the three axes unequal and inclined at oblique angles. 2 relating to the system classifying such substances.

tricolour (trī´kŭlə, trik´ələ), (N Am.) **tricolor** n. a flag or banner having three colours, esp. arranged in equal stripes, such as the national standard of France of blue, white and red, divided vertically. ~a. three-coloured. **tricoloured** a.

tricorn (trī´kawn), **tricorne** a. (of a hat) having three corners. ~n. a three-cornered hat.

tricot (trē´kō) n. a hand-knitted woollen fabric or a machine-made imitation.

tricycle (trī´sikəl) n. 1 a three-wheeled cycle. 2 a three-wheeled vehicle used by a disabled driver. ~v.i. to ride on this. **tricyclist** n.

tricyclic (trīsī´klik) a. (of a compound) having three rings in its molecule. ~n. any antidepressant drug with this molecular structure.

trident (trī´dənt) n. a three-pronged implement or weapon, esp. a fish-spear. **tridentate** (-den´tāt) a. having three teeth or prongs.

Tridentine (trīden´tīn) a. of or relating to Trent, or the Council held there 1545–63. **Tridentine mass** n. the liturgy used by the Roman Catholic Church 1570–1964.

tried TRY.

triennial (trīen´iəl) a. 1 lasting for three years. 2 happening every three years. **triennially** adv. **triennium** (-iəm) n. (pl. **triennia** (-iə), **trienniums**) a period of three years.

trier TRY.

trifid (trī´fid) a. (Biol.) divided wholly or partially into three.

trifle (trī´fəl) n. 1 a thing, matter, fact etc. of no value or importance. 2 a small amount of money etc. 3 a light confection of whipped cream or white of egg, with cake, jam, wine etc. 4 something of little value, bauble, trinket. 5 a small amount of something. ~v.i. 1 to act or talk with levity. 2 to sport, to jest, to fool. ~v.t. to waste, fritter or fool away (time) in trifling. **to trifle with** 1 to treat with levity, disrespect or lack of proper seriousness. 2 to flirt with. **trifler** n. **trifling** a. 1 insignificant, trivial. 2 frivolous. 3 (of a sum of money) very small. **triflingly** adv. **triflingness** n.

trifocal (trīfō´kəl) a. having three focuses or focal lengths. **trifocals** n.pl. trifocal spectacles.

trifoliate (trīfō´liət), **trifoliated** (-ātid) a. (Bot.) 1 three-leaved, consisting of three leaflets. 2 (of a plant) having such leaves.

triforium (trīfaw´riəm) n. (pl. **triforia** (-riə)) a gallery or arcade in the wall over the arches of the nave or choir, or sometimes the transepts, in a large church.

triform (trī´fawm), **triformed** (-fawmd) a. having three shapes, parts or divisions.

trifurcate (trī´fœ´kət, trīfur´-), **trifurcated** (-kātid) a. having three branches or forks. ~v.t., v.i. to divide into three.

trig[1] (trig) n. (coll.) trigonometry.

trig[2] (trig) a. (esp. dial.) neat, trim, spruce. ~n. a dandy. ~v.t. (pres.p. **trigging**, past, p.p. **trigged**) to make trim.

trigamous (trig´əməs) a. 1 married three times. 2 having three wives or three husbands at once. 3 (Bot.) having male, female and hermaphrodite flowers on the same head. **trigamist** n. **trigamy** n.

trigger (trig´ə) n. 1 a catch or lever for releasing the hammer of a gunlock. 2 any similar device for releasing a spring etc. in various forms of mechanism. 3 anything that initiates a process, sequence of events etc. ~v.t. 1 to cause to happen, to set off. 2 to activate, to put into operation. 3 to fire (a gun). **triggered** a. **triggerfish** n. (pl. in general **triggerfish**, in particular **triggerfishes**) any usu. tropical fish of the family Balistidae which live in tropical and temperate seas. **trigger-happy** a. 1 too eager to fire (a gun etc.). 2 too eager to take action.

triglyceride (trīglis´ərīd) n. (Chem.) any ester of glycerol and three acid radicals.

trigonometry (trigənom´itri) n. the branch of mathematics treating of the relations of the sides and angles of triangles, and applying these to astronomy, navigation, surveying etc. **trigonometric** (-nəmet´-), **trigonometrical** a.

trigram (trī´gram) n. 1 a group of three letters representing a single sound, a trigraph. 2 a set of three straight lines in one plane not all intersecting in the same point.

trigraph (trī´grahf) n. 1 a group of three letters representing a single sound. 2 a figure of three lines.

trihedron (trīhē´drən) n. (pl. **trihedra** (-drə), **trihedrons**) a figure having three sides. **trihedral** a.

trihydric (trīhī´drik) a. (Chem.) containing three hydroxyl groups.

trike (trīk) n., v.i. (coll.) short for TRICYCLE.

trilabiate (trīlā´biət) a. (Bot., Zool.) three-lipped.

trilateral (trīlat´ərəl) a. 1 of or having three sides. 2 involving three parties or people. ~n. a three-sided figure. **trilaterally** adv.

trilby (tril´bi) n. (pl. **trilbies**) a man's soft felt hat with a dent in the middle. **trilbied** a.

trilinear (trīlin´iə) a. consisting of three lines.

trilingual (trīling´gwəl) a. 1 able to speak three languages. 2 of, relating to or expressed in three languages. **trilingualism** n.

trilith (trī´lith), **trilithon** (-on) n. a megalithic monument usu. consisting of two uprights supporting an impost. **trilithic** (-lith´-) a.

trill (tril) v.i. to sing or emit a sound with a tremulous vibration. ~v.t. to sing or utter with a quavering or shake. ~n. 1 a tremulous or quavering sound. 2 a consonant pronounced with a trilling sound, such as r. 3 a shake, a rapid alternation of two notes a tone or semitone apart.

trillion (tril´yən) n. (pl. **trillion**, **trillions**) 1 a million million. 2 (esp. Hist.) the product of a million raised to the third power. 3 (pl., coll.) an indefinite large number. **trillionth** (-th) a., n.

trillium (tril´iəm) *n.* any herbaceous plant of the genus *Trillium*, with a single central flower above three leaves.

trilobite (trī´ləbīt, tril´-) *n.* any of the Palaeozoic group of articulates with a three-lobed body. **trilobitic** (-bit´-) *a.*

trilogy (tril´əji) *n.* (*pl.* **trilogies**) a group of three plays, operas, novels etc., each complete in itself, but connected.

trim (trim) *v.t.* (*pres.p.* **trimming**, *past, p.p.* **trimmed**) **1** to put in good order, to make neat and tidy. **2** to remove irregularities, excrescences or superfluous or unsightly parts from. **3** to cut, lop, or clip (those) away or off. **4** to reduce (e.g. costs). **5** to decorate, to ornament (with trimmings etc.). **6** to adjust (sails, yards etc.) to the wind. **7** to adjust (a ship) by arranging the cargo, ballast etc. **8** (*coll.*) to reprove sharply; to chastise, to flog. **9** to decorate (e.g. a piece of clothing) esp. round the edges. ~*v.i.* to adopt a middle course, between parties, opinions etc. ~*a.* (*comp.* **trimmer**, *superl.* **trimmest**) **1** properly adjusted, in good order. **2** well-equipped, neat, tidy, smart. **3** good condition. ~*n.* **1** (esp. of a ship or her cargo, ballast, masts etc.) a state of preparation or fitness, order, condition. **2** dress or equipment. **3** material used to trim clothes etc. **4** an act of trimming, esp. hair. **5** the angle at which an aeroplane flies in given conditions. **6** the interior panels, decorative fascia, etc. of a vehicle. **in trim** (*esp. Naut.*) looking smart or neat. **trimly** *adv.* **trimmer** *n.* **trimming** *n.* **1** the act of a person who trims. **2** material sewn on a garment for ornament. **3** (*pl., coll.*) accessories to a dish. **4** (*pl.*) anything additional to the main item. **5** (*pl.*) pieces trimmed off. **trimness** *n.*

trimaran (trī´məran) *n.* a sailing vessel with three hulls.

trimer (trī´mə) *n.* (*Chem.*) a polymer whose molecule is formed from three molecules of a monomer. **trimeric** (-mer´-) *a.* **trimerous** (trim´-, trī´-) *a.* having three parts, joints, members etc.

trimester (trimes´tə) *n.* **1** a period of three months. **2** any of the three divisions of the academic year. **trimestral** *a.* **trimestrial** *a.*

trimeter (trim´itə) *n.* a verse consisting of three measures of two feet each. ~*a.* consisting of three measures. **trimetric** (trīmet´-), **trimetrical** *a.*

trimmer, trimming TRIM.

Trinidadian (trinidad´iən, -dā´-) *n.* a native or inhabitant of Trinidad. ~*a.* of or relating to Trinidad or its inhabitants.

trinitrotoluene (trīnītrōtol´uēn), **trinitrotoluol** (-ol) *n.* a chemical compound, usually known as TNT, largely used as a high explosive.

trinity (trin´iti) *n.* (*pl.* **trinities**) **1** a group or union of three individuals, a triad. **2** the state of being three or threefold. **3** (*Theol.*) (**Trinity**) the union of three persons (the Father, the Son and the Holy Ghost) in one Godhead. **4** a symbolical representation of the Trinity frequent in art, such as the triangle or three interlacing circles.

Trinitarian (-teə´ri-) *a.* of or relating to the doctrine of the Trinity. ~*n.* a person who believes in this. **Trinitarianism** *n.* **Trinity Sunday** *n.* the Sunday next after Whit Sunday.

trinket (tring´kit) *n.* **1** a small personal ornament of no great value as a jewel, esp. a ring. **2** any small ornament or fancy article. **trinketry** (-ri) *n.*

trinomial (trīnō´miəl) *a.* consisting of three terms, esp. connected by the signs + or -. ~*n.* a trinomial name or expression.

trio (trē´ō) *n.* (*pl.* **trios**) **1** a set of three. **2** (*Mus.*) **a** a musical composition for three voices or three instruments. **b** a set of three singers or players. **c** the second part of a minuet, march etc.

triode (trī´ōd) *n.* **1** a thermionic valve with three electrodes. **2** any electronic device with three electrodes.

trioxide (trīok´sīd) *n.* (*Chem.*) an oxide having three oxygen atoms.

trip (trip) *v.i.* (*pres.p.* **tripping**, *past, p.p.* **tripped**) **1** to move, step, walk or run lightly or nimbly. **2** (of rhythm etc.) to go lightly or evenly. **3** to catch the foot (over something) so as nearly to fall, to make a false step, to stumble. **4** to make a short journey. **5** (*coll.*) to be under the influence of a hallucinogenic drug. **6** to err, to go wrong. **7** to be activated. ~*v.t.* **1** to cause to fall by catching or obstructing the feet etc. **2** to catch or detect in a fault, mistake or offence. **3** to release (a part of a machine) by unfastening. **4** to activate, to set off. ~*n.* **1** a short excursion, voyage or journey. **2** a stumble, a false step. **3** a failure, a mistake. **4** a light nimble step. **5** a leaping movement of the feet. **6** (*coll.*) a period spent under the influence of a hallucinogenic drug. **7** any device for activating a mechanism. **to trip the light fantastic** (*facet.*) to dance. **tripmeter** *n.* an instrument in a vehicle used for recording the distance of an individual journey. **tripper** *n.* **1** a person who goes on a trip, an excursionist. **2** (*coll.*) a person under the influence of a hallucinogenic drug. **trippingly** *adv.* **trippy** *a.* (*comp.* **trippier**, *superl.* **trippiest**) (*coll.*) producing an effect similar to that of taking hallucinogenic drugs. **tripwire** *n.* a wire that trips a mechanism when pulled.

tripartite (trīpah´tīt) *a.* **1** consisting of three parts. **2** divided into three corresponding parts or copies. **3** made or concluded between three parties. **tripartitely** *adv.* **tripartition** (-tish´ən) *n.*

tripe (trīp) *n.* **1** a part of the stomach of ruminating animals prepared for food. **2** (*coll.*) silly stuff, rubbish, nonsense.

triphthong (trif´thong) *n.* a combination of three vowels forming one sound. **triphthongal** (-thong´gəl) *a.*

triplane (trī´plān) *n.* an aeroplane with three supporting planes.

triple (trip´əl) *a.* **1** consisting of three parts or three things united, threefold. **2** multiplied by three. **3** (of musical rhythm) having three beats to the bar. ~*n.* **1** a threefold quantity. **2** three of anything. **3** (*pl.*) a peal of changes on seven bells.

~*v.t.* to treble, to make threefold. ~*v.i.* to become three times as large or as many. **triple acrostic** *n.* an acrostic which uses the first, middle and last letters to make words. **triple crown** *n.* **1** the crown or tiara worn by the Pope. **2** the act of winning all three of a series of matches, races etc. **triple jump** *n.* an athletic event in which the competitor performs a hop, a step and a jump in succession. **triple play** *n.* in baseball, the act of getting three players out with one ball. **triple point** *n.* (*Physics*) the temperature and pressure at which the solid, liquid and vapour phases of a substance are in equilibrium. **triple rhyme** *n.* a rhyme using three syllables. **triplet** *n.* **1** a set or group of three. **2** any one of three children born of the same mother at one birth. **3** three verses rhyming together. **4** (*Mus.*) three notes performed in the time of two. **triple time** *n.* a musical rhythm of three beats in a bar. **Triplex**® (-leks) *n.* a type of laminated glass. **triplex** *a.* triple or threefold. **triplicate**[1] (-likət) *a.* made three times as much or as many, threefold. ~*n.* a copy, document or other thing corresponding to two others of the same kind. **in triplicate** written out or copied three times. **triplicate**[2] (-likāt) *v.t.* to make triplicate, to treble. **triplication** (-kā´shən) *n.* **triplicity** (-plis´-) *n.* (*pl.* **triplicities**) **1** the state of being triple. **2** a group of three things. **triploid** (-loid) *a.* (*Biol.*) having three times the haploid number of chromosomes. ~*n.* a triploid organism. **triploidy** *n.* **triply** *adv.*

tripod (trī´pod) *n.* **1** a three-legged stand, stool, utensil, seat, table etc. **2** a three-legged support for a camera etc. **tripodal** (trip´ədəl) *a.*

tripoli (trip´əli) *n.* rotten-stone, a friable siliceous limestone.

tripos (trī´pos) *n.* (*pl.* **triposes**) either part of the examination for an honours BA at Cambridge University.

tripper TRIP.

triptych (trip´tik) *n.* **1** a picture, carving or other representation, on three panels side by side, frequently used for altarpieces. **2** a group of three associated pictures etc. **3** a writing-tablet in three leaves.

trireme (trī´rēm) *n.* a war-galley with three benches of oars.

trisaccharide (trīsak´ərīd) *n.* (*Chem.*) a sugar that consists of three monosaccharide molecules.

trisect (trīsekt´) *v.t.* to divide into three (esp. equal) parts. **trisection** *n.* **trisector** *n.*

trishaw (trī´shaw) *n.* a three-wheeled rickshaw.

triskaidekaphobia (triskīdekəfō´biə) *n.* fear of the number 13.

trismus (triz´məs) *n.* (*Med.*) lockjaw.

trisomy (tris´əmi) *n.* (*Med.*) a condition in which one chromosome type is represented three times instead of twice.

trisyllable (trīsil´əbəl) *n.* a word of three syllables. **trisyllabic** (-lab´-) *a.* **trisyllabically** *adv.*

trite (trīt) *a.* **1** commonplace, hackneyed, stale. **2** worn out. **tritely** *adv.* **triteness** *n.*

tritium (trit´iəm) *n.* (*Chem.*) an isotope of hydrogen with a mass three times that of ordinary hydrogen.

tritone (trī´tōn) *n.* (*Mus.*) an augmented fourth, containing three whole tones.

triturate (trit´ūrāt) *v.t.* **1** to rub or grind down to a fine powder. **2** to masticate with the molar teeth. **triturable** *a.* **trituration** (-rā´shən) *n.* **triturator** *n.*

triumph (trī´əmf) *n.* **1** the state of being victorious. **2** victory, success. **3** joy or exultation at a success. **4** a great example. ~*v.i.* **1** to gain a victory, to prevail (over). **2** to enjoy a triumph. **3** to boast or exult (over). **4** to exult. **triumphal** (-ŭm´-) *a.* of or relating to a triumph. **triumphalism** *n.* an arrogant pride in one's own success. **triumphalist** *n.*, *a.* **triumphant** (-ŭm´-) *a.* **1** victorious, successful. **2** exultant. **triumphantly** *adv.* **triumpher** *n.*

triumvir (trīŭm´viə) *n.* (*pl.* **triumvirs, triumviri** (-rī)) any one of three men united in office, esp. a member of the first or second triumvirate in ancient Rome. **triumviral** *a.* **triumvirate** (-ərət) *n.* **1** the office of a triumvir. **2** a coalition of three men in office or authority, esp. the first triumvirate, of Pompey, Julius Caesar and Crassus in 60 BC, or the second, of Mark Antony, Octavian, and Lepidus, in 43 BC. **3** a party or set of three men.

triune (trī´ūn) *a.* three in one. **triunity** (-ū´niti) *n.* (*pl.* **triunities**).

trivalent (trīvā´lənt) *a.* (*Chem.*) having a valency or combining power of three. **trivalence, trivalency** *n.*

trivet (triv´it) *n.* a three-legged stand, esp. a metal tripod or movable bracket for supporting a cooking vessel or kettle. **trivet table** *n.* a table that has three feet.

trivia (triv´iə) *n.pl.* trifles, inessentials.

trivial (triv´iəl) *a.* **1** of little value or importance, trifling, inconsiderable. **2** concerned with trivia. **trivialism** *n.* **triviality** (-al´-) *n.* (*pl.* **trivialities**). **trivialize, trivialise** *v.t.* to cause to seem trivial, to minimize. **trivialization** (-zā´shən) *n.* **trivially** *adv.* **trivialness** *n.*

tri-weekly (trīwēk´li) *a.* happening, issued or done three times a week or once every three weeks.

-trix (triks) *suf.* (*pl.* **-trices** (trisez, trī´-), **-trixes**) forming feminine agent nouns.

tRNA *abbr.* transfer RNA.

trocar (trō´kah) *n.* (*Med.*) an instrument for draining an internal part of fluid, used in dropsy, hydrocele etc.

trochee (trō´kē) *n.* a metrical foot of two syllables, long and short. **trochaic** (-kā´-) *a.*, *n.*

trochlea (trok´liə) *n.* (*pl.* **trochleae** (-liē)) (*Anat.*) a pulley-like anatomical part or surface, esp. that of the humerusarticulating with the ulna. **trochlear** *a.*

trod, trodden TREAD.

trog[1] (trog) *v.i.* (*pres.p.* **trogging**, *past*, *p.p.* **trogged**) (*sl.*) to walk, esp. wearily.

trog[2] (trog) *n.* (*sl.*) a lout or hooligan.

troglodyte (trog´lədīt) *n.* **1** a cave dweller. **2** a hermit. **3** (*derog.*) an eccentric or old-fashioned person. **troglodytic** (-dit´-), **troglodytical** *a.* **troglodytism** *n.*

trogon (trō´gon) *n.* any of a family of tropical American insectivorous birds, the Trogonidae, with brilliant plumage.

troika (troi´kə) *n.* **1** a team of three horses harnessed abreast. **2** a vehicle drawn by this. **3** a group of three people, esp. a triumvirate.

troilism (troi´lizm) *n.* sexual activity involving three people of both sexes.

Trojan (trō´jən) *a.* of or relating to ancient Troy. ~*n.* **1** an inhabitant of ancient Troy. **2** a person of pluck or determination. **Trojan horse** *n.* **1** any subterfuge intended to undermine an organization etc. from within. **2** (*Comput.*) (*also* **trojan**) a program designed to harm a computer system, which gains access to the system by being inserted into a legitimate program, and differs from a virus in that it cannot replicate itself.

troll[1] (trōl) *v.t.* **1** to roll or reel out (a song) in a careless manner. **2** to fish (water) by trailing or spinning a revolving bait, esp. behind a boat. **3** to sing the parts of (a song) in succession. ~*v.i.* **1** to fish in this way. **2** to sing in a free and easy way. **3** to walk, to stroll. ~*n.* **1** the act of trolling for fish. **2** a reel on a fishing rod. **3** a spinning or other bait used in trolling for fish. **troller** *n.*

troll[2] (trōl) *n.* **1** a giant or giantess in Scandinavian mythology, endowed with supernatural powers. **2** a familiar but impish dwarf.

trolley (trol´i), **trolly** *n.* (*pl.* **trolleys**, **trollies**) **1** a set of shelves with wheels, used for moving things, e.g. trays of food, around. **2** a basket on wheels used for containing goods to be purchased in a grocery shop, supermarket etc. **3** (*also* **trolley-wheel**) a grooved wheel on a pole used for conveying current to the motor on electric railways, tramways etc. **4** (*N Am.*) a trolley-car. **5** a trolleybus. **off one's trolley** (*sl.*) crazy, insane. **trolleybus** *n.* a bus deriving its motive power through a trolley from overhead wires. **trolley-car** *n.* (*N Am.*) a tramcar.

trollop (trol´əp) *n.* **1** a careless, slovenly woman, a slattern. **2** a woman of bad character; a prostitute.

trombone (trombōn´) *n.* **1** a large and powerful wind instrument of the trumpet kind usu. played by means of a sliding tube. **2** a trombone-player. **3** an organ stop with the quality of a trombone. **trombonist** *n.*

trompe (tromp) *n.* an apparatus worked by a descending column of water for producing a blast in a furnace.

trompe l'œil (tromp lœy´, trōp) *n.* (*pl.* **trompe l'œils** (lœy´)) (a painting etc. giving) a very deceptive appearance of reality.

-tron (tron) *suf.* (*Physics*) **1** elementary particle, as *plectron*. **2** particle accelerator, as *cyclotron*. **3** thermionic valve, as *klystron*.

troop (troop) *n.* **1** an assemblage of persons or animals, a crowd, a company. **2** (*pl.*) soldiers. **3** the unit of cavalry formation, usu. consisting of 60 troopers, commanded by a captain. **4** a group of Scout patrols. **5** a unit of artillery and armoured formation. ~*v.i.* **1** to come together, to assemble, to come thronging (up, together etc.). **2** to move (along a way etc.) in a troop. **3** to hurry (off etc.). ~*v.t.* to form (a squadron etc.) into troops. **troop carrier** *n.* a ship, aircraft or vehicle for carrying troops. **trooper** *n.* **1** a cavalry soldier. **2** a private in a cavalry regiment. **3** a troopship. **4** (*N Am., Austral.*) a mounted policeman. **5** a cavalry horse. **to swear like a trooper** to swear strongly or excessively. **trooping the colour** *n.* a ceremonial parade at which the colour is carried between the files of troops. **troopship** *n.* a ship transporting soldiers.

Usage note See note under TROUPE.

tropaeolum (trəpē´ələm) *n.* (*pl.* **tropaeolums**, **tropaeola** (-lə)) a S American climbing plant of the genus *Tropaeolum*, with trumpet-shaped flowers.

trope (trōp) *n.* a figurative use of a word.

-trope (trōp) *comb. form* forming nouns indicating a turning towards or affinity for. **-tropic** *comb. form* forming adjectives.

trophic (trof´ik) *a.* of or relating to nutrition.

-trophic (trō´fik, trof´-) *comb. form* **1** relating to nutrition. **2** relating to regulation, esp. by a hormone. **-trophism** *comb. form* forming nouns.

trophoblast (trof´ōblast, trō´-) *n.* a membrane enclosing the mammalian embryo which absorbs nourishment from the uterine fluids.

trophy (trō´fi) *n.* (*pl.* **trophies**) **1** anything, esp. a cup, preserved as a memorial of victory or success. **2** an ornamental group of typical or symbolical objects placed on a wall etc. **trophied** *a.* (*alsoin comb.*)

-trophy (trəfi) *comb. form* a specified form of nourishment or growth.

tropic (trop´ik) *n.* **1** (*also* **tropic of Cancer**) the parallel of latitude 23° 26´ north of the equator. **2** (*also* **tropic of Capricorn**) the parallel of latitude 23° 26´ south of the equator. **3** (**Tropics**) the regions of the torrid zone between these. **4** either of the corresponding parallels of declination on the celestial sphere. ~*a.* of or relating to the tropics, tropical. **tropical** *a.* **1** of, relating to, lying within or characteristic of the Tropics. **2** (of the weather) very hot. **3** of the nature of a trope, figurative, metaphorical. **tropical cyclone** *n.* a cyclone over a tropical ocean with hurricane-force winds. **tropically** *adv.* **tropical storm** *n.* a tropical cyclone. **tropical year** *n.* a solar year. **tropic bird** *n.* any seabird of the family Phaethontidae.

tropism (trō´pizm) *n.* (*Biol.*) the direction of

growth in a plant or other organism that is due to an external stimulus.

tropology (trəpol´əji) *n.* (*pl.* **tropologies**) **1** the use of tropical or figurative language. **2** interpretation of the Scriptures in a figurative sense. **tropological** (tropəloj´-) *a.*

tropopause (trop´əpawz) *n.* the boundary between the troposphere and the stratosphere.

troposphere (trop´əsfiə) *n.* the hollow sphere of atmosphere surrounding the earth, bounded by the stratosphere, in which temperature varies and the weather functions. **tropospheric** (-fer´ik) *a.*

troppo[1] (trop´ō) *adv.* (*Mus.*) too much, excessively.

troppo[2] (trop´ō) *a.* (*Austral., sl.*) affected mentally by a tropical climate; crazy.

Trot (trot) *n.* (*coll., often derog.*) a Trotskyite or other left-winger.

trot (trot) *v.i.* (*pres.p.* **trotting**, *past, p.p.* **trotted**) **1** (of a horse or other quadruped) to move at a steady rapid pace by simultaneously lifting one forefoot and the hind foot of the opposite side alternately with the other pair, the body being unsupported at intervals. **2** to run with short brisk strides. **3** (*coll.*) to walk or go. **4** to fish using a trotline. ~*v.t.* **1** to cause to trot. **2** to cover (a distance etc.) by trotting. ~*n.* **1** the pace, motion or act of a horse etc. in trotting. **2** a brisk steady pace. **3** (*pl., Austral., coll.*) trotting races. **on the trot** (*coll.*) one after the other, successively. **the trots** (*sl.*) diarrhoea. **to trot out 1** to cause (a horse) to trot to show its paces. **2** (*coll.*) to utter (esp. something familiar or trite). **trotter** *n.* **1** a person who or animal which trots, esp. a horse trained for fast trotting. **2** (*pl.*) sheep's or other animals' feet used as food. **3** (*pl., facet.*) a human foot. **trotting** *n.* harness racing for trotting horses.

†troth (trōth) *n.* faith, fidelity, truth.

Trotskyism (trot´skiizm) *n.* the political theories of Trotsky, esp. that of worldwide proletarian revolution.

trotter, trotting TROT.

troubadour (troo´bədaw) *n.* **1** any one of a class of lyric poets who flourished in Provence in the 11th cent., writing chiefly of love and chivalry. **2** a singer or poet.

trouble (trŭb´əl) *v.t.* **1** to agitate, to disturb. **2** to annoy, to molest. **3** to distress, to afflict. **4** to inconvenience, to put to some exertion or pains. ~*v.i.* **1** to be agitated or disturbed. **2** to take trouble or pains. **3** to be subjected to inconvenience. ~*n.* **1** affliction, distress, worry, perplexity, annoyance, misfortune. **2** labour, exertion, inconvenience. **3** a cause of this. **4** a fault; something amiss. **5** fighting or unrest. **6** disagreement. **7** an illness. **in trouble 1** liable to suffer punishment or misfortune. **2** (*coll.*) pregnant when not married. **to ask for trouble** (*coll.*) to lack caution. **to be no trouble** not to cause any difficulty, inconvenience etc. **to go to**

the trouble to go out of one's way to do something. **to look for trouble 1** (*coll.*) to try to cause trouble. **2** (*coll.*) to behave in a way that invites trouble. **to take (the) trouble** to go out of one's way to do something. **trouble and strife** *n.* wife (rhyming slang). **troubled** *a.* **troublemaker** *n.* a person who stirs up discontent, strife etc. **trouble-making** *n., a.* **troubler** *n.* **troubleshooter** *n.* a person who finds the causes of problems and solves them. **troubleshoot** *v.i., v.t.* (*past, p.p.* **troubleshot**). **troubleshooting** *n.* **troublesome** *a.* **1** giving trouble. **2** annoying, vexatious. **3** tiresome, wearisome, importunate. **troublesomely** *adv.* **troublesomeness** *n.* **trouble spot** *n.* a place where there is frequent disturbance, e.g. strikes or fights.

trough (trof) *n.* **1** a long, narrow, open receptacle of wood, iron etc., e.g. for holding water, fodder etc., for domestic animals. **2** a deep narrow channel, furrow, or depression (in land, the sea etc.). **3** an area of low atmospheric pressure. **4** a hollow between the crests of a wave of radiation. **5** a low point, e.g. in economic activity, in demand etc. **6** the part of a curve of variation of a quantity that is around the minimum. **7** a state of low spirits.

trounce (trowns) *v.t.* **1** to beat severely. **2** to inflict a decisive defeat upon. **3** to punish severely. **trouncer** *n.*

troupe (troop) *n.* a company of actors, performers etc. **trouper** *n.* **1** a member of such a company. **2** a reliable person.

Usage note Actors and performers form a *troupe*, and other people (especially soldiers) or animals a *troop*, and the spellings of the two should not be confused.

trousers (trow´zəz) *n.pl.* **1** a two-legged outer garment reaching from the waist to the ankles; also called *pair of trousers*. **2** (*sing., used attrib.*) (**trouser**) of or relating to trousers. **to wear the trousers** to be in the position of authority, esp. in a family. **trouser-clip** *n.* BICYCLE CLIP (under BICYCLE). **trousered** *a.* **trouserless** *a.* **trouser suit** *n.* a suit of a jacket and a pair of trousers, worn by a woman.

trousseau (troo´sō) *n.* (*pl.* **trousseaux** (-sōz), **trousseaus**) the clothes and general outfit of a bride.

trout (trowt) *n.* (*pl. in general* **trout**, *in particular* **trouts**) **1** any of various freshwater fishes of the genus *Salmo* or *Salvelinus*, esp. *Salmo trutta*. **2** any of various unrelated fishes. **3** (*sl., derog.*) an unprepossessing woman, esp. an old one. **trouting** *n.* trout-fishing. **troutlet, troutling** *n.* **trouty** *a.*

trove (trōv) *n.* TREASURE TROVE (under TREASURE).

trover (trō´və) *n.* (*Law*) **1** the acquisition or appropriation of any goods. **2** an action for the recovery of personal property wrongfully converted by another to their own use.

trowel (trow´əl) *n.* **1** a flat-bladed, usu. pointed, tool used by masons etc., for spreading mortar etc. **2** a scoop-shaped tool used in digging up plants etc. *~v.t.* (*pres.p.* **trowelling**, (*N Am.*) **troweling**, *past, p.p.* **trowelled**, (*N Am.*) **troweled**) to apply or dress with a trowel. **to lay it on with a trowel** to flatter grossly.

troy (troi), **troy weight** *n.* a system of weights (based on the grain, in which one pound troy equals 12 oz. av. (340 g) or 5760 grains) used chiefly in weighing gold, silver and gems.

truant (troo´ənt) *n.* **1** a child who stays away from school without leave. **2** a person who shirks or neglects duty. *~a.* shirking, idle, loitering. *~v.i.* to play truant. **to play truant** to stay away from school without leave. **truancy** *n.* **truantly** *adv.*

truce (troos) *n.* a temporary cessation of hostilities.

truck[1] (trŭk) *n.* **1** a strong, usu. four-wheeled vehicle for conveying heavy goods; a lorry. **2** an open railway wagon for freight. **3** a framework and set of wheels for supporting the whole or part of a railway carriage etc. **4** (*Naut.*) a small wooden disc at the top of a mast with holes for the halyards etc. **5** an axle unit on a skateboard. *~v.t.* to convey in or on a truck. *~v.i.* (*esp. N Am.*) **1** to work as a lorry driver. **2** (*sl.*) to go or stroll. **truckage** (-ij) *n.* **trucker** *n.* **1** a lorry driver. **2** a firm transporting goods by lorry. **truckie** *n.* (*coll.*) a lorry driver. **trucking** *n.* (*N Am.*) transportation of goods by lorry. **truckload** *n.* **1** the amount contained in or carried in a truck. **2** (*coll.*) a large quantity or number. **by the truckload** in large quantities or numbers. **truck stop** *n.* (*esp. N Am.*) a transport café.

truck[2] (trŭk) *n.* **1** exchange of commodities. **2** commodities suitable for barter, small wares. **3** (*N Am.*) fresh vegetables etc. from a market garden. **4** (*coll.*) rubbish. **5** dealings. **to have no truck with** to have no dealings with. **truck system** *n.* (*Hist.*) the practice of paying wages in goods instead of money.

truckle (trŭk´əl) *v.i.* **1** to give way obsequiously (to the will of another), to cringe, to be servile (to). **2** to sleep in a truckle-bed. *~n.* **1** (*also* **truckle-bed**) a low bed on castors or wheels for rolling under another. **2** (*orig. dial.*) a small barrel-shaped cheese. **truckler** *n.*

truculent (trŭk´ūlənt) *a.* **1** defiant or sullen. **2** aggressive. **3** savage, ferocious, barbarous, violent. **truculence, truculency** *n.* **truculently** *adv.*

trudge (trŭj) *v.i.* to travel on foot, esp. with labour and fatigue. *~v.t.* to cover (a distance) in this manner. *~n.* a walk of this kind. **trudger** *n.*

true (troo) *a.* (*comp.* **truer**, *superl.* **truest**) **1** conformable to fact or reality, not false or erroneous. **2** in accordance with appearance, not deceptive, counterfeit, or spurious, genuine. **3** in accordance with right or law, legitimate, rightful. **4** corresponding to type or standard. **5** correctly positioned; level. **6** accurate; exact. **7** (of a voice etc.) in perfect tune. **8** faithful, loyal, constant. **9** (of a compass bearing) determined in relation to

the earth's geographical, rather than its magnetic pole. *~v.t.* (*3rd pers. sing. pres.* **trues**, *pres.p.* **trueing, truing**, *past, p.p.* **trued**) to make true, exact or accurate. *~adv.* **1** truly. **2** accurately. **3** without variation from the ancestral type. **in true** correctly aligned. **out of true** not correctly aligned. **to come true** to happen. **true to type** normal, what might be expected. **true-blue** *a.* **1** staunch, faithful, genuine. **2** loyal to the British Conservative Party. *~n.* a true-blue person. **true-born** *a.* **1** of legitimate birth. **2** such by birth or blood. **true-bred** *a.* of genuine or right breed. **true coral** *n.* a marine coelenterate of the reef-forming order Madreporaria. **true horizon** *n.* CELESTIAL HORIZON (under CELESTIAL). **true love** *n.* **1** a person truly loved or loving. **2** one's sweetheart. **true-love knot, true-lover's knot** *n.* a kind of double knot with two interlacing bows on each side and two ends. **trueness** *n.* **true north** *n.* north according to the earth's axis. **true rib** *n.* any of the upper seven pairs of ribs, joined directly to the breastbone.

❌ **truely** common misspelling of TRULY.

truffle (trŭf´əl) *n.* **1** any fleshy fungus of the order Tuberales, used for seasoning etc. **2** a sweet flavoured with rum or chocolate, resembling a truffle in shape.

trug (trŭg) *n.* a wooden basket used by gardeners, greengrocers etc.

truism (troo´izm) *n.* **1** a self-evident or unquestionable truth. **2** an obvious statement, a platitude. **truistic** (-is´-) *a.*

truly (troo´li) *adv.* **1** sincerely. **2** genuinely. **3** in reality. **4** faithfully, honestly, loyally. **5** really, indeed. **6** in accordance with truth, accurately. **7** rightly, properly.

trump[1] (trŭmp) *n.* **1** any card of a suit ranking for the time being above the others. **2** (*pl.*) this suit. **3** an advantage, esp. involving surprise. **4** (*coll.*) a generous or reliable person. **5** (*Austral.*) someone in authority. *~v.t.* **1** to take with a trump. **2** to outdo. *~v.i.* to play a trump card. **to come up trumps** (*coll.*) to be useful or helpful at an opportune moment. **to trump up** to invent or fabricate (a charge etc.). **trump card** *n.* **1** the card turned up to determine which suit is to be trumps. **2** any card of this suit. **3** (*coll.*) an infallible expedient.

†**trump**[2] (trŭmp) *n.* a trumpet blast.

trumpery (trŭm´pəri) *n.* (*pl.* **trumperies**) **1** worthless finery. **2** a worthless article. **3** rubbish. *~a.* **1** showy but worthless. **2** delusive, rubbishy.

trumpet (trŭm´pit) *n.* **1** a musical wind instrument, usu. consisting of a long, straight, curved or coiled tube with a wide termination, usu. of brass, with a cup-shaped mouthpiece. **2** a trumpet-player. **3** a thing resembling a trumpet in shape, such as a funnel. **4** an organ stop with a bright sound. **5** a sound of or as of a trumpet, e.g. that made by an elephant. **6** the horn of an old gramophone. **7** an ear-trumpet. *~v.t.* (*pres.p.* **trumpeting**, *past, p.p.* **trumpeted**) to proclaim by or as by a trumpet. ~*v.i.* (esp. of the elephant) to make a loud sound like a trumpet. **trumpet call** *n.* **1** a call sounded by a trumpet. **2** an imperative call to action. **trumpeter** *n.* **1** a person who sounds a trumpet, esp. a soldier giving signals on the trumpet in a cavalry regiment. **2** a person who proclaims, publishes or denounces. **3** a variety of the domestic pigeon, with a prolonged coo. **4** a S American bird of the genus *Psophia*, allied to the cranes. **5** a trumpeter swan. **trumpeter swan** *n.* a large N American wild swan, *Cygnus buccinator.* **trumpet major** *n.* the head trumpeter in a cavalry regiment.

truncal TRUNK.

truncate[1] (trŭngkāt´, trŭng´-) *v.t.* **1** to cut the top or end from. **2** to replace (an angle) by a plane. **truncation** (-kā´shən) *n.*

truncate[2] (trŭng´kāt) *a.* **1** cut short, truncated. **2** (*Bot., Zool.*) terminating abruptly, as if a piece had been cut off. **truncately** *adv.*

truncheon (trŭn´shən, -chən) *n.* **1** a short staff, club or cudgel, esp. one carried by a police officer in Britain. **2** a baton, a staff of authority. ~*v.t.* to beat with a truncheon.

trundle (trŭn´dəl) *v.t., v.i.* to move heavily (as if) on wheels. ~*n.* (*N Am.*) (*also* **trundle-bed**) a low bed on castors or wheels or for rolling under another, a truckle-bed.

trunk (trŭngk) *n.* **1** the main stem of a tree, as opposed to the branches or roots. **2** the body of an animal apart from the limbs, head and tail. **3** the main body of anything. **4** a box or chest with a hinged lid for packing clothes etc. in for travel. **5** (*N Am.*) the boot of a motor car. **6** a ventilating shaft, conduit, chute, flume etc. **7** the proboscis of an elephant or any analogous organ. **8** the main body of an artery etc. **9** (*pl.*) men's shorts for swimming. **truncal** *a.* **trunk call** *n.* a long-distance telephone call. **trunkful** *n.* (*pl.* **trunkfuls**). **trunking** *n.* **1** a system of ventilation shafts, conduits etc. **2** the use or arrangement of trunk lines. **trunkless** *a.* **trunk line** *n.* the main line of a railway, canal, telephone etc. **trunk road** *n.* any major road for long-distance travel.

truss (trŭs) *v.t.* **1** to support or brace with a truss. **2** to fasten (a fowl or the wings of a fowl etc.) with a skewer or twine before cooking. **3** to tie up securely, to bind. ~*n.* **1** a timber or iron supporting and strengthening structure in a roof, bridge etc. **2** a large corbel. **3** (*Naut.*) a heavy iron ring securing a lower yard to the mast. **4** a padded belt or other apparatus worn round the body for preventing or compressing a hernia. **5** a bundle of hay or straw. **6** a compact terminal cluster of flowers or fruit. **to truss up 1** to make up into a bundle. **2** to bind or tie up. **3** to hang.

trust (trŭst) *n.* **1** confident reliance on or belief in the integrity, veracity, justice, friendship, power, protection etc. of a person or thing. **2** confidence, firm expectation (that). **3** the person or thing on which reliance is placed. **4** reliance on (assumed honesty etc.) without examination. **5** commercial credit. **6** (*Law*) confidence reposed in a person to whom property is conveyed for the benefit of another. **7** (*Law*) the right to or title in such property as distinct from its legal ownership. **8** (*Law*) the property or thing held in trust. **9** (*Law*) the legal relation between such property and the holder. **10** something committed to one's charge or care. **11** the obligation of a person who has received such a charge. **12** care, safekeeping. **13** a combination of a number of businesses or companies under one general control for the purpose of defeating competition, creating a monopoly etc. **14** a body of trustees. ~*v.t.* **1** to place confidence in, to believe in, to rely upon. **2** to believe, to have a confident hope or expectation. **3** to commit to the care of a person, to entrust. **4** to entrust (a person with a thing). **5** to give credit to. ~*v.i.* **1** to have trust or confidence. **2** to sell goods on credit. **in trust** (*Law*) held for safekeeping or as a trustee. **on trust 1** on credit. **2** without questioning. **to take on trust** to accept without questioning. **trustable** *a.* **trustbuster** *n.* (*esp. N Am.*) a person who breaks up business trusts. **trust company** *n.* a company performing the functions of a trustee or dealing with trusts. **trustee** (-tē´) *n.* **1** (*Law*) a person to whom property is committed in trust for the benefit of another. **2** a member of a body of people, often elective, managing the affairs of an institution. **3** a state governing a trust territory. **trusteeship** *n.* **truster** *n.* **trustful** *a.* **1** full of trust, esp. when this is naive. **2** trusting, confiding. **trustfully** *adv.* **trustfulness** *n.* **trust fund** *n.* money etc. held in trust. **trustie** TRUSTY (under TRUST). **trusting** *a.* **trustingly** *adv.* **trustingness** *n.* **trust territory** *n.* a territory governed by another country by the authority of the United Nations. **trustworthy** *a.* deserving of trust or confidence. **trustworthiness** *n.* **trusty** *a.* (*comp.* **trustier**, *superl.* **trustiest**) **1** †trustworthy, reliable, not liable to fail in time of need. **2** †loyal. ~*n.* (*pl.* **trusties**) (*also* **trustie**) a prisoner trusted with a certain amount of liberty to do jobs etc. **trustily** *adv.* **trustiness** *n.*

truth (trooth) *n.* (*pl.* **truths** (troodhz, -ths)) **1** the state or quality of being true. **2** that which is true, a fact, a verity. **3** a principle or statement that is generally considered true. **in truth** in reality, in fact, truly. **to tell the truth** to be frank. **truth drug** *n.* any drug used to make a person more liable to tell the truth when being interrogated. **truthful** *a.* **1** habitually speaking the truth. **2** veracious, reliable, conformable to truth. **truthfully** *adv.* **truthfulness** *n.* **truth table** *n.* (*Logic*) a table indicating the truth or falsity of propositions by the binary digits 0 and 1.

try (trī) *v.t.* (*3rd pers. sing. pres.* **tries**, *pres.p.* **trying**, *past, p.p.* **tried**) **1** to test, to examine by experiment. **2** to determine the qualities etc. of by reference to a standard. **3** to find out by experiment or experience. **4** to attempt, to endeavour (to do etc.). **5** to subject to a severe or undue test, to strain. **6** to subject to hardship, suffering etc., as if for a test, to afflict. **7** to investigate (a charge, issue etc.) judicially, to subject (a person) to judicial trial. **8** to prove or settle by a test or experiment. *~v.i.* to endeavour, to make an attempt, to make an effort. *~n.* (*pl.* **tries**) **1** an attempt. **2** in rugby, the right to carry the ball and try to kick a goal from in front, earned by touching the ball down behind the opponents' goal line. **3** in American football, an attempt to score an extra point after a touchdown. **to try for size** to try out. **to try it on 1** (*coll.*) to see how far one can go before provoking someone. **2** (*coll.*) to try to deceive, outwit or seduce someone. **to try on** to put (clothes) on to see if they fit. **to try one's hand** to try to do something new requiring skill. **to try out** to test. **tried** *a.* shown to be effective, durable etc. by testing or use, proven. **trier** (trī´ə) *n.* **1** a person who tries, examines or tests in any way. **2** a person who keeps on endeavouring or persisting. **3** (*also* **trior**) a person appointed to determine whether a challenge to a juror or jurors is well founded. **trying** *a.* **1** irritating, annoying. **2** difficult, demanding. **tryingly** *adv.* **try-on** *n.* (*coll.*) an act of trying it on. **try-out** *n.* a trial, e.g. of a new method. **trysail** (trī´səl) *n.* a fore-and-aft sail set on a gaff abaft the foremast and mainmast.

Usage note In spoken and informal written English, *try and do* (something) can be used for *try to do* (something), though only where the verb takes the form *try* itself (not *tries, tried, trying*). It is not usual in negative contexts (*did not try to do* not *did not try and do*).

trypanosome (trip´ənəsōm, -pan´-) *n.* (*Med.*) any protozoan parasite of the genus *Trypanosoma*, causing sleeping sickness and other diseases. **trypanosomiasis** (-mī´əsis) *n.* any of several diseases caused by an infection with a trypanosome.

†tryst (trist, trīst) *n.* **1** an appointed meeting, an appointment. **2** a rendezvous. *~v.i.* to agree to meet. *~v.t.* to appoint (a time or place) for meeting. **tryster** *n.*

tsar (zah), **czar, tzar** *n.* **1** (*Hist.*) the emperor of Russia. **2** a very powerful person. **tsardom** *n.* **tsarevich, tsarevitch** *n.* (*Hist.*) the son of a tsar, esp. the eldest son. **tsarina** (-rē´nə), **tsaritza** (-rit´sə), **tsaritsa** *n.* (*Hist.*) an empress of Russia, the wife of a tsar. **tsarism** *n.* **tsarist** *n., a.*

tsessebi (tsəsā´bi), **sassaby** (s-) *n.* (*pl.* **tsessebis, sassabies**) a large S African antelope, *Damaliscus lunatus.*

tsetse (tset´si) *n.* any fly of the genus *Glossina*, the bite of which is often fatal to cattle, horses, dogs etc., and transmits to humans the trypanosomes of sleeping sickness.

tsk (tsk), **tsk tsk** *int., n., v.i.* TUT-TUT.

tsp *abbr.* teaspoon(ful).

tsps *abbr.* teaspoon(ful)s.

tsunami (tsoonah´mi) *n.* (*pl.* **tsunamis**) a very

large wave at sea caused by a submarine earthquake, volcanic eruption etc.

Tswana (tswah´nə) *n.* (*pl.* **Tswana, Tswanas, Batswana** (bətswah´nə)) **1** a member of a southern African people living chiefly in Botswana. **2** the Bantu language of this people, Setswana. *~a.* of or relating to the Tswana or Setswana.

TT *abbr.* **1** teetotal(ler). **2** Tourist Trophy. **3** tuberculin-tested.

TU *abbr.* trade union.

Tu. *abbr.* Tuesday.

tuatara (tooətah´rə) *n.* the largest New Zealand reptile, the lizard-like *Sphenodon punctatum*, now the last survivor of the class Rhyncocephalia.

tub (tŭb) *n.* **1** an open wooden (usu. round) vessel constructed of staves held together by hoops, used for washing, holding butter etc. **2** the amount (of butter etc.) that a packing tub holds. **3** a small cask. **4** a small, usu. plastic, container for ice cream, margarine etc. **5** (*coll.*) a bathtub, a sponge bath, a bath in a tub. **6** (*Mining*) a bucket, box or truck for bringing up ore etc. from a mine. **7** (*coll.*) a short clumsy boat. **8** (*coll.*) a boat for practising rowing in. *~v.t.* (*pres.p.* **tubbing**, *past, p.p.* **tubbed**) **1** to place or set in a tub. **2** to bathe in a tub. **3** to line (a mine shaft) with a casing. *~v.i.* **1** to take a bath in a tub. **2** to row in a tub. **tubbable** *a.* **tubby** *a.* (*comp.* **tubbier**, *superl.* **tubbiest**) **1** tub-shaped, corpulent. **2** (*Mus.*) sounding like an empty tub when struck, lacking resonance. **tubbiness** *n.* **tub chair** *n.* a chair which has solid arms and usu. a semicircular back. **tubful** *n.* (*pl.* **tubfuls**). **tub-thumper** *n.* (*coll.*) a ranting preacher. **tub-thumping** *a.*

tuba (tū´bə) *n.* (*pl.* **tubas, tubae** (-bē)) **1** a brass wind instrument of the saxhorn kind, with a low pitch. **2** a tuba player. **3** a powerful reed-stop in an organ.

tube (tūb) *n.* **1** a long hollow cylinder for the conveyance of fluids and various other purposes, a pipe. **2** a cylindrical vessel of thin flexible metal for holding pigment, toothpaste etc. **3** the main body of a wind instrument. **4** (*Zool., Bot. etc.*) a tubular vessel in an animal or plant for conveying air, fluids etc. **5** (*coll.*) an underground railway. **6** (*also* **tube train**) an underground train. **7** a cathode ray tube. **8** (*N Am., coll.*) a television set. **9** (*N Am.*) a thermionic valve. **10** (*N Am.*) a radio valve. **11** an inner tube. **12** (*esp. Austral., sl.*) a can of beer. *~v.t.* to furnish with or enclose in a tube or tubes. **tubal, tubar** *a.* **tubectomy** (-bek´təmi) *n.* (*pl.* **tubectomies**) the cutting or removal of a Fallopian tube. **tubeless** *a.* **tubelike** *a.* **tube worm** *n.* a worm that makes and lives in a tube of sand, lime etc. **tubing** *n.* a length or quantity of tubes.

tuber (tū´bə) *n.* **1** a short, thick portion of an underground stem, set with eyes or modified buds, as in the potato. **2** a similar root, as of a dahlia. **3** (*Anat.*) a swelling or prominence.

tuberous *a.* **1** having prominent knobs or excrescences. **2** like or bearing tubers. **tuberousness** *n.*
tuberous root *n.* a thick root like a tuber but not having buds or eyes.
tubercle (tū'bəkəl) *n.* **1** a small prominence, esp. in bone. **2** a small granular non-vascular tumour or nodule formed within the substance of an organ, esp. such a lesion characteristic of tuberculosis of the lungs. **3** a small tuber, a warty excrescence. **tubercle bacillus** *n.* a bacterium that causes tuberculosis. **tubercular** (-bœ'kū-) *a.* of or relating to tubercles or tuberculosis. ~*n.* a person suffering from tuberculosis. **tuberculate** (-lət), **tuberculated** (-lātid) *a.* **tuberculation** (-lā'shən) *n.* **1** formation of tubercles. **2** a system of tubercles. **tuberculin** (-lin) *n.* **1** a ptomaine produced by the action of the tubercle bacillus. **2** a fluid used hypodermically in the diagnosis of tuberculosis. **tuberculin test** *n.* an injection of tuberculin to test for tuberculosis or immunity to it. **tuberculin-tested** *a.* (of milk) produced by cows tested and found free of infection and tuberculosis. **tuberculosis** (-lō'sis) *n.* a diseased condition caused by the bacillus *Mycobacterium tuberculosis*, characterized by the presence of tubercles in the tissues, esp. pulmonary tuberculosis or consumption. **tuberculous** (-ləs), **tuberculose** (-lōs) *a.*
tuberose[1] (tū'bərōs) *a.* tuberous. **tuberosity** (-ros'-) *n.*
tuberose[2] (tū'bərōz) *n.* a bulbous plant, *Polianthes tuberosa*, with fragrant white flowers.

Usage note Sometimes pronounced (tūb'rōz), as if from *tube, rose*.

tubifex (tū'bifeks) *n.* (*pl.* **tubifex, tubifexes**) any reddish annelid worm of the genus *Tubifex*, used as food for aquarium fish.
tubiform (tū'bifawm) *a.* having the shape of a tube.
tubing TUBE.
tubular (tū'būlə) *a.* **1** tube-shaped. **2** having or consisting of a tube or tubes. **3** made of tube-shaped pieces. **tubular bells** *n.pl.* an orchestral percussion instrument consisting of metal tubes suspended vertically and struck to produce a bell-like sound. **tubular tyre**, (*N Am.*) **tubular tire** *n.* a tyre that is cemented on to the wheel rim, used esp. on racing bicycles. **tubule** (-ūl) *n.* a small pipe or fistular body.
TUC *abbr.* Trades Union Congress.
tuck (tŭk) *v.t.* **1** to press close together or press, fold, or roll those loose ends or parts of compactly (up, in etc.). **2** to wrap or cover (up or in) closely or snugly. **3** to gather up, to fold or draw together or into a small area. **4** to push or press, to cram, to stuff, to stow (away, into, etc.). **5** to gather or stitch (a dress etc.) in folds. **6** to hit (a ball) to the place where one wants it to go. ~*n.* **1** a horizontal fold in a dress etc., esp. one of a series made for ornament or to dispose of loose material. **2** (*coll.*) food, esp. sweets, pastry etc. **3** (*Naut.*) the after

part of a ship where the ends of the bottom planks meet. **4** a dive or gymnastic move in which the knees are bent and held close to the chest. **to tuck away** **1** to eat heartily. **2** to place somewhere hidden or isolated. **to tuck in** (*coll.*) to eat heartily. **to tuck into** (*coll.*) to eat heartily. **tucker**[1] *n.* **1** a person who or thing which tucks. **2** (*esp. Austral., coll.*) food. **tucker-bag, tucker-box** *n.* (*Austral., coll.*) a food container. **tuck-in, tuck-out** *n.* (*coll.*) a hearty meal, a spread. **tucking** *n.* a series of tucks. **tuck-net, tuck-seine** *n.* a net or seine used for removing fish from a larger net. **tuck position** *n.* the position for a tuck in diving or gymnastics. **tuck shop** *n.* a shop, esp. in a school, where food is sold.
tucker[1] TUCK.
tucker[2] (tŭk'ə) *n.* (*Hist.*) an ornamental frilling of lace or muslin round the top of a woman's dress, covering the neck and shoulders, worn in 17th 18th cents.
tucker[3] (tŭk'ə) *v.t.* (*esp. N Am., coll.*) to exhaust (often with *out*).
-tude (tūd) *suf.* forming abstract nouns, as *altitude, beatitude, fortitude*.
Tudor (tū'də) *a.* **1** of or relating to the English royal line (from Henry VII to Elizabeth I) founded by Owen Tudor of Wales, who married the widow of Henry V. **2** of or relating to their period. ~*n.* a member of the Tudor royal family. **Tudor rose** *n.* a five-lobed flower adopted as a badge by Henry VII.
Tue., Tues. *abbr.* Tuesday.
Tuesday (tūz'dā, -di) *n.* the third day of the week, following Monday. ~*adv.* (*coll.*) on Tuesday. **Tuesdays** *adv.* (*coll.*) every Tuesday.
tufa (tū'fə, too'-) *n.* **1** a soft calcareous rock deposited by springs and streams. **2** TUFF. **tufaceous** (-fā'shəs) *a.*
tuff (tŭf) *n.* an earthy, sometimes fragmentary, deposit of volcanic materials of the most heterogeneous kind. **tuffaceous** (-ā'shəs) *a.*
tuffet (tŭf'it) *n.* **1** a tuft of grass etc. **2** a low mound or seat.
tuft (tŭft) *n.* **1** a cluster, a bunch, a collection of hairs, threads, feathers, grass etc. held or fastened together at one end. **2** (*Anat.*) a bunch of small blood vessels etc. ~*v.t.* **1** to adorn with or as with tufts. **2** to pass thread through (a mattress etc.) at regular intervals and fasten a button or tuft in the depression thus made. ~*v.i.* to grow in tufts. **tufted** *a.* **tufted duck** *n.* a small duck, *Aythya fuligula*, the male of which has a long black drooping crest. **tufty** *a.*
tug (tŭg) *v.t.* (*pres.p.* **tugging**, *past, p.p.* **tugged**) **1** to pull or draw with great effort or with violence. **2** to haul, to tow. ~*v.i.* to pull violently (at). ~*n.* **1** the act or a spell of tugging. **2** a vigorous or violent pull. **3** a violent effort, a severe struggle. **4** (*also* **tugboat**) a small powerful boat for towing others. **5** an aircraft towing a glider. **6** a loop hanging from the saddle in harness supporting a shaft or trace. **tugger** *n.* **tuggingly** *adv.* **tug of love**

n. (*coll.*) a dispute between parents or guardians over custody of a child. **tug-of-war** *n.* **1** a contest between two sets of persons pulling a rope from opposite ends across a line marked on the ground. **2** a struggle between two sides.

tugrik (too´grēk), **tughrik** *n.* the standard unit of currency in Mongolia.

tui (too´ē) *n.* (*pl.* **tuis**) a New Zealand honeyeater, *Prosthemadura novaeseelandiae.*

tuition (tūish´ən) *n.* **1** teaching, instruction, esp. in a particular subject or group of subjects and separately paid for. **2** a fee for this. **tuitional**, **tuitionary** *a.*

tulip (tū´lip) *n.* any plant of the genus *Tulipa*, bulbous plants of the lily family, with bell-shaped flowers of various colours. **tulip-root** *n.* a disease which affects oats, causing swelling of the base of the stems. **tulip tree** *n.* any N American tree of the genus *Liriodendron*, bearing greenish-yellow, tulip-like flowers. **tulipwood** *n.* the wood of *Liriodendron tulipifera.*

tulle (tūl) *n.* a fine silk net, used for veils etc.

tum¹ (tŭm) *n.* (*coll.*) the stomach. **tum-tum** *n.* (used by or to children).

tum² (tŭm), **tum-tum** (-tŭm) *n.* the sound of a stringed musical instrument like the banjo.

tumble (tŭm´bəl) *v.i.* **1** to fall (down etc.) suddenly or violently. **2** to roll or toss about. **3** to walk, run, or move about in a careless or headlong manner. **4** to perform acrobatic feats, esp. without special apparatus. **5** to decrease quickly. **6** (*coll.*) to (begin to) comprehend (often with *to*). **7** to turn over in flight. *~v.t.* **1** to toss or fling forcibly. **2** to throw or push (down etc.). **3** to cause to tumble or fall. **4** to throw into disorder, to rumple. **5** to dry (clothes) in a tumble-dryer. **6** to clean (gemstones etc.) in a tumbling-barrel. *~n.* **1** a fall. **2** a state of disorder. **3** an acrobatic feat, esp. a somersault. **4** a sudden sharp decrease. **tumbledown** *a.* dilapidated. **tumble-dry** *v.t.* (*3rd pers. sing. pres.* **tumble-dries**, *pres.p.* **tumble-drying**, *past, p.p.* **tumble-dried**) to dry (clothes) in a tumble-dryer. **tumble-dryer**, **tumble-drier** *n.* an appliance with a revolving cylinder into which damp clothes are placed and dried by having warm air blown through them as they turn. **tumbleweed** *n.* a plant such as *Amaranthus albus*, that breaks away from its roots in autumn and is blown around by the wind. **tumbling** *n.* **tumbling-barrel**, **tumbling-box** *n.* a revolving box etc. in which castings are cleaned by friction. **tumbling-bay** *n.* the outfall of a river or reservoir, or the pool into which this flows. **tumbly** *a.*

tumbler (tŭm´blə) *n.* **1** a person who or thing which tumbles. **2** a person who performs somersaults, an acrobat. **3** a variety of pigeon (from its habit of turning over in flight). **4** a stemless drinking glass, orig. with a rounded base, so that it fell on the side when set down. **5** a springlatch (usu. one of several) in a lock, that engages a bolt unless lifted by the key. **6** a part of the lock in a

firearm attached to the hammer and engaging with the trigger. **7** (*also* **tumbler-dryer**) a tumble-dryer. **8** a tumbling-barrel. **tumblerful** *n.* (*pl.* **tumblerfuls**). **tumbler switch** *n.* a simple form of switch used for electric light connections.

tumbril (tŭm´brəl, -bril), **tumbrel** *n.* (*Hist.*) an open cart which conveyed victims to the guillotine during the French Revolution.

tumid (tū´mid) *a.* **1** swollen, enlarged, distended. **2** pompous, bombastic, turgid. **tumefy** (-mifī) *v.t.* (*3rd pers. sing. pres.* **tumefies**, *pres.p.* **tumefying**, *past, p.p.* **tumefied**) **1** to cause to swell. **2** to inflate. *~v.i.* **1** to swell. **2** to rise in or as in a tumour. **tumefacient** (-fā´shənt) *a.* **tumefaction** (-fak´shən) *n.* **tumescent** (-mes´ənt) *a.* **1** swollen, enlarged. **2** becoming swollen or enlarged. **tumescence** *n.* **tumescently** *adv.* **tumidity** (-mid´-) *n.* **tumidly** *adv.* **tumidness** *n.*

tummy (tŭm´i) *n.* (*pl.* **tummies**) (*coll.*) the stomach. **tummy button** *n.* the navel.

tumour (tū´mə), (*N Am.*) **tumor** *n.* a swelling on some part of the body, esp. if due to an abnormal growth of tissue. **tumorous** *a.*

tumult (tū´mŭlt) *n.* **1** the commotion, disturbance or agitation of a multitude, esp. with a confusion of sounds. **2** a confused outbreak or insurrection. **3** excitement, agitation or confusion of mind. **tumultuous** (-mŭl´-) *a.* **tumultuously** *adv.* **tumultuousness** *n.*

tumulus (tū´mūləs) *n.* (*pl.* **tumuli** (-lī)) a mound of earth, sometimes combined with masonry, usu. sepulchral, a barrow. **tumular** *a.*

tun (tŭn) *n.* **1** a large cask, esp. for alcoholic liquors. **2** a wine measure, 216 imperial gal. or 252 US gal. (11.46 hl). **3** a brewer's fermenting-vat.

tuna (tū´nə) *n.* (*pl.* **tuna**, **tunas**) **1** (*Zool.*) any marine fish of the family Scombridae found in warmer waters; also called *tunny.* **2** (*also* **tuna fish**) its flesh as food.

tundra (tŭn´drə) *n.* a marshy treeless plain in the Arctic and subarctic regions, with permanently frozen subsoil and covered largely with mosses and lichens.

tune (tūn) *n.* **1** a melodious succession of musical tones forming a coherent whole, an air, a melody, esp. as a setting for a song, hymn etc. **2** correct intonation in singing or playing. **3** proper adjustment of an instrument for this. **4** a distinctive intonation pattern in speech. *~v.t.* **1** to put in tune. **2** to adjust, to adapt, to attune. **3** to adjust (an engine) for optimum performance. **4** to adjust (a radio, TV set) for optimum reception of an incoming signal. **5** (*poet.*) to sing, to produce (a song, music etc.). **in tune 1** at the correct pitch. **2** correctly adjusted for pitch. **3** in harmony, sympathy, agreement (with). **out of tune 1** not at the correct pitch. **2** not in harmony, sympathy or agreement (with). **to call the tune** to give orders, to say what is to be done. **to change one's tune** to alter one's attitude or tone. **to the tune of** (*coll.*) to the sum or amount of. **to tune in 1** to adjust a radio circuit to obtain resonance at a required frequency. **2** to switch on a radio or TV set and start listening or watching. **to tune up 1** (of a group of musicians) to adjust (instruments) to a common pitch before playing. **2** to start to play or sing. **3** to improve the performance of (an engine) by tuning. **tuned in (to)** (*coll.*) up to date (with); acquainted (with); knowledgeable (about). **tunable, tuneable** *a.* **tuneful** *a.* melodious, musical. **tunefully** *adv.* **tunefulness** *n.* **tuneless** *a.* **1** not in tune. **2** unmusical, inharmonious. **3** silent, without voice. **tunelessly** *adv.* **tunelessness** *n.* **tuner** *n.* **1** a person who tunes, esp. one whose occupation is to tune musical instruments. **2** a knob, dial etc. by which a radio or TV set is tuned to different wavelengths. **3** an electronic device used to tune a guitar etc. **tuning** *n.* **1** the act of putting something in tune. **2** (*Mus.*) a set of pitches to which (the strings of) stringed instruments are tuned. **3** the state of adjustment of an engine, radio receiver etc. **tuning fork** *n.* a two-pronged steel instrument giving a fixed note when struck, used to measure the pitch of musical tones etc. **tuning peg** *n.* a peg attached to the strings of an instrument, by which it can be tuned.

tung (tŭng), **tung tree** *n.* a tree of the genus *Aleurites.* **tung oil** *n.* the oil of the seeds of this tree, used in paints, varnishes etc.

tungsten (tŭng´stən) *n.* (*Chem.*) a heavy, greyish-white metallic element, at. no. 74, chem. symbol W, of unusually high melting point; also called *wolfram.* **tungstate** (-stāt) *n.* a salt of tungstic acid. **tungsten carbide** *n.* a very hard black powder used in the manufacture of dies, drill bits etc. **tungstic** *a.* **tungstous** *a.*

tunic (tū´nik) *n.* **1** a military or police officer's jacket. **2** (*Hist.*) a short-sleeved body-garment reaching nearly to the knees, worn by the ancient Greeks and Romans. **3** a modern loose coat or short overskirt gathered in or belted at the waist, now worn only by women and children. **4** (*Anat.*) a membrane or envelope covering some part or organ. **5** (*Bot.*) a membranous skin. **6** (*Zool.*) the outer coat of an ascidian etc. **tunicate** (-kət) *a.* having or covered with a tunic. ~*n.* (*Zool.*) any marine animal of the subphylum Urochordata, including the sea squirts.

tuning TUNE.

tunnel (tŭn´əl) *n.* **1** an artificial underground passage or gallery, esp. one under a hill, river etc., for a railway, road or canal. **2** a passage dug by a burrowing animal. **3** a mining level, an adit. **4** a main flue of a chimney. ~*v.t.* (*pres.p.* **tunnelling,** (*N Am.*) **tunneling,** *past, p.p.* **tunnelled,** (*N Am.*) **tunneled**) to make a tunnel through (a hill etc.). ~*v.i.* to cut or make a tunnel. **tunnel diode** *n.* a type of semiconductor diode capable of giving amplification. **tunnel-kiln** *n.* a kiln in which articles for firing are carried along a heated passage on trucks. **tunneller,** (*N Am.*) **tunneler** *n.* **tunnel-net** *n.* a fishing net with a

wide mouth narrowing towards the other end. **tunnel vision** *n.* **1** a medical condition in which peripheral vision is largely lost and a person can only see objects directly in front of them. **2** (*coll.*) extreme narrowness of viewpoint due to concentration on a single issue.

tunny (tŭn´i) *n.* (*pl.* **tunny, tunnies**) TUNA.

tup (tŭp) *n.* **1** a ram or male sheep. **2** the striking-part of a steam hammer. ~*v.t., v.i.* (*pres.p.* **tupping,** *past, p.p.* **tupped**) to copulate with (a ewe), to cover, as a ram.

tupelo (tū´pilō) *n.* (*pl.* **tupelos**) **1** a N American or Asian tree of the genus *Nyssa*, living in swampy conditions. **2** the wood of this.

tuppence (tŭp´əns) *n.* (*coll.*) TWOPENCE (under TWO). **tuppenny** (tŭp´ni) *a.* TWOPENNY (under TWO).

Tupperware® (tŭp´əweə) *n.* a range of plastic kitchen equipment, esp. food containers.

tuque (took) *n.* a Canadian cap made by tucking in one end of a knitted cylindrical bag both ends of which are closed.

turban (tœ´bən) *n.* **1** a (Muslim or Sikh) man's headdress consisting of a sash or scarf wound round a cap or the head. **2** a woman's headdress imitating this. **turbaned** *a.*

turbellarian (tœbəleə´riən) *n.* any flatworm of the class Turbellaria, with ciliated skin. ~*a.* of or relating to this class.

turbid (tœ´bid) *a.* **1** muddy, discoloured, thick, unclear. **2** disordered, unquiet, disturbed. **turbidity** (-bid´-), **turbidness** *n.* **turbidly** *adv.*

Usage note The adjectives *turbid* and *turgid* should not be confused: *turbid* means muddy or unclear, and *turgid* means swollen or bombastic.

turbinate (tœ´binət) *a.* **1** top-shaped, like an inverted cone. **2** spiral, whorled. **3** (*Anat.*) shaped like a scroll. **turbinal** *a.* **turbination** (-ā´shən) *n.*

turbine (tœ´bīn, -bin) *n.* **1** a waterwheel or motor enclosed in a case or tube in which a flowing stream acts by direct impact or reaction upon a series of vanes or buckets. **2** a similar wheel or motor driven by steam, gas or air.

turbo (tœ´bō) *n.* (*pl.* **turbos**) **1** a model of car etc. incorporating a turbocharger. **2** a turbocharger.

turbo- (tœ´bō) *comb. form* having or driven by a turbine. **turbocharger** *n.* a supercharger, esp. for motor car engines, driven by exhaust gas turbines. **turbocharge** *v.t.* **turbocharged** *a.* **turbodiesel** *n.* **1** a turbocharged diesel engine. **2** a vehicle powered by this. **turbofan** *n.* **1** a gas-turbine aero-engine with a large fan which forces air out with the exhaust gases, thus increasing thrust. **2** an aircraft powered by this. **turbojet** *n.* **1** a turbojet engine. **2** an aircraft powered by this. **turbojet engine** *n.* an engine with a turbine-driven compressor for supplying compressed air to the combustion chamber. **turboprop** *n.* **1** an engine with a turbine-driven propeller. **2** an aircraft powered by this. **turboshaft** *n.* a gas turbine that powers a shaft. **turbosupercharger** *n*. a turbocharger.

turbot (tœ´bət) *n*. (*pl. in general* **turbot**, *in particular* **turbots**) **1** a large European flatfish, *Scophthalmus maximus*, with bony tubercles, highly valued as food. **2** any of various similar or related fishes such as the halibut.

turbulent (tœ´būlənt) *a*. **1** disturbed, tumultuous. **2** (of a flow of air) causing disturbance. **3** insubordinate, disorderly. **turbulence, turbulency** *n*. **turbulently** *adv*.

Turco- (tœ´kō), **Turko-** *comb. form* Turkish; Turkish and

turd (tœd) *n*. (*taboo sl*.) **1** a lump of excrement or dung. **2** a contemptible person.

tureen (tūrēn´, tər-) *n*. a deep covered dish or vessel for holding soup etc.

turf (tœf) *n*. (*pl.* **turfs, turves** (tœvz)) **1** surface earth filled with the matted roots of grass and other small plants. **2** a piece of this, a sod. **3** greensward, growing grass. **4** peat. ~*v.t*. to cover or line with turfs or sods. **the turf 1** the racecourse. **2** the occupation or profession of horseracing. **to turf out** (*coll*.) to throw out, to eject forcibly. **turf accountant** *n*. a bookmaker. **turfless** *a*. **turfman** *n*. (*pl.* **turfmen**) (*esp. N Am*.) a person devoted to or making a living from horseracing. **turfy** *a*. (*comp.* **turfier**, *superl.* **turfiest**). **turfiness** *n*.

turgid (tœ´jid) *a*. **1** swollen, bloated, morbidly distended, tumid. **2** (esp. of writing) pompous, boring and difficult to understand. **turgescence** (-jes´əns) *n*. **turgescent** *a*. **turgidity** (-jid´-), **turgidness** *n*. **turgidly** *adv*. **turgor** (-gə) *n*. (*Bot*.) the rigid state of a cell caused by pressure of the contents against the cell wall.

Usage note See note under TURBID.

Turk (tœk) *n*. **1** a native or inhabitant of Turkey. **2** a native speaker of a Turkic language. **3** (*offensive*) a violent or troublesome person, esp. a boy. **Turk's cap** *n*. **1** a martagon lily. **2** any of various cacti of the genus *Melocactus*. **Turk's head** *n*. an ornamental knot suggestive of a turban.

turkey (tœ´ki) *n*. (*pl.* **turkeys**) **1** a large gallinaceous bird, *Meleagris gallopavo*, allied to the pheasant, orig. introduced from America. **2** the flesh of this as food. **3** (*Austral*.) any of various birds resembling the turkey, as the brush turkey, *Alectura lathami*, or the mallee bird. **4** (*esp. N Am., sl*.) a flop. **5** (*esp. N Am., sl*.) a stupid person. **to talk turkey** (*esp. N Am., coll*.) to come to the point, to talk business. **turkey buzzard, turkey vulture** *n*. an American vulture, *Cathartes aura*. **turkeycock** *n*. **1** a male turkey. **2** a conceited, pompous person.

Turkey carpet (tœ´ki) *n*. TURKISH CARPET (under TURKISH). **Turkey red** *n*. **1** a brilliant red dye orig. obtained from madder. **2** cotton cloth dyed with this. **Turkey-red** *a*.

Turki (tœ´ki) *a*. of or relating to the Turkic

languages or their speakers. ~*n*. (*pl.* **Turki**) **1** a Turkic speaker. **2** the Turkic languages collectively. **Turkic** *a*. of or relating to the branch of the Altaic languages to which Turkish belongs. ~*n*. the Turkic languages collectively.

Turkish (tœ´kish) *a*. of or relating to Turkey or the Turks or their language. ~*n*. the language of the Turks. **Turkish bath** *n*. **1** a hot-air bath in which one is sweated, washed, rubbed, massaged etc. and conducted through a series of cooling-rooms. **2** a building for this. **Turkish carpet** *n*. a soft velvety woollen carpet, orig. made in Turkey. **Turkish coffee** *n*. very strong black coffee. **Turkish delight** *n*. a gelatinous sweet, coated in powdered sugar. **Turkish towel** *n*. a rough loose-piled towel made of cotton terry.

turmeric (tœ´mərik) *n*. **1** an Asian plant, *Curcuma longa*, of the ginger family. **2** the powdered rhizome of this used as a dyestuff, stimulant or condiment, esp. in curry.

turmoil (tœ´moil) *n*. a commotion, disturbance, tumult.

turn (tœn) *v.t*. **1** to cause to move round on or as on an axis, to give a rotary motion to. **2** to cause to go, move, aim, point, look etc. in a different direction. **3** to expose the other side of, to invert, to reverse. **4** to bring (lower soil) to the surface by digging or ploughing. **5** to revolve in the mind. **6** to perform (a somersault). **7** to apply or devote to a different purpose or object, to give a new direction to. **8** to bend, to adapt, to change in form, condition, nature etc. **9** to cause to change (into), to convert, to transform, to transmute. **10** to translate, to paraphrase. **11** to pass, go or move to the other side of, to go round. **12** to reach or pass beyond (a certain age, time). **13** to cause to ferment, to make sour. **14** to nauseate. **15** to infatuate, to unsettle, to make giddy. **16** to cause to go, to send, to put by turning. **17** to shape in a lathe or on a potter's wheel. **18** to give a shapely form to, to mould, to round (a sentence etc.). **19** to cause (an enemy agent) to become a double agent. **20** to twist or sprain. **21** to make (a profit). ~*v.i*. **1** to have a circular or revolving motion, to rotate, to revolve, to move round or about. **2** to move the body, face or head in a different direction, to change front from right to left etc. **3** to change in posture, attitude or position. **4** to reverse direction. **5** to return. **6** to take a particular direction. **7** to give one's attention to, set about. **8** to be changed in nature, form, condition etc. **9** to change colour. **10** to become sour or spoiled. **11** to become unsettled, infatuated or giddy. **12** to become nauseated. **13** to result, to terminate. **14** to undergo the process of turning on the lathe. **15** in cricket, to spin, to deviate from line. **16** in cricket, (of a wicket) to assist spin bowling. **17** to become. **18** to change sides. ~*n*. **1** the act of turning, rotary motion. **2** a revolution. **3** the state of being turned. **4** a change of direction, position or tendency, a deflection. **5** a bend, a curve, a winding, a corner. **6** a single round or coil of a rope etc. **7** a change, a vicissitude. **8** a turning point. **9** a point of change in time. **10** a short walk, a stroll, a promenade. **11** a performance, bout or spell (of doing something). **12** an occasion, opportunity or time (for doing something) coming in succession to each of a number of persons. **13** a purpose. **14** succession, alternation, rotation. **15** (*coll.*) a nervous shock. **16** shape, form, mould, character, disposition, temper. **17** (*Mus.*) a melodic embellishment consisting of the principal tone with those above and below it. **18** (the performer of) a short, theatrical act. **19** character or disposition. **20** an action or deed. **at every turn** 1·constantly. **2** everywhere. **by turns** 1 alternately. **2** at intervals. **done to a turn** cooked exactly right. **in one's turn** when one's turn, chance etc. comes. **in turn** in order of succession, in rotation. **not to know which way to turn** to be unsure what to do, where to go etc. **on the turn** 1 (of the tide) just turning. **2** beginning to go sour. **3** on the point of changing. **out of turn** 1 out of the proper order of succession. **2** at an inappropriate time. **to serve one's turn** 1 to serve one's purpose. **2** to help or suit one. **to take turns** to alternate, to perform or participate in rotation or succession. **to turn about** 1 to turn the face in another direction. **2** to turn round. **to turn against** 1 to (cause to) become hostile to. **2** to use against. **to turn around** (*esp. N Am.*) to turn round. **to turn aside** 1 to deviate. **2** to divert, to avert. **to turn away** 1 to turn to face the other way. **2** to reject. **3** to send away, dismiss. **to turn back** 1 to send back. **2** to begin to go back. **3** to fold back. **to turn down** 1 to fold or double down. **2** to lower (a light, the volume on a radio etc.). **3** to lay (a card) face downwards. **4** to reject. **to turn in** 1 to direct or incline inwards. **2** to fold or double in. **3** to send, put or drive in. **4** to hand over, to surrender. **5** to give, to execute (a performance etc.). **6** (*coll.*) to go to bed. **7** to achieve (a score). **8** to hand in. **9** (*coll.*) to abandon (a plan etc.). **to turn off** 1 to deflect. **2** to deviate. **3** to dismiss. **4** to shut or switch off. **5** to achieve, to produce, to accomplish. **6** (*coll.*) to cause to lose interest in, esp. sexually. **to turn on** 1 to open a way to (gas etc.) by turning a tap. **2** to switch on. **3** to direct, to aim. **4** to hinge or depend upon. **5** to attack. **6** (*coll.*) to excite, to arouse the interest of, esp. sexually. **7** (*sl.*) to introduce to drugs. **8** (*sl.*) to take and get high on drugs. **to turn one's hand to** to undertake; to apply oneself to. **to turn out** 1 to drive out, to expel. **2** to point or to cause to point outwards. **3** to turn (pockets etc.) inside out. **4** to clean (a room) thoroughly. **5** to bring to view. **6** to produce, as the result of labour. **7** to prove to be. **8** to switch off. **9** to dress, to groom, to look after the appearance of. **10** (*coll.*) to gather, to assemble. **11** (*coll.*) to go out. **12** (*coll.*) to get out of bed. **13** (*Mil.*) to call (a guard) from the guardroom. **14** to become. **to turn over** 1 to change the position of, to invert, to reverse. **2** (of an engine) to (cause to) start or run at low revolutions. **3** to surrender, to hand over. **4** to transfer (to), to put under other control. **5** to cause to turn over, to upset. **6** to do business to the amount of. **7** to consider, to ponder. **8** (*sl.*) to rob. **to turn round** **1** to face about. **2** to adopt a new view, attitude, policy etc. **3** to complete the processing of. **4** to complete the unloading and reloading of (a ship, aircraft). **5** to restore to profitability. **to turn the tide** to reverse the course of events. **to turn to** 1 to have recourse to. **2** to change or be changed into. **3** to direct towards. **4** to find (a page) in a book. **5** to set to work. **6** to seek the help of. **to turn up** 1 to bring to the surface. **2** to unearth, to bring to light. **3** to place (a card etc.) with the face upwards. **4** to tilt up. **5** to find and refer to (a passage) in a book. **6** to point upwards. **7** to come to light. **8** to happen. **9** to make one's appearance. **10** to shorten (a garment etc.). **11** to increase (the brightness or a light, the volume of a radio etc.). **to turn upon** 1 to hinge on. **2** to attack. **3** to direct or aim at. **turn and turn about** alternately, successively. **turnabout** *n.* **1** the act of facing in an opposite direction. **2** a complete reversal (of opinion, policy etc.). **turnaround** *n.* **1** a turnabout. **2** turnround. **turnback** *n.* REVERS. **turncoat** *n.* a person who deserts their party or principles. **turndown** *n.* **1** a rejection. **2** a downturn. ~*a.* folded or doubled down. **turned** *a.* **turner** *n.* a person who turns, esp. one who turns articles in a lathe. **turnery** *n.* **1** turning articles in a lathe. **2** articles turned in a lathe. **turning** *n.* **1** the act of a person who or of a thing which turns. **2** a bend, a corner, the point where a road meets another. **3** such a road. **4** the use of a lathe. **5** (*pl.*) shavings from a lathe. **turning circle** *n.* the smallest circle in which a vehicle can turn round. **turning point** *n.* the point in place, time etc. on or at which a change takes place, the decisive point. †**turnkey** *n.* (*pl.* **turnkeys**) a person who has the charge of the keys of a prison, a warder. ~*a.* being in its entirety the responsibility of a single contractor or supplier. **turn-off** *n.* **1** a turning off a main road. **2** (*coll.*) something that repels or makes one lose interest. **turn of speed** *n.* the ability to go fast. **turn-on** *n.* (*coll.*) a person who or thing which excites one, esp. sexually. **turnout** *n.* **1** a turning out for duty. **2** an assembly, a large party. **3** a showy or well-appointed equipage. **4** dress, get-up. **5** a quantity of articles or products manufactured in a given time. **6** the number of people attending something. **turnover** *n.* **1** the act or an instance of turning over. **2** a semicircular pie or tart made by turning over half the crust. **3** the amount of money turned over in a business in a given time. **4** the rate at which stock in trade is sold and replenished. **5** the rate at which employees leave and have to be replaced. **6** (*N Am.*) in sport, loss of the possession of the ball. **turnpike** *n.* **1** (*Hist.*) a gate set across a road to stop carriages etc. from passing till the toll is paid, orig. a frame set with spikes to prevent passage. **2** (*Hist.*) a turnpike road. **3** (*N Am.*) a motorway on which a toll is payable. **turnpike road** n. (*Hist.*) a road on which turnpikes or toll gates were established. **turnround** n. **1** (the time taken by) the process of unloading a ship or aircraft and reloading it ready for its next trip. **2** (the time taken by) the complete processing of anything. **3** a change to an opposite and usu. better state. **turnstile** n. a post with four horizontal revolving arms, set at the entrance to an enclosure, building etc., allowing persons to pass through one at a time often after a toll or fee is paid. **turnstone** n. any small wading bird of the genus *Arenaria*, which looks for small animals under stones. **turntable** n. **1** the rotating table which supports a gramophone record or CD while being played. **2** a platform rotating in a horizontal plane used for shifting rolling stock from one line of rails to another. **turn-up** n. **1** a turned-up fold at the bottom of a trouser leg. **2** (*coll.*) a sudden and unexpected (fortunate) occurrence. **turn-up for the book, turn-up for the books** n. (*coll.*) a sudden and unexpected (fortunate) occurrence.

turnip (tœ´nip) n. **1** a plant, *Brassica rapa*, with a fleshy globular root used as a vegetable and for feeding sheep. **2** a similar plant such as a swede. **turnip-tops,** (*N Am.*) **turnip greens** n.pl. the green sprouts of a turnip used as a vegetable. **turnipy** a.

turpentine (tœ´pəntīn) n. **1** an oleoresin exuding naturally or from incisions in several coniferous trees, esp. the terebinth. **2** a volatile oil distilled from turpentine used for mixing paint, varnishes etc. and in medicine; oil of turpentine. **3** (*also* **turpentine substitute**) white spirit. **4** the turpentine tree. ~*v.t.* **1** to put turpentine in. **2** to saturate with turpentine. **turpentine tree** n. a tree from which turpentine is obtained, esp. the terebinth. **turpentinic** (-tin´-) a. **turps** n. (*coll.*) oil of turpentine.

turpitude (tœ´pitūd) n. (*formal*) baseness, depravity.

turquoise (tœ´kwoiz, -kwahz) n. **1** a sky-blue or bluish-green translucent or opaque precious stone. **2** a pale greenish-blue. ~*a.* of the colour turquoise.

turret (tŭr´it) n. **1** a small tower attached to a building, and rising above it. **2** a low flat cylindrical or conical armoured tower, usu. revolving, so that the guns command a wide radius on a warship, tank or fort. **3** a similar structure on an aircraft. **4** a rotatable holder for cutting tools etc. on a lathe, milling machine etc. **turret lathe** n. CAPSTAN LATHE (under CAPSTAN).

turtle (tœ´təl) n. **1** a marine reptile of the order Chelonia, encased in a carapace, like a tortoise, with flippers used in swimming. **2** the flesh of a chelonian, esp. the green turtle, *Chelonia mydas*, used for soup. **3** turtle soup. **4** (*Comput.*) a device or cursor which can be instructed to draw graphics. **to turn turtle** to turn completely over,

to capsize. **turtleneck** n. **1** (a sweater with) a round, high, close-fitting neck. **2** (*N Am.*) POLO NECK (under POLO). **turtler** n. **turtle shell** n. tortoiseshell, esp. the darker and less valuable kind, used for inlaying. **turtleshell** a. made of turtle shell.

†**turtle-dove** (tœ´təl dŭv) n. any wild dove of the genus *Streptopelia*, esp. *S. turtur*, noted for its soft cooing and its devotion to its mate and young.

turves TURF.

Tuscan (tŭs´kən) n. **1** a native or inhabitant of Tuscany. **2** the Italian dialect of Tuscany. **3** the Tuscan order. ~*a.* of or relating to Tuscany of the Tuscan order. **Tuscan order** n. (*Archit.*) the simplest of the five classic orders, a Roman modification of Doric. **Tuscan straw** n. a yellow straw used for hats etc.

†**tush**[1] (tŭsh) *int.* used to express contempt or impatience.

tush[2] (tush) n. (*N Am.*, *sl.*) the buttocks.

tusk (tŭsk) n. **1** a long pointed tooth, esp. one permanently protruding from the mouth as in the elephant, narwhal etc. **2** a toothlike point, spike, projection etc., as in a harrow, lock etc. ~*v.t.* to gore, mangle or root up with tusks. **tusked, tusky** a. **tusker** n. an elephant or wild boar with well-developed tusks.

tussle (tŭs´əl) *v.i.* to struggle, to scuffle (with or for). ~*n.* **1** a difficult struggle. **2** a fight, a scuffle.

tussock (tŭs´ək) n. a clump, tuft or hillock of growing grass. **tussock grass** n. a grass, esp. of the genus *Poa*, *Nassella* or *Deschampsia*, forming tufts 5–6 ft. (1.7–2.0 m) high. **tussocky** a.

tussore (tŭs´aw), **tusser** (-ə), (*N Am.*) **tussah, tussur** n. **1** an Indian silkworm moth, *Antheraea mylitta*, feeding on the jujube tree etc. **2** a Chinese oak-feeding silkworm moth, *A. pernyi*. **3** (*also* **tussore-silk**) a strong, coarse silk obtained from these.

tut TUT-TUT.

tutee TUTOR.

tutelage (tū´təlij) n. **1** guardianship. **2** the state of being under a guardian. **3** the period of this. **4** tuition. **tutelar, tutelary** a. **1** having the care or protection of a person or thing, protective. **2** of or relating to a guardian.

tutor (tū´tə) n. **1** a private teacher, esp. one having the general care and instruction of a pupil in preparation for a university etc. **2** an officer directing the studies of undergraduates in a university college and charged with discipline etc. **3** a college or university teacher who teaches and holds discussions with students in small groups. **4** an instruction book. ~*v.t.* **1** to act as a tutor to. **2** to discipline, to correct. ~*v.i.* **1** to work as a tutor. **2** (*N Am.*) to receive tuition. **tutee** (-tē´) n. a student or person being tutored. **tutorage** n. **tutorial** (-taw´ri-) a. of a tutor or tuition. ~n. **1** a teaching session or conference with a tutor. **2** an explanation of a subject used by someone studying privately. **tutorially** *adv.* **tutorship** n.

tutti (tut´i) *adv.* (*Mus.*) all together. ~*n.* (*pl.* **tuttis**) a composition or passage for singing or performing all together.

tutti-frutti (tootifroo´ti) *n.* (*pl.* **tutti-fruttis**) a confection, such as ice cream, made of or flavoured with different fruits.

tut-tut (tŭttŭt´), **tut** *int.* used to express disapproval, impatience or contempt. ~*n.* an utterance of 'tut-tut', an exclamation of disapproval etc. ~*v.i.* (*pres.p.* **tut-tutting, tutting**, *past, p.p.* **tut-tutted, tutted**) to exclaim 'tut-tut', to express or show disapproval etc.

tutu[1] (too´too) *n.* a New Zealand shrub, *Coriaria arborea*, with poisonous berries.

tutu[2] (too´too) *n.* a ballet dancer's short, stiff skirt that spreads outwards.

tu-whit tu-whoo (təwit təwoo´) *int., n.* used to imitate the cry of an owl.

tuxedo (tŭksē´dō) *n.* (*pl.* **tuxedos, tuxedoes**) (*N Am.*) **1** a dinner jacket. **2** a suit including this. **tux** *n.* (*coll.*) a tuxedo.

TV (tēvē´) *n.* (*pl.* **TVs**) **1** television. **2** a television set. **TV dinner** *n.* a complete, ready-packaged and frozen dinner that only needs reheating before being eaten.

TVP® *abbr.* textured vegetable protein.

twaddle (twod´əl) *v.i.* **1** to talk unmeaningly. **2** to prate, to chatter. ~*n.* meaningless talk, silly chatter, nonsense. **twaddler** *n.*

†**twain** (twān) *a.* two. ~*n.* a pair, a couple. **in twain** in two, asunder.

twang (twang) *v.i.* **1** to make a ringing metallic sound as by plucking the string of a musical instrument. **2** (*usu. derog.*) to play (on) in this way. **3** to speak or be uttered with a nasal sound. ~*v.t.* **1** to cause to sound with a twang. **2** to play (an instrument) in this way. **3** to utter or pronounce with a nasal sound. ~*n.* **1** a ringing metallic sound. **2** a nasal tone (in speaking etc.). **twangy** *a.*

†'**twas** (twoz) *contr.* it was.

twat (twat, twot) *n.* (*taboo sl.*) **1** the female genitals. **2** a stupid or contemptible person.

twayblade (twā´blād) *n.* any orchid of the genus *Listera* etc., with two broad, ovate, radical leaves, and green or purplish flowers.

tweak (twēk) *v.t.* **1** to pinch and twist or pull with a sudden jerk, to twitch. **2** to make fine adjustments to; to tune. ~*n.* a sharp pinch or pull, a twitch.

twee (twē) *a.* (*comp.* **tweer** (twē´ə), *superl.* **tweest** (twē´ist)) (*usu. derog.*) **1** excessively dainty and prettified. **2** sentimentally sweet. **tweely** *adv.* **tweeness** *n.*

tweed (twēd) *n.* **1** a twilled woollen or wool-and-cotton fabric with an unfinished surface, used chiefly for outer garments. **2** (*pl.*) garments made of tweed. **tweedy** *a.* (*comp.* **tweedier**, *superl.* **tweediest**) **1** of or resembling tweed. **2** of a hearty, outdoor type. **tweedily** *adv.* **tweediness** *n.*

tweet (twēt), **tweet tweet** *n.* the chirp of a small bird. ~*int.* used to imitate the sound made by a small bird. ~*v.i.* to make this sound. **tweeter** *n.* a loudspeaker used to produce higher frequencies.

tweezers (twē´zəz) *n.pl.* a small pair of pincers for picking up minute things, plucking out hairs etc.

twelfth (twelfth) *n.* **1** any one of twelve equal parts. **2** (*Mus.*) an interval of an octave and a fifth. **3** (*Mus.*) a note separated from another by this interval. ~*n., a.* **1** the last of 12 (people, things etc.). **2** the next after the 11th. **Twelfth Day** *n.* the 12th day after Christmas, the festival of the Epiphany, 6 Jan. **twelfthly** *adv.* **twelfth man** *n.* a player selected as a reserve in a cricket team. **Twelfth Night** *n.* **1** the eve of Twelfth Day, 5 Jan. **2** Twelfth Day.

twelve (twelv) *n.* **1** the number or figure 12 or XII. **2** the age of 12. **3** midnight or midday. **4** (**12**) a film for over 12-year-olds only. ~*a.* **1** 12 in number. **2** aged 12. **twelvefold** *a., adv.* **1** twelve times as much or as many. **2** consisting of 12 parts. **twelvemo** (-mō) *n.* (*pl.* **twelvemos**) duodecimo, 12mo. †**twelvemonth** *n.* a year. **twelve-note, twelve-tone** *a.* (*Mus.*) of, relating to or using the 12 chromatic notes of the octave, esp. as developed by Arnold Schönberg.

twenty (twen´ti) *n.* (*pl.* **twenties**) **1** the number or figure 20 or XX. **2** the age of 20. **3** (*coll.*) a large but indefinite number. ~*a.* **1** 20 in number. **2** aged 20. **3** a large but indefinite number of. **twenties** *n.pl.* **1** the period of time between one's 20th and 30th birthdays. **2** the range of temperature between 20 and 30 degrees. **3** the period of time between the 20th and 30th years of a century. **twentieth** (-tiəth) *n.* any one of 20 equal parts. ~*n., a.* **1** the last of 20 (people, things etc.). **2** the next after the 19th. **twenty-first, twenty-second** etc. *n., a.* the ordinal numbers corresponding to twenty-one etc. **twentyfold** *a., adv.* **twenty-one, twenty-two** etc. *n., a.* the cardinal numbers between twenty and thirty. **twenty-pence (piece)** *n.* a British coin worth 20p. **twenty-twenty, 20/20** *a.* **1** (of vision) normal. **2** (*coll.*) denoting clear perception or hindsight.

twerp (twœp), **twirp** *n.* (*sl.*) a contemptible or silly person.

twice (twīs) *adv.* **1** two times. **2** doubly.

twiddle (twid´əl) *v.t.* **1** to rotate. **2** to twirl idly, to fiddle with. ~*v.i.* **1** to twirl. **2** to fiddle or trifle (with). ~*n.* **1** an act of twiddling. **2** a curly mark. **to twiddle one's thumbs 1** to rotate one's thumbs around each other, as a gesture of nervousness or boredom. **2** to sit idle, to have nothing to do but wait. **twiddler** *n.* **twiddly** *a.*

twig[1] (twig) *n.* **1** a small shoot or branch of a tree, bush, etc., a branchlet. **2** (*Anat.*) a small branch of an artery or other vessel. **twigged** *a.* (*also in comb.*) **twiggy** *a.* (*comp.* **twiggier**, *superl.* **twiggiest**) **twigless** *a.*

twig[2] (twig) *v.t.* (*pres.p.* **twigging**, *past, p.p.* **twigged**) (*coll.*) **1** to understand, to comprehend, to catch the drift of. **2** to see, to notice. ~*v.i.* to understand what is happening or being said.

twilight (twī′līt) *n.* **1** the diffused light from the sky appearing a little before sunrise and after sunset. **2** the period of this. **3** a faint light, shade, obscurity. **4** indistinct or imperfect perception, revelation or knowledge. **5** a period of decay, decline etc. *~a.* **1** of, relating to, happening or done in the twilight. **2** dim, shady, obscure. *~v.t.* (*past, p.p.* **twilit** (-lit), **twilighted**) to illuminate dimly. **twilight zone** *n.* **1** a transitional or intermediate zone. **2** a decaying urban area esp. between the commercial centre and the residential suburbs. **twilit** *a.*

twill (twil) *n.* a fabric in which the weft threads pass alternately over one warp thread and then under two or more, producing diagonal ribs or lines. *~v.t.* to weave in this way. **twilled** *a.*

†**'twill** (twil) *contr.* it will.

twin (twin) *a.* **1** being one of two born at a birth. **2** being one of a similar or closely related pair of things, parts etc. **3** (*Bot.*) growing in pairs or divided into two equal parts. *~n.* **1** either of two children or young produced at a birth. **2** a person or thing very closely resembling or related to another. **3** an exact counterpart. **4** a compound crystal having symmetrical halves separated by a plane that is not a plane of symmetry. *~v.t.* (*pres.p.* **twinning**, *past, p.p.* **twinned**) **1** to couple, to pair (with). **2** to pair, to mate. **3** officially to link (a town etc.) with another town in a foreign country, for civic and cultural exchanges etc.; to link (two towns) in this way. *~v.i.* **1** to give birth to twins. **2** to be born at the same birth. **3** to be mated or paired (with). **4** to grow as a twin crystal. **5** to forge a link with another town in a foreign country, for civic and cultural exchanges etc. **twin bed** *n.* either of a matching pair of single beds. **twin-bedded** *a.* **twin-cam** *a.* (esp. of an engine) having two camshafts. **twin-engined** *a.* having two engines. **twinning** *n.* **twin-screw** *a.* (of a steamer) having two propellers twisted in opposite directions. **twinset** *n.* a jumper and cardigan made to match. **twinship** *n.* **twin town** *n.* a town which has twinned with a town in a foreign country.

twine (twīn) *v.t.* **1** to twist. **2** to form (thread etc.) by twisting together. **3** to wind or coil round, to embrace. **4** to form by interweaving. *~v.i.* **1** to be interwoven. **2** to entwine, to coil (about, round etc.). **3** to wind, to meander. *~n.* **1** strong string made of two or three strands twisted together. **2** a twist, a convolution, a coil. **3** an interlacing, a tangle. **twiner** *n.*

twinge (twinj) *v.t.* (*pres.p.* **twingeing**, **twinging**) to affect with a sharp, sudden pain. *~v.i.* to feel or give a sharp, sudden pain. *~n.* **1** a sharp, sudden, shooting pain. **2** a pang, as of remorse or sorrow.

twinkle (twing′kəl) *v.i.* **1** to shine with a broken quivering light, to gleam fitfully, to sparkle. **2** (of eyes) to look bright and lively, esp. in amusement. **3** to open and shut rapidly, to blink, to wink. **4** (of the feet in dancing) to move lightly. *~v.t.* **1** to flash or emit (light) in rapid gleams.

2 to blink or wink. *~n.* **1** a tremulous gleam, a sparkle. **2** a bright and lively look in the eyes, esp. of amusement. **3** a glimmer. **4** a blink, a wink. **in a twinkle** in a twinkling. **twinkler** *n.* **twinkling** *n.* **1** a twinkle. **2** the time taken to twinkle, an instant. **in a twinkling** in an instant. **in the twinkling of an eye** in an instant. **twinkly** *a.*

twirl (twœl) *v.t.* **1** to cause to rotate rapidly, esp. with the fingers, to spin. **2** to whirl (round). **3** to twiddle, to twist, to curl (the moustache etc.). *~v.i.* to revolve or rotate rapidly, to whirl (round). *~n.* **1** a rapid circular motion. **2** a quick rotation. **3** a twist, a curl, a flourish. **twirler** *n.* **twirly** *a.*

twirp TWERP.

twist (twist) *v.t.* **1** to wind (a thread, filament, strand etc.) round another. **2** to form (a rope or threads etc., into a rope etc.) in this way, to intertwine (with or in with). **3** to give a spiral form to by turning the ends in opposite directions or turning one end only. **4** to turn round. **5** to wrench, to distort. **6** to pervert, to misrepresent. **7** to twine, to wreathe. **8** to make (one's way) in a winding manner. **9** (*sl.*) to cheat. **10** to sprain or wrench. *~v.i.* **1** to be turned or bent round and round upon itself. **2** to be or grow in a spiral form. **3** to move in a curving, winding or irregular path. **4** to turn round. **5** to writhe, to squirm. **6** to dance the twist. **7** to be distorted. *~n.* **1** an act or the manner of twisting. **2** the state of being twisted. **3** a quick or vigorous turn, a whirling motion given to a ball etc. **4** a sharp bend. **5** (*usu. derog.*) a peculiar tendency, a bent, an idiosyncrasy. **6** an unexpected development in, or conclusion to, the plot of a story. **7** a twisting strain. **8** the angle or degree of torsion of a rod etc. **9** forward motion combined with rotation. **10** thread, cord, string, rope etc. made from twisted strands, esp. strong silk thread or cotton yarn. **11** a twisted roll of bread. **12** twisted tobacco. **13** a paper packet with twisted ends. **14** a small piece of lemon etc. rind. **15** a dance, popular in the 1960s, in which the dancer gyrates their hips in time to the music while remaining more or less on the same spot. **16** (*sl.*) a swindle. **round the twist** (*coll.*) crazy. **to twist off** to remove or break off by twisting. **to twist someone's arm** to use force or psychological pressure to persuade someone. **twistable** *a.* **twisted** *a.* emotionally unbalanced. **twister** *n.* **1** a person who or thing which twists. **2** a ball delivered with a twist at cricket, billiards etc. **3** (*esp. N Am.*) a tornado, a waterspout. **4** (*coll.*) a cheat, a rogue. **twisty** *a.* (*comp.* **twistier**, *superl.* **twistiest**).

twit[1] (twit) *v.t.* (*pres.p.* **twitting**, *past, p.p.* **twitted**) to reproach, taunt or upbraid (with some fault etc.).

twit[2] (twit) *n.* (*coll.*) a fool. **twittish** *a.*

twitch[1] (twich) *v.t.* **1** to pull with a sudden or sharp jerk. **2** to snatch. *~v.i.* **1** to pull or jerk (at). **2** to move with a spasmodic jerk or contraction.

~n. **1** a sudden pull or jerk. **2** a sudden involuntary contraction of a muscle etc. **3** a cord twisted by a stick, fastened to the upper lip of a refractory horse for controlling it. **twitcher** n. **1** a person who or thing which twitches. **2** (pl.) tweezers. **3** (sl.) a birdwatcher who is interested in spotting rare birds. **twitchy** a. (comp. **twitchier**, superl. **twitchiest**) nervous. **twitchily** adv. **twitchiness** n.

twitch² (twich) n. QUITCH. **twitch grass** n. couch grass.

twite (twīt) n. a N European finch, Acanthis flavirostris, which resembles the linnet.

twitter (twit′ə) v.i. **1** to utter a succession of short, tremulous, intermittent notes. **2** to talk idly. **3** to have a tremulous motion of the nerves, to be agitated. ~v.t. to utter with tremulous, intermittent sounds. ~n. **1** such a succession of sounds; idle talk. **2** (coll.) (also **twitteration**) a state of excitement or nervous agitation. **3** a chirping. **twitterer** n. **twittery** a.

†**'twixt** (twikst) prep. between.

twizzle (twiz′əl) v.i., v.t. (coll., dial.) to twist round and round, to spin. ~n. a twist or turn.

two (too) n. **1** the number or figure 2 or II. **2** the age of two. **3** the second hour after midnight or midday. **4** a size denoted by two. **5** a set of two. **6** a card with two pips. ~a. **1** two in number. **2** aged two. **in two 1** into two parts. **2** asunder. **or two** denoting several. **to put two and two together** to draw inferences. **two by two** in pairs. **two or three** a few. **two-bit** a. (NAm., coll.) insignificant, small-time. **two-by-four** n. untrimmed timber, 2 in. by 4 in. (approx. 5 cm by 10 cm)in cross-section (somewhat less when dressed). **two-dimensional** a. **1** having two dimensions. **2** lacking (the appearance of) depth. **two-dimensionality** n. **two-edged** a. **1** (of a knife etc.) having an edge on both sides. **2** cutting both ways. **two-faced** a. **1** having two faces. **2** deceitful, insincere. **twofold** a. **1** double. **2** composed of two parts. ~adv. doubly. **two-handed** a. **1** having two hands. **2** requiring both hands for use. **3** played, worked etc. by two persons. **4** using both hands with equal dexterity, ambidextrous. **twoness** n. the state of being two, duality. **twopence** (tŭp′əns) n. **1** the sum of two pence. **2** (coll.) a thing of little value. **twopenn'orth** (toopen′əth) n. **1** as much as is worth or costs twopence. **2** an insignificant amount. **to put in one's twopenn'orth** (coll.) to give one's views. **twopenny** (tŭp′ni) a. **1** worth twopence. **2** (coll.) cheap, worthless, common, vulgar. **twopenny-halfpenny** a. **1** paltry, insignificant. **2** (Hist.) worth or costing twopence-halfpenny. **two-piece** n., a. (a garment) consisting of two usu. matching parts. **two-ply** a. having two strands (as cord) or two thicknesses (as carpets, cloth etc.). ~n. two-ply wool, wood etc. **two-seater** n. **1** a vehicle or aeroplane with seats for two people. **2** a sofa for two people. **two-sided** a. having two sides or aspects. **twosome** (-səm) n. **1**

a couple. **2** a dance, game of golf etc. involving two people. **two-step** n. a kind of round dance in march or polka time. **two-stroke** a. being or having an internal-combustion engine with a cycle of two strokes. ~n. **1** a two-stroke engine. **2** a vehicle having a two-stroke engine. **two-time** v.t. (coll.) **1** to be unfaithful to. **2** to double-cross. **two-timer** n. **two-timing** a. **two-tone** a. having two colours or shades. **two-up** n. an Australian gambling game in which two pennies are tossed in the air and bets made on whether they fall two heads or two tails; also called swy. **two-way** a. **1** arranged to allow movement in either of two directions. **2** (of a radio) able to send and receive. **3** reciprocal. **two-way mirror** n. a sheet of glass that is a mirror on one side but translucent when viewed from the other.

Usage note See note under TOO.

-ty¹ (ti) suf. forming abstract nouns, as bounty, cruelty, fealty.

-ty² (ti) suf. denoting tens, as fifty, twenty.

tycoon (tīkoon′) n. **1** a financial or political magnate. **2** (Hist.) a title given to the shogun of Japan, from 1857 to 1868.

tying TIE.

tyke (tīk), **tike** n. **1** a dog. **2** a cur. **3** an ill-mannered person. **4** a small child. **5** (sl.) a Yorkshireman.

tympan (tim′pən) n. **1** a frame stretched with paper cloth or parchment, used for equalizing the pressure in some printing presses. **2** any thin sheet or membrane tightly stretched. **3** (Archit.) a tympanum.

tympani TIMPANI.

tympanum (tim′pənəm) n. (pl. **tympanums**, **tympana** (-nə)) **1** (Anat.) **a** the middle ear. **b** the tympanic membrane or eardrum. **2** (Zool.) the membrane covering the hearing organ of an insect. **3** (Archit.) a triangular area, usu. recessed, in a pediment, the space between the lintel of a doorway and the arch enclosing it. **4** a wheel in the form of a drum for scooping up water from a stream. **tympanic** (-pan′-) a. **1** like a drum. **2** acting like a drumhead. **3** (Anat.) of or relating to the tympanum. **tympanic membrane** n. the membrane separating the outer ear and middle ear.

type (tīp) n. **1** a kind, a class, a category. **2** any person or thing that stands as an illustration, pattern, characteristic example or representative specimen of another thing or class of things. **3** an original conception, object or work of art, serving as a model or guide to later artists. **4** (coll.) a person (of a specified kind). **5** a piece of metal or hard wood bearing a letter or character usu. in relief, for printing with. **6** such pieces collectively. **7** characters produced by type. ~v.t. **1** to prefigure, to be a type of. **2** to write with a typewriter. **3** to typecast. **4** (esp. Biol., Med.) to assign to a type. ~v.i. to write with a typewriter. **in type** set in type. **typal** a. **-type** comb. form of the kind specified, resembling. **typecast** *v.t.* (*past, p.p.* **typecast**) **1** to cast (an actor) in a role for which they are suited by nature. **2** to cast continually in the same kind of part. **typeface** *n.* **1** the printing surface of type. **2** a design of printing type. **typescript** *n.* **1** typewritten matter or form. **2** a typewritten document. **typesetter** *n.* (*Print.*) **1** a compositor. **2** a machine for setting type. **typeset** *v.t.* (*pres.p.* **typesetting**, *past, p.p.* **typeset**). **typesetting** *a., n.* **type size** *n.* a named size of printing type. **typewrite** *v.i.* (*pres.p.* **typewriting**, *past* **typewrote**, *p.p.* **typewritten**) to write with a typewriter. **typewriter** *n.* a machine with keys for producing printed characters on individual sheets of paper inserted round a roller. **typewriting** *n.* **typewritten** *a.* **typist** *n.* a person who works at a typewriter, typing letters, documents etc.

typhoid (tī´foid) *a.* of, relating to or resembling typhus. ~*n.* **1** (*also* **typhoid fever**) an infectious fever characterized by an eruption of red spots on the chest and abdomen, severe intestinal irritation, inflammation, diarrhoea etc.; also called *enteric fever.* **2** a similar disease of animals. **typhoidal** (-foi´-) *a.*

typhoon (tīfoon´) *n.* a violent cyclonic hurricane occurring in the China Seas and the West Pacific. **typhonic** (-fon´-) *a.*

typhus (tī´fəs) *n.* a contagious rickettsial fever marked by an eruption of dark purple spots, great prostration, stupor and delirium. **typhous** *a.*

typical (tip´ikəl) *a.* **1** of the nature of or serving as a type. **2** representative, emblematic, symbolic (of). **3** embodying the characters of a group, class etc. **4** characteristic (of). **5** normal, average. **typicality** (-kal´-), **typicalness** *n.* **typically** *adv.* **typify** (-fī) *v.t.* (*3rd pers. sing. pres.* **typifies**, *pres.p.* **typifying**, *past, p.p.* **typified**) **1** to be a type of, to exemplify. **2** to betoken, to prefigure. **3** to represent by a type. **typification** (-fīkā´shən) *n.* **typifier** *n.*

typist TYPE.

typo (tī´pō) *n.* (*pl.* **typos**) (*coll.*) **1** a typographical error. **2** a typographer.

typography (tīpog´rəfi) *n.* **1** the art of printing. **2** the arrangement, character or appearance of printed matter. **typographer** *n.* **typographic**

(-pəgraf´-), **typographical** *a.* **typographically** *adv.*

tyrannical, tyrannicide etc. TYRANT.

tyrannosaurus (tīranəsaw´rəs),**tyrannosaur** (-ran´əsaw) *n.* a large flesh-eating dinosaur, *Tyrannosaurus rex*, which had small front legs and powerful hind legs.

tyrant (tī´rənt) *n.* **1** an arbitrary or despotic ruler. **2** a person who uses authority oppressively or cruelly. **tyrannical** (tiran´-) *a.* acting like or characteristic of a tyrant, despotic, arbitrary, imperious. **tyrannically** *adv.* **tyrannicalness** *n.* **tyrannicide** (tiran´isīd) *n.* **1** the act of killing a tyrant. **2** a person who kills a tyrant. **tyrannicidal** (-sī´-) *a.* **tyrannize** (tir´ə-), **tyrannise** *v.i.* to behave tyrannically, to rule despotically or oppressively (over). ~*v.t.* to rule (a person etc.) despotically or oppressively. **tyrannous** (tir´ə-) *a.* **tyrannously** *adv.* **tyranny** (tir´əni) *n.* (*pl.* **tyrannies**) **1** arbitrary or oppressive exercise of power. **2** an arbitrary, despotic or oppressive act. **3** the office or rule of a tyrant. **4** the period of this. **5** harshness, severity.

tyre (tīə), (*N Am.*) **tire** *n.* **1** an air-filled rubber casing round the outside of a wheel. **2** a strip of solid rubber or a band of metal surrounding a wheel. **tyre gauge** *n.* a device for measuring the air pressure in a tyre.

Usage note The British spelling of the noun *tyre* (around a wheel etc.) and the verb *tire* (to exhaust) should not be confused.

Tyrian (tir´iən) *a.* of or relating to ancient Tyre. ~*n.* a native or inhabitant of Tyre. **Tyrian dye, Tyrian purple** *n.* a purple dye formerly prepared from shellfish, esp. species of *Murex*.

tyro (tī´rō), **tiro** *n.* (*pl.* **tyros, tiros**) (*sometimes derog.*) a beginner, a novice.

Tyrolean (tirəlē´ən), **Tirolean** *a.* of or relating to the Tyrol, in Austria. ~*n.* a native or inhabitant of the Tyrol. **Tyrolese** (-lēz´) *a., n.* (*pl.* **Tyrolese**).

tyrosine (tī´rəsēn, -sin) *n.* (*Chem.*) an amino acid formed by the decomposition of proteins.

tzar TSAR.

tzatziki (tsatsē´ki) *n.* a Greek dip of yogurt flavoured with cucumber, garlic etc.

tzigane (tsigahn´), **tzigany** (tsig´əni) *n.* (*pl.* **tziganes, tziganies**) a Hungarian gypsy. ~*a.* of or relating to the Hungarian gypsies or their music.

U

U¹ (ū), **u** (*pl.* **Us, U's**) the 21st letter of the English and other versions of the Roman alphabet. It has five principal sounds: (1) long, back and rounded as in *rule*, marked in this dictionary oo; (2) short, back and rounded as in *bull*, unmarked, u; (3) short, central and unrounded as in *but*, marked ŭ; (4) long, central and unrounded, where historically modified by the letter *r*, as in *bur*, marked œ; (5) diphthongal as in *due*, marked ū. In unstressed syllables it is often obscured, as in *success*, marked ə. In conjunction with other vowels *u* also represents a variety of sounds, as in *pour, due, should* etc. *~symbol* (**u**) a factor of one millionth, micro- (originally μ). *~n.* a U-shaped thing or part. **U-turn** *n.* **1** a U-shaped turn made by a motor vehicle which takes it back in the direction from which it has come. **2** a complete reversal of policy etc.

U² *a.* (*coll.*) (of words, phrases, behaviour etc.) associated with the so-called upper classes.

U³ *abbr.* **1** university. **2** universal (of a film certified for viewing without age limit).

U⁴ *chem. symbol* uranium.

U⁵ (ū) *n.* a Burmese (Myanmar) title of respect used before a man's name.

UAE *abbr.* United Arab Emirates.

UB40 (ūbēfaw'ti) *n.* (*pl.* **UB40s**) **1** a card issued to a person registered as unemployed. **2** (*coll.*) an unemployed person.

-ubility (ūbil'iti) *suf.* forming nouns that correspond to adjectives in *-uble*, as *dissolubility*.

ubiquitous (ūbik'witəs) *a.* **1** present everywhere or in an indefinite number of places at the same time. **2** frequently encountered. **ubiquitously** *adv.* **ubiquitousness, ubiquity** *n.*

-uble (ūbəl) *suf.* that can or must be, as *dissoluble, voluble*. **-ubly** *suf.* forming adverbs.

U-boat (ū´bōt) *n.* a German submarine used in World Wars I and II.

UBR *abbr.* uniform business rate.

u.c. *abbr.* upper case.

udder (ŭd´ə) *n.* the milk-secreting organ of a cow, ewe etc., having several teats. **uddered** *a.*

UDI *abbr.* unilateral declaration of independence.

UFO (ūefō´, ū´fō) , **ufo** *n.* (*pl.* **UFOs, ufos**) an unidentified flying object. **ufology** (ūfol´əji) *n.* the study of UFOs. **ufologist** *n.*

ugh (ŭkh, ŭh, uh) *int.* **1** used to express disgust or horror. **2** used to represent a grunt or a cough.

Ugli® (ŭg´li), **ugli fruit** *n.* (*pl.* **Ugli, ugli fruit**) a cross between a grapefruit and a tangerine.

ugly (ŭg´li) *a.* (*comp.* **uglier**, *superl.* **ugliest**) **1** unpleasing to the sight or ear, not beautiful (*an ugly building*; *an ugly tone*). **2** morally repulsive. **3** threatening, unpleasant (*Things turned ugly*; *ugly scenes*). **to raise/ rear its ugly head** to appear, often after an absence, and start to cause problems. **uglify** (-fī) *v.t.* (*3rd pers. sing. pres.* **uglifies**, *pres.p.* **uglifying**, *past, p.p.* **uglified**) to make ugly. **uglification** (-fikā´shən) *n.* **uglily** *adv.* **ugliness** *n.* **ugly customer** *n.* an unpleasant and rather aggressive person. **ugly duckling** *n.* an unpromising person or thing that turns out surprisingly successful etc.

Ugric (ū´grik) *a.* **1** of or relating to the Magyars and other eastern Finnic peoples. **2** of or relating to the group of Finno-Ugric languages including Hungarian. *~n.* the Ugric family of languages.

UHF *abbr.* ultra-high frequency.

uh-huh (ŭ´hŭ) *int.* (*coll.*) used to express assent or show understanding.

UHT *abbr.* ultra heat-treated (of milk).

UK *abbr.* United Kingdom.

ukase (ūkāz´) *n.* **1** an edict or decree of the Imperial Russian Government. **2** any arbitrary decree.

Ukrainian (ūkrā´niən) *n.* **1** a native or inhabitant of Ukraine. **2** the language of Ukraine, similar to Russian. *~a.* of or relating to Ukraine, its people or language.

ukulele (ūkəlā´li) *n.* a small four-stringed instrument resembling a guitar.

-ular (ūlə) *suf.* forming adjectives, as *corpuscular, avuncular*. **-ularity** (ūlar´iti) *suf.* forming nouns, as *angularity*.

ulcer (ŭl´sə) *n.* **1** an open sore on the outer or inner surface of the body, often accompanied by a secretion of pus or other discharge. **2** a source of corruption or moral pollution. **ulcerate** *v.t.* to affect with or as with an ulcer. *~v.i.* to form an ulcer. **ulceration** (-ā´shən) *n.* **ulcerative** (-rətiv) *a.* **ulcered** *a.* **ulcerous** *a.* **ulcerously** *adv.* **ulcerousness** *n.*

-ule (ūl) *suf.* forming diminutive nouns, as *globule, pustule*.

ulema (oo´limə) *n.* **1** a body of Muslim doctors of law and interpreters of the Koran. **2** a member of this body.

-ulent (ūlənt) *suf.* forming adjectives meaning full of, abounding in, as *succulent*. **-ulence** *suf.* forming nouns.

ullage (ŭl´ij) *n.* **1** the quantity by which a cask falls short of being full. **2** loss of liquid by evaporation or leakage.

ulna (ŭl´nə) n. (pl. **ulnae** (-nē), **ulnas**) **1** the longer and thinner of the two bones in the forearm. **2** (Zool.) a corresponding bone in an animal's foreleg or in a bird's wing. **ulnar** a.

-ulous (ūləs) suf. forming adjectives, as querulous, nebulous.

ulster (ŭl´stə) n. a long, loose overcoat, usu. with a belt, made of rough cloth.

Ulsterman (ŭl´stəmən) n. (pl. **Ulstermen**) a native or inhabitant of Ulster. **Ulsterwoman** n. (pl. **Ulsterwomen**).

ult (ŭlt) adv. (formal) ultimo.

ulterior (ŭltiə´riə) a. **1** lying behind or beyond what is admitted or disclosed; hidden (ulterior motives). **2** more remote or distant. **3** lying beyond or on the other side of any line or boundary. **ulteriorly** adv.

ultimate (ŭl´timət) a. **1** last, final. **2** beyond which there is nothing existing or possible, incapable of analysis (the ultimate achievement). **3** fundamental, elementary, primary. **4** maximum (ultimate tensile stress). ~n. **1** (**the ultimate**) the best achievable or conceivable. **2** something final or fundamental. **ultimacy** (-əsi) n. (pl. **ultimacies**). **ultimately** adv. **ultimateness** n.

ultimatum (ŭltimā´təm) n. (pl. **ultimatums**, **ultimata** (-tə)) **1** a final proposal or statement of conditions by one party, the rejection of which may involve rupture of diplomatic relations of a declaration or war etc. **2** anything final, essential, or fundamental.

ultimo (ŭl´timō) a. (formal) in or during last month (the 7th ultimo).

ultra (ŭl´trə) a. extreme; advocating extreme views or measures. ~n. an extremist.

ultra- (ŭltrə) pref. **1** beyond, on the other side of, as ultramundane. **2** beyond the ordinary limit or range of, as ultrasonic. **3** beyond the reasonable, excessive(ly); extreme(ly), as ultra-efficient, ultramodern.

ultra- (+ a–l words) ultraconservative a. extremely conservative. **ultra-high** a. (of radio frequencies) between 300 and 3000 megahertz. **ultraist** (ŭl´-) n. an extremist in religion, politics etc. **ultraism** n.

ultra- (+ m–u words) ultramicroscope n. a microscope with a light source at the side, for examining particles too small to be seen with an ordinary microscope. **ultramicroscopic** a. **1** too small to be visible under an ordinary optical microscope. **2** of or relating to an ultramicroscope. **ultramicroscopy** n. **ultramontane** (-mon´-tān) a. **1** being or lying beyond the mountains, esp. the Alps. **2** supporting the supremacy of the Pope. ~n. **1** a person who resides south of the Alps. **2** a supporter of ultramontanism. **ultramontanism** (-mon´tən-) n. in the Roman Catholic Church, the principle that all ecclesiastical power should be concentrated in the hands of the Pope. **ultramontanist** (-mon´tə-) n. **ultramundane** (-mŭn´-) a. external to the world or the solar system. **ultrasonic** a. of, relating to, or

using, sound waves of higher than audible frequency. **ultrasonically** adv. **ultrasonics** n. the branch of physics dealing with ultrasonic waves and their applications. **ultrasound** (ŭl´-) n. **1** ultrasonic waves, used esp. for medical diagnosis. **2** sound that has an ultrasonic frequency.

ultramarine (ŭltrəmərēn´) a. deep blue. ~n. **1** a deep-blue pigment formerly obtained from lapis lazuli. **2** a synthetic form of this made from clay, sodium carbonate, sulphur and resin. **3** the colour of this.

ultra- (+ v–z words) ultraviolet a. (Physics) of or relating to the part of the electromagnetic spectrum having wavelengths shorter than the violet end of the visible spectrum but longer than X-rays.

ultra vires (ŭltrə vīə´rēz, vē´rāz) a., adv. beyond one's legal power or authority.

ululate (ū´lūlāt) v.i. **1** (of a dog, wolf etc.) to howl. **2** to make a hooting cry. **ululant** a. **ululation** (-lā´shən) n.

um (əm) int. used to express hesitation or a pause in speaking.

-um -IUM.

umbel (ŭm´bəl) n. (Bot.) an inflorescence in which the flower stalks spring from one point and spread like the ribs of an umbrella forming a flattish surface, as in parsley. **umbellar** a. **umbellate** (-lət), **umbellated** (-lātid) a. **umbellifer** (-bel´ifə) n. any plant of the Umbelliferae family, bearing umbels and including parsley and carrot. **umbelliferous** (-lif´-) a.

umber (ŭm´bə) n. **1** a dark yellowish-brown pigment derived from a mineral ferric oxide containing manganese. **2** a dark brown colour. ~a. **1** of the colour of umber. **2** dark, dusky.

umbilical (ŭmbil´ikəl) a. **1** of, relating to or situated near the navel. **2** linking. **3** inseparably connected. ~n. a long flexible line, tube etc. supplying or controlling something otherwise difficult to access. **umbilical cord** n. **1** the ropelike structure of vessels and tissue connecting the foetus with the placenta. **2** a cable carrying electricity, air etc., from a servicing point to a spacecraft, astronaut, diver etc. **umbilically** adv. **umbilicate** (-kət) a. **1** having the shape of a navel. **2** having an umbilicus. **umbilication** (-ā´shən) n. **umbilicus** (-kəs, -lī´-) n. (pl. **umbilici** (-sī), **umbilicuses**) **1** (Anat.) the navel. **2** (Biol.) a navel-shaped depression or other formation. **3** (Geom.) a point through which all cross-sections have the same curvature. **umbiliform** (-bil´ifawm) a.

†umbles (ŭm´bəlz) n.pl. the entrails of a deer.

umbra (ŭm´brə) n. (pl. **umbras**, **umbrae** (-brē)) **1** the darker part of a shadow cast by an opaque object, esp. that cast by the moon on to the earth during a solar eclipse. **2** (Astron.) the dark central area of a sunspot. **umbral** a.

umbrage (ŭm´brij) n. a sense of injury; offence (to take umbrage).

umbrella (ŭmbrel´ə) n. **1** a light screen of fabric,

stretched on a folding frame of radiating ribs on a stick, for holding above the head as a protection against rain or sun. **2** protection. **3** an organization which protects or coordinates the activities of a number of separate groups (*umbrella group*). **4** (*Zool.*) the umbrella-shaped disc of a jellyfish etc. that enables it to move through water. **5** a screen of aircraft or of gunfire covering a military movement. **6** a general heading etc. encompassing several individual ones. **umbrella bird** *n.* a S American bird of the genus *Cephalopterus*, with a large erectile spreading crest. **umbrellaed** (-ləd) *a.* **umbrella-like** *a.*

umiak (oo´miak), **oomiac, oomiak** *n.* an Eskimo (Inuit) boat made of skins stretched on a framework, used by women.

umlaut (um´lowt) *n.* **1** a change of the vowel in a syllable through the influence of an *i*, *r* etc. (now usu. lost or modified) in the following syllable. **2** (*Print.*) the diaeresis mark (¨) used over German vowels. *~v.t.* to sound with or modify by an umlaut.

ump (ŭmp) *n.* (*esp.* N Am., *sl.*) an umpire.

umpire (ŭm´piə) *n.* **1** a person chosen to enforce the rules and settle disputes in a game, esp. cricket or football. **2** a person chosen to decide a question of controversy. *~v.t.* to act as umpire in. *~v.i.* to act as umpire (for, at etc.). **umpirage** (-rij), **umpireship** *n.*

umpteen (ŭmptēn´) *a.* very many. *~pron.* an indefinitely large number. **umpteenth** *a.* **umpty** (ŭmp´ti) *a.*

UN *abbr.* United Nations.

un-¹ (ŭn) *pref.* **1** giving a negative sense to adjectives, adverbs and nouns, as *unappealing, unerringly, unpretentiousness.* **2** denoting the reversal or annulment of an action, state or quality (sometimes ambiguous, thus *unrolled* may mean 'not rolled up' or 'opened out after having been rolled up'. **3** denoting an absence of, as *untruth.* **4** denoting dispossession or separation, as *uncrown.* **5** denoting release from something, as *unfetter.*

un-² (ŭn) *pref.* (*Chem.*) denoting 'one' and used in combination with other numerical roots to form names of elements based on their atomic number, as *unnilpentium*, at. no. 105.

'un (ən) *n.*, *pron.* (*coll.*, *dial.*) one.

un- (+ a– words) **unabashed** *a.* not abashed; shameless. **unabashedly** *adv.* **unabated** *a.* **unable** *a.* not able (to); not having sufficient power or ability. **unabridged** *a.* **unabsorbed** *a.* **unacademic** *a.* **unaccented** *a.* **unacceptable** *a.* **unacceptableness, unacceptability** *n.* **unacceptably** *adv.* **unaccommodating** *a.* **unaccompanied** *a.* **1** unattended. **2** (*Mus.*) without accompaniment. **unaccomplished** *a.* **1** unfinished; not carried out or effected. **2** lacking accomplishments. **unaccountable** *a.* **1** not accountable or responsible. **2** inexplicable. **3** puzzling and strange. **unaccountability** *n.* **unaccountableness** *n.* **unaccountably** *adv.* **unaccounted** *a.* of which there

is no account. **unaccounted for** not explained; not included in an account or list. **unaccustomed** *a.* **1** not usual or familiar. **2** not used (to). **unaccustomedly** *adv.* **unacknowledged** *a.* **unacquainted** *a.* **unadopted** *a.* **1** not adopted. **2** (of a road etc.) not taken over by the local authority. **unadorned** *a.* not adorned, without decoration. **unadulterated** *a.* **1** not adulterated, unmixed. **2** pure, genuine (*unadulterated joy*). **unadventurous** *a.* **unadventurously** *adv.* **unadvised** *a.* **1** not having been given advice. **2** not prudent or discreet, rash. **unadvisedly** *adv.* **unadvisedness** *n.* **unaffected** *a.* **1** not influenced or affected. **2** without affectation, sincere, genuine. **unaffectedly** *adv.* **unaffectedness** *n.* **unaffiliated** *a.* **unafraid** *a.* **unaided** *a.* **unaligned** *a.* **1** NON-ALIGNED (under NON- (+ A– WORDS)). **2** not in physical alignment. **unalike** *a.* **unalleviated** *a.* **unalloyed** *a.* **1** not alloyed. **2** sheer; utter. **unalterable** *a.* **unalterability, unalterableness** *n.* **unalterably** *adv.* **unaltered** *a.* **unambiguous** *a.* plain, clear. **unambiguity** *n.* **unambiguously** *adv.* **unambiguousness** *n.* **unambitious** *a.* **unambitiously** *adv.* **unambitiousness** *n.* **unambivalent** *a.* **unambivalently** *adv.* **un-American** *a.* **1** not in accordance with American ideals, characteristics etc. **2** contrary to US interests. **un-Americanism** *n.* **unamiable** *a.* **unamused** *a.* **unannounced** *a.* **unanswerable** *a.* that cannot be satisfactorily answered or refuted. **unanswerableness** *n.* **unanswerably** *adv.* **unanswered** *a.* **unanticipated** *a.* **unapologetic** *a.* **unapologetically** *adv.* **unapparent** *a.* **unappealing** *a.* **unappealingly** *adv.* **unappeased** *a.* **unappetizing, unappetising** *a.* **unappetizingly** *adv.* **unappreciated** *a.* **unappreciative** *a.* **unapproachable** *a.* **1** that cannot be approached, inaccessible. **2** reserved, distant in manner. **unapproachability** *n.* **unapproachableness** *n.* **unapproachably** *adv.* **unapproved** *a.* **unapt** *a.* **unaptly** *adv.* **unaptness** *n.* **unarguable** *a.* **unarguably** *adv.* **unarm** *v.t.*, *v.i.* to disarm. **unarmed** *a.* **unarresting** *a.* uninteresting. **unartistic** *a.* **unartistically** *adv.* **unashamed** *a.* **1** not embarrassed or ashamed. **2** blatant. **unashamedly** *adv.* **unashamedness** *n.* **unasked** *a.* **1** not requested. **2** not invited. **unasked-for** *a.* not requested. **unassailable** *a.* **1** incapable of being assailed. **2** incontestable. **unassailability, unassailableness** *n.* **unassailably** *adv.* **unassailed** *a.* **unassertive** *a.* **unassertively** *adv.* **unassertiveness** *n.* **unassigned** *a.* **unassimilable** *a.* **unassimilated** *a.* **unassisted** *a.* **unassuaged** *a.* **unassuageable** *a.* **unassuming** *a.* not arrogant or presuming; modest. **unassumingly** *adv.* **unassumingness** *n.* **unattached** *a.* **1** not attached (to a club, organization etc.). **2** not married or having a partner. **unattainable** *a.* **unattainableness** *n.* **unattainably** *adv.* **unattempted** *a.* **unattended** *a.* **1** not attended (to). **2** not accompanied; not cared for. **unattractive** *a.* **unattractively** *adv.* **unattractiveness** *n.* **unattributable** *a.* **unattributably** *adv.* **unattributed** *a.*

unauthenticated *a.* unavailable *a.* unavailability, unavailableness *n.* unavailing *a.* ineffectual; vain; useless. unavailingly *adv.* unavoidable *a.* inevitable. unavoidably *adv.* unaware *a.* 1 not aware, ignorant (of). 2 careless, inattentive. ~*adv.* unawares. unawareness *n.* unawares *adv.* 1 without warning; by surprise, unexpectedly. 2 undesignedly.

unanimous (ūnan´iməs) *a.* 1 being all of one mind, agreeing in opinion. 2 (of an opinion, vote etc.) formed, held, or expressed with one accord. unanimity (-nim´-), unanimousness *n.* unanimously *adv.*

☒ **unatural** common misspelling of UNNATURAL (under UN- (+ M—N WORDS)).

un- (+ b–c words) unbacked *a.* 1 (of a horse) not taught to bear a rider, unbroken. 2 unsupported, having no backers. 3 without a back. unbalance *v.t.* to throw off balance. unbalanced *a.* unban *v.t.* (*pres.p.* unbanning, *past, p.p.* unbanned) to remove a ban from. unbar *v.t.* (*pres.p.* unbarring, *past, p.p.* unbarred) 1 to remove a bar or bars from. 2 to open, to unlock. unbearable *a.* unbearableness *n.* unbearably *adv.* unbeatable *a.* that cannot be beaten; unsurpassable. unbeaten *a.* 1 not beaten. 2 not surpassed. unbecoming *a.* 1 not becoming, not suited (to). 2 not befitting; improper. unbecomingly *adv.* unbeknown, unbeknownst *adv.* without the knowledge of (*Unbeknownst to us he had already left*). ~*a.* not known (to). unbelief *n.* lack of belief or disbelief (in, esp. divine revelation). unbelievable *a.* unbelievability, unbelievableness *n.* unbelievably *adv.* unbeliever *n.* unbelieving *a.* unbend *v.t.* (*past, p.p.* unbent) to change or free from a bent position; to straighten. ~*v.i.* 1 to become straightened. 2 to relax from constraint, formality etc.; to be affable. unbending *a.* 1 unyielding, resolute. 2 yielding oneself to relaxation or amusement; affable. unbendingly *adv.* unbendingness *n.* unbiased, unbiassed *a.* †unbid, unbidden *a.* 1 not commanded; not called for; spontaneous. 2 uninvited. unbind *v.t.* (*past, p.p.* unbound) 1 to untie, to unfasten. 2 to free from bonds, to release. unbirthday *a.* (*coll., facet.*) (of a present) given on an occasion other than a birthday. unbleached *a.* unblemished *a.* unblinking *a.* 1 not blinking. 2 showing no surprise or other emotion. 3 not hesitating or wavering. unblinkingly *adv.* unblock *v.t.* to remove a blockage from. unblushing *a.* 1 not blushing. 2 shameless, barefaced, impudent. unblushingly *adv.* unbolt *v.t.* to undo the bolts of; to open. unbolted *a.* 1 not fastened by a bolt. 2 (of flour etc.) not bolted or sifted. unborn *a.* 1 not yet born. 2 never to come into being. unbosom *v.t.* (*pres.p.* unbosoming, *past, p.p.* unbosomed) 1 to disclose (one's feelings etc.). 2 (*reflex.*) to open one's heart. unbothered *a.* unbound *a.* 1 not constrained. 2 (of a book) not bound. 3 (of a particle etc.) in a free state. unbounded *a.* 1 boundless, not bounded (by). 2 infinite, not subject to check or

control. unboundedly *adv.* unboundedness *n.* unbowed (-bowd´) *a.* not bowed; unconquered. unbreakable *a.* unbreathable *a.* unbridgeable *a.* unbridle *v.t.* to remove the bridle from. unbridled *a.* 1 freed from the bridle. 2 unrestrained; unruly. unbroken *a.* 1 not broken. 2 not subdued. 3 uninterrupted, regular. 4 (of a horse) not broken in, not accustomed to the saddle. 5 (of a record) not bettered. unbrokenly *adv.* unbrokenness *n.* unbruised *a.* unbuckle *v.t.* to unfasten the buckle of. unbuild *v.t.* (*past, p.p.* unbuilt) to demolish. unbuilt *a.* 1 not built. 2 (of land) not yet built upon. unbundle *v.t.* 1 to unpack. 2 to price and sell (goods or services) separately. 3 to divide (a company) into separate businesses. unbundler *n.* unburden *v.t.* 1 to free from a load or burden. 2 to relieve (oneself) by disclosure or confession. unburdened *a.* unbury *v.t.* (*3rd pers. sing. pres.* unburies, *pres.p.* unburying, *past, p.p.* unburied) 1 to remove from the ground after burial. 2 to bring (a secret etc.) into the open. unburied *a.* unbusinesslike *a.* unbutton *v.t.* to unfasten the buttons of. ~*v.i.* (*coll.*) to talk without restraint. uncalled *a.* not called or summoned. uncalled for not necessary; not asked for; gratuitous. uncanny *a.* (*comp.* uncannier, *superl.* uncanniest) weird, mysterious. uncannily *adv.* uncanniness *n.* uncanonical *a.* uncap *v.t.* (*pres.p.* uncapping, *past, p.p.* uncapped) to remove a cap or cover from. uncapped *a.* (of a sportsperson) never having been selected to play for their national team. uncared-for *a.* not cared for; neglected. uncaring *a.* uncarpeted *a.* uncashed *a.* uncaught *a.* unceasing *a.* not ceasing; incessant, continual. unceasingly *adv.* uncensored *a.* uncensured *a.* unceremonious *a.* 1 without ceremony or formality. 2 brusque, abrupt. unceremoniously *adv.* uncertain *a.* 1 not certain or sure; doubtful. 2 not to be relied on. 3 undecided; changeable; capricious. in no uncertain terms forcefully and unambiguously. uncertainly *adv.* uncertainty *n.* (*pl.* uncertainties) 1 the state of being uncertain. 2 something that is uncertain. unchain *v.t.* unchallengeable *a.* unchallenged *a.* unchallenging *a.* unchangeable *a.* unchangeableness *n.* unchangeably *adv.* unchanged *a.* unchanging *a.* unchangingly *adv.* unchaperoned *a.* uncharacteristic *a.* uncharacteristically *adv.* uncharitable *a.* censorious; judging harshly. uncharitableness *n.* uncharitably *adv.* uncharted *a.* unmapped. unchartered *a.* 1 not having a charter. 2 not authorized or legal. unchaste *a.* unchastity *n.* unchecked *a.* 1 not checked or repressed. 2 unrestrained, uncontrolled. 3 not examined. unchivalrous *a.* unchivalrously *adv.* unchristian *a.* not Christian; not according to or befitting the spirit of Christianity. uncircumcised *a.* uncivil *a.* 1 discourteous; ill-mannered. 2 not contributing to the civic good. uncivilized, uncivilised *a.* unclad *a.* unclaimed *a.* unclasp *v.t.* 1 to unfasten the clasp of. 2 to release from a grip. unclassified *a.* **1** not divided into categories. **2** (of information) not restricted. **unclassifiable** *a.* **unclean** *a.* **1** not clean. **2** lewd, unchaste. **3** not ceremonially clean. **4** (*Bible*) wicked. **uncleanly**[1] (-klēn´-) *adv.* †**uncleanly**[2] (-klen´-) *a.* (*also formal*) unclean. **uncleanliness** *n.* **uncleanness** *n.* **uncleared** *a.* **unclench** *v.t., v.i.* **unclimbed** *a.* not ever climbed. **unclog** *v.t.* (*pres.p.* **unclogging**, *past*, *p.p.* **unclogged**) to remove an obstruction from. **unclose** *v.t.* **1** to open. **2** to reveal. ~*v.i.* to open. **unclothe** *v.t.* **1** to take the clothes off. **2** to lay bare; to expose. **unclothed** *a.* **unclouded** *a.* **1** not obscured by clouds; clear, bright. **2** untroubled. **uncluttered** *a.* **uncoil** *v.t., v.i.* to unwind. **uncollected** *a.* **1** waiting to be collected. **2** (of money) not claimed or collected in. **3** (of literary writings) not brought together into a collection for publication. **uncoloured**, (*N Am.*) **uncolored** *a.* **1** not coloured. **2** told with simplicity or without exaggeration. **3** impartial. **uncomfortable** *a.* **uncomfortably** *adv.* **uncommercial** *a.* **1** not commercial. **2** not consistent with commercial principles or usage. **uncommitted** *a.* **1** not committed. **2** not pledged to support any particular policy, party etc. **uncommon** *a.* **1** not common, unusual, remarkable. **2** unusually great. **uncommonly** *adv.* remarkably, to an uncommon degree. **uncommunicative** *a.* reserved, taciturn. **uncommunicatively** *adv.* **uncommunicativeness** *n.* **uncompetitive** *a.* **uncomplaining** *a.* **uncomplainingly** *adv.* **uncompleted** *a.* **uncomplicated** *a.* **uncomplimentary** *a.* **uncomprehending** *a.* **uncomprehendingly** *adv.* **uncompromising** *a.* not compromising; determined; inflexible. **uncompromisingly** *adv.* **uncompromisingness** *n.* **unconcealed** *a.* **unconcern** *n.* absence of concern or anxiety; indifference; apathy. **unconcerned** *a.* **unconcernedly** *adv.* **unconditional** *a.* not conditional; absolute. **unconditionally** *adv.* **unconditionality** *n.* **unconditionalness** *n.* **unconditioned** *a.* **1** (of behaviour) not learned or conditioned, innate. **2** without conditions. **unconditioned reflex** *n.* an innate response to a stimulus. **unconfined** *a.* **unconfirmed** *a.* **uncongenial** *a.* **unconnected** *a.* **1** not linked, connected or joined. **2** (of ideas etc.) disconnected. **unconnectedly** *adv.* **unconnectedness** *n.* **unconquerable** *a.* **unconquerably** *adv.* **unconquered** *a.* **unconscionable** *a.* **1** not reasonable, inordinate. **2** not influenced or restrained by conscience; unscrupulous. **3** (*Law*) grossly unfair, inequitable. **unconscionably** *adv.* **unconscious** *a.* **1** ignorant, unaware (of). **2** temporarily deprived of consciousness. **3** not perceived by the mind. ~*n.* (*Psych.*) the part of the mind including instincts, impulses etc. which lies hidden from the conscious mind. **unconsciously** *adv.* **unconsciousness** *n.* **unconsecrated** *a.* **unconsidered** *a.* **1** not taken into consideration. **2** (of a reply etc.) not considered; immediate. **unconstitutional** *a.* not authorized by or contrary to the principles of a constitution. **unconsti-**

tutionality *n.* **unconstitutionally** *adv.* **unconstrained** *a.* **unconstricted** *a.* **unconsumed** *a.* **unconsummated** *a.* **uncontaminated** *a.* **uncontentious** *a.* **uncontested** *a.* **uncontradicted** *a.* **uncontrollable** *a.* **uncontrollably** *adv.* **uncontrolled** *a.* **uncontroversial** *a.* **uncontroversially** *adv.* **unconventional** *a.* not fettered by convention or usage; unusual. **unconventionality** *n.* **unconventionally** *adv.* **unconverted** *a.* **unconvinced** *a.* **unconvincing** *a.* **unconvincingly** *adv.* **uncooked** *a.* **uncool** *a.* **1** (*sl.*) not cool; unfashionable. **2** (of jazz) not cool. **uncooperative** *a.* **uncoordinated** *a.* **uncork** *v.t.* **1** to take the cork out of (a bottle). **2** to give vent to (one's feelings etc.). **uncorrected** *a.* **uncorroborated** *a.* **uncountable** *a.* immeasurable; immense. **uncountable noun** *n.* (*Gram.*) a noun that has no plural forms, takes only a singular verb and cannot be used with an indefinite article. **uncountably** *adv.* **uncounted** *a.* **1** not counted. **2** innumerable. **uncount noun** *n.* UNCOUNTABLE NOUN (under UN- (+ B–C WORDS)). **uncouple** *v.t.* to disconnect. **uncoupled** *a.* **uncover** *v.t.* **1** to remove a covering from. **2** to make known, to disclose. **3** to expose (a line of troops behind) by wheeling to right or left. **uncovered** *a.* **1** not covered. **2** not wearing a hat, esp. as a sign of respect. **uncreative** *a.* **uncredited** *a.* not acknowledged as the originator, author etc. **uncritical** *a.* **1** not critical. **2** not according to the rules of criticism. **uncritically** *adv.* **uncross** *v.t.* to change from a crossed position. **uncrossed** *a.* **1** (of a cheque) not crossed. **2** not opposed. **uncrowded** *a.* **uncrown** *v.t.* **1** to dethrone. **2** to take a position from (someone). **uncrowned** *a.* **1** not yet crowned. **2** having the power of royalty without the title of king or queen. **3** having high status within a particular group (*the uncrowned king of jazz*). **uncultivable** *a.* **uncultivated** *a.* **uncultured** *a.* **uncurl** *v.t., v.i.* **uncut** *a.* **1** not cut. **2** (of a book) having the margins untrimmed or not having the pages cut open. **3** (of a film etc.) not shortened or abridged. **4** (of a diamond) not shaped and faceted by cutting. **5** (of fabric) not having its pile-loops cut.

uncial (ŭn´shəl) *a.* denoting a kind of majuscule writing somewhat resembling modern capitals, used in manuscripts of the 4th 8th cents. ~*n.* an uncial letter, style or manuscript.

uncle (ŭng´kəl) *n.* **1** the brother of one's father or mother. **2** the husband of one's aunt. **3** (*coll.*) a name that children sometimes give to a male friend of the family. **4** (*sl.*) a pawnbroker. **Uncle Sam** *n.* (*coll.*) the government, a typical representative or the people of the US. **Uncle Tom** *n.* (*offensive*) a black man considered to be servile in his manner towards white people.

uncouth (ŭnkooth´) *a.* lacking in refinement, culture or manners. **uncouthly** *adv.* **uncouthness** *n.*

unction (ŭngk´shən) *n.* **1** the act of anointing with oil or an unguent, as a symbol of consecration or for medical purposes. **2**

something which is used for anointing; an oil or ointment. **3** anything soothing. **4** ingratiating words; excessive flattery. **5** a quality in speech conveying deep religious or other fervour. **6** effusive or affected emotion, gush. **unctuous** *a.* **1** greasy, oily, soapy to the touch. **2** full of unction. **3** (of words, behaviour etc.) oily; full of effusive, insincere flattery. **unctuously** *adv.* **unctuousness** *n.*

un- (+ d– words) undamaged *a.* **undated** *a.* not marked or provided with a date. **undaunted** *a.* **undauntedly** *adv.* **undead** *a.* (of a vampire, ghost etc. in fiction) dead but not at rest. **the undead** those who are undead. **undeceive** *v.t.* to free from deception or error; to open the eyes of. **undecided** *a.* **1** not decided or settled. **2** irresolute, wavering. **undecidedly** *adv.* **undecipherable** *a.* **undeclared** *a.* **undecorated** *a.* **undefeated** *a.* **undefended** *a.* **undefiled** *a.* not defiled; pure. **undefined** *a.* **1** not defined. **2** indefinite, vague. **undefinable** *a.* **undefinably** *adv.* **undelivered** *a.* **undemanding** *a.* **undemocratic** *a.* **undemocratically** *adv.* **undemonstrative** *a.* not demonstrative; reserved. **undemonstratively** *adv.* **undeniable** *a.* **1** not capable of being denied; indisputable. **2** decidedly good, excellent (*of undeniable character*). **undeniably** *adv.* **undenied** *a.* **undependable** *a.* not to be depended on. **undeserved** *a.* **undeservedly** *adv.* **undeserving** *a.* **undesigned** *a.* not designed, unintentional. **undesirable** *a.* not desirable; unpleasant; inconvenient. *~n.* an undesirable person. **undesirability** *n.* **undesirably** *adv.* **undesired** *a.* **undesirous** *a.* **undetectable** *a.* **undetectably** *adv.* **undetected** *a.* **undetermined** *a.* **1** not determined; not fixed; indeterminate. **2** irresolute. **undeterred** *a.* **undeveloped** *a.* **undiagnosed** *a.* **undifferentiated** *a.* **undigested** *a.* **1** not digested. **2** (of facts etc.) not arranged in a systematic or convenient form. **undignified** *a.* **undiluted** *a.* **1** not diluted. **2** complete (*undiluted nonsense*). **undiminished** *a.* **undiplomatic** *a.* **undiplomatically** *adv.* **undischarged** *a.* **undisciplined** *a.* **undisclosed** *a.* **undiscoverable** *a.* **undiscoverably** *adv.* **undiscovered** *a.* **undiscriminating** *a.* **undiscussed** *a.* **undisguised** *a.* **undisguisedly** *adv.* **undismayed** *a.* **undisputed** *a.* **undissolved** *a.* **undistinguished** *a.* **undisturbed** *a.* **undivided** *a.* **undo** *v.t.* (*3rd pers. sing. pres.* **undoes**, *pres.p.* **undoing**, *past* **undid**, *p.p.* **undone**) **1** to reverse (something that has been done); to annul. **2** to unfasten, to untie. **3** to unfasten the buttons, garments etc. of (a person). **4** to bring ruin to; to destroy. **undoer** *n.* **undoing** *n.* **1** ruin or downfall; the cause of this. **2** the action of reversing something that has been done. **3** the action of unfastening. **undone** *a.* **1** not done. **2** unfastened. **3** †ruined. **undocumented** *a.* **1** not documented. **2** (*NAm.*) not having the necessary documents. **undoer, undoing** UNDO (under UN- (+ D– WORDS)). **undomesticate** *v.t.* **undomesticated** *a.* **undone** UNDO (under UN-

(+ D– WORDS)). **undoubted** *a.* not called in question, not doubted. **undoubtedly** *adv.* **undreamed, undreamt** *a.* not imagined or thought of (*advances undreamed of only 20 years ago*). **undress** *v.t.* to remove the clothes from; to strip. *~v.i.* to undress oneself. *~n.* **1** the state of being partly or completely undressed. **2** ordinary dress, as opposed to full dress or uniform. **3** informal dress. *~a.* of or relating to everyday dress. **undressed** *a.* **1** partly or completely naked. **2** (of food) without a dressing. **3** (of leather etc.) not fully processed or treated. **undrinkable** *a.* **undue** *a.* **1** excessive, disproportionate. **2** not yet due. **unduly** *adv.* **undyed** *a.* **undying** *a.* **1** unceasing. **2** immortal.

under (ŭn′də) *prep.* **1** in or to a place or position lower than, below (*It's under the chair*; *He crawled under the bed*). **2** at the foot or bottom of (*under the cliff*). **3** covered by, on the inside of, beneath the surface of (*She wore a T-shirt under her jumper*). **4** beneath the appearance or disguise of (*under the guise of*). **5** inferior to or less than in quality, rank, degree, number etc. (*under 30 years*). **6** subject or subordinate; governed or controlled (*to live under a dictatorship*; *born under Scorpio*). **7** liable to; on condition or pain of; in accordance with (*under oath*). **8** in the time of (*under the Romans*). **9** planted or sown with (a crop). **10** because of. **11** in the process of (*The building is under repair*). **12** in a group consisting of (*It comes under biochemistry*). **13** powered by (*under steam*). *~adv.* **1** in or into a lower or subordinate place, condition or degree. **2** (*coll.*) in or into a state of unconsciousness. *~a.* lower, inferior, subordinate. **under age** not old enough to do an activity legally. **under one's breath** in a low voice, in a whisper. **under sentence** having received sentence or judgement. **under separate cover** in another envelope. **under water** beneath the surface of the water. **underling** (-ling) *n.* (*usu. derog.*) an inferior agent or assistant. **under-the-counter** *a.* (of black-market goods etc.) secretly obtained.

under- (ŭndə) *pref.* **1** under, below, as *underpass*. **2** lower than in rank, position etc.; subordinate, as *under-sheriff*. **3** insufficiently, incompletely, as *underplay*, *underexpose*.

under- (+ a–s words) underachieve *v.i.* to fail to achieve as much (esp. academically) as might be expected. **underachievement** *n.* **underachiever** *n.* **underarm** (ŭn′-) *a., adv.* **1** in cricket etc., with the arm below shoulder level. **2** under the arm. **3** in the armpit. *~n.* the armpit. **underbelly** (ŭn′-) *n.* (*pl.* **underbellies**) **1** the underside of an animal, usually its most vulnerable part. **2** any vulnerable part or aspect (of an organization etc.). **underbid** *v.t.* (*pres.p.* **underbidding**, *past*, *p.p.* **underbid**) **1** at an auction etc., to bid less than (someone). **2** in bridge etc., to make a bid on (one's hand) that is less than is warranted by its strength. *~n.* **1** such a bid. **2** the act of underbidding. **underbrush** (ŭn´-) *n.* (*N Am.*) undergrowth. **undercarriage** (ŭn´-) *n.* **1** the main landing gear of an aircraft. **2** the frame supporting the body of a vehicle. **undercharge** *v.t.* **1** to charge less than the fair price for. **2** to put an insufficient charge in (a gun, battery etc.). **underclass** (ŭn´-) *n.* a social class below the standard scale, very deprived in economic, educational etc. terms. **undercliff** *n.* a terrace formed by material that has fallen from a cliff. **underclothes** (ŭn´-) *n.pl.* clothes worn under others, esp. next to the skin. **underclothing** *n.* underclothes in general. **undercoat** (ŭn´-) *n.* **1** a layer of fine fur underneath an animal's main coat. **2** a coat of paint serving as a base for the main coat. **3** the paint used for this. ~*v.t.* to apply an undercoat of paint to. **undercoating** *n.* **undercook** *v.t.* to cook too little. **undercover** *a.* **1** done in secret. **2** engaged in espionage. **undercroft** (un´-) *n.* a vault, esp. under a church or large building; a crypt. **undercurrent** *n.* **1** a current beneath the surface. **2** an underlying tendency, influence etc. **undercut** (ŭn´-) *v.t.* (*pres.p.* **undercutting**, *past, p.p.* **undercut**) **1** to sell at a lower price than that of (a competitor). **2** to work for lower wages than (a competitor). **3** to cut away the part under (something). **4** to cut away the material beneath (a carved design) to give greater relief. **5** in golf, to hit (a ball) so as to make it rise high. ~*n.* **1** the act or effect of undercutting. **2** the underside of a sirloin. **underdeveloped** *a.* **1** not sufficiently or adequately developed. **2** (of a country) not economically advanced. **3** (of a photograph) not sufficiently developed to give a clear image. **underdevelopment** *n.* **underdo** *v.t.* (*3rd pers. sing. pres.* **underdoes**, *pres.p.* **underdoing**, *past* **underdid**, *p.p.* **underdone**) **1** to cook insufficiently. **2** to do inadequately. **underdone** *a.* **1** insufficiently cooked. **2** not adequately done. **underdog** (un´-) *n.* **1** a person in a contest or fight who stands little chance of winning. **2** an oppressed person. **underdress** *v.t., v.i.* to dress insufficiently or too plainly. **underemphasis** *n.* (*pl.* **underemphases**) a lack of emphasis. **underemphasize, underemphasise** *v.t.* **underemployed** *a.* not fully or adequately employed. **underemployment** *n.* **underestimate** *v.t.* to estimate at too low a level. ~*n.* an inadequate estimate. **underestimation** *n.* **underexpose** *v.t.* to expose (a photographic film) with insufficient light or for too short a time. **underexposure** *n.* **underfeed** *v.t.* (*past, p.p.* **underfed**) to feed insufficiently. **underfed** *a.* **underfelt** (ŭn´-) *n.* a felt underlay. **under-fives** *n.pl.* children of less than five years of age. **underfloor** *a.* situated or installed under the floor (*underfloor heating*). **underflow** (ŭn´-) *n.* an undercurrent. **underfoot** *adv.* **1** under one's feet. **2** on the ground. **3** in the way. **4** in a position of subjection. **underfund** *v.t.* to fund inadequately. **underfunded** *a.* **underfunding** *n.* **undergarment** (ŭn´-) *n.* an item of underclothing. **underglaze** (ŭn´-) *a.* **1** (of painting on ceramics

etc.) done before the application of the glaze. **2** (of pigments etc.) suitable for painting with before the glaze is applied. ~*n.* a pigment etc. used in this way. **undergo** *v.t.* (*3rd pers. sing. pres.* **undergoes**, *pres.p.* **undergoing**, *past* **underwent**, *p.p.* **undergone**) to suffer; to endure; to bear up against. **undergrad** *n.* (*coll.*) an undergraduate. **undergraduate** *n.* a member of a university who has not yet taken a degree. **underground**[1] (-grownd´) *adv.* **1** below the surface of the earth. **2** into secrecy or hiding. **underground**[2] (ŭn´-) *a.* **1** situated below the surface of the earth. **2** secret; unperceived by those in authority. **3** ignoring or subversive of established trends; avant-garde. ~*n.* **1** an underground railway. **2** a secret or subversive group or organization. ~*v.t.* to lay (cables) below the ground. **undergrowth** (ŭn´-) *n.* small trees or shrubs growing under larger ones. **underhand** (ŭn´-) *adv.* **1** secretly, clandestinely. **2** slyly; unfairly; by fraud. **3** underarm. ~*a.* **1** secret, clandestine. **2** sly; unfair; fraudulent. **3** underarm. **underhanded** *a., adv.* underhand. **underlay**[1] (-lā´) *v.t.* (*past, p.p.* **underlaid**) to lay something under (a thing), e.g. as a support. **underlay**[2] (ŭn´-) *n.* **1** felt or rubber laid under a carpet. **2** a piece of paper etc. placed beneath a forme or block to bring it to the proper level for printing. **underlie** *v.t.* (*3rd pers. sing. pres.* **underlies**, *pres.p.* **underlying**, *past* **underlay**, *p.p.* **underlain**) **1** to lie under or beneath. **2** to be the basis or foundation of. **3** (of a feeling, attitude etc.) to lie hidden beneath. **underline**[1] (-līn´) *v.t.* **1** to draw a line under, esp. for emphasis. **2** to emphasize. **underline**[2] (ŭn´-) *n.* **1** a line drawn under a word etc. **2** a caption. **underlinen** (ŭn´-) *n.* linen underclothing. **underling** UNDER. **underlip** *n.* the lower lip. **underlying** *a.* **1** basic; fundamental. **2** lying beneath. **undermanned** *a.* having an insufficient number of crew members or members of staff. **undermentioned** *a.* mentioned below or in a later place. **undermine** *v.t.* **1** to injure or harm by secret or underhand means. **2** to weaken (one's health etc.) by imperceptible degrees. **3** (of the wind, a river etc.) to wear away the base or bottom of (a bank, cliff etc.). **4** to dig a mine or excavation under. **underminer** *n.* **underneath** *prep.* **1** beneath, below. **2** within. ~*adv.* **1** under; beneath. **2** inside. ~*n.* an underside. ~*a.* lower. **undernourish** *v.t.* **undernourished** *a.* **undernourishment** *n.* **underpaid** *a.* **underpants** (ŭn´-) *n.pl.* a men's or boys' undergarment covering the body from the waist to the thighs. **underpart** (ŭn´-) *n.* a lower part. **underpass** (ŭn´-) *n.* **1** a road passing under a railway or another road. **2** a pedestrian crossing beneath a road. **underpay** *v.t.* (*past, p.p.* **underpaid**) to pay inadequately. **underpayment** *n.* **underperform** *v.i.* to perform less well than expected. ~*v.t.* to perform less well than. **underperformance** *n.* **underpin** *v.t.* (*pres.p.* **underpinning**, *past, p.p.* **underpinned**) **1** to support (a wall etc.) by propping up with timber, masonry, etc. **2** to strengthen the foundations of (a building). **underplay** *v.t.* **1** to play down. **2** to play (a part) with deliberate restraint or subtlety. *~v.i.* to underplay a part. **underpopulated** *a.* **underpowered** *a.* lacking sufficient electrical etc. power. **underprice** *v.t.* to price (something) at too low a level. **underprivileged** *a.* lacking the economic and social privileges enjoyed by most members of society. *~n.* (*as pl.*) underprivileged person. **underproduction** *n.* lower or less production than the normal or the demand. **underrate** *v.t.* to rate or estimate too low. **underrepresent** *v.t.* to represent insufficiently. **underrepresented** *a.* **underscore**[1] (-skaw´) *v.t.* to underline. **underscore**[2] (ŭn´-) *n.* an underline. **undersea** *a.* below the surface of the sea. **underseal** (ŭn´-) *v.t.* to coat the exposed underparts of (a vehicle) with a corrosion-resistant substance. *~n.* such a substance. **under-secretary** *n.* (*pl.* **undersecretaries**) **1** a senior civil servant or junior minister. **2** (*N Am.*) the principal assistant to the secretary in charge of a government department. **undersell** *v.t.* (*past, p.p.* **undersold**) **1** to sell cheaper than (another seller). **2** to sell (an article) at less than its true value. **undersexed** *a.* having a weaker sex drive than is considered normal. **undershirt** *n.* (*esp. N Am.*) a vest or singlet. **undershoot**[1] (-shoot´) *v.t.* (*past, p.p.* **undershot**) **1** (of an aircraft) to land short of (a runway). **2** to shoot something so that it falls short of or below. **undershoot**[2] (ŭn´-) *n.* the act of undershooting; an instance of this. **undershorts** (ŭn´-) *n.pl.* (*N Am.*) men's or boys' underpants. **underside** (ŭn´-) *n.* a lower side or surface. **undersign** *v.t.* to sign under or at the foot of. **the undersigned** the person or persons signing a document etc. **undersized, undersize** *a.* below the normal or average size. **underskirt** (ŭn´-) *n.* a skirt worn under another. **underslung** *a.* **1** (of a motor vehicle chassis) with the frame below the axles. **2** supported from above. **underspend**[1] (-spend´) *v.i.* (*past, p.p.* **underspent**) to spend less than expected or allowed for. *~v.t.* to spend less than (a particular amount). **underspend**[2] (ŭn´-) *n.* **1** the act of underspending or an instance of this. **2** the amount by which a particular sum is underspent. **understaffed** *a.* **understaffing** *n.* **understate** *v.t.* **1** to express (something) in a deliberately restrained way, often for ironic effect. **2** to represent as less, inferior etc., than the truth. **understated** *a.* restrained, simple. **understatement** (-stāt´-, ŭn´-) *n.* **understeer** (ŭn´-) *n.* a tendency in a motor vehicle to turn less sharply than expected. *~v.i.* to have this tendency. **understorey**, (*N Am.*) **understory** *n.* (*pl.* **understoreys**, (*N Am.*) **understories**) **1** a layer of small trees and shrubs that grows beneath the main canopy of a forest. **2** the plants, trees etc. that make up this. **understudy** (ŭn´-) *v.t.* (*3rd pers. sing. pres.* **understudies**, *pres.p.* **understudying**, *past, p.p.* **understudied**) **1** to study (a part) in order to play it if the usual actor is unable to. **2** to study the acting

of (an actor or actress) in this way. *~n.* (*pl.* **understudies**) a person who understudies another. **undersubscribed** *a.* **undersurface** (ŭn´-) *n.*

understand (ŭndəstand´) *v.t.* (*past, p.p.* **understood** (-stud´)) **1** to take in, know or perceive the meaning of (*I can't understand what he's saying*). **2** to perceive the force or significance of (*I don't understand what the fuss is about*). **3** to be sympathetic to (*I can understand your dilemma*). **4** to take as meant or implied, to gather or infer (*I understand you're looking for volunteers*). **5** to be informed or told (*She's in line for promotion, I understand*). **6** to supply (a word, explanation etc.) mentally. *~v.i.* to have or exercise the power of comprehension. **to understand each other 1** to know and be sympathetic to each other's feelings. **2** to have an agreement with each other. **understandable** *a.* **understandability** (-bil´-) *n.* **understandably** *adv.* **understander** *n.* **understanding** *a.* **1** intelligent and perceptive. **2** sympathetic, tolerant. *~n.* **1** the act of understanding; comprehension. **2** the power or faculty of apprehension; the faculty of thinking or of apprehending relations and drawing inferences. **3** clear insight and intelligence in practical matters. **4** a personal judgement or perception of a situation etc. **5** union of minds or sentiments, accord. **6** an informal agreement or compact. **on the understanding that** provided that. **understandingly** *adv.*

under- (+ t–z words) undertenant (ŭn´-) *n.* a tenant under another tenant. **underthings** (ŭn´-) *n.pl.* (*coll.*) underclothes. **undertone** (ŭn´-) *n.* **1** a low or subdued tone, esp. in speaking. **2** an unstated meaning or emotional tone. **undertow** (ŭn´-) *n.* an undercurrent flowing in the opposite direction to the current on the surface; the backward flow under waves breaking on a shore. **underuse**[1] (-ūs´) *n.* **underuse**[2] (-ūz´) *v.t.* **undervalue** *v.t.* (*3rd pers. sing. pres.* **undervalues**, *pres.p.* **undervaluing**, *past, p.p.* **undervalued**) **1** to value at too low a level; to despise. **2** to underestimate. **undervaluation** *n.* **underwater** *a., adv.* **underwear** (ŭn´-) *n.* underclothing. **underweight**[1] (-wāt´) *a.* of less than the average or expected weight. **underweight**[2] (ŭn´-) *n.* too little weight. **underwhelm** *v.t.* (*coll., facet.*) to fail to impress, to disappoint (formed from *overwhelm*). **underwing** (ŭn´-) *n.* **1** the hind wing of an insect. **2** the inner side of a bird's feather. **3** a nocturnal moth with conspicuous markings on the hind or under wings. **underwood** (ŭn´-) *n.* undergrowth. **underwork** *v.t.* to give too little work to. *~v.i.* to work inadequately. **underworld** (ŭn´-) *n.* **1** the criminal class of society. **2** the nether world, the infernal regions. **underwrite** *v.t.* (*past* **underwrote**, *p.p.* **underwritten**) **1** to execute and deliver (an insurance policy, accepting liability should certain losses occur). **2** to accept (liability) in an insurance policy. **3** to engage to buy all the stock in (a new company etc.) not subscribed for by the public. **4** to undertake the financing of. **5** to write beneath, to subscribe. *~v.i.* to act as an underwriter of insurance policies. **underwriter** (ŭn´-) *n.*

undertake (ŭndətāk´) *v.t.* (*past* **undertook** (-tuk´), *p.p.* **undertaken** (-kən)) **1** to take upon oneself, to assume, to engage in, to enter upon (a task, enterprise, responsibility etc.). **2** to engage oneself, to promise (to do). **3** to guarantee, to affirm (that). **undertaker** (ŭn´-) *n.* **1** a person who manages funerals. **2** a person who undertakes something. **undertaking** (ŭn´-) *n.* **1** the act of undertaking any business. **2** something which is undertaken, a task, an enterprise. **3** an agreement; a promise; a stipulation. **4** the business of managing funerals.

undies (ŭn´diz) *n.pl.* (*coll.*) women's underwear.

undine (ŭn´dēn) *n.* a female water spirit without a soul, but capable of obtaining one by marrying a mortal and bearing a child.

undulate (ŭn´dūlāt) *v.i.* **1** to have a wavy motion. **2** (of water) to rise and fall. *~v.t.* to cause to have a wavy motion. **undulation** (-lā´shən) *n.* **1** the act of undulating. **2** a wavy or sinuous form or motion; a gentle rise and fall; a wavelet. **3** a set of wavy lines. **undulatory** *a.* **1** rising and falling like waves. **2** of, relating to or due to undulation.

un- (**+ e–g words**) **unearned** *a.* **unearned income** *n.* income from rents, investments etc. as distinct from salary or wages. **unearth** *v.t.* **1** to bring to light, to find out through searching or rummaging. **2** to dig up. **unearthly** *a.* **1** not earthly. **2** not of this world, supernatural. **3** (*coll.*) ridiculous and unreasonable (*at an unearthly hour*). **unearthliness** *n.* **unease** *n.* lack of ease; anxiety; discomfort. **uneasy** *a.* (*comp.* **uneasier**, *superl.* **uneasiest**) **1** troubled, anxious or uncomfortable. **2** disturbing, disquieting. **3** awkward, stiff, constrained. **uneasily** *adv.* **uneasiness** *n.* **uneatable** *a.* **uneaten** *a.* **uneconomic** *a.* not economic, not financially viable. **uneconomical** *a.* not economical; profligate. **uneconomically** *adv.* **unedifying** *a.* **unedifyingly** *adv.* **unedited** *a.* **uneducable** *a.* **uneducated** *a.* **unelectable** *a.* **unelected** *a.* **unembarrassed** *a.* **unemotional** *a.* **unemotionally** *adv.* **unemphatic** *a.* **unemphatically** *adv.* **unemployed** *a.* **1** having no paid work; not in work. **2** not in use. *~n.* (*as pl.*) people who are out of work. **unemployable** *a., n.* **unemployability** *n.* **unemployment** *n.* **1** the state of being out of work. **2** the number of unemployed people in a country or region. **unemployment benefit** *n.* a regular payment by the State to an unemployed worker. **unencumbered** *a.* **1** not encumbered. **2** (of an estate etc.) having no liabilities on it. **unending** *a.* having no end, endless. **unendingly** *adv.* **unendingness** *n.* **unendowed** *a.* **unendurable** *a.* **unendurably** *adv.* **unenforceable** *a.* **un-English** *a.* **1** not English. **2** not characteristic of English people. **unenjoyable** *a.* **unenlightened** *a.* **unenterprising** *a.* **unenthusiastic** *a.* **unenthusiastically** *adv.* **unenviable** *a.* **unenviably** *adv.* **unequal** *a.* **1** not equal (to). **2**

uneven; varying. **3** (of a contest etc.) not evenly balanced. **unequalled**, (*N Am.*) **unequaled** *a.* **unequally** *adv.* **unequipped** *a.* **unequivocal** *a.* not equivocal, not ambiguous; plain. **unequivocally** *adv.* **unerring** *a.* **1** committing no mistake. **2** not missing the mark, certain, sure. **unerringly** *adv.* **unessential** *a.* **1** not essential, not absolutely necessary. **2** not of prime importance. *~n.* something or part not absolutely necessary or indispensable. **unestablished** *a.* **unethical** *a.* **unethically** *adv.* **uneven** *a.* **1** not even, level or smooth. **2** not uniform, regular or equable. **3** (of a contest etc.) not equal. **unevenly** *adv.* **unevenness** *n.* **uneventful** *a.* **uneventfully** *adv.* **uneventfulness** *n.* **unexamined** *a.* **unexceptionable** *a.* to which no exception can be taken; unobjectionable; faultless. **unexceptionably** *adv.* **unexceptional** *a.* not exceptional, ordinary. **unexceptionally** *adv.* **unexcitable** *a.* **unexcitability** *n.* **unexciting** *a.* **unexpected** *a.* **unexpectedly** *adv.* **unexpectedness** *n.* **unexpired** *a.* not having come to an end or termination. **unexplainable** *a.* **unexplainably** *adv.* **unexplained** *a.* **unexploded** *a.* **unexplored** *a.* **unexposed** *a.* **unexpressed** *a.* **unexpurgated** *a.* **unfading** *a.* **unfailing** *a.* **1** not liable to fail or run short. **2** unerring, infallible. **3** reliable, certain. **unfailingly** *adv.* **unfailingness** *n.* **unfair** *a.* **1** not equitable; not impartial. **2** dishonourable, fraudulent. **unfairly** *adv.* **unfairness** *n.* **unfaithful** *a.* **1** not faithful to a promise, vow etc. **2** adulterous. **unfaithfully** *adv.* **unfaithfulness** *n.* **unfamiliar** *a.* **unfamiliarity** *n.* **unfamiliarly** *adv.* **unfashionable** *a.* **unfashionably** *adv.* **unfasten** *v.t.* **unfastened** *a.* **1** not fastened. **2** that has been loosened, untied or opened. **unfatherly** *a.* **unfathomable** *a.* **unfathomably** *adv.* **unfathomed** *a.* **1** of unknown depth. **2** not completely explored or known. **unfavourable**, (*N Am.*) **unfavorable** *a.* **unfavourably** *adv.* **unfazed** *a.* (*coll.*) not troubled or perturbed. **unfeasible** *a.* **unfeasibility** *n.* **unfeasibly** *adv.* **unfed** *a.* **unfeeling** *a.* **1** insensible. **2** hard-hearted, unsympathetic towards others. **unfeelingly** *adv.* **unfeigned** *a.* **unfeignedly** *adv.* **unfeminine** *a.* **unfemininity** *n.* **unfenced** *a.* **1** not enclosed by a fence. **2** not fortified. **unfermented** *a.* **unfertilized**, **unfertilised** *a.* **unfetter** *v.t.* to free from fetters or restraint. **unfettered** *a.* **unfilled** *a.* **unfinished** *a.* **1** not finished, incomplete. **2** not having been through a finishing process. **unfit** *a.* **1** not fit (to do, to be, for etc.). **2** unsuitable (for). **3** not in good physical condition. *~v.t.* (*pres.p.* **unfitting**, *past, p.p.* **unfitted**) to make unfit or unsuitable. **unfitness** *n.* **unfitted** *a.* **1** not fitted. **2** unfit. **3** not fitted up, not furnished with fittings. **unfitting** *a.* **unfittingly** *adv.* **unfix** *v.t.* **unfixed** *a.* **unflagging** *a.* **unflaggingly** *adv.* **unflappable** *a.* (*coll.*) not readily upset or agitated, imperturbable. **unflappability** *n.* **unflattering** *a.* **unflatteringly** *adv.* **unfledged** *a.* **1** (of a bird) not yet fledged. **2** inexperienced and immature. **unflinching** *a.* **unflinchingly** *adv.* **unfocused**, **unfocussed** *a.* **un-**

fold *v.t.* **1** to open the folds of; to spread out. **2** to discover; to reveal. *~v.i.* **1** to spread open; to expand. **2** to develop. **unfoldment** *n.* (*N Am.*) **unforced** *a.* **1** not forced, not constrained. **2** natural, easy. **unforeseeable** *a.* **unforeseen** *a.* **unforgettable** *a.* that cannot be forgotten; highly memorable. **unforgettably** *adv.* **unforgivable** *a.* **unforgivingly** *adv.* **unforgiven** *a.* **unforgiving** *a.* **unforgivingly** *adv.* **unforgivingness** *n.* **unforgotten** *a.* **unformed** *a.* **1** not formed. **2** shapeless, amorphous, structureless. **3** not yet fully developed, immature. **unformulated** *a.* **unforthcoming** *a.* **unfortified** *a.* **unfortunate** *a.* **1** not fortunate, unlucky. **2** unhappy. **3** regrettable. **4** unsuccessful; disastrous. *~n.* a person who is unfortunate. **unfortunately** *adv.* **1** unluckily. **2** I'm sorry to say. **3** in an unfortunate manner. **unfounded** *a.* **1** having no foundation in fact or reason, groundless. **2** not yet established. **unframed** *a.* (of a picture etc.) not set in a frame. **unfree** *a.* **unfreedom** *n.* **unfreeze** *v.t.* (*past* **unfroze,** *p.p.* **unfrozen**) **1** to cause to thaw. **2** to relax restrictions on (assets, credit etc.). *~v.i.* to thaw. **unfriendly** *a.* (*comp.* **unfriendlier,** *superl.* **unfriendliest**) not friendly. **unfriendliness** *n.* **unfrock** *v.t.* to deprive of the character and privileges of a priest. **unfruitful** *a.* **1** not productive or producing good results. **2** not producing fruit. **unfruitfully** *adv.* **unfruitfulness** *n.* **unfulfillable** *a.* **unfulfilled** *a.* **unfulfilling** *a.* **unfunded** *a.* (of a debt) not funded, floating. **unfunny** *a.* (*comp.* **unfunnier,** *superl.* **unfunniest**) not funny. **unfunnily** *adv.* **unfunniness** *n.* **unfurl** *v.t.* to open or spread out (a sail, banner etc.). *~v.i.* to be opened and spread out. **unfurnished** *a.* without furniture. **ungallant** *a.* **ungallantly** *adv.* **ungenerous** *a.* **ungenerously** *adv.* **ungenerousness** *n.* **ungentlemanly** *a.* not becoming a gentleman; rude, ill-bred. **ungentlemanliness** *n.* **unget-at-able** *a.* (*coll.*) difficult of access. **unglamorous** *a.* **unglazed** *a.* **ungodly** *a.* **1** not godly; wicked. **2** (*coll.*) outrageous (*at an ungodly hour of the night*). **ungodliness** *n.* **ungovernable** *a.* not governable; unruly; wild. **ungovernability** *n.* **ungovernably** *adv.* **ungraceful** *a.* **ungracefully** *adv.* **ungracefulness** *n.* **ungracious** *a.* **1** discourteous; unkind. **2** not attractive. **ungraciously** *adv.* **ungraciousness** *n.* **ungrammatical** *a.* not according to the rules of grammar. **ungrammaticality** *n.* **ungrammatically** *adv.* **ungrammaticalness** *n.* **ungrateful** *a.* **1** not thankful. **2** unpleasant; unrewarding. **ungratefully** *adv.* **ungratefulness** *n.* **ungreen** *a.* **1** not supporting environmental conservation. **2** not environmentally-friendly. **ungrounded** *a.* **1** unfounded, baseless. **2** not earthed. **3** not having a good grounding (in a subject). **4** (of an aeroplane, ship etc.) not grounded. **ungrudging** *a.* **ungrudgingly** *adv.* **unguarded** *a.* **1** not guarded. **2** careless, incautious. **unguardedly** *adv.* **unguardedness** *n.*

❌ **unecessary** common misspelling of UNNECESSARY (under UN- (+ M–N WORDS)).

ungainly (ŭngān'li) *a.* (*comp.* **ungainlier,** *superl.* **ungainliest**) clumsy, awkward. **ungainliness** *n.* **unguent** (ŭng'gwənt) *n.* any soft composition used as an ointment or for lubrication. **ungula** (ŭng'gūlə) *n.* (*pl.* **ungulae** (-lē)) a hoof, claw or talon. **ungulate** (-lət) *a.* hoofed. *~n.* an ungulate animal.

un- **(+ h–i words)** **unhallowed** *a.* **1** unconsecrated. **2** unholy, profane. **unhampered** *a.* **unhand** *v.t.* (*formal or facet.*) **1** to take one's hand or hands off. **2** to let go from one's grasp. **unhappy** *a.* (*comp.* **unhappier,** *superl.* **unhappiest**) **1** not happy, miserable, wretched. **2** unlucky, unfortunate. **3** inappropriate. **4** causing bad luck. **5** disastrous. **6** not propitious. **unhappily** *adv.* **unhappiness** *n.* **unharmed** *a.* **unharness** *v.t.* to remove a harness from. **unhatched** *a.* (of eggs) not hatched. **unhealthy** *a.* (*comp.* **unhealthier,** *superl.* **unhealthiest**) **1** not enjoying or promoting good health. **2** (*coll.*) dangerous. **unhealthily** *adv.* **unhealthiness** *n.* **unheard** *a.* not heard. **unheard-of** *a.* not heard of; unprecedented. **unheated** *a.* **unheeded** *a.* **unheeding** *a.* **unheedingly** *adv.* **unhelpful** *a.* **unhelpfully** *adv.* **unhelpfulness** *n.* **unheralded** *a.* **unheroic** *a.* **unheroically** *adv.* **unhesitating** *a.* **unhesitatingly** *adv.* **unhindered** *a.* **unhinge** *v.t.* **1** to take (a door) off the hinges. **2** to unsettle (the mind etc.). **unhinged** *a.* **unhitch** *v.t.* to unfasten or release from a hitched state. **unholy** *a.* (*comp.* **unholier,** *superl.* **unholiest**) **1** not holy, not hallowed. **2** impious, wicked. **3** (*coll.*) hideous, frightful. **unholily** *adv.* **unholiness** *n.* **unhook** *v.t.* **1** to remove from a hook. **2** to open or undo by disengaging the hooks of. **unhoped** *a.* not hoped (for). **unhorse** *v.t.* **1** to remove from horseback. **2** (of a horse) to throw (a rider). **3** to dislodge, e.g. from a powerful position. **unhouse** *v.t.* **1** to drive from a house. **2** to deprive of shelter. **unhuman** *a.* **1** not human. **2** superhuman. **3** inhuman, savage. **unhung** *a.* **1** not hung. **2** (of paintings etc.) not hung up. **unhurried** *a.* **unhurriedly** *adv.* **unhurt** *a.* **unhygienic** *a.* **unhygienically** *adv.* **unhyphenated** *a.* **unidentifiable** *a.* **unidentified** *a.* **unilluminated** *a.* **1** not illuminated; dark. **2** ignorant. **unillustrated** *a.* **unimaginable** *a.* that cannot be imagined; inconceivable. **unimaginably** *adv.* **unimaginative** *a.* **unimaginatively** *adv.* **unimaginativeness** *n.* **unimpaired** *a.* **unimpeachable** *a.* beyond reproach; blameless. **unimpeachably** *adv.* **unimpeded** *a.* **unimportant** *a.* **unimportance** *n.* **unimposing** *a.* **unimposingly** *adv.* **unimpressed** *a.* **unimpressionable** *a.* **unimpressive** *a.* **unimpressively** *adv.* **unimpressiveness** *n.* **unimproved** *a.* **1** not improved. **2** (of land) not tilled, cultivated, drained etc. **3** (of resources etc.) not made use of. **uninflected** *a.* **1** (*Gram.*) (of a language) not inflected. **2** not varying. **uninfluenced** *a.* **uninfluential** *a.* **uninformative** *a.* **uninformed** *a.* **1** not informed (about). **2** ignorant generally. **uninhabitable** *a.* **uninhabited** *a.* **uninhibited** *a.* **uninhibitedly** *adv.* **unin-**

hibitedness *n.* uninitiated *a.* uninjured *a.* uninspired *a.* uninspiring *a.* uninspiringly *adv.* uninsurable *a.* uninsured *a.* unintelligent *a.* unintelligently *adv.* unintelligible *a.* unintelligibility *n.* unintelligibleness *n.* unintelligibly *adv.* unintended *a.* unintentional *a.* unintentionally *adv.* uninterested *a.* **1** not taking any interest (in). **2** indifferent; unconcerned. **uninteresting** *a.* uninterestingly *adv.* uninterestingness *n.* uninterpretable *a.* uninterrupted *a.* uninterruptedly *adv.* uninvited *a.* uninviting *a.* not inviting, not attractive, repellent. **uninvitingly** *adv.* uninvolved *a.*

uni (ū´ni) *n.* (*pl.* **unis**) (*coll.*) a university.

uni- (ūni) *comb. form* one, single, as *unisex, unipolar.*

uni- (+ a–c words) uniaxial *a.* having a single axis. **unicameral** *a.* (of a legislative body) consisting of a single chamber. **unicellular** *a.* consisting of a single cell. **unicycle** (ū´ni-) *n.* a one-wheeled cycle, esp. used by circus performers. **unicyclist** *n.*

Uniate (ū´niāt), **Uniat** (-ət) *n.* a member of any of the Eastern Churches acknowledging the supremacy of the Pope but retaining their own liturgy, rites and ceremonies. *~a.* of or relating to the Uniates.

unicorn (ū´nikawn) *n.* **1** a fabulous animal like a horse, but with a long, straight, tapering horn. **2** (*Her.*) a one-horned horse with a goat's beard and lion's tail.

uni- (+ d–f words) unidirectional *a.* moving, operating etc. in only one direction. **unidirectionality** *n.* **unidirectionally** *adv.* **uniflow** (ū´ni-) *a.* involving only one direction of flow.

uniform (ū´nifawm) *a.* **1** having an unchanging form, appearance, quality, character etc.; the same, not varying, not changing. **2** conforming to one rule or standard applying or operating without variation with time or place. *~n.* clothing of the same kind and appearance as that worn by other members of the same body, esp. the regulation dress of soldiers, sailors etc. *~v.t.* to make uniform. **uniformed** *a.* dressed in uniform. **uniformity** (-faw´-) *n.* (*pl.* **uniformities**) the quality or state of being uniform; consistency, sameness. **uniformly** *adv.*

unify (ū´nifī) *v.t.* (*3rd pers. sing. pres.* **unifies**, *pres.p.* **unifying**, *past*, *p.p.* **unified**) **1** to make one. **2** to regard as one. **3** to reduce to uniformity. **unifiable** *a.* **unification** (-fikā´shən) *n.* **unificatory** *a.* **unifier** *n.*

uni- (+ l–o words) unilateral *a.* **1** applied by or affecting one side or party only. **2** of, occurring on or restricted to one side only. **3** (*Bot.*) arranged on or turned towards one side only. **unilateralism** *n.* **1** unilateral action; esp. unilateral disarmament. **2** (*esp. N Am.*) the pursuit of an independent foreign policy. **unilateralist** *n.* **unilaterally** *adv.* **uninucleate** *a.* (*Biol.*) having only one nucleus. **uniovular** (ūniov´ūlə) *a.* of, relating to or developed from one ovum.

union (ūn´yən) *n.* **1** the act of uniting; the state of being united. **2** a combination of parts or members forming a whole; an amalgamation; a confederation or league. **3** the political unit formed by such a combination, esp. the UK or US. **4** a trade union. **5** agreement or concord of mind, will, affection, or interests. **6** marriage. **7** (**Union**) a students' club at some universities; the building housing such a club. **8** (*Math.*) a set containing all the members of two or more sets. **9** in plumbing, a device for connecting pipes. **10** a fabric made of two different yarns, such as linen and cotton. **11** a device emblematic of union borne in the upper corner next to the staff of a flag. **12** (*Med.*) the growing together of parts separated by injury. **Union flag** *n.* the national flag of the United Kingdom composed of the crosses of St George, St Andrew and St Patrick. **unionist** *n.* **1** a member of a trade union. **2** a promoter or advocate of trade unionism. **3** (*usu.* **Unionist**) a member of a political party formed to uphold the legislative union between Great Britain and Northern Ireland (before 1920 Great Britain and Ireland). **unionism** *n.* **unionistic** (-nis´-) *a.* **unionize, unionise** *v.t.* to organize into a trade union. *~v.i.* to become organized into a trade union. **unionization** *n.* **Union Jack** *n.* **1** UNION FLAG (under UNION). **2** (**union jack**) in the US, a ship's flag consisting only of a union. **union suit** *n.* (*N Am.*) an undergarment combining vest and long pants; men's combinations.

uni- (+ p– words) uniparous (ūnip´ərəs) *a.* **1** (of a woman, of certain animals) producing a single offspring at a birth. **2** (*Bot.*) having one axis or stem. **uniped** (ū´niped) *a.* having only one foot. *~n.* a one-footed person or animal. **uniplanar** *a.* lying or occurring in one plane. **unipod** (ū´ni-) *n.* a one-legged support, e.g. for a camera. **unipolar** *a.* **1** (*Biol.*) (of nerve-cells etc.) having only one process. **2** exhibiting only one kind of polarity. **unipolarity** *n.*

unique (ūnēk´) *a.* **1** having no like or equal; unmatched, unparalleled. **2** very unusual or remarkable, extraordinary. **uniquely** *adv.* **uniqueness** *n.*

Usage note It is best to avoid uses of *unique* which imply or allow more than one (for example with qualifying adverbs, as *most unique*, or simply with the meaning extraordinary).

uni- (+ s– words) unisex (ū´ni-) *a.* that can be used, worn, etc. by both sexes. **unisexual** (-sek´-) *a.* **1** of one sex only. **2** (*Bot.*) having either stamens or pistils. **3** unisex. **unisexuality** *n.* **unisexually** *adv.*

unison (ū´nisən) *n.* **1** (*Mus.*) coincidence of sounds proceeding from equality in rate of vibrations; unity of pitch. **2** an interval of one or more octaves. **3** the act or state of sounding together at the same pitch (*to sing in unison*). **4** concord, agreement, harmony. *~a.* sounding

unit together; coinciding in pitch. **unisonal** (ŭnis´-), **unisonant, unisonous** *a.*

unit (ū´nit) *n.* **1** a single person, thing, or group, regarded as one and complete for the purposes of calculation. **2** each one of a number of things, persons etc., forming a plurality. **3** a quantity adopted as the standard of measurement or calculation. **4** a part of a machine which performs a particular function. **5** a piece of furniture which forms part of a set, designed for a particular use in a kitchen etc. **6** a group of workers that has a particular job in an organization. **7** a part of a larger military formation. **8** a quantity of a drug, vitamin etc., which produces a specific effect. **9** the smallest share in a unit trust. **10** a group of buildings in a hospital with a particular function (*the burns unit*). **11** the number one. **Unitarian** (-teə´ri-) *n.* a member of a Christian body that rejects the doctrine of the Trinity and believes that God is one person. ~*a.* of or relating to the Unitarians. **Unitarianism** *n.* **unitary** *a.* **1** of or relating to a unit or units. **2** of the nature of a unit, whole, integral. **unitarily** *adv.* **unit cell** *n.* in crystallography, the smallest group of atoms, ions or molecules which characterizes the lattice of a given crystal. **unit cost** *n.* the cost of producing one item. **unit-holder** *n.* a person who has a holding in a unit trust. **unit trust** *n.* an investment company which invests contributions from many individuals by purchasing holdings in a range of different enterprises and pays out dividends according to the amount invested.

unite (ūnīt´) *v.t.* **1** to join together so as to make one. **2** to combine, to amalgamate. **3** to join in marriage. **4** to cause to adhere. ~*v.i.* **1** to become one. **2** to become consolidated, to combine, to cooperate. **3** to join in marriage. **4** to adhere. **united** *a.* **United Kingdom** *n.* Great Britain and Northern Ireland. **unitedly** *adv.* **United Reformed Church** *n.* a Church formed in 1972 from the union of the Presbyterian and Congregational Churches in England and Wales. **United States, United States of America** *n.* (*sing. or pl.*) a federal republic consisting of 50 states, mostly in N America. **uniter** *n.*

unity (ū´niti) *n.* (*pl.* **unities**) **1** the state or condition of being one or individual, oneness as opposed to plurality or division. **2** the state of being united, union. **3** an agreement of parts or elements, harmonious interconnection, structural coherence. **4** concord, agreement, harmony. **5** a thing forming a coherent whole. **6** (*Math.*) the number one, a factor that leaves unchanged the quantity on which it operates.

Univ. *abbr.* University.

uni- (**+ v– words**) **univalent**[1] (ūnivā´lənt) *a.* **1** (*Chem.*) having a valence or combining to the power of one. **2** (*Biol.*) (of a chromosome) remaining unpaired during meiosis. **univalent**[2] (ūniv´ələnt) *n.* (*Biol.*) a chromosome which remains unpaired during meiosis.

univalve (ū´ni-) *a.* (*Zool.*) having only one valve. ~*n.* (*Zool.*) a univalve mollusc.

universal (ūnivœ´səl) *a.* **1** of or relating to the whole world or all persons or things in the world or in the class under consideration; common to all cases; all embracing, general. **2** (*Logic*) in which something is asserted of all the individuals in a class. ~*n.* **1** (*Logic*) a universal proposition. **2** (*Philos.*) a universal concept. **3** (*Philos.*) universal term. **universal agent** *n.* an agent who is authorized to do anything that can be delegated. **universal compass** *n.* a compass with legs that can be extended for drawing large circles. **universalism** *n.* **1** the quality of being universal. **2** (*Theol.*) the doctrine that all human beings will eventually be saved. **universalist** *a.*, *n.* **universalistic** (-lis´-) *a.* **universality** (-sal´-) *n.* **universalize, universalise** *v.t.* **universalizability** (-bil´-) *n.* **universalization** (-zā´shən) *n.* **universal joint, universal coupling** *n.* a device for connecting two rotating shafts allowing freedom of movement in any direction. **universal language** *n.* a specially created language intended for use by all nations. **universally** *adv.* **universalness** *n.* **universal suffrage** *n.* the right to vote extended to all adults.

universe (ū´nivœs) *n.* **1** all existing things; all created things viewed as constituting one system or whole, the cosmos. **2** all humankind. **3** in logic and statistics, all the objects that are the subjects of consideration.

university (ūnivœ´siti) *n.* (*pl.* **universities**) **1** an educational institution for both instruction and examination in the higher branches of knowledge with the power to confer degrees, often comprising subordinate colleges, schools etc. **2** the members of this collectively. **at university** studying at a university.

un- (**+ j–k words**) **unjust** *a.* not just, not conformable to justice. **unjustly** *adv.* **unjustness** *n.* **unjustifiable** *a.* **unjustifiableness** *n.* **unjustifiably** *adv.* **unjustified** *a.* **unkempt** *a.* **1** (of a promise etc.) not kept. **2** not tended. **unkind** *a.* **1** not kind. **2** harsh, hard, cruel. **3** not pleasant. **unkindly** *adv.* **unkindness** *n.* **unknot** *v.t.* (*pres.p.* **unknotting**, *past, p.p.* **unknotted**) to undo the knot or knots of. **unknowable** *a.* that is not knowable. ~*n.* something that is unknowable. **unknowability** *n.* **unknowing** *a.* **1** not knowing. **2** ignorant or unaware (of). **unknowingly** *adv.* **unknowingness** *n.* **unknown** *a.* not known. ~*n.* an unknown person, thing or quantity. **unknown to** without the knowledge of (*Unknown to me she'd already gone*). **unknown quantity** *n.* a person, thing or number whose importance or value is unknown. **Unknown Soldier, Unknown Warrior** *n.* an unidentified soldier whose body is buried in a memorial as a symbol of all soldiers killed in war.

unkempt (ŭnkempt´) *a.* **1** (of hair) uncombed. **2** scruffy and untidy. **unkemptly** *adv.* **unkemptness** *n.*

un- (+ l– words) unlabelled, (*N Am.*) **unlabeled** *a.* **unlace** *v.t.* **1** to undo the lace or laces of. **2** to loosen or unfasten by undoing the lace or laces of. **unladen** *a.* **unladen weight** *n.* the weight of a lorry etc. when not laden with goods etc. **unladylike** *a.* **unlamented** *a.* **unlatch** *v.t.* **1** to unfasten the latch of (a door etc.). **2** to open in this way. ~*v.i.* to be opened in this way. **unlawful** *a.* **unlawfully** *adv.* **unlawfulness** *n.* **unleaded** *a.* **1** (of petrol) without added lead compounds. **2** not weighted, covered etc. with lead. **3** (*Print.*) (of lines of typesetting) not spaced with leads. **unlearn** *v.t.* (*past, p.p.* **unlearnt, unlearned**) **1** to forget the knowledge of. **2** to get rid of something learned. **unlearned**[1], **unlearnt** *a.* not learnt. **unlearned**[2] (-nid) *a.* not learned, uneducated. **unleash** *v.t.* **1** to set free from a leash. **2** to set free from control or restraint. **unleavened** *a.* **unliberated** *a.* **unlicensed,** (*N Am.*) **unlicenced** *a.* **unlighted** *a.* unlit. **unlike** *a.* **1** not like. **2** dissimilar. ~*prep.* **1** not like (*Unlike Shubhu, I found the exhibition disappointing*). **2** not characteristic of. **unlikeness** *n.* **unlikeable, unlikable** *a.* **unlikely** *a.* (*comp.* **unlikelier,** *superl.* **unlikeliest**) **1** improbable. **2** unpromising. **3** not likely (to do something). **unlikelihood, unlikeliness** *n.* **unlimited** *a.* **1** not limited; having no bounds; indefinite; unnumbered. **2** unconfined, unrestrained. **unlimitedly** *adv.* **unlimitedness** *n.* **unline** *v.t.* to remove the lining from. **unlined**[1] *a.* (of a garment, curtain etc.) not lined. **unlined**[2] *a.* without lines. **unlisted** *a.* **1** not on a list. **2** (of securities) not listed on the Stock Exchange. **3** (*N Am.*) (of a telephone number) ex-directory. **unlit** *a.* **unlivable** *a.* not able to be lived or lived in. **unlived-in** *a.* **1** not lived in. **2** over-tidy. **unload** *v.t.* **1** to discharge the load from. **2** to discharge (a load). **3** to withdraw the charge from (a gun etc.). **4** (*coll.*) to get rid of. **5** (*coll.*) to disclose (information). **6** (*coll.*) to give vent to (one's troubles, feelings etc.). ~*v.i.* to discharge a load or freight. **unloader** *n.* **unlock** *v.t.* **1** to unfasten the lock of (a door, box etc.). **2** to disclose. **unlocked** *a.* **unlooked-for** *a.* not looked for, unexpected. **unloose, unloosen** *v.t.* **1** to unfasten, to loose. **2** to set at liberty. **unlovable, unloveable** *a.* **unloved** *a.* **unlovely** *a.* not lovely; not beautiful or attractive. **unloveliness** *n.* **unloving** *a.* **unlovingly** *adv.* **unlovingness** *n.* **unlucky** *a.* (*comp.* **unluckier,** *superl.* **unluckiest**) **1** not lucky or fortunate; unsuccessful. **2** disastrous. **3** inauspicious, ill-omened. **4** not well considered or judged. **unluckily** *adv.* **unluckiness** *n.*

unless (ŭnles´) *conj.* if it be not the case that; except when (*I'm not giving it to you unless you promise me something*; *We used to meet in the park unless it was raining*).

un- (+ m–n words) unmade *a.* **1** not made or not yet made. **2** undone; annulled. **unmake** *v.t.* (*past, p.p.* **unmade**) to destroy; to annihilate; to depose. **unman** *v.t.* (*pres.p.* **unmanning,** *past, p.p.* **unmanned**) **1** to deprive of maleness or manly qualities. **2** to deprive of courage or fortitude. **3** to deprive of men. **unmanned** *a.* **1** not manned, having no crew. **2** caused to lose one's self-control and become emotional etc. **unmanageable** *a.* not manageable; not easily controlled. **unmanly** *a.* **unmanliness** *n.* **unmannerly** *a.* not mannerly; rude, ill-bred. **unmannerliness** *n.* **unmapped** *a.* **1** not shown on a map. **2** unexplored. **unmarked** *a.* **1** not marked. **2** not noticed, unobserved. **unmarketable** *a.* **unmarried** *a.* **unmask** *v.t.* **1** to remove the mask from. **2** to expose. ~*v.i.* to take one's mask off. **unmasker** *n.* **unmatched** *a.* **unmeaning** *a.* **1** having no meaning; senseless. **2** expressionless, vacant. **unmeaningly** *adv.* **unmeant** *a.* not meant, not intended. **unmediated** *a.* perceived directly with no intervention. **unmemorable** *a.* **unmemorably** *adv.* **unmentionable** *a.* not mentionable, not fit to be mentioned. ~*n.* **1** (*pl., facet.*) underwear. **2** a person or thing that is not to be mentioned. **unmentionability, unmentionableness** *n.* **unmentionably** *adv.* **unmerciful** *a.* **unmercifully** *adv.* **unmercifulness** *n.* **unmerited** *a.* **unmet** *a.* (of a goal, target etc.) not achieved. **unmethodical** *a.* **unmethodically** *adv.* **unmindful** *a.* not mindful, heedless (of). **unmindfully** *adv.* **unmindfulness** *n.* **unmissable** *a.* that cannot be missed; that is too good to miss. **unmistakable, unmistakeable** *a.* that cannot be mistaken; manifest, plain. **unmistakability, unmistakableness** *n.* **unmistakably** *adv.* **unmistaken** *a.* **unmitigated** *a.* **1** not mitigated. **2** unqualified (*an unmitigated disaster*). **unmitigatedly** *adv.* **unmixed** *a.* **unmixed blessing** *n.* something that has advantages and no disadvantages. **unmodified** *a.* **unmolested** *a.* **unmoral** *a.* non-moral; outside morality. **unmorality** *n.* **unmotherly** *a.* **unmotivated** *a.* lacking in motive or incentive. **unmounted** *a.* **1** not on horseback. **2** (of a drawing, gem etc.) not mounted. **unmourned** *a.* **unmoved** *a.* **1** not moved. **2** not changed in purpose, unshaken, firm. **3** not affected emotionally. **unmoving** *a.* **1** motionless. **2** unaffecting. **unmown** *a.* **unmusical** *a.* **1** not pleasing to the ear, discordant. **2** not interested or skilled in music. **unmusicality** *n.* **unmusically** *adv.* **unmuzzle** *v.t.* **1** to remove a muzzle from (a dog etc.). **2** to allow to speak, report etc. again (*to unmuzzle the press*). **unnameable** *a.* **unnamed** *a.* **unnatural** *a.* **1** not natural; contrary to nature. **2** not in accordance with accepted standards of behaviour. **3** monstrous, inhuman. **4** artificial. **5** forced, strained, affected. **unnaturally** *adv.* **unnaturalness** *n.* **unnecessary** *a.* **1** not necessary. **2** needless, superfluous. ~*n.* (*pl.* **unnecessaries**) (*usu. in pl.*) something which is unnecessary. **unnecessarily** *adv.* **unnecessariness** *n.* **unneeded** *a.* **unneighbourly,** (*N Am.*) **unneighborly** *a.* **unneighbourliness** *n.* **unnerve** *v.t.* to deprive of nerve, strength or resolution. **unnerved** *a.* **unnerving** *a.* **unnervingly** *adv.* **unnoticeable** *a.* **unnoticeably** *adv.* **unnoticed** *a.* **unnumbered** *a.* **1**

not marked with a number or numbers. **2** countless. **3** not counted.

un- (+ o–p words) unobjectionable *a.* **unobjectionableness** *n.* **unobjectionably** *adv.* **unobservable** *a.* **unobservant** *a.* **unobservantly** *adv.* **unobserved** *a.* **unobstructed** *a.* **unobtainable** *a.* **unobtrusive** *a.* **unobtrusively** *adv.* **unobtrusiveness** *n.* **unoccupied** *a.* **unoffending** *a.* not offending; harmless, innocent. **unoffended** *a.* **unofficial** *a.* **1** not having official character or authorization. **2** not typical of officials. **unofficially** *adv.* **unofficial strike** *n.* a strike that does not have the formal backing of the strikers' trade union. **unopened** *a.* **unopposed** *a.* **unorganized, unorganised** *a.* **1** not organized or arranged. **2** not unionized. **unoriginal** *a.* not original, derived, lacking originality. **unoriginality** *n.* **unoriginally** *adv.* **unorthodox** *a.* **unorthodoxly** *adv.* **unorthodoxy** *n.* **unostentatious** *a.* **unostentatiously** *adv.* **unostentatiousness** *n.* **unpack** *v.t.* **1** to open and take out the contents of. **2** to take (things) out of a package etc. **unpacker** *n.* **unpaged** *a.* not having the pages numbered. **unpaid** *a.* **1** (of a debt) not paid, not discharged. **2** not having received the payment due. **3** working without pay. **unpainted** *a.* **unpaired** *a.* **1** not paired, not matched. **2** not forming one of a pair. **unpalatable** *a.* **unpalatability, unpalatableness** *n.* **unparalleled** *a.* not paralleled; unequalled, unprecedented. **unpardonable** *a.* **unpardonableness** *n.* **unpardonably** *adv.* **unparliamentary** *a.* contrary to the rules or usages of Parliament. **unparliamentarily** *adv.* **unparliamentariness** *n.* **unparliamentary language** *n.* abusive language. **unpasteurized, unpasteurised** *a.* **unpatriotic** *a.* **unpatriotically** *adv.* **unpaved** *a.* **unpeeled** *a.* **unperceived** *a.* **unperceptive** *a.* **unperforated** *a.* **unperformed** *a.* **unperfumed** *a.* **unperson** (ŭn´-) *n.* a person whose existence is officially ignored or denied. **unpersuaded** *a.* **unpersuasive** *a.* **unpersuasively** *adv.* **unperturbed** *a.* **unperturbedly** *adv.* **unpick** *v.t.* **1** to undo (the stitches) of. **2** to take out the sewing of (a garment). **unpicked** *a.* **1** not picked. **2** not picked out or selected. **unpin** *v.t.* (*pres.p.* **unpinning,** *past, p.p.* **unpinned**) **1** to remove the pins from. **2** to unfasten (something held together by pins). **3** in chess, to free (a piece that has been pinned). **unpitied** *a.* **unpitying** *a.* **unpityingly** *adv.* **unplaceable** *a.* **unplaced** *a.* **1** not placed. **2** not among the first three at the finish of a race. **unplanned** *a.* **unplayable** *a.* **1** that cannot be played. **2** (of a ball) that is impossible to return, strike etc. **unpleasant** *a.* not pleasant; disagreeable. **unpleasantly** *adv.* **unpleasantness** *n.* **unpleasantry** *n.* (*pl.* **unpleasantries**) **1** lack of pleasantness. **2** (*pl.*) unpleasant comments, events etc. **unpleasing** *a.* **unpleasingly** *adv.* **unplug** *v.t.* (*pres.p.* **unplugging,** *past, p.p.* **unplugged**) **1** to remove a plug or obstruction from. **2** to disconnect (an electrical appliance) from a source of electricity. **unplumbed** *a.* **1** not plumbed. **2** not fully explored

or known. **unpointed** *a.* **1** not having a point. **2** not punctuated. **3** not having the vowel-points or diacritical marks. **4** (of masonry) not pointed. **unpolished** *a.* **unpolitical** *a.* not related to or interested in politics. **unpolitically** *adv.* **unpolluted** *a.* **unpopular** *a.* **unpopularity** *n.* **unpopularly** *adv.* **unpopulated** *a.* **unposed** *a.* **unpowered** *a.* (of a vehicle) powered by other means than fuel. **unpractical** *a.* **1** (of a person, proposal etc.) not practical. **2** not possessing practical skill. **unpracticality** *n.* **unpractically** *adv.* **unpractised,** (*N Am.*) **unpracticed** *a.* **1** not put in practice. **2** unskilful, inexperienced. **unprecedented** *a.* **1** being without precedent, unparalleled. **2** new. **unprecedentedly** *adv.* **unpredictable** *a.* that cannot be predicted. **unpredictability** *n.* **unpredictably** *adv.* **unpredicted** *a.* **unprejudiced** *a.* **unpremeditated** *a.* not premeditated, not planned beforehand; unintentional. **unpremeditatedly** *adv.* **unprepared** *a.* **1** not prepared, impromptu. **2** not ready (for etc.). **unpreparedly** *adv.* **unpreparedness** *n.* **unprepossessing** *a.* **unpresentable** *a.* not presentable; not fit to be seen. **unpressed** *a.* **unpressurized, unpressurised** *a.* **unpresuming** *a.* **unpretending** *a.* unpretentious. **unpretentious** *a.* **unpretentiously** *adv.* **unpretentiousness** *n.* **unpriced** *a.* not having a price or prices fixed, quoted or marked up. **unprincipled** *a.* not dictated by moral principles; immoral. **unprintable** *a.* that cannot be printed (because obscene or libellous). **unprintably** *adv.* **unprinted** *a.* **unprivileged** *a.* **unproblematic** *a.* **unproblematically** *adv.* **unprocessed** *a.* **unproductive** *a.* **unproductively** *adv.* **unproductiveness** *n.* **unprofessional** *a.* **1** not of or relating to a profession. **2** contrary to the rules or etiquette of a profession. **unprofessionally** *adv.* **unprofitable** *a.* **unprofitableness** *n.* **unprofitably** *adv.* **unprogressive** *a.* not progressive, conservative. **unprogressiveness** *n.* **unpromising** *a.* not likely to be successful. **unpromisingly** *adv.* **unprompted** *a.* of one's own free will or initiative. **unpronounceable** *a.* **unpronounceably** *adv.* **unpropitious** *a.* **unpropitiously** *adv.* **unprotected** *a.* not protected. **unprotectedness** *n.* **unprotesting** *a.* **unprotestingly** *adv.* **unprovable** *a.* **unprovability** *n.* **unproved, unproven** *a.* **unprovided** *a.* not provided or furnished (with supplies etc.). **unprovoked** *a.* **unpublished** *a.* (of books etc.) not published. **unpublishable** *a.* **unpunctual** *a.* **unpunctuality** *n.* **unpunctuated** *a.* **unpunished** *a.* **unpurified** *a.* **unputdownable** *a.* (*coll.*) (of a book) too exciting to put down before it is finished.

un- (+ q–r words) unqualified *a.* **1** not qualified; not fit, not competent. **2** not having passed the necessary examination etc. **3** not limited by conditions or exceptions, absolute (*unqualified support*). **unquantifiable** *a.* **unquantified** *a.* **unquestionable** *a.* not to be questioned or doubted, indisputable. **unquestionability, unquestionableness** *n.* **unquestionably**

adv. **unquestioned** *a.* **1** not called in question, not doubted. **2** having no questions asked, not interrogated. **unquestioning** *a.* **1** not questioning, not doubting. **2** implicit. **unquestioningly** *adv.* **unquiet** *a.* **1** restless, uneasy, agitated. **2** anxious. **unquietly** *adv.* **unquietness** *n.* **unquote** *v.i.* to close a quotation. *~int.* used to indicate the end of a (spoken) quotation. **unquotable** *a.* **unravel** *v.t.* (*pres.p.* **unravelling,** (*esp. N Am.*) **unraveling,** *past, p.p.* **unravelled,** (*esp. N Am.*) **unraveled) 1** to separate the threads of; to disentangle, to untwist. **2** to solve, to clear up (a mystery, the plot of a play etc.). **3** to undo (a knitted fabric etc.). *~v.i.* to become disentangled. **unreachable** *a.* **unreachably** *adv.* **unread** (-red´) *a.* **1** not read. **2** not well-read, unlearned. **unreadable** *a.* **1** illegible. **2** dull or difficult to read. **unreadability, unreadableness** *n.* **unreadably** *adv.* **unready** *a.* **1** not ready. **2** not prompt to act etc. **unreadily** *adv.* **unreadiness** *n.* **unreal** *a.* **1** not real. **2** unsubstantial, visionary, imaginary. **3** (*N Am., Austral., sl.*) amazing. **unrealism** *n.* **unrealistic** *a.* **unrealistically** *adv.* **unreality** *n.* **unrealizable, unrealisable** *a.* **unrealized** *a.* **unreally** *adv.* **unreason** *n.* **1** lack of reason. **2** folly, absurdity. **unreasonable** *a.* **1** not reasonable; exorbitant, extravagant. **2** not listening to reason. **unreasonableness** *n.* **unreasonably** *adv.* **unreasoned** *a.* not reasoned or thought out rationally. **unreasoning** *a.* not reasoning; irrational. **unreasoningly** *adv.* **unreceptive** *a.* **unreciprocated** *a.* **unrecognized, unrecognised** *a.* **1** not recognized. **2** not acknowledged. **unrecognizable** *a.* **unrecognizably** *adv.* **unreconciled** *a.* **unreconstructed** *a.* **1** clinging to old-fashioned social or political notions. **2** not rebuilt. **unrecordable** *a.* **unrecorded** *a.* **unredeemed** *a.* **1** not redeemed, not fulfilled. **2** not taken out of pawn. **3** not counterbalanced by any redeeming quality, unmitigated. **unredeemable** *a.* **unreel** *v.t.* to unwind. *~v.i.* to become unwound. **unrefined** *a.* **1** not refined; not purified. **2** of unpolished manners, taste etc. **unreflecting** *a.* not reflecting or thinking. **unreflectingly** *adv.* **unreflectingness** *n.* **unreflective** *a.* **unreformed** *a.* **unregarded** *a.* **unregenerate** *a.* not regenerate; unrepentant. **unregeneracy** *n.* **unregenerately** *adv.* **unregistered** *a.* **unregulated** *a.* **unrehearsed** *a.* **unrelated** *a.* **unrelatedness** *n.* **unrelaxed** *a.* **unrelenting** *a.* **unrelentingly** *adv.* **unrelentingness** *n.* **unreliable** *a.* **unreliability, unreliableness** *n.* **unreliably** *adv.* **unrelieved** *a.* **unrelievedly** *adv.* **unremarkable** *a.* **unremarkably** *adv.* **unremembered** *a.* **unremitting** *a.* not relaxing; incessant, continued. **unremittingly** *adv.* **unremittingness** *n.* **unremunerative** *a.* not profitable. **unremuneratively** *adv.* **unrenewable** *a.* **unrenewed** *a.* **unrepeatable** *a.* **1** that cannot be done or said again. **2** (of language) too rude to repeat. **unrepeatability** *n.* **unrepentant** *a.* **unrepentantly** *adv.* **unreported** *a.* **unrepresentative** *a.* **unrepresentativeness** *n.* **unrepresented** *a.* **unrequited** *a.* (of love etc.) not requited. **unrequitedly** *adv.*

unrequitedness *n.* **unreserved** *a.* **1** not reserved. **2** open, frank. **3** given, offered or done without reservation. **unreservedly** *adv.* **unreservedness** *n.* **unresisting** *a.* **unresistingly** *adv.* **unresolved** *a.* **1** not resolved, undecided, irresolute. **2** unsolved, not cleared up. **unresolvedly** *adv.* **unresolvedness** *n.* **unresponsive** *a.* **unresponsively** *adv.* **unresponsiveness** *n.* **unrest** *n.* restlessness, agitation, uneasiness. **unrestful** *a.* **unrestfully** *adv.* **unresting** *a.* **unrestingly** *adv.* **unrestored** *a.* **unrestrained** *a.* **unrestrainedly** *adv.* **unrestrainedness** *n.* **unrestricted** *a.* **unrestrictedly** *adv.* **unreturned** *a.* **unrevealed** *a.* **unrevealing** *a.* **unrevised** *a.* **unrevoked** *a.* **unrewarded** *a.* **unrewarding** *a.* **unridden** *a.* **unrideable, unridable** *a.* that cannot be ridden. **unrighteous** *a.* **1** not righteous, not just. **2** evil, wicked, sinful. **unrighteously** *adv.* **unrighteousness** *n.* **unripe** *a.* not ripe; not mature. **unrivalled,** (*N Am.*) **unrivaled** *a.* having no rival; unequalled, peerless. **unroadworthy** *a.* **unroll** *v.t.* **1** to unfold (a roll of cloth etc.). **2** to display, to lay open. *~v.i.* **1** to be unrolled. **2** to be displayed after being unrolled. **unromantic** *a.* **unromantically** *adv.* **unroof** *v.t.* to strip the roof off. **unruffled** *a.* not ruffled, unperturbed. **unruled** *a.* **1** not governed. **2** (of paper etc.) not ruled with lines. **unruly** *a.* (*comp.* **unrulier,** *superl.* **unruliest**) not submitting to restraint; ungovernable; disorderly. **unruliness** *n.*

un- (**+ s–t words**) **unsaddle** *v.t.* **1** to remove the saddle from. **2** to unseat. **unsafe** *a.* **1** dangerous, perilous, risky. **2** (*Law*) (of a verdict, conclusion etc.) not based on sufficient evidence. **unsafely** *adv.* **unsafeness** *n.* **unsaid** *a.* not said, unspoken. **unsalaried** *a.* **unsalted** *a.* **unsanctified** *a.* **unsanctioned** *a.* **unsanitary** *a.* unhealthy. **unsatisfactory** *a.* **1** not satisfactory; unacceptable. **2** (*Law*) (of a verdict, conviction etc.) not based on sufficient evidence. **unsatisfactorily** *adv.* **unsatisfactoriness** *n.* **unsatisfied** *a.* **unsatisfiedness** *n.* **unsatisfying** *a.* **unsatisfyingly** *adv.* **unsaturated** *a.* **1** not saturated. **2** (of fats) having a high proportion of fatty acids containing double bonds. **3** (*Chem.*) (of a compound) having double or triple bonds and thus capable of undergoing further reactions. **unsavoury,** (*N Am.*) **unsavory** *a.* **1** unattractive, repellent, disgusting. **2** morally offensive. **unsavourily** *adv.* **unsavouriness** *n.* **unsay** *v.t.* (*past, p.p.* **unsaid**) to retract or withdraw (what has been said). **unsayable** *a.* **unscalable** *a.* that cannot be climbed. **unscarred** *a.* **unscathed** *a.* not scathed, uninjured. **unscented** *a.* **unscheduled** *a.* **unscholarly** *a.* **unscholarliness** *n.* **unschooled** *a.* **1** not having received an education. **2** not sent to school. **3** having received no training. **4** (of talent etc.) natural. **unscientific** *a.* **1** not in accordance with scientific principles or methods. **2** lacking scientific knowledge. **unscientifically** *adv.* **unscramble** *v.t.* **1** to restore to order from a scrambled state. **2** to make (a scrambled message) intelligible. **unscrambler** n. **unscrew** v.t. **1** to withdraw or loosen (a screw). **2** to unfasten in this way. ~v.i. to become unscrewed. **unscripted** a. **1** not using a script. **2** unplanned, unrehearsed. **unscrupulous** a. having no scruples of conscience; unprincipled. **unscrupulously** adv. **unscrupulousness** n. **unseal** v.t. to break or remove the seal of; to open. **unsealed** a. **unseasonable** a. **unseasonableness** n. **unseasonably** adv. **unseasonal** a. **unseasoned** a. **1** not flavoured with seasoning. **2** (of wood) not seasoned. **3** not experienced. **unseat** v.t. **1** to remove from a seat. **2** to throw from one's seat on horseback. **3** to deprive of a parliamentary seat or political office. **unseaworthy** a. **unsecured** a. **unseeded** a. in a sporting tournament, not put with the best players in the competition draw. **unseeing** a. **1** blind. **2** unobservant, unsuspecting. **unseeingly** adv. **unseemly** a. (comp. **unseemlier**, superl. **unseemliest**), adv. **unseemliness** n. **unseen** a. **1** not seen. **2** invisible. **3** (of a text to be translated) not seen previously. ~n. an unseen translation. **unsegregated** a. **unselective** a. **unselfconscious** a. **unselfconsciously** adv. **unselfconsciousness** n. **unselfish** a. concerned for the interests of others rather than one's own. **unselfishly** adv. **unselfishness** n. **unsentimental** a. **unsentimentally** adv. **unserviceable** a. **unserviceability, unserviceableness** n. **unsettle** v.t. **1** to change from a settled state or position; to make uncertain. **2** to derange, to disturb. ~v.i. to become unsettled. **unsettled** a. **1** not settled, fixed or determined. **2** undecided, hesitating; changeable. **3** unpaid. **4** not settled, uncolonized. **unsettledness** n. **unsex** v.t. to deprive (someone, esp. a woman) of the typical qualities of their sex. **unshackle** v.t. **unshakeable, unshakable** a. **unshakeability** n. **unshakeably** adv. **unshaken** a. not shaken; firm, steady. **unshakenly** adv. **unshaven** a. **unsheathe** v.t. to draw (a knife etc.) from its sheath. **unshelled** a. **unsheltered** a. **unshockable** a. **unshockability** n. **unshockably** adv. **unshod** a. **unshorn** a. not shorn, clipped or shaven. **unshrinkable** a. (of fabric) that will not shrink. **unshrinkability** n. **unshrinking** a. not recoiling, undaunted, unhesitating. **unshrinkingly** adv. **unsighted** a. **1** not sighted, not seen. **2** having one's view blocked. **unsightly** a. unpleasing to the sight, ugly. **unsightliness** n. **unsigned** a. **unsinkable** a. **unsinkability** n. **unsized**[1] a. **1** not arranged by size. **2** not made according to a size. **unsized**[2] a. not sized, not stiffened. **unskilled** a. **1** lacking skill or special knowledge or training. **2** produced without or not requiring special skill or training. **unskilful, (N Am.) unskillful** a. **unskilfully** adv. **unskilfulness** n. **unsleeping** a. **unsleepingly** adv. **unsliced** a. **unsmiling** a. **unsmilingly** adv. **unsmoked** a. **1** (of bacon etc.) not smoked. **2** (of a cigarette etc.) not consumed by smoking. **unsociable** a. not sociable, solitary. **unsociability, unsociableness** n. **unsociably** adv. **un-**

social a. **1** not social, solitary. **2** (of hours of work) falling outside the usual working day. **3** antisocial. **unsocialist** a. **unsoiled** a. **unsold** a. **unsolicited** a. **unsolvable** a. **unsolved** a. **unsophisticated** a. **1** simple, artless; not worldlywise. **2** not corrupted or adulterated, pure, genuine. **unsorted** a. **unsought** a. **1** not sought for. **2** without being asked. **unsound** a. **1** diseased. **2** weak, decayed. **3** unreliable. **4** ill-founded, not valid, fallacious. **5** unorthodox. **6** wicked. **of unsound mind** mentally unbalanced. **unsoundness** n. **unsparing** a. **1** liberal, profuse, lavish. **2** unmerciful. **unsparingly** adv. **unsparingness** n. **unspeakable** a. **1** inexpressible. **2** inexpressibly bad or evil. **unspeakableness** n. **unspeakably** adv. **unspeaking** a. silent. **unspecialized, unspecialised** a. **unspecific** a. **unspecified** a. **unspectacular** a. **unspectacularly** adv. **unspilt** a. **unspoiled** a. not spoiled. **unspoilt** a. **1** unspoiled. **2** not plundered. **unspoken** a. **1** understood without being spoken. **2** not uttered. **unsponsored** a. **unspool** v.t. **1** to unwind from a spool. **2** to show (a film) on a screen. ~v.i. **1** to be unwound from a spool. **2** (of a film) to be screened. **unsporting** a. **unsportingly** adv. **unsportsmanlike** a. unsporting; not generous. **unspotted** a. **1** free from spots. **2** unblemished; morally pure. **3** not spotted or noticed. **unsprayed** a. (esp. of crops) not sprayed. **unstable** a. (comp. **unstabler**, superl. **unstablest**) **1** not stable, not firm. **2** liable to sudden shifts of moods. **3** changeable. **4** (of a chemical compound, atom etc.) decaying or decomposing rapidly or easily. **unstained** a. not stained; unblemished, unsullied. **unstamped** a. **1** not having a stamp affixed. **2** not marked by a stamp. **unstarched** a. **unstated** a. **unsteady** a. (comp. **unsteadier**, superl. **unsteadiest**) **1** not steady, not firm. **2** changeable, variable. **3** irregular, not uniform. **4** irregular in habits or conduct. **unsteadily** adv. **unsteadiness** n. **unsterile** a. **unstick** v.t. (past, p.p. **unstuck**) **1** to separate (two things stuck together). **2** (coll.) to cause (an aircraft) to take off. ~v.i. (coll.) (of an aircraft) to take off. **to come unstuck** (coll.) (of a plan etc.) to go wrong or fail. **unstinted** a. **unstintedly** adv. **unstinting** a. generous and ungrudging. **unstintingly** adv. **unstitch** v.t. to open by unpicking the stitches of. **unstop** v.t. (pres.p. **unstopping**, past, p.p. **unstopped**) **1** to free from obstruction. **2** to remove the stopper from, to open. **unstoppable** a. **unstoppability** n. **unstoppably** adv. **unstopper** v.t. to remove the stopper from. **unstrained** a. **1** not strained, not filtered. **2** not subjected to strain. **3** not forced; easy, natural. **4** not injured by excessive use. **unstreamed** a. (of schoolchildren) not streamed. **unstressed** a. **1** not subjected to stress. **2** unaccented. **unstring** v.t. (past, p.p. **unstrung**) **1** to take away the string or strings of. **2** to loosen the string or strings of. **3** to remove (pearls etc.) from a string. **unstructured** a. **1** not having a formal or rigid structure. **2** relaxed, unceremonious. **unstrung** *a.* unnerved. **unstudied** *a.* not studied; easy, natural. **unstuffy** *a.* unstylish *a.* **1** without style. **2** not fashionable. **unsubstantial** *a.* **1** not substantial. **2** having little solidity or validity. **3** unreal. **unsubstantiated** *a.* **unsubtle** *a.* **unsubtly** *adv.* **unsuccessful** *a.* unsuccessfully *adv.* **unsuitable** *a.* **unsuitability, unsuitableness** *n.* **unsuitably** *adv.* **unsuited** *a.* **1** not suited, not fit. **2** not adapted (to). **unsullied** *a.* **unsung** *a.* **1** not acclaimed or recognized. **2** not sung. **unsupervised** *a.* **unsupportable** *a.* **1** that cannot be endured. **2** unjustifiable. **unsupportably** *adv.* **unsupported** *a.* **unsupportive** *a.* **unsure** *a.* **unsurely** *adv.* **unsureness** *n.* **unsurpassable** *a.* **unsurpassably** *adv.* **unsurprised** *a.* **unsurprising** *a.* **unsurprisingly** *adv.* **unsusceptible** *a.* **unsuspected** *a.* **unsuspecting** *a.* **unsuspectingly** *adv.* **unsustainable** *a.* **unsustainably** *adv.* **unsustained** *a.* **unswayed** *a.* not swayed, biased or influenced. **unsweetened** *a.* **unswept** *a.* **unswerving** *a.* **1** constant, steadfast. **2** not veering to one side. **unswervingly** *adv.* **unsymmetrical** *a.* **1** out of symmetry. **2** lacking in symmetry. **unsymmetrically** *adv.* **unsympathetic** *a.* **unsympathetically** *adv.* **unsystematic** *a.* **unsystematically** *adv.* **untainted** *a.* **untalented** *a.* **untameable, untamable** *a.* **untameableness** *n.* **untamed** *a.* **untangle** *v.t.* to disentangle. **untanned** *a.* **untapped** *a.* **untarnished** *a.* **untaught** *a.* **1** not instructed, ignorant. **2** natural, spontaneous. **untaxed** *a.* not having to pay or not subject to taxes. **unteachable** *a.* **untechnical** *a.* **untenable** *a.* **untenability, untenableness** *n.* **untenably** *adv.* **untended** *a.* **untender** *a.* not tender, unkind. **untendered** *a.* not offered. **untenured** *a.* **untested** *a.* **untether** *v.t.* **untethered** *a.* **unthankful** *a.* **untheorized, untheorised** *a.* not evolved from a fundamental theory. **unthink** *v.t.* (*past, p.p.* **unthought**) **1** to retract in thought. **2** to cease to think about. **unthinkable** *a.* **1** incapable of being thought or conceived. **2** (*coll.*) highly improbable. **unthinkability, unthinkableness** *n.* **unthinkably** *adv.* **unthinking** *a.* **1** heedless, careless. **2** unintentional. **unthinkingly** *adv.* **unthinkingness** *n.* **unthread** *v.t.* **1** to take a thread out of (a needle etc.). **2** to find one's way out of (a maze). **unthreatening** *a.* **unthrone** *v.t.* **untidy** *a.* (*comp.* **untidier,** *superl.* **untidiest**). **untidily** *adv.* **untidiness** *n.* **untie** *v.t.* (*3rd pers. sing. pres.* **unties,** *pres.p.* **untying,** *past, p.p.* **untied**) **1** to undo (a knot), to unfasten. **2** to loose from bonds. ~*v.i.* to become untied. **untied** *a.* **untilled** *a.* **untimely** *a.* **1** unseasonable, inopportune. **2** premature. **untimeliness** *n.* **untiring** *a.* never tiring; indefatigable. **untiringly** *adv.* **untold** *a.* **1** not told, revealed or communicated. **2** not counted, innumerable; not able to be measured. **untouchable** *a.* that cannot be touched. ~*n.* a Hindu belonging to one of the lowest castes or to no caste and whom members of the higher castes were formerly forbidden to touch. **untouchability, untouchableness** *n.* **untouched** *a.* un-

untoward *a.* **1** unlucky, unfortunate. **2** awkward. **3** improper or unseemly. **untowardly** *adv.* **untowardness** *n.* **untraceable** *a.* **untraceably** *adv.* **untraced** *a.* **untracked** *a.* **1** unmarked by tracks. **2** that has no previously trodden path. **3** not traced. **untraditional** *a.* **untrained** *a.* **untrainable** *a.* **untrammelled,** (*N Am.*) **untrammeled** *a.* **untranslatable** *a.* **untranslatability, untranslatableness** *n.* **untranslated** *a.* **untravelled,** (*N Am.*) **untraveled** *a.* **1** not having travelled. **2** not travelled over. **untreatable** *a.* **untreated** *a.* **untried** *a.* **1** not tried; untested. **2** not tried by a judge. **untrodden** *a.* **untroubled** *a.* not disturbed by care, sorrow etc.; calm, unruffled. **untrue** *a.* **1** not in accordance with facts, false. **2** not faithful, disloyal (to). **3** not conforming to a rule or standard. **untruly** *adv.* **untruss** *v.t.* **untrusting** *a.* **untrustworthy** *a.* **untrustworthiness** *n.* **untruth** *n.* **1** the state of being untrue. **2** a falsehood, a lie. **untruthful** *a.* **untruthfully** *adv.* **untruthfulness** *n.* **untuck** *v.t.* to cause (blankets etc.) to no longer be tucked in. **untuned** *a.* **1** (of a musical instrument) that has not been tuned. **2** (of a radio etc.) not tuned to a particular frequency. **3** not in harmony. **unturned** *a.* **untutored** *a.* uninstructed. **untwine** *v.t., v.i.* **untwist** *v.t., v.i.* **untypical** *a.* **untypically** *adv.*

until (ŭntĭl´) *prep.* **1** up to the time of. **2** as late as. ~*conj.* up to the time when.

Usage note The forms *until* and *till* are largely interchangeable, but *until* tends to be used especially at the beginning of sentences and in formal contexts.

†**unto** (ŭn´tu) *prep.* to.

un- (**+ u–w words**) **unused**[1] (ŭnūzd´) *a.* not having been or not being used. **unused**[2] (ŭnūst´) *a.* not accustomed (to). **unusual** *a.* **1** not usual. **2** remarkable. **unusually** *adv.* **unusualness** *n.* **unutterable** *a.* inexpressible, indescribable. **unutterably** *adv.* **unvaccinated** *a.* **unvalued** *a.* **1** not esteemed. **2** not appraised, not estimated. **unvanquished** *a.* **unvaried** *a.* **unvarnished** *a.* **1** not covered with varnish. **2** not embellished, plain, simple. **unvarying** *a.* **unvaryingly** *adv.* **unveil** *v.t.* **1** to remove a veil or covering from, esp. to remove a covering from (a statue etc.) with public ceremony. **2** to reveal, to disclose. ~*v.i.* to take one's veil off. **unveiling** *n.* **unventilated** *a.* **unverifiable** *a.* **unverified** *a.* **unversed** *a.* not versed or skilled (in). **unviable** *a.* **unvoiced** *a.* **1** not spoken, not uttered. **2** in phonetics, not voiced. **unwaged** *a.* not paid a wage; unemployed or not doing paid work. **unwanted** *a.* **unwarlike** *a.* **unwarrantable** *a.* not defensible or justifiable, inexcusable. **unwarrantably** *adv.* **unwarranted** *a.* **1** not authorized. **2** not justified. **unwary** *a.* **1** not cautious. **2** not aware of danger. **unwashed** *a.* not washed. **unwatchable** *a.* **unwatered** *a.* **unwavering** *a.* steady, steadfast, firm. **unwaveringly** *adv.* **unweaned** *a.* **unwearable** *a.* **unwearied** *a.* **1**

not wearied. **2** tireless. **3** incessant. **unweariedly** *adv.* **unweary** *a.* **unwearying** *a.* **1** incessant; persistent. **2** not causing weariness. **unwed, unwedded** *a.* **unweeded** *a.* **unwelcome** *a.* **unwelcomed** *a.* **unwelcomely** *adv.* **unwelcomeness** *n.* **unwelcoming** *a.* **unwell** *a.* **1** not well; sick. **2** indisposed. **unwholesome** *a.* **1** having a harmful physical or moral effect. **2** (esp. of food) unhealthy. **3** of unhealthy appearance. **unwholesomely** *adv.* **unwholesomeness** *n.* **unwieldy** *a.* (*comp.* **unwieldier,** *superl.* **unwieldiest**) **1** that cannot be easily handled owing to size or weight. **2** bulky, ponderous, clumsy. **unwieldiness** *n.* **unwilling** *a.* not willing; averse; reluctant. **unwillingly** *adv.* **unwillingness** *n.* **unwind** *v.t.* (*past, p.p.* **unwound**) **1** to free (something that has been wound). **2** to free from entanglement. **3** (*coll.*) to relax (a person). ~*v.i.* **1** to become unwound. **2** (*coll.*) to relax. **unwinking** *a.* **1** not winking. **2** watchful, vigilant. **unwinnable** *a.* **unwisdom** *n.* lack of wisdom; folly. **unwise** *a.* **1** not wise, without judgement. **2** foolish. **unwisely** *adv.* **unwished** *a.* not desired; not sought (for). **unwomanly** *a.* **unwonted** *a.* not accustomed; unusual. **unwontedly** *adv.* **unwontedness** *n.* **unworkable** *a.* **unworkability, unworkableness** *n.* **unworkably** *adv.* **unworked** *a.* **1** not shaped. **2** not exploited. **unworldly** *a.* **1** not worldly, spiritually minded. **2** of or relating to spiritual things. **unworldliness** *n.* **unworn** *a.* never worn, new; not impaired by use. **unworried** *a.* **unworthy** *a.* (*comp.* **unworthier,** *superl.* **unworthiest**) **1** not worthy, not deserving (of). **2** not becoming, not seemly, discreditable. **3** contemptible. **unworthily** *adv.* **unworthiness** *n.* **unwound** (-wownd) *a.* not wound. **unwounded** (-woon´-) *a.* **unwoven** *a.* **unwrap** *v.t.* (*pres.p.* **unwrapping,** *past, p.p.* **unwrapped**) **1** to take the wrapping off (something). **2** to unfold or unroll. ~*v.i.* to become unwrapped. **unwritten** *a.* **1** not written. **2** traditional. **unwritten law** *n.* a law not formulated in statutes etc., esp. one based on custom and judicial decisions.

unwitting (ŭnwit´ing) *a.* **1** unconscious. **2** unintentional, inadvertent. **unwittingly** *adv.* **unwittingness** *n.*

un- (+ y–z words) unyielding *a.* **1** unbending, stiff. **2** firm, obstinate. **unyieldingly** *adv.* **unyieldingness** *n.* **unzip** *v.t.* (*pres.p.* **unzipping,** *past, p.p.* **unzipped**) to undo the zip of.

up (ŭp) *adv.* **1** to or at a higher place or position. **2** to a capital city, university, a place farther north, or other place regarded as higher (*up to Edinburgh*). **3** at or to the time or place referred to (*I went up to them; Everything had been going well up till then*). **4** off the ground. **5** to or in an erect position or standing posture. **6** to or in a position or condition for action. **7** out of bed. **8** (*coll.*) to the front or in front (*I went up ahead*). **9** to or in a prepared or required state (*We put the tent up*). **10** to or at a higher price (*Petrol is up again*). **11** in a stronger position or better off

(*They're two goals up; £20 up on the deal*). **12** (of a computer) switched on and ready for use. **13** more loudly (*You'll have to speak up*). **14** (of the sun) above the horizon. **15** indicating completion or the end of something (*Five minutes are up*). **16** completely, entirely, effectually (*drink up; tear up*). **17** appearing in court as a defendant. **18** indicating a tightly closed or compact state (*to sew up; tied up; to roll up*). **19** indicating accumulation (*mount up*). **20** knowledgeable (*She's well up in English literature*). **21** (of a road) undergoing repairs. **22** towards the source of a stream or river. **23** inland. **24** in baseball, to one's turn at batting. **25** (of points in a game) gained so far or shown on a scoreboard. **26** upstairs. **27** (of a theatre curtain) raised. ~*prep.* **1** from a lower to a higher place or point of. **2** in an ascending direction on or along, towards the higher part of. **3** towards the source of (a river). **4** towards the interior of. **5** at or in a higher part of. ~*a.* **1** moving, sloping or directed towards a higher or more central part. **2** towards the capital (*the up train*). ~*n.* a period of good fortune. ~*v.t.* (*pres.p.* **upping,** *past, p.p.* **upped**) to raise or increase, esp. suddenly. ~*v.i.* **1** to do something suddenly and unexpectedly (*She upped and left him*). **2** to pick up (*He upped his bags*). **all up with** doomed or hopeless. **on the up and up 1** (*coll.*) becoming steadily more successful. **2** (*esp. N Am., coll.*) straight, honest. **something is up** (*coll.*) something unusual or strange is happening. **to up sticks** (*coll.*) to move house, to go and live elsewhere, to make off. **up against 1** confronting, having to deal with. **2** close to. **3** touching. **up against it** (*coll.*) facing stiff opposition or great difficulties. **up and about** having got out of bed. **up and doing** active and busy. **up and down 1** alternately backwards and forwards. **2** alternately upwards and downwards. **3** in every direction. **4** (*coll.*) varying in moods or states of health. **up and running** functioning. **up for** put forward for or being considered for (office). **up front 1** at the front. **2** (of payments) in advance. **up to 1** until (*up to now*). **2** as far as (*up to my shoulder*). **3** as many or as much as (*up to five goes*). **4** incumbent upon (*It's not up to me to decide*). **5** capable of; equal to (a task etc.). **6** occupied with (*What are you up to?*). **up with** used to express support for something (*Up with the republic!*). **up yours** (*sl., offensive*) used to express contempt, defiance etc. **what's up?** (*coll.*) what is going on? **2** (*coll.*) what is the matter? **up-and-coming** *a.* (*coll.*) (of a person) enterprising and promising. **up-and-comer** *n.* **up-and-over** *a.* (of a door) opened by pulling it upwards to a horizontal position. **up-and-under** *n.* in rugby, a high kick to give fellow team players time to get to the spot where the ball will come down. **up to date, up-to-date** *a.* recent, modern, abreast of the times. **up-to-the-minute** *a.* most recent or modern.

up- (ŭp) *pref.* up; upwards; upper.

up- (+ b– words) upbeat (ŭp´-) *n.* (*Mus.*) an unaccented beat, on which the conductor raises his baton. ~*a.* (*coll.*) cheerful, optimistic. **upbringing** (ŭp´-) *n.* bringing up, education.

upbraid (ŭpbrād´) *v.t.* to reproach (with, for); to reprove with severity. **upbraider** *n.* **upbraiding** *n.* **upbraidingly** *adv.*

up- (+ c–h words) upcoming *a.* (*esp. N Am.*) forthcoming. **up-country** (ŭp´-, -kŭn´-) *adv., a.* towards the interior of a country, inland. **update**[1] (-dāt´) *v.t.* to bring up to date. **update**[2] (ŭp´-) *n.* **1** a bringing up to date. **2** something which has been updated. **updraught** (ŭp´-), (*N Am.*) **updraft** *n.* an upward current of air. **upend** *v.t.* **1** to turn over on its end. **2** to transform or affect greatly. ~*v.i.* to rise on end. **upfield** *adv.* in football etc., in or towards the opposing team's end of a field. **upfront** *a.* (*coll.*) **1** honest, straightforward. **2** (of money) paid out in advance. **3** at the front or forefront. ~*adv.* up front. **upgrade**[1] (-grād´) *v.t.* **1** to raise (a worker or a job) to a higher grade or status. **2** (*Comput. etc.*) to improve (a computer, piece of machinery etc.), e.g. by buying new components. **upgrade**[2] (up´-) *n.* **1** an act or instance of upgrading. **2** a piece of machinery etc. that has been upgraded. **on the upgrade** improving, advancing or progressing. **upgradeable, upgradable** *a.* **upheaval** *n.* **1** a violent disturbance, revolution etc. **2** (*Geol.*) an elevation of part of the earth's crust. **3** the act or process of heaving up. **uphill**[1] (ŭp´-) *a.* **1** leading or going up a hill. **2** difficult, arduous, severe. ~*n.* an upward incline. **uphill**[2] (-hil´) *adv.* in an ascending direction, upwards. **uphold** *v.t.* (*past, p.p.* **upheld**) **1** to support, to sustain, to maintain. **2** to approve, to countenance. **upholder** *n.*

upholster (ŭphōl´stə) *v.t.* **1** to provide (chairs etc.) with stuffing, cushions, coverings etc. **2** to furnish with curtains, carpets, furniture etc. **upholsterer** *n.* a person who upholsters furniture professionally. **upholstery** *n.* **1** the stuffing, cushions,coverings etc. of a piece of furniture. **2** the work of an upholsterer.

up- (+ k–m words) upkeep (ŭp´-) *n.* (cost of) maintenance. **upland** (ŭp´-) *n.* (*also* **uplands**) high ground or the higher part of a district. ~*a.* of or relating to or situated on the uplands. **uplift**[1] (-lift´) *v.t.* **1** to lift up, to raise. **2** to raise morally or spiritually. **uplift**[2] (ŭp´-) *n.* **1** a lifting up. **2** (*coll.*) spiritual or moral improvement. **3** (*Geol.*) the raising of land to a higher level. **4** a brassiere designed to support and lift the bust. ~*a.* uplifted or providing uplift. **uplifter** *n.* **uplifting** *a.* **uplighter** (ŭp´-) *n.* a light designed to cast light upwards. **upmarket** *a.* of or relating to the more expensive sector of the market. ~*adv.* towards this sector of the market.

upon (ŭpon´) *adv.* on.

upper[1] (ŭp´ə) *a.* **1** higher in place (*the upper jaw*). **2** superior in rank or status (*the upper classes*). **3** (**Upper**) situated on higher land. **4** (**Upper**) situated to the north or further upstream (*Upper Nile*). **5** (*Geol.*) (*sometimes* **Upper**) designating the late part of a period, formation etc. ~*n.* the part of a boot or shoe above the sole. **on one's uppers** (*coll.*) destitute. **upper case** *n.* (*Print.*) capital letters. **upper class** *n.* the economically and socially most powerful class in a society. ~*a.* (*also* **upper-class**) of or relating to this class. **upper crust** *n.* (*coll.*) the upper class. **uppercut** *n.* in boxing, a punch delivered in an upwards direction with a bent arm. ~*v.t.* (*pres.p.* **uppercutting**, *past, p.p.* **uppercut**) to punch (someone) in this way. **upper deck** *n.* (*Naut.*)the full-length deck of a shipabove thewater level. **upper hand** *n.* the superior position, mastery. **Upper House** *n.* the higher house in a bicameral legislature, esp. the House of Lords. **uppermost** *a.* **1** highest in place, rank, authority etc. **2** predominant. ~*adv.* at or to the highest place or position.

upper[2] (ŭp´ə) *n.* (*sl.*) a stimulant drug.

uppish (ŭp´ish) *a.* (*coll.*) self-assertive, pretentious or snobbish. **uppishly** *adv.* **uppishness** *n.*

uppity (ŭp´iti) *a.* (*coll.*) **1** uppish. **2** not amenable to persuasion or control.

up- (+ r– words) uprate *v.t.* **1** to raise to a higher rank, rate or value. **2** to upgrade. **uprising** (ŭp´-) *n.* an insurrection, a rising, a riot. **upriver** *adv.* towards the source of a river. ~*a.* near the source of a river. **uproot** *v.t.* **1** to tear up by or as by the roots. **2** to displace (a person) from their usual surroundings. **3** to eradicate. ~*v.i.* to move away from one's familiar or usual surroundings. **uprooter** *n.* **uprush** (ŭp´-) *n.* an upward rush.

upright (ŭp´rīt) *a.* **1** erect, perpendicular. **2** righteous, honest. **3** (of a book etc.) being taller than it is wide. ~*adv.* erect, vertically. ~*n.* **1** an upright timber, pillar, post etc. **2** an upright piano. **uprightly** *adv.* **uprightness** *n.* **upright piano** *n.* a piano with a vertical case for the strings.

uproar (ŭp´raw) *n.* a noisy tumult; a violent disturbance; bustle and clamour. **uproarious** (-raw´-) *a.* **1** noisy and disorderly. **2** extremely funny. **uproariously** *adv.* **uproariousness** *n.*

up- (+ s– words) upshift (ŭp´-) *v.i.* to move to a higher gear. ~*v.t.* (*esp. N Am.*) to increase. ~*n.* a movement to a higher gear. **upshot** (ŭp´-) *n.* the final issue, result or conclusion (of a matter). **upside** (ŭp´-) *n.* **1** the positive aspect of a situation that is generally bad. **2** an upward movement, e.g. of share prices. **3** the upper part. **upstage** *adv.* at the rear of a stage. ~*a.* **1** situated upstage. **2** stand-offish. ~*v.t.* **1** to force (an actor) to face away from the audience by taking a position upstage of them. **2** to draw attention away from (a person) to oneself. **upstairs** (ŭp´-) *a.* (*also* **upstair**) of or relating to or in an upper storey. ~*n.* an upper storey or storeys. ~*adv.* on or to an upper storey. **upstanding** *a.* **1** erect. **2** honest, upright. **3** of strong and upright build. **upstart** (ŭp´-) *n.* **1** a person who rises suddenly from humble origins to wealth, power or consequence. **2** a person who assumes an arrogant bearing. ~*a.* **1** who is an upstart. **2** characteristic of an upstart. **upstate** (ŭp´-) *n.* (*N Am.*) part of a state of the US which is away from, and usu. to the north of, the principal city or cities. ~*adv.* to or in this part. ~*a.* in or relating to this part. **upstater** *n.* **upstream** *a., adv.* **1** against the current. **2** (situated) higher up a river. **upstroke** (ŭp´-) *n.* an upward line in writing. **upsurge** (ŭp´-) *n.* a sudden, rapid rise. **upswept** *a.* **1** swept or brushed upwards. **2** curved upwards. **upswing** (ŭp´-) *n.* **1** an upward rise. **2** an increase or improvement, esp. in economic terms.

ups-a-daisy UPSYDAISY.

upset[1] (ŭpset´) *v.t.* (*pres.p.* **upsetting**, *past, p.p.* **upset**) **1** to overturn. **2** to put out of one's normal state, to disconcert, to distress. **3** to make slightly ill (*Something upset my stomach*). **4** to disrupt. ~*v.i.* to be overturned. **upsetter** *n.* **upsettingly** *adv.*

upset[2] (ŭp´set) *n.* **1** the act of upsetting. **2** the state of being upset. **3** an unexpected reversal in a game etc. ~*a.* physically disturbed (*an upset stomach*).

upside down (ŭpsīd down´) *a., adv.* **1** with the upper part under. **2** in complete disorder and confusion.

upsilon (ŭp´silon) *n.* the 20th letter in the Greek alphabet (υ, Y).

upsydaisy (ŭp´sidāzi), **ups-a-daisy, oops-a-daisy** *int.* used as a reassuring expression to accompany the lifting up of someone, esp. a child, who has stumbled or fallen.

up- (**+ t– words**) **uptake** (ŭp´-) *n.* **1** the act of taking or lifting up. **2** the process of taking, absorbing or accepting what is on offer. **quick on the uptake** quick to understand or learn. **uptempo** *a., adv.* at a fast tempo. **upthrow** (ŭp´-) *n.* **1** a throwing up, an upheaval. **2** (*Geol.*) the upward displacement on one side of a fault. **upthrust** (ŭp´-) *n.* (*esp. Geol.*) an upward thrust, esp. a geological upheaval. **uptick** (ŭp´-) *n.* (*esp. N Am.*) a small increase. **uptime** (ŭp´-) *n.* the time during which a machine, esp. a computer, is actually working. **uptown** (ŭp´-) *n.* (*esp. N Am.*) the upper, or residential, part of town. ~*a.* of or in this part. ~*adv.* into or towards this part. **up-turn**[1] (ŭp´-) *n.* **1** an upward trend or turn towards improved conditions, higher prices etc. **2** an upheaval. **upturn**[2] (-tœn´) *v.t.* **1** to turn up or over. **2** to direct upwards.

uptight (ŭptīt´) *a.* (*coll.*) **1** tense, nervy. **2** nervous, irritated. **3** conventional, strait-laced.

UPVC *abbr.* unplasticized polyvinyl chloride.

up- (**+ w– words**) **upwarp** (ŭp´-) *n.* (*Geol.*) an anticline. **upwind** (-wind´) *adv., a.* **1** against the wind. **2** (to or) on the windward side of.

upward (ŭp´wəd) *a.* directed, turned or moving towards a higher place. ~*adv.* upwards. **up-wardly** *adv.* upwards. **upwardly mobile** *a.* aspiring to improve one's lifestyle, social status etc. **upward mobility** *n.* movement to a position

of higher social or professional status. **upwards** *adv.* **1** towards a higher place or level; in an upward direction. **2** towards the source or spring. **3** more. **upwards of** more than.

ur- (uə) *comb. form* original, primitive, as *Urtext*.

Ural-Altaic (ūrəlaltā´ik) *a.* **1** of or relating to the Ural and Altaic mountain ranges or the people inhabiting them. **2** denoting a family of Mongolian, Finnic and allied languages of agglutinative structure spoken in N Europe and Asia. ~*n.* this family of languages.

uranium (ūrā´niəm) *n.* (*Chem.*) a radioactive, fissionable, silvery-white metallic element, at. no. 92, chem. symbol U, found in pitchblende, and used as a source of nuclear energy. **uranic** (-ran´-), **uranous** (ū´-) *a.*

urano- (ū´rənō) *comb. form* **1** sky, the heavens. **2** uranium.

urban (œ´bən) *a.* of or relating to, situated or living in a city or town. **urban guerrilla** *n.* a guerrilla operating in a town or city. **urbanism** *n.* **1** the character of urban life. **2** the study of urban life. **urbanist** *n.* **urbanite** (-nīt) *n.* a town-dweller. **urbanize, urbanise** *v.t.* **1** to make townlike. **2** to ruin the rural character of. **urbanization** (-zā´shən) *n.*

urbane (œbān´) *a.* courteous, polite; suave; refined. **urbanely** *adv.*

urbanity (œban´iti) *n.* **1** the quality of being urbane. **2** urban life.

urchin (œ´chin) *n.* **1** a roguish, mischievous child, esp. one dressed in rags. **2** SEA URCHIN (under SEA).

Urdu (uə´doo) *n.* a language closely related to Hindi but with many Persian and Arabic words, an official language of Pakistan, also widely used in India esp. by Muslims.

-ure (ūə, yə, ə) *suf.* **1** forming nouns indicating process or action, as *censure, portraiture, seizure*. **2** indicating result, as *caricature*. **3** forming collective nouns, as *architecture*. **4** indicating office or function, as *judicature*.

urea (ūrē´ə) *n.* (*Chem.*) a soluble crystalline compound contained in urine, esp. of mammals. **ureal** *a.*

ureter (ūrē´tə) *n.* the duct conveying the urine from the kidneys into the bladder. **ureteral** *a.* **ureteric** (-ter´-) *a.* **ureteritis** (-ī´tis) *n.*

urethane (ū´rəthān) *n.* (*Chem.*) **1** a crystalline amide, $NH_2COOC_2H_5$, used esp. in plastics and as an anaesthetic. **2** polyurethane.

urethra (ūrē´thrə) *n.* (*pl.* **urethrae** (-rē), **urethras**) the duct by which the urine is discharged from the bladder. **urethral** *a.* **urethritis** (ūrithrī´tis) *n.*

urge (œj) *v.t.* **1** to drive or impel; to force on-wards. **2** to press earnestly with argument, entreaty etc., to importune. **3** to press the acceptance or adoption of. **4** to cite forcefully as a reason or justification. ~*n.* **1** a strong impulse. **2** an inner drive or compulsion. **urgency** (-jənsi) *n.* the quality or state of being urgent. **urgent** *a.* **1** pressing, demanding early attention. **2**

demanding or soliciting with importunity. **urgently** adv. **urger** n.

-uria (ū´riə) comb. form indicating a diseased condition of the urine, as dysuria.

uric (ū´rik) a. of or relating to urine. **uric acid** n. a white, tasteless and inodorous, almost insoluble compound found chiefly in excrement of birds and reptiles, and in small quantities in the urine of mammals.

urinal (ūrī´nəl, ū´rin-) n. **1** a receptacle fixed to a wall for men to urinate into. **2** a public or private room, building, enclosure etc. containing these.

urine (ū´rin) n. a pale-yellow fluid with an acid reaction, secreted from the blood by the kidneys, stored in the bladder, and discharged through the urethra, the chief means for the removal of nitrogenous and saline matters resulting from the decay of tissue. **urinalysis** (ūrinal´isis) n. (pl. **urinalyses** (-ēz)) the analysis of urine, esp. in order to diagnose disease. **urinary** a. of or relating to urine or the urinary system. **urinate** v.i. to pass urine. **urination** (-ā´shən) n. **urinous** a.

urn (œn) n. **1** a vase with a foot and a usu. rounded body used for preserving the ashes of the dead, for holding water, as a measure, and other purposes. **2** a vase-shaped vessel with a tap, and usually a spirit lamp or other heater, for making tea, coffee etc. or keeping it hot. **urnful** n. (pl. **urnfuls**).

uro- (ū´rō) comb. form urine.

urogenital (ūrōjen´itəl) a. of or relating to the genital and urinary organs.

urology (ūrol´əji) n. the branch of medicine concerned with the study of the urinary system. **urologic** (-əloj´-), **urological** a. **urologist** n.

Ursa (œ´sə) n. Ursa Major. **Ursa Major** n. the constellation, the Great Bear or Plough, visible in the northern sky and containing seven bright-stars. **Ursa Minor** n. the small constellation, the Little Bear, containing the north celestial pole and the pole star.

ursine (œ´sīn) a. of or relating to or resembling a bear.

urticaceous (œtikā´shəs) a. (Bot.) of or having the character of nettles. **urticaria** (-keə´riə) n. (Med.) nettle-rash. **urticate** v.t. to sting with or as with nettles. **urtication** (-ā´shən) n.

US abbr. **1** United States. **2** unserviceable.

us (ŭs) pron. **1** objective (acc. and dat.) of WE. **2** (coll.) me. **3** (formal) objective of WE as used by newspaper editors and monarchs.

USA abbr. United States of America.

usage (ū´sij, ū´zij) n. **1** the manner of using or treating, treatment. **2** customary or habitual practice, esp. as authorizing a right etc. **3** (an instance of) the way a language is actually used.

use¹ (ūs) n. **1** the act of using. **2** the state of being used (The lift is in constant use). **3** employment in or application to a purpose (I'm sure you'll find some use for it). **4** occasion, need, or power to use (He regained the use of his left arm). **5** the quality of being useful or serving a purpose (It's no use complaining now). **6** custom, practice, usage. **to have no use for 1** to dislike, to disapprove of. **2** to find no use for. **to make use of 1** to use, to employ. **2** to take advantage of. **useful** a. **1** of use, serving a purpose. **2** good, beneficial, profitable, advantageous. **3** (coll.) competent or highly satisfactory. **to make oneself useful** to be of service to someone. **usefully** adv. **usefulness** n. **useless** a. **1** not of use, serving no useful end or purpose. **2** (coll.) ineffectual, weak (useless at tennis). **uselessly** adv. **uselessness** n.

use² (ūz) v.t. **1** to employ, to apply to a purpose, to put into operation. **2** to turn to account, to avail oneself of (Use your common sense). **3** to treat in a specified way (They used him badly). **4** to exploit for one's own purposes. **5** to use up, to wear out. **6** (usu. p.p.) to accustom, to habituate (I'm not used to getting up early in the morning). ~v.i. (usu. in past) to be accustomed, to make it one's constant practice to (We used to play football here). **could use** (coll.) would appreciate having. **to use up 1** to finish; to consume completely. **2** to find some use or purpose for (something left over). **3** to exhaust or wear out. **usable, useable** a. capable of being used. **usability** (-bil´-) n. **used** a. **1** already made use of. **2** second-hand. **3** exploited. **used-up** a. exhausted, finished. **user** n. **1** a person who uses something. **2** (coll.) a person who takes drugs. **user-friendly** a. (esp. Comput.) (esp. of computers) easy to operate or understand. **user-friendliness** n.

usher (ŭsh´ə) n. **1** a seat-attendant at a cinema, theatre etc. **2** an officer or servant acting as doorkeeper (esp. in a court or public hall). **3** a person whose job it is to introduce strangers or to walk before a person of rank. ~v.t. **1** to act as usher to. **2** to introduce, as a forerunner or harbinger; to bring or show (in etc.). **usherette** (-ret´) n. a woman usher at a cinema or theatre.

usquebaugh (ŭs´kwibah, -baw) n. **1** (Sc., Ir.) whisky. **2** an Irish liqueur made of brandy, spices etc.

USSR abbr. (Hist.) Union of Soviet Socialist Republics.

usual (ū´zhūəl) a. such as ordinarily occurs; customary, habitual. ~n. a person's usual drink, meal etc. **as per usual** as usually happens. **usually** adv. **usualness** n.

usurer (ū´zhərə) n. a person who lends money at (esp. exorbitant) interest. **usurious** (ūzhuə´riəs) *a.* **1** practising usury, exacting exorbitant interest. **2** of or relating to or of the nature of usury. **usuriously** *adv.* **usury** (-ri) *n.* **1** (*esp. Law*) the practice of lending money at interest, esp. higher than that allowed by law. **2** exorbitant interest.

usurp (ūzœp´) *v.t.* to seize or take possession of without right. *~v.i.* to encroach (upon). **usurpation** (-pā´shən) *n.* **usurpatory** *a.* **usurper** *n.*

Utd *abbr.* United.

utensil (ūten´sil) *n.* an implement, esp. one used in cookery or domestic work.

uterus (ū´tərəs) *n.* (*pl.* **uteri** (-rī)) the womb. **uterine** (-rīn) *a.* **1** of or relating to the womb. **2** born of the same mother but not the same father. **uteritis** (-ī´tis) *n.*

utilitarian (ūtilitee´riən) *a.* **1** concerned with or made for practical use rather than beauty. **2** of or relating to utility or to utilitarianism. *~n.* an advocate of utilitarianism. **utilitarianism** *n.* **1** the ethical doctrine that actions are right in proportion to their usefulness or as they tend to promote happiness. **2** the doctrine that the end and criterion of public action is the greatest happiness of the greatest number.

utility (ūtil´iti) *n.* (*pl.* **utilities**) **1** usefulness, serviceableness. **2** something which is useful. **3** utilitarianism, the greatest happiness of the greatest number. **4** a public service, such as the supply of water or electricity. *~a.* **1** designed or adapted for general use. **2** practical, utilitarian. **utility program** *n.* (*Comput.*) a program for carrying out a routine task. **utility room** *n.* a room (in a private house) used for storage, laundry etc. **utility vehicle, utility truck** *n.* a small truck or van, esp. a pick-up.

utilize (ū´tilīz), **utilise** *v.t.* to make use of, to turn to account. **utilizable** *a.* **utilization** (-zā´shən) *n.* **utilizer** *n.*

utmost (ŭt´mōst) *a.* being or situated at the farthest point or extremity; extreme; greatest. *~n.* the utmost extent or degree. **to do one's utmost** to do everything that one can.

Utopia (ūtō´piə), **utopia** *n.* a place or state of ideal perfection. **Utopian, utopian** *a.* of or relating to or resembling Utopia; ideal or highly desirable but impracticable. *~n.* an ardent and visionary political or social reformer. **Utopianism** *n.*

utter[1] (ŭt´ə) *a.* total, absolute. **utterly** *adv.* **uttermost** *a.* utmost. **utterness** *n.*

utter[2] (ŭt´ə) *v.t.* **1** to emit audibly (*She uttered a surprised cry*). **2** to give expression to. **3** (*Law*) to put (esp. forged notes or coins) into circulation. **utterable** *a.* **utterance** *n.* **1** the act of uttering; vocal expression. **2** a spoken word, statement etc. **3** the power of speaking. **4** a way of speaking. **utterer** *n.*

UV *abbr.* ultraviolet.

UVA *abbr.* ultraviolet radiation with a range of 320–380 nanometres.

UVB *abbr.* ultraviolet radiation with a range of 280–320 nanometres.

UVC *abbr.* ultraviolet radiation of very short wavelengths.

uvula (ū´vūlə) *n.* (*pl.* **uvulae** (-lē)) (*Anat.*) the fleshy tissue hanging from the posterior margin of the soft palate at the back of the throat. **uvular** *a.* **1** of or relating to the uvula. **2** (of a sound, letter) articulated with the uvula and the back of the tongue. *~n.* a uvular consonant.

uxorious (ŭksaw´riəs) *a.* excessively fond of one's wife. **uxoriousness** *n.*

V¹ (vē), **v** (*pl.* **Vs, V's**) the 22nd letter of the English and other versions of the Roman alphabet. It is usually pronounced as a voiced labiodental fricative. *~symbol* 5 in Roman numerals. *~n.* a V-shaped object or mark. **V-neck** *n.* **1** the neck of any garment when it is shaped like the letter V. **2** a garment, esp. a pullover, with such a neck. **V-necked** *a.* **V-sign** *n.* **1** a sign made with the index and middle fingers in the form of a letter V and the back of the hand facing outwards, to indicate scorn, contempt, defiance etc. **2** a sign made similarly but with the palm of the hand outwards, to signify victory.

V² *abbr.* **1** volume. **2** volt. **3** voltage.

V³ *chem. symbol* vanadium.

v, v. *abbr.* **1** velocity. **2** verse. **3** verso. **4** versus. **5** very. **6** L *vide*, see.

vac (vak) *n.* (*coll.*) a vacation, esp. a university holiday.

vacant (vā´kənt) *a.* **1** unfilled, empty, unoccupied. **2** having no occupant, tenant, holder or incumbent. **3** showing no awareness or mental activity. **4** unintelligent, empty-headed, silly, inane. **5** (of time) not being used. **vacancy** *n.* (*pl.* **vacancies**) **1** the state of being vacant, emptiness. **2** an unfilled or vacant post or office. **3** an unoccupied room in a hotel, boarding house etc. **4** empty space, a gap, a chasm. **5** a lack of thought or interest. **vacantly** *adv.* **vacant possession** *n.* availability of a house or other property for immediate occupation.

vacate (vəkāt´) *v.t.* **1** to make vacant, to give up occupation or possession of (a room, property). **2** to give up one's tenure of (a post, position). **3** (*Law*) to annul, to make void.

vacation (vəkā´shən) *n.* **1** a period of cessation of legal or other business, or of studies at university etc. **2** (*N Am.*) a holiday. **3** the act of vacating. *~v.i.* (*N Am.*) to take a holiday. **vacationer, vacationist** *n.* (*N Am.*) a holidaymaker.

vaccinate (vak´sināt) *v.t.* **1** to inoculate with the modified virus of any disease so as to produce a mild form of the disease and prevent a serious attack. **2** (*Hist.*) to immunize against smallpox with cowpox virus. **vaccinal** (-sin´-), **vaccinic** *a.* **vaccination** (-ā´shən) *n.* **vaccinationist** *n.* **vaccinator** *n.* **vaccine** (-sēn) *a.* of or relating to vaccination. *~n.* **1** any agent used for inoculation and immunization. **2** (*Hist.*) the virus of cowpox prepared for use in vaccination. **vaccinia** (-sin´iə) *n.* (*Med.*) cowpox, esp. as produced by inoculation.

vacillate (vas´ilāt) *v.i.* **1** to oscillate from one opinion or resolution to another, to be irresolute. **2** to sway to and fro, to waver. **vacillatingly** *adv.* **vacillation** (-ā´shən) *n.* **vacillator** *n.*

❌ **vacinate** common misspelling of VACCINATE.

vacuole (vak´ūōl) *n.* (*Biol.*) a minute cavity in a cell, containing air, fluid etc. **vacuolar** (-ūələ) *a.* **vacuolation** (-ələā´shən) *n.*

vacuous (vak´ūəs) *a.* **1** showing no signs of feeling or intelligence. **2** unintelligent, inane, fatuous. **3** empty, unfilled, void. **vacuity** (vəkū´-) *n.* (*pl.* **vacuities**). **vacuousness** *n.*

vacuum (vak´ūəm, -ūm) *n.* (*pl.* **vacuums, vacua** (-ūə)) **1** a space completely devoid of matter. **2** a space or vessel from which the air has been exhausted to the furthest possible extent by an air pump or analogous means. **3** a partial diminution of pressure, as in a suction pump, below the normal atmospheric pressure. **4** an emptiness or void caused by the removal or absence of a person or thing; a feeling of emptiness. **5** (*pl.* **vacuums**) a vacuum cleaner. *~v.t., v.i.* to clean with a vacuum cleaner. **vacuum cleaner** *n.* a machine for removing dirt by suction. **vacuum-clean** *v.t., v.i.* **vacuum flask** *n.* a flask constructed with two walls between which is a vacuum, for the purpose of keeping the contents hot or cold. **vacuum gauge** *n.* a gauge indicating the pressure consequent on the production of a vacuum. **vacuum-packed** *a.* sealed in a container from which most of the air has been removed. **vacuum pump** *n.* an airpump used to remove air or other gas, and so create a vacuum. **vacuum tube** *n.* (*N. Am.*) an electronic valve.

vade-mecum (vahdimā´kəm, vādimē´-) *n.* (*pl.* **vade-mecums**) a pocket companion or manual for ready reference.

vagabond (vag´əbond) *n.* **1** a person who wanders about without any settled home, a wanderer, esp. an idle or disreputable one, a vagrant. **2** (*coll.*) a scamp, a rogue. *~a.* **1** wandering about, having no settled habitation, nomadic. **2** driven or drifting to and fro, aimless. *~v.i.* to wander about as a vagabond. **vagabondage** (-dij), **vagabondism** *n.*

vagal VAGUS.

vagary (vā´gəri) *n.* (*pl.* **vagaries**) a whimsical idea, an extravagant notion, a freak. **vagarious** (-geə´ri-) *a.*

vagi VAGUS.

vagina (vəjī´nə) *n.* **1** the genital passage of a female from the vulva to the uterus. **2** a sheath, a sheathlike envelope or organ, esp. a sheath or semi-tubular part, as at the base of a stem.

vaginal (-jī´-, vaj´i-) *a.* **vaginismus** (vajiniz´məs) *n.* painful spasmodic contraction of the vaginal sphincters. **vaginitis** (vajinī´tis) *n.*

vagrant (vā´grənt) *n.* 1 a person wandering about without a settled home or visible means of subsistence, a tramp. 2 a bird that has strayed outside its normal area or from its normal migratory route. ~*a.* 1 wandering about without a settled home. 2 itinerant, strolling. 3 unpredictable, erratic, wayward. **vagrancy** *n.* **vagrantly** *adv.*

vague (vāg) *a.* 1 of doubtful meaning or application; not expressed or understood clearly. 2 (of a shape or outline) not clear. 3 uncertain about what to do. 4 (of a person) lacking clarity of thought, expression etc.; absent-minded; disorganized. **vaguely** *adv.* **vagueness** *n.* **vaguish** *a.*

vagus (vā´gəs) *n.* (*pl.* **vagi** (-jī, -gī)) (*Anat.*) the tenth cranial nerve, which regulates the heartbeat, rhythm of breathing etc. **vagal** *a.*

vain (vān) *a.* 1 excessively proud of one's appearance or attainments, conceited, self-admiring. 2 empty, unsubstantial, unreal, worthless. 3 not achieving the desired result. **in vain** unsuccessfully, without result. **to take someone's name in vain** 1 to use someone's name, esp. God's, profanely or without due respect. 2 to mention someone's name. **vainglory** *n.* 1 excessive vanity. 2 pride, boastfulness. **vainglorious** *a.* **vaingloriously** *adv.* **vaingloriousness** *n.* **vainly** *adv.* **vainness** *n.*

valance (val´əns), **valence** (vā´-) *n.* a short curtain or hanging round the frame or tester of a bedstead, along a shelf, above a window etc. to conceal structural details. **valanced** *a.*

vale (vāl) *n.* (*poet.*) a valley. **vale of tears** *n.* human life, existence, the world.

valediction (validik´shən) *n.* 1 the act or an instance of bidding farewell. 2 a farewell, an adieu. **valedictory** *a.* 1 bidding farewell. 2 of the nature of a farewell. ~*n.* (*pl.* **valedictories**) a parting address or oration, esp. at graduation in an American university. **valedictorian** (-taw´ri-) *n.* (*N Am.*) a student who delivers a valedictory.

valence[1] (vā´ləns) *n.* (*Chem.*) the combining or replacing power of an element or radical reckoned as the number of monovalent elements it can replace or combine with. **valence electron, valency electron** *n.* an electron in the outermost shell of an atom, responsible for forming chemical bonds. **valency** *n.* (*pl.* **valencies**) 1 a unit of combining capacity. 2 valence.

valence[2] VALANCE.

valentine (val´əntīn) *n.* 1 a letter or card of an amatory or satirical kind sent to a person, often anonymously, on St Valentine's day. 2 a sweetheart chosen to receive a greeting on St Valentine's day.

valerian (vəliə´riən) *n.* 1 a herbaceous plant of the genus *Valeriana*, esp. *V. officinalis*, with clusters of pink or white flowers. 2 a preparation from the root of *V. officinalis* used as a mild

stimulant etc. 3 a related Mediterranean plant with red spurred flowers, *Centranthus ruber*; red valerian. **valeric** (-ler´ik) *a.* **valeric acid** *n.* (*Chem.*) pentanoic acid, a fatty acid with a disagreeable smell obtained from valerian.

valet (val´it, val´ā) *n.* 1 a manservant who acts as a personal attendant to his employer, looking after his clothes, serving his meals etc. 2 a person employed in a hotel, liner etc. to perform similar functions. ~*v.t.* (*pres.p.* **valeting**, *past, p.p.* **valeted**) 1 to act as valet to. 2 to clean the interior of (a car). ~*v.i.* to act as a valet.

valeta VELETA.

valetudinarian (valitūdinee´riən), **valetudinary** (-tū´dinəri) *a.* 1 morbidly anxious about one's state of health. 2 sickly, infirm, delicate. 3 seeking to recover health. ~*n.* (*pl.* **valetudinarians, valetudinaries**) 1 a valetudinarian person. 2 an invalid. **valetudinarianism** *n.*

valiant (val´iənt) *a.* brave, daring. **valiantly** *adv.*

valid (val´id) *a.* 1 based on sound reasoning. 2 (*Law*) legally sound, sufficient, and effective; legally binding. 3 not having reached its expiry date. **validate** *v.t.* 1 to make valid, to ratify, to confirm, to make binding. 2 to prove that something is true. **validation** (-ā´shən) *n.* **validity** (-lid´-), **validness** *n.* **validly** *adv.*

valise (vəlēz´) *n.* 1 a bag or case, usu. of leather, for holding a traveller's clothes etc., esp. one for carrying in the hand, a travelling bag. 2 a kitbag.

Valium® (val´iəm) *n.* the tranquillizer diazepam.

Valkyrie (val´kiri, -kiə´ri) *n.* in Norse mythology, each of 12 maidens of Valhalla who were sent by Odin to select those destined to be slain in battle and to conduct their souls to Valhalla.

valley (val´i) *n.* (*pl.* **valleys**) 1 a depression in the earth's surface bounded by hills or mountains, and usu. with a river or stream flowing through it. 2 any hollow or depression between higher ground or elevations of a surface. 3 (*Archit.*) the internal angle formed by two inclined sides of a roof.

valorize (val´əriz), **valorise** *v.t.* to increase or stabilize the price of (an article) by an officially organized scheme. **valorization** (-zā´shən) *n.*

valour (val´ə), (*N Am.*) **valor** *n.* personal bravery, courage esp. as displayed in fighting. **valorous** *a.* **valorously** *adv.*

value (val´ū) *n.* 1 worth, the desirability of a thing, esp. as compared with other things. 2 the qualities that are the basis of this. 3 worth estimated in money or other equivalent, the market price. 4 the equivalent of a thing in terms of something else to be substituted for it. 5 valuation, estimation, appreciation of worth. 6 the usefulness of a thing within a specific context or to achieve a particular end. 7 (*pl.*) moral principles, standards; those things which a person or group sets most store by for the achievement of goodness or excellence in any sphere of life. 8 the quality of a speech sound represented by a particular letter. 9 (*Math.*) the amount or quantity denoted by a symbol or expression. **10** (*Mus.*) the relative duration of a tone as indicated by the note. **11** rank, in terms of the rules of a game, of a particular card, piece etc. **12** (*Physics, Chem.*) a number or numerical measure denoting magnitude or quantity on a conventional scale. *~v.t.* (*3rd pers. sing. pres.* **values**, *pres.p.* **valuing**, *past, p.p.* **valued**) **1** to estimate the value of, to appraise. **2** to consider special or important. **3** to fix the value of. **valuable** *a.* **1** having great value, worth or price, costly, precious. **2** very useful or important. **3** considered special or important. *~n.* (*usu. pl.*) an object of high value, esp. a valuable piece of personal property. **valuably** *adv.* **valuate** (-āt) *v.t.* (*esp. N Am.*) to value; to evaluate. **valuation** (-ā´shən) *n.* **1** the act of valuing or appraising. **2** estimation of the value of a thing. **3** estimated value or worth, the price placed on a thing. **valuator** *n.* an appraiser. **value added** *n.* **1** the amount by which the value of an article is increased in the process of production; the difference between the final value of an article and the cost of manufacturing and marketing it. **2** improvement or benefit acquired during a process. **value-added** *a.* **value added tax** *n.* in Britain, a tax levied at each stage of production and distribution of a commodity or service and paid by the buyer as a purchase tax. **valued** *a.* **value for money** *n.* something that gives adequate or abundant satisfaction in return for the money spent on it. **value judgement** *n.* a subjective and personal estimate of merit in a particular respect. **valueless** *a.* of no value, worthless, futile. **valuelessness** *n.* **valuer** *n.* a person who values, an appraiser, esp. of property, jewellery etc.

valve (valv) *n.* **1** an automatic or other contrivance for opening or closing a passage or aperture so as to permit or prevent passage of a fluid, such as water, gas or steam. **2** (*Anat.*) a membraneous part of a vessel or other organ preventing the flow of liquids in one direction and allowing it in the other. **3** (*Physics*) a vacuum tube or bulb containing electrodes and exhibiting sensitive control by one or more electrodes of the current flowing between the others. **4** (*Mus.*) a device to increase the effective length of the tube of a brass instrument, allowing the full chromatic range of notes to be played. **5** (*Zool.*) one of the parts or divisions of a shell. **6** (*Bot.*) one of the segments into which a capsule dehisces; either half of an anther after its opening. **valvate** (-vāt) *a.* **valved** *a.* **valveless** *a.* **valvular** (-vū-) *a.* **1** having a valve or valves; operated by valves. **2** having the shape or function of a valve.

vamoose (vəmoos´) *v.i.* (*N Am., sl.*) to decamp, to be gone, to be off.

vamp[1] (vamp) *n.* **1** the part of a boot or shoe upper in front of the ankle seams. **2** a patched-up or reworked thing. **3** (*Mus.*) an improvised

accompaniment. *~v.t.* **1** (*often* **vamp up**) to give a new appearance to, to repair, to renovate. **2** (*usu.* **vamp up**) to put together from odds and ends. **3** (*Mus.*) to improvise an accompaniment to. **4** to put a new vamp on (a boot etc.). *~v.i.* to improvise accompaniments.

vamp[2] (vamp) *n.* an adventuress, a woman who exploits her sexual attractiveness to take advantage of men. *~v.t.* to fascinate or exploit (men). *~v.i.* to act as a vamp.

vampire (vam´pīə) *n.* **1** a ghost of a heretic, criminal or other outcast, supposed to leave the grave at night and suck the blood of sleeping persons. **2** a person who preys upon others, a bloodsucker. **3** (*also* **vampire bat**) a bat of the family Desmodontidae, which sucks the blood of man and other animals, esp. while they are asleep. **4** in a theatre, a small trapdoor used for sudden entrances and exits. **vampiric** (-pir´ik) *a.* **vampirism** (vam´pir-) *n.* **1** belief in vampires. **2** bloodsucking. **3** extortion.

van[1] (van) *n.* **1** a motor vehicle, usu. covered, for conveying goods, furniture etc. **2** a closed railway carriage for luggage or for the guard. **3** a caravan.

van[2] (van) *n.* **1** the foremost division of an army or fleet, the advance guard. **2** the leaders of a movement, the forefront. **3** the leading position in a movement etc.

van[3] (van) *n., int.* (*coll.*) in tennis, advantage.

vanadium (vənā´diəm) *n.* (*Chem.*) a rare, silver-white metallic element, at. no. 23, chem. symbol V, used to give tensile strength to steel and, in the form of its salts, to produce an intense permanent black colour.

vandal (van´dəl) *n.* **1** a person who wilfully or ignorantly destroys or damages anything. **2** (**Vandal**) a member of a Germanic people from the shores of the Baltic that overran Gaul, Spain, and N Africa and Rome in the 5th cent., destroying works of art etc. *~a.* (**Vandal**) of or relating to the Vandals. **Vandalic** (-dal´-) *a.* **vandalism** *n.* deliberate destruction or defacement of property. **vandalistic** (-is´-) *a.* **vandalistically** *adv.* **vandalize, vandalise** *v.t.* to destroy or damage deliberately and senselessly.

vandyke (vandīk´) *n.* **1** any one of the series of points forming an ornamental border to lace, linen etc. **2** a collar or cape with these points. *~a.* (**Vandyke**) applied to the style of dress, esp. ornamented with vandykes, worn by the figures in Van Dyck's portraits. **Vandyke beard** *n.* a pointed beard. **Vandyke brown** *n.* a reddish-brown colour or pigment. **Vandyke collar, Vandyke cape** *n.* a collar or cape ornamented with vandykes.

vane (vān) *n.* **1** a weathercock, flag or arrow pointing in the direction of the wind. **2** the arm of a windmill. **3** the blade of a propeller, turbine etc. **4** the sight on a quadrant, compass etc. **5** a horizontal part on a surveyor's levelling-staff for moving up and down to the line of sight of the telescope. **6** the broad part of a feather. **vaned** *a.* **vaneless** *a.*

vanessid (vənes´id) *n.* a butterfly with notched wings, belonging to any of several brightly coloured species, such as Camberwell Beauty, red or white admiral, tortoiseshell etc.

vanguard (van´gahd) *n.* **1** the troops who march in the front or van of an army, an advance guard, the van. **2** the leaders or leading position in a movement etc.

vanilla (vanil´ə) *n.* **1** any member of a genus, *Vanilla*, of tall, epiphytal orchids, natives of tropical Asia and America, bearing fragrant flowers. **2** the pod of *Vanilla planifolia* and other species used to flavour food. **3** an extract from this used for flavouring ices, syrups etc. *~a.* flavoured with vanilla. **vanillate** (-lət) *n.* **vanillin** *n.* the aromatic principle of vanilla, a white crystalline aldehyde.

vanish (van´ish) *v.i.* **1** to disappear suddenly. **2** to become imperceptible, to be lost to sight, to fade away, to dissolve. **3** to pass away, to pass out of existence. **4** (*Math.*) to become zero. *~v.t.* to cause to disappear. **vanishing** *a.*, *n.* **vanishing point** *n.* **1** in perspective views, the point in which all parallel lines in the same plane tend to meet. **2** a point in space or time at which something disappears or ceases to exist.

vanity (van´iti) *n.* (*pl.* **vanities**) **1** the quality or state of being vain. **2** empty pride, conceit about one's personal attainments or attractions. **3** ostentation, show. **4** emptiness, futility, unreality, worthlessness. **5** something which is visionary, unreal or deceptive. **vanity bag, vanity case** *n.* a small bag or case used to carry a woman's make-up and toiletries. **vanity publisher** *n.* a company that publishes books at the authors' expense, often with little prospect of selling copies of the works. **vanity publishing** *n.* **vanity unit** *n.* a piece of furniture consisting of a washbasin built into a dressing table or set of cupboards.

vanquish (vang´kwish) *v.t.* to conquer, to overcome, to subdue. **vanquishable** *a.* **vanquisher** *n.*

vantage (vahn´tij) *n.* **1** (*formal*) superiority or elevation, esp. such as to give a commanding view. **2** (*formal*) a situation, condition or opportunity favourable to success. *~v.t.* to profit, to advantage. **vantage ground** *n.* superiority of position or place. **vantage point** *n.* a position or place that affords a good view of a scene or event.

vapid (vap´id) *a.* lacking interest or excitement. **vapidity** (-pid´-), **vapidness** *n.* **vapidly** *adv.*

vapour (vā´pə) (*N Am.*) **vapor** *n.* **1** moisture in the air, light mist. **2** any visible diffused substance floating in the atmosphere. **3** (*Physics*) the gaseous form of a substance that is normally liquid or solid. **4** an unreal or unsubstantial thing, a vain imagination. **5** a medicinal preparation applied by inhaling. **6** (*pl.*) †depression of spirits, hypochondria. *~v.i.* **1** to give out vapour.

2 to boast, to brag, to bluster. **vaporific** (-rif´-) *a.* **1** of or relating to vapour. **2** causing vapour or vaporization. **3** tending to become vapour. **vaporimeter** (-rim´itə) *n.* an instrument for measuring the pressure of vapour. **vaporize, vaporise** *v.t.* to convert into a vapour, gas or fine spray. *~v.i.* to be converted into a vapour etc. **vaporizable** *a.* **vaporization** (-zā´shən) *n.* **vaporizer** *n.* a device that vaporizes a substance, esp. a medicinal spray. **vaporous** *a.* **vaporosity** (-ros´-) *n.* **vaporously** *adv.* **vaporousness** *n.* **vapourish** *a.* **vapourishness** *n.* **vapour trail** *n.* a white trail of condensed vapour left in the sky after the passage of an aircraft.

VAR *abbr.* value-added reseller.

var. *abbr.* variety.

varactor (vərak´tə) *n.* a two-electrode semiconductor device in which capacitance varies with voltage.

varec (var´ik) *n.* kelp or the ash obtained from kelp.

variable (veə´riəbəl) *a.* **1** capable of varying, liable to change. **2** changeable, unsteady, fickle, inconstant. **3** able to be varied, adapted or adjusted. **4** quantitatively indeterminate, susceptible of continuous change of value, esp. assuming different values while others remain constant. **5** (of winds, currents) tending to change in direction and intensity. **6** (*Astron.*) applied to stars whose apparent magnitudes are not constant. *~n.* **1** a thing which is variable. **2** (*Math.*) a variable quantity. **3** (*Naut.*) **a** a shifting wind. **b** (*pl.*) the region between the northerly and southerly trade winds. **variability** (-bil´-), **variableness** *n.* **variable gear** *n.* a gear that is designed to give varying speeds. **variably** *adv.*

variance (veə´riəns) *n.* **1** the fact of varying, the state of being variant, disagreement, difference of opinion, dissension, discord. **2** (*Law*) disagreement between the allegations and proof or between the writ and the declaration. **3** a statistical measure of the dispersion of a set of observations. **at variance 1** conflicting, not in accord (with one another). **2** (of people) in disagreement or dispute. **variant** *a.* **1** showing variation, differing in form, character, or details. **2** tending to vary, changeable. *~n.* a variant form, reading, type etc.

variation (veəriā´shən) *n.* **1** the act, process or state of varying. **2** the extent to which a thing varies. **3** something that differs from a norm, standard etc. **4** (*Mus.*) a repetition of a theme with fanciful elaborations and changes of form. **5** (*Astron.*) deviation of a heavenly body from the mean orbit or motion. **6** the angle of deviation from true north or of declination of the magnetic needle. **7** the deviation in structure or function from the type or parent form. **8** (*Math.*) a change in a function due to small changes in the values of constants etc. **variational** *a.*

varicella (varisel´ə) *n.* (*Med.*) **1** chickenpox. **2**

(*also* **varicella zoster**) a virus that causes chickenpox and shingles.

varices VARIX.

varicoloured (veə'rikŭləd), (*N Am.*) **varicolored** *a.* variously coloured, variegated, particoloured.

varicose (var'ikōs) *a.* (of veins) permanently dilated, affected with varix. **varicosed** *a.* **varicosity** (-kos'-) *n.*

varied VARY.

variegate (veə'rigāt) *v.t.* **1** to diversify in colour, to mark with patches of different hues, to dapple, to chequer. **2** to give variety to. **variegated** *a.* (*Bot.*) having leaves with two or more colours. **variegation** (-gā'shən) *n.*

variety (vərī'əti) *n.* (*pl.* **varieties**) **1** the quality or state of being various; diversity, absence of sameness or monotony, many-sidedness, versatility. **2** a collection of diverse things. **3 a** a minor class or group of things differing in some common peculiarities from the class they belong to. **b** a member or example of such a class or group. **4** a kind, a sort; a thing of a particular sort or kind. **5** (*Biol.*) an individual or group differing from the type of its species in some transmittable quality but usually fertile with others of the species; a sub-species. **6** (*Bot.*) a cultivar. **7** a form of entertainment consisting of a number of unrelated acts or short performances, usu. with singing, dancing, comic or acrobatic turns, conjuring etc. ~*a.* consisting of or relating to this type of entertainment. **varietal** *a.* **varietally** *adv.*

varifocal (veərifō'kəl) *a.* having a variable focal length, allowing the focusing range to alter gradually to accommodate near, intermediate and far vision. ~*n.* (*pl.*) varifocal spectacles.

variform (veə'rifawm) *a.* varying in form, of different shapes.

variola (vərī'ələ) *n.* (*Med.*) smallpox. **variolar** *a.* **variole** (veə'riōl) *n.* a shallow pitlike depression. **variolous** (vərī'ələs) *a.*

variometer (veəriom'itə) *n.* **1** a device for varying the inductance in an electric circuit. **2** an instrument indicating rate of climb or descent in an aircraft. **3** an instrument for measuring variations in a magnetic field.

variorum (veəriaw'rəm) *a.* **1** (of an edition of a work) with notes of various commentators inserted. **2** including variant readings. ~*n.* a variorum edition. **variorum edition** *n.* an edition of a classic etc. with comparisons of texts and notes by various editors and commentators.

various (veə'riəs) *a.* **1** differing from each other, diverse. **2** several. **3** (*poet.*) variegated. **variously** *adv.* **variousness** *n.*

Usage note The construction *various of* (after *several of, some of*) is best avoided.

varistor (vərist'ə) *n.* a semiconductor with two electrodes which has a resistance dependent on the strength of the voltage applied.

varix (veə'riks) *n.* (*pl.* **varices** (-isēz)) **1** (*Med.*) **a** a permanent dilatation of a vein or other vessel. **b** a varicose vessel. **2** any of the ridges traversing the whorls of a univalve shell.

varlet (vah'lit) *n.* **1** (*Hist.*) a page, an attendant preparing to be a squire. **2** †a menial. **3** (*facet.*) †a knave, a rascal.

varmint (vah'mint) *n.* (*N Am. or dial.*) a troublesome or mischievous person or animal.

varnish (vah'nish) *n.* **1** a thin resinous solution for applying to the surface of wood, metal etc., to give it a hard, transparent, shiny coating. **2** a similar solution or preparation giving a glossy surface. **3** an application of varnish. **4** any lustrous or glossy appearance on the surface of leaves etc. **5** superficial polish. **6** gloss, palliation, whitewash. ~*v.t.* **1** to cover with varnish. **2** to give an improved appearance to, to gloss over, to whitewash. **varnisher** *n.*

varsity (vah'siti) *n.* (*pl.* **varsities**) **1** (*coll.*) university. **2** (*N Am.*) the principal team representing a university, college, school etc. in a sports or other competition.

vary (veə'ri) *v.t.* (*3rd pers. sing. pres.* **varies**, *pres.p.* **varying**, *past, p.p.* **varied**) **1** to change, to alter in appearance, form or substance. **2** to modify, to diversify. **3** to make variations of (a melody etc.). ~*v.i.* **1** to be altered in any way. **2** to undergo change. **3** to be different or diverse, to differ, to be of different kinds. **4** to increase or decrease proportionately with or inversely to the increase or decrease of another quantity. **varied** *a.* **1** possessing or showing variety, diverse. **2** consisting of many different kinds of things or people. **3** variegated.

vas (vas) *n.* (*pl.* **vasa** (vā'sə)) (*Anat.*) a vessel or duct. **vasal** (vā'-) *a.* **vas deferens** (def'ərenz) *n.* (*pl.* **vasa deferentia** (defərən'shiə)) the spermatic duct.

vascular (vas'kūlə) *a.* (*Anat.*) **1** of, consisting of, or containing vessels or ducts for the conveyance of blood, chyle, sap etc. **2** containing or rich in blood vessels. **vascularity** (-lar'i-) *n.* **vascularize**, **vascularise** *v.t.* (*Med., Anat.*) to make vascular, to develop blood vessels in. **vascularization** (-zā'shən) *n.* **vascularly** *adv.*

vasculum (vas'kūləm) *n.* (*pl.* **vascula** (-lə), **vasculums**) a botanist's collecting case, usu. of tin.

vase (vahz) *n.* **1** a vessel of pottery etc., of various forms but usu. circular with a swelling body and a foot or pedestal, used for various ornamental and other purposes, esp. holding flowers. **2** a sculptured ornament in imitation of an ancient vase, used to decorate cornices, gateposts, monuments etc. **vaseful** *n.* (*pl.* **vasefuls**).

vasectomy (vəsek'təmi) *n.* (*pl.* **vasectomies**) excision of the vas deferens or part of it to produce sterility. **vasectomize**, **vasectomise** *v.t.*

Vaseline® (vas'əlēn) *n.* a soft, medicated paraffin jelly employed as a lubricant etc. **vaseline** *v.t.* to treat, lubricate etc. with Vaseline.

vasiform (vā´zifawm) *a.* **1** having the form of a vas. **2** having the form of a vase.

vaso- (vā´zō) *comb. form* relating to a vas, vessel or duct.

vasoactive (vāzōak´tiv) *a.* vasomotor.

vasoconstrictor (vāzōkənstrik´tə) *a.* causing constriction of a blood vessel. ~*n.* a nerve, drug or other agent causing this. **vasoconstriction** *n.* **vasoconstrictive** *a.*

vasodilator (vāzōdilā´tə) *a.* causing dilatation of a vessel. ~*n.* a nerve or drug causing this. **vasodilation, vasodilatation** (-dīlətā´shən) *n.*

vasomotor (vāzōmō´tə) *a.* causing constriction or dilatation in a vessel. ~*n.* a vasomotor nerve, agent or drug.

vassal (vas´əl) *n.* **1** (*Hist.*) a person holding land under a superior lord by feudal tenure, a feudatory. **2** a slave, a humble dependant, a low wretch. ~*a.* servile. **vassalage** (-lij) *n.*

vast (vahst) *a.* **1** of great extent, immense, huge, boundless. **2** very great in numbers, amount, degree etc. ~*n.* (*poet.*) a boundless expanse. **vastitude** (-titūd) *n.* **1** vastness. **2** a vast expanse of space. **vastly** *adv.* **vastness** *n.*

VAT (vat, vē ā tē´) *abbr.* VALUE ADDED TAX (under VALUE). **VATman** *n.* (*pl.* **VATmen**) (*coll.*) a customs and excise officer responsible for the administration, collection etc. of VAT.

vat (vat) *n.* **1** a large tub, tank or other vessel used for holding mash or hop liquor in brewing and in many manufacturing operations in which substances are boiled or steeped. **2** a liquor containing a reduced, colourless, soluble form of an insoluble dye in which textiles are steeped, the colour appearing when the textiles are afterwards exposed to the air. ~*v.t.* (*pres.p.* **vatting**, *past*, *p.p.* **vatted**) to put into or treat in a vat.

vatic (vat´ik) *a.* (*formal*) prophetic; oracular.

Vatican (vat´ikən) *n.* the papal government.

vatu (vah´too) *n.* (*pl.* **vatus, vatu**) the standard monetary unit of Vanuatu.

vaudeville (vaw´dəvil) *n.* **1** (*N Am.*) a miscellaneous series of sketches, songs etc., a variety entertainment. **2** a slight dramatic sketch or pantomime interspersed with songs and dances. **3** a topical or satirical song with a refrain. **vaudevillian** (-vil´-) *a.* of or relating to vaudeville. ~*n.* a person who performs in vaudeville.

vault[1] (vawlt) *n.* **1** (*Archit.*) an arched roof; a continuous arch or semi-cylindrical roof; a series of arches connected by radiating joints. **2** an arched chamber, esp. underground; a cellar. **3** a strongroom for the deposit and storage of valuables. **4** a place of interment built of masonry under a church or in a cemetery. **5** any vault-like covering or canopy, such as the sky. **6** (*Anat.*) an arched roof of a cavity. ~*v.t.* **1** to cover with, or as with, a vault or vaults. **2** to construct in the form of a vault. **vaulting** *n.* an arched ceiling or roof or the arched work that supports or composes it.

vault[2] (vawlt) *v.i.* to leap, to spring, esp. with the hands resting on something or with the help of a pole. ~*v.t.* to leap over (a gate, obstacle etc.) by vaulting. ~*n.* such a leap. **vaulter** *n.* **vaulting horse** *n.* a wooden horse or frame for vaulting over in a gymnasium.

vaunt (vawnt) *v.i.* to boast, to brag. ~*v.t.* to boast of. ~*n.* a boast. **vaunter** *n.* **vauntingly** *adv.*

vb *abbr.* verb.

VC *abbr.* **1** Vice-Chairman. **2** Vice-Chancellor. **3** Vice-Consul. **4** Victoria Cross.

VCR *abbr.* video cassette recorder.

VD *abbr.* venereal disease.

VDU *abbr.* visual display unit.

VE *abbr.* Victory in Europe.

veal (vēl) *n.* the flesh of a calf as food. **vealy** *a.*

vector (vek´tə) *n.* **1** (*Physics, Math.*) a quantity having both magnitude and direction (e.g. velocity), but not temperature. **2** a line in space or in a diagram representing the magnitude and direction of a quantity. **3** a course to be taken by an aircraft. **4** an agent (such as an insect) that carries a disease or parasite from one host to another. **5** an agent which can be used to transfer a fragment of DNA from one organism to another. **6** a force or influence. ~*v.t.* to direct (an aircraft) to a particular point. **vectorial** (-taw´ri-) *a.* **vectorize, vectorise** *v.t.*

vedette (videt´), **vidette** *n.* a sentinel (usu. mounted) stationed in advance of an outpost.

vee (vē) *n.* **1** the letter V, v. **2** anything in the shape of this letter.

veep (vēp) *n.* (*N Am.*, *coll.*) a vice-president.

veer[1] (viə) *v.i.* **1** to change direction, esp. (of the wind) in the direction of the sun (i.e. clockwise in the northern hemisphere and anticlockwise in the southern hemisphere). **2** to change direction esp. suddenly. **3** to shift, to change about, esp. in opinion, conduct etc. **4** (*Naut.*) (of a ship) to turn away from the wind, to wear. ~*v.t.* **1** to change the direction of. **2** (*Naut.*) to wear (a ship). **veeringly** *adv.*

veer[2] (viə) *v.t.* to let out or slacken (a rope etc.).

veery (viə´ri) *n.* (*pl.* **veeries**) a tawny N American thrush, *Catharus fuscescens*.

veg (vej) *n.* (*pl.* **veg**) (*coll.*) a vegetable.

vegan (vē´gən) *n.* a person who uses no animal products whatsoever for food, clothing etc. ~*a.* containing no animal products.

Vegeburger® (vej´ibœgə) *n.* a veggie burger.

vegetable (vej´təbəl, vej´i-) *n.* **1** (*Bot.*) a plant, esp. a herbaceous one, used for culinary purposes or for feeding cattle etc. **2** (*coll., sometimes offensive*) a person who, usu. through brain damage, has limited awareness and has lost control of bodily functions. **3** (*coll., derog.*) a very sluggish, idle or apathetic person; a person who leads a very monotonous life. ~*a.* **1** of the nature of, relating to or resembling, a plant. **2** made of or relating to culinary vegetables. **3** (of a person's existence) dull, sluggish, inactive; very monotonous. **vegetable butter** *n.* any number of vegetable fats that have the consistency of butter. **vegetable marrow** *n.* a large edible gourd with white flesh from the plant *Cucurbita pepo*. **vegetable oil** *n.* an oil obtained from seeds or plants, used in cooking etc. **vegetable oyster** *n.* salsify. **vegetable parchment** *n.* a type of paper made to resemble parchment. **vegetable spaghetti** *n.* a variety of marrow that has flesh resembling spaghetti; its flesh. **vegetable sponge** *n.* a loofah. **vegetable wax** *n.* a waxy substance exuded by certain plants, e.g. the sumac, to prevent moisture loss. **vegetal** (vej´i-) *a., n.* **vegetarian** (-itea´ri-) *n.* a person who abstains from eating meat, and sometimes also other animal products and fish. ~*a.* **1** excluding meat and other animal products to a greater or lesser extent. **2** of or relating to vegetarians and vegetarianism. **vegetarianism** *n.* **vegetate** (-itāt) *v.i.* **1** to grow in the manner of a plant, to fulfil the functions of a vegetable. **2** to live an idle, passive, monotonous life. **vegetation** (-ā´shən) *n.* **1** vegetables or plants collectively, plant life. **2** the act or process of vegetating. **vegetative** *a.* **1** concerned with development and growth as distinct from sexual reproduction. **2** of or relating to vegetation, plant life or plant growth. **3** (*Med.*) (of the state of e.g. a person in a coma) alive but without responsiveness or apparent brain activity. **vegetatively** *adv.* **vegetativeness** *n.*

veggie (vej´i) *n.* **1** short for VEGETABLE. **2** (*coll.*) short for VEGETARIAN (under VEGETABLE). **veggie burger** *n.* a flat cake of minced or chopped seasoned vegetables, soya etc., resembling and prepared and eaten like a hamburger.

vehement (vē´əmənt) *a.* **1** proceeding from or exhibiting intense fervour or passion, ardent, passionate, impetuous. **2** acting with great force, energy or violence. **vehemence** *n.* **vehemently** *adv.*

vehicle (vē´ikəl) *n.* **1** any kind of carriage or conveyance for use on land, having wheels or runners. **2** any liquid etc. serving as a medium for pigments, medicinal substances etc. **3** any person or thing employed as a medium for the transmission of thought, feeling etc. **4** a space rocket or launcher. **vehicular** (-hik´ū-) *a.*

veil (vāl) *n.* **1** a more or less transparent piece of cloth, muslin etc., usu. attached to a hat or headdress, worn to conceal, shade or protect the face. **2** a piece of linen worn as part of a nun's headdress, framing the face and falling over the shoulders. **3** a curtain or other drapery for concealing or protecting an object. **4** a piece of cloth used to conceal, cover or protect something. **5** a mask, a disguise, a pretext. ~*v.t.* **1** to cover with a veil. **2** to hide, to conceal, to disguise. **beyond the veil** in the unknown state that follows death. **to draw a veil over 1** to conceal discreetly. **2** to refrain from mentioning. **to take the veil 1** to assume the veil according to the custom of a woman when she becomes a nun. **2** to retire to a

convent. **veiled** *a.* **veiling** *n.* a light fabric used for making veils. **veilless** *a.*

vein (vān) *n.* **1** any of the tubular vessels in animal bodies conveying blood to the heart. **2** (*loosely*) any blood vessel. **3** a rib or nervure in an insect's wing or a leaf. **4** a fissure in rock filled with material deposited by water. **5** a seam of any substance. **6** a streak or wavy stripe of different colour, in wood, marble or stone. **7** a distinctive trait, quality, tendency or cast of mind. **8** a particular mood or humour. ~*v.t.* to fill or cover with, or as with veins. **veining** *n.* a pattern or network of veins, streaks etc. **veinless** *a.* **veinlet** *n.* **veinlike** *a.* **veiny** *a.* (*comp.* **veinier**, *superl.* **veiniest**) having or covered with veins.

vela VELUM.

velar (vē´lə) *a.* **1** of or relating to a velum. **2** (of a speech sound) articulated with the back of the tongue close to or in contact with the soft palate, as in *k* or *g*. ~*n.* a velar sound or consonant. **velarize, velarise** *v.t.* **velarization** (-zā´shən) *n.*

Velcro® (vel´krō) *n.* a fastening for clothes etc. which consists of two nylon strips, one consisting of hooks and the other of loops, which stick together when pressed. ~*v.t.* (*3rd pers. sing. pres.* **Velcroes**, *pres.p.* **Velcroing**, *past, p.p.* **Velcroed**) **1** to attach Velcro to. **2** to fasten with Velcro.

veld (velt, felt), **veldt** *n.* (*S Afr.*) open country suitable for pasturage, esp. the high treeless plains in N Transvaal and NW Natal.

veleta (vəlē´tə), **valeta** *n.* a dance or dance tune in slow waltz time.

vellum (vel´əm) *n.* **1** a fine parchment orig. made of calfskin. **2** a manuscript written on this. **3** a superior quality of paper made to imitate vellum. ~*a.* made of or resembling vellum. **vellumy** *a.*

velocimeter (veləsim´itə) *n.* an apparatus for measuring velocity.

velocipede (vilos´ipēd) *n.* **1** an early kind of bicycle propelled by the feet. **2** (*N Am.*) a child's tricycle. **velocipedist** *n.*

velociraptor (vilos´iraptə) *n.* a small carnivorous dinosaur of the Cretaceous period which stood upright and had a large curved claw on each hind foot.

velocity (vilos´iti) *n.* (*pl.* **velocities**) **1** swiftness, rapidity, rapid motion. **2** a measure of the rate of motion, esp. of inanimate things, in a given direction.

velodrome (vel´ədrōm) *n.* a building containing a cycle-racing track.

velour (viluə´), **velours, velure** (-ūə´) *n.* velvet, velveteen or other fabric resembling velvet. **velouté** (-oo´tā) *n.* a thick creamy sauce or soup. **velutinous** (-loo´ti-) *a.* velvety, covered with short, soft hairs.

velum (vē´ləm) *n.* (*pl.* **vela** (-lə)) a membrane, a membraneous covering, envelope etc., esp. the soft palate.

velvet (vel´vit) *n.* **1** a closely-woven fabric, usu. of silk, with a short, soft nap or cut pile on one side. **2** anything soft and smooth or resembling velvet. **3** the furry skin covering the growing antlers of a deer. ~*a*. **1** velvety. **2** as soft as velvet. **on velvet** (*coll.*) in a position of comfort, luxury, wealth etc. **velvet ant** *n*. a downy-bodied, parasitic wasp of the family Mutillidae, the female of which is wingless. **velveted** *a*. **velveteen** (-tēn´) *n*. **1** a cotton velvet or cotton fabric with a velvet pile. **2** (*pl.*) trousers made of this. **velvet glove** *n*. gentleness concealing strength. **velvety** *a*.

Ven. *abbr.* Venerable.

vena (vē´nə) *n*. (*pl.* **venae** (-nē)) (*Med.*) a vein. **vena cava** (kā´və) *n*. (*pl.* **venae cavae** (-vē)) (*Med.*) either of the two large veins conveying oxygen-depleted blood to the heart. **venation** (-nā´shən) *n*. the arrangement of the veins on leaves, insects' wings etc. **venational** *a*. **venepuncture** (vē´nipŭngkchə, ven´-), (*N Am.*) **venipuncture** *n*. (*Med.*) the piercing of a vein, esp. with a hypodermic needle. **venesection** (venisek´shən) *n*. (*Med.*) an incision into a vein, a phlebotomy.

venal (vē´nəl) *a*. **1** ready to be bribed or to sacrifice honour or principle for sordid considerations. **2** characterized by mercenary motives. **venality** (-nal´-) *n*. **venally** *adv*.

Usage note The adjectives *venal* and *venial* should not be confused: *venal* means mercenary or sordid, and *venial* excusable or (of sin) not mortal.

vend (vend) *v.t.* **1** (*Law*) to sell. **2** to offer (small wares) for sale (as a costermonger etc.). **vendee** (-dē´) *n*. (*Law*) a person who buys something, esp. property. **vendible** *a*., *n*. **vending machine** *n*. a slot machine dispensing goods, e.g. cigarettes, drinks, sweets. **vendor** *n*. **1** (*Law*) a person who sells something, esp. property. **2** a vending machine. **vendue** (-dū´) *n*. (*N Am.*) a public auction.

vendace (ven´dās) *n*. a small and delicate whitefish, *Coregonus albula*, found in some lakes.

vendetta (vendet´ə) *n*. **1** a blood feud, often carried on for generations, in which the family of a murdered or injured man seeks vengeance on the offender or any member of his family, prevalent esp. in Corsica, Sardinia and Sicily. **2** this practice. **3** a feud, private warfare or animosity.

vendeuse (vondœz´) *n*. a saleswoman, esp. in a fashionable dress shop.

veneer (viniə´) *v.t.* **1** to cover with a thin layer of fine or superior wood. **2** to put a superficial polish on, to disguise, to gloss over. ~*n*. **1** a thin layer of superior wood for veneering. **2** superficial polish, a superficial appearance (*a veneer of politeness*). **3** any surfacing or facing material that is applied to a different backing. **4** a layer in plywood. **veneering** *n*.

venepuncture VENA.

venerable (ven´ərəbəl) *a*. **1** worthy of reverence, esp. on account of old age and good character. **2** rendered sacred by religious or other associations. **3** ancient. **4** applied as a title to archdeacons in the Church of England, and to a person who has attained the first of three degrees in canonization in the Roman Catholic Church. **venerability** (-bil´-), **venerableness** *n*. **venerably** *adv*.

venerate (ven´ərāt) *v.t.* to regard or treat with profound deference and respect, to revere. **veneration** (-rā´shən) *n*. **venerator** *n*.

venereal (viniə´riəl) *a*. **1** of or relating to, or produced by sexual intercourse. **2** of or relating to venereal disease. **venereal disease** *n*. (*Med.*) a disease conveyed by sexual intercourse, esp. gonorrhoea, syphilis and chancroid. **venereology** (-ol´-) *n*. the study of venereal diseases.

venesection VENA.

Venetian (vinē´shən) *a*. of or relating to the city or province of Venice, in N Italy. ~*n*. **1** a native or inhabitant of Venice. **2** the Italian dialect spoken in Venice. **3** (*usu.* **venetian**) a venetian blind. **venetian blind** *n*. a blind made of thin slats on braid or webbing arranged to turn so as to admit or exclude light. **Venetian red** *n*. **1** a pigment made from ferric oxide. **2** a reddish-brown colour. **Venetian-red** *a*. **Venetian window** *n*. a window with three separate apertures, of which the centre one is largest and arched.

vengeance (ven´jəns) *n*. punishment inflicted in return for an injury or wrong, retribution. **with a vengeance** to a greater degree than was anticipated or wished; forcibly, emphatically, undoubtedly, extremely. **vengeful** *a*. vindictive, revengeful. **vengefully** *adv*. **vengefulness** *n*.

Usage note *Vengeance* implies greater justification and less purely personal motivation than *revenge*.

venial (vē´niəl) *a*. **1** that may be pardoned or excused. **2** in the Roman Catholic Church, (of some sins) not mortal. **veniality** (-al´-), **venialness** *n*. **venially** *adv*.

Usage note See note under VENAL.

venipuncture VENA.

venison (ven´isən, ven´izən) *n*. the flesh of deer as food.

Venn diagram (ven) *n*. a diagram in which sets and their relationships are represented by intersecting circles or other figures.

venom (ven´əm) *n*. **1** a poisonous fluid secreted by snakes, scorpions etc., and injected by biting or stinging. **2** extreme anger or hatred. **venomed** *a*. **venomous** *a*. **1** containing poison. **2** able to inject poison by bite or sting. **3** full of extreme anger or hatred. **venomously** *adv*. **venomousness** *n*.

venose (vē´nōs) *a*. **1** veiny, having many or very marked veins. **2** venous. **venosity** (-nos´-) *n*.

venous (vē´nəs) a. **1** of, relating to or contained in veins. **2** having veins. **venously** adv.

vent¹ (vent) n. **1** (also **vent-hole**) a hole or aperture, esp. for the passage of air, water etc. into or out of a confined place, to allow air to enter while liquid is being drawn. **2** a means or place of passage, escape etc., an outlet. **3** (Zool.) the opening of the cloaca, the anus in animals below mammals. **4** the mouth of a volcano or other aperture through which lava and gases can escape through the earth's surface. **5** (Mus.) a finger-hole in a wind instrument. **6** a touch-hole in a gun. **7** the flue of a chimney. ~v.t. **1** to make a vent in. **2** to give vent to; to utter, to pour forth. **to vent one's spleen** to berate angrily or spitefully, often without just cause. **ventless** a.

vent² (vent) n. a slit in a garment, esp. in the back of a coat or jacket. ~v.t. to make a vent or vents in.

venter (ven´tə) n. the belly, the abdomen, any large cavity containing viscera. **ventral** a. **1** (Anat.) of or relating to the venter. **2** (Zool. etc.) of, relating to or situated on the anterior surface or point (of fins etc.). **ventrally** adv.

ventiduct (ven´tidŭkt) n. (Archit.) a passage or conduit, esp. subterranean, for ventilation.

ventifact (ven´tifakt) n. a pebble shaped or polished by wind-blown sand.

ventil (ven´til) n. (Mus.) **1** a valve in a wind instrument. **2** a shutter for regulating the admission of air in an organ.

ventilate (ven´tilāt) v.t. **1** to supply with fresh air, to cause a circulation of air in (a room etc.). **2** to give publicity to, to throw open for discussion etc. **3** (Med.) **a** to oxygenate (the blood). **b** to supply or force air into (the lungs). **ventilation** (-ā´shən) n. **ventilative** a. **ventilator** n. **1** a device for admitting or introducing fresh air into a place, room etc. **2** (Med.) a machine that supplies air to the lungs of a person with breathing difficulties.

ventouse (ven´toos) n. in obstetrics, a vacuum suction cup that may be placed on the baby's head to assist the delivery.

ventral VENTER.

ventricle (ven´trikəl) n. (Anat.) a cavity or hollow part in an animal body, esp. in the heart and brain. **ventricular** (-trik´ū-) a.

ventriloquism (ventril´əkwizm), **ventriloquy** (-kwi) n. the act or art of speaking or producing sounds so that the sound appears to come not from the person speaking but from a different source. **ventriloquial** (-lō´-), **ventriloquistic** (-kwis´-) a. **ventriloquist** n. **ventriloquize**, **ventriloquise** v.i.

venture (ven´chə) n. **1** the undertaking of a risk, a hazard. **2** an undertaking of a risky nature. **3** a commercial speculation. **4** a stake, that which is risked. ~v.t. **1** to (dare to) express (an opinion, guess). **2** to expose to hazard or risk, to hazard, to stake. **3** to brave the dangers of. ~v.i. **1** to dare; to have the courage or presumption (to do etc.). **2** to

(dare to) go (out, forth etc.). **3** to undertake a risk. **at a venture** at random; without planning, preparation, forethought etc. **to venture on/ upon** to (dare to) enter upon or engage in etc. **venture capital** n. money supplied by investors or organizations, usu. other than the owners, to launch a new commercial enterprise. **Venture Scout** n. a senior member of the Scout Association usu. over 15 years old. **venturesome** a. **1** adventurous. **2** risky. **venturesomely** adv. **venturesomeness** n.

venturi (ventū´ri) n. (pl. **venturis**) a tube or duct, wasp-waisted and expanding at the ends, used in measuring the flow rates of fluids, as a means of accelerating air flow, or to provide a suction source for vacuum-operated instruments. **venturi tube** n.

venue (ven´ū) n. a place chosen as the site of an organized event or meeting.

Venus (vē´nəs) n. **1** a beautiful woman. **2** (poet.) sensual love. **Venus flytrap, Venus's flytrap** n. an insectivorous herb of the sundew family, Dionaea muscipula, with hinged leaves that close on its prey. **Venus's comb** n. an annual herb of the parsley family, Scandex pecten-veneris, with spiny fruit set like comb teeth; shepherd's needle. **Venus's looking-glass** n. any plant of the genus Legousia, with small blue flowers.

veracious (virā´shəs) a. (formal) **1** habitually speaking or disposed to speak the truth. **2** characterized by truth and accuracy. **veraciously** adv. **veracity** (-ras´-) n. **1** truthfulness, honesty. **2** accuracy.

veranda (viran´də), **verandah** n. **1** a light external gallery or portico with a roof on pillars, along the front or side of a house. **2** (Austral., New Zeal.) a roof or canopy over the pavement in front of a shop.

verb (vœb) n. (Gram.) that part of speech which predicates, a word or group of words that denotes an action performed or state undergone by something else (the subject).

verbal (vœ´bəl) a. **1** of or relating to words. **2** respecting words only, not ideas etc. **3** oral, spoken, not written. **4** (Gram.) of or relating to or derived from a verb. **5** literal, word for word. ~n. **1** (Gram.) a word derived from a verb, esp. a verbal noun or adjective such as an English word ending in -ING¹. **2** an oral statement.**3** (pl.,sl.) an admission of guilt made by a suspect when arrested. **4** (sl.) insults, abuse. **verbalism** n. **1** exaggerated attention to words, e.g. in the form of minute criticism of wording, excessive literalism or a fondness for rhetoric. **2** a merely verbal expression, a statement lacking real content. **verbalist** n. **verbalistic** (-lis´-) a. **verbalize**, **verbalise** v.t. **1** to express in words. **2** (Gram.) to convert or change into a verb. ~v.i. to use many words, to be verbose. **verbalizable** a. **verbalization** (-zā´shən) n. **verbalizer** n. **verbally** adv. **verbal noun** n. (Gram.) a form of a verb functioning as a noun.

Usage note In some contexts *verbal* may be ambiguous, as it can refer to words generally, or specifically to spoken words: *oral* can be used instead if the opposition to written words is important.

verbatim (vœbā´tim) *adv., a.* word for word.

verbena (vœbē´nə) *n.* any of a large genus of plants, *Verbena*, of which *V. officinalis*, the common vervain, is the type.

verbiage (vœ´biij) *n.* **1** an excess of words, unnecessary words. **2** the use of many words unnecessarily, verbosity, wordiness.

verbose (vœbōs´) *a.* using or containing more words than are necessary, prolix. **verbosely** *adv.* **verboseness** *n.* **verbosity** (-bos´-) *n.*

verboten (vœbō´tən, fœ-) *a.* forbidden by authority.

verdant (vœ´dənt) *a.* **1** green. **2** covered with growing plants or grass. **3** fresh, flourishing. **4** green, inexperienced, unsophisticated, easily taken in. **verdancy** *n.* **verdantly** *adv.*

verd-antique (vœdantēk´) *n.* **1** an ornamental stone composed chiefly of serpentine, usu. green and mottled or veined. **2** a green incrustation on ancient bronze.

verdict (vœ´dikt) *n.* **1** the decision of a jury on an issue of fact submitted to them in the trial of any cause, civil or criminal. **2** an official decision.

verdigris (vœ´digrēs) *n.* **1** a green crystalline substance formed on copper by the action of dilute acetic acid, used as a pigment and in medicine. **2** greenish rust on copper etc.

verdure (vœ´dyə) *n.* **1** greenness of vegetation. **2** fresh vegetation or foliage. **3** (*poet.*) freshness. **verdured** *a.* **verdurous** *a.*

verge[1] (vœj) *n.* **1** an edge, border or boundary. **2** the extreme edge, brink, border or margin. **3** the grass edging of a bed or border or alongside a road. **4** (*Archit.*) the edge of the tiles projecting over a gable etc. **5** a rod, wand or staff, carried as an emblem of authority, esp. before a bishop or other dignitary. **6** (*Archit.*) the shaft of a column. *~v.t.* to form the edge or verge of. **to verge on 1** to border on, to be next to. **2** to come near to, to nearly be.

verge[2] (vœj) *v.i.* to move or incline in a particular direction, esp. downwards.

verger (vœ´jə), **virger** *n.* **1** an official in a church acting as caretaker, attendant, usher etc. **2** an officer carrying the verge or staff of office before a bishop or other dignitary. **vergership** *n.*

verglas (veə´glah) *n.* a film of ice on rock.

veridical (virid´ikəl) *a.* **1** (*formal*) truthful, veracious. **2** (*Psych.*) (of a vision, dream) that corresponds with reality or is confirmed by subsequent events. **veridically** *adv.*

verify (ver´ifī) *v.t.* (*3rd pers. sing. pres.* **verifies**, *pres.p.* **verifying**, *past, p.p.* **verified**) **1** to confirm the truth of. **2** to inquire into the truth of, to authenticate. **3** to fulfil (a prediction, promise). **4** (*Law*) to append an affidavit to (pleadings), to

support (a statement) by testimony or proofs. **verifiable** *a.* **verifiability** (-bil´-) *n.* **verifiably** *adv.* **verification** (-fikā´shən) *n.* **verifier** *n.*

†verily (ver´ili) *adv.* in very truth, assuredly.

verisimilitude (verisimil´itūd) *n.* **1** the appearance of or resemblance to truth. **2** probability, likelihood. **3** something apparently true or a fact. **verisimilar** (-sim´-) *a.*

verism (ver´izm, viə´-) *n.* extreme naturalism in art or literature. **verismo** (veriz´mō) *n.* realism, esp. in late 19th-cent. opera.

verity (ver´iti) *n.* (*pl.* **verities**) **1** truth, correspondence (of a statement) with fact. **2** a true statement, truth. **3** a thing really existent, a fact. **veritable** *a.* **1** rightly or justifiably so called. **2** real, genuine. **veritably** *adv.*

verjuice (vœ´joos) *n.* **1** an acid liquid expressed from crab apples, unripe grapes etc. and used in cooking and for other purposes. **2** sourness of temper, crabbiness. **verjuiced** *a.*

vermeil (vœ´mil) *n.* **1** silver gilt. **2** an orange-red garnet. **3** (*poet.*) vermilion. *~a.* (*poet.*) vermilion.

vermi- (vœ´mi), **verm-** *comb. form* of or relating to worms.

vermicelli (vœmichel´i, -sel´i) *n.* **1** a pasta in the form of long slender tubes or threads like macaroni. **2** CHOCOLATE VERMICELLI (under CHOCOLATE).

vermicide (vœ´misīd) *n.* a medicine or drug that kills worms, an anthelmintic.

vermicular (vəmik´ūlə) *a.* **1** (*Med.*) of or relating to worms; caused by intestinal worms. **2** resembling the motion or track of a worm. **3** tortuous, marked with intricate wavy lines (of reticulated work etc.). **4** vermiform. **vermiculate** (-lət) *a.* **1** worm-eaten. **2** vermicular. **vermiculite** (vœmik´ūlīt) *n.* **1** any of a group of hydrated silicates resulting from the alteration of mica, which expand and exfoliate when heated. **2** flakes of this material used as insulation or a medium for growing plants.

vermiform (vœ´mifawm) *a.* worm-shaped. **vermiform appendix** *n.* a small wormlike organ of no known function situated at the extremity of the caecum.

vermifuge (vœ´mifūj) *n.* a medicine or drug that destroys or expels intestinal worms, an anthelmintic.

vermilion (vəmil´yən) *n.* **1** a brilliant red pigment consisting of mercuric sulphide, obtained by grinding cinnabar or by the chemical treatment of mercury and sulphur. **2** the colour of this. **3** cinnabar. *~a.* of a brilliant red colour. *~v.t.* to colour with or as with vermilion.

vermin (vœ´min) *n.* **1** (*collect.*) certain harmful or troublesome animals, such as the smaller mammals or birds injurious to crops or game, noxious or offensive insects, grubs or worms, esp. lice, fleas etc. **2** (*collect.*) low, despicable or repulsive persons. **3** an obnoxious person. **verminous** *a.* **1** infested with vermin. **2** like vermin, troublesome, repulsive, obnoxious. **verminously** *adv.*

vermouth (vœ´məth) *n.* a drink consisting of wine flavoured with wormwood and other aromatic herbs.

vernacular (vənak´ūlə) *n.* **1** the native language or dialect of a particular place or country. **2** the language or idiom of a particular group of people. **3** plain, unvarnished speech. **4** a vernacular style of building. ~*a.* **1** of or relating to the vernacular language. **2** (*Archit.*) in the indigenous style of ordinary houses rather than of monumental buildings. **3** (of the names of plants and animals) common, not Latin. **vernacularism** *n.* **vernacularity** (-lar´i-) *n.* **vernacularize, vernacularise** *v.t.* **vernacularization** (-zā´shən) *n.* **vernacularly** *adv.*

vernal (vœ´nəl) *a.* **1** of or relating to, prevailing, done or appearing in spring. **2** of or relating to youth. **vernal equinox** *n.* the spring equinox. **vernal grass** *n.* a fragrant grass, *Anthoxanthum odoratum*, sown among hay. **vernalize, vernalise** *v.t.* to treat (seeds), usu. by cooling, before sowing in order to hasten flowering. **vernalization** (-zā´shən) *n.* **vernally** *adv.* **vernation** (-nā´shən) *n.* (*Bot.*) the arrangement of the young leaves within the leaf bud.

vernier (vœ´niə) *n.* a movable scale for measuring fractional portions of the divisions of the scale on a measuring instrument, a barometer, theodolite etc. **vernier engine, vernier rocket** *n.* a thruster for making slight adjustments to the movement or direction of a space vehicle.

Veronal® (ver´ənəl) *n.* a hypnotic drug, diethyl-barbituric acid, also called barbitone.

veronica (vəron´ikə) *n.* **1** a herb or shrub of the genus *Veronica*, with blue, purple or white flowers; the speedwell. **2** a handkerchief or cloth bearing a portrait of Christ, esp. that of St Veronica said to have been miraculously impressed with the image of his face. **3** in bullfighting, a movement of the matador's cape away from the onrushing bull.

verruca (vəroo´kə) *n.* (*pl.* **verrucae** (-sē), **verrucas**) **1** a wart, esp. a contagious wart on the sole of the foot. **2** (*Biol.*) a wartlike growth. **verrucose** (-kōs), **verrucous** *a.*

vers (veə) *n.* verse. **vers libre** (lē´brə) *n.* free verse.

versatile (vœ´sətīl) *a.* **1** readily adapting or applying oneself to new tasks, occupations, subjects etc., many-sided. **2** (of a device) having many different uses. **3** (*Zool., Bot.*) (of anthers, antennae etc.) moving freely round or to and fro on its support. **versatilely** *adv.* **versatility** (-til´-) *n.*

verse (vœs) *n.* **1** metrical composition as distinct from prose. **2** a particular type of metrical composition. **3** a metrical line consisting of a certain number of feet. **4** a group of metrical lines, a stanza. **5** any one of the short divisions of a chapter of the Bible. **6** a short sentence in a liturgy etc. ~*v.t.* to express in verse. **verset** (-sit) *n.* (*Mus.*) a short organ interlude or prelude. **versicle** (-sikəl) *n.* a short verse, esp. one of a series recited in divine service by the minister alternately with the people. **versicular** (-sik´ū-) *a.* **versify** (-sifī) *v.t.* (*3rd pers. sing. pres.* **versifies,** *pres.p.* **versifying,** *past, p.p.* **versified**) **1** to turn (prose) into verse. **2** to narrate or express in verse. ~*v.i.* to make verses. **versification** (-fikā´shən) *n.* **versifier** *n.*

versed (vœst) *a.* **1** skilled, familiar, experienced, proficient (in). **2** (*Math.*) (of sines) turned about, reversed. **versed sine** *n.* (*Math.*) a trigonometric function equal to one minus the cosine.

versin (vœ´sin), **versine** (-sīn) *n.* (*Math.*) a versed sine.

version (vœ´shən) *n.* **1** a statement, account or description of something from a person's particular point of view. **2** a variant form of something. **3** a translation of a work from one language into another. **4** the adaptation of a work of art into another medium. **5** a piece of translation, esp. the rendering of a passage into another language as a school exercise. **6** (*Med.*) the turning of a child in the womb to facilitate delivery. **versional** *a.*

verso (vœ´sō) *n.* (*pl.* **versos**) **1** a left-hand page of a book lying open. **2** the back of a sheet of printed or manuscript paper. **3** the other side of a coin or medal to that on which the head appears.

verst (vœst) *n.* a Russian measure of length, 3500.64 ft., nearly two-thirds of a mile (about 1 km).

versus (vœ´səs) *prep.* against.

vertebra (vœ´tibrə) *n.* (*pl.* **vertebrae** (-brē)) **1** any one of the bony segments of which the spine or backbone consists. **2** (*pl.*) the backbone. **vertebral** *a.* **vertebrally** *adv.* **vertebrate** (-brət) *n.* an animal with a backbone belonging to the subphylum Vertebrata, which includes fishes, amphibians, reptiles, birds and mammals. ~*a.* of or relating to the Vertebrata. **vertebrated** (-brātid) *a.* **vertebration** (-brā´shən) *n.* division into vertebrae or segments resembling vertebrae.

vertex (vœ´teks) *n.* (*pl.* **vertices** (-tisēz), **vertexes**) **1** the highest point, the top, summit, or apex. **2** (*Geom.*) **a** the meeting point of the lines of an angle. **b** each angular point of a polygon, polyhedron etc. **c** the point of intersection of a curve with its axis. **3** (*Anat.*) the top of the arch of the skull.

vertical (vœ´tikəl) *a.* **1** perpendicular to the plane of the horizon. **2** extending in a perpendicular direction, running from the top to the bottom of something. **3** of, relating to, or situated at the vertex or highest point. **4** situated at or passing through the zenith. **5** (*Anat.*) of or relating to the vertex of the head. **6** involving the various successive stages in a production process or all the various levels in a hierarchical structure. ~*n.* a perpendicular line or plane. **vertical angles** *n.pl.* (*Math.*) either pair of opposite angles made by two intersecting lines. **vertical fin** *n.* (*Zool.*) any of the fins situated in the median line, the dorsal, anal and caudal fins. **verticality** (-kal´-), **verticalness** *n.* **vertically** *adv.* **vertical plane** *n.* a plane passing through the zenith perpendicular to the horizon. **vertical take-off** *n.* the take-off of an aeroplane without a preliminary run or taxiing. **vertical thinking** *n.* deductive reasoning. **verticil** (vœ´tisil) *n.* (*Bot., Zool.*) a whorl, an arrangement of parts in a circle round a stem etc. **vertigo** (vœ´tigō) *n.* giddiness, dizziness, a feeling as if one were whirling round. **vertiginous** (-tij´i-) *a.* **1** of, relating to or causing vertigo. **2** dizzy, giddy. **vertiginously** *adv.* **vertiginousness** *n.*

vertu VIRTU.

vervain (vœ´vān) *n.* a wild plant or weed, with small purplish flowers, of the genus *Verbena*, esp. *V. officinalis*, formerly credited with medical and other properties.

verve (vœv) *n.* spirit, enthusiasm, energy, esp. in literary or artistic creation.

vervet (vœ´vit) *n.* a small S African monkey, *Cercopithecus aethiops*, usu. black-speckled greyish-green, with reddish-white face and abdomen.

very (ver´i) *adv.* **1** (used as an intensifier) in a high degree, greatly, extremely. **2** (used for emphasis with superlative adjective or *own, same*) absolutely, truly, as in *at the very earliest, their very own words, the very same day.* ~*a.* (*comp.* †**verier,** *superl.* †**veriest**) **1** actual, precise (*her very words, this very day, the very thing we needed*). **2** absolute (*the very bottom*). **3** mere (*the very thought, his very name struck terror into their hearts*). **very good** used to indicate assent or approval. **very well** used to indicate assent or approval. **very high frequency** *n.* a radio frequency between 30 and 300 megahertz; this frequency band. **very low frequency** *n.* a radio frequency between 3 and 30 kilohertz; this frequency band. **Very Reverend** *n.* the title of a dean and of the superiors of some religious orders. **Very light** (ver´i) *n.* a flare for lighting up the surroundings or for signalling. **Very pistol** *n.* a pistol for firing Very lights.

vesica (ves´ikə, vē´-) *n.* (*pl.* **vesicae** (-sē)) **1** (*Anat.*) a bladder, cyst etc., the gall bladder, the urinary bladder. **2** a vesica piscis. **vesical** *a.* **vesicant, vesicatory** *n.* (*pl.* **vesicants, vesicatories**) **1** a blister-producing counterirritant. **2** a poison gas that causes blisters. ~*a.* producing blisters. **vesica piscis** (pis´kis), **vesica piscium** (pis´kium) *n.* the elliptic aureole with which medieval painters or sculptors sometimes surrounded the figures of Christ or the saints. **vesicle** (ves´ikəl, vē-) *n.* **1** (*Anat., Biol.*) a small fluid-filled bladder or sac. **2** (*Bot.*) a bladder-like cavity in seaweed, filled with air. **3** (*Geol.*) a rounded cavity in a rock, formed by the expansion of gases present in the original magma. **4** (*Med.*) a blister. **vesicular** (-sik´ūlə) *a.* **vesiculation** (-lā´shən) *n.*

vesper (ves´pə) *n.* **1** (*poet.*) evening. **2** (*pl.*) in the Roman Catholic and Greek Churches, the sixth of the seven canonical hours. **3** (*pl.*) the evening service. ~*a.* of or relating to the evening or to vespers.

vessel (ves´əl) *n.* **1** a hollow receptacle, esp. for holding liquids, as a jug, cup, dish, bottle, barrel etc. **2** a ship or craft of any kind, esp. one of some size. **3** (*Anat.*) a tube, a duct, or canal in which the blood or other fluids are conveyed. **4** (*Bot.*) a canal or duct formed by the breaking down of the partitions between cells. **5** (*formal or facet.*) a person regarded as receiving or containing a particular thing (grace, wrath etc.).

vest (vest) *n.* **1** an undergarment for the upper part of the body, a singlet. **2** (*N Am., Austral.*) a waistcoat. **3** a (usu. V-shaped) piece on the front of the bodice of a dress. ~*v.t.* **1** to invest or endow (with authority, etc.). **2** to confer an immediate fixed right of present or future possession of (property in a person). **3** (*poet.*) to clothe with or as with a garment. ~*v.i.* **1** (of property, a right etc.) to come into the possession (of a person). **2** (of a priest etc.) to put on vestments. **vested** *a.* (*Law*) held by or fixed in a person, not subject to contingency. **vested interest** *n.* **1** (*Law*) an existing and disposable right to the immediate or future possession of property. **2** a particular and personal interest in something, often in the continuance of an existing state of affairs, usually involving an expectation of financial gain. **3** (*often pl.*) a person or group having such an interest. **vestee** (-tē´) *n.* (*N Am.*) a vest of a bodice or dress. **vest-pocket** *a.* (*N Am.*) small enough to fit into a waistcoat pocket; very small.

vesta (ves´tə) *n.* (*pl.* **vestas**) (*Hist.*) a wax match igniting by friction.

vestal (ves´təl) *a.* **1** of or relating to the goddess Vesta or the vestal virgins. **2** pure, chaste. ~*n.* **1** a vestal virgin. **2** a woman of spotless chastity. **vestal virgin** *n.* any one of the virgin priestesses, vowed to perpetual chastity, who had charge of the temple of Vesta at Rome, and of the sacred fire which burned perpetually on her altar.

vestibule (ves´tibūl) *n.* **1** a small hall, lobby or antechamber next to the outer door of a house, from which doors open into the various inner rooms. **2** a porch. **3** (*N Am.*) a covered passage between the cars in a corridor train. **4** (*Anat.*) a chamber, cavity or channel communicating with others, such as the central chamber of the labyrinth of the ear. **vestibular** (-tib´-) *a.* **vestibuled** *a.*

vestige (ves´tij) *n.* **1** a sign, a mark or trace of something no longer present or in existence. **2** a small piece, a particle. **vestigial** (-tij´-) *a.* **1** of or being a vestige, very small or slight. **2** (*Biol.*) (of an organ) having degenerated and nearly or entirely lost its function in the course of evolution.

vestment (vest´mənt) *n.* **1** any of the ritual garments of the clergy, choristers etc., esp. a chasuble. **2** a garment, esp. a robe of state or office.

vestry (ves´tri) *n.* (*pl.* **vestries**) **1** a room or place attached to a church in which the vestments are kept and in which the clergy, choristers etc. robe. 2 a room attached to a church, used for meetings, Sunday schools etc. **vestral** a.

vet[1] (vet) n. short for VETERINARY SURGEON (under VETERINARY). ~v.t. (pres.p. **vetting**, past, p.p. **vetted**) 1 to subject to careful scrutiny and appraisal. 2 to treat or cure (an animal) as a vet.

vet[2] (vet) n. (N Am.) short for VETERAN.

vetch (vech) n. a plant of the genus Vicia of the bean family, including several wild and cultivated species used for forage, esp. the common vetch or tare. **vetchling** (-ling) n. a plant of the genus Lathyrus, allied to the vetches. **vetchy** a.

veteran (vet´ərən) a. 1 grown old or experienced, esp. in the military service. 2 of or relating to veterans. ~n. 1 a person who has had long experience in any service, occupation or art, esp. as a soldier. 2 (N Am.) an ex-serviceman or ex-servicewoman. **veteran car** n. a motor car built before 1916 (and esp. before 1905).

veterinary (vet´ərinəri) a. of or relating to treatment of the diseases of animals, esp. domestic or farm animals such as cows, horses, dogs etc. ~n. (pl. **veterinaries**) a veterinary surgeon. **veterinarian** (-neə´ri-) n. (N Am.) a veterinary surgeon. **veterinary surgeon** n. a person qualified to diagnose and treat diseases and injuries in animals.

Usage note Pronunciation as (vet´nəri) is best avoided.

vetiver (vet´ivə) n. khus-khus grass and root.

veto (vē´tō) n. (pl. **vetoes**) 1 the power or right of a sovereign, president, or branch of a legislature to negative the enactments of another branch. 2 the act of exercising such right. 3 a document or message conveying a rejection. 4 any authoritative prohibition, refusal, negative, or interdict. ~v.t. (3rd pers. sing. pres. **vetoes**, pres.p. **vetoing**, past, p.p. **vetoed**) 1 to refuse approval to (a bill etc.). 2 to prohibit, to forbid. **vetoer** n. **vetoless** a.

vex (veks) v.t. 1 to cause trouble or annoyance to, to irritate. 2 (poet.) to agitate, to throw (the sea etc.) into commotion. **vexation** (-ā´shən) n. 1 the act of vexing or the state of being vexed, irritation, annoyance, trouble. 2 that which causes irritation, an annoyance. **vexatious** (-ā´shəs) a. 1 making one feel annoyed. 2 (Law) (of a legal action) undertaken on insufficient grounds merely to harass or cause annoyance, embarrassment etc. to the defendant. **vexatiously** adv. **vexatiousness** n. **vexed** a. 1 annoyed, worried, filled with vexation. 2 (of a question or doctrine) much debated or contested. **vexedly** (-sid-) adv. **vexer** n. **vexing** a. **vexingly** adv.

VG abbr. Vicar-General.

vg abbr. very good.

VGA abbr. video graphics array.

vgc abbr. very good condition.

VHF abbr. very high frequency.

VI abbr. Virgin Islands.

via (vī´ə, vē´ə) adv. by way of, through.

viable (vī´əbəl) a. 1 likely to become actual or to succeed, practicable, feasible. 2 (Biol.) capable of normal growth and development. 3 (Med.) (of a foetus etc.) capable of maintaining independent existence, able to survive. **viability** (-bil´-) n.

viaduct (vī´ədŭkt) n. 1 a bridgelike structure, esp. one composed of masonry and a considerable number of arches carrying a road or railway over a valley etc. 2 a road or railway on such a structure.

vial (vī´əl) n. a small vessel, usu. cylindrical and of glass, for holding liquid medicines etc.

viand (vī´ənd) n. (formal) 1 an article of food. 2 (pl.) provisions, victuals.

viaticum (vīat´ikəm) n. (pl. **viatica** (-kə), **viaticums**) the Eucharist as given to a person at the point of death.

vibes (vībz) n.pl. (coll.) 1 feelings, intuitions or sensations experienced or communicated. 2 the vibraphone.

vibrant (vīb´rənt) a. 1 vibrating, tremulous. 2 thrilling, exciting. 3 resonant. 4 (of colour) very bright and eye-catching. **vibrancy** n. **vibrantly** adv.

vibraphone (vīb´rəfōn) n. a percussion instrument similar to a xylophone but with metal bars placed over electronic resonators. **vibraphonist** n.

vibrate (vībrāt´) v.i. 1 to move to and fro rapidly, to swing, to oscillate. 2 to thrill, to quiver, to throb. 3 (Physics) to move to and fro ceaselessly, esp. with great rapidity. 4 (of a sound) to resound, to ring. ~v.t. 1 to cause to swing, oscillate or quiver. 2 to send out or give off in vibrations. **vibration** (-rā´shən) n. 1 the act of vibrating. 2 oscillation. 3 (Physics) rapid motion backward and forward, esp. of the parts of an elastic solid or of a liquid the equilibrium of which has been disturbed. 4 one such complete movement. 5 (pl., coll.) feelings communicated instinctively or occultly from person to person; an atmosphere communicated or feelings aroused by a person, place etc. 6 a trembling movement. 7 the resounding or ringing of a sound. **vibrational** a. **vibrative** (vī´-) a. **vibrator** n. 1 a vibrating electrical apparatus used in massage or to provide sexual stimulation. 2 a vibrating conductor used to chop a continuous current and thus produce an alternating current. 3 (Mus.) a reed, as in a reed-organ. **vibratory** (vī´-) a.

vibrato (vibrah´tō) n. (Mus.) a pulsating effect, esp. in singing or string-playing, produced by the rapid variation of emphasis on the same tone.

vibrio (vib´riō) n. (pl. **vibrios**, **vibriones** (-ō´nēz)) (Biol., Med.) a bacterium of the genus Vibrio, more or less screw-shaped with a filament at each end, such as that causing cholera.

viburnum (vībœ´nəm) n. (pl. **viburnums**) a shrub or small tree of a genus Viburnum, containing the guelder rose and the laurustinus etc., of the honeysuckle family.

vicar (vik´ə) n. **1** in the Church of England, the priest in charge of a parish. **2** in other Anglican Churches, a member of the clergy deputizing for another. **3** in the Roman Catholic Church, a bishop's deputy or representative. **4** a substitute or deputy. **vicarage** (-rij) n. **1** the house or residence of a vicar. **2** the benefice of a vicar. **vicar apostolic** n. in the Roman Catholic Church, a titular bishop appointed where no episcopate has been established etc. **vicar-general** n, (pl. **vicars-general**) **1** in the Roman Catholic Church, an officer appointed by a bishop as his assistant, esp. in matters of jurisdiction. **2** in the Church of England, an officer assisting a bishop or archbishop in ecclesiastical causes and visitations. **vicarial** (-keə´ri-) a. **vicarship** n.

vicarious (vikeə´riəs, vī-) a. **1** experienced at second hand by imaginative or sympathetic participation in the pleasure, satisfaction etc. of someone else. **2** performed, done or suffered for or instead of another. **3** deputed, delegated. **4** acting on behalf of another. **vicariously** adv. **vicariousness** n.

vice[1] (vīs) n. **1** an evil or immoral practice or habit. **2** evil conduct, gross immorality, depravity. **3** a particular form of such conduct, esp. prostitution. **4** a fault, a blemish, a defect. **5** a bad habit or trick in a horse. **vice ring** n. a group of criminals involved in organizing prostitution. **vice squad** n. a police department assigned to enforce the law on prostitution, gambling etc.

vice[2] (vīs), (NAm. also) **vise** n. an instrument with two jaws, brought together by a screw or lever, between which an object may be clamped securely. ~v.t. to secure in or as in a vice. **vicelike** a.

vice- (vīs) pref. forming nouns denoting a person acting or qualified to act in place of another or next in rank below another. **vice-admiral** n. a naval officer next in rank below an admiral, and next above a rear-admiral. **vice-chamberlain** n. a deputy chamberlain, esp. the Lord Chamberlain's deputy. **vice-chancellor** n. **1** a deputy chancellor. **2** the chief administrative officer at most British universities. **vice-president** n. an official ranking next below a president and often serving as the latter's deputy. **vice-presidency** n. (pl. **vice-presidencies**). **vice-presidential** a.

vicegerent (vīsjer´ənt) a. having or exercising delegated power. ~n. an officer exercising delegated authority, a deputy. **vicegerency** n. (pl. **vicegerencies**).

viceroy (vīs´roi) n. a ruler exercising authority in a colony, province etc. in the name of a sovereign or government. **viceregal** (-rē´-) a. of or relating to a viceroy. **vicereine** (vīs´rān) n. **1** the wife of a viceroy. **2** a woman viceroy. **viceroyalty** n. (pl. **viceroyalties**) **1** the office of a viceroy. **2** the territory governed by a viceroy. **3** the term of office of a viceroy. **viceroyship** n.

vice versa (vīsi vœ´sə, vīs) adv. the order or relation being inverted, the other way round.

vichyssoise (vēshiswahz´) n. a cream soup usu. served chilled, with ingredients such as leeks and potatoes. **Vichy water** n. an effervescent mineral water found at Vichy.

vicinage (vis´inij) n. (formal) **1** neighbourhood, vicinity, surrounding places, environs. **2** nearness, closeness. **vicinal** a. **1** near, neighbouring. **2** of or relating to a particular neighbourhood.

vicinity (visin´iti) n. (pl. **vicinities**) **1** the neighbourhood, the adjoining or surrounding district. **2** the state of being near, proximity. **3** near relationship (to). **in the vicinity** nearby.

vicious (vish´əs) a. **1** likely, disposed or intended to attack, hurt or wound. **2** bad-tempered, spiteful, malignant. **3** ferocious, violent. **4** characterized by some vice, fault or blemish; imperfect, defective, incorrect, corrupt. **5** (formal) addicted to vice, depraved, wicked. **6** (formal) contrary to moral principles or to rectitude. **vicious circle** n. **1** a situation in which progressing from cause to effect or from problem to solution merely brings one back to one's starting point and aggravates the original state of things. **2** circular reasoning, providing a proof or explanation for something which depends for its truth or validity on the truth or validity of the thing one is setting out to prove or explain. **viciously** adv. **viciousness** n.

vicissitude (visis´itūd) n. **1** a change of condition, circumstances or fortune, a mutation, a revolution. **2** (poet.) regular change or mutation. **vicissitudinary** (-tū´-), **vicissitudinous** (-tū´-) a.

victim (vik´tim) n. **1** a person killed or injured as a result of an event such as an accident or epidemic. **2** a person or thing destroyed or injured in the pursuit of some object. **3** a dupe, a prey. **4** a living creature sacrificed to some deity or in the performance of some religious rite. **victimize, victimise** v.t. **1** to single out for harsh treatment or unfair punishment. **2** to make a victim of. **victimization** (-zā´shən) n. **victimizer** n.

victor (vik´tə) n. a person, organization, nation etc. that conquers in battle or wins in a contest. **victorious** (-taw´ri-) a. **1** having conquered in a battle or any contest, triumphant. **2** associated or connected with victory. **victoriously** adv. **victoriousness** n. **victor ludorum** (loodaw´rəm) n. the overall champion in a sports competition, esp. at a school. **victory** n. (pl. **victories**) the defeat of an enemy in battle or war, or of an opponent in a contest. **victory roll** n. a roll performed by an aircraft to celebrate a victory in aerial combat. **victory sign** n. the first and second fingers extended in the form of a V. **victress** (-tris), **victrix** (-triks) n. (pl. **victresses**, **victrices** (-trisēz, -trī´sēz), **victrixes**) (formal) a female victor. **victrix ludorum** n. a female victor ludorum.

victoria (viktaw´riə) n. **1** a four-wheeled carriage

with a raised seat for the driver, seats for two persons over the back axle and a low seat for two persons over the front axle, and a collapsible top. **2** (*also* **victoria plum**) a large red plum. **Victoria Cross** *n.* a British military decoration in the shape of a Maltese cross, instituted by Queen Victoria (1856), bestowed for conspicuous bravery or devotion in the presence of the enemy. **Victorian** *a.* of, relating to, flourishing or living in the reign of Queen Victoria. ~*n.* **1** a person, esp. a writer, living or flourishing then. **2** a native of Victoria, Australia. **Victorianism** *n.* **victoriana** (-ah´nə) *n.pl.* objects, ornaments etc. of the Victorian period. **Victoria sandwich, Victoria sponge** *n.* a cake consisting of two layers of sponge with jam in between.

victual (vit´əl) *n.* (*usu. in pl.*) food, provisions. ~*v.t.* (*pres.p.* **victualling,** (*N Am.*) **victualing,** *past, p.p.* **victualled,** (*N Am.*) **victualed**) to supply or store with provisions. ~*v.i.* **1** to lay in provisions. **2** to take food, to eat. **victualler,** (*N Am.*) **victualer** *n.* **1** a person who supplies victuals, esp. an innkeeper. **2** a victualling ship. **victualless** *a.*

vicuña (vikoon´yə), **vicuna** (vikū´nə) *n.* **1** a S American animal, *Vicugna vicugna*, allied to the camel, a native of the Andean regions of Bolivia and N Chile. **2** a fine cloth made from its wool or an imitation made of worsted yarn.

vide (vid´ā, vē´-, vī´di) *int.* (as an instruction in a book) see, consult.

videlicet (vidē´liset, -dā´liket) *adv.* namely, that is to say, to wit (usu. abbreviated to *viz.*).

video (vid´iō) *n.* (*pl.* **videos**) **1** a video recorder. **2** a video recording. **3** the process of recording, reproducing or broadcasting visual images on magnetic tape or disc. **4** the visual elements of television. **5** (*N Am., coll.*) television. ~*a.* **1** relating to the process of recording, reproducing or broadcasting visual images on magnetic tape or disc. **2** relating to or employed in the transmission or reception of a televised image. ~*v.t., v.i.* (*3rd pers. sing. pres.* **videos,** *pres.p.* **videoing,** *past, p.p.* **videoed**) to make a video recording (of). **video camera** *n.* a camera which records its film on videotape or transmits images to a monitor. **video cassette** *n.* a cassette containing videotape. **video cassette recorder** *n.* a video recorder that takes cassettes. **videoconference** *n.* a live discussion between participants in different locations who are linked by audio and video communications. **videoconferencing** *n.* **video diary** *n.* a record of events filmed on videotape usu. by a layperson with a camcorder. **videodisc** *n.* a disc from which television pictures and sound can be played back. **video film** *n.* a film recorded on videotape. **videofit** *n.* a picture similar to an Identikit constructed on a screen by selecting and combining facial features in accordance with witnesses' descriptions, usu. of a suspect sought by the police. **video game** *n.* an electronically operated

game played by means of a visual display unit. **video nasty** *n.* (*pl.* **video nasties**) a video film which includes horrific or gruesome scenes of violence, sexual outrage or other atrocities. **videophone, video telephone** *n.* a telephone which can also transmit a picture of each speaker. **video recorder** *n.* a machine for recording and playing back television broadcasts or for playing films made on videotape. **video recording** *n.* **videotape** *n.* **1** magnetic tape used for recording television pictures and sound for subsequent transmission or reproduction. **2** a length of this tape, esp. a video cassette. **3** a recording made on this tape. ~*v.t.* to record on videotape.

vie (vī) *v.i.* (*3rd pers. sing. pres.* **vies,** *pres.p.* **vying,** *past, p.p.* **vied**) **1** to strive for superiority, to contend, to compete (with). **2** to rival, to be equal or superior (with or in). **vying** *a.*

Viennese (vēənēz´) *a.* of or relating to Vienna or its inhabitants. ~*n.* (*pl.* **Viennese**) **1** a native or inhabitant of Vienna. **2** (*pl.*) the people of Vienna.

Vietnamese (vietnəmēz´) *a.* of or relating to Vietnam in SE Asia, its people or their language. ~*n.* (*pl.* **Vietnamese**) **1** a native or inhabitant of Vietnam. **2** (*pl.*) the people of Vietnam. **3** the language of Vietnam.

view (vū) *n.* **1** sight, range of vision. **2** that which is seen, a scene, a prospect. **3** a picture or drawing of this. **4** survey or examination by the eye. **5** an intellectual or mental survey. **6** the manner or mode of looking at things, considering a matter etc. **7** judgement, opinion, theory. **8** intention, purpose, design. **9** inspection by a jury etc. ~*v.t.* **1** to examine with the eye, look over, inspect. **2** to survey mentally or intellectually. **3** to consider, to form a mental impression or judgement of. **4** to watch on television. ~*v.i.* to watch television. **in view 1** in sight. **2** in mind when forming an opinion. **3** as one's object or aim. **in view of** considering, having regard to. **on view** open to public inspection. **with a view to 1** with the intention of. **2** in hopes or anticipation of. **viewable** *a.* **1** able to be seen or inspected. **2** worth watching. **viewdata** *n.* a communications system by which data can be transferred through a telephone line and displayed on TV or video. **viewer** *n.* **1** a person who views something. **2** a person who watches television; a member of a particular television audience. **3** a device with a magnifying lens for looking at transparencies. **viewership** *n.* the (estimated) audience watching a particular TV programme or channel. **viewfinder** *n.* a device of mirrors in a camera which shows the view to be taken. **viewgraph** *n.* a graph produced on a transparency for projection on to a screen or use in a videoconference. **view halloo** *n.* a huntsman's shout on seeing the fox break cover. **viewing** *n.* **1** an opportunity to view, inspect or look over. **2** watching television. **viewless** *a.* **1**

not affording a view or prospect. **2** not having an opinion. **viewpoint** *n.* **1** a point of view. **2** a place for viewing.

vigesimal (vijes´iməl) *a.* **1** relating to or based on the number twenty. **2** taking place or proceeding by intervals of twenty.

vigil (vij´il) *n.* **1** keeping awake during the customary hours of rest, watchfulness. **2** a period of watchfulness. **3** a demonstration in support of a cause in which the demonstrators usu. stand in silence for a long time in or outside a particular place. **4** the eve of a festival. **5** a religious service held at night, esp. on the eve of a festival, orig. the watch kept on the night before a feast. **vigilance** *n.* the state of being vigilant. **vigilance committee** *n.* (*N Am.*) a self-organized committee for maintaining order or inflicting summary justice in an ill-ordered community or district. **vigilant** *a.* **1** awake and on the alert. **2** watchful, wary, circumspect. **vigilantly** *adv.* **vigilante** (-lan´ti) *n.* **1** a self-appointed upholder of law and order or administerer of justice. **2** (*N Am.*) a member of a vigilance committee. **vigilantism** (-lan´tizm) *n.*

vigneron (vēn´yərō) *n.* a wine-grower.

vignette (vinyet´) *n.* **1** a short descriptive essay or sketch. **2** a similar descriptive or evocative scene in a film or play. **3** an engraving not enclosed within a definite border, esp. on the title page of a book. **4** a photograph, drawing or other portrait showing the head and shoulders with a background shading off gradually. ~*v.t.* **1** to shade off (a portrait, drawing etc.) gradually. **2** to make a photograph or portrait of in this style. **vignettist** *n.*

vigour (vig´ə), (*N Am.*) **vigor** *n.* **1** active physical or mental strength or energy. **2** healthy condition or growth, robustness. **3** force, power, intensity. **4** forcefulness, trenchancy. **vigorous** *a.* **1** active, vital and strong. **2** healthy, robust. **3** energetic and enthusiastic in undertaking an activity. **4** (of an activity) undertaken with great energy and enthusiasm. **vigorously** *adv.* **vigorousness** *n.* **vigourless** *a.*

Viking (vī´king) *n.* any of the Scandinavian seafaring warriors of the 8th 11th cents., who raided and colonized large parts of N and W Europe.

vile (vīl) *a.* **1** foul, disgusting. **2** depraved, abominably wicked, odious. **3** morally base, despicable, abject. **4** (*coll.*) very bad or unpleasant, abominable. **vilely** *adv.* **vileness** *n.*

vilify (vil´ifī) *v.t.* (*3rd pers. sing. pres.* **vilifies**, *pres.p.* **vilifying**, *past, p.p.* **vilified**) to say unpleasant things about. **vilification** (-fikā´shən) *n.* **vilifier** *n.*

villa (vil´ə) *n.* **1** in ancient Rome, a country house or farmhouse with subsidiary buildings on an estate. **2** a large detached or semi-detached suburban house. **3** a large house in the country. **4** a sizeable property usu. in a holiday resort, for rent as a holiday home.

village (vil´ij) *n.* **1** a small assemblage of houses, smaller than a town or city and larger than a hamlet. **2** the inhabitants of such a community. **3** any area or community within a town or city having a distinctive character and some of the close-knit qualities of a village. **4** (*N Am.*) an incorporated municipality smaller than a town. **5** (*Austral.*) an upmarket suburban shopping centre. **village idiot** *n.* (*offensive*) a person in a village community noted for mental disability, stupidity etc. **villager** *n.* an inhabitant of a village.

villain (vil´ən) *n.* **1** a person guilty or capable of crime or great wickedness. **2** the principal wicked character in a play, book, film etc. **3** (*coll., usu. facet.*) a rogue, a rascal. **4** (*sl.*) a criminal. **villain of the piece** *n.* the principal wicked character. **villainous** *a.* **1** worthy or characteristic of a villain, depraved, vile. **2** very bad. **villainously** *adv.* **villainousness** *n.* **villainy** *n.* (*pl.* **villainies**) **1** villainous behaviour. **2** a villainous act.

Usage note See note under VILLEIN.

-ville (vil) *comb. form* (*sl.*) a place, condition or quality with a character as specified, e.g. *dullsville, dragsville, squaresville.*

villein (vil´ən, -ān) *n.* (*Hist.*) a feudal serf, a bondsman attached to a feudal lord or to an estate. **villeinage** (-ij) *n.* **1** the status or condition of a villein. **2** the form of tenure whereby a villein held land.

Usage note The spellings of the nouns *villein* (a feudal serf) and *villain* (a scoundrel) should not be confused.

villus (vil´əs) *n.* (*pl.* **villi** (-lī)) **1** (*Anat.*) any of the short hairlike or finger-like processes on certain membranes, such as those on the inner surface of the small intestine. **2** (*pl., Bot.*) long, close, soft hairs. **villose, villous** *a.*

vim (vim) *n.* (*coll.*) energy, vigour.

vinaigrette (vinigret´) *n.* **1** (*also* **vinaigrette sauce**) a salad dressing consisting of oil, vinegar and seasoning. **2** (*also* **vinegarette**) an ornamental bottle or perforated case of gold or other metal etc. for holding aromatic vinegar etc., a smelling-bottle.

vinca (ving´kə) *n.* any plant of the periwinkle genus, *Vinca.*

vincible (vin´sibəl) *a.* (*formal*) capable of being conquered, not invincible. **vincibility** (-bil´-), **vincibleness** *n.*

vindaloo (vindəloo´) *n.* a type of hot Indian curry.

vindicate (vin´dikāt) *v.t.* **1** to clear from blame, suspicion, criticism etc. **2** to prove to be true or valid, to justify. **3** to maintain (a claim, statement etc.) against attack or denial. **4** to defend (a person) against reproach, accusation etc. **vindicable** *a.* **vindication** (-ā´shən) *n.* **vindicative** (-dikātiv, -dik´ətiv) *a.* **vindicator** *n.*

vindicatory a. 1 tending to vindicate or justify. 2 punitory.

vindictive (vindik´tiv) a. 1 characterized or prompted by a desire for revenge. 2 spiteful, rancorous. **vindictive damages** n.pl. (Law) damages given to punish the defendant. **vindictively** adv. **vindictiveness** n.

vine (vīn) n. 1 a slender climbing plant of the genus Vitis, esp. V. vinifera, the grapevine. 2 any plant with a slender climbing or trailing stem. 3 the stem of such a plant. **vine-dresser** n. a person who dresses, trims or prunes vines. **vinery** (-əri) n. (pl. **vineries**) a greenhouse for vines. **vineyard** (vin´yahd, -yəd) n. a plantation of grapevines. **viny** a.

vinegar (vin´igə) n. 1 an acid liquid obtained by oxidation or acetous fermentation from wine, cider etc., used as a condiment and as a preservative in pickling. 2 anything sour or soured, as a disposition etc. **vinegarette** VINAIGRETTE. **vinegary, vinegarish** a. 1 like or flavoured with vinegar. 2 sour.

vingt-et-un (vantæœ´) n. a card game in which the object is to make the aggregate number of the pips on the cards as near as possible to 21 without exceeding this; pontoon.

vinho verde (vēnyō veə´di) n. any of a number of light, immature, sharp-tasting Portuguese wines.

vini- (vin´i), **vin-** comb. form of or relating to wine or vines.

viniculture (vin´ikŭlchə) n. the cultivation of grapevines. **vinicultural** (-kŭl´-) a. **viniculturist** (-kŭl´-) n.

vinify (vin´ifī) v.t. (3rd pers. sing. pres. **vinifies**, pres.p. **vinifying**, past, p.p. **vinified**) to convert (grape juice) into wine. **vinification** (-fikā´-shən) n.

vino (vē´nō) n. (pl. **vinos**) (coll.) wine, esp. cheap wine.

vinous (vī´nəs) a. 1 of, relating to or resembling wine. 2 indulging in or resulting from indulgence in wine. **vinosity** (-nos´iti) n.

vintage (vin´tij) n. 1 the yield of grapes or wine from a vineyard or vine district for a particular season, esp. the wine obtained in a particularly good year. 2 the process of gathering grapes. 3 the season of gathering grapes. 4 a time of origin. 5 a group of things, people etc. of the same period. 6 (poet.) wine. ~a. 1 (of wine) produced in a particularly good year. 2 representative of what is best and most typical, esp. in a person's work. 3 of an earlier period but of continuing interest. **vintage car** n. an old motor car (esp. one built between 1919 and 1930).

vintner (vint´nə) n. a wine merchant.

vinyl (vī´nil) n. 1 (Chem.) a an organic radical CH₂CH-, derived from ethylene. b any vinyl resin or plastic, esp. PVC. 2 (coll.) a gramophone record (as opposed to a tape or CD); gramophone records collectively. ~a. of or made of a vinyl resin. **vinyl resin, vinyl plastic** n. any of various thermoplastic resins, polymers or copolymers of vinyl compounds.

viol (vī´əl) n. any of a family of medieval stringed musical instruments, the predecessor of the violin family, that had six strings and were held on or between the knees and played with a curved bow. **violist**[1] (vī´əlist) n. a player on a viol.

viola[1] (viō´lə) n. 1 an instrument like a large violin, the alto instrument in the violin family tuned an octave above the cello. 2 a viola player. 3 a viol. **viola da gamba** (də gam´bə) n. a viol held between the player's legs, esp. the tenor viol from which the modern cello was developed. **viola d'amore** (damaw´rā) n. an instrument of the viol family with sympathetic strings under the fingerboard and a particularly sweet tone. **violist**[2] (viō´list) n. a player of the viola.

viola[2] (vī´ələ) n. a plant or flower of the genus Viola, containing the violet and pansy.

violate (vī´əlāt) v.t. 1 to infringe or transgress, to break, to disobey (a law, obligation, duty etc.). 2 to treat irreverently, to profane, to desecrate. 3 to break in on, to disturb rudely or violently. 4 to ravish, to rape, to subject to sexual assault. **violable** a. **violation** (-ā´shən) n. **violative** a. **violator** n.

violence (vī´ələns) n. 1 the state or quality of being violent. 2 violent treatment; the use of physical force to inflict injury or damage. 3 vehemence, intensity or impetuosity of feeling, action etc. 4 (Law) the illegal exercise of physical force; an act of intimidation by the show or threat of force. 5 stormy or windy weather. **to do violence to** 1 to do a physical injury to. 2 to distort the meaning or intent of. **violent** a. 1 acting with, or characterized by, the exertion of great physical force. 2 (of a person) tending to resort to physical force, aggressive. 3 vehement, impetuous, furious. 4 intense, abrupt, immoderate. 5 (of death etc.) produced by or resulting from extraneous force or poison, not natural. 6 involving an unlawful use of force. 7 (of weather) stormy or windy. **violently** adv.

violet (vī´ələt) n. 1 a plant or flower of the genus Viola, esp. the sweet violet, V. odorata, the dog-violet, V. riviniana, and some other species with small blue, purple or white flowers. 2 a colour seen at the opposite end of the spectrum to red, produced by a slight mixture of red with blue. 3 a pigment of this colour. ~a. of the colour of violet.

violin (vīəlin´) n. 1 a musical instrument with four strings, held under the chin and played with a bow, the most important of modern string instruments and the one with the highest pitch. 2 a player on this. **violinist** n.

violist[1] VIOL.

violist[2] VIOLA¹.

violoncello (vīələnchel´ō) n. (pl. **violoncellos**) (formal) a cello. **violoncellist** n.

VIP abbr. (a) very important person.

viper (vī´pə) *n.* **1** a venomous snake of the family Viperidae, esp. the European viper or adder, the only poisonous British snake. **2** a treacherous or malignant person. **viperiform** (-rifawm), **viperine** (-rīn), **viperous** *a.* **viper's bugloss** *n.* a bristly blue-flowered plant, *Echium vulgare*, of the borage family.

virago (virah´gō) *n.* (*pl.* **viragoes, viragos**) a bad-tempered, violent or scolding woman, a termagant, a shrew. **viraginous** (-raj´-) *a.*

viral (vī´rəl) *a.* of, relating to or caused by a virus.

virement (vīə´mənt) *n.* a transfer of funds from one account to another.

vireo (vir´iō) *n.* (*pl.* **vireos**) any American passerine insectivorous songbird of the genus *Vireo*.

virgate (vœ´gət, -gāt) *a.* (*Bot., Zool.*) long, straight and erect, rodlike.

virger VERGER.

virgin (vœ´jin) *n.* **1** a person, esp. a woman, who has never had sexual intercourse. **2** (*usu.* **Virgin**) a madonna. **3** a female insect that produces eggs without fertilization. **4** (*coll.*) a person who is inexperienced in a specified sphere or activity. ~*a.* **1** being a virgin; pure, chaste, undefiled. **2** befitting a virgin; maidenly, modest. **3** unworked, untried, not brought into cultivation. **4** (of insects) producing eggs without impregnation. **5** (of oil) obtained from the first pressing. **6** (of clay) unfired. **7** (of metal) made from ore by smelting. **8** (of wool) not yet, or only once, spun or woven. **virginal** *a.* **1** of, relating to or befitting a virgin. **2** pure, chaste, maidenly. **3** untouched, undefiled. ~*n.* (*often pl.*) a keyed musical instrument, shaped like a box, used in the 16th–17th cents., also *pair of virginals*. **virginally** *adv.* **virgin birth** *n.* **1** parthenogenesis. **2** (**Virgin Birth**) (the doctrine of) the birth of Jesus Christ from a virgin mother. **virgin forest** *n.* forest in its natural state, unexplored and unexploited by humans. **virginhood** *n.* **virginity** (-jin´iti) *n.* (*pl.* **virginities**) the state of being a virgin, purity, innocence.

Virginia (vəjin´iə) *n.* **1** tobacco from Virginia. **2** a cigarette of Virginia tobacco. **Virginia creeper** *n.* a woody vine, *Parthenocissus quinquefolia*, with ornamental foliage that turns red in autumn. **Virginian** *a.* of or relating to the state of Virginia. ~*n.* a native or inhabitant of Virginia. **Virginia reel** *n.* an American country dance; music written for this. **Virginia stock, Virginian stock** *n.* a Mediterranean cruciferous plant, *Malcolmia maritima*, that has white or pink flowers.

Virgo (vœ´gō) *n.* (*pl.* **Virgos**) **1** (*Astron.*) one of the 12 ancient zodiacal constellations, the Virgin. **2** (*Astrol.*) **a** the sixth sign of the zodiac, which the sun is in from about 23 August to 22 September. **b** a person born under this sign.

virgule (vœ´gūl) *n.* a slanting line used as a division within or between words, a solidus.

viridescent (virides´ənt) *a.* **1** greenish. **2** becoming slightly green. **viridescence** *n.* **viridian**

(-id´iən) *n.* **1** a green pigment made from a hydrated form of chromium oxide. **2** a bluish-green colour. ~*a.* of this colour.

virile (vir´īl) *a.* **1** characteristic of a man, masculine, manly; strong, forceful, vigorous. **2** (of a male) sexually potent. **3** of or relating to adult men or the male sex. **virility** (-ril´-) *n.*

viroid, virology VIRUS.

virtu (vœtoo´), **vertu** *n.* **1** a taste for or knowledge of the fine arts. **2** rare, old or beautiful objects collectively. **3** the quality of rareness or beauty. **4** intrinsic goodness or worth.

virtual (vœ´tūəl) *a.* **1** being such in effect or for practical purposes, though not in name or by strict definition; near, practical. **2** (*Comput.*) computer-simulated. **3** (*Comput.*) (of memory, storage) apparently internal but in fact consisting of data automatically transferred from back-up storage, such as a disk, into the core memory as required. **4** in mechanics, relating to an infinitesimal displacement of a point in a system. **virtuality** (-al´iti) *n.* **virtually** *adv.* **1** almost, nearly, practically. **2** in effect. **virtual reality** *n.* an image or environment generated by computer software that closely resembles reality and with which a user can interact by using a helmet, joystick or various other items of special equipment.

virtue (vœ´choo) *n.* **1** moral excellence, goodness, uprightness, rectitude. **2** a particular moral excellence. **3** a good quality or feature. **4** inherent power, goodness or efficacy. **5** (*pl.*) the seventh order of the celestial hierarchy. **by virtue of** by or through the efficacy or authority of, on the strength of. **to make a virtue of necessity** to attempt to derive some benefit from consciously opting to undertake, or undertaking with a good grace, something that one is in any event compelled to do. **virtueless** *a.* **virtuous** *a.* **1** characterized by virtue, morally good. **2** chaste. **virtuous circle** *n.* a chain of cause and effect that has beneficial consequences. **virtuously** *adv.* **virtuousness** *n.*

virtuoso (vœtūō´sō, -zō) *n.* (*pl.* **virtuosos, virtuosi** (-sē, -zē)) **1** a skilled performer in some fine art, esp. music. **2** a connoisseur of articles of virtu. ~*a.* showing great skill. **virtuosic** (-os´-) *a.* **virtuosity** (-os´-), **virtuosoship** *n.*

virulent (vir´ulənt) *a.* **1** extremely poisonous. **2** (of a micro-organism) highly infectious. **3** (of a disease) having a rapid course and severe effects. **4** extremely bitter, acrimonious or malignant. **virulence, virulency** *n.* **virulently** *adv.*

virus (vī´rəs) *n.* (*pl.* **viruses**) **1** a very small infective agent capable of self-propagation only in living matter, the causative agent of many diseases, consisting of a single nucleic acid molecule in a protein coat. **2** (*coll.*) a disease caused by this. **3** (*Comput.*) a computer virus. **4** moral taint or corrupting influence. **viroid** *n.* an infectious agent, similar to a virus but without a protein coat, known to cause certain plant diseases. **virology** (-rol´-) *n.* the study of viruses and virus diseases. **virological** (-əloj´-) *a.* **virologist** *n.*

Vis. *abbr.* viscount.

visa (vē´zə) *n.* an official endorsement on a passport showing that it has been examined and found correct, esp. one enabling the holder to travel to or through a particular country.

visage (viz´ij) *n.* (*formal*) the face, the countenance. **visaged** *a.*

vis-à-vis (vēzahvē´) *prep.* **1** in relation to. **2** opposite to; face to face with. *~adv.* face to face. *~n.* (*pl.* **vis-à-vis**) **1** a person facing another as in certain dances, e.g. a quadrille. **2** one's counterpart or opposite number.

viscacha (viskah´chə), **vizcacha** *n.* a S American burrowing rodent of the genus *Lagostomus* or *Lagidium*, related to the chinchilla.

viscera (vis´ərə) *n.pl.* the internal organs of the great cavities of the body, such as the skull, thorax, and abdomen, esp. those of the abdomen, the intestines. **visceral** *a.* **1** of or relating to the viscera. **2** instinctive or intuitive rather than reasoned.

viscid (vis´id) *a.* **1** sticky, adhesive. **2** semi-fluid in consistency. **viscidity** (-sid´-) *n.*

viscometer (viskom´itə), **viscosimeter** (-kōsim´-) *n.* an apparatus for determining the viscosity of liquids. **viscometry** (-kom´itri) *n.*

viscose (vis´kōz, -kōs) *n.* **1** the highly viscous cellulose sodium salt used in the manufacture of artificial silk. **2** rayon made from this. *~a.* viscous.

viscount (vī´kownt) *n.* a British peer ranking next below an earl, and above a baron. **viscountcy** (-si) *n.* (*pl.* **viscountcies**). **viscountess** *n.* **1** a viscount's wife. **2** a woman holding the rank of a viscount. **viscounty** *n.* (*pl.* **viscounties**).

viscous (vis´kəs) *a.* **1** (of liquids) thick and sticky. **2** semi-fluid. **3** having a high viscosity, not flowing freely. **viscosity** (-kos´iti) *n.* (*pl.* **viscosities**) **1** the fact of being viscous, stickiness, thickness. **2** (*Physics*) the extent to which a fluid or semifluid resists the tendency to flow owing to the interactive force between its molecules. **3** a quantity expressing this.

viscus (vis´kəs) *n.* any of the viscera.

vise VICE².

visible (viz´ibəl) *a.* **1** capable of being seen, perceptible by the eye. **2** apparent, evident, obvious. **visibility** (-bil´-) *n.* **1** the state of being visible, visibleness. **2** the range or possibility of vision, esp. as determined by atmospheric conditions and weather. **visible exports** *n.pl.* goods exported and sold abroad. **visible horizon** *n.* SENSIBLE HORIZON (under SENSIBLE). **visibleness** *n.* **visibly** *adv.*

vision (vizh´ən) *n.* **1** the act or faculty of seeing, sight. **2** a mental representation of a visual object, esp. in a dream or trance. **3** a supernatural or prophetic apparition. **4** something vividly perceived by the imagination or fancy. **5** foresight, an appreciation of what the future may hold, wise or imaginative planning for the future. **6** imaginative insight. **7** a person or thing of great beauty. **8** the image on a television screen; television pictures collectively. *~v.t.* **1** to see in or as in a vision. **2** to imagine. **3** to present as in a vision. **visional** *a.* **visionary** *a.* **1** characterized by or capable of vision or foresight. **2** capable of or given to seeing visions. **3** of the nature of or seen in a vision. **4** existing in a vision or in the imagination only. **5** unreal and existing only in the mind. **6** given to daydreaming, fanciful theories etc. *~n.* (*pl.* **visionaries**) **1** a person who sees visions, a seer. **2** an impractical daydreamer or schemer. **visionariness** *n.* **visionless** *a.* **vision mixer** *n.* a person who blends or combines different camera shots in television or films.

visit (viz´it) *v.t.* **1** to go or come to see, as an act of friendship, civility, business, curiosity etc. **2** to come or go to for the purpose of inspection, supervision, correction of abuses etc. **3** to reside temporarily with or in. **4** (of diseases etc.) to come upon, to overtake, to afflict. *~v.i.* **1** to call on or visit people. **2** (*N Am., coll.*) to converse or chat (with). *~n.* **1** the act of visiting or going to see a person, place or thing; a call. **2** a stay or sojourn (with or at). **3** a formal or official call or inspection. **visitable** *a.* **visitant** *n.* **1** a migratory bird that visits a country at certain seasons. **2** a supernatural visitor, a ghost, apparition. **3** (*poet.*) a visitor, a guest. **visitation** (-ā´shən) *n.* **1** a formal or official visit for the purpose of inspection, correction etc., esp. by a bishop to the churches of his diocese. **2** a divine dispensation, esp. a chastisement or affliction; any catastrophic occurrence. **visiting** *n.*, *a.* **visiting card** *n.* a small card, bearing one's name etc., to be left in making a call. **visiting hours** *n.pl.* the period or periods of the day during which visitors are allowed, esp. to see a patient in hospital. **visitor** *n.* **1** a person who makes a call. **2** a person who visits a place. **3** a visiting migratory bird, a visitant. **4** an officer appointed to make a visitation to any institution. **visitors' book** *n.* a book in which visitors' names are entered, esp. in which visitors to a hotel, boarding house, museum etc. write remarks.

visor (vī´zə), **vizor** *n.* **1** the movable perforated part of a helmet defending the face. **2** a projecting part on the front of a cap, for shielding the eyes. **3** a small movable flap or shield used to protect the eyes from strong light, esp. a sun visor in a motor vehicle. **visored** *a.* **visorless** *a.*

vista (vis´tə) *n.* **1** a long view shut in at the sides, as between rows of trees. **2** a mental view far into the past or future. **vistaed** *a.*

visual (vizh´ūəl) *a.* of, relating to or used in sight or seeing. *~n.* **1** (*often pl.*) a picture, photograph etc. as distinct from the words accompanying it. **2** a sketch of the layout of an advertisement. **visual aid** *n.* a picture, film, photograph, diagram etc. used as an aid to teaching or imparting information. **visual display unit** n. (*Comput.*) a device, usu. with a keyboard, which displays characters etc. representing data stored in a computer memory. **visual field** n. a field of vision. **visualize, visualise** v.t. 1 to picture in the mind, to call up a visual image of. 2 to make visible to the eye. **visualization** (-zā´shən) n. **visualizer** n. **visually** adv.

vital (vī´təl) a. 1 very important and necessary. 2 extremely important, decisive. 3 of, relating to, necessary to or supporting organic life. 4 full of life and activity, lively, dynamic, energetic. ~n.pl. the parts or organs of animals essential to life, such as the heart, brain etc. **vital force** n. a force assumed as accounting for the development and evolution of organic life, operating independently of physical and chemical forces. **vitalism** n. (*Biol.*) the doctrine that life is derived from something distinct from physical forces. **vitalist** n. **vitalistic** (-lis´-) a. **vitality** (-tal´-) n. (*pl.* **vitalities**) 1 physical or mental energy; liveliness, dynamism. 2 the ability to continue to live, function or flourish. **vitalize, vitalise** v.t. 1 to give life to. 2 to animate, to make more lively. **vitalization** (-zā´shən) n. **vitally** adv. **vitalness** n. **vital power** n. the power to sustain life. **vital statistics** n.pl. 1 those relating to birth, marriage and mortality. 2 (*coll.*) the measurements of a woman's bust, waist and hips.

vitamin (vit´əmin) n. any of a number of naturally occurring substances which are necessary, though in minute quantities, for normal metabolism. **vitamin A** n. a liquid hydrocarbon obtained from resin, used in pharmacy etc. **vitamin B₁** n. THIAMINE. **vitamin B₂** n. RIBOFLAVIN. **vitamin B₆** n. PYRIDOXINE (under PYRIDINE). **vitamin B₁₂** n. CYANOCOBALAMIN. **vitamin B complex** n. a large group of vitamins, chemically unrelated but often found together esp. in liver and yeast. **vitamin C** n. ASCORBIC ACID. **vitamin D** n. any of a group of fat-soluble vitamins occurring in fish-liver oils, milk, butter and eggs, essential for calcium absorption and the prevention of rickets. **vitamin D₂** n. CALCIFEROL. **vitamin D₃** n. CHOLE-CALCIFEROL. **vitamin E** n. TOCOPHEROL. **vitamin H** n. (*esp. N Am.*) BIOTIN. **vitaminize, vitaminise** v.t. to add vitamins to. **vitamin K** n. any of a group of vitamins, found mainly in green leaves, essential for normal coagulation of the blood. **vitamin K₁** n. PHYLLOQUINONE. **vitamin K₂** n. MENAQUINONE. **vitamin M** n. (*esp. N Am.*) FOLIC ACID.

vitellus (vitel´əs) n. (*pl.* **vitelli** (-lī)) yolk of egg; the protoplasmic contents of the ovum. **vitellin** (-in) n. (*Chem.*) the chief protein constituent of egg yolk. **vitelline** (-īn) a. 1 of or relating to the yolk of an egg. 2 having the yellow colour of egg yolk.

vitiate (vish´iāt) v.t. 1 to impair the quality of; to render faulty or imperfect. 2 to corrupt. 3 to render invalid or ineffectual. **vitiation** (-ā´shən) n. **vitiator** n.

viticulture (vit´ikŭlchə) n. 1 the cultivation of the grapevine. 2 the science or study of this. **viticultural** (-kŭl´-) a. **viticulturist** (-kŭl´-) n.

vitreous (vit´riəs) a. 1 consisting of or resembling glass. 2 obtained from glass. **vitreosity** (-os´-), **vitreousness** n. **vitreous humour, vitreous body** n. (*Anat.*) the jelly-like substance filling the posterior chamber of the eye, between the lens and the retina. **vitrify** v.t. (*3rd pers. sing. pres.* **vitrifies**, *pres.p.* **vitrifying**, *past, p.p.* **vitrified**) to convert into glass or a glassy substance by heat and fusion. ~v.i. to be converted into glass. **vitrifiable** a. **vitrifiability** (-bil´-) n. **vitrification** (-fikā´shən), **vitrifaction** (-fak´-) n.

vitriol (vit´riol) n. 1 sulphuric acid as made from copperas. 2 any salt of this, a sulphate. 3 malignancy, caustic criticism etc. **vitriolic** (-ol´-) a. (of language) very cruel and hurtful.

vituperate (vītū´pərāt) v.i. to use violently abusive language. ~v.t. to upbraid, to abuse, to rail at. **vituperation** (-ā´shən) n. **vituperative** a. (of criticism) angry and cruel. **vituperator** n.

viva¹ (vē´və) n. an exclamation of joy or applause. ~int. long live.

viva² (vī´və) n. a viva voce examination. ~v.t. (*3rd pers. sing. pres.* **vivas**, *pres.p.* **vivaing**, *past, p.p.* **vivaed, viva'd**) to subject to an oral examination.

vivace (vivah´chā) adv. (*Mus.*) in a brisk, lively manner.

vivacious (vivā´shəs) a. lively, animated, sprightly, high-spirited. **vivaciously** adv. **vivacity** (-vas´-), **vivaciousness** n.

vivarium (vīveə´riəm) n. (*pl.* **vivariums, vivaria** (-riə)) a park, enclosure or other place artificially prepared in which animals etc. are kept alive as nearly as possible in their natural state.

vivat (vī´vat, vē´-) n., int. (a shout of) long live.

viva voce (vīvə vō´chi) adv. by word of mouth, orally. ~a. oral. ~n. an oral examination.

viverrid (viver´id, vī-) n. any of the Viverridae, a family of carnivorous mammals containing the civets, genets, mongooses etc. ~a. of or relating to this family.

vivid (viv´id) a. 1 (of colour, light) very bright, intense, brilliant. 2 (of a description) evolving a very clear and striking mental picture. 3 (of a memory) very distinct and fresh. 4 (of the imagination) creating very clear, lifelike and striking images, often too prolifically. 5 intense, powerful. 6 (of a person etc.) vigorous, lively. 7 clear and detailed. **vividly** adv. **vividness** n.

vivify (viv´ifī) v.t. (*3rd pers. sing. pres.* **vivifies**, *pres.p.* **vivifying**, *past, p.p.* **vivified**) to give life to, to quicken, to animate, to enliven. **vivification** (-fikā´shən) n. **vivifier** n.

viviparous (vivip´ərəs, vī-) a. (*Zool.*) giving birth to young alive, as distinct from *oviparous* and *ovoviviparous*. **viviparity** (vivipar´i-), **viviparousness** n. **viviparously** adv.

vivisection (vivisek´shən) n. 1 the dissection of, or performance of inoculative or other experiments on, living animals. 2 minute and merciless examination or criticism. **vivisect** (viv´-) *v.t.* to dissect (a living animal). **vivisectional** *a.* **vivisectionist** *n.* **vivisector** (viv´-) *n.*

vixen (vik´sən) *n.* **1** a female fox. **2** a shrewish, quarrelsome woman. **vixenish, vixenly** *a.*

Viyella® (vīe´lə) *n.* a soft woven fabric made from cotton and wool, used esp. for blouses and shirts.

viz. *abbr.* VIDELICET.

Usage note Primarily a written form, and read aloud as 'namely'.

vizcacha VISCACHA.

vizier (vizie´) *n.* a high officer or minister of state in some Muslim countries, esp. in the former Ottoman empire.

vizor VISOR.

VJ *abbr.* Victory over Japan.

VLF *abbr.* very low frequency.

VO *abbr.* Royal Victorian Order.

vocable (vō´kəbəl) *n.* a word, esp. as considered phonologically.

vocabulary (vəkab´ūləri) *n.* (*pl.* **vocabularies**) **1** a list or collection of words used in a language, science, book etc., usu. arranged in alphabetical order, and explained. **2** all the words contained in a particular language. **3** the stock of words at a particular person's command. **4** (of forms, techniques) range, repertoire.

vocal (vō´kəl) *a.* **1** of or relating to the voice or oral utterance. **2** uttered or produced by the voice. **3** having a voice. **4** outspoken, freely expressing an opinion. **5** eloquent. **6** (*Mus.*) written for the voice or voices. **7** resounding with or as with voices. ~*n.* **1** (*often pl.*) the part of a musical, esp. a jazz or pop composition that is sung. **2** a performance of this. **vocal cords, vocal folds** *n.pl.* the elastic folds of the lining membrane of the larynx around the opening of the glottis. **vocalese** (-lēz´) *n.* a style of esp. jazz singing in which the singer improvises words to a tune or instrumental solo. **vocalic** (-kal´-) *a.* of, relating to or consisting of vowel sounds. **vocalise**¹ (-lēz, -lēz´) *n.* (*Mus.*) **1** a musical exercise consisting of a passage sung on one vowel sound. **2** a vocal passage or composition consisting of a melody without words. **3** (*derog.*) a display of vocal expertise. **vocalise**² VOCALIZE (under VOCAL). **vocalism** *n.* **1** the exercise of the vocal organs. **2** singing technique. **3** a vowel sound or system. **vocalist** *n.* a singer, as distinct from an instrumental performer, esp. of jazz or popular music. **vocality** (-kal´-), **vocalness** *n.* **vocalize, vocalise** *v.t.* **1** to form or utter with the voice. **2** to articulate, to express. **3** to change (a consonant) to a vowel or semivowel. ~*v.i.* **1** to utter a vocal sound. **2** to exercise the voice. **3** (*Mus.*) to sing several notes to one vowel. **vocalization** (-zā´shən) *n.* **vocally** *adv.* **vocal score** *n.* a musical score showing the singing parts in full but with the instrumental parts reduced or omitted.

vocation (vəkā´shən) *n.* **1** a call or sense of

fitness for and obligation to follow a particular career. **2** a divine call or spiritual injunction or guidance to undertake a duty, occupation etc. **3** a person's calling or occupation. **vocational** *a.* **1** of or relating to an employment, occupation or vocation. **2** (of training, qualifications) relating to the skills needed for a particular occupation. **vocationally** *adv.*

vocative (vok´ətiv) *a.* used in addressing a person or thing. ~*n.* (*Gram.*) the case of a noun used in addressing a person or thing.

vociferate (vəsif´ərāt) *v.i.* **1** to cry loudly, to bawl, to shout. **2** to make one's views known loudly and strongly. ~*v.t.* to cry, to shout, to express or utter loudly and vehemently. **vociferation** (-ā´shən) *n.* **vociferator** *n.* **vociferous** *a.* **1** making an outcry, expressing oneself loudly and insistently. **2** clamorous, noisy. **vociferously** *adv.* **vociferousness** *n.*

vocoder (vōkō´də) *n.* an electronic device, similar to a synthesizer, that produces synthetic speech.

Vodafone® (vō´dəfōn) *n.* a British cellular telephone system; a handset used for this.

vodka (vod´kə) *n.* a strong spirituous liquor distilled from rye, orig. from Russia.

vogue (vōg) *n.* **1** a fashion prevalent at any particular time. **2** currency, popular acceptance or usage. **in vogue** fashionable, currently popular or widespread. **vogue word** *n.* a word much used at a particular time or period. **voguish** *a.*

voice (vois) *n.* **1** the sound uttered by the mouth, esp. by a human being, in speaking, singing etc. **2** the characteristic sound made by an individual when speaking or singing. **3** the faculty or power of vocal utterance. **4** a sound suggestive of human speech. **5** expression of the mind or will in words, whether spoken or written etc. **6** one's opinion or judgement; one's right to express this; one's choice, vote or suffrage. **7** someone who expresses the will or judgement of others, a spokesperson, a mouthpiece. **8** sound produced by the breath acting on the vocal cords, sonancy. **9** (*Gram.*) the verb form expressing the relation of the subject to the action, as active, passive or middle. ~*v.t.* **1** to give utterance to, to express. **2** to give voice or sonancy to. **3** to regulate the tones of, to tune. **in good voice** in a condition to sing or speak well. **in voice** in good voice. **to give voice to** to utter, to express, to make known. **with one voice** unanimously. **voice box** *n.* (*coll.*) the larynx. **voiced** *a.* **1** produced with vibration of the vocal cords. **2** having a voice (*usu. in comb.*, as *loud-voiced*). **voiceless** *a.* **1** speechless, mute. **2** of a speech sound, not voiced. **3** having no say or vote. **voicelessness** *n.* **voice-over** *n.* **1** the voice of an unseen narrator, actor etc. in a film etc. **2** the text spoken by a voice-over. **voiceprint** *n.* an electronically recorded graphic representation of a person's voice.

void (void) *a.* **1** empty, unfilled, vacant. **2** lacking, destitute (of). **3** (*Law*) having no legal force, null, invalid. **4** useless, ineffectual. **5** having no holder, occupant or incumbent. ~*n.* **1** an empty space. **2** a vacuum, a feeling of loss or emptiness. **3** an unfilled space in a wall or building. ~*v.t.* **1** to invalidate, to nullify. **2** to empty (contents); to make empty. **3** to discharge, to emit from the bowels. **voidable** *a.* **voidance** *n.* **1** the act of nullifying; an annulment. **2** (of an office or benefice) the state of being vacant. **voider** *n.* **voidly** *adv.* **voidness** *n.*

voile (voil) *n.* a thin, semi-transparent dress material.

vol. *abbr.* volume.

volatile (vol´ətīl) *a.* **1** readily evaporating. **2** (of a person) liable to change their mind quickly or to become angry suddenly. **3** (of a situation) unpredictable, liable to sudden violent change, explosive. **4** short-lived, transient. **5** (of a computer memory) not retaining data when the power is switched off. ~*n.* a volatile substance. **volatility** (-til´-) *n.* **volatilize** (volat´-), **volatilise** *v.t.* to cause to pass off in vapour. ~*v.i.* to evaporate. **volatilizable** *a.* **volatilization** (-zā´shən) *n.*

vol-au-vent (vol´ōvã) *n.* a small, round puff pastry case filled with a filling, often savoury.

volcano (volkā´nō) *n.* (*pl.* **volcanoes**) **1** an opening in the earth's surface through which lava, cinders, gases etc. are ejected from the interior, esp. at the top of a hill or mountain formed by the successive accumulations of ejected matter. **2** such a hill or mountain. **3** any situation where danger, upheaval etc. seems likely. **volcanic** (-kan´-) *a.* of or relating to, produced by, or of the nature of a volcano. **volcanic glass** *n.* rock without a crystalline structure, such as obsidian, pumice etc. produced by the rapid cooling of molten lava. **volcanicity** (volkənis´-) *n.* volcanism. **volcanism** (vol´-), **vulcanism** (vŭl´-) *n.* volcanic activity and phenomena collectively. **volcanology** VULCANOLOGY (under VULCANITE).

vole (vōl) *n.* a mouselike or ratlike rodent of the family Cricetidae, with a stocky body, blunt nose, short tail and inconspicuous ears.

volition (vəlish´ən) *n.* **1** exercise of the will. **2** the power of willing. **of**/ **by one's own volition** voluntarily. **volitional**, **volitionary** *a.* **volitionally** *adv.* **volitionless** *a.* **volitive** (vol´-) *a.*

volley (vol´i) *n.* (*pl.* **volleys**) **1** a simultaneous discharge of missiles. **2** the missiles thus discharged. **3** a noisy outburst or emission of many things at once. **4** a return of the ball at tennis and similar games before it touches the ground. **5** in cricket, a ball bowled close to the wicket without hitting the ground. **6** in football, a kick delivered before the ball has hit the ground. ~*v.t.* (*3rd pers. sing. pres.* **volleys**, *pres.p.* **volleying**, *past, p.p.* **volleyed**) **1** to discharge in or as in a volley. **2** to return, kick or bowl in a volley. ~*v.i.* **1** to discharge a volley. **2** (of missiles etc.) to fly in a volley. **3** (of guns) to fire together.

4 to return a ball before it touches the ground. **on the volley** before the ball hits the ground. **volleyball** *n.* **1** a game in which a large ball is hit back and forward over a high net by hand, played between two teams. **2** the ball used in this game.

volplane (vol´plān) *v.i.* to glide down to earth in an aircraft with the engine shut off. ~*n.* such a descending flight.

volt[1] (vōlt) *n.* the SI unit of electric potential or potential difference, the difference of potential between two points in a conductor carrying a current of 1 ampere when the power dissipated between them is 1 watt. **voltage** (vōl´tij) *n.* electromotive force or potential difference as measured or expressed in volts. **voltaic** (voltā´ik) *a.* of or relating to electricity produced by chemical action or contact, galvanic. **voltameter** (-tam´itə) *n.* an instrument for measuring an electric charge. **voltmeter** *n.* an instrument for measuring electromotive force directly, calibrated in volts.

volt[2] (volt) *n.* **1** (*also* **volte**) a circular tread, the gait of a horse going sideways round a centre. **2** a sudden leap to avoid a thrust in fencing. ~*v.i.* to make a volte in fencing.

volte-face (voltfas´) *n.* **1** a complete change of opinion, attitude etc. **2** a turn round.

voluble (vol´ūbəl) *a.* **1** producing or characterized by a flow of words, fluent, glib, garrulous. **2** (*Bot.*) twisting, twining, climbing by winding round a support. **volubility** (-bil´-), **volubleness** *n.* **volubly** *adv.*

volume (vol´ūm) *n.* **1** a collection of (usu. printed) sheets of paper, parchment etc., bound together forming a book or work or part of one. **2** a book, a tome. **3** (*Hist.*) a roll or scroll of papyrus, vellum etc. constituting a book. **4** the complete set of issues of a periodical over a specified period, usu. a year. **5** cubical content. **6** mass, bulk. **7** a (large) amount or quantity. **8** (*usu. pl.*) a rounded, swelling mass, a wreath, a coil. **9** loudness, or the control for adjusting it on a radio, television etc. **10** (*Mus.*) fullness or roundness of tone. **volumed** *a.* **volumetric** (-met´-), **volumetrical** *a.* of or relating to the measurement of volume. **volumetrically** *adv.*

voluminous (vəloo´minəs) *a.* **1** of great volume, bulk or size. **2** (of a dress, drapery) loose-fitting and using large quantities of fabric. **3** consisting of many volumes. **4** (of a writer) producing many or bulky books. **voluminosity** (-nos´-), **voluminousness** *n.* **voluminously** *adv.*

voluntary (vol´əntəri) *a.* **1** acting, performed, given etc. of one's own free will or choice, not under external constraint. **2** unpaid. **3** (of an organization, institution) brought about, established or supported by voluntary action. **4** (of muscles, movement etc.) subject to or controlled by the will. **5** endowed with or exercising the power of willing. **6** (*Law*) done without constraint or by consent, without valuable consideration. ~n. (pl. **voluntaries**) **1** an organ solo played in a church etc. before, during or after a service. **2** a routine, piece etc. chosen for performance by a competitor in a competition. **voluntarily** adv. **voluntariness** n. **voluntarism** n. **1** (also **voluntaryism**) the principle of relying on voluntary action rather than compulsion. **2** (Philos.) the theory that the will is the fundamental or dominant principle in any individual or in the universe. **voluntarist, voluntaryist** n. **voluntary-aided** a. (of a school) originally established by a voluntary organization but funded mainly by a local authority. **voluntary-controlled** a. (of a school) established by a voluntary organization, but wholly funded by a local authority. **voluntaryism** VOLUNTARISM (under VOLUNTARY). **voluntary school** n. in the UK, a school established by a voluntary organization, usu. a religious denomination, but partly or wholly maintained by a local authority. **Voluntary Service Overseas** n. in the UK, an organization which sends volunteers overseas, usu. to underdeveloped countries, to use and teach their skills.

volunteer (voləntiə´) n. **1** a person who undertakes a job etc. voluntarily. **2** a person who enters into any service of their own free will, esp. orig. a member of a military body in the United Kingdom superseded by the Territorial Force in 1907. ~a. **1** voluntary. **2** (Bot.) self-sown. ~v.t. **1** to offer or undertake voluntarily. **2** to offer or commandeer the services of (another person). ~v.i. to offer one's services voluntarily, esp. orig. to offer to serve (for a military campaign etc.) as a volunteer. **volunteerism** n.

voluptuary (vəlŭp´chuəri) n. (pl. **voluptuaries**) a person given to luxury or sensual pleasures. ~a. relating to, promoting or devoted to sensual pleasure. **voluptuous** a. **1** of or relating to, contributing to or producing sensuous or sensual gratification. **2** (of a woman) sexually alluring because of shapeliness or fullness of figure. **voluptuously** adv. **voluptuousness** n.

volute (vol´ūt, -lūt´) n. **1** a spiral, a whorl. **2** (Archit.) a spiral scroll used in Ionic, Corinthian and Composite capitals. **3** a marine gastropod of the genus Voluta, usu. of tropical seas and having a beautiful shell. **4** the shell of one of these. ~a. (Bot.) rolled up. **voluted** a. **volution** (-ū´shən, -oo´shən) n. **1** a revolving movement. **2** a spiral turn. **3** a whorl of a spiral shell. **4** (Anat.) a convolution.

vomer (vō´mə) n. (Anat.) a small thin bone forming the chief portion of the partition between the nostrils in human beings.

vomit (vom´it) v.t. (pres.p. **vomiting**, past, p.p. **vomited**) **1** to eject from the stomach by the mouth. **2** to eject or discharge violently, to belch out. ~v.i. to eject the contents of the stomach by the mouth, to spew, to be sick. ~n. matter ejected from the stomach by the mouth. **vomitory** (-təri) a. emetic.

voodoo (voo´doo) n. **1** a cult involving animistic deities, witchcraft and communication in trances practised by Creoles and blacks in Haiti and other parts of the W Indies and in the southern US. **2** a sorcerer or conjurer skilled in this. **3** a charm, spell or fetish used in this. ~v.t. (3rd pers. sing. pres. **voodoos**, pres.p. **voodooing**, past, p.p. **voodooed**) to put a spell on or bewitch with voodoo. **voodooish** a. **voodooism** n. **voodooist** n.

voracious (vərā´shəs) a. **1** greedy in eating. **2** ravenous, gluttonous, ready to swallow up or devour. **3** insatiable, very eager. **voraciously** adv. **voracity** (-ras´-) n.

-vore (vaw) comb. form forming nouns denoting creatures that live on a certain type of food, as carnivore, herbivore. **-vorous** (vərəs) comb. form feeding on, living on, as carnivorous, herbivorous.

vortex (vaw´teks) n. (pl. **vortices** (-tisēz)) **1** a whirling or rotating mass of fluid, esp. a whirlpool. **2** any whirling motion or mass. **3** a situation, activity, way of life etc. which seems likely to engulf anyone who becomes involved in it. **4** (Physics) a portion of fluid the particles of which have a rotary motion. **vortex ring** n. a vortex on the axis of which is a closed curve. **vortical** a. of or relating to a vortex, whirling. **vortically** adv. **vorticism** (vaw´tisizm) n. a school of early 20th-cent. painting which seeks to represent nature in formal designs of straight and angular patterns. **vorticist** n. **vorticity** (-tis´-) n. **vorticose** (-kōs), **vorticular** (-tik´ū-) a.

votary (vō´təri) n. (pl. **votaries**) **1** a person who is devoted or consecrated by a vow or promise. **2** a person who is devoted to some particular service, study, pursuit etc. **votaress**, †**votress** n. a female votary.

vote (vōt) n. **1** a formal expression of opinion, will or choice, in regard to the election of a candidate, the passing or rejection of a resolution, law etc., usu. signified by voice, gesture or ballot. **2** anything by which this is expressed, such as a ballot, ticket etc. **3** something which is approved by a vote, such as a grant of money. **4** the aggregate votes of a party etc. **5** the right to vote, the suffrage. ~v.i. **1** to give one's vote (for or against). **2** to express one's allegiance, preference etc. by voting. ~v.t. **1** to give one's vote for. **2** to enact, resolve, ratify or grant by a majority of votes. **3** to cause to be in a specified condition by voting. **4** (coll.) to declare by general consent. **5** (coll.) to suggest, propose. **to put to a/ the vote** to obtain a decision regarding (a proposal) by holding a vote. **to vote down** to defeat or suppress by vote. **to vote in** to elect. **to vote off** to remove from (a committee etc.) by voting. **to vote out** to dismiss from office by voting. **to vote with one's feet** to indicate one's dissatisfaction with a situation or conditions by leaving. **votable** a. **voteless** a. **vote of no confidence, vote of censure** n. the legal method of forcing the resignation of a government or governing body or person. **voter** *n.* **1** a person entitled to vote. **2** a person who actually casts a vote. **voting** *n.* **voting machine** *n.* a machine that automatically registers and records votes cast at an election. **voting paper** *n.* a paper by means of which one votes, esp. by ballot in a parliamentary election. **voting stock** *n.* stock that entitles a shareholder to vote.

votive (vō′tiv) *a.* **1** given, paid or dedicated in fulfilment of a vow. **2** (of a Mass etc.) being a voluntary offering, performed for some particular purpose. **votively** *adv.*

vouch (vowch) *v.t.* to uphold or guarantee by assertion, proof etc., to confirm, to substantiate. ~*v.i.* to be a surety or guarantee, to answer (for). **voucher** *n.* **1** a ticket, card etc. substitutable or exchangeable for goods or cash. **2** a document etc. serving to confirm or establish something, as a payment, the correctness of an account etc. **3** a person who vouches or acts as security for another.

vouchsafe (vowchsāf′) *v.t.* (*formal*) to condescend to grant. ~*v.i.* to deign, to condescend (to).

voussoir (vooswah′) *n.* any of the wedge-shaped stones forming an arch.

vow (vow) *n.* **1** a solemn promise or pledge, esp. made to God or to a saint etc., undertaking an act, sacrifice, obligation etc. **2** a promise of fidelity. ~*v.t.* **1** to promise solemnly. **2** to dedicate by a vow. ~*v.i.* to make a vow. **to take vows** to enter a religious order and commit oneself to the vows of chastity, poverty and obedience. **under a vow** having made a vow.

vowel (vow′əl) *n.* **1** a sound able to make a syllable or to be sounded alone; an open and unimpeded sound as distinct from a closed, stopped or mute sound or consonant. **2** a letter representing this, esp. the simple vowels, *a*, *e*, *i*, *o*, *u*. **vowel gradation** *n.* ablaut. **vowelled,** (*N Am.*) **voweled** *a.* having (many) vowels. **vowelless** *a.* **vowelly** *a.* **vowel mutation** *n.* umlaut. **vowel point** *n.* any of the marks indicating the vowels in Hebrew etc.

vox (voks) *n.* (*pl.* **voces** (vō′sēz)) a voice. **vox pop** *n.* (*coll.*) public attitudes or opinion as represented by comments by ordinary people; radio or TV interviews to elicit these. **vox populi** (pop′ūlī) *n.* the voice of the people, public opinion, the popular verdict.

voyage (voi′ij) *n.* **1** a journey by water or air or through space, esp. to a distant place. **2** an account of such a journey. ~*v.i.* to make a voyage. ~*v.t.* to travel over or through. **voyageable** *a.* **voyager** *n.*

voyeur (vwahyœ′) *n.* **1** a person who derives sexual gratification from watching sexual acts, people undressing etc. **2** an obsessive observer of the sordid or unpleasant. **voyeurism** *n.* **voyeuristic** (-ris′-) *a.* **voyeuristically** *adv.*

VP *abbr.* Vice-President.

VR *abbr.* **1** variant reading. **2** Victoria Regina (Queen Victoria). **3** virtual reality.

vroom (vroom) *v.i.* **1** (of an engine) to make a loud revving noise. **2** (of a vehicle) to travel at speed. ~*v.t.* to rev (an engine). ~*n.* the roaring sound of an engine being revved. ~*int.* used to represent this sound.

vs. *abbr.* versus.

VSO *abbr.* Voluntary Service Overseas.

VSOP *abbr.* Very Special Old Pale (used to indicate that brandy or port is between 20 and 25 years old).

VTO *abbr.* vertical take-off.

VTOL (vē′tol) *abbr.* vertical take-off and landing, a system by which aircraft take off and land without taxiing.

VTR *abbr.* videotape recorder.

vulcanism VOLCANISM (under VOLCANO).

vulcanite (vŭl′kənīt) *n.* vulcanized rubber, ebonite. **vulcanize, vulcanise** *v.t.* to treat (rubber) with sulphur at a high temperature so as to increase its strength and elasticity, producing vulcanite (the hard form) or soft and flexible rubber. **vulcanization** (-zā′shən) *n.* **vulcanology** (vŭlkənol′əji), **volcanology** (vol-) *n.* the scientific study of volcanoes. **vulcanological** (-əloj′-) *a.* **vulcanologist** *n.*

vulgar (vŭl′gə) *a.* **1** of, relating to or characteristic of the common people. **2** plebeian, common, coarse, low, unrefined. **3** rude, boorish. **4** ordinary, in common use. **5** referring to sex in a rude or offensive way. **vulgar fraction** *n.* a fraction having the numerator less than the denominator. **vulgarian** (-geə′ri-) *n.* a vulgar person, esp. a rich person with low ideas, manners etc. **vulgarism** *n.* **1** a word or expression in coarse or uneducated use. **2** vulgarity. **vulgarity** (-gar′i-) *n.* (*pl.* **vulgarities**) **1** the condition of being vulgar; lack of good manners, refinement etc. **2** a vulgar action or expression. **vulgarize, vulgarise** *v.t.* **1** to debase by making vulgar or commonplace. **2** to make (a person) coarse or crude. **3** to popularize, to make more generally accessible. **vulgarization** (-zā′shən) *n.* **vulgarizer** *n.* **vulgar Latin** *n.* colloquial Latin. **vulgarly** *adv.* **vulgar tongue** *n.* the vernacular.

Vulgate (vŭl′gət) *n.* **1** the Latin translation of the Bible made by St Jerome, 383–405. **2** the official Latin text of the Bible used in the Roman Catholic Church, revised from St Jerome's version in 1592.

vulnerable (vŭl′nərəbəl) *a.* **1** capable of being wounded physically or emotionally. **2** susceptible or liable to injury, attack etc. **3** in bridge, subject to higher penalties and bonuses having won a game towards rubber. **vulnerability** (-bil′-), **vulnerableness** *n.*

Usage note Pronunciation as (vŭn′-), without the first (l), is best avoided.

vulpine (vŭl′pīn) *a.* **1** of or relating to or characteristic of a fox. **2** crafty, cunning.

vulture (vŭl´chə) *n.* **1** a large bird of the family Accipitridae (Old World) or Cathartidae (New World) with head and neck almost naked, feeding chiefly on carrion. **2** a rapacious person. **vulturine** (-rīn), **vulturish, vulturous** *a.*

vulva (vŭl´və) *n.* (*pl.* **vulvas**) (*Anat.*) the external female genitals, esp. the opening of the vagina. **vulval, vulvar, vulvate** (-vət) *a.* **vulvitis** (-vī´tis) *n.*

vv. *abbr.* **1** verses. **2** volumes.

vying VIE.

W

W¹ (dŭb´əlū), **w** (pl. **Ws, W's**) the 23rd letter of the English and other versions of the Roman alphabet, taking its form and name from the union of two V's (V and U formerly being variants of one letter and sharing the name now given to U). It is pronounced as a bilabial semivowel, as in *was, will, forward.*

W² *abbr.* **1** watt. **2** West, Western. **3** women. **4** women's size.

W³ *chem. symbol* tungsten.

w, w. *abbr.* **1** week. **2** weight. **3** white. **4** wicket. **5** wide. **6** width. **7** wife. **8** with.

wacko (wak´ō) *a.* (*esp. N Am., sl.*) crazy, eccentric. *~n.* (*pl.* **wackos, wackoes**) a crazy or eccentric person.

wacky (wak´i), **whacky** *a.* (*comp.* **wackier, whackier,** *superl.* **wackiest, whackiest**) (*sl.*) crazy, eccentric, absurd. *~n.* (*pl.* **wackies, whackies**) a wacky person. **wackily** *adv.* **wackiness** *n.*

wad (wod) *n.* **1** a small, compact mass of some soft material, used for stopping an opening, stuffing between things etc. **2** a felt or paper disc used to keep the charge in place in a gun, cartridge etc. **3** a bundle of currency notes, documents etc. **4** (*sl.*) a bun or sandwich. **5** (*coll.*) a large amount, esp. of money. *~v.t.* (*pres.p.* **wadding,** *past, p.p.* **wadded**) **1** to compress into a wad. **2** to stuff, line or protect with wadding. **3** to pack, stop up or secure with a wad. **wadding** *n.* **1** a soft spongy material, usu. composed of cotton or wool, used for stuffing garments, cushions etc. **2** material for gun wads.

waddle (wod´əl) *v.i.* to walk with an ungainly rocking or swaying motion and with short, quick steps, as a duck or goose does. *~n.* a waddling gait. **waddler** *n.*

waddy (wod´i) *n.* (*pl.* **waddies**) **1** an Australian war club, usu. bent like a boomerang or with a thick head. **2** (*Austral., New Zeal.*) any club or stick.

wade (wād) *v.i.* **1** to walk through water or a semi-fluid medium, such as snow, mud etc. **2** to make one's way with difficulty and labour. *~v.t.* **1** to pass through or across by wading. **2** to ford (a stream) on foot. **to wade in/ into** (*coll.*) to tackle or attack vigorously. **to wade through** to read (a book etc.) with difficulty or effort. **wadable, wadeable** *a.* **wader** *n.* **1** a person who wades. **2** (*usu. pl.*) a high, waterproof boot or trouser-like garment, worn by anglers etc. for wading. **3** a wading bird. **wading bird** *n.* any long-legged bird that wades, esp. one of the order Ciconiiformes, including the storks, herons etc.

wadi (wod´i), **wady** *n.* (*pl.* **wadis, wadies**) the valley or channel of a stream that is dry except in the rainy season.

WAF (waf) *abbr.* (*N Am.*) Women in the Air Force. *~n.* a member of the WAF.

wafer (wā´fə) *n.* **1** a small, thin, sweet biscuit, esp. one eaten with ice cream. **2** a thin disc of unleavened bread used in the Eucharist, the Host. **3** a thin disc of adhesive paper or dried paste used for sealing letters, fastening documents etc. **4** in electronics, a thin disc of silicon or other semiconductor material on which integrated circuits are formed before being cut into individual chips. *~v.t.* to seal or attach with a wafer. **wafer-thin** *a.* very thin. *~adv.* very thinly. **wafery** *a.*

waffle¹ (wof´əl) *n.* a thin batter cake baked in a waffle-iron. **waffle-iron** *n.* a utensil with hinged plates for baking waffles.

waffle² (wof´əl) *v.i.* **1** (*coll.*) to talk or write aimlessly and at length. **2** (*coll.*) to waver. *~n.* (*coll.*) vague or inconsequential talk or writing. **waffler** *n.* **waffly** *a.*

waft (wahft, woft) *v.t.* **1** to carry or convey through the air. **2** to carry lightly or gently along. *~v.i.* to float or be borne on the air. *~n.* **1** an act of wafting. **2** a breath or whiff of odour etc.

wag¹ (wag) *v.t.* (*pres.p.* **wagging,** *past, p.p.* **wagged**) **1** to shake up and down or backwards and forwards lightly and quickly, esp. in playfulness, reproof etc. **2** to move (the tongue etc.) in chatter or gossip. *~v.i.* **1** to move up and down or to and fro, to oscillate. **2** (of the tongue etc.) to move in chatter or gossip. *~n.* an act or a motion of wagging, a shake.

wag² (wag) *n.* **1** a facetious person, a wit, a joker. **2** (*sl.*) a truant. **waggery** *n.* jocularity, playful merriment, practical joking. **waggish** *a.* **waggishly** *adv.* **waggishness** *n.*

wage (wāj) *n.* **1** (*often pl.*) payment for work done or services rendered, esp. fixed periodical pay for labour of a manual kind. **2** (*usu. pl.*) recompense, reward, requital. **3** (*pl.*) in economics, the part of the national income that accrues to labour rather than to capital. *~v.t.* to engage in, to carry on (a battle, war etc.). **wage bill** *n.* the total amount paid to employees. **waged** (wājd) *a.* earning a wage. **wage earner** *n.* **1** a person who earns a wage, esp. as opposed to a salary. **2** a person who earns money to support a household. **wage-earning** *a.* **wageless** *a.* **wages council** *n.* a body of employers' and workers' representatives that determines wage levels in an industry. **wage**

slave n. (coll. or iron.) a person dependent on a wage or salary.

wager (wā´jə) n. **1** something staked or hazarded on the outcome of a contest etc., a bet. **2** an act or instance of betting. **3** something on which bets are laid. ~v.t., v.i. to bet. **wagerer** n.

waggery, waggish etc. WAG².

waggle (wag´əl) v.t., v.i. (coll.) to wag or swing to and fro, esp. quickly and frequently. ~n. a short, quick wagging motion. **waggly** a. **1** waggling. **2** unsteady.

waggon WAGON.

Wagnerian (vahgniə´riən) a. of, relating to or in the style of Wagner's music or operas.

wagon (wag´ən), **waggon** n. **1** a strong four-wheeled vehicle for the transport of heavy loads, usu. with a rectangular body, often with a removable cover, usu. drawn by two or more horses. **2** a railway truck, esp. an open one. **3** (coll.) a car, esp. an estate car. **off the wagon** (coll.) no longer abstaining from alcohol, off the water wagon. **on the wagon** (coll.) abstaining from alcohol, on the water wagon. **wagoner** n. (esp. Hist.) a person who drives or leads a wagon. **wagonload** n.

wagon-lit (vagōlē´) n. (pl. **wagons-lits** (vagōlē´), **wagon-lits** (-lēz´)) a sleeping car on a Continental train.

wagtail (wag´tāl) n. any of various small, long-tailed birds, chiefly of the genus Motacilla (from the wagging of their tails).

wahoo¹ (wah·hoo´), **wahoo elm** n. (N Am.) a N American elm, Ulmus alata, also called winged elm.

wahoo² (wah·hoo´) n. (N Am.) a N American shrub or small tree, Euonymus atropurpureus.

wahoo³ (wah·hoo´) n. (N Am.) a fast-swimming food fish, Acanthocybium solanderi, of tropical seas.

waif (wāf) n. **1** a homeless wanderer, esp. a forsaken child. **2** any person or thing found astray, ownerless or cast up by or adrift on the sea. **waifish** a. **waiflike** a. **waifs and strays** n.pl. **1** homeless or forsaken children. **2** odds and ends.

wail (wāl) v.i. **1** to lament. **2** to utter wails. **3** (of the wind etc.) to make a plaintive sound. ~v.t. (poet.) to lament loudly over, to bewail. ~n. **1** a loud, high-pitched lamentation, a plaintive cry. **2** a sound like this. **wailer** n. **wailful** a. **wailing** n., a. **wailingly** adv.

wain (wān) n. (poet.) a four-wheeled vehicle for the transportation of goods, a wagon.

wainscot (wān´skət) n. **1** a wooden, usu. panelled, lining or casing of the walls of a room. **2** the lower part of the walls of a room when lined or finished differently from the upper part. ~v.t. (pres.p. **wainscoting, wainscotting**, past, p.p. **wainscoted, wainscotted**) to line with a wainscot. **wainscoting, wainscotting** n. **1** a wainscot or wainscots. **2** material for this.

waist (wāst) n. **1** the part of the human body below the ribs or thorax and above the hips. **2** this part as normally narrower than the rest of the trunk. **3** the circumference of this. **4** the part of a garment encircling the waist. **5** the constriction between the abdomen and thorax of a wasp etc. **6** the part of a ship between the quarterdeck and the forecastle. **waistband** n. a band worn round the waist, esp. a strip of fabric forming the upper part of a skirt, trousers etc. **waistcoat** (wāst´kōt, wās´kōt, wās´kət) n. a short garment, usu. without sleeves or collar, extending from the neck to the waist. **waisted** a. (also in comb.) **waistless** a. **waistline** n. **1** the size or outline of a person's waist. **2** the waist of a dress etc., not necessarily corresponding with the wearer's natural waist (a low waistline).

wait (wāt) v.i. **1** to remain inactive or in the same place until some event or time for action, to stay. **2** to be in a state of expectation or readiness (for). **3** to be on the watch (for). **4** to be ready or in a fit state for use etc. **5** to wait at table. **6** to be postponed or delayed (Can it wait?). ~v.t. **1** to wait for, to await, to bide (to wait one's turn). **2** to postpone, to defer, to delay. ~n. **1** the act of waiting. **2** a period of waiting. **3** watching, ambush. **to wait and see** to wait patiently for some future event. **to wait at table** to act as a waiter in a hotel, restaurant etc. **to wait on/ upon 1** to attend on as a waiter or servant. **2** to pay a visit to deferentially. **3** to await. **4** (of consequences etc.) to follow. **to wait up** to remain out of bed waiting (for). **wait for it! 1** do not begin too soon. **2** used to introduce an unexpected remark, a punchline etc. **you wait!** used to threaten or warn. **waiter** n. **1** a person who waits. **2** an attendant on guests at a table in a restaurant etc. **waiting** n. **1** parking for a short time at the side of a road (no waiting). **2** official attendance at court. **3** the act of a person who waits. **in waiting** in attendance, esp. on the sovereign. **waiting list** n. a list of people waiting for a vacancy, treatment etc. **waitperson** n. (esp. N Am.) a waiter or waitress. **waitress** (-ris) n. a female waiter in a restaurant etc. **waitressing** n. the occupation or work of a waitress.

waive (wāv) v.t. **1** to decide officially that something can be ignored (to waive the rules). **2** to defer, to postpone. **waiver** n. (Law) **1** the act of waiving a claim, a right etc. **2** a written statement of this.

Usage note The spellings of the verbs waive (to forgo) and wave (to move to and fro) should not be confused (as is especially easily done in wave aside, which means something similar to waive). Waiver, the noun from waive, should also be distinguished from the unrelated verb waver.

wake¹ (wāk) v.i. (past **woke** (wōk), **waked**, p.p. **woken** (wō´kən), **waked**) **1** to be aroused from sleep, to cease to sleep. **2** to revive from a trance, death etc. **3** to be awake, to be unable to sleep. **4** to be roused or to rouse oneself from inaction, inattention etc. (He must wake up to his responsibilities). ~v.t. **1** to rouse from sleep, to awake.

2 to revive, to resuscitate, to raise from the dead. **3** to arouse, to stir (up), to excite, to alert. **4** to break the silence of, to disturb. ~*n.* **1** a vigil. **2** the watching of a dead body, prior to burial, by friends and neighbours of the deceased, with lamentations often followed by a merrymaking. **wakeful** *a.* **1** not disposed or unable to sleep, restless. **2** (of a night) passed without sleep. **3** watchful, alert. **wakefully** *adv.* **wakefulness** *n.* **waker** *n.* **wakey-wakey** *int.* used to rouse a person from sleep, inattention etc. **waking** *a.* awake. **waking dream** *n.* a waking experience of involuntary vision; a hallucination.

wake² (wāk) *n.* **1** the track left by a vessel passing through water. **2** the track or path left after something has passed. **in the wake of** following.

waken (wā´kən) *v.t.* **1** to rouse from sleep. **2** to rouse to action etc. ~*v.i.* to wake, to cease from sleeping. **wakener** *n.*

wale (wāl) *n.* **1** a ridge on the skin, a weal. **2** a ridge on the surface of cloth, such as corduroy. **3** (*Naut.*) a wide plank extending along a ship's side. **4** a strong band around a woven basket.

waler (wā´lə) *n.* (*Austral.*) a riding horse (orig. as supplied by military authorities in New South Wales).

walk (wawk) *v.i.* **1** to go along by raising, advancing and setting down each foot alternately, never having both feet off the ground at once. **2** (of a quadruped) to go along with a slow gait keeping at least two feet on the ground at any time. **3** to go at the ordinary pace, not to run, not to go or proceed rapidly. **4** to go or travel on foot. **5** (*sl.*) to depart, to be off, to be dismissed or released. **6** (of a batsman in cricket) to leave the wicket before being declared out. **7** in baseball, to go to first base after not hitting four illegally pitched balls. ~*v.t.* **1** to walk over, on or through, to perambulate, to tread. **2** to cause to walk; to lead, drive or ride at a walking pace (*to walk a dog*). **3** to accompany on foot. **4** to move (an object) by alternately lifting one side then the other. **5** in baseball, to allow to walk. ~*n.* **1** the act of walking. **2** the pace, gait or step of a person or animal that walks. **3** a distance walked (*five minutes' walk from the station*). **4** an act of walking for pleasure, exercise etc. (*to go for a walk*; *a sponsored walk*). **5** the route chosen for this. **6** a piece of ground laid out for walking, a footpath, a promenade etc. **7** the district or round of a hawker, postman etc. **8** (*also* **walk of life**) one's profession, occupation, sphere of action etc. **to walk all over 1** (*coll.*) to defeat easily or conclusively. **2** (*coll.*) to take advantage of. **to walk away from 1** to go much faster than, esp. in a race. **2** to refuse to deal with (*to walk away from one's responsibilities*). **3** to survive without serious injury (*to walk away from an accident*). **to walk away with** to win or gain easily. **to walk in** to enter. **to walk in on** to interrupt. **to walk into 1** to enter or encounter unwittingly (*to walk into a trap*). **2** to gain easily (*to walk into a job*). **to**

walk it (*coll.*) to win or achieve something without effort. **to walk off 1** to depart abruptly. **2** to get rid of by walking (*to walk off one's depression*). **3** to get rid of the effects of (a meal etc.) by walking. **to walk off with 1** (*coll.*) to carry off, to steal. **2** to walk away with. **to walk out 1** to depart suddenly, esp. in anger. **2** to stop work as a protest. **to walk out on** to abandon. **to walk over 1** (*coll.*) to walk all over. **2** to walk or go slowly over (a racecourse etc.) because one is the only competitor, or because one's opponents are weak. **to walk someone off their feet** to make a person walk so far or so fast that they are exhausted. **to walk tall** (*coll.*) to feel proud. **to walk the boards** to be an actor. **to walk the streets 1** to be a prostitute. **2** to wander round a town or city, esp. in search of work, accommodation etc. **to walk the wards** to be a medical student in a hospital. **to walk up to** to approach. **walk up!** used to invite spectators to a circus etc. **walkable** *a.* **walkabout** *n.* **1** a wandering journey in the bush by Australian Aborigines. **2** an informal walk to meet the public by a politician, member of royalty etc. **walkathon** *n.* a long-distance walk to raise funds for charity. **walker** *n.* **1** a person who walks, esp. for pleasure, exercise etc. **2** a frame for supporting a baby, disabled person etc. when walking. **walkie-talkie** (-taw´ki) *n.* a portable combined transmitter and receiver. **walk-in** *a.* (of a wardrobe etc.) large enough to walk into and move around in. **walking** *n., a.* **walking frame** *n.* a frame for supporting a disabled person when walking. **walking shoe** *n.* a strong shoe suitable for walking a long distance. **walking stick** *n.* a stick carried in walking, esp. for support. **walking tour** *n.* a holiday on foot in a particular area (*a walking tour of the Highlands*). **walking wounded** *n.* (*pl.* **walking wounded**) **1** (*usu. pl.*) an injured person who is able to walk. **2** (*coll.*) a person with mental or emotional problems. **Walkman®** *n.* (*pl.* **Walkmans, Walkmen**) a small portable stereo with headphones. **walk-on** *n.* **1** a walk-on part. **2** an actor playing such a part. **walk-on part** *n.* a small, non-speaking part in a play etc. **walkout** *n.* a sudden departure in anger, esp. of workers. **walkover** *n.* an easy victory. **walkway** *n.* **1** a path etc. for pedestrian use only. **2** a passage connecting buildings.

wall (wawl) *n.* **1** a continuous structure of stone, brick etc. forming an enclosure, a side or internal partition of a building etc. **2** the inner or outer surface of this (*to paper the walls of a room*). **3** (*usu. pl.*) a rampart, a fortification. **4** anything resembling a wall, such as a cliff, a mountain range etc. **5** the enclosing sides of a vessel, cavity etc. (*the cell wall*). **6** a defence or obstacle (*a wall of silence*). ~*v.t.* **1** to enclose, surround or defend with a wall. **2** to separate or divide with a wall. **3** to block (up) or seal (off) with a wall. **off the wall** eccentric, unexpected. **to go to the wall 1** (*coll.*) to be defeated in a contest. **2** (*coll.*) to be pushed aside. **up the wall** (*coll.*) in or into a state of distraction or exasperation (*to go up the wall*; *This work is driving me up the wall*). **wall bars** *n.pl.* a set of parallel horizontal bars fixed to a wall, used for gymnastics. **wallchart** *n.* a chart designed to be displayed on a wall as a source of information etc. **wallcovering** *n.* any material used to cover interior walls, such as wallpaper. **walled** *a.* **wallflower** *n.* **1** any of various sweet-smelling plants of the genera *Cheiranthus* or *Erysimum*, esp. *E. cheiri*, with yellow, brown and crimson flowers. **2** (*coll.*) a person who is excluded from the main social activity, esp. a woman without a partner at a dance. **wall game** *n.* a kind of football played only at Eton. **wall-hung** *a.* wall-mounted. **walling** *n.* **wall-less** *a.* **wall-mounted** *a.* attached to a wall, esp. by a bracket or brackets. **wallpaper** *n.* **1** paper, usu. with decorative patterns or texture, for pasting on the walls of rooms. **2** (*often derog.*) bland background music etc. ~*v.t.* to cover or decorate with wallpaper. **wall space** *n.* space on the surface of a wall to hang a picture, mount a cupboard etc. **Wall Street** *n.* the New York Stock Exchange and money market. **wall-to-wall** *a.* **1** (of carpet etc.) covering all the floor. **2** (*coll.*) continuous, non-stop.

wallaby (wol'əbi) *n.* (*pl.* **wallabies**) a marsupial of the family Macropodidae, similar to but smaller than the kangaroo.

wallah (wol'ə), **walla** *n.* (*coll.*) **1** (*often in comb.*) an agent, worker or any person concerned with a usu. specified thing (*You'd better ask the computer wallah*). **2** (*sometimes derog.*) a person, a fellow.

wallaroo (woləroo') *n.* (*pl.* **wallaroos**) a large species of kangaroo, *Macropus robustus*.

wallet (wol'it) *n.* **1** a small case for carrying paper money, credit cards etc. **2** a folder for papers, documents etc.

wall-eye (wawl'ī) *n.* **1** a condition of the eye characterized by opacity of the cornea. **2** an eye with a very light-coloured iris, esp. due to this. **3** an eye that squints outwards. **wall-eyed** *a.*

Walloon (wəloon') *n.* **1** a member of a French-speaking people in SE Belgium and the adjoining parts of France. **2** their language. ~*a.* of or relating to the Walloons or their language.

wallop (wol'əp) *v.t.* (*pres.p.* **walloping**, *past*, *p.p.* **walloped**) (*coll.*) **1** to thrash, to flog. **2** to defeat or beat decisively. ~*n.* **1** (*coll.*) a blow, a punch. **2** (*coll.*) forceful impact, power. **3** (*sl.*) beer. **walloper** *n.* **1** a person or thing that wallops. **2** (*Austral.*, *sl.*) a police officer. **walloping** *n.* (*coll.*) a thrashing. ~*a.* big, thumping, whopping.

wallow (wol'ō) *v.i.* **1** to roll or tumble about in mud, water etc. **2** to revel grossly or self-indulgently (in) (*to wallow in self-pity*). ~*n.* **1** the act of wallowing. **2** a mudhole or other place in which animals wallow. **wallower** *n.*

wally (wol'i) *n.* (*pl.* **wallies**) (*sl.*) an incompetent or stupid person.

walnut (wawl'nŭt) *n.* **1** a tree of the genus *Juglans*, esp. *J. regia*, bearing a nut enclosed in a green fleshy covering. **2** the unripe fruit of this used for pickling. **3** the ripe nut. **4** the timber of this or other species of the same genus used in cabinetmaking etc.

Usage note Pronunciation as (waw'nŭt), without the (l), is best avoided.

walrus (wawl'rəs, wol'-) *n.* (*pl.* **walruses**) a large, amphibious, long-tusked, seal-like mammal of the Arctic seas, *Odobenus rosmarus*. **walrus moustache**, (*N Am.*) **walrus mustache** *n.* a thick moustache with long drooping ends.

Usage note Pronunciation as (waw'rŭs) without the (l) is best avoided.

waltz (wawlts, wawls, wols) *n.* **1** a dance in triple time in which the partners pass round each other smoothly as they progress. **2** the music for such a dance. ~*v.i.* **1** to dance a waltz. **2** (*coll.*) to move quickly, confidently or casually (*She waltzed in and announced she was leaving*). ~*v.t.* to move (a person) in or as in a waltz (*He waltzed her across the floor*). **waltzer** *n.* **1** a person who waltzes. **2** a type of fairground ride with spinning cars.

wampum (wom'pəm) *n.* small beads made of shells, used by N American Indians formerly as money, or for decorating belts, bracelets etc.

wan (won) *a.* (*comp.* **wanner**, *superl.* **wannest**) **1** pale or sickly in hue, pallid. **2** lacking vigour or liveliness, worn. **3** (of light etc.) dim, faint. **wanly** *adv.* **wanness** *n.* **wannish** *a.* **wanny** *a.*

wand (wond) *n.* **1** a long, slender rod, esp. one used by conjurors or as a staff of office. **2** (*coll.*) a conductor's baton. **3** a light-pen used for reading bar codes.

wander (won'də) *v.i.* **1** to travel or go here and there without any definite route or object, to rove, ramble or roam. **2** to follow an irregular or winding course. **3** to lose one's way, to go astray. **4** to talk or think in a confused or unclear way, to be delirious. **5** to digress from the subject in hand. ~*v.t.* to wander over, to traverse in a random way. ~*n.* a short relaxed walk without any definite route or object. **wanderer** *n.* **wandering** *a.*, *n.* **wandering Jew** *n.* **1** a legendary character condemned, for an insult to Christ, to wander from place to place until the Day of Judgement. **2** any of various trailing or climbing plants, esp. *Tradescantia albiflora* or *Zebrina pendula*. **wanderingly** *adv.* **wanderlust** *n.* the desire to travel.

wane (wān) *v.i.* **1** (of the illuminated portion of the moon) to diminish in size and brilliance. **2** to decrease in power, strength etc., to decline. ~*n.* **1** the act or process of waning, decrease, diminution. **2** the period when the moon wanes. **on the wane** waning.

wangle (wang'gəl) *v.t.* (*coll.*) **1** to achieve or gain by devious means (*She wangled herself a pay* *rise*). **2** to falsify (accounts etc.). ~*n.* the act or an instance of wangling. **wangler** *n.*

wank (wangk) *v.i., v.t.* (*taboo sl.*) to masturbate. ~*n.* an instance of masturbating. **wanker** *n.* **1** a person who masturbates. **2** a worthless, incompetent or contemptible person.

wannabe (won´əbē), **wannabee** *n.* (*sl.*) a person anxious to be like somebody, esp. a famous person, or to become something.

want (wont) *n.* **1** the state or condition of not having, lack, deficiency, absence (of). **2** need, privation, penury, poverty. **3** a longing or desire for something that is necessary or required for happiness etc. **4** something so desired. ~*v.t.* **1** to wish, to desire (*I want to go home*). **2** to feel a desire or longing for, to crave (*I want a drink*). **3** to desire or request the presence or assistance of (*You're wanted in reception*). **4** to need, to require. **5** to be without, to lack, to be deficient in. **6** to be short by, to require in order to be complete. **7** (*coll.*) ought (to) (*You want to try this new diet*). ~*v.i.* **1** to be in need, to be in want (for). **2** to be deficient (in), to fall short (in). **3** to be lacking, to have need (for). **4** (*esp. N Am., coll.*) to desire to be (*He wants out*). **not to want to** to be unwilling to. **wanted** *a.* **1** sought by the police. **2** sought by a person advertising in a newspaper, magazine etc. **wanter** *n.* **wanting** *a.* **1** absent, missing. **2** not meeting the required or expected standard. **3** lacking (in), deficient (in). **to be found wanting** to fail to meet the required or expected standard.

wanton (won´tən) *a.* **1** behaving in a licentious manner, with uncontained immorality. **2** random, heedless, reckless, purposeless (*wanton destruction*). **3** extravagant, luxuriant. **4** unrestrained, loose, wild, unruly. **wantonly** *adv.* **wantonness** *n.*

wapiti (wop´iti) *n.* (*pl.* **wapitis**) a N American stag, *Cervus canadensis*, related to the red deer.

War. *abbr.* Warwickshire.

war (waw) *n.* **1** a contest carried on by force of arms between nations, or between parties in the same state (*a world war; a civil war*). **2** a state of armed hostilities with suspension of ordinary international relations (*to declare war*). **3** (*also* **War**) a specific armed conflict (*They moved to Sussex after the war*). **4** hostility, enmity, strife. **5** a conflict, feud, struggle or campaign (*the war against crime*). ~*v.i.* (*pres.p.* **warring**, *past, p.p.* **warred**) **1** to make or carry on war. **2** to contend, to strive, to compete. **3** to be in opposition, to be inconsistent. **at war** engaged in hostilities (with). **in the wars** (*coll.*) bruised or injured as from fighting or quarrelling. **to go to war 1** to begin a war. **2** to begin active service in a war. **war chest** *n.* (*esp. N Am.*) a fund for a war or other campaign. **war crime** *n.* a crime committed in violation of the accepted rules of war. **war criminal** *n.* **war cry** *n.* (*pl.* **war cries**) **1** a name or phrase formerly shouted when charging into battle etc., a rallying cry. **2** a watchword. **3** a party slogan. **war damage** *n.* damage caused to property etc.

by bombs or shells during a war. **war dance** *n.* a dance practised, as by some N American Indian tribes, as a preparation for battle or in celebration of victory. **warfare** (-feə) *n.* **1** a state of war, hostilities. **2** conflict, strife. **warfarer** *n.* **war game** *n.* **1** a simulated military battle or campaign. **2** an enactment of a battle using models. **war gaming** *n.* **warhead** *n.* the head of a torpedo, aerial bomb, rocket etc., charged with explosive. **warhorse** *n.* **1** (*Hist.*) a charger, a horse used in battle. **2** (*coll.*) a veteran of war, politics etc. **warlike** *a.* **1** threatening war, hostile. **2** martial, soldier-like, military. **3** fit or ready for war. **war loan** *n.* a loan raised to meet the cost of a war. **warlord** *n.* a military leader or commander. **war memorial** *n.* a monument to those killed in a war. **warmonger** *n.* a person who promotes or traffics in war. **warmongering** *n., a.* **war of attrition** *n.* a long-drawn-out conflict in which each side tries to wear down the other. **warpaint** *n.* **1** paint put on the face and body, esp. by N American Indians, before going into battle. **2** (*coll.*) make-up. **warpath** *n.* **1** the path taken by an attacking party of N American Indians. **2** a warlike expedition. **on the warpath 1** ready for or engaged in conflict. **2** (*coll.*) thoroughly roused or incensed. **warplane** *n.* a military aircraft for use in war. **warring** *a.* **1** at war, fighting. **2** rival (*warring factions*). **3** conflicting, inconsistent. **warship** *n.* an armed ship for use in war. **Wars of the Roses** *n.pl.* (*Hist.*) the civil wars between the houses of York and Lancaster in the 15th cent. **wartime** *n.* a period of war. **war-torn** *a.* devastated by war. **war widow** *n.* the widow of a man killed in a war.

warble[1] (waw´bəl) *v.i.* **1** (esp. of birds) to sing in a continuous quavering or trilling manner. **2** (of streams etc.) to make a continuous melodious sound. **3** to sing (with trills and variations etc.). ~*v.t.* to sing or utter thus. ~*n.* **1** the act or sound of warbling. **2** a song. **3** a trill. **warbler** *n.* **1** a person or thing that warbles. **2** a member of the Sylviidae, a family of small birds including the nightingale, blackcap, robin etc. **warbling** *a.* **warblingly** *adv.*

warble[2] (waw´bəl) *n.* **1** a small hard tumour on a horse's back caused by the galling of the saddle. **2** a small tumour under the skin of cattle produced by the larva of the warble fly. **warble fly** *n.* (*pl.* **warble flies**) any of various flies of the genus *Hypoderma*.

ward (wawd) *n.* **1** an administrative or electoral division of a town or city. **2** a separate division of a hospital, prison etc. **3** a minor or other person under the care of a guardian. **4** (*also* **ward of court**) a person placed under the protection of a court, esp. a minor or a mentally handicapped person. **5** guardianship, protection, control. **6** (*usu. pl.*) a projection inside a lock that prevents the turning of any but the right key. **to ward off 1** to parry, to turn aside, to keep off. **2** to avert. **wardroom** *n.* a room on a warship for commissioned officers below the rank of commander. **wardship** n.

-ward (wəd), **-wards** (wədz) suf. used to form adjectives and adverbs expressing direction, as backward, forward, homeward, inwards, outwards etc.

warden (waw´dən) n. 1 a keeper, a guardian. 2 a governor. 3 the head of a college, school or hostel. 4 (esp. N Am.) a prison governor. 5 a person who keeps watch. 6 any of various public officials (a traffic warden). **wardenship** n.

warder (waw´də) n. 1 a keeper. 2 a jailer, a prison officer. 3 a guard, a sentinel. **wardress** (-dris) n. a female warder.

wardrobe (waw´drōb) n. 1 a tall cupboard with rails, shelves etc. where clothes are hung up. 2 a person's stock of clothes. 3 the costumes of a theatre or film company. 4 the department in charge of these. 5 the department of a royal household concerned with clothing etc. **wardrobe master, wardrobe mistress** n. a person in charge of the costumes of a theatre or film company.

-wards -WARD.

ware (weə) n. 1 (usu. in comb.) **a** manufactured articles of a specified kind, as tableware, glassware, silverware, hardware etc. **b** pottery of a specified kind, as Wedgwood ware. 2 (pl.) **a** articles of merchandise, articles for sale, goods. **b** a person's skills or talents.

warehouse[1] (weə´hows) n. 1 a building in which goods are stored, kept for sale or in bond. 2 a wholesale or large retail store. **warehouseman** n. (pl. **warehousemen**) a person who keeps or is employed in a warehouse. **warehouse party** n. (pl. **warehouse parties**) a large organized party for young people, often illegal, held in a disused warehouse or similar building.

warehouse[2] (weə´hows, -howz) v.t. 1 to deposit, secure or store (furniture, bonded goods etc.) in a warehouse. 2 (N Am., coll.) to shut up in a hospital, prison or similar establishment and forget about.

warfare WAR.

warfarin (waw´fərin) n. a compound used as a rodent poison and to prevent blood clotting.

†warlock (waw´lok) n. a wizard, a sorcerer.

warm (wawm) a. 1 at a rather high temperature. 2 having heat in a moderate degree. 3 promoting, emitting or conveying heat (warm clothing). 4 having the body or skin temperature raised by exercise etc. 5 ardent, zealous, enthusiastic. 6 friendly, cordial (a warm welcome). 7 sympathetic, emotional, affectionate (a warm nature). 8 amorous, erotic. 9 animated, heated, vehement, passionate (a warm debate). 10 (of colours) predominantly red or yellow. 11 (of a scent) fresh, strong. 12 (coll.) unpleasant, hot, uncomfortable. ~v.t. 1 to make warm. 2 to make ardent or enthusiastic, to excite. 3 (sl.) to thrash. ~v.i. 1 to become warm. 2 to become animated, enthusiastic or sympathetic (to or towards) (She warmed to

our suggestion). ~n. 1 an act of warming (I'll give the plates a warm). 2 a warm place or condition (Stay in the warm). **to warm up 1** to make or become warm. 2 to reheat (cooked food). 3 to prepare for a contest, performance etc., esp. by exercising or practising. 4 to make (an audience) more receptive to a show or act by a preliminary entertainment. **warm-blooded** a. 1 (of animals etc.) having warm blood, esp. between 98° and 112°F (36.6 and 44.4°C). 2 emotional, passionate, excitable. **warm-bloodedness** n. **warmed** a. **warmed-over** a. (N Am.) warmed-up. **warmed-up** a. 1 (of food) reheated. 2 stale, unoriginal. **warmer** n. **warm front** n. the advancing edge of a mass of warm air. **warm-hearted** a. having warm, affectionate or kindly feelings. **warm-heartedly** adv. **warm-heartedness** n. **warming-pan** n. a closed pan, usu. of brass with a long handle, for holding live coals, formerly used to warm a bed. **warmish** a. **warmly** adv. **warmness** n. **warmth** n. **warm-up** n. the act or an instance of warming up.

warn (wawn) v.t. 1 to give notice to, to inform beforehand. 2 to caution, to make aware of danger. 3 to put (a person) on their guard (against)(We warned him against accepting their offer). 4 to expostulate with, to admonish. 5 to tell or order to go or stay (away, off etc.). **warner** n. **warning** n. 1 the act of cautioning or making aware of danger etc. 2 previous notice (without warning). 3 something serving to warn. ~a. serving to warn (a warning sign). **warningly** adv.

warp (wawp) n. 1 the state of being twisted or distorted, a twist or distortion in timber etc. 2 a perversion or aberration of mind or disposition. 3 the threads running the long way of a woven fabric, crossed by the weft or woof. 4 a rope, usu. smaller than a cable, used in towing a vessel. ~v.t. 1 to turn or twist out of shape, to make crooked, to distort. 2 to pervert, to bias, to turn awry. 3 to tow or move (a ship) with a line attached to a buoy, anchor or other fixed point etc. 4 to prepare (yarn) as a warp for weaving. ~v.i. 1 to become twisted, crooked or distorted. 2 to become perverted. 3 (of a ship) to be towed or moved by warping. **warpage** (-ij) n. **warped** a. 1 distorted (warped timbers). 2 perverted (a warped mind). **warper** n. **warping** n.

warrant (wor´ənt) v.t. 1 to answer or give an assurance for, to guarantee. 2 to give authority to, to sanction. 3 to serve as grounds or justification for. ~n. 1 anything that authorizes a person to do something. 2 authorization, sanction. 3 reason, grounds, justification. 4 an instrument giving power to arrest a person, search premises etc. 5 a certificate of office held by a warrant officer. 6 any person or thing that warrants. **I warrant** I am sure. **warrantable** a. **warrantee** (-tē´) n. a person to whom a warranty is given. **warranter** n. **warrant of attorney** n. a written authority by which one person authorizes another to act in their stead. **warrant officer** n. an officer ranking below a commissioned officer and above a non-commissioned officer in the army or air force. **warrantor** *n.* **warranty** *n.* (*pl.* **warranties**) **1** a promise or undertaking from a vendor to a purchaser that the thing sold is good and fit for use etc. **2** an express or implied undertaking in a contract that a fact is as stated. **3** a warrant, an authorization. **4** a justification.

warren (wor´ən) *n.* **1** a piece of ground with a network of underground tunnels where rabbits live and breed. **2** an overcrowded district. **3** a maze of interconnecting streets or passages.

warring WAR.

warrior (wor´iə) *n.* a person experienced or distinguished in war, a distinguished soldier.

wart (wawt) *n.* **1** a small hard excrescence on the skin of the hands etc. due to irregular growth of the papillae, caused by a virus. **2** a spongy excrescence on the hind pastern of a horse. **3** a small protuberance on the surface of a plant. **warted, warty** *a.* **warthog** *n.* a large-headed African wild pig, *Phacochoerus aethiopicus*, with warty excrescences on the face. **wartless** *a.*

wary (weə´ri) *a.* (*comp.* **warier**, *superl.* **wariest**) **1** cautious, watchful against deception, danger etc. **2** circumspect. **3** done with or characterized by caution. **warily** *adv.* **wariness** *n.*

was BE.

wash (wosh) *v.t.* **1** to cleanse with water or other liquid (*to wash one's hair; to wash the dishes*). **2** to remove or take out, off, away etc. thus. **3** to pass water or other liquid through or over. **4** (of waves, the sea etc.) to fall upon, cover or dash against. **5** to carry along, to sweep away etc., to scoop (out) by or as by the action of moving liquid. **6** to cover with a thin coat of colour. **7** to overlay with a thin coat of metal. ~*v.i.* **1** to cleanse oneself, one's hands, one's face etc. with water etc. **2** to wash clothes, dishes etc. (*I'll wash, you can dry*). **3** (of clothes etc.) to stand washing without fading or being damaged in any way. **4** (*coll.*) (of a story etc.) to stand examination, to be accepted or believed (*It won't wash*). **5** (of water etc.) to move or splash or sweep along. **6** to drift or be carried along on water. ~*n.* **1** the act or process of washing. **2** the state of being washed. **3** a quantity of clothes etc. washed at one time. **4** the motion of a body of water or air, esp. that caused by the passage of a ship or aircraft. **5** soil removed and accumulated by water, alluvium. **6** land washed by the sea or a river. **7** waste from the kitchen often used as food for pigs. **8** thin liquid food, slops. **9** a liquid used for cleansing, healing or cosmetic purposes, a lotion. **10** a thin coating of colour spread over broad masses of a painting, pen-and-ink drawing etc. **11** a thin liquid for coating a wall etc. **12** a thin coat of metal. **to come out in the wash 1** to be removed in washing. **2** (*coll.*) to be resolved or revealed in the end. **to wash down 1** to wash the whole of. **2** to accompany (food) with a drink. **to wash off** to remove or be removed by washing. **to wash**

one's hands (*euphem.*) to go to the lavatory. **to wash one's hands of** to disclaim any responsibility for. **to wash out 1** to remove or be removed by washing. **2** to wash free of something unwanted. **3** to cause to be cancelled because of rain. **4** (*coll.*) to cancel, to annul. **5** to erode. **6** (of a flood etc.) to cause a breach in. **to wash over** to happen around, without affecting (a person) (*His parents are always arguing, but it just washes over him*). **to wash up 1** to wash dishes etc. **2** (*esp. N Am.*) to wash one's hands and face. **washable** *a.* **washability** (-bil´-) *n.* **washbasin** *n.* a basin for washing the hands etc., forming part of the furnishings of a toilet, bathroom, some (hotel) bedrooms etc. **washboard** *n.* **1** a board with a ribbed surface for scrubbing clothes on. **2** such a board used as a musical instrument. **washday** *n.* the day on which domestic washing is done or sent to the laundry. **washed** *a.* **washed out, washed-out** *a.* **1** limp, exhausted, worn out. **2** pale, wan. **3** faded, colourless. **washed up, washed-up** *a.* (*sl.*) no longer successful or effective, finished, failed. **washer** *n.* **1** a ring or perforated disc of metal, rubber etc. for placing under a nut etc. to tighten the joint or spread the load. **2** a person or thing that washes. **3** a washing machine. **washer-dryer, washer-drier** *n.* a combined washing machine and tumble-dryer. **washerwoman** *n.* (*pl.* **washerwomen**) a laundrywoman or laundress. **washeteria** (-ətiə´riə) *n.* a launderette. **washing** *n.* **1** the act of cleansing by water etc. **2** clothes etc. washed or to be washed together. **washing machine** *n.* an electrical machine in which clothes etc. are washed automatically. **washing powder** *n.* a preparation of detergent or soap used in washing clothes etc. **washing soda** *n.* crystalline sodium carbonate. **washing-up** *n.* **1** the washing of dishes etc., esp. after a meal. **2** dishes, cutlery etc. to be washed. **wash-leather** *n.* a chamois leather or an imitation of this. **wash-out** *n.* **1** (*coll.*) a failure, a fiasco. **2** (*coll.*) an incompetent person. **3** (*Geol.*) (*also* washout) a scooping out or sweeping away of rock, earth etc. by a rush of water. **washroom** *n.* (*N Am.*) a bathroom or lavatory. **washstand** *n.* (*Hist.*) a piece of furniture for holding a ewer or pitcher, basin etc. for washing one's face and hands etc. **washtub** *n.* a tub in which clothes etc. are washed. **washy** *a.* (*comp.* **washier**, *superl.* **washiest**) **1** watery, too much diluted, weak, thin. **2** lacking solidity, intensity or vigour, feeble. **washily** *adv.* **washiness** *n.*

wasn't (woz´ənt) *contr.* was not.

Wasp (wosp), **WASP** *n.* (*N Am., usu. derog.*) an American of N European descent, considered in N America as belonging to a privileged class. **Waspy** *a.*

wasp (wosp) *n.* a predatory hymenopterous insect of solitary or social habits, esp. the common wasp, *Vespula vulgaris*, a European insect with a slender waist, black and yellow stripes and a powerful sting. **waspish** *a.* bad-tempered

and critical. **waspishly** *adv.* **waspishness** *n.*
wasplike *a.* **wasp-waist** *n.* a very thin waist.
wasp-waisted *a.*

†**wassail** (wos´āl, -əl) *n.* **1** a festive occasion, a
drinking-bout. **2** spiced ale or other liquor prepared for a wassail. ~*v.i.* to carouse, to make
merry. **wassailer** *n.*

waste (wāst) *v.t.* **1** to consume, to spend, to use
up unnecessarily, carelessly or lavishly, to
squander. **2** to fail to use to advantage. **3** (*often
pass.*) to use or bestow (advice, talent etc.) without effect or where appreciation is lacking (*Sarcasm is wasted on her*). **4** to wear away gradually.
5 to cause to lose weight, strength and health.
6 (*poet.*) to devastate, to lay waste. **7** (*sl.*) to kill.
~*v.i.* **1** to wear away gradually, to dwindle, to
wither. **2** to lose weight, strength and health. **3** to
be wasted. ~*a.* **1** superfluous, left over as useless
or valueless. **2** desolate, desert, unoccupied, uncultivated, devastated. **3** barren, unproductive.
~*n.* **1** the act or an instance of wasting, squan-
dering or throwing away. **2** the state or process of
being wasted or used up, gradual diminution of
substance, strength, value etc. **3** material, food
etc. rejected as superfluous, useless or valueless;
refuse. **4** a desolate or desert region, a wilderness. **to go/ run to waste** to be wasted. **to lay
waste 1** to render desolate. **2** to devastate, to ruin.
wastage (-ij) *n.* **1** loss by use, decay, leakage etc.
2 avoidable loss of something useful. **3** NATURAL
WASTAGE (under NATURAL). **wastebasket** *n.* (*esp.
N Am.*) a waste-paper basket. **waste bin** *n.* a
receptacle for waste paper and other refuse.
wasted *a.* **1** used up unnecessarily or carelessly.
2 not used to advantage. **3** (*sl.*) exhausted. **4** (*sl.*)
showing the effects of alcohol or drug abuse.
waste disposal *n.* the process of disposing of
waste, rubbish, refuse etc. **waste disposal unit** *n.*
an electrically operated device fitted to a kitchen
sink that breaks up waste, food refuse etc. before
it goes down the waste pipe. **wasteful** *a.* **1** extravagant, spending or using recklessly, unnecessarily or too lavishly. **2** causing waste. **wastefully**
adv. **wastefulness** *n.* **waste ground** *n.* a patch of
undeveloped or unused land, esp. in an urban
area. **wasteland** *n.* **1** a desolate or unproductive
area of land. **2** any time, place etc. considered
spiritually or intellectually desolate (*a cultural
wasteland*). **wasteless** *a.* **waste paper** *n.* spoiled,
used or discarded paper. **waste-paper basket** *n.* a
receptacle for waste paper. **waste pipe** *n.* a discharge pipe for used or superfluous water. **waste
product** *n.* (*often pl.*) **1** material produced by a
process as a useless by-product. **2** an unusable
product of metabolism. **waster** *n.* **1** a person who
wastes. **2** a prodigal, a spendthrift. **3** (*coll.*) a
good-for-nothing, a wastrel.

wastrel (wās´trəl) *n.* **1** a wasteful person. **2** a
good-for-nothing.

watch (woch) *n.* **1** a state of alertness, vigilance,
close observation or attention. **2** a small timepiece activated by a spring or battery, for

carrying on the person. **3** a period of watching or
of keeping guard. **4** (*Naut.*) **a** the period of time
during which each division of a ship's crew is
alternately on duty (four hours except during
the dogwatches of two hours). **b** either of two
halves into which a ship's officers and crew
are divided, taking duty alternately. ~*v.i.* **1** to be
vigilant, observant or expectant. **2** to look out
(for). **3** to act as a protector or guard (over). **4** to
keep awake at night, to keep vigil. ~*v.t.* **1** to
guard. **2** to observe closely, to keep one's eye or
eyes on. **3** to monitor or keep under observation
(*to watch one's weight*). **4** to look at, to view (*to
watch television*). **5** to tend, to look after. **6** to be
careful of. **on the watch** vigilant, on the lookout.
on watch on duty, esp. as a lookout. **to watch out
1** to be on the lookout (for). **2** to take care. **watchable** *a.* **watch-chain** *n.* a metal chain for securing
a pocket watch to the clothing. **watchdog** *n.* **1** a
dog kept to guard premises etc. **2** a person or
group that monitors the activities of an organization etc. to guard against illegal or undesirable practices and protect the rights of others.
~*v.t.* (*pres.p.* **watchdogging**, *past, p.p.* **watch-
dogged**) to guard, to keep under surveillance.
watcher *n.* **watchful** *a.* **1** careful to notice what
is happening. **2** cautious, wary. **watchfully** *adv.*
watchfulness *n.* **watch-glass** *n.* a glass covering
the face of a watch. **watching brief** *n.* **1** a brief
issued to a barrister instructed to watch a case on
behalf of a client not directly concerned in the
action. **2** observation of or interest in a proceeding with which one is not directly concerned.
watchmaker *n.* a person who makes or repairs
watches etc. **watchmaking** *n.* **watchman** *n.* (*pl.*
watchmen) **1** a person who guards a large building etc. at night. **2** (*Hist.*) a guard, a sentinel, esp.
a member of a body formerly employed to patrol
or guard the streets of a town at night. **watch
spring** *n.* the mainspring of a watch. **watch strap**
n. a strap for securing a watch round the wrist.
watchtower *n.* a tower of observation or one on
which sentinels are placed. **watchword** *n.* **1** a
motto, word or phrase symbolizing or epitom-
izing the principles of a party etc. **2** (*Hist.*) a
word given to sentinels etc. as a signal that one
has the right of admission etc., a password.

water (waw´tə) *n.* **1** (*Chem.*) a colourless, transparent liquid, without taste or smell, possessing
a neutral reaction, a compound of two parts by
weight of hydrogen with one of oxygen. **2** an
impure form of this found in rivers, lakes, oceans
etc. **3** (*often pl.*) a (natural) body of water, such as
a sea, a lake, a river. **4** a liquid consisting chiefly
or partly of water, such as various solutions
or products of distillation. **5** (*usu. pl.*) mineral
water at a spa. **6** tears, sweat, urine or another
bodily secretion. **7** (*usu. pl.*) the amniotic fluid
surrounding a foetus. **8** the state of the tide (*at
low water; an hour before high water*). **9** the
transparency or lustre of a diamond, pearl etc.
~*a.* **1** living or growing in, on or near water (*a

water plant). **2** of, for or relating to water (*a water pipe*). **3** involving water (*water sports*). *~v.t.* **1** to apply water to, to moisten, sprinkle, irrigate or supply with water. **2** to dilute or adulterate with water. **3** to provide with water for drinking. **4** (*usu. in p.p.*) to give an undulating sheen to the surface of (silk etc.) by moistening, pressing and heating in manufacture (*watered silk*). *~v.i.* **1** (of the mouth, eyes etc.) to secrete, shed or run with water in the form of saliva, tears etc. **2** to get or take in water. **3** (of cattle etc.) to drink. **like water** lavishly (*spending money like water*). **to hold water** to be sound or valid, to stand scrutiny. **to keep one's head above water** to avoid financial ruin. **to make one's mouth water 1** to stimulate one's appetite. **2** to make one very desirous. **to water down 1** to dilute with water. **2** to make less forceful, offensive, harsh, vivid etc. **water avens** *n.* the pinkish-flowered *Geum rivale*. **water bailiff** *n.* an officer employed to watch a river or other fishery to prevent poaching. **waterbed** *n.* a bed with a rubber or plastic mattress filled with water. **waterbird** *n.* an aquatic bird, esp. one living on or near fresh water. **water biscuit** *n.* a thin plain biscuit made from flour and water. **water blister** *n.* a blister containing watery fluid without pus or blood. **water-bloom** *n.* a rapid growth of microscopic algae in water. **water-boatman** *n.* (*pl.* **water-boatmen**) an aquatic insect of the family Notonectidae or Corixidae, with paddle-like hind legs. **water-buck** *n.* an African antelope, *Kobus ellipsiprymnus*, found near rivers, lakes and swamps. **water buffalo** *n.* (*pl.* **water buffalo, water buffaloes**) the common domesticated Asian buffalo, *Bubalus arnee*. **water bus** *n.* a river craft carrying passengers on a regular service. **water-butt** *n.* a large open-headed barrel for catching and preserving rainwater. **water-cannon** *n.* a device that ejects a jet of water at high pressure, used for quelling riots etc. **water chestnut** *n.* **1** an aquatic plant, *Trapa natans*, with an edible nutlike fruit. **2** the Chinese water chestnut, *Eleocharis tuberosa*, or its tuber used in cooking. **water closet** *n.* **1** a toilet with a water supply for flushing the basin. **2** a room containing this. **watercolour**, (*N Am.*) **watercolor** *n.* **1** a pigment ground up with water etc. instead of oil. **2** a painting done with watercolours. **3** (*often pl.*) the art of painting with watercolours. **watercolourist** *n.* **water-cool** *v.t.* to cool by (circulating) water. **water-cooled** *a.* **water-cooler** *n.* a device for cooling drinking water. **watercourse** *n.* **1** a stream, a brook. **2** a channel for the conveyance of water or in which a natural stream etc. flows. **watercraft** *n.* ships, boats etc. **watercress** *n.* a creeping aquatic plant, *Nasturtium officinale*, eaten as salad. **water-diviner** *n.* a dowser. **waterer** *n.* **waterfall** *n.* a steep or perpendicular descent of a river etc., a cascade, a cataract. **water flea** *n.* a minute freshwater crustacean of the genus *Daphnia*. **waterfowl** *n.* (*pl.* **waterfowl**) a bird that frequents rivers, lakes etc. **waterfront**

n. the part of a town facing or bordering a sea, harbour, lake, river etc. **watergate** *n.* **1** a gate for confining or releasing water, a floodgate. **2** a gate giving access to a river etc. **water hemlock** *n.* a poisonous marsh plant, *Cicuta maculata*, the cowbane. **water hen** *n.* the moorhen. **waterhole** *n.* a hole where water collects, esp. a pool in a dried-up river bed. **water hyacinth** *n.* an aquatic plant, *Eichhornia crassipes*, which floats in the waterways of tropical countries. **water ice** *n.* a frozen confection made from water, sugar etc. **watering** *n.* the act of obtaining or supplying water. **watering can** *n.* a vessel with a long spout and usu. a perforated nozzle for sprinkling water on plants etc. **watering hole** *n.* **1** a water-filled pool or hollow where animals can drink. **2** (*sl.*) a pub, bar etc. **water jump** *n.* a ditch, stream etc. to be jumped, esp. in a steeplechase. **waterless** *a.* **water lily** *n.* (*pl.* **water lilies**) an aquatic plant of the family Nymphaeaceae, with large floating leaves and white or coloured flowers. **waterline** *n.* **1** the line up to which the hull of a vessel is submerged in the water. **2** a line marking the level of a body of water. **waterlogged** *a.* **1** saturated with water. **2** (of a vessel) flooded with water so as to be unmanageable. **water main** *n.* a main pipe in a system of water supply. **waterman** *n.* (*pl.* **watermen**) **1** a boatman plying for hire on rivers etc. **2** a (good or bad) oarsman. **watermanship** *n.* **watermark** *n.* a translucent design stamped in paper in the process of manufacture to show the maker, size etc. *~v.t.* to stamp (paper) with a watermark. **water-meadow** *n.* a meadow fertilized by being flooded at certain seasons from an adjoining stream. **water measurer** *n.* an aquatic insect of the family Hydrometridae, which walks on the water. **watermelon** *n.* **1** a large trailing plant, *Citrullus lanatus*. **2** its edible fruit, with green rind and watery red flesh. **water meter** *n.* a device for measuring a water supply. **watermill** *n.* a mill driven by water or a waterwheel. **water moccasin** *n.* a large venomous snake, *Agkistrodon piscivorus*, of American swamps. **water nymph** *n.* a naiad, a nymph of the water in Greek mythology etc. **water ouzel** *n.* the dipper, *Cinclus cinclus*. **water pipe** *n.* **1** a pipe for conveying water. **2** a hookah. **water pistol** *n.* a toy pistol that shoots a jet of water. **water plantain** *n.* a plant of the genus *Alisma* found in marshes and ditches. **water polo** *n.* a game in which swimmers throw or dribble a ball like a football, aiming to put it in a goal. **waterproof** *a.* impervious to water. *~n.* **1** a waterproof coat or other garment. **2** cloth rendered waterproof. *~v.t.* to render waterproof. **waterproofer** *n.* **waterproofing** *n.* **waterproofness** *n.* **water rail** *n.* the common European rail, *Rallus aquaticus*. **water rat** *n.* a water vole. **water rate** *n.* a rate or charge for the supply of water. **water-repellent, water-resistant** *a.* resistant but not impervious to water. **water-resistance** *n.* **watershed** *n.* **1** a ridge or other line of separation between two river basins or drainage systems. **2** any dividing line or turning point. **waterside** n. the margin of a river, stream, lake or the sea. **water-ski** n. (pl. **water-skis**) a type of ski used for planing over water in water-skiing. ~v.i. (3rd pers. sing. pres. **water-skis**, pres.p. **water-skiing**, past, p.p. **water-skied**) to plane over water on water-skis; to go water-skiing. **water-skier** n. **water-skiing** n. the sport of being towed on water-skis at great speed by a motor boat. **water slide** n. a long slide down which water runs, usu. into a swimming pool. **water sports** n.pl. sporting activities that take place on or in water, such as windsurfing, water-skiing, swimming etc. **waterspout** n. a phenomenon which occurs during a tornado over the sea, in which water appears to be drawn up from the sea in a whirling column, sometimes connecting sea and cloud. **water-table** n. **1** the level below which the ground is saturated with water. **2** a projecting ledge or string course for throwing off the water on a building. **water taxi** n. (pl. **water taxis**) a small boat, usu. a motor boat, for transporting passengers over short distances. **watertight** a. **1** so tightly fastened or fitted as to prevent the passage of water in or out. **2** (of an argument etc.) unable to be attacked or refuted. **water torture** n. a form of torture involving water, esp. one in which water is dripped on to the victim's forehead. **water tower** n. an elevated building carrying a large tank or reservoir for giving pressure to a water supply. **water vole** n. a large semiaquatic vole, esp. *Arvicola terrestris*, a water rat. **water wagon** n. a vehicle for transporting water. **off the water wagon** (coll.) no longer abstaining from alcohol. **on the water wagon** (coll.) abstaining from alcohol. **waterway** n. **1** a navigable channel, a fairway. **2** a route for travel or transport by boat or ship. **3** the thick planks along the edge of a deck in which a channel is hollowed for conducting water to the scuppers. **waterweed** n. **waterwheel** n. a wheel moved by water and used to drive machinery etc. **water wings** n.pl. floats worn by a person learning to swim. **waterworks** n. **1** an establishment for the collection, storage and distribution of water for the use of communities, driving machinery etc. **2** an artificial fountain. **3** (as pl., coll.) the urinary system. **4** (as pl., coll.) crying, tears (to turn on the waterworks). **watery** a. **1** containing too much water (watery soup). **2** wet, sodden. **3** suffused or running with water. **4** thin, transparent or pale, like water. **5** rainy-looking. **6** of or consisting of water. **7** tasteless, insipid, vapid. **wateriness** n.

Waterloo (wawtəloo´) n. a downfall, a decisive defeat (to meet one's Waterloo).

watt (wot) n. a unit of power or rate of doing work, equal to a rate of working of one joule per second or the power available when the electromotive force is one volt and the current is one ampere. **wattage** (-ij) n. an amount of power in watts. **watt-hour** n. a unit of (electrical) energy

equal to a power of one watt operating for one hour. **wattmeter** n. a meter for measuring electrical power in watts.

wattle (wot´əl) n. **1** a construction of interwoven twigs or wickerwork used to make fences, walls etc. **2** the twigs etc. used for this. **3** the fleshy lobe under the throat of the domestic fowl, turkey etc. **4** a barbel of a fish. **5** any of various Australian and Tasmanian species of acacia, the bark of which is used in tanning. **6** the national flower of Australia. ~v.t. **1** to interweave, to interlace, to plait. **2** to construct from wattle. **wattle and daub** n. a method of constructing walls of interwoven twigs or wickerwork covered with mud or clay. **wattled** a. **wattling** n.

wave (wāv) v.i. **1** to move to and fro with a sinuous or sweeping motion like a flag in the wind, to flutter or undulate. **2** to have an undulating shape or conformation, to be wavy. **3** to greet or signal (to) by waving the hand etc. ~v.t. **1** to cause to move to and fro (to wave a hand; to wave a flag). **2** to give an undulating motion to. **3** to brandish (a weapon etc.). **4** to give an undulating surface, conformation or appearance to, to make wavy. **5** to indicate, direct or command by a waving signal (She waved him away). **6** to express by waving (to wave goodbye). ~n. **1** a moving ridge or long curved body of water or other liquid, esp. one formed on the surface of the sea, rising into an arch and breaking on the shore. **2** (often pl., poet.) the sea, water. **3** (Physics) **a** a disturbance of the equilibrium of a fluid medium continuously propagated from point to point without a corresponding advance of the particles in the same direction, by which motion, heat, light, sound, electricity etc. are transmitted. **b** a single curve or cycle in such a motion. **4** a curve or series of curves, an undulation. **5** a waviness of the hair. **6** the process of producing this (a permanent wave). **7** the act or gesture of waving, as a greeting, signal etc. **8** a heightened volume or intensity of some force, influence, emotion, activity etc. (a wave of panic). **9** a movement like that of a wave on the sea. **10** a widespread advance or influx. **11** a prolonged spell of hot or cold weather. **12** a waveform. **13** a rhythmical electromagnetic disturbance propagated through space. **14** a wavelike stripe or streak. **to make waves 1** (coll.) to cause trouble. **2** (coll.) to make an impression. **to wave aside** to dismiss with or as with a wave of the hand. **to wave down** to wave as a signal to (a driver or vehicle) to stop. **waveband** n. a range of frequencies or wavelengths which is allocated for radio transmissions of a particular type. **wave equation** n. (Physics) a differential equation describing wave motion. **waveform** n. **1** (Physics) the graph of a wave, showing the variation in a varying quantity against time. **2** the shape of this. **wavelength** n. **1** the distance between the crests of two adjacent waves. **2** the space intervening between corresponding points, such as the maximum positive points of two successive waves. **3** (*coll.*) a way of thinking, feeling, communicating etc. (*to be on the same wavelength*). **waveless** *a.* **wavelet** *n.* a small wave. **wavelike** *a.*, *adv.* **wave mechanics** *n.* quantum mechanics based on the wavelike properties and behaviour of particles. **waving** *a.* **wavy** *a.* (*comp.* **wavier**, *superl.* **waviest**) **1** rising or swelling in waves. **2** having an alternately concave and convex outline, undulating (*a wavy line*). **3** (of hair) having an undulating surface or loose curls. **wavily** *adv.* **waviness** *n.*

Usage note See note under WAIVE.

waver (wā′və) *v.i.* **1** to be in a state of indecision, to hesitate, to vacillate. **2** to become less certain. **3** to reel, to be unsteady. **4** to flicker, to quiver. **waverer** *n.* **wavering** *a.* **waveringly** *adv.* **waveringness** *n.* **wavery** *a.*

Usage note See note under WAIVE.

wax[1] (waks) *n.* **1** a yellow, mouldable, fatty substance excreted by bees and used for the cells of honeycombs; beeswax. **2** this substance purified and bleached, used for candles, modelling and pharmaceutical and other purposes. **3** any of various plant or animal substances that are principally esters of fatty acids or alcohols. **4** a mineral substance, such as ozocerite, composed of hydrocarbons. **5** any of various substances resembling beeswax, such as sealing wax. **6** cerumen, earwax. ~*a.* made of wax. ~*v.t.* **1** to smear, rub, polish, treat or join with wax. **2** to apply wax to (the legs etc.) and peel it away, thereby removing unwanted hair. **waxbill** *n.* a small bird of the family Estrildidae with a bill resembling red sealing wax in colour. **waxcloth** *n.* oilcloth. **waxed** *a.* **waxed jacket** *n.* a jacket made of cotton fabric waterproofed with wax. **waxen** *a.* **1** with a surface resembling wax. **2** like wax, impressible, plastic. **3** †made or consisting of wax. **waxer** *n.* **wax myrtle** *n.* the candleberry or bayberry shrub. **waxwing** *n.* any bird of the genus *Bombycilla*, the secondary and tertiary quills in some of which terminate in horny tips resembling pieces of red sealing wax. **waxwork** *n.* **1** modelling in wax, esp. in close imitation of living persons. **2** a wax figure or other object modelled in wax. **3** (*pl.*) an exhibition of wax figures. **waxworker** *n.* **waxy** *a.* (*comp.* **waxier**, *superl.* **waxiest**) resembling wax in appearance or consistency. **waxily** *adv.* **waxiness** *n.*

wax[2] (waks) *v.i.* **1** to increase gradually in size and brilliance, as the illuminated portion of the moon between new and full. **2** (*poet.*) to become larger, to grow in numbers, strength, intensity etc. **3** to pass into a specified condition, to become gradually (*to wax lyrical*).

way (wā) *n.* **1** a road, path, track or other place of passage. **2** a length of space passed over, a distance to be traversed (*a long way*). **3** the course or route followed or to be followed between two

places or to reach a place (*to ask the way*). **4** a place of entrance, exit etc. (*the way in*). **5** the direction in which a thing or place lies or in which motion etc. takes place. **6** a particular or specified direction (*Come this way*). **7** the method, plan or manner of doing something, or proceeding to carry out some purpose. **8** a line or course of action. **9** a usual or habitual mode of action or conduct, a personal peculiarity, an idiosyncrasy (*to change one's ways*). **10** the usual course of events. **11** condition, state (*in a bad way*). **12** relation, respect, point. **13** onward movement, progress, advance, impetus (*to make one's way*). **14** room for passage or advance, ground over which one would proceed. **15** the state of being in transit (*on the way*). **16** (*pl.*) parts, portions (*The money was split four ways*). ~*adv.* (*coll.*) far, much (*It's way too expensive*). **across the way** opposite, on the other side of the road etc. **all the way 1** the full distance. **2** completely. **by the way** in passing, parenthetically. **by way of 1** by the route of, via. **2** for the purpose of. **3** as a form of or substitute for, to serve as (*by way of introduction*). **in a way 1** to some degree. **2** from one point of view. **in its way** considered from an appropriate standpoint. **in no way** by no means. **in the way** in a position or of a nature to obstruct or hinder. **in the way of 1** so as to fall in with or obtain (*I can put you in the way of a good deal*). **2** as regards, by way of. **on the way 1** in progress. **2** travelling or in transit. **3** (*coll.*) not yet born (*She's got four kids and another one on the way*). **on the way out** going out of fashion or favour. **to be on one's way 1** to set off. **2** to be travelling or in transit. **to come someone's way 1** to become available to someone. **2** to fall to someone's lot (*You must take whatever comes your way*). **to find a way** to discover a means (of). **to get/ have one's (own) way** to get what one wants. **to go one's own way** to follow one's own plan, to act independently. **to go one's way** to depart. **to go out of one's way** to take great trouble (to), to make a special effort (to). **to go someone's way 1** to travel in the same direction as someone. **2** (of events etc.) to be in someone's favour. **to have it both ways** to have or alternate between two incompatible things. **to make one's way 1** to proceed. **2** to prosper, esp. by one's own exertions. **under way 1** (of a ship etc.) in motion. **2** in progress. **way back** (*coll.*) a long time ago. **waybill** *n.* a list of passengers in a public conveyance or of goods sent by a carrier. **wayfarer** *n.* a traveller, esp. on foot. **wayfaring** *n.*, *a.* **wayfaring tree** *n.* a large shrub, *Viburnum lantana*, with white flowers and black berries, found by roadsides. **waylay** *v.t.* (*pres.p.* **waylaying**, *past*, *p.p.* **waylaid**) **1** to wait for and stop, accost or intercept. **2** to lie in wait for and attack or rob. **waylayer** *n.* **way-leave** *n.* a right of way over the land of another, esp. rented by a company etc. **waymark** *n.* a post or other marker for guidance along a route, esp. on a footpath. **waymarked** *a.*

way of thinking n. an opinion (to my way of thinking). **way-out** a. 1 (coll.) out of the ordinary, unconventional, experimental. 2 (sl.) excellent. **waypoint** n. 1 a stopping place on a journey. 2 the coordinates of a stage on a sea journey, flight etc., used in navigation. **ways and means** n.pl. 1 methods of doing or achieving something. 2 methods of raising money, esp. government revenue. **wayside** n. the side of the road. ~a. situated or growing by the wayside. **to fall by the wayside** to fail or drop out during the course of an undertaking. **way station** n. (N Am.) 1 a railway halt. 2 a stage of progress in a course of action.

-ways (wāz), **-way** (wā) suf. forming adverbs of position, direction, manner etc., as always, lengthways.

wayward (wā´wəd) a. 1 selfish, stubborn and difficult to control. 2 freakish, unpredictable, capricious. **waywardly** adv. **waywardness** n.

Wb abbr. weber.

WC abbr. 1 water closet. 2 West Central.

W/Cdr abbr. Wing Commander.

we (wē) pron. 1 the plural of I², denoting the person speaking and others associated with or represented by that person. 2 I (used by a sovereign, a newspaper editor etc.). 3 people in general. 4 (coll.) you (How are we today?).

weak (wēk) a. 1 deficient in physical strength, not robust, vigorous or powerful. 2 feeble, infirm, sickly, easily exhausted or fatigued. 3 deficient in mental or moral strength, feeble-minded, lacking strength of will, resolution etc. 4 characterized by or showing lack of resolution or willpower. 5 deficient in strength, durability, force or efficiency. 6 fragile, brittle, pliant. 7 unreliable, ineffective, inefficacious. 8 deficient in number, quantity, weight etc. 9 lacking in flavour, watery (weak coffee). 10 poor, inadequate. 11 unsustained, unconvincing, controvertible (a weak argument). 12 (Gram.) (of verbs) inflected by the addition of -ed, -d or -t to the stem in forming the past tense and p.p., not by internal vowel change. 13 (of a syllable) unaccented, unstressed. 14 (of light) difficult to see; dim or faint. 15 (of sound) difficult to hear. **weaken** v.t. 1 to make weak or weaker. 2 to reduce the force of. 3 to add water or another liquid to. ~v.i. 1 to become weak or weaker. 2 to begin to change one's opinion. **weakener** n. **weaker** a. **weaker sex** n. (derog.) the female sex, women. **weakish** a. **weak-kneed** a. giving way easily, lacking in resolution. **weakling** n. a feeble person. **weakly** adv. in a weak manner. ~a. (comp. **weaklier**, superl. **weakliest**) not strong in constitution; feeble, infirm, sickly. **weakliness** n. **weak-minded** a. feeble in intelligence or in resolution. **weak-mindedness** n. **weakness** n. 1 the state or condition of being deficient in physical strength. 2 the state or condition of being infirm or sickly. 3 the state or quality of being unreliable or ineffective. 4 the state or quality of being deficient in number,

quantity, weight etc. 5 the state or quality of being unconvincing. 6 dimness or faintness of light. 7 a particular defect, failing or fault, a weak point. 8 a lack of resisting power. 9 a self-indulgent fondness (a weakness for cream cakes). **weak point, weak spot** n. 1 a place where defences are weak. 2 a failing or fault. 3 a trait by which a person is most easily influenced.

weal¹ (wēl) n. 1 a ridge or raised streak made by a rod or whip on the flesh. 2 (Med.) a raised or inflamed area of the skin. ~v.t. to mark with a weal or weals.

weal² (wēl) n. (poet.) a sound, healthy or prosperous state of persons or things.

wealth (welth) n. 1 riches, large possessions of money, goods or lands. 2 the state of being rich, affluence. 3 an abundance, a profusion (of) (a wealth of information). **wealthy** a. (comp. **wealthier**, superl. **wealthiest**) rich, affluent, having many possessions. **wealthily** adv. **wealthiness** n.

wean¹ (wēn) v.t. 1 to accustom (a child or animal) to nourishment other than its mother's milk, to teach to feed other than from the breast or bottle. 2 to detach or estrange from a habit, indulgence, desire etc. (I'm trying to wean him off computer games).

wean² (wān) n. (Sc., North.) a child.

weapon (wep´ən) n. 1 an instrument of attack or defence, a thing used to inflict bodily harm. 2 any means used for attack or defence. **weaponed** a. **weaponless** a. **weaponry** n. weapons collectively.

wear¹ (weə) v.t. (past **wore** (waw), p.p. **worn** (wawn)) 1 to have on the person as clothing, ornament etc. 2 to be dressed in, esp. habitually. 3 to arrange (hair or clothes) in a specified manner. 4 to bear, to carry, to maintain. 5 to exhibit, to display (to wear a smile). 6 to consume, diminish, impair, efface or alter by rubbing or use. 7 to make thinner or weaker because of continuous use. 8 to produce (a hole, channel etc.) by attrition. 9 to exhaust, fatigue or weary. 10 (coll.) to stand for, to tolerate, accept (Do you think she'll wear it?). 11 to pass (time) slowly or gradually. ~v.i. 1 to be consumed, diminished, effaced, altered etc. by rubbing or use. 2 to become thinner or weaker because of continuous use. 3 to be exhausted, to be tired (out). 4 to stand continual use (well, badly etc.). 5 to resist the effects of use, age, attrition etc., to endure, to last. 6 to pass slowly or gradually (away etc.) (as the day wore on). ~n. 1 the act of wearing. 2 the state of being worn. 3 something worn or to be worn, clothing. 4 damage or diminution by rubbing, use etc. 5 durability, fitness for use. **in wear** being worn regularly. **to wear off** 1 to efface or diminish by attrition; to rub off. 2 to be effaced or diminished by attrition. 3 to decline or pass away gradually (when the effects of the drugs wear off). **to wear out** 1 to use until no longer of use, to consume or render worthless by use. 2 to exhaust, to tire out.

3 to be used up, consumed or rendered worthless by attrition and use. **to wear thin 1** to become thin through use. **2** (of patience) to diminish. **3** (of excuses) to become less convincing or acceptable. **-wear** *comb. form* forming names of categories of clothing, as in *menswear, swimwear*. **wearable** *a.* **wearability** (-bil´-) *n.* **wear and tear** *n.* waste, diminution or damage caused by ordinary use. **wearer** *n.* **wearing** *a.* **1** tiresome. **2** tiring. **wearingly** *adv.*

wear² (weə) *v.t.* (*past, p.p.* **wore** (waw)) to bring (a ship) about by turning the bow away from the wind. *~v.i.* (of a ship) to come round thus.

weary (wiə´ri) *a.* (*comp.* **wearier**, *superl.* **weariest**) **1** tired, fatigued, exhausted. **2** expressing weariness or exhaustion (*a weary smile*). **3** impatient or sick (of). **4** tiresome, tedious. **5** exhausting, irksome. *~v.t.* (*3rd pers. sing. pres.* **wearies**, *pres.p.* **wearying**, *past, p.p.* **wearied**) **1** to tire, to fatigue. **2** to make impatient or sick (of). *~v.i.* **1** to become tired or fatigued. **2** to become impatient or sick (of). **weariless** *a.* **wearily** *adv.* **weariness** *n.* **wearisome** *a.* tedious, tiresome, causing weariness. **wearisomely** *adv.* **wearisomeness** *n.* **wearyingly** *adv.*

weasel (wē´zəl) *n.* **1** a small reddish-brown, white-bellied mammal, *Mustela nivalis*, related to the stoat, ferret etc., with a long lithe body and short legs, preying on small birds, mice etc. **2** (*coll.*) a sly, deceitful, furtive or treacherous person. *~v.i.* (*pres.p.* **weaselling**, (*N Am.*) **weaseling**, *past, p.p.* **weaselled**, (*N Am.*) **weaseled**) (*coll.*) **1** to evade or extricate oneself from a responsibility, obligation etc. (*He tried to weasel out of the deal*). **2** (*esp. N Am.*) to equivocate. **weaselly** *a.* **weasel word** *n.* (*usu. pl.*) a word designed to mislead or to be evasive.

weather (wedh´ə) *n.* **1** the state of the atmosphere, esp. at a given time or place, with reference to cold or heat, humidity, rain, pressure, wind, electrical conditions etc. **2** (*usu. pl.*) change, vicissitude. *~v.t.* **1** to encounter and pass through (a storm etc.) in safety. **2** to endure and come through (a crisis etc.) in safety. **3** to expose to the action of the weather. **4** (*usu. p.p.*) to wear, disintegrate or discolour (rock, cliffs, masonry etc.) by this. **5** (*Naut.*) to get to windward of (a cape etc.) in spite of inclement weather. *~v.i.* **1** to stand the effects of weather. **2** to become worn or discoloured by exposure to weather. *~a.* situated towards the wind; windward (*the weather side*). **to keep a/ one's weather eye open 1** (*coll.*) to be on the alert. **2** (*coll.*) to have one's wits about one. **to make heavy weather of** to exaggerate the difficulty of. **under the weather 1** poorly, unwell. **2** depressed, in low spirits. **3** drunk, intoxicated. **weather-beaten** *a.* seasoned or tanned by exposure to weather, storms etc. **weatherboard** *v.t.* to furnish with weatherboarding. *~n.* **1** a board used for weatherboarding. **2** a board fastened to the bottom of a door to keep out rain, snow etc. **weatherboarding** *n.* a series of sloping

boards fastened together so as to overlap and to throw off rain, snow etc. from roofs, walls etc. **weathercock** *n.* **1** a weathervane, esp. in the shape of a cock. **2** an inconstant person. **weatherglass** *n.* a barometer. **weathering** *n.* **1** exposure to the weather. **2** disintegration etc. through this. **weatherman** *n.* (*pl.* **weathermen**) a man who reports on the weather on television etc., a meteorologist. **weathermost** *a.* furthest to windward. **weatherproof** *a.* proof against the weather, esp. against rain. *~v.t.* to make weatherproof. **weatherproofed** *a.* **weather station** *n.* a place where meteorological observations are taken or recorded. **weatherstrip** *n.* a piece of board, rubber etc. fastened across a door, window etc. to keep out wind or rain. **weathervane** *n.* a revolving vane mounted on the top of a steeple or other high point to show the direction of the wind.

weave¹ (wēv) *v.t.* (*past* **wove** (wōv), *p.p.* **woven** (wō´vən), **wove**) **1** to form (threads, yarns etc.) into fabric by interlacing. **2** to produce (fabric or an article) thus (*to weave a rug*). **3** to construct by intertwining canes, rushes etc. **4** (of a spider) to form (a web). **5** to interweave (facts, details etc.) into a story, theory etc. **6** to construct (a scheme, plot etc.) thus. *~v.i.* **1** to make fabric by interlacing threads etc. **2** to work at a loom. **weavable** *a.* **weaver** *n.* **1** a person who weaves, esp. one whose occupation is to weave cloth etc. **2** a weaver-bird. **weaver-bird** *n.* a finchlike bird of the family Ploceidae, of the warmer parts of Asia, Africa and Australia, that constructs elaborate nests of woven grass.

weave² (wēv) *v.i.* (*past, p.p.* **weaved**) **1** to take a zigzag course, esp. to avoid obstructions (*to weave through the traffic*). **2** (*coll.*) to take evasive action. **to get weaving 1** (*sl.*) to begin. **2** (*sl.*) to hurry.

web (web) *n.* **1** a network of threads constructed by spiders to catch their prey, a cobweb. **2** a similar structure spun by insect larvae etc. **3** a woven fabric, a piece of woven cloth. **4** any complex network or similar structure. **5** an artfully contrived plot, trap etc. **6** the membrane between the toes of swimming birds etc. **7** the vane of a feather. **8** a large roll of paper for printing etc. as it comes from the mill. **the Web** the World Wide Web. **webbed** *a.* **1** (of a bird's foot etc.) having the toes connected by a membrane. **2** connected or covered with or as with a web. **webbing** *n.* **1** a strong woven band of fibre etc., used for belts, straps, the bottoms of seats or beds etc. **2** any strong woven tape or edging. **webfoot** *n.* (*pl.* **webfeet**) a webbed foot. **web-footed** *a.* having the toes connected by a web. **web offset** *n.* offset printing using a continuous roll of paper. **Web site** *n.* a locus of packaged resources made available for access on the World Wide Web. **web-toed** *a.* webfooted.

weber (vā´bə, web´ə) *n.* the SI unit of magnetic flux.

Wed. *abbr.* Wednesday.

wed (wed) *v.t.* (*pres.p.* **wedding**, *past, p.p.* **wedded, wed**) **1** (*usu. formal*) **a** to marry. **b** to join in marriage. **2** to unite, to attach firmly. ~*v.i.* (*usu. formal*) to marry. **wedded** *a.* **1** married, of or relating to matrimony. **2** intimately united. **3** strongly attached (to). **wedding** *n.* a marriage ceremony, usu. with the accompanying festivities. **wedding breakfast** *n.* a celebratory meal given after a wedding ceremony. **wedding cake** *n.* an iced cake distributed to the guests at a wedding, portions being afterwards sent to absent friends. **wedding day** *n.* the day of a marriage or its anniversary. **wedding night** *n.* the night after a wedding, esp. as the time when the marriage is consummated. **wedding ring** *n.* a plain ring given by one partner to the other during the marriage ceremony, and worn thereafter.

we'd (wēd) *contr.* **1** we had. **2** we would.

wedge (wej) *n.* **1** a piece of wood or metal thick at one end and tapering to a thin edge at the other, used for splitting wood, rocks etc., for exerting great pressure, for fixing or fastening etc. **2** an object or portion of anything that is thick at one end and tapers to a thin edge at the other. **3** something that causes a separation or divide (*Politics drove a wedge between them*). **4** a shoe without an instep, having the heel and sole together forming the shape of a wedge. **5** (*also* **wedge heel**) the heel of such a shoe. **6** a golf club with a wedge-shaped head. ~*v.t.* **1** to fix or fasten with a wedge or wedges. **2** to split or separate with or as with a wedge. **3** to squeeze or push, esp. in or into a narrow space (*I was wedged between two fat men*). **the thin end of the wedge** a relatively unimportant first step, measure or change that is likely to lead to something more important, serious etc. **wedgelike** *a.* **wedgewise** *adv.*

Wedgwood® (wej'wud) *n.* Wedgwood blue. **Wedgwood blue** *n.* a light greyish-blue. ~*a.* of this colour.

wedlock (wed'lok) *n.* matrimony, the married state. **born in wedlock** legitimate. **born out of wedlock** illegitimate.

Wednesday (wenz'di, wed'ənzdā) *n.* the fourth day of the week, following Tuesday. ~*adv.* (*coll.*) on Wednesday. **Wednesdays** *adv.* (*coll.*) every Wednesday.

Weds. *abbr.* Wednesday.

wee[1] (wē) *a.* (*comp.* **weer** (wē'ə), *superl.* **weest** (wē'ist)) **1** (*esp. Sc.*) little. **2** (*coll.*) very small, tiny.

wee[2] WEE-WEE.

weed (wēd) *n.* **1** a useless or troublesome plant in cultivated land, a wild plant springing up where not wanted in a garden etc. **2** (*coll.*) a weak or weedy person. **3** (*sl.*) a cigar or cigarette. ~*v.t.* **1** to clear (ground) of weeds. **2** to pull up (a troublesome or intrusive plant). **3** to clear of anything harmful or offensive. **4** to sort (out) (useless or inferior elements, members etc.) for removal or elimination (*to weed out the troublemakers*). **5** to

rid of these. ~*v.i.* to pull up weeds from a garden etc. **the weed 1** (*sl.*) tobacco. **2** (*sl.*) marijuana. **weeder** *n.* **weedkiller** *n.* a chemical or other substance (usu. poisonous) for destroying weeds. **weedless** *a.* **weedy** *a.* (*comp.* **weedier,** *superl.* **weediest**) **1** containing weeds. **2** (*coll.*) thin, weak, lacking stamina. **weediness** *n.*

week (wēk) *n.* **1** a period of seven days, esp. from Sunday to Saturday inclusively. **2** the five or six working days, excluding Sunday or Saturday and Sunday. **3** the time spent working (*a 40-hour week*). **4** (*pl.*) a long time, several weeks (*weeks later*). **5** a week after or before (the day specified) (*Thursday week*; *yesterday week*). **weekday** *n.* any day of the week except Sunday and usu. also Saturday. **weekend** *n.* the days at the end of the working week, usu. Saturday and Sunday, esp. as a time for leisure, holiday etc. ~*v.i.* to spend a weekend, esp. on holiday (*We weekended by the sea*). **weekender** *n.* a person who spends a weekend on holiday. **week-long** *a.* lasting a week. **weekly** *a.* **1** happening, issued or done once a week or every week. **2** lasting a week. **3** of, relating to or reckoned by the week (*weekly wages*). ~*adv.* **1** once a week. **2** week by week. ~*n.* (*pl.* **weeklies**) a weekly periodical. **weeknight** *n.* a night of a weekday.

weeny (wē'ni) *a.* (*comp.* **weenier,** *superl.* **weeniest**) (*coll.*) very small, tiny.

weep (wēp) *v.i.* (*past, p.p.* **wept** (wept)) **1** to shed tears. **2** to lament, to mourn (for). **3** to drip, to exude liquid, to run or be suffused with drops of moisture. **4** (*usu. pres.p.*) to have pendulous branches (*weeping ivy*; *a weeping ash*). ~*v.t.* **1** to utter with tears. **2** to shed (tears). **3** to exude. ~*n.* a spell of weeping. **weeper** *n.* **weepie** *n.* (*coll.*) a sentimental film, play, book etc. **weeping willow** *n.* a willow, *Salix babylonica,* with delicate pendulous branches. **weepy** *a.* (*comp.* **weepier,** *superl.* **weepiest**) tearful. ~*n.* (*pl.* **weepies**) (*coll.*) a weepie. **weepily** *adv.* **weepiness** *n.*

weever (wē'və) *n.* any marine fish of the genus *Trachinus,* such as *T. vipera,* inflicting painful wounds with their dorsal and opercular spines.

weevil (wē'vəl) *n.* **1** a small beetle, esp. of the family Curculionidae, with the head prolonged into a rostrum or proboscis, feeding on grain, nuts, roots, leaves etc. **2** any insect that is a pest of grain. **weevily** *a.*

wee-wee (wē'wē), **wee** (wē) *v.i.* (*3rd pers. sing. pres.* **wee-wees, wees,** *pres.p.* **wee-weeing, wee-ing,** *past, p.p.* **wee-weed, weed**) (*sl.*) to urinate (used esp. by or to children). ~*n.* **1** an act of urinating. **2** urine.

weft (weft) *n.* **1** the threads passing through the warp from selvedge to selvedge, the woof. **2** woven cloth.

weigh (wā) *v.t.* **1** to find the weight of by means of scales etc. **2** to be equivalent to in weight. **3** to weigh out (a particular amount). **4** to hold in the hands to or as to guess the weight of. **5** to ponder, to consider carefully. **6** to estimate the relative value, advantages etc. of, to compare. **7** to raise (an anchor). *~v.i.* **1** to have weight. **2** to be considered important, to have influence. **3** to be burdensome or oppressive (on or upon). *~n.* the act or process of weighing. **to weigh down 1** to cause to sink by weight, to force down. **2** to hold or keep down by weight. **3** to oppress. **to weigh in 1** (of a jockey, boxer etc.) to be weighed before a race, contest etc. **2** (*coll.*) to intervene (with) (*She weighed in with an argument about traffic congestion*). **to weigh into** to attack. **to weigh one's words** to choose one's words carefully. **to weigh up 1** (*coll.*) to assess, to judge. **2** (*coll.*) to consider carefully (*to weigh up the pros and cons*). **weighable** *a.* **weighbridge** *n.* a machine with an iron platform, on which lorries etc. are weighed. **weigher** *n.* **weigh-in** *n.* the act of weighing in a boxer, jockey etc. **weighing** *n.* **weighing machine** *n.* a machine for weighing people, animals, loaded vehicles etc.

weight (wāt) *n.* **1** (*Physics*) the force with which bodies tend towards a centre of attraction, esp. the centre of the earth; the downward tendency caused by gravity less the centrifugal tendency due to the earth's rotation. **2** the relative mass or quantity of matter contained in a body, heaviness, esp. as expressed in terms of some standard unit. **3** the amount that something or someone weighs or should weigh. **4** a piece of metal etc. of known weight used with scales for weighing goods etc. **5** a heavy object or mass used for mechanical purposes, as in a clock, or for weight training etc. **6** a heavy load, a burden. **7** pressure, oppressiveness. **8** importance, consequence, influence. **9** preponderance. **10** the density of cloth, paper, type etc. *~v.t.* **1** to attach a weight or weights to. **2** to hold down with a weight or weights. **3** to add weight to. **4** to burden, to oppress. **5** to bias. **6** to assign a handicap weight to. **to carry weight** to be important or influential. **to lose weight** to become lighter or thinner. **to pull one's weight** to take one's due share of work or responsibility. **to put on weight** to become heavier or fatter. **to throw one's weight about/ around** (*coll.*) to act in a domineering or aggressively self-assertive way. **weighting** *n.* an allowance paid in addition to the basic salary to offset the higher living costs of a particular area. **weightless** *a.* having no apparent weight, esp. because unaffected by gravity, as in an orbiting spacecraft. **weightlessly** *adv.* **weightlessness** *n.* **weightlifting** *n.* the sport of lifting barbells of increasing weight using standard lifting techniques. **weightlifter** *n.* **weight training** *n.* physical training using weights to strengthen and tone muscles. **weighty** *a.* (*comp.* **weightier**, *superl.* **weightiest**) **1** having great weight, heavy. **2** important, serious, momentous. **3** convincing, cogent, influential. **4** serious. **5** difficult to deal with; worrying. **weightily** *adv.* **weightiness** *n.*

weir (wiə), **wear** *n.* **1** a dam across a river or stream for raising the level of the water above it.

2 a ̲l̲e̲.̲.̲.̲ or enclosure of stakes, nets etc. set in a stream or river to catch fish.

weird (wiəd) *a.* **1** supernatural, unearthly, uncanny. **2** (*coll.*) strange, peculiar. **weirdly** *adv.* **weirdness** *n.* **weirdo** (-dō) *n.* (*pl.* **weirdos**) (*coll.*) a strange or eccentric person.

welch WELSH.

welcome (wel'kəm) *a.* **1** admitted or received with pleasure and cordiality. **2** producing satisfaction or gladness (*a welcome sight*). **3** gladly permitted (to) (*You're welcome to borrow my calculator*). **4** (*often iron.*) gladly permitted to have (*You're welcome to it!*). *~n.* **1** a salutation or act of saying 'welcome' to a newcomer etc. **2** a kind or cordial reception or entertainment of a guest etc. **3** a willing acceptance of an offer etc. *~int.* used to express cordial reception of a guest etc. *~v.t.* **1** to greet cordially. **2** to receive or entertain with kindness or cordiality. **3** to receive or accept with pleasure. **4** to greet or receive in a particular way. **to make welcome** to receive in a kind or hospitable way. **to outstay one's welcome** to stay too long. **you're welcome!** used in response to thanks. **welcomeness** *n.* **welcomer** *n.* **welcomingly** *adv.*

weld (weld) *v.t.* **1** to unite or join (pieces of metal) together by heat or by compressing, esp. after they have been softened by heat. **2** to unite (pieces of plastic) similarly. **3** to make, produce or repair thus. **4** to unite into a coherent mass, body etc. *~v.i.* to unite (well or badly) by this process. *~n.* a joint or junction made by welding. **weldable** *a.* **weldability** (-bil'-) *n.* **welder** *n.*

welfare (wel'feə) *n.* **1** prosperity, success. **2** health, well-being. **3** financial and other aid given to those in need. **welfare state** *n.* **1** a system in which the government promotes and assumes responsibility for the general welfare of the population, usu. by introducing social security measures. **2** a state operating such a system. **welfare work** *n.* efforts to improve living conditions for the very poor, elderly etc. **welfare worker** *n.*

well[1] (wel) *adv.* (*comp.* **better**, *superl.* **best**) **1** in a good or right manner, properly, satisfactorily. **2** kindly. **3** skilfully (*He cooks well*). **4** prosperously, successfully. **5** happily, fortunately. **6** adequately, amply, sufficiently. **7** fully, perfectly, thoroughly. **8** to a considerable extent. **9** closely, intimately. **10** heartily, cordially. **11** favourably, with approval, in good terms (*She spoke well of you*). **12** justly, fairly, reasonably, wisely. **13** very possibly, indeed. **14** comfortably, liberally (*to live well*). *~a.* (*usu. pred.*) **1** in good health. **2** in a satisfactory state, position or circumstances. **3** sensible, advisable (*It would be well to check*). **4** fortunate (*It is well that you noticed*). *~int.* **1** used to express astonishment, expectation, resignation, concession etc. **2** used in resuming one's discourse. **as well 1** in addition. **2** equally, as much (as), not less than. **3** proper, right, not unadvisable (to) (*It's as well to switch it off first*).

(just) as well just as reasonably, with no worse results (*We might as well go home*). **well and good** used to express calm or dispassionate acceptance. **well and truly** completely, utterly. **well away 1** making or having made rapid progress. **2** (*coll.*) drunk. **3** (*coll.*) fast asleep. **well in** (*coll.*) on good terms (with). **well worth** certainly worth (*well worth the trouble*; *well worth avoiding*). **well-adjusted** *a.* **1** mentally stable. **2** properly adjusted. **well advised** *a.* prudent, judicious, wise (*You would be well advised to leave*). **well-appointed** *a.* fully furnished or equipped. **well aware** *a.* fully aware (of). **well-balanced** *a.* **1** sensible, sane. **2** having the parts well-matched. **well-behaved** *a.* having or displaying good behaviour or manners. **well-being** *n.* the state of being healthy, happy etc. **well-born** *a.* of good birth. **well-bred** *a.* having good breeding or manners. **well-built** *a.* **1** sturdy, robust, muscular. **2** of sound construction. **well-chosen** *a.* selected with judgement (*a few well-chosen words*). **well-connected** *a.* related to rich or socially powerful people. **well-defined** *a.* clearly determined. **well-deserved** *a.* thoroughly merited. **well-designed** *a.* skilfully or practically designed. **well-developed** *a.* **1** fully developed. **2** large. **well disposed** *a.* of favourable and kindly feeling (to or towards). **well done** *a.* (of food) cooked thoroughly. *~int.* used to express congratulation. **well-dressed** *a.* dressed in fashionable or elegant clothes. **well-earned** *a.* thoroughly deserved (*a well-earned rest*). **well-educated** *a.* having a good education. **well-endowed** *a.* **1** having plenty of money, talent etc. **2** (*coll.*) **a** (of a man) having a large penis. **b** (of a woman) having large breasts. **well-equipped** *a.* fully equipped, having all the necessary equipment, resources etc. **well-established** *a.* of long standing. **well-fed** *a.* **1** having a good diet. **2** having had plenty to eat. **well-formed** *a.* **1** attractively shaped. **2** correctly constructed (*a well-formed sentence*). **well-found** *a.* well-appointed. **well-founded** *a.* based on certain or well-authenticated grounds. **well-groomed** *a.* neat and elegant in dress and appearance. **well-grounded** *a.* **1** well-founded. **2** having all the basic knowledge of a subject etc. **well-heeled** *a.* (*coll.*) wealthy. **well-hung** *a.* **1** (*coll.*) (of a man) having large genitals. **2** (of meat, game etc.) hung for the right length of time. **well-informed** *a.* **1** having ample information. **2** having knowledge of numerous subjects. **well-intentioned** *a.* having good intentions (usu. with unsatisfactory results). **well-judged** *a.* skilfully, tactfully or accurately done, aimed, contrived etc. **well-kept** *a.* well looked after, well-maintained (*a well-kept garden*). **well-known** *a.* **1** known to many people, familiar, notorious. **2** thoroughly known. **well-liked** *a.* liked by many people, popular. **well-loved** *a.* regarded with affection by many people. **well-made** *a.* **1** skilfully made, strongly constructed. **2** well-built, well-proportioned.

well-mannered *a.* well-bred, polite. **well-matched** *a.* evenly matched, compatible. **well-meaning** *a.* having good intentions. **well-meant** *a.* showing good intentions. **wellness** *n.* **well-nigh** *adv.* almost, nearly. **well off** *a.* **1** in good circumstances. **2** wealthy, prosperous. **3** having plenty of. **well-oiled** *a.* (*coll.*) **1** drunk. **2** (of an operation etc.) running smoothly. **well-ordered** *a.* arranged in a methodical or tidy manner; properly or correctly arranged. **well-paid** *a.* **1** (of a person) receiving ample remuneration. **2** (of a job) that pays well. **well placed** *a.* **1** in a good or advantageous position. **2** in a suitable position (to) (*She is well placed to find out what is going on*). **well-prepared** *a.* **1** carefully prepared. **2** having prepared carefully (*He was well-prepared for their questions*). **well-preserved** *a.* young-looking for one's age. **well-qualified** *a.* **1** having many good qualifications. **2** thoroughly able (to), through experience etc. **well-read** *a.* having read extensively, having wide knowledge gained from books. **well received** *a.* having a favourable reception. **well-rounded** *a.* **1** pleasantly curved or rounded. **2** symmetrical, complete. **3** broad in scope, full, varied. **4** well expressed. **well spent** *a.* used effectively or profitably (*money well spent*). **well-spoken** *a.* **1** speaking well, eloquent. **2** well-mannered, of good disposition. **well-stocked** *a.* containing a wide or plentiful range of items (*a well-stocked fridge*; *a well-stocked garden*). **well-structured** *a.* having a clear or well-thought-out structure. **well-supported** *a.* **1** (of an event) attended by many people. **2** (of an argument etc.) supported by much sound evidence. **well-taken** *a.* **1** skilfully done (*a well-taken catch*). **2** accepted. **well-thought-of** *a.* respected, esteemed. **well-thought-out** *a.* carefully planned. **well-thumbed** *a.* (of a book) marked from much handling. **well-timed** *a.* opportune. **well-to-do** *a.* well off. **well-travelled** *a.* **1** (of a person) having travelled widely. **2** (of a path etc.) much used. **well-tried** *a.* often tried or tested with satisfactory results. **well-trodden** *a.* much used or frequented. **well-turned** *a.* **1** shapely. **2** aptly expressed. **well-used** *a.* **1** much used. **2** worn. **well-wisher** *n.* a person who wishes one well, a benevolent, charitable or sympathetic person. **well-worn** *a.* **1** worn out. **2** trite, hackneyed.

Usage note Compounds of *well* are conventionally hyphenated when in front of the noun qualified, but written as two separate words after the verb *to be* (*a well-read person*, *He was well read*).

well² (wel) *n.* **1** a shaft bored in the ground to obtain water, oil, gas etc. **2** a space in the middle of a building enclosing the stairs or a lift or left open for light and ventilation. **3** a source (*a well of knowledge*). **4** a spring, a fountain. **5** a natural pool fed by this. **6** the receptacle holding the ink in an inkstand. **7** any space or depression for holding something, esp. a liquid. ~*v.i.* to spring or issue (forth etc.) as from a fountain (*Tears welled up in her eyes*). **well-head** *n.* **1** the source of a river etc. **2** (*fig.*) a source or fountainhead. **wellspring** *n.* **1** a source of continual supply. **2** a well-head.

we'll (wēl) *contr.* we will, we shall.

wellington (wel´ingtən), **wellington boot** *n.* a waterproof boot, usu. rubber, coming up to the mid-calf or knee.

welly (wel´i), **wellie** *n.* (*pl.* **wellies**) (*coll.*) a wellington boot.

Welsh (welsh) *a.* of or relating to Wales, its inhabitants or their language. ~*n.* **1** the Celtic language of Wales. **2** (*pl.*) the people of Wales. **Welsh corgi** *n.* a corgi. **Welsh dresser** *n.* a dresser with open shelves above drawers and cupboards. **Welshman, Welshwoman** *n.* (*pl.* **Welshmen, Welshwomen**) a native or inhabitant of Wales. **Welshness** *n.* **Welsh rabbit, Welsh rarebit** *n.* cheese mixed with seasonings, melted and spread over toasted bread.

welsh (welsh), **welch** (welch) *v.i.* **1** (of a bookmaker) to make off from a racecourse without paying up bets. **2** to evade an obligation, esp. to fail to pay a debt. **welsher** *n.*

welt (welt) *n.* **1** a strip of leather sewn round a boot or shoe between the upper and the sole to attach them together. **2** a ribbed or strengthened border or trimming of a garment. **3** a weal.

welter¹ (wel´tə) *v.i.* **1** to roll, to tumble about, to wallow. **2** to lie or be steeped (in a liquid, esp. blood). ~*n.* **1** a turmoil, a confusion. **2** a confused mixture (*a welter of opinions*).

welter² (wel´tə) *n.* a heavy boxer or rider. **welterweight** *n.* **1** a boxer, wrestler, weightlifter etc. in the weight category intermediate between lightweight and middleweight. **2** this weight category.

wen (wen) *n.* **1** a sebaceous cyst, frequently occurring on the scalp or neck. **2** (*fig.*) an excrescence, an abnormal growth.

wench (wench) *n.* **1** (*now esp. facet.*) a girl or young woman. **2** †a prostitute. ~†*v.i.* to keep company with prostitutes. †**wencher** *n.* †**wenching** *n.*

wend (wend) *v.t.* (*esp. poet.*) to go or direct (one's way) (*We wended our way home*). ~*v.i.* to go.

Wendy house (wen´di) *n.* a small toy house for children to play in.

went GO¹.

wept WEEP.

were BE.

we're (wiə) *contr.* we are.

weren't (wœnt) *contr.* were not.

werewolf (weə´wulf, wiə´-, wœ´-), **werwolf** (wœ´-) *n.* (*pl.* **werewolves, werwolves**) a person turned into or supposed to have the power of turning into a wolf.

Wesleyan (wez´liən) *a.* of or belonging to the Church founded by John Wesley. ~*n.* a member of this, a Wesleyan Methodist. **Wesleyanism** *n.*

west (west) *adv.* at, in or towards the quarter opposite the east, or where the sun sets at the equinox. ~*n.* **1** that one of the four cardinal points exactly opposite the east. **2** (*also* **West**) the region or part of a country or of the world lying opposite to the east, esp. the western part of England, Europe or the US. **3** the Occident. **4** in bridge etc., the player in the position corresponding to that of west on the compass. ~*a.* **1** being, lying or living in or near the west. **2** moving or facing towards the west. **3** (blowing) from the west. **the West 1** the culture or civilization of Europe, N America etc. as opposed to that of oriental countries. **2** (*Hist.*) the non-Communist countries of Europe and N America. **to go west 1** (*sl.*) to die. **2** (*sl.*) to be destroyed. **westbound** *a.* going, travelling or leading towards the west (*a westbound train*). **West Country** *n.* the SW part of England. **westerly** *a.* **1** in, situated or directed towards the west. **2** (blowing) from the west. ~*n.* (*pl.* **westerlies**) a wind from the west. ~*adv.* towards the west. **West Indian** *n.* **1** a native or inhabitant of the West Indies. **2** a person whose family came from the West Indies. ~*a.* of or relating to the West Indies. **West Indian satinwood** *n.* a satinwood tree, *Fagara flava*. **west-north-west** *n.* the direction or point of the compass between west and north-west. **west-south-west** *n.* the direction or point of the compass between west and south-west. **westward** (-wəd) *a., adv.* **westwards** *adv.*

western (wes´tən) *a.* **1** in, facing or directed towards the west. **2** belonging to or to do with the west. **3** (blowing) from the west. **4** (**Western**) of or relating to the West. ~*n.* a film, play or novel dealing with the western states of the US in the wilder periods of their history. **westerner** *n.* a native or inhabitant of the west. **western hemisphere** *n.* the half of the globe that contains the Americas. **westernize, Westernize, westernise, Westernise** *v.t.* to influence with the customs and culture of the West. **westernization** (-zā´-shən) *n.* **westernizer** *n.* **westernmost** *a.*

wet (wet) *a.* (*comp.* **wetter,** *superl.* **wettest**) **1** moistened, soaked, saturated or covered with water or other liquid. **2** rainy (*wet weather*). **3** not yet dry or hard (*wet paint*). **4** using or used with a liquid. **5** (*coll.*) feeble, characterless, foolish, sentimental. **6** (*esp. N Am., sl.*) (of a state etc.) allowing or favouring the sale of alcoholic beverages, not prohibitionist. **7** (of a young child) incontinent. ~*n.* **1** wetness, moisture. **2** anything that wets, esp. rain. **3** rainy weather. **4** (*coll.*) a feeble or foolish person. ~*v.t.* (*pres.p.* **wetting,** *past, p.p.* **wet, wetted**) **1** to make wet; to moisten, drench or soak with liquid. **2** to urinate on or in. **3** (*reflex.*) to urinate involuntarily. **the wet** (*Austral.*) the monsoon season. **to wet one's whistle** (*coll.*) to have a drink. **to wet the baby's head** to have a celebratory drink after the birth of a child. **wet behind the ears** immature, inexperienced. **wet through** thoroughly soaked. **wetback**

n. (*N Am.*, *coll.*) an illegal immigrant to the US from Mexico. **wet blanket** *n.* (*coll.*) a person who damps enthusiasm, zeal etc. **wet dock** *n.* a dock in which vessels can float. **wet dream** *n.* an erotic dream with emission of semen. **wetland** *n.* (*often pl.*) swamp, marshland. **wet look** *n.* **1** a shiny finish given to fabrics etc. **2** a shiny appearance given to the hair by the application of a gel. *~a.* (*usu.* **wet-look**) having a shiny finish or appearance. **wetly** *adv.* **wetness** *n.* **wet-nurse** *n.* a woman employed to suckle a child not her own. *~v.t.* **1** to act as wet-nurse to. **2** (*coll.*) to coddle. **wet pack** *n.* (*Med.*) a wet sheet in which a patient is wrapped. **wet rot** *n.* **1** a type of rot that affects damp timber. **2** the fungus that causes this, esp. *Coniophera puteana*. **wetsuit** *n.* a tight-fitting usu. rubber garment for divers etc. that allows water in whilst retaining body heat. **wettable** *a.* **wetting** *n.* **wetting agent** *n.* a substance added to a liquid to help it spread or penetrate. **wettish** *a.* **wet-weather** *a.* of, used in, suitable for or occurring in rainy weather.

wether (wedh´ə) *n.* a castrated ram.

we've (wēv) *contr.* we have.

Wg. Cdr. *abbr.* Wing Commander.

whack (wak) *v.t.* to strike heavily. *~n.* **1** a heavy or resounding blow. **2** (*sl.*) a share, a portion. **3** (*sl.*) an attempt. **out of whack** (*N Am.*, *Austral.*, *sl.*) out of order. **(the) full whack** the maximum rate, price etc. **whacked** *a.* (*coll.*) exhausted. **whacker** *n.* **whacking** *n.* a beating, a thrashing. *~a.* (*coll.*) large, whopping, thumping. *~adv.* (*coll.*) very.

whacko (wak´ō) *int.* (*sl.*) used to express delight. **whacky** WACKY.

whale (wāl) *n.* **1** any large marine fishlike mammal of the order Cetacea, several of which are hunted chiefly for their oil and whalebone. **2** (*coll.*) something very big, good, exciting etc. (*We had a whale of a time*). *~v.i.* to engage in whaling. **whaleboat** *n.* a boat sharp at both ends, such as those formerly used in whaling. **whalebone** *n.* a horny, elastic substance occurring in long, thin plates, found in the palate of certain whales. **whalebone whale** *n.* a baleen whale. **whale-headed stork** *n.* an African stork, *Balaeniceps rex*, with grey plumage and a large, clogshaped bill. **whale oil** *n.* oil obtained from the blubber of whales. **whaler** *n.* **1** a person employed in whaling. **2** a ship employed in whaling. **3** a whaler shark. **4** (*Austral.*, *sl.*) a tramp. **whaler shark** *n.* a large Australian shark, *Carcharinus brachyurus*. **whale shark** *n.* a large tropical shark, *Rhincodon typus*. **whaling** *n.* the catching and processing of whales.

wham (wam) *n.* **1** a forceful blow. **2** the noise of this. *~v.i.* (*pres.p.* **whamming**, *past*, *p.p.* **whammed**) to strike or crash with a loud, forceful blow. *~v.t.* to cause to do this.

whammy (wam´i) *n.* (*pl.* **whammies**) (*coll.*) **1** (*esp. N Am.*) an evil influence, a curse. **2** a particularly severe setback, blow or misfortune (*a double whammy*).

whang (wang) *v.t.* to beat noisily, to bang. *~v.i.* (of a drum etc.) to make a noise as if whanged. *~n.* a whanging blow, a bang.

whap WHOP.

wharf (wawf) *n.* (*pl.* **wharfs, wharves** (wawvz)) a landing place for cargo beside a river, harbour, canal etc., usu. consisting of a platform, pier or quay of timber, masonry etc. *~v.t.* **1** to moor at a wharf. **2** to deposit or store (goods) on a wharf. **wharfage** (-ij) *n.* **1** the use of a wharf. **2** the charge for this. **wharfie** *n.* (*Austral.*, *New Zeal.*, *coll.*) a worker at a wharf. **wharfinger** (-finjə) *n.* a person who owns or has charge of a wharf.

what (wot) *pron.* **1** (*interrog.*) which thing or things. **2** (*rel.*) that which, those which. **3** how much. **4** (*dial.*) that or which. *~a.* **1** (*interrog.*, *rel.*) which thing, kind, amount, number etc. **2** how great, remarkable, ridiculous etc. (*What a shame!*). **3** (*rel.*) such as, as much or as many as, any that. *~adv.* (*interrog.*) to what extent, in what respect. **and what not** (*coll.*) and anything else of the kind. **or what have you** (*coll.*) or anything else of the kind. **to give someone what for** (*coll.*) to give someone a severe reprimand or punishment. **what about** what do you think, feel, know etc. about; what is the position concerning (*What about Jonathan?*). **what ever** what at all (*What ever is she talking about?*). **what for** for what reason, purpose etc. **what if 1** what would happen if (*What if it rains?*). **2** what does it matter if (*What if I am being selfish?*). **what is more** moreover. **what of** what is the news about. **what of it?** why does that matter? **what's what** (*coll.*) the real or important thing or situation. **what with** (*coll.*) because of. **what-d'you-call-it** *n.* (*coll.*) a whatsit. **whatever** (-ev´ə), (*poet.*) **whate'er** (-eə´) *pron.* **1** anything at all that. **2** all that which. **3** at all (*of no use whatever*). **4** no matter what (*whatever you say*). *~a.* no matter what (thing or things). **or whatever** (*coll.*) or some similar unspecified thing (*Use a knife, a screwdriver or whatever*). **whatnot** *n.* **1** a trivial or unspecified thing. **2** a piece of furniture with shelves for ornaments, books etc. **whatsit** (-sit), **what's-its-name** *n.* (*coll.*) a person or thing whose name is unknown or temporarily forgotten. **whatsoever**, (*poet.*) **whatsoe'er**, †**whatso** *pron.*, *a.* whatever.

wheat (wēt) *n.* **1** any annual cereal grass of the genus *Triticum*, cultivated for its grain which is ground into flour for bread. **2** its grain. **to separate the wheat from the chaff** to separate or distinguish good things from bad or useless things. **wheat belt** *n.* an area where wheat is extensively cultivated, such as the area east of the Rocky Mountains in Canada and the US. **wheaten** *a.* made of wheat. **wheatgerm** *n.* the embryo of the wheat grain, rich in vitamins. **wheatgrass** *n.* couch grass. **wheatmeal** *n.* flour containing much of the original wheat grain. *~a.* made from such flour.

wheatear (wē´tiə) *n.* a small white-rumped bird of the genus *Oenanthe*, esp. *O. oenanthe*.

whee (wē) *int.* used to express delight or excitement.

wheedle (wē'dəl) *v.t.* **1** to entice, to win over, to persuade by coaxing or flattery. **2** to cheat by cajolery. **3** to obtain from or get (out of) by coaxing and flattery. **wheedler** *n.* **wheedling** *a.* **wheedlingly** *adv.*

wheel (wēl) *n.* **1** a circular frame or solid disc turning on its axis, used in vehicles, machinery etc. to reduce friction and facilitate motion. **2** a machine, implement, device etc. consisting principally of a wheel, such as a spinning wheel, potter's wheel, steering wheel etc. **3** an object resembling a wheel, a disc. **4** (*pl., coll.*) a car. **5** (*N Am., coll.*) a bicycle. **6** a Catherine wheel. **7** a turn, a revolution. **8** the turning or swinging round of a body of troops or a line of warships as on a pivot. **9** a set of short lines at the end of a stanza. ~*v.t.* **1** to move or push (a wheeled vehicle etc.) in some direction. **2** to cause to wheel. ~*v.i.* **1** to turn or swing round as on a pivot. **2** to change direction or objective, to face another way. **3** to go round, to circle, to gyrate. **at the wheel 1** driving a motor vehicle. **2** steering a vessel. **3** directing, in control, in charge. **to wheel and deal** to be a wheeler-dealer. **wheels within wheels 1** intricate machinery. **2** (*coll.*) concealed reasons or interdependent circumstances. **wheelback** *a.* (of a chair) having a back shaped like a wheel. **wheelbarrow** *n.* a barrow device supported on a single wheel, with two handles by which it is wheeled. **wheelbase** *n.* the distance between the front and rear axles of a vehicle. **wheelchair** *n.* a chair on wheels, esp. for invalids or disabled people. **wheel clamp** *n.* a clamp fixed on to the wheel of an illegally parked car to prevent it from being driven away before a fine is paid. **wheel-clamp** *v.t.* **wheeled** *a.* having wheels (*usu. in comb.*, as *four-wheeled*). **wheeler** *n.* **1** a person who wheels. **2** a wheelwright. **3** (*in comb.*) a vehicle with the specified number of wheels (*a three-wheeler*). **wheeler-dealer** *n.* a person who operates shrewdly and often ruthlessly in business, politics etc. **wheeler-dealing** *n.* **wheelhouse** *n.* a shelter for the steersman on a boat. **wheelie** *n.* (*sl.*) a manoeuvre in which a bicycle or motorcycle is briefly supported on the rear wheel alone. **wheelie bin, wheely bin** *n.* (*coll.*) a large plastic dustbin with two wheels so that it can be tilted and wheeled to the dustcart, where it is emptied automatically. **wheelless** *a.* **wheelspin** *n.* the revolution of wheels without a grip of the road. **wheelwright** *n.* a person whose occupation is to make or repair wheels etc. **wheely** *a.*

wheeze (wēz) *v.i.* to breathe hard and with an audible sound, as in asthma. ~*v.t.* to utter thus. ~*n.* **1** a wheezing sound. **2** (*coll.*) a joke, a trick. **3** (*coll.*) a design, a scheme. **wheezer** *n.* **wheezy** *a.* **wheezily** *adv.* **wheeziness** *n.*

whelk (welk) *n.* a marine spiral-shelled gastropod of the family Buccinidae, esp. the common whelk, used for food.

whelp (welp) *n.* **1** the young of a dog, a pup. **2** †the young of a beast of prey, a cub. **3** an offensive or ill-bred child or youth. **4** (*usu. pl.*) a ridge on the drum of a capstan or windlass. ~*v.i.* (of a bitch etc.) to give birth to young. ~*v.t.* **1** to give birth to (a pup or cub). **2** (*derog.*) to originate or produce.

when (wen) *adv.* **1** (*interrog.*) at what or which time? **2** (*rel.*) at which (time). ~*conj.* **1** at the time that, at any time that. **2** as soon as. **3** just after the time that. **4** after which, and then. **5** although. **6** considering that. **7** while (*often with pres.p.*). ~*pron.* what or which time. ~*n.* the time or date. **whenever** (-ev'ə), (*poet.*) **whene'er** (-eə´) *adv., conj.* at whatever time. **or whenever** (*coll.*) or at any similar or suitable time. **whensoever**, (*poet.*) **whensoe'er** *adv., conj.* (*formal*) whenever.

whence (wens) *adv.* (*formal*) **1** (*interrog.*) from what place? where from? how? **2** (*rel.*) from which place, origin, source etc. ~*conj.* **1** to or at the place from which. **2** for which reason, wherefore. ~*pron.* what or which place or starting point.

Usage note The use of *from whence*, instead of simple *whence* or *from where*, is sometimes disapproved of, on the grounds that *whence* already contains the notion 'from'.

---

where (weə) *adv.* **1** (*interrog.*) at or in what place, situation, case, circumstances? **2** (*interrog.*) to what place? in what direction? **3** (*rel.*) in which (place or places). ~*conj.* **1** in or to the place, direction etc. in which. **2** whereas. ~*pron.* what or which place. ~*n.* the place (*the where and when*). **whereabouts** *adv.* near what or which place roughly? ~*n.* the approximate location of a person or thing. **whereafter** (weərahf´tə) *conj.* (*formal*) after which. **whereas** (weəraz´) *conj.* **1** the fact on the contrary being that, when in reality. **2** in legal preambles etc., the fact or case being that, considering that. **whereby** (-bī´) *conj.* by which. **wherefore** †*adv.* **1** for what reason? why? **2** for which reason, on which account. ~*n.* (*coll.*) the reason why. **wherein** (weərin´) *adv.* (*formal*) in what place or respect? ~*conj.* in which thing, place, respect etc. **whereof** (weərov´) *adv.* (*formal*) of what? ~*conj.* of which or whom. **wheresoever**, (*poet.*) **wheresoe'er** *adv., conj.* (*formal*) wherever. **whereupon** (weərəpon´) *conj.* **1** upon which. **2** in consequence of or immediately after which. **wherever** (weərev´ə), (*poet.*) **where'er** (-eə´) *adv., conj.* at, in or to whatever place. **or wherever** (*coll.*) or in any similar or suitable place. **wherewith** (-widh´) *adv.* (*formal*) with what? ~*conj.* with which. **wherewithal** *adv., conj.* wherewith. ~*n.* (*coll.*) the necessary means or resources, esp. money.

wherry (wer´i) *n.* (*pl.* **wherries**) **1** a light shallow rowing boat for plying on rivers. **2** a type of barge.

whet (wet) *v.t.* (*pres.p.* **whetting**, *past, p.p.* **whetted**) **1** to sharpen by rubbing on a stone or similar substance. **2** to excite, to stimulate (*to whet the appetite*). ~*n*. **1** the act of whetting. **2** anything taken to whet or stimulate the appetite. **3** a small quantity. **whetstone** *n*. **1** a piece of stone used for sharpening cutlery etc. **2** anything that sharpens or stimulates. **whetter** *n*.

whether (wedh´ə) *conj*. introducing (an indirect question in the form of) an alternative clause followed by an alternative *or*, *or not*, or *or whether*, or with the alternative unexpressed (*whether you like it or not*). **whether or no 1** in any case. **2** which (of two opposite cases).

whew (hwū, fū) *int*. used to express relief, astonishment or consternation.

whey (wā) *n*. the watery part of milk that remains after the curds have formed and been separated. **whey-face** *n*. a pale-faced person. **whey-faced** *a*.

which (wich) *pron*. **1** (*interrog*.) what person, thing or persons or things of a definite number. **2** (*rel*.) used in a subordinate clause to represent a noun expressed or understood in the principal sentence or previous clause. **3** (*rel*.) used after a preposition or after *that* (*the ladder on which she was standing*). ~*a*. **1** (*interrog*.) what (person, thing etc.) of a definite number. **2** (*rel*.) used with a noun defining an indefinite antecedent. **which is which** used when people or things are difficult to tell apart. **whichever, †whichsoever** *pron*. **1** which person or thing of two or more. **2** no matter which person or thing. ~*a*. **1** which of two or more. **2** no matter which.

whiff (wif) *n*. **1** a sudden expulsion of smoke etc., a puff, a light gust, esp. one carrying an odour. **2** a small amount, a trace. ~*v.i*. **1** to puff or blow lightly. **2** (*coll*.) to smell (unpleasant). ~*v.t*. **1** to puff or blow lightly. **2** to detect a faint odour of, to sniff, to smell. **whiffy** *a*. (*comp*. **whiffier**, *superl*. **whiffiest**) (*coll*.) smelly.

whiffle (wif´əl) *v.i*. **1** (of the wind etc.) to veer about. **2** to change from one opinion or course to another, to prevaricate, to equivocate. **3** to flicker, to flutter. ~*v.t*. to blow lightly. **whiffler** *n*.

Whig (wig) *n*. (*Hist*.) a member of the British political party that contended for the rights and privileges of Parliament in opposition to the Tories, supported the Revolution of 1688 and the principles it represented, and was succeeded by the Liberals. **Whiggery, Whiggism** *n*. **Whiggish** *a*.

while (wīl) *n*. a space of time, esp. the time during which something happens or is done. ~*conj*. **1** during the time that, as long as, at the same time as (*often used ellipt. with pres.p.*). **2** whereas (*One group had learning difficulties, while the other group were of average ability*). **3** despite the fact that (*While I disapprove of gambling in general, I do occasionally buy a lottery ticket*). **4** (*dial*.) until. ~*adv*. (*rel*.) during which. **a good while** a long time (*a good while later*). **for a while** for some time. **in a while** soon. **to be worth (someone's) while** to be worth the time, labour or expense involved. **to while away**

to pass (time etc.) pleasantly or in a leisurely manner. **whilst** (wīlst) *conj*., *adv*. while.

whim (wim) *n*. a sudden fancy, a caprice. **whimsy** (-zi), **whimsey** *n*. (*pl*. **whimsies, whimseys**) **1** a whim, a fancy. **2** whimsical humour. **whimsical** (-zikəl) *a*. **1** full of whims, capricious. **2** oddly humorous. **whimsicality** (-kal´-), **whimsicalness** *n*. **whimsically** *adv*.

whimper (wim´pə) *v.i*. **1** to cry with a soft, broken, whining voice. **2** to whine. ~*v.t*. to utter in such a tone. ~*n*. **1** a soft, querulous or whining cry. **2** a feeble note. **whimperer** *n*. **whimperingly** *adv*.

whin (win) *n*. furze, gorse. **whinchat** *n*. a small thrushlike bird, *Saxicola rubetra*.

whine (wīn) *v.i*. **1** to make a plaintive, long-drawn cry. **2** to complain or find fault in a peevish way. ~*v.t*. to utter with a whine or in a peevish way. ~*n*. **1** a whining cry, sound or tone. **2** a peevish complaint. **whiner** *n*. **whiningly** *adv*. **whiny** *a*. (*comp*. **whinier**, *superl*. **whiniest**).

whinge (winj) *v.i*. (*pres.p*. **whingeing**, *past*, *p.p*. **whinged**) (*coll*.) **1** to cry fretfully. **2** to complain peevishly, to whine. ~*n*. a complaint. **whingeing** *n*., *a*. **whingeingly** *adv*. **whinger** *n*.

whinny (win´i) *v.i*. (3rd *pers. sing. pres*. **whinnies**, *pres.p*. **whinnying**, *past*, *p.p*. **whinnied**) to neigh, esp. in a gentle or delighted way. ~*n*. the act or sound of whinnying.

whip (wip) *v.t*. (*pres.p*. **whipping**, *past*, *p.p*. **whipped**) **1** to lash, to flog. **2** to drive or urge (on) with a whip. **3** to beat (out of etc.). **4** to strike forcefully as if with a whip (*The wind whipped our faces*). **5** to beat (eggs, cream etc.) into a froth. **6** to move suddenly and quickly, to snatch, to jerk (out, away etc.) (*She whipped out her camera*). **7** (*sl*.) to beat, to overcome, to defeat. **8** (*sl*.) to steal. **9** to manage or discipline (the members of a political party). **10** to stir up the emotions of. ~*v.i*. to move or start suddenly, to dart (out, in etc.). ~*n*. **1** an instrument for driving horses, punishing people etc., consisting of a lash tied to a handle or rod. **2** a member of a political party appointed to enforce discipline in Parliament and to summon the members of the party to divisions etc. **3** a summons sent out by a whip to ensure such attendance. **4** a whipping motion. **5** a dessert made with whipped eggs, cream etc. **to whip in** to bring (hunting hounds) together. **to whip on** to urge forward or into action. **to whip up 1** to excite, arouse, stimulate. **2** to produce hurriedly. **3** to summon (*to whip up attendance*). **whipcord** *n*. **1** a hard twisted cord for making a whip. **2** a very durable corded cloth made from worsted yarns. **whip hand** *n*. **1** the hand holding the whip. **2** the advantage or control (*to have the whip hand*). **whiplash** *n*. **1** the lash of a whip. **2** a blow with a whip. **3** a sudden, sharp reaction. **4** whiplash injury. ~*v.t*., *v.i*. to jerk or move like the lash of a whip. **whiplash injury** *n*. an injury to the neck caused by a sudden uncontrolled forwards and backwards movement of

the unsupported head. **whipless** *a.* **whiplike** *a.*
whipper *n.* **whipper-in** *n.* (*pl.* **whippers-in**) a person employed to assist the huntsman by looking after the hounds. **whippersnapper** *n.* **1** a young child. **2** a noisy, presumptuous, insignificant person. **whipping** *n.* **whipping boy** *n.* a scapegoat. **whipping-top, whip-top** *n.* a top kept spinning with a whip. **whippy** *a.* flexible, springy. **whippiness** *n.* **whip-round** *n.* (*coll.*) an informal or impromptu collection of money (*to have a whip-round*). **whipsaw** *n.* a narrow saw blade with the ends fastened in a frame. **whip snake** *n.* a slender snake of the family Colubridae.

whippet (wip'it) *n.* **1** a racing-dog similar to but smaller than a greyhound. **2** this breed of dog.

whippoorwill (wip'əwil) *n.* a small N American nocturnal bird, *Caprimulgus vociferus*, allied to the nightjars.

whir (wœ), **whirr** *v.i.* (*pres.p.* **whirring**, *past, p.p.* **whirred**) to revolve, move or fly quickly with a buzzing or whizzing sound. ~*n.* a whirring sound.

whirl (wœl) *v.t.* **1** to swing round and round rapidly. **2** to cause to revolve or fly round with great velocity. **3** to carry (away or along) rapidly. **4** to hurl or fling. ~*v.i.* **1** to turn round and round rapidly, to rotate, to gyrate, to spin. **2** to be carried or to travel rapidly in a circular course. **3** to move along swiftly. **4** (of the brain etc.) to be giddy or confused, to seem to spin round. ~*n.* **1** a whirling motion. **2** a confused state, giddiness. **3** commotion, bustle. **4** (*coll.*) an attempt, a trial (*I'll give it a whirl*). **whirler** *n.* **whirligig** (wœ'-ligig) *n.* **1** a child's spinning or rotating toy. **2** a merry-go-round. **3** a freshwater beetle of the family Gyrinidae that darts about in a circular manner over the surface of pools etc. **whirling** *n.*, *a.* **whirling dervish** *n.* a member of a Muslim ascetic order whose physical exercises take the form of wild, ecstatic, whirling dances. **whirlingly** *adv.* **whirlpool** *n.* an eddy or vortex. **whirlwind** *n.* **1** a funnel-shaped column of air moving spirally round an axis, which at the same time has a progressive motion. **2** a confused or rapid motion or process. ~*a.* developing or moving very rapidly (*a whirlwind romance*). **to reap the whirlwind** to suffer the consequences of a bad or foolish action. **whirlybird** *n.* (*coll.*) a helicopter.

whisht (wisht), **whist** (wist), **whish** (wish) *int.* (*esp. Sc., Ir., dial.*) hush! silence! ~*v.t.* to quieten.

whisk (wisk) *v.t.* **1** to sweep, brush or flap (away or off). **2** to carry (off) or take (away) swiftly or suddenly. **3** to shake, flourish or wave with a quick movement. **4** to beat up (eggs etc.). ~*v.i.* to move or go swiftly or suddenly. ~*n.* **1** a whisking movement. **2** a small bunch of grass, straw, feathers, hair etc., used as a brush or for flapping away flies, dust etc. **3** an instrument for beating up cream, eggs etc.

whisker (wis'kə) *n.* **1** any one of the bristly hairs growing round the mouth of a cat or other animal. **2** (*usu. pl.*) hair growing on the cheeks of

a narrow margin (*to win by a whisker*). **to have whiskers** (*coll.*) to be very old. **whiskered** *a.* **whiskery** *a.*

whisky (wis'ki), **whiskey** *n.* (*pl.* **whiskies, whiskeys**) **1** a spirit distilled usu. from malted barley, sometimes from wheat, rye etc. **2** a drink of this.

Usage note The Scottish product is conventionally spelt *whisky*, and the Irish and American *whiskey*.

whisper (wis'pə) *v.i.* **1** to speak with articulation but without vocal vibration. **2** to converse privately or in a whisper. **3** to plot, to gossip. **4** to make a soft rustling sound. ~*v.t.* **1** to tell or utter in a whisper or privately. **2** to hint or suggest privately or secretly. ~*n.* **1** a whispering tone or voice. **2** a whispered remark or speech. **3** a hint, an insinuation, a rumour. **4** a soft rustling sound. **5** a very small amount of something. **whisperer** *n.* **whispering** *n.* **whispering gallery** *n.* (*pl.* **whispering galleries**) a gallery, corridor etc. in which the faintest sounds made at particular points are audible at other distant points though inaudible elsewhere. **whisperingly** *adv.*

whist[1] (wist) *n.* a card game, usu. for four persons, played with the entire pack of 52 cards. **whist drive** *n.* a social occasion involving a competitive series of games of whist.

whist[2] WHISHT.

whistle (wis'əl) *v.i.* **1** to make a shrill musical sound by forcing the breath through a small opening of the lips or with an instrument, an appliance on a steam engine etc. **2** (of an instrument, engine etc.) to emit this sound. **3** (of birds etc.) to make a similar sound. **4** (of a missile, the wind etc.) to make such a sound by swift motion. ~*v.t.* **1** to emit or produce (a tune etc.) by whistling. **2** to call or give a signal to thus. ~*n.* **1** a whistling sound, note or cry. **2** an instrument for producing such a sound. **3** (*sl.*) the throat. **clean/ clear/ dry as a whistle** very clean, clear etc. **to whistle for** to seek or ask for in vain, to stand little or no chance of getting. **whistle-blower** *n.* a person who informs on someone or brings something to an end. **whistler** *n.* **whistle-stop** *n.* **1** (*N Am.*) a small station where trains stop only on request. **2** a brief visit to a town, e.g. by a political candidate. ~*a.* (*attrib.*) rapid, with only brief pauses (*a whistle-stop tour*).

Whit WHITSUN.

whit (wit) *n.* a jot, the least amount, an iota (*not a whit*).

white (wīt) *a.* **1** being of the colour produced by reflection of all the visible rays in sunlight, as of pure snow, common salt etc. **2** approximating to the colour of pure snow; pale, pallid, bloodless, transparent, colourless. **3** silvery, whitish-grey. **4** (*also* White) belonging to a light-complexioned people. **5** of or relating to such people. **6** white-haired as from age etc. **7** pure, clean, stainless. **8** spotless, innocent. **9** (of coffee) containing milk or cream. **10** having snow (*a white Christmas*).

11 clothed in white. **12** not malicious or malevolent. **13** fair, happy, propitious. ~*n.* **1** a white colour. **2** a white paint or pigment. **3** (*also* **White**) a white person or a member of one of the paler peoples, esp. a European. **4** a white animal, esp. a butterfly. **5** the sclerotic coat of the eye surrounding the iris. **6** the albuminous material surrounding the yolk of an egg. **7** white clothing (*dressed in white*). **8** (*pl.*) white clothes (*tennis whites*). **9** (*pl.*) leucorrhoea. **10** in chess, snooker etc., a white piece, ball etc., or a player using such a piece or pieces. **11** a blank space in printed matter etc. **to bleed white** to drain of money, resources etc. **white admiral** *n.* a butterfly, *Limenitis camilla*, with white markings on its wings. **white ant** *n.* a termite. **whitebait** *n.* (*pl.* **whitebait**) (*usu. pl.*) the fry of herrings, sprats etc. eaten when about 2 in. (5 cm) long. **white (blood) cell** *n.* a leucocyte. **whiteboard** *n.* a board with a white surface used by teachers, lecturers etc. to write and draw on with coloured felt-tip pens. **whitecap** *n.* **1** a bird with a light-coloured head, such as the male redstart. **2** a white-crested wave. **white-collar** *a.* of or relating to nonmanual employees, esp. administrative and clerical workers. **white corpuscle** *n.* a leucocyte. **white currant** *n.* a cultivated shrub, *Ribes sativum*, with white edible berries. **whited sepulchre** *n.* a hypocrite (from Christ's allusion to the scribes and Pharisees, Matt. xxiii.27). **white dwarf** *n.* a type of small, very faint, dense star. **white elephant** *n.* a useless and expensive possession (alluding to the cost of an elephant's keep). **white feather** *n.* a symbol of cowardice (from a white feather in the tail of a game bird of bad breeding). **white fish** *n.* any food fish with pale flesh, esp. whiting, haddock, plaice, cod etc. **whitefish** *n.* (*pl. in general* **whitefish**, *in particular* **whitefishes**) a N American salmonoid food fish of the genus *Coregonus*. **white flag** *n.* FLAG OF TRUCE (under FLAG¹). **whitefly** *n.* (*pl.* **whiteflies**) any small insect of the family Aleyrodidae, a pest of plants. **White Friar** *n.* a Carmelite monk (from the white cloak). **white gold** *n.* a whitish alloy of gold with palladium, nickel etc. **white goods** *n.pl.* large kitchen appliances, such as freezers and cookers. **whitehead** *n.* a white-topped pustule on the skin. **white heat** *n.* **1** the degree of heat at which bodies become incandescent and appear white. **2** a high pitch of excitement, passion etc. **white hope** *n.* a member of a group, team, organization etc. who is expected to achieve much or bring glory. **white horehound, white hoarhound** *n.* the labiate herb *Marrubium vulgare*. **white horses** *n.pl.* foamcrested waves. **white-hot** *a.* at the temperature of white heat. **white-knuckle** *a.* (*attrib.*) causing fear and excitement (*a white-knuckle ride at an amusement park*). **white lie** *n.* a pardonable fiction or misstatement. **white light** *n.* light containing more or less equal intensities of all wavelengths in the visible spectrum. **whitely**

adv. **white magic** *n.* **1** magic used for good. **2** magic not involving the Devil. **white meat** *n.* meat that appears white after cooking, such as poultry, veal or pork. **white metal** *n.* a tin- or sometimes lead-based alloy used for bearings, domestic utensils etc. **whiten** *v.t.*, *v.i.* **whitener** *n.* **whitening** *n.* **1** the act of making white. **2** the state of becoming white. **3** powdered chalk used in whitewashing etc., whiting. **whiteness** *n.* **white night** *n.* a sleepless night. **white noise** *n.* noise containing more or less equal intensities of many frequencies. **white-out** *n.* **1** a condition of uniform whiteness occurring in polar or similar snow-covered regions in heavy cloud. **2** a dense blizzard. **White Paper** *n.* a government report on a matter recently investigated. **white pepper** *n.* pepper made by removing the skin from *Piper nigrum* berries by rubbing etc. before grinding. **white poplar** *n.* the abele. **white rose** *n.* (*Hist.*) the emblem of the House of York in the Wars of the Roses. **White Russian** *n.*, *a.* BELORUSSIAN. **white sauce** *n.* a thick sauce made with flour and milk or a fish or white-meat stock. **white slave** *n.* a woman or child procured, and usu. exported, for prostitution. **white slaver** *n.* **white slavery** *n.* **white spirit** *n.* a distillate of petroleum used as a paint solvent and thinner. **white sugar** *n.* refined sugar. **whitethorn** *n.* the hawthorn. **whitethroat** *n.* any small warbler of the genus *Sylvia*, with a white throat, esp. *S. communis*. **white tie** *n.* **1** a white bow tie worn by men as part of full evening dress. **2** full evening dress for men. **whitewash** *n.* **1** a mixture of quicklime and water or of whiting and size used for whitening walls, ceilings etc. **2** a false colouring given to the reputation of a person or institution to counteract allegations of disreputableness. ~*v.t.* **1** to cover with whitewash. **2** to cover up or conceal (a misdemeanour etc.). **3** to clear (a person's name) thus. **4** (*coll.*) to defeat decisively. **whitewasher** *n.* **white water** *n.* foaming water in breakers, rapids etc. **white wedding** *n.* a wedding in which the bride wears white, orig. as a symbol of purity. **white whale** *n.* the beluga. **white wine** *n.* any wine of a light colour, as opposed to red, made from white grapes or from black grapes with their skins removed. **whitewood** *n.* **1** any of various trees yielding light-coloured timber. **2** such timber. **whitey, Whitey** *n.* (*pl.* **whiteys**, **Whiteys**) (*offensive*) **1** a white person. **2** white people collectively. **whitish** *a.*

Whitehall (wĭt′hawl) *n.* **1** the British Government. **2** its central administration, offices or policy.

†**whither** (widh′ə) *adv.* **1** (*interrog.*) to what or which place, where. **2** (*rel.*) to which. ~*conj.* **1** to whatever place. **2** and to that place.

whiting¹ (wī′ting) *n.* (*pl.* **whiting**) a sea fish, *Merlangus merlangus*, used for food.

whiting² (wī′ting) *n.* fine chalk pulverized, washed and prepared for use in whitewashing, polishing etc.

whitlow (wit´lō) *n*. a pus-filled inflammation, esp. round the nail of a finger or toe.

Whitsun (wit´sən), **Whit** (wit) *a*. of or relating to Whit Sunday or Whitsuntide. ~*n*. Whitsuntide. **Whit Sunday** *n*. the seventh Sunday after Easter, a festival commemorating the day of Pentecost. **Whitsuntide** *n*. Whit Sunday and the following days.

whittle (wit´əl) *v.t*. **1** to trim, shave or cut pieces or slices from with a knife. **2** to shape thus. **3** to thin down. **4** (*with away or down*) to reduce, pare or bring down in amount etc., gradually or by degrees. ~*v.i*. to keep on paring, shaving or cutting (at a stick etc.) with a knife.

whiz (wiz), **whizz** *v.i*. (*pres.p.* whizzing, *past, p.p.* whizzed) **1** to make or move with a hissing sound, like an arrow or ball flying through the air. **2** to move about rapidly. ~*n*. **1** a whizzing sound. **whiz-bang** *n*. **1** a small high-velocity shell. **2** a type of firework. ~*a*. lively, spectacular. **whiz-kid** *n*. (*coll*.) a person who is outstandingly successful or clever, esp. at a relatively young age. **whizzingly** *adv*.

who (hoo) *pron*. (*obj.* **whom** (hoom), *poss.* **whose** (hooz)) **1** (*interrog*.) what or which person or persons? **2** (*rel*.) that (identifying the subject or object in a relative clause with that of the principal clause). **who goes there?** used as a challenge by a sentry etc. **whodunnit** (-dŭn´it), (*esp. N Am*.) **whodunit** *n*. (*coll*.) a detective or mystery story. **whoever** (-ev´ə), (*poet*.) **whoe'er** (-eə´) *pron*. (*obj.* **whomever**, *poet*.) **whome'er**, *poss*. **whosever**, (*poet*.) **whose'er**) **1** any person without exception who, no matter who. **2** (*coll*.) who at all. †**whosoever** (-ev´ə), **whosoe'er** (-eə´) *pron*. (*obj.* **whomsoever, whomsoe'er**, *poss*. **whosesoever, whosesoe'er**) whoever. **who's who** *n*. **1** who each person is (*to find out who's who*). **2** a directory of famous people.

Usage note (1) *Whom* is sometimes used instead of *who* in relative clauses of the type *the man who she said is her father, the woman who I believed was his wife*, but this is best avoided. (2) The subjective pronouns *who* and *whoever* are the everyday choice for direct objects in questions (direct and indirect) and as relatives, even though the objective forms (*whom* etc.) are required by strict grammatical rule. So *Who did you hit?, You asked who I hit, the policeman who I hit* are generally acceptable, with *Whom did you hit?, You asked whom I hit* etc. more formal equivalents. (3) The spellings of the pronoun *whose* and the contraction *who's* (who is) should not be confused.

whoa (wō), **wo** *int*. stop! (used chiefly to horses).

who'd (hood) *contr*. **1** who had. **2** who would.

whole (hōl) *a*. **1** complete or entire. **2** containing the total number of parts, undivided, undiminished. **3** unimpaired, uninjured, not broken, intact. **4** integral, composed of units, not fractional. **5** having no constituents removed (*whole milk*).

~*n*. **1** a thing complete in all its parts, units etc. **2** all that there is of a thing, the entirety. **3** a complete system, a complete combination of parts, an organic unity. **as a whole** considered as an organic unity. **on the whole 1** all things considered. **2** in most cases. **the whole of** everybody in (*The whole of the village heard the explosion*). **wholefood** *n*. food that has undergone little or no processing or refining. **wholegrain** *a*. made from or containing complete grains with no parts removed (*wholegrain bread*). **wholehearted** *a*. done or intended with all one's heart, hearty, generous, cordial, sincere. **wholeheartedly** *adv*. **wholeheartedness** *n*. **wholemeal** *a*. made from flour ground from the entire wheat grain. ~*n*. such flour. **wholeness** *n*. **whole number** *n*. an integer. **wholesale** *n*. the sale of goods in large quantities, as distinct from *retail*. ~*a*. **1** buying or selling thus. **2** done in the mass, on a large scale, indiscriminate (*wholesale destruction*). ~*adv*. **1** by wholesale, in large quantities. **2** by the mass, on a large scale. ~*v.t*. to sell wholesale. **wholesaler** *n*. **wholesome** *a*. **1** tending to promote physical health, salutary, salubrious. **2** promoting moral or mental health. **3** indicating health. **wholesomely** *adv*. **wholesomeness** *n*. **whole-tone scale** *n*. (*Mus*.) a scale in which each interval is a tone, with no semitones. **wholewheat** *a., n*. wholemeal. **wholly** (hō´li) *adv*. **1** entirely, completely. **2** totally, exclusively.

wholism HOLISM.

whom, whomever etc. WHO.

whoop (woop, hoop) *v.i*. **1** to utter a 'whoop'. **2** to shout or cry out loudly in excitement, encouragement, exultation etc. ~*v.t*. **1** to utter with a whoop. **2** to urge (on) with whoops. ~*n*. **1** the cry 'whoop'. **2** a loud shout of excitement, encouragement etc. **3** the sound made in whooping cough. **to whoop it up 1** (*coll*.) to engage in riotous enjoyment. **2** (*coll., N Am*.) to stir up enthusiasm etc. **whoopee** (wupē´) *int*. (*coll*.) used to express excitement or delight. ~*n*. (*coll*.) riotous enjoyment. **to make whoopee 1** (*coll*.) to whoop it up. **2** (*coll*.) to make love. **whooper** *n*. **whooper swan** *n*. a large swan, *Cygnus cygnus*, with a whooping call. **whooping cough** (hoo´-) *n*. an infectious disease, esp. of children, characterized by a violent cough followed by a loud convulsive respiration; pertussis. **whooping crane** (hoo´-, woo´-) *n*. a large white crane, *Grus americana*, of N America. **whoops** (wups), **whoops-a-daisy** *int*. (*coll*.) used to express surprise or apology.

whoosh (wush), **woosh** *n*. a rushing or hissing sound as of something moving swiftly through the air. ~*v.i*. to make or move with such a sound.

whop (wop), **whap** *v.t*. (*pres.p.* **whopping, whapping**, *past, p.p.* **whopped, whapped**) (*sl*.) **1** to beat, to thrash. **2** to defeat. ~*n*. a heavy blow or thud. **whopper** *n*. (*sl*.) **1** anything uncommonly large etc. **2** a monstrous lie. **whopping** *a*. (*sl*.) uncommonly large.

whore (haw) *n.* **1** a prostitute. **2** (*derog.*) a promiscuous woman. ~*v.i.* **1** to be a whore. **2** to have sexual relations with a whore or whores. ~*v.t.* to prostitute (a person or oneself). **whorehouse** *n.* a brothel.

whorl (woel, wawl) *n.* **1** a circular set or ring of leaves, sepals or other organs on a plant. **2** one convolution or turn of a spiral, as in a univalve shell. **3** a circular pattern in a fingerprint. **whorled** *a.*

whortleberry (woe´təlberi) *n.* (*pl.* **whortleberries**) the bilberry.

whose, whosever etc. WHO.

whump (wŭmp, wump) *n.* a dull thud or thump.

why (wī) *adv.* **1** (*interrog.*) for what reason or purpose? **2** (*rel.*) on account of which. ~*n.* (*pl.* **whys**) the reason, explanation or purpose of anything. ~*int.* used to express surprise, impatience etc.

WI *abbr.* **1** West Indies. **2** Women's Institute.

Wicca (wik´ə) *n.* the cult or practice of modern witchcraft. **Wiccan** *n., a.*

wick (wik) *n.* a piece or bundle of fibrous or spongy material used in a candle or lamp to convey the melted grease or oil by capillary action to the flame. **to get on one's wick** (*coll.*) to annoy or irritate one.

wicked (wik´id) *a.* (*comp.* **wickeder,** *superl.* **wickedest**) **1** sinful, addicted to evil or vice, immoral, depraved. **2** mischievous, roguish. **3** harmful, injurious. **4** (*coll.*) very bad. **5** (*sl.*) very good. **wickedly** *adv.* **wickedness** *n.*

wicker (wik´ə) *n.* twigs or osiers plaited into a material for baskets, chairs etc. ~*a.* made of this material. **wickered** *a.* **wickerwork** *n.*

wicket (wik´it) *n.* **1** a set of three stumps surmounted by two bails at which the bowler directs the ball in cricket. **2** the ground on which this is set up. **3** the innings or turn of each batsman at the wicket. **4** the pitch between the wickets, esp. as regards condition for bowling. **5** a small gate, door or other entrance, esp. one close beside or forming part of a larger one. **6** (*N Am.*) a small aperture in a door or wall, having a grille or opened and closed by means of a sliding panel. **on a good wicket** (*coll.*) in a favourable situation. **on a sticky wicket** (*coll.*) in an unfavourable situation. **to keep wicket** in cricket, to be wicketkeeper. **to take a wicket** in cricket, to get a batsman out. **wicketkeeper** *n.* the fielder who stands behind the batsman's wicket in cricket. **wicketkeeping** *n.*

widdershins WITHERSHINS.

wide (wīd) *a.* **1** having a great relative extent from side to side, broad, as opposed to *narrow.* **2** having a specified degree of breadth. **3** extending far. **4** vast, spacious, extensive. **5** not limited or restricted, free, liberal, comprehensive, catholic. **6** distant or deviating by a considerable extent or amount from a mark, point, purpose etc. **7** fully open or expanded. **8** (*sl.*) crafty, shrewd. **9** (of clothes) hanging losely. ~*adv.* **1** widely. **2** to a great distance, extensively. **3** far from the mark

or purpose. **4** to the fullest extent, fully (*wide open*). ~*n.* **1** in cricket, a wide ball. **2** the wide world. **the wide world** all the world. **to the wide** completely, absolutely. **-wide** *comb. form* extending throughout, as *nationwide.* **wide-angle lens** *n.* a camera lens with an angle of up to 100° used for photographing buildings etc. **wideawake** *n.* a soft felt hat with a broad brim. **wide awake** *a.* **1** fully awake. **2** (*coll.*) alert, wary. **3** (*coll.*) keen, sharp, knowing. **wide ball** *n.* in cricket, a ball bowled too far to the side and out of the batsman's reach. **wide boy** *n.* (*sl.*) a crafty, shrewd man, inclined to sharp practice. **wide-eyed** *a.* **1** surprised, astonished. **2** naive. **widely** *adv.* **1** to a wide extent or degree. **2** by many people (*widely accepted*). **widen** *v.t., v.i.* **widener** *n.* **wideness** *n.* **wide open** *a.* **1** fully open. **2** open to attack. **3** of indeterminate or unpredictable outcome. **wide-ranging** *a.* extending over a wide range. **wide-screen** *a.* of or for a screen that has much greater width than height (*wide-screen film projection*). **widespread** *a.* widely disseminated. **widish** *a.*

widget (wij´it) *n.* **1** a gadget. **2** a thingumajig, a whatsit.

widow (wid´ō) *n.* **1** a woman who has lost her husband by death and has not remarried. **2** a woman whose husband devotes much time to a (sporting) activity that takes him away from home (*a golf widow*). **3** (*Print.*) a short final line of a paragraph etc. at the top of a printed column or page. **4** in some card games, an extra hand of cards dealt separately. ~*v.t.* **1** to bereave of a spouse, to make a widow or widower. **2** to bereave, to deprive (of). **widower** *n.* a man who has lost his wife by death and has not remarried. **widowhood** *n.* **widow's cruse** *n.* an unfailing source of supply (I Kings xvii.16). **widow's mite** *n.* a small but ill-afforded contribution (Mark xii.42). **widow's peak** *n.* the natural growth of hair to a point in the middle of the forehead.

width (width, witth) *n.* **1** the extent of a thing from side to side, breadth, wideness. **2** a large extent. **3** a piece of material cut from the full width of a roll etc. **4** comprehensiveness of mind, liberality, catholicity. **widthways, widthwise** *adv.*

wield (wēld) *v.t.* **1** to handle, hold, use or employ (*to wield a hammer*). **2** to have, exert, command or maintain (power etc.). **3** to brandish or wave. **wieldable** *a.* **wielder** *n.* **wieldy** *a.* (*comp.* **wieldier,** *superl.* **wieldiest**) that may be wielded, manageable.

Wiener schnitzel (vēnə-shnit´səl) *n.* a cutlet of veal or pork, coated with a breadcrumb mixture and fried.

☒ **wierd** common misspelling of WEIRD.

wife (wīf) *n.* (*pl.* **wives** (wīvz)) **1** a married woman, esp. in relation to her husband. **2** (*in comb.*) a woman engaged in a specified occupation (*a housewife; a fishwife*). †**to have/ take to wife** to marry. **wifely** *a.* **wifeliness** *n.*

wig[1] (wig) *n.* a covering for the head composed of false hair, worn to conceal baldness, as a disguise, for ornament or as part of an official costume, esp. by judges, lawyers etc. **wigged** *a.* **wigless** *a.*

wig[2] (wig) *v.t.* (*pres.p.* **wigging**, *past*, *p.p.* **wigged**) (*coll.*) to reprimand, to scold. **wigging** *n.* a scolding.

wigeon (wij´ən), **widgeon** *n.* a wild duck of the genus *Anas*, esp. *A. penelope* or *A. americana*.

wiggle (wig´əl) *v.i.* to move (oneself) jerkily, esp. from side to side. ~*v.t.* to move (someone or something) jerkily, esp. from side to side. ~*n.* **1** an act of wiggling. **2** a bend or undulation in a line etc. **wiggler** *n.* **wiggly** *a.* (*comp.* **wigglier**, *superl.* **wiggliest**).

wigwam (wig´wam) *n.* **1** a N American Indian hut or cabin, usu. consisting of a framework covered with bark, matting, hides etc. **2** a similar structure for children, used as a tent etc.

wild (wīld) *a.* **1** living in a state of nature, esp. inhabiting or growing in the forest or open country. **2** (esp. of animals) not tamed or domesticated. **3** (esp. of plants) growing naturally; uncultivated. **4** not civilized, savage. **5** (of land etc.) unsettled, uncultivated, irregular, desert, uninhabited. **6** wayward, disorderly, lawless. **7** reckless, incautious, rash. **8** ill-considered, imprudent, extravagant, inordinate. **9** ungoverned, unchecked, unrestrained. **10** turbulent, stormy, furious. **11** expressing very strong uncontrolled feelings e.g. anger or excitement. **12** excited, enthusiastic (about). **13** (*coll.*) angry. **14** (*coll.*) exciting. **15** (of horses etc.) shy, easily startled, given to shying. **16** very untidy. **17** (of a guess) made without much thought or knowledge. ~*n.* **1** an uninhabited and uncultivated tract. **2** a desert. ~*adv.* in a wild manner or state. **in the wild** in its natural state. **(out) in the wilds** (*coll.*) a long way from human habitation (*to live out in the wilds*). **to run wild 1** to grow or become unrestrained or uncontrolled. **2** to grow unchecked. **3** to behave in an uncontrolled way. **wild arum** *n.* the cuckoo pint. **wild boar** *n.* the male of the wild swine, *Sus scrofa*. **wild card** *n.* **1** a playing card that can have any value or rank chosen by the holder. **2** (*Comput.*) a character or symbol that will match any character or group of characters. **3** an unpredictable element. **4** in sport, an extra player or team allowed to take part in a competition at the organizers' discretion. **wildcat** *n.* **1** (*usu.* **wild cat**) an undomesticated species of cat, such as *Felis sylvestris*. **2** a quick-tempered, fierce person. **3** an exploratory drilling for oil or natural gas. ~*a.* speculative or risky (*a wildcat scheme*). **wildcat strike** *n.* a sudden strike not approved by the relevant union, or undertaken in breach of a contract. **wildfire** *n.* **1** (*Hist.*) a combustible material formerly used in warfare. **2** ignis fatuus. **to spread like wildfire** to spread very quickly. **wildfowl** *n.* (*pl.* **wildfowl**) (*usu. pl.*) any of various birds pursued as game,

esp. waterfowl. **wildfowler** *n.* **wildfowling** *n.* **wild-goose chase** *n.* a foolish or hopeless enterprise. **wild hyacinth** *n.* the bluebell, *Hyacinthoides nonscripta*. **wildish** *a.* **wildlife** *n.* wild animals and plants. **wildly** *adv.* **wild marjoram** *n.* the herb *Origanum vulgare*. **wildness** *n.* **wild oat** *n.* **1** a type of grass, *Avena fatua*, growing as a weed in cornfields. **2** (*pl.*) youthful excesses, esp. sexual ones. **wild rice** *n.* any plant of the genus *Zizania*, with edible grains. **wild silk** *n.* **1** silk produced by wild silkworms. **2** silk made from short fibres in imitation of this. **wild spaniard** *n.* any of various sharp-leaved plants of the New Zealand *Aciphylla*. **Wild West** *n.* the N American West during the lawless period of its early settlement. **wildwood** *n.* (*poet.*) a tract of natural wood or forest.

wildebeest (wil´dibēst) *n.* (*pl.* **wildebeest**, **wildebeests**) a gnu.

wilderness (wil´dənis) *n.* **1** an uninhabited or uncultivated land, a desert. **2** a portion of a garden left to run wild. **in the wilderness** out of office, not wielding power.

wile (wīl) *n.* (*usu. pl.*) a trick, an artifice, a stratagem or deception. ~*v.t.* to entice, to cajole (into, away etc.).

wilful (wil´fəl), (*N Am.*) **willful** *a.* **1** intentional, voluntary, deliberate. **2** obstinate, self-willed, headstrong, perverse. **wilfully** *adv.* **wilfulness** *n.*

wilily, **wiliness** WILY.

will[1] (wil) *v.t.* (*past* **would** (wud), *2nd pers. sing. pres.* †**wilt** (wilt), *2nd pers. sing. past* †**wouldst** (wudst)) **1** to desire, to wish, to choose, to want (a thing, that etc.) (*Will you have another cup of tea?*). **2** to be induced, to consent, to agree (to etc.) (*Will you close the door, please?*). **3** to be in the habit or accustomed (to). **4** to be able (to). **5** (*in 1st pers.*) to intend, desire or have a mind to. ~*v.aux.* **1** (*esp. in 2nd and 3rd pers.*) to be about or going to (expressing simple futurity or conditional action). **2** (*esp. in 1st pers.*) to intend, desire or have a mind to. **3** to be certain or probable as a natural consequence, must. **will do** (*coll.*) used to express willingness to comply. **would-be** *a.* (*attrib.*, *often derog.*) desirous, vainly aspiring to be.

Usage note See note under SHALL.

will[2] (wil) *n.* **1** the mental power or faculty by which one initiates or controls one's activities, as opposed to *impulse* or *instinct*. **2** the exercise of this power, an act of willing, a choice of volition, an intention, a fixed or authoritative purpose. **3** determination, the power of carrying out one's intentions or dominating others. **4** that which is willed, resolved or determined upon. **5** arbitrary disposal, discretion or sufferance. **6** inclination or disposition towards others. **7** the legal declaration of one's intentions as to the disposal of one's property after one's death, embodied in a written instrument (*to make a will*). **8** a wish or desire (*What is your will?*). **at will 1** at one's pleasure or discretion. **2** (*Law*) (of a tenant) that can be evicted without notice. **with a will** heartily, zealously. **with the best will in the world** no matter how good one's intentions are, however determined one is. **willed** *a.* **will-less** *a.* **will of one's own** *n.* a wilful disposition. **will-power** *n.* control exercised deliberately over impulse or inclinations.

will[1] (wil) *v.t.* **1** to intend or bring about by the exercise of one's will, to resolve, to determine. **2** to direct, control or cause to act in a specified way by the exercise of one's will-power. **3** to bequeath or devise by will. ~*v.i.* to exercise will-power.

willful WILFUL.

willie WILLY.

willies (wil'iz) *n.pl.* (*coll.*) nervousness, apprehensiveness (*It gives me the willies*).

willing (wil'ing) *a.* **1** inclined, ready, not averse or reluctant (to). **2** cheerfully acting, done, given etc. **to show willing** to indicate a readiness to help, comply etc. **willingly** *adv.* **willingness** *n.*

will-o'-the-wisp (wiledhewisp') *n.* **1** an ignis fatuus. **2** an illusory hope, goal etc. **3** an elusive person.

willow (wil'ō) *n.* **1** (*also* **willow tree**) any tree or shrub of the genus *Salix*, usu. growing near water, characterized by long, slender, pliant branches, largely yielding osiers and timber used for cricket bats etc. **2** a cricket bat. **willowherb** *n.* any plant of the genus *Epilobium*, esp. one with leaves like a willow's. **willow-pattern** *n.* a decorative pattern of Chinese style in blue on a white ground, introduced in 1780 and used for china, earthenware etc. **willow warbler, willow wren** *n.* a small woodland bird, *Phylloscopus trochilus*. **willowy** *a.* **1** abounding with willows. **2** lithe, slender or graceful, like a willow.

willy (wil'i), **willie** *n.* (*pl.* **willies**) (*coll.*) the penis.

willy-nilly (wilinil'i) *adv.* willingly or unwillingly. ~*a.* happening whether it is desired or not.

wilt (wilt) *v.i.* **1** to wither, to droop. **2** to lose freshness or vigour. **3** to lose freshness or vigour. ~*v.t.* to cause to wilt. ~*n.* a disease of plants that causes them to wilt.

Wilts. *abbr.* Wiltshire.

wily (wī'li) *a.* (*comp.* **wilier**, *superl.* **wiliest**) using or full of wiles, cunning, crafty. **wilily** *adv.* **wiliness** *n.*

wimp (wimp) *n.* (*coll.*) a feeble, ineffectual person. **wimpish** *a.* **wimpishly** *adv.* **wimpishness** *n.* **wimpy** *a.*

wimple (wim'pel) *n.* a covering of silk, linen etc., worn over the head, neck and sides of the face by some nuns and formerly by other women.

win (win) *v.t.* (*pres.p.* **winning**, *past*, *p.p.* **won** (wŭn)) **1** to gain, obtain, achieve or attain by fighting or superiority in a contest, competition, wager etc. (*to win a prize*). **2** to gain by effort, work etc., to earn. **3** to be victorious (*to win a battle*). **4** to make one's way to, to reach. **5** to win over. **6** to get or extract (ore etc.) by mining,

smelting etc. **7** to attract or charm. ~*v.i.* **1** to be successful or victorious in a fight, contest, wager etc. **2** to make one's way by struggle or effort (through etc.). ~*n.* a success, a victory. **to win out** to win through. **to win over** to persuade, to secure the support, favour or assent of. **to win through** to be successful, to prevail. **winless** *a.* **winnable** *a.* **winner** *n.* **1** a person or thing that wins. **2** (*coll.*) a person or thing that is bound to succeed. **winning** *a.* **1** that wins. **2** attractive, charming. ~*n.* (*pl.*) the amount won in betting, gambling etc. **winningly** *adv.* **winningness** *n.* **winning post** *n.* a post marking the end of a race.

wince (wins) *v.i.* to shrink, recoil or flinch, as from pain, trouble or a blow. ~*n.* the act of wincing. **wincer** *n.* **wincingly** *adv.*

wincey (win'si), **winsey** *n.* (*pl.* **winceys, winseys**) a cotton cloth with wool filling. **winceyette** (-et') *n.* a lightweight cotton cloth with a raised nap on both sides.

winch (winch) *n.* **1** a windlass, a hoisting machine. **2** a crank or handle for turning an axle etc. ~*v.t.* to pull or hoist with a winch. **wincher** *n.*

Winchester (win'chiste) *n.* **1** (*also* **Winchester rifle**) a breech-loading repeating rifle. **2** (*Comput.*) (*also* **Winchester disk, Winchester drive**) a type of hard disk drive in a sealed unit.

wind[1] (wind) *n.* **1** air in motion, a natural air current, a breeze, a gale. **2** air set in motion artificially. **3** the wind instruments in an orchestra etc. or their players. **4** breath as required by the body in exertion, speech etc. **5** the power of breathing in exertion etc., lung power. **6** breath expended in words, meaningless talk or rhetoric. **7** the gas produced in the stomach during digestion etc., flatulence. **8** a hint, suggestion or indication. **9** the windward position (of). ~*v.t.* (*past*, *p.p.* **winded**) **1** to perceive the presence of by scent. **2** to cause to be out of breath. **3** to enable to recover breath by resting etc. **4** to bring the wind up from the stomach of (a baby) after feeding. **5** to expose to the wind, to ventilate. **between wind and water** in a vulnerable place or position. **how the wind blows** the position or state of affairs. **in the wind** showing signs of occurring. **like the wind** very swiftly. **to break wind** to discharge wind from the anus. **to get the wind up** (*coll.*) to get nervous, to become frightened. **to get wind of 1** (*coll.*) to hear about. **2** (*coll.*) to smell out. **to put the wind up** (*coll.*) to frighten. **to sail close to/ near the wind 1** to keep a vessel's head as near the direction from which the wind is blowing as possible while keeping the sails filled. **2** to take risks. **to take the wind out of someone's sails 1** to sail to the windward of someone. **2** to frustrate someone's plans, to disconcert someone. **to take wind** to become known. **to the (four) winds 1** in all directions. **2** into a state of abandonment (*to cast caution to the winds*). **which way the wind blows** the position or state of affairs. **windbag** *n.* a person who says much of little value, a long-winded speaker. **windbreak** *n.* a screen, fence, line of trees etc. that provides protection from the wind. **Windbreaker®** *n.* (*N Am.*) a windcheater. **windburn** *n.* skin irritation caused by the wind. **windcheater** *n.* a close-knitted pullover or close-textured garment to keep out the wind. **wind-chill** *n.* the combined chilling effect of low temperature and wind. **winded** *a.* **windfall** *n.* 1 something blown down by the wind, esp. an apple or other fruit. 2 a piece of unexpected good fortune, esp. a sum of money. **wind farm** *n.* a group of windmills or wind turbines for generating electric power. **windflower** *n.* an anemone, esp. the wood anemone. **wind-gauge** *n.* an anemometer. **windhover** *n.* the kestrel. **wind instrument** *n.* a musical instrument in which the tones are produced by the vibration of an air column forced into the pipes, reeds etc., esp. by the mouth. **windless** *a.* **windlessness** *n.* **windmill** *n.* 1 a mill driven by the action of the wind on sails. 2 a toy with curved plastic or paper vanes that revolve in the wind. ~*v.t., v.i.* to move like a windmill. **windpipe** *n.* the breathing passage, the trachea. **windscreen** *n.* a glass screen at the front of a car to protect the driver and passengers from the wind caused by the speed of the car. **windscreen wiper** *n.* an electrically-operated device fitted with a rubber blade to keep a windscreen clear of rain, snow etc. **wind shear** *n.* a variation in wind speed at right angles to its direction. **windshield** *n.* (*N Am.*) a windscreen. **wind-sleeve** *n.* a windsock. **windsock** *n.* an open-ended fabric sleeve flying from a mast, serving as an indicator of the strength and direction of the wind. **windstorm** *n.* a storm with strong winds but no rain. **windsurfing** *n.* the sport of sailing on water standing upright on a sailboard. **windsurf** *v.i.* **windsurfer** *n.* **windswept** *a.* 1 exposed to the wind. 2 blown by the wind (*windswept hair*). **wind tunnel** *n.* a tunnel-like device for producing an airstream of known velocity for testing the effect of wind on the structure of model vehicles, aircraft etc. **windward** (-wəd) *n.* the direction from which the wind blows. ~*a.* lying in or directed towards this. ~*adv.* in the direction from which the wind blows. **windy**¹ *a.* (*comp.* **windier**, *superl.* **windiest**) 1 having much wind, stormy, boisterous (*a windy day*). 2 exposed to the wind. 3 flatulent, caused by flatulence. 4 verbose, loquacious, empty. 5 (*coll.*) scared, frightened, apprehensive. **windily** *adv.* **windiness** *n.*

wind² (wīnd) *v.i.* (*past, p.p.* **wound** (wownd)) 1 to turn, move or be twisted or coiled in a spiral, curved or tortuous course or shape. 2 to be circular, spiral, tortuous or crooked. 3 to meander. 4 to be wrapped spirally (round, into etc.). ~*v.t.* 1 to cause to turn spirally, to wrap, twine or coil. 2 to encircle, to coil round, to entwine. 3 to pursue (one's course) in a spiral, sinuous or circuitous way. 4 to twist (one's way) or insinuate oneself (into etc.). 5 to hoist or move by means of

a windlass, capstan etc. 6 to wind up (*to wind a watch*). ~*n.* 1 a bend or curve. 2 a single turn in winding. 3 the act or an instance of winding. **to wind down** 1 to lower by winding. 2 to reduce gradually. 3 to relax. 4 to unwind. 5 gradually to reduce the amount of work in (something), before it stops completely. **to wind off** to unwind. **to wind up** 1 to coil up. 2 to coil or tighten up the spring of (a watch etc.). 3 (*coll.*) to put into a state of tension or readiness for activity. 4 (*coll.*) to irritate, to annoy. 5 (*sl.*) to tease. 6 to bring to a conclusion, to conclude. 7 to come to a conclusion. 8 to arrange the final settlement of the affairs of (a business etc.). 9 to go into liquidation. 10 (*coll.*) to end up in a certain state or situation (*They wound up in hospital*). **wind-down** *n.* (*coll.*) a gradual reduction. **winder** *n.* **winding-sheet** *n.* the sheet in which a corpse is wrapped. **wind-up** *n.* 1 the act or an instance of winding up. 2 an end or conclusion. ~*a.* operated by a winding mechanism (*a wind-up toy*). **windy**² *a.*

wind³ (wīnd) *v.t.* (*past, p.p.* **winded, wound** (wownd)) (*poet.*) to sound (a horn, bugle etc.) by blowing.

windlass (wind'ləs) *n.* a machine consisting of a cylinder on an axle turned by a crank, used for hoisting or hauling. ~*v.t.* to hoist or haul with this.

window (win'dō) *n.* 1 an opening in the wall or roof of a building, vehicle or other structure, usu. with the wooden or metal glazed framework filling it, for the admission of light or air. 2 the glass filling this (*to break a window*). 3 the sash of a window frame. 4 the space behind the large front window of a shop, used for display. 5 an aperture in a wall or screen separating customers from staff in a bank, ticket office etc. 6 any opening resembling a window, as in a window envelope. 7 (*Comput.*) a rectangular area on a VDU where information can be displayed. 8 a brief period of time when the conditions allow a particular activity. 9 any opportunity for action etc. **window box** *n.* a box for growing flowers on a window sill. **window cleaner** *n.* 1 a person whose job is cleaning windows, esp. outside. 2 a substance or device used to clean windows. **window-dresser** *n.* a person employed to arrange goods for display in a shop window. **window-dressing** *n.* 1 the arrangement of goods for display in a shop window. 2 deceptive display, insincere argument. **windowed** *a.* **window frame** *n.* the framework in a window that supports the glass. **windowing** *n.* (*Comput.*) the use of windows to display information from different files etc. simultaneously. **window ledge** *n.* a window sill. **windowless** *a.* **window pane** *n.* a sheet of glass in a window. **window seat** *n.* 1 a seat in the recess of a window. 2 a seat beside a window in a train, bus, aeroplane etc. **window-shop** *v.i.* (*pres.p.* **window-shopping**, *past, p.p.* **window-shopped**) to idly gaze at the displays in shop windows. **window-shopper** *n.* **window-shopping**

n. **window sill** *n.* a ledge at the bottom of a window, inside or outside.
Windsor (win´zə) *a.* of or relating to the British royal family from 1917. **Windsor chair** *n.* a strong, plain wooden chair with a back curved into supports for the arms.
windy[1] WIND[1].
windy[2] WIND[2].
wine (wīn) *n.* **1** the fermented juice of grapes. **2** the juice of certain fruits etc. prepared in imitation of this. **3** a dark red colour. *~v.i.* to drink wine. *~v.t.* to serve or entertain with wine. **to wine and dine** to entertain with food and alcohol. **wine bar** *n.* a bar that serves mostly wine, esp. with food. **wine box** *n.* a cardboard box with a plastic lining, usu. with a three-litre capacity, filled with wine and fitted with a tap for dispensing it. **wine cellar** *n.* **1** a cellar where wine is stored. **2** its contents. **wineglass** *n.* **1** a small glass for drinking wine from. **2** a wineglassful. **wineglassful** *n.* (*pl.* **wineglassfuls**) **1** the capacity of a wineglass, esp. a sherry glass, about 2 fl. oz (6 cl). **2** the contents of a wineglass. **wine-grower** *n.* a person who grows grapes for winemaking. **wineless** *a.* **wine list** *n.* a list of the wines available in a restaurant, from a supplier etc. **winepress** *n.* **1** an apparatus in which grapes are pressed. **2** the place in which this is done. **wine red** *n.* a dark red colour. *~a.* of this colour. **winery** *n.* (*pl.* **wineries**) a place where wine is made. **wineskin** *n.* a skin, usu. of a goat, sewn into a bag for holding wine. **wine taster** *n.* a person who samples wine to judge its quality. **wine tasting** *n.* **1** an occasion when people can sample various wines. **2** the act of sampling wine to judge its quality. **wine vinegar** *n.* vinegar made from wine. **wine waiter** *n.* a waiter in a restaurant, hotel etc. who is responsible for serving customers with wine. **winey, winy** *a.* (*comp.* **winier,** *superl.* **winiest**) resembling wine.
wing (wing) *n.* **1** each of the limbs or organs of flight in birds, insects etc. **2** each of the supporting parts of an aircraft. **3** a part of a building, fortification, army, bone, implement etc. projecting laterally. **4** a part of a building that extends from the main part. **5** in football and similar games, a player on one or other extreme flank. **6** the position in which such a player plays. **7** an extreme faction of a party, group etc. **8** a part of a car or other motor vehicle above the wheels. **9** an RAF unit of three squadrons. **10** (*pl.*) the sides of a stage or pieces of scenery placed there. **11** (*pl.*) the mark of proficiency a pilot qualified in the RAF is entitled to wear on his uniform. *~v.t.* **1** to enable to fly or move with swiftness. **2** to traverse or travel on wings. **3** to wound in the wing or the arm. *~v.i.* to fly. **in the wings** waiting in readiness. **on a wing and a prayer** with no more than a slight chance of success. **on the wing 1** flying. **2** in motion. **to spread/ stretch one's wings** to develop or make full use of one's powers, abilities etc. **to take under one's wing** to

take under one's protection. **to take wing 1** to begin flying, to fly away. **2** to disappear. **wing-beat** *n.* a complete stroke of the wing in flying. **wing-case** *n.* the horny cover or case, consisting of a modified wing, protecting the flying wings of some insects. **wing collar** *n.* a stiff upright shirt collar with the points turned down. **wing commander** *n.* a commissioned officer in the RAF ranking below a group captain and above a squadron leader. **wing covert** *n.* any of the small feathers covering the insertion of a bird's flight feathers. **winged** *a.* **1** having wings. **2** going straight to the mark, powerful, rousing (*winged words*). **winged elm** *n.* WAHOO[1]. **winger** *n.* **1** a football player etc. positioned on the wing. **2** (*in comb.*) a member of a specified wing of a political party etc. (*left-winger, right-winger*). **wing forward** *n.* in rugby, a forward positioned on the wing. **wingless** *a.* **winglet** *n.* **winglike** *a.* **wing nut** *n.* a nut that is tightened by two flat winglike projections on its sides. **wingspan, wingspread** *n.* the distance from one wing-tip of a bird, aircraft etc. to the other.
wink (wingk) *v.i.* **1** to close and open one eye quickly. **2** to close and open both eyes quickly, to blink. **3** (of an eye) to close and open. **4** to twinkle, to flicker, to flash intermittently. *~v.t.* to close and open (an eye or the eyes). *~n.* **1** the act of winking, esp. as a signal. **2** (*coll.*) a moment of sleep. **in a wink** very quickly. **to wink at 1** to pretend not to see. **2** to connive at. **winker** *n.* **winking** *n., a.* **winkingly** *adv.*
winkle (wing´kəl) *n.* an edible marine mollusc of the genus *Littorina,* a periwinkle. **to winkle out 1** (*coll.*) to extract with difficulty. **2** (*coll.*) to elicit (information etc.) with difficulty. **winkle-pickers** *n.pl.* (*sl.*) shoes with long pointed toes.
winnable, winner etc. WIN.
winnow (win´ō) *v.t.* **1** to separate and drive the chaff from (grain). **2** to fan (chaff) (away, out etc.). **3** to sift, to sort, to examine or analyse thoroughly. **winnower** *n.* **winnowing** *n.*
wino (wī´nō) *n.* (*pl.* **winos**) (*sl.*) an alcoholic, esp. one who drinks mainly wine.
winsome (win´səm) *a.* engaging, winning, charming, attractive. **winsomely** *adv.* **winsomeness** *n.*
winter (win´tə) *n.* **1** (*Astron.*) the coldest season of the year, astronomically from the winter solstice to the vernal equinox, usu. regarded in northern latitudes as including December, January, February. **2** a period of inactivity, a cheerless or depressing state of things. **3** (*poet.*) a year of life. *~a.* **1** of, relating to or suitable for the winter. **2** lasting throughout the winter. **3** (of fruit) ripening late. **4** (of crops) sown in autumn (*winter wheat*). *~v.i.* **1** to pass the winter. **2** to hibernate. *~v.t.* to keep, feed or maintain through the winter. **winter aconite** *n.* a yellow-flowered plant of the genus *Eranthis.* **winter garden** *n.* **1** a large conservatory or glasshouse for plants not hardy enough to withstand the climate outside

during winter. **2** a garden of plants that flourish in winter. **wintergreen** *n.* **1** a low plant of the genus *Pyrola*, keeping green throughout the winter. **2** the checkerberry, *Gaultheria procumbens*. **3** OIL OF WINTERGREEN (under OIL). **winter heliotrope** *n.* a plant of the daisy family, *Petasites fragrans*, which produces light purple flowers in winter. **winterize, winterise** *v.t.* (*esp. NAm.*) to prepare or adapt for use in cold winter weather. **winterization** (-zā´shən) *n.* **winter jasmine** *n.* a yellow-flowered jasmine, *Jasminum nudiflorum*. **winterless** *a.* **winter solstice** *n.* (*Astron.*) one of the times (about 22 Dec. in the northern hemisphere) and points at which the sun is farthest from the celestial equator. **winter sport** *n.* (*usu. pl.*) a sport practised on snow and ice, usu. outdoors, e.g. skiing, skating. **wintertime**, (*poet.*) **winter-tide** *n.* the season of winter. **wintry** (-tri), **wintery** *a.* (*comp.* **wintrier**, *superl.* **wintriest**) **1** of or like winter. **2** (of a smile, look etc.) cold and cheerless. **wintrily** *adv.* **wintriness** *n.*

winy WINE.

wipe (wīp) *v.t.* **1** to rub with something soft in order to clean or dry. **2** to rub (a cloth, hand etc.) over something for this purpose. **3** to remove (dirt etc.) by wiping. **4** to apply (grease etc.) by wiping. **5** to clear (a magnetic tape or videotape) of recorded material. **6** to remove (recorded material, data etc.) in this way. ~*n.* **1** an act of wiping. **2** something used for wiping, esp. a disposable cloth or tissue treated with a cleansing substance. **to wipe down** to clean (a wall, door etc.) by wiping. **to wipe out 1** to clean out by wiping. **2** to efface, to obliterate. **3** to destroy, to annihilate. **4** (*sl.*) to murder. **to wipe up 1** to remove (a liquid etc.) by wiping. **2** to dry (dishes etc.). **wipeable** *a.* **wipe-out** *n.* **1** an act or instance of wiping out. **2** interference that renders impossible the reception of other radio signals. **3** (*sl.*) a fall from a surfboard or skateboard. **wiper** *n.* **1** a cloth etc. used for wiping. **2** a windscreen wiper.

wire (wīə) *n.* **1** metal drawn out into a slender and flexible rod or thread of uniform diameter. **2** a piece or length of this, esp. used to carry electric current. **3** (*dated, coll.*) the electric telegraph, a telegram message. ~*a.* made of wire. ~*v.t.* **1** to apply wire to, to fasten, secure, bind or stiffen with wire. **2** to install electrical wiring in. **3** to snare with wire. **4** (*coll.*) to telegraph to. ~*v.i.* (*coll.*) to send a telegram. **by wire** by telegraph or telegram. **wire brush** *n.* **1** a brush with wire bristles used e.g. for scraping rust off metal. **2** a brush with wire strands used in playing cymbals. **wired** *a.* **1** provided with or connected by (electrical) wires. **2** (*sl.*) highly nervous, stressed. **3** (*sl.*) intoxicated, high on drugs or alcohol. **wire gauge** *n.* **1** an instrument for measuring the diameter of wire. **2** a standard system of sizes designating the diameter of wire. **wire gauze** *n.* a textile fabric made of wire, used for very fine

sieves, respirators etc. **wire-haired** *a.* (of a dog) having stiff, wiry hair (*a wire-haired terrier*). **wire netting** *n.* a mesh of interwoven wire used for fencing, reinforcement etc. **wirer** *n.* **wire stripper** *n.* (*often pl.*) a tool for stripping the insulation from electric wires. **wire-tap** *v.t.* (*pres.p.* **wire-tapping**, *past, p.p.* **wire-tapped**) to tap (a telephone). **wire-tapper** *n.* **wire-tapping** *n.* **wire wheel** *n.* a wheel with wire spokes, esp. on a sports car. **wire wool** *n.* an abrasive material consisting of a mass of very fine wires, used for cleaning etc. **wireworm** *n.* the vermiform larva of a click beetle, destructive to roots of vegetables, cereals etc. **wiring** *n.* **1** a system of wires, esp. one carrying electric current. **2** the act of installing such a system. **wiry** *a.* (*comp.* **wirier**, *superl.* **wiriest**) **1** made of or resembling wire. **2** tough and flexible. **3** (of a person) lean but sinewy. **4** (of hair etc.) stiff. **wirily** *adv.* **wiriness** *n.*

wireless (wīə´lis) *n.* (*dated*) **1** any process or method whereby messages, music or other sounds can be transmitted by electromagnetic waves without the intervention of wires; radio. **2** an instrument for receiving such messages etc.; a radio. **3** the programmes of entertainment etc. thus transmitted. **4** wireless telegraphy. ~*a.* not having or requiring wires. **wireless telegraphy** *n.* radio-telegraphy.

wisdom (wiz´dəm) *n.* **1** the quality or state of being wise. **2** knowledge and experience together with the ability to make proper use of them, practical discernment, sagacity, judgement, common sense. **3** a collection of wise sayings. **wisdom tooth** *n.* (*pl.* **wisdom teeth**) the third molar, usu. appearing about the age of 20.

wise¹ (wīz) *a.* **1** having or showing the power or faculty of discerning or judging rightly; sagacious, sensible, discreet, prudent, judicious. **2** having or showing knowledge and experience together with the ability to apply them rightly. **3** informed, aware. **4** (*N Am., coll.*) insolent, cocksure. **none the wiser** having no more knowledge or understanding than before. **to put someone wise** to inform someone. **to wise up 1** (*esp. NAm., coll.*) to be or become aware or informed. **2** (*esp. N Am., coll.*) to make aware, to inform. **wise to** aware of, alert to. **without anyone being the wiser** without anyone knowing, without detection. **wisecrack** *n.* (*coll.*) **1** a smart but not profound epigram. **2** a witty comment. ~*v.i.* to make a wisecrack. **wisecracker** *n.* **wise guy** *n.* (*esp. N Am., coll.*) an insolent or cocksure person. **wisely** *adv.* **wise man** *n.* (*pl.* **wise men**) **1** a wizard. **2** each of the Magi. **wiseness** *n.*

†**wise²** (wīz) *n.* a manner, way or mode of acting, behaving etc. **in no wise** not at all.

-wise (wīz) *suf.* **1** forming adverbs of manner, as *lengthwise, likewise*. **2** with regard to, concerning, as *jobwise, weatherwise*.

wiseacre (wī´zākə) *n.* a person pretending to learning or wisdom.

wish (wish) *v.t.* **1** to have a desire, aspiration or craving (for). **2** to want (*I wish to stay*). **3** to frame or express a desire or wish concerning (*She wished him well*). **4** to invoke, to bid (*I wish you to leave*). *~v.i.* **1** to have a desire (for). **2** to make a wish. *~n.* **1** a desire, a longing, an aspiration. **2** an expression of this, a request, a petition, an invocation. **3** that which is desired. **wishbone** *n.* the forked bone in the breast of a bird, which when broken by two persons is supposed to entitle the holder of the longer part to the fulfilment of some wish. **wisher** *n.* **wishful** *a.* **wishfully** *adv.* **wishfulness** *n.* **wishful thinking** *n.* belief based on desires rather than facts. **wishfulfilment,** (*NAm.*) **wish-fulfillment** *n.* the fulfilment of a subconscious wish in fact or fantasy. **wishing** *n.* **wishing-well** *n.* a well into which coins are dropped in the hope of making wishes come true. **wish-list** *n.* a usu. mental list of desires.

wish-wash (wish´wosh) *n.* thin weak liquor or drink. **wishy-washy** (wish´iwoshi) *a.* **1** vague, ill-defined. **2** lacking strength, forcefulness etc. **3** watery, insipid. **4** (of colours) pale, not bright or dark.

wisp (wisp) *n.* **1** a small bunch or handful of straw, hay etc. **2** a piece, a strand, a small quantity (*a wisp of hair*). **3** a thin band or streak (*a wisp of smoke*). **wispy** *a.* (*comp.* **wispier,** *superl.* **wispiest**). **wispily** *adv.* **wispiness** *n.*

†**twist** WIT².

wisteria (wistiə´riə), **wistaria** (-teə´-) *n.* any leguminous climbing shrub of the genus *Wisteria*, with racemes of lilac-coloured flowers.

wistful (wist´fəl) *a.* **1** full of vague yearnings, esp. for unattainable things, sadly longing. **2** thoughtful in a melancholy way, pensive. **wistfully** *adv.* **wistfulness** *n.*

wit¹ (wit) *n.* **1** (*often pl.*) intelligence, understanding, sense, sagacity. **2** (*pl.*) sanity. **3** the power of perceiving analogies and other relations between apparently incongruous ideas or of forming unexpected, striking or ludicrous combinations of them. **4** a person distinguished for this power, a witty person. **at one's wits' end** at a complete loss as to what further steps to take, in a state of despair or desperation. **out of one's wits** mad. **to have/ keep one's wits about one** to be alert. **to live by one's wits** to live by cunning or ingenuity rather than regular employment. **witless** *a.* foolish, stupid. **witlessly** *adv.* **witlessness** *n.* **witted** *a.* **witticism** (-sizm) *n.* a witty phrase or saying, a jest. **witty** *a.* (*comp.* **wittier,** *superl.* **wittiest**) showing or characterized by wit or humour. **wittily** *adv.* **wittiness** *n.*

†**wit²** (wit) *v.t., v.i.* (*1st & 3rd pers. sing. pres.* **wot** (wot), *2nd pers. sing. pres.* **wottest** (wot´əst), *past, p.p.* **wist** (wist)) to know. **to wit** namely.

witch¹ (wich) *n.* **1** a woman having dealings with evil spirits or practising sorcery. **2** an ugly old woman, a hag. **3** a bewitching or fascinating woman. **witchcraft** *n.* **1** the practices of witches.

2 sorcery, magic. **3** bewitching charm. **witch doctor** *n.* in some tribal societies, a person who invokes supernatural powers, esp. to cure people. **witchery** *n.* witchcraft. **witch-hunt** *n.* **1** the searching out and public exposure of opponents accused of disloyalty to a state, political party etc. **2** (*Hist.*) the searching out and persecution of witches. **witch-hunting** *n.* **witchlike** *a.* **witchy** *a.*

witch² (wich) *a.* (*attrib.*) WYCH. **witch alder** *n.* an American shrub, *Fothergilla gardenii*. **witch elm** *n.* WYCH ELM (under WYCH). **witch hazel** *n.* **1** an American or E Asian shrub of the genus *Hamamelis*, esp. *H. virginiana*. **2** a medicinal lotion derived from the leaves and bark of *H. virginiana*, used to treat bruises etc.

with (widh) *prep.* **1** in or into the company of, in or into the relation of accompaniment, association, simultaneousness, cooperation, harmoniousness etc. **2** having, marked or characterized by. **3** in the possession, care or guardianship of. **4** by the means, instrumentality, use or aid of. **5** by the addition or supply of. **6** because of, owing to, in consequence of. **7** in regard to, in respect of, concerning, in the case of. **8** in separation from. **9** in opposition to, against. **10** in spite of, notwithstanding. **to be with someone 1** to support someone. **2** to agree with someone. **3** (*coll.*) to understand someone, to follow what someone is saying (*I'm not with you*). **with it** *a.* (*coll.*) **1** up to date, fashionable. **2** alert to what is being done or said. *~adv.* besides, in addition.

withdraw (widhdraw´) *v.t.* (*past* **withdrew** (-droo´), *p.p.* **withdrawn** (-drawn´)) **1** to draw back, aside or apart. **2** to take away, to remove (*to withdraw an accusation*). **3** to state officically that something which one said previously is not true. **4** to take (money) from an account. *~v.i.* **1** to retire, to go away. **2** to move back, away or aside. **3** to retract a statement, accusation etc. **4** to discontinue one's involvement (*to withdraw from a competition*). **withdrawal** *n.* **1** the act or an instance of withdrawing. **2** the act of offically stating that something which one said previously is not true. **3** the act of leaving a place. **4** the act of no longer doing something. **5** the process or period following termination of the use of addictive drugs etc. **6** coitus interruptus. **withdrawer** *n.* **withdrawn** *a.* very shy or reserved, socially isolated, emotionally detached etc.

withe (widh, with, wīdh) *n.* a tough, flexible branch, esp. of willow or osier, used in binding things together.

wither (widh´ə) *v.t.* **1** to cause to fade, shrivel or dry, to shrivel and dry (up). **2** to cause to lose freshness, soundness, vitality or vigour. *~v.i.* **1** to become dry and shrivelled, to dry and shrivel (up). **2** to fade away, to languish, to droop, to decline. **withering** *a.* scornful. **witheringly** *adv.*

withers (widh´əz) *n.pl.* the ridge between the shoulder blades of a horse.

withershins (widh´əshinz), **widdershins** (wid´-ə-) *adv.* anticlockwise, in the contrary direction, esp. to the left or opposite to the direction of the sun.

withhold (widh·hōld´) *v.t.* (*past, p.p.* **withheld** (-held´)) **1** to keep back, to refuse to grant or give; to deduct. **2** to keep from action, to hold back, to restrain. **withholder** *n.*

within (widhin´) *adv.* (*poet.*) **1** inside, in or to the inside, in the inner part or parts, internally. **2** indoors. **3** in the mind, heart or spirit. ~*prep.* **1** in or to the inner or interior part or parts of, inside. **2** in the limits, range, scope or compass of. **3** not beyond, not further off than. **4** in no longer a time than (*within three days*). **within reach** close enough to be reached. **within sight** close enough to be seen.

☒ **withold** common misspelling of WITHHOLD.

without (widhowt´) *adv.* (*poet.*) **1** in, at or to the outside. **2** outside, outwardly, externally. **3** out of doors. ~*prep.* **1** not having, not with, having no, destitute of, lacking, free from. **2** not accompanied by, in the absence of. **3** neglecting to (*They left without saying goodbye*).

withstand (widhstand´) *v.t.* (*past, p.p.* **withstood** (-stud´)) to stand up against, to resist, to oppose. **withstander** *n.*

withy (widh´i) *n.* (*pl.* **withies**) **1** a withe. **2** a willow.

witness (wit´nis) *n.* **1** a person who has seen an incident etc., a spectator, a person present at an event. **2** a person who gives evidence in a law court or for judicial purposes, esp. on oath. **3** a person who affixes their name to a document to testify to the genuineness of the signature. **4** attestation of a fact etc., testimony, evidence. **5** a thing or person serving as testimony to or proof of. ~*v.t.* **1** to see or know by personal presence, to be a spectator of. **2** to attest (a signature), to sign (a document) as witness. **3** to indicate, to show, to prove. **4** (*in imper.*) used to introduce evidence (*She is a caring person: witness her devotion to her invalid father*). **to bear witness 1** to give testimony. **2** to be a sign of (*Their response bears witness to their lack of concern*). **to call to witness** to summon, appeal to or ask for confirmation or testimony. **witnessable** *a.* **witness box,** (*N Am.*) **witness-stand** *n.* (*Law*) an enclosure in a law court for witnesses to give evidence from.

witter (wit´ə) *v.i.* (*coll.*) to talk without purpose or at length, to chatter or babble (*He wittered on about his car*).

witticism, wittiness etc. WIT¹.

witting (wit´ing) *a.* conscious, knowing, intentional. **wittingly** *adv.*

witty WIT¹.

wives WIFE.

wizard (wiz´əd) *n.* **1** a sorcerer, a magician, a conjuror. **2** a person who works wonders, a genius, an expert. ~*a.* **1** (*dated sl.*) wonderful, marvellous. **2** magic, enchanting, enchanted. **wizardly** *a.* **wizardry** *n.*

wizen (wiz´ən) *v.t., v.i.* to wither, to dry up, to shrivel. ~*a.* wizened. **wizened** *a.* withered or shrivelled, esp. with age.

wk *abbr.* week.

wks *abbr.* weeks.

WNW *abbr.* west-north-west.

WO *abbr.* Warrant Officer.

wo WHOA.

woad (wōd) *n.* **1** a plant, *Isatis tinctoria*, yielding a blue dye. **2** this dye formerly used for staining the body, esp. by the ancient Britons. **woaded** *a.*

wobble (wob´əl), **wabble** *v.i.* **1** to incline to one side and then the other alternately, as when not properly balanced. **2** to oscillate. **3** to go unsteadily, to stagger. **4** to waver, to be inconsistent or inconstant. **5** to quaver or tremble (*Her voice wobbled*). ~*v.t.* to cause to wobble. ~*n.* **1** a wobbling movement, sound etc. **2** a rocking, uneven motion. **3** an act of hesitation, inconsistency or vacillation. **wobbler** *n.* **wobbly** *a.* (*comp.* **wobblier,** *superl.* **wobbliest**) **1** inclined to wobble. **2** unsteady. **3** wavy. **4** vacillating. ~*n.* (*pl.* **wobblies**) (*coll.*) a fit of nerves, a tantrum (*to throw a wobbly*). **wobbliness** *n.*

woe (wō), †**wo** *n.* **1** (*poet.*) sorrow, affliction, distress, overwhelming grief. **2** (*often pl.*) calamity, trouble, misfortune (*a tale of woe*). **woe betide** may misfortune befall; used to warn of unpleasant consequences (*Woe betide anyone who touches my new computer!*). **woebegone** (-bigon) *a.* overcome with woe, sorrowful-looking, dismal. **woeful** *a.* **1** sorrowful, miserable. **2** pitiful, inadequate, very poor. **3** causing sorrow. **woefully** *adv.* **woefulness** *n.*

wog (wog) *n.* (*offensive*) any dark-skinned person.

wok (wok) *n.* a large metal bowl with curved sides and handles used in Chinese cooking.

woke, woken WAKE¹.

wold (wōld) *n.* a tract of open country, esp. downland or moorland.

wolf (wulf) *n.* (*pl.* **wolves** (wulvz)) **1** a grey, tawny-grey, reddish or white carnivorous quadruped, esp. *Canis lupus*, closely allied to the dog, preying on sheep, calves etc. and hunting larger animals in packs. **2** a rapacious, ravenous, greedy or cruel person. **3** (*coll.*) a man who is rapacious in the pursuit of women for sexual purposes. ~*v.t.* to devour ravenously, to gulp or swallow (down) greedily. **to cry wolf** to raise a false alarm, esp. repeatedly. **to keep the wolf from the door** to keep off starvation. **to throw to the wolves** to send to certain destruction, to sacrifice or abandon without scruple or remorse. **wolfhound** *n.* a large powerful dog formerly used to hunt wolves. **wolf in sheep's clothing** *n.* a person who disguises malicious intentions behind a pretence of innocence. **wolfish** *a.* **wolfishly** *adv.* **wolfishness** *n.* **wolflike** *a.* **wolfsbane** *n.* a species of aconite, esp. *Aconitum lycoctonum*. **wolf spider** *n.* any spider of the family Lycosidae, which hunts its prey. **wolf whistle** *n.* a whistle made usu. by a male at the sight of an attractive female. **wolf-whistle** *v.i.*

wolfram (wul´frəm) *n.* **1** tungsten. **2** wolframite. **wolframite** *n.* a native tungsten ore composed of tungstate of iron and manganese.

wolverine (wul´vərēn), **wolverene** *n.* a small carnivorous animal, *Gulo gulo*, also called the glutton or carcajou.

wolves WOLF.

woman (wum´ən) *n.* (*pl.* **women** (wim´in)) **1** an adult human female. **2** womankind, the female sex. **3** (*coll.*, *often offensive*) a wife, mistress or girlfriend. **4** (*coll.*) an effeminate or timid and tender man. **5** (*coll.*) a female servant, esp. a domestic help. ~*a.* female. **to be one's own woman** (of a woman) to be of independent mind. **womanhood** *n.* **womanish** *a.* **1** (*usu. derog.*) having the characteristics or qualities of a woman, weak, effeminate. **2** suitable for a woman. **womanishly** *adv.* **womanishness** *n.* **womanize**, **womanise** *v.i.* (of a man) to have casual sexual relationships with many women. **womanizer** *n.* **womankind** *n.* women collectively, the female sex. **womanlike** *a.* **womanly** *a.* having the qualities associated with a woman, feminine. **womanliness** *n.* **woman of the moment** *n.* a woman who is important or famous at the present time. **woman of the streets** *n.* a prostitute. **woman of the world** *n.* a woman knowledgeable about or experienced in the ways of the world. **womenfolk** *n.* **1** the women of a household or family. **2** women collectively. **womenkind** *n.* womankind. **Women's Institute** *n.* a non-political and non-sectarian organization of women in Britain, esp. in rural areas, meeting regularly for domestic, social and cultural activities. **women's liberation**, (*coll.*) **women's lib** *n.* the social, sexual and psychological emancipation of women from the dominance of men. **women's rights** *n.pl.* the rights of women, esp. for social, occupational and legal equality with men. **womenswear** *n.* clothing for women.

womb (woom) *n.* **1** the organ in a woman or other female mammal in which the young is developed before birth, the uterus. **2** the place where anything is engendered or brought into existence. **womb-like** *a.*

wombat (wom´bat) *n.* any burrowing Australian marsupial of the family Vombatidae, resembling a small bear.

women, womenfolk etc. WOMAN.

won[1] WIN.

won[2] (won) *n.* the standard monetary unit in N and S Korea.

wonder (wŭn´də) *n.* **1** a strange, remarkable or marvellous thing, person, event, action etc., a miracle, a prodigy. **2** the emotion excited by that which is unexpected, strange, extraordinary or inexplicable. **3** surprise mingled with admiration. ~*a.* having amazing, extraordinary or miraculous qualities (*a wonder drug*). ~*v.i.* **1** to be struck with wonder or surprise. **2** to look with

wonder or admiration (at). **3** to feel doubt or curiosity (about etc.). ~*v.t.* **1** to speculate about. **2** to feel doubt or curiosity about. **3** to be surprised (that). **I wonder** I doubt it. **no wonder** it is not surprising (that). **to work/ do wonders** to achieve remarkable or miraculous results. **wonderer** *n.* **wonderful** *a.* **1** remarkable, marvellous, admirable. **2** exciting wonder or astonishment. **wonderfully** *adv.* **wonderfulness** *n.* **wonderland** *n.* **1** a land of marvels. **2** a place or scene of great beauty. **wonderment** *n.* **1** amazement, awe. **2** curiosity. **wondrous** (-drəs) *a.* (*poet.*) wonderful, marvellous, strange. ~*adv.* wonderfully, exceedingly. **wondrously** *adv.* **wondrousness** *n.*

wonky (wong´ki) *a.* (*comp.* **wonkier**, *superl.* **wonkiest**) (*sl.*) **1** askew, crooked. **2** unsteady, shaky. **3** unreliable. **wonkily** *adv.* **wonkiness** *n.*

wont (wōnt) *a.* (*poet.*) **1** used, accustomed (to). **2** using or doing habitually. ~*n.* (*formal or facet.*) custom, habit, use (*as is her wont*). **wonted** *a.* customary, habitual, usual.

won't (wōnt) *contr.* will not.

wonton (wonton´) *n.* a small Chinese dumpling with a savoury filling, usu. served in soup.

woo (woo) *v.t.* (*3rd pers. sing. pres.* **woos**, *pres.p.* **wooing**, *past, p.p.* **wooed**) **1** to court, esp. with a view to marriage. **2** to seek to gain or attain. **3** to solicit, to coax, to importune. ~*v.i.* to go courting. **wooable** *a.* **wooer** *n.*

wood (wud) *n.* **1** the fibrous substance of a tree between the bark and the pith. **2** timber. **3** (*often pl.*) a large and thick collection of growing trees, a forest. **4** in bowls, a wooden bowl. **5** a golf club with a wooden head. **6** wooden casks or barrels, esp. for wine (*aged in the wood*). **not to see the wood for the trees** to be prevented by excessive details from getting an overall view. **out of the wood** out of danger or difficulty. **out of the woods** (*esp. N Am.*) out of the wood. **wood anemone** *n.* a wild anemone, *Anemone nemorosa*. **wood avens** *n.* herb bennet. **woodbine, woodbind** *n.* **1** the wild honeysuckle. **2** (*N Am.*) the Virginia creeper. **woodblock** *n.* a die cut in wood for taking impressions or woodcuts from. **woodcarver** *n.* a person who carves designs etc. on wood. **woodcarving** *n.*, *a.* **woodchip** *n.* **1** a chip of wood. **2** (*also* **woodchip paper**) a type of wallpaper containing woodchips for texture. **woodcock** *n.* (*pl.* **woodcock**) a game bird of the genus *Scolopax* or *Philohela*. **woodcraft** *n.* (*esp. N Am.*) **1** skill in anything relating to life in the woods or forest. **2** skill in woodwork. **woodcut** *n.* **1** an engraving on wood, a woodblock. **2** a print or impression from this. **3** the technique of making such prints or engravings. **woodcutter** *n.* **1** a person who cuts wood or timber. **2** an engraver on wood. **wooded** *a.* covered with trees or woods. **wooden** *a.* **1** made of wood. **2** resembling wood. **3** stiff, clumsy, awkward, stilted. **4** spiritless, expressionless. **wooden-head** *n.* (*coll.*) a stupid person, a blockhead. **wooden-headed** *a.*

wooden-headedness n. **woodenly** adv. **woodenness** n. **wooden spoon** n. **1** a spoon made of wood, used in cooking. **2** a booby prize, esp. in sports competitions. **wood fibre,** (N Am.) **wood fiber** n. fibre obtained from wood, used for papermaking etc. **wood-grain** a. having a pattern imitating that of the grain of wood (a wood-grain finish). **woodgrouse** n. the capercaillie, Tetrao urogallus. **wood hyacinth** n. the bluebell, Hyacinthoides nonscripta. **woodland** n. land covered with woods, wooded country. ~a. of or relating to this, sylvan. **woodlander** n. **woodlark** n. a European lark, Lullula arborea, smaller than the skylark. **woodless** a. **woodlouse** n. (pl. **woodlice**) any small isopod crustacean of the genera Oniscus, Porcellio etc., infesting decayed wood etc. **woodman** n. (pl. **woodmen**) **1** a forester. **2** a person who fells timber. **wood mouse** n. (pl. **woodmice**) a field mouse. **wood nymph** n. a dryad. **woodpecker** n. a bird of the family Picidae living in woods and tapping trees to discover insects. **wood pigeon** n. the ring-dove, Columba palumbus, a Eurasian pigeon whose neck is nearly encircled by a ring of whitish-coloured feathers. **woodpile** n. a pile of wood. **wood pulp** n. wood fibre pulped in the process of manufacturing paper. **woodruff** n. a woodland plant with fragrant white flowers of the genus Galium, esp. G. odoratum. **woodscrew** n. a metal screw for fastening pieces of wood together. **woodshed** n. a shed for storing wood, esp. firewood. **something nasty in the woodshed** (coll.) something unpleasant or shocking, esp. from a person's past, kept hidden or secret. **woodsman** n. (pl. **woodsmen**) **1** a person who lives in the woods. **2** a woodman. **3** a person who is skilled in woodcraft. **woodsmoke** n. the smoke produced by a wood fire. **wood sorrel** n. a creeping woodland plant, Oxalis acetosella, with acid juice and small white flowers. **wood spirit** n. crude methyl alcohol. **woodturning** n. the process of shaping wood on a lathe. **woodturner** n. **wood warbler** n. **1** a European woodland bird, Phylloscopus sibilatrix. **2** any American warbler of the family Parulidae. **woodwasp** n. a wasplike insect of the family Siricidae that lays its eggs in wood, esp. Urocerus gigas, a pest of conifers. **woodwind** (-wind) n. (Mus.) **1** the wind instruments in an orchestra etc. orig. made of wood, such as the flute, oboe and clarinet. **2** any of these instruments or their players. ~a. of or relating to these instruments. **woodwork** n. **1** the art or process of making things from wood. **2** things made of wood. **3** the part of a building or other structure which is composed of wood. **to crawl out of the woodwork** (of something unpleasant or undesirable) to appear, to come to light, to become known. **woodworker** n. **woodworking** n., a. **woodworm** n. **1** any of various insect larvae that bore into furniture, wooden beams etc., esp. the larvae of the furniture beetle, Anobium punctatum. **2** the damage caused by such larvae.

woody a. (comp. **woodier,** superl. **woodiest**) **1** abounding in woods, well wooded. **2** of the nature of or consisting of wood (woody fibre; woody tissue). **3** of, relating to or found in woods. **woodiness** n. **woody nightshade** n. a poisonous trailing plant, Solanum dulcamara, with purple flowers and brilliant red berries. **woodyard** n. a yard where wood is cut or stored.

woodchuck (wud´chŭk) n. a N American marmot, Marmota monax.

woof[1] (wuf) n. the sound of a dog barking or growling. ~v.i. to produce this sound. **woofer** n. a loudspeaker used to reproduce low audio frequencies.

woof[2] (woof) n. **1** the threads that cross the warp, the weft. **2** woven cloth. **3** texture.

wool (wul) n. **1** the fine, soft, curly hair forming the fleece of sheep, goats and some other animals, used as the raw material of cloth etc. **2** yarn, fabric or clothing made from this. **3** short, thick or curly hair, underfur or down, resembling wool. **4** any fibrous or fleecy substance resembling wool (steel wool). ~a. **1** made of wool. **2** of or relating to wool (the wool trade). **to pull the wool over someone's eyes** to deceive someone. **woolen** WOOLLEN (under WOOL). **wool-fat** n. lanolin. **wool-gathering** a. absent-minded, daydreaming. ~n. absent-mindedness, inattention. **wool-grower** n. a person who keeps or breeds sheep for wool. **woollen,** (N Am.) **woolen** a. made or consisting of wool. ~n. **1** a cloth made of wool. **2** (pl.) woollen goods, esp. woollen clothing. **wool-like** a. **woolly** a. (comp. **woollier,** superl. **woolliest**) **1** bearing or naturally covered with wool, or with hair resembling wool. **2** consisting of or resembling wool in texture. **3** resembling wool in appearance, fleecy (woolly clouds). **4** lacking clear definition, firmness or incisiveness. **5** with hazy ideas, muddled. ~n. (pl. **woollies**) (coll.) a woollen pullover etc. **woolliness** n. **woolly-bear** n. **1** a hairy caterpillar, esp. of the tiger moth. **2** the hairy larva of a carpet beetle. **woolman** n. (pl. **woolmen**) **1** a wool merchant. **2** a wool-grower. **wool-oil** n. the natural grease of wool. **woolshed** n. (Austral., New Zeal.) a building for shearing, packing and storing wool. **wool-sorter** n. a person who sorts wool according to quality etc. **wool-sorter's disease** n. pulmonary anthrax due to the inhalation of dust from infected wool. **wool staple** n. the fibre of wool. **wool-stapler** n. a wool-sorter.

woosh WHOOSH.

woozy (woo´zi) a. (comp. **woozier,** superl. **wooziest**) (coll.) **1** suffering from giddiness, nausea etc. **2** dazed, confused, e.g. with drink. **3** vague. **woozily** adv. **wooziness** n.

wop (wop) n. (sl., offensive) any person of S European origin, esp. an Italian.

Worcester sauce (wus´tə), **Worcestershire sauce** (-shə) n. a dark sauce made by mixing soy sauce, vinegar, spices etc.

Worcs. abbr. Worcestershire.

word (wœd) *n*. **1** an articulate sound or combination of sounds uttered by the human voice or written, printed etc., expressing an idea or ideas and usu. forming a constituent part of a sentence. **2** speech, discourse, talk. **3** something said, a remark. **4** news, intelligence, information, a message. **5** a command, an order, an injunction. **6** a password, a watchword, a motto. **7** one's assurance, promise or definite affirmation. **8** (*pl*.) the text of a song, speech etc. (*I've forgotten the words*). **9** (*pl*.) talk or remarks exchanged expressive of anger, contention or reproach. **10** a rumour. ~*v.t*. to express in words, to phrase, to select words to express. **by word of mouth** by actual speaking, orally. **in a/ one word 1** briefly, in short. **2** to sum up. **in other words** expressing the same thing in a different way. **in so many words** explicitly, precisely, bluntly. **of one's word** able to be relied upon to do what one says one will do (*a man of his word*). **on my word (of honour)** used to make a promise or give a solemn assurance. **to have a word with** to have a brief conversation with. **to have words with** to have a dispute with, to reproach. **too...for words** extremely..., too... to describe (*This is too ridiculous for words*). **to put into words** to express in speech or writing. **to take someone at their word** to assume that someone means what they say. **to take someone's word for it** to believe someone without proof or further investigation. **(upon) my word!** used to express surprise, indignation etc. **word for word** in exactly the same words, verbatim. **wordage** (-ij) *n*. **word-blind** *a*. unable to understand written or printed words owing to a cerebral lesion. **word-blindness** *n*. **wordbook** *n*. a vocabulary or dictionary. **word-deaf** *a*. unable to understand spoken words owing to a cerebral lesion. **word-deafness** *n*. **word division** *n*. the dividing of words between lines in printing. **word game** *n*. any game involving the formation, alteration etc. of words. **wording** *n*. **1** choice of words, phrasing etc. **2** the contents of a document, advertisement etc. **wordless** *a*. **wordlessly** *adv*. **wordlessness** *n*. **word of honour** *n*. a solemn promise, assurance or undertaking. **word of mouth** *n*. spoken communication. **word order** *n*. the order in which words are arranged in a sentence etc. **word-perfect** *a*. able to repeat something without a mistake. **wordplay** *n*. playing on words, making puns, witty repartee. **word processor** *n*. an electronic device used for the automatic typing, editing and often printing of texts in various formats, usu. equipped with a VDU. **word-process** *v.t*. **word processing** *n*. **word-search** *n*. a type of puzzle involving words hidden in a grid of letters. **wordsmith** *n*. a person skilled in the use of words, esp. a writer. **word-square** *n*. a series of words so arranged that the letters spell the same words when read across or downwards. **word wrap** *n*. (*Comput*.) the automatic shifting of a word from the end of one line to the beginning of the next. **wordy** *a*. (*comp*.

wordier, *superl*. **wordiest**) **1** using more words than necessary to express oneself, verbose. **2** consisting of words, verbal. **wordily** *adv*. **wordiness** *n*.

wore[1] WEAR[1].

wore[2] WEAR[2].

work (wœk) *n*. **1** the exertion of physical or mental energy, effort or activity directed to some purpose. **2** an undertaking, a task. **3** the materials used or to be used in this. **4** employment as a means of livelihood, occupation. **5** an action, deed, performance or achievement. **6** a thing made. **7** a product of nature or art. **8** a book or other literary composition, a musical or other artistic production (*an orchestral work*; *the works of Shakespeare*). **9** a large engineering structure, esp. a piece of fortification. **10** a place of employment. **11** (*Physics*) the exertion of force in producing or maintaining motion against the action of a resisting force. **12** (*pl*., *often sing. in constr.*) an industrial establishment, a factory. **13** (*pl*.) building operations, esp. carried out under the management of a public authority. **14** (*pl*.) the working part or mechanism (of a watch etc.). **15** (*in comb*.) making things or things made with a specified material, tool, pattern etc., as *metalwork*, *needlework*, *fretwork*. **16** skill in making things. ~*v.i*. (*past, p.p.* **worked**, †**wrought** (rawt)) **1** to exert physical or mental energy for some purpose, to be engaged in labour or effort, to do work. **2** to be employed or occupied. **3** to be in activity, to act, to operate, to function, to run. **4** to take effect, to be effective, to exercise influence (*Their plan won't work*). **5** to be in a state of motion or agitation, to ferment. **6** to make way with effort or difficulty. **7** to reach a certain condition gradually (*to work loose*). ~*v.t*. **1** to exert energy in or on. **2** to cause to do work, to keep in operation, to employ, to keep busy. **3** to carry on, to manage, to run, to operate. **4** to cultivate (land). **5** to bring about, to effect, to produce as a result (*to work miracles*). **6** to prepare or alter the condition, shape or consistency of by some process, to knead, to mould, to fashion. **7** to make or embroider with needlework. **8** to earn through paid work. **9** to cause to progress with effort or difficulty. **10** to treat, to investigate, to solve. **11** to excite. **12** to arrange something in a clever and skilful way so that one benefits from it. **at work 1** doing work, in action or operation. **2** at one's place of employment. **in work** in paid employment. **out of work** not in paid employment, unemployed. **the works 1** (*coll*.) everything. **2** (*coll*.) the appropriate treatment. **3** (*coll*.) a violent beating (*to give someone the works*). **to have one's work cut out** to have a hard task. **to work in 1** to introduce or combine by manipulation. **2** to find space or time for. **to work it** (*coll*.) to arrange things, to bring it about (*She worked it so that he couldn't refuse*). **to work off 1** to get rid of, esp. by effort, activity etc. **2** to pay off (a debt etc.) by working. **to work out 1** to

compute, to solve, to find out, to understand.
2 to accomplish, to effect. **3** to devise, to formulate (*to work out a plan of action*). **4** to have a result (*It didn't work out as well as we'd hoped*). **5** to undertake a series of exercises to get fit. **6** to be successful. **7** to add up to (a certain amount). **to work over 1** to examine carefully. **2** (*coll.*) to beat severely, to mug. **to work to rule** to follow working rules so strictly that productivity is reduced, esp. as a form of industrial action. **to work up 1** to elaborate, to bring gradually into shape or efficiency. **2** to excite gradually, to stir up, to rouse. **3** to advance or increase gradually. **4** to mingle together. **5** to study (a subject) perseveringly. **workable** *a.* **1** capable of being worked, practicable. **2** that will work or operate. **3** worth working or developing. **workability** (-bil´-), **workableness** *n.* **workably** *adv.* **workaday** (-ədā) *a.* of, relating to or suitable for workdays, everyday, common, ordinary, plain, practical. **workaholic** (-əhol´ik) *n.* (*coll.*) a person addicted to working. **workaholism** *n.* **workbasket, work-bag** *n.* a basket or bag used for holding materials etc. for work, esp. for sewing. **workbench** *n.* a bench specially designed for woodworking, metalworking etc. **workbook** *n.* **1** a book containing exercises for students, often with spaces for answers. **2** a book for recording work done. **work-box** *n.* a box used for holding materials etc. for work, esp. for sewing. **work camp** *n.* a camp at which voluntary community work is done, esp. by young people. **workday** *n.* (*esp. N Am.*) a working day, a day on which work is ordinarily done. **worked up** *a.* excited, agitated or angry (*to get worked up*). **worker** *n.* **1** a person who works, esp. a member of the working class. **2** an employee. **3** a sterile female insect in a colony of insects that specializes in gathering food, caring for the young etc. **4** a person who works in a specified job or manner (*a social worker; a dedicated and reliable worker*). **5** a person who works hard. **6** a performer or doer. **work experience** *n.* short-term experience in a workplace given to young people before they leave school. **workfare** *n.* a welfare scheme in which those receiving benefits are required to undergo training, do community work etc. **workforce** *n.* the total number of workers employed or available for employment. **workhorse** *n.* a person or thing that does or is capable of doing a great deal of work. **workhouse** *n.* **1** (*Hist.*) a public establishment maintained by a parish or union for paupers. **2** (*N Am.*) a penal institution for petty offenders. **workless** *a.* **workload** *n.* the amount of work expected from or done by a person, machine etc. **workman** *n.* (*pl.* **workmen**) any man employed in manual labour, an operative. **workmanlike** *a.* done in the manner of a good worker. **workmanship** *n.* **1** comparative skill, finish or execution shown in making something or in the thing made. **2** the result of working or making. **Workmate®** *n.* a portable collapsible

workbench. **workmate** *n.* a person with whom one works. **work of art** *n.* **1** a painting, sculpture or other piece of fine art. **2** anything skilfully or beautifully constructed or composed. **workout** *n.* a series of exercises for physical fitness. **workpeople** *n.pl.* workers. **workpiece** *n.* any item on which work is being done, esp. with a tool or machine. **workplace** *n.* a place where people work, such as an office or factory. **works council** *n.* a group of workers representing the employees of a factory etc. in negotiations with management. **worksheet** *n.* **1** a sheet of paper on which the progress of work is recorded. **2** a list of work to be done, questions to be answered by students etc. **workshop** *n.* **1** a building in which manual work, esp. making or repairing things, is carried on. **2** a room in which manual work, esp. making or repairing things, is carried on. **3** a meeting for discussion, training, practical work etc. (*a creative writing workshop*). **work-shy** *a.* reluctant or disinclined to work. **worksite** *n.* the site of an industry or manual labour. **workspace** *n.* **1** a space in which work can be done. **2** (*Comput.*) a temporary memory storage facility. **workstation** *n.* **1** the place in an office, factory etc. where one person works. **2** (*Comput.*) a unit consisting of a VDU and keyboard for use by one worker. **work study** *n.* the investigation of the methods and practice of a particular type of work with a view to getting the best results for all concerned. **work surface** *n.* a worktop. **work table** *n.* a table on which work can be done, usu. with drawers etc. for keeping sewing or writing materials in. **worktop** *n.* a flat board covered with laminate and often fixed to the top of kitchen units, used to prepare food. **work-to-rule** *n.* the act or an instance of working to rule. **workwear** *n.* clothes for working in.

working (wœ´king) *a.* **1** engaged in work, esp. manual labour. **2** during which work is done or business discussed (*a working lunch; working hours*). **3** functioning or able to function. ~*n.* **1** the act of labouring. **2** operation, mode of operation. **3** a mine or quarry or a portion of it which has been worked or in which work is going on. **4** fermentation, movement. **working capital** *n.* funds employed for the actual carrying on of a business. **working class** *n.* the class of people who earn their living by manual labour. **working-class** *a.* **working day** *n.* **1** any day on which work is ordinarily performed, as distinguished from Sundays and holidays. **2** the period daily devoted to work. **working drawing** *n.* a scale drawing or plan of a work prepared to guide a builder, engineer etc. in executing work. **working hypothesis** *n.* a hypothesis on the basis of which plans are made or action is taken. **working knowledge** *n.* sufficient knowledge to work with (*I have a working knowledge of the system*). **working man** *n.* (*pl.* **working men**) a man in paid employment. **working order** *n.* the condition in which a machine functions as it should (*in working order*). **working party** *n*. (*pl.* **working parties**) a committee set up specifically to investigate a particular issue. **working woman** *n*. (*pl.* **working women**) a woman in paid employment.

world (wœld) *n*. **1** the earth with its lands and seas. **2** a celestial body regarded as similar to this. **3** a large natural or other division of the earth. **4** the human inhabitants of the earth, humankind. **5** the whole system of things, the universe, everything. **6** a system of things, an orderly or organic whole, a cosmos. **7** human affairs, the ways, customs, opinions etc. of people, active life, social life and intercourse. **8** human society, the public. **9** fashionable or prominent people. **10** a particular section or class of people, animals or things (*the world of fashion*). **11** a particular area of activity, a realm, a domain. **12** a vast quantity, amount, number, degree etc. (of) (*a world of difference*). **13** all things external to oneself as related to the individual. **14** any time, state or sphere of existence (*the prehistoric world*). **15** secular interest as opposed to *spiritual*. **16** the ungodly or unregenerate portion of humankind. ~*a*. of or relating to all nations of the world. **dead to the world** (*coll.*) fast asleep. **for all the world** exactly, precisely (*It sounded for all the world like an explosion*). **in the world** at all, possibly (*How in the world did that happen?*). **out of this world 1** (*coll.*) remarkable, striking. **2** (*coll.*) excellent. **the best of both worlds** the benefits of two different or incompatible things, ways of life, sets of ideas etc. (*to get the best of both worlds*). **the world to come** the hereafter, life after death. **to bring into the world 1** to give birth to. **2** to deliver (a baby). **to think the world of** to love or respect greatly. **world without end** to all eternity, everlastingly. **world-beater** *n*. a person or thing that is the best of its kind in the world. **world-beating** *a*. **world-class** *a*. of the highest class in the world. **World Cup** *n*. an international football or other sporting competition. **world fair** *n*. an international exhibition of achievements in industry, science, technology, the arts etc. **world-famous** *a*. famous throughout the world. **worldling** *n*. a worldly person. **world music** *n*. rock or pop music incorporating elements from a variety of national (esp. Third World) styles. **world order** *n*. a system for preserving international political stability (*the new world order*). **world power** *n*. a sovereign state so strong as to be able to affect the policy of every civilized state in the world. **world's end** *n*. the remotest part of the earth. **World Series** *n*. a series of baseball games played in the US between the winners of major leagues to decide the professional championship. **world war** *n*. a war involving most of the earth's major nations, esp. the 1914–18 or 1939–45 wars. **world-weary** *a*. tired of existence. **world-weariness** *n*. **world-wide** *a*. **1** spread over the whole world. **2** existing everywhere. ~*adv*. throughout the world. **World**

Wide Web *n*. a network of files from all round the world available over the Internet.

worldly (wœld'li) *a*. (*comp.* **worldlier**, *superl.* **worldliest**) **1** of or relating to the present, temporal or material world. **2** earthly, secular, material, not spiritual. **3** practical, sophisticated, worldly-wise. **worldliness** *n*. **worldly-wise** *a*. wise in the ways or things of this world. **worldly wisdom** *n*.

worm (wœm) *n*. **1** any of various invertebrate creeping animals with a long limbless segmented body. **2** any long creeping animal with very small or undeveloped feet, such as larvae, grubs, caterpillars or maggots. **3** an intestinal parasite. **4** (*pl.*) any disease caused by parasitic worms, esp. in the intestine. **5** any of various other animals such as the blindworm or slow-worm. **6** (*coll.*) a poor, grovelling, debased or despised person. **7** a wormlike or spiral part or thing. ~*v.i.* **1** to crawl, creep, wriggle or progress with a wormlike motion. **2** to work stealthily or underhandedly. ~*v.t.* **1** to insinuate (oneself), to make (one's way) in a wormlike manner (*He wormed his way into our favour*). **2** to draw (out) by craft and perseverance (*I wormed the secret out of her*). **3** to free (a dog etc.) from worms. **worm-cast** *n*. a cylindrical mass of earth voided by an earthworm. **worm-eaten** *a*. **1** gnawed or bored by worms. **2** rotten, decayed. **3** dilapidated. **4** antiquated. **wormer** *n*. **worm-fishing** *n*. fishing with worms for bait. **worm-gear** *n*. a gear having a toothed or cogged wheel engaging with a revolving spiral. **wormhole** *n*. **1** a hole made by a worm in wood, fruit, the ground etc. **2** (*Physics*) a hypothetical tunnel connecting different regions of space-time. **wormholed** *a*. **wormless** *a*. **wormlike** *a*. **worm's-eye view** *n*. a view from below, low down or from a humble position. **worm-wheel** *n*. the toothed wheel of a worm-gear. **wormy** *a*. (*comp.* **wormier**, *superl.* **wormiest**) **1** full of worms. **2** resembling a worm. **3** worm-eaten. **worminess** *n*.

wormwood (wœm'wud) *n*. **1** a shrub of the genus *Artemisia*, esp. *A. absinthium*, having bitter and tonic properties, used in the manufacture of vermouth and absinthe and in medicine. **2** bitterness, gall, mortification.

worn (wawn) *a*. **1** tired, exhausted. **2** well worn. **worn out**, **worn-out** *a*. **1** thoroughly tired, exhausted. **2** rendered useless by long wear.

worried, **worriment** etc. WORRY.

worry (wŭr'i) *v.t.* (*3rd pers. sing. pres.* **worries**, *pres.p.* **worrying**, *past, p.p.* **worried**) **1** to cause mental distress to. **2** (*also reflex.*) to tease, harass, bother or importune. **3** (of dogs etc.) to bite or keep on biting, to shake or pull about with the teeth. ~*v.i.* **1** to be unduly anxious or troubled, to fret. **2** (of dogs etc.) to bite, pull (at) etc. ~*n*. (*pl.* **worries**) **1** the act of worrying. **2** a cause or source of worry. **3** the state of being worried; anxiety, care, solicitude, vexation. **not to worry** (*coll.*) there's no need to worry. **worried** *a*.

anxious, troubled. **worriedly** adv. **worrier** n. **worriless** a. **worriment** n. (esp. N Am.) **1** the state of being worried. **2** the act of worrying. **3** a cause of worry or trouble. **worrisome** a. causing worry. **worrisomely** adv. **worry beads** n.pl. a string of beads that are fingered in order to relieve tension. **worrying** a. causing anxiety or mental distress (worrying news). **worryingly** adv.

worse (wœs) a. **1** more bad, bad in a higher degree. **2** (pred.) in a less favourable state, position or circumstance. **3** (pred.) in a poorer state of health. ~adv. **1** more badly. **2** into a poorer state of health etc. ~n. a worse thing or things. **or worse** or some even worse eventuality. **the worse for** damaged or harmed by. **the worse for drink** (coll.) drunk. **the worse for wear 1** shabby, worn. **2** (coll.) tired, untidy etc. **worse off** in a poorer condition or financial situation. **worsen** v.i. to grow worse. ~v.t. to make worse.

worship (wœ´ship) n. **1** the act of paying divine honour to God or some other deity, esp. in religious services. **2** the rites or ceremonies associated with this. **3** an act or feeling of adoration, admiring devotion or submissive respect to a person, principle etc. ~v.t. (pres.p. **worshipping**, (N Am.) **worshiping**, past, p.p. **worshipped**, (N Am.) **worshiped**) **1** to pay divine honours to. **2** to perform religious service to. **3** to reverence with supreme respect and admiration. **4** to treat as divine. ~v.i. **1** to take part in a religious service. **2** to be filled with adoration etc. **Your Worship** a title of respect or honour used in addressing mayors, certain magistrates etc. **worshipful** a. (usu. **Worshipful**) a title of respect or honour used to or of various people or organizations. **worshipfully** adv. **worshipfulness** n. **worshipper**, (N Am.) **worshiper** n. **1** a person who worships. **2** an attender at a place of worship.

worst (wœst) a. most bad, bad in the highest degree. ~adv. most badly. ~n. **1** the worst thing or things. **2** the most bad or severe part, event, state, possibility etc. (while the storm was at its worst). ~v.t. to get the better of in a contest etc., to defeat, to best. **at (the) worst 1** in the worst circumstances. **2** in the least favourable view. **if the worst comes to the worst** if the worst of all possible things happens. **worst-case** a. of or relating to the worst of all possible situations, conditions, circumstances etc. (a worst-case scenario).

worsted (wus´tid) n. **1** a fine woollen yarn used for making fabric, knitting stockings etc. **2** fabric made from this. ~a. made of worsted.

wort (wœt) n. **1** a plant, a herb (usu. in comb., as moneywort, soapwort). **2** an infusion of malt for fermenting into beer.

worth (wœth) a. (pred.) **1** equal in value or price to. **2** deserving, worthy of. **3** having property to the value of, possessed of. **4** †estimable, valuable. ~n. **1** that which a person or thing is worth, value, the equivalent of anything, esp. in money. **2** usefulness or importance. **3** high character,

excellence. **for all one is worth** (coll.) with all one's strength, energy etc. **for what it's worth** used to express doubt about the truth or value of something. **worthless** a. **worthlessly** adv. **worthlessness** n. **worthwhile** (-wīl´) a. worth the time, expense or effort involved. **worthwhileness** n.

worthy (wœ´dhi) a. (comp. **worthier**, superl. **worthiest**) **1** having worth, estimable. **2** deserving of or entitled to respect, praise or honour, respectable. **3** deserving (of, to be etc.). **4** fit, suitable, adequate, appropriate or equivalent to the worth (of). ~n. (pl. **worthies**) **1** a worthy person. **2** a person of some note or distinction in their time, locality etc. **worthily** adv. **worthiness** n.

-worthy (wœ´dhi) comb. form **1** safe or suitable for, as seaworthy. **2** deserving of, as praiseworthy.

†wot WIT².

would, would-be WILL¹.

wouldn't (wud´ənt) contr. would not.

wound¹ (woond) n. **1** an injury caused by a cut or blow to the skin and flesh of an animal or the bark or substance of plants, esp. one involving disruption of the tissues. **2** any damage, hurt or pain to feelings, reputation etc. ~v.t. **1** to inflict a wound on. **2** to make (someone) feel very unhappy or upset. ~v.i. to cause a wound. **woundable** a. **wounded** a. injured, hurt (wounded soldiers; wounded pride). ~n.pl. injured people (The wounded were taken to hospital). **wounder** n. **woundingly** adv. **woundless** a.

wound² WIND².

wound³ WIND³.

wove¹ WEAVE¹.

wove² (wōv) a. (of paper) having a uniformly smooth surface.

woven WEAVE¹.

wow¹ (wow) int. used to express astonishment, wonder etc. ~n. (sl.) a sensational or spectacular success. ~v.t. (sl.) to cause to feel great enthusiasm, to impress greatly.

wow² (wow) n. a variation in pitch occurring at low frequencies in sound-reproducing systems.

WP abbr. **1** (also **w.p.**) weather permitting. **2** word processing. **3** word processor.

wpb abbr. waste-paper basket.

WPC abbr. woman police constable.

wpm abbr. words per minute.

wrack (rak) n. **1** seaweed thrown upon the shore. **2** moving or driving clouds, cloud rack. **3** rack, destruction, ruin. **4** a wreck, wreckage.

wraggle-taggle RAGGLE-TAGGLE.

wraith (rāth) n. **1** the double or phantom of a living person. **2** an apparition, a ghost appearing after death. **wraithlike** a.

wrangle (rang´gəl) v.i. to dispute, argue or quarrel angrily, peevishly or noisily, to brawl. ~v.t. (N Am.) to herd (cattle or horses). ~n. an angry or noisy dispute or quarrel, an altercation, a brawl. **wrangler** n. **1** a person who wrangles. **2** (esp. N Am.) a cowboy, herder or horsebreaker. **wranglership** n.

wrap (rap) *v.t.* (*pres.p.* **wrapping**, *past, p.p.* **wrapped**) **1** to fold or arrange so as to cover or enclose something. **2** to enfold, envelop, muffle, pack or surround in some soft material. **3** to fold paper round (a present). **4** to hide, to conceal, to disguise. **5** (*Comput.*) to move (a word etc.) from the end of one line to the beginning of the next. ~*v.i.* **1** to fold, to lap. **2** (*Comput.*) to be wrapped. ~*n.* something intended to wrap, such as a cloak or shawl. **to take the wraps off** to reveal or disclose. **to wrap up 1** to fold paper etc. round (*to wrap up a present*). **2** to dress warmly. **3** to bring to a conclusion. **4** (*usu. in p.p.*) to absorb, to engross (*wrapped up in her work*). **5** (*usu. imper., sl.*) to be quiet. **under wraps** secret, in secrecy. **wraparound** *a.* **1** (of a garment) designed to be wrapped round the body. **2** (of a windscreen etc.) curving round at the sides. ~*n.* something that wraps or is wrapped round. **wrap-over** *a.* (of a skirt etc.) designed to be wrapped round the body and fastened with the open edges overlapping. ~*n.* such a skirt etc. **wrapped** *a.* **1** that has been wrapped (*wrapped sweets*). **2** finished. **3** (*Austral., coll.*) delighted, rapt. **wrapper** *n.* **1** a person who wraps. **2** that in which anything is wrapped, esp. an outer covering. **3** the outer paper covering of a book. **wrapping** *n.* **1** that which wraps. **2** (*often pl.*) that in which something is wrapped or packaged. **3** a wrapper, a cloak, a shawl, a rug. **wrapping paper** *n.* paper used to wrap parcels, esp. decorative paper for wrapping gifts.

wrasse (ras) *n.* a sea fish of the family Labridae, having thick lips and strong teeth.

wrath (roth) *n.* (*poet.*) deep or violent anger, indignation, rage. **wrathful** *a.* **wrathfully** *adv.* **wrathfulness** *n.* **wrathless** *a.* **wrathy** *a.* (*N Am.*) wrathful. **wrathily** *adv.*

wreak (rēk) *v.t.* **1** to carry out, to inflict, to execute (*to wreak vengeance*). **2** to cause (*to wreak havoc*). **3** to vent, express or satisfy (*to wreak one's anger*). **wreaker** *n.*

wreath (rēth) *n.* (*pl.* **wreaths** (rēdhz, rēths)) **1** a band or ring of flowers or leaves tied, woven or twisted together for wearing on the head, decorating statues, walls, graves etc. **2** a representation of this in wood, stone etc. **3** a ring, a twist, a curl (of cloud, smoke etc.). **4** a garland, a chaplet. **wreathless** *a.* **wreathlike** *a.*

wreathe (rēdh) *v.t.* **1** to form (flowers, leaves etc.) into a wreath. **2** to surround, encircle, entwine (as if) with a wreath or with anything twisted. **3** to decorate with a wreath. ~*v.i.* **1** to be curled, folded or entwined (round etc.). **2** (of smoke etc.) to move in twists or curls. **wreather** *n.*

wreck (rek) *n.* **1** destruction, ruin, esp. of a ship. **2** a vessel dashed against rocks or otherwise destroyed, seriously crippled or shattered. **3** the remains of anything irretrievably shattered or ruined. **4** a dilapidated or worn-out person or thing (*a nervous wreck*). **5** wreckage. **6** (*Law*) goods etc. cast ashore from a wreck. ~*v.t.* **1** to

ruin or destroy. **2** to destroy or shatter (a vessel etc.) by collision, driving ashore etc. **3** to involve in shipwreck. ~*v.i.* **1** to suffer shipwreck. **2** (*N Am.*) to demolish or break up wrecked vehicles etc. **wreckage** *n.* **1** the debris, remnants or material from a wreck. **2** the act of wrecking or the state of being wrecked. **wrecker** *n.*

Wren (ren) *n.* (*Hist.*) a member of the Women's Royal Naval Service.

wren (ren) *n.* **1** a small songbird of the family Troglodytidae, esp. *Troglodytes troglodytes*, with a short erect tail and short wings. **2** any of various warblers or other birds resembling the wren.

wrench (rench) *n.* **1** a violent twist or sideways pull. **2** an injury caused by twisting, a sprain. **3** pain or distress caused by a parting, loss etc. **4** a tool for twisting or untwisting screws, bolts, nuts etc., a spanner. ~*v.t.* **1** to pull, wrest or twist with force or violence. **2** to pull (off or away) thus. **3** to strain, to sprain. **4** to pervert, to distort.

wrest (rest) *v.t.* **1** to pull or wrench (away) forcibly. **2** to take or obtain (from) with force, effort or difficulty. **3** to twist, to turn aside by a violent effort. **4** to pervert, to distort, to twist or deflect from its natural meaning. ~*n.* a violent wrench or twist.

wrestle (res'əl) *v.i.* **1** to fight by grappling with and trying to throw one's opponent, esp. in a sporting contest under recognized rules. **2** to struggle, to contend, to strive vehemently (with). ~*v.t.* **1** to contend with in a wrestling match. **2** to move with difficulty, to manhandle. ~*n.* **1** a sporting contest in which two opponents wrestle, a wrestling match. **2** a struggle. **wrestler** *n.* **wrestling** *n.*

wretch (rech) *n.* **1** a miserable or unfortunate person. **2** a despicable, mean or contemptible person. **wretched** (-id) *a.* (*comp.* **wretcheder**, *superl.* **wretchedest**) **1** miserable, unhappy, sunk in deep affliction or distress. **2** calamitous, pitiable. **3** worthless, poor, contemptible. **4** extremely unsatisfactory or unpleasant. **to feel wretched 1** to feel ill. **2** to feel embarrassed or ashamed. **wretchedly** *adv.* **wretchedness** *n.*

wrick (rik) *v.t.* to sprain or strain. ~*n.* a sprain or strain.

wrier, wriest WRY.

wriggle (rig'əl) *v.i.* **1** to turn, twist or move the body to and fro with short motions. **2** to move or go (along, in, out etc.) with writhing contortions or twistings. **3** to manoeuvre by clever or devious means. ~*v.t.* **1** to move (one's body etc.) with a wriggling motion. **2** to make (one's way etc.) by wriggling. ~*n.* a wriggling motion. **to wriggle out of** (*coll.*) to evade, avoid or shirk. **wriggler** *n.* **wriggly** *a.*

wring (ring) *v.t.* (*past, p.p.* **wrung** (rŭng)) **1** to twist and squeeze or compress (*to wring the neck of a chicken*). **2** to turn, twist or strain forcibly. **3** to twist, press or squeeze (out) thus (*to wring *out a cloth; to wring water out of a cloth).* **4** to pain, to torture, to distress. **5** to extract, to extort. *~n.* an act of wringing, a twist, a press, a squeeze. **to wring one's hands** to press one's hands together convulsively, as in great distress. **to wring someone's hand** to clasp or squeeze someone's hand with great force or emotion. **wringer** *n.* **1** a person or thing that wrings. **2** a wringing machine, a mangle. **wringing** *n., a.* **wringing machine** *n.* a machine for wringing water out of newly-washed clothes etc. **wringing wet** *a.* so wet that moisture can be wrung out.

wrinkle (ring'kəl) *n.* **1** a small ridge, crease or furrow caused by the folding or contraction of a flexible surface. **2** such a crease or furrow in the skin, esp. as a result of age. *~v.t., v.i.* to fold or contract into furrows, creases or ridges. **wrinkly** *a.* (*comp.* **wrinklier**, *superl.* **wrinkliest**) marked with wrinkles, having many wrinkles. *~n. (pl.* **wrinklies**) *(sl., derog.)* an old person.

wrist (rist) *n.* **1** the joint uniting the hand with the forearm. **2** the part of a sleeve over the wrist. **wristband** *n.* a band or part of a sleeve, esp. a shirtsleeve, covering the wrist; a cuff. **wristlet** *n.* **1** a band worn round the wrist to strengthen it, hold up a glove, carry a watch etc. **2** a bracelet. **wristwatch** *n.* a watch worn on a strap round the wrist. **wristy** *a.* (of a shot or style of play in cricket, tennis, golf etc.) making much use of the wrist or wrists.

writ (rit) *n.* **1** a written command or precept issued by a court to a person commanding them to do or refrain from doing some particular specified act (*to serve a writ on someone*). **2** a document ordering the election of a Member of Parliament, summoning a peer to Parliament etc.

write (rīt) *v.t.* (*past* **wrote** (rōt), †**writ** (rit), *p.p.* **written** (rit'ən), †**writ**) **1** to form or trace (words, a sentence etc.) in letters or symbols, with a pen, pencil or the like on paper or other material. **2** to trace (signs, characters etc.) thus. **3** to set (down), record, describe, state or convey by writing. **4** to compose or produce as an author. **5** to cover or fill with writing (*to write a cheque*). **6** (*usu. pass.*) to impress or stamp (guilt etc.) on a person's face. **7** (*esp. N Am., coll.*) to send a letter to. **8** to communicate in writing. **9** (*Comput.*) to record (data) in a storage device. **10** to state in writing. *~v.i.* **1** to trace letters or symbols representing words on paper etc. **2** to write or send a letter (to). **3** to compose or produce articles, books etc. as an author or journalist (*to write for a newspaper*). **to write down 1** to put in writing, to record. **2** to depreciate, to criticize unfavourably in writing. **3** to write in such a way as to appeal to low standards of taste, intelligence etc. **4** in accounting, to reduce the book value of. **to write in** to send a letter, request, query, suggestion etc. to a magazine, radio station etc. **to write off 1** to write and send a letter etc. **2** to cancel (a debt etc.) from a written record. **3** to consider (a loss etc.)

as irrecoverable. **4** to damage (a car) beyond repair. **5** to discard as useless, insignificant etc. **to write out 1** to write the whole of. **2** to write in finished form. **3** to remove (a character, episode etc.) from a drama series, book etc. **to write up 1** to praise in writing. **2** to bring (a diary, account book etc.) up to date. **3** to give full details of in writing. **writ large 1** set down or recorded in large letters. **2** magnified, emphasized, very obvious, on a large scale. **writable** *a.* **write-down** *n.* in accounting, the act of reducing the book value of stocks, assets etc. **write-off** *n.* something written off, esp. a badly damaged car. **writer** *n.* **writerly** *a.* **1** characteristic of an accomplished writer. **2** literary. **writer's block** *n.* a total lack of ideas, inspiration or creativity affecting a writer, usu. temporarily. **writer's cramp** *n.* a spasmodic pain in the fingers or hand caused by prolonged writing. **writership** *n.* **write-up** *n.* (*coll.*) **1** a review. **2** a written account. **writing** *n.* **1** the act of a person who writes. **2** that which is written. **3** handwriting. **4** a book, article or other literary composition. **5** an inscription. **6** a legal instrument. **in writing** in written form. **the writing on the wall** a solemn warning (Dan. v.5). **writing pad** *n.* a number of sheets of writing paper fastened together at the edge. **writing paper** *n.* paper with a smooth surface for writing on.

writhe (rīdh) *v.i.* **1** to twist, turn or roll the body about, as in pain. **2** to shrink, to squirm (at, with shame etc.). *~v.t.* to twist or distort (the limbs etc.). *~n.* an act of writhing. **writhingly** *adv.*

wrong (rong) *a.* **1** false, inaccurate, incorrect, mistaken, erroneous. **2** not that which is required, intended, proper, best etc. **3** not morally right, contrary to morality, conscience or law, wicked. **4** out of order, in bad condition etc. **5** not according to truth or reality. *~adv.* **1** wrongly. **2** unjustly. *~n.* **1** that which is wrong. **2** a wrong act, an injustice, an injury or hurt. **3** deviation from what is right. **4** wrongness, error. *~v.t.* **1** to treat unjustly, to do wrong to. **2** to impute evil motives to unjustly. **in the wrong 1** guilty, responsible. **2** in error. **the wrong side of the tracks** an undesirable or less prestigious area, esp. of a town or city (*to live on the wrong side of the tracks*). **to get on the wrong side of** to fall into disfavour with. **to get wrong 1** to misunderstand (*Don't get me wrong, I'm not criticizing you*). **2** to fail to give or obtain the correct answer to. **to go down the wrong way** (of food or drink) to pass into the windpipe instead of the gullet. **to go wrong 1** to fail morally, to fall into sin. **2** to fail to operate correctly. **3** to fall into error. **4** to take the wrong road, path etc. **wrong side out** inside out. **wrong way round** back to front, in reverse of the proper sequence. **wrongdoer** *n.* a person who does wrong. **wrongdoing** *n.* **wrong end of the stick** *n.* the contrary to what is meant. **wronger** *n.* **wrong-foot** *v.t.* (*coll.*) **1** to cause to be off balance. **2** to gain an advantage over. **3** to take by surprise, to catch unprepared. **wrongful** *a.*

1 injurious, unjust, wrong. **2** illegal. **3** not entitled to the position held. **wrongfully** *adv.* **wrongfulness** *n.* **wrong-headed** *a.* perverse, obstinate. **wrong-headedly** *adv.* **wrong-headedness** *n.* **wrongly** *adv.* **wrongness** *n.* **wrong side** *n.* the side (of fabric, paper etc.) not intended for use.

wrote WRITE.

wrought (rawt) *a.* **1** worked, formed or fashioned (*often in comb.*, as *well-wrought*). **2** decorated or ornamented. **3** (of metal) shaped by hammering or bending. **4** (of timber) planed on one or more sides. **wrought iron** *n.* **1** iron made malleable by having non-metallic impurities burned out of it. **2** iron made malleable by forging or rolling. **wrought-up** *a.* very tense or excited.

wrung WRING.

WRVS *abbr.* Women's Royal Voluntary Service.

wry (rī) *a.* (*comp.* **wryer, wrier,** *superl.* **wryest,**

wriest) **1** twisted, distorted, crooked. **2** showing distaste, disgust, mockery etc. (*a wry smile*). **3** (of humour) dry or sardonic. **4** wrong, false, perverted. **wryly** *adv.* **wryness** *n.*

WSW *abbr.* west-south-west.

wt. *abbr.* weight.

wunderkind (vun´dəkint) *n.* (*pl.* **wunderkinds, wunderkinder** (-kində)) (*coll.*) **1** a child prodigy. **2** a person who is outstandingly successful or clever at a relatively young age.

WWW *abbr.* World Wide Web.

WX *abbr.* women's extra large size.

wych (wich) *a.* (*attrib.*) drooping. **wych elm** *n.* a rough-leaved Eurasian elm, *Ulmus montana*. **wych hazel** *n.* WITCH HAZEL (under WITCH²).

WYSIWYG (wiz´iwig), **wysiwyg** *a.* (*Comput.*) denoting or relating to a computer or word processor which can print out exactly what is shown on the screen.

X (eks), x (*pl.* **Xs, X's**) the 24th letter of the English and other versions of the Roman alphabet, corresponding to the Greek xi (ξ, Ξ). It has three principal sounds: (1) *ks*, medially and finally, as in *axis*, *tax*; (2) *gz*, medially, as in *exhaust*, *exult*; (3) *z*, initially, chiefly in words of Greek origin, as in *xylophone*. ~*symbol* **1** (*Math.*) the first unknown quantity or variable in an algebraic expression. **2** 10 in Roman numerals (xx 20, xxx 30, xc 90). **3** an unknown thing or person. **4** a kiss. **5** an error. **6** a choice. **7** before 1983, a film for over-18-year-olds only. **x-axis** *n.* the horizontal axis, along which coordinates of the first unknown quantity are plotted in graphs, histograms etc. **X chromosome** *n.* (*Biol.*) a sex chromosome which is found paired in women, and paired with the Y chromosome in men. **X-rated** *a.* **1** (of films etc.) indecent, pornographic, excessively violent. **2** (*Hist.*) relating to films given an X classification prior to 1983. **X-ray, x-ray** *n.* **1** an electromagnetic ray of very short wavelength, used in producing a photographic image of internal parts of the body, such as organs or bones, and used in medical diagnosis. **2** a picture thus produced. ~*v.t.* **1** to produce such an image of (part of the body). **2** to treat with X-rays. **X-ray astronomy** *n.* the branch of astronomy concerned with the observation of celestial bodies by detecting and measuring their X-ray emissions. **X-ray crystallography** *n.* the study of crystal structure through the diffraction pattern produced by X-rays. **X-ray tube** *n.* an evacuated tube in which electrons are beamed on to a metal target to produce X-rays.

-x (z) *suf.* forming the plural of many nouns from French, as in *plateaux*, *beaux*.

xanthate (zan´thāt) *n.* a salt or ester of xanthic acid.

xanthic (zan´thik) *a.* of a yellowish colour. **xanthic acid** *n.* (*Chem.*) a colourless oily liquid, prepared by decomposing potassium xanthate with sulphuric or hydrochloric acid. **xanthine** (-thēn, -thīn), **xanthin** (-thin) *n.* **1** the part of the yellow colouring matter of flowers that is insoluble in water. **2** a crystalline compound found in blood, urine, the liver etc.

Xe *chem. symbol* xenon.

xeno- (zen´ō), **xen-** *comb. form* **1** strange, foreign; foreigner. **2** other.

xenolith (zen´əlith) *n.* (*Geol.*) a fragment of rock enclosed in a different type of rock.

xenon (zen´ən) *n.* (*Chem.*) an inert gaseous element, at. no. 54, chem. symbol Xe, found in the atmosphere and solidifying at the temperature of liquid air.

xenophobia (zenəfō´biə) *n.* fear or hatred of strangers or foreigners. **xenophobe** (zen´-) *n.* **xenophobic** *a.*

xeranthemum (ziəran´thiməm) *n.* an annual plant of the genus *Xeranthemum*, with everlasting flowers.

xero- (ziə´rō), **xer-** *comb. form* dry.

xeroderma (ziərōdœ´mə), **xerodermia** (-miə) *n.* (*Med.*) an abnormal dryness of the skin.

xerography (ziərog´rəfi) *n.* a photographic process in which the plate is sensitized electrically, and the latent image developed by a resinous powder. **xerograph** (ziə´rōgrahf) *n.* a copy produced in this way. **xerographic** (-graf´-) *a.* **xerographically** *adv.*

xerophilous (ziərof´iləs, zer-) *a.* (*Bot.*) (of a plant) adapted to living in a hot, dry climate. **xerophile** (ziə´rəfil) *n.*

xerophyte (ziə´rōfīt, zer´-) *n.* a plant adapted to living in a region of little moisture, such as a cactus, a xerophile. **xerophytic** (-fit´-) *a.*

Xerox® (ziə´roks) *n.* **1** a xerographic copying process. **2** the copy produced by this process. **3** the machine used for this process. **xerox** *v.t.* to produce a copy of (an original document) by this process.

Xhosa (kō´sə, kaw´-) *n.* (*pl.* **Xhosa, Xhosas**) **1** a member of one of the Bantu-speaking peoples in the Cape Province, S Africa. **2** their language, which is characterized by a sound system involving a series of clicks. ~*a.* of or relating to the Xhosa or their language.

xi (zī, ksī, sī, ksē) *n.* the 14th letter of the Greek alphabet (ξ, Ξ).

-xion (kshən) *suf.* used to form nouns from Latin participial stems in -x-, usu. involving action, as *crucifixion*, *connexion*.

Xmas (eks´məs, kris´-) *n.* (*coll.*) Christmas.

xu (soo) *n.* (*pl.* **xu**) a unit of currency in Vietnam, equal to one-hundredth of a dong.

xylem (zī´ləm) *n.* (*Bot.*) woody tissue, wood parenchyma, as opposed to *phloem*.

xylene (zī´lēn) *n.* (*Chem.*) any one of three isomeric colourless, volatile, liquid hydrocarbons distilled from coal or wood tar.

xylo- (zī´lō), **xyl-** *comb. form* relating to wood.

xylophone (zī´ləfōn) *n.* (*Mus.*) an instrument consisting of a graduated series of wooden or metal bars vibrating when struck or rubbed. **xylophonic** (-fon´-) *a.* **xylophonist** (-lof´-) *n.*

Y

Y¹ (wī), **y** (*pl.* **Ys, Y's**) the 25th letter of the English and other versions of the Roman alphabet, corresponding to the Greek upsilon (υ, Y). It is pronounced both as a vowel and as a palatal semivowel: as a vowel it has the same value as *i*; at the beginning of syllables and followed by a vowel, it corresponds to the Latin *i* or *j*, as in *ye, you*. ~*symbol* (*Math.*) the second unknown quantity or variable in an algebraic expression. ~*n.* a Y-shaped branch, pipe, fork, coupling, figure etc. **y-axis** *n.* the vertical axis along which coordinates of the second unknown quantity are plotted in graphs, histograms etc. **Y chromosome** *n.* (*Biol.*) a sex chromosome which is found paired with the X chromosome in men, and is not present at all in women. **Y-fronts®** *n.pl.* men's or boys' underpants with an inverted Y-shaped front opening.

Y² *chem. symbol* yttrium.

Y³, Y. *abbr.* yen.

y *abbr.* years.

-y¹ (i) *suf.* **1** forming adjectives from nouns and adjectives, as *lucky, pricey.* **2** forming adjectives from verbs, as *wobbly.*

-y² (i) *suf.* **1** forming abstract nouns etc., as *memory, remedy.* **2** forming nouns expressing action or result, as *army, treaty.*

-y³ (i), **-ey, -ie** *suf.* forming diminutives, pet names etc., as *laddy, Jimmy, sonny, Mickey, nightie.*

yacht (yot) *n.* **1** a light sailing vessel, esp. one designed for racing. **2** a power-driven vessel, used for pleasure trips, cruising, travel or as a state vessel to convey members of royalty or government officials. **3** a light vessel for travelling on sand or ice. ~*v.i.* to sail or cruise about in a yacht. **yacht club** *n.* a club for yacht racing etc. **yachting** *n.* **yachtsman, yachtswoman** *n.* (*pl.* **yachtsmen, yachtswomen**) a person who keeps or sails a yacht.

yack YAK².

yackety-yack YAK².

yah¹ (yah) *int.* used to express dismissal, scepticism or derision.

yah² (yah) *int.* (*coll., esp. facet.*) yes.

yahoo (yah´hoo, yəhoo´) *n.* (*pl.* **yahoos**) a coarse, brutish person, a lout.

Yahweh (yah´wā), **Yahveh** (-vā), **Jahveh** *n.* the Hebrew name for God in the Old Testament, Jehovah.

yak¹ (yak) *n.* a long-haired ox, *Bos grunniens*, from the mountainous regions of Central Asia.

yak² (yak), **yack** *n.* (*coll., often derog.*) noisy, unceasing, trivial chatter. ~*v.i.* (*pres.p.* **yakking,**

yacking, *past, p.p.* **yakked, yacked**) to talk in this way. **yackety-yak** (yakəti-) *n.* trivial, persistent chatter.

Yale® (yāl), **Yale lock** *n.* a type of lock with a revolving barrel, turned by a flat key with a serrated edge.

y'all YOU-ALL (under YOU).

yam (yam) *n.* **1** the fleshy edible tuber of various species of the genus *Dioscorea*, tropical climbers orig. from India. **2** the plant yielding this. **3** (*N Am.*) the sweet potato.

yammer (yam´ə) *v.i.* (*coll. or dial.*) to cry out, to whine, to complain peevishly. ~*n.* **1** a complaint. **2** nonsense. **3** a whining sound. **yammerer** *n.* **yammering** *n., a.*

yang (yang) *n.* the masculine, positive, bright principle in nature, according to Chinese philosophy, which interacts with its complement, *yin.*

Yank (yangk) *n.* (*often derog.*) an American, a native or inhabitant of the US.

yank (yangk) *v.t.* to pull sharply, to twitch, to jerk (off, out of etc.). ~*v.i.* to jerk vigorously. ~*n.* a sharp jerk, a twitch.

Yankee (yang´ki) *n.* **1** (*sometimes derog.*) an American, a native or inhabitant of the US. **2** an inhabitant of New England or other Northern states. **3** (*Hist.*) a Federal soldier or Northerner in the American Civil War (1861–65). **4** a type of multiple bet on four or more horses in different races. ~*a.* of or relating to America or the Yankees. **Yankee Doodle** *n.* an American.

yap (yap) *v.i.* (*pres.p.* **yapping,** *past, p.p.* **yapped**) **1** to yelp or bark snappishly. **2** to talk constantly in a shrill, foolish manner. ~*n.* **1** a snappish yelp or bark. **2** foolish chatter. **yapper** *n.* **yappy** *a.* (*comp.* **yappier,** *superl.* **yappiest**)

yard¹ (yahd) *n.* **1** a unit of length, 3 ft. or 36 in. (0.9144 m). **2** a measuring rod of this length, or this length of material. **3** (*Naut.*) a cylindrical spar tapering each way from the middle slung horizontally or slantwise on a mast to extend a sail. **4** a square yard, a cubic yard. **5** (*pl., coll.*) great lengths (of). **by the yard 1** in great quantities. **2** at great length. **yardage¹** (-dij) *n.* an amount of material in cubic yards. **yardarm** *n.* (*Naut.*) either half of a sailyard from the centre to the end. **yard of ale** *n.* **1** a tall, narrow drinking glass for beer or ale. **2** the amount of beer or ale in such a glass. **yardstick** *n.* **1** a known and trusted entity against which to assess other things. **2** a stick, 3 ft. in length and usu. graduated in feet, inches etc. used for measuring.

yard² (yahd) *n.* **1** a small piece of enclosed ground, esp. adjoining or enclosed by a house or other building. **2** such an enclosure used for some specified manufacture or other purpose, such as a dockyard, graveyard, timber yard etc. **3** a series of tracks near a railway used for the storage and maintenance of rolling stock. **4** (*N Am.*) a garden. ~*v.t.* to collect or pen (cattle etc.) in a yard. **yardage²** (-dij) *n.* **1** the use of a yard as a cattle enclosure. **2** the charge levied for such a use. **yardbird** *n.* (*N Am.*, *sl.*) **1** a military recruit. **2** a convict. **Yardie** *n.* (*sl.*) a member of a W Indian gang etc., usu. associated with drug-dealing or related crime (from Jamaican Eng. use of *yard* to mean house, home). **yardman** *n.* (*pl.* **yardmen**) **1** a person employed in a railway yard, timber yard etc. **2** (*N Am.*) a household gardener, odd-job man etc.

yardage¹ YARD¹.

yardage² YARD².

yarmulke (yah´mulkə), **yarmulka** *n.* a skullcap worn all the time by Orthodox Jewish men, and during prayer by others.

yarn (yahn) *n.* **1** any spun fibre prepared for weaving, knitting, rope-making etc. **2** (*coll.*) a long or rambling story, esp. one of doubtful truth or accuracy. ~*v.i.* to tell a yarn, to spin yarns.

yarrow (yar´ō) *n.* a perennial herb of the genus *Achillea*, esp. *A. millefolium*, the milfoil, with white flowers, a pungent odour and astringent properties.

yashmak (yash´mak) *n.* the veil worn by many Muslim women in public.

yatter (yat´ə) *v.i.* (*coll.*) to talk at length, gossip, chatter, esp. irritatingly.

yaw (yaw) *v.i.* (of a ship, aircraft etc.) to steer out of the direct course, to move unsteadily, esp. from side to side. ~*n.* **1** an unsteady motion or temporary deviation from a course. **2** the motion of an aircraft about its vertical axis.

yawl¹ (yawl) *n.* **1** a small two-masted sailing boat with a small jigger-mast towards the stern. **2** a small boat, esp. a ship's jollyboat.

yawl² (yawl) *v.i.* to howl, to yell, to yowl. ~*n.* a howl or yell, a yowl.

yawn (yawn) *v.i.* **1** to open the mouth wide or to have the mouth open involuntarily through drowsiness, boredom, bewilderment etc., to stand agape. **2** to be or stand wide open. ~*v.t.* to express or utter with a yawn. ~*n.* **1** the act of yawning. **2** (*coll.*) something that is boring or tedious. **yawner** *n.* **yawning** *a.*, *n.* **yawningly** *adv.*

yawp (yawp) *n.* a hoarse or raucous cry. ~*v.i.* **1** to cry harshly or noisily. **2** (*N Am.*) to talk foolishly.

yaws (yawz) *n.* (*Med.*) an infectious tropical disease whose symptoms include sores, caused by spirochaetes; also called *framboesia*.

Yb *chem. symbol* ytterbium.

yd *abbr.* yard (measure).

yds *abbr.* yards (measure).

†ye¹ (yē, yi) *pron.* pl. of THOU¹, you people (orig. nom. or subjective).

ye² (yē) *a.* (*facet.*) THE.

†yea (yā) *adv.* (*also formal*) **1** yes. **2** verily, truly, indeed. **3** not only so but also. ~*n.* **1** an affirmative. **2** a person who votes in the affirmative.

yeah (ye, yeə) *adv.* (*coll.*) yes. **oh yeah?** used to express incredulity.

year (yiə) *n.* **1** the period of time occupied by the revolution of the earth round the sun, the time taken by the sun in returning to the same equinox, in mean length, 365 days, 5 hrs., 48 min. and 46 sec. **2** the sidereal year. **3** the calendar year. **4** any period of about 12 months taken as a unit of time (*during the last year*). **5** a body of students who enter a school or university in the same year. **6** (*coll.*) age, length or time of life, a long time. **7** (*poet.*) old age. **in the year of Our Lord** in a specified year AD (*in the year of Our Lord 1665*). **of the year** outstanding in a particular year (*sports personality of the year*). **the year dot** as long ago as can be remembered. **year in, year out** constantly over a very long period, without cessation. **yearbook** *n.* a book published annually giving information up to date on some subject liable to change. **year-end** *n.* the end of the (fiscal) year. **yearling** *n.* **1** an animal more than one and less than two years old. **2** a colt a year old dating from 1 Jan. of the year of foaling. ~*a.* **1** being one year old. **2** terminating after one year. **year-long** *a.* lasting a year. **yearly** *a.* **1** happening or recurring once a year or every year, annual. **2** lasting a year. ~*adv.* **1** annually. **2** once a year, by the year. **year of grace** *n.* a year AD. **year-round** *a.* open or operating all year. **years of discretion** *n.pl.* the age when one is considered capable of exercising one's own judgement.

yearn (yœn) *v.i.* to feel a longing desire, tenderness, compassion etc. (for, after etc.). **yearner** *n.* **yearning** *n.*, *a.* **yearningly** *adv.*

yeast (yēst) *n.* **1** a yellowish, viscous substance consisting of a growth of fungous cells developed in contact with saccharine liquids and producing alcoholic fermentation by means of enzymes, used in brewing, distilling etc. and for raising dough for bread etc. **2** any unicellular fungus which reproduces by budding or fission. **yeastless** *a.* **yeastlike** *a.* **yeasty** *a.* (*comp.* **yeastier**, *superl.* **yeastiest**) **1** containing or resembling yeast, esp. in causing or being characterized by fermentation. **2** frothy, foamy. **3** unsubstantial, empty, superficial. **yeastily** *adv.* **yeastiness** *n.*

☒ **yeild** common misspelling of YIELD.

yell (yel) *v.i.* **1** to cry out with a loud, sharp or inarticulate cry as in rage, agony, terror or uncontrollable laughter. **2** to shout. ~*v.t.* to utter or express by yelling. ~*n.* **1** such a cry or shout, esp. a war cry. **2** (*N Am.*) a distinctive shout used by college students etc. for encouragement, applause etc. **3** (*sl.*) a cause of hilarity or yelling.

yellow (yel'ō) *a.* **1** of a colour between green and orange in the spectrum or like that of gold, brass, sulphur, lemon or, the duller form, like that of discoloured old paper etc. **2** (*coll.*) cowardly. **3** (*poet.*) jaundiced, jealous, envious. **4** (of a newspaper etc.) sensational, outrageous. **5** (*often offensive*) having a yellowish skin or complexion. ~*n.* **1** this colour, a yellow pigment, dye etc. **2** a yellow butterfly or moth. **3** the yellow ball in snooker. **4** the yellow counter in a board game etc.; the person playing with this. **5** (*pl.*, *N Am.*) a disease attacking peach trees etc. and turning their leaves yellow. **6** egg yolk. ~*v.t.* to make (something) yellow. ~*v.i.* to turn yellow. **yellow archangel** *n.* a Eurasian nettle, *Lamistrum galeobdolon*, with yellow helmet-shaped flowers. **yellow arsenic** *n.* orpiment. **yellow-belly** *n.* (*pl.* **yellow-bellies**) **1** (*coll.*) a coward. **2** any animal with yellow underparts. **yellow-bellied** *a.* **yellowcake** *n.* (*Chem.*) semi-refined uranium oxide obtained during the processing of uranium ore. **yellow card** *n.* in soccer, a yellow card shown as a caution by a referee to a player who has violated a rule. **yellow fever** *n.* a malignant tropical fever caused by the bite of the mosquito, characterized by jaundice and black vomit. **yellowfin** *n.* any of several fishes with yellow fins, esp. the yellowfin tuna. **yellowfin tuna** *n.* the edible tuna, *Thunnus albacares*, found in warm seas. **yellowhammer** *n.* a bunting, *Emberiza citrinella*, with a yellow head, neck and breast. **yellowish** *a.* **yellow jersey** *n.* a jersey worn by the overall leader in a cycle race lasting several days. **yellowlegs** *n.* either of two N American migratory sandpipers, *Tringa flavipes* and *T. melanoleuca*, having yellow legs. **yellow line** *n.* a line painted at the side of a road showing parking restrictions. **yellowly** *adv.* **yellowness** *n.* **Yellow Pages**® *n.pl.* a telephone directory, printed on yellow paper, which lists subscribers according to business. **yellow pepper** *n.* a variant of the red pepper *Capsicum annuum.* **yellow spot** *n.* the area at the centre of the retina where vision is acutest in daylight. **yellow streak** *n.* (*coll.*) a tendency towards cowardice. **yellowy** *a.*

yelp (yelp) *v.i.* to utter a sharp, quick cry, as a dog in pain, or in fear or anticipation. ~*n.* such a bark or cry. **yelper** *n.*

Yemeni (yem'əni) *n.* a native or inhabitant of the Republic of Yemen. ~*a.* of or relating to Yemen or its people.

yen[1] (yen) *n.* (*pl.* **yen**) the standard unit of currency of Japan.

yen[2] (yen) *n.* (*coll.*) ambition, yearning, desire, longing. ~*v.i.* (*pres.p.* **yenning**, *past*, *p.p.* **yenned**) to yearn.

yeoman (yō'mən) *n.* (*pl.* **yeomen**) **1** (*Hist.*) a freeholder not ranking as one of the gentry. **2** (*Hist.*) a man qualified to serve on juries and to vote etc., as holding free land of £2 annual value. **3** (*Hist.*) a member of the yeomanry force. **4** (*Hist.*) a farmer, esp. a freeholder. **5** a yeoman of signals. **yeomanlike** *a.* **yeomanly** *a.* **yeoman of signals** *n.* a petty or non-commissioned officer who carries out signalling or clerical duties in the navy. **Yeoman of the Guard** *n.* (*pl.* **Yeomen of the Guard**) **1** a Yeoman Warder. **2** a member of the British sovereign's ceremonial bodyguard. **yeomanry** (-ri) *n.* (*pl.* **yeomanries**) **1** yeomen collectively. **2** (*Hist.*) a British force of volunteer cavalry consisting largely of country gentlemen and farmers. **yeoman service, yeoman's service** *n.* good service, hearty support. **Yeoman Warder** *n.* (*pl.* **Yeoman Warders**) a warder at the Tower of London, a beefeater.

yep (yep), **yup** (yŭp) *adv.* (*coll.*) yes.

-yer (yə) *suf.* forming nouns, esp. from words in *-w*, denoting an agent, as *lawyer*, *sawyer*.

yes (yes) *adv.* **1** as you say, it is true, agreed (indicating affirmation or consent). **2** I hear (in answer to a summons etc.). ~*n.* (*pl.* **yeses**) **1** the word 'yes'. **2** an affirmative reply. **yes?** **1** what do you want? **2** is that so?, really? **yes and no** a response indicating that what has been said is partly true but also partly untrue. **yes-man** *n.* (*pl.* **yes-men**) (*coll.*) an unquestioning follower, a sycophant.

yester- (yes'tə) *comb. form* (*poet.*) of or relating to yesterday (*yesteryear*). **yesterday** (yes'tədi) *n.* **1** the day immediately before today. **2** time in the immediate past. ~*adv.* **1** on or during yesterday. **2** in the recent past. **yesterday afternoon** during the afternoon of yesterday. **yesterday morning** during the morning of yesterday. **yesteryear** *n.*, *adv.* (*poet.*) **1** last year. **2** the recent past.

yet (yet) *adv.* **1** still, up to this or that time (*They had yet to mature*). **2** by this or that time, so soon or early as the present, so far (*Are you up yet?*). **3** in addition, further, besides (*yet another soap opera*). **4** eventually, at some future time, before all is over (*They may yet arrive*). **5** even (*with comp.*) (*yet more*). **6** nevertheless, in spite of that (*Yet, we must remember*). ~*conj.* nevertheless, notwithstanding, but still (*We were beaten, yet we were proud of our efforts*). **as yet** up to this or that time, so far. **nor yet** and also not (*He had not finished the exam nor yet started the last question*). **not yet** not up to the present time.

yeti (yet'i) *n.* (*pl.* **yetis**) a hypothetical manlike, apelike or bearlike creature, whose tracks are alleged to have been found in the snows of the Himalayas, also called *Abominable Snowman*.

yew (ū) *n.* **1** a dark-leaved evergreen shrub or tree of the genus *Taxus*, esp. *T. baccata*, a large tree with spreading branches, the wood of which has long been valued for making bows and used in cabinetmaking. **2** its wood. **yew tree** *n.*

Yiddish (yid´ish) *n.* a language spoken by Jews of E Europe and N America, based on a Hebraized Middle German, with an admixture of Polish, French and English, and usually written in Hebrew characters. *~a.* of or relating to this language. **Yid** *n.* (*sl., offensive*) a Jew. **Yiddisher** *n.* a Yiddish speaker. *~a.* **1** of or relating to Yiddish. **2** Yiddish-speaking, Jewish. **Yiddishism** *n.* **1** a word, idiom etc. derived from Yiddish. **2** support for the use of Yiddish.

yield (yēld) *v.t.* **1** to produce, to bear, to bring forth as fruit, reward or result. **2** to give up, to surrender, to concede, to relinquish, to resign. *~v.i.* **1** to give a return, to repay one's labour in cultivation etc., to bear fruit, to be productive (beneficially or otherwise). **2** to give way, to assent, to submit, to comply, to surrender. **3** to give place, to yield precedence or admit inferiority (to). *~n.* **1** something that is yielded or produced, output, return. **2** annual return from an investment. **yieldable** *a.* **yielder** *n.* **yielding** *a.* **1** compliant. **2** able to bend, pliable. **yieldingly** *adv.* **yieldingness** *n.*

yikes (yīks) *int.* (*sl.*) used to express surprise, astonishment, alarm etc.

yin (yin) *n.* the feminine, passive, dark principle in nature, according to Chinese philosophy, which interacts with its complement and opposite, *yang*.

yip (yip) *n.* a short sudden cry, a yelp. *~v.i.* (*pres.p.* **yipping**, *past, p.p.* **yipped**) to give a short sudden cry, to yelp.

yippee (yipē´) *int.* used to express delight, pleasure, exuberant anticipation etc.

yips (yips) *n.pl.* (*coll.*) an attack of nerves, particularly in sport and esp. when putting in golf.

-yl (il, īl) *suf.* (*Chem.*) denoting a radical, as *ethyl, methyl.*

ylang-ylang (ēlangē´lang), **ilang-ilang** *n.* **1** a Malayan tree, *Cananga odorata*, of the custard-apple family. **2** an oil from the flowers of this tree, used in perfumes, aromatherapy etc.

-yne (īn) *comb. form* (*Chem.*) denoting a triple bond, as *alkyne.*

yo (yō) *int.* (*sl.*) used as a greeting, to gain someone's attention, etc. (*Yo, dudes!*).

yob (yob) *n.* an aggressive, loutish youth, a hooligan. **yobbish** *a.* **yobbishly** *adv.* **yobbishness** *n.* **yobbo** (-ō) *n.* (*pl.* **yobbos, yobboes**).

yod (yod) *n.* **1** the tenth letter of the Hebrew alphabet. **2** its sound, a palatal semivowel.

yodel (yō´dəl) *v.t., v.i.* (*pres.p.* **yodelling**, (*N Am.*) **yodeling**, *past, p.p.* **yodelled**, (*N Am.*) **yodeled**) to sing or shout in a musical fashion with alternation from the natural voice to the falsetto. *~n.* such a shout or musical cry, used esp. by Swiss and Tyrolese mountaineers. **yodeller**, (*N Am.*) **yodeler** *n.*

yoga (yō´gə) *n.* **1** a Hindu system of abstract meditation and rigid asceticism by which the soul is supposed to become united with the eternal spirit of the universe. **2** certain exercises and practices assisting this, HATHA YOGA. **yogi** (yō´gi) *n.* (*pl.* **yogis**) a devotee or adept of yoga. **yogic** *a.* **yogism** *n.*

yogurt (yog´ət, yō´-), **yoghurt, yoghourt, yogourt** *n.* a custard-like food made from milk fermented in a special way.

yo-heave-ho (yōhēvhō´) *int., n.* HEAVE-HO (under HEAVE).

yoke (yōk) *n.* **1** a frame or crossbar fitting over the necks of two oxen or other draught animals and attaching this to a plough or vehicle. **2** a device resembling this. **3** a frame fitting a person's shoulders for carrying a pair of buckets suspended from the ends. **4** a part of a garment made to support the rest, as at the shoulders or hips. **5** (*pl.* **yoke, yokes**) a pair of draught animals, esp. oxen yoked together. **6** servitude, slavery, submission. *~v.t.* **1** to put a yoke upon. **2** to unite by a yoke. **3** to join, to link. **4** to enslave. *~v.i.* to go or work (well or badly together etc.).

yokel (yō´kəl) *n.* a rustic, a country bumpkin. **yokelish** *a.*

yolk (yōk), (*dial.*) **yelk** (yelk) *n.* the yellow part of an egg, the contents of the ovum, esp. that nourishing the embryo, the vitellus. **yolked** *a.* **yolkless** *a.* **yolky** *a.*

yomp (yomp) *v.i.* to trek, often with heavy equipment, over heavy terrain.

yon (yon) *a., adv.* (*Sc.*) yonder. *~pron.* **1** yonder person, thing or place. **2** that.

yonder (yon´də) *a.* **1** that over there (*yonder tree*). **2** being at a distance, but in the direction looked at or pointed out. *~adv.* **1** over there. **2** at a distance but within view, or where one is looking or pointing.

yonks (yongks) *n.pl.* (*coll.*) a long time, ages.

yoo-hoo (yoo´hoo) *int.* used to attract someone's attention.

yore (yaw) *n.* (*poet.*) †long ago, old time. **of yore** (*poet.*) formerly, of old time, long ago (*days of yore*).

yorker (yaw´kə) *n.* in cricket, a ball bowled so as to pitch immediately under the bat. **york** *v.t.* to bowl (out) with a yorker.

Yorkist (yaw´kist) *a.* (*Hist.*) of or relating to the house descended from Edmund Duke of York, son of Edward III, or the White Rose party supporting this in the Wars of the Roses. *~n.* an adherent of this house or party.

Yorks. (yawks) *abbr.* Yorkshire.

Yorkshire (yawk´shə) *a.* of or derived from Yorkshire. **Yorkshireman** *n.* (*pl.* **Yorkshiremen**). **Yorkshire pudding** *n.* a baked batter pudding, often served with roast beef. **Yorkshire terrier** *n.* a small shaggy variety of toy terrier. **Yorkshirewoman** *n.* (*pl.* **Yorkshirewomen**).

Yoruba (yor´əbə) *n.* **1** a member of a people

living in the coastal regions of W Africa, esp. SW Nigeria. **2** the Kwa language of this people.

you (ū, yu) *pron.* (*sing. and pl.*) **1** the person, animal, thing or persons etc. addressed. **2** (*reflex.*) yourself, yourselves. **3** (*indefinite*) one, anyone, people generally. **you and yours** you and your family, property etc. **you-all, y'all** *pron.* (*N Am., coll.*) you (usu. more than one person). **you'd** (yud) *contr.* **1** you had. **2** you would. **you-know-what, you-know-who** *n.* something or someone unspecified known to both speaker and hearer. **you'll** (yul) *contr.* you will, you shall. **you're** (yaw) *contr.* you are. **youse** (ūz, yuz), **yous** *pron.* (*coll., dial.*) you (usu. more than one person). **you've** (yuv) *contr.* you have.

Usage note See note under YOUR.

young (yŭng) *a.* (*comp.* **younger** (yŭng´gə), *superl.* **youngest** (yŭng´gist)) **1** being in the early stage of life, growth or development. **2** of recent birth or beginning, newly formed, produced, come into action or operation etc. **3** not infirm or decayed with age, vigorous, fresh. **4** of, relating to or characteristic of youth. ~*n.* **1** offspring, esp. of animals. **2** those who are young. **with young** pregnant. **young blood** *n.* a new accession of vigour or enterprise. **younger** *a.* **1** less in age, growth etc. **2** that is the younger of two people of the same name. **younger hand** *n.* in cards, the second player of two. **young fogey** *n.* a young person with old-fashioned tastes, attitudes, mannerisms etc. **young hopeful** *n.* **1** a person with good prospects of success. **2** a person with misplaced expectations of success. **youngish** *a.* **young lady** *n.* (*pl.* **young ladies**) **1** a young woman, esp. one unmarried. **2** a girlfriend. **youngling** *n.* **young man** *n.* (*pl.* **young men**) **1** a young man or boy. **2** a boyfriend. **youngness** *n.* **young offender** *n.* (*Law*) a young criminal between 14 and 17 years of age. **young person** *n.* (*Law*) someone aged between 14 and 17. **youngster** *n.* **1** a young person, a child. **2** a young animal, such as a young horse. **young thing** *n.* (*coll.*) a young person. **young woman** *n.* (*pl.* **young women**) **1** a young woman or girl. **2** a girlfriend.

your (yaw, yə, ūə) *a.* **1** possessive of YOU. **2** (*coll., usu. derog.*) well-known, familiar, much talked of (*Take your yuppies, for example*). **your humble servant, your obedient servant** *n.* (*formal*) used preceding the signature of a letter, often now used ironically. **yours** (-z) *pron.* **1** something which belongs to you or is associated with you. **2** your letter. **3** someone at your service (in a formula ending a letter) (*yours ever*). **of yours** of or belonging to you. **yours truly** I, this person (*Of course, yours truly came last!*). **yourself** (-self´) *pron.* (*pl.* **yourselves** (-selvz´)) **1** you and not others, you alone. **2** your own person, you in particular. **3** you in your normal condition, health etc. (*You don't look yourself today*). **by yourself/ yourselves 1** alone. **2** unaided. **to be yourself/**

yourselves to act normally, without affectation etc.

Usage note (1) The spellings of the adjective *your* and the contraction *you're* (you are) should not be confused. (2) The pronoun *yours* does not have an apostrophe (not *your's*).

you're, youse etc. see YOU.

youth (ūth) *n.* (*pl.* **youths** (ūdhz)) **1** the state of being young. **2** the period of life from infancy to manhood or womanhood. **3** youthfulness, the vigour, freshness, inexperience etc. of this period. **4** a young man. **5** young men and women collectively. **youth club, youth centre,** (*N Am.*) **youth center** *n.* a club which provides leisure time and social activities for young people. **youthful** *a.* **youthfully** *adv.* **youthfulness** *n.* **youth hostel** *n.* an organized establishment where hikers etc. may stay for the night. **youth hosteller,** (*N Am.*) **youth hosteler** *n.* **youth hostelling** *n.*

you've see YOU.

yowl (yowl) *n.* a howl or yell of distress. ~*v.i.* to cry out in this way.

yo-yo (yō´yō) *n.* (*pl.* **yo-yos**) a toy which consists of a spool winding up and down on a string. ~*v.i.* (*3rd pers. sing. pres.* **yo-yoes,** *pres.p.* **yo-yoing,** *past, p.p.* **yo-yoed**) **1** to move up and down rapidly, to fluctuate rapidly. **2** to play with a yo-yo.

yr. *abbr.* **1** year. **2** younger. **3** your.

yrs. *abbr.* **1** years. **2** yours.

ytterbium (itoe´biəm) *n.* (*Chem.*) a rare metallic element, at. no. 70, chem. symbol Yb, used to improve the mechanical properties of steel.

yttrium (it´riəm) *n.* (*Chem.*) a rare metallic element, at. no. 39, chem. symbol Y, belonging to the cerium group, used in alloys, lasers and in making superconductors. **yttria** (-riə) *n.* a white earth, yttrium oxide. **yttriferous** (-rif´-) *a.*

yuan (yuahn´) *n.* (*pl.* **yuan**) the standard monetary unit of China.

yucca (yŭk´ə) *n.* any liliaceous subtropical American flowering plant of the genus *Yucca*, with rigid lanceolate leaves and an erect cluster of white flowers, many species of which are grown for ornament.

yuck (yŭk), **yuk** *int.* (*sl.*) used to express disgust or distaste. ~*n.* (*sl.*) something unpleasant or messy. **yucky, yukky** *a.* (*comp.* **yuckier, yukkier,** *superl.* **yuckiest, yukkiest**) (*coll.*) disgusting, unpleasant.

Yugoslav (yoo´gəslahv), **Jugoslav** *a.* **1** of or relating to the southern Slav peoples or countries, esp. the former Yugoslavia. **2** of Yugoslavian descent. ~*n.* a native or inhabitant of the former Yugoslavia. **Yugoslavian** (-slah´-) *a.*

Yule (yool), **Yuletide** (yool´tīd) *n.* Christmas time or the festival of Christmas. **yule log** *n.* **1** a large log formerly burned on Christmas Eve. **2** a chocolate cake shaped and decorated like a log, eaten at Christmas.

yum-yum (yŭmyŭm´) *int.* (*coll.*) used to express

pleasure, esp. anticipation of delicious food.
yummy (yŭm´i) *a.* (*comp.* **yummier,** *superl.*
yummiest) delicious, tasty.
yup YEP.
yuppie (yŭp´i), **yuppy** *n.* (*pl.* **yuppies**) (*sometimes
derog.*) a young financially successful profes-
sional person who spends much money on their
lifestyle. ~*a.* of, relating to or designed to appeal

to yuppies. **yuppiedom** *n.* **yuppify** *v.t.* (*3rd pers.
sing. pres.* **yuppifies,** *pres.p.* **yuppifying,** *past,
p.p.* **yuppified**) to make suitable for or typical of
yuppies. **yuppification** (-fikā´shən) *n.*
yurt (yuət, yœt) *n.* **1** a circular, collapsible tent
made of skins and used by nomads in Central
Asia. **2** a hut built partially underground and
covered with turf or earth.

Z

Z (zed), **z** (pl. **Zs, Z's**) the 26th and last letter of the English and other versions of the Roman alphabet, corresponding to the Greek zeta (ζ, Z). It is pronounced as a voiced alveolar continuant (like a voiced *s*), as in *zeal, lazy, reason*, or as a voiced affricate (like a voiced *sh*), as in *azure*. **~symbol** (*Math.*) the third unknown quantity or variable in an algebraic expression. **z-axis** *n.* a reference axis in the Cartesian coordinate system.

zabaglione (zabalyō´ni) *n.* a warm whipped dessert of egg yolks, sugar and marsala.

zag (zag) *n.* a sharp change of direction in a zigzag course. **~v.i.** (*pres.p.* **zagging**, *past, p.p.* **zagged**) to move in this way.

Zairean (zīiə´riən), **Zairian** *n.* a native or inhabitant of Zaire in central Africa (now Congo). **~a.** of or relating to Zaire. **zaire** *n.* the standard unit of currency of Zaire.

Zambian (zam´biən)´ *n.* a native or inhabitant of the central African republic of Zambia. **~a.** of or relating to Zambia.

zany (zā´ni) *a.* (*comp.* **zanier**, *superl.* **zaniest**) outrageous, comical, absurd (e.g. of a comedy show). **~n.** (*pl.* **zanies**) **1** a person who acts the fool. **2** (*Hist.*) a buffoon in old theatrical entertainments who mimicked the clown. **zanily** *adv.* **zaniness** *n.* **zanyism** *n.*

zap (zap) *v.t.* (*pres.p.* **zapping**, *past, p.p.* **zapped**) **1** (*coll.*) to hit, smack, strike suddenly. **2** to kill or destroy. **3** to cause to go quickly. **4** (*Comput.*) to delete or change (an item on screen, in a program etc.). **~v.i.** **1** to move suddenly or quickly. **2** to switch rapidly between television channels using a remote control. **~n.** **1** energy, go, vitality. **2** a powerful emotional effect. **~int.** used to express a sudden action. **zapper** *n.* **1** a remote control for television, video etc. **2** (*coll.*) a person who habitually switches rapidly between television channels. **zappy** *a.* (*comp.* **zappier**, *superl.* **zappiest**) (*coll.*) **1** energetic, fast-moving. **2** punchy, snappy.

Zarathustrian (zarəthus´triən) *a., n.* ZORO-ASTRIAN. **Zarathustrianism** *n.*

zarzuela (zahzwā´lə) *n.* **1** a traditional Spanish form of musical comedy or comic opera. **2** a Spanish seafood stew.

zeal (zēl) *n.* **1** ardour, earnestness, enthusiasm. **2** intense and eager pursuit or endeavour to attain or accomplish some object. **zealot** (zel´ət) *n.* **1** a fanatical partisan. **2** (*Hist.*) (**Zealot**) a member of a militant Jewish sect opposing the Roman occupation of the Holy Land until AD 70. **3** a person

full of zeal, esp. one carried away by it. **zealotism** *n.* **zealotry** (-tri) *n.* **zealous** (zel´-) *a.* **zealously** *adv.* **zealousness** *n.*

zebra (zeb´rə, zē´-) *n.* (*pl. in general* **zebra**, *in particular* **zebras**) **1** a black and white striped, asslike mammal of the genus *Equus*, esp. *E. burchelli*, from the mountainous regions of S Africa. **2** (*attrib.*) denoting other kinds or species of plant, bird, fish or mammal with similar markings, including the *zebra antelope*, *zebra caterpillar*, *zebra fish*, *zebra mouse*, *zebra woodpecker* and *zebra wood*. **zebra crossing** *n.* a street-crossing marked by stripes where pedestrians have precedence over all other traffic. **zebra finch** *n.* an Australian waxbill, *Poephila guttata*, having black and white stripes on the face.

zebu (zē´boo) *n.* (*pl.* **zebus**) the humped Indian ox, *Bos indicus*.

zed (zed) *n.* the letter Z.

zee (zē) *n.* (*N Am.*) the letter Z, zed.

Zeitgeist (tsīt´gīst) *n.* the spirit, or moral and intellectual tendency, of the times.

Zen (zen) *n.* a form of Mahayana Buddhism teaching that truth is in one's heart and can be learned only by meditation and self-mastery. **Zenist, Zennist** *n.*

zenith (zen´ith) *n.* **1** the point in the heavens directly overhead to an observer, as opposed to *nadir*. **2** the highest or culminating point (*the zenith of his career*). **zenithal** *a.*

zeolite (zē´əlīt) *n.* **1** any one of a group of hydrous silicates found in cavities of eruptive rocks, which gelatinize in acid owing to the liberation of silica. **2** any of various synthetic silicates resembling this. **zeolitic** (-lit´-) *a.*

zephyr (zef´ə) *n.* (*poet.*) any soft, gentle breeze.

Zeppelin (zep´əlin), **zeppelin** *n.* (*Hist.*) a large dirigible airship.

zero (ziə´rō) *n.* (*pl.* **zeros**) **1** the figure 0, a cipher, nothing, nought, nil. **2** the point on a scale from which positive or negative quantities are reckoned, esp. on a thermometer (e.g. on the Fahrenheit scale 32° below the freezing point of water; on the Celsius and Réaumur scales zero is the freezing point). **3** the lowest point in any scale or standard of comparison, the nadir, nullity. **4** zero hour. **~a.** **1** having no measurable quantity, size etc. **2** (of a cloud ceiling) limiting visibility to 15 m (approx. 50 ft.) or less. **3** (of horizontal visibility) limited to 50 m (approx. 165 ft.) or less. **4** (*coll.*) not any, nothing. **~v.t.** (*3rd pers. sing. pres.* **zeroes**, *pres.p.* **zeroing**, *past, p.p.* **zeroed**) to adjust or set (an instrument, scale, gauge etc.) to zero. **to zero in on 1** to focus attention on, to fix on. **2** to aim for. **3** to converge upon, to home in on. **zero hour** *n.* **1** the precise hour for the commencement of a pre-arranged military movement or other action, operation etc. **2** the crucial time. **zero option** *n.* a proposal that both sides in international nuclear arms negotiations agree to limit or remove shorter-range nuclear missiles. **zero-rated** *a.* denoting goods on which the buyer need pay no value added tax, but on which the seller can claim back any value added tax they have already paid. **zero-rate** *v.t.* **zero tolerance** *n.* total intolerance, esp. of street crime by police authorities.

zest (zest) *n.* **1** keen enjoyment. **2** that which makes a thing enjoyable, piquancy, relish. **3** a piece of lemon, lime or orange peel, or the oil extracted from this, used to give a flavour to soups, wines etc. **zester** *n.* a kitchen utensil for scraping or peeling citrus fruits to obtain zest. **zestful** *a.* **zestfully** *adv.* **zestfulness** *n.* **zesty** *a.* (*comp.* **zestier,** *superl.* **zestiest**).

zeta (zē'tə) *n.* the sixth letter of the Greek alphabet (ζ, Z).

zeugma (zūg'mə) *n.* (*Gram.*) a figure in which a verb or adjective governs or modifies two nouns to only one of which it is logically applicable. **zeugmatic** (-mat´-) *a.*

zidovudine (zidō'vūdēn, -dov´-) *n.* (*Med.*) a drug derivative of thymine used to alleviate the symptoms of Aids sufferers, AZT.

zig (zig) *n.* a sharp change of direction in a zigzag course. *~v.i.* (*pres.p.* **zigging,** *past, p.p.* **zigged**) to move in this way.

ziggurat (zig´ərat) *n.* an ancient Mesopotamian temple tower of a rectangular or tiered design.

zigzag (zig´zag) *a.* having or taking sharp alternate turns or angles to left and right. *~n.* a zigzag line, road, path, pattern, moulding, series of trenches, stitches etc. *~adv.* in a zigzag course or manner. *~v.t.* (*pres.p.* **zigzagging,** *past, p.p.* **zigzagged**) to form or do in a zigzag fashion. *~v.i.* to move in a zigzag course. **zigzagedly** *adv.*

zilch (zilch) *n.* (*sl.*) nothing, zero.

zillion (zil´yən) *n.* (*coll.*) a huge unspecified amount, quantity or number. **zillionth** *a.*

Zimbabwean (zimbahb´wiən) *n.* a native or inhabitant of the southern African republic of Zimbabwe. *~a.* of or relating to Zimbabwe.

Zimmer® (zim´ə), **Zimmer frame** *n.* a metal walking frame used as a means of support by those with walking difficulties.

zinc (zingk) *n.* (*Chem.*) a bluish-white metallic element, at. no. 30, chem. symbol Zn, used in the manufacture of brass and other alloys, for coating sheet iron, as roofing material, in electric batteries etc. *~v.t.* (*pres.p.* **zincing,** *past, p.p.* **zinced**) to coat or cover with zinc. *~a.* of or containing zinc. **zinc blende** *n.* native zinc sulphide, sphalerite. **zinced** *a.* **zincic** *a.* **zincoid** (-koid) *a.*

zinc ointment *n.* a medical preparation of zinc oxide in an ointment base such as petroleum jelly. **zinc oxide** *n.* a powder used as a white pigment, and in cements, ointments etc. **zincy** *a.*

zing (zing) *n.* **1** energy, go, zest. **2** (*coll.*) a shrill buzzing noise as of a bullet or a vibrating rope. *~v.i.* (*coll.*) to move very quickly esp. with a high-pitched humming sound. **zinger** *n.* (*N Am., sl.*) **1** a quip, wisecrack, gag etc. **2** an unexpected turn of events. **3** a person or thing with zing, an outstanding person or thing. **zingy** *a.* (*comp.* **zingier,** *superl.* **zingiest**).

zinnia (zin´iə) *n.* a plant of the genus *Zinnia* (daisy family) with showy rayed flowers in single terminal heads.

Zion (zī'ən), **Sion** (sī´-) *n.* **1** the ancient Hebrew theocracy, the Christian Church, the heavenly Jerusalem, heaven. **2** the Jewish homeland or people. **Zionism** *n.* orig. a movement for establishing the resettlement of Palestine as the Jewish homeland, and now one promoting the development of the state of Israel. **Zionist** *n., a.* **Zionistic** (-nis´-) *a.*

zip (zip) *n.* **1** a zip fastener, a zipper. **2** the sharp sound made by a bullet or other missile striking an object or flying through the air. **3** (*coll.*) energy, zest. *~v.i.* (*pres.p.* **zipping,** *past, p.p.* **zipped**) to move or fly at high speed. **to zip through** to finish quickly. **to zip up** to fasten by means of a zip. **zip fastener, zipper** *n.* a fastening device, with interlocking teeth, which opens or closes with a single motion. **zippy** *a.* (*comp.* **zippier,** *superl.* **zippiest**) (*coll.*) energetic, speedy. **zippily** *adv.* **zippiness** *n.* **zip-up** *a.* able to be fastened with a zip.

Zip code (zip), **ZIP code, zip code** *n.* (*N Am.*) a postal code.

zircon (zœ´kən) *n.* a translucent, variously-coloured zirconium silicate, some varieties of which are cut into gems. **zirconium** (-kō´niəm) *n.* (*Chem.*) an earthy metallic element, at. no. 40, chem. symbol Zr, found chiefly in zircon.

zit (zit) *n.* (*sl.*) a spot, a pimple. **zitty** *a.* (*comp.* **zittier,** *superl.* **zittiest**).

zither (zidh´ə) *n.* (*Mus.*) a simple stringed instrument consisting of a flat sounding-board and strings plucked by the fingers. **zitherist** *n.*

zizz (ziz) *n.* (*coll.*) **1** a nap, a short sleep. **2** a whizzing sound. *~v.i.* to doze.

zloty (zlot´i) *n.* (*pl.* **zloty, zlotys, zloties**) a coin and monetary unit of Poland.

Zn *chem. symbol* zinc.

zodiac (zō´diak) *n.* **1** the zone or broad belt of the heavens, extending about 8° to each side of the ecliptic, which the sun traverses during the year. **2** a representation of the signs of the zodiac. **3** a complete circuit or revolution. **zodiacal** (-dī´ə-) *a.*

zoetrope (zō´itrōp) *n.* (*Hist.*) an optical instrument in which a series of pictures on the inner face of a rotating cylinder gives an impression of continuous motion when viewed through slits in the cylinder.

zoic (zō´ik) *a.* **1** of or relating to animals or animal life. **2** (*Geol.*) (of rocks) containing fossils or other evidence of plant or animal life.

zombie (zom´bi), **zombi** *n.* (*pl.* **zombies, zombis**) **1** (*coll.*) a stupid, apathetic or slow-moving person. **2** in W Indian voodooism, a reanimated dead person capable of slow automatic movements. **3** the supernatural spirit regarded as animating such a person's body. **zombielike** *a.* **zombiism** *n.*

zone (zōn) *n.* **1** an area sectioned off for a particular function (*a smoke-free zone*). **2** an area characterized by a particular form of government, business practice etc. (*a duty-free zone*). **3** any one of the five great divisions of the earth bounded by circles parallel to the equator (the torrid, temperate and frigid zones). **4** any well-defined belt or tract of land distinguished by climate, the character of its organisms etc. **5** TIME ZONE (under TIME). **6** (*poet.*) a well-marked band or stripe encircling an object. **7** the part of the surface of a sphere or of a cone or cylinder enclosed between two parallel planes perpendicular to the axis. **8** (*Geol.*) a stratum or area of rock distinguished by particular fossil remains. ~*v.t.* **1** to divide into zones. **2** to encircle with or as with a zone. **3** to allocate to certain districts or zones. **zonal** *a.* **zonally** *adv.* **zonation** (-ā´shən) *n.* arrangement or division into zones. **zoned** *a.* **zoner** *n.* **zoning** *n.* **1** division into, or allocation to, zones. **2** the marking off in town planning of certain areas for specific purposes, e.g. residence, shopping etc.

zonk (zongk) *v.t.* (*sl.*) to hit sharply or suddenly. ~*n.* **1** a sharp blow. **2** the sound of a sudden impact. **to zonk out** to overcome with sleep, alcohol, drugs etc. **zonked** (zongkt) *a.* **1** intoxicated by drugs or alcohol, extremely drunk or stoned. **2** tired out, exhausted. **zonked out** *a.* **zonked**.

zoo (zoo) *n.* (*pl.* **zoos**) a place with a collection of living wild animals on public display or kept in captivity as a conservation measure. **zookeeper** *n.* **1** a person responsible for the welfare of animals in a zoo. **2** the owner etc. of a zoo.

zoo- (zoo´ō, zō´ō), **zo-** (zō) *comb. form* of or relating to animals or to animal life.

zooid (zō´oid) *n.* (*Zool.*) **1** a more or less independent invertebrate organism developed by fission or budding. **2** a member of a compound invertebrate organism. **zooidal** (-oi´-) *a.*

zoology (zoo-ol´əji, zōol´-) *n.* the natural history of animals, the branch of biology dealing with the structure, physiology, classification, habits and distribution of animals. **zoological** (-loj´-) *a.* **zoological garden, zoological gardens** *n.* a public garden or park in which a collection of wild and other animals is kept, a zoo. **zoologically** *adv.* **zoologist** *n.*

zoom (zoom) *v.i.* **1** to move quickly (as) with a deep loud buzzing noise. **2** (of prices etc.) to rise rapidly, to soar. **3** in photography etc., to zoom in. **4** to turn an aircraft upwards suddenly at a very sharp angle. ~*n.* **1** an act, instance or sound of zooming. **2** a zoom lens. **3** in cinematography, video etc., a shot taken with a lens whose focal length is adjusted during the shot. **to zoom in** with a zoom lens, to go from long shot to close-up, when taking a photograph, a film shot etc. **to zoom out** with a zoom lens, to go from close-up to long shot when taking a photograph, a film shot etc. **zoom lens** *n.* a lens in a camera or microscope which has a variable focal length and can increase or decrease the size of an image continuously without changing position.

zoomorphic (zōəmaw´fik) *a.* **1** (*Zool.*) of, relating to or exhibiting animal forms. **2** having religious symbols representing animals. **3** having gods represented in the form of animals. **zoomorphism** *n.*

zoonosis (zōōn´əsis, zōənō´-) *n.* (*pl.* **zoonoses** (-sēz)) a disease which can be transmitted to humans by animals, e.g. rabies.

zoophyte (zō´əfīt) *n.* (*Zool.*) an invertebrate animal presenting many external resemblances to a plant, such as a coral, sea anemone, sponge etc. **zoophytic** (-fit´-), **zoophytical** *a.*

Zoroastrian (zorōas´triən) *a.* of or relating to Zoroaster (or Zarathustra) or the religious system expounded by him and his followers in the Zend-Avesta, based on the dual principle of Ormazd, the god of light and good, and Ahriman, the god of darkness and evil. ~*n.* a follower of Zoroaster, an adherent of Zoroastrianism. **Zoroastrianism** *n.*

Zouave (zooahv´) *n.* **1** a soldier belonging to a French light infantry corps, orig. composed of Algerian recruits and still wearing an Oriental uniform. **2** (*pl.*) trousers with wide tops tapering to a narrow ankle, worn by women.

zouk (zook) *n.* a kind of lively music combining Latin American, African and Western influences, originating in the French Caribbean.

ZPG *abbr.* zero population growth.

Zr *chem. symbol* zirconium.

zucchetto (tsuket´ō) *n.* (*pl.* **zucchettos**) the skullcap of a Roman Catholic ecclesiastic, black for a priest, purple for a bishop, red for a cardinal, white for a pope.

zucchini (zukē´ni) *n.* (*pl.* **zucchini, zucchinis**) a courgette.

Zulu (zoo´loo) *n.* (*pl.* **Zulus, Zulu**) **1** a member of a branch of the Bantu-speaking people of SE Africa. **2** the language of this people. ~*a.* of or relating to this people or their language.

zwieback (zwē´bak, tsvē´-) *n.* a type of biscuit or rusk.

zydeco (zī´dikō) *n.* a kind of Afro-American dance music, orig. from S Louisiana.

zygo- (zī´go, zig´ō), **zyg-** *comb. form* union, pairing.

zygoma (zīgō´mə, zig-) *n.* (*pl.* **zygomata** (-mətə)) (*Anat.*) the arch joining the cheekbone and temporal bone. **zygomatic** (-mat´-) *a.* **zygomatic arch** *n.* the zygoma. **zygomatic bone** *n.* the cheekbone.

zygospore (zī´gəspaw) *n.* a spore formed by conjugation of two similar gametes within certain fungi or algae.

zygote (zī´gōt) *n.* (*Biol., Zool.*) the product of the fusion between the oocyte and the spermatozoon, the fertilized ovum. **zygotic** (-got´-) *a.* **zygotically** *adv.*